P9-BZV-445

Britannica 1996 Book of the Year

Encyclopædia Britannica, Inc. Chicago • Auckland • London • Madrid • Manila • Paris • Rome • Seoul • Sydney • Tokyo • Toronto

Library of Congress Catalog Card Number: 38-12082
International Standard Book Number: 0-85229-628-2
International Standard Serial Number: 0068-1156

BRITANNICA BOOK OF THE YEAR

Britannica Online may be accessed on the Internet at http://www.eb.com.

(Trademark Reg. U.S. Pat. Off.) Printed in U.S.A.

FOREWORD

On behalf of the staff of Encyclopædia Britannica, I am happy to present the 1996 edition of the *Britannica Book of the Year.* This covers a year in which a great deal happened not only in the United States and in the rest of the English-speaking world but everywhere on the globe. The conclusion of the O.J. Simpson trial lessened but did not end the fascination it had for the American people. Not only did it lay bare the now-undeniable gulf between black and white Americans and raise troubling questions about the country's police forces, but it had its resonance overseas as well.

In the U.S. the Republican Party took control of both houses of Congress for the first time in 40 years and began an attack on the past 60 years of American domestic politics. It remained to be seen, of course, whether the Republicans could consolidate their self-proclaimed revolution or would simply remind voters, in the words of one wag, of the reasons they kept them out for so long. The Republican speaker of the House of Representatives, Newt Gingrich, had become so unpopular by the end of the year that he was taking a determinedly low profile in the fierce struggles over the budget.

One of the centrepieces of the Republican agenda was the "Contract with America," and we thought it might be interesting to examine it from the standpoint of contract law. Attorney and author Nina Massen agreed to write a special report for us that discusses the fate of the contract, generally over the first 100 days of the new Congress. As the year ended, only three of the Contract's provisions had become law, and two major items—term limits for members of Congress and a constitutional amendment mandating a balanced budget—had been defeated.

In this year we perhaps could begin to see the outline of the new world that was replacing the world of the Cold War. In a special report on the 1946 *Britannica Book of the Year,* we use excerpts from that volume to see from their vantage point some things that the people of 1945 thought were important for the present and the future. More than that, we get a sense of how things seemed to those on the brink of a new age.

We too are on such a brink, and John Kenneth Galbraith gives us in his Commentary some thoughts on the new world. We trust these ideas will be as interesting in 50 years as they are now. Like those of 1945, the people of 2045 are in our thoughts, and perhaps your world too is changing radically. We hope that as you read this, you are well.

Of the things that happened this past year, we commissioned special reports on those that seemed most compelling, in addition to the "Contract with America" mentioned above. We explore the concept of cyberspace, examine the use of financial derivatives, review postmodernism in Latin-American literature, and look at the worldwide crisis in child care. In this year of the collapse of the venerable Barings PLC and the many troubles of Japan's Daiwa Bank Ltd., we have added a new regular report on U.S. and international banking.

This 1996 edition of the *Britannica Book of the Year* also contains coverage of individual topics, known in the publishing trade as sidebars. We examine the past year's developments and controversies on the plundering of art, ubiquitous infomercials, POGs, El Niño, the emergence of new viruses and the strange behaviour of familiar ones, the Smithsonian Institution and charges of historical revisionism, *Ebony* magazine after 50 years of publication, John Peters Humphrey, the new professionalism in sports, senior golf, the situation in sub-Saharan Africa, the UN Fourth World Conference on Women, and the participation of Vietnam in the global economy.

We also turn our spotlight on the Berbers of North Africa, the multilateral conflict over the Spratly Islands, the recent French elections, secularism in South Asia, the crises in Mexico, communism's legacy of pollution in Eastern Europe, and the move by Native Americans to retain or regain their cultural legacies.

The Sports and Games section has been rearranged to include the Sporting Record tables from the *Micropædia,* which we update each year and which had heretofore been included in a separate section. For the first time, then, all sports reports and their appropriate tables will be available in the same place. We added new tables for Australian rules football, Latin-American baseball, and sumo wrestling, and we are covering once more events of the year in archery, curling, and fencing.

This is my debut volume as editor of the *Britannica Book of the Year,* and I would like to use the editor's privilege to thank all of those at Britannica who have done such a splendid job of producing it. You now hold in your hands the best 1996 *Britannica Book of the Year* we could provide. I trust you will enjoy and profit by it.

Glenn M. Edwards, Editor

CONTENTS

Oklahoma City bombed by terrorists, page 21

Cal Ripken sets record, page 302

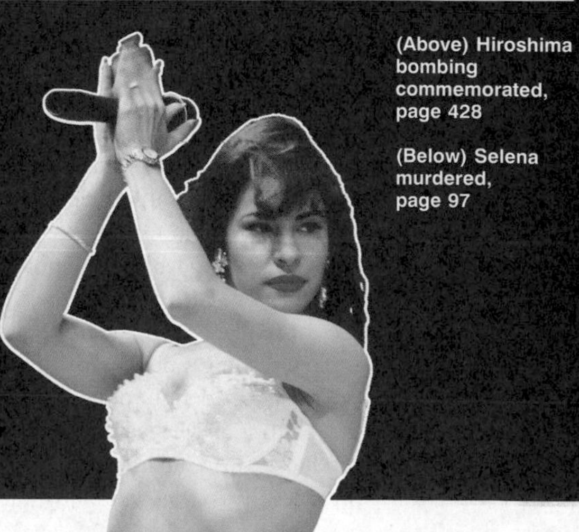

(Above) Hiroshima bombing commemorated, page 428

(Below) Selena murdered, page 97

The musical drama *Broken Birds* premieres, page 264

The Outlines of an Emerging World

by John Kenneth Galbraith

SEBASTIÃO SALGADO

Looking back on 1995, I am led to reflect, first of all, on the larger currents of history that have a controlling influence in these times, including the year just past. The first of these is the continuing effect of the release from the international tension that after World War II, a full half century ago, came to be called the Cold War. This, in turn, has given time for attention to the myriad of lesser conflicts, foreign and domestic, that afflict the modern world. Once these would have been assigned a lesser, even minor role except as they might bear on the larger confrontation. They have now come to bulk large in thought and expression.

Two world focal points in 1995 were former Yugoslavia and the impoverished peoples of Africa. There was also the continuing tension in the former republics of the Soviet Union, most notably in Chechnya, and, in lesser measure, in Mexico and Haiti. One is led, first of all, to consider the causes of conflict.

The most obvious of these is the continuing righteous and angry assertion of ethnic, religious, racial, and national identity. Even in the rich countries—in Western Europe and the United States, on the Pacific Rim, and notably in Canada—these conflicts exist. Race, however denied by many citizens, is still a source of continuing and bitter dissension in the United States, on which I will have a later word. In Canada there is continuing debate and action involving Quebec separatism and the French language, which was temporarily decided in 1995 but remains wholly unresolved. In Western Europe there is assertion of national identity and difference and, in particular, an adverse reaction to the large numbers of foreign workers who staff the industrial establishments and otherwise do the work to which native-born sons and daughters are no longer inclined or for which they are unavailable.

The singular aspect of this tension and conflict is that in the fortunate countries it is contained. Relative well-being, one cannot doubt, is a major solvent of social tension. Well-off people become angry, but not to the extent of jeopardizing their comfort. So it is between the rich countries, and so within them. In the United States it is taken for granted

John Kenneth Galbraith is well known not only as one of the major economists of the 20th century but also as an energetic crusader for liberal causes. Currently the Paul M. Warburg professor of economics, emeritus, at Harvard University, he also has held a number of U.S. governmental positions ranging from department administrator in the Office of Price Administration during World War II to adviser to Pres. John F. Kennedy and ambassador to India. Professor Galbraith consequently has been able to advance the study of economics, explain the field to those who are not specialists, and implement policies based on his extensive knowledge. He is a prolific author whose books include American Capitalism *(1952),* Almost Everyone's Guide to Economics *(1978), and* A Short History of Financial Euphoria *(1993).*

that the better sections of the cities and the affluent suburbs will be peaceful and benign. Disorder and crime are the bitter legacy of the impoverished, usually relegated to the central cities.

I would like to offer here a general guide to the larger world polity of 1995. The rich and the modestly affluent nations were at peace, not only internally but also with each other. There was still tension in the Middle East, culminating as the year came to a close in the cruel and senseless murder of Yitzhak Rabin. This was a deep, unforgivable tragedy to which the leaders and peoples of the whole world responded, not because Rabin was a leader in war but because he was a force for peace. It was in the relatively poor countries of the Balkans, in the poverty-ridden countries of Africa, in the poorest state of Mexico, and among the Kurds in Turkey and Iraq that deprivation, fighting, and death were commonplace.

Although in and between the fortunate countries there was peace, there were also defining crises leading to political tensions. In the United States there were two such crises: there was a major renewal and deepening of the issue of race, and there was a strong reaction against the seemingly solid benefits and services of the welfare state. Each calls for a comment.

The prime focus of the question of race in the United States in 1995 was the televised O.J. Simpson trial, continuing from the previous year and ending with his exceptionally prompt acquittal. This raised the question whether the criminal justice system could be overridden by racial consciousness and commitment, especially when intensified by the incompetent and deeply prejudicial behaviour of the police.

The other factor bringing race onto the national scene was, in substantial and even encouraging measure, the social and economic gains of the African-American community. Once, and indeed until relatively recent times, blacks lived in silent anonymity in the rural South or in enclaves in New York City, Chicago, Detroit, Mich., and other large cities. There was peace because they were not seen. In recent times and strongly manifest in 1995 was the emerging economic, political, and social strength of the black community. In consequence of this, where there was once indifference in the white community, there was now a sense of competition, even economic fear. Affirmative action programs were seen as enhancing this competition—as taking employment from white job seekers. This was not an issue when blacks were sharecroppers or menials in the big cities. So, while definitely not recognized as such, the black and white tension evident in 1995 was a mark of social and civilized progress. The deeper improvement in race relations had its more superficial price.

Rwandan refugees, driven to a camp in neighbouring Zaire by vicious fighting between Hutu and Tutsi, prepare to return to their homes. It was in the Balkans and in parts of Africa in 1995 that the world saw the most violent conflicts arising out of ethnic and religious differences.

RADHIKA CHALASANI—GAMMA LIAISON

The greatly publicized case, of course, was former Yugoslavia. Here the ethnic, religious, and territorial commitments were especially deep—some of many centuries' standing. These people sacrificed a modest well-being for the deprivation of many or all. This, and the efforts to bring peace there, dominated the headlines of the year. There were times when one read or heard the news from the Balkans and all but wished for the stable relationships of the Cold War.

But the Balkans were not, in fact, the worst case of the year. That was in Africa, in Rwanda, Burundi, and neighbouring Zaire, with the residual effects of conflict in Somalia and Liberia. There starvation, so far from being an episodic affliction, was the norm. Out of poverty came the forces of disorder and conflict that ensured further poverty—and death. Here, more than anywhere else in the world, was the dark side of 1995.

When Americans were not watching the Simpson trial in Los Angeles or the "Million Man March" on Washington, D.C., they were the silent, approving, or concerned audience for the great political revolt in Washington—the attack on government as a social instrument, more generally on the welfare state. And, as ever, Americans saw the manifestation of extremist popular attitudes, one appalling example being the bombing of the federal office building in Oklahoma City, Okla. In other countries of the industrial world—in Canada and France and in some measure in Germany, Spain, Italy, and The Netherlands—the welfare state was also, at least marginally, under siege. The United States was, as usual, the extreme case. A new Congress, led by young Republican radicals, came to power in Washington in January 1995. There was no reticence as to their aim. Welfare legislation—health care, regulatory restraints, varied government services, and, above all, aid to the poor—was to be rolled back. The word *capitalism* being no longer politically quite correct, the *market system,* in the preferred reference, was to be accorded its pristine freedom and power.

The problem was not that simple. Much welfare legislation, it was being discovered, was the offspring of history, not of politics or ideology. Once the poor in the United States, as observed earlier, were invisible as long as they stayed on the sharecropper plantations of the South or deep in the valleys of the Appalachian Plateau. It was their movement to the cities and away from their primitive sources of support that made welfare, education, crime, law enforcement, and much else public issues and the basis for public action. Once, a predominantly farm population had little need for Social Security and unemployment compensation. On the farm the next generation took care of the one before. Times could be bad, and often were, but there was no unemployment on a farm. Health care, until relatively recent times, was wonderfully inexpensive because the local doctor had very little to sell. It was the enormous advances in medicine and surgery that made health care an issue. The costs of keeping people alive could now range from considerable to huge, and a civilized society, or one with such claim, could not allow people to be sick and die merely because they had no money. From this came the intense debate over health care and how to pay for it. The problem was thought to have been given by ideology; in fact, it was the result of the great thrust of history.

In the modern economy and polity inflation is more feared than unemployment, and a reserve army of the unemployed, to use an old Marxian phrase, is now seen as a protection against price increases.

So it was with much of the political debate this past year in the United States Congress, and this fact goes far to explain why the oratory so far has substantially exceeded the action. What was readily seen as a revolt against costly and intrusive government became, on closer examination, a reaction to larger forces not easy and, indeed, on occasion not possible to reverse.

The year 1995 was also one in which narrower economic issues became obtrusively evident. In general, with Japan being somewhat of an exception, it was a time of favourable economic performance. Economic growth, as it is called—the broad increase in the production of goods and the rendering of services—was generally favourable. Prices were mostly stable. But there were also some very dark spots on the world economic scene.

The darkest was in the former communist countries, notably Russia. Here it was still being discovered that the transition to a market system was far more difficult, far more cruel, than once imagined. A poor economic system, defective especially in its meeting of the varied and changing needs of consumers, was replaced in some measure by no system at all. Instead, there were idle factories, badly disorganized agriculture and food supply, continuing if less severe inflation, and a new entrepreneurial class deeply and profitably committed to forthright crime and corruption.

The economic disorder in Russia and its political consequences cast the blackest shadows on the world scene. When World War II ended, the winning nations, led by the United States, united in a major effort at repair and reconstruction. It was wonderfully successful for both victors and vanquished. Alas, the end of the Cold War brought no such effort, invoked no such generosity, no such intelligence. In international affairs increasing intelligence cannot be assumed.

Within the fortunate countries in 1995, two economic factors were a lasting reason for concern. One was the continuing high and enduring level of unemployment in the United States and Canada and, notably, in Europe. This has two causes, neither as yet fully recognized and appreciated. There is, first, the fact that in the modern economy and polity inflation is more feared than unemployment, and a reserve army of the unemployed, to use an old Marxian phrase, is now seen as a protection against price increases. Second, the modern welfare state has within its structure factors that are adverse to worker employment. Each of these matters needs to be examined.

The modern economy and polity has a very large number of people living on fixed or more or less stable incomes and also a big minority who have bank savings or other fixed-income assets. To these, inflation, even a mild increase in prices, is a most unwelcome expropriation. Thus the fear of inflation as it affects a large and articulate community. And thus the acceptance of unemployment, which is now seen as a necessary stabilizing force against the wage increases that might, in turn, drive up prices. We have come close to saying and often now do say that a too great reduction in unemployment is economically adverse, even dangerous. It may be asked if this is not a cruel resolution of a difficult situation: idle workers suffering the pain and deprivation of idleness as a stabilizing factor in the economy. It is, but for a fairly obvious reason: inflation is feared by a wide, articulate, and influential public. Unemployment is suffered by an anonymous and relatively inarticulate community. It is for someone else.

The other cause of unemployment is deep in the modern structure of the welfare state. This places on the employer a substantial labour cost in addition to wages, the provision of pension and health benefits in particular but other costs as well. These costs can be lessened by not hiring new workers and by resorting to overtime, temporary workers, or labour-saving technology. In the modern factory the computer and the machinery it controls do to industrial workers what the tractor once did to the horse. The time may well come when more of the welfare costs now placed upon the employer will have to be taken over by the state. The cost of hiring a new worker will not have to be so severely calculated. But that is for the future.

There is an undoubted tendency for an economist to dwell on the controlling role of economics in larger life. Causation is still large in all economic thought. This is not wholly an error. Economic well-being allows, as it always has allowed, opportunity for the higher orders of life. The visual arts have always been the particular opportunity and pleasure of the affluent. So also the theatre, music, and entertainment in general. A strong current of effort has sought, never without success, to find artistic expression in the work and attitudes of the poor. Thus the past and continuing celebration of the folk arts, as they are sometimes compulsively called. This is good, but the larger fact remains: the arts flourish, and from ancient times have flourished, when sustaining well-being and wealth are available. The Medicis would not still be known to us had they been poor. Shakespeare lived a life of more than modest well-being.

So it is now in a greatly diversified fashion. In the year just passed, a major, even dominant discussion was of music and entertainment, much of it centring, needless to say, on music groups and on television. Heavily involved as they are with sex and violence, music and television were thought to be deeply damaging to the young, who are enthusiastic listeners and viewers. The discussion is one that I, at least, have listened to with a certain detachment. Whatever the adverse effects, they are almost certainly less than those from any efforts at control. The remarkable fact, indeed, is how intense is the discussion of contemporary music and television and how little emerges by way of action. For better or worse, a society with the income and leisure that allows for a major indulgence of entertainment and the arts must all too evidently accept the defective or allegedly damaging along with the good.

Students at the University of California, San Francisco, protest the decision to end affirmative action programs in higher education. This was seen as one of many indications that racial divisions were deepening in the U.S.

LISA QUINONES—BLACK STAR

To any discussion of entertainment and the arts, one must add a word on the economic change and development of which they are a part. Once, and in all orthodox discussion, economics was concerned with the production of things—of food, clothing, steel, automobiles. So, in much thought, it remains. The true worker is the man on the assembly line. That is industry.

With economic development this is no longer the case. As the production and consumption of goods expand, attention turns to design and also to the means of persuading people to buy. Here enters the artist or, in any case, someone with artistic instinct. Design was the basis of the great economic success of Italy in the years after World War II. Italian products became synonymous with good design. Automobiles and shoes had Italian names. There was no Nebraska, Dakota, or Jones.

But that is only the beginning. After products please as to design and are duly advertised and promoted, itself a large occupation, people go on to entertainment, which becomes a centrally important industry. We are reluctant to admit it, but no country can compete with the United States in the production of television programs, often, no doubt, morally depraved. We do not like to think of entertainment as a solidly based industry such as a steel mill. However, it is inherent in economic advance, as are also, at an undoubtedly higher level, painting, sculpture, architectural design, the fine arts generally, and, I hasten to add, health care. When we view the economic life of 1995, our attention should be as much on the arts and entertainment and the health industry as on industrial production, including its technological advances. We reflect regularly and even compulsively on the workers replaced by robots and computers; we do not reflect on the number who have moved onward, and most would say upward, to the higher claims of employment and enjoyment.

I conclude with the most discussed, most publicized technological development of the year and the time. Its words and phrases are with us every day—the Internet, the information superhighway, the information revolution. We are to be informed as never before; much of the means by which we once communicated is on its way to obsolescence. I personally have read this and listened with attention, but I am not completely impressed. Others will respond with more enthusiasm.

In modern times our problem has not been in conveying information. It has been in providing the original knowledge and in deciding what is good, bad, or purely fraudulent. That problem remains. So, I think, it will.

And so will the basic means for communicating knowledge. When I need some information, my first thought is still of a book—and the library. When I have an inquiry, I still turn first to the telephone. The latter has served with improvement but no basic change for rather more than a century; books have survived for far longer. They will endure the information revolution; they will not be lost on that superhighway. The problem will still be finding the relevant and sorting out the true from the false. Our problem, to repeat, is not a shortage of information or in its transfer. It is in deciding what is useful and what is right.

Chronicle of 1995

1

Cardoso assumes office

Having won some 54% of the ballots cast in the October 1994 election, Fernando Cardoso took the oath of office as president of Brazil. As chief executive of South America's largest nation, Cardoso was committed to bringing inflation under control and revitalizing the economy through foreign investments and expanded trade. Before seeking the presidency, Cardoso had served both as foreign minister and as minister of finance.

2

Mercosur to expand

One day after the Southern Cone Common Market (Mercosur) had become operational, Chile and Bolivia approved plans to seek membership in the trade organization, which presently included Argentina, Brazil, Paraguay, and Uruguay. More than 90% of the goods that were traded within the market would be exempt from tariffs, and standardized tariffs would be imposed on imports from countries that were outside the Mercosur trade zone.

3

AIDS cases increase

The World Health Organization (WHO) announced that the number of AIDS cases reported to its headquarters in Geneva had officially passed the one million mark. WHO officials, however, believed that the actual number of cases was probably four times that number because many cases had not been properly diagnosed and others went unreported. The most severely affected area was Africa, where more than 70% of the cases were thought to exist. Statistics indicated that 9% of the cases occurred in the United States, 9% in other parts of the Western Hemisphere, 6% in Asia, 4% in Europe, and 2% in other parts of the world. On January 30 the U.S. Centers for Disease Control and Prevention reported that in 1993 AIDS had become the leading cause of death for both American men and women 25–44 years old.

•

Cease-fire in Sri Lanka

The Liberation Tigers of Tamil Eelam and the government of Sri Lanka agreed to suspend hostilities on January 8 while a new effort was made to end the 12-year-old civil conflict. The Tiger rebels were promised $800 million in economic aid to help reverse the effects of the economic sanctions and trade embargoes that had been imposed on them by previous administrations. The Tamils, who were mostly Hindus in a predominantly Buddhist country, comprised 18% of the total population. They had taken up arms to secure autonomy for a homeland in the northern and northeastern regions of the country.

Kenyan children stand beneath an AIDS-prevention poster. In a report on January 3, the World Health Organization stated that some 70% of all AIDS cases were found in Africa.

WENDY STONE—GAMMA LIAISON

4

PDP to govern Uzbekistan

The national election committee in Uzbekistan reported that according to incomplete returns, members of the People's Democratic (former Communist) Party of Uzbekistan would form a solid majority in the 250-seat Supreme Assembly. The National Progress Party, which participated in the election with the approval of Pres. Islam Karimov, was the only other party that had been allowed to nominate candidates for the Dec. 25, 1994, election. Nonetheless, nonparty candidates captured 20 seats, and the Progress of the Fatherland party, which advocated accelerated economic reforms, won 6 seats. Karimov's decision to allow token political opposition was apparently prompted by a desire to have the nation's first post-Soviet election viewed abroad as a multiparty contest.

6

France annoys allies

Following a meeting in Paris with Iraqi Deputy Prime Minister Tariq Aziz, French Foreign Minister Alain Juppé announced that his country would resume limited diplomatic ties with Iraq. Relations had soured because French troops had been part of the successful UN-sponsored military force that defeated Iraq after its attempt to annex Kuwait in 1990. The U.S. and Great Britain vigorously opposed France's decision because Iraq was still in violation of UN Security Council resolutions and under an oil embargo. France, however, reportedly hoped that improved relations with Iraq now would help secure for France a major role in rebuilding that nation's oil industry when the time was ripe. Before the Persian Gulf War, the two countries had been major trading partners.

8

Use of CFZ curtailed

The Australian Cotton Foundation announced that the nation's cotton industry would suspend use of the chemical pesticide chlorfluazuron (CFZ) until further studies had been completed. Although CFZ was considered to have low toxicity, the U.S. and Japan had banned the importation of Australian beef in 1994 after learning that some cattle had been fed cotton waste contaminated with the chemical.

10

Rubin replaces Benson

The U.S. Senate unanimously approved (99–0) the appointment of Robert Rubin as secretary of the treasury. The former cochairman of Goldman, Sachs & Co. investment bank had won wide respect as chairman of the National Economic Council, which Pres. Bill Clinton had created. In that capacity he had coordinated the economic policies of various White House and federal agencies and was the chief architect of the government's federal deficit-reduction program.

11

Refugees to go home

Germany revealed that Vietnam had finally agreed to accept the return of some 40,000 of its citizens residing illegally in Germany. The 55,000 Vietnamese who had earlier acquired legal residence in Germany would not be affected. Following the

A man walks through the rubble of a building that collapsed in the January 17 earthquake that struck the Kobe area, one of the most densely populated parts of Japan. The earthquake killed about 6,000 people, and it was estimated that in all some 100,000 buildings were destroyed.

PHILLIP J. GRIFFITHS—MAGNUM

reunification of Germany in 1990, nearly 40% of the 155,000 Vietnamese then living in Germany had voluntarily returned to their native land. For agreeing to accept the returnees, Vietnam would receive more than $65 million in development funds and an equal amount in export credit guarantees.

•

Cubans to leave Panama

Pentagon officials announced that 3,000 soldiers would be sent to Panama and Cuba to reinforce security while some 8,000 Cuban refugees, who were confined in Panamanian camps, were transferred to the U.S. Guantánamo Bay Naval Base in Cuba. More than 21,000 Cubans were already housed there. The U.S. sought to minimize the possibility of violent resistance because the refugees had long hoped to join friends and relatives in Florida.

12

British patrols trimmed

Sir Hugh Annesley, head of security in Northern Ireland, announced that British troops would no longer accompany the Royal Ulster Constabulary on daytime patrols in Belfast after January 15. During peace talks with British officials, Sinn Fein, the political arm of the Irish Republican Army, had repeatedly demanded that the troops leave Northern Ireland. Encouraged by the fact that a five-month-old cease-fire was holding firm, Annesley expressed hope that British troops would also, in time, be withdrawn from night patrols.

13

Dini to govern Italy

Lamberto Dini became Italy's prime minister-designate three weeks after Silvio Berlusconi resigned under fire. The new head of government, who took the oath of office on January 17, was expected to use his extensive knowledge of banking and finance to stabilize Italy's financial markets. Berlusconi indicated that his powerful Forza Italia party was prepared to give Dini and his politically neutral Cabinet short-term support while the government initiated political and election reforms. Dini suggested that these goals could be reached within a few months.

•

Wolves returned to park

Eight North American gray wolves were returned to Yellowstone National Park under a provision of the Endangered Species Act. Four others were scheduled to be set free in a wilderness area of Idaho. Ranchers, fearful that the wolves would attack their sheep and cattle, had successfully impeded implementation of the government program until a federal court in Colorado permitted the restoration to begin.

15

Pope arrives in Manila

Pope John Paul II celebrated the Roman Catholic Church's 10th World Youth Day in Manila with a public mass attended by an estimated four million people. The gathering was twice as large as the one that welcomed the pontiff when he returned home to Cracow, Poland, in 1979. During his 33,500-km (20,800-mi) tour, John Paul also visited Papua New Guinea, Australia, and Sri Lanka. Buddhist leaders in Sri Lanka, offended by written remarks the pope had made about Buddhism's "perfect indifference to the world," declined to meet the pope, who ended the 63rd overseas journey of his pontificate on January 21.

•

Niger vote challenged

The state radio in Niger reported that the four opposition parties had won a total of 42 of the 83 seats in the national legislature in the election held on January 12. The five parties supporting Pres. Mahamane Ousmane captured 40 seats, with the remaining seat going to the candidate of an independent party. Because Ousmane's backers claimed that the balloting had been fraudulent, it was not immediately clear who would fill the post of prime minister.

17

Quake devastates Kobe

Kobe, Japan's sixth largest city and one of the country's most vital ports, suffered immense damage when a powerful early-morning earthquake occurred about 10 km (6 mi) beneath Awaji Island in Osaka Bay. The Great Hanshin Earthquake—the worst since the 1923 temblor that leveled Tokyo—killed about 6,000 people, injured more than 30,000, and left more than 300,000 homeless. The collapse of elevated highways and major buildings severely impeded efforts to reach the victims. The government later acknowledged that its initial response to the crisis was slow and inadequate. Final estimates of the damage were about $150 billion, approximately one-fifth of Japan's 1994 national budget.

18

Ancient cave art found

French Minister of Culture and Francophone Affairs Jacques Toubon confirmed that cave paintings and engravings believed to be 17,000–20,000 years old had been discovered near the town of Vallon-Pont-d'Arc in southern France in December 1994. (Late in the year scientists estimated that the art work was more likely some 30,000 years old.) The find had been kept secret until the site could be physically and legally protected. Archaeologists reported that the drawings rivaled in importance the prehistoric art previously found in Spain and France. The newly discovered art treasures included the first known Paleolithic depictions of a panther, a hyena, and owls.

•

Algerians still at odds

A plan drawn up by militant Islamists to end the three-year-old civil strife in Algeria was rejected by the government because, among other things, it called for the recognition of the outlawed Islamic Salvation Front. The seeds of violence had been sown in January 1992 when the government canceled the second round of elections that would almost certainly have given the Muslims a majority in the National People's Assembly and paved the way for the establishment of an Islamic state. On January 30 a car bomb was detonated near the main police station in Algiers, the capital; 42 persons were killed and nearly 300 injured.

21

Mubarak visits Jordan

Egyptian Pres. Hosni Mubarak traveled to Jordan, where he and King Hussein reaffirmed the friendship that had traditionally marked the relationship between their two nations. It was the first time the two leaders had met since tensions developed over Jordan's support for Iraqi Pres. Saddam Hussein during the Persian Gulf War. Egypt and Jordan, however, had come to recognize that they had much in common: both had signed peace treaties with Israel, and both had discussed with Syrian Pres. Hafez al-Assad his refusal to establish diplomatic relations with Israel until it abandoned the occupied Golan Heights. On January 30 Israel withdrew its forces from a desert area south of the Dead Sea and thereby restored Jordanian sovereignty over the territory. The transfer of authority satisfied one more element of the peace treaty that the two nations had signed.

•

Eritrea backs U.S. role

After arriving in the U.S. for a two-week visit, Isaias Afwerki, president of the newly (1993) independent nation of Eritrea, told reporters that the U.S. had to continue its policy of active involvement in African affairs despite the problems it had encountered in its mission to Somalia. Many African nations, he said, needed U.S. financial and diplomatic assistance in order to maintain peace, foster democracy, and alleviate poverty.

28

Turmoil in Sierra Leone

Officials in Guinea reported that as many as 30,000 refugees had entered their country from neighbouring Sierra Leone when rebel troops attacked the town of Kambia. The Revolutionary United Front, led by Foday Sankoh, had been attacking the government from bases inside Liberia since 1991. According to officials of the UN World Food Programme, nearly one-fifth of Sierra Leone's 4.6 million people had been forced to flee their homes because of the fighting. At the end of 1993, the military government had announced a schedule to return the country to civilian rule. Voters were to be registered, a new constitution drawn up, and general elections held after the election of a president in November 1995. The fighting, however, continued.

30

Floods inundate Europe

Sections of Belgium, France, Germany, and The Netherlands were under a state of emergency after torrential rains and melting Alpine snow buried vast expanses of northwestern Europe under spreading sheets of water. One measure of the disaster was provided by the Rhine River, which crested at a point not seen since the 18th century. The Dutch found themselves in an especially perilous situation because so much of the land reclaimed from the sea lies below sea level. More than 100,000 people had to be evacuated from land lying between the Waal and Meuse rivers.

31

UN to bypass ex-leaders

A spokesman for UN Secretary-General Boutros Boutros-Ghali announced that neither of the two living former heads of the organization would be invited to attend the 50th-anniversary celebration in the U.S. The decision prevented a possible confrontation with the U.S. Department of Justice, which barred Kurt Waldheim from U.S. soil. Waldheim, an Austrian who directed the UN from 1972 to 1981, had served in a German army unit that had been accused of war crimes in the Balkans during World War II. Boutros-Ghali's decision meant that his immediate predecessor, Javier Pérez de Cuéllar of Peru, would also be absent from the official celebration.

AP/WIDE WORLD

Newly found cave paintings in France depict a Stone Age menagerie that includes bears, bison, mammoths, and woolly rhinoceroses. The discovery was announced only after the site, accessible only from the Mediterranean Sea, had been secured.

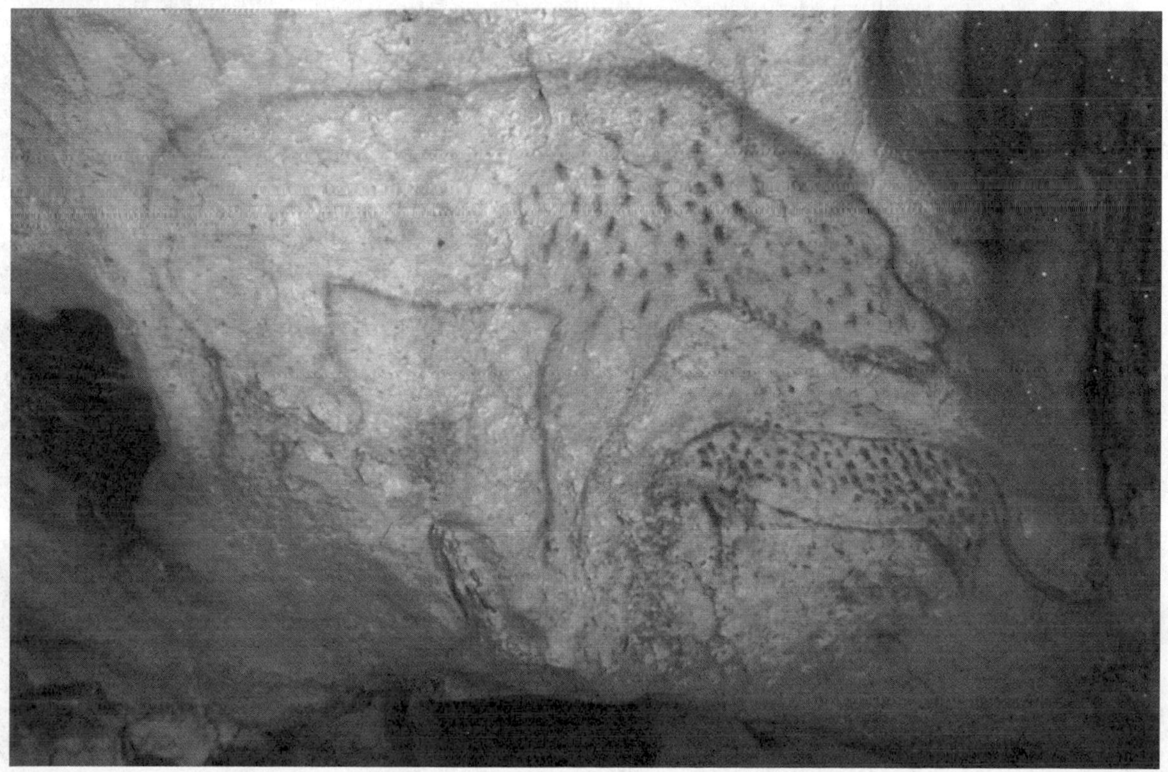

(LEFT) FORREST ANDERSON; (BELOW) MASAO ENDO—SABA

(Left) Chinese look over pirated CDs in Beijing, an example of the copyright violations that led the U.S. to threaten tariffs on selected Chinese exports. (Below) A member of the Taleban, a mostly student army of religious fundamentalists, stands guard in Afghanistan after the group's refusal to join in negotiations helped doom an accord announced on February 11.

1

Report on human rights

John Shattuck, head of the human rights section of the U.S. State Department, discussed with reporters the just-released U.S. annual report on the observance of human rights in 160 countries. As in past years, the report, which covered calendar year 1994, denounced the "flagrant and systematic abuses of basic human rights" that took place under the regimes controlling Cuba, Iran, Iraq, North Korea, and Myanmar (Burma). China was singled out for special condemnation for its "widespread and well-documented human rights abuses." In unusually harsh language, the report deplored China's use of "arbitrary and lengthy incommunicado detention, torture, and mistreatment of prisoners." The report also cited unfair trials, labour camps, and suppression of free speech.

3

New wage rate proposed

President Clinton proposed that over a period of two years the minimum wage be increased to $5.15 an hour from the current $4.25. In terms of real buying power, Clinton said, a minimum wage of $4.25 in 1996 would place the hourly wage at its lowest level in 40 years. He argued that if the nation hoped to reform the welfare system successfully, employment would have to be made more attractive. Many Republicans vigorously opposed Clinton's plan on the grounds that numerous businesses were striving to control costs and that mandatory wage increases would result in untold numbers losing their jobs. An estimated 4.2 million workers were currently earning the minimum wage.

4

China facing high tariffs

Mickey Kantor, the chief U.S. trade representative, announced that the Clinton administration would impose punitive tariffs as high as 100% on a wide variety of Chinese goods effective February 26. During long negotiations China had rejected U.S. demands that effective measures be taken to end the flagrant pirating of copyrighted U.S. intellectual property, notably computer software, movies, and music. China reacted to Kantor's announcement by imposing similar tariffs on imports from the U.S. A trade war, however, was averted at the last minute when China, after 11 more days of intense bargaining in Beijing, agreed to launch a serious crackdown on the pirating and marketing of material protected by international and domestic copyrights. Though pleased, U.S. business leaders cautioned that the problem would be solved only if China implemented the agreement.

7

Pakistan extradites suspect

Ramzi Ahmed Yousef, believed to have masterminded the Feb. 26, 1993, bombing of the World Trade Center in New York City, was arrested by police in Islamabad, Pak. The FBI had offered a $2 million reward for his capture. The following day Yousef was extradited to New York, where he faced charges of having purchased and prepared the chemicals used in the bombing and of actually having helped to put the bomb in place. In 1994 four other Islamic terrorists had been convicted of conspiracy in the case. Each was sentenced to 240 years in prison.

•

Oleksy to lead Poland

Warned by Polish Pres. Lech Walesa that he would dissolve the Sejm (parliament) unless Waldemar Pawlak, a member of the Polish Peasant Party, was replaced as prime minister, the ruling two-party coalition government nominated Jozef Oleksy, a member of the Democratic Left Alliance, head of government. Walesa had grown impatient with Pawlak's slow implementation of economic reforms, but it was not certain how much or how quickly the situation would change under Oleksy. The party that he represented had formerly been the Communist Party, and it already dominated the ruling coalition.

8

Peacekeepers enter Angola

With Jonas Savimbi, leader of the rebel National Union for the Total Independence of Angola (UNITA), showing a new willingness to terminate the civil war in Angola, the UN Security Council voted unanimously to dispatch 7,000 peacekeeping troops to the area. In 1992 a UN-sponsored presidential election had been expected to restore order and stability to the country, but UNITA refused to accept the election results. Two years later, when Pres. José Eduardo dos Santos' Popular Movement for the Liberation of Angola (MPLA) and UNITA came together to sign their third peace agreement since 1989, Savimbi failed to appear. Santos then also declined to

sign the document. The first critical test of the new peace initiative would come when rebel troops were scheduled to report to quartering areas and give up their arms. Because Savimbi had recently confessed to UNITA associates that their cause was all but lost, there was a feeling of optimism that the civil strife was coming to an end. The conflict had claimed some 500,000 lives since Angola won independence from Portugal in 1975.

11

Afghan foes compromise

A UN mediator in the Afghan civil war reported that most of the militias had agreed to establish a multiparty council that would hold temporary power until a new government structure had been created. Pres. Burhanuddin Rabbani, who had reportedly dismissed earlier demands that he resign, advanced the fragile peace effort by promising to step aside at an unspecified date. A brutal war had erupted in 1979 when Soviet troops invaded the country to preserve the communist regime. Unable to subdue the guerrillas, they withdrew in 1989. The fall of the communist government three years later was followed by bitter fighting between various Muslim groups, each vying for political ascendency.

14

New court in South Africa

Nelson Mandela, president of South Africa, and other dignitaries attended the formal inauguration of the country's first Constitutional Court. He and a panel of judges had selected seven whites, three blacks, and one Indian as Supreme Court justices. The chief justice would be Arthur Chaskalson, who had helped draft the nation's interim constitution. The court's first order of business would be to determine the constitutionality of the death penalty. The fate of 400 prisoners on death row would be decided when the 1990 moratorium on executions was rendered moot by the court's ruling.

•

Zürich drug market closed

Swiss police, responding to the complaints of residents in the once respectable Letten quarter of Zürich, began closing off the area, which had become an open market for illegal drugs. The government had chosen to abide the situation in the hope that social workers could help the addicts and inhibit the spread of AIDS by supplying clean needles to heroin users. Inexorably, the problem reached intolerable proportions as addicts from other parts of Switzerland—as well as foreigners—flocked to Letten. The police then cordoned off the market, which was an abandoned train depot, and detained hundreds of addicts and dealers. A similar situation had developed in 1992 in the Platzspitz public park in the centre of Zürich. When the police sealed off that area, the drug addicts moved across town.

17

Peru-Ecuador dispute ends

Three days after declaring a cease-fire in their three-week-old border war, Peru and Ecuador signed a peace accord that each side hailed as a victory. The remote 77-km (48-mi) stretch of land along their mountainous border had long been under dispute and would remain so until politicians, military personnel, and cartographers agreed on lines of demarcation. Meanwhile, international observers would oversee the demilitarization of the contested area.

•

U.S. trade deficit soars

The U.S. Commerce Department reported that the U.S. trade deficit in 1994 reached $108.1 billion, about 42% higher than in 1993. Analysts attributed the deficit mainly to the relatively stagnant economies of Japan and Europe, major U.S. trading partners, and a concomitant reluctance on the part of their citizens to seek U.S. products and services. A stronger U.S. economy, conversely, was an incentive for U.S. customers to make purchases more readily, including foreign goods and services. During 1994 the U.S. gross domestic product had grown at an inflation-adjusted rate of 4%, the highest it had been in 10 years.

18

NAACP gets new leader

By the margin of a single vote, the National Association for the Advancement of Colored People (NAACP) elected Myrlie Evers-Williams chairperson of its board. The widow of Medgar Evers, a civil rights activist slain in 1963, assumed the office at a critical time in the organization's history. Its debt had escalated beyond $4 million, and nearly half the board had wanted William Gibson, who had headed the board for 10 years and sought reelection, to continue in office. Evers-Williams said that her top priority, aside from seeking the help of those who had opposed her, was to find a new executive director to replace the Rev. Benjamin Chavis, Jr., who had been dismissed by the board in August 1994 after he had held the job for only 15 months. He had been accused of financial mismanagement, discrimination, and sexual harassment.

ANIBAL SOLIMANO—GAMMA LIAISON

Peruvian soldiers guard the border with Ecuador. On February 17, after three weeks of fighting, the two countries announced a cease-fire in their latest border skirmish.

FEBRUARY

19

Andreotti linked to Mafia

According to reports not yet made public, Gioacchino Pennino, a surgeon and confessed member of the Sicilian Mafia, was providing Italian authorities with evidence that Giulio Andreotti had close ties to the Mafia. The powerful politician, who was under intense investigation, had been prime minister seven times and held the post of foreign minister for six years. The dramatic testimony being given by Pennino, who had been arrested in Croatia in 1994, was said to include direct and persuasive evidence of collusion between Cosa Nostra and prominent politicians and professionals. About 70% of those polled after listening to Andreotti's two-hour defense on television said that they found his explanations unconvincing. On March 2 he was formally indicted and ordered to stand trial in September.

21

Mexico accepts aid terms

Faced with virtually no other alternative, Mexico accepted the tough terms the United States had set down as conditions for receiving an aid package worth $20 billion. The International Monetary Fund, which insisted on the same conditions, agreed to disburse an additional $17.8 billion. The Swiss-based Bank for International Settlements also pledged a substantial contribution. All told, Mexico would receive $52 billion from foreign sources. The money was intended principally to stabilize Mexico's peso and prevent the country from defaulting on its debt. To secure the financial help it needed, Mexico agreed, among other things, to post the revenues of its state-owned oil company as collateral and to reduce government spending.

•

Military shake-up in Haiti

Haitian Pres. Jean-Bertrand Aristide purged the nation's military leadership by forcing 43 senior officers into retirement. With the removal of all four army generals and others of high rank who were in uniform when the military ousted Aristide in 1991, the armed forces were effectively brought under civilian control. The army, which was simultaneously reduced to a force of only 1,500 soldiers, had earned a reputation for brutality and corruption.

•

Sandinista loses post

During a formal ceremony in Managua, Nicaragua, Gen. Joaquin Cuadra replaced Gen. Humberto Ortega, a Sandinista, as commander in chief of the armed forces. After Violeta Barrios de Chamorro ousted the Sandinista government by defeating Daniel Ortega Saavedra in the 1990 presidential election, she allowed the Sandinistas a share of power by confirming General Ortega (the former president's brother) as head of the military. With the delicate period of political readjustment behind her, Chamorro gave her blessing to the removal of the last Sandinista to hold a position of significant power in the country.

24

Iran to get reactors

After two days of intense discussions in Washington, D.C., Russian officials refused to reverse their decision to build four nuclear reactors in Iran. Even though the units were designed for commercial use, the U.S. insisted that such facilities could be used to produce nuclear weapons. Russia's determination to fulfill the contract, worth nearly $1 billion in hard currency, elicited a warning from Speaker of the House Newt Gingrich and other members of Congress that U.S. aid to Russia could be drastically reduced or terminated unless the deal was voided.

25

Rebels bomb train in India

At least 22 soldiers and 5 civilians were killed when two bombs exploded on a passenger train traveling through Assam province, India. The soldiers were returning to their base after voting in the Manipur state election. Government officials tended to blame the terrorist attack on a tribal group that had been struggling for decades to gain an independent homeland. Despite a series of military offensives against their stronghold near the Myanmar (Burma) border, the rebels continued to present a formidable challenge to the government.

Mexican and U.S. officials sign an agreement guaranteeing loans to rescue the Mexican economy. On February 21 Mexico agreed to U.S. terms for the aid, including reduced spending.
TERRY ASHE—GAMMA LIAISON

26

Barings Bank collapses

Eddie George, governor of the Bank of England, stunned the financial world by announcing that Barings PLC, Britain's oldest merchant bank, was bankrupt. The venerable institution was destroyed virtually overnight when one of its British employees in Singapore lost over $1 billion through apparently unauthorized transactions in risky futures contracts. Peter Baring, chairman of the bank, which was founded in 1762, told the *Financial Times* that 1994 profits were expected to exceed $150 million. He also reassured Barings customers that none of them would suffer financial losses because of the bankruptcy. On March 1, six days after fleeing Singapore, 28-year-old Nicholas Leeson, the man held responsible for Barings' collapse, was traced to Frankfurt, Germany, where he was later detained by authorities.

•

Old treaty ends dispute

An Arabian Peninsula border conflict subsided when Saudi Arabia and Yemen reaffirmed the Treaty of at-Ta'if, which they had signed in 1934, and agreed to use it as a basis for settling a border dispute that had persisted for some 60 years. Meanwhile, both sides made pledges of nonaggression and promised to resolve their differences through negotiations. The 1934 treaty had demarcated the border running from the Red Sea to Najran, Saudi Arabia, but the rest of the 1,500-km (950-mi) border was never defined.

28

Denver airport opens

The world's most technologically sophisticated international airport finally opened outside Denver, Colo., some 16 months behind schedule. The 137-sq km (53-sq mi) facility was the first major U.S. airport opened to traffic since the Dallas-Fort Worth (Texas) International Airport began operations in 1974. Virtually everyone praised the new terminal's architecture, but many were unhappy with the $4.9 billion price tag—substanially more than the original estimated budget. Initially, the innovative but complex baggage-handling system was an embarrassing disaster as engineers sought ways to prevent the luggage from being damaged by the machinery. Those who were most critical of the project wondered why the city's Stapleton Airport could not have been expanded, at considerably less expense, to meet the region's air transportation needs for the foreseeable future.

2

Chinese test free speech

A group of 12 well-known Chinese intellectuals, including two former senior editors of the Communist Party's official *People's Daily,* urged the National People's Congress to use its constitutional powers to curb abuses by the police. It was the second time in less than a week that the group had used petitions to test the limits of free speech in China. Those who signed the petitions were also implicitly denouncing the monolithic influence of the Communist Party over all branches of government.

•

Scientists find top quark

Two teams of particle physicists, working independently and using different equipment at the Fermi National Accelerator Laboratory in Batavia, Ill., announced that their experiments had revealed the top quark, the last of six quarks that are believed to be the ultimate building blocks of all matter. The findings confirmed theories postulated in the 1960s, namely, that matter is made up of two kinds of fundamental particles: leptons, which include electrons, and six types of quarks. One of the teams measured the mass of the top quark at 176 GeV (billion electron volts); the other team, at 199 GeV. In view of the margin of error inherent in both measurements, scientists accepted the two reports as mutual confirmation.

3

UN ends Somalia mission

With a seven-nation UN force of 23 ships, 80 aircraft, and more than 14,000 soldiers ready to face any eventuality, the last 2,400 UN peacekeeping troops left Somalia. Several days earlier some 1,800 U.S. marines and 400 Italian soldiers had gone ashore to enhance security during the withdrawal. UN relief workers and persons associated with private organizations chose to remain in Somalia. In December 1992 the UN had launched a successful international effort to prevent massive starvation in the East African nation, but it was unable to establish a functioning government because it could not bring an end to factional fighting, most notably between forces loyal to Muhammad Farah Aydid and those supporting Ali Mahdi Muhammad.

•

War crimes revealed

During an interview published in *Pagina 12,* Adolfo Scilingo, a former commander in the Argentine navy, confessed that during the late 1970s he had been among those who murdered between 1,500 and 2,000 "dissidents." The doomed men, already in custody, were forced aboard aircraft, drugged, stripped, and then dumped into the ocean. Scilingo, who claimed that high-ranking naval officers had ordered the death flights, filed a formal complaint against the navy chief of staff for covering up the crimes. Between 1976 and 1983 some 10,000 Argentines were "disappeared." It was widely believed that they were killed by junta death squads. On March 28 Pres. Carlos Menem called for an end to public disclosures of atrocities committed during the country's "dirty war." Such things, he said, were best forgotten.

SCOTT D. PETERSON—GAMMA LIAISON

These soldiers, among the last UN troops to leave Somalia, board a plane on March 3. Although the effort to stave off mass starvation succeeded, attempts to restore political stability failed.

12

New Mormon president

The Church of Jesus Christ of Latter-day Saints, popularly known as the Mormon Church, elevated Gordon B. Hinckley to the status of president. He succeeded Howard Hunter, who had led the nine million-member church for only nine months before his death. Hinckley had initiated the Utah-based church's use of television and public relations to spread its religious message.

14

Thagard rides Soyuz rocket

After spending a year training near Moscow, Norman Thagard became the first U.S. astronaut ever to head for space aboard a Russian Soyuz rocket. He and two Russian companions were scheduled to spend two days in orbit before their capsule docked with Russia's *Mir* space station. The flight, which was hailed as historic because two former foes were now committed to a joint exploration of space, was launched from the former secret Baikonur Space Centre. Two momentous events at that site had inaugurated the Space Age: the 1957 launching of Sputnik, the first artificial Earth satellite; and the first manned spaceflight, by Yury Gagarin in 1961. U.S. pilot Gary Powers was shot down by the Soviets while on a supersecret mission to photograph the launch site in 1960.

17

Clinton and Adams meet

For the second time in as many days, President Clinton met with Gerry Adams, leader of Sinn Fein, the political arm of the outlawed Irish Republican Army (IRA). The cordiality that marked the meetings and Clinton's earlier decision to allow Adams to collect money in the U.S. infuriated British Prime Minister John Major. His government had insisted that it was critical to the peace process not only that the IRA observe the cease-fire, which was already in place, but that it also lay down its arms. While politicians wrangled, Catholics and Protestants in Armagh, Northern Ireland, were marching side by side in a St. Patrick's Day parade. That had not happened since "the troubles" began in Northern Ireland a quarter of a century earlier.

•

Singapore executes Filipino

Flor Contemplacion, a Filipino maid, was hanged in Singapore for the 1991 murders of another Filipino maid and a four-year-old Singaporean boy in her care. Although Contemplacion had confessed to the murders, her attorneys contended that she had been framed and that the confessions had been coerced. News of the execution sparked emotional demonstrations throughout the Philippines and focused attention on the often pitiful conditions of millions of other Filipino maids working overseas, some 75,000 of them in Singapore alone. On April 17 Philippine Foreign Minister Roberto Romulo was forced to resign for having failed to prevent the execution.

19

Finns replace government

Prime Minister Esko Aho, whose Centre Party had led Finland's four-party coalition government, lost his post when the Social Democratic Party (SDP) gained 15 seats in national parliamentary elections. The SDP's plurality of 63 seats in the 200-seat Eduskunta (parliament) guaranteed that Paavo Lipponen would be the leader of a new coalition government. The Centre Party's loss of 11 of its 55 seats was attributed to voter discontent over the nation's weak recovery from a long recession. During the campaign both leading candidates promised substantial reductions in the national budget and the introduction of other measures to hasten economic recovery.

20

Rabin to resume talks

A spokesman for Israeli Prime Minister Yitzhak Rabin announced that his government had no intention of changing its plans to resume talks with the Palestine Liberation Organization (PLO) or to prevent Palestinians from gradually returning to daytime jobs in Israel, even though two Israeli settlers had been killed in Hebron the previous day. Rabin chose not to condemn the murders publicly, however, apparently fearing that any harsh words would merely intensify public anger and create another obstacle on the road to peace. Rabin was clearly committed to implementing terms of the 1993 Israeli-PLO peace accord, which included a gradual extension of Palestinian self-rule in occupied Gaza and the West Bank, but in January he had suspended talks with the PLO and sealed Israel's border to the Palestinians after 21 Israelis were killed in a suicide-bomb attack.

•

Ukraine's debt eased

In an effort to help Ukraine inaugurate a program of economic reforms, Russia agreed to reschedule about 50% of the $4.4 billion it was owed. During its three years of independence since the breakup of the Soviet Union, Ukraine had accumulated some $7 billion in foreign debts and could no longer operate about 60% of its factories, in large part because its supply of natural gas had been cut off by Turkmenistan for nonpayment of bills. The rescheduling of Ukraine's debt, partly negotiated by the International Monetary Fund, extended the period over which various payments had to be made after a grace period of several years.

•

Gas attack panics Tokyo

In a coordinated operation, Japanese terrorists released sarin, a deadly nerve gas, on five Tokyo subway cars traveling three different lines at the height of the morning rush hour. Twelve persons were killed and more than 5,500 injured. Within a few days police had discovered incriminating evidence, including tons of chemicals used to produce nerve gas, at a training camp operated by Aum Shinrikyo, a religious sect. Its principal deity was Shiva, the Hindu god of destruction and regeneration. Intense efforts to track down Shoko Asahara, the founder and leader of Aum Shinrikyo, finally succeeded on May 16 when he was found hiding in the Aum compound in Kamikuishiki, Yamanashi prefecture.

•

Mandela welcomes queen

South African Pres. Nelson Mandela officially welcomed Queen Elizabeth II and Prince Philip to South Africa upon their arrival in Cape Town. It was the British queen's first visit since 1947, when as a princess she toured the African continent with other members of the royal family. The following year South Africa adopted apartheid, a policy of racial separation that was so widely criticized abroad that South Africa withdrew from the Commonwealth in 1961. The abolition of apartheid in 1993, however, and the establishment of a multiracial government paved the way for South Africa's return to the Commonwealth and for a visit by Queen Elizabeth. Addressing the nation's leaders, the queen spoke in glowing terms of the transformation that had taken place and said that South Africa had set an example for the rest of the world with its spirit of reconciliation.

ASASHI SHIMBUN—SYGMA

A victim of the toxic nerve gas sarin receives aid in the Tokyo subway. Terrorists belonging to a Japanese religious sect, Aum Shinrikyo, released the gas in subway cars on March 20.

22

CIA accused of cover-up

Robert Torricelli, a member of the Intelligence Committee in the U.S. House of Representatives, accused the CIA of covering up its ties to two murders in Guatemala. He alleged that a Guatemalan army officer on the payroll of the CIA had ordered the murder of a U.S. hotel owner in 1990 and of a native guerrilla leader married to a U.S. citizen. The latter victim was reportedly tortured by the military before being killed in 1992. Torricelli called the murders "the single worst example of the intelligence community being beyond civilian control and operating against our national interest." Although the CIA denied that it had any knowledge of the murders "at the time the deaths occurred," steps were apparently taken as early as 1992 to conceal the CIA's connection to what had taken place.

Rwandan refugees leave a camp in Burundi to escape ethnic violence. It was reported on March 26 that tens of thousands of Burundians also had fled the capital.
MARIELLA FURRER—REA/SABA

•

Mandates restricted

President Clinton signed into law a bill that deterred the federal government from requiring states to observe financially burdensome laws or regulations without providing funds for their enforcement. The Congressional Budget Office would be required to make a public report on the costs of implementing any such new legislation. If the costs exceeded $50 million and were not federally funded, a special majority vote in Congress was required for validation. The restrictions on "unfunded mandates" were supported in the Senate by a vote of 91–9 and in the House 394–28. Opponents of the bill contended that it would, among other things, severely restrict legislation designed to protect the environment.

25

Iraq sentences Americans

Two U.S. citizens employed in Kuwait by McDonnell Douglas Corp. were sentenced to eight years in prison after they were convicted by an Iraqi court for having entered the country illegally on March 13. U.S. officials insisted that the two men had accidentally strayed across the border at nightfall while on their way to visit friends in the demilitarized zone. Earlier that day the U.S. had persuaded other members of the UN Security Council not to remove or weaken the sanctions it had imposed on Iraq.

26

Violence surges in Burundi

Sylvestre Ntibantunganya, president of Burundi, reported that tens of thousands of people had fled the capital of Bujumbura as Hutu and Tutsi tribesmen intensified their attacks on one another. There was international concern that a civil war was in the offing and that it could rival in ferocity the violence that had occurred in neighbouring Rwanda in 1994. In that outburst of mayhem, at least 500,000 people had been killed during a period of four months.

27

Canadian rail strike ends

Some 30,000 Canadian railroad workers returned to work after Parliament forced an end to a nation-crippling strike that had begun on March 18. Some of the workers had been locked out by management after their co-workers went on strike because no settlement could be reached on such central concerns as wages and job security. During the nine-day shutdown, Canadian industries that could not use the railroads to ship their products lost billions of dollars in revenues. The return-to-work order stipulated that a federally appointed mediator would impose a contract on both sides if they were unable to resolve their differences within 70 days.

28

Japan plans huge bank

Mitsubishi Bank and the Bank of Tokyo announced that they planned to merge and become the world's largest bank, with combined assets of about $800 billion. Together the two institutions operated 380 branch offices in Japan and had substantial holdings outside the country. If the proposed deal became a reality, the new bank would have triple the assets of Citicorp, the largest bank in the U.S. Analysts generally agreed that the impact of the merger outside Japan would not be significant because Japanese banks had long been among the wealthiest in the world and had far less global influence than, for example, Crédit Suisse, Deutsche Bank, or Morgan Guaranty Trust Co. of New York.

30

UN rebuffs Libya

The UN Security Council sanctions imposed on Libya in April 1992 were extended another 120 days without a formal vote because Col. Muammar al-Qaddafi still refused to hand over two suspects sought for trial in the 1988 bombing of a Pan Am Boeing 747 over Lockerbie, Scotland. All 259 persons aboard the flight and 11 persons on the ground were killed. Strenuous U.S. efforts to persuade the council to impose a mandatory total boycott of Libyan oil won little support, in part because Germany, Italy, Spain, and other industrial nations relied heavily on imported Libyan oil.

31

U.S. troops leave Haiti

The U.S. formally turned over its peacekeeping duties in Haiti to 6,900 UN soldiers and police drawn from more than 30 nations. The UN would continue the task of keeping order while Haiti struggled to establish democratic institutions and a functioning economy. One of the most difficult problems Haiti faced was the creation of jobs for half of the workforce, which was unemployed. The UN mission was expected to end in February 1996 with the inauguration of a new president.

•

Chechen cities captured

Superior Russian forces gained control of the last important urban centres in Chechnya, a Russian province that was fighting to become independent. After coming under heavy artillery and air attacks, local troops began their withdrawal, carrying ammunition and other matériel with them. Far from preparing to surrender, the Chechen soldiers vowed to initiate a guerrilla war from bases in the Caucasus mountains, where rough terrain precluded the effective use of tanks and heavy armoured vehicles.

4

Cabinet ousted in Ukraine

With near unanimous consent (292–15), members of Ukraine's Supreme Council (parliament) voted to oust the Cabinet of Pres. Leonid Kuchma. The vote of no confidence cast by numerous former communist legislators was generally interpreted as an expression of dissatisfaction with Kuchma's reforms. Some analysts, however, suggested that the president may have been pleased that ministers who opposed his programs had been removed from positions of influence. That same day, in a state of the nation address, Kuchma vowed to accelerate economic reforms despite political opposition because the economy, he said, could not survive without implementation of measures that he knew were unpopular.

7

Police raid Claes's home

Demands that Willy Claes resign as secretary-general of NATO intensified after Belgian police raided his home and office. The authorities were searching for evidence that the Flemish Socialist Party had accepted a BF 50 million bribe in 1988, when Claes was the party's economic affairs minister. The money was reportedly turned over to the coalition government's senior partner after helicopters worth $285 million were purchased from Agusta SpA, an Italian company. The scandal had already forced five government ministers to resign.

•

House GOP holds rally

Republican members of the U.S. House of Representatives held a rally on the steps of the Capitol to celebrate the completion of legislative action on their party's "Contract with America." Under the leadership of House Speaker Newt Gingrich, the Republicans had fulfilled their promise to bring 10 initiatives to a floor vote before April 13—100 days after the 104th Congress had convened. The only item that had failed to win approval was a limit on the number of terms a representative could serve. Other laws affected such things as crime, welfare, taxes, social security, and military affairs.

9

Fujimori coasts to victory

Having succeeded in stabilizing Peru's economy by controlling inflation and in restoring public tranquillity by virtually destroying the Sendero Luminoso (Shining Path) guerrilla movement, Alberto Fujimori won a second five-year term as president by capturing nearly two-thirds of the popular vote. The strongest of his 13 opponents was Javier Pérez de Cuéllar, the former secretary-general of the United Nations, who got the support of about 22% of the vote. Although Fujimori had temporarily suspended the constitution, the national legislature, and the courts in 1992, his authoritarian methods were seen by many as having improved the well-being of ordinary citizens.

10

Palestinians hold trials

A new court established by the Palestine Authority in Gaza sentenced a member of the Islamic Jihad to 15 years in prison for having trained youths to kill Israelis. Yasir Arafat, chairman of the Palestine Liberation Organization, appeared determined to crack down on those who challenged his authority or sought to undermine efforts to achieve peace in the Middle East. Numerous arrests followed by secret trials and severe sentences appeared to be Arafat's strategy to quell violence in his homeland.

11

Taipei officials resign

The Taipei city council in Taiwan was thrown into turmoil when one of its members accused the vice mayor of being a foreigner. Chen Shih-ming was in fact a U.S. citizen by birth, but he had renounced his citizenship at the U.S. embassy in Thailand on January 31. A female councillor who belonged to the Nationalist Party (Kuomintang) then denounced Mayor Chen Shuibian, a member of the Progressive Party, for allowing foreigners to run the city government. The directors of finance and transportation for the city had both become naturalized U.S. citizens and were technically in violation of the nation's law that prohibited elected officials, government representatives, and civil servants from holding dual nationalities. The two men consulted with the mayor behind closed doors, then submitted their resignations.

•

ZANU-PF wins easily

Election officials announced that candidates of the ruling Zimbabwe African National Union-Patriotic Front (ZANU-PF) had won 63 of the 65 seats contested in the parliamentary elections held April 8–9. The ZANU-PF also won 55 uncontested seats in the 150-seat House of Assembly. Pres. Robert Mugabe, whose term was due to expire in 1996, directly controlled 20 additional seats through personal appointments. The remaining 10 seats were reserved for tribal chiefs. Some opposition groups boycotted the election, and they and others insisted that there had been blatant election fraud and that government harassment had made it impossible for their parties to campaign effectively.

AFP

A Spanish trawler, which had been seized by Canadian authorities, receives a welcome home. On April 16 the European Union announced resolution of a fishing dispute between the two countries.

16

Fishing dispute settled

Acting on behalf of Spain, the European Union settled a bitter fishing dispute with Canada. The six-week-long confrontation over fishing rights in international waters off Newfoundland had reached such intensity that both Spain and Canada had sent gunboats into the area. Canadian authorities, claiming that fish stocks of turbot were dwindling because of overfishing, had taken matters into their own hands on March 9 by seizing a Spanish trawler at gunpoint. Canadians also cut the fish nets of another Spanish trawler, contending that it was exceeding international fishing quotas and hauling in too many small fish. The dispute was settled when both sides agreed to observe in the future the quotas assigned to each country by the Northwest Atlantic Fisheries Organization.

18

Bolivia faces crisis

With labour unions refusing to return to work until the government agreed to their demands, the Bolivian government reacted by declaring a 90-day state of siege. To stifle civil unrest, soldiers were deployed in the streets of major cities, public gatherings were proscribed, the right to bear arms was suspended, and travel within the country was restricted. The government also imposed a midnight-to-6 AM curfew. There was a report the following day that some 380 union members had been arrested.

19

Federal building destroyed

In the worst act of terrorism in U.S. history, a huge car bomb virtually destroyed the Alfred P. Murrah Federal Building in Oklahoma City, Okla. Six other nearby buildings were also heavily damaged by the explosion. The bodies of a dozen or more small children who had been in a second-floor day-care centre were among those confirmed dead shortly after rescue teams arrived at the scene. As many as 200 others were believed to be trapped beneath the wreckage, but firefighters had to proceed with great caution because the damaged structure was so unstable. Attorney General Janet Reno pledged to seek the death penalty if those who had committed the crime were apprehended. Just about 90 minutes after the bombing, Timothy McVeigh, a 27-year-old army veteran, was stopped by county police some 100 km (60 mi) from Oklahoma City for driving a car that had no license plates. Soon afterward, the FBI had reason to consider McVeigh a prime suspect in the bombing.

•

Terrorists strike again

More than 300 people were rushed to hospitals in Yokohama, Japan, after poisonous phosgene was released on a crowded train. The gas quickly spread throughout the city's main train station. Two days later several persons were overcome by acrid fumes in a nearby shopping centre. In both instances the victims complained of dizziness and had difficulty breathing. Police were unable to identify the perpetrators immediately, but suspicions centred on members of the Aum Shinrikyo religious sect, which was being intensely investigated in connection with the March 20 sarin attack in a Tokyo subway that had killed 12 persons and injured more than 5,500.

A firefighter holds a baby rescued after the bombing of a federal office building in Oklahoma City, Okla., on April 19. The baby, who had been in the building's day-care centre, soon died.
CHARLES H. PORTER IV—SYGMA

21

Stolen uranium seized

Four Slovaks, three Hungarians, and two Ukrainians were arrested near Poprad, Slovakia, and charged with the illegal possession of radioactive material. Evidence indicated that the 17 kg (37.4 lb) of uranium were being transported from Ukraine to a location somewhere in Hungary. Laboratory tests would be used to determine whether the Slovak authorities had intercepted weapons-grade material. Past instances of smuggling radioactive material out of countries that were once part of the Soviet Union had caused international concern.

22

Rwandan Hutu massacred

Thousands of Hutu in the Kibeho refugee camp in southwestern Rwanda were shot, bayoneted, or trampled to death when members of the Tutsi-dominated Rwandan Patriotic Army tried to force them to return to the homes they had abandoned when tribal warfare engulfed their country. Hoping to avoid being killed or maimed, a huge number of Rwandans had fled into neighbouring countries, but hundreds of thousands of others were housed in nine refugee camps set up by the French army. Violence had reached an unprecedented level in 1994. During April–August more than a million Rwandans were killed in the worst case of mass slaughter in African history. The Hutu, who comprised about 90% of the population, had tried to obliterate the Tutsi. The slaughter at Kibeho was attributed in large measure to fear on both sides of what the other might do.

•

Denktash wins reelection

In a runoff election, Rauf Denktash won a third term as president of the Turkish-controlled section of Cyprus. His opponent was Dervis Eroglu, former prime minister of the self-declared Turkish Republic of Northern Cyprus (TRNC). The nation was divided along ethnic lines in 1974 when Turkish troops intervened in order to prevent ethnic Greeks from seizing control of the entire island in a coup. Few governments, however, had recognized the TRNC as a legitimate political entity. In February the Greek Cypriot national assembly had voted unanimously to change the name of the divided capital of Nicosia to Lefkosia, the Greek pronunciation of the name Lefkosha, already used by Turkish Cypriots.

23

New coalition in Iceland

Davíd Oddsson, the prime minister of Iceland, announced that he had formed a new coalition government with the Progressive Party as junior partner. In the April 8 general election, his Independence Party had won a plurality of 25 seats in the 63-seat Althing (parliament), and the Progressives had gained control of 15. Oddsson's new Cabinet included Halldor Asgrimsson, a Progressive, who was given the post of foreign affairs minister. Like Oddsson, Asgrimsson was opposed to Iceland's entry into the European Union.

•

Sudanese envoy expelled

According to a Kampala radio report, Uganda broke off diplomatic relations with its neighbour The Sudan and ordered its ambassador to leave the country. The diplomat, whose residence had been surrounded by Ugandan police for several days, allegedly held a cache of weapons, which he refused to surrender. Tensions between the two nations had been gradually escalating over accusations that each country was supporting rebels trying to overthrow the other's government.

25

Mahathir retains power

In general elections the 14-party National Front, headed by Prime Minister Mahathir bin Mohamad, captured 162 of the 192 seats in Malaysia's House of Representatives. The landslide victory registered by the Front, which had dominated politics in Malaysia ever since the country became independent in 1957, meant that Mahathir's party could amend the constitution without being encumbered by dissenting views. The Front also swept to victory on the local level by winning two-thirds majorities in 10 of 11 state legislatures.

26

Churchill papers are sold

The British government announced that it was purchasing Winston Churchill's pre-1945 papers for £12.5 million. The money would come largely from Britain's national lottery, with a small additional contribution from an American philanthropist. Those who opposed the sale argued that the writings of Britain's World War II prime minister properly belonged to the government. Churchill's widow, who disagreed, had already given her husband's post-1945 writings to the University of Cambridge, but she retained earlier papers as part of a family trust.

29

Nazarbayev to stay on

In a national referendum, Kazakh voters agreed to extend the term of Pres. Nursultan Nazarbayev to the year 2000. The president had already dissolved Kazakhstan's Parliament and postponed the presidential election scheduled for 1996. Critics, however, scoffed at a report that more than 95% of the voters had supported the referendum. They declared that Nazarbayev, who was the only president the nation had had since it became independent of the Soviet Union in 1991, had now become a dictator.

PAUL LOWE—MAGNUM PHOTOS

The grounds of a refugee camp at Kibeho, in southwestern Rwanda, are strewn with the bodies of Hutu after a massacre by Tutsi-dominated government troops on April 22. The government was trying to force the refugees back to their homes.

2

Refugee policy changed

With the consent of the Cuban government, the Clinton administration adopted a new policy regarding Cuban refugees seeking admission to the U.S. Henceforth, all Cuban boat people would be immediately returned to their homeland, but most of the 21,000 refugees currently detained by the U.S. at its Guantánamo Bay naval base in Cuba would be allowed to enter the U.S. Cubans could also apply for immigration visas at a U.S. government office in Havana. Cuban-American groups were overjoyed that the Guantánamo detainees would be heading for the U.S., but they angrily denounced the government's decision to turn its back on others hoping to leave the communist country. The new U.S. policy was designed to discourage a mass exodus from Cuba comparable to the one in 1994.

6

V-E Day commemorated

Scores of international leaders gathered in Europe to commemorate the 50th anniversary of V-E (Victory in Europe) Day. Most European nations celebrated the end of World War II on May 8, but Russia preferred May 9, the day Nazi Germany's surrender was ratified in Berlin. Before traveling to Paris, Berlin, and Moscow, the dignitaries attended the opening of a three-day ceremony in London that featured Queen Elizabeth, the Queen Mother.

7

Chirac replaces Mitterrand

In a runoff presidential election, French voters chose former prime minister Jacques Chirac, the mayor of Paris and leader of the neo-Gaullist Rally for the Republic party, over the Socialist Party candidate, Lionel Jospin. In two previous attempts (1981, 1988) to win the presidency, Chirac had been defeated by François Mitterrand, a Socialist, who held office an unprecedented 14 years. While on the campaign trail, Chirac pledged to reduce unemployment, which exceeded 12%, and to make greater use of national referenda to decide government policies, especially regarding France's role in the European Union. On May 17, inauguration day, Chirac named Alain Juppé prime minister. Under Mitterrand he had been minister of foreign affairs.

(Top) Jets fly over the Arc de Triomphe in Paris in a ceremony marking the 50th anniversary of the Allied victory in Europe in World War II. World leaders began the observances in London on May 6. (Above) Jacques Chirac, elected president of France on May 7, waves to the crowd at his inauguration. Formerly mayor of Paris, Chirac faced difficult economic problems.

(TOP) AFP; (BOTTOM) LANGEVIN—SYGMA

•

Ethiopia's future at risk

Millions of Ethiopians cast ballots in national and regional elections that would radically change the political structure of their nation. Because four of the seven national political parties boycotted the election on the grounds that the process was unfair, Pres. Meles Zenawi was assured of reelection to another five-year term. His Ethiopian People's Revolutionary Democratic Front also was in a position to exercise its political power without being seriously challenged. Political analysts viewed Ethiopia's political experiment as a risky gamble with unpredictable consequences. The new federal system was designed to mitigate ethnic violence and end civil conflict by granting regional and ethnic groups the right to secede if they so desired. Although Zenawi had been denounced as dictatorial and chastised for violating human rights, he had allowed political parties to multiply and independent newspapers to flourish. He had also cooperated with the World Bank to control inflation and foster open markets.

•

China attacks corruption

Chinese Pres. Jiang Zemin, using his authority as head of the Communist Party, continued his assault on official corruption with an order to arrest or investigate a wide range of party members associated with the powerful party organization in Beijing. On April 27 Chen Xitong, the party secretary in Beijing, had been dismissed from his post. Earlier that month the executive deputy mayor had died, an apparent suicide. In the latest purge numerous city officials, their secretaries, and in some instances their relatives faced charges of corruption. A similar crackdown in Guizhou province earlier in the year had led to the dismissal of the party secretary and the execution of his wife. China publicly acknowledged that corruption had become endemic throughout the country.

8

Filipinos back reforms

Philippine Pres. Fidel Ramos' plans to revitalize the nation's economy through continued deregulation of industry and a dismantling of monopolies gained momentum when voters backed members of his Lakas-Laban coalition in national and local elections. Half the 24 Senate seats and all 200 elected seats in the House of Representatives were filled, as were thousands of positions in local governments. The government's most conspicuous defeat occurred in Manila, where Alfred Lim won reelection as mayor despite a vigorous effort to unseat him. Ferdinand Marcos, Jr., son of the former dictator, was soundly defeated in his bid to gain a Senate seat, but his mother, Imelda, won a place in the House. Violence by Muslim groups in Mindanao forced the closure of many polls, but about 100,000 voters were allowed to cast their ballots on May 27. This and other factors delayed an official report on the election results.

9

Hungary to sell utilities

After debating the merits of various proposals for nearly a year, Hungary's National Assembly passed legislation that facilitated the sale of state-owned companies and utilities. Opposition to privatization came mainly from socialist legislators and from members of trade unions, who argued forcefully that the state should never relinquish its monopoly on electricity or sell off certain other enterprises currently under its control.

10

Chinese delegates defect

The Royal Canadian Mounted Police and Canada's immigration department began to search for about 75 of the 87 Chinese officials who had arrived in the country on April 17 to study the economy of southern Ontario. The number of those attending a one-week business seminar declined so dramatically that those placed in charge had to cancel many of the scheduled events. Authorities presumed that the missing delegates planned to remain in Canada illegally.

11

Nuclear treaty extended

After more than three weeks of debate at UN headquarters in New York City, representatives of 174 nations agreed to extend the Nuclear Non-proliferation Treaty indefinitely. Many viewed the original treaty, which was valid for 25 years beginning in 1970, as a guarantee against the spread of nuclear weapons. Before backing the extension, however, many nonnuclear powers had lobbied hard for certain compromises, including an extension for only a limited time period. Three of the five permanent members of the UN Security Council—Great Britain, Russia, and the U.S.—had signed the treaty in 1968; China and France did not add their names until 1992. Under the terms of the treaty, nuclear nations were obliged to destroy their arsenals gradually and nonnuclear nations to refrain from developing a nuclear capability.

•

Landmark in trouble

Faced with serious financial problems, the owners of Rockefeller Center, a prestigious complex of 12 Art Deco buildings in the heart of New York City, were forced to declare bankruptcy to protect themselves from creditors. The Mitsubishi Estate Co., a Japanese real estate giant, had acquired an 80% interest in the property over a three-year period at a cost of $1.4 billion. Under Chapter 11 of the federal bankruptcy laws, the owners were free to wage a battle to retain ownership of the centre. Any resolution of the problem would necessarily involve Rockefeller Center Properties, Inc., a publicly held real estate investment trust, which held a $1.3 billion mortgage on the property.

14

Menem reelected

Carlos Menem avoided a runoff election by easily defeating 13 other candidates seeking to replace him as president of Argentina. His closest rival, Sen. José Octavio Bordón of the left-leaning coalition Frente Grande, finished with about 20% fewer votes. The president's Justicialist National Movement (Peronist) party (PJ) did equally well, capturing majorities in the Senate and Chamber of Deputies and winning control of 12 of the 23 provincial legislatures. Political analysts gave Domingo Cavallo, Menem's economic minister, substantial credit for the PJ's solid victory. Under the Menem-Cavallo economic program, the inflation rate had fallen to 4% (compared with 5,000% in 1989), foreign investments had multiplied, and the local currency had been strengthened by backing each peso with one U.S. dollar in reserves. Billions of dollars had also been committed to public works projects to increase employment, especially in some of the poorest sections of the country.

15

Ancient tomb discovered

Kent R. Weeks poses by a relief of Osiris in a tomb built by Ramses II. On May 15 he reported on the complex, which apparently had been undisturbed for 3,000 years.
PATRICK LANDMANN—SYGMA

Kent R. Weeks, a professor of Egyptology at the American University in Cairo, gave a detailed report on an enormous royal mausoleum recently explored in the Valley of the Kings some 500 km (300 mi) south of Cairo. Archaeologists believed the site contained the tomb of the sons of Ramses II, one of ancient Egypt's greatest pharaohs. Despite its incredible size and unquestionable value to historians, the elaborate burial site was not expected to yield treasures comparable to those found in the tomb of Tutankhamen.

•

Dow Corning bankrupt

Lawsuits filed by hundreds of thousands of women claiming to have suffered health problems as a result of silicone breast implants forced Dow Corning to seek protection from its creditors under Chapter 11 of the U.S. bankruptcy code. The company, which had been the largest manufacturer of breast implants until the Food and Drug Administration severely restricted their use in 1992, hoped to continue operations after a financial reorganization. According to a study reported in the June 22 issue of the *New England Journal of Medicine*, researchers at Harvard University and Brigham and Women's Hospital found no evidence linking silicone breast implants to connective tissue disorders. The result of the study was the same as that reached in several earlier studies by other scientists.

16

Iran to get 100 tanks

Poland confirmed that it intended to complete delivery of some 100 Soviet-designed T-72 tanks to Iran despite U.S. pleas that no nation "engage in arms related trade with terrorist supporting states like Iran." A week earlier Poland had informed the UN that 34 of the tanks already had been shipped. The sale, estimated to be worth between $30 million and $40 million, was not considered to be strategically important in that part of the world. During the Cold War, Poland had ranked among the top 10 arms producers in the world, but after the collapse of the Soviet Union, about half of the workforce in its largest tank factory joined the ranks of the unemployed.

21

Syria supports Hariri

The Lebanese National Assembly, by a margin of 2–1, voted to retain Rafiq al-Hariri as prime minister. The decision had in effect been made by Syria, which had some 35,000 troops in the country and had long been a power broker in Lebanon. Frustrated by his political opponents, Hariri had resigned on May 19 after consultation with Syrian officials, who agreed to support his nomination to a second term. As expected, members of Hariri's new Cabinet were more in tune with his plans to rebuild Lebanon, which had been devastated by 15 years of civil war. According to the terms of the 1990 peace accord that had ended the conflict, the prime minister always would be a Sunni Muslim, the president a Maronite Christian, and the speaker of the Assembly a Shi'ite Muslim.

•

Dehaene coalition wins

Jean-Luc Dehaene was assured of another term as prime minister of Belgium when members of his four-party centre-left coalition won 81 of 150 seats in the House of Representatives. It was Belgium's first national election since the adoption of a new constitution, which reduced the size of the House by 62 seats and transferred significant powers from the federal government to the nation's four regional assemblies. The outcome of the election was viewed as somewhat surprising because prominent members of the ruling coalition had been implicated in an ongoing corruption scandal.

22

Court rejects term limits

The U.S. Supreme Court, in a 5–4 vote, denied individual states the right to limit the number of terms their representatives could serve in Congress. The ruling instantly voided laws that had been passed by 23 states. If the court had endorsed what appeared to be the wishes of a majority of U.S. citizens, 72 current members of the House, representing seven different states, could not have sought reelection in 1996. There remained the possibility of limiting congressional terms by amending the Constitution, which would involve a long and complicated process.

•

Israel placates Arabs

Prompted by a desire to defuse tensions at home and respond to international concerns, the Israeli Cabinet suspended a government plan to confiscate 55 ha (135 ac) of mainly Arab-owned land in East Jerusalem. The territory, which the Arabs envisioned as the capital of a future Palestinian state, was to have become the site of several hundred homes for Jews and a police station. With the plan at least temporarily dead, the Israelis and Palestinians were once again able to concentrate on the next phase of a plan to grant self-rule to Palestinians living in Jewish-occupied territories.

23

East German spies cleared

Germany's highest court ruled 5–3 that former spymasters in East Germany could not be prosecuted because they were now citizens of a united Germany. As a consequence, charges of treason against more than 6,300 individuals were dropped. The court also recommended leniency for spies who had operated in West Germany during the Cold War because such activities were carried on by virtually all nations. Markus Wolf, who had been convicted of treason in 1993 and sentenced to prison for six years, was among those directly affected by the court's ruling. He had headed the spy branch of East Germany's secret police (Stasi) from 1958 to 1987.

25

Euthanasia approved

After 14 hours of intense debate, the legislature in Australia's Northern Territory voted 15–10 in favour of a bill called the Rights of the Terminally Ill. It granted patients who were at least 18 years old and "of sound mind" the right to request that they be put to death if they were suffering. Two doctors, at least one of whom had to be a psychiatrist, were required for verifying that the patient was terminally ill. The new law was believed to be the first in the world that sanctioned voluntary mercy killing.

30

Ebola virus kills 153

The World Health Organization announced that according to the latest available statistics, 153 persons had died in Zaire after being infected with the Ebola virus. The death toll included seven Italian nuns who became infected while treating patients suffering from the infection. When the epidemic erupted early in the year in Kikwit, a city with a population of some 600,000, local health care workers were overwhelmed and ill-equipped to stem the tide of the infection or help the victims, whose symptoms included vomiting, diarrhea, fever, and profuse hemorrhaging. There was no known cure for the disease, which was believed to be carried by unidentified insects, rodents, or other animals.

LIZ GILBERT—SYGMA

In Zaire workers wearing protective clothing transport a victim of the Ebola virus. It was reported on May 30 that 153 people in Zaire had died from the outbreak.

7

Australia weighs presidency

Paul Keating, prime minister of Australia, outlined a plan to sever his nation's constitutional ties to Great Britain by having a president replace the British monarch as head of state. Even though Australia was already self-governing, many shared Keating's view that such a change was needed to "permit the full and unambiguous expression of Australia's national identity." To change the constitution, a majority of voters in at least four of Australia's six states had to approve a referendum. If this was accomplished by the year 1999, Australia's present ties to the British crown would be severed in 2001, the centennial of the union of the nation's states. Following popular referenda in 1898–99, the Commonwealth of Australia was proclaimed on Jan. 1, 1901.

9

Lee visits alma mater

Lee Teng-hui, president of the Republic of China on Taiwan, delivered an address to the alumni of Cornell University, Ithaca, N.Y., where he had obtained a doctoral degree in agricultural economics in 1968. Even though Lee was technically visiting the U.S. as a private citizen, China was furious that the U.S. had issued a visa because Lee was, in fact, the head of a government that was not recognized by China, the U.S., or the UN. In early May the U.S. House of Representatives forced the issue by unanimously approving (396–0) a nonbinding resolution urging the State Department to reverse its earlier decision and allow Lee to attend a reunion at his alma mater. The Senate later approved (97–1) a similar resolution. The congressional vote added another item to the growing list of differences causing tension between China and the U.S., but it also signaled a desire to make amends for what most members of Congress felt was the humiliating treatment Lee had received in 1994 when he was not allowed to step on U.S. soil when his plane made an overnight stop in Hawaii on its way to Latin America.

•

Black Sea Fleet divided

Control of the Black Sea Fleet, which had been a bone of contention between Ukraine and Russia ever since the demise of the Soviet Union in 1991, was finally settled when the leaders of the two nations met face to face. The highly complicated issue, which was far more political than military (the fleet was small and aging), was resolved when both parties agreed to split the fleet. Russia would then purchase a large part of the Ukrainian fleet, leaving it with 82% of the vessels. In Russia's view it was vitally important to have a presence in the Black Sea to counter Turkish influence in the area. The two leaders also reached agreement on what rights each had at the Sevastopol naval base, but neither side felt it was an appropriate time to discuss the future status of Crimea.

12

Affirmative action curtailed

In a decision with far-reaching consequences, the U.S. Supreme Court ruled 5–4 that federal programs that classified people by race, even to broaden opportunities for minorities, were unconstitutional unless they were "narrowly tailored" to satisfy "compelling government interests." Speaking for the majority, Justice Sandra Day O'Connor argued that because all members of society have equal rights and equal protection under the Constitution, race could not be a decisive factor in making decisions except in very special circumstances. The court's decision, among other things, effectively ended programs that set aside a certain percentage of contracts for minorities solely on the basis of their ethnicity. It also had important ramifications on affirmative action policies that had been adopted by many institutions.

•

Dominica changes course

After 15 years in power, Prime Minister Eugenia Charles, the "Iron Lady" of the Caribbean, was forced to relinquish the reins of government when the opposition United Workers' Party won 11 of 21 contested seats in the House of Assembly. Charles, who had founded the Dominica Freedom Party, announced that she was retiring after 27 years in politics. The new government, under the leadership of Edison James, took office on June 14.

13

UN hostages set free

The Bosnian Serbs, who had taken 370 UN peacekeepers hostage in Bosnia and Herzegovina after NATO planes launched air strikes against them on May 25–26, released most of the 144 UN personnel they still held. The first group of hostages had been set free on June 2. Contradicting the Bosnian Serb foreign minister, UN officials flatly denied that the hostages had been released only after Western negotia-

RAUPACH—ARCUS/SABA

Spectators flock to see Christo's "Wrapped Reichstag" in Berlin. The artist and his wife, Jeanne-Claude, presented the work, which used silver fabric, on June 25.

tors had pledged that there would be no more bombing. Despite gargantuan efforts to end the massacres of Croats, Muslims, and Serbs, the UN had been unable to work out a peace settlement. The process had been hampered by UN and NATO differences over tactics and strategy and by the fact that UN troops on the ground could not be protected if the bombings continued.

15

Nicaraguan crisis eases

A four-month-long political crisis in Nicaragua abated when Pres. Violeta Barrios de Chamorro yielded to the National Assembly and agreed to promulgate the 66 amendments to the constitution it had approved. The changes substantially strengthened the power of the Assembly at the expense of the executive branch of government. The political standoff, which was solved with the mediation of the Roman Catholic cardinal, had put foreign aid in jeopardy and had precluded agreement on appointments to the Supreme Court.

•

Military coup in Iraq fails

U.S. officials revealed, without naming their source of information, that a military coup against Iraqi Pres. Saddam Hussein had failed when loyal Republican Guards suppressed a mutiny organized by Guard tank troops. The showdown occurred in Abu Ghraib, the site of a military camp, a prison, and a government radio station some 20 km (12 mi) from Baghdad, the capital. The significance of the uprising, the second such in recent weeks, was difficult to assess, but some days later there were unconfirmed reports that about 150 soldiers and officers had been executed.

25

Haitians flock to polls

Some eight months after the military junta departed Haiti and democratically elected Pres. Jean-Bertrand Aristide returned from forced exile in the U.S., Haitians went to the polls to elect 18 of the nation's 27 senators, all 83 members of the Chamber of Deputies, and hundreds of mayors and municipal councils. Among the 28 parties seeking representation were the Lavalas Political Organization, supported by Aristide; the National Front for Change and Democracy, Aristide's original coalition; and the National Congress for Democratic Movements, which had been expelled from the Front. Despite predictable confusion, numerous delays, and charges of voting irregularities, international observers reported that Haiti had taken a positive step toward democratic rule.

A voter's thumb is marked to prevent fraud in Haiti's elections on June 25. Observers called the balloting "chaotic," but it took place without the violence of previous elections.
REGNAULT—GAMMA LIAISON

•

Reichstag under wraps

Bulgarian-U.S. artist Christo and his wife, Jeanne-Claude, presented the German people with a unique work of art: Berlin's former and future Parliament building wrapped in silver fabric that was tied down with bright blue rope. For more than 20 years the couple had sought permission to undertake the project, but the controversial undertaking was not sanctioned by Parliament until February 1994. The cost of materials and labour, estimated at some $10 million, was expected to be covered through sales of memorabilia.

26

Mubarak survives attack

Egyptian Pres. Hosni Mubarak was unscathed when five or six gunmen fired automatic weapons at his three-car motorcade as it moved down a street in Addis Ababa, the capital of Ethiopia. During the exchange of gunfire, two gunmen who had leaped from their jeep after it smashed into the lead car were killed, as were two native policemen. Other gunmen had taken up positions on rooftops and on the street. Mubarak, who claimed to have remained calm because he was in a bulletproof car, immediately canceled plans to attend the opening session of the Organization of African Unity summit. Upon his arrival in Cairo, he vowed that the attackers would pay dearly for their actions. It was widely believed that Arabs bent on establishing an Islamic state in Egypt had plotted the failed assassination.

27

Qatar prince ousts father

Hamad ibn Khalifah ath-Thani, the crown prince of the gas-rich emirate of Qatar, forced the abdication of his father, Sheikh Khalifah ibn Hamad ath-Thani, with whom he had been feuding for several years. Five other members of the Gulf Cooperation Council, including Saudi Arabia, immediately recognized Hamad as Qatar's new ruler. He had in fact already been using the considerable authority granted him by his father to restore relations with Iraq (which had been a foe during the Persian Gulf War), extend friendship to Iran, move toward normal relations with Israel, and sign a defense pact with the U.S.

28

U.S.-Japan dispute settled

Just hours before the U.S. was scheduled to impose billions of dollars in punitive tariffs on imported Japanese automobiles, negotiators for the two countries signed a broad but ambiguously worded accord in Geneva that ended an often bitter two-year-long trade dispute. Mickey Kantor, the U.S. trade representative, was demanding, among other things, that Japanese markets for U.S.-made auto parts and car dealerships be expanded. His goal was to reduce Japan's trade surplus in automobiles and auto parts, which exceeded $36 billion in 1994. Ryutaro Hashimoto, Kantor's counterpart, vigorously opposed any agreement that smacked of quotas because, he said, quantifiable numbers contravened the principles of free trade. Although the text of the accord was not released immediately, it appeared that Japan had merely agreed to make a good-faith effort to solve the problem.

Drug king José Santacruz Londono sits in the custody of Colombian officials after his arrest on July 4. Santacruz reportedly controlled the Cali cartel's operations in major U.S. cities.
CARLOS ANGEL—GAMMA LIAISON

unconditional. Before her confinement on July 20, 1989, Suu Kyi had been the nation's chief spokesperson for democracy. Even though she was not allowed to leave her compound to participate in the 1990 election campaign, her National League for Democracy party won a stunning victory. The military nullified the results and later offered Suu Kyi her freedom if she agreed to leave the country. She refused. When she reappeared in public after an absence of six years, she surprised nearly everyone by professing a willingness to cooperate with the military during a transition period leading to democracy. Asked why she harboured no ill will toward those who had taken away her freedom, she explained that her father, a hero in Burma's struggle for independence, had been an army general.

3

Caribbean nation votes

Kennedy Simmonds, who had been prime minister of the Caribbean federation of St. Kitts (St. Christopher) and Nevis from the time it gained independence from Great Britain in 1983, lost his post to Denzil Douglas, leader of the Labour Party. In the parliamentary election, the outgoing People's Action Movement won only one of the seats assigned to St. Kitts, the other seven going to Douglas supporters. For Nevis, the Concerned Citizens' Movement captured two of the three seats and the Nevis Reformation Party the other. The 11 elective seats and four nonelective seats constituted Parliament.

4

John Major risks career

British Prime Minister John Major, who had resigned as leader of the ruling Conservative Party on June 22, was reelected party leader by fellow Conservatives in Parliament. In secret balloting he received 218 votes; John Redwood, his only challenger, got 89. Major had become so frustrated with fellow Conservatives who challenged his approach to integration into the European Union (the so-called Euroskeptics) that he decided on a showdown. By resigning as party leader, Major effectively forced his colleagues to either reaffirm his leadership or replace him as party leader and prime minister.

•

Banharn takes over

With his Chart Thai party holding a plurality of 92 seats in the House of Representatives after the July 2 elections and with five other parties promising their support, Banharn Silpa-archa announced that he would be heading a new coalition government in Thailand. His position was bolstered by a seventh party, which gave him control of 233 of the 391 seats in the national legislature. Former prime minister Chuan Leekpai had been forced to call new elections because of a land-reform scandal involving leading members of Chuan's Democrat Party.

•

Colombia nabs drug king

In an ongoing offensive to curtail the nation's illegal drug trade, Colombian officials arrested José Santacruz Londono, who reportedly controlled the Cali cartel's network in such major U.S. cities as Los Angeles, Chicago, and Miami, Fla. He also was believed to control large cocaine-processing laboratories in the U.S. There was, however, little likelihood that he would ever be tried in the U.S. for these and other crimes, including murder, because Colombia did not permit its citizens to be extradited to the U.S.

5

Turkey attacks Kurds

In the second such offensive of the year, Turkish military aircraft, heavy artillery, and some 3,000 troops attacked the strongholds of separatist Kurdish guerrillas in the eastern part of the country. The rebels had been fighting for years to achieve their dream of an independent Kurdistan. The territory that they laid claim to extended into northern Iraq and southwestern Iran as well as into Turkey and a small area of Armenia. The movement for independence was led by the Kurdish Workers' Party, whose members reportedly had killed 20 Turkish soldiers in June in a hit-and-run attack launched from Iraq.

10

Aung San Suu Kyi freed

The military junta in Myanmar (Burma) revoked the house arrest of Daw Aung San Suu Kyi, winner of the 1991 Nobel Peace Prize. Government officials confirmed that her release was

11

U.S. renews Vietnam ties

In a brief ceremony at the White House, President Clinton announced that the U.S. was reestablishing full diplomatic relations with Vietnam. Two prominent senators, both casualties of the Vietnam War, were among those who supported the president by their presence. The American Legion, the largest veterans association in the country, was adamantly opposed to normalizing relations before the fate of U.S. soldiers missing in action had been satisfactorily determined. Senate Majority Leader Bob Dole, who had been permanently injured in World War II, backed the American Legion. Trent Lott, the Senate majority whip, reflected the sentiments of other conservatives in Congress when he vowed to block funding for a U.S. embassy in Hanoi. (The Senate also would have to ratify any bilateral agreement granting each country most-favoured-nation trade status.)

•

Srebrenica falls to Serbs

Undeterred by a 1993 UN declaration that its peacekeeping forces in Bosnia and Herzegovina would protect civilian refugees in six specific "safe areas" of the region, Bosnian Serb forces met only token resistance when they took over the safe area of Srebrenica. A little more than one week later, Zepa, another safe area, fell to the Serbs. The future of the remaining safe areas (Gorazde, Tuzla, Bihac, and Sarajevo) largely depended on what action the United Nations would take to counter the current Serb offensives and on the ability of Muslim and Croat military units to continue fighting.

14

Nigeria holds secret trials

The military government of Nigeria confirmed that in secret trials 40 persons had been convicted and sentenced, some to death, on charges of supporting a coup to overthrow Gen. Sani Abacha. According to unconfirmed rumours, Gen. Olusegun Obasanjo, the country's former leader, was put on trial and sentenced to 25 years in prison for concealing information about the plot. There was growing international condemnation of Abacha, who had seized power in 1993, for suppressing political dissent and violating human rights.

23

Election weakens SDPJ

Japanese Prime Minister Tomiichi Murayama and the Social Democratic Party of Japan (SDPJ) faced an uncertain future following national elections to the upper house of the Diet. The SDPJ had lost 6 of the 22 seats it had held, but the two other members of the ruling coalition, the Liberal-Democratic Party and the New Party Sakigake, fared much better in the election. As a consequence, the coalition won enough seats in the upper house to preserve its majority. All three parties agreed that for the time being at least, Murayama would continue to head the government with a revamped Cabinet.

24

Terrorist strikes in Israel

In an apparent attempt to disrupt peace negotiations between Israel and the Palestine Liberation Organization (PLO), a suicide bomber, believed to be a Palestinian, killed himself and six Israelis when he detonated a pipe bomb on a bus near Tel Aviv. Israeli Prime Minister Yitzhak Rabin tried to reassure outraged Israelis that their government and the PLO were both doing all in their power to prevent innocent people from being killed. He also promised that no act of terrorism would deter him in his search for peace.

Daw Aung San Suu Kyi stands outside her home after the military government of Myanmar (Burma) lifted its six-year house arrest on July 10.

D. AUBERT—SYGMA

25

Paris bomb causes panic

A bomb explosion on a crowded commuter train in Paris killed 4 people outright and injured more than 80, some critically. No person or group claimed responsibility, but officials strongly suspected that the attack was the first case of terrorism in France since a series of bombings in the mid-1980s. Possible suspects included militant Muslims who were fighting to establish an Islamic state in Algeria, a former overseas province of France; Bosnian Serbs who had been angered when the French government called for a buildup of UN troops to protect designated "safe areas" in Bosnia and Herzegovina; and environmental groups that were at odds with the French government over its decision to resume testing nuclear devices in the Pacific.

27

Transgenic organ test

With the approval of the U.S. Food and Drug Administration, researchers at the Duke University Medical Center, Durham, N.C., and the Nextran Corp. announced that they were preparing to test the viability of mixed-species organs in human beings. The aim of the research was to develop two new medical technologies; the first of these would use genetically altered animal organs outside the human body, and the other would implant such organs inside the body. In the first case, a pig liver laced with human genes would be linked outside the body to the circulatory system of a comatose patient who was near death and incapable of receiving a transplant. The hope was that the pig liver would function as a normal human liver. The possibility of using transgenic organs for transplants was being investigated because the demand for human organs far exceeded the supply.

30

Peace in Chechnya

Nine days after the Russian central government and the secessionist republic of Chechnya agreed to end their conflict, the two parties signed an accord guaranteeing that Chechnya would enjoy the "broadest form of statehood" but not total independence. In December 1994 Russia had triggered a bloody confrontation by dispatching some 40,000 Russians to Chechnya to prevent it from leaving the Russian Federation. Even though the peace accord ended hostilities, the future was still uncertain.

31

Merger stuns Wall Street

Michael Eisner, chairman and chief executive officer of the Walt Disney Co., announced that his company was acquiring Capital Cities/ABC. Investors were stunned by the news and the sheer magnitude of the deal, estimated to be worth $19 billion. The merger would bring together Disney's film and television operations, its theme parks, its animation studio, its film-distribution outlets, the highly marketable cast of characters Disney had created, the nation's most profitable television network (ABC), the ESPN sports network, radio and television stations, newspapers, home videos, and multimedia products. While some expressed a belief that the union of these two giants would result in more creative entertainment, others feared that the growing concentration of ownership would limit diversity in both culture and politics.

AUGUST

2

Thai workers held captive

In a predawn raid in El Monte, Calif., U.S. immigration officials freed about 70 Thai workers who had been held captive in a clothes factory surrounded by barbed wire fences. They were locked up and guarded at night and threatened with bodily harm if they tried to escape. The workers, moreover, had little or no hope of ever paying the debt they had incurred for being smuggled into the U.S. On August 15 state authorities reported that many of the manufacturers who had bought from the sweat shops were themselves operating illegally. Seven were fined $35,000 each, but twice that number were likely to face penalties before the investigation concluded. In similar raids on other factories in the Los Angeles area, federal officials found evidence that Asian gangs were controlling the operations.

7

Croatians retake Krajina

In a lightning offensive that began on August 4, Croatian government troops recaptured the region of Krajina, which had fallen to Serbian troops several years earlier. Although the territory had been the home of ethnic Serbs for some five centuries, it became part of Croatia during World War II and remained in Croatian hands until the Serbs reclaimed it during the current conflict. Following the successful Croatian offensive, as many as 150,000 Serb civilians were forced to leave Krajina and seek refuge in Serbia or Serb-held areas in Bosnia and Herzegovina. There were reports of large-scale human rights violations on the part of Croatian soldiers seeking revenge for the atrocities their own people had endured at the hands of their enemies.

8

Defections shock Iraq

Two of Pres. Saddam Hussein's sons-in-law were given political asylum in Jordan after fleeing Iraq with their wives and other senior military officers. Lieut. Gen. Hussein Kamel Hasan al-

Lieut. Gen. Hussein Kamel Hasan al-Majid, son-in-law of Iraqi Pres. Saddam Hussein, meets the press after defecting with other relatives of Hussein on August 8.
SYGMA

Majid, husband of the president's eldest daughter, had been responsible for building up Iraq's arsenal before the Persian Gulf War. His brother, Col. Saddam Kamel Hasan al-Majid, had been in charge of presidential security forces. Both had left Iraq on the pretext that they were traveling on an official visit to Bulgaria by way of Jordan. According to an unconfirmed report, another of Hussein's sons-in-law also defected with his wife. Jordanian King Hussein I, who had supported Iraq during the Persian Gulf War, announced that he would protect the defectors. On August 17 a Saudi newspaper reported in a front-page story that on the evening before the Kamel brothers left Iraq, a family feud had ended in gunfire. Six bodyguards were slain, and Hussein's half-brother was seriously wounded.

10

"Jane Roe" changes mind

Norma McCorvey, who under the name "Jane Roe" had been the central figure in a landmark 1973 Supreme Court ruling that permitted abortions, stunned both pro-choice and pro-life advocates by revealing during a radio interview in Dallas, Texas, that she no longer supported the right to abortion. She remarked, "I think I have always been pro-life. I just didn't know it." Two days earlier McCorvey had been baptized by the national leader of Operation Rescue, an antiabortion organization. Sarah Weddington, one of the lawyers who had represented McCorvey in the class-action suit argued before the Supreme Court in 1973, expressed the dismay of many proponents of abortion rights: "I'm shocked. At a time when we are working so hard . . . and not having much luck, I didn't need this one."

•

Bombing suspects charged

A federal grand jury in Oklahoma City, Okla., indicted Timothy McVeigh and Terry Nichols, prime suspects in the April bombing of a federal building in Oklahoma City that killed 169 persons. The two

men had become friends in the army and reportedly shared antigovernment views. The 11-count indictment included a charge that the suspects had robbed a gun dealer in Arkansas to help finance their operation. Michael Fortier, another of McVeigh's friends from army days, pleaded guilty to lesser charges and agreed to reveal in court testimony what he knew about the bombing.

11

Nepal dam canceled

Plans to construct a hydroelectric dam in eastern Nepal had to be shelved when the World Bank decided not to grant a promised $175 million loan. Its chief concern was that Nepal would not be able to find other backers for the $1 billion project, which was designed to generate 200 MW of power. Those who opposed the construction of Arun III argued that the cost of electricity would be prohibitive, that indigenous people would be displaced, and that endangered species would lose their habitats.

SEBASTIÃO SALGADO

Serbs flee Krajina after Croatian troops recaptured the region on August 7. As many as 150,000 Serbs fled to Serbia or Serb-held areas of Bosnia and Herzegovina.

•

Perot is host of convention

Eager to win the political support of voters committed to former independent presidential candidate Ross Perot, virtually every important national politician except President Clinton attended a weekend convention at which Perot served as host in Dallas, Texas. All those invited to address 3,000 members of Perot's United We Stand America organization endorsed many of Perot's principles. Analysts viewed the gathering as a political phenomenon and an acknowledgment that it was politically risky to ignore the political force that Perot represented.

15

Murayama apologizes

On the 50th anniversary of Japan's surrender at the end of World War II, Japanese Prime Minister Tomiichi Murayama delivered a nationally televised speech that included an apology for his nation's wartime aggression. At one point he remarked, "Japan, following a mistaken national policy, advanced along the road to war, only to ensnare the Japanese people in a fateful crisis, and through its colonial rule and aggression caused tremendous damage and suffering to the people of many countries, particularly to those of Asian nations." Going well beyond the declaration of "deep remorse" that Japanese officials had previously expressed, Murayama declared, "In the hope that no such mistake be made in the future, I regard, in a spirit of humility, these irrefutable facts of history, and express here once again my feelings of deep remorse and state my heartfelt apology."

•

Brazilian peasants slain

A Roman Catholic cleric reported by phone that landless peasants in the west central Brazilian state of Rondônia had been killed in a clash with police on August 9. A bishop in the area believed that the death toll could be as high as 75. There were reasons to suspect that the bodies of the victims had been burned and then buried. Violence had erupted when police attempted to evict some 1,300 landless labourers from a jungle estate they had taken over. Witnesses claimed that police had arrested the leader of the peasants, Sérgio Rodrigues Gomes, but there was no record that he had been jailed.

16

Bermuda remains colony

Voters in the self-governing British colony of Bermuda rejected a referendum that would have made the territory an independent nation. Only one-quarter of the voters backed Prime Minister John Swan, who had pledged to resign if independence was not approved. Those favouring the status quo argued that a British presence enhanced stability, which contributed to Bermuda's expanding financial services sector and fostered tourism, the island's principal source of income.

•

Three Indonesians freed

On the eve of Indonesia's 50th anniversary of independence, President Suharto ordered the release of three political prisoners who had been jailed for nearly 30 years. The group included Subandrio, who had been the country's foreign minister; Omar Dhani, former air force commander; and Raden Sugent Sutarto, the former head of intelligence. All had been accused of supporting a pro-communist movement that led to a bloody upheaval in 1965. The violence caused some 300,000 deaths and led to Sukarno's political demise and Suharto's rise to power.

17

McDougals indicted

James McDougal and his ex-wife, Susan, were indicted by a federal grand jury in Little Rock, Ark., on charges of bank fraud and conspiracy. President Clinton and his wife, Hillary, had been their partners in the Whitewater Development Corp., a real estate venture that was under investigation. Arkansas Gov. Jim Guy Tucker, who had already been charged in June with irregularities in the Whitewater affair, was further charged with fraud in the new indictment. A total of 14 people had thus far either pleaded guilty or been indicted, but the Clintons had not been charged with any crime. One of the prime goals of the investigation was to determine whether funds from Madison Guaranty Savings and Loan, which McDougal owned before its collapse, had been illegally diverted to the Clinton gubernatorial campaigns in Arkansas in the 1980s.

18

Female quits academy

Shannon Faulkner, who had waged a legal battle for more than two years to become the first female cadet at the Citadel, withdrew from the Charleston, S.C., military academy just five days after being enrolled. Some 30 other cadets also acknowledged during the first week of training that they could not meet the physical demands of the academy, but Faulkner got all the attention. While recognizing that many men as well as women would be disappointed that she had failed, Faulkner expressed a hope that other young women would seek admission to the Citadel.

19

Liberia embraces peace

During negotiations in Abuja, Nigeria, the leaders of various Liberian factions agreed to end five years of hostilities. A major obstacle to peace was removed when all consented to have Wilton Sankawulo serve as chairman of the Council of State in place of nonagenarian Chief Tamba Tailor. Of equal importance was an agreement that Charles Taylor, rebel leader of the National Patriotic Front of Liberia, would have a role in the interim government. The council would also include, besides Chief Tailor, Alhaji Kromah, leader of the Ulimo-K faction and chief rival of Taylor; George Boley, head of the Liberia Peace Council; and Oscar Quiah of the Liberian National Conference. Hopes rose that democratic elections would bring an end to the fighting, which had already claimed some 150,000 lives.

21

Deane to represent queen

Australian Prime Minister Paul Keating announced that he would nominate Sir William Deane to succeed Bill Hayden when he retired as governor-general on Feb. 15, 1996. The governor-general, who represented Queen Elizabeth II, Australia's head of state, had no significant power, but Deane, whose appointment was certain to win royal approval, would be involved in the current debate over whether Australia should retain its ties to the British throne or become a republic. Deane, a High Court judge, had no political affiliation and was highly regarded by members of all political parties.

23

Sudan to free detainees

The state radio of The Sudan reported that the National Security Council, headed by Pres. Omar Hassan Ahmad al-Bashir, had decided to release all political prisoners within a few days. The most prominent detainee was former prime minister Sadiq al-Mahdi, whose elected government had been toppled by Bashir in a June 1989 bloodless coup. Mahdi subsequently had been accused of involvement in an antigovernment plot but was never charged. Promising that parliamentary and presidential elections would be held in 1996, the government urged all opposition leaders living abroad to return home so they might be able "to contribute to security and stability in the country."

24

China expels Harry Wu

After being convicted of "spying, illegally obtaining, buying, and providing state secrets to overseas institutions, organizations, and people, and of passing himself off as a government worker for deceptive activities," Harry Hongda Wu, a naturalized U.S. citizen, was sentenced to 15 years' imprisonment by a court in Wuhan, China, and then expelled. He was put on a Chinese plane and flown to San Francisco. Wu had immigrated to the U.S. in 1985 after spending 19 years (1960–79) in Chinese labour camps for criticizing the Communist Party and the 1956 Soviet invasion of Hungary. Posing as a businessman, Wu returned to China for the first time in 1991 to make secret videotapes of prison conditions and inmates producing products for export. On his latest trip he was identified and detained when he tried to enter China from Kazakhstan. His U.S. passport was stamped with a valid Chinese visa.

•

Windows 95 debuts

Amid much fanfare and a multimillion-dollar worldwide advertising campaign, U.S. software maker Microsoft Corp. released Windows 95, the long-awaited upgrade to its popular Windows computer operating environment. Customers in some countries stood in line for hours waiting for stores to admit them, and many retailers opened at midnight. Windows 95, which incorporated 32-bit addressing, preemptive multitasking, a revamped graphic user interface, and other enhancements, faced resistance from those who were reluctant to buy the hardware upgrades needed to take full advantage of Windows 95's capabilities. By year's end, however, Microsoft had sold an estimated 18 million–20 million copies.

Bill Gates, head of Microsoft Corp., speaks at the launch of Windows 95 on August 24. Among other features, the computer operating system boasted a friendlier graphic user interface.
JIM LEVITT—IMPACT VISUALS

25

Criminal court on hold

After two weeks of discussions, the United Nations decided that the formation of an international criminal court needed to be studied more carefully during the fall session of the General Assembly. The jurisdiction and functions of the new tribunal would differ from those of the International Court of Justice in The Hague and would be concerned with war crimes, genocide, and other crimes against humanity. Currently, these ad hoc tribunals were authorized to deal with only those atrocities that were committed in Rwanda and former Yugoslavia.

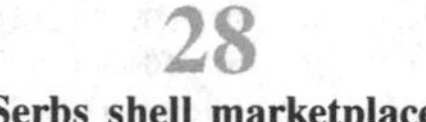

28

Serbs shell marketplace

Despite dire warning from NATO that it would bomb Serb military targets if Sarajevo, the capital of Bosnia and Herzegovina, or any other UN-designated "safe area" came under attack, the Bosnian Serbs fired mortar into the city's crowded marketplace. At least 37 civilians were killed and more than 80 wounded. On August 30 and 31, 60 NATO aircraft carried out bombing missions against Serb positions on the outskirts of Sarajevo. UN and NATO leaders had agreed that retaliation was their only option if they hoped to retain their credibility. President Clinton described the air strikes as "the right response to the savagery in Sarajevo."

29

Shevardnadze targeted

A large car bomb was detonated in the inner courtyard of the Parliament building in Tbilisi, Georgia, in an attempt to kill Eduard Shevardnadze, Georgia's de facto head of state and leader of Parliament. He survived the attempted assassination with only minor injuries. Shevardnadze had traveled to the legislature to affix his signature to a new constitution that restored the presidency and invested it with enhanced powers. He had already disclosed that he would seek the presidency in the November election. Following the attack, tanks and armoured personnel carriers patrolled the streets of the capital, but Parliament declined to follow the advice of many and declare a state of emergency.

1

Libya bars Palestinians

Col. Muammar al-Qaddafi, Libya's de facto head of state, announced that he was expelling all 30,000 Palestinians working in his country. The decision was meant to punish Yasir Arafat and his Palestine Liberation Organization for seeking to reach a peace settlement with Israel. Hundreds of Palestinians were subsequently stranded at the Egyptian border because they were not holding permits allowing them to enter Gaza after passing through Egypt. Thousands more were reported to have been denied entrance into Lebanon when they arrived by ship.

•

Music hall of fame opens

An estimated 50,000 people attended the official opening of the Rock and Roll Hall of Fame and Museum in Cleveland, Ohio. The $92 million structure, designed by architect I.M. Pei, was opened to the general public the following day. Among many other things, the complex featured exhibits about the more than 120 performers who had been inducted into the hall of fame during the previous decade. To qualify, a candidate had to have begun his or her career at least 25 years earlier. Expectations were high that at least 750,000 tourists would visit the site each year, adding tens of millions of dollars to the local economy.

5

Nuclear tests denounced

Ignoring demands that it cancel a series of planned nuclear tests, France detonated a device at Mururoa atoll in the South Pacific. The underground explosion, which was equivalent to nearly 20,000 tons of TNT, was detected as far away as Australia. Tahitians vented their anger at the action by setting fire to the international airport terminal in Papeete, the capital. Greenpeace, an environmental organization, called the test "an obscene outrage." Australian Prime Minister Paul Keating called the event "an act of stupidity." Protesters in The Netherlands attempted to block access to the French embassy in The Hague. In Vienna police had to use tear gas to repel demonstrators attempting to climb over the walls of the French embassy. On September 6 New Zealand and Chile called their ambassadors home for consultation. Objections to the tests were also voiced by Denmark, Italy, Japan, Russia, and the U.S. In an attempt to quiet the storm of criticism, French Pres. Jacques Chirac announced that the tests would end well before the end of May 1996 if adequate information was gained from the early explosions.

U.S. Sen. Bob Packwood listens to reporters' questions about allegations of sexual misconduct and other wrongdoing. Packwood resigned his Senate seat on September 7.

TOM HORAN—SYGMA

•

Cuba seeks investments

Cuba's National Assembly of the People's Power passed legislation that reversed long-standing economic policies by opening the door to greater foreign investments. For the first time, Cuban exiles and foreigners could become sole owners of property and businesses. Special zones, moreover, would be created as free-trade and free-export manufacturing centres, where foreign-owned assembly plants would operate, using local workers hired from state-run employment agencies. Cuba's move toward a free-market economy was necessitated in great part by the collapse of the Soviet Union, which had been its chief supporter.

7

Senator Packwood resigns

Facing charges of sexual misconduct, influence peddling, and obstruction of the Senate Ethics Committee investigation of his conduct, Sen. Bob Packwood of Oregon announced his resignation. The previous day the committee had voted 6–0 to recommend to the entire Senate that Packwood be expelled. During a 33-month-long investigation, the bipartisan committee had studied thousands of pages of evidence, including Packwood's private diaries, before concluding that there was credible evidence of misconduct.

10

Nepal ousts Marxists

By a vote of 107–88, the Parliament of Nepal passed a vote of no-confidence in the government of Prime Minister Man Mohan Adhikari, leader of the United Marxist-Leninist Party. He had held office for less than 10 months. King Birendra then appointed Sher Bahadur Deuba prime minister. His centrist Nepali Congress Party enjoyed the support of the National Democratic and Goodwill parties and of others who considered themselves independents.

13

Dalai Lama visits U.S.

One day before ending his 10-day visit to the U.S., the Dalai Lama met privately with Vice Pres. Al Gore in the White House. The Senate had earlier voted unanimously in favour of a meeting between President Clinton and the Dalai Lama, but Clinton, apparently unwilling to risk antagonizing China, merely paid a courtesy call during the Dalai Lama's visit with Gore. The Dalai Lama, who had been the temporal ruler of Tibet as well as spiritual leader of the country's largest Buddhist sect before China occupied his country in 1950, used the occasion to ask Clinton to assist Tibetan refugees. An estimated two-thirds of the population had left the country after an unsuccessful revolt against Chinese rule in 1959. Many had accompanied the Dalai Lama to India, where he set up a government-in-exile.

14

Eurotunnel losing money

The Anglo-French company operating the Channel Tunnel (Eurotunnel), which connects France and England, announced that interest payments on its £8 billion debt would be suspended for 18 months while it worked out a financial restructuring plan with 225 creditor banks. Its daily revenues of £600,000 fell far short of the £2 million needed to cover interest payments. Long before the tunnel was operational, the project had faced serious financial difficulties. Because of delays and cost overruns, the project had to be refinanced three times.

15

Women gather in China

The UN Fourth World Conference on Women ended its 12-day convention in Beijing

Women demonstrate at the UN Fourth World Conference on Women, which concluded its sessions in Beijing on September 15. Attempts by the Chinese government to curb public protests by conference delegates were not wholly successful.
DONNA BINDER—IMPACT VISUALS

with most delegates, representing some 180 countries, endorsing a Platform for Action designed to promote women's rights around the world. Special attention was paid to the need to fund and promote programs to halt all forms of violence against women and to increase their economic and political power. Some 35 nations, however, went on record as opposing certain parts of the platform. In a speech to the delegates on September 5, Hillary Rodham Clinton declared that it was "no longer acceptable to discuss women's rights as separate from human rights." She also noted: "It is a violation of human rights when women are denied the right to plan their own families, and that includes being forced to have abortions or being sterilized against their will." Though she did not mention China by name, the practices were part of the government's one-child-per-family program. Her list of human rights abuses also included the burning of brides whose dowries were deemed inadequate, the mutilating of female genitals, and the raping of women in wartime. Clinton also addressed the UN-sponsored Nongovernmental Organizations Forum on Women held in Huairou, a remote suburb of Beijing. The participants complained that they were repeatedly harassed by security forces.

17

Hong Kong holds election

Despite a warning from China that it would abolish an anti-China legislature in Hong Kong when it resumed sovereignty over the British crown colony on July 1, 1997, voters seated 29 prodemocracy candidates on the Legislative Council. It was the first time that voters representing various constituencies had had an opportunity to fill all 60 seats. The Democratic Party, which under the leadership of Martin Lee advocated greater democracy, won a plurality of 19 seats. The Democratic Alliance for the Betterment of Hong Kong (DAB), which was strongly pro-China, captured only six seats. The DAB's top three leaders were all defeated.

•

Haiti concludes voting

Final tallies after the third and final round of balloting in Haiti gave Lavalas, a three-party coalition supported by Pres. Jean-Bertrand Aristide, an overwhelming victory over its opponents. Lavalas won 17 of the 18 contested seats in the 27-seat Senate and 67 of the 83 seats—all were contested—in the Chamber of Deputies. Lavalas scored equally impressive victories at the local level, winning a large majority of the races for mayor and local councils. Haiti's fledgling democracy would face its greatest test when voters went to the polls to elect a president early in 1996.

•

Swedes oppose EU

Even though in a 1994 referendum Swedish voters had narrowly approved their country's participation in the European Union, vocal opponents of membership in the EU undermined that support when the Greens, an environmental group, and the Left Party won 7 of the nation's 22 seats in the European Parliament. Having won control of nearly one-third of their government's seats in an organization they did not believe in, they called for a new national referendum.

20

AT&T to break up

In order to increase the efficiency of its various operations and to adapt more quickly to changing conditions, AT&T, the world's largest telecommunications company, announced that it would become three separate entities. The first would retain the name AT&T and be responsible for basic telephone services, wireless communication items, and credit cards. The second would take over communications equipment, including telephone network switching, answering machines, computer chips, and business telephone systems. The computer-manufacturing unit would become the third company. AT&T expected that about 20% of the 43,000 jobs in this segment of the business eventually would be eliminated.

22

Hashimoto to lead LDP

Japan's Liberal-Democratic Party (LDP), the largest group in the three-party coalition that ruled Japan under the leadership of Prime Minister Tomiichi Murayama, a socialist, elected Ryutaro Hashimoto leader of their party. During complicated negotiations that ended a bitter Japanese-U.S. trade dispute, Hashimoto had gained international prominence as his country's minister for international trade and industry. There was widespread belief that Hashimoto's elevation to the top post in the LDP made him the leading candidate to succeed Murayama as prime minister.

•

TBS accepts merger

The world's largest mass media company was created when the Turner Broadcasting System (TBS) agreed to merge with Time Warner. For the deal to become final, federal regulators would first have to be satisfied that the merger did not violate antitrust laws. Under terms of the agreement, Time Warner would purchase TBS in an all-stock deal estimated to be worth $7.5 billion. Each TBS share would be worth three-quarters of one Time Warner share. During 1994 the combined revenues of the two companies came to $18.5 billion; their current combined debt was about $19 billion. Several observers expressed concern that the new company would be large enough to stifle diversity.

23

Albania bans ex-officials

The People's Assembly (parliament) in Albania passed a law that banned members of the former communist government from holding public office or positions with the mass media until the year 2002. Those who had collaborated with the secret police during the years of communist rule also fell under the ban. Opposition parties claimed that the law was a ruse to eliminate Pres. Sali Berisha's main opposition when he ran for reelection in March 1996.

25

Three labs to stay open

After evaluating the findings of a special review board that had studied the work performed by three U.S. nuclear weapons research laboratories, President Clinton ordered the Department of Energy to keep the laboratories open. The board's investigation of the Lawrence Livermore National Laboratory (Livermore, Calif.), the Los Alamos (N.M.) National Laboratory, and the Sandia National Laboratories (Albuquerque, N.M., and Livermore) indicated that all three were providing "essential services to the nation in fundamental science, national security, environmental protection and cleanup, and industrial competitiveness." A special commission had issued a report in February questioning the need for all three laboratories.

26

Peace plan for Bosnia

After years of brutal conflict, the warring factions in Bosnia and Herzegovina accepted a peace plan negotiated in large measure by U.S. Assistant Secretary of State Richard Holbrooke. The foreign ministers of Bosnia, Croatia, and Yugoslavia (representing the Serbs) accepted, among other things, that the republic would continue to exist within its present borders and that 51% of the territory would belong to a federation consisting of Muslims and Croats. The country would be governed by a collective presidency and a parliament, with their respective powers still to be determined. All persons would be allowed to move freely through the region, and displaced persons could repossess their property or receive appropriate compensation. Internationally recognized human rights, including freedom of speech, would be respected. Following elections, a parliament would be established with one-third of the seats occupied by Serbs. Although numerous details still had to be worked out, including the delineation of borders, there was a growing belief that the large-scale fighting in the region had finally come to an end.

28

PLO-Israel accord

During a ceremony at the White House, the Palestine Liberation Organization (PLO) and Israel signed a pivotal accord that significantly advanced the cause of peace in the Middle East. The Israeli Cabinet and PLO Executive Committee had previously approved the complex document. After prolonged negotiations both sides had agreed on terms governing the second stage of Israel's military withdrawal from occupied Palestinian territory in the West Bank and the transfer of administrative responsibility to the Palestinian National Authority. At a date to be determined later, elections would be held to form a legislative council. Among both Israelis and Palestinians, there were some who bitterly opposed making peace with their longtime foes. Israeli Prime Minister Yitzhak Rabin, however, restated his commitment to peace and acknowledged that withdrawal from occupied Arab lands was an indispensable condition for reaching that goal. He declared that the settlement reached with the PLO marked "the end of the hallucination of a Greater Israel."

PETER TURNLEY—NEWSWEEK/BLACK STAR

Children in Hebron throw rocks to protest the Israeli-Palestinian accord signed in Washington, D.C., on September 28. The pact provided for further Israeli withdrawals from the West Bank.

1

Abdel Rahman convicted

A federal jury in New York City convicted Sheikh Omar Abdel Rahman and nine codefendants on 48 of 50 charges of seditious conspiracy to wage "a war of urban terrorism" in the U.S. Abdel Rahman, a blind Muslim cleric from Egypt, was accused of masterminding plans to bomb the United Nations headquarters and other sites in New York City and to assassinate political leaders, including Egyptian Pres. Hosni Mubarak. Abdel Rahman was also found guilty of directing a terrorist group that murdered Rabbi Meir Kahane in 1990. Most of the evidence against the accused came from more than 100 hours of conversations secretly recorded by a paid government informer who had infiltrated the group.

•

Portugal's Socialists win

Portuguese voters ended the 10-year tenure of Prime Minister Aníbal Cavaco Silva's centre-right Social Democratic Party when they gave the Socialist Party (PS) 112 of the 230 seats in the nation's Assembly of the Republic. With António Guterres leading the party, the PS increased its share of the popular vote by almost 15%. The PSD gained 40 seats in the national assembly (the weighted formula for rural and urban representation was used in the figuring of results). Both parties had campaigned on similar platforms, promising to support the European Union's (EU's) economic and monetary systems, to adhere to austere budgets, and to oppose higher taxes. While head of government, Cavaco Silva had brought Portugal into the EU and had revitalized the nation's economy. When he announced in January that he would not seek another term, many believed he had set his sights on the presidency.

3

O.J. Simpson acquitted

A Los Angeles Superior Court jury found former football star O.J. Simpson not guilty of the murders of his ex-wife Nicole Brown Simpson and her friend Ronald Goldman on June 12, 1994. Race was a predominant issue during the trial, which received more mass media coverage than any other trial in history. This was attributed to the celebrity of the defendant, the fact that he was African-American and the victims white, the formidable "dream team" of expensive lawyers Simpson had hired, and the fact that the trial was televised live. Although the rule of double jeopardy prevented Simpson from ever being tried again on the same charges, he still faced wrongful death suits filed by the families of the deceased. In those civil proceedings Simpson could be forced to take the witness stand, an option his defense attorneys chose not to take during the murder trial.

Alberto Dahik, vice president of Ecuador, defends himself against allegations of misusing state funds. He fled the country on October 11 after the Supreme Court charged him.
CLAUDIA DAUT—REUTERS

•

Assassination fails

Kiro Gligorov, president of the Republic of Macedonia, was seriously injured when a car bomb tore apart his armoured automobile as it moved down the street near the presidential offices in Skopje. Gligorov had returned to the capital the previous day after a meeting in Yugoslavia with Serbian Pres. Slobodan Milosevic. The two had discussed the conditions that would have to be met to normalize relations, which had been disrupted when Macedonia made its declaration of independence from Yugoslavia in 1991.

9

Sam Nunn to retire

During a news conference in Atlanta, Ga., Sen. Sam Nunn announced that he would not seek election to a fifth term in the Senate in 1996. He thus became the ninth senator, and the eighth Democrat, in recent months to announce that he would be leaving Congress. Nunn, who had gained wide respect as chairman of the Senate Armed Services Committee before being replaced when the Republicans gained control of both houses of Congress, said that he had lost much of his enthusiasm for the job and was discouraged by the way "big money" and "saturation television ads" were influencing politics.

10

Palestinians set free

Fulfilling a commitment it had made with the Palestine Liberation Organization (PLO), Israel released some 900 incarcerated Palestinians and began a military withdrawal from Palestinian towns. This second phase of an agreement to expand Palestinian self-rule gradually beyond the enclave of Jericho to seven other cities and about 450 towns in the West Bank would, it was hoped, lead to a peaceful withdrawal of all Israeli troops from the area by March 1996. The PLO, led by its chairman, Yasir Arafat, had formed the Palestinian National Authority with responsibility for local administration. It was in the process of formalizing plans to elect a Palestinian executive and a legislature.

11

Dahik flees Ecuador

After Ecuador's Supreme Court charged Vice Pres. Alberto Dahik with misuse of state funds and ordered his arrest, he fled to Costa Rica and asked for political asylum. On August 23, one week after the court had charged Dahik with bribery, embezzlement, and illicit use of government money, it issued a subpoena ordering him to appear in court to respond to the charges. Then, on October 6, an attempt was made in the National Congress to impeach Dahik, but the vote fell short of the needed two-thirds majority. During the impeachment hearings, Dahik had blamed his troubles on the government of Pres. Sixto Durán Ballén, saying that it had resorted to bribing legislators and judges in order to win support for its economic reforms.

•

Scandal rocks Estonia

Estonian Prime Minister Tiit Vahi and his entire Cabinet resigned in the wake of a wiretapping scandal involving Minister of the Interior Edgar Savisaar. When police raided the Security Intelligence Agency, a company allegedly run by former KGB agents and linked to organized crime, they discovered recordings of conversations between Savisaar and other politicians, including the prime minister. The Centre Party rejected demands that it force Savisaar, one of its members, to resign. He was then fired by Pres. Lennart Meri at Vahi's request. Although Vahi himself was never implicated in the scandal, he said that he felt obliged to resign because his partners in the coalition had refused to disassociate themselves from wrongdoing.

13

Austria's coalition fails

One day after reaching an impasse on a 1996 fiscal budget, Austria's parliament dissolved itself and paved the way for new national elections in December. The two-party ruling coalition had been led by Chancellor Franz Vranitzky, a Social Democrat, whose party had proposed tax increases to reduce the projected 1995 deficit of nearly $12.4 billion by 26% in 1996. The Austrian People's Party, led by Wolfgang Schüssel, preferred drastic cuts in social security benefits. Agreement on a budget was rendered more difficult because the right-wing Austrian Freedom Party had made significant gains in the 1994 elections and hoped to enhance its power through new elections.

14

Russian kidnaps Koreans

An armed Russian seized a bus in Moscow's Red Square and took some 25 South Korean tourists hostage. During negotiations with police, the man gradually reduced his demand from $10 million to $1 million and released all but four of the Koreans. He was killed early the next morning when commandos stormed the bus, which had been moved by riot police to a nearby bridge.

16

Black men hold rally

Responding to a call issued by Louis Farrakhan, leader of the Nation of Islam, hundreds of thousands of black men from all across the nation traveled to Washington, D.C., to take part in the "Million Man March," a rally that had been promoted as a "holy day of atonement and reconciliation." The participants were urged to make a promise that they would unite and take responsibility for themselves, their families, and their communities. The event was organized by the Rev. Benjamin F. Chavis, Jr., who had been executive director of the National Association for the Advancement of Colored People. Numerous blacks, some of whom decided to join the rally, found themselves in a quandary. They endorsed the message of the rally, but they did not want to imply that they also endorsed the racist statements Farrakhan had repeatedly made.

CHRISTOPHER SMITH—IMPACT VISUALS

A participant in the "Million Man March" carries his own version of the American flag. The rally of black men, held in Washington, D.C., on October 16, included pledges of unity and responsibility.

17

Chief minister resigns

Mayawati, chief minister of Uttar Pradesh state in northeastern India, and her Bahujan Samaj Party relinquished control of the state government after the Bharatiya Janata Party (BJP) withdrew from the ruling coalition. The following day the national government, headed by Prime Minister P.V. Narasimha Rao of Congress (I), took over direct administration of the state. The move deprived the BJP of an opportunity to strengthen its political base in the country's most politically important state before the 1996 general elections. Mayawati was the first member of India's Dalit ("Untouchables") social caste to head a state government.

20

Claes quits NATO post

One day after the Belgian Parliament voted to remove Willy Claes's immunity (as a former Cabinet member) from prosecution, he resigned as secretary-general of NATO to face charges of corruption, fraud, and forgery in connection with what had come to be known as the Agusta scandal. The Italian aviation company Agusta SpA allegedly paid the ruling Flemish Socialist Party a bribe of $1.7 million in 1988 to secure a contract for 46 military helicopters. At the time, Claes was minister of economic affairs and was one of the officials who approved the contract.

22

Ivorians reelect Bédié

In Côte d'Ivoire's second multiparty election, Pres. Henri Konan Bédié of the Democratic Party handily defeated his only opponent, Francis Wodie of the Ivorian Workers' Party; he had gained prominence as head of Amnesty International. The low voter turnout was blamed on the two major opposition parties, the Popular Front and the Rally of Republicans, which had called for a boycott at the polls. Critics of the government had charged that voter lists had been rigged and that Bédié had used other unfair tactics to ensure his victory, including a revision of the election code that effectively barred his strongest opponent, Alassane Dramane Ouattara, from entering the race. Ouattara, the current deputy director of the International Monetary Fund, was defeated when he ran for the presidency in 1993.

23

Minorities lose contracts

Following a U.S. Supreme Court ruling in June that it was unconstitutional to award government contracts to minorities solely on the basis of race, and after a review of government practices in light of that ruling, the Defense Department announced that it was ending a program designed to help minority-owned firms secure such contracts. The Clinton administration had directed the Defense Department to make the announcement after the Justice Department concluded that the federal government's affirmative action policy was almost certainly unconstitutional. In 1994 about $6.1 billion in prime contracts had been awarded to minority firms; of that amount, $1 billion had been awarded in competitions that excluded white-owned firms.

24

UN marks anniversary

Delegates from all over the world began to return home after a three-day celebration in New York City commemorating the 50th anniversary of the United Nations. It had been the largest gathering of world leaders in history. Before adjourning, member nations endorsed a new document that reaffirmed the principles of the UN Charter, which had taken effect on Oct. 24, 1945. It also took into account the criticism that had been leveled at the organization and acknowledged that reforms were needed. At the same time, there was overwhelming confidence in the UN's ability to promote peace and social development around the world. During speeches by 178 national delegates and by 23 others with only observer status, there were calls for an end to such things as lavish spending, nuclear testing, and trade in arms. There were also pleas for more help to less developed nations and for timely payment of assessments to the United Nations.

26

Yeltsin hospitalized

Russian Pres. Boris Yeltsin was hospitalized for the second time in less than four months after suffering chest pains caused by a deficiency of oxygenated blood to the heart. The doctors reported that Yeltsin was in stable condition but would need six weeks to recover. Three days after Yeltsin was admitted to the hospital, the Russian election committee used a technicality to bar Yabloko, the country's most popular reformist party, and other political groups from participating in the December parliamentary elections. From his hospital bed, Yeltsin demanded an explanation.

•

Islamic leader slain

Fathi ash-Shiqaqi, the leader of Islamic Jihad, was killed when five shots were fired into his head at point-blank range. The assassination, carried out by two gunmen on a motorcycle, took place in Sliema, a seaside town in Malta. Shiqaqi, who was traveling home to Syria after holding meetings with Col. Muammar al-Qaddafi in Libya, was not positively identified until October 29 because he was carrying a Libyan passport and was using an alias. The Islamic Jihad, which had taken responsibility for terrorist attacks against Israel in the past, accused the Israeli secret service of plotting the assassination and vowed to take revenge.

28

Vietnam gets civil code

By an overwhelming margin, Vietnam's National Assembly approved the nation's first civil code. The landmark legislation was considered to rival the nation's constitution in importance. Over a period of 10 years, lawmakers had studied the civil codes of other nations while drafting legislation that was compatible with Vietnam's social conditions. Several days earlier the assembly had approved a fundamental change in the government bureaucracy. It replaced eight existing ministries with three superministries. The move toward greater efficiency was expected to eliminate at least one-third of the jobs in the affected ministries.

30

Quebec keeps status quo

In an election that had the potential to divide Canada into two separate nations, voters in the predominantly French-speaking province of Quebec rejected by the narrowest of margins a referendum that could have separated Quebec from the rest of Canada. Final tallies showed that 50.6% of the valid ballots favoured union with the rest of Canada, but an analysis of the vote showed that about 60% of French-speaking Quebeckers (who comprised 82% of the province's total population) supported independence. Many of these said that they felt the rest of Canada was insensitive to their deep attachment to their native language and French cultural heritage and that their insistence on greater autonomy had fallen on deaf ears.

A. MCINNIS—GAMMA LIAISON

Four young Quebec voters supporting union with Canada celebrate their narrow victory in the referendum held on October 30. Only 50.6% of the voters opposed a separate Quebec.

At the entrance to the Knesset, a young Israeli woman lights a candle in memory of Yitzhak Rabin, who was assassinated on November 4. A right-wing Israeli was charged with killing the prime minister for seeking peace with the Palestinians.
LIZ GILBERT—SYGMA

2

Daiwa Bank indicted

The U.S. Justice Department indicted Japanese-owned Daiwa Bank on 24 counts of conspiracy and fraud after concluding that top-ranking bank officials had tried to cover up more than $1 billion in losses it had incurred as a result of illegal bond trading at its New York City offices. Federal and state officials then ordered the bank to close down all of its U.S. operations by February 1996.

4

Rabin assassinated

Israeli Prime Minister Yitzhak Rabin was shot and killed in Tel Aviv as he was about to enter his car after attending a late-evening rally held to gain support for a peace settlement with the Palestinians. The assailant, Yigal Amir, was seized by security agents as Rabin collapsed with bullets lodged in his chest, back, and abdomen. The young Jewish law student, an ultranationalist vigorously opposed to the peace initiative, said he had acted on orders from God and had no regrets for what he had done. Most Israelis were stunned to learn that their leader had been killed by a fellow Jew, but there were right-wing extremists who declared Amir a hero. On November 6 numerous world leaders attended Rabin's funeral in Jerusalem. Three days later Yasir Arafat, visiting Israel for the first time, offered his personal condolences to Rabin's widow, Leah. In public statements she asserted that the inflammatory rhetoric of the Likud party, led by Benjamin Netanyahu, had created an atmosphere that made her husband's assassination possible.

•

Andreotti called murderer

Giulio Andreotti, who had been elected prime minister of Italy seven times, became the first European leader in modern times to be accused of murder. He was charged with involvement in the 1979 Mafia assassination of Carmine Pecorelli, a journalist, who reportedly had been trying to blackmail Andreotti with information about his alleged ties to Sicilian organized crime figures. Four others, including Italy's former foreign trade minister, were also indicted. The government's case was said to rest on information given it by former mafiosi.

5

Shevardnadze elected

Voters supported Eduard Shevardnadze by a margin of 3–1 in his bid to win the presidency of the Republic of Georgia. Under the nation's new constitution, Shevardnadze, who had been chairman of Parliament and Georgia's de facto head of state, would hold office for five years. Incomplete results of the parliamentary election indicated that Shevardnadze's Citizens' Union would have substantial representation in the 235-seat national legislature.

7

Rape case angers Japan

In a courtroom in Naha, Okinawa, three U.S. servicemen pleaded guilty to charges of conspiring to abduct and rape a 12-year-old girl. While all three men admitted that they had actively participated in the crime, only one acknowledged that he had raped the girl. The incident, which had occurred in September, received worldwide coverage. The Japanese were not alone in expressing their outrage and demanding to know why 26,000 U.S. troops were allowed to occupy about one-fifth of the total area of Okinawa's principal island.

8

Powell declines to run

During a crowded press conference in Alexandria, Va., retired army general Colin Powell declared that he would not seek the U.S. presidency or any other elective office in 1996. He also announced, for the first time, that he was a member of the Republican Party. Powell remarked that he had looked deep into his soul before reaching a decision and recognized that he did not feel "the passion and commitment" needed to run a successful campaign. Nonetheless, he added, he would "speak out forcefully" on political issues in the months ahead. On October 20 Powell had ended a book tour undertaken to promote his memoirs, *An American Journey.* The enthusiastic crowds that greeted him at each stop underscored his appeal to ordinary Americans and explained why

Accompanied by his wife, Alma, Gen. Colin Powell announced on November 8 that he would not run for the U.S. presidency in 1996. The retired general's decision disappointed many.
WIN MCNAMEE—REUTERS

leaders of both major political parties had tried to persuade him to join their ranks.

9

McNamara meets Giap

During a three-day visit to Vietnam, Robert McNamara, who had been the U.S. secretary of defense during the war in that country, traveled to Hanoi to meet Gen. Vo Nguyen Giap, the wartime commander of North Vietnam's forces. In answer to a question posed by McNamara, Giap denied that Vietnam had attacked the U.S. destroyer *Maddox* in the Gulf of Tonkin for a second time on Aug. 4, 1964. The U.S. Congress, assured at the time that the attack had indeed taken place, passed the Gulf of Tonkin Resolution authorizing an escalation of the war. McNamara later said he was no longer certain that the attack had actually taken place. In a recently published book, he conceded in retrospect that the U.S. war policy had been a mistake.

•

Panday assumes office

The political standoff that was created in Trinidad and Tobago by the November 6 parliamentary elections was resolved when the United National Congress (UNC) party agreed to form a coalition with the much smaller National Alliance for Reconstruction (NAR) party. Basdeo Panday then took the oath of office as prime minister, the first person of East Indian descent to hold that position. The UNC and the ruling People's National Movement (PNM) party had both won 17 seats in the election, but the PNM, which had governed the two-island Caribbean nation for all but five years since 1956, had found its support deteriorating in recent years.

11

Commonwealth meets

On the second day of their four-day meeting in New Zealand, members of the Commonwealth voted to suspend Nigeria's membership in the organization because of its abuse of human rights. The previous day the military government of Gen. Sani Abacha had hanged the author and environmentalist Ken Saro-Wiwa and eight other political activists despite worldwide pleas that they be spared. During the meeting the Commonwealth nations also spent considerable time discussing France's testing of nuclear devices in the Pacific, which had been condemned by a great many nations.

13

Six killed in Riyadh

A military training and communications centre in Riyadh, Saudi Arabia, was rocked by two explosions that killed six people, five of whom were Americans. About 60 other people were injured. The first blast, a car bomb, was targeted at a three-story building that housed members of the Saudi National Guard. Although two different groups quickly took credit for the attack, the only thing that appeared somewhat certain was that the perpetrators opposed Saudi Arabia's ties to the West and possibly harboured resentment against the royal family.

15

Guatemalans split vote

The Guatemalan government reported that a newly completed tally of the ballots cast in the November 12 presidential election indicated that none of the 19 candidates had come close to winning 50% of the vote, a requirement for outright victory. As a consequence, Alvaro Arzú of the centre-right National Advancement Party (PAN), who finished in first place, would face runner-up Alfonso Portillo of the far-right Guatemalan Republican Front (FRG) in a runoff election in early January 1996. Ramiro de León Carpio, the incumbent president, was constitutionally barred from seeking reelection.

•

Hungarian-Slovak row

The National Council (parliament) of Slovakia passed (108–17, with 17 abstentions) a law declaring that Slovak was the official language of the republic and that it alone could be used in official communications, ceremonies, broadcasting, and advertising. On November 28 Pres. Michal Kovac signed the legislation, which revoked the right of ethnic minorities to use their own languages in public administration where they comprised more than 20% of the population. Hungarians, who made up 10.7% of the country's population, were outraged. Hungary recalled its ambassador after the council vote, and its foreign minister said he would take the matter before the European Union, the Council of Europe, and NATO.

16

Roh Tae Woo arrested

South Korean police arrested Roh Tae Woo on charges of accepting millions of dollars in bribes during his five-year term as president. In 1988 Roh had become the country's first democratically elected president after promising voters that he would end the corruption that pervaded the outgoing military government of Chun Doo Hwan. In late October uncontrollable circumstances had forced Roh to admit that he had amassed a slush fund of more than $650 million in secret political donations and that about one-third of the money was still in his personal bank accounts. When the news became public, Kim Dae Jung, South Korea's most prominent critic of the government, reported that he had received about $250,000 from Roh during the 1992 presidential campaign. He also contended that Kim Young Sam, who won the election, had received many times that amount in illegal contributions during the same period. Kim quickly denied the charge. Roh told reporters that he took full responsibility for his actions and was prepared to accept whatever punishment was meted out to him.

•

Zeroual wins election

In the first contested presidential election in Algeria since the country gained independence from France in 1962, Liamine Zeroual appeared to have received more than 60% of the popular vote. The former army general had been appointed president by the military government in January 1994, two years after it had canceled the final round of legislative elections that had been expected to give the fundamentalist Islamic Salvation Front (FIS) a majority in the legislature and turn Algeria into an Islamic state. The FIS had urged Algerians to boycott the latest election and in some instances had issued death threats to those who went to the polls. After the election opposition groups claimed that the government's report of a 75% turnout was utterly false.

19

Walesa meets defeat

In a close runoff presidential election, Aleksander Kwasniewski, leader of the former communist Democratic Left Alliance (SLD), defeated incumbent Lech Walesa by capturing 51.7% of the vote. Analysts reported that Kwasniewski had greater support among young voters who apparently discounted Walesa's warning that a victory by his opponent would mean a revival of communism in Poland. During Walesa's five-year term, the nation had adopted a free-market economy, but the president seemed incapable of building a consensus and had lost the lustre he had acquired as the spokesman for Solidarity, the federation of trade unions that had loosened the communists' hold on the country. Both candidates favoured admission into NATO and membership in the European Union, but they differed sharply when Walesa defended the right of the Roman Catholic Church to have a say in determining certain government policies.

•

APEC meets in Japan

Representatives of the 18 economic powers that constituted the Asia-Pacific Economic Cooperation (APEC) organization met in Osaka, Japan, to sign a declaration outlining general principles for achieving free trade among themselves by the year 2020. The blueprint, drafted by Japan, contained no sanctions because participation was voluntary and each state was allowed to work out its own policies for achieving APEC's ultimate goals. Industrialized nations were to strive to reach the goal by the year 2010. Together the members of APEC represented more than one-third of the world's population and accounted for more than 50% of the world's economic production and 40% of the value of world trade. The two most affluent members of APEC were Japan and the U.S.

21

Wei Jingsheng arrested

The Chinese government formally placed Wei Jingsheng, one of the country's best-known dissidents, under arrest and charged him with attempting to overthrow the government. After spending nearly 15 years in prison for his role in the 1979 Democracy Wall movement, Wei was paroled in September 1993. Because he continued to openly criticize the government's disregard for human rights, and because he had met with John Shattuck, a human rights official with the U.S. State Department, he was taken into custody at an undisclosed location and held incommunicado. The same day that the New China News Agency announced that Wei had been formally arrested, a spokesman for the U.S. State Department said, "We have maintained consistently that Mr. Wei should not be subject to prosecution for the peaceful expression of his political views. We are not aware that Mr. Wei has ever advocated violence." On December 13, after a secret trial that lasted less than a day, Wei was sentenced to 14 years in prison.

22

OPEC retains quotas

Before concluding a two-day meeting in Vienna, oil ministers of the 12 nations that constitute OPEC agreed to retain for at least an additional six months the level of production it had established in 1994. The members were reminded that exceeding assigned production quotas would depress oil prices and reduce revenues. Total output had been fixed at a little more than 24.5 million bbl a day.

23

CBC cuts U.S. programs

Recognizing his responsibility "to ensure that Canadian voices continue to be heard in Canadian homes," Perrin Beatty, president of the publicly funded Canadian Broadcasting Corporation (CBC), announced that all U.S.-produced television programs would be eliminated from CBC's prime-time schedules. Beatty felt that the change would stimulate the production of more programs by local talent, even though U.S. programs would still be accessible to Canadians through other channels. The cancellation of popular U.S. programs was expected to diminish CBC's revenues by nearly $9 million a year.

24

Irish sanction divorce

Irish voters were so evenly divided on a referendum allowing divorce that a recount was needed the following day before officials could confirm that 50.3% of the 1.6 million who had cast valid ballots approved removal of the constitutional ban on divorce. If the vote was not challenged in court, in December the ban would no longer have legal standing. Couples who had lived apart for a period of four years could then apply for divorce if they affirmed that there was no hope of reconciling. Under current law couples could legally separate, but they could not remarry.

29

Panchen Lama identified

In a move that was clearly designed to undercut the authority of Tibet's Dalai Lama, who opposed China's occupation of his country, the Chinese government held an elaborate religious ceremony in Lhasa during which a six-year-old child was declared the 11th Panchen Lama. The Chinese authorities had injected an element of legality into the proceedings by allowing co-operative Buddhist monks to select a new Panchen Lama from among three children selected by the government. On May 14 the spiritual leader of Tibetan Buddhism, the Dalai Lama, had exercised his traditional authority by certifying that a different child was the 11th incarnation of the Panchen Lama. The whereabouts of that child were not generally known.

HOCINE ZAOURAR—AFP

Women walk past posters for Liamine Zeroual, who won the presidency in the Algerian elections held on November 16. He had been appointed to the post by the military government in 1994.

1

Defense bill passed

Facing the possibility that Congress would refuse to fund the deployment of U.S. troops in Bosnia and Herzegovina if he adhered to his promise to veto a defense bill that was far larger than he wanted, President Clinton allowed the $243.3 billion 1996 Defense Department bill to become law automatically without his signature. On November 16 the House of Representatives had passed the bill by a vote of 270–158 and the Senate by a vote of 59–39.

2

KMT loses ground

Under the leadership of Lee Teng-hui, president of the Republic of China on Taiwan, the ruling Kuomintang (KMT; Nationalist Party) lost ground in an election to fill seats in the Legislative Yuan. The KMT captured 85 of the 164 seats, the opposition Democratic Progressive Party (DPP) 54, the New Party 21, and independents 4. Following the election a proposal was made to abandon the practice of assigning all three top seats in the Legislative Yuan to the ruling party. Instead, the president would come from the ranks of the KMT, the vice president from the DPP, and the secretary-general from the New Party. To free the top two legislators from political pressure, it was suggested that they temporarily resign their party membership. Attention, however, was already shifting to March 1996, when the president would, for the first time, be directly elected by the people.

3

Chun Doo Hwan arrested

South Korean police arrested former president Chun Doo Hwan on charges of having orchestrated the December 1979 military coup that brought him to power. Roh Tae Woo, an old friend of Chun's from their days in the military and his successor as president, had recently been indicted on charges of bribery. He was also being questioned about his and Chun's roles in the May 1980 massacre of pro-democracy protesters in the city of Kwangju. An investigation of the incident already had been concluded and a decision made not to prosecute either man. Pres. Kim Young Sam then declared the matter finished, but popular resentment kept the incident alive. After his arrest Chun became defiant and went on a hunger strike. On the 26th day he collapsed and was placed on a life-support system.

CHOI HANG YOUNG—REUTERS/ARCHIVE PHOTOS

South Koreans burn an effigy of Chun Doo Hwan, arrested on December 3 for crimes allegedly committed during his presidency. Chun's successor, Roh Tae Woo, also faced charges.

4

UAW ends long strike

Despite vociferous objections by some 8,700 striking union employees, officials of the United Automobile Workers union (UAW) called an end to a strike against Caterpillar that had lasted 17 months without significantly affecting the Peoria, Ill.-based firm's production or profits. In June 1994 about 14,000 union workers had walked off their jobs after being without a contract since 1991. Temporary hires, administrative personnel, and eventually some 4,000 former employees who decided to cross the picket lines were able to produce the company's earthmoving equipment. When the strike ended, Caterpillar promised that all those who had been on strike could return to work, but it was not clear what each one's assignment would be.

5

Solana to head NATO

After weeks of wrangling, NATO's ministers formally agreed that Javier Solana Madariaga would replace Willy Claes as secretary-general of the organization. As the foreign minister of Spain, Solana had been involved in all the discussions that had taken place about NATO's role in the post-Cold War period and about requests to expand NATO's membership to include countries that had belonged to the Eastern bloc. During the meeting, France announced that it was rejoining NATO's military committee, which it had left in 1966 on orders from Pres. Charles de Gaulle. His policy of "national independence" had excluded all agreements except those between nation-states.

6

Egypt holds election

In the second round of parliamentary elections, Egypt's governing National Democratic Party (NDP) solidified its hold on power by reportedly adding 193 seats to the 124 it had won in the first round of balloting on November 29. The nation's interior minister announced on December 7 that independents would occupy 114 seats, leaving only 13 seats for members of minor parties. Because the NDP had unchallenged control of the People's Assembly, Pres. Hosni Mubarak was in a position to run unopposed when he sought reelection in 1997.

7

Strike cripples France

Hundreds of thousands of French public-sector workers continued the strike they had initiated on November 24 to protest Prime Minister Alain Juppé's plan to cut welfare spending in order to balance the federal budget. As time passed, the transportation union received growing support from teachers, hospital workers, bank employees, airline personnel, and others sympathetic to their cause. With trains, subways, and buses not operating, most students were unable to get to their schools, and workers had no way to reach their jobs. Virtually every aspect of French life was affected one way or another. During a huge rally in Paris

Striking workers protest the French government's proposals for economic and social reform. On December 7 strikes affected cities throughout the country.

GARY MATOSO—CONTACT PRESS IMAGES

on December 5, protesters overturned cars and clashed with police. On December 10 Juppé made another effort to settle the strike by offering to meet face to face with union leaders. Nothing had been definitively solved when by December 15 many workers had decided to return to their jobs. Neither side had achieved all it had hoped for.

8

Religious law tightened

During a plenary session of Japan's House of Councillors, the nation's Religious Corporation Law was revised to allow the government to scrutinize religious groups more intently. Among other things, jurisdiction over religious corporations operating in more than one prefecture would shift to the Education Ministry, and all religious corporations would be required to submit annual reports listing their senior officers and financial assets. The Education Ministry, moreover, had the right to grant authorities permission to question, and demand reports from, a religious group when its activities came under suspicion and there was reason to consider ordering it to disband. Soka Gakkai, the nation's largest lay Buddhist organization, vigorously opposed the new law, as did also Shinshinto, the main opposition party, which received substantial support from Soka Gakkai.

9

Mfume gets NAACP post

The board of the National Association for the Advancement of Colored People (NAACP) unanimously elected Kweisi Mfume its top executive officer. Mfume said that in February 1996 he would resign from Congress, where he had been chairman of the Congressional Black Caucus, to assume responsibility for the "financial, political, and spiritual health" of the NAACP. The group's reputation had been sullied by financial scandals involving former top executives, and the organization was more than $3 million in debt. Mfume asked for and received the title president and chief executive officer as well as the enhanced authority he felt was needed to carry out his responsibilities.

11

PNA to govern Nabulus

With the approval of Shimon Peres, who had replaced the late Yitzhak Rabin as prime minister of Israel, responsibility for the local administration of Nabulus, the largest city in the West Bank, was turned over to the Palestinian National Authority (PNA). The departure of Israeli troops after 28 years of occupation kept the peace process on course and assured everyone that Peres would continue the policies Rabin had established. Nabulus, known as a centre of ardent nationalism, was in fact the fourth West Bank city to gain limited autonomy. The enclave of Jericho had been the first, in May 1994. In recent weeks Janin and then Tulkarm had been turned over to the PNA.

•

Terrorists admit guilt

Two Japanese men, former members of the religious cult Aum Shinrikyo, admitted in court that they had released toxic sarin gas in Tokyo subway trains in March with the intention of committing indiscriminate murder. The gas killed 12 persons and injured thousands of others. Prosecutors had concluded that 10 persons were directly involved in the attack, 5 who released the gas and 5 who drove them to the subway stations. The men said they had acted on orders from Shoko Asahara, who was in prison charged with murder and other crimes.

13

EU–Turkey trade pact

During a meeting in France, the European Parliament, the legislative branch of the European Union (EU), approved a customs pact with Turkey. By adopting many of the regulations governing trade within the EU, Turkey would be allowed to participate in the EU market as an outsider. Critics cited Turkey's treatment of separatist Kurds as evidence of its disregard for human rights and argued that such conduct should exclude it from membership in the EU. Others, however, pointed to the reforms Turkey had initiated and argued that membership in the EU would bolster its fledgling democracy.

14

Peace agreement signed

During a ceremony in Paris, the four-year civil war in Bosnia and Herzegovina officially came to an end when the presidents of Bosnia and Herzegovina, Serbia, and Croatia affixed their signatures to a peace agreement. A vital provision of the accord called for the deployment of 60,000 NATO troops, whose mission would be to maintain peace by keeping the former combatants apart. The U.S. contingent of 20,000 men was the largest single military group, but numerous other nations, notably Great

A U.S. Army camp stands in floodwater in Croatia. The troops, who were building a bridge across the Sava River to Bosnia and Herzegovina, were part of a NATO force.

PETR JOSEK—REUTERS

Britain and France, were contributing military support. The U.S. Congress held heated debates about U.S. participation, which President Clinton insisted was absolutely essential to keep the peace initiative from total collapse. Congress finally supported the measure, but in some cases congressmen—believing that Clinton had the authority to dispatch the troops with or without congressional approval—indicated that their vote was a gesture of support for the troops but not for Clinton's policy.

15

ASEAN is nuclear-free

The seven members of the Association of Southeast Asian Nations (ASEAN) concluded a two-day meeting in Bangkok, Thailand, after signing a pact declaring their region a nuclear-free zone. The declaration prohibited the "possession, manufacture, and acquisition" of nuclear weapons in Brunei, Indonesia, Malaysia, the Philippines, Singapore, Thailand, and Vietnam. Cambodia and Laos, which had only observer status, and Myanmar (Burma), which hoped to obtain that status, also signed the document.

17

Russians elect Duma

Incomplete tallies of the votes cast in an election to fill the 450 seats in Russia's State Duma indicated that the Communist Party of the Russian Federation, under the leadership of Gennady Zyuganov, had won control of a large percentage of the seats. Its candidates blamed the government for Russia's decline. The second largest bloc was expected to be the Liberal Democratic Party, led by ultranationalist Vladimir Zhirinovsky. Although the reformists—followers of Pres. Boris Yeltsin and Prime Minister Viktor Chernomyrdin—did not have the strength to challenge the major political blocs in the State Duma, government policies were not likely to be much affected by the election because the Russian president had constitutional powers that far exceeded those of the State Duma.

•

Austrians go to polls

Following the breakup of Austria's ruling coalition, voters gave the Social Democrats of Chancellor Franz Vranitzky 38.3% of the vote (an increase of 3.4% over 1994) and the People's Party 28.3% (a 0.6% increase). The Freedom Party retained the 22.1% it had before the election. Losses were suffered by the environmentalist Greens and the Liberal Party. It appeared that the Social Democratic Party and the People's Party would reunite in a new coalition early in 1996.

18

Security pact signed

With Indonesian President Suharto and Australian Prime Minister Paul Keating presiding over the ceremony, the foreign ministers of their two countries signed a mutual security pact in Jakarta, Indonesia's capital. The two nations agreed to foster "such cooperation as would benefit their own security and that of the region," but the treaty did not oblige either country to assist the other militarily during an emergency. There was heated criticism of Keating, both at home and abroad, for signing a treaty with a nation whose annexation of the former Portuguese colony of East Timor had never been recognized by the United Nations and whose military operations against East Timorese dissidents had been denounced repeatedly by human rights organizations.

•

Seal quotas raised

Brian Tobin, Canada's minister of fisheries, announced in Nova Scotia that beginning in 1996, seal hunters would be allowed to harvest up to 250,000 seals annually along Canada's Atlantic coast. The new quota amounted to an increase of about 30% over the present limit. Dismissing protests from animal rights protesters, Tobin said that the country's harp seal population had doubled to 4.8 million since 1982 and that seals were at least partly responsible for shrinking stocks of cod and other fish in Canada's coastal waters. The shortage had led to a moratorium on fishing certain species, which in turn resulted in financial losses for commercial fishermen.

20

Queen urges divorce

Buckingham Palace confirmed that earlier in the month Queen Elizabeth II had sent letters to her son, Prince Charles, and to his wife, Diana, urging them to seek a divorce as quickly as possible. The royal couple's failed marriage had been almost daily fodder for tabloids all over the world. After the two announced their separation, they were hounded everywhere they went. In November Diana had violated royal protocol by granting a television interview without the queen's knowledge or consent. Diana's on-camera admission that she had had an affair reportedly shocked the queen and caused her to advise an immediate divorce.

31

U.S. agencies shut down

A final effort to reach a federal budget compromise that would allow several hundred thousand federal workers to return to their jobs after New Year's Day failed when Republicans and Democrats in the Senate and House of Representatives and President Clinton rejected the others' conditions for ending the stalemate. The shutdown of government offices that resulted when budgets were unfunded or underfunded had created chaos in some quarters and serious inconveniences in others. The U.S. Postal Service, however, continued to operate because it functioned independently. The budget crisis had little to do with money. It was rather the result of deep philosophical differences over the role of government in people's lives. With virtually every avenue of compromise already explored and neither side indicating a willingness to abandon its principles, it was impossible to predict how long the stalemate would last.

Disasters

The loss of life and property from disasters in 1995 included the following:

Aviation

January 5, Near Isfahan, Iran. A C-140 JetStar carrying the commander of the Iranian air force and 11 other top military officers, including 4 other generals, crashed on the tarmac when it returned to the airport after experiencing mechanical difficulties; all aboard perished.

January 11, Near Cartagena, Colombia. A DC-9 aircraft carrying 53 persons crashed and broke apart in a field, apparently as the pilot attempted to make a crash landing in a nearby swamp; a nine-year-old girl, who was pushed out of the plane by her mother and landed on a soft pile of seaweed some 9 m (30 ft) from the wreckage, was the only survivor.

March 31, Near Bucharest, Rom. A Romanian Tarom Airlines Airbus 310 with 60 persons aboard crashed during a sleet storm shortly after takeoff, but investigators blamed a faulty engine mechanism for the crash; there were no survivors.

April 28, Jaffna province, Sri Lanka. A military transport plane carrying troops to Colombo crashed moments after takeoff; none of the 38 persons aboard survived.

May 24, Near Harrogate, England. A commuter plane with 12 persons aboard crashed in a field during a violent thunderstorm, presumably after being struck by lightning; all aboard the aircraft perished.

Late June, Lagos, Nigeria. An airliner making a domestic flight from Kaduna skidded off a rain-soaked runway while attempting to land and burst into flames in a nearby field; of the 80 persons aboard, at least 16 lost their lives.

Mid-July, Antananarivo, Madagascar. A military transport plane crashed upon landing at the airport; 34 passengers, including 21 doctors from a humanitarian aid group, were killed.

August 9, San Salvador, El Salvador. An airliner making its approach to the airport inexplicably slammed into the side of a volcano; all 65 persons aboard were killed.

Early September, Near Jalalabad, Pak. An Afghan airliner with 46 persons aboard crashed; there were no survivors.

September 10, Shacklefords, Va. A plane carrying parachutists went into a steep dive before crashing into a house; all 11 persons aboard the craft and one person on the ground were killed. Investigators concluded that the plane had been improperly loaded and had exceeded its maximum takeoff weight.

September 13, Near Colombo, Sri Lanka. A military transport plane with 75 persons aboard crashed during a thunderstorm while simultaneously experiencing instrument failure; there were no survivors.

September 15, Borneo. A Malaysian airliner carrying 53 persons plowed through a shantytown and exploded near the town of Tawau, where it was attempting to land; 37 persons aboard the plane were killed, and 9 persons on the ground were injured, two critically.

September 21, Near Moron, Mongolia. A Mongolian airliner with 41 persons aboard went down after taking off from Ulan Bator; one person survived the crash.

September 22, Near Elmendorf Air Force Base, Alaska. An air force airborne warning and control system jet equipped with one of the world's most sophisticated surveillance systems and carrying 24 crewmen (22 Americans and 2 Canadians) crashed in a forest shortly after takeoff when its left engine suddenly caught on fire; all aboard perished.

October 4, Kyrgyzstan. A helicopter that was ferrying workers from a gold mine to the capital crashed in the Tien Shan mountains; all 15 persons aboard perished.

November 8, Central Argentina. A military aircraft en route to an aviation school ceremony crashed in a mountainous area during a raging storm; none of the 53 persons aboard survived.

December 3, Near Douala, Cameroon. A Cameroon jetliner clipped some trees and crashed into a swamp, apparently after the pilot tried to abort the landing when the right engine began emitting sparks; of the 78 persons aboard the craft, only 6 survived.

December 6, Near Nakhichevan, Azerbaijan. A twin-engine plane went down shortly after takeoff, apparently after experiencing engine problems; 49 persons were killed, and 33 were injured.

December 7, Russia. A Russian aircraft with 97 persons aboard vanished from radar screens while it was en route from Sakhalin Island to Khabarovsk; the wreckage of the craft was discovered 11 days later, and all aboard were found dead.

December 7, Near Belle-Anse, Haiti. A twin-engine plane with 20 persons aboard, 16 of them Haitians bound for repatriation, inexplicably crashed; there were no survivors.

December 13, Near Verona, Italy. A Romanian charter plane carrying at least 45 persons crashed shortly after take-off from Villafranca Airport; all aboard perished.

December 18, Near Jamba, Angola. A Zairean-based plane that was carrying at least 136 persons went down in a remote area; only 5 persons survived the crash.

December 20, Near Buga, Colombia. An American Airlines 757 jet with 164 persons aboard crashed into a mountain shortly before it was due to land in Cali; the accident, which was attributed to pilot error, claimed the lives of 160 and was the deadliest crash involving a U.S. jetliner since 1988.

Fires and Explosions

January 5, Jinan, Shandong province, China. An underground pipeline explosion blasted apart a 2-km (1.25-mi) expanse of pavement and killed at least 10 persons.

February 7, Pusan, South Korea. A fire that erupted in the engine room of a cargo ship that was docked for repairs killed 18 persons and seriously injured 7.

February 15, T'ai-chung, Taiwan. An explosion touched off a fire in a restaurant/karaoke complex, which was gutted by the blaze; at least 64 patrons were killed, many of them trapped behind iron-barred windows and a locked rear-door exit.

Mid-April, Urumqi, Xinjiang Uygur, China. A fire that ripped through a movie theatre and karaoke bar claimed the lives of 51 persons and injured countless others.

April 17, Gdansk, Poland. A powerful explosion caused by a ruptured gas main in the basement of an 11-story building obliterated the first 3 floors

JOSE MIGUEL GOMEZ—REUTERS

A fisherman rows past a wing from an airliner that was carrying 52 persons when it crashed near Cartagena, Colombia, on January 11. The only survivor of the crash was a nine-year-old girl who had been pushed from the plane by her mother and who landed on a pile of seaweed.

Women in Mandi Dabwali in northern India mourn the deaths of family members killed in a fire on December 23. More than 500 people attending a school ceremony died in the blaze.
KAMAL KISHORE—REUTERS

of the structure and destabilized the remaining 8 levels; 7 persons were killed in the blast, and 20 were missing and presumed dead.

April 17, Taiwan. A predawn fire at a nightclub claimed the lives of 11 persons, 10 of whom died after being hospitalized for smoke inhalation; the blaze, which was possibly the work of an arsonist, also injured 13 of the 39 persons on the premises.

April 23, Lao Cai province, Vietnam. A jeep crammed with some 20 persons exploded when its cargo of explosives ignited; the vehicle and its passengers were incinerated.

April 28, Taegu, South Korea. A thunderous rush-hour explosion that was precipitated by a leaking gas main at a subway construction site hurled huge metal plates serving as a temporary roadway atop cars and buses loaded with schoolchildren, tossed some 100 cars and city buses into the excavation site, and damaged about 70 buildings; 110 persons were believed killed, at least half of them schoolchildren.

Late May, Northern India. A fire at a fireworks factory claimed the lives of 23 persons, including 13 women and 6 children.

June 23, Belgrade, Yugos. A powerful explosion rocked a chemical factory during the production of a new but unidentified product; 10 persons were killed, and 11 were injured seriously.

August 21, Near Seoul, South Korea. A fire in a church-run reformatory for women was deliberately started by prostitutes and runaways who tried to escape; at least 38 women perished behind barred windows and doors.

October 27, Near Kosice, Slovakia. A ruptured gas pipeline that was oozing carbon monoxide gas exploded at a steel mill; 11 workers were fatally injured.

October 28, Baku, Azerbaijan. A fire that enveloped a subway car as it was traveling between stations claimed the lives of more than 300 persons and injured some 200; most of the victims were felled by carbon monoxide fumes emanating from burning materials, and others were electrocuted as they tried to grasp cables to escape the blazing train.

November 3, Córdoba province, Arg. A powerful explosion at an Argentine munitions factory in the town of Río Tercero killed at least 13 persons and left 200 missing; the initial blast, which injured some 330 others, also touched off a fire that threatened to spread to an underground heavy artillery depot.

December 7, Shaqlawah, Iraq. A fuel tanker that was taking oil to a UN gasoline station exploded; at least 10 persons, including two UN guards, lost their lives in the blast.

December 23, Mandi Dabwali, India. A fire that engulfed a tent that had been erected in a walled courtyard for a school ceremony claimed the lives of more than 500 persons, mostly youths but also some entire families gathered for the occasion, and severely burned hundreds of others; the official cause of the blaze was linked to an electrical short circuit that ignited a fire in the tent's synthetic fabric.

Marine

Early January, Constanta, Rom. Two bulk carriers, the Maltese-flagged *Paris* and the Hong-Kong-registered *You Xiu,* lost power in heavy seas and a blizzard and sank after hitting the port's breakwater; 54 seamen were feared drowned.

February 25, Off the northwestern coast of Australia. Three small fishing boats apparently sank after being battered by ferocious winds; 11 persons were lost at sea.

March 2, Off the coast of Angola. A coaster carrying some 227 persons, many of them women and children, ran aground and sank; about 45 persons survived.

Late March, South China. An overloaded boat carrying nearly twice its capacity sank; some 42 Buddhist pilgrims lost their lives.

Mid-May, Off the coast of the Philippines. An interisland ferry erupted in flames, causing panicked passengers to jump into the sea without their life jackets; 42 persons drowned, and 23 others were missing.

Late May, Central India. Three boats carrying festival revelers capsized in the Narmada River; 22 persons drowned, and 100 suffered injuries.

Early June, Zambezia province, Mozambique. A boat sank in the Ligonha River; 12 of the craft's occupants were killed by crocodiles, and several others were missing.

Mid-June, Bangkok, Thailand. A floating pier that was loaded with commuters capsized on the Chao Phraya River; at least 20 persons lost their lives, and as many as 80 were injured.

Early July, Gulf of Guinea. A passenger boat traveling between Cameroon and Nigeria sank in choppy waters; at least 100 persons were feared drowned.

Mid-August, Western Bangladesh. A ferryboat capsized on the Chitra River; about 150 persons were believed drowned.

August 17, Southeastern Venezuela. A tourist boat plummeted over a 91.5-m (300-ft) waterfall; 11 children and a priest who was accompanying them were killed.

August 18, Off the coast of Yemen. A strong tide upended a boat carrying Eritreans sailing to Yemen; at least 92 persons lost their lives when the craft sank.

Early September, Bihar state, India. A boat capsized after slamming into a bridge on the rain-swollen Ganges River; at least 40 of the 150 persons aboard perished.

October 29, Near Patna, India. A boat brimming with a group of Hindu pilgrims capsized while attempting to cross the Ganges River; at least 60 persons drowned.

November 8, Off the coast of Oregon. A charter fishing boat en route to Alaska was missing after experiencing engine problems during a spell of bad weather; the fate of the 11 persons aboard was unknown.

November 10, Off the coast of Bangladesh. A fierce storm battered fishing boats in the Bay of Bengal; at least 21 trawlers and nearly 200 fishermen were missing.

Mining and Tunneling

January 1–March 15, China. A total of 92 mining accidents killed 573 persons during the 10-week period.

February 26, Near Quetta, Pak. A methane gas explosion in a coal mine caused part of the mine to collapse; more than 27 workers were buried alive.

March 13, Yunnan province, China. A gas explosion in a poorly ventilated mine killed 32 workers and injured 12; the mine, which had operated in violation of safety regulations, was closed by the government.

March 26, Sorgun, Turkey. An explosion trapped at least 40 miners and injured 5.

March 30–31, Near Vorkuta, Russia. Two separate gas explosions that occurred in the same mine on successive days resulted in the deaths of a total of 15 persons.

May 10, Near Johannesburg, South Africa. A runaway underground locomotive at the Vaal Reefs gold mine plowed through a safety mechanism, plunged down a mine shaft, and crushed more than 100 miners who were descending in a cage; all were killed.

August 31, Mieres, Spain. A gas explosion in a deep coal mine killed 14 miners.

September 4, Kemerovo, Russia. A planned explosion in a coal mine, where 81 miners were working, claimed the lives of 15 miners who were killed when the cage in which they were riding collapsed as a result of the blast.

Late September, Near Jos, Nigeria. A cave-in buried 80 persons who were illegally mining for tin; the dead were mostly teenagers and farmers in need of employment.

September 27, Near Dhanbad, India. Two coal mines were flooded with water that surged into the shaft after a river overflowed; at least 70 miners drowned.

PATRICK DE NOIRMONT—REUTERS

Relatives and friends attend a memorial service for workers killed at a gold mine near Johannesburg, South Africa, on May 10. A runaway locomotive crushed the miners.

Natural

Early January, Northern Bangladesh. A bitter cold snap, the worst in 30 years, killed at least 120 persons.

Early–mid-January, California. A series of violent storms deluged much of the state, claimed at least 11 lives, and caused some $300 million in damages to crops, homes, businesses, and roads; 34 rain-drenched counties were declared disaster areas, and the community of Rio Linda, just north of Sacramento, was one of the worst affected after a channel named Dry Creek burgeoned into a lake and inundated hundreds of homes.

January 16, Súdhavík, Iceland. A predawn avalanche roared down upon a sleeping fishing village during a raging storm accompanied by gale-force winds; 14 persons were entombed in their homes.

January 16–19, Kashmir, India. A thundering Himalayan avalanche trapped more than 5,000 motorists in their vehicles on the Jammu-Srinagar highway; more than 200 persons were known dead, 400 were taking temporary refuge in a tunnel, and 5,000 were rescued.

January 17, Kobe, Japan. The Great Hanshin Earthquake, a cataclysmic temblor of magnitude 7.2, devastated the city, claimed some 6,000 lives, injured more than 30,000 persons, left some 300,000 persons homeless, and temporarily closed the world's busiest port. Hundreds of streets buckled or caved in, nearly 200,000 buildings were destroyed or badly damaged, and kilometres of train tracks were mangled. It was estimated that the reconstruction of Kobe would cost around $120 billion, which would make the quake the costliest natural disaster in history.

Late January–early February, Belgium, France, Germany, The Netherlands. Torrential rains and melting snow caused massive flooding as overflowing rivers, notably the Rhine, Main, Mosel, Meuse, Waal, and Nahe, unleashed their waters and submerged surrounding towns; the northern half of France was almost completely under water, German city dwellers navigated by boat, and The Netherlands, which was hardest hit of all, fortified stressed earthen dikes that were protecting low-lying farmlands with some 15,000 sandbags while more than 250,000 residents evacuated the already saturated areas. Some 30 deaths were attributed to the flooding, which inflicted damages in excess of $2 billion.

February 8, Pereira, Colombia. An earthquake of magnitude 6.4 rocked the area, toppled cement and brick structures, and claimed at least 38 lives; 230 persons were injured, and at least 3,000 were left homeless after some 700 homes were destroyed.

Early March, California. Record-setting relentless rains pummeled the state, destabilized twin Interstate 5 bridges, which collapsed and resulted in the closure of a 290-km (180-mi) stretch of highway, closed other roads, and isolated the communities around Monterey, which resembled a soggy bog. The storm also disrupted electrical and telephone services, submerged vineyards in the Napa and Sonoma valleys, and destroyed crops in some of the nation's most fertile farmlands. At least 12 fatalities were attributed to the violent weather.

March 27, Kalluq, Afghanistan. Heavy rains triggered a mud slide that obliterated a remote mountain village; 354 persons were killed, and 64 were injured.

Early May, Northern Sumatra, Indon. Floods and landslides caused by heavy rains killed at least 55 persons and left some 17,500 homeless.

May 5, Dallas and Fort Worth, Texas. A string of drenching storms packing high winds and accompanied by hailstones the size of softballs pounded the northern part of the state and claimed the lives of 17 persons.

May 17, Southeastern Bangladesh. A vicious rainstorm and a tidal surge claimed the lives of nearly 100 persons; some 10,000 shanties were destroyed, and at least 120 passengers aboard two boats were spilled into the waters after the crafts capsized.

May 28, Sakhalin Island, Russia. An earthquake of magnitude 7.5 nearly wiped out the town of Neftegorsk, where only 1,208 persons out of some 3,200 survived.

A woman on Sakhalin Island searches through the ruins of a house belonging to relatives. Nearly 2,000 people were killed when a powerful earthquake struck the Russian island on May 28.

VLADIMIR VELEGURIN—AFP

Late May, Central Angola. Torrential rains washed away a feeding centre; 25 children were among the 33 fatalities.

Early June, Northern and central India. A sweltering heat wave with temperatures in excess of 46° C (115° F) tormented residents in the states of Uttar Pradesh, Rajasthan, Bihar, and Madhya Pradesh; though the official death toll was placed at 550, more than 1,200 corpses were prepared for burial.

Early–mid-June, Bangladesh and Nepal. Heavy premonsoon rains produced severe flooding and landslides; at least 50 deaths were reported in Bangladesh, 60 persons were confirmed dead in Nepal, and 35 were missing.

Early June–early July, Hunan, Hubei, and Jiangxi provinces, China. Severe rains touched off massive flooding and swelled the Chang Jiang (Yangtze River) to a dangerously high level; at least 1,200 persons perished in the flooding, some 5.6 million were stranded, and 1.3 million were relocated after some 900,000 homes were destroyed and some 4 million damaged.

June 3, Puerto Lempira, Honduras. An electrical storm claimed the lives of at least 17 soccer fans who were struck by a bolt of lightning as they sought protection in a nearby shelter.

June 15, Egion, Greece. An earthquake of magnitude 6.1 reduced an apartment building and a hotel to heaps of rubble; at least 17 persons were killed, 59 were injured seriously, and some 500 buildings were damaged.

June 30, Near Kuala Lumpur, Malaysia. A landslide buried more than 15 cars and 2 buses traveling on a highway leading to a resort; at least 20 persons lost their lives, and 23 were injured.

July, U.S. A scorching heat wave that stalled over the Midwest and then gripped the East with suffocating temperatures hovering around 38° C (100° F) claimed the lives of nearly 1,000 persons nationwide; Chicago reported a record 733 heat-related deaths, while the other fatalities were scattered across the nation.

July 13, Western Turkey. Flash floods triggered massive mud slides that descended on the town of Senirkent; at least 50 persons perished, and some 200 homes were destroyed.

Mid-July, Bangladesh. Chest-deep floodwaters inundated at least 27 districts and claimed the lives of more than 150 persons.

Mid-July, Pakistan. Relentless monsoon rains touched off severe flooding; nearly 600 persons perished.

Mid-July, Southwestern China. Weeks of heavy rains triggered a landslide that buried a sleeping village; 26 deaths were reported.

Mid-July, South Korea. Typhoon Faye lashed the country with heavy rain and high winds; at least 16 persons were known dead, and 25 were missing.

Mid-July, Spain. A stifling heat wave, with temperatures soaring to 44° C (111° F), was blamed for the deaths of 10 persons.

August 17, Morocco. A downpour in the drought-stricken Atlas Mountains triggered flash flooding and landslides, which swept away homes and cars carrying vacationers; more than 230 persons were killed, and some 500 were missing.

Early September, Northern India. Heavy monsoon rains were blamed for the deaths of at least 40 villagers.

Early September, Morocco. A new round of flooding killed 31 persons.

September 4–6, Northeastern Caribbean islands. Hurricane Luis, one of the most powerful storms of the 20th century and packing winds of 225 km/h (140 mph), brutalized Antigua and Barbuda, St. Kitts and Nevis, the Dutch and French island of St. Martin, Dominica, Montserrat, Anguilla, Saint-Barthélemy, and Guadeloupe before grazing the northern coast of Puerto Rico and losing force; though Antigua was hardest hit, the other islands sustained heavy damage, and at least 15 persons, 9 of them on St. Martin, lost their lives.

September 6, Southern Philippines. Waist-high floodwaters descended on towns in Cotabato province after the rim of Parker Volcano collapsed, causing the crater's lake waters to overflow; 26 persons were killed, and more than 100 were missing and feared dead.

September 14, Mexico. Hurricane Ismael hammered the northwestern Pacific states and claimed the lives of at least 107 persons, many of them fishermen caught at sea.

Mid-September, Thailand. Extensive flooding affected 52 of the country's 76 provinces and claimed the lives of at least 62 persons.

September 15–16, U.S. Virgin Islands and eastern Puerto Rico. Hurricane Marilyn unleashed its fury on St. Thomas with winds in excess of 160 km/h (100 mph) and destroyed 80% of its buildings, battered St. John and ripped off 60% of the roofs there, and bashed St. Croix before destroying 50 homes and damaging some 200 others on Puerto Rico; at least nine fatalities were attributed to the storm, which caused some $875 million in damages.

Late September–early October, Bangladesh. Five days of heavy rains created severe flooding that trapped more than one million persons in their homes and claimed the lives of more than 100.

October 1, Western Turkey. An earthquake of magnitude 6 rocked the area and reduced to

Damaged boats lie on the shore of the island of St. Martin. Hurricane Luis, one of the most powerful storms of the 20th century, moved through the Caribbean on September 4–6.
SYLVRE SELBONNE—AFP

rubble more than 60% of the buildings in Dinar; at least 84 persons were known dead, dozens of others were buried under debris and feared dead, and more than 190 were injured.

October 1, The Philippines. Tropical storm Sybil ravaged at least 29 provinces and 27 cities and helped unleash floods, landslides, and volcanic mudflows; more than 100 fatalities were reported, and 100 were missing and feared dead.

October 4, Florida, North Carolina, Georgia, and Alabama. Hurricane Opal pummeled the Florida panhandle along a 195-km (120-mi) stretch of land with wind gusts of up to 200 km/h (125 mph), ruptured sewer and water lines, caused $50 million in damages to recreational boats, inflicted at least $1.8 billion in property damages, and claimed the lives of at least 19 persons.

October 7, Sumatra, Indon. An earthquake of magnitude 7 claimed the lives of at least 100 persons and injured at least 700.

October 9, Mexico. An earthquake of magnitude 7.6 rocked the country's Pacific coast, toppling two hotels (one in the resort town of Manzanillo, Colima state, and the other in Jalisco state); the temblor claimed the lives of more than 65 persons and injured scores of others.

October 24, Yunnan province. An earthquake of magnitude 6.5 struck during a torrential downpour, demolished hundreds of buildings and homes, killed at least 40 persons, and injured at least 70.

October 26, Flateyri, Iceland. A massive predawn snowslide, preceded by days of blizzards and storms, engulfed 19 homes and claimed the lives of 20 persons in the fishing village.

Late October, The Philippines. Tropical storm Zack roared through the country and forced at least 60,000 persons to flee their homes; the brutal storm claimed at least 100 lives.

November 3, The Philippines. Typhoon Angela, with punishing winds of 225 km/h (140 mph), blasted the northern part of the country and left a trail of destruction that included $77 million in damages to crops, roads, and bridges; the death toll of more than 700 was expected to rise, as many persons remained missing.

November 11–12, Nepal. Heavy snow in the Himalayas triggered a series of snowslides and mudflows that killed at least 49 persons and trapped scores of others; more than 500 persons were rescued.

November 22, Middle East. A powerful earthquake shook Egypt, Israel, Lebanon, Jordan, and Saudi Arabia and claimed at least 10 lives across the region.

December 25, KwaZulu/Natal province, South Africa. Flash floods caused by incessant rains killed at least 130 persons, many of them swept away in their corrugated iron shacks.

Late December, Europe and Asia. A series of blizzards and spells of extreme cold that stretched from the U.K. to Kazakhstan and Bangladesh took the lives of over 350 people, many of whom froze to death in Moscow while intoxicated.

Late December, Brazil. Severe rains and attendant flooding resulted in the deaths of some 60 people.

Railroad

January 13, Near Hilli, Bangladesh. A speeding passenger train collided with a stationary passenger train; more than 150 lives were lost, and at least 300 were injured in the high-speed crash.

April 2, Prachuap Khiri Khan, Thailand. A 10-ton truck slammed into the locomotive of a passenger train at an unmarked railroad crossing, causing the train to derail; 14 persons were killed, including the truck driver, the train engineer, a mechanic, and 11 passengers, and at least 109 were injured.

Mid-May, Tamil Nadu, India. A freight train collided head-on with an express passenger train near the town of Salem after barreling through a stop signal; at least 50 fatalities and some 200 injuries were reported.

August 20, Firozabad, India. An express train that hit a cow and came to a complete stop after its braking system was damaged was rammed from behind by another express train when signaling problems developed; the worst rail accident in the country's history killed 348 persons and injured scores of others.

October 24, Near Tasikmalaya, Indon. A passenger train carrying between 300 and 400 persons left the tracks and tumbled into an area filled with ravines and volcanic mountains; at least 17 persons were killed, and 100 were injured.

December 21, Near Cairo. A commuter train traveling at high speed in thick fog rammed into the rear of a passenger train, propelling one car of the passenger train atop another of its cars and derailing two other cars; the official toll was placed at 75 dead and 76 injured, but eyewitnesses reported that many more were killed.

Traffic

January 3, Near Echague, Phil. A bus that was racing with another bus fell off a bridge into a ravine; 31 persons were killed, and 38 were injured.

January 7, Hao Binh province, Vietnam. A passenger bus, which experienced brake problems while the driver's son was at the wheel, left the road and plunged into a ravine; 21 passengers were killed, but the boy survived the crash.

February 3, Near Jhumsa, Nepal. A bus rolled off a mountain road and fell some 100 m (330 ft); 43 persons lost their lives in the accident.

March 12, Near Madras, India. An oil truck collided with a bus after attempting to pass a tractor-trailer filled with wedding guests; at least 110 persons were killed when all three vehicles burst into flames.

Early March, Côte d'Ivoire. A bus traveling on the Abidjan-Touba coastal route left the roadway and plowed into a village; 14 persons were killed, and 54 were injured.

April 9, Near Bowie, Ariz. A swirling dust storm blinded motorists traveling on Interstate 10 and resulted in a 24-car pileup; 10 persons were killed in the crash.

April 17, India. A bus filled with Buddhist pilgrims was traveling on a mountain road when it fell off a cliff on Adam's Peak; 14 persons were killed, and 34 were injured.

April 25, Southern India. A truck veered off a road and dived into a deep irrigation ditch; at least 29 Hindu pilgrims aboard the vehicle were killed.

Early May, Near Chongqing, China. A bus collided with a truck and fell into a river; 12 persons lost their lives.

Mid-May, Eastern Spain. A bus carrying some 40 senior citizens collided head-on with a tractor-trailer truck; 13 passengers were killed.

May 23, Near Bristol, England. A bus carrying British Legion members spun off the M4 roadway, landed in a culvert, and burst into flames, apparently after the driver swerved to avoid wooden pallets strewn across the pavement; 12 retirees were killed in the crash.

Early June, Near Kalubathan, India. An express train collided with a freight train; 48 persons perished, and 76 were injured.

June 4, Maharashtra, India. A truck overturned and plunged into a deep valley near Kohlapur; 23 persons perished, and 10 were injured.

July 10, Near Roquemaure, France. A bus transporting Spanish students from Amsterdam to Barcelona, Spain, swerved wildly and rolled over several times after the bus driver apparently dozed off; at least 22 persons were killed and 32 injured when the driver, who was abruptly awakened after the vehicle's side mirror scraped a truck, tried frantically to steer the bus back on course.

Miscellaneous

January 2, Tajikistan. Locally brewed champagne mixed with cyanide claimed the lives of 10 revelers celebrating the New Year.

Mid-January, Laghouat, Alg. A perfume that was laced with a toxic substance killed at least 27 persons, including 10 victims who blended wine with the scent, and hospitalized some 40 others; it was not known if all of those afflicted had drunk the adulterated concoction or if some merely had worn it.

February 24, Rasht, Iran. A stampede at a mosque on the last Friday of the Muslim month of Ramadan claimed the lives of 14 persons; additional details of the tragedy were not made available.

March 16, Kigali, Rwanda. At least 22 of the 74 Hutu prisoners being held on suspicion of genocide suffocated after being incarcerated in a cramped cell built to hold between 5 and 10 inmates.

April 28, South Island, New Zealand. A viewing platform above a spectacular cavern in the Paparoa National Park, built to support 10 persons, collapsed under the weight of 18 visitors; of the 14 persons who were hurled to their deaths on the rocks below, 13 were students.

June 29, Seoul, South Korea. A five-story department store collapsed in a heap of rubble, causing a fire in an underground parking garage where cars crushed by falling debris leaked gasoline, which ignited and sent acrid smoke billowing through the complex; more than 500 shoppers were killed, and 400 were missing amid tons of concrete and metal debris. Investigators attributed the tragedy to shoddy construction.

July 15, Near Gyor, Hung. An abandoned truck that had a faulty ventilation system became a death chamber for 18 Sri Lankan Tamils, who suffocated when the driver disappeared without opening the sealed trailer.

People of 1995

NOBEL PRIZES

Prize for Peace

Partly as a protest against nuclear testing by China and France, the Norwegian Nobel Committee awarded the 1995 Nobel Prize for Peace to the physicist and antinuclear activist Joseph Rotblat and the Pugwash Conferences on Science and World Affairs that he had headed for many years. A physicist who had helped develop the atomic bomb, Rotblat left the project to pursue peaceful uses of nuclear energy. Recognition of the efforts of these supporters of nuclear disarmament and arms limitations came in the year that marked the 50th anniversary of the bombings of the Japanese cities of Hiroshima and Nagasaki during World War II.

Born on Nov. 4, 1908, in Warsaw and educated in Poland, Rotblat went to the University of Liverpool, England, as a lecturer in 1939. He then became a member of the British team that joined U.S. scientists at Los Alamos, N.M., to work on the Manhattan Project. Although he was uncomfortable about participating in the creation of an atomic bomb, Rotblat initially believed that the weapon would be used only to deter a German threat. After learning in 1944 that it would be used to contain the Soviet Union, a World War II ally, he left the project and returned to Liverpool. After the war Rotblat became a British citizen, and he dedicated himself to peaceful applications of physics, primarily in nuclear medicine. He directed research in nuclear physics at the University of Liverpool (1945–49) and was a professor at the University of London's St. Bartholemew's Hospital Medical College (1950–76).

In 1955 Rotblat joined a group of scientists in signing a manifesto advanced by Bertrand Russell and Albert Einstein that urged an end to nuclear arms. "Such weapons," it said, "threaten the continued existence of mankind." No fewer than 10 of the signatories were past or future Nobel laureates. From the group's commitment came the first of the annual Pugwash Conferences, named for the village in Nova Scotia where the first meeting was held in 1957. Some 25 invited participants, mostly scientists, met each year to hear and read papers and to discuss critical issues on arms control. They were encouraged to take the antinuclear message home with the hope of influencing policy changes in their respective countries. Hiroshima was the site of the 1995 meeting. Rotblat served as secretary-general of the London-based organization from 1957 to 1973 and as president after 1988.

One purpose of the conferences was to foster a dialogue between opposing sides in the arms race, and the speakers often included scientists and government officials in charge of the nuclear arms programs in their own countries. During the Cold War years, some U.S. officials criticized the Pugwash Conferences as dupes of the Soviet Union.

While there was no clear evidence that the conferences directly led to arms reduction, it was thought that the discussions were not without influence. There was evidence that contacts made in the meetings contributed to the resolution of events such as the Cuban missile crisis in 1962.

Rotblat's published works include *Science and World Affairs* (1962), *Pugwash* (1967), *Scientists in the Quest for Peace* (1972), *Scientists, the Arms Race and Disarmament* (1982), *Coexistence, Co-operation and Common Security* (1989), *Building Global Security Through Co-operation* (1990), *Towards a Secure World in the 21st Century* (1991), and *A World at the Crossroads* (1994). Many of the works reflected his commitment to engaging scientists of all nations to work for world peace.

(MARGARET BARLOW)

Prize for Economics

In 1995 the University of Chicago faculty added another Nobel laureate to its growing list of notables. For the fifth time in six years, one of its professors was awarded the Nobel Memorial Prize for Economic Science. The latest recipient, Robert Emerson Lucas, Jr., was honoured for having developed and applied the hypothesis of rational expectations.

Ever since the Great Depression of the 1930s, whenever the U.S. government wanted to correct the direction of the economy, it did so by raising or lowering taxes or interest rates. However, during the recession of the 1970s, lowering interest rates and infusing money into the economy resulted in higher, not lower, unemployment and excessive inflation.

Lucas offered an explanation of this unexpected result based on a simple observation: that business and industry, workers, and consumers were too smart to be manipulated over and over again. According to his theory, people had learned to anticipate government policies to direct the economy and then adjusted their own course of action on the basis of those "rational expectations." For example, during the recession the government had lowered taxes because in the past when businesses expected increased profits, they hired more workers and paid them higher wages. The government economists knew that this policy also caused prices to rise, but the increased inflation was viewed as a trade-off for higher employment. In the 1970s, though, the government's strategy backfired. Workers demanded even higher wages to offset rising prices, which caused inflation and unemployment to skyrocket.

Despite interest in Lucas' early publications, such as *Rational Expectations and Econometric Practice* (1981; coauthored with colleague Thomas J. Sargent) and *Studies in Business-Cycle Theory* (1981), government economists during the 1980s persisted in trying to apply the old models.

In its announcement of the 1995 prize, worth $1 million, the Swedish Academy said that Lucas, through his development and application of the rational expectations hypothesis, had "transformed macroeconomic analysis and deepened our understanding of economic policy." (Macroeconomics is the study of an economic system as a whole, involving how various sectors of an economy interrelate.) Rational expectations had become "a standard part of the macroeconomic toolbox," according to the Swedish Academy. Lucas' theory changed the way government policy makers around the world discussed and developed economic tactics.

Lucas was born Sept. 15, 1937, in Yakima, Wash. He received a B.A. in history (1959) and a Ph.D. in economics (1964) from the University of Chicago, where he was a student of 1976 Nobel laureate Milton Friedman. Lucas taught economics from 1963 to 1974 at Carnegie Mellon University, Pittsburgh, Pa., after which he joined the department of economics faculty at his alma mater. Lucas' later publications, some coauthored by various colleagues, revealed his interest in other aspects of macroeconomics.

(MARGARET BARLOW)

Prize for Literature

The Irish poet Seamus Heaney, long considered a chief contender for the award, won the Nobel Prize for Literature in 1995. The Swedish Academy praised Heaney for "works of lyrical beauty and ethical depth, which exalt everyday miracles and the living past." It also commended his treatment, without political rhetoric, of the conflict in his native Northern Ireland. A highly popular poet and well-liked man, Heaney was the fourth Irish writer, after William Butler Yeats (1923), George Bernard Shaw (1925), and Samuel Beckett (1969), to win the Nobel.

Many critics called Heaney the greatest Irish poet since Yeats. Given their different backgrounds and approaches to poetry, the two appeared to have little in common, yet they shared an experience that was deeply rooted both in the Western classics and in Irish myth and history. Too, their works were similarly rich with cadences unique to Irish speech. For his use of everyday language and rural imagery to frame universal themes, Heaney sometimes was also compared to the American poet Robert Frost and the English poet and novelist Thomas Hardy.

Born on April 13, 1939, in County Londonderry, northwest of Belfast, Heaney was the eldest of nine children in a tight-knit Roman Catholic family. Their farm bordered a large Protestant estate, and from his childhood he felt "symbolically placed" between the two clashing cultures. Heaney studied and later lectured at Queen's University, Belfast. In his first major collection of poems, *Death of a Naturalist* (1966), he established his dual roots in the Irish soil and the literary realm. In one of his best-known poems, "Digging," he endowed his father and grandfather's digging of peat with a universal richness that became a metaphor for his own writing of poetry. Indeed, much of Heaney's early work sprang from his happy childhood experiences and his life on a farm and from his home and family, including his wife and three children.

In 1972 Heaney moved to the Irish republic. He later came to divide his time between Dublin, the University of Oxford, where he was professor of poetry from 1989 to 1994, and Harvard University, where from 1985 he was Boylston professor of rhetoric and oratory. Many of the poems published after his move, such as those in *North* (1975) and *Field Work* (1979), expressed the struggles of living in the political strife of Northern Ireland. The power of Heaney's words, never loud, never preaching, was in their subtlety, and the power of his images was in their familiarity. Again and again he referred to an individual's experience as the basis of poetry.

As the translator of *Sweeney Astray* (1983), about a legendary Irish king who is cursed by a Christian cleric and wanders the land as a mad beast, half bird and half man, Heaney revitalized an ancient poem with contemporary themes. In the title poem of *Station Island* (1984), Heaney used a narrative form, influenced by the work of Dante, to describe a journey set against the agonizing background of Northern Ireland's politics. As a teacher Heaney also explored the role of poetry. In his lectures, recorded in volumes that

Joseph Rotblat

Seamus Heaney

Christiane Nüsslein-Volhard

Martin Perl

include *The Place of Writing* (1989) and *The Redress of Poetry* (1995), he examined writing under every condition, from creative freedom to imprisonment. Underlying the lyricism of his work was a belief that poetry's purpose should be in the service of language, not of a narrow political philosophy. (MARGARET BARLOW)

Prize for Chemistry

The 1995 Nobel Prize for Chemistry was awarded to Paul Crutzen, a Dutch citizen with the Max Planck Institute for Chemistry, Mainz, Germany; F. Sherwood Rowland of the University of California, Irvine; and Mario Molina of the Massachusetts Institute of Technology. The scientists' research alerted the world to the possibility that human-manufactured gaseous compounds could destroy the stratospheric ozone layer, which protects life on Earth from damaging solar ultraviolet (UV) radiation. "By explaining the chemical mechanisms that affect the thickness of the ozone layer, the three researchers have contributed to our salvation from a global environmental problem that could have catastrophic consequences," the Royal Swedish Academy of Sciences said in its citation.

The ozone layer is a region of the atmosphere, roughly 15–48 km (9–30 mi) in altitude, that contains small quantities of ozone. Ozone is a form of oxygen that comprises three atoms (O_3) rather than the two atoms (O_2) found in ordinary molecular oxygen. Despite its sparse distribution, ozone absorbs most of the Sun's UV light, which otherwise would cause severe sunburn and skin cancer in people and adversely affect other organisms.

In 1970 Crutzen took some of the first steps in calling attention to the ozone layer's vulnerability. He showed that the nitrogen oxides NO and NO_2 act as catalysts to speed decomposition of ozone. Those compounds form in the atmosphere from nitrous oxide (N_2O) released naturally at the surface by soil bacteria. A year later the U.S. scientist Harold Johnston warned that a planned fleet of commercial supersonic transport (SST) aircraft would release nitrogen oxides directly into the ozone layer and thus could damage it. Crutzen's and Johnston's work sparked strong debate among scientists and decision makers and marked the beginning of intensive research into the chemistry of the atmosphere.

The next major advance came in 1974, when Rowland and Molina published a study of the threat posed by chlorofluorocarbon (CFC) gases. They showed that CFCs, which were widely used as aerosol-spray propellants, air-conditioning refrigerants, and foaming agents in plastics manufacture, were transported to the ozone layer. There, under the influence of UV light, they participated in reactions that destroyed ozone molecules. Rowland and Molina wrote that continued use of CFCs would seriously deplete the ozone layer within decades. That prediction triggered strong scientific controversy. CFCs were a mainstay of modern society, and no substitutes were available. Chemists knew that CFCs were extremely nonreactive at the Earth's surface and thus believed that they posed no environmental threat. "Many were critical of Molina and Rowland's calculations, but yet more were seriously concerned by the possibility of a depleted ozone layer," the Swedish Academy said. "Today we know that they were right in all essentials. It was to turn out that they had even underestimated the risk."

In 1985 concerns about ozone depletion intensified after English researchers detected the Antarctic ozone hole, a region of the atmosphere that becomes seriously depleted in ozone every austral spring. The work by Crutzen, Rowland, Molina, and other scientists led to a 1987 treaty, the Montreal Protocol, in which the industrialized countries agreed to phase out the production of CFCs.

Crutzen was born Dec. 3, 1933, in Amsterdam and received a Ph.D. in 1973 from Stockholm University. Rowland was born June 28, 1927, in Delaware, Ohio, and earned a Ph.D. in 1952 from the University of Chicago. Molina, born March 19, 1943, in Mexico City, took his Ph.D. in 1972 from the University of California, Berkeley. (MICHAEL WOODS)

Prize for Physics

Frederick Reines of the University of California, Irvine, and Martin L. Perl of Stanford University shared the 1995 Nobel Prize for Physics for their respective discoveries of the neutrino and the tau lepton, members of the family of fundamental subatomic particles that make up all matter in the universe. Reines worked with the late Clyde L. Cowan, Jr., at Los Alamos (N.M.) National Laboratory in the 1950s to confirm the existence of the neutrino. Perl and collaborators at the Stanford Linear Accelerator Center (SLAC) identified the tau lepton in the 1970s.

Reines and Perl discovered what the Royal Swedish Academy of Sciences termed in its citation "two of nature's most remarkable fundamental particles." Both discoveries were critical in developing the so-called standard model that physicists used to describe the subatomic particles that make up the cosmos and the interactions, or forces, between them. The standard model maintained that all matter consists of 12 kinds of particles. Six are leptons, a group that includes electrons—the negatively charged particles that orbit the central nucleus of atoms—as well as the muon, three kinds of neutrinos, and the tau lepton. Six others are quarks, which combine to make up the protons and neutrons in the nucleus. The 12 particles are divided into three families, each of which contains two leptons and two quarks.

The work by Reines and Cowan in making the first definitive detection of neutrinos was critical for initial development of the standard model. Physicists first invoked the existence of the neutrino in the 1930s in order to uphold the law of conservation of energy, one of the most sacrosanct principles in physics. Although the law states that energy can be neither created nor destroyed, energy did seem to disappear in a certain form of radioactive decay called beta decay. To preserve the law, the Austrian-born physicist Wolfgang Pauli proposed that the missing energy is carried off by a particle that has no electric charge and rarely interacts with matter. The Italian-born physicist Enrico Fermi named the ghostly particle the neutrino, for "little neutral one."

Although physicists quickly accepted the neutrino as reality, the detection of a particle that seems to shun interactions was a formidable challenge. In 1956 Reines and Cowan "succeeded in a feat considered to border on the impossible" and "raised the neutrino from its status as a figure of the imagination to an existence as a free particle," according to the Swedish Academy. Reins and Cowan built a simple detector that identified the interactions of neutrinos emanating from a nuclear reactor as they passed through a tank containing half a cubic metre (130 gal) of water. The interactions were visible as faint flashes of light that registered on electronic devices monitoring the water. Their small neutrino detector was the forerunner of the huge detectors of the 1980s and '90s, which attempted to catch the elusive neutrinos that emanate from the Sun and other stars in huge water tanks, large volumes of the sea, and even Antarctic ice.

Before Perl and his colleagues discovered the tau lepton in experiments carried out between 1974 and 1977, physicists thought that there were only two families of fundamental particles. The tau was the first evidence for a third family, which proved essential for completing the standard model. Perl and co-workers discovered the signature of the new lepton in particle debris produced when electrons were smashed into their antimatter counterparts, positrons, in a particle collider at SLAC. They named it tau, the first letter of the Greek word *tritos,* which means "third."

Reines, born March 16, 1918, in Paterson, N.J., received a Ph.D. degree from New York University in 1944. Perl was born June 24, 1927, in New York City and received a Ph.D. degree from Columbia University, New York City, in 1955. (MICHAEL WOODS)

Prize for Physiology or Medicine

Three developmental biologists—the Americans Edward B. Lewis and Eric F. Wieschaus and the German Christiane Nüsslein-Volhard—won the 1995 Nobel Prize for Physiology or Medicine. They were honoured for their discoveries about a family of master genes that determine body architecture early in an embryo's development. The work, done between the 1940s and the 1970s, showed that a small number of critical genes map out the body's form. The biologists also identified genes that determine which organs form inside individual body segments, telling an insect embryo, for instance, where to grow wings, a fish where to build gills, or a human embryo to form eyes in the head rather than in the abdomen. The experiments cited by the Nobel Assembly at the Karolinska Institute in Stockholm involved the vinegar fly, or fruit fly, *Drosophila melanogaster.* It was the first Nobel Prize honouring basic research in developmental biology since 1935.

The Nobel Committee remarked in its announcement of the award that the decision of Nüsslein-Volhard and Wieschaus to join forces on this project "was a brave decision by two young scientists at the beginning of their scientific careers. Nobody before had done anything similar and the chances of success were very uncertain." Wieschaus responded at a press conference in Princeton by saying, "We were young and foolish, and it was worth trying."

Lewis, of the California Institute of Technology, did his research independently at that institution in the 1940s. Wieschaus, of Princeton University, and Nüsslein-Volhard, of the Max Planck Institute for Developmental Biology, Tübingen, Germany, collaborated on their research as young scientists in the 1970s. Others researchers later determined that what Lewis, Wieschaus, and Nüsslein-Volhard had discovered in *Drosophila* also applies to humans.

Lewis studied genetic mutations that cause sections of a fly's body to develop abnormally. One such mutation, for instance, resulted in adult flies with an extra set of wings. By collecting and crossbreeding flies with other mutations and altered segments, he discovered a cluster of genes that control how individual body segments develop. The genes were arranged in head-to-tail fashion on the chromosomes, in the same order as the body segments they controlled. First came genes that controlled the development of the head region, next those that determined the architecture of the thorax, and, finally, those for the posterior. Lewis identified a family of such genes, which later were named homeotic selector genes.

Wieschaus and Nüsslein-Volhard focused on earlier developmental stages in their research, which began in the late 1970s at the European Molecular Biology Laboratory, Heidelberg, West Germany. Because Lewis' research did not explain the key genetic events that cause an embryo to begin dividing into body segments and activate the homeotic genes, they set out to determine how a newly fertilized *Drosophila* egg developed into a segmented embryo. They treated flies with mutagens, chemicals that cause changes in genes. The mutated genes, in turn, caused the formation of abnormal body segments. Using a microscope with which two people could simultaneously study the same embryo, Wieschaus and Nüsslein-Volhard spent more than a year examining and classifying defects caused by the mutations. They eventually identified a small number of genes—out of the fly's 20,000—that are critical for determining the body plan. It was believed that the work of the three biologists would eventually help explain certain types of congenital malformations in humans.

Lewis was born on May 20, 1918, in Wilkes-Barre, Pa., and received his Ph.D. degree from the California Institute of Technology, where he remained active in research. Wieschaus was born on June 8, 1947, in South Bend, Ind., and received a Ph.D. from Yale University, where he became professor of biology. Nüsslein-Volhard, who was born on Oct. 20, 1942, in Magdeburg, Germany, and received her Ph.D. from the University of Tübingen, was affiliated with that city's Max Planck Institute. (MICHAEL WOODS)

(OPPOSITE PAGE, CLOCKWISE FROM TOP)
SIMON WALKER—THE TIMES NEWSPAPERS LTD.; BERND WEISSBROD—DPA/PHOTOREPORTERS; LEA SUZUKI—GAMMA LIAISON; PACEMAKER PRESS

BIOGRAPHIES

Adams, Scott
Cartoonist Scott Adams was asked one question so many times that he came up with a stock answer. It began, "I don't work at your company." People could not be blamed for asking. The comic strip "Dilbert" continuously seemed to be reflecting the events of everyone's workplace. Its lead character, a computer programmer and engineer for a high-tech company with no apparent purpose, was buffeted daily by the illogical projects and business decisions of his clueless boss and the corporation's equally inept management. Dilbert, readily recognized by his perpetually curled necktie (the subject of another frequently asked question), survived the indignities of his existence with the assistance of his pet, Dogbert, who often seemed to have his own self-serving agenda.

Adams was born June 8, 1957, and grew up in Windham, N.Y., in the Catskill Mountains. He was valedictorian of his high-school class (because, he said, "the other 39 people in my class couldn't spell *valedictorian*") and went on to earn a B.A. in economics from Hartwick College, Oneonta, N.Y., in 1979 and an M.B.A. from the University of California, Berkeley, in 1986. From 1979 to 1986 he was employed at Crocker National Bank in San Francisco (while working as a teller, Adams was robbed twice at gunpoint). From 1986 until June 1995 he worked for Pacific Bell in San Ramon, Calif., in a number of jobs involving technology and finances.

Dilbert, a composite of Adams' co-workers over the years, became the main character of Adams' doodles and made his first public appearances in business presentations. The comic strip was first published in 1989, and by 1995 it had been syndicated to some 600 newspapers, was being read in at least 15 countries, and found its own corner on the Internet. A few years after "Dilbert" appeared, Adams began publishing his E-mail address in the strip. He personally read and answered each message, and he credited his correspondents for suggesting many of the situations that Dilbert encountered.

(BARBARA WHITNEY)

Allende, Isabel
Author of four novels, including the critically acclaimed and popular *La casa de los espíritus* (1982; *The House of the Spirits,* 1985), Isabel Allende wrote in the style of magic realism, which incorporated fantastic and mythical elements into realistic fiction. Her work included some of the most spiritual and highly charged literature of the late 20th century. Sometimes compared to Gabriel García Márquez, Octavio Paz, and Carlos Castaneda, Allende was one of the few female Latin-American authors whose name was well known and whose works (translated into more than two dozen languages) could be found on bookshelves worldwide. She considered herself part of a feminist literary awakening, one that tied together minority writers with a shared "dimension of emotion, passion, obsession and dream."

Born on Aug. 2, 1942, in Lima, Peru, Allende spent her adolescence in Chile, where her uncle, Pres. Salvador Allende, was assassinated in 1973 in a military coup. With her husband, Miguel Frias, and children, Paula and Nicolás, Allende immediately fled to Venezuela, where she lived in exile for the next several years. She and Frias divorced around the time her maternal grandfather was diagnosed as being terminally ill. It was the divorce, coupled with her deep respect for her grandfather, that spurred her first novel, *La casa de los espíritus*. The book was a retelling of much of her family history, and it was later made into a motion picture. After immigrating to the United States in 1987, Allende took up residence outside San Francisco with her second husband, William Gordon, a lawyer who claimed to have fallen in love with her through her novels. Allende said that it was writing her fourth novel, *El plan infinito* (1991; *The Infinite Plan,* 1993), that brought her closest to her husband and to an America she had grown to respect deeply. Her other works include *De amor y de sombra* (1984; *Of Love and Shadows,* 1987), *Eva Luna* (1987; Eng. trans., 1988), and *Cuentos de Eva Luna* (1989; *The Stories of Eva Luna,* 1991), a collection of short stories.

Allende's first nonfiction work, *Paula* (1994; Eng. trans., 1995), was written as a letter to her daughter. After falling into a coma resulting from a hereditary blood disease, the daughter died in 1992. During the year of her illness, Allende found solace by "writing" to her daughter every day, often about a long legacy of female endurance: "I think of my great-grandmother, of my clairvoyant grandmother, of my own mother, of you, and of my granddaughter who will be born in May, a strong female chain going back to the first woman, the universal mother." It was partly this legacy that made Allende's such a strong and passionate literary voice.

(SARA N. BRANT)

Isabel Allende
MARCIA LIEBERMAN

Asahara, Shoko
At the end of 1995, self-styled messiah Shoko Asahara was in prison facing charges of having masterminded a series of crimes that included murder, kidnapping, and manufacturing sarin, the poisonous nerve gas that caused thousands of casualties when released in a Tokyo subway.

Chizuo Matsumoto, who changed his name to Shoko Asahara, was born in Kumamoto prefecture, Japan, on March 2, 1955. At the age of six, he was sent to a school for the blind to learn how to cope with severely impaired vision. After graduating in 1975, he failed to gain admission to the School of Medicine at Kumamoto University, so he studied acupuncture and pharmaceuticals.

In 1975 he tried to enter Tokyo University but was unsuccessful. He then opened his own pharmacy, specializing in Chinese medicaments, in nearby Chiba. In 1982 he was arrested for selling fake remedies. After his business went bankrupt, he started a yoga school and sold health drinks.

Asahara, assisted by his wife, set up Aum Shinrikyo (Supreme Truth) in 1987 and began producing numerous books that included a prediction that Armageddon would come with a gas cloud from the United States as early as 1997. By 1989, when the Tokyo metropolitan government granted Aum Shinrikyo legal status as a religious organization, Asahara had begun calling himself the "Holy Pope," "Saviour of the Country," and "Tokyo's Christ." He usually dressed in satiny pajamas, expressed admiration for Adolf Hitler and Mao Zedong, and boasted that he could levitate and bestow superpower on his disciples. The cult, which honoured Shiva, the Hindu god of destruction and regeneration, claimed to have 10,000 followers in Japan and 20,000 abroad, mainly in Russia, and regional offices in the U.S., Germany, and Sri Lanka. Many of Asahara's followers came from prosperous families and were well educated. The top Aum leaders held degrees in such fields as law, biotechnology, medicine, chemistry, computer science, and rocket technology. All were expected to donate everything they owned to the cult. Cult members ate rice and stewed vegetables once or twice a day, often fasting in Buddhist fashion. They performed yoga exercises, and some acolytes at the Yamanashi training centre wore helmets equipped with electrodes, which were reported to increase their alpha waves. Devoted worship was rewarded with a drink from the "miracle pond"—Asahara's bathwater. Asahara dispatched trusted lieutenants to buy chemicals, obtain licenses to fly Russian military helicopters, and buy the aircraft and secondhand weaponry. His attempt to gain a voice in national politics failed miserably when all 25 Aum Shinrikyo candidates who ran for seats in the lower house of the Diet in 1990 were defeated.

(KAY K. TATEISHI)

Baiul, Oksana
Displaying a technical mastery and artistic flair far in advance of her age, Ukrainian figure skater Oksana Baiul won gold medals at both the 1993 world figure skating championships in Prague and the 1994 winter Olympic Games in Lillehammer, Norway, to emerge in 1995 as one of the world's most gifted athletes. The fact that she had competed at the international level for only two seasons, when she was 15 and 16, made her feat even more incredible. Behind her delicate-looking elfin appearance was a fierce determination that was evidenced at the Olympics. After the opening technical segment, Baiul was placed second and needed a remarkable free-skate performance to challenge the leader, U.S. skater Nancy Kerrigan. During a practice session on the eve of the finals, Baiul and a German skater were involved in a collision, in which Baiul bruised her back and received a nasty shin wound that required three stitches. Fortified with two injections of painkillers, she took the ice to the music of Tchaikovsky's *Swan Lake* and landed five triple jumps that—combined with her artistic aplomb—helped her capture the gold and the hearts of those who dubbed her "the swan of Odessa."

Her life was not always likened to a fairy tale. Baiul was born on Nov. 16, 1977, in Dnipropetrovsk, Ukraine, then part of the U.S.S.R. After her father's unexplained disappearance, she was raised by her mother, who together with her grandparents gave her emotional support. Baiul's grandfather bought her skates when she was about four so she could exercise to lose weight. Her mother died in 1991 after both grandparents had died, and Baiul was orphaned. Her coach, Stanislav Korytek, briefly gave her shelter until he left for a job in Canada. Skating coach Galina Zmiyvskaya, at the request of her eldest daughter, Nina, took Baiul as a pupil and welcomed the orphan into her cramped, three-room apartment.

Baiul was also taken under the wing of countryman Viktor Petrenko, Nina's husband.

Under Zmiyvskaya's direction, Baiul was transformed into a world-class skater in one year. She finished second to Surya Bonaly of France at both the 1993 and 1994 European championships but finished first at the 1993 world championships and the 1994 Olympics. In 1994 she was unable to defend her world title owing to injury. Subsequently she moved to the U.S. with Zmiyvskaya to live and train in Simsbury, a suburb of Hartford, Conn.

In 1995 she participated in professional ice shows and competitions and starred in the touring production of *Nutcracker on Ice.* Olympics enthusiasts were left wondering whether Baiul, who counted teddy bears and Snickers candy bars among her favourite things, would ever return to amateur skating, a possibility open to her under existing rules. (HOWARD BASS)

Banderas, Antonio

With 43 movies under his belt, Antonio Banderas in 1995 was on his way to becoming America's next "Latin lover." His undeniable sexuality and European flair made this Spanish actor a full-fledged Hollywood film star.

Banderas was born on Aug. 10, 1960, in Málaga, Spain. After seeing a performance of *Hair* at the age of 15, he said of acting, "I want to be part of this ritual; I want to do this forever." In 1981 he embarked on a five-year acting stint with the Spanish national theatre in Madrid. There he was discovered by movie director Pedro Almodóvar, who offered him roles in films. In his first movie with Almodóvar, Banderas played the first of several roles as a homosexual. Under Almodóvar's direction the young actor was able to express his talent fully through unconventional roles such as rapist, mental patient, and kidnapper.

This experience proved valuable for Banderas after he moved to Hollywood in 1989. There in 1992 he landed a role in *The Mambo Kings,* playing a young Cuban musician living in New York City. Although he spoke almost no English, Banderas was able to learn his lines phonetically and later took intensive English courses, which helped him land the role of Tom Hanks's lover in the box office hit *Philadelphia* in 1993. Wanting to take the U.S. by storm, Banderas then embarked on a whirlwind acting spree. His movies include *The House of the Spirits* (1993), *Interview with the Vampire* (1994), *Miami Rhapsody* (1995), *Desperado* (1995), *Assassins* (1995), and *Never Talk to Strangers* (1995). There also were plans for the release of the big-screen musical version of *Evita* starring singer-actress Madonna as Eva Perón and Banderas as the Latin-American revolutionary Che Guevara. Banderas conceded to being ambitious but said that in Spain actors prove their success by making one film after another.

Success for Banderas came with a price. His personal life recently became public when he fell in love with costar Melanie Griffith from the film *Two Much,* which was expected to be released in early 1996. Gossip columns across the country were filled with news about the breakup of his eight-year marriage to a Spanish actress. Banderas insisted that his marriage had been unstable for some time and said of Griffith, "I love this woman, and I want to make her happy—that is my only purpose." (MARIA OTTOLINO RENGERS)

Barnett, Gary

Gary Barnett in 1995 played the fairy godmother in the most compelling Cinderella story to come along in years. As head coach he guided the Northwestern University football team, longtime lovable losers of the Big Ten Conference, to a national top-10 ranking.

When Barnett arrived on the campus of Northwestern in Evanston, Ill., in 1992, the Wildcats had not had a winning season since 1971. Between 1979 and 1982 they lost 34 consecutive games, setting the all-time futility mark in the history of National Collegiate Athletic Association (NCAA) Division I-A football. Northwestern had not won a Big Ten title since 1936, and in its entire football history the team had played in only one bowl game, the 1949 Rose Bowl. During Barnett's first three seasons, the Wildcats turned in typically poor performances, winning only 8 games while losing 24 and tying one. Through those years, however, he recruited a high calibre of student-athlete and built the confidence of the coaching staff and players. The results of his patience and dedication shone through in the very first game of the 1995 season, when Northwestern surprised Notre Dame 17–15; it was its first win there in 34 years. A disappointing loss to Miami (Ohio) the next week seemed to erase all the promise of the Notre Dame victory. But, playing rugged and fundamentally sound football, the Wildcats won the next nine games, including victories over two national powerhouses, Michigan and Penn State.

Barnett's squad finished the Big Ten schedule without a loss, and after Michigan defeated Ohio State in the last week of the regular season, Northwestern claimed sole possession of the conference title and a trip to the Rose Bowl in Pasadena, Calif. Though Northwestern lost 41–32 to Southern California in the Rose Bowl, it was ranked eighth in the final national poll and had captured the nation's attention as the biggest story of the year in NCAA football.

Barnett was born May 23, 1946, in Lakeland, Fla. He attended the University of Missouri at Columbia, where he played wide receiver on the football team and earned a bachelor's degree in 1969. He remained at Missouri, taking a master's degree in education in 1971 and working as a graduate assistant coach for the football team. After a decade as a successful high-school coach, Barnett became head coach at Fort Lewis College, Durango, Colo., in 1982. He moved in 1984 to the University of Colorado at Boulder, where he served as an assistant coach and was offensive coordinator of the 1990 national championship team. After Northwestern's success Barnett received many different Coach of the Year honours, including the Bear Bryant Award.

(JAMES HENNELLY)

Benetton, Luciano

A duck drenched with crude oil, a man's naked derriere stamped "HIV Positive," the blood-soaked uniform of a soldier killed in Bosnia and Herzegovina: these were not the sort of images one generally associated with fashionable clothing—unless one happened to be Luciano Benetton, the driving force behind the Benetton Group, the billion-dollar family-run apparel empire that conquered the fashion world in the 1980s with its bright-coloured knitwear. Self-described "tastemaker" Benetton and creative director Oliviero Toscani conducted a "shock" advertising campaign that focused not on the company's products but on controversial social issues. Benetton argued that the ads reflected the company's social consciousness and advocacy of tolerance and diversity; others branded them immoral. By mid-1995 the Benetton Group had lost lawsuits in France (a court ruled that the "HIV Positive"-stamped flesh "evoked Nazi barbarity") and in Germany.

Born in Treviso, Italy, on May 13, 1935, Benetton left school at age 14 to work in a clothing store after the death of his father, a businessman. In 1965 he, his brothers, Carlo and Gilberto, and his sister, Giuliana, formed the company—now based in Ponzano Veneto, Italy—that would eventually have more than 7,000 retail outlets in some 120 countries. Reputedly, the sale of Luciano's bicycle had raised the money needed to buy the company's first knitting machine. More important, the implementation of a wool-softening process that he had encountered in Scotland helped establish a pattern of productivity and innovation that would become the company's trademark. Under a "system of services," Benetton contracted out most manufacturing to smaller textile producers and specialized in design, dying, and cutting. It also established an unusual franchise arrangement whereby independent retailers stocked only Benetton clothing. Franchises proliferated wildly and, helped by favourable exchange rates, the firm prospered during the 1980s and early '90s even as its primary market, Western Europe, suffered a recession. During this period the Benetton family began to diversify its holdings, but by 1994 the core apparel business was struggling owing to the continuing recession. A group of store owners in Germany refused to pay for stock, claiming that the controversial advertising had caused sales to drop by 30–50%. Blaming poor local management for the losses, the Benetton Group sued the rebellious stores for nonpayment and in February 1995 won a case in a German court. In July, however, a German appellate court ruled that the advertising violated the standards of fair competition because it exploited human suffering by using compassion for commercial purposes. Wary of shock advertising, Benetton's siblings appeared to be wresting control of the company from the man who had once posed naked for a poster to raise money for the homeless.

(JEFF WALLENFELDT)

Björk

Already unique among pop stars because of her unlikely origins, Björk went a step farther in 1995 and created for herself a distinct musical identity that transcended mere geographic boundaries. The Iceland native, employing spectacular vocal gymnastics and an insatiable desire for experimentation, forged a career that by 1995 had catapulted her from the punk-rock clubs of Reykjavík to international recognition and critical acclaim.

Björk Gudmundsdottir was born in Reykjavík on Nov. 21, 1965. She recorded her first solo album, a collection of cover versions of popular songs, as an 11-year-old music student in

TIBOR BOZI—LGI AGENCY

Björk

1977. Although she never took voice lessons, the diminutive singer credited her vocal technique to breath control learned while studying karate. Throughout her teens she performed with various short-lived bands, ending up at age 18 with Kukl, a punk group that eventually became the Sugarcubes. With Björk as lead vocalist the Sugarcubes won acclaim in the U.K. with the single "Birthday" and their first album, *Life's Too Good* (1986). After recording two more albums, *Here Today, Tomorrow, Next Week!* and *Stick Around for Joy*, over the next five years, the band broke up, and Björk embarked on a solo career.

In 1993 she released *Debut,* her first international solo album. *Debut* produced a number of hit singles—"Human Behaviour," "Venus as a Boy," "Big Time Sensuality," and "Violently Happy"—and won Björk the Best International Newcomer and Best International Female Artist awards at the 1994 Brit awards. The album sold more than 2.5 million copies. It was a departure from the harder-edged sound of the Sugarcubes and included a wide variety of musical styles ranging from techno-pop to jazz.

Never content to conform—even to her own standards—Björk sought to challenge herself even more for her next album because, she said, pop music should reflect the varying moods of the "emotional roller coaster" of everyday life. After two years she produced *Post.* The 1995 release opened with the single "Army of Me," a characteristically throbbing, synthesized track accompanied by the singer's now-familiar breathy yodel. Farther into the album, however, Björk traveled a strange musical journey, accompanied at times by strings and even a harpsichord. Ironically, the futuristic musical journey of *Post* reached perhaps its wildest moment with "It's Oh So Quiet," the cover of a 1940s big-band tune originally performed by the movie star Betty Hutton. Björk's shrill version of the song included a 20-piece orchestra. Critics and fans praised the new album and wondered where Björk's musical whims would take her next. (ANTHONY G. CRAINE)

Blake, Sir Peter James

A knighthood beats every other distinguishing mark in New Zealand. When the South Pacific nation of 3.5 million people wrested the America's Cup from the U.S. in mid-May, in the challenge series off San Diego, Calif., Peter Blake served as "grunt" aboard the winning yacht, *Black Magic.* On board he was a "mainsheet traveler," assisting a trimmer in the gut-wrenching task of supplying sail as signaled by the shipboard hierarchy. Ashore, however, Blake was in charge of the whole Team New Zealand operation. When the final gun sounded the victory, he was acclaimed as the vital factor. Back home supporters, who had bought 100,000 pairs of Blake's "lucky" red socks to raise money for the team, made him a national hero.

Russell Coutts, *Black Magic*'s young skipper, had put it this way: "We all think we've sailed a lot, but Peter has sailed more.... Everyone on this boat respects Peter." At 46, Blake was the master of round-the-world odysseys (including many Whitbread races), two-man races, Fastnet Cups, and even a catamaran charging round the world.

In previous attempts to win the America's Cup, Sir Michael Fay, a businessman interested in yachting, had established himself as the Kiwi patron and manager, without bringing all the pieces together on the water or any of the pieces home in victory. Blake came aboard after circling the world in a catamaran—a 90-footer—and capturing the 1994 Jules Verne Trophy for completing that course in 74 days, 22 hours. He was used to crowds—and solitude. "This is the toughest thing I have ever been involved with.... There is always something else to consider.... In the Whitbread you were off on your own.... Here it's the time on the boat, sailing, that I look forward to."

Blake was born in Auckland, N.Z., on Oct. 1, 1948. He was interested in learner yachts at age 8 and built his first ocean racer (a 24-footer) at 18. Blue water beckoned the following year when he won a New Zealand junior off-shore championship. By 1979 he had participated in a number of international classics, including the first two Whitbreads round-the-world.

Blake was made a Member of the Order of the British Empire (MBE) in 1983 and an Officer of the Order of the British Empire (OBE) in 1991. In the Queen's Birthday Honours in June 1995, for his contribution to yachting over the years, he was awarded the title Knight Commander of the Civil Division of the Most Excellent Order of the British Empire. At year's end he was planning New Zealand's America's Cup defense, scheduled for 2000. (JOHN A. KELLEHER)

Boyz II Men

By 1995 the vocal quartet Boyz II Men had harmonized their way into the record books and earned many of the music industry's top prizes, including multiple Grammy awards for best rhythm and blues vocal group performance. In 1992 their recording of "End of the Road," from the movie sound track of *Boomerang,* spent 13 consecutive weeks in the number one slot on *Billboard*'s pop chart, eclipsing by two weeks the previous record set by Elvis Presley—"Don't Be Cruel" backed with "Hound Dog"—in 1956. In 1994 after Whitney Houston broke their record by spending 14 weeks at number one with "I Will Always Love You," Boyz II Men came back to tie her record with "I'll Make Love to You." Then, as if to punctuate their success with an exclamation point, the release of their follow-up single, "On Bended Knee," put them with an elite group of artists (Elvis Presley and the Beatles) who succeeded themselves at the number one spot.

The members of Boyz II Men included Wanya (pronounced wan-YAY) Morris and Nathan Morris (the group's founder and no relation to Wanya), who were born in 1973 and 1971, respectively, and Shawn Stockman and Michael McCary, who were both born in 1972. They grew up in separate neighbourhoods of Philadelphia and came together as high-school friends at the Philadelphia High School for the Performing Arts, where they studied classical music and vocal arts.

The name Boyz II Men came from a song that had been recorded by the pop quintet New Edition. In 1989 the quartet managed to meet Michael Bivins—who had been a member of New Edition—and gave him an impromptu audition. Bivins later signed on as their manager and helped define their gentlemanly image. In 1991 Boyz II Men debuted on Motown records with the album *Cooleyhighharmony,* which went on to sell more than seven million copies. That success led to the enormous popularity of "End of the Road," and in 1994 the group helped write and produce the album *II,* which included the hits "I'll Make Love to You" and "Water Runs Dry." As 1995 drew to a close, singles continued to be released from *II,* a Spanish version of the album was planned, and the quartet pondered what future musical direction they would take. Said Stockman, "We don't want to limit ourselves creatively. . . . We don't want to be considered just R&B singers." (ANTHONY L. GREEN)

Bussell, Darcey Andrea

When the Royal Ballet's fall season began in London in October 1995, the star of the season opener, *Swan Lake,* was to have been Darcey Bussell. For the second year in a row, however, injury deprived her of that opportunity. It deprived the audience as well. In her few years with the company, she had come to be regarded as one of the finest ballerinas in the world, equally at home in such dramatic classical ballets as *Giselle* and *Romeo and Juliet* and the more modern works of George Balanchine. Her fame was not confined to the ballet stage, however. With the beauty, height, and long legs of a supermodel, Bussell found her way onto the pages of *Vogue* and *Vanity Fair.* In addition, she appeared on television with, for example, Dawn French and Jennifer Saunders (*q.v.*); her portrait was hung in the National Portrait Gallery; and she screen-tested with Harrison Ford for the remake of the classic movie *Sabrina* (though the part finally went to an actress believed to have greater name recognition).

Bussell was born April 27, 1969, in London. When she began attending White Lodge, the Royal Ballet's lower school, at the age of 13, she had difficulty with the strenuous exercises and dance routines. Though she had been studying ballet since she was a small child, she had started her serious training later than most students at the school. She persevered nevertheless, and in 1986, when she was 17, she was chosen for the lead in a school performance at Covent Garden's Royal Opera House. She also won the Prix de Lausanne that year. After Bussell graduated in 1987, she was taken into the Sadler's Wells Royal Ballet (later Birmingham Royal Ballet). A year later she was back at the Royal Ballet as a soloist, having been selected to create the role of Princess Rose in Sir Kenneth MacMillan's new version of *The Prince of the Pagodas.* She was promoted to principal dancer the day after its premiere in 1989, and in 1990 she was named *Dance & Dancers* magazine's Dancer of the Year.

Bussell went on to perform every major role in the Royal Ballet's repertoire and made frequent guest appearances with such companies as the New York City Ballet, the Paris Opéra Ballet, and the Frankfurt (Germany) Ballet. She was praised especially for the purity and radiance of her dancing, her strength and dynamism, and the intelligence and passion with which she portrayed her characters. Her intelligence was also evident in her attitude about injuries. Even after being sidelined for more than six months in 1994, Bussell felt that the time off had been valuable for her mental growth and had brought a new maturity and confidence to her work. Her audience was delighted when recovery from her latest injury enabled her to return to the stage late in the year. (BARBARA WHITNEY)

Chan, Jackie

Since crashing onto the martial-arts movie scene in the late 1970s, Hong Kong actor-director Jackie Chan had been a smash. The popular film star broke box-office records in Asia, along with many of the bones in his body, by performing his own outrageous acrobatic stunts that gave his adventure-comedy films a kinetic blend of over-the-top action and engaging physical humour. Although he had cracked movie markets in Europe, Australia, and South America, he had had little impact in the U.S.—the film capital of the world. If 1995 was any indication, however, he was poised for his big American break; in June he received the Lifetime Achievement Award from the U.S. cable network MTV. His blockbuster films *Rumble in the Bronx* and *Thunderbolt* were released in Asia in January and August, respectively. Although *Rumble in the Bronx* had limited U.S. distribution in 1995, it was slated for broad U.S. release in 1996, along with some of his classic titles.

Reportedly, Chan's impoverished parents nearly sold him for a pittance to the British doctor who delivered him in Hong Kong on April 7, 1954. When he was six years old, his family moved to Canberra, Australia, but the following year they sent him back alone to Hong Kong to attend a strict boarding school for Peking opera. From 7 to 17 he studied acrobatics, singing, martial arts, and mime—skills that launched him into a professional tumbling troupe and landed him bit roles as a child actor and, later, as a stuntman. He was discovered by independent film producer Lo Wei, who, hoping to find a successor to the late Bruce Lee, cast him in a series of lacklustre kung fu movies in 1976–78. Chan soon traded in Lee's gritty persona for a hero more in the mold of silent-film star Harold Lloyd. This penchant for physical comedy first emerged in the 1978 films *Snake in the Eagle's Shadow* and *Drunken Master,* in which he played a bumbling but talented student of martial arts.

In 1980 Chan made his directorial debut in *Young Master* with the production company Golden Harvest, which he subsequently helped to transform into Hong Kong's largest movie conglomerate. In the early 1980s, at the time when he was making an unsuccessful foray into English-language cinema, he moved beyond traditional martial arts period movies to modern action-adventure films, such as *Project A* (1983) and *Police Story* (1985) and their sequels. These films, which brought him newfound stardom, showcased his directorial talent for fight and stunt choreography. His own stunts were literally death-defying; he nearly perished from a fall in *Armour of God* (1986) that fractured his skull and impaired his hearing. Because of their spectacular nature, Chan's films were often interrupted by shots of the same stunt in succession from different angles, and mishaps were generally arranged in a montage of outtakes that appeared as the credits rolled. (TOM MICHAEL)

Chirac, Jacques René

On his third attempt to win the French presidency, Mayor Jacques Chirac of Paris at last succeeded in May 1995. First topping his friend and fellow Gaullist Prime Minister Édouard Balladur, Chirac then was pitted against the Socialist Party (PS) candidate, Lionel Jospin. With France facing a soaring budget deficit and steadily rising unemployment, Chirac convinced voters that a change was needed and that he was the man for the job.

Two times the prime minister of France (1974–76 and 1986–88), Chirac had twice before run for president. His first attempt, in 1981, split the conservative vote with Valéry Giscard d'Estaing and resulted in the election of François Mitterrand of the PS. When a strong conservative coalition won a slight majority in the National Assembly in 1986, Mitterrand appointed Chirac prime minister. This power-sharing arrangement, known as cohabitation, gave Chirac the lead in domestic affairs. He ran against Mitterrand in 1988 but was defeated in runoff elections.

Chirac was born on Nov. 29, 1932. He graduated from the Institut d'Études Politiques de Paris in 1954, served as an army officer in Algeria (1956–57), and earned a graduate degree from the École Nationale d'Administration in 1959. He then became a civil servant and rose rapidly through the ranks, serving as a department head and a secretary of state before becoming minister for parliamentary relations in 1971–72 under Pres. Georges Pompidou. He was elected to the National Assembly as a Gaullist successively from 1967. After serving as minister of agriculture (1972–74) and the interior (1974), Chirac was appointed prime minister by newly elected President Giscard. Citing personal and professional differences with Giscard, Chirac resigned that office in 1976 and set about reconstituting the Gaullist Union of Democrats for the Republic into a neo-Gaullist group, the Rally for the Republic. With the new party firmly under his control, Chirac was elected mayor of Paris in 1977. He proceeded to build up his political base among France's several conservative parties, and it was this power base that ultimately led to his victory.

One of his first moves in office was to name Alain Juppé prime minister. Soon Juppé was embroiled in a scandal over his distribution of city-owned apartments to friends and cronies, a scandal that threatened to involve Chirac as well. In a decision of more far-reaching proportions, Chirac insisted upon the resumption of nuclear tests in the South Pacific. He remained undaunted by the international protests pouring into his office. On the home front, at year's end he faced workers' strikes of major proportions.

(KATHLEEN KUIPER)

Cho, David Yonggi

The flourishing Christian church in South Korea owed much of its vitality to the Rev. David Yonggi Cho, who in September 1995 was unanimously reelected in Jerusalem to serve as chairman of the Executive Committee of the World Assemblies of God Fellowship.

Cho Yonggi was born on Feb. 14, 1936, in a country village of Kyongsang Namdo, Korea. At the age of 17, when he was dying from tuberculosis, he experienced a healing from God and was led into the Christian faith. After graduating from Full Gospel Theological Seminary in 1958, he opened a tent church on a hillside near Seoul.

At that time many Koreans were homeless and jobless as a consequence of the Korean War. Cho's hopeful message and reports of faith healing attracted many of the unfortunate to his church.

As the congregation grew, the church was moved to a downtown area of Seoul and in 1973 to a new sanctuary known as Yoido Island. By 1981 Cho's congregation was said to include 200,000 people, and by 1995 it numbered an incredible 700,000.

The central philosophy of Pastor Cho's ministry was the fivefold message of the gospel: rebirth, fullness of the Holy Spirit, blessings, healing, and the return of Jesus Christ to Earth; and the threefold message of salvation: spiritual, circumstantial, and physical blessings, presented as the nucleus of the gospel. Characteristic elements of his message were: the presence of God's kingdom, God's absolute sovereignty, total redemption and salvation through the cross of Jesus Christ, and walking together with the Holy Spirit.

Fluent in English and Japanese, Cho had preached the gospel through television and radio in the U.S., Japan, Africa, and elsewhere. The church had sent more than 700 missionaries to 472 churches in 48 nations, including some in the Third World. Cho was also chairman of the *Kookmin Daily,* a newspaper he founded on Christian principles in 1988.

The social work of the church included Elim Social Welfare Town, which cared for senior citizens who had no supporting families. Poverty-stricken young men and women were also trained there in a choice of four occupations. With funds earned from wastepaper collected for recycling, the Yoido Full Gospel Church had been able to give 2,000 children a new lease on life through open-heart surgery. The Bread of Grace an ongoing coin-collection campaign, supported Food for the Hungry programs throughout the world. Recently rice, clothes, medicine, and medical vehicles were given to some of the world's poorest nations. On Oct. 3, 1994, Cho led the World Prayer Rally via satellite, linking Korea's one million Christians with delegates from 133 nations gathered on Seoul's Yoido Plaza as they prayed for world peace and the preservation of the environment. (KANG SUK-KYU)

Christo and Jeanne-Claude

On June 25, 1995, when the last panel of silver fabric fell into place, the biggest artwork of the year was completed in Berlin by site artists Christo and his wife, Jeanne-Claude. But this was a veiling, not an unveiling; "Wrapped Reichstag" covered the 101-year-old German parliament building with 100,000 sq m (1,076,000 sq ft) of fabric held in place by nearly 16 km (10 mi) of blue rope. In a now-familiar pattern, skeptics wary of the concept delighted in the execution, seeing in the wrapped structure a monumentality and mystery that symbolized . . . something, perhaps the end of one historical era and the beginning of another or the transformation of control to freedom. All this monumentality carried an equally impressive price tag—some $10 million.

Christo Javacheff was born in Gabrovo, Bulg., on June 13, 1935, the son of a textile mill owner and the general secretary of an art academy. After attending the Fine Arts Academy in Sofia, Bulg., he went to Prague. His family had already run afoul of the communist government; the 1956 Hungarian uprising led him to flee, with Paris as his ultimate destination. While working there as a portrait artist, Christo met Jeanne-Claude de Guillebon, whom he married in 1959. Jeanne-Claude, who was born in Casablanca, Morocco, on the same day in 1935 as her husband, was once described as her husband's publicist and business manager. She later received equal billing with him in all creative and administrative aspects of their work.

Christo began his Dadaist wrapping on a small scale—bottles, motorcycles, a girl, a tree—and created shrouded and packaged forms. Then in 1968 he and Jeanne-Claude wrapped the Kunsthalle (art museum) in Bern, Switz., and in 1969 the Museum of Contemporary Art in Chicago. They created huge plastic packages of "wrapped air" in Eindhoven, Neth.; Minneapolis, Minn.; and Kassel, West Germany. They hung the "Valley Curtain" across Rifle Gap in the Colorado Rockies (1972), and they wrapped a beach in Australia (1969) and the Pont Neuf in Paris (1985). The couple surrounded 11 Florida islands with pink skirts (1983), ran a 39.5-km (24.5-mi)-long white fabric fence through Marin and Sonoma counties in California (1976), and, in a 1991 project, installed 1,340 giant blue umbrellas across the Sato River valley in Japan and 1,760 giant yellow ones in Tejon Pass, California.

As the scope of their projects widened, increased time was needed for planning and construction phases, the securing of permits, and environmental impact research. For each project they formed a corporation, which secured financing and sold the primary models and sketches. Most installations were documented in print and on film, and the materials that created them were sold or given away after the projects were dismantled. (ANITA WOLFF)

Close, Glenn

On July 2, 1995, Glenn Close took her final bow as the delusional former film star Norma Desmond in Andrew Lloyd Webber's theatrical production of *Sunset Boulevard.* Critics had hailed Close's definitive portrayal of the murderous, manipulative Desmond as an artistic triumph, an opinion shared by Close's peers, who presented her with the 1995 Tony award for best actress in a musical.

Although best known for her work in films, for which she had received five Academy Award nominations, Close was no stranger to the footlights. She had a long and distinguished theatrical résumé and had received Tony awards in 1984 and 1992 for her work in *The Real Thing* and *Death and the Maiden.* One of the few performers to be nominated for the top awards in film, theatre, and television, Close also earned an Emmy award for her 1995 role in *Serving in Silence: The Margarethe Cammermeyer Story.*

Close was born on March 19, 1947, in Greenwich, Conn., a town that her ancestors had helped found in the 17th century. Her father was a well-known surgeon who, when Close was 13, left the mansions and well-manicured lawns of Greenwich to open a medical clinic in the Belgian Congo (now Zaire). Close spent several years in Africa and at boarding schools in Switzerland before returning to Connecticut to live with her grandmother and attend Rosemary Hall, an exclusive girl's school in Greenwich.

Following her high-school graduation in 1965, Close spent several years touring Europe and the U.S. with the musical group "Up with People." In 1970 she enrolled at the College of William and Mary, Williamsburg, Va. After graduating in 1974 with a degree in drama and a Phi Beta Kappa key, she joined the New Phoenix Repertory Company and made her Broadway debut that same year. A succession of other theatre roles followed, and Close's reputation grew. In 1980 she received a

MICHAEL GRECCO—SYGMA

Glenn Close

Tony award nomination for her role in *Barnum,* drawing the attention of motion-picture director George Roy Hill, who offered her a role in *The World According to Garp* (1982), for which she received an Academy Award nomination as best supporting actress.

Following her film debut in *Garp,* Close was nominated for Oscars in 1983 and 1984 as best supporting actress for roles in *The Big Chill* and *The Natural.* In 1987 and 1989 she received best actress Academy Award nominations for her roles as a psychopathic temptress in the thriller *Fatal Attraction* and as the scheming Marquise de Merteuil in *Dangerous Liaisons*, but she again failed to win. Although theatre remained her first love, Close continued to accept television and film roles—but only if they were interesting.

(JOHN H. MATHEWS)

Davies, Paul Charles William

On May 3 the mathematical physicist Paul Davies was awarded the 1995 Templeton Prize for Progress in Religion. Professor of natural philosophy at the University of Adelaide, Australia, Davies received the honour, which carried a monetary award of $1 million, for his efforts to resolve the dichotomy between science and religion. With his acceptance he became one of an elite group of people, which includes Mother Teresa, Billy Graham, and Aleksandr Solzhenitsyn, who had been given the prize since its establishment by Wall Street wizard John Templeton in 1972.

Throughout his career Davies had sought to bring an understanding of the universe to the general public. To Davies the presence of the laws of physics suggested a meaningful design to the universe, and the ability of humans to comprehend mathematics and science was their connection with that design and the designer. As he stated in his award acceptance speech in Westminster Abbey, "Although we are not at the centre of the universe, human existence *does* have a powerful wider significance. Whatever the universe as a whole may be about, . . . we, in some limited yet ultimately profound way, are an integral part of its purpose."

Davies was born in London on April 22, 1946. He graduated from University College, London, in 1967 with a bachelor's degree and remained to earn a Ph.D. in theoretical physics. Upon graduation in 1970 he worked as a research fellow at the University of Cambridge and two years later accepted a position at King's College, London, as a lecturer in applied mathematics.

Davies became interested in the theory of quantum fields in curved space-time and focused much of his research in that area. He published *The Physics of Time Asymmetry* (1974), the first of more than 20 books directed to either his professional colleagues or the general public. Davies then joined physicists Stephen Hawking and Roger Penrose, who were researching the thermodynamic properties of black holes.

In the 1980s Davies served as professor of theoretical physics at the University of Newcastle-upon-Tyne. During those years he published such books as *The Edge of Infinity* (1981), on the topic of black holes; *God and the New Physics* (1983); and *Superstrings: A Theory of Everything?* (1988), based on his BBC documentary on the topic.

Davies moved to Australia in 1990 to accept the chair of mathematical physics at the University of Adelaide. A year later he published *The Matter Myth,* an argument against the idea of a Newtonian clockwork universe. In 1992 appeared one of his most influential works, *The Mind of God,* which explores the connectedness of science and religion. The following year the university created the position of professor of natural philosophy for him. Davies' most recent publications were *About Time: Einstein's Unfinished Revolution* and *Are We Alone?* (both 1995). The latter examines the implications for humanity should extraterrestrial life be found.

(AMANDA E. FULLER)

Deutch, John Mark

In 1995 U.S. Pres. Bill Clinton appointed John Deutch the new director of central intelligence. Although once considered one of the prime jobs in government, this directorship was now viewed as such a difficult and unrewarding position that Deutch had originally turned it down; a personal plea from the president persuaded him to accept the post. Deutch's foremost task was to rebuild the morale and efficiency of what many viewed as an agency in serious trouble.

The years following the collapse of the Soviet Union and the subsequent end of the Cold War had not been kind to the CIA. Some critics questioned its purpose in the 1990s; others assailed the agency for its intelligence failures. Meanwhile, the CIA was shaken by internal dissension, which was reflected in a growing rate of resignations among younger officers and in the uncomfortable publicity of a sexual discrimination suit. This followed the scandal that ensued early in 1994 when it was revealed that Aldrich Ames, a career counterintelligence officer, had been a Soviet mole, passing along information that resulted in the deaths of at least 10 agents working on behalf of the U.S.

Deutch was born in Brussels, Belgium, on July 27, 1938, and was naturalized in 1945. He received bachelor's degrees from Amherst (Mass.) College and the Massachusetts Institute of Technology in 1961 and a doctorate in chemistry from MIT in 1965. Deutch worked at the Department of Defense and taught at Princeton University before returning to MIT as a faculty member in 1970. He became chairman of the chemistry department in 1976 and was appointed provost of the university in 1982. He left MIT in 1993 to return to the Department of Defense, and in 1994 he was appointed deputy secretary of defense. Deutch gained praise and political support for his handling of the touchy issue of military base closings while at the Pentagon.

One of Deutch's first official actions as director of central intelligence was to begin a thorough overhaul of the CIA's upper ranks, replacing most top officials with candidates from outside. He also responded swiftly to allegations of human rights abuses by a Guatemalan army colonel who was also a CIA agent. Deutch fired the former head of Latin-American covert operations and the station chief at the time of the abuses and demoted and reprimanded eight other CIA officers. While Deutch's first steps were popular with many politicians, including members of the influential Senate and House intelligence oversight committees, some veteran CIA officers were disturbed by what they perceived as the sacrifice of their fellow agents for political gain and by the influx of outsiders who were now largely responsible for the direction the agency was taking.

(JOHN H. MATHEWS)

Devi, Phoolan

After her release from prison in 1994, India's folk hero Phoolan Devi abandoned her life of crime, married, and converted to a form of Buddhism. In June 1995 she launched a new political party for the lower castes, Eklavya Manch, and opened the prospect of a new career in politics. But the news reported in the West was the release (over Devi's objections) of *Bandit Queen,* a movie based on her life. To Westerners its plot—including rape, murder, and retribution—was characteristic of high Hollywood style.

Devi was born in 1957, the second daughter of a low-caste illiterate farmer. At the age of 11, she was sold by her hapless father into marriage for the price of a bicycle and a cow. Ill, much abused, and humiliated, she soon returned home. As an errant married woman, she was shunned by the villagers, but she could not seem to stay out of trouble. Picked up on trumped-up charges and further humiliated by the police, she was eventually returned to her husband. Ultimately, at the age of 20, she was abandoned. Shortly thereafter she was kidnapped by one of the many *dacoit* (armed bandit) gangs that roamed the ravines of Uttar Pradesh's Chambal River valley. The episode took an unexpected turn when Devi became one of them, finding herself more at home in the company of bandits than she had ever been elsewhere.

She became the mistress of Vikram Mallah, one of the gang's leaders, and learned to defend

RAVEENDRAN—AFP

Phoolan Devi

herself. After a year, however, Mallah was treacherously killed by a former friend, who also had Devi captured. She was held for several weeks in a hut in the village of Behmai and nightly was raped and humiliated by several men of the high Thakur caste. When she escaped, she was taken in by another gang, and her notoriety grew. After participating in robberies and ambushes (and badly beating her abusive first husband), Devi had become both one of India's most wanted criminals and a heroine of the oppressed, who called her Dasyu Sundari ("Beautiful Bandit"). She underlined her defiance by her involvement in the Feb. 14, 1981, shooting of 22 Thakur men of Behmai, all but two of whom died. She and her gang taunted the authorities, evading capture for two years. Finally, after negotiating terms, she surrendered on Feb. 12, 1983, in a dramatic ceremony witnessed by thousands of her admirers.

While imprisoned for 11 years in Gwalior Central Jail in Madhya Pradesh, she was befriended by Mala Sen, who wrote her story in *India's Bandit Queen* (1991), the basis of 1995's most-talked-about foreign movie release.

(KATHLEEN KUIPER)

Drewermann, Eugen

"This is not the church Jesus would want," proclaimed the Catholic priest and psychotherapist Eugen Drewermann. His basic postulate that the image procedes the word, because for thousands of years the human psyche "thought" solely in images and symbols, was expressed in his highly esteemed three-volume doctoral and habilitation thesis *Structures of Evil* (1976–78). Here he combined the philosophy of Søren Kierkegaard, current psychoanalytic knowledge, and exegesis to lay the foundation for his later works.

Drewermann was born on June 20, 1940, in Bergkamen, Germany. He studied philosophy at the University of Münster, theology in Paderborn, and neopsychoanalysis in Tiefenbrunn, not formally completing a degree in the latter. He went on to teach Catholic dogmatics at the Faculty of Theology in Paderborn.

Drewermann's first conflict with the Roman Catholic Church hierarchy arose in 1983 when he criticized its anthropocentrism as regards our natural environment. He was subsequently barred from offering courses for teachers of religious education. In 1986 the Vatican Congregation addressed the archbishop of Paderborn, Johann Joachim Degenhardt, concerning Drewermann. As a consequence, the German Bishops' Conference prepared a dossier on Drewermann in 1987–88. The main accusation was that he denied the historicity of revelation and that Jesus was the son of God and that he doubted man's need for redemption. On Oct. 7, 1991, the archbishop of Paderborn withdrew Drewermann's right to teach religion. He was, however, explicitly allowed to continue his activities as priest and to publish. Most probably as a result of an interview that appeared in *Der Spiegel* on Dec. 23, 1991, Archbishop Degenhardt the next month withdrew Drewermann's right to preach.

A prolific author and lecturer, having written some 40 books that sold a total of about one million copies, Drewermann held that anthropocentrism, rationality, and morality must be understood in less absolute terms and that repression of sexuality must be overcome. At the same time, he described the possibilities of a properly understood religiousness that calms human aggressiveness, "spiritualizes" conflicts, and is able to pacify the alienated unconscious mind. He felt that only when people have learned to be in harmony with themselves will they be able to fulfill moral requirements. Advocating more tolerance, Drewermann stated in an interview that religions are "like medicines for particular illnesses, and not every medicine is suitable for every illness."

(JOHN CHINNERY)

Evers-Williams, Myrlie

In a dramatic illustration of how every vote does indeed count, on Feb. 18, 1995, Myrlie Evers-Williams was elected chairperson of the board of the National Association for the Advancement of Colored People (NAACP) by the closest of margins, 30 to 29. Plagued with accusations of impropriety, the NAACP, the oldest civil rights organization in the U.S., hoped that Evers-Williams would be able to give it a shot of new life. Reluctant to run because of her second husband's battle with cancer, she eventually acquiesced, admitting, "I just could not imagine us as a people, as a country, not having the NAACP as a strong and viable organization."

Myrlie Louise Beasley was born on March 17, 1933, in Vicksburg, Miss. Her parents separated shortly afterward, and she was reared by her grandmother and an aunt. In 1950 Myrlie Beasley entered Alcorn A & M College in Lorman, Miss., to major in education. She met upperclassman Medgar Evers, and they married the following year. In 1952 Medgar Evers accepted a job as an insurance agent in a depressed area of the Mississippi Delta. So disgusted was the couple by the poor conditions in which some of the local African-Americans had to live that they became active in the NAACP in order to make a change. Resistance to the then-young civil rights movement was especially virulent in the South, however, and the Evers family, which by 1960 included three children, began to receive death threats. In the early hours of the morning of June 12, 1963, Medgar Evers was fatally shot on his front porch as he returned from an NAACP meeting. Segregationist Byron De La Beckwith was tried for the murder but was set free when a jury failed to reach a verdict. (Not until February 1994 was Beckwith convicted and sentenced to life in prison.) In 1964 Myrlie Evers moved her family to California.

Myrlie Evers-Williams
NICOLE BENGIVENO—MATRIX

Vowing not to become a "professional widow," Evers continued the fight for equality. In 1967 her book, *For Us, the Living,* (written with William Peters), chronicled her husband's life; it was later made into a television movie. She earned a degree in sociology in 1968, and in 1970 she ran, unsuccessfully, for Congress. She served as commissioner of the Los Angeles Board of Public Works. In 1976 she married another civil rights activist, Walter Williams.

A longtime board member of the NAACP, Evers-Williams watched support for the organization wane as the leadership of the organization was rocked by a series of financial scandals. Following a vote of no confidence for the incumbent leadership, elections were held and Evers-Williams emerged the victor. Walter Williams died four days later. (ANTHONY L. GREEN)

Fanini, Nilson do Amaral

At the August 1995 meeting of the Baptist World Congress meeting in Buenos Aires, Arg., the Rev. Nilson do Amaral Fanini was elected to a five-year term as president of the Baptist World Alliance (BWA), a world body composed of 40 million Baptists.

Prior to his appointment, Fanini had for 31 years been pastor of the 7,000-member First Baptist Church of Niteroi, Brazil, one of the largest evangelical churches in South America, and had served as president of the Brazilian Baptist Convention and vice president of the BWA. He had preached in 87 nations and was the first evangelist allowed to give a sermon in communist Angola and Mozambique. As president, Fanini placed his greatest emphasis on evangelism; he wanted to see the number of Baptist churches double to 300,000 during his tenure.

Fanini also was the president of Reencontro, which, in addition to taking an active role in evangelism and the worldwide distribution of Bibles, operated 19 clinics where both medical and psychological assistance were offered free, an orphanage, a vocational training program, a food-distribution centre, and child-care agencies. The group recently distributed 120 tons of food and clothing and helped rebuild many homes for the poor. Reencontro, the largest benevolent institution in the state of Rio, functioned in a nation where an estimated 60% of the population was under the age of 28. Fanini said, "The children have a special place in my heart. It's easier to help a child than to transform a criminal in prison." In 1994 the church adopted 3,000 babies from the slums.

Fanini preached weekly on 52 radio and 110 television stations that reached 40 million people in Brazil and six other South American countries. The Brazilian Bible League, sponsored by Fanini, provided 25 million Bibles to Brazil alone. His church had launched 28 new churches and sponsored 92 missions.

Fanini was born on March 18, 1932, in Curitiba, Paraná, Brazil. He held a theological degree from Southwestern Baptist Theological Seminary (affiliated with the Southern Baptist Convention), Fort Worth, Texas, and a law degree from the Fluminense Federal University of Rio de Janeiro. He also was a graduate of the prestigious Superior School of War, a unique privilege reserved for the nation's outstanding leaders.

When asked about his five-year plan in the BWA, Fanini viewed its primary role as defending human rights, attacking social injustice, promoting peace, and helping those who were hungry and those with desperate needs, but he placed evangelism at the heart of the BWA.

(NORMAN R. DE PUY)

Fischer, Joschka (Joseph Martin)

Joschka Fischer, Germany's Green Party (Die Grünen) leader, steered his party from its anti-nuclear image during the 1990s and in 1995 accomplished his goal of having the Greens replace the Free Democratic Party (FDP) as the third force in German politics. Earlier, in May 1994, the Green Party had won 10% of Germany's vote while the FDP failed to win the minimum 5% needed for seats in Parliament. In 1990 when the Green Party was knocked out of the Bonn Parliament by a euphoric tidal wave that followed reunification, few would have taken seriously Fischer's plan to run the country in 1998. In 1995 few doubted it.

Fischer was born on April 12, 1948, in the town of Gerabronn, Baden-Württemberg. His political views were galvanized in 1967 when a student was shot dead by police following a political demonstration in Berlin. In 1983, at the height of the protest movement against the U.S. deployment of Pershing II and cruise missiles, he was elected one of the Green Party's first MPs in Bonn on a platform advocating the immediate shutdown of nuclear plants, a shorter workweek, withdrawal from NATO, and the dismantling of the German army. From his seat in the Bundestag (lower house of Parliament), Fischer was a gadfly, often heckling the government with wicked and humorous remarks.

Fischer emerged as the clear leader of the Greens after the party failed to win seats in the legislature in 1990. His realist (Realo) faction, composed largely of Bundestag members, wanted the Greens to work within the political system, pursuing environmental goals but with more flexibility. The fundamentalist (Fundi) faction, which dominated the party's nonparliamentary executive committee, advocated a purist ideological posture and pushed to maintain its extraparliamentary roots and campaign for change at the local level. Fischer's Realo ideologies moved the Green Party beyond grass roots environmentalism. The party worked to curb automatic entitlements and to cut government bureaucracy, appealing to young professionals whose parents, holding the same jobs 10 years earlier, would never have voted Green. Fischer saw Germany bound militarily to the West, if not through NATO, then through a European alliance. That seemed to some a betrayal, but it returned the Greens to Bonn in 1994 with 7.3% of the vote. Fischer asserted that the Greens were no longer radical, as demonstrated by the party's pragmatic shift toward the centre that had been spurred by his leadership.

(DANIEL LATHAM)

Friel, Brian

The 1995 revival of Brian Friel's *Translations* at New York City's Plymouth Theatre demonstrated the continuing power of Irish drama. In the tradition of such Irish playwrights as John Millington Synge and Sean O'Casey, Friel rooted his works firmly in the history and culture of the Irish people yet still spoke to the universal problems affecting the human condition.

Friel was born on Jan. 9, 1929, outside the town of Omagh in County Tyrone in Northern Ireland. When he was 10, his family moved to Londonderry, Northern Ireland, where his father served as a school principal. Friel studied for the priesthood at St. Patrick's College, Maynooth, Ireland, and earned a B.A. in 1948. After deciding against entering the priesthood, Friel returned to Northern Ireland, where he studied at St. Joseph's Teacher Training College, Belfast. In 1950 he accepted a teaching position in Londonderry, and he taught there for 10 years. During this period Friel started to write, and his short stories began appearing in *The New Yorker.*

In 1960 Friel left teaching to write full time, concentrating on short stories but also turning his attention toward drama. In 1963 he went to the U.S. and spent six months working at the Tyrone Guthrie Theatre in Minneapolis, Minn. When he returned to Northern Ireland, Friel wrote the play that became his first critical and commercial success, *Philadelphia, Here I Come!* It was first produced at the Dublin Theatre Festival in 1964 and focused on a young Irish immigrant, Gar O'Donnell, as he prepared to leave for the U.S. The play was well received by both the public and the critics, who hailed Friel's unconventional approach: he used two actors to convey the public and private sides of the main character.

Following the success of *Philadelphia, Here I Come!*, Friel moved to County Donegal, Ireland. There, over two decades, he produced an impressive output; he wrote plays at the rate of almost one a year. In 1980 Friel and actor Stephen Rea formed the Field Day Theatre Company in Londonderry. The new company's first production was *Translations,* a play that addressed the existing troubles in Northern Ireland by focusing on the collision between English and Irish culture and language in 19th-century Donegal. By 1990 Friel had firmly established himself as one of Ireland's leading dramatists. The Abbey Theatre's production of *Dancing at Lughnasa* was hailed by critics in every city it played. Although some of his other works, notably *Wonderful Tennessee,* did not meet with the same critical acclaim, the 1995 revival of *Translations* proved to be a critical and commercial success, demonstrating Friel's continuing appeal.

(JOHN H. MATHEWS)

Fudge, Ann Marie

With an outstanding reputation as a manager and a proven record for reviving languishing brands, Ann Marie Fudge, president of the $1.4 billion Maxwell House Coffee, ranked among the top 20 women in corporate America. Many predicted that this ambitious executive would need all her skills to counter the competition facing the 100-year-old firm.

Ann Marie Brown was born on April 23, 1951, in Washington, D.C. At the age of 19, while attending Simmons College in Boston, she married Richard Fudge. By the time she received her B.A. in 1973, she had given birth to the first of their two sons. After graduating with an M.B.A. from Harvard University in 1977, Fudge worked nine years for General Mills in Minneapolis, Minn. She advanced from marketing assistant to marketing director and was instrumental in the development and introduction of Honey Nut Cheerios, one of the nation's best-selling breakfast cereals.

Fudge joined General Foods USA (GFUSA), Kraft General Foods' largest operating unit, in 1986 as associate director of strategic planning. She soon moved into marketing positions, where her innovative coupon campaign targeting children boosted Kool-Aid's flagging sales. As vice president of marketing and development (1989–91) for GFUSA's Dinners and Enhancers Division, Fudge and her team, appealing to Americans' growing health consciousness, developed the "Why fry?" slogan for Shake 'N Bake, another product that was on shaky ground. Sales increased at double-digit rates the following year. After her promotion in 1991 to executive vice president of the $6 billion GFUSA, Fudge oversaw the manufacture, promotion, and sales of such familiar name brand products as Minute Rice, Log Cabin Syrup, and Good Seasons Salad Dressing.

Fudge was named to head Maxwell House in 1994. Under her leadership, the company tried to turn its age into an advantage. Advertising campaigns featured jazz renditions of the venerable jingle ("ba ba ba ba bup bup"), and the longtime slogan "Good to the last drop" was emblazoned in neon above Times Square. To appeal to the "20-something" crowd, the company marketed a line of instant cappuccino drinks that promised to deliver "the magic without the machine."

Fudge's honours included the Black Achievers award from the Harlem YMCA in 1988 and the Candace award from the National Coalition of 100 Black Women in 1991. She sat on the boards of Liz Claiborne, Inc., and Allied Signal, Inc. Her long history of community service included positions on the boards of the Women's Economic Development Corp., the Partnership for a Drug Free America, the allocations panel of the United Way, and the Executive Leadership Council.

(DANIEL LATHAM)

Gandhi, Sonia

Throughout 1995 a single question held out hope for—or haunted—political life in India: What would Sonia Gandhi choose to do? The Italian-born Sonia was the widow of one Indian prime minister, Rajiv Gandhi; daughter-in-law of another, Indira Gandhi; and granddaughter-in-law of India's first prime minister, Jawaharlal Nehru. When Rajiv was assassinated in 1991, Sonia was seen by many as the natural heir to the Nehru-Gandhi dynasty, and she was offered the leadership of the Congress (I) Party. The party's elders had concluded that the right to assume responsibility for the party—and by implication India—was hers. She rejected the offer and remained at home in New Delhi, seldom appearing in public and refusing to discuss politics publicly. She did not visit Rajiv's former constituency in Amethi, Uttar Pradesh, until 1993—but the crowds cheered her. Subsequently, she traveled throughout the country on behalf of trusts and committees devoted to Indian public life.

She was born Sonia Maino in Turin, Italy, on Dec. 9, 1947. While studying English at the University of Cambridge, she met Rajiv Gandhi, a mechanical engineering student. They married in 1968 and lived at India's official residence, although Rajiv eschewed politics for a career as a commercial airline pilot. Sonia quickly adopted Indian ways and journeyed all over the country with Indira. She accepted her husband's entry into politics after the death of his brother, Sanjay, in 1980, and when Indira was assassinated in 1984, it was Sonia who rushed to her side. Though she campaigned for Rajiv during his years in politics, Sonia chose to remain in the background, studying art restoration and working to preserve India's artistic treasures.

In May 1995 she finally broke her long silence and telephoned Prime Minister P.V. Narasimha Rao to urge him to allow two leading dissidents back into the party in time for the 1996 elections. In August she and her daughter, Priyanka, went to rural Amethi to dedicate a medical camp. There Sonia delivered an eight-minute address in which she praised Rajiv's dedication to the welfare of the people and expressed her anguish over the lack of progress into the investigation of his assassination. Resounding applause and shouts of antigovernment slogans greeted this apparent criticism of Rao's leadership: Sonia Gandhi had at last spoken out. Political commentators had a field day speculating on her talk and on her family's future, but at year's end the regal Sonia Gandhi was continuing to be as enigmatic as ever.

(JOHN LITWEILER)

George, Eddie

Governors of the Bank of England had always been powerful people, but traditionally they exercised their power in private. When Eddie George, a hard-line advocate of low inflation at all costs, was appointed governor in 1993, he quickly proved his determination to retain that power. The difference was that he was prepared to be more forthright in public than his predecessors, both about economic policy in general and about his differences with the U.K.'s chancellor of the Exchequer. In 1995 a decision to start publishing minutes of George's monthly meetings with Chancellor Kenneth Clarke revealed the scale of a dispute about interest rates that was at the heart of the government machine.

Edward Alan John George was born on Sept. 11, 1938, at Carshalton, outside London. After studying economics at Emmanuel College, Cambridge, he served briefly in the Royal Air Force. He joined the Bank of England in 1962 and worked mainly in its international section. He was seconded to the Bank of International Settlements in the mid-1960s and the International Monetary Fund in the early 1970s. George was promoted to executive director in 1982 and to deputy governor in 1990.

During the 1980s George came into regular contact, and conflict, with government ministers. In 1984, when he was responsible for the money markets division, he warned then chancellor Nigel Lawson to keep out of market operations. In 1991, as deputy governor, George faced criticism for his role in the collapse of the Bank of Credit and Commerce International. An official inquiry uncovered a series of failures in the Bank of England's systems of supervision and communication. George retrieved his reputation by his adept handling of the U.K.'s embarrassing withdrawal from the European Communities' exchange rate mechanism in September 1992. Withdrawal—which amounted to a forced devaluation of sterling—was a political disaster for the Conservative government, but George managed the technical side of the crisis with consummate skill.

His reward was promotion to governor in July 1993. In that position he lost no opportunity to expound his view that the U.K.'s economy could sustain more rapid growth only if it kept inflation down by keeping interest rates high. By the end of 1995, as signs of an economic slowdown became clear, George acknowledged that Clarke had been right to overrule him and hold rates down. This setback did not deter George from his longer-term aim, of securing full independence for the Bank of England, along the lines of Germany's Bundesbank.

(PETER KELLNER)

Gingrich, Newt

On Jan. 4, 1995, Newt Gingrich became speaker of the U.S. House of Representatives, the first Republican in 40 years to hold the powerful position. A blunt, outspoken partisan, he advocated policies that seemed outrageous to some but resonated deeply with others. Gingrich was seen as the architect of the stunning Republican victory in the 1994 congressional elections. As speaker he tried to reduce the size and influence of the federal government and to redirect the U.S. away from what he called a "welfare state" to an "opportunity society."

Newton Leroy Gingrich was born in Harrisburg, Pa., on June 17, 1943. After graduating from Emory University, Atlanta, Ga., in 1965, he went to Tulane University, New Orleans, La., where he received M.A. (1968) and Ph.D. (1971) degrees in modern European history. He began teaching at West Georgia College in 1970.

After unsuccessful runs for Congress in 1974 and 1976, Gingrich in 1978 won a seat from a district outside Atlanta. From the beginning he was confrontational. In the 1980s he led a group of conservatives who used the "special orders" period following House sessions to read highly charged material into the *Congressional Record,* all televised on C-SPAN. In 1987 Gingrich began an assault on Speaker of the House Jim Wright for questionable financial dealings. The charges forced Wright to resign in 1989.

That same year, Gingrich was elected House minority whip by a vote of 87–85. In 1994 he helped draft the "Contract with America," a document outlining legislation to be enacted by the House within the first 100 days of the 104th Congress. (*See* WORLD AFFAIRS: *United States:* Special Report.) In December 1994 he was chosen by the majority Republicans as House speaker. With one exception, all parts of the "Contract with America" were passed by the House within 100 days, as promised.

During the course of his career, Gingrich had at times come under attack for his own behaviour. Perhaps the most publicized controversy involved a $4.5 million advance from the publisher HarperCollins, owned by Rupert Murdoch's News Corp., Ltd., for two books. Because Murdoch, who had met with Gingrich, was under investigation by the Federal Communications Commission, the deal appeared to many to be a clear conflict of interest, and Gingrich was forced to give up the advance. The first of the books, *To Renew America* (1995), was briefly a best-seller.

Potentially more damaging to the speaker was the decision of the House ethics committee in December to appoint a special counsel to investigate charges that the political organization GOPAC, which the speaker long headed, had violated tax laws. Nonetheless, Gingrich continued to take tough stands on ideological questions and policy issues, including the matter of a balanced budget, which resulted in partial government shutdowns in November and December. For his influence on the government, *Time* magazine named Gingrich its Man of the Year. (ROBERT RAUCH)

Grass, Günter Wilhelm

In 1995 Günter Grass, Germany's best-known living author, published *Ein weites Feld* ("A Broad Field"), an ambitious novel dealing with German reunification. The work became an instant best-seller, as much for the fierce controversy surrounding the author's view that reunification was a mistake as for its literary interest.

Grass was born on Oct. 16, 1927, in Danzig (now Gdansk), Poland. The son of a small grocery owner, he observed the process of Nazification among the people of Danzig, and at age 16, during World War II, he was drafted and made a tank gunner. He was wounded and became a prisoner of war. After the war Grass embarked on art studies but, encouraged by the association Gruppe 47, began to write poems and plays. His literary reputation was established with his first novel, *Die Blechtrommel* (1959; *The Tin Drum,* 1959), regarded by many to be his most important work. An imaginative re-creation of his experiences in Danzig during the war, *Die Blechtrommel* condemned Germany's Nazi experience and led to the author's becoming known as the "conscience of his generation."

A prolific writer, Grass soon published *Katz und Maus* (1961; *Cat and Mouse,* 1963) and *Hundejahre* (1963; *Dog Years,* 1963), completing a trilogy set in Danzig. His later books treated both social and political themes. These include, among many others, *Örtlich Betäubt* (1969; *Local Anaesthetic,* 1969), a protest against the Vietnam War; *Der Butt* (1977; *The Flounder,* 1978), an interpretation of the relationship between the sexes throughout history; *Die Rättin* (1986; *The Rat,* 1986), a vision of the end of the human race that expressed Grass's fear of nuclear holocaust and environmental disaster; and *Unkenrufe* (1992; *The Call of the Toad,* 1992), an examination of German-Polish relations.

Ein weites Feld was one of the first major novels to tackle the issue of German reunification. The work was highly anticipated, but when it appeared in August, many of Germany's leading critics vehemently attacked it, denouncing Grass's portrayal of reunification as "misconstrued" and "unreadable." Grass, whose leftist political views were often not well received, was outspoken in his belief that Germany lacked "the politically organized power to renew itself," and in his novel he portrayed a country quickly and carelessly thrown together. Partly because of the controversy surrounding *Ein weites Feld,* public interest in the novel was intense. (SHERMAN HOLLAR)

Gusinsky, Vladimir

Few figures in contemporary Russia better embodied the ambiguities and contradictions of the country's erratically evolving capitalist democracy than Vladimir Gusinsky. Believed to be among the wealthiest of Russia's nouveau riche, Gusinsky headed the Most Group, a powerful business conglomerate anchored by the Most Bank. It also included the nation's only independent television network and an influential Moscow newspaper.

Little was known of his past. By his own account, Gusinsky was an only child, born in Moscow in 1952 to a Jewish family that suffered the anti-Semitism of the late Stalin period. At age 17 he entered a technical institute; a tour of duty in the army followed. Gusinsky spent the next five years in Moscow as a theatre director while moon-lighting as a taxi driver.

Gusinsky's big break came in 1986, when Mikhail Gorbachev launched a period of reform. Gusinsky quickly formed one of the first Soviet-American joint ventures, from which evolved the Most Group (named after the U.S. automatic teller machine). By 1993 the group controlled several dozen companies and had moved into the media. The exact sources of Gusinsky's vast fortune remained murky, however. Many speculated that the Most Group profited from lucrative business contacts with the Moscow city government, and especially from Gusinsky's personal relationship with Moscow's mayor.

Although Gusinsky flatly dismissed charges of impropriety, his special relationship with Luzhkov, whom many saw as a potential political challenger to the Russian president, Boris Yeltsin, was undoubtedly the source for one of the most talked about incidents in recent Russian history. In December 1994 Gusinsky's driver and several members of his security team were roughed up by a squad of armed men belonging to the president's official security service. Menacing remarks from the Kremlin followed, and Gusinsky fled with his family to the West, where he remained in self-imposed exile until May 1995. Late in the year he was reportedly negotiating to open a London affiliate.

Gusinsky's treatment illuminated the precariousness of Russia's emerging democracy, just as the shadowy accumulation of his fortune pointed to the seamy side of Russia's transition to capitalism. Gusinsky was nevertheless a steadfast supporter of political and economic reform, and his newspaper, *Segodnya* ("Today"), and his television network, NTV, remained among the best examples of independent media in contemporary Russia. NTV in particular distinguished itself with hard-hitting reporting during the Russian war in Chechnya, an achievement that brought home to Russians the horror of the conflict—and that undoubtedly exacerbated the tensions between Gusinsky and the Kremlin. (STEPHEN FOYE)

Harris, Mike

On June 26, 1995, Mike Harris was sworn in as the 22nd premier of Ontario. His Progressive Conservative Party (PCP) had won a legislative majority in the provincial election of June 8. Harris' administration represented a sharp change from the socialism of the previous New Democratic Party government to conservatism. Perceived as a small-town man with the common touch, he had gained a reputation as a crusader for tax relief and for a smaller, less interventionist government. Thus, he began immediately to implement what he called his "Common Sense Revolution," and his policy changes in the first months of his administration were significant. The government reduced welfare benefits payments by more than 20% and repealed the anti-scab labour legislation passed by the previous government. Harris centralized the administration of the government, and his 20-member Cabinet was the smallest in modern Ontario history.

Harris was first elected to the Ontario legislature in the general election of 1981 to represent the riding of Nipissing. He served as parliamentary assistant to the minister of the environment and was chairman of public accounts. He sat on the General Government and the Resources Development committees. In 1985 Harris was appointed minister of natural resources and minister of energy. From 1985 to 1990 he was the leader of the PCP in the legislature. After the defeat of the Progressive Conservative government in 1987, Harris served as critic for the Revenue, Labour, Housing, Finance, and Northern Development ministries. It was as finance critic that he developed his party's fiscal policy. In May 1994 he released his *Common Sense Revolution*, a plan to cut taxes and reduce the size and the cost of government. On May 12, 1990, Harris was elected leader of the Ontario PCP.

Born on Jan. 23, 1945, in Toronto, Michael Deane Harris grew up in North Bay, Ont. He attended classes at Waterloo (Ont.) Lutheran University (now Wilfrid Laurier University), Laurentian University at Sudbury, Ont., and Nipissing University College, North Bay, and received a teaching certificate from North Bay Teachers' College. For several years he taught seventh- and eighth-grade mathematics in North Bay before joining his father in business. He owned and operated tourism and recreation businesses in the Nipissing and Parry Sound areas of Ontario.

In 1975 Harris was elected to the Nipissing Board of Education; he served as chairman of the board from 1977 to 1981. For one term he was president of the Northern Ontario Trustees Association (1980–81), after which he entered provincial politics. (DIANE LOIS WAY)

Jerusalem, Siegfried

Siegfried Jerusalem's name and voice were both well suited to a Wagnerian heldentenor. Strong, clear, and expressive, with a slight vibrato to give it richness, his voice was, Jerusalem believed, perfect for the role of Siegmund in *Die Walküre.* He also was praised for his effortless phrasing and seductive tone. In addition, Jerusalem had the good looks and athletic build that fit such roles.

Jerusalem did not begin his singing career in earnest until the age of 37. Once having begun, however, he rose rapidly, singing nearly every heldentenor role to acclaim and appearing on nearly every major operatic stage. He sang Lohengrin at the Metropolitan Opera (1980) and La Scala (1981) and sang Parsifal at the Vienna Staatsoper (1979) and at the Metropolitan (1992). He appeared for several seasons as Siegmund at the Wagner festival at Bayreuth, Germany, and he also sang the role at Zürich, Switz. (1988), and at the Lyric Opera of Chicago (1994). He first appeared at Bayreuth, however, in 1977 as Froh in *Das Rheingold,* and in 1988 and 1989 he appeared there as Siegfried in both *Siegfried* and *Götterdämmerung.* In 1990 Jerusalem appeared in a production of *Der Ring des Nibelungen* at the Metropolitan that was televised nationally. For this production he sang Loge in *Das Rheingold* and the title role in *Siegfried.* He also performed in four complete recordings of the *Ring,* including the role of Loge in James Levine's 1991 recording of *Das Rheingold,* which won a Grammy award. Other Wagnerian roles included Walther von Stolzing in *Die Meistersinger von Nürnberg* and Erik in *Der fliegende Holländer.*

Born in Oberhausen, Germany, on April 17, 1940, Jerusalem began his musical career as a bassoonist. He played with orchestras in Germany from 1961 to 1977, his last position being with the Stuttgart Radio Symphony Orchestra. It was in Stuttgart that he began to study voice seriously, and his singing career began there in 1976. In the same year, when the orchestra played for a television production of Johann Strauss's *The Gypsy Baron* and the scheduled tenor did not appear, Jerusalem performed the role of Sandor Barinkay. For a year he continued as a bassoonist while taking small parts with the Stuttgart State Opera. When his performances as Lohengrin in Stuttgart, Hamburg, and Zürich led to offers from Berlin, Vienna, and Munich, Jerusalem decided to pursue his singing career full-time.

Jerusalem credited his clear diction to his singing of lieder. He gave his first lieder recital at Bayreuth in 1982, and he later recorded Schumann's *Dichterliebe* and *Liederkreis.* He also recorded selections from Mahler's *Des Knaben Wunderhorn* and the Rückert, as well as *Das Lied von der Erde.*

Although he was known primarily as a Wagnerian tenor, Jerusalem's repertoire also included Mozart and Italian operas. His Mozartean roles included Tamino in *The Magic Flute* and the title role in *Idomeneo.* He had a particular talent and fondness for Italian opera, notably for Verdi, and he had sung the tenor part in Verdi's *Requiem.*

(DIANE LOIS WAY)

Johnson, Michael Duane

In 1995 U.S. track star Michael Johnson gave further proof that he was the finest sprinter in the world. He did not lose a single race at the distances of 400 and 200 m all year and was clocked under 44 seconds in the 400 m four times and under 20 seconds in the 200 m six times—an unprecedented feat. Indeed, he had not lost a 400-m race outdoors in more than 50 contests since 1988, and his second-place finishes in the 200 m were scarce. Johnson began his undefeated season by breaking the indoor world record at 400 m twice, in February (44.97) and then again in March (44.63). At the outdoor national championships in June, Johnson could not choose between the 200 m and the 400 m, so he ran them both. He repeated this grueling double in August at the world championships, where he matched a personal best time in the 200 m (19.79) and set a personal record in the 400 m (43.39), narrowly missing both world records. He capped his achievements by running the anchor leg for the first-place U.S. 4 × 400-m relay team.

The 200-m/400-m double was rare among world-class sprinters, who traditionally chose to double at 100-m/200-m distances. Johnson's double victory in the long sprints at the world championships—which never before had been accomplished in a major nonboycotted meet—was a feat he hoped to repeat at the 1996 Olympic Games, but at year's end it was still uncertain if the conflicting race schedules would be changed to accommodate him. As the world's top-rated runner of the decade at 200 m and 400 m, he was named the American Athlete of the Year by *Track and Field News* four times (1990, 1993–95).

Johnson, who was born Sept. 13, 1967, in Dallas, Texas, first entered track competition when he was 11 years old. He took second place in the 200 m at the 1986 high-school state championships but did not run the 400 m until his freshman year at Baylor University, Waco, Texas. In 1989 he set an indoor U.S. record at 200 m (20.59) with a victory in the national collegiate championships, a title he successfully defended both indoors and outdoors in 1990. In 1991 he lowered the 200-m indoor record (20.55) and raced undefeated at both 200 m and 400 m outdoors, logging a 200-m victory at the world championships. He qualified for the 1992 Olympic Games in the 200 m but was slowed by illness during the competition, although he did recover to win a gold medal as part of the U.S. 4 × 400-m relay team, which set a world record (2:55.74). In 1993 the U.S. relay team lowered the world mark again (2:54.29), and Johnson's anchor leg of 42.94 seconds became the fastest relay split ever. (TOM MICHAEL)

Michael Duane Johnson
MIKE POWELL—ALLSPORT

Katzenberg, Jeffrey

In September 1994 Jeffrey Katzenberg, chairman of Walt Disney Studios, resigned in a dispute with his longtime boss, Michael Eisner, head of Walt Disney Co. Within days Katzenberg founded DreamWorks SKG with his friends filmmaker Steven Spielberg and record impresario David Geffen. Together they shared two-thirds of the equity in the new entertainment studio, planning to make movies, animation, television shows, and records and produce interactive computer-based entertainment.

Katzenberg's strained relationship and eventual split with Eisner was widely viewed as familial strife engendered by his desire to break from the mold cast by his mentor-father. He was born in 1950 and attended New York University for one year. He worked as a political organizer and held odd jobs (including talent agent) before securing a position at Paramount Pictures. While Eisner was president of Paramount (1976–84), Katzenberg became his protégé, working his way up from the mail room to president of production of motion pictures and television. When Eisner took over the reins at the moribund Disney with Frank Wells from Warner Brothers in 1984, Katzenberg joined them as a junior partner.

Over the next decade Eisner, Katzenberg, and Wells built Disney from a beleaguered $2 billion not-so-magical kingdom into a $22 billion empire. Katzenberg oversaw film and television production, with special responsibility for Disney's animation division and Touchstone Pictures, Disney's first adult feature subsidiary. A ruthless cost cutter, he expanded studio revenues from $320 million to $3.7 billion and pretax profits from $2 million to $800 million. The highly profitable animation features he produced—*The Little Mermaid, Aladdin, Beauty and the Beast,* and *The Lion King*—fueled Disney's growth. Moreover, they made Disney once more a weaver of richly textured fantasies comparable to those of the 1930s, '40s, and '50s.

Katzenberg quit when it became clear Eisner would not bestow wider-ranging responsibilities on him following Wells's accidental death in April 1994. Only six business days after he left, the contracts were signed with Spielberg and Geffen for their new entertainment studio, wherein Katzenberg would run animation and television production. Given the fusion of talent and vision, Hollywood was optimistic about their success. Katzenberg's first animated feature, *The Prince of Egypt*, was scheduled to be released for Christmas 1998. (DANIEL LATHAM)

Kemal, Yashar

Stating that regardless of the consequences he would continue to express his thoughts, 71-year-old Turkish novelist Yashar Kemal was brought to trial in mid-July 1995. Kemal, whose name often appeared on the shortlist for the Nobel Prize for Literature, stood accused of "separatist propaganda" for the publication of his essay "Campaign of Lies" in the German weekly newsmagazine *Der Spiegel.* In his "terrorist" essay, he accused the government of waging a war of oppression against the Kurdish Workers' Party and the Kurdish people that had cost the lives of some 15,000 people over the past 11 years. Listing the myriad acts of violence and humiliation, he accused the government of practicing "the Oriental art of disguise and double talk" to conceal its "unbearable cruelties and coercions." Like more than 8,000 journalists, academics, and intellectuals, he was accused of "crimes of expression." His essay was a clear violation of the eighth article of the Turkish Law Against Terrorism, which forbids "written or spoken propaganda" that undermines the "indivisible integrity of the state."

Kemal, himself of Kurdish descent, did not advocate a separate Kurdish state, the charges against him notwithstanding. He was born Kemal Sadik Gogceli in 1922 in Hemite, a small village in the Taurus Mountains of southwestern Turkey. At the age of five he saw his father murdered in a mosque and, during the same incident, was blinded in one eye. He left secondary school after two years and worked in a variety of jobs. He published two books of folklore in the early 1940s. Arrested in 1950 and 1971 for his political activism, he began to find a natural place for himself as a journalist. In the 1950s he also began to write fiction.

He published a novella, *Teneke* ("The Tin Pan"), and what proved to be the first of a series of novels, *İnce Memed* ("Thin Memed"), in 1955. The latter, a popular tale about a bandit and folk hero, was translated into more than 20 languages—including English, as *Memed, My Hawk* (1961)—and made into a movie in 1987. It remained one of the best-known Turkish novels, and it established Kemal's mastery of the "village novel." Other novels of the type followed, including the trilogy *Ortadirek* (1960; *The Wind from the Plain,* 1960), *Yer demir, gök bakır* (1963; *Iron Earth, Copper Sky,* 1974), and *Ölmez otu* (1968; *The Undying Grass,* 1977); and *İnce Memed II* (1969; *They Burn the Thistles,* 1972). He also wrote short stories, essays, and several more volumes of folktales. Coastal villages and urban settings provided the backdrop for many of Kemal's later works, notably the novella *Yılanı Öldürseler* (1976; *To Crush the Serpent*, 1991).

(KATHLEEN KUIPER)

Khaled

Beyond the borders of its Algerian birthplace, the exotic sounds of rai music continued to attract listeners in 1995, primarily through the rich, passionate voice of the "king of rai," Khaled. The Algerian singer was not only one of the best-known voices of rai but an embodiment of its spirit of youth, pleasure, and sexual freedom. His celebration of this lifestyle, however, put him at risk. Islamic extremists viewed this music as a corrupting influence on the young and issued a *fatwa,* or death sentence, against those espousing this message. As a result, Khaled moved to France and had not returned to Algeria since 1990.

Nevertheless, Khaled was a man who exuded happiness, especially when performing. Khaled Hadj Brahim was born on Feb. 29, 1960, in the western Algerian city of Oran. By the age of 10 he was playing a variety of instruments, including the accordion, guitar, and harmonica, and at 14 he recorded his first single, "La Route de lycée" ("The Road to School").

Rai—from the Arabic word meaning "opinion" or "advice"—blossomed in Oran in the 1920s. The port city, known as "little Paris," was a melting pot of various cultures, full of nightclubs and bordellos, the place to go for a bawdy good time. Out of this milieu, female Muslim singers called cheikhas emerged. They stood the poetic and classical lyrics of traditional Algerian music on its head, singing instead about the real conditions of urban life in a raw and gritty language reminiscent of American blues.

Modern rai built on the music of these women, retaining the plain speaking and the flaunting of accepted mores while incorporating the sounds of Western rock, Jamaican reggae, Egyptian and Moroccan pop, and other innovative styles that made their way into Algeria. In the 1980s Khaled and other singers added drum machines, synthesizers, and electric guitars to the mix. By the time the first international rai festival was held in Algeria in 1985, Khaled was the central figure; his name had become virtually synonymous with rai.

In the 1990s his music evolved beyond the synthesized sounds of his earlier period. His most recent recording, "N'ssi N'ssi," included pedal steel guitars and Asian string arrangements. Although extremely popular in North Africa, the Middle East, India, and Europe, Khaled was not as well known in the United States. With the inclusion of his music on the sound track of the 1994 film *Killing Zoe,* however, and the production of an upcoming album by U.S. producer Don Was, he could yet capture an American audience.

(MARY JANE FRIEDRICH)

Kieslowski, Krzysztof

Little was heard from Polish film director Krzysztof Kieslowski in 1995 after he publicly declared his retirement in 1994, just when his work was reaching its widest audience and receiving its greatest acclaim. But his swan song, the *Trois Couleurs* (*Three Colors*) trilogy, still resonated clearly as the voice of one of the most talented filmmakers in Europe. The trilogy, which depicts characters linked only by coincidence, was thematically arranged around the colours of the French flag and the revolutionary slogan of "liberty, equality, and fraternity." One theme, the frailty of human relationships, emerged from the lonely awakening in *Bleu* (1993; *Blue*) and permeated the grim humour of *Blanc* (1993; *White*) before providing the symbolic epiphany in *Rouge* (1994; *Red*).

Kieslowski was born on June 27, 1941, in occupied Warsaw. There he attended a school specializing in theatre technology (1957–62) before studying film directing in Lodz at the School of Cinema and Theatre (1964–69). His early works were mostly television films and documentaries about daily life in communist Poland. He began shooting short feature films in the mid-1970s, but his first feature to reach an international audience was *Amator* (1979; "The Camera Buff"), which shows the powerful impact that camera images can make on lives. *Przypadek* ("The Accident," or "Blind Chance"), which was completed in 1981 but not released until 1987, marked Kieslowski's shift from real-life, political issues to deterministic, psychological themes. The film traces three fateful directions the protagonist's life may take as he rushes to board a train.

In 1982 Kieslowski met Krzysztof Piesiewicz, a lawyer who defended Solidarity activists arrested during the period of martial law in Poland. Piesiewicz would coauthor the remainder of Kieslowski's films, beginning with *Bez konca* (1984; "No End"), the story of a woman who searches for meaning in her life after the death of her husband. Kieslowski also directed *Dekalog* ("Decalogue"), a 1988 series of 10 films for television, each based on one of the Ten Commandments. That same year two of the episodes were expanded into feature-length films—*Krotki film o zabi janiu* ("A Short Film About Killing") and *Krotki film o miłosci* ("A Short Film About Love").

With his next film, *La Double Vie de Véronique* (1991), Kieslowski began working outside Poland, primarily with French studios. The film compares the lives of two women with similar backgrounds and uses an unorthodox narrative style to communicate how the sufferings of Weronika of Poland have mysteriously influenced the life of Véronique of France. After releasing *Rouge* Kieslowski announced his retirement—for reasons known only to himself.

(TOM MICHAEL)

FRANCOIS DARMIGNY—SYGMA

Khaled

Kwasniewski, Aleksander

On Dec. 23, 1995, Aleksander Kwasniewski, a former Communist Party apparatchik, was sworn in as the second president of postcommunist Poland. Though utilizing Western-style craft, Kwasniewski rode the wave that returned former party officials to the shores of power throughout Eastern Europe. In a narrow runoff victory that was seen by many as a political watershed, he dunked the sitting president and past reigning hero of Polish anticommunism, Lech Walesa, who had won the nation's first direct presidential election in 1990. Ironically, both men were baptized in the same political waters. Kwasniewski entered politics in the 1970s as a member of the ruling Communist Party at the same time that Walesa came of age, engineering the party's collapse while a leader of the Solidarity trade union. From a distance, the close election race pitted two political archetypes. Indeed, Kwasniewski's slick campaign and polished, noncontroversial image appealed to young voters unaffected by negative communist symbols and to others, mainly in northern and western towns, unimpressed by recent market reforms instituted on Walesa's watch.

Kwasniewski was born on Nov. 15, 1954, in the town of Bialogard in northwestern Poland. He studied economics at the University of Gdansk, where he was chairman of a student group. He joined the Polish United Workers' Party (*i.e.,* the Communist Party) in 1977 and moved to Warsaw to edit two of the party's youth newspapers—the weekly *Itd* ("Etc.") (1981–84) and the daily *Sztandar Mlodych* ("Youth Standard") (1984–85). He steadily rose up the party ranks, with appointments to the Council of Ministers in 1985 and as minister of youth affairs and physical culture in 1987. He was invited to take part in the round-table discussions that resulted in the end of communist rule in the late 1980s, heading the committee that dealt with trade unions. After the fall of communism, Kwasniewski founded a new party, the Democratic Left Alliance, which captured a plurality of seats in the parliamentary elections of 1993. Subsequently, he formed a ruling coalition with the Polish Peasant Party, which was similarly composed of former communists. In the closing days of the 1995 presidential election campaign, Kwasniewski had to face widespread accusations of dishonesty for inaccurately reporting his wife's earnings and for falsely claiming to have received his college degree. Ultimately, he capitalized on the waning popularity of Walesa, but he pledged to continue with less austerity and dislocation Walesa's reform efforts toward a market economy and membership in NATO and the European Union.

(TOM MICHAEL)

Lawrence, Carmen Mary

When Carmen Lawrence joined the Australian Cabinet as minister of health on March 25, 1994, less than two weeks after she entered the federal Parliament, it seemed only a matter of time before she became the nation's first woman prime minister. Lawrence had previously been the Australian Labor Party (ALP) premier of the state of Western Australia, and she had seized the opportunity to enter national politics at an unexpected by-election. The Conservative state government led by Premier Richard Court, however, pursued her from Perth to Canberra and set up a royal commission, which, many observers agreed, soon turned into a witch-hunt intended to destroy Lawrence's political career. Court instructed the royal commissioner to seek to establish the facts surrounding the tabling (formal submission) of a petition in the Western Australian Parliament in November 1992. This petition, which involved allegations of perjury against lawyer Penny Easton (who committed suicide a few days later), was the last salvo in an acrimonious divorce between Easton and her husband, Brian Easton, a state government official against whom she had brought unsuccessful charges of corruption and financial impropriety. The commission was ordered to investigate the tangled case to see if then premier Lawrence had made improper use of executive power in the matter.

Lawrence was born March 2, 1948, to a wheat farming family in Northam, Western Australia. She studied psychology at the University of Western Australia. After being elected to the Western Australian Parliament in 1986, she was chosen to lead the party and served as premier and treasurer of Western Australia until the ALP was defeated at the 1993 elections. After a very short stint in opposition as shadow treasurer and shadow minister for employment, she entered the federal Parliament on March 12, 1994. Prime Minister Paul Keating put her on the fast track into the Cabinet, but from that time forward she was under constant fire from her former political enemies in the west.

Before the royal commission began its hearings, Lawrence had a reputation for being "Teflon tough." While public opinion was primarily concerned about the huge cost of her legal proceedings, Lawrence herself admitted she had been reduced to tears by her ordeal. She was driven to the brink of resignation and blamed her political woes on her sex. As the only woman in Keating's Cabinet, Lawrence complained that she was "hot political property" and a clearly identifiable target for the opposition. "If you're initially anointed with the saintly stereotype that I was," she said, "only one course of action can follow—the halo will eventually become tarnished."

(A.R.G. GRIFFITHS)

Lobo, Rebecca

On Oct. 22, 1995, Rebecca Lobo received the National Collegiate Athletic Association's (NCAA's) Woman of the Year award for her outstanding achievements in athletics, academics, and community leadership. This capped a year in which the 1.9-m, 81-kg (6-ft 4-in, 180-lb) centre-forward Lobo led the University of Connecticut women's basketball team to its first NCAA title and a perfect 35–0 record through postseason play.

While Lobo had help from fellow All-American Jennifer Rizzotti and future star Kara Wolters, she anchored the team with her season average of 17.3 points, 10.3 rebounds, 3.4 blocked shots, and 3.8 assists. In addition to her 2,133 career points and two University of Connecticut records—1,268 rebounds and 227 blocked shots—she finished college as a Phi Beta Kappa with a 3.6 grade-point average in political science. But Lobo had heart as well as brains and brawn, making time for charitable causes and, always, her fans.

For her efforts she was named Most Outstanding Player at the NCAA Final Four competition, the Associated Press's Player of the Year, and the Naismith National Player of the Year. She also won the Wade Trophy for her leadership on and off the court. Lobo appeared on David Letterman's television show, had a street named after her in her hometown, and signed multiyear agreements with the Reebok and Spalding athletic equipment firms. In 1995 she joined the women's national team and hoped to earn a place on the 1996 Olympic team. If Lobo were a man, she would have been among the top picks in the National Basketball Association draft. As a woman, her professional choices were limited unless the attention and admiration fueled, in part, by Lobo got the new Women's Major Basketball League off the ground. Otherwise, she might play professionally in Europe.

Born Oct. 6, 1973, in Southwick, Mass., Lobo was part of a close-knit family. Her sister, Rachel, was a basketball coach at Salem (Mass.) State College, and her brother, Jason, now a lawyer, played basketball for Dartmouth College, Hanover, N.H. Lobo began breaking records at Southwick-Tolland High School, becoming the all-time leading scorer—male or female—in Massachusetts state history while also managing to star in field hockey, track, softball, and academics.

(ELLEN FINKELSTEIN)

Lomu, Jonah

South Africa may have won the 1995 Rugby Union World Cup final, but the man of the year was undoubtedly Jonah Lomu. The giant New Zealand wing dominated the World Cup and became the most talked-about player in generations.

At 1.95 m (6 ft 5 in) and weighing 19 stone (119 kg; 266 lb), the 20-year-old Lomu could have played just about any position, having clocked 10.8 seconds for the 100-m sprint. In less than 12 months, however, he had become one of the most devastating wing threequarters ever to set foot on a rugby pitch. Born of Tongan parents in Mangere, N.Z., on June 1, 1975, Lomu weighed in at a massive 5 kg (11 lb) at birth.

As a youngster he played Rugby League before switching to Union. He regularly won every school athletics event he entered and held records for sprint, hurdles, shot put, and discus. In Rugby Union he played in the forwards, usually as a flanker but sometimes at lock.

It was the 1994 Hong Kong Sevens tournament that brought him to the attention of the New Zealand national selectors, and they decided that his best position would be wing. He became the youngest-ever All Black when he made his debut against France in June 1994 at age 19, but his defensive naïveté was exposed and he lost his place.

Lomu bounced back, thrilling the crowds once again at the 1995 Hong Kong Sevens, and the New Zealand management decided to take a gamble and include him in their World Cup squad. They knew he had all the attributes to be a great player, but they needed to see if he had the mental discipline and ability to cope with pressure. Their faith was rewarded when he turned in a series of stunning performances in South Africa.

The All Black management wisely kept him under wraps, and the legend of Jonah Lomu grew as the tournament progressed. Against England he turned out to be virtually unstoppable—destroying them in the semifinals almost single-handedly, scoring four tries, and trampling many of England's finest players underfoot in the process.

Performances like that soon had the big Rugby League clubs knocking on his door, and even the U.S. football Dallas Cowboys were rumoured to have made him an offer. But the shy, unassuming giant elected to stay in Rugby Union, thanks to probably the biggest deal ever struck for a Union player.

Away from the media glare he was a simple soul, professing a liking for fast food and loud music. A keen surfer, he loved swimming in the sea, and he claimed his favourite film was *Forrest Gump*. Not a bad role model!

(DAVID LAWRENSON)

Lukas, D(arrell) Wayne

In 1995 D. Wayne Lukas made history when he became the first trainer to win thoroughbred horse racing's Triple Crown with different horses and the first to win five consecutive Triple Crown races. A thoroughbred among trainers, Lukas possessed an unorthodox style, achieving rapid results at the most opportune times. He produced herds of champions, though few that had gone the extra furlong to receive the Horse of the Year award.

Lukas was born on Sept. 2, 1935, in Antigo, Wis. At the age of eight he was buying, selling, and training horses. He continued training and trading horses while at the University of Wisconsin, where he received a master's degree in 1961, and later while coaching high-school basketball throughout the 1960s. Lukas began training quarter horses full-time in 1967 and won 73 races in 1970. In 1975 his 150 victories doubled the record for most quarter horse wins in a year by a trainer. He produced 23 champions in 1976–77 and captured all six major California stakes of $100,000 or more for three consecutive years (1975–77).

Lukas began training thoroughbreds full-time in 1978. He led the nation's trainers in earnings for eight consecutive years (1983–90). While setting a record with 92 stakes winners in 1987, he became the first trainer in history to amass more purse earnings than the nation's leading jockey. His horses won $17.8 million in 1988, more than double the amount ever won in a single year by any other trainer. Lady's Secret earned 1986 Horse of the Year, as did Criminal Type in 1990. Lukas won the Eclipse Award as the nation's best trainer for three consecutive years (1985–87). He held the Breeder's Cup record with 12 wins. In 1988 Winning Colors gave Lukas his first Kentucky Derby victory. She was only the third filly in history to claim that jewel.

Before rewriting the record books again in 1995, Lukas himself might have considered retiring. He was not winning as he once did and was stung by criticism that he was causing his horses to break

PATRICK DE NOIRMONT—HULTON DEUTSCH/REUTERS

Jonah Lomu

down by running them too frequently. His financial empire, moreover, unraveled when investors backed off in 1989, and he lost millions of dollars in 1991 with the bankruptcy of Calumet Farms. Probably the heaviest blow came in December 1993 when his son and chief assistant, Jeff Lukas, was knocked comatose and nearly killed by the rogue horse Tabasco Cat.

Possibly only the eccentric and controversial Lukas would have cajoled that renegade horse into a Triple Crown champion. Tabasco Cat took both the Preakness and Belmont Stakes in 1994, pulling Lukas out of a 2½-year slump. He added to his legendary status in 1995 when Thunder Gulch claimed victory in both the Kentucky Derby and the Belmont Stakes and Timber Country took the Preakness. Thunder Gulch, however, lost his bid to be named Horse of the Year when he fractured a cannon bone in the Jockey Club Gold Cup Stakes and could not run in the Breeder's Cup. (DANIEL LATHAM)

McFerrin, Bobby

Imagine a symphony orchestra performing Rossini's *William Tell* overture not on their instruments but by singing. Imagine, in fact, an album of orchestral works by Mozart, Bach, and other masters with the melodies sung instead of played. If you were the American vocal virtuoso Bobby McFerrin, to imagine it would be to do it, as he and the St. Paul (Minn.) Chamber Orchestra did on the 1995 album *Paper Music* and as he went on to do in concert.

McFerrin had sung classical music, as written and in his own improvisations, since the mid-1980s, and he did an album with cellist Yo-Yo Ma in 1992. Earlier he had become known as an original jazzman who sang a cappella, providing his own percussion accompaniment by tapping his chest. He also sang standards and folk songs, 1960s rock and soul tunes, and jazz themes with original lyrics. He had always preferred to sing without fixed lyrics, sounding like a trumpet, a bass, or a guitar, with a full-bodied voice that ranged from bass to falsetto. In concert he might wander through the auditorium singing, make up songs on listeners' names, conduct his audience in spontaneous choirs, or burst into a condensed version of *The Wizard of Oz*, complete with tornado sounds and munchkin, witch, and scarecrow voices. On record he could improvise all the parts in a vocal group himself, as in his hit "Don't Worry, Be Happy." If a McFerrin performance was anything, it was spontaneous. "Improvisation," he said, "is the courage to move from one note to the next," and the word *courage* provided a clue to the force behind his career.

Born in New York City on March 11, 1950, McFerrin had parents with distinguished vocal careers. His mother, a soprano, was a Metropolitan Opera judge who chaired the vocal department at Fullerton College, near Los Angeles, and his father, who sang at the Met, dubbed Sidney Poitier's singing on the 1959 *Porgy and Bess* sound track. In McFerrin's youth he was inclined to become a minister of music, but after attending California State University at Sacramento and Cerritos College, Norwalk, Calif., he instead became a pianist and organist with the Ice Follies and with pop music bands. In 1977 he auditioned for and won a singing job.

As a swinging jazz and ballad vocalist by 1980, McFerrin was touring with popular jazz singer Jon Hendricks. Inspired by Keith Jarrett's improvised piano concerts, in 1983 he worked up the nerve to sing alone. His had been a triumphant career ever since. Among other projects, he recorded television commercials and the "Cosby Show" theme; improvised music for a dance troupe and to actor Jack Nicholson's readings of Rudyard Kipling's children's stories; coped with audience guests such as comedian Robin Williams and saxman Wayne Shorter on his *Spontaneous Inventions* album and video, and won a string of Grammy awards. Clearly, McFerrin had gone far beyond the customary jazz vocal boundaries; he said, "People are always asking me to describe what I do, and to me it's just singing, but one of the reviews called it . . . McFerrining."

(JOHN LITWEILER)

Bobby McFerrin
MICHAEL JANG—LGI AGENCY

Maddux, Gregory Alan

Greg Maddux of the Atlanta Braves established himself in 1995 as the best pitcher of his day and one of the greatest in baseball history. Maddux won the National League's Cy Young Award—given annually to the league's top pitcher—for the fourth consecutive year. Only one other pitcher had won four Cy Young Awards, and none had ever won the award more than two years in a row. In leading the Braves to the National League pennant, Maddux won a league-best 19 games while losing only 2. His league-leading earned-run average (ERA) of 1.63, along with a 1994 mark of 1.57, made him the first pitcher since the legendary Walter ("Big Train") Johnson in 1918–19 to post an ERA of less than 1.80 in consecutive seasons. At 1.8 m and 77 kg (6 ft and 170 lb), Maddux was smaller than the average ballplayer. He did not have a blazing fastball or a devastating curve; instead, he was able to dominate hitters by studying their tendencies and then baffling them with the amazing accuracy and varying speeds of his pitches.

Maddux was born on April 14, 1966, in San Angelo, Texas. From a young age he and his older brother, Mike (who also became a major league pitcher), were drilled in the fundamentals of the game by their father. Greg earned all-state honours in both his junior and senior years as a pitcher for Valley High School in Las Vegas, Nev., and upon his graduation in 1984 he was drafted by the Chicago Cubs and assigned to the minor league system.

Late in the 1986 season, Maddux, just 20 years old, was called up to the big leagues. His performance that season (two wins, four losses, 5.52 ERA) and the next (6–14, 5.61) was anything but masterful. Known as an overly emotional player who often taunted umpires and opposing hitters, Maddux, by his own later admission, was not a thinking pitcher but a "brain-dead heaver." All that began to change, however, when he adjusted the mechanics of his delivery. In 1988 he won 15 of his first 18 decisions and finished 18–8 with a 3.18 ERA. In 1989, as the ace of the Chicago pitching staff when the Cubs won the East Division crown, he went 19–12 with a 2.95 ERA. The next two seasons, pitching for losing teams, he won 30 games and lost 26. In 1992, with a 20–11 record and a 2.18 ERA, Maddux won his first Cy Young Award.

A contract dispute with the Cubs left him a free agent, and he signed a five-year, $28 million contract with Atlanta. Maddux then went to work to dispel the notion that high salaries ruined players' incentive to perform; during the first three years of his contract, he won the Cy Young Award three times while compiling a 55–18 record. At the age of 29 and with a large part of his career still ahead of him, Maddux was already virtually assured of a spot in baseball's Hall of Fame.

(ANTHONY G. CRAINE)

Marcos, Subcommandante

On Feb. 9, 1995, Mexico's Pres. Ernesto Zedillo Ponce de León broke a cease-fire and ordered thousands of Mexican troops into the area of Chiapas state held by the Zapatista National Liberation Army (EZLN), the group that had launched a rebellion on New Year's Day 1994 to demand indigenous rights and greater democracy, liberty, and justice. The stated purpose of the crackdown was to prevent further violence by capturing Zapatista leaders, in particular Subcommandante Marcos, their eloquent but elusive spokesperson. As part of the offensive, Zedillo unmasked Marcos as Rafael Sebastián Guillén Vicente, a middle-class "maverick philosopher and university professor," in an attempt to discredit him as the voice of the peasant-led EZLN and to strip him of the charismatic guerrilla mystique that had captured the imagination of many. Pictures of Guillén juxtaposed with those of the masked Marcos appeared worldwide. One of the EZLN's few non-Indian fighters, Marcos had become internationally known for his literate communiqués, issued in the name of the Revolutionary Indigenous Clandestine Committee of the General Command (CCRI-CG) of the EZLN. These letters to the Mexican people often combined humour, poetry, and storytelling with sharp political critiques.

Marcos, the EZLN, and the population of many villages faded into the Lacandón jungle as troops moved into the area, while the press was kept out. Meanwhile, more than 100,000 demonstrators in Mexico City and elsewhere answered Zedillo by proclaiming, "We are all Marcos." The government move to isolate the rebels politically thus met with limited success. The military push and reported abuse of civilians galvanized the support of students, union leaders, human rights advocates, and leftists outside Chiapas. While Zedillo proclaimed Marcos a terrorist, the National Autonomous University awarded him Mexico's highest honour—an honorary degree. By mid-March the troops had been pulled out of the area, and peace talks limped along. Marcos continued to communicate via the Internet from the rain forest. In October he emerged to participate in

WESLEY BOCXE—JB PICTURES
Subcommandante Marcos

talks, doing so with his usual dramatic flair—on horseback with armed, masked Zapatistas to the sounds of conch shells blowing and a cheering crowd of peasants.

Guillén, the man Zedillo identified as Marcos, was the Jesuit-trained 37-year-old son of the owner of a furniture chain in Tampico who had moved to the mountains of Chiapas in 1984 to work with Mayan peasants. After going to school in Tampico, Guadalajara (Jalisco), and Monterrey, Guillén attended the national university in Mexico City. In 1981 he was one of five students from the department of philosophy and letters to receive a national medal of excellence from Pres. José López Portillo. He taught aesthetics part-time at a working-class school known as a left-wing activist centre before resigning in 1984. As his mother said, "[For some he] is a delinquent, and for many others, he's a hero."

(ELLEN FINKELSTEIN)

Masekela, Hugh

The 1995 album *Johannesburg* surely was a surprise to trumpeter Hugh Masekela's longtime fans. The title promised South African-styled music by that country's most popular instrumentalist. The content, however, was American-sounding rap, hip-hop, and contemporary urban pop selections, with the ostensible leader's contribution limited to jazzy trumpet introductions and backgrounds (and on some pieces he apparently did not even play). After the 1994 *Hope,* which offered Masekela's South African band reviving his biggest hits over the decades, *Johannesburg* was a new direction. He now appeared as a mentor for young South African performers, the youngest being the 16-year-old rapper Anansa.

It was as if Masekela were enjoying a second career in music. His first career came to an end in 1990 when he received a telephone call that he had been awaiting for 30 years: Come home. The caller was his sister Barbara, in Johannesburg, reporting that the South African government had declared amnesty for political exiles; herself an exile, she had returned home to become Nelson Mandela's chief of staff. An outspoken opponent of apartheid, Masekela had lived in the U.S., Europe, and Africa while bringing his own country's unique rhythms and harmonies to international stages.

Born on April 4, 1939, in Johannesburg, Masekela was the son of the chief health inspector of Sharpeville township, a sculptor in wood who owned an extensive jazz record collection. Records by the American trumpeters Dizzy Gillespie and Clifford Brown inspired the son to play bop with the Jazz Epistles in 1959, a group that included the noted pianist Abdullah Ibrahim (then Dollar Brand) and that was the first black band in the country to record an album. When the grip of apartheid tightened the following year, Masekela immigrated to the U.S., where he attended the Manhattan School of Music in New York City and began forming his own bands. In the 1960s he arranged for and accompanied his then wife, the singer Miriam Makeba; he also wrote and played songs in the *kwela* style, the pop-folk music of the South African townships.

With his 1970s travels in Africa, Masekela became involved in the continent's varieties of music, teaching for a year in Guinea, playing in the popular Nigerian performer Fela Anikulapo Kuti's band, and recording five albums and touring with the band Hedzolleh Soundz. In the 1980s, after starring in outdoor concerts in Lesotho and Botswana that drew throngs of black and white South Africans, he settled in Botswana and set up a mobile recording studio near the South African border to be able to record that country's musicians; he also played on Paul Simon's "Graceland" world tour. When the call came from his sister, who later became South Africa's ambassador to France, he was ready: "We had both been abroad only physically. Spiritually we'd never left for one second."

(JOHN LITWEILER)

Mercredi, Ovide

In 1995 the elected (June 12, 1991) national chief of the Assembly of First Nations, Ovide Mercredi—representing some 1.5 million Indians from more than 600 bands across Canada—repeatedly espoused his belief that "aboriginal people, as the land's original inhabitants, have inherent rights to self-government." He warned that aboriginals would not allow their concerns to be ignored in discussions taking place in the wake of the October defeat of the Quebec referendum on sovereignty. Mercredi had participated in talks formulating the 1992 Charlottetown accord, which, had it been adopted, would have supported self-government and treaty review for Canada's Indian population.

A Cree, Mercredi was born in 1946 in Grand Rapids, Man. He lived outside the reservation because his mother was stripped of her Indian status when she married a métis of mixed Indian and European descent. After receiving in 1977 a law degree from the University of Manitoba, Mercredi practiced criminal law. He was appointed a member of the Manitoba Human Rights Commission, and in 1989 he became the Assembly of First Nations' vice-chief for Manitoba.

Mercredi had been an advocate for native peoples' rights for over 20 years. He was involved with the Cree of Northern Quebec in their efforts to stop the Great Whale hydroelectric project. In June 1990 he was one of the tacticians who helped Manitoba legislator Elijah Harper defeat the Meech Lake accord because it did not address the rights of native people.

Influenced by the teachings of Gandhi, Mercredi took a path of civil disobedience, passive resistance, and nonviolence. While acting as a mediator in confrontations between the government and Indians at Oka in Quebec (1990) and at Gustafsen Lake in British Columbia (1995), he argued against the use of violence.

Mercredi and the Assembly favoured distinct status for Indians, with the right of self-government, mainly so that aboriginal people could deal with their problems according to traditional laws and values. The Assembly also opposed the federal Indian Act, which allowed the government to dictate who had status as an Indian. Mercredi himself did not have status as an Indian until 1985 because his father was not one.

As national chief, Mercredi spoke for a diverse group of status Indians who embraced differing traditions and at times represented conflicting interests. In his efforts to find consensus for policies and to foster unity, he spent much of his time traveling across Canada to meet people and to learn firsthand of their problems. Mercredi cowrote the book *In the Rapids: Navigating the Future of First Nations* (1993).

(DIANE LOIS WAY)

Muster, Thomas

With his 7–5, 6–2, 6–4 victory over Michael Chang of the U.S. in the final of the 1995 French Open, Thomas Muster, the first Austrian ever to win a Grand Slam tournament, joined the elite of the tennis world. Perhaps more impressive than his rise to stardom, however, was the fact that he could even play professional tennis; six years earlier a drunken driver had nearly ended his career.

Muster was born on Oct. 2, 1967, in Leibnitz, Austria. After finishing 10th in the 1984 world junior rankings, he turned pro in 1985. Four tournament titles in 1988 raised his world ranking to 16th. On a March night in 1989, having just defeated Yannick Noah of France to advance to the finals of the Lipton International in Key Biscayne, Fla., and poised to solidify a spot in the top 10, Muster was unloading gear from the trunk of his car when it was struck in the front by another car. The rear bumper hit Muster's left knee, severing the ligaments. Surgery repaired the knee, but Muster's ability to play professional tennis—or even walk comfortably—was uncertain.

Determined to return to the game, Muster, with the help of his coach, Ronald Leitgeb, designed a special chair from which he could hit tennis balls while his leg healed. Within six months Muster was back on the tour, and he finished the year ranked 21st in the world. With his career back on track, he began to establish a pattern: except for a 1990 title on the hard-court surface at Adelaide, Australia, every tournament he won was played on clay, where the slower pace of the game seemed to lessen the disadvantage of his weakened knee. He finished 1990 ranked seventh in the world, but his mastery of the clay court was just beginning. His 1995 victory over Chang in Paris extended his clay-court winning streak to 35 matches, and he would carry that string to 40, third best in the Open era, behind Bjorn Borg (44) and Guillermo Vilas (53). Success in the French Open also lifted Muster to his highest ranking ever, third in the world, which was where he would finish the season after winning a record 12 titles on the Association of Tennis Professionals tour, the last one coming at the Eurocard Open in Essen, Germany, for his first-ever win indoors.

Though he won more than $2.5 million in prize money, Muster's 1995 season was not without its negative moments. Many observers questioned his resolve when he chose—presumably to preserve his high ranking—not to compete at Wimbledon, where he had lost in the first round in each of his four previous appearances. Near the end of the 1995 season, however, Muster announced that he planned to play at Wimbledon in 1996.

(ANTHONY G. CRAINE)

Nachtwey, James

Photojournalist James Nachtwey followed his instincts when deciding where to travel for the stories he worked on, and those instincts took him all over the world, often to scenes of violent conflict and social upheaval. The haunting images he recorded in those places appeared in a number of the most respected international publications—*National Geographic, Life, Time, El País,* and *L'Express*—and he received numerous awards for them. In 1995 he became the first photographer to win three of the profession's most prestigious awards in a single year. For his work in South Africa in the period leading up to the April 1994 elections, he was given the Robert Capa Gold Medal, his fourth, and for pictures taken on assignment in Rwanda, he received both the Magazine Photographer of the Year award, his sixth, and the World Press Photo of the Year, his second, for a portrait showing the mutilation inflicted upon a Hutu man who refused to take part in the brutality against the Tutsi.

The danger inherent in Nachtwey's work became especially apparent during his assignment in South Africa, when a group of journalists was fired upon. Nachtwey was attempting to aid his friend and colleague Ken Oosterbroek, who had been shot, when a bullet came so close to Nachtwey that it parted his hair. Oosterbroek had been fatally wounded.

Nachtwey was born on March 14, 1948, in Syracuse, N.Y. He graduated from Dartmouth College, Hanover, N.H., with a degree in art history and political science and then served in the merchant marine. Influenced by the work of still photographers during the Vietnam War and impressed by the power of photos to communicate the reality of a situation, he became a self-taught student of photography. After serving four years as a newspaper photographer in New Mexico, he moved to New York City in 1980 to become a freelance magazine photographer. Following his first assignment, in Northern Ireland in 1981, Nachtwey worked in Central America, the Middle East, Africa, and Eastern Europe. In 1984 he became a contract photographer with *Time* magazine and in 1986 joined the Magnum cooperative for photojournalists. His books include *Deeds of War* (1989) and *The Inferno* (1995).

(BARBARA WHITNEY)

Nakauchi, Isao

Isao Nakauchi was a retailer who had always wanted to end the traditional right of Japanese manufacturers to determine what products made it to the market and how much they would cost. Pushing for change and the interests of consumers, Nakauchi became not only a maverick in the retail establishment but chairman and controlling shareholder of the country's largest supermarket chain.

Nakauchi's severe criticism of the government's inept response to the Great Hanshin Earthquake, which struck the Kobe area on Jan. 17, 1995, was well in keeping with his long-held views on the need for deregulation. Ordering his employees to immediately deliver relief goods to the disaster area, Nakauchi earned praise and respect. To be sure, it was a cause close to his heart as well as his pocketbook.

Nakauchi was born in Kobe on Aug. 2, 1922, and it was in the nearby town of Senri that he opened his first Daiei Housewives Store in 1957. The Great Hanshin Earthquake caused about $500 million in damage to his outlets and inflicted the first financial loss ever on the Daiei empire. Nakauchi soon had his business on the road to recovery by keeping his stores open round-the-clock in defiance of regulations. Fearful that the Great Hanshin disaster might reverse the trend toward the liberalization he eagerly championed, he resigned from the prestigious post of vice-chairman of Keidanren (the Federation of Economic Organizations). He explained that he was fed up with making proposals to a government in whose ability to act he no longer had any confidence. The bureaucrats "hold meetings but nobody assumes responsibility," he complained.

Nakauchi's views were shaped by his constantly battling authorities, making them eventually accept his markdowns and unorthodox trading activities. By pioneering the development of private-brand products as a strategy for checking large manufacturers, he changed the power relationship between providers and retailers. Some chose to categorize Nakauchi's business philosophy as ruthless "survival of the fittest," but by his own accord he wanted to double disposable incomes by slashing consumer prices in half. That, he believed, could be accomplished in less than 20 years by removing government regulations that stifled competition and increased costs. While maintaining that "only manufacturers worry about price-cutting," Nakauchi proposed that the Japanese would have to start learning how to acquire interests other than their jobs if falling prices produced a shift in industrial structure and unemployment. "We must discard our conventional ways of thinking," he insisted. (GERD LARSSON)

Ngema, Mbongeni

With the inauguration of Nelson Mandela as president of South Africa in 1994, a new era dawned for the theatre in that nation. As proof, there was *Mama! The Musical of Freedom,* a 1995 work by the Zulu playwright, composer, director, and choreographer Mbongeni Ngema. *Mama!* was based on Ngema's experiences with Committed Artists, a theatre troupe he founded in Johannesburg in 1983; it was a story about the youngsters who joined the troupe, and the determined title character from the all-black urban complex Soweto was based on Mandela's wife, Winnie, who had helped Committed Artists. Most of all, *Mama!* was packed with songs and vivacious dancing. If some of the purportedly Zulu-inspired music resembled contemporary African-American music, and if the dancers included one Indian and three white women, these too reflected the changes in today's South Africa. After a six-week run in Durban, *Mama!* went on tour to Germany, Switzerland, and The Netherlands.

MICHELINE PELLETIER—SYGMA

Mbongeni Ngema (right), with his wife, actress Leleti Khumalo

Mama! was the first nonpolitical production for Ngema, whose previous works reflected the spirit of South Africa's blacks under apartheid. Born in Natal, South Africa, in 1955, Ngema worked as a manual labourer and guitarist before he began acting in local theatre groups in the late 1970s. With actor Percy Mtwa he wrote the satirical play *Woza Albert!* (1981), which imagines the second coming of Christ, this time in South Africa; the government first tries to exploit him and then banishes him to a notorious prison for blacks. Ngema's next show, the musical *Asinamali!* (1983), dealt with police violence, forced separations from families, and constricting racist laws as experienced by five prisoners; soon after it opened, police raided a performance and arrested Ngema's actors. Despite its serious theme, *Asinamali!* is filled with music and comedy.

The success of both productions in the U.S. paved the way for Ngema's international triumph with the musical *Sarafina!* in 1987. The title character is a black teenager who at first wants to become a superstar; instead, inspired by a teacher, she becomes a revolutionary in the 1976 student uprisings in Soweto. Ngema and Hugh Masekela (*q.v.*) wrote the score, which features *mbaqanga,* the fusion of traditional South African music with modern American gospel, jazz, and rock. In 1990 Ngema, inspired by a violent strike by South African railway workers, wrote the musical *Township Fever.* "When I did *Township Fever,* I was moving away from protest to the theatre of enlightenment," he said. (JOHN LITWEILER)

Pagels, Elaine

Only a few academics are read by both their peers and the general public. Elaine Pagels, the Harrington Spear Paine professor of religion at Princeton University, was part of that elite group. Throughout her career she was lauded for her concise elucidations of early Christian texts, and her books are a happy marriage of elegant scholarship and lucid prose.

Elaine Hiesey was born in Palo Alto, Calif., on Feb. 13, 1943. She received her B.A. from Stanford University in 1964 and went on to earn a master's degree in Greek. She then entered Harvard's graduate program of religious studies in 1965, married physicist Heinz Pagels in 1969, and was awarded her Ph.D. in 1970. Her main area of scholarship was the history of the early Christians, and she published two books about the Gnostics, *The Johannine Gospel in Gnostic Exegesis* (1973) and *The Gnostic Paul* (1975). Pagels then joined an international team of scholars that issued an English edition of the Nag Hammadi manuscripts in 1977. Her work with the documents resulted in *The Gnostic Gospels* (1979), which achieved enormous popularity among both academics and the public at large. Her exploration of the documents exploded the myth of a solid unity within the early Christian movement and also explored the feminine imagery and ideology prevalent in the Gnostic texts. The book was awarded the National Book Critics Circle Award and the National Book Award, although Pagels' interpretations received sharp criticism from traditionalists who felt her claims were not supported by the texts and who objected to her feminist interpretation of Scripture.

During this period Pagels taught at Barnard College, Columbia University, New York City. In 1974 she was appointed chairperson of the religion department at Barnard, a position she held for eight years. Pagels was awarded a Rockefeller fellowship in 1978 and a Guggenheim fellowship the following year. The Pagelses had a child named Mark whose birth in 1980 was followed by Pagels' receipt of the prestigious MacArthur Prize fellowship in 1981. Two years later she accepted a position at Princeton University. She then turned her keen eye to the Bible creation stories and published *Adam, Eve, and the Serpent* (1988).

Pagels' six-year old son died of a respiratory ailment in 1987, and 15 months later her husband died while hiking in Colorado. Their deaths led her to reflect upon how humans cope with catastrophe and who is blamed for tragedy. Her thoughts found their way into *The Origin of Satan* (1995), an account of the tendency in Christian tradition to demonize one's opponents. Again, some critics claimed that Pagels was "scavenging at the edges of tradition" to prove her theories. It was unlikely, however, that criticism would silence Pagels' scholarship and reflections upon early Christian history. (AMANDA E. FULLER)

Pärt, Arvo

Dubbed a "Holy Minimalist" by one reviewer and described as neo-Baroque by others, Arvo Pärt in 1995 continued to captivate classical music listeners. In 1995 the Estonian Philharmonic Chamber Choir and Tallinn Chamber Orchestra, on their first North American tour, featured Pärt's works in concert. Their program's particular draw was Pärt's *Te Deum*, which they had recorded (1993) on the ECM label and which had topped the classical music charts. Ten years earlier few Americans had heard Pärt's name, much less his music. Since that time, however, something about his simplicity and medieval liturgical sound appeared to have struck a chord throughout the Western world.

Born on Sept. 11, 1935, in Paide, Estonia, Pärt showed an early interest in music. After putting in the requisite time in military service, he enrolled in 1958 at the music conservatory in Tallinn. From 1958 to 1967 he worked for the music division of Estonian Radio. He won recognition in Eastern Europe by taking first place in the All-Union Young Composers' Competition for an early popular work, *Meie aed* (1959; "Our Garden"), a cantata for children's choir and orchestra, and also for the oratorio *Maailma samm* (1960; "The World's Stride"). Developing an interest in the contemporary 12-tone system (an early 20th-century composing method generally credited to Arnold Schoenberg), he experimented with the system in his own striking composition *Nekrolog* (1960), the first 12-tone piece written in Estonia. Pärt graduated from the conservatory in 1963. Soon afterward he composed his *Symphony No. 1* (1964) and *Symphony No. 2* (1966), the latter including quotations from the music of other composers. He also used this collage technique in *Credo* (1968), a work for piano, mixed chorus, and orchestra. Banned in the U.S.S.R. because of its religious text, *Credo* also signaled the end of Pärt's experimentation with the 12-tone system.

Eight years of intensive music study followed. Pärt composed little but film scores during this time, immersing himself in the examination of such forms as the Gregorian chant and Orthodox liturgical music. The first sign of his new musical direction was his *Symphony No. 3* (1971), one of the few works he produced during his "years of silence." But it was with the release of his works for strings during the late 1970s—especially *Fratres* (1977)—that his compositions began to take on the sound most U.S. listeners identified as distinctly Pärtian.

Pärt's first work written in this new, austere style was a piano piece entitled *Für Alina* (1976), the work in which he discovered the triad series, which he made his "simple, little guiding rule." Describing the sound of the triad as like that of pealing bells, he called his new method of composition "tintinnabuli style." But whatever he called his style, Pärt produced a simple, intense, and ravishing sound that seemed to communicate directly to a new generation in search of spiritual connection. (KATHLEEN KUIPER)

Pelli, Cesar

In 1995 Cesar Pelli continued to solidify his position as one of the 20th century's preeminent architects. The Argentine-born designer was known for the lightweight, almost tentlike, appearance of his buildings, which were often surfaced in glass or a thin stone veneer. His projects displayed a fascination with abstract, crystalline glass shapes shot through with lines of coloured stone or metal. Among his best-known works were the Pacific Design Center in Los Angeles, the United States embassy in Tokyo, the expansion and renovation of the Museum of Modern Art in New York City, the World Financial Center and Winter Garden in New York City, the Canary Wharf Tower in London, and the Carnegie Hall Tower in New York City. The Pacific Design Center, notable for its reflective, opaque blue-glass exterior and geometric design, gained Pelli early recognition. His Museum of Modern Art gallery expansion and residential tower was hailed as an innovative reworking of an important cultural landmark. His most recent projects were the two circular, step-tapered Petronas Towers in Kuala Lumpur, Malaysia. Upon completion in 1996 they would, at 450 m (1,476 ft), be among the tallest buildings in the world. Critics described his work as "poetic" and "fresh" and noted his diversity, sensitivity to site, and innovative solutions to architectural problems.

Pelli was born in Tucumán, Arg., on Oct. 12, 1926. After earning a bachelor's degree in architecture at the National University of Tucumán, he moved to the U.S. to attend the University of Illinois at Champaign-Urbana, where he received a master's degree in 1954. He began his professional career with the firm of Eero Saarinen and Associates in Bloomfield Hills, Mich., and Hamden, Conn., where, among other projects, he worked on the Trans World Airlines Terminal at the John F. Kennedy International Airport in New York City. Pelli was director of design at Daniel, Mann, Johnson, & Mendenhall in Los Angeles from 1964 to 1968 and at Gruen Associates, also in Los Angeles, from 1968 to 1977. During those years he perfected the technology of glass skins, producing buildings of lightweight, translucent quality. He served as dean of the School of Architecture at Yale University from 1977 to 1984 and established his own practice in New Haven, Conn. In this period the taut style of his early work evolved into stone-clad buildings of greater sculptural quality.

Throughout his career Pelli lectured and published extensively. He won more than 80 awards for design excellence, including the American Institute of Architects' 1995 Gold Medal, its highest honour. (ANN M. BELASKI)

Rifkind, Malcolm Leslie

When he reshuffled the United Kingdom's Cabinet in July 1995, Prime Minister John Major promoted Malcolm Rifkind to become his foreign secretary. Rifkind had long supported greater cooperation with the rest of Europe, but he had to devise policies that would not cause too much offense to those fellow Conservatives who opposed European integration.

Rifkind was born in Edinburgh on June 21, 1946. A lawyer by training, he entered the House of Commons in February 1974 as Conservative MP for Edinburgh Pentlands. One year later Margaret Thatcher, the newly elected leader of the Conservative Party—then in opposition—appointed Rifkind as one of the party's spokesmen on Scottish affairs. The following year, however, he resigned in protest against Thatcher's hostility to a proposal (later dropped) on the creation of a Scottish assembly.

On winning the 1979 general election, Prime Minister Thatcher forgave Rifkind his earlier defiance and appointed him to a succession of middle-ranking ministerial posts. As minister of state at the Foreign Office (1983–86), he played a significant role in persuading a reluctant Thatcher to accept plans to create a single market in Europe, which involved removing all barriers to movements of goods, services, and people throughout the European Community (now European Union) and coordinating a number of fiscal and commercial laws.

Rifkind entered Thatcher's Cabinet in 1986 as secretary of state for Scotland. (By this time he had lost his earlier enthusiasm for Scottish devolution.) In 1990 he was promoted to be transport secretary, and after the 1992 general election Major appointed him defense secretary. In this post Rifkind faced two difficult tasks: to oversee the deployment of British troops in former Yugoslavia without provoking diplomatic trouble within the Atlantic alliance and to manage a succession of reductions in the U.K.'s defense budget without provoking hostility from the chiefs of the armed forces. Neither policy was popular with all sections of his party or of the wider British public. By applying himself to detail and refusing to descend into partisan hectoring, Rifkind won praise for his efforts on both fronts.

On Douglas Hurd's retirement in July 1995, Rifkind was the obvious successor at the Foreign Office. Rifkind immediately made it clear that he would maintain Hurd's broadly pro-European policies, although to pacify Conservative Euroskeptics, Rifkind also promised "a stalwart defence of British interests." Rifkind also made it clear that he would maintain the U.K.'s even-handed stance toward the Middle East. (PETER KELLNER)

Ripken, Cal, Jr.

On Sept. 6, 1995, at Oriole Park at Camden Yards in Baltimore, Md., the Baltimore Orioles had a night game against the California Angels. After the national anthem was sung, Oriole player Cal Ripken, Jr., ran out to his usual spot at shortstop; in the fifth inning of the game, he broke Lou Gehrig's 56-year-old major league record of 2,130 consecutive games played. There was, of course, all the hoopla one would expect for such historical occasions, but none of it could outshine the simple grace of Ripken, who seemed the very model of the soft-spoken, hard-nosed ballplayer. His new record of 2,131 consecutive games played underscored the youthful heart of the game—just playing.

Great achievements in sport do not come easily, and Ripken's streak was no exception. It began on May 30, 1982, and over the course of the next 13 seasons, Ripken played through injuries, slumps (both personal and team), and personnel changes, including the dismissals of his father, Cal Sr., as manager of the Orioles in 1988 and of his brother, Billy, a second baseman in 1992. His streak even survived the players strike of 1994–95. Some critics felt he was unfit to replace the great Gehrig as baseball's "Iron Horse," but Ripken, who was not the storied hitter that Gehrig was, proved his worth both at shortstop, where he set the record for consecutive innings played at 8,243 (1982–87) and won two Gold Glove awards (1991–92), and at the plate, where his career batting average of .276 included 327 home runs, 1,267 runs-batted-in, and 2,371 hits. In 1983 and 1991 he won the American League's Most Valuable Player award.

Calvin Edwin Ripken, Jr., was born on Aug. 24, 1960, in Havre de Grace, Md. Much of his youth was spent in ball parks with his father, who was a minor league catcher and manager in the Oriole organization, and Ripken chose early on to be a ballplayer. He was selected in the second round of the 1978 free-agent draft by the Orioles and after four seasons in the minor leagues made his major league debut in August 1981. The following year, his first full season in the majors, Ripken won the American League Rookie of the Year award. During his career he played in the All-Star Game 12 years in a row and was named that game's Most Valuable Player in 1991. Ripken also held major league single-season records in highest fielding percentage by a shortstop (.996 in 1990), fewest errors by a shortstop (3 in 1990), and most consecutive games without an error by a shortstop (95 in 1990). (JAMES HENNELLY)

Ruggiero, Renato

When the dust finally settled in a three-way regional struggle to determine the first director-general of the newly established World Trade Organization (WTO), Renato Ruggiero, a longtime Italian diplomat, assumed the post on May 1, 1995. The successor to the General Agreement on Tariffs and Trade (GATT), the WTO was cast as the United Nations of world trade, with considerably greater scope and power than the "provisional" accord that had been the centre of world trade negotiations for more than four decades. By the time the WTO officially came into being on Jan. 1, 1995, three candidates remained serious competitors for the post of director-general. South Korean economist Kim Chul Su was favoured by many Asian countries; former Mexican president Carlos Salinas de Gortari was championed by the U.S. government; and Ruggiero was the choice of most European governments. Even when Salinas' candidacy was scuttled by a political scandal, the U.S. remained leery of Ruggiero because it feared he would support protectionism. The U.S. agreed to endorse him only after winning the concession that Ruggiero would serve a single four-year term and be succeeded by a non-European.

Ruggiero was born on April 9, 1930, in Naples and earned (1953) a law degree from the University of Naples. He entered the Italian diplomatic service in 1955 and was posted to São Paulo, Brazil; Moscow; Washington, D.C.; and Belgrade, Yugos., before taking on a series of European Community (EC) assignments, beginning in 1969. In 1978 he took the first of several senior posts in the Italian Foreign Ministry. Following a stint (1980–84) as Italy's permanent representative to the EC, Ruggiero rose to the post of minister of foreign trade. During his tenure (1987–91), he helped plan a number of Group of Seven economic summits and played an important role in Italy's involvement in the European Monetary System. After leaving public service in 1991, he took a position with the automaker Fiat.

Notwithstanding the initial fears of the U.S. government, Ruggiero was seen by many as a genuine free trader who was determined to prevent a slide into the sort of protectionism that had characterized European economic leadership for so long. Taking the reigns of the 125-member WTO, he was faced with implementing a 27,000-page treaty, comprising 28 major provisions. Ruggiero, the tenacious "Rocky" of the British press, sought to establish a sound framework for an organization that he hoped would eventually replace bilateral economic brinkmanship with enforcement of multilaterally established rules of trade. Additionally, he was committed to a global economy in which less developed countries were seen as equal partners. (JEFF WALLENFELDT)

RuPaul

After immortalizing the phrase "You better work" in the 1993 hit song "Supermodel (You Better Work)," cross-dresser RuPaul took his own advice and did just that. By 1995 his flamboyant, blond-bewigged alter ego (a transformation that took him about three hours each time to attain) had done the television talk-show circuit, commercial product endorsements, and movie and television roles and had had success on the dance and video charts with a multiplatinum-selling debut album, *Supermodel of the World.* Then in mid-1995 his autobiography, *Lettin It All Hang Out,* was published.

RuPaul Andre Charles was born in San Diego, Calif., on Nov. 17, 1960, to parents who divorced

RuPaul
TIM MOSENFELDER—LGI AGENCY

by the time he was seven. In what was probably one of his earliest gender-bending ventures, RuPaul reportedly sawed the breasts off of a Barbie doll at the age of five. At age 15 he moved in with one of his older sisters in Atlanta, Ga., and attended a performing arts high school. Among his personal heroes he cited the popular singers Diana Ross and Cher, who RuPaul had said were "oddballs" who made it big, and that if they could do it, so could he. "When I was a little boy I wanted to become a drag racer. Instead I became a drag queen," he said. So in 1987, armed with a flair for playing dress-up, he headed for New York City to seek stardom.

His show business career began in go-go bars and on television on "The Gong Show" and MTV. Despite his overwhelming appearance—elaborate makeup and gowns and a height of more than 2.13 m (7 ft) in high heels and massive hair—RuPaul was determined to convey that he was a person just like everyone else, saying, "I may look different, but I put my panty hose on one leg at a time," and "You can't get satisfaction by living your life according to someone else's rules." He had noticed that people were often unable to see beyond images and responded to him differently depending on whether he was in or out of drag. "I feel very powerful when I'm in drag . . . but as an African-American male, I can walk into an elevator and have people clutch their handbags."

With barely time to bat a false eyelash, RuPaul appeared in several films in 1995: *Blue in the Face, The Brady Bunch Movie,* and two drag-themed films, *To Wong Foo, Thanks for Everything, Julie Newmar* and *Wigstock: The Movie;* he flipped his wig to play a male character in a made-for-cable-television movie, *A Mother's Prayer.* Toward the end of the year, his fans were anxiously awaiting his second album. (ANTHONY L. GREEN)

Sacks, Oliver Wolf

Consciousness and brain function have been examined through the lens of many disciplines, including philosophy, biology, psychology, and artificial intelligence. One of the most insightful approaches, however, was that of neurologist Oliver Sacks, who crafted artistic case histories of neurologically damaged persons that illuminated the existential as well as pathological condition of the patient. An empathetic, humane approach to treating persons afflicted with some of the most macabre neurological conditions known was the hallmark of Sacks's writings. In his sixth book, *An Anthropologist on Mars* (1995), Sacks continued to relate the stories of his patients, as he had done in such earlier works as *The Man Who Mistook His Wife for a Hat* (1986).

That patients must be listened to and the accounts of their illnesses respected was one of Sacks' most ardently held tenets. His own experience as a patient only strengthened that concern. Having injured a leg in a mountaineering accident, Sacks learned firsthand how a physician's dismissal of a patient's condition could hinder recuperation, a saga he recounted in *A Leg to Stand On* (1984).

Sacks was born July 9, 1933, in London. His choice of careers was not surprising, given that both his parents were general practitioners trained as neurologists. His three older brothers also pursued medical careers. Sacks received a B.A. in physiology from Queen's College, Oxford, in 1954 and continued at the college for several other degrees. On completing his M.D. in 1960 at Middlesex Hospital, Sacks left England for the U.S. to study neurology at the University of California, Los Angeles. While in California he won a state championship in weight lifting and rode briefly with the motorcycle group Hell's Angels.

In 1965 Sacks left the West Coast to become an instructor at Albert Einstein College of Medicine in the Bronx borough of New York City, where he remained, eventually becoming clinical professor of neurology. A year later he also joined Beth Abraham Hospital, a charity institution in the Bronx, as a staff neurologist. There he met a group of patients who had contracted a sleeping sickness, encephalitis lethargica, during an epidemic that broke out between 1917 and 1927. The patients had survived only to develop a type of parkinsonism that caused varying degrees of immobility, speechlessness, and depression. Sacks recounted the brief cure that the patients experienced after receiving the drug L-dopa and the drug's subsequent side effects in his 1973 book *Awakenings,* which was made into a motion picture in 1990.

Sacks was a somewhat shy, self-effacing man who lived alone in a red house in the Bronx. He was an avid swimmer and had a passion for ferns and invertebrate animals. A self-proclaimed eccentric, Sacks believed that his unconventional nature helped him to identify with his patients, whose symptoms placed them outside the norm as well. (MARY JANE FRIEDRICH)

Saunders, Jennifer

In the summer of 1995, the season premiere of "Absolutely Fabulous," a seemingly unlikely television series, brought the U.S. cable channel Comedy Central its largest audience ever; its first episodes had doubled that station's prime-time ratings the previous summer. The Emmy award-winning series—known as "AbFab" to its fans—was a wacky, over-the-top BBC production that, since its debut in Britain in 1992, had attracted a worldwide cult following by maintaining its sophistication while reveling in outrageous comments and behaviour that were decidedly *not* politically correct. Written by and starring Jennifer Saunders, "AbFab" featured the antics and misadventures of two role models in reverse—Edina (Saunders) and her best friend, Patsy (Joanna Lumley)—as they attempted to experience all things trendy, strenuous exercise excepted. Meanwhile, Edina's disapproving superstraight daughter, Saffron (Julia Sawalha), was forced by necessity to take on the role of mothering her mother, as Edina concerned herself more with wearing designer-label clothing (though she wore them in ensembles the designers never intended) than with providing for the needs of her daughter.

Saunders was born July 6, 1958. She attended London's Central School of Speech and Drama with the intention of becoming a teacher. After graduation, she saw an audition notice for the Comic Strip, a London comedy club. She and Dawn French had performed as a team in college, so they auditioned together. They were accepted, and the club proved an excellent training ground. French and Saunders went on to TV appearances in Comic Strip productions, the "Girls on Top" series, and several seasons of their own series, "French and Saunders," as well as starring roles in the 1993 West End stage production *Me & Mamie O'Rourke.* In 1993 the BBC signed a five-year, £2 million contract with them so they would not defect to independent television. When French took a year off from performing, Saunders created "AbFab," basing it on the "French and Saunders" sketch "Modern Mother and Daughter."

By 1995 U.S. television had already begun trying to copy aspects of "AbFab." Roseanne, who had purchased the U.S. rights to the format, was preparing the American version, and Saunders had a motion-picture version in the works. In addition, even though there were no new episodes of "AbFab," reruns would likely continue to be broadcast indefinitely, and the show's favourite term of endearment, "Sweetie darling," would go on being heard throughout the land. (BARBARA WHITNEY)

Schneider, Vreni

The French called her "La Legende." To the Germans she was "wunderbar." For the Italians, "Vreni, vidi, vici" said it all. In any language Vreni Schneider, the Swiss Alpine ski racer, was the toast wherever ski fans congregated, and they followed her across the Alps in droves, armed with mountain cowbells and Swiss national flags. In a glorious career of 11 seasons in the top flight, the consistent Schneider accumulated a massive collection of honours. At the end of the 1994–95 season, she announced her retirement from competitive skiing.

She was overall World Cup victor three times, in 1989, 1994, and 1995, and for 10 successive years was never out of the top six in the final ratings despite inevitable knee injuries. Her six titles in slalom and five in giant slalom were unmatched. In one season, 1988–89, she won a record 13 World Cup races and a combined event, including all seven slaloms held that winter. Her career included 55 cup race wins, seven short of the Austrian downhiller Annemarie Moser-Proell.

Undoubtedly the best woman slalomer and giant slalomer of all time, Schneider won the most Olympic women's titles in Alpine skiing, three both giant slalom and slalom at Calgary, Alta., in 1988 and slalom again at Lillehammer, Norway, in 1994. In the world championships she gained two giant slalom titles, at Crans-Montana, Switz., in 1987 and at Vail, Colo., in 1989, and one in slalom, at Saalbach, Austria, in 1991. Also in the world championships, she claimed a runner-up place in slalom and second and third spots in Alpine combination.

A shoemaker's daughter born on Nov. 26, 1964, in the tiny village of Elm in the eastern Swiss canton of Glarus, Schneider, a down-to-earth nature lover, remained modest and unaffected notwithstanding extensive media coverage and the devotion of her fans. A characteristic of her slalom racing was a relatively cautious first descent, to minimize the chance of elimination through an early mishap. Afterward, throwing caution to the wind, she often spectacularly came from behind with a sizzling risk-all second burst to clinch a winning two-run aggregate. This was seldom better exemplified than in the final race of her career, in March 1995 at Bormio, Italy, when a slalom victory was needed to clinch her third World Cup triumph. She responded to the challenge with a superb second run to win the overall title by only six points, the smallest-ever margin. It was a perfect swan song.

Essentially a slalom specialist, Schneider disliked the downhill but was not averse to taking part when World Cup points were vital. Despite ever-increasing commercialization at the sport's top level, she always raced because she loved it—and that, perhaps, was the key to her consistent success. Summoning total concentration and complete commitment, she demonstrated a flawless technical fluency that commanded worldwide admiration. (HOWARD BASS)

Schwimmer, David

David Schwimmer was a member of an American television elite: the single, attractive, 20-something crowd that hung out in a New York coffee bar and talked primarily about themselves during 1995. He was a member of the cast of the top-rated sitcom "Friends"—one that harvested its jokes from the lives of six generation-Xers, young and unfocused characters who spent most of their time "hanging around" together. Schwimmer, who played Ross Geller on the show, had a considerable part in its success. Described by cast members Jennifer Aniston and Courteney Cox as "the father figure" of the show, Schwimmer played a paleontologist (one of the few characters with a steady job) whose pregnant wife left him for a woman during the first season (1994–95).

Schwimmer was considered the runaway hit of the ensemble, and he had garnered both a commercial and a motion-picture offer by 1995. He played a goofy caller in an AT&T commercial, and he spent the summer of 1995 in New York shooting the movie *The Pallbearer,* which also starred Barbara Hershey and Carol Kane and was scheduled to open in the spring of 1996. Schwimmer said that he was deeply serious about his comic craft. "Friends" producers David Crane and Marta Kauffman contended that they hired Schwimmer "for his vulnerability. He's both emotional and smart." He brought these traits to his portrayal of Geller, who was arguably the most sensitive character on the show.

Born in the New York City borough of Queens on Nov. 2, 1966, Schwimmer was raised by his parents—both prominent attorneys—in Los Angeles. He said that he could have used help fitting in at Beverly Hills High School, where he was a self-proclaimed "fat, ugly geek." By the time he entered the theatre department of Northwestern University in Evanston, Ill., in 1984, he was a 1.9-m, 79-kg (6-ft 2-in, 175-lb) heartthrob, and he found inspiration and success on the Chicago stage. In his junior year he mounted an off-campus production of *Alice in Wonderland* that eventually led to the launching of the Lookingglass Theater Company, which Schwimmer co-founded with seven other Northwestern alumni following graduation in 1988. After commuting between Chicago and Los Angeles for a time, Schwimmer decided to concentrate on achieving success in Hollywood. He landed several small parts on television shows such as "The Wonder Years," "Monty," and "NYPD Blue" before being successfully cast in "Friends." He found friendship in the cast of "Friends" as well, all of whom considered Schwimmer to be the one they would go to in a crisis because "he's real easy to talk to. He cares." It seemed that despite the stereotype that most generation-Xers led a disconnected existence, Schwimmer was one who had found his niche. (SARA N. BRANT)

MICHAEL GRECCO—SYGMA

David Schwimmer

Shields, Carol

Novelist Carol Shields fashioned the type of fiction she had wanted to read but could not find: stories about women's friendships and their inner moral and intellectual lives. In 1995 *The Stone Diaries* (1993) was awarded the Pulitzer Prize for Fiction after having won the 1993 Canadian Governor General's Literary Award and the 1994 National Book Critics Circle Award for fiction. The novel, a portrait of an ordinary woman whose life spanned most of the 20th century, was written in a semiautobiographical style and contained quotations from letters, newspapers, and characters in the novel—it even had a section of photographs.

The way people appeared and related to one another was the theme throughout Shields's fiction and poetry. Two collections of her poetry, *Others* (1972) and *Intersect* (1974), concerned relationships and distances between people. Her first two novels, *Small Ceremonies* (1976) and *The Box Garden* (1977), were about two women who were the third generation of twins. *A Celibate Season* (1991), coauthored with Blanche Howard, told the story of a modern marriage in which the characters were separated by their work. In *The Republic of Love* (1992), Shields told a love story set amid the details of ordinary life. She specialized in depicting the careful, contented lives of the middle class and was an expert at evoking the feelings and concerns of ordinary people.

Shields believed that telling a story from a single perspective was too limiting. In the novels *Happenstance* (1980) and *A Fairly Conventional Woman* (1982), she examined the marriage of a middle-aged couple living in a small U.S. city. In these novels she developed the plot through overlapping narratives of the husband and the wife. In *Swann: A Mystery* (1987), four characters explore their individual interpretations of the life and work of a murdered poet.

She was born Carol Warner in Oak Park, Ill., on June 2, 1935. She received a B.A. in English from Hanover College, Hanover, Ind., in 1957, the same year she married and moved to Canada. After taking a course in creative writing at the University of Toronto, Shields won (1965) a young writers contest sponsored by the Canadian Broadcasting Corporation and received (1975) an M.A. in English literature from the University of Ottawa. In 1977 she published her thesis on Susanna Moodie, a 19th-century pioneer in Ontario, and after moving to Winnipeg taught English at the University of Manitoba.

Shields's first novel, *Small Ceremonies,* won the Canadian Authors Association Award for fiction. For *Swann: A Mystery,* she received the Arthur Ellis Award for crime writing. Shields won the Marian Engel Award, given to a Canadian woman writer for her body of work. In spite of these awards, Shields's work was often underrated by critics because of the domestic setting of her stories. With *The Stone Diaries,* the literary world gained new appreciation for Shields's well-crafted, quiet books. (DIANE LOIS WAY)

Stewart, Martha

Whether one saw her as a champion of the skills and values of the traditional homemaker or as a driven, obsessive businesswoman, Martha Stewart loomed as large as the Statue of Liberty on the American horizon in 1995. She was everywhere—on a syndicated weekly television show with an audience of five million, in the pages of her magazine, *Martha Stewart Living,* in 15 books and 6 videos, in self-spoofing television commercials, and in two parodies of her magazine. Smiling, competent, and in control, she was at home wielding a band saw, a hedge trimmer, a rolling pin, or her signature glue gun. Not since the 1950s had domesticity been so celebrated—or so debated.

Martha Kostyra was born in Jersey City, N.J., on Aug. 3, 1941, and grew up in a Polish-American household where the traditional arts of cooking, sewing, preserving, housekeeping, and gardening were practiced. She started planning birthday parties for neighbour children while she was in grammar school, and she paid her college tuition by modeling. While at Barnard College, New York City, she married law student Andrew Stewart; their daughter, Alexis, was born in 1965. Martha became a successful stockbroker at a Wall Street firm, but she left New York in 1973 for Westport, Conn., where she and Andrew began the transformation of Turkey Hill, a Federal-style farmhouse. With yeoman labour they gardened, restored, and decorated, acquiring the skills and the setting for books and TV shows, but their marriage ended in a bitter divorce in 1990. A house in the Hamptons and a Manhattan apartment later provided further raw material.

In 1976 she started a catering business with a partner, Norma Collier, and Stewart's talent for innovation and presentation soon brought her a string of prestigious clients. Her first book, *Entertaining* (1982; with Elizabeth Hawes), set the tone for subsequent publications: superb art direction, gorgeous settings, labour-intensive recipes and decorating projects, and a smiling Martha to show how easy it all was. Other books include *Martha Stewart's Hors d'Oeurves* (1984), *Weddings* (1987), and *The Martha Stewart Cookbook* (1995). In addition, she oversaw the CBS Masterworks Classics, a series of music compilations that could provide the appropriate background for a picnic, a cocktail party, Sunday brunch, or exotic meals. In 1994 she reached a zenith of sorts with a pricey line of interior paints that imitated the colours of the eggs laid by her flock of Araucana chickens.

Stewart's perfectionism, encyclopaedic knowledge, and bottomless capacity for work were not universally admired. She was censured for setting an impossible model for harried working mothers, and her glorification of a home-centred existence seemed to some a step backward for women. But her fans were legion, and criticism and analysis were both swept away by the rising tide of her commercial success. (ANITA WOLFF)

Stine, R.L.

Unless you have young children or baby-sit frequently, you may not be likely to know the name R.L. Stine. But children and book publishers worldwide do. The humour-writer-turned-horror-novelist by the end of 1995 had sold about 100 million copies of his novels in some 20 languages, an unprecedented phenomenon in the world of children's book publishing. In the fast-paced world of video games, television, and interactive software, Stine's work gave children a charge in the old-fashioned way: through reading. Remarkably, boys returned to a market dominated traditionally by girls. The unpredictability, plot twists, and cliff-hanger endings of his books relied on surprise, avoided the seriously threatening topics of modern urban life, and delivered kids what Stine termed "a safe scare."

Robert Lawrence Stine was born Oct. 8, 1943, in Columbus, Ohio. He graduated from Ohio State University in 1965, having served three years as editor of the campus humour magazine. After teaching junior high school for a year, he went to New York City, where he eventually landed an editorial job with Scholastic Books. He worked there for 16 years on various children's magazines, notably *Bananas,* a humour magazine for older age groups. The first of Stine's more than 40 humour books for children, *How to Be Funny,* was published in 1982. It was a short step to his first scary novel, *Blind Date* (1986), a big seller that launched Stine's career as a horror writer. His Fear Street series of stories for young teens began with *The New Girl* (1989); the Goosebumps series for 8- to 11-year-olds was launched with *Welcome to Dead House* (1992). Stine wrote one 120-page book a month for each series. Their runaway popularity—they sold between one million and two million copies in retail sales monthly—rocked the publishing world.

As if writing two books a month were not enough, Stine was working on two new spin-off series of books for 8- to 12-year-olds: The Ghosts of Fear Street and Give Yourself Goosebumps, a choose-your-own-scary-adventure line. Moving out of the book market, Stine developed Goosebumps Theater, a live-action television series that premiered in October and was broadcast in a prime-time-for-kids' TV slot. Stine also broke into the adult horror market with *Superstitious* (1995), a graphic hardcover book, and a movie was expected to follow. With contracts signed for three more years of Fear Street and Goosebumps, Stine was showing no sign of slowing down. "I'm writing more books than Stephen King, and no one over 14 has ever heard of me," he says. "I like that." (ANN M. BELASKI)

Stoichkov, Hristo

In leading Bulgaria to a best-ever fourth place finish in the 1994 World Cup, Hristo Stoichkov showed fans worldwide what those in Bulgaria and Spain (where he starred for Barcelona) already knew—that he had become one of the most potent offensive weapons in association football (soccer). In the process, the explosive striker was named 1994 European Player of the Year. While his battles of will with the Barcelona coach, Johann Cruyff, were well known, many were stunned when Stoichkov shifted teams in the middle of the 1994–95 season, moving to Parma in the Italian first division. That move brought a transfer fee of some $16 million (half to Stoichkov, half to the club he had led to four consecutive Spanish league championships and the 1991–92 European Cup of Champion Clubs).

Born on Feb. 8, 1966, in Plovdiv, Bulg., Stoichkov began his soccer career early. By age 12 he was playing for Maritza Plovdiv in the Bulgarian second division, where his goal-scoring prowess earned him a contract with the powerful CSKA Sofia in 1984. Lifetime bans were imposed upon Stoichkov and five others in 1985 for fighting during a match; however, the bans were lifted 10 months later, after Bulgaria qualified for the 1986 World Cup. Stoichkov did not play for that World Cup team, but in 1987 he made the first of 60 appearances as a Bulgarian international. His professional career skyrocketed in 1989 when he tallied 38 goals for Sofia, sharing the award for Europe's leading scorer.

In 1991 Stoichkov took his dangerous left foot and fierce competitiveness to Spain. The emotional intensity that earned "the Raging Bull" a two-month suspension (for kicking a referee) during his four years with Barcelona also made him a huge fan favourite.

Stoichkov was at his best during Bulgaria's remarkable 1994 World Cup run. In five previous appearances, Bulgaria had failed to gain a World Cup victory (10 losses, 6 ties), but after the fall of the communist regime in 1989, the country's best players were free to hone their talents against the world's finest in leagues in Western Europe. Although the 1994 competition looked promising for Bulgaria, it was forced to play heavily favoured France in a do-or-die match in Paris to qualify. Doubting his team's chances, Stoichkov promised to walk to Barcelona should the Bulgarians pull off the upset. They did; he did not. Instead, he became the World Cup's leading scorer (six goals) as Bulgaria advanced to the final 16 by defeating Greece and Argentina. Then Stoichkov led the way to a semifinal victory over defending champion Germany. Only a hard-fought loss to Italy kept Bulgaria from reaching the finals. (JEFF WALLENFELDT)

Swan, Sir John William David

In August 1995 Bermuda did what no other British colony had done during the 20th century: it voted against independence—and by a three-to-one margin. In so doing, Bermuda's voters delivered a sharp rebuff to their premier, Sir John Swan, who promptly resigned.

Swan was born in Bermuda on July 3, 1935. Educated in Bermuda and West Virginia, he entered Bermuda's parliament in 1972. As minister for home affairs from 1978 to 1982, Swan played a key role in introducing social reforms following race riots in 1977. Coming from the black community himself, Swan achieved widespread popular support for a series of housing and education initiatives while at the same time reassuring Bermuda's mainly white business leaders.

Swan received his reward in 1982, when he became Bermuda's premier. Few political leaders around the world could have enjoyed a better inheritance: prosperity, low taxes, and little crime. Although Bermuda remained a British colony, London exercised its powers with the lightest of touches. Britain's governor-general retained theoretical responsibility for external affairs, defense, internal security, and the police. In practice, successive governors-general had intervened little.

Yet for some Bermudans, especially in the black community, the idea of independence remained a potent one. Swan sought to harness this and called a referendum for August 1995 to seek public support. His move backfired badly. The opposition Progressive Labour Party, seeing its chance to unseat a man they accused of wanting to amass power for himself rather than for the people of Bermuda, called on voters to either abstain or oppose independence. Swan's own party, the United Bermuda Party, belied its name by dividing along racial lines.

In the event, just 58% of Bermuda's 38,000 registered voters took part in the referendum (compared with a normal turnout of 70% in general elections), and they divided 74–26% against independence. More than 310 years after becoming a British colony, Bermuda voted to remain so for at least a few years more and to retain its status as an offshore tax haven, within the political orbit of the British crown and the economic orbit of the U.S. dollar. Opinion polls showed that not only had white voters opted overwhelmingly against independence, but so had a majority of black voters. Swan announced on the radio that "I'm satisfied with the result"; he implemented his promise—or threat—to resign and return to his family business. (PETER KELLNER)

Takahashi, Hisako

In February 1994 Morihiro Hosokawa exercised his right as prime minister to select Hisako Takahashi to fill a vacancy on Japan's Supreme Court. Takahashi, who was introduced to the media as "a present to the people," became the first woman ever appointed to that prestigious group.

The amiable bureaucrat and career woman was born in Yokohama on Sept. 21, 1927. After graduating from Ochanomizu University, she did postgraduate work in economics at Tokyo University. In 1953 she entered the Women's Bureau of the Ministry of Labour, where she was immediately named chief of the employment statistics section. She was then reassigned to head the women and youth section, where she was appalled to find that women employees were still required to perform such menial tasks as cleaning desks and serving tea. This and other instances of gender discrimination prompted Takahashi to assume personal responsibility for improving the status of Japanese women. Years later she won a significant victory when the government passed a bill affirming equal rights for women.

Two years after representing Japan at the 1980 meeting of the Organisation for Economic Co-operation and Development, Takahashi resigned from government service and became director of the Asian Women's Interchange Research Forum, a government affiliate established to further relations and interchange among women of Asia. This was one of her fondest dreams, bringing women of Asia closer together. The following year she was named president of a related group known as the 21st Century Occupational Foundation. Takahashi, an acknowledged expert in the field of economics, frequently voiced concern about the absence of women in Japan's judiciary system, especially the lack of representation on the Supreme Court. She pointedly noted that in the U.S. two of the nine Supreme Court justices were women.

That difference was partially obliterated and the cause of women's rights significantly advanced when Takahashi joined 14 male colleagues as a member of the nation's highest court. Although she expressed surprise on learning that the court handled at least 4,000 cases a year, she declared herself committed to reviewing every case with great care.

The petite new justice was a dedicated calligrapher and had a pleasant disposition and friendly smile behind her steel-rimmed glasses. To keep physically fit, she took up swimming, played golf, and even skipped rope until her dog (and possibly her university professor husband, Shozo) loudly complained. On weekends the couple played tennis for three hours and at their mountain hideaway in Yatsutatake took frequent hikes far from the hectic life they were compelled to live in rambunctious Tokyo. (KAY K. TATEISHI)

Turner, Ted

Ted Turner once commented, "I am the right man in the right place at the right time." That statement could not have been more true than in September 1995, when it was announced that Turner Broadcasting System, Inc. (with 1994 revenues of nearly $3 billion), would merge with Time Warner, Inc. The deal, with a value of at least $7 billion, would make Turner the new vice-chairman of Time Warner and was expected to earn him more than $100 million over the next five years and more than $2.5 billion in Time Warner stock.

Robert Edward Turner III was born in Cincinnati, Ohio, on Nov. 19, 1938. When he was nine years old, his father moved the family to Georgia and began the Turner Advertising Co. Young Turner later attended Brown University, Providence, R.I., where he was commodore of the school yachting club and vice president of the debating union. After his father's suicide in 1963, he took over the company. In 1970 he bought a small independent Atlanta television station (WJRJ, which later became WTBS), making it the flagship of the fledgling Turner Broadcasting System. In 1976 WTBS began beaming via satellite to cable systems nationwide and was dubbed the first "superstation," reaching some two million households. (As of October 1995 the station boasted an audience of nearly 67 million.) That same year, Turner purchased the Atlanta Braves baseball team. He took time off to pursue an old interest—yachting—and in September 1977 skippered *Courageous* to victory in the America's Cup.

In June 1980 Turner launched his biggest risk (and biggest success) to date—the Cable News Network (CNN). With its in-depth, 24-hour, all-news format and worldwide broadcasting capabilities, CNN prospered as the first station that provided instantaneous coverage of any event worldwide, including live coverage of the Persian Gulf War.

Not all of Turner's ventures proved successful. In the mid-1980s he made an unsuccessful bid for the CBS television network in an attempted hostile takeover that cost him $20 million. He later acquired the MGM Entertainment Co., although analysts said he overpaid by nearly half a billion dollars. In an effort to widen the appeal of the MGM film library, Turner had many of its black-and-white films electronically colourized, a move he defended against considerable criticism.

Ted Turner
RICK MAIMAN—SYGMA

Many wondered if Turner, who had accomplished so much and had been completely in charge over the years, would be content playing second fiddle at Time Warner. Turner rejoined, "I've been a CEO for 33 years and that's a long time for anyone. I'm married to Jane Fonda, so I know what it's like to be number two."
(ANTHONY L. GREEN)

Valdivieso, Alfonso
For two decades life in Colombia had been carried out in the ever-present shadow of the violence and corruption engendered by narcotics trafficking. The infamous Medellín and Cali drug cartels exerted their influence over every element of society, corrupting individuals and institutions alike through a combination of bribery and threats. No area seemed secure from the malignant power of the drug lords, so it was perhaps no great surprise when in 1995 revelations emerged that the 1994 election of Pres. Ernesto Samper Pizano had been aided by money funneled to him from the Cali cartel. What was surprising were the efforts of the nation's top prosecutor, Attorney General Alfonso Valdivieso, in uncovering the scandal and the courage and determination he showed in bringing charges against some of the most powerful men in the country despite the threat of assassination.

In 1994 a tape recording of a telephone conversation between members of the Cali cartel discussing financial contributions to Samper's election coffers was made public. Samper and his defense minister and former campaign manager, Fernando Botero Zea, admitted that financial support had been offered, but they denied that any money had been received. On June 21, 1995, however, following a government crackdown on narcotics traffickers, the fugitive Cali leaders announced that they had information linking the government to the cartel. The next day Valdivieso announced that his office was beginning a large-scale investigation.

By August, Valdivieso's investigation had implicated members of Samper's administration. Santiago Medina, the former campaign treasurer of Samper's Liberal Party, had admitted receiving about $6 million from the Cali cartel. Following his arrest in July, Medina had implicated Botero and Samper himself in the conspiracy, claiming that they had authorized him to accept money from the cartel and that the funds were kept in a secret bank account in New York City. Following Medina's revelations, Valdivieso focused his investigation on Samper's administration, authorizing the Supreme Court to review the evidence against Botero, who then resigned from his office.

Samper continued to deny his involvement in the scandal, but to many his protestations seemed suspect. He previously had asserted that his administration was innocent of any wrongdoing; he now claimed that he had no personal knowledge of any drug money being accepted. By year's end Botero had been charged with illicit enrichment and falsification of documents, while a congressional committee halted the investigation of Samper on drug charges, which could have led to his impeachment. Valdivieso's actions were viewed as a courageous step in a nation where official corruption and narcotics trafficking had long been accepted as a fact of life. (JOHN H. MATHEWS)

Venter, J. Craig
Little more than 100 years ago, genetics research was about as interesting as counting peas. In fact, pea counting—by the monk Gregor Mendel—was state-of-the-art genetics. Fast forward to 1995, a time in which the study of genes was in full bloom. Not a monk but an ex-surfer, the biochemist J. Craig Venter, in collaboration with molecular geneticist Hamilton Smith of Johns Hopkins University, Baltimore, Md., determined the DNA sequence of the entire genome (all the genetic material of an organism) of *Hemophilus influenzae,* a bacterium that causes earaches and meningitis in humans. The achievement marked the first time that the complete sequence of a free-living organism had been deciphered, and it was accomplished in less than a year.

Venter's work was significant for several reasons. First, the sequence information would aid in the development of a vaccine against the bacterium and illuminate the mechanisms of the infection process. Second, as the genomes of other organisms were decoded, it would contribute to the study of evolution at the DNA level. Finally, the time- and money-saving strategy developed to sequence the genome was expected to benefit the genetic research process in general.

Venter was born Oct. 14, 1946, in Salt Lake City, Utah. Soon thereafter, his family moved to the San Francisco area, where swimming and surfing occupied his free time. After high school Venter joined the U.S. Naval Medical Corps and served in Vietnam. On returning to the U.S., he earned a B.A. in biochemistry (1972) and then a doctorate in physiology and pharmacology (1975) at the University of California, San Diego. In 1976 he joined the faculty of the State University of New York at Buffalo, where he was involved in neurochemistry research. In 1984 Venter moved to the National Institutes of Health (NIH), Bethesda, Md., studying genes involved in signal transmission between nerve cells.

While at the NIH, Venter became frustrated with traditional methods of gene identification, which were slow and time-consuming. He developed an alternative technique that he used to identify thousands of human genes much more quickly. Although first received with skepticism, the approach later gained increased acceptance; in 1993 it was used to identify the gene responsible for a type of colon cancer. Venter's attempts to patent the gene fragments that he identified, however, created a furor among those in the scientific community who believed that such information belonged in the public domain.

Venter left the NIH in 1992 and, with the backing of the for-profit company Human Genome Sciences, Gaithersburg, Md., established a research arm, the Institute for Genomic Research. Another genome, that of the microorganism *Mycoplasma genitalium,* was completely sequenced at the institute by a team headed by Claire Fraser, Venter's wife. (MARY JANE FRIEDRICH)

Villeneuve, Jacques
In 1994, his first year as a driver on the IndyCar racing circuit, Jacques Villeneuve placed second in the Indianapolis 500 race. He finished the season in sixth place in the overall points standing and was named Rookie of the Year. His second season on the circuit was even better. He won the Indianapolis 500, becoming the first Canadian to do so. At the end of the season, he had the highest overall points total and thereby won the PPG IndyCar World Series Championship; he was the youngest driver to have won that prize.

Born on April 9, 1971, Villeneuve was the son of Gilles Villeneuve and the nephew of Jacques Villeneuve, both Canadian race car drivers. He spent much of his early childhood traveling on the racing circuit with his parents, first in North America and then in Europe. His father became successful in European racing and moved the family from Quebec to Monaco in 1978. Jacques attended boarding school in Switzerland for six years and then decided to become a race car driver. In 1986 he took lessons at the Jim Russell Driving School in Quebec—the same school that his father had attended. The next year he went to the Spenard-David Racing School in Shannonville, Ont. There he was given lessons by his father's former teammate, Richard Spenard.

Villeneuve began his racing career at the age of 17, driving in three events in the Alfa Italian Tourism Championship. From 1989 to 1991 he drove on the Italian Formula Three racing circuit, and then in the 1992 season he raced Formula Three cars in Japan. There he won three races and finished second in the overall points standing. He spent the 1993 season driving on the Formula Atlantic racing circuit in North America, winning 5 of his 15 races there and gaining Rookie of the Year honours. In 1994 he joined the IndyCar racing circuit. The car he drove there had a Reynard chassis and a Ford-Cosworth engine.

Villeneuve was a cool, mature, and consistent driver who kept his emotions in check behind the wheel and took risks only when he thought them justified. This was unlike his father who, according to his son, "always drove like crazy." In the main, Jacques disliked comparisons between his style and that of his father, who was killed in a racing accident in 1982. He admitted, however, that the Villeneuve name had made his career path easier. (DIANE LOIS WAY)

Wahid, Abdurrahman
One could say that Abdurrahman Wahid was born to lead the world's largest Muslim organization, the 25 million-member Nahdatul Ulama (NU), founded by his grandfathers and a third Muslim teacher in Jombang, Java, in 1926. As NU chief since 1984, Wahid was one of the most respected figures in Indonesian Islam and the most politically active. The stout, soccer-loving Wahid also headed Forum Demokrasi, which welcomed dissidents and human-rights advocates. From behind his thick spectacles, Wahid spoke frankly on national issues to ministers, diplomats, journalists, and others who consulted him. Many admired his defense of Indonesia's Christian minority. Even the powerful military was keen to maintain good ties to a perceived bulwark against radical Islam. Honoured in 1993 with the Magsaysay Award, Wahid was elected the following year to lead the World Council for Religion and Peace.

Deviating from conventional Muslim positions, Wahid suggested normalizing ties with Israel and contended that the conflict in Bosnia and Herzegovina was not religious. That unorthodox streak hailed from childhood. Wahid, who was born on Aug. 4, 1940, studied the Qur'ān intensively at East Java *pesantren,* religious boarding schools pioneered by his paternal grandfather, and at institutes in Jakarta when his father was Indonesia's first Cabinet minister for religion. Instead of studying more scripture during his years at Egypt's venerable al-Azhar University, Wahid devoured New Wave movies, French and English books, and Marxism. Finding Cairo's teachings irrelevant, he moved to Baghdad, Iraq, and soon began attracting attention with his religious writings.

After returning to Indonesia in the late 1960s, Wahid became a scholar; he was elevated to the post of general chairman of NU in 1984. The organization then severed links to a Muslim-based party and concentrated on social work and education. The owners of 6,500 *pesantren* nationwide—NU's backbone—opposed any antigovernment moves. Wahid, nonetheless, was widely perceived

Jacques Villeneuve
AL BEHRMAN—ASSOCIATED PRESS

to present a threat to authority. His vision that Nahdatul Ulama "should move toward the transformation of society, socially and culturally," meant involvement in such political issues as poverty, corruption, and injustice.

In 1990 he declined to join the new Association of Muslim Intellectuals, accusing its chairman, B.J. Habibie, protégé of President Suharto and the nation's research and technology minister, of using Islam to gain power. Critics and even relatives conceded, however, that Wahid could not separate his own political stance from NU's needs. In 1994 pro-Suharto forces tried in vain to end Wahid's chairmanship. One of Wahid's problems was that many of his staunchest backers were outside NU. Still, he did not fear reprisals because, he pointed out, "I have never attempted to support or oppose anyone in the government."

(RICARDO L. SALUDO)

Warne, Shane Keith

If any sportsman could be said to have made his name in an instant, it was cricketer Shane Warne, the Australian leg spinner whose love of taking wickets was equaled only by his love of surfing. During 1995 Warne confirmed himself as a bowler of guile, accuracy, and devastating spin, defying critics who feared he might be more of a passing comet than a permanent star in cricket's firmament, and on December 11 he claimed his 200th Test wicket in only 42 Test matches, the fourth quickest to reach that achievement. But, however many wickets he took in his career, he would be remembered for one ball, bowled to England's Mike Gatting at Old Trafford, Manchester, in the series of 1993. The ball was a perfect example of the leg-spinner's art, pitching on leg stump and spinning viciously past the bat to hit Gatting's off stump. It was Warne's first ball in a Test in England and established a huge psychological advantage for Warne and the Australian team, which lasted into the next Ashes series in the southern summer of 1994–95.

By the end of that series, just three and a half years after his Test debut in the third Test against India at Sydney in 1991–92, Warne had taken 176 Test wickets at an average of 24.08. He had played just seven matches in the Sheffield Shield before being selected for Australia, and after he had three Tests with figures of one wicket for 300 runs to his name, there were plenty of critics who said he had been blooded too early. But match figures of 7 for 86 in an innings victory over New Zealand early in 1993 were proof that Australia had unearthed an exceptional talent from the most unlikely background.

Warne was born on Sept. 13, 1969, in Ferntree Gully, near Melbourne. Only relatively late in his teenage years did he decide that cricket might be his game, and even then the Victorian's free surfing spirit threatened to end a career before it had begun. Warne's relaxed manner—allied to his bleached hair and stud earring—made him a folk hero round the world. When Test cricket seemed in danger of becoming more blood sport than noble game, Warne's success promoted the forgotten art of leg-spin, showed that brain can be as important as brawn in winning Test matches, and brought a delightful variety to the recent tedious diet of fast bowling, with good disguise on his top-spinner and fine control on two or three different googlies. Like most Australians, Warne saved his best for England, the old enemy. In the Ashes series of 1993, he took 34 wickets in six Tests at an average of 25.79; in the 1994–95 return series he took 27 wickets at 20.33, including a match-winning 8 for 71 in the second innings of the first Test and a hat trick in the second Test.

(ANDREW LONGMORE)

White, Tim D.

Did scientists take a giant step toward finding the elusive link between humans and apes? Paleoanthropologist Tim D. White and his team of fossil hunters thought so in 1994 when they described what they interpreted to be the oldest, most apelike hominid fossils yet found. White named the 4.4 million-year-old bones *Australopithecus ramidus,* which classified the new primate among the australopithecine hominids and gave it the status of a potential root species for the human family. In May 1995, however, after finding more bones and hearing his colleagues' criticisms, White appeared less sure and changed its name to *Ardipithecus ramidus*, thus creating a new genus for it. Even if *A. ramidus* proved not to be a direct human ancestor, it was certain to be a significant piece of the puzzle of human evolution.

White, along with Gen Suwa of the University of Tokyo and Berhane Asfaw of the Ethiopian government's Paleoanthropology Laboratory, unearthed *A. ramidus* near the town of Aramis, which lies in the Middle Awash region of northern Ethiopia. The first fragments—teeth and pieces of skull, jawbone, and arm bones—were discovered in 1992, and later excavations yielded bones of the pelvis, leg, ankle, and foot, fragments necessary to determine whether the species walked upright.

The passion for hunting ancient remains came to White at a young age. Born on Aug. 24, 1950, in Los Angeles, he spent much time in his early years around Lake Arrowhead, California, scouring Native American campsites for artifacts. After studying anthropology and biology at the University of California, Riverside, he earned a Ph.D. in biological anthropology in 1977 from the University of Michigan. After that he had several teaching posts, and in 1986 he became a professor at the University of California, Berkeley.

White's research led him naturally to Africa. As a graduate student he was part of an expedition to Tanzania headed by anthropologist Richard Leakey. He also worked with Leakey's mother, Mary, studying fossilized hominid footprints. Some of White's most significant finds, however, were made in Ethiopia in the Middle Awash Valley. In the early 1990s at Maka, a town to the west of Aramis, he uncovered the 3.4 million-year-old remains of *Australopithecus afarensis,* a hominid species for which specimens (including the famous partial skeleton Lucy) had been discovered earlier in Ethiopia and Tanzania. White's find helped quell the controversy over whether the specimens from the two countries were indeed of one species.

Although White's *A. ramidus* was found in the same region as his *A. afarensis,* its physical characteristics, many of them chimpanzee-like, left little doubt that it was different. Whether its humanlike characteristics gave it sufficient claim to being an early hominid, however, remained unresolved.

(MARY JANE FRIEDRICH)

Wilson, Edward O.

A worldwide erosion of biological diversity is occurring that bodes ill for the Earth's remaining inhabitants—so warned Harvard University biologist Edward Osborne Wilson, 1995 winner of the Audubon Medal for contributions to conservation and environmental protection. That solemn message, eloquently expounded three years earlier in his best-seller *The Diversity of Life,* thrust Wilson into the scientific spotlight in the 1990s.

No stranger to notoriety, Wilson had earlier found himself enmeshed in controversy after the publication in 1975 of *Sociobiology: The New Synthesis,* in which he attributed the development of social behaviours to genetic as well as cultural factors. That idea was denounced by some who perceived implications of genetic determinism in the book. Wilson's argument, however, was that genetic predispositions exist upon which cultural forces operate and that the outcome entails the interplay of biology and culture, not the supremacy of one over the other. Twenty years later evidence for that view was mounting.

Wilson's career was decidedly tumultuous for a myrmecologist, otherwise known as an ant biologist. His life's work, detailed in the 1994 autobiography *Naturalist,* emerged from what he described as "biophilia," an inherited affinity for nature that he believed exists in all humans. Wilson developed his own love of nature early on, as it was the one constant in a world of change. Born June 10, 1929, in Birmingham, Ala., he was an only child whose parents divorced when he was seven. Because of the road assignments of his father, a government accountant, he moved from town to town throughout the southeastern U.S. Especially fascinated by insects, Wilson chose to study ants while a high-school senior, and he went on to obtain bachelor's and master's degrees (1949, 1950) from the University of Alabama. He received a doctorate in biology from Harvard in 1955 and joined the faculty a year later. As his career advanced, he was named Frank B. Baird Jr. professor of science in 1976 and Pellegrino university professor in 1994. Wilson also served as curator of entomology at Harvard's Museum of Comparative Zoology.

Among highlights of Wilson's impressive early research was the discovery in the 1950s of chemicals, known as pheromones, by which ants communicate. In the 1960s, in collaboration with ecologist Robert H. MacArthur, he outlined the theory of island biogeography, which describes how environmental factors determine the number and distribution of species in a circumscribed area. He tested the theory in a series of experiments on mangrove islands off southern Florida, work that led to an interest in conservation.

A prolific writer, Wilson won two Pulitzer Prizes, one in 1979 for *On Human Nature,* a book expanding the ideas in *Sociobiology,* and the other in 1991 for *The Ants,* co-written with Bert Hölldobler.

(MARY JANE FRIEDRICH)

Winton, Timothy John

Australia's most successful author since Nobel laureate Patrick White, Tim Winton put another feather in his cap in 1995 when his novel *The Riders* became an international best-seller and was short-listed for the Booker Prize. His precocious talent had been recognized by the time he was 21, when he won the *Australian*/Vogel Literary Award for his first novel *An Open Swimmer.* His second, *Shallows,* won the Miles Franklin Award in 1984. By the time he was nominated for the Booker, Winton had written more than 10 other books, including *Scission; That Eye, the Sky; Minimum of Two; Lockie Leonard, Human Torpedo; Cloudstreet,* which won the 1992 Miles Franklin Award; *The Bugalugs Bum Thief;* and *Land's Edge.*

Born near Perth, Western Australia, on Aug. 4, 1960, Winton had decided by the age of 10 to be a writer. He studied creative writing at the Western Australian Institute of Technology, but his down-to-earth hobbies—sports and recreational surfing, fishing, camping, and "hanging out" in the old whaling port of Albany—gave him an inexhaustible supply of anecdotes that appealed initially to teenage readers.

Although his earlier books were set mainly

in Western Australia, for 18 months in 1987–88 Winton gathered material for *The Riders* while living with his wife and son in France, Greece, and Ireland. In a picaresque plot, the novel's Australian hero, Fred Scully, is shocked by the unexplained desertion of his wife, who fails to arrive at Dublin's Shannon Airport to rendezvous with Scully and join him in a new life in a restored Irish croft. The tension in the novel builds as Scully and his seven-year-old daughter travel across Europe, revisiting old family haunts in a fruitless hunt for an explanation and reconciliation. The calculated naiveté of style in the novel mirrors the unlikely background to the hero's apocalyptic adventures. "I guess deep down I'm one of these people who's not particularly articulate," said Winton, an observation that could explain his wide and popular attraction to readers of all ages and backgrounds and not just the nominators of the Booker Prize.

(A.R.G. GRIFFITHS)

Wolfensohn, James D.

"I have learned that the real test of development can be measured not by the bureaucratic approval process but by the smile on a child's face when a project is successful," said James Wolfensohn, the new president of the World Bank, in addressing that organization's annual meeting in October 1995. Yet Wolfensohn—who became the Bank's ninth president on June 1, 1995, when Lewis Preston retired because of ill health—desperately needed the approval of a budget-minded U.S. Congress, which appeared ready to slash contributions to the Bank's "soft loan" window, the International Development Association. The IDA, which financed development projects for the world's poorest nations on extremely generous terms, made up more than $6.6 billion of the $22.5 billion the Bank lent less developed countries in fiscal 1995. (The Bank's International Bank of Reconstruction and Development lent money at market rates.) Having seen firsthand the invaluable benefits provided by IDA-funded projects while traveling to 24 countries during his first months in office, Wolfensohn lobbied hard against the congressional spending cuts. He feared that if the U.S. reduced its contributions to the IDA's replenishment fund, other donor nations would follow suit, putting the "whole field of development in turmoil."

Wolfensohn, who was born on Dec. 1, 1933, in Sydney, Australia, became a naturalized U.S. citizen in 1980. He was a veteran of the Royal Australian Air Force and a member of the 1956 Australian Olympic fencing team and was educated at the University of Sydney (B.A., 1954; LL.B, 1957) and Harvard University (M.B.A., 1959). During a distinguished career in investment banking, he oversaw the restructuring of the Chrysler Corp. while working at Salomon Brothers, and for 14 years he served as president and chief executive officer of James D. Wolfensohn Inc., an investment company that did between $8 million and $10 million of business annually. A philanthropist as well as an accomplished cellist, Wolfensohn served as the chairman (1980–91) of New York City's Carnegie Hall, overseeing its remodeling, and as chairman (1990–95) of the board of trustees of the John F. Kennedy Center for the Performing Arts, Washington, D.C.

As president, his goal was to become the Bank's first president since Robert McNamara (1968–81) to serve more than one five-year term and to change the culture of the institution. Rather than measuring success by the volume of loans, he tried to shift the Bank's emphasis back to alleviating poverty, creating sustainable development, and attaining social justice.

(JEFF WALLENFELDT)

Wu, Harry Hongda

When human rights activist Harry Wu was sentenced to 15 years in prison, then expelled from China on Aug. 24, 1995, the worsening of relations between China and the U.S. eased ever so slightly. Wu had been arrested by Chinese customs officials on June 19 at a remote northwestern border station when he attempted to enter China from Kazakhstan. While his American assistant was detained for only four days, Wu (a naturalized U.S. citizen) was charged with "entering China under false names, illegally obtaining state secrets, and conducting criminal activities."

Wu had spent 19 years as a political prisoner in China—building roads, mining coal, and farming—before immigrating to the U.S. in 1985. Haunted by his experiences and deeply disturbed by the 1989 Tiananmen Square massacre of prodemocracy students in Beijing, he assumed personal responsibility for exposing *laogai* ("reform through labour"), "a vast prison machine that crushes all vestiges of humanity—not only flesh and blood but spirit and ideals as well."

Wu's books—*Laogai: The Chinese Gulag* (1992) and *Bitter Winds: A Memoir of My Years in China's Gulag* (1994)—are a scathing condemnation of the way the Chinese government treats dissidents and political foes. The author, however, was destined to become more widely known for his daredevil return trips to China: twice in 1991, again in 1994, and the failed attempt in 1995. Risking arrest, Wu had posed as a prison guard, a tourist, and an American businessman to gain the documentary footage that later was shown on "60 Minutes" and the BBC. Wu most recently had focused on the harvesting of organs from executed prisoners, a practice roundly condemned by various groups. China responded aggressively to criticism, condemning a BBC-produced documentary on the lot of prisoners in China. Wu freely admitted that several specific scenes were faulty representations of the true state of affairs, but such groups as Amnesty International wondered about the virulence of the condemnation of China by those in the U.S. who supported the death penalty. Wu acknowledged that no one not previously scheduled for execution had been killed in order to obtain organs for transplants.

Wu Hongda was born Feb. 8, 1937, in Shanghai to a homemaker and a banker. He attended Beijing College of Geology (1955–60). His criticism of the 1956 Soviet invasion of Hungary led to his imprisonment in 1960. After his release in 1979, he taught at China Geoscience University, Wuhan (1980–85). He was a visiting scholar (1985–87) at the University of California, Berkeley, before becoming a research fellow at the Hoover Institution, a conservative think tank at Stanford University. He founded the Laogai Research Foundation in 1992 and served as its executive director.

(ELLEN FINKELSTEIN)

Yi Mun Yol

Yi Mun Yol may have been unhappy in his early years, but he so superbly turned this to his advantage that he became a commanding presence in the world of Korean literature. Once his works had been translated into major European and Asian languages, his literary talents also received wide praise overseas.

Yi was born on May 18, 1948, in Yongyang, Kyongsang-pukto. Two years later, at the outbreak of the Korean War, his father defected to North Korea. As a consequence, his family had to contend with poverty, social stigma, and police surveillance. These factors came into play when Yi decided to drop out of school. Suffering from deep depression, he came close to committing suicide. During these dark days he helped to save himself by reading omnivorously, never dreaming that at the same time he was laying the foundation of his future career.

Yi proved himself a master of the short story, novella, and novel. After making his debut in 1979 with realistic stories centred on social problems, he quickly went on to reveal the many faces of his talent one by one. In *Son of Man* (1979), he explored numerous Western and Oriental theologies in the course of tracing a young man's determined quest for transcendence. *Youth* (1981), a trilogy of novellas, recorded a young man's Herculean efforts to overcome his romantic nihilism and his impulse to commit suicide. *Hail to the Emperor* (1983), a jeu d'esprit, is a rambunctious satire on imperial delusions that showcases the author's incredible erudition. In *The Age of Heroes* (1984), Yi imaginatively reconstructed what he imagined his father's life might have been like after his defection to communist North Korea. In each of the 16 short stories making up *You Can't Go Home Again* (1986), Yi examines one aspect of hometown life, a spiritual space that has vanished beyond recall. It evokes nostalgia, fury, or pained amusement. In *Odysseia Seoul* (1992), readers travel through the maze of Seoul's underworld, encountering evils and corruption every step of the way. In "The Bird with Golden Wings" a master of calligraphy becomes the central figure in a discussion of Eastern and Western aesthetics. In *The Foot* a 19th-century vagabond poet is torn between his political commitments to the people and the pursuit of his artistic ideals. He suffers, moreover, from a distrust of his own motives.

Yi produced 12 novels and 52 novellas and short stories, besides numerous other kinds of writing. The range and force of his works were even more impressive than their volume. Yi, still in his late 40s and apparently at the height of his power, was certain to continue to enrich Korean literature and delight and enlighten his enthusiastic readers worldwide for years to come.

(SUH JI-MOON)

J. PATRICK FORDEN—SYGMA

Harry Hongda Wu

OBITUARIES

Abadi, Agha Hasan, Indian-born Pakistani financier who founded the Bank of Credit and Commerce International (b. May 14, 1922—d. Aug. 5, 1995).

Abbott, George Francis, U.S. theatrical director, producer, playwright, actor, and motion-picture director (b. June 25, 1887, Forestville, N.Y.—d. Jan. 31, 1995, Miami Beach, Fla.), as the dean of Broadway showmen, brought a no-nonsense approach, a flair for establishing pacing and humour, and an exceptional ability to maintain action effectively to the staging of some of the most popular Broadway musicals and farces that appeared from the 1920s to the '60s. His more than 120 productions over an eight-decade career bore his unmistakable touch, often as a play doctor. From 1948 through 1962 Abbott's shows garnered a remarkable 40 Tony awards, including five for him. (He received a special lifetime achievement Tony award in 1976.) After graduating (1911) from the University of Rochester, N.Y., Abbott studied drama at Harvard University before making his acting debut in *The Misleading Lady* (1913). He performed until the 1920s, when he turned to playwriting. Abbott scored a huge success with *Broadway* (1926) and followed that with such plaudit-gathering melodramas as *Chicago* (1926), *Four Walls* (1927), and *Coquette* (1927). He established a reputation as a master of farce with *Twentieth Century* (1932), *Three Men on a Horse* (1935), and *Boy Meets Girl* (1935). Among his directorial efforts were *Jumbo* (1935), *On Your Toes* (1936), *The Boys from Syracuse* (1938), *Pal Joey* (1940), *On the Town* (1944), *Where's Charley?* (1948), *Call Me Madam* (1950), *A Tree Grows in Brooklyn* (1951), *The Pajama Game* (1954), *Damn Yankees* (1955), *Fiorello!* (1959), and *A Funny Thing Happened on the Way to the Forum* (1962). He also collaborated on the screenplay for *All Quiet on the Western Front* (1930) and directed the film versions of *The Pajama Game* (1957) and *Damn Yankees* (1958). Abbott's autobiography, *Mister Abbott*, appeared in 1963. At 100 years of age he directed a revival of *Broadway*, and he collaborated on a Broadway revival of *Damn Yankees* shortly before his death at the age of 107.

Alfvén, Hannes Olof Gösta, Swedish astrophysicist (b. May 30, 1908, Norrköping, Sweden—d. April 2, 1995, Djursholm, Sweden), was one of the founders of the field of plasma physics and shared the 1970 Nobel Prize for Physics "for fundamental work in magnetohydrodynamics with fruitful applications in different parts of plasma physics." Alfvén was educated at Uppsala University (Ph.D., 1934) and taught at the Royal Institute of Technology, Stockholm, from 1940. His early research into auroras and atmospheric magnetic fields led him to theorize in 1942 that plasma (ionized matter in a semigaseous state) passing through magnetic fields in space would create electromagnetic waves (later called Alfvén waves). He also proposed an alternative to the big-bang model of the universe, postulating that the continuous interaction between matter and antimatter would produce an eternal oscillation between expansion and contraction. In 1963 Alfvén was named the Royal Institute's first professor of plasma physics. In 1967, in protest against the Swedish government's plans to build nuclear power plants, he left the institute and his job as a national science adviser and went to the U.S. to teach at the University of California at San Diego. He later reconciled with the Royal Institute and divided his time between San Diego and Stockholm. He retired in 1989. Alfvén's books include *Cosmical Electrodynamics* (1950), *Structure and Evolutionary History of the Solar System* (1975; with Gustaf Arrhenius), and a science-fiction novel written under a pseudonym.

Allen, Walter Ernest, British novelist, academic, and critic, best known for his 1954 study *The English Novel* (b. Feb. 23, 1911—d. Feb. 28, 1995).

Almeida, Laurindo, Brazilian virtuoso classical and jazz guitarist who helped popularize the bossa nova in the U.S. and who, as a guitarist and a composer of film sound-track music, notably *The Godfather*, won five Grammy awards (b. Sept. 2, 1917—d. July 26, 1995).

Amis, Sir Kingsley William, British novelist and poet (b. April 16, 1922, London, England—d. Oct. 22, 1995, London), created about 40 books—over 20 novels as well as several volumes of poetry, short stories, and miscellaneous other works—but remained best known for his first published novel, *Lucky Jim* (1953), which launched his literary career. A satire of academic life, it was regarded by some as one of the funniest books in the English language. It won the Somerset Maugham Award and gained Amis fame as one of Britain's Angry Young Men, a label he rejected. Amis also was considered representative of the so-called Movement poets of the 1950s. After Amis' education at St. John's College, Oxford, was interrupted by service in the Royal Corps of Signals during World War II, he graduated in 1947. He taught (1949–61) at universities in Wales and the U.S. and then accepted a post as fellow at Peterhouse College, Cambridge. He resigned in 1963 and thereafter—with the exception of a visiting professorship at Vanderbilt University, Nashville, Tenn. (1967–68)—concentrated on his writing. Among his notable novels were *That Uncertain Feeling* (1955), *Take a Girl like You* (1960), *The Green Man* (1969), *Girl, 20* (1971), *Ending Up* (1974), *Jake's Thing* (1978), and *The Old Devils* (1986), which won the Booker Prize. In addition, Amis also wrote a James Bond novel, *Colonel Sun* (1968), under the pseudonym Robert Markham. His last book was *The Biographer's Moustache* (1995). Though his early novels were considered liberal in tone, he had become increasingly conservative by the late 1960s, and some considered him an irascible curmudgeon. Nonetheless, he had the status of a British institution and remained one of the best of the moral satirists. Amis was made a Commander of the Order of the British Empire in 1981 and was knighted in 1990.

Andrews, Maxene, U.S. singer and entertainer (b. Jan. 3, 1916, Minneapolis, Minn.—d. Oct. 21, 1995, Hyannis, Mass.), formed, with her two sisters, Patty and LaVerne, the Andrews Sisters, whose blended harmonies and energetic style made them favourites of audiences. The group rocketed to fame in 1937 with their rendition of "Bei Mir Bist du Schön." During World War II the trio entertained U.S. troops overseas, belting out such hits as "Boogie Woogie Bugle Boy," "Don't Sit Under the Apple Tree," and "Rum and Coca-Cola." The Andrews Sisters became a cherished American icon and were hugely successful, selling more than 50 million records from the late 1930s to the early '40s. They appeared in scores of films and worked with the Glenn Miller Orchestra and Bing Crosby. Their relationships with one another, however, were fragile. In 1953 they disbanded, and Maxene and Patty went on to pursue solo careers. Three years later they reunited, but LaVerne died in 1967. In 1970 Maxene became dean of women at Tahoe Paradise College of Fine Arts, Lake Tahoe, Nev., and she eventually became its vice president. She and Patty teamed up in 1974 to make their Broadway debuts in *Over Here!* The show ran for more than a year, but the two became estranged and never sang together again. Maxene wrote a memoir, gave lectures, and performed in concerts, nightclubs, and musicals.

Andrews, Michael James, British painter (b. Oct. 30, 1928, Norwich, Norfolk, England—d. July 19, 1995, London, England), had a relatively small output of sizable, delicately wrought figurative paintings, each of which might consume months of careful planning and slow, painstaking brushwork. While Andrews was still a student at the Slade School of Fine Art in London (1949–53), his works were selected for inclusion in the 1952 exhibition "Young Painters" at the Institute of Contemporary Arts, London. One of his earliest paintings, "A Man Who Suddenly Fell Over," was later acquired by the Tate Gallery. He had his first successful solo exhibitions in 1958 and 1963. Andrews often grouped a series of enormous paintings around a single theme or variations of a single image. This technique was especially notable in his paintings of the Scottish Highlands, London nightlife, Ayers Rock in Australia, fish in water, and a solitary balloon floating above vast expanses of the bucolic English countryside. His canvas "A View from Uamh Mhor," a panoramic study of the Perthshire hills that had taken more than two years to complete, was named Picture of the Year at the Royal Academy's 1992 Summer Exhibition. Andrews' final completed painting was the second in a planned series on the River Thames.

STEVE SHIPMAN—IMPACT

Kingsley Amis

Anfinsen, Christian Boehmer, U.S. biochemist (b. March 26, 1916, Monessen, Pa.—d. May 14, 1995, Randallstown, Md.), concentrated on research into the structure of enzymes, proteins that serve to promote biochemical reactions, and was co-winner with Stanford Moore and William H. Stein of the 1972 Nobel Prize for Chemistry for fundamental work on correlating the structural properties of proteins with their physiological functions. Anfinsen, who conducted his research while serving as chief of the laboratory of chemical biology at the National Institutes of Health (NIH), Bethesda, Md., was honoured for having discerned how the protein enzyme ribonuclease folds to form a characteristic three-dimensional structure that determines its biochemical properties. His pioneering thinking on the interrelation of protein chemistry and genetics was set out in his innovative book *The Molecular Basis of Evolution* (1959). Anfinsen earned (1943) a Ph.D. from Harvard University and held a teaching position there and also at the University of Pennsylvania and the Nobel Medical Institute in Stockholm. He stayed at the NIH from 1950 to 1981 (except in 1962, when he taught at Harvard), when he joined Johns Hopkins University, Baltimore, Md., and began work examining the proteins of hyperthermophilic (extreme heat loving) bacteria taken from hydrothermal vents located on the floor of the Mediterranean Sea and the Pacific Ocean. He served as editor of the journal *Advances in Protein Chemistry* and was the author of some 200 original scientific articles.

Anwarul, Haq, Pakistani jurist who, as chief justice of the Pakistan Supreme Court, cast the deciding vote upholding former prime minister Zulfikar Ali Bhutto's death sentence for conspiracy to murder (b. May 11, 1917—d. March 3, 1995).

Aspin, Les(lie), Jr., U.S. politician (b. July 21, 1938, Milwaukee, Wis.—d. May 21, 1995, Washington, D.C.), was a Democrat from Wisconsin who won election in 1970 to the U.S. House of Representatives as an opponent of the Vietnam War. Later, while serving (1985–92) as chairman of the House Armed Services Committee, he supported the development of the multi-warhead MX missile and U.S. funding for the contra rebels attempting to overthrow the Marxist government in Nicaragua. Aspin also served as Pres. Bill Clinton's embattled defense secretary for 11 months until his resignation in 1994. In the latter post Aspin gained a reputation for indecisiveness. While attempting to implement Clinton's campaign promise to allow homosexuals to serve openly in the military, Aspin developed the unsatisfactory "don't ask, don't tell" compromise. He broadened the combat role of women and was widely praised for his initiative to restructure the U.S. military in a post-Cold War climate, but he failed to fortify U.S. troops in Somalia just weeks before 18 U.S. soldiers died there in a raid, an inaction that led to his resignation under pressure. Aspin, who earned a Ph.D. in economics from the Massachusetts Institute of Technology, served as one of Secretary of Defense Robert McNamara's "whiz kids" at the Pentagon. He then returned to Wisconsin and was elected to the House of Representatives. After earning a position on the Armed Services Committee, Aspin made a name for himself by issuing frequent bulletins about financial mismanagement in the Pentagon. At the time of his death, Aspin was chairman of the president's Foreign Intelligence Advisory Board, a committee established to scrutinize U.S. intelligence agencies.

Atanasoff, John Vincent, U.S. physicist (b. Oct. 4, 1903, Hamilton, N.Y.—d. June 15, 1995, Frederick, Md.), was belatedly credited (1973) with developing the first electronic digital computer. That acknowledgment followed a lawsuit that resulted in a judge's voiding a patent owned by Sperry Rand Corp. on the Electronic Numerical Integrator and Computer (ENIAC), an invention that had been recognized as the first electronic digital computer. Though Atanasoff gained legal stature for his achievement, many historians continued to credit ENIAC's inventors, J. Presper Eckert, Jr. (*q.v.*), and John W. Mauchly, as the founding fathers of the modern computer. With Clifford Berry, Atanasoff developed (1937–42) a fragile prototype, the Atanasoff-Berry Computer (ABC), at Iowa State University. The limited-function vacuum-tube device lacked a central processing unit and was not programmable but could solve differential equations using binary arithmetic. The machine was historically important because it contained design components of what would become the basic architecture of a computer, and the computer controversy stemmed from a 1941 visit that Mauchly made to Atanasoff and their discussion about the design of the ABC. Atanasoff abandoned his computer work to become chief of the acoustics division of the Naval Ordnance Laboratory, Washington, D.C., and later headed two engineering firms. His contributions to computing were detailed in two 1988 books, *The First Electronic Computer: The Atanasoff Story* and *Atanasoff: Forgotten Father of the Computer*. He was the recipient in 1981 of the Computer Pioneer Medal and was honoured in 1990 with the National Medal of Technology.

Ballantine, Ian Keith, U.S. pioneer paperback book publisher (b. Feb. 15, 1916—d. March 9, 1995).

Bambara, Toni Cade (TONI CADE), U.S. writer, civil rights activist, and teacher who penned short stories and other works that were written in distinctive dialects, featured sharply drawn characters, and chronicled the concerns of African-Americans living in the rural South and urban North (b. March 25, 1939—d. Dec. 9, 1995).

Barrow, Dame (Ruth) Nita, Barbadian public health official and diplomat (b. Nov. 15, 1916, St. Lucy, Barbados—d. Dec. 19, 1995, Bridgetown, Barbados), capped a long and distinguished career with her appointment in 1990 as the first woman governor-general of Barbados. Barrow, who was the sister of the country's first prime minister, Errol Barrow, studied nursing in Barbados, at the Universities of Toronto and Edinburgh, and at Columbia University, New York City. During the 1940s and '50s, she held a variety of nursing and public health posts in Barbados and Jamaica, and in 1964 she became an adviser to the World Health Organization (WHO). She rapidly gained international stature as nursing adviser (1967–71) to the Pan American Health Organization, medical commissioner (1971–80) and a president (1983) of the World Council of Churches, president (1975–83) of the World YWCA, health consultant (1981–86) to WHO, president (1982–90) of the International Council for Adult Education, and Barbadian ambassador (1986–90) to the UN. Barrow presided at the 1985 international women's conference in Nairobi, Kenya, and was the only woman named to the Eminent Persons Group set up to investigate racism in South Africa. In 1988 she lost a bid for the presidency of the UN General Assembly. Barrow was made Dame of the Order of St. Andrew in 1980.

Bazargan, Mehdi, Iranian political leader (b. September 1907?, Tehran, Iran—d. Jan. 20, 1995, Zürich, Switz.), as a longtime leader of the Muslim opposition to Mohammad Reza Shah Pahlavi, was named the first prime minister of the Islamic Republic of Iran on Feb. 5, 1979. His calls for moderation and order failed to stem the tide of violent fundamentalism under Ayatollah Ruhollah Khomeini, however, and he resigned on November 6, two days after extremists captured the U.S. embassy in Tehran. Barzargan was the son of an Azerbaijani merchant and was educated in thermodynamics and engineering at the École Centrale des Arts et Manufactures in Paris. He returned to Iran to teach engineering at the University of Tehran, where he eventually became dean of the College of Technology. In 1951 he was made director of the newly nationalized oil industry by Prime Minister Mohammad Mosaddeq. In 1953 Mosaddeq was ousted and the shah restored to power in a Western-backed coup. Despite being arrested and jailed several times, Bazargan continued to campaign against the shah, cofounding the opposition National Resistance Movement (1953) and the National Liberation Movement of Iran (1961). After Khomeini finally replaced the shah in 1979, Bazargan was appointed head of the provisional government. He complained that he had little real power, however, and resigned after only nine months when Khomeini supported the seizure of the U.S. embassy and the taking of more than 50 American hostages.

Belladonna, Giorgio, Italian contract bridge player who led the Italian Squadra Azzura, or Blue Team, to 10 European championships and 16 world titles between 1957 and 1975 (b. June 7, 1923—d. May 12, 1995).

Bemberg, Maria Luisa, Argentine motion-picture director (b. April 14, 1922, Buenos Aires, Arg.—d. May 7, 1995, Buenos Aires), challenged tradition when she embarked on a directing career after expressing disappointment at the way her semi-autobiographical screenplays were interpreted by male directors and later emerged as Latin America's foremost female director. Bemberg, who was raised in a patrician family, married and bore four children but felt unfulfilled in that role and secured a divorce. She found her feminist voice as a screenwriter when she was 48 and financed her first feature-length film, *Momentos* (1981), at the age of 59. In her six films she explored—in a context of political oppression—women's struggles to assume their rightful place in a patriarchal society. Her second film, *Senora de Nadie* (1982), focused on the friendship between a woman separated from her husband and a gay man. *Camila* (1984), a true story about a woman who fell in love with a priest and was executed, was followed by *Miss Mary* (1987), an examination of the influences of a British governess on her charges. Another film, *Yo, la peor de todas* (*I, the Worst of All*; 1990), was considered by many her best work and told the story of the 17th-century nun Juana Ines de la Cruz, a poet and thinker whose ideas were too radical for her times. Bemberg's last film was *We Don't Want to Talk About It* (1992), a fairy tale starring Marcello Mastroianni as an elderly gentleman who loves a dwarf.

Bernays, Edward L., U.S. publicist (b. Nov. 22, 1891, Vienna, Austria—d. March 9, 1995, Cambridge, Mass.), monitored, modified, and molded public opinion as the astute "father of public relations." He profoundly influenced the commercialization of American culture and shaped attitudes by relying on tradition, the testimony of experts, and the results of surveys to help endorse products. As the nephew of psychoanalyst Sigmund Freud, Bernays also recognized the importance of using psychology and drawing on the social sciences to influence the opinions of a particular audience. After graduating (1912) from Cornell University, Ithaca, N.Y., with a degree in agriculture, Bernays soon abandoned the grain market and found his niche as a publicist. When the producer of the play *Damaged Goods* found that the taboo theme of venereal disease was limiting support for his production, Bernays secured endorsements from civic leaders, a move that ensured the play's success. He then worked as a propaganda agent for the U.S. government during World War I before opening his own office with his future wife, Doris Fleischman. He used his expertise to promote a wide range of products for such clients as General Electric, General Motors, Time, CBS, and NBC. For Procter & Gamble's Ivory soap, he sponsored children's soap-carving competitions; for Venida hairnets, he stressed the safety aspects for women who worked in factories near machinery and the sanitary aspects for women dealing with food in restaurants; and for the American Tobacco Co.'s Lucky Strike cigarettes, he helped gain acceptance for women to smoke in public. In later years, however, he opposed smoking and participated in antismoking campaigns. Bernays, whose counsel was sought even after he celebrated his 100th birthday, divulged his insights into public relations in more than a dozen books.

Berque, Jacques Augustin, French sociologist, Orientalist, author of many books on the Arab world, and translator of the Qur'an into French (b. June 4, 1910—d. June 27, 1995).

Bhatia, Prem, Indian journalist, newspaper editor, political commentator, and diplomat (b. Aug. 11, 1911—d. May 8, 1995).

Birla, Aditya Vikram, Indian industrialist who headed the Birla Group, an international business empire that included interests in aluminum, textiles, petrochemicals, and telecommunications (b. Nov. 14, 1944—d. Oct. 1, 1995).

Birney, (Alfred) Earle, Canadian poet and writer (b. May 13, 1904, Calgary, Alta.—d. Sept. 3, 1995, Toronto, Ont.), was one of the most highly esteemed poets in Canada. He was especially well-known for his controversial poem "David" (1941), about the mercy killing of a young mountain climber badly injured in a fall. It was included in most Canadian high-school literature studies and was featured in *David, and Other Poems* (1942), which earned (1943) Birney the first of two Governor-General's awards. The second, in 1946, was for *Now Is Time* (1945). Birney earned a B.A. (1926) from the University of British Columbia and an M.A. (1927) and a Ph.D. (1936) from the University of Toronto. He taught at the University of California, Berkeley (1927–30), the University of Utah (1930–34), and the University of Toronto (1936–42), and from 1936 to 1940 he was literary editor of *Canadian Forum,* which showcased works of newly discovered young poets. His experiences while serving in the army during World War II provided material for one of his novels, *Turvey* (1949), for which he won the Stephen Leacock Memorial Medal for Humour. After the war Birney worked for the Canadian Broadcasting Corporation for a short time before returning (1946) to academe, at the University of British Columbia. From 1965 to 1984 he taught at a number of campuses in Canada and the U.S. In the late 1950s he began giving lectures and readings all over the world. His travels influenced his poetry, in which he adopted the viewpoint of a stranger in the observation of cultures. His poems were published in at least 15 languages. Birney also wrote verse plays, radio plays, short stories, and essays on literary criticism. His poetry collections include *Selected Poems, 1940–1966* (1966), *The Collected Poems of Earle Birney* (1975), *Ghost in the Wheels* (1977), *Copernican Fix* (1985), and *Last Makings* (1991).

Blaine, Vivian, U.S. actress of stage and screen who was best remembered for her showstopping rendition of "Adelaide's Lament" in both the Broadway and film productions of *Guys and Dolls* (b. Nov. 21, 1921—d. Dec. 9, 1995).

Blake, Hector ("Toe"), Canadian hockey player and coach (b. Aug. 21, 1912, Victoria Mines, N.S.—d. May 17, 1995, Montreal, Que.), was a strict disciplinarian and brilliant strategist who helped the Montreal Canadiens secure 11 Stanley Cup victories, 3 of them as a player and a record 8 as a coach. Blake joined the team in 1936 after two seasons with the Montreal Maroons. As a Canadien he played left wing on the "Punch Line" with Maurice ("the Rocket") Richard and Elmer Lach, two other deadly scorers. In the 1938–39 season Blake was the recipient of both the Art Ross Trophy and the Hart Trophy as the National Hockey League's leading scorer and most valuable player, respectively. After breaking his ankle in 1948, he retired as a player but found a new career in 1955 when he returned to the team as its coach. Blake was defined by an ever-present fedora, a tough yet fair coaching style, and an impressive 13-year record that included nine first-place finishes, eight Stanley Cup trophies, and a .634 winning percentage. After his retirement in 1968, Blake remained a guiding force as a team vice president and as the proprietor of a beer hall that served as the club's unofficial headquarters.

Blane, Ralph, U.S. Tin Pan Alley songwriter of such all-time favourites as "Have Yourself a Merry Little Christmas," "The Boy Next Door," and "Trolley Song" (b. July 26, 1914—d. Nov. 13, 1995).

Bolt, Robert Oxton, British dramatist (b. Aug. 15, 1924, Sale, near Manchester, England—d. Feb. 20, 1995, near Petersfield, Hampshire, England), drew international acclaim for his play *A Man for All Seasons* (1960; filmed 1966), in which he used the clash between King Henry VIII and Sir Thomas More to explore the struggle by which a man of honour and integrity achieves a kind of heroism in the face of moral ambiguity and historic upheaval. He continued to explore this issue in the screenplays for *Lawrence of Arabia* (1962) and *Doctor Zhivago* (1965), as well as the scripts for the films *Ryan's Daughter* (1970), *Lady Caroline Lamb* (1972), *The Bounty* (1984), and *The Mission* (1986). Bolt attended Victoria University of Manchester (B.A.; 1949) after completing his World War II military service. He began writing radio dramas while working as a schoolteacher, but the success of his first major play, *Flowering Cherry* (1957), allowed him to write full-time. Other plays include *The Tiger and the Horse* (1960), *Gentle Jack* (1963), *Vivat! Vivat Regina!* (1970), and *State of Revolution* (1977). His career was disrupted in 1979 by a near-fatal stroke. Bolt won Academy Awards for the screenplays of *A Man for All Seasons* and *Doctor Zhivago* and was made Commander of the Order of the British Empire in 1972.

Borsos, Phillip, Canadian film director (b. May 5, 1953, Hobart, Tasmania, Australia—d. Feb. 1, 1995, Vancouver, B.C.), was a visionary perfectionist who captured the haunting beauty of the Canadian landscape in films that featured a poetic storytelling style. While in high school he was given a 16-mm Bolex camera, which sparked a lifelong obsession with filmmaking. After making a series of short documentary films about workers and craftsmen, notably *Cooperage* (1976), *Spartree* (1977), and the Academy Award-nominated *Nails* (1979), Borsos made an extraordinary feature-film debut with *The Grey Fox* (1982), a romantic saga about Bill Miner, a stagecoach bandit who turned to robbing trains in turn-of-the-century British Columbia. That film won a Genie award as best picture at the Canadian Film Awards. Borsos directed four other feature films—*The Mean Season* (1985), *One Magic Christmas* (1985), *Bethune: The Making of a Hero* (1988), and *Far from Home: The Adventures of Yellow Dog* (1995)—before succumbing to acute myeloid leukemia.

Botvinnik, Mikhail Moiseyevich, Soviet chess grandmaster (b. Aug. 17 [Aug. 4, Old Style], 1911, Kuokkala, near St. Petersburg, Russia—d. May 5, 1995, Moscow, Russia), was the first Soviet world chess champion (1948–57, 1958–60, 1961–63). Botvinnik learned chess at the relatively advanced age of 12, but within two years he had defeated the reigning world champion, José Raúl Capablanca of Cuba, in an exhibition match. In 1931 he won the first of seven national championships. He graduated in electrical engineering from the Leningrad Polytechnic Institute (1932) and worked as an engineer during World War II, although he was allowed to concentrate on chess three days a week. After the death of Alexander Alekhine of France left the world title open, Botvinnik defeated four other grandmasters in a championship tournament (1948). He successfully defended his title in 1951 and 1954. He lost in 1957 (to Vasily Smyslov) and 1961 (to Mikhail Tal), but both times he regained the championship in the mandatory rematch. When he lost to Tigran Petrosyan in 1963, rematches were no longer obligatory. He retired from competition in 1970. Botvinnik was known as a brilliant tactician and an intimidating competitor who could withstand the most distracting conditions. He also wrote several books on chess tactics, worked on a computer chess program, and ran a chess school, where his students included future world champions Anatoly Karpov and Garry Kasparov.

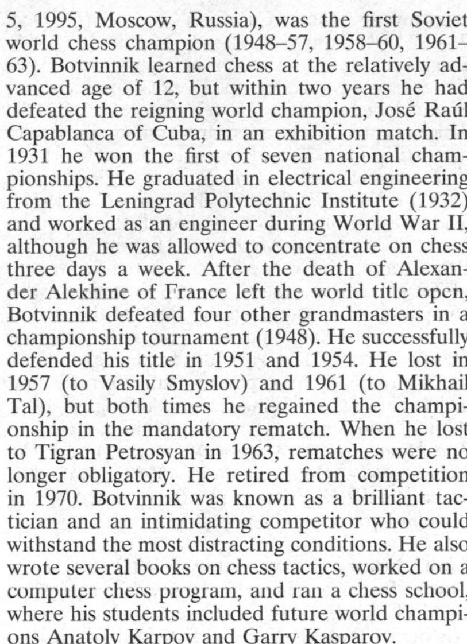

Boutin, François, French racehorse trainer (b. Jan. 21, 1937, Beaunay, France—d. Feb. 1, 1995, Paris, France), in a 31-year career as one of France's leading Thoroughbred trainers, won more than 1,880 races, including 17 French classics and major races in Britain and the U.S. Boutin was the son of a farmer in Normandy and showed a flair with horses even as a boy. He drove in trotting races and rode in cross-country and flat-track races, as well as show-jumping and events competitions. He apprenticed as a trainer, obtained his license in 1964, and established his own stable in 1966. Although Boutin never won the three most prestigious races—the Prix de l'Arc de Triomphe (France), the Derby (England), and the Kentucky Derby (U.S.)—his horses captured most of the other Group 1 races and made him France's leading money winner seven times (1976, 1978–81, and 1983–84). Outside France, Boutin was perhaps best known as the trainer of Sagaro, which won the Ascot Gold Cup three times (1975–77); Nureyev, which triumphed in the 1980 English Two Thousand Guineas before being disqualified for jockey interference; Miesque, which won the Breeders' Cup Mile and the Turf female title in two consecutive years (1987 and 1988); and Arazi, which recovered from 20 lengths off the pace to capture a spectacular come-from-behind victory in the 1991 Breeders' Cup Juvenile.

EXPRESS PHOTOS/ARCHIVE PHOTOS

Mikhail Moiseyevich Botvinnik (Right)

Braithwaite, Max, Canadian author (b. Dec. 7, 1911, Nokomis, Sask.—d. March 19, 1995, Brighton, Ont.), drew on his humorous experiences as a teacher in Depression-era rural Saskatchewan in *Why Shoot the Teacher?* (1965), which was made into an award-winning film of the same title in 1977 and became part of a trilogy that includes *Never Sleep Three in a Bed* (1969) and *The Night We Stole the Mountie's Car* (1971). The latter volume was awarded the Stephen Leacock Memorial Medal for Humour in 1972. Braithwaite, who was educated at the University of Saskatchewan, was a superb craftsman who compassionately captured the spirit of the prairie people and the hardships they endured during the "Dirty Thirties." His work as a freelance included writing radio dramas, film and stage scripts, and articles for Canadian magazines. Among his more than 20 books was a series for children, including *The Mystery of the Muffled Man* (1962) and *The Valley of the Vanishing Birds* (1963). An adult book, *All the Way Home* (1986), returned to the theme of poverty.

Brett, Jeremy (PETER JEREMY WILLIAM HUGGINS), British actor who began his career in classical theatre and portrayed dashing young aristocrats, notably Freddie Eynsford-Hill in the 1964 film *My Fair Lady,* but found his signature role as the quintessential Sherlock Holmes onstage and in Granada Television's 41-part series, 1984–95 (b. Nov. 3, 1935—d. Sept. 12, 1995).

Brophy, Brigid Antonia, British novelist (b. June 12, 1929, London, England—d. Aug. 7, 1995, Louth, Lincolnshire, England), enjoyed a dual career as a writer and as a crusader for feminist issues, animal rights, and increased royalty payments for writers. Her campaign for establishing lending rights for authors resulted (1979) in a law that provided government royalty payments to authors whenever one of their books was checked out of a British library. Brophy attended (1947–48) St. Hugh's College, Oxford, but was expelled. A volume of short stories, *The Crown Princess,* was published in 1953, but it was the publication later that year of her first novel, the imaginative fantasy *Hackenfeller's Ape,* that brought her to the public's attention. It won (1954) the Cheltenham Literary Festival's prize for first novel. Brophy went on to write such novels as *Flesh* (1962), *The Snow Ball* (1964), *In Transit* (1969), and *Palace Without Chairs* (1978), her last novel. She also wrote the play *The Burglar* (1967), contributed to the controversial *Fifty Works of English and American Literature We Could Do Without* (1967), and, in one of her many other nonfiction works, the essay collection *Baroque 'n' Roll* (1987), described her battle with multiple sclerosis. Even after the disease confined her to her house, she continued to champion causes. Brophy became a fellow of the Royal Society of Literature in 1973.

Brunner, John Kilian Houston, British science-fiction writer whose popular novels include *The Sheep Look Up, The Shockwave Rider,* and the Hugo Award-winning *Stand on Zanzibar* (b. Sept. 24, 1934—d. Aug. 25, 1995).

Burger, Warren Earl, U.S. Supreme Court chief justice (b. Sept. 17, 1907, St. Paul, Minn.—d. June 25, 1995, Washington, D.C.), presided (1969–86) as the 15th chief justice of the United States. Burger, who attended night school to earn a law degree (1931) from St. Paul (now William Mitchell) College of Law, joined a prominent law firm in his hometown while gradually becoming active in Republican Party politics. After helping Dwight D. Eisenhower secure the 1952 presidential nomination, Burger was rewarded with the post of assistant attorney general. In 1956 he was elevated to the U.S. Court of Appeals, where he acquired a reputation as a conservative and came to the attention of Pres. Richard M. Nixon, who needed to replace retiring liberal Chief Justice Earl Warren. Though Burger and three other Nixon appointees were expected to reverse the activist thrust that characterized the Warren legacy on civil rights issues and criminal law, they upheld both the 1966 Miranda decision, requiring that a criminal suspect under arrest be informed of his rights, and the decision to validate busing as a means of racially desegregating public schools. Though generally steering a conservative course, Burger voted with the majority in the court's landmark 1973 decision (*Roe* v. *Wade*) that established a woman's constitutional right to have an abortion, and in 1974 he wrote the legal opinion for the 8–0 decision that struck down executive privilege and forced Nixon to surrender White House tapes containing conversations about the Watergate scandal. Burger also unsealed court records that named Nixon an "unindicted co-conspirator" in the Watergate affair. Nixon was then forced to resign. Burger was noted for taking an activist role in the administration of the court. He modernized and computerized the court and overhauled the entire judicial system, though his campaign to create a new level of appellate courts to lighten the Supreme Court's caseload failed to gain support. In 1986 Burger, the longest-serving chief justice in the 20th century, unexpectedly resigned to assume the chairmanship of the commission planning the bicentennial celebration of the U.S. Constitution (1987). He was awarded the Presidential Medal of Freedom in 1988. His book, *It Is So Ordered* (1995), examined 14 cases that helped shape constitutional interpretation.

Burri, Alberto, Italian artist (b. March 12, 1915, Città di Castello, Italy—d. Feb. 13, 1995, Nice, France), devised collages and abstractions by using such unorthodox materials as old rags, sackcloth, burnt wood, cellophane, rusted metal, and brightly coloured plastic, often scorched or partially melted. Burri trained as a physician at the University of Perugia and served in the army medical corps in North Africa during World War II. He began painting while interned in a prisoner-of-war camp in Texas and abandoned medicine entirely when he was repatriated to Rome about 1946. Although Burri's earliest works were conventional landscapes and still lifes, he quickly moved in a new direction with a series of pieces in which he used burlap sacks—stitched together, torn, patched, and splashed with red paint—to evoke powerful images of bloodstained wartime field dressings. His first major exhibition was in Rome in 1947. From the early 1950s, Burri divided his time between Europe and the U.S., where his work influenced young American abstract painters and collagists.

Butenandt, Adolf Friedrich Johann, German biochemist (b. March 24, 1903, Bremerhaven-Lehe, Germany—d. Jan. 18, 1995, Munich, Germany), was the co-winner (with Leopold Ruzicka) of the 1939 Nobel Prize for Chemistry for pioneering work (1929–34) on sex hormones, primarily the isolation of estrone (a hormone that influences development of the female reproductive tract), progesterone (a female hormone that primarily regulates the condition of the inner lining of the uterus), and the male hormone androsterone. Butenandt also synthesized testosterone, which stimulates the development of masculine characteristics. He isolated estrone about the time that biochemist Edward Doisy accomplished the same feat in the U.S. Butenandt, who was also the first to explain the role of these hormones, found that they are closely related to steroids. Forbidden by Germany's Nazi government to receive the Nobel Prize when it was awarded him, he accepted the gold medal and diploma in 1949. His discoveries about hormones influenced the large-scale production of cortisone and laid the groundwork for the development of birth control pills. Butenandt, the first to crystallize an insect hormone, ecdysone, also was the first to isolate a pheromone, bombykol, the sex attractant of the female silkworm moth. After earning (1927) a Ph.D. from the University of Göttingen, he taught there and at the Danzig (now Gdansk, Poland) Institute of Technology (1933–36). He was director (1936–45) of the Kaiser Wilhelm Institute for Biochemistry, Berlin-Dahlem (now Tübingen), and professor of physiological chemistry there from 1945 to 1956. When the institute (after World War II renamed the Max Planck Institute for Biochemistry) moved to Munich in 1956, he retained those posts. Butenandt also served (1960–72) as president of the Max Planck Society for the Advancement of Science.

Cairncross, John, British government official who was identified in 1991 as the long-sought "fifth man" in the notorious Soviet spy ring that included Kim Philby, Guy Burgess, Donald MacLean, and Anthony Blunt (b. July 27, 1913—d. Oct. 8, 1995).

Caro Baroja, Julio, Spanish Basque anthropologist and historian who was best known for his ethnographic studies of Basque and Spanish traditional cultures and folklore (b. Nov. 13, 1914—d. Aug. 18, 1995).

Cash, Rosalind, U.S. stage and screen actress who performed with the Negro Ensemble Company and was especially noted for her portrayal of the daughter in *Ceremonies in Dark Old Men,* 1969, a role she reprised for television in 1975 (b. Dec. 31, 1938—d. Oct. 31, 1995).

Chadwick, Florence, U.S. swimmer who in 1950 broke the women's record for swimming the English Channel from France to England and in 1955 broke the world record for swimming from England to France (b. Nov. 9, 1918—d. March 15, 1995).

Chandrasekhar, Subrahmanyan, Indian-born U.S. astrophysicist (b. Oct. 19, 1910, Lahore, India [now in Pakistan]—d. Aug. 21, 1995, Chicago, Ill.), shared with William A. Fowler the 1983 Nobel Prize for Physics for his theory on the later stages of stellar evolution, work that subsequently led to the discovery of neutron stars and black holes. This theory, which contradicted the then current belief that all dying stars end their lives by contracting into extremely dense white dwarfs, predicted that stars with masses greater than 1.4 times that of the Sun (the Chandrasekhar limit, eventually revised to 1.2 solar masses) would collapse into objects smaller and denser than white dwarfs—neutron stars and black holes. Chandrasekhar received (1930) a B.A. from Presidency College, University of Madras, India, and completed (1933) his doctorate in theoretical physics at the University of Cambridge. In 1937 he joined the University of Chicago at Yerkes Observatory, Williams Bay, Wis., becoming (1952) the Morton D. Hull distinguished service professor of astrophysics, a post he held until 1986, when he became professor emeritus. During this time the focus of his research shifted among such topics as stellar structure, the transfer of energy in stellar atmospheres, and black holes. From 1952 to 1971 he served as editor of the *Astrophysical Journal,* which became the national journal of the American Astronomical Society. The recipient of numerous awards, including the 1953 Gold Medal of the Royal Astronomical Society, Chandrasekhar was also the author of 10 books; his last, *Newton's "Principia" for the Common Reader,* was published in 1995.

Chang, Eileen (CHANG AI-LING), Chinese writer (b. Sept. 30, 1920, Shanghai, China—found dead Sept. 8, 1995, Los Angeles, Calif.), wrote sad, bitter love stories that gained her a large devoted audience in Chinese communities as well as critical acclaim as one of the giants of modern Chinese literature. Her outlook was shaped partly by the cruelty of her father, who subjected her to mental torture, and her unhappiness with her first husband, who collaborated with the Japanese during World War II and was unfaithful to her. After Chang's education at the University of Hong Kong was halted by the Japanese invasion, she returned to Shanghai and pursued a writing career, beginning with film scripts and romantic works. Her novella *Chinsuo chi* (1943, "The Golden Cangue"; *The Rouge of the North,* 1967) was her first critical success. It was one of many works that were later made into motion pictures. Chang moved to Hong Kong in 1952 and to the U.S. three years later. Two of her most widely known novels were published during that period: *Yang-ko* (1954; *The Rice-Sprout Song,* 1955), which was written first in English

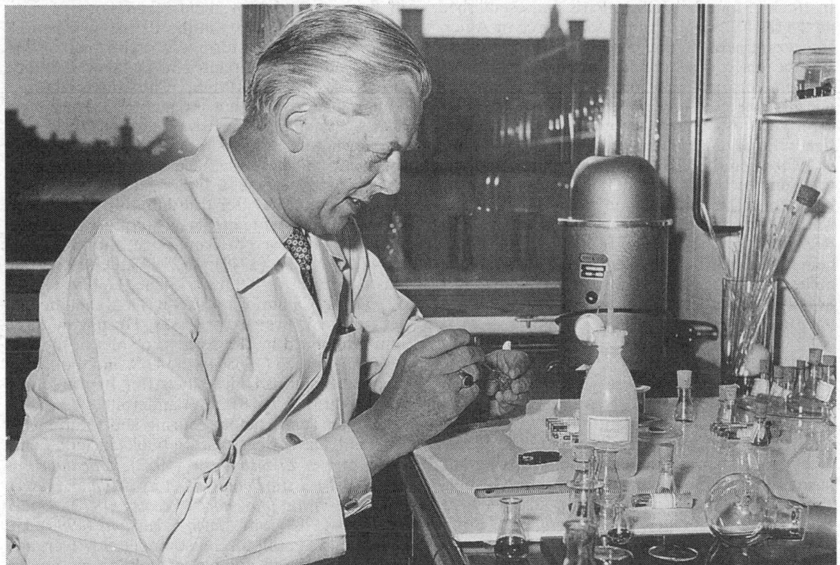
Adolf Butenandt
GERHARD GRONEFELD

but published first in Chinese and which brought Chang her audience in the West, and *Chih-ti chih lien* (1954; *Naked Earth,* 1956). Though Chang held visiting positions at several U.S. universities over the years, she became increasingly reclusive. She refused interviews with editors who wanted to meet with her, communicated with her editor in Taiwan via a fax machine installed at a neighbourhood store, and—when she received a major Taiwanese literary award in 1994—sent a selection of photographs of herself in lieu of appearing in person.

Chen Yun (Ch'en Yün; LIAO CH'EN-YÜN), Chinese revolutionary (b. 1905?, Shanghai, China—d. April 10, 1995, Beijing, China), was one of the last surviving members of the fledgling Communist Party's 10,000-km (6,000-mi) Long March (1934–35) from southeastern to northwestern China to escape Chiang Kai-shek's Nationalist troops. During his entire life Chen, who had no formal education, remained a highly influential conservative Marxist; during the 1980s he opposed the full implementation of paramount leader Deng Xiaoping's program of modernization and economic reforms. His eventual endorsement of reforms was tempered by a stern admonition that the state must never permit "the bird to leave the cage." At Deng's urging, Chen relinquished his posts in 1987 as a member of the Political Bureau and of its Standing Committee and as a member of the Communist Party of China Central Committee, but he continued to back younger hard-liners who shared his conservative ideology and distrust of Western democracy and culture.

Cherkassky, Shura, Ukrainian-born concert pianist whose idiosyncratic performances were alternately brilliant and erratic; he was particularly admired for his interpretations of Romantic music (b. Oct. 7, 1911—d. Dec. 27, 1995).

Cherry, Donald Eugene, U.S. jazz trumpeter (b. Nov. 18, 1936, Oklahoma City, Okla.—d. Oct. 19, 1995, Málaga, Spain), was a pioneer of free jazz as a member of the Ornette Coleman Quartet and later joined jazz with elements of African, Asian, Middle Eastern, and European music, thereby becoming a pioneer of world music as well. Cherry, who grew up in Los Angeles, hailed from a musical family. He had already achieved some local success as a trumpeter in the conventional bop idiom by the time he met alto saxophonist Coleman in 1956. After Cherry joined Coleman's quartet, the group abandoned standard harmonic structures in favour of improvisation wholly on melodic material. Cherry played trumpet and Pakistani pocket trumpet in Coleman's classic recordings of 1958–61 and evolved into a melodic improviser of rare rhythmic freedom and poise. The free jazz idiom was highly controversial when Cherry left Coleman to join Sonny Rollins' quartet in 1962. While Cherry performed with the New York Contemporary Five, his trumpet provided a lyric contrast to the drastically intense sonic explorations of tenor saxophonist Albert Ayler when they played and recorded in Europe in 1964. Cherry's own albums began appearing the next year. He traveled widely and mastered ethnic instruments as well, including African and Indian flutes in his 1968 ensemble composition *Eternal Rhythm* and in duets with drummer Edward Blackwell. During the 1970s Cherry began playing in Old and New Dreams, a quartet comprising Coleman veterans devoted to his repertoire. Though the most influential of free jazz trumpeters also played with rock and reggae groups, he was principally known as a jazz artist.

Christiansen, Godtfred Kirk, Danish toy manufacturer who engineered the growth of Legos into an international sensation and made Legoland, a theme park built out of the tiny, brightly coloured plastic building blocks, into one of Denmark's leading tourist attractions (b. July 8, 1920—d. July 13, 1995).

Church, Alonzo, U.S. mathematician (b. June 14, 1903, Washington, D.C.—d. Aug. 11, 1995, Hudson, Ohio), was a pioneer in the field of mathematical logic. His contributions to number theory and the theories of algorithms and computability laid the theoretical foundations of computer science. Church was educated at Princeton University (A.B., 1924; Ph.D., 1927) and spent a year as a fellow at Harvard University and a year at the University of Göttingen, Germany, before returning to his alma mater to teach (1929–67) mathematics and philosophy. Just before reaching retirement age at Princeton, he took (1967–90) a professorship at the University of California, Los Angeles. In 61 years of teaching, he supervised 31 doctoral students, including such notable mathematicians as Alan M. Turing, Stephen Cole Kleene, John G. Kemeny, Raymond M. Smullyan, and Martin Davis. Many of Church's innovations originated in the 1930s, such as his creation of λ (lambda) calculus, which later became an important tool for computer scientists. He was probably best known for a thesis, proposed independently by Turing, that holds that a function is calculable if it is recursive (able to be repeated) and, therefore, that problems are either solvable or unsolvable by mechanical methods of computation. The so-called Church-Turing thesis helped to extend the work of Kurt Gödel, who in 1931 theorized that there are truths in elementary mathematics that cannot be proved or disproved on the basis of the axioms within that system. In 1936 Church helped found the *Journal of Symbolic Logic,* compiling an exhaustive bibliography on logic for its first issue; he remained editor until 1979. He also wrote the textbook *Introduction to Mathematical Logic* (1956).

Cioran, Emil Mihai, Romanian-born writer (b. April 8, 1911, Rasinari, Rom.—d. June 20, 1995, Paris, France), was the author of elegantly written philosophical essays in which he displayed a sense of alienation and pessimism that was, according to one critic, "so profound and ironic as to almost meet a serious optimism at the other end of its arc." Cioran received a degree in philosophy (1932) from the University of Bucharest, Rom., having written his thesis on the French philosopher Henri Bergson. His first book, *Pe culmile disperării* (1933; *On the Heights of Despair,* 1992), won a prize for young writers from the Romanian Royal Academy. Over the next four years he studied philosophy in Berlin, taught briefly in Bucharest, and wrote three more volumes of essays. In 1937 Cioran went to Paris on a grant from the French Institute in Bucharest. There his philosophy of futility and despair found a suitable home among French existentialist and nihilist writers. He lived in Paris for the rest of his life and wrote 10 books in French, beginning with *Précis de décomposition* (1949; *A Short History of Decay,* 1975). Later books include *La Tentation d'exister* (1956; *The Temptation to Exist,* 1968) and *De l'inconvénient d'être né* (1973; *The Trouble with Being Born,* 1976).

Clark, Sir (John) Grahame Douglas, British archaeologist and authority on the prehistoric age in northwestern Europe known as the Mesolithic Period, which dates from about 8000 until about 2700 BC (b. July 28, 1907—d. Sept. 12, 1995).

Clayton, Jack, British motion-picture director whose nine films ranged from the social realism of *Room at the Top* to the psychological ghost story *The Innocents* (b. March 1, 1921—d. Feb. 25, 1995).

Close, Robert, Australian novelist (b. July 15, 1903, Camberwell, Victoria, Australia—d. July 17, 1995, Palma de Mallorca, Spain), in a sensational 1946 trial before the Victoria Supreme Court, was charged under an 18th-century law with having committed an obscene libel with his novel *Love Me Sailor* (1945). Although mild by later standards, the book, which dealt with the chaos wrought by a seductive woman passenger aboard a windjammer full of men, was banned as immoral, and copies were publicly burned. Close was sentenced to three months' imprisonment and fined £100, a sentence that was altered on appeal to time served (10 days) and £150. A few months later he left Australia for France, where he and his novel were enthusiastically received. Close set nearly all of his later novels in Australia, notably *Eliza Callaghan* (1957) and *The Voyage Continues* (1969). After a quarter of a century in Europe, he was welcomed back to Australia with his reputation restored, but he remained only two years before returning to Europe. Close also published two autobiographical works, *Morn of Youth* (1949?) and *Of Salt and Earth* (1977).

Coleman, James Samuel, U.S. sociologist (b. May 12, 1926, Bedford, Ind.—d. March 25, 1995, Chicago, Ill.), conducted landmark scientific studies that significantly influenced U.S. education policies. After earning a Ph.D. (1955) in sociology from Columbia University, New York City, he held a fellowship (1955–56) at the Center for Advanced Study of Behavioral Science, Palo Alto, Calif.; assistant professor of sociology (1956–59) at the University of Chicago; professor (1959–73) at Johns Hopkins University, Baltimore, Md.; and senior study director (from 1973) of the University of Chicago's National Opinion Research Center. Coleman's controversial findings—that disadvantaged black children learned better in integrated classes when mixed with a majority of middle-class children—provided the impetus for busing during the 1960s and '70s, a practice that created a furor and led to violent confrontations in some cities. When Coleman claimed in 1975 that busing had been a failure because it had contributed to white flight from public schools, critics assailed him for seemingly reversing himself. Some members of the American Sociological Association launched proceedings to revoke Coleman's membership, but the move was not successful, and Coleman eventually became president of the association in 1991. Another study by Coleman in 1981 caused a stir when he concluded that private and Roman Catholic schools provided a superior education to public schools, but he soon retracted his findings, citing flaws in the data. Among his writings are *The Adolescent Society* (1961), *Youth, Transition to Adulthood* (1975), *The Asymmetric Society* (1982), and *Foundations of Social Theory* (1990), which he viewed as his most important sociological work.

Cook, Elisha, Jr., U.S. character actor who often portrayed villains, most notably the psychotic Wilmer in *The Maltese Falcon* (b. Dec. 26, 1902—d. May 18, 1995).

Cook, Peter Edward, British entertainer (b. Nov. 17, 1937, Torquay, Devon, England—d. Jan. 9, 1995, London, England), gained international fame in the 1960s in the hit satirical revue *Beyond the Fringe* (with Alan Bennett, Jonathan Miller, and Dudley Moore) and for his longtime comedy partnership with Moore on stage, screen, television, and comedy records. He also founded The Establishment, a London comedy club where many younger comedians got their start, and published the satirical magazine *Private Eye.* Cook studied modern languages at Pembroke College, Cambridge, where he began writing and performing irreverent sketches with fellow students Bennett, Miller, and Moore. The quartet's efforts evolved into *Beyond the Fringe,* which they took to London's West End in 1961 and to Broadway a year later. Cook's tall, lean frame and droll, deadpan delivery of even the most absurd dialogue made him a perfect foil for the short, energetic Moore, and the two created a series of comic duos, notably the inane working-class philosophers Pete 'n' Dud, on their long-running television program, "Not Only . . . But Also" (1965–66 and 1970–73), and their two-man shows *Behind the Fridge* (1971–72) and *Good Evening* (1973–75). The pair's films included the Faustian *Bedazzled* (1967), a spoof version of *The Hound of the Baskervilles* (1977) with Cook as Sherlock Holmes, and *Derek and Clive* (1980), a variation on the original Pete 'n' Dud. After Moore moved to Hollywood in the 1980s, Cook concentrated on *Private Eye,* although he made a few more films and was a frequent guest on TV talk shows.

Cooper, Susan Vera Barker ("SUSIE"), British ceramic designer whose elegant but utilitarian household pottery was prized by royalty, private collectors, and museums (b. Oct. 29, 1902—d. July 28, 1995).

Coposu, Corneliu, Romanian politician who was jailed for anticommunist activities, 1947–64, and was harassed for years afterward but went on to lead the centrist Christian and Democratic National Peasants' Party in the postcommunist parliament (b. May 20, 1916—d. Nov. 11, 1995).

Cornfeld, Bernard, U.S. financier (b. Aug. 17, 1927, Istanbul, Turkey—d. Feb. 27, 1995, London, England), was the flamboyant jet-setting head of Investors Overseas Services (IOS) and its Fund of Funds, a Geneva-based international mutual-fund investment firm that was allegedly worth some $2.5 billion dollars until the company collapsed amid financial panic and allegations of fraud in 1970. Cornfeld was born in Turkey to a Romanian father and a Russian mother. The family moved to the U.S., where the young boy grew up in Brooklyn, N.Y. He studied psychology at Brooklyn College and social work at Columbia University, New York City, but he quit social work to become a mutual-fund salesman in Philadelphia. In 1955 he founded IOS in Paris and established an aggressive, highly trained sales force of American expatriates. The company skirted U.S. and European securities regulations and grew rapidly in the booming stock market of the 1960s, especially after Cornfeld moved the headquarters from Paris to Geneva (reportedly to avoid investigation by French authorities). The bubble burst in 1970 when the U.S. stock market fell; IOS and the Fund of Funds lost millions of dollars in investments. Cornfeld lost control of the company, which was taken over by the American financier Robert L. Vesco, who fled the U.S. in 1973 after being accused of having defrauded IOS of $224 million. Although Cornfeld spent 11 months in a Swiss jail on a different charge of fraud, he was later acquitted.

Corrigan, Douglas ("WRONG WAY"), U.S. aviator who became a folk hero when he turned his authorized coast-to-coast (New York to California) flight into a transatlantic one (to Ireland) after U.S. authorities refused to approve his solo flight across the Atlantic; he insisted that he had misread his compass and earned the moniker "Wrong Way Corrigan" (b. Jan. 22, 1907—d. Dec. 9, 1995).

Cosell, Howard (HOWARD WILLIAM COHEN), U.S. sportscaster (b. March 25, 1918, Winston-Salem, N.C.—d. April 23, 1995, New York, N.Y.), reached the pinnacle of his career as the audacious commentator on television's "Monday Night Football" (1970–83) and was simultaneously crowned the nation's most loved and most hated sports broadcaster. Cosell's foray into broadcasting in 1956 followed a legal career representing sports and entertainment figures. Before he moved to television with his twangy Brooklyn monotone, he became the host of a radio show that featured Little League players questioning major league baseball stars. His determination to "tell it like it is" often created controversy or criticism, but he reveled in the attention his trenchant observations drew. Cosell, who sported a trademark toupee and, by his own admission, had been variously described as "arrogant, pompous, obnoxious, vain, cruel, verbose, and a show-off," willingly embraced those characterizations as a form of homage. He was remembered as the first to defend Muhammad Ali when the boxer was stripped of his heavyweight title after refusing to be drafted into the army because of religious reasons, and he voiced his approval of the black-power salutes made by sprinters John Carlos and Tommie Smith at the 1968 summer Olympic Games. In 1982 he refused to cover boxing matches after viewing a particularly brutal bout between Larry Holmes and Tex Cobb, and the following year he left his chair at "Monday Night Football," complaining that pro football had become "a stagnant bore." After the publication of his 1985 book, *I Never Played the Game,* which featured uncomplimentary portraits of his former colleagues at ABC, the network dropped his "Sportsbeat" program, ending his presence on television. He returned to radio until he retired from broadcasting in 1992, six months after surgery to remove a cancerous chest tumour. Cosell was posthumously awarded a Sports Emmy for lifetime achievement.

Costello, John Edward, Scottish-born World War II historian and author who gained access to the U.S. national and Soviet KGB archives and subsequently wrote several controversial books on the international espionage community (b. May 3, 1943—d. Aug. 26, 1995).

Curtis, Jean-Louis (LOUIS LAFFITTE), French novelist, translator, and member of the French Academy who won the Prix Goncourt in 1947 for his novel *Les Forêts de la nuit* (b. May 22, 1917—d. Nov. 11, 1995).

Davie, Donald Alfred, British poet and critic (b. July 17, 1922, Barnsley, Yorkshire, England—d. Sept. 18, 1995, Exeter, Devon, England), was one of the most prolific and influential poet-critics of his generation and was considered a major force in the so-called Movement, champions of anti-romantic British poetry in the 1950s. He espoused the view that poetic form and precise use of language were directly related to personal morality. Davie began studies at St. Catharine's College, Cambridge, in 1940 but interrupted them after a year for service in the Royal Navy in World War II, which took him to the Soviet Union. While there he taught himself Russian and developed what would become a lifelong interest in Russian literature; he later translated works of Boris Pasternak and wrote on Slavic literature. After the war Davie returned to Cambridge, earning a B.A. (1947), an M.A. (1949), and a Ph.D. (1951). He was a lecturer at Trinity College, Dublin (1950–57), and at Cambridge (1958–64) and then helped set up the University of Essex. He taught there until, disgusted by the student revolts of the late 1960s, he moved (1968) to the U.S. and took a position at Stanford University. After 10 years there he taught (1978–88) at Vanderbilt University, Nashville, Tenn., before retiring and returning to England. Davie's best-known books include *Purity of Diction in English Verse* (1952), *Articulate Energy* (1955), *Ezra Pound: Poet as Sculptor* (1964), *The Poet in the Imaginary Museum* (1977), *Under Briggflats* (1989), and *Slavic Excursions* (1990). He considered himself foremost a poet, however, and produced a large number of collections, among them *Brides of Reason* (1955), *A Winter Talent* (1957), *Essex Poems, 1963–67* (1969), *In the Stopping Train & Other Poems* (1977), and *To Scorch or Freeze* (1988). *The Psalms in English* would be published in 1996.

Davies, (William) Robertson, Canadian writer (b. Aug. 28, 1913, Thamesville, Ont.—d. Dec. 2, 1995, Orangeville, Ont.), was considered one of the finest and most important literary figures of his generation. Though his works comprised plays, essays, and criticism in addition to fiction, he was thought of primarily as a storyteller whose plots, dealing with moral conflict and self-discovery, were influenced by his interest in Jungian psychology. Davies earned (1938) a bachelor's degree from Balliol College, Oxford, and then spent two years in London as a teacher, actor, and director at the Old Vic before returning to Canada to work for his father's newspaper business. He was literary editor (1940–42) of *Saturday Night* and then served for some 20 years as editor and publisher of the *Peterborough* (Ont.) *Examiner.* For the *Examiner* he was ghostwriter for a column supposedly contributed by a humorous curmudgeon named Samuel Marchbanks, and he wrote many of his plays during this period. Davies became professor of English at the University of Toronto's Trinity College in 1960 and in 1963 was appointed master of its new Massey College. He was given emeritus status when he retired in 1981. Of all his works, which were translated into 17 languages, Davies was best known for his three trilogies. The Salterton trilogy, a comedy of small-town social manners, includes Davies' first novel, *Tempest-Tost* (1951), *Leaven of Malice* (1954), which won the Stephen Leacock Medal for Humour, and *A Mixture of Frailties* (1958). The first volume of the Deptford trilogy, *Fifth Business* (1970), brought Davies international acclaim. It and the trilogy's two other novels, *The Manticore* (1972) and *World of Wonders* (1975), dealt with the effects of a tragic event on the lives of three men. The Cornish trilogy—*The Rebel Angels* (1981), *What's Bred in the Bone* (1985), which was short-listed for the Booker Prize, and *The Lyre of Orpheus* (1988)—further cemented his reputation. His last book, *The Cunning Man,* was published in 1994. Davies, the recipient of many awards and honorary degrees, was a member of the American Academy and Institute of Arts and Letters, the first Canadian to be so honoured.

Davis, William Strethen ("WILD BILL"), U.S. jazz organist and arranger who popularized the Hammond organ as a jazz instrument (b. Nov. 24, 1918—d. Aug. 22, 1995).

Day, Leon, U.S. baseball player (b. Oct. 30, 1916, Alexandria, Va.—d. March 13, 1995, Baltimore, Md.), was a phenomenal right-handed pitcher whose fastball and change-up pitches secured his place as a strikeout artist; he held the strikeout record in the Negro National League, the Puerto Rican League, and the East-West All-Star game. Besides specializing in delivering no-windup speedballs, Day was a lightning-quick base runner, exceptional fielder, exemplary hitter, and capable bunter. The versatile athlete played every position (with the exception of catcher) during his tenures with such Negro leagues teams as the Baltimore Black Sox (1934), Brooklyn Eagles (1935), Newark Eagles (1936–39, 1941–43, 1946), and Baltimore Elite Giants (1949–50). In 1937 he finished the season with a perfect 13–0 record, and even after his career was interrupted by military service (1944–46), he returned to the mound on opening day to hurl a no-hitter. Day, who emerged victorious in three of four matchups with the legendary pitcher Satchel Paige, was elected to the Baseball Hall of Fame about a week before his death.

de Vaucouleurs, Gerard Henri, French-born U.S. astronomer whose pioneering studies of distant galaxies contributed to knowledge of the age and large-scale structure of the universe (b. April 25, 1918—d. Oct. 7, 1995).

Deane, Edna (EDNA MORTON SEWELL), British and world champion ballroom dancer, choreographer, author, and cofounder of the Deane School of Dance and Drama (b. Oct. 15, 1905—d. Nov. 22, 1995).

Delany, Annie Elizabeth ("BESSIE"), noted U.S. centenarian and co-writer with her older sister, Sadie, of *Having Our Say* (1993), which became the basis of a Broadway play and chronicled the changes the African-American sisters faced during over a century of living (b. Sept. 3, 1891—d. Sept. 25, 1995).

Deleuze, Gilles, French antirationalist philosopher best known for his 1972 book *Anti-Oedipus,* co-written with the radical psychiatrist Félix Guattari (b. Jan. 18, 1925—d. Nov. 4, 1995).

Denner, Charles, Polish-born French motion-picture actor who was best known for his role as the lascivious title character in François Truffaut's 1977 film *The Man Who Loved Women* (b. May 28, 1926—d. Sept. 10, 1995).

Desai, Morarji Ranchhodji, Indian politician (b. Feb. 29, 1896, Bhadeli, Gujarat, India—d. April 10, 1995, Bombay, India), as prime minister of India (1977–79), was the austere and uncompromising leader of that nation's first non-Congress Party government. Desai was educated at the University of Bombay and joined the civil service in Bombay state in 1918. A staunch nationalist and follower of Mohandas K. Gandhi, Desai was imprisoned several times during the 1930s and '40s. During and after India's move toward independence (1947) from the U.K., Desai served in the Bombay Provincial Cabinet as home and revenue minister (1946–52) and chief minister (1952–56). He joined the central government in 1956, and in 1967 he was named deputy prime minister and finance minister under Prime Minister Indira Gandhi. Two years later he resigned to lead the opposition. He was arrested when Gandhi declared a state of emergency in 1975, and when the Congress Party lost the 1977 general election to a coalition headed by the Janata Party, Desai was named prime minister. Within two years factional fighting inside Janata had brought down the government. Desai resigned from office on July 15, 1979. His published works include the three-volume *The Story of My Life* (1974–79).

POPPERFOTO/ARCHIVE PHOTOS

Morarji Desai

Desir, Wilson, Haitian freedom fighter and exiled consul general, 1991–95, who maintained an office in New York City to deal with the social and financial problems of thousands of Haitian refugees (b. 1938?—d. Sept. 13, 1995).

Dickson, Dorothy Schofield, U.S.-born British actress and dancer who was a phenomenal success on the London stage in a series of long-running musical comedies in the 1920s and '30s (b. July 25, 1893—d. Sept. 25, 1995).

Dietz, Robert Sinclair, U.S. geophysicist and oceanographer (b. Sept. 14, 1914, Westfield, N.J.—d. May 19, 1995, Tempe, Ariz.), plumbed the ocean depths and set forth (1961) a theory of seafloor spreading, the process in which new crustal material continually upwells from the Earth's depths along the mid-ocean ridges and spreads outward at a rate of several centimetres per year. He later helped incorporate that theory into the broader, revolutionary concept of plate tectonics, which describes the Earth's surface as a mosaic of more than a dozen crustal plates in relative motion. Dietz also was noted for demonstrating that asteroidal and meteoritic impacts have been important geologic processes acting on the Earth and Moon for billions of years. He conceived and organized the manned deep-diving expedition to the Pacific Ocean's Challenger Deep in the bathyscaphe *Trieste,* the descent of which on Jan. 23, 1960, set a submarine depth record of 10,912 m (35,800 ft). Dietz was educated at the University of Illinois (B.S., 1937; M.S., 1939; Ph.D., 1941). During World War II he rose to the rank of lieutenant colonel in the U.S. Army Air Corps, and following the war he served (1946–54 and 1959–63) as a civilian scientist with the U.S. Navy. In this capacity he oversaw the oceanographic research on Adm. Richard E. Byrd's last Antarctic expedition (1946–47). Dietz was also associated with such organizations as the U.S. Coast and Geodetic Survey (1958–65) and the Atlantic Oceanography and Meteorology Laboratories (1970–77). From 1977 until his retirement in 1985, he served as professor of geology at Arizona State University.

Djilas, Milovan, Yugoslav politician and writer (b. June 12, 1911, Podbisce, Montenegro—d. April 20, 1995, Belgrade, Yugos.), was a communist revolutionary and top aide to Josip Broz Tito in the 1930s and '40s; he later repudiated Karl Marx, denounced Joseph Stalin and other communist leaders as self-serving hypocrites, and became one of Eastern Europe's leading dissidents. Djilas joined the Communist Party while studying law at the University of Belgrade and was imprisoned (1933–35) for antimonarchist activities. By 1938 he was a close colleague of Tito (then the Communist Party's secretary-general) and a full member of the Politburo. Djilas fought with the Partisans during World War II, joined Tito's postwar government as a Cabinet minister and chief of propaganda, and was sent to Moscow to meet with Stalin when Yugoslavia broke from the Soviet orbit in 1948. In 1954, however, Djilas, increasingly disillusioned with communism in general and with Tito's regime in particular, resigned from the government and the party. He was imprisoned in 1956 for openly supporting the Hungarian uprising and was released in 1961, despite the furor over his book *The New Class* (1957), which was published in the U.S. from a smuggled manuscript. Imprisoned again after the appearance of the scathing *Conversations with Stalin* (1962), he was released in a general pardon (1966). Djilas renounced communism entirely in *The Unperfect Society* (1969). He later opposed both the breakup of Yugoslavia and the nationalist warfare that followed. Djilas also published biographies, fiction, poetry, essays, four volumes of autobiography, and translations of John Milton and Maksim Gorky.

Douglas-Home, Sir Alec, *see* Home of the Hirsel, Alexander Frederick Douglas-Home, Baron, of Coldstream.

Duke, Angier Biddle, U.S. heir to the American Tobacco Co. fortune, diplomat, and chief of protocol to Presidents John F. Kennedy and Lyndon B. Johnson (b. Nov. 30, 1915—d. April 29, 1995).

Durrell, Gerald Malcolm, British naturalist (b. Jan. 7, 1925, Jamshedpur, India—d. Jan. 30, 1995, St. Helier, Jersey), gained international stature among conservationists for his pioneering yet sometimes controversial role in preserving and breeding endangered species by housing them in zoos with the intention of eventually returning them to the wild. He was also a prolific author, producing more than 35 amusing and informative books about the animal kingdom and his adventures in pursuit of threatened species. Durrell's love of animals began when he was a boy living on the Greek island of Corfu. After his family returned to Britain, he became an assistant at the Whipsnade Zoological Park in Bedfordshire and was encouraged by his brother, novelist Lawrence, to write about his passion for nature. Durrell's first book, *The Overloaded Ark* (1953), was a best-seller and was followed by such popular successes as *Three Singles to Adventure* (1954), *My Family and Other Animals* (1956), *A Zoo in My Luggage* (1960), and *Birds, Beasts, and Relatives* (1969), the sales of which helped support his expeditions and conservation efforts. An inheritance and loan financed the founding on Jersey, one of the Channel Islands, of the Jersey Zoological Park in 1959 and the Jersey Wildlife Preservation Trust in 1963. Besides writing about his extensive travels to such locales as Argentina, Paraguay, Sierra Leone, Mexico, Australia, Mauritius, and Madagascar (where he captured a thought-to-be-extinct lemur, the aye-aye), Durrell produced a series of television programs, among them "Two in the Bush" (1962), "The Amateur Naturalist" (1983), and "Ourselves and Other Animals" (1987). In 1976 he erected, adjacent to the Jersey zoo, the International Training Centre, an educational facility that trained more than 700 scientists and field-workers from 80 countries. In 1983 Durrell was made an Officer of the Order of the British Empire in recognition of his wildlife conservation work.

Eazy-E (ERIC WRIGHT), U.S. gangsta rapper and founding member of the influential group N.W.A (b. Sept. 7, 1963—d. March 26, 1995).

Eckert, J(ohn) Presper, Jr., U.S. engineer (b. April 9, 1919, Philadelphia, Pa.—d. June 3, 1995, Bryn Mawr, Pa.), was widely recognized with John W. Mauchly as the inventor of the first general-purpose electronic digital computer, the Electronic Numerical Integrator and Computer (ENIAC). In 1973 a patent lawsuit resulted in John V. Atanasoff's (*q.v.*) being legally recognized as the developer of the first electronic computer when a judge revoked Sperry Rand's patent on the ENIAC. Historians, however, continued to regard Eckert and Mauchly as the founding fathers of the computer because of the complexity and programmability inherent in ENIAC's design as opposed to Atanasoff's limited-function Atanasoff-Berry Computer (ABC). On the basis of correspondence and meetings between Mauchly and Atanasoff about the ABC, the judge ruled that key components of the ABC, which was designed in the late 1930s, had been incorporated into the ENIAC. Eckert was educated (B.S., 1941; M.S., 1943) at the Moore School of Electrical Engineering at the University of Pennsylvania. It was there in 1943 that he began work on an electronic digital computer for the U.S. government. The massive ENIAC, which weighed 30 tons and filled an entire room, used some 18,000 vacuum tubes, 70,000 resistors, and 10,000 capacitors. The machine could be programmed to perform different kinds of calculations at high speed and in December 1945 solved its first problem—calculations for the hydrogen bomb. After its official unveiling on Feb. 14, 1946, the ENIAC was used to prepare artillery-shell trajectory tables and perform other military and scientific calculations. Eckert and Mauchly founded their own company in 1946, and the two ushered in the modern age of computers with the introduction of the Binary Automatic Computer (BINAC), which stored information on magnetic tape rather than punched cards, and the Universal Automatic Computer (UNIVAC I), which was built for the U.S. Census Bureau and found widespread applications in commerce. Eckert, who received 87 patents, remained in executive positions as the Eckert-Mauchly Computer Corp. was acquired (1950) by Remington Rand and that firm, in turn, merged (1955) to form the Sperry Rand Corp. and later merged again to form Unisys Corp. Eckert retired from Unisys in 1989.

Eddington, Paul, British character actor who excelled at light comedy, notably in the BBC television series "The Good Life," 1975–79, "Yes, Minister," 1980–85, and "Yes, Prime Minister," 1986–90 (b. June 18, 1927—d. Nov. 4, 1995).

Eisenstaedt, Alfred, German-born U.S. photojournalist (b. Dec. 6, 1898, Dirschau, West Prussia [now Tczew, Poland]—d. Aug. 23, 1995, Oak Bluffs, Mass.), was best known for his work with *Life* magazine during a career that spanned some 70 years and lasted until shortly before his death. As a member of the staff from its beginning, he contributed about 2,500 stories and nearly 90 covers to that publication. Eisenstaedt's interest in taking pictures was sparked by the gift of a camera when he was 14. After service in the German army in World War I, he took up photography as a hobby but turned professional after he sold a photograph for publication. Eisenstaedt's acquisition of a Leica 35-mm camera freed him from the limitations that previous cameras, with their cumbersome glass plates and metal holders, had imposed, and he was able to take more easily the candid shots that were his specialty. A 1933 picture of Nazi propaganda minister Joseph Goebbels glaring directly at the camera remained one of his best-known images. Eisenstaedt achieved international recognition in 1935 with his shot of the bare, cracked feet of an Ethiopian soldier fighting against the fascists. Later that year he left Nazi Germany for the U.S., and he began his career with *Life* the next year. Eisenstaedt photographed a great number of celebrities, but his most enduring images were those of more ordinary people: children joyously

PHOTOGRAPHS, ALFRED EISENSTAEDT—LIFE MAGAZINE/TIME INC.

Photographs by Alfred Eisenstaedt: (right) children following a drum major; (bottom left) Pennsylvania Station in New York City; (bottom right) Nazi official Joseph Goebbels

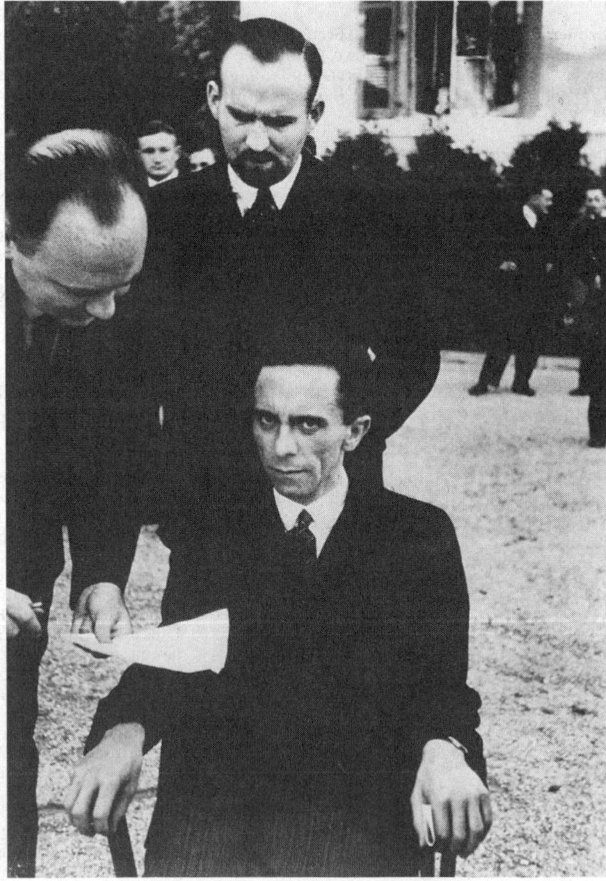

parading behind a drum major; a young audience enjoying a puppet theatre performance; and, his most famous—and *Life*'s most-reproduced—photograph, a U.S. sailor exuberantly kissing a nurse in the midst of V-J Day celebrations in New York City's Times Square. His books include *Witness to Our Time* (1966), *The Eye of Eisenstaedt* (1969), and *Eisenstaedt on Eisenstaedt* (1985).

Elkin, Stanley, U.S. novelist and educator (b. May 11, 1930, New York, N.Y.—d. May 31, 1995, St. Louis, Mo.) was praised for his comic wit and insightful, lyric prose, which was showcased in 17 novels and several works of short fiction, including an early and highly acclaimed collection of short stories, *Criers and Kibitzers, Kibitzers and Criers* (1966). He began writing in Chicago as a boy, completed (1961) a doctorate from the University of Illinois at Urbana-Champaign, and then began his lifelong work, teaching writing at Washington University, St. Louis. Elkin was perhaps best identified with one of his characters, Ben Flesh from *The Franchiser* (1976). Like Elkin, Flesh suffers from debilitating multiple sclerosis, which for him was both an enlightenment and a burden. As with many of Elkin's characters, Flesh is often preoccupied with illness and how it relates to the American industrial ideal. Central to all of his novels, including *The Dick Gibson Show* (1971), *The Living End* (1979), and *Magic Kingdom* (1985), were Elkin's darkly comic cultural portraits and an innovative style expressing his postmodernist belief that alienation was a phenomenon inherent in American mass culture. Elkin, who was thrice nominated for the National Book Award, was given the honour in 1982 for the novel *George Mills.* His final novel, *Mrs. Ted Bliss,* was published posthumously.

Ende, Michael Andreas Helmuth, German children's writer who was best known for his fantasy stories *Jim Button and Luke the Engine Driver, Momo,* and *The Neverending Story* (b. Nov. 12, 1929—d. Aug. 28, 1995).

Endfield, Cy Raker, U.S. blacklisted film director who took residence in Britain, after which he made such films as *Hell Drivers* and *Zulu* (b. Nov. 10, 1914—d. April 16, 1995).

Escobar Bethancourt, Rómulo, Panamanian politician (b. Sept. 5, 1927, Panama City, Panama—d. Sept. 28, 1995, Panama City), as chief negotiator for the 1977 Panama Canal Treaties, helped his country regain control of the Canal Zone and partial ownership of canal operations, with an agreement to assume full ownership from the United States by the year 2000. The U.S. had gained canal rights in November 1903, just two weeks after Panama was established as an independent republic. Escobar was an able diplomat and a pro-Panama polemicist, who, despite his leftist political orientation, served under a succession of right-wing military regimes. Trained as a criminal lawyer, he ascended the ranks of Communist Party leadership and, as a result, was jailed when Omar Torrijos orchestrated a military coup in 1968. Escobar soon became a valuable political adviser to Torrijos, however, notably in the mid-1970s, during the difficult canal negotiations with U.S. diplomats under Pres. Jimmy Carter. Escobar also served as rector of the University of Panama and one of the founders, in 1979, and president of the Democratic Revolutionary Party (PRD), the civilian arm of the military. He recounted the Torrijos regime in his book *Torrijos: ¡Colonia americana no!* (1981). With the rise to power of Manuel Noriega in 1983, Escobar remained in his post as chief political adviser and aggressively defended the dictator when the U.S. military forced his removal from power in 1989; Escobar was jailed after the U.S. invasion. When the PRD returned to power after the 1994 elections, Escobar became an adviser to the minister of foreign relations.

Everett, Kenny (MAURICE JAMES CHRISTOPHER COLE), British radio disc jockey and television comedian known for his zany and irreverent humour (b. Dec. 25, 1944—d. April 4, 1995).

Ewart, Gavin Buchanan, British poet of light verse, including limericks, clerihews, and poetic parodies (b. Feb. 4, 1916—d. Oct. 23, 1995).

Fangio, Juan Manuel, Argentine race-car driver (b. June 24, 1911, Balcarce, Arg.—d. July 17, 1995, Buenos Aires, Arg.), was an endurance specialist and precision technician who combined quick reflexes, strength, and tenacity to dominate automobile-racing competitions during the 1950s. He was a record five-time winner (1951, 1954, 1955, 1956, and 1957) of the world driving championship, a feat unequaled in modern times. His victories came during a period when drivers donned leather helmets and raced at dangerously high speeds without wearing seat belts. (At least 30 drivers died during Fangio's career.) After competing in South American long-distance races, Fangio joined (1948) the grand prix circuit and won world titles driving for Alfa Romeo, Mercedes-Benz, Ferrari, and Maserati. His most spectacular win was in 1957; Fangio trailed the leaders by almost a minute but challenged them late in the race and crossed the finish line 3.6 seconds ahead of them, precariously holding himself in the cockpit with his knees because the bolt that fastened his seat had broken. Although averse to taking risks, he had broken the lap record 10 times during that race. At the time of his retirement in 1958, he had won 24 of his 51 grand prix races and earned the admiration of his peers as well as the adulation of his countrymen. He settled in Argentina and became an executive for Mercedes-Benz.

Ferrell, Richard Benjamin ("RICK"), U.S. baseball player, 1929–47, and Hall of Fame catcher who covered home plate while his younger brother, Wes, ruled the pitcher's mound for the Boston Red Sox, 1934–37, and Washington Senators, 1937–38 (b. Oct. 12, 1905—d. July 27, 1995).

Finney, Walter Braden ("JACK"), U.S. writer (b. 1911, Milwaukee, Wis.—d. Nov. 14, 1995, Greenbrae, Calif.), was the author of 10 novels as well as short stories and plays, but his fame rested on 2 novels that were especially well known. *The Body Snatchers* (1955; republished as *Invasion of the Body Snatchers,* 1961), about humans being replicated by alien seed pods, was filmed three times, and *Time and Again* (1970), concerning an advertising artist who is recruited for a government project involving time travel, became a cult classic. Finney attended Knox College, Galesburg, Ill., and then worked in advertising in New York City. He began writing short stories, and many were published in such magazines as *Collier's, The Saturday Evening Post,* and *McCall's.* His first, "The Widow's Walk" (1946), won a special prize in an *Ellery Queen's Mystery Magazine* contest. Finney's first novel, *5 Against the House* (1954), as well as *Assault on a Queen* (1959) and *Good Neighbor Sam* (1963) were adapted for the cinema. Another notable book was *The Woodrow Wilson Dime* (1968), which created a parallel world in which much is familiar yet striking differences exist. In 1995 *From Time to Time,* Finney's long-awaited sequel to *Time and Again,* was published.

Fischer, Annie, Hungarian pianist who was particularly admired for her interpretations of Mozart, Beethoven, Schubert, and Schumann (b. July 5, 1914—d. April 10, 1995).

Fleetwood, Susan Maureen, British actress who was a mainstay of the British classical theatre for almost 30 years, particularly in dozens of acclaimed roles with the Royal Shakespeare Company and the National Theatre (b. Sept. 21, 1944—d. Sept. 29, 1995).

Flores, Lola (DOLORES FLORES RUIZ), Spanish flamenco performer and motion-picture actress (b. Jan. 21, 1923, Jerez de la Frontera, Spain—d. May 16, 1995, Madrid, Spain), embodied the excitement and beauty of the Andalusian Gypsy folk art for millions of fans in Spain and Latin America. Flores, who was one-quarter Gypsy, began dancing as a child in her father's local bar. The family moved to Madrid in 1940, and there, paired with the popular performer Manolo Caracol, she became a star. Flores acquired a variety of nicknames, including "Lola de España" ("Lola of Spain") and "La Faraona" ("the female pharaoh"), and was as famous for her succession of glamorous lovers and, later, for her marriage to a flamenco guitarist known as "El Pescailla" as for her talent. Her significant films include *Estrella de la Sierra Morena* (1952) and *El balcón de la luna* (1961). In 1994 Flores was awarded a gold medal from the Spanish government for her life's work.

Fordham, Michael Scott Montague, British analytical psychologist who applied Jungian analysis to the study of development in children (b. Aug. 4, 1905—d. April 14, 1995).

Fowler, William Alfred, U.S. nuclear astrophysicist (b. Aug. 9, 1911, Pittsburgh, Pa.—d. March 14, 1995, Pasadena, Calif.), formulated the widely accepted theory that almost all the chemical elements in the universe, including those that make up humans, were created in stars from primordial hydrogen and helium, and with Subrahmanyan Chandrasekhar (*q.v.*) won the 1983 Nobel Prize for Physics for contributing to the understanding of stellar evolution. Fowler, who earned (1936) a Ph.D. in physics from the California Institute of Technology, spent his entire professional career there, becoming professor emeritus in 1982. He and colleagues Fred Hoyle, Margaret Burbidge, and Geoffrey Burbidge used particle accelerators at the university's Kellogg Radiation Laboratory to demonstrate that nuclear processes in stars could manufacture virtually all the elements. Fowler and Hoyle set forth this theory in the seminal paper "Synthesis of the Elements in Stars" (1957), and the two collaborated on the 1965 book *Nucleosynthesis in Massive Stars and Supernovae.* Fowler described a process in stars called nucleosynthesis, in which heavier elements are made progressively from lighter ones, beginning with hydrogen and helium in the nuclear reactions that produce a star's light and heat. The heaviest elements are created during the death of more massive stars in explosions called supernovas, which then scatter the elements far into interstellar space. Fowler also helped design proximity fuses during World War II, conducted work with Hoyle in radio astronomy, and studied quasars, pulsars, and neutrinos. He was the recipient in 1974 of the U.S. National Medal of Science.

Franklin, Melvin (DAVID ENGLISH), U.S. bass singer with the Temptations (b. Oct. 12, 1942—d. Feb. 23, 1995).

Freleng, Isadore ("FRIZ"), U.S. animator (b. Aug. 21, 1906, Kansas City, Mo.—d. May 26, 1995, Los Angeles, Calif.), was a pioneering producer and director of more than 300 cartoons, most of them for Warner Brothers (later Warner Bros. Inc.), and gave life to such cartoon characters as Bugs Bunny, Daffy Duck, Sylvester, Tweety Pie, Porky Pig, and Yosemite Sam, a mustachioed, gun-slinging, raspy-voiced creation that he modeled after himself. Freleng, who joined the company as head animator in 1930 and drew the first Warner cartoon, *Sinkin' in the Bathtub,* won four Academy Awards during his more than 30-year tenure with the studio. After Warner closed its animation department in 1963, he created the Pink Panther and garnered his fifth Academy Award for *The Pink Phink* (1964), the premier cartoon of that series. He also helped form DePatie-Freleng Enterprises, which made animated television and theatrical shorts. During the 1980s Freleng directed television specials for Warner Bros. and helped produce compilation features.

Friedrichs, Hanns Joachim, German television journalist (b. 1926?—d. March 27, 1995).

Frondizi, Arturo, Argentine politician (b. Oct. 28, 1908, Paso de Los Libres, Corrientes, Arg.—d. April 18, 1995, Buenos Aires, Arg.), was a political firebrand who participated in hundreds of demonstrations against the dictatorial regime of

Juan Perón while a law student at the University of Buenos Aires. Yet he adopted a pragmatic approach in his presidential election campaign by calling for democratization while at the same time incorporating Peronists into the political process. This philosophy caused a split in Frondizi's Radical Civic Union, and in the 1958 elections he represented the leftist faction of that party, defeating the rightist candidate, Ricardo Balbín. As president, Frondizi implemented a series of austerity measures that placed a severe burden on the poor and middle class, resulting in strikes, demonstrations, and confrontations with police. Though his economic policies were harsh, they would eventually lead to rapid industrialization and economic resurgence. His political undoing occurred when he attempted to lift a ban on Peronist parties and candidates and secretly met with Ernesto ("Che") Guevara, an emissary of Cuban dictator Fidel Castro. The military withdrew its support, and Frondizi was forced to resign in March 1962. Frondizi, who continued to take a keen interest in economics, formed a small party, the Movement for Integration and Development, which promoted state protection for industrialization.

Frossard, André, French Roman Catholic journalist (b. Jan. 14, 1915—d. Feb. 2, 1995).

Fukuda, Takeo, Japanese statesman (b. Jan. 14, 1905, Gumma prefecture, Japan—d. July 5, 1995, Tokyo, Japan), was a pragmatic politician whose career during the 1970s was dominated by a battle with Kakuei Tanaka for the leadership of the Liberal-Democratic Party (LDP). After graduating (1929) from Tokyo University, Fukuda entered the Finance Ministry, where he remained until 1950, when he was indicted on charges of taking bribes from the Showa Denko K.K. Co. (He was cleared of the charge in 1958.) In 1952 he was elected a member of Japan's House of Representatives, and by the early 1960s he was a major figure within the LDP. After gaining the LDP leadership, Fukuda automatically became prime minister and served in that post from 1976 to 1978. During his tenure he issued (1977) the Fukuda Doctrine, which pledged that Japan would never again strive to become a military power and that the country would provide economic aid to Southeast Asian countries. In 1978 he helped formalize a treaty of peace and friendship with China. He was also at the centre of international trade disputes, especially with the U.S., that erupted because of Japan's annual trade surplus, which reached $12 billion while he was prime minister. Fukuda was forced to dissolve his Cabinet (1978) when some LDP members were implicated in the Lockheed bribery scandal. He then became a mentor to younger politicians.

Fulbright, James William, U.S. politician (b. April 9, 1905, Sumner, Mo.—d. Feb. 9, 1995, Washington, D.C.), was the congressional sponsor (1946) of the international foreign-exchange program that by 1995 had provided Fulbright educational scholarships to some 250,000 persons and served with distinction as a U.S. Democratic senator from Arkansas (1945–74) and influential chairman of the Foreign Relations Committee (1959–74). After graduating from the University of Arkansas, Fulbright attended Oxford as a Rhodes scholar, earning two degrees. In the U.S. he received a law degree from George Washington University, Washington, D.C., before teaching at the University of Arkansas, where he served as president (1939–41). In 1942 he was elected to the U.S. House of Representatives, and in the following year he introduced a resolution that led to U.S. approval of participation in what became the United Nations. In the Senate he cast (1954) the lone vote of dissent against financing Sen. Joseph R. McCarthy's anticommunist investigations and later that year helped compose the bill of particulars attached to the censure motion that effectively ended McCarthy's communist witch-hunt and his political career. A pragmatist with an eye toward reelection, Fulbright consistently voted against integration and civil rights bills. He made his most notable mark in foreign affairs, advising Pres. John F. Kennedy not to invade Cuba

James William Fulbright

GEORGE TAMES—THE NEW YORK TIMES

in 1961 and opposing Pres. Lyndon B. Johnson's 1965 intervention in the Dominican Republic. Though Fulbright voted in favour of the 1964 Gulf of Tonkin Resolution, which allowed Johnson to wage war in Vietnam with congressional approval, he later regretted the action. His opposition to the war was set forth in *The Arrogance of Power* (1967). His committee's televised hearings on U.S. policy toward Vietnam and China gave respectability to antiwar protests. When Fulbright was unseated in the 1974 primary election after his opponent maintained that new blood was needed in Washington, he joined a law firm and worked as a lobbyist. In 1993 Pres. Bill Clinton bestowed the Medal of Freedom on his mentor.

Gabor, Eva, U.S. actress (b. Feb. 11, 1921, Budapest, Hung.—d. July 4, 1995, Los Angeles, Calif.), was the youngest (behind Magda and Zsa Zsa) of the glamorous Gabor sisters and together with Zsa Zsa, to whom she bore a striking resemblance, had achieved worldwide celebrity status by the 1950s; the two often made headlines as a result of their many marriages (Eva married five times). Gabor was best remembered for her television portrayal of a New York City socialite who had to adapt to farm life on "Green Acres" (1965–71). Her striking features helped her land a Hollywood contract in 1939, but her career in show business did not ignite until she played an unemployed acrobat on Broadway in *The Happy Time* (1950). She appeared in such films as *The Wife of Monte Cristo* (1946), *The Last Time I Saw Paris* (1954), and *Gigi* (1958), and she was the voice of Miss Bianca in the two animated films *The Rescuers* and *The Rescuers Down Under.* The dazzling star also ran a multimillion-dollar wig company.

Gallagher, Rory, Irish blues-rock guitarist, singer, and composer (b. March 2, 1948—d. June 14, 1995).

Garcia, Jerome John ("JERRY"), U.S. musician (b. Aug. 1, 1942, San Francisco, Calif.—d. Aug. 9, 1995, Forest Knolls, Calif.), personified the hippie counterculture for three decades as the mellow leader of the rock band the Grateful Dead. Garcia was the singer, songwriter, and lead guitarist of the San Francisco-based group that emerged from the Haight-Ashbury psychedelic-drug-and-music scene in the mid-1960s. Known for his gentle, laid-back stage presence and soulful extended guitar improvisations, he became the portly patriarch of a devoted legion of nomadic fans called the Deadheads, who followed the band on tour in spirited makeshift communities. Garcia, whose father was a jazz musician, was raised amid a variety of musical influences, including folk, bluegrass, country, rock, and rhythm-and-blues. The band gained notoriety as the party band for Ken Kesey's Acid Tests, featuring revelers experimenting with the then-legal hallucinogen LSD, and fame for performing at such high-profile rock concerts as the Monterey (Calif.) Pop Festival in 1967 and Woodstock, N.Y., in 1969. Although the Grateful Dead regularly released albums, they made only one top-10 single. They became, however, one of the most successful touring bands in the nation, as much for the spectacle of their Deadhead entourage as for Garcia's marathon four-hour musical meanderings. Garcia and the band discovered newfound fame in the late 1980s, when baby-boomer nostalgia combined with a new generation of young fans to make the Grateful Dead more popular than ever before. Garcia was in ill health for the last decade of his life and had long struggled with heroin addiction. He died of a heart attack at a drug rehabilitation centre.

Gardner, Beatrix Tugendhut, Austrian-born U.S. psychologist who with her husband, R. Allan Gardner, taught a chimpanzee sign language (b. July 13, 1933—d. June 5, 1995).

Gellner, Ernest André, Czech-born British philosopher, social anthropologist, and director of the Centre for the Study of Nationalism at the Central European University in Prague (b. Dec. 9, 1925—d. Nov. 5, 1995).

Gernsheim, Helmut Erich Robert, German-born British photographer, collector, and photographic historian (b. March 1, 1913, Munich, Germany—d. July 20, 1995, Switzerland), was central to the evolution of the history of photography as an academic discipline in his roles as one of the art's first serious collectors and as coauthor, with his wife Alison, of the authoritative reference work *The History of Photography from the Earliest Use of the Camera Obscura in the Eleventh Century up to 1914* (1955), which was revised twice. Gernsheim studied art history and photography in Munich before finding employment (1937) as a commercial photographer in London. At the outbreak of World War II, he was interned in Australia as an enemy alien, but he was allowed to return to London in 1942 as a member of an official team chosen to photograph historic buildings that were at risk of destruction. After the war Gernsheim devoted much of his time to researching

ARCHIVE PHOTOS

Eva Gabor

and collecting the work of early photographers, which many had previously deemed unworthy of serious study. His collection, which eventually exceeded 33,000 images in addition to hundreds of books and pieces of antique photographic equipment, was purchased by the University of Texas at Austin in 1964. Gernsheim's other books include *Julia Margaret Cameron* (1948) and *Historic Events, 1839–1939* (1960; with Alison Gernsheim).

Giles, Carl Ronald, British cartoonist (b. Sept. 29, 1916, London, England—d. Aug. 27, 1995, Ipswich, Suffolk, England), for some 50 years created cartoons that made political or social statements by showing the impact of events on ordinary people. His cartoon family, especially the indomitable Grandma with her ever-present umbrella, became part of British folklore. After working as an office boy for a London film company, Giles became a cartoon animator and was a principal animator on Britain's first full-length animated colour cartoon with sound, *Fox Hunt* (1936). Giles continued producing animated films even after becoming a newspaper cartoonist, first for *Reynolds News* (1937–43) and from 1943 for the *Daily Express* and *Sunday Express.* Giles's work was treasured for its richness of detail in both characters and backgrounds and for its affection for human foibles. His cartoons were internationally syndicated and used in advertisements and reproduced on posters. Beginning in 1946 collections of his cartoons were issued annually. In 1993 London's National Museum of Cartoon Art presented a one-man exhibition of his work. Giles was made an Officer of the Order of the British Empire in 1959.

Gilmore, John E., U.S. jazz drummer and tenor saxophonist whose improvisations highlighted the Sun Ra trio (b. Sept. 28, 1931—d. Aug. 20, 1995).

Gingold, Josef, Russian-born U.S. violinist and teacher (b. Oct. 28, 1909—d. Jan. 11, 1995).

Glennan, T. Keith, U.S. government official (b. Sept. 8, 1905, Enderlin, N.D.—d. April 11, 1995, Mitchellville, Md.), as the first director (1958–61) of NASA, coordinated and incorporated the spaceflight efforts of the various laboratories working in the U.S. armed services and merged them into one agency. One of Glennan's first actions was to recruit controversial German rocket engineer Wernher von Braun, who was working on U.S. army missiles, to work on space projects. Glennan's vision was a cautionary one—he wanted to keep NASA small and did not want to compete with the U.S.S.R. in a race into space. A graduate of Yale University with a B.S. (1927) in electrical engineering, Glennan first used his technological training to convert the U.S. and British film industry to the emerging sound technology. During World War II he served as administrator of the U.S. Navy's underwater sound laboratory, New London, Conn., where he developed new methods of detecting submarines—later known as sonar. In 1947 Glennan became president of the Case Institute of Technology (now Case Western Reserve University), Cleveland, Ohio, and turned the facility into one of the nation's premier engineering schools. He temporarily left Case in 1950 to serve as a commissioner of the Atomic Energy Commission but left that post on Oct. 30, 1952, one day before the first hydrogen bomb was tested in the Pacific. After retiring from Case in 1966, Glennan became the U.S. representative to the International Atomic Energy Agency in Vienna.

Godunov, Alexander (ALEKSANDR BORISOVICH GODUNOV), Russian ballet dancer and actor (b. Nov. 25/28, 1949, Sakhalin Island, U.S.S.R.—d. May 18?, 1995, Los Angeles, Calif.), had a successful career with Moscow's Bolshoi Ballet before defecting to the U.S. during the company's 1979 engagement in New York City. The incident became even more dramatic when his wife attempted to return to the Soviet Union; U.S. authorities prevented the plane from departing for three days while they tried to determine whether she was being forced to leave. Godunov began his dance training in Riga, Latvia, at age nine. At 17 he joined Igor Moiseyev's Young Ballet, and three years later he joined the Bolshoi, becoming the company's youngest principal dancer. Maya Plisetskaya, one of the Bolshoi's most famous ballerinas, selected Godunov for the role of Karenin in *Anna Karenina* (1972), and he soon became her regular partner. His strength and flamboyance made him an audience favourite, and he won a gold medal at the 1973 Moscow International Ballet Competition. After his defection he joined American Ballet Theatre, but he left (1982) after a falling out with artistic director Mikhail Baryshnikov. Following a series of guest appearances with other companies, a tour with an ensemble he put together, and his own television show, "Godunov: The World to Dance In" (1983–84), Godunov embarked on an acting career. He made an impressive debut in *Witness* (1985) and had notable roles in *The Money Pit* (1986) and *Die Hard* (1988), but his film career then faltered, and his more recent efforts were largely ignored.

Goetz, Walter, German-born British illustrator and cartoonist whose amusing perspectives on the English and on Anglo-French relations delighted the public in the *Daily Express* cartoon strips "Colonel Up and Mr. Down" and "Dab and Flounder," 1934–54, and in Pierre Danino's "Major Thompson" books, 1954–57 (b. Nov. 24, 1911—d. Sept. 13, 1995).

Golombek, Harry, British international chess grandmaster, writer, and chess correspondent for *The Times,* 1945–85, and *The Observer,* 1955–79 (b. March 1, 1911—d. Jan. 7, 1995).

Gonzales, Richard Alonzo ("PANCHO"), U.S. tennis player (b. May 9, 1928, Los Angeles, Calif.—d. July 3, 1995, Las Vegas, Nev.), was a fiery-tempered tennis ace whose deadly right-handed power serves crushed opponents and made him one of the world's toughest competitors. During the late 1950s and early 1960s, he won the U.S. professional championship in men's singles eight times, seven consecutively (1953–59, 1961), and captured the U.S. men's doubles championship five times (1953, 1954, 1957, 1958, and 1969, with various partners). At the age of 12 Gonzales taught himself to play with a 50 cent racket and became so obsessed with the sport that he was frequently charged with truancy. Following military service, he was sponsored by the Southern California Tennis Association and began playing in big tournaments. After winning the U.S. singles title at Forest Hills, N.Y., in 1948 and 1949, Gonzales turned professional in 1949 and relinquished his chance to compete in amateur events. By the time professionals were allowed to play in those competitions (1968), Gonzales was 40 years old. Nonetheless, in 1969 he won the longest match in Wimbledon history—a 112-game marathon, lasting five hours over two days. The following year he beat Rod Laver, who had won the Grand Slam of tennis in 1969, in a $10,000 winner-take-all match. Gonzales then served (1969–89) as the tennis director at a hotel in Las Vegas.

Goodman, Linda, U.S. astrologer and best-selling author of the 1968 book *Sun Signs,* which sparked mass-market interest in the occult (b. April 19, 1925?—d. Oct. 21, 1995).

Gordone, Charles, U.S. playwright who became the first African-American to win the Pulitzer Prize with the Broadway production of his gritty barroom drama *No Place to Be Somebody,* based on his work at a bar in New York City's Greenwich Village (b. Oct. 12, 1925—d. Nov. 17, 1995).

Gould, Laurence McKinley, U.S. polar explorer who participated in a landmark expedition to Antarctica and served (1945–62) as president of Carleton College, Northfield, Minn. (b. Aug. 22, 1896—d. June 20, 1995).

Grant, James, U.S. international organization executive (b. May 12, 1922, Beijing, China—d. Jan. 28, 1995, Mount Kisco, N.Y.), was UNICEF's executive director for 15 years and was credited with making it the UN's most respected specialized agency. Grant earned a degree in economics from the University of California at Berkeley (1943) and a law degree from Harvard University (1951). After World War II he served in China with the UN Relief and Rehabilitation Administration, and after practicing law (1951–54) in Washington, D.C., he served in such agencies as the International Cooperation Administration (1958–62), the Agency for International Development (1967–69), and the Overseas Development Council (1969–79) before becoming head of UNICEF in 1980. That year he began to issue *The State of the World's Children,* an annual report that spotlighted the world's successes and failures in meeting its children's needs. Leading what he considered a child survival revolution, Grant campaigned tirelessly around the world to bring easy, low-cost solutions to children's health problems. He was never without a supply of oral rehydration salts, a simple mixture of baking soda, glucose, and salt used for treating diarrhea, a leading child killer. The UN estimated that he had helped save 25 million young lives. Grant also organized the World Summit for Children (1990), the largest gathering of world leaders that had ever met to discuss a single topic. More than 100 countries made a commitment to achieving the summit's goals by the year 2000. Grant was awarded the U.S. Presidential Medal of Freedom in 1994. Even after cancer forced him to retire from UNICEF only a week before his death, Grant continued his campaign for U.S. ratification of the 1989 Convention on the Rights of the Child, a legal guarantee of children's basic rights. At his memorial service, first lady Hillary Rodham Clinton announced that the U.S. would become the 178th country to sign it.

Pancho Gonzales
HULTON DEUTSCH

Graves, Nancy Stevenson, U.S. Postminimalist artist and sculptor of offbeat, abstract forms, especially camels (b. Dec. 23, 1940—d. Oct. 21, 1995).

Greco, Emilio, Italian sculptor (b. Oct. 11, 1913, Catania, Italy—d. April 5, 1995, Rome, Italy), created graceful bronze and marble figures and reliefs that reflected both the self-conscious elegance and the artificial, even distorted, poses common to 16th-century Italian Mannerism. Greco was born into a poor Sicilian family and was apprenticed to a funerary stonecutter. He studied at the Academy of Art in Palermo and began taking small commissions for extra money during his World War II military service. His first solo exhibition was held in Rome in 1946. Although Greco was best known for his sensuous female nudes, his major commissions include the semi-abstract monument to Pinocchio in Collodi, Italy (1953–56), a set of bronze doors for the cathedral at Orvieto (1961–64), and a monument to Pope John XXIII in Saint Peter's Basilica in Rome (1965–67). Greco's work was particularly popular in Japan, where a Greco Garden in Hakone was dedicated in 1974.

Grinkov, Sergey, Russian figure skater (b. Feb. 4, 1967, Moscow, U.S.S.R.—d. Nov. 20, 1995, Lake Placid, N.Y.), was a member of one of the greatest pairs in ice-skating history. Known to skating aficionados as simply G and G, he and his partner (and eventually his wife), Yekaterina Gordeyeva, won two Olympic gold medals and four world championships as amateurs and numerous competitions as professionals. Grinkov began as a singles skater when he was 9, but in 1982, when he was 15, Soviet skating authorities paired him with the tiny 11-year-old Gordeyeva. In 1984 the pair won the world junior championship, followed by their first world championship in 1986 and an Olympic gold medal two years

Sergey Grinkov, with his wife and daughter
G. DE KEERLE—SYGMA

later. They won three more world championships (1987, 1989, 1990) before turning professional in 1990. The difference in their sizes made the lifts and throws of pairs skating easy, and audiences came to expect one spectacular throw in particular, a quadruple twist. The two had an almost unmatched style, notable for its elegance, fluidity, precision, and purity of line, and Grinkov was the perfect partner, willing to use his strength to draw the focus to Gordeyeva. After G and G married in 1991 and became the parents of a daughter, Daria, in 1992, their skating took on a new emotional harmony. When Olympic rules were changed to allow professionals to apply for reinstatement as amateurs, G and G took advantage and skated in the 1994 Games, winning their second gold medal with a program that reflected their passion and maturity. Their last public performance was in Albany, N.Y., in November for the "Skates of Gold III" television special. As they were practicing their routine for Stars on Ice, Grinkov collapsed and died of a heart attack.

Gruber, Karl, Austrian politician and diplomat who served as foreign minister in the years immediately following World War II (b. May 3, 1909—d. Feb. 1, 1995).

Gucci, Maurizio, Italian business executive who oversaw the resurrection of the family fashion empire in the 1980s until he was forced off the board of directors in 1993 (b. Sept. 26, 1949—d. March 27, 1995).

Gucci, Paolo, Italian designer and businessman whose ongoing legal and personal disputes with various relatives contributed to the sale of the family-owned fashion company in 1993 (b. 1931—d. Oct. 10, 1995).

Gustafson, Ralph Barker, Canadian poet (b. Aug. 16, 1909, Lime Ridge, Que.—d. May 29, 1995, North Hatley, Que.), was renowned for his exquisitely crafted verse, which in its simplicity defines a Canadian sense of place while celebrating the country's geography and examining European influences that shaped the nation. Other recurring themes include travel and music, respectively in *Ixion's Wheel* (1969) and *Visions Fugitive,* an unpublished volume and his last work. Gustafson was educated at Bishop's University, Lennoxville, Que., and the University of Oxford. During the early 1930s he was a music instructor in Ontario and later a freelance writer in London. He settled in New York and worked for British Information Services (1942–46) but returned to Canada to teach (1963–79) at Bishop's University, where he remained until his retirement. His early poetry, including such volumes as *The Golden Chalice* (1935), *Lyrics Unromantic* (1942), and *Flight into Darkness* (1944), showed a progressive individuality of style. Later works such as *Rocky Mountain Poems* (1960), *Sift in an Hourglass* (1966), and *Selected Poems* (1972) were sometimes obscure but were considered among his best works. Gustafson was also a founding member in 1966 of the League of Canadian Poets, the editor of several poetry anthologies, and the author of short story collections, including *The Brazen Tower* (1974) and *The Vivid Air* (1980). In 1974 he won the Governor-General's Award for *Fire on Stone,* and in 1994 he published his latest book of poetry, *Tracks in the Snow,* which deals with the end of life.

Gutiérrez Mellado, Manuel Gutiérrez Mellado, MARQUÉS DE, Spanish lieutenant general and government official who, in his role as first prime minister for defense, 1976–81, resisted an attempted military coup in 1981 and reorganized the military in Spain to serve the civilian government of King Juan Carlos (b. April 30, 1912—d. Dec. 15, 1995).

Gwala, Harry, South African communist and a leader of the African National Congress who never accepted the more conciliatory approach taken by the ANC after Nelson Mandela's release from prison (b. July 30, 1920—d. June 20, 1995).

Haberler, Gottfried von, Austrian-born U.S. economist and educator (b. July 20, 1900, Purkersdorf, Austria—d. May 6, 1995, Washington, D.C.), was an expert on international trade and a staunch advocate of free-market principles. Haberler was educated (B.A., 1923; Ph.D., 1925) at the University of Vienna, where he adopted an "Austrian" school of thought that was identified with a generation of top economists who attended that university. Haberler sought to dispel the notion that governments and politicians should serve as guardians of economic life and set forth in his writings that methodological individualism—which examines all human conduct as a result of personal instincts, judgments, and decisions—was the proper approach to the study of government, its bureaucracy, and the political processes that influence economics. He studied in London and the U.S. before returning to the University of Vienna to teach (1928–36) economics and statistics. Haberler also served as consultant (1935–36) to the League of Nations and wrote the classic *Prosperity and Depression* (1937) for that organization. From 1936 to 1971 he taught at Harvard University, and from 1971 until his death he presided as resident scholar at the American Enterprise Institute, Washington, D.C., a think tank devoted to free-market approaches to public policy issues. Haberler was also noted for his reformulation of the theory of comparative costs in terms of opportunity cost, for helping to revive the influence of the purchasing power parity doctrine, and for such works as *The Theory of International Trade* (1937), *Money in the International Economy* (1965), and *Inflation and the Unions* (1972).

Hackett, Albert, U.S. screenwriter and playwright (b. Feb. 16, 1900, New York, N.Y.—d. March 16, 1995, New York), collaborated with his first wife, Frances Goodrich, on more than 30 screenplays, many of them comedies and musicals, before the couple won a Pulitzer Prize for drama for *The Diary of Anne Frank,* a moving adaptation of the best-selling book *Anne Frank: The Diary of a Young Girl.* Their play opened on Broadway in 1955 and became an overnight sensation, and their screenplay was used for the 1959 film. Soon after the two were married in 1931, they moved to Hollywood. They made their debut as screenwriters with *The Secret of Madame Blanche* (1933) and followed that with such hits as *The Thin Man* (1934) and two of its five sequels, *Lady in the Dark* (1944), *The Virginian* and *It's a Wonderful Life,* both in 1946, *Easter Parade* (1948), *In the Good Old Summertime* (1949), *Father of the Bride* (1950), *The Long, Long Trailer* (1954), and *Seven Brides for Seven Brothers* (1954). Their last offering was in 1962.

Hajek, Igor, Czech writer, translator, teacher, and foreign literary editor, 1964–69, of the radical Czechoslovak Writers' Union's *Literarni Noviny* (b. March 22, 1931—d. April 19, 1995).

Halas, John, British motion-picture animator and producer (b. April 16, 1912, Budapest, Hung.—d. Jan. 20/21, 1995, London, England), was, with his wife, Joy Batchelor (died 1991), the force behind the largest cartoon film studio in Great Britain and creator of some 2,000 animated films, notably *Animal Farm* (1954), the first British full-length colour feature cartoon. Halas was educated in Budapest and at the Academy of Fine Arts in Paris. After studying with the Hungarian-born director and special-effects expert George Pal, he moved to London (1936), where he met Batchelor, who was already a movie animator. They later married, and in 1940 they founded Halas and Batchelor Animation, Ltd. In later years the company experimented with holography, three-dimensional graphics, and computer animation, and they eventually produced the first fully digitalized cartoon, *Dilemma* (1982). Halas was president of the British Federation of Film Societies (1980–95) as well as president (1975–85) and honorary president (1985–95) of the International Animated Film Association. He also served as a UN adviser and wrote numerous books, including *The Technique of Film Animation* (1959), *Computer Animation* (1974), and *Graphics in Motion* (1981). Halas was made an Officer of the Order of the British Empire in 1972.

Hall, Emmett Matthew, Canadian lawyer and judge (b. Nov. 29, 1898, St-Colomban, Que.—d. Nov. 12, 1995, Saskatoon, Sask.), had a long legal career but had a larger impact outside the courtroom as an adviser to government leaders. He became known as the father of Canadian medicare after a commission he chaired at the request of his friend and former schoolmate John Diefenbaker, then Canada's prime minister, made radical recommendations in its 1964 report that led in 1968 to Canada's system of government-paid health insurance. A graduate of the University of Saskatchewan, Hall was called to the Saskatchewan bar in 1922. His first appearance before Canada's Supreme Court came in 1928, and he became a king's counsel in 1935, continuing to appear before the court. He became (1957) chief justice of the Court of Queen's Bench for Saskatchewan and (1961) chief justice of Saskatchewan before being appointed (1962) to the Supreme Court of Canada. He retired in 1973. Among the other reports Hall made for the government were those on the Ontario educational system (1968) and grain handling and transportation (1977). He also served as a mediator in several labour conflicts and even at the age of 90 helped settle a logging dispute. In addition, he continued speaking out on government issues. Hall was a Companion of the Order of Canada, and the University of Ontario awarded him the only honorary medical degree ever given in Canada.

Hanai, Masaya, Japanese businessman who as director (1959–78) and chairman (1978–82) of Toyota Motor Corp. turned the firm into one of the world's most competitive car producers (b. Aug. 1, 1912—d. June 10, 1995).

Hardy, Albert ("BERT"), British photojournalist who covered the world as chief photographer for *Picture Post* magazine, 1941–57 (b. May 19, 1913—d. July 3, 1995).

Hargreaves, Alison, British mountaineer who died in a blizzard while descending from an apparently successful assault on the Himalayan peak K2 only weeks after she had become the first woman to scale Mt. Everest alone and without bottled oxygen (b. Feb. 17, 1962—d. Aug. 13, 1995).

Harrington, Oliver Wendell, African-American cartoonist and illustrator who used humour and satire to criticize racism and other social problems in the U.S.; he immigrated to France in the late 1940s and settled in East Berlin in 1961 (b. Feb. 14, 1912—d. Nov. 2, 1995).

Harris, Maxwell Henley, Australian avant-garde poet, editor, and publisher (b. April 13, 1921—d. Jan. 13, 1995).

Harris, Phil, U.S. singer and bandleader who as a member, 1936–52, of Jack Benny's radio ensemble played the part of Benny's bourbon-swigging foil; he later starred with his wife, Alice Faye, on his own show from 1946 to 1954 (b. Jan. 16, 1904—d. Aug. 11, 1995).

Hatton, Ragnhild Marie Hanssen, Norwegian historian and author of important biographical studies of Kings Charles XII of Sweden, Louis XIV of France, and George I of England (b. Feb. 10, 1913—d. May 16, 1995).

Havard-Williams, Peter, Welsh librarian and international library management consultant whose more than 40-year career included influential posts at university libraries in England, New Zealand, Northern Ireland, Canada, and Botswana (b. July 11, 1922—d. Aug. 16, 1995).

Hemphill, Julius Arthur, U.S. saxophonist and composer (b. *c.* 1940, Fort Worth, Texas—d. April 2, 1995, New York, N.Y.), elicited a varied, reedy sound that was punctuated by rhythmic improvisations and produced compositions that drew on such musical forms as gospel and cool jazz but remained firmly rooted in blues. The accomplished alto saxophonist released two influential albums in 1972, *Dogon, A.D.* and *'Coon Bid'ness.* He also cofounded (1976), composed prolifically for, and performed until 1989 with the World Saxophone Quartet, which featured the precision instrumentation of David Murray, Hamiet Bluiett, and Oliver Lake. Other compositions include "The Orientation of Sweet Willie Rollbar," "Obituary: Cosmos for 3 Parts," and "Long Tongues: A Saxophone Opera." In 1991 he founded the Julius Hemphill Sextet, an ensemble that experimented with black musical forms and showcased Hemphill's provocative style.

Herriot, James (JAMES ALFRED WIGHT), Scottish-born veterinarian and writer (b. Oct. 3, 1916, Glasgow, Scotland—d. Feb. 23, 1995, Thirlby, near Thirsk, Yorkshire, England), beginning with the U.S. publication of *All Creatures Great and Small* (1972), charmed millions of fans around the world with humorous fictionalized reminiscences of his life as a rural veterinarian in the Yorkshire Dales, particularly in the years just before and after World War II. After training at Glasgow Veterinary College, "Alf" Wight joined the practice of Donald and Brian Sinclair, two brothers who treated mainly farm animals in and around the

James Herriot
PAUL CONKLIN—ARCHIVE PHOTOS

village of Thirsk (fictionalized as Darrowby). At the age of 50 Wight was goaded by his wife into writing down a collection of personal anecdotes with which he had long entertained his family and friends. *If Only They Could Talk* (1970), published under the pen name James Herriot, had some success, as did the follow-up, *It Shouldn't Happen to a Vet* (1972). In 1972 a U.S. publisher issued the two volumes as *All Creatures Great and Small.* This "omnibus" edition was an instant best-seller and brought fame and fortune to the quiet country vet, who maintained his practice until he retired in the late 1980's. The series continued with *All Things Bright and Beautiful* (1974), *All Things Wise and Wonderful* (1977), and *The Lord God Made Them All* (1981). Other books include *James Herriot's Yorkshire* (1979), *Every Living Thing* (1992), and several children's stories. Herriot's tales were adapted for two films and a long-running series broadcast on the BBC and on American television. He was made an Officer of the Order of the British Empire in 1979. Donald Sinclair, who was immortalized in Herriot's books as Siegfried Farnon, died on June 28.

Highsmith, (Mary) Patricia, U.S. writer (b. Jan. 19, 1921, Fort Worth, Texas—d. Feb. 4, 1995, Locarno, Switz.), crafted suspense-filled psychological thrillers that summoned a mounting feeling of apprehension, beginning with *Strangers on a Train* (1950; filmed 1951) and continuing with some 20 novels, 5 of them featuring the chilling psychopath Tom Ripley, an amoral gentleman murderer. In many of her works, seemingly harmless activities often foreshadowed violence. Highsmith's ingeniously written novels and her compelling short stories earned her a cult following in Europe, where she moved in 1963. She surrounded herself with cats and lived as a recluse in Italy, France, and finally Switzerland. Among her other books are *The Price of Salt* (1952; written under the pseudonym Claire Morgan), a tale of a love affair between a young girl and a married woman; *The Animal-Lover's Book of Beastly Murder* (1975), about the killing of humans by animals; and *Ripley Under Water* (1991), the last work featuring her popular central character.

Hobby, Oveta Culp, U.S. newspaper executive and public servant (b. Jan. 19, 1905, Killeen, Texas—d. Aug. 16, 1995, Houston, Texas), was the first U.S. secretary of health, education, and welfare and later, through family media holdings, became one of the country's wealthiest women. Culp served as parliamentarian of the Texas House of Representatives (1925–31) and as assistant to the city attorney of Houston (1930) before marrying William Pettus Hobby, the publisher of the *Houston Post,* in 1931 and going to work for that paper. By 1938 her organizational skills had earned her the position of executive vice president. In 1941 Hobby was asked to organize and head a women's division of the War Department's Bureau of Public Relations. The next year she was put in charge of the new Women's Auxiliary Army Corps, which was given full army status in 1943 and renamed the Women's Army Corps. Hobby remained in command, with the rank of colonel, until she left the army in 1945 and returned to Houston and her work at the *Post.* In 1953 she was appointed administrator of the Federal Security Agency, and later that year, with the agency's elevation to Cabinet status as the Department of Health, Education, and Welfare, Hobby became the second woman to hold a U.S. Cabinet post. She resigned in 1955 to look after her seriously ill husband in Houston, and she helped him run the business until his death in 1964. She became chairman of the board of the *Post* the next year, and in 1983 she sold the paper, which was subsequently resold and later closed. Other family media outlets were sold in 1992.

Home of the Hirsel, Alexander Frederick Douglas-Home, BARON, OF COLDSTREAM (SIR ALEC DOUGLAS-HOME), British politician and statesman (b. July 2, 1903, London, England—d. Oct. 9, 1995, Coldstream, Berwickshire, Scotland), as Sir Alec Douglas-Home, served as prime minister from Oct. 19, 1963, to Oct. 16, 1964. Lord Dunglass—the courtesy title he held before he succeeded his father as the 14th Earl of Home—was educated at Eton College and Christ Church, Oxford. He was defeated in his first political contest (1929) but was successful two years later and sat in the House of Commons as a Unionist (1931–45, 1950–51). While serving (1937–39) as parliamentary private secretary to Prime Minister Neville Chamberlain, he accompanied the prime minister to the meeting with Adolf Hitler in Munich, Germany, that resulted in Czechoslovakia's partition, and he supported the policy of appeasement, claiming that it gave Britain time to rearm. In Winston Churchill's "caretaker" government (May–July 1945), he served as undersecretary of state for foreign affairs. After becoming (1951) the Earl of Home, he entered the House of Lords. He was minister of state for Scotland (1951–55), secretary of state for Commonwealth relations (1955–60), deputy leader (1956–57) and leader (1957–60) of the House of Lords, lord president of the council (1957–60), and foreign secretary (1960–63) before becoming prime minister. Four days after his appointment, he legally relinquished his hereditary titles, retaining the knighthood he had received in 1962. Home held office for only one year before the Conservatives' narrow defeat in the 1964 election led to his resignation. He remained in the House of Commons, functioning as the opposition spokesman for foreign affairs, and from 1970 to 1974 he once again served as foreign secretary. In 1974 he was given a life peerage, and he retired from active politics. Home's books include his autobiography, *The Way the Wind Blows* (1976), *Border Reflections* (1979), and *Letters to a Grandson* (1983).

Hordern, Sir Michael Murray, British actor (b. Oct. 3, 1911, Berkhamsted, Hertfordshire, England—d. May 2, 1995, Oxford, England), as a stage, screen, and television actor for more than 60 years, used his distinctive voice, careworn features, and wry humour in a remarkable variety of character roles—ranging from Mr. Toad to King Lear. He was particularly adept at deadpan comedy, notably as the dithering philosopher George Moore in Tom Stoppard's play *Jumpers* (1972). Hordern worked as a salesman until a stint in amateur theatricals induced him to take up the profession in his 20s. He made his London stage debut in *Othello* in 1937 and his Broadway debut in 1959. Hordern's memorable stage appearances included the title roles in Shakespeare's *King John* and Anton Chekhov's *Ivanov,* but he also excelled in comedies by Harold Pinter, Alan Ayckborn, John Mortimer, Evelyn Waugh, George Bernard Shaw, and Sir Arthur Pinero, among others. He made his first motion picture in 1939 and later appeared in such films as *Passport to Pimlico* (1949), *A Funny Thing Happened on the Way to the Forum* (1966), and *The Missionary* (1982). His television work (mainly in the 1970s and '80s) included a reprise of *King Lear,* and he also provided the voice of Paddington Bear. Hordern was knighted in 1983.

Horgan, Paul, U.S. novelist, historian, and biographer who won two Pulitzer Prizes for works about the American Southwest (b. Aug. 1, 1903—d. March 8, 1995).

Houston, Lawrence Reid, U.S. lawyer and intelligence officer who served as CIA general counsel, 1947–73, and was known as one of the founding fathers of that agency (b. Jan. 4, 1913—d. Aug. 15, 1995).

Humphrey, Percy, U.S. jazz trumpeter and bandleader who became a fixture in New Orleans, La., performing both with bands he fronted and with the Preservation All Stars, with whom he played at Preservation Hall until early 1995 (b. Jan. 13, 1905—d. July 22, 1995).

Hunter, Howard William, U.S. religious leader and president, June 1994–March 1995, of the Church of Jesus Christ of Latter-day Saints (b. Nov. 14, 1907—d. March 3, 1995).

Hyman, Phyllis, U.S. jazz and rhythm-and-blues singer whose commanding stage presence and husky low alto defined a singing career that later embraced rap; she was best remembered for precise timing in interpreting love songs and for a starring role in the Broadway musical *Sophisticated Ladies* (b. July 6, 1950—d. June 30, 1995).

Ioann (IVAN MATVEYEVICH SNYCHEV), Russian Orthodox archbishop and metropolitan of St. Petersburg and Ladoga, 1990–95, whose extreme nationalist statements were criticized as xenophobic and anti-Semitic (b. Oct. 9, 1927—d. Nov. 2, 1995).

Ives, Burl Icle Ivanhoe, U.S. singer and actor (b. June 14, 1909, Hunt, Ill.—d. April 14, 1995, Anacortes, Wash.), was the portly, goateed entertainer whose mellifluous renditions of such folk ballads and popular songs as "The Blue Tail Fly," "Big Rock Candy Mountain," "Holly Jolly Christmas," and "Frosty the Snowman" endeared him to both children and adults and whose stage and screen performances brought him renown as a dramatic performer. Ives originated the role of the domineering Big Daddy in the 1955 Broadway play *Cat on a Hot Tin Roof,* and he reprised his powerful performance for the 1958 screen version. It was his role as a stubborn feuding landowner in *The Big Country,* however, that earned him an Academy Award for best supporting actor. Ives began performing in public at the age of four and learned hundreds of American ballads of Scottish, English, and Irish origin from his pipe-smoking grandmother. He attended Eastern Illinois State Teachers College for three years before abandoning his studies to hitchhike around the U.S., collecting songs from hobos and drifters and chronicling his adventures in the autobiographical *Wayfaring Stranger* (1948). In 1945, after having served in the military during World War II, he made his folk concert debut at Town Hall in New York City. He made his first film appearance in *Smoky* (1946). During the next 50 years Ives, who was hailed by poet Carl Sandburg as "the mightiest ballad singer of this or any other century," recorded more than 100 albums. He was remembered for his interpretations of such songs as "I Know an Old Lady (Who Swallowed a Fly)," "The Foggy, Foggy Dew," and "A Little Bitty Tear" and starred in such films as *East of Eden* (1955) and *Desire Under the Elms* (1958). He also appeared in 13 Broadway productions and numerous television shows. His last recording, *The Magic Balladeer,* was released in 1993.

Iyer, Raghavan Narasimhan, Indian-born political philosopher, Hindu scholar, and founder of the Institute of World Culture, Santa Barbara, Calif. (b. March 10, 1930—d. June 20, 1995).

Jeakins, Dorothy, U.S. Academy Award-winning costume designer whose striking creations for *Joan of Arc, Samson and Delilah,* and *Night of the Iguana* merited her three Oscars (b. Jan. 11, 1914—d. Nov. 21, 1995).

Jonassaint, Émile, Haitian politician (b. 1913, Port-de-Paix, Haiti—d. Oct. 24, 1995, Port-au-Prince, Haiti), served as president of Haiti for five months in 1994 as the puppet of the military regime that had overthrown the elected president, Jean-Bertrand Aristide, in 1991. He oversaw some of the regime's harshest human rights abuses. Jonassaint agreed to step down when a U.S. peace mission negotiated a compromise that averted an imminent invasion by U.S. forces. Instead, a peaceful occupation began the next morning, and Aristide was restored to office the next month. Jonassaint's career in politics began in the 1950s when he was a senator in Gen. Paul Magloire's dictatorship. During the years of the Duvalier family's rule, however, he withdrew from political life and practiced law and worked as a classics professor. Jonassaint was picked (1986) to be president of a constituent assembly organized to draft a new constitution after the ouster of Jean-Claude Duvalier. He served on the Supreme Court until Aristide ordered him to retire in 1991 because of his age, but he was placed back on the court later that year when the military took over. Jonassaint was a firm believer in voodoo, sprinkled his speeches with spiritual references, and often invoked the name of Agaou, a voodoo god.

Jouhaud, Gen. Edmond, Algerian-born French air force chief of staff who, with three other French generals, staged an abortive coup in Algiers, 1961–62, in an attempt to prevent Algerian independence; he was sentenced to death but eventually served only a five-year prison term (b. April 2, 1905—d. Sept. 4, 1995).

Kay, Ulysses Simpson, U.S. composer (b. Jan. 7, 1917, Tucson, Ariz.—d. May 20, 1995, Englewood, N.J.), produced hundreds of neoclassical works that were marked by vibrant harmonic and orchestral colouring, complex polyphony, melodic lyricism, and tonal orientation supplemented by chromaticism. He composed hundreds of choral, chamber, and film compositions, most notably *An Essay on Death* (1964), a tribute to John F. Kennedy. He dealt with the abolition of slavery in two of his five operas, *Jubilee* (1976) and *Frederick Douglass* (1991). Kay, a nephew of New Orleans jazz trumpeter Joe ("King") Oliver, played jazz saxophone before turning to piano, violin, and composition. He earned (1938) a B.A. at the University of Arizona and studied at the Eastman School of Music, the Berkshire Music Center, Yale University (with composer Paul Hindemith), and Columbia University, New York City. In 1968 he was named professor of music at Lehman College of the City University of New York, and he was made distinguished professor of music there in 1972. Among his more than 200 works were such orchestral pieces as *Symphony* (1967) and *Southern Harmony* (1975); cantatas, notably *Song of Jeremiah* (1945); organ and piano music; and two one-act operas, *The Boor* (1955) and *The Juggler of Our Lady* (1956).

Keene, Christopher, U.S. musician (b. Dec. 21, 1946, Berkeley, Calif.—d. Oct. 8, 1995, New York, N.Y.), was an influential conductor and arts administrator who harboured a special enthusiasm for contemporary opera. In his 26 years with the New York City Opera and especially as general director from 1989, he strove to extend its repertoire beyond the lavish, more traditional type of productions typical of the Metropolitan Opera. Keene began studying music as a child and organized neighbourhood opera and theatrical productions. At the University of California, Berkeley, he majored in history, claiming that he had already learned all about music. He spent much of his time and energy, however, directing and conducting operas—both student and semiprofessional—and he dropped out of school in 1967. He had made his public conducting debut with Benjamin Britten's *The Rape of Lucretia* in 1965 and was an assistant conductor at the San Francisco Opera in 1966 and the San Diego (Calif.) Opera in 1967. Keene made (1968) his European debut at the Festival of the Two Worlds in Spoleto, Italy, when Gian Carlo Menotti invited him to conduct *The Saint of Bleecker Street.* He later served as music director (1972–76) of that festival and director (1977–80) of the Spoleto Festival U.S.A., Charleston, S.C. Keene's association with the New York City Opera began when he became (1969) the first Julius Rudel fellow in the company's training program. His conducting debut there was in 1970, and his Metropolitan Opera bow was the following year. While continuing to conduct at the New York City Opera, he took the posts of music director of the Artpark Festival, Buffalo, N.Y. (1974–89), the Syracuse (N.Y.) Symphony (1975–84), and the Long Island (N.Y.) Philharmonic Orchestra (1979–90), which he founded. Keene was music director (1982–86) of the New York City Opera, and when Beverly Sills retired as general director (1989), he succeeded her. Keene also made numerous guest appearances—conducting many world premieres—and wrote and translated libretti.

Kennedy, Rose Elizabeth Fitzgerald, U.S. personality (b. July 22, 1890, Boston, Mass.—d. Jan. 22, 1995, Hyannis Port, Mass.), as the matriarch of the Kennedys, a family that created a political dynasty in the U.S., drew on her Roman Catholic faith to endure what she characterized as a life of agonies and ecstasies. The daughter of John Francis ("Honey Fitz") Fitzgerald, she was propelled into public life when her father embarked on a political career and became (1906) mayor of Boston. When she was 16, she began to accompany him to public functions, taking the place of

BERT AND RICHARD MORGAN—ARCHIVE PHOTOS

Rose Kennedy, with her husband

her shy mother. In 1914 Rose married Joseph P. Kennedy, a banker who became a multimillionaire by making shrewd investments. The Kennedy parents instilled in their nine children a competitive and ambitious spirit, which, together with the family fortune, helped propel three of four sons to high political offices. Tragedy stalked the family: their first son, Joseph P., Jr., was killed during World War II. In 1948 daughter Kathleen was killed in a plane crash. Their second eldest son, John F., served as president of the U.S. for almost three years before being assassinated in 1963. Another son, Robert F., served as U.S. attorney general and as a senator from New York before he too was assassinated during his 1968 presidential campaign. The youngest son, Edward, became a U.S. senator from Massachusetts but was touched by scandal in 1969 when he admitted leaving the scene of a car accident in which a female passenger drowned. It was Rose, however, who urged him to seek reelection, and she participated in his successful campaign. Her husband, who had suffered a debilitating stroke in 1961, died in 1969. Daughters Eunice, Patricia, and Jean largely remained out of the public eye. Another daughter, Rosemary, was institutionalized for retardation from early adulthood after undergoing a lobotomy. Her condition inspired her mother to become a benefactor for the mentally handicapped. When Kennedy died of pneumonia at age 104, her extended family included 28 grandchildren and 41 great-grandchildren, a number of whom were active in politics.

Khomeini, Hojatoleslam Seyed Ahmad, Iranian political leader who was a close aide of his father, Ayatollah Ruhollah Khomeini, and a member of Iran's Supreme National Security Council (b. March 15, 1946?—d. March 17, 1995).

Kingsley, Sidney (SIDNEY KIRSHNER), U.S. playwright (b. Oct. 18, 1906, New York, N.Y.—d. March 20, 1995, Oakland, N.J.), explored the social ills of the Depression era in exhaustively researched and realistic plays, notably the Pulitzer Prize-winning *Men in White* (1933; filmed 1934), which chronicled the lives of medical interns and proselytized in favour of legalizing abortion, and *Dead End* (1935; filmed 1937), an indictment against slums as a haven for crime. After earning a B.A. from Cornell University, Ithaca, N.Y., Kingsley embarked on a brief acting career while at the same time writing plays. Both *Men in White* and *Detective Story* (1949; filmed 1951), a compelling melodrama focusing on the way that the personal life of a detective influenced his professional judgment, became narrative models for future hospital and police dramas. Another play, *The Patriots* (1943), examined the ideologies of Thomas Jefferson and Alexander Hamilton and won the New York Drama Critics Circle plaque as best play. Some of Kingsley's later plays, including *Darkness at Noon* (1951; a dramatization of Arthur Koestler's novel) and *Night Life* (1962), were poorly received.

Kipkoech, Paul, Kenyan runner who captured the 10,000-m race at the 1987 world championships and was the first Kenyan gold medalist in a world track championship (b. Jan. 6, 1963—d. March 13, 1995).

Köhler, Georges J.F., German immunologist (b. April 17, 1946, Munich, Germany—d. March 1, 1995, Freiburg im Breisgau, Germany), shared the 1984 Nobel Prize for Physiology or Medicine for his contribution to the discovery (1975) of a method of producing unlimited amounts of extremely pure proteins known as monoclonal antibodies, each of which could be directed against a specific antigen. These antibodies—and the subsequent developments based on the work done by Köhler and his partner and colaureate, César Milstein—revolutionized the diagnosis and treatment of many immunologic diseases, including some forms of cancer and AIDS. In 1974 Köhler received his doctorate in biology from the University of Freiburg and joined Milstein at the Medical Research Council Laboratory of Molecular Biology, Cambridge, England. Within months they had made their antibody breakthrough. Köhler left to conduct research (1977–84) at the Basel (Switz.) Institute for Immunology, where colaureate Niels K. Jerne had first proposed his Nobel Prize-winning theories on antibodies and the human immune system. Köhler was appointed a director of the Max Planck Institute of Immunobiology in Freiburg in 1985.

Krasner, Louis, Ukrainian-born U.S. violinist and music teacher who was best remembered for having commissioned Alban Berg to write his 1934 *Violin Concerto* (b. June 21, 1903—d. May 4, 1995).

Kray, Ronald ("RONNIE"), British gangster who, with his twin brother, Reggie, ruled the East End of London from 1957 until 1969, when they were convicted of murder and imprisoned for life (b. Oct. 24, 1933—d. March 17, 1995).

Kronstam, Henning, Danish ballet dancer (b. June 29, 1934, Copenhagen, Den.—d. May 28, 1995, Copenhagen), during his performing career with the Royal Danish Ballet, was an outstanding interpreter of roles in a variety of choreographic styles. In some 130 roles he excelled in ballets ranging from the traditional works of the noted 19th-century Danish choreographer August Bournonville to such more modern ones as George Balanchine's *Apollo* and José Limón's *The Moor's Pavane.* Kronstam received his dance training at the Royal Danish Ballet School—being especially influenced by the Russian teacher Vera Volkova, who had begun teaching there in 1951—and joined the company in 1952. In 1955 he was chosen to create the role of Romeo in Frederick Ashton's *Romeo and Juliet,* the first non-Soviet choreography to the Prokofiev score. Another role that especially displayed his style and technique was James in *La Sylphide,* which also showcased his partnership with Kirsten Simone. Kronstam moved into character roles as he grew older, notably Lord Capulet in *Romeo and Juliet* and Peppo in *Napoli.* He also became a teacher at the company's school and later its director, and from 1978 to 1985 he served as the artistic director of the company. The Bournonville festival he organized (1979) to commemorate the 100th anniversary of the choreographer's death attracted an international audience. All of Bournonville's complete surviving ballets were presented. Kronstam was named a Knight of the Order of Dannebrog in 1964.

Krugman, Saul, U.S. award-winning pediatrician whose studies of hepatitis, rubella, and measles resulted in the development of vaccinations for these debilitating diseases (b. April 7, 1911—d. Oct. 26, 1995).

Kuhn, Margaret E. ("MAGGIE"), U.S. activist (b. Aug. 3, 1905, Buffalo, N.Y.—d. April 22, 1995, Philadelphia, Pa.), was the vivacious cofounder (1970) of the Gray Panthers, a group initially dedicated to championing causes of the elderly, including challenging age discrimination and lobbying for government health care coverage, but the organization soon embraced wider causes and helped raise opposition to the Vietnam War. After her retirement from a position with the Presbyterian Church in New York City became mandatory when she reached age 65, Kuhn used her energy and inspirational speeches to attract members to the Gray Panthers. She made no apologies for her age, wrinkles, and gray hair, reminding those her junior that "Everyone of us is growing old." The indomitable spokesperson for peace and social justice joined a picket line of transit workers just two weeks before her death. Kuhn published her autobiography, *No Stone Unturned,* in 1991.

Kunstler, William Moses, U.S. lawyer (b. July 7, 1919, New York, N.Y.—d. Sept. 4, 1995, New York), was a flamboyant radical who defended a number of controversial clients in high-profile cases. He gained national renown during the trial of the "Chicago Seven" on charges of having conspired to incite riots in Chicago during the 1968

William Kunstler

FRED R. CONRAD—THE NEW YORK TIMES

Democratic national convention. The disruptive antics of the defendants and Kunstler's spirited battles with the judge led to hundreds of contempt citations. Kunstler himself was sentenced to 4 years and 13 days, but most of the counts were dismissed on appeal, and he was not imprisoned. After graduating (1941) from Yale University, Kunstler saw World War II army service in the Pacific and was awarded a Bronze Star. He then attended Columbia University School of Law, New York City, graduating in 1948. His law practice was unremarkable until, in the mid-1950s, he represented a State Department employee whose travel to China as a freelance writer had resulted in the confiscation of his passport. Kunstler became involved with the American Civil Liberties Union and with such clients as the antisegregationist Freedom Riders in the South and the Rev. Martin Luther King, Jr., not only defending them in court but becoming active in their respective causes. Later cases that reflected his political leanings were those in which he represented black power activists Stokely Carmichael and Bobby Seale, antiwar activist Daniel Berrigan, and prisoners accused in the aftermath of the deadly 1971 riot at the Attica (N.Y.) state prison. Most controversial was his defense of such clients as alleged Mafia boss John Gotti and, in his most recent case, Sheikh Omar Abdel Rahman and other suspected terrorists linked to the bombing of New York City's World Trade Center in 1993. Kunstler's books include *Beyond a Reasonable Doubt?* (1961; editor) and *The Case for Courage* (1962).

Laborit, Henri Marie, French neurologist and discoverer of some of the earliest known tranquilizing drugs, including chlorpromazine (b. Nov. 21, 1914—d. May 18, 1995).

Lamont, Corliss, U.S. humanist philosopher, author, and socialist, who was the son of the chairman of the J.P. Morgan investment bank but devoted his life to fighting for radical causes (b. May 28, 1902—d. April 26, 1995).

Larwood, Harold, British cricketer (b. Nov. 14, 1904, Nuncargate, Nottinghamshire, England—d. July 22, 1995, Sydney, Australia), pummeled the Australian side with his fast, short-pitched bowling in the infamous "bodyline" tour of 1932–33. Larwood worked in the coal mines from age 14, but four years later he quit to join the ground staff at Trent Bridge, Nottingham. He made his debut for Nottinghamshire in 1925 and was selected to play for England against Australia in 1926. Although he was a physically small man,

Harold Larwood
HULTON DEUTSCH

Larwood was a fearsome bowler, with tremendous speed and accuracy. He distinguished himself in Tests against Australia (1926, 1928, and 1930), West Indies (1928), South Africa (1929), and New Zealand (1931). On the 1932–33 tour to Australia, the England captain, Douglas Jardine, ordered Larwood and Bill Voce to use bodyline, or fast-leg theory, bowling and aim their deliveries directly at the Australian batsmen in an effort to intimidate their opponents. The tactic worked; England took the series 4–1, and Larwood took 33 wickets at an average of 19 runs apiece. The casualties, however, included Larwood, who splintered a bone in his foot during the final Test. The bodyline strategy was widely denounced as unsportsmanlike, and Larwood, who refused to apologize, never played for England again. He remained with Nottinghamshire until 1938, when he retired with a 14-year career total of 1,427 first-class wickets (average 17.51), including 78 wickets (average 28.53) in 21 Tests. He was also a useful middle-order batsman, with 7,290 first-class runs and three centuries. Larwood immigrated to Australia in 1950. He was made a Member of the Order of the British Empire in 1993.

Lawson, Yank (John Rhea Lausen), U.S. jazz trumpeter (b. May 3, 1911—d. Feb. 18, 1995).

Lenihan, Brian Joseph, Irish politician (b. Nov. 17, 1930, Dundalk, County Louth, Ireland—d. Nov. 1, 1995, Dublin, Ireland), was a leading member of the Fianna Fail party for more than 30 years, notably while serving as Ireland's deputy prime minister (1987–90) and as foreign minister three times. Though Lenihan was expected to win the 1990 presidential election in keeping with the Fianna Fail party's historic domination of that contest, he narrowly lost to coalition candidate Mary Robinson, partly owing to alleged political wrongdoing in 1982. Lenihan grew up in Athlone and moved to Dublin to attend University College and study law at King's Inns. After practicing law for a short time, he was elected to the Seanad (Senate) in 1957 and to the Dail (House of Representatives) in 1961. Well regarded for his affable manner, he was seen as one of the rising stars of the Fianna Fail party, along with his ally Charles Haughey—later prime minister—whom he succeeded as minister of justice in 1964. In this position Lenihan softened the nation's strict censorship laws. He then held successive ministerial posts in education, transportation, foreign affairs, and fisheries before serving in Haughey's Cabinet as foreign minister (1979–81, 1987–89), minister of agriculture (1982), and minister of defense (1989–90). As foreign minister Lenihan attempted to stabilize relations with Britain and with Northern Ireland during a series of crises. In 1990 his party nominated him as its candidate for the presidency, and he was an early favourite despite poor health (he had received a liver transplant in 1989). Following his defeat, he remained active in foreign affairs and domestic politics, helping to form a coalition between the Fianna Fail and Labour parties in 1992. He also wrote book reviews and articles on Irish history.

Lever of Manchester, Harold Lever, Baron, British millionaire, Labour Party politician, and economic adviser to Labour Prime Ministers Harold Wilson and James Callaghan (b. Jan. 15, 1914—d. Aug. 6, 1995).

Lévinas, Emmanuel, Lithuanian-born French philosopher who combined the ideas of the German Phenomenologists Edmund Husserl and Martin Heidegger; after World War II he was admired as a scholar of Judaism, especially the Talmud (b. Dec. 30, 1905 [Jan. 12, 1906, Old Style]—d. Dec. 25, 1995).

Li Zhisui (Li Chih-sui), Chinese physician (b. 1919, Beijing, China—d. Feb. 13, 1995, Carol Stream, Ill.), was the personal physician and confidant of Chairman Mao Zedong and author of *The Private Life of Chairman Mao* (1994). Li received his medical degree from the West Union University Medical School in Sichuan province in 1945 and five years later was named director of the private medical facility that treated China's top leaders. Beginning in 1954, when Mao chose Li as his personal physician, the two men began to develop a close relationship that lasted until Mao's death in 1976. During those years, Li compiled a series of diaries. Following Mao's death, Li held several medical posts before joining his two sons in the U.S. in 1988. Li's biography of Mao honoured the memory of his late wife, who had urged her husband to share his knowledge with the rest of the world. Relying partly on memory (some 40 diaries were deliberately destroyed during the perilous Cultural Revolution), Li set forth a detailed account of the man he had served for 22 years. Li's unflattering portrait of Mao characterized him as ruthless, uncaring, treacherous, corrupt, intolerant of dissent, unwilling to acknowledge failures, indifferent to personal hygiene, addicted to barbiturates, and enamoured of young mistresses. The book, which was banned in China as slanderous but became a best-seller in English and several other languages, also provided important details, previously unknown, about many of Mao's colleagues and of pivotal events that occurred during Mao's rule.

Lincoln, Evelyn Norton, U.S. personal secretary to and confidante of Pres. John F. Kennedy (b. June 25, 1909—d. May 11, 1995).

Lindfors, Viveca (Elsa Viveca Torstensdotter Lindfors), Swedish-born actress who enjoyed successful stage and screen careers in both Sweden and the U.S. (b. Dec. 29, 1920—d. Oct. 25, 1995).

Listyev, Vladislav Nikolayevich, Russian journalist and television personality (b. 1956—d. March 1, 1995, Moscow, Russia), as an investigative journalist, a popular game-show host, and a tough network executive, was central to the emergence of a more independent, Westernized style of television during and after the breakup of the Soviet Union. Listyev studied journalism at the Moscow State University and began his career in radio. In 1987 he was chosen to be a presenter on "Vzglyad" ("View"), a lively new weekly television newsmagazine on which he took advantage of the era of glasnost ("openness") to cover many previously taboo political, economic, and social subjects. When the show was dropped in 1990, he became host of "Pole chudes" ("Field of Wonders"), a Russian version of the U.S. show "Wheel of Fortune." As the head of his own production company from 1992, he produced and served as host of the political interview program "Chas pik" ("Rush Hour"). In early 1995 he was named to head state-run Ostankino television and was responsible for overseeing its conversion to a partially privatized station, Russian Public Television (ORT). Listyev was assassinated outside his apartment in what was widely believed to be a contract killing by organized crime figures who objected to a proposed ban on lucrative commercial advertising on ORT.

Lowe, Edward, U.S. entrepreneur and marketer of the absorbent clay granules that he sold under the name Kitty Litter, an invention that made him a multimillionaire (b. 1920—d. Oct. 4, 1995).

Lupino, Ida, U.S. film and television actress, director, and screenwriter (b. Feb. 4, 1918?, London, England—d. Aug. 3, 1995, Burbank, Calif.), first gained fame through her portrayals of strong, worldly-wise characters and went on to become one of the first women film directors in Hollywood. Lupino was born into a theatrical dynasty of several generations' duration. As a child she acted in a model theatre built by her father, and she entered the Royal Academy of Dramatic Art at age 13. After her film debut in *Her First Affaire* (1932), she appeared in several inconsequential roles before being cast as a vengeful prostitute in *The Light That Failed* (1939). That led to meaty roles in such films as *They Drive by Night* (1940), *High Sierra* (1941), *The Sea Wolf* (1941), *Ladies in Retirement* (1941), and *The Hard Way* (1942), for which she won a New York Film Critics award. With her second husband, Collier Young (her first husband was actor Louis Hayward), Lupino founded (1949) a production company and began writing scripts, tackling such controversial topics as rape, unmarried mothers, and bigamy. When the director of *Not Wanted* (1949) had a heart attack three days after filming began, she took over. Her official directing debut came a year later with *The Young Lovers,* and she followed that with several other gritty features. Especially notable were the 1953 films *The Bigamist* and *The Hitch-Hiker.* Lupino was a star (1952–56) of the dramatic television anthology "Four Star Playhouse" and appeared with her third husband, Howard Duff, in the situation comedy "Mr. Adams and Eve" for three seasons in the late 1950s. She also directed episodes of numerous television series, among them "The Untouchables," "Have Gun, Will Travel," "The Fugitive," "The Twilight Zone," and "Alfred Hitchcock Presents." The most notable of her later motion-picture performances came in *Junior Bonner* (1972).

Lyttleton, Raymond Arthur, British mathematician and theoretical astronomer whose many books include *The Comets and Their Origin* (b. May 7, 1911—d. May 16, 1995).

McClure, Doug, U.S. actor (b. May 11, 1935, Glendale, Calif.—d. Feb. 5, 1995, Sherman Oaks, Calif.), was a onetime broncobuster whose engaging looks and winning smile earned him television stardom first as William Bendix's sidekick in the series "The Overland Trail" (1960) and then as Trampas, a happy-go-lucky cowpoke, on "The Virginian" (1962–70), TV's first 90-minute western series. He also starred with James Drury, the title character in "The Virginian," in a spin-off called "The Men from Shiloh" (1971). Earlier McClure appeared in the taut naval thriller *The Enemy Below* (1957) and in the western *The Unforgiven* (1960). Other film credits include *Shenandoah* (1965), *The Land That Time Forgot* (1975), and a walk-on in *Maverick* (1994). McClure succumbed to lung cancer less than two months after unveiling his star on the Hollywood Walk of Fame in December 1994.

McCluskie, Samuel Joseph, British trade unionist who wielded great power as general secretary of the National Union of Seamen, 1986–90; executive officer of the Rail, Maritime and Transport Union, 1990–91; a member of the Labour Party

National Executive Committee, 1974–95 (treasurer, 1984–92); and chairman of the Labour Party, 1983 (b. Aug. 11, 1932—d. Sept. 15, 1995).

McKinley, Raymond Frederick, U.S. Dixieland drummer, vocalist with the Glenn Miller Orchestra, and bandleader of the ensemble after Miller's death (b. June 8, 1910—d. May 7, 1995).

MacPherson, Stewart Myles, Canadian-born British broadcaster and commentator who became one of the best-known voices on British radio during World War II (b. Oct. 29, 1908—d. April 16, 1995).

McQueen, Thelma ("BUTTERFLY"), U.S. character actress who often portrayed maids and was forever identified with the film role of Prissy, the befuddled slave who confessed, "Miss Scarlett, I don't know nothin' 'bout birthin' babies!" in *Gone with the Wind* (b. Jan. 8, 1911—d. Dec. 22, 1995).

Maksimov, Vladimir Yemelyanovich (LEV ALEKSEYEVICH SAMSONOV), Russian writer (b. Dec. 10, 1930, Moscow, U.S.S.R.—d. March 26, 1995, Paris, France), was a dissident novelist and poet, editor of the Communist literary journal *Oktyabr* (1967–68), and a senior member of the Soviet Writers' Union. Lev Samsonov lived on the streets as a boy after his parents were sent to the labour camps; he was often jailed as a juvenile delinquent. Most of his early poetry and plays, written from 1952 under the name Maksimov, were well received. In 1968 he resigned from the editorial staff at *Oktyabr* in protest over the Soviet invasion of Czechoslovakia. Thereafter, his work became increasingly critical of the Soviet political system. Maksimov was eventually committed to psychiatric hospitals for his dissident activities. He was dismissed from the union in 1973, and the next year he was deprived of his citizenship while in Paris, where he settled and edited (1974–92) the influential émigré quarterly *Kontinent.* His novels *Sem dney tvoreniya* (1971; *The Seven Days of Creation,* 1975) and *Karantin* (1973; "Quarantine") were smuggled out of the country and published to acclaim in Germany. Later books include the novels *Kovcheg dlya nezvanykh* (1979; *Ark for the Uncalled,* 1984) and *Zaglyanut v bezdnu* (1986; "To Glance into the Abyss") and the two-volume autobiography *Proshchaniye iz niotkuda* (1974, 1982; *Farewell from Nowhere,* 1979). Maksimov's Soviet citizenship was restored in 1990, and the offices of *Kontinent* were moved to Moscow shortly thereafter.

Malle, Louis, French film director (b. Oct. 30, 1932, Thumeries, France—d. Nov. 23, 1995, Beverly Hills, Calif.), was internationally known for films that often explored difficult—and sometimes controversial—subjects in a cool, reflective, and nonjudgmental manner. His diverse themes included suicide (*Le Feu follet* [1963; *The Fire Within*]), incest (*Le Souffle au coeur* [1971; *Murmur of the Heart*]), collaboration (*Lacombe, Lucien* [1973]), and child prostitution (*Pretty Baby* [1978; his first U.S. film]). Malle, who was educated at the Jesuit College at Fontainebleau, the Sorbonne, and the Institute of Advanced Cinematographic Studies, Paris, went to work in 1953 for the oceanographer Jacques-Yves Cousteau. He served as codirector with Cousteau on the documentary *Le Monde du silence* (1956; *The Silent World*) and was largely responsible for the underwater photography. It won an Academy Award and the Palme d'Or at the Cannes Film Festival. He also worked as an assistant to the director Robert Bresson. Malle's first feature, *Ascenseur pour l'échafaud* (1957; *Frantic*), was followed by *Les Amants* (1958; *The Lovers*), which established his reputation in the film industry. After making a few more motion pictures, Malle went to India, where he took enough footage to produce the feature-length documentary *Calcutta* (1969) and seven films that were combined into the six-hour documentary *L'Inde fantôme* (1972; *Phantom India*). After his marriage (1980) to actress Candice Bergen, Malle divided his time between Los Angeles and Paris. His later credits include *Atlantic City* (1980) and *My Dinner with André* (1981), which featured an intellectual discussion between two men in a restaurant. His last motion picture was *Vanya on 42nd Street* (1994). The film Malle wanted most to be remembered for was *Au revoir les enfants* (1987; *Goodbye, Children*), an autobiographical story set at a Catholic school where Jewish children were concealed from the Nazis. It won the Grand Prize at the Venice Film Festival.

Mandel, Ernest, German Marxist economist, Trotskyist academician, and author of such works as *Late Capitalism* and *Power and Money* (b. April 5, 1923—d. July 20, 1995).

Mansholt, Sicco Leendert, Dutch politician (b. Sept. 13, 1908, Ulrum, near Groningen, Neth.—d. June 30, 1995, Wapserveen, Neth.), was the guiding force behind the Mansholt Plan, a proposed radical restructuring of Western European agriculture that became the basis for the Common Agricultural Policy of the European Economic Community (EEC) and its successor, the European Community (EC). Mansholt, who was born into a dairy-farming family, studied at the School for Tropical Agriculture in Deventer, Neth., and, after gaining experience in farming (1924–34), worked for three years on a tea plantation on Java in the Dutch East Indies (now Indonesia). After fighting with the Dutch resistance forces during World War II, he helped rebuild domestic food production as minister of agriculture, fisheries, and food (1945–58). In 1946 he represented The Netherlands at the UN and in the negotiations for the creation of the Benelux Economic Union with Belgium and Luxembourg. In 1953 he introduced the original guidelines for the Mansholt Plan, and he later served as vice president (1958–67) of the EEC Commission and as vice president (1967–72) and president (1972–73) of the EC Commission.

Mantle, Mickey, U.S. professional baseball player (b. Oct. 20, 1931, Spavinaw, Okla.—d. Aug. 13, 1995, Dallas, Texas), displayed tremendous power as a switch-hitting centre fielder for the New York

AP/WIDE WORLD PHOTOS

Mickey Mantle

Yankees (1951–68), slugging both right- and left-handed a career total of 536 home runs. Mantle was a cultural icon in the postwar U.S., leading the Yankees to 12 World Series and leading the American League repeatedly in home runs, runs scored, and runs batted in. Mantle was reared in Commerce, Okla.; his father, a zinc miner and semiprofessional baseball player, taught him how to bat from both sides of the plate at an early age. After two years in the minor leagues, he made his major league debut in 1951, eventually succeeding the great Joe DiMaggio as the Yankee centre-fielder. Mantle was noted for his strength, speed, and durability. During 18 seasons he batted 8,102 times in 2,401 games despite constant battles with knee injuries and the aftereffects of osteomyelitis, a bone disease contracted as a teenager—ailments that three times led to his exemption from military service. His rifle-shot home runs, among the longest in the game, inspired the adoption of a new recording method, the tape-measure home run, an estimate of the distance of the ball's flight. In 1956 he captured the coveted triple crown with a league-leading .352 batting average, 52 home runs, and 130 runs batted in. In 1961, when teammate Roger Maris broke Babe Ruth's season home-run record with 61 homers, Mantle hit a personal best of 54 before an abscessed hip brought his season to a premature end. (He did break Ruth's record for lifetime strikeouts, however, with 1,710.) After his last season in 1968, the Yankees retired his uniform number, 7, in 1969, and he was elected to the Baseball Hall of Fame in 1974. Diagnosed as having cirrhosis of the liver in 1994, he publicly acknowledged his longtime problem of alcoholism and sought treatment. His condition worsened the following year and, despite a high-profile and controversial liver transplant, he succumbed to cancer shortly thereafter.

Marcus, Jacob Rader, U.S. Jewish historian who published his findings in hundreds of books and articles and was both a teacher and a father figure to some 2,000 rabbinical students (b. March 5, 1896—d. Nov. 14, 1995).

Marin, Jean (YVES-ANDRÉ-MARIE MORVAN), French journalist, Free French radio commentator during World War II, and head of the international news agency Agence France-Presse, 1954–75 (b. Feb. 24, 1909—d. June 3, 1995).

Marshall, David Saul, Singaporean lawyer, politician, and diplomat (b. March 12, 1908, Singapore—d. Dec. 12, 1995, Singapore), was one of the founding fathers of the city-state of Singapore and, after the authoritarian People's Action Party (PAP) took over (1959), consistently and unequivocally spoke out against the government's repressive policies. Though he was quick to praise the economic progress achieved by the PAP, he condemned what he saw as the resultant loss of a sense of humanity. Marshall earned a law degree in Britain and was called to the bar in 1937. After service in the colonial army in World War II, during which he was captured (1942) by the Japanese and forced to work in the coal mines in Hokkaido, Japan, he became a successful criminal defense lawyer. He had the reputation of never losing, and his courtroom effectiveness was cited as a reason the PAP abolished the jury system. In the early 1950s during Singapore's struggle for independence, Marshall entered politics and cofounded the Labour Front. He was elected (1955) to the Legislative Assembly and, after forming a coalition government, became Singapore's first chief minister. Following the failure of two missions to London for independence talks, Marshall resigned (1956) his position. He remained active in politics until 1972 and practiced law until 1978. For the next 15 years, he served as ambassador to France (1978–93), Portugal (1981–93), Spain (1981–93), and Switzerland (1990–93). Upon his return to Singapore, Marshall resumed his law practice—and his outspoken criticism of the government. In 1994 he was one of the very few citizens publicly to oppose the caning of the U.S. teenager Michael Fay as punishment for vandalism.

Martin, Charles Elmer, U.S. artist whose cartoons and drawings appeared in the pages of such magazines as *The New Yorker, Time, Life, Punch,* and *Esquire* (b. Jan. 12, 1910—d. June 18, 1995).

Martin, Dean (DINO PAUL CROCETTI), U.S. singer-actor (b. June 17, 1917, Steubenville, Ohio—d. Dec. 25, 1995, Beverly Hills, Calif.), was a member for 10 years of one of the most popular comedy teams on stage and television and in motion pictures before moving on to a successful solo career as singer, actor, and television variety show host. In the Steubenville area Martin worked in steel mills, delivered bootleg liquor, and was a prizefighter and a casino croupier before becoming a pop crooner. After appearing in local nightspots, he was hired by bandleader Sammy Watkins and began to tour. During an engagement in Atlantic City, N.J., in 1946, he and another performer, comedian Jerry Lewis, began clowning around during each other's acts. This led to an immensely successful comedy partnership that featured Martin as a suave straight man and Lewis as an immature clown. Before long the two were making $5,000 a week at New York City's Copacabana. They made 16 motion pictures together, beginning with *My Friend Irma* (1949) and ending with *Hollywood or Bust* (1956). Despite predictions of doom, Martin's career prospered after he ended the partnership with Lewis. Martin struck gold with such hit records as "That's Amore" (1953), "Memories Are Made of This" (1955), and "Everybody Loves Somebody" (1964). He starred in such films as *The Young Lions* (1958), *Some Came Running* (1958), *Bells Are Ringing* (1960), *Toys in the Attic* (1963), and *Airport* (1970), as well as several with his fellow Hollywood clique members (dubbed the Rat Pack), among them *Sergeants Three* (1962) and *Robin and the Seven Hoods* (1964). "The Dean Martin Show," a television variety show, began an eight-year run in 1965 and was followed by "The Dean Martin Comedy Hour" (1973–74) and a number of celebrity roasts and touring appearances thereafter. Though Martin often seemed to be intoxicated during his television and nightclub performances, an impression aided by his easygoing manner and slurred singing style, he and his friends insisted it was part of his act.

Maruki, Iri, Japanese painter with his wife, Toshi, of 15 murals and panels that depicted the bombing of Hiroshima (b. June 20, 1901—d. Oct. 18 or 19, 1995).

Mata, Eduardo, Mexican conductor (b. Sept. 5, 1942, Mexico City, Mexico—d. Jan. 4, 1995, Cuernavaca, Mexico), as music director (1977–93) of the Dallas (Texas) Symphony Orchestra, elevated the ensemble's performance standard to such a level that it enjoyed both national and international acclaim, and he vigorously lobbied for the construction of the Morton H. Meyerson Symphony Center, which opened in Dallas in 1989. Mata's interpretations of contemporary music and such Latin-American composers as Silvestre Revueltas, Alberto Ginastera, and Heitor Villa-Lobos were the hallmark of his career, though he also conducted and recorded works by other 20th-century composers as well as by Mozart and Schumann. After studying at the Mexican National Conservatory with composers Carlos Chávez and Julián Orbón, Mata received (1964) a Koussevitzky fellowship to continue his studies in the U.S. At the Berkshire Music Center at Tanglewood, Lenox, Mass., he studied conducting under Max Rudolf and Erich Leinsdorf and composition with Gunther Schuller. Mata returned to Mexico to become music director of the Guadalajara Symphony Orchestra, and he held directorial posts at the University of Mexico and the National Symphony of Mexico. After leaving Dallas, Mata became principal guest conductor of the New Zealand Symphony and the artistic director of the Solistas de Mexico. He was killed when the plane that he was piloting crashed.

Matthews, Victor Collin Matthews, BARON, British self-made millionaire business executive whose Trafalgar House PLC served as the base for an empire that included Cunard Steam-ship Co. PLC, the Ritz Hotel, and Express Newspapers (b. Dec. 5, 1919—d. Dec. 5, 1995).

Mau, Carl, U.S. religious leader and general secretary, 1974–85, of the Lutheran World Federation (b. June 22, 1922—d. March 31, 1995).

Maxwell, Vera (VERA HUPPÉ), U.S. fashion designer (b. April 22, 1901, New York, N.Y.—d. Jan. 15, 1995, Rincón, P.R.), was dubbed "the American Chanel" as the creator of timeless fashions that were comfortable yet chic, and she was one of the first U.S. designers to introduce sportswear for women. A onetime dancer (1919–24) with the Metropolitan Opera Ballet, Maxwell became interested in designing while working as a model. After studying tailoring in London, she joined the U.S. sportswear house of Adler and Adler, Inc., as a designer of tailored day wear. She founded her own company, Vera Maxwell Originals, in 1947 and gained prominence during the 1950s with a loyal clientele that included U.S. first lady Pat Nixon, dancer Martha Graham, and actress Lillian Gish. Maxwell's innovations included a "weekend wardrobe," comprising two jackets, two skirts, and a pair of trousers; the wraparound jersey blouse; a riding-jacket suit; and a "speed suit," a zipperless, buttonless, and snapless pull-on dress with a stretch bodice. The latter could be donned in seconds. Though her designs were sold in some 700 stores nationwide, by the 1960s London designers had come to dominate the fashion spotlight. Maxwell continued to produce classic suits, coats, and dresses until her retirement in 1985.

Mazar, Benjamin (BINYAMIN MAISLER), Russian-born Israeli biblical archaeologist (b. June 28, 1906, Ciechanowiec, Poland, Russian Empire—d. Sept. 9, 1995, Jerusalem, Israel), excavated Temple Mount, Jerusalem (1968–77), and other sites in Palestine; his work was embraced by Israeli nationals who sought to validate the recovery of a Jewish homeland. Upon completing his studies at the German universities of Berlin and Giessen, Mazar immigrated to Palestine in 1929 and became a member of the Jewish Palestine Exploration Society. He directed excavations at Ramat Rahel (1932) and Bet She'arim (1936–40), unearthing remains of the Herodian dynasty (*c.* 55 BC–*c.* AD 93). In 1943 he joined the faculty of Hebrew University of Jerusalem, where he was a professor (1951–77), rector (1952–61), and president (1953–61); he oversaw the university's transfer from Mount Scopus to Giv'at Ram during the first Arab-Israeli War in 1948–49. Mazar's digs at Tell Qasile and 'En Gedi uncovered artifacts of the Philistine (12th century BC) and Byzantine (7th century BC) periods, respectively. His most famous excavation, however, was of the southern and western walls of Temple Mount, a site first made available to Jewish archaeologists after the Six-Day War in 1967. The 10-year excavation uncovered many historical finds, notably at the stratum dating from the Herodian period. His work had political significance as well, attracting praise from Jewish patriots and criticism from Muslim leaders who protested his treatment of sacred Islamic ruins on the site; these protests brought the project to a halt in the mid-1970s. Mazar was noted for his scholarship, and he published more than 300 works, including *Historical Atlas of Palestine: Israel in Biblical Times* (1941), *The Mountain of the Lord* (1975), and *Biblical Israel: State and People* (1992).

Meade, James Edward, British economist (b. June 23, 1907, Swanage, Dorset, England—d. Dec. 22, 1995, Cambridge, England), influenced Britain's economic policies during World War II and served two years as the chief economist in the postwar Labour government. For his pioneering research in international trade, he was awarded the 1977 Nobel Prize for Economics, together with Bertil Ohlin of Sweden. Meade, who held liberal views on public policy issues, also played a leading role in the establishment (1948) of the General Agreement on Tariffs and Trade and made important studies on national income accounting. His most important work, *The Theory of International Economic Policy,* was published in two volumes—*The Balance of Payments* (1951) and *Trade and Welfare* (1955). In the first of these, he sought to synthesize Keynesian and neoclassical elements in a model designed to show the effects of various monetary and fiscal policies on the balance of payments. In the second volume, Meade explored the effects on economic welfare of various kinds of trade policy. This early work also led to studies on trade discrimination and effective protection. Meade, who was educated at Malvern College and at Oriel College, Oxford, earned first-class honours in 1928 and undertook (1930–31) postgraduate studies at Trinity College, Cambridge. There he joined a circle of economists associated with John Maynard Keynes. During this period Meade's policy work gained its distinctly Keynesian and somewhat leftist flavour. He also held professorships at the London School of Economics (1947–57) and at Cambridge (1957–68), where he remained as a resident fellow until 1974. In the 1980s he was an adviser to the Social Democratic Party.

Merrill, James Ingram, U.S. poet (b. March 3, 1926, New York, N.Y.—d. Feb. 6, 1995, Tucson, Ariz.), perfected the technique of wittily using rhyme and meter to produce lyric and epic poems that dealt with love and loss. His superb craftsmanship was showcased in a body of work that celebrated his eclectic and elegant style, securing him renown as one of the most important figures in American literature. In 15 volumes of verse he mastered such diverse forms as sonnet, haiku, and epigram, besides publishing novels, plays, and essay collections. He was the son of Charles E. Merrill, a founder of the investment firm now known as Merrill Lynch & Co., Inc. While attending Amherst (Mass.) College, Merrill privately printed *Jim's Book: A Collection of Poems and Short Stories* (1942). His education was interrupted by military service during World War II, but he earned a B.A. in 1947, after which he devoted himself to writing. He produced several volumes of poetry before achieving critical acclaim with *Water Street* (1962), followed by *Nights and Days* (1967), for which he won the first of two National Book Awards. *The Fire Screen* (1969) and *Braving the Elements* (1972) appeared before Merrill was awarded the Bollingen Prize in 1973 and a Pulitzer Prize for *Divine Comedies* (1976), a poetry collection. *Mirabell: Books of Number* (1978) earned him a second National Book Award. The last two volumes and a third, *Scripts for the Pageant* (1980), were republished as a trilogy with a new epilogue in *The Changing Light at Sandover* (1982), which was particularly notable because Merrill admitted using a Ouija board to summon and converse with spirits as diverse as W. H. Auden and the archangel Gabriel. As his work became more introspective, Merrill explored such themes as wealth, homosexuality, AIDS, and senility. His last collection of poems, *A Scattering of Salts* (1995), was published posthumously.

Messina, Francesco, Italian sculptor whose monumental bronzes include a statue of Pope Pius XII in Saint Peter's Basilica in Rome and a remarkable figure of a horse outside the Rome headquarters of RAI-TV, the Italian national broadcasting corporation (b. Dec. 15, 1900—d. Sept. 13, 1995).

Michelangeli, Arturo Benedetti, Italian pianist (b. Jan. 5, 1920, Brescia, Italy—d. June 12, 1995, Lugano, Switz.), combined superb technique, clarity of tone, and a talent for delicate shadings in his interpretations, particularly of pieces by Beethoven, Brahms, Schumann, Debussy, and Ravel. His demanding perfectionism and reclusive nature, however, often drove him to cancel scheduled performances on short notice or to leave the stage in the middle of a concert. Although Michelangeli played violin from the age of three, he concentrated on piano when he entered the Milan Conservatory seven years later. He abandoned a proposed medical career after winning the grand prize at the Geneva International Piano Competition in 1939. During World War II Michelangeli's playing career was interrupted for several years while he served as a pilot in the Italian air force. He began teaching in the early 1950s when ill health forced him to stop touring for a time. He was also director (1964–69) of an international pianists' academy in Brescia.

Mitarai, Hajime, Japanese industrialist who, as president of Canon Inc., introduced nonconformist marketing strategies that turned the electronics manufacturer into one of the world's most innovative companies (b. Oct. 5, 1938—d. Aug. 31, 1995).

Moncion, Francisco, U.S. principal dancer and charter member, 1948–95, of the New York City Ballet (b. July 6, 1922—d. April 1, 1995).

Montgomery, Elizabeth, U.S. actress (b. April 15, 1933, Los Angeles, Calif.—d. May 18, 1995, Beverly Hills, Calif.), as the comely, green-eyed star of television's "Bewitched" (1964–72), portrayed Samantha, a resourceful suburban witch who promised her "mortal" husband, an advertising executive, that she would not resort to witchcraft yet nevertheless found herself engaging in sorcery, usually to extricate him from precarious situations. Her modus operandi was a twitch of her nose, an action that unleashed her supernatural powers. On that sitcom she also appeared as Serena, Samantha's identical-looking cousin. Montgomery, who attended the American Academy of Dramatic Arts in New York City, made her television debut on her father's playhouse series, "Robert Montgomery Presents." During the 1950s and '60s she appeared on such television shows as "Wagon Train" (1959), "The Untouchables" (1960), and "Rawhide" (1963) and in films, including *The Court-Martial of Billy Mitchell* (1955) and *Johnny Cool* (1963). Montgomery later appeared as a dramatic actress and starred in such made-for-television films as *A Case of Rape* (1974), *The Legend of Lizzie Borden* (1975), and *Black Widow Murders: The Blanche Taylor Moore Story* (1993). She was also the narrator of the Academy Award-winning *The Panama Deception* (1993) and on TV portrayed crime reporter Edna Buchanan in *The Corpse Had a Familiar Face* (1994) and *Deadline for Murder* (1995).

Monzon, Carlos, Argentine undisputed world middleweight boxing champion, 1970–74, and World Boxing Association middleweight champion, 1974–77 (b. Aug. 7, 1942—d. Jan. 8, 1995).

Morrison, (Holmes) Sterling, U.S. guitarist of the rock group the Velvet Underground (b. Aug. 29, 1942—d. Aug. 30, 1995).

Muir, Jean Elizabeth, British dressmaker (b. July 17, 1928, London, England—d. May 28, 1995, London), as a champion of "the little black dress," created classically elegant, deceptively simple women's fashions for three decades. Muir taught herself to sew at boarding school, and she later took a job in the stockroom of Liberty's department store in London. She apprenticed as a designer at Jaeger Ltd. (1956–62) and Jane & Jane (1962–66) before she started her own label in 1967. Using such soft fabrics as jersey, crepe, suede, and cashmere, Muir paid minute attention to detail, a hallmark of her excellent craftsmanship. Her designs, which emphasized perfect tailoring, featured graceful shapes that flattered almost any woman's silhouette. Her creations proved to be equally successful in the "swinging '60s" and the more conservative '80s. Muir's many honours include the British Fashion Industry Award (1984), the Australian Bicentennial Award (1988), and election to the British Fashion Hall of Fame (1994). She was made Commander of the Order of the British Empire in 1984.

Müller, Heiner, East German dramatist and director whose plays transcended the conventions of Socialist Realism with episodic, experimental structures and complex, often flawed characters facing the everyday problems and ambiguities of modern life (b. Jan. 9, 1929—d. Dec. 30, 1995).

Nearing, Helen, U.S. author who with her husband, Scott, turned out at least 50 books that glorified the back-to-the-land movement (b. Feb. 23, 1904—Sept. 17, 1995).

Needham, (Noël) Joseph (Terence Montgomery), British biochemist and scientific historian (b. Dec. 9, 1900, London, England—d. March 24, 1995, Cambridge, England), published *Science and Civilisation in China,* a remarkable multivolume study of nearly every branch of Chinese medicine, science, and technology over some 25 centuries. Needham matriculated at Gonville and Caius College, Cambridge (Ph.D., 1924; Sc.D., 1932). Although he traveled extensively and held numerous teaching positions, he spent most of his academic career at Caius, as a fellow (1924–66), president (1959–66), master (1966–76), and senior fellow (from 1976). He was also university demonstrator (1928–33) and Sir William Dunn reader (1933–66) in biochemistry and director of the Needham Research Institute. Needham's early research was mainly in embryology, and his published works include the massive three-volume *Chemical Embryology* (1931) and *Biochemistry and Morphogenesis* (1942). In 1942 his longtime interest in Chinese language and scholarship led to his appointment as a scientific adviser to China. Four years later he helped found UNESCO. Initially, Needham planned to write a short book on the differences between Western and Chinese scientific principles and traditions. By the time the first volume appeared in 1954, however, the project had expanded to seven volumes. Eventually he supervised a staff of dozens of writers and researchers; the work was still incomplete at the time of his death. Needham was elected a fellow of the Royal Society (1941) and of the British Academy (1971). He was made a Companion of Honour in 1992.

Nesin, Aziz (MEHMET NUSRET), Turkish satirist and militant secularist novelist and short-story writer who published over 90 books and plays attacking bureaucracy and hypocrisy from a left-wing perspective (b. Dec. 20, 1915—d. July 6, 1995).

Netting, Robert McCorkle, U.S. anthropologist who established cultural ecology as a scientific discipline (b. Oct. 14, 1934—d. Feb. 4, 1995).

Neumann, Vaclav, Czech conductor and proponent of the music of Gustav Mahler and of both classical and contemporary Czech composers, such as Bohuslav Martinu and Leos Janacek (b. Sept. 29, 1920—d. Sept. 2, 1995).

Nu, U (THAKIN NU), Burmese independence leader and politician (b. May 25, 1907, Wakema, Burma [now Myanmar]—d. Feb. 14, 1995, Yangon [Rangoon], Myanmar), was named the first prime minister of independent Burma in 1948; he was briefly out of office in 1956–57 and 1958–60 and was finally ousted in a military coup (1962) led by Gen. Ne Win. U Nu graduated (B.A., 1929) from the University of Rangoon, taught school for several years, and then returned to the university to study law. In 1936 he and fellow militant Aung San gained national prominence at the centre of anti-British protests and a subsequent student strike. U Nu was arrested at the outbreak of World War II. Released during the Japanese occupation of Burma (1942–45), he served (1943) in a pro-Japanese puppet government. After the assassination of Aung San (1947), U Nu oversaw the transition to independence, at which time he became prime minister. A devout Buddhist and a respected leader, he was reelected in 1952, 1956, and 1960, but his administration was plagued by economic difficulties, political factionalism, and armed rebellion. From 1958 to 1960 he was replaced by a "caretaker" government under Ne Win, and he was arrested when the military took full control in 1962. U Nu led the opposition from exile (1969–80), then returned in a general amnesty and tried unsuccessfully (1988) to form a civilian government. He was placed under house arrest in 1990 (soon after Aung San's daughter, Daw Aung San Suu Kyi) but was released in 1992.

O Jin U, North Korean defense minister, commander of the army, and influential member of the Communist Party (b. 1918?—d. Feb. 25, 1995).

O'Shea, Tessie, British music-hall entertainer of the 1930s and '40s who gained new popularity on the stage and screen in the 1960s (b. March 13, 1914—d. April 21, 1995).

Okada, Eiji, Japanese actor who starred in such films as the Japanese *Woman in the Dunes,* the French *Hiroshima, Mon Amour,* and the U.S. *The Ugly American* (b. June 13, 1920—d. Sept. 14, 1995).

Onganía, Juan Carlos, Argentine general and politician (b. March 17, 1914, Buenos Aires, Arg.—d. June 8, 1995, Buenos Aires), served (1966–70) as president of Argentina during a period of harsh repression and authorized (1966) riot police to storm the University of Buenos Aires and forcibly eject students and professors in what became known as the Night of the Long Truncheons. Onganía, who graduated from the National Military College as a second lieutenant in 1934, rose quickly through the ranks. He was promoted to brigadier general in 1959 and briefly served as commander of the Cavalry Corps before leading a revolt against an opposing army faction and becoming (1962) army commander in chief. He helped quell a coup meant to oust Pres. Arturo Illía, a liberal democrat, but he later became disillusioned—like many others who wearied of the ineffectiveness of a democratic government in the face of resurgent Peronism and economic troubles—and resigned his commission to take power himself. Following Onganía's installation by the military, he tried to bolster the economic sector and instituted such authoritarian measures as dismantling Congress and all political parties, assuming full legislative and executive power, and depriving universities of their autonomy. This last action led to violent clashes between students and police, which escalated in 1969 and eventually led to Onganía's own ouster in 1970, when a three-man ruling military junta unseated him. He then retired. In February 1995 Onganía was placed under house arrest for two weeks after he charged the government with corruption.

Onoe Baiko VII (SEIZO TERASHIMA), Japanese Kabuki actor (b. Aug. 31, 1915, Tokyo, Japan—d. March 24, 1995, Tokyo), was revered as the country's leading postwar *onnagata* (female impersonator) and was designated a Living National Treasure in 1968. Baiko captivated audiences with his exquisite style, sensitive yet riveting portrayals, and masterful interpretations. In keeping with the ancient art of Kabuki, in which the tradition is passed from father to son, Baiko, the illegitimate heir of Kikugoro VI, was adopted by him to preserve the family heritage. Baiko first performed at the age of six and after moving up in rank was named Kikunosuke III in 1935. He was given the honorific stage name of Onoe Baiko VII in 1947. Baiko performed the *Fujimusume* ("Daughter of Fuji") dance more than 1,000 times and became a household name by appearing on the television drama "Gengizai" ("The Well of Righteousness"). Baiko also appeared in male roles, notably as a samurai, but after the death of his father in 1949, he helped found the Kikugoro acting company and performed only female roles. In 1994 he was awarded the Order of the Rising Sun.

Oppenheimer, Sir Philip Jack, British entrepreneur and chairman, 1948–93, of the De Beers Mining Co.'s international diamond-marketing cartel (b. Oct. 29, 1911—d. Oct. 8, 1995).

Parrish, Robert, U.S. child actor who appeared as a newsboy in Charlie Chaplin's *City Lights* and later earned an Academy Award for film editing for *Body and Soul* and plaudits for his direction of such films as *Cry Danger* and *The Purple Plain* (b. Jan. 4, 1916—d. Dec. 4, 1995).

Patrick, John, U.S. Pulitzer Prize-winning playwright of *Teahouse of the August Moon* and screenwriter of such hits as *Three Coins in the Fountain, Love Is a Many Splendored Thing,* and *High Society* (b. May 17, 1905—d. Nov. 7, 1995).

Patterson, Clair Cameron, U.S. geochemist who in 1953 made the first precise measurement of the Earth's age, 4.6 billion years (b. June 2, 1922—d. Dec. 5, 1995).

Peierls, Sir Rudolf Ernst, German-born British physicist (b. June 5, 1907, Berlin, Germany—d. Sept. 19, 1995, Oxford, England), laid the theoretical foundations for the creation of the first atomic bomb. In 1940 he and Otto Frisch, a colleague at the University of Birmingham, England, issued a three-page memorandum that correctly theorized that a highly explosive but compact bomb could be fashioned out of small amounts of the rare element uranium-235. This memo ignited the race to develop the bomb in Britain and the United States, advancing it from an issue of academic speculation to an Allied war project of the highest priority. Peierls studied and conducted research at universities in Berlin, Munich, and Leipzig, Germany; Zurich, Switz.; and Manchester and Cambridge, England, before becoming a professor of mathematical physics at Birmingham in 1937. His early work in quantum theory led to studies in nuclear physics. Despite the fact that it was his research that gave rise to the British bomb effort, he was initially excluded from official proceedings because of his German origins. In 1943 his British atomic research group joined the Manhattan Project in the United States. After the war he reassumed his professorship at Birmingham, working there until 1963, when he joined the University of Oxford. He retired from Oxford in 1974 and taught for three years at the University of Washington. Among his books are *The Laws of Nature* (1955), *Surprises in Theoretical Physics* (1979), and *More Surprises in Theoretical Physics* (1991); he also wrote on nuclear disarmament for the Pugwash Conference. He became a British citizen in 1940 and was knighted in 1968. His autobiography, *Bird of Passage,* was published in 1985.

Penick, Harvey, U.S. golf instructor and coauthor at 87 of *Harvey Penick's Little Red Book: Lessons and Teachings from a Lifetime in Golf,* the best-selling sports book of all time (b. Oct 23, 1904—d. April 2, 1995).

Pépin, Jean-Luc, Canadian statesman who held important Cabinet posts—energy, mines, and resources; industry, trade, and commerce; transport—in the Liberal administration of Prime Minister Pierre Trudeau and was cochairman of the Task Force on Canadian Unity, 1977–79 (b. Nov. 1, 1924—d. Sept. 6?, 1995).

Perry, Frank, U.S. director of such wide-ranging films as *David and Lisa, Diary of a Mad Housewife, Mommie Dearest,* and *On the Bridge,* which dealt with his battle against prostate cancer (b. Aug. 21, 1930—d. Aug. 29, 1995).

Perry, Frederick John ("FRED"), British tennis player (b. May 18, 1909, Stockport, Cheshire, England—d. Feb. 2, 1995, Melbourne, Australia), during the period 1933–36 led England to victory in four consecutive Davis Cup finals and won eight Grand Slam singles titles: three straight All-England (Wimbledon) championships (1934, 1935, and 1936), three U.S. championships (1933, 1934, and 1936), the Australian title in 1934, and the 1935 French championship. Perry taught himself to play table tennis at the local YMCA and, at the age of 20, won the World Table Tennis Championship. He switched to lawn tennis at the urging of his father, a cotton spinner, and within two years he had been named to the Davis Cup team. Despite his achievement as the first player to win all four events in the Grand Slam, Perry was often criticized for his working-class background and his "ungentlemanly" aggression on the court, as well as for his decision to turn professional. He won the world professional title in 1937 and 1941 and settled in the U.S., where he became a citizen. After retiring from active play, Perry was a tennis commentator on BBC radio and a cofounder of the Fred Perry Sportswear Co. He published an autobiography in 1984, the same year the All-England Club erected a statue and renamed a gate in his honour at Wimbledon.

Peters, Ellis (EDITH MARY PARGETER), British novelist (b. Sept. 28, 1913, Horsehay, Shropshire, England—d. Oct. 14, 1995, Madeley, Shropshire), wrote scores of detective novels and other fiction, but she was probably best known as the creator of Brother Cadfael, a middle-aged Welsh Benedictine monk who uses his skill as the abbey herbalist and his vast knowledge of the world from his years as a youthful Crusader to solve murders and other crimes in 12th-century England and Wales. She was born Edith Mary Pargeter and trained as a pharmacist's assistant. Beginning in the mid-1930s she wrote (using her own name and several pseudonyms, most notably Ellis Peters) crime novels and historical fiction in her spare time, including a novel based on her World War II experiences in the Women's Royal Naval Service, *She Goes to War* (1942). She gained a wider audience with a series of 13 contemporary crime novels (1951–78) featuring the Felse family—Police Inspector George Felse, his wife, Bunty, and their son, Dominic. In 1977 Peters published *A Morbid Taste for Bones: A Mediaeval Whodunnit,* the first of 20 Brother Cadfael novels. (She also wrote a volume of shorter pieces.) Starting with *One Corpse Too Many* (1979), she concentrated on producing the Brother Cadfael books, several of which were later filmed for television with Derek Jacobi in the title role. A 21st novel remained unfinished at her death. She was also an accomplished translator of Czech-language literature and was the winner of the 1968 Czechoslovak Society for International Relations Gold Medal and Ribbon. She was made an Officer of the Order of the British Empire in 1994.

Pietrangeli, Carlo, Italian director-general of the monuments, museums, and pontifical galleries of the Vatican, 1978–95 (b. Oct. 20, 1912—d. June 23, 1995).

Pilkington, Sir Alastair (SIR LIONEL ALEXANDER BETHUNE PILKINGTON), British industrialist and inventor of the float glass process (b. Jan. 7, 1920—d. May 5, 1995).

Pineau, Christian Paul, French politician who, in his role as foreign minister, 1956–58, signed the Treaty of Rome (b. Oct. 14, 1904—d. April 5, 1995).

Pinson, Vada, U.S. centre fielder with the Cincinnati Reds for 11 of his 18 major league seasons and two-time all-star who was one of only six baseball players to hit 250 home runs and steal 300 bases (b. Aug. 11, 1938—d. Oct. 21, 1995).

Pleasence, Donald, British actor (b. Oct. 5, 1919, Worksop, Nottinghamshire, England—d. Feb. 2, 1995, St.-Paul-de-Vence, France), was one of Britain's most enduring character actors on stage, screen, and television for more than 50 years; his greatest triumph was as the manipulative tramp, Davies, in Harold Pinter's *The Caretaker,* a character he created in London in 1960 and molded into his own on Broadway in 1961, in the 1963 film adaptation, and in the 1991 London revival. Pleasence ran the gamut from Shakespeare to the *Halloween* horror movies, and he was equally believable as the sinister Blofeld in the James Bond film *You Only Live Twice* (1967) and as the mild Rev. Septimus Harding in the television production of "The Barchester Chronicles" (1982). Pleasence made his professional debut in 1939 and his London debut in 1942. During World War II he served in the Royal Air Force, and he spent more than a year in a German prison camp, an experience he drew on for *The Great Escape* (1963). Other notable stage roles included William Mossop in *Hobson's Choice* (1952), Bitos in *Poor Bitos* (1963–64), and Arthur Goldman in *The Man in the Glass Booth* (1967–68). He appeared in scores of motion pictures, including *The Beachcomber* (1954), *Dr. Crippen* (1963), *Fantastic Voyage* (1966), *The Eagle Has Landed* (1976),

Donald Pleasence
HULTON DEUTSCH

and *Shadows and Fog* (1992). He also wrote children's books. Pleasence was made an Officer of the Order of the British Empire in 1994.

Porter, Eric Richard, British classical actor who found success on television in such roles as Count Bronowsky in "The Jewel in the Crown" and, especially, Soames Forsyte in the 26-part drama "The Forsyte Saga" (b. April 8, 1928—d. May 15, 1995).

Possony, Stefan Thomas, Austrian-born U.S. military theorist who conceived the U.S. Strategic Defense Initiative, known as "Star Wars" (b. March 15, 1913—d. April 26, 1995).

Powell, (Elizabeth) Dilys, British motion-picture critic (b. July 20, 1901—d. June 3, 1995, London, England), as the outspoken film critic for *The Sunday Times* (1939–79) and *Punch* (1979–92) and then as *The Sunday Times*'s reviewer for movies shown on British television (1976–95), wielded enormous power over the success or failure of virtually every screen actor and every film shown in Britain for more than half a century. Powell studied modern languages at Somerville College, Oxford, began writing for *The Sunday Times* in 1928, and joined the staff full-time in 1936. Her first movie review appeared on March 26, 1939. Although Powell seldom analyzed the technical aspects of filmmaking, she was generally praised for her clear insights, her passionate love for the industry, and her willingness to fight for films, actors, and directors she admired. She was also one of the first British critics to champion such highly technical directors as Orson Welles, John Ford, Alfred Hitchcock, and Steven Spielberg. Many of her reviews were collected into book form, as were her personal recollections and memoirs. Powell was made Commander of the Order of the British Empire in 1974.

Pramoj, Kukrit, Thai politician, writer, and actor (b. April 20, 1911, Phitsanulok, Thailand—d. Oct. 9, 1995, Bangkok, Thailand), saw life imitate art when he became prime minister of Thailand several years after portraying the leader of a fictitious Southeast Asian country in the Marlon Brando film *The Ugly American* (1963). The son of a prince, Kukrit had the title Mom Rajawong. He was educated in Thailand and England and graduated from Queen's College, Oxford, with a degree in politics, philosophy, and economics. When he returned to Thailand, he worked in the Finance Ministry and the central bank. He also began writing stories and poems. Kukrit served (1946–47) in the parliament and then, during a period of military rule (1947–73), focused mainly on promoting and preserving Thai culture. He also founded (1950) the newspaper *Siam Rath* and used it to attack the regime. When a student uprising overthrew the regime, Kukrit returned to politics. He helped create a new constitution and formed the Social Action Party. His brother Seni was named prime minister, but the government failed, and in 1975 Kukrit gained the office. To maintain Thailand's independence and prevent it from falling under communism, as was happening in neighbouring countries, he established diplomatic relations with China and arranged the withdrawal of U.S. forces from the Thai bases from which much of the Vietnam War had been mounted. An unpopular proposal for raising the price of rice in Bangkok led to the downfall of his government in 1976. Even after the military regained power, Kukrit continued to speak his mind, and he enjoyed the role of elder statesman. A number of his books were considered modern classics in his country.

Preston, Lewis Thompson, U.S. bank executive (b. Aug. 5, 1926, New York, N.Y.—d. May 4, 1995, Washington, D.C.), served (1991–95) as president of the World Bank during the critical period when 23 new member nations entered the institution following the breakup of the former Soviet Union. While Preston was at the helm, he approved the financing of programs to alleviate poverty and initialed a sharp increase in loans for environmental projects, health, education, and family planning. He also attempted to broaden the bank's role in an advisory capacity, especially in the restructuring of public sectors of client nations. He tried to increase cost-effectiveness, slashed some 240 senior positions from the staff shortly after arriving in 1991, and announced a 6% budget cut in 1994. Before his appointment, the Harvard-educated banker had spent 40 years at J.P. Morgan and Co., successively serving as vice president, president, and chairman and chief executive. He was instrumental in persuading the company, which had acquired the Guaranty Trust Co., to trade in the new but unknown Eurodollar market, a move that led to prosperity for Morgan. After leaving Wall Street's most distinguished bank, where his annual salary reportedly had been $2 million, Preston was invited by U.S. Pres. George Bush to head the World Bank, with an annual salary of $285,000. Preston, who was being treated for cancer, resigned his post in March 1995.

Price, George, U.S. cartoonist (b. June 9, 1901, Coytesville, N.J.—d. Jan. 12, 1995, Englewood, N.J.), as a longtime contributor (1926–95) to *The New Yorker* magazine, depicted the absurdities of human nature in distinctive drawings that were characterized by bold lines and a minimal use of shading; these images were usually accompanied by a clever, succinct caption. His attention-grabbing cartoons, which featured feuding couples often beset by domestic mishaps or victims of natural disasters coping with tragedy in an amusing way, helped modernize the magazine cartoon. Another theme—totally unreasonable persons stubbornly clinging to power—was a hallmark of his work. Price honed his craft while working as a freelance illustrator, advertising artist, and printmaker. His fresh approach to the changing mores of society during his six-decade career kept him in the vanguard of his profession. His priceless witticisms were collected in 11 volumes, including *Good Humor Man* (1940), *Who's in Charge Here?* (1943), *The People Zoo* (1971), *Browse at Your Own Risk* (1977), and his last, *The World of George Price: A 55-Year Retrospective* (1988).

Pullen, Don, U.S. jazz pianist (b. Dec. 25, 1941—d. April 22, 1995).

Rabin, Yitzhak, Israeli soldier, politician, and statesman (b. March 1, 1922, Jerusalem—d. Nov. 4, 1995, Tel Aviv, Israel), was for some five decades a central figure in shaping his country's history while serving as both a brilliant military strategist and a peace-seeking prime minister. In one of the more memorable moments in recent history, Rabin, at the urging of U.S. Pres. Bill Clinton, shook the hand of Palestine Liberation Organization leader Yasir Arafat—once his avowed enemy—on the White House lawn in 1993 after they signed an accord on Palestinian self-rule. Rabin, Arafat, and Shimon Peres, then Israeli foreign minister, were awarded the 1994 Nobel Prize for Peace for their efforts to bring peace to the Middle East. As a young man Rabin had intended to become a farmer and graduated from Kadourie Agricultural School, Kfar Tabor. Instead, however, he joined (1941) the Palmach, the commando unit of the Jewish Defense Forces. He saw action during World War II and developed skills that made him an excellent military tactician. During Israel's war of independence (1948), Rabin directed Jerusalem's defense. He became army chief of staff in 1964 and, though Gen. Moshe Dayan received most of the publicity, planned the strategy that helped Israel win the Six-Day War (1967). Rabin served as ambassador to the U.S. (1968–73) and then, on his return home, entered politics. Elected to the Knesset (parliament) as a member of the Labour Party in December 1973, he became minister of labour in Prime Minister Golda Meir's Cabinet the following March. A month later she resigned, and in June he became Israel's first native-born prime minister. It was Rabin who ordered the 1976 raid that resulted in the rescue of over 100 hostages, most of them Israelis, being held by Palestinian terrorists at the airport at Entebbe, Uganda. During an election campaign in 1977, however, he was forced to resign when it was revealed that he and his wife had violated Israeli law by maintaining bank accounts in the U.S. Peres became the leader of the Labour Party. Rabin returned to government in 1984 and served as defense minister until 1990. He regained the party leadership from Peres in 1992, and after elections later that year, he again became prime minister. His government thereupon initiated secret talks that led to the historic agreement between Israel and the Palestinians. Rabin was assassinated by a right-wing Jewish activist as he was leaving a peace celebration rally at which he had spoken and had joined in singing the Hebrew song of peace.

Rachid, Mimouni, Algerian French-language novelist (b. Nov. 20, 1945—d. Feb. 12, 1995).

Randolph, Theron G., U.S. pioneering allergist who founded the field of environmental medicine and characterized environmental illness as one that included such symptoms as chronic headache, fatigue, and mental depression (b. 1906?—d. Sept. 29, 1995).

Raney, James Elbert ("JIMMY"), U.S. musician (b. Aug. 20, 1927, Louisville, Ky.—d. May 10, 1995, Louisville), was one of the most influential, lyrical jazz guitarists of his generation. As an improviser he was uniquely committed to melody, a devotion emphasized by his muted, lightly amplified electric guitar tone. He played with unusual rhythmic poise and freedom, constructing original solos with contrasting developments, often in long phrases, and a stimulating harmonic imagination. The son of a newspaperman and a guitarist mother, he began playing guitar at age 10, studied with a classical guitar teacher, and was inspired by the jazz recordings of Charlie Christian. During the 1940s Raney played with small groups and big bands, most notably the Woody Herman band; he then joined tenor saxophonist Stan Getz, helping him to achieve (1951–53) a unique quintet sound. His work with Getz, the Red Norvo Trio (1953–54), and pianist Jimmy Lyon's New York supper club trio (1954–60) and his frequent recordings identified Raney with the cool jazz idiom. His concentration on melody, ideal for cool jazz, was less suitable for the more extroverted jazz idioms that dominated the '60s, a decade that he also spent performing in Broadway show bands and as a studio musician. Alcoholism interrupted Raney's career, and he returned to Louisville. By the '80s he was again touring and recording, and he was also performing with his son Doug, a guitarist. Severe recurring deafness gradually diminished Raney's performing career.

Redenbacher, Orville, U.S. agricultural scientist and cocreator of a new hybrid of popcorn, "snowflake," which was lighter and fluffier than traditional popped kernels; he achieved celebrity status when his hayseed image—complete with bow tie and horn-rimmed glasses—appeared on the labels of the popcorn that bore his name (b. July 16, 1907—d. Sept. 19, 1995).

Reston, James Barrett ("SCOTTY"), U.S. journalist (b. Nov. 3, 1909, Clydebank, Scotland—d. Dec. 6, 1995, Washington, D.C.), was considered one of the nation's most influential journalists during his 50-year association with the *New York Times.* He broke a number of his era's most important stories and counted two Pulitzer Prizes among his honours. After Reston graduated (1932) from the University of Illinois, former Ohio governor James Cox, for whom he had caddied at the Dayton Country Club, gave him a job on the *Springfield* (Ohio) *Daily News,* a Cox newspaper. That was followed by positions as publicity director for the Cincinnati Reds baseball team and sportswriter for the Associated Press in New York City and London. In 1939 he joined the London bureau of the *New York Times.* Reston was transferred to Washington in 1941 and, except for a leave in 1942 to set up the London bureau of the Office of War Information and 13 months in New York City as executive editor (1968–69) of the *Times*, spent the rest of his life there. He served in such positions as national correspondent (1945–48), diplomatic correspondent (1948–53), and Washington bureau chief (1953–64) and wrote a nationally syndicated column from 1953 to 1987. Reston's first big scoop came when he discovered the proposals for the formation of the UN being discussed at the Dumbarton Oaks Conference (1944). His coverage won him his first Pulitzer Prize (1945). His second Pulitzer (1957) was awarded for his articles on the impact of Pres. Dwight D. Eisenhower's illness on the functioning of the government. Other media issues in which Reston figured were the Bay of Pigs invasion (1961); the Cuban missile crisis (1962), coverage of which he helped delay in the interest of national security; and the secret Pentagon Papers (1971) on the Vietnam War, the publication of which he supported. Reston was also instrumental in recruiting and nurturing journalistic talent and in the creation (1970) of the first op-ed page in a U.S. newspaper. He retired in 1989 on his 80th birthday. Among his honours was the Medal of Liberty; he was also made a Commander of the Order of the British Empire and a chevalier of the French Legion of Honour. His memoirs, *Deadline,* appeared in 1991.

Rich, Ben R., U.S. engineer (b. June 18, 1925, Manila, Phil.—d. Jan. 5, 1995, Los Angeles, Calif.), conducted top-secret research on advanced military aircraft while working at Lockheed Aircraft Corp. under an alias, which he was required to adopt for security reasons. Rich, known as Ben Dover, helped develop more than 25 airplanes, notably the F-117A Stealth fighter-bomber, which eluded detection on enemy radar screens and inflicted a disproportionate share of damage on Iraqi targets during the 1991 Persian Gulf War; the SR-71 Blackbird, a reconnaissance craft that cruised at three times the speed of sound; and the U-2, the spy plane that flew missions over the Soviet Union from 1956 to 1960. After earning a B.S. (1949) from the University of California, Berkeley, and an M.S. (1950) from the University of California, Los Angeles, Rich joined Lockheed at its Burbank, Calif., "Skunk Works," so named both because of its location near a malodorous plastics factory and because it was a secret installation, much like the operation of similar name portrayed in the "Li'l Abner" comic strip. In his 1994 autobiography Rich recounted that the technology for his crowning achievement, the Stealth fighter-bomber, virtually "fell into my lap" after a Soviet scientist openly published (1975) an idea that led to the technology for the Stealth. Rich, who retired in 1991 as president of Lockheed Advanced Development Co., was a member of the National Academy of Engineering from 1981 and the 1994 recipient of the Distinguished Service Medal, the highest U.S. military honour for a civilian.

Rich, Charlie, U.S. country singer (b. Dec. 14, 1932, Colt, Ark.—d. July 25, 1995, Hammond, La.), vaulted to the top of the country music charts in 1973 with the release of two million-selling records, "Behind Closed Doors" and "The Most Beautiful Girl." The Silver Fox (so nicknamed because his hair was prematurely gray) receded into the shadows, however, when his "countrypolitan" sound—a lush, easy-listening blend of country music with jazz and blues influences—fell out of vogue with country-western fans. During the 1950s Rich formed his first band, the Velvetones, a group influenced by the Stan Kenton sound. He achieved solo success in 1960 with "Lonely Weekends" but struggled for another five years before "Mohair Sam" made him a household name. Rich, a gifted instrumentalist who played tenor saxophone and piano, was an expressive singer whose deep baritone voice crooned such romantic songs as "There Won't Be Anymore," "A Very Special Love Song," "Every Time You Touch Me (I Get High)," and "I Love My Friend." After such hits as "I Still Believe in Love" (1978) and "Even a Fool Would Let Go" (1980), Rich, the Country Music Association's 1974 Entertainer of the Year, went into semiretirement. He resurfaced in 1992 with *Pictures and Paintings,* one of his finest albums.

Rie, Dame Lucie, Austrian-born British studio potter (b. March 16, 1902, Vienna, Austria—d. April 1, 1995, London, England), created graceful, elegant domestic pottery characterized by minimal ornamentation and unique glazes in a wide range of vivid colours and textures. She was born Lucie Gomperz, the daughter of a prominent Viennese doctor who was a close friend and colleague of Sigmund Freud. She studied at the Vienna Arts and Crafts School and won awards across Europe for her richly textured earthenware pots. In 1938 she moved to Britain with her husband, Hans Rie. The marriage soon failed, however, and she established a private studio-workshop in London. Rie, who spurned the rustic and classical Oriental pottery styles that were popular at the time, supported herself during World War II by crafting ceramic buttons and jewelry. In the late 1940s she formed a lifelong partnership with a German-born ceramist, Hans Coper, and began experimenting with distinctive glazes fired in a high-temperature electric kiln. Rie's later stoneware and porcelain pieces, including tea sets, bowls, and vases, often commanded high prices, and many were exhibited at the Victoria and Albert Museum and New York City's Metropolitan Museum of Art. Rie was the subject of a BBC television documentary in the early 1980s and was created Dame Commander of the Order of the British Empire in 1991.

Rifkind, Simon Hirsch, Russian-born U.S. lawyer and judge (b. June 5, 1901, Meretz, Russia—d. Nov. 14, 1995, New York, N.Y.), in a career of more than 60 years, represented clients ranging from the Municipal Assistance Corp., which rescued New York City from bankruptcy in the mid-1970s, to Jacqueline Kennedy Onassis in two well-publicized lawsuits. Renowned for his versatility in legal matters, he held several political appointments, notably as Gen. Dwight D. Eisenhower's adviser on Jewish affairs in post-World War II Europe. He subsequently was awarded a Medal of Freedom. In 1910 Rifkind's family emigrated from Russia to New York City, where he later attended City College of New York (B.S., 1922) and Columbia University (LL.B., 1925). He began his career serving as the legislative secretary (1927–33) of Sen. Robert F. Wagner—one of the leading sponsors of New Deal legislation—later joining him as a partner in his law firm (1930–41). He was a federal district court judge for southern New York from 1941 until 1950, when he joined the firm that would later become known internationally as Paul, Weiss, Rifkind, Wharton & Garrison. In 1956 the Supreme Court chose him to arbitrate the rival claims of Western states to the water of the Colorado River, and Pres. John F. Kennedy selected him to examine (1961–62) labour disputes in the railroad industry. Rifkind also held prominent posts on the New York City Board of Higher Education, the American Jewish Committee, the Jewish Theological Seminary, and the American College of Trial Lawyers.

Riggs, Robert Larimore ("BOBBY"), U.S. tennis player (b. Feb. 25, 1918, Los Angeles, Calif.—d. Oct. 25, 1995, Leucadia, Calif.), was one of the top-ranked U.S. players in the 1930s and '40s but was best known for his participation in the 1973 "Battle of the Sexes" with Billie Jean King. After making disparaging comments regarding women's tennis, Riggs, a self-proclaimed "chauvinist pig," challenged Margaret Smith Court to a match and won it. His subsequent challenge to King produced a quite different result, however. Before a record crowd of 30,472 spectators at the Houston (Texas) Astrodome and a television audience of some 50 million, King won all three sets in an event that helped to elevate women's tennis to the status of a major sport. Riggs began taking tennis lessons at age 12 and progressed rapidly. At 18 he was ranked fourth in the U.S., and in 1939, at the age of 21, he was first in the world. Riggs was on the 1938 and 1939 Davis Cup teams, and in 1939, at Wimbledon, he won the singles, men's doubles, and mixed doubles titles. He also won the first of his U.S. championships in 1939. After turning professional (1941), Riggs won the 1942 and 1947 U.S. doubles titles, with Don Budge, and the 1946, 1947, and 1949 U.S. singles titles. He quit professional tennis in 1951, although he later played in senior events. He was inducted into the International Tennis Hall of Fame in 1967. In 1994 Riggs formed the Bobby Riggs Tennis Museum Foundation to promote awareness of prostate cancer.

Ritchie, Charles Stewart Almon, Canadian diplomat and diarist (b. Sept. 23, 1906, Halifax, Nova Scotia—d. June 7, 1995, Ottawa, Ont.), served with distinction as ambassador to Germany (1954–58), the United Nations (1958–62), the U.S. (1962–66), and NATO (1966–67) before reaching the pinnacle of his career as high commissioner to London (1967–71). He was best remembered, however, for a deliciously revealing series of four diaries, which recorded both his private and professional life. The first volume, *The Siren Years* (1974), vividly captured the climate of London during the Blitz, when Ritchie served (1939–45) as a junior officer there. The book won the Governor-General's Award for nonfiction. A gifted raconteur who delighted in recounting juicy tidbits about celebrities and politicians, he found appreciative audiences for *An Appetite for Life*

(1977), *Diplomatic Passport* (1981), and *Storm Signals* (1983). He also penned a memoir of his youth called *My Grandfather's House* (1987).

Roblès, Emmanuel François, Algerian-French novelist and playwright (b. May 4, 1914, Oran, Alg.—d. Feb. 22, 1995, Boulogne, France), portrayed the struggle of the individual to find fulfillment, a sense of purpose, and happiness, however short-lived, in the face of political and social oppression and violence. Roblès was reared by his widowed mother and grandmother in a bilingual (French and Spanish) household in the Roman Catholic section of Oran, and he drew on his Spanish heritage as well as the French North African milieu in which he spent his childhood for the settings and themes of his best works. He attended teachers college and began his first novel, *L'Action* (1938), while employed as a teacher in Oran. During his World War II service as a Spanish translator and special war correspondent, he met Albert Camus, who encouraged him to contribute articles to *Alger-Républicain,* the liberal daily of which Camus was editor, and to write his second novel, *La Vallée du paradis* (1941). After the war Roblès moved between Paris and Algiers, but in 1958 he settled in Paris permanently to escape the rapidly escalating Algerian war. Roblès' novels include *Travail d'homme* (1943; *The Angry Mountain,* 1948), the Prix Fémina-winning *Les Hauteurs de la ville* (1948), *Le Vésuve* (1961; *Vesuvius*, 1970), and *L'Herbe des ruines* (1992). He also wrote short stories and several plays, notably *Montserrat* (1948) and *Plaidoyer pour un rebelle* (1965; *Case for a Rebel,* 1977). Roblès was elected to the Académie Goncourt in 1973.

Rodger, George, British photojournalist who was a World War II correspondent, 1939–45, for *Life* magazine and cofounder, 1947, of the Magnum cooperative photographic agency (b. March 19, 1908—d. July 24, 1995).

Rogers, Ginger (Virginia Katherine McMath), U.S. dancer and actress (b. July 16, 1911, Independence, Mo.—d. April 25, 1995, Rancho Mirage, Calif.), was a vision of elegance as her fluid dance steps wittily complemented those of her celebrated partner, Fred Astaire, in 10 unforgettable Hollywood musicals. Although she was better remembered for her wisecracking repartee in a string of light romantic comedies, she won an Academy Award as best actress for a dramatic performance in *Kitty Foyle* (1940). The golden-haired Rogers, whose career was carefully orchestrated by her mother, appeared with Eddie Foy's vaudeville troupe before winning a Charleston contest that would ultimately lead her to the Broadway stage. By the time she was 19, Rogers had introduced George Gershwin's "Embraceable You" and "But Not for Me" in the 1930 Broadway hit *Girl Crazy*. She made her motion-picture debut in *Young Man of Manhattan* (1930), in which she immortalized the catchphrase, "Cigarette me, big boy." Her gum cracking and good-natured wholesomeness typified *42nd Street* (1933) and *Gold Diggers of 1933,* while her stately beauty and sophisticated charm fueled the on-screen chemistry with Astaire in such films as *Flying Down to Rio* (1933), *The Gay Divorcée* (1934), *Top Hat* (1935), *Follow the Fleet* (1936), *The Story of Vernon and Irene Castle* (1939), and *The Barkleys of Broadway* (1949), their last collaboration. Her dramatic skills were evidenced in *Stage Door* (1937) and *Primrose Path* (1940), while her comedic gifts were showcased in *Bachelor Mother* (1939), *Tom, Dick and Harry* (1941), and *The Major and the Minor* (1942), in which her character pretended to be a 12-year-old girl. Some of her other 70 films include *Roxy Hart* (1942), *Lady in the Dark* (1944), and *Monkey Business* (1952). After appearing in her last film as the mother in *Harlow* (1965), Rogers maintained a busy theatre schedule, appearing in the title role of *Hello, Dolly!* from 1965 to 1967 and introducing *Mame* to London audiences in 1969. Rogers' autobiography, *Ginger: My Story* (1991), touched on her five failed marriages and explored her lifestyle as a Christian Scientist. She was also a 1992 recipient of the Kennedy Center Honors for lifetime achievement.

Ginger Rogers
HULTON DEUTSCH

Rome, Esther, U.S. women's health advocate and one of the authors of the best-seller *Our Bodies, Ourselves* (b. Sept. 8, 1945—d. June 24, 1995).

Romney, George Wilcken, U.S. politician and business executive who promoted compact cars while presiding as chairman, 1954–62, of American Motors Corp.; served as Republican governor, 1963–69, of Michigan; and derailed his bid for the U.S. presidential nomination by remarking in 1967 that he had been "brainwashed" by the military into supporting the Vietnam War (b. July 8, 1907—d. July 26, 1995).

Rosen, Nathan, U.S.-born Israeli theoretical physicist who in 1935 collaborated with Albert Einstein and Boris Podolsky on a much-debated refutation of the theory of quantum mechanics; he later came to accept the theory (b. March 22, 1909—d. Dec. 18, 1995).

Roth, Henry, U.S. teacher and author (b. Feb. 8, 1906, Tysmenica, Galicia, Austria-Hungary [now in Ukraine]—d. Oct. 13, 1995, Albuquerque, N.M.), published a critically acclaimed first novel, *Call It Sleep* (1934), then sank into a literary silence that lasted for decades until it was broken near the end of his life. Roth was the son of Jewish immigrants who lived in an area of New York City where life was dominated by Jewish culture. After they moved to a mixed neighbourhood of Irish and Italian immigrants, Roth discovered the sense of isolation reflected in his first novel. *Call It Sleep* was a portrayal of immigrant life in New York City as seen through the eyes of a young Jewish boy. In 1928 Roth graduated from the College of the City of New York, where he met Eda Lou Walton, an academic, critic, and poet 12 years his senior. She supported him while he worked on his book, which he dedicated to her. After it was published, he started work on another novel but became discouraged, and it was never completed. Roth had joined the Communist Party in the 1930s, and he seemed unable to resolve the conflict between his writings and his politics. He and Walton ended their relationship in 1938, and Roth married composer Muriel Parker the following year. He held a variety of blue-collar jobs before moving to Maine, where he bought a farm and taught. He was rediscovered in the early 1960s when *Call It Sleep* was issued in paperback. He published a few short stories, but he was most affected by the outbreak of the Six-Day War (1967). When the Communist Party supported the Arabs, his enthusiasm for the party disappeared. After moving to Albuquerque, Roth started work in 1979 on *Mercy of a Rude Stream,* a series of six related novels about immigrant life in New York City. Despite crippling arthritis, Roth managed before his death to complete the work he had started so many years before.

Rowling, Sir Wallace Edward ("Bill"), New Zealand politician (b. Nov. 15, 1927, Motueka, N.Z.—d. Oct. 31, 1995, Motueka), led the New Zealand Labour Party throughout the 1970s and served an embattled 15-month tenure as prime minister in 1974–75. Rowling, whose father was a founding member of the Labour Party, received a master's degree in economics in 1952 from the University of Canterbury, where he subsequently lectured. He was serving as an education officer in the army when he entered politics, joining Parliament in 1962. He was president (1970–72) of the Labour Party and held the post of minister of finance (1972–74). His abrupt entrance into the nation's top political post came after the sudden death of Prime Minister Norman Kirk in 1974. Rowling, the youngest prime minister of the century, helped shape a foreign policy that included a strong anti-nuclear stance. His detractors, such as Robert Muldoon, leader of the rival National Party, criticized his low-key style of management as irresolute and ineffective. Owing to his waning popularity and continuing economic troubles, Rowling lost reelection to Muldoon, yet he maintained leadership of the opposition party until 1983, parrying challenges from deputy party leader David Lange. In 1984 he retired from Parliament and was awarded a knighthood. He later served as ambassador to the United States (1985–88), president of the New Zealand Institute of International Affairs (1990–95), and chairman of a committee to construct a national museum in Wellington.

Royal, Marshall, U.S. alto saxophonist and clarinetist, who served as music director, from 1950 to 1970, of the Count Basie Orchestra (b. May 12, 1912—d. May 8, 1995).

Rudolf, Max, German-born U.S. conductor (b. June 15, 1902, Frankfurt am Main, Germany—d. Feb. 28/March 1, 1995, Philadelphia, Pa.), was conductor (1945–58) and music administrator (1950–58) at the Metropolitan Opera in New York City and music director of the Cincinnati (Ohio) Symphony (1958–70), but he was perhaps best known for his long association (1970–95) as a teacher, adviser, and head of the opera and conducting departments at the Curtis Institute in Philadelphia. Rudolf studied piano, organ, cello, trumpet, and composition as a child. He began to compose chamber music at age 12 and made his debut as assistant conductor of the Stadtische Theater in Freiburg, Germany, in 1923. After serving as associate conductor of the German Theatre in Prague (1929–35) and guest conductor for the Berlin Philharmonic (1929–30), he left Germany for Göteborg, Sweden. He moved to the U.S. in 1940 and taught in Chicago before joining the Met in 1945. Rudolf's highly influential textbook, *The Grammar of Conducting,* was published in 1950.

Runcorn, Stanley Keith, British geophysicist (b. Nov. 19, 1922, Southport, Lancashire, England—d. Dec. 5, 1995, San Diego, Calif.), was the first to discover evidence of the periodic polar reversals of the Earth's magnetic field. In the 1950s he was a pioneer in the fledgling discipline of paleomagnetism, or remanent magnetism, the study of the residual magnetism in rocks. Magnetic minerals within rocks generally align their magnetic domains permanently to the Earth's field at the time of the rock's formation and deposition, which thereby provides a lasting chronology of geomagnetism. Through this line of study he helped to establish the theories of polar wandering, the migration of the Earth's magnetic poles over time; continental drift, the slow horizontal shifting of continents in relation to one another and to the ocean basins; and plate tectonics, the independent movement of the Earth's outer shell relative to its underlying mantle. In the 1960s he suggested that the Moon, generally thought to be an inactive celestial object, had once possessed a magnetic field. Runcorn was educated at the University of Cambridge (B.A., 1944; M.A., 1948) and the University of Manchester (Ph.D., 1949), where he studied under the Nobel Prize-winning physicist Patrick M.S. Blackett. During 1950–56 Runcorn conducted research at Cambridge that paralleled Blackett's work at Manchester. From 1956 to 1988 he was director of the physics department at King's College, a part of the University of Durham that was reorganized as the University of Newcastle upon Tyne in 1963. At the end of his career, he held a chair (1989–95) at the University of Alaska.

Sa'id, Aminah as-, Egyptian journalist and writer (b. 1914, Cairo, Egypt—d. Aug. 13, 1995, Cairo), was one of her country's leading feminists and was a founder (1954) and editor (1954–69) of *Hawa'* ("Eve"), the first women's magazine to be published in Egypt. Throughout her entire career she worked fervently to fight injustice and to promote the cause of women's rights. At the age of 14, Sa'id joined the youth section of the Egyptian Feminist Union, and in 1931 she became one of the first women to attend the Egyptian University (now Cairo University). After graduation (1935) she joined the staff of the journal *al-Musawwar* and began writing columns, work that she would continue until shortly before her death. She became that publication's editor in 1973, and in 1976 she became chair of the publishing group that produced it, a position she held until 1985. Sa'id also served in such capacities as secretary-general of the Pan-Arab League Women's Union (1958–69) and vice president of the Egyptian Union of Journalists (1959–70). She also was Egypt's representative at a number of international conferences. Among the awards she received were the First Order of the Republic (1975), the Universal Star (1979), and the National Arts Award (1982).

Salk, Jonas, U.S. physician and medical researcher (b. Oct. 28, 1914, New York, N.Y.—d. June 23, 1995, La Jolla, Calif.), was the creator of the first effective vaccine against poliomyelitis (infantile paralysis). Salk first conducted research on viruses in the 1930s when he was a medical student at New York University, and in the 1940s he helped develop flu vaccines at the University of Michigan. He began his studies of polio at the University of Pittsburgh, Pa., where in 1947 he had become head of viral research. Polio epidemics had been intensifying until in 1952, the worst year, about 58,000 cases were reported in the U.S. alone, and more than 3,000 died from the disease. It had been thought that live forms of the poliovirus were necessary for successful immunization, but Salk was convinced that inactivated virus would work. With financial help from the March of Dimes campaign of the National Foundation for Infantile Paralysis, he developed an injectable inactivated-virus vaccine. He conducted the first human trials on former polio patients and on himself and his family, and then in 1954 clinical trials began on some 1.8 million U.S. schoolchildren. On April 12, 1955, the announcement was made that the vaccine was effective and safe. A nationwide inoculation campaign began, and by 1962 the number of new cases of polio had dropped to approximately 1,000. Although in the U.S. the Salk vaccine was superseded about that time by the oral live-virus vaccine developed by Albert B. Sabin, the former remained in use in many countries. By 1995 polio had been eliminated from the entire Western Hemisphere and was targeted for global eradication. In 1963 Salk opened the Salk Institute for Biological Studies in La Jolla. In later years he began research aimed at developing vaccines for multiple sclerosis and AIDS, and at the time of his death a vaccine to prevent the development of AIDS in HIV-infected persons was being tested in a small clinical trial. Among the many awards Salk received during his career were the French Legion of Honor (chevalier, 1955; officer, 1976), the Albert Lasker Award (1956), and the Presidential Medal of Freedom (1977).

Salkey, (Felix) Andrew (Alexander), West Indian writer (b. Jan. 30, 1928, Colón, Panama—d. April 28, 1995, Amherst, Mass.), was part of the community of influential West Indian writers living in post-World War II London. Salkey was born in Panama to Jamaican parents and was educated in Jamaica and at the University of London (B.A., 1955). In 1955 he won the Thomas Helmore Poetry Prize for "Jamaica Symphony," which was finally published as *Jamaica* in 1973. His first novel, *A Quality of Violence* (1959), set the tone for much of his later work with its Jamaican setting, sombre themes, and distinctive use of island dialect. It was quickly followed by a prodigious output of novels, poetry, radio plays, children's books, travel journals, and short stories, notably two volumes of stories about the Caribbean folk character Anancy. Salkey was also instrumental in helping other West Indian writers in his roles as a radio interviewer for BBC World Service, a contributing editor of the expatriate journal *Savacou,* and the editor of several anthologies, including *West Indian Stories* (1960), *The Poetry of the Caribbean* (1973), and *Writing in Cuba Since the Revolution* (1977). He was a professor of writing at Hampshire College, Amherst, Mass., from 1976.

Samuel, Athanasius Yeshue, Syrian-born archbishop and primate of the Syrian Orthodox Church of the United States, who first brought the Dead Sea Scrolls to the attention of the world (b. Dec. 25, 1907—d. April 16, 1995).

Sánchez, Ricardo, U.S. ex-convict turned poetic dean of Chicano literature, a genre that featured writings fraught with descriptions of misery and embittered cries for social justice (b. March 29, 1941—d. Sept. 3, 1995).

Saro-Wiwa, Kenule Beeson ("KEN"), Nigerian author and environmentalist (b. Oct. 10, 1941, Bori, near Port Harcourt, Nigeria—d. Nov. 10, 1995, Port Harcourt), used his popular standing as a journalist, playwright, novelist, and poet to speak out aggressively against the Nigerian military regime and the Anglo-Dutch petroleum company Shell for causing environmental damage to Ogoni tribal lands in his native Rivers state. His execution by hanging, along with eight fellow activists, aroused international condemnation and led to calls for economic sanctions against Nigeria as well as to its suspension from the Commonwealth, which was formally voted. In a trial by special tribunal that was denounced by foreign human rights groups, Saro-Wiwa was found guilty for alleged complicity in the 1994 murders of four Ogoni chiefs who were killed at a political rally. As leader of the Movement for the Survival of the Ogoni People, he criticized the destructive impact of the oil industry—the main source of Nigeria's national revenue—on the Niger delta region and demanded a greater compensatory share of oil profits for the Ogoni. Saro-Wiwa was educated at Government College, Umuahia, and at the University of Ibadan. He taught briefly before joining federal forces in the civil war of the late 1960s; afterward he worked as a government administrator until 1973, when he left to concentrate on his literary career. One of his most notable works, the novel *Sozaboy* (1985), was written in pidgin English and satirized the corruption in Nigerian society. He reached his largest audience, however, with *Basi and Company,* a comedic television series that ran for some 150 episodes in the 1980s. From about 1991 he devoted himself full-time to the causes of the Ogoni, a minority tribe that numbered about 500,000 people. In mid-1992 he broadened the reach of his organization internationally, particularly in Britain, where Shell had one of its headquarters; as a result of mounting protest, Shell suspended operations in Ogoni lands in 1993. Despite the outcry, however, Shell announced in late 1995 its commitment to a nearly $4 billion natural-gas project, one of the largest foreign investments in Nigerian history.

Sarton, Eléanore Marie ("MAY"), U.S. poet and author (b. May 3, 1912, Wondelgem, Belgium—d. July 16, 1995, York, Maine), explored the human condition, ranging from love and individual uniqueness to social justice and aging, in some 50 books. Her works include volumes of poetry, novels, screenplays, autobiographies, and journals. Though Sarton did not receive critical acclaim until late in her career, she gained a huge following among students and feminists as her reputation grew, largely by word of mouth. Sarton's family moved to England after the outbreak of World War I, and two years later they moved to the U.S., settling in Cambridge, Mass. Sarton's name was anglicized to Eleanor May Sarton. She became an actress with Eva Le Gallienne's theatre in 1929 and, when that company disbanded (1933), formed her own troupe, which lasted until 1936. Sarton then began to concentrate on her writing—she had had some sonnets published—and her first volume of poetry, *Encounter in April,* appeared in 1937. Her first novel, *The Single Hound,* followed in 1938 and another poetry volume, *Inner Landscape,* in 1939. She supplemented her income over the years by teaching, writing book reviews, scripting U.S. Office of War Information films during World War II, and lecturing at colleges and universities. After Sarton revealed her lesbianism in what was perhaps her best-known and most interesting book, *Mrs. Stevens Hears the Mermaids Singing* (1965), she became a U.S. cult figure in feminist circles. Later works include the journal *After the Stroke* (1988) and a collection of poems, *Coming into Eighty* (1992). Sarton was awarded some 18 honorary degrees and was a member of the American Academy of Arts and Sciences.

Sasakawa, Ryoichi, Japanese businessman, philanthropist, and suspected World War II criminal who used his vast wealth, amassed from a gambling empire, to aid international charitable organizations (b. May 4, 1899—d. July 18, 1995).

Scali, John A., U.S. news correspondent who served as an unofficial go-between during what became known as the Cuban missile crisis and thus helped defuse tensions between the U.S. and the U.S.S.R. (b. April 27, 1918—d. Oct. 9, 1995).

Schaeffer, Pierre, French composer, writer, and teacher (b. Aug. 14, 1910, Nancy, France—d. Aug. 19, 1995, Aix-en-Provence, France), devel-

CAMERA PRESS

Ryoichi Sasakawa

oped musique concrète, a montage form using assemblages of recorded sounds. Educated as an engineer, he began a long affiliation with the French state radio in 1936. During World War II, Schaeffer helped found the Studio d'Essai, which became an important centre of resistance activity and of research in the medium of radio and where he developed a reputation as an innovative programmer. Among other organizations he founded was the Groupe de Recherche de Musique Concrète, which later became the Groupe de Recherches Musicales. From the beginning of his career, Schaeffer was interested in the analysis of sounds, both natural and man-made, and in the 1940s he developed procedures for using recorded sounds, first on disc and then on tape, as the basic components of what he began to call musique concrète. Unlike traditional music, this method of composing did not depend on performers to interpret or realize what had been set down in notation. One of Schaeffer's best-known compositions was *Symphonie pour un homme seul* (1950), written with his colleague Pierre Henry. From 1968 Schaeffer taught electronic composition at the Paris Conservatory. Among his wide-ranging interests were philosophy, literature, the theatre, and the visual arts; he created music for ballet, film, and the stage. He also was the creator of a popular animated cartoon series with original music. His writings include novels, short stories, and essays, as well as theoretical works in music. Among his books on music are *À la recherche d'une musique concrète* (1952), *Traité des objets musicaux* (1966), and the two-volume *Machines à communiquer* (1970–72).

Scharrer, Berta Vogel, U.S. research scientist who conducted pioneering research on the physiology of cockroaches, work that helped establish neuroendocrinology as a scientific discipline (b. Dec. 1, 1906—d. July 23, 1995).

Scribner, Charles, Jr., U.S. publisher who was head, 1952–84, of the Charles Scribner's Sons book publishing company, which had been founded by his great-grandfather, and personal editor of Ernest Hemingway's works (b. July 13, 1921—d. Nov. 11, 1995).

Seldes, George, U.S. author, journalist, and self-styled "progressive" critic of the mainstream press who argued in his writings that commercial censorship posed a greater danger to press freedom in the U.S. than the government did and turned out the weekly *In Fact,* a muckraking newsletter that delivered "the real inside news" (b. Nov. 16, 1890—d. July 2, 1995).

Selena (SELENA QUINTANILLA PEREZ), U.S.-born Hispanic singer (b. April 16, 1971, Lake Jackson, Texas—d. March 31, 1995, Corpus Christi, Texas), was dubbed the Latin Madonna and was poised to achieve crossover success with the release of her first English-language album before being murdered, apparently by the founder of her fan club, who was suspected of embezzlement. Selena, who had performed from the age of nine with the family band, was a vivacious entertainer whose fluid voice celebrated the sound of Tejano, a fast-paced accordion-based Latin dance music that combined elements of jazz, country, and German polka and was rooted in South Texas. Selena's Tex-Mex popularity earned her laurels as the queen of Tejano, and she won a 1994 Grammy award for best Mexican-American album for *Selena Live.* Another album, *Amor Prohibido,* sold more than 400,000 copies and was nominated for a 1995 Grammy award. At the time of Selena's shooting death, her song "Fotos y Recuerdos" was number four on *Billboard*'s Latin chart.

Shils, Edward, U.S. sociologist who conducted research on the role of intellectuals in society during his five-decade association with the University of Chicago (b. July 1, 1910—d. Jan 23, 1995).

Siad Barre, Muhammad (MAXAMED SIYAAD BARRE), Somali general and political leader (b. *c.* 1919, Ganane, Italian Somaliland—d. Jan. 2, 1995, Lagos, Nigeria), held dictatorial rule over

Selena
RENO—SYGMA

Somalia from October 1969, when he led a bloodless military coup against the elected government, until January 1991, when he was overthrown in a bloody civil war. Siad was born about 1919 (or earlier) into a nomadic family in the small Marehan clan of the Daarood clan group in southern Somaliland. He joined the Somali police force after the British took control in 1941 and rose to the post of chief inspector. When Somalia was returned to Italian sovereignty in 1950, Siad was sent to the military academy in Italy. He transferred to the Somali national army when it was formed (1960), and by 1966 he held the rank of major general and had become commander in chief. After taking state power on Oct. 22, 1969, Siad made himself head of a Supreme Revolutionary Council and imposed autocratic rule through a personality cult and the harsh enforcement of an official ideology called "Scientific Socialism." He strengthened relations with the Soviet Union, officially outlawed clan loyalties (while using clan elders to establish order in rural areas), and promoted literacy with a newly introduced Roman alphabet. He later renounced his ties with the Soviets and sought U.S. aid, but allegations of human rights abuses hurt his international standing. By 1990 fighting among clans and between clan militias and the government forced Siad to promise reforms, including free elections. He was forced out of office in January 1991 and in 1992 went into exile in Nigeria.

BENOIT GYSEMBERGH—CAMERA PRESS

Muhammad Siad Barre

Simon, Barney, South African theatre director (b. April 13, 1932, Johannesburg, South Africa—d. June 30, 1995, Johannesburg), was a longtime force behind the growth of indigenous South African black drama and served as the artistic director of the nonracial Market Theatre in Johannesburg from its founding in 1976 until his death. Simon, the son of working-class Lithuanian immigrants, became an opponent of racial inequality at an early age. He discovered a love of theatre while working under director Joan Littlewood in London in the 1950s. After returning to Johannesburg, he supported himself by working as an advertising copywriter while he produced and directed plays, notably Athol Fugard's *The Blood Knot* (1961). Simon spent a year (1969–70) in the U.S., where he introduced South African plays to a wider audience and edited the journal *New American Review.* In 1976 Simon and Mannie Manim opened the Market Theatre in a converted fruit market. There he nurtured dramatists such as Fugard, Percy Mtwa, and Mbongeni Ngema—in spite of recurring financial difficulties and the constant threat of arrest for staging controversial contemporary plays performed by multiracial casts in front of multiracial audiences. Simon's own published works include the play *Born in the R.S.A.*

Slonimsky, Nicolas, Russian-born U.S. musicologist, lexicographer, conductor, pianist, and composer who compiled such indispensable reference works as *Music Since 1900, A Lexicon of Musical Invective*, and several editions of *Baker's Biographical Dictionary of Musicians* besides composing short, mostly witty pieces of music (b. April 27, 1894—d. Dec. 25, 1995).

Slovo, Joe (YOSSEL MASHEL SLOVO), Lithuanian-born South African lawyer and political activist (b. May 23, 1926, Obelai, Lithuania—d.

Jan. 6, 1995, Johannesburg, South Africa), as spokesman, chairman (1984–87 and 1991–95), and general secretary (1987–91) of the South African Communist Party (SACP), was the chief white leader in the struggle against apartheid for more than 40 years. He was also the first white member (1985) of the National Executive Committee of the African National Congress (ANC). Slovo's family immigrated to South Africa in 1935. He left school at age 13 and joined the SACP three years later, in part because it was the nation's only nonracial political organization. After completing his military service, he studied law at the University of Witwatersrand, where he became friends with Nelson Mandela. The SACP was outlawed in 1950, and Slovo was banned from political activity in 1954. He continued to provide legal counsel for black dissidents, helped to draft (1955) the ANC's Freedom Charter, and worked to form (1961) the group's military wing, *Umkhonto we Sizwe* ("Spear of the Nation"). Slovo was out of the country when the ANC leadership was arrested in 1963. For 27 years he campaigned to solicit money and raise international awareness from bases in London, Zambia, and Mozambique. The activities of Slovo's first wife, Ruth First, who maintained the struggle in South Africa until she joined him in exile, was the basis for the 1987 film *A World Apart.* He returned to Johannesburg when Mandela was released from prison in 1990. Slovo was named minister of housing in the first multiracial government in 1994.

Smith, Margaret Chase, U.S. politician (b. Dec. 14, 1897, Skowhegan, Maine—d. May 29, 1995, Skowhegan), was an independent-minded Republican who became the first of her party to condemn Sen. Joseph McCarthy's anticommunist witch-hunts and was the first woman to win election and serve in both houses of Congress. Her remarkable career also included a nomination (1964) to the U.S. presidency. Smith, the daughter of the town barber, excelled on the high-school basketball court but was an indifferent student. After graduation she taught school and worked as a telephone operator before joining the staff of the local *Independent Republican* as a girl Friday. There she met her future husband, publisher Clyde Smith. After he was elected to Congress in 1936, she served as his secretary, but when he suffered a heart attack in 1940, he urged voters to elect her in his stead. Smith served for eight years in the House of Representatives before winning election in 1948 to the Senate, where she established a reputation as the conscience of that body. She was a staunch anticommunist and regretted that Pres. John F. Kennedy did not have the courage to use nuclear weapons against the Soviet Union, a view that prompted Soviet leader Nikita Khrushchev to dub her "the devil in disguise of a woman." The opinionated Smith also backed New Deal legislation proposed by Democratic Pres. Franklin D. Roosevelt and rejected two of Republican Pres. Richard M. Nixon's Supreme Court nominees. In her 1972 bid for a fifth term in the Senate, Smith, by then 74 and moving about the Capitol corridors in a small yellow cart, was defeated by William D. Hathaway. She retired from politics and returned to her hometown. In 1989 she was the recipient of the Presidential Medal of Freedom.

Soukop, Wilhelm Josef ("Willi"), Austrian-born British sculptor (b. Jan. 5, 1907—d. Feb. 8, 1995).

Souphanouvong, Prince, Laotian revolutionary and political leader (b. July 13, 1909, Luang Prabang, Laos—d. Jan. 9, 1995, Laos), fought against French colonial rule in post-World War II Indochina and then against the U.S.-backed government of independent Laos, notably as founder-leader of the procommunist Pathet Lao guerrilla movement. He eventually served (1975–86) as the first president of the Lao People's Democratic Republic. Souphanouvong studied civil engineering in France and returned to Indochina to build roads and bridges for the colonial administration. He was foreign minister (1947–48) in the Free Lao government-in-exile, but he broke with it in 1950 to form the revolutionary Pathet Lao in alliance with Ho Chi Minh's forces in neighbouring Vietnam. Although he joined a short-lived coalition government (1962–63) with his half brother Prince Souvanna Phouma as prime minister, Souphanouvong was arrested when the coalition collapsed. He escaped and resumed the civil war in the north. After the Pathet Lao seized control in 1975, Souphanouvong was named to the largely ceremonial post of president.

Prince Souphanouvong
UPI/BETTMANN

Southern, Terry, U.S. screenwriter and satirical novelist who collaborated on *Dr. Strangelove* and *Easy Rider,* 1960s films that reflected society's anger and unease during that era, and co-wrote *Candy,* a scandalous erotic fantasy (b. May 1, 1924—d. Oct. 29, 1995).

Spender, Sir Stephen Harold, British poet and critic (b. Feb. 28, 1909, London, England—d. July 16, 1995, London), was one of the preeminent English poets of the 1930s and a member of the "Oxford generation," a small group of youthful literary aesthetes whose innovative, socially committed work in that decade gave a new direction to English literature and left a lasting effect on later generations. While Spender was an undergraduate at University College, Oxford, he developed lifelong friendships with C. Day-Lewis and W.H. Auden, whose first collection of poems Spender printed in 1928. He also coedited *Oxford Poetry* (1929) with Louis MacNeice, and he lived with the novelist Christopher Isherwood for several months during a sojourn (1930–33) in Germany. *Poems* (1933), Spender's first important verse collection, was followed in quick succession by another, *Vienna* (1934); a volume of literary criticism, *The Destructive Element* (1935); and a collection of short stories, *The Burning Cactus* (1936). Although he remained a committed liberal, Spender joined the Communist Party but quickly left after becoming disenchanted with Marxism. He was coeditor (1939–41) of the literary journal *Horizon* and of *Encounter* (1953–67) until he learned of that periodical's links to the CIA. His total output included fiction, essays, plays, criticism, journals, translations, and several volumes of poetry, notably *Dolphins* (1994), which was published on his 85th birthday. He also held several academic positions, in particular as a professor of English at University College, London (1970–77, emeritus from 1977). Spender was the first non-American to serve (1965) as consultant in poetry in English to the U.S. Library of Congress. He was made Commander of the Order of the British Empire in 1962 and knighted in 1983.

Stennis, John Cornelius, U.S. politician (b. Aug. 3, 1901, De Kalb, Miss.—d. April 23, 1995, Jackson, Miss.), as a formidable Mississippi Democrat and the second longest-serving U.S. senator (1947–89), behind Carl Hayden of Arizona, exerted vast influence over the U.S. military while serving as chairman of both the Armed Services Committee and the defense subcommittee of the Appropriations Committee during the 1970s; he was especially admired for his sterling integrity, a trait that led colleagues to select him to head numerous political inquiries. One year after earning (1927) a law degree from the University of Virginia, Stennis was elected to the Mississippi legislature. He served as a district attorney and circuit judge before winning the Senate seat left vacant by the death of Theodore Bilbo. Stennis' Senate record also was marked by his opposition to integration, although late in his career he supported some civil rights measures. The indomitable Stennis, who was nicknamed the "conscience of the Senate" for his work on the Senate's ethics code, exhibited personal fortitude in 1973 when he made a remarkably swift recovery after being shot by robbers and left bleeding on the sidewalk in front of his home. In 1984, after losing a leg to cancer, Stennis returned to his desk sooner than expected. He remained a staunch advocate of a strong military throughout his career and during the final years of his tenure became a mentor to junior senators.

Stephens, Sir Robert, British actor who was a star with the National Theatre in the 1960s; after a period of personal and professional decline following a divorce from actress Maggie Smith in 1975, he made a spectacular comeback in the 1990s playing Falstaff and King Lear for the Royal Shakespeare Company (b. July 14, 1931—d. Nov. 12, 1995).

Stevens, Brooks, U.S. industrial designer (b. June 7, 1911, Milwaukee, Wis.—d. Jan. 4, 1995, Milwaukee), was the creative genius behind the design of the immensely popular 1949 Harley-Davidson motorcycle, a lavishly appointed, chrome-laden, rugged machine that became an American classic and served as the prototype for the company's modern-day Heritage Classic series. Stevens first

Stephen Spender
HULTON DEUTSCH

began drawing while suffering from childhood polio. He studied architecture at Cornell University, Ithaca, N.Y., but decided to pursue a career in design when the stock market crash of 1929 and the following Great Depression put a halt to most construction projects. Some of his most notable designs included the Lawn Boy, the world's first rotary mower; a Hamilton tumble dryer (notable for a porthole viewing window positioned in the appliance's front door); and the 1958 Oscar Mayer Wienermobiles, vehicles that were fashioned in the shape of hot dogs. Stevens was also one of 10 pioneering designers who founded (1944) the Society of Industrial Designers to gain status for industrial design as a profession. Among Stevens' other innovations were the 1948 Willys Jeepster, a jazzed-up civilian version of the army Jeep; the 1964 Excalibur two-seat sports car; and Studebaker's 1962 Hawk GT and 1963 Lark.

Stibitz, George Robert, U.S. mathematician (b. April 30, 1904, York, Pa.—d. Jan. 31, 1995, Hanover, N.H.), was regarded by many as the "father of the modern digital computer." While serving as a research mathematician at Bell Telephone Laboratories in New York City, Stibitz worked on relay switching equipment used in telephone networks. Because he and his colleagues were unable to quickly perform the complex mathematical calculations needed for this work, Stibitz began tinkering at home and devised a primitive binary adder comprising dry-cell batteries, metal strips from a tobacco can, and flashlight bulbs connected to two old telephone relays. Stibitz and co-worker Samuel Williams, an engineer, expanded this desktop electrical device into the closet-size Model I Complex Calculator, which became operational at Bell Labs on Jan. 8, 1940. The machine remained in use until 1949 and was considered a forerunner of the digital computer. A replica of Stibitz' first rudimentary adder later was housed in the Smithsonian Institution, Washington, D.C. In 1940 Stibitz also achieved what was believed to have been the first remote computer operation when he transmitted problems to be solved over a teletypewriter from Dartmouth College, Hanover, N.H., to a Bell Labs Model I computer in New York City and received the answers back in the same way. After earning (1930) a Ph.D. in mathematical physics from Cornell University, Ithaca, N.Y., Stibitz joined Bell Labs, where he remained until 1941. During World War II he served on the U.S. National Defense Research Committee and also conducted research on binary computers for military use. He then worked as a private consultant until joining (1964) the faculty of Dartmouth Medical School as professor of physiology. There he pioneered computer applications in such biomedical areas as the movement of oxygen in the lungs, brain-cell anatomy, the diffusion of nutrients and drugs in the body, and capillary transport. In 1973 he became professor emeritus, but he continued to conduct research into the 1980s. Stibitz, who held 38 patents, was inducted into the Inventors Hall of Fame in 1983 and was elected to the National Academy of Engineering in 1981.

JACK VARTOOGIAN, 1989
Sunnyland Slim

Stoutt, H(amilton) Lavity, chief minister of the British Virgin Islands five times from 1967 to 1995 and a member of the Legislative Council from 1957, the longest-serving parliamentarian in the region (b. March 7, 1929—d. May 14, 1995).

Sunnyland Slim (ALBERT LUANDREW), U.S. blues musician (b. Sept. 5, 1907, Vance, Miss.—d. March 17, 1995, Chicago, Ill.), introduced his own powerful brand of Mississippi Delta-blues piano and helped build post-World War II Chicago into a major centre for the performance and recording of classic and electrified blues music. The son of a preacher and the grandson of a slave, he learned to play organ and piano in his father's church. He ran away in his early teens and drifted, working odd jobs and playing piano in roadhouses, juke joints, and silent cinemas. In the mid-1920s Sunnyland Slim settled in Memphis, Tenn., where his shouting, boogie-woogie style became a fixture in local blues clubs. After moving to Chicago in the early 1940s, he signed with Aristocrat (later called Chess Records), which became a force in the recording and promotion of blues. In 1947 he helped to secure the future of Chess and the Chicago blues scene when he arranged for a recording contract for a friend from his days in Memphis: Muddy Waters. In addition to his solo music, Sunnyland Slim often worked as an accompanist or as backup for other bluesmen, and in the 1970s he founded his own label, Airways Records. He recorded more than 200 songs and 20 albums, variously using the name Sunnyland Slim (allegedly acquired from one of his songs, "Sunnyland Train"), Sunny Land Slim, Delta Joe, and Dr. Clayton's Buddy.

Swayze, John Cameron, U.S. pioneering newscaster who gained fame "hopscotching the world for headlines" on "Camel News Caravan" and

Timex watch pitchman who assured consumers that "it takes a licking and keeps on ticking" (b. April 4, 1906—d. Aug. 15, 1995).

Tagliavini, Ferrucio, Italian opera tenor and motion-picture actor (b. Aug. 14, 1913—d. Jan. 28, 1995).

Tang Yee-ming, Dominic, Chinese Roman Catholic priest who served (1951–58) as titular bishop and apostolic administrator of Guangzhou (Canton) diocese before spending 22 years in various prisons for refusing to break contact with the Vatican as ordered by the government; he served (1981–95) as archbishop of Canton while in exile in Hong Kong (b. May 13, 1908—d. June 27, 1995).

Tansi, (Marcel) Sony Labou, Congolese writer (b. June 5, 1947, Kimwanza, Moyen-Congo, French Equatorial Africa—d. June 14, 1995, Brazzaville, Congo), explored issues of past colonial exploitation and contemporary political corruption through complex fables that showed elements of satire, dark humour, and fantasy akin to Latin-American magic realism. Tansi's first published novel, *La Vie et demie* (1979), was admired in West Africa and in Europe. That volume won the special jury's prize in 1979 at the international festival for Francophone literature held in Nice, France. By that time, however, he already had a small stockpile of other works, including *L'État honteux,* which was published in 1981. In the 1980s Tansi wrote novels, plays, and poetry while employed by the Congolese Ministry of Culture. He was also founder and director of the Rocado Zulu Theatre in Brazzaville. Elected to the National Assembly in 1993 as a member of the opposition, he refused to take his seat as a political protest and was placed under house arrest. In early 1995 Tansi and his wife were allowed to travel to Paris for medical treatment for AIDS.

Tarasov, Anatoly, Russian ice hockey coach who introduced aggressive, Canadian-style play to his country and led the Soviet national team to 11 European championships and 10 world titles, including three Olympic gold medals, 1962–72 (b. *c.* 1918—d. June 23, 1995).

Tax, Sol, U.S. anthropologist (b. Oct. 30, 1907, Chicago, Ill.—d. Jan. 4, 1995, Chicago), was instrumental in establishing anthropology as a global discipline, especially as the founding editor (1957–74) of *Current Anthropology*, an international journal devoted to the exchange of ideas and discussion of important issues in the field. He was also an expert on the cultures of North and Middle American Indians, especially the Fox (Mesquakie) and Sauk. From 1948 to 1962 he served as director of the Fox Indian Project in Tama, Iowa, and he was coordinator of the 1961 American Indian Chicago Conference, at which some 700 Native Americans from more than 80 tribes drafted a "Declaration of Indian Purpose." The document urged the government to respect native customs and to include Native Americans in economic and social development projects. Tax received a Ph.D. (1935) from the University of Chicago and was an ethnologist (1934–48) for the Carnegie Institution in Washington, D.C. At the University of Chicago he served as a research associate (1940–44), associate professor (1944–48), and professor of anthropology from 1948 until his retirement in 1974. He was also department chairman (1955–58) and dean (1963–68) of the University Extension. Tax conducted anthropological studies in Guatemala, Mexico (training a number of anthropologists there), and the U.S., where he established "action anthropology." This approach was meant to incorporate the work of anthropologists in matters of practical concern and involve them in solving the problems identified by the people they were studying. Tax was president of the American Anthropological Association (1958–59) and was the recipient in 1962 of the Viking Fund Medal and Award for his outstanding anthropological achievements. His writings include *Heritage of Conquest: The Ethnology of Middle America* (1952; with others), *Penny Capitalism: A Guatemalan Indian Economy* (1953), and contributions to Encyclopædia Britannica's *Yearbook of Science and the Future.*

Taylor, Art, U.S. jazz drummer and bandleader (b. April 6, 1929—d. Feb. 6, 1995).

Tembo, Biggie (Rodwell Marasha), Zimbabwean musician who found international popularity in the early 1980s as a member of the Bhundu Boys "jit-jive" dance band (b. Sept. 30, 1958—d. July 30, 1995).

Teng, Teresa (Teng Li-chün), Chinese singer (b. Jan. 29, 1953, Yün-lin county, Taiwan—d. May 8, 1995, Chiang Mai, Thailand), was a superstar throughout East Asia and was especially admired in her homeland, where she earned the affection of fans by entertaining troops with her renditions of Mandarin love songs. Although she repeatedly declined invitations to visit the People's Republic of China, pirated recordings of her songs could be found even in remote villages. The government's effort to ban Teng's songs as "spiritual pollution" proved futile. Her popularity was so great that it was said to rival that of Deng Xiaoping (Teng Hsiao-p'ing), China's paramount leader, with whom she shared a surname. A popular saying was that Old Deng ruled the day and Little Teng the night. Her transnational success was attributed to her multilingualism (she sang in Mandarin, Cantonese, Japanese, and English), her clear and sweet vocals, and her heart-rending love songs, which appealed to both young and old in such far-flung locations as China, Malaysia, Singapore, Indonesia, and Japan, where in 1975 she was crowned the best new artist and won top prize at the 18th Album Awards. Some of her most popular albums include *Faded Feelings* (1983), *I'm in Your Debt* (1984), and *The Unforgettable Teresa Teng* (1992). Before her death Teng had taken up residence in France, where she was able to live comfortably off her Japanese royalties. She was vacationing in Thailand when she suffered a fatal asthma attack.

Tinsley, Marion, U.S. world checkers champion, 1955–58 and 1975–92 (b. Feb. 3, 1927—d. April 3, 1995).

Tisch, Harry, East German chairman of the Free German Trade Union Federation, 1975–89, and the first member of the East German Politboro to be tried for corruption in reunified Germany (b. March 18, 1927—d. June 18, 1995).

Toeplitz, Jerzy Bonawentura, Ukrainian-born Polish motion-picture historian who was the first director of the Polish national film school at Lodz, 1949–52 and 1957–68, and of the Australian Film and Television School in Sydney, 1973–79 (b. Nov. 24, 1909—d. July 24, 1995).

Torga, Miguel (Adolfo Correia da Rocha), Portuguese poet and diarist (b. Aug. 12, 1907, São Matinho de Anta, Port.—d. Jan. 17, 1995, Coimbra, Port.), wrote poetry and fiction that reflected his love for Portugal—in particular, for his boyhood home in Trás-os-Montes, a harsh, poverty-stricken rural province in northern Portugal—and his more universal concerns about human suffering and despair in the modern world. He graduated with a degree in medicine from the University of Coimbra (1933) and went on to establish a private practice in otolaryngology in that city. While still a medical student, he founded a literary magazine, *Presença*, and published his first book of poetry, *Ansiedade* (1928), under his real name. Later verse collections, which were published under his pen name, include *Libertação* (1944), *Orfeu rebelde* (1958), and *Poemas ibéricos* (1965). He also wrote short stories, plays, and novels, notably *Contos da montanha* (1941; *Tales from the Mountain*, 1991) and the autobiographical novel *A criação do mundo* (1935). Torga was particularly admired among young Portuguese for his 16-volume *Diário* (1941–94), which he began in 1938 and in which he mixed poetry and stories amid the details and personal musings about daily life.

Townshend, Peter Wooldridge, British Royal Air Force group captain and royal equerry whose controversial romance with Princess Margaret ended in 1955 when she publicly renounced him because his earlier divorce was not sanctioned by the Church of England (b. Nov. 22, 1914—d. June 19, 1995).

Trevor, Elleston (Trevor Dudley Smith), British novelist who published dozens of mysteries, thrillers, and adventure books under several pseudonyms; his best-known novels were *The Flight of the Phoenix* and *The Quiller Memorandum* (b. Feb. 17, 1920—d. July 21, 1995).

Truitte, James, U.S. lead dancer with the companies of Lester Horton and Alvin Ailey who promoted and taught Horton's technique and choreography (b. 1923—d. Aug. 21, 1995).

Turner, Lana (Julia Jean Turner), U.S. actress (b. Feb. 8, 1920, Wallace, Idaho—d. June 29, 1995, Los Angeles, Calif.), was a sultry Hollywood glamour queen whose shapely figure was featured in a series of "Sweater Girl" films, vehicles that made her one of the most popular pinups among U.S. servicemen in World War II. Her screen roles often mirrored her tumultuous private life, which was headlined by eight marriages and the sensational 1958 stabbing death of her gangster boyfriend, Johnny Stompanato, by her 14-year-old daughter. As legend has it, the golden-haired starlet was in high school when she was "discovered" at a soda fountain by a Hollywood film journalist. After making her film debut in *They Won't Forget* (1937), Turner appeared as a showgirl in *Ziegfeld Girl* (1941) before starring opposite Clark Gable in two films, *Honky Tonk* (1941) and *Somewhere I'll Find You* (1942). She played a gangster's moll in *Johnny Eager* (1942) but was best remembered for her sizzling sex appeal as a murdering adulteress in *The Postman Always Rings Twice* (1946). Turner portrayed an alcoholic actress in *The Bad and the Beautiful* (1952) and earned an Academy Award nomination for her role as a neurotic mother in the blockbuster *Peyton Place* (1957). She had two other box-office smash hits, *Imitation of Life* (1959) and *Madame X* (1966), before her career began to slide. She made a steady stream of melodramas and turned to television soap operas in the 1970s and '80s, with roles in "The Survivors" and "Falcon Crest."

Tynan, Kathleen Jeanette Halton, British novelist and biographer who won acclaim for a 1987 biography of her late husband, drama critic Kenneth Tynan (b. Jan. 25, 1937—d. Jan. 10, 1995).

VerMeulen, Michael, U.S. magazine editor who boosted the circulation of the premier men's magazine *GQ* by 40% while serving, 1992–95, as editor (b. Dec. 10, 1956—d. Aug. 28, 1995).

Victor, Paul-Émile, French polar explorer and ethnologist who led more than 60 expeditions to the Arctic and Antarctic regions (b. June 28, 1907—d. March 7, 1995).

Vlachos, Helen (Elena Vlakhou), Greek newspaper publisher who shut down two daily papers and a weekly picture magazine before she fled to England in protest against the military junta imposed on Greece in 1967 (b. Dec. 18, 1911—d. Oct. 14, 1995).

Volkogonov, Dmitry Antonovich, Russian colonel general and Soviet military historian who gained access to archival material and published scathing exposés on V.I. Lenin, Joseph Stalin, Leon Trotsky, and other formerly sacrosanct Soviet leaders (b. March 22, 1928—d. Dec. 6, 1995).

Walker, Junior (Autry DeWalt), U.S. rhythm-and-blues tenor saxophonist and leader of Motown's Junior Walker and the All Stars, the group that scored such hits as "These Eyes" and "How Sweet It Is" (b. 1942—d. Nov. 23, 1995).

Walker, Patric William, U.S.-born British astrologer whose syndicated newspaper and mag-

Lana Turner
COLLECTION OF LOU VALENTINO

azine columns were read by millions of avid followers in the U.S. and Britain (b. Sept. 25, 1931—d. Oct. 8, 1995).

Walton, Ernest Thomas Sinton, Irish physicist (b. Oct. 6, 1903, Dungarvan, County Waterford, Ireland—d. June 25, 1995, Belfast, Northern Ireland), was corecipient, with Sir John Douglas Cockcroft of England, of the 1951 Nobel Prize for Physics for their fundamental work on "the transmutation of atomic nuclei by artificially accelerated atomic particles," work they accomplished by means of a primitive nuclear particle accelerator known as the Cockcroft-Walton generator. Walton, the son of a Methodist minister, studied mathematics and experimental science at Trinity College, Dublin, and nuclear physics at Trinity College, Cambridge, where he worked with Cockcroft in Lord Rutherford's Cavendish Laboratory. In April 1932 Walton and Cockcroft, using a device they had constructed from glass cylinders, vacuum tubes, and car batteries, shot a beam of protons into a target of lithium, splitting the lithium atom into two helium atoms. The news that Walton and Cockcroft had split the atom without the use of radioactive elements spread quickly, but by the time the results of their experiment were formally announced, they had split the nuclei of 15 different elements. In 1934 Walton returned to Trinity College, Dublin, as a fellow in the physics department. He was appointed Erasmus Smith's professor of natural and experimental philosophy in 1946, and he retired in 1974.

Watanabe, Michio, Japanese politician (b. July 28, 1923, Tochigi prefecture, Japan—d. Sept. 15, 1995, Tokyo, Japan), had a long career as an influential Liberal Democratic politician, though he never attained the prime ministership, the office he especially aspired to and made three attempts to win. His many accomplishments were often overshadowed, however, by blunt, tactless, and ill-considered comments. At various times during his career, he caused furors by, for example, stating that U.S. blacks had too casual an attitude about their debts, that many Chinese lived in holes, and that Korea had consented to its annexation by Japan in 1910. Watanabe became an accountant after graduating from Tokyo University of Commerce (now Hitotsubashi University) and later decided to enter politics. He was elected to the prefectural assembly in 1955 and to the national House of Representatives in 1963. He was reelected eight times and held that seat for the rest of his life. During his career Watanabe rose quickly through party ranks and headed most of the senior Cabinet ministries, among them Health and Welfare (1976–77), Finance (1980–82), and International Trade and Industry (1985–86). He became foreign minister and deputy prime minister, the last positions he held, in 1991, but a bout of ill health forced him to resign those posts. In 1995 Watanabe led two delegations to North Korea; one was attempting to normalize relations, and the other negotiated a deal for Japan to provide 300,000 tons of rice in emergency aid to North Korea.

Waters, Frank, U.S. novelist and biographer whose works concentrated on the American Southwest (b. July 5, 1902—d. June 3, 1995).

Wayne, David (WAYNE JAMES MCMEEKAN), U.S. actor (b. Jan. 30, 1914, Traverse City, Mich.—d. Feb. 9, 1995, Santa Monica, Calif.), took Broadway by storm as the leprechaun Og in *Finian's Rainbow* (1947), a performance that earned him the first-ever Tony award for acting, and he went on to score another stage triumph and win a second Tony as the wily Sakini in *The Teahouse of the August Moon.* A wiry character actor who demonstrated his versatility in a range of roles, Wayne appeared onstage as Ensign Pulver in *Mister Roberts* (1948), an eccentric uncle in *The Ponder Heart* (1956), and a hypochondriac in *Send Me No Flowers* (1960). Some of his most notable film credits were as a barber in *Wait Till the Sun Shines, Nellie* (1952), a music impresario in *Tonight We Sing* (1953), and the husband of a woman with a multiple personality in *The Three Faces of Eve* (1957). On television Wayne appeared as the Mad Hatter in the "Batman" television series of the 1960s, in the title role in "Norby" (1955), as a tycoon in "The Good Life" (1971–72), as inspector Richard Queen in "The Adventures of Ellery Queen" (1975–76), as Willard ("Digger") Barnes in "Dallas" (1978), and as Dr. Amos Weatherby in "House Calls" (1980–82).

White of Hull, Vincent Gordon Lindsay White, BARON, British business tycoon and ruthless takeover expert who used his formidable skills to build Hanson PLC into one of the U.K.'s largest international conglomerates (b. May 11, 1923—d. Aug. 23, 1995).

Wigner, Eugene Paul, Hungarian-born U.S. physicist (b. Nov. 17, 1902, Budapest, Hung.—d. Jan. 1, 1995, Princeton, N.J.), was the joint winner of the 1963 Nobel Prize for Physics (with Maria Goeppert Mayer and Johannes Hans Jensen) for his insight into quantum mechanics, especially the principles governing the interaction of protons and neutrons in the nucleus. Wigner determined that the nuclear force that binds neutrons and protons together is necessarily short-range and independent of any electric charge. In his work Wigner used the abstract mathematical concept of group theory to investigate problems of atomic structure. He gathered information by focusing on the symmetries, rather than the dynamics, among subatomic particles in a physical system such as an atomic nucleus. He detailed this work in the classic book *Gruppentheorie und ihre Anwendung auf die Quantenmechanik der Atomspektren* (1931; *Group Theory,* 1959). Wigner was initially trained as an engineer and earned a Ph.D. (1925) in that field from the Berlin Institute of Technology. He immigrated to the U.S. in 1930 and began working part-time at Princeton University. In 1937 he became a U.S. citizen and the next year a permanent faculty member at Princeton, where he remained until his retirement in 1971. When he perceived in 1939 that German scientists might be on the brink of achieving a nuclear chain reaction and thus the capability of developing nuclear weapons, Wigner and fellow Hungarians Leo Szilard and Edward Teller persuaded Albert Einstein to write to Pres. Franklin D. Roosevelt and outline the potential threat. Einstein's historic letter was instrumental in setting up the wartime Manhattan Project, thereby launching the U.S. into the nuclear age. This prompted Wigner to interrupt his career at Princeton, beginning in 1942, to help Enrico Fermi at the University of Chicago with work on the top-secret atomic bomb. There they explored the technology needed for nuclear reactors to produce plutonium for the first atomic bomb. After the war Wigner briefly served as director of research and development at the Clinton Laboratories (later Oak Ridge [Tenn.] National Laboratory). He later became a supporter of the Atoms for Peace movement. Among Wigner's other publications are *Dispersion Relations and Their Connection with Causality* (1964) and *Symmetries and Reflections* (1967). A member of the National Academy of Sciences, he was the recipient of numerous awards, including the Atoms for Peace Award (1960), the Max Planck Medal (1961), the Einstein Award (1972), and the Order of Merit (1994), Hungary's highest award, for scientific achievement.

Willingham, Calder, U.S. novelist and screenwriter (b. Dec. 22, 1922, Atlanta, Ga.—d. Feb. 19, 1995, Laconia, N.H.), was lionized at the age of 24 after the publication of the explicit *End as a Man* (1947), a graphic and lurid account of life at a southern military school resembling South Carolina's Citadel, where Willingham was enrolled for one year. The novel, which achieved commercial success after the publisher was unsuccessfully prosecuted for obscenity, was made into a film called *The Strange One* (1957). Willingham was grouped with such other young writers as Gore Vidal, Norman Mailer, and Truman Capote, all of whom employed the same gritty realism. His success was not repeated in his other novels, however, and he explored that theme in his last book, *The Big Nickel* (1975). In later years Willingham gained success as a screenwriter with such credits as *Paths of Glory* (1957), *The Vikings* (1958), *One-Eyed Jacks* (1961), *The Graduate* (1967), *Little Big Man* (1970), and *Rambling Rose* (1991), an adaptation of his same-titled 1972 novel. Shortly before his death he finished an original screenplay for Steven Spielberg.

Wilson of Rievaulx, (James) Harold Wilson, BARON, British politician (b. March 11, 1916, Huddersfield, Yorkshire, England—d. May 24, 1995, London, England), as the pragmatic leader of the British Labour Party for 13 years (1963–76), held together the disparate wings of the party, modified Labour's socialist rhetoric to win the trust of the voters in four general elections, and served as prime minister for eight years (1964–70 and 1974–76). Wilson studied politics, philosophy, and economics at Jesus College, Oxford. He taught economics at New College before accepting a fellowship to University College, where he was research assistant (1938–39) to Sir William (later Lord) Beveridge. Wilson's work with Beveridge on social welfare reforms had great influence on future Labour Party domestic policies, as did the

TOM NORTHEY—CAMERA PRESS
Harold Wilson

study on the mining industry that he produced during his World War II stint as director of economics and statistics at the Ministry of Fuel and Power. Elected to Parliament in 1945, he served in the Ministry of Works (1945–47) and was president of the Board of Trade (1947–51). Wilson allied himself with left-wing challenges to the party leader, Hugh Gaitskell, in 1951 and 1960. When Gaitskell died in 1963, Wilson was elected Labour leader. Under his guidance, Labour won the 1964 election after 13 years in opposition. A natural conciliator, Wilson sought to prevent the unilateral declaration of independence by the Rhodesian white minority government and to improve Anglo-American relations by endorsing U.S. involvement in Southeast Asia. At home, however, he oversaw an unpopular devaluation of the pound and struggled to manage proposed trade union reforms. Labour lost the 1970 and March 1974 general elections to the Conservative Party, but when the Tories were unable to form a workable coalition government in 1974, Wilson was recalled to office. He called another general election in October of that year and won a slight majority. One of his administration's major accomplishments came in 1975 when he defied leftist opposition and put the question of British membership in the European Economic Community to the voters in a successful referendum. Ongoing intraparty strains, combined with additional trade union reforms and increasing budget difficulties, induced Wilson to resign from office unexpectedly on March 16, 1976. He did not stand for reelection to Parliament in 1983; shortly afterward he was made a life peer.

Wolfman Jack (ROBERT WESTON SMITH), U.S. rock-and-roll radio disc jockey whose gravel-throated voice and wolf howls made him a cult personality on the nighttime airwaves until he was elevated to international fame after appearing in the 1973 film classic *American Graffiti* (b. Jan. 21, 1938—d. July 1, 1995).

Wood, Evelyn, U.S. educator who developed a speed-reading technique that came to be recommended by presidents and used by politicians and students; she lent her name in 1959 to a Reading Dynamics Institute that promised to boost reading speed from 250 words per minute to 1,500 or more (b. Jan. 8, 1909—d. Aug. 26, 1995).

Woodcock, George, Canadian poet, critic, historian, travel writer, playwright, scriptwriter, and editor (b. May 8, 1912, Winnipeg, Man.—d. Jan. 28, 1995, Vancouver, B.C.), was a prolific man of letters who philosophized that anarchism—the mutual noninvolvement of the individual and the state—would transform society, a view reflected especially in his poetry. Though born in Canada, Woodcock was an infant when his family moved to England. He was educated there and later worked as a railway clerk. Woodcock became involved in left-wing politics and sat out World War II as a conscientious objector while editing his own magazine, *Now* (1940–47). After returning to Canada in 1949, he led a hardscrabble existence, shoveling manure for a living. Soon Woodcock gained a steady income as a writer and broadcaster. He taught from 1954 to 1955 at the University of Washington and from 1956 to 1963 at the University of British Columbia, where he founded (1959) the journal *Canadian Literature.* As editor (until 1977) of that quarterly, he showcased the works of Canadian writers. He also established a fund for impoverished Canadian authors. The breadth of his writings was enormous and included historical travelogues: *Faces of India* (1964), *South Sea Journey* (1976), and *The Canadians* (1979); political writings: *The Anarchist Prince: A Biographical Study of Peter Kropotkin* (1950; with Ivan Avakumovic) and *Anarchism* (1962), the movement's bible; literary criticism: *Dawn and the Darkest Hour: A Study of Aldous Huxley* (1972), *Thomas Merton, Monk and Poet* (1978), and *The Crystal Spirit* (1966), an award-winning biography about George Orwell; and three volumes of memoirs.

Wright, Peter Maurice, British intelligence officer (b. Aug. 9, 1916, Chesterfield, Derbyshire, England—d. April 27, 1995, Tasmania, Australia), was at the centre of a lengthy international legal battle when Prime Minister Margaret Thatcher's government banned the publication or sale of his memoirs, *Spycatcher: The Candid Autobiography of a Senior Intelligence Officer* (1987), and filed suit (1985) in Australia in a prolonged but ultimately unsuccessful attempt to prevent the book's publication there. Wright worked as an electronics technician for the Admiralty Research Laboratory during World War II. He was an unpaid scientific adviser to MI-5, the counterintelligence branch of the British Security Service, from 1949 until 1954, when he was recruited as MI-5's director of technological improvement. He served as head of the research division in the counterintelligence department from 1964 until his retirement to Tasmania in 1976. In the early 1980s Wright, who claimed that the infiltration of communist spies in the British intelligence community was more widespread than previously thought and who allegedly was angry over the small size of his government pension, cooperated in the writing of Chapman Pincher's exposé *Their Trade Is Treachery* (1982) and *Spycatcher.* The U.K. government banned *Spycatcher,* prosecuted British newspapers and magazines for printing excerpts or reviews, and filed suit in Australia, charging that Wright had violated the Official Secrets Act. The government's actions triggered accusations of censorship and of hypocrisy since Pincher's book had not been suppressed. By 1988 the case in Australia had been lost and the U.S. edition of *Spycatcher* was already an international best-seller. Four years later the House of Lords ruled that the ban had become meaningless and overturned it. Wright also published *The Spycatcher's Encyclopedia of Espionage* (1991) and reportedly was writing a fictional spy thriller at the time of his death.

Wyatt, Robert Elliott Storey ("BOB"), British cricketer (b. May 2, 1901, Milford, Surrey, England—d. April 20, 1995, Treliske, Cornwall, England), in a first-class career (always as an amateur) that lasted from 1923 to 1957, was a reliable middle-order batsman and medium-fast bowler, scoring 39,405 runs (average, 40.04), including 85 centuries, and taking 901 wickets (average, 32.84). Between 1927 and 1937 he made 40 Test appearances for England (16 as captain), scored 1,839 runs (average, 31.70), and took 18 wickets (average, 35.66). Wyatt was educated in Coventry and in 1923 made his first-class debut with Warwickshire, which he captained from 1930 to 1937. After his World War II military service, he transferred to Worcestershire, where he played regularly until 1951 (as captain in 1950–51); he made his last first-class appearance at the age of 56. Although Wyatt was a controversial choice to lead England against Australia in 1930, he proved to be a tough competitor and was named vice-captain for the infamous "bodyline" tour to Australia in 1932–33. Wyatt also served as an England selector (1949–53) and as chairman of selectors (1950).

Yglesias, José, U.S. author and journalist (b. Nov. 29, 1919, Tampa, Fla.—d. Nov. 7, 1995, New York, N.Y.), wrote fiction about Latinos and nonfiction about life in Latin America and Spain, the latter of which was particularly concerned with revolutions and how they affect individuals. In addition to penning about a dozen novels and works of nonfiction, he contributed articles to leading magazines, translated books from Spanish, and tried his hand at writing for the theatre. Yglesias, whose ethnic background was Cuban and Spanish, was raised in Ybor City, a Hispanic neighbourhood of Tampa. He relocated to New York City in 1936, served in the navy during World War II, attended college for a year, and worked as a journalist. He held an executive position at a pharmaceutical company from 1953 until 1963, when his first novel—*A Wake in Ybor City*—was published. Afterward, both he and his wife, Helen, became full-time novelists. *The Goodbye Land* (1967) traced his family roots in Galicia, Spain, where his father had returned to die. In the work *In the Fist of the Revolution* (1968), he chronicled the hopes of the townspeople of Mayarí, Cuba, in response to the communist revolution. In these and other nonfiction works—*Down There* (1970) and *The Franco Years* (1977)—Yglesias used a sympathetic but impartial technique to convey the zeal of foreign revolutionaries. He focused on the histories of Cuban-American families in the novels *The Truth About Them* (1971), *The Kill Price* (1976), *Home Again* (1987), and *Tristan and the Hispanics* (1989). His other novels include *An Orderly Life* (1968), *Double Double* (1974), and *Widower's Walk* (1996).

Young, Marguerite Vivian, U.S. author who published several volumes of poetry before spending nearly two decades crafting *Miss MacIntosh, My Darling,* a 1,198-page novel that examined illusion and reality (b. 1909—d. Nov. 17, 1995).

Yun, Isang, Korean-born German composer (b. Sept. 17, 1917, Tongyong, Korea [now Chungmu, South Korea]—d. Nov. 3, 1995, Berlin, Germany), used contemporary Western techniques to express an Asian sensibility in more than 150 musical works, including four operas and five symphonies. Although he was notable in music circles in Japan and Germany, his name became more widely known in 1967 when he and his wife were abducted from their home in West Germany by the South Korean secret police. They were taken to Seoul, where Yun was tried for treason as a communist and sentenced to life in prison; his wife received a three-year prison sentence. Protests by the West German government and by a group of high-profile musicians led by Igor Stravinsky helped to bring about their release in 1969. The son of a poet, Yun began composing at the age of 14 and, in the early 1940s, studied music in Japan at Osaka and Tokyo. Returning to Korea, he was active in the resistance movement against the Japanese during World War II and afterward taught music in Tongyong, Pusan, and Seoul. In the late 1950s he pursued further study in Paris and in Germany in Darmstadt and Berlin, where he eventually settled. His musical style matured in the 1960s with such chamber pieces as *Loyang* (1962), *Gasa* (1963), and *Garak* (1963). With *Réak* (1966) he established his pattern of dividing the orchestra into three parts: softly played strings, aggressive brass, and fluttering woodwinds. This is exemplified in *Piri* (1971), in which a lonely oboe wanders between the gentle tones of the strings and the hard sounds of the brass. In addition to illustrating the precepts of Taoist philosophy, he wrote in the idiom of protest, such as in the cello concerto of 1976, which drew upon his imprisonment, and in his 1981 orchestral memoriam to the victims of the Kwangju massacre. His later works helped develop his concept of *Haupttöne* ("main notes"), in which sweeping movements pivot on a central melodic tone.

Zawawi, Qais ibn ʿAbd al-Munim az-, Omani politician who was an effective and influential minister of state for foreign affairs, 1973–82, and deputy prime minister for financial and economic affairs, 1982–95 (b. Aug. 27, 1935—d. Sept. 11, 1995).

Zelazny, Roger, U.S. science-fiction writer (b. May 13, 1937, Cleveland, Ohio—d. June 14, 1995, Santa Fe, N.M.), first became prominent in the 1960s as one of the best of the "new wave." Rather than optimistically celebrating new technologies as the earlier generation of science-fiction writers had, his works explored the implications for humanity of the changes that technology had brought to the 20th century. Though Zelazny was the winner of many awards for such books as *Lord of Light* (1967) and *Eye of Cat* (1982), his later works were less successful with critics and the public.

Zuse, Konrad, German engineer who in 1941 constructed the first fully operational program-controlled electromechanical binary calculating machine, or digital computer, called the Z3 (b. June 22, 1910—d. Dec. 18, 1995).

Events of 1995

Agriculture and Food Supplies

The major world food developments in 1995 involved declining grain production per capita and increasing meat production. Both developments were continuations of multiyear trends. It was estimated that global grain stocks declined to record low levels in 1995, and they were expected to decline further by the end of the 1995–96 marketing year. In response, world grain prices increased sharply. The world food system continued to be affected by the two major regions that were moving in opposite directions. In China personal incomes were rising rapidly, and the population demanded more meat in its diet. In the republics of the former Soviet Union, however, incomes and meat consumption had dropped dramatically. These longer-run changes had major impacts on world food production and consumption in 1995. As in past years, nature and humans continued to create food emergencies in many countries—notably in Africa. The most important agricultural policy event of the year, however, may have been the creation of the World Trade Organization (WTO).

The gap between world food-aid needs and food-aid deliveries from donor nations widened in 1995, and the gap was expected to grow in 1996. Global food-aid needs increased, while aid shipments from donor nations declined. Aid needs existed in Africa, Asia, the former Soviet republics, Bosnia and Herzegovina, and Latin America. Chronic food shortages and emergencies were caused by a combination of natural and man-made disasters in 1995. Conditions were made worse by higher prices for grain imports and lower grain export subsidies from the United States and the European Union (EU). The decline in food-aid shipments was caused by smaller aid budgets, mainly in the United States, and higher grain prices.

INTERNATIONAL ISSUES

Food-Aid Needs. According to a study by the Economic Research Service of the U.S. Department of Agriculture (USDA), poor countries would need about 14 million tons of food aid during the 1995–96 marketing year, an increase of 12% from the previous year. The estimate was obtained by examination of the needs of more than 60 less developed countries (LDCs). Aid needs for each country were defined as the difference between a target level of food consumption and what could be grown and commercially imported. The target was defined as the average level of food consumption per person over the previous five years. For many countries the target fell well below what would be considered minimum nutritional needs.

The Food and Agriculture Organization (FAO) of the United Nations estimated that 36 million people faced severe food shortages in 1995, with more than 23 million of these people living in sub-Saharan Africa. Many more faced the insecurity of chronically scarce and uncertain food supplies. Somewhat smaller global grain supplies and higher prices added to the insecurity. With the exception of war-torn Bosnia and some countries of the former Soviet Union, most food-aid needs were in Africa, southern Asia, and Latin America.

Food emergencies persisted in Africa in 1995, with drought, civil strife, and refugees adding to the chronic problems of poverty and food shortages. A severe drought hit southern Africa, and grain harvests there were down for the second consecutive year. The FAO estimated that 10 million people needed emergency assistance in the region. Mozambique, Zambia, and Zimbabwe had the greatest food-aid needs. Access to food in Angola and Mozambique was hampered by the disruptions caused by the civil strife of previous years.

Civil strife also continued to disrupt food supplies elsewhere in Africa. Conflicts in Rwanda and Burundi created food emergencies at home and in the refugee camps in neighbouring Zaire and Tanzania. More than one million people in The Sudan needed food aid, primarily because of civil war. Civil war also increased food needs in Liberia and Sierra Leone. Even though Ethiopia expected an average harvest, its food-aid needs were expected to top one million tons in 1995. The country's poverty and limited potential to produce food caused its chronic food shortages.

Afghanistan and Bangladesh accounted for most of the food-aid needs in Asia. Poverty in both countries, along with the lingering effects of war in Afghanistan, created chronic food shortages. Floods in North Korea devastated crops in 1995, and by the end of the year major food shortages were arising. Most other Asian countries had experienced sustained economic growth in recent years and had been able to reduce their needs for aid by importing food through commercial channels.

Food shortages were reported in Transcaucasia and Central Asia in 1995, primarily because of poor harvests, local civil strife, and the disruption of former distribution channels. Armenia, Azerbaijan, Georgia, Kyrgyzstan, Tajikistan, and the Russian republic of Chechnya all required some food aid. In general, however, the average caloric consumption in these areas was high relative to other countries with food-aid needs.

Although most Latin-American countries experienced impressive economic growth in 1995, chronic food shortages persisted in Bolivia, Guatemala, Honduras, and Peru. Haiti, the poorest country in Latin America, continued to suffer from widespread poverty and poor crop production.

Food-Aid Supplies. Food-aid shipments fell by one-third in 1994–95 relative to the previous year. The United States accounted for virtually all of the drop. (*See* Table II.) The FAO expected a further decline in 1995–96. Shipments in 1994–95 and aid commitments for 1995–96 were the lowest since the mid-1970s and fell well below the minimum target of 10 million tons established by the World Food Conference in 1974.

Not all food-aid shipments went to the poorest countries. Those countries classified as low-income food-deficit countries (with an average income below $1,345 in 1993) received 10% less food aid in 1994–95. (*See* Table II.)

Though their needs probably would expand, they were likely to receive less aid in 1995–96.

Low Grain Stocks. In December the USDA estimated that the global supply of grain at the end of the 1995–96 marketing year (called year-end, or carryover, grain stocks) would fall to about 229 million tons—down 23% from the end of the previous year and down 37% from 1992–93. The totals included wheat, rice, and coarse grains such as corn (maize), sorghum, oats, and barley.

The data on year-end stocks provided an indication of the world's reserve that would be available to meet potential shortages in the following year. A carryover of 229 million tons would at first appear to be an adequate amount, since the world had never experienced a one-year shortfall of that magnitude. The figure could be misleading, however, since, because of trade barriers, grain does not flow freely between all countries. The USDA estimate of year-end stocks represented 13% of the annual world consumption, a record low. The percentage was less than that available during the world grain crisis of the early 1970s, when grain prices more than doubled and world conferences were required for addressing fears of food shortages.

Global grain stocks declined steadily beginning in 1992. Most of the decline came from the major grain-exporting countries: the United States, the countries of the EU, Canada, Argentina, and Australia. Stocks in the former Soviet republics also declined sharply. The remainder of the world typically carried relatively few stocks—less than 4% of their annual consumption—and relied on grain from exporting countries to cover emergencies.

The decline in grain stocks was alarming on world markets because it was concentrated in exporting countries—especially the United States and the EU. Importers such as Japan and Egypt relied on these countries for a dependable supply of grain. Stocks in exporting countries were much more effective in buffering the world grain market against shortages than were stocks in other countries. Exporters sold to the highest bidders anywhere in the world. Other countries tended to use their grain stocks only to meet domestic needs.

China, for example, was expected to have nearly 30% of the world's grain stocks by the end of the 1995–96 marketing year. This development would appear surprising, since China was a major grain importer in 1995–96. China's grain stocks, however, were mainly stored in interior locations, where they were produced. Because of domestic transportation difficulties, it would typically be more difficult for coastal cities to get grain from China's interior than for them to get it from abroad. China's large stocks of grain provided food security to China's interior, but they provided little security for the rest of the world.

The low levels of grain stocks in major exporting countries at the end of the 1995–96 marketing year likely would consist only of grain in the marketing channels from producers to processors and feeders. Virtually no reserve would be left to meet possible shortages the following year. In response to these conditions, grain prices on world markets increased sharply in 1995. Higher prices caused grain consumption to decline, especially grain fed to livestock.

The FAO estimated that global grain production would have to increase 4% in 1996 to provide a minimum level of food security. If the shortage experienced on grain markets during the 1970s was repeated, high prices in 1995 and beyond would be expected to encourage production and discourage consumption around the world. Grain stocks would thus be replenished in several years.

Declining Grain Consumption. World grain use in 1995 was 305 kg per person (1 kg = 2.2 lb). The amount was a drop of 2.6% from the previous year and a decline of 8% from the peak in 1986. Before 1986 grain use per person had increased, although somewhat unsteadily, for many years. The decline in per capita consumption in 1995 was partly a result of the temporary drop in grain supplies and the increase in population. The decline was also the result of longer-run dynamic changes that were taking place in world agriculture, however. Though it might first have seemed that there was some cause for concern, these changes did not necessarily imply that the world was becoming less capable of feeding its people. Rather, two forces explained most of the decline: more efficient meat production, and the restructuring of the economies of the countries of the former Soviet Union and of Eastern Europe.

About 37% of the world's grain crop was fed to livestock—including cattle, hogs, poultry, sheep, horses, and goats. Although the quantity of grain fed to the world's livestock had not increased since 1986, world meat production had increased 22%. This increase was explained by an increase in the efficiency of converting grain to meat. Improved breeds and improved management explained part of the increase in feeding efficiency. Shifting to the production of poultry and pork rather than beef was also an important factor. It took about 11 kg of grain equivalent to produce one kilogram of beef, including the feed necessary to maintain the breeding herd. Approximately six kilograms of grain produced one kilogram of pork, and only three kilograms of grain were needed for one kilogram of poultry.

Since 1986 world beef production had increased little. Nearly all of the increase in meat production was due to increased pork and poultry meat. China accounted for virtually all the increase in pork production. The net result was that since 1986 the quantity of grain consumed per person in the form of meat had declined 18 kg, while meat production per person had increased between one and two kilograms.

About half of the global decline in grain consumption per person since 1986 was explained by the major decline in consumption in Eastern Europe and the former Soviet

HOLT STUDIOS INTERNATIONAL—PHOTO RESEARCHERS, INC.

These young pigs are being raised in modern feeding pens in the U.K. The shift from grain-fed beef to pork and poultry, both of which can be produced more efficiently, has helped to conserve grain stocks and raise meat consumption in many parts of the world.

Union. Over the past 10 years, grain consumed as human food had dropped 6 million tons in these countries, while grain consumed as livestock feed had dropped 64 million tons. The combined decline was equivalent to 4% of the world grain consumption. There also was a sharp decline in the production of meat and milk. Political and economic restructuring led to higher retail prices for cereals and meat and to much lower incomes. As a result, there was a small reduction in demand for grain for human food and a large reduction in meat consumption.

The trends of more efficient feeding of livestock and of the shift from grain-fed beef to poultry and pork should help meet the growing world demand for meat without greatly increasing the use of grain for livestock feed. As the countries of Eastern Europe and the former Soviet Union restored economic growth, they likely would increase their demand for meat, but they also had the potential to increase their output of grain and livestock significantly.

China. China's meat production increased 14% in 1995, accounting for most of the growth in world production. China's meat production was up 80% above 1990 levels. Most of the increase came from hogs, which supplied more than 70% of China's meat. About half of the world's pork was produced in China. Poultry production also expanded rapidly, but from a much smaller base.

The rapid expansion of meat production had a major impact on China's grain consumption. About one-fourth of the grain in China was fed to livestock. Although the production and human consumption of grain in 1995 were about the same as in 1990, consumption by livestock was up more than 50%. The additional grain came from higher imports and a reduction in year-end stocks. Between 1993 and 1995, China shifted from being a major grain exporter to being a major importer.

Rapid economic growth and the associated increases in personal income were the main forces behind the expansion of meat consumption in China. The country's economy grew about 8–9% in 1995 after experiencing an extraordinarily high 50% growth over the previous four years. In addition, the annual population growth was about 14 million.

In the future China could play a major role in shaping the world's supply and distribution of food. A large increase in grain production in China was not expected. If, however, rapid economic growth did continue and China's leaders permitted meat production to expand at recent rates, China—the world's leading grain producer—could quickly become the world's leading importer of grain. On the other hand, China's leaders could make a policy decision to curtail grain and meat imports. Political resistance to the growth of grain imports was evident in 1995.

Former Soviet Republics. In 1995 the 15 republics of the former Soviet Union continued their trend of producing and consuming much less meat. Meat production was down 10% from 1994 and down more than 50% from 1990. The decline was about equally distributed among beef, pork, sheep, and poultry. The decline in milk production slowed in 1995, but production was still 46% below 1990.

The reduction in meat production in these countries greatly reduced the domestic demand for grain. In 1995 grain consumed as livestock feed was down 12% from 1994, while its use as human food was down 6%. Grain used for feed and food since 1990 was down 47% and 13%, respectively. As a result, the production and importation of grain also declined. Production in 1995 was down 8% from 1994 and 36% from 1990. Net imports (imports minus exports) of grain were only 6 million tons in 1995, compared with 42 million tons in 1990. These striking changes in livestock and grain production had a major impact on world trade and food supply-demand balances in the early 1990s.

Recovery was slow from the massive disruptions to the economies of these countries following the collapse of the Soviet Union. The sharp drop in personal income and the higher prices for food forced people to reduce their consumption of meat and milk from the high levels of earlier years and switch to more bread, potatoes, and vegetables. Although the command system had collapsed, by 1995 a new infrastructure to get production inputs to farmers, to get farm produce to consumers, and to get everyone properly reimbursed had not developed. Basic questions of who owned the land also continued to block progress. Private

Table I. Selected Indexes of World Agricultural and Food Production

(1979–81 = 100)

	Total agricultural production					Total food production					Per capita food production				
Region or country	1991	1992	1993	1994	1995	1991	1992	1993	1994	1995	1991	1992	1993	1994	1995
Developed countries	**108**	**108**	**103**	**106**	**. . .**	**108**	**108**	**101**	**106**	**. . .**	**100**	**100**	**95**	**97**	**. . .**
Canada	127	124	121	126	127	129	126	123	127	128	112	109	105	107	107
Europe	110	109	106	102	103	110	107	106	103	103	106	103	102	98	98
Japan	91	96	81	100	91	93	99	83	103	94	88	93	78	97	88
South Africa	174	189	197	209	215	107	85	101	107	91	82	84	74	76	84
United States	105	114	104	120	112	104	114	104	120	112	94	102	91	105	97
Former U.S.S.R.	106	94	94	88	. . .	108	96	96	89	. . .	98	102	90	99	. . .
Less developed countries	**145**	**149**	**151**	**154**	**. . .**	**145**	**150**	**153**	**156**	**. . .**	**115**	**117**	**117**	**118**	**. . .**
Argentina	112	115	112	118	122	112	115	112	119	122	98	97	94	98	100
Bangladesh	129	130	130	123	133	130	132	132	125	135	104	103	101	93	100
Brazil	132	140	146	153	155	136	146	152	160	164	109	115	118	122	123
China	167	171	180	187	188	163	170	180	189	189	139	143	150	156	155
Egypt	144	153	158	156	162	157	185	170	171	179	119	122	123	122	124
Former Ethiopia	110	115	113	113	. . .	111	116	116	115	. . .	83	84	81	78	. . .
India	152	159	162	168	171	154	161	164	169	174	122	125	126	127	127
Indonesia	161	171	174	172	175	165	176	179	177	181	134	141	141	137	138
Malaysia	188	204	224	219	226	244	255	285	279	288	184	187	204	195	197
Mexico	119	117	125	126	123	120	119	128	130	125	93	90	96	95	89
Nigeria	174	189	197	209	215	174	189	197	208	214	128	133	134	138	188
Philippines	116	118	120	122	123	116	118	120	123	124	90	90	90	90	89
Turkey	134	134	135	133	139	136	135	136	135	140	106	103	101	99	100
Venezuela	135	140	137	151	156	135	142	140	154	158	102	104	101	108	109
Vietnam	153	161	170	176	183	152	160	168	173	181	120	123	127	100	100
Zaire	148	147	151	135	138	143	148	152	135	138	100	100	100	86	85
World	**129**	**129**	**130**	**133**	**133**	**126**	**129**	**131**	**135**	**135**	**105**	**106**	**105**	**106**	**105**

Source: Food and Agriculture Organization of the United Nations, *FAO Quarterly Bulletin of Statistics.*

ownership of farmland increased very slowly, with less than 5% of all agricultural land on privately owned farms by 1995.

If a Western-style agricultural sector were to develop in the republics of the former Soviet Union, farm production could greatly expand and the region could be a significant exporter of grains. Such exports could help offset the growing demand for grain in other parts of the world.

World Trade Organization. After six years of negotiations, known as the Uruguay round, member nations in 1994 agreed to significant modifications of the General Agreement on Tariffs and Trade (GATT), the set of rules governing international trade. One component of the agreement was the creation of the World Trade Organization, effective in January 1995, to oversee the implementation of the trade rules.

The new rules would have major long-term implications for agricultural trade and world food security. A reliable trading system was essential for moving food efficiently from food-surplus to food-deficit countries. Most countries had erected barriers to trade of agricultural products, to protect either their farmers or their consumers. The net effect of each country's actions was an inefficient global system of agriculture, in which some countries overproduced, others underproduced, and trade was more difficult than it needed to be. Past trade agreements greatly reduced barriers to trade in manufactured products, and as a result trade flourished. Little progress was made in agriculture, however. The Uruguay round agreement, for the first time, provided a framework for halting the escalation of agricultural trade barriers and for gradually bringing them down. The long-term effect should be an improved global food system.

The basic principles of the trade rules were as follows: (1) trading should take place between countries without discrimination; (2) there should be predictable and growing access to each country's markets; (3) fair trade should be promoted; and (4) industrial countries were encouraged to assist the trade of LDCs. The main components of the GATT agreement on agriculture were the following principles. All nontariff barriers to trade were to be converted to equivalent tariffs, with all tariffs reduced an average of at least 36% over six years. Countries must allow duty-free imports of at least 3% to 5% of the domestic consumption of agricultural products. Export subsidies were to be reduced at least 36% and the volume of subsidized exports reduced at least 21% over six years. Subsidies to domestic producers of traded products would be reduced at least 20% over six years. Sanitary and phytosanitary regulations (human health standards and plant and animal safety standards) were to be based on science rather than on arbitrary rules that tended to discriminate against imports.

AGRICULTURAL COMMODITIES

Grains. World grain consumption in 1995–96 was again expected to exceed production, further depleting year-end stocks. In December 1995 production of all grains was estimated to be down nearly 4% from the previous year. Although wheat production was up slightly from the poor harvest of 1994–95 and rice remained about the same, coarse grain production was expected to be down 9%. The decline in coarse grain production was caused by poor harvests in the United States (down one-fourth) and the former Soviet republics (down one-fifth). Grain production in 1995–96 was forecast to be higher in many of the LDCs.

Because of tight supplies in the major grain-exporting countries, world grain trade in 1995–96 was forecast to continue at the level of the two previous years. A decline in coarse grain imports to Japan was expected as a result of declining livestock production and increased meat imports. China and drought-stricken Morocco were expected to increase their grain imports.

Oilseeds. Global oilseed production in 1995–96 was forecast to decline about 2% from the record crop of 1994–95. Soybeans, which represented half of the world's oilseed crop, accounted for the decline. A record amount was forecast to be crushed in 1995–96 to produce vegetable oil and meal (a livestock feed). As a result of lower production and higher consumption in 1995–96, year-end stocks of oilseeds were forecast to decline by about 20% from the previous

Table II. Shipment of Food Aid in Cereals

In 000-metric ton grain equivalent

Region and country	Average 1990–91 to 1992–93	1993–94	1994–95	1995–96[1]
Australia	303	219	240	300
Canada	949	712	525	400
European Union[2]	3,477	2,671	2,735	3,000
By members	938	1,086	782	. . .
By organizations	2,539	1,585	1,953	. . .
Japan	419	378	402	300
Norway	60	56	74	20
Sweden	126	85	99	. . .
Switzerland	70	58	41	40
United States	7,593	8,258	4,190	3,200
Others	545	178	130	. . .
Total	13,542	12,615	8,436	7,600
To LIFDC[3]	10,291	8,226	7,407	6,000
Sub-Saharan Africa	4,301	3,690	3,074	. . .
To other countries	3,251	4,389	1,029	1,600

[1] Estimated, partly based on minimum commitments under the Food Aid Convention.
[2] Up to 1994, 12 member countries; from 1995, 15 member countries.
[3] Low-income food-deficit countries with per capita incomes under U.S. $1,305 in 1992.
Source: FAO, *Food Outlook*, August–September 1995.

Table III. World Cereal Supply and Distribution

In 000,000 metric tons

	1992–93	1993–94	1994–95[1]	1995–96[2]
Production				
Wheat	562	559	522	533
Coarse grains	865	790	863	787
Rice, milled	352	353	361	359
Total	1,779	1,702	1,746	1,679
Utilization				
Wheat	550	563	549	550
Coarse grains	837	831	850	832
Rice, milled	355	357	362	365
Total	1,742	1,751	1,761	1,747
Exports				
Wheat	124	118	111	113
Coarse grains	107	99	102	104
Rice, milled	16	16	20	17
Total	247	233	233	234
Ending stocks[3]				
Wheat	145	141	114	97
Coarse grains	163	122	134	89
Rice, milled	54	50	49	43
Total	362	313	297	229
Stocks as % of utilization				
Wheat	26.4%	25.0%	20.8%	17.6%
Coarse grains	19.5%	14.7%	15.8%	10.7%
Rice, milled	15.2%	14.0%	13.5%	11.8%
Total	20.8%	17.9%	16.9%	13.1%
Stocks held by U.S. in %				
Wheat	9.9%	11.0%	12.1%	10.8%
Coarse grains	38.7%	22.4%	33.7%	22.3%
Stocks held by EU in %				
Wheat	16.6%	11.5%	10.9%	10.3%
Coarse grains	12.7%	15.0%	10.0%	11.6%

[1] Estimated.
[2] Forecast.
[3] Data not available for all countries.
Source: USDA, Foreign Agricultural Service, December 1995.

year. World prices of oilseeds increased throughout the last half of 1995 as supplies became tighter.

The United States continued to produce about half of the world's soybeans. Its output in 1995 was estimated to be down 13% from the record harvest of 1994, as the average yield per hectare declined to a more normal level (1 ha = 2.47 ac). Soybean production was also expected to be down in China and Brazil.

Livestock and Meat. World meat production continued to expand more rapidly than population in 1995, especially in the LDCs. The FAO estimated that meat consumption per person in the LDCs would be 4% higher than in 1994, with the largest gains in East Asia and Latin America. North America and Western Europe would have small gains, and contractions would occur in the republics of the former Soviet Union, in Africa, and in the Middle East.

The continued expansion of meat production in China and reductions in the former Soviet republics affected global meat statistics in 1995. Elsewhere, Brazil expanded its cattle herd by 3.7 million head in response to growing domestic demand and farmers' expectations of higher profits. The economic crisis combined with a drought to force Mexican farmers to cut back on their cattle and hog numbers. Australia continued to switch from grass-fed to grain-fed beef to supply the expanding Asian import market. Australia also began rebuilding its sheep herd in 1995 after the devastation left by drought. Poland increased its pork production more than 10% because of ample feed supplies and increased demand.

The world's livestock farmers continued to increase their efficiency throughout 1995. In major producing countries beef and veal increased 2–3%, but cattle and buffalo herds increased less than 1%. World pork production increased more than 6%, but there was virtually no increase in hog inventories.

Dairy. Milk production in 1995 continued to decline slowly in developed countries (except in North America and Oceania) and increase in the LDCs. In the United States and Canada, the number of milk cows remained about the same, but more milk was obtained per cow. In spite of dry weather, Australia and New Zealand continued to expand

Table IV. World Production of Major Oilseeds and Products

In 000,000 metric tons

	1993–94	1994–95[1]	1995–96[2]
Total production of oilseeds	**227.4**	**259.4**	**253.2**
Soybeans	**117.4**	**136.7**	**124.5**
U.S.	50.9	68.5	59.4
China	15.3	16.0	14.5
Argentina	12.3	12.2	12.5
Brazil	24.7	25.5	23.3
Cottonseed	**29.8**	**32.9**	**34.6**
U.S.	5.8	6.9	6.6
Former Soviet republics	3.8	3.7	3.7
China	6.4	7.7	7.6
Peanuts	**23.8**	**26.4**	**25.5**
U.S.	1.5	1.9	1.6
China	8.4	9.7	9.6
India	7.6	8.4	7.6
Sunflower seed	**20.8**	**23.7**	**25.4**
U.S.	1.2	2.2	2.1
Former Soviet republics	5.3	4.4	6.7
Argentina	3.8	5.8	5.3
European Union[3]	3.4	4.1	3.3
Rapeseed	**26.7**	**30.2**	**33.6**
Canada	5.5	7.2	6.6
China	6.9	7.5	9.0
European Union[3]	5.9	7.3	8.5
India	5.5	5.5	5.6
Copra	**4.8**	**5.0**	**4.8**
Palm kernel	**4.2**	**4.6**	**4.8**
Oilseeds crushed	**188.4**	**206.6**	**211.9**
Soybeans	101.5	110.2	109.6
Oilseed ending stocks	**19.5**	**25.1**	**20.0**
Soybeans	16.7	21.7	16.6
World production[4]			
Total fats and oils	**75.3**	**81.1**	**. . .**
Edible vegetable oils	61.1	66.7	69.1
Soybean oil	18.1	19.8	19.8
Palm oil	13.4	14.5	15.4
Animal fats	13.0	13.1	. . .
Marine oils	1.2	1.3	1.3
High-protein meals[5]	**129.8**	**141.4**	**144.2**
Soybean meal	80.7	87.1	86.9
Fish meal	6.4	6.7	6.6

[1] Preliminary.
[2] Forecast.
[3] Expanded from 12 countries to 15 countries in 1994–95.
[4] Processing potential from crops in year indicated.
[5] Converted, based on product's protein content, to weight equivalent of soybeans of 44% protein content.
Source: USDA, Foreign Agricultural Service, November 1995.

Table V. Livestock Inventories and Meat Production in Major Producing Countries[1]

In 000,000 head and 000,000 metric tons (carcass weight)

Region and country	1994[2]	1995[3]	1994	1995[2]
	Cattle and buffalo		Beef and veal	
World total[4]	**1,043.6**	**1,052.0**	**45.57**	**46.77**
Canada	12.7	13.1	0.90	0.96
United States	103.3	105.4	11.19	11.54
Mexico	30.2	27.8	1.81	1.85
Argentina	54.2	53.7	2.60	2.56
Brazil	148.1	151.8	4.48	4.65
Uruguay	10.3	10.4	0.37	0.37
European Union	83.4	82.7	7.75	7.84
Eastern Europe[5]	13.4	13.1	1.04	0.98
Former Soviet republics				
Kazakhstan	8.1	6.8	0.58	0.50
Russia	43.9	39.7	3.10	2.76
Ukraine	19.6	17.7	1.42	1.35
Australia	26.0	26.4	1.84	1.72
India	274.2	276.1	1.05	1.10
China	123.3	133.0	3.30	4.50
	Hogs		Pork	
World total[4]	**762.2**	**767.1**	**70.12**	**74.70**
Canada	11.2	11.1	1.23	1.26
United States	60.0	59.1	8.03	8.11
Mexico	12.5	11.1	0.90	0.96
European Union	116.3	115.4	15.32	15.20
Eastern Europe[6]	37.1	38.3	3.33	3.23
Former Soviet republics				
Kazakhstan	n.a.	n.a.	n.a.	n.a.
Russia	25.0	22.1	2.26	1.94
Ukraine	13.9	12.3	0.91	0.82
Japan	10.2	10.1	1.39	1.35
China	414.6	426.0	32.05	37.00
	Poultry		Poultry meat	
World total[4]	**. . .**	**. . .**	**43.21**	**44.45**
United States	. . .	. . .	13.21	13.86
Brazil	. . .	. . .	3.49	3.89
European Union	. . .	. . .	7.36	7.51
Eastern Europe[7]	. . .	. . .	0.80	0.88
Former Soviet republics				
Russia	. . .	. . .	1.17	1.10
Ukraine	. . .	. . .	0.40	0.38
Japan	. . .	. . .	1.30	1.28
China	. . .	. . .	7.55	7.50
	Sheep		Sheep, goat meat	
World total[4]	**876.2**	**888.3**	**6.28**	**6.49**
			All meat	
Total[4]	**. . .**	**. . .**	**165.18**	**172.41**

[1] Livestock numbers at year's end.
[2] Preliminary.
[3] Forecast.
[4] Total of major producing countries.
[5] Bulgaria, Czech Republic, Poland, and Romania.
[6] Bulgaria, Czech Republic, Hungary, Poland, and Romania.
[7] Hungary, Poland, and Romania.
Source: USDA, Foreign Agricultural Service, October 1995.

their dairy herds in 1995. Their combined output was forecast to equal their record production of 1994.

In the EU milk production remained about the same as in 1994. In Eastern Europe and the republics of the former Soviet Union, production continued to decline. Most of the decline in milk production in Russia occurred on former state and collective farms because of the lack of profits from commercial sales. Private farms apparently increased their production of milk, but mainly for local consumption. Throughout the LDCs increased demand, favourable weather conditions, and improved management combined to increase milk production in 1995.

World prices of dairy products, including cheese, butter, and nonfat dry milk, increased substantially in the latter part of 1994 and in 1995. The increase was caused by limited export supplies by major exporters (the United States, countries of the EU, Australia, and New Zealand) and increased demand by importers.

Sugar. World sugar production in 1995–96 was forecast in November at a record 118 million tons. Production was expected to exceed consumption for the second consecutive year, allowing some rebuilding of world stocks. World sugar stocks were at record low levels at the beginning of the 1994–95 crop year. Driven by low stocks and strong demand, world sugar prices increased throughout 1994 and early 1995. Prices then declined as the prospects for a large harvest in 1995 became apparent.

The strong growth in the demand for sugar continued in 1995. Growth in the population and personal income in Latin America, the Middle East, and Asia caused these areas to increase their demand for soft drinks and processed foods containing sugar. In the industrialized countries, however, there was little growth. Consumers in these countries continued to switch to alternative sweeteners such as high-fructose corn syrup and low-caloric sweeteners.

Cuba's sugar production in 1995–96, forecast at four million tons, was expected to rebound from the extremely poor harvest of the previous year. The figure remained, however, well below the seven million to eight million tons harvested annually during the late 1980s and early 1990s, when Cuba's sugar industry was supported by the countries of Eastern Europe and the Soviet Union. It was thought that Cuba's export prospects may have improved when it reached a multiyear agreement in 1995 with Russia to barter sugar for oil.

Coffee. Poor weather conditions in Brazil had a major impact on world coffee production and prices in 1995–96. World production in 1995–96 was forecast to be down 8% from the previous year. Brazil's harvest was expected to be off by one-third, the lowest since 1986–87. Increased production in Mexico and Central America would only slightly offset Brazil's lowered output.

Severe frosts in June and July 1994 combined with an extended dry spell to greatly reduce the 1995 yields of coffee in the major producing regions of Brazil. As a result, world coffee prices increased. The International Coffee Organization's monthly indicator price increased to $2.02 per pound in September 1994 from $1.08 in May. By mid-1995, however, prices had declined significantly.

Cocoa. World cocoa production in 1995–96 was expected to exceed the record 1994–95 harvest by 4%. Côte d'Ivoire and Ghana, which accounted for half of the world's cocoa production, enjoyed record harvests in 1994–95 because

Table VI. World Production of Milk

In 000,000 metric tons

Region and country	1993	1994[1]	1995[2]
Developed countries	**350.0**	**345.0**	**342.0**
United States	68.3	69.7	71.4
Canada	7.5	7.6	8.0
Europe	159.0	157.0	156.0
European Union	120.3	120.4	120.4
France	25.0	25.3	25.8
Germany	28.1	28.0	28.7
Italy	10.4	10.2	10.0
Netherlands, The	11.0	10.9	10.9
United Kingdom	14.6	14.9	14.6
Eastern Europe			
Poland	12.6	11.9	11.6
Romania	3.8	4.0	4.2
Former Soviet republics			
Russia	46.5	42.8	40.5
Ukraine	18.1	18.2	17.5
Australia/New Zealand[3]	16.3	18.0	18.0
Japan	8.6	8.4	8.5
Less developed countries	**178.0**	**180.0**	**184.0**
Latin America	46.0	47.0	48.0
Brazil	15.3	15.7	16.1
Africa	19.0	19.0	19.0
Asia	113.0	114.0	117.0
China	5.0	5.0	5.1
India[4]	30.6	30.0	31.2
World total	**528.0**	**525.0**	**526.0**

[1] Preliminary.
[2] Forecast.
[3] Year ended June 30 for Australia and May 31 for New Zealand.
[4] Year begun April 1.
Sources: FAO, *Food Outlook*, May–June 1995; USDA, Foreign Agricultural Service, September 1995.

Table VII. World Production of Centrifugal (Freed from Liquid) Sugar

In 000,000 metric tons raw value

Region and country	1993–94	1994–95	1995–96[1]
North America	**10.8**	**11.9**	**11.3**
United States	6.9	7.2	6.9
Mexico	3.8	4.6	4.2
Caribbean	**5.1**	**4.2**	**5.0**
Cuba	4.0	3.3	4.0
Central America	**2.4**	**2.6**	**2.8**
Guatemala	1.1	1.3	1.3
South America	**15.5**	**18.3**	**19.2**
Argentina	1.1	1.2	1.5
Brazil	9.9	12.4	13.0
Colombia	1.8	2.0	2.1
Europe	**22.1**	**19.6**	**20.6**
Western Europe	18.6	16.6	17.1
European Union	18.4	16.5	17.0
France	4.7	4.4	4.6
Germany	4.7	4.0	4.2
Eastern Europe	3.5	3.0	3.5
Poland	2.2	1.5	1.8
Former Soviet republics[2]	**7.5**	**5.7**	**6.4**
Russia	2.7	1.7	1.9
Ukraine	4.2	3.6	4.0
Africa and Middle East	**9.8**	**10.2**	**10.2**
South Africa	1.2	1.8	1.8
Turkey	2.2	1.7	1.6
Asia	**31.8**	**37.4**	**36.9**
China	6.5	6.0	6.5
India	11.7	16.3	15.2
Pakistan	3.1	3.2	3.2
Philippines	1.8	1.6	1.8
Thailand	4.0	5.4	5.7
Oceania	**4.9**	**5.7**	**5.5**
Australia	4.4	5.1	5.0
Totals			
Beginning stocks	21.1	18.4	19.4
As % of consumption	18.8%	16.1%	16.6%
Production	109.8	115.6	118.0
Imports[3]	30.0	30.5	31.3
Consumption	112.5	114.5	116.6
Exports[3]	30.0	30.5	31.3

[1] Preliminary.
[2] Includes Estonia, Latvia, and Lithuania.
[3] Exports may not equal imports because "Totals" are a composite of slightly differing marketing years, not all beginning in the same months.
Source: USDA, Foreign Agricultural Service, November 1995.

of favourable growing conditions, improved management practices, and more trees reaching their peak performance years. The 1995–96 cocoa season, which began in October, was expected to produce another record-breaking harvest in Côte d'Ivoire.

Because of drought and disease, Brazil's 1994–95 harvest was much smaller than had been forecast and the smallest in 18 years. The 1995–96 crop was expected to rebound, although not to the levels of the early 1990s. Malaysia's cocoa production was forecast to be down 7% from the previous year, a continuation of a longer-run decline. Government-owned land in Malaysia continued to be shifted from cocoa to oil-palm production.

World consumption of cocoa products continued its upward trend in 1994–95 as a result of higher personal incomes in much of the world. In the United States, however, consumption had declined in recent years.

TOMAS STARGARDTER—AFP

A Costa Rican worker prepares coffee husks to be used as fuel.

Table VIII. World Green Coffee Production

In 000 60-kg bags

Region and country	1993–94	1994–95[1]	1995–96[2]
North America	**16,679**	**17,248**	**18,423**
Costa Rica	2,475	2,492	2,500
El Salvador	2,361	2,314	2,425
Guatemala	3,078	3,500	[illegible]
Honduras	2,050	2,295	2,400
Mexico	4,200	4,030	4,600
South America	**44,577**	**44,500**	**35,705**
Brazil	28,500	26,000	16,800
Colombia	11,400	13,000	13,500
Ecuador	2,150	2,400	2,150
Africa	**15,051**	**17,877**	**17,410**
Cameroon	1,250	1,300	1,300
Côte d'Ivoire	2,700	3,733	3,000
Ethiopia	3,000	3,500	3,700
Kenya	1,230	1,572	1,600
Uganda	2,700	3,000	3,000
Zaire	1,100	1,300	1,000
Asia and Oceania	**16,930**	**16,368**	**16,688**
India	3,465	3,185	3,800
Indonesia	7,400	6,000	5,800
Vietnam	2,500	3,500	3,500
Total production	**93,237**	**95,993**	**88,226**
Exportable	70,019	72,061	. . .
Beginning stocks[3]	42,570	35,534	. . .
Exports[4]	77,609	77,297	. . .

[1] Preliminary.
[2] Forecast.
[3] Production minus domestic use.
[4] In exporting countries.
Source: USDA, Foreign Agricultural Service, December 1995.

Cotton. World cotton production in 1995–96 was forecast to be up 4% over that of 1994–95. Production was expected to exceed consumption, and for the second consecutive year the world's carryover stocks of cotton were expected to increase. Production increases were expected in countries in Africa and in Pakistan, but a smaller crop was expected in the United States.

Farmers in the United States increased the area planted to cotton in 1995 by nearly 20%, but production fell short of early expectations as the yield per hectare dropped more than 20% from the relatively high 1994 yield. Cotton production in Central Asia leveled off in 1995 after several years of large declines. As was typical of many agricultural products after the collapse of the Soviet Union, the production of cotton had dropped by one-fourth between 1989 and 1994. During that same period domestic cotton consumption dropped by two-thirds. It was more profitable to export the cotton than to use it in domestic mills.

(JERRY A. SHARPLES)

See also Business and Industry Review: *Textiles;* The Environment: *Gardening.*

This article updates the *Macropædia* article The History of AGRICULTURE.

Table IX. World Cocoa Bean Production

In 000 metric tons

Region and country	1993–94	1994–95	1995–96[1]
North and Central America	**111**	**113**	**116**
South America	**451**	**405**	**451**
Brazil	281	234	276
Ecuador	80	81	85
Africa	**1,423**	**1,475**	**1,540**
Cameroon	105	100	100
Côte d'Ivoire[2]	850	905	970
Ghana	312	315	315
Nigeria[3]	130	130	130
Asia and Oceania	**541**	**496**	**492**
Indonesia	280	280	290
Malaysia	204	162	150
Total production	**2,525**	**2,489**	**2,599**
Net production	2,500	2,464	2,573
Cocoa grindings	2,483	2,526	2,573
Change in stocks	+17	−62	0

[1] Forecast.
[2] Includes some cocoa marketed between Ghana and Côte d'Ivoire.
[3] Includes cocoa marketed through Benin.
Source: USDA, Foreign Agricultural Service, October 1995.

Table X. World Cotton Production and Consumption

In 000,000 480-lb bales

Region and country	1993–94	1994–95[1]	1995–96[1]
Production	**77.0**	**85.5**	**89.3**
Western Hemisphere	20.5	25.6	25.7
United States	16.1	19.7	18.8
Brazil	1.9	2.5	2.6
Europe	1.7	1.8	1.8
Former Soviet republics	9.6	9.0	9.0
Uzbekistan	6.2	5.8	5.9
Africa	5.8	5.6	6.5
Asia and Oceania	44.9	43.6	46.3
China	17.2	9.0	9.0
India	9.6	10.8	11.0
Pakistan	6.3	6.5	8.5
Consumption	**85.3**	**84.4**	**86.0**
United States	10.4	11.2	11.0
China	21.2	19.7	20.5
India	9.9	10.3	10.5
Pakistan	6.7	6.8	6.8
European Union	5.5	5.5	5.6
Southeast Asia	4.6	4.6	4.8
Russia	2.2	1.3	1.5

[1] Forecast.
Source: USDA, Foreign Agricultural Service, November 1995.

FISHERIES

World fish catches reached record levels in 1993, with over 100 million mt (metric tons) produced by fisheries and aquaculture. The new record total of 101,417,500 mt was up from 98,785,200 mt the year before and was over a million tons more than the previous record, which was set in 1989. The figures reported by the Food and Agriculture Organization showed that although most of the rise over 1992 was due to continuing increases in production from aquaculture, the country figures showed that results in many fisheries were consistent, with improvements showing on some of them.

With more than 17% of world production—17,567,907 mt—China again topped the table. Sea fisheries produced over 10 million mt, but increased aquaculture accounted for most of the country's staggering 2.5 million-mt jump over the previous year.

Emerging pelagic giant Peru knocked Japan from the number two spot with an 8,450,000-mt catch. Japan recorded 8.1 million mt to continue its steady decline since 1988, when it caught 12 million mt. Chilean catches also decreased in the face of stiff competition from Peru. One-time leading fisheries nation Russia fell to sixth place with 4,460,000 mt.

U.S. catches continued to increase steadily and in 1993 were at 5.9 million mt, a rise from 5.6 million mt in 1992. That was enough to knock Russia, which had been in decline since the demise of the communist system, out of fifth place. The decay of the Russian fleet had left hundreds of thousands of tons of catching capacity rusting away in harbours around the world with insufficient funds to operate.

A massive doubling in anchoveta catches to 8.3 million mt since 1991 accounted for Peru's climb in the ranks. Anchoveta was the most-caught species in the world for the second consecutive year, followed by Alaskan pollock, which totaled 4.6 million mt in 1993.

Aquaculture rose dramatically over 1992 production, and wild fish catches may actually have dropped. Silver carp and grass carp were the main aquaculture species, accounting for 1.9 million and 1.5 million mt, respectively. Seaweed production, which was not included in the total, had increased by one million metric tons to 7.2 million. China again dominated, producing 4.5 million mt.

Despite the international community's efforts over the past 10 years, there was little improvement in the conservation and management of the world's fisheries. The political dimension of fisheries conservation and management had been seriously underestimated. In an effort to deal with certain major issues facing the industry, in 1993 the United Nations set up the UN Conference on Straddling Fish Stocks and Highly Migratory Fish Stocks to identify, assess, and find solutions to the long-standing problems of high-seas fisheries. Conferees met six times at UN headquarters in New York City before August 1995 brought the much-anticipated culmination: the approval of a 48-article draft agreement relating to the conservation of depleted fish stocks and the management of high-seas fisheries.

The agreement was built on three essential pillars:

- Principles for conservation and management should be based on a precautionary approach and the best scientific information available. In other words, states were obliged to act conservatively when there was doubt about the vulnerability of stocks.
- Conservation measures must not be undermined by those who fished for vulnerable stocks.
- Disputes should be settled peacefully.

It was this last area, fishing disputes, that often made the international news in early 1995. In March the international press had a field day when Canadian government vessels and Spanish trawlers were involved in a row that threatened to boil over into a dramatic showdown over the straddling fishery for groundfish, such as cod, American flounder, and Greenland halibut, on the Grand Banks off Canada.

The roots of the problem went back to the reemergence of Spain in waters off Newfoundland in the late 1980s. The stocks of cod and other groundfish collapsed, which led to a moratorium inside Canada's 200-mi exclusive economic zone in 1992 and to the loss of 50,000 fishing and onshore jobs. This placed a fresh emphasis on conserving straddling stocks, which migrate between the Canadian zone and international waters.

During 1994 Canada had extended laws that allowed the high-seas arrest of vessels that bore state flags and were suspected of breaking conservation rules to cover the Spanish and Portuguese fleets, which accounted for most of the European Union's (EU's) presence in the northwestern Atlantic. Ultimatums followed stating that ships in international waters could be arrested, and in March 1995 the Spanish vessel *Estai* was boarded, arrested, and escorted

Table I. Top 10 Species Landed, 1993

In order of tonnage

Species	Metric tons
Anchoveta	8,299,944
Alaskan pollock	4,641,630
Chilean Jack mackerel	3,349,569
Silver carp	1,912,645
Japanese pilchard	1,796,132
Caplin	1,742,149
South American pilchard	1,624,362
Atlantic herring	1,622,560
Grass carp	1,487,196
Skipjack tuna	1,476,996

Table II. World Fisheries, 1993[1]

	Catch in 000 metric tons		Trade in $000,000	
Country	Total	Inland	Imports	Exports
China	17,567,907	7,507,413	575,930	1,542,426
Peru	8,450,600	40,500	818	685,004
Japan	8,128,121	176,191	14,187,149	766,952
Chile	6,037,985	17,773	18,505	1,124,679
United States	5,939,339	344,954	6,290,233	3,179,474
Russian Federation	4,461,375	307,002	19,074	1,471,446
India	4,232,060	1,837,424	4,497	810,645
Indonesia	3,637,700	907,000	99,820	1,419,492
Thailand	3,348,149	263,150	830,480	3,404,268
South Korea	2,648,977	30,246	545,518	1,335,419
Norway	2,561,771	435	310,352	2,302,346
Philippines	2,263,789	575,394	94,601	478,086
North Korea	1,780,000	111,900	1,700	65,815
Iceland	1,718,495	907	23,374	1,137,638
Denmark	1,534,058	35,490	1,094,253	2,150,665
Taiwan	1,414,834	176,652	544,243	2,369,422
Spain	1,290,000	30,550	2,629,799	813,750
Mexico	1,200,686	165,004	128,026	430,774
Canada	1,171,851	36,228	821,404	2,055,438
Vietnam	1,100,000	275,200	—	368,435
Bangladesh	1,047,170	734,455	160	168,290
Argentina	930,690	12,703	44,763	709,292
United Kingdom	901,025	15,287	1,628,852	1,036,916
Myanmar (Burma)	836,878	211,628	—	46,362
France	830,000	56,780	2,556,151	857,752
Brazil	780,000	215,000	200,567	191,633
Malaysia	680,000	20,000	265,032	306,845
Morocco	622,411	1,812	7,775	538,688
Pakistan	621,695	122,536	185	184,591
South Africa	563,228	2,375	90,038	199,030
World Total	**101,417,500**	**17,168,500**	**44,621,848**	**41,193,392**

[1]Excludes aquatic mammals, crocodiles and alligators, pearls, corals, sponges, and aquatic plants.

Source: United Nations Food and Agriculture Organization, *Yearbook of Fishery Statistics*, vol. 76 and 77.

into St. John's harbour before a cheering crowd of thousands. The EU branded the Canadian action an act of "high seas piracy."

This game of brinkmanship led to feverish activity between the two parties involved and finally resulted in a compromise. The two countries agreed to the reallocation of their catch quotas on groundfish species. Canada also agreed to repeal the law allowing authorities to board and arrest Spanish and Portuguese vessels and to drop all charges against the *Estai*. (MARTIN J. GILL)

This article updates the *Macropædia* article Commercial FISHING.

FOOD PROCESSING

In 1995, as people in Western nations came to realize that "there are no unhealthful foods, only unhealthful diets," sales of low-fat and diet foods declined slightly, and a shift toward traditional full-flavoured products was noted, as was the growing tendency of people to consume more fatty foods. Sales of butter and butter-based products increased. In Japan "functional foods"—containing ingredients claimed to promote health—gained ground. That market, worth an annual $7 billion, was aided by advertising laws that were less stringent than those in most other countries and that permitted unsubstantiated health claims to be made. Meat consumption was rising by 3% annually in less developed countries, contrasting with a 1% fall in developed countries, where there was an increase in vegetarianism.

It was believed that nearly half of all consumers in the West did not bother to read nutritional information on labels and that between half and three-quarters neither read nor followed manufacturers' cooking instructions. Young people showed the greatest ignorance. Significantly, this group suffered most from food poisoning, the worldwide incidence of which continued to grow. In the U.K. 7.5% of people said they had suffered from food poisoning, up one-third from the previous year; working days lost as a result could have cost the British economy alone some $1 billion.

A spate of food-poisoning outbreaks across the U.S. left many Americans worried about food safety. This benefited sales of kosher foods, which increased 12% in a year marked by an overall static food market. Over 26,000 products in the U.S. carried the kosher designation, including mainstream products such as Coca-Cola, Tropicana orange juice, and many canned fruits and vegetables. It was estimated that up to 70% of those buying kosher foods were not Jewish.

Business Trends. The 10 biggest emerging markets identified by the U.S. government were China, Indonesia, India, South Korea, Mexico, Argentina, Brazil, South Africa, Poland, and Colombia. If trends continued, by 2010 this market group could be bigger than the combined markets of the European Union (EU) and Japan. Some African, Caribbean, and Pacific states expressed alarm at EU proposals to allow the use of vegetable fats other than cocoa butter in the manufacture of chocolate, saying this could cost them $125 million a year in lost cocoa bean exports.

Major restructuring took place among European food businesses, with large companies continuing to shift from national to regional and global operations. The completion of the General Agreement on Tariffs and Trade had opened the way to increased cheese imports into Europe, particularly affecting Denmark, Europe's biggest cheese exporter. Japan's food industry experienced unprecedented changes, notably the establishment of an open pricing system, which made that country's complex food-distribution system more accessible to imports.

Penetration of private-label food products in the European market reached 15%. This was greatest in the U.K., where 35% of food and 28% of drinks were sold under private labels, closely followed by France, and with Spain lowest at 5%. Kellogg, Mars, and some other large companies stated they would not manufacture private-label goods, but PepsiCo, owners of the U.K.'s leading brand of potato chips, took the plunge. Heinz announced it would supply private-label baked beans to leading supermarket chains, in contrast to Nestlé's subsidiary Crosse & Blackwell, which withdrew from supplying private-label baked beans and began eliminating canned-goods sales in the U.K. because of competitive price cutting by supermarkets. Coca-Cola Co.'s dominance of the British cola drink market was hit by soaring sales of private-label colas manufactured by Cott Corp. of Canada and sold by Sainsbury and Tesco, the U.K.'s two largest supermarket chains.

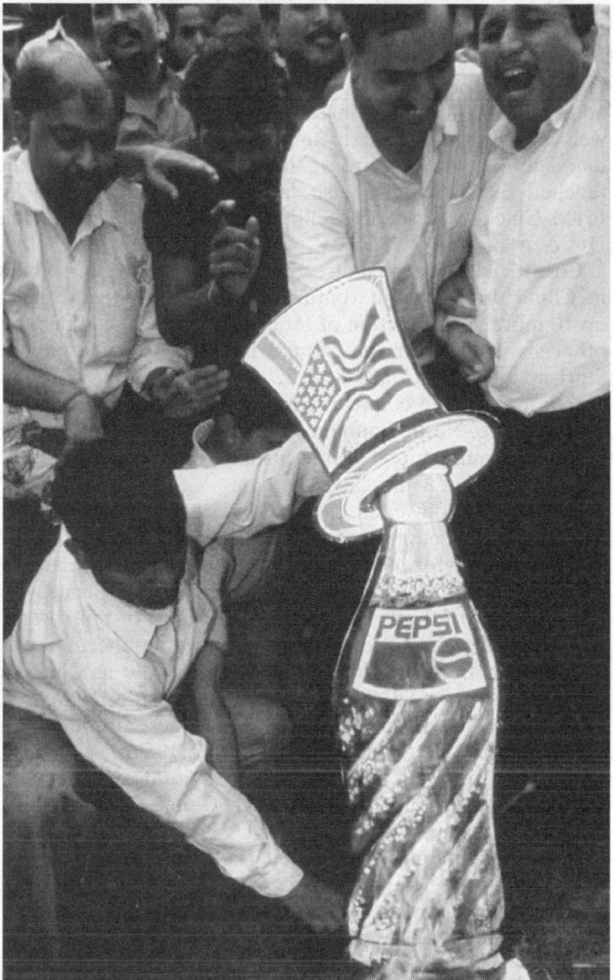

Protesters show their opposition to multinational investments in India. PepsiCo, the U.S.-based beverage and food giant, continued to expand its operations in India, controlling almost one-third of the soft-drink market and opening Kentucky Fried Chicken and Pizza Hut outlets.
ROBERT NICKELSBERG—TIME MAGAZINE

In the U.K. a large increase in the price of milk followed the abolition of the Milk Marketing Board and its replacement by Milk Marque, a cooperative owned by 60% of the country's dairy farmers. This led to declining milk sales and a shortage of milk for processing at a time when milk prices were falling in the rest of Europe.

Company Developments. The first phase of Florida's first new orange juice processing plant in nearly 20 years started in Clewiston. The plant, which would be operated by U.S. Sugar Corp.'s affiliate Southern Gardens Citrus Processing, would process more than 20 million boxes of oranges into 450 million litres (120 million gal) of juice a year.

PepsiCo, which over five years had invested $200 million in building local bottling plants in India, announced an additional $100 million investment in soft drinks there, as well as $80 million to set up some 60 restaurants in India. The company's share of the Indian soft drinks market reached 32%. PepsiCo also launched the first Kentucky Fried Chicken outlet in Delhi, followed by the first Pizza Hut outlet.

Coca-Cola Co., which already operated 13 bottling plants in China through joint ventures, announced plans to start up 10 more. Construction of four began during the year; the other six would bring investment in China to $500 million. Start-up of Coca-Cola's new $20 million bottling plant in Hanoi marked the company's return to Vietnam after a 20-year absence. Nestlé announced plans to build a $24 million plant to manufacture Nescafé instant coffee and Milo malt drink in Ho Chi Minh City, Vietnam.

Tetra Laval of Sweden, the world's largest privately owned food packaging and processing company, supplied most of the equipment for Anchor Products' new cheese plant in Lichfield, N.Z. It was the world's largest cheese plant, with a throughput of 3 million litres (790,000 gal) of milk a day.

Fosters Brewing Group of Australia announced it was withdrawing from brewing in the U.K. and sold its Courage brewing assets for $825 million to the Scottish & Newcastle PLC, which thus became the U.K.'s largest brewer, with nearly a third of the country's beer market. Bass, with 23% of the British beer market, formed a joint venture with Ginsber Beer Group of Siping City, China, in which Bass held a 55% share.

New Products and Ingredients. The number of innovative new products in the U.S. and Europe declined in 1995. Japan was at the forefront in developing new ingredients for processors and consumers, mostly in the "functional foods" category. Among new products in Japan was Yakult, a fermented milk drink that was also being made in The Netherlands and marketed in France, where Chambourcy launched a range of lactic fermented products that claimed to enhance the body's defense mechanisms. Previously confined to Japan, a number of products appeared in Europe that contained oligosaccharides, claimed to promote the growth of beneficial gut bacteria. Inulin, an oligofructose extracted from chicory, was the basis of a number of fermented milk drinks and yogurts launched by Mona and Nutricia of The Netherlands. Such products were increasingly being targeted at children, the elderly, and pregnant women.

A powdered natural honey said to retain the typical character of the original product was introduced by Food Ingredient Specialities of the U.K. From SmithKline Beecham came a juice and dietary fibre drink under the Ribena brand name. Also in the U.K., Boots launched a fortified flavoured milk drink for mothers-to-be.

Trends in new product development in the U.S. largely mirrored those in Europe, with low-fat introductions continuing, although at a reduced rate. The vast majority of new products were actually line extensions. Noteworthy was the mainstreaming of vegetarian foods. A new Green Giant product, Harvest soy-based burgers, was one among many new vegetable offerings introduced for the growing vegetarian market. Aseptically packed long-life milk in cartons, available in Europe for 20 years, was successfully introduced in the U.S. by Italian manufacturer Parmalat under the name Today's Milk; a few months after it was launched, sales soared to 3 million litres (790,000 gal) per month.

Technology. PurePulse Technologies, Inc., of San Diego, Calif., collaborated with Tetra Laval to develop a sterilization system called PureBright, which would produce a rapid succession of high-intensity light flashes 20,000 times brighter than sunlight to kill microorganisms on food and packaging materials. The system was being evaluated by the American Meat Institute for use in sterilizing or extending the shelf life of chicken, hot dogs, and prepackaged cuts of beef.

The first milk-fractionation plant in the U.S. started up in the Center for Dairy Research in Madison, Wis., using equipment made by Tirtiaux of Belgium. Funded by the Wisconsin Milk Marketing Board, the plant was initially providing milk fat fractions—widely used by European bakers for making croissants and flaky pastry—to researchers and food companies in the U.S.

Packaging. An 80% increase over 18 months in the world price of aluminum forced beverage manufacturers to go back to using steel or plastic containers. Prices of other packaging materials were rising fast.

Chris-Craft Industries Inc. of the U.K. launched an edible, water-soluble cellulose film for packaging premeasured ingredients. The packets, which accurately measured and protected ingredients from dust, were time-savers and ensured safe handling.

During the year Hans Rausing, then head of Tetra Laval, bitterly attacked Europe's packaging-recycling policy in general and Germany's stringent packaging laws in particular, claiming they actually increased waste instead of reducing it. More than 200 local authorities in Germany restricted the sale and use of plastic cups. At least 100 German towns were considering a local tax on disposable packaging; Frankfurt and Kassel had already imposed one. Europe's packaging industry was skeptical that recovery of used materials would be profitable but glad that the laws allowed the extra costs to be passed on to the consumer.

Government Action. EU regulations that became effective January 1995 required new machinery to carry a mark signifying compliance with safety laws by designers, manufacturers, purchasers, and installers. An EU sweeteners directive, effective from the end of 1995, permitted the use of six intense sweeteners—aspartame, acesulfame K, saccharin, cyclamate, thaumatin, and neohesperidin DC—and prescribed an acceptable daily intake limit for each. This changed the food law in some countries and permitted cyclamate to be used in food in France and the U.K. after a ban of many years.

Wide abuse of the cross-border EU trade system, which relied on the integrity of health certificates accompanying animal products, caused the European Parliament to endorse countermeasures that included outlawing the signing of blank certificates and maintaining a register of sample signatures of veterinarians and authorized health officials.

(ANTHONY WOOLLEN)

See also Business and Industry Review: *Beverages; Tobacco;* The Environment; Health and Disease.

This article updates the *Macropædia* article FOOD PROCESSING.

Anthropology and Archaeology

ANTHROPOLOGY

Physical. Evidence was offered in 1995 for a possible evolutionary radiation of primates, near the beginning of the Pliocene (*i.e.,* roughly four million to five million years ago), that were bipedal but more apelike than human in other anatomic features. Tim White (*see* BIOGRAPHIES) of the University of California, Berkeley, who in 1994 had announced *Australopithecus ramidus* as a newly discovered species of hominid, renamed that fossil *Ardipithecus ramidus.* The change in genus was based on additional fossil discoveries indicating that the primate, although it walked on two feet, had dentition more like that of chimpanzees than australopithecines. The concept of a new genus that is bipedal but not a hominid generated debate among the experts.

Meave Leakey of the National Museums of Kenya and colleagues announced a new find from that country, named *Australopithecus anamensis,* that was bipedal but, again, had apelike teeth. It was perhaps significant that both it and *A. ramidus* evidently once lived in a forest or woodland environment in East Africa more than four million years ago. Other clues came from South African fossil bones that were excavated in 1980 but only recently analyzed. Phillip Tobias and Ronald Clarke of the University of Witwatersrand, Johannesburg, South Africa, described the fossils as the first connected foot bones ever found of a presumed australopithecine (nicknamed "Little Foot"). The biped, which may have lived as early as 3.5 million years ago, had a humanlike ankle and heel but apelike toes, as observed in the articulation of the big toe. The new finds and interpretations may indicate that the capacity for upright walking had selective value for more than the direct human ancestral line.

Because there will never be enough fossil material from any epoch to settle all questions concerning relationships, scientists have pursued complementary approaches. One major technique, molecular dating, is based on the assumption that the degree of difference in the sequences of noncoding DNA (DNA that does not specify functional proteins) of modern species can be directly translated into years since the species diverged from a common ancestor. The validity of the assumption depends on the regularity of the mutation rate of the noncoding DNA, the so-called molecular clock. During the year population geneticist Wen-Hsiung Li of General Hospital of PLA, Beijing (Peking), showed from an analysis of many different sequences of DNA that mutation rate varies by species. For example, New World monkeys have a slightly faster rate than Old World monkeys and twice the rate of humans. Such variance of the molecular clock between species had interesting implications in the calculation of taxonomic relationships.

JOHAN REINHARD—NATIONAL GEOGRAPHIC SOCIETY

This Inca girl, whose body was frozen in ice, is thought to have died a ritual death on Mt. Ampato in Peru. After anthropologists had discovered the well-preserved 500-year-old, other experts began testing the tissues and body fluids to identify pathogens existing at the time.

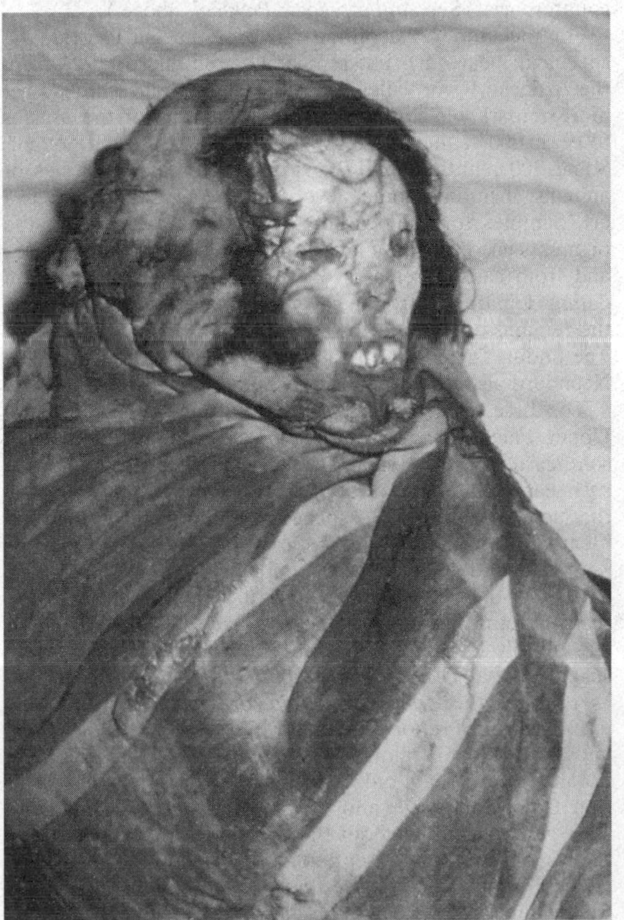

Ongoing analysis of DNA sequences for different human populations, enhanced by the application of sophisticated statistical techniques, yielded evidence for population contractions and expansions over the last 200,000 years. One result is support for the "weak Garden of Eden" model promoted in the early 1990s by Alan Rogers of the University of Utah and Henry Harpending of Pennsylvania State University. It suggests that the original modern human population—not large to begin with—split into separate populations as it spread slowly over the Old World starting about 100,000 years ago. Those populations remained small (and perhaps dangerously close to extinction) for tens of thousands of years until finally, between 80,000 and 30,000 years ago, they rapidly expanded. The model best explained the small amount of genetic diversity seen in modern human populations. Looking at nuclear DNA, Maryellen Ruvolo of Harvard University showed that two lowland gorillas from the same forest are more genetically diverse than two humans from separate continents. All this supported the theory that whereas all humans ultimately descend from *Homo erectus,* they have a much more recent common ancestry.

An intriguing report of early human behaviour came from John Yellen of the U.S. National Science Foundation and co-workers, who discovered carved bone points resembling harpoons at a site in Zaire at least 75,000 years old. The sophistication of the tools, implying truly modern human activity, would not be seen in Europe for about another 50,000 years.

Evidence presented in 1994 from a redating of fossils from Java that human ancestors left Africa far earlier than a million years ago was strengthened by the dating of an *H. erectus* mandible from Dmanisi, Georgia, at 1.8 million years and the discovery of 1.9 million-year-old hominid bones and stone tools, apparently from a species more primitive than *H. erectus,* in a cave in central China. In addition, the date for the earliest known occurrence of hominids in Europe was pushed back about 300,000 years to at least 780,000 years ago by the discovery of fossil bones and tools in a cave in northern Spain. Initial descriptions of the fossil hominids at the site indicate similarities to some *H. erectus* forms from Africa but also enough differences to require a new species designation. The discovery, added to other findings, had some experts suggesting that *H. erectus* be split into at least two species. (HERMANN K. BLEIBTREU)

Cultural. Cultural anthropologists in 1995 struggled to reconcile research interests with strongly held ethical commitments to human rights and scholarly integrity as they debated the effects of exponential population growth, global warming, AIDS, the collapse of old political orders, and the rise of new ethnic, gender, and race coalitions. Increasingly aware of the potential of their research and particular points of view to affect their subjects, who often were people fighting for cultural or physical survival, they argued whether their discipline is an art or a science, whether they had the ability or the right to represent other cultures, and whether it was appropriate to involve themselves in issues affecting the people that they studied.

In a review of Adam Kuper's *The Chosen Primate: Human Nature and Cultural Diversity,* ethnologist Roy A. Rappaport of the University of Michigan at Ann Arbor framed the central problem of anthropological development in his characterization of humanity as a species that must construct meaningful symbol systems "in a world devoid of intrinsic meaning but subject to natural law." Emphasizing the dynamically complex nature of meaning systems in *After the Fact: Two Countries, Four Decades, One Anthropologist,* ethnologist Clifford Geertz of the Institute for Advanced Studies, Princeton, N.J., urged colleagues to focus efforts on interpretive cultural understandings. Impressed by the influence of natural laws on culture, anthropologist Robin Fox of Rutgers University, New Brunswick, N.J., in *The Challenge of Anthropology: Old Encounters and New Excursions,* called on ethnologists to direct their attention toward scientific explanations of regularities crossing cultural boundaries.

The debate over whether anthropology is a science or one of the humanities progressed from a simple "either-or" argument to considerably more nuanced examinations of the relative merits of scientific and humanistic approaches, such as those presented in the books by Geertz and Fox cited above. This more balanced perspective was mirrored in the call by David J. Hess of Rensselaer Polytechnic Institute, Troy, N.Y., in his book *Science and Technology in a Multicultural World: The Cultural Politics of Facts and Artifacts,* for renewed efforts to build creatively upon anthropology's tradition as the most humanistic of sciences.

Anthropologists and their subjects throughout the world increasingly questioned both the abilities and the rights of outside observers to represent their cultures. While few objected to the efforts of support groups to protect indigenous knowledge and resources from foreign exploitation, controversy continued to swirl around anthropological representations of other cultures. For example, in his 1992 book *The Apotheosis of Captain Cook: European Mythmaking in the Pacific,* Princeton University professor Gananath Obeyesekere claimed that his perspective as a Sri Lankan enabled him to expose the fallacies underlying University of Chicago anthropologist Marshall Sahlins' hypothesis that mythic thinking caused Hawaiians to confuse British explorer James Cook with the god Lono. Maintaining that Hawaiians, like Sri Lankans, were fully capable of rational thought, Obeyesekere turned Sahlins' argument on its head with the assertion that the actual mythmongers were British writers perpetuating "white god" legends. In his 1995 book *How "Natives" Think: About Captain Cook, For Example,* Sahlins responded by questioning the privileged position of "native" informant assumed by Obeyesekere. He pointed out that Indo-European-speaking Sri Lankan people had long been in close contact with Eurasian nation-states and that they had more in common with Western European cultures than with the isolated and more traditional Hawaiian chiefdoms. Reaffirming the need to view the actions of the Hawaiians from the perspective of their own cultural logic, Sahlins went on to show that mythic thinking did not obstruct Hawaiian rationality any more than Western belief in a Judeo-Christian God precluded scientific understanding.

More and more use was being made of the vast amounts of information already amassed in previous fieldwork. In *Yanomami Warfare,* for instance, anthropologist R. Brian Ferguson of Rutgers University showed how competition for Western manufactures, rather than innate ferocity, could account for the bellicose nature of Venezuelan and Brazilian native people who belonged to what was regarded as one of the world's most violent cultures. Western psychiatrists increasingly consulted anthropological studies for insights in treating patients who suffered from syndromes afflicting members of particular cultures. Two examples were *susto,* a state of unhappiness and sickness, caused by "soul loss," that afflicts Latin Americans in the U.S. and the Caribbean, and *latah,* a trancelike condition characterized by giddily inappropriate behaviour and mimicry that strikes Malaysian, Indonesian, and Thai people. (ROBERT S. GRUMET)

ARCHAEOLOGY

Eastern Hemisphere. Prevailing political turmoil continued to close off the possibility for archaeological fieldwork in many parts of the Old World during 1995. One notable exception was Lebanon, where the end of political strife allowed archaeological clearances to be conducted on the war-torn ruins of broad areas of the city of Beirut. Another impediment to archaeological research, one of worldwide concern, was the increasing resistance to excavation of the remains—either artifactual or physical—of indigenous inhabitants. In Israel, Australia, and the Americas, religious officials and descendants of the ancient inhabitants strove to prevent further excavations and were demanding the return of previously exhumed bones and artifacts.

Increasingly, evidence showed that the earliest traces of human activity come from Africa. Dating of stone tools recently recovered in Ethiopia showed them to be about 2.6 million years old. By contrast, the oldest known tools found in Europe, reported during the year for a site in north-central Spain, yielded dates of about 780,000 years. Even carved bone points recently recovered in Zaire were found to be about 75,000 years old, far older than their European counterparts. (See *Anthropology: Physical,* above.)

For the Upper Paleolithic range of the Old World, the spectacular cave art first reported at the end of 1994 from the Ardèche River valley in southeastern France proved yet more remarkable after dating showed some of the images to be 30,000 years old, 10,000 years older than first thought. Some 300 paintings and engravings show many species of animals, including some never before represented in cave art. Samples for radiocarbon dating were taken from the pigments used for the images, from the soot of torch marks, and from carbon remains on the cave floor. Radiocarbon dating of materials from a cave in southern Spain containing the remains of Neanderthals yielded an age of 30,000 years. The finding fueled the debate over the degree to which late Neanderthals and early modern human beings interrelated.

The June issue of *Antiquity* featured an account of early Upper Paleolithic (about 45,000-year-old) materials from southeastern Siberia near Lake Baikal. The production of such early flint blade tools so far to the east and toward the New World tempted speculation about the timing and identity of the first humans to arrive in the Americas.

In England studies were conducted on hair from the 5,000-year-old remains of a man, nicknamed Ötzi and the Iceman, found frozen in an Alpine glacier in 1991. The hair was heavily contaminated with copper and arsenic, which suggested that Ötzi was associated with copper smelting.

Although the *American Journal of Archaeology* provided useful regional reports on fieldwork in southwestern Asia and the Aegean region, the contents of the reports were usually several years old. A lack of archaeological information from Iran, Iraq, and southeastern Turkey tended to skew generalizations about the origin of food production in the region. For the present, some archaeologists seemed to take for granted that the settled-village–farming-community way of life, based on livestock and cultivated grains, began

New evidence suggests that this section of the frieze on the Parthenon may show Erechtheus, king of Athens, preparing to sacrifice his three daughters to save the city. The scene had traditionally been thought to show a festival commemorating the birth of Athena.

ALISON FRANZ COLLECTION, AMERICAN SCHOOL OF CLASSICAL STUDIES, ATHENS, GREECE

in the Levant (southern and western Syria, Lebanon, Jordan, and Israel).

Fruitful fieldwork persisted in the central and western portions of Turkey. Excavations at various sites of the more developed time range were renewed after some years, including work by Italian and British teams at Mersin and Catalhuyuk, while joint German and American excavations continued at Troy. The Oriental Institute of the University of Chicago was returning after 57 years to its old excavations in the Plain of Antioch in southern Turkey. Work by its so called Amouq expedition, interrupted by World War II, had yielded important materials over a 6,000-year time frame. The new Amouq team was headed by Aslihan Yener.

In northern Syria a Dutch team continued its work at an important early site, Hammam el-Turkman. Excavations were reported from Jordan covering a time frame that stretched from fully prehistoric to early Christian. On Mt. Gerizim Yitzhak Magen, Israel's chief archaeologist for the West Bank, located what was claimed to be an exact replica of the Second Temple of Jerusalem.

Big news from Egypt was anticipated as archaeologists worked to finish clearing a large multichambered mausoleum found in the Valley of the Kings. The structure was believed to be the burial place of many of the sons of the great pharaoh Ramses II, who fathered more than 100 children. Egyptologist Kent R. Weeks of the American University in Cairo made the discovery.

During 1995 items of clothing belonging to the boy pharaoh Tutankhamen, including dozens of loincloths, tunics, gloves, and shawls, were under study for the first time. They had lain in wooden chests in a Cairo Museum storeroom and remained ignored since the discovery of Tut's tomb in 1922. A claim made by archaeologists early in the year that the grave of Alexander the Great had been found near Siwa in the western desert of Egypt was discounted by other researchers sent to investigate.

In recent years archaeological activity in Cyprus increased, as did fieldwork in Crete. News of the activities was covered in the *American Journal of Archaeology*'s October 1994 and April 1995 issues. An article by L. Vance Watrous offered an excellent general review of Cretan prehistory through the end of the protopalatial period (about 3500–1800 BC).

The various national "schools" in Greece were active, but direct information was long delayed. The most fascinating news from Greek archaeology concerned the analysis of a scene from the frieze of the Parthenon. The text of a papyrus found in the wrapping of an Egyptian mummy stimulated Joan B. Connelly of New York University to reason that the scene showed Erechtheus, king of Athens, about to follow the Delphic oracle's request that he sacrifice his three daughters in order for Athens to be saved from an impending attack. Not all authorities accepted the interpretation.

A compact U.S. Navy nuclear submarine originally designed for Cold War missions was made available for deep-sea inspection and recovery of archaeological remains. It was capable of diving to 800 m (2,600 ft), and its first use was to be in the Mediterranean along the ancient Greco-Roman-Carthaginian trade route, where it would search for and recover materials from ancient sunken ships.

One highlight among the scant news of eastern Asia was the success of radar images taken from space during a U.S. space shuttle mission in late 1994 in delineating the whole complex of the ancient Cambodian city of Angkor. The region is so covered with tropical forest that surface-based mapping had never been addressed. In China vast new development of the region around the so-called Three Gorges of the Chang Jiang (Yangtze River), stimulated by an enormous dam-construction project, attracted archaeological attention, and several U.S. universities were involved.

The loss of one of archaeology's foremost figures in later European prehistoric studies came with the death of Sir Grahame Clark (*see* OBITUARIES) of the University of Cambridge. Another death of note was that of Benjamin Mazar (*see* OBITUARIES), a Russian-born Israeli biblical archaeologist who excavated the southern and western walls of Temple Mount, Jerusalem, in the late 1960s and early '70s.

(ROBERT J. BRAIDWOOD)

Western Hemisphere. Of all the controversies in New World archaeology, none has engendered such passionate debate as that over the nature and date of first settlement of the Americas. Most experts believed that the first human settlers crossed from Siberia over the Bering land bridge into Alaska near the end of the last ice age, before sea levels began rising about 15,000 years ago. The earliest widely accepted dates for human arrival in the Americas were in the 14,000–12,000-year range, after which time human populations rapidly increased with the appearance of the Clovis cultural tradition about 11,000 years ago.

For years claims for much earlier settlement centred on the controversial Pedra Furada, a rock shelter in northeastern Brazil. French archaeologist Niède Guidon maintained that the lower levels of the site contain hearths and stone artifacts, which radiocarbon dating showed to be as old as 48,000 years, contemporary with the Neanderthals in Europe and western Asia. In 1994 three U.S.-based experts on North American Paleo-Indians, James Adovasio, Thomas Dillehay, and David Meltzer, visited Pedra Furada for a firsthand look at the evidence. They concluded that the early "occupation deposits" and associated stone "artifacts" were probably formed by natural geologic phenomena. If they were correct, Pedra Furada was no longer an anomaly—the only 50,000-year-old archaeological site in the Western Hemisphere. Recent DNA studies tended to collaborate a somewhat later date for human settlement, for they identified at least three genetic strains of Native American ancestry dating back to the end of the last ice age.

Not only genetics but also medical science worked increasingly closely with archaeology. The frozen body of a girl that was found buried in a subterranean house near Barrow, Alaska, promised to throw light on endemic diseases among the Thule whaling people who lived in the region about AD 1200. The girl, who probably died of starvation between four and eight years of age, suffered from a congenital respiratory disease, alpha-1 antitrypsin deficiency. Rare among modern Americans, the disease may have been more common in the far north in ancient times.

In the 1950s and '60s, archaeologist Richard MacNeish's excavations in the dry caves of Mexico's Tehuacán Valley yielded early maize (corn) cobs from levels that were dated by standard radiocarbon techniques—measuring the concentration of radioactive carbon-14 atoms in an organic sample by their decay—to about 5000 BC. That figure became the long-accepted date for the beginning of maize agriculture in Mesoamerica. In recent years archaeologists benefited from a technological refinement called accelerator mass spectrometry (AMS), which allows radiocarbon dating to be carried out with greater precision and on much smaller samples, even individual seeds, by the direct counting of carbon-14 atoms rather than radioactive disintegrations. When early Tehuacán cobs found in levels previously dated to 5000 BC were analyzed with AMS, they yielded dates of about 2600 BC, placing early maize farming some 2,500 years later than long assumed. Thus, maize agriculture apparently preceded the appearance of Olmec and Maya civilizations in the Mesoamerican lowlands by only about a millennium.

AMS dating also produced convincing evidence for the widespread cultivation of native tubers and grasses in the river valleys of eastern North America by at least 2000 BC. It confirmed that experimentation with the deliberate cultivation of many native grasses was widespread in pre-Columbian North America at least 4,500 years ago.

The decipherment of Maya glyphs, which had advanced particularly rapidly in the past two decades, was one of the great triumphs of archaeology in the 20th century. As recently as the 1960s, the Maya were considered a peaceful civilization ruled by calendar-obsessed priests. Decoding their complex script, however, painted an entirely different portrait of a society of powerful militaristic states ruled by bloodthirsty shaman-rulers. Maya civilization was seen to be a mosaic of small centres that vied diplomatically and on the battlefield. Many rose to prominence, then fell into obscurity with bewildering rapidity. Recently, with ongoing decipherment, perceptions were changing again. From a study of numerous inscriptions, Simon Martin of University College, London, and Nikolai Grube of the University of Bonn, Germany, found that most settlements in the core of the Maya lowlands were allied politically with two powerful kingdoms, Tikal in the Petén region of Guatemala and Calakmul in southern Campeche state, Mexico, each of which competed ferociously for vassal centres. Thus, the real political power lay in only a few hands.

By no means were all Maya excavations concerned with cities. Investigations at Talgua Cave in northeastern Honduras by James Brady of George Washington University, Washington, D.C., and other American and Honduran scholars revealed a Maya ossuary, used between about 980 and 800 BC. Twenty-three deposits of human skeletal material were found in the cave, many of them communal bone

MEDFORD TAYLOR—THE DISCOVERY CHANNEL

A skull from a cave in Honduras glows from the calcite deposited by rainwater that seeped through the limestone walls. The skeletal remains found in the burial chamber were dated to 980 BC and were thought to be the remains of a farming society based on manioc (cassava).

collections arranged in natural depressions, topped with ceramic jars. The interred individuals probably were all from a nearby village of manioc (cassava) farmers, and Brady believed that they were all from the same lineage.

About AD 900 Maya civilization in the southern Yucatán lowlands collapsed rapidly. The cause has long been a controversial subject, with experts invoking such factors as environmental degradation, warfare, internal rebellion, and disease. A large-scale settlement survey at the ancient Maya city of Copán in Honduras examined more than 135 sq km (1 sq km is about 0.39 sq mi) around the urban core and documented the collapse in dramatic detail. A combination of aerial photography, on-foot inspection, and test excavations recorded more than 1,425 archaeological sites in the Copán Valley. The survey revealed an urban core, a densely occupied area surrounding the core, and a rural region with a much lower settlement density. By using hydration dating on artifacts made of obsidian (volcanic glass), the investigators were able to date the sampled sites quite precisely and reconstruct the changing demography of the Copán Valley.

From AD 550 to 700, the Copán state expanded rapidly, with most of the population concentrated in the core and immediate periphery. Between 700 and 850, the valley reached its greatest sociopolitical complexity, experiencing a rapid population increase that peaked at 18,000–20,000 people. Those figures, calculated from site size, suggested that the local population was doubling every 80–100 years. About 80% lived in or near the city, while rural settlement remained relatively scattered. At the time, people were farming foothill areas to support a population density that reached more than 8,000 per square kilometre in the urban core and about 500 per square kilometre in the periphery. About 80% of the population lived in relatively humble dwellings, an indication of the extreme stratification of Copán society. Then, after AD 850, a few decades following the end of Copán's ruling dynasty, depopulation occurred. The urban core and periphery lost about half their populations, while the rural population increased by almost 20%. Small regional settlements replaced the scattered villages of earlier times, a response to cumulative deforestation, overexploitation of even marginal agricultural soils, and sheet erosion near the capital. By 1150 the Copán Valley population had fallen to 5,000–8,000 people. (BRIAN FAGAN)

This article updates the *Macropædia* articles Human EVOLUTION; The Study of HISTORY: *Archaeology;* The SOCIAL SCIENCES: *Cultural Anthropology*.

Architecture and Civil Engineering

ARCHITECTURE

The most talked-about work of architecture and engineering in 1995 was what some called "the Crossroads of Europe," the immense new cluster of buildings at the entrance to the Channel Tunnel (Eurotunnel) in Lille, France.

The complex, known as Euralille, was one hour from Paris and two hours from London by train. It was to be linked by high-speed rail to Amsterdam; Brussels; Cologne, Germany; and other parts of Europe in the future and would likely serve as the nerve centre for a multinational community of 100 million people. Parts of Euralille opened in 1994 and 1995, but much was still under construction. Dutch architect Rem Koolhaas created the master plan for Euralille. He also designed the vast Grand Palais, or Congrexpo, which included a conference centre, an exhibit hall, and an arena for rock concerts. Koolhaas gave each of them a different architectural appearance, using industrial materials such as corrugated polyester and aluminum, in order to create a sense of random collision and congestion—qualities that he admired and that were described in his book *Delirious New York.*

Other buildings, straddling the station for the TGV (Train à Grande Vitesse), included a slope-sided Credit-Lyonnais bank tower by French architect Christian de Portzamparc and Euralille Centre, a vast complex by Frenchman Jean Nouvel that included stores, restaurants, theatres, a business school, a sports centre, and residential apartments. Hotels, parks, and a world trade centre were also planned for Euralille.

Awards. Tadao Ando of Japan was the 1995 winner of the most prestigious international award in the field, the $100,000 Pritzker Architecture Prize. Already widely honoured, Ando was known for an austere, almost monastic type of architecture, usually built of beautifully finished raw concrete, often in simple geometric shapes, and without any ornament or historic detail. "I do not believe architecture should speak too much," Ando had said. "It should remain silent and let nature in the guise of sunlight and wind speak." A believer in solid construction, Ando proudly announced that after the destructive January 17 Great Hanshin Earthquake in the Kobe, Japan, area, all of his 30 buildings in the quake zone remained intact. (*See* EARTH AND SPACE SCIENCES: *Geophysics*.) One of the architect's major works was the Suntory Museum in Osaka, which opened during 1995 and contained spaces for housing contemporary art and for staging performing arts.

In an unusual move the Royal Institute of British Architects gave its Gold Medal to a teacher and critic rather than an architect: Colin Rowe, a British-born professor of architecture at Cornell University, Ithaca, N.Y. The triennial Aga Khan Awards for Architecture were presented for 12 works of Islamic architecture, ranging from the reconstruction of historic neighbourhoods to the design of an environmentally sensitive office tower. The Mies van der Rohe Pavilion Award for European Architecture was given to Nicholas Grimshaw's Waterloo International Terminal, the British link to the Channel Tunnel. The American Institute of Architects did not award its Gold Medal in 1995. The winner of the AIA's Twenty-Five Year Award for 1996 was announced. Given annually to a building that has proved its worth over time, the award went to the 1962 Air Force Academy Cadet Chapel in Colorado Springs, Colo., by Skidmore, Owings, & Merrill. The AIA also chose 13 buildings for its annual Honor Awards for good design. Among the more prominent of the 1995 winners were Westendstrasse 1, an office tower in Frankfurt am Main, Germany, by Kohn Pedersen Fox; Seiji Ozawa Hall, a concert space in Massachusetts by William Rawn; Arrow International, a corporate headquarters in Pennsylvania by Kallmann, McKinnell & Wood; Jacobs Field baseball park in Cleveland, Ohio, and Hong Kong Stadium in Hong Kong, both by the firm of HOK; and the Center for the Arts Theater in San Francisco, by James Polshek.

Cultural Buildings. Buildings intended for music or books tended to dominate world architecture in 1995. The construction of libraries was somewhat puzzling because some people were predicting that books would soon be made obsolete by electronic media. Many new libraries, however, were being envisioned as community centres, replete with day-care facilities, art galleries, and restaurants.

The most prominent and controversial library was the National Library of France. It was completed in 1995 but was not expected to be open to the public until 1997, which allowed a two-year time frame for moving 12 million books

The interior spaces of the Contemporary Art Museum in Barcelona, Spain, are bathed in natural light. The all-white structure, designed by architect Richard Meier and referred to by some as the "pearl," made a dramatic contrast with the surrounding buildings in old Barcelona.

onto the library's 435 km (270 mi) of shelves. Designed by Dominique Perrault and erected on the Left Bank of the Seine River in Paris, the structure was much criticized for being "upside down." The books, which were to be housed in glass towers that resembled office buildings, would be bathed in sunlight, while the patrons would be relegated to underground reading rooms.

Israeli-Canadian architect Moshe Safdie's Library Square opened in Vancouver, B.C. A dramatic building in the shape of an oval, it resembled the ancient Colosseum in Rome. In Denver, Colo., a new main library by U.S. architect Michael Graves also employed a round shape, this time a circular rotunda set between symmetrical wings in a manner that vaguely recalled such neoclassical buildings as the U.S. Capitol. Both libraries tried to achieve a sense of grandeur by evoking memories of great buildings of the past. In San Antonio, Texas, by contrast, a new main library by Mexican architect Ricardo Legoretta was a bold modern structure in bright colours of red, yellow, and blue.

In Cleveland the long-awaited Rock and Roll Hall of Fame and Museum opened. It was designed by famed U.S. architect I.M. Pei, who, at age 79, admitted to journalists that in his attempts to appreciate rock music, he had progressed as far as Bruce Springsteen but could not continue any farther. Sited on the shore of Lake Erie, the Rock Hall looked like a frozen explosion, with solid chunks in the shape of cubes and cylinders seeming to blast outward from a central glass pyramid. The pyramid reminded many of Pei's more famous pyramid at the Louvre Museum in Paris. The exhibits, designed by the Burdick Group, were a wild mix of celebrity memorabilia on the one hand and serious displays on the history of rock on the other. The actual Hall of Fame was a windowless room at the top of the building, with walls made of black glass onto which were projected the images of the stars, in a manner that recalled the stained glass windows of a cathedral.

In Paris the final phase of the Cité de la Musique opened at the edge of the Parc de la Villette. Designed by Portzamparc, it included a 2,700-seat concert hall and a museum that housed more than 4,500 historic instruments. In Japan the Kirishima International Concert Hall, in a remote mountain setting, was designed by Fumihiko Maki. Sheathed in the architect's trademark glowing brushed-silver surfaces, it peaked in one of his "cloud" roofs: a mound of folded planes in stainless steel, looking rather like Japanese origami paper. In the countryside of Britain, a new hall for the famed Glyndebourne Opera, by Michael Hopkins, featured a horseshoe-shaped interior finished in reclaimed 150-year-old pine. Critics said the hall resembled a huge, beautifully crafted and polished instrument, such as a violin.

Other Buildings. A Korean War Veterans' Memorial opened on the Mall in Washington, D.C. It included a wall of dark granite, on which were engraved ghostlike images of soldiers and other veterans. The European Court of Human Rights in Strasbourg, France, was designed by British architect Richard Rogers in the high-tech style of his earlier Pompidou Centre, with huge curving wings of gleaming stainless steel. In Houston, Texas, Renzo Piano of Italy, Rogers' partner in the Pompidou design, created a small gem of a museum for the work of U.S. artist Cy Twombly. Piano also was the architect of the vast Kansai International Airport in Osaka, Japan, which opened in late 1994.

Competitions. With most of the German government moving to Berlin, a major design competition was held for a new U.S. embassy to be built next to the landmark Brandenburg Gate. Six prominent American architects were asked to propose designs for the embassy, with a winner to be selected by a jury of architects and diplomats. The jurors completed their work in September, but no result was announced by year's end. In London a competition for a design to convert a riverfront power plant into a new branch of the Tate Gallery was won by the Swiss firm of Jacques Herzog and Pierre de Meuron.

Exhibitions. The year's most significant architectural exhibition was undoubtedly the wrapping of the Reichstag in Berlin. Artist Christo and his wife, Jeanne-Claude (*see* BIOGRAPHIES), swaddled this former home of the German Parliament in translucent polypropylene. The magical effect was to convert the grim old building, for one week, into an architectural cloud formation. After the wraps came off, construction crews began the task of renovating the Reichstag, which would become, again, the German capitol. The architect for the renovation was Sir Norman Foster of Britain.

The Museum of Modern Art in New York City mounted a show of the work of Koolhaas. It included drawings and models of Koolhaas' work for Euralille, as well as other urban design plans and the architect's unchosen but memorable proposal for the National Library of France. The Art Institute of Chicago displayed the work of Bruce Goff, an idiosyncratic follower of Frank Lloyd Wright.

Controversies and News Events. Times Square in New York City was again a topic of controversy, thanks to a proposal for a 47-story hotel for the Disney Co. designed by the Miami firm Arquitectonica. In cartoon fashion, the tower would be split by a curved glass "bolt of light." Disney, which planned to renovate other properties along 42nd Street, was also at work in Florida. The company opened a sales office there for Celebration, an entire new town that the company was building near Disney World and for which it was employing a star list of architects, including Robert Venturi, Philip Johnson, Michael Graves, Cesar Pelli, Robert A.M. Stern, and Jaquelin Robertson. With no buildings yet built, Disney instead erected full-size billboards of the future houses to entice prospective buyers. Critics noted that while the town celebrated the architecture of the American small town and evoked its vision of democracy, the community actually would be carefully controlled by the Disney corporation.

After more than a year of delay caused by technical glitches, the Denver International Airport finally opened in February, at a cost of $4.9 billion. Occupying a larger area than the entire city of Paris, the airport featured a terminal building roofed by a tent made of white membrane stretched over steel masts. It looked to some like the snowcapped Rockies, to others like a teepee encampment. In Chicago a losing battle was waged to save from demolition the Arts Club, an interior by Ludwig Mies van der Rohe.

Two catastrophes during the year were expected to influence the architecture of the future. The April 19 bombing of a federal building in Oklahoma City, Okla., which also damaged some 70 other buildings, was likely to lead to stricter security requirements for government architecture. Some feared the rise of a fortress mentality, ill suited to a democracy, a fear that was reinforced by a decision to close off a section of Pennsylvania Avenue in Washington, D.C., to protect the White House. The Great Hanshin Earthquake was the first major quake ever to strike a modern downtown. It was even more devastating than the Oklahoma City bombing—many buildings toppled over into the streets, and about 6,000 people died—but it was noted that little damage was suffered by the most recently constructed buildings, which were erected according to strict earthquake codes. The problem remained of how to protect Japan's older cities—and cities located on earthquake fault lines in other countries, such as the U.S.—from similar catastrophes in the future.

Among those who died during the year were Wolf von Eckardt, former architecture critic of the *Washington* (D.C.)

The Rock and Roll Hall of Fame and Museum, a dramatic structure designed by I.M. Pei, stands on Lake Erie in Cleveland, Ohio. The museum, which opened to great fanfare in September, included multimedia displays as well as memorabilia from a number of rock stars.

Post, at 77. A death of another kind was the demise of the Architects Collaborative (TAC) in Cambridge, Mass., founded in 1946 by legendary architect Walter Gropius with a group of young partners. Once one of the largest and most successful firms in the U.S., TAC collapsed under debt in April. (ROBERT CAMPBELL)

See also Business and Industry Review: *Building and Construction*.

This article updates the *Macropædia* article The History of Western ARCHITECTURE.

BRIDGES

The year 1995 started with a celebration and a shock. Fanfares were for the official opening in January of the Pont de Normandie, the world's longest cable-stayed type, with elegant A-frame towers carrying a motorway across the Seine estuary on France's northern coast. The 856-m-long (1 m = 3.3 ft) central composite steel and concrete span took technology a huge step forward.

The shock, quite literally, was to the world's biggest bridge project on January 10. The earthquake in Japan looked as if it might also have damaged the half-built 500 billion yen Akashi Kaikyo suspension bridge, just 10 km (1 km = 0.62 mi) from the quake's epicentre. The bridge's 1,990-m main span passes over the Akashi Strait, which contains one of the main fault lines in the Kobe area.

Work stopped on the bridge, but no damage was found. Still, surveys showed the quake had pushed the towers apart by 1.1 m—only 0.005% of the total span but enough to mean that suspension hangers and deck needed redesigning.

Seismic resistance was also a major design concern for other bridges as well, particularly in California, where many thousands of ordinary road bridges as well as larger crossings needed expensive retrofit strengthening to come up to modern standards. For example, the Golden Gate suspension bridge at San Francisco was now deemed unsafe even in a magnitude-7 quake. Some $175 million in upgrades would be needed to permit it to carry emergency traffic within 24 hours of a magnitude-8.5 earthquake. Portugal's new Tagus II bridge also got a substantial working over for seismic resistance. The 420-m centre span cable-stayed bridge, on which construction began in 1994, was part of an 18-km viaduct crossing of repeated concrete spans.

Other examples of this trend in bridge building—very long composite multispan bridges, usually featuring a single main span over a shipping channel—included the bridge section on the Øresund link between Sweden and Denmark, begun in November, with its spectacular 1,200-m cable-stayed central section and a 492-m main span; the Store Bælt interisland link in Denmark, which included a tunnel and an artificial island centre point as well as the bridge with a 1,620-m main span (it would hold the world record briefly in 1997); and the second Severn crossing in Great Britain, which ran 5.2 km across the estuary, using a cable-stayed 456-m centre bridge and repeated concrete box spans between 2,000-ton caisson piers for the remainder. Canada's Prince Edward Island project had no main bridge but rather used 250-m-long precast concrete spans to form the 11-km viaduct. The bridge piers, of special superstrength concrete to withstand ice floes, were also of interest. At 1,377 m the main span of the Tsing Ma suspension bridge in Hong Kong was shorter than Store Bælt, but the bridge was double-decked to carry rail and road traffic; cable spinning for this bridge had been completed by early summer. Part of the series of bridges linking the Japanese islands of Honshu and Shikoku, the Akashi Kaikyo Bridge itself was yet another sample of contemporary composite multispan bridge projects.

The world's largest concrete barge, 220 m (720 ft) long and weighing 70,000 metric tons, nears completion at Marseille, France. Designed to be used as an oil-production platform, the barge was scheduled to enter into service late in the year off the west coast of Africa.
PETER REINA

Indeed, the Far East was where the most exciting projects were planned for coming years. China had several giant projects under consideration for crossing its big rivers, including the Chang Jiang (Yangtze), Huang Ho (Yellow River), and Zhu Jiang (Pearl River). India had three large bridges planned for the south. A hint for the next century came perhaps from a tiny five-metre slab footbridge in Oxfordshire, England. For the first time ever, plastic reinforcement was used in the concrete instead of steel.

(ADRIAN LEE GREEMAN)

BUILDINGS

The world's tallest buildings were being developed in Asia in 1995. Construction of the Petronas Towers in Kuala Lumpur, Malaysia, was under way, and completion was expected toward the end of 1996. At 450 m, it would be overtaken in height by the 460-m Chongqing Tower, Chongqing, China, which was expected to be completed in 1997. A Hong Kong developer, however, was planning to complete a 468-m-tall building, the Nina Tower, by 1997. This skyscraper was to be square in plan and would feature a composite steel and concrete construction with splayed corners to reduce wind drag.

Construction on Hong Kong's new airport at Chek Lap Kok began in 1995 with the main terminal contract awarded early in the year. A Y-shaped footprint was selected from some 50 possible designs for the building. It was 1.2 km long and accommodated 38 pier gates. The design incorporated modular steel framed barrel vaults supported on high columns, with a partially glazed roof in an attempt to create a feeling of light and space.

Mid-1995 saw the tragic collapse of a six-year-old multistory department store in Seoul, South Korea, where more than 500 people were killed. The building, a reinforced-concrete slab construction, was supported by columns 10.8 m apart. The collapse was attributed to a failure around a column at roof level that then led to the progressive failure of other columns. The debris load on floors below then caused a collapse of the entire building.

The reunification of Germany resulted in increased construction in the former East Germany. In Leipzig, a centuries-old trading hub, a new conference and exhibition centre was being built to the north of the city to replace the outdated exhibition facilities. The focal point of the development was a 250 × 80-m steel-framed, glass-clad hall. The main structure included external arch trusses rising 28 m and spaced 25 m apart. Supported by these was a grid of steel tubes arranged in squares that, in turn, supported the glazing envelope. A smooth, highly transparent glass surface was presented internally, and efforts were also made to keep the degree of natural daylight virtually uninterrupted by the steel structure.

In Nottingham, England, a novel form of prefabrication was used to combine high quality with quick construction. An architect chose this technique to match a facades' brickwork construction with that of other buildings in the area. Over 1,000 one-story brick piers were prefabricated. The building was also designed to reduce solar gain (increase in heat in structures with large areas of glass) and maximize the use of ambient energy in an attempt to avoid the need for air conditioning. (GEOFFREY M. PINFOLD)

DAMS

Throughout the world in 1995 there were over 60,000 dams more than 15 m high, holding back some 6,000 cu km of water. Since 1975 the rate of dam construction had slowed worldwide, with only about 300 dams being built each year. This decrease was attributed to a recognition of the damage caused to ecosystems and of the social impact of population displacement.

Less developed countries were under pressure for continued economic development, however, and believed that the alternatives, nuclear and fossil-fuel energy sources, also had objectionable environmental impacts. The growing need for food and energy called for a balance to be achieved between preservation and exploitation of the environment. Many governments had opted for dam construction.

Along this line, Pres. Nelson Mandela opened the Durban, South Africa, meeting of the International Commission on Large Dams with a reminder that more than 12 million people in South Africa were without access to reliable drinking water and that without its large dams the country would not have been able to grow as it had.

In China the controversial Three Gorges Dam was going ahead in spite of the World Bank's withdrawal of financial aid because of environmental and resettlement concerns. In Southeast Asia the Mekong River project was revived by Thailand, Laos, Cambodia, and Vietnam. (China and Myanmar [Burma] also had been invited to join.) Thailand was expected to be the principal producer and user of the power, amounting to 80%, with Vietnam, Laos, and Cambodia sharing the rest. In Nepal the Arun III Dam was being proposed at a site in the Himalayan region, but there too the World Bank withdrew its funding after pressure from environmental groups.

India's first private dam project, the Baspa II Dam, got under way, although debates over resettlement issues caused a slowdown in construction. Turkmenistan started its third dam since it became independent. The Madav Dam would form a 250 million-cu m reservoir to regulate the flooding of the Tedzhen River. The national plan called for seven new reservoirs by the year 2004. Despite economic and financial boycotts, Iran pushed forward its dam program, with the 120-m-high Zanjan Dam and the 126-m-high Kowsar Dam, the latter of which was to store 450 million cu m of irrigation and drinking water.

Ethiopia accelerated its dam building program to increase the supply of potable water, and Oman was responding to its water shortage by building numerous aquifer recharge dams, which, although small, would store water that would otherwise be lost.

South Africa and Swaziland embarked on a joint venture to develop a series of dams to regulate the waters of the Komati River. Five dams would be involved, with the Maguga Dam to be started in 1996. Morocco announced an ambitious program to provide a million hectares under irrigation by the year 2000. The Itaipú Dam, the largest in the world in both output and size, was completed in Brazil.

In the U.S. the extensive drought helped gain approval for the Domenigoni Valley off-stream dam project, intended to create a reservoir with a capacity of 1,010,000,000 cu m of water serving the Los Angeles and San Diego areas. Also in California, the Auburn Dam, which had been stopped in 1975 because of fears of earthquakes, was revived as a solution to flood threats on the American River. A final decision was not expected soon because alternatives were being presented. On the Santa Ana River near Los Angeles, the Seven Oaks Dam was being built to provide flood control and was scheduled to be completed in the year 2000.

(T.W. MERMEL)

COURTESY OF NORSKE SHELL, REPRINTED FROM *OIL AND GAS JOURNAL*

A ship tows an oil-drilling platform, owned by Norske Shell and named *Troll A*, from its construction site out to sea. It was claimed that the platform, which had a 142-m (465-ft) freeboard and was 430 m (1,410 ft) tall, was the largest object ever to be moved.

ROADS

One of the abiding images of 1995 was the crumpled section of the Hanshin Expressway in the Japanese city of Kobe, which collapsed during the January 17 earthquake. Once again questions were raised about the wisdom of constructing elevated highways in earthquake-prone regions.

Massive highway projects were being planned throughout Asia. China was increasing its road network at the rate of about 13,000 km (1 km = 0.6 mi) each year, providing both urban and long-distance routes. The Shanghai ring road, a 48-km four-lane highway, was opened, helping to ease congestion in one of the world's largest and busiest cities. Three major expressways running north-south and three running east-west would provide the country with a basic network. South Korea announced plans to triple its expressway system to over 4,500 km within 30 years. A $1.2 billion plan to provide a road network linking China, Vietnam, Laos, Cambodia, Thailand, and Myanmar (Burma)—was agreed upon between the governments of those six countries. The project would be paid for by tolls, with initial funding from the Asian Development Bank.

The use of tolls to pay for new infrastructure, usually through a build-operate-transfer (BOT) contract arrangement, was becoming increasingly common throughout the world. Under these arrangements a private company would build the highway and then be permitted to charge tolls for a designated period of years, after which the highway would revert to government ownership. Indonesia invited bids for the construction of 770 km of toll roads worth an estimated $2.7 billion, mostly on the island of Java. India invited similar proposals for eight highways and nine bridges, together valued at $300 million. The Pakistan National Highway Authority announced plans for 754 km of highways—the largest being a 270-km two-lane expressway linking the Karachi port with Hub Chauki—which were to be offered as BOT contracts.

In Russia a 700-km highway to link Moscow with St. Petersburg was being studied, as were highways to link Moscow with Warsaw, Poland, and Kiev, Ukraine. It was estimated that 1% of all road bridges in Russia collapsed each year. Hungary was seen as a good example of the use of BOT contracts, with the first privately funded highway—the 42-km, $370 million M1 motorway—opened in 1995. Five further motorway sections totaling 580 km were under construction and were scheduled to open between 1996 and 2003.

In the United Kingdom a novel form of private finance was being planned. Under a design-build-finance-operate contract, a private company would assume all responsibility for the construction of a highway but would not collect tolls. Instead, costs would be paid by so-called "shadow tolls"; the road would be free for motorists, but the government would compensate the builder as if tolls had been charged.

In Toronto construction began on Highway 407, the world's first all-electronic tolled highway. In order to use the highway, drivers would be required to use transponding equipment fitted with "smart cards," and all tolls would be charged automatically. A similar project was begun in Melbourne, Australia.

In the U.S. the first privately owned and operated highway constructed in the 20th century was completed and opened to traffic. The 22.5-km Dulles Greenway connected Leesburg, Va., to Dulles International Airport near Washington, D.C. State Route 91 in California was the first highway in the U.S. to employ "congestion pricing," where motorists were charged higher tolls at busier times of day.

(RUSS SWAN)

TUNNELS

New tunneling techniques were introduced in 1995 to cope more efficiently with difficult ground conditions or logistically difficult projects. Odd as it may sound, the injection of foam into the excavation chamber of soft-ground earth pressure balance (EPB) pressurized tunnel-boring machines (TBMs) was being used as a soil-conditioning agent to counterbalance the pressure within the water-bearing soils. The purpose behind this operation was to decrease the permeability of the soil and give it a homogeneous consistency for more favourable extrusion through the screw conveyor of the EPB technique. Consisting mostly of air, the foam bubbles eventually would disappear, leaving a slightly moist, easily handled soil.

Major mechanical advances took place in Japan, where a triple-headed TBM was launched to excavate the three chambers of a 17-m-wide × 7.5-m-high underground station for the Osaka Metro all in one pass, and segment robots on the eight TBMs working on the Trans-Tokyo Bay Highway project were lifting and placing the eleven 10-metric ton precast concrete segments in each 1.5-m-wide × 650-mm-thick ring of segmental lining. These robots also fitted and tightened the 110 bolts in each bolting ring, all totally automatically. Such developments were yet to be employed outside Japan. In London the technique of compensation grouting was developed to sophisticated levels to control surface settlement and prevent damage to buildings as the tunnels for the new Jubilee Line Extension of the Underground network passed close by such famous landmarks as Big Ben and the Houses of Parliament. The technique compensated for the predicted amount of settlement by injecting thin horizontal lenses of grout or mortar into the ground above the tunnel alignment and below the foundations of the sensitive structures. When grout was applied gently and skillfully, settlement was effectively eliminated, which restored the slight declivities back to normal level ground.

Large-scale excavation for metro systems also continued during 1995 beneath Lisbon, Paris, Cairo, Munich, Washington, and Los Angeles, where in June a section of tunnel collapsed, leaving a gaping hole in Hollywood Boulevard.

The tunneling industry awaited official reports from the British Institution of Civil Engineers and the U.K. Health and Safety Executive concerning the safe use of NATM (New Austrian Tunneling Method), or shotcrete-supported tunneling, in urban areas following the collapse of NATM tunneling at Heathrow Airport in October 1994. A full year later the exact cause of the collapse was not known. Despite the delayed reports, NATM work was resumed on the Heathrow Express Railway project and on London's Jubilee Line Extension. NATM work also continued on the Munich Metro following a collapse in 1994 that claimed three lives.

Urgent remedial work to a London underground tunnel under the River Thames was delayed by more than six months when an injunction initiated by historical societies prevented the application of shotcrete to strengthen the interior of the structure. The brick-lined tunnel, finished in the mid-1800s, was the first-ever subaqueous tunnel in soft ground. Covering the interior with layers of shotcrete was adopted as the most appropriate and cost-effective method of renovating the tunnel and ensuring public safety. Historical societies wanted to preserve the interior as a monument of English heritage even though there was no public access into the tunnel nor could the interior be seen from within the passing trains. (SHANI WALLIS)

This article updates the *Macropædia* articles BUILDING CONSTRUCTION; PUBLIC WORKS.

Notable Civil Engineering Projects (in work or completed, 1995)

Name	Location		Year of completion	Notes
Airports		**Area (ha)**		
Chek Lap Kok	Chek Lap Kok Isl., Hong Kong	1,248	1997	Artificial island, terminal, bridge, tunnel links
Sepang International Airport	near Kuala Lumpur, Malaysia		1998	Project includes high-speed rail link to Kuala Lumpur
Aqueducts		**Length (m)**		
Lesotho Highlands Water Project	Maluti Mts., Lesotho-South Africa	82,000	2020	Breakthrough (Phase 1) March 3
TARP: Calumet Tunnel	Chicago, U.S.	18,700	1995	TARP: Deep Tunnel and Reservoir Plan
Great Manmade River	Sarir/Tazerbo wellfields, Libya			Water supply to coastal agriculture, cities, industries
Bridges		**Length (main span; m)**		
Akashi-Kaikyo	Honshu-Awaji Isls., Japan	1,991	1998	World record (suspension) upon completion
Store Baelt (Great Belt) (East)	Great Belt (Channel), Denmark	1,624	1997	World record (suspension) upon completion
Jiangyin Yangtze	China	1,385	1999	4th longest in world (suspension) upon completion
Tsing Ma	Tsing Yi-Ma Wan Isls., Hong Kong	1,377	1997	Cable spinning finished 1995
Tatara (Great)	Japan	890	1999	World record (cable-stayed) upon completion
Normandie	Le Havre, France	856	1995	World record (cable-stayed), opened January
Trans-Tokyo Bay Highway	Kisarazu, Japan	590	1997	Includes 10-km tunnel to Kawasaki
Oresund	Flinterenden, Denmark-Sweden	492	2000	18-km road/rail tunnel/bridge link; 3,750-m tunnel
Severn II	Severn Estuary, U.K.	456	1996	U.K. record (cable-stayed)
Guangdong Shantou Bay	Shantou, China	452	1995	To be opened early 1996
Tagus II	Lisbon, Portugal	420	1997	Total length 18.0 km
Wuhan Yangtze II	Wuhan, China	400	1995	Opened June 18
Glebe Island	Sydney, Australia	345	1996	Australia record (cable-stayed), opened December 2
Northumberland Strait	NB-PEI, Canada	250	1997	250-m single spans, 12.9-km total length
Buildings		**Height (m)**		
Chongqing Tower	Chongqing, China	457	1997	World record upon completion
Petronas I and II	Kuala Lumpur, Malaysia	450	1996	Twin towers, world record upon completion
Jin Mao	Shanghai, China	420	1997	
Shun Hing Square	Shenzhen SEZ, China	[illegible]	1996	Asian record, January 1996 completion
T&C Tower	Kaohsiung, Taiwan	347	1997	
Atlanta Olympic Stadium	Atlanta, Ga., U.S.		1996	85,000 seats; to be converted to 49,000-seat baseball park
Cities		**Area (ha)**		
Putrajaya	near Kuala Lumpur, Malaysia	4,400	1998	Planned national capital; government transfer 2000
Dams		**Crest length (m)**		
Yacyretá-Apipe	Paraná River, Argentina-Paraguay	69,600	1998	Hydroelectric power, navigation, irrigation
New China (Three Gorges)	Yangtze River, China	1,983	2009	Stage 1: 1993–97; 2: 1998–2003; 3: 2004–09
Xiaolangdi	Huang Ho (Yellow River), China	1,317	2001	Flood, ice, silt control; irrigation; power
Bakun	Balui, Bakun Rapids, Malaysia	900	2002	2,400 MW
Seven Oaks	Santa Ana River, U.S.	802	1999	
Ertan	Yalong River, China	763	1998	2nd largest hydroelectric project in China
Katse	Malibamatso, Lesotho	700	1996	Part of Lesotho Highlands Water Project; see above
Rogun	Vakhsh River, Tajikistan	600	...	World's highest (335 m) upon completion
Tehri	Bhagirathi River, India	575	1997	World's 6th highest upon completion
Manwan	Lancang (Mekong) River, China	132	1995	1,500 MW
Offshore production platforms		**Length (m)**		
Troll A	North Sea, Norway	472	1995	Emplaced May 17, largest structure ever moved
Barge (unnamed)	Marseille, France	220	1995	World-record floating concrete platform
Railways		**Length (km)**		
Beijing–Kowloon	Beijing–Kowloon, China	2,536	1997	Beijing–Fuyang (900-km) opened September
Konkan	Bombay–Mangalore, India	740	1995	High-speed, 83 tunnels, 143 major bridges
Bafq–Bandar Abbas	Bafq–Bandar Abbas, Iran	630	1995	Final section opened March
Seoul–Pusan	Seoul–Pusan, South Korea	426	2002	High-speed; environmental controversy over Kyongju segment
Subways		**Length (m)**		
Seoul Metro (extensions)	Seoul, South Korea	61,500	1997	Lines 6, 7, 8
Bangkok: MRTA Red Line (BERTS)	Bangkok, Thailand	60,000	1999	Bangkok Elevated Road and Train System
Taipei	Taipei, Taiwan	55,000	1995	Mucha line to open December
Pusan Metro (Line 2 extension)	Pusan, South Korea	39,100	1996	Phase 1: 22.4 km, phase 2: 16.7 km
Medellín Metro	Medellín, Colombia	23,200	1995	Line A: 23.2 km; line B: 5.6 km
Warsaw	Warsaw, Poland	23,100	1995	First 12 km opened April
Guangzhou (Canton) Subway: Line 1	Guangzhou, China	18,200	1997	Phase II: 18-km north-south line
Shanghai Subway: Line 1	Shanghai, China	16,100	1995	Revenue service began April 12
London Metro (Jubilee Extension)	London, U.K.	15,600	1998	Twin tunnels
Buenos Aires (Tren de la Costa)	Buenos Aires, Argentina	15,400	1995	Rehab of line closed in 1961
Towers		**Height (m)**		
Oriental Pearl Television Tower	Shanghai, China	478	1995	
Vegas World (Stratosphere) Tower	Las Vegas, Nev., U.S.	308	1995	Includes observation deck, restaurant, roller coaster
Tunnels		**Length (m)**		
Pinglin Highway	near Taipei, Taiwan	12,900	1999	
Trans-Tokyo Bay I and II	Tokyo, Japan	9,300	1997	Twin tunnels
Store Baelt	Great Belt, Denmark	8,000	1995	Twin tunnels

1 m = 3.28 ft; 1 km = 0.62 mi; 1 ha = 2.47 ac

Art, Antiques, and Collections

In 1995 the world of fine art and antiques was highlighted by the exhibition of 74 paintings, including many major "lost" Impressionist works, at the Hermitage in St. Petersburg. Degas's "Place de la Concorde" was perhaps the most notable of the paintings from German collections believed lost or destroyed during World War II and hidden in Russia for the past 50 years. The fate of these paintings—the subject of ongoing litigation—brought to international attention the issue of ownership of works that were stolen during the war. (*See* Sidebar.)

The major international auction houses posted annual earnings that pointed to a healthy art market, though one not as robust as that of the frenetic 1980s. At the annual spring Impressionist, modern, and contemporary sales in New York City, collectors posted record bids for several works. Two paintings from Christie's May sale of the Ralph and Georgia Colin collection established record prices at auction for two artists; Modigliani's "Nu assis au collier" went for $12.4 million, and Miró's "La Poetesse" sold for $4.7 million. Latin-American paintings from the IBM collection set records at Sotheby's in May. A rare Blue Period portrait by Picasso, from the collection of Donald and Jean Stralem, "Angel Fernandez de Soto," brought $29.2 million (the highest price for a painting at auction since 1990).

London's big June auctions matched the cautious optimism seen earlier in New York, with strong contemporary sales. Francis Bacon's "Study for a Portrait of John Edwards" fetched £1.2 million—the first contemporary work to command such a high price in London since 1990.

International art fairs and shows continued to flourish. The Whitney Biennial and Venice Biennale garnered particular attention. The Whitney show—widely expected to return to traditional displays after a 1993 exhibit was lambasted as too radical—mixed the radical and the traditional; while one installation relied heavily on doughnuts, other, more standard works were also in evidence.

Two major events in Germany were the wrapping of the Reichstag in silver fabric by artist Christo and his wife, Jeanne-Claude (*see* BIOGRAPHIES), and, in October, Sotheby's 15-day auction of 25,000 objects from the collection of the Margrave of Baden.

In June the collectibles market showed particular vigour. At Christie's in New York City, the white polyester suit worn by John Travolta in *Saturday Night Fever* commanded a record $145,500, making it the most expensive film costume ever sold.

(REBECCA KNAPP)

DENVER ART MUSEUM, THE HELEN DILL COLLECTION (1935.14) [W 1666]

This 1904 "Water Lilies," one of Claude Monet's earlier paintings of the subject, was inspired by the garden he constructed at his home at Giverny, France. The Art Institute of Chicago's Monet retrospective, which was the largest collection of the painter's works ever to be exhibited together, drew record crowds and was highly successful commercially.

ART EXHIBITIONS

By 1995 the digital chip and CD-ROM—technologies not usually associated with art exhibitions—were promising to usurp the role of audio headsets in prerecorded tours and to provide innovative features that could change the way museums and works of art were perceived.

Since 1993 a number of art museums and galleries had offered handheld "wands" that allowed visitors to listen to commentaries about various displays or to access interactive computer stations to receive additional information at random and in greater or less detail, as desired. These and other developing technologies inevitably ignited a debate whether the technology was being used as an educational tool or seen as an end in itself. Though some feared that the technology could distract from the objects on view, to others the new horizons opened by technology promised exciting developments.

In New York City the Solomon R. Guggenheim Museum mounted a retrospective of German artist Georg Baselitz that demonstrated some new possibilities. Many of the show's 100 paintings were labeled with codes that matched recordings by various commentators, including observations by the artist. Visitors could rent a "soundtrack," a telephone-like wand, and selectively listen to these comments by entering the appropriate code. A diverse group of museum patrons with different tastes, backgrounds, or interests could gain differing, and perhaps more appropriate, appreciations of Baselitz' figurative paintings and inverted canvases.

Permanent museum and gallery collections were making use of new technology as well. The National Gallery in London offered for rental a portable CD-ROM player with recorded comments on works in the permanent collection. The National Gallery of Art in Washington, D.C., opened a Micro Gallery, which featured computer terminals with touch screens. Visitors could access information about the museum's collection (organized by subject, period, artist, or geography) and make use of sound, pictures, and text. After the Michael C. Carlos Museum of Emory University, Atlanta, Ga., developed a "virtual museum" on the Internet, larger numbers of patrons were able to "visit" by using home-based computer technology.

Art created on computers was a popular subject of discussion. Though such art appeared mostly in private galleries rather than in public museums, the tide was shifting as new opportunities offered by digital technology intrigued artists, curators, and visitors. The Institute of Contemporary Arts in London held a series of shows and talks devoted to computer art entitled "Access All Areas: Visions of the Future."

In September at the Serpentine Gallery in London, an exhibition entitled

Stitched figures adorn the border of a mantle that was buried with the dead in Peru some 2,000 years ago. Several pre-Columbian fabrics, all showing the rich array of colours in which the ancient Peruvians worked, were exhibited at New York City's Metropolitan Museum of Art.
COURTESY OF THE METROPOLITAN MUSEUM OF ART, NEW YORK

"The Maybe" offered fuel for the perennial debate "What is art?" Enormous publicity brought more than 20,000 people in one week to the show, which featured possessions of famous personalities from the past and a Sleeping Beauty-like display. Artist Cornelia Parker and actress Tilda Swinton collaborated on the exhibit, which showcased Swinton lying in repose in a glass box for eight hours per day. This display attracted far more attention than such inanimate objects as a 50-year-old cigar that had belonged to Winston Churchill, a quill pen that had been used by Charles Dickens, or ice skates that had been owned by the late Duchess of Windsor. The show demonstrated how performance art—though lacking in paint, canvas, design, colour, or line—could stimulate emotional response as thoroughly as conventional visual art. But many asked nonetheless if it was art.

Conventional shows proliferated, especially those devoted to the Impressionists and dealing with familiar themes. Paul Cézanne was the subject of a comprehensive exhibition, the first large show of his work in 60 years, on view at the Grand Palais in Paris and then at the Tate Gallery in London. In 1996 the exhibit would travel to the Philadelphia Museum of Art. The London show included nearly 100 of about 800 known paintings by Cézanne as well as about 60 watercolours and drawings borrowed from public and private collections worldwide. Two of the three paintings from his "Bathers" series were on loan from the National Gallery in London and the Philadelphia Museum of Art; the third canvas, belonging to the Barnes Foundation, Merion, Pa., was not part of the exhibition. Although smaller shows mounted in the 1970s and '80s explored specific aspects of Cézanne's work, this was the largest show to allow a full study of his influence, genius, and evolution as an artist.

"Impressionism in Britain," an exhibition at the Barbican Art Gallery in London and later mounted in Dublin, included more than 200 works by 100 artists and covered works painted in Britain by visiting French artists and Impressionist paintings created by British artists. Such French artists as Claude Monet, Alfred Sisley, and Camille and Lucien Pissarro were represented. Works by English painters influenced by Impressionism formed a less coherent stylistic group. The works of Wilson Steer and Laura Knight were featured, along with a section devoted to American painter James McNeill Whistler and his followers.

An exhibition entitled "Landscapes of France: Impressionism and Its Rivals" was mounted at the Hayward Gallery in London and later traveled to the Museum of Fine Arts in Boston. The show illustrated styles ranging from the academic mode of the 1860s to the more abstract and colourful Pont-Aven school of the 1880s. Many of the works, which were on loan from French regional museums, showed the wide divergence between officially sanctioned art and that of the more avant garde. The Impressionists were represented by such artists as Sisley, Berthe Morisot, Monet, and eventually Cézanne.

A major Monet exhibition at the Art Institute of Chicago was the most comprehensive retrospective ever held of the artist's work and drew record crowds to the museum during its stay (July 22–November 26). The assemblage included 161 masterpieces drawn from private and public collections around the globe.

One of the lesser-known Impressionists, Gustave Caillebotte, was the subject of a retrospective at the Grand Palais, Paris, that was later shown at the Art Institute of Chicago. The exhibition included a number of works from U.S. museums, including the 1877 "Paris Street: Rainy Day," owned by the Art Institute.

An exhibition devoted to the work of Pierre-Auguste Renoir was seen in a number of Australian cities. The exhibit, which began in the Queensland Art Gallery, Brisbane, in mid-1994, traveled to the National Gallery of Victoria in Melbourne before closing in early 1995 at the Art Gallery of New South Wales, Sydney. The works, which included 51 paintings and one sculpture, were part of European and American collections and covered most of the major aspects of the artist's career. An Australian show comprising more than 150 works by Henri Matisse was on view at the Australian National Gallery, Canberra, and the National Gallery of Victoria. The exhibition, which was on loan, included items drawn from collections throughout the world. It was the first antipodean show devoted to Matisse.

Whistler, who spent most of his life in England, was the subject of a comprehensive exhibition at the Tate late in 1994. The show, which encompassed the entire range of Whistler's life and work—drawings in several different mediums, paintings, and examples of decorative schemes—was also mounted at the Orsay Museum in Paris and at the National Gallery of Art in Washington, D.C. Whistler's famous portraits were well represented and familiar, but some of his later paintings, including some splendid examples of fireworks, were less well-known. One of these, "Nocturne in Black and Gold: The falling rocket," came under such harsh criticism by John Ruskin when it was first exhibited (1877) in London that Whistler filed and won a celebrated lawsuit for libel.

"Whistler and Japan," an exhibition at the Freer Gallery of Art in Washington, D.C., focused on Whistler's works in the museum's own collections and the Japanese influence on his work during the 1860s and '70s. The Freer Gallery works—never loaned—were therefore not among the paintings represented in the large Whistler show.

A number of interesting shows concentrated on manuscript illumination. Italian book illustration was the focus of an exhibition in London at the Royal Academy of Arts and later on view in New York City at the Pierpont Morgan Library. The show, entitled "The Painted Page: Italian Renaissance Book Illustration 1450–1550," included 137 superb examples covering such diverse themes as classical and humanist texts, liturgical and biblical manuscripts, and patrons of the Italian Renaissance. The show, which was organized by subject rather than chronologically, encompassed a very wide range of beautiful objects and covered a subject less well-known than other examples of Italian Renaissance painting.

Plundering Art

While the strategy and tactics of warfare changed significantly throughout the centuries in response to technological and cultural developments, one rule had remained constant—"To the victor belong the spoils." Though the acquisition of loot was no longer the primary motivation for engaging in warfare, the seizure of the cultural treasures of a conquered nation—whether by individual soldiers looking for trophies or as part of an officially sanctioned plan—remained a common occurrence during conflicts taking place in the 20th century. As events in 1995 demonstrated, the question of whether such plunder should remain with the captors or be returned to its original owners had yet to be satisfactorily resolved.

During World War II both the Soviet and German armies employed special "trophy brigades," whose main purpose was to seize paintings, sculpture, and other cultural artifacts taken from conquered nations. The Germans, in keeping with the Nazi disdain for non-German culture, destroyed much of the art seized in the countries they overran. The Soviets, however, kept many of the cultural treasures that they had confiscated. An estimated 24,000 works of art from private collections were looted by German forces during World War II, and the defeat of Germany and its subsequent partition led to situations of Byzantine complexity. The Soviets seized art that the Nazis had stolen from occupied countries, for example, and then returned it to the East German government.

In March 1995 an exhibition at the Hermitage Museum in St. Petersburg captivated the attention of the art world. Entitled "Hidden Treasures Revealed," the exhibition featured 74 masterworks by such artists as Vincent van Gogh, Edgar Degas, and Henri Matisse. These paintings had not been viewed publicly for more than 50 years and had been stored undisturbed since the end of World War II, when the Soviet army seized them from German museums and private collectors. Amazingly, the Hermitage's director, Mikhail Pyotrovsky—whose father had served as museum director for 26 years—had no knowledge of the paintings until 1991.

The existence of some of the paintings was first revealed in 1993, when the Hermitage reached an agreement with the heirs of German collector Otto Gerstenberg, whose collection included the Degas masterpiece *Place de la Concorde,* one of the standouts of the Hermitage exhibit. The Hermitage agreed to return half of Gerstenberg's collection, including *Place de la Concorde,* to his heirs. The return of the art, however, was still contingent upon the approval of the Russian government, and many Russians felt that the collection should remain in Russia as reparation for the damage and suffering inflicted upon the Russian people in World War II and as a replacement for Russian art destroyed by the Germans during the war. At the end of 1995 the collection remained in Russian hands, and the controversy over the rightful ownership of plundered art was left unresolved. (JOHN H. MATHEWS)

Edgar Degas's "Place de la Concorde" was one of 74 paintings in the Hermitage show "Hidden Treasures Revealed." The paintings were among works taken from Germany by the Soviets at the end of World War II and not seen by the public for 50 years.

Some 100 items, including painted panels and manuscript illuminations, were included in the exhibition "Painting and Illumination in Early Renaissance Florence" at the Metropolitan Museum of Art, New York City. Illuminated manuscripts were also displayed in a series of exhibitions at the J. Paul Getty Museum in Malibu, Calif. One show running in late winter and early spring featured animal mythology and included illustrations of fables and games.

"The Art of Devotion" at the Rijksmuseum in Amsterdam comprised 44 works—paintings, prints, books, sculpture, and objects in gold and silver—some of which were borrowed from foreign collections. Most were made in monasteries to be used by monks for private devotion and were therefore relatively small. Most of the images and objects, which dated from 1300 to 1500, were portable, and a series of miniature prints could easily be carried within the pages of a book. Objects from the show were displayed in darkened rooms and illuminated in isolated cases that were lit in such a way that the contents seemed to float in space.

An exhibition devoted to the 15th-century Flemish artist Hans Memling was enormously popular when it was shown in late 1994 in Bruges, Belgium. The show consisted of 88 paintings (nearly half were attributed to Memling) and a subsidiary exhibition comprising textiles, manuscripts, and goldwork from this period. Aside from Memling's works, there were copies of lost works and works by his predecessors, followers, and contemporaries. The Louvre, Paris, also held a show celebrating Memling's quincentenary, with an exhibition drawn from French museums and pieces loaned from Italian and Dutch collections.

An exhibition focusing on 16th-century French drawings from the École des Beaux-Arts in Paris was shown there and later at both the Arthur M. Sackler Museum at Harvard University and the Metropolitan Museum of Art. The show featured glasswork, silver work, and examples of decorative architectural projects. Though the emphasis of the show was on the school of Fontainebleau, there were many works by little-known artists, including some exquisite miniatures. Architectural drawings also were well represented.

An exhibition, "The Italian Metamorphosis, 1943–1968," at the Guggenheim Museum was devoted to Italian art after World War II. More than 1,000 items drawn from this seminal era of Italian art and covering an important period in Italian history included objects related to photography, crafts, fashion, and film. Parallels were drawn between the works of such filmmakers as Luchino Visconti, Roberto Rossellini, and Vittorio De Sica and images created in the other arts, including the designs of both Fiat, the Italian automobile manufacturer, and architect Gio Ponti.

The exhibition also noted, through the work of such artists as Alberto Burri and Lucio Fontana, the important influence of the Futurism movement, which emphasized the power of the machine and the restlessness of modern life in general. The show highlighted the inventive and sometimes experimental use in both painting and sculpture of such everyday material as industrial-waste products and wire mesh.

The paintings and sculptures of the period, somewhat unusually, were probably less well-known, particularly outside Italy, than the designs and fashions. A notable aspect of the exhibition, which was also seen in Milan and Wolfsburg, Germany, was the way in which the duality of Italian modern art was expressed in its modern form, frequently relying on images from past artistic history, events, myths, or recollections.

The main summer exhibition at the Victoria and Albert Museum in London was devoted to the history of the Wedgwood factory and the English stoneware produced by Josiah Wedgwood and his colleagues. The show, "The Genius of Wedgwood," commemorated the 200th anniversary of his death and included important items on loan from the Hermitage in St. Petersburg, notably dinner pieces from the Frog Service, which was made for Catherine the Great. It was only the second time (the other was in 1909) that the Frog Service had been shown in England since it was commissioned in 1773. The wares in the exhibition were limited to those produced by Wedgwood's factory before his death in 1795.

The bicentenary of Wedgwood's death also was marked by an exhibition at the City Museum and Art Gallery in Stoke-on-Trent, England. "Josiah Wedgwood: The Man and his Mark" featured 195 pieces of Wedgwood drawn from public and private collections as well as works by Wedgwood's competitors and contemporaries. In Melbourne, the National Gallery of Victoria displayed "Three Centuries of Wedgwood."

The marking of 100 years of trade between Japan and Brazil was recognized in an exhibition at the Fuji Art Museum in Tokyo. The show consisted of a collection of paintings on loan from the Museum of Art in São Paolo, Brazil, and included works by El Greco, Jean-Baptiste-Simeon Chardin, and Vincent van Gogh.

In Ljubljana, Slovenia, a large show, which opened in three separate venues in May, gathered the important examples of Gothic art from 1250 to 1450. Paintings, sculptures, and manuscripts were shown in the National Art Gallery, the minor arts were housed in the National Museum, and conservation techniques and materials and architecture appeared at the Cekinov Grad. The show covered cultural links with Italy and northern Europe, social history, and patronage.

At the Hermitage, "Hidden Treasures Revealed" showed 74 works, including ones by Picasso and Edgar Degas, that had been removed from Germany at the end of World War II and since hidden in the museum. (*See* Sidebar.)

(SANDRA MILLIKIN)

PHOTOGRAPHY

The purchase in 1995 of the huge Bettmann Archive by software billionaire Bill Gates underscored a potentially revolutionary trend taking place in museums, archives, and libraries: the conversion of visual images to digitized form for electronic storage, access, and distribution. Gates's privately owned company, Corbis Corp., also had acquired electronic rights to 500,000 images, including work from individual photographers and art from the National Gallery of London, the Philadelphia Museum, and the Barnes Foundation. The Bettmann Archive—established in the 1930s by Otto L. Bettmann, who fled to New York from Hitler's Germany with $5 in cash and two steamer trunks of images on 35-mm film—now housed some 16 million images that, taken together, constituted an unmatched visual chronicle of the 20th century. The acquisition of this collection placed Gates at the forefront of photographic image digitization for use by new electronic imaging and communications technologies.

An exhibition at the J. Paul Getty Museum in Malibu, Calif., "Vision in Motion: The Photographs of Laszlo Moholy-Nagy," celebrated the centennial of the birth of this protean photographer, painter, filmmaker, and designer, who had powerfully influenced modern art in Europe and the United States between World Wars I and II. Some 50 vintage photograms (camera images and photographic collages made in Germany between 1923 and 1930) displayed his dynamic structures disciplined by elegant formalism.

"An American Century of Photography from Dry Point

to Digital" traveled to several venues and surveyed a familiar field but gave an unusually fresh and lively historical look at American photography from the mid 1880s to the early 1990s. More than 300 works, including many rare, less well-known, or virtually forgotten images, were selected from the notable Hallmark Photographic Collection of some 2,600 prints taken by 400 photographers.

Another traveling exhibition, "The Garden of Earthly Delights: Photographs by Edward Weston and Robert Mapplethorpe," provoked controversy with its pairings for comparison of 82 prints by these two photographers. Though each artist was a rebel and a sensualist, some questioned whether they shared a common vision, as the exhibition seemed to suggest. Some critics, however, found a striking commonality of perception and style in the paired portraits, nudes, and erotic shapes of plant life. Others found the attempt superficial and unconvincing, arguing that the photographic genres for which each man was famous—landscapes for Weston and homoerotic images for Mapplethorpe—were too unalike for paired comparison.

In this photograph by Javier Bauluz, a Rwandan man carries two orphans found on the road. Bauluz and three colleagues from the Associated Press—Jacqueline Artz, Jean-Marc Bouju, and Karsten Thielker—won the Pulitzer Prize for feature photography for their coverage of events in Rwanda.

JAVIER BAULUZ

"Dirty Windows," an exhibition by Merry Alpern, tested the limits of artistic expression, with photographs that some felt bordered on the merely sensational or pornographic. By photographing across an air shaft through the grimy window of a Manhattan sex-club bathroom, Alpern framed anonymous yet startling fragments showing sexual encounters and drug transactions taking place there. Though her project was selected to receive a grant by a peer-review panel of the National Endowment for the Arts, the National Council on the Arts, which reviews such recommendations, rejected it. Collectors, galleries, and leading museums were quick to acquire her pictures, however, which also appeared in book form.

News of a rare daguerreotype unveiled by Sotheby's created a stir among collectors and aficionados of such works. Made in 1846 and tentatively attributed to early American photographer John Plumbe, Jr., the half-plate daguerreotype depicts the U.S. Capitol building with the Bullfinch-designed dome that replaced the original destroyed by fire during the War of 1812. Rumoured to have been purchased in the 1960s for about $5, it was estimated by Sotheby's to be worth between $100,000 and $150,000.

The 1995 Pulitzer Prize for spot news photography was awarded to Carol Guzy of the *Washington* (D.C.) *Post* for her series of photographs illustrating the Haitian crisis. For their coverage of Rwanda, the Pulitzer for feature photography went to four Associated Press photographers: Jacqueline Artz, Javier Bauluz, Jean-Marc Bouju, and Karsten Thielker. At the 52nd Annual Pictures of the Year Competition sponsored by the National Press Photographers Association and the University of Missouri School of Journalism, James Nachtwey (*see* BIOGRAPHIES) of *Time* magazine/Magnum Photos was named Magazine Photographer of the Year, while Michael Williamson of the *Washington Post* took the title of Newspaper Photographer of the Year. At the 38th Annual World Press Photo contest, the World Press Photo of the Year award was given to Nachtwey. The primary W. Eugene Smith Grant in Humanistic Photography went to Russian photographer Vladimir Syomin for his ongoing documentation of life in areas of Russia left untouched by industrial development. A secondary grant went to Fabio Ponzio of Rome so he could continue photographing life in Eastern Europe for his project "The Other Europe."

Alfred Eisenstaedt, one of *Life* magazine's first four photographers and probably the most famous photojournalist of the 20th century, died at age 96. (*See* OBITUARIES.) "Eisie," as he was known to friends and associates, left a memorable montage of evocative photographs that chronicled his early years in Weimar Germany and Hitler's Third Reich, World War II, and postwar life in the U.S.

(ARTHUR GOLDSMITH)

ART AUCTIONS AND SALES

The recovery from a five-year market slump finally arrived in 1995. In 1990 art prices, in response to a worldwide recession and an overheated, speculative market, had dropped precipitously and remained at low levels.

Although spotty evidence of a comeback could be seen in some collecting areas as early as mid-1994, sales were relatively lacklustre for most of that year. Even so, many market observers predicted an imminent recovery based on improving economic conditions and a growing demand for high-quality works of art.

During the spring and summer of 1995, a series of unusually successful public sales pointed, at last, to a substantial recovery. A cooperating economy drew collectors back into the market at a time when an abundance of fresh, high-priced pictures was emerging.

The Impressionist and modern art market consistently strengthened, fueled by some of the most exciting and important offerings in years. In May, Sotheby's and Christie's, major international auction houses, each offered important single-owner sales. The extraordinarily fine collection of Donald and Jean Stralem at Sotheby's and the estate of Ralph and Georgia Colin at Christie's tempted collectors with rare opportunities that they enthusiastically embraced.

The Stralems' major Picasso portrait "Angel Fernandez de Soto," from his Blue Period, brought a startling $29.2 million, well above the expected $10 million–$20 million, placing it among the 10 most expensive paintings ever sold at auction. At the same sale, Matisse's "La Pose hindoue" provoked intense bidding and resulted in a $14.9 million sale, a new record for the painter. From the Colin estate, Modigliani's superb seated nude, "Nu assis au collier," reached $12.4 million, a record price for the artist.

At another spring sale at Christie's, a portrait by van Gogh, "Jeune Homme à la casquette," commanded $13.2 million, well above the $7 million–$9 million estimate. It was the first portrait by van Gogh auctioned since Christie's sold "Portrait of Dr. Gachet" for $82.5 million in 1990. When the Neoclassical Picasso "Mère et enfant" of Pamela Harriman, the U.S. ambassador to France, brought $11.9 million (a sum considerably higher than an unpublished estimate of $7 million–$10 million), some viewed the sale as a gauge of market strength.

Monet's "La Cathédrale de Rouen: effet d'après-midi," unseen publicly since 1924 and, by all accounts, a stunning example of his work, went to a collector for $12.1 million at a Christie's London sale in June.

Art of the 19th century, which had been spared the worst ravages of the market slump in 1990, continued a steady upward spiral that, according to some, had begun as early as 1992. Romantic pictures that were executed with technical perfection continued to find enthusiastic buyers willing to pay good prices.

Sotheby's May sale of 19th-century paintings fetched a respectable $18.7 million, but its specialty sale, La Belle Epoque, was not as successful. Price records were set for a large number of artists, however, and the top works sold well. James Tissot's "Le Printemps" brought $1.1 million, and a portrait by Jules Bastien-Lepage of Sarah Bernhardt went to an American buyer for $706,500.

Christie's sold a late work by Sir Lawrence Alma-Tadema, "The Finding of Moses." Although somewhat atypical of the artist's best work, it found a buyer for $2.8 million. Tissot's appealing portrait of his mistress, Kathleen Newton, created considerable interest and sold for $2.5 million.

Beginning in late 1994 and continuing into 1995, both dealers and buyers cheerfully noted the sudden influx of high-quality American paintings. Buyers, who had been anticipating the moment that the market would change, responded with high bids. "A sudden match of supply and demand," quipped one New York dealer. Realists applauded the number of exceptional works while recognizing that the cache of such stellar art would continue to dwindle.

Sotheby's also sold a number of works that had been part of the IBM collection. Frank Weston Benson's "The Sisters," a charming portrait of the artist's two daughters playing beside a lake, commanded a stunning $4.2 million. An unusually fine George Bellows, "Easter Snow (Easter Sunday)," brought $2.8 million, and "Diamond Shoal," the last dated watercolour by Winslow Homer, fetched a record $1.8 million.

Christie's, whose sales of American pictures increased by 37% in 1995, sold Frederick Frieseke's "Garden in June" for $937,500, much higher than the estimate of $350,000–$450,000.

Contemporary art, which, along with Impressionism, was hardest hit by the 1990 decline in art sales, showed a less spectacular recovery. Nonetheless, many considered the market strong but complained about the scarcity of available great works; many of the high-priced stars of the 1980s were conspicuously absent.

Sotheby's realized the highest price for a contemporary work when it sold Bacon's "Study for a Portrait of John Edwards" to a European collector for £1.2 million. It was the first painting to be sold in London for more than £1 million in almost five years. Other notable sales were Yves Klein's "IKB 103," which went for $369,000, considerably higher than the expected $127,000–$159,000, and Lucio Fontana's 1965 "Concetto spaziale attese," which brought $682,000.

The market for fine prints echoed the one for paintings; top examples brought top dollar, while lesser works saw little increase over previous years. Notable sales included a large Maurice Prendergast monotype, "Figures in the Park," which was energetically bid up at Christie's to $244,500—more than double the presale estimate. The contemporary art of Jasper Johns, Frank Stella, and Andy Warhol also commanded good prices.

British watercolours and drawings had remained strong relative to other markets during the previous five years. Sales of early British watercolours, generally considered the domain of connoisseurs, suffered from a dearth of quality in an area in which condition was critical. For rare and outstanding examples, buyers paid high prices. Sotheby's sale of Samuel Palmer's "A Cornfield, Shoreham at Twilight" fetched $256,490, double its presale estimate. Pleasant Victorian genre pictures continued to find a broader popular market.

Early in the year, Old Master sales received a boost when Sotheby's sold the New-York Historical Society's impressive collection, and Christie's offered works from the collections of both Alice Tully and Rudolf Nureyev. Crowded sales rooms reflected an interest rarely seen in Old Master sales, and the bidding matched the excitement. The auspicious beginnings did not carry over to the spring sales, which failed to confirm a trend.

At the end of a successful season (August 1994–July 1995), Sotheby's reported sales of $1,480,000,000, up 7% over the previous season. Christie's sold $1,410,000,000, an increase of 20%. The first half of 1995 was even more promising, with Sotheby's and Christie's reporting advances of 20% and 23%, respectively.

Art dealers and others in the trade generally agreed that the nature of the art market was considerably different from that of the high-flying 1980s. The "autograph collectors" and investment speculators had left the market, buyer confidence had returned to a preslump level, and a more sophisticated and selective market had emerged.

(JOHN HANLON)

ANTIQUARIAN BOOKS

Steady but not spectacular performance defined the 1995 market for antiquarian books. With books and manuscripts having less accessibility to a broad market, their prices remained relatively stable, with fewer of the wrenching price movements seen in other collecting areas.

Still, big names inspired big prices in 1995 as new buyers interested in acquiring the works of famous authors entered the market in increasing numbers. Previously active collectors, who had curbed their buying in the early 1990s while recovering from personal financial reversals, were beginning to buy once more. Money seemed readily available for top-quality lots, but a plethora of other material kept prices down for less-than-great items.

Christie's auction house reported a number of notable sales. Among them was the sale of George Washington's personal copy of the Acts of the First Congress (sessions 1–3), containing copies of the Constitution, the Bill of Rights, the Treaty of Paris, and other legislative acts. It sold for an impressive $310,500. At the same sale, a second Madrid edition of *Don Quixote* was purchased for $85,000, nearly triple the estimated selling price, and a three-volume first edition of Herman Melville's *The Whale* (later titled *Moby Dick*) fetched $74,000. In April Winston Churchill's pre-1945 papers were sold by his family to the British government for £12.5 million in spite of protests that the writings already were the property of the government. Part of the purchase price was provided by an American philanthropist.

A late 15th-century French translation of Giovanni Boccaccio's important *De casibus virorum illustrium* was bought for $200,500, just short of the low estimate.

During the summer the auction giant Sotheby's conducted in London the second in a series of sales from the Otto Schafer collection. The lot, called "the most important collection of books assembled in Europe since the second World War," sold for $4.5 million.

In another important single-owner sale, Sotheby's offered the 500-volume library of the 5th Earl of Rosebery, prime minister of England from 1894 to 1895. The London sale, estimated at $1.7 million, realized $2.4 million.

The library of Sir Karl Popper, noted philosopher of science, was sold to the Republic of Austria and the state of Kärnten (Carinthia) in a private sale negotiated by Sotheby's. The collection contained Popper's annotated copies of his own work, letters to him from Albert Einstein, and antiquarian books.

An early printing of Clement Moore's *Account of a Visit from St. Nicholas,* which was expected to bring $800 to $1,200, sold at Sotheby's for an astounding $29,900. Some felt that the sale of Moore's original manuscript for $255,500 just six months prior prompted the high price.

Market observers speculated that continuing economic improvement and successful public sales were fueling a new interest in books and manuscripts as collectibles. Some, fearing a duplication of the market swings that had afflicted certain art markets, considered the prospect a mixed blessing. (JOHN HANLON)

PHILATELY

Renewed efforts in Great Britain to promote stamp collecting among the general public included an initial donation of £60,000 from Royal Mail National to support the British Philatelic Trust's Strategic Plan, including the appointment of a full-time coordinator. Meanwhile, the 1995 market for major collections and single rarities of stamps and postal history continued to gain strength. In September, Royal Mail deepened its commitment by announcing that it was "championing" the international Stamp World exhibition that would be held at Earls Court, London, in the year 2000.

In July the "Rare Stamps of the World" exhibition was held at Claridge's Hotel, London, and showcased exhibits from the Royal Collection at Buckingham Palace, the National Postal Museum, and private collections from Britain, the U.S., and South Africa. Highlighted were the unique Swedish 3-skilling error of colour, a Mauritius 1847 1*d* "Post Office" on cover (sold late in 1993 for £900,000), and the Cape of Good Hope 1861 "Woodblock" 4*d* red error of colour.

In May both Christie's and Sotheby's held auctions in Hong Kong, with respective sales totaling HK$13,151,035 (£1,051,914) and HK$5,273,555 (£421,817). Top prices included HK$735,000 (£58,790) for a Hong Kong 1882 2 cents rose (S.G. 32*b*—only six were known to exist) and HK$276,000 (£22,076) for a mint example of China's 8 fen Cultural Revolution stamp that was "prepared but not officially issued." This Far Eastern philatelic activity was followed in September by the first, and enormously successful, international stamp exhibition held in Singapore. It was there that the Feldman Group, based in Zürich, Switz., established David Feldman Pte. Ltd. to handle its fast-developing Far East business.

In New York City, Sotheby's sold the Koenig collection of Mexico for $565,783; the 1921 10 centavos blue and brown inverted centre brought $25,300, three times the estimate. Sotheby's in London sold the famous France 1849 unused 40 centimes orange strip of five with retouched "4" on two stamps (ex-Ferrari) for a record £34,000, more than double the estimate. Collections sold in London by Phillips included the George Hollings Belgium for £164,012, double the estimate, and the R.P. Towers Grenada for £104,493.

In London, Frank Staff's collection of Treasury Essays 1839–40 (the most extensive collection held in private hands) made £120,000 at Christie's. Included in that sale was a cover with both the black and red Chalmers essays, which brought £16,000. Cavendish Philatelic Auctions (Derby, England) sold Staff's philatelic ephemera and library for £172,700. Top price at that sale was a record £3,080 for a privately produced Valentine of 1805. Christie's in Zürich sold the Rudi Oppenheimer Bavaria collection for Sw F 1,178,925 (£624,830) and the second part of the Gary Ryan Hungary collection for Sw F 762,600 (£404,178). Outstanding individual items included the Bavarian entire letter franked with an 1862 1Kr yellow and 1Kr rose, which brought Sw F 11,500 (£6,097), and a single Hungary 1867 3Kr red error of colour, which fetched Sw F 63,250 (£33,536).

The most remarkable "find" of the year was a House of Lords envelope, which was discovered between some worthless modern stationery that lined a dog basket. The envelope, which was addressed by the Duke of Wellington and postmarked Feb. 13, 1840, commanded £11,000 at Sotheby's in London.

After serving 27 years as keeper of the Royal Philatelic Collection, John Marriott retired in September and was knighted by the queen. He was succeeded by Charles Goodwyn, most recent past president of the Royal Philatelic Society, London. (KENNETH F. CHAPMAN)

NUMISMATICS

Coin collectors searched their pocket change for 1995 Lincoln cents with doubled lettering on the "head side"—the most widely publicized U.S. Mint error in several years. Some dealers paid $150 or more for the coin soon after the mistake was discovered in February, but prices dropped after thousands of the cents turned up in circulation. All of the errors were created by one malformed die in Philadelphia. Overall, the U.S. Mint was expected to produce about 19.5 billion coins in 1995—nearly 25% more than it made just two years earlier and almost even with the production record of 1982—as a growing economy fueled demand.

At congressional hearings in May and July, coinage experts debated proposed legislation that would force the U.S. government to replace dollar bills with $1 coins. Proponents argued that coins would reduce the cost of making money because they would last 30 years as opposed to $1 bills, which were estimated to wear out in less than 18 months. Others contended that the public would not support a switch. U.S. Mint Director Philip N. Diehl announced in May that the U.S. Treasury opposed a change, in part because he said savings estimates were exaggerated. Meanwhile, Treasury officials prepared for the 1996 debut of restyled $100 notes that would be more difficult to counterfeit. The new bills would include an enlarged, off-centre portrait and some colour-shifting ink, the first extensive U.S. currency redesign since the 1920s.

Tajikistan became the last of the republics of the former Soviet Union to issue its own money, a ruble note dated 1994, and Georgia replaced monetary coupons with a new national currency, the lari. On January 1 the National Bank of Poland introduced a revalued zloty—worth 10,000 times more than the old zloty—to keep up with inflation. Several countries minted coins commemorating the end of World War II and the 50th anniversary of the UN, while Denmark, Norway, and Sweden marked the 1,000th anniversary of coinage in their respective countries.

During 1995 the U.S. Mint sold several types of commemorative coins to collectors amid growing complaints about rising prices and the large number of new issues. The most controversial was a silver dollar that raised money for the 1995 Special Olympics World Games. It featured the profile of Eunice Kennedy Shriver, sister of former president John F. Kennedy and founder of the Special Olympics movement. She became the first living woman and just the fifth living American to have been depicted on a U.S. coin. Even though four others (Alabama Gov. Thomas E. Kilby, U.S. Pres. Calvin Coolidge, Virginia Sen. Carter Glass, and Arkansas Sen. Joseph T. Robinson) had been so honoured, a Mint advisory committee recommended that the Shriver motif be rejected because no living person should appear on a coin.

In 1994 the worldwide market for gold bullion coins was the lowest in two decades, and sales in the first half of 1995 remained at depressed levels. According to a *Coin World* survey that tracked 16,576 coin values, U.S. rare-coin prices edged up 2.9% in the 12 months ended August 31. One of about 10 known 1870-S silver dollars, which had been part of the James A. Stack, Sr., collection since 1944, commanded $462,000 in a March auction. Three months later a 1927-D $20 gold piece sold for $390,500 at auction and a 1927-S $20 gold piece brought $181,500; both coins had been owned by the Museum of Connecticut History. A Spanish gold coin minted between 1469 and 1504 in Seville went for $364,550 in January, reportedly a record auction price for a medieval coin. (ROGER BOYE)

This article updates the *Macropædia* article COINS AND COINAGE.

COLLECTIBLES

In 1995 buyers took new notice of 18th-century American and Victorian furniture, Tiffany lamps, arcade machines, rock-and-roll memorabilia, and art pottery.

The Eddy Nicholson collection of 18th-century American furniture fetched record prices. The Philadelphia Chippendale piecrust tea table that sold for $1,045,000 in 1986 shattered that record, making $2,422,500. A Queen Anne carved and inlaid walnut dressing table, Portsmouth, N.H., 1735–60, went for $103,700, while a Federal carved mahogany settee attributed to Samuel McIntire, Salem, Mass., 1800–11, fetched $134,500. Some pieces did not match earlier sales prices, but the receipts for the total collection exceeded the original cost.

Victorian furniture sold well. A six-piece Rococo Revival-style Belter parlour set, *c.* 1850, was auctioned for $134,750, and a Herter Brothers carved oak console, *c.* 1881, brought a record $288,500. Pieces by Thomas Molesworth, a 20th-century western-style furniture designer, brought high prices—$85,000 for a credenza, $51,750 for twin beds with cowboy trim, and $25,300 for a set of four open armchairs with carved Indian teepee motif.

Prices for American art pottery also increased; a Weller Aurelian vase decorated with red and yellow roses, 1899, was auctioned for $36,300, while a Weller Eocean vase with chrysanthemums brought $20,900. Record prices for Rookwood included $4,510 for a set of 1933 bookends showing Union Terminal and $62,700 for a 1911 black iris vase. A four-colour Newcomb vase decorated by Lenore Nicholson brought $29,700, and a rare grand feu 10.5-in green, brown, and mahogany vase made in Los Angeles (*c.* 1910) $8,250.

Rare beer stein prices shot up: a Mettlach stein, No. 2106, brought $5,500; a No. 2717 fetched $3,520; and a student character stein by Sarreguemines realized $5,390. Typical auction prices for majolica included $1,265 for a Holdcroft dolphin-footed lily bowl, $990 for a George Jones floral strawberry serving dish, $2,970 for a rope and fern cheese keeper, and $4,180 for a Minton four-tier oyster server.

Mickey and Minnie Mouse take a ride on a windup motorcycle authorized by Walt Disney and made by Tipp & Co. in Germany in the 1930s. The 25-cm (10-in)-long toy, complete with "Dunlop Cord" tires, sold for $30,800, a record for an item based on a cartoon character.
JAMES D. JULIA, INC.

Prices continued to climb for art glass, Depression glass, cut glass, and better glassware of the 1930s–1960s by Fenton, Pairpoint, and Fry. A record $23,100 was set for an 18th-century American pitcher with gadrooned design, olive amber glass. Two paperweights set records; an American weight with a parrot on latticinio ground brought $34,500, while a French pear weight on red ground fetched $22,500.

A Tiffany Favrile Virginia creeper lamp with glass beads (*c.* 1900) sold for $1,102,500. Sales of lamps with reverse painted shades included a Handel lamp with a domed shade showing ruins along the Nile River ($5,750) and a Pairpoint lamp with a shade depicting a jungle bird ($4,025).

Interest in the baseball card market dropped, but older memorabilia, game-worn uniforms, and autographs sold for top prices. A 1952 Mickey Mantle Topps rookie card in mint condition sold for $24,150—less than half the 1992 price of $55,000. Prices rose for Mantle memorabilia after his death, however. (*See* OBITUARIES.)

Interest appeared for 20th-century photographs by name photographers and for early historic daguerreotypes. A sixth plate daguerreotype of the interior of a dry goods store sold for a record $16,000. Vintage textiles and clothing were also popular—a 1940s Adrian evening dress of lavender and peach satin fetched $7,187, while a Rudi Gernreich "Kabuki" wool knit dress brought $4,370.

Sales were brisk for 20th-century steel toys, including pieces by Buddy L, cars and trucks of all types, and farm toys. Hot Wheels, vehicles made only since 1968, sold for more than their original price as soon as they reached the market. A 1969 Volkswagen Beach Bomb with surfboards reportedly sold for $1,500. A windup motorcycle that was made during the 1930s by Tipp & Co. of Germany and featured Mickey and Minnie Mouse sold for a record $30,800. Record prices also were set for marbles.

Miscellaneous sales included $22,000 for a Superman Action Comics premium ring dating from 1940, $112,500 (was paid in 1994) for a King Kong poster, $84,000 for the typewriter used to write the James Bond stories, $17,250 for an Uncle Sam grip tester from 1904, and a record $107,000 for a Beverly Machine Co. Standard Grip Testing Machine made about 1897. (RALPH AND TERRY KOVEL)

See also Libraries and Museums; Performing Arts.

This article updates the *Macropædia* articles COINS AND COINAGE; The History of Western PAINTING; PHOTOGRAPHY; The History of Western SCULPTURE.

Business and Industry Review

With very few exceptions, 1994 was an excellent year. The world economy finally put a lingering recession behind it, and a vigorous recovery, accompanied by low inflation, was in train. Led by an unexpected double-digit growth in world trade volumes, output expanded rapidly, with manufacturing, buoyed by export-led growth, outperforming gross domestic product (GDP) in most economies.

Manufacturing increased its production by 4.6% in 1994, a welcome recovery from two years of recession and stagnation. In the industrialized countries, which had been the worst affected, growth was 4.4%; in the less developed economies, where the slowdown had been barely perceptible, growth picked up to over 5%.

The main industrialized economies were at different phases of the economic cycle. At one extreme the U.S. was into its fourth year of a recovery that retained its vigour through 1995; at the other Japan, beset by financial difficulties and with an exchange rate pushed to new levels of uncompetitiveness, was struggling to reorient its economy away from the traditional dependency on exports. U.S. industrial production rose more than 5% in 1994 (up from 4% in 1993), while in Japan growth was 0.8%, contrasted with a decline of more than 10% in 1992–93 combined.

In between these two extremes the U.K., lagging a year behind the U.S. in recovery and helped by another strong year of North Sea oil production, attained a 5% increase in industrial production. In continental Europe, where the cycle lagged yet another year, growth was typically slower than in the U.S. and the U.K. Because they were also driven by exports, it was the devaluing economies such as Italy that

Table I. Annual Average Rates of Growth of Manufacturing Output, 1980–94

Percent

Area	1980–86	1987–91	1992	1993	1994
World[1]	2.0	1.9	−1.0	0.1	4.6
Industrial countries	1.7	1.5	−1.8	−0.8	4.4
Less industrialized countries	4.3	3.9	3.5	4.5	5.1

[1] For definition, *see* Table IV.
Source: UN, *Monthly Bulletin of Statistics.*

Table II. Manufacturing Production in Eastern Europe[1]

1980 = 100

Country	1990	1991	1992	1993	1994	%[3]
Bulgaria[2]	116	90	76	74	78	5
Hungary	101	76	63	65	71	9
Poland	80	70	71	78	89	14
Romania	106	81	58	57	59	4

[1] Former Czechoslovakia and former Soviet Union not available.
[2] All industries.
[3] % change, latest year shown from previous year.
Source: UN, *Monthly Bulletin of Statistics.*

Table III. Pattern of Output, 1991–94

Percent change from previous year

	World[1]				Developed countries				Less developed countries			
	1991	1992	1993	1994	1991	1992	1993	1994	1991	1992	1993	1994
All manufacturing	**−1**	**−1**	**0**	**5**	**−2**	**−2**	**−1**	**4**	**4**	**4**	**5**	**5**
Heavy industries	−1	−1	**0**	**5**	**−2**	**−2**	**0**	**5**	4	4	**6**	**6**
Base metals	−3	−3	0	4	−4	−4	−1	4	2	2	7	6
Metal products	−2	−3	0	6	−2	−3	−1	6	6	3	6	7
Building materials, etc.	−3	−1	1	3	−5	−2	−1	3	6	5	5	6
Chemicals	0	3	1	5	−1	2	0	4	1	6	5	6
Light industries	**0**	**0**	**−1**	**3**	**−1**	**−1**	**−2**	**3**	**4**	**3**	**3**	**4**
Food, drink, tobacco	2	1	0	3	1	0	−1	2	4	3	3	4
Textiles	−2	−1	−2	1	−4	−2	−4	0	2	1	3	3
Clothing, footwear	−4	−3	−2	0	−6	−4	−4	−1	1	0	2	3
Wood products	−2	1	1	4	−3	0	1	3	5	3	2	5
Paper, printing	0	0	−1	4	0	−1	−2	4	5	3	5	3

[1] Excluding Albania, China, North Korea, Vietnam, former Czechoslovakia, former Soviet Union, and former Yugoslavia.
Source: UN, *Monthly Bulletin of Statistics.*

Table IV. Index Numbers of Production, Employment, and Productivity in Manufacturing Industries

1980 = 100

Area	Relative importance[1] 1980	1994	Production 1993	1994	Employment 1993	1994	Productivity[2] 1993	1994
World[3]	1,000	1,000	125	131	...	...	...	...
Industrial countries	861	812	118	123	...	...	...	...
Less industrialized countries	139	188	171	188	...	...	...	...
North America[4]	282	315	136	146	...	...	...	...
Canada	22	21	119	128	98	...	121	...
United States	260	293	143	152	89	90	161	169
Latin America[5]	79	73	115	121	...	...	...	...
Brazil	26	21	99	107	...	...	...	...
Mexico	18	...	131	135	160	157	82	86
Asia[6]	183	249	173	178	...	...	...	...
India	11	...	214	231	...	...	...	...
Japan	131	136	135	136	120	118	112	115
South Korea	6	19	380	421	166	171	229	247
Europe[7]	422	343	103	106	...	...	...	...
Austria	9	9	132	138	78	75	169	184
Belgium	13	11	118	121	...	...	...	...
Denmark	5	0	134	...	94	...	143	...
Finland	6	6	127	142	65	66	195	215
France	75	63	104	109	79	76	132	143
Former West Germany	114	105	115	120	97	92	118	131
Greece	4	3	97	98	...	...	...	...
Ireland	2	4	234	264	85	88	275	300
Netherlands, The	14	14	123	128	...	...	...	...
Norway	5	5	113	121	76	79	149	154
Portugal	3	3	140	139	98	...	142	...
Sweden	13	13	116	128	...	...	...	...
Switzerland	13	13	122	132	...	...	...	...
United Kingdom	58	54	115	120	63	...	183	...
Rest of the world[8]	34	...	...	...	...	...	...	...
Oceania	15	14	121	126	...	...	...	...
South Africa	8	6	104	106	99	...	106	...

[1] The 1980 weights are those applied by the UN Statistical Office.
[2] This is 100 times the production index divided by the employment index, giving a rough indication of changes in output per person employed.
[3] Excluding Albania, China, North Korea, Vietnam, former Czechoslovakia, former Soviet Union, and former Yugoslavia.
[4] Canada and the United States.
[5] South and Central America (including Mexico) and the Caribbean islands.
[6] Asian Middle East and East and Southeast Asia, including Japan, Israel, and Turkey.
[7] Excluding Albania, former Czechoslovakia, former Yugoslavia, and European countries of the former Soviet Union.
[8] Africa and Oceania.
Source: UN, *Monthly Bulletin of Statistics.* ILO, *Yearbook of Labour Statistics.*

enjoyed the lion's share of buoyant intra-European trade. Even the high-exchange-rate economies such as Germany, however, were boosted by a surge in investment demand, concentrated on high-tech capital goods.

The dynamic economies of Asia enjoyed another successful year. In terms of GDP, double-digit growth was achieved in China and Singapore, while South Korea, Malaysia, Thailand, and Vietnam were not far short of the 10% mark. In industrial production, the main impetus behind the expansion, growth was as high as 20% in China. Such a pace of advance did not, however, prove sustainable. Inflationary pressures emerged in a number of economies—prices rose 24% in China and 14% in Vietnam in 1994—and monetary policy was tightened, which resulted in Chinese industrial production slowing to a growth rate of 16%.

Such rates of growth were the envy of the rest of the less industrialized world, particularly in the formerly communist countries of Eastern Europe and in those of the former Soviet Union. In Eastern Europe, however, the corner was turned. Output rose in 1994 in all economies, with those more advanced in the reform process, notably Hungary and Poland, beginning to pick up speed. In Russia, in contrast, there was little good news. Output fell 15% in 1994 (after a 12% decline in 1993), and the Organisation for Economic Co-operation and Development forecast that Russia would suffer another decline, of 5%, in 1995.

For Latin America 1994 was generally a good year. With the exception of Brazil, inflation fell to lower, more sustainable levels throughout the region, which underpinned stronger output. Fundamental problems, exemplified by the Mexican financial crisis, were still prevalent, however. In most economies output growth slowed in 1995, while in Mexico output fell.

On a sectoral basis the pattern of output in 1994 reflected the nature of the cycle. Led by exports and investment, heavy industries outperformed the lighter industries more dependent on consumer demand. Textiles and clothing and footwear missed out on the upturn, and in the industrialized economies these sectors stagnated. Across the less industrialized group, output expanded on a broad front.

In retrospect, 1994 appeared to have been the peak of the cycle in the world economy. In 1995 demand slowed, producing an inventory buildup that took its toll on manufacturing. The impetus from trade also diminished. With inflationary pressures modest in most countries, however, there was scope for policy to adjust.

(GEOFFREY R. DICKS)

ADVERTISING

Despite concerns about the economy, spending on advertising surged ahead in 1995, with large companies spending aggressively to get their messages to the public. Industry forecaster Robert J. Coen predicted that overall advertising expenditures in the U.S. in 1995 would top $157.7 billion, a 5.1% increase over the $150 billion spent in 1994. He estimated that spending outside the U.S. would top $193 billion, up 8.2% from $178.4 billion in 1994, led by strong growth in large ad markets like Britain, France, and Germany and with double-digit percentage gains in emerging markets like China and Vietnam.

U.S. advertisers, optimistic that consumers would continue spending through much of 1996, invested heavily in network television's "upfront," or advance sales, market. More than $5.6 billion was committed to shows for the 1995–96 season, up 27.3% from the $4.4 billion worth of commercial time sold in advance of the 1994–95 season. Advertisers doled out up to $1 million per minute for commercials that aired during "Seinfeld," NBC's top-rated comedy. "Seinfeld" was the first regularly scheduled series to come close to the $1 million-a-minute mark, something that previously had been attained only by events such as the Super Bowl. NBC sold a record $600 million in advertising for its coverage of the 1996 Olympic Games in Atlanta, Ga., a 20% increase from the $500 million the network had sold for the 1992 Summer Games in Barcelona, Spain.

One of the biggest advertising splashes in 1995 was the worldwide introduction of Microsoft Corp.'s Windows 95. Supported by an estimated $700 million in advertising, $200 million from Microsoft itself, and most of the rest from retailers and hardware and software companies, the launch on August 24 more closely resembled the release of a blockbuster movie than a computer operating system. Microsoft estimated that more than one million copies of Windows 95 were purchased by consumers in retail stores in the software's first four days on the market. The enthusiasm for new computer software came during a rush by consumers and advertisers alike to gain a toehold on the Internet. Through on-line services such as America Online, CompuServe, and Prodigy as well as through direct links to the Internet, approximately 24 million people in the U.S. and Canada signed onto the worldwide network. Some 17.6 million people regularly used the World Wide Web, a subset of the Internet designed for multimedia use, where many corporations and advertising agencies had created "home pages" for their products and services.

An unprecedented effort by U.S. Pres. Bill Clinton and the Food and Drug Administration to outlaw cigarette ads pitched at young people drew an immediate response from advertising and tobacco groups, which filed suits in a U.S. district court in Greens-

Infomercials

In 1964 a gadget inventor and salesman named Ron Popeil started a company named Ronco and became instrumental in creating the television infomercial industry in the U.S. Poised between superficial talk shows and the strident tones of Madison Avenue, the half-hour ads originally existed in a kind of television netherworld—shown only late at night after most consumers had gone to bed. By 1995, however, infomercials were no longer limited to appliances such as Veg-O-Matics and the Ronco food dehydrator. Their products ranged from high-priced Barbie dolls to citrus fruit, from skin- and hair-care products to diet regimens, and from investment advice to methods for improving interpersonal relationships.

Modern infomercials usually relied on celebrity endorsements rather than high-pressure salesmen to lend credibility to their products. Singer Dionne Warwick had been affiliated with the "Psychic Friends Network" for almost a decade, while actresses Meredith Baxter and Ali McGraw both appeared in popular infomercials for Victoria Jackson cosmetics. Covert Bailey, a familiar face on public television, advertised an exercise machine, and veteran actress Angela Lansbury brought children's literature to infomercials by promoting a series of Beatrix Potter stories on videotape.

Infomercials also showed they had great potential for profit. The National Infomercial Marketing Association International (NIMA), the trade association for the industry, estimated that in 1994 the ads brought in $1 billion in product sales. NIMA played an important role in reinforcing marketing guidelines and in holding the companies accountable for the claims they made for their products. NIMA also presented yearly awards for excellence within the industry. In 1995 fitness expert Jake Steinfeld swept the field, winning infomercial of the year, best product, and best product offer.

More recently, program-length commercials gained in popularity among mainstream products. Many companies opined that a standard 60-second television commercial was not long enough to present their products thoroughly, so they began turning to an offspring of infomercials called "documercials" to fill the need for more in-depth advertising. Documercials generally concentrated on promoting a product or company image rather than on direct sales. Familiar names included the Toyota and Ford motor companies, Sears, Roebuck and Co., American Airlines, and Eastman Kodak. In a bid for a younger audience, Sega of America released an infomercial describing new software for its Genesis video game machine, running the ad for four weeks during the 1994 holiday season.

Industry executives predicted a metamorphosis of the infomercial, which would be crucial to its survival in the second half of the decade. There was an effort to make infomercials more sophisticated by making various technical improvements. Some political candidates had begun to use documercial-like programs to promote themselves and their policies. The ads had even found their way onto the Internet. Direct-response marketers often made the claim that infomercials were the first interactive medium, and their appearance on the information superhighway seemed to many to be a natural step in their evolution.

(AMANDA E. FULLER)

boro, N.C., challenging the agency's right to regulate tobacco as well as alleging violations of the First Amendment protection of free speech. Federal regulators asserted that aggressive tobacco marketing was the most influential factor in persuading young people to start smoking.

In September the FBI and the U.S. Department of Justice launched an investigation of designer Calvin Klein's controversial jeans campaign that featured young people in suggestive poses, even though the ads had been pulled from distribution. The legal issue was whether any of the models were under the age of 18, which was found not to be the case.

Vietnam continued to expand its consumer markets, and advertisers and agencies from the West poured into the country. Advertising had already helped some American brands such as Pepsi, Kodak film, and Oral B toothbrushes become dominant with Vietnamese consumers. American brands also were becoming popular in China, although advertising continued to be sporadic and concentrated on the three largest markets—Shanghai, Beijing, and areas in southern Guangdong province.

After being squeezed out of Saatchi & Saatchi Co., the ad agency he and his brother had cofounded, Maurice Saatchi opened the New Saatchi Agency, with billings of more than $211 million from former clients such as British Airways, Dixons consumer electronics, Qantas, and Mirror Group Newspapers. Actress Candice Bergen was ranked again in 1995 as the top entertainer in Video Storyboard Tests' 10th annual rating of celebrity presenters. For the seventh time in eight years, basketball star Michael Jordan was the top-rated athlete for commercial endorsements.

A study by Yankelovich Partners found that only 25% of 1,000 consumers questioned said a television ad would induce them to try a new product or brand. Only 15% said that a newspaper ad would entice them to buy, while only 13% said that a magazine ad would influence them. A global survey by Roper Starch Worldwide found that 73% of consumers believed that advertisers regularly misled or exaggerated a product's benefits. Consumers in the former Soviet Union proved to be the most suspicious of advertising. Only 9% of Russian and Ukrainian consumers felt that advertising provided accurate information, while 10% said that they felt advertisers respected their intelligence.

(LAURIE FREEMAN)

Table V. Most Valuable Brands Worldwide in 1994

1994 rank (1993 rank)	Brand name	Brand value
1 (1)	Coca-Cola	$39,050,000,000
2 (2)	Marlboro	$38,714,000,000
3 (282)	IBM	$17,147,000,000
4 (8)	Motorola	$15,284,000,000
5 (10)	Hewlett-Packard	$13,167,000,000
6 (7)	Microsoft	$11,740,000,000
7 (3)	Kodak	$11,594,000,000
8 (5)	Budweiser	$11,353,000,000
9 (4)	Kellogg's	$11,003,000,000
10 (6)	Nescafé	$10,340,000,000
11 (14)	Intel	$ 9,712,000,000
12 (9)	Gillette	$ 9,672,000,000
13 (11)	Pepsi	$ 7,806,000,000
14 (18)	GE	$ 7,420,000,000
15 (13)	Levi's	$ 6,922,000,000
16 (17)	Frito-Lay	$ 6,919,000,000
17 (30)	Compaq	$ 6,895,000,000
18 (16)	Bacardi	$ 6,535,000,000
19 (20)	Campbell's	$ 5,961,000,000
20 (15)	Pampers	$ 5,919,000,000

Source: *Financial World*, Aug. 1, 1995.

AEROSPACE

The dilution of revenues and profits resulting from overcapacity and duplication of products in the aerospace sector in the West was aggravated in 1995 by the growing influence of capable players from Asia, Russia, and the countries of the Commonwealth of Independent States (CIS) as they jostled for markets. In the U.S. and Europe the industrial shakeout continued, with buyouts, mergers, and partnerships proliferating in efforts to reduce costs, streamline production, exploit common resources, and facilitate access to new opportunities. As an example, Daimler-Benz Aerospace of Germany and Alenia of Italy sought an alliance to consolidate work and to alleviate their financial difficulties. Western companies increasingly sought new business through joint ventures with CIS countries and by expanding coproduction with China, the latter seen as a huge but tough market. The industries of both France and Germany declined, in Germany's case largely because of the high costs of reunification and in France because of severe military budget cuts.

The airline sector generally continued a slow recovery in 1995, taking with it the world's three major airframe companies, Boeing, Airbus Industrie, and McDonnell Douglas. Of the airlines themselves, TWA sank into bankruptcy again for two months in the summer and remained in a weak financial state and saddled with the oldest fleet of aircraft of any U.S. operator. The mostly state-owned European airlines—apart from the privatized and now sharply competitive British Airways—recorded sluggish business as a result of financial weakness, a shortage of slots, and nationalistic protection. Air France's situation was characterized as "dreadful" by its chairman, Christian Blanc. The global freight business continued to grow, however. In 1994 it increased by 12%, and similar growth was anticipated for 1995.

Boeing maintained its status as the number one commercial transport supplier. Its 777 "big-twin" rival to Airbus's A330, the first all-new Boeing design since the 767 and 757 of 1982 and 1983, entered service in June and was demonstrated at the Paris Air Show during the same month. Predictions were that 1995 sales would reverse a company decline that had begun in 1991. This was borne out in November when Boeing won a record $12.7 billion contract from Singapore Airlines, which was followed in December by a large order from Philippine Airlines. Prospects were helped by two large orders placed by the California-based aircraft leasing company ILFC and by the Saudi Arabian airline Saudia. In the latter case U.S. Pres. Bill Clinton personally intervened to secure a sale over Airbus. Airbus, however, was set to nearly match Boeing's 1995 orders. In a policy statement Airbus managing director Jean Pierson set a goal of securing 50% of the global market for large transport aircraft. McDonnell Douglas struggled with its small product base of MD-11s and the MD-90 family. Launch of the short/medium-range MD-95, seen as essential to the company's viability, was threatened when SAS—a longtime customer—and Saudia both chose Boeing. The MD-95 finally went ahead, however, with a 50-aircraft, $1 billion order from Valujet.

Anticipating an eventual upturn, the three major players continued to investigate new aircraft of jumbo-plus size. Boeing looked to "stretch" its currently biggest transport into the 747-500, along with developing a longer-range, higher-capacity 777, the pair to be launched more or less simultaneously. It was also studying a 600-seat project called the New Large Aircraft. At the same time, Boeing and Airbus suspended their collaborative examination of the Very Large Commercial Transport project because the U.S. company wanted more time to study the market. Airbus continued to refine its own proposal for an 850-seat transport called the A3XX.

Meanwhile, Russia continued to probe Western markets with its Tupolev Tu-204 airliner and heavyweight Antonov An-124 freighter, both built at the vast new Ulyanov production plant. Certification to Western standards and the substitution of U.S. and European power plants and avionics were held to enhance the appeal to Western and Pacific Rim airlines. Britain responded to intense lobbying by industry and the Royal Air Force by becoming the launch customer for both a new version of the 40-year-old Lockheed C-130 Hercules and Europe's Future Large Aircraft (FLA), a replacement for the C-130. Previously a supplier exclusively of airliners, Airbus began establishing a military subsidiary to manage and market the FLA.

The U.S. Joint Advanced Strike Technology program, intended to demonstrate the technology for a next-generation strike fighter to replace the F-16 AV-8B and F/A-18, was restructured to become the Joint Strike Fighter. The program was no longer concerned with just technology, since an actual aircraft was now in view, for entry into service in about 2007–2010. Military aircraft upgrades continued, with earlier fighter types such as Douglas Skyhawk, Northrop F-5, General Dynamics F-16, and Mikoyan MiG-21 being favourite candidates for new avionics to extend their life and effectiveness. An extraordinary demonstration of how far East-West rapprochement had developed since the end of the Cold War was the dialogue between Russia and the U.S. regarding the acquisition by the U.S. Department of Defense of the former's AA-11 Archer short-range air-to-air missile for top U.S. fighters such as the F-15 and F/A-18. The AA-11 was widely regarded as the world's most effective such weapon, and with export versions being sold to less developed countries, the U.S. and other Western nations equipped only with the Sidewinder would face serious threats.

The civil war in Bosnia and Herzegovina provided an opportunity for NATO to deploy new or upgraded aircraft and systems, in particular the "smart" weapons that could be guided by radio and laser links to their targets. Amid controversy, Tomahawk cruise missiles were used against Bosnian Serb targets. Most of the weapons displayed improved target accuracy over earlier versions used in the Persian Gulf War. Bosnia also saw the introduction, after some 25 years of equivocation by the U.S. military, of a full-fledged American unmanned air vehicle (UAV) system for reconnaissance and target spotting. Predator UAVs could monitor movements of the warring parties for up to 24 hours at a time and remain largely undetected. A growing intelligence gap, however, forced plans to bring the Mach 3 Lockheed SR-71 strategic reconnaissance aircraft back into service five years after it had been retired.

(MICHAEL WILSON)

APPAREL

Clothing. In 1995 the apparel industry continued its slump as consumers directed discretionary income toward the purchase of cars and home-related and electronic products. Both Martha Stewart (*see* BIOGRAPHIES), who was held responsible for the "Martha Stewartization" of America, and the aging of the baby-boom generation were cited as reasons for the shift. Also, women—who continued to make nearly 80% of all clothing purchases—seemed less susceptible to fashion fads and preferred to use personal and household disposable income for family-oriented purchases.

Women's intimate apparel sales surged, however, following the introduction of the Wonder Bra and its many competitors. Brassiere sales rose more than 25% from 1992 to 1994, while sales of other intimate apparel also increased substantially. Fibres like DuPont's Lycra improved the comfort and appearance of foundation garments, causing a resurgence of interest in "body slimmers" and other body-control garments. Swimwear also benefited from the use of these new fibres and a growing emphasis on figure-flattering designs.

Corporate culture's acceptance of "casual Friday" also sparked apparel sales. Men, especially, bought casual sport slacks and shirts at an unprecedented rate, which caused a decline in sales for men's suits. Levi Strauss, which boasted annual sales of about $800 million from its Dockers men's line of casual pants and shirts, added a Docker footwear line and Docker lines for women and children.

The retail industry underwent significant changes as consumer price sensitivity resulted in more sales at discount stores, as financially troubled retailers were absorbed by larger companies, and as apparel companies struggled to compete for fewer retail accounts as bankruptcies and plant closures loomed in 1994 and 1995.

In 1994 U.S. consumers spent $172 billion on apparel, half of which was imported. U.S. apparel manufacturers, competing with the low-wage producers in the Far East, stayed competitive by relying on automation and technology to streamline production—a concept known as quick response—and by moving some assembly operations to the Caribbean Basin and Mexico, where labour was less costly. Though some jobs were created despite these changes, the overall result was a loss of 100,000 manufacturing jobs from 1994 to 1995 and the lowest level of employment since 1939.

Shrinking membership in the International Ladies' Garment Workers' Union and the Amalgamated Clothing and Textile Workers Union prompted a merger of the two into the Union of Needleworkers, Industrial and Textile Employees. Both that union and John Sweeney, the newly elected head of the AFL-CIO, called for the eradication of garment industry sweatshops that were again proliferating.

(ALLISON WHEELER WOLFF)

Footwear. In 1995 such name brands as Timberland, Reebok, and Keds recorded losses, while Nike Inc. and Nine West Group Inc. posted record gains. In May Nine West purchased U.S. Shoe Corp. for over $600 million, creating a footwear empire boasting eight fashion and three comfort brands, over 850 retail stores, and nearly 14,000 employees. Nine West projected that 1995 sales would total $1.5 billion. Meanwhile, athletic footwear giant Nike reported record-shattering sales of $4,760,000,000 and a 34% increase in earnings for fiscal 1994, ended May 31. In October Nike sealed a deal with the National Football League (NFL), worth $200 million over five years, to outfit several NFL teams and sell NFL-licensed merchandise.

Others posting gains were: Wolverine World Wide, maker of Hush Puppies, Caterpillar, and Wolverine Wilderness, with earnings up 52.4% through the third quarter; and Italian shoe and apparel manufacturer Fila, which scored a marketing/sales coup with the introduction of a shoe worn and endorsed by Grant Hill of the Detroit Pistons professional basketball team.

Reebok International Ltd. entered an earnings slump amid an executive shuffle at the top; the Timberland Co. posted second- and third-quarter losses totaling $32 million; Converse Inc. folded licensed apparel manufacturer Apex One three months after acquiring it; and the Stride Rite Corp. was beset by sagging sales and the fallout from a 1994 distribution snafu in its Keds division.

In retailing, Woolworth Corp., parent of Foot Locker and Kinney, brought in department store guru Roger Farah as chairman and Payless ShoeSource veteran Dale Hilpert as president of a reorganized shoe division. J. Baker Inc. pulled the plug on its 357-store Fayva chain; Melville Corp., parent of Thom McAn and FootAction and the operator of shoe departments in 2,176 Kmart stores, planned to spin off its footwear operations; and the 2,700-store Edison Bros., operator of Bakers, the Wild Pair, and Precis stores, filed for Chapter 11 bankruptcy. In the U.S., Brown Group Inc., the Timberland Co., and Vans Inc. closed their remaining footwear factories.

(DONNA HEIDERSTADT)

Furs. Mild winter weather in 1994–95 put a major damper on the retail fur season in the U.S., where sales remained near the 1993–94 level of $1.1 billion. As a result, the international industry adopted a less-than-optimistic mood for the remainder of 1995 because retailers left with stock were expected to curb spending on new merchandise and the unpredictability of the weather was expected to deter spending among consumers accustomed to making purchases when needed and to taking advantage of year-round discounts.

Pelt merchants and manufacturers, however, received huge orders from South Korea, Russia, and China. The developing Korean market gained new momentum after Jan. 1, 1995, when South Korea slashed its heavy taxes on luxury items. Although Russia and China traditionally had used furs as trimmings and accessories, relied on their own ample domestic supplies, and exported their surplus to earn hard currencies, both countries became fur importers after economic changes brought an increase in consumer disposable income and unleashed a pent-up desire for luxuries. As a result of the increased demand, prices of virtually all types of skins held steady or increased. Some, including blue fox and certain colours of ranched mink, experienced extraordinary price increases because of limited supply. By year's end, stocks were almost depleted of ranch-raised furs and wild furs. The generally higher prices encouraged ranchers to increase production and trappers to expand traplines.

AD VAN DENDEREN

Authorities look for illegal immigrants in a raid on a factory in The Netherlands. A number of countries, including the U.S., were attempting to clamp down on sweatshops, which were often found in the apparel industry and which employed illegal immigrants and violated labour laws.

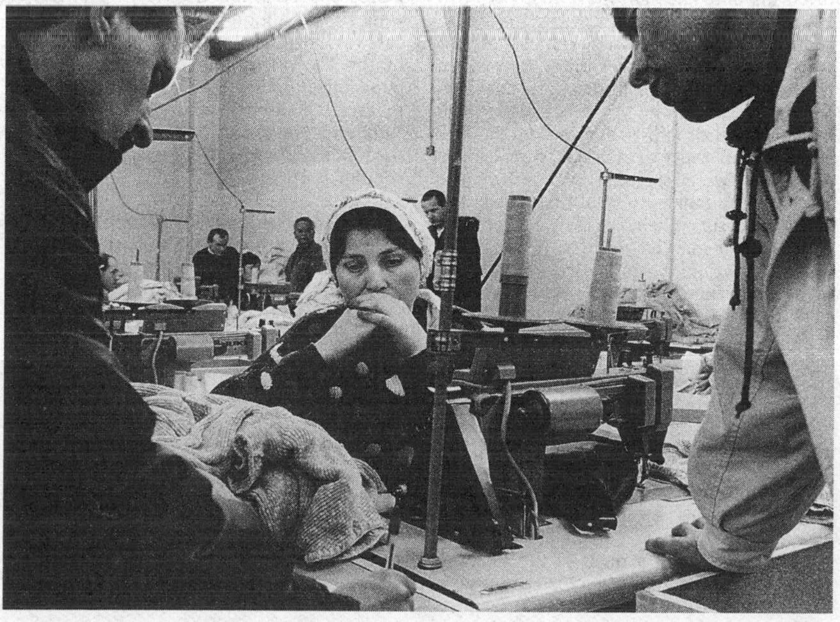

As the year ended, the international fur trade was gearing for an upheaval as a result of a ban, scheduled to take effect on Jan. 1, 1997, on imports of wild furs into the member countries of the European Union. The ban affected the skins and products of 13 animal species from countries that either permitted the use of steel leghold traps or had shown little progress in developing more humane harvesting methods. The principal countries affected were the U.S., Canada, and Russia, and the banned furs included beaver, otter, coyote, wolf, lynx, bobcat, sable, raccoon, muskrat, fisher, badger, marten, and ermine. (SANDY PARKER)

AUTOMOBILES

In many ways, 1995 was a major disappointment for the automobile industry. The Chrysler Corp. predicted that sales in the U.S. market would top 16 million units, while Ford Motor Co. projected sales of 15.9 million and General Motors (GM) Corp. 15.6 million. In the event, the industry's high expectations were not met, and sales for the year fell 1.7% behind 1994. The so-called Big Three were not alone in their disappointment. In Mexico the collapse of the peso crippled the market. In South America, especially in Brazil and Argentina, the "tequila effect" of Mexico's crisis stalled the economy. Europe also showed surprising weakness, despite what looked like a good start to the year. Only in Japan, where sales increased about 5% from their weak levels of the year before—thanks largely to sales of multipurpose vehicles—did the industry show any sign of strength. Even so, Japanese automakers continued to run with at least 3.5 million units of overcapacity, which caused most of them to post losses.

This poor performance forced the industry to focus on expansion in less developed countries. Ford and Chrysler announced plans to begin building cars in Vietnam. Chrysler announced that it was developing a $3,600–$6,000 minicar for developing markets. Toyota began building an assembly plant to make 20,000 Hilux trucks per year in Argentina. GM began assembling Blazers from kits in Indonesia, with plans to increase production gradually to 16,000 units annually. Ford announced plans to build small cars (the Fiesta and Escort) in conjunction with Mahindra & Mahindra Ltd. in India, and Volkswagen (VW) AG, Honda, and Hyundai announced their intentions to enter the Indian market.

Virtually all automakers fought to get into or expand their presence in the Chinese market. For every winner, however, there was a loser. In 1994 China had announced its plans to permit three or four automakers to build large assembly operations and three or four to establish small ones. In the melee that followed, Chinese authorities proved adept at pitting one automaker against another. Mercedes-Benz landed a major contract to build minivans (the Viano), beating out Chrysler. General Motors beat out Ford to build an executive-class passenger car (the Buick Regal). Ford was not left out of the market, however, as it landed a contract to build a truck version of its Transit van in China in 1997, and Chrysler maintained a toehold with its joint-venture Beijing Jeep. In a move that could provide a backdoor entry to China, Toyota doubled its equity holding in Daihatsu to 33.4%. Daihatsu made 50,000 small cars annually in China, while Toyota had no presence there. Analysts speculated that Toyota would begin building its own car in China, using Daihatsu's operations there to gain entry to the market.

A vehicle is assembled at a Ford Motor Co. plant in Mexico using the most modern manufacturing techniques. Automakers that had invested in Mexican operations felt the shock of the peso's collapse in 1995 as domestic sales of motor vehicles fell dramatically.

ROB SCHOENBAUM—BLACK STAR

Chinese authorities were specifically interested in selecting automakers that promised to produce large numbers of components in China and not just assemble vehicles from imported parts. They also prodded automakers to transfer their latest technology and commit to exporting their Chinese-made vehicles to other markets. Some industry observers warned that Chinese exports could undermine a world market already saddled with overcapacity.

Automakers also learned that developing markets operated in a state of flux. The collapse of the Mexican peso, for example, caught the industry completely by surprise. Car and truck prices skyrocketed as credit dried up, and sales fell more than 75%. In Brazil import taxes doubled to 70%, which reduced the country's trade deficit but also caused Toyota to cancel plans to build a major assembly plant there. Ford and VW terminated their joint venture, called Autolatina, in Brazil and Argentina. In the late 1980s, when the two markets were closed and sales were stagnant, it made sense for both companies to pool their resources and split costs. When Brazil and Argentina opened their markets to more competition, however, the joint venture proved slow in introducing new products, which allowed GM and Fiat SpA to gain market share. It was not clear if Ford and VW would maintain AutoEuropa, their joint venture in Portugal.

For all the clamour to get into developing markets, the U.S. proved to be an attractive place to build cars. Toyota announced that it would build a new assembly plant in Indiana to make pickup trucks, and it increased engine production in Kentucky. Peugeot SA continued to make rumblings that it would build a plant in the U.S. capable of making 200,000 vehicles annually. Adding fuel to the rumours were reports that Peugeot had begun testing its sedans, minivans, and convertibles in Chicago, California, and Texas.

Mercedes-Benz announced studies on building a passenger car in its plant in Alabama, which would build its All Activity Vehicle. The company cited the strong value of the Deutsche Mark and rising labour costs in Germany as reasons for moving more production to the U.S. beginning in 1998. The E-class and C-class, which sold about 25,000 units annually in the U.S., were considered prime candidates.

When Japan's currency hit 90 yen to the U.S. dollar early in the year, Japanese automakers took drastic measures to reduce their production at home and build more vehicles overseas. Toyota, Nissan, and Honda all announced plans to increase production in Europe. Toyota said that it would double its capacity in Britain, and Honda and Nissan said that they would increase production there by 50%. Meanwhile, Ford announced that it would build cars for Mazda in Europe (a Mazda version of the Fiesta) to help the Japanese company offset the strong yen without having to invest in its own manufacturing facility.

The increasing Japanese presence in Europe was not always welcome, however. European suppliers formulated plans to force Japanese automakers to buy more parts from them. The Paris-based supplier organization known as CLEPA (Liaison Committee of the European Automotive Components and Equipment Industry) specifically issued demands for Japan to import more parts from Europe and for Japanese transplants in Europe to buy more parts from its members. In a show of solidarity, the British SMMT Components Group and Swedish Automotive Suppliers organization voiced their support for CLEPA's efforts.

The U.S. and Japan collided once again on trade talks, with automobiles playing a major role in the negotiations. The administration of Pres. Bill Clinton threatened to impose 100% tariffs on 13 Japanese luxury cars—a move that would almost certainly have driven Lexus, Acura, and Infiniti dealers out of business. The administration demanded that Japan open its markets to more U.S. cars and parts, while the Big Three demanded more dealerships. For their part, Japanese negotiators countered that their market was already open, and they refused to accept U.S. demands to set quotas as a yardstick for measuring trade progress. A new agreement was reached, at the eleventh hour, with both sides declaring victory. Japanese negotiators trumpeted the fact that the accord did not include numerical targets, while U.S. negotiators hailed the accord as a breakthrough for their "get-tough" policies. Meanwhile, the Big Three began to take advantage of the weakening dollar by cutting the prices of the vehicles they sold in Japan. Chrysler, for example, cut the price of a Cherokee in Japan by 10% and service parts by 30%.

At the 1995 Tokyo Motor Show, Toyota unveiled the Cavalier—a car made by GM in the U.S. to be sold by Toyota dealers in Japan. Toyota's desire to sell the car was widely regarded as an effort to reduce trade tensions. Toyota, however, said that it planned to use the Cavalier to attract Japanese buyers who preferred imported cars with bigger engines and more flamboyant styling. The move could be an important strategy. Toyota's market share in Japan had sagged to historically low levels (38%), and sales of imported cars represented the greatest growth segment in Japan.

U.S. automakers, showing increasing willingness to use their political muscle in trade disputes, also got the Clinton administration to pry open the South Korean market, which was more closed than Japan's. South Korea shipped more than 200,000 vehicles to the U.S. during the year, while U.S. exports to Korea numbered fewer than 2,000. Meanwhile, South Korea demonstrated that its aggressive investments in new capacity were beginning to pay off. Production increased to about 2.6 million units, and South Korea surpassed Canada as the fifth largest automotive producer in the world.

As the average price of a new vehicle in the U.S. rose to more than $20,000, the issue of affordability emerged as a major issue. The 1995 Harbour Report, an annual study that compared the manufacturing efficiency of each automaker in North America, showed that the Big Three still had ample opportunity to cut costs. If Chrysler ran at Toyota's level of manufacturing efficiency, for example, it would cut costs by $1.4 billion. Ford would save $1.7, billion and GM would save $4.1 billion. Even so, when all costs were taken into account, the Big Three had lower costs than Toyota or the other Japanese automakers.

Ford launched its global reorganization, known as Ford 2000, with a goal of cutting costs by at least $3 billion a year. The Big Three also jointly announced a program to use common design standards for simple parts such as light bulbs, jacks, and radiator caps. By eliminating duplicate engineering and development on parts on which they did not compete, GM, Ford, and Chrysler hoped to reduce investment and achieve greater economies of scale.

The need to cut costs even led Toyota to modify its famous lean production system. The new process chopped the traditional long assembly line into 11 smaller production lines, with only 15 to 20 workers on each subline. Similar or related tasks, such as installing all electrical wiring, were performed in each line. To compensate for the speed it took to complete the tasks in the different lines, a slight amount of inventory was allowed to accumulate between them. Though the system might not be as "lean," the buffers allowed the line to move faster.

In Brazil, VW executive Inaki López introduced a radical new assembly process at a bus plant near Rio de Janeiro. The bus was assembled from modules that suppliers built inside the VW plant. Each module was put together in a manufacturing cell that was totally managed by the supplier. As the bus moved down the assembly line, the supplier bolted its module onto the vehicle. While a typical assembly plant employed 2,000 to 3,000 people, López said that his new system would need only 200 to 300. While this clearly would reduce costs, it was not expected to spread quickly through the industry because of resistance from labour unions.

The growth in the used car market in the U.S. persuaded one large retailer to open franchised outlets. The retailer, called CarMax, began building outlets that offered hundreds of used cars of many brands. Each vehicle came with a 30-day warranty and a nonnegotiable price that eliminated the haggling many buyers found distasteful. Owners were also allowed to return their cars for a full refund within five days if they had not driven them more than 400 km (250 mi). CarMax caused considerable concern among new car dealers, who thought that it could steal their used car business. Automakers were also concerned that CarMax could become an outlet for new automakers trying to break into the U.S.

Brand management became the industry's hottest buzzword in 1995. While brand management was a marketing technique that had been around for decades and had been honed to perfection by companies such as Procter & Gamble, it had not been used by mass-market automakers. When using the technique, automakers planned to emphasize each nameplate in their marketing, such as Mustang or Camaro, rather than the name of the company or division that sold the vehicle. To launch its brand management program, GM reorganized its North American operations to establish more than 30 brand managers. Not to be outdone, Ford established brand managers for every model in each country where it was sold. Ford had to face a disappointing consumer response to the redesign of its Taurus, which had been the best-selling car in the U.S.

Chrysler faced a major issue when billionaire Kirk Kerkorian, chairman of Tracinda Corp., made a bid to buy the company. At first, because he had no line of credit and no financial backers, few people treated his effort seriously. That later changed, however, when Kerkorian hired Chrysler's former chief financial officer, Jerry York, to lead his takeover attempt. Kerkorian also enlisted former Chrysler chairman Lee Iacocca.

Kerkorian claimed that he was out to protect stockholder interests and accused Chrysler's management of hoarding too much money for a future recession ($7.5 billion). He also berated the company's quality as below average. (Almost as if to underscore his point, Chrysler was forced into a safety recall to fix faulty rear latches on the liftgates of about 4.5 million minivans.) After conducting a detailed financial analysis of the automaker, York announced that Chrysler was hoarding at least $2.5 billion too much, a fact that caused institutional investors on Wall Street to sit up and take notice. As the year drew to a close, Kerkorian was demanding that York be given a seat on the Chrysler board.

Kerkorian and York were not the only ones eyeing Chrysler's cash hoard. Steve Yokich, who replaced Owen Bieber as president of the United Automobile Workers, promised that the union would make sure a portion of the cash ended up in the pockets of its members when negotiations began on the 1996 contract.

An announcement by Englehard Corp. about a system that would reduce air pollution from automobiles attracted considerable attention. Called PremAir, it consisted of a specially coated radiator that converted ozone and carbon monoxide into oxygen and carbon dioxide. The coating was made from materials similar to those used in catalytic converters and was sprayed onto the radiator. As a vehicle traveled along, it cleaned the air passing through the radiator, more than offsetting the emissions discharged through the tailpipe. Ford entered into a long-term evaluation test with Englehard to verify the system's capabilities. (JOHN MCELROY)

BEVERAGES

Beer. With the ongoing success of craft brewing in 1995, Anheuser-Busch, Miller, and Coors continued their efforts to convince consumers that their products were just as good as those of their tiny competitors. For Anheuser-Busch, the world's largest beer purveyor, the effort manifested itself in American Originals, a trio of beers said to hark back to recipes from the turn of the century. Miller Brewing took on partners with pedigrees in microbrewing, inking strategic alliances with Celis Brewing of Texas and Shipyard Brewery of Maine. Miller spent much of the year, however, trying to revive the fortunes of Miller Lite, which had lost its number one ranking in light beers to Bud Light in late 1994. Coors Brewing, whose Coors Light also was a competitor, tried to carve its niche among little beers with a product dubbed Blue Moon, which was distributed by Coors but made by the much smaller F.X. Matt.

Microbrewers themselves capitalized on the 50% rise in business of 1994. There were some 600 craft breweries operating in North America by the end of 1995, about 20 times more than a decade earlier. The most successful among them—Boston Beer, Redhook Ale Brewery, Pete's Brewing Co.—found themselves the darlings not only of drinkers but also of investors when each made public stock offerings. The fever even spread as far as the Pacific Rim, where Asia's first independent craft brewer, South China Brewing, opened in Hong Kong.

The most significant global transaction in 1995 involved Belgium's Interbrew, which purchased Canada's John Labatt Ltd. Heineken continued to reach beyond Dutch borders, buying Interbrew Italia from Labatt's new owner and a majority stake in Zlaty Bazant of Slovakia. From the U.K. came word that Guinness would make its world-famous stout in China after having exported it there for 15 years. Leaving England was Australia's Foster's, which sold its Courage brewing unit to Scottish & Newcastle. The profits of China's Tsingtao beer unexpectedly fell 49% in the first half of 1995.

The U.S. beer industry struggled toward year's end to mount a 1% increase over 1994 sales and volume totals. Europe, on the other hand, saw volume decreasing from that of the previous year at about a 1% rate. (GREG W. PRINCE)

Spirits. The demographics of the 20-something generation that so fascinated marketers of products during the 1990s got the attention of the distilled spirits industry as well. Conventional wisdom had it that this attractive age group might be beyond the reach of a business whose reputation was rather stodgy, but companies in the spirits industry were intent on turning that thinking around in 1995.

Tradition got shaken up in several ways. The leading distiller Bacardi had not disturbed its basic rum recipe since its creation in 1862. In 1995, however, the company introduced Bacardi Limón, a 70-proof citrus spirit, whose flavour came from a blend of lemon, lime, and grapefruit. Bacardi called its release a matter of "being in touch with the marketplace of today's consumers." Likewise, another grand old spirit marketer, Brown-Forman, gave its product line a new treatment with the introduction of low-alcohol Tropical Freezes, the first blended freezer cocktails designed to give drinkers "an easy, convenient way to enjoy great-tasting slushy bar drinks" at home.

Jim Beam, a proud name in the pantheon of spirits, celebrated its 200th anniversary in 1995. Eager to prove that it had not reached its bicentennial without keeping up with trends, Beam subsidiaries introduced a pair of alcoholic beverages that would have been most out of place in the late 18th century: Mad Melon Watermelon Schnapps and After Shock Liqueur. The latter promised drinkers "an initial blast of hot, fiery cinnamon followed by an icy cool sensation when you inhale." After Shock proved hot indeed, selling one million bottles after only three months on the U.S. market.

Reaching into the past also proved popular. Mexico's most notable export was Encantado Mezcal, a spirit whose heritage dated to the 19th century, when the "cognac of Mexico" was imbibed solely by the colonial aristocracy. Mexico was also the focus of an industrywide controversy, namely a debate over what could and could not be called margaritas. Mexican officials wanted companies like E&J Gallo and Seagram to stop marketing items as margaritas if they continued to make them without tequila. In Russia a court was no more generous with its heritage, keeping Grand Metropolitan from using the Smirnoff name to sell vodka there, where the name had originated in the tsarist era.

The U.S. spirits market continued to sag, suffering a 1.8% decline in 1994. The prospects appeared brighter in Asia, however, where the demand for liquor translated into a 50% sales increase between 1991 and 1995. (GREG W. PRINCE)

Wine. The 1995 harvest reports indicated mixed results. French producers were mildly optimistic for wines of good to superior quality, with moderate yields after an extremely hot summer and a harvest troubled by early rains. Bordeaux and Burgundy producers who were able to harvest after the rains were not greatly affected. Alsace and Loire producers were able to take advantage of late summer conditions to bring their grapes to ripeness, conditions that were repeated in Germany.

Italy, however, had an off vintage, leaving producers concerned about the size and quality of the crop or wondering whether they would be able to produce vintage wines at all. The early season experienced drought conditions, which stressed the vines, followed by high summer heat and humidity. Later, hailstorms further damaged vineyards. The Italian press tried to save the reputation of the vintage, saying that growers who had waited harvested a small crop of superior quality, but only time would tell.

In California the early season was plagued by flooding, but this gave way to a moderate summer and a harvest later than usual, with the promise of another vintage of high-quality wines. The demand for certain varieties continued to drive grape prices upward, particularly in merlot and bulk juice.

In sales, auctions continued their strong performance for wines of high price or limited availability, with older Bordeaux setting new price records. In London a case of 1945 Mouton-Rothschild in pristine condition brought the incredible price of $46,630. New York City showed a great increase in auction activity in 1995 owing to relaxed sales restrictions.

Exports of wine continued to show growth on a worldwide basis as more countries sought markets beyond their borders. Wines from South America, New Zealand, Australia, and South Africa became widely available and gained acceptance for quality. Late in the year a major wine publication gave an Australian wine its top honour as wine of the year. Eastern European wines grew in distribution with a reputation for acceptable wines at moderate prices. At the same time, the so-called wine lake in Europe continued to shrink, owing in part to restrictions on production by the European Union. A surprisingly mild backlash occurred against French exports as a result of that country's nuclear tests in the Pacific. (HOWARD HERING)

Soft Drinks. The Pepsi-Cola Co. extended its reach farther beyond carbonated soft drinks in 1995 than ever before. Among the products it tested were Smooth Moos, a flavoured dairy drink; Aquafina, a bottled water; Mazagran sparkling coffee, part of a joint venture with Starbucks; Josta, a high-caffeine drink based on the South American guarana berry; and Sierra, billed as a nontraditional "ice soda." The Coca-Cola Co., meanwhile, relied more on tradition, trying to add even more to the already global recognition enjoyed by its flagship product. Just as it had adapted the original contour shape to an updated Coke bottle in 1994, the company took packaging a step farther in 1995, experimenting with a similarly curved can in Germany. The Arizona brand of iced teas and fruit drinks attempted to challenge both Coke and Pepsi by introducing carbonated drinks: three flavoured colas and a root beer in its "Cowboy Cola" line. Observers were uncertain whether Arizona would be able to find a profitable market niche in this venture, though the company felt its unique marketing strategy would make it a competitor.

While Coke was not as quick as Pepsi to develop new products, it was not shy about buying other soft drinks, acquiring Barq's Inc., a root beer specialist based in Baton Rouge, La. The biggest acquisition in soft drinks, however, was the long-awaited transaction that saw London's Cadbury Schweppes complete its takeover of Dr Pepper/Seven-Up. The deal immediately made Cadbury a serious competitor in the U.S. for the first time. Both Coke and Pepsi tried to gain advantage outside the U.S. Coke decided that one of the best ways to build its business was through establishing "anchor bottlers," franchisees that would serve as the springboard for inundating entire regions with their product. Coke created such ventures with Panamco in Latin America and Sabco in southern Africa.

Other companies were willing to do the same thing. Cadbury took Dr Pepper to Argentina for the first time. In the U.K. the private-label producer Cott made real inroads by supplying the concentrate for Sainsbury's Classic, the country's leading store brand, which through lower prices grabbed a 7% share of the market in just one year. Another Cott client, the Virgin Group, infiltrated Japan with its private-label offering.

As 1995 came to a close, the U.S. soft drink market was growing in retail estab-

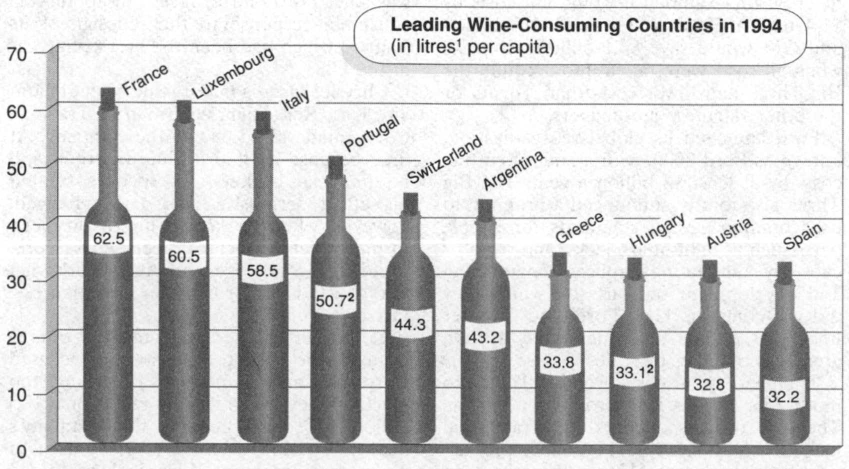

[1] One litre =1.0567 U.S. quarts = 0.8799 imperial quart.
[2] Estimated from production data.

Source: *World Drink Trends*, in association with Produktschap voor Gedistilleerde Dranken, Schiedam, Neth.

lishments at an annual rate of about 1.5%, while the industry as a whole was expected to increase by 2% over 1994. North America was estimated as accounting for 46% of soft drink consumption during the previous year, with Western Europe representing 31% and Asia 18%. (GREG W. PRINCE)

BUILDING AND CONSTRUCTION

The pace of U.S. construction trailed off in 1995. Housing starts declined sharply during the first quarter before rebounding in the second and third quarters. The U.S. Department of Commerce adjusted the annual rate to 1.4 million units, the same number as in 1994. The U.S. government reported the value of all new construction as of August at an annual level of $530.4 billion, a 5% increase over the previous year's level. In nonresidential construction the overall pattern was essentially flat compared with a steady 8–9% increase during 1992–94.

The U.S. Congress pushed for reduced federal spending, which threatened to tie up public-works funding for infrastructure. Delays in appropriations slowed plans for bridges and highways. Upgrades of water and sewer systems in Boston, Los Angeles, Miami, Fla., and Houston, Texas, worth at least $1 billion in each case, continued, but many other localities waited to see if federal legislation would rewrite environmental standards to shift financial responsibility to the states. Sports and hotel construction continued their robust trends of recent years, and the $4.2 billion Denver (Colo.) International Airport finally opened, $2.1 billion over budget and 16 months late.

In Canada a nationwide construction strike in July dampened housing starts, but the number rebounded by 11% in August. Economists predicted 163,000 monthly starts for the year, below the average for the previous 10 years. Although tight fiscal policy restrained massive public-works start-ups, a number of innovative engineering and construction endeavours already under way continued. In Newfoundland the Can$6.2 billion Hibernia offshore oil production platform, the first concrete gravity-base structure of its type to be built in North America, continued to take shape.

As Mexico's economy had its worst performance since 1941, private citizens deferred spending on residential construction. The government cautiously continued a privatization initiative aimed at attracting foreign investment in infrastructure projects. Japanese, British, French, and U.S. firms invested in water and sewer projects in Mexico City and other municipalities.

With aggressive construction in most major cities, China expected private development to add 137,000 MW of new power capacity by the year 2000. Despite a reputation for imposing bureaucratic obstacles, the government was showing greater willingness to consider what were called build-operate-transfer projects. The national strategy was based on large coal-fired generating units in the north, nuclear plants along the eastern seaboard, and hydropower in the south. China and Britain also smoothed out financial agreements that allowed continued construction of the $20.9 million Hong Kong airport project, which had begun in 1991.

The January earthquake that struck the Kobe area of Japan was expected to stimulate construction, but the overall effects proved marginal at best. After a first-quarter surge pushed residential construction up 8.6%, housing starts quickly trailed off to 1994 levels. The heady expansion of the 1980s was only a memory for most major Japanese contractors, who looked offshore for work on large projects. One impressive exception was the Tokyo International Forum, a $1,650,000,000 convention centre and theatre complex designed by the New York architect Rafael Viñoly.

(ANDREW G. WRIGHT)

A new building goes up in Shanghai, one of China's most prosperous cities. Despite a tightened money supply, designed to curb inflation, construction in China's major cities continued at a brisk pace in 1995.

PETER TURNLEY—BLACK STAR

CHEMICALS

Despite the good records compiled in 1994, the world's chemical industry began 1995 with a cautious attitude, largely because of worries about the economies of the U.S. and Europe. As the year wore on, however, the industry became more confident that both output and profits would be strong. Among encouraging signs were projections of continued stability in the Middle East, relatively low oil and gas prices, and political stability in China, Indonesia, and Malaysia.

In 1994 Europe's growth rate had generally caught up to that of the U.S., and data for the first three-quarters of 1995 showed Europe again to be roughly matching the pace of the U.S.

The seven major European countries in the chemical industry—Germany, France, the United Kingdom, Italy, Belgium, Spain, and The Netherlands—expected to raise their output in 1995 by 4% and sales by 10%, with the U.S. anticipating about the same rates of growth. This followed a strong 1994, when the major European nations had hiked their output by 5.9% and sales by 8.7%, while the U.S. racked up a 4.2% growth in output and an 8.8% sales gain. There were indications that countries in Eastern Europe were improving production and increasing sales.

Japan, hobbled by the high yen and a variety of internal problems, nonetheless found 1995 to be a decided improvement after a disappointing and essentially flat 1994. Elsewhere in Asia many nations—particularly Indonesia, Singapore, Malaysia, India, the Philippines, and even Vietnam—had plans for developing their domestic petrochemical strength to a point where they could export products as well as meet domestic needs. As an engineering company executive reflected, "Asia in 1995 is involved in 40 percent of the world's expansion contracts in petrochemicals, while it made up just 25 percent two years ago."

Germany's BASF AG planned to make major investments in Southeast Asia in the next 15 years, expecting the area to grow at double the rate of the worldwide chemical market. Within a short time, according to an international market consultant, Asia would represent almost 25% of the world's petrochemical capacity. Further, it was predicted that Asia would be the largest producing and consuming area of the world, although Japan would lose its dominance there. Even China, despite its unresolved leadership problems, its lack of capital, and its poor roads, rails, power, and transport, had posted a 15.8% rise in the value of its chemical output in 1994.

Because the chemical industry was increasingly becoming global, the importance of chemical producers in areas of low-cost hydrocarbons continued to grow. Sold the best technology by international engineering firms, nations in the Middle East such as Saudi Arabia and Kuwait (and, potentially, Iran) often were able to offer commodity chemicals at lower prices than established makers in the U.S. and Europe.

The chemical industry encompassed a wide range of products, however, not just a handful of high-volume commodities, and for that reason both the U.S. and Europe continued to have powerful import and export markets worldwide. In 1994 the nations of the European Union, for example, built the value of their exports to $204 billion, 15% more than in 1993, and their imports rose to $163 billion. In the same year, the U.S. expanded its export market to $52 billion, while its imports were $33 billion. Midyear data supplied by the Chemical Manufacturers Association of the U.S. showed that by mid-1995 the U.S. chemical industry had exports of $30.5 billion and imports of $20.3 billion, increases of roughly 15% in both categories.

Nonetheless, the chemical industry was continuing to become important in other regions of the world. In Central and South America, for example, the prospect of increasing the number of participants in the North American Free Trade Agreement (NAFTA) was encouraging countries such as Argentina and Chile to expand their industries. Only Brazil, however, had a substantial chemical industry, including such basic facilities as large ethylene crackers that could compete with those in the U.S. and elsewhere in the Western world.

In this climate of growth, several important technological changes had taken place. Perhaps the most significant were two developments affecting the production of polyethylene, the most common plastic. A new method of altering processing conditions (called "super condensing") had the potential for almost doubling the capacity of gas-phase production plants (as most in the industry were). The other innovation, which applied to polyethylene, polypropylene, polystyrene, and some other lower-volume polymers, involved new catalysts. The so-called single-site, or metallocene, catalysts, which had been expanding their commercial base from specialty grades into commodity-grade materials, were the centre of growing interest among companies. These catalysts had the advantage of allowing producers to tailor products to meet highly specific needs. This development could lead to the manufacture of better plastics, since the lower-cost polyethylenes and polypropylenes, for example, might be able to compete against other, more expensive and complex specialty plastics.

One of the characteristics of the chemical industry was that, as it increased the productivity of its plants, used more advanced equipment, and pushed its profits to new highs, its need for personnel declined. The total employment of major chemical companies was down 41% from that of a decade before. (J. ROBERT WARREN)

ELECTRICAL

The significant rises in raw material prices that began in 1994 continued to hit the electrical manufacturing industry in 1995. Copper, the industry's most important raw material, cost 60% more in January 1995 than 12 months earlier; aluminium almost doubled its 1993 price; and polyvinyl chloride, a major insulating material, reached twice its mid-1991 price.

Manufacturers were forced to absorb the bulk of these price hikes because intense competition kept output prices low. Heinrich von Pierer, president and chief executive officer (CEO) of Siemens, the world's largest multinational electrical manufacturer, blamed rapid globalization of the market. He noted that the cost of skilled labour in Germany was very high at DM 44 per hour, while in the neighbouring Czech Republic the cost was DM 5 per hour. Wages were even lower in Southeast Asia, Pierer said, and the competitiveness of that region was enhanced by innovation and regular replacement of old plants with new equipment.

Innovation was the single most important key to success, Pierer claimed, and he pointed to Siemens' sales history: in 1980 barely half of the company's worldwide sales were of products that had been developed less than five years previously, and in 1995 the figure was two-thirds.

Siemens and another large company, ABB Asea Brown Boveri Ltd. (ABB), continued to spend a large proportion of their revenues on research and development (R and D). ABB had 17,000 scientists and engineers employed in R and D and in 1994 spent about 8% of revenue, approximately $2.4 billion. Siemens spent around 8.5% of its revenue, about $5,280,000,000. In contrast, R and D spending by General Electric (GE) fell by 11% in 1994 to $1,741,000,000.

Competition and technological changes continued to reduce employment in the industry. GE, for example, which had been downsizing to become more globally competitive, announced on Jan. 1, 1995, that the total number of employees was 221,000, a net loss of 77,000 over five years. At Westinghouse jobs declined 18% in 1994.

Employment in the electrical industry had been subject to a geographic shift as well. ABB reported that personnel costs had been reduced from 34% of total sales in 1991 to 30% in 1994, a result of a 6% improvement in productivity and a shift in production to low-wage countries in Asia and Central and Eastern Europe. ABB's total number of employees on Jan. 1, 1995, was 207,557.

Another employment trend that had recently hit the industry was the decrease in full-time positions. Siemens reported phasing out 21,000 full-time jobs from its worldwide workforce in 1994 while increasing part-time employees by the same number. Siemens' total workforce was 382,000 on Sept. 30, 1994.

Both ABB and GE reported an increase of 7.5% in the sale of power-generation, transmission, and distribution plants during 1994. Total sales at Siemens fell by 9.9%, which reflected the exceptionally high activity of the previous year and signaled the end of the boom generated by Germany's reunification. Sales in Westinghouse's energy systems sector (mainly nuclear) fell by 6%, and its power-generation-sector sales dropped by 4% in 1994.

Overall, the worldwide electrical market expanded by around 7% in 1994. While demand rose by about 14% in North and South America and Southeast Asia in 1995, sales in Europe rose by a more modest 3%. ABB predicted that more than half the world's investments in electrical power generation over the next 10 years would be made in Asia.

Significant innovation in power generation, following the recent trend toward the small combined-cycle gas-fired power plant, came from a small Californian company, Exergy, which developed a technique, the Kalina Cycle, that used a mixture of working fluids with different boiling points. This was said to boost efficiency by up to 40%. GE already had a license to use the technology in combined-cycle plants, and Ansaldo Energia of Italy planned to use it in geothermal plants. ABB and a Japanese power utility, Ebara, agreed to collaborate with Exergy to develop the cycle for use in direct-fired plants.

Siemens predicted that output prices were likely to fall farther in the immediate future and, although sales would rise, pressure on employment would continue. Percy Barnevik, president and CEO of ABB, agreed that low-wage countries would remain very competitive for a long time and was looking to new markets stimulated by the economic reemergence of South Africa. (T.C.J. COGLE)

ENERGY

Petroleum. A continuing surge in oil production from outside OPEC was the dominant feature of world oil markets in 1995. Much of the growth in non-OPEC supplies came from offshore fields in the Norwegian and British sectors of the North Sea. There was, however, a worldwide trend toward greater production from many existing oil-producing countries, as well as new supplies from countries not normally thought of as oil producers. The increase in non-OPEC output was such that the organization was forced to maintain the production ceiling of 24,520,000 bbl a day it had imposed on its members in September 1993. Total world oil production in 1995 was about 70 million bbl a day.

The rise in oil production during 1995 could be explained by a number of factors, with technological progress foremost among them. New seismic techniques offered geologists a three-dimensional view of oil fields, which in turn gave them greater confidence about where to drill new wells. Advanced drilling techniques enabled much more oil to be recovered from reservoirs. Recovery rates had jumped from about 25% or so 10 years earlier to more than 50% in some cases. Some industry executives believed recovery rates might eventually reach 70% or so as new ways were found to enhance oil production in both older and new fields. Rising recovery rates and the lower cost of technology also enabled oil companies to tap smaller fields. This was one of the main reasons for the growth in output from the North Sea, Western Europe's largest oil-producing area.

The impact of such developments could be seen in the U.S., where a rapid decline in oil production in the 1990s had been predicted. Oil output had fallen at a rate of 2–3% for some years, with the Department of Energy estimating 1995 production at 6,520,000 bbl a day, compared with peak production of about 9 million bbl 10 years earlier. The government predicted that production could fall to 5,350,000 bbl a day by the year 2000, although industry experts expected that technological progress would substantially slow the rate of decline in key fields, such as those located on Alaska's North Slope. In addition, new fields in the deep water of the U.S. sector of the Gulf of Mexico had proved particularly prolific, a development that could slow the decline in what was the biggest producing area in the continental U.S.

Another trend during the year was the change in attitude of many governments toward the international oil industry. Countries that had previously been closed to the industry because of the Cold War, or that had nationalized Western oil interests in the 1970s and 1980s, welcomed new foreign involvement in their oil industries. Competition to attract international investment was fierce, and many countries relaxed tax laws and introduced liberal regulatory regimes to encourage exploration and production. Success at attracting foreign investment was not universal, however. New legislation in Russia that would allow a number of large Western-sponsored projects to proceed became bogged down in bitter debates in the parliament. Other former Soviet republics, such as Azerbaijan, were more successful in encouraging new investment. An $8 billion project to develop three offshore oil fields in the Caspian Sea passed a major milestone in October when the companies and the countries involved agreed on the export routes for the initial oil from the area to Western markets. During the year other big international oil companies moved into the Caspian region, and some industry executives predicted that it could rival the Persian Gulf within the next 20 years or so.

The liberalizing trend extended to OPEC countries, many of which were finding it hard to balance the need to fund additional investment in their oil industries with other demands for state revenues. Venezuela, for example, a founding member of OPEC, signed agreements with Western producers to develop existing fields and explore for new ones. Many smaller OPEC producers entered into similar deals, although Saudi Arabia, OPEC's dominant member, showed no sign of allowing international oil companies to operate there other than as technical advisers to Saudi Aramco, the state oil giant.

During the year Iraq announced that it would rely on international oil companies to help rehabilitate its industry once UN sanctions had been removed. Agreements in principle were reached with French and Russian oil companies to develop existing oil fields. Iraqi oil exports had been banned since Pres. Saddam Hussein invaded Kuwait in 1990. The UN said that it would allow Iraq to export $1 billion worth of oil every three months to fund purchases of food and other humanitarian supplies, but the government refused to accept the conditions attached to the offer. The oil embargo was due to be lifted fully when the UN determined that the Iraqi government was in complete compliance with demands that it dismantle all capability to manufacture weapons of mass destruction.

Oil also figured in other foreign policy moves during the year. In May U.S. Pres. Bill Clinton ordered Conoco, the oil subsidiary of E.I. du Pont de Nemours & Co., to abandon plans to invest in an offshore oil and gas field in Iran, which the U.S. government said was guilty of supporting terrorism in the Middle East. Clinton later banned U.S. companies from buying Iranian crude oil, although his appeal for broader international support for the embargo was largely ignored. There were also moves late in the year to organize an oil embargo against Nigeria, Africa's largest oil producer, after the military government executed nine minority rights activists from Ogoniland, one of the centres of Nigeria's onshore oil industry. Initial attempts to impose a full oil embargo did not appear to have international support, however.

Oil prices remained within a narrow range, with the price for the benchmark Brent Blend trading between $16 and $18.50 a barrel for much of the year. Such prices were seen as soft by many in the industry, but they did not prevent large international companies from reporting strong growths in profits during the year. Most U.S. and European companies had gone through large-scale corporate restructurings in which tens of thousands of jobs and millions of dollars in costs and overhead had been eliminated.

Environmental issues continued to pose problems for the industry. In June the Royal Dutch/Shell Group found itself at the centre of a bitter controversy over its plan to dump *Brent Spar,* an obsolete oil-storage installation, in deep water off the Atlantic coast of Britain. (*See* ENVIRONMENT: *Sidebar.*) The environmental group Greenpeace led a successful campaign against the dumping. Greenpeace activists occupied the installation as it was being towed out to sea, while violent attacks were launched by environmental extremists against Shell stations in Germany and elsewhere in Europe. Shell's decision to abandon the sinking defused the confrontation, but the issue of how to dispose of oil platforms located in deep water was likely to remain controversial.

(ROBERT CORZINE)

Natural Gas. Demand for natural gas outside the former Soviet Union continued to grow strongly in 1995. The increasing use of gas for power generation was one reason behind a surge in consumption in North America, which accounted for a third of total world demand. U.S. consumption rose by 3.9% in 1995, according to the American Gas Association. Asia, however, remained the fastest-growing market, with much of the supply being in the form of liquefied natural gas.

Trade in liquefied natural gas continued to be buoyant in spite of the relatively high prices needed to justify the liquefaction process. In 1994 world trade in liquefied natural gas increased by 5%, although demand grew by 11% in the Asia-Pacific region. Proposals were made, however, for new long-distance pipelines that might eventually link the vast gas reserves in the Middle East and central Asia to the fast-growing markets in South and Southeast Asia.

(ROBERT CORZINE)

Coal. World hard coal production in 1995 was estimated to be about 3.7 billion metric tons, about 200 million tons higher than in 1994. It was estimated that production would grow to nearly four billion tons by 2010. The reversal of coal's fortunes with the transition from a buyer's to a seller's market was maintained through 1995.

The U.S. was expecting record production of 1,033,100,000 short tons (1 short ton = 0.9 metric ton) and an increase in coal exports to 77 million tons from 72 million tons in 1994. Output also continued to increase in other major producers, including China (1.2 billion tons raw coal) and India (240 million tons). South Africa produced more than 235 million tons in 1995, with exports at about 60 million tons. Australia remained the world's largest coal exporter, with 137 million tons exported in 1994–95. Production in the European Union and in Eastern Europe (with the exception of Poland) continued to fall.

(ROBERT J.M. WYLLIE)

Nuclear. Statistical data released by the International Atomic Energy Agency in 1995 indicated that at the beginning of 1994 there were a total of 432 units operating in nuclear power stations in 31 countries, with a total capacity of 340,347 MW. There were 48 units under construction in 15 countries, 4 of which were connected to grids for the first time during the year. No new reactor construction was started during 1994. The total number of reactors shut down throughout the world increased to 70. Worldwide, nuclear power units had a total net production of 26,054.1 TWh (terawatt-hours; 1 terawatt-hour = 1 billion kilowatt-hours).

Lithuania continued to be the country most heavily dependent on nuclear power, with 76.4% of its production of electricity coming from the two nuclear units at Ignalina (2,370 MW net). Nonetheless, the government announced the start of a decommissioning program and set 2010 as the target for completing the closure of the station. France had a 76.3% stake in nuclear power amounting to 58,493 MW from 56 units, followed by Belgium (55.8%) and Sweden (51.1%).

Slovakia decided to finance continued work and guarantee existing loans on the four-unit Mochovce station. Discussions with the European Bank for Reconstruction and Development ended because of the bank's condition that Slovakia close two pressurized-water reactor (PWR) units at Bohunice. The units were of an earlier Soviet design and were widely considered by Western engineers to be unsafe. (Ukraine agreed in late December to close the plant at Chernobyl.) China's negotiations with Russia over the building of two 1,000-MW reactors in Liaoning province reached the concluding stages, and China ordered two 985-MW PWR units from Framatome of France to be built at Lin-ao. China also signed a memorandum of understanding with Atomic Energy of Canada Ltd. for the construction of two 700-MW Candu-type reactors and began building its own high-temperature reactor.

Japan's 280-MW fast breeder reactor at Monju began producing electricity during commissioning tests, but it was not due to produce full power until 1996. A water leak at the Onagawa reactor led to a shutdown of operations in December. Meanwhile, in France further problems at the 1,200-MW Creys-Malville fast breeder reactor, Superphénix, kept the plant shut down for more than half the year. Prolonged delays over the Tennessee Valley Authority's construction at Watts Bar, Tenn., and Bellefonte, Ala., ended with the announcement that the three units would not be completed. The two Bellefonte units could, however, be completed after conversion to another fuel, probably natural gas.

In Germany Siemens decided to close its fuel fabrication plant at Hanau in Lower Saxony and move the operation to its plant in Richland, Wash. The company blamed the closure on excessively strict licensing requirements. PreussenElektra decided to decommission the Würgassen station, where the GE-designed 640-MW boiling-water reactor had a troubled history.

Changes in Germany's policies on irradiated fuel reprocessing, allowing direct storage of spent fuel, resulted in cancellation of contracts with British Nuclear Fuels Ltd. (BNFL). Cancellation penalties with four German stations protected their contracts. The loss of business for the controversial new British reprocessing plant spurred sales efforts by the company to win contracts in the growing Asian markets. A long-awaited deal between BNFL and Nuclear Electric was signed, however, giving BNFL long-term contracts worth $20 billion. Final plans for the privatization of Britain's nuclear industry were announced. The two existing state-owned companies, Nuclear Electric and Scottish Nuclear, would be privatized subsidiaries of a holding company, whose headquarters would be in Scotland. The new company would take over the 14 advanced gas-cooled reactors and the newly commissioned Sizewell B PWR, while a new government company would take responsibility for the Magnox stations.

(RICHARD A. KNOX)

Alternative Energy. It was predicted in 1995 that the increasing economic competitiveness of energy sources such as solar, biomass, wind, geothermal, and tidal barrages would not be dependent on technological breakthroughs. Within 20 years, it was thought, some alternative energy sources should reach competitive parity with oil priced at $15 a barrel. Limited market demand and the economics of production continued to restrict the large-scale development of alternative sources in 1995, however.

Commercial applications of alternative

A construction crew works on a Petróleos Mexicanos (Pemex) refinery being built in Tula, in east-central Mexico, to produce gasoline from petroleum waste products. A joint Italian-Mexican venture, the refinery was one of the latest projects of the state-owned oil company.
ROB SHOENBAUM—BLACK STAR

energy generally remained confined to remote locations or areas in which it had a distinct competitive advantage, as in solar-powered heating or the generation of electricity in sunny climates. Even the international oil industry, however, began to use alternative energy to bring down operating costs. The U.S. oil company Amoco, for example, began installing wind-powered electrical generators on offshore natural gas platforms in the North Sea. There also was growing interest in combining alternative energy sources with more conventional methods of power generation. In the U.S. there was interest in using the high-quality gas produced at urban landfills, and natural gas companies were looking into ways in which biomass gathered from land or aquatic plant material could be processed to produce gas energy. (ROBERT CORZINE)

See also Architecture and Civil Engineering; Transportation.

This article updates the *Macropædia* articles ENERGY CONVERSION; FOSSIL FUELS.

GAMES AND TOYS

There was no doubt that 1995 would go down in history as the year the Mighty Morphin Power Rangers refused to lie down and die. It would also be remembered as the year the toy industry tied the knot with the wider world of children's entertainment. Television and movies dominated the toy scene, and the industry's major manufacturers rushed to forge strategic alliances and partnerships with the so-called content providers, those companies responsible for creating the shows that continued to enthrall children the world over.

Sky Dancer flying fairies and the toys introduced in the film *Toy Story,* notably the action figures of Woody, the cowboy, and Buzz Lightyear, the spaceman, were runaway hits. The Power Rangers were supposed to have bowed out gracefully in 1995. Buoyed by a hit movie, however, they hung on to record yet another year of tremendous sales the world over.

In their bid to knock Bandai Co.'s Power Rangers off their lofty pedestal, two toy companies announced that they were going into show biz. The first, Hasbro, Inc., forged a strategic partnership with DreamWorks SKG, the new entertainment studio created by Steven Spielberg, Jeffrey Katzenberg (*see* BIOGRAPHIES), and David Geffen. Although the deal would not produce any toy products until at least 1997, few people were willing to bet against the fledgling studio's coming up with the entertainment and Hasbro's reaping the game and toy rewards. In the second deal a resurgent Lewis Galoob Toys, Inc., profitable again because of the hit girls concept Sky Dancers, announced that it had first option to market toys based on Fox Entertainment properties, beginning with a forthcoming television sci-fi series called "Space: Above and Beyond" and a full-length animated movie titled *Anastasia.*

Elsewhere in the U.S., *Star Wars* again hit the headlines. Hasbro's line of action figures and vehicles based on the famous trilogy of movies—remastered and rereleased on video during the year—raced out of stores as the year came to an end, and Lewis Galoob produced *Star Wars* miniature figures and vehicles under its successful Micro Machines brand. The race was now on between the two companies to land the master toy license for the eagerly awaited trilogy of new *Star Wars* movies to be made by George Lucas back-to-back in 1997 and set for release one every 12 months until the year 2000.

It was another movie that kept the Mattel Inc. show on the road in 1995. With Barbie sales still growing rapidly all over the world and the preschool Fisher-Price brand producing real results since its acquisition in 1993, Mattel confirmed its position as the world's largest toy maker and was able to sit back and bask in the reflected glory of the Disney movie *Pocahontas,* for which it was master toy licensee, producing dolls and action figures based on the Native American princess.

Saban Entertainment, producers of the Power Rangers programming, failed to emulate the success of its first major toy venture with the disappointing VR Troopers but ended the year with another new spin-off series called the Masked Rider. Again, Bandai was the master toy licensee. Other key licenses for the year included Batman, flying high on the back of the third and, in terms of toys, best movie to date; Spider Man, which made a triumphant return to television animation; and even Barbie, which got in on the act with a doll based on the television series "Baywatch," which proved to be even more successful in Europe than in the U.S.

In retailing, Toys "Я" Us still led the way around the world but faced stiff competition in Europe and in the U.S., where Wal-Mart Stores, Inc., increased its market share. Taking the attack to its competitors, Toys "Я" Us announced details of plans to open a new chain of Babies "Я" Us stores and a new megastore concept, the latter designed as the ultimate children's shop.

Toys "Я" Us also learned a valuable lesson in Europe when it took on shop employees unions in Sweden and found itself on the receiving end of a boycott by staff members who refused to participate in collective bargaining. Although finally resolved satisfactorily, the dispute did little to engender a warm feeling toward the U.S.-based multinational toy giant.

Computer games came back with a vengeance in 1995 after a lean 18-month period. PC-based products got a firm grip in households the world over, and Sega Enterprises launched its Saturn system and Sony its PlayStation platform. Nintendo Co. was to join the fray with its next-generation machine, the Ultra 64, in 1996.

The jury was still out on the likely impact of new computer games on traditional playthings. Market analysts would be brave indeed, however, if they were to predict the demise of traditional toys after having witnessed the phenomenal sales that powerful concepts like Cabbage Patch Kids, Teenage Mutant Ninja Turtles, and Mighty Morphin Power Rangers had recorded over the years. (JONATHAN M. SALISBURY)

GEMSTONES

Though the recession was beginning to lift in Europe and the U.S. by early 1995, the jewelry trade showed little increase in revenues and profits. Activity levels remained brisk in the salesroom, however.

De Beers Consolidated Mines Ltd., the South African concern controlling approximately 80% of the world trade in uncut diamonds, faced twin threats to its long domination of that market. In Angola maverick operators smuggled uncut stones out of the northern provinces and took advantage of a fragile cease-fire that had left the fate of diamond mining uncertain. In Russia a large number of diamonds were mined in the Sakha (Yakutia) area and sold through a centralized Russian organization. Though De Beers contracted in both instances to buy and market most of the stones, the firm feared that this uncontrolled production along with major alterations in the existing system of price maintenance could seriously affect the world diamond trade.

Vietnam continued to produce good-quality rubies and blue sapphires; Thailand exported some $300 million in rubies, almost all smuggled from Vietnam via Cambodia or Laos; and Myanmar (Burma) introduced high-quality rubies from its newly opened Mong Hsu mine. Pakistan and Tanzania both produced fine green peridot, while the latter also offered good-quality rubies from the Morogoro area and zircons in a variety of unusual colours.

A "diamond rush" in Canada lost impetus in August 1994 when RTZ/Kennecott indicated that the quality of diamonds in the Lac de Gras area of the Northwest Territories would be low-grade. Investors on the Canadian markets lost an estimated Can$500 million. In March 1995 De Beers abandoned exploration in Lac de Gras.

Top salesroom news included $16,548,750 paid for the 100.10-carat Star of the Season, the largest D-colour (top-colour), internally flawless pear-shaped diamond ever to be sold at auction; £4.7 million for a 19.66-carat pink diamond, a new record for that colour stone; £4 million for a 19.2-carat blue diamond; Sw F 1,131,000 for a 10.37-carat fancy heart-shaped intense yellow diamond; and Sw F 1,323,500 for a 12.34-carat cushion-shaped ruby from Myanmar.

Jewelry regulators remained undecided about a disclosure policy regarding gems that underwent an artificial colour-enhancement treatment. (MICHAEL O'DONOGHUE)

HOME FURNISHINGS

Furniture. If a single piece of furniture could serve as a symbol for an entire year, the 1995 furniture industry could be visualized in the Coda, an origami chair designed by Dakota Jackson for Lane. Jackson chose

POG Power

The game of POGs, which had been played since the 1920s when Hawaiian dairy workers at the Haleakala Dairy on Maui flipped milkcaps during their lunch breaks, was reinvented in 1991 by a Hawaiian schoolteacher who brought the old-fashioned rules to a new generation that by 1995 had raised the game's popularity to new heights and spawned a big business in the process. The cardboard disks that were coined POGs, an acronym formed from Haleakala Dairy's popular drink made from (P)assion fruit and (O)range and (G)uava juices, turned up with designs that ranged from revolting (psychedelic one-eyed skeletons) to religious (Pope John Paul II's image adorned one). The craze quickly swept from Hawaii to the mainland and across the Atlantic Ocean into Europe. Part of the game's charm was that its rules were spread by word of mouth. Children were playing the game with their own milkcaps long before toy companies had recognized the marketing potential of POGs. Now laminated and about the size of a poker chip, POGs were produced in hundreds of designs, with depictions of skulls or cartoon characters especially coveted and usually selling for a higher price, though most POGs cost just 25 cents each and could be purchased at specialized kiosks as well as toy and department stores. The McDonald's food chain even joined in, packaging POGs with their "Happy Meals" for children in the hope of appealing to the 4–14-year-olds who had caught the fever. The World POG Federation, a California-based firm that had bought the rights to the POG name in 1993, boasted profits exceeding $140 million in 1995.

Compared with the high-tech computer-generated games that evolved during the late 1980s and early '90s, POGs were conceptually simple and unique in the marketplace. To play, all a child needed was a stack of milkcaps; a slammer (also called a kini), which was slightly heavier and was used to turn the POGs; and a flat playing surface. Each player took an equal number of milkcaps, stacking them facedown, and used a slammer to strike the stack of POGs. Any milkcaps that were flipped over to show their emblems belonged to that player. Once each player had taken a turn, the one with the most POGs was the winner. Though these were the basic rules there were several variations, such as starting with the milkcaps faceup.

Partly as a result of the nature of the game, the disks quickly became collectibles. POGs, like stamps and sports cards before them, were the most hotly traded items of 1995. Children began to play for "keepsies" and built huge collections of their favourite POGs. Once milkcap trading had caught on, some school systems banned the game, maintaining that it contributed to rowdy play and disagreements between students. Many parents felt, however, that POGs had brought back to playtime an innocence that had been missing for quite some time. (SARA N. BRANT)

A POG at actual size

the name because *coda* is the musical term for a concluding section of a piece that serves to summarize what has gone before. The Coda chair, created by folding paper, demonstrated innovative technology and styling that looked forward to the 21st century.

Similarly, the industry as a whole embraced new technology and focused on the future. The major new design trends were strong colour instead of natural and neutral shades (exemplified by Craftique's painted mahogany and vivid upholstery from Preview, Directional, and Stanley) and "contemporized" traditional rather than the long-popular country and Americana (Lexington's Arnold Palmer Home Collection, Bassett's Bermuda Run, Drexel Heritage's Bel-Aire, and a most important group, Baker's Archetype Collection).

Computer capabilities were applied to advancing the industry instead of being used solely as a tool within the industry; Lexington produced the first CD-ROM press kit, and for the first time, a handful of retailers (Furnitureland South, Hickory, Furniture Mart) and manufacturers (Lexington, Hickory Chair, and Bernhardt, among others) established World Wide Web on-line services. The year also saw the first-ever technological conference, which focused on new strategies for the 21st century.

Another novel development was that major manufacturers were divesting instead of consolidating (LADD and Masco), and major retailers were buying and expanding (Heilig-Meyers, Haverty's, Rhodes). Case goods manufacturers expanded their lines by adding upholstery (Millennium and Stickley). AKTRIN, a furniture research company, foresaw continuing movement toward globalization and growth of ready-to-assemble furniture.

The American Furniture Manufacturers Association reported that economic indicators rose for the fourth year in a row. The trade group projected at the end of the third quarter of 1995 that revenues would reach $19,693,000,000, an increase of 3.4%. Exports were up by 8%. Business was soft, however, and there was much discussion about the decreasing margin of profit in light of discounting practices and speculation that this would be standard operating procedure for the future.

Furniture/Today's surveys of top manufacturers and stores showed no repositioning. Levitz ($1,036,000,000 in revenues) was still in the number one spot, followed by the burgeoning Heilig-Meyers ($697.2 million), with over 600 stores, Pier 1 Imports ($442.5 million), and Art Van ($385 million). Its survey of top manufacturers placed Masco ($1,945,000,000) first, with a 14.5% increase, followed by Broyhill/Lane ($1,072,700,000) and La-Z-Boy ($856.9 million).

Home-office and home-theatre furniture represented a growing share of the market; an environmentally conscious new material, water hyacinth, was introduced (Bernhardt and Hickory Chair); and a relatively new industry showcase in Tupelo, Miss., garnered attention. The four inductees into the Furniture Hall of Fame were Charles Tomlinson, Patrick Norton, Hyman Meyers, and Harold Braun. (ABBY CHAPPLE)

Housewares. In 1995 U.S. consumers spent more than $50 billion on housewares such as furnishings, appliances, kitchenware, storage and cleaning items, and personal-care products. As incomes declined, however, shoppers also made a point of looking for value; one-third of houseware purchases were made in discount stores. Consumers were willing to pay for cooking products that would last longer, especially those made of commercial-grade stainless steel and those having premium nonstick surfacing. Products that were designed for durability and space efficiency and served an "essential" purpose had the highest appeal, though such specialty items as bread makers, which evoked a sense of nostalgia, made a strong showing.

Though high-tech styling still had appeal, buyers were looking for dual-purpose and multifaceted products. The 46 million Americans who worked full- or part-time at home (the self-employed, moonlighters, and telecommuters) found a need for such desktop items as electric pencil sharpeners, calculators, and telephone answering machines. And, though the overall home consumption of coffee was declining, some 32 million adults at home were drinking more than five cups per day, spurring the market for specialty coffee products. Interest in cooking sparked sales of rotisserie grills and pressure cookers, while avid gardeners caused sales to blossom for seed-storage bins and ergonomically designed garden tools. Closet organization systems and space maximizers, including boxes, crates, and shelf dividers, remained popular. (KIRA GOULD)

The Coda chair by Dakota Jackson owes its dramatic shape and look to a metal frame covered with wicker in a diamond pattern. The chair, manufactured by Lane Venture, was one of the year's hottest items in home furnishings.
COURTESY OF LANE VENTURE

INSURANCE

Sharp price and product competition characterized the private insurance world in 1995, enhanced by company consolidations and restructurings to reduce expenses. Catastrophes of many kinds tested the loss-paying abilities of insurers, from devastating earthquakes in Japan and Mexico to an unusually large number of hurricanes in the Americas. The Caribbean islands were badly hit, and Hurricane Opal, with insured losses exceeding $2 billion, became the third worst windstorm loss in U.S. history. Only Hurricane Hugo, at $4 billion in 1989, and Hurricane Andrew, at $15 billion in 1992, were larger. The most severe flood losses ever occurred in California.

First-half results for U.S. property-liability insurers were quite favourable, with net income up 270%, surpluses up 17% (with large realized capital gains), and net underwriting losses down 39%. Catastrophes for the first nine months were costly, a record 29 totaling $5.7 billion in insured losses. After several decades of spiraling losses in workers' compensation, state reforms lowered costs by 5%.

Universal life insurance premiums in the U.S. for the first half of 1995 gained 18% over the same period in 1994, while variable life premiums were down an equal percentage. AIDS deaths curtailed improvements in longevity, but the $5 billion in AIDS-related life insurance claims paid up to 1995 were much less than earlier predictions, and health claims dropped to $450 million. For the first time in many years, general health care costs rose less than inflation.

The number one insurance issue noted in a survey by the Society of Insurance Research was the debate over banks in insurance. The issue continued to cause rifts between both businesses, and federal legislation proposed a five-year moratorium on actions by the comptroller of the currency. Banks in several states, including Florida and Connecticut, gained the right to sell annuities. New automated underwriting systems using credit-risk evaluations were gaining favour. Insurance companies led 10 industry groups surveyed in their use of telecommuting with personal computers and modems. At the same time, high-technology thieves were costing insurers $8 billion a year. Environmental-impairment liability insurance rates were down 5–20%, and the expanding market offered wider coverage options.

Term life insurance rates sank to all-time lows. Better information for policyholders was the aim of a new questionnaire recommended by Chartered Life Underwriters to determine whether existing policies should be canceled. Life insurers moved substantial surpluses to fund requirements for new "asset valuation reserves." In the U.K. telephone marketing of motor and household insurance increased competition. Some 25 companies, including subsidiaries of all the principal groups, were doing such business. The market leader, Direct Line, owned by the Bank of Scotland, was highly profitable.

Mergers continued at a record pace for insurers around the world. In the U.S. consolidations under way or completed included Metropolitan and New England Life, Massachusetts and Connecticut Mutual Life, Jefferson-Pilot and Alexander Hamilton Life, Manulife and North American Life, Phoenix Home Life and Duff and Phelps, CNA and Continental Insurance, Kemper and Zurich, Humana and Emphesys, and MetraHealth and United Health Care. A new insurer, Prudential Select Life, began to sell level-commission life insurance contracts. Risk Capital Holdings, a new reinsurer, traded publicly after raising $240 million. Two large reinsurers, General Re and Employers Reinsurance, bought German reinsurers. Cigna boosted its asbestos and environmental liability reserves by $1.2 billion following sizable increases by other companies, including Aetna Life and Casualty, Fireman's Fund, and Swiss Re America.

Lloyd's of London showed improving results in 1995, but turbulence continued. As the number of individual underwriting members and syndicates fell amid the market restructuring, corporate risk takers provided 23% of the coverage. Bermuda's international market readied for a renewed boom with a new premier and a vote rejecting independence.

In the U.S. bitter debates raged over how to contain the burgeoning costs of Medicare. Related issues included the projected savings of managed-care plans, cuts in benefits, medical malpractice liability limits, and tax changes. Extension beyond year-end of Superfund financing for environmental cleanup was also a major controversy involving insurers, centring on who should pay for future and retroactive costs. Life insurers rallied to oppose legislation that would have taken away the tax deductibility of interest on loans for company-owned policies. Insurance commissioners in various states weighed legislative action to alleviate problems such as new limits in California earthquake insurance, overwhelming growth in the Florida windstorm market, and insurance fraud. Tort reform bills made slow progress in some states, restricting claims for noneconomic, punitive, and product liability awards. The bills were attacked as limiting the right of injured consumers to redress.

Elsewhere, regulations aimed to protect insurance policyholders by promoting reasonable competition. The U.K., for example, sought to control growing national health service deficits by encouraging private insurance, which 11% of the population already had for medical and hospital expenses. (DAVID L. BICKELHAUPT)

MACHINERY AND MACHINE TOOLS

The world's leading producer of machine tools in 1994, the last year for which figures were available, was Japan, with a total output worth $6.7 billion, followed by Germany with $5.3 billion. The United States, at $3.7 billion, was third in total value. Italy was estimated to have built machine tools worth $2.3 billion, while the countries of Switzerland, China, Taiwan, and the United Kingdom were each reported to have produced machines worth a total in excess of $1 billion.

Of Japan's $6.7 billion machine-tool production in 1994, $5.4 billion was in metal-cutting machines and $1.3 billion was in metal-forming machines. Japan exported metal-cutting machines worth $3.2 billion and metal-forming machines worth $1.1 billion. Consumption by Japan (the value of machines installed in Japanese factories) totaled $2.7 billion in 1994.

Of the U.S. total of $3.7 billion in 1994, $2.4 billion, or approximately 65%, was accounted for by metal-cutting machines, and the rest, $1.3 billion, was attributed to machines used for metal forming. During the year the United States imported machine tools valued at $2.6 billion and exported machines worth $1.1 billion. The value of machine tools installed in U.S. factories in 1994 was $5.2 billion, a record high for installations by U.S. manufacturers. Imported machine tools accounted for 50% of the installations, which was also a historical high.

In 1994 the principal export markets for U.S.-built machine tools were Canada, China, and Mexico, with the United Kingdom, South Korea, Germany, and Japan also being important buyers. Exports to Canada more than doubled from a year earlier, to $380 million. Imports to the U.S. in 1994 were mainly from Japan, which sold three times as much in the United States as did second-place Germany. In third place was Switzerland, followed by Taiwan.

(JOHN B. DEAM)

MATERIALS AND METALS

Glass. Worldwide economic recession in 1993 and 1994 meant continuing difficult times for the glass industry overall in 1995. Slight growth was evident from the second half of 1994. While production capacity exceeded demand, price levels continued to be depressed, although less severely than in 1993. Currency fluctuations and inexpensive imports adversely influenced price levels and profitability in Europe. Although many could point to strong growth areas in 1994, most believed that the market in 1995 would show little, if any, change. In addition, the price of raw materials in 1995 was expected to increase, creating an inflationary situation within the industry.

Manufacturers of expensive crystal glassware were in recession much earlier and to a far greater extent than producers of low-priced noncrystal glassware. This sector was also the slowest to show signs of recovery. In the domestic sector this was partly because the Western world succumbed to cheap imports, particularly from the Far East and Eastern Europe.

Glass container production in Europe rose by 6% in 1994 (from a 2.4% decline in 1993). In response to the substantial overcapacity in Europe that had affected this sector in 1992, manufacturers took the steps necessary (closure of lines and even the shutdown of furnaces) to achieve a better balance between supply and demand. These efforts started to bear fruit in 1993, the overcapacity and stock situation having improved, but results were unsatisfactory overall. The situation improved in 1994, however, reflecting the sector's recovery. European production in 1994 stood at almost 25 million metric tons, and the industry employed over 208,000 workers.

Legislative matters continued to dominate in Europe, and in December 1994 the Directive on Packaging and Packaging Waste was finally adopted in the U.K. Among its many provisions, the directive called for packaging-recovery targets of 50–60% by June 2001; packaging-recycling targets of 25–45%, with a minimum of 15% for each packaging material, by 2001; concentration limits set for heavy metals in packaging and their release into the environment from incinerator emissions or from leaching in landfill from waste glass; and provision for a committee to decide on the identification and marking of packaging.

In the flat-glass sector, world demand was expected to increase annually by 5% until 1998. The key to this growth would be healthy expansion in the major end-use industries of construction and motor vehicles. The flat-glass market also benefited from demand created by an array of new products, such as solar control glass. Flat-glass demand remained steady in North America, Western Europe, and the developed nations of Asia and Oceania. In North America the market was benefiting from strong growth following the recession of 1991. In Western Europe and Japan flat-glass markets enjoyed a rebound. The industrializing nations of South America and the Pacific Rim (especially Brazil, China, and South Korea) provided the most rapid increases in flat-glass demand. In Eastern Europe the outlook was also favourable owing to an infusion of Western and Japanese capital and technology dedicated to upgrading outdated flat-glass capacity. New, upgraded float plants were already in operation in the Czech Republic, Hungary, and Poland.

(THERESA GREEN)

Ceramics. In 1994 the ceramics industry continued to show strong sales in products such as tile and sanitaryware, primarily because of the strength in building construction and in the overall economy. Worldwide sales of ceramic materials in 1994 were estimated at $88 billion by *Ceramic Industry*, with the U.S. market share at approximately one-third of the total. Because the survey did not include much of the production of China and the former Soviet bloc, however, its sales estimate was low. Ceramic Forum International, for example, estimated worldwide whiteware sales alone at $34 billion, three times the *Ceramic Industry* total.

The U.S. market for advanced ceramics in 1994 was estimated at $4.9 billion by the Business Communications Co. The market was expected to grow at a rate of 9.8% to $8.5 billion by the year 2000. It was further estimated that the electronic segment of the market would be 79% of the total, with advanced ceramic coatings 11% and advanced structural ceramics 10%.

Multilayer ceramic capacitors were gaining market share by improving their cost-effectiveness through a reduction in thickness, which increased their dielectric efficiency. Multilayer multicomponent (MLMC) electronic packages were also beginning to enter the market. This technology permitted several electronic components, such as capacitors and inductors, to be built into a multilayer ceramic package, thereby producing circuits for use in the large-volume consumer market. Fuzzy-logic circuits, for example, which had already been used in military equipment, could become available for use in consumer products since MLMCs significantly reduced the cost of such devices.

Porcelain enamel sales were flat in 1994 at approximately $6 billion. Because of customers' preferences in North America, the U.S. enjoyed an estimated 75% of the world market. The volume depended heavily on the sales of home appliances. U.S. sales of whitewares (including tile, dinnerware, sanitaryware, and electrical porcelain) remained strong in 1994, with a total of approximately $3 billion.

One of the interesting developments in ceramic fabrication was solid freeform fabrication, also known as rapid prototyping. This new technology allowed net-shaped ceramics to be formed directly from a computer-aided design (CAD) file. Several different techniques were being developed under contracts from the U.S. Department of Defense. One of the techniques was the fused deposition of ceramics, being developed jointly by AlliedSignal and the Center for Ceramic Research at Rutgers University, New Brunswick, N.J. This technique, by building the part one layer at a time, could be used to fabricate complex-shaped components of advanced ceramics such as silicon nitride engine components or advanced functional ceramic components. One of the advantages of the technique was that an experimental design could be fabricated from a CAD file in a few days. Using conventional technology, it might take several weeks to fabricate the same component.

Another interesting development in advanced ceramic research was bio-inspired processing. This research was based on discovering the way in which plants and animals designed and built materials and structures. For example, some animals were known to be capable of growing single oriented crystals of inorganic materials. Considerable progress had been made in the understanding of the organic and inorganic chemistry by which animals grow such crystals, opening up a whole new direction in advanced materials research that was expected to lead to exciting new materials and processes. (DALE E. NIESZ)

Rubber. Amid increasing demand for rubber products worldwide, numerous expansions began or were announced in 1995. Spurred by strong growth in the Asian and Pacific regions and by moderate growth in North America, worldwide consumption of rubber was expected to reach nearly 15 million metric tons, a 4% increase over 1994 levels.

China continued to pace the Asian region, with expansion projects for eight tire-manufacturing facilities and four new plants announced. Among these undertakings were a $120 million radial light truck and truck and bus tire plant by Nan Jing Kumho, which was to produce three million units a year; a $50 million tire plant in Shanghai by Cheng Shin Rubber; and a $120 million project by Tianjin Kumho Tire to modernize and add off-road radial capacity at its Tianjin facility. Sumitomo announced that it would build a $120 million passenger tire and golf ball facility in Indonesia with the capacity to produce 1.5 million tires annually. In Malaysia, Sime Tyres was expanding production by 66% for passenger radials.

Strong activity was under way in India as well, with four new plants and six expansions announced during the year. New plants were announced by Dunlop India (a $235 million facility with an annual capacity of 1.2 million passenger and truck tires), Modi Rubber (a $97 million truck tire plant with a capacity for 500,000 units a year), and Modistone (a $21 million truck tire plant). In addition, Apollo Tyres announced that it would build a $161 million passenger tire plant and purchase Premier Tyres, with plans to modernize the Premier facility and double its radial output. In Egypt Pirelli opened the largest truck tire plant in North Africa and the Middle East. The Alexandria facility cost $150 million and had a capacity of 350,000 tires annually.

The world's largest tire company, Michelin, announced that it would build two tire plants in France and undertake a number of expansions at facilities worldwide. Michelin also was negotiating a joint venture with Germany's Continental AG to manufacture low-end tires, with the alliance under review by the European Union. Goodyear, the third-ranked tire company in terms of sales, announced expansions for its facilities in Lawton, Okla., Quebec, and Luxembourg. The Luxembourg expansion was tied to an attempt to put the factory on a seven-day work schedule, a practice being adopted by tire manufacturers throughout Europe but one that was meeting resistance from unions and some governments. With funds nearly depleted from the strike against Bridgestone/Firestone and with the company hiring replacement workers, the United Rubber Workers of America called off its action and later announced a merger with the United Steelworkers of America.

Suppliers were active in 1995 in trying to alleviate tight supplies and in creating better processes. Metallocene catalysts, which enabled chemical engineers to create tailor-made elastomers based on ethylene or propylene, were having an impact. Two joint ventures, one involving Dow Chemical and Du Pont and the other joining Exxon and DSM, had metallocene chemistry as a basis. Another joint venture, between Akzo Nobel of The Netherlands and Monsanto and titled Flexsys LP, created the top supplier of rubber chemicals and instruments, with expected sales of $700 million for 1995.

There were significant additions to suppliers in the rubber industry in 1995. Bayer AG was constructing an accelerator plant and expanding antiozonant production by 50% at a South Carolina facility and was adding synthetic rubber capacity for polybutadiene at two North American sites and doubling hydrogenated nitrile rubber production in Orange, Texas. Goodyear announced a 10% increase in polybutadiene capacity at its Beaumont, Texas, facility, and Du Pont was increasing worldwide production of fluoroelastomers by 50%. Exxon increased the capacity for polyisobutylene at its Bayway, N.J., facility by 50%. Synthomer Chemie of Frankfurt, Germany, and Doverstrand of Harlow, England, merged to form a company with 200,000 metric tons of capacity for styrene-butadiene rubber (SBR) and natural latex. Taiwan Synthetic Rubber increased its thermoplastic elastomer (TPE) output to 100,000 metric tons, ChiMei opened a 120,000-metric ton TPE plant in China, and Taiwan Synthetic Rubber was building a 100,000-metric ton SBR plant in China.

Prices for natural rubber peaked during the first quarter of 1995 and plateaued during the fourth quarter. Synthetic rubber prices rose throughout the year as tightness for the major feedstocks was felt throughout the world. The International Natural Rubber Agreement (INRA), the UN-brokered pact to stabilize natural rubber prices and encourage continued cultivation, was renegotiated during 1995 but not ratified. Both producers and suppliers were debating the efficacy of the agreement.

(DONALD SMITH)

Plastics. Although economic growth continued in both the U.S. and Europe in 1995, with plastics somewhat outpacing the overall trend, the materials manufacturing industry was again taken by surprise by an unexpected reversal of the balance between supply and demand. The year began with acute shortages of the major thermoplastics and with prices at very high levels. By midyear, however, stability had largely returned, with improved product availability and rebuilt inventories. An upturn in prices was expected after the summer slowdown, but instead they fell sharply through the autumn as plastics converters, which had earlier had acute difficulty in passing on increased costs to endusers and now had adequate stocks, felt the weaker position of their suppliers.

This radical change in the business climate was especially noticeable in Europe. In May the Chinese government suddenly decided to effect a major cutback in plastics imports. The loss, even if temporary, of this important market served to upset the delicate global supply balance. At the same time, the pricing structure of the European industry was destabilized by internal currency fluctuations, while many of its products seemed comparatively expensive to the rest of the world. As a consequence, exports from Europe fell and imports diverted from the Asian-Pacific region rose.

Much was done in 1995 toward the continued rebuilding of the polymers industry in eastern Germany, technically outdated and environmentally unsound at the time of the country's reunification. By agreement with the German government, the U.S. company Dow Chemical was in the process of acquiring 80% of BSL Olefinverbund, an olefins/polyolefins complex formed by the merger of three major chemicals combines in the former East Germany. Another important move was the further development by BASF AG of its large Schwarzheide complex in the east for compounding engineering plastics.

The most interesting development in the materials sector during 1995 was the emergence of metallocene catalysts, which enable grades of polyolefins (both polypropylene and polyethylene) to be manufactured with more uniform polymer chain lengths. The molecular weight distribution is consequently narrower, which leads to improved properties—for example, in toughness, clarity, and processibility. Metallocene-based polyolefins were produced on a pilot scale by the Exxon Corp. in 1995, and several firms indicated their interest at the K'95 exhibition in Düsseldorf, Germany. It was predicted that by the year 2005 such materials would gain a 10% share of the market for polypropylene, now produced with the original Ziegler-Natta type of catalyst.

Among other significant advances in polymers technology shown at K'95 were cyclic olefin copolymers, developed jointly by Hoechst AG of Germany and Mitsui of Japan. Shell Chemical introduced aliphatic polyketones with characteristics unlike those of earlier ether-containing aromatic polyketones and displaying a broad range of engineering properties. BP Chemicals International Ltd. also entered the field, with a new pilot plant at Grangemouth, Scotland. In processing K'95 demonstrated the growing importance of injection moulding machines constructed without tiebars, which facilitated access to the mould area and allowed the use of smaller equipment. (ROBIN C. PENFOLD)

Advanced Composites. During 1995 polymer matrix composites (PMCs) continued to be the most widely used advanced composites. It was projected that by the end of the 20th century, the industry would produce 90,000 metric tons of PMCs worldwide, with gross sales totaling $5 billion. Although the high costs of raw materials had been faulted for the slow growth of PMCs, materials typically accounted for only 8–10% of the overall cost of composite components. In fact, the processing of composite components was the single largest contributor to overall costs. Thus, the development of innovative processing technology, along with affordable materials, could significantly reduce PMC costs. Promising processing technology for producing continuous fibre-reinforced components included advanced tow placement, pultrusion, resin-transfer molding, resin-film infusion, in situ consolidation, and out-of-autoclave curing. Whether sufficient reduction could be made to meet the demands of large-scale applications remained uncertain.

The low number of applications for metal matrix composites (MMCs), especially for continuously reinforced MMCs, continued to fail to stimulate the development and implementation of low-cost manufacturing methods. One exception was discontinuously reinforced aluminum. MMC specialty materials, such as titanium matrix composites, would enable significant advancements in high-performance applications, such as advanced gas turbine engine components. The use of MMCs would surge considerably if an automotive application (*e.g.,* a brake caliper, piston, or engine valve) became cost-effective. MMCs were forecast to develop into a billion-dollar industry by the end of the 20th century.

The development of ceramic matrix composites (CMCs), which had advanced significantly during the past 10 years, continued to lack a mature technical foundation. As a result, the industrial base had not reached the level at which competitive market forces prevailed. CMCs were being developed for critical hot section components that could reliably operate in severe environments beyond the capability of existing metallic materials. The market for such a material was not expected to be large, but CMCs would permit important new products, such as highly efficient heat exchangers and high-performance turbine engines. A few large companies had decided to commit substantial resources to CMC development to commercialize existing technology. The market for CMCs was projected to develop to $500 million by the end of the 20th century. (ROBERT E. SCHAFRIK; THOMAS F. MUNNS)

Iron and Steel. Steel consumption in the U.S. in 1994 increased by 14% from the previous year to reach 103 million metric tons, a level not achieved since 1974. With domestic steel producers operating close to capacity, the result was a rise in imports, from 11 million to 27 million metric tons. Demand from the automotive sector was particularly strong, reinforced by the fact that booming demand for vehicles was being met increasingly by cars produced in the U.S.

In Western Europe the automotive sector also led the revival in several countries, although the construction sector remained weak. Vehicle exports were an important element in the U.K. recovery, and France and Spain tried to encourage the purchase of new cars. The German recovery was export-driven, with the machinery sector benefiting from strong Asian demand. Apparent consumption of steel products in the European Union recovered by 13% from the low 1993 figure, to 108 million metric tons. The EU's production of crude steel rose by 5%. Turkish steel use suffered a setback owing to that country's economic difficulties.

In Eastern and Central Europe 1994 brought an 8% recovery in steel consumption, after years of precipitous decline, which continued in the countries of the former Soviet Union, where steel consumption dropped to around 43 million metric tons.

The Japanese economy grew by less than 1% in 1994, and steel consumption remained depressed. The high yen was a handicap for Japan's steel-using manufacturing sector, which now tended to build capacity outside Japan. Although the residential-construction sector was firm, the civil engineering sector remained weak.

Taiwan's residential sector was in a downturn, and there was slippage in civil engineering contracts, but elsewhere in South

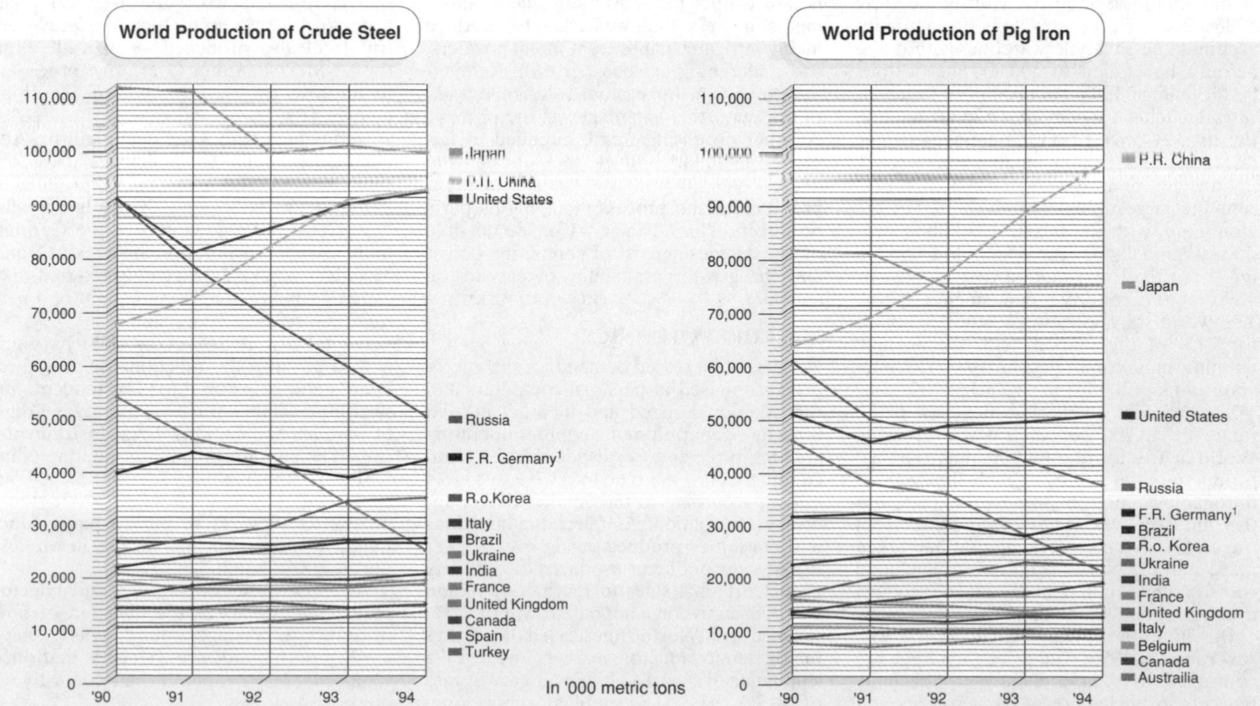

[1] Includes the former East Germany from 1991.
Source: *International Iron and Steel Institute*

east Asia strong growth continued in steel demand, notably in South Korea, which registered 20% growth.

Authorities in China let it be known that inventories of steel were very high, and imports were expected to fall to around 10 million to 12 million metric tons. As it turned out, almost 25 million metric tons were imported, and apparent consumption remained above 100 million metric tons. It became clear that there had been a considerable buildup of inventories.

Australia and New Zealand saw an 11% growth in steel consumption, and the growth in steel consumption in Latin America averaged 14%, with Mexico posting a 25% rise. Before the financial crisis began in December 1994, Argentina and Brazil experienced increases in steel demand of 21% and 14%, respectively. (ANTHONY TRICKETT)

Light Metals. For the light metals, 1995 proved to be a year of recovery. The group continued to be dominated by aluminum, with 1995 world production of 15 million metric tons, followed by magnesium at 300,000 metric tons, titanium at 33,000 metric tons (U.S. ingot), and beryllium at 6,800 metric tons.

The aluminum industry had largely recovered from the oversupply that began in 1992 with a massive surge in exports from the Commonwealth of Independent States, whose internal markets, particularly in the defense industry, had collapsed. In early 1994 the market price of aluminum fell to its lowest level in history (when adjusted for inflation), at $1,035 per metric ton. In response, the governments of the world's six major producing regions (Australia, Canada, the European Union, Norway, Russia, and the U.S.) agreed to reduce production for a two-year period, and by early 1995 the price of aluminum had recovered, to $2,100 per metric ton.

Speculation on the London Metal Exchange (LME) complicated the problems in the aluminum industry. During the early 1990s, 2.6 million metric tons of aluminum accumulated in LME warehouses, but the amount had fallen to 500,000 metric tons by the end of 1995. As producers began to restart smelter capacity that had been idled, the market price of aluminum settled into the range of $1,700 per metric ton.

Cans for beverages continued to represent the largest single product market for aluminum, with the nearly 100 billion produced annually in the U.S. alone utilizing more than two million metric tons, or 50%, of the country's new smelter metal. The world transportation sector accounted for 24% of the market, with the average amount in automobiles in 1995 reaching about 90 kg (200 lb) per vehicle.

The price of magnesium hovered in the range of $3,700 per metric ton in 1995. World figures for titanium ingot and sponge production were not available because of unreliable data from some producers, but the industry was clearly recovering from the cuts in defense spending that had taken place earlier. Newer applications included roofs, domes, golf clubs, tennis racquets, eyeglasses, and watch cases.

Beryllium production remained in a narrow range in 1995. The price ($352 per kg) continued to restrict its use to speciality markets in nuclear reactors, aerospace, alloys, and electronic components.

(GEORGE J. BINCZEWSKI)

Metalworking. Metal parts sales continued to increase in 1995 because of the ongoing demand for consumer goods. Capital equipment production and a weak U.S. dollar kept the demand for parts sturdy, the supply tight, and lead times lengthy. Mill shipments of castings, forgings, powder metal parts, and extrusions, which had improved 9% in 1993 and 11% in 1994, were expected to grow 2% in 1995. Open market sales of ferrous and nonferrous metal castings rose 5%, to almost 9.1 million tons. Sales of forged steel, aluminum, titanium, and high-temperature alloys grew by almost 10% in 1994, to 1,250,000 tons, and they grew another 5% in 1995. Similar growth was seen in extruded aluminum shapes, an industry that was benefiting from the adoption of technology that previously had been developed for military aircraft. Much of the growth in powder metal shipments was due to the expanding use of powder metal bearing caps and powder forged connecting rods by the three major U.S. automobile manufacturers. The auto industry's consumption of steel for frame and sheet metal parts was expected to increase by at least 60,000 tons in 1996, following the continuing trend toward upsizing, strengthening, enhancing comfort, and providing greater performance.

It was announced that a consortium of 32 steel companies would invest $20 million to construct ultralight auto bodies, demonstrating steel's continuing viability in the automotive industry. In a move that reflected the auto industry's shift from cast iron to wrought steel drivetrain components, International Crankshaft was doubling its steel crankshaft forging capacity to 1.5 million per year at its Georgetown, Ky., plant. Alcoa was building a $32.5 million facility in Hungary to produce forged aluminum wheels. Cerro Copper Tube Co. combined its cold pilger rolling mills with a 4,000-ton extrusion press, which produced defect-free hollow copper tubes. Metal injection molding, a process that was used to produce highly intricate shapes from metal powders, was undergoing explosive growth. Remington Arms Co., for example, designed a .22 rifle around the advantages of the process. Another promising trend, intended to improve the quality and the speed of delivery of new components, was the use of rapid prototyping and process modeling by parts producers. This advance was made possible by the decreasing cost of computing power and the greater availability of easy-to-use software. (HOWARD A. KUHN)

MICROELECTRONICS

Because of increased demand for the microprocessors used in personal computers and the additional speed and memory needed for a new generation of computer operating systems, projected worldwide sales of semiconductors in 1995 rose by 43.7% to $146.4 billion, according to the Semiconductor Industry Association. As telecommunications and consumer products made ever-greater use of semiconductor products, the industry expected global sales to reach $261 billion by 1998, an average annual growth of 21%.

Once again North America led the world's major semiconductor markets, with 1995 shipments of over $47 billion, a growth rate of 40.2%. The U.S. supplied almost one-third of the world's supply; the Japanese supplied another 27.7%, up 38% from 1994. The Asian Pacific market, including South Korea, Taiwan, and Singapore, replaced the European market as the third largest provider, with a growth rate of more than 57%. The two largest growth products were memory at a 66.7% growth rate and microprocessors at a 41.4% rate.

To keep pace with this increasing demand, chip manufacturers were planning modern plants. Motorola, Inc., planned to spend over $700 million to build a wholly owned semiconductor plant in the city of Tianjin, China. The 280,000-sq m (3 million-sq ft) plant would manufacture chips used in cellular phones, pagers, personal computers, and other electronic products produced in China. A similar plant was planned for Hong Kong to serve the Southeast Asian market. Motorola also announced plans to build a $3 billion plant near Richmond, Va., to produce its PowerPC chip and was considering a joint venture with General Motors' Delco Electronics Corp. for a $1 billion plant in Israel. Intel Corp. anticipated spending $3.2 billion for plants in Ireland and Malaysia in addition to a scheduled expansion in Israel. IBM expected to spend $1 billion to expand its existing chip facility in Essonnes, France, and Japanese firms Hitachi, Ltd., and Mitsubishi, Ltd., planned to spend $400 million and $3 million, respectively, for expanding facilities in Irving, Texas, and Durham, N.C.

In late 1994 Intel had reluctantly admitted that its new Pentium chip had a problem in its floating point unit. After IBM and other computer manufacturers decided to replace the chips, Intel finally agreed in January 1995 to replace defective chips at a cost estimated to be $475 million. Surviving that setback, the Pentium quickly replaced the 486 family of chips in new computers. Intel also introduced the next-generation chip, the Pentium Pro (formerly known by the code name P6), in 1995. This new chip, priced under $1,000, would be available at speeds up to 200 MHz and had 5.5 million transistors—80% more than its predecessor. Intel also produced an upgrade chip, the 83-MHz Pentium OverDrive processor to improve the performance of 486 chips by over 50%.

In the meantime, Intel's competitors, Advanced Micro Devices, Inc., and NexGen, Inc., merged and planned to produce a Pentium Pro alternative by the late 1990s.

In October IBM, Motorola, the German multinational corporation Siemens AG, and Toshiba Corp. of Japan confirmed that they were discussing joint development of a new random-access memory chip.

Digital Signal Processors (DSP) continued to advance the functionality of add-on boards and chips used for fax, modem, answering machine, graphics, sound, and digital wireless applications. Texas Instruments, Inc. (TI), announced a 32-bit floating point DSP for under $10. TI also reached an agreement with Motorola to share technology to allow TI to embed pager functionality into microchips for use in wireless portable computers.

Another challenge for the semiconductor industry in 1995 was the question of how to reduce the voltage requirements of chips used in portable devices. Devices that once required 12 v to operate had come to require 3.3 v or less.

MPEG-2 (Moving Picture Experts Group), a digital video compression-decompression standard for high-definition television (HDTV) and other high-speed-transmission applications, had been imbedded into chips that would be used in HDTV and other digital video applications, in the future.

Smart cards, credit card-sized microcontrollers with memory, were being used to provide added features, such as encryption, to cellular technology. These cards, which were also used for phone cards and identity cards, were already popular in Europe and were expected to grow in popularity in the U.S. (THOMAS E. KROLL)

MINING

The mining industry enjoyed a good year in 1995. The economic recovery that had got under way in the United States in 1994 continued, Europe staged a strong recovery, and Japan's recession proved to be shallower than anticipated. Consequently, the demand for mineral commodities held up well, outpacing production in some sectors, and this helped to reduce surplus stocks substantially. The strength of the demand also helped offset the debilitating impact on the market, experienced in recent years, of large-volume, low-priced exports of metals and minerals from China and Russia.

Although such exports continued, in Russia—for the first time since the collapse of the former Soviet Union—there were signs that the economy was beginning to recover. In China rapid economic growth made it an increasingly important commodity importer as well as an exporter. Both countries were seeking to attract foreign investment into their mineral sectors, as were many of the former Soviet Asian republics. For international mining companies, the opportunities had become truly global.

Exploration. Activity continued at a high level in the less developed countries in 1995, particularly in South America, where Chile and Peru headed the list. Argentina, a comparatively new entrant in mineral exploration, also proved a major attraction in the first nine months of 1995, when more than 180,000 m (590,500 ft) of exploration drilling were completed, mainly for base and precious metals. Only three years earlier, prior to new mining legislation, the annual total drilled by private companies had been near 7,000 m (23,000 ft). A welcome development in Brazil was the long-awaited revision of the 1988 legislation that had restricted foreign mining activity.

West African countries, including Ghana, Guinea, Burkina Faso, and Mali, proved popular destinations for exploration teams, although in these countries the focus was almost entirely on gold. Indonesia, too, attracted interest, much of the excitement being directed toward Irian Jaya, where the American company Freeport-McMoRan Copper & Gold Inc. was exploiting one of the largest and richest copper and gold deposits ever discovered. The U.K.-based mining giant RTZ purchased a substantial interest in the company during 1995. In addition to metals, Indonesia's coal resources continued to attract much exploration activity. The country had rapidly emerged as a significant coal producer, with three-quarters of the production being exported.

Among the developed countries, Australia's gold-exploration boom continued, but Canada stole the limelight; initial reports late in 1994 of a significant discovery of nickel, copper, and cobalt in Labrador were rapidly confirmed, and the deposit at Voisey Bay proved to be the biggest base metals find in Canada in decades. Previously ignored by the exploration fraternity, Labrador was witnessing one of Canada's biggest-ever claim-staking rushes. The activity largely eclipsed the diamond rush in the Northwest Territories.

Within the less developed countries, the competition to attract risk capital for exploration was intense. Some 75 nations had revised or introduced new mineral legislation tailored to attract the foreign investor, and during 1995 the Philippines and Pakistan were significant additions to the list. The wealth of mineral opportunities evident, particularly in the Southeast Asian and the Pacific regions, was one of the reasons RTZ and its Australian associate, CRA, announced in October their intention to merge. The combined group would have a market capitalization in excess of $20 billion.

Few countries continued to insist on majority government equity participation in mining projects, and several, like Peru, moved farther along the road to privatization of state-owned mining companies. A new entrant in 1995 was Indonesia's state-owned PT Tambang Timah, the world's largest tin mining company. The government chose to retain 65% ownership and sold the balance to domestic and international investors.

In Brazil, however, a government plan to privatize the country's mining giant Companhia Vale do Rio Doce met with opposition. The company not only was the world's largest iron ore miner and a substantial producer of other important minerals, such as bauxite and gold, but also operated railways and had its own oceangoing fleet of ore carriers. Its operations were efficient and highly profitable, and for many Brazilians selling the company was an emotional issue.

Privatization was not on the agenda for the world's largest copper producer, Codelco in Chile. Approval was being sought, however, for the company to undertake new mining projects in joint venture with private partners on ground it held.

State-owned copper companies in central Africa had long been starved for investment. Production was falling, and many saw privatization as the solution to the problem. Zambia Consolidated Copper Mines urgently needed funding in order to embark on a new deep mine project, as reserves at its existing mines would be depleted by the end of the decade. The government had indicated its wish to privatize, but the timing and form remained unclear. In Zaire economic and political problems continued to deter investor interest.

In South Africa the government was giving priority to the minerals sector, and new mineral legislation was being prepared. Mineral rights ownership remained a key issue. The government was concerned that ground held by the major mining houses was not being explored fully. The mining companies contended that the transfer of mineral rights to the state would severely dent investor confidence. Analysts predicted that the gold industry in South Africa was heading for one of its worst years ever, with output dropping 10% from 1994.

In West Africa mineral sands mining in Sierra Leone was halted at the end of January when the operations were overrun by rebels opposed to the government. The mine, operated by Sierra Rutile, Ltd., was the world's largest producer of the titanium mineral rutile. The operation remained closed throughout the year, and the world price of rutile rose by 50%.

Indexes of Production, Mining and Mineral Commodities

(1980 = 100)

	1990	1991	1992	1993	1994
Mining (total)					
World[1]	100.2	97.8	101.4	101.3	108.2
Developed market economies[2]	106.3	107.3	107.6	100.2	113.4
North America[3]	96.2	95.5	94.2	93.0	95.7
European Economic Community[4]	90.4	91.9	91.7	92.9	99.9
Less developed market economies[5]	96.0	91.3	97.1	96.6	104.6
Coal					
World[1]	100.2	99.0	95.5	91.5	90.5
Developed market economies[2]	95.7	93.1	88.1	82.8	81.2
North America[3]	129.2	124.7	119.3	117.7	128.1
European Economic Community[4]	75.9	72.5	67.1	58.7	50.9
Less developed market economies[5]	181.4	203.2	226.2	247.2	256.2
Petroleum and natural gas					
World[1]	93.6	90.8	95.8	97.1	105.5
Developed market economies[2]	99.0	103.5	106.9	111.9	122.3
North America[3]	80.6	81.3	80.6	80.8	82.3
European Economic Community[4]	101.3	108.5	114.0	125.3	146.8
Less developed market economies[5]	91.4	85.8	91.4	91.2	98.9
Metals					
World[1]	136.4	136.9	137.8	135.3	135.2
Developed market economies[2]	148.1	147.7	148.1	146.8	144.2
North America[3]	139.8	142.0	144.1	140.1	135.6
European Economic Community[4]	72.0	69.5	64.9	49.3	47.3
Less developed market economies[5]	116.0	118.3	119.9	115.1	119.5
Manufacturing (total)	127.6	126.2	125.1	125.2	130.9

[1] Excluding Albania, China, former Czechoslovakia, North Korea, former U.S.S.R., Vietnam, and former Yugoslavia.
[2] Includes North America (Canada and the United States), Europe (excluding former Czechoslovakia and the European countries of the former U.S.S.R.), Australia, Israel, Japan, New Zealand, and South Africa.
[3] Canada and the United States.
[4] Now European Union; includes Belgium, Denmark, France, Germany, Greece, Ireland, Italy, Luxembourg, The Netherlands, Portugal, Spain, and the United Kingdom.
[5] Includes Caribbean nations, Central and South America, Africa (excluding South Africa), Asia (excluding China, North Korea, Israel, Japan, Vietnam, and Asian countries of the former U.S.S.R.), and Oceania (excluding Australia and New Zealand).

Commodities. The recovery in demand for metals and minerals that had developed in 1994 continued into 1995, and although the base metals markets lost some of their lustre when speculative interest by investment funds faltered, the recovery from economic recession in Europe and elsewhere ensured that consumer demand was sustained. Demand outpaced supply for a number of metals, and the huge surpluses accumulated during the recessionary years continued to decline, thereby ensuring that prices for most base metals stayed high in the first eight months of the year. The average prices received by some copper and nickel producers were as much as 40% above those received in the equivalent period in 1994.

Nickel and other steel-alloying metals enjoyed good demand. Molybdenum was a spectacular performer. The price of the metal had been trading at close to historic lows for much of the 1990s, when many mines were forced to close. A severe squeeze on supplies saw prices spiral in early 1995, however, and the average price for the year was expected to be double that of 1994. The demand for stainless steel showed signs of faltering during the final quarter of 1995, with oversupply in the Asian market and with consumers in North America and Europe beginning to reduce their stocks.

The demand for aluminum in 1995 was such that the high stock levels that had severely depressed prices only two years before depleted rapidly. This called into question whether the voluntary two-year agreement reached in early 1994 between several major producing countries, including Russia, to cut annual production was still necessary.

There were similar sentiments in the tin market. Since the price of tin collapsed 10 years earlier, leading producing countries had agreed on annual export quotas as a means of limiting supplies and reducing surplus stocks. Prices improved markedly in 1995, and producers agreed to end the export quota system in June 1996.

Despite strong demand, zinc prices continued to languish against a background of high stocks and large amounts of metal reaching the market from China. Nevertheless, substantial new production capacity was planned. One of the largest new mines, McArthur River in Australia's remote Northern Territory, came on stream in September. The project cost $A 250 million and would produce 160,000 metric tons of zinc annually over a mine life of 30 years. The mine was operated by MIM Holdings, which had discovered the deposit 30 years earlier. In Queensland, BHP announced that it would develop a major silver-zinc-lead mine at Cannington, and CRA was expecting a favourable decision for its huge Century zinc deposit.

In the precious metals sector, gold had a quiet year in 1995. The price showed little movement, but at around $380 an ounce, compared with an average cost to produce it near $240 an ounce, it still offered one of the best and most rapid investment returns. South Africa remained the largest gold producer, and it contributed about 25% of the world output.

Because of platinum's growing use as a catalyst to reduce exhaust emissions in motor vehicles, the demand for it rose to record levels in 1994, and in 1995 the demand rose again, albeit less sharply. South Africa and Russia continued to dominate the supply. In South Africa two companies, Lonrho and Gencor, merged their platinum interests to rival Rustenburg as the world's largest producer. Russia's ability to maintain the production of platinum at a high level was doubted in some quarters, and much of its sales in 1995 were believed to have been from government stocks. The size of the stockpile, however, remained a closely guarded secret.

The South African company De Beers Consolidated Mines maintained a monopoly on the marketing of uncut diamonds through its Central Selling Organisation, which bought about 80% of the world's production, but its ability to control supply and hence prices was becoming more difficult. Its marketing agreement with Russia, the source of 25% of the world's diamond production by value, came under strain. The agreement came up for renewal at the end of 1995, and there was uncertainty whether it would be extended. Russia was seeking better terms, and during 1995 substantial quantities of Russian rough diamonds, estimated to be worth as much as $800 million, "leaked" onto the world markets outside the De Beers' marketing channel.

Because of record steel output, the demand for iron ore saw world exports reach a new peak in the first half of 1995, with imports into Japan during the period jumping by 10%. In 1994 world iron ore production and exports both rose by 30 million metric tons to 970 million and 430 million metric tons, respectively. Australia and Brazil remained the dominant exporters, providing almost 60% of the total.

In contrast, a report published in 1995 by the International Energy Agency (IEA) noted that the coal trade was essentially local. The proportion traded internationally amounted only to about 11% but was expected to increase significantly. The Asian and Pacific markets would grow in importance, and the IEA suggested that by the year 2010 the region could account for 70% of the world's imports, or some 500 million metric tons. Colombia, Venezuela, and possibly Vietnam could all post significant export increases, but Australia should remain the dominant supplier.

In 1994, after four years of decline, world coal consumption staged a modest recovery, and production rose by nearly 2% to 3.2 billion metric tons, with China and the United States consuming 50% of the output. The improved consumption appeared to have been maintained during 1995.

Safety and the environment. Cave-ins, rockslides, flooding, and methane gas explosions all took their toll during 1995. One of the worst mine accidents occurred in May at the Vaal Reefs gold mine in South Africa, where more than 100 people died when an underground locomotive plunged down a shaft.

The safe storage and disposal of waste material continued to be one of the industry's principal environmental problems. Conventionally, the liquid waste, or tailings, from mining had been impounded in ponds behind a retaining wall made from compacted earth and rock. When a tailings dam at a large gold mine in Guyana failed in 1995, the local river was polluted by some four billion litres (about a billion gallons) of cyanide-bearing waste, and although the cyanide concentrations were low and were rapidly diluted, the incident was quickly labeled an environmental disaster. The mine remained closed pending investigations into the cause and appropriate remedial action.

In Papua New Guinea a large copper and gold mine located in a remote mountainous area where construction of a tailings dam proved impracticable had dumped waste into the local river for years. Landowners campaigned for compensation for the pollution and damage caused, and in a new departure an Australian legal firm launched a $A 4 billion damages suit on behalf of the landowners against the Australian majority owner of the operation.

The threat, perceived or real, of environmental pollution had halted development of one of Canada's largest unworked copper deposits, in northwestern British Columbia, in 1994. The provincial government halted the project by the simple expedient of converting the area into a national park. In 1995 the project operators received compensation.

During 1995 the environment was also an issue in Madagascar. Plans by a multinational company to mine mineral sands for titanium in an ecologically unique coastal area spurred strong opposition from outside the country.

Technology. Much of the new technology being developed within the mining industry had environmental benefits. In mineral processing the use of solvents to extract copper directly from ore, which obviated the need for smelting, was gaining in popularity, while in the gold sector the use of bacterial cultures to recover the metal without recourse to roasting became a reality. Bio-oxidation to recover gold was being employed at a large new project at the Ashanti mine in Ghana, and in South Africa, Gencor, the company that pioneered the process, was developing the technology to process nickel ores.

It also was thought that biological techniques might be used to clean up old mine sites. The use of bacteria to prevent or tackle the problem of acid mine drainage was being investigated, as was the use of certain types of plants able to absorb metals for the extraction of heavy metals from waste dumps. (ROGER ELLIS)

See also Earth and Space Sciences.

This article updates the *Macropædia* article Extraction and Processing INDUSTRIES.

PAINTS AND VARNISHES

For paint manufacturers 1995 marked a return to economic equilibrium. In the U.S., after a record year in 1994, paint output rose 2.6% during the first half of 1995. In Europe demand from the automotive and building markets boosted volume, though not necessarily profits. Asia and the Pacific regions, however, continued on their course of hearty growth, with China the main magnet for foreign investment. Only the Japanese paint industry remained in the doldrums.

Raw material prices exploded everywhere. The price of xylene jumped by 60% in January alone, and titanium dioxide prices soared as well. Prices peaked in the first quarter of the year but began to level off thereafter. Paint prices failed to keep pace with those of raw materials. Shortages of some chemicals reached crisis proportions. Methyl methacrylate was tight, as was phthalic anhydride.

In the U.S. a contest between Sherwin-Williams and ICI ensued over the Grow Group. By raising Sherwin-Williams' $320 million bid to $350 million, ICI won Grow and thus became the fifth largest paint company in the U.S. Sherwin-Williams, in turn, made several smaller purchases—FLR Paints, White Lightning Products, Con-Lux Coatings—before acquiring Pratt & Lambert, the company that itself had taken over United Coatings only a year earlier. Not only did this strengthen Sherwin-Williams' architectural coatings and distribution businesses on the East Coast, but it also gave it a stake in general industrial, powder, and aerospace coatings.

There were two notable acquisitions in Europe. The merger of Kalon with Total's paint interests brought Kalon, Johnstone's, Manders, and Windeck in the U.K. and Euridep and La Seigneurie in France under a single umbrella. ICI purchased PPG's architectural coating business in France. In the Pacific Rim expansion proceeded via joint ventures. Nippon Paint (Japan), PPG (U.S.), and ICI (U.K.) were among the companies establishing paint factories in China, a second plant in the case of ICI. ICI also moved into the markets of the Philippines and Pakistan. Akzo Nobel entered the Vietnamese market by acquiring a 51% share in Sapina Denzo Saigon Co. Ltd.

The course of new technologies in paints appeared more uncertain in 1995. Earlier projections of the growth of waterborne and other coatings that complied with environmental regulations underwent a radical revision. A new European study predicted that as much as 53% of industrial coatings would still be solvent-based by the year 2004. The U.K. industry reported that compliant products were 5 to 10 years away. Investments in water-based automotive coatings continued, with Herberts and BASF pointing the way. At the same time, voluntary initiatives acquired a new urgency. A program initiated by the International Paint and Printing Ink Council was being developed both in Europe and in the U.S. to ensure consistency in what had become a global industry. (HELMA JOTISCHKY)

PHARMACEUTICALS

In the United States in 1995, the pharmaceutical industry faced reform in the private sector driven by the growth of managed care. Moreover, Congress planned to trim spending on Medicare and Medicaid. The industry seemed to be entering an era of increasing pressures.

Meanwhile, the pharmaceutical industry supported congressional calls to rein in the U.S. Food and Drug Administration (FDA). Some industry groups called for the end of the FDA or a ban on its regulation of the promotion of pharmaceuticals. The Pharmaceutical Research and Manufacturers of America proposed measures that would speed review of new drugs and allow companies more freedom to disseminate product information.

In Europe, however, pressure on the industry grew. Germany and France cut consumption and prices, and only Britain adopted pro-industry policies. Still, regulatory relief loomed as the European Medicines Evaluation Agency set up shop in London. Worldwide, the industry began to face the rise of new health threats such as antibiotic-resistant diseases.

Despite tightening market conditions throughout the year, the pharmaceutical industry accomplished a major rebound on the U.S. stock market by climbing an average of 44% by November. Leading companies posted healthy earnings, with growth and profits in the double digits, thanks to a combination of restructuring, partnering, and new products.

The industry pursued two new approaches—vertical partnering and regionalization—to the problem of adapting to a customer base that showed ever-greater power and complexity. Rather than acting merely as suppliers of medicines, companies offered managed-care organizations (MCOs) additional services and collaborations, including evidence of their products' cost-effectiveness, educational programs for patients and professionals, and risk-sharing contracts that compensated companies on a per-patient basis. To get closer to their customers, large companies created regional or strategic business units. Companies such as Bayer of Germany also began to apply the U.S. model to their global operations.

Some companies encountered problems over their mergers with pharmacy benefits management organizations (PBMs) and over other vertical initiatives. Medco settled with 17 states that sued the PBM for favouring products of its owner, Merck. MCOs also remained skeptical of new "disease-management" programs offered by pharmaceutical companies or by separate entities such as Lilly's Integrated Disease Management subsidiary. Zeneca went beyond offering such programs into actual care with its $195 million purchase of oncology company Salick Health Care, Inc.

Backed by a weak dollar, European acquisitions of U.S. companies led industry consolidations. Germany's Hoechst AG bought Marion Merrell Dow for $7 billion, and Switzerland's Roche Holding AG completed its absorption of Syntex Corp. Upjohn and Pharmacia formed a $7 billion transatlantic merger. Marrying two British companies, Glaxo purchased Wellcome for about $15 billion. Companies also made many smaller investments to capture new technologies and markets. Sandoz AG entered a host of alliances in gene therapy, and Bayer repurchased its U.S. aspirin line and extended an alliance with the generics company Schein. (WAYNE KOBERSTEIN)

PHOTOGRAPHY

In 1995 two photo industry giants, Eastman Kodak and Fuji Photo Film, clashed over alleged marketing restrictions in Japan. Kodak filed a petition in May under section 301 of the Trade Act of 1974 and requested that the U.S. government investigate and remedy "decades of anti-competitive trade practices in the Japanese market for consumer photographic film and paper." The charge of abuses included price-fixing, anticompetitive rebate schemes, and the "systematic denial of access to essential distribution channels." According to Kodak, the practices particularly involved Fuji and at times were conducted with the knowledge and participation of the Japanese government. Fuji vigorously denied the charges and blamed Kodak's "own poor business decisions in Japan" for the company's less-than-10% share of the Japanese film and photographic paper market, compared with Fuji's 70%. The U.S. government promised an investigation, and as the year ended, both parties were aggressively defending their positions with barrages of documentation.

Photographic manufacturers continued efforts to exploit the explosively growing field of digital imaging with 35-mm still-camera models adapted for electronic image capturing. Canon in conjunction with Kodak introduced its EOS DCS 3 in three configurations: colour, black and white, and infrared. It linked its multifeatured Canon EOS-1N single-lens-reflex (SLR) camera with Kodak's DCS digital-imaging camera back and a high-resolution (1.3 million-pixel) charge-coupled device (CCD) imaging sensor. Chinon introduced an ES-3000 digital still camera with autofocus and a 3 × zoom lens; it was available in three models delivering a range of resolution from normal (76,800 pixels) to superfine (179,200 pixels). Kodak's relatively low-priced DC 40 digital camera was a compact electronic "snapshooter" for real estate agents and other commercial users. It provided a resolution of 381,024 pixels, had a speed corresponding to ISO 84 (*i.e.,* approaching ISO 100 film), and stored up to 48 images.

Camera design for conventional photography showed little that was strikingly novel. Canon introduced the EOS-1N RS, which was claimed to provide the fastest continuous shooting speed—10 frames per second—of any 35-mm autofocus SLR as well as the shortest shutter-release lag time (six milliseconds) while maintaining constant visibility through the viewfinder. Those superlatives were achieved with the aid of a fixed pellicle mirror, which passed some of the light to the film plane and reflected the rest to the viewfinder—a method used for an earlier SLR and revived by Canon for its current top of the line model.

The trend among point-and-shoot cameras was to extend zoom range while maintaining compactness. The 28–90-mm *f*/3.5–9 lens of the Pentax IQZoom 928 was claimed to be the longest 28-mm-to-telephoto zoom available on a compact 35-mm camera, while the Pentax IQZoom 140 had an *f*/4.1–10.2 lens that zoomed from 38 mm to an impressive 140 mm. Konica's Big Mini Zoom TR, with a 28–70-mm *f*/3.5–8.4 lens offered an unusual feature: a built-in folding minipod for supporting the camera during self-portraits. Leica entered the elite category of titanium-clad point-and-shoot compacts with its Minilux, manufactured in Japan and having a six-element 40-mm *f*/2.4 lens that revived the classic Summarit name, a top shutter speed of 1/400 second, and numerous automatic and electronic features. Canon introduced its Sure Shot del Sol, advertised as the first fully automatic solar-powered camera. A 35-mm compact with a 32-mm *f*/3.5 lens and a 1/250-second top shutter speed, the new model used an array of amorphous silicon solar cells to charge a secondary lithium ion battery.

A factor leading to a wait-and-see attitude from photographic manufacturers during the year was the anticipated introduction in 1996 of the Advanced Photo System (APS) from Kodak, Fuji, Canon, Nikon, and Minolta. The group released a brochure that revealed some new facts and emphasized expected benefits for consumers and photofinishers. Smaller than the current 35-mm cartridge and containing 24-mm film, the APS cartridge was designed to be completely lightproof and provide foolproof loading. Other advantages included data-carrying magnetic strips on the film for camera and processor use and improvements in various processing and reordering steps. (ARTHUR GOLDSMITH)

PRINTING

The worldwide printing industry continued its expansion in 1995 even though the U.S. was troubled by shortages of paper in some markets. The international DRUPA exhibition in Germany in May saw the introduction of advanced computer-to-plate and digital printing technology as well as highly automated presses at virtually every level.

Over 30 new digital plates for laser imaging were announced, especially "thermal" plates from Eastman Kodak and Presstek that had the potential for dry, nonchemical processing. Other dry-film products were shown by Eastman Kodak, Polaroid, and Xerox.

Worldwide installations of Indigo (Israel) and Agfa/Xeikon (Belgium) digital colour-printing systems totaled 800 units. New digital printers were shown by Scitex/Fuji-Xerox (Israel and Japan) and Canon (Japan), ushering in the second wave of high-productivity digital colour printers. High-speed ink-jet printing was shown by Scitex on-line with web and sheetfed presses for customized printing as well.

The increasing ability to output directly to film, plate, and paper was supported by the worldwide trend to on-demand digital document production. Over 65% of all printed pages were now produced on electronic workstations and output as page description coding based on the PostScript language developed by Adobe Systems, Inc.

Digital page production also had advanced because of the proliferation of high-quality image scanners, the availability of digital cameras, and advanced software for art creation, image manipulation, and page design and production. New digital proofing devices, such as Polaroid DryJet ink jet, Scitex Iris ink jet, 3M Rainbow dye sublimation, and Eastman Kodak Approval ablation technologies provided simulated representations of colour printing prior to film, plate, or paper output.

Although worldwide print volume was growing, there appeared to be challenges to traditional print on the horizon. In 1995 more encyclopaedias were distributed on CD-ROM than in print, and most major publishing companies had created new media divisions to develop products for interactive multimedia. The growth in desktop colour printers was significant—pundits predicted the future might see the reproduction of one page on a million printers instead of a million pages on one press.

(FRANK J. ROMANO)

RETAILING

For many of the world's biggest retailers in 1995, the real action was in the boardroom and not on the sales floor. Numerous chief executives resigned or were forced out, hundreds of stores were closed, and entire divisions were sold. Growth had come easily in the spendthrift 1980s. With the 1990s having ushered in an era marked by frugal consumers and intense competition, however, it was time to retrench and refocus.

Shoppers choose from a variety of merchandise in a Dutch-owned Makro store in Malaysia. A number of major U.S. and European retailers continued to enter new markets in Asia and other parts of the world, many of them building warehouse stores and superstores.
MUNSHI AHMED

Nowhere was the trend more apparent than at Kmart Corp. as the second biggest U.S. retailer struggled to revive its sagging fortunes. Under fire from shareholders for declining market share and profits, Joseph Antonini resigned as Kmart president and chief executive officer (CEO) in March after having been ousted as chairman in January. He was replaced by Floyd Hall, a retailing veteran who in the early 1980s had served as CEO of the successful discount merchant Target Stores. Hall faced a herculean task at Kmart. Plagued by outdated stores, sloppy customer service, and chronic stock problems, Kmart was losing ground rapidly as competitor Wal-Mart Stores Inc. raced ahead. In 1987 Wal-Mart's sales were roughly half of Kmart's. By fiscal 1995, however, Wal-Mart's annual sales of $82.5 billion were more than double Kmart's, at $34 billion.

Kmart's turnaround strategy was to shed noncore assets and use the proceeds to spruce up its discount stores and to build more Super Kmarts, which featured a discount store and supermarket under one roof. Kmart sold its 860 auto service centres and its stake in three specialty retailers, Borders Group (books and music), OfficeMax (office products), and Sports Authority (sporting goods). It also announced the closing of nearly 200 of its more than 2,100 discount stores. Over 18 months Kmart raised approximately $3 billion, a sum that seemed sure to rise as it considered selling a fourth chain, Builders Square (home-improvement goods). As Kmart's troubles mounted and its stock plunged, the corporation avoided bankruptcy by reorganizing its debt and forgoing a common-stock dividend.

Kmart was coming to grips with its troubles just as Sears, Roebuck and Co. was putting the finishing touches to its own sweeping restructuring. The third-ranked U.S. retailer sold its 80.3% stake in insurer Allstate Corp. for nearly $10 billion, the biggest in a string of asset sales that returned Sears to its roots as a department store retailer. Much of the credit for Sears's successful turnaround, which began in 1993 with the closing of more than 100 stores and the venerable Sears catalog, went to Arthur Martinez, who had been hired away from Saks Fifth Avenue to head Sears's retailing operations. He was rewarded with a promotion to chairman and CEO, replacing Edward Brennan, who retired after 39 years with the company.

The revolving door to the executive suite was spinning outside the U.S. as well, often pushed by institutional shareholders who were unhappy with the way companies were being run. In Canada, for example, one of the biggest specialty clothing store operators, Dylex Ltd., filed for court protection from creditors after years of losses. Nearly 200 of its 877 stores were closed, and Dylex's controlling shareholder, the Posluns family, was pushed out, its investment reduced to almost nothing. In Australia institutional investors forced the resignation of Solomon Lew, chairman of the country's largest retailer, Coles Myer Ltd. Lew, who remained a significant shareholder, had been dogged by controversy arising from questionable transactions between his private companies and Coles.

Around the world consumer spending rebounded somewhat, but shoppers remained cautious. Many Japanese retailers endured their worst year in recent memory in 1995 as consumers, their confidence already shaken by the sputtering economy, faced the horror of terrorist attacks and a powerful earthquake that devastated the city of Kobe. Japan's biggest supermarket operator, Daiei Inc., posted its first-ever loss for the year that ended in February.

After a burst of expansion in the early 1990s, many retailers paused to catch their breath. Home Depot Inc., the U.S. home-improvements chain, put a planned foray into Mexico on hold and said that it would add 5 instead of 10 stores in Canada in 1996. The U.K.'s Body Shop International PLC said that it would slow the pace of U.S. expansion. Not everyone was scaling back, however. Wal-Mart, the world's largest retailer, with about 3,000 stores, forged ahead with plans to open more than 200 discount stores, supercentres, and Sam's Club stores in 1996 in the U.S. and abroad. Meanwhile, the U.S.-based Toys "Я" Us Inc. said that it would open a chain called Babies "Я" Us to sell everything from bibs to cribs, going head-to-head with Baby Superstore Inc. and others. (JOHN HEINZL)

SHIPBUILDING

By the second quarter of 1995, according to figures produced by Lloyd's Register of Shipping, there were 2,367 ships of 44.1 million gt (gross tons) in the world order book, of which the cargo-carrying component was 1,800 ships of 43.7 million gt. Nearly 400 of the latter were dry-bulk carriers. The preponderance of dry-bulk carriers in the order book was perhaps explained by the previous year's shipping activity. During 1994 there had been an increase in ore and bulker orders because of a firming of freight rates in the dry-bulk markets.

These developments were reflected in the 1995 second-quarter cargo-carrying order book figure of 43.7 million gt, with the largest categories by ship type as follows: 398 dry bulk carriers of 14.3 million gt, 245 oil tankers of 11.8 million gt, 315 container ships of 7.4 million gt, 59 liquefied-gas ships of 2.2 million gt, 388 general cargo ships of 1.8 million gt, 125 chemical carriers of 1.6 million gt, and 108 passenger ships of 1.8 million gt. The delivery schedule of the 1,800 cargo ships in the order book was, in 1995, 844 ships of 14.4 million gt; in 1996, 720 ships of 20.5 million gt; and, in 1997 and beyond, 236 ships of 8.6 million gt.

The principal shipbuilding areas continued to be Asia and Europe, though Denmark's Burmeister & Wain was forced to close. For the second quarter of 1995, South Korea, with 30% of the world's order book in terms of gross tonnage, overtook Japan, which had 29%. Together these two Asian shipbuilding countries accounted for nearly 60% of the total world order book. In contrast, Western Europe took 17.6% and Eastern Europe 13.1%.

South Korea overtook Japan in 1995 both in the volume of its order book and in the number of orders reported, perhaps as a result of expanding its shipbuilding facilities. This development obviously affected the competitive position of Japan, as did the value of the yen. The very large crude carrier and bulker markets appeared to have been left by European shipbuilders to Asia, while Europeans concentrated their efforts on sophisticated high-value tonnage such as cruise ships, container ships, liquefied-gas carriers, chemical carriers, and refrigerated cargo ships.

Efforts were in hand to revive the fortunes of U.S. shipyards, which had previously relied heavily on defense contracts, to make them internationally competitive for new commercial building. The Maritech program, coordinated by the U.S. government's Advanced Research Projects Agency, awarded a number of research projects to 18 U.S. shipbuilding companies. Another measure to assist U.S. shipyards was the introduction of Title XI financing, which provided a federal guarantee for up to 87.5% of a project's financing over 25 years at attractive interest rates.

The expanding shipbuilders of South Korea and Japan continued to be challenged by China. Shanghai's Pudong area was to be the site of the largest shipyard in China, capable of building six 150,000-dwt (deadweight ton) vessels a year. The yard would have facilities for steel processing, hull welding, pipe production, painting, and computer-aided design. The owners were Jiangnan Shipyard, which had been building ships for 130 years.

Chinese banks were behind an operation to finance the building in China of six ships for the merchant fleet of The Sudan. The combined tonnage of the ships would be 23,000 dwt, and they would be built over a six-year period. Wang Rongsheng, general manager of the China Shipbuilding Corporation, forecast that the country would be building 2.5 million gt of ships by the end of the 20th century. (EDWARD CROWLEY)

TELECOMMUNICATIONS

AT&T surprised the telecommunications industry in 1995 when it announced that it would voluntarily split itself into three publicly held companies. Occurring just 11 years after the breakup of the old Bell System, when AT&T divested itself of its regional telephone companies, this latest restructuring represented the largest voluntary breakup in U.S. history and isolated AT&T's profitable core business—long-distance and wireless communications. It also paved the way for AT&T to enter into the local phone service market. Two new companies would be formed from its equipment manufacturing and its AT&T Global Information Solutions (GIS), formerly NCR Corp. By spinning off its computer division, AT&T retreated from its attempts over the previous 10 years to become a major player in the computer business. AT&T also kept its profitable AT&T Universal Card Services, which in five years had grown to more than 15 million credit card accounts. Also in 1995, AT&T announced that it was the first U.S. long-distance company to offer service from the U.S. to every country in the world.

The U.S. Federal Communications Commission (FCC) continued its public airwave auction in 1995. After announcing bids of almost $500 million for 30 regional advanced paging, or narrowband personal communications services (NPCS), licenses in late 1994, its March 1995 auction for 99 personal communications services (PCS) spectrum licenses brought in more than $7 billion. This next generation of portable telephone service saw bids from 18 different companies go as high as $493.5 million for the Los Angeles region and a bid price per potential customer of almost $32 for one Chicago license.

As the largest spenders, the Sprint Corp., in partnership with cable firms Tele-Communications, Inc., Comcast Corp., and Cox Cable Communications, formed Wirelessco and bid more than $2 billion for 29 licenses. AT&T Wireless was the next highest bidder, at $1.6 billion, for 21 licenses. Only the right to use the spectrum was awarded, and winning companies had to provide the equipment needed to deliver the services as well as the cost of moving the current users of the spectrum to other areas. Additional PCS auctions aimed at small businesses were scheduled to take place in 1996. MCI Communications Corp., the number two long-distance carrier without partners in the bidding for PCS licenses, announced its plans to purchase Nationwide Cellular Services, Inc., a reseller of cellular service, for $190 million.

In September, SkyTel Corp. introduced the first NPCS product—SkyTel 2-Way—a two-way paging service that allowed customers to respond to paging messages with 500-character messages. Also in September human error rendered millions of pagers useless when thousands of satellite receivers were inadvertently turned off.

Modems with speeds of 28.8 kilobits per second became available at prices below $500 in 1995. Future modems were expected to be able to transmit video over analog phone lines. The Internet and its World Wide Web pages were the most dynamic telecommunications service of 1995. In addition to providing text-based information, the Internet was providing sound, animation, and electronic commerce. It was also being used to place long-distance telephone calls between the U.S. and Israel. Integrated Services Digital Network, a digital switching technology, surfaced as a high-speed alternative to modems for Internet access.

Because of the increased use of fax machines, modems, and cellular phones, countries such as the United States and Britain found themselves running out of phone numbers. In North America the middle digit of the area codes, once restricted to 0 and 1, was expanded to allow other digits. By the end of 1996, 22 new area codes were planned. Because toll-free 800 numbers were also being used up, an 888 prefix was added, to be followed by 877, 866, and so on down to 822. The U.K. increased from two digits to three its geographic area code.

The U.S. House and Senate passed their own versions of telecommunications reform bills in 1995, and disputes over the final shape of the legislation continued through December. It was expected that the final bill would provide long-distance companies access to the local-exchange market, until now monopolized by the Regional Bell Operating Companies, and would allow the RBOCs to provide long-distance services. In addition, telephone numbers would become "portable" so that customers could change service providers without changing their telephone numbers.

New products introduced in 1995 included a 110-g (3.9-oz) cellular telephone, a pager the size of a fountain pen, a cross between a cordless and a cellular phone, and a wireless programmable sign that provided news, stock quotes, and sports results in public places. (THOMAS E. KROLL)

TEXTILES

Problems in the world textile trade continued in 1995, although in the United States there was some upturn in the retail trade. American manufacturers continued to search for partners to participate in joint ventures, usually aimed at making products that would find a ready market in the United States but that could be produced in Mexico or elsewhere at a lower cost. In Europe there was a continuing decline in the numbers employed in textiles. The liberalization of trading conditions in Asia, however, had led to explosive growth. Vietnam, emerging from virtual isolation, continued its ambitious plans to develop textile production, one such scheme being a project in partnership with South Korean interests to build a polyester fibre plant and then to convert its production into goods, most of which would be exported.

There was movement among textile machine builders to transfer their production to be nearer customers in the Pacific and Indian Ocean areas. Production of shuttleless looms had started in Pakistan, for example, with technical assistance provided by a South Korean partner. In Indonesia one large textile-manufacturing company was now building its own looms. In India partnerships with various European equipment makers were being forged, and one Austrian company had transferred all its production of drive belts to that country, while a German machinery maker neared completion of a plant in India to make ring spinning machinery.

Despite the talk of automation replacing people and contributing to a more level playing field in terms of competition, labour costs remained a key factor throughout the world textile industry. Although the trend toward complex and sophisticated electronically programmed automation continued in garment making, it remained very much a cottage industry. It was a labour-intensive industry, but it did not demand particularly high skills or high capital investment to produce quality products.

Man-Made Fibres. Figures issued by the International Rayon and Synthetic Fibres Committee showed that in 1994, the most recent year for which figures were available, man-made-fibre production was 21,102,000 metric tons, compared with cotton at 18,982,000 metric tons and wool at 1,544,000 metric tons. Asia showed no slowdown in the production of the major synthetic fibres.

There was a constant flow of news in 1995 about projects to build new fibre plants, almost all for the making of polyester filament yarns and the staple fibres that emulate silk, cotton, and wool. Almost unnoticed, however, was the astonishing rise in the production of olefin fibres, particularly polypropylene. Although the output of nylon in 1994 in Western Europe rose slightly, it was matched almost exactly by polypropylene. Based on a polymer made by converting the inflammable waste gases (propylene) from oil refineries into a meltable polymer, the fibre could be extruded in comparatively simple plants.

Polypropylene producers thus tended to be comparatively small companies, often units within large organizations that used all the fibre they could make within their own company. Very low in its specific weight, the fibre floated in water and had immense strength and durability, making it ideal for marine uses such as ropes, hawsers, and fishing nets. Because it did not rot or otherwise degrade, even in damp environments, polypropylene also had largely supplanted jute as the backing material for carpets.

In the developed countries there had been a move away from making fibres such as polyester, acrylic, and nylon and toward highly complex fibres. In Britain, for example, an acrylic fibre had been made that incorporated microcapsules containing phase-change materials, which absorbed and released heat as they changed from one environmental state to another. The development was seen as having potential for use in making lighter-weight blankets.

In Switzerland one maker had started to produce a synthetic fibre based on starch, which, being biodegradable, might have uses in agriculture. Exotic fibres continued to be developed for highly specialized applications such as the aerospace sector, where high cost was not as important as performance. (PETER LENNOX-KERR)

Wool. The year 1995 started well for wool. Prices had risen strongly in 1994, with Australia's representative eastern market indicator (EMI) accelerating from its 1993 recession low of less than 400 cents (Australian) per kilogram (1 kg = 2.2 lb) to exceed 800 cents in September 1994. It held on to most of the increase into the opening weeks of 1995. By then China, the leading customer for Australian wool, had become an active buyer, and an EMI price peak of 842 cents was reached in April. Even when Chinese buying later declined because of stricter import duties and credit restrictions, there was no immediate loss of confidence. Wool-production estimates were down, and Chinese interest was expected to revive later in the year.

Wool prices declined at an accelerating pace during the opening months of the 1995–96 season, which began in July. Further reductions in Australian production estimates failed to check the decline. A later forecast for Australia in 1995–96 was 448,000 metric tons clean, compared with 477,000 metric tons in 1994–95. World wool supply, including stocks, was estimated at 1,647,000 metric tons in 1995–96, compared with 1,658,000 metric tons in 1994–95.

Australia's stockpile-disposal policy, with Wool International required by legislation to sell a quarterly quota of about 190,000 bales, proved disruptive in a falling market. Stockpile wool was offered privately at a discount, and it failed to sell adequately when offered at auction in October. The EMI reached a low point of 582 cents before demand revived and stockpile sales improved.

Apart from China's erratic and uncertain situation, Western Europe and Japan were affected by disappointing retail sales and orders. The year ended with the market outlook difficult but with hopes of a steadier price trend. The longer-term outlook—with wool supplies declining and the stockpile liquidated and with the Commonwealth of Independent States becoming a consumer instead of a maverick supplier of wool—was for improving demand and rising prices. (H.M.F. MALLETT)

Cotton. Despite a somewhat gloomy outlook, there was a general increase in cotton consumption in 1995. According to the International Cotton Advisory Committee, economic growth was expected to lead to higher levels of cotton use, with world consumption estimated at 19 million metric tons in 1995–96.

The disaster among cotton farmers in Pakistan, where heavy rains and flooding caused immense damage in Punjab and Sindh provinces, continued in 1995. It was estimated that farmers lost about $4 million over the season and that about half the entire crop was damaged. There also were serious insect infestations of cotton fields. Another area hit by bad weather was southern Africa, where, in contrast to Pakistan, the problem was drought. In the 1994–95 season, production in South Africa dropped by 5,000 metric tons to 22,000 metric tons, while in Zimbabwe the fall was far worse, by 21,000 metric tons to only 39,000 metric tons. There was also a serious shortfall in Tanzania.

A worker takes a rest on drying cotton in Pakistan. Heavy rains and flooding caused extensive damage to the cotton crops of the country's Punjab and Sindh provinces during the 1995 growing season.

J. HAMES—PANOS

The adjustments following the collapse of the Soviet Union continued to be reflected in low cotton crops. In Russia alone the consumption of cotton by mills was only 350,000 metric tons in 1994–95, a fall of 100,000 metric tons. Uzbekistan was granted a World Bank credit worth $66 million to develop cotton farming. The money was to be used in the production of cotton seed, in the resolution of irrigation difficulties, for treatment of plants, and in the marketing and certification of cotton. In Syria a drop in production was blamed on a lack of irrigation together with excessively high summer temperatures.

In Australia, however, where the area under cotton cultivation in 1994–95 declined, an increase in yield resulted in an overall rise of 6,000 metric tons to a total of 335,000 metric tons. In the United States, expansion continued in the cultivation of very long-fibre Pima cottons in the Southwest.

In Peru, after years of serious political problems, the economy was beginning to recover, with special attention being given to revitalizing cotton growing.

(PETER LENNOX-KERR)

Silk. The worldwide supply of and demand for silk were nearly in balance during 1995, as concern about a drop in demand was followed by news of a poor cocoon crop in China that resulted in a shortage of the high-grade silk needed for modern processing machinery.

The industry malaise in Europe came to an end. Old stocks were absorbed in Italy and France, and demand for such silk accessories as ties and scarves was good. The restriction on silk garment imports imposed by the European Union (EU) in March 1994 did not appear to create a shortage and resulted in an improvement in the quality of imported silk and an enhanced image for the fibre.

In January 1995 China and the EU signed trade agreements regarding future silk quota levels and licensing arrangements. More Chinese goods were allowed into the EU than in 1994 but fewer than in 1993.

China remained both the largest consumer and the largest producer of silk, while in Japan, for the first time, silk used in the manufacture of Western-style clothing exceeded that used for making kimonos. The Indian industry continued to flourish, and raw silk was imported to meet demand. Brazilian quality continued to improve, and certain grades of silk were priced 25% higher than Chinese silk.

Silk waste and noils continued to be scarce, while the market for knitted garments from noil yarn contracted. World silk production for 1994 was estimated at 100,935 metric tons. The top three producers were China (72,500 metric tons), India (13,500 metric tons), and Brazil (2,535 metric tons). (ANTHONY H. GADDUM)

TOBACCO

Contrary to expectations, the antismoking movement reduced neither world manufacture nor consumption of tobacco products in 1995. The world consumed 5,342,991,000,000 cigarettes during the year, almost as many as in 1990, the year of peak consumption. The downward drift in some markets—notably the United States—showed a temporary reversal. World production of raw tobacco, however, was lower in 1995, at 6.4 million metric tons because of large carryover stocks from previous harvests.

There were profound changes continuing in the structure of the world market for tobacco products in 1995. The large private tobacco groups in the West had formerly been denied entry to the huge market in the Soviet bloc. With the breakup of the Soviet Union, these companies positioned themselves to purchase controlling interests in what had been monopoly government enterprises. In new and modernized factories throughout the former Soviet empire, they were producing modern-style cigarettes, including many bearing international brand names. While Western manufacturers had been largely restricted to domestic trade and a small export business, they now were virtually global, although China slowed their spread there.

The most significant change this westernization was bringing to Eastern Europe was the introduction of milder tobacco blends. State monopolies previously had made cigarettes of whatever local farmers grew and what the factories could import cheaply. The result was rough, harsh cigarettes (many without filters), with no pretensions to elegance or modernity. National tastes were changing, however, to favour blends in which mild flue-cured and Burley tobaccos were dominant and the role of pungent dark tobaccos diminished. Together with consumers' preference for cigarettes with low tar and nicotine, this affected the leaf market by increasing the demand for mild tobaccos.

The industry's critics lauded the decision of the U.S. Food and Drug Administration in 1995 to begin the process of classifying nicotine as an addictive drug, a status that would allow the agency to assert jurisdiction over the sale of cigarettes. The move was part of a larger program proposed by U.S. Pres. Bill Clinton to put further restrictions on the tobacco industry.

(MICHAEL F. BARFORD)

A group of hikers in the Drakensberg range in South Africa pause to enjoy the spectacular scenery. Several African countries, particularly those south of the Sahara, had significant increases in the numbers of tourists in 1995, with South Africa alone boasting a 24% jump.

CHRIS VAN LENNEP—A.B.P.L.

TOURISM

World tourism saw only moderate growth in 1995 when compared with record levels in the previous year. Consumer caution and a slow climb out of recession in main origin countries, including the U.S., Japan, Germany, the U.K., and France, explained this trend. Prospects for international air travel looked bright, however; the International Air Transport Association estimated scheduled passenger growth at 7% for 1995, with Asia-Pacific the fastest-growing region. While the world's largest tour operator, Touristick Union International of Germany, showed an 8% growth in clients and a 9% growth in revenue for 1995, U.K. majors such as Thomson and Airtours found that flat demand put growth in jeopardy.

A regional analysis showed that Africa's tourism industry was showing good growth in 1995. Sub-Saharan Africa showed the most promise, with South Africa's arrivals up by 24%. Tunisia welcomed 6% more tourists than the previous year, but Morocco, the region's leading destination, continued to decline.

The U.S. expected a 4% decline in visitor numbers owing primarily to weakness in neighbouring markets Canada and Mexico. Canada, however, moved ahead by 8%, and Mexico grew 2%. Greg Farmer, undersecretary for travel and tourism in the U.S. Department of Commerce, reported that while international visitors would spend $77 billion in the U.S. during 1995, poor advertising undermined tourism potential. Argentina's tourism expanded by 5% and Jamaica's by 7%. Caribbean destinations were repeatedly battered by hurricanes during the fall, which damaged facilities at Antigua, St. Martin, and St. Thomas. Costa Rica, visited by 800,000 tourists annually, remained Central America's prime ecotourism destination, welcoming visitors to its 28 parks and reserves. Guatemala, Honduras, and Mexico cooperated in the development of the "Maya Trail" linking of the archaeological sites in the three countries.

India's tourism market grew 3%, Sri Lanka's 5%, and Maldives' 15%. Myanmar (Burma) relaxed entry formalities to welcome tourists during "Visit Myanmar Year 1996." Generally there was strong growth in Pacific Rim countries: the Philippines 18%, Thailand 15%, Australia 11%, China 8%, South Korea 5%, and Singapore 3%. Japan's tourism fell by 4%, however. Australia's Tourism Minister Michael Lee announced a $550 million investment in new tourist accommodations, as well as help for ecotourism development on Pacific islands.

With the apparent arrival of peace in the region and despite continued security problems, the Middle East reaped a sizable tourism dividend; Egypt expected three million tourists in 1995, a 20% increase over 1994. Israel and Jordan anticipated 20% and 16% growth in tourist numbers, respectively. Syria began to market its rich history and scenery with $900 million for new hotel investment in 1995.

In Europe tourism continued to decline in

Leading International Tourist Destinations

Number of tourist arrivals from abroad

Destination	1993	1994
France	61,300,000	60,840,000
United States	45,793,000	45,504,000
Spain	40,600,000	43,232,000
Italy	25,700,000	27,480,000
Hungary	22,800,000	21,425,000
China	19,452,000	21,070,000
United Kingdom	19,400,000	20,855,000
Poland	...	18,800,000
Austria	18,257,000	17,894,000
Mexico	16,860,000	17,113,000
Czech Republic	7,479,000	17,000,000
Canada	15,021,000	15,971,000
Germany	15,200,000	14,494,000
Switzerland	12,750,000	12,200,000
Greece	9,384,000	10,072,000
Hong Kong	7,896,000	9,331,000
Portugal	8,993,000	9,132,000
Malaysia	6,800,000	7,197,000
Singapore	5,848,000	6,268,000
Netherlands, The	5,404,000	6,178,000

Source: World Tourism Organization, Madrid, 1995.

Austria, Germany, and Switzerland. Despite excellent snowfall in the Alps, Switzerland's winter sports season weathered a 6% drop. Spain saw a 3% growth in arrivals, France 6%, the United Kingdom 7%, and Turkey 15%. The U.K. welcomed a record 2.6 million visitors during an exceptionally warm July and promoted London as a good tourist value. Fierce competition between English Channel ferries and the new Channel Tunnel (Eurotunnel) continued as Eurostar announced lower fares and hourly shuttles on its London–Paris/Brussels services. Starting July 1 seven countries (Germany, Spain, Portugal, Belgium, The Netherlands, Luxembourg, and France) were grouped in a border-free zone in the hope of increasing tourism within the European Union.

On Sept. 5, 1995, the World Tourism Organization (WTO), the World Travel and Tourism Council (WTTC), and the Earth Council launched Agenda 21 for travel and tourism in London. The WTO secretary-general, Antonio Enríquez Savignac, the WTTC president, Geoffrey Lipman, and the Earth Council chairman, Maurice Strong, revealed priority issues for governments and the industry to address in order to meet Rio de Janeiro Earth Summit guidelines. In October the WTO general assembly in Cairo celebrated the 20-year anniversary of the intergovernmental tourism association, whose membership numbered some 130 states and 304 private-sector affiliates in 1995. During the Cairo conference, the WTO adopted a declaration for the prevention of organized sex tourism. Germany was host to an international meeting to combat the growing problem of sex tourism and juveniles. Australia, France, Germany, Norway, Sweden, and the U.S. had already adopted laws allowing tourists to be prosecuted for traveling abroad and committing sex crimes. (PETER SHACKLEFORD)

WOOD PRODUCTS

Wood. The global wood supply remained tight in 1995, prompting producers to rely more on wood products such as panels that used wood residues and on smaller-diameter trees. U.S., European, and Asian markets looked to South America and Russia for alternative forest resources.

Environmental restrictions continued to force lumber mills to close in the western United States as companies struggled to find sufficient raw materials. In 1994 there were 421 sawmills operating in the western U.S.; in 1995 the number had fallen by 9% to 383 mills. Some companies were moving to the southeastern U.S., where the timber supply from private plantations was more stable.

The wood panel industry enjoyed increasing production and plant capacity in 1995. Construction of medium-density fibreboard plants rose globally, with 51 expansion projects in Asia, 25 in North America, 18 in Europe, and 7 in Oceania. European and U.S. producers hoped that Asia's furniture industry would absorb much of the new capacity. Taiwan, Japan, China, and South Korea alone generated an import demand of 1 million–1.2 million cu m (1 cu m = 423.8 bd-ft) per year. Natural disasters, such as the earthquake that struck the Kobe, Japan, area, was also expected to raise the demand for prefabricated homes using structural laminated lumber, which had withstood the quake well.

Tight wood supplies in the United States and Europe, coupled with strong demand in Asia, led to increased interest in the forest resources of South America and Russia. Brazilian softwood log exports—mostly to Europe—reached 780,000 cu m in 1995, up from 185,000 cu m in 1993. Chile's forest products exports were expected to grow by 50% in 1995. Russia's vast Asian timber resources attracted U.S. investors, but political instability and the lack of data and infrastructure remained strong impediments.

The movement to certify timber from sustainable forests gained momentum internationally. Movements in the U.K. and the U.S. spawned several certification initiatives in Indonesia, Brazil, Africa, Scandinavia, Italy, and Canada. The International Standards Organization was working on the establishment of international certification criteria. Other efforts were more local, with individual groups setting standards for specific regions of the world. Although the forest products industry was starting to explore certification, it was unclear whether consumers would pay more for certified wood products.

There also were developments in the international regulation of the forest products trade. Japan approved the abolition of regulations affecting a wide range of wood products. With new membership in the European Union, Finland and Sweden, Europe's largest exporters of wood products, would have voting rights in deciding future wood-trade policies for EU countries. A long-standing dispute over Canadian exports of softwood lumber to the U.S. was resolved after a bilateral consultation process was established, although there were indications that the U.S. might file another complaint. Canada offered in December to cut such shipments to the U.S. by imposing an export tax on lumber companies in British Columbia. Their share of the U.S. market was expected to decline.

(WORLD FOREST INSTITUTE)

JEFFREY AARONSON—NETWORK ASPEN

A Chilean worker measures logs to be used for paneling. The remaining wood chips would be made into other products. Demand for the forest resources of the South American countries and of Russia increased during 1995.

Paper and Pulp. The North American pulp and paper industry in 1995 was enjoying the best market conditions in five years. All sectors of the marketplace, from newsprint to recycled fibre, saw price increases. Pulp moved to record demand and prices, and several factors indicated that the market would remain strong well into 1996.

World pulp, paper, and board production in 1994, the last year for which complete figures were available, was 268.5 million metric tons, an increase of 16,840,000 metric tons, or 6.7%, over 1993. Western Europe showed an impressive 8.2% increase in total production in 1994, with Germany taking the lead. Germany would no doubt increase production again in 1995 as three new newsprint machines reached full capacity. Eastern Europe appeared to have reached bottom as Asia rose sharply, with production increases in 1994 of 27.3% in Thailand and 17.5% in Indonesia. China produced 21.4 million metric tons in 1994, up from 18.7 in 1993. Asia as a whole recorded an 8.4% increase in 1994 and was steadily expanding capacity.

Pulp production rose to 171.5 million metric tons in 1994, a 5.4% increase over 1993. The share of pulp in papermaking, however, continued its steady decline of 1% a year. The trend toward the use of recycled fibre in deinked pulp would undoubtedly continue, but obtaining even recyclable fibre proved to be more difficult as it became a premium-priced product.

The start-up of recycling operations in North America and Europe continued to affect the availability of wastepaper for export, as evidenced by the record prices for all grades of wastepaper. The increase in North American and European demand was not likely to be offset by a significant increase in recycling rates, since the supply was not building fast enough.

As demand continued to exceed supply, pulp mills in both North America and elsewhere were running at full capacity, with many customers on waiting lists. Worldwide pulp capacity was expected to grow by less than 1% in 1996 and by 2% in 1997, with Indonesian and South American projects starting up. The biggest impediment to expansion was the lack of the wood fibre, which had become increasingly difficult to obtain, needed to supply existing mills. Because of the shortage of raw materials, the industry was looking at low-fibre and even at "tree-free" paper.

The U.S. industry was awaiting the final outcome of the Environmental Protection Agency's cluster rules. The industry claimed that the regulations, as written, would impose significant economic hardships on pulp producers, forcing them to install unproven, expensive technology with no significant environmental benefits.

(H. CLAUDE LAVALLÉE)

This article updates the *Macropædia* articles BEVERAGE PRODUCTION; BUILDING CONSTRUCTION; DRESS AND ADORNMENT; ELECTRONICS; ENERGY CONVERSION; FORESTRY AND WOOD PRODUCTION; INDUSTRIAL GLASS AND CERAMICS; Chemical Process INDUSTRIES; Extraction and Processing INDUSTRIES; Manufacturing INDUSTRIES; Textile INDUSTRIES; INSURANCE; MARKETING AND MERCHANDISING; PHOTOGRAPHY; PRINTING, TYPOGRAPHY, AND PHOTOENGRAVING; TELECOMMUNICATIONS SYSTEMS; TOOLS.

Computers and Information Systems

Two forces dominated developments in the computer industry in 1995—the arrival of Microsoft Corp.'s new Windows 95 personal computer (PC) operating system and the overnight ascendancy of the Internet (*see* SPECIAL REPORT) and the World Wide Web, a subset of the Internet designed for multimedia use.

Events in 1995 drew so much attention to both Windows and the Web that by year's end the computer mouse had become almost as well known to the world's population at large as the television set remote control. In fact, the trends that played out during 1995 led many to argue that a computer mouse might soon be used as much as the TV remote control to call up everything from computer-served movies on demand to news stories and E-mail from friends and families. The decline of the well-known supercomputer company Cray Computer Corp., which filed for bankruptcy in March, was further evidence of the growing dominance of the PC industry.

Windows 95, which made its world debut on August 24 accompanied by a $300 million global advertising campaign, was a major overhaul of Microsoft's Windows operating environment, which added a "point-and-click" operating system known as a graphic user interface, or GUI, to the text-based disk operating system, or DOS, used in most PCs.

The graphic World Wide Web evolved in academic computer laboratories during the early 1990s as software originally developed by the European particle physics consortium CERN, headquartered in Geneva, was adapted to allow people using the global Internet computer network to use the same sort of graphic manipulations available in systems such as Microsoft Windows and Apple Computer, Inc.'s Mac OS. Until the Web appeared, the Internet itself had been used virtually exclusively by business, scientific, government, and academic professionals rather than by the public at large.

This image of tyrannosaur skeletons at tea owes its realism to new three-dimensional simulation techniques available on computers. Applications of 3-D computing ranged from medical diagnosis and scientific modeling to architectural design and military training exercises.
COURTESY OF COLOR ASSOCIATES

Both Windows 95 and the Web were mileposts on what clearly emerged during the year as the road toward something that industry analysts started calling "convergence." The term pointed toward the coming integration of all forms of information from simple text to moving video as digital data that could be processed, stored, and manipulated by computers using a graphic interface.

By year's end it was clear that PC operating systems, led by Mac OS and Windows 95, had evolved into easy-to-use tools capable of working with converging audio and video material, as well as with the text and photographic images of the past. It also was clear that in the future the medium of exchanging digital information ranging from grocery lists sent via E-mail to full-length Hollywood-type motion pictures would be the World Wide Web. Thus did convergence cross the divide between prediction and reality. Encyclopædia Britannica, Inc., was one of many companies that joined the rush toward convergence in 1995 when it announced that the entire text of its reference work would be available to individual subscribers through the Web, as well as in its 32-volume print set and in a new CD-ROM version.

Businesses such as computing network giants Oracle Systems Corp. and Novell Inc. began adapting the networks used in corporate computing enterprises to use the same software and communications protocols that made convergence with things such as digital movies possible at the home-entertainment level. Executives and computer scientists at both of these companies, as well as their counterparts all across the industry, increasingly adapted business computer enterprises to operate under the Internet-developed procedures known as Transmission Control Protocol/Internet Protocol (TCP/IP), which was the key technology needed to bring about convergence across computer networks.

TCP/IP can convert any type of data moving from computer to computer via long-distance communications lines into small packets of data that can be transmitted in quick bursts over whatever communications line is available at any given time. For example, one packet, or part of a computer file, might be transmitted from New York City to London by undersea cable, while a second packet is sent via microwave to Los Angeles, Singapore, and Paris before reaching London, depending upon the traffic patterns on the Internet. TCP/IP thus allows computers to communicate easily, regardless of geographic distances.

Seizing on this power, companies such as Oracle began setting up TCP/IP networks for their business clients to allow customers to reach into the companies' databases from remote points as part of the course of doing business. Such links would allow a company to set up databases to handle product-support calls and to establish systems that would allow remote customers to scan data banks showing what products are in stock and to order them on-line, as well as to perform numerous other efficiencies. Oracle executives

Special Report

Cyberspace

BY ROBERT EVERETT-GREEN

Like the Land of Oz, cyberspace was originally the invention of a writer, the science-fiction novelist William Gibson. While Oz remains the domain of a wizard and a little girl from Kansas, however, cyberspace has leapt off the page to become a subject of wide public interest and debate. As both a dream and a reality, it has sparked renewed discussion about the social and economic assumptions underlying our present means of communication, as well as the role of technology in our lives. By the beginning of 1995, there was a growing consensus that cyberspace had become a region that could significantly affect the structure of our economies, the development of our communities, and the protection of our rights as free citizens.

Gibson's cyberspace, as described in his book *Neuromancer* (1984) and several later novels, was an artificial environment created by computers. Unlike a motion picture, which presents moving images on a flat surface, a cyberspatial environment would convey realistic detail in three dimensions and to all five senses. It would also allow for a degree of face-to-face intimacy between people in remote places. In one of Gibson's novels, for instance, a woman "meets" a mysterious financier outside a cathedral in Barcelona, Spain, though in fact she is sitting alone in an office in Brussels. Research continues into ways of realizing this type of cyberspatial experience, which has come to be known as virtual reality. By 1994 virtual reality machines had begun to appear in amusement parks and shopping malls, though a full experience of Gibson's vision has so far been frustrated by the crude state of the technology and by the physical disorientation, bordering on nausea, that some machines provoke. Moreover, users of virtual reality devices are usually communicating not with others but only with the computer.

Robert Everett-Green is senior features writer and Internet columnist of the Globe and Mail, *Toronto.*

Cyberspace as a present reality has come to be associated primarily with networks of computers linked through telephone lines. The biggest and most familiar of these, the Internet, was developed in the 1970s to assist U.S. military and academic research. As recently as 1990, the Internet was almost unknown to the general public. By the end of 1995, however, the network had absorbed millions of users with no affiliations to defense institutions or universities. The volume of exchanges between these users, who numbered at least 20 million–30 million in 1995, surpassed 30 terabytes per month, or enough information to fill 30 million books of 700 pages each. For many of those involved in these exchanges—and for millions more who have no experience of computer networks—cyberspace and the Internet have become nearly synonymous terms.

The Internet is a hybrid medium, combining aspects of the printing press, the telephone, the public bulletin board, and the private letter. It also permits crude radio, and television transmission without the physical plant required by conventional broadcasting. Indeed, some commentators have predicted that the Internet or a successor network will eventually absorb the functions of television, telephone, and conventional publishing. They speak of an "information superhighway," a term coined in 1992 by then senator Al Gore, Jr., to refer to a unified, interactive system of electronic communication. The prospect of such a system, with the capacity to deliver an unprecedented range of informational services to the home, school, or office, has provoked a flurry of strategic alliances between major commercial interests in the telephone, software-programming, and entertainment industries. By 1995 the business world was beginning to regard the largely noncommercial Internet as the electronic equivalent of China: a huge, ever-growing, and virtually untapped market.

For some commentators, however, the social implications of cyberspace far outstrip its commercial potential. Unlike television, which beams its messages to a passive and isolated audience, the Internet depends upon its users to supply and share content and to act cooperatively to aid its dispersal. Since resource sharing and mutual aid are age-old traits of successful social groupings, some Internet advocates argue that the medium may help repair a social fabric badly weakened by television. They claim that cyberspace encourages the formation of "virtual communities," without hindrance from national or geographic boundaries. They also view the

noted that the company also set up TCP/IP networks that would allow customer companies to handle their own internal affairs, such as in-house messaging, publishing training materials, and tracking everything from inventory to vacation schedules.

Meanwhile, with Internet computers pervading traditional corporate business environments, 1995 saw a marked acceleration of a trend that surfaced in 1994 as many of the world's leading media companies, including Time Warner Inc., Viacom Inc., and the Walt Disney Co., began forging alliances and consummating mergers with enterprises in the computer and telecommunications industries. Driving the mergers was the clear need of companies with one part of the convergence formula to join forces with companies owning other parts. In each case the combined enterprise was positioned to seize on the opportunities inherent in reducing the totality of the world's information, education, and entertainment content into computer-ready digital form and then selling it through distribution channels pegged to the GUIs of PC operating systems and of the Web.

The largest of the 1995 convergence-related mergers linked the Walt Disney Co. with Capital Cities/ABC, Inc., a $19 billion acquisition plan geared toward a marriage of Capital Cities' holdings in television networks, television stations, cable television systems, newspapers, and radio stations with the huge studios and cable networks used by Disney to produce and sell programming.

Shortly after the Disney-Capital Cities merger was announced, Time Warner announced it would acquire Turner Broadcasting System, Inc., owned by the media magnate Ted Turner. (*See* BIOGRAPHIES.) Time Warner combined the largest magazine publishing company in the U.S. with Warner Bros. Inc., the world's top producer and distributor of movies and TV programming. Subsidiaries included a major music recording company, book publisher Little, Brown & Co. Inc., and Home Box Office, the largest cable TV movie provider. Time Warner also owned cable television systems that reached nearly 15 million households by the end of 1995. Turner Broadcasting owned the worldwide CNN news organization along with four cable television entertainment networks in the U.S. and four others in Latin America, Asia, and Europe.

Internet as the harbinger of a renaissance in free speech. Since the network gives everyone the tools to become a publisher, they say, cyberspace offers a potent means of freeing public discourse from the control of private newspaper companies and broadcasters.

Similarly optimistic predictions have greeted the appearance of every major electronic medium, including the telephone, radio, and television. Often, announcements of the new utopia have proved less correct than the statements of dissenting voices. One of the earliest and most prescient warnings about electronic media was delivered by Fedor Dostoyevsky in his novel *The Brothers Karamazov* (1879–80). "We are assured that the world is becoming more and more united, is being formed into brotherly communion, by the shortening of distances, by the transmitting of thoughts through the air," he wrote. In the novelist's view, however, the devices responsible for these transmissions would only stimulate "meaningless and foolish desires." Dostoyevsky's novel was published only about four years after Alexander Graham Bell secured his patent on the telephone, which may be regarded as the first instrument of cyberspace.

More recent critics have warned that electronic networks, far from creating a true global village, will only exaggerate disparities between rich and poor. Users may turn away from their television sets only to withdraw into narrow communion with other residents of their exclusive "cyburbia." Other commentators have warned of the danger lurking in the great potential for violations of civil and privacy rights through the use of computer networks. As citizens perform more social and commercial transactions in cyberspace, it becomes easier to track their spending habits, private interests, and political beliefs. Advocacy groups such as the Electronic Frontier Foundation have called for vigorous protection of privacy rights in cyberspace. The U.S. government has proposed that a device known as the Clipper Chip be accepted as a standard means for encrypting and decoding messages on the Internet, which would thus protect privacy. Critics observe, however, that the Clipper Chip would feature a "back door" to which the government would retain the only key, allowing it to intercept and decode private messages at will.

Further debate has surrounded the issue of how existing laws affect cyberspace as a public space. A University of Michigan student who published on the Internet a violent rape fantasy in which he named a fellow classmate as his victim was arrested in 1995 by the FBI on suspicion of using interstate communications to threaten another person with injury or kidnap. The charge was eventually dismissed on the grounds that the student's writing did not constitute a threat to do real harm. Some observers regarded the case as an awkward application of a law designed for other, more private media. Fear of a flood of pornographic material cascading onto the screens of young Internet users gripped many a politician and journalist in 1995, even though pornographic images represented less than one-half of one percent of all images on the Internet. Some U.S. legislators proposed new laws requiring strict screening of unregulated computer networks for pornographic materials—a measure critics contended would be comparable to asking telephone companies to monitor their lines for discussions that may assist criminal activity.

Perhaps the thorniest legal issue of all is that of copyright, which forbids unauthorized duplication of another's original work. The mere act of viewing a document on the Internet, however, offends against this principle since the document is literally copied to the viewer's screen. If the document is then copied onto a storage device such as a floppy disk, the viewer may alter the document and republish it in a form that may not be readily distinguishable from the work of the original author. Some writers and artists have greeted this situation as a new impetus for collective creativity, but for defenders of intellectual property rights it is a problem of unprecedented scale. Some have suggested that the very notion of copyright, which was unknown before the invention of printing, may not survive the advent of cyberspace.

The most intriguing aspect of cyberspace, however, may have more to do with the evolving relationship of humankind with its technologies. At the root of Gibson's notion of computer-simulated worlds and electronically assisted experience is the prospect of a meeting of machine and human at a near-organic level. Some commentators have spoken of a coming "bionic convergence" through which we may all someday be fitted with computer implants that shunt messages directly to and from our brains and that may have the capacity to stimulate electronically our creativity or our response to pleasure. At that level of cyberspatial experience, to borrow a phrase from media theorist Marshall McLuhan, "man becomes, as it were, the sex organs of the machine world." Whether we shall be content with that status, if indeed it becomes ours, remains to be seen.

Turner also had formed a strategic relationship with the world's leading maker of PC microprocessor chips, Intel Corp., to provide television programming to desktop computers equipped with television circuit boards built by Intel. In November Intel announced that its new chip, the Pentium Pro, would include the ability to serve as a digital television set within the circuitry of every PC equipped with the chip.

The merger mania extended from the media giants into the more traditional computer industry, which saw a wave of mergers, acquisitions, and consolidations that dramatically altered the industry's power structure and dynamics. Apple Computer, which faced increased competition from Windows 95 and from newly released Macintosh clones, remained the subject of takeover rumours.

By far the largest of the completed mergers involved the $3.5 billion acquisition of Lotus Development Corp. by IBM Corp., an alliance that most analysts viewed as a strategy to position IBM, the world's largest computer company, as a participant in the same convergence linking the media companies.

The chief asset of Lotus was an Internet-capable computer networking package called Lotus Notes, designed to let businesses move digital data across multiple types of machines, including IBM's large mainframe computers, mid-range business computers such as IBM's AS/400 and RS/6000 lines, and PCs using Windows, Mac OS, IBM's competing OS/2 GUI operating system, and the UNIX operating system long in use by business and academic computing experts. By acquiring Lotus Notes, which worked across multiple computing platforms and was capable of handling the full range of digital content being developed elsewhere, IBM hoped to counter Microsoft, which reigned as the world leader in personal computing, both with its Windows operating system and with a number of projects under development designed to use desktop computers as servers capable of sending cable television programming and movies on demand to other computers linked via the World Wide Web.

Oracle, which previously had focused much of its enterprise toward huge business networks running databases for Fortune 500 companies, took steps to put the company into position as a server of the digital data, such as movies and archived television programs, that the media mergers were geared toward developing and marketing.

In order for virtually all of the other developments to work, however, computers would have to be linked by much faster data-transmission links than the telephone lines that accounted for the great bulk of on-line traffic. There was a strong consensus that achieving this speed was only a matter of time because the technology for the speed needed to send movies along with text down a wire already existed in the form of cable television systems and the fibre-optic cables that phone companies installed in much of the U.S. In fact, much of the merger activity of the year involved owners of these high-bandwidth transmission facilities (such as Time Warner and Capital Cities) joining forces with content providers.

Companies producing the software needed to manage the developing digital communications networks when, and if, they became a reality also benefited from this dynamic. The most visible players were a pair of competing companies, Netscape Communications, Inc., and Spyglass, Inc., both producers of the software called Web servers and Web browsers needed to let people actually use the digital data that came in over their wires to the World Wide Web.

Early in 1995 Microsoft licensed Spyglass' Web browser, Mosaic; changed its name to Microsoft Internet Explorer; and made it the centre of the company's own on-line service, the Microsoft Network. The three largest on-line computer services—America Online, CompuServe, and Prodigy—charged that this Microsoft business initiative gave the company an unfair monopoly because the software needed to access the Microsoft Network was built into the Windows 95 operating system itself.

Netscape, however, proved to be a hugely popular competitor, more than holding its own against Microsoft as some surveys showed that more than 80% of those using the World Wide Web were using Netscape's browser, the Netscape Navigator. Netscape started selling stock to the public in the summer of 1995, and its shares proved to be one of the hottest issues in the history of trading, which thereby underscored the volatility of 1995 computer industry developments. Netscape shares went on sale below $20 each, and a frenzy of trading drove the new issue well above $80 per share within hours. At the close of trading during its first day on the market, Netscape, which had recorded less than $20 million earnings in its entire history, had a market value above $2 billion. This prompted *USA Today*'s editors to note that thanks to excitement over the so-called information superhighway that dominated the 1995 media business scene, Netscape had risen overnight to the point where its market value was greater than that of Maytag Corp. Late in the year, Spyglass announced a stock split to compensate for the quadrupling of its own share price.

(JAMES COATES)

This article updates the *Macropædia* articles COMPUTERS; INFORMATION PROCESSING AND INFORMATION SYSTEMS.

Earth and Space Sciences

GEOLOGY AND GEOCHEMISTRY

In 1995 significant developments took place in the realm of geologic mapping, which provides the foundation for the presentation and comparison of data in the Earth sciences. The most important observational development of the past decade was the appearance of a new map of the topography of the world's ocean floors based in part on formerly classified satellite data. In the late 1980s the U.S. Navy's Geosat satellite measured the heights of the ocean surface with a radar altimeter for the purpose of aiding submarine navigation and missile guidance. The measurements yielded maps of gravity anomalies at sea level that mimic the topography of the ocean floor below. With the declassification of the data between 1990 and 1995, researchers were able to combine the Geosat data with those from the European Space Agency's ERS-1 remote-sensing satellite to produce the new topographic map. David Sandwell of the Scripps Institution of Oceanography, La Jolla, Calif., and Walter Smith of the U.S. National Oceanic and Atmospheric Administration employed a complex modeling algorithm to resolve the topography to a precision 30 times better than that in previous maps. Their map revealed in detail the enormous transform fracture zones that record the history of plate motions over millions of years, new underwater volcanoes and faults, and even structures buried under sediments. (See *Oceanography,* below.)

Improved maps of the continents were promised during the year in a report from Tom Farr of the Jet Propulsion Laboratory, Pasadena, Calif., and seven coauthors. The many scientific applications of high-resolution topographic data have been severely limited by the relatively poor quality of the global digital topographic database for continents. According to the report, a Joint Topographic Science Working Group appointed by NASA and the Italian Space Agency was developing a strategy for improving data quality, the most promising approach being a combination of satellite radar interferometry and laser altimetry. A proposed Global Topographic Mission (TOPAC) would improve the best available global digital coverage by more than two orders of magnitude. The recently developed technique of differential radar interferometry, which was capable of measuring topographic changes of less than a centimetre (0.4 in) that occur rapidly over broad regions, had already been used to map surface changes caused by an earthquake, to show the flow of a glacier, and to detect the deformation of a volcano.

The promise of a substantially improved understanding of kinematic and dynamic processes that affect regions of continental deformation was offered in a report from M. Burc Oral and six coauthors from the U.S. and Turkey. Slow movements of the crustal plates covering the Earth's surface and their deformation at places where they meet were being measured by the Global Positioning System (GPS), a precise satellite-based navigation and location system developed for U.S. military use. A plate-tectonic theoretical framework for understanding deformation in the eastern Mediterranean area had first been formulated 25 years earlier and was subsequently developed on the basis of the analysis of global oceanic spreading, fault systems, and earthquake slip. The new space-based GPS measurements supported that basic framework—with an important modification. Western, central, and east-central Turkey and the southern Aegean region and Greece were now seen to be moving as a single tectonic plate, whereas the previous interpretation had called for independent Aegean and Turkish plates that were separated by a zone of north-south extension in western Turkey. The new model had considerable geologic implications.

A 25-year debate about the source and origin of mid-ocean-ridge basalts (MORBs) appeared to have been resolved. The generation and eruption of these lavas at the sites of seafloor spreading, where new crust is being formed, are fundamental processes in the origin of the oceanic crust and the evolution and chemical differentiation of the Earth. According to one hypothesis, MORBs are generated by partial melting of rocks of the Earth's mantle at a depth of about 40 km (25 mi) and are separated from the mantle source at that depth (batch melting). According to the opposing hypothesis, partial melting of the mantle at considerably greater depths generates hotter, magnesium-rich basalt, which precipitates olivine crystals as it ascends and transforms into lavas having the compositions of MORBs.

During the year Michael Baker and Edward Stolper of the California Institute of Technology, using a novel technique developed independently by Ikuo Kushiro of the University of Tokyo, reported experimental results showing that neither hypothesis was satisfactory. They demonstrated that the first hypothesis is impossible—the lavas must have been formed at greater depths—and that the second hypothesis is inadequate—olivine precipitation alone during uprise of the lava from greater depths could not change its composition to that of MORBs. More complicated processes were indicated, and the new model involved upwelling of mantle beneath mid-ocean ridges accompanied by partial melting through a range of depths, with melts of various compositions separating rapidly almost as soon as they form. The melts rise through the rock matrix, and the different melt fractions become aggregated at several depths en route to the surface. Blending and crystal fractionation occurs in magma chambers beneath the ridge before eruption.

Bill Collins of the University of Newcastle, Australia, similarly demonstrated that the history of the granitic rocks forming the continents is more complex than many geologists had believed. A classification system based on origin had been in vogue for 20 years, ever since the granitic rocks of the Lachlan fold belt in Australia were identified as consisting of two contrasting chemical groups and, thus, interpreted to be derived from partial melting of two distinct source rocks in the lower crust. The S-type granites had geochemical characteristics indicating derivation from sedimentary rocks, whereas the I-type granites had characteristics indicating derivation from igneous rocks that had been emplaced in the crust from a mantle source. That classification was widely accepted and the principles applied to granitic rocks worldwide.

Collins pointed out that such a classification led to a paradox: the geochemical differences between S- and I-type granites are not reflected in the composition of their isotopes. Instead, the complete set of S- and I-type granitic rocks shows a continuous range of variation in the isotopes of strontium, neodymium, lead, and oxygen, as if all the rocks of both types had been formed by simple mixing of basalt from the mantle and granite from the crust. Similar arguments had been rejected previously on other geochemical grounds. Collins then showed that his combined field and geochemical data could be explained with a mixing scheme involving three, rather than two, source components. According to Collins, the I-type granites are themselves the products of mixing of mantle-derived basalt with siliceous magma that was formed by partial melting of igneous rocks in the lower crust; subsequent crystallization of the mix produced all the I-type granites. On the other hand, the S-type granites do contain a major sedimentary component, which was identified as Ordovician sediment from mid-crustal levels. The isotopic compositions and the other geochemical characteristics of all the various S-type granites appeared to be explained by the blending of magma derived from the sedimentary source with the magma mix for the I-type granites described above. The new geochemical and petrological interpretations had significance for interpreting the tectonic history of a given region.

Renewed interest in the once-disdained idea that catastrophic events can cause profound changes to the physical Earth and the course of biological evolution had focused during the past 15 years on the relationship of asteroid or comet impacts and mass extinctions during the past 540 million years. In contrast, Andrew Glikson of Parkes, Australia, considered the effects of such impacts on Precambrian rocks, those older than 540 million years. He pointed out that existing models of the geologic evolution of the Precambrian crust fail to explain the episodic nature of major igneous and rifting events seen in the crustal record and also ignore the tectonic and thermal effects of the large-scale extraterrestrial impacts that came after the heavy asteroid bombardment of the young Earth, which ended about 3.9 billion years ago. Estimates of cratering rates left no doubt that the Earth continued to experience many major extraterrestrial impacts between 3.9 billion and 540 million years ago. The possible correlation between the impact that formed the Chicxulub crater in Mexico's Yucatán Peninsula and the massive outpouring of basalt in India (the Deccan Traps)—both of which occurred about 65 million years ago, when the dinosaurs became extinct—led Glikson to seek connections between giant impacts and Precambrian rifting, igneous activity, and other major geologic events. He summarized the correlations of Precambrian impact events with major thermal and tectonic episodes and also concluded that the geochemical signatures of more recent impacts need to be sought in sedimentary rocks distant from the impact structures. Such signatures might take the form of anomalies in the concentrations of platinum-group elements, similar to the iridium anomaly caused by the Chicxulub impact, which appears globally in sediment marking the 65 million-year-old boundary between the Cretaceous and Tertiary periods.

(PETER JOHN WYLLIE)

GEOPHYSICS

The most deadly earthquake of 1995, having a magnitude of 7.2, struck January 17 in the vicinity of Kobe, Japan. Named the Great Hanshin Earthquake, it killed some 6,000 persons and injured more than 30,000. Nearly 200,000 buildings were destroyed or seriously damaged, and more than 300,000 people had to be housed in temporary shelters. Ground effects included liquefaction of the surface in the vicinity of the epicentre and a nine-kilometre surface fracture, with horizontal displacements reaching 1.5 m. (One kilometre is about 0.62 mi; one metre is about 3.3 ft.) Another high-fatality earthquake, having a magnitude of 7.5, occurred May 28 in and around the town of Neftegorsk, Sakhalin Island, in the Sea of Okhotsk off eastern Russia; nearly 2,000 people lost their lives.

Scientists from Oregon State University mapped a blind thrust fault in Ventura county, Calif. The structure, named the Oak Ridge Fault, was designated as blind because it does not reach the surface but is overlaid by the Santa Susana thrust fault. It is the site of the Jan. 17, 1994, Northridge earthquake, which caused more than 60 deaths and major destruction throughout the stricken area. During the Northridge quake both sides of the Santa Susana Fault were displaced owing to the movement on the fault hidden beneath it. It was postulated that if a fault runs through the mountains, rather than along the edge of a valley, as is the case with the Santa Susana Fault, then it is probable that a blind fault lies beneath it.

The physical mechanism by which energy is suddenly released in deep-focus earthquakes—*i.e.,* those that occur below about 400 km depth—has long been a puzzle to seismologists. At such depths high temperature and pressure should cause rock under stress to flow smoothly rather than rupture suddenly, as it does in earthquakes near the surface. Recent studies by researchers at the University of California, Santa Cruz, showed that on average the deeper the focus, the more symmetrical the pattern of energy release over time. As recorded on a seismograph, the disturbances caused by a deep-focus earthquake tend to begin abruptly, build to a maximum, and then end relatively quickly and smoothly. The researchers believed that such a pattern is due to the uniformity of the material at the focus but could not determine whether it is the result of a rupture or a geochemical transformation that releases a burst of energy.

A strong impetus to the search for an acceptable theory for deep-focus earthquakes resulted from the occurrence of the great Bolivian earthquake of June 9, 1994. At magnitude 8.2 it was the largest shock on record to have had a focus more than 600 km below the surface, at the base of the upper mantle. Upon analysis by investigators of the Carnegie Institution of Washington, D.C., and the University of Arizona, the rupture zone was found to be many times too large—it covered a horizontal area 30 × 50 km—to fit the currently accepted olivine–spinel transformation theory. According to that explanation, transformation under pressure of the mineral olivine into a more stable mineral, spinel, causes microfissures, which permit an earthquake to occur. Because deep-focus earthquakes generally take place beneath areas of active subduction, where the edge of one of a pair of colliding crustal plates is descending beneath the edge of the other plate, it was thought that such quakes have their origin in subducted crustal slabs that have survived the descent to deep-focus depths. Because the slab supposedly erodes and thins as it descends, however, at 600 km or deeper it would be much thinner than the size of the fracture zone calculated for the Bolivian earthquake. Several studies were under way to test various alternative theories. One speculative idea was that under the extremes of temperature and pressure at depth, some kind of nuclear reaction occurs that releases energy directly, with little or no physical deformation.

As was happening in other spheres of science, geophysics was benefiting greatly from high technology. Developments in computers and instrumentation were increasing accuracies and resolution manyfold. Two techniques for exploring beneath the Earth's surface recently gained recognition. One, called cross-borehole seismology, was first used by scientists at the French Petroleum Institute in the early 1970s but did not attain wider acceptance until advances in instrumentation made it feasible. Seismic studies on the surface collect data on wavelengths of 20–100 m, while well logs (records made during well drilling) register wavelengths of 0.3–1 m and measure the environment immediately around the borehole. In contrast, cross-borehole seismology covers the range of wavelengths from two to five metres. Instruments are set up in an array, with receivers vertically spaced in one borehole and signal generators placed in surrounding boreholes at distances of 100–300 m. The generated signals are tailored so as not to damage the borehole but still be strong enough for reception. By means of multiple receivers and multistation receiver cables, it is possible to record as many as 25,000 seismograms in a few days. The analysis of the data is quite complex, combining the techniques of medical X-ray computed tomography and more conventional wave-tracing techniques of exploration seismology with enhancement from standard reflection imaging. The dramatic enhancement of rock-structure definition gained by the technique was expected to increase the detection of high-porosity zones and permeability barriers and thus help identify oil reservoirs and their dimensions.

The second technique, geophysical diffraction tomography, is similarly derived from medical tomography. First developed in the early 1980s, it involves the mathematical combination of many individual signals from a specifically designed array of instruments to produce a three-dimensional image of the region traversed by the signals. As of 1995 it had been used to detect underground tunnels across the demilitarized zone between North Korea and South Korea; to trace the outline of the still unexcavated fossil bones of *Seismosaurus,* an enormous dinosaur discovered in the southwestern U.S.; and to map the remains of ancient underground settlements in the Negev region of Israel.

Using data collected by satellites of the Global Posi-

NATSUKO UTSUMI—GAMMA LIAISON

Part of Kobe, Japan, lies in ruins following the earthquake that struck the area on January 17. Although there were more powerful shocks during the year, the Great Hanshin Earthquake was the most damaging in terms of injuries and deaths and in destruction of property.

tioning System (GPS), researchers from the University of Colorado and Stanford University found that Australia is moving north-northeast with respect to Antarctica at a rate of five to eight centimetres (two to three inches) per year. The detection of that heretofore unknown movement was made possible by means of weekly measurements of the relative positions of points all over Antarctica, Australia, Hawaii, New Zealand, Tahiti, and Tasmania carried out by GPS satellites and disseminated on the Internet. The GPS system was capable of measuring positional variations of less than 2 mm (0.08 in).

Work carried out on Legs 152 through 158 of the International Ocean Drilling Program (ODP), which studied the crust beneath the world's oceans by means of the coring and extraction of rock samples from below the seafloor, was confined to the Atlantic Ocean. Exploration proceeded from sites on or near the continental shelf southeast of Greenland (Leg 152) to the Mid-Atlantic Ridge south of the Kane Fracture Zone (Leg 153), to a transept across the Ceara Rise in the western equatorial Atlantic (Leg 154), to the Amazon River deep-sea fan (Leg 155), to the deformation front of the North Barbados Ridge (Leg 156), to the Canary Basin (Leg 157), and finally to the Mid-Atlantic Ridge at latitude 26° N (Leg 158). The ODP expeditions collected data relevant to paleoceanography (study of the ocean in past ages), seafloor spreading, and the evolution of the Mid-Atlantic Ridge at those critical sites.

(RUTLAGE J. BRAZEE)

HYDROLOGY

Floods and drought again played a large role in global hydrology during the year. Although flooding in the U.S. Midwest was less severe than that experienced in 1993, it continued to raise questions about the need for flood-management policy in the major river basins. California pursued its recovery from the multiyear drought of the late 1980s and early '90s with a vengeance as storms and floods hit throughout the state early in the year.

In northwestern Europe flooding of the Rhine, Main, Meuse, Waal, and other major rivers during January and February was as great as it had ever been in the past 40 years. Valley residents evacuated as rivers rose throughout the subcontinent; the Rhine reached the highest level witnessed since the 18th century. Paradoxically some of the same areas later endured a summer that was among the hottest and driest on record. Flooding also plagued Morocco and Egypt, and North Korea was so badly affected that it requested aid from the UN.

Drought persisted in the northeastern U.S. and the Caribbean, including Puerto Rico. Scientists speculated that the Caribbean islands were experiencing a Sahel-like dry period that recurred about every 25 years. Desperate farmers in northern Mexico watched their fields wither once again under the onslaught of a third year of drought.

Water-management efforts around the globe continued to effect large-scale geologic changes and thus to raise concerns about environmental problems. Dam-building projects in India promised to create large amounts of water-storage capacity and hydroelectric power within three years, but opponents objected on environmental and social grounds since the reservoirs would flood many villages and much farmland and inundate thousands of hectares of riverside habitat. In the face of both local and worldwide criticism over population displacement and environmental damage, construction continued on the nearly 2-km (1¼-mi)-wide Three Gorges Dam on the Chang Jiang (Yangtze River) in China, which would form a reservoir 600 km (370 mi) long when completed. In Germany a plan to alter the flow of the Danube River with locks in order to move more commercial traffic met with vehement objections from residents all along the river.

A chronically disappearing lake was caught in the act of reappearing. Lake Merzbacher in the Tien Shan Mountains of Kyrgyzstan, in Central Asia, mysteriously drains and refills on an annual, or sometimes biannual, cycle. Aerial photographic studies in 1995 recorded the lake as it returned. Interest also was focused on another hydrologic mystery in Central Asia, the rise in the level of the Caspian Sea, which has persisted since the late 1970s despite the presence of numerous hydroelectric dams and reservoirs on its inflowing rivers. As the world's largest inland sea encroached on towns and industrial sites along its shores, experts debated various explanations, including changing weather patterns, tectonic activity affecting the seafloor, increased influx from the Volga River, and even an underground shift of water from the shrinking Aral Sea, which lies about 500 km (300 mi) to the east.

(N. EARL SPANGENBERG)

METEOROLOGY AND CLIMATE

An abnormally strong and southward-displaced jet stream across the Pacific Ocean, partially fueled by an unprecedentedly prolonged El Niño warming of the eastern tropical Pacific (*see* Sidebar), steered strong storms into the western United States that produced excessive precipitation and severe flooding across California in January and again in March. In stark contrast, a relatively mild, dry winter prevailed over the eastern United States, while a severe drought, also influenced by the El Niño, afflicted Hawaii from October 1994 to March 1995.

As spring progressed, the displaced jet stream pushed strong storms into the Midwest, bringing precipitation more than twice normal to many areas between mid-April and mid-June. Water levels along the middle and upper Mississippi River, the lower and middle Missouri, and their tributaries approached but did not exceed those reached during the 1993 floods. In contrast, the aforementioned atmospheric pattern kept much of the Atlantic Seaboard unusually dry, and during the summer subnormal rainfall persisted across the Northeast and Middle Atlantic states. In July a short-lived but intense heat wave enveloped the central and eastern U.S., accounting for nearly 1,000 heat-related deaths from the High Plains to the Atlantic Seaboard, including more than 700 in the Chicago area alone.

One of the most active Atlantic hurricane seasons in history, featuring 17 storms of at least tropical-storm strength through mid-October, abetted wetness across parts of the Caribbean islands, Florida, and the southern U.S. Allison, the first June hurricane in 10 years, tracked through western Florida and the south Atlantic states. In August remnants of Tropical Storm Dean inundated southeastern Texas and parts of the Great Plains, while Hurricane Erin pushed through The Bahamas before striking Florida twice, once along the central Atlantic coast and again along the western Panhandle. Subsequently, Hurricane Felix buffeted Bermuda with strong winds and heavy rain and then stalled in the western Atlantic, which resulted in prolonged high winds, rough surf, and beach erosion along the U.S. East Coast. In late August and September Hurricanes Iris, Luis, and Marilyn all battered parts of the eastern Caribbean islands. The latter two storms hit the northeastern Leeward Islands head on, causing widespread damage. All three storms stayed away from the eastern U.S., but the coastline again took a prolonged beating from rough surf and very high tides. In October yet another hurricane, Opal, struck the western Florida Panhandle with winds gusting to 232

(continued on page 165)

What's Happening to El Niño?

Most of the year-to-year variability in climate in the tropics—and much of it worldwide—is related through a phenomenon called El Niño. The term originally applied to an annual warm ocean current that runs along the coast of Peru about Christmastime; in Spanish, El Niño refers to the Christ child. Today, however, it designates a much larger anomalous ocean warming that stretches westward to the international date line. It is this phenomenon that is linked with the unusual global climate patterns that occur every few years. El Niño is not solely oceanic but couples intimately with an atmospheric component termed the Southern Oscillation. Scientists often refer to the two together as the El Niño–Southern Oscillation, or ENSO.

ENSO is a natural phenomenon that appears to have been going on for millennia. Conditions in the tropical Pacific actually are seldom average but, instead, fluctuate irregularly between the warm El Niño phase and a cooling phase, dubbed La Niña. A complete ENSO cycle runs about three to six years, with the most intense El Niño phase lasting about a year. Although no two ENSOs are alike, 11 have been identified since 1950. The warm phase of the most recent cycle persisted from 1990 to mid-1995, a duration unprecedented in the last 114 years of instrumental records—clearly a signal that something very unusual is happening.

The stage for an El Niño is set by a distinctive pattern of sea-surface temperatures in the Pacific. Key features include a pool of warm water in the western tropical Pacific and much colder waters in the eastern Pacific. Easterly trade winds pile up the warm waters in the west, while wind-driven surface currents allow cooler nutrient-rich waters to upwell along the Equator and western coasts of the Americas, favouring plankton growth and thus fish. In time the increased convection and rainstorms that tend to occur over warmer waters affect atmospheric heating, which in turn influences the winds. The easterly trades weaken, and the warm waters in the west migrate eastward. This shifts the pattern of tropical rainstorms, further weakening the trades and reinforcing the eastward flow of warm waters.

The atmospheric changes, however, are not confined to the tropics. They extend globally and affect the temperate latitudes, typically bringing dryness to some regions and heavy rainfall to others. The effects of an El Niño on society can be large, with losses often overshadowing gains. The oceanic changes can be disastrous for fish and seabirds and thus for the fishing and guano industries along the South American coast. The atmospheric changes act to suppress tropical storms and hurricanes in the tropical Atlantic. Consequently, the return to normal Pacific conditions in mid-1995 unleashed numerous devastating Atlantic tropical storms.

Recent research has clarified ENSO's cyclic nature, showing that the moisture content and enormous heat capacity of the ocean make it the flywheel that drives the system through an essentially self-sustained seesawing sequence in which the ocean and atmosphere are never in equilibrium. Tropical warm water is redistributed, depleted, and restored during an ENSO cycle such that much of what is to come is determined by the previous one to two years. Consequently, the future becomes predictable for several seasons in advance.

ENSO's recent abnormal behaviour has scientists wondering. Is it a natural variation, or is it related to human activity—in particular, to global warming associated with increases in greenhouse gases in the atmosphere? A computer model using a century of modern ENSO records to simulate cycles for a million years suggests that the 1990–95 El Niño is very unusual and that the climate indeed may be changing in a way that will make such behaviour more likely. Increased greenhouse gases trap more heat in the atmosphere—clearly a potential source of interference with ENSO.

What does this mean for the future? Because greenhouse gases are likely to continue increasing, the climate can be expected to continue to change, sometimes in ways unexpected. A challenge for scientists is to capitalize on their improved understanding of ENSO to make seasonal predictions of temperatures, rainfalls, and the way that the risk of extreme conditions varies from year to year. (KEVIN E. TRENBERTH)

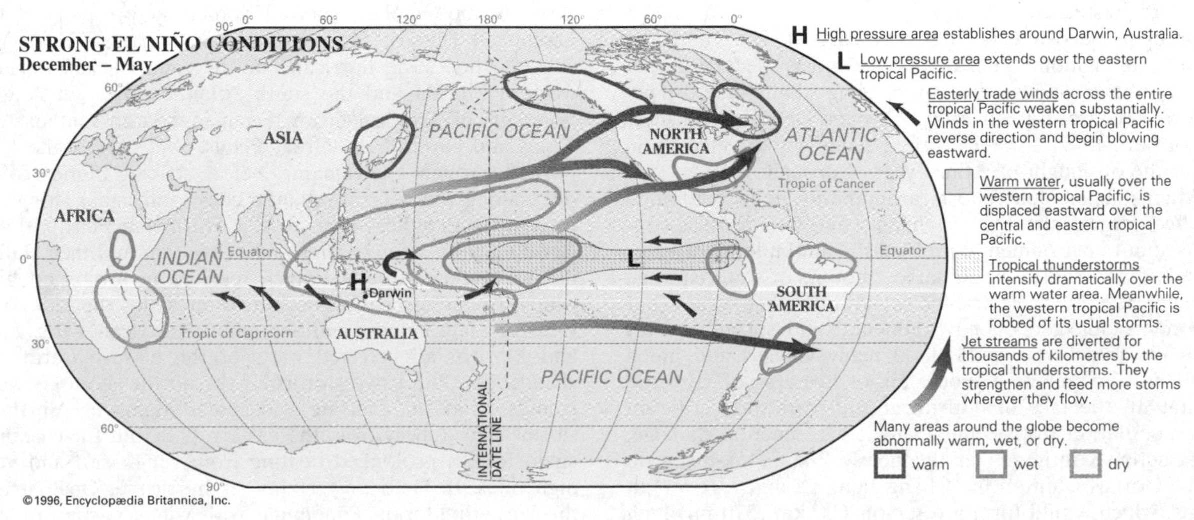

Boats at a yacht club in Manila are battered by the winds of approaching Typhoon Angela, which struck the Philippines on November 3. It was estimated that the storm, which was the strongest to hit the islands since 1984, killed more than 600 people and left more than 600,000 homeless.
ROMEO RANOCO—REUTERS

(continued from page 163)
km/h (144 mph). Opal's remnants spawned locally heavy rains and tornadoes in the East but brought much-needed rainfall to the Northeast. The storm also took 10 lives on Mexico's Yucatán Peninsula, which then was hit by Hurricane Roxanne a week later.

During January and February heavy rains caused localized flooding and crop damage in south-central Brazil. In contrast, almost eight months of exceptionally dry weather were reported across east-central Brazil. April brought beneficial rains to those regions, but heavy rains farther south soaked northeastern Argentina and produced brief but severe flash flooding near Buenos Aires.

Between 100 and 250 mm (4 and 10 in) of precipitation fell on saturated ground across much of central and western Europe during the last two weeks of January, pushing several rivers to levels rivaling those observed during the December 1993 "Flood of the Century." In June hot, dry weather enveloped the British Isles, eastern Europe, and western Asia. The conditions expanded across most of Europe and northwestern Africa through July and August and were particularly extreme in the British Isles. Dryness dominated many areas of southern Africa in late January and February, and above-normal temperatures further stressed crops. Late-March rains finally brought relief to most locations, although heavy rains evaded Zambia and northern Zimbabwe, where soil-moisture shortages persisted. The African Sahel wet season (May–September) was rather uneventful, with most areas receiving near-normal rains.

A heat wave overspread Pakistan and northern India during June. Temperatures reached 50° C (122° F) at some locations, causing hundreds of deaths. By month's end, however, monsoonal showers had begun advancing through the region, and torrential rains fell on many locations throughout July and early August, causing sporadic river flooding. For the Indian subcontinent as a whole, the summer of 1995 was the seventh wettest since 1934.

Conditions varied markedly with time and location across the Far East. Between mid-April and mid-July, heavy rains doused parts of northern Hunan and Jiangxi provinces in China, leading to severe flooding that claimed more than 1,000 lives. In addition, heavy rains during an 11-week period that ended in early September spawned severe flooding across lower northeastern China and North Korea. Beginning in April unusually wet weather also dominated southeastern China (through August) and western Japan (into late July), punctuated by Typhoon Faye, which lashed southern South Korea and western Japan in mid-July. From late July through early October, eight tropical storms or typhoons pummeled parts of the Philippines, Taiwan, southern China, and northern Vietnam. By contrast, much of central and east-central China endured abnormally dry summer conditions. Summer dryness also plagued south-central and eastern Japan before Typhoon Oscar soaked the region, including Tokyo, in September.

After a rather dry start to Australia's 1994–95 wet season, the year commenced with subnormal January rains along the northwestern and eastern coastlines, but at least twice the normal January rain pelted areas from central Queensland southward through eastern Tasmania, resulting in localized flooding. Farther west, Cyclone Bobby brought rare heavy rains and locally severe flash flooding to much of Western Australia. Subnormal precipitation during March and April adversely affected agriculture in Queensland, but widespread beneficial rains fell on the eastern half of Australia during May. (ELBERT W. FRIDAY, JR.)

OCEANOGRAPHY

One of the most important themes in oceanography in 1995 was exploration. Some of it was conducted in the traditional mode, from ships, but much was done from Earth-orbiting satellites. Remarkably, satellite radar measurements were able to tell scientists not only about the motion of the ocean's surface waters but also about the shape of the underlying seafloor. Radar measurements of the distance from the satellite to the sea surface provided a picture of the shape of the Earth that was accurate to a few centimetres once the effects of waves and tides had been removed. (A centimetre is about 0.4 in.) Such determinations were possible because the solid material beneath the seafloor gravitationally attracts the water above it in a way that mirrors seafloor topography. For example, the sea surface near a seamount is a few metres farther from the Earth's centre than is the sea surface far from the seamount, and the sea surface over a submarine trench is a few metres closer than is the sea surface far from the trench. (A metre is about 3.3 ft.) Satellite radar easily measures such differences in sea level and thus, in principle, can map the seafloor.

The U.S. Navy had made such global satellite radar measurements in the late 1980s, but the data only gradually became available to researchers. In 1995 the last of the data were released and combined with similar radar measurements from other satellites to form a global database. The most exciting result was a map of the global seafloor. Because much of the seafloor previously had been only sparsely surveyed, the new map revealed many new features. The large-scale features of the seafloor continued to be understandable in terms of the theory of plate tectonics, according to which the global seafloor is divided into about a dozen plates of crust that move rigidly away from mid-ocean ridges toward regions of subduction (where one plate is plunging beneath another), such as deep-ocean trenches, or sometimes directly collide with one another. Nevertheless, the new map showed features suggesting that the plates are not entirely rigid but, rather, are compressed or pulled apart as they approach different subduction regions. Because the gravitational attraction of seafloor material depends on how heavy it is, such satellite maps of the seafloor also contained information about the density and temperature of the material underlying the seafloor and thus should aid in understanding of the global distribution of mineral resources on the seafloor. (See *Geology and Geochemistry*, above.)

The sea surface is not exactly where one would expect to find it solely on the basis of knowledge of the way that seafloor material distorts the Earth's gravity field. The discrepancy is small, generally a few tens of centimetres or less, but it can be determined by a comparison of satellite radar measurements of sea-surface shape with the shape calculated from the very best estimates of the Earth's total gravity field. The difference directly reflects the motion of the water in the upper ocean. For example, because of the rapidly flowing Gulf Stream, the sea surface along the U.S. east coast is about a metre closer to the centre of the Earth than that in the Sargasso Sea. During the year researchers continued to study the circulation of the oceans, using satellite measurements made for the joint U.S.-French Topex/Poseidon project. Launched in 1992, the Topex/Poseidon satellite made radar measurements of sea level along the same geographic track once every 10 days and thus provided a unique view of fluctuations in upper-ocean flow over months, seasons, and years. It could resolve variations in sea level ranging from waves that traverse the tropical ocean over a period of months to sea-level differences between different years associated with the anomalous tropical Pacific Ocean warming known as El Niño. (*See* Sidebar.) Researchers were also using the satellite to look directly for the slow sea-level rise associated with hypothesized ongoing global warming.

Despite the strides in satellite oceanography, more traditional measurements made from ships were needed in order to understand the deep flow of the ocean. The World Ocean Circulation Experiment (WOCE), which began in 1990, was a multinational study of ocean circulation. Many different kinds of measurements were made as part of WOCE, but the central field program around which they were organized was a series of hydrographic transects by ship that traversed the major ocean basins. The central measurements made on each transect were of the temperature and salinity of the water from the top to the bottom of the ocean; they were supplemented by measurements of nutrients and dissolved gases as well as by underwater acoustic profiles of currents below the ship. At the very end of 1994, WOCE researchers began a series of research cruises in the Indian Ocean that continued through 1995. The goals of that work were to learn how deep waters flow into the Indian Ocean from around Antarctica and how they rise and then return southward at shallower depths, to learn how the Indian Ocean contributes to the global transport of heat, and to provide a background picture of the deep flow underlying the surface circulation that was being studied by satellite radar and other techniques. (MYRL C. HENDERSHOTT)

ASTRONOMY

The year 1995 presented astronomers with another set of exciting discoveries. As insights into cometary dynamics and gas-planet atmospheric physics continued to emerge from the spectacular crash of Comet Shoemaker-Levy 9 into the planet Jupiter in 1994, a new comet was detected that could turn out to be even more spectacular. Perhaps the biggest newsmaker in astronomy was the announcement of the discovery of a planet outside the solar system orbiting a star much like the Sun. Other noteworthy reports ranged from the discovery of new satellites of the planet Saturn to a better understanding of the nature of intergalactic matter at the most distant reaches of the universe.

Solar System. Saturn is best known for the beautiful rings encircling the planet. Just beyond the main ring system lies the so-called F ring, a wispy band of material sometimes described as braided or clumped. In 1980 and 1981, as the two Voyager spacecraft flew by Saturn, they discovered two moons, later dubbed Prometheus and Pandora, which appear to "shepherd" material into the clumps observed in the F ring. The glare of sunlight reflected off the rings usually makes direct observation from Earth of Saturn's many small moons difficult. Every 14 to 16 years, however, the rings appear edge-on as seen from Earth, and in 1995 astronomers had their first opportunity to use the Earth-orbiting Hubble Space Telescope (HST) to observe the Saturnian environment free of ring glare. Amanda Bosh of the Lowell Observatory, Flagstaff, Ariz., and Andrew Rivkin of the University of Arizona reported finding two, and perhaps as many as four, new satellites of Saturn. Later it was determined that one of the objects was indeed a previously unknown moon. Designated 1995 S4, it is no more than 70 km (45 mi) across and lies just outside the F ring. On the other hand, the other objects were thought to be the previously seen moons Pan, Atlas, or Prometheus. The confusion may have arisen as a result of the complex dynamics between the moons and the rocky debris of the rings, leading to unforeseen motions of the moons. At year's end astronomers counted at least 19 moons around Saturn, though there may well be more. Unfortunately, the next good opportunity to search for such moons from Earth, when the rings will be edge-on and Saturn will be far enough from the Sun's glare, will not occur until the year 2038.

Between July 16 and 22, 1994, 21 fragments of Comet Shoemaker-Levy 9 collided with the giant gas planet Jupiter. Months later Earth-based infrared telescopes continued to detect dark markings on Jupiter at the planetary latitudes of the impact sites. A new estimate placed the size of the original comet, before it had been tidally fragmented by Jupiter's gravity, at about 2 km (1.2 mi) in diameter. Whether the resulting markings on Jupiter arose from the original cometary material or from compounds synthesized in the impact explosions was still hotly debated.

Just as public interest in comets began to wane, a new comet was reported that, according to some predictions, could become the brightest since the so-called Great Comet of 1811. Discovered on July 22 by two amateur astronomers, Alan Hale and Thomas Bopp, Comet Hale-Bopp was first spotted at a distance of about seven times that of the Earth from the Sun, beyond the orbit of Jupiter and farther out than any other comet detected to date by amateurs. Given its distance and brightness, astronomers estimated it to be about 5–10 times the size of Halley's Comet, which is roughly 15 km in diameter. When it made its closest approach to the Sun in early 1997, it could be the brightest object in the night sky other than the Moon and Venus, and its tail could stretch as much as a third of the way across the sky.

Comets made more news in 1995 when scientists led by Anita L. Cochran of the University of Texas, using the HST, discovered 30 objects lying in a region beyond the orbits of the outermost planets Pluto and Neptune. In the past few years, searches with ground-based telescopes had revealed about 20 such trans-Neptunian objects. The newly discovered bodies appeared to be members of the Kuiper Belt, a ring or shell of objects at the outer reaches of the solar system, which is thought to be the source of most comets. The objects detected by the HST were thought to be about 20 km in diameter, compared with the estimated 200-km diameters of the previously detected trans-Neptunian objects. On the basis of the size of the region surveyed by the HST, astronomers calculated that the Kuiper Belt may hold as many as 100 million objects. According to current thinking, occasional passing stars gravitationally perturb the Kuiper Belt objects, kicking some into the inner solar system and nearer the Sun, where they become visible as comets when their ices and gases evaporate.

Stars. The announced detection of a planet orbiting a Sun-like star, if confirmed, may well turn out to be the most exciting astronomical discovery of 1995. Michael Mayor and Didier Queloz of the Geneva Observatory announced the discovery of an object having roughly the mass of Jupiter in orbit around the solar-type star 51 Pegasi, which lies only about 42 light-years from the Sun. Their claim was based on a year and a half of precise observations of the star's velocity. A periodic variation detected in the velocity was interpreted as being due to the gravitational tug of an unseen companion orbiting 51 Pegasi. Although certain unknowns prevented the astronomers from calculating a mass for the companion, they were able to determine a minimum value—about one-half the mass of Jupiter. The unseen object orbits 51 Pegasi with a period of 4.2 days at a distance of only 1/20 the Earth-Sun distance; *i.e.,* the planet must lie inside the hot corona of its star. If the detected velocity variations in 51 Pegasi indeed are due to a companion, the observations raise a number of questions. How could a planet have formed so near to its parent star? Is it gaseous (like Jupiter) or rocky (like Mercury)? Is it really small enough to be a planet, or is it a more massive object such as a brown dwarf, a stellar object too small to produce energy by nuclear reactions?

Other reports of objects around stars were made during the year. Interpreting near-infrared images and spectra, Shrinivas Kulkarni and collaborators at the California Institute of Technology announced their detection of an object about 20 times the mass of Jupiter orbiting the tiny star GL 229, which lies about 30 light-years from the Sun. The observed infrared spectrum indicated the presence of methane, a molecule unlikely to exist in the atmosphere of a normal star. Though the dividing line between a planet and a brown dwarf was unclear, the companion object to GL 229 is either a massive planet or arguably the best case yet for a brown dwarf.

Since 1991 evidence had been accumulating that a pulsar (a rapidly spinning neutron star) designated PSR B1257+12 was orbited by at least two planets. Continuing observations of the system in 1995 revealed at least three planets having masses that ranged from a few percent of that of Earth to about 3.4 Earth masses. The three planets orbit the pulsar at distances between 19% and 47% of the Earth–Sun distance. Intriguingly, the ratio of the orbital radii follows precisely the same relation, called Bode's law, as do most of the planets in the solar system.

Another promising candidate for a brown dwarf was discovered in the Pleiades star cluster, a comparatively young (100 million-year-old) star-forming region lying about 400 light-years from the Sun. From observations with a ground-based telescope in the Canary Islands and other instruments, astronomers concluded that the object, dubbed Teide 1, probably has a mass about 20 times that of Jupiter, although a somewhat higher value could not be ruled out.

During the year research continued on two remarkable objects lying within the Milky Way Galaxy and exhibiting energetic outbursts. One, called GRS 1915+105, is in a class of objects known as X-ray novas. They produce an X-ray outburst, which then fades away, somewhat akin to the much more energetic outbursts observed in active galaxies and quasars. Also like quasars, the GRS 1915+105 outburst was followed by the ejection of two radio-emitting blobs

Earth Perihelion and Aphelion, 1996

Jan. 1	Perihelion, 147,000,000 km (91,390,000 mi) from the Sun
July 5	Aphelion, 152,000,000 km (94,510,000 mi) from the Sun

Equinoxes and Solstices, 1996

March 20	Vernal equinox, 08:03[1]
June 21	Summer solstice, 02:24[1]
Sept. 22	Autumnal equinox, 18:00[1]
Dec. 21	Winter solstice, 14:06[1]

Eclipses, 1996

April 3–4	Moon, total (begins 21:16[1]), the beginning visible in extreme eastern North America, South America east of the Andes, southern and eastern Greenland, Europe, western and central Asia, Africa, the Indian Ocean, and extreme western Australia; the end visible throughout the Western Hemisphere except for the western United States and western Canada and in Europe, western Asia, and Africa.
April 17–18	Sun, partial (begins 22:05[1]), the beginning visible in the South Pacific Ocean south of Tasmania, Australia; the end visible in the South Pacific west of South America (south of the Galapagos Islands).
Sept. 27	Moon, total (begins 03:06[1]), the beginning visible in central and eastern regions of Canada and the United States, much of Mexico, South America, Greenland, Europe, western Asia, and Africa; the end visible in the entire Western Hemisphere, western and central Europe, and western Africa.
Oct. 12	Sun, partial (begins 13:24[1]), the beginning visible south of Hudson Bay (near Winnipeg) and in northern Greenland; the end visible in northeastern Africa (near Khartoum).

[1]Universal time.
Source: *The Astronomical Almanac for the Year 1996* (1995).

Dust and hydrogen gas were sculpted into pillarlike clouds by "photoevaporation" under the intense light emitted from nearby newborn stars (off the top edge of the image). The clouds, part of a star-forming region known as the Eagle Nebula (M16), were photographed by the Hubble Space Telescope in April.
JEFF HESTER AND PAUL SCOWEN—UNIVERSITY OF ARIZONA/NASA

that were observed to be moving transverse to the line of sight from Earth. Six months of observations indicated that the blobs were moving at 92% of the speed of light.

Another transient X-ray source, called GRO J1655−40, which lies some 10,000 light-years from the Sun in the constellation Scorpius, was first detected by the Earth-orbiting Compton Gamma Ray Observatory in 1994. Subsequent radio observations with the Very Long Baseline Array in New Mexico revealed ejected material racing away from the central object with the highest rate of angular motion found to date for any object outside the solar system. Although that rate, combined with the distance to the source, yields an apparent speed for the ejected material that is 50% greater than the speed of light, the observations can be understood as arising from motion at less than the speed of light but in a direction nearly along the line of sight to Earth.

Galaxies and Cosmology. One of the most remarkable predictions of Einstein's general theory of relativity is that gravity bends light. That effect was first demonstrated during a total solar eclipse in 1919, when the positions of stars near the Sun were observed to be slightly shifted from their usual positions—an effect due to the pull of the Sun's gravity as the stars' light passed close to the Sun. In the 1930s Einstein predicted that a mass distribution could act as a gravitational "lens," not only bending light but also distorting images of objects lying beyond the gravitating mass. In 1995 the HST recorded one of the most spectacular examples of a gravitationally lensed astronomical system. An image of the relatively close galaxy cluster Abell 2218 showed a collection of spiral and elliptical galaxies, along with about 120 filamentary arcs. The arcs are light from galaxies lying much farther away than Abell 2218. Theoretical analysis of the shape and distribution of the arcs suggested that they are images of galaxies formed at a time when the universe was only about one-fourth its present age, only a few billion years after its beginning.

The presence of the same lensing effect appeared to have misled astronomers four years earlier into claiming that they had detected the brightest object in the universe. The galaxy, called FSC 10214+4724, had been estimated to be about 100 trillion times more luminous than the Sun, or 1,000 times brighter than the entire Milky Way. However, in two independent studies that made use of the giant W.M. Keck Telescope in Hawaii and the HST, astronomers found that a galaxy in the foreground acts as a gravitational lens to increase the apparent brightness of FSC 10214+4724. Their observations, made in the near-infrared, suggested that the galaxy is only about as bright as other giant elliptical galaxies that lie relatively close to the Milky Way.

A major prediction of the big-bang model of cosmology, which hypothesizes that the universe began with a hot explosion, is that most of the helium observed today was synthesized from hydrogen in nuclear reactions occurring during the universe's fiery first few minutes. In 1995 the spectroscopic signature of helium filling intergalactic space was seen in data from the Astro 2 Observatory carried aloft on the U.S. space shuttle *Endeavour* in March. Using the space observatory's Hopkins Ultraviolet Telescope, Arthur F. Davidson and collaborators of Johns Hopkins University, Baltimore, Md., reported finding absorption lines characteristic of helium in the spectrum of the quasar HS 1700+64, which lies about 10 billion light-years from the Sun. Detection of intergalactic matter had eluded scientists for more than three decades. Analysis of the observations suggested that intergalactic hydrogen and helium constitute more matter than had been detected in all the visible stars and galaxies seen to date. The exact amount of intergalactic gas was uncertain, however, since it was not clear whether it resides in clumps as intergalactic clouds or as diffuse matter uniformly filling intergalactic space. In either case, the amount of gaseous matter detected, while significant, does not contribute enough mass to the universe to slow its expansion to a halt in the future and then cause it to collapse. (*See* MATHEMATICS AND PHYSICAL SCIENCES: *Physics*.)

(KENNETH BRECHER)

This article updates the *Macropædia* articles The COSMOS; GALAXIES; The PHYSICAL SCIENCES: *Astronomy;* The SOLAR SYSTEM; STARS AND STAR CLUSTERS.

SPACE EXPLORATION

Space station practice missions dominated space news during 1995 as the United States and Russia prepared to start building an international space station that could cost a total of $100 billion through the year 2012. By contrast, unmanned exploration took a turn for the smaller and cheaper as the U.S. initiated a low-cost program for planetary exploration. Meanwhile, NASA faced a drastic downsizing on

May 19 when Administrator Daniel Goldin announced a cut of 3,560 civil service jobs and up to 25,300 contractor jobs—30% of the NASA-based workforce—by the year 2000. Goldin also revealed that space shuttle operations would be turned over to a single private contractor.

Manned Spaceflight. The highlight of the year was the docking of the U.S. space shuttle *Endeavour* with Russia's space station *Mir.* The rendezvous came almost 20 years after the Apollo-Soyuz Test Project, the first docking of manned spacecraft from two separate countries. Before the 1995 docking, a practice rendezvous was flown by the space shuttle *Discovery* in February to demonstrate the shuttle orbiter's ability to approach and maneuver safely around *Mir.* Despite a leaky thruster that might have damaged *Mir*'s solar arrays, rendezvous occurred on schedule on February 6 at an altitude of 392 km (245 mi). *Discovery* came within 11.3 m (37 ft) of *Mir* at speeds as low as 0.03 m (0.1 ft) per second. *Discovery* then moved into a separate orbit for another week of operations, including a space walk by mission specialists who tested new gloves on the space suits.

Following the *Discovery* rendezvous, U.S. astronaut Norman Thagard rode the Soyuz TM-21 on March 14 with commander Vladimir Dezhurov and flight engineer Gennady Strekalov to rendezvous with and board *Mir.* Thagard stayed aboard for three months to start developing U.S. expertise in long-term space operations, including biomedical experiments.

The shuttle docking with *Mir* was achieved by *Atlantis* on June 29 and continued until July 4. The mission included the exchange of crew members as Thagard (who set a U.S. space record of 115 days), Strekalov, and Dezhurov returned to Earth aboard *Atlantis.* They were replaced by Anatoly Solovyev and Nikolay Budarin, who rode up on *Atlantis.* The docking was made possible with a special module similar to the one that was to be used to link shuttles with the international space station when it was completed.

Endeavour carried the Astro-2 cluster of three telescopes to observe the heavens in ultraviolet light. Information on the mission, on March 2–18, was available in real time via the Internet, and more than 350,000 requests were logged during its three-day availability.

The launch of *Discovery* in July had been delayed for several weeks to repair damage by woodpeckers. This odd "space first" happened when northern flicker woodpeckers mistook the shuttle's external tank's reddish-coloured foam insulation for rotting wood and bored numerous holes in the foam. Once in orbit, the crew launched the last Tracking and Data Relay Satellite to replace the one that was lost when *Challenger* was destroyed in 1986. During the mission NASA started trial operations with its new Consolidated Control Center, which used advanced computer workstations in place of the familiar 1960s-era digital television displays.

After a delay of more than a month because of defective booster nozzles and a generator malfunction, *Endeavour* was launched on September 7. Attempts to operate the specialized Wake Shield Facility (WSF) satellite were frustrated. After being launched from the shuttle, the WSF flew for several orbits to process special electronics materials in the ultrahard vacuum created in its own wake, although it was pointed in the wrong direction for part of the flight. Two days after launching the satellite, the shuttle crew retrieved it and found that it had shut down automatically. Two crew members walked in space to test tools and techniques for assembling a space station. The crew also launched the Spartan 201 solar observatory.

On one of the longest missions of the year, from October 20 to November 5, *Columbia* carried the U.S. Microgravity Laboratory-2. Experiments included the growth of crystals and other materials and the first use by astronauts of the Geophysical Fluid Flow Facility, which was designed to simulate the flow of the atmosphere of Jupiter. During a flight on November 12–20, astronauts aboard *Atlantis* attached to *Mir* a docking module for use by future shuttle missions.

The 10-year-old *Mir* continued to operate, thanks to frequent repairs and the concerted efforts of ground and flight crews. Going into 1995, *Mir* was crewed by Aleksandr Viktorenko, Yelena Kondakova, and Valery Polyakov. Viktorenko and Kondakova had been launched aboard Soyuz TM-20 on Oct. 3, 1994, along with European Space Agency (ESA) astronaut Ulf Merbold. The craft returned to Earth on March 22 with Viktorenko, Kondakova, and Polyakov after they were replaced by the Soyuz TM-21 crew (Merbold had returned on Soyuz TM-19 on Nov. 4, 1994). Polyakov set the world record for duration in space: 439 days on this mission and a career total of 680 days. Kondakova set a women's record of 174 days. On September 3 ESA astronaut Thomas Reiter was launched along with Sergey Avdeyev and Yury Gidzenko aboard Soyuz TM-22 for a 133-day stay aboard *Mir.* The TM-21 crew returned to Earth on September 11. *Mir* was expanded with the addition of the 20-ton Spektr experiment module, launched on May 26. Spektr carried experiment gear plus new solar arrays to extend the space station's operating life.

The U.S. space shuttle *Atlantis* (bottom) begins to undock from the Russian *Mir* space station on July 4. The photograph was taken from the Soyuz spacecraft, which had separated from *Mir* in order to perform a brief flight around the space station and *Atlantis*.
RUSSIA SPACE AGENCY/NASA

With its design settled, work moved ahead quickly on the international space station (the earlier name, Alpha, had been dropped), and flight hardware started taking shape. In Huntsville, Ala., the Boeing Co. completed the main structure for the laboratory module and for the first of two nodes that would join the lab and habitat modules.

Space Probes. In mid-July the Galileo spacecraft, nearing the end of its six-year odyssey to Jupiter, released a probe that plunged into the atmosphere of Jupiter in early December 1995 and provided the first direct measurements of the composition and structure of the gas giant planet. After plunging through the planet's atmosphere, the probe jettisoned its heat shield and deployed a parachute for a slower descent through the atmosphere while it measured winds, clouds, and atmospheric conditions. The probe collapsed when it was so close to Jupiter that the outside pressure equaled 100 times that of Earth's atmosphere at sea level.

The probe's data were received by the Galileo spacecraft for retransmission to Earth. Galileo flew past two of Jupiter's moons, Europa and Io, on December 7, about the same time the probe entered Jupiter's atmosphere and then went into orbit around the planet on December 8. Galileo was scheduled to spend at least a year taking pictures of Jupiter and its moons. However, because the spacecraft's large parabolic antenna resisted all attempts to deploy completely, pictures had to be transmitted through a slower antenna. This reduced by 80% the number of pictures that scientists would receive during the mission.

Scientists during the year were preparing to launch the Discovery program, designed to achieve one planetary mission a year at a total cost of less than $250 million. Three missions were scheduled, and selection was under way for a fourth. In most cases NASA would allow universities and corporate laboratories to develop the spacecraft with minimum supervision and without reporting through a NASA field centre.

Unmanned Satellites. One of the most interesting events of the year was the release of information about satellites that had flown more than 30 years earlier. Following directions from U.S. Pres. Bill Clinton, the CIA on February 24 declassified details of spy satellites it operated from 1960 through 1972 and started releasing some 800,000 photographs. During those years the CIA developed a series of "keyhole" satellites, starting with KH-1, that ultimately could resolve details just a few meters across. Pictures were recorded on film magazines that were returned to the Earth in small reentry capsules. The KH-series satellites were free to roam across the entire Soviet Union, and they returned millions of images of Soviet military and civil installations. Among other revelations, the U.S. discovered that the Soviets had built only 25 ballistic-missile launchpads, about a tenth of what had been estimated by other means.

Europe and Israel entered the spy satellite business during the year. On July 7 ESA launched Europe's first spy satellite, Helios 1, a joint venture of the French, Spanish, and Italian governments. Germany was expected to participate in the Helios 2 mission. On April 5 Israel launched the Ofeq 3 (Horizon 3) satellite, which was believed to be a forerunner of more sophisticated craft.

Exploration of the space environment around Earth intensified with the launches of several satellites under the International Solar Terrestrial Physics program. NASA's Wind spacecraft, launched Nov. 1, 1994, was to move into a "halo orbit" between the Sun and Earth by late 1995. On August 2 Russia launched its Interbol 1 to study the structure of Earth's magnetosphere. On December 2 ESA's Solar Heliospheric Observatory was launched into a halo orbit, where it would constantly monitor the Sun.

In space astronomy, ESA launched its Infrared Observatory (ISO) in November atop an Ariane 4 rocket. ISO carried a telescope and instruments cooled to −270° C (−454° F) to observe the coldest and darkest objects in the universe.

Launch Vehicles. The DC-X "Delta Clipper" vertical takeoff and landing rocket flew two tests, June 12 and July 7, for the U.S. Air Force and then was transferred to NASA for refurbishment and further test flights as the DC-XA. Many of the technologies tested in the DC-X program were to be applied to the X-33 project to demonstrate "single stage-to-orbit" launch capability. Three teams, led by Boeing and McDonnell Douglas Corp., Rockwell International, and Lockheed Martin Corp., were to develop competing concepts. Each would take off vertically, but only the Boeing/McDonnell Douglas concept would land vertically; the others would land like an aircraft.

The X-33 should lead to an unmanned Reusable Launch Vehicle capable of resupplying the space station faster and more cheaply than the shuttle. In a related program, Rockwell International and Orbital Sciences Corp. won a NASA contract to develop the X-34. It was to have a reusable first stage that would boost a satellite and its orbital insertion stages to an altitude of 96 km (60 mi) and then glide back to the airstrip for reuse. The first flight was expected in 1998.

ESA moved into the final phases of developing its new Ariane 5 launch vehicle. Testing problems with the Vulcain main engine delayed the first launch until February 1996. Japan's H-2 launch vehicle made its third flight on March 18. The payload included the Space Flyer Unit (to be retrieved by the U.S. space shuttle in 1996) and a weather satellite. The Space Flyer carried an infrared telescope plus life sciences and materials sciences experiments.

Despite a failure in March, Russia started marketing a small satellite launcher based on its SS-26 ballistic missile. China lost a U.S.-built communications satellite, Apstar-2, in a launch accident in January that killed six people on the ground as debris fell from the sky. (DAVE DOOLING)

See also Business and Industry Review: *Aerospace; Energy; Mining; Telecommunications;* Chronicle: *Disasters;* The Environment; Life Sciences; Media and Publishing: *Radio; Television;* Military Affairs.

This article updates the *Macropædia* articles ATMOSPHERE; CLIMATE AND WEATHER; DINOSAURS; The EARTH; The EARTH SCIENCES; EARTHQUAKES; EXPLORATION: *Space Exploration;* GEOCHRONOLOGY; The HYDROSPHERE; OCEANS; PLATE TECTONICS; RIVERS; TELESCOPES; VOLCANISM.

Manned Spaceflights, 1995

Flight	Date	Crew	Mission
STS-63, *Discovery*	February 3–12	James D. Wetherbee,* Eileen M. Collins, Bernard A. Harris, Jr., C. Michael Foale, Vladimir Titov, Janice Voss	Demonstrate the shuttle orbiter's ability to approach and maneuver around *Mir*
STS-67, *Endeavour*	March 2–18	Stephen S. Oswald,* William G. Gregory, Wendy B. Lawrence, John M. Grunsfeld, Tamara Jernigan, Samuel Durrance, Ronald Parise	Carry cluster of three telescopes to observe the sky in ultraviolet light
Soyuz TM-21	March 16	Vladimir Dezhurov,* Gennady Strekalov, Norman Thagard	Transport crew to *Mir*
STS-71, *Atlantis*	June 27–July 7	Robert L. Gibson,* Charles Precourt, Ellen S. Baker, Bonnie Dunbar, Gregory J. Harbaugh, Anatoly Solovyev, Nikolay Budarin	Dock with *Mir* and exchange crew members; conduct biomedical experiments
STS-70, *Discovery*	July 13–22	Terence Henricks,* Kevin Kregel, Nancy Currie, Donald Thomas, Mary Weber	Launch final Tracking and Data Relay Satellite
Soyuz TM-22	September 3	Sergey Avdeyev,* Yury Gidzenko, Thomas Reiter	Transport crew to *Mir*
STS-69, *Endeavour*	September 7–18	David Walker,* Kenneth Cockrell, James Voss, James Newman, Michael Gernhardt	Operate Wake Shield Facility satellite; test equipment for assembling a space station
STS-73, *Columbia*	October 20–November 5	Kenneth D. Bowersox,* Kent Rominger, Kathryn Thornton, Catherine Coleman, Michael Lopez-Alegria, Fred Leslie, Albert Sacco	Carry Microgravity Laboratory-2 to study the growth of material in space
STS-74, *Atlantis*	November 12–20	Ken Cameron,* James Halsell, Jerry Ross, William McArthur, Chris Hadfield	Attach docking module to *Mir*

*Mission commander.

Economic Affairs

In 1995 the world economy experienced another year of robust growth. According to International Monetary Fund (IMF) estimates, total output expanded by about 3.5%, largely unchanged from the previous year's level, which in turn was the best performance since 1988. This strong overall performance, however, disguised a pronounced slowdown in the developed countries as a group.

The pace of economic expansion in the developed countries slowed to an estimated 2.5% in 1995 from the previous year's 3.1%. Measures taken in 1994, which included preemptive rises in interest rates to prevent an upturn in inflation and higher taxes to rein in budget deficits, contributed to this moderation, as did turbulence on foreign exchange markets. Growth moderated most in those countries where the recovery had been strong and long established. Thus, U.S. growth fell back to 2.5% (4.1% in 1994) as interest-sensitive sectors, including residential investment and consumer consumption, reacted adversely early in the year before recovering later on. Because of its close links with the U.S., Canada experienced a similar moderation in growth. In Australia and New Zealand the economic growth rate also slowed sharply. In Europe, with the exception of the U.K., the slowdown was fairly mild. In the U.K. the rate of economic growth moderated from 4% in 1994 to 2.7% in 1995. The Japanese economy did not pull out of the long economic slowdown, despite the government's introduction of several packages to stimulate activity in both 1994 and 1995. The deflationary effect of the appreciating yen prevailed for most of the year, as did a lack of confidence in the financial system since the high (often overvalued) prices of real estate and other assets of the 1980s collapsed. Economic output in Japan in 1995 expanded at 0.5%, the same rate as in 1994.

Once again, the economies of the less developed countries (LDCs) grew much faster than those of the developed countries. Total growth at 6% was twice as fast as in the developed countries. As this growth rate exceeded the birthrate, there was a small gain in living standards. Regionally, Asia, led by China, experienced the fastest economic growth. The economic growth rate in Latin America slowed rapidly as a result of the financial crisis in Mexico (*see* SPOTLIGHT: *Accelerating Changes in Mexico*), which led to the introduction of stabilization measures in the region. By contrast, there was a welcome pickup in economic activity rates in Africa and the Middle East.

Exchange-rate instability was an important development that produced a negative impact in the early part of the year. The Mexican crisis, which started in December 1994 with the collapse of the peso, had repercussions outside the region. Initially, there was an outflow of capital funds from many LDCs as the weakening of investor confidence led to reassessment of investment risk in those countries. This was accompanied by wider but short-lived exchange-rate volatility among the exchange rates of LDCs.

The Mexican crisis coincided with concern in the international markets about the large balance of payments deficit in the U.S. and uncertainty relating to the future direction of interest rates in the U.S., Japan, and Germany. This led to a sharp decline in the value of the U.S. dollar against the Japanese yen and the Deutsche Mark during the first half of 1995. The yen appreciated by 15% against the dollar and the Deutsche Mark by 9%. The other European currencies that were closely tied to the Deutsche Mark appreciated similarly. However, as a result of coordinated intervention by central banks and lower interest rates in Japan, the U.S., and Germany, the misalignment of the key currencies had been adjusted by the autumn. By that time the yen, for example, which had strengthened from 100 yen to the dollar to 80 yen to the dollar, had receded back to the level it had at the beginning of 1995.

As economic growth slowed, central banks in North America and Germany changed their previously counter-inflationary stance and allowed short-term interest rates to fall. The German Bundesbank cut its discount rate by 0.5% as early as March. Japan followed suit by cutting its interest rates twice to curb the strength of the yen. A 0.75% cut in April was followed by a further 0.5% reduction in September. This took the Japanese interest rates to a record-low 0.5%. In the U.S. the Federal Reserve Board (Fed) cut the Fed funds rate by 0.25% to 5.75% in July, which enabled a similar reduction in the banks' prime rate to 8.75%. On December 19 the Fed announced another 0.25% cut, and the prime fell accordingly to end the year at 8.5%.

In the U.K. a 0.5% increase in February was the last increase in this cycle and meant interest rates peaked at 6.75%. A faster-than-expected slowdown in the British economy led to a change of attitude in the summer and heightened expectations of an interest-rate cut early in 1996. In contrast to the relaxation in monetary policy, many governments in the developed world continued to reduce their budget deficits. This meant another year of tight government spending and tax reforms instead of tax giveaways. Partly as a result of the prior year's measures to rein in public spending and higher revenues arising from taxation and continued economic recovery, budget deficits in many countries narrowed. In the U.S. the deficit for the 1994–95 fiscal year (ended October) narrowed to $164 billion, the smallest gap since 1988–89 ($203 billion the year before). The administration of Pres. Bill Clinton bowed to pressure from the Republican-controlled Congress, however, and agreed to the principle of a balanced budget over the next seven years, although the exact details of how this was to be achieved remained unresolved at year's end.

In the U.K. progress was slower than expected, and the public-sector deficit narrowed to £29 billion, £7 billion less than the year before but £6 billion above the target set in November 1994. This slippage effectively deferred the projected date of a balanced budget by a year to 1999. An austerity package of reduced public spending, higher taxes, and social security reforms proposed by French Prime Minister Alain Juppé caused widespread discontent and strikes. A key aim of this package was to reduce the public-sector deficit to 3% of gross domestic product (GDP) by 1999 in order to meet the convergence criterion stipulated in the Maastricht Treaty. Good progress was made in Germany as well as in other countries, including Italy, Canada, Spain, and The Netherlands, in reducing public-sector deficits.

Table I. Real Gross Domestic Products of Selected OECD Countries

% annual change

Country	1991	1992	1993	1994	1995[1]
United States	−0.6	2.3	3.1	4.1	2.5
Japan	4.3	1.1	−0.2	0.6	0.5
Germany[2]	5.0	2.2	−1.2	2.9	2.5
France	0.8	1.3	−1.5	2.7	2.4
United Kingdom	−2.0	−0.5	2.2	3.8	2.5
Canada	−1.8	0.6	2.2	4.5	3.2
Italy	1.2	0.7	−1.2	2.2	2.6
All developed countries	1.0	1.7	1.2	2.9	2.5
Seven major countries above	1.0	1.6	1.3	3.0	2.7
European Union	1.6	1.0	−0.6	2.7	2.5

[1]Estimated. [2]From 1991, figures include former East Germany.
Sources: OECD, *The Economist*.

Japan once again went against the trend. To stimulate the flat economy, the government announced three packages containing a mixture of tax cuts and higher public spending. To pay for the proposed spending, the government issued additional bonds. This added to the public-sector deficit, which was heading for 4% of GDP in 1995–96.

Employment growth was disappointing in 1995, and the rate at which jobs were created slowed in both North America and Europe. Although there was a reduction in the average unemployment rate in countries belonging to the Organisation for Economic Co-operation and Development (OECD), to 7.9% from 8.1% in 1994, this meant that 33.6 million people were searching for work in OECD countries during 1995. The official figures excluded those who failed to register as unemployed because of poor prospects or because they believed they were too old or lacked necessary skills.

In Japan the unemployment rate, at 3.2%, remained the lowest among developed countries, but it was up from the 1994 rate of 3%. In the U.S. continuing economic recovery reduced the unemployment rate, which at the end of 1995 stood at 5.6%, compared with 5.8% a year earlier. Europe still had the highest rate of unemployment and the slowest job-creation rate. The average unemployment rate in Europe, at 11.1%, barely improved from the previous year's 11.3%. The highest unemployment rate was in Spain, at 22.7%, only a slight improvement on the 24% rate in 1994.

Inflationary pressures remained subdued in most regions and countries. In OECD countries, with the exception of Turkey and Mexico, average inflation for 1995 was about 2.5%, compared with 2.2% in 1994. No significant upturn was expected in the near future. The median inflation rate moderated to 8% in the LDCs (11.5% in 1994). By region, Latin America, the Middle East, and Europe continued to experience above-average inflation rates.

World trade remained buoyant during 1995 and expanded at a rapid pace of 8%, close to the rate in 1994. The strength of world trade was largely due to increasing trade between the developed countries and recovery of trade in the former communist countries in Europe. Large regional trade surpluses and deficits remained. Despite some improvement in the U.S. because of the economic slowdown and currency appreciation, a large deficit of about $200 billion remained. In Japan the trade surplus narrowed in yen terms but was largely unchanged in dollar terms at about $145 billion.

With the exception of Africa, the IMF expected the debt burdens of the LDCs to remain manageable. As a result of a large proportion of capital inflows being non-debt-creating, the overall debt levels of LDCs was rising gently. Although in absolute terms their debt was rising, as a proportion of exports of goods and services, it was declining.

Table II. Consumer Prices in OECD Countries

% change from preceding year

Country	1991	1992	1993	1994	1995[1]
United States	4.2	3.0	3.0	2.6	2.8
Japan	3.3	1.7	1.3	0.7	−0.6
Germany[2]	3.5	4.0	4.1	3.0	1.8
France	3.2	2.4	2.1	1.7	1.8
United Kingdom	5.9	3.7	1.6	2.5	3.2
Canada	5.6	1.5	1.8	0.2	2.4
Italy	6.5	5.3	4.2	3.9	6.0
Austria	3.3	4.0	3.6	3.0	1.9
Belgium	3.2	2.4	2.8	2.4	1.5
Denmark	2.4	2.1	1.3	2.0	1.9
Finland	4.3	2.9	2.2	1.1	1.0
Greece	19.5	15.9	14.4	10.9	8.5
Iceland	6.8	4.0	4.0	1.6	1.3
Ireland	3.2	3.1	1.4	2.3	2.7
Luxembourg	3.1	3.2	3.6	2.2	2.3
Netherlands, The	3.2	3.2	2.6	2.8	1.3
Norway	3.4	2.3	2.3	1.4	2.7
Portugal	11.4	8.9	6.5	5.2	4.0
Spain	5.9	5.9	4.6	4.7	4.3
Sweden	9.3	2.3	4.6	2.2	2.7
Switzerland	5.8	4.0	3.3	0.8	2.0
Turkey	66.0	70.1	66.1	106.3	88.5
Australia	3.2	1.0	1.8	1.9	5.0
New Zealand	2.6	1.0	1.3	1.8	4.6
OECD Total	6.1	4.8	4.2	4.3	4.5

[1]Twelve-month rate of change in October 1995. [2]Western Germany only.
Sources: OECD, *The Economist.*

NATIONAL ECONOMIC POLICIES

United States. Economic growth slowed sharply in the first half of 1995, but a recovery in the second half put the U.S. economy on a sustainable growth rate. GDP for the year as a whole expanded at about 2.5%, down from 4.1% the year before, which in turn was the best performance for a decade. In view of the slowing economy and the relatively low inflation rate, the Fed cut short-term interest rates by 0.25% in July, signaling an easing in its tight money policy.

The slowing of the U.S. economy early in 1995 was largely due to the reaction of interest-sensitive sectors—residential investment and private consumption—to the rise in interest rates over the previous 18 months. Consumer spending fell by 3.4% in the opening quarter, led by a slump in automobile sales. Retail sales were also weak. As longer-term interest rates fell in the spring and the effects of the higher taxes introduced in the November 1993 budget dissipated, spending recovered, ending the year 2.6% up (3.5% in 1994). Retail spending at Christmas proved to be a disappointment, which indicated shaky consumer confidence. Government spending recovered in the second half of the year, reversing declines recorded in the opening quarter.

Industrial production mirrored the trend in domestic demand. As demand weakened, manufacturers reduced output to prevent an excessive buildup in inventories. After four months of decline, output stabilized and rose in the second half of the year, registering a 2% gain for the year as a whole. Likewise, capacity utilization, having reached a 15-year high of 85.5% in January, fell back to below 83%.

For the second year running, nonresidential investment climbed at a double-digit rate, encouraged by healthy corporate profits, high-capacity utilization, and a drop in long-term interest rates, as well as by good export prospects. Residential investment did not fare so well and fell after a strong gain in 1994.

The labour market improved in the autumn, but job creation remained relatively low. Payrolls grew by a monthly average of 226,000 in the first quarter, 82,000 in the second, and 114,000 in the third. As in past years, most of the new jobs were in low-paid, part-time service sectors. From a peak of 5.8% in April, the unemployment rate improved in the summer and autumn and stood at 5.5% in November.

Against the background of economic slowdown, inflation remained subdued. Year-on-year inflation moderated to 2.8% by November from a two-year high of 3.2% in May. The rise in the inflation rate earlier in the year was largely due to the decline in the external value of the dollar. Wages and salaries grew by an average of 3% during 1995. This meant there was hardly any real growth (inflation adjusted) in the take-home pay of most employees.

After a slow start in early 1995, export growth picked up and expanded by about 9% for the year as a whole. Export growth was largely due to the strong demand from industrial countries and LDCs, with Asia leading the way. The lower value of the dollar early in the year also boosted exports during the summer and autumn.

Once again, imports grew faster and the trade deficit widened. The current-account deficit (which includes trade balances on invisible and capital movements) was expected to rise by a record $176 billion, up from $151 billion the year before.

Economic policy during 1995 was characterized by two main features: the easing of the Fed's monetary policy and disagreement between the Congress and the Clinton administration on future spending cuts and tax reform. Given the sharp economic slowdown earlier in the year, coupled with low inflationary pressures and a money supply expanding at the low end of the target range, the easing of monetary policy was a relief to businesses and consumers. Following the 0.25% reduction in the Fed funds rate to 5.75% in July, banks cut their prime rates by 0.25%, to 8.75%. Late in the year both rates were cut another 0.25%. Further reductions in interest rates during 1996 were widely expected.

In contrast to an easier monetary policy, there was a move toward a tighter fiscal policy. The budget planned by the Clinton administration in February intended a nominal fall in the real value of the budget deficit. The Republican-controlled Congress passed a budget resolution to reduce spending over the next seven years on various federal programs, however, including social security, Medicare, and Medicaid. Tax cuts of $245 billion were also proposed. It was claimed that this proposal would have balanced the budget by the year 2002. Clinton subsequently proposed an alternative plan, to balance the budget in 10 years. The differences between the two proposals proved difficult to resolve, and the new fiscal year started without an agreement. With presidential elections due in 1996, neither side wanted to back down first. Following a partial shutdown of some government services in mid-November and the furloughing of some 800,000 "nonessential" federal employees, a compromise was reached to balance the budget in seven years, but it failed to hold. Another shutdown in December left 280,000 government workers idle and thousands of contractors without pay. Clinton and the Congress remained at an impasse at year's end. Treasury Secretary Robert Rubin, who juggled funds to prevent a default on interest payments on the national debt in November, indicated that a default on interest due in February 1996 was still a possibility.

Inflation Rate
Percentage change from December to December

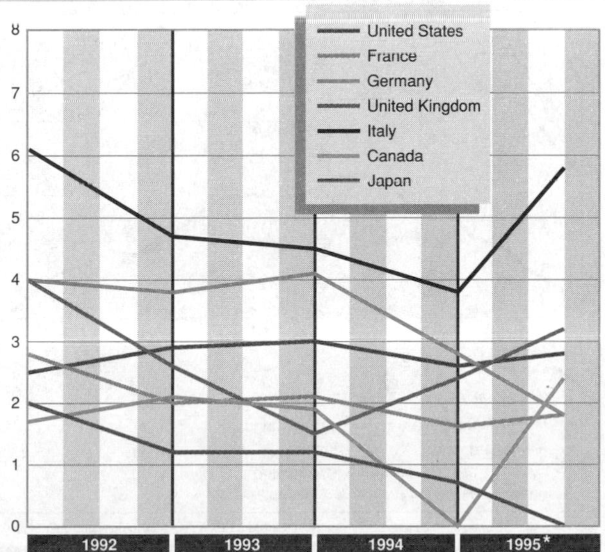

*Percentage change from October 1994 to October 1995.
Source: International Monetary Fund, *International Financial Statistics*

Industrial Production
semiannual averages; 1990 =100

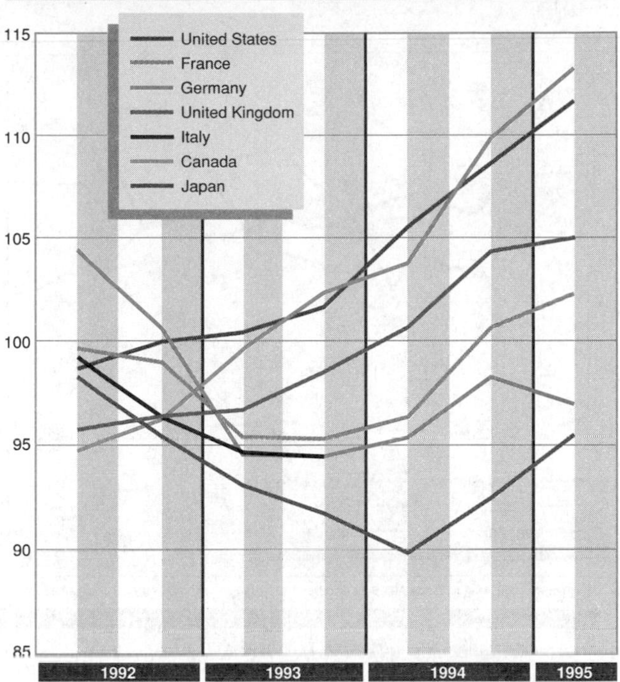

Source: International Monetary Fund, *International Financial Statistics.*

Japan. The recovery from the long economic slowdown in Japan failed to take root during 1995. Although the recession had touched bottom nearly two years earlier, the upturn was so feeble that 1995 marked the fourth consecutive year of negligible growth. Renewed economic downturn in evidence in the closing months of 1994 continued into 1995, and GDP in the opening quarter registered zero growth. Economic growth picked up a little in the second and third quarters, helped by the reconstruction in the Kobe area after the Great Hanshin Earthquake, reversal of the earlier rise in the yen, lower interest rates, and higher government spending. On the basis of incomplete data, GDP was likely to have grown by 0.5% for 1995, unchanged from the previous year's growth rate.

In part, the continuing weakness of the economy was due to unfavourable developments in the value of the yen and the Japanese stock market in the first half of the year. By the summer the yen had appreciated by 17% against the U.S. dollar, or by about 15% against a basket of currencies, and share prices on the Tokyo stock market had fallen by 25%. The strong yen, by making Japanese exports more expensive and imported goods cheaper, undermined domestic production and weakened consumer confidence and investment. The prolonged weakness in asset prices (share prices had fallen by 60% from their peak level and land prices were down by 50%) affected the balance sheet and profitability of many banks. This weakened the banks' ability to extend new loans and threatened a financial crisis.

To help boost the stagnant economy, the economic policy makers announced various measures during the year. The Bank of Japan cut the discount rate twice to curb the strength of the yen. A cut of 0.75% in April was followed by a further 0.5% cut in September to a record low of 0.5%. This, together with concerted moves by the authorities in the U.S. and Germany, succeeded in moving the yen against the U.S. dollar to about 100 yen to the dollar, back to the level it had been at the beginning of the year.

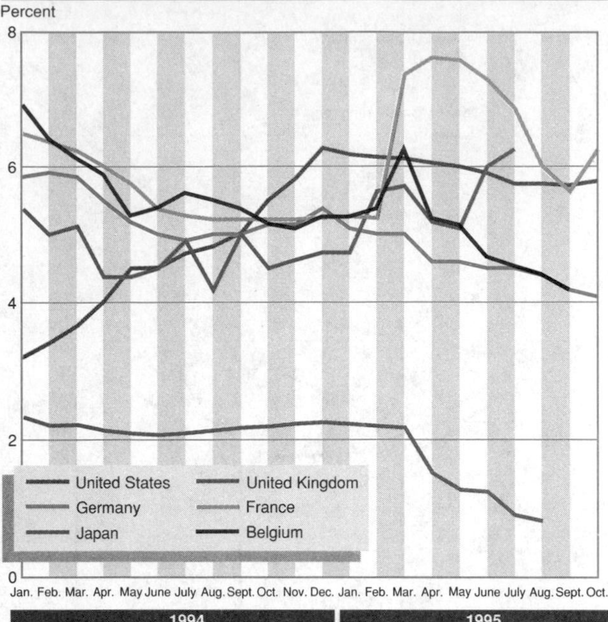

Source: International Monetary Fund, *International Financial Statistics.*

In addition to interest-rate cuts, the government announced three fiscal packages. The first one was in April in the aftermath of the Great Hanshin Earthquake, and it was quickly followed by another one in June. As both were modest and were seen by economists to have had only a limited impact on the weak economy, a third attempt in September to kick start the economy came as no surprise. This sixth package in three years proposed 14.2 trillion yen in extra spending. About one-third was earmarked for public works projects, 15% for Kobe, and a smaller amount for land purchase to improve property prices. Given the unresolved problems surrounding the Japanese financial system, trade barriers, and land and tax reform, the long-term effectiveness of the latest package was also questioned.

Despite these measures to boost domestic demand, private consumption, in particular retail sales, remained weak. Early in the year, consumption was affected by the Kobe disaster. High unemployment and low wage increases also made consumers cautious. Excluding the effect of the opening of new stores, retail sales during the first nine months of the year were about 1.5% down from the same period in 1994. Although the strength of the yen reduced the prices of imported goods in the shops, it did not encourage consumers to change their spending habits and bring forward into 1995 purchases that they had intended to defer until a later date.

The labour market, having begun to improve in late 1994, stalled in early 1995, reflecting the renewed weakness of the economy. The strong yen increased production costs and encouraged firms to shift manufacturing abroad. The unemployment rate in November stood at a record level of 3.2%. At this level 2,170,000 workers were seeking employment. If unemployment were to be defined in the same way as in other industrialized countries, it would be considerably higher than the official figures suggested—perhaps about 9%. Despite the rise in unemployment, wages rose by nearly 2.5% in 1994, but both overtime working and bonuses declined. Because the inflation rate was close to zero, however, the small increase in wages meant there was a real rise in earnings, after adjusting for inflation.

The underlying investment trend strengthened a little. Stronger expenditure on plant and equipment, boosted by reconstruction at Kobe, was partly offset by a reduction in housing investment. Government investment recovered, too. Thus, total investment was nearly 2% up in 1995.

The strong yen in the first half of the year reduced the trade deficit by depressing exports and making imports cheaper. Although the sharp weakening of the yen from the summer eased the burden of the exporters, in yen terms exports were only 3% higher than a year earlier, but imports increased by nearly 10%. In dollar terms the trade balance was likely to have been close to the 1994 figure of $146 billion, but as a result of a larger deficit on invisible items, such as services and foreign travel, the current-account surplus fell a little to $177 billion ($129 billion in 1994). Although this was still high in absolute terms, Japan's trade partners, the U.S. in particular, welcomed the downward trend.

United Kingdom. Under the impact of higher taxes and interest rates introduced in 1994, combined with a slackening in world economic growth, the pace of economic activity slowed in the U.K. Following a GDP growth of 4% in 1994, the economy expanded at an annual rate of 2.5% in 1995.

Concerned with a likely upturn in inflation later in the year, the chancellor of the Exchequer, Kenneth Clarke, and the governor of the Bank of England, Eddie George (*see* BIOGRAPHIES), extended their policy of preemptive rises in interest rates. The Bank rate went up by 0.5%, to 6.75%, in February. This was the third increase since the previous September. Although the Bank of England urged a further rise in interest rates, Clarke's wait-and-see approach proved to be a more accurate assessment of the underlying trends. Given a rapid slowdown in economic activity, coupled with subdued inflationary pressures, the Bank of England changed its view in the autumn, which paved the way for lower interest rates before the end of the year.

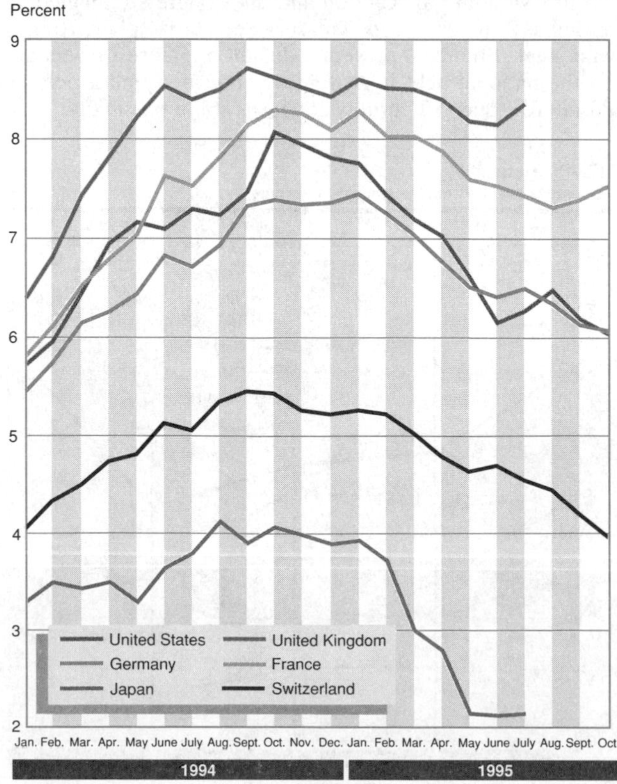

Source: International Monetary Fund, *International Financial Statistics.*

The chancellor also faced a dilemma in framing the government's fiscal policy because he came under pressure for substantial tax cuts in the November 1995 budget to restore the electoral fortunes of the government. The difficulty for Clarke was that the public-sector deficit for 1995–96 turned out to be £6 billion higher than the revised target of £23.5 billion. The overshoot was largely due to lower tax revenue, reflecting the economic slowdown. In the event, Clarke produced a cautious tax-cutting budget, reducing taxes by £3,250,000,000—less than expected. This was balanced by reductions in public spending.

The economic slowdown was largely caused by a fall in exports rather than by developments in the domestic economy. By the autumn the three-month average growth rate of exports was down to 2%, from 8% at the beginning of the year. The lull in world economic growth was the main cause of this adverse trend.

Consumer spending weakened under the cumulative impact of higher taxes and interest rates introduced in the previous years. Retail sales increased by just over 1% in real terms, compared with over 3% in 1994. The weak housing market, a hot summer, and continuing gloom about job security also led consumers to spend less and save more. There was no significant contribution to economic growth from investment spending. Total gross fixed investment rose by an estimated 3%, down from nearly 4% in the previous year. The weakest areas were private housing and new industrial and commercial buildings. Investment into new plant and equipment was more encouraging. Against this background of weaker domestic and external demand, industrial production weakened. For the year as a whole, total output expanded by an average of 2.7% (5% in 1994). As the year drew to a close, however, the underlying growth rate of industrial production was 0.5%, compared with 5.5% at the beginning of the year.

The trend in the number of unemployed closely reflected the overall economic slowdown. After a steady two-year decline in the number of people out of work, there was a small increase in unemployment in October. Even so, the unemployment rate of 8.1% was below the previous year's 9%. Both wage and price inflation remained restrained. Average earnings growth remained about 3.5% for most of the year. The headline annual inflation rate peaked at 3.9% in September and fell sharply to 3.2% in October.

Germany. The unexpectedly strong economic growth seen in Germany during 1994 continued into 1995 but lost momentum as the year unfolded. During the first half of the year, GDP in Germany as a whole expanded by 2.5% (3% for 1994). The result for the full year was about 2.1% (1.8% in western Germany and 6% in eastern Germany). As the German national account statistics were revamped in 1995 to show GDP components for the first time on a pan-German basis, the early estimates were subject to greater uncertainty than usual. The overall slowdown, however, was unmistakable. Growth in eastern Germany remained stronger than in the west, with investment and manufacturing output the most dynamic components. Because the region was still heavily dependent on transfers and subsidies from western Germany, however, growth in eastern Germany was not yet self-sustaining.

One of the main reasons for the economic slowdown was a loss of competitiveness arising from the relatively high wage settlements and the appreciation of the Deutsche Mark. Wage settlements, at about 4%, were above the inflation rate, but they were partly offset by some productivity gains. The appreciation in the Deutsche Mark, at 6%, was large and potentially more serious. Slower world growth was another cause of this slowdown.

Economic growth was underpinned by growth in investment activity and higher export volumes. Gross capital investment during the year was 6% higher (4.5% in 1994). Investment in machinery and equipment was relatively modest. Despite higher capacity utilization, manufacturer's investment was targeted at efficiency improvements instead of adding to manufacturing capacity and facilities. Construction activity trends were mixed, too. Industrial and residential construction were comparatively weak in western Germany but buoyant in the east.

The volume of exports expanded by about 5%, a little slower than the year before. The loss in competitiveness was to some extent offset by a relatively strong external demand from Germany's main trading partners and by productivity gains. Surprisingly, private consumption recovered in 1995 and grew a little faster than the year before. The squeeze on consumers' disposable income by the reintroduction of the 7.5% Solidarity levy and lower unemployment benefits was partly offset by wages and salaries growing well above the moderating inflation rate. Increased consumer spending went on housing-related expenditures and on holidays. Retail spending remained flat.

Against a background of sustained higher economic activity, there was no real improvement in the labour market. A small decline in unemployment for all of Germany was more than offset by a natural rise in the labour market. Thus, the unemployment rate toward the close of the year stood at about 9.2%, compared with 8.2% the year before. The employment rate in eastern Germany rose faster than in recent years as a result of higher industrial output in the east. Further progress was made in stabilization of prices. After an upward surge about the turn of 1994–95, the inflationary pressures eased. In November the year-on-year rise in consumer prices was just under 2% (2.8% the year before) in western Germany and 2.5% in eastern Germany (3.2% a year earlier).

As the inflationary pressures abated, money supply expanded well below the target rate, and economic growth slackened, monetary policy was eased. At the end of March, the Bundesbank cut the discount rate by half a percentage point. This was followed by a similar cut in August, reducing the discount rate to 3.5% and the Lombard rate to 5.5%. The fiscal policy, on the other hand, remained tight. As a result of higher taxes (voted the year before), additional revenue arising from economic upturn, and expenditure restraints, the total public-sector deficit for 1995 shrank to about DM 100 billion from the previous year's DM 145 billion. The 1996 budget, approved in the summer, envisaged a 7.6% real reduction in the federal government's spending. Some of these savings were offset by tax cuts forced on the government by the Constitutional Court's decision that child benefits and tax thresholds of those close to the

Table III. Standardized Unemployment Rates in Selected Developed Countries

% of total labour force

Country	1991	1992	1993	1994	1995[1]
United States	6.6	7.3	6.7	6.0	5.5
Japan	2.1	2.2	2.5	2.9	3.2
Germany[2]	4.2	4.6	6.1	6.9	9.2[3]
France	9.4	10.4	11.6	12.5	11.5
United Kingdom	8.8	10.1	10.5	9.6	8.1
Canada	10.3	11.3	11.2	10.3	9.4
Italy	9.9	10.5	10.2	12.0	11.3[4]
All developed countries	6.7	7.4	7.8	7.8	7.5
Seven major countries above	10.2	11.2	11.1	6.9	6.5
European Union	8.7	9.5	10.6	11.5	11.4

[1]October, national definitions. [2]Western Germany only. [3]September.
[4]Not seasonally adjusted.
Sources: OECD, *The Economist*.

minimum subsistence level were too low. As a result, the federal government's deficit was likely to widen in 1996, but the total public-sector deficit, as a proportion of GDP, was expected to remain unchanged at about 2.9%.

France. The steady economic recovery experienced in 1994 continued in 1995 but at a slightly weaker pace. As a result, GDP expanded by close to 2.5%, compared with 2.7% in 1994. Against the background of political uncertainty arising from the presidential elections in the spring, currency weakness that prompted higher interest rates, and a higher tax burden, this was a creditable economic performance.

The year's economic growth was largely investment-led, with some assistance from export growth. The role of consumer spending was not as important as in the previous year because of sluggish growth in incomes, continuing high levels of unemployment, and higher taxation. Although both capacity utilization and industrial output improved during 1995, manufacturers used industrial capacity more efficiently and deferred some of their planned investment. Nonmanufacturing sectors experienced higher levels of new investment. As there was no improvement in the price competitiveness of French exports, growth was largely due to stronger demand from foreign markets. The 7% improvement in export volume was largely offset by a similar rise in imports, however.

Unemployment, which had been a source of concern for several years, declined a little in 1995 but not as much as the government had hoped. As the year drew to a close, the unemployment rate stood at 11.5%, marginally down from the 12.2% of the year before. The incoming government of Pres. Jacques Chirac (*see* BIOGRAPHIES) introduced a package of measures in June providing assistance to the long-term unemployed. Employment subsidies of F 2,000 per month and exemption from social security contributions for two years were the main planks of this program. Independent observers thought that in the absence of higher economic growth, Prime Minister Juppé's target of 700,000 new jobs to be created by this package was far too optimistic. The high level of unemployment was one of the reasons hourly wage rates grew by only 2% during 1995. Although a wage freeze was imposed on the civil servants, built-in contractual increments provided for an automatic 2% rise. Despite repeated protests by the trade unions, the government and the employers did not bend. Against this background, inflation remained subdued; the average rise of 1.8% was largely unchanged from the previous year.

Even though there was a change in government, economic policy remained largely unchanged, contrary to references made by Chirac during his election campaign. An "alternative" economic policy, designed to produce faster economic growth and drastically cut unemployment, was soon ditched in favour of an austerity program aimed at cutting the public-sector deficit to ensure that France could join the European economic and monetary union in 1999. Thus, a minibudget, introduced in June, raised the standard rate of the value-added tax by 2 percentage points to 20.6%. A 10% surcharge was also introduced on corporate tax liabilities and personal wealth taxation. Measures to raise taxes were accompanied by a cut in government spending. Continuing the drive to reduce government spending, in particular the spiraling social security spending, in November a new income tax of 0.5% was levied, together with a wide-ranging reform of the welfare system. This triggered another wave of protests and strikes from the public-service unions, paralyzing the transport system.

The tightening of the fiscal policy, together with the reduction in German interest rates, led to a temporary easing of monetary policy. As the franc came under pressure in the autumn, however, largely because of the financial market's concern over the high level of public-sector deficit, short-term interest rates were raised to defend the currency. This reignited fears that the *franc fort* strict monetary policy and the accompanying high interest rates could choke off economic growth.

The Former Centrally Planned Economies. While the economic decline in the former centrally planned economies persisted for the fifth consecutive year, the rate fell sharply to 2%. This compared with 9.5% in 1994, and the prospect was for real growth of over 3.5% in 1996.

The performance across the region was by no means uniform. In Central and Eastern Europe, the economy expanded very slightly following a 38% economic decline in 1994. If Belarus and Ukraine were excluded, output showed much stronger growth of 4%, which compared favourably with the better-than-had-been-expected 2.8% advance in 1994. In much of the Transcaucasus and Central Asia, however, restructuring and stabilization measures were less advanced, and here there was a contraction of 5.9% following on from a 16% decline in 1994.

In Russia there were signs by the end of the year that the recession had bottomed. Output fell by about 4% during the year after the 1994 decline of 15%. Russia faced special difficulties in adjusting to the requirements of a market-based economy. The breakup of the Soviet Union had disrupted its trade and payments system. Its military and enterprise infrastructure had been dictated by strategic rather than economic considerations, and there were particular problems and costs involved in dismantling them.

The most successful individual economies—including Poland, the Czech Republic, Slovakia, Hungary, Slovenia, and Albania—were those that were most advanced in their structural reforms. This resulted in strong and productive investment and impressive trade performances. These countries achieved growth rates in the 4–6% range.

Overall inflation in the region was expected to average 150%, less than half the 1994 rate. Across the region the performances were mixed. The rate for Central and Eastern Europe—once again excluding Belarus and Ukraine, where prices were still soaring by over 700% and 300%, respectively—was only 64%, down from 87% in 1994. In the Transcaucasus and Central Asia, where reforms were generally much less advanced, inflation was running at over 200%, with the average being forced up by the very high rates of inflation that persisted in Azerbaijan (464%) and Tajikistan (389%). Nevertheless, this was well down from the 1,583% average rate in 1994.

Consumer price inflation in most countries rose much more slowly than in 1994. Hungary, partly as a result of the March devaluation, and Tajikistan were notable exceptions. Many of the falls in inflation rates were dramatic, as in Georgia, where prices rose by under 200% after increasing by 7,380% in 1994, and in Armenia, where they declined

Table IV. Changes in Output in Less Developed Countries

% annual change in real gross domestic product

Area	1991	1992	1993	1994	1995[1]
All less developed countries	4.9	5.9	6.1	6.2	6.0
Oil-exporting countries	5.1	3.9	0.4	0.1	1.9
Non-oil-exporting countries	4.9	6.1	6.8	6.8	6.5
Africa	−1.0	−1.9	−1.8	−0.1	0.4
Asia	4.7	6.5	7.0	6.8	7.0
Middle East and Europe	2.0	−0.3	1.4	−2.4	−0.3
Western Hemisphere	1.6	0.7	1.3	2.7	−0.9

[1]Estimated.
Sources: International Monetary Fund, *World Economic Outlook*, October 1995.

from over 5,000% to under 200%. The lowest inflation was experienced by Albania, Croatia, the Czech Republic, Slovakia, and Slovenia, where prices were rising at an annual rate of less than 10%.

By the end of 1995, 10 Central and Eastern European countries (CEECs) had signed association agreements with the European Union (EU). They were Bulgaria, Estonia, the Czech Republic, Hungary, Latvia, Lithuania, Poland, Romania, Slovakia, and Slovenia. The CEECs, which had already received EU assistance worth ECU 38.7 billion in 1990–94, were told by the European Council that they could join the EU when the necessary economic and political conditions required had been met and when the EU institutions were able to cope with a larger membership. The promise had stimulated liberalization, economic restructuring, and commercial activity. By the end of 1995, more than half the CEECs' trade was with the EU.

Early accession to the EU was not expected, however, given EU concerns about sensitive sectors that accounted for 40% of imports from the CEECs. The EU was concerned about the adverse effects on its own industries if it opened its markets completely. A 1995 EU study of the CEECs' agricultural sectors highlighted the difficulties and vulnerabilities, with 25% of the CEEC workforce dependent on agriculture, compared with only 6% in the EU. Despite its greater efficiency, EU prices were much higher, and the group had no intention of abolishing its subsidy mechanism, the common agricultural policy.

Six years after the end of the Cold War, there were signs that many formerly communist countries were gradually being integrated into the global trade and payments system. Until the late 1980s, the state had been responsible for nearly all aspects of activity, but by the end of 1995, the impetus was firmly shifting to the private sector. In many of those countries that had implemented comprehensive and large-scale privatization programs, the private sector accounted for more than half of GDP and employment. In the Czech Republic, for example, the privatization program was almost complete, and some 80% of all assets were in the private sector. Unemployment, at 3%, was by far the lowest in the region and well below Western European levels. Elsewhere, unemployment was often understated, and there was no easy solution in sight.

Financial-sector reforms continued to be made, with help from international institutions, but they remained inadequate and an obstacle to enterprise restructuring and investment finance. Banking reforms were under way, with new private banks being established and gaining significant market shares. By the middle of 1995, for example, there were 220 banks in Ukraine, with only two owned by the government. The banking systems remained fragile, however. Local institutions lacked experience in risk evaluation, and the allocation of financial resources and the inappropriate regulation and supervision of the banks reflected this. As a result, many banks became insolvent in 1995. Notably, in August the Russian banking sector suffered a liquidity and confidence crisis. Interbank lending came to a halt and spiraled overnight interest rates to 1,000% a year. In Latvia the largest commercial bank collapsed, and the government took over its management. Throughout the region better supervision and monitoring, as well as appropriate accounting standards, were required.

Less Developed Countries. Despite a slowdown in the industrial countries, real economic growth in the LDCs remained strong and averaged an estimated 6%. The rapid pace of economic activity in 1995 was sustained by the ongoing benefits of economic reforms, steady interest rates, export growth, and an inflow of capital funds. The impact of the Mexican financial crisis on capital flows was short-lived, as confidence returned fairly quickly.

As in previous years, the region with the fastest growth rate was Asia, in particular South Asia. This was a welcome offset to the weakness in Japan. Once again, China experienced the fastest rate of growth in the region, but as a result of earlier measures, growth stabilized at about 11%, compared with around 10% in 1994 and nearly 14% in 1993. In several countries in the region, including South Korea, Malaysia, Thailand, and Vietnam, GDP grew by over 8%, assisted by a combination of strong export growth, investment, and domestic demand. Hong Kong, Indonesia, and the Philippines lagged behind the region's growth rate. The recovery in India remained intact, and economic output grew by 5.5%, thanks to earlier economic reforms and inflow of capital. Latin America was adversely affected by the financial crisis in Mexico, and overall regional growth slowed to an estimated 1.5% from 4.5% in 1994. Not surprisingly, Mexico and Argentina were particularly affected by a loss of confidence, decline in capital inflows, and restrictive measures that were introduced. The growth rate in both Africa and the Middle East picked up considerably in 1995, despite some weakness in oil prices.

The inflation rate continued to moderate among the LDCs, reflecting the worldwide downward trend. The IMF expected a median inflation rate of 8% in 1995, down from 11.5% the year before. Even so, inflation remained high in some countries and regions. In Latin America the regional average was over 30%, but remarkable progress was made in controlling the hyperinflation in Brazil. The overall inflation rate was almost as high in the Middle East and Europe. Turkey was the worst problem spot, with an inflation rate over 75%. In Asia inflation remained relatively high at about 12% but was steady, despite high capacity utilization in many export-oriented South Asian countries.

Following a sharp improvement in the trade performance of the LDCs during 1994, thanks to the rapid expansion in world trade, there was no significant change in their trade or current-account balances. With the exception of Africa, the debt burden of the LDCs was expected to ease during 1995.

INTERNATIONAL TRADE

Following a rapid growth in the volume of world trade in goods and services in 1994, the momentum was maintained in 1995. IMF projections pointed to a growth rate of about 8%, largely unchanged from the previous year's upswing. This represented another year of strong performance, well above the long-term growth rate of 5%.

The buoyancy in world trade during 1995 was largely attributed to demand from countries with strong exchange rates, rising trade among the LDCs, and continued recovery among the former communist countries in Europe.

Reflecting the sharp slowdown in economic activity rates in the developed countries, growth in their export volumes fell to about 6.5% from the previous year's 8%. Import

Table V. Changes in Consumer Prices in Less Developed Countries

% change from preceding year

Area	1991	1992	1993	1994	1995[1]
All less developed countries	33.5	35.8	43.1	48.1	19.5
Oil-exporting countries	19.4	21.0	24.8	30.5	26.7
Non-oil-exporting countries	35.2	37.6	45.3	50.0	18.8
Africa	25.0	28.2	27.9	32.9	20.8
Asia	7.6	7.1	9.4	13.5	12.0
Middle East and Europe	25.9	25.7	24.5	32.3	25.3
Western Hemisphere	129.4	152.7	212.2	226.7	38.2

[1]Estimated.
Sources: International Monetary Fund, *World Economic Outlook*, October 1995.

growth slowed even more and rose by an estimated 7%, compared with more than 9% in 1994. The slowdown in the developed countries as a group was largely offset by a higher volume of trade by the LDCs, however. The export growth of this group as a whole, at 11%, was largely unchanged from the previous year, while their import growth rose from an estimated 8.5% in 1994 to 11% in 1995.

Changes in exchange rates usually affect the trade pattern and flows after a time lag. Consequently, the changes in exchange rates, particularly the weakening of the yen and Deutsche Mark in the second half of the year, did not significantly influence the outcome in 1995. The changes that occurred the previous year and in the opening months of 1995 were more influential. Loss of competitiveness in Japan, as a result of a 15% appreciation in the trade-weighted value of the yen during the first half of the year on top of a 7% appreciation in 1994, reduced the volume of export growth from Japan to 2.5% from 5% the year before. The strong yen made imported goods cheaper and accelerated the growth in the volume of imports to over 9%, despite the stagnant economic background. In the early months of the year, the Great Hanshin Earthquake affected exports more than imports because the Kobe port was more important for shipment of exports than handling imports. As in previous years, Japan came under pressure to open its markets, and this prompted imports to grow faster than they would otherwise have done.

Conversely, the weakness of the dollar encouraged U.S. exports. IMF estimates pointed to an 11% increase during 1995, compared with 9% in 1994, which, in turn, was the fastest growth rate since 1989. As the economic growth slowed sharply in the first half of the year, imports into the U.S. faltered, cutting the growth rate to under 10% from the previous year's 14%.

Export growth in Germany and the U.K. slowed appreciably for different reasons. German exports were affected by the strength of the Deutsche Mark, as well as by economic slowdown in the developed countries. The British exports were not so much handicapped by an unfavourable exchange rate but could not escape being dragged down by the economic slowdown experienced by its major trading partners. Although the trading volumes in the other European countries varied less between 1994 and 1995, because of the relative importance of Germany and the U.K., the EU's overall export volumes slowed to 6% (8% in 1994). Import volumes into the EU slowed by a similar amount and declined to 5% from 7.5% in 1994.

Despite the slowdown in the developed world, the pace of export growth from the LDCs was maintained at a high rate of 11%. Coincidentally, imports by the LDCs expanded at a similar rate. Import growth by this group during 1995 was 2.5 percentage points higher as a result of improved imports by Asian countries, including China. Regionally, trade volumes were most buoyant in Asia, with a 13–14% increase over 1994. There was a good upswing in Africa, too, leading to 8% volume gains. By contrast, trade in the Middle East and Latin America was subdued. The sharp devaluation and austerity measures in many Latin-American countries following the Mexican crisis drastically reduced the imports into the region.

In spite of a small decline in commodity prices, favourable currency movements in the first half of 1995 enabled the LDCs to improve their terms of trade. According to IMF estimates, the terms of trade of the LDCs as a group improved by 0.2 point, somewhat below the previous year's 0.5-point improvement. Oil exports suffered a large drop in their terms of trade, largely because international oil prices traded within a narrow range during the year. More important, as oil is priced in dollars, the decline in the value of the dollar early in 1995 reduced the effective value of the LDCs' import revenues.

Following the successful conclusion of the Uruguay round of the General Agreement on Tariffs and Trade in 1994, the World Trade Organization (WTO) was established on Jan. 1, 1995. Within months of its birth, the U.S. and Japan moved to the brink of a trade war over automobiles, a topic that had not been satisfactorily concluded in the Uruguay round. A last-minute truce in June avoided the imposition of huge tariffs on luxury Japanese cars and enabled both countries to claim victory. Regulatory changes were agreed upon. The Japanese market would be opened up for U.S. automobiles, but as a face-saver for the Japanese, there would be no numerical targets. The U.S. announced its own forecasts regarding the impact of the agreement, but the Japanese did not endorse the report.

A more important development was the agreement by China to cut its import tariffs so that it could join the WTO. The agreement was announced at the 18-nation Asia-Pacific Economic Cooperation (APEC) meeting in Osaka, Japan, in November. Chinese Pres. Jiang Zemin told delegates that from 1996 Beijing would reduce its overall tariff level by 30%. Up to 4,000 items were expected to be covered, and average tariffs were projected to decline to about 25% from 35%.

To the disappointment of the Western markets of APEC, notably the U.S. and Australia, insufficient progress was made in an agreement on more liberalism in agricultural products. East Asian countries—China, Japan, South Korea, and Taiwan—voted to move cautiously and protect their domestic markets. The Western members wanted greater liberalization in order to expand the market for their agricultural produce.

INTERNATIONAL EXCHANGE AND PAYMENTS

A year of two halves is an apt description of the sharp variation in exchange rates during 1995. A sharp fall in the value of the dollar against the yen and Deutsche Mark in the opening months was largely reversed in the late summer and early autumn. Against foreign currencies the dollar ended the year close to the levels at the end of 1994 and more in line with the level suggested by the underlying economic situation.

The turbulence in foreign-exchange rates in the spring was caused by a combination of various factors. The Mexican crisis following the collapse of the peso at the end of 1994 turned sentiment against the dollar. This coincided with signs of a sharp slowdown in the U.S. economy and a continuing current-account deficit. In turn, this put a question mark on the future direction of U.S. interest rates. Yet another adverse development was reduced investment by Japanese investors in dollar-denominated assets. Given the earlier rises in the yen against the dollar, which reduced the value of Japanese assets in the U.S., this was understandable. The combination of these adverse developments triggered a sharp dollar decline against the yen and the Deutsche Mark. In the spring the dollar fell to a record low of just under 80 against the yen and slightly less than 1.35 against the Deutsche Mark. This represented a swing of 17% and 9%, respectively.

In August the dollar began to strengthen against the yen and Deutsche Mark as the central banks in all three countries reduced their interest rates. There was also a coordinated intervention on the foreign-exchange markets in support of the rising dollar. Following these concerted moves and lower interest rates, stability returned to foreign-exchange markets, and during the second half earlier dollar gains were held. As the year drew to a close, the dollar traded at about 103 yen and DM 1.44.

During the early summer, when the dollar was at its weakest, its effective rate (trade-weighted) was only 1% down on previous year-end levels. The strength of the dollar and the yen was offset by the weakness of the Canadian dollar and the Mexican peso. Both currencies had large weights in the calculation of the effective rate. At the year-end the dollar was showing a small gain on its effective rate. By contrast, during the spring the Deutsche Mark was showing a 5% appreciation in its effective rate before the summer correction. It ended the year still showing a small overall gain. A number of European currencies, including the Italian lira, the Swedish krona, and the British pound sterling, depreciated against the Deutsche Mark during 1995, particularly in the early months. The French franc experienced periods of strong turbulence against the Deutsche Mark. In October the French interest rates were raised to defend the franc as it fell on concerns relating to the adequacy of measures proposed to bring down the budget deficit to meet the Maastricht criterion.

The distortions in exchange rates in the early months of the year did not last long enough to seriously affect the relative competitive positions or the balance of payments of the countries concerned. The balances on the current accounts of the developed countries as a group were projected by the IMF to show a wider deficit in 1995—$19 billion, compared with $6 billion the year before. This was largely due to a wider deficit in the United States and a smaller surplus in Japan. The continued recovery in the U.S. encouraged imports to grow faster than exports and led to a wider trade deficit. The current-account deficit widened as well (IMF forecasts pointed to $176 billion in 1995, up from $150 billion in 1994), reflecting a larger shortfall in invisibles and transfers. The IMF was forecasting a reduction in Japan's balance of payments surplus to $116 billion, compared with $129 billion in 1994. If confirmed, this would be the first reduction since 1990, but it was unlikely to satisfy demands by the U.S. that Japan open its domestic markets more and increase its transfer payments. The continued buoyancy in global trade enabled the EU to increase its current-account surplus to a projected $52 billion, up from $27 billion in 1994.

The current-account deficit of the LDCs as a whole, at $64 billion, was expected to be smaller than the previous year, continuing the improvement seen in 1994. Higher exports from the Latin-American countries contributed to this improvement. The currencies of these countries declined

FRED CHARTRAND—CANAPRESS

On the waterfront of Halifax, Nova Scotia, G-7 leaders and aides gather around Canadian Prime Minister Jean Chrétien, host of their June meeting. Russian Pres. Boris Yeltsin joined the group for the last part of its meeting, which centred on economics but also touched on various political issues.

Effective Exchange Rates*
average rates, 1990 = 100

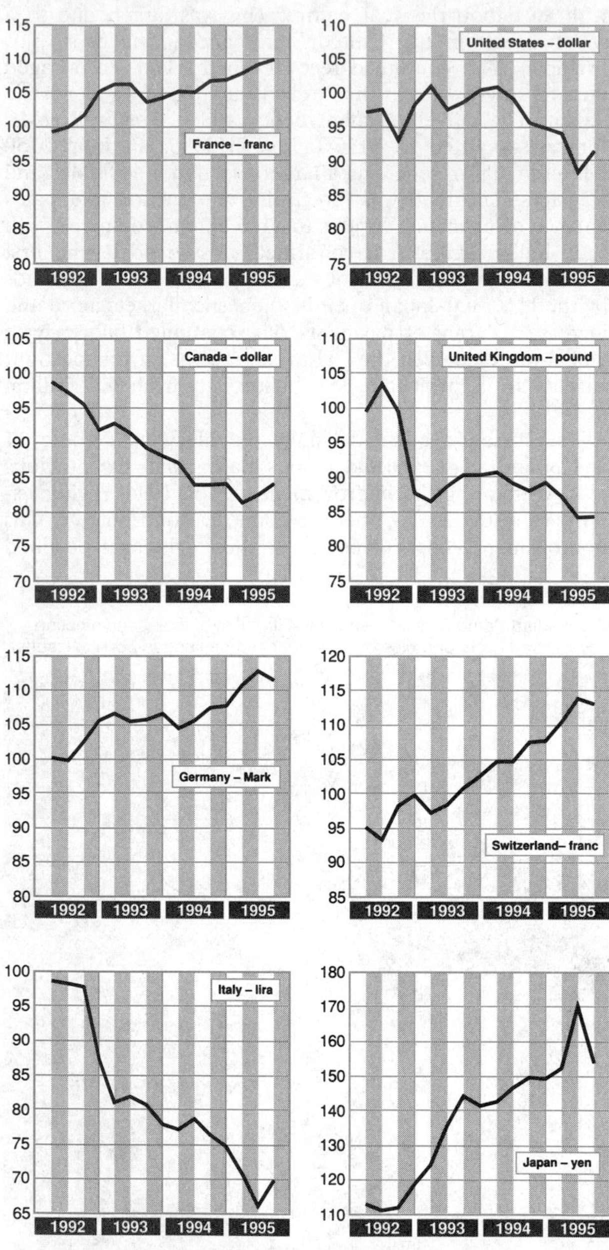

*Measure of a currency's value relative to a weighted average of the values of the currencies of the country's principal trading partners.

Source: International Monetary Fund, *International Financial Statistics.*

against the dollar, giving them a competitive advantage in exporting to the U.S., Japan, and Europe. Regionally, the current-account deficit in Africa and Asia worsened, while the Middle East and Europe remained unchanged.

The total external debt of the LDCs was expected by the IMF to rise by 8% in 1995 to $1,852,000,000,000. This was broadly in line with the increase in the previous two years. With the exception of Africa, the debt burden of the LDCs continued to ease as growth in export earnings outpaced growth in debt. (IEIS)

This article updates the *Macropædia* articles ECONOMIC GROWTH AND PLANNING; GOVERNMENT FINANCE; INTERNATIONAL TRADE.

STOCK EXCHANGES

The world's stock exchanges in 1995 were characterized by an accelerated rise, following an earlier stagnation or fall. Despite this uneven performance, most investors had a vintage year. The *Financial Times*/Standard & Poor's (FT/S&P) World Index gained 26%, in dollar terms, over the year, thanks to the strong performance of Wall Street. Europe, led by the U.K., was 18% higher, in dollar terms, while the Pacific Basin made no headway. (*See* Table I.)

Early in the year, European stock markets were held back by two main concerns, uncertainty about the future direction of interest rates and the weakness of the dollar against the Deutsche Mark. In addition to similar concerns, investors' confidence in the Asia-Pacific region was further undermined by Japan's economic weakness, the Great Hanshin Earthquake, and the aftershocks of the Mexican crisis. The latter caused a run on some currencies tied to the dollar and led to a temporary rise in short-term interest rates.

The trigger for the recovery and the robust rise from the summer was the investors' perception that global interest rates had peaked. In early 1995 economic indicators in North America, the U.K., Australia, and, to a lesser extent, continental Europe indicated a slowing economy with inflation under control. It was expected that economic policy makers would reduce interest rates to support moderating economic activity. In the event, interest rates came down three times in Germany and twice in Japan and the U.S. In the U.K., after a rise of 0.5% in February, interest rates were held steady until December, when they were eased down by the same amount. Initially, government fixed-income securities (bonds) responded to these developments. Sharp rises in bond prices reduced the yields and made equities look more attractive. Prospects of lower interest rates also reduced the attractions of holding cash deposits. Further stimulation came from a series of corporate takeovers in both the New York and the London stock markets.

As in previous cycles, the U.S. led the way, and the positive sentiment spilled over into other markets. Led by technology shares, the Dow Jones industrial average (DJIA) outperformed the rest of the world, setting almost daily new records from June. As the year drew to a close, there was no decline in global investors' enthusiasm for equities, though few expected to see the same superlative gains in the U.S. repeated in 1996. The prospects looked more encouraging in Japan, however, than they had for a long time. (IEIS)

United States. The stock market had a record-breaking year in 1995 as the bull market continued its longest and strongest performance on record. By year-end the upward move in the S&P 500 index was in its 62nd month, with not so much as a 10% pullback in the process. Stocks were trading at three times book value; dividend yields were at a 100-year low of 2.4%; and the number of initial public offerings (IPOs) reached an all-time high. The price of a seat on the New York Stock Exchange (NYSE) was back to the pre-October 1987 level of $1 million. There was great enthusiasm for mutual funds and technology stocks, especially biotechnology, which was the year's best Dow Jones industry group. (*See* Table III.) The DJIA achieved new highs more than 65 times in a steady rise throughout the year. By the close of 1995, the DJIA was up more than 33% from the beginning of the year; the S&P 500 was up nearly 35%; and the National Association of Security Dealers automated quotation (Nasdaq) composite index, with its heavy weighing of technology stocks (especially high tech), was up just under 40%.

Low interest rates, low inflation, a healthy economic climate, high corporate profits, and huge pools of liquidity in the form of net cash inflows into mutual funds helped fuel the bull market. Productivity gains due to radical restructuring and globalization of business were also credited for some of the upward momentum. Expectations of a lower rate of taxation on realized capital gains in 1996 caused investors to defer selling appreciated securities at the higher tax rates of 1995.

The DJIA began the year at a level of about 3830, rose to 4000 by the end of the month, dipped slightly after the collapse of Barings PLC, the oldest British investment bank, in late February, declined in early March as the dollar hit a post-World War II low against the Deutsche Mark, and climbed through April, despite falling slightly to about 4200 in mid month as the dollar reached a new low against the Japanese yen. A strong rally kept the upward momentum through July, passing 4700, when the Federal Reserve (Fed) cut the discount rate 0.25%, its first cut in nearly three years. The index fell briefly to 4600 in August and then moved above the 5000 mark on November 21, just nine months after crossing the 4000 barrier. The positive trend continued through the end of the year. The broader averages also gained, with the S&P 500 hitting a record 621.69 before easing to 615.93 at year's end and the NYSE composite index rising to a record 331.17 and ending 1995 at 329.51. Other indexes showed similar increases. (*See* Table II.)

During the first half of 1995, there were concerns that the economy had turned sluggish, and many economists anticipated lower interest rates because of the threat of a recession. These concerns were dissipated in the second half as the growth rate in gross domestic product (GDP) accelerated.

Despite the euphoria of the bull market at year-end, many securities analysts expected that a correction in the equities market could come from overenthusiasm about the likelihood of an imminent interest-rate reduction and a belief that the single-digit earnings growth likely to be experienced in 1996 was insufficient to support the market. The price-earnings ratio on the S&P 500 was 15 in 1995, considered high by historical standards.

Stock ownership by Americans was valued at about $5 trillion in 1995, passing, for the first time, equity in homes, which aggregated approximately $4.5 trillion. This massive shift into the stock market was largely due to a slowing of inflation in house prices and a major flow of cash into mutual funds and retirement plans.

There were more than 425 new stock issues in 1995, collectively raising more than $26.7 billion in fresh capital for a widely diverse group of corporations. This was below the record of 1993, when there were 543 equity offerings, which raised more than $33.2 billion. The most dramatic IPO was Netscape Communications, a designer of Internet-browsing computer software, which went public in August at $28 per share and rapidly climbed to $171, or 20 times 1997's projected revenues. The average gain for 1995's IPOs was 37.4%. More than 25% of all common stocks brought to market were trading below their initial offering prices, however, while roughly 5% remained unchanged. Among the new issues were 227 spin-offs, 29 reverse leveraged buyouts, and 34 U.S. underwritings by foreign entities. Technology offerings accounted for 164 transactions, or 40% of all new issues floated. The average communications issue rose 114%; computer-equipment offerings averaged a 70%

Table I. Selected Major World Stock Market Indexes[1]

Country and index	1995 range[2] High	1995 range[2] Low	Year-end close	Percent change from 12/31/94
Australia, Sydney All Ordinaries	2226	1823	2203	15
Austria, Credit Aktien	395	329	345	−13
Belgium, Brussels BEL20	1560	1272	1559	12
Canada, Toronto Composite	4745	3991	4714	12
Denmark, Copenhagen Stock Exchange	375	330	366	5
Finland, HEX General	2332	1555	1712	−7
France, Paris CAC 40	2017	1721	1872	0
Germany, Frankfurt FAZ Aktien	847	709	816	4
Hong Kong, Hang Seng	10,073	6968	10,073	23
Ireland, ISEQ Overall	2261	1814	2227	20
Italy, Milan Banca Comm. Ital.	681	548	590	−7
Japan, Nikkei Average	20,012	14,485	19,868	1
Mexico, IPC	2834	1448	2791	17
Netherlands, The, CBS All Share	322	265	322	16
Norway, Oslo Stock Exchange	1292	1036	1261	10
Philippines, Manila Composite	2958	2196	2594	−7
Singapore, SES All-Singapore	559	473	555	4
South Africa, Johannesburg Industrials	7991	6222	7987	14
Spain, Madrid Stock Exchange	320	264	320	12
Sweden, Affarsvarlden General	1872	1440	1736	18
Switzerland, SBC General	1136	871	1132	22
Taiwan, Weighted Price	7051	4503	5159	−27
Thailand, Bangkok SET	1472	1136	1281	−5
Turkey, Istanbul Composite	54,654	24,644	40,025	47
United Kingdom, FT-SE 100	3689	2954	3689	20
United States, Dow Jones Industrials	5216	3832	5117	33
World, MS Capital International	735	596	619	0

[1] All numbers are rounded. [2] Based on daily closing price.
Source: *Financial Times.*

New York Stock Exchange Common Stock Index Closing Prices
Stock prices (Dec. 31, 1965 = 50)

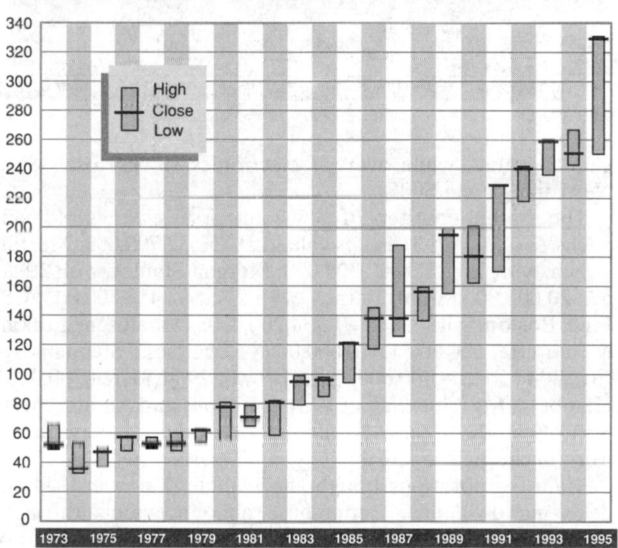

Number of shares sold
In billions of shares

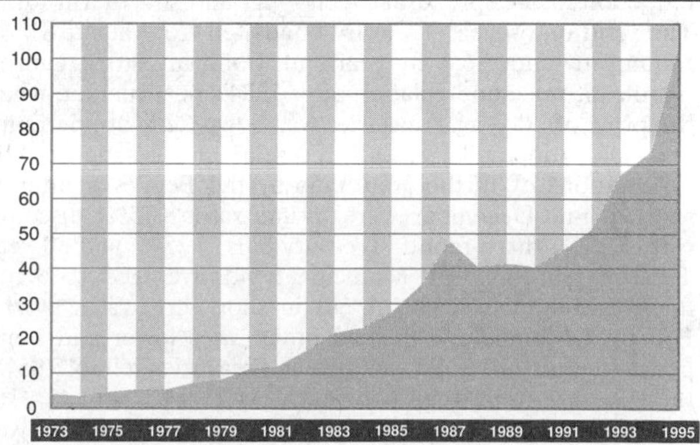

Sources: *Barron's National Business and Financial Weekly; The Wall Street Journal.*

New York Stock Exchange Composite Index, 1995
Stock prices (Dec. 31, 1965 = 50)

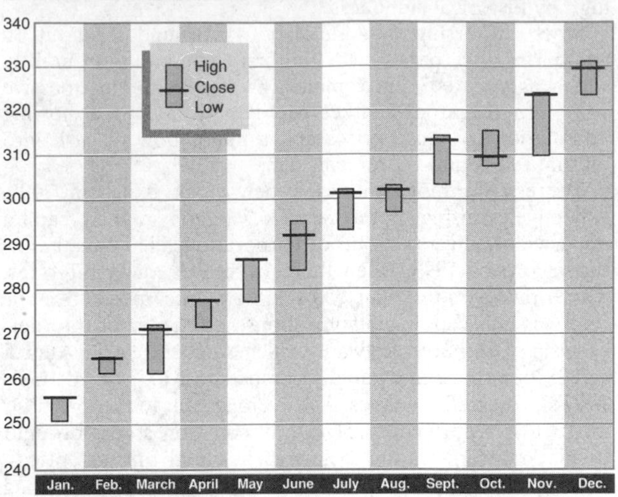

Average daily share volume
In thousands of shares

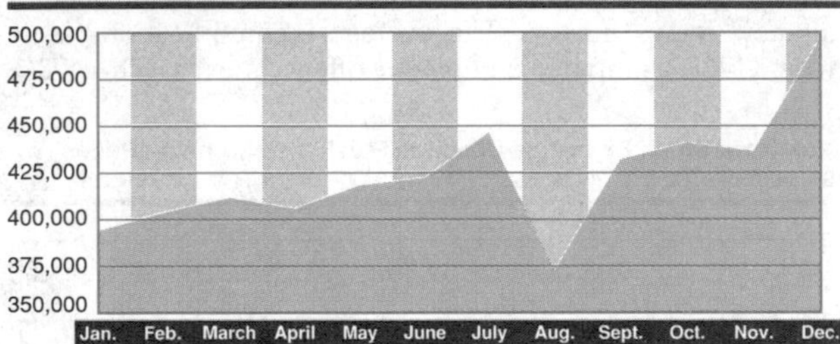

Sources: *Barron's National Business and Financial Weekly; The Wall Street Journal.*

gain in value, while average electronics stocks rose 38%. Netscape gained 500%.

The top underwriters of new equity issues were Goldman Sachs & Co., with 31 issues valued at $5,632,700,000; Merrill Lynch, with 24 at $3,162,300,000; Morgan Stanley, with 29 at $2,520,000,000; Smith Barney, with 27 at $2,413,800,000; CS First Boston, with 11 at $1,734,200,000; Donaldson, Lufkin & Jenrette, 23 at $1,570,000,000; Robertson, Stephens & Co., 30 at $1,208,100,000; Alex Brown, 29 at $1,114,300,000; Hambrecht & Quist, 25 at $781.1 million; and Montgomery Securities, 16 at $699.1 million. The major underwritings were in the fields of technology and health care.

Many corporations bought back their shares instead of declaring dividends. Repurchase announcements through mid-October soared to a record $72.5 billion, surpassing all of 1994's $69 billion.

Interest rates declined during 1995, with a pronounced reduction in the spread between long- and short-term rates. The yield on 30-year Treasury bonds fell from about 8% in January to under 6% by year-end. Bond investors realized significant price appreciation after 1994's bear market, when the price of 30-year Treasuries was down 22% at one point and yields topped 8.1%. Bullish sentiment was supported by expectations of further rate cuts by the Fed. Key interest rates in mid-December were: prime rate, 8.75%; discount rate, 5.25%; three-month Treasury bills, 5.25%; and 30-year Treasury bonds, 6.08%. Municipal bonds averaged 5.7% and telephone bonds 7.25%. A cut in short-term rates by the Fed on December 20 pushed other rates lower and bond prices higher. The yield on 30-year Treasuries fell to 5.95%, the lowest in more than two years.

Mid-December year-to-date volume on the NYSE was 84,033,762,400 shares, up 18.6% from the year-earlier figure of 70,844,452,600. December 15 saw a record one-day volume of 653.2 million shares, eclipsing a mark that had stood since the market crash of October 1987. The extraordinary day's trading was accounted for by expiring stock options, stock index futures, and options on futures, a so-called triple witching day, and year-end portfolio adjustments. Average daily trading volume on the NYSE was a record 346 million shares, up from 291 million a day in 1994. In a reversal of 1994, advances outnumbered declines 2,751 to 788, with 82 of the 3,621 issues traded on the NYSE left unchanged. For the second consecutive year, Teléfonos de México was the most active stock. (*See* Table IV.) Year-to-date bond sales at mid-December were $6,788,205,000, slightly below the prior-year level of $6,959,179,000.

Big Board member firms posted record pretax profits in the first three quarters of 1995. Pretax earnings for member firms increased 72% to $5.7 billion from $3.3 billion in 1994. Revenue increased 28% to $68.7 billion from $53.3 billion a year earlier. Strong trading activity, asset-management fees, and declining interest rates were factors.

Trading volume for stocks on the American Stock Exchange (Amex) by mid-December was 4,865,780,300, up 11.6% from the previous year. Out of 1,058 Amex stocks 661 advanced, 375 declined, and 22 held unchanged for the year. Bond sales were off sharply.

Nasdaq (6,597 issues) became the largest U.S. stock market on the basis of turnover in 1995, with average daily volume of some 400 million shares, compared with the Big Board's 346 million average. By comparison, the Amex traded an average of only 20 million shares a day. Nasdaq's volume, which was 36% above 1994's average daily volume, was accounted for in large measure by its many technology company shares. Year-to-date volume by mid-December was 98,095,081,900, up from 71,886,448,100 shares traded in the corresponding period of 1994. At year's end 2,898 stocks had advanced, 1,380 had declined, and only 62 were unchanged.

The National Association of Securities Dealers (NASD), a self-regulatory organization for the brokerage industry and the operator of Nasdaq, was under investigation by the Department of Justice and by the Securities and Exchange Commission (SEC) for alleged antitrust violations. An independent committee headed by former U.S. senator Warren

***Financial Times* Industrial Ordinary Share Index**
Annual averages, 1973–95

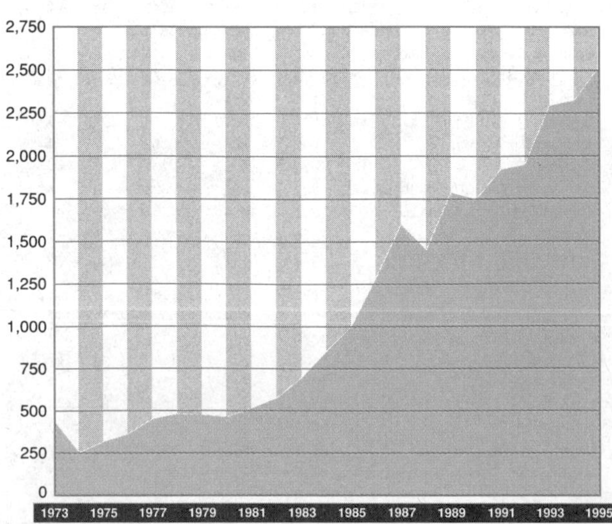

Source: *Financial Times.*

Rudman also issued a report, which led to a reorganization of the NASD, with Nasdaq being spun off as an independent subsidiary with its own board of directors, separate from the regulatory functions of the parent organization.

The five regional exchanges—Cincinnati (Ohio), Boston, Philadelphia, Chicago, and Pacific—traded an aggregate of 36.5 million shares a day but provided significant competition for the larger exchanges by offering better services to investors, including superior handling, cleaner trade executions, potentially better pricing, and longer hours.

Mutual funds had their best year ever as money market fund assets rose to $766,390,000,000 by mid-December 1995 from about $640 billion in a steady rise during the course of the year. No-fee fund "supermarkets" evolved that permitted investors to trade mutual funds without incurring commission or transaction fees. Initiated by Charles Schwab & Co., the movement grew rapidly in 1995 with entry into the field by major brokerage firms. The first nine months were the best since 1957, with a year-to-date total rate of return of 25.2%. Funds specializing in health and biotechnology stocks returned 15.37%, science and technology 14.95%, and financial services 15.37%. At mid-October, U.S. stock funds were up 25.34% year-to-date, and U.S. bond funds were up 11.81%.

In index options trading, the ranges for underlying indexes at mid-December 1995 were S&P 100(OEX) closed at 591.75, up 162.12 or 38.1% from the beginning of the year; the S&P 500(SPX) closed at 616.92, up 34.3%; and the S&P Midcap(MID) closed at 213.38, up 25.9%. The Commodity Futures Trading Commission (CFTC) and the National Futures Association (NFA) studied ways of curbing the incidence of fraud in the sales of futures contracts through "blind" advertisements. The CFTC reviewed its statutory enforcement powers, while the NFA increased its surveillance of member firms promoting blind pools.

The SEC filed more than 500 enforcement cases, an all-time high, in 1995. Among its priorities was a scrutiny of order-flow fees and related order-handling practices on Wall Street because of their potential to reduce competition based on published quotes. The SEC also eased limits on the use of computer technology in communicating with investors, allowing financial documents to be sent via E-mail or downloaded from an Internet site. Legislation introduced would eliminate controls over how much stock institutional investors could buy on margin; scrap rules that required brokers to give investors a prospectus before a stock purchase, free brokers of their duty to recommend only "suitable" investments to institutional clients, including state and local governments; and, most controversially, preempt "blue sky" laws, under which states police securities and mutual fund sales within their borders. The SEC dropped a proposal to allow companies to delete financial footnotes from annual reports sent to shareholders.

Canada. Canadian stocks were up 12% in 1995, according to the Dow Jones World Stock Index, as contrasted with the DJIA gain of 33.5%. The Toronto Stock Exchange (TSE) index of 300 stocks closed at 4713.5, a gain for the year of 11.8%. The TSE 300 rose from about 4000 in January to within a narrow range of 4600 in July, eased to 4500 in October, and dipped sharply to 4300 before climbing to a high of 4745.1 in early December. Trading during October included the sixth largest one-day decline ever, as the separatists in Quebec gained ground before the separatist referendum, and the largest single-day increase in eight years, following the razor-thin victory by the federalists. There were concerns that the Canadian government might relax its fiscal discipline as its main priority in order to appease the Quebeckers. Corporate profits were up, particularly for forest product concerns, especially those producing pulp and paper; petroleum concerns; and base-metal miners. Industrial companies performed well, but gold-mining stocks declined on average.

Total rates of return on Canadian bonds in U.S. dollars were up 20.5%. Because of political uncertainties and a declining growth rate in GDP early in 1995, both Moody's Investors Service and S&P downgraded Canadian government bonds. The government sold bonds at auction without the benefit of a top rating. Following the referendum on the constitution, the bond market rallied.

Merger mania swept the Canadian stock market in the third quarter, pushing the value of deals in 1995 to a record with three months left. The value of mergers and acquisitions in the first three quarters was Can$64.5 billion, a 76% increase from the corresponding period of 1994 and well above the 1994 full-year record of Can$48.4 billion. The top-valued deal announced in the third quarter was a hostile takeover, valued at Can$1,770,000,000, begun by a Canadian company, the Moore Corp., for Wallace Computer Services, Inc., of Schaumburg, Ill. Second was the Canadian govern-

Table II. Selected U.S. Stock Market Indexes[1]

	1995 range[2] High	1995 range[2] Low	Year-end close	Percent change from 12/31/94
Dow Jones Averages				
30 Industrials	5216	3832	5117	33
20 Transportation	2002	1455	1981	36
15 Utilities	225	182	225	24
65 Composite	1736	1274	1693	33
Standard & Poor's				
500 Index	622	459	616	34
Industrials	732	546	721	32
Utilities	203	150	203	35
Others				
NYSE Composite	331	251	330	31
Nasdaq Composite	1070	744	1052	40
Amex Market Value	554	433	548	26
Wilshire 5000	6085	4539	6057	00

[1] All numbers are rounded. [2] Based on daily closing price.
Source: *Wall Street Journal.*

Table III. Performance of Selected Dow Jones Industry Groups in 1995

Best		Worst	
Industry	Percent change from 12/31/94	Industry	Percent change from 12/31/94
Biotechnology	81.5	Trucking	−14.5
Oil drilling	72.4	Steel	−8.5
Aerospace and defense	70.7	Transportation equipment	−4.6
Banks in western states	67.4	Specialty retailers	−3.6
Semiconductors	64.5	Coal	2.7
Banks in eastern states	64.5	Precious metals	3.7

Source: *Wall Street Journal.*

Table IV. Most Active U.S. Stocks in 1995

	Volume of shares traded (in 000,000)		Volume of shares traded (in 000,000)
New York Stock Exchange		Nasdaq	
Teléfonos de México	1,202.4	Intel	2,106.3
Micron Technology	1,114.3	Microsoft	1,204.2
Motorola	877.1	Novell	1,106.6
Ford Motor	855.8	Cisco Systems	1,082.1
Compaq	811.9		
Wal-Mart	801.7	American Stock Exchange	
IBM	780.5	Viacom Var	479.9
Kmart	774.3	Viacom "B"	367.7
AT&T	688.0	XCL Ltd.	208.1
Merck	654.0	Echo Bay Mining	161.4

Source: *Wall Street Journal.*

ment's sale of most of its stake in Petro-Canada. The value of mergers in the third quarter was 46% higher than a year before. The transaction value was $18.5 billion on 260 deals, compared with $12.6 billion on 323 deals in 1994.

After a close brush with recession early in the year (GDP, which had grown 4.5% in 1994, fell to about 2%), the Canadian economy appeared likely to resume growing until the end of 1997, according to a report by the Royal Bank of Canada. GDP was expected to rise by 2.2% in 1995 and 2.3% in 1996. The Bank of Canada reduced its overnight lending rate by 25 basis points in July.

The Investment Funds Institute of Canada proposed a sales code that would limit "trailer fees" that kick in only when brokers and other mutual fund salespeople have sold a minimum of a fund. The concern was that there would be undue incentives to oversell investors.

Market sentiment was bullish by year-end, with strong expectations that the Canadian stock market would perform well into 1996 in tandem with its U.S. counterpart. The U.S. accounted for 8% of all Canadian foreign trade, and the two economies were closely integrated. (IRVING PFEFFER)

Western Europe. Many European stock exchanges turned in a good performance in 1995. During the first five months of the year, Western European stock markets made little headway. Investor confidence was undermined with the strength of the Deutsche Mark against the dollar. In order to protect their currencies from weakening against the Deutsche Mark, France, Italy, Sweden, and Spain kept their short-term interest rates high. Political uncertainty in France and Italy also had an adverse impact, as did fears that interest rates might go up again in the U.S. However, beginning in May the sentiment changed, and share prices rose in many markets. This was largely triggered by lower interest rates in Deutsche Mark bloc countries. Another push came from the U.S., where Wall Street was reaching new highs. As measured by the FT/S&P Euro top 100 index, European stock markets as a whole were 12.3% up from the beginning of the year. Some of the best performers were peripheral markets. Switzerland, with a gain of 22%, led the field. Other good performers included Ireland (20%), the U.K. (20%), and Sweden. Austria, with a decline of 13%, was the worst European performer. France was nearly flat.

The London Stock Exchange, the largest and the most influential market in Europe, started the year concerned with a poor inflation outlook and the prospect of higher interest rates. The Mexican crisis and the collapse of Barings PLC also affected sentiment. By mid-March the *Financial Times* Stock Exchange 100 (FT-SE 100) index was close to the psychologically important 3000 level, having been above 3100 a month earlier and 3066 at the end of 1994. However, encouraging prospects for corporate profits, export growth, and increasing takeover activity started moving the market higher. It was also encouraged by Wall Street's reaching new highs. By early summer economic statistics pointed to a slowing in the economy but, with inflation not yet under complete control, Chancellor Kenneth Clarke surprised the markets and held interest rates unchanged. Bond prices were stimulated, and new strength spilled into the equity markets. In mid-June, by the time Prime Minister John Major resigned the Conservative Party leadership, the FT-SE 100 had gained 400 points, or 13%, since the lowest point of the year. After Major's reelection as party leader, the market regained its strength and reached 3500, close to an all-time high, by August. For the next three months it drifted sideways, and it fell a little in late October on concerns that the weakening economy and faltering export growth could reduce corporate profitability in 1996. The market rallied again in November when a prudent budget signaled that lower interest rates were on the way. The continued strength of Wall Street, speculation on further takeovers, and traditional year-end buying buoyed up the market. It ended the year at an all-time high of 3689.30.

Among the larger markets on the European continent, Germany and France started the year on a weak note. The German DAX Index fell by 10% to 1910.96 by the end of March. The combination of a strong Deutsche Mark against the dollar, relatively high wage settlements in the engineering sector, and a poor outlook for corporate profits drove the market down. In May, as short-term interest rates were cut and the Deutsche Mark weakened against the dollar, the market rallied, and it reached a record high of 2317 in mid-September. The summer rally was sustained by a further cut in interest rates and the new highs reached by most foreign stock markets. After that, however, the DAX Index slid to around the 2260 level because of concern about a sharp economic slowdown and poor corporate profitability. It closed the year at 2253.88. The FAZ Aktien Index followed a similar pattern and ended the year at 815.66, up just over 4% for the year.

The Paris Bourse experienced a volatile and disappointing year. In the early months of 1995, the French bourse fell steeply as interest rates were temporarily raised in response to a decline in the franc. Subsequent lower interest rates in Germany and France, as the currency turbulence subsided, pushed the CAC 40 Index to the year's high of 2017.27. The optimism surrounding Jacques Chirac's presidential victory in May soon evaporated as it became clear that France's problems were deep seated. The continuation of the *franc fort* policy effectively kept interest rates too high in France, given the depressed state of the economy. Widespread strikes and protests in December against proposed reductions in public spending and welfare reforms also adversely affected sentiment. The CAC 40 closed the year at 1871.97, just below its level at the beginning of the year.

The Nordic countries were among the best performers in Europe. Sweden led the way with an 18% rise. Across the border Norway gained 10%, and Denmark was 5% up on the year. Finland, an earlier star performer, gave up all its gains in the second half of the year. These countries benefited from a combination of global enthusiasm for telecommunications stocks and high prices for paper and forestry products. The performance of the southern European bourses was lacklustre. An economic boom in Spain led by strong export growth pushed share prices up by 12% during 1995. Italy and Portugal performed badly, and share prices fell by around 7% and 14%, respectively.

Other Countries. After experiencing considerable volatility, particularly in the opening months, the Asian equity markets, with the exception of Hong Kong, were flat throughout the year as whole. The Japanese market, until the autumn, was held back by pessimism over the economy and the strength of the yen. The FT/S&P Pacific Index (excluding Japan) rose by 6%, in dollar terms, over the year. This lacklustre performance was initially due to shock waves from the Mexican crisis. Interest rates in Hong Kong and Thailand were temporarily raised to defend the Hong Kong dollar and Thai baht from speculative attacks. At the same time, there was substantial selling by local investors. As the direction of interest rates in the U.S. became clearer, international investors' interests in the summer and the autumn were focused on the rising markets in the U.S., Europe, and Japan. Little interest was shown in the Pacific Basin stock markets. Although economic growth was two to three times as fast as in the developed countries, the risk of overheating and low growth in earnings per share of companies in the

(continued on page 186)

Special Report

The Concern over Derivatives

BY PATRICIA TEHAN

Derivatives had been acquiring a bad name even before the collapse of the London-based merchant bank Barings PLC in February 1995 rocked the world's banking community. But the failure of Barings brought derivatives into the public spotlight after Nicholas Leeson, a 28-year-old trader in Singapore, accumulated losses of over $1 billion by trading futures contracts on Asian markets.

Derivatives are contracts that have value that is linked to, or derived from, another asset (known as the underlying asset), which can include stocks, bonds, currencies, interest rates, commodities, and related indexes. Purchasers are essentially wagering on the future performance of that asset. The economic rationale of derivatives is that they provide a means of transferring and spreading risk and of accommodating risk-management needs more accurately and economically than conventional financial instruments. Though they can offer substantial advantages to those seeking to reduce financial exposure to a fall in prices, derivatives also can be very risky. Initial reaction to the Barings debacle was that given the growing use of such products, it would have been only a matter of time before they led to such a disaster.

In the 1980s the case of some U.K. local authorities' involvements in options-based derivatives contracts first brought them into bad repute. The highest profile was London's Hammersmith and Fulham council, which suffered huge losses on derivatives contracts as interest rates moved against it. The contracts proved to be unenforceable, however, when the House of Lords ruled that local authorities did not have the power to enter into swaps contracts.

There had been some high-profile corporate losses involving derivatives in 1994, involving Procter & Gamble (P&G), the U.S. consumer-products company, Metallgesellschaft AG of Germany, and Orange county in southern California. In early 1995 U.S. regulators started to raise concerns about the way derivative products were being sold to investors. This was the issue behind the argument between P&G and Bankers Trust, which designed its investments, and between Orange county and its broker, Merrill Lynch & Co.

Despite the bad name that derivatives were beginning to acquire, the collapse of Barings was due to losses caused by a lack of adequate internal controls over an employee's proprietary trading activities. The highly publicized corporate disasters were caused by different circumstances. Ironically, it was the collapse of Barings, caused by trading in the tightly controlled futures market, that served as a means to focus attention on the products and prompted market participants to consider certain national and cross-border issues related to the structure and operation of the international markets for derivatives trading.

Derivatives are not a new concept, but growth in their use has been dramatic over the past 20 years. This growth reflected a globalization of—and an increase in volatility in—financial markets, as well as a reduction in foreign-exchange controls. Volatility in interest rates, exchange rates, and asset prices created a climate of uncertainty. By using derivatives, corporations, foreign-exchange traders, and other investors were able to manage, control, and hedge risk.

Derivatives include such widely accepted products as futures, options, and swaps. Standard derivatives contracts—those involving standard maturity, contract size, and delivery terms—are traded on exchanges such as the Chicago Board of Trade, the London International Financial Futures and Options Exchange, the Marché à Terme des Instruments Financiers (the French exchange), the Singapore International Monetary Exchange, the Deutsche Terminbörse (the German exchange), and the Tokyo International Financial Futures Exchange. Once the transaction has taken place, the contractual relationship is between each original counterparty and the exchange or clearing house. Customized contracts—those tailored to meet a specific customer's needs—are unregulated and traded in over-the-counter (OTC) arrangements. In OTC contracts the counterparties remain exposed to each other for the life of the contract.

Debate in the months preceding the collapse of Barings was over how much derivatives were a tool to be used to provide flexibility in an investment portfolio and to reduce the risks being taken on by investment banks and their customers and how much they were becoming a threat to the stability of markets. The debate after the Barings failure focused the attention of investors on risk. The popularity of more complex derivatives contracts waned, while turnover in simple, less complicated futures and options products increased. After several months of panic, which saw a reduction in the volume of derivatives trading and a subsequent reduction of the number of players on some trading floors, markets settled down by the end of the year. Meanwhile, institutional and corporate derivatives users took a fresh look at their controls and revised their practices.

At a 1994 meeting in Windsor, England, securities regulators from 16 countries agreed on measures to strengthen supervision of futures exchanges and improve the flow of information across international markets and to ensure that any problems that did arise could be contained locally to prevent an international domino effect. The initiative, brought about by the Securities and Investments Board of the U.K. and the Commodity Futures Trading Commission of the U.S., recognized that no one market supervisor has the full picture about traders who are operating globally.

In a separate move, the Basle Committee of International Banking Supervisors published proposals designed to help banks avoid losses from adverse market movements. It also joined forces with the International Organization of Securities Commissions to issue new joint guidelines on derivatives for national regulators. The effect has been a gradual tightening of monitoring and enforcement.

The horror stories of 1994 and 1995 resulted from imprudent use, lack of understanding, or lack of proper control of derivatives products and activities. In the case of Barings, inappropriate risk exposures were taken without proper guidelines or management controls. There was a complete failure to note the level of derivatives trading. In other cases there was a lack of understanding of the relationship between client and counterparty. All served to identify two issues in using the derivatives markets. The first was that players should examine the legal issues, including the nature of the relationships between the counterparties, ensuring proper documentation of transactions and ensuring that each side has the authority to deal. The second was a management issue, that those running an organization should have an understanding of risks being taken and be satisfied that proper operational controls are in place.

Patricia Tehan is banking correspondent for The Times, *London.*

(continued from page 184)
region reduced their attractions. Hong Kong's 23% gain over the year was in stark contrast to sharp declines in some other countries, including Taiwan (down 27%), South Korea (down 14%), and Thailand (off 5%). Indonesia, Singapore, and Malaysia bucked the trend and rose by 9%, 4% and 2.5%, respectively, over the year.

The Japanese stock market fell sharply from January until July before recovering strongly in response to a weaker yen, lower interest rates, and increased government spending. The poor performance of the Japanese stock market in the first half of 1995 caused the Nikkei 225 Index to plunge to 14,485 in July, a decline of 26% from the level at the beginning of the year. As the Bank of Japan moved to reduce interest rates, the market surged, and it continued to move upward. Its path was eased by the weakness of the yen against the dollar and a third economic stimulus package introduced in September. Surveys also showed that the profits of Japan's top 1,500 nonfinancial businesses improved by 20% in the half year to September. During 1995 the Japanese market was driven by foreign buying. Local investors preferred to sell selectively. The Nikkei approached the year's end on a strong note and closed at 19,868.15, just above its level of a year earlier. Lower interest rates, rapid economic growth, and good demand for commodities helped the Australian market to rise by 15% over the year. The New Zealand stock market benefited less from these trends and rose by just over 12%.

The emerging markets were very volatile during 1995. Following a loss of confidence caused by the Mexican crisis in January 1995, equity markets in the emerging markets regained their poise. A good recovery began in March, particularly in Latin America, and continued, albeit at a slower pace.

Commodity Prices. The sharp gains seen in commodity prices during 1994 were partly reversed during 1995. Economic slowdown in the developed world and lack of speculative activity were the main reasons for the weakening in commodity prices during the year. *The Economist* Commodity Price Index of spot prices for 28 internationally traded foodstuffs, nonfood agricultural products, and metals fell by nearly 5% during the first 11 months of the year. In sterling terms the decline was slightly smaller, at 3.5%.

The price of crude oil, which is not included in *The Economist* Index, rose by 8% over the year and was trading at around $17 per barrel in early December. For most of the year, it traded in a narrow range between $16 and $18 a barrel. Oil prices were stronger early in 1995. In response to seasonal demand and anticipated continued recovery in the industrialized countries, it touched $19 per barrel. Prices weakened in the summer, however, as production continued to run ahead of demand and OPEC decided not to change the quotas. A short-lived price recovery gave way to renewed weakness, which continued into the autumn, reflecting below-average seasonal temperatures and lower demand. Following the November meeting of OPEC, the market firmed and oil prices increased by 6%.

Both sectors of *The Economist* Index declined during 1995. The food index fell by 5.5% and the industrials by 3.3%. Lead, with a gain of 15% over the year, was one of the few metals to rise strongly. Reduced exports from the former Soviet Union and Eastern Europe, coupled with stronger industrial demand, particularly from auto battery manufacturers, boosted prices. Copper, tin, and zinc were broadly steady during 1995 following strong rises the year before. Nickel prices declined by over 10%.

Cereal prices increased 10–20%. Bad weather, which disrupted grain production in the U.S. and Russia, was largely responsible for the upward pressure on prices. The prices of other agricultural commodities were mixed. Coffee prices fell by 25% from the previous year's peak after the crops in Brazil were not damaged by rainfall and output was higher than anticipated. Cotton was up by 7%, while wool prices declined by 10% under the weight of surplus stock. Gold prices in 1994 traded within a range of $374 to $394 per troy ounce and ended the year at $388, barely above the level of a year earlier. (IEIS)

This article updates the *Macropædia* article MARKETS.

BANKING

International. The biggest story in international banking in 1995 was the collapse of the London-based merchant bank Barings PLC in late February. Nicholas Leeson, a trader in the 233-year-old bank's Singapore office, had run up losses of more than $1 billion trading futures contracts on the Asian markets. Barings management claimed that Leeson was carrying out unauthorized transactions and then covering up his losses in a secret account. Inspectors in Singapore, however, alleged that bank officials, anxious to participate in the lucrative derivatives market, had allowed the 28-year-old trader to use highly risky instruments without adequate supervision. (*See* Special Report.) In March Barings was acquired by a Dutch financial group, Internationale Nederlanden Groep NV. Leeson, who was arrested after fleeing to Germany, was returned to Singapore for trial and sentenced to 6½ years in prison.

Unauthorized trading by a single individual was also blamed for the $1.1 billion in losses accumulated by Daiwa Bank Ltd. of Japan. In September Toshihide Iguchi, a U.S. Treasury bond trader based in New York City, was charged with falsifying records to conceal the deficit, which he had incurred through some 30,000 unauthorized trades over an 11-year period. Unlike Barings, Daiwa, one of the world's 25 largest banks (*see* Table), was able to absorb the enormous losses. However, state and federal bank regulators discovered that Iguchi had confessed to Daiwa executives two months before U.S. authorities were notified. In November the authorities ordered Daiwa to close its operations in the U.S. within three months, while the Japanese Finance Ministry demanded that the bank cut back all of its international operations.

In August the Bank of Japan announced that it would liquidate the Hyogo Bank, which had built up $6 billion in debts through unwise property speculation, rather than arrange a bailout, as had been expected. It was the first time since World War II that the Japanese government had allowed a commercial bank to fail. The government of Fiji approved a taxpayer-financed bailout of the National Bank of Fiji (NBF). Critics accused politicians of having benefited from the NBF's questionable loan practices. In the United Arab Emirates, the emirs of Ajman and al-Fujayrah agreed to pay $10 million to settle claims against them resulting from the 1991 collapse of the Bank of Credit and Commerce International. In June the Chinese government agreed to allow five foreign banks to open branches in Beijing, including the Bank of Tokyo and Citibank of the U.S.

The British banking industry saw several mergers and acquisitions in 1995. In May S.G. Warburg accepted a bid from Swiss Bank Corp. for its investment banking arm. In September the Bank of Scotland paid $A 900 million to acquire 100% ownership of the Bank of Western Australia. The merger of Lloyds Bank PLC and TSB Group PLC, announced in October, was completed at year's end. The new institution, called Lloyds-TSB Group PLC, would form the largest retail bank in the U.K., with assets of £150 billion.

(MELINDA C. SHEPHERD)

United States. They called it the "Goldilocks economy" in the banking industry—not too hot, not too cold, just the right temperature. U.S. banks made very good profits in 1995 as loan losses remained low, borrowing picked up at a modest pace, and their huge bond portfolios increased in value. The big news for banks was a tidal wave of mergers and takeovers. About $73 billion worth of mergers and acquisitions were announced in the U.S. banking community. Fifteen deals exceeded $1.1 billion in value, including the three largest takeovers of all time. There were two forces driving the takeover movement: the high stock prices of the acquiring banks, which made it relatively cheap for them to offer stock to the shareholders of the banks being taken over, and the realization that the good times of 1995 were unlikely to last forever.

Police escort Nicholas Leeson from the airport in Singapore upon his extradition from Germany on November 23 to stand trial on charges of fraud and forgery. It was alleged that Leeson's activities in trading securities futures in Singapore had led to the collapse of Britain's Barings PLC in February.
JOHN MACDOUGALL—AFP

Increasingly, big banks were merging in hopes of cutting costs by reducing payrolls and closing buildings. In a flurry of activity, deals were announced between First Union Corp. of Charlotte, N.C., and First Fidelity Bancorp of Newark, N.J., and First Chicago Corp. and NBD Bancorp Inc. of Detroit, Mich., among others. The biggest example of this phenomenon in 1995 was the merger of Chase Manhattan Corp. and Chemical Banking Corp., both of New York. The combined bank, which would surpass Citicorp as the nation's largest, with assets of nearly $300 million, would retain the Chase name. There was no question, however, that the transaction was a takeover by Chemical, which paid Chase stockholders about $10 billion worth of Chemical Bank stock in exchange for all their shares. While Wall Street cheered the Chase/Chemical merger, it was clear that thousands of employees soon would be laid off.

World's 25 Largest Banks*

	Bank	Country	Assets (in U.S.$000,000)
1	Dai-Ichi Kangyo Bank	Japan	520,335
2	Fuji Bank	Japan	518,101
3	Sumitomo Bank	Japan	510,272
4	Sakura Bank	Japan	508,736
5	Sanwa Bank	Japan	506,416
6	Mitsubishi Bank	Japan	471,968
7	Norinchukin Bank	Japan	443,708
8	Industrial Bank	Japan	397,057
9	Deutsche Bank	Germany	365,774
10	Mitsubishi Trust & Banking	Japan	333,858
11	Credit Lyonnais	France	328,331
12	Credit Agricole	France	328,147
13	Tokai Bank	Japan	318,443
14	HSBC Holdings	U.K.	315,312
15	Industrial & Commercial Bank	China	311,866
16	Long-Term Credit Bank	Japan	309,118
17	Sumitomo Trust & Banking	Japan	306,443
18	Mitsui Trust & Banking	Japan	301,984
19	Bank of China	China	291,856
20	ABN Amro Holdings	Netherlands	290,686
21	Societe Generale	France	277,914
22	Banque Nationale de Paris	France	271,548
23	Asahi Bank	Japan	268,351
24	Daiwa Bank	Japan	262,815
25	Dresdner Bank	Germany	257,548

*Ranked by assets as determined by Worldscope; figures are based on each company's 1994 fiscal-year results.
Source: *Wall Street Journal.*

Loans to individuals at commercial banks, which had been growing at around 15% a year in 1993 and 1994, increased at a much slower pace in the last part of 1995 and were heading down to an annual rate of 5% to 6% as the year closed. Americans, who had seen little if any growth in income in 1995, were maintaining their standard of living by borrowing more on their credit cards. This effect had to slow down and reverse, and this "reliquification" process was already in sight at the end of 1995. Bankers and the Wall Street investment community were expecting a big increase in loan losses on those credit cards in 1996. In an economic slowdown, the losses could rise from about 3.25% of the credit card loans outstanding to 4% or higher, a significant increase in an industry where net interest margins were only a little over 4% before taxes and other expenses. The growth of bank loans to commerce and industry was also declining. "C & I" loans peaked in May 1995 at an annual rate of 17.7% and by the end of 1995 were about 12% over the year-earlier level.

The other mainstay of bank earnings, the bond market, performed extremely well in 1995. The decline in interest rates led to a rise in the price of bonds. Since U.S. Treasury bonds represented around 20% of the total loans and securities held by banks, this was a good source of profit. If interest rates rose in 1996, however, bond prices could fall, and there was a risk that any inflationary threat in 1996 could turn bond profits into losses.

U.S. banks may have made good profits in 1995, but they still faced an uncertain future. The record level of mergers and acquisitions was a symptom of competitive pressures and the need to reduce costs, and bankers knew that "Goldilocks" was, in the end, a fairy tale.

(JOHN W. DIZARD)

This article updates the *Macropædia* article BANKS AND BANKING.

LABOUR-MANAGEMENT RELATIONS

In 1995 the economic environment improved in most of the industrialized countries, the main exception being Japan, which had another lacklustre year. There was healthy growth in world trade, and inflation was low. Unemployment tended to fall, but it was still high in many countries.

Europe. Unemployment was a major concern in the European Union (EU), where in December 1994 the European Council had adopted a five-point plan to improve the functioning of labour markets. The creation of jobs was prominent in the European Commission's Social Action Programme for 1995–97, put forward in April. The program reflected the reaction against the heavy concentration on legislation in recent years and contained few significant new proposals. It was mainly a program of consolidation, of ensuring that existing legislation was implemented, and of providing for analyses and consultation about future work.

In the U.K. there were a number of minor disputes and a series of strikes in the railways in the summer, but on the whole it was a quiet year for labour-management relations. The most notable event was the abolition in July of the Department of Employment. There had been a government department for labour matters since 1893 and a full ministry since 1917. The functions of the department were distributed among other departments, mainly Education—which became the Department of Education and Employment—and Trade and Industry.

In two decisions the European Court of Justice found that the U.K. had failed to implement fully EU directives on large-scale layoffs and workers' acquired rights, which required consultation with workers' representatives. In response the government put forward regulations in October requiring such consultation where 20 or more employees were to be dismissed at one establishment during a 90-day period. How to consult was left to the employer, but consultation had to be with employee representatives whether or not the employees were unionized.

British law required workers wishing to appeal their dismissal to an industrial tribunal to have at least two years' service with their employer to do so. Two women, dismissed by different employers and each having only 15 months' service, were refused access to the tribunal. They turned to the courts on the basis that women tended to change jobs more frequently than men and were therefore less likely to have as much as two years' service, which made British law incompatible with EU law on equal treatment. In July the Court of Appeal ruled in favour of this view. The case could go to the highest British court, the House of Lords, which in turn might refer it to the European Court of Justice.

In German industry the annual wage round generally passed without much strife, but the resultant pay increases were criticized by the Organisation for Economic Co-operation and Development (OECD) as being "disappointingly high." A lengthy series of negotiations with Volkswagen ended in September with the company's concession of a postdated 4% wage increase and commitment to guaranteeing jobs for its workers in Germany (about 100,000) for two years. In return, the union (IG Metall) made concessions increasing the flexibility of working time, though not as extensive as the company had wanted. An important judgment of the Federal Constitutional Court confirmed the government's stance on the interpretation of a section of the Work Promotion Act that refused state temporary jobs and unemployment benefits to employees temporarily laid off on account of a strike in their sector, even if it was not in their region. Unions had counted on benefits being paid to laid-off members to lower their costs in industrial

Members of IG Metall, Germany's largest labour union, demonstrate against Volkswagen. In September, after concessions on both sides, the workers accepted a 4% wage increase and a two-year job guarantee and in return agreed to more flexibility in working hours.
EPA

disputes. In the former communist part of the country, wage rates continued to move closer to those in the west. Unemployment, though still severe—and much higher than in the west—was declining.

In France the main central employers and trade union organizations signed a declaration in February expressing their intention to establish a continuing social dialogue. Talks started in March and were particularly concerned with encouraging employment and with fighting unemployment, which continued to hover around 11% to 12% in spite of an economic recovery that seemed to stall late in the year. Among other matters discussed were the vocational integration of young people, flexibility of working time, and ways to articulate collective bargaining at the national-central, industrywide, and enterprise levels. In July the parties agreed to set up a joint intervention fund to improve the functioning of the labour market. The fund would be used particularly to help workers who might wish—subject to their employer's agreement—to retire early and who had already paid pension contributions for at least 40 years and whose jobs could then be filled by the unemployed. The government also introduced the Employment Initiative Contract to subsidize employers who hired certain classes of people, such as the long-term unemployed. By mid-August 23,000 such contracts had been effected. Beginning in August, however, labour troubles increased. The government proposed to reduce public expenditures, including the costs of civil service pensions and health care and the debts of the railways. Starting with a well-supported one-day strike in October, union opposition grew, with strikes causing massive disruption in November and December and, at one time or another, involving civil servants, workers on the railways and the Paris transport system, and employees in power supply, telecommunications, and schools.

The thorny question of modifying Italy's overly generous pension arrangements was settled, at least for the present, by a comprehensive agreement on May 29 between the government and the three main union confederations. The agreement formed the basis of a law published on August 17. A wave of protests against limits on pensions broke out by year's end, however. A series of issues put to a national referendum on June 11 included questions concerning the legal obligation of employers to facilitate the deduction of union dues from pay, when requested by workers, and concerning the representational rights of trade unions in an enterprise. The referendum went in favour of repealing the obligation to deduct union dues and of reducing the monopoly of the three main union confederations as representative bodies. The government was also active in the area of employment, promoting bills to encourage optimal flexibility in employment contracts and to create the new National Agency for Employment. In Spain the main trade union and employers confederations agreed in April on the establishment of conciliation, mediation, and arbitration procedures to replace the services run by the state.

In an unusual move, Sweden's trade union confederations set an objective of negotiating wage increases in 1995 corresponding to the European norm, considered to be 3.5%. In the event, after gaining annual increases of 3.8% a year in a two-year agreement in the paper and pulp industry and even more in a three-year agreement with hotels and in catering, the unions did better than expected. In the metal industry the union secured a 12-minute cut in the 40-hour workweek to be added to vacation time, as well as wage increases. There were also institutional changes; union mergers reduced the number of Swedish Trade Union Confederation affiliates from 23 to 21, but the central employers organizations were unable to merge into a single body.

United States. The report of the Dunlop Commission on the Future of Worker-Management Relations became available in January 1995. Though the commission made a number of recommendations, the report was widely viewed as a disappointing document that failed to address a number of problems affecting American labour-management relations. Admittedly, any radical proposals would have had little chance of being legislated in the present Congress. The commission's most disputed proposal was one that would ensure that cooperative labour-management bodies could be constituted in the workplace without running afoul of the section of the National Labor Relations Act that forbids company unionism. On March 8, Pres. Bill Clinton signed an executive order sanctioning federal contractors who hired permanent striker replacements.

It was an important year for U.S. trade unions. On June 12, following lengthy controversy within the American Federation of Labor–Congress of Industrial Organizations (AFL–CIO), Pres. Lane Kirkland announced his retirement, after 16 years in office, effective August 1. Thomas R. Donahue, secretary-treasurer, took over the presidency until the election scheduled for October 25, when he contested the office against John J. Sweeney, president of the Service Employees International Union. Sweeney, a dissident leader in the AFL–CIO, defeated Donahue.

The continued decline of U.S. trade union membership in recent years was the major factor prompting a number of union mergers. The mergers included those between the International Ladies' Garment Workers' Union and the Amalgamated Clothing and Textile Workers Union, the United Steelworkers of America and the United Rubber Workers of America, and (to be effective by the year 2000) the United Automobile Workers, the United Steelworkers, and the International Association of Machinists and Aerospace Workers. The Department of Labor estimated that labour contracts for 42% of workers under major agreements would expire or reopen during the year. With employers tending to take a tough line, it was not surprising that a number of negotiations ended in strikes, several of which hinged on meeting the ever-rising costs of health care, while others concerned work rules and antiunion action by employers.

Canada. In the populous and industrially important province of Ontario, the conservative government moved to replace significant parts of the industrial relations legislation of its New Democratic Party predecessor. The government added new provisions that reversed a ban on the permanent replacement of striking workers and that required secret ballots in cases of certification of a union, in ratifying a collective agreement, or in calling a strike. A general strike in London, Ont., in December protested the government's pro-business policies.

South Africa. The new South Africa stood in need of revised labour legislation, and much of 1995 was taken up with preparing a comprehensive labour relations measure. Progress was slow and difficult, but agreement was reached by the National Economic Development and Labour Council in July and was carried into law in October as the Labour Relations Act. It provided for a Labour Court, with a more refined role than the existing Industrial Court; a Commission for Conciliation, Mediation, and Arbitration; and Workplace Forums (a form of works council). A union demand for centralized collective bargaining was not taken up, but the act did make provision for bargaining councils.

(R.O. CLARKE)

See also Business and Industry Review.

This article updates the *Macropædia* article WORK AND EMPLOYMENT.

CONSUMER AFFAIRS

Consumer concerns were significantly addressed in 1995 when the UN Economic and Social Council (ECOSOC) passed a landmark resolution calling for extensive revision and updating of the 1985 UN Guidelines for Consumer Protection. The guidelines, which covered consumer safety and product standards and education, provided both a framework and a benchmark for governments, particularly those in less developed countries, to establish a legal basis for consumer protection. The impact made by the guidelines could be seen in India, where a consumer forum was set up to resolve problems outside the legal system, and in Eastern Europe and the states of the former Soviet Union, where there was an explosion of activity in consumer affairs. The 10-year anniversary marking the establishment of the guidelines was celebrated on World Consumer Rights Day, held annually on March 15. The 1995 ECOSOC resolution was the most significant broadening of the guidelines in the past decade and was expected to lead to a sustainable level of consumption.

The World Trade Organization (WTO), a court set up by the 1994 General Agreement on Tariffs and Trade to arbitrate international trade disputes, officially opened its doors on Jan. 1, 1995. The WTO, headed by Renato Ruggiero (*see* BIOGRAPHIES), had several cases in its docket, but none was heard during 1995.

Consumers International (formerly the International Organization of Consumers Unions) launched a Consumer Charter for Global Business for transnational corporations. Those signing the charter would agree to abide by consumer-friendly standards in such areas as competition, advertising, and environmental impact.

Most consumer activity in 1995 took place at the grassroots level and often against great odds. As democratic reforms and market liberalization spread in Africa, consumer movements also emerged, particularly in Western Africa. Yet Africa as a whole remained mired in deep economic crisis, which had taken its toll on humans through increased malnutrition, reduced social services, lowered incomes, and higher unemployment.

The consumer movement—working with very limited resources—was swamped with issues needing urgent attention. Fewer than 10 African countries had organizations with permanent offices and staffing, and 21 had no identified consumer groups at all. Most of the offices were operating at capacity and were working to open new centres to handle the high volume of consumer complaints. Attempts also were made to assess the impact of economic structural adjustment programs on Africans. In January, 27 consumer leaders from 17 West and Central African countries attended a conference on the subject.

The African Office of Consumers International was studying the state of consumer protection legislation in Africa and was in the process of drafting a model consumer protection law, which was expected to be completed by year's end.

Eastern Europe also was struggling to build a consumer movement virtually from ground zero. Six years after the fall of the Berlin Wall, nearly every country in Eastern and Central Europe had formed some type of consumer organization. Macedonia, Armenia, and Georgia joined the group in 1995.

Most countries in Central and Eastern Europe instituted, at the minimum, basic consumer protection laws and, with an eye toward joining the European Union (EU) by the end of the century, many were working hard to bring their laws in line with those of Western Europe. As a sign of how rapidly times were changing, Albania was hoping to have a consumer protection law in place in 1996.

Overall, a major concern was to educate consumers who had little experience with savings and investment so they could make wise investments with their earnings. Newspapers reported numerous scandals in Eastern and Central Europe and the republics of the former Soviet Union, where fraudulent and incompetent banks and financial service companies were operating.

Western Europeans faced different problems, many of them related to the EU, which included 15 members after Sweden, Finland, and Austria were admitted in 1995. (Norway rejected membership.) The single market—the world's largest trading bloc—was intended to remove all trade barriers across member countries. Consumer groups, however, continued to confront the European Commission (EC) in areas they felt—despite promises of trade liberalization—continued to hurt consumers. (For example, automobile distributors were still excluded from EC competition rules and could maintain monopolies across Europe.) In 1995, however, consumer groups scored a victory by persuading the EC to allow competing car manufacturers to advertise where monopolies existed.

Consumer organizations lobbied the EC regarding pending legislation about after-sales services and guarantees. Consumer representatives argued that in a single market, guarantees should be honoured across borders—guarantees on goods bought in France should be honoured in Spain, and services on products purchased in Germany should be available in the United Kingdom.

In Latin America, improving economies and expanding trade signaled an end to a long period of economic isolation and recession. Yet very few benefits appeared to be trickling down to the 165 million Latin Americans classified as poor—80 million of whom were living in dire poverty, according to the World Bank. An estimated 19% of Latin Americans lacked access to clean drinking water, while 32% had no electricity and 43% were without drainage or sanitary services. Low-income consumers were especially vulnerable to hazardous or substandard products and such abusive practices as false advertising and adulterated weights and measures.

Nonetheless, consumers fought back; 16 Latin-American countries established national consumer protection laws. In 1995 the governments of Argentina and Colombia added consumer protection to their respective constitutions.

In November, with the help of a manual published by Consumers International, more than 100 organizations involved in adult education planned to introduce consumer education into their curriculum.

In Asia the consumer scene was characterized by glaring contrasts both within the region and within individual countries. Though foreign investment poured into the area, Asia's booming growth produced greater economic disparity; millions of impoverished consumers were confronted by higher prices, unregulated markets, and an influx of substandard imported goods. As a result, more than 60 consumer representatives from Malaysia, India, Thailand, the Philippines, and Vietnam attended a conference in Malaysia to discuss "Consumerism in Developing Economies: Agenda for the Future."

In the South Pacific, consumers banded together to halt the dumping of both toxic wastes and poor-quality food. Since 1992 Papua New Guinea and the Solomon Islands had passed consumer protection laws, and Western Samoa and Tonga were expected to follow suit by the end of 1995.

(ALINA TUGEND)

In the United States the Federal Aviation Administration concluded in May 1995 that legislative efforts to mandate the use of child safety seats during air travel for children under two would not accomplish its intended goal of saving lives. Strapping children into safety seats—as opposed to the more common practice of allowing them to sit on the lap of a parent—would increase the cost of flying and cause some families to choose less-safe modes of travel.

A cost-benefit approach to safety regulations was a central theme in congressional legislation introduced during the year. In July two major bills on regulatory reform—both requiring the federal government to provide evidence that the benefits of proposed regulations justified their costs—were postponed indefinitely. The new Republican-majority Congress effectively changed the tenor of the policy debate concerning a number of food-, drug-, and pesticide-safety regulations.

In February new meat-inspection regulations proposed by the U.S. Department of Agriculture recommended instituting Hazard Analysis and Critical Control Points, an inspection procedure in which key stages of meat production would be targeted to prevent the spread of pathogens. Although the procedure was considered an important advance in food inspection, critics in the industry charged that imposing it without dismantling the traditional system would raise costs without bringing about a commensurate improvement in safety.

At the state level, a groundswell of consumer and physician complaints prompted lawmakers in New Jersey and Maryland to pass the first state legislation requiring minimum maternity stays in hospitals. In some states women were routinely discharged 12 hours after giving birth, down from the typical 2 and 3 days of recovery time traditionally paid for by insurers. Groups such as the American College of Obstetricians and Gynecologists warned that early discharges presented a health hazard, especially when women and infants went home before complications could be observed or child-care guidance provided. Health insurers and managed-care groups maintained that one-day stays with follow-up home-care visits met the needs of most maternity patients. The laws guaranteed women 48-hour stays after delivery and 4 days of hospitalization for deliveries by cesarean section.

Action against fraudulent and misleading auto-leasing deals took place in Florida, Maryland, Washington, and New York. Each state passed a law aimed at increasing dealer disclosure of the various costs incurred by consumers in leasing. The Federal Reserve Board also drafted new disclosure standards under the federal law that governed leasing. Law-enforcement officials who were tracking the recent upward growth of auto leasing reported widespread deceptive leasing practices. Frequently, consumers were persuaded to sign leasing agreements that apparently carried low monthly payments, but lessees were not furnished with important basic information such as the amount of principal upon which payments were based.

The U.S. General Accounting Office (GAO) questioned the reliability of the government's automobile crash-test scores as a source of consumer information. The results of the New Car Assessment Program—undertaken by the National Highway Traffic Safety Administration and widely disseminated by the news media and consumer publications—improved the overall crashworthiness of cars. But the GAO determined that individual car scores were not reliable and could mislead consumers to purchase less-safe cars.

(PETER L. SPENCER)

See also Business and Industry Review: *Advertising; Retailing*; The Environment.

Education

Significant educational news in 1995 included comparisons of educational achievement between countries, plans to increase schooling opportunities, the expansion of private schools, the resolution of ethnic and religious issues, educational transition in Eastern Europe, educational financing, the transfer of credits in higher education, and university promotion practices.

Primary and Secondary Education. Downsizing of the U.S. government adversely affected federal education programs, while the number of difficult tasks facing educators continued to multiply in 1995. Voicing his concern, U.S. Secretary of Education Richard W. Riley noted that the Information Age requires an "Education Age."

The new Republican-controlled Congress sought to cut spending in many programs as part of its "Contract with America" (*see* Special Report) and to return control over most education to the states. The Department of Education was initially in danger of elimination, but Pres. Bill Clinton proposed less-drastic changes in Cabinet-level departments.

The president sought to retain adequate federal support for safe and drug-free schools, adult job programs, and AmeriCorps—the national-service program.

Enrollments in the U.S. for the 1995–96 school year increased at all levels of education. Preschool and kindergarten numbers rose by some 250,000 students to more than 7.7 million. Elementary and secondary enrollments reached 51 million students, surpassing even the peak levels of 1971. The number of minority students was expected to reach 32.8%, a 4.6% increase over the previous year. High-school graduates for the academic year were expected to number 2.6 million.

There were some three million teachers in U.S. elementary and secondary schools, with a smaller number of educators serving in collegiate faculty positions. About 4.2 million individuals held administrative, various other professional, and support positions in educational institutions.

A judicial ruling on drug testing that could have wider ramifications was handed down by the U.S. Supreme Court, which upheld random drug testing of high-school athletes. The justices ruled that athletes must submit to testing at the beginning of a sports season and to random tests thereafter. Results would be available only to school officials.

It was possible that the drug ruling could be applied to random testing of all students, as part of a school's general responsibility to protect young people's well-being. Under the decision, school officials were not required to have a specific suspicion of drug use, unlike a Fourth Amendment requirement for adult testing.

The high court left some issues unsettled with regard to prayer in school. It overturned a 1994 ruling by the Court of Appeals for the 9th Circuit stating that student-initiated prayers during graduation ceremonies were unacceptable and left intact an earlier ruling by the Court of Appeals for the 5th Circuit that upheld the constitutionality of student-led graduation prayers.

The Supreme Court found that a federal judge had exceeded constitutional limits in a long-standing Missouri desegregation case. The judge had ruled that school officials had to pay additional salaries to minority employees as part of an effort to undo the effects of past segregation. The supervised district had undertaken the most expensive desegregation plan in the U.S. The court ruled that under the Constitution, officials were not bound to pay higher salaries to minorities to meet the requirements of desegregation.

The Supreme Court also found that school gun-free zones, authorized in a 1990 federal act, were an unacceptable extension of the interstate commerce clause of the Constitution, a provision that had been used for decades to extend federal jurisdiction in many areas.

Scholastic Assessment Test (SAT) scores reached their highest levels in many years, especially math scores, which were the highest in 20 years. White and Asian students topped the rankings, while minority students continued to make gains. Male students again outscored females, who continued to improve their performance.

Voucher plans to permit public funding of private schools continued to be widely advocated around the nation. The Wisconsin Supreme Court overturned a legislative act that permitted Milwaukee schools to provide up to $3,600 for private, even sectarian, school tuition for families whose annual income was less than $26,000.

Pres. Albert Shanker of the American Federation of Teachers (AFT) found recent achievement levels reported by the National Center for Education Statistics both "surprising and encouraging." Shanker noted that student course selections and graduation requirements had become more rigorous than they had been a decade previously, when the publication of *A Nation at Risk* (1983) sounded an education-crisis alarm. The government publication had focused on low educational achievement and called for massive changes, many of which subsequently were implemented, said the veteran AFT leader.

Poverty and alcoholism were tied to many school-age children's problems. Researchers from the Centers for Disease Control and Prevention (CDC) in conjunction with Emory University, Atlanta, Ga., reported that women in poverty were more likely to have retarded children who would probably have more difficulty in getting an education. CDC researchers also found that the percentage of babies born with fetal alcohol syndrome (FAS) had increased sixfold between 1979 and 1993. FAS babies experience mental retardation and central nervous system problems, which make their education more difficult.

Violence in the media remained a nationwide concern. The Television Violence Monitoring Report, based at the University of California, Los Angeles, claimed that in 1995 motion pictures and children's television programs had more violence than could be found on prime-time television. Harvard University's Robert D. Putnam proposed the idea that the introduction of television notably weakened the nation's social and educational fabric. He theorized that the advent of television led to declines in social trust and group participation, which he claimed were crucial to maintaining social and educational standards in a democracy. He held that this decline brought on by TV possibly contributed more to an overall social change in the United States than did such factors as divorce, the rise in the number of working women, and the spread of the welfare state.

The increase in the numbers of children who did not speak English as their primary language was attributed to the increased number of immigrants to the country. The National Association for Bilingual Education's executive director said that one child in six entered school speaking a language other than English.

In 1995 a comparison of educational levels in 21 member nations of the Organisation for Economic Co-operation and Development showed that in most OECD countries over half of the adult population had completed secondary school. In Germany, Switzerland, Norway, and the United States, the level rose to more than 80%. In Europe, where 19 of the OECD nations are located, there were marked disparities in educational achievement between northern and southern countries. More than 60% of adults had earned a high-school diploma in Austria, Finland, Germany, Norway, Sweden, Switzerland, and the United Kingdom, while fewer than one-third had completed high school in Greece (32%), Italy (25%), Spain (25%), Portugal (15%), and Turkey (15%). In only two of the OECD countries had more than one-fifth of the population between ages 25 and 64 completed college—The Netherlands (21%) and the United States (24%).

A World Bank report urged governments to furnish all citizens with at least six years of schooling as a means of stimulating economic growth and reducing poverty in less developed nations. The report noted that the proportion of children attending school in less developed countries had risen from below 50% in 1960 to 76% in 1995, and it concluded that a still higher proportion of citizens with basic education would be needed to keep pace with predicted shifts in labour markets caused by technological innovations and economic reform.

A variety of sub-Saharan African governments adopted plans to cooperate with other countries to improve educational systems. In one effort research teams from nine nations launched a joint assessment of education sponsored by the Southern African Consortium for Monitoring Educational Quality. Participating countries included Kenya, Malawi, Mauritius, Namibia, Swaziland, mainland Tanzania and Zanzibar, Zambia, and Zimbabwe. The primary aim of the research was to identify the major influences on students' reading achievement. In a separate effort, education ministries in Lesotho and Swaziland sought to become independent of Great Britain's influence over the Cambridge Overseas School Certificate by localizing the assessment of test papers.

JIMMY DORANTES

Students in a southern California school recite the pledge of allegiance. In parts of the U.S., children whose native language was not English made up a large part, or even a majority, of the enrollment in local public schools, which gave rise to disagreements about the best way to teach them.

In Kenya a plan adopted in 1985 to vocationalize education at all levels had proved too complicated and too costly to implement; a similar plan was rejected in Botswana.

A Nicaraguan study of 6,600 school-age children from 2,500 homes indicated that males took a year longer than females to complete primary school and two years longer to finish secondary school. More than 20% of pupils repeated grades because of poor academic performance or ill health, and the main cause of school delinquency was economic, with the dropout rate for males far higher than that for females. Pupils in Nicaragua were more likely to succeed in school if they came from homes of married couples, their families had few children, they had attended preschool, and they had started school at age five.

Cuba's economic crisis contributed to a deterioration of the nation's highly centralized school system and discouraged an increasing number of qualified people from entering the teaching profession.

The extent to which technological advances were adopted in schools was investigated in Great Britain, where a survey of the popularity of educational broadcasts among 1,500 teachers in 700 British schools revealed that most primary teachers took advantage of television programs but only half used educational radio. In secondary schools television broadcasts were employed most often for studying geography and history and least often for mathematics. Secondary teachers rarely used radio programs, with the exception of modern-language classes, where radio was used fairly often.

The privatization of schools increased in various parts of the world. In Canada increased enrollments in private schools continued into 1995, with many of the students coming from middle-class families that traditionally had patronized public schools. Part of the appeal of the private institutions was their low teacher-student ratios.

Economic reforms in Vietnam that created greater wealth for the private sector led to cutbacks in public moneys for education, and thus the traditional school system became drastically underfunded. As a consequence, secondary schools that charged tuition grew increasingly popular with the country's expanding middle class. Such schools attracted well-qualified teachers and provided higher-quality education than did the impoverished public schools attended by the rural poor.

In Pakistan the network of private schools continued to expand as a result of the underfunding of state schools and corruption in the public education system.

Several nations announced plans to expand educational opportunities. Thailand's government intended to invest $1.5 billion toward several educational initiatives, including an extension of compulsory schooling from six to nine years, a refinancing of private schools outside the capital city of Bangkok, and an increase in the availability of loans for economically disadvantaged students. The purpose was to improve younger workers' skills in order to sustain the country's economic boom.

A new education law in China, drafted over 10 years, went into effect September 1. The law provided a framework for future legislation and outlined a revised educational system focusing on moral and intellectual development. Subsequently, the nation's State Education Commission issued regulations governing the establishment of schools jointly operated by Chinese and foreign sponsors. Although no religious affiliates would be allowed to conduct school, nonreligious groups would be permitted to do so as long as they provided high-quality education as defined in the commission's guidelines. As the government increased its investment in economic development, however, its financial support of education continued to decline. As a consequence, schools at all levels of the educational system were obliged to launch cottage industries or other moneymaking ventures to sustain their operations.

Mexico's Pres. Ernesto Zedillo pledged that before the close of his administration, all children would have the opportunity to advance through secondary school. This commitment was considered highly optimistic for a country in which 75% of rural pupils traditionally did not complete the six years of primary education. Economic needs were cited as the main cause of high dropout rates, particularly in subsistence-farming regions, where children were needed for their labour. Critics also charged that the primary- and secondary-school curriculum had long been ill-suited to regional needs. Because of this, many pupils found schooling irrelevant and either dropped out or were not motivated to study. This problem also extended to the 10% of pupils in Mexico (nine million) who spoke only an Indian dialect.

Malaysia's Prime Minister Datuk Seri Mahathir bin Mohamad had begun to stress the importance of the English language in the country's national curriculum, thereby initiating a shift from the policy of the past three decades, which emphasized the Malaysian national language. He said that knowledge of English was vital to international trade, and he hoped that prestigious overseas universities would consider establishing branches in Malaysia. Datuk Francis Yeoh Sock Ping, a prominent business leader, confirmed that he would like to build a local campus for the University of London, a proposal that until recently would not have been considered.

A number of countries took steps to resolve racial conflicts and to offer equal educational opportunities for ethnic groups. The South African government sought to reverse years of inequality by committing itself to furnishing every child, regardless of racial background, with 10 years of education at government expense. Educational segregation was officially abolished, and new school-construction plans and improved training for black teachers were announced.

Many Australian schools expanded their Asian studies curricula in an attempt to integrate and promote a greater appreciation of Australia's Asian population. Classes in magnet schools included Asian languages, geography, literature, and religious history.

Educational authorities in France were criticized by Islamic leaders for not permitting women students to wear head scarves in the public schools. Officials claimed that displaying the traditional Islamic head coverings violated France's law banning religion in schools, even though Catholic students were still allowed to wear crosses.

Higher Education. A UNESCO report on higher education disclosed that annual attendance in postsecondary institutions throughout the world grew from 28 million students in 1970 to 65 million in 1991 and would continue to increase, reaching 79 million by 1999 and 97 million by 2015. In less developed countries enrollments over the 1970–91 period rose from 7 million to 30 million. The proportion of students at private universities increased, particularly in less developed regions, with the numbers of nondegree and part-time students also rising. According to the report, the financial burden of rapid growth tempted officials to limit spending on higher education. UNESCO's director general, Federico Mayor, warned that yielding to that temptation would simply widen the gap between industrialized and nonindustrialized societies. Sub-Saharan Africa had the fewest educational resources and opportunities of any region. Students in Africa were four times less likely to pursue postsecondary education than those in other less developed areas and 17 times less likely than those in the industrialized countries.

Public and private postsecondary enrollments in the U.S. were projected to increase slightly, to 15.4 million students. More than half of the students—nine million—were expected to attend four-year institutions. Two-year colleges were set to enroll an estimated six million. Proprietary schools and postsecondary programs were expecting one million enrollees, and degrees earned were projected to reach record levels. Federal officials expected seven million students to receive some type of financial aid by 1996.

Spending in the U.S. for public elementary, secondary, and collegiate education was projected to reach $433 billion in 1995. The cost of a private education was predicted to reach $104 billion, and the head of the U.S. College Board said that most college students faced a heavily mortgaged future. His assessment was made in response to rising tuition and a decline in available federal grants and loans. Tuition increased at a 6% rate for the third year in a row, an increase greater than the pace of inflation. The annual cost of tuition, room and board, books, and personal expenses averaged $19,762 per student at four-year private colleges and $9,285 at state colleges. To make matters worse, Congress had been hammering out an agreement to trim billions of dollars from student loan programs as part of its move toward balancing the federal budget by 2002.

A schoolgirl in Ethiopia stands at her desk to answer a question in mathematics. One of four girls in a class of 18 students, she and other children had walked for an hour from their village to reach the school, which offered primary instruction in the Amharic language.

MELISSA FARLOW—MATERIAL WORLD WOMEN'S PROJECT. PICTURES FROM *WOMEN IN THE MATERIAL WORLD* BY FAITH D'ALUISIO AND PETER MENZEL TO BE PUBLISHED BY SIERRA CLUB BOOKS IN THE FALL OF 1996

By 1995 the European Union's (EU's) plan for transferring academic credits across country borders had resulted in 5,546 students' receiving credit for foreign study pursued in 145 institutions in 18 countries. The initial program was limited to the subject areas of business administration, chemistry, history, mechanical engineering, and medicine. Plans were laid to double the number of cooperating institutions and increase the diversity of disciplines in 1996.

Ireland's system of 46 nonuniversity postsecondary institutions adopted a system that permitted students to earn a national degree by combining studies completed at different institutions. A national computerized database, containing 6,000 registered courses, kept track of all students' completed courses, certificates, and degrees.

The number of Canada's aboriginal peoples—Indians and Inuits—enrolled in higher education increased fourfold over the decade between 1985 and 1995, owing largely to financial aid from the federal government and a growing number of academic programs designed precisely for the nation's indigenous ethnic groups. Focused on providing indigenous youths with opportunities to study their own cultures, Canada's first aboriginal higher-education institution, the Saskatchewan Indian Federated College, enrolled 1,300 students in 1995, most of them women.

Former communist nations faced problems of transition. Russian institutions suffered from insufficient funds; only 3.65% of the national budget was allocated for education in 1995, over 80% of the country's schools lacked proper experimental facilities, the number of students in specialized programs declined, and skilled personnel continued to emigrate. Student admission policies were changing in such institutions as Moscow State University and Plekhanov Russian Academy of Economics, where well-trained, academically apt students from preparatory schools were being admitted without an entrance examination or tuition fee. Critics charged that such admission practices were unfair to students who could not afford to attend quality preparatory schools.

In 1995 Romanian academicians were concerned that the quality of higher education was threatened by the hasty establishment of more than 60 private universities set up to meet a rapidly rising demand. At the same time, efforts to reform the curricula in state universities were hampered by a shortage of funds. In the neighbouring state of Moldova, government leaders endeavoured to assert their nation's independence, but students and faculty members of most of Moldova's 15 higher-education institutions went on strike when the government changed the title of a common university course from "The History of the Romanian People" to "The History of Moldova."

New legislation in Estonia inaugurated the most dramatic changes in the nation's six universities since the former Russian system was discarded in 1990. By 1995 Estonia's universities had revamped their budgetary system and completed their changeover to an American-style structure in which course work was measured by credits earned and bachelor's, master's, and doctoral degrees were awarded by institutions.

Four years after the former Yugoslav republic of Macedonia achieved independence, representatives of the nation's ethnic Albanians announced the establishment of an Albanian-language university in the town of Tetovo. The plan was denounced by government authorities, who felt that Albanians were entitled only to primary and secondary education in their native language. Founders of the university vowed to conduct classes anyway, even if the government refused the institution official recognition.

In Israel political conflicts between Palestinians and Israelis continued to disrupt university life. Early in the year, Israeli military forces arrested 21 Islamic students at a college near Jerusalem on charges of anti-Israeli propaganda and stockpiling weapons. The Israeli civil administration also stopped granting entry permits to Palestinian students, a measure intended to discourage Palestinian nationalistic activism. Because tuition charges doubled at some Palestinian universities in the West Bank, many students were forced to drop out.

Recent emergency legislation enabled Peru's military forces to take control of three universities where members of the Marxist Sendero Luminoso (Shining Path) organization had disrupted the educational process. One institution, Hermilio Valdizán National University of Huánuco, had been adrift since 1994, when its rector, Abner Chávez Leandro, had confessed to abetting Sendero Luminoso terrorists.

Ways to raise revenue in support of higher education were a concern throughout the world. In China financial problems prompted the government to urge universities to generate their own funds. A shortage of money also led institutions in several countries to admit wealthy, less-qualified students in preference over poor but talented applicants.

The French government's handling of the financial plight of universities drew sharp criticism from university presidents and faculty organizations. The Conference of French University Presidents, representing 83 institutions, charged that the 1995 increase of 5% in research funds and 2.8% in operating expenses was far short of what was needed in view of rapidly growing enrollments. The presidents sought greater latitude in raising money from private sources and recommended a gradual increase in student registration fees, which traditionally had been extremely low. The nation's largest faculty union claimed that inadequate support for basic research, libraries, and undergraduate teaching had reached a crisis level. The union also criticized the government's tightened immigration policy, which resulted in a growing number of foreign students—particularly Algerians—being forced to leave France.

Requiring students to pay tuition continued to be a controversial issue in Eastern Europe, where the cost of attending a university had long been borne entirely by the government. The Czech Republic's new higher-education law set fees ranging from $95 to $380 per year, depending on which academic specialty a student pursued. In mid-March thousands of Hungarian students demonstrated in Budapest following the government's announcement that tuition would be charged in the fall term.

Swiss students protested a tuition increase from $60 to $450 per semester and proposed instead that the needed funds be raised through the savings achieved by the hiring of associate professors rather than full professors. Academics in Switzerland had been among the highest paid in the world, with salaries of associate professors ranging from $97,000 to $133,000 and of full professors from $121,000 to $166,000.

The issue of tuition also set off street demonstrations in Australia, where protesters demanded that the government abolish fees for graduate students and revoke the deferred-payment system that required students to pay about 20% of their educational costs.

At the same time, in a bold move the Australian government allotted a record high of U.S. $12 billion for state higher education programs over the 1997–99 period. The funds would equip institutions to serve an additional 11,000 students in regions with growing populations, to provide more research facilities, to increase vocational education offerings, and to strengthen the Australian Research Council. The government's new performance-based funding system led to a transfer of funds from existing institutions to newly established universities. The plan provided nearly $248 million annually to new institutions, on the basis of their success in obtaining research grants from industries, on their levels of publication, and on the number of graduate students completing their studies.

Concern over bureaucratic meddling in the hiring and promotion of professors was voiced in Japan and Italy. At a conference of Japanese academics, the nation's Ministry of Education was accused of contributing to a decline in the quality of teaching in universities by preventing higher education institutions from individually evaluating faculty members. Critics charged that the ministry's strict bureaucratic control over appointments served to keep ineffective professors in their posts and thereby led to a lower quality of instruction.

In Italy the practice of basing professorial appointments on political patronage rather than on candidates' accomplishments was attacked by delegates at a conference on recruitment and academic promotion in European universities held at the University of Bologna. Speakers claimed that the patronage system, in which assignments were made nationally rather than by individual institutions, damaged the image of Italian academics in international circles and caused Italy to perform poorly in the competition for European Union research grants. In contrast to the Italian model, promotion schemes operating in France, The Netherlands, Austria, and the United Kingdom were said to include continuous assessment of merit in both teaching and research, student evaluations of professors' teaching effectiveness, and faculty-selection committees including representatives from various departments of the university.

(JOEL L. BURDIN; ROBERT MURRAY THOMAS)

See also Libraries and Museums.

This article updates the *Macropædia* articles History of EDUCATION; TEACHING.

The Environment

INTERNATIONAL ENVIRONMENTAL ACTIVITIES

International Cooperation. The threat of global warming continued to dominate environmental concerns in 1995, and for the first time, climatologists were confident they had detected conclusive evidence of it. Some progress was made by European countries toward curbing traffic pollution. What was said to be the third largest oil spill ever recorded, in the Russian Arctic, caused less damage than had been feared. Most of the oil was contained, and an effective cleanup operation was launched. In June Greenpeace protesters drew worldwide attention to an obsolete oil-storage platform, *Brent Spar,* which was to have been sunk in the Atlantic Ocean, and succeeded in persuading the owner, the Royal Dutch/Shell Group, to opt instead for disposal on land. Many scientists, however, believed deep-sea disposal would have been preferable from an environmental standpoint, and Greenpeace eventually discovered an error in the sampling on which it based its objections. The controversy over what constitutes "safe" disposal lasted throughout the year. (*See* Sidebar.)

At a meeting on toxic-waste exports held in Dakar, Senegal, in March, Denmark offered to serve as host for further discussions on the substances covered by the Basel Convention on international trade in hazardous wastes. This deflected attempts to prevent an extension of the ban—agreed upon in 1994 on exports of waste from countries in the Organisation for Economic Co-operation and Development to non-OECD countries—to the export of substances intended for recycling. The U.S. government was delaying ratification of the convention until it was amended to permit such shipments, provided the countries involved agreed and the waste was handled by internationally agreed upon and environmentally sound methods. The U.S. Chamber of Commerce also opposed the ban, which it said would affect the $2.2 billion a year the U.S. earned from trade in recyclable materials. In September, however, the 89 signatory countries to the convention agreed to the extension, forbidding the 25 OECD members to ship wastes to non-OECD members for recycling after 1997.

At a meeting of members of the OECD held in Paris in June, Canada and Australia blocked an agreement, proposed by the U.S. and the European Commission, to reduce the amount of lead in the environment by phasing out lead in such products as gasoline, solder used in food and beverage cans, and paint used on toys and to reduce exposure to lead from paint, ceramics, and crystalware. Australia and Canada favoured a "voluntary action plan" in which the lead-producing industry would finance a database on lead and its health risks and advise governments on ways to reduce exposure. European and U.S. officials said this was inadequate unless incorporated in an agreement committing member states to recognizing the need to reduce exposure.

United States. In proposals for the fiscal 1996 budget presented to Congress by the White House on February 6, the Environmental Protection Agency (EPA) requested $7.4 billion, $138 million more than its 1995 budget. The Office of Research and Development asked for an $84 million increase, to $630 million, some of which would come from reclassifying research funds from elsewhere in the EPA. The EPA, which celebrated its 25th anniversary during the year, sought approval for an additional $42 million to be spent on external research grants and $5 million for more graduate student fellowships.

On April 18 Vice Pres. Al Gore introduced the National Environmental Technology Strategy, a document describing environmental progress made in the U.S. since the first Earth Day, in 1970, and setting goals for the 50th, in 2020. On April 22 (Earth Day 1995), 30 environmental groups launched a major campaign opposing congressional plans to weaken environmental regulation.

Western Europe. In the European Union (EU), Ritt Bjerregaard, a Social Democrat from Denmark, was appointed environment commissioner in the newly appointed European Commission announced on Oct. 19, 1994.

In November 1994 negotiators for the European Parliament and Council of Ministers agreed on new limits of 35 g per cu m for volatile organic compounds (VOC) released during the loading and unloading of gasoline tankers. The limit would apply initially to new installations but would be phased in at existing plants and garages. Two additional directives being drafted by the Commission would limit VOC emissions at the pump and from solvents, such as those in paint and dry-cleaning fluid.

On January 4 the Commission announced a directive reducing by 80% the maximum permitted levels of lead in drinking water. The directive followed a World Health Organization (WHO) recommendation by reducing the limit from 50 to 10 micrograms per litre at a total cost of almost $64 billion over 15 years.

The first shipment of high-level radioactive waste to be transported from Europe to Japan sailed from Cherbourg, France, on February 23 under commando guard. The cargo, comprising 28 steel 100-ton flasks containing 14 metric tons of Japanese spent reactor fuel that had been reprocessed and vitrified at Cap De La Hague, was carried on the *Pacific Pintail.* Greenpeace sought to prevent the shipment, and on February 21 the group was ordered by a Cherbourg court not to approach within five miles of the *Pacific Pintail* while it was in French waters or to blockade it or interfere with the loading of its cargo. On the day the ship sailed, a French tugboat rammed the Greenpeace vessel *Moby Dick.* Commandos boarded the *Moby Dick* and a trawler chartered by another environmental group. Twenty Greenpeace protesters on three inflatables were captured by commandos when they tried to approach the *Pacific Pintail.* On April 25 the *Pacific Pintail* arrived, to more protests, at Mutsu Ogawara, Japan, near Rokkasho, where its cargo was to be stored for 50 years.

In the German Bundestag (lower house of Parliament) election in October 1994, the Greens won 7.3% of the vote, which entitled them to 49 seats, after a four-year absence from the chamber. In the *Land* (state) elections held in Mecklenburg-Vorpommern and Thuringia, however, they received fewer votes than the 5% needed to gain seats, despite their ties with the Alliance '90 civil rights group.

A court in Lüneberg, Germany, ruled in November 1994 that no nuclear waste could be transported from the Phillipsburg power station in Baden-Württemberg to the Gorleben interim storage depository near Hamburg until a decision had been reached on a challenge by local residents to the repository's right to operate. The ruling bought time for the antinuclear movement, which was using opposition to storage at Gorleben in its efforts to prevent the continued use of nuclear power in Germany. Permission was later given for the depository to receive its first consignment of spent fuel rods. After clashes that began on April 22, 6,500 police were brought in on April 25 to disperse demonstrators attempting to block the delivery. Border guards rode on the train carrying the waste, and five helicopters landed more guards inside the Gorleben site to prevent demonstrators from storming the entrance when the gates were opened. Protesters set fire to a railway car, set up a road and rail barricade, pulled up rail track, and threw grappling hooks onto power lines. More than 20 people were injured and nearly 200 arrested.

On July 26 Germany introduced a nationwide ban on cars without catalytic converters, which would be enforced when at least three monitoring stations reported ozone levels higher than 240 micrograms per cubic metre. Commuters able to prove they had no other means of transport, vacationers, and commercial traffic were excluded.

In the Swedish election for the European Parliament held on September 16–17, the Greens, who were opposed to EU membership, won 17.2% of the vote, which entitled them to four seats.

On Oct. 13, 1994, British Environment Secretary John Gummer published the Environment Agencies Bill, which would combine the National Rivers Authority (NRA), the Inspectorate of Pollution, and local authority waste regulators into a single agency. Environmental groups said the bill would weaken existing legislation because of its requirement that the agency take costs and benefits into account before exercising its powers. The NRA issued a statement that the proposed agency would be weak and unable to deliver promises made by ministers. It was particularly concerned that the agency's duty to conservation would be replaced by a duty to "have regard to the need for conservation" and objected strongly to the requirement that environmental improvement costs be justified in advance by benefits that would accrue from them.

New regulations to reduce pollution by vehicles were announced on Feb. 27, 1995, by British Transport Secretary Brian Mawhinney in a speech to a conference organized by the pressure group Transport 2000. Curbside checks would be introduced in 23 cities, covering all types of vehicles. Failure to comply with the regulations would lead to automatic prosecution and fines of up to £2,500. On June 13 Environment Minister Robert Atkins introduced powers, added as an amendment to the bill, allowing ministers to instruct local authorities to establish car-free zones or fine drivers of vehicles without catalytic converters entering cities when pollution levels were high. On July 25 Transport Secretary Sir George Young said spot checks over three months on more than 46,000 cars, vans, and taxis in 23 towns showed that the number causing unacceptable pollution had more than halved in a year. Prohibition notices were issued to 7.2% of the 4,203 light freight vehicles tested, 4.5% of cars, 4.1% of trucks, and 2.8% of public service vehicles.

The Environment Act became law on July 20, obliging local authorities to monitor and curb air pollution. A new set of targets for substances harmful to health—including benzene, volatile organic compounds, carbon monoxide, ozone, and nitrogen oxides—were being prepared, and the number of monitoring stations was to be increased from 26 to 36 by the end of 1996.

The British Inspectorate of Pollution announced a change in policy to allow teams of inspectors to make random checks at factories. In its annual report, published on July 21, the inspectorate said it responded to 2,200 reports of pollution incidents in 1994–95 and issued 106 prohibition, improvement, and enforcement notices, compared with 56 in 1993–94. Pollution complaints in England and Wales increased 30%.

Eastern Europe. Since the breakup of the Soviet Union in 1991, Eastern European countries had begun the arduous task of cleaning up environmental pollution. (*See* SPOTLIGHT: *Pollution in Eastern Europe*.) The third Ministerial Conference of the "Environment for Europe" Process, held in Sofia, Bulg., on October 23–25, addressed environmental challenges and opportunities facing the region and the progress made in improving the European environment. At the conference a "debt for environment" agreement was signed between Bulgaria and Switzerland, under which Switzerland canceled some of the debt owed it by Bulgaria in return for Bulgarian financial support for environmental projects in Bulgaria. The conference was attended by environment ministers from 57 countries, including the U.S., Canada, and Japan. Key donor agencies were also represented, including the World Bank, the European Bank for Reconstruction and Development, and the UN Economic Commission for Europe.

An emergency was declared in Russia's northern Komi Republic in October 1994 when rain washed away a dike built to contain oil leaking from a badly corroded 19-year-old pipeline, spilling nearly 200,000 tons of crude. The pipeline, carrying oil from the Arctic to refineries in central Russia, had ruptured in February 1994. When the cleanup halted at the onset of winter, Anatoly Yakovlev, of the Ministry of Protection of the Environment and Natural

Brent Spar

During 1995 an abandoned North Sea oil-storage platform known as *Brent Spar* was at the centre of an international dispute over the safe disposal of waste material. In the spring, members of the environmental group Greenpeace occupied *Brent Spar* for 23 days to protest the proposed sinking of the rig by its owner, the Royal Dutch/Shell Group. The British government was criticized at the North Sea Protection Conference, held in June in Esbjerg, Den., for granting permission for the platform to be towed from the North Sea to the Atlantic Ocean and sunk in the 2,000-m (6,560-ft)-deep North Feni Ridge, which is part of the Rockall Trough and well clear of the continental shelf. The row erupted again later in June at the Group of Seven summit in Halifax, Nova Scotia, when German Chancellor Helmut Kohl raised the subject with British Prime Minister John Major, and other German ministers discussed it with their British counterparts.

GREENPEACE—GAMMA LIAISON

Water cannons spray the oil platform *Brent Spar* in the North Sea after an unmarked helicopter delivered supplies to two Greenpeace activists. Greenpeace persuaded the Shell Oil Co. to abandon plans to dispose of the platform by sinking it.

The controversy continued as part of a well-publicized Greenpeace campaign. Its vessel *Altair* shadowed the platform as it moved north of the Shetland Islands, and on June 16 two activists boarded it by helicopter. *Solo,* a 66-m (218-ft) Greenpeace tug with a helicopter landing pad was also sent into the area. Environmentalists picketed Shell gasoline stations internationally, and in Germany six shots were fired at a Shell station outside Frankfurt and a Hamburg station was firebombed. Shell sales fell 15–20% in Germany. British, Danish, Dutch, and Swiss Shell stations were also picketed. The British government supported Shell, but the company backed down and said the platform would be dismantled on land. In July the Norwegian government agreed to store it for up to a year while Shell found a way to dispose of it, and the platform was taken to Erfjord, a deep inlet on Norway's west coast.

As the year progressed, however, the issue proved to be more complex than first thought. Most scientists actually favoured deep-sea disposal, regarding disposal on land as more difficult and potentially environmentally hazardous. At a parliamentary briefing in July, John Krebs, director of the Natural Environment Research Council, said the platform contained 68,000 metric tons of concrete ballast chemically similar to rust, 100 tons of bituminous sludge, 30 tons of low-level radioactive scale, and small amounts of heavy metals and polychlorinated biphenyls, which would pose a negligible threat to marine life. Greenpeace had claimed that the platform contained some 5,000 tons of crude oil mixed with radioactive waste and other contaminants. On September 5, Greenpeace admitted its assessment had been incorrect and issued a public apology to Shell. In October an independent study confirmed Shell's original assessment. By year's end, the fate of *Brent Spar* remained undecided, but the possibility of deep-sea disposal had not been abandoned. (MICHAEL ALLABY)

Resources, said the extent of the contamination had not been determined, but the oil was almost entirely contained within a layer of swamp above the permafrost, and isolated from the water table, along a 51-km (1 km = 0.62 mi) stretch of the pipeline. Rivers were not seriously affected, although a small amount of oil had been detected in the Kolva River. Aleksandr Avdoshin, of the Ministry of Civil Defense, Emergencies, and Natural Disasters, said 80% of the oil had been cleaned up, and there was no risk of polluting the Pechora River basin or the Barents Sea. On the other hand, Valerian Silabok, of the Committee for Nature Protection at Usinsk, said the containment barrier was ineffective, the Pechora had been contaminated, and fishermen were removing large lumps of oil from the river. In April 1995 the World Bank approved loans of $99 million to the Komineft company that managed the pipeline to help mitigate the damage. The cleanup resumed in March 1995, but it was hampered by an early thaw and delays in reinforcing earth dikes to protect the Kolva River.

A UN conference on the condition of the Aral Sea opened on Sept. 18, 1995, in Uzbekistan and was attended by delegates from littoral republics. They had inherited from the former Soviet Union financial responsibility for reversing environmental damage in the region. Formerly the fourth largest body of inland water in the world, the Aral Sea had shrunk to about half its original surface area, and its depth had decreased from 69 m (1 m = 3.28 ft) at the deepest point to 54 m, exposing about 36,200 sq km of the bed and almost tripling the salinity of the remaining water.

Central America. At a meeting of the American Chemical Society, held in April at Anaheim, Calif., Donald Blake and Sherwood Rowland of the University of California, Irvine, reported that up to 25% of low-level ozone in Mexico City was produced by leaks of liquefied petroleum gas used for heating and cooking. Stopping all these leaks could reduce ozone levels by 25%.

Asia and the Pacific. In December 1994 Chinese Premier Li Peng inaugurated the Three Gorges Dam, due to be completed in 2009, on which construction work had already commenced. The dam would power 26 sets of 700-MW turbines with a planned capacity of 18.2 gigawatts. The project was budgeted at $22 billion to $34 billion, not all of which had been raised. Doubts also remained over how more than a million people living in the area to be inundated by the 600-km-long reservoir were to be relocated and how sewage contamination and sedimentation would be minimized in large cities upstream, including Chongqing.

There were fears in India in July that a leak of cesium-137 and other isotopes from the Tarapur nuclear-waste-immobilization plant had contaminated wells and ponds around Ghivali, a village of 3,000 people about a kilometre away. The plant had been closed on April 15 when a leak of steam from defective pipes was discovered. Officials said the isotopes would be immobilized in the soil and any contamination would be negligible and harmless.

ENVIRONMENTAL ISSUES

Climate Change. In September the Intergovernmental Panel on Climate (IPCC) made novel use of a World Wide Web page on the Internet to post a draft of its final report for "peer review." In the draft the panel concluded that the observed increase in global mean temperature of 0.3°–0.6° C (0.5°–1° F) was unlikely to be entirely due to natural causes. This was the first time climatologists had claimed to have detected a clear sign of global warming.

A team led by Thomas Karl at the National Climatic Data Center in Asheville, N.C., combined data gathered since 1910 on summer droughts, wet winters, drenching rainstorms, and other extremes of weather in the U.S. to produce a Climate Response Index. Karl reported in April that this had remained at a high level since the late 1970s. Although the trend to more unsettled weather over a 15-year period did not prove global warming had begun, it revealed a pattern consistent with that possibility.

On February 6, delegates from the countries that signed the 1992 UN Framework Convention on Climate Change (FCCC) in Rio de Janeiro met in New York City to prepare for the first full post-Rio meeting. That meeting, the Conference of the Parties (*i.e.,* the 116 signatories that had ratified the Rio convention), opened in Berlin on March 28 and lasted two weeks. OPEC countries opposed the setting of targets for fear it would harm their oil revenues, and the 36 members of the Alliance of Small Island States (AOSIS) regarded a 20% reduction in carbon dioxide emissions by the year 2005 as only a first step. After all-night negotiations, agreement was reached on April 7 on the "Berlin Mandate," which accepted that the target agreed upon at the Rio Summit—of returning carbon dioxide emissions to their 1990 levels in the industrialized countries by the year 2000—was inadequate and further reductions would be needed after 2000. A permanent secretariat was to be established in Bonn, Germany, with a staff building to 50 over two years, a £12 million budget over two years, and a negotiating group representing major power blocs, including AOSIS, OPEC, the EU, China, India, and some other less developed countries. The signatories to the FCCC would meet annually, and the negotiating group would report to the 1996 meeting. Firm proposals produced by then would be discussed at the 1997 meeting and, if approved, would become international law by 2000. The IPCC would remain the principal advisory body.

Evidence emerged of the climatic effect of atmospheric aerosols. In May another study by Karl found that aerosols reduced temperatures by approximately 0.5° C (0.9° F) over the Northern Hemisphere, about equal to the global warming observed over the past century. A projection by the Hadley Centre for Weather Prediction and Research based at the U.K. Meteorological Office in Bracknell, Berkshire, England, suggested that the sulfate aerosol cooling effect would offset about 30% of greenhouse warming, but with no reduction in emissions, the atmosphere would warm by about 0.2° C (0.36° F) per decade. The combined effect of aerosols, increased mid-level cloudiness produced by them, and greenhouse warming were believed to account for the disparity between changes in maximum and minimum temperatures. Between 1951 and 1990 average daily maximum temperatures at the land surface increased 0.28° C (0.5° F) and average daily minimum temperatures by 0.84° C (1.51° F). Clouds reduce temperatures during the day and raise them at night.

It was reported in March that an iceberg measuring about 78 by 37 km and 200 m thick had broken away from the Larsen Ice Shelf on the Antarctic Peninsula. Argentine scientists reported that there was a 64-km crack in the shelf and that a channel had opened, allowing the circumnavigation of Ross Island at the tip of the peninsula. The calving was believed to be due to rapid warming in recent decades. Robert Crawford of the University of St. Andrews, Scotland, reported on March 22 that Blomstrandhaloya, an Arctic peninsula, had become an island because the ice linking it to the Spitsbergen mainland had melted. He found that flowering plants had colonized a larger area than ever before. Analysis of two consecutive series of data by a team at the Nansen Environmental and Remote Sensing Centre in Bergen, Norway, reported in August, showed that since 1978 sea ice had been melting around Antarctica, and Arctic pack ice was melting faster than previously, at 2.5–4.3% per decade. Tree-ring studies by Keith Briffa of the climate research institute at the University of East Anglia, Norwich, England, and colleagues in Switzerland, the U.S., and Russia showed that on average Siberian summers over the past 90 years were the warmest for 1,000 years.

Ozone Layer. The Second European Stratospheric Arctic and Mid-Latitude Experiment found that in the early spring of 1995, ozone levels at 16–18 km above the Arctic and northern Europe were 50% lower than any previously observed. It was not clear how much thinning was due to chemical depletion and how much to the mixing of air masses at different levels, but exceptionally cold winter weather had caused a polar vortex to form.

Thinning of the Antarctic ozone layer, beginning in October and lasting until February, was reported in August to have increased in severity, duration, and extent for each of the past 10 years. Austral spring values at the Halley Research Station of the British Antarctic Survey were less than 40% of their 1960s values. The World Meteorological Organization reported that ozone levels over Europe and North America had fallen 10–15% since the 1980s and that the Antarctic "ozone hole" had doubled in size in the preceding year, to twice the size of Europe.

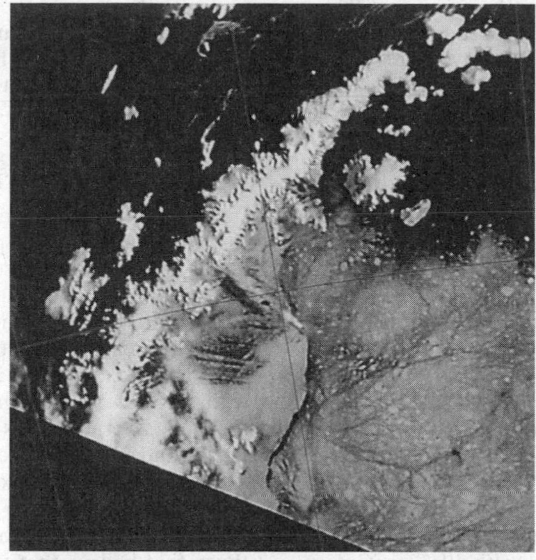

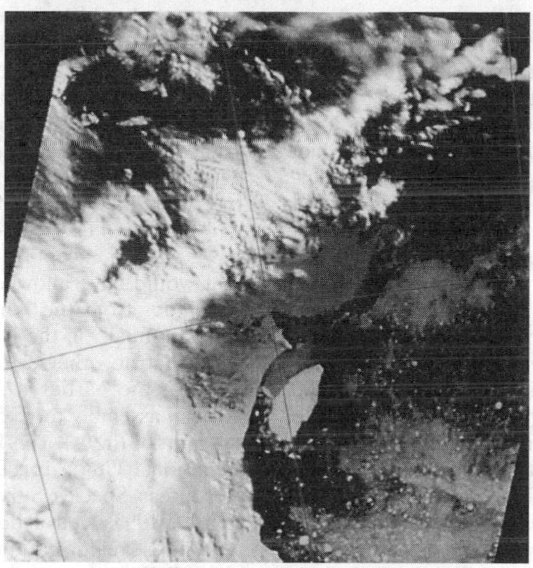

These two photographs show the effects of warming in Antarctica. The top photo, taken in January 1995, shows Ross Island (upper right), known for at least 100 years to have been connected to the Antarctic Peninsula by an ice shelf, now surrounded by water. The bottom photo, taken in February, shows a large iceberg (centre) that has broken off.
PHOTOGRAPHS, BRITISH ANTARCTIC SURVEY

Air Pollution. A report by the World Wide Fund for Nature, published in July, found that more than half the prime nature reserves in Europe were being damaged by acid rain. The most seriously affected area, where more than 90% of ecosystems were being damaged, was in a belt stretching from Liverpool, England, to Moscow.

The reduction of industrial emissions of sulfur dioxide was reported in September to be producing signs of sulfur deficiency in vegetation across Europe. Sulfur deposition on fields fell by 80% from the late 1970s to 1995. Trees were dying, crop yields were falling, and crop diseases were increasing, with oilseed rape and other brassicas the worst affected. Grain crops, which are more tolerant of sulfur shortage than rape, were starting to show signs of distress. It was also possible that sulfur shortages were causing plants to emit smaller amounts of hydrogen compounds, such as hydrogen sulfide, which reduce atmospheric ozone. This might make them more vulnerable to ozone damage and be linked to increasing ozone pollution.

Buses in London, Lyons, France, and Dresden, Germany, were reported in November 1994 to be testing exhaust-gas filters that might reduce small particulate (PM10) emissions by 90% and nitrogen oxide emissions by about 10%. The filter used nitrogen dioxide in the exhaust to oxidize carbon to carbon monoxide over a platinum catalyst, then oxidized carbon monoxide and hydrocarbons to carbon dioxide and reduced nitrogen dioxide to nitrogen.

A hot, dry summer brought pollution alerts to several European cities. In an attempt to combat pollution, for four hours on the morning of April 10 the centre of Athens was closed to all traffic except vehicles used by residents or carrying tourists to three city-centre hotels, free minibuses, and delivery vans. On May 5, smog levels reached high levels in England and Wales. In central London they were almost double the guideline limits.

In Paris on July 25, Police Chief Philippe Massoni asked drivers to leave their cars at home over the weekend to reduce pollution. Mayor Jean Tiberi announced that when heavy pollution was forecast, city parking would be free and public transport fares would be reduced or waived, depending on the seriousness of the pollution. Pollution forecasts would be displayed publicly, cars would be checked to make sure they complied with emission standards, and more bus lanes and cycle paths would be provided. The French Ministry of Environment issued more than three times as many ozone alerts in 1994 as in 1993 (1,316 against 357). Part of the increase was the result of a growth in the number of monitoring stations from 64 to 90, but even allowing for this the number at least doubled.

Fresh Water. A study by The Lindsay Museum in Walnut Creek, Calif., reported in late May, found that up to 70% of chemical pollutants in San Francisco Bay originated in ordinary activities rather than from industrial discharges. Pollutants included oil leaked from cars, dust containing copper from brake pads, and garden fertilizers and pesticides.

In a study of 34,000 water samples, the most extensive ever undertaken in the U.S., reported in September, the U.S. Geological Survey found that water in 9% of all domestic wells and 21% of shallow wells beneath farmland had more than the accepted safety level of 10 mg of nitrate per litre. Previous studies had found only 2.4% of wells exceeding the limit. The survey studied data from 1970 to 1992 and found nitrate levels increasing steadily in all wells where data were comparable throughout the period.

Marine Pollution. Russian scientists warned in January that chemical weapons dumped off the British coast after World War II were in danger of leaking from their containers. The British Ministry of Defence said the weapons had been sealed in ships and sunk at depths of up to 6,000 m in four locations: 400 km southwest of Land's End, 130 km northwest of Northern Ireland, and two sites off the coast west of the Hebrides. Armed Forces Minister Nicholas Soames said 120,000 tons of material, mainly mustard gas and phosgene, were disposed of between 1945 and 1949 and an additional 25,000 tons of British and German weapons, containing Tabun, were dumped in the Atlantic Ocean between 1955 and 1957. Weapons dumped in the Irish Sea were blamed in March for elevated levels of arsenic found in plaice caught in Liverpool Bay, and 700 containers, some of flares and some of blistering gas, had been washed up on the coasts of the former County Antrim, Ireland, the Isle of Man, and the west coast of Scotland.

A European Commission report published on June 14 said that in 1994, 82% of water at 457 British bathing beaches met mandatory EU standards for coliform bacteria. In Germany the figure was 80%, in The Netherlands 63.5%, and in Ireland 100%. This was an improvement for the U.K., from 76% in 1991, but a rise in enteroviruses caused concern. Only 33.7% of British beaches met the more stringent guideline standards, compared with 91% in Greece, 89% in Ireland, and 81% in Italy.

Pesticides. In 1990 burbot and trout in Lake Laberge, Yukon, were found to contain toxaphene, a volatile pesticide widely used in tropical Asia and Latin America, at 10 times Canadian health limits. Some burbot contained up to 2,330 parts per billion. It was reported in July that a Canadian study had found that the pesticide resulted from air pollution, not dumping. Levels of toxaphene, polychlorinated biphenyls (PCBs), dioxins, and heavy metals were higher in northern than in southern lakes, seemed to be increasing, and—according to David Schindler of the University of Alberta, who led the study—resulted from biomagnification.

Toxic Wastes. Stanford University agreed in October 1994 to pay nearly $1 million in fines for mishandling hazardous-waste materials. The university would pay $460,000 in penalties to the state, $235,000 in costs, and $300,000 to environmental groups, after admitting liability for 40% of the 1,600 violations of which it had been accused. These involved spills of toxic material, mislabeling of containers, and inadequate waste storage between 1988 and 1992.

A new containment technology was being developed in July at Cape Cod, Massachusetts, where compounds including trichloroethylene (TCE) and tetrachloroethylene (PCE) were leaching from a nearby military base. Migrating at one metre every two to three days, they had already forced the closure of a well supplying 25% of the public water supply to a nearby town and were within 300 m of another well. The new technique involved sealing the contaminants inside a wall made from steel sheets sunk several metres into the ground and funneling groundwater into a small opening filled with sand mixed with iron filings. The iron would supply electrons to reduce chlorinated compounds, and a corrosion reaction would strip chlorine atoms from such compounds as TCE and PCE, breaking them into harmless ethene and ethane gases.

Chernobyl. WHO reported on March 25 that the screening of 70,000 children under the age of 15 had found an incidence of nearly one in 10,000 of thyroid cancer in the Homel region of Belarus, probably due to exposure to iodine-131. There was also a 100-fold increase in northern Ukraine and an 8-fold increase in the Bryansk and Kaluga regions of Russia. In a letter to the *British Medical Journal,* Keith Baverstock, a WHO radiation scientist, and his colleagues said up to 2.3 million children may have been exposed. By the end of 1993, 418 cases of thyroid cancer had been diagnosed in Ukraine in people aged 18 and under at the time of the accident. Of these cases, 170 were among people 14 and under at the time of the accident and 248 in people over 15. In Pripyat, 3.5 km from Chernobyl, six cases of thyroid cancer were found in 1990–92 among 14,580 people under 18 at the time of the accident.

(MICHAEL ALLABY)

WILDLIFE CONSERVATION

In the wildlife conservation community, the debate over the sustainable use of wild species became both widespread and intense in 1995 as pressures increased on wild animals and their habitats. Conservationists were divided over the issue; some advocated that the sustainable use of a species can be used to ensure its conservation, while others argued that sustainable use can be a guise for exploiting wild animals with no conservation gain. This important issue was the focus of several articles published in *Oryx* (the Journal of Fauna and Flora International) during the year.

The most dramatic example of this split in the conservation world was the case of the African elephant. Countries with elephant populations generally fall into two groups: those that believe that sales from ivory and other elephant products should be used to raise revenue for conservation and those that argue that any resumption in trade would result in an upsurge in elephant poaching. Since the ban on international trade in elephant products came into force in 1990, a group of the former exporting countries had pressed for a resumption in carefully controlled trade, but this had been resisted at the biennial meetings of the Convention on International Trade in Endangered Species of Wild Fauna and Flora (CITES). The ninth meeting, held in November 1994, was no exception. South Africa withdrew a proposal that would have allowed it to trade internationally in meat and hides from the hundreds of elephants that had to be culled annually in the Kruger National Park when it became clear that no other elephant range states would support it. Instead, the parties to CITES agreed to set up an intra-African assembly to review the issue of ivory stockpiles with the help of the African Elephant Specialist Group of the International Union for Conservation of Nature and Natural Resources Species Survival Commission (IUCN-SSC). On Feb. 9, 1995, Kenya burned 10 metric tons of confiscated ivory in a "reaffirmation of its commitment to save the elephant." Kenya's management policy for elephants did not include culling. To help reduce conflict between people and elephants, the Kenya Wildlife Service established a Problem Animal Management Unit and adopted an early strike policy on marauding elephants to reduce human deaths.

The situation did not improve for the tiger in 1995. Poaching accelerated, and there were extensive, well-organized illegal trade networks operating. Seizures by law-enforcement authorities showed that hundreds of tigers were being killed every year in India alone, primarily for use in traditional Chinese medicines. Peter Jackson, chairman of the IUCN-SSC Cat Specialist Group, said that the tiger would be virtually extinct in the wild by 1999 unless India and other range states declared open war on poachers and illegal traders.

Illegal wildlife trade continued to affect many other species adversely. In some countries of the former U.S.S.R., poaching escalated, driven by economic problems and made easy by a breakdown in law enforcement and border controls. There were reports of snow leopards and lynx being poached for their skins and of argali (a species of wild sheep) being killed for their horns, as well as an extensive trade in rare amphibians and reptiles.

In March poachers killed four mountain gorillas in Bwindi Impenetrable Park in Uganda, probably to capture a young animal for the illegal trade. In 1995 only about 600 of these animals were left in the world. Until these deaths, the International Gorilla Conservation Programme (run as a partnership between the African Wildlife Foundation, Fauna and Flora International, and World Wide Fund for Nature) had been pleased to report that during the previous decade not one mountain gorilla was known to have been killed. This was largely due to the efforts of the program and the commitment to the conservation of the gorillas and their habitat by the governments of Rwanda, Uganda, and Zaire. More deaths followed in August, this time in Zaire, where three more mature gorillas were killed in two separate incidents. A baby also was captured, but it was later found abandoned and was restored to its family group. The gorillas that died were in two groups that were regularly visited by tourists, and the killings dealt a blow to gorilla-based tourism, which brought in much-needed foreign earnings. Gorilla protection was stepped up, especially in Zaire, where the national park, home to the gorillas, was being severely damaged because of its proximity to Rwandan refugee camps.

In April *Oryx* carried the results of a survey that found that the saola, or spindlehorn antelope (*Pseudoryx nghetinhensis*), which had been discovered in Vietnam in 1992, also lived in Laos. Plans were made to extend conservation areas in its range. On June 16 more than 60 nations signed the Agreement for the Conservation of Migratory Waterbirds under the Bonn Convention on the Conservation of Migratory Species of Wild Animals. Conservationists welcomed the agreement but expressed concern that it allowed hunting of some birds that had uncertain conservation status.

Several new species were described in 1995, including a mountain goat (*Pseudonovibos spiralis*) from Vietnam, a nightjar (*Caprimulgus solala*) from Ethiopia, a nighthawk (*Chordelies vielliardi*) from Brazil, and a pygmy owl (*Glaucidum parkeri*) from Ecuador. Reported extinctions included the river pipefish from South Africa and the Formosan flying fox (*Pteropus dasymallus formosus*) in Taiwan. The last Spix's macaw (*Cyanopsitta spixii*) in the wild—a male in northern Brazil—was given a mate (one of 30 or so in captivity) in the hope that they would breed. The release followed months of research and preparation by the Spix's Macaw Recovery Committee, led by the Brazilian wildlife authorities. A golden conure (*Aratinga guarouba*) hatched at Sorocaba Zoo in Brazil, the first time that the endangered species had bred in a zoo. The birds continued to be captured illegally, however, with specimens smuggled out of Brazil fetching as much as $1,800 each.

The first comprehensive UN report on biodiversity, released on November 14, estimated that there were as many as 15 million animal and plant species in the world, of which only 1,750,000 had been identified. A minimum of 5,400 animal species were considered endangered. (JACQUI M. MORRIS)

ZOOS

The worst zoo tragedy in U.S. history occurred on Christmas eve when smoke from a fire in the World of Primates building at the Philadelphia Zoo, the nation's oldest, killed 23 primates—six western lowland gorillas (including two infants and an unborn fetus), three Bornean orangutans, four white-handed gibbons, six ring-tailed lemurs, two ruffed lemurs, and two mongoose lemurs. All were considered endangered species, and several were among the few remaining wild-born animals. The personal grief of the zoo staff and the city's zoogoers was overwhelming, but the loss to the primate gene pool was especially catastrophic. In addition, the incident seemed likely to give added momentum to the animal rights activists, who recently had been instrumental in closing the Vancouver, B.C., zoo.

In 1995 many "new zoo" programs designed to breed and preserve the various species were in place around the world. The Europäisches Erhaltungszucht Programme (EEP) coordinated 112 species programs involving 117 species and 137 taxa. They also identified 26 working Taxon Advisory Groups (TAGs) and 21 studbooks encompassing 29 taxa. The American Zoo and Aquarium Association (AZA) ad-

JESSIE COHEN—NATIONAL ZOOLOGICAL PARK/SMITHSONIAN INSTITUTION

At the National Zoological Park in Washington, D.C., an animal moves over the Orangutan Transit System. The system permitted movement between the Ape House and a centre for experiments.

ministered 70 Species Survival Plans (SSPs) covering 117 species. They also coordinated 43 TAGs, 240 studbooks, and a variety of other scientific advisory groups. In 1995 the AZA formed a field conservation committee to focus the attention and energy of North American zoos and aquariums on field conservation efforts.

Globally, species management programs based on the EEP and SSP models were being developed to coordinate worldwide efforts to preserve species. In 1995 the Australian Species Management Program developed a zoo-collection-planning software system for international circulation.

Despite this emphasis on cooperative species management, there was a shift in the overall planning process. Worldwide, there was a limited amount of space available to house the captive-bred animals, and native habitats were disappearing so rapidly that there was no real "wild" in which animals could be reintroduced. In order to address this, researchers began to develop programs that would encompass a more "holistic" approach to conservation of endangered species.

In some areas the holistic approach also called for the designation of a "flagship species" to represent a specific habitat. This concept advocated employing an animal that is well-loved by the general public to represent an entire ecosystem. For example, if a conservation and education program was based upon the preservation of habitat for the giant panda, in theory not only would the panda be saved but so also would the other plants and animals that inhabit the ecosystem.

In early October 1995 the World Zoo Organization (officially the International Union of Directors of Zoological Gardens) published *Zoo Future 2005,* an action plan derived from the 1995 Futures Search Workshop, held in Cologne, Germany. This innovative document outlined the "ideal future" for a world-class zoo, the constraints and opportunities, an ambitious plan of action, and task assignments.

(JANE COYLE BALLENTINE)

BOTANICAL GARDENS

In 1995 emphasis was placed on developing networks among botanical gardens and organizations involved in the research and protection of plants. That theme pervaded the fourth International Botanic Gardens Conservation Congress, which was organized by Botanic Gardens Conservation International and held in Perth, Australia. At the Planta Europa meeting in Hyères, France, the principal resolution involved the creation of a Planta Europa Network to coordinate efforts to save Europe's wild plants and their habitats. The Auckland Plant Collection Network was formed to create a structure to improve the effectiveness of botanical gardens in New Zealand.

Celebrations were held marking the 50th anniversary of the Main Botanical Garden of the Russian Academy of Sciences in Moscow. It was founded in April 1945 as a methodological and coordinating centre for the country's botanical gardens. In January a large electrical storm inflicted considerable damage on the Mt. Coot-tha Botanic Gardens, Brisbane, Australia; more than 100 mature trees were uprooted or snapped. In July the Montreal Botanic Gardens was the site of the American Association of Botanic Gardens and Arboreta annual conference, which highlighted the progress made in the biodiversity of plants in public gardens and ways in which public gardens could attract larger and more diverse audiences.

The Royal Botanic Gardens, Kew, near London, secured £1.5 million from the Ministry of Agriculture to redevelop the deteriorating Jodrell Laboratory and herbaceous greenhouses. Plans were developed to establish a new national botanical garden in Nairobi, Kenya. The centre would focus on education and conservation of native plant taxa outside their natural habitat. The Missouri Botanical Garden, St. Louis, received a grant to support the establishment of a seed-storage and germination laboratory. The National Botanic Gardens in Limbé, Cameroon, opened a centre devoted to research and fieldwork based on the larger Mount Cameroon Project.

Botanical gardens in Bonn, Germany, and Göteborg, Sweden, returned 150 clones of the extinct tree *Sophora toromiro* to Easter Island; the last such tree had been seen there in 1958. Worldwide, individual specimens of *S. toromiro* were identified in a number of botanical gardens, increasing the confirmed number of surviving trees. The Kings Park and Botanic Garden in Perth launched a new A$ 230,000 plan intended to conserve 11 endangered plants in that city and three *Eucalyptus* species elsewhere in the western part of the country. Botanic Gardens Conservation International, in conjunction with its regional office at Utrecht (Neth.) University Botanic Gardens, launched the Dutch Plant Charter Group as a forum for business and industry to lend support and voice concern for the conservation of plants.

(PETER J. ATKINSON)

GARDENING

In a rare coup, *Salvia farinacea* Strata, a newly introduced bedding plant, captured the triple crown of flower breeders in 1995. It won both the All-America Selections gold medal and the Fleuroselect (the European-based seed-testing cooperative) gold medal and was named 1996 Plant of the Year by the British Bedding and Pot Plant Association. This well-proportioned plant was 45–61 cm (18–24 in) tall and almost as broad, with thin, smooth foliage typical of its species. Its sweep of the awards was attributed to its entirely new colour: bicolour flowers, with grayish white calyxes that contained mid-blue corollas just touched with white in the throat.

The All-America bedding plant winner was a cultivar: *Petunia* Fantasy Pink Morn, which represented a new class of petunias called "milliflora." The pink flowers with creamy white throats were small, 2.5–3.8 cm (1–1½ in), but in scale with dwarf plants that naturally grow only 30 cm (12 in) high and up to 45 cm (18 in) across. The natural growth habit of dwarfs was prized by growers, who were able to avoid the use of growth retardants to prevent crowding and stretching during plant production. This easy commercial production—referred to as pack performance—was not considered an indicator of actual garden performance; however, garden maintenance probably would be minimized.

Fleuroselect, which would also include pack performance as a criterion for future awards, decided to expand its testing program to North America but in a nonvoting form. The organization also announced that it would hold its 1996 meeting in California, the first time the event would convene outside Europe.

Two other Fleuroselect gold medal winners were *Ammobium alatum* Bikini, rewarded for its compact habit, and *Petunia x hybrida* Lavender Storm, chosen for its tolerance of rainy weather.

The Perennial Plant Association named *Perovskia atriplicifolia,* commonly known as Russian sage, its Plant of the Year. The specimen had a long growing season and light blue flowers that added a striking ornamental effect to gardens.

An Australian study that tracked the worldwide purchase of garden products found that middle-aged married couples with relatively high incomes purchased the largest number of garden products and did their shopping at independent garden centres, while retirees made the highest dollar volume of purchases at mass-market discount stores.

In the U.S., where enthusiasm for gardening continued to grow, gardeners "chatted over the fence" by using such online services as America Online, Prodigy, and CompuServe. Such new software programs as Key Home Gardener, Design Your Own Home-Landscape, Landscape Design, FLOWERscape, Mum's the Word, and Better Homes and Gardens Complete Guide to Gardening moved gardening into the high-tech world of home computers. While some of the programs concentrated on hardscape aspects of landscape design (fences, patios, and decks), others focused on the plants themselves and included a database of hundreds of ornamentals, vegetables, trees, shrubs, herbs, and grasses.

In Central and Eastern Europe the well-established practice of community gardening came into conflict with land privatization. In the Czech Republic many long-established garden communities found that their plots rested on land scheduled to be returned to those who owned the property before communist governments seized it. In Prague, where real estate values were high, those who had had ownership restored to them and wished to sell were not in a position to settle with all of the current occupants. The problem created insecurity for gardeners, who depended on their community plot for food, and headaches for the government, which had to accommodate all interests.

(SHEPHERD OGDEN; KAY MELCHISEDECH OLSON)

See also Agriculture and Food Supplies; Business and Industry Review: *Energy;* Life Sciences.

This article updates the *Macropædia* articles CONSERVATION OF NATURAL RESOURCES; GARDENING AND HORTICULTURE.

Fashions

Conservative chic—the new look for women in 1995—was a pretty, elegant, and feminine style that featured simply tailored yet luxurious clothes. The dressed-up glamour look of 1994 was still popular but with a significant change—a new emphasis on refinement.

At the Paris spring/summer haute couture shows, models parading down nearly every catwalk appeared in clothes reminiscent of those worn by such style icons of the 1950s and early '60s as actress Audrey Hepburn, model Suzy Parker, Princess Grace Kelly, and U.S. first lady Jacqueline Kennedy. Models Kristen McMenamy and Kate Moss, former grunge torchbearers, looked groomed and metamorphosed in the ubiquitous look—a fitted, figure-hugging suit matched with such accessories as satin gloves, small earrings, a cabochon brooch, and a clutch purse. The deep red lipstick of 1994 was replaced by a shade of coral.

Though some viewed conservative chic as a reaction to a political shift to the right in the West, the new mood was more a reflection of a change within the industry. For the first time in three decades, haute couture (the very costly custom-made designs shown twice yearly in Paris) became the barometer of fashion change. Traditionally, styles worn on the street were the work of ready-to-wear designers.

A renewed interest in the craft of couture accompanied the big news of the year—Hubert de Givenchy's retirement after 43 years as designer in chief of his eponymous Paris fashion house. Givenchy's replacement, announced in July, was the 35-year-old Paris-based British designer John Galliano. His designs, mainly favoured by young women, would presumably attract a younger clientele to haute couture, traditionally patronized by older women.

Even before Galliano's appointment, haute couture fashions were worn by young high-profile women. At the Academy Awards ceremony in Los Angeles, actress Uma Thurman wore a long lavender gown fashioned by Prada, the Milanese design house. Viscountess Linley appeared at Ascot in a lace dress made by French designer Hervé Léger. In New York City, British actress Elizabeth Hurley wore a simple yellow Gianni Versace fitted couture suit to the ceremony at which she accepted the contract to represent Estée Lauder cosmetics. For the July 1 wedding in London of Marie-Chantal Miller and Crown Prince Pavlos of Greece, Valentino made 62 outfits for the wedding party, including the bridal gown.

At the international shows it was clear that many designers had run out of original ideas after they delivered a chaotic series of ready-to-wear designs for spring/summer 1995. Though sharply tailored clothes could be found on runways in every fashion capital, refined, feminine looks were overpowered by gimmicky fads—not fashion. The glamour of the '70s, an inspiration for autumn/winter 1994, was still a popular theme in Milan, where Bianca Jagger-style tuxedo suits, tube tops, and tight trousers appeared. Mariuccia Mandelli, the designer behind the Krizia line, celebrated 40 years in fashion by reviving the hot pants (short shorts) that she had made fashionable in the early '70s. Giorgio Armani in Milan and Valentino in Paris also reinvented them.

Other retro influences included knee-length skirts and flimsy floral mid-calf-length tea dresses from the '40s. The design duo Dolce & Gabbana revived underwear as outerwear, pairing pencil skirts with bustiers. Also prominent was the corset, which appeared underneath sheer organza blouses as an evening look. Its structured shape also provided the basis for jackets and evening dresses.

In Paris a record 81 international designers unveiled spring/summer collections, which resulted in fashion confusion. Retro styles—borrowed from every decade of the 20th century—mixed with elements of '70s glamour and bizarre manifestations of classic tailoring. Jean-Paul Gaultier mixed denim with early 20th-century tailoring, producing a Pygmalion-styled full-length frilled skirt and fitted jacket. Rifat

This Shetland coat from Prada's autumn/winter line exemplifies the sharply tailored style of its 1995 fashions. With traditional styling combined with modern sleekness, Prada continued to be highly influential.

P. LINDBERGH—PRADA/GRAZIA NERI SRL

Ozbek designed a neck corset in rhinestones. Underneath Vivienne Westwood's knee-length wool and piqué cotton skirts were metal "bum cages," her reinterpretation of the Victorian bustle. A number of designers in New York and Paris experimented with futuristic themes. Prada delivered such accessories as a clear-plastic purse in the shape of a shopping bag and shoes with high heels made from Perspex, both reminiscent of the space-age styles introduced by André Courrèges in the late '60s. The London-based Canadian-born shoe designer Patrick Cox reintroduced jellies—inexpensive, clear-plastic sandals popular in the early '80s—adding high heels and glitter effects.

Expanding on this theme, designers shaped traditional styles such as pantsuits and evening dresses from such high-tech and synthetic fabrics as plastic, laminates, Lurex, and vinyl. Donna Karan made a prom dress from olefin-treated paper (the same material used for FedEx envelopes), and Jil Sander used silk as lining for an iridescent nylon pantsuit.

The international men's wear spring/summer collections delivered a range of upbeat but unorthodox clothes, with an emphasis on colour and texture. Casual looks such as trousers, sweaters, and jean jackets were made from satin, polyvinyl chloride (PVC), and terry cloth. Pastel shades—powder blue, candy floss pink, and light yellow—appeared alongside stronger colours—red, blue, and lemon yellow. Slim suits were cut from an iridescent fabric known as two-tone. Such designers as Armani, Sonia Rykiel, Gaultier, and Dries van Noten produced the boxer-style zoot suit, which complemented the '40s revival in women's wear, with its six-button double-breasted jacket.

A general lack of consumer confidence in the West combined with news that women were losing all interest in fashion, especially European women who disliked such elements of glamour as high heels and accessories, cast a scare throughout the industry. Though *Clueless,* a film about a crew of clothes-crazy Beverly Hills, Calif., teenage girls, was viewed as a sign that young people cared about high-fashion designs, *Women's Wear Daily* reported that U.S. teenagers were buying basics: overalls, flannel shirts, and backpacks. Shops selling such items—the Gap, Urban Outfitters, and Eddie Bauer—were quite popular among young people.

As spring arrived, U.S. department stores reported a slump in the sale of dresses, due to both the cool weather and the new knee-length skirt, which was unpopular. *Fortune* claimed that a lack of strong, saleable fashion ideas had hurt retailers such as the Limited and Broadway. Department stores Bloomingdale's and Bergdorf Goodman reported that the sartorial elements of glamour—satin clothes, knee-length slip skirts, corset jackets, and patent leather accessories—intimidated female customers. Prada, controlled by Miuccia Prada and known as "the Gap for the superrich," was the choice for high-spending customers, both men and women. Prada was the first designer to use Pocono nylon (the material of military tents) to make such fashion items as handbags, trench coats, and knee-length skirts. Designers Donna Karan and Calvin Klein also used nylon.

Prada, proclaiming that "dressing truly bad is an exclusive art," presented a collection that flew in the face of high-fashion glamour. Idiosyncratic elements of style—that could be labeled "bad taste"—were prominent on Prada's seasonal runways: plastic handbags, white leather shoes for winter, and colour combinations of orange and brown. Her look proved popular; fashion magazines depicted high-profile actors, models, fashion editors, and photographers wearing the company's sharply tailored, stark styles adorned with Prada accessories. Prada's expansion throughout the year also reflected its popularity. The company reported a net worth of $210 million.

At the autumn/winter men's collection, fashion's mood of frivolity showed no sign of abating. Decadent styles, deemed downright camp by many fashion critics, dominated runways in Milan, Florence, and Paris. Billowing shirts, big dark "Jackie O." sunglasses, floral silk head scarves knotted at the neck, and frilly shirts were the feminine influences designers felt were right for the '90s man.

The focus changed during the international women's ready-to-wear shows for autumn/winter '95. Model Claudia Schiffer appeared on the cover of *Time* magazine in a fitted off-white Versace skirt suit, displaying the "simply beautiful classics" designers had produced.

Fashion's autumn/winter ready-to-wear designs were sensible and uncomplicated and followed the sober mood of the haute couture shows. The fitted skirt suit reappeared alongside the "boxy suit," an equally slim but squarely tailored style. Both were more popular than pantsuits.

Winter coats and suits appeared in strong shades of camel, red, and navy, as well as tones of lavender and burnt orange. The designers that had experimented with high-tech fabrics just a season before opted for the pure, classic materials couturiers favoured—cashmere, taffeta, gazar, radzimir, and Harris Tweed. The stiletto, the shoe of 1994, was replaced by a demure low, slim heel—a copy of the look Audrey Hepburn wore in the 1954 film *Sabrina*. A *Breakfast at Tiffany's*-style cocktail dress, made in light shades of satin and basic black, was the option for evening.

In Milan and New York, mod was the inspiration for designers who copied the neat, clean style of dressing popularized by British middle-class youth during the '60s. Authentic mod looks such as hipster belts, mid-calf go-go boots, checkerboard prints, collarless coats, and narrow-tailored pantsuits were introduced by Gucci, Prada, and Marc Jacobs, as well as by Istante and CK, the diffusion lines produced by Versace and Calvin Klein, respectively. The hairdresser Garren cut Linda Evangelista's hair into a shape similar to the five-point geometric bob, a haircut originated in 1964 by Vidal Sassoon.

Leather, once reserved for hard-edged clothes worn by motorcyclists, became a mainstay of the new mod wardrobe. Leather appeared in gentle colours—snow white and matte black—and soft cuts. Anna Sui made black leather cocktail dresses and white leather collarless coats. Helmut Lang created sexy belted trench coats from leather, and Karan produced them for her DKNY line.

Early reports on the sale of refined clothes were positive. Bloomingdale's and Saks Fifth Avenue both reported that sales of designer fashions were up from the previous year.

The conservative mood stymied Calvin Klein's ad campaign for his signature line of jeans. He and photographer Steven Meisel had devised a print and television ad campaign that featured young male and female models (some nonprofessional) posing in suggestive positions. In August—under pressure from retailers, TV stations, and watchdog groups—Klein withdrew the campaign.

Maurizio Gucci—grandnephew of Guccio Gucci, the founder of the Italian fashion house of that name—was assassinated in Milan by an unknown gunman. He was the last family member to work for Gucci before Investcorp, a Bahrain-based investment group, purchased it in 1993. Maurizio's cousin Paolo died in October, leaving a tangled estate. He had left the family firm in 1987 and declared bankruptcy. The deaths underscored the financial difficulties this once family-run business had faced.

(BRONWYN COSGRAVE)

See also Business and Industry Review: *Apparel.*

This article updates the *Macropædia* article DRESS AND ADORNMENT.

Health and Disease

Celebrities attracted international attention to a variety of medical causes in 1995. The announcement in late 1994 that former U.S. president Ronald Reagan was suffering from Alzheimer's disease led to the establishment of a new institute to conduct research into this brain disorder. Baseball legend Mickey Mantle's liver transplant and subsequent death promoted public awareness of the acute need for donor organs and the ethical issues involved in deciding who is to receive them. (*See* OBITUARIES.) *Superman* star Christopher Reeve's paralysis following a fall from a horse publicized the devastating consequences of spinal cord injuries. The murder trial of former football great O.J. Simpson focused attention on the problem of domestic violence.

A deadly tickborne illness known as human granulocytic ehrlichiosis was reported in the United States, an outbreak of the killer Ebola virus surfaced in Zaire, and health officials from Central and South America launched an emergency plan to combat a major epidemic of dengue hemorrhagic fever, which is spread by the *Aedes aegypti* mosquito.

Chronic diseases continued to take the greatest toll in the industrialized world, however. A mid-decade report from the U.S. Department of Health and Human Services found that Americans were making progress in some respects (living longer, smoking less, and cutting deaths from heart disease, stroke, and alcohol-related automobile crashes) but that setbacks had occurred in efforts to reduce obesity and in the prevention of violence, teen pregnancy, and deaths from pneumonia and influenza.

Genetics. The Human Genome Project, an international effort to identify and analyze the 100,000 or so genes that make up the entire human genetic complement, was progressing faster than expected. Laboratories in the U.S., France, and Britain reported that detailed mapping efforts already had determined the approximate location of about 75% of the human genes, and more than 50% had been sequenced (*i.e.,* broken down into their constituent parts). Experts predicted that 99% of the genome may be sequenced by the year 2002. The first-ever sequencing of the full genome of a free-living organism, the infectious bacterium *Hemophilus influenzae,* was reported by J. Craig Venter (*see* BIOGRAPHIES) and co-workers.

Efforts to isolate specific disease-related genes also raced ahead. Researchers at the University of Texas Health Science Center at San Antonio reported that the *BRCA1* gene, isolated in 1994 in women with a family history of breast cancer, also plays a role in the more common nonfamilial form of the disease. Another study found that a significant proportion of Ashkenazi, or Eastern European, Jews carry a particular mutation of *BRCA1* that puts them at a much greater than average risk of breast and ovarian cancer. British scientists announced in December the discovery of a second gene linked to breast cancer, *BRCA2.* Still another piece of the breast cancer puzzle may have been supplied by the discovery of the gene defect responsible for ataxia telangiectasia (AT), a progressive, fatal neurological disorder. AT first becomes apparent as an unsteady gait in toddlers. Affected individuals, who have two copies of the mutated gene, usually die in their teens or 20s. Carriers—those who inherit only one copy of the mutated gene—have three to five times the normal risk of cancer, and women who carry the mutated gene may have as much as six times the normal risk of breast cancer. About 1% of the U.S. population—2.5 million people—may be carriers.

Back-to-back reports identified two genes responsible for early-onset forms of Alzheimer's disease, which tend to run in families. A University of Toronto team announced in June that a gene on chromosome 14 appears to be responsible for as many as 80% of familial cases. In August investigators from Seattle, Wash., and Boston simultaneously reported that a similar gene on chromosome 1 may account for most other such cases. Scientists hoped these findings would speed the understanding of all forms of Alzheimer's disease.

In New York City, Rockefeller University investigators, who cloned an obesity gene in 1994, reported in July 1995 that the protein product of the gene dramatically reduced body weight in mice after only two weeks of treatment. Additional research published in October suggested that the protein, dubbed leptin (from the Greek root *leptos,* "thin"), plays a role in regulating fat storage in the body.

The first clear evidence that a gene plays a role in non-insulin-dependent diabetes mellitus (NIDDM), a disorder that usually develops in later life, was announced by researchers in France. Scientists in Sweden, France, and the U.S. reported in August that they had pinpointed another gene that was associated with both obesity and earlier-than-usual onset of NIDDM in some populations.

Dean Hamer and his colleagues at the National Institutes of Health (NIH) confirmed and extended their 1993 work suggesting that a particular region of the X chromosome influences the development of homosexuality in males. Other "finds" included the gene believed responsible for Batten disease, the most common neurodegenerative disorder afflicting children; a mutation that increases susceptibility to venous thrombosis (blood clots in the veins); and two genes that cause the heart disorder known as long QT syndrome.

Pioneering gene therapy protocols were evaluated and found to have produced mixed results. Treatment of a rare condition called adenosine deaminase deficiency was beneficial, while no therapeutic improvements were seen in patients with cystic fibrosis or Duchenne muscular dystrophy.

Cardiovascular Disease. Although heart transplantation is an accepted procedure, its success is compromised in some recipients by the development of high blood cholesterol levels. Elevated cholesterol, in turn, may cause fatty deposits, blocking the coronary arteries and producing the symptoms that necessitated the operation in the first place. Researchers at the University of California, Los Angeles, School of Medicine and Brigham and Women's Hospital, Boston, showed that the cholesterol-lowering drug pravastatin markedly reduces the risk of restenosis (*i.e.,* renarrowing of the arteries) after heart transplantation. Patients given pravastatin had much lower cholesterol levels a year after transplantation than those not receiving the drug. They were also much less likely to reject their new hearts, and their survival rate was significantly higher.

Several studies raised concerns about the safety of calcium channel blocking drugs used in treating millions of patients in the U.S. and elsewhere with hypertension (high blood pressure) and certain heart disorders. The National Heart, Lung, and Blood Institute issued a warning in September that one of these drugs, short-acting nifedipine, should be used with great caution, if at all, but declared that more research was needed on other calcium channel blockers.

Evidence of the role of diet in cardiovascular disease continued to accumulate. A University of Washington study showed that eating as little as one serving per week of "fatty" fish, such as salmon, tuna, or mackerel, can reduce the risk of cardiac arrest. These kinds of fish are rich in omega-3 fatty acids. Another report from the same institution concluded that folic acid, a B vitamin already known to play a part in preventing birth defects, also helps prevent coronary heart disease. Paralleling an earlier finding

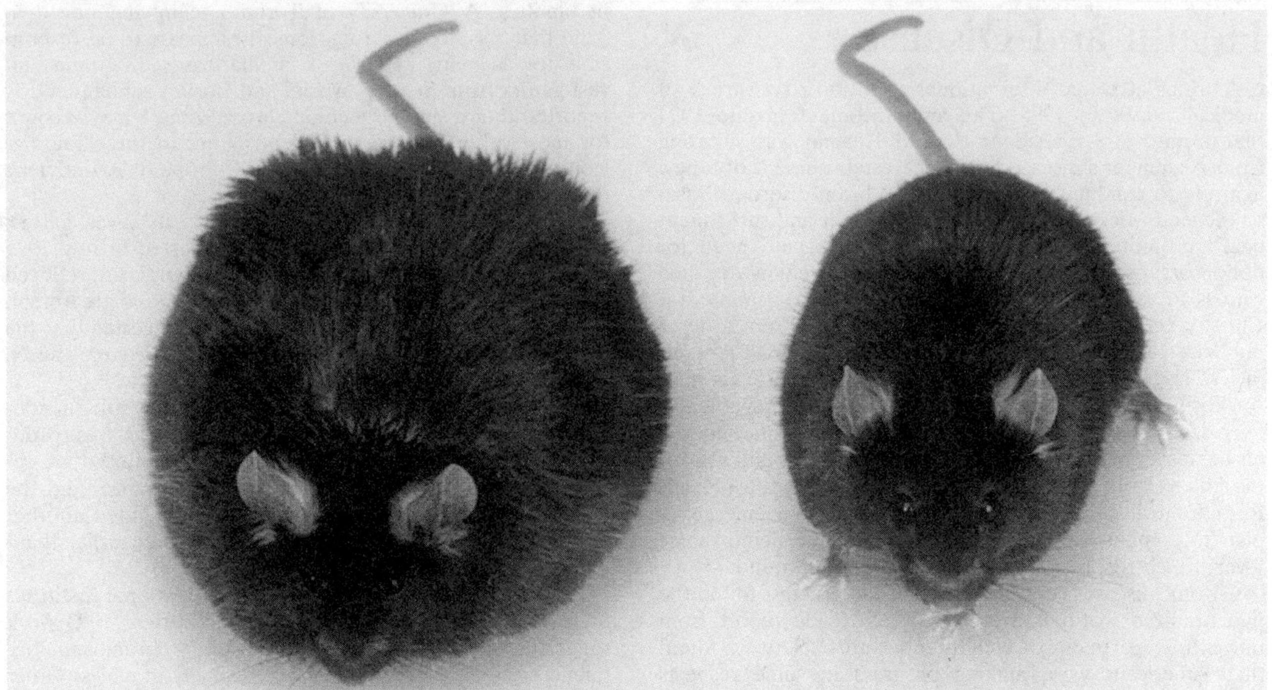

Both of these mice have a defect of the *ob* (for "obesity") gene. After daily injections with leptin, the protein product of the normal *ob* gene, the mouse on the right lost nearly half its body weight in four and a half weeks. The implications for human obesity were not yet clear, however.
JOHN SHOLTIS, THE ROCKEFELLER UNIVERSITY, NEW YORK, NEW YORK

in women, a report by investigators at Harvard Medical School demonstrated that men who eat a diet high in fruits and vegetables have a significantly reduced risk of stroke compared with men who consume less of these antioxidant-rich foods.

Cancer. A report issued in February by the National Cancer Institute found that the rate of new cancer cases in the U.S. had risen nearly 19% in men and 12% in women from the mid-1970s to the early '90s, largely because of more widespread early detection of prostate and breast cancers and increased incidence of smoking-related lung cancers. The rates of several less common cancers, such as non-Hodgkin's lymphoma and skin, kidney, testicular, and brain cancers, also had increased.

The form of leukemia known as adult T-cell leukemia-lymphoma, which is associated with a virus similar to the one that causes AIDS, is one of the most difficult cancers to treat. In 1995, however, studies in several hospitals in both France and the U.S. showed that alpha interferon, combined with zidovudine (which is also used to combat AIDS), was effective even in patients in whom conventional therapies had failed.

Infectious Diseases. The incidence of tuberculosis (TB) increased in several countries, especially among economically disadvantaged groups. Research in England and Wales established that TB cases had risen by 35% in the poorest tenth of the population over four years and by 13% in the next two-tenths; there was no change in incidence among the remaining 70% of the population. Investigators concluded that socioeconomic factors (such as crowded living conditions) were the major reason for the increase, the immigration of infected persons making only a minor contribution.

Physicians in The Netherlands expressed concern that TB was spreading more rapidly than expected from high-risk groups to the general population. The number of cases reported in Amsterdam in 1995 rose by 37% over the previous year's total to reach the highest figure since 1966. Although there was a 20% increase in TB incidence among immigrants from countries with high TB rates, new cases rose by 74% among people born in The Netherlands.

A study in New York City, a locale hard hit by the recent resurgence of TB, suggested that in that city, at least, the tide may have been turned; reported cases had declined by 21% over a two-year period. Reasons for the change included measures to reduce the spread of infection in institutions such as jails and to ensure that patients complete the prolonged (up to one year) course of drug treatment. Failure to complete antibiotic therapy was a factor in the continued spread of the disease, as well as in the rise of drug-resistant strains of the tubercle bacillus.

Strains of the bacillus insensitive to once-effective antibiotics such as streptomycin posed ongoing problems, however. Especially alarming was the emergence in New York City of organisms resistant to fluoroquinolones—drugs hitherto effective against tubercle bacilli that had become resistant to other agents.

The emergence of drug-resistant forms of a bacterium that causes pneumonia, *Streptococcus pneumoniae,* aroused particular concern in the U.S. A survey in metropolitan Atlanta, Ga., showed that a quarter of the strains isolated from both children and adults suffering from invasive pneumonia were resistant to penicillin, formerly the first-choice antibiotic for this disease. This finding prompted calls for more widespread use of the vaccine against *S. pneumonia.*

Studies published during the year confirmed that combination therapy is more effective than monotherapy (*i.e.,* use of a single drug) in combating HIV. Scientists at Wellcome Research Laboratories in Kent, England, found that when the drugs AZT (zidovudine) and 3TC (lamivudine) were administered together, they were far more effective in reducing the level of circulating virus particles and protecting vulnerable immune cells than either drug used singly. Patients were also less likely to develop drug resistance. In November 3TC was approved for sale in the U.S. under the trade name Epivir.

A new class of anti-HIV drugs, called protease inhibitors, was showing promise in clinical trials. These agents attack the virus at a different stage in its life cycle than drugs like AZT. In a finding that had implications for both AIDS vaccine and drug therapy research, researchers at the Macfarlane Burnet Centre for Medical Research in Victoria, Australia, reported in *Science* in November that they had found a genetically weakened strain of HIV in a small cluster of patients who remained healthy despite having been infected for more than a decade.

Health Behaviours. Male former smokers gain about 4.5 kg (10 lb) and females 5 kg (11 lb) in the decade after they quit, but according to the U.S. Centers for Disease Control and Prevention, the decline in smoking in recent years accounted for less than one-fourth of the overall weight gain in the U.S. population in the 1980s. During this period the proportion of Americans who were overweight rose nearly 10% in men and 8% in women.

U.S. teenagers were engaging in unhealthy behaviours in greater numbers than before and at ever-younger ages. Data published in July based on a 1992 government survey of more than 10,000 youths aged 12 to 21 showed that more than one-fourth were current smokers, one-fourth said they had indulged in "binge drinking" (five or more drinks in a row), one in 10 had smoked marijuana, and one in 7 had carried a weapon in the previous month. Six out of 10 never-married youths had engaged in sexual intercourse. In August the administration of Pres. Bill Clinton launched an unprecedented attack on teen smoking, proposing curbs on advertising and vending machine sales and mandating new antismoking education campaigns. Tobacco companies responded by taking the government to court.

Women and Infants. An international consensus emerged as to the most effective way of dealing with eclampsia—the occurrence of convulsions (not attributable to a condition such as epilepsy) in women who develop high blood pressure during pregnancy. In what the *British Medical Journal* described as "the most important obstetric trial of the 20th century," researchers at 23 centres in eight countries assessed the different therapies currently in use worldwide

New, Resurgent, and Surprising Viruses

The smallest of the microbes, the viruses, provoked the greatest concern in 1995. Australian scientists reported in April that they had identified the cause of a puzzling 1994 outbreak that killed several horses and their trainer. The culprit was a new virus, a member of the family that includes the measles virus and the organism responsible for canine distemper.

An epidemic of Ebola virus in Africa prompted increased awareness of the potential dangers of so-called hot viruses, which cause deadly and virtually untreatable diseases in humans and other animals. Between January and April, 189 people in southwestern Zaire developed an acute illness marked by fever, vomiting, and bloody diarrhea. About a third of them died. Epidemiologists from the World Health Organization (WHO) soon incriminated the Ebola virus and initiated

CHRISTOPHE CALAIS—GAMMA LIAISON

In the hospital in Kikwit where Zaire's outbreak of the Ebola virus began in April, patients try to protect themselves by covering their faces. It was only the fourth recorded outbreak of the virulent disease, which killed as many as 90% of those who contracted it.

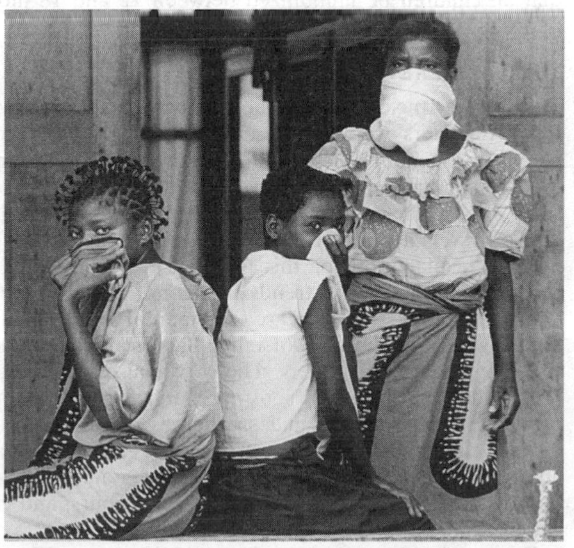

measures to prevent further spread of the infection. By August, when WHO announced that the epidemic was over, 315 people had become ill, and 77% of them were dead.

In 1989 a fatal disease among laboratory monkeys imported into the U.S. from the Philippines had been linked to an Ebola-type virus. In their search for the origin of the Zaire outbreak, the WHO investigators captured over 3,000 birds, rodents, and other animals, plus several thousand insects, but failed to pinpoint the source of the virus.

Firm evidence of a link between primates and Ebola virus infection in humans did come to light, however. In May French scientists reported that they had isolated a new strain of the virus from a researcher who became infected in Côte d'Ivoire while performing an autopsy on a chimpanzee. The troop in the wild to which the animal belonged had recently been decimated by a hemorrhagic disease similar to that caused in humans by the Ebola virus.

That even relatively familiar viruses are capable of surprises was underlined by a report from Sweden of the mysterious spread of hepatitis C virus among 37 patients in a hospital ward. Although this virus is usually transmitted by intravenous drug abuse or through contaminated blood or donor organs, the Swedish scientists were convinced that it had not been spread via the usual routes or as a result of any lapse in hygiene. They concluded that the virus had been transmitted by some other, as-yet-unrecognized route—possibly through the air.

Another surprise in 1995 was the publication of research from London and Glasgow, Scotland, indicating that childhood diabetes is related to infection with Coxsackie B viruses (relatives of the poliovirus). Although diabetes involves a genetic predisposition, environmental factors are also thought to play a role. The researchers found the genetic material of Coxsackie viruses in blood samples from 9 of 14 children at the onset of diabetes but in only 2 of 45 healthy children. This finding did not prove causation but was highly suggestive. (BERNARD DIXON) and concluded that magnesium sulfate (rather than the formerly widely used phenytoin or diazepam) should be the treatment of choice in the future.

In the wake of complaints that the medical problems of women had received short shift in the past, basic and clinical research in the field of women's health continued to grow. A Harvard Medical School study of more than 115,000 women found that even being mildly to moderately overweight is hazardous to health. In this study a gain of 6.8–9.1 kg (15–20 lb) after age 18 was associated with an increased risk of heart attack in later life. Even being of "average" weight increased a woman's risk of dying prematurely. As a result of these and other data, government agencies were revising—downward—the weight guidelines for adults.

A three-year NIH study of healthy women aged 45 to 64 found that taking any one of four hormone regimens significantly increased blood levels of high-density lipoprotein (HDL), the "good" cholesterol, and decreased low-density lipoprotein (LDL), the harmful form. HDL increases had been shown to reduce the risk of coronary heart disease, the number one killer of men and women alike in most Western countries. Women who took estrogen alone (as opposed to a combination of estrogen and progestin) had the greatest heart benefits but were also at increased risk of uterine cancer. Thus, women who still had a uterus were advised to opt for combination therapy.

Studies evaluating the breast cancer risk of hormone replacement therapy came to conflicting conclusions. Data from the Nurses' Health Study, a long-term epidemiological investigation of more than 100,000 female nurses, found a slightly increased rate of breast cancer among women who used hormones for five or more years after menopause. A smaller study published almost simultaneously found no link between hormone use and breast cancer.

A survey commissioned by the Henry J. Kaiser Family Foundation found that the number of U.S. doctors, particularly younger ones, willing to do surgical abortions was declining. Overall only about one-third of practicing obstetrician-gynecologists said they currently performed such procedures. These findings gave added impetus to the search for nonsurgical approaches to ending early-stage pregnancies. In September the New York City-based Population Council completed the clinical part of a U.S. study that could clear the way for government approval of mifepristone, or RU 486, an abortifacient drug already used extensively in Europe.

Calling it a "silent violent epidemic," the American Medical Association (AMA) issued new guidelines to help physicians become more involved in preventing and treating sexual assault. The AMA said that about 6 out of 10 female victims were under age 18, and three-quarters of sexual assaults were committed by someone known to the victim, such as a friend, acquaintance, partner, or family member. Male victims represented only about 5% of reported sexual assaults.

Other Developments. A clue to understanding and treating chronic fatigue syndrome (CFS), a puzzling condition most common in young women but also found in men and women of all ages and occasionally reported in localized outbreaks, came from two small studies at Johns Hopkins Hospital in Baltimore, Md. Doctors identified an abnormality in blood pressure regulation, known as neurally mediated hypotension, that may increase an individual's vulnerability to CFS. Preliminary results suggested that drugs to treat the abnormality and increased salt in the diet could help reduce CFS symptoms. A larger government-funded study was planned for 1996.

(BERNARD DIXON; CRISTINE RUSSELL)

In additional developments worthy of note:

• Investigators at Boston University School of Medicine found that excessive vitamin A intake—more than 10,000 international units per day (the amount found in two to three multivitamin pills)—early in pregnancy increases the risk of birth defects.

• Epidemiologists comparing 200 infants who had died of sudden infant death syndrome, or SIDS, with 200 healthy controls found that exposure to secondhand smoke was strongly associated with sudden unexplained death in otherwise healthy babies.

• A study from the University of Kentucky suggested that soy protein can lower elevated blood cholesterol levels, especially levels of LDL.

• An NIH trial demonstrated that daily doses of hydroxyurea, a drug used for some years to treat certain cancers, significantly reduced the number of painful episodes in patients with sickle-cell disease. Those taking the drug also required fewer hospitalizations and fewer transfusions than their untreated counterparts.

• One of the largest studies ever to evaluate air quality in the U.S. concluded that the risk of death was 15% higher in those cities with the dirtiest air. The higher death rates were attributed to the respiratory effects of microscopic particles in automobile exhaust and industrial emissions.

• A team led by scientists at Yale University School of Medicine confirmed what many had long suspected—that men and women think differently. The Yale investigators used functional magnetic resonance imaging to compare the brain function of men and women while reading; they found that male and female subjects used different parts of their brains while performing the task.

• A report from Denmark indicated that drinking wine—but not beer or liquor—reduces the incidence of deaths from all causes. The beneficial effects were particularly evident with respect to mortality from cardiovascular disease.

• Scientists at Memorial Sloan-Kettering Cancer Center in New York City announced that they had slowed the growth of prostate cancer in laboratory mice by cutting the amount of fat in the animals' diets. They reduced the percentage of fat the mice consumed by nearly half, to 21%. (The average American diet is about 36% fat.)

• The first vaccine to prevent chicken pox was licensed for use in the U.S. The Advisory Committee on Immunization Practices of the U.S. Public Health Service recommended that all children be immunized between 12 and 18 months of age.

MENTAL HEALTH

Depression, suicide, suicidal behaviours, and other psychosocial disorders were all increasing rapidly among young people throughout Europe and North America, according to a major international survey conducted in 1995. The study group, chaired by Sir Michael Rutter of the Institute of Psychiatry at the University of London, could find no clear explanation for this growing problem, which was accompanied by similar trends in alcohol and drug dependence. Virtually the only area of mental health that did not show unambiguously worsening figures among teenagers was that of eating disorders. The survey also indicated that the incidence of suicide, substance abuse, and crime was particularly high among males, whereas depression, eating disorders, and suicidal behaviours were especially prevalent among females; however, the male and female rates for depression, substance abuse, suicidal behaviours, and crime were beginning to converge.

From a global perspective, the outlook appeared no more optimistic. In a report issued in May at United Nations headquarters in New York City, a team of health authorities from 30 countries warned that increasing rates of mental illness in less developed countries threatened the social stability of the Third World. The group cited not only neuropsychiatric disorders such as epilepsy and schizophrenia but also behavioral problems such as substance abuse and violence. It noted that war and political upheaval were responsible for an increased risk of depression, anxiety disorders, and other forms of mental distress among the world's more than 40 million refugees and displaced persons.

Concern about rising suicide rates among men under 35 in Europe prompted researchers in Helsinki, Finland, to assess the incidence of mental disorders in such individuals. The results showed that significantly more of these men had suffered from a psychotic illness, compared with those aged 35–59 who had committed suicide. The latter had higher rates of alcohol dependence and depression. The prevalence of psychotic disorders in the under-35 age group was much higher (25%) than in previous studies in similar groups in Canada (9%) and in Sweden and the U.S. (17%). However, the prevalence of personality disorders (43%) was about the same as in earlier surveys conducted elsewhere.

Researchers in Edinburgh reported a disturbing trend in the rate of suicide during the first 28 days after discharge from psychiatric hospitals in Scotland during the years 1968–92. They found that although the incidence of suicide had declined by 40% among discharged male patients, the rate among female patients had almost trebled. The investigators pointed out that this development had occurred during a period when mental health services had changed from largely institutional to predominantly community-based programs, the number of psychiatric beds for adults having declined by 60%.

A strong association between suicide and parasuicide (an act of self-injury not motivated by a genuine desire to die) emerged from work carried out in Bristol, England. Despite the difference in motivation between the two types of acts, socioeconomic deprivation emerged as a common element.

A report by the Royal College of Psychiatrists and Royal College of Physicians of London focused on the importance of paying attention to the psychological needs and difficulties of medical patients. People with appreciable physical illness have at least twice the rate of psychiatric disorder of the population at large, yet many hospitals fail to provide appropriate services to assist with these problems, which include depression, mood disorders, and cognitive impairment. In addition to citing direct benefits to the patient, the report included evidence from the U.S. of economic benefits—for example, orthopedic patients in the U.S. who received psychiatric counseling had shorter hospital stays than those not offered such assistance. The report advocated integrated physical and psychiatric care for all patients with significant physical illness.

Research published during the year contributed to the understanding of auditory verbal hallucinations ("hearing voices") in patients with schizophrenia. The investigators, psychiatrists and neurologists in New York City and London, used brain scanning to study patients with schizophrenia who complained of hearing voices. They also studied schizophrenics who did not hear voices, as well as a group of normal, healthy individuals (controls). The scans were designed to reveal alterations in blood flow as various parts of the brain became active. The procedure showed that there were no differences in blood flow between the hallucinators and the controls when they were asked to "think in sentences." There were differences, however, when the subjects were asked to imagine sentences being spoken in another person's voice—a task that required them to both generate and monitor so-called inner speech. In the latter case one brain region in the hallucinators functioned normally, but abnormally low responses occurred in two other regions, which were activated in both the controls and the nonhallucinating schizophrenics. This finding strongly suggested that a predisposition to "hearing voices" is associated with a failure to activate areas of the brain that play a role in monitoring inner speech. Those who are affected may misperceive such verbal thoughts as coming from external sources, or they may simply be unaware of having them.

(BERNARD DIXON)

This article updates the *Macropædia* article MENTAL DISORDERS and Their Treatment.

VETERINARY MEDICINE

Japan was host to the 1995 World Veterinary Congress in September. The event, which was opened in Yokohama by Emperor Akihito, attracted representatives from 82 countries. The emperor noted that veterinary scientists, with their deep understanding of and rich experience with animals, had provided "many suggestions regarding the optimal relationship between human beings and animals."

Speakers included Jean Blancou of the International Office of Epizootics, who reviewed the often devastating consequences of past disease outbreaks associated with the movement of animals between countries. As international trade in animals and animal products was likely to increase as a result of the newly established World Trade Organization, Blancou observed, a strengthening of veterinary surveillance arrangements and increased research on animal vaccines were called for.

At the World Small Animal Veterinary Association Congress, which was held concurrently, the association's president, Peter Bedford of London, announced that the group's Eastern Europe continuing education program, which aimed to update veterinarians in former Eastern bloc countries, would be extended to help less developed nations elsewhere.

Bovine viral diarrhea is a disorder that affects cattle worldwide and has serious adverse effects on health and productivity. The virus is passed from dam to fetus in the womb, and the calf is born with the infection. Calves often show no signs of disease until they acquire a form of the virus that rapidly causes mucosal disease and death. In the absence of any effective treatment, vaccination of female cattle before they are bred has been recognized as the route to control. Live vaccines have been developed and used in some countries, including the U.S., but have not eradicated the problem. In 1995 a new inactivated vaccine was shown to protect heifers exposed to the virus, and calves subsequently born to them, unlike control animals, were free from infection.

The production of identical calves potentially would be valuable to the livestock industry by increasing the number of offspring from high-quality parents and to scientific research by providing genetically identical animals for comparative studies. Embryo-transfer and cell-division techniques have been used to this end, but the maximum number of calves produced by these methods was three. In 1995, however, W.H. Johnson and colleagues at the University of Guelph, Ont., succeeded in producing four identical calves from a single embryo. The embryo was divided at the four-cell stage and transferred to two recipients, which resulted in the births of two sets of identical twins—four genetically identical animals.

(EDWARD BODEN)

See also Life Sciences: *Molecular Biology.*

This article updates the *Macropædia* articles DIAGNOSIS AND THERAPEUTICS; DISEASE; INFECTIOUS DISEASES; MEDICINE.

Law, Crime, and Law Enforcement

LAW

There were two dominant themes in international law in 1995: adjudication and the United Nations. In the background was the steady development of regional economic organizations, as well as treaties containing laws governing the conduct of private parties. In spite of the occasional eruption of violence between nations and the insistent refusal of the U.S. to subordinate itself to international structures or to external adjudication, a powerful impression was emerging that the old sovereign separateness of the members of the family of nations, on which classic international law had been based, was being diluted as part of the process of constructing a genuine world order. In addition, international law was altering its character to become more of a mix of public and private law, matching the change in international conflict from military to political-economic.

International Adjudication. By mid-1995 the International Court of Justice had a load of 13 pending cases, including two requests for advisory opinions, submitted by the World Health Organization and by the UN General Assembly, on the legality of the use of nuclear weapons. Of the 13 cases, one involved the lawfulness of Indonesia's occupation of Timor Timur (the former Portuguese colony of East Timor). Portugal claimed that Indonesia was not entitled to conclude a treaty on behalf of Timor Timur. The court, however, held that it had no jurisdiction and dismissed the case.

The decision by France to carry out a series of nuclear tests between September 1995 and May 1996 on Mururoa atoll in the Pacific led to an action brought in August by New Zealand, seeking an examination of its legality in accordance with the court's 1974 judgment in the *Nuclear Tests Case* between the same parties. That case had involved atmospheric tests, whereas the present test series was to be carried out underground. Because there was no link between the 1974 undertaking and the present tests, the court said that it had no jurisdiction to consider the matter, and the action was dismissed.

The court accepted jurisdiction in *Qatar* v. *Bahrain* in February 1995, following an interim judgment the previous July, in a case related to maritime limits. Despite Bahrain's objections, the court held that it had jurisdiction over the dispute and that the relevant texts allowed either party to make a unilateral application, so Bahrain's consent was not necessary. The other cases pending before the court included *Iran* v. *U.S.* (aerial incident of July 3, 1988), *Guinea-Bissau* v. *Senegal* (sea boundaries), *Libya* v. *U.K.* and *Libya* v. *U.S.* (Lockerbie air disaster), *Iran* v. *U.S.* (oil platforms), *Hungary* v. *Slovakia* (Gabcikovo-Nagymaros river diversion), *Cameroon* v. *Nigeria* (land and sea boundaries), *Bosnia and Herzegovina* v. *Yugoslavia* (genocide), and *Spain* v. *Canada* (fishery jurisdiction).

Like the rest of the United Nations, the court celebrated its 50th anniversary in 1995. It renewed the mandate of its special chamber on environmental matters until 1997. The court received its first woman judge, Rosalyn Higgins, who replaced Sir Robert Jennings on his retirement. Another highly respected veteran of the court, Roberto Ago, died during the year and was replaced by Luigi Ferrari-Bravo, who had been head of the Italian legal team at the European Court of Justice.

Apart from the already-existing regional tribunals, a number of new initiatives came to fruition during the year. The World Trade Organization's new Dispute Settlement Body was completed by the swearing in of the seven members of its appellate body in mid-December. The newly created Court of Conciliation and Arbitration of the Organisation for Security and Co-operation in Europe held its first meeting in Geneva in May. The entry into force of the Law of the Sea Convention in November 1994 paved the way for the establishment of the International Tribunal for the Law of the Sea, with the parties agreeing that the members of the tribunal would be appointed in August 1996 and hold their first organizational session the following October. A U.S. proposal at the Group of Seven summit in mid-1995 for an international bankruptcy court did not, however, find broad favour.

The established European courts continued to work through their ever-increasing caseloads. The Court of the European Free Trade Association (EFTA) lost three of its members at the beginning of the year when Austria, Finland, and Sweden joined the European Union, but the court continued with its 1994 judges (except for the Finnish president, who became a judge on the European Court of Justice) until the end of June 1995 in order to clear up outstanding cases. Thereafter, it was reconstituted with only three judges (Norway, Iceland, and Liechtenstein, the last having joined the European Economic Area and hence the EFTA Court two months earlier). The court also moved its headquarters to Luxembourg.

Other Issues. That not all disputes were susceptible to peaceful means of settlement was shown when a sudden border war flared up between Peru and Ecuador in January over a 77-km (48-mi) stretch of disputed land along the Cenepa River. The hostilities, which involved ground and air troops, were ended by a treaty signed in Brasília, Brazil, on February 17 providing for negotiations toward a definitive agreement on the frontier. Tension also increased during the first half of the year between China and the Philippines in relation to the long-running dispute regarding sovereignty over the Spratly Islands in the South China Sea. (*See* SPOTLIGHT: *The Spat over the Spratlys*.) Growing concern over the effects of antipersonnel mines left strewn over battle areas, which kill and injure civilians for years after the end of hostilities, found expression in a large number of resolutions and proposals. The one serious attempt to deal with the problem, by banning their manufacture and use, was discussed at a UN conference in Vienna during October, but there was no agreement.

Other events of the year included a memorandum of understanding issued in March on an interorganizational program for the management of chemicals that was stimulated by the UN Conference on Environment and Development. Russia adopted a new law on international treaties in June, and a treaty was signed in April between Cambodia, Laos, Thailand, and Vietnam on cooperation for the sustainable development of the Mekong River basin.

International Criminal Courts. The International War Crimes Tribunal for the Former Yugoslavia, established at The Hague in 1994, began work in earnest during 1995. The trial of the one defendant who was actually in custody, Dushan Tadic, which was to have started in November, was postponed to May 1996 at the request of his counsel in order for defense witnesses located in Bosnia and Herzegovina to be contacted. The tribunal began public hearings of witnesses in connection with other suspects in preparation for the issuing of international arrest warrants, to include Radovan Karadzic and Gen. Ratko Mladic, the civil and military leaders, respectively, of the Bosnian Serbs, and Dario Kordic and Gen. Tihomir Blaskic, leaders in Croat-held Bosnia. The tribunal expressed fears that the financial difficulties that the United Nations as a whole was facing would affect the tribunals efficacy, particularly in view of the high expenses involved in tracking down witnesses and defendants.

The International Criminal Tribunal for Rwanda was running about a year later than the Bosnia tribunal. With the same prosecutor, Richard Goldstone, and the same appellate body, it was formally inaugurated in The Hague in June. Its operational premises were relocated to Arusha, Tanzania, where, having adopted its rules of procedure, it expected to be ready to hold hearings by the end of the year. By the end of the autumn, it was facing difficulties over funding, bureaucratic cooperation, and inexperienced investigators. In addition, governments were being less cooperative, and one, Kenya, was openly hostile, refusing to hand over any Rwandan suspects and threatening to arrest any tribunal investigator entering the country to serve a summons on behalf of the tribunal.

A number of prosecutions for war crimes in Bosnia and Ethiopia took place before national courts. The New Zealand International War Crimes Tribunal Act of 1995 provided for assistance not only to the two tribunals on Bosnia and Rwanda but also to any other ad hoc tribunal that the UN Security Council might institute in connection with other violations of international humanitarian law. Proposals for a permanent international criminal court continued to be made, based on the draft statute for a criminal tribunal produced by the International Law Commission in 1993. (NEVILLE MARCH HUNNINGS)

Other Court Decisions. People around the world in 1995 watched the televised trial of former football star O.J. Simpson, who was found not guilty of charges that he had murdered his former wife Nicole Brown Simpson and her acquaintance Ronald Goldman. The verdict was celebrated by many black Americans and condemned by a majority of whites, but there was general agreement that the state of race relations in the U.S. had been highlighted by the case. The racial composition of the jury convinced many in the legal community from the start that conviction would not be possible, no matter how strong the evidence of guilt, especially after testimony indicated deep-seated racism in the Los Angeles Police Department. Whatever the correctness of this view, it convinced some that justice might be better served by adoption of the approach taken in most European countries of letting a panel of judges decide at least major criminal cases.

In the Simpson case the jury was sequestered from family members and the public so as to shield it from media coverage. The confinement lasted 266 days, believed to be a record in the U.S. Some legal scholars blamed the long confinement for the quick verdict, with deliberations lasting only four hours. In this view the jury was tired of the case and wanted to get it over with as quickly as possible. Others, however, were of the opinion that the jury had decided the case long before it ended and had no need to sort through the mountain of evidence entrusted to it. In any case, many scholars believed that sequestration was a bad idea that rarely, if ever, should be used. They pointed out that it did not necessarily provide airtight isolation because conjugal visits, for example, broke the seal. Moreover, if trials were not televised, many argued, there would be less need to shield a jury from the media, since television tended to generate an excessive amount of other media interest. In addition, some experts claimed that televised trials encouraged posturing by lawyers and judges and thus inevitably lengthened proceedings.

More important decisions from a legal point of view were handed down by tribunals in various countries. As usual, these cases centred on questions of sex and age discrimination, civil rights, the regulation of business, and politics.

Only one prominent case involving abortion was handed down in 1995. The Supreme Court of Ireland rendered an advisory opinion to the country's president that the Regulation of Information Act, dealing with providing information for abortion services abroad, was constitutional. The court also ruled that abortion was permissible in Ireland when it had been established as a matter of probability that the life of the pregnant woman could be saved only by a termination of the pregnancy. In *U.S.* v. *X-Citement Video, Inc.,* the U.S. Supreme Court upheld the constitutionality of the Protection of Children Against Sexual Exploitation Act, which banned the interstate shipment of child pornography. A majority on the court found that the act required proof of "scienter"—that is, knowledge by the defendant that the person performing the pornographic act was a minor—and that it was reasonable to read the statute as containing such a requirement.

In *R.* v. *Ministry of Defence, ex parte Smith,* an English divisional court held that the policy of dismissing homosexuals from the armed forces, while not related to national security, was, nevertheless, not unreasonable and did not violate English constitutional principles or Article 8 of the European Convention on Human Rights. The U.S. Supreme Court, in *Hurley* v. *Irish-American Gay Group,* also dealt a blow to claimants of homosexual rights by declaring unconstitutional a Massachusetts law that required a private parade sponsor to include, as marching units, organizations of gays, lesbians, and bisexuals. The court said that the law violated the free-speech rights of the sponsor, in this case an

NAJLAH FEANNY—SABA

A crew prepares for work on an airport construction project. The U.S. Supreme Court in 1995 restricted the interpretation of affirmative action law by ruling that federal as well as state programs must be limited to the correction of specific wrongs suffered in the past.

association of people who traditionally organized Boston's Saint Patrick's Day parade.

In another significant case, the Japanese Court of Grand Bench, with 5 dissents out of the 15 judges, held constitutional a civil code provision that limited inheritance for illegitimate children to one-half of that available to legitimate children.

The UN Human Rights Committee handed down three important civil rights decisions in 1995. In *Kome* v. *Senegal* it held that the pretrial detention of a person for more than four years by the Senegalese government violated Article 9 of the International Covenant on Civil and Political Rights (ICCPR), which guaranteed freedom of expression. In *Coeriel and Aurik* v. *Netherlands,* the committee ruled that The Netherlands' refusal to allow a Dutch national to change his name violated the right to privacy guaranteed by Article 17 of the ICCPR. Finally, it decided in *Lansman* v. *Finland* that Finland had not violated Article 27 of the ICCPR, which guaranteed the right of minorities to enjoy their own culture, when it granted a license to a company to do quarrying on a mountain that had religious and other cultural significance for a minority group.

Meanwhile, the U.S. Supreme Court resolved several notable civil rights cases during the year. The most important of the decisions may have been in *Adarand Constructors* v. *Pena*. The case concerned the constitutional validity of federal contracts that were required to contain provisions giving financial incentives for hiring subcontractors certified as small businesses controlled by socially and economically disadvantaged individuals, presuming that such individuals included minorities found by the Small Business Administration to be disadvantaged. The court held that "strict scrutiny" must be exercised when any classification imposed by the federal, state, or local government was based on race. That is to say, such a classification was constitutional only if it was narrowly tailored to further a compelling government interest. Under this test the court held that the contracts in question were unconstitutional.

In *Harris* v. *Alabama* the court ruled that an Alabama law allowing judges to impose the death sentence in spite of a jury's recommendation of life imprisonment was constitutional. In *McIntyre* v. *Ohio Elections Commission,* it ruled that a statute barring anonymous campaign literature was unconstitutional. In *Veronia School District* v. *Acton,* the court held that a school's policy requiring drug testing of students who participated in athletic programs did not violate the U.S. Constitution. In *Capitol Square Review Board* v. *Pinette,* it held that Ohio had violated the Constitution when it denied an application by the Ku Klux Klan to display an unattended cross on the statehouse square.

Although it was less active in 1995 than in previous years, the European Court on Human Rights (ECHR) handed down a decision that, in the view of many legal experts, could have far-reaching importance for Europe's judicial tribunals. In *Hiro Balani* v. *Spain,* the ECHR held that Spain had violated Article 6 of the European Convention on Human Rights, which guaranteed the right to a fair trial, by the failure of its Supreme Court to give a reasoned decision when it handed down its ruling on the merits of the case. Legal experts noted that while in the U.S. appellate courts were required to deliver long, written opinions justifying their decisions, the practice in Europe was different. The ECHR stated that the obligation of appellate courts to give reasoned decisions varied according to the kind of case involved and other circumstances, but it apparently would require such decisions when the applicant's submission was relevant, stated in a precise manner, and supported by evidence.

The Supreme Court of Israel clarified its views on the protection of intellectual property by holding in the case of *David Geva* v. *The Walt Disney Corporation* that there was copyright infringement by an Israeli cartoonist who used the character Donald Duck in a comic book. The cartoonist had contended that his use of the Disney character was satirical criticism and thus within fair use. The court emphatically recognized the fair use exemption, but it found that the requirements had not been met in this case since the use was commercial and did not constitute criticism. In *Publishers Association* v. *Commission,* the European Court of Justice struck down the Net Book Agreement promulgated by the U.K. under which standard conditions were set for the sale of books at fixed prices. It held that the arrangement violated competition rules of the European Union.

The U.S. Supreme Court resolved an issue that had pitted the insurance industry against commercial banks. Under banking legislation, largely enacted through the lobbying efforts of insurance companies, national banks were prohibited from selling insurance. In *NationsBank* v. *Variable Annuity Life Insurance Co.,* the hotly debated question arose whether annuities were insurance for purposes of the exclusion. In a victory for commercial banks, the court ruled that annuities were not insurance and that they could be sold by national banks.

The frequent-flyer programs of U.S. airlines, under which passengers could receive free tickets and other benefits, came under attack. In the past few years, some carriers had canceled or curtailed the programs retroactively, with the result that a number of lawsuits were filed against them. The airlines, in turn, contended that their actions were legal under the Airline Deregulation Act of 1978. The U.S. Supreme Court held in *American Airlines* v. *Wolens* that the federal statute did not shield the airlines from actions for breach of contract but did protect them from claims of fraud.

The U.S. Supreme Court in 1995 also dealt with two sensitive political issues, term limits and congressional redistricting. In *U.S. Term Limits, Inc.* v. *Thornton,* it declared unconstitutional an Arkansas law that denied ballot access to congressional candidates who had been elected to two terms in the Senate or three terms in the House of Representatives. The decision, however, did not prohibit the states from imposing term limits on those running for state office. In *Miller* v. *Johnson* the court held that a Georgia redistricting plan based predominantly on race violated the equal protection clause of the Constitution.

(WILLIAM D. HAWKLAND)

See also World Affairs: *Multinational and Regional Organizations; United Nations.*

This article updates the *Macropædia* articles CONSTITUTIONAL LAW; INTERNATIONAL LAW.

CRIME

Terrorism. On April 19, 1995, a bomb explosion in Oklahoma City, Okla., destroyed any illusion that the world's most powerful nation was immune from the scourge of domestic terrorism. The bomb, placed in a truck parked outside a federal office building, ripped the structure apart and left 169 dead and more than 500 injured. The two prime suspects turned out to be former U.S. Army comrades Timothy J. McVeigh and Terry L. Nichols. In August a federal grand jury indicted both men on bombing and murder charges that were punishable by death. A third man, Michael Fortier, pleaded guilty to lesser charges and was expected to become a key government witness. The alleged participants in the bombing were believed to have links to self-styled right-wing paramilitary groups. The Oklahoma

City bombing occurred on the second anniversary date of the FBI's ending of the siege at Waco, Texas, in which some 80 members of the Branch Davidians, a religious cult, had died.

On October 9, in what seemed to be a further domestic terrorist attack, an Amtrak passenger train derailed in a remote part of the Arizona desert, reportedly as a result of track sabotage. One person was killed and some 100 injured. A note found at the scene said that the attack was the work of the Sons of the Gestapo and referred to the federal siege at Waco and to another at Ruby Ridge, Idaho.

In Japan the members of the religious cult Aum Shinrikyo (Supreme Truth) were accused of having masterminded the worst terrorist attack in that nation's history. The group was said to have been responsible for the March 20 release of sarin, a deadly nerve gas, in the Tokyo subway during the morning rush hour. Twelve people died as a result of the gas attack, and more than 5,500 were injured. Subsequent police raids on premises occupied by cult members uncovered large caches of chemicals capable of being used to manufacture poison gas and explosives. Japanese authorities prepared a case against more than 100 cult members, including leader Shoko Asahara, held on suspicion of involvement in the subway attack and a number of related incidents.

The commuter train system in Paris was also the target of terrorist attacks. On July 25 a bomb exploded during the evening rush hour on a crowded train near Notre-Dame cathedral. The blast killed 7 people and injured more than 80. Another bombing of a Paris commuter train, on October 17, injured 29 people. Between July and late September, further bombs were planted in Paris and other locations, all seemingly designed to cause casualties and fear among civilians during the peak months of the European tourist season. A group of Algerian Islamic militants claimed responsibility. In late September French police claimed the first major success in their hunt for the bombers when security forces killed Khaled Kelkal, an Algerian fugitive who was said to have been involved in at least three of the terrorist incidents.

In Algeria the struggle between Islamic militant groups and the military-backed government for control of the country continued unabated. Since the violent revolt began in early 1992 with the cancellation by the military of elections that the Islamic movement seemed certain to win, more than 30,000 people were believed to have been killed, with security officers, government officials, foreigners, and prominent citizens the main targets of the militants. Islamic fundamentalist groups also continued their terrorist activities in the Middle East. On June 26 Pres. Hosni Mubarak of Egypt survived an assassination attempt in the Ethiopian capital, Addis Ababa. Egypt blamed the fundamentalist government of The Sudan, but responsibility was claimed by the Islamic Group, an Egyptian terrorist organization. In New York City on October 1, Sheikh Omar Abdel Rahman and nine codefendents were convicted of conspiracy to destroy U.S. targets and to kill Mubarak. A right-wing Israeli man was charged with the assassination of Israeli Prime Minister Yitzhak Rabin on November 4 in Tel Aviv.

A series of deadly suicide bombing attacks, directed against soldiers and civilians in Israel and the Gaza Strip by the fundamentalist groups Hamas and Islamic Jihad, failed to derail the ongoing peace talks between the Palestine Liberation Organization (PLO) and Israel. In October PLO Chairman Yasir Arafat, in an attempt to end the attacks, sent a new truce proposal to leaders of the militant groups following the signing of an accord with the Israeli government to expand Palestinian self-rule in the West Bank. It seemed by year's end that the peace process continued in spite of Rabin's death. In Northern Ireland the cease-fire declared by Roman Catholic and Protestant paramilitary organizations continued to hold, but peace talks with the British government to resolve the long-standing conflict remained deadlocked.

War Crimes. A Bosnian Serb, Dusan Tadic, became the first defendant to face an international war crimes hearing since the Nürnberg and Tokyo trials at the end of World War II. Appearing in The Hague in April 1995 before a UN tribunal established by the Security Council in 1993 to deal with violations of international humanitarian law in former Yugoslavia, Tadic pleaded not guilty to a list of charges that included the murder, rape, and torture of Muslims and Croats during Serb "ethnic cleansing" campaigns in the Bosnian region of Prijedor. Following a hearing before one of the members of the tribunal, Tadic was detained at a Dutch prison.

In July the tribunal issued 24 new indictments against alleged war criminals, including Bosnian Serb leader Radovan Karadzic and the Bosnian Serb army commander, Gen. Ratko Mladic. Despite these indictments, 22 issued earlier, and 6 more indictments in November, Tadic remained the only defendant to be held in custody.

Drug Trafficking. In August 1995, responding to strong pressure from the U.S. government, Colombian police captured Miguel Rodríguez Orejuela, reputed to be the second in command in the world's most powerful cocaine supply group, the Cali cartel. Rodríguez was the sixth cartel leader to be arrested over a two-month period. The Colombian government itself, however, was shaken by allegations brought by Prosecutor General Alfonso Valdivieso (*see* BIOGRAPHIES) of drug-related corruption that reached into the office of Pres. Ernesto Samper Pizano.

U.S. and Latin-American experts reported that Mexican drug groups, who for years had acted as transshippers for Colombian cartels, were now operating as independent entities. As in Colombia, where the Medellín and Cali cartels had built up a huge cocaine supply business through the use of violence and bribes, Mexican criminal organizations were operating in a similar way with the protection of members of the government, police, and judiciary. In an attempt to curb the flow of narcotics across the border with Mexico, U.S. customs officials announced in February the start of Operation Hard Line, a new antidrug push to increase agent strength on the border by 20%. Extra surveillance equipment was also to be brought in.

Murder and Other Violence. In May 1995 the FBI reported that the U.S. crime rate had dropped 3% overall in 1994, posting a decline for the third year in a row. Violent crimes reported to the police fell by 4%. Many large U.S. cities saw their murder rates decline by more than 10%. Accelerating a four-year trend, the murder rate in New York City over the first six months of 1995 plunged to its lowest level in 25 years. Other crimes were also down over the same period, including robbery, with a 22% decrease. Criminologists urged caution in interpreting these figures, however.

The U.S. was not alone in reporting a decreasing rate of crime. In Canada the Department of Justice reported in August that the nation's crime rate had dropped by 5% in 1994, its third consecutive annual decrease, while in September the British government hailed figures revealing the biggest drop in crime in the 20th century. Recorded crimes in England and Wales had fallen by 10% in the two-year period ended June 1995, with the number of violent offenses down for the first time in nearly 50 years.

Observed live on television by millions in the U.S. and around the globe, the trial of former football player and television and movie figure O.J. Simpson in Los Angeles attracted unprecedented interest. Following nine months of testimony, during which the jury had been sequestered, they took less than four hours to reach a verdict, announced on October 3, finding Simpson not guilty of the killing of his former wife Nicole Brown Simpson and her companion Ronald Goldman on June 12, 1994. The trial included tape-recorded claims of brutality, fabrication of evidence, and abuse of minorities made by a prosecution witness, former Los Angeles detective Mark Fuhrman. It was a stark reminder of the gulf between blacks and whites in U.S. society, with the majority of African-Americans believing, unlike their white counterparts, that Simpson was the victim of a police conspiracy to link him to the killings. In another much-publicized U.S. trial, in July Susan Smith was sentenced to life in prison for the drowning of her two young sons in South Carolina in 1994.

The FBI continued its manhunt for the serial mail bomber and killer known as the Unabomber. The Unabomber was believed responsible for 16 bombings since 1978 that had killed 3 people and injured 23, many of them seriously. His latest victim was Gilbert Murray, a timber industry executive, who was killed by a parcel bomb in Sacramento, Calif., on April 24. That bomb and four letters, including one addressed to the *New York Times,* was sent on April 20, the day after the Oklahoma City bombing. The Unabomber subsequently sent a 35,000-word manifesto to the *New York Times* and *Washington Post* expounding his views on the evils of modern society and calling for a revolution against the industrial-technological world. The Unabomber vowed to end his terror campaign if one of the papers published his manifesto. In September the *Washington Post* published the entire manifesto at the request of the U.S. attorney general and the director of the FBI, while the *New York Times* published excerpts. Critics argued that publication would lead to copycat requests and allowed the government to dictate what was printed in the nation's media; supporters suggested that publication might assist in the capture of the Unabomber.

The rape in September of a 12-year-old girl by three U.S. servicemen based in Okinawa sparked anger among the Japanese, much of it triggered by the fact that although both the Americans and Japanese agreed that a crime had been committed, the U.S. military did not immediately allow Japanese police to take the alleged offenders into custody. Following the issue of a formal indictment as required under the Status of Forces Agreement governing the presence of U.S. military forces in Japan, the three servicemen were handed over to Japanese prosecutors.

Political Crime and Espionage. In September 1995 Giulio Andreotti, the Christian Democratic leader who was Italy's prime minister in seven governments, went on trial in Palermo on charges that he had acted as a protector and friend to the Sicilian Mafia during his years in power. In November additional charges were brought against him. The prosecution's case against Andreotti was believed to rely substantially upon evidence that had been given by several Mafia turncoats, or *pentiti,* who had broken their vows of silence in return for leniency. Italian authorities also continued their efforts to bring other former prominent politicians, businessmen, and government officials to justice as part of the far-reaching Operation Clean Hands, an anticorruption investigation launched by prosecuting magistrates in Milan in February 1992. Since that time more than 700 persons had been sent to trial in connection with bribes paid for government contracts.

The secretary-general of NATO, Willy Claes, resigned his post in October following revelations of a corruption scandal in Belgium. A special Belgian parliamentary commission was considering whether Claes should face charges related to his involvement, as the country's economic affairs minister, in alleged kickbacks paid in 1988 by an Italian company to the ruling Flemish Socialist Party to secure a contract to supply the Belgian army with 48 helicopters. Claes denied any knowledge of the BF 50 million bribe.

Russia's fledgling democracy came under threat during the year as a flood of candidates with criminal records sought election to all levels of government in order to evade

VLADISLAV LISTIEV—GAMMA LIAISON

Mourners lay flowers on the coffin of Vladislav Listyev, a popular Russian television journalist and head of the state-run television system, who was murdered, apparently by hired killers, on March 1. Murder and other violent crimes were sweeping Russia.

prosecution. More than 230 elected Russian officials were reported to have been investigated in the previous two years for criminal offenses as serious as murder. In almost 160 cases prosecutors said that they had enough evidence to file charges against the elected officials, but the politicians were protected by parliamentary immunity. The State Duma, the lower house of the Russian parliament, began a crackdown to rid itself of the worst offenders in its midst.

White Collar Crime and Theft. Fraud and malfeasance led to the collapse in February 1995 of Britain's oldest merchant bank, Barings PLC. The bank, which included members of the British royal family among its clients, was forced into receivership after Nicholas Leeson, a trader in its Singapore office, had accumulated losses of over $1 billion in the futures market. (*See* ECONOMIC AFFAIRS: *Special Report*.) According to a Bank of England report, Leeson was able to conceal the losses from his employers as they turned a blind eye to what they believed was a risky yet highly profitable trading operation. Just prior to the collapse, Leeson fled Singapore, but he was detained on March 2 by German police in Frankfurt aboard a flight bound for London. Leeson was extradited and pleaded guilty to reduced charges. He was sentenced to over six years in prison.

One of the world's biggest financial corporations, Daiwa Bank Ltd. of Japan, suffered one of history's largest fraud losses in September. Authorities charged Toshihide Iguchi, a bond trader at the bank's New York City branch, with having falsified records to conceal $1.1 billion in losses incurred through 30,000 unauthorized trades over the previous 11 years. Iguchi pleaded guilty in October as senior officials of the bank were implicated. In November the government banned operations by the bank in the U.S., and Japan's Finance Ministry ordered Daiwa to curtail its international operations.

LAW ENFORCEMENT

In the wake of the Oklahoma City bombing, law-enforcement officials in the U.S. began to review the security measures taken to protect vulnerable targets against possible terrorist attack. In May 1995 security at the White House was heightened by the closing of Pennsylvania Avenue in front of the building to deter would-be truck bombers. Questions also were raised about the adequacy of measures to monitor domestic groups that advocated violence. At U.S. Senate hearings, FBI Director Louis Freeh claimed that for two decades the agency had been at a disadvantage with regard to such groups. "We have no intelligence or background information on them until their violent talk becomes deadly action," he said. Freeh said that the agency needed a broader interpretation of existing laws and regulations, including guidelines dating from the 1970s that barred the surveillance or infiltration of domestic organizations unless there was a "reasonable indication" they were prepared to resort to violence to achieve their goals. The guidelines had been written in response to FBI excesses under the long stewardship of J. Edgar Hoover.

Law-enforcement officials in Italy reported success in their struggle to break the power of the Mafia. In June they arrested Leoluca Bagarella, a convicted murderer and one of the country's most sought-after criminals who was accused of being responsible for some of the most striking Mafia crimes of recent years. These included the 1992 bombing that killed anti-Mafia magistrate Giovanni Falcone, his wife, and three bodyguards and the bombing in 1993 of the Uffizi Gallery in Florence, in which five people died. The Florence bombing was believed to have been part of a Mafia terror campaign that followed the arrest in January 1993 of Salvatore ("the Beast") Riina, the alleged head of the infamous Sicilian-based Corleonese Mafia clan. It was thought that the Mafia's aim was to frighten Italians into supporting a relaxation of tough anti-Mafia laws passed in 1992, which included legal benefits to Mafia members who became turncoats. The terror campaign did not work, and the new laws, designed to break *omertà,* the Mafia code of silence, were said to have resulted in close to 1,000 Mafiosi applying for protection in return for their collaboration with prosecutors.

Members of the European Union signed a convention in July opening the way for Europol, the EU's police agency, to come into full operation. The move came after France dropped its hard-line opposition to providing powers to Europol to collect and analyze criminal intelligence outside the control of national police forces. While further hurdles remained to be cleared regarding the scope of the supervisory powers that the EU's Court of Justice would have over Europol, the agency was now able to conduct its own investigation of drug cartels, car-theft syndicates, and other forms of organized crime within Europe. EU members also agreed, at Spain's urging, that Europol's mandate should be extended in the near future to cover international terrorism.

Police in New Delhi reported considerable success with their newly established Anti-Eve-Teasing Squad, designed to prevent a host of sexual harassment offenses ranging from catcalls to physical assault. Members of the squad, working undercover on New Delhi's vastly overcrowded buses, apprehended many gropers, pinchers, and molesters who made travel for commuting women a daily nightmare. The squad was just one of a number of policing innovations used by South Asian police to combat a dramatic increase in crime against women. In New Delhi alone the number of rapes and molestation cases reported to police by women had nearly doubled over the previous five years. The trend reflected dramatic changes in conservative South Asian societies, where until recently women had held few professional jobs and seldom ventured out alone.

The use of advanced technology to assist in the detection of crime took a major step forward with the establishment in Britain of a national library of DNA profiles. In April, using new and controversial powers, British police began the routine collection of blood, saliva, and hair samples from any suspect charged with or even warned for an imprisonable offense. The British government said that the DNA library would have five million entries by the year 2000. DNA samples would then be widely available for matching with bodily fluids found at a crime scene. Police were enthusiastic about the advance in forensic science, which was described as the most significant step forward since the establishment of fingerprint databases more than a century earlier.

(DUNCAN CHAPPELL)

PRISONS AND PENOLOGY

Internationally, the scope of criminal law was widened and the sentencing powers of the courts strengthened during 1995. As a result, criminal justice systems were placed under ever-increasing strain. Romania instituted prison sentences of between one and five years for various homosexual acts and imprisoned, for up to three years, those who flew foreign national flags or played national anthems of other states. Iraq added to its list of punishments branding and the amputation of hands, feet, and ears and televised before-and-after images of the punishment, mainly to deter desertion from the army. In the U.S. 30 states acted upon or were considering "three strikes and you're out" sentencing provisions that typically ensured life imprisonment for an offender convicted of a third felony. In a California referendum voters strongly backed such a proposition, even though it would cause the percentage of state funds allocated to the state prison system to double within eight years. Alabama restored the chain gang, a practice that had been abolished some 30 years earlier. Prisoners were manacled together in groups of five with 2.4-m (8-ft) lengths of chain as they worked alongside state highways. In October 1995 the Washington state judge who in 1994 suspended the sentences of two Native American teenagers on charges of robbery and assault and gave a Native American tribal court a chance to rehabilitate them revoked his decision. After hearing conflicting testimony on the effectiveness of their banishment to separate corners of an uninhabited island off the Alaskan coast, he sent the two to prison (for 55 and 31 months, with each earning a 12-month credit for time served).

Prison populations worldwide continued to grow; the number of those incarcerated between 1991 and 1994 rose in 13 of 14 Eastern and Central European countries, with populations doubling in the Czech Republic and Belarus. Russia and the U.S. again had the world's largest prison populations, with rates per 100,000 of 590 and 555, respectively.

Severe crowding and other appalling prison conditions were reported worldwide. Amnesty International, reporting on Mongolia, attributed one-third of 90 prisoner deaths in the first nine months of 1994 to starvation. Bulgarian prisons were overflowing and operating with minimal levels of sanitation. At the Stara Zagora penitentiary, cells were dark and grossly overcrowded. In Cambodia a UN-sponsored centre found that prisoners were frequently shackled and kept in darkened solitary confinement for lengthy periods; many were reportedly dying from malnutrition and other diseases. In Phnom Penh prison, inmates were held in large rooms with only one open latrine and water trough for their use. The Combinado del Este prison in Cuba, with a capacity of 3,000, reportedly held over 5,000 prisoners. The Glendiary prison in Barbados, with a capacity of 245, held 724 men and women, often for lengthy periods without light and with little ventilation. At Kresty Prison, St. Petersburg, some 8,000 were jailed in accommodations designed for 3,500. Conditions at a special unit of the Korydallos Psychiatric Centre in Greece were so abysmal that the government closed it. That country's prisons held 6,700 inmates in a system designed for 3,900. In the U.S. a federal judge condemned ill treatment of prisoners at the "supermax" Pelican Bay facility in California. There, naked men were confined in tiny metal cages during bitter weather, while others were handcuffed wrists-to-ankles for up to 19 hours in that "hog-tied" position. The world's worst conditions were undoubtedly found in Rwanda, where 23,000 Hutu prisoners, many of them under investigation for the massacre of Tutsi, were forced to stand in space designed to hold 4,000.

In 1995 a new facility in Florence, Colo., was called the most secure prison ever built. In January three prisoners serving life sentences escaped from Parkhurst top-security prison in Britain shortly after a critical report had been issued on a breakout by six men (five of whom had been convicted for terrorist offenses) from Whitemoor Prison four months earlier. A mutiny in February at the Serkadji prison in Algeria left 95 prisoners and 4 officers dead.

Death Penalty. In 1994 in China, where as many as 65 offenses—ranging from bicycle theft to political dissent—were punishable by death, authorities reported that 1,991 prisoners had been executed, though the number was believed to be much higher. Several prostitutes were executed just prior to the 1995 UN Fourth World Conference on Women, which was held in Beijing. In May two refugees testified before a U.S. Senate committee that the Chinese authorities systematically removed organs from executed prisoners in order to sell them for medical transplants. They also reported that some executions were arranged in order to meet particular transplant demands. In Iran a reported 139 persons were put to death during 1994, but the actual figure was thought to be much higher. In Bangladesh the buying and selling of women and children became a capital offense, while in Nigeria a dramatic increase occurred in the number of executions by firing squad. In the U.S.—where 56 people were put to death in 1995—New York became the 38th state since 1976 to adopt capital punishment; 10 types of murder were punishable by lethal injection.

Being held for court appearances on charges of genocide, inmates in an overcrowded prison in Kigali line up to receive food rations. The disease-ridden facility, which was built to house 2,000 but was holding many times that number, was typical in Rwanda's prisons.
MALCOLM LINTON—BLACK STAR

In March the hanging of a Filipina maid in Singapore prompted a serious rift between that country and the Philippines. In Singapore 32 people were executed in 1994, many of them for drug-related offenses, and it was seen that ancient penalties were still sometimes imposed when a man who had been convicted of rape in Somalia was put to death by stoning. Two Christians in Pakistan, one of them a 14-year-old, were acquitted on appeal after having been sentenced to death for blasphemy. Though capital punishment became the mandatory sentence for blasphemy in 1991, the only other person so convicted had had his sentence overturned in 1994.

In South Africa opponents of capital punishment welcomed the unanimous decision of an 11-member constitutional court in June to declare the death penalty for murder unconstitutional. More than 1,000 persons had been hanged in that country during the past two years, and some 450 persons were on death row at the time of the court's decision.

(ANDREW RUTHERFORD)

See also World Affairs: *Multinational and Regional Organizations; United Nations.*

This article updates the *Macropædia* articles CONSTITUTIONAL LAW; CRIME AND PUNISHMENT; INTERNATIONAL LAW; POLICE.

Libraries and Museums

LIBRARIES

During 1995 various events demonstrated the uncertainties facing libraries in a rapidly changing world. Two commonly held, but fully opposed, notions about libraries aptly articulated those uncertainties. One held that libraries serve a totemic function, that architecturally grand and massive library buildings stand as symbols of the wisdom and culture of the organizations that create them. The second notion stated that physical libraries would cease to exist; the library of the future would be a television set capable of retrieving all of the world's wisdom and culture through the Internet.

Supporting the totemic view was the 1995 dedication of the new Perpustakaan Negara Malaysia, that country's national library. The Kuala Lumpur facility employed architectural treatments, particularly in the shape of its blue roof, that reflected the cultural heritage of Malaysia. Reviled by Britain's Prince Charles and legions of others, and becoming a metaphor for national disarray, the new British Library at St. Pancras station was now—after some 30 years of work, delay, cost overruns, and controversy—completely visible. In 1995 some critics cautiously announced that the building may be not an architectural abomination but rather an exciting and edifying edifice. Meanwhile, across the English Channel, France rushed, nearly successfully, to complete the construction of the National Library of France during Pres. François Mitterrand's term of office because Mitterrand considered the library, located on the Left Bank of the Seine, to be a part of his legacy. The design employed four L-shaped glass towers, each resembling an open book. Reading areas were located below. The design outraged many bibliophiles because exposure to sunlight makes preservation of materials problematic.

The new public library in San Antonio, Texas, also caused architectural controversy; Denver, Colo., and Phoenix, Ariz., also opened new downtown central libraries in 1995. The New York Public Library celebrated its centennial on May 20 and in November announced the receipt of $15 million—the largest one-time benefaction in its history—to renovate the historic Main Reading Room. On the last day of the year, San Francisco's Main Library closed. The books would be moved to a new building across the street.

The Oklahoma City, Okla., downtown library was closed for just over a month following the explosion that devastated the nearby federal office building on April 19. The bomb blew out 90% of the library's windows as well as causing extensive ceiling damage on the upper floors.

Even as countries, cities, and universities built grand symbols of culture and learning, librarians worked to create an electronic future that might make those structures obsolete. Worldwide, budgets lagged behind demands for materials and services, and librarians, particularly in less-developed nations, knew that a computer and an Internet connection were less expensive than a large collection. North America and Western Europe continued to lead, but many of the fastest-growing computerized library networks were in Latin America, Eastern Europe, and the Pacific.

This page is from a 14th-century manuscript commissioned by the poet Petrarch. Scholars were horrified by reports that an Ohio State University art history professor had removed this and another leaf from the manuscript at the Vatican Library and tried to sell them.

JAMES MARROW—AP/WIDE WORLD

Cooperative ventures abounded. The 1995 General Conference of the International Federation of Library Associations and Institutions, held in August in Istanbul, focused on turning the global promise of the Internet into a reality. The European Union was funding projects that promoted resource sharing within and across borders. A record-breaking 13,178 paid registrants at the American Library Association's 114th annual conference in Chicago heard new ALA Executive Director Elizabeth Martinez announce "ALA Goal 2000," a five-year plan to position the association for the Information Age. In February the U.S. Library of Congress unveiled Thomas, a new computer system (named for Thomas Jefferson) giving citizens Internet access to information on the workings of Congress. The library came under attack when it closed an exhibit on slavery the day after it opened. Several black officers and staff members had complained.

Amid charges of a cover-up of recent book mutilations at the Library of Congress, the U.S. General Accounting Office planned to conduct a review of the library's management as well as oversee a federal investigation of the damage. Public library circulation in the U.S. showed a modest decline of 3% in 1994, while expenditures leveled off to keep pace with inflation, according to the annual University of Illinois survey. In the face of declining circulation and diminishing advertising revenues, the 81-year-old *Wilson Library Bulletin* ceased publication in June.

(GORDON FLAGG; THOMAS GAUGHAN)

This article updates the *Macropædia* article LIBRARIES AND LIBRARY SCIENCE.

MUSEUMS

The year 1995 saw the "information superhighway" become part of the mainstream of museum work. Systems for transmitting and receiving high-quality graphic images were developing rapidly, and museums throughout the world began to exploit the great potential of publication and communication on the World Wide Web. By midyear the Virtual Library museums Web site, originated by Jonathan Bowen at the University of Oxford, had received a quarter of a million "hits" (electronic visits), and an average of one new museum site was being added every day. Some, like the Vatican Museums and Galleries, even offered a "virtual museum visit." Some feared that virtual visits could replace real museum visits, but initial evidence suggested the opposite. The International Council of Museums (ICOM) also established an electronic presence during the year, supported by the Swedish National Museum of Natural History.

The triennial ICOM World Congress of Museums in July in Stavanger, Norway, focused attention on the "economic liberalization" policies of many governments that had resulted in major reductions in the level of public funding or in the privatization of museums—or even outright closures. For example, the government of Zimbabwe decided to phase out subsidies for its national museums and monuments service and replace them with capital investments in income-generating initiatives. Likewise, major collections in Russia were developing video and CD-ROM products with an eye to replacing moneys not forthcoming from the state.

A June 1995 advisory from a mission of museum experts from Quebec to Armenia recommended that all available funds be earmarked for saving a few national museums and creating a secure storage facility for the remaining collections.

In one of the most remarkable openings of 1995, the national Museum of Arts and Crafts in Zagreb, Croatia, completely reconstructed the famous Secessionist building. The new Museum of Sydney, Australia, explores the interaction between the British settlers and the Aboriginal population over two centuries. The Rock and Roll Hall of Fame and Museum brought a spectacular building designed by I.M. Pei to a lakeside setting in Cleveland, Ohio. The new San Francisco Museum of Modern Art, designed by Swiss architect Mario Botta, was expected to anchor a revitalized museum centre that would include a Jewish museum and a Mexican museum, which launched a fivefold expansion into a new $15 million facility. That city's M.H. de Young Memorial Museum undertook a $61 million bond measure to construct earthquake-proof galleries.

The Smithsonian

On June 28, 1995, following over a year of public controversy, the Smithsonian Institution's National Air and Space Museum, the most attended museum in the world, opened its *Enola Gay* exhibit, which featured a section of the B-29 that dropped the atomic bomb on Hiroshima, Japan, in August 1945. That plane was the main attraction in a commemoration of the bombing and the Allied victory over Japan. In addition, the exhibit featured a 16-minute video in which the crew members stated why they believed that the bombing was both necessary and justifiable.

The exhibit was very different from the one planned by the museum curators. In addition to the *Enola Gay* section, they had intended to display a number of artifacts from Hiroshima and Nagasaki that dramatized the horror of nuclear war—one of them the burned lunch box of a Japanese child who had been killed by the bomb. Their planned exhibit, with about a 35,000–40,000-word text to be placed on placards and wall panels, had sought to summarize the dominant historical interpretation of the bombing and note some of the ongoing disputes about why the bomb was dropped.

That original plan had been initially attacked by the Air Force Association, a veterans group and aerospace lobby, and by other veterans organizations, most notably the 3 million-member American Legion. These critics charged that the exhibit was bad history, anti-American, and antinuclear. They claimed that the exhibit treated the Japanese as "victims" and thus implicitly suggested that the atomic bombings were "atrocities." Fundamentally, most of the critics asserted, there was no question that the use of the atomic bombs had been necessary and just and that the bombs had saved many American and Japanese lives by ending the war before the November 1945 invasion of Kyushu, Japan.

In 1994 and early 1995, the museum had been unable to reach a compromise with its critics. In January 1995, amid mistrust on each side, the museum's director, astrophysicist Martin Harwit, stated that he was going to insert new material into the text noting the army chief of staff's forecast in June 1945 that U.S. forces in the Kyushu operation would suffer no more than 63,000 casualties (dead, wounded, and missing). The Legion was outraged, and veterans organizations soon demanded Harwit's resignation. (He did resign in May 1995.)

In late January 1995 his superior, Smithsonian secretary (director) Ira Michael Heyman, had announced that he was taking over the planned exhibit, canceling the earlier text and Japanese artifacts, and that the scaled-back exhibit would feature the *Enola Gay* and commemorate the atomic bombings and the end of the war. It had been a mistake, he asserted, to try to mix academic analysis with historical commemoration, especially on the 50th anniversary of the bombings. Often critics then charged that Heyman was "selling out," destroying "good history," and yielding to the veterans organizations and Congress. His defenders, in contrast, argued that he had rescued history from severe misinterpretation and was helping save the museum, which depended heavily upon federal funding.

Participants on each side in the controversy had maintained that the dispute was basically about what was good history, who should define it, and how it should be defined. Some on each side agreed that the differences reflected a deep cultural divide in the U.S. Critics of the final exhibit sneeringly called it "patriotically correct," as many of the critics of the earlier planned exhibit had termed that one "politically correct."

(BARTON J. BERNSTEIN)

The new "punk architecture" art museum in the old city centre of Groningen, Neth., masterminded by Alessandro Mendini (designer of the Swatch watch), and the new home of the Bonnefanten Museum in Maastricht, Neth., designed by Aldo Rossi, also won acclaim. The Brooklyn (N.Y.) Museum opened its reinstallation of the African Galleries, and Philadelphia's Museum of Art concluded its three-year-long reinstallation of 80 European art galleries. University museum-expansion projects included the Henry Art Gallery at the University of Washington and the Lowe Art Museum at the University of Miami, Fla. In Egypt the former Nile-side villa of politician and art collector Mahmoud Khalil, which housed his collection of European masters, opened. Other world museums announcing major renovation and expansion plans included London's Tate Gallery, Madrid's Prado, and New York City's American Museum of Natural History and the Whitney Museum of American Art.

New York's Metropolitan Museum of Art received a surprise gift of $35 million—one of the largest in its history—from Frank A. Cosgrove, Jr., while Olga Hirshhorn, widow of the founder of the Hirshhorn Museum and Sculpture Garden in Washington, D.C., promised her 700-work modern art collection to another Washington institution, the Corcoran Gallery of Art. For much of the year, the Smithsonian Institution in Washington was involved in the debate about the *Enola Gay* exhibit. (*See* Sidebar.)

The Los Angeles-based nonprofit Lannan Foundation announced that it would end its exhibition program and disperse its 1,500 works of 20th-century modernist art to the Los Angeles Museum of Contemporary Art, the Chicago Museum of Contemporary Art, and the Art Institute of Chicago. The Boston Museum of Fine Arts met its fiscal deficit by cutting 20% of its personnel and scaling back exhibition activities. The museum also finalized a plan to establish its first foreign branch. In exchange for a 20-year loan of art works, Nagoya, Japan, offered a facility and a $50 million donation to the Boston Museum.

(PATRICK J. BOYLAN; JOSHUA B. KIND)

See also Art, Antiques, and Collections.
This article updates the *Macropædia* article MUSEUMS.

Life Sciences

ZOOLOGY

A keener awareness of global conservation issues emerged during 1995 from research involving a variety of animal groups. In addition, scientists discovered new reproductive traits related to mate selection, parental care, and the induction of egg hatching in several species.

To examine factors that control the presence and absence of animal species on islands and that contribute to the success of colonization, Thomas W. Schoener and David A. Spiller of the University of California, Davis, conducted a difficult but informative experiment. Their objective was to test the relative influence of island size and the presence of predators on the colonization success of prey species. They selected islands from a chain in The Bahamas, of which five each were large ones with predatory lizards, *Anolis sagrei;* large ones without lizards; and small ones without lizards. They selected a common orb spider, *Metepeira datona,* native to the region but absent on all of the test islands, as the artificially introduced prey species. In the first year of the experiment, spiders of both sexes were released on each of the 15 islands, and in the following year three times as many were released. By the end of the five-year experiment, the introduced spiders were extinct on all islands with lizards. One small island still had spiders, and three of the large lizardless islands had enormous spider populations. The investigators concluded that the presence of predators strongly influenced survival success and persistence of spiders. In some ways island size was less important, suggesting that more emphasis in conservation ecology should be given to studying predation effects on islands.

Zoological studies in temperate climates offered evidence that threats to biological diversity and to the environment are global in scale and not confined to tropical terrestrial ecosystems or restricted to less developed countries. Charles Lydeard and Richard L. Mayden of the University of Alabama reported on imperiled aquatic animals of the rivers and streams of the Mobile Basin in the southeastern U.S. They showed that the biodiversity of native fish, aquatic snails, mussels, and turtles in the temperate-zone ecosystem rivals that of many higher-profile tropical systems. The extraordinarily high species diversity found there was attributed to circumstances of the area's surface features and river-drainage history. Many species in the region remained undescribed, and the ecology and life history of the majority were poorly known. Numerous snails and mussels and at least two fish species in the region were known to have become extinct in the past century. Because declines and extirpations of species populations can be directly attributed to general habitat degradation, Lydeard and Mayden emphasized the importance of strengthening environmental protection regulations to safeguard entire ecosystems rather than just particular species.

Karen A. Kidd and David W. Schindler of the University of Alberta and colleagues offered an explanation for the presence of unusually high levels of the pesticide toxaphene in fish from a subarctic lake. The use of toxaphene as an agricultural insecticide and fish-killing agent was discontinued in the U.S. and Canada in the 1980s but continued in Mexico, parts of South America, Africa, and Asia. The chlorinated compound is transported via the atmosphere to Arctic regions and in 1991 was detected in lake trout (*Salvelinus namaycush*), burbot (*Lota lota*), and whitefish (*Coregonus clupeaformis*) from Lake Laberge, Yukon Territory, at levels considered hazardous to human health. Although the same fish species in other lakes in the region also contained toxaphene, levels in the Lake Laberge fish were higher. Kidd, Schindler, and co-workers showed that the higher levels were caused by biological concentration, or biomagnification, of toxaphene up an unusually long food chain. In the other lakes the fish in question eat mostly invertebrates, whereas those in Lake Laberge feed heavily on other fish. By occupying the top of a longer food chain, the Lake Laberge fish accumulate more toxaphene than do the same fish species in other regional lakes.

Bill Amos of the University of Cambridge and colleagues found evidence of mate fidelity in the gray seal (*Halichoerus grypus*), generally considered a purely polygynous species in which males compete with each other for territories and mates. Seals born on the island of North Rona, Scotland, were genetically analyzed to determine which pups were full siblings—*i.e.,* shared the same father and mother. The number was high, although dominant males in the breeding colony fathered an unexpectedly small proportion of the full sibs, indicating significant partnering between females and subordinate males. The investigators concluded that although some males are polygynous, many show partner fidelity, mating with the same female year after year. Partner fidelity should increase survival rates of seal pups by reducing fights between males over females, which by disturbing the clan are often a major cause of pre-weaning deaths.

Rudolf Diesel and Gernot Bäurle of the University of Bielefeld, Germany, and Peter Vogel of the University of the West Indies, Kingston, Jamaica, reported the first known instance in which frogs breed in caves and transport their fully developed young to the outside. The investigators observed male Jamaican frogs (*Eleutherodactylus cundalli*) calling from as far back as 87 m (285 ft) from the cave entrance to attract females. After mating, females laid eggs in the cave in total darkness, attended them for about a month, and then carried the hatchlings out of the cave on their backs. Egg laying in caves and the subsequent transport of newborn frogs were theorized to have evolved as a way to maintain developing eggs in a relatively predator-free environment and then to place the young in a productive habitat after birth.

Karen M. Warkentin of the University of Texas reported the first known instance in which egg hatching is induced by a predator. The red-eyed tree frog (*Agalychnis callidryas*) of Middle America lays eggs on leaves overhanging temporary ponds. At hatching, which occurs 5 to 10 days after the eggs are laid, the tadpoles drop into the water below. The primary predator of the eggs is the cat-eyed snake (*Leptodeira septentrionalis*), whereas fish and other animals prey on the tadpoles. Older hatchlings were found to be less vulnerable to aquatic predators than younger ones; therefore, later hatching favoured the survival of tadpoles. In experiments comparing the timing of hatching, most undisturbed eggs hatched late, but eggs under attack by snakes were seen to hatch within minutes, sometimes seconds. The escaping tadpoles entered the water at a more vulnerable stage but managed to avoid egg predators. Such plasticity in an animal's life history can be highly advantageous. A hatching age that changes with conditions to maximize survivorship should increase fitness in a variable environment.

(J. WHITFIELD GIBBONS)

WALTER GEHRING—SCIENCE

An extra eye grows from the antenna (below the normal eye) of a fruit fly. Scientists announced in 1995 that they had found the "master control gene" for eye development and had been able to demonstrate its effects by activating the gene in various tissues of the fly embryo.

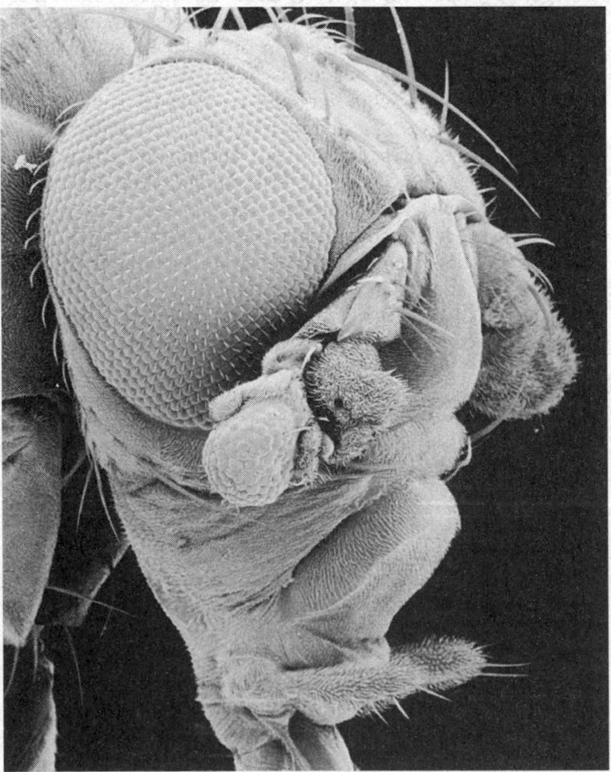

Entomology. Most modern insects possess wings and can fly. The evolutionary development of wings and flight in insects, however, is obscure because of the lack of transitional forms between earlier wingless and later winged forms in the fossil record. To demonstrate a possible intermediate step in wing evolution, James H. Marden and Melissa G. Kramer of Pennsylvania State University investigated primitive aquatic insects called stoneflies that have wings but do not fly. *Taeniopteryx burksi* move across water by surface skimming, with the body supported by water but propelled forward by the wings. *Allocapnia vivipara* sail across water by raising their wings to catch the wind. In experiments comparing surface-skimming and sailing abilities in stoneflies having artificially shortened wings of various sizes, the researchers found that greater wing area generally resulted in greater speed. They proposed that ancestral stoneflies and other semiaquatic insects used gill structures to move across the water's surface and that over time the advantages of faster surface skimming or sailing favoured an increase in the size of those structures, ultimately leading to wings and wing-powered flight.

The defensive behaviour with which some honeybees (genus *Apis*) respond to attacks by hornets may be an example of coevolution, according to a study carried out in Japan by Masato Ono and colleagues of Tamagawa University, Tokyo. Giant hornets (*Vespa mandarinia japonica*) make orchestrated attacks on other social hymenopterans such as honeybees, which they kill with their mandibles and feed to their larvae. The investigators confirmed that an individual giant hornet marks a bee colony with a pheromone (chemical attractant) from specialized glands. Additional giant hornets then congregate and initiate a slaughter attack. Introduced European honeybees (*A. mellifera*) appear defenseless against the hornets and are killed at rates as high as 40 per minute. Native Japanese honeybees (*A. cerana japonica*), however, can detect the hornet pheromone and change their behaviour by increasing the number of defending bees. More than 500 bees swarm around an attacking hornet, forming a ball whose internal temperature reaches 47° C (117° F), high enough to kill the hornet but not the bees. European bees seem unaware of the hornet pheromone and do not respond effectively to the hornet attacks. The differential responses of the two bee species suggest that the Japanese honeybees have coevolved with the predator and developed an effective defense.

The evolutionary history of symbiotic relationships between fungus-growing ants (tribe Attini) and their fungi was investigated by Ulrich G. Mueller and colleagues of Cornell University, Ithaca, N.Y., and the U.S. Department of Agriculture. Using ribosomal DNA analysis and morphological characteristics to compare phylogenies, or evolutionary family trees, for the ants and their fungi, they concluded that whereas the ants originated from a single ancestral form, the cultivated fungi had more than one ancestral line, which indicated that ants developed symbiotic relationships with different fungal lineages. They also found that the less primitive, generally more specialized species, including the leaf-cutting ants, have been associated with the same fungal lineage for at least 23 million years. In a related study Mitchell Sogin of Woods Hole (Mass.) Marine Biological Laboratory and colleagues, using ribosomal RNA analysis, concluded that the less-primitive leaf-cutting ant species and their fungal symbionts have undergone long-term coevolution. A notable feature of the relationship that exists between ants and fungi is that one symbiont may be inconspicuous yet be essential to the survival of the other.

(ANNE R. GIBBONS)

This article updates the *Macropædia* article INSECTS.

Ornithology. Identifying the factors that regulate the number of birds of a particular species breeding in a particular area has been a difficult task but is one of fundamental importance in the study of the natural regulation of animal numbers. I. Newton of the Institute of Terrestrial Ecology, part of the U.K. Natural Environment Research Council, reviewed the results of experiments on the limitation of the densities of breeding birds. In general, densities can be limited by resources such as food or suitable nest sites or held at a lowered level by predators, parasites, or other natural enemies. Among a group of 18 experiments in which supplementary winter food was provided by the experimenter, 11 showed an increase in nesting-season densities compared with control areas. Four experiments in which the summer food of insect-eating forest birds was depleted by the use of insecticides resulted in no reduction in the density of nesting pairs. In a third group of experiments in which additional nest sites (boxes) were provided, density increased in 30 cases out of 32. Among experiments in which natural predators of the birds were removed, 14 out of 15 led to increased hatching success, 4 out of 8 to higher post-breeding numbers, and 6 out of 11 to increased breeding density. Taken together, the experiments confirmed that all major potential external limiting factors can affect breeding density of one bird species or another. They also confirmed that a particular species limited by one factor in certain years or areas may be limited by a different factor in other years or areas.

It was well known that birds act as important dispersers of plant seeds by voiding not only the seeds of consumed fruit but also the remains of the fruit material, which has been converted into useful fertilizer. That a fruit has evolved to contain a laxative for speeding the seed through the bird's digestive system was revealed for the first time by Greg Murray of Hope College, Holland, Mich. He showed that the fruits of *Witheringia solanacea,* a Central American bush, pass quickly through the gut of the black-faced solitaire (*Myadestes melanops*) of Panama and Costa Rica and are thus more likely to germinate.

Newly discovered bird species included the chestnut-bellied cotinga (*Doliornis remseni*), a thrush-sized fruit eater from the Andes of Ecuador, and the diademed tapaculo (*Scytalopus schulenbergi*), a small, secretive, fast-running bird of the cloud forest, which was discovered near La Paz, Bolivia, but later was shown to be common at 900 m (3,000 ft) altitude and above in Bolivia and neighbouring Peru. In a semideciduous Brazilian forest was found a previously unknown member of the Tyrannidae (the tyrant flycatcher family), which was named the Bahia tyrannulet (*Phylloscartes beckeri*). Brazil also yielded a new nighthawk, *Chordeiles viellardi,* a bird of the caatinga vegetation common in the state of Bahia. From Africa was reported a new nightjar (a close relative of the nighthawk, both groups being insect feeders active at dawn and dusk) dubbed the Nechisar nightjar (*Caprimulgus solala*). Nechisar is a plain in southern Ethiopia. The Indian Ocean revealed a new long-winged seabird, the Mascarene shearwater (*Puffinus atrodorsalis*).

The monumental, nine-volume *The Birds of the Western Palearctic* (*i.e.,* Europe, North Africa, and the Middle East), easily the most detailed reference to the birds of any major region of the Earth, was completed with publication of its last two volumes. The first volume had appeared in 1977. In total the series covered 770 species. (JEFFERY BOSWALL)

This article updates the *Macropædia* article BIRDS.

MARINE BIOLOGY

Studies reported from the Finnish research vessel *Aranda* in 1995 demonstrated a reversal of a recent trend detected in the Gotland Basin of the Baltic Sea toward reduced oxygen and increased hydrogen sulfide concentrations in the water of the basin. In 1993 a major inflow of North Sea water had occurred, and it was thought that the event created favourable preconditions for even small subsequent inflows to increase oxygen concentration drastically in the basin. Another report focusing on northern Europe presented the results of a comprehensive analysis of the effects of offshore gas and oil exploration and production on bottom-living animals of the Norwegian continental shelf. The study showed that oil-based drilling fluid resulted in severe depletion of key species, some of which serve as food for bottom-living fish. Whereas replacement organisms were abundant, they were too small and too deeply burrowing to serve as substitute food for fish. In work in the U.S., researchers reported that the oyster population in the Maryland portion of Chesapeake Bay had fallen 50-fold since the early 1900s. The decline was blamed on habitat destruction and overfishing, not on worsening water quality and disease, as had been previously thought.

Phytoplankton is the plantlike part of the community of the generally minute, drifting organisms called plankton that live at or near the water's surface. Japanese workers showed for the first time that phytoplankton growth can be inhibited by cell-to-cell contact with another organism. The phytoplanktonic flagellate *Gyrodinium instriatum* was observed to be killed by contact with a species of *Heterocapsa,* one of the dinoflagellates responsible for the toxic blooms called red tides that occasionally discolour the ocean. A recently described dinoflagellate, *Pfiesteria piscicida,* was implicated as a causative agent of major fish kills in the southeastern U.S. *Pfiesteria* responded to as-yet-unidentified substances secreted from fish schools by producing toxins that in laboratory assays proved lethal to 19 species of native and exotic finfish and shellfish. U.S. scientists reported a severe decline (80% since 1951) in the biomass of zooplankton, the animal-like component of plankton, in the ocean off southern California. The decline was correlated with a rise in ocean surface temperatures of more than 1.5° C (2.7° F) in some areas. The warming was thought to have caused zooplankton reduction, and a consequent decline in abundance of fish and some birds in the region, by slowing cold-water upwellings that replenish the surface waters with nitrates and other nutrients.

In a U.K. study miniature acoustic transponders wrapped in bait were released on the seafloor from an autonomous vehicle at depths of 1,500–4,000 m (4,900–13,100 ft) in the Porcupine Sea Bight of the North Atlantic. Photographs of deep-sea fish taking the baits and sonar records of signals from the swallowed transponders showed that the fish moved out of range of the sonar in three to nine hours, which indicated that they had no home range or territorial behaviour. New threats to the survival of the so-called living fossil known as the coelacanth (*Latimeria chalumnae*) were reported. In its protected habitats around the island of Grande Comore in the Comoros, the rare lobe-finned fish was being illegally taken by local fishermen who were unable to move their motorized canoes out from shore beyond the designated coelacanth-protection zone.

Maltese studies revealed the first occurrence in the Mediterranean Sea of "imposex," a phenomenon observed in marine snails whereby females became masculinized and unable to reproduce. This threat to species survival was caused by tributyl tin, until recently a commonly used antifoulant compound in marine paints. Such findings continued to spur searches for less toxic antifoulants, including compounds made naturally by marine organisms. The presence of such a natural antifoulant was suggested in studies in the U.K. of the egg cases of a shark species, the dogfish *Scyliorhinus canalicula,* which were found to survive cleanly in the sea for as long as 300 days before hatching. Similar properties of resistance to marine fouling were also reported for ascidians, marine animals commonly called sea squirts.

In Australia the large herbivorous marine mammals known as dugongs (*Dugong dugon*) were seen to practice "cultivation grazing." They fed intensively in large herds in a manner that favoured rapidly growing, nutritious algae such as *Halophila ovalis*. As a result, those algal species thrived at the expense of slower growing, normally dominant species such as *Zostera capricorni,* which the dugongs favoured less. A female green turtle (*Chelonia mydas*) was fitted with a radio transponder and tracked by satellite in the South China Sea from its nesting beach to its normal foraging grounds more than 600 km (370 mi) away. The final 475-km (295-mi) leg of the journey brought the turtle directly to its goal with pinpoint accuracy, the animal maintaining constant speed and direction by day and night. The best explanation for such precise orientation seemed to be a geomagnetic compass similar to that previously reported in birds, honeybees, and other animals. (ERNEST NAYLOR)

This article updates the *Macropædia* articles CRUSTACEANS; FISHES; MOLLUSKS; etc.

BOTANY

The publication in June of *Botany for the Next Millennium* by the Botanical Society of America (BSA) was a landmark in the history of botany. The report, the result of a collaboration of the BSA and nine other scientific societies that represented diverse interests ranging from mycology and lichenology to taxonomy and chemical ecology, established a framework for identifying research and educational goals, priorities, and opportunities in the botanical sciences on the eve of the 21st century. One set of goals addressed what the report called "vigor of the profession" and suggested actions that would help maintain botany's record of achievement and discovery. A second set addressed "continuity of the profession" and included actions designed to attract future botanists and support their training. A third set spoke to "integration into the community" in order to broaden the relevance of botanical knowledge beyond academia. The report was needed because, although plants and plant products were ubiquitous in daily life, botany was underemphasized in biology curricula at all levels of education. The brief (54-page), easily readable publication was expected to spur improvements in botanical education and help focus research efforts in the coming years.

Within the space of eight months, the U.S. journal *Science* produced two special issues focusing on subjects important to botany. One reviewed recent discoveries in plant biotechnology, and the other dealt with aspects of developmental biology. By 1995 plant biotechnology had become an emerging and rapidly expanding field in which the techniques of the molecular biologist were being applied to practical problems in plant science. Reports in one of the special issues included descriptions of plants that had been genetically engineered to synthesize specific substances that stimulate the animal immune system, with the eventual goal of making plant-produced vaccines against human diseases. There was even speculation that vaccines could be built into plants that then would be eaten as part of a normal diet. Other reports described ways in which biotechnology was helping to transform the concept of plant-based raw materials. For instance, researchers engineered cotton plants to produce natural fibres incorporating some of the desired characteristics of synthetic polyesters. Other potential products from engineered plants included naturally produced biodegradable plastics and industrial lubricants. Among the more promising studies were those aimed at a better understanding of plant disease-resistance mechanisms and the pertinent genes so that plants might be better equipped to protect themselves against the wide array of disease organisms that attack them. At the very least, such studies could lead to novel strategies for plant-disease control and less reliance on traditional chemical pesticides.

No matter how complex the form of a mature organism, all sexually reproducing organisms, after fertilization, begin as single cells called zygotes, which are nearly spherical in shape. In higher plants, once fertilization has been achieved, the zygote begins to differentiate into an embryo. Polarity, the development of recognizably different ends, begins with the first cell division. Although the precise genetic and molecular mechanisms that result in embryo formation and polarity were still poorly understood, major insights were gained from recent studies of plant embryo mutants and others that used molecular approaches. These were summarized in the *Science* special issue on development by Robert Goldberg and collaborators of the University of California, Los Angeles. Taken together, the research suggested that the structure of a developing plant embryo is modular, with several regions forming independently.

Parasitism, an association between two different organisms in which one benefits at the expense of the other, is widespread in nature. Mutualism, an association in which both organisms benefit, is also widespread although less commonly noticed. Mutualism is a characteristic of a large group of plantlike organisms called lichens, which develop as an association between an alga and a fungus. The alga photosynthesizes and produces food for the fungus, which in turn absorbs water and perhaps supplies other benefits to the algal partner. It had been accepted by many that lichen associations probably started as parasitic associations, which in the course of evolution transformed into mutualistic ones. A collaborative study among scientists of the Smithsonian Institution, Washington, D.C., Graz (Austria) University, and the University of Stockholm challenged that idea. By comparing DNA sequences taken from different fungus species, including lichen-derived fungi, and using the relationships to construct a fungal family tree, they showed that the alga-fungus association originated independently at least five times and involved very different groups of fungi whose lifestyles range from benign to parasitic. On the basis of such results, the authors found no support for the frequently expressed notion that mutualism must begin with parasitism. (PHILIP D. REID)

MOLECULAR BIOLOGY

Mitochondria, Aging, and Disease. Aptly called the powerhouses of the cell, mitochondria are the organelles responsible for most of the cell's respiration and energy production. They possess their own DNA that is distinct from that which makes up the chromosomes of the cell nucleus. In 1995 more evidence of the importance of this "other genome" came to light as researchers continued studying mitochondrial genetics and its role in aging and disease.

About the size and shape of bacilli, mitochondria are bound by two membranes, as are some bacteria. Indeed, it is likely that mitochondria arose from an ancient symbiosis between a bacterium and a primitive amoeba-like cell. As befits an association that has lasted a billion years, there have been accommodations. For example, the bacterial symbiont lost its cell wall, which was superfluous in the protected environment provided by the host cell. Also, its inner membrane became corrugated, increasing greatly in surface area to accommodate the extra molecular machinery required for meeting the energy needs of the host cell. The host cell, for its part, took over most of the biochemical chores for the symbiont's replication and maintenance. The host benefited from the ability of the symbiont to trap the abundant energy released during aerobic respiration—the oxygen-dependent breakdown of foodstuff molecules—while the symbiont benefited from the stable environment and nutrients supplied by its host. The association has proved highly successful, as evidenced by its numerous and diverse progeny, which constitute all macroscopic life on Earth.

There are hundreds of mitochondria in the average cell. Perhaps as a relic of its symbiotic origin, each mitochondrion retains a bit of its own DNA, which codes for 13 different proteins and 24 different RNA molecules that assist in protein synthesis. It retains the ability to replicate its DNA and make its proteins, which are essential components of its energy-producing and energy-trapping functions.

Both egg and sperm cells contain mitochondria. During fertilization in humans and in nearly all other animal species, however, the mitochondria of the sperm are not incorporated into the fertilized egg. Consequently, mitochondrial genes are transmitted to offspring only by the mother.

DNA, the repository of the genetic information of the cell, is not a perfectly stable storage medium, and changes can creep in for a variety of reasons. Cells go to great lengths to minimize such changes and to repair those that do occur. Yet some changes persist and, if they are transmitted to progeny, are the cause of mutations, which often are deleterious.

Mitochondrial DNA is at greater risk of mutation than is nuclear DNA. The reasons remained to be fully understood, but it was clear that damage accumulates in mitochondrial DNA 10–20 times faster. Such damage, as investigators were learning, is involved in senescence—*i.e.,* the biological changes related to aging—and disease.

A decrease in the usable energy available to cells and tissues as they age would necessarily undermine their function, and a decline in mitochondrial integrity would certainly curtail that energy supply. When researchers looked for evidence to support the idea that mitochondrial integrity declines with age, they found it. Mitochondria isolated from aged animals were seen to be enlarged, full of cavities (vacuoles), and lacking in the degree of inner-membrane corrugation seen in the mitochondria of young animals. Senescent mitochondria also were fragile and less likely to survive the isolation procedure itself, which means that the most severely affected mitochondria were likely underrepresented in the observations.

In spite of the difficulty in isolating senescent mitochondria, scientists detected a number of age-related losses of function, including less-efficient coupling of respiration to the production of useful energy and a decline in the activities of enzymes crucial to respiration. Furthermore, they found that mitochondrial DNA from aged animals contain a variety of genetic damage, which can reduce or destroy mitochondrial function.

How is it that the cell can tolerate such damage at all? The answer lies in the large numbers of mitochondria in each cell and of DNA molecules in each mitochondrion. Damage thus has a graded effect, with a little cumulative damage causing little loss of function for the cell and more damage causing more loss. Different tissues are dependent to different degrees on the metabolic energy production by mitochondria and will reflect to different degrees the cumulative damage to their mitochondria. Whereas damage to mitochondrial DNA in somatic (nonreproductive) cells may be a problem for the individual, it will not be passed on to offspring. On the other hand, damage that occurs in egg cells may or may not be transmitted to progeny. Why is this the case?

The fertilized egg contains about 200,000 molecules of mitochondrial DNA. In the early stages of development, however, cells divide without replicating their mitochondrial DNA; consequently, the number of copies per cell falls dramatically. Each cell destined to give rise to different tissues in the developing embryo thus receives a relatively small number of molecules of mitochondrial DNA. If that DNA is seriously defective, the result is death; if it is moderately defective, the result is transmission of a genetic disease.

The first mitochondrial disease was described in the 1960s by investigators who were attempting to understand the symptoms of an extremely emaciated, weak, feverish patient who consumed enormous amounts of food and liquids and sweated profusely. Her basal metabolic rate was nearly double the normal value. After eliminating hyperthyroidism as the possible cause, the investigators realized that her symptoms might be explained by "uncoupled" mitochondria—that is, mitochondria in which respiration was liberating energy from foodstuffs but not trapping it in metabolically useful form. Indeed, when mitochondria from muscle tissue of the patient were isolated, they were found to be uncoupled.

This pioneering discovery opened the door to the field of mitochondrial diseases. Other investigators followed the lead, linking mitochondrial defects with maladies such as Kearns-Sayre syndrome, chronic external opthalmoplegia, and myoclonic epilepsy and ragged red-fibre disease. In 1995 medical science knew of about 120 mitochondrial diseases. As expected, they are maternally inherited, and they tend to affect specific tissues because of the different dependence of various tissues on mitochondrial energy production. Many make their appearance only later in life because the defects that accumulate with age add to those that are inherited and must reach a critical threshold level before symptoms appear.

Knowledge of the cause of a problem often leads to a solution. Consequently, researchers were optimistic that their growing appreciation of the complexities of mitochondrial genetics would eventually produce practical benefits.

(IRWIN FRIDOVICH)

Telomeres: New Beginnings from Old Ends. A major distinction between prokaryotes, or bacteria, and eukaryotes, or so-called higher organisms made of nucleated cells, is the manner in which they arrange the DNA of their genetic endowment, or genome. Bacteria generally maintain their genomes as circular molecules, whereas animals and plants maintain their nuclear genomes as collections of linear molecules, called chromosomes. Although a linear architecture has its benefits, it also presents problems—perhaps most notably, what to do about the ends.

The trouble with having ends is at least twofold. First, free ends on DNA molecules are notoriously unstable; they degrade chemically and undergo recombination much more often than their non-end, protected counterparts. Second, the DNA polymerase enzyme that is responsible for replicating the nuclear genome during cell proliferation has difficulty copying the very ends of DNA molecules, so without special precaution the end molecular sequences tend to be lost in the copies. To circumvent the problems, eukaryotic cells cap their chromosomes at both ends with specialized structures called telomeres. New evidence gathered in a number of laboratories suggests that telomeres and the enzyme or enzymes that create and maintain them play key roles in cellular aging and the immortalization of cells so often associated with cancer.

The first telomere was isolated in the 1970s from the single-celled ciliated protozoan *Tetrahymena thermophila*. It was found to consist of 50–70 tandem copies of the short DNA base sequence TTGGGG (T is the base thymine; G is guanine). Both the structure and sequence were considered peculiar at the time, but subsequent work with many different organisms served to validate and extend the observations. For example, all mammals examined as of 1995, including humans, carry the repeated sequence TTAGGG (A is adenine) in their telomeres. Indeed, not only do telomeric sequences from different organisms look alike, but they also may function alike. This was first demonstrated when linear pieces of DNA carrying ciliate-derived telomeres were put into cells of yeast, an extremely distant relative of ciliates. The ends of the DNA remained stable; in other words, the ciliate telomeres worked in yeast. With time, however, the ciliate-derived telomeric sequences eroded and were replaced by the corresponding yeast sequences.

The gradual erosion of the ciliate-derived telomeric sequences suggested that telomeres do not escape the fate of unprotected DNA ends during cell replication; they simply buffer the loss. Indeed, telomeric sequences made of multiple repeats are, in retrospect, very logical; such sequences can be at least partially sacrificed without losing genetic information. That the eroded ciliate sequences were replaced by yeast counterparts indicated that the repeats are not only expendable but also renewable by means of a cellular activity that is independent of the sequence of existing repeats. That activity was found to be carried out by a most unusual enzyme, named telomerase, that consists of both RNA and protein. Subsequent experiments involving the ciliate *Tetrahymena* revealed that if telomerase is inactivated (by a mutation, for example), the telomeres in the mutant cells grow shorter and shorter; moreover, the single-celled organisms, which normally do not have a finite life span, eventually die. In other words, in the absence of functional telomerase, the length of a cell's telomeres appears to have an inverse relationship to its age.

The mortality of human beings and most other living creatures is a characteristic not only of the body as a whole but also of most of the body's cells, even cultured cells. Although aging is clearly a complex process that likely reflects the interactions of many genes and environmental factors, a variety of recent observations imply a role for telomeres and telomerase in the replicative senescence of cells. For example, it was found that proliferating cultured human fibroblasts, which normally die after a finite number of divisions, lack telomerase activity; as they age, their telomeres become gradually, and ultimately profoundly, shorter. Similar observations were made for somatic cells functioning normally in the body; in other words, chromosomes from the cells of younger people tend to have longer telomeres, while those from older people tend to have shorter ones. This is consistent with the general observation that cells taken from younger donors tend to live longer in culture than do cells from older donors. Indeed, in a study of cultured fibroblasts from 31 donors ranging from newly born to 93 years in age, investigators saw a striking correlation between initial telomere length in the donated cells and ultimate proliferative capacity. In addition, they found that telomeres from fibroblasts donated by Hutchinson-Gilford progeria patients, who experience abnormally rapid aging, were unusually short.

In contrast to the findings in somatic cells, studies of normal human and nonhuman cells that are naturally "immortal," namely, germ, or reproductive cells, revealed that the telomeres of those cells appear to be stable with time. For example, telomeres from normal human sperm do not shorten with age, which suggests that some mechanism such as telomerase activity maintains telomere length. Consistent with this idea, telomerase activity was directly observed in frogs' eggs. All this information taken together suggests that telomerase activity is generally absent from normal mortal cells, which thus experience replicative telomere shortening, but is found in normally immortal cells, such as protozoans or germ cells. If this is true, what then of normally mortal cells that become immortalized, such as cancer cells?

The potential role of telomeres and telomerase in cancer has been revealed in at least two ways. First, experiments were conducted in which normal cultured cells, which lacked telomerase activity, were exposed to oncogenic (cancer-inducing) DNA sequences derived from tumour viruses. Whereas most of the cells died after a number of replications, some continued to divide without limit, presumably owing to transformation by the viral DNA. Under examination the telomeres of the newly immortalized populations were found to be stable with time, and telomerase activity was observed. The results suggested that the switching on of telomerase activity, presumably by activation of one or more otherwise silent genes, might be part of the process whereby normal cells are transformed into cancer cells.

A second line of information came from studies of cells taken directly from tumours removed from patients. Again, in sets of matched cells derived either from tumours or from the corresponding normal tissues, telomerase activity was found in tumour cells but not in normal cells.

These studies offered considerable food for thought about how telomere shortening interacts with other factors involved in the aging process, for both replicating and nonreplicating cells. On a much more practical note, they pointed to telomerase as a possible new target for anticancer drugs. Indeed, during the year researchers worked to develop specific and effective inhibitors against the enzyme, following the logic that if telomerase can be inactivated in tumour cells, the cells may become mortal again and eventually die. Because most normal cells already lack telomerase activity, a truly specific inhibitor should cause them little if any harm. (JUDITH FRIDOVICH-KEIL)

PALEONTOLOGY

Paleontological discoveries during the year shed light on the phylogeny of living and extinct organisms. Neil H. Shubin of the University of Pennsylvania and Farish A. Jenkins, Jr., of Harvard University reported the discovery of the fossilized remains of a jumping frog from the Early Jurassic Kayenta formation of Arizona. The species, which the investigators named *Prosalirus bitis,* lived about 190 million years ago. Although the fossil retained some of the primitive characters of earlier amphibians, certain features of the pelvic girdle, legs, and feet were clearly indicative of saltatory, or leaping, locomotion. The investigators concluded that the species unquestionably belonged within the Anura, the frog and toad order, and was the order's earliest known member.

The question of whether dinosaurs were endothermic or ectothermic (warm-blooded or cold-blooded) has long been an issue of intense debate. The physiology of endothermic animals enables them to maintain a nearly constant body temperature in the face of varying environmental conditions and, as a result, to maintain high levels of activity. Among ectothermic animals, on the other hand, body temperature and, consequently, level of activity vary significantly under changing conditions. Although dinosaurs originally had been thought to be ectothermic, like living reptiles, some paleontologists had argued, largely on the basis of skeletal characteristics, that they were endothermic, like birds and mammals.

John Ruben of Oregon State University and his former student Williem Hillenius took a stride toward possibly resolving the issue. They proposed that the key lay in the respiratory turbinates, which are found in the nasal passages of living mammals and birds but are absent in living reptiles. These bony plates, which in life are covered with a thin membrane, provide a large surface of exposed tissue. The tissue and the blood that it contains are cooled by inhaled air and then are reheated as warm air is exhaled, thus providing an important mechanism for maintaining body temperature. Because the turbinates are delicate, they are seldom preserved in fossils. According to Ruben and Hillenius, however, the turbinates are attached to a distinct ridge of bone in the nasal passage, which the investigators identified in fossil mammals dating back to the origin of the class in the Jurassic Period some 160 million years ago. On the other hand, they found no such evidence in the dinosaur fossils that they examined. Opponents argued that dinosaurs still may have had turbinates or may have evolved other mechanisms of thermoregulation. Whatever the outcome of the debate over dinosaurs, the findings of Ruben and Hillenius were an important contribution to scientific knowledge of the physiology of fossil vertebrates.

Paleontologists have long been puzzled by the so-called Cambrian explosion some 540 million years ago, when most of the great phyla that were to dominate the subsequent history of life appeared, in geologic terms, quite suddenly. Whereas many Precambrian fossils were known, none of them contributed much to an understanding of the remarkable increase in animal diversity at the start of the Cambrian Period. During the year a report drawn from knowledge of developmental biology offered an explanation for the lack of any evidence that would presage the dramatic events that were to occur at the beginning of the Cambrian. E. Davidson and R.A. Cameron of the California Institute of Technology and K. Peterson of the University of California, Los Angeles, argued that before such wide diversification could occur, organisms had to overcome a barrier that limited their size and complexity by restricting to about 10 the number of times a fertilized egg could divide. According to the authors, the solution lay in the appearance of cells, of a kind found in the embryos of some organisms living today, that are not destined to develop into a particular kind of tissue. It was those cells, the authors contended, that may have provided an opportunity for the evolution of much larger and more complex organisms. Davidson and his colleagues concluded that this crucial development would have taken place in soft-bodied, embryolike animals, which almost never would have left any trace, hundreds of millions of years before the Cambrian explosion.

Clusters of fossil dinosaur eggs presumed to be the remains of nests have been known for decades. A discovery in south central Mongolia, however—an example of the recent continuing Chinese-U.S. cooperation—appeared to demonstrate that dinosaurs not only laid eggs in clutches but tended to them as well. In a press conference at the American Museum of Natural History, New York City, it was announced that the skeletal remains of an oviraptor, a toothless predaceous dinosaur about the size of an ostrich, were found positioned with at least 15 eggs in such a way as to suggest that the animal had been sitting on the eggs when it was killed in some catastrophic event, perhaps a sandstorm, in the late Cretaceous Period about 80 million years ago. The eggs, which measured about 18 cm (7 in) long, were found arranged in a circular pattern under the skeleton. Mark Norell of George Washington University, Washington, D.C., who found the specimen, pointed out that, judging from the skeleton, oviraptors were more closely related to birds than to other meat-eating dinosaurs—which perhaps accounted for the birdlike brooding behaviour.

(DAVID B. KITTS)

See also Earth and Space Sciences; The Environment; Libraries and Museums; Mathematical and Physical Sciences: *Chemistry*.

This article updates the *Macropædia* articles Animal BEHAVIOUR; BIOCHEMICAL COMPONENTS OF ORGANISMS; The BIOLOGICAL SCIENCES; BIOSPHERE; CANCER; CELLS; CONSERVATION OF NATURAL RESOURCES; DISEASE; The Theory of EVOLUTION; The Principles of GENETICS AND HEREDITY; GEOCHRONOLOGY; GROWTH AND DEVELOPMENT; MAMMALS; PLANTS; REPRODUCTION AND REPRODUCTIVE SYSTEMS; SENSORY RECEPTION.

MARK A. PURNELL AND PHILLIP DONOGHUE

A model of the feeding apparatus of an extinct conodont suggests how the separate elements may have functioned as teeth in the primitive vertebrate. Scientists interpreted wear marks found on fossil conodont elements as evidence that the first vertebrates were predators.

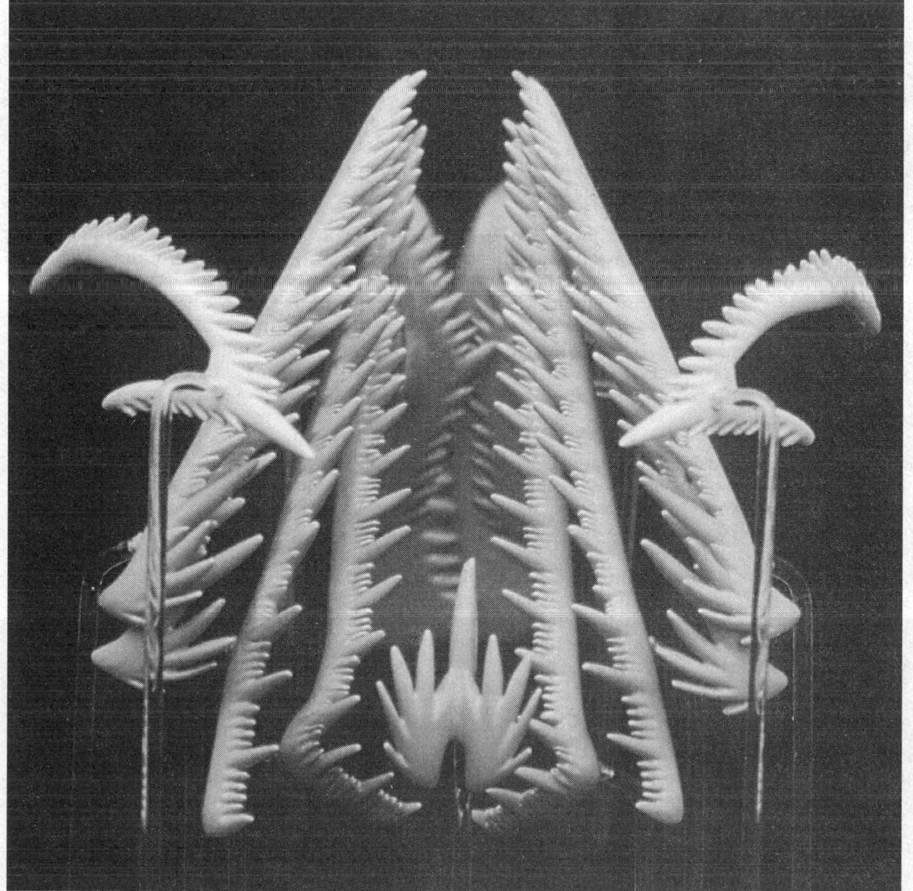

Literature

The 1995 Nobel Prize for Literature was awarded to the Irish poet Seamus Heaney. (*See* NOBEL PRIZES.) Heaney had moved his home from Northern Ireland, part of the United Kingdom, across the border to the Irish republic. Nevertheless, he remained perhaps the most respected and admired poet in the U.K., better known than any other poet of the flourishing Northern Irish school. His award was generally reckoned to be associated with the recent successes in furthering peace in the troubled island. Earlier in the year, John Redmond had written in the *London Review of Books* about the continuing achievements of Northern Irish poetry, observing that the poetry displayed "the kind of integrity and intertextuality which English poetry last had in the Thirties." He recognized that some attributed the phenomenon to "the concentrating pressure of 'The Troubles' "—that being the euphemistic term for the political violence that had, for so long, disfigured Ireland. Redmond held, however, that an equally important factor was "the symbolic coherence of Northern Irish poetry"—"poets as diverse as Heaney, [Paul] Muldoon and [Derek] Mahon are to a certain degree sustained by a single symbolic world." Asked by an interviewer about the Troubles, the prizewinning Heaney replied, "That's all over now." Some, however, remembered his poetic reference to an atrocity committed by the Irish rebels as the "tribal, intimate revenge" and held that Heaney was too tolerant of such activities.

Wole Soyinka, the Nobel laureate of 1986, drew attention to the troubles of his own homeland, Nigeria, from which he was exiled. His play *The Beatification of Area Boy* had been banned by the Nigerian military government, and it received its world premiere in Britain at the West Yorkshire Playhouse. The production, a comedy about petty rogues and large-scale corruption in Nigeria, was broadcast by BBC radio. Soyinka, a strong opponent of several Nigerian governments since the nation gained independence in 1960, expressed his sympathy for another Nigerian playwright, his friend Ken Saro-Wiwa (*see* OBITUARIES), who with eight others was executed for alleged complicity in the murders of four chieftains in the oil-rich Ogoni territory.

Saro-Wiwa had long been a leader of the Ogoni protest movement against the spoliation of the area by the oil company Shell and its friends in the government. Although many held him to be innocent of the murder charges, it was his status as a writer that seemed to stimulate international opinion against his execution. At a meeting of Commonwealth heads of government, Nigeria was formally suspended from membership. Saro-Wiwa's best-known novel was *Sozaboy* ("Soldier Boy"), a satire on the military government, and he also developed the highly popular television series *Basi and Company,* which was shown on British television. Doubts about Saro-Wiwa's innocence were expressed publicly by a few Britons, including Auberon Waugh, the editor of *Literary Review.*

In France the Prix Goncourt was awarded to Andreï Makine, a 38-year-old Russian novelist living in Paris. His latest novel, *Le Testament français,* concerned a boy trapped between the cultures of France and Russia. It seemed ironic that Makine's application for French citizenship had recently been rejected. It was generally expected, however, that Makine's success, not only in winning the Goncourt but also in sharing the Prix Médicis, would induce the immigration authorities to review their unfavourable decision.

ENGLISH

United Kingdom. The 50th anniversary of the conclusion to World War II, though well marked by public ceremonies, attracted less attention in the world of literature and publishing than might have been expected. The Allied victory, suggested Hew Strachan in the *Times Literary Supplement,* had been overshadowed by the collapse of one of those victorious allies, the Soviet Union; "Thus the notion of the 'short' twentieth century, begun in 1914 and concluded in 1989, diminishes the importance of 1945." Strachan was reviewing *The Oxford Companion to the Second World War,* edited by I.C.B. Dear and M.R.D. Foot, which he described as "an outstanding guide, as sensible and cogent on the big questions as it is instructive and informed on the lesser ones." There were, of course, other compendious new accounts of the war. Martin Gilbert's *The Day the War Ended* was reviewed without enthusiasm by Richard Overy, who himself published a book called *Why the Allies Won. Armageddon: The Second World War,* by Clive Ponting was also received with disfavour in the *Times Literary Supplement* on the grounds that its studied objectivity looked too much like a discreditable neutrality. Such arguments seemed rather narrow and esoteric to the general public. It was interesting to note that Strachan was engaged in writing a history of World War I, for there were indications that 1914–18 had become as fascinating a period for the general reader as 1939–45.

The U.K. publishing world was "convulsed," according to David Sexton in the *Sunday Telegraph,* by the collapse of the price-fixing mechanism known as the Net Book Agreement. Best-sellers were discounted in the shops, and there was a general fear that more ambitious books, with less commercial appeal, would become more difficult to publish. The apparently pleasurable prospect of cheaper books was seen to be accompanied by unexpected disadvantages.

The rumours of a revival of interest in poetry proved to be greatly exaggerated, despite a notable increase in the sales of Heaney's work after he won the Nobel Prize. The bicentenary of the birth of John Keats was marked by several essays in journals and numerous radio broadcasts, but it drew little attention from book publishers. The poet laureate, Ted Hughes, wrote an admiring poem about the Queen Mother on her 95th birthday, comparing her to a six-rooted oak tree, but his verse was received in a mocking spirit. One poet who was accorded serious attention was Robert Graves (1895–1985), a veteran of World War I, a mythopoeic fantasist, and a historical novelist as well as a pure-voiced poet of erotic love. His long, strange life, with his wives and his lovers, was recorded once more in a new biography by Miranda Seymour, while his nephew, R.P. Graves, proffered the third volume of his own biography—*Robert Graves and the White Goddess, 1940–85.* An earlier biography by Martin Seymour-Smith also reappeared in a new edition. The Carcanet Press began a 21-volume reprint program of the poet's work, starting with the first volume of *Collected Poems, Complete Short Stories,* and *Collected Writings on Poetry.* The press also offered *The Centenary Selected Poems,* which was found too limited by Neil Powell in the *Times Literary Supplement,* who called it "rather perverse" in omitting many admired poems. Perplexed by Graves's life, Powell remained impressed by his verse. Mark Ford, on the other hand, writing in the *London Review of Books,* was inclined to dismiss Graves's claim to universal significance and to see his poems only as "symptoms of his personal problems."

The death of Kingsley Amis (*see* OBITUARIES), shortly after the publication of his latest novel, *The Biographer's Moustache,* seemed to mark the end of a significant genre of British fiction, the novel of snobbery. Amis had been the most accomplished writer of these class-conscious comedies since Evelyn Waugh, as interested as Nancy Mitford in the ways a choice of words and their pronunciation could be used to distinguish between "common" people and those thought to be "posh." Such distinctions, made to seem very old-fashioned, lingered on, quite credibly, in *The Biographer's Moustache,* which told of a rather charming elderly novelist confronted by an ambitious young biographer, somewhat dubious about the novelist's worth. The biographer, clever and common, seemed to resemble Amis in his youth, while the novelist, posh and snobbish, reflected certain apparent characteristics of the older Amis. Observant, subtle, and comical, the novel concluded straightforwardly, with a modern girl saying, "Oh, they're really there, all those distinctions are, but . . . it isn't class differences that keep people apart, it's thinking they bloody *matter.*" This might be read as Amis' apologia.

Amis had been a previous winner of the Booker Prize, but his novel did not appear on the shortlist for 1995. Nor did new novels by seven other previous winners, including Penelope Fitzgerald, whose historical novel about the German poet Novalis, *The Blue Flower,* had been much admired. Also omitted, to the surprise of many, was the new novel by Amis' son, Martin Amis, a writer whose career, marital situation, and dealings with publishers attracted great interest among journalists. His book *The Information,* another study of a conflict between two writers, did not appeal to the Booker judges, however.

The Booker candidate most generally favoured was Salman Rushdie, with a new novel about the history of an Indian family in Bombay from the last days of the British Empire to the 1970s. *The Moor's Last Sigh* was an extravagant saga—"a triumph of unnaturalism and a feast for anyone with a strong literary digestion," according to Victoria Glendinning in the *Daily Telegraph.* Though it did not win, Rushdie's novel was nominated for the Whitbread Book of the Year Award, and it was the winner in the fiction section. Barry Unsworth—like Rushdie a previous Booker Prize winner—was another strong contender with a historical novel, *Morality Play,* about a priest in

14th-century England who joins a company of traveling actors; it develops into a sort of detective story, its sombre realism vitiated by rather heavy moralizing.

Justin Cartwright, born in South Africa, was nominated for his sour novel set in London, *In Every Face I Meet,* concerning a failing businessman, who was bred in Africa, and his dealings with a young London prostitute. "Deeply depressing," commented Patrick Gale, "as though Kingsley Amis had turned his hand to tragedy." A fourth contender, from Australia, was Tim Winton (*see* BIOGRAPHIES), who published *The Riders,* an eerie but perhaps sentimental tale of an Australian and his small daughter searching throughout Europe for a missing wife and mother. In the *London Review of Books,* Jonathan Coe called it a "bruising, exultant novel." The winner of the Booker Prize, however, was a woman writing about men at war. *The Ghost Road* was the third volume of Pat Barker's trilogy of World War I. In the book she dealt with the psychological traumas of the ex-combatants and the attempts to heal them. Barker's grasp of military systems and her understanding of the period were much admired. The chairman of the Booker Prize judges, however, after reading 141 new novels, remarked despondently, "Our art hankers after the past. Very few people write with any conviction about the present."

NEIL GRAHAM

Martin Amis

This impression of a fin de siècle world yearning for the past did not receive much support from the year's crop of biographies. There were several lives of writers who had clearly lost their old appeal. Three modern playwrights—Terence Rattigan, William Douglas Home, and Dennis Potter—were rather defensively appreciated. Before Amis' novel *The Biographer's Moustache* was published, a biography of the novelist appeared, written by his genial friend Eric Jacobs. D.J. Taylor, writing in the *Times Literary Supplement,* took strong objection to the book and to its subject: "It would be a brave man who suggested that the life outlined here was particularly edifying or attractive." Margaret Drabble attempted to revive the reputation of a suddenly neglected novelist in her biography of Angus Wilson. "The conflict between Wilson's generous humanity and his apparently selfish delight in extravagant behaviour, in the crazy crowd, is a persistent theme of this large and satisfying biography," wrote Frank Kermode in the *London Review of Books.* He admired Drabble's handling of "the theme of male homosexual social relations" and noted that "there was a freakishness, a habit of clowning, an ebullience that was to become an ingredient of Wilson's huge but, as it turned out, transient popular success." It seemed that Wilson's reputation would not be revived.

The detective story writers Arthur Conan Doyle and Dorothy L. Sayers each received another appraisal, as did that biographers' favourite Lewis Carroll (Charles Lutwidge Dodgson). More contentious perhaps was Ian MacKillop's biography *F.R. Leavis: A Life in Criticism.* The once-authoritative scholar and critic, born a century earlier, was gravely appreciated, his pugnacity and his sense of persecution comprehended. "Notwithstanding MacKillop's avowedly personal attachment to his subject," wrote Dan Jacobson in the *Times Literary Supplement,* "he does as much as anyone could to be fair-minded alike to friends, enemies and friends-late-revealed-as-enemies."

Biographies of an encomiastic sort were published by two senior politicians with once-powerful reputations in the Labour Party. One was Roy Jenkins, who had broken with that party to become cofounder, in 1981, of the Social Democrats; he offered a new life of the scholarly Victorian statesman W.E. Gladstone, who broke with the Conservatives to become a Liberal prime minister. Jenkins was already recognized as an accomplished political biographer, and it was evident that his own ministerial experience had been of value to him in writing the book. The work was much admired, and it was the winner of the biographical section of the Whitbread Award.

The other senior statesman-biographer was Michael Foot, former leader of the Labour Party, who further strengthened his literary credentials with *H.G.: The History of Mr. Wells.* Foot had known H.G. Wells and supported him in many of his political and social campaigns, and the biographer appeared as an advocate for Wells's utopian objectives and achievements. For those readers who had come to think of Wells primarily as a science-fiction romancer and a brilliant comic novelist, Foot's use of long quotations from his half-forgotten pamphlets and fiction supported the appreciation of the literary merits and modern relevance of this prolific author.

(D.A.N. JONES)

United States. Despite a marketplace in turbulent transition, with more and more publishers' advances rising in amount and going to fewer and fewer writers and with large chain stores squeezing out venerable independent bookshops around the nation and these same chains seeming to narrow the range and depth of books available on their shelves, the quality of fiction in the U.S. in 1995 never seemed higher. Looking back on the year's production of novels and stories, one might even detect a shifting of ground, with the writers of the old guard falling back a bit to give way to the vital work of a newer generation.

Among older established American novelists, the prolific Philip Roth produced a powerful book in 1995. After having published his prizewinning novel *Operation Shylock* only two years earlier, Roth brought out *Sabbath's Theater,* as raw and raucous a piece of work as anything in his already prodigious canon. The protagonist of the book was an aging New Jersey-born Jewish puppeteer named Mickey Sabbath who suffered from arthritis in his hands, a nearly constant attack of priapic fever, and a deep self-loathing and an abiding desire to end his life. In scenes ferociously offensive in a sexual way and in soliloquies dark with suicidal menace, Sabbath bullies through the aftermath of a lover's death and, like a drowning man, makes an accounting to himself of his failed life as lover, husband, artist, and son. Roth turned his portrait of the puppeteer as an old roué into a triumph on the side of life—an accomplishment the reader had to applaud and admire. The posthumously published *Mrs. Ted Bliss,* another novel on Jewish motifs, by Stanley Elkin (*see* OBITUARIES) seemed gentle—almost genteel—by comparison.

In a serene sequel to his superb novel *The Sportswriter,* Richard Ford brought back narrator Frank Bascombe in *Independence Day* to tell of the next part of his life. A crafty fusion of subtlety and rampant emotion, Ford's new book showed off the increasing powers of one of the country's best fiction writers.

For other American writers of reputation, the news was not as good in 1995. Anne Tyler in *Ladder of Years* gave readers lacklustre work on the familiar motif of a middle-aged woman groping toward some sort of self-discovery. In *Rule of the Bone,* Russell Banks attempted to produce a modern-day Huckleberry Finn but, despite a promising first half, fell far short of his goal. In *The Tortilla Curtain,* T. Coraghessan Boyle seemed to yearn toward making a contemporary version of *The Grapes of Wrath;* his work was a bold but flawed novel about the clash of new immigrants and the southern Californian middle class. Among commercial writers with household names, Pat Conroy showed up once again on the best-seller lists with his gabby, flabby beach-reading production called, appropriately enough, *Beach Music.* Michael Crichton offered *The Lost World,* a sequel to his best-seller *Jurassic Park,* with much greater success.

Several powerful new works emerged out of the ranks of younger American novelists in 1995. In *All Souls' Rising,* Madison Smartt Bell went back to the events of the Haitian revolution (1791–1804) to create a historical novel of great force and erudition, a book that immediately pushed him into recognition as one of the most serious and accomplished American writers under the age of 40. Turning to the history of her native Puerto Rico for the material of her latest novel, Rosario Ferré in *The House on the Lagoon* made an evocative and sensuous portrait of the island commonwealth with all of the flavour of magical realism and none of the rhetorical excesses. *Wonder Boys* by Michael Chabon appeared to wonderful critical notices and more than fulfilled the promise of the writer's debut novel, *The Mysteries of Pittsburgh.*

Maria Flook, a New England fiction writer and poet, came out with *Open Water,* her second novel, an impressive treatment of the underclass of the Rhode Island coastline. Chris Bohjalian issued *Water Witches,* another novel with a regional locus—the setting was Vermont—that won fine national notices. Hollywood was the setting for Christopher Bram's biographical novel, called *Father of Frankenstein,* on the life of horror movie director James Whale. Susanna Moore's *In the Cut* was a flashy, finely sculptured version of an erotic thriller. Craig Lesley's *The Sky Fisherman* turned some distinctive twists on the western coming-of-age novel set against the Oregon forests.

Among short-story collections, *Skinned Alive,* Edmund White's subtle tales of homosexual life in Europe and the United States, stood out as beautifully polished work. Octogenarian Harriet Doerr's collection of fiction and memoir, *The Tiger in the Grass,* glowed with the incandescence of masterfully measured prose. Lucy Jane Bledsoe demonstrated her powers in a debut volume of stories titled *Sweat,* on female erotic themes. Haitian-American writer Edwidge Danticat won a nomination for a National Book Award with her fresh tales of Caribbean life titled *Krik? Krak!* A first collection by New Jersey writer Rick Moody, *The Ring of Brightest Angels Around Heaven,* showed off a gifted new talent in the short-story form.

Adrienne Rich's latest collection, *Dark Fields of the Republic,* displayed her seemingly ever-increasing gift for the short poem. Her collection also included a number of powerful narrative sequences and once again alerted critics and fellow poets to the richness of her mature work. *A Scattering of Salts* by James Merrill (*see* OBITUARIES) appeared posthumously, signaling the end of the work of one of the U.S.'s elder statesmen of poetry. From others of his generation there were *New & Selected Poems* by Donald Justice, *Collected Poems, 1945–1990* by Barbara Howes, and *Passing Through,* new and selected poems by Stanley Kunitz.

Carol Shields
GERRY KOPELOW

Odd Mercy, a new collection of poetry by Gerald Stern, appeared during the year, as did Deborah Digges's *Rough Music,* William Matthews's *Time & Money,* and Charles Wright's *Chickamauga.* Mark Doty brought out *Atlantis,* Lynda Hull *The Only World,* Billy Collins *The Art of Drowning,* and Gary Soto *New and Selected Poems.* In his new collection *The Hunger Wall,* James Ragan showed off musicality tied to social themes.

In the realm of biography, autobiography, and memoir, 1995 was a year of the master. Norman Mailer published two books, one a massive study of the life of Lee Harvey Oswald—*Oswald's Tale*—half of it based on exclusive access gained by Mailer to the files of the KGB on Oswald. The other book of Mailer's was his work on one of the 20th-century's greatest painters, *Portrait of Picasso as a Young Man. Palimpsest,* the memoir Gore Vidal promised that he would never write, was published in 1995. Vidal took the title from the word for a writing material that has been reused, a revision, or, as he put it in his own words, "a second seeing, an afterthought, erasing some but not all of the original while writing something new over the first layer of text." As gossip *Palimpsest* was titillating; as a portrait of the writer's mind sifting through the shards of memory, it was fascinating. *The Diaries of Dawn Powell, 1931–1965,* edited by Tim Page, was a more conventional, if just as caustic, record of one 20th-century writer's days and nights on the town. Alfred Kazin's *Writing Was Everything* offered an intimate portrait of one of the century's best literary critics. In *All Rivers Run to the Sea,* the English version of Nobel laureate Elie Wiesel's 1994 memoir published

NANCY CRAMPTON
Philip Roth

in French, presented a traditional memoir of his life as a Jew, a refugee, and a writer on historical and sublime themes. Poet and fiction writer Al Young gathered his three volumes of "musical memoirs" under the omnibus title of *Drowning in the Sea of Love* and added additional essays. Novelist Victor Perera successfully traced his Sephardic roots from medieval times onward in *The Cross and the Pear Tree.*

Poet Li-Young Lee brought out a memoir titled *The Winged Seed,* and Garrett Hongo returned to his Hawaiian roots in *Volcano.* In *The Liars' Club,* Mary Karr wrote beautifully about the pain of her early life with her Texas family. Scott Russell Sanders celebrated family life in many of the superb essays in *Writing from the Center.*

Among literary biographies Lyle Leverich's *Tom* turned the spotlight on Tennessee Williams in a book whose publication had been held up for years because of legal battles between the biographer and the Williams estate. Robert D. Richardson, Jr., published *Emerson: The Mind on Fire,* a biography of Ralph Waldo Emerson, to much critical acclaim. Poet Robert Polito demonstrated how much could be made of a minor literary figure in *Savage Art,* a biography of genre writer Jim Thompson. Frederick R. Karl focused on a major British writer in *George Eliot, Voice of a Century.*

Two American painters received lavish attention in books during the year. In *Edward Hopper* art critic Gail Levin produced a 700-page study of the life and work of a subject she had been working on for years. She employed previously unpublished material from diaries kept by Hopper's wife of 43 years. John Loughery's *John Sloan: Painter and Rebel,* on the Armory Show artist, also was published in 1995.

In literary criticism and belles lettres, several poets had books that stood out in 1995, among them David Lehman's *The Big Question,* a collection of intelligent and interesting reviews; Pulitzer Prize-winner Mary Oliver's *Blue Pastures,* essays on poets, poetry, and the natural world; and Donald Hall's *Principal Products of Portugal.* Two book-length essays on the question of evil appeared to copious notices: Elaine Pagels' *The Origin of Satan* (*see* BIOGRAPHIES) and Andrew Delbanco's *The Death of Satan.* Jack Miles offered his highly praised *God: A Biography.*

Greil Marcus, one of the most perceptive (and idiosyncratic) critics of American culture, gathered his reviews and occasional essays on music, literature, and life under the title *The Dustbin of History.* Joe David Bellamy, formerly the program consultant of the literature program at the National Endowment for the Humanities, wrote with vigour about contemporary fiction in *Literary Luxuries: American Writing at the End of the Millennium.* Novelist and poet Kelly Cherry published her essays and reviews in *Writing the World.*

Simon Schama embraced grand themes in *Landscape and Memory.* Inveterate traveler-novelist Paul Theroux entertained his public with *The Pillars of Hercules: A Grand Tour of the Mediterranean.* The novelist and nature writer Rick Bass narrated a trek into the Colorado wilderness in *The Lost Grizzlies.* In *Desert Quartet* the nature writer Terry Tempest Williams took the reader on an erotic journey across the sensuous Utah landscape.

The 1995 Pulitzer Prize for Fiction went to Carol Shields (*see* BIOGRAPHIES), a writer of dual U.S. and Canadian citizenship, for her novel *The Stone Diaries.* The book also won the National Book Critics Circle Award for fiction. The PEN/Faulkner Award for Fiction was given to Puget Sound writer David Guterson for his first book-length work of fiction, *Snow Falling on Cedars.* Robert Pinsky won the *Los Angeles Times* prize for poetry for his translation of Dante's *Inferno.* The winner of the National Book Award in poetry was Kunitz for his *Passing Through.* In fiction the award went to Roth for *Sabbath's Theater.* Historian David McCullough, whose biography of U.S. Pres. Harry S. Truman won the 1993 Pulitzer Prize, received the National Book Foundation's medal for distinguished contributions to American letters. Poet Kenneth Koch won the Bollingen Prize for his 1994 collection *One Train* and his lifetime achievements.

Science-fiction writer Octavia E. Butler received a MacArthur Foundation Award in 1995. Robert Hass, whose works include *Field Guide,* was named U.S. poet laureate by the Library of Congress.

(ALAN CHEUSE)

Canada. A number of important novels were published in Canada in 1995. The theme of Abraham Boyarsky's *A Gift of Rags* was that the short, terrible history of the Holocaust could never be forgotten by those who survived it or by their children. Dennis E. Bolen focused on the Holocaust from an opposite angle in *Stand in Hell,* the story of a teacher with his own sins to contend with who searches for the truth about his grandfather's complicity in Nazi war crimes. Audrey Thomas used the lost wax art of Ghana as a central metaphor for the influence of the past on the future in *Coming Down from Wa,* and in *The Piano Man's Daughter* Timothy Findley, through a meticulous rendering of a madwoman's life, analyzed the play of fate in the lives of four generations.

Hugh Hood used two linked novellas in *Dead Men's Watches* to observe how the forces of love, at war and in play, could influence the course of people's lives. *Mother Love* by L.R. Wright chronicled a woman's journey from madness back into the ongoing histories of her husband and daughter, while Evelyn Lau's *Other Women* portrayed a woman defying both past and future with the reckless power of naive passion. Joy Kogawa's *The Rain Ascends* recounted how a woman's world turns upside down with her discovery that her father has a history of abusing small boys. Poet Nicole Markotic took on history as biography in *Yellow Pages,* a novel based on the life of Alexander Graham Bell, whereas history as fiction infused *The Macken Charm,* Jack Hodgins' tale of an infamous family on Vancouver Island.

Collections of short Canadian fiction in 1995 presented history as mosaic, in fragments, as in *Sleeping with the Insane* by Jennifer Mitton, which offered a gallery of madness that ranged from the mildly, even humorously, deranged to the chilling. Steven Heighton's prose in *On Earth as It Is* leaped from mind to place to memory, in and out of time, in a dizzy spiral of lies and myths retold from generation to generation. The stories in Olive Senior's *Discerner of Hearts,* set in Jamaica, were also spun around a thread of madness and the infections of the sun. Priscilla Galloway's gallows wit twisted familiar fairy tales in wickedly new ways in her *Truly Grim Tales.*

Poetry proliferated in Canada in 1995. Margaret Atwood's 11th collection, *Morning in the Burned House,* treated disaster and triumph with her usual mordant wit, while in his gentler, yet acerbic fashion Ray Souster proclaimed *No Sad Songs Wanted Here.* George Amabile was prepared for everything and nothing in *Rumours of Paradise, Rumours of War;* Gary Geddes used a modern image to express ancient conundrums in *The Perfect Cold Warrior;* and Elizabeth Brewster, in *Footnotes to the Book of Job,* annotated sorrow in the language of survival. Liliane Welch's *Dream Museum* exhibited the shards of a lifetime in strange, stark patterns.

Poetry in 1995 seemed to be a craft for many different journeys. Lesley Choyce's *The Coastline of Forgetting* was a journal of hiking through Nova Scotia, while Robin Skelton took a hike through *The Edge of Time* and relativity, and the relativity of the dead to the living fueled Zoë Landale's *Burning Stone.* Rhea Tregebov surveyed the universe with a steely eye in *Mapping the Chaos.* Judith Fitzgerald managed to go with the flow in *River,* while in the end Lorna Crozier found that *Everything Arrives at the Light.*

Selected works were a milestone of their own. Robert Bringhurst brought out *The Calling: Selected Poems 1970–1995;* Paulette Jiles offered *Flying Lessons: Selected Poems;* and Mary di Michele winnowed 20 years of work for *Stranger in You: Selected Poems.*

The 1995 Governor General's Literary Award for fiction went to Greg Hollingshead for his story collection *The Roaring Girl.* The U.S.-born Canadian writer Carol Shields (*see* BIOGRAPHIES), who had won the 1993 Governor General's Literary Award for *Stone Diaries,* won the 1995 Pulitzer Prize for the same book. Robertson Davies (*see* OBITUARIES), prolific novelist and playwright and one of Canada's best-known literary figures, died during the year.

(ELIZABETH WOODS)

Other Literature in English. Writers from Australasia and Africa made particularly important contributions in English in almost every genre in 1995.

In Australia the renowned novelist, dramatist, and screenwriter Thomas Keneally (*Schindler's List*) published *A River Town,* a novel based on events in the life of his grandfather in which the protagonist's compassion triumphs over prejudice. Patricia Shaw published an engaging romance-adventure, *Cry of the Rain Bird,* set in 19th-century Australia. The unusual settings of Tasmanian hop farms and of Vietnam and Cambodia in the 1960s and 1970s served as the backdrop for Christopher Koch's latest war correspondent story, *Highways to a War.* The young and highly acclaimed writer Tim Winton (*see* BIOGRAPHIES) brought out his 11th book of fiction, *The Riders,* shortlisted for the 1995 Booker Prize, which portrayed—mostly unsympathetically—the Australian male through a series of folkloric stereotypes.

Also highlighting the year in Australian fiction was Alex Miller's novel *The Sitters* and Peter Carey's *Collected Stories,* which included three works not previously published in book form. Noteworthy in poetry

Wole Soyinka

FREDERIC REGLAIN—GAMMA LIAISON

was the publication of verse anthologies by three of Australia's internationally recognized poets: Chris Wallace-Crabbe's *Selected Poems 1956–1994,* Kevin Hart's *New and Selected Poems,* and David Malouf's *Selected Poems 1959–1989.* In nonfiction, *The First Stone* by the feminist writer Helen Garner provided a balanced reflection on a controversial 1992 Melbourne harassment case.

A furor erupted in Australia over the revelation that Helen Demidenko, purportedly the author of *The Hand That Signed the Paper,* was not Ukrainian as she had claimed but actually Helen Darville, the daughter of British immigrants. Winner of the prestigious Miles Franklin Award in 1995, the book falsely claimed to be based on the experiences of the author's family during World War II.

Another social issue, that of land development and the suffering of native peoples at the hands of imperialist oppressors, was the subject of the novel *Potiki* by New Zealand's Patricia Grace. The author presented the story through skillful characterization and elegant prose.

Works of outstanding quality and great diversity also characterized literature from Africa in 1995. Nobel laureates Wole Soyinka of Nigeria and Nadine Gordimer of South Africa, for example, each had new releases. Soyinka, a political exile, added to his string of plays *The Beatification of Area Boy,* published to coincide with its world premiere in October at the West Yorkshire (England) Playhouse. In *Writing and Being,* drawn from lectures she had delivered at Harvard University, Gordimer mused on the connection between life and literature and offered reflections on writers from South Africa and elsewhere. V.Y. Mudimbe of Zaire examined culture, politics, and history in *The Idea of Africa,* his sequel to *The Invention of Africa* (1988). Important fiction from Africa included *Astonishing the Gods* and *Adjusted Lives* by the Nigerians Ben Okri and Odun Balogun, respectively, as well as two new works by South Africans: Mike Nicol's *Horseman* and Lindsey Collen's controversial novel *The Rape of Sita,* winner of the Commonwealth Writers Prize for best fiction in Africa. There was an international outcry when the Nigerian military government executed writer Ken Saro-Wiwa (*see* OBITUARIES) in November.

(DAVID D. CLARK)

GERMANIC

German. Nothing in German literature received more publicity in 1995 than the novel *Ein weites Feld* by Günter Grass. (*See* BIOGRAPHIES.) Although he was by no means the only person to denounce the work, critic Marcel Reich-Ranicki's ripping up the book on national television incurred the ire of the author and of many others. In the novel, which dealt with the events of 1989–91, Grass attempted to forge a link across the events of a century by comparing the reunification of modern Germany with Bismarck's unification of the country in 1871. Grass made his protagonist (Theo Wuttke) a descendant of the 19th-century author Theodor Fontane and an employee of Treuhand, the controversial agency established to privatize the economy of the former German Democratic Republic. The author was unsparing in his attack on what he saw as the forced incorporation of the GDR into the Federal Republic.

Tabu I, by the poet and essayist Peter Rühmkorf, was a novel-style journal of 1989–91. Rühmkorf welded notes, essays on poetics, poems, polemics, and diverse articles into an entertaining text that gave an ironic account of the period while keeping the larger world context in view through television. Similar to Grass, he gathered up the events of 1989–91 and all those who spoke and acted in those days into a gay, apocalyptic cavalcade that, despite the diary form, told less about the author than it did about the sudden and startling end of the old Federal Republic. Peter Wawerzinek recounted the end of the GDR in his novel *Mein Babylon.* Here also, autobiographical minutiae were in the foreground as the author related the comical progress of the protagonist as art student, cemetery gardener, cabinetmaker's apprentice, chauffeur, and writer and as he looked at everyday life in East Berlin's artists' quarter.

In his riotous and willful novel *Abschied von den Feinden,* the romancer Reinhard Jirgl told an East-West story of a very special type: a woman has been murdered and her body left in a field. Seeking to clear up the murder are two brothers, one from the East, the other having immigrated years earlier to the West, both of whom were in love with the woman. The story develops into a tragedy involving the Stasi (the East German secret police), psychiatric treatments, and the craft of writing. Christoph Ransmayr's *Morbus Kitahara* speculated as to the consequences for Germany after World War II had U.S. Pres. Harry S. Truman listened to those who wanted to reduce Germany to a preindustrial condition by transforming it into a pastoral country of sheepherders and goatherds. In a ravaged landscape of iron and mud, Ransmayr showed three people struggling to survive in a nightmare worthy of Kafka.

Suspenseful and funny at once, *Langer Samstag* by Burkhard Spinnen told of a lawyer who meets a woman in a supermarket, goes with her to a soccer game, and then goes to bed with her. It told of an average life in the provinces, but it was a virtuoso work full of humour and irony. Of equal note was the picaresque novel *Unbekannt verzogen* by Michael Schulte, whose hero is always moving from one city to the next and from one continent to another. Along the way the radical flaneur dreams up bizarre tales of faith healers, thieving hoteliers, and opera divas, all told in a sharp and lively manner.

The most noteworthy lyrical work of the year was Hans Magnus Enzensberger's *Kiosk,* his first volume of poetry in a good while. Laconic, fractured, and ironic in style, the work was in the tradition of the late poetry of Gottfried Benn, the state of the world being depicted with a cheerful melancholy. Yet behind the mature equanimity of the gracile and minimalist Enzensberger lurked the trenchant poet who, armed with pointed aphorisms, was never afraid to take on contemporary issues—only no longer in an instructional way, as he had in the 1960s. Other works of poetry included Raoul Schrott's *Hotels* and Barbara Köhler's second book, *Blue Box: Gedichten.*

With Thomas Mann's *Tagebücher, 1953–1955,* Inge Jens completed the 10-volume project begun more than 15 years earlier by the Thomas Mann biographer Peter de Mendelssohn. The private life and sorrows of Mann in the years before his death, his doubts that he had created a significant and lasting work, and the secret passions of the "magician" could now be read by interested laypersons and experts alike. Equally important were the journal entries of the novelist Victor Klemperer, *Ich will Zeugnis ablegen bis zum letzten,* culled from his bequest. In this work, like nowhere else, the everyday life of a Jew in Hitler's Third Reich was meticulously documented. It supplemented Klemperer's 1947 work *LTI; Notizbuch eines Philologen,* in which he analyzed the language of the National Socialists. Playwright Heiner Müller died on December 30. (*See* OBITUARIES.)

(DANIEL A. HAUFLER)

Netherlandic. A substantial number of new novels in Dutch were written either by immigrants or by Dutch novelists writing about immigration. Together, these categories reflected the changing nature of the population of The Netherlands and the adjustment of the Dutch people to it. Representative of the first group was Naima El Bezaz, who, in *De weg naar het Noorden,* described the emotions of a young Moroccan who leaves his fatherland and attempts, unsuccessfully, to settle as an illegal immigrant in The Netherlands. The Iranian Kader Abdolah's *De meisjes en de Partizanen,* another example of what might be termed immigrant writing, focused on the immigrant's sad but apparently unavoidable loss of identity. Dutch authors writing about the same topic were represented by Joost Zwagerman, who, in *De buitenvrouw,* described the relationship between a married high-school teacher and his black female colleague. Typical of many modern Dutch novels, the erotic element of the relationship dominated the narrative.

International awareness was given a different dimension in several books related to the loss of the former Dutch colony of Indonesia. In *Indische lessen: Nederland en de koloniale ervaring,* J.A.A. van Doorn demonstrated the inability of the Dutch to sever their emotional ties with Indonesia, in contrast to the Indonesians, who never looked back after gaining independence following World War II. The renowned South African author Etienne van Heerden's novel *De Stoetmeester,* which might well constitute one of the last novels on apartheid, was translated into Dutch.

Adding a historical perspective to the theme of internationalism was Imme Dros's highly original series on Odysseus, of which the latest volume, *Odysseus: Een man van verhalen,* was published in 1995. Though primarily written for young people, it could be enjoyed by readers of all ages. Charles Vergeer's *Een verlies van vleugels* argued that the idea that the Romans slavishly imitated the Greek philosophers was unfounded.

Dutch literature suffered a loss with the death of the leading novelists Annie M.G. Schmidt and W.F. Hermans. Hermans had completed *Ruisend gruis* only weeks before his death. (MARTINUS A. BAKKER)

Danish. The year 1995 saw the eagerly awaited final volume of Ib Michael's *Vanillepigen* trilogy, *Brev til månen,* bringing his autobiographical fantasy into the present. Otherwise, thrillers seemed to be in vogue in Denmark. Michael Larsen published his highly successful *Uden sikker viden,* about murder and the pornography trade, in which all evidence was gradually subject to doubt because of the possibility of doctoring by computer. Bjarne Reuter's *Langebro med løbende figurer* was a book about a serial murderer in which the two main figures hunted each other. Helle Stangerup, after her historical novels, returned to the thriller with *Stedfar.* Hans Lyngby Jepsen moved in a similar direction with *Sin lykkes smed,* once more showing psychological insight.

The same author's *Endnu en god dag* was in a completely different vein, a reflective diary on his wife's life after she was affected by a stroke. Poul Ørum, also known for his thrillers, changed course and published his memoirs in *Den magiske dimension: Et barns oplevelsesverden.* The reflective note was continued in Jens Christian Grøndahl's collection of essays entitled *Ved flodens munding,* an attempt to overcome what the author saw as the lethargy of the 1990s. In *Datter af* Henrik Stangerup wrote about the often tense relationship with his mother, the actress Betty Söderberg. The occupation, which figured in these memoirs, also was featured in those of the graphic artist Lars Bo, *En underlig dreng.*

One of the younger writers, also acclaimed for her poetry, produced another volume of short stories. Naja Marie Aidt's *Tilgang* centred on the relationships between people close to each other—parents and children, siblings and lovers—and was written in a style reminiscent of her poetry. Kim Fupz Aakeson, a leading literary experimenter, also contributed a collection of short stories, *Sidemanden.*

Benny Andersen wrote lighthearted poetry about the Danes in *Verdensborger i Danmark,* published at the same time in English as *Cosmopolitan in Denmark.* Poetry was well represented in volumes by Henrik Nordbrandt, *Ormene ved himlens port;* Per Højholt, *Lynskud;* Marianne Larsen, *Chance for at danse;* Morti Vizki, *Eliksir;* and Rolf Gjedsted, *Lorcas hus.*

(W. GLYN JONES)

Norwegian. The year 1995 confirmed the strong position of the short story in Norway. Lack of communication was a central theme in Sigmund Jensen's debut collection *Antikvarens datter,* and human relationships were subtly analyzed in Sidsel Mørck's *Svevet og andre noveller.* Øystein Lønn carried the enigmatic to extremes in *Hva skal vi gjøre i dag og andre noveller.*

In the novel, Finn Carling analyzed the writer's art in his *Matadorens hånd.* In Tove Nilsen's metanovel *Lystreise,* an author's pregnancy parallels her planned novel about Rembrandt's mistress Hendrickje Stoffels. Terje Stigen's *Allegretto* depicted the last weeks in the life of a middle-aged teacher, diagnosed as incurably ill, who returns to his childhood world in northern Norway to die.

The 18th-century western Norwegian farming and fishing community was brilliantly brought to life in Johannes Heggland's *Jordparadiset. Vårherres nedfallsfrukt,* whereas upper-middle-class eastern Norway and Copenhagen in the same period were portrayed in Sissel Lange-Nielsen's *Tryllefløyten.* Marital, economic, and political problems in farming as well as in rural industry around 1930 were central in Anne Karin Elstad's best-seller *Som dine dager er.* Ebba Haslund's *I mangel av sverd* was a recapitulation of the German occupation as seen through the eyes of an Oslo family.

Jan Erik Vold combined humour and biting satire in his collection of poems *Kalenderdikt.* The late Hans Børli's collected poems, *Samlede dikt,* were also published.

Hans Aaraas' monograph *Peer Gynt* gave a detailed analysis of the dream motifs in Henrik Ibsen's play, and Merete Morken Andersen provided a detailed guide to Ibsen's dramas in her illustrated *Ibsenhåndboken. Knut Hamsuns brev, 1896–1907,* edited by Harald Næss, contained 374 letters showing the author troubled by financial difficulties, partly caused by gambling and by bohemian escapades, and pestered by defamatory anonymous letters received by people Hamsun knew. The tempestuous life of Finn Alnæs was documented in Truls Gjefsen's *Finn Alnæs. Titan og sisyfos,* and the trouble-filled existence of Olaf Bull was presented by Fredrik Wandrup in his *Olaf Bull og hans samtid.* The value of Janneken Øverland's *Cora Sandel. En biografi* was enhanced by its excellent illustrations, including nine colour reproductions of Sandel's paintings.

The Norwegian Literary Critics' Prize for 1995 was awarded to Torgeir Schjerven for his novel *Omvei til Venus.* The Brage Prize for poetry went to Øyvind Berg for his collection *Forskjellig* and for prose to Ingvar Ambjørnsen for his novel *Fugledansen.* The poet Halldis Moren Vesaas died in 1995.

(TORBJØRN STØVERUD)

Swedish. The short story experienced a renaissance in Sweden in 1995. Inger Edelfeldt's *Den förunderliga kameleonten* revolved around feminine identity, Ninni Holmqvist's *Kostym* depicted relationships with impressive control and detachment, and Kerstin Strandberg's *Undangömda berättelser* opened up the mysteries of character and milieu.

Similar themes preoccupied many novelists, with some producing texts also formulating a critique of society. Kjell Espmark's *Hatet,* narrated by a murdered prime minister, traced the end of an era, with political illusions finally being laid to rest, while Torgny Lindgren's *Hummelhonung* was a haunting tale of hatred and the need for love. Family relationships, memory, and death were the themes of Lars Gyllensten's *Ljuset ur skuggornas värld.* Feminine identity was explored in Eva Adolfsson's *Till Moskva* and Ellen Mattson's *Vägen härifrån.* Marie Hermanson's *Värddjuret* ventured into a context of dissolving boundaries, and Birgit Häggkvist's *Den blödiga* enforced the perspective of a young girl. Peter Nilson's *Rymdväktaren* was an elegant and learned novel set in the 21st century that focused on an apocalyptic theme recurring in Maria Gummesson's *Jordens sång till månen,* while Lars Andersson's *Artemis* drew on myth and technology to investigate the relationship between humankind and landscape. Stig Claesson's *Eko av en vår* and P.C. Jersild's *En gammal kärlek* told of love in middle age. Margareta Ekström's *En levande och en död* formulated a daughter's sense of loss on the death of her mother. With *Tanten och krokodilen,* Merete Mazzarella tantalizingly transcended conventional genre categories.

It was a major year for poetry in Swedish. Birgitta Lillpers' *Propolis* asserted the role of poetry in an uncertain world. The voices in Ernst Brunner's *Mr Skylight* conveyed the horrors of a ferry disaster, while the sharp image in Bo Carpelan's *I det sedda* centred on love, old age, and death. While Magnus William-Olsson's *Att det ur din eld* drew on classical metres to state the certainty of death and Bruno K. Öijer's *Det förlorade ordet* defined a sense of abandonment in carefully controlled stanzas, the formless verbosity of Stig Larsson's *Matar* had the effect of undermining the texts. Bengt Emil Johnson's selection of poetry from 1958 to 1993, *Vittringar,* made a rewarding collection. Krister Gidlund's *Hallonens röda konster,* Catharina Rysten's *Ormsömn,* and Mats Söderlund's *Lyfter din kropp till sist* were other notable volumes.

Lars Norén's *De döda pjäserna* consisted of four volumes containing 14 plays, sketches, and fragments from the period 1989–94. The volumes significantly enhanced readers' understanding of the work of this leading playwright.

(HELENA FORSÅS-SCOTT)

FRENCH

France. The year was particularly rich in the realm of fiction. The two grandes dames of French literature, Nathalie Sarraute and Marguerite Duras, each published a book in 1995 that perfectly encapsulated her art and unique talent. In *Ici,* Sarraute continued her work on "tropisms," first begun in 1939. The short pieces that made up her latest book, however, should be—must be—read slowly, like poems, and, as in *Enfance* or *Tu ne t'aimes pas,* she further revealed a hidden side of her personality. In *C'est tout,* a book born of illness, Duras entranced the reader with simple and pure words that conveyed her vision of loving passion and the force of writing. It was a remarkable book, undoubtedly the last Duras would write and one that would make some laugh and others weep.

Also in the area of fiction, in *C'était toute une vie,* François Bon succeeded in capturing the expression of misery without becoming maudlin or clichéd. The writing studios in the south of France were brought to life through his portrayal of a small village devastated by unemployment. Through these studios literature seemed to become a refuge. In *Hier,* Agota Kristof also explored a universe of implacable hardness and continued to examine a theme dear to her: exile.

Childhood and mother and father figures appeared in numerous novels. In Héctor Bianciotti's beautiful autobiographical work, *Le Pas si lent de l'amour,* unanimously hailed by the critics, the character of the mother occupied a central place. The same was true for *L'Ingratitude* by Ying Chen, which strongly and humorously denounced maternal love. In *La Folle allure,* Christian Bobin told the story of a little girl born in a circus who spends her time running away, to the great despair of her mother. In *Russe blanc,* Jean-Pierre Milovanoff subtly portrayed his Russian-born father. In *La Puissance des mouches,* Lydie Salvayre showed a man on the brink of madness who wants nothing more than to murder his own father. Finally, *La Maladie de la chair,* by the poet Bernard Noël, was a splendidly written work in the form of a long letter addressed to his father.

In philosophical essays, *Petit Traité des grandes vertus* by André Comte-Sponville was remarkable more for its unforeseen success than for the relevance of its thesis. In *Journal* by Jean Baudrillard, the philosopher continued to examine the world—and its fixed destiny—with his customary irony. Finally, in *Ce que l'homme fait à l'homme,* Myriam Revault d'Allonnes, who was very much influenced by the work of Hannah Arendt, questioned the power of evil in politics.

Biographies included a work by Pierre Daix on the historian Fernand Braudel, who had died 10 years earlier. Daix clearly illuminated the adventurous thought and originality of the author of *La Méditerranée,* who believed that "history always repeats itself." Also noteworthy was *Descartes,* an important work by Geneviève Rodis-Lewis on the philosopher whose 400th birthday would be observed in 1996. The magnificent work *Dante* by Jacqueline Risset should also be noted, in which all the modernity of the author of *The Divine Comedy* was shown. In addition, notice should be given to Josyane Savigneau's passionate book on Carson McCullers.

The year was filled with surprises for those concerned with literary prizes. In an unprecedented move, Andreï Makine received both the Prix Goncourt and the Prix Médicis *ex æquo* for his *Le Testament Français,* in which he portrayed the picturesque life of a French-Russian family through several generations. Lacking great originality in both form and style, the book nevertheless pleased a large number of readers. Vassilis Alexakis received the Prix Médicis *ex æquo* for *La Langue maternelle,* an overtly autobiographical story. The judges thus honoured two writers born outside of France who chose to write in French. Finally, the Prix Fémina went to Emmanuel Carrère for *La Classe de neige,* a story of suspense and terror set among children. The book was published by a small, high-quality press, P.O.L., and not by one of the three big publishers (Gallimard, B. Grasset, Seuil) that usually shared the literary prizes. P.O.L. also published *Lambeaux,* an emotional work by Charles Juliet about his adoptive mother, as well as *Quel ange n'est terrible?,* a highly successful book on incest by Marc Le Bot. Incest was also the theme of the latest book by Claude Louis-Combet, *Blesse, ronce noire.* Once again his prose, much unappreciated, was dazzling in its magnificently engaging fiction, poetry, and mysticism. (FRANÇOIS POIRIÉ)

Canada. In French Canada 1995 was marked by the works of women writers who reached new heights in their careers. Rachel Leclerc's novel *Noces de sable* clearly illustrated this phenomenon. The novel was set in a Gaspesian fishing village in historic lower Canada, in which the conflict between a French-Canadian and a British merchant crystallized in the marriage of a worker to his employer's daughter. The tale was written in a poetic prose far removed from a realistic style. With *La Démarche du crabe,* Monique LaRue combined high formal standards with the desire to re-create the Québécois past. The protagonist, a dentist, embodies the generation that grew up in the 1960s; he was filled with ideals but found that his life as a middle-aged man was barren. *L'Ingratitude* was the third book published by Ying Chen, a young writer of Chinese background. Considered for France's Prix Fémina, the novel placed the mingled love and hatred a young woman feels for her mother in a Chinese cultural frame. After her own death, the narrator retraces the major events of her life as she witnesses the rituals of her funeral. The internationally known author Marie-Claire Blais published *Soifs,* in which AIDS, racism, capital punishment, and other modern themes formed an impressive picture that flowed for 300 pages without a single paragraph break.

Mysticism continued to inspire French-Canadian writers. Yolande Villemaire's *Le Dieu dansant* arose from a vision the author allegedly experienced when visiting India. It was a convincing portrait of that country during the 11th century, as much for its description of social institutions as for its handling of personal spiritual experience. Serge-Patrice Thibodeau offered, in the form of the long poem *Le Quatuor de l'errance,* an account of an actual initiation journey that took him from New Delhi to Jerusalem via the countries of Nepal, Pakistan, and Iran.

TOSEE LAMBERT—PONOPRESSE/PHOTOREPORTERS

Monique LaRue

It should also be mentioned that many major Quebec writers published during 1995. These included Michel Tremblay, Anne Hébert, André Major, Nicole Brossard, and Madeleine Gagnon. (PATRICK NICOL)

ITALIAN

In the climate of deepening institutional crisis, weakening political debate, and increasing ideological disorientation, the general public in Italy seemed to show a marked appetite in 1995 for ordinary tales of good feelings and "true" emotions, preferably told in a traditional style. That may be why Umberto Eco's third novel failed to make more than a passing impact on the literary scene. The problem with *L'isola del giorno prima*—a story of love and adventure set in 17th-century Europe with perhaps too few events and, in true baroque fashion, too many words—was that the tale it told was hardly as compelling as its telling was clever and interesting. (The novel was published in English during the year as *The Island of the Day Before.*) On the contrary, the homespun matrilinear theme continued to steal the limelight, and Susanna Tamaro's *Va' dove ti porta il cuore* triumphed, for a second year, on the best-seller list. It was closely followed by another 1994 favourite, Antonio Tabucchi's *Sostiene Pereira,* which enjoyed continuing success, thanks also to its much-publicized film version.

The triumph of the ordinary was confirmed with the awarding of the Strega Prize to the posthumously published *Passaggio in ombra* by the hitherto unknown Mariateresa Di Lascia, who died in 1994 at the age of 40. The work was an intensely lyrical and painful first-person account of the experiences of a woman and her southern Italian family from the 1940s to the present. In this evocation there was no room for joy unless marred by impending anguish and doom. The destiny of sorrow that ruled over its main characters (the narrator's mother, her aunt, and her great-aunt) was avoided by the protagonist and narrator only at the cost of social marginalization and total loneliness.

At least on the surface, nothing seemed more distant from this work than *Jack Frusciante è uscito dal gruppo* by the 20-year-old Enrico Brizzi. The book was an amusing portrait of a "late teenager," epitomizing all the ties and tastes of his generation. The most striking feature of the novel—one already widely exploited by a number of recent young writers—was its language, a new type of Italian modeled entirely on the real-life jargon of teenagers' subculture. The story it told and its narrative form, however, had little that was transgressive, the protagonist's irony being no more than a device to keep at bay an underlying sentimentality that often came to dominate the story. Nonetheless, with his mixture of bold language, good heartedness, and social conscience, Brizzi cleverly managed to appeal to both his contemporaries and older generations of readers.

Another novel full of good intentions was *Voci* by Dacia Maraini, a writer who for many years had been actively engaged in giving artistic expression to some of

Enrico Brizzi

M. GIARDI—GRANATA/PHOTOREPORTERS

the most pressing problems of our time. In *Voci* these social and moral concerns (including violence against women, ecological degradation, and social marginalization) were once again at the fore, but they coexisted somewhat uncomfortably in what was a typical whodunit, ultimately failing to coalesce into an imaginative and coherent narrative unity.

A serious attempt to move out of and to challenge the everyday was made by Sebastiano Vassalli in his work *3012: L'anno del Profeta,* an interesting and provocative narrative meditation. Conjuring up a future, upside-down world in which the present was, however, transparently recognizable, Vassalli probably intended to challenge his reader at various levels, ironically envisaging hatred and war, rather than love and peace, as humanity's vital force. It was unfortunate that the form in which the provocation was realized—an uneasy blend of science fiction, fable, prophecy, and pseudoacademic prose—was inadequate to bear its ideological ambition, and for this reason the book failed to convince either the critics or the public.

One of the most widely acclaimed books of the year was Daniele Del Giudice's *Staccando l'ombra da terra,* which, rather unusual for the Italian literary tradition, was entirely focused on a technical subject: flying. It included eight prose pieces, one of which was a conventional short story that enacted a national mystery, the still-unexplained crash of passenger flight Itavia 870 in waters off Sicily. The other pieces were accounts of different flights, mostly by the same amateur pilot with, occasionally, the company of his laconic instructor. What was particularly memorable in Del Giudice's writing was his ability to communicate to the reader the sense that the technical error, the wrong command that causes an irreversible chain of events, was never far away from the pilot's fingertips and that the instruments were ready to register it with impassible objectivity. This sense was made more compelling by the use of a vocabulary that, in keeping with the writer's past novels—especially *Atlante occidentale*—was so precise and technical as to seem to be inspired by a flying manual. Del Giudice's style convincingly managed to convey the sense of almost total symbiosis, in which the pilot and his aircraft hung suspended in the air, and without making any concessions to sentimentality and earthly matters, it achieved in its intense, almost astringent purity a kind of severe, geometric lyricism.

(LINO PERTILE)

SPANISH

Spain. A surprising number of established Spanish novelists, all men, wrought fictions in 1995 through first-person female narrators who transcended or merely endured the tedium of their existence. Fernando Delgado won the Planeta Prize with *La mirada del otro,* an erotically charged story of obsessive marital jealousy told by a woman well placed in the Madrid business establishment of the 1980s. In *Telepena de Celia Cecilia Villalobo,* Álvaro Pombo offered a compelling monologue by a shy middle-aged widow as she pondered herself on a videotaped television interview speaking about her famous departed husband. José María Guelbenzu's *El sentimiento* explored the crisscrossing destinies of a bored housewife and her husband's predatory female business partner. A prostitute in Javier Tomeo's *El crimen del cine Oriente* coarsely recounted her foredoomed attempt to escape solitude and squalor through honest love; and a Sevillian aristocrat, faced with the collapse of her family, remade her life through rediscovered sensuality, personal sacrifice, and high adventure in *Más allá del jardín,* Antonio Gala's runaway best-seller.

Julián Ríos voiced a more purely literary fascination for women in *Amores que atan o Belles Lettres,* a cryptically encoded gallery—from *A* (Marcel Proust's Albertine) to *Z* (Raymond Queneau's Zazie)—of unnamed fictional heroines fondly remembered by a jilted narrator whose one true love, all along, was literature itself. Readers expecting a commentary on Ríos' *Larva* cycle appreciated the author's *Álbum de Babel,* an illustrated multilingual punhouse of polysemous compositions.

Ana Rossetti's new poetry (*Punto umbrío*) and fiction (*Mentiras de papel*) were well received, as was Fanny Rubio's complex narrative *La casa del halcón.* In *Ardor guerrero,* Antonio Muñoz Molina offered a grotesquely comic and morally troubling depiction of army life, based on the author's experiences as a bewildered recruit, and Juan Madrid prowled the capital's roughest neighbourhoods in *Cuentas pendientes* and *Crónicas del Madrid oscuro.*

Gonzalo Torrente Ballester published a new novel, *La boda de Chon Recalde,* and in *Diario de un jubilado* Miguel Delibes eased an autobiographical character from two earlier novels into retirement. The *Obras completas* of Spain's most distinguished dramatist, Antonio Buero Vallejo, appeared in a two-volume set. In December the Cervantes Prize, the top award in Hispanic letters worldwide, went to the Spanish novelist Camilo José Cela.

(ROGER L. UTT)

Latin America. Nobel laureate Gabriel García Márquez' novel *Of Love and Other Demons* was published in English in 1995. His 13th book of fiction to appear in English, it re-created the exotic and magical world of his writings. The novel had originally appeared in Spanish in 1994.

Other Colombian writers also had books published. Darío Jaramillo Agudelo's second novel, *Cartas cruzadas,* was an epistolary work dealing with destiny and chance in human relationships. Rodrigo Parra Sandoval published *Tarzan y el filósofo desnudo,* a satire of Colombian academics and intellectual traditions. R.H. Moreno-Durán published *Cartas en el asunto* and *Como el halcón peregrino.* His seventh book of fiction, *Cartas en el asunto* consisted of short narratives connected by letters. In *Como el halcón peregrino* the author recounted his experiences with the Latin-American writers of the 1960s and '70s and of his own generation. Arturo Alape published *La hoguera de las ilusiones,* dealing with one of Bogotá's neighbourhoods. Alberto Duque López issued the novel *Muriel, mi amor,* essayist and novelist Alvaro Pineda Botero published the novel *Cárcel por amor,* and Raimundo Gómez Cásseres published his second novel, *Días así.*

A new so-called TV generation of writers, born in the 1950s, appeared in Colombia. Three of them—Philip Potdevin, Octavio Escobar Giraldo, and José Gabriel Baena—published their first novels after having won prizes for short fiction. Potdevin's *Metatrón* was an experimental book full of history, alchemy, music, theology, and a plethora of esoteric subjects. Escobar Giraldo's *El último diario de Tony Flowers* offered a rewriting of North American literary and popular culture. Baena published the experimental novel *El amor eterno es un sandwich express* in late 1994. Edgar Torres Arias, of the same generation, wrote a popular fictionalization of the Medellín cartel's underground life, *Los mercaderes de la muerte.*

Mexican writer Carlos Fuentes' latest novel appeared in English under the ti-

Special Report

Postmodern Literature in Latin America

BY RAYMOND LESLIE WILLIAMS

Latin-American literature blossomed and received international acclaim in the 1960s and 1970s with the so-called boom in the novel, a movement signaled by the publication of major works by the Colombian Gabriel García Márquez, the Mexican Carlos Fuentes, the Peruvian Mario Vargas Llosa, the Argentine Julio Cortázar, and the Chilean José Donoso. (More recently, the Chilean Isabel Allende [*see* BIOGRAPHIES] has become one of the most widely read Latin-American novelists.) The rise of these writers was anticipated by the master who served as father figure for them all: Jorge Luis Borges. The cultural importance of the region also became evident in the awarding of the Nobel Prize for Literature to several Latin-American writers beginning in the 1960s: the Guatemalan novelist Miguel Ángel Asturias (in 1967), the Chilean poet Pablo Neruda (1971), García Márquez (1982), and the Mexican poet and essayist Octavio Paz (1990).

The Latin-American literature of the 1990s includes some of the writers from the 1960s, for Vargas Llosa, Fuentes, García Márquez, and Donoso have continued their brilliant literary careers. Cortázar died in 1984, but his heirs have published several of his writings posthumously. Beyond these novelists, however, a new generation of Latin-American writers has surfaced, and these writers are creating a heterogeneity in literature never seen before in the Hispanic world. This new generation includes the Argentine Ricardo Piglia, the Chilean Diamela Eltit, the Colombian R.H. Moreno-Durán, the Venezuelan José Balza, the Puerto Rican Luis Rafael Sánchez, and the Mexican José Emilio Pacheco.

The writing of the 1990s in Latin America exhibits a trend toward postmodern experimentation, with Piglia, Eltit, Moreno-Durán, Balza, Sánchez, and Pacheco its most prominent exponents. Piglia and Eltit are the most radically experimental, and the fiction of Piglia is one of the most aesthetically innovative and politically significant since the writings of Cortázar. Piglia's fictional works consist of *Nombre falso* (1975; *Assumed Name,* 1995), *Respiracíon artificial* (1980; *Artificial Respiration,* 1994), *Prisión perpetua* (1988), and *La ciudad ausente* (1992). The four works can be seen as an outgrowth of Borges' writings, for they are fictional meditations that can also be read as essays. Piglia's fiction is a major rewriting of Argentine history and literature in a fictional world of provisional truths. Along with the work of Piglia and Fuentes' *Terra nostra* (1975), Eltit's total writing represents one of the most ambitious, challenging, and profound searches for historical origins published in Latin America. Her project consists of the four novels *Lumpérica* (1983), *Por la patria* (1986), *El cuarto mundo* (1988; *The Fourth World,* 1995), and *Vaca sagrada* (1991). As her first three books were written under the dictatorship of Augusto Pinochet, Eltit joined other young novelists in the creation of a writing of resistance.

Raymond Leslie Williams is professor of Spanish at the University of Colorado. His writings include The Postmodern Novel in Latin America.

LATIN FOCUS

Diamela Eltit

Moreno-Durán and Balza are less experimental in their writing, but they are concerned with much the same aesthetic and political program as are Piglia and Eltit. The roots of Moreno-Durán's hermetic trilogy of the 1980s, *Fémina suite,* are found not in the empirical reality of Colombia but rather, as is the case in much postmodern fiction, in modernist literature. The subjects of Moreno-Durán's seven books of fiction are writing and language; with his later novels he has assumed the role of the chronicler of postmodern Bogotá. Balza has published numerous volumes of fiction in various forms, including several books of different variations and combinations that he, like Moreno-Durán, considers his "exercises." Like Moreno-Durán, Piglia, and other postmodern writers with whom he closely identifies, Balza often blurs the line between fictional and essayistic discourses, writing fictions about literature and essays in a fictional mode.

After having previously published short fiction and plays, Sánchez brought postmodern fiction to the forefront of Puerto Rican culture with the publication in 1976 of *La guaracha del macho Camacho* (*Macho Camacho's Beat,* 1980). He continued his postmodern writings with a second novel, *La importancia de llamarse Daniel Santos* (1989). After the breakdown of the frontiers between popular and high culture already effected by Guillermo Cabrera Infante and Severo Sarduy, Sánchez's novelization of the popular culture of Caribbean music and American television in *Macho Camacho's Beat* was a logical step in the Caribbean postmodern.

Pacheco is just one of a group of postmodern writers in Mexico that includes Salvador Elizondo, Luis Arturo Ramos, and Carmen Boullosa. Signs of early postmodernism were evident in Mexico as early as the late 1960s, and Pacheco's novel *Morirás lejos* (1967, *You Will Die in a Distant Land,* 1987) has some of the qualities of such writing. The postmodern character of the novel betrays and subverts the unity suggested in reading it as an ultimately harmonious, modernist text. In the 1980s and 1990s, Ramos and Boullosa have published high-quality postmodern fiction.

Thus, there are numerous postmodern tendencies in the Latin-American fiction of the past two decades. The centres of this literary production are Mexico, the Caribbean, and the Southern Cone nations. Never constituted to be a repetition or a duplication of the boom of the 1960s, this heterogeneous and often political fiction marks several directions for Latin-American literature at the end of the century.

---

tle *Diana, the Goddess Who Hunts Alone.* In the novel Fuentes continued his exploration of the relationships between literature, history, and life. The writer Federico Campbell published his first book in English, *Tijuana.* Set on the border between Mexico and the United States, the stories engaged the reader with several types of borders—geographic, psychological, cultural, and spiritual.

The major novels to appear in Mexico included *La viuda* by María Luisa Puga, *La corte de los ilusos* by Rosa Beltrán, *La ceremonia perfecta* by Federico Patán, and *Olvídame* by Sergio Fernández. *La viuda* told the story of a woman's discovery of a new identity. *La corte de los ilusos* was set in 19th-century Mexico. *La ceremonia perfecta* dealt with changes in a married couple's life with black humour. *Olvídame* demonstrated an impressive control of narrative technique. Novelist Ignacio Solares published a volume of short stories, *Muérete y sabrás.*

Writing in London, Cuban Guillermo Cabrera Infante created fictional memoirs of life in Havana in *Delito por bailar el chachachá.* Lisandro Otero's *La travesía* portrayed a protagonist who was obsessed with a variety of erotic activities but had difficulties establishing authentic human relationships. René Vázquez Díaz' *La isla del Cundeamor* had been written in exile.

Diario de Andrés Fava, a short work by Argentine novelist Julio Cortázar, appeared posthumously. Alicia Borinsky, whose novel

Mean Woman had appeared in English in 1993, published *Sueños de un seductor abandonado* in Argentina. The novel dealt with the labyrinthine, nocturnal urban life of grotesque characters.

Other major writers who published novels during the year included José Donoso, Adriano González León, and Sergio Ramírez. Donoso's *Donde van a morir los elefantes* recounted the story of a Chilean writer who accepts a position in an American university and then becomes fascinated with a female student and embroiled in academic politics. Venezuelan writer Adriano González León, who had not published a novel for many years, issued *Viejo,* dealing with a writer's attempts to confront his solitude and inactivity. Nicaraguan Sergio Ramírez published *Un baile de máscaras.*

Several of Latin America's most renowned writers published notable books of nonfiction. Nobel laureate Octavio Paz, who lived in India in the 1960s, wrote about his relationship with that nation in *Vislumbres de la India.* Elena Poniatowska's *Luz y luna, las lunitas* was an insightful set of chronicles about the lives of Mexican women. Puerto Rican writer Luis Rafael Sánchez issued a set of literary essays, *La guagua aérea. Memoria y olvido (1920–1946)* was the title of Juan José Arreola's autobiography. The Mexican celebrity painter José Luis Cuevas published his observations in *Gato macho.*

(RAYMOND LESLIE WILLIAMS)

PORTUGUESE

Portugal. One trend in Portuguese fiction was an interest in subjects of a historical character. These were treated, however, with a freedom and sweep of imagination that had little to do with the conventional historical novel, bound as that form had been by the rules of chronological plausibility. National history provided most of the inspiration, giving the opportunity of rethinking the country's past and its present predicament. Mário de Carvalho's new novel, *Um deus passeando pela brisa da tarde,* broke with this trend, however. The author set the story in Lusitania, on the Iberian Peninsula, in the 3rd century of the Christian era, when the region formed part of the Roman Empire. His choice of time and place tended to give the allegory a universal meaning. The book was considered to be a remarkable achievement, and the Association of Portuguese Authors awarded it the prize as best novel of the year.

The novel tells of a Roman town's hard-pressed governor, who is harassed by marauding groups of North African invaders as he tries to restore the town's walls to resist an imminent siege. His plans clash with the interests of the townspeople, and his military reasoning is passively resisted by them. Faced with this dilemma, the governor decides that he would rather sacrifice human life than surrender the besieged town or compromise with the enemy. Seeing signs of the fall of the empire, he argues with an adherent of Christianity who chooses martyrdom over tolerance of Roman law. In the end the governor finds himself alone, secretly in love with the Christian woman whose attitudes he despises and wondering whether his own integrity is not as disgusting as hers.

Sofia Ferreira's *Mulheres de sombra,* which examined the question of the inner solitude of the human being as a malaise of modern civilization, was an impressive first novel. Spreading over a period of three generations, the narrative encompassed many incidents and extended to many different places, but everything was secondary to the inner pursuit that reached the depths of despair in the women referred to in the title and that led to madness. The circular development of the narrative, which took a tragic instant wherever it might lead, made the novel compulsive reading.

The Association of Portuguese Authors awarded the Great Prize for Poetry to Nuno Júdice's *Meditação sobre ruínas.* The work used a severe poetic diction to serve the anger of critical reason. (L.S. REBELO)

Brazil. New fiction published in Brazil during 1995 included *O xangô de Baker Street,* a novel by the eminent comic and cultural commentator Jô Soares. The work was set in 1886, with Sarah Bernhardt bringing the British detective to aid Emperor Pedro II in solving a series of crimes. Truly comic detective fiction, the novel highlighted figures, traditions, and events of the last years of the empire. Luiz Vilela published a polemical short novel, *Te amo sobre todas as coisas,* which included explicit sex scenes. Ana Miranda dealt with the life of the Brazilian "poet of death," Augusto dos Anjos, in her historical novel *A última quimera;* the novel was narrated through the thoughts and opinions of the deceased writer's friends.

Anjos' complete poetry was published in an edition organized by the critic Alexei Bueno. The critic and novelist Silviano Santiago published *Cheiro forte,* his first volume of poetry since the late 1950s.

Theatre activity in Brazil was intense during 1995. A play based on the poetry of Ana Cristina César's *A teus pés* ran for most of the year. In *Pérola,* Mauro Rasi once again turned to family themes: his childhood in the interior of São Paulo. Aderbal Freire Filho's *Ao terceiro dia* dealt with the depressing life of the early 20th-century novelist Lima Barreto in the form of a tragicomedy. Miguel Falabella was active as dramatist, director, and actor. Antônio Callado's *A revolta da cachaça,* published in 1983 and describing a 17th-century rebellion in Rio against the Portuguese crown's imposition of wine over the native *cachaça,* was finally staged. Also of note was Vinícius Vianna's narration of his strained relationship with his father, the playwright Oduvaldo Vianna Filho (Vianinha), in *Esta ave estranha e escura.*

NANCY CRAMPTON

Jorge Amado

Other important cultural events of the year included Nélida Piñón's first volume of memoirs; a study of the cultural impact of Antônio Cândido's literary criticism; Darcy Ribeiro's *A gestação do Brasil,* the new volume in his ongoing study of Brazilian civilization; and Hermano Vianna's *O mistério do samba,* which insisted that the development of the samba was, in fact, a cooperative effort between elite and popular musicians. Jorge Amado was awarded the Camões Prize for 1995. (IRWIN STERN)

RUSSIAN

In commemoration of the 50th anniversary of the end of World War II, the Russian literary scene in 1995 was dominated by works that looked to the past. Several new titles reflected the country's struggle with the legacy of war and with communist rule. Mikhail Kurayev's semiautobiographical novel *Blokada* ("Blockade"), about the siege of Leningrad, represented a whole series of works that depicted the horrors of the Stalinist era. Sergey Bondlevsky's autobiographical work *Trepanatsiya cherepa* ("The Trepanation of the Skull"), analyzing the generation of the 1920s, reflected the trend toward historical and personal introspection. Vasily Aksyonov published *Negativ polozhitelnogo geroya* ("A Negative of a Positive Hero"), a series of 12 short stories with lyrical interludes that takes place in Moscow and the U.S. in the past and in the present. Noteworthy works of fiction in a more contemporary vein included Lyudmila Petrushevskaya's *Tayna doma* ("The Secret of the House"), Lyudmila Ulitskaya's *Bednye rodstvenniki* ("Poor Relatives"), Aleksandr Melikhov's *Gorbatye atlanty* ("Hunchbacked Atlantis"), and Daniil Granin's *Begstvo v Rossiyu* ("Escape to Russia").

Absorbed with Russia's past, Aleksandr Solzhenitsyn published several new short stories. "Ego," for example, was thematically related to *Krasnoe koleso* ("The Red Wheel"), and "Na krayakh" ("Far Away") continued the theme of peasant insurrections in Tambov. Treated principally as a news maker rather than a writer, Solzhenitsyn was followed more closely by journalists than by literary critics. In addition, the writer's silence about the war in Chechnya added to the controversy surrounding his political views.

The need to revisit the past was also reflected in the Russian Booker Prize nominations. Only 3 of the 36 writers nominated ended up on the shortlist, and the choices showed the judges' preference for traditional and realistic prose. On the shortlist were Georgy Vladimov's *General i yego armiya* ("A General and His Army"), a novel about the war on the Eastern Front and a voice in the ongoing Russian debate over the historical roles played by Gener-

Yevgeny Yevtushenko
RICK CHARD

als Georgy Zhukov and Andrey Vlasov in World War II; Oleg Pavlov's literary debut, *Kazyonnaya skazka* ("An Official Tale"), a novel about a unit guarding prisoners in the depths of Kazakhstan that, in both realistic and grotesque terms, presented the horrors and absurdities of contemporary Russian army life; and Yevgeny Fyodorov's account of his time in the Stalinist Gulag, entitled *Ilyada Zheni Vasyaeva* ("The Odyssey"). The prize went to Vladimov's *General i yego armiya*.

The so-called little Booker was established to honour the journal considered to have done the most to promote Russian literature in any of the countries of the former Soviet Union other than the Russian Federation itself. The 1995 award went to *Rodnik* (Riga, Latvia).

The Pushkin Prize for poetry was awarded to Semen Lipkin for his life's work, which included fiction, historical prose, poetry, and translations of Eastern literature. Noteworthy new collections of poetry included Joseph Brodsky's *Peresechyonnaya mestnost* ("Broken Country"), reflecting on the multitude of places the poet had lived; Inna Bliznetsova's *Zhizn ognya* ("The Life of a Fire"); and Vladlen Gavrilchik's *Izdeliya dukha* ("The Goods of the Spirit"). *Gadaniye po knige* ("Fortune Telling by the Book"), a collection by the esteemed poet Andrey Voznesensky, was criticized by some for what was considered its lack of genuine poetry. Known for the use of videos in his poetry, Voznesensky this time had a pair of dice supplied with the book so that the reader might throw them to determine the page and poetic line corresponding to his or her fortune, somewhat like the *I Ching*.

A return to the past was also reflected in biography and criticism. The reading public expressed interest in many newly published memoirs: diaries by Mikhail Prishvin and Yury Nagibin, Varlam Shalamov's *Iz zapisnykh knizhek* ("Pages from the Notebooks"), and Dmitry Likhachev's *Vospominaniya* ("Memoirs"). The first Russian biography of Vladimir Nabokov, *Mir i dar Vladimira Nabokova* ("The World and the Gift of Vladimir Nabokov"), was published by Boris Nosik.

In criticism, Yevgeny Yevtushenko stirred controversy with his anthology of 20th-century Russian poetry, *Strofy veka* ("The Verses of the Century"). *Vernutsya v Rossiyu stikhami* ("Returning to Russia in Verse") was an anthology of Russian émigré poetry of the first and second wave, together with biographies and with commentaries by Vadim Kreyd. An almanac, *Rubezh* ("Border"), published in Vladivostok, provided an overview of Russian émigré literature in China before World War II.

(EDWARD J. CZERWINSKI; AGNIESZKA PERLINSKA)

EASTERN EUROPEAN

Perhaps the most eagerly awaited publication of the past decade in Poland was Jerzy Giedroyć's *Autobiografia na cztery ręce* ("Autobiography for Four Hands"). It was an amazing revelation of the events that had inspired the monthly *Kultura* ("Culture") and the Publishing House of the Literary Institute, which published hundreds of banned books. At the same time, it was an intimate portrait of the writer. This was supplemented by Giedroyć's collection of letters, *Listy 1950–1987* ("Letters 1950–1987").

Marek Nowakowski, a member of the so-called angry generation of the 1960s, regained his popularity with the younger audience with *Powidoki: Chłopcy z tamtych lat* ("Afterimages: Young Men from Those Years"). As in his earlier works, the 72 sketches were populated with pimps, prostitutes, crooks, beggars, and a panoply of the insulted and humiliated. Hanna Krall's new volume of 10 tales, *Dowody na istnienie* ("Proofs of Existence"), explored the Jewish experience in Poland in a prose style reminiscent of Tadeusz Borowski. In his novel *Trzy razy* ("Three Times"), Dariusz Bitner once again demonstrated his skill as a modern-day spinner of tales, replete with strong language and colourful situations. In the third volume of her memoirs, *Wspomnienia i podróże* ("Reminiscences and Travels"), Monika Zeromska lightheartedly related her thoughts about visiting England, Israel, and Italy. Science fiction and parapsychology formed the basis of three popular novels, Andrzej Sapkowski's *Oko Yrrhedesa* ("The Eye of Yrrhedes"), Jacek Natanson's *MIB* ("Men in Black"), and Joanna Chmielewska's *Ladowanie w Garwolinie* ("Landing in Garwolin").

At age 66 Serbia's greatest contemporary playwright, Aleksandar Popovic, had three premiers during the 1995 season: *Ružičnjak* ("The Rose Garden"), *Čarlama, zbogom* ("Farewell, Liars"), and *Mrtva tačka* ("The Dead Spot"). A number of his earlier works were revived, including *Razvojni put Bore Šnajdera* ("The Evolutionary Road of Bore the Tailor"). His antiwar play *Tamna je noč* ("Dark Is the Night") was premiered in New York City in September. Two additions to the theme of World War II appeared: Nikola Moravčević's *Albion Albion*, offering a rich mixture of historical authenticity and high literary quality, and Sava Janković's first volume of the epic, *Na prelomu* ("Turning Point"), a semihistorical account of the war years.

With the distribution of print in the hands of government officials, Romania was still experiencing technical censorship. Even after six years of restricted freedom, television and newspaper coverage depended primarily on the vagaries of the print distributor. The appointment of Viorel Marginean as minister of culture was viewed skeptically by the country's intelligentsia. His predecessor, Marin Sorescu, was implicated in various financial scandals and was forced to resign.

With the lifting of the embargo by Greece, Macedonia was quickly recovering from the shocks of economic and political turmoil. Nowhere was the change more evident than in the field of publishing. Ante Popovski's collection *Prividenija* ("Providence") won the Braća Miladinović Award at the Struga poetry festival as the best book of poetry. The worlds of history and theosophy were intimately intertwined in these poems, which contained mysterious messages from the forefathers to posterity. Petre M. Andreevski's collection of short stories *Site lica na smrtta* ("All the Faces of Death") was considered his finest work. The stories, combining both modernity and folk wisdom, were read as metaphors for Macedonian life today. Dragi Mihajlovski's collection of short stories *Skok so stap* ("Pole Vault") won the Račin Recognition Award for the best book of fiction. The stories displayed an interesting union of the grotesque and fantastic, used to create insight into the nature of reality. The historical novel was also represented by Slobodan Mičković's *Aleksandr i smrtta* ("Alexander and Death"). The novel was written in the form of notes that Alexander's armourer sends to Aristotle and covered the final two years of the Macedonian ruler's life.

In the Czech Republic, Antonín Brousek was awarded the Seifert Prize for his collection of poems *Vteřinové smrti* ("Deaths by Seconds"), a pessimistic view of the human condition at the end of the 20th century. Jan Trefulka's novel *Svedený a opuštěný* ("Misled and Abandoned") described the conflict between two approaches to life. Zdena Frýbová's *Polda* ("Cop"), the best-seller of 1995, recounted the illegal activities of various entrepreneurs and of the Mafia after 1989. Lenka Procházková's *Zvrhlé dny* ("Perverted Days"), a collection of short stories, presented life in a society that recently had discovered the meaning of freedom. Karel Steigerwald's drama *Nobel* was notable for its topicality and its attempt to explore the Czech past.

(EDWARD J. CZERWINSKI; AGNIESZKA PERLINSKA)

JEWISH

Hebrew. Several veteran writers published novels in 1995 that did not match their previous achievements. Among them were Savyon Liebrecht's *Tsarikh Sof le-Sipur Ahavah* ("On Love Stories and Other Endings"), Judith Katzir's *LeMatisse Yesh et haShemesh baBeten* ("Matisse Had the Sun in His Belly"), Yitzhak Ben-Ner's *Dubim veYa'ar* ("Bears and Forests"), and David Schütz's *Sheva Nashim* ("Seven Women"). Even Orly Castel-Bloom's *HaMina Liza* ("The Mina Lisa") was less intriguing than her previous novels. The only novel that rose above this tendency was Ronit Matalon's *Ze Im haPanim Eileinu* ("The One Facing Us"). Originality and promise could be found in the first novels of Benny Ziffer (*Marsh Turki* ["La Marche Turque"]), Ronit Yedaya (*Vacuum*), Dorit Rabinyan (*Simtat* *haShkediot beOmerijan* ["The Almond Tree Alley in Omerijan"]), and Masha Waisel (*Michtavim leMartha* ["Letters to Martha"]).

The main publications in Hebrew poetry were Dalia Rabikovitch's *Kol haShirim Ad Ko* ("The Complete Poems So Far"), Meir Wieseltier's *Mahsan* ("Storage"), and Aharon Shabtai's *HaLev* ("The Heart"). Others included Rahel Halfi's *Ahavat haDrakon* ("Love of the Dragon"), Nathan Yonathan's *Re'ul Panim haZman* ("Veiled Face Is the Time"), Agi Mishol's *HaShfeila haPnimit* ("The Interior Plain"), and Admiel Kosman's *Ma Ani Yakhol* ("What I Can").

Among works of literary scholarship were Dan Miron's studies in classical Jewish fiction (*Harofe haMedume* ["La Médicin Imaginaire"]), Yitzhak Laor's *Anu Kotvim Otakh Moledet* ("Narratives with No Natives"), and Hillel Barzel's *Dramah Shel Matsavim Kitsoniyim: Milhamah ve-Sho'ah* ("Drama of Extreme Situations: War and Holocaust"). Avraham Balaban examined postmodern trends in Hebrew fiction in *Gal Aher baSiporet haIvrit* ("A Different Wave of Hebrew Fiction"). Dan Laor studied aspects of Shmuel Yosef Agnon's fiction in *S.Y. Agnon: Hebetim Hadashim* ("S.Y. Agnon: New Perspectives"), and Avraham Holtz published an edition of Agnon's *Hakhnasat Kala* ("The Bridal Canopy"). Zvia Ben-Yosef Ginor discussed Abba Kovner's poems in *Ad Ketz haBedaya* ("Beyond the Legend"). The Israel Prize was awarded to the poet Nathan Zach and the novelist A.B. Yehoshua. (AVRAHAM BALABAN)

Yiddish. Among new publications was Moyshe Bernshteyn's *Shlofloze nekht* ("Sleepless Nights"), a volume of elegiac poems. The verse in Eli Beyder's *Troymen un vor* ("Dreams and Reality") was evocative and autobiographical. The anthology *A libe-regn* ("A Shower of Love"), by Mikhal Felzenbaum, demonstrated a meditative spirit. Daniel Galay hovered over his subjects with brief but penetrating reflections in *Oyer-siluetn* ("Audio-Silouettes"). The poet Ktsiye Ratner-Margolin's *Oyf mayne vegn fun vander* ("On My Wandering Path") provided an array of settings for her interior monologue. Aleksander Royzin wrote of Jewish life under Soviet rule in *Mayne lider, vi di toybn* ("My Poems, Like Doves"). Aaron Kramer translated and edited a bilingual anthology of Dore Taytlboym's poems, *Ale mayne nekhtn zaynen shtign* ("All My Yesterdays Were Steps").

Among prose works *Nyu-yorker adresn* ("New York Addresses") included more than 20 short stories by Yoni Fayn. The prose sketches, tales, and short novel in Shire Gorshman's *Vi tsum ershtn mol* ("As Though for the First Time") gave an enigmatic vision of modern times. Yisroel Kaplan penned a series of prose sketches in *Onhalt* ("Support"). *Misnagdishe mayses* ("Stories of the Misnagdim") was the third of H.-D. Meynkes' collections. Shloyme Vorzoger published the sophisticated and powerful novel *Libshaft* ("Love"), about the Eastern European community in Israel.

Herts Grosbard was the subject of a monograph, *Der bal-tfile fun der yidisher literatur* ("The Coryphaeus of Yiddish Literature"), by Mordkhe Tsanin. Avrom Lis compiled a collection of correspondence, including previously unpublished items, in his *Briv fun Sholem Aleikhem* ("The Letters of Sholem Aleichem"). Yoysef Bulof's *Fun altn mark-plats* ("From the Old Market-Place"), published as a book nearly 10 years after the author's death, was an imaginative memoir of childhood and adolescence written by a figure of the stage. Miriam Krant's essays in *Geflekht fun tsvaygn* ("A Skein of Branches") offered reflections on leading writers and poets. (THOMAS E. BIRD)

Yashar Kemal
ULF ANDERSON—GAMMA LIAISON

TURKISH

For Turkish literature 1995 was a lack-lustre year in which no major works saw print. Yashar Kemal (*see* BIOGRAPHIES) published no new book in 1995, but he did stir controversy with his relentless criticism of human rights violations in the *Index on Censorship*, *Stern*, and the *New York Times*. Orhan Pamuk rested on the laurels of his 1994 blockbuster *Yeni hayat* ("New Life") and the English translation of his novel *Kara kitap* (*The Black Book*). He also attracted attention with essays and interviews published in Europe and with his first-page critical essay on Salman Rushdie in the *Times Literary Supplement*.

Hundreds of books of poetry were published in 1995. Noteworthy were new and republished collections by Ilhan Berk and *Toplu siirler* ("Collected Poems") by Ahmet Oktay, who also published a 1,300-page first volume of his critical anthology of the literature of the Turkish republic. There were dazzling achievements in translation—from Chaucer's *The Canterbury Tales* to the poetry of Hilda Doolittle.

Nedim Gürsel, who lived in Paris, produced *Boğazkesen* ("Bosphorus Fortress"), one of the best Postmodernist novels in Turkish, which integrated the fall of Constantinople and the coup d'état of 1980. Necati Cumali received the Orhan Kemal and the Yunus Nadi prizes for his novel *Viran dağlar* ("Ruined Mountains").

Turkey's most popular satirist of all time, Aziz Nesin (*see* OBITUARIES), who had been a controversial figure since the mid-1940s, died in 1995 at the age of 79. He left behind more than 90 books of fiction, poetry, plays, essays, and other works, in addition to hundreds of uncollected newspaper articles. Bilge Karasu, a prominent novelist, who had won the Pegasus Prize in 1991 for his *Gece* (1985; *Night*, 1994), also died during the year. (TALAT S. HALMAN)

PERSIAN

Despite tensions over literature and culture, many works were published in Iran in 1995, and literature continued to enjoy the privileged social position it had occupied historically. Two novels, *Farar-e Faravahar* ("Faravahar's Escape") by Esma'il Fasih and *Hekayat-e ruzegar* ("The Story of the Times") by Farideh Golbu, won the Golden Plume prize for fiction established by *Gardun*, a monthly literary journal, as did Ghazaleh Alizadeh's short-story collection entitled *Chahar-rah* ("Crossroads"). A state-supported literature glorifying Muslims and demonizing enemies of Islam continued to present idealized images in countless poems and stories. Popular and journalistic fiction, headed by two serial works by Fahimeh Rahimi, a prolific writer, continued to outsell works of far greater aesthetic merit. Afghan and Tajik writers also published works in Tehran, mostly in anthologies.

Presses in Europe and the United States published several important works of Persian literature in 1995, among them Abbas Saffari's collection of poems titled *Dar moltaqaye dast va sib* ("At the Crossing of Hands and Apples") and Naser Shahinpar's short-story collection *Labas-e rasmi-ye tars* ("Fear's Official Uniform"). *Edges of Poetry,* a selection of Esma'il Kho'i's poems in Persian with English on facing pages, led the way in translations of Persian poetry into English.

The Society for Iranian Studies established a prize in the name of the late Iranian writer Ali-Akbar Sa'idi-Sirjani. Iranian poets, novelists, and critics, both those living in Iran and in exile, conducted reading tours sponsored by various Iranian community organizations in Europe, Canada, and the United States, and a variety of scholarly and academic exchanges between Iran and its expatriates proceeded unaffected by the embargo imposed by the U.S. government. (AHMAD KARIMI-HAKKAK)

ARABIC

The 19th congress of the General Union of Arab Writers (GUAW), held in Casablanca, Morocco, in January 1995, voted unanimously to readmit Egypt. Readmission was conditional, however, on Egypt's Writers Union's adhering to the GUAW policy of opposition to normalization of relations with Israel. The GUAW split over the issue of its general secretariat, finally deciding to reelect its general secretary and maintain its headquarters in Amman, Jordan. Some members supported the head of the host Moroccan Writers Union, one of the few independent unions in the Arab world, and moving the secretariat to Rabat. The disagreement illustrated the conflict between the old centres of modern Arabic culture, in Egypt and the Levant, and the vibrant literature in North Africa and elsewhere.

The debate over opposition to the Middle East peace treaties erupted again when the Syrian Writers Union suspended the membership of the poet Adūnīs for his call for normalization of relations with Israel and his participation with Israelis in several conferences. Several Algerian writers, dramatists, and journalists were assassinated by Islamic extremists in 1995. In Lebanon the three major works of the secular Libyan writer as-Sādiq an-Nayhūm, who died on Nov. 15, 1994, were banned.

The only Arabic magazine devoted to the literature of women and their cultural concerns faltered in 1995 and then ceased publication altogether. After its phenomenal early success, *An-Kātibah* ("The Woman Writer"), which was published in London, was censored and banned in several Arab countries and encountered financial problems. The literary monthly *An-Nāqid* ("The Critic") also was forced to close down. A platform for experimentation and an independent journal championing freedom of expression, it too was censored and banned.

A number of outstanding novels appeared in 1995. The towering achievement was Bahā' Ṭāhir's *Al-Ḥubb fi al-manfā* ("Love in Exile"), an insightful reexamination of one of the recurring themes in Arabic literature, the relationship between the Arab "self" and the Western "other." It established its author as Egypt's most outstanding novelist after Naguib Mahfouz. *An-Nakhkhās* ("The Slave Merchant") by the Tunisian novelist Ṣalāḥ ad-Dīn Būjāh was a remarkably innovative novel, praised for its profound dialogue in traditional Arab prose and its rich lyricism. *'Azīzi as-Sayyid Kawabata* ("Dear Mr. Kawabata") by Rashīd ad-Ḍa'īf stood out for its poetic vision and its sensitive rendering of childhood in a Christian village in Mount Lebanon. Other important novels included, in Egypt, the erotic work *Bayḍat an-na'āmah* ("The Ostrich's Egg") by Ra'ūf Mus'ad, *Ṭa'm al-Ḥrīq* ("The Taste of Fire") by Maḥmūd al-Wirdāni, *An-Naml al-Abyaḍ* ("White Ants") by 'Abd al-Wahhāb al-Aswānī, and *Laḥn as-Ṣabāḥ* ("Morning Tune") by Muḥammad Nājī; in Lybia, *As-Saḥarah* ("The Sorcerers") by Ibrāhīm al-Kūnī; in Syria, *Inānah wa 'n-nahr* ("Inanah and the River") by Halīm Barakāt; and in Iraq, *Khātim ar-raml* ("The Sand Ring") by Fu'ād at-Takarlī.

Novels published by women included, in Lebanon, *Ahl al-hawa* ("The Lovers") by Hudā Barakāt, *Al-Jamr al-ghāfi* ("The Slumber Ember") by Emily Naṣrallah, and *Ḥayāt wa ālām Ḥamad ibn Silānah* ("The Life and Pains of Hamad the Son of Silanah") by Najwā Barakāt; in Iraq, *Al-Wala'* ("Obsession") by 'Āliyah Mamdūḥ; in Egypt, *Ṣāḥib al-Bayt* ("The Landlord") by Laṭīfah az-Zayyāt, *Maryamah wa 'r-raḥīl* ("Maryamah and the Departure") by Raḍwā 'Āshūr, and *Muntahā* ("Muntaha") by Hālah al-Badrī; and, in Tunisia, *Tamās* ("Contact") by 'Arūsīyah an-Nālūtī.

The poetry collection *Limādhā ayuhā al-māḍi tanām fi ḥadīqati* ("Oh! Past Why Do You Sleep in My Garden"), by the Egyptian poet 'Abd al-Mun'im Ramaḍān, was published during the year. The new collection by Adūnīs was immodestly entitled *Al-Kitāh* ("The Book"), normally reserved in Arabic for the Qur'ān. (SABRY HAFEZ)

CHINESE

Fiction continued to dominate the Chinese literary scene in 1995. There was a trend toward promotion and "packaging" while taking care not to surfeit the reader with ideologies or avant-gardism. A fiction series labeled "Cloth Tiger" (a pun on "Paper Tiger") that was launched by Shenyang's Spring Breeze Literary Press met with an enthusiastic reception. Wang Meng's *Ansha 3322* ("Assassination 3322"), one notable work in the series, entertained while not losing sight of the need for moral relevance. The story dramatized the ruinous aftereffects of a "crime" on a bright young man's future. Also in the series was Tie Ning's *Wuyuzhi cheng* ("The Rainless City"), a feminist work that pitted men's self-preserving instincts against women's capacity for self-sacrifice in their assertion of love.

The popular success of "Cloth Tiger" spawned a number of imitators. Not to be outdone, literary journals also tried to rally the reader by casting an aura of mystique on their fiction selections. *Beijing wenxue* "Beijing Literature"), for instance, installed "xintiyan xiaoshuo" ("fiction of new experientialism") as a special feature.

The desire to be noted, to reach a larger audience, and to secure a better financial return for his labour seemed to affect Yu Hua, a postmodern fabulist known for elliptical writing. In the eyes of common readers, he became a born-again storyteller with the publication of *Huozhe* ("To Live"), an old-fashioned narrative celebrating the virtue of the will to live. The novel was adapted by director Zhang Yimou into a movie. *Baiye* ("Pallid Night"), Jia Pingwa's first novel since the sensational *Feidu* ("The Ruined Capital"), documented the lethargic and purposeless existence of Xi'an's middle and lower classes. Su Tong's *Chengbei didai* ("North of the City") revisited the eruption of violence and manifestations of depravity on the legendary Xiangchun Street during the Cultural Revolution. Howard Goldblatt's translations of *Tiantang suandaizhige* (*The Garlic Ballads*) and *Mi* (*Rice*), novels by Mo Yan and Su Tong, respectively, were published in the U.S.

In Taiwan the *Chung-kuo Shih-pao* (*China Times*) chose Chu T'ien-wen as the first recipient of its prize for fiction. Narrated from the perspective of a gay male, her *Huang-jen shou-chi* ("Notes of the Misbegotten") was a daring attempt to probe homosexuality both as an exquisite anguish and as an aesthetic experience. Su Wei-chen won an award for her *Ch'en-mo-chih tao* ("The Silent Isle"), essentially a tale about a career woman in conflict with herself. In Hong Kong the first part of the latest work by Xi Xi, *Feizhan* ("The Flying Carpet"), was serialized in *Lianhe wenxue* ("Unitas"). Framed in settings at once fantastic and realistic, the episodic work evoked memories of the British colony in its early days. (JOSEPH S.M. LAU)

JAPANESE

Two voluminous and remarkable novels, *Saigyō kaden* ("The Glorious Life of Saigyō") by Kunio Tsuji and *Nejimaki-dori kuronikura* ("The Chronicle of the 'Screw-turning' Bird") by Haruki Murakami, were published in 1995. Tsuji's novel was awarded the Jun'ichirō Tanizaki Prize. Murakami's trilogy was especially popular among young readers, but the critics were divided.

Tsuji's biographical novel of Saigyō, a 12th-century samurai turned priest-poet, was impressive for its evocative prose and rich texture in describing the historical milieu. Saigyō had long been an appealing character to the Japanese imagination, and many legends and much academic research had accumulated on him, but Tsuji's narration, which made use of multiple points of view, revived interest in the enigmatic figure.

Murakami's trilogy was remarkable for its curious mixture of fantasy and realism. The central story was the abrupt, mysterious disappearance of a young wife and the search by her husband, Tōru, nicknamed Nejimaki-dori (hence the title). In his search he comes across various interruptions and unexpected encounters, sometimes in dreams, sometimes in reality. Some of the characters he happens across are ominous and violent, and some of them, especially women, sexually liberated or endowed with prophetic visions.

There were two charming collections of short stories, both by women novelists, published in 1995. Nobuko Takagi's *Suimyaku* ("Vein of Water"), winner of the Women Writers' Prize, was successful in evoking a curiously sensuous mood with rich overtones by interweaving apparently unrelated short stories around the central motif of water. Mizuko Masuda's *Kazekusa* ("Wind Grass") was a straightforward, even prosaic, account of various aspects of family relationships in contemporary Japan. Masuda's stories were not simply gloomy and depressing but rather revealed an unexpected sense of family solidarity.

The Sakutarō Hagiwara Prize in Poetry was awarded to Sachiko Yoshihara, whose *Hakkō* ("Radiation") was remarkable for its limpid, pure lyricism, something quite rare in contemporary Japanese poetry. Mutsuo Takahashi's *Ane no shima* ("Island of My Elder Sister") was half mythical and half autobiographical; it tried to fuse the mythical motifs of an ancient island in Kyushu with the memories of a deceased sister.

Hiroko Takenishi's *Nihon no bungakuron* ("Literary Criticism in Japan") was an analysis of classical poetics that revealed insights by traditional poet-critics. Eisuke Nakazono's *Torii Ryūzō-den* ("Life of Torii Ryūzō") was a remarkable contribution to biography, dealing with the explorer-archaeologist (1870–1953) who, even though he did not finish grade school, came to teach at the University of Tokyo and whose researches covered wide areas in East Asia. (SHOICHI SAEKI)

Mathematics and Physical Sciences

MATHEMATICS

The long-running saga of Fermat's last theorem was finally concluded in 1995. The nearly 360-year-old conjecture states that $x^n + y^n = z^n$ has no positive integer solutions if x, y, z, and n are positive integers and n is three or more. In 1993 Andrew Wiles of Princeton University announced a proof, based on new results in algebraic number theory. By 1994, however, a gap in the proof had emerged. The gap was repaired—or, more accurately, circumvented—by Wiles and former student Richard Taylor of the University of Cambridge. The difficulty in Wiles's proof arose from an attempt to construct a so-called Euler system. The new approach involves making a detailed study of algebraic structures known as Hecke algebras, a task in which Taylor's contribution proved crucial. The complete proof was confirmed by experts and published in the *Annals of Mathematics.*

Fruitful revisionism of a different kind took place in the important area of gauge field theory, in which ideas originating in mathematical physics for the purpose of describing subatomic particles and their interactions were being applied to topology—the study of the properties that a region of space retains under deformation—with spectacular consequences. Paramount among them was the discovery, made in 1983 by Simon Donaldson of the University of Oxford, that the properties of four-dimensional Euclidean space are exceptional compared with those of the spaces of all other dimensions. Donaldson's discovery was based on the Yang-Mills field equations in quantum mechanics, introduced in the 1950s by the physicists Chen Ning Yang and Robert L. Mills to describe the interactions between particles in the atomic nucleus. The equations possess special solutions known as instantons—particle-like wave packets that occupy a small region of space and exist for a tiny instant. Donaldson observed that instanton solutions of the Yang-Mills equations encode topological information about the space for which the equations are posed. But just as mathematics was adjusting to the powerful new techniques arising from that insight, Edward Witten of the Institute for Advanced Study, Princeton, N.J., developed an entirely new system of equations that can be substituted for those of Yang and Mills. Witten's ideas, far from supplanting the earlier approach, were shedding light on how the Yang-Mills equations work. Witten's equations replace instantons with magnetic monopoles, hypothetical particles possessing a single magnetic pole—mathematically a far more tractable setting. The early payoff included proofs of several long-standing conjectures in low-dimensional topology.

A long-standing question in dynamical systems theory, *i.e.,* the genuineness of the chaos observed in the Lorenz equations, was answered. The equations were developed by the meteorologist Edward Lorenz in 1963 in a model of atmospheric convection. Using a computer, he showed that the solutions were highly irregular—small changes in the input values produced large changes in the solutions, which led to apparently random behaviour of the system. In modern parlance such behaviour is called chaos. Computers, however, use finite precision arithmetic, which introduces round-off errors. Is the apparent chaos in the Lorenz equations an artifact of finite precision, or is it genuine? Konstantin Mischaikow and Marian Mrozek of the Georgia Institute of Technology showed that chaos really is present. Ironically their proof was computer-assisted. Nevertheless, that fact did not render the proof "unrigorous" because the role of the computer was to perform certain lengthy but routine calculations, which in principle could be done by hand. Indeed, Mischaikow and Mrozek justified using the computer by setting up a rigorous mathematical framework for finite precision arithmetic. Their main effort went into devising a theory to pass from finite precision to infinite precision. In short, they found a way to parlay the computer's approximations into an exact result.

A famous problem in recreational mathematics was solved by political scientist Steven Brams of New York University and mathematician Alan Taylor of Union College, Schenectady, N.Y. The problem is to devise a proportional envy-free allocation protocol. An allocation protocol is a systematic method for dividing some desired object—traditionally a cake—among several people. It is proportional if each person is satisfied that he or she is receiving at least a fair share, and it is envy-free if each person is satisfied that no one is receiving more than a fair share. This area of mathematics was invented in 1944 by the mathematician Hugo Steinhaus. For two people the problem is solved by the "I cut, you choose" protocol; Steinhaus' contribution was a proportional but not envy-free protocol for three people. In the early 1960s John Selfridge and John Horton Conway independently found an envy-free protocol for three people, but the problem remained open for four or more people. Brams and Taylor discovered highly complex proportional envy-free protocols for any number of people. Because many areas of human conflict focus upon similar questions, their ideas had potential conflict-resolving applications in economics, politics, and social science. (IAN STEWART)

This article updates the *Macropædia* articles ANALYSIS; NUMBER THEORY; Principles of PHYSICAL SCIENCE; TOPOLOGY.

CHEMISTRY

Chemical Nomenclature. Responding to criticism from chemists around the world, the International Union of Pure and Applied Chemistry (IUPAC) in 1995 decided to reconsider the definitive names that it had announced the previous year for elements 101–109. The decision was unprecedented in the history of IUPAC, an association of national chemistry organizations formed in 1919 to set uniform standards for chemical names, symbols, constants, and other matters. IUPAC's Commission on Nomenclature of Inorganic Chemistry had recommended adoption of names for the elements that, in several cases, differed significantly from names selected by the elements' discoverers.

The extremely heavy elements were synthesized between the 1950s and 1980s by researchers in the U.S., Germany, and the Soviet Union. Although the discoverers had exercised their traditional right to select names, the names never received IUPAC's stamp of approval because of disputes over priority of discovery. The conflicting claims were resolved by an international commission in 1993, and the discoverers submitted their chosen names to IUPAC. An international furor ensued after the IUPAC nomenclature panel ignored many of the submissions and made

Names and Symbols for Elements 101–109

Atomic number	IUPAC proposals	ACS differences
101	mendelevium (Md)	—
102	nobelium (No)	—
103	lawrencium (Lr)	—
104	dubnium (Db)	rutherfordium (Rf)
105	joliotium (Jl)	hahnium (Ha)
106	rutherfordium (Rf)	seaborgium (Sg)
107	bohrium (Bh)	nielsbohrium (Ns)
108	hahnium (Hn)	hassium (Hs)
109	meitnerium (Mt)	—

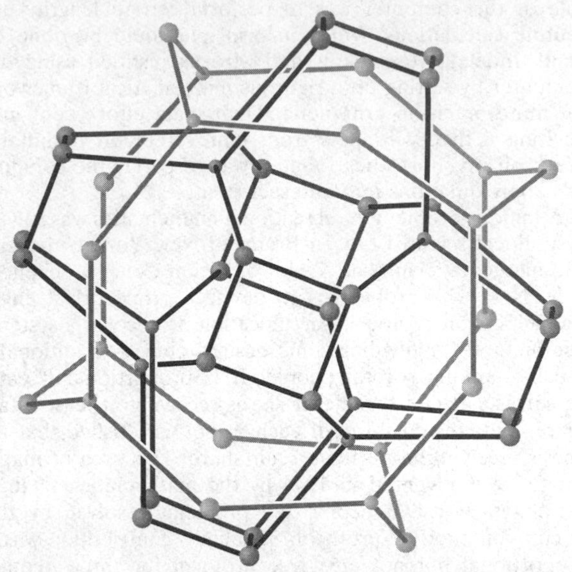

Two interlocking structures form a molecular cage in a representation of a new crystalline material discovered by Richard Robson and co-workers at the University of Melbourne, Australia. The material may prove useful in trapping molecules for novel chemical reactions.

ADAPTED WITH PERMISSION FROM S. BATTEN, B. HOSKINS, R. ROBSON, *JOURNAL OF THE AMERICAN CHEMICAL SOCIETY*, VOL. 117 (MAY 17, 1995), PP. 5385–86; © 1995; AMERICAN CHEMICAL SOCIETY

its own recommendations. IUPAC's rejection of the name seaborgium for element 106 caused particular dismay in the U.S. Discoverers of the element had named it for Glenn T. Seaborg, Nobel laureate and codiscoverer of plutonium and several other heavy elements. In response, IUPAC's General Assembly decided that names for elements 101–109 would revert to provisional status during a five-month review process scheduled to begin in January 1996. Chemists and member organizations were to submit comments on the names for IUPAC's reconsideration.

The American Chemical Society (ACS) directed its publications to continue using the recommendations of its own nomenclature committee for the duration of IUPAC's review. All of the ACS's names for elements 104–108 differed from those on IUPAC's list. (*See* Table on p. 239.)

Inorganic Chemistry. People treasure gold mainly because it resists tarnishing and discoloration better than any other metal. Iron rusts and silver tarnishes when in contact with oxygen in the air. Gold remains bright and glistening, however, even in the presence of acids and other highly corrosive chemicals. Scientists have never fully understood gold's inertness. It is not a simple matter of gold's inability to form chemical bonds, since it does form stable compounds with many elements. The real mystery is why gold does not react with atoms or molecules at its surface, at the interface with gases or liquids.

Bjork Hammer and Jens Nørskov of the Technical University of Denmark, Lyngby, used calculations run on a supercomputer to explain gold's stature as the noblest of the noble metals. Those elements, known for their inertness, are gold, silver, platinum, palladium, iridium, rhodium, mercury, ruthenium, and osmium. The Danish scientists found that gold's surface has electronic features that make reactions energetically unfavourable. Molecules form very weak attachments to gold's surface and quickly lose their tendency to break up into reactive chemical species. As a result, they simply slide away without forming long-lasting electronic or molecular attachments.

Hammer and Nørskov studied a simple reaction involving the breakup, or dissociation, of molecular hydrogen (H_2) into its constituent atoms on the surface of gold and other metals. Of all the metals studied, gold had the highest barrier for dissociation and the least-stable chemisorption state—*i.e.,* the least tendency to take up and hold atoms or molecules by chemical bonds. The properties result, in part, from an overlap of the electron orbitals, the clouds of electrons that surround atoms, between gold and the adsorbed molecule. The overlapping orbitals oscillate out of phase with each other, a situation that makes bond formation unlikely.

Physical Chemistry. Chemists long have sought better techniques for studying individual reactions between molecules in solutions. Such information about reaction dynamics can contribute to a basic understanding of chemical reactions and to the search for ways of improving the yield of industrial processes. Molecules in solution tend to move around rapidly, making it difficult to observe how the molecules react to yield a product. In contrast, molecules in solids undergo relatively little movement, and well-established techniques exist for studying interactions between molecules in gases. Recent efforts at improving the picture for molecules in solutions involved focusing on extremely small volumes of solution, thus reducing the number of molecules to be observed.

R. Mark Wightman of the University of North Carolina at Chapel Hill and Maryanne M. Collinson of Kansas State University reported a new technique for confining and observing molecules in solution that combines spectroscopy and electrochemistry. Wightman and Collinson studied reactions of oppositely charged ions of 9,10-diphenylanthracene (DPA) in an electrochemical cell containing a gold electrode. By rapidly reversing the electrical potential in the cell, the researchers produced batches of DPA cations and then anions—DPA ions with, respectively, positive and negative electrical charges. When a pair of oppositely charged ions interact, one of them emits a photon of light that can be detected with a photomultiplier tube. The researchers restricted the motion of DPA molecules by making the electrode only 10 micrometres (0.0004 in) in diameter, which produced small quantities of ions. They also observed the reactions in 50-microsecond time steps, which gave the DPA ions little time for movement.

Materials. Fibre-reinforced composite materials are a fixture in modern society. Tiny fibres of glass or silicon carbide, for instance, can be mixed into batches of plastic, ceramics, or other material. The combination yields lightweight, superstrong composites used in aircraft, automobiles, sports equipment, and many other products. Generally, the thinner the fibre, the stronger the material. Thin fibres provide a greater surface area to bond with the plastic or ceramic matrix and are less likely to have weakening defects in their crystal structure. Tensile strength increases as the size of the fibres decreases.

Charles M. Lieber and his associates of Harvard University reported synthesizing carbide whiskers 1,000 nm (nanometres; billionths of a metre) long and less than 30 nm in diameter—one-thousandth the size of those used in today's superstrong composites. Their ultrafine whiskers, or "nanorods," of silicon carbide—and carbides of boron, titanium, niobium, and iron—could lead to a new generation of superstrong composites. Lieber's carbide nanorods have the same properties as the bulk materials. Nanorods of silicon carbide, for instance, are semiconductors, those of niobium carbide are superconducting, and those of iron carbide are ferromagnetic. Nanorods thus could have additional practical applications in electronics. Lieber synthesized carbide nanorods from carbon nanotubes, which are hollow, nanometre-diameter tubes of graphitic carbon. They used the nanotubes as templates, heating the tubes with volatile oxides such as silicon monoxide (SiO) or halides such as silicon tetraiodide (SiI_4) in sealed quartz tubes at temperatures above 1,000° C (1,800° F).

Charles R. Martin and co-workers of Colorado State University reported the synthesis of metal membranes that are spanned by nanometre-sized pores and that can selectively pass, or transport, ions, an ability similar to that possessed by ion-exchange polymers. The electrical charge on the membranes can be varied such that they reject ions of the same charge and transport ions of the opposite charge. Existing porous membranes can transport either anions or cations, but they are fixed in terms of ion selectivity and pore size. Martin suggested that the new membranes could serve as a model for studying biological membranes, which exhibit the same ion selectivity. They also could be used in commercial separation processes—for example, for separating small anions from a solution containing both large and small anions and cations.

Martin's group made the membranes by gold-plating commercially available polymer filtration membranes, which have cylindrical pores about 50 nm in diameter. The researchers originally planned to plate the pores full of gold to make gold nanofibres. Serendipitously they discovered that the membrane became ion selective when its pores were lined with gold but not completely filled.

Researchers at the University of Bath, England, reported a method for synthesizing hollow porous shells of crystalline calcium carbonate, or aragonite, from a self-organizing reaction mixture. The shells resemble the so-called coccospheres synthesized by certain marine algae and could have important applications as lightweight ceramics, catalyst supports, biomedical implants, and chemical separations material. Stephen Mann and his associates made the complex, three-dimensional structures from emulsions consisting of microscopic droplets of oil, water, and surfactants (detergents) and supersaturated with calcium bicarbonate. The pore size of the resulting material was determined by the relative concentrations of water and oil in the emulsion, with micrometre-sized polystyrene beads serving as the substrate.

Organic Chemistry. Polyethylene plastics are the world's most popular type of plastic, widely used in packaging, bags, disposable diapers, bottles, coatings, films, and innumerable other products. Chemical companies make polyethylene by means of a polymerization reaction that involves linking together thousands of molecular units of ethylene (C_2H_4) into enormous chains.

Researchers at BP Chemicals, a division of British Petroleum, London, reported development of a simple modification in their widely used polyethylene process that can more than double output from each reactor. During conventional polymerization, reactor temperatures rise, and heat removal becomes a bottleneck that limits production capacity. The new reactor design overcomes the problem by using gases given off during polymerization to cool the reactor. Gases are collected, cooled, liquefied, and injected back into the reactor. The liquids immediately vaporize and, in so doing, absorb enough heat to permit a doubling of polyethylene output.

Chemists have grown adept at enclosing single atoms of different elements inside molecular cages like the 60-carbon molecules known as buckminsterfullerenes, or buckyballs. The spaces inside those soccer-ball-shaped molecules are relatively small, however, which has spurred researchers to develop bigger molecular cages that can accommodate larger molecules or groups of molecules. Held together in close quarters, such confined molecules might undergo commercially important reactions.

Richard Robson and his associates at the University of Melbourne, Australia, reported their development of a crystalline lattice containing a regular array of comparatively huge cagelike compartments. Each cage is about 2.3 nm in diameter, large enough to house as many as 20 large molecules. Robson and co-workers developed the cages by accident while trying to make new types of zeolites, highly porous minerals used as catalysts and molecular filters. Into an organic solvent they mixed ions of nitrate, cyanide, zinc, and molecules of tri(pyridyl)-1,3,5-triazine, hoping to create a new zeolite. Instead, the components self-assembled into two interlocking structures that formed a lattice of large cagelike cells.

Light-emitting diodes (LEDs) have become a ubiquitous part of modern life, widely used as small indicator lights on electronic devices and other consumer products. LEDs are semiconductors that convert electricity directly into light. The most common commercial LEDs are made from gallium arsenide phosphide and emit red light. Nevertheless, chemists and materials scientists also have developed LEDs that emit light of other colours, a notable exception being true, bright white light.

Junji Kido's group at Yamagata (Japan) University reported progress in making such an LED, which could have major commercial applications—for example, as a backlight source for extremely thin, flat television screens, computer displays, and other devices. Kido made the LED by stacking layers of three different light-emitting organic compounds between two electrodes. The bottom layer, made from triphenyldiamine, emits blue light. The middle layer is made from tris(8-quinolinolato)aluminum(III) and emits green light. The top layer is a red emitter made from tris(8-quinolinolato)aluminum(III) combined with small amounts of the organic dye nile red. Kido added a layer of another material between the blue and green to enhance production of blue light. The combination of red, green, and blue emission results in a bright white light. Kido's device shone with a record intensity for an LED, 2,000 candelas per square metre, which is about half the intensity of an ordinary fluorescent room light. (MICHAEL WOODS)

This article updates the *Macropædia* articles CHEMICAL COMPOUNDS; CHEMICAL ELEMENTS; CHEMICAL REACTIONS; ELECTRONICS; Chemical Process INDUSTRIES; The PHYSICAL SCIENCES: *Chemistry*.

PHYSICS

Confirmation of the discovery of a long-sought elementary particle delighted physicists in 1995, while the possible identification of another, unexpected type of particle gave them pause for thought. Cosmologists and astronomers were pleased with the finding of strong evidence for dim, small, starlike objects called brown dwarfs, which represent some of the so-called dark matter that is believed to make up perhaps 90% of the universe, but were baffled by conflicting determinations of the age of the universe. In the strange world of quantum physics, an intriguing proposal was made for an experiment using DNA, the molecule of life, in a modern version of a famous thought experiment outlined 60 years earlier.

The biggest development of the year was the confirmation of a claim tentatively put forward in 1994 that the top quark had been detected in particle-collision experiments at the Fermi National Accelerator Laboratory (Fermilab) near Chicago. Data in 1995 from two separate detectors at Fermilab's Tevatron proton-antiproton collider provided what appeared to be unequivocal evidence for this last piece in the jigsaw puzzle of the so-called standard model of particle physics. The standard model explains the composition of all matter in terms of six leptons (particles like the electron and its neutrino) and six quarks (constituents of particles like protons and neutrons), five of which had already been detected. Results from one detector indicated a mass for the top quark of 176 GeV (billion electron volts), with an uncertainty of 13 GeV; results from the other detector gave a mass of 199 GeV, with an uncertainty of 30 GeV. The two values were consistent with each other, given the overlap in their uncertainties.

Further experiments were expected to pin down the mass of the top quark more precisely, which in turn would provide insight into the nature of a theoretical entity called the Higgs field. The Higgs field is thought to pervade all of space and, through its interaction with all the matter particles, to give the particles their masses. A major shortcoming of the standard model is that it does not account for the way in which the quarks and leptons come to have the masses that they do.

Confirmation of the existence of the top quark by no means closed the book on the mysteries of particle physics. In mid-1995 researchers working with the HERA accelerator at DESY, the German national accelerator laboratory in Hamburg, announced that they had found something completely different. Their work built on earlier evidence that mysterious showers of particles are sometimes produced in so-called soft collisions, wherein a proton and an electron, or a pair of protons, strike each other a glancing blow rather than colliding head-on. Almost tongue in cheek, physicists had suggested that one of the colliding particles might emit a new kind of particle, dubbed a pomeron, that is actually responsible for the effects observed in a soft collision. The problem has been that the standard model, which relies on the theory of quantum chromodynamics (QCD) to explain the strong force that binds the quarks in the protons and neutrons of the atomic nucleus, is inaccurate for low energies. QCD is much less useful for calculating what happens in soft collisions than in the more energetic collisions like those used to search for the top quark. Nevertheless, the results from HERA did suggest that pomerons are involved in soft collisions. When, for example, an electron and a proton approach one another, the proton emits a pomeron, which then interacts with the electron to produce a shower of other particles, while the proton itself proceeds unscathed.

FERMILAB VISUAL MEDIA SERVICES

A computer-generated image depicts a potential top-quark signature—a distinctive set of particle tracks—emerging from the collision of a proton and an antiproton. In 1995, after analyzing billions of collisions for such signatures, Fermilab scientists confirmed the existence of the top quark.

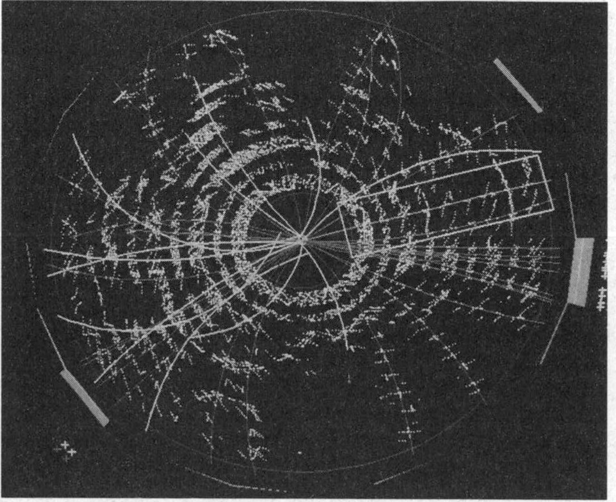

The questions to be answered were whether the pomeron indeed does exist, what it is made of, and what its properties are.

Physicists found the possibility of a particle like the pomeron exciting because it was something not predicted by theory. On the other hand, two teams of researchers were no less excited by their success in obtaining a new form of matter that had actually been predicted 70 years earlier, as a result of theoretical work by Albert Einstein and the Indian physicist Satyendra Bose. The old calculations had predicted that if atoms in the form of a dilute gas could be made cold enough, they would merge and become, in a quantum sense, a single entity much larger than any individual atom. The challenge was to produce the phenomenal cooling required for achieving this state, called the Bose-Einstein condensate. The atoms must be chilled to less than 200 billionths of a degree above absolute zero, −273.15° C (−459.67° F). The trick was at last achieved during the year, first by scientists from the National Institute of Standards and Technology, Boulder, Colo., and the University of Colorado and then by a team at Rice University, Houston, Texas. Both used similar techniques of slowing the atoms down with laser beams, trapping them in a magnetic field, and allowing the hottest, fastest individuals to escape. The resulting Bose-Einstein condensates were made up of several thousand atoms in a ball about 30 micrometres (0.001 in) across, behaving as a single quantum entity thousands of times bigger than an atom. The first experiment to achieve this state cost only about $50,000 for the hardware, plus months of intense and skillful effort, and opened up a whole new area of investigation of the predictions of quantum theory.

Investigations of quantum phenomena like Bose-Einstein condensation gained new importance from recent work highlighting the baffling nature of quantum physics. Sixty years after the quantum theory pioneer Erwin Schrödinger devised his famous cat paradox to illustrate his dissatisfaction with the more absurd aspects of the standard interpretation of quantum theory, two Indian researchers went one better. They conceived a version of this thought experiment using DNA, which is particularly apposite since Schrödinger's book *What Is Life?,* written in the 1940s as an attempt to use quantum physics to explain the stability of genetic structure, was instrumental in setting Francis Crick on the trail that lead to his identification of the structure of DNA with James Watson in 1953.

The absurdity that Schrödinger wished to emphasize was the part of quantum theory that says that the outcome of any quantum experiment is not real until it has been observed, or measured by an intelligent observer. He scaled an imaginary experiment up from the quantum world of particles and atoms to a situation in which a cat exists in a 50:50 "superposition of states," both dead and alive at the same time, and definitely takes on one or the other state only when somebody looks to see if it is dead or alive. Whereas carrying out such an experiment with a real cat would present tremendous difficulties, the experiment proposed by Dipankar Home and Rajagopal Chattapadhyay of the Bose Institute, Calcutta, really could be done.

To bring out the quantum measurement paradox in sharp relief, they picked up on a comment made by Alastair Rae in his book *Quantum Physics* (1986) that a single particle is all that is required for producing a mutation in a DNA molecule. In the proposed experiment a gamma-ray photon (a particle-like packet of electromagnetic energy) is directed into a cesium iodide crystal, producing a shower of photons with wavelengths in the ultraviolet (UV) range around 250 nanometres (billionths of a metre). The photon shower then passes through a solution containing DNA and an enzyme known as photolyase. Any DNA molecule that is damaged by absorption of a UV photon changes its shape in such a way that molecules of photolyase bind to it. In principle, an observer could then measure the enzyme binding.

The point of the experiment is that absorption of a single UV photon, a quantum event, causes a microscopic displacement in the molecular structure of the DNA, which in turn produces a macroscopically measurable (*i.e.,* a nonquantum, or classical) effect through its chemical interaction with the enzyme. The standard interpretation of quantum theory says that each DNA molecule should exist in a superposition of states, a mixture of being damaged and not damaged, until an intelligent observer looks at it. On the other hand, common sense says that each molecule is either damaged or not damaged, and that the enzyme is perfectly capable of telling the state of the DNA without assistance from a human observer. In a Bose Institute preprint, the two researchers came down on the side of common sense, arguing that an individual DNA molecule could be regarded as definitely either damaged or not damaged "regardless of whether or when an experimenter chooses to find this out." Thus, in their view some other interpretation of quantum physics was required. Sixty years on, Schrödinger would be delighted to see which way the quantum wind was blowing.

One of the more eagerly anticipated discoveries of relevance to cosmology was made by researchers using the William Herschel Telescope on La Palma, one of the Canary Islands. They found the best evidence yet for a brown dwarf, a small, extremely faint substellar object, in the Pleiades star cluster. It has only a small percentage of the mass of the Sun and less than 100 times as much as the planet Jupiter. Because they are so small, brown dwarfs could exist in the Milky Way Galaxy in huge numbers without contributing much to its overall mass. The new discovery suggested that about 1% of the mass of the Milky Way (and, by extension, other galaxies) is in the form of brown dwarfs. That value still leaves plenty of scope for other, as yet unidentified, entities to make up the rest of the "missing mass" of the universe, the dark, or nonluminous, matter whose presence is suggested through its gravitational effects on the observed rotation of galaxies and their movement in clusters. (*See* EARTH AND SPACE SCIENCES: *Astronomy*.)

In another tour-de-force Earth-based observation, astronomers at the Cerro Tololo Inter-American Observatory in Chile discovered the most distant supernova—an explosion of a dying star—yet seen. It lies in a galaxy about six million light-years from the Earth. Because supernovas, depending on their type, have much the same absolute brightness (they are "standard candles," in astronomical terms), if more can be found at such great distances, it may be possible to use them to measure how quickly the rate at which galaxies are moving apart is decreasing—*i.e.,* how fast the expansion of the universe is decelerating. If the absolute brightness of a supernova is known, then its apparent brightness can be used to calculate its true distance. This value then can be combined with the red shift of the supernova's parent galaxy, which is a measure of how fast the galaxy is receding from the Earth.

This ability would be a great boon because it is one way to determine the time that has elapsed since the big bang—*i.e.,* the age of the universe. The age is calculated in terms of a number called the Hubble parameter, or Hubble constant (H_0), a constant of proportionality between the recessional velocities of the galaxies and their distances from the Earth. H_0 is the rate at which the velocity of the galaxies increases with distance and is conventionally expressed in kilometres per second per megaparsec (a parsec is 3.26 light-years). The reciprocal of H_0, $1/H_0$, yields the time that has elapsed since the galaxies started receding. Various techniques for making the galaxy-distance measurements that were needed to calculate H_0 had seemed for some years to be converging on a value for H_0 that yielded an age for the universe of 15 billion to 20 billion years, and it had been anticipated that measurements for distant galaxies made with the Hubble Space Telescope (HST) would give a definitive value. To the surprise of many, measurements with the HST in late 1994 determined a value for H_0 that implied an age of 8 billion to 12 billion years. In 1994 and 1995 other determinations made with the HST or ground-based telescopes gave a range of values for H_0, some indicating a relatively young universe and others an old one. The new measurements put clear water between two sets of numbers that were, at face value, impossible to reconcile.

Raymond Chiao of the University of California, Berkeley, reported using the quantum phenomenon known as tunneling to make photons of light appear to move, paradoxically, faster than the speed of light itself. Scientists were divided over the interpretation of the bizarre result.
JAMES D. WILSON—NEWSWEEK

Apart from the embarrassment of the disagreement itself, some of the measurements implied that the age of the universe is less than the accepted ages of the oldest stars, which are at least 15 billion years old. Clearly something was wrong. A major consolation, however, was that some of the most significant progress in science eventually comes from investigations in areas where theory and observation are in conflict rather than in agreement. (JOHN GRIBBIN)

This article updates the *Macropædia* articles The COSMOS; MECHANICS: *Quantum Mechanics;* Principles of PHYSICAL SCIENCE; Principles of THERMODYNAMICS; SUBATOMIC PARTICLES; The PHYSICAL SCIENCES: *Physics.*

Media and Publishing

TELEVISION

In much of the world, capital from new partners fueled television expansion in 1995, while governments acted against both monopolies and "foreign" incursions. In the U.S. there were mergers and buyouts, along with a relaxation of federal regulations.

Organization. As NHK (Nippon Hoso Kyokai; Japan Broadcasting Corporation) celebrated its 70th anniversary on March 22, Japan Satellite Systems (JSAT) launched a second satellite, carrying 50 digital channels. Sumitomo and Tele-Communications, Inc. (TCI), of the U.S. launched Jupiter pay-TV, and Itochu, with Time Warner Inc. and US West Communications, Inc., set up Titus. Beginning in April, Rupert Murdoch's STAR Television and Turner Entertainment Networks Asia were permitted to broadcast in Japan.

Thailand launched its third cable network in 1995, while in Australia Sydney and Melbourne were offered 25 new channels on a third pay-TV service, Foxtel (owned equally by Murdoch's News Corp. and Telstra). Earlier, Optus Vision had launched 11 cable channels that carried, like Foxtel, CNN International, Turner Broadcasting System, Inc.'s entertainment and cartoon networks, and a country music channel while sharing Australian racing broadcasts and coproducing a news channel. Satellite and microwave system Australis Media Galaxy secured exclusive rights to films from Sony's Columbia/Tristar, MCA/Universal, and Paramount Pictures. Over protests the Australian Broadcasting Corporation joined pay-TV with a 24-hour news and current affairs channel and a channel for children's programs, comedy, and documentaries.

In Taiwan, where TV advertising revenues were the third highest in the region (after Japan and South Korea), only large companies purchased programming: United Communications of the powerful Koo Group, Po-Hsin Entertainment, and Rebar Communications. India's smaller cable operators, suffering price undercutting, were bought up by more powerful players: the Hinduja group, RPG Enterprises, and Zee TV (49.9% STAR-owned). Cableview Services Pty. Ltd. started Mega TV, Malaysia's first multichannel cable television service, offering ESPN, the Discovery Channel, CNN, the Cartoon Network, and HBO. The Singapore government issued to the Walt Disney Co. the country's first private-user uplink-downlink license for communicating directly via satellite. Taiwan received Disney's first broadcast, followed by Singapore Cable Vision (SCV). Asia Business News became a 24-hour service on SCV. MTV Asia, the seventh global music TV network, inaugurated its Singapore headquarters, transmitting Mandarin and English programs to 18 million households in 30 countries.

Italian media magnate Silvio Berlusconi sold 20% of Fininvest's Mediaset for 1.8 trillion lire to Germany's Leo Kirch (10%), South African Johann Rupert's Swiss-based Richemont group (5.9%), and King Fahd's nephew, Prince al-Walid ibn Talal of Saudi Arabia (4.1%). Another 1.8 trillion lire gave a bank consortium 20%, and a further 20% was to go into the stock market during 1996, which would leave Berlusconi with 40%. Although he won the June 11 referendum on media ownership, Berlusconi had until August 1996 to comply with the constitutional court's ruling that no single entity could own more than 20% of the country's TV market. Mediaset included three national TV channels (Canale 5, Italia 1, and Rete 4), a program library, and Publitalia advertising (with a 60% share of the country's TV ad market).

Sixteen German states moved to permit media companies to own majority stakes in TV stations. Bavaria and North Rhine–Westphalia, having big media industries, insisted on allowing firms to own up to 100% of one channel, and smaller stakes in others, without exceeding 30% of the total market. Bertelsmann and France's Canal Plus bought 47.5% of Monagesque des Ondes (MDO), the manager of Monaco's family TV station TMC.

An agreement between Télévision Française 1 (TF1) and China Central Television (CCTV), the first between China

Cast members of MTV's "The Real World" are filmed having dinner at their home in London. The popular show, in its fourth year and set for the first time outside the U.S., presented the daily lives of a group of seven college and postcollege young people living together.

and a Western public-service channel, allowed TF1 a permanent correspondent post in Beijing and CCTV the right to buy documentaries and fiction series produced by Télédiffusion de France. Ad agency France Espace would sell advertising spots for CCTV.

A "green book" issued by the British state secretary for national heritage and communications, Stephen Dorrell, ruled that only groups possessing less than 20% of the written press would be allowed to invest in TV, as long as these did not exceed a 15% audience share. The ruling hit Murdoch, owner of the satellite TV chain BSkyB and News Corp.'s five English newspapers, with 40% of the national circulation.

In the U.S. in 1995, consolidation swept the TV industry. On July 31 the Walt Disney Co. announced the purchase of Capital Cities/ABC, Inc., for $18.5 billion. In the same week, Westinghouse Electric Corp., which had pioneered commercial radio broadcasting 75 years earlier at KDKA in Pittsburgh, Pa., announced a deal to buy CBS for $5.6 billion. Frustrated by his inability to buy one of the networks, Ted Turner (*see* BIOGRAPHIES) merged his Turner Broadcasting System (CNN, CNN Headline News, Turner Network Television, superstation WTBS, and the Cartoon Network) with Time Warner in a deal that would net Turner shareholders more than $7 billion in Time Warner stock.

As the year ended, Microsoft Corp. and NBC announced that they would create a new all-news cable channel to compete with CNN. Despite claims that the market could not support this new venture, it was hailed as an opportunity for Microsoft to gain access to the content it needed and a chance for General Electric Co., the parent company of NBC, to gain an effective entry to the Internet and the World Wide Web.

Station groups also competed fiercely to buy available TV stations, which drove prices to new highs. In August longtime broadcasting executives were awed by Tribune Broadcasting's $70.5 million bid for KTTY in San Diego, Calif., and by the $207 million that Dow Jones & Co., Inc., and ITT Corp. were willing to pay for New York's WNYC-TV. Driving the consolidation were the loosening of federal ownership restrictions and the anticipated loosening of others, along with a red-hot advertising market. In the spring, advertisers ponied up a record $5.6 billion for the best spots on the networks' fall schedules. Even though the market later showed signs of softening, estimated TV broadcasting revenues in 1995 topped $30 billion, up from $29 billion in 1994.

The U.S. House of Representatives and Senate passed sweeping telecommunications reform legislation in 1995 aimed at encouraging competition between cable and local telephone companies as well as between local and long-distance telephone companies. Work resumed on the bills in early November, with proponents hopeful that differences between the House and Senate versions could be reconciled. The administration of Pres. Bill Clinton had problems with certain provisions, however, principally those that would relax broadcast ownership restrictions and deregulate cable TV rates. Conferees agreed in December to keep the rate regulations in place for three years.

Although its executives complained about government regulation, U.S. cable enjoyed a good year. Subscriptions grew 4.3%, to about 62.3 million homes (63.4% of all homes with TV). At the same time, rates increased 4.1%. Revenues for the year were projected to hit $26.2 billion, up nearly $2 billion from 1994. Tempering cable's good news, however, were concerns about competition. The large telephone companies continued to make plans to challenge cable for its subscribers by building parallel networks. Hoping to get a head start, Pacific Telesis Group, NYNEX, and Bell Atlantic Corp. invested heavily into "wireless cable," which delivered services to subscribers via microwave channels. To receive the service, subscribers' televisions had to be equipped with a special antenna and a set-top tuner and descrambler. At year's end it was estimated that 200 systems served more than 800,000 subscribers in the U.S.

A more immediate threat to cable, however, was satellite-delivered pay-TV. After 16 months on the market, Hughes Electronics Corp.'s DirecTV and United States Satellite Broadcasting claimed in November that more than one million consumers had purchased the 18-inch dish and other equipment needed to subscribe. Hoping to launch a similar service, the nation's largest cable operators, led by TCI, agreed to buy the satellite channels of another company. The FCC nixed the deal, however, saying that the cable venture—Primestar Partners—would have to bid for the channels at an open auction in January 1996.

There were two new broadcast networks in 1995, each hoping to repeat Fox's remarkable success. Both debuted in January, with abbreviated prime-time schedules. The United Paramount Network (UPN), the creation of Paramount and the Chris-Craft/United station group, offered programming on Mondays and Tuesdays. The WB Network, a partnership of Warner Bros. Inc. and the Tribune Broadcasting station group, began broadcasting on Wednesdays and added a slate of sitcoms on Sundays in the fall. UPN had the better ratings, primarily on the strength of "Star Trek: Voyager."

Programming. The European Commission adopted for 10 years the directive "Television sans Frontiers," which obligated general audience channels to broadcast a majority of European works. Thematic channels could opt to invest in European production by using quotas.

France 3 and Television Suisse Romande (TSR) created the first transborder newscast. Lasting five to seven minutes, "Genève-Region" (over Suisse 4)/"Genève le journal" (France 3) was produced by eight reporters from each country and financed equally by the two stations. Chaine Metco, patterned after the U.S. Weather Channel and the Canadian Meteo Media, started giving 24-hour forecasts on TMC and Serie Club. It was the first in France entirely dedicated to weather. At the 11th Mediaville convention of satellite and cable specialists, it was announced that Arab-language programs would be allowed on cable despite tensions with Algeria.

After a two-year negotiation, the Council Superior Audiovisual authorized Canal Plus to broadcast until the year 2000. Listed in the convention were restrictions in announcing and broadcasting films not suitable for children below 16 years of age on Wednesdays (when there was no school), Saturday mornings, and Sunday mornings. Pornographic films broadcast once a month could be rerun three times.

CNN disappeared from Berlin's cable service, and MTV Europe also appeared to be on its way out in favour of local competitors, the NTV news channel and VIVA rock music station. Media authorities pointed to an acute shortage of frequencies caused by Deutsche Telekom's monopoly of cable infrastructure. Targeting 14–49-year-old German women, TM3 aired in August. The business news service Bloomberg LP started the 24-hour channel Bloomberg Information Television Europe to compete with CNN Business News Europe, NBC Super Channel, and Dow Jones & Co.'s European Business News over Britain's Sky Channel.

Russian Public Television (ORT), which was 51% state-owned, dropped the twice-monthly "Meetings with Solzhenitsyn." Writer Aleksandr Solzhenitsyn's wife, Natalya, suggested that criticism was being stifled before the parliamentary elections held on December 17. On a scale unheard of in Russia, journalists protested the March 1 killing of ORT's newly appointed executive director, Vladislav Listyev (*see* OBITUARIES), one of Russia's most popular journalists.

After an outcry the Romanian government rescinded its ban on tobacco advertising on TV. Women's groups forced the withdrawal of a TV ad for Malaysia's first sports car, Bufori. The ad, featuring four women in a marriage bureau, had one woman list ownership of a Bufori as a criterion for a spouse.

AsiaSat 2's launching in late 1995 expanded the STAR movie channels' capacity to broadcast in Mandarin, Hindi, English, Bahasa Indonesia, Tagalog, Cantonese, and Japanese. A contractual dispute between STAR and Viacom resulted in MTV's pullout and Channel V's creation. Featuring rock videos by singers from Taiwan, Hong Kong, and India, the channel sent different transmissions to India and the Middle East from those to East Asia and Taiwan. MTV returned to India on Doodarshan, while the British media conglomerate Pearson (which acquired 10% of Hong Kong's Television Broadcast, TVB) took a stake in *The Hindustan Times* to produce Hindi-language programs.

India's Supreme Court ruled the government's broadcasting monopoly unconstitutional on February 9. The Board of Cricket Control India had wanted to sell world broadcast rights to the 1996 World Cup to ESPN; earlier the Cricket Association of Bengal tangled with the Ministry of Information and Broadcasting over another tournament. Although the constitution allowed business monopolies, broadcasting, as a means of expression, could not be monopolized.

The big three U.S. networks (ABC, CBS, and NBC) saw their share of the prime-time audience drop to an all-time low of 57% in the 1994–95 season, down four points from the previous season's 61% and three points off the previous low, of 60%, in 1992–93. The culprits were Fox, the new networks, cable's increased investment in original programming, and the O.J. Simpson trial, which was covered extensively on cable and drew huge audiences.

ABC was the most watched network during the 1994–95 season, with a 12 rating and a 20 share, according to the A.C. Nielsen Co. (A rating was the percentage of the 95.9 million U.S. homes with TV sets, a share the percentage of TV homes with their sets on at the time of a program.) NBC came in second (11.5 rating/18 share), and CBS, which had dominated prime time for several seasons, finished third (11.1 rating/18 share). Fox was again fourth (7.7 rating/12 share), but it gained ground against the older networks, especially with the younger audiences that advertisers sought. ABC had four of the top 10 shows: "Home Improvement," "Grace Under Fire," "NFL Monday Night Football," and "NYPD Blue." In "Seinfeld" and "ER," however, NBC had the top two shows.

The networks tried to stem their prime-time slide by introducing 42 new shows in September. Two months later, however, it appeared that the season was something of a bust. Of the newcomers, only NBC's "Caroline in the City" and "Single Guy" cracked the top 10.

By November it was clear that David Letterman had lost his grip on the lead in late-night TV ratings. While his CBS audience drifted away, Jay Leno's fans on NBC stayed faithful. By August, Leno was regularly outscoring Letterman in the ratings.

While NBC prepared to cover the 1996 summer Olympic Games in Atlanta, Ga., in 1996, in August it secured the TV rights to the 2000 Summer Games in Sydney, Australia, and the 2002 Winter Games in Salt Lake City, Utah, for $1,270,000,000. In addition, in December NBC bought the rights to the 2004 and 2008 Summer Games, as well as the 2006 Winter Games.

Mickey Mouse, grown to plutocratic proportions, brandishes a cigar to celebrate the Walt Disney Co.'s purchase of Capital Cities/ABC, Inc. The merger generated concern over the concentration of information in a shrinking number of media giants.

CHARLES BURNS

Fox, which had acquired TV rights to National Football Conference games prior to the 1994–95 season, captured a piece of major league baseball in November. Fox was to share coverage of regular and postseason baseball with NBC, ESPN, and Liberty Media through the 2000 season. Under the five-year multinetwork deal, baseball teams would divvy up $1.7 billion in network rights payments.

Television programming became a political target in 1995. Republican presidential candidates Robert Dole and Richard Lugar made alleged excesses of TV an early campaign theme, with Dole warning in an April speech that TV was guilty of "bombarding our children with destructive messages of casual violence and even more casual sex." Three months later President Clinton called for legislation that would require every TV set to include so-called V-chip technology, allowing parents to block out programming rated as objectionable, and Congress added its support to the idea. In October former secretary of education William Bennett and Senators Sam Nunn and Joe Lieberman took aim at sensationalistic talk shows. They cited a "Jenny Jones" show that some said had prompted a murder; a male guest became so upset when another man declared his love for him during a taping of the program that he later shot and killed him. With the support of congressional Democrats and children's advocates, Reed Hundt, chairman of the Federal Communications Commission, called for rules requiring TV stations to air a minimum amount of children's programming. Opposed by the broadcasting industry, he was unable to persuade a majority of his fellow commissioners to adopt the requirement.

Technology. Europe launched its first digital satellite, Astra 1E, in 1995. Using digital compression technology in transmitting 500 channels, it gave customers using a decoder or a set-top box access to global news and sports events and services like teleshopping and telebanking. South African Multichoice Ltd.'s pay-TV Nethold started a 24-channel digital satellite service for 200 subscribers who paid for decoders. Using the Eutelsat Hot Bird l, Canal Horizons (the African version of Canal Plus) attracted 90,000 subscribers.

Sales of Japanese TV sets with oblong screens wide enough to show films reached 1.5 million in 1994 and 3 million in 1995 and led to the issuance of specially made "extended-definition" films. Sony Corp. stopped exporting Japanese-made colour TVs by the end of 1995 because the strong yen made them too expensive overseas. Sony's production from factories in the U.S., South America, Europe, and Asia reached nine million, up 10% from 1994. Matsushita Electric, the world's largest consumer electronics firm and maker of Panasonic sets, competed with its own factories in Wales, Mexico, and Malaysia.

RADIO

Radio worldwide in 1995 was marked with excesses. Four days before the sovereignty referendum in Quebec, the Montreal talk show host Pierre Brassard (posing as Prime Minister Jean Chrétien) telephoned Queen Elizabeth II. The French disc jockey François Meunier was fired from Skyrock and sued by several unions for saying four times "A dead policeman is more or less good news" after announcing the assassination of Nice policeman Georges Janvier.

Set up discreetly on Berlin's FM band since September 13, 1994, Radio France International (RFI) was officially installed on May 17, 1995. The more popular France Inter had ceased broadcasting on Dec. 31, 1994, upon the departure of Allied troops after German reunification. Radio Free Europe/Radio Liberty (RFE/RL), a symbol of the Cold War, moved from Munich, Germany, where it was first set up in 1951, to Prague after the U.S. Congress reduced its budget.

In Canada, Vancouver's alternative radio station (1040 AM or 88.5 Cable FM) introduced a program featuring unusual international recordings. It was the first of its kind in Vancouver, and the Filipino journalist Mel Tobias served as its host.

In the U.S. nationally syndicated talk shows proliferated. Among the newcomers was former New York governor Mario Cuomo, who provided a liberal counterweight to popular conservatives like Rush Limbaugh. In the wake of the bombing of the federal office building in Oklahoma City, Okla., in April, Pres. Bill Clinton condemned "loud and angry voices" for fostering civil unrest, and conservative talk-show hosts complained that the president was unjustly referring to them. Catching much of the flak was the Watergate conspirator who had turned radio host, G. Gordon Liddy, who told listeners that he used drawings of President and Mrs. Clinton for target practice and who discussed on the air how to shoot federal agents.

Infinity Broadcasting agreed in September to pay the government about $1.7 million to settle a host of outstanding indecency complaints against Howard Stern. Infinity did not concede that its star was indecent, saying that it agreed to the settlement only to clear the way for the approval of station acquisitions.

Anticipating the relaxation of federal ownership restrictions, the big radio station groups got bigger by buying up other groups. Prices also increased. In November the Spanish Broadcasting System agreed to pay $83.5 million for the New York FM station WPAT. Undergirding the rising prices was the strong advertising market, with total revenues predicted to grow 8–9% in 1995 and top $11 billion.

(RAMONA MONETTE S. FLORES; HARRY A. JESSELL; LAWRENCE B. TAISHOFF)

Amateur Radio. When telephone service was disrupted by the terrorist bomb that ripped apart a federal building in Oklahoma City, amateur radio operators were soon on the scene providing emergency communications. They were also on call to aid rescue workers and displaced families as a series of hurricanes battered the southeastern U.S. and the Caribbean area throughout the late summer and early fall.

According to the American Radio Relay League, some two million people around the world—680,000 in the U.S. alone—held licenses to transmit voice or data over private noncommercial amateur channels. In the U.S. the Federal Communications Commission ruled in February that hams could choose their own call signs, but squabbles over who could apply and how to apply for the "vanity" signs held up implementation. The FCC also ruled that amateurs operating in the high-frequency band could use automatic control systems for data communications.

(HARRY A. JESSEL; LAWRENCE B. TAISHOFF)

See also Business and Industry Review: *Advertising; Telecommunications;* Performing Arts: *Motion Pictures; Music.*
This article updates the *Macropædia* article BROADCASTING.

NEWSPAPERS

A series of price rises for newsprint wreaked havoc in the newspaper industry worldwide in 1995. Between March and the end of the year, newsprint prices rose about 50%. It brought to an abrupt end the decade-long trend toward larger papers and special-interest supplements and encouraged a switch to more economical tabloid formats.

One of the worst-hit companies was Rupert Murdoch's News International and its five U.K. titles (*The Times, Sunday Times, Sun, News of the World,* and *Today*). The company was forced to cut pages and print runs in March and April. Its weakest newspaper, the Labour-leaning *Today,* founded in 1986, was most seriously hit; it suffered a marked fall in circulation, was at one point put up for sale, and in November was closed. The rising costs resulted in the abatement of a fierce two-year price war in Britain, which had been initiated by Murdoch, and cover prices started to edge up. In August *The Times* was given away free for one day, courtesy of Microsoft Corp., which sponsored the entire issue to mark the launch of its Windows 95.

The money-losing *Independent,* founded shortly after *Today* in 1986, was briefly famous for its fresh and fearless approach to reporting. By 1995, however, it had become the sickest of the British papers, and it endured another round of refinancing in March, which resulted in Tony O'Reilly's Irish Independent Newspapers group and Mirror Group Newspapers more than doubling their stakes, to 43% each. The paper was relaunched with a tabloid second section in June, but it was still below the target of 300,000 copies per day as the year ended. Its editor, Ian Hargreaves, was forced out by the two dominant owners in November.

In such competitive markets there was an unusually large number of changes of editors during the year, as new leadership was established at *The Guardian, Daily* and *Sunday Telegraph, Daily* and *Sunday Express, Daily Mirror,* and *News of the World.* In September *The Observer,* which had suffered two decades of decline, was relaunched by new editor Andrew Jaspan and the new owner, the Guardian Media Group, but as the year ended it had yet to show a significant improvement in sales.

The Thomson Corp. withdrew from the British industry by putting its Scottish newspapers up for sale, as well as its English regional newspaper chain. In November the *Scotsman,* flagship of the company, a morning daily famous for speaking up for Scottish interests from Edinburgh, was sold for an estimated £90 million to property tycoons David and

Frederick Barclay. The brothers also salvaged the *European,* an English-language weekly founded by the late Robert Maxwell. In December *Lloyd's List and Shipping Gazette,* the daily paper serving the shipping industry, was sold to its staff via a management buyout by the troubled insurance market owners, Lloyd's of London.

Ireland's debt-laden Irish Press Newspapers group, which published the *Irish Press, Sunday Press,* and *Evening Press,* was placed in liquidation. The papers stopped publication on May 26, but efforts to salvage the titles continued, unsuccessfully, until August.

In Hong Kong the *South China Morning Post* suffered editorial cuts and gained a new editor, Jonathan Fenby (former editor of *The Observer* in London). It also dropped its "Lily Wong" cartoon strip in what some criticized as a self-censorship move in preparation for China's taking control in 1997. Murdoch struck a deal with the communist *People's Daily* to develop information services.

In Singapore the *International Herald Tribune* was in the spotlight in the ongoing struggle over how far American news organizations were prepared to compromise with governments that rejected Western concepts of free speech. In July the paper was ordered to pay record damages of S$950,000 to Prime Minister Goh Chok Tong and to Lee Kuan Yew (Singapore's founding father and senior minister) and his son, Lee Hsien Loong, the deputy prime minister. The damages arose from an article by Philip Bowring, a former editor of the *Far Eastern Economic Review,* which suggested that the son had been appointed deputy prime minister because of his father.

In India the English-language press, led by the *Times of India,* became more popular in tone in an effort to fend off competition from rapidly growing Indian-language papers. The Bombay (Mumbai)-based Audit Bureau of Circulation said that with five main titles (*Times of India, Indian Express, Hindu, Hindustan Times,* and *Economic Times*), there was a saturation of English-language papers.

In Australia there was a buildup of pressure on the government from three media magnates, Murdoch, Kerry Packer, and Conrad Black, all seeking a relaxation in rules limiting foreign interests in Australian companies. Control of the media group John Fairfax Holdings was one of the most coveted prizes. (MAGGIE BROWN)

Newspapers in the U.S. also were affected by the skyrocketing cost of newsprint in 1995, with some forced to take drastic measures. The *Washington Post* limited the amount of foreign travel by reporters and cut back on space in some sections. Other papers, including the *Wall Street Journal* and the *Los Angeles Times,* laid off staffers. The *New York Times* raised its newsstand prices both in and out of town. Sunday magazines at papers such as the *Dallas* (Texas) *Morning News* and the *Providence* (R.I.) *Journal* were folded. *USA Today* cut its news space by 5%, and California's *Orange County Register* reduced the width of its pages.

Houston, Texas, became the nation's largest one-newspaper city with the abrupt closing of the *Houston Post.* The 111-year-old paper was sold to the Hearst Corp.'s *Chronicle,* which immediately shut it down. There was no final commemorative issue. The *Evening Sun,* an 85-year-old institution in Baltimore, Md., was closed by its Los Angeles-based owner, the Times Mirror Co. Most famous as H.L. Mencken's forum for 30 years, the paper was known for its coverage of local issues and its blue-collar readership. The 10-year-old *New York Newsday* also closed during the year.

The nation's largest newspaper publisher, Gannett Co., became even larger with its acquisition of Multimedia Inc. Gannett, which already owned 82 newspapers, including *USA Today,* would add another 11 dailies and 49 nondaily papers, increasing its circulation to more than 6.4 million a day. The purchase also allowed Gannett to expand its holdings in television and radio as well as branch out to cable TV. The newly acquired papers were located in medium to small markets, and all were in states where Gannett owned no newspapers.

A survey found that fully half the newspapers in the U.S. were initiating or exploring the possibility of starting on-line services. Eight of the largest newspaper companies banded together to create a national network of local newspapers on-line. The participating companies were Gannett Co. Inc., Knight-Ridder Inc., Advance Publications Inc., Times Mirror Co., Tribune Co., Cox Newspapers Inc., Hearst Corp., and Washington Post Co. They collectively owned 185 daily papers with a circulation of about 20 million. The goal of the partnership was to get greater numbers of papers on-line, establishing a coast-to-coast network. Two New Hampshire dailies got a jump on the 1996 presidential election by setting up a site on the World Wide Web. *Foster's Democrat* in Dover and the *Citizen* of Laconia would cover the New Hampshire primary, offering analysis and on-line discussion between citizens and candidates.

The *Wall Street Journal* added a sports page and a travel page to its Friday edition. The *New York Daily News* launched *El Daily News,* a bilingual edition published Monday through Friday. The *Evening Bulletin* in Providence, started in 1863 to provide late-breaking news from the Civil War front, merged with the city's morning paper, the *Providence Journal.* The owner of the *Milwaukee* (Wis.) *Journal* and the *Milwaukee Sentinel* combined the two papers in April as the *Journal Sentinel.* In Michigan the *Detroit News* and *Detroit Free Press* continued to publish despite a strike that began in July.

The *Virgin Islands Daily News* won the 1995 Pulitzer Prize for public service with a 10-part series on crime and the criminal justice system. The Gannett newspaper, based on St. Thomas, had only 18 full-time editors and reporters. The prize for spot news reporting went to the staff of the *Los Angeles Times.* Using manual typewriters, emergency phones, and flashlights, the staff managed to publish a paper capturing the drama and devastation of the 1994 Los Angeles earthquake. Two *New York Newsday* reporters won the prize for investigative reporting for stories about the abuse of disability pensions by police officers. Other Pulitzers went to *Washington Post* reporter Leon Dash and photographer Lucian Perkins, who won for explanatory journalism for their series on a welfare family in Washington, D.C. The prize for beat reporting went to David M. Shribman of the *Boston Globe* for his insights on the national political scene. Tony Horwitz of the *Wall Street Journal* took the award for national reporting for his stories on the oppressive conditions that workers in low-wage and low-skill fields were forced to endure. For his graphic and moving coverage of the ethnic violence in Rwanda, Mark Fritz of the Associated Press won the prize for international reporting. The feature writing award went to Ron Suskind of the *Wall Street Journal* for a series on inner-city honours students in Washington, D.C. Jim Dwyer of *New York Newsday* won the prize for commentary. Margo Jefferson of the *New York Times* took the award for criticism. The winner for editorial cartooning was Mike Luckovich of the *Atlanta* (Ga.) *Constitution,* and the award for editorial writing went to Jeffrey Good of Florida's *St. Petersburg Times* for his editorials urging reform of the state probate system. The award for spot news photography went to Carol Guzy of the *Washington Post* for her work in Haiti, and the prize for feature photography went to the Associated Press for staff coverage of the Rwanda tragedy. (MELANIE ANNE COOPER)

James Nachtwey photographs a gunman engaged in a firefight in South Africa. For his work in South Africa, Nachtwey won the Robert Capa Gold Medal, and for his subsequent work in Rwanda he received the Magazine Photographer of the Year award, while his shot of a Hutu man (inset) mutilated with a machete because of suspected sympathy with the Tutsi was named the World Press Photo of the Year.

DAVID TURNLEY—DETROIT FREE PRESS/BLACK STAR; (INSET) JAMES NATCHWEY—MAGNUM PHOTOS

MAGAZINES

There was only limited growth in new magazines in 1995, with launches generally aimed at exploiting existing gaps. *Wired,* the U.S computer magazine, had a troubled launch in the U.K. and had to revise its format and marketing. The American magazine *Men's Health,* owned by Rodale, launched a customized U.K. edition, while the U.K. computer magazine company Dennis Publishing launched *Maxim,* also aimed at mainstream male readers. Rather than risking start-ups, large publishers such as Condé Nast sought new business by taking on contract publishing. Condé Nast set up a U.K. on-line editorial team to establish computerized versions of its products. National Magazines, the U.K. arm of the Hearst Corp., changed the editors of five of its six titles. (MAGGIE BROWN)

Americans traveling abroad were more likely to find their favourite magazines on a European newsstand. Companies like Reader's Digest, Condé Nast, Playboy, and Hearst published their titles in more than 80 countries and more than a dozen languages. Most of the articles were generated by local editorial staffs, with translations of material that had appeared in the original American editions.

Many U.S. newsstand magazines, including *Time* and *Newsweek,* offered both on-line and print copies in 1995. Less popular magazines, from esoteric underground titles to more than 300 scholarly and literary journals, were available only as computer journals. More items became available on the Internet, and some libraries were checking in e-journals just as they did printed journals. Publishers saw this as the beginning of what would develop into centralized information sources for periodicals. Several publishers, librarians, and editors warned, however, that the rush to go on-line often overlooked the need for careful planning for the new format. Others expressed fears that the new technologies threatened the future of all magazines, on or off line. There might be, such critics said, so much information available that the traditional magazine would be crowded out altogether.

According to the Faxon Co., the prices for U.S. magazines would rise by about 15% in 1995–96. By mid-1995 the average annual price of a physics journal was $1,126, contrasted with an average price of $35.58 for a popular newsstand magazine. The hikes were caused by increases in the costs of paper and postage and by a shaky U.S. dollar. Faced with a 12% increase in postal rates as well as close to a 40% jump in paper prices, Hearst decided to control its costs by producing fewer copies, thereby reducing the number of readers; some 15 titles, from *Good Housekeeping* to *Cosmopolitan,* had their circulation cut. Other publishers were expected to follow the Hearst lead.

Two new political magazines appeared in the U.S. in 1995: *The Weekly Standard,* a conservative journal edited by William Kristol and backed by Rupert Murdoch, and the liberal entertainment-oriented *George,* edited by John F. Kennedy, Jr., and supported by the Paris conglomerate Hachette. With all of the money behind them, both were expected at least to last out 1996. Among other new titles

A page from the CD-ROM magazine *Launch,* which made its debut in May, carries advertising likely to appeal to its youthful, computer-literate audience. One of a small number of CD-ROM magazines available in the U.S., *Launch* focused on music, movies, and computer games.
LAUNCH MAGAZINE

were *Double Take,* a documentary magazine with photographs introduced by the child psychiatrist Robert Coles; *Civilization,* a bimonthly from the Library of Congress that had a multicultural approach; and *Legacy,* an Afro-American history magazine published by American Heritage.

The highest honours in the 1995 National Magazine Awards went to *GQ* (*Gentlemen's Quarterly*) for special interest and features. The general excellence award for magazines with a circulation of more than one million went to *Entertainment Weekly,* followed by *The New Yorker* (400,000–1 million) and *I.D. Magazine* (less than 100,000), a publication on culture and design. Among other winners were *The Atlantic Monthly* for reporting and *The New Republic* for public interest. (WILLIAM A. KATZ)

BOOK PUBLISHING

The European book industry continued to suffer a period of considerable uncertainty in 1995. In the U.K. a variety of strategic responses were adopted in response to sluggish sales, the breakdown of the Net Book Agreement (NBA), rapidly increasing paper prices, and bad debts arising from the Dillons book chain receivership.

In July Reed Elsevier offered for sale its consumer book publishing business, including the Hamlyn, Octopus, and Heinemann imprints. This reflected a decision to concentrate on the relatively profitable specialist imprints such as Butterworth and on-line information services. By contrast, Hodder Headline announced its intention to expand the number of titles published in 1995 by 55%, targeting nontraditional outlets such as supermarkets and gasoline (petrol) stations. Dorling Kindersley successfully built up its CD-ROM business, and HarperCollins restructured into two superdivisions while shedding roughly 100 staff members. Layoffs also were announced at Penguin.

The independent publishing sector in the U.K. was again reduced in size. The largest independent, Macmillan, agreed in April to sell 65% of the company to Holtzbrinck, one of Germany's biggest publishing groups, and in July André Deutsch was bought by the VCI video group.

The longer-term prospects for reference books and other traditional strengths of established imprints appeared to be in question as multimedia versions took their place. In 1995 the trend toward electronic publishing was apparent everywhere, with Bonnier of Sweden, for example, setting up a multimedia operation. Even the print version novel was under threat from new technology; Penguin published its first electronic version in November.

The cult of the author began to bridge the divide between "literary" and "popular" fiction. The payment of a $750,000 advance to Martin Amis appeared to indicate a fresh impetus to market "highbrow" authors in a manner little

Ebony at 50

It was 1945 and World War II had ended when the premiere issue of *Ebony* magazine hit the newsstands in November. The brainchild of Johnson Publishing Co. founder John Johnson, *Ebony* (so christened by Johnson's wife) was the second publication to evolve from the company that had begun just three years earlier with $500 and a dream. As a 24-year-old newspaper editor in 1942, Johnson borrowed the money to produce *Negro Digest,* the flagship publication of his fledgling company. The magazine chronicled a sampling of events taking place within the black community that went largely unreported by the mass media. Three years later *Ebony,* a sister publication, was born.

"*Ebony,*" explained Johnson, "was founded to project all dimensions of the Black personality in a world saturated with stereotypes.... Blacks needed positive images to fulfill their potentialities." Never intended as a black version of such weeklies as *Time* or *Newsweek, Ebony* was a monthly with a photo-editorial format and was designed to infuse a much-needed sense of self-esteem into the black community by illustrating in words and pictures the varied accomplishments of the African-American populace, thereby replacing negative images with positive ones. In the 50 years from the magazine's inception, it annually claimed the number one position as the most widely circulated and popular magazine of its kind.

Ebony's original press run was 25,000 copies (but another 25,000 copies had to be quickly printed in order to meet demand). By 1995 *Ebony* was available in more than 40 countries, reported a monthly circulation of two million copies, and gauged its overall monthly readership at 11 million people. Linda Johnson Rice, Johnson's daughter, served from 1987 as president and chief operating officer of the corporation, which had annual revenues in excess of $250 million in 1995 and reached, through its publications, more than half of all African-American adults across a broad spectrum. Rice once remarked, "I guess we have been successful and have been number one for so long that I believe fundamentally we must be doing something right."

In addition to the magazine's focus on family, relationships, fitness, and finances, *Ebony* had over the years featured articles written by such well-known figures as first lady Eleanor Roosevelt, U.S. Supreme Court Justice Thurgood Marshall, and poet Gwendolyn Brooks. In keeping with this tradition, the magazine's 50th-anniversary issue contained articles written by Coretta Scott King, Maya Angelou, and four U.S. presidents, including Bill Clinton. (ANTHONY L. GREEN) seen since the days of Charles Dickens. A further sign of the times was the decision by the Booker Prize-nominated author Timothy Mo to publish his new novel on his own.

Access to Dickens through libraries or cheap paperback reprints remained secure, but the same could no longer be said of H.G. Wells or George Orwell. The combination of rising paper prices and the extension of copyright protection in the European Union from 50 to 70 years looked certain to spell the end of the cheap paperback classic, of which Wordsworth Editions, which pioneered the concept in the U.K., had sold 30 million since 1992.

Needless to say, the U.K. NBA remained constantly in the news. With investigations under way by the European Commission and the U.K. Restrictive Practices Court, Hodder Headline chose in May to discount John Le Carré's new hardback novel, *Our Game.* Stocked by many supermarket chains at discounts of up to 50% off the list price, the book sold well enough to induce Hodder to follow up with a new Rosamunde Pilcher novel. Hodder's determination to move to the top of the publishing industry was also reflected in its purchase of Moa Beckett of New Zealand in January for $5.3 million. (PETER J. CURWEN)

In June 1994 the publishing community had been shocked by the ouster of Richard E. Snyder, Simon & Schuster's legendary chief executive officer, by Viacom, the company that took over Simon & Schuster's parent company, Paramount Communications, Inc. In September 1995 Snyder sought to make a comeback by acquiring a majority interest in Western Publishing, the largest children's book publisher in the U.S. The collapse of the deal in October, combined with Western's poor earnings performance, caused the company's share price to fall precipitously.

The sensational murder trial of O.J. Simpson, the former football star who was accused of stabbing to death his ex-wife Nicole Brown Simpson and her friend Ronald Goldman, ended with Simpson's controversial acquittal in October. The intense scrutiny propelled a number of titles. Nicole Simpson's friend Faye Resnick started the frenzy off with *Nicole Brown Simpson: The Private Diary of a Life Interrupted* (Dove Books), which became a national best-seller. Then Simpson himself wrote (with Larry Schiller) from his cell *I Want to Tell You* (Little, Brown), which also was a best-seller, though his second book, with the working title *Now I Can Tell You,* was unable to find a buyer even after the asking price of $6 million reportedly had been reduced by half. *Raging Heart: The Intimate Story of the Tragic Marriage of O.J. and Nicole Brown Simpson* by Sheila Weller (Pocket Books) was published at the same time in January and rose up the best-seller lists. Barbara Cochran Berry, the ex-wife of Simpson's legal team leader, Johnnie Cochran, weighed in with *Life After Johnnie Cochran: Why I Left the Sweetest-Talking, Most Successful Black Lawyer in L.A.* (Basic), which accused him of physical abuse. Still to come were books on the case by noted authors who were under contract with various houses: Dominick Dunne (Crown), Joseph Bosco (Morrow), Joe McGinniss (Crown), and Jeffrey Toobin (Random House). Los Angeles prosecutor Marcia Clark sold world rights to her memoir to Viking for $4.2 million, while HarperCollins bought the memoir of Clark's legal partner Christopher Darden for $1.3 million.

Republican Speaker of the House Newt Gingrich (*see* BIOGRAPHIES) also grabbed a few headlines when, in January, he signed with HarperCollins to write two books for $4.5 million. Following a storm of criticism surrounding speculation that HarperCollins' owner, media mogul Rupert Murdoch, was angling for political favours, Gingrich refused the advance, opting instead for $1 against royalties. The House Ethics Committee began looking into the matter. The first book, *To Renew America,* was expected to net Gingrich $1.4 million. Gingrich raised a storm again when he was asked to speak at the American Booksellers Association (ABA) convention in June. Members of the ABA events committee sent a letter of protest to ABA management over the selection. During Gingrich's speech at the convention, a bookseller was arrested for distributing leaflets, but criminal charges against her were later dropped.

In 1994 the ABA had filed an antitrust suit against five publishers, claiming they had offered illegal "secret" deals, prices, and promotions to various chain bookstores and discount outlets. A week before the suit was to be heard in a New York court, the ABA settled with one of the publishers charged, Hugh Lauter Levin. While denying wrongdoing, Levin agreed to abide by the Robinson-Patman Act in terms of its pricing. Houghton Mifflin settled with the ABA in late October, agreeing to pay $270,000 and revise its discount and display allowance structure. Penguin USA later settled on similar terms, but the remaining cases were still in litigation.

In another major lawsuit the seven authors of the textbook *Merrill Mathematics* won a $3.2 million suit against a variety of publishers, including Macmillan and Macmillan/McGraw-Hill; it was thought to be one of the largest settlements ever won by authors in a suit against a publisher. (Because of several mergers, Macmillan, Macmillan/McGraw-Hill, Merrill, and Bell & Howell were all named in the suit.) The conflict arose when Macmillan decided not to publish the third edition of the book and refused to return the manuscript to the authors, which thus prevented them from finding another publisher. In addition, the company held that the noncompetition clause in their contracts prohibited them from working on similar projects with other publishers. The authors then filed a lawsuit charging breach of contract and alleging that the publishing companies refused to publish the third edition in order to eliminate market competition. An out-of-court settlement was reached with Maxwell Proceeds Trust, which handled monies resulting from sales of Maxwell companies, including Macmillan. The authors also were given back their publishing rights and production materials.

Setting off fears for the survival of the Canadian book trade industry, Borders, the U.S. bookstore chain, announced it would open its first Canadian superstore in Toronto in the spring of 1996.

The 1995 Pulitzer Prize for Fiction was awarded to Carol Shields, author of *The Stone Diaries* (Viking). (*See* BIOGRAPHIES.) Jonathan Weiner won for nonfiction for *The Beak of the Finch: A Story of Evolution in Our Time* (Knopf). Fiction best-sellers for 1994, as reported by *Publishers Weekly,* were *The Chamber* by John Grisham (3,189,893), *Debt of Honor* by Tom Clancy (2,302,529), and *The Celestine Prophecy* by James Redfield (2,092,526). The nonfiction best-sellers were *In the Kitchen with Rosie* by Rosie Daley (5,487,369), *Men Are from Mars, Women Are from Venus* by John Gray (1,853,000), and *Crossing the Threshold of Hope* by Pope John Paul II (1,625,883). Total book sales in the U.S. rose more than 4% in 1994 to $18.8 billion.

The National Book Award for fiction went to Philip Roth for *Sabbath's Theater,* for nonfiction to Tina Rosenberg for *The Haunted Land: Facing Europe's Ghosts After Communism,* and for poetry to Stanley Kunitz for *Passing Through: The Later Poems, New and Selected.* David McCullough received the 1995 National Book Foundation Medal for Distinguished Contribution to American Letters.

(BETH S. LEVINE)

See also Literature.

This article updates the *Macropædia* article PUBLISHING.

Military Affairs

In 1995 the Allies of World War II celebrated the 50th anniversary of their victories over Nazi Germany and Japan, but not without some controversy and angst. (*See* Special Report.) In Washington, D.C., the Smithsonian Institution's planned exhibit of the *Enola Gay*—the B-29 from which the atomic bomb was dropped on Hiroshima—was criticized by veterans groups and others as being a revisionist history of that event. (*See* LIBRARIES AND MUSEUMS: *Sidebar*.) In Moscow world leaders joined Russian politicians and Soviet military veterans in commemorating the end of the war in Europe, while a demoralized Russian army was bogged down in a humiliating and bitter war in the breakaway Russian republic of Chechnya. Talk of a half century of peace in Europe had a hollow ring during most of the year in former Yugoslavia, where the conflicts entered a new stage marked by the military resurgence of the Bosnian Muslims, a stunning Croatian offensive, and the dramatic escalation of NATO military pressure on the Bosnian Serbs. The NATO strikes triggered strong negative reactions in Moscow and, when coupled with fears of NATO's eastward expansion, soured the relations between Russia and the alliance. Serbia, Croatia, and Bosnia and Herzegovina finally signed a peace agreement, and the first troops of the NATO-led (IFOR) were in place as the year ended.

The spectre of nuclear weapons proliferation continued to be a major concern. United Nations inspectors discovered that Iraq had been much closer to assembling a nuclear bomb in 1991 than previously estimated. In May the delegates to the Nuclear Non-proliferation Treaty (NPT) Review and Extension Conference adopted by acclamation a decision to extend the treaty indefinitely, an outcome that had been in some doubt. Terrorist use of weapons of mass destruction moved from theory to reality in March when a Japanese cult released nerve gas in the Tokyo subway system, killing 12 and sending more than 5,500 to the hospital. Despite strong pressure from the United States, Russia refused to back away from a deal to provide Iran with nuclear reactors. The 1994 agreement in which North Korea pledged to give up its existing nuclear program in return for receiving two modern reactors was slowly being implemented and in June the U.S. and North Korea reached an agreement on the type of reactors that would be provided.

After the painful decision had been taken to withdraw all of the United Nations Mission in Somalia II (UNOSOM II) forces, a combined international task force with contributions from seven countries successfully covered the withdrawal in early March of the last 2,400 UN peacekeepers from Mogadishu. Some 57,000 UN peacekeepers were deployed around the world in 16 other forces and missions. In January UN Secretary-General Boutros Boutros-Ghali appealed for the formation of a UN rapid-reaction force as a strategic reserve for future emergencies but found few countries willing to contribute.

Arms Control and Disarmament. The two treaties considered to be the linchpins of nuclear and conventional arms control came under some pressure in 1995. Continuing U.S. efforts to develop defense systems against theatre ballistic missiles raised strident objections in Moscow that Washington planned to abandon the 1972 antiballistic missile (ABM) treaty. Russian Pres. Boris Yeltsin sent the Strategic Arms Reduction Talks II (START-II) treaty to the State Duma (parliament) in June for ratification, but in both Washington and Moscow, other security and political concerns pushed the START-II ratification process into the background. Implementation of the START-I treaty continued without any major difficulty, with baseline on-site inspections completed in June. In April Russian and Kazakh officials announced that all former Soviet strategic nuclear weapons had been removed from Kazakhstan and repatriated to Russia. All such weapons were scheduled to be transferred from Belarus during the year also, but Belarusian Pres. Alyaksandr Lukashenka in July "temporarily suspended" the removal of the last 18 SS-25 mobile intercontinental ballistic missiles from Belarusian territory. Ukraine continued to download warheads from the missiles on its territory. By year's end it had shipped an estimated 700 strategic warheads to Russia. Both Russia and the U.S. continued to dismantle their surplus warheads.

The numerical ceilings on offensive conventional arms mandated by the Conventional Armed Forces in Europe (CFE) treaty became effective on November 17, and most—but not all—of the 30 states party to the treaty had eliminated their excess weapons by that date. A more serious challenge to the treaty was Russia's refusal to meet the so-called "flanks" limitations placed upon it by the treaty. In September NATO offered to allow Russia to redraw the boundaries of its North Caucasus military district so as to partially offset the treaty's restrictions, but Turkey balked at a Russian counterproposal that called for even more territorial concessions.

The commitment on the part of the nuclear powers to negotiate a Comprehensive Test Ban Treaty (CTBT) in 1996 at the UN Conference on Disarmament (CD) had been an important factor in approval of the indefinite extension of the NPT. Thus, many were dismayed when China conducted an underground test less than three days after the conference had adjourned. Protests were even louder when incoming French Pres. Jacques Chirac announced that France would conduct up to six nuclear tests before the end of May 1996. On September 5 the first test took place at Mururoa atoll in the South Pacific. France conducted four additional tests during the year but joined with China in pledging to work for an unconditional CTBT in 1996. By the end of the year, 182 states had signed the NPT, with Brazil, India, Israel, and Pakistan the most significant absentees.

In March the U.S. Senate finally ratified the 1980 Convention on Conventional Weapons, which, inter alia, places restrictions on the use of antipersonnel landmines. In September a UN review conference met in Vienna with the goal of tightening the convention's restrictions on the use

REUTERS/ARCHIVE PHOTOS

A U.S. surveillance photograph shows what were thought to be mass graves in an area near Srebrenica, in eastern Bosnia and Herzegovina. Bosnian Serbs were accused of having executed thousands of civilians following the capture of Srebrenica in July.

of such mines, but the 42 participants adjourned without an agreement. The 1993 Chemical Weapons Convention continued to limp toward implementation. Of the 160 signatories, only 47 (of the required 65) had deposited their instruments of ratification by year's end. Neither of the two admitted chemical weapons states—signatories Russia and the U.S.—had yet ratified the convention. In contrast, there was some progress in replacing the defunct Coordinating Committee for Multilateral Export Controls with a broader regime, informally called the New Forum, to guide the export of conventional weapons and technology in the future.

United States. Congress approved a national defense budget authority of $263.5 billion for fiscal year 1995 and supplemented this with $3.1 billion to pay for contingency costs related to the operations in Haiti, former Yugoslavia, and the Persian Gulf. The Clinton administration's Future Year's Defense Program for 1996 differed significantly from the 1995 version, with a shift from procurement to readiness and improving the quality of military life. While parsimonious in most other budget areas, the Republican-controlled Congress was inclined to be generous to the Department of Defense in the fiscal year 1996 budget, although the impasse between the president and the Congress over eventually balancing the budget meant that nothing had been resolved as that fiscal year began. In November Congress passed a $243.3 billion defense appropriations bill that was $7 billion larger than Pres. Bill Clinton had requested. It called for the continued construction of B-2 strategic bombers, financed a third Seawolf attack submarine, provided for continued development of the F-22 fighter, and added $529 million to Clinton's $2.9 billion missile defense request. A national missile defense program received $745.6 million, more than twice the amount requested by the administration, while the conflict between such a program and the ABM treaty was postponed by compromise wording that directed the Department of Defense to "develop" a national system by the end of 2003 rather than "deploy" one, as called for in the original Senate bill. Clinton reluctantly signed the appropriations bill but vetoed the $275 billion defense authorization bill because it again called for the design of an ABM system by 2003.

In September the Department of Defense established the policy of prohibiting the use of lasers specifically designed to blind enemy personnel. Several new weapons systems were unveiled in 1995, among them the Seawolf fast attack submarine, the prototype of the army's RAH-66 Comanche armed reconnaissance helicopter, and the navy's F/A-18E "Super Hornet" strike fighter.

John White, who chaired the Commission on Roles and Missions of the Armed Forces, a congressionally mandated panel, was appointed deputy secretary of defense to replace John Deutsch, who left to head the CIA. (*See* BIOGRAPHIES.) The commission report released on May 24 skirted many of the roles and missions issues. It recommended the creation of a joint training command, a larger planning and policy role for overseas commanders, and a new agency to develop doctrine for joint operations.

In March a federal district court declared unconstitutional the administration's "don't ask, don't tell" policy regarding homosexuals in the military. The government said it would appeal. After studying 10,000 Persian Gulf War veterans suffering from the so-called Gulf War syndrome, the Department of Defense concluded that there was no single or unique illness involved. Four Army Ranger trainees died of exposure during an exercise in February at Eglin Air Force Base, Florida; nine instructors were disciplined. When none of the personnel involved in the tragic April 1994 downing by U.S. fighters of two U.S. Army helicopters over northern Iraq were convicted of any wrongdoing, Air Force Chief of Staff Gen. Ronald Fogleman in August wrote derogatory "letters of evaluation" on seven officers involved in the incident, effectively ending their military careers. An army counterintelligence officer, Capt. Lawrence Rockwood, was dismissed from the service in May after a court-martial found him guilty of disobeying orders while serving in Haiti in September 1994. He had left his post to investigate possible human rights abuses in the Port-au-Prince prison. After a long legal battle, in August Shannon Faulkner became the first woman to be admitted to the Citadel, a military college in Charleston, S.C., only to drop out during initiation week, citing severe stress. In October the Supreme Court declined to hear an appeal filed on her behalf.

NATO. NATO's "Partnership for Peace" (PfP) program continued to expand, with Austria, Belarus, Malta, and Macedonia joining in 1995. Non-NATO membership stood at 27, with Tajikistan the only successor state to the U.S.S.R. not a participant. The scope and frequency of multilateral PfP peacekeeping exercises picked up and included the first such maneuvers to be held in the U.S. While Russia approved its individual PfP program with NATO in May, its relations with the alliance became increasingly strained as the states of Central Europe repeated their desire to join NATO. In September NATO released its study on enlargement, and while it stressed that such a move would threaten no one, the study failed to ease Russian concerns, especially when officials in Poland, the Czech Republic, and Hungary said they would be ready to accept NATO nuclear weapons on their soil as part of their membership obligations.

NATO Secretary-General Willy Claes was forced to resign in October after the Belgian Parliament lifted his immunity in connection with a procurement scandal that took place when he was economics minister. His deputy, Italian diplomat Sergio Balanzino, took over as acting secretary-general as the alliance searched for a permanent replacement. He was succeeded by Javier Solana, the Spanish minister of foreign affairs.

In January the Canadian government ordered the disbanding of its Airborne Regiment, an elite unit often used in peacekeeping missions. Nine members of the regiment were put on trial in connection with the torture and killing of a civilian in Somalia in 1993. The four partners in the Eurofighter 2000 project, Germany, Italy, Spain, and the U.K., continued negotiations on how they would divide the production. Eight countries were also cooperating in the Future Large Aircraft (FLA) project, a program to provide a new military transport by 2002. On March 28 Belgium and The Netherlands signed an agreement to merge the operational staffs of their navies into an integrated centre in Den Helder by the end of the year. Belgium became the second European NATO country, after the U.K., to end conscription.

France, Italy, and Spain signed the founding documents for the creation of an army joint rapid reaction force (EUROFOR) and a European maritime force (EUROMARFOR) to provide extra security in the Mediterranean at a time of mounting concern over the security situation in the region. Portugal asked to join both. The 50,800-strong European Corps, answerable to the Western European Union and made up of troops from Germany, France, Belgium, and Spain, officially became operational on October 1.

As peace talks on Bosnia and Herzegovina in Dayton, Ohio, bore fruit in mid-November, NATO military authorities were working out plans for deploying as many as 60,000 troops to guarantee the peace. Russian participation was deemed crucial, but the Russians made it clear they would not serve under NATO command, while the U.S. and other

NATO members were equally insistent that NATO be in charge of the peace force. Ultimately, the Russians agreed to provide a brigade that would serve in a U.S. division but receive orders through a Russian general. The Bosnian peace agreement was signed on December 14, and six days later the UN turned over control of military operations in Bosnia and Herzegovina to NATO. By the end of the year, it had more than 17,000 troops in Bosnia.

United Kingdom. In May, Defence Secretary Malcolm Rifkind announced that a new permanent Joint Headquarters would be established at Northwood by April 1, 1996. It would both plan for and execute joint operations, responsibilities presently handled on a temporary, ad hoc basis. A new Headquarters, Land Command, was established for all army units at home and overseas. In Prime Minister John Major's June Cabinet reshuffle, Michael Portillo was named to replace Rifkind.

HMS *Vigilant,* the third Vanguard-class Trident missile submarine, was rolled out on October 14; it was scheduled to enter operational service in 1998. By the end of 1998, the Trident submarines would be Britain's only nuclear delivery system, as the government announced in April that the Royal Air Force would loose its nuclear capability by that date with the withdrawal from service of the WE-177 free-fall nuclear bomb. In November the United States agreed to provide U.S.-built Tomahawk convention-

Approximate Strengths of Selected Regular Armed Forces of the World

	Military personnel in 000s				Warships: Submarines				Combat aircraft[1]				
Country	Total	Army	Navy	Air Force[2]	Nuclear	Diesel	Aircraft Carriers/ Cruisers	Destroyers/ Frigates	Bombers and fighter-ground attack	Fighters	Recon-nais-sance	Tanks[3]	Defense expenditure as % of 1994 GDP
I. NATO													
Belgium	47.2[4]	30.1	2.8	12.3	—	—	—	2	133	—	—	334	1.7
Canada	70.5[4]	20.3	10.0	17.1	—	3	—	12	122	—	18	114	1.7
Denmark	33.1	19.1	6.0	8.0	—	5	—	3	66	—	—	411	1.9
France	409.0[4]	241.4	64.2[5]	89.2	11	7	3	39	484	91	191	1,016	3.3
Germany	339.9[4]	234.0	28.5	75.3	—	20	—	13	326	181	51	2,695	2.0
Greece	171.3	125.0	19.5	26.8	—	8	—	13	179	150	22	2,268	5.7
Italy	328.7[4]	175.0	44.0	67.8	—	9	2	30	222	111	36	1,309	2.1
Netherlands, The	74.4[4]	43.2	14.3	12.5	—	4	—	18	164	—	19	740	2.1
Norway	30.0[4]	14.7	6.4	7.9	—	12	—	4	59	15	6	170	3.1
Portugal	54.2[4]	29.7	12.5	7.3	—	3	—	11	97	—	6	198	2.6
Spain	206.0	144.7	31.9[5]	29.4	—	8	1	17	42	131	15	684	1.6
Turkey	507.8	400.0	51.0[5]	56.8	—	16	—	21	204	194	49	4,280	3.2
United Kingdom	236.9	116.0	50.5[5]	70.4	15	—	3	35	407	148	26	506	3.4
United States	1,547.3	524.9	613.7[5]	408.7	100	—	44	95	4,267	43	300	12,516	4.3
II. NON-NATO EUROPE													
Albania	73.0	60.0	2.5	10.0	—	2	—	—	47	51	—	859	2.7
Armenia	60.0[4]	51.8	—	7.4	—	—	—	—	5	1	—	128	3.1
Austria	55.7	51.5	—	4.2	—	—	—	—	24	24	—	169	0.9
Azerbaijan	86.7	73.3	2.2	11.2	—	—	—	—	16	30	—	325	8.7
Belarus	98.4[4]	50.5	—	25.7	—	—	—	—	141	166	42	2,348	2.2
Bosnia and Herzegovina	92.0	92.0	—	—	—	—	—	—	—	—	—	31	69.2
Bulgaria	101.9[4]	51.6	3.0	21.6	—	2	—	1	169	82	21	1,786	2.5
Croatia	105.0	99.6	1.1	4.3	—	1	—	—	28	—	—	176	10.2
Czech Republic	86.4[4]	37.4	—	18.5	—	—	—	—	156	68		1,011	2.6
Finland	31.1	25.7	2.5	2.9	—	—	—	—	—	108	—	232	2.0
Hungary	70.5	53.7	—	16.8	—	—	—	—	—	133	14	1,016	1.6
Ireland	12.9	10.9	1.0	1.0	—	—	—	—	20	—	4	—	1.2
Moldova	11.8	10.5	—	1.3	—	—	—	—	—	27	—	—	3.8
Poland	278.6	188.2	17.8	72.6	—	3	—	2	119	265	28	1,752	2.5
Romania	217.4[4]	128.8	19.0[5]	54.0	—	1	—	6	169	222	11	1,843	2.9
Slovakia	47.0	33.0	—	14.0	—	—	—	—	34	69	8	912	2.5
Sweden	64.0	43.5	9.0	11.5	—	13	—	—	158	185	50	708	2.5
Ukraine	452.5[4]	212.6	16.0[5]	151.0	—	—	—	4	252	482	112	4,775	2.1
Yugoslavia	126.5	90.0	6.0	29.0	—	4	—	4	140	113	29	639	23.1
III. RUSSIA													
Russia	1,520.0[4]	670.0	200.0	430.0[6]	119	64	26	124	1,435	1,295	406	19,850	9.6
IV. MIDDLE EAST AND NORTH AFRICA; SUB-SAHARAN AFRICA; LATIN AMERICA													
Algeria	121.7	105.0	6.7	10.0	—	2	—	3	61	100	9	960	2.7
Egypt	436.0	310.0	16.0	110.0	—	4	—	7	160	384	20	3,500	5.9
Iran	513.0[4]	345.0	18.0[5]	30.0	—	2	—	5	170	125	14	1,440	3.8
Iraq	382.5	350.0	2.5	30.0	—	—	—	1	136	180	—	2,700	14.6
Israel	172.0	134.0	6.0	32.0	—	2	—	—	222	205	22	4,095	9.5
Jordan	98.6	90.0	0.6	8.0	—	—	—	—	50	32	—	1,141	7.1
Kuwait	16.6[4]	10.0	2.5	2.5	—	—	—	—	68	8	—	220	12.2
Lebanon	44.3	43.0	0.5	0.8	—	—	—	—	—	3	—	300	4.4
Libya	80.0	50.0	8.0	22.0	—	4	—	2	200	209	11	2,210	3.7
Morocco	195.5	175.0	7.0	13.5	—	—	—	1	84	15	2	224	4.3
Oman	43.5[4]	25.0	4.2	4.1	—	—	—	—	46		—	91	15.9
Saudi Arabia	105.5	70.0	13.5[5]	22.0	—	—	—	8	163	122	10	1,055	11.2
Sudan, The	118.5	115.0	1.5	3.0	—	—	—	—	27	23	2	320	3.5
Syria	423.0	315.0	8.0	100.0	—	1	—	2	234	331	14	4,600	8.6
Tunisia	35.5	27.0	5.0	3.5	—	—	—	—	32	—	—	84	1.4
United Arab Emirates	70.0	65.0	1.5	3.5	—	—	—	—	61	28	8	133	5.7
Yemen	39.5	37.0	1.5	1.0	—	—	—	—	35	34	—	1,125	5.2

ally armed cruise missiles for the Royal Navy's nuclear-powered attack submarines.

In September the Ministry of Defence announced that it would review all aspects of its policy of excluding homosexuals from the armed forces after the High Court ruled that the current policy was lawful but urged that it be reviewed. Major and French Pres. Jacques Chirac signed a new bilateral defense agreement on October 30 in which they agreed to exchange technical information on their nuclear weapons.

France. Chirac, who took office on May 17, named Charles Millon as his minister of defense, and in June the new government announced an 8.5% cut in 1995 weapons procurement. Millon said that no major programs would be terminated, but he admitted that the previous year's 1995–2000 procurement blueprint was no longer credible. In September the government announced that it would limit military procurement spending in the 1996 budget to F 95 billion, a 15% cut. Reports indicated that the government planned to abandon the land-based missile leg of its nuclear triad by closing down the base on the Plateau d'Albion in southeastern France. The controversial nuclear tests in the South Pacific served to certify the new TN-75 warhead for the next generation of M-45 submarine-launched ballistic missiles. In addition, France planned to develop a new long-range air-launched cruise missile with a nuclear warhead

(continued on page 260)

Approximate Strengths of Selected Regular Armed Forces of the World (continued)

Country	Military personnel in 000s				Warships: Submarines		Warships		Combat aircraft[1]				Defense expenditure as % of 1994 GDP
	Total	Army	Navy	Air Force[2]	Nuclear	Diesel	Aircraft Carriers/ Cruisers	Destroyers/ Frigates	Bombers and fighter-ground attack	Fighters	Recon-nais-sance	Tanks[3]	
Angola	82.0	75.0	1.5	5.5	—	—	—	—	88	21	3	200	8.7
Kenya	24.2	20.5	1.2	2.5	—	—	—	—	28	—	—	76	2.2
Madagascar	21.0	20.0	0.5[5]	0.5	—	—	—	—	12	—	—	—	0.8
Mozambique	34.8	30.0	0.8	4.0	—	—	—	—	43	—	—	80	7.1
Nigeria	77.1	62.0	5.6	9.5	—	—	—	1	92	—	—	210	3.1
South Africa	136.9[4]	118.0	4.5	9.0	—	3	—	—	243	—	13	250	3.3
Tanzania	34.6	30.0	1.0	3.6	—	—	—	—	—	24	—	65	3.5
Zaire	49.1[4]	25.0	1.3[5]	1.8	—	—	—		22	—	—	60	1.9
Zimbabwe	45.0	41.0	—	4.0	—	—	—	—	23	14	15	40	3.5
Argentina	67.3	40.4	18.0[5]	8.9	—	3	—	13	271	0	12	296	1.7
Brazil	295.0	195.0	50.0[5]	50.0	—	5	1	20	257	16	13	—	1.6
Chile	99.0	54.0	31.0[5]	14.0	—	4	—	9	91	15	20	119	3.5
Colombia	146.4	121.0	18.1[5]	7.3	—	4	—	4	74	—	—	—	2.3
Cuba	105.0	85.0	5.0[5]	15.0	—	2	—	3	14	116	—	1,575	2.7
Ecuador	57.1	50.0	4.1[5]	3.0	—	2	—	2	58	14	—	—	3.2
El Salvador	30.5	28.0	0.5[5]	2.0	—	—	—	—	21	—	—	—	1.9
Mexico	175.0	130.0	37.0[5]	8.0	—	—	—	5	90	11	9	—	0.7
Peru	115.0	75.0	25.0[5]	15.0	—	6	2	9	70	20	7	300	1.8
Uruguay	25.6	17.6	5.0[6]	3.0	—	—		3	36	—	6	—	2.5
Venezuela	79.0[4]	34.0	15.0[5]	7.0	—	2	—	6	119	—	4	70	1.6
V. SOUTH AND CENTRAL ASIA; EAST ASIA AND OCEANIA													
Australia	56.1	23.7	15.0	17.4	—	4	—	11	102	—	23	90	2.3
Bangladesh	115.5	101.0	8.0	6.5	—	—	—	4	30	27	—	140	1.8
Cambodia	88.5[4]	36.0	2.0	0.5	—	—	—	—	6	19	—	250	2.3
China	2,930.0	2,200.0	260.0[5]	470.0	6	46	—	50	1,675	4,000	310	8,000	5.6
India	1,145.0	980.0	55.0[5]	110.0	—	15	2	23	487	372	62	2,400	2.8
Indonesia	274.5	214.0	40.5[5]	20.0	—	2	—	13	61	12	21	—	1.4
Japan	239.5[4]	151.2	43.7	44.6	—	18	—	63	140	290	130	1,160	1.0
Kazakhstan	40.0	25.0	—	15.0	—	—	—	—	69	69	27	624	3.5
Korea, North	1,128.0	1,000.0	46.0	82.0	—	25	—	3	509	—	—	3,400	26.6
Korea, South	633.0	520.0	60.0[5]	53.0	—	6	—	40	303	130	51	2,110	3.6
Kyrgyzstan	7.0	7.0	—	—	—	—	—	—	96	—	—	204	1.4
Laos	37.0	33.0	0.5	3.5	—	—	—	—	31	—	—	30	7.9
Malaysia	114.5	90.0	12.0	12.5	—	—	—	4	86	29	12	—	3.9
Mongolia	21.1	20.0	—	1.1	—	—	—	—	15	—	—	650	2.8
Myanmar (Burma)	286.0	265.0	12.0[5]	9.0	—	—	—	—	55	36	—	62	3.1
New Zealand	10.0	4.5	2.2	3.3	—	—	—	4	37	—	6	—	1.1
Pakistan	587.0	520.0	22.0[5]	45.0	—	9	—	11	168	243	16	2,050	6.9
Philippines	106.5	68.0	23.0[5]	15.5	—	—	—	1	36	7	8	—	1.4
Singapore	53.9	45.0	2.9	6.0	—	—	—	—	109	38	6	60	4.8
Sri Lanka	125.3	105.0	10.3	10.0	—	—	—	—	27	—	6	25	4.7
Taiwan	376.0	240.0	68.0[5]	68.0	—	4	—	38	424	—	38	570	5.0
Thailand	259.0	150.0	66.0[5]	43.0	—	—	—	10	175	43	28	253	2.6
Turkmenistan	11.0	11.0	—	—	—	—	—	—	89	82	—	530	1.1
Uzbekistan	25.0[4]	20.4	—	4.0	—	—	—	—	52	64	10	179	2.4
Vietnam	572.0	500.0	42.0[5]	30.0	—	—	—	7	65	125	4	1,300	5.7

Note: Data exclude most paramilitary, security, and irregular forces. Naval data exclude vessels of less than 100 tons standard displacement. Figures are for June 1995. Because of substantive changes in national forces and reassessments of evidence, data may not be comparable with previous editions.

[1]Includes combat aircraft from all services, including naval and air defense. Light strike/counterinsurgency aircraft are included in bomber/fighter-ground-attack category. Reconnaissance includes maritime reconnaissance and antisubmarine warfare aircraft.

[2]Includes air defense troops.

[3]Main battle tanks (MBT), weighing at least 16.5 metric tons with gun of at least 75-mm calibre.

[4]Some countries have staffs, centrally controlled units, support services, military police, regular armed forces not responsible to the Ministry of Defense, and the like, which means total armed forces are greater than the sum of the three armed forces.

[5]Includes marines or naval infantry.

[6]Includes strategic missile forces.

Source: International Institute for Strategic Studies, 23 Tavistock Street, London, *The Military Balance 1995–1996*.

1945—A Watershed Year

The year 1995 has been called "the 50th anniversary of almost everything," and the hyperbole is arguably slight. The only world many of us have known came into existence in the period from 1945 to 1947. Although that world may have come to its end with the breakup of the Soviet Union—and even though Eric Hobsbawm recently has published a history of the "short" 20th century that he claims ran from 1914 to 1991—the contours of some new world are by no means evident.

The following are extracts from articles published in the 1946 edition of the *Britannica Book of the Year* and were chosen to illuminate the way people thought then about the great events that were defining their lives and that now can be seen as seminal to the age that was beginning. In chronological order, they are: the Yalta Conference, the death of Franklin D. Roosevelt, the surrender of Germany, the Holocaust, the formation of the United Nations, the development and use of the atomic bomb, and the surrender of Japan.

• [From "United States"] At a meeting between Roosevelt, Churchill and Stalin at Yalta on the Black sea in February plans were discussed for the most effective co-operation of the Allies in bringing about the unconditional surrender of Germany and the treatment of that country in respect to occupation and reparations when the victory should be won. On his return from Yalta President Roosevelt addressed the nation (March 1), reporting the close accord of the Allies and declaring, "this time we are not making the mistake of waiting until the end of the war to set up the machinery of peace." Four days later the governments of the United States, Great Britain and Russia, with the concurrence of China, issued invitations to 39 nations (later increased to 51) to attend a United Nations conference at San Francisco to draft a Security charter on the basis of the Dumbarton Oaks proposals of Oct. 1944.

• [From "Roosevelt, Franklin Delano"] **Roosevelt, Franklin Delano** (1882–1945) devoted the last few months of his life to preparing for a victory over the axis and a difficult postwar era which he did not live to experience. When he died suddenly on April 12, 1945, at his Warm Springs cottage in Georgia, the armed forces he had mobilized as commander in chief were beating at the gates of Berlin and bombarding the shores of Japan's home islands.

His death caused universal shock. Despite obvious evidence of his physical strain through 1944, the state of his health had been a carefully guarded secret. In late Feb. 1945, Vice-Adm. Ross T. McIntyre, White House physician, gave public assurances that his condition was "excellent." But when he continued to lose weight early in March, Dr.

ED CLARK—LIFE MAGAZINE © TIME WARNER INC.

Graham Jackson, a U.S. Navy musician who often performed at presidential parties, cries as he plays "Going Home" while the body of Pres. Franklin D. Roosevelt is taken from the "Little White House" in Warm Springs, Ga., to the railroad station. The wartime leader died on April 12, 1945.

McIntyre prescribed a rest in the south. On March 30 he left for the infantile paralysis centre which he founded.

At one o'clock of the fatal day he was sitting before the fireplace of the "Little White House" while a New York artist sketched him. Suddenly he exclaimed to Commander Howard G. Bruen, a naval physician: "I have a terrific headache!" The stricken president was carried into his bedroom, where he died at 3:55 PM, Georgia time, of a massive cerebral haemorrhage without regaining consciousness. The White House announced his death at 5:48 PM, eastern war time, and at 7:09 PM Vice-President Harry S. Truman was sworn in as president in the cabinet room.

Quiet, sorrowing crowds lined the railroad tracks as the funeral train brought the body to Washington, where simple ceremonies were held in the east room at 4 PM, April 14. For three days the nation and the world paid him a tribute which no other U.S. president, in life or in death, had received. He was given a military burial on Sunday morning, April 15, in a hedge-enclosed rose garden on the ancestral estate at Hyde Park, N.Y.

Almost as if he had a premonition that the end was near, even the energetic Roosevelt had rarely laboured so ceaselessly as he did during those last few months. It seemed as if he were consciously striving to write a last will and testament for what he knew might be a free but chaotic universe.

• [From "World War II"] **The Surrender of Germany.**—The death of Hitler, the fall of Berlin and the junction of the United States and soviet armies at Torgau were all factors that quickened the beginning of the end of the long German reign of terror on the continent. The armies of the western Allies and the soviet union were overrunning the entire reich. German resistance was rapidly fading and failure of their military strategy to halt the invading armies led the nazi high command to lay greater stress on political tactics. Their hope was to divide the western Allies and the soviet union. Doenitz, who succeeded Hitler as fuehrer, said in a broadcast May 1 that as long as the western Allies obstructed achievement of his aim to save Germany from "bolshevik" destruction, his forces would carry on the "defensive" struggle against Britain and the United States as well as against the soviet union. This appeal was ignored by Churchill and Truman. They insisted on the full and unconditional surrender of the German armies to the soviet as well as the British and United States forces. Consequently the war dragged on.

But the defeat of Hitler's Germany was not far distant. . . .

Significantly, in the final months of the battle of Germany, most of the major fighting was carried on against the soviet forces. After the crossing of the Rhine, German resistance to the armies of the western Allies was relatively light.

With German resistance now virtually nonexistent, Doenitz had no choice but to accept the Allied ultimatum that he surrender to all three forces—United States, British and Russian—simultaneously. He dispatched two emissaries, Gen. Adm. Hans Georg von Friedeburg and Col. Gen. Alfred Jodl, to Gen. Eisenhower's headquarters in Reims, France, where Jodl signed (May 7) the final surrender document. The following day (May 8), Friedeburg, Field Marshal Gen. Wilhelm Keitel, chief of staff of the German high command and Gen. Hans Jürgen Stumpff signed similar documents in Berlin in the presence of Marshal Zhukov. While the cease-fire order was given May 8, the actual signing of the Berlin document did not take place until shortly after midnight May 9.

Some fighting continued in Czechoslovakia after the prescribed surrender date but by May 12, all fighting in Europe had ended and peace was restored to the continent.

• [From "Jewish Religious Life"] The end of World War II revealed how disastrous to Judaism had been the atrocities of Hitlerism. In continental Europe, few Jewish children survived, and the exhausted adult survivors in the underground movements or in displaced persons camps were seen to be for the most part without communities, synagogues, religious or Jewish educational institutions or ritual articles. Outside of soviet Russia, only 1,500,000 Jews remained in Europe; 5,000,000 were destroyed. A typical figure is that from Leipzig, Germany, where of 16,000 Jews, 16 survived, and they only because they were married to Christians and were bringing up their children as Christians. Of the 3,500,000 Jews of prewar Poland, there remained but 80,000, scattered, starved and still being pogromized. In western Europe there was some hope of rebuilding Jewish communities; but in central and eastern Europe the shadow of extinction loomed over what were before the war the greatest centres of Jewish learning and of intensely lived Judaism.

There were some encouraging incidents during 1945. Thus, when the first service was held in the reopened Amsterdam synagogue, four-fifths of the congregation was made up of Christians who came to show their sympathy with the Jewish survivors. In Bergen, Oslo and Trondheim, Norway, the surviving Jews were given money seized from German accounts to help them repair their synagogues. But attempts to reorganize Jewish life were generally hampered by the utter poverty that gripped so much of Europe, indoctrinated nazi anti-Semitism, and the unwillingness to give back to Jews seized Jewish property. Thus, at Maastricht, Netherlands, the community planned for U.S. Jewish soldiers a celebration of the Biblical festival of Purim; but it was disapproved of lest it stir up additional anti-Semitism. When at Dachau, Germany, a U.S. Jewish chaplain attempted to hold an open-air religious service, the Jewish displaced persons declared that it would lead to disorders. In the Belsen camp, Polish internees smashed the synagogue set up by the Jewish displaced persons and desecrated the Torahs and prayer books.

This atmosphere in postwar Europe tended to drive the surviving Jews to one of two extremes—either a flight from Judaism, dramatized by the conversion to Catholicism of the chief rabbi of Rome, or an intensification of Jewishness which makes the overwhelming majority of the Jewish displaced persons want to settle down only in Palestine. The failure of the British Labour government to live up to British pledged policy of facilitating the establishment in Palestine of a Jewish national home stirred a reaction of a far more militantly determined Zionism in Palestine, in the Jewish people generally, and in the congress of the United States which by an overwhelming vote called for the fulfillment of the international pledge to make a reality of Zionism.

• [From "United Nations Conference"] **The Procedure of the Conference.**—The conference opened on April 25 with an address of welcome from President Truman, who spoke from Washington.

During the first eight plenary sessions the heads of 37 delegations addressed the conference, stating the general views of their respective states concerning the nature and functions which should be possessed by the future United Nations organization. Many of these delegates took the opportunity to point out what they believed to be basic shortcomings of the League of Nations which must be corrected if the new organization were to achieve its stated goal of maintaining international peace and security. . . .

As the committees plunged into their work, it soon became apparent that the major line of cleavage on issues was between the sponsoring powers and their smaller satellites, on the one hand, and those small and middle-sized states which, having no political ties such as to limit their freedom of action, were vocal in criticizing the draft charter because of its substantial departures from the principle of state equality. Australia and New Zealand assumed strong positions of leadership in the latter group, but the Netherlands, Belgium, Norway and many others joined vigorously in the fray. The sponsoring powers followed the general policy of trying to reach agreement on controversial issues outside the committee rooms, so as to present a united front in defense of the Dumbarton draft, or at least in defense of a compromise offer to which they could agree.

The position of France was somewhat equivocal. Though not a participant in the Dumbarton Oaks conversations or the Yalta conference, France was assured a permanent seat on the Security council. In a sense, therefore, the French were torn between a desire to go along with the other great powers and the desire to force a greater recognition of their status of equality by taking an independent stand on debatable issues. The policy which they generally followed was that of supporting the great powers' positions but indicating at the same time that they had made their decisions entirely for individual reasons. The Latin-American states, for the most part, vacillated between approval of the United States positions and support of the small-power stand. Czechoslovakia, Yugoslavia, the Byelorussian S.S.R. and the Ukrainian S.S.R. generally sided with the U.S.S.R. . . .

Women known as "burners" operate acetylene torches at a steelworks in Gary, Ind., producing plating to be used on tanks for the U.S. Army in World War II. When the war ended in 1945, many women left their industrial jobs, but the nature of the U.S. workforce had forever been changed.

When the final printed texts in the five official languages of the charter and the new statute of the court of international justice were officially signed on June 26, the day President Truman addressed the closing session of the conference, the delegates also placed their signatures on another document, the Interim agreement, which set forth the subsequent procedure to be followed in establishing the United Nations organization. This agreement established a new executive committee, consisting of the same states as those which had served on the executive committee of the conference and a preparatory commission, composed of one representative of each national delegation. The new executive committee was directed to assist the preparatory commission in making arrangements for the holding of the first general assembly meeting of the U.N.O., to make plans for the secretariat of the organization and to canvass the whole problem of taking over those properties and functions of the League of Nations which were desired by the new organization. These bodies were directed to make their temporary headquarters in London. As a result of their work during the months of November and December it was agreed that the first general assembly meeting should be held in London in Jan. 1946.

• [From "Atomic Bomb"] Atomic bomb is the name given to a bomb which obtains its explosive violence from the release of atomic energy, or more exactly, the conversion of matter into energy by an atomic transformation known technically as nuclear fission. No comparable weapon has existed in the history of the world. The first one dropped had more power than 20,000 tons of T.N.T.

Based on the discovery of uranium fission by O. Hahn and F. Strassman in Germany in 1939, the atomic bomb was perfected in the United States during World War II as a joint venture of the United States, British and Canadian governments. The first bomb was exploded in a test on the New Mexico desert on July 16, 1945. Two atomic bombs were dropped on Japan from U.S. aeroplanes, the first on Hiroshima on Aug. 6, 1945 (Japanese time), the second on Nagasaki on Aug. 9 (Japanese time). Japan surrendered on Aug. 14. Former Prime Minister Winston Churchill estimated that by shortening the war, the atomic bomb had saved the lives of 1,000,000 U.S. soldiers and 250,000 British soldiers.

The release of atomic energy is one of the greatest triumphs in the history of science, perhaps the most significant development in the progress of mankind after the discovery of the use of fire. It has equally vast potentialities for good and for evil. . . .

The Atomic Bomb Project. The story of the production of the atomic bomb is in many ways as unique as the bomb itself. At the centre of the enterprise was a brilliant group of United States, British and refugee scientists. While engaged in one war in Europe and another in the Pacific, the United States marshaled the manpower and resources needed to complete in four years a project that otherwise might have taken half a century. The cost of the project, $2,000,000,000, indicates its magnitude.

It is difficult to assign credit to all those who took part in the venture. The brilliant group of research scientists formed its heart. But later, as the project developed and vast plants had to be built and tens of thousands of workers employed, the co-operation of a large number of the nation's chief industrial corporations as well as that of the war department and other branches of the government was required. The decision to embark on the project had to be made by President Roosevelt himself, and he and his advisers, both civil and military, deserve the highest praise for their courage and foresight. . . .

The Explosion of the Bombs. A total of three atomic bombs were set off prior to the surrender of Japan, one in a test in New Mexico, two in actual warfare.

The Test.—The first atomic bomb in the history of mankind was exploded at 5:30 A.M. on July 16, 1945, at the Alamogordo air base in the desert 120 mi. southeast of Albuquerque, N.M. The bomb had been placed on a tall steel tower while scientists and military experts occupied observation posts placed at distances ranging from 10,000 to 17,000 yd. from the tower. They had been instructed to lie down with their feet toward the tower and to protect their eyes from the blinding flash of the explosion. The skies were dark and it was raining. An occasional lightning flash illumined the sandy desert and the distant mountains.

The explosion caused a flash that lit up the mountain peaks 10 mi. away. Then came a tremendous, sustained roar accompanied by a tornadolike burst of wind. Where the tower had stood there was a great boiling, surging cloud of many colours rising into the stratosphere, more than 40,000 ft. in height. When the cloud had disappeared, it was noted that the steel tower was gone. The heat of the explosion, estimated at several millions of degrees, had completely vaporized it. In place of the tower there was a huge crater, the floor of which consisted of a glass formed by the fusion of the sand.

The Bombing of Hiroshima.—The first atomic bomb to be used in warfare was dropped on Hiroshima, a Japanese army base and city of 343,000 inhabitants, at 9:15 A.M., Aug. 6 (Japanese time), 1945. The bomb was dropped from a B-29 Superfortress, the "Enola Gay." Col. Paul W. Tibbets, Jr., was the pilot and Major Thomas W. Ferebee the bombardier. Capt. Parsons, who had helped design the bomb, went along as the "weaponeer." The flash of the explosion was seen by a reconnaissance plane 170 mi. away. Those in the "Enola Gay" reported that a black cloud rose over Hiroshima to a height of 40,000 ft. Aerial photographs taken after the smoke and dust had cleared away showed a scene of destruction unlike any before witnessed. The entire business section at the centre of the town had disappeared except for the skeletons of three concrete buildings. It was estimated by the Japanese government that the bomb killed 60,000 persons, wounded 100,000 and rendered an additional 200,000 homeless.

The Bombing of Nagasaki.—The second bomb to be used against Japan was dropped on Nagasaki at 12:01 P.M., Aug. 9 (Japanese time), from a B-29 Superfortress, the "Great Artiste," piloted by Major Charles W. Sweeney. It was said that the construction of this bomb was so superior to that used at Hiroshima as to render that model obsolete. This second bomb created a considerable crater. Its toll of human life was smaller due to the smaller population of Nagasaki. The Japanese government estimated that 10,000 persons were killed, 20,000 wounded, and an additional 90,000 made homeless.

The skeletal remains of Hiroshima show the devastation caused by the atomic bomb dropped on the Japanese city on Aug. 6, 1945, the first use of the weapon developed by the U.S. during World War II. Three days later the U.S. dropped a second atomic bomb, this time on the city of Nagasaki.
WAYNE MILLER—MAGNUM

The Future of Atomic Energy. Following a message from President Truman on Oct. 3, 1945, a bill sponsored by the war department and known as the May-Johnson bill was introduced into congress. The purpose of this bill was to keep the atomic bomb a secret and to set up a commission charged with the administration and control of all research in the field of atomic energy and the formation of security regulations stipulating what might or might not be made public. The bill aroused the immediate antagonism of the great majority of scientists who had worked on the bomb and they made their opinions public through hastily formed organizations such as the Atomic Scientists of Chicago, the Association of Oak Ridge Scientists, and the Federation of Atomic Scientists. This sudden entrance of scientists into the arena of public affairs was unique in United States history.

The Scientists' Viewpoint.—The scientists were convinced that any attempt to keep the bomb a secret was futile because all the fundamental scientific facts were known throughout the world in 1940. They believed that the only result of the attempt would be to embark the world upon an international atomic bomb race certain to end in World War III and the destruction of civilization. Moreover, they regarded the proposed controls over scientific research as contrary to the basic principles of U.S. democracy and inimical to scientific progress.

The scientists advocated instead a policy of international cooperation with a return to the classic freedom of scientific research and the creation of an international inspection committee by the United Nations Organization charged with the task of seeing that no nation set up plants for the manufacture of atomic bombs or the concentration of fissionable materials in forms and amounts suitable for quick conversion into bombs.

• [From "World War II"] The first reaction in the United States to the use of the atomic weapon was elation. The popular impression was that it had brought the war that much nearer to its end. Subsequently, more sober appraisals lent strength to the view that the United States, in employing this dangerous explosive without warning, set a grave precedent fraught with risk in the event of future wars. It was pointed out that a future aggressor might justify use of atomic weapons against the United States, arguing that as the U.S. forces were the first to use it without advance notice, they were therefore deprived of the moral right to protest in the event it were turned against them under similar circumstances. . . .

On Aug. 8, three months after the reich's surrender, the soviet union declared war on Japan. The Red armies starting the attack the following day (Aug. 9) at 12.01 A.M., launched a three-ply invasion of Japanese-held Manchuria. . . .

End of World War II.—The atomic bombings and the soviet invasion of Manchuria convinced the Japanese that further resistance was futile and the Japanese government decided to accept the surrender offer as laid down at the Potsdam conference by Great Britain, the United States and China, July 26. Under these terms, Japan was to be stripped of its vast empire and reduced to the home islands. While Emperor Hirohito was permitted to retain his throne, he was made subject to the authority of the commander of the Allied occupation armies. Hirohito announced acceptance of the Potsdam terms, Aug. 14, and on Sept. 2, Japanese emissaries signed the formal surrender document in a ceremony aboard the U.S. battleship "Missouri" in Tokyo bay, thus concluding World War II, six years and one day after it was launched by the German invasion of Poland, Sept. 1, 1939.

Residents of the Japanese island of Okinawa protest the alleged rape of a schoolgirl by three U.S. servicemen in September. The incident inflamed Japanese public opinion and led to calls by some for changes in the agreement by which U.S. forces were stationed on Japanese territory.
KYODO NEWS SERVICE

(continued from page 255)
to provide a nuclear capability for the new Rafale fighter-bombers. In December France agreed to rejoin NATO's military wing. Some 900 French troops were sent to the former French territory of the Comoros in October to put down a coup by army rebels and white mercenaries.

Germany. On January 1 the operational forces of the Bundeswehr in the former East Germany were assigned to NATO, completing a four-year effort to integrate the units in the new states into the national forces. On March 15 Defense Minister Volker Rühe announced plans to trim the armed forces by 32,000 to 338,000 and to reduce conscription to 10 months. The new Crisis Reaction Forces would include 37,000 army, 12,300 air force, and 4,300 navy personnel. A Special Forces Command would be established at Calw, near Stuttgart. There would be 22 peacetime brigades—a drop of two—and one of the present eight divisions was to be abolished. German Tornadoes flew reconnaissance and air-defense suppression missions in Bosnia and Herzegovina in support of NATO's Rapid Reaction Force, and the government announced that it would contribute as many as 6,000 men to the Bosnian peace implementation force.

Turkey. Beginning on March 20, 35,000 Turkish troops, backed by tanks and planes, marched into part of northern Iraq to crush Kurdish rebels of the outlawed Kurdish Workers' Party. The Turks withdrew in early May. A second five-day incursion by some 3,000 troops took place in July. These events strained Turkish relations with its NATO allies and prompted Norway, The Netherlands, and Germany to halt arms transfers to Turkey for a time.

Commonwealth of Independent States (CIS). Russia signed military-basing agreements with Armenia and Georgia, and Russian border troops patrolled the external borders of most CIS members. Russian peacekeeping troops were active in Moldova, Tajikistan, and the Georgian region of Abkhazia. Russia and Ukraine agreed to divide the rusting Black Sea Fleet, with 82% of the ships going to Russia. Sevastopol, in Ukraine, would be the Russian base.

After the failure of the New Year's Eve attack on Grozny, the Chechen capital, Russian Defense Minister Pavel Grachev called in elite units from throughout Russia to bolster the federal government's military contingent in the breakaway republic. Still, the stubborn Chechen militants continued to expose the weaknesses in morale, leadership, and equipment of the Russian troops, who could not drive Dzhokhar Dudayev's supporters out of the capital until February 8. Fierce fighting continued in other parts of the republic for months more. The bungled military intervention revealed deep fissures in Russia's military leadership. More than 500 military officers refused to take part in the Chechen operations. Yeltsin ultimately fired four deputy defense ministers, including Boris Gromov, the popular last commander of Soviet troops in Afghanistan. Another military critic of the operation was Lieut. Gen. Aleksandr Lebed, the charismatic leader of the Russian 14th Army deployed in the Transdniestr region of Moldova. Lebed resigned to enter politics after his command was downgraded.

The reputation of Russia's military and security forces was further sullied in June when army and elite Interior Ministry antiterrorist troops were unable to dislodge a Chechen separatist band from a hospital in the southern Russian town of Budennovsk, where they had holed up with over 1,000 hostages. Prime Minister Viktor Chernomyrdin on June 18 negotiated an end to the siege by offering a truce in Chechnya and freedom for the attackers. On July 30 Russian and Chechen negotiators signed an agreement calling for the disarmament of the Chechen separatists and the withdrawal of most of the federal troops. An Organization for Security and Cooperation in Europe mission went to Grozny to observe compliance with the agreement. Shooting incidents continued to take a steady toll of Russian troops. On October 9 the disarming and withdrawal were suspended following the attempted assassination of the commander of federal forces in Chechnya.

Tajikistan was another spot where Russian servicemen suffered regular casualties, mainly border troops trying to prevent Tajik dissidents from entering the country from Afghanistan. Inside Tajikistan two brigades of the Tajikistan army came to blows as they competed for influence in the Kurgan-Tyube region.

In an incident reminiscent of a Soviet response at the height of the Cold War, Belarus air defense forces on September 13 shot down a hot-air balloon that had drifted into Belarusian airspace while participating in a prestigious international race; the two American crew members were killed.

The Rest of Europe. Fortune in the conflicts in former Yugoslavia turned against the Serbs in 1995, with impressive gains by the Bosnian government and Croatian armies and forceful military actions rather than their usual bluffs and threats by the frustrated NATO forces. In March the Bosnian government went on the offensive in the central and northern parts of the country. Croatian forces, in a 48-hour blitzkrieg that began on May 1, seized the territory in western Croatia that had been held by the self-proclaimed Republic of Serbian Krajina (RSK). On May 25–26 NATO aircraft struck a Bosnian Serb ammunition dump near Pale at the request of the UN Protection Force (UNPROFOR) following Bosnian Serb shelling of UN safe areas. The Serbs retaliated by taking several hundred UNPROFOR soldiers hostage. On June 2 U.S. Air Force Capt. Scott F. O'Grady's F-16C was shot down over western Bosnia and Herzegovina by a Bosnian Serb SAM-6 missile. O'Grady was rescued six days later, having used his survival training to evade searching Serbs, and returned to a hero's welcome in the U.S. The U.K., France, and The Netherlands contributed the troops for an 8,700-man Rapid Reaction Force that began to arrive in the region in mid-June. More mobile and with heavy weapons, this force was to back up the 20,500 UNPROFOR troops already deployed. In July the Bosnian Serb forces took Srebrenica, one of the UN's declared "safe areas," after humiliating the 400 Dutch UN peacekeepers stationed there. This prompted a debate on whether to reinforce or withdraw the NATO and UN forces. In mid-July the U.S. deployed its newest unmanned reconnaissance aircraft to Grader, Albania, to support the UN and NATO forces. Two of these "Predator" spy drones were lost within a four-day period in August. In early August the Serbs captured Zepa, another of the UN safe areas, and attacked Bihac. This was to be their high-water mark. On the morning of August 4, Croatia launched an offensive with its 100,000-man army along the entire 1,125-km (700-mi) front separating the RSK from the rest of Croatia and in a five-day blitz regained control over almost all of the country. This was the largest army to fight in Europe in 50 years. On August 10 NATO and UN commanders signed a memorandum of agreement concerning NATO air operations to protect the remaining safe areas, and on August 30 NATO began Operation Deliberate Force, a massive application of air and artillery power aiming to force the Bosnian Serbs to respect the safe areas. After a brief pause, the strikes continued on September 5, and five days later they included the firing of 13 Tomahawk Land Attack Missiles against Bosnian Serb air defense installations by a U.S. cruiser in the Adriatic Sea. The parties to the conflict in Bosnia and Herzegovina agreed to a 60-day cease-fire, which began on October 11.

Middle East. The UN Security Council retained the economic sanctions against Iraq after determining that Saddam Hussein's government had failed to fulfill all its Persian Gulf War cease-fire obligations. On August 8 Lieut. Gen. Hussein Kamel Hassan, one of Hussein's sons-in-law and director of Iraq's Military Industrialization Corporation, defected to Jordan. This prompted the Iraqi government to provide a large amount of additional data to the UN Special Commission. This material and Hassan's revelations showed that Iraq had three separate biological weapons programs and had filled 191 bombs, artillery shells, and missiles with biological agents for possible use in the 1991 war. It had also launched a crash program in 1990 to test a nuclear bomb by April 1991, had produced its own rocket engines for its Scud and al-Hussein ballistic missiles, and was working on a radiological weapon.

Convinced that Iran was pursuing a program to build nuclear weapons, President Clinton in April imposed a total ban on U.S. trade with Iran. He could not, however, convince Russian President Yeltsin to cancel the deal to sell a nuclear reactor to Iran.

Despite the efforts of the radical groups Hamas and Hezbollah to disrupt it, the Israeli-Palestinian peace process moved slowly forward. On September 28 the two parties signed an interim agreement in Washington, D.C. One of its terms provided for the withdrawal of the Israeli Defense Forces (IDF) from most of the towns and villages of the West Bank by the end of March 1996. The IDF would still be responsible for the external security of the West Bank. Less progress was made between Israel and Syria, although their chiefs of staff met in Washington in June and again in late December. In November, Israel's High Court of Justice ordered the air force to accept women as fighter pilots, overturning a long-standing ban on women in combat roles. In December Yemen and Eritrea clashed over the ownership of a disputed island in the Red Sea.

On July 1 the U.S. Navy recommissioned the 5th Fleet in the Persian Gulf. In October Bahrain agreed to be host to 18 U.S. warplanes until the end of the year in the absence of a U.S. aircraft carrier in the region, while in November the United Arab Emirates indicated it would allow the equipment for one U.S. armoured brigade to be stored on its territory. Approximately 200 U.S. aircraft were also based in Kuwait and Saudi Arabia.

South and Central Asia. In troubled Afghanistan the long civil war took a new twist as the Taleban, a movement made up of fundamentalist religious students turned warriors, swept out of the southwest to the very gates of Kabul after first having driven rebel leader Gulbuddin Hekmatyar from his headquarters at Charasyab. In mid-March, after a week of heavy fighting, they were pushed out of the capital's suburbs by government forces only to fight their way back later in the year. At the end of October, the northern Afghan warlord 'Abd ar-Rashid Dostam said he was willing to ally his ethnic Uzbek forces with the Taleban.

Resumption of U.S. arms aid to Pakistan threatened to fuel an arms race on the subcontinent. Congress agreed to permit the delivery of $368 million in embargoed U.S. military equipment sold to Pakistan prior to the imposition of sanctions against Pakistan's nuclear program. The equipment included three P-3C maritime patrol aircraft, Sidewinder air-to-air missiles, howitzers, antitank guided missiles, and Mk 46 torpedoes. Congress specifically excluded the 28 F-16s purchased and paid for by Pakistan. The U.S. tried unsuccessfully to sell the F-16s to a third country and reimburse Pakistan with the proceeds. In January Pakistani and Indian soldiers exchanged fire across the Kashmir border. Although both countries denied it, analysts believed that Pakistan had acquired several M-11 ballistic missiles from China, and India used this rumour to justify its further development of the nuclear-capable Prithvi and Agni missiles. While India and the U.S. signed a defense cooperation document in January, India strengthened its traditional military-procurement ties with Russia.

A truce between the Sri Lankan government and the Liberation Tigers of Tamil Eelam was broken in April when Tamil guerrillas blew up two government navy vessels and then shot down two military transport planes, killing over 100 people. In July government forces launched a major offensive to drive the Tamil Tigers from their strongholds on the Jaffna Peninsula. A second major drive that began in October culminated in the capture of Jaffna by the government forces, but the rebels continued to fight elsewhere.

East and Southeast Asia, Oceania. Bucking the worldwide trend, defense spending in Asia was generally up. Western analysts continued to argue about the size of China's defense budget, with estimates running from 4 to 20 times the official figure. China figured in two of the three potential flash points in the region: the South China Sea and Taiwan. In January Chinese troops removed Filipino fishermen from Mischief Reef in the disputed Spratly Islands, which prompted reactions from the Philippine navy and air force. Vietnam and Taiwan, two of the other claimants to the islands, also were involved in military incidents in the area. (*See* SPOTLIGHT: *The Spratly Spat.*) While China's Pres. Jiang Zemin on January 30 said that his country would not use force against Taiwan, the Chinese test-fired six M-9 and M-11 surface-to-surface missiles into the East China Sea to the north of Taiwan in July during exercises interpreted as an attempt to intimidate Taiwan. During the year China took delivery of three Kilo-class diesel submarines from Russia. On May 30 the Chinese tested their new Dongfeng-31 truck-launched intercontinental ballistic missile, estimated to have an 8,000-km (5,000-mi) range.

The Korean demilitarized zone remained the region's third potential flash point. For the second year running, the U.S. and South Korea canceled their annual "Team Spirit" joint military exercises as a gesture to North Korea. In October South Korean soldiers killed a North Korean infiltrator and captured another in separate incidents. Russia began to deliver military equipment—including T-80 tanks, BMP-3 armoured infantry fighting vehicles, and antitank missiles—to South Korea in partial repayment of the former Soviet Union's debt to Seoul. The deliveries were to continue for two more years.

In a Pentagon report issued in February, the U.S. pledged to maintain a force of 100,000 troops in Asia at least through the end of the decade. These included 48,000 in Japan and 37,000 in Korea. The alleged rape of a 12-year-old Okinawan girl by three U.S. servicemen in September sparked a number of protests against the U.S. military presence in Japan, and specifically on Okinawa, where some 28,000 U.S. servicemen were based. U.S. defense officials indicated some of the troops on Okinawa might be moved to other bases in Japan. Late in the year the Japanese National Security Council issued a new Defense Program Outline to replace the one adopted in 1976. It called for cuts in personnel and weapons of roughly 20%. The Air Self-Defense Force would cut its 350 fighters by 10%. The new FSX fighter-bomber made its first flight in October; the joint Japanese-American project was expected to enter serial production in 1996.

Malaysia received the 18 MiG-29s it had ordered from Russia in 1994. Singapore announced in September that it was purchasing a used submarine from Sweden. Burmese troops gained a major victory against the Karen rebels when they overran the Manerplaw headquarters of the Karen National Union in January. Thailand continued to acquire modern, sophisticated military equipment, receiving the first element of its second squadron of F-16 fighters.

The U.S., Britain, and France on October 20 announced they would sign the 1985 South Pacific Nuclear Free Zone Treaty. China and Russia had already signed.

Caribbean and Latin America. Peru and Ecuador engaged in a monthlong conflict early in the year over an unmarked 77-km (48-mi) stretch of jungle border. The Peruvians officially admitted losing 46 soldiers and several aircraft, and Ecuador reported 30 dead and at least 300 wounded, but unofficial reports placed the casualty toll higher. Despite a peace agreement in February that called for the demilitarization of the area, skirmishes between the two sides continued. The Sendero Luminoso (Shining Path) guerrillas in Peru, dormant for some time, killed 16 government soldiers in a July ambush.

At the end of March, the U.S.-led occupation force in Haiti turned over the country's security responsibilities to a 6,000-member UN peacekeeping force. Earlier in the year, Haiti's Pres. Jean-Bertrand Aristide had abolished the army. Ministers of defense from 34 nations in the Americas attended the first annual Ministerial of the Americas at Williamsburg, Va., in July. In March Cuba, which had been the last holdout in the region, signed the Treaty of Tlatelolco banning the proliferation of nuclear arms in Latin America and the Caribbean.

Africa South of the Sahara. The bloody civil war in Liberia paused in August with a power-sharing agreement between the battling parties but flared again on December 31. At the same time, the four-year rebellion in neighbouring Sierra Leone blazed up again. Civilians were once again the principal victims as fighting broke out between the Rwandan army and Hutu militia infiltrating back into the country from refugee camps in Zaire. Ethnic Tutsi soldiers in Burundi were accused of massacring hundreds of Hutu villagers in late October, and they launched a large offensive against Hutu rebels in December. In Nigeria the military government arrested 29 military officers and civilians in March for plotting a coup. In October the rebel Sudan People's Liberation Front carried out its biggest offensive in several years. The Sudanese government accused Uganda of sending troops and tanks into southern Sudan to help the rebels. Once the pariah of Africa, South Africa embarked upon a profitable campaign to export both its military equipment and its expertise. In October the South African government arrested former defense minister Gen. Magnus Malan and 10 other high-ranking military officers in connection with the slaying of 13 people in Natal in 1987. He was charged with murder on December 1.

New Technology. In February Sweden launched a conventionally powered submarine equipped with an air-independent propulsion system. The U.S. Air Force agreed with the Federal Railroad Administration to jointly develop magnetic levitation technologies. The service would use the technology to conduct realistic hypersonic tests of weapons.

(DOUGLAS L. CLARKE)

This article updates the *Macropædia* article The Technology of WAR.

Performing Arts

MUSIC

Classical. The world of classical music found its usual causes for celebration in 1995—birthdays, milestones, appointments, and awards—but the year's defining events were more sombre and reflective than they were festive as musicians everywhere joined a worldwide 50th-anniversary commemoration of the end of World War II. Composers, conductors, and concert organizers did their part to bring together those forces and sensibilities that the war had so tragically diffused.

The single blemish on the spirit of cooperation and reconciliation was the tussle between Germany and Poland over a cache of some 400 music manuscripts once held by the Prussian State Library in Berlin but moved to Poland for safekeeping during the war. At stake were not only a number of important scores valued at hundreds of millions of dollars, including symphonies by Mozart and Beethoven, but also the cultural heritage of one side pitted against the sense of violation and desire for reparation on the other. Bitter politics were the exception rather than the rule, however, in a year that saw the premiere of the *Requiem of Reconciliation,* a setting of the Latin requiem mass commissioned by the International Bach Academy in Stuttgart, Germany, with individual sections composed by 14 different composers representing countries involved in the war. The collaborators included Luciano Berio, John Harbison, György Kurtag, Arne Nordheim, Krzysztof Penderecki, Wolfgang Rihm, Alfred Schnittke (although a stroke prevented him from finishing his section), and Judith Weir. The work was premiered in Stuttgart by the Israel Philharmonic, conducted by Helmuth Rilling.

The Royal Philharmonic Orchestra embarked on an extended international tour as the official orchestra of the 50th birthday of the United Nations, and three U.S. orchestras—those of Chicago, Pittsburgh, Pa., and St. Louis, Mo.—toured Japan. In Amsterdam the Royal Concertgebouw, the Vienna Philharmonic, and the Berlin Philharmonic collaborated in a Mahler festival to celebrate the 50th anniversary of the liberation of The Netherlands. Meanwhile, the Wagner festival in Bayreuth, Germany, kept a decidedly low profile.

The anniversaries of 1995 were not all causes for sombre reflection. Festivals and performances commemorated the 300th anniversary of the death of Henry Purcell and the 100th anniversary of the birth of Paul Hindemith. The eminent African-American composer William Grant Still, born in the same year as Hindemith, was celebrated with a concert that included a performance of his unjustly neglected Third Symphony by the Brooklyn (N.Y.) Philharmonic, conducted by Gunther Schuller. Another series of concerts and lectures honoured the enigmatic and reclusive Paul Bowles, who made a rare public appearance at the event in New York City. On the other end of the publicity spectrum, Pierre Boulez celebrated his 70th birthday with a 20-concert tour conducting the London Symphony, seeming to assume and embrace the post of elder statesman conductor-composer that had been vacant since the death of Leonard Bernstein.

Boulez also was named principal guest conductor of the Chicago Symphony. In addition, two other high-profile U.S. posts were filled: Mariss Jansons, the Latvian conductor especially noted for his recordings with the Oslo (Norway) Philharmonic, was appointed Lorin Maazel's successor as music director of the Pittsburgh Symphony (effective in 1997), and the Dutch conductor Hans Vonk was named to replace Leonard Slatkin in St. Louis (in 1996). While Europeans continued to maintain their stranglehold on U.S. directorships, two Americans were named to important posts in Europe: James Conlon as principal conductor at the Paris National Opera, and Lawrence Foster, formerly the director of the Aspen (Colo.) Music Festival and School, as music director of the Barcelona Symphony and National Orchestra of Catalonia in Spain. Daniele Gatti, the music director of the Accademia Nazionale di Santa Cecilia in Rome and principal guest conductor of the Royal Opera in London, was appointed music director of the Royal Philharmonic Orchestra, and Robert Spano was named to succeed Dennis Russell Davies as music director of the Brooklyn Philharmonic.

Morton Gould was awarded the Pulitzer Prize for *Stringmusic,* written for and premiered (in 1994) by the National Symphony of Washington, D.C., under Mstislav Rostropovich. Other important prizes included the Grawemeyer Award for Music Composition, given to John Adams for his Violin Concerto, and the William Schuman Award, given to Hugo Weisgall for a lifetime of achievement and contributions. The first-ever Carnegie Hall Composer's Chair was filled by Ellen Taaffe Zwilich, who planned to use the opportunity to compose a work for the Emerson String Quartet. Deaths included those of the composer Ulysses Kay, conductors Christopher Keene, Eduardo Mata, and Max Rudolf, pianists Annie Fischer and Shura Cherkassky, and violinists Josef Gingold and Louis Krasner. (*See* OBITUARIES.) The conductors Charles Bruck and Efrem Kurtz and the music patron Edward S. Naumburg, Jr., also died in 1995.

Of several new operas, perhaps the most ballyhooed in 1995 was *Harvey Milk* (Houston [Texas] Grand Opera, commissioned by the San Francisco and New York City operas), Stewart Wallace and Michael Korie's portrayal of events surrounding the homosexual San Francisco politician. Also drawing a lot of attention was the premiere of *Modern Painters,* an account of events in the life of the art critic John Ruskin, with music by David Lang and a libretto by the Pulitzer Prize-winning critic Manuela Hoelterhoff, at Santa Fe, N.M. Noteworthy premieres in Europe included Rolf Liebermann's *Freispruch für Medea* (Hamburg [Germany] State Opera) and Alexander Goehr's *Arianna* (Royal Opera, Covent Garden, London). Other world premieres included Thea Musgrave's *Simon Bolivar* (Virginia Opera, Norfolk), Arnold Saltzman's *Touro* (Washington [D.C.] Opera), about the oldest synagogue in North America, Stephen Paulus' *The Woman at Otowi Crossing* (Opera Theatre of Saint Louis), and Evan Chen's *Bok Choy Variations* (Minnesota Opera, Minneapolis), about the lives of Chinese immigrants following a perilous journey to America.

Operagoers also witnessed a renewed interest in older works by composers who seemed to fall by turns into and out of favour. The operas of Nikolay Rimsky-Korsakov attained a new visibility, thanks to productions by the Bolshoi Theatre in Moscow (*The Maid of Pskov*) and the Kirov Opera in St. Petersburg (*Kashchey the Immortal* and others). The Hindemith centennial was celebrated with separate productions of *Mathis der Maler* by the New York City Opera and by the Royal Opera, Covent Garden, the latter directed by Peter Sellars and conducted by Esa-Pekka Salonen. Other older works emerging into the spotlight included Purcell's *King Arthur* (Châtelet, Paris), Franz Schubert's *Des Teufels Lustschloss* (Opernhaus, Zürich, Switz.), and Albert Lortzing's *Zar und Zimmerman* (Deutsche Oper, Berlin). Opera producers also continued to program works of more recent vintage, such as Penderecki's *Ubu Rex* and Hans Werner Henze's *Der junge Lord* (both Bavarian State Opera, Munich, Germany), György Ligeti's *Le Grand Macabre* (Opernhaus,

Zürich), Fabio Vacchi's *La Station thermale* (La Scala, Milan), Samuel Barber's *Vanessa* (Washington [D.C.] Opera), and Toshiro Mayuzumi's *Kinkakuji* (New York City Opera).

The summer festival circuit was a series of postwar commemorations and tributes. Dresden, Germany, reflected on the 50 years since the bombs had fallen with performances of Bernd Alois Zimmermann's *Die Soldaten,* a powerful proclamation against the horrors of war, Richard Strauss's *Friedenstag,* a work first heard under Nazi auspices in 1938, and Benjamin Britten's *War Requiem*. Berlin dedicated its festival to composers associated with Berlin or Moscow whose work had been suppressed by dictatorships in the first half of the 20th century: Hindemith, Ernst Krenek, Arthur Lourie, Nikolay Roslavetz, Erwin Schulhoff, Dmitry Shostakovich, and Igor Stravinsky. Lucerne, Switz., also presented music of wartime composers, including Berthold Goldschmidt, who was forced to flee Germany and lived in exile in England, and Viktor Ullmann, who organized a group of Jewish musicians at the concentration camp at Theresienstadt. Vienna offered a performance of *Der ewige Frieden,* a sardonic operetta by Kurt Schwertsik. The Salzburg (Austria) Festival looked back 75 years to its founding in 1920 with performances of Mozart's *Marriage of Figaro* and other favourites but narrowed its focus especially to the war years with a production of Zimmermann's monumental *Requiem für einen jungen Dichter,* a chaotic tour through the evils and ills of contemporary society. In the U.S. the Santa Fe Chamber Music Festival presented music of Marc Neikrug and Tomiko Kohjiba, and the Aspen Festival held concerts of music that had been composed during the war (Olivier Messiaen's *Quartet for the End of Time,* Aaron Copland's Third Symphony, Bela Bartok's *Concerto for Orchestra*) and of music by Czech composers killed at Theresienstadt (Hans Drasa, Pavel Haas, Gideon Klein, and Ullmann).

During the regular concert season, orchestral programming was more diverse, and many new works continued the trend of adding more and more concerti to the contemporary solo repertoire. Among the composers introducing new concerti were Steven Mackey (for electric guitar, Los Angeles Philharmonic), Harbison (flute, American Composer's Orchestra), Oliver Knussen (horn, Cleveland [Ohio] Orchestra), and Joseph Schwantner (percussion, New York Philharmonic). Schwantner also introduced a new orchestral work, *Evening Land* (Saint Louis Symphony). The Philadelphia Orchestra under Wolfgang Sawallisch premiered two important new pieces: Frank Martin's *Die Weise von Liebe und Tod des Cornets* and Christoph Rilke and Bernard Rands's *Canzoni per Orchestra*. Among other important premieres were Christopher Rouse's Second Symphony (Houston Symphony), Toru Takemitsu's *Family Tree* (New York Philharmonic), and *Reckoning Time: A Song of Walt Whitman,* a dramatic oratorio by Peter Child and the playwright Alan Brody (John Oliver Chorale). The National Symphony (Washington, D.C.) began to premiere a series of 18 fanfares by various composers, heralding the arrival of Slatkin as its new music director starting in 1996. John Adams collaborated with the poet June Jordan and director Sellars to premiere *I Was Looking at the Ceiling and Then I Saw the Sky* (as part of the Serious Fun Festival in New York), and Karlheinz Stockhausen premiered his *Helicopter Quartet,* a work mixing sounds and movements of four helicopters with sounds made by musicians inside them (Holland Festival, Amsterdam).

MUNSHI AHMED

A dancer performs in the musical drama *Broken Birds: An Epic Longing.* Ong Keng Sen, director of the TheatreWorks in Singapore, based the drama on his research into *karayuki-san,* the Japanese women who from the 1870s to the 1920s were forced to work in brothels throughout Asia.

In the area of recordings, EMI Classics did an admirable job preserving on both compact disc (CD) and video Rostropovich's performances of the Bach Cello Suites at an abbey church in Burgundy. Another important new video was a rerelease of Sergey Eisenstein's film *Alexander Nevsky* with a newly performed sound track of Sergey Prokofiev's music. The recording industry brought out its usual commemorative sets, including two collections of Purcell, one an eight-CD set from Erato with performances conducted by John Eliot Gardiner and the other a six-CD set from Harmonia Mundi containing many of the composer's best-known works, and a compilation from Decca/London of music by Jewish composers targeted by Nazis in Germany in the 1930s, including Franz Schreker's opera *Die Gezeichneten* and Erwin Schulhoff's First Symphony. Several of Boulez's earlier recordings were rereleased, even while the composer was newly recording many of the same works.

Among the year's encyclopedic reissues were EMI Classics' 10-CD set of recordings made by Otto Klemperer and the Philharmonia Orchestra in London between 1955 and 1970, BMG Classics' 10-CD set of Yevgeny Mravinsky's recordings made with the Leningrad Philharmonic between 1965 and 1982, Philips' 21-CD set of performances by the reclusive Russian pianist Svyatoslav Richter, and the same label's 78-CD set of performances by the Belgian violinist Arthur Grumiaux. Vox reissued its set of music by Louis Moreau Gottschalk to complement a new biography of the composer, Frederick Starr's *Bamboula*. Noteworthy new recordings included a release of all of the Beethoven symphonies performed by Gardiner conducting the Orchestre Révolutionnaire et Romantique (Archiv) and a performance of all of the Beethoven piano concerti by Maurizio Pollini, accompanied by Claudio Abbado and the Berlin Philharmonic (Deutsche Grammophon). *Gramophone* magazine awarded its Record of the Year prize to Teldec's disc of the first violin concerti of Prokofiev and Shostakovich by the young Russian violinist Maksim Vengerov and the London Symphony, led by Rostropovich.

Among the more interesting of the year's new books were Henry-Louis de La Grange's long-awaited second and concluding volume in his biography of Mahler (*Gustav Mahler: Vienna: The Years of Challenge [1897–1904]*), Maynard Solomon's psychobiographical study *Mozart: A Life,* and a new book by Charles Rosen, about music of the Romantic period (*The Romantic Generation*). (PHILIP LAMBERT)

Jazz. As events in 1995 demonstrated, New York City's importance in jazz, while still primary, had diminished considerably. One sign of this was the attention attracted by jazz in the San Francisco Bay Area, where homegrown fusions of jazz and rock by young musicians became popular, while explorations by a variety of free musicians increased. Hip-bop and acid jazz are terms applied to San Francisco fusion music, which included jazz-rap groups and others that rearrange the jazz repertoire to fit the high volumes, metallic electric guitar sounds, and simpler, repeated rhythms of rock. Some of these fusion bands began to appear on recordings, the most noted of them probably being T.J. Kirk, named for Thelonious Monk, James Brown, and Rahsaan Roland Kirk. Meanwhile, bassist Lisle Ellis and guitarist Henry Kaiser; the ROVA Saxophone Quartet, especially Larry Ochs; the big band of tenor saxophonist Glenn Spearman, which fused jazz and classical elements; Jon Jang's Pan-Asian Arkestra, which included traditional Chinese instruments and musical materials; and the Afro-Danish tenor saxophonist John Tchicai were catalysts in daring Bay Area explorations of free improvisation and composition. Like the established Berlin and Chicago festivals, the San Francisco Jazz Festival had become a forum for introducing native musicians to an international jazz audience. The 1995 festival featured a variety of young fusion bands as well as Spearman's 40-piece orchestra led by Cecil Taylor, one of the most influential jazz pianists, performing his complex compositions.

There were a number of prominent anniversaries in 1995. The longest-running continuous jazz club, New York's Village Vanguard, was 60 years old. The famous jazz broadcaster Washington, D.C.-based Willis Conover celebrated his 40th year of spreading jazz throughout the world on the Voice of America. Two leading jazz record companies, both Europe-based, had their 20th anniversaries: Italy's Black Saint/Soul Note, which concentrated largely on American musicians, and the Swiss hatART (formerly hatHut), which documented Europeans such as flugelhornist Franz Koglmann and the Vienna Art Orchestra as well as Americans such as multi-instrumentalists Joe McPhee and Anthony Braxton, Taylor, and soprano saxophonist Steve Lacy at valuable length and which reissued important small-label LPs on CD as well. London-based Leo Records, which had begun by releasing jazz albums by underground Soviet musicians, was 15 years old.

Among festivals the largest, the 20-year-old North Sea Jazz Festival, drew 67,000 listeners to three days of concerts by 1,300 musicians on 15 stages in The Hague. The Vancouver (B.C.) Jazz Festival celebrated its 10th anniversary, as did the Lionel Hampton Jazz Festival at the University of Idaho. The most prominent jazz musicians cooperative, the Association for the Advancement of Creative Musicians, presented a 30th-anniversary festival in Chicago, where it had been born.

As support for jazz from U.S. state and federal arts endowments continued to dwindle in 1995, the most prominent private supporter, the Lila Wallace Reader's Digest Fund, granted $5.1 million to underwrite its Jazz Network for another five years. The network represented six regional arts organizations throughout the U.S., among other projects, and the fund had donated nearly $19 million to jazz projects since 1991. The New England Conservatory of Music, Boston, which had a unique history of teaching and supporting jazz, joined with the Thelonious Monk Institute of Jazz to establish a new curriculum, with teaching residencies by trumpeter Wynton Marsalis, and pop-jazz saxophonist Grover Washington, Jr., along with long-established senior artists such as swing tenor saxophonist Illinois Jacquet, pioneer bop drummer Max Roach, and pioneer free jazz bassist Charlie Haden.

The major record companies' search for young lions yielded two prominent players, pianist Jacky Terrasson and a 21-year-old New Orleans, La., trumpeter with an unusually rich tone and a fabulous technique, Nicholas Payton, whose approach wavered between swing and bop. Payton released two albums and played at the Chicago Jazz Festival with pianist Ellis Marsalis. Marsalis' trio made up half of the album *Joe Cool's Blues* (Columbia), music from "Charlie Brown" television cartoon specials, and Marsalis' son Wynton led his septet on the other half. Another Marsalis, tenor saxophonist Branford, fired insults at host Jay Leno when he quit leading NBC's "Tonight Show" band, where the quantity of jazz had dwindled severely. He was replaced by jazz guitarist Kevin Eubanks. Composer-multiwoodwind player Anthony Braxton was the subject of a three-night festival at New York's Kitchen, at which he presented multimedia works for orchestra, medleys of big band compositions, and operatic compositions with singers and shifting ensembles; some of the pieces dated from the 1970s, and a number received their first public performances at the festival. His valuable *Creative Orchestra (Köln) 1978* (hatART) was released, as was his *Composition No. 174,* for 10 percussionists, speakers, and controlled environment (Leo). The first release of alto saxophone giant Ornette Coleman's Harmolodic label was *Tone Dialing,* by his electric Prime Time band. While fellow saxophonist Henry Threadgill proved more successful in integrating Coleman's harmolodic principles with rock-influenced guitars and rhythms in his band Very Very Circus, his *Carry The Day* (Columbia) often sounded unfocused amid a welter of singers and instrumentalists.

There were no misgivings about the joyous hard bop of tenor saxophonist Johnny Griffin on *Chicago, New York, Paris* (Verve), with trumpeter Roy Hargrove, about the solo piano of Randy Weston on *Marrakech in the Cool of the Evening* (Verve), or about the trio of tenor saxophonist Fred Anderson, pianist Marilyn Crispell, and drummer Hamid Drake on *Destiny* (Okkadisk). Among other releases, Drake appeared with Brötzmann on *The Dried Rat-Dog* (Okkadisk), alto saxophonist Roscoe Mitchell presented his lyrical side on *Hey, Donald* (Delmark), tenor saxophonist Joe Lovano and composer-arranger Gunther Schuller collaborated on *Rush Hour* (Blue Note), and a pair of younger free musicians, Joe Morris (guitar) and Rob Brown (alto saxophone), offered *Illuminate* (Leo). Although the quantity of important reissues declined, Blue Note offered Bob Graettinger's 1951 massive, atonal *City of Glass* by the Stan Kenton Orchestra, and Mosaic's boxed sets included *The Complete Capitol Recordings of Duke Ellington* and *The Complete Blue Note Andrew Hill Sessions* on both LP and CD. As Columbia issued Miles Davis' *The Complete Plugged Nickel Sessions* from 1965 on CD, Mosaic issued it on LP.

While drummer Albert "Tootie" Heath replaced the late Connie Kay in the Modern Jazz Quartet, Atlantic released *Dedicated to Connie,* from an outstanding 1960 MJQ concert held in Ljubljana, Slovenia, Yugos. The death of lyric trumpeter Don Cherry (*see* OBITUARIES), a pioneer of free jazz, was keenly felt. The year's other deaths included arranger-saxophonist Julius Hemphill, pianist Don Pullen, lyric guitarist Jimmy Raney, drummer Art Taylor, bandleader and saxophonist Junior Walker (*see* OBITUARIES), and critic Frederic Ramsey. (JOHN LITWEILER)

Popular. British popular music had a great year in 1995. A whole batch of new guitar-based bands took attention away from American pop and generated such media interest and excitement that the new "Britpop" scene was being compared to the golden age of the British music industry of the mid-1960s. The best-known and most publicized of the newcomers were the Manchester band Oasis and the London-based Blur, whose rivalry was likened to the north-south clash between the Beatles and the Rolling Stones 30 years earlier (though in musical terms Blur sounded more like the Kinks or Small Faces, while Oasis sounded like the Stones attempting to imitate the Beatles). When both bands released a new single in the same week in August, the contest to see which would be the most popular became a national obsession. Blur won on this occasion with the song "Country House," but the commercial success of the second Oasis album, *(What's the Story) Morning Glory?,* which went straight to the top of the chart in the first week of its release, showed that they retained an enormous following.

There were many other new bands snapping at their heels, from Pulp to Suede (known as London Suede in the U.S., they caused something of a stir when they were given top billing over Bob Dylan at a summer festival). The youngest of the bunch, Supergrass, led by 18-year-old Gaz Coombes, sold enough copies of their first album, *I Should Coco,* for it to be awarded platinum status just one month after its release, something their record label, Parlophone, had not experienced since the Beatles released their debut album, *Please Please Me,* in the 1960s. Like the early Beatles, Supergrass had a knack for writing catchy and hummable pop tunes, though the lyrics to hit singles such as "Caught by the Fuzz" and "Alright" tended to deal with getting into trouble with the police or with youthful lust.

Female newcomers included members of bands such as Echobelly and Elastica, as well as PJ Harvey, a striking-looking performer who mixed her brooding, bluesy rock songs with a sense of menace and unease. The more experimental side of the new music was represented by Tricky and Portishead, who were classified as dance artists but who produced records that were languid yet gently unnerving and edgy. Portishead, fronted by singer Beth Gibbons, won the year's Mercury Music Prize for the album *Dummy,* which mixed samples taken from recordings by anyone from Weather Report to Isaac Hayes into their own pained and eerie soulful songs.

Away from the new Britpop there were further experiments by more established artists. David Bowie was reunited with producer Brian Eno, with whom he had recorded such classic albums as *Low* in the 1970s, and the resulting *Outside* was a marked improvement on much of Bowie's recent work. Eno also collaborated with the Irish band U2, not just as producer but also as a comember of Passengers, a new group they had formed. Their album *Original Soundtracks 1* was remarkable for the song "Miss Sarajevo," a drifting, atmospheric piece on which they were joined by opera star Luciano Pavarotti. With British music in such a vibrant state, it was appropriate that veteran heroes also should make a comeback. The Rolling Stones continued their Voodoo Lounge world tour and for the first time allowed one of their songs to be used on a commercial. Microsoft Corp. paid them a record £8 million for the use of the 1981 hit "Start Me Up" as part of the campaign to launch Windows 95.

Even so, it seemed that the Rolling Stones would be upstaged by the three remaining members of the Beatles. Twenty-six years after their last recording session together, the three announced plans to release 150 Beatles tracks that had never been heard before, enough for three double CDs. These would include remixed alternative versions of well-known Beatles classics, studio outtakes, home recordings, and cover versions. Most intriguing of all was the promise of three new songs, including one by John Lennon. He had recorded "Free as a Bird" in the 1970s, accompanying himself on piano, and the track was now transformed as Paul McCartney, George Harrison, and Ringo Starr added bass, guitar, and percussion backing. All this was timed to coincide with a major television history of the band, "The Beatles Anthology," and it was predicted that 15 years after Lennon's murder, the Fab Four would once again be the biggest act in the world.

Outside Britain the best European album came from France, where Les Negresses Vertes proved that they had survived the death of their leader, Helno, by releasing *Zig-Zague,* a delightful mixture of French balladry, flamenco, and North African *rai* styles. From Africa there were strong albums from the Zairean veteran Papa Wemba, from the South African reggae star Lucky Dube, and from Salif Keita, "the golden voice of Mali," who moved away from Western jazz-funk and back toward African influences on *Folon.*

(ROBIN DENSELOW)

Hootie and the Blowfish, a racially mixed rock band from Columbia, S.C., sold more than 10 million copies of its debut album, *Cracked Rear View,* and spent eight weeks at the top of the U.S. album sales charts during 1995. Led by vocalist-guitarist Darius Rucker, the four-piece group undertook a successful tour of major concert venues, playing to larger, more diverse audiences than the college fraternity fans who

The members of the rock band Hootie and the Blowfish, who met in college and had both a white and black following, undertook a national tour in 1995. Their debut album, *Cracked Rear View*, was the year's best-selling album.
DANA FRANK—LGI PHOTO AGENCY

had first embraced the band's music. "Hootie embodies the liberal dream of a successful civil rights movement," wrote one reviewer. Alanis Morissette, a native of Canada, rose to prominence with *Jagged Little Pill*, an album of highly personal, sometimes angry songs describing emotional upheaval. A dance-pop recording artist at age 14, Morissette collaborated with songwriter and pop producer Glen Ballard to create her more mature rock-oriented sound. Released by Madonna's record label, Maverick, Morissette's album sold more than three million copies with help from the brassy, confrontational pop hit "You Oughta Know."

The Georgia-based rock group R.E.M., which first rose to prominence in the early 1980s, reaffirmed its status as a pioneer of alternative college rock with a successful world tour in support of its late-1994 release, *Monster*. A slightly younger generation of alternative rock bands, including Hole (led by Courtney Love, widow of Nirvana's Kurt Cobain), Sonic Youth, Beck, and the British group Elastica, joined the 1995 lineup of Lollapalooza as the traveling alternative rock festival moved into its fifth year.

The $92 million Rock and Roll Hall of Fame and Museum opened its doors in Cleveland, Ohio, in early September with gala festivities and a concert featuring rock and pop stars past and present, including Bruce Springsteen, Bob Dylan, Jerry Lee Lewis, Chuck Berry, Melissa Etheridge, and Al Green. Earlier in the year, Green joined the Hall of Fame along with new members the Allman Brothers Band, Janis Joplin, Led Zeppelin, Martha and the Vandellas, Neil Young, Frank Zappa, the Orioles, and journalist Paul Ackerman.

Jerry Garcia (*see* OBITUARIES), Rock and Roll Hall of Fame member and singer and guitarist for the Grateful Dead, died on August 9 at age 53 in Forest Knolls, Calif. Garcia's band had placed great emphasis on musical improvisation in performance. Many of the band's fans, known as "Deadheads," followed the group from concert to concert during its frequent tours. In December the Grateful Dead announced that they would disband. Equally devastating to fans was the March 31 murder, by a disgruntled employee, of Tejano superstar Selena Quintanilla Perez, known professionally as Selena. (*See* OBITUARIES.) Just over a month before her death, the 23-year-old native of Lake Jackson, Texas, had captured 6 of 15 honours at the 15th annual Tejano Music Awards in San Antonio, Texas. Selena's posthumously released album, *Dreaming of You*, a mix of mainstream pop and Spanish-language Tejano selections, debuted at number one on *Billboard* magazine's Top 200 chart, the first album by a Latino artist to achieve the distinction.

Alison Krauss, a 24-year-old fiddler and singer, stunned the country music world by winning four awards at the 29th annual Country Music Association awards. An Illinois native, Krauss initially built her reputation by playing and singing a traditional bluegrass repertoire for Rounder Records, a company based in Cambridge, Mass., and not affiliated with the larger Nashville, Tenn.-based country record labels. Reba McEntire mounted the most elaborate stage show and drew the largest audiences in the country field in 1995. Garth Brooks, the best-selling country artist in history, released *Fresh Horses*, his first studio album in two years, with $4.5 million in marketing support from his record company. Singer-songwriter Roger Miller and the former executive director of the Country Music Association, Jo Walker-Meador, were elected as members of the Country Music Hall of Fame. Country and pop artist Charlie Rich died in Hammond, La., while on a trip to hear his son perform, and the popular crooner, actor, and comedian Dean Martin died on Christmas Day. (*See* OBITUARIES.) Oscar Brand's radio broadcast "Folk Song Festival" celebrated its 50th anniversary.

Michael Jackson paired a disc of his past hits with a second disc of new songs on *HIStory: Past, Present and Future Book 1*, and his sister Janet Jackson also assembled a best-selling retrospective, *Design of a Decade 1986/1996.* African-American vocal harmony groups Boyz II Men (*see* BIOGRAPHIES) from Philadelphia and TLC from Atlanta, Ga., continued to score hits in both the pop and the rhythm-and-blues fields. The fortunes of rap acts declined somewhat and rap records included more singing, but rap fans continued to greet warmly new releases by artists such as Naughty by Nature, Bone Thugs-N-Harmony, and Tupac Shakur. Rapper Eric ("Eazy-E") Wright, a founding member of the seminal Los Angeles-based gangsta rap group N.W.A, died from complications related to AIDS.

(JAY ORR)

This article updates the *Macropædia* article The History of Western MUSIC.

DANCE

North America. In 1995 dance in North America mostly looked back to anniversaries or forward to big-scale arts festivals, to an inaugural festival planned for the summer of 1996 at New York City's Lincoln Center for the Performing Arts, for example, or to high-profile events that would include dance, such as the 1996 summer Olympic Games. The year began, however, not with a dance event itself but rather with controversy over an essay on dance aesthetics. *The New Yorker* published critic Arlene Croce's "Discussing the Undiscussable," an analysis of what she called "victim art." The essay was built around Bill T. Jones and his work *Still/Here.* Croce discussed what she viewed as performances bent on gaining audience responses by way of foregone sympathy for their dying subjects, often graphically portrayed. She concluded that works wielding such emotional blackmail were unreviewable. Partly because she had not seen Jones's work, her essay stirred wide and heated debate, far more than *Still/Here* ever could have in and of itself. All this helped make Jones even more of a cause célèbre and made what some saw as his undistinguished work in dance theatre into a subject of even greater interest during its 1995 tour.

American Ballet Theatre's (ABT's) annual New York spring season managed to interweave a focus on its past with a pleasing fix on its present. Besides celebrating the 10th anniversary of ballerina Alessandra Ferri's connection to the troupe and honouring veteran Fernando Bujones with a farewell performance, ABT made a point of showcasing the newest dances of Twyla Tharp. An all-Tharp triple bill made up a gala performance, with one-time-only ballets framing an ABT commission, *How Near Heaven,* to the music of Benjamin Britten. Tharp's diffuse Britten work stayed in the repertoire without, however, ever really making a satisfactory impression. New ABT dancers Vladimir Malakhov and Angel Corella added to the excitement already in evidence from other company performers. The mature and dragonfly-like Malakhov was riveting in all he did, and the teenage Corella was endearing in the way prodigious youth always is. Dancer Paloma Herrera was amazing, even though, especially opposite the overwrought Julio Bocca, she seemed to be in need of guidance regarding artistic restraint.

The most worthy news from New York City Ballet (NYCB) centred around its presentation of Jerome Robbins' *West Side Story Suite* during the spring season. In the preceding winter season, the company had acquired Robbins' *2 + 3 Part Inventions,* made in 1994 for the School of American Ballet. Both works were impeccably presented, although *Inventions* seemed a little thin on the company's maturer dancers. *West Side Story Suite,* on the other hand, proved entertaining and moving, with especially touching performances from the Danish-born-and-bred Nikolaj Hübbe, who not only danced the part of a streetwise New Yorker but successfully sang it as well. *Adams Violin Concerto* by Peter Martins, NYCB's ballet master in chief, was new to the repertoire but seemed overfamiliar to the eye.

Dance Theatre of Harlem (DTH) played a season at the Brooklyn Academy of Music (BAM) in March. Besides unveiling *Joplin Dances,* a charming showcase for DTH dancers by the company's own Robert Garland, the troupe offered its first staging of *The Prodigal Son* by George Balanchine. Coached in part by the former Balanchine ballerina Suzanne Farrell, the DTH dancers made the 1929 ballet come to life. Farrell's more wide-ranging guidance helped the Kennedy Center for the Performing Arts in Washington, D.C., begin a yearlong celebration of its 25th anniversary. In October the ballerina-turned-ballet-mistress put on a weeklong season billed as "Suzanne Farrell Stages Balanchine." Producing seven Balanchine works with an ensemble from the Washington Ballet and with handpicked leading dancers from companies familiar to her from staging ballets in the U.S. and elsewhere, Farrell created a luminous season with what looked like a little Balanchine company.

In May Helgi Tomasson arranged for his San Francisco Ballet (SFB) to act as host of a festival celebrating the 50th anniversary of the UN. With participants from near and far, though without the participation of most of the world's major ballet companies, the festival was regarded more for its goodwill than for its good works. Modern dance's Mark Morris was generally credited with providing the event, in the form of an SFB premiere, with its most winning work, *Pacific* (to music of Lou Harrison).

At year's end Morris' own troupe gave all-Morris programs in BAM's "Next Wave Festival," offering audiences a look at numerous works the prolific choreographer had made outside New York in the recent past. When SFB played a fall week in New York, the dancers, especially the newly acquired Yury Possokhov, stood out, while the repertoire proved largely disappointing. St. Petersburg's Mariinsky (Kirov) Ballet played a two-week New York summer season that featured the Russian troupe's first stagings of the now-classic *Firebird* and *Schéhérezade* by its own Michel Fokine. Financial constraints prevented the troupe from returning in the fall for a multiple-city conclusion to its U.S. tour.

After formalizing the appointment of Roy Kaiser as its artistic director, Pennsylvania Ballet spent the year mostly shoring up its organization and presenting fairly standard and familiar repertoire. Pacific Northwest Ballet continued to present its mix of homegrown works and those of Balanchine, a solid sampling of which made up the troupe's appearances in Australia's Melbourne International Festival of the Arts. Peter Anastos continued to set his stamp on the Cincinnati (Ohio) Ballet, with a mix of original choreographies and Balanchine favourites. Edward Villella marked the 10th season of his Miami (Fla.) City Ballet with a debut presentation of Balanchine's *Jewels* at the Kennedy Center. Boston Ballet's Bruce Marks put together a triple bill, entitled "Happily Ever After," that featured works based on fairy tales. Ballet Concierto de Puerto Rico played a successful weeklong season in New York. In January, with a pickup ensemble of her own, Tharp gave a successful week of work-in-progress performances at BAM. In September the Joffrey Ballet, which had spent most of the year trying to hold itself together, announced a move out of New York to Chicago.

New York's experimental Dance Theater Workshop celebrated its 30th anniversary in the spring, and in the fall, after a year's hiatus, it reinstated its Bessie awards for outstanding performance in dance and performance. Among the Bessie awardees was Tina Ramirez, whose Ballet Hispanico marked its 25th anniversary in 1995. Bocca's Ballet Argentino made its U.S. debut in November. The Merce Cunningham Dance Company gave a two-week season that featured two new works by the maestro of innovation, who was still performing. Paul Taylor also gave a two-week season, to taped music, featuring *Offenbach Overtures,* a wicked and witty look at oompah dances. The Martha Graham Dance Company presented the world premiere of its Robert Wilson commission, *Snow on the Mesa,* at the Kennedy Center. The vital Alvin Ailey American Dance Theater celebrated associate artistic director Masazumi Chaya during its year-end season in New York. The Japanese-born husband and wife team Eiko & Koma performed *River,* a powerful site-specific work, in the Delaware River before celebrating their 20th anniversary with performances at the Japan Society.

Toronto Dance Theater made a good New York showing under the guidance of its newly appointed artistic director, Christopher House. Les Grands Ballets Canadiens commissioned a new ballet from the American Kevin O'Day, whom NYCB also commissioned for two works. Montreal's Festival International de Nouvelle Danse included the participation of international troupes. The most anticipated was William Forsythe's Frankfurt (Germany) Ballet, but even some of the choreographer's most avid admirers found the presentation, *Eidos: Telos,* to be shapeless and uneven. Artistic director Reid Anderson of the National Ballet of Canada (NBC) was given the John Cranko award from the Stuttgart (Germany) Ballet, while his company ended its year with a new production of *The Nutcracker* by James Kudelka.

Dancers from the Bill T. Jones company perform in *Still/Here*. The work by dancer and choreographer Jones, which included videotapes of gravely ill and dying people, was denounced in a *New Yorker* article by critic Arlene Croce, who called it "victim art" and said that it was unreviewable.

BEATRIZ SCHILLER

Because of illness the U.S. ballerina Marie Jeanne was unable to work with NBC dancers on a videotape project about Balanchine's *Concerto Barocco* for the Interpreter's Archive of the George Balanchine Foundation. Earlier in the year, ballerina Maria Tallchief had worked on a related project. Other video and film projects appeared during the year. Nonesuch Records released five videocassettes of *The Balanchine Library,* an ongoing series of releases of recordings of Balanchine's dances and dance technique. Five more were scheduled for release in 1996. Frederick Wiseman's 170-minute documentary about ABT, called *Ballet,* was released and aired on public television. The 33rd New York Film Festival screened Carlos Saura's *Flamenco.* Dance publications of note included *Massine: A Biography* by Vicente García-Márquez, *Costumes by Karinska* by Toni Bentley, and *Following Balanchine* by Robert Garis.

Modern dance veteran Anna Sokolow was given a stellar 85th birthday celebration in 1995, with Robbins and Taylor among those paying tribute. Repertory seasons, touring, and symposia marked the 100th anniversary of the birth of the late modern dance pioneer Doris Humphrey.

Two years after his death, to benefit the Rudolf Nureyev Foundation, the longtime superstar recaptured the public's and the media's attention when his contested estate was finally auctioned amid some frenzy by Christie's (in January in New York; November in London).

Deaths in 1995 included the Russian dancer and Hollywood actor Alexander Godunov and the dancers Francisco Moncion and James Truitte. (*See* OBITUARIES.) Among others who died were dancer Keith McDaniel, choreographer Loyce Houlton, dancer Jean-Louis Morin, dance journalist Joseph Mazo, dance photographer Fred Fehl, Dance Films Association founder Susan Braun, dancer and teacher Salvatore Aiello, and dancer and dance educator Martha Hill.

(ROBERT J. GRESKOVIC)

Europe. Intrigue and upheaval within Russia's two most celebrated ballet companies turned 1995 into a year dominated more by politics than by artistic achievement. In Moscow simmering feuds at the Bolshoi erupted into turmoil, with publicly voiced fears that the company was being torn apart, while in St. Petersburg a serious shortage of funds, coupled with increasing dependence on income from foreign touring, found the Mariinsky Ballet in grave trouble.

At the Bolshoi autocrat Yury Grigorovich had for many of his 31 years as artistic director run an ensemble that in style and achievement was the envy of the rest of the world. Yet it was becoming apparent that he had held on to power for too long and that the company was stagnating. He and the old guard at the Bolshoi Theatre had failed to recognize the importance of sweeping reforms of perestroika, money was cripplingly short, the bureaucracy had become stifling, and the theatre itself was found to be crumbling.

Battles behind the scenes broke into the public domain when the introduction of Western-style contracts for the ballet company put an end to the practice of lifetime security that had long been a perk of employment. Such was the importance to Russia of the Bolshoi that Pres. Boris Yeltsin felt compelled to intervene, and ultimately Grigorovich was left with no option but to resign. This shocked some of the dancers, who called a strike, and for the first time in the Bolshoi Ballet's 219-year history, a performance was canceled. The ringleaders—chief among them Grigorovich's wife, ballerina Natalya Bessmertnova—found themselves in serious trouble: they were fined and sacked.

Vladimir Vasilyev, a former star of the Grigorovich regime who had once openly protested directorial policy, was brought in as his replacement. Vasilyev was one of the greatest male dancers of his generation and had gone on to a career as a choreographer and director; he launched his directorship of the Bolshoi with a reminder to his dancers that it was their duty to serve the audience and not to engage in political intrigue. Vasilyev promised to lead in a spirit of openness and democracy, but he warned that he might sometimes find it necessary to act as a dictator for the sake of artistic achievement. One of his first initiatives was to invite the French choreographer Maurice Béjart, renowned for modern ballets with mass appeal, to create a work for the company.

Meanwhile, the Mariinsky's artistic director, Oleg Vinogradov, who acknowledged that during his 18 years in office he had made enemies, became a victim of death threats and street muggings and found himself obliged to hire a bodyguard. Furthermore, he took the unexpected step of appointing two assistants (dancers Farukh Ruzimatov and Makharbek Vaziyev) to help run the company, thereby diluting his power. Vinogradov increasingly was forced to regard foreign tours as lifelines for the financially strapped company. Nonetheless, in the autumn an important tour to the U.S. was called off at the eleventh hour, following accusations from an impresario that Vinogradov had been pocketing touring funds, and he was briefly imprisoned. He was released to continue directing the company while awaiting trial, but the Mariinsky's financial and artistic problems deepened.

While the Russians' problems captivated the world's press, the year brought several less-publicized changes to company leadership. At the Paris Opéra Ballet, mutual agreement was reached between the management and Patrick Dupond that he would relinquish the directorship to concentrate on his career as one of the company's star dancers. He was replaced by his administrator, Brigitte Lefèvre, who had previously run the Théâtre du Silence.

Less than a year into a seven-year contract with the Royal Danish Ballet (RDB), Peter Schaufuss fell out with the management and departed. It was a blow to the company, which in preparation for Copenhagen's 1996 assignation as the European City of Culture had planned tours to London and Paris in 1995 to enhance its international standing. (Following Danish outrage at France's nuclear testing in the Pacific, Paris was eventually canceled.) Rifts were patched over speedily, however, Schaufuss agreeing to continue to stage certain works for the company and Johnny Eliasen appointed acting artistic director. Ironically, when in the summer the British director of the Royal Swedish Ballet, Simon Mottram, resigned, the man chosen to replace him was Frank Andersen, who in 1994 had himself been forced to hand over the reigns of the RDB to Schaufuss.

The year's most carefully planned departure was that of Sir Peter Wright, director of the Birmingham (England) Royal Ballet (BRB). He retired in the summer after producing a new version of *Coppélia* as his swan song and winning a welter of tributes from colleagues, critics, and audiences. His relocation of the then Sadler's Wells Royal Ballet to Birmingham and the five years in which he had guided the company in its new home had secured for it a strong new identity, a major achievement.

Notable anniversaries in 1995 included the 35 years of the Netherlands Dance Theatre (NDT) and the 20 years during which Jiri Kylian had directed the company. Both were celebrated through Kylian's lighthearted *Arcimboldo,* a work that not only brought together for the first time all three NDT companies but also drew on resources of light and space never previously experienced in the company's specially built theatre in The Hague.

Attention was focused in 1995 on works by leading choreographers produced by companies other than their own. Martins, the Danish-born director of NYCB, returned to the RDB to mount an evening of his ballets selected from the more than 50 works he had created for his American company. The Britisher David Bintley turned to an English monarch as inspiration for *Edward II,* a new work for the Stuttgart Ballet, and he produced *Carmina Burana* for the BRB in October, by which time he had taken up his new position as artistic director in succession to Wright. At year's end Tharp, whose choreographic reputation had been forged through her own company and her collaborations with Mikhail Baryshnikov, created her first work for Britain's Royal Ballet, a full evening to Rossini's music.

Yet despite the activity of Europe's great dance institutions, it was doubtful whether 1995 brought any significant developments. Radical thinking went on, however, among the vast networks of independent and experimental work extending throughout Europe. The development of new technologies and the potential for creative application pointed toward expanding horizons, as did increasing emphasis on multicultural work. Ageism became a topic for debate. On the one hand there was increasing concern over how to extend audience expectations beyond the confines of youth and beauty (especially in ballet), and on the other a seminar in Lausanne, Switz., addressed the difficulties of helping to prepare dancers, both practically and psychologically, for second careers.

British deaths during the year included two dancers from the early years of Ballet Rambert: Prudence Hyman (who went on to dance with Colonel W. de Basil's Ballet Russe de Monte Carlo and the Markova-Dolin Ballet) and Annette Chappell (who also danced in Munich, Germany, and later taught there and in Stuttgart). Travis Kemp, a celebrated dancer with the Camargo Society and the Vic-Wells Ballet who had danced with the Markova-Dolin company and done much to stimulate ballet in Turkey, died during the year. Three writers and editors who contributed significantly to dance's wider appreciation and understanding also died: Peter Brinson, whose writings and lectures helping establish a better working climate for dancers and choreographers won him an international following; Chris de Marigny, founder-editor of *Dance Theatre Journal;* and Peter Williams, founder-editor of *Dance & Dancers.*

Other deaths included the Dane Henning Kronstam (*see* OBITUARIES), a leading dancer with the RDB who went on to serve as artistic director of the company for seven years; the Dutch Carel Birnie, the driving force behind the founding of the NDT; the German Jürgen Schneider, a distinguished teacher of ballet in Europe and the U.S.; the Russian-French Youly Algaroff, a dancer and impresario; the Russian dancer and choreographer Wazlaw Orlikowsky, a director of ballet companies in Oberhausen, Germany, and Basel, Switz., and the producer of spectacular classical ballets; two former Austrian dancers of the central European style, Rosalia Chladek and Bettina Vernon; and the New Zealander Bryan Ashbridge, formerly principal dancer with the Royal Ballet and associate artistic director of the Australian Ballet. In addition, there were many deaths from AIDS-related illnesses among young men just beginning to make names for themselves in dance. (ANN NUGENT)

This article updates the *Macropædia* article The History of Western DANCE.

THEATRE

Great Britain and Ireland. There were strange, troubled times in 1995. The brilliant actor Mark Rylance, who questioned the authenticity of the authorship of William Shakespeare's plays, was appointed artistic director of the new Globe Theatre, the Shakespearean shrine under construction at bankside on the River Thames. In a year of *Macbeth*s all over the country—the play was on the British school system's examination syllabus—Rylance himself played the murderous Scottish thane as a rotten apple among the orange people—a deviant in a cult faction. It was a brilliant notion that addressed, in a serious contemporary fashion, the pervasive atmosphere of magic and superstition in the play. Rylance's Lady Macbeth, played by Jane Horrocks, was a vicious innocent whose idea of fancy dress at the feast—the entire play was set around Halloween—was to go as a nun. In the sleepwalking scene, stripped to her childish underwear, Horrocks actually urinated on stage.

As the Royal Shakespeare Company (RSC) confirmed that it would vacate the Barbican Centre in London for at least six months of each year from 1997 and concentrate on touring (while retaining the Stratford-upon-Avon stronghold), the Shakespearean initiatives were clearly happening elsewhere. The RSC's main stage Stratford productions of *Romeo and Juliet, The Taming of the Shrew,* and *Julius Caesar* were intellectually arid, under-cast, and physically dull.

Easily the best Stratford Shakespeare was *Richard III* with new RSC star David Troughton, directed with imagination and verve by Steven Pimlott. At the Swan at Stratford, Adrian Noble directed Anton Chekhov's *The Cherry Orchard* to general acclaim, while Matthew Warchus was responsible for one of the most gleeful and vigorous Ben Jonson revivals in living memory, *The Devil Is an Ass.*

Rylance's vivid *Macbeth* was almost matched by a brave, bold version at the Birmingham Rep directed by former

RSC associate Bill Alexander. The same play was imaginatively treated by the English Touring Theatre—one of the medium-scale touring companies that were maintaining the transformation of the classic repertoire begun by Cheek by Jowl and Shared Experience in the 1980s—and also at the Tricycle in Kilburn, north London, in a fast, furious production by Nicolas Kent with a black Macbeth (Lenny James) and an outstanding Lady Macbeth (Helen McCrory), lit continuously by flaming torches, fires, and candles.

The team of actress Fiona Shaw and director Deborah Warner, having made headlines in 1994 with their controversial production of Samuel Beckett's *Footfalls,* which was banned by the author's estate, presented a *Richard II* in the Royal National Theatre's (RNT's) small Cottesloe auditorium that was equally divisive. Shaw played the monarch as a gender-free hysteric wrapped like a mummy in white bandages, but it was impossible to ignore the conceit. Warner's exciting production was played through the middle of the audience, and the idea was to consider notions of monarchy aside from personality, as indeed Richard himself does on many occasions in the play. This task, in the end, proved self-defeating, and Shaw consoled herself with a fascinating, but deliberately unfrivolous, performance as Millamant in the RNT's modern-dress revival of William Congreve's masterpiece *The Way of the World,* in which Geraldine McEwan as Lady Wishfort had a field day in a rose pink tutu, clinging desperately to her carnal instincts. McEwan's achievement was deservedly recognized with the *Evening Standard* (ES) best actress award.

The RNT once again cleaned up in the ES awards, notching four of the seven prizes: in addition to McEwan, best actor for Michael Gambon in the leading role in *Volpone,* whose director, the shooting star Warchus again, was named best director; and best comedy for Patrick Marber's *Dealer's Choice,* an astoundingly confident debut by a well-known young television comedy writer set around a poker school in a London restaurant. A special award was made to Richard Eyre, artistic director of the RNT, who was planning to move on in 1997.

The race for Eyre's succession was already heating up. Obvious nominees, such as the actor Sir Ian McKellen and Stephen Daldry, the director of the Royal Court and of the worldwide blockbuster hit revival of J.B. Priestley's *An Inspector Calls,* denied any interest in the job. This left the field clear for the very young Sam Mendes, Eyre's favoured contender, who had made a spectacular job of running the Donmar Warehouse in Covent Garden, or possibly Jonathan Kent of the Almeida Theatre.

Kent's RNT revival of Bertolt Brecht's *Mother Courage* in a new text by David Hare, with an acclaimed performance by Dame Diana Rigg in the title role, would not have damaged his chances. Kent also directed the very fine, romantically old-fashioned *Hamlet* of Ralph Fiennes at the Hackney Empire and on Broadway. Kent's work was given a gloss and sheen uncomplicated by the sort of innovative daredevilry Rylance brought to Shakespeare.

The RNT mounted excellent revivals of Joe Orton's *What the Butler Saw,* Rodney Ackland's *Absolute Hell,* Eduardo de Filippo's *La Grande Magia,* and (an RSC discovery of the 1970s) John O'Keeffe's *Wild Oats.* Best of all, perhaps, was Sean Mathias' revival of Stephen Sondheim's 1973 *A Little Night Music* with the entire action whirling in waltz time around a brilliant gray/gauze design by Stephen Brimson Lewis.

The RNT's major new play of the year was Hare's *Skylight,* directed by Eyre and starring Gambon and Lia Williams, in which a long-exhausted affair between a shambling, thuggish restaurateur and his former employee, now an overworked schoolteacher in the deprived East End of London, is revisited, and re-created, in a present crisis. Technically, the writing was superb, and Hare's debate about a collision between the insensitive entrepreneurial spirit and the incensed reality of a society falling apart—refracted through the romance—was brilliantly joined.

The other outstanding new play of the year was *The Steward of Christendom* by the Irish writer Sebastian Barry, directed by Max Stafford-Clark in a coproduction between his own touring company, Out of Joint, and the Royal Court. This was a memory play concerned with a crucial period of Irish history reenacted in a mental home by a retired Catholic policeman, Thomas Dunne, in 1932.

Dunne, a real-life ancestor of Barry, switched allegiance from the British Crown to the revolutionary republican Michael Collins, who signed the treaty with London for Irish independence and was later assassinated. Deranged and confused like King Lear, Dunne was surrounded by his daughters and accumulative regrets, retreating finally to jibbering, childlike helplessness. The play was powerful enough, but it became a veritable sensation through the performance of Donal McCann.

Other new plays of note were Jonathan Harvey's *The Rupert Street Lonely Hearts Club,* a superior situation comedy of modern sexuality and quirkiness presented by the English Touring Theatre and the Contact Theatre, Manchester, at the Donmar Warehouse and finally at the Criterion in the West End; and Harry Gibson's *Trainspotting,* a hilarious, devastating adaptation of Irvine Welsh's cult novel about junkies and no-hopers in Edinburgh that seized the popular imagination all year in cities from Glasgow and Liverpool to Manchester and London. *Trainspotting,* like *Rupert Street,* came to rest in the West End at the end of the year, a sure indication that in order to survive, the theatre must exist enthusiastically in its own times.

In its first year the National Lottery elicited differing views on the propriety—or otherwise—of a government actively encouraging gambling as a form of taxation; it also produced millions of pounds for the arts. The Royal Court was a chief beneficiary, securing £16 million toward a comprehensive redesign and refurbishment of the famous old theatre in Sloane Square to begin in 1996. Under Daldry the artistic policy had been at its liveliest since the first flush of John Osborne and the Angry Young Men in the 1950s. The first "first play" to be mounted on the main stage since Osborne's *Look Back in Anger* was a riotous gangland comedy set in the Soho of the 1950s, *Mojo* by Jez Butterworth (ES most promising playwright).

Also memorable were Sam Shepard's haunting *Simpatico* and Phyllis Nagy's *The Strip,* a seriously underrated, beautifully written adventure story ranging from Las Vegas, Nev., to Earl's Court, London, with one of the best opening lines in modern drama: "Female impersonation is a rather curious career choice for a woman, Miss Coo." Nagy's other play was *Disappeared,* a fascinating thriller of escape and mystery that toured the country and contained one of the year's best performances, by Kerry Shale.

In the Royal Court's little Theatre Upstairs, a first play by young Sarah Kane, *Blasted,* created one of the year's big controversies. Scenes of molestation, buggery, baby-munching, and Bosnia-in-your-front-room violence had critics frothing at the mouth with rage. Not since Edward Bond's *Saved* in 1964 with its baby-stoning scene had there been such a furor. But there was also a disturbing sense of a dysfunctional relationship between a cynical journalist and his underage girlfriend, and Bond himself joined Harold Pinter and others in defending the play and hailing a talented new theatrical voice.

Pinter directed *Taking Sides,* a fine new play by Ronald Harwood, at Chichester and in the West End. This posed a confrontation between a coarse American officer played by Michael Pennington and the mystical conductor Wilhelm Furtwängler (Daniel Massey) during the denazification of Berlin at the end of World War II. *Taking Sides* arrived in town from the Chichester Festival, where producer Duncan Weldon first capitalized the show for £25,000. Had he presented it first in the West End, the costs would have been at least £200,000, an amount, he said, that would be virtually impossible to recoup on a serious play.

Thus, like Broadway, London's commercial theatre was becoming barren of creativity, except in musical theatre. The difference was that in the U.K. so many plays came from the subsidized sector, and from venues like Chichester, the problem was virtually disguised. Julie Christie shimmered mysteriously in Pinter's *Old Times,* an import from the Theatre Clyd at Mold, near Chester, and Pinter appeared, hilariously, as a demented administrator of a mental home in a revival of one of his own early plays, *The Hothouse,* which also began life in Chichester. The same address provided a superb revival of Harold Brighouse's *Hobson's Choice* for Shaftesbury Avenue, with the cast led by Leo McKern. Alan Ayckbourn's *Communicating Doors,* like his other plays, was first seen at the Stephen Joseph Theatre in Scarborough. Its three interlocking time scales were ingeniously managed in the one hotel bedroom, and the leading role was taken by the musical comedy star Julia McKenzie.

The West End was fortified by the dazzling solo comedy of Eddie Izzard and by a season of Royal Court "classics" at the Duke of York's—Ron Hutchinson's *Rat in the Skull,* starring Rufus Sewell, followed by Terry Johnson's farce *Hysteria.* Alan Bates gave a leisurely reading of Solness in Henrik Ibsen's *The Master Builder,* directed by Peter Hall, but his Hilde Wangel, newcomer Victoria Hamilton, made an indelible first impression. Tom Stoppard adapted a radio play for his less-than-brilliant *Indian Ink* at the Aldwych; the year closed with a revival of his first hit, *Rosencrantz and Guildenstern Are Dead,* at the RNT.

One of the most curious events of the year was the defection of the actor Stephen Fry—who made his name in university and television revue with Hugh Laurie and Emma Thompson and his fortune by rewriting the "Lambeth Walk" musical *Me and My Girl*—from Simon Gray's play *Cell Mates.* The defection was doubly ironic, given that Fry was playing the British spy George Blake. The notices were admittedly mixed and the play undoubtedly poor, but Fry seemed poised on the brink of a personal crisis, and he simply disappeared three days after the opening. He resurfaced in Brugge, Belgium, and faxed his friends that he was all right, but he was unable to allay the wrath of the playwright or the producing management, who entered legal proceedings against him.

The musical cupboard was virtually bare with a continuing proliferation of undistinguished cabaret-style entertainments. An attempt to jazz up Gilbert and Sullivan, *The Hot Mikado,* gave pleasure to some but was, in truth, an enterprise of hollow worth. Jerry Herman and the late Michael Stewart's eagerly anticipated *Mack and Mabel* (ES best musical) arrived 20 years after its Broadway premiere in a sadly underfinanced production first mounted at the Leicester Haymarket. The second-act narrative problems had not been solved, the songs were reasonably effective and well-upholstered (especially when they were reminiscent of *Hello, Dolly!* or *Mame,* Herman's big hits), while the acting and choreography were undistinguished.

Much livelier was *Jolson*, which mixed elements of the biomusical and compilation show to powerful effect. The politically tricky issue of Jolson's blackface stage persona was neither ducked nor celebrated; otherwise, Brian Conley's magnificent performance, possibly the most extraordinary performance of the year on any British stage, gave a warts-and-all portrait of the superstar monster, and his lungs and personality gave full justice to the wonderful repertoire of songs.

This reminder of the great actor's supremacy over all other theatrical components only underlined the sadness of so many departures during the year. John Osborne's death on Christmas Eve 1994 seemed to trigger a spate of casualties (*see* OBITUARIES): the grand old character actor Sir Michael Hordern, the finical classicist Eric Porter, the immensely popular light comic actor and Ayckbourn specialist Paul Eddington, the fascinating elder juvenile Jeremy Brett, the blazing RSC star Susan Fleetwood, and Sir Robert Stephens, a founding member of both the modern Royal Court and the RNT. Stephens had made a remarkable comeback in recent years as Falstaff and King Lear with the RSC and, though debilitated by illness following a liver and kidney transplant operation, had managed to complete his autobiography, a recording of Shakespearean speeches at the command of Prince Charles, and a television appearance as the poet John Dryden in Tony Palmer's TV film about the composer Henry Purcell.

The glorious but politically and economically threatened tradition of weekly repertory theatre continued in Leeds, Birmingham, Manchester, Leicester, Glasgow, and Nottingham. All those cities' theatres had productive years. The Edinburgh Festival triumphed with Philip Prowse's Glasgow Citizens' production of Friedrich von Schiller's *Don Carlos,* the long-awaited return of the Pina Bausch dance company, and a double bill of delightful, bitter Sacha Guitry sex plays from the Schaubühne, Berlin, directed by Luc Bondy, which forged a missing link in European light comedy between Ferenc Molnár and Noël Coward.

In Ireland the most significant production was Marie Jones's *A Night in November,* which toured incessantly under the banner of Dubbeljoint (a joining of Dublin and Belfast) and charted the personal history of an association football (soccer) fanatic and Protestant bigot who is transformed and converted by his enthusiasm for the Republic of Ireland's success on the international soccer stage. The solo role was memorably taken by Dan Gordon, whose passionate performance diverted the audience from the slight worries of implausibility surrounding the narrative premise. The Dublin Festival premiered a new Barry play, *The Only True History of Lizzie Finn,* at the Abbey, but this failed to fulfil the expectations engendered by the massive impact of *The Steward of Christendom.* (MICHAEL COVENEY)

U.S. and Canada. Political events on both sides of the 49th parallel—the threatened evisceration of the National Endowment for the Arts by the conservative-controlled U.S. Congress and the unsuccessful but culturally charged push by Quebec for independence from Canada—cast shadows of discord and apprehension on the arts in North America during 1995. Theatre in the U.S. and Canada, labouring to rise above economic and artistic uncertainties, offered audiences a mix of the tried-and-true and the cautiously innovative.

In the U.S. it was a year with something for everyone. Impoverished by the closure of Tony Kushner's acclaimed sociopolitical epic *Angels in America* (which continued to draw record audiences in a flurry of regional productions and on national tour), Broadway turned its attention to what it does best: the dispensation of glamour. Propelled by a small tornado of publicity, a bevy of female stars of a certain age returned to the New York stage, some in creaky vehicles that depended for survival entirely on the legendary leading ladies' marquee power.

Julie Andrews, who last had appeared on Broadway as Guenevere in *Camelot* in 1961, returned in the sex-reversed title role of *Victor/Victoria,* a noisy, charmless musical directed by her husband, Blake Edwards, and based on his 1982 film. Comedienne Carol Burnett chose a new play, Ken Ludwig's less-than-riotous farce *Moon over Buffalo,* for her comeback. Carol Channing, who at age 74 claimed to have played the role of Dolly Levi some 4,500 times, was at it again in a revival of *Hello, Dolly!* In the unusual case of a sellout hit drama on Broadway, Zoe Caldwell earned critical adulation (and a $1 million advance before previews began) in the role of diva Maria Callas in Terrence McNally's *Master Class.* Off-Broadway, acting doyenne Uta Hagen offered a rare appearance as a scarifying psychoanalyst in Nicholas Wright's psychodrama *Mrs. Klein.*

Star power also was the driving force behind a number of New York productions, including the Public Theater's expensive shift from Central Park to Broadway of George C. Wolfe's Afro-Caribbean-flavoured *The Tempest,* with the classically trained British actor (and TV icon) Patrick Stewart as a howlingly anguished Prospero, and the arrival in New York City of film actor and writer Steve Martin's ingenious 1993 comedy *Picasso at the Lapin Agile,* under the direction of Randall Arney, who had helmed the piece's premiere at his own Steppenwolf Theatre Company in Chicago. Brian Dennehy starred with Rufus Sewell in a flawed revival of *Translations* by the Irish playwright Brian Friel. (*See* BIOGRAPHIES.)

Veteran theatre, film, and television writer Horton Foote (in a surprise upset over McNally, whose gay-themed *Love! Valour! Compassion!* garnered wide attention) won the 1995 Pulitzer Prize for Drama for his oblique, resolutely uneventful drama *The Young Man from Atlanta,* which debuted at New York City's Signature Theatre Company. The Signature, which devoted each season to the work of a different playwright, moved on in the fall to the plays of Adrienne Kennedy, beginning with the justly celebrated-but-seldom-produced writer's haunting 1964 phantasmagoria *Funnyhouse of a Negro.*

Love! Valour! Compassion! did go on to win the 1995 Tony award for best play, however. Tonys also went to Andrew Lloyd Webber's *Sunset Boulevard* (best musical, best book, and best score) and to its star, Glenn Close (*see* BIOGRAPHIES), for her portrayal of the aging movie star Norma Desmond. Other acting awards went to Ralph Fiennes (leading actor in a play) for *Hamlet,* Cherry Jones (leading actress in a play) for her triumph as the loveless spinster in the revival of *The Heiress,* and Matthew Broderick (leading actor in a musical) in the rousing revival of *How to Succeed in Business Without Really Trying.* Channing received a lifetime achievement award. The Tony for best regional theatre went to the Goodspeed Opera House in East Haddam, Conn.

In the year in which the O.J. Simpson trial became a media obsession, theatres across the U.S. offered a number of resonant treatments of racial issues. In January Chicago's Goodman Theatre presented the world premiere of August Wilson's *Seven Guitars.* The play, a tragicomic study of a blues musician and his friends in 1948 Pittsburgh, Pa., went on to Boston and San Francisco in preparation for its Broadway opening in 1996. At California's Sacramento Theatre Company, *Uncle Bends: a home-cooked negro narrative* by Bob Devin Jones fleshed out cultural symbols like Aunt Jemima; at Connecticut's Hartford Stage Company, Robert Alexander's *I Ain't Yo' Uncle* (originally scripted for the San Francisco Mime Troupe) imagined a spirited confrontation between Hartford's own Harriet Beecher Stowe and the characters she indelibly imprinted on black history; Alexander's *Servant of the People,* a biographical drama about Huey P. Newton staged in Atlanta, Ga., St. Louis, Mo., and Oakland, Calif., was one of several plays about the controversial Black Panther leader. Many theatres reached into the historic repertoire of African-American plays for pertinent material: the Guthrie Theater in Minneapolis, Minn., reassessed Theodore Ward's Federal Theatre Project drama *Big White Fog,* about Marcus Garvey's ill-fated back-to-Africa movement, seldom seen since its landmark debut in 1938; Douglas Turner Ward's 1965 fable *Day of Absence,* in which life in a small Southern town grinds to a halt when blacks go on strike, was mounted in Baltimore, Md., by Center Stage.

Institutional theatres across the country continued to serve as a testing ground for emerging playwrights and as the locus of vigorous new work by established writers. Among the promising young American playwrights who came into their own with major new works were Octavio Solis, whose *Santos & Santos,* a powder-keg drama about the downfall of an immigrant family, attracted youthful and ethnically diverse audiences at the Dallas (Texas) Theater Center; and Chay Yew, whose *A Language of Their Own* at New York's Public Theater adventurously examined the relationship of identity and language. Sondheim took a break from the musical form to indulge his other obsession—esoteric puzzles—by coauthoring (with familiar collaborator George Furth) an intricate comedy thriller, *The Doctor Is Out,* which premiered at San Diego, Calif.'s Old Globe Theatre. Garland Wright capped his farewell season as artistic director of the Guthrie Theater with an adaptation of a Franz Kafka novel titled *K: Impressions of "The Trial,"* which proved a tour de force of precision, timing, and clarity.

With the British megamusical firmly ensconced as a staple of Broadway and the commercial touring circuit, it was refreshing to witness a steady flow of important new plays from British writers as well. On the heels of a Stoppard doubleheader—the philosophical spy thriller *Hapgood* and the expansive historical romance *Arcadia*—Lincoln Center Theater offered Hare's rigorously intelligent *Racing Demon,* in which the internecine squabbles of a group of Anglican clerics reflect the unsettled state of English religious life. *Moonlight,* Pinter's first full-length play since 1978, was given a luminous production by director Karel Reisz at New York's Roundabout Theater. New Haven, Conn.'s Yale

JOAN MARCUS

Blair Brown and Robert Sean Leonard play two of the contemporary characters in Tom Stoppard's *Arcadia,* which also features a set of characters living in 1809. The play was one of a number of works by British authors that moved to the New York stage during 1995.

Repertory Theatre offered the U.S. debut of David Edgar's *Pentecost,* a baroque attack on Eurosupremacy that won the London ES award.

In January legendary producer-director George Abbott died at the age of 107. Other theatrical luminaries lost during the year included actress Vivian Blaine, playwright John Patrick, and actor David Wayne. (*See* OBITUARIES.)

In Canada diminishing government and corporate support sent theatres scurrying in several directions. Winnipeg's venerable Manitoba Theatre Centre ensured the sellout of its season subscriptions by programming a production of *Hamlet* starring the solidly wooden but wildly popular film actor Keanu Reeves. Toronto's Harbourfront Centre turned to the East, serving as host to a grand-scale nine-week exposition called "Today's Japan," in which more than 200 Japanese artists brought theatre, dance, music, visual arts, and film to the city. Distressed by the constraints of reduced rehearsal periods—often as little as two and a half weeks—creative Toronto companies such as Da Da Kamera and Sound Image Theatre announced that they would take up the model of Robert Lepage's Quebec-based Ex Machina, which developed works over long periods, perhaps several years, and invited audiences in periodically during the works' development.

Lepage, the French-Canadian experimentalist known for his audacious culture-bridging vision and arresting visual style, marked the theatrical year with an authentic masterwork. The director's project on the theme of Hiroshima, titled *The Seven Streams of the River Ota,* made its Canadian debut at the "Today's Japan" festival after some three years of development and in-progress performances at nine international sites, including Tokyo. It was expected in the U.S. at the Brooklyn (N.Y.) Academy of Music in late 1996. With its intermingling of 30-odd characters (portrayed by a cast of 10) and its sweep across continents, generations, and cultures, *The River Ota* was a monumental, impressionistic comment on the bombing of Japan, which the play connects to two other of the century's formidable calamities: the Jewish Holocaust and the AIDS epidemic. Clocking in at more than five hours (with more material to come, according to Lepage), the play made dazzling use of film and sound and leavened its pageantlike seriousness with episodes of sly, hip humour. It was Lepage's most ambitious work in a decade, surpassing even his epic about Canadian expansion, *The Dragon's Trilogy,* in its emotional impact and theatricality.

(JIM O'QUINN)

This article updates the *Macropædia* article The History of Western THEATRE.

MOTION PICTURES

The year 1895 saw a race between experimenters in the U.S., France, Britain, and Germany to find a means to project the animated films of Thomas Edison's peep show kinetoscope onto a screen. The race had no clear winner, but the date generally accepted as the birth of cinema is Dec. 28, 1895, when the Lumière brothers began regular projections for a paying public in the basement of the Grand Café on the boulevard des Capucines in Paris.

The centenary of motion pictures was widely celebrated in 1995 with exhibitions, publications, and television programs. For a French film, *Lumière and Company*, a group of contemporary filmmakers—ranging from Theo Angelopoulos of Greece and Zhang Yimou of China to James Ivory of the U.K. and Spike Lee of the U.S.—were each invited to make a one-shot film, using an original 1896 Lumière camera and working in the same conditions as their earliest antecedents. The commemoration inevitably inspired reflection on the achievements of the first century, and many were left to conclude that, sadly, motion pictures had failed to fulfill the promise of their early years.

English-Speaking. The only common factor among younger U.S. filmmakers was a fairly general desire to emulate the mannerisms of the world's currently most modish film director, Quentin Tarantino—fast, stylish, gaudy, violent, and self-consciously insubstantial. As the antithesis of this, however, adaptations of two children's books—Frances Hodgson Burnett's *A Little Princess,* by the Mexican director Alfonso Cuarón and Lynne Reid Banks's *The Indian in the Cupboard,* directed by Frank Oz—struck a blow for the well-made film and enjoyed popular success. Among the bigger box-office winners was Joel Schumacher's *Batman Forever,* with Val Kilmer taking over the title role. The troubled production of *Waterworld*—a persuasive fantasy about an anarchic future-world where land masses have been covered in water—escalated its budget to an estimated $175 million, making it the most costly film in history. Time travel from a plague-ravaged future was the subject of Terry Gilliam's apocalyptic *12 Monkeys*.

The James Bond series was triumphantly revived in *GoldenEye,* with a new team of producers and writers, a new director (Martin Campbell), and a dashing new Bond, Pierce Brosnan. Bryan Singer's *The Usual Suspects* was an outstanding crime thriller, handling its complicated plot and rich character observation with great skill. Other good crime thrillers included Michael Mann's *Heat;* David Fincher's *Seven;* and a tense, tough remake of Henry Hathaway's 1947 *Kiss of Death* directed by Barbet Schroeder. Martin Scorsese's violent study of organized crime, *Casino,* was a disappointing companion piece to his earlier *GoodFellas*.

The Walt Disney studios explored American history with their 33rd cartoon feature, *Pocahontas,* directed by Mike Gabriel and Eric Goldberg. Disney also enjoyed commercial successes during the year with the first full-length, completely computer-animated feature, *Toy Story,* directed by John Lasseter, as well as a live-action version of *The Jungle Book,* directed by Stephen Sommers.

James Ivory's *Jefferson in Paris* was a decorative but heavy-handed biographical essay. Oliver Stone's three-hour *Nixon* was a diligent biopic rather than the sensational exposé anticipated after the director's *JFK*. Ron Howard made a reverential dramatic reconstruction of the near-disastrous 1970 space mission, *Apollo 13*. Ancient Scottish lore came into its own. Mel Gibson directed and starred in the swashbuckling 13th-century epic *Braveheart,* about William Wallace's fight against the English, while Michael Caton-Jones made a dour *Rob Roy* on authentic Scottish locations.

Romantic drama and comedy had their place, notably in Clint Eastwood's adult version of Robert James Waller's sentimental best-seller *The Bridges of Madison County* and Rob Reiner's amiable romantic comedy *The American President*. A more sardonic view of romance appeared in Jeremy Leven's *Don Juan DeMarco,* which updated the Byronic legend, with Marlon Brando as psychiatrist to the deluded great lover (Johnny Depp). Tim Robbins wrote and directed *Dead Man Walking,* an intelligent examination of the relationship between a nun and the rapist-murderer she visits on Death Row in the prison meeting room. Mike Figgis' *Leaving Las Vegas* told the poignant love story of a self-destructive alcoholic and a prostitute. Hollywood and its ethics were satirized in Barry Sonnenfeld's *Get Shorty,* based on the Elmore Leonard novel, and in Gus Van Sant's black comedy *To Die For.*

African-American filmmakers and themes were strongly represented. Lee shed some of his earlier belligerence in *Clockers,* a thriller about drug dealers. Allen and Albert Hughes's *Dead Presidents* offered a portrait of a middle-class black youth in the early 1970s drifting into crime after military service in Vietnam. Carl Franklin treated the difficulties of a black man returning from World War II in his thriller *Devil in a Blue Dress*. Forest Whitaker's *Waiting to Exhale* observed four black women searching for love. John Singleton's *Higher Learning* grappled with issues of race and sexual identity in American college life. Preston A. Whitmore II's *The Walking Dead* paid tribute to the black combat soldiers of the Vietnam War. In *Panther,* the father-son/writer-director team of Melvin and Mario Van Peebles related the rise of the Black Panther movement.

Among more offbeat and independent productions must be noted Wayne Wang's *Smoke,* from a story by Paul Auster, and its companion piece, *Blue in the Face*, improvised by the same cast. Edward Burns's *The Brothers McMullen,* winner of the main prize at the Sundance Film Festival, was a beautifully observed portrait of the emotional crises of an Irish Catholic family.

Two longtime leading ladies of the screen, Lana Turner and Ida Lupino, died during the year. (*See* OBITUARIES.)

British cinema was in bullish mood with the confidence inspired by the international success of a number of recent low-budget films, notably *Four Weddings and a Funeral.* Investment, production, and average budgets rose; further exceptional new productions resulted. Notable among these were Ken Loach's *Land and Freedom,* the story of the disillusion of a communist believer in the Spanish Civil War; and Nicholas Hytner's elegant, intelligent period piece *The Madness of King George.* Another successful essay in historical biography, *Carrington,* marked the directorial debut of writer Christopher Hampton.

Comedies of note were Peter Chelsom's macabre black fantasy about professional comedians, *Funny Bones,* and John Schlesinger's stylish version of Stella Gibbons' 1930s parody novel *Cold Comfort Farm.* Benjamin Ross's *The Young Poisoner's Handbook,* based on the real story of a juvenile murderer, achieved both grotesque comedy and wry reflections on British social habits.

Thrillers included Michael Winterbottom's disturbing *Butterfly Kiss;* Anthony Waller's *Mute Witness,* an effective story about Americans caught up in the underworld of the new Russia; and Scott Michell's *The Innocent Sleep,* set in London locations and the world of the homeless. Terence Davies went to the U.S. to film John Kennedy Toole's novel *Neon Bible* in Georgia. Another established filmmaker, Nicolas Roeg, made *Two Deaths,* a chilling psychological drama set in 1989 Romania.

Jane Austen suddenly became the screen's favourite author, with adaptations for big screen or television of all her major novels, including Roger Michell's *Persuasion* and Amy Heckerling's *Clueless,* a lively version of Austen's *Emma* set among modern Beverly Hills teens. The best was *Sense and Sensibility,* Hollywood-financed, directed by the Taiwanese Ang Lee, and scripted by its star, Emma Thompson.

The long-cherished project of one of the world's finest draftsmen-animators, Canadian-born Richard Williams, emerged after a quarter of a century's gestation. Sadly, in its final stages *The Thief and the Cobbler* had hit financial problems, and the version that finally emerged, as a U.S. release under the title *Arabian Knights,* showed signs of having been finished rapidly and with compromises. Also during the year British cinema lost the Oscar-winning screenwriter Robert Bolt. (*See* OBITUARIES.)

Irish cinema continued to demonstrate an independent national style. The Irish conflict provided the subject of Thaddeus O'Sullivan's painfully authentic *Nothing Personal.* Gerard Stembridge's *Guiltrip* was a powerful, unsparing portrait of the tensions in a marriage in a traumatized society. Cathal Black's *Korea* was the story of a strained father-and-son relationship in the rural Ireland of the 1950s.

The international success of a generally unremarkable year in Australian cinema was Chris Noonan's *Babe,* a fable, treated with wit and charm, of a pig adopted by a sheepdog. A new film version of a popular literary subject, *Dad and Dave: On Our Selection,* cast Dame Joan Sutherland as an early 20th-century working-class mother.

Actors (clockwise from left) Tom Hanks, Kevin Bacon, and Bill Paxton play the crew of the spacecraft in *Apollo 13.* The film, directed by Ron Howard, was praised for its portrayal of the bravery and skill of the astronauts who narrowly averted disaster in the 1970 mission.

R. BATZDORFF—UNIVERSAL/SHOOTING STAR

Production in Canada was plentiful, but few Canadian films attracted a great deal of international notice in 1995. In *Rude* writer-director Clement Virgo made a forceful debut in his music-driven picture of life in black, inner-city Toronto. Mort Ransen's *Margaret's Museum* dramatized a woman haunted by the coal mine that took her husband's life. Kal Ng's visionary *The Soul Investigator* confronted and questioned Chinese Confucianism with the story of a Canadian Chinese estate agent who developed stigmata. A French-language production, Robert Lepage's *The Confessional,* set its scary thriller plot in Quebec City in 1952, at the moment when director Alfred Hitchcock was there shooting *I Confess.*

Continental Europe. In France the biggest commercial film of the year was Jean-Paul Rappeneau's visually dazzling adaptation of Jean Giono's *The Horseman on the Roof.* Pierre Boutron, a former theatre director, adapted José Luis de Villalonga's antiwar novel *Fiesta* with great style and a masterly performance by Jean-Louis Trintignant.

Emir Kusturica's *Underground,* winner of the Palme d'Or at the Cannes Film Festival, was officially a Franco-German-Hungarian coproduction. Its setting was the chaos of former Yugoslavia, which Kusturica presented as an epic dance of death, with astounding set pieces.

The year saw a rash of French films about juvenile delinquents. The most notable of these was Mathieu Kassovitz's *La Haine,* a black-and-white film that showed a vicious circle of violence escalating between police and youngsters from a deprived housing complex. Bertrand Tavernier's *The Bait* (*L'Appat*) effectively deglamourized crime in its story of a trio of none-too-bright working kids whose robbery for kicks gets them involved in murder.

Several older directors remained active in France during the year. Jacques Rivette conceived a whimsical musical, *Haut bas fragile*. At age 87 Jean Delannoy directed *Mary of Nazareth.* Agnes Varda contributed a whimsical all-star cavalcade, *A Hundred and One Nights.* Eric Rohmer's *Les Rendez-vous de Paris* was a collection of three garrulous antiromantic episodes. Claude Sautet's admirable *Nelly et Monsieur Arnaud* related the passion of an elderly man for a young woman. Claude Chabrol was back in form with *La Cérémonie,* an adaptation of Ruth Rendell's thriller *A Judgment in Stone.* For Claude Lelouch, Hugo's *Les Misérables* provided the jumping-off point for a contemporary epic. One of France's outstanding directors, Louis Malle, died in November. (*See* OBITUARIES.)

The Italian octogenarian Michelangelo Antonioni, speechless and partly paralyzed, returned to activity to direct a collection of four stories, *Par dela les nuages* (*Beyond the Clouds*), with the collaboration of Wim Wenders. Another great director was recalled in Marco Tullio Giordana's *Pasolini, un delitto italiano* (*Pasolini, an Italian Crime*), a dramatic reconstruction of director Pier Paolo Pasolini's murder in 1975 and the investigation that followed.

Among the few other outstanding works produced during the year, the standouts were Giuseppe Tornatore's *The Star Man,* about a confidence man traveling the countryside in the 1950s; Michele Placido's re-creation of the downfall of a Sicilian banking tycoon, *Un eroe borghese;* Daniele Luchetti's *La scuola,* the story of a nonfunctioning school in suburban Rome; Mario Martone's psychological mystery story *L'amore molesto;* and a talented first film by Stefano Incerti, *Il verificatore (The Gas Inspector)*.

Two of the most striking German films of the year were Joseph Vilsmaier's riveting screen version of Robert Schneider's 1992 best-seller *Brother of Sleep,* about a 19th-century peasant tormented by his own musical genius; and Margarethe von Trotta's first German production in a decade, *The Promise,* the story of a romance that fails to survive 30 years of separation brought about by the divisions of communist-era Germany.

Sweden's biggest box-office hit was *One in a Million,* a black comedy about unemployment, coscripted and directed by Mans Herngren and Hannes Holm. The year's most ambitious Norwegian production was Liv Ullmann's medieval epic *Kristin Lavransdatter,* adapted from Sigrid Undset's novel. A Norwegian first feature, Bent Hamer's whimsical tale of the domestic life of two elderly brothers, *Eggs,* enjoyed success at international festivals.

Marleen Gorris' *Antonia's Line,* a Dutch-Belgium-British coproduction, offered an intimate saga of a rural matriarchy, rich in atmosphere, finely played, and touched with magic realism. Belgium offered Frank Van Passel's *Manneken Pis,* a strange little fable about a young man who (with justification) believes he brings ill fortune to those he loves. In Spain, Carlos Saura celebrated the national art of dance in *Flamenco,* while one-time *enfant terrible* Pedro Almodóvar made a surprisingly restrained and unmelodramatic study of family life and marital breakdown, *The Flower of My Secret.* One of the most active actors of the year, starring in four English-language movies, was Almodóvar's protégé Antonio Banderas. (*See* BIOGRAPHIES.)

The veteran Portuguese Manuel de Oliveira devised a curious moral reflection in *The Convent,* while João César Monteiro played the leading role in his own bizarre and scabrous farce *God's Comedy*. Greece enjoyed a homegrown box-office success with Antonis Kokkinos' nostalgic recollection of high-school days at the end of the 1960s, *End of an Era.* Angelopoulos' *Ulysses' Gaze* used an anecdote of an émigré filmmaker in the Balkans as the motive for a survey—part visionary, part realistic—of geographic borders and national identities.

The most notable Russian productions of the year were Savva Kulish's costly four-hour saga *The Iron Curtain,* about a boy growing up in post-World War II Stalinist years, and two absurdist satires, Vladimir Menshikov's *What a Mess. . .* and Dmitry Astrakhan's *Everything Will Be O.K.* Yana Drouz's *Side by Side* viewed the disintegration of contemporary Moscow society through the eyes of a resourceful German shepherd dog. Vladimir Khotinenko's *A Moslem* used the story of a prisoner of war returning from Afghanistan to his Russian village, a convert to Islam, as a metaphor for many of the preoccupations of the new Russia.

In Poland, Krzysztof Kieslowski, director of the acclaimed *Trois Couleurs* (Three Colours) trilogy, announced his retirement in late 1994 (*see* BIOGRAPHIES), while the veteran Kazimierz Kutz released a new film, *Colonel Kwiatkowski.* In Hungary, Judit Elek's *The Awakening* was a sensitive study of a lonely, observant Jewish girl during the Stalinist 1950s, while Peter Gothar's *The Outpost* was a Kafkaesque story of a woman "posted" to a bleak, remote outpost. The elegance and invention of Joseph Pacskovszki's *The Wondrous Journey of Kornel Esti,* adapted from two stories by Dezso Kosztolanyi, belied its impoverished budget.

From Slovakia, Martin Sulik's whimsical, stylized, yet human comedy *The Garden* proved a major success at the 30th Karlovy Vary Festival. From the Czech Republic, Jan Sverak's road movie, *The Ride,* made up for minimal resources with invention and observation. A Romanian-German coproduction, Bogdan Dumitrescu's *Thalassa, Thalassa, Return to the Sea,* was a lively description of the journey of discovery by seven underprivileged children in a "borrowed" car.

Middle East and North Africa. In Israel the two hits of the year were Savi Gabinon's *Lovesick on Nana Street,* with star comic actor Moshi Ivgi as a sweet fantasist who ends up confined to a mental hospital, and Eytan Fox's debut feature *Song of the Siren,* a witty romantic comedy set against the background of the Persian Gulf War and Scud missile attacks on Tel Aviv. Other successes were Shmuel Hasfari's *Sh'hur,* based on the writer Hana Azulay-Hasfari's autobiographical reminiscence of the Jewish Moroccan subculture, and Eli Cohen's *Under the Domin Tree,* which described a group of children coping with trauma in a camp for Holocaust survivors in the 1950s.

Iran's outstanding contemporary director Abbas Kiarostami scripted Aliraisa Raisian's *The Journey,* about the psychological adventures of a middle-class family fleeing from the Iraq-Iran war, and provided the story for Jafar Panahi's prizewinning *The White Balloon,* about the adventures of a small girl and a lost bank note.

Far East. Though the favourite commercial genre in Japan was fast-paced thrillers (Kazuyoshi Okuyama's *The Mystery of Rampo* was an unusually inventive example of the

(continued on page 278)

Selected Film Awards 1995

Golden Globes, awarded in Beverly Hills, Calif., in January 1995	
Best drama	*Forrest Gump* (U.S.; director, Robert Zemeckis)
Best musical or comedy	*The Lion King* (U.S.; directors, Roger Allers, Rob Minkoff)
Best director	Robert Zemeckis (*Forrest Gump,* U.S.)
Best actress, drama	Jessica Lange (*Blue Sky,* U.S.)
Best actor, drama	Tom Hanks (*Forrest Gump,* U.S.)
Best actress, musical or comedy	Jamie Lee Curtis (*True Lies,* U.S.)
Best actor, musical or comedy	Hugh Grant (*Four Weddings and a Funeral,* U.K.)
Best foreign-language film	*Farinelli* (Italy/Belgium; director, Gérard Corbiau)

Sundance Film Festival, awarded in Park City, Utah, in January 1995	
Grand Jury Prize, dramatic film	*The Brothers McMullen* (U.S.; director, Edward Burns)
Grand Jury Prize, documentary	*Crumb* (U.S.; director, Terry Zwigoff)
Audience Award, dramatic film	*Picture Bride* (U.S.; director, Kayo Hatta)
Audience Award, documentary	*Ballot Measure 9* (U.S.; director, Heather MacDonald) *Unzipped* (U.S.; director, Douglas Keeve)

Berlin International Film Festival, awarded in February 1995	
Golden Bear	*The Bait* (France; director, Bertrand Tavernier)
Special Jury Prize	*Smoke* (U.S.; director, Wayne Wang)
Best director	Richard Linklater (*Before Sunrise,* U.S./Germany)
Best actress	Josephine Siao (*Summer Snow,* Hong Kong)
Best actor	Paul Newman (*Nobody's Fool,* U.S.)

Césars (France), awarded in February 1995	
Best film	*Les Roseaux sauvages* (France; director, André Techiné)
Best director	André Techiné (*Les Roseaux sauvages,* France)
Best actress	Isabelle Adjani (*La Reine Margot,* France)
Best actor	Gérard Lanvin (*Le Fils préféré,* France)
Best first film	*Regarde les hommes tomber* (France; director, Jacques Audiard)

Academy of Motion Picture Arts and Sciences (Oscars, U.S.), awarded in Los Angeles in March 1995	
Best film	*Forrest Gump* (U.S.; director, Robert Zemeckis)
Best director	Robert Zemeckis (*Forrest Gump,* U.S.)
Best actress	Jessica Lange (*Blue Sky,* U.S.)
Best actor	Tom Hanks (*Forrest Gump,* U.S.)
Best supporting actress	Dianne Wiest (*Bullets over Broadway,* U.S.)
Best supporting actor	Martin Landau (*Ed Wood,* U.S.)
Best foreign language film	*Burnt by the Sun* (CIS; director, Nikita Mikhalkov)

British Academy of Film and Television Arts, awarded in London in April 1995	
Best film	*Four Weddings and a Funeral* (U.K.; director, Mike Newell)
Best director	Mike Newell (*Four Weddings and a Funeral,* U.K.)
Best actress	Susan Sarandon (*The Client,* U.S.)
Best actor	Hugh Grant (*Four Weddings and a Funeral,* U.K.)
Best supporting actress	Kristin Scott Thomas (*Four Weddings and a Funeral,* U.K.)
Best supporting actor	Samuel L. Jackson (*Pulp Fiction,* U.S.)
Best foreign-language film	*To Live* (China; director, Zhang Yimou)

Cannes International Film Festival, France, awarded in May 1995	
Palme d'Or	*Underground* (France/Germany/Hungary; director, Emir Kusturica)
Grand Jury Prize	*Ulysses' Gaze* (Greece/France/Italy; director, Theo Angelopoulos)
Special Jury Prize	*Carrington* (U.K.; director, Christopher Hampton)
Best director	Mathieu Kassovitz (*La Haine,* France)
Best actress	Helen Mirren (*The Madness of King George,* U.K.)
Best actor	Jonathan Pryce (*Carrington,* U.K.)
Caméra d'Or	*The White Balloon* (Iran; director, Jafar Panahi)
International Critics' Prize	*Land and Freedom* (U.K.; director, Ken Loach) *Ulysses' Gaze* (Greece/France/Italy; director, Theo Angelopoulos)

Moscow International Film Festival, Russia, awarded in July 1995	
Best film	not awarded
Best director	Régis Wargnier (*Une Femme française,* France) Milan Steindler (*I Thank You for Each New Morning,* Czech Republic)
Best actress	Emmanuelle Béart (*Une Femme Française,* France)
Best actor	Gabriel Barylli (*Une Femme française,* France)

Montreal World Film Festival, awarded in September 1995	
Best film (Grand Prix)	*Georgia* (French-U.S.; director, Ulu Grosbard)
Best actress	Jennifer Jason Leigh (*Georgia*)
Best director	Xie Fei (China-Hong Kong, *A Mongolian Tale*) Goran Markovic (Yugoslavia, *Burlesque Tragedy*)
Grand Prix of the Jury	*A Moslem* (Russia; director, Vladimir Khotinenko)
Best actor	Fabrizio Bentivoglio (Italy, *Ordinary Hero*)
Best screenplay	Shemi Zarhin (Israel, *Passover Fever*)
People's choice most popular film	*Don't Die Without Telling Me Where You're Going* (Argentina; director, Eliseo Subiela)
People's choice best Canadian film	*Behind the Blue* (director, Robert Menard)
Best first fiction feature	*Cross My Heart and Hope to Die* (Norway; director, Marius Holst) *Manneken Pis* (Belgium; director, Frank Van Passel)
International cinematographic press award	(in competition): *Like It Never Was Before* (Sweden; director, Susanne Bier) (out of competition): *Manneken Pis* (Belgium; director, Frank Van Passel)

Toronto International Film Festival, awarded in September 1995	
Best Canadian Feature Film	*Live Bait* (director, Bruce Sweeney)
Special Jury Citations	*Rude* (director, Clement Virgo) *Curtis's Charm* (director, John L'Ecuyer)
Best Canadian Short Film	Laurence Green (*Reconstruction*)
Special Citations	Guy Maddin (*Odilon Redon*) John L'Ecuyer (*Use Once and Destroy*)
Metro Media Award	*La Cérémonie* (France; director, Claude Chabrol)
International Cinematographic Press Award	*Eggs* (Norway; director, Bent Hamer) *Desolation Angels* (U.S.; director, Tim McCann)
People's Choice Award	*Antonia's Line* (The Netherlands; director, Marleen Gorris)

Venice Film Festival, Italy, awarded in September 1995	
Golden Lion	*Cyclo* (France/Vietnam; director, Tran Anh Hung)
Special Jury Prize	*God's Comedy* (Portugal; director, Joao Cesar Monteiro)
Silver Lion	*The Star Man* (Italy; director, Giuseppe Tornatore)
Volpi Cup, best actress	Sandrine Bonnaire, Isabelle Huppert (*La Cérémonie,* France)
Volpi Cup, best actor	Goetz George (*The Deathmaker,* Germany)
International Film Critics' Prize	*Cyclo* (France/ Vietnam; director, Tran Anh Hung) *Beyond the Clouds* (France/Italy/Germany; director, Michelangelo Antonioni)

Chicago International Film Festival, awarded in October 1995	
Best feature film	*Maborosi* (Japan; director, Koreeda Hirokazu)
Special Jury Prize	*L'amore molesto* (Italy; director, Mario Martone)
Best actress	Anna Bonaiuto (*L'amore molesto,* Italy)
Best actor	Jean-Louis Trintignant (*Fiesta,* France)
Best first feature	*Cross My Heart and Hope to Die* (Norway, Marius Holst)
Best screenplay	Marleen Gorris (*Antonia's Line,* The Netherlands)
Best documentary	*Anne Frank Remembered* (U.K., Jon Blair)

San Sebastián International Film Festival, Spain, awarded in October 1995	
Best film	*Margaret's Museum* (Canada; director, Mort Ransen)
Best director	Mike Figgis (*Leaving Las Vegas,* U.S.)
Best actress	Victoria Abril (*Nobody Will Talk About Us When We're Dead,* Spain)
Best actor	Nicolas Cage (*Leaving Las Vegas,* U.S.)
Special Jury Prize	*Nobody Will Talk About Us When We're Dead,* (Spain; director, Agustin Díaz Yanes)

Tokyo International Film Festival, awarded in October 1995	
Grand Prix	not awarded
Gold Prize	*The Usual Suspects* (U.S.; director, Bryan Singer) *The White Balloon* (Iran; director, Jafar Panahi)

Vancouver International Film Festival, Canada, awarded in October 1995	
Federal Express Award	*Margaret's Museum* (Canada; director, Mort Ransen)
Air Canada Award	*Carrington* (U.K.; director, Christopher Hampton)
Rogers Award	Robert Lepage (*Le Confessional*)
NFB Award	*Your Name in Cellulite* (Gail Noonan)
Best Western Canadian Short Film	*The Land of Cain* *The Shaper*
Best Documentary	*Caught in the Act* (France) *Jupiter's Wife* (U.S.)
Dragons and Tigers Award for Young Cinema	*Goldfish* (China; director, Wu Di) *Maborosi* (Japan; director, Koreeda Hirokazu)

European Film Awards (Felix), awarded in Berlin in November 1995	
Best European film of the year	*Land and Freedom* (U.K.; director, Ken Loach)
Best young European film of the year	*La Haine* (France; director, Mathieu Kassovitz)

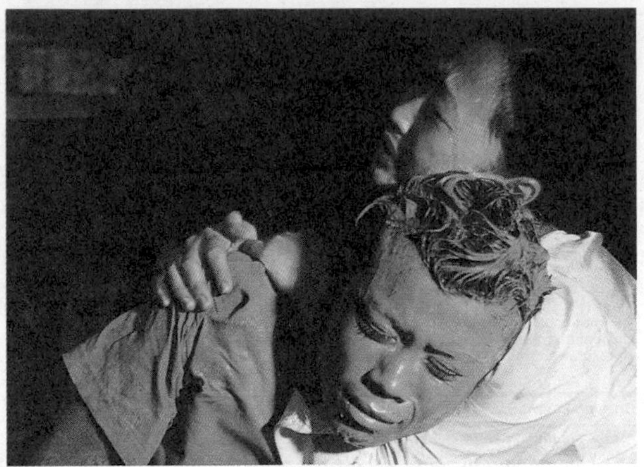

Le Van Loc played the title role in *Cyclo,* a Vietnamese film that shockingly portrayed the brutality of everyday life in Ho Chi Minh City.
LAURENCE TREMOLET—LUMIERE PICTURES

(continued from page 276)
genre), some of the best films dealt with intimate, private subjects—Yun Ichikawa's elegiac study of a family relationship, *Tokyo Koydai;* Junichi Suzuki's *Sukiyaki,* about a family disrupted by the matriarch's Alzheimer's disease and her granddaughter's epilepsy; and two fine first films, Makoto Shinozaki's *Okaeri* and Koreeda Hirokazu's *Maborosi*.

Despite official repression, Chinese directors continued to produce varied and interesting work. Xie Fei's *A Mongolian Tale* surpassed its political function in China's delicate power game with Mongolia to relate a warm and human story. He Jianjun's *The Postman* dealt with a character whose own spiritually impoverished life leads him to intervene in other people's lives. Zhang Yimou, whose recent films had experienced political difficulties, dealt with a safer subject in the beautifully staged period gangster drama *Shanghai Triad.* A woman director, Ning Ying created a riveting wry comedy about the uneventful daily grind of a suburban Beijing police station, *On the Beat.* A Chinese-Hong Kong coproduction, Li Shaohong's *Blush* was an observant story of two prostitutes after the communist takeover of China.

In *Summer Snow* Ann Hui of Hong Kong observed with humour and tenderness a woman's relationship with her father-in-law as he degenerates as a result of Alzheimer's disease. Stanley Kwan's *Red Rose, White Rose* was a sardonic study of a man's relationships with two women. Hong Kong actor-director Jackie Chan (*see* BIOGRAPHIES) continued his long and successful career with two new films, *Rumble in the Bronx* and *Thunderbolt.*

Directors explored Taiwan's troubled 20th-century history: Hou Hsiao-hsien in *Good Men, Good Women;* Hsu Hsiao-ming in *Heartbreak Island,* about a former urban political terrorist released from prison after 10 years; and Wan Jen in *Super Citizen Ko,* which describes an old man grappling with the legacy of guilt and of 16 years' imprisonment for political offenses committed in the 1950s.

Having established an international reputation with his first film, *The Scent of Green Papaya,* Vietnamese filmmaker Tran Anh Hung took the Golden Lion at the Venice Film Festival with *Cyclo,* a dazzling stylized study of the lives of the underprivileged, driven into corruption and vice in Ho Chi Minh City. From Malaysia came U-Wei Bin Haji Saari's *Kaki Bazaar,* which adapted a William Faulkner story about an arsonist to modern Malaya.

In India controversy and censorship threats ensured commercial success for Mani Rathnam's *Bombay,* a drama set against the background of the sectarian troubles of the early 1990s. Sandip Ray successfully filmed *Target,* a script by his late father, Satyajit Ray, about a feudal lord who finds himself reliant upon untouchables. From Assam, Jahnu Barua's *It's a Long Way to the Sea* told of a ferryman whose livelihood is threatened by a new bridge.

Latin America. Mexico alone continued to maintain a substantial commercial production in 1995, and one of the year's best films was Jorge Fons's *Midaq Alley,* which had its unlikely origins in a novel by Egyptian author Naguib Mahfouz. Films of note from other Latin-American countries included Carla Camurati's historical extravaganza *Carlota Joaquina, Princess of Brazil;* Walter Salles' *Foreign Land,* a love story that highlighted the economic hardship and exile of young Brazilians after the return of democracy in 1990; Jorge Sanjines' *The Bird's Singing,* a satirical film about a crew filming among the Indian communities of the Bolivian high plateau; and, from Cuba, Tomás Gutiérrez Alea and Juan Carlos Tabio's satirical comedy *Guantanamera.*

Africa. Burkina Faso continued to prove itself the most film-conscious of the African countries, with notable pictures from Drissa Touré (*Haramuya*), the newcomer Dani Kouyaté (*Keita, Voice of the Griot*), and Idrissa Ouedraogo (*Africa, My Africa*). In Mali, Cheik Oumar Sissoko made a political satire, *Guimba, a Tyrant and His Age.* In Cameroon, Bassek Ba Kkobhio's *The Great White of Lambarene* offered an African view of the great humanitarian Albert Schweitzer. From Guinea, Laurent Chevallier's *L'Enfant noir* (*The African Child*) was based on the autobiography of Guinean writer Laye Camara.

In South Africa, Ralph Zimat made an assured debut with *Hearts and Minds,* based on a true story of a white policeman's attempt to assassinate an African National Congress leader. Darrell James Roodt directed a new adaptation of Alan Paton's classic novel *Cry, the Beloved Country.* It was the first major motion picture made in the new South Africa and boasted an international cast headed by James Earl Jones and Richard Harris. (DAVID ROBINSON)

Nontheatrical Films. In 1995 tens of thousands of nontheatrical films and videos were made worldwide, and three-fourths were sponsored by industry. A Swedish film took the grand prize on two continents—at the International Industrial Film and Video Congress (Europe's largest festival) and at the U.S. International Film and Video Festival in Chicago. *Everywhere I Go* was a Volvo promotional film that superimposed various scenes on the shiny body of a speeding car traveling through the countryside.

A film sponsored by the Shriners Hospitals for Crippled Children in the U.S. was a CINE Golden Eagle selection, won the City of Torino (Italy) prize, and took a Gold Medal at the New York Film Festival. *Dreams of Gold* told the remarkable story of Tony Volpentest, a boy born without hands or feet who grew up to set a world record in track.

Bui doi: Life like Dust, a documentary about a Vietnamese refugee, took the grand prize at the USA Film Festival, Dallas, Texas, was chosen best documentary at the Santa Barbara (Calif.) International Documentary Festival, and was chosen a CINE Golden Eagle selection.

A Belgium film titled *Mrs. Foucault's Pendulum* was awarded 13 top honours. The film focused on a couple whose orderly life is tragically interrupted by an intruder.

Three U.S. student films won awards in 1995. *Heat Spell* and *Chaos in Congerville,* by undergraduate students at Florida State University, and *Sportster,* by a University of Southern California graduate student, were awarded prizes at international film festivals. (THOMAS W. HOPE)

See also Art, Antiques, and Collections: *Photography;* Media and Publishing: *Radio; Television*.

This article updates the *Macropædia* article MOTION PICTURES.

Population and Human Relations

DEMOGRAPHY

At midyear 1995, world population stood at 5,702,000,000, according to estimates prepared by the Population Reference Bureau. The 1995 figure was about 700 million higher than in 1987, when world population first reached 5 billion. The 1995 figure represented an increase of about 88 million over the previous year. The annual rate of population increase declined to about 1.54% in 1995 from 1.6% in 1994, a result of birthrate declines in both developing and industrialized nations. If the 1995 growth rate continued, the world's population would double in the next 45 years. In 1995, 139 million babies were born, 125 million (90%) in developing countries. Each day, world population increased by 242,000, the result of 382,000 births and 140,000 deaths. More than 85% of the population growth in industrialized countries occurred in the United States. New data from censuses in 26 countries and territories were reported to the United Nations in 1995. (*See* WORLD DATA: *Area and population*.)

Worldwide, contraceptive use for all methods stood at 58% of married couples in 1995. Fully 49% of couples reported using a "modern" method such as clinically supplied contraceptives or sterilization. In less developed countries (LDCs) 55% were practicing some form of family planning and 49% were using a modern one. The percentage of couples who used contraceptives in LDCs was significantly low, however, except in China, where a vigorous family-planning program had raised contraceptive usage to high levels. When China was excluded, only 33% of couples in LDCs were using a modern method. Sub-Saharan Africa reported the lowest level of usage, 11%, while Latin America had the highest figure among LDCs, 51%.

In 1995, 32% of the world's population was below the age of 15 in 1995, but the figure was 38% in LDCs outside China. In more developed countries (MDCs), 20% were below age 15, and the figures dropped as low as 16% for Germany, Japan, and Switzerland. (The younger age distribution of LDCs in 1995 was expected to result in a large number of youths entering the childbearing ages in the near future, which should offer considerable potential for population growth.) Only 5% of the population in LDCs was over the age of 65, compared with 13% in MDCs. Sweden, with 18%, remained the country with the highest percentage above age 65.

Nearly half—43%—of world population in 1995 lived in urban areas. In LDCs 35% of the population was classified as urban, compared with 74% in MDCs. Among the world's least urbanized countries was Burundi, with only 6% urban population in 1995.

On average, life expectancy at birth was 64 years for males and 68 for females. In MDCs the same figures were 70 and 78 and in LDCs 62 and 65, respectively. In 1995 males could expect to live one year less than in 1994; this statistic was due primarily to rapidly declining health conditions in the republics of the former Soviet Union. The 1995 world infant mortality rate stood at 62 infant deaths per 1,000 live births—10 in MDCs and 67 in LDCs.

Less Developed Countries. The share of world population growth occurring in LDCs increased to 98% in 1995. Of the 88 million people added annually, about 86.5 million were in the world's poorer nations. At the 1995 pace of childbearing, women in LDCs were averaging about 3.5 children each during their lifetime, slightly more than double that of MDCs. In LDCs, excluding the large statistical effect of China's 1.2 billion population, women averaged four children each. This was far from the "two-child family" essential to slowing population growth to zero and stabilizing world population size.

The release of the first national fertility survey of India, the world's second most populous country, made major demographic news. India's total fertility rate (TFR), the average number of children a woman would bear during her lifetime, assuming that the rate of childbearing in a given year remains constant, fell to 3.4 children per woman. The State Statistical Bureau of China, the world's most populous country, reported that the TFR had dropped to 1.86 in the previous year.

In 1995 life expectancy in Africa was the world's lowest, at 53 years for males and 56 for females. Even so, because that continent reported the world's highest birthrate—a TFR of 5.8 (6.2 in sub-Saharan Africa)—its population growth was the world's fastest, at 2.8% annually. Overall, Africa's population stood at 720 million.

Latin America's population stood at 481 million in 1995, with an annual growth rate of 1.9%, down from 2% in 1994. The TFR in this region remained a comparatively modest 3.1, ranging from 5.4 in Guatemala to 1.8 in Cuba, the same as it was in 1994. Life expectancy rose to 66 for males and 72 for females.

Asia's population grew from 3.4 billion in 1994 to 3.5 billion in 1995, although its growth rate of 1.7% was the lowest of the developing regions. China's population reached 1,219,000,000, but the growth rate continued falling, to 1.1%. Population growth rates in the Pacific Rim countries of East Asia fell to historically low levels. This region was close to approaching the low birth and death rates characteristic of industrialized countries.

Despite the fact that birthrates were declining and growth rates were lower in many developing countries, an important distinction had to be drawn between lower growth rates in 1995 and future prospects. Even at the current lower birthrates, world population would soar to well over 50 billion by the end of the 21st century and increase very rapidly thereafter. Mathematically, this placed great impor-

World's 25 Most Populous Urban Areas[1]

		City proper		Metropolitan area	
Rank	City and country	Population	Year	Population	Year
1	Tokyo, Japan	8,021,943	1994 est.	26,518,000	1994 est.
2	Seoul, South Korea	10,873,055	1991 est.	17,588,000	1989 est.
3	New York City, U.S.	7,333,253	1994 est.	16,271,000	1994 est.
4	Osaka, Japan	2,575,042	1994 est.	16,210,000	1990 est.
5	São Paulo, Brazil	9,393,753	1991 cen.	16,110,000	1994 est.
6	Mexico City, Mexico	9,815,795	1990 cen.	15,525,000	1994 est.
7	Los Angeles, U.S.	3,448,613	1994 est.	15,302,000	1994 est
8	Shanghai, China	8,930,000	1993 est.	14,709,000	1994 est.
9	Bombay (Mumbai), India	9,925,891	1991 cen.	14,496,000	1994 est.
10	Moscow, Russia	8,570,200	1994 est.	13,150,000	1991 est.
11	Buenos Aires, Arg.	2,960,976	1991 cen.	12,582,321	1991 cen.
12	London, U.K.	6,933,000	1993 est.	12,275,600	1989 est.
13	Beijing, China	6,690,000	1993 est.	12,030,000	1994 est.
14	Calcutta, India	4,399,819	1991 cen.	11,485,000	1994 est.
15	Jakarta, Indonesia	8,259,266	1990 cen.	11,017,000	1994 est.
16	Tianjin, China	5,000,000	1993 est.	10,376,000	1994 est.
17	Rio de Janeiro, Brazil	5,473,909	1991 cen.	9,817,000	1994 est.
18	Karachi, Pakistan	5,208,132	1981 cen.	9,500,000	1994 est.
19	Delhi, India	7,206,704	1991 cen.	9,500,000	1994 est.
20	Paris, France	2,156,766	1991 est.	9,400,000	1994 est.
21	Cairo, Egypt	6,849,000	1994 est.	9,400,000	1994 est.
22	Manila, Philippines	1,894,667	1991 est.	9,000,000	1994 est.
23	Chicago, U.S.	2,731,743	1994 est.	8,527,000	1994 est.
24	Nagoya, Japan	2,153,293	1994 est.	8,432,000	1990 est.
25	Istanbul, Turkey	7,331,927	1993 est.	7,490,342	1993 est.

[1]Ranked by population of metropolitan area.

tance on the birthrates in developing countries declining to about two children per woman if world population size was to stabilize.

More Developed Countries. In 1995 Europe recorded its first negative rate of natural increase in modern history, −0.1%. This change was largely the result of the steeply declining birthrate in the European republics of the former Soviet Union. Deaths outnumbered births in Russia by more than 700,000. The TFR dropped to between 1.3 and 1.5 in Belarus, Estonia, Latvia, Russia, and Ukraine. The principal reasons given for the dramatic reduction in childbearing among women surveyed were the confused state of the economy and the uncertain prospects for recovery in the foreseeable future. Prior to the dissolution of the Soviet Union, birthrates were relatively high. All of these countries now faced the prospect of population decline and accelerated aging. Italy now had the world's lowest TFR, 1.21, reclaiming that distinction from Spain, which had a TFR of 1.24. Life expectancy for females in Japan continued to set records at 83. Males in Iceland enjoyed the longest life expectancy, 76.9 years.

United States. The population of the U.S. was 263,057,000 in July 1995, up from 260,651,000 a year earlier. This represented an increase of 2,406,000 Americans, or 0.92%. The National Center for Health Statistics (NCHS) reported that during the 12 months ended in March 1995, natural increase—which is calculated as births minus deaths—amounted to 1,675,000, the net result of 3,955,000 births and 2,280,000 deaths. During that period the birthrate dropped to 15.1 births per 1,000 population, compared with 15.6 in the 12 months ended in March 1994. Preliminary estimates indicated that the U.S. TFR decreased slightly to 2.05 in 1994, from 2.08 in 1990. The natural increase through March 1995 was 74,000 less than in the 12-month period ended March 1994, a result of the gradual aging of women born during the baby boom and a real decline in the birthrate since the 1990 peak.

The age-adjusted death rate for the 12-month period ended in February 1995 declined 3% from the same period ended in February 1994. The age-adjusted rate was 504.7 per 100,000 population. The NCHS reported that in 1992 life expectancy at birth rose to a new high, 75.8 years. Female life expectancy was 79.1, a slight increase over 1991, while that of males rose to 72.3 from 72. Life expectancy for white females stabilized at 79.8, a small increase over the previous year. Black men had a life expectancy of only 65 years in 1992. The 15 major causes of death accounted for 85% of all deaths in the year ended in February 1995, about the same as one year earlier.

Table II. Causes of death in the United States
(year ended February)

Rank in 1995		Rate per 100,000 population 1994	1995
1.	Diseases of the heart	290.4	276.5
2.	Malignant neoplasms	207.2	206.2
3.	Cerebrovascular diseases	58.9	58.9
4.	Chronic obstructive pulmonary diseases	40.9	38.3
5.	Accidents and adverse effects	34.1	33.9
6.	Pneumonia and influenza	33.5	29.6
7.	Diabetes mellitus	21.7	21.3
8.	HIV infection	14.5	15.7
9.	Suicide	11.7	11.6
10.	Chronic liver disease and cirrhosis	9.7	10.0
11.	Nephritis, nephrotic symptoms, and nephrosis	9.6	9.5
12.	Homicide and legal intervention	9.6	9.0
13.	Septicemia	8.0	7.7
14.	Atherosclerosis	6.8	6.4
15.	Certain conditions of the perinatal period	6.1	5.4

There were 2,356,000 marriages in the U.S. in the 12-month period ended in March 1995, slightly up from 2,329,000 one year earlier. The marriage rate was 9 marriages per 1,000 population, the same as in the previous 12-month period. The number of divorces decreased by 3,000 to 1,180,000. The U.S. infant mortality fell to a historic low of 7.9 infant deaths per 1,000 live births in the 12-month period ended in March 1995. Legal immigration to the U.S. declined in fiscal year 1994 to 804,416, down from 880,014 in 1993. In 1995 immigration accounted for roughly 33% of U.S. net population growth. (CARL V. HAUB)

See also World Data.

INTERNATIONAL MIGRATION

Governments throughout the world made renewed efforts in 1995 to reduce the number of arrivals of illegal immigrants and asylum seekers. In the U.S. the anti-immigrant backlash that had been reflected in the results of the November 1994 elections continued to be a major political theme. Patrick Buchanan, a candidate for the Republican Party's presidential nomination, made the curbing of immigration part of his message of economic nationalism.

Opposition to immigration also had been part of the message of California Gov. Pete Wilson, whose state had voted in 1994 to deny illegal aliens access to medical and social services. Wilson's presidential campaign quickly failed because of his inability to raise the funds needed to continue.

The U.S. Immigration and Naturalization Service (INS) fortified the Mexican border with additional floodlights and steel fences and introduced more sophisticated computer and tracking technology. More than $500 million had been budgeted in 1994 by the Clinton administration to halt illegal crossings of the U.S.-Mexico border. The assessments after one year were mixed, with arrests declining in some areas and rising in others. It became known in 1995 that the U.S. had been granting asylum to Mexicans. This tacit recognition of political repression in Mexico was a further cause of tension between the governments of the two countries. The INS also streamlined procedures to expedite the deportation of unqualified asylum seekers. More than 147,000 asylum applications were filed during the year, the largest numbers coming from Guatemalans and Salvadorans.

The Republican-controlled Congress in September introduced bills that would crack down on illegal immigration and reduce, for the first time since 1924, the number of foreigners allowed to enter the U.S. The Congress proposed, among other measures, to cut legal immigration by one-third and reduce by one-half the number of people granted political asylum. These proposals came under attack not only from groups that had long supported the rights of immigrants but, more unexpectedly, from businessmen who claimed they needed to bring into the country workers, such as computer programmers, who supplemented the insufficient number of U.S. citizens with these skills.

The number of asylum applications submitted in Western Europe during 1994 dropped to 320,000 from 550,000 in 1993. The largest reduction was recorded in Germany, where 127,000 applications were received, compared with 323,000 a year earlier. Belgium, Denmark, Norway, Sweden, and Switzerland all reported significantly fewer applicants. Only The Netherlands and the United Kingdom experienced significant increases. The reductions resulted primarily from the introduction of more restrictive immigration and asylum regulations that were designed to deny entry to foreign nationals originating or arriving from safe countries in Central and Eastern Europe. In response, trafficking in illegal immigrants increased. Romania and Bulgaria were believed to be the most common entry point for illegals from Africa and

Two elderly women and two young sisters are among the Tibetans who have fled to Ladakh, in eastern Kashmir, to escape Chinese rule. After China occupied Tibet in 1950 and later imposed harsh rule over the people, hundreds of thousands fled to neighbouring countries.

PHOTOGRAPHS, PHIL BORGES

Asia, while immigrants from Central Asia generally moved from Moscow through the Baltic states, and into Scandinavia. European police agencies were concerned about the growing involvement of international criminal syndicates in these operations. A report by the U.K. Home Office immigration intelligence service claimed that the British government's "light touch" policy on visitors from other European countries had led to massive welfare fraud costing millions of pounds.

Rapid social and economic change in China, particularly in the coastal provinces Fujian and Guangdong, continued to spur a major exodus of international migrants. The total number of Chinese living illegally in other countries was estimated to have reached at least 500,000. In April 1994 the U.S. State Department estimated that 100,000 illegal Chinese immigrants would enter the U.S. during the year, many of them transported by criminal syndicates and other professional smugglers.

The movement of Vietnamese boat people to the countries of Southeast Asia came to an effective halt in 1994 as a result of improved economic and political conditions within Vietnam and declining opportunities for resettlement in the West. In 1994, of the roughly 52,000 Vietnamese citizens who legally emigrated by using assistance from an internationally supervised Orderly Departure Program, the vast majority went to the U.S. Some 13,000 Vietnamese boat people returned to their homeland in 1994, about half of them from Hong Kong. More than 40,000, however, remained in camps throughout Southeast Asia at the end of the year.

South Africa, which completed its transition to majority rule in 1994, was confronted very quickly with a growing influx of immigrants from such less prosperous and stable countries as Liberia, Rwanda, Somalia, and Zaire. The number of illegal immigrants in South Africa stood at some two million; many of them were unskilled workers who provided cheap and nonunion labour. This caused growing public concern about the social and economic impact of the new arrivals, which the South African government responded to by deporting over 90,000 foreigners in 1994.

(JEFF CRISP)

REFUGEES

Although the worldwide refugee population had decreased to 14.5 million by early 1995, the total number of persons of concern to the Office of the United Nations High Commissioner for Refugees (UNHCR) had risen to 27.4 million. That number, however, did not include the 2.8 million Palestinian refugees who fell under the mandate of the United Nations Relief and Works Agency for Palestinian Refugees in the Near East or the estimated 26 million other displaced persons. UNHCR continued to implement a core mandate by providing international refugee protection and by seeking permanent solutions to their dislocation, preferably through voluntary repatriation. As a reflection of the increasingly complex displaced-population crisis, UNHCR also expanded its activities to assist 4 million returning refugees, 5.4 million internally displaced persons (those who had a refugee-like status but had not crossed an international border), and 3.5 million others of humanitarian concern.

The humanitarian crisis, provoked in 1994 by the flight of over two million Rwandans and Burundians in the African Great Lakes region, continued to fester. While disease was kept under control and nutrition remained sufficient, security concerns, environmental degradation, and ethnic imbalances strained the generosity of those African countries that had traditionally welcomed refugees. Zaire, host to the largest number of Rwandan refugees, began forcibly repatriating them. Tanzania, an asylum country for African refugees even before its independence, sealed the border against further arrivals. Meanwhile, an estimated 750,000 refugees, mostly Tutsi who had left in the early 1960s, returned to Rwanda. Many of the former exiles took over houses abandoned by more recent refugees, a move that complicated the return of the new caseload. A meeting of these countries plus Uganda produced in November an agreement to return the refugees to Rwanda. In southern Africa the voluntary repatriation of 1.6 million Mozambicans was successfully completed in June. UNHCR turned its focus to helping their long-term integration into a devastated country. A duplication of the Mozambican repatriation was hoped for in Angola, where a fragile peace prevailed after 20 years of civil war that had spawned 311,000 refugees and 2 million internally displaced persons. In the Horn of Africa, Ethiopia was host nation to some 350,000 Somali, Sudanese, Djiboutian, and Kenyan refugees. Somalia witnessed the return of some 127,000 of its nationals over a 54-month period. UNHCR assisted their reintegration by means of small-scale projects intended to bridge the gap between emergency relief and long-term development. Repatriation to Eritrea faltered in the face of limited donor support. In West Africa the formation of a new government in Monrovia ushered in prospects for an end to five years of fighting and the return of 794,000 Liberian refugees. Violence in neighbouring Sierra Leone resulted in an additional 275,000 Sierra Leonean refugees.

In former Yugoslavia aggressors and victims changed roles as lightning gains and attritional battles bloated the displaced-person population. By the fall of 1995, fighting had displaced an estimated 500,000 people, adding to the 3.5 million refugees, displaced persons, and others of concern. The peace treaty signed in December raised the possibility that in the short term more people could be displaced to accommodate territorial adjustments. As a token of this, some 750 rebels against the Bosnian government, fearful of their reception, returned from Croatia. In Russia the year opened with a heavy-handed war in the self-declared independent republic of Chechnya. UNHCR assisted the 210,000 persons who had escaped to the neighbouring republics of Ingushetia and Dagestan, while the International Committee of the Red Cross worked to succour those within Chechnya. The cease-fire agreed to by Armenia and Azerbaijan in May 1994 continued to hold, and some 450,000 of the most needy of those displaced by the dispute in the enclave of Nagorno-Karabakh were assisted by UNHCR. UNHCR and concerned governments of the Commonwealth of Independent States (CIS) developed a regional approach to the problems affecting refugees, returnees, displaced persons, and migrants in the CIS and relevant neighbouring states. In 1994 Western Europe experienced a 40% decline in asylum applications compared with the previous year. Of the 338,000 persons who applied, 47,000 were granted refugee status and another 58,000 were allowed to stay for humanitarian reasons. By early 1995 some 700,000 persons from former Yugoslavia had been granted temporary protection.

The Afghan refugees who streamed out of their country after the 1979 invasion by Soviet forces were the largest refugee caseload of concern to UNHCR. About 2.7 million persons fled to Iran and Pakistan. As Afghanistan remained divided into regions of relative peace and ongoing combat, UNHCR attempted to encourage repatriation and mitigate further outflows by intensifying its activities in safer areas within the country. A major impediment to return and rehabilitation—as was the case also in Angola, Cambodia, and Mozambique—was the presence of indiscriminately sown land mines. Although most of the 500,000 internally displaced Tajiks and 60,000 Tajik refugees had returned to their places of origin within Tajikistan or in Afghanistan, some 34,000 Tajiks remained displaced. In a departure, UNHCR supported the Tajikistan authorities in protecting returnees and attempted to resolve conflicts. The 15,000 Turkish Kurd refugees in Iraq endured further displacement and uncertainty when their camps were targeted during a Turkish operation against suspected Kurd militants. More than 600,000 Iraqi refugees, mostly Kurds and Arab Shi'ites, combined with 1.6 million Afghan refugees to make Iran the top country of asylum. In Yemen, Somali refugees, many of whom had previously found themselves on the front line between warring sides of Yemeni, fell prey to a campaign

SEBASTIÃO SALGADO

Vietnamese children crowd a cage at a detention centre in Hong Kong. Despite the return of many of the boat people to their homeland, it was estimated that at the beginning of 1995 some 40,000 Vietnamese refugees continued to live in camps throughout Southeast Asia.

of forced repatriation. Two years after the signing of a declaration of principles between Israel and the Palestine Liberation Organization, Palestinian refugees were forcibly pushed out of Libya and put under increasing pressure to leave Lebanon as well.

In Asia more than 200,000 Burmese Muslim refugees had repatriated from Bangladesh since September 1992, and 50,000 remained in camps in Bangladesh. The repatriation of Sri Lankan Tamil refugees from southern India ebbed and flowed in tandem with developments in Sri Lanka. More than 10,000 Sri Lankans returned in the first half of 1995, but 54,000 remained in camps in India. Some 85,000 Bhutanese refugees remained in camps in Nepal as efforts to resolve their plight proved fruitless. Plans to settle Indo-Chinese asylum seekers met a temporary roadblock when 41,000 Vietnamese nonrefugees refused to repatriate in the hope that proposed legislation would allow them to resettle in the United States. Nearly a million Vietnamese had fled after the fall of the Saigon government in 1975, and the vast majority had resettled in other countries. Under the Comprehensive Plan of Action for Indo-Chinese Refugees (CPA), those who had left for reasons other than a well-founded fear of persecution were designated for repatriation. Of the more than 73,000 persons who had returned to Vietnam since the implementation of the CPA in 1989, UNHCR found no significant cases of persecution.

The plight of Cubans and Haitians who had taken to the high seas and then been apprehended and sequestered at the United States naval base at Guantánamo Bay, Cuba, was resolved. Following a political breakthrough in Haiti and the reinstatement of Pres. Jean-Bertrand Aristide, Haitians were repatriated, involuntarily in many cases. Most of the 21,000 Cubans at Guantánamo were allowed to enter the U.S., but any Cubans picked up at sea would be returned to Cuba after Pres. Bill Clinton revoked a long-standing U.S. policy of granting asylum to all Cubans. The repatriation of the more than 40,000 Guatemalan refugees in Mexico proceeded cautiously; the deliberate killing of returnees by paramilitary groups, notably in the fall, amplified the wariness of potential returnees. The United States issued guidelines to help immigration officers grant asylum to women who were threatened with sexual violence, which was used as political persecution in their homeland. The new guidelines did not change the criteria needed for refugee status but rather educated asylum officers about gender-based discrimination and provided them with procedures and methods for evaluating refugee standards for individual claims.

(UNHCR)

This article updates the *Macropædia* article POPULATION.

RACE AND ETHNIC RELATIONS

Worldwide, the catalog of race and ethnic problems continued to be long and grim in 1995.

Europe. Russia's Human Rights Commission reported that 24,000 civilians had been killed in Grozny after 40,000 Russian troops entered the republic of Chechnya in December 1994 to quell a rebellion by Chechen separatists.

Croatian and Bosnian Muslim forces routed Bosnian Serbs to retake much of the territory lost in the bloody three-year civil war in Bosnia and Herzegovina. While retaliatory "ethnic cleansing" continued, the U.S. brokered a cease-fire between all parties—Croats, Serbs, and Muslims—and helped negotiate a peace agreement in November. Thousands of ethnic Georgians were expelled from the autonomous republic of Abkhazia by February 1995. The war in the Azerbaijani enclave of Nagorno-Karabakh, where Armenians formed the bulk of the population, had so far claimed 20,000 lives and left 600,000 people homeless.

In France radical Algerian Islamists were suspected of a 1994 airline hijacking and repeated bombings of civilian targets, primarily in Paris. Neo-Nazi extremists were suspects in the February bomb explosion that killed four Gypsies in Austria and in the firebombing of Turkish mosques, travel agencies, and German cultural centres in Cologne, Gelsenkirchen, and Erlenbach. During the week in early May when the 50th anniversary of V-E (Victory in Europe) Day was commemorated, a fire was set in a synagogue in Lübeck, tombstones of Nazi victims were toppled in Berlin, and that city's New Synagogue was rededicated.

In Spain, Basque terrorists kidnapped a Madrid businessman. The government opened an inquiry into the deaths in 1993 of Basque guerrillas, apparently at the hands of death squads employed by the Ministry of Interior. Britain engaged in peace talks held in Washington, D.C., with Sinn Fein, the political arm of the Irish Republican Army, over the fate of Northern Ireland. A vote of the Slovak parliament curbing the use of the Hungarian language angered citizens of Hungarian descent and led Prime Minister Gyula Horn of Hungary to protest. He claimed that this action violated the European Convention on Human Rights and could jeopardize the entry of each country into the European Union.

North America. In the U.S. in October, some 835,000 blacks peacefully participated in the "Million Man March" in Washington, D.C., to demonstrate solidarity among black males and to bring about a spiritual renewal that would instill a sense of personal responsibility for improving the condition of African-Americans. The event was organized by Louis Farrakhan, leader of the Nation of Islam, and directed by Benjamin F. Chavis, Jr., the former executive director of the National Association for the Advancement of Colored People. The NAACP, under the chairmanship of Myrlie Evers-Williams (*see* BIOGRAPHIES), did not endorse the march. The march and the not-guilty verdict in the trial of former football star O.J. Simpson, a black, accused of murdering his estranged wife and one of her friends, both white, elicited vastly different reactions among blacks and whites and placed race relations, the plight of black youth, and the condition of black urban neighbourhoods at the centre of a national policy debate. Kweisi Mfume of Maryland resigned his congressional seat to take over as president and chief executive officer of the NAACP. Mfume vowed to revitalize the nation's oldest and largest civil rights organization, which had been troubled by scandal and controversy for over two years.

The results of several studies conducted by the *New York Times* over two decades suggested that although blacks were victims in one-half of all murders committed each year, 85% of those executed had killed a white, while 11% had murdered a black. The results indicated that the death penalty was imposed more often when the victim was white, whether the killer was black or white.

In Canada, Quebec's governing party, the Parti Québécois, held an October referendum on sovereignty. After the measure was narrowly defeated, Quebec Premier Jacques Parizeau dealt a blow to the separatist movement's pledge to ethnic pluralism and diversity by remarking in a concession speech that the defeat was caused by "money and the ethnic vote."

In Mexico's Chiapas state, representatives of the federal government and Zapatista guerrillas held peace talks in January, April, and October to end an almost two-year insurgency over demands for better living conditions for Mayan Indian peasants, the poorest in Mexico.

South America. Macushi Indians in Roraima state, Brazil, demanded that the government fulfill a promise to set aside

Defendant O.J. Simpson smiles as the jury's not guilty verdict is read in court on October 3. The trial raised a number of troubling issues, including the way law officials handle domestic violence, the gulf between races in the U.S., and live television coverage of trials.
SYGMA

10,460 sq km (6,500 sq mi) of ancestral land as an official reserve, a move vigorously opposed by local settlers. In a nearby area, civil rights advocates filed a complaint with the Inter-American Commission on Human Rights, claiming that Yanomamö Indians had been the victims of genocidal killings when gold miners had camped on their land two years earlier.

Asia. A force of 35,000 Turkish troops crossed the border into Iraq in March to crush Iraqi Kurdish guerrillas who were assisting Turkish Kurds in their long-simmering rebellion.

The Israeli government and the Palestinians completed negotiations for the withdrawal of Israeli troops from about 30% of the territory of the occupied West Bank, giving the Palestinians control of the seven largest towns there. In Israel bombings continued by such extremist groups as Hamas and Islamic Jihad. Muslim guerrillas of the Hezbollah launched attacks on Israeli troops in southern Lebanon and on Israeli civilians in northern Israel. Negotiations with Syria over the disposition of the Israeli-occupied Golan Heights remained deadlocked, but in December U.S. Secretary of State Warren Christopher indicated that talks might soon resume.

India remained troubled by religious and ethnic conflict. Hindu extremists advocated suppression of the country's Muslims, Sikhs sought a separate state in Punjab, and Muslim rebels in Jammu and Kashmir opposed India's rule over the country's only state with a Muslim majority. In Pakistan, Sunni Muslim gunmen fired into Shi'ite mosques in Karachi in February, killing 20 worshipers. By October more than 2,500 persons had been killed in sectarian clashes in Karachi alone. The Mohajir Qaumi Movement stepped up efforts to gain greater autonomy in Karachi for Muslims who fled India in 1947. Tamil separatist rebels broke a three-month cease-fire with Sri Lankan government troops in April, ending negotiations over possible concessions toward Tamil autonomy in the northern part of the country. Attacks on military bases and bombings in villages over several months resulted in hundreds of Tamil and Sinhalese deaths. (*See* SPOTLIGHT: *Secularism in South Asia.*)

In January troops of Myanmar's (Burma's) military junta captured the headquarters and last stronghold of the Karen National Union on the Thai-Burmese border. The ethnic-based movement had been fighting for independence from Myanmar since 1948. Several months later Burmese troops, joined by dissident Karens, attacked Karen refugee camps in Thailand.

Africa. Virtually all African countries south of the Sahara exhibited ethnopolitical divisions. Rwanda struggled in the aftermath of the deaths of an estimated 500,000 persons, mostly Tutsi, at the hands of Hutu soldiers and militia. The Tutsi-dominated government engaged in vigilante justice and attempts at legal retribution. In neighbouring Burundi, where a long-standing Tutsi government ruled over an ethnic population comprising 15% Tutsi and 85% Hutu, clashes between Hutu and Tutsi occurred regularly.

Clan rivalry and violence continued sporadically in Somalia. Northern clans cooperated to administer a self-styled "Republic of Somaliland"; no central government had returned to southern Somalia. The execution of prominent writer Ken Saro-Wiwa (*see* OBITUARIES) in November brought charges by Human Rights Watch of genocide against the Ogoni people by the military government of Nigeria.

A cease-fire was negotiated between the Sudanese government, now dominated by Islamic fundamentalists, and southern rebels (Christian and animists) who had been fighting for independence or autonomy since 1983. In Mali, Tuareg rebels, who also operated in neighbouring Niger, attacked settlements and government outposts near Timbuktu and other towns on the edge of the Sahara desert. Liberia's six-year civil war between factions originating in ethnoregional groups that spanned the country's borders came to a negotiated end.

Racial division narrowed in South Africa, five years after the official end of apartheid, with racial integration the rule in all public institutions. Majority black rule seemed to have brought a decline in political and racial violence, although KwaZulu/Natal province remained the primary scene of political killings and unrest within the Zulu population. Threats from the "white right" and calls for a separate *volkstaat* (Afrikaner enclave) were diluted considerably by mainstream politics, which promoted cross-racial alliances. The National Party made gains among Coloureds in Western Cape province, and the African National Congress attracted many white liberals.

Islamic militants assaulted government officials and foreigners in Egypt and Algeria. While visiting Addis Ababa, Eth., in June, Egyptian Pres. Hosni Mubarak survived an assassination attempt, which he blamed on Sudanese Islamic fundamentalists. The government of Algeria continued a counterterrorist campaign against several militant Islamic groups after hard-line police and army officials rejected a peace plan put together by the opposition leadership. In the mountainous Kabylie region, armed Berber groups fought militant Islamists. (*See* SPOTLIGHT: *The Berbers of North Africa.*) (HARVEY GLICKMAN)

SOCIAL PROTECTION

Efforts were made throughout most parts of the world in 1995 to ease the strain brought about by widespread unemployment and to restructure and reform benefit programs. Social security benefits and programs in Western Europe were used to promote the introduction of new and flexible forms of employment. Countries in Central and Eastern Europe followed the lead of their Western neighbours, but they were primarily concerned with ensuring that large segments of the population did not fall below a minimum standard of living. In industrialized Asia and the Pacific, efforts were made to combat discrimination in the distribution of social security benefits. Major reforms were proposed but not implemented in emerging and less developed countries. In North America the U.S. and Canada initiated a massive restructuring of social policy, as did Mexico, where a 52-year-old social security system was on the brink of collapse.

North America. The first U.S. Republican-controlled Congress in 40 years moved to cut back and dismantle welfare, health care, and other social policies launched during Pres. Franklin D. Roosevelt's New Deal and expanded under Pres. Lyndon B. Johnson's Great Society.

The Republicans wanted to reduce federal spending and administrative involvement by turning more control over to states and ending entitlements, which guaranteed benefits to every eligible individual. Opponents called the changes "social regression" and charged that critical assistance would end for large numbers of children and other needy and disadvantaged persons. At the end of the year, portions of the government were shut down in the impasse between the two sides.

Congress began its revision of social programs by overhauling the $23 billion, 60-year-old welfare program that had supported 4.7 million families and more than 9 million children with cash benefits, child care, child protection, school meals, and nutritional aid. The House of Representatives passed a welfare-reform measure in March, and the Senate followed in September. The two versions agreed on the general thrust of reform but differed in some important aspects, with the House clamping down harder than the Senate. Both bills called for replacing the existing entitlement program with lump-sum block grants to the states, which would run their own programs and take responsibility for determining eligibility and the establishment of job training and child-care assistance.

Certain limitations were set, requiring most recipients to work within two years of receiving benefits and limiting them to a lifetime maximum of five years on welfare rolls. The bills denied noncitizens access to a variety of services. The House version barred states from using federal funding to provide cash assistance to unwed teenage mothers or children born to welfare recipients. The Senate proposal made those restrictions optional. The House measure did not include provisions to expand education, job training, and federally subsidized jobs, which were part of the Senate bill.

The changes would reduce federal welfare spending over seven years by an estimated $66 billion (Senate) to $90 billion (House). Critics estimated that the cuts would end benefits for more than 100,000 children. President Clinton, who had called for "an end to welfare as we know it" during his 1992 election campaign, vetoed the Republican bill in December. His counterproposal promised additional education, job training, and child-care assistance to help cushion the transition.

Even before Congress acted, some states obtained or requested waivers to revamp their welfare programs. Wisconsin, Michigan, New Jersey, and Massachusetts were among those experimenting with policies that required beneficiaries to work and limited the time they could remain on welfare. Several states reported reductions in welfare rolls and spending, but some observers questioned the extent and lasting effects of the gains.

In terms of the number of people affected and potential savings, the most significant social program targeted for reform by the Congress was Medicare, the federal health-insurance program, begun in 1965, that covered 37.2 million elderly and disabled. Soaring costs prompted trustees of the fund to forecast that Medicare would be insolvent by the year 2002 if nothing was done. The Congressional Budget Office estimated that without significant changes, the cost of Medicare would rise to $455 billion, or 18.6% of the federal budget, in 2005 from $178 billion, or 11.7%, in 1995. Citing these concerns, the House of Representatives approved a plan that would reduce projected Medicare spending by $270 billion over the next seven years. Democrats, while acknowledging the need to slow Medicare costs, contended that the Republicans wanted to gut the program in order to fund a tax cut for the wealthy. They offered their own plan for a $90 billion, seven-year cut.

Most of the savings in the Republican plan would be realized from smaller increases in payments to doctors, hospitals, and other health-care providers and from limiting malpractice awards and cracking down on fraud and abuse. Premiums would be raised for most beneficiaries, with larger increases for the wealthiest. Seniors would be encouraged to move into private health maintenance organizations and other managed-care plans, but they could choose to keep their existing fee-for-service Medicare coverage.

John Peters Humphrey

In 1968 French jurist René Cassin was honoured with the Nobel Peace Prize as the author of the Universal Declaration of Human Rights, adopted and proclaimed by the UN General Assembly on Dec. 10, 1948. This document, which served as "a common standard of achievement for all peoples of all nations," was vitally important in focusing global attention on human rights, a term that previously had not been defined in any act of international law. Although some nations routinely violated the principles of the declaration, most countries not only accepted its precepts but adhered to them. In 1988, however, John Hobbins of the law library at McGill University, Montreal, examined the original document and found that it had been written not in the hand of Cassin but in that of John Peters Humphrey.

Humphrey, a Canadian lawyer, diplomat, and scholar, died in Montreal, on March 14, 1995, having been belatedly recognized as the architect of the "Magna Carta of mankind." He was born April 30, 1905, in Hampton, N.B. His childhood was unfortunate. At the age of six he lost his left arm in a fire, and from the age of 11 he was raised in orphanages. Humphrey entered Mount Allison University, Sackville, N.B., at 15 and was called to the Quebec bar in 1929. He practiced law until 1936, when he joined the faculty of McGill, specializing in international law. In 1946 he was appointed the first director of the Division of Human Rights for the UN Secretariat, a post he held for two decades. It was there that he penned the Declaration.

In 1966 he returned to McGill, and he remained active as a human rights crusader, helping to establish both the Canadian Human Rights Foundation and the Canadian branch of Amnesty International. Humphrey was the author of numerous books, notably *Human Rights and the United Nations: A Great Adventure* (1984) and *No Distant Millennium: The World Law of Human Rights* (1989). (KAREN J. SPARKS)

Medicaid—a medical assistance program jointly financed by state and federal governments for qualified low-income individuals—was also targeted for reform. Under a new proposal, the main responsibility for running Medicaid would be shifted to the states, which would receive lump-sum payments from Congress and the responsibility to decide, within flexible guidelines, whom to cover and at what level.

Proponents of the overhaul said it would save the federal government $182 billion over seven years. Foes denounced it as an assault on children and the elderly and noted that 39.7 million Americans did not have health insurance.

Republicans pushed for cutbacks, stricter regulations, greater state responsibility, and changes in such other programs as food stamps, subsidized housing, legal aid, job training, and supplemental security income for the aged, blind, and disabled. They also sought to tighten eligibility standards and to reduce the cost of the earned income tax credit, which provided $25 billion in direct tax refunds to about 20 million low-income working families.

The only changes scheduled in social security for 1996 were the annual adjustments in benefits and taxes. However, major revisions were proposed, including a rise in the retirement age and a reduction in the annual cost-of-living adjustment in benefits, in anticipation of an influx into the system of retired baby boomers. The automatic annual increase would boost benefits by 2.6% in 1996, raising the average monthly payment for a retired worker from $702 to $720 and from $1,184 to $1,215 for couples. The social security tax rate would remain at 12.4%, but it would be levied on the first $62,700 of workers' salaries, up from $61,200 in 1995. An additional 2.9% Medicare tax (one-half of which was paid by employers and the other half paid by employees) would continue to apply to all wages.

Social program retrenchments in Canada were significant, though not as broad as in the U.S. Canada had been considered socially more responsive than the U.S., with a comprehensive national health plan and generous welfare benefits. The federal government announced in February that payments transferred to the provinces for health, welfare, and postsecondary education, which amounted to nearly $30 billion in 1995, would be cut by $2.5 billion in 1996–97 and $4.5 billion in 1997–98. Starting in 1996, federal funds that had been allocated for those three areas would be lumped together in a new Canada Social Transfer Fund. Prime Minister Jean Chrétien's goal was to cut health spending by about $10 billion each year, and he was expected to push for budget cuts in pensions, child care, services for the homeless, legal aid, and help for the disabled. The Ottawa government also announced plans to review old-age security and the Canada Pension Plan and said it would consider new approaches to government-run job-training programs and the unemployment insurance system.

Some provinces, in an effort to balance budgets and cut taxes, acted to slash health and welfare benefits by imposing workfare, closing and merging hospitals, and cutting back on universal coverage that paid for doctor and hospital visits. In October the welfare rates in Ontario were reduced by 21.6%. British Columbia became the first province to impose, as of December 1, a residency requirement for those seeking welfare. These actions came at a time when the National Council of Welfare (NCW) reported that poverty rates in Canada had grown dramatically. The number of those living in poverty, as defined by the NCW, rose to 4.8 million in 1993 from 4.3 million in 1992, bringing the poverty rate to 17.4%. Children were hardest hit, with 20.8% of those under age 18 living in poverty, compared with 20.5% of people 65 and older.

(continued on page 288)

Special Report

Child Welfare Crisis

BY DAVID TOBIS

The United Nations Convention on the Rights of the Child, adopted by the General Assembly in 1989, affirmed the rights of the world's children to be protected against all forms of abuse, neglect, and exploitation. By 1995 it had been ratified by 180 nations, which made it the most widely adopted convention in human rights history. The agreement recognized the family as the primary caregiver, responsible for the growth and well-being of children. It asserted that families should receive the necessary assistance to fulfill this responsibility so that children could remain with their parents except when doing so would not be in their best interest. It also stated that children should be entitled to special protection by the state if their families could not care for them.

UNICEF uses the designation "children in especially difficult circumstances" to describe those youngsters who require the special protection outlined in the convention. Although systematic data do not exist, hundreds of millions of the world's two billion children are living in especially difficult circumstances. Ironically, it appeared in 1995 that more children were living in such conditions than when the Convention on the Rights of the Child came into force. This increase was one of the main factors contributing to the child welfare crisis.

Traditionally the family, the clan, and the community were the primary sources of assistance for children in need. Increasingly, however, government had assumed the responsibility of caring for these children, providing child welfare services—either direct help to families or substitute (*i.e.,* foster) care—when traditional sources of help were unavailable. In recent years fewer government resources relative to need were made available for these children, a situation that exacerbated the crisis.

The conditions that placed children at risk and the assistance provided varied widely from one country to another. For purposes of comparison, four areas could be identified: the industrialized nations, Eastern Europe and the former Soviet Union, the less developed nations, and those countries experiencing civil war or internal disintegration.

Industrialized Nations. In the industrialized world increased unemployment and poverty resulted in an increase in the number of children needing special protection. Policy shifts and budgetary problems unraveled social safety nets, contributing simultaneously to an increase in the number of children placed in substitute care and a deterioration in the conditions of care.

The United States, one of the wealthiest industrialized nations, historically provided very limited financial assistance or child welfare services to families; generally, help was given only after children and families had encountered severe problems, and then most funding went for out-of-home care rather than for family preservation. In 1995 many U.S. states further restricted the conditions under which mothers and children could receive financial assistance (no

David Tobis is director of social welfare research, Center for the Study of Family Policy, Hunter College, New York City, and a consultant to UNICEF and the World Bank.

state provided benefits for families at or above the poverty level), and both houses of Congress approved the elimination of the 50-year-old entitlement to financial assistance for individuals living in poverty, though the change had not yet become law. The number of children found to be abused or neglected was increasing, reaching 1,036,000 in 1994, 1.6% of the child population. In the absence of adequate assistance for families, the number of children in foster care also increased, from a low of 250,000 in 1983 to 460,000 in 1995.

As political support for child welfare programs diminished, funding—which for years was inadequate for meeting the growing need—also was reduced, forcing state agencies to cut or curtail services. In New York, for example, limits were placed on the amount of time children in need could remain in substitute care.

In contrast to the situation in the U.S., a number of European countries and Japan succeeded in protecting or improving essential child welfare services in spite of fiscal pressure of varying degrees of severity.

Eastern Europe and the Former Soviet Union. The demise of communism resulted in the elimination, privatization, or reduction of many social services and family supports, which, although of inconsistent quality, had been widely available and virtually free. The loss of these programs, coupled with an unprecedented peacetime deterioration in the standard of living, resulted in increases in several countries in the number of children abandoned in maternity wards and hospitals, placed in custodial institutions, living on the street, or involved in acts of delinquency.

Less Developed Nations. The essential focus of human development efforts in less developed nations had long been on basic health care, education, nutrition, and survival rather than on special protection for children at risk. In recent years increased poverty in large parts of the less developed world had endangered more children than ever before. At the same time, rapid urbanization and industrialization undermined the extended family and the community, institutions through which child welfare problems were formerly resolved.

The practice of child labour accounted for perhaps the greatest proportion of children in especially difficult circumstances. The International Labor Organization estimated that as many as 200 million children under the age of 15 were out of school and working to support themselves and their families. Working youngsters in African cities, many of them "street children," represented as much as 20% of the urban child population. Thailand, Sri Lanka, and the Philippines had an estimated 500,000 child prostitutes.

The HIV/AIDS pandemic not only caused the death of large numbers of parents in the less developed world but also affected those who might otherwise provide substitute care for orphans. According to the World Health Organization, by the year 2000, 10 million children would be without one or both parents as a result of AIDS. In Uganda alone, at least 150,000 children were orphaned by AIDS.

Placing children in institutions continued to be favoured in most less developed countries over informal foster care by relatives. These facilities were generally austere and regimented and sheltered only a small portion of the children in need of protection. Defence for Children International estimated that between six million and eight million children worldwide lived in institutions. Very few needed to be in such restrictive settings. Most could be better cared for by extended families or community networks, in temporary family foster care, or in permanent adoptive homes.

Nations Experiencing Civil War or Internal Disintegration. With the end of the Cold War, the number of children affected by armed conflict and social disintegration, rather than decreasing, increased significantly, particularly in Africa but also in Asia, Central and Eastern Europe, and Latin America. Half of the 23 million refugees and 25 million displaced persons in the world were children. In Rwanda alone 114,000 children were separated from their families or orphaned as a result of mass killings, exodus, and epidemics in 1994.

Relief agencies increasingly worked toward strengthening vulnerable families and promoting family reunification. Restoring families became nearly impossible in some areas, however, as many countries with large refugee populations made their immigration policies more restrictive.

The Future. The conditions that caused children to live in especially difficult circumstances did not appear likely to diminish, and few new resources would be devoted to remedying such problems. UNICEF estimated that countries would devote only a small amount—an annual addition of $1.05 per child to the end of the century—toward the conditions of children at risk. Although industrialized nations pledged at least 0.7% of their gross national product in official development assistance to the less developed world, only Norway, Sweden, Denmark, and The Netherlands had followed through on this commitment.

Nevertheless, in the 1990s there was a gradual acceptance worldwide that children had legal rights, and children themselves were increasingly aware of these rights. Until 1995 the main focus of UN agencies had been universal ratification of the Convention on the Rights of the Child. With this goal near, the focus shifted to implementation of the convention, which would truly benefit children.

LAURENT VAN DER STOCKT—GAMMA LIAISON

Children have bread and tea at an orphanage in Kabul, capital of Afghanistan. As in other countries suffering from civil warfare, the destruction of families in Afghanistan, with its resultant suffering among children, has created unprecedented needs for foster care.

(continued from page 286)

In the U.S. the Census Bureau reported that the number of people living in poverty dropped by 1.2 million in 1994, to 38.1 million, the first year-to-year decline since 1989. The proportion of those below the poverty line, defined as $15,141 for a family of four, fell from 15.1% in 1993 to 14.5% in 1994.

Western Europe. In this region, where 10% of the economically active population suffered from unemployment, a number of governments promoted alternative jobs that made working life more flexible and provided a possible way of preventing additional job losses and of reducing unemployment. Social security benefits were used by employers to entice employees to accept part-time work, reduced weekly or annual work hours, night or weekend work, fixed-term employment, and participation in job-sharing and extended-leave programs. Denmark's special-leave program—launched to encourage employees to take time off work and thereby allow temporary employment for some of the unemployed—proved so popular that it had to be curtailed by 10%. Under the old plan, employees were paid 80% of the maximum unemployment benefit when they took time off for job training, sabbaticals, or parental leave.

Belgium introduced a program that entitled employees to take up to two months off work to care for an elderly parent or someone with an incurable disease. During this time social security coverage continued without interruption and the employee was granted a pay allowance.

As alternative working practices spread, a number of countries recognized a need to avoid discrimination. In the United Kingdom both full- and part-time workers would receive the same benefits in cases of layoffs and wrongful dismissal. In The Netherlands one of the largest funds announced that it would grant pensions to part-time workers and, in compliance with a ruling by the European Court of Justice, would credit service back to 1976. The European Commission drafted a directive to eliminate sex discrimination affecting occupational pension benefits.

Most social security payments in Western Europe were made on an individual basis, rather than as a joint benefit payment to couples. Switzerland abolished a joint benefit for couples and introduced provisions for early retirement. It also raised the retirement age for women from 62 to 63, effective in 2001, and to 64 in 2005. The retirement age for men remained unchanged at 65.

In an effort to reduce the absentee rate due to sickness, the Dutch government considered privatizing sick leave by obligating employers to cover the costs on the basis of civil law. During the summer Italy passed a long-awaited pension reform that was similar to the Swedish plan, which linked retirement benefits to life expectancy and gave incentives to those who purchased private coverage.

In France, however, attempts by the government to change the social security system led to a series of strikes that forced a renegotiation of the plan.

Central and Eastern Europe. Countries in Central and Eastern Europe faced difficulties in implementing their social security systems owing to persistently high levels of inflation and unemployment. Governments made efforts, however, to maintain minimum standards of living and to continue the payment of benefits.

In Russia minimum wages and pensions were more than doubled, while Lithuania launched a program granting special income support to families in need. After the approval in May of an austerity package in Hungary, the government planned to reduce allowances for child care, maternity, and families as of July 1, 1995. The Constitutional Court decided against these cuts, ruling that those concerned would not have enough time to prepare for the changes and that the protection of families, mothers, and children was guaranteed under the constitution. The Ministry of Social Affairs of Estonia was preparing a new law that would introduce a supplementary earnings-related pension. Attempts were made in Bulgaria to combat long-term unemployment with the introduction of a national part-time employment program that would encourage employers to hire the unemployed on a short-term, part-time basis. Romania sought to reduce its unemployment problem by offering early retirement.

Industrialized Asia and the Pacific. In Japan there was continued concern about the effects of an aging population on economic and social systems. A group of experts commissioned by the Ministry of Health and Welfare proposed long-term-care insurance that would cover persons aged 65 and older and would be funded by additional contributions to social security. The ministry projected that within five years the aging population and growing medical costs would require an increase of up to 25% in contributions made to social security health insurance.

Hong Kong launched an improved social security package that included increases in existing benefits and the introduction of new ones, notably a special supplement to single-parent families. In Taiwan new national health insurance legislation came into force, covering employed persons and their dependents; the latter did not qualify for benefits under previous regulations.

Australia continued to pay social security benefits on an individual basis rather than making combined payments to couples or families. A parenting allowance was introduced for spouses of welfare recipients or low-wage earners whose main responsibility was caring for dependent children under age 16. It was paid to the primary caregiver for a dependent child but was subject to an income threshold. In New Zealand pension plans were required to obtain independent legal counsel to comply with the 1993 Human Rights Act.

Emerging and Less Developed Countries. Though no major social security reforms were reported, debate centred on the elements of reform that should be addressed prior to a comprehensive overhaul of the system. In Brazil the Commission on Constitution and Justice removed a major obstacle to reform by ruling that the revision of the "long-service pension" was permitted under the constitution. The pension, which could be paid to an employee of any age after 30 years of service, was one of the main financial drains on the country's social security system. In June Uruguay's president drafted a social security reform plan that included a mixed system of pay-as-you-go and capitalization. Pension reform stemming from changes made since 1993 to both the health and workers' compensation plans was under discussion in Nicaragua.

Problems of inadequate coverage and financial imbalances continued to plague many emerging and less developed countries. Nevertheless, Bahrain and Iran offered coverage to the self-employed, and the Philippines adopted legislation that extended health coverage to all citizens. In China individual cities and provinces introduced social security reforms and experimented with plans for retirement, health, work injury, and unemployment. The Caribbean nations of Dominica, Grenada, and St. Vincent and the Grenadines increased the levels of benefits paid to the insured and introduced additional benefits. Malawi announced that it would establish a workers' compensation fund followed by a comprehensive social security plan.

(CHRISTIANE KUPTSCH; DAVID M. MAZIE)

See also Business and Industry Review: *Insurance;* Education; Health and Disease.

This article updates the *Macropædia* article SOCIAL WELFARE.

Religion

During 1995 religious groups faced challenges in relating to one another and to government policies in various countries. Internally, many continued to grapple with the role of women in the ordained ministry and whether to accept certain sexual practices among adherents. It was a year of restructuring and leadership changes for some, and the impact of science on faith—and the uses of technology in its propagation—gained renewed attention.

In an encyclical in May titled *Ut unum sint* ("That They May Be One"), Pope John Paul II called for greater efforts to overcome the differences separating Roman Catholics from Orthodox Christians and Protestants while insisting that the office of the papacy had to remain the prime authority on the faith. A month later the pope joined with Orthodox Ecumenical Patriarch Bartholomew I in celebrating a liturgy at the Vatican and in describing the role of the papacy as one of service, not power.

In the interfaith sphere Vatican and Muslim officials announced in June the formation of a Joint Liaison Committee to explore their respective positions on religious and social issues. Earlier during the month the opening of a mosque in Rome was welcomed by the Vatican, and an official of the Holy See said it would be desirable for a Catholic church to be built in Saudi Arabia "as soon as possible." While the mosque made history on the European continent, what was described as the biggest Hindu temple in the Western world opened in the Neasden district of London. It was sponsored by the Swaminarayan sect, which was founded in the 19th century in the Indian province of Gujarat and had a strong following in London.

Britain's religious diversity also was highlighted when Prince Charles declared in a television interview that if he became the sovereign he wanted to be known as "Defender of Faith" in general rather than accepting the traditional title of "Defender of the Faith," referring to that of the Church of England.

In the United States the Supreme Court broke new ground in a 5–4 ruling stating that the refusal of the University of Virginia to give money for a student Christian magazine while subsidizing other student publications was a violation of free-speech rights. The decision marked the first time that the high court had approved public money for a religious activity. While Justice David Souter said in a dissenting opinion that the decision violated the First Amendment's establishment clause, Justice Anthony Kennedy wrote for the majority that no public money would have gone directly to the periodical since the subsidy would have gone to an outside printer.

In another case the court ruled 7–2 that government must afford private religious speech as much public access as secular speech. It upheld the Ku Klux Klan's right to erect a cross in front of the Ohio statehouse on the ground that the area had become a public forum.

In April a federal judge ruled in Oxford, Miss., that organized prayer in public schools is unconstitutional even if organized by students. During the same month, a broad national coalition of religious and legal groups issued a set of guidelines for accommodation of religion in the public schools. Pres. Bill Clinton and Secretary of Education Richard Riley drew on the document in issuing a similar one in August for the nation's 15,000 public school districts.

The Internal Revenue Service revoked the tax-exempt status of the Church at Pierce Creek in Conklin, N.Y., because of ads the church had taken out in 1992 urging Christians not to vote for Clinton. The IRS action was believed to be the first of its kind taken against a local congregation. The General Council of the Assemblies of God found itself hit with a sexual discrimination lawsuit by the U.S. Equal Employment Opportunity Commission in response to an allegation that male employees of its headquarters in Springfield, Mo., who had engaged in extramarital affairs were disciplined more leniently than females.

The Minnesota Court of Appeals ruled in April that a $9 million punitive damages award against the mother church of the Christian Science faith was unconstitutional because it sought to force the church to give up its belief in spiritual healing. The 1993 decision, resulting from the death of an 11-year-old boy whose Christian Scientist mother refused to provide him with medical care, had been the first civil verdict against the church.

The Chinese government accused the Dalai Lama of breaking the rules of his own faith by proclaiming a six-year-old boy as the reincarnation of the Panchen Lama, the second most important monk in Tibetan Buddhism, claiming that this was done improperly. The government installed its own claimant in December.

In response to a decision by Lutheran Archbishop Janis Vanags to stop ordaining women because of the negative effect it had on relations with the Roman Catholic and Orthodox churches, the council of the Lutheran World Federation called on its 122 member churches to support female clergy, saying that "ordination should not become a bargaining tool" in relationships with other churches.

The General Synod of the 215,000-member Christian Reformed Church (CRC), meeting in Grand Rapids, Mich., gave district governing bodies the option of declaring the denomination's male-only requirement for the offices of pastor and elder to be inoperative. That action led the 239,000-member Presbyterian Church in America to urge the North American Presbyterian and Reformed Council to expel the CRC.

A survey of 4,900 clergy in 16 Protestant denominations conducted by Hartford (Conn.) Seminary found that the percentage of female clergy had declined over eight years in denominations that were once at the forefront of women's ordination. The study found that only 11% of the clergy were female, despite a near doubling of female seminary enrollment since 1980.

Although the Vatican moved no closer toward the ordination of women in 1995, John Paul surprised many feminists when he issued a letter apologizing for Catholic involvement in policies that had relegated women to the margins of society. Harvard law professor Mary Ann Glendon was selected to chair the 20-member Vatican delegation to the United Nations Fourth World Conference on Women in Beijing in September; this made her the first woman to take the leadership role for the church at a major international gathering.

Conservative Rabbi Bea Wyler became Germany's first female rabbi since the Holocaust when she was named in August to head two congregations in Lower Saxony state. The appointment was sharply criticized by Ignatz Bubis, an Orthodox Jew who headed the Central Conference of Jews in Germany and whose branch of Judaism did not recognize women rabbis.

The 36 archbishops of the Anglican Communion said in a pastoral letter in March that patterns of human sexuality by church members "at variance with the received Christian moral tradition" posed issues that

PAOLO COCCO—REUTERS

Patriarch Bartholomew I (left) and Pope John Paul II celebrate mass in St. Peter's Basilica at the Vatican. The religious leaders held historic meetings in June to discuss relations between the Orthodox and Roman Catholic churches, as well as ecological problems and other concerns.

"do not always admit of easy, instant answers." A study published in June by the Church of England's Board for Social Responsibility said couples who lived together without marrying should not be viewed as "living in sin" and that the church should welcome single, married, separated, or cohabiting couples, in either heterosexual or homosexual relationships.

In the U.S. the 2.5 million-member Episcopal Church announced that retired bishop Walter C. Righter of Iowa would be put on a church trial for having knowingly ordained a noncelibate homosexual, Barry Stopfel, as a deacon in 1990. Righter denied having violated church law, and before the charges were brought against Righter, a five-bishop panel appointed by Presiding Bishop Edmond Browning ruled that "there is no provision of the Constitution or Canons of the church which prohibits the ordination of homosexuals." The Rev. Jeanne Audrey Powers, a prominent ecumenical leader in the United Methodist Church, became the highest-ranking official in the 8.6 million-member denomination to announce that she was gay. The church's rules declared the practice of homosexuality incompatible with Christian teaching. Powers refused to say whether she was a practicing homosexual but said her July announcement was "an act of resistance to false teachings that have contributed to heresy and homophobia within the church itself."

After the 150th meeting of the Southern Baptist Convention in Atlanta, Ga., repented of its racist roots, the 15.6 million-member denomination approved a restructuring plan that was designed to reduce the number of its national agencies from 19 to 12 and that included its first-ever comprehensive mission statement. An ad hoc committee of U.S. Catholic bishops proposed several changes for the U.S. Catholic Church, including combining its two major national organizations into one and pressing for a more collegial relationship with the Vatican.

The Worldwide Church of God suffered losses of membership and income after a January sermon by Pastor General Joseph W. Tkach, Sr., in which he said that tithing and observing the sabbath on Saturday were no longer mandatory. Tkach, who succeeded church founder Herbert W. Armstrong, moved the group closer to Christian orthodoxy before he died in September. A drop in income led to cutbacks in the church's headquarters staff in Pasadena, Calif., and in its magazine, *The Plain Truth*. More than 100 dissident clergy gathered in Indianapolis, Ind., in April to form a breakaway group called the United Church of God.

Nearly 200 leaders from a broad spectrum of religious faiths issued a statement in Washington, D.C., in May urging an end to the patenting of human and animal life forms for profit. Jeremy Rifkin, a biotechnology critic and organizer of the religious coalition, said the statement presaged "a great historical debate about to unfold between religion and commerce."

Australian physicist Paul Davies (*see* Biographies), who once wrote that science "offers a surer path to God than religion," won the $1 million Templeton Prize for Progress in Religion in 1995. Davies, whose works include *The Mind of God* (1992), said when the award was announced that "I do not like to think of God as another object or another force at work in the universe. When I use the word 'god' I use it probably rather in the same way Einstein used the word 'god'—to mean something which underpins this ordered universe."

Less than a year after assuming the presidency of the Church of Jesus Christ of Latter-day Saints, 87-year-old Howard W. Hunter died in March (*see* Obituaries). Other notable deaths in 1995 included Carl Mau, former general secretary of the Lutheran World Federation (*see* Obituaries), and Patriarch Volodymyr of the Ukrainian Orthodox Church. The Rev. Nilson Fanini of Brazil (*see* Biographies) became president of the Baptist World Alliance, and the Rev. H. George Anderson, president of Luther College, Decorah, Iowa, was elected presiding bishop of the Evangelical Lutheran Church in America. Archbishop Iakovos, who had led the Greek Orthodox Church in the Western Hemisphere since 1959, announced that he would retire in 1996.

(DARRELL J. TURNER)

PROTESTANT CHURCHES

Anglican Communion. The Anglican Church of Mexico became the newest province in the Anglican Communion in 1995. Previously a missionary district of the U.S. Episcopal Church, the 1994 Episcopal Convention granted the five Mexican dioceses permission to withdraw in order to become an autonomous province effective Jan. 1, 1995. The Mexican church held its first General Synod in February and elected Bishop José G. Saucedo of Cuernavaca as its first primate and leader.

In England, Bishop David Hope was named archbishop of York, the second highest post in the Church of England. Hope, an Anglo-Catholic, had been bishop of London since 1991. His appointment was seen as a move to balance the more evangelical style of Archbishop of Canterbury George Carey.

A new 900-page volume, *A Prayer Book for Australia,* was authorized by an overwhelming majority during the Anglican Church of Australia's General Synod in July. Meanwhile, the diocese of Sydney postponed voting on a proposal allowing deacons and laypersons to preside at Holy Communion. The measure breaks a 450-year-old Anglican tradition of allowing only ordained priests and bishops to celebrate Holy Communion.

The Episcopal Church in the U.S. survived a year of scandals that included an embezzlement by its national treasurer, a suicide of a leading bishop, and an ecclesiastical trial against a bishop. Presiding Bishop Edmund Browning announced in May that former national treasurer Ellen Cooke had diverted $2.2 million from church funds during a five-year period. Cooke, who had resigned in January, had been the second highest paid national member. A grand jury indictment on embezzlement and theft charges was expected.

In January, 10 bishops filed a formal "letter of presentment" charging Bishop Walter C. Righter with "holding and teaching doctrine contrary to that of the Episcopal Church" because he ordained an avowed practicing homosexual to the diaconate. Righter, the retired bishop of Iowa, was currently assistant bishop of Newark, N.J. By August the required one-fourth of the 297-member House of Bishops had consented to allow the presentment charges to proceed to a trial. The trial, scheduled for February 1996, would be the first ecclesiastical trial of a bishop in the Episcopal Church since 1924.

Bishop David Johnson of Massachusetts, the largest diocese in the Episcopal Church, died in January of a self-inflicted gunshot wound. The diocese later revealed that the bishop, who had already announced his retirement, had been involved in extramarital affairs over several years and had made at least one previous attempt to take his life.

On the brighter side, Episcopal Church membership increased in 1994 for the fourth consecutive year, reversing a decline that had begun in 1966. Baptized church membership topped 2.5 million for the first time since 1986. (DAVID E. SUMNER)

Baptist Churches. At its annual meeting, the Southern Baptist Convention (SBC), the largest Protestant denomination in the U.S., adopted a resolution renouncing its racist roots. The body took action, apologizing for its past defense of slavery. The resolution called for the assembly "to unwaveringly denounce racism, in all its forms, as deplorable sin" and to "lament and repudiate historic acts of evil such as slavery from which we continue to reap a bitter harvest."

Minorities continued to be the main source of growth in the SBC, as they had been since 1980. Currently about 500,000 were African-American, with another 300,000 being ethnic minorities.

Aidsand F. Wright-Riggins III, executive director of the American Baptist National Ministries (Northern Baptists), noted in response, "Isn't it ironic that 150 years after the split of the Baptist denomination over slavery, the sons of former slave owners must now come to the table to apologize to a son and daughter of former slaves. The arc of the universe is long but it does indeed bend toward justice." Wright-Riggins went on to say, "It would be wrong to single out the SBC as the only predominantly white denomination doing too little too late. Only a handful of denominations have launched intentional strategies to seriously deal with racial justice and the growing racial/ethnic diversity of mainline denominations."

More than 20,000 "messengers" from the 15.6 million-member Southern Baptist denomination met on June 20–22, 1995, in Atlanta's Georgia Dome.

The question of acceptance of homosexuals was raised in the American Baptist Churches USA when its Board of National Ministries severed ties with the Baptist Peace Fellowship of North America "until such times as the BPF's stated aims, goals and resolutions are consistent with the American Baptist policies." The action followed a February 11 meeting of the BPFNA's Board of Directors in which that group decided to "take an active role at denominational meetings to defeat denominational resolutions that prevent gay, lesbian, and transgendered persons from becoming members of churches, being ordained, being credentialed for chaplaincy and pastoral counseling, and being employed in denominational structures." Wright-Riggins said, "We regret the truly partisan position BPFNA has taken. Many of us hoped that they would play a role of reconciler among

Christian people who have differing positions on issues related to homosexuality."

In Saudi Arabia two Philippine Baptists were jailed for holding private Bible studies. Colleagues insisted, however, that the Bible studies were not evangelistic efforts to convert Muslims.

The international membership of the Baptist World Alliance kept growing, according to a recent BWA report. The alliance included 150,619 congregations and more than 38,540,000 members, an increase over 1994 of 2,841 congregations and more than 437,000 members. The alliance marked its 90th anniversary in 1995.

(NORMAN R. DE PUY)

Christian Church (Disciples of Christ). The Christian Church (Disciples of Christ) built a dwelling place for an inner-city congregation, took several actions strengthening its ecumenical witness, and elected new leaders during its 1995 General Assembly in Pittsburgh, Pa. The biennial gathering convened under the theme "Becoming a Dwelling Place for God." Disciples members donated hundreds of hours of volunteer service and thousands of dollars toward erecting a new worship space and community centre for East Hills Community Christian Church, a 140-member congregation located in one of Pittsburgh's most impoverished neighbourhoods.

The assembly elected as its leaders for the next two years the Rev. Janet Long, moderator; Saundra Bryant, first vice moderator; and Paul Rivera, second vice moderator. The trio would preside over the General Board and Administrative Committee and the next General Assembly, which was scheduled to meet in 1997 in Denver, Colo.

The plenary body also endorsed a plan to "reconcile ordained ministries" with the church's ecumenical partner, the United Church of Christ. This action eased the way for Disciples and United Church congregations to receive each other's ordained clergy. The Disciples and the UCC declared the churches to be in "full communion" in 1989. Another highlight was the approval of "Churches in Covenant Communion," a wide-ranging church unity plan that linked the Disciples with eight other U.S. mainline denominations. Besides the Disciples and the UCC, the participants included the United Methodist and Episcopal churches and three predominantly black Methodist bodies. The assembly also backed several "mission imperatives" for the denomination that involved strengthening ministries to children and youth, nurturing faith, and engaging in mission and congregational renewal. Voting representatives also reaffirmed the denomination's commitment to affirmative action. (CLIFFORD L. WILLIS)

Churches of Christ. The international newspaper *The Christian Chronicle* highlighted world evangelism, disaster relief, efforts for worship renewal, and programs to nurture "Generation X" in 1995. There was a revival of interest across the nation in vacation Bible schools for children and a new emphasis on men and their spiritual role in the family. Ministries for seniors and families multiplied. Abilene (Texas) Christian University held its fifth workshop on "Equipping Women for Ministry," which correlated with the increasing use of women in the work of the church while reserving the roles of elder and preacher for men.

Annual Bible lectureships on each of the 21 colleges and universities associated with Churches of Christ drew thousands to study the Bible's answers to current issues. Ten thousand from primarily African-American churches attended the Crusade for Christ in Atlanta, Ga. The 51st national lectureship was sponsored by the Harlem Church in New York City. Two other national forums, the International Soul Winning Workshop in Tulsa, Okla., and Jubilee in Nashville, Tenn., were attended by thousands.

In May gifts poured into Oklahoma City, Okla., churches after the bombing of a federal building there. A task force from 29 congregations led rescue work and provided relief, housing, and counseling.

Thousands joined Manna International in a day of fasting and prayer, and gifts were provided for the hurting and helpless in Haiti, Ethiopia, Croatia, Rwanda, El Salvador, and Ghana.

At the end of five years of full-scale mission work, there were 100 churches in the former Soviet Union and 40 in Eastern Europe and the Balkans. In Haiti a Center for Biblical Studies began to train ministers and other leaders, while a church-run orphanage operated in Cap-Haïtien. Nigerian Christian Bible College began a bachelor's degree program. After 33 years Sunset School of Preaching in Lubbock, Texas, became International Bible Institute.

(M. NORVEL YOUNG)

Church of Christ, Scientist. At the 100th annual meeting of the First Church of Christ, Scientist, held in Boston on June 5, 1995, members were invited to include one another and humankind in the love and healing of scientific Christianity. Incoming church president David C. Driver of Seattle, Wash., spoke to the members about the importance of loving one's neighbour as a collective responsibility. "No one is exempt from being defined as our neighbour—no one in our family, our church, our community, our country, our world," he pointed out. "And no one is exempt from the demand to love this neighbour from the same spiritual standpoint as ourselves. This is the love that breaks down walls of division."

The meeting included presentations by the officers of the Mother Church as well as reports from members bringing out the vital role of Christian Science Reading Rooms in communities throughout the world. Virginia S. Harris, the publisher of the writings of Mary Baker Eddy, reported on the unprecedented public interest in spirituality and healing. "This surge continues," she pointed out, "and observers are predicting further growth in the next few years. In every heart there's a natural inclination toward the spiritual, the real." In speaking of the Christian Science textbook, *Science and Health with Key to the Scriptures* by Eddy, Harris added, "The increasing demand for a greater understanding of spiritual existence is a direct result of the leavening action of this book's message."

(M. VICTOR WESTBERG)

Church of Jesus Christ of Latter-day Saints. Howard W. Hunter, who became president of the church on June 5, 1994, died on March 3, 1995, after having served only nine months. (*See* OBITUARIES.) Sustained as the new president was Gordon B. Hinckley, 84, who had been an apostle since 1961 and a member of the church's First Presidency since 1981. Born in Salt Lake City, Utah, Hinckley had devoted most of his life to church public relations and pioneered in adapting modern electronic media to church uses. His counselors were Thomas S. Monson and James E. Faust. New apostles were Jeffrey R. Holland, former president of Brigham Young University, Provo, Utah, and Henry B. Eyring, former commissioner of the Church Education System.

New temples were under construction in Hong Kong; Bogotá, Colombia; Preston, England; Nashville, Tenn.; St. Louis, Mo.; Vernal and American Fork, Utah; Hartford, Conn.; Cochabamba, Bolivia; and Recife, Brazil.

Substantial welfare assistance was given to those suffering from the floods in southern Georgia and Texas and from the earthquake in Kobe, Japan. More than 28,000 food packages and several tons of clothing were sent to needy and hungry people in Albania, Croatia, Bosnia and Herzegovina, Russia, and Haiti.

With a membership of nine million by 1995, the church had 2,024 stakes (dioceses), 21,800 wards (congregations), and 310 missions in 156 nations and territories. There had been a heavy growth of membership in Mexico, Brazil, Colombia, Chile, the Philippines, and Eastern Europe.

The church celebrated the centennial of the Family History Library on Nov. 13, 1994. The largest library of its kind in the world, the collection included 2 million reels of microfilmed genealogical records, 200,000 books, and more than 300,000 microfiches.

The Mormon Tabernacle Choir performed four concerts in Washington, D.C., and New York City as part of events commemorating the 50th anniversary of the end of World War II.

(LEONARD J. ARRINGTON)

Jehovah's Witnesses. "*You* are to be Bible educators," explained Albert D. Schroeder, a member of the Governing Body of Jehovah's Witnesses. He spoke these words to the graduating missionary class of the Watchtower Bible School of Gilead that in April was the first to use the new Watchtower Educational Center in Patterson, N.Y. This complex of 28 buildings—including school facilities, an office building, and residence buildings for 1,500 was built entirely by volunteers. Since ground was broken in 1988, more than five million hours of labour had gone into the project. The centre coordinated the work of more than 1,000 translators in 93 countries, making it possible to publish literature in various languages, currently numbering 271.

On Sept. 29, 1994, a daylong program at the United States Holocaust Memorial Museum, Washington, D.C., focused on the Witnesses' integrity in the face of the Nazi terror and also on their outspokenness at a time when many other religions were silent. Michael Berenbaum, director of the museum's Research Institute, explained: "The Witnesses are in a very real sense the only voluntary victims. They are the only people who were persecuted, not because of what they did [or who they were], but because of what they refused to do. They would not swear allegiance to the state . . . and they would not utter the words 'Heil Hitler.' " Historian Christine King, chancellor of Staffordshire (England) University, added: "Those Witnesses were a rock in the mud. [One prisoner] said that they were the only people who didn't spit when the guards walked past. They were the only people who didn't deal with all of this by hatred, but by love and hope—feeling that there was a purpose. . . . [They] brought morally to their knees the might of that Gestapo power." In contrast to others, King said, "They spoke out from the beginning. They spoke out with one voice. And they spoke out with a tremendous courage, which has a message for all of us."

(MILTON HENSCHEL)

Lutheran Communion. The Council of the Lutheran World Federation (LWF) met in Windhoek, Namibia, in June 1995. This was the first meeting held under the leadership of Ishmael Noko of Zimbabwe, elected general secretary in 1994. Resolutions were adopted noting the importance of Jerusalem in the Middle Eastern peace process, calling upon the International Tribunal for Rwanda to begin its work, and urging all governments to desist from the testing of nuclear weapons. The council accepted a proposal for joint cooperation between the LWF and the World Council of Churches for emergency relief work. The council also admitted two new member churches to the LWF, bringing its membership to 122. The council confirmed its commitment to the ordination of women. About 70% of the LWF member churches were prepared to ordain women. This confirmation was made in view of the decision of the archbishop of the Latvian Lutheran Church to halt the ordination of women.

The council devoted attention to the ninth assembly of the LWF to be held in July 1997 in Hong Kong, shortly after the territory reverted to China. The theme was to be "In Christ—Called to Witness." The assembly also would observe the 50th anniversary of the LWF.

A synod of the official Swedish Lutheran Church meeting in Sigtuna, Sweden, in late August agreed on a constitutional separation of the church from the state effective in the year 2000. Ecumenical progress continued between a number of Nordic and Baltic Lutheran churches and several Anglican churches in the U.K. with the acceptance of the Porvoo Report, which recommended closer Anglican-Lutheran relations. This report had the approval of the Lutheran churches in Estonia, Norway, and Sweden and of Anglican churches in England, Ireland, and Scotland. A process continued by which certain condemnations expressed between Lutherans and Roman Catholics in the 16th century would be declared in 1997 as inapplicable.

The assembly of the Evangelical Lutheran Church in America (ELCA), the second largest Lutheran church in the world, elected H. George Anderson, a former seminary and college president, its second churchwide bishop. Anderson succeeded Herbert W. Chilstrom, who retired. On the final ballot Anderson defeated April Ulring Larson, a bishop of a synod of the ELCA; this marked the first time a woman had been a finalist in an election to head a U.S. Lutheran church. A statement on peace was approved by the assembly.

At its convention in 1995, the Lutheran Church—Missouri Synod reelected Alvin L. Barry to his second term as president. At the convention the church accepted several proposals for restructuring and formally joined the International Lutheran Council.

(WILLIAM G. RUSCH)

Men and boys demonstrate their commitment at a rally of Promise Keepers at the Silverdome in Pontiac, Mich. The all-male fundamentalist movement, founded by former University of Colorado football coach Bill McCartney, required adherents to make seven promises governing behaviour.

DONNA BINDER—IMPACT VISUALS

Methodist Churches. The officers of the World Methodist Council met in Cambridge, England, in October 1995 to finalize plans for the 17th World Methodist Conference, which was to be held in Rio de Janeiro on Aug. 7–14, 1996. The conference theme was to be "Holy Spirit: Giver of Life." A new feature of the conference program would be a choice, on the second and third days, of 11 seminars focusing on world evangelism, international social concerns, family life issues, ecumenical relationships, Christian education, Wesleyan heritage and history, theological education, the renewal of church life for Methodist men, international publishing, worship, and Bible study. It would be the first time that the World Methodist Council had met in South America. The council, which had representatives from each of the 77 member churches, was scheduled to meet during the conference. The World Federation of Methodist Women planned an Assembly on July 27–August 4, also in Rio de Janeiro.

In 1996, also, there were to be celebrations at the Methodist Central Hall, Westminster, London, to mark 50 years since the first meeting of the General Assembly of the United Nations, which was held there in 1946. Representatives of the World Federation of Methodist Women took part in the United Nations Forum on Women in Huairou, near Beijing, on Aug. 30–Sept. 8, 1995.

The Preliminary Commission for Dialogue between the Ecumenical Patriarch and the World Methodist Council held its third meeting in March 1995. A proposal regarding the inauguration of a full dialogue went for decision to the Ecumenical Patriarch and through the Patriarch to the 13 autocephalous Orthodox Churches. The World Methodist Council would make its decision in Rio de Janeiro in 1996.

The World Methodist Council approved Methodist participation in the planning for an ecumenical event in Bethlehem at Christmas in the year 1999 to welcome the new millennium.

The Christian Conference of Asia, a body that represented more than 120 churches in that region, decided to keep its headquarters in Hong Kong after the British colony reverted to Chinese sovereignty on July 1, 1997.

The British Methodist Conference, meeting in Bristol, England, in June 1995, voted to "discourage" churches and church organizations from applying to the National Lottery for funds. The conference also established an annual Youth Conference and received a report on substance abuse encouraging a sensitive awareness of the pressures faced by many young people and commended it for discussion. The conference adopted a statement on political responsibility that underlines the church's pastoral role toward people engaged in legitimate political activity and encourages Christians to proclaim their convictions boldly.

(JOHN C.A. BARRETT)

Pentecostal Churches. The "Toronto Blessing" attracted hundreds of thousands of visitors to the Airport Vineyard Church throughout 1995, including many Pentecostals. The movement broke out in many other countries and in many North American cities, but in December the Toronto church was excommunicated for failing to de-emphasize "exotic" manifestations such as roaring and barking.

On March 31 the Church of God in Christ mourned the death of Presiding Bishop Louis Henry Ford of Chicago. Succeeding Ford as head of the eight million-member predominately black church was Bishop Chandler Owens of Atlanta, Ga. In June some 4,000 blacks and whites gathered in Greensboro, N.C., for "Bondfire '95," the first gathering of the newly constituted Pentecostal/Charismatic Churches of North America; racial reconciliation was the theme. Some 10,000 Pentecostals and charismatics met in July at the "Orlando '95" congress sponsored by the North American Renewal Service Committee. Over half of the registrants were Catholic charismatics. Plans also were made for thousands of young people to travel to Atlanta in 1996 as Christian witnesses to the Olympic Games.

In August the Assemblies of God conducted their biennial General Council in St. Louis, Mo., reelecting Thomas Trask as general superintendent. He reported that membership in the Assemblies of God throughout the world had surpassed 30 million during the previous year.

The 17th Pentecostal World Conference gathered in Jerusalem in September for a triennial conference that attracted over 6,500 registered delegates from around the world, the largest Christian conference in the history of the city. Featured speakers were Chairman Ray Hughes, David Yonggi Cho (*see* BIOGRAPHIES), Reinhard Bonnke, and Pat Robertson. (VINSON SYNAN)

Reformed, Presbyterian, and Congregational Churches. Can we arrive at a more comprehensive understanding of the Reformation to enrich the ecumenical discussion today? This was the central question in a consultation organized by the World Alliance of Reformed Churches (WARC) in Geneva at the end of 1994. The meeting brought together theologians from the Church of the Brethren, the Czech Hussite Church, the Evangelical Church of Czech Brethren, Hutterites, Mennonites, Moravians, Society of Friends, and Waldensians, as well as representatives of the Reformed and Lutheran traditions. In March 1995 Reformed and Anglican representatives agreed to survey the development of Anglican-Reformed relations since the appearance of *God's Reign and Our Unity* (1984) and to publish case studies on Anglican-Reformed cooperation at local and congregational levels. In July, Alliance and Pentecostal representatives agreed that international Reformed-Pentecostal dialogue should begin in May 1996.

The first in a series of regional WARC consultations on Reformed faith and economic justice was held in Manila in March. While the Asian economy showed great dynamism, participants reported, there were significant human, social, and ecological costs involved. "Growth and poverty, the insolent wealth of the few and the misery of the many, go hand in hand." A second consultation took place in Zambia in October.

The first meeting of the WARC European Area Council since the fall of the Berlin Wall took place in Edinburgh in August. Representatives of 40 WARC member churches condemned all forms of "ethnic cleansing" in former Yugoslavia and expressed their solidarity with churches throughout Central and Eastern Europe in the struggle against "nationalism, chauvinism and xenophobia." Nuclear testing by France and China came in for fierce criticism as "a retrograde step in the search for a peaceful and nuclear-free future."

Discussions about unity in the Dutch Reformed family of churches in South Africa proceeded slowly as the white Dutch Reformed Church undertook an extended consultation of its synods and congregations.

Under the aegis of the John Knox International Reformed Centre (Geneva), an ambitious project was launched in 1995 to produce a handbook on all the Reformed churches in the world. The Reformed family had a peculiar genius for division. A detailed survey of the reality of Reformed church life should underline the need to work toward greater cooperation and unity.

Five churches were admitted to WARC membership in 1995: the Christian Reformed Church of Nigeria, the Church of Christ in the Sudan among the Tiv (Nigeria), the Congregational Federation (U.K.), the Evangelical Church of Christ in Mozambique, and the Presbyterian Church in Korea (Hap Dong Chung Tong). WARC now linked over 70 million Christians in 198 churches in 99 countries.

(PÁRAIC RÉAMONN)

Religious Society of Friends. Like so many others, Quakers in Rwanda and Burundi were getting caught up in the devastating, persistent intertribal warfare. Several Quaker pastors in those countries were working in their communities and nationally to resolve conflicts and bring about understanding and reconciliation between Hutu and Tutsi and to deliver aid to refugees.

In preparation for the United Nations Fourth World Conference on Women held in Beijing in September 1995, the Quaker UN Office in New York ran colloquiums to help negotiators focus on the issues so that decisions made at the conference might effectively be implemented. Representatives from each of the five world regions who had been giving leadership on the issues were invited, as were representatives from some of the emerging democracies.

A cooperative group of Quakers from Western Europe, Russia, and the United States was planning a Friends House in Moscow, a centre for peace. Since there were a variety of visions of how such a venture might best serve the changing community and many practical difficulties to be considered, the work was proceeding with patient caution.

Friends in Great Britain, the country that gave rise to the Quaker movement in the mid-17th century, agreed at their annual business sessions to change their name from London Yearly Meeting to Britain Yearly Meeting (BYM). At the meeting, British Friends also agreed on the text of the new edition of the YM's *Quaker Faith & Practice: The Book of Christian Discipline of the YM of the Religious Society of Friends (Quakers) in Britain.* This was the result of nine years of work by a committee of 30 Friends. As with the previous edition (1959), the new BYM *Faith & Practice* would be used in many parts of the Quaker world.

(THOMAS F. TAYLOR)

Salvation Army. The work undertaken in 1995 by the Salvation Army undoubtedly provided the year's unofficial theme: fighting to improve the lives of people unable to help themselves.

Addressing the Religious Alliance Against Pornography conference in February, Gen. Paul A. Rader acknowledged that pornography was a global problem that the churches of the world had a responsibility to fight. The conference, including 162 of the world's most prominent religious leaders, concluded with an action plan uniting churches against pornography, heightening government awareness, and passing legislation.

Later in the year General Rader, together with the Christian Council of Social Service, launched an AIDS awareness campaign in Hyderabad, India. While AIDS was a worldwide problem, lack of facilities, finance, and education meant that the less developed nations were often the worst equipped to cope. The Salvation Army believed that AIDS might be combated through better understanding and prevention, and these factors were central to the theme of the campaign.

During late summer a delegation of female Salvation Army officers attended the UN Forum on Women in Huairou, near Beijing. The officers were from Europe, Southeast Asia, Africa, the South Pacific, East Asia, the Americas, and the Caribbean.

Salvation Army emergency teams provided assistance and spiritual comfort during the devastating earthquake in Kobe, Japan, the bomb blast in Oklahoma City, Okla., and the floods in Brazil. In postwar Rwanda the Army continued its vital relief work: caring for orphans and undertaking food-distribution, education, and health programs. Housing-for-the-homeless programs progressed in France and in the United Kingdom, combining accommodation with rehabilitation and employment training. In 1995 as always, wherever there was a need, the Salvation Army provided inspiration, hope, and practical assistance.

(CHARMAINE FLETCHER)

Seventh-day Adventist Church. Meeting in Utrecht, Neth., June 29 to July 8, 1995, the General Conference session of the Seventh-day Adventist Church, the world assembly that convened every five years, voted major changes to the constitution and bylaws of the church. Delegations to future General Conference sessions would include more lay members and field-workers and fewer administrators. The General Conference Executive Committee, which governed the church between sessions, became more international with a sharp decrease in the proportion of representatives from the U.S. As of Dec. 31, 1994, membership stood at 8,382,558, drawn from 208 countries.

One controversial item discussed in Utrecht concerned the ordination of women ministers. This topic had come to the floor of the previous two sessions (1985, 1990). The session of 1990 voted not to proceed with the ordination of women clergy but granted them authority to function as pastoral leaders of local churches. In 1995 the North American Division of the church presented a request that each division of the world church be granted permission to decide for itself the issue of gender-inclusive ordination. After lively debate the session voted down the request by a two-to-one margin. With some 2,341 delegates and more than 50,000 Adventists attending weekend services, the Utrecht event was the largest of the 56 General Conference sessions that the church had conducted.

Two major evangelistic projects were launched in 1995. In North America nearly 700 sites were downlinked to receive via satellite a five-week program of public evangelism originating in Chattanooga, Tenn. Total attendance averaged about 44,000 each night. "Hands Across the World," which called for the establishment of 2,000 strategically placed new congregations in various lands by the year 2000, was inaugurated for the world church.

(WILLIAM G. JOHNSSON)

Unitarian (Universalist) Churches. An International Council of Unitarians and Universalists—the first in history—was founded near Boston on March 22–26, 1995, by delegates from Asia, Africa, Europe, North America, and Australia/New Zealand. It was the culmination of a process begun with a British General Assembly resolution in 1987. Although the council was taking over responsibilities formerly assumed by the U.S. Unitarian Universalist Association (UUA)—with little fiscal support so far and apparently relying on a lay-led structure—the act still created a strong euphoria in the delegates.

The 1995 North American General Assembly of the UUA attracted more than 2,600 clergy and laypersons to Spokane, Wash., June 15–20. Its theme was "Building Our Future: Generation by Generation." "Study resolutions" from 1994 were passed, including "Oppose the Marketing of Violence," "Criteria for U.S. Health Care Reform," and "A Job, a Home, a Hope." Among resolutions approved by the British General Assembly was one urging Queen Elizabeth II and European governments to strengthen and uphold humanitarian laws regarding the export of live animals. Another related to drug abusers and suppliers and to dangers in "letter of the law" application to drug abusers that do not address their addiction.

Meadville/Lombard Theological School, Chicago, celebrated its 150th anniversary May 26–28. The denomination's Church of the Larger Fellowship reported that its 2,200 members lived in every U.S. state and Canadian province, as well as in 65 other countries.

The Unitarian Universalist Service Committee worked on three continents to create a more just world, with emphasis on the rights of women, children, and minorities. It was supported by more than 20,000 individuals and over 600 congregations.

(JOHN NICHOLLS BOOTH)

The United Church of Canada. Perhaps the most notable event for the United Church of Canada in 1995 was the relocation of its national offices in March to rented facilities in the western suburbs of Toronto.

Financial concerns continued to plague Canada's largest Protestant denomination, and the church expended much of its energy on budget issues. The proportion of money that was given for the work of the wider church continued to shrink in comparison with that given for local concerns. Anticipated deficits and new spending needs forced heavy program cuts early in the year. National office staff cuts were anticipated in 1996. Meanwhile, the denomination grappled with the need to set mission priorities so that cuts could be made with integrity and in response to constituency needs. The denomination at large raised CAN$308,276,194 in 1994 for all purposes. Approximately 90% of this money was directed to local church work.

The denomination's new hymn book, *Voices United,* was to be published early in 1996. A new body to support ethnic ministries within the church was established in 1995. The church released statements on issues such as the church's budget, human rights and the Lubicon peoples, U.S. involvement in Haiti, Rwandan relief, and support for Canada's criminal code in relation to the sentencing of those convicted of crimes motivated by hate, bias, or prejudice.

A major report issued through the church, "The Unitrends '94 Survey," generated widespread interest. This stewardship survey of church members and personnel clearly indicated that the trend in the church was to direct more of its resources toward supporting congregational life.

(DOUGLAS L. FLANDERS)

United Church of Christ. The General Synod of the 1.5 million-member United Church of Christ (UCC), meeting in Oakland, Calif., in July 1995, took historic steps to change the church's structure in the national setting. Three proposed ministry units—Local Church, Justice and Witness, and Wider Church—along with an Office of the General Minister and President formed the core of the new structure. Delegates affirmed a transition process to be implemented in 1999.

The delegates furthered the church's ecumenical commitments by affirming "the Church of Christ Uniting" proposal to establish full communion between the UCC and eight other denominations and by voting to "reconcile" ordained ministries with the UCC's ecumenical partner, the one million-member Christian Church (Disciples of Christ).

Other significant actions of the General Synod included the introduction and dedication of the recently published *New Century Hymnal;* reaffirmation of the church's commitment to be multiracial and multicultural; efforts to reduce violence in media and society; and renewed calls for solidarity with the poor and exploited in the United States and around the globe. Edith A. Guffey was reelected to a four-year term as secretary of the church; David Dean was elected moderator of the General Synod; and Margaret MacDonald and Frank Thomas were elected assistant moderators.

Throughout the year the church continued its season of Theological Reflection on "A Church Attentive to the Word." The introduction of a new church school curriculum, "The Word Among Us," supported this effort. Continued attention was given to evangelism and stewardship concerns in light of continuing membership losses and reduced financial support at the regional and national levels. "Make a Difference," a major fund-raising campaign currently under way, thus far had raised almost $17 million toward a final goal of $30 million.

(PAUL H. SHERRY)

ROMAN CATHOLIC CHURCH

Vatican missionary officials reported that for the first time, the world Catholic population exceeded one billion. Africa continued to be the area of most dynamic growth, its Catholic population having increased to more than 122 million from 2 million in 1900. Asia, with about two-thirds of the world's population, was less than 3% Catholic and continued to receive the greatest proportion of the church's missionary effort. A large meeting was held in Rome June 16–18, 1995, to explore more effective missionary strategies and to discover expanded roles for women in the process of evangelization.

Pope John Paul II issued a major letter to the world's women on July 10. Responding to critics of the church's all-male clergy, the pope said that the male priesthood does not detract from the dignity of the role of women or signify male domination of the church. His words evoked some criticism on this topic and promised to remain controversial. Very favourable reactions met the pope's condemnation of prostitution, rape, torture, and the oppression of women by political and economic authorities. John Paul's forthright condemnation of abortion and defense of motherhood received mixed reviews.

Another flurry of criticism came in November when the Vatican announced that the doctrine for forbidding the ordination of women was "infallibly" taught. There was some controversy over the meaning of the declaration because it had not been issued by the pope nor did it seem to meet the requirements for what is called ordinary infallibility. This does not involve a papal pronouncement but holds that basic doctrines taught universally by the church are to be considered infallible.

The letter on women was intended as the first papal pronouncement before the UN Fourth World Conference on Women that met in Beijing in September. For the first time, a woman, Mary Ann Glendon of Harvard Law School, was appointed to head a Vatican delegation to a major international conference. Glendon, a self-proclaimed economic liberal and social conservative, had written on several topics, including abortion. Glendon's views were in accord with those of the Vatican on most issues, and her appointment was meant to show that many roles outside the priesthood could be filled by women.

Responding to the question "How can Cain's hand be stayed?" the pope issued on March 30 an encyclical entitled *Evangelium vitae* ("Gospel of Life"), a powerful and moving statement of the value of human life in the face of the threats against it all over the world. The letter pointed explicitly to a Jubilee year in 2000 and called for a deep transformation by then of human aggressiveness brought about through a renewed awareness of the horrors of killing.

On May 30 the pope issued the encyclical *Ut unum sint* ("That They May Be One") on the general theme of ecumenism. Following in the tradition of the decree on ecumenism of the Second Vatican Council (1962–65), the pope stressed the need for unity in Christ, for an authentic change of heart on the part of all believers, and for a true spirit of brotherhood. These aspects of the letter met with almost universal approval. Controversial were the pope's insistence on the need for the papacy as both a symbol and an institution representing authority and unity. On June 29, at the end of Patriarch Bartholomew I's historic visit to the Vatican, the pope and patriarch, the leaders of the Roman and Orthodox branches of the Christian world, respectively, issued a joint statement on the need for continued ecumenical work between their two traditions and for more theological understanding and collaboration.

John Paul traveled extensively in 1994, in part to dispel rumours concerning his health. Besides producing numerous major letters, he journeyed to Asia and Australia, Central Europe, Africa, and the United States.

The 50th anniversary of the end of World War II did not pass unnoticed by Catholic authorities. On June 11 the pope delivered a homily at St. Peter's in which he said that "every war is contrary to the covenant of peace" and that "we are aware of the exterminated ranks of war victims." In a spirit of reconciliation, the pope singled out no parties for praise or censure. He called on all to seek true peace. Bishops in

Japan called for the elimination of nuclear weapons as a fitting memorial to those who died in the war. Pax Christi, the international Catholic peace organization, used its 50th anniversary celebration in Assisi, Italy, in May to orient its strategies away from the prevention of nuclear war among Cold War opponents. Now Pax Christi would address itself to human rights and to the peaceful mediation of domestic conflicts.

In Western Europe and the United States, there was controversy over what type of consultation should take place between local churches and the Vatican. American bishops, promoting more collegial models of church government, found themselves thwarted by a Vatican unwillingness to countenance changes in the rituals of worship or to accept, for use in worship, "inclusive" scriptural translations.

In November the Canon Law Society of America cautiously endorsed the ordination of women as deacons in the church, but the chairman of the bishops' committee on the permanent diaconate expressed disagreement with the report. Responding to attempts by right-wing religious and political groups to reach out to Catholics, U.S. bishops issued a statement rejecting "religious leaders telling people how to vote."

Irish Bishop Brendan Comiskey continued to call for an end to mandatory celibacy, and Bishop Victor Guazzelli of Westminster called for thorough debate on the subject. In January the Vatican deposed Bishop Jacques Gaillot of Évreux, France, who called for an end to mandatory celibacy and also demanded the ordination of women and the distribution of condoms to control the spread of AIDS. Bishop David Konstant of Leeds, England, who was less radical, also called for full exploration of the issue of women's ordination. Polls showed that Bishop Comiskey enjoyed the support of three-quarters of Irish Catholics, and former bishop Gaillot also possessed widespread support.

Another issue was the prevalent conviction that the Vatican should undertake wider consultation with the local clergy and even with the laity. Austrians were particularly outraged when the archbishop of Vienna, Hans Hermann Cardinal Groer, was accused of having molested seminarians 20 years earlier. Groer was unpopular with the majority of Austrian Catholics and many Austrian bishops and priests. It was felt that wider consultations in 1986 might have prevented his appointment. This belief was seen as part of a wider theological movement typified by such writers as Eugen Drewermann. (*See* BIOGRAPHIES.)

On June 22 the Dominican priest and world-famous theologian Yves Congar died in Paris. Congar was the last surviving practitioner of the "New Theology" that was condemned by Rome in 1950 but that reigned triumphant at the Second Vatican Council. The 19th century had seen an affirmation of the church's long-standing commitment to scholastic theology. In the 1930s a group of theologians—Congar, Henri de Lubac, Jean Daniélou, and Hans Urs von Balthasar—began to call for a new theology that was less rooted in Aristotelian logic, more grounded in the Bible, and closer to actual human experience. Congar's passing marked the end of an era.

See WORLD AFFAIRS: *Vatican City State.*

(THOMAS F.X. NOBLE)

THE ORTHODOX CHURCH

At a meeting convened in December 1994 in Ligonier, Pa., by the Standing Conference of Canonical Orthodox Bishops in America (SCOBA), 29 bishops, representing 10 Orthodox jurisdictions in the Americas, pledged cooperation toward jurisdictional unity. Statements made subsequently by some of the hierarchs provoked a negative reaction early in 1995 by the Ecumenical Patriarchate of Constantinople, which interpreted the event as a step toward severing relationships, though this was denied by SCOBA leaders.

On June 29, the Feast of St. Peter and St. Paul in both the Orthodox and Roman Catholic churches, Patriarch Bartholomew I of Constantinople and Pope John Paul II of Rome marked the day together in an extraordinary set of observances at the Vatican and signed a document pledging increased efforts at overcoming the division between their respective churches. The statement also called on the churches' membership to address such social and economic issues as the severe ecological problem facing the contemporary world. The meeting was held in the face of mixed Orthodox response to the pope's May 30th encyclical, *Ut unum sint,* which, in part, reiterated aspects of papal authority unacceptable to the Orthodox. At a service in St. Peter's Basilica in Rome, however, both leaders spoke about moving toward unity, exchanged the "kiss of peace," and blessed the congregation.

In Kiev, Ukraine, Patriarch Volodymyr, the leader of one faction of the Ukrainian Orthodox Church—Kiev, which was opposed to the official Ukrainian Orthodox Church under the Moscow Patriarchate, died on July 14. His funeral procession turned violent when it diverged from its approved path to the Baykovoye Cemetery and supporters sought to inter the patriarch's body in the 11th-century St. Sophia Cathedral, now a museum. Prohibited by police from entering, the mourners dug a grave in front of the cathedral, where the coffin was buried.

On July 18 Patriarch Aleksey II of Moscow protested actions by the Ecumenical Patriarchate relating to Ukrainian Orthodox in the diaspora. The Ecumenical Patriarchate received under its protection the Ukrainian Orthodox Church in Canada in 1990 and the Ukrainian Orthodox Church in Exile in March 1995. Representatives of Constantinople met with Estonian Orthodox leaders earlier in the year to discuss problems in their relationships with Moscow's Patriarchate. Aleksey's letter indicated concern with the legitimacy of the actions and threatened the breaking of liturgical communion.

In the United States, Archbishop Iakovos of the Greek Orthodox Archdiocese of North and South America submitted to the Ecumenical Patriarchate his decision to retire for reasons of age and health. That decision was received and accepted on August 21 with high words of praise for Archbishop Iakovos' life of service and commitment to the church. The action would become effective on July 29, 1996, Iakovos' 85th birthday—following the 1996 Biennial Clergy-Laity Congress of the Archdiocese.

A five-month series of events marked the 1,900-year celebration of the writing of the New Testament Book of Revelation on the island of Patmos, Greece. On September 25–26 the leaders of the canonical self-governing Orthodox Churches of the world met on Patmos, with Patriarch Bartholomew I presiding, to discuss concerns of world Orthodoxy.

The longest-standing continuous dialogue between the Orthodox and Roman Catholic churches celebrated its 50th continuous meeting in Milwaukee, Wis., October 26–28. The dialogue met twice annually. Sponsors were SCOBA and the U.S. Conference of Catholic Bishops.

(STANLEY S. HARAKAS)

ORIENTAL ORTHODOX CHURCH

Succeeding the catholicos of Echmiadzin, Vazgen I, who died in August 1994, was Syrian-born Karekin I (secular name, Neshan Sarkisian). He was elected the 131st supreme head of the Armenian Orthodox Church at the church's council held in Echmiadzin on April 4, 1995. His prior position was catholicos of Cilicia, Lebanon. The election was widely interpreted as a step in overcoming the rivalries between the two centres of Armenian church life. In his first encyclical the new catholicos of Echmiadzin announced a six-point program of action for church renewal.

On June 28 the vacant see of the catholicos of Cilicia was filled with the election of Archbishop Aram Keshishian of the diocese of Lebanon. Keshishian had been serving as moderator of the Central Committee of the World Council of Churches. He was consecrated catholicos on July 1 in Antelias, Lebanon. Present at the consecration were Catholicos Karekin I of Echmiadzin and the Armenian patriarchs of Constantinople and Jerusalem, an event unprecedented in modern times.

The Coptic Church in Egypt reported that harassment by Muslims continued. A female convert from Islam whose conversion was deemed a crime of "denigrating Islam" was arrested in November 1994. A priest and laymen also arrested in the incident were released in January 1995.

An influx of proselytizing Protestants provoked Orthodox reaction in Addis Ababa, Eth., in April. After a group of about 100 Orthodox protested a crusade led by a California-based evangelist, the city council relocated the event.

(STANLEY S. HARAKAS)

JUDAISM

The top item on the agenda for world Jewry in 1995—peace in the Middle East—received a severe blow in early November with the murder in Tel Aviv of Israeli Prime Minister Yitzhak Rabin (*see* OBITUARIES); the shock was felt more strongly because the assassin was himself a Jew.

Before the attack, world Jewish support for the peace process had diminished in reaction to continuing terrorist attacks. The withdrawal of Israeli troops from the West Bank had brought to the fore a religious issue concerning the "settlers," some of whom believed they were performing a religious duty by maintaining Jewish possession of territories that the Bible says God promised to the "People of Israel." A group of Jewish settlers joined by Knesset members called for armed resistance against the Israeli army should the government act to remove their settlements. Some extremist

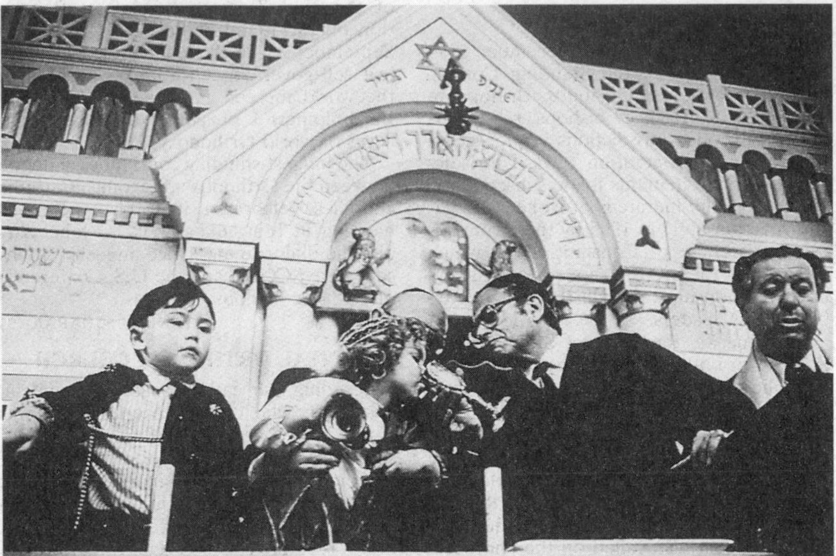

Jews celebrate the festival of Purim at a synagogue in Berlin. The years following the dissolution of the Soviet Union in 1991 had seen a widespread renewal of religious activity among Jews, particularly by the young, in a number of the countries of Central and Eastern Europe.
EDWARD SEROTTA—TIME MAGAZINE

rabbis in New York called the leaders of the Israeli government "traitors" and declared it acceptable under Jewish law to assassinate them. The tragedy in November seemed consistent with this line of thought.

Former president Chaim Herzog of Israel called a meeting in April with world Jewish leaders on relations between Israel and the Diaspora. Though Herzog himself regarded the conference as a success, it ended acrimoniously, with delegates expressing doubts whether any real dialogue had taken place. Herzog had taken a negative stance toward the Diaspora, arguing that the only future for Jews outside Israel lay in *aliya* (immigration) to Israel. Avraham Burg, on the other hand, urged that Zionism today should be concerned with Jewish education, wherever it might take place. In July Burg, a Religious Zionist who identified strongly with the Peace Now movement, was elected chairman of the Jewish Agency and the General Zionist Council. His manifesto *Brit Am* placed great emphasis on the need to "return to the sources" in Jewish education and for a separation of state and religion in Israel.

The monopoly on the determination of Jewish status, held by the Orthodox rabbinate since 1953, was challenged when the Israeli Supreme Court ruled that conversions under the auspices of Conservative and Reform rabbis were valid, though the government would not be required to recognize such converts as Jews.

Jews in many countries participated in ceremonies marking the 50th anniversary of the Allied victory over Japan. Comparisons drawn between the Holocaust and the dropping of the atomic bombs on Hiroshima and Nagasaki caused resentment and vigorous debate in some Jewish circles.

In the U.K. the conservative Masorti movement opened a new congregation in Manchester, England, and continued to make headway elsewhere, despite vociferous Orthodox opposition and attempts to deny them a public platform. The U.K. also was the scene for serious controversies surrounding the attempt to secure equality for women in religious affairs. There was considerable disappointment at the failure of the Chief Rabbinate to act positively on the recommendations of the 1994 report, "Women in the Community," produced partly on its own initiative. In October women demonstrated outside the office of Chief Rabbi Jonathan Sacks.

The Second African Christian/Jewish Consultation took place in Johannesburg, South Africa, on June 26–29 under the joint auspices of the World Council of Churches and the International Jewish Committee on Interreligious Consultations. Delegates were greatly inspired by the breakdown of apartheid that had occurred since the first consultation, in Nairobi, Kenya. An independent group of Christians, Jews, and Muslims headed by the Duke of Edinburgh, Sir Evelyn de Rothschild, and Crown Prince Hassan of Jordan promoted a code of ethics on international business for Christians, Muslims, and Jews intended to reflect the ethical basis common to the three religions. (NORMAN SOLOMON)

BUDDHISM

The self-immolation of a Buddhist monk in May 1994 and demonstrations led by Buddhist monks in major cities symbolized the deepening conflict between the Vietnamese government and the outlawed Unified Buddhist Church of Vietnam (UBCV) during 1994–95. In December 1994 Thich Huyen Quang, the UBCV's supreme patriarch, was arrested for staging a hunger strike, and in January 1995 his chief deputy was also arrested.

The Dalai Lama's government-in-exile continued to challenge the Chinese occupation of Tibet during 1995. In March, shortly after hundreds of Tibetans marched from Dharmshala to New Delhi to mark the anniversary of the failed 1959 uprising against China, Beijing announced new regulations for Tibetan Buddhism, including limitations on the number of monks per temple. In May the Dalai Lama designated six-year-old Gedhun Choekyi Nyima the reincarnation of the 10th Panchen Lama, who died in 1989, thereby defying Beijing's claim of authority to select Tibet's second highest leader. Denying the legality of the Dalai Lama's selection method, Beijing refused to recognize the boy as the 11th Panchen Lama. In June Chinese officials placed under house arrest the deputy abbot of Tashilhunpo Monastery, traditional seat of the Panchen Lama, whom they accused of collaborating with the Dalai Lama. In a ceremony held in Beijing in December, the Chinese government installed its own candidate as Panchen Lama.

In December 1994 the Mahanayakas of Sri Lanka's main Buddhist monastic orders protested against characterizations of Buddhism in a recent book by Pope John Paul II, which they called an "unprovoked and uncalled-for insult." Despite an official apology and the pope's own conciliatory remarks, they boycotted an interreligious dialogue convened for the January 1995 papal visit to Sri Lanka. In February, during a three-month truce in the decade-long Sri Lankan civil war, Buddhist monks led 2,000 people on a peace march to rebel-held Jaffna. In June, however, Sinhalese mobs attacked Tamil-owned shops in the south after the funeral of K. Silalankara, revered chief priest of the Dimbulagala temple.

The release of Nobel Peace Prize winner Aung San Suu Kyi in July had been anticipated since September 1994, when a Myanmar monk living in England successfully negotiated a meeting between the influential Buddhist democrat and leading Myanmar generals. Throughout the year refugee Rohingya Muslims in Bangladesh balked at repatriation to Myanmar, citing fear of Arakanese Buddhists who had occupied their lands and razed many of their mosques.

During March 1995 Thailand's Sangha Supreme Council enacted a new measure to defrock a popular monk accused of violating his celibacy vow. Leaders of the Japanese Aum Shinrikyo movement, which claimed to incorporate many Buddhist elements, were arrested in April for releasing poisonous gas in the Tokyo subway. (*See* CHRONOLOGY: *March 20.*) In February India's notorious "Bandit Queen" Phoolan Devi converted to Ambedkar-style Buddhism as part of her ongoing advocacy for low-caste Indians. (*See* BIOGRAPHIES.)

(JONATHAN S. WALTERS)

HINDUISM

During January and February 1995, an estimated 18 million Hindu pilgrims from around the world journeyed to Allahabad to bathe in the sacred Ganges River as part of the triennial Kumbh Mela, "Festival of the Pot." Allahabad is regarded as particularly holy because it lies at the confluence of three sacred rivers: the Ganges, Yamuna, and the mythical, subterranean Saraswati. Ten thousand police were needed to preserve order as pilgrims arrived at the rate of 150,000 an hour on the eve of January 30, which astrologers had fixed as the most propitious day to bathe.

Concern about the future of the Ganges brought together Hindu leaders and environmentalists in opposition to a proposed government project to construct a hydroelectric dam just north of the pilgrimage site of Rishikesh near the glacial source of the river. During the summer a leading environmentalist, Sunder Lal Bahuguna, fasted 49 days to pressure India's Prime Minister P.V. Narasimha Rao to appoint a commission to study the project, and Hindu leaders mounted a protest to preserve the course and flow of the river.

The potent interaction of Hinduism and politics in India was prominent during the year. A 39-year-old outcast female lawyer, Mayawati, who had served in both houses of India's Parliament, became chief minister of Uttar Pradesh, India's most populous state. Mayawati had outraged many Hindus in 1994 when she denounced Mohandas Gandhi as the "worst enemy of the Dalits" (outcasts). The Hindu nationalist Bharatiya Janata Party (BJP) also experienced stunning election successes in other states during the year.

In the March elections an alliance of the BJP and the radical Hindu Shiv Sena ("Army of Shiva") Party—both of which advocated the end of India's constitutional status as a secular state and the adoption of Hinduism as the nation's official religion—was successful. The Shiv Sena gained political control of Maharashtra, the state in which Bombay is located and the scene of violent conflicts between Hindus and Muslims attributed to the Shiv Sena. In August Bombay was renamed "Mumbai" after the goddess Mumbhadevi, the name by which the city is known in the regional language of Marathi. The Bombay Shiv Sena leader, Bal Thackeray, was satirized by Salman Rushdie in a new novel, *The Moor's Last Sigh,* which, when released in September, was banned in Maharashtra.

More than 600 Hindu leaders from 38 countries gathered in South Africa during July for the World Hindu Conference, a highlight of which was an address by South African Pres. Nelson Mandela to a crowd of 40,000 of his country's 1.1 million Hindus. In August the Swaminarayan Hindu Mission consecrated a large cultural complex and temple in London, and in Chicago more than 3,000 Hindus celebrated the ancient Vedic Asvamedha Yajna fire ritual.

The year saw the death on June 20 in California of Raghavan Narasimhan Iyer, the Indian-born philosopher and founder of the Institute of World Culture in Santa Barbara, Calif., whose many writings were directed at showing connections between Eastern and Western thought. (*See* OBITUARIES.) In April the McDonald's Corp. announced plans to open restaurants in Bombay and New Delhi that, out of deference to the Hindu belief in the sanctity of the cow, would not serve beef hamburgers.

(H. PATRICK SULLIVAN)

ISLAM

By the 1990s disproportions of wealth, intractable poverty, unemployment, feelings of almost total insecurity, rising expectations, overwhelmingly rapid social and cultural change, alienation of youth, disintegration of traditional values—all these concerns were turning Muslims of all ages, educational attainments, and social classes toward trusting Islam to provide a solution.

What that solution should be, however, was not clear. Observers referred to Islamic fundamentalism and saw aspects of it as part of the worldwide fundamentalist movements evident in many countries, such as the United States, where groups had similar feelings of alienation in a too rapidly changing, unstable world.

Concerns about the radical aspects of Islam, however, were taking up so much attention that another important development tended to be overlooked, namely, the quiet but ever-increasing presence and spread of Islam in various parts of the world, especially Western countries. New mosques and Islamic centres continued to be built and to present attractive programs in such symbolic places as Rome and the university city of Cambridge, Mass. Specific developments in Muslim lands should be seen in the context of the broader developments.

Violence continued in Afghanistan and Algeria throughout the year; Algerian extremist attacks occurred in France as well. Pakistan suffered violence in its cities, as did India, and the Kashmir situation remained unsettled. (*See* SPOTLIGHT: *Secularism in South Asia.*) Attempts to bring the warfare in Bosnia to a halt resulted in the signing of a peace treaty in December, though many feared it could not be maintained. In the southern Philippines younger radicals violently challenged what they saw as weakness or accommodation by the older Moro leadership. Violent outbreaks occurred in Turkey, involving both the ongoing fighting between Kurds and Turks and a March attack on Alawites, a Muslim minority group, some of whom lived in Istanbul. In late June, Pres. Hosni Mubarak of Egypt escaped an assassination attempt in Ethiopia, which Egyptians claimed was the responsibility of The Sudan's Muslim extremists, and which caused a brief border skirmish between The Sudan and Egypt. Egypt continued to suffer outbreaks of violence throughout the year as Islamic militants continued their attacks. Egypt accused The Sudan of supporting the militants and of aiding many who were said to be residents of Upper Egypt. In June an Egyptian judge ordered a wife divorced from her husband because the man's writings were judged anti-Islamic; he was declared an apostate to whom a proper Muslim woman could no longer be married. The couple was subsequently reported to have left the country. In other Muslim countries a number of writers and intellectuals were attacked or charged as anti-Islamic.

There were positive developments in the Muslim world as well. The growing prominence of charismatic Muslim leaders and social reformers such as Indonesia's Abdurrahman Wahid (*see* BIOGRAPHIES) was encouraging. The Aga Khan IV continued his efforts to assist the Ismailis, the Shi'ite sect of which he was the head, with announced support to those living in the Pamirs. In Iran a group of Muslim clerics began making accessible on computers a substantial amount of traditional Islamic legal writing, including thousands of responses to religious questions. Before the hajj in the spring, the United Nations lifted its ban on flights from Libya to allow Egyptian airliners to fly Libyan pilgrims to Saudi Arabia.

In the United States the trial of 10 terrorists (including Sheikh Omar Abdel Rahman) accused of terrorist conspiracy in the World Trade Center bombing in 1993 concluded at the end of September with a guilty verdict. That bombing had apparently fueled the initial report that Islamic terrorists were responsible for the bombing of the federal building in Oklahoma City, Okla., in April. Although the report was quickly found to be erroneous, once again U.S. Muslims found themselves offended and put on the defensive. Louis Farrakhan, the leader of the Nation of Islam, called for a mass march of all African-American men, regardless of religious background, in Washington, D.C., in October to dramatize their need for understanding and solidarity. His apparent anti-Jewish remarks continued to alienate large numbers of people, however.

(REUBEN W. SMITH)

This article updates the *Macropædia* articles The Buddha and BUDDHISM; CHRISTIANITY; EASTERN ORTHODOXY; HINDUISM; Muhammad and the Religion of ISLAM; JUDAISM; PROTESTANTISM; The Study and Classification of RELIGIONS; ROMAN CATHOLICISM; and *Micropædia* entries on the various denominations.

DAVID CHURCHILL—ARCAID

The gleaming Swaminarayan temple, the largest Hindu temple outside India, stands in suburban London. The ornate structure, part of a complex that includes cultural facilities, opened in August. It was built of Bulgarian limestone and of Indian and Italian marble carved by Indian craftsmen.

Worldwide Adherents of All Religions by Six Continental Areas, Mid-1995

	Africa	Asia	Europe	Latin America	Northern America	Oceania	World	%	Number of countries
Christians	348,176,000	306,762,000	551,892,000	448,006,000	249,277,000	23,840,000	**1,927,953,000**	33.7	260
Roman Catholics	122,108,000	90,041,000	270,677,000	402,691,000	74,243,000	8,265,000	**968,025,000**	16.9	249
Protestants	109,726,000	42,836,000	80,000,000	31,684,000	123,257,000	8,364,000	**395,867,000**	6.9	236
Orthodox	29,645,000	14,881,000	165,795,000	481,000	6,180,000	666,000	**217,948,000**	3.8	105
Anglicans	25,362,000	707,000	30,625,000	1,153,000	6,819,000	5,864,000	**70,530,000**	1.2	158
Other Christians	61,335,000	158,297,000	4,795,000	11,997,000	38,478,000	681,000	**275,583,000**	4.8	118
Atheists	427,000	174,174,000	40,085,000	2,977,000	1,670,000	592,000	**219,925,000**	3.8	139
Baha'is	1,851,000	3,010,000	93,000	719,000	356,000	75,000	**6,104,000**	0.1	210
Buddhists	36,000	320,691,000	1,478,000	569,000	920,000	200,000	**323,894,000**	5.7	92
Chinese folk religionists	12,000	224,828,000	116,000	66,000	98,000	17,000	**225,137,000**	3.9	60
Confucians	1,000	5,220,000	4,000	2,000	26,000	1,000	**5,254,000**	0.1	12
Ethnic religionists	72,777,000	36,579,000	1,200,000	1,061,000	47,000	113,000	**111,777,000**	2.0	104
Hindus	1,535,000	775,252,000	1,522,000	748,000	1,185,000	305,000	**780,547,000**	13.7	94
Jains	58,000	4,804,000	15,000	4,000	4,000	1,000	**4,886,000**	0.1	11
Jews	163,000	4,294,000	2,529,000	1,098,000	5,942,000	91,000	**14,117,000**	0.2	134
Mandeans	0	44,000	0	0	0	0	**44,000**	0.0	2
Muslims	300,317,000	760,181,000	31,975,000	1,329,000	5,450,000	382,000	**1,099,634,000**	19.2	184
New-Religionists	19,000	118,591,000	808,000	913,000	956,000	10,000	**121,297,000**	2.1	27
Nonreligious	2,573,000	701,175,000	94,330,000	15,551,000	25,050,000	2,870,000	**841,549,000**	14.7	226
Parsees	1,000	184,000	1,000	1,000	1,000	1,000	**189,000**	0.0	3
Sikhs	36,000	18,130,000	490,000	8,000	490,000	7,000	**19,161,000**	0.3	21
Shintoists	0	2,840,000	1,000	1,000	1,000	1,000	**2,844,000**	0.0	4
Spiritists	4,000	1,100,000	17,000	8,768,000	300,000	1,000	**10,190,000**	0.2	30
Other religionists	88,000	98,000	443,000	184,000	1,068,000	42,000	**1,923,000**	0.0	182
Non-Christians	**379,898,000**	**3,151,195,000**	**175,107,000**	**33,999,000**	**43,564,000**	**4,709,000**	**3,788,472,000**	**66.3**	**262**
Total population	**728,074,000**	**3,457,957,000**	**726,999,000**	**482,005,000**	**292,841,000**	**28,549,000**	**5,716,425,000**	**100.0**	**262**

Continents. These follow current UN demographic practice, which divides the world into the 6 major areas shown above and 21 regions (1994). *See* United Nations, *World Population Prospects: The 1994 Revision* (1995), with populations of all continents, regions, and countries covering the period 1950–2025. The table above therefore combines its former columns "East Asia" and "South Asia" into one single continental area, "Asia," which also now includes the former U.S.S.R. Central Asian republics. Note also that "Europe" now extends eastward to Vladivostok, the Sea of Japan, and the Bering Strait.
Countries. The last column enumerates sovereign and nonsovereign countries in which each religion or religious grouping has a numerically significant following.
Rows. The list of non-Christian religions is arranged in alphabetical order.
Adherents. As defined and enumerated for each of the world's countries in *World Christian Encyclopedia* (1982), projected to mid-1995, adjusted for recent data.
Christians. Followers of Jesus Christ affiliated with churches (church members, including children: 1,791,227,000) plus persons professing in censuses or polls though not so affiliated.
Other Christians. This term in the above table denotes Catholics (non-Roman), marginal Protestants, crypto-Christians, and adherents of African, Asian, black, and Latin-American indigenous churches.
Atheists. Persons professing atheism, skepticism, disbelief, or irreligion, including antireligious (opposed to all religion).
Buddhists. 56% Mahayana, 38% Theravada (Hinayana), 6% Tantrayana (Lamaism).
Chinese folk religionists. Followers of the traditional Chinese religion (local deities, ancestor veneration, Confucian ethics, Taoism, universism, divination, some Buddhist elements).
Confucians. Non-Chinese followers of Confucius and Confucianism, mostly Koreans in Korea.
Hindus. 70% Vaishnavites, 25% Shaivites, 2% neo-Hindus and reform Hindus.
Jews. Adherents of Judaism. For detailed data on "core" Jewish population, *see* "World Jewish Populations" in the American Jewish Committee's *American Jewish Year Book.*
Muslims. 83% Sunnites, 16% Shi'ites, 1% other schools. Up to 1990 the ethnic Muslims in the former U.S.S.R. who had embraced communism were not included as Muslims in this table. After the collapse of communism in 1990–91, these ethnic Muslims were once again enumerated as Muslims in cases where they have returned to Islamic profession and practice.
New-Religionists. Followers of Asian 20th-century New Religions, New Religious movements, radical new crisis religions, and non-Christian syncretistic mass religions, all founded since 1800 and most since 1945.
Nonreligious. Persons professing no religion, nonbelievers, agnostics, freethinkers, dereligionized secularists indifferent to all religion.
Other religionists. Including 70 minor world religions and a large number of spiritist religions, New Age religions, quasi religions, pseudo religions, parareligions, religious or mystic systems, religious and semireligious brotherhoods of numerous varieties.
Total population. UN medium variant figures for mid-1995, as given in *World Population Prospects: The 1994 Revision* (1995).

Religious Adherents in the United States of America, AD 1900–2000

Adherents	Year 1900	%	mid-1970	%	mid-1990	%	Annual change, 1990–95 Natural	Conversion	Total	Rate (%)	mid-1995	%	mid-2000	%
Christians	**73,270,000**	**96.4**	**186,120,000**	**90.8**	**214,979,000**	**86.0**	**2,167,500**	**-317,900**	**1,849,600**	**0.83**	**224,457,000**	**85.3**	**233,475,000**	**84.9**
Professing Christians	73,270,000	96.4	186,120,000	90.8	214,979,000	86.0	2,167,500	-317,900	1,849,600	0.83	224,457,000	85.3	233,475,000	84.9
Unaffiliated Christians	18,845,000	24.8	32,920,000	16.1	40,996,000	16.4	413,337	167,563	580,900	1.33	43,963,000	16.7	46,805,000	17.0
Affiliated Christians	54,425,000	71.6	153,200,000	74.7	173,983,000	69.6	1,754,160	-485,463	1,268,700	0.71	180,494,000	68.6	186,670,000	67.9
Roman Catholics	10,775,000	14.2	48,391,000	23.6	53,495,000	21.4	539,357	-244,757	294,600	0.54	55,259,000	21.0	56,441,000	20.5
Protestants	35,000,000	46.1	70,653,000	34.5	78,742,000	31.5	793,907	-401,107	392,800	0.49	80,678,000	30.6	82,670,000	30.0
Evangelicals	26,598,000	35.0	50,688,000	24.7	67,743,000	27.1	683,011	224,189	907,200	1.26	72,363,000	27.5	76,815,000	27.9
Anglicans	1,600,000	2.1	3,234,000	1.6	2,500,000	1.0	25,206	-54,906	-29,700	-1.26	2,350,000	0.9	2,203,000	0.8
Orthodox	400,000	0.5	4,387,000	2.1	4,999,000	2.0	50,402	75,698	126,100	2.27	5,631,000	2.1	6,260,000	2.3
Black Christians	5,750,000	7.6	19,679,000	9.6	23,998,000	9.6	241,957	1,343	243,300	0.97	25,261,000	9.6	26,431,000	9.6
Black Evangelicals	5,320,000	7.0	13,551,000	6.6	17,248,000	6.9	173,901	56,099	230,000	1.26	18,420,000	7.0	19,548,000	7.1
Catholics (non-Roman)	100,000	0.1	472,000	0.2	500,000	0.2	5,041	59	5,100	0.98	526,000	0.2	551,000	0.2
Other Christians	800,000	1.1	6,384,000	3.1	9,749,000	3.9	98,293	138,207	236,500	2.20	10,789,000	4.1	12,114,000	4.4
Non-Christians	**2,724,800**	**3.6**	**18,928,000**	**9.2**	**34,942,000**	**14.0**	**352,300**	**317,900**	**670,200**	**1.77**	**38,791,000**	**14.7**	**41,644,000**	**15.1**
Atheists	1,000	0.0	200,000	0.1	750,000	0.3	7,562	12,138	19,700	2.36	870,000	0.3	947,000	0.3
Baha'is	2,800	0.0	138,000	0.1	250,000	0.1	2,521	8,979	11,500	3.86	300,000	0.1	365,000	0.1
Buddhists	30,000	0.0	200,000	0.1	700,000	0.3	7,058	29,942	37,000	4.33	780,000	0.3	1,070,000	0.4
Chinese folk religionists	70,000	0.1	90,000	0.0	80,000	0.0	807	-1,807	-1,000	-1.33	76,000	0.0	70,000	0.0
Hindus	1,000	0.0	100,000	0.0	500,000	0.2	5,041	64,959	70,000	9.15	910,000	0.3	1,200,000	0.4
Jews	1,500,000	2.0	6,700,000	3.3	5,515,000	2.2	55,604	-36,904	18,700	0.33	5,602,000	2.1	5,702,000	2.1
Muslims	10,000	0.0	800,000	0.4	4,500,000	1.8	45,371	77,629	123,000	2.45	5,100,000	1.9	5,730,000	2.1
Black Muslims	0	0.0	200,000	0.1	1,250,000	0.5	12,603	27,397	40,000	2.82	1,400,000	0.5	1,650,000	0.6
New-Religionists	0	0.0	110,000	0.1	750,000	0.3	7,562	24,838	32,400	3.66	947,000	0.4	1,074,000	0.4
Nonreligious	1,000,000	1.3	10,069,000	4.9	20,702,000	8.3	208,726	133,674	342,400	1.54	22,928,000	8.7	24,126,000	8.8
Sikhs	0	0.0	1,000	0.0	150,000	0.1	1,512	7,488	9,000	4.81	190,000	0.1	240,000	0.1
Tribal religionists	100,000	0.1	70,000	0.0	45,000	0.0	454	-1,954	-1,500	-3.97	38,000	0.0	30,000	0.0
Other religionists	10,000	0.0	450,000	0.2	1,000,000	0.4	10,082	-1,082	9,000	0.87	1,050,000	0.4	1,090,000	0.4
Total population	**75,995,000**	**100.0**	**205,048,000**	**100.0**	**249,921,000**	**100.0**	**2,519,800**	**0**	**2,519,800**	**0.97**	**263,248,000**	**100.0**	**275,119,000**	**100.0**

Methodology. This table depicts the United States, the country with the largest number of adherents to Christianity, which is the world's largest religion. Statistics for five times in the 20th century are presented. Also analyzed is each religion's *Annual change* by: *Natural* increase (births minus deaths, plus immigrants minus emigrants) per year and *Conversion* (new converts minus new defectors) per year, which together constitute the *Total* increase per year. *Rate* is then computed as percentage per year.
Structure. Vertically the table lists 27 major religious categories. The 12 major religions (including nonreligion) in the U.S. are listed alphabetically, except the largest (Christians) is first. Indented names of groups in the "Adherents" column are subcategories of the groups above them and are also counted in these unindented totals, so they are not added into the column total. Figures for Christians in 1970 are built upon detailed head counts by churches, usually to the last digit. The 1990 figures are current estimates, rounded to the nearest 1,000. Because of rounding, the corresponding percentage figures may sometimes not total exactly 100%. Figures for AD 2000 are projections based on current long-term trends.
Christians. Professing Christians are all persons who profess publicly (in censuses or polls) to follow Jesus Christ as Lord and Saviour. This category is subdivided into **affiliated Christians** (church members) and **unaffiliated (nominal) Christians** (professing Christians not affiliated with any church).
Evangelicals. Churches, agencies, and individuals that call themselves by this term usually emphasize five or more fundamental doctrines (salvation by faith, personal acceptance, verbal inspiration of Scripture, depravity of man, Virgin Birth, miracles of Christ, atonement, evangelism, Second Advent).
Black Christians. Members of denominations initiated by African-Americans.
Other Christians. This term here denotes members of denominations and churches that regard themselves as outside mainline Protestant/Catholic/Orthodox Christianity.
Non-Christians. Followers of non-Christian religions or of no religion; the 12 largest such varieties are listed.
Jews. Core Jewish population relating to Judaism, excluding Jewish persons professing a different religion but including immigrants from the former U.S.S.R., Eastern Europe, Israel, and other areas.
Other categories. Definitions as given above under the Worldwide Adherents table.

(DAVID B. BARRETT)

Sports and Games

After the huge success of the association football (soccer) World Cup in 1994, the spotlight in 1995 turned to rugby, with the Union World Cup won by South Africa, the host, and the League World Cup, staged in Britain, confirming the supremacy of Australia. If there was an image to be treasured from all the sporting achievements of the year, it was the sight of Nelson Mandela, in his South African number 6 rugby jersey, handing the Webb Ellis Trophy to the real number 6, François Pienaar, the captain of South Africa, after his team had pulled off the surprise of the tournament by beating heavily favoured New Zealand in the final in Johannesburg. After three decades of sporting isolation of South Africa, the moment captured the triumphant fusion of sport and politics. The Rugby League World Cup was a more sedate affair marked by the joyous play of the Pacific Island teams of Tonga, Fiji, Western Samoa, and Papua New Guinea but lacking the individual brilliance that Jonah Lomu (*see* BIOGRAPHIES) brought to Rugby Union.

Another outsize performer, John Daly, produced the biggest shock in golf by winning the British Open. The controversial American, though, deserved his victory, earned in a play-off with Costantino Rocca of Italy. Daly was left off the U.S. team for the Ryder Cup, which was won by Europe amid scenes of high emotion at Rochester, N.Y. With Corey Pavin winning the U.S. Open and Ben Crenshaw the Masters, only Steve Elkington of Australia, with his victory in the U.S. Professional Golfers' Association Championship, broke the American stranglehold on the four major tournaments.

In tennis Pete Sampras won his third consecutive Wimbledon title, and Andre Agassi briefly defied all predictions by gaining the top ranking in the world. Of individual feats, though, none could match that of baseball player Cal Ripken, Jr. (*see* BIOGRAPHIES), whose 2,131st consecutive game for the Baltimore Orioles, on September 6, beat the record set in 1939 by Lou Gehrig. Ripken said modestly that he had just gone to the office every day just like most of his countrymen. He could not quite understand the fuss, but baseball, still desperately trying to recover its balance after the 1994 major league strike, was thankful for his achievement. (ANDREW LONGMORE)

The New Professionals

During 1995 more of the traditional barriers in sports between amateurs and professionals crumbled beneath the weight of commercial pressure. Chief among the sports to profit, or suffer, whichever way one looked at it, was Rugby Union. The World Cup in South Africa effectively marked the end of an era characterized by the old-fashioned idea that games should be played for fun. In truth, such countries as New Zealand, Australia, and France had been paying their players for years, and so, for all the cries of the diehards that the game would never be the same, the advent of professionalism was merely a recognition of the status quo, at least at the international level.

Conversely, tennis, one of the most lucrative of all sports, put limits on its professionalism after the well-publicized troubles experienced by the teenage prodigy and 1992 Olympic Games singles champion Jennifer Capriati, who made her debut at the age of 13 but took leave from the tour after four years. The Women's Tennis Association, which ran the women's world tour, ruled that no girl would be allowed to play in a leading tournament before her 16th birthday. The new ruling did not apply to several young players who had already made their debuts or stated their intention of doing so.

Even the Olympic Games, which had accepted the professional basketball players of the 1992 Dream Team and the expedient reinstatement of professional figure skaters to amateur status, found it increasingly difficult to compete with the lure of money. In 1995 Ukrainian figure skater Oksana Baiul (*see* BIOGRAPHIES), who had captured the 1993 world championship at age 15 and the Olympic gold medal less than a year later, announced that she would not seek to defend her Olympic title in 1998. The 17-year-old Baiul said she preferred the relative freedom of professional skating as much as the high fees paid for ice shows and professional competitions.

The movement to professionalism in sports was so pervasive that 19-year-old golfer Eldrick ("Tiger") Woods attracted considerable attention during the year when he chose not to turn pro after winning his second U.S. amateur championship. (ANDREW LONGMORE)

ARCHERY

FITA Outdoor World Target Archery Championships

Year	Men's individual		Men's team	
	Winner	Points	Winner	Points
1987	V. Esheyev (U.S.S.R.)	329	West Germany	891
1989	S. Zabrodsky (U.S.S.R.)	332	U.S.S.R.	985
1991	S. Fairweather (Austl.)	334	South Korea	998
1993	Park Kyung Mo (S.Kor.)	113	France	249
1995	**Lee Kyung Chul (S.Kor.)**	**109**	**South Korea**	**255**
Year	**Women's individual**		**Women's team**	
	Winner	Points	Winner	Points
1987	Ma Xiangjun (China)	330	U.S.S.R.	884
1989	Kim Soo Nyung (S.Kor.)	338	South Korea	995
1991	Kim Soo Nyung (S.Kor.)	333	South Korea	1,030
1993	Kim Hyo Jung (S.Kor.)	104	South Korea	236
1995	**N. Valeyeva (Moldova)**	**113**	**South Korea**	**247**

At the 1995 world outdoor target archery championships, held in Jakarta, Indon., August 1–6, the United States won the combined team men's trophy, and Sweden took the women's prize. For the first time since the formation of the sport's governing body in 1931, a new bow division, the Compound, was included in the competition. The tournament had particular significance because it was the qualifying meet for the 1996 Olympic Games.

Individual men's winners included, in the Olympic Division, Lee Kyung Chul of South Korea and, in the Compound Division, Gary Broadhead of the U.S. The women's champions were Natalya Valeyeva of Moldova in the Olympic Division and Angela Moscarelli of the U.S. in the Compound. Men's team winners were South Korea in the Olympic Division and France in the Compound. The champion women's teams were South Korea in the Olympic Division and the U.S. in the Compound. The U.S. gained the most medals in the tournament, with three golds, two silvers, and two bronzes. South Korea placed second with three golds and two bronzes.

In March the U.S. National Field Archery Association (NFAA) held its annual indoor championship in Tulsa, Okla. When all 1,000 archers had shot their last arrow, Carolyn Elder and Jason Street were the Limited winners. Linda Klosterman won the women's Unlimited title, and Kenny Young won his first national Unlimited championship with a strong perfect second round.

The 1995 NFAA National Field outdoor champions were crowned in July at Wausau, Wis. The 1995 Limited titles were won by Carolyn Elder and Steve Gibbs. Nancy Zorn won the women's Unlimited championship and Mike Leiter won his seventh men's Unlimited title. The highlight of the weeklong tournament was the first-ever perfect 560 Hunter round shot by Terry Ragsdale. (LARRY WISE)

AUTOMOBILE RACING

Grand Prix Racing. Michael Schumacher began the 1995 International Formula One racing season as the world champion driver, the first German to hold the title, but the Williams-Renaults, to be raced by Damon Hill and newcomer David Coulthard of Scotland, were regarded as better cars than Schumacher's Benetton-Renaults. As the season unfolded, Schumacher proved himself the finest exponent of this exacting and dangerous sport, and four races before the end of the season, he had again clinched the world championship and had ousted Williams from the constructors' title.

The season opened in São Paulo, Brazil, where Schumacher finished first and Coulthard was second. At the Argentine Grand Prix in Buenos Aires, Hill retrieved his reputation, winning the 305-km (190-mi) race for Williams.

Formula One Grand Prix Race Results, 1995

Race	Driver	Average speed (km/h)	Car
Brazilian GP	M. Schumacher	187.001	Benetton B195-Renault V10
Argentine GP	D. Hill	162.449	Williams FW17-Renault V10
San Marino GP	D. Hill	181.199	Williams FW17-Renault V10
Spanish GP	M. Schumacher	201.404	Benetton B195-Renault V10
Monaco GP	M. Schumacher	137.666	Benetton B195-Renault V10
Canadian GP	J. Alesi	172.247	Ferrari 412T2-Ferrari V12
French GP	M. Schumacher	186.417	Benetton B195-Renault V10
British GP	J. Herbert	195.722	Benetton B195-Renault V10
German GP	M. Schumacher	222.220	Benetton B195-Renault V10
Hungarian GP	D. Hill	172.326	Williams FW17-Renault V10
Belgian GP	M. Schumacher	190.291	Benetton B195-Renault V10
Italian GP	J. Herbert	233.920	Benetton B195-Renault V10
Portuguese GP	D. Coulthard	182.396	Williams FW17-Renault V10
European GP	M. Schumacher	183.266	Benetton B195-Renault V10
Pacific GP	M. Schumacher	169.546	Benetton B195-Renault V10
Japanese GP	M. Schumacher	192.469	Benetton B195-Renault V10
Australian GP	D. Hill	168.232	Williams FW17-Renault V10

WORLD DRIVERS' CHAMPIONSHIP: Schumacher 102 points, Hill 69 points, Coulthard 49 points.
MANUFACTURERS' WORLD CHAMPIONSHIP: Benetton-Renault 137 points, Williams-Renault 112 points, Ferrari 73 points.

Michael Schumacher of Germany, in a Benetton-Renault (right), moves ahead of the Williams-Renault driven by Damon Hill of the U.K. in the Pacific Grand Prix, held at Aida, Japan, in October. Schumacher won his second straight world drivers' championship in 1995.

PASCAL RONDEAU—ALLSPORT

The third round took place in San Marino. Schumacher led until crashing on the wet course. Coulthard pressed Hill, but the latter gained the victory. In the Spanish Grand Prix at Barcelona, the Benettons placed first and second, with Schumacher ahead of Britain's Johnny Herbert.

The inimitable "round-the-streets" race at Monaco was the fifth round of the championship series. Schumacher won after one refueling stop, with Hill second. The Schumacher-Hill battle seemed likely to be continued at Montreal, but in the Canadian Grand Prix there, a faulty gearbox dropped the former to fifth place and Hill fell behind the Ferraris, slowed by hydraulic maladies. Jean Alesi of France in a Ferrari won his first Grand Prix.

At Magny-Cours in the French Grand Prix, Schumacher and Hill again dueled for the lead, with the latter making a good start, but the two fuel stops that each one made decided the race, Schumacher winning by 31.3 seconds. In the British Grand Prix at Silverstone, a collision between Schumacher and Hill 15 laps from the finish allowed Herbert to win in the other Benetton. Alesi placed second.

In the German Grand Prix at Hockenheim, Hill made a blazing start, only to go off at the first corner on lap two; a worn driveshaft was blamed. Even though Schumacher made two stops to Coulthard's one, he established such an advantage that he was able to come in for his second stop without losing the lead.

Hill returned to the winner's circle at the Hungarian Grand Prix, with Coulthard coming in second. In the Belgian Grand Prix, Schumacher started far back but had made up eight places by the third lap. Then, when rain caused Hill to change to "wet" tires, Schumacher stayed on "dry" ones, and owing to his wonderful display of skill, his strategy paid off with a victory in the race.

In the Italian Grand Prix at Monza, Hill shunted Schumacher out of the race as they were overtaking Japanese driver Taki Inoue. Herbert was the winner.

International Cup for Formula One Manufacturers

Year	Car	Year	Car
1990	McLaren/Honda	1993	Williams/Renault
1991	McLaren/Honda	1994	Williams/Renault
1992	Williams/Renault	**1995**	**Benetton/Renault**

World Championship of Drivers

Year	Winner	Car
1991	A. Senna (Braz.)	McLaren/Honda
1992	N. Mansell (U.K.)	Williams/Renault
1993	A. Prost (Fr.)	Williams/Renault
1994	M. Schumacher (Ger.)	Benetton/Ford
1995	**M. Schumacher (Ger.)**	**Benetton/Renault**

Le Mans 24-Hour Grand Prix d'Endurance

Year	Car	Drivers
1991	Mazda	V. Weidler, J. Herbert, B. Gachot
1992	Peugeot	Y. Dalmas, M. Blundell, D. Warwick
1993	Peugeot	G. Brabham, C. Bouchut, E. Helary
1994	Dauer Porsche	Y. Dalmas, H. Haywood, M. Baldi
1995	**McLaren**	**Y. Dalmas, J.J. Lehto, M. Sekiya**

Monte-Carlo Rally

Year	Car	Driver, codriver
1991	Toyota Celica	Sainz, Moya
1992	Lancia Delta Integrale	Auriol, Occelli
1993	Toyota Celica	Auriol, Occelli
1994	Ford Escort	Delecour, Grataloup
1995	**Subaru Impreza**	**Sainz, Moya**

In Portugal Coulthard drove a sound race to win from Schumacher. The European Grand Prix at the Nurburgring was frustrating for Hill, who crashed in pursuit of Coulthard, his hopes for the world championship expiring at that moment. Schumacher again made a great overtaking pass three laps from the finish to win.

The competition then moved to Japan. The Pacific Grand Prix at Aida became a race of clever tactics by Benetton, resulting in a victory for Schumacher. In the Japanese Grand Prix at Suzuka, Schumacher equaled Nigel Mansell's nine wins in one season when he finished first.

In the season finale, the Australian Grand Prix at Adelaide, Hill drove a well-calculated race to win for Williams. Schumacher was rammed by Alesi's Ferrari, both cars retiring. (WILLIAM C. BODDY)

U.S. Racing. Two Canadians, Jacques Villeneuve (*see* BIOGRAPHIES) and Scott Goodyear, figured in another astonishing finish at the 1995 Indianapolis 500. Goodyear, in a Reynard-Honda, was in the lead when he passed the Chevrolet Corvette pace car illegally just after the 190th lap of the 200-lap race; officials stopped scoring his laps on the 196th, and Goodyear finished 14th. Ironically, Villeneuve earlier in the race had been penalized two laps for the same infraction but had battled back into contention. Driving a Reynard-Ford, he averaged 247.221 km/h (153.616 mph) to beat Christian Fittipaldi of Brazil by 2.481 sec and win $1,312,019 of the $8,063,550 purse. The race was unusual because neither defending champion Al Unser, Jr., nor 1993 winner Emerson Fittipaldi (Christian's uncle) qualified for the final.

Villeneuve also won the Championship Auto Racing Teams (CART) IndyCar PPG

Indy Car Champions	
Year	Driver
1990	A. Unser, Jr.
1991	Mi. Andretti
1992	B. Rahal
1993	N. Mansell
1994	A. Unser, Jr.
1995	**J. Villeneuve**

Indianapolis 500		
Year	Winner	Avg. speed in mph
1991	R. Mears	176.457
1992	A. Unser, Jr.	134.479
1993	E. Fittipaldi	157.207
1994	A. Unser, Jr.	160.872
1995	**J. Villeneuve**	**153.616**

National Association for Stock Car Auto Racing (NASCAR) Winston Cup Champions	
Year	Winner
1990	D. Earnhardt
1991	D. Earnhardt
1992	A. Kulwicki
1993	D. Earnhardt
1994	D. Earnhardt
1995	**J. Gordon**

World Series season championship over Unser, with Bobby Rahal third and Michael Andretti fourth. Unser could not overcome Villeneuve's early lead and also was disqualified after apparently winning at Portland, Ore.

The other Indianapolis classic, the Brickyard 400 of the National Association for Stock Car Auto Racing (NASCAR), contested in U.S. stock cars, paid a $4,447,015 purse. Defending Winston Cup champion Dale Earnhardt, in his black Goodwrench Chevrolet Monte Carlo, won over four Ford Thunderbirds led by Rusty Wallace. The average speed was 249.780 km/h (155.206 mph), and the margin of victory was only 0.37 sec. Despite this and four other NASCAR victories, Earnhardt lost his Winston Cup crown to Jeff Gordon, who clinched it in the last race by 34 points, 4,614–4,580. And, for the 11th time in a row, Earnhardt failed to win NASCAR's most prestigious race, the Daytona 500, finishing second to defending champion Sterling Marlin by 0.67 sec.

Gordon won 7 of the 31 races in the Winston Cup series, becoming the first NASCAR driver to earn $4 million ($4,347,-343) in a single season.

NASCAR during the year began a new SuperTruck series for race trucks on small tracks. Chevrolet dominated this competition easily, just as it had in winning the Winston Cup national manufacturers' crown. The trucks basically had Winston Cup engines in full-size pickup bodies. Mike Skinner was crowned champion.

In the Sports Car Club of America's Trans-Am, the oldest continuous racing series in the U.S., Tom Kendall, driving a Roush Mustang, won the title by 24 points, 305–281, despite a late charge by Ron Fellows of Canada. In the International Race of Champions, Unser edged NASCAR's Mark Martin for the title, contested in identically prepared Dodge Avengers.

(ROBERT J. FENDELL)

BADMINTON

China defeated Indonesia 3–1 in the world mixed team championships at Lausanne, Switz., May 17–21, 1995, and thereby took home its first Sudirman Cup. China's victory emphasized its reemergence as a world power in badminton. The women's doubles pair of Ge Fei and Gu Jun started the barrage for China by defeating Indonesia's Elisa and Rosiana Zelin 15–9, 15–10. Indonesia's Olympic and world champion, Susi Susanti, failed to live up to expectations, being crushed by China's Ye Zhaoying 11–2, 11–3 in a match that took only 20 minutes and gave China a crucial 2–0 lead. All hope for victory was lost for Indonesia following the men's singles competition, in which China's Sun Jun defeated Heryanto Arbi 15–7, 9–15, 15–11. Indonesia's top-ranked men's doubles team of Ricky Subagja and Rexy Mainaky then prevented a shutout by defeating China's Jiang Xin and Huang Zhanzhong 11–15, 15–11, 15–6. The final mixed doubles match was not contested.

Held in conjunction with the Sudirman Cup in Lausanne were the world championships. In the men's singles Arbi avenged his loss in the Sudirman Cup by defeating South Korea's Park Sung Woo 15–11, 15–8 to take the title. In women's singles Ye Zhaoying again easily defeated Susanti 5–11, 11–8, 11–2 in the semifinals and then went on to defeat Han Jingna of China 11–7, 11–10 in the final. Subagja and Mainaky again demonstrated that they were the best men's doubles pair in the world, defeating Jon Holst-Christensen and Thomas Lund of Denmark 15–5, 15–2. Gil Young Ah and Jang Hye Ock of South Korea defeated Indonesia's Lili Tampi and Finarsih 3–15, 15–11, 15–10 for the women's title. It was all Denmark in the mixed doubles final as Lund and Marlene Thomsen defeated fellow Danes Jens Eriksen and Helene Kirkegaard 15–2, 15–6.

(PAUL PAWLACZYK)

FABRICE COFFRINI—AFP

Sun Jun of China returns the birdie in the men's singles competition during a Sudirman Cup match in May in Lausanne, Switz. Sun's 15–7, 9–15, 15–11 victory over Heryanto Arbi of Indonesia clinched the cup for China, the first time it had won the world mixed team championships.

World Badminton Championships

Year	Men's singles	Women's singles	Men's doubles	Women's doubles
1987	Yang Yang (China)	Han Aiping (China)	Li Yongbo, Tian Bingyi (China)	Lin Ying, Guan Weizhen (China)
1989	Yang Yang (China)	Li Lingwei (China)	Li Yongbo, Tian Bingyi (China)	Lin Ying, Guan Weizhen (China)
1991	Zhao Jianhua (China)	Tang Jiuhong (China)	Park Joo Bong, Kim Moon Soo (S.Kor.)	Guan Weizhen, Nong Qunhua (China)
1993	J. Suprianto (Indon.)	S. Susanti (Indon.)	R. Subagja, R. Gunawan (Indon.)	Nong Qunhua, Zhou Lei (China)
1995	**H. Arbi (Indon.)**	**Ye Zhaoying (China)**	**R. Subagja, R. Mainaky (Indon.)**	**Gil Young Ah, Jang Hye Ock (S.Kor.)**

All-England Championships—Singles

Year	Men	Women
1991	A. Wiranata (Indon.)	S. Susanti (Indon.)
1992	Liu Jun (China)	Tang Jiuhong (China)
1993	H. Arbi (Indon.)	S. Susanti (Indon.)
1994	H. Arbi (Indon.)	S. Susanti (Indon.)
1995	**P.-E. Hoyer-Larsen (Den.)**	**Lim Xiao Qing (Swed.)**

Uber Cup (Women)

Year	Winner	Runner-up
1985–86	China	Indonesia
1987–88	China	S.Korea
1989–90	China	S.Korea
1991–92	China	S.Korea
1993–94	Indonesia	China

Thomas Cup (Men)

Year	Winner	Runner-up
1985–86	China	Indonesia
1987–88	China	Malaysia
1989–90	China	Malaysia
1991–92	Malaysia	Indonesia
1993–94	Indonesia	Malaysia

BASEBALL

Despite the absence of a collective bargaining agreement between the team owners and the players, major league baseball was played in 1995, though the season was shortened. The schedule was reduced from the usual 162 games to 144. There was an extra round of play-offs during the postseason, as established in the 1994 realignment of the divisions.

World Series. The Atlanta Braves, who had been on the verge of a championship during the last few years, finally won the World Series by defeating the Cleveland Indians four games to two in the best-of-seven series. The Braves clinched their first title in 30 years, since moving from Milwaukee, Wis., by beating the Indians 1–0 before 51,875 fans in Atlanta-Fulton County Stadium in the final game on October 28. David Justice provided the Braves' run with a sixth-inning home run off Cleveland relief pitcher Jim Poole. Atlanta left-hander Tom Glavine, the pitcher with the most victories in baseball for the last five seasons, pitched masterfully. He allowed just one single—to Tony Pena in the sixth inning—to the hard-hitting Indians over eight innings before Mark Wohlers closed the triumph with a perfect ninth inning.

Glavine was voted Most Valuable Player for the series. He was the veteran of the vaunted Atlanta pitching staff, which restricted the Indians to a .179 batting average through six games, well below their regular season .291 average, which led the major leagues.

Greg Maddux (*see* BIOGRAPHIES), the number one starter in the Braves' strong rotation, opened the series with a 3–2 triumph at Atlanta, Ga., on October 21. He surrendered unearned runs in the first and the ninth innings but permitted only two hits in his complete-game performance. The Braves scored their winning run in a two-run seventh inning on a squeeze bunt by Rafael Belliard. Orel Hershiser, who began the inning by walking the first two batters, was the losing pitcher.

The next night the Braves won 4–3 on a two-run homer by catcher Javier López. Glavine yielded a two-run homer to Cleveland's Eddie Murray in the second inning but worked six innings and received credit for the victory.

The series then moved to Cleveland's new Jacobs Field, where an emotional crowd of 43,584 fans cheered the Indians to a 7–6 conquest in 11 innings on October 24. The Indians jumped to a 4–1 lead against John Smoltz, but the Braves went ahead 6–5 before the Indians tied it 6–6 in the eighth

Final Major League Standings, 1995

AMERICAN LEAGUE East Division				Central Division				West Division			
Club	W.	L.	G.B.	Club	W.	L.	G.B.	Club	W.	L.	G.B.
Boston	86	58	–	Cleveland	100	44	–	California	78	66	–
New York	79	65	7	Kansas City	70	74	30	Seattle	78	66	–
Baltimore	71	73	15	Chicago	68	76	32	Texas	74	70	4
Detroit	60	84	26	Milwaukee	65	79	35	Oakland	67	77	11
Toronto	56	88	30	Minnesota	56	88	44				
NATIONAL LEAGUE East Division				Central Division				West Division			
Club	W.	L.	G.B.	Club	W.	L.	G.B.	Club	W.	L.	G.B.
Atlanta	90	54	–	Cincinnati	85	59	–	Los Angeles	78	66	–
New York	69	75	21	Houston	76	68	9	Colorado	77	67	1
Philadelphia	69	75	21	Chicago	73	71	12	San Diego	70	74	8
Florida	67	76	22½	St. Louis	62	81	22½	San Francisco	67	77	11
Montreal	66	78	24	Pittsburgh	58	86	27				

World Series*

Year	Winning team	Losing team	Results
1991	Minnesota Twins (AL)	Atlanta Braves (NL)	4–3
1992	Toronto Blue Jays (AL)	Atlanta Braves (NL)	4–2
1993	Toronto Blue Jays (AL)	Philadelphia Phillies (NL)	4–2
1994	not held		
1995	**Atlanta Braves (NL)**	**Cleveland Indians (AL)**	**4–2**

*AL—American League; NL—National League.

SCOTT WACHTER—SPORTS ILLUSTRATED

Setting a new record on September 6 by playing in his 2,131st consecutive game, Baltimore Orioles shortstop Cal Ripken, Jr., receives the congratulations of fans in Camden Yards. The previous record had been set by Lou Gehrig of the New York Yankees and had stood for 56 years.

inning and won the four-hour nine-minute marathon on Murray's single off Alejandro Pena in the 11th. Cleveland's ace relief pitcher, José Mesa, was the winner.

The Braves, however, assumed a commanding 3–1 lead in games the next night by downing the Indians in Cleveland 5–2. Left hander Steve Avery, the winning pitcher, restricted the Indians to three hits over six innings, while the Braves mounted a three-run rally in the seventh. Ken Hill was the losing pitcher.

The Braves then sent their ace Maddux to the mound on October 26, but the Indians averted elimination. Albert Belle stroked a two-run homer in the first inning, and Hershiser pitched eight excellent innings toward a 5–4 triumph. The winning margin was a long home run by Cleveland third baseman Jim Thome off Atlanta reliever Brad Clontz in the eighth.

The Braves, needing only one victory to clinch, secured it upon returning home to end their recent string of frustrations. They had lost the World Series to the Minnesota Twins in 1991 and the Toronto Blue Jays in 1992 and then were upset by the Philadelphia Phillies in the 1993 National League Championship Series.

Tom Glavine of the Atlanta Braves delivers a pitch in the second game of the World Series. Glavine, with more wins than any other pitcher during the past five years, was voted the Most Valuable Player of the series, which the Braves won over the Cleveland Indians in six games.

RICK STEWART—ALLSPORT

Play-offs. With the 1995 season, a new play-off format was instituted whereby a wild-card team with the best second-place record in each league joined the six division-winning teams.

The Colorado Rockies, in only their third year, earned wild-card honours in the National League. But they drew the powerful Braves in the best-of-five division series and were eliminated in four games.

The New York Yankees achieved the wild-card berth in the American League. They won the first two games at home in their best-of-five division series against the upstart Seattle Mariners, but the Mariners swept three games at home to advance in dramatic fashion.

After defeating Colorado, the Braves claimed their third National League pennant since 1991 by sweeping the Cincinnati Reds four games to none in the best-of-seven National League Championship Series. The Reds had swept the Los Angeles Dodgers in the division series. The Braves stunned the Reds with two extra-inning victories in Cincinnati and then went home to win twice, by scores of 5–2 and 6–0.

The Indians swept the Boston Red Sox in the division series. They then lost the opener of the American League Championship Series in Seattle and also lost their first home game to fall behind 2–1 in the series. But they won the next three games—by scores of 7–0, 3–2, and 4–0—to seize their first pennant since 1954.

After the Mariners and California Angels tied for first place in the American League West division, they had a one-game playoff, won by the Mariners. The Angels, who had led the division for most of the summer, also lost out on a wild-card spot, because the Yankees posted a better second-place record in the American League East.

Regular Season. The Braves cruised to a first-place finish in the National League East with a 90–54 record, 21 games better than Philadelphia and the New York Mets. Cincinnati won the Central division by nine games over the Houston Astros, and Los Angeles captured the West division by one game over Colorado.

Cleveland posted the best record in either league, winning 100 of 144 games and romping to a first-place finish in the American League Central by 30 games over the Kansas City Royals. Boston outdistanced New York by seven games in the East, while the Mariners, who appeared hopelessly out of contention in August, caught up with the slumping Angels.

Despite the new play-off format, interest in baseball was down throughout the major leagues. Overall attendance dropped about 20% after the strife of the previous season, when play was halted in mid-August because of a player strike.

Individual Accomplishments. The highlight of the season occurred on September 6 in Baltimore, Md., where Orioles' shortstop Cal Ripken, Jr. (*see* BIOGRAPHIES), played his 2,131st consecutive game, breaking the 56-year-old record of New York Yankee Hall of Famer Lou Gehrig. Ripken's streak spanned more than 13 seasons, and he celebrated the historic evening by hitting a fourth-inning home run in a 4–2 victory over California.

Despite the abbreviated schedule, Belle of the Indians became the 12th player ever to hit 50 home runs in a season. He also tied Boston's Mo Vaughn for the American League lead in runs batted in with 126. Edgar Martínez of Seattle won the batting championship with an average of .356, and teammate Randy Johnson led pitchers with a 2.48 earned-run average (ERA) and struck out 294 batters, the most in either league. Baltimore's Mike Mussina won 19 games, one more than Johnson and David Cone of the Yankees. Mesa of Cleveland led relief pitchers with 46 saves.

In the National League, Tony Gwynn of the San Diego Padres won the batting title with an average of .368. Dante Bichette of Colorado hit the most home runs, 40, and batted in the most runs, 128. Maddux crafted a brilliant ERA of 1.63 while compiling a 19–2 record. Randy Myers of the Chicago Cubs had the most saves, 38. Ramón Martínez of the Dodgers pitched the only no-hitter, a 7–0 victory over the Florida Marlins.

Cincinnati shortstop Barry Larkin was named the National League's Most Valuable Player, and first baseman Vaughn won the honour in the American League. The Cy Young Awards for best pitcher went to Maddux for a record fourth consecutive year in the National League and Johnson in the American. Los Angeles pitcher Hideo Nomo was the National League's Rookie of the Year, and Minnesota outfielder Marty Cordova won in the American. Managers of the Year were Don Baylor of Colorado in the National League and Lou Piniella of Seattle in the American.

Other Developments. The National League beat the American League 3–2 in the annual All-Star Game at Arlington, Texas, on July 11. Jeff Conine of Florida hit a pinch home run in the eighth inning and was named Most Valuable Player. Dodger rookie star Nomo started the game for the National League, marking the first time a Japanese-born player had ever appeared in an All-Star Game.

In January former Phillies third baseman Mike Schmidt was the only player elected to the Hall of Fame. Mickey Mantle, the former New York Yankee star, died in August of liver cancer. (*See* OBITUARIES.) Sparky Anderson, who had managed the Detroit Tigers for 17 seasons, resigned at the end of the year.

Management-Labour Situation. With the impasse still existing after a winter of restless and occasionally acrimonious negotiations, owners opened spring training camps in mid-February to replacement players. Regular players were also welcome, but the union proved strong. Exhibition games began without the major leaguers but were not warmly received by fans.

On March 26 the National Labor Relations Board, which had been investigating unfair labour practices, authorized its general counsel to seek a preliminary injunction against owners for the purpose of restoring 1994 work rules. On March 31, U.S. District Court Judge Sonia Sotomayor issued the injunction in New York City, at which time the union announced it would end its strike.

Latin-American National Champions*

Country	Champion
Dominican Republic	Este Sugar Growers
Mexico	Hermosillo Orange Growers (PL) Monterrey Sultans (ML)
Puerto Rico	San Juan Senators
Venezuela	Caracas Lions

*ML—Mexican League; PL—Pacific League.

Japan Series*

Year	Winning team	Losing team	Results
1991	Seibu Lions (PL)	Hiroshima Tōyō Carp (CL)	4–3
1992	Seibu Lions (PL)	Yakult Swallows (CL)	4–3
1993	Yakult Swallows (CL)	Seibu Lions (PL)	4–3
1994	Yomiuri Giants (CL)	Seibu Lions (PL)	4–2
1995	**Yakult Swallows (CL)**	**Orix Blue Wave (PL)**	**4–1**

*CL—Central League; PL—Pacific League.

The owners' request for a stay of the injunction was denied, and shortly thereafter interim commissioner Bud Selig declared that regular players should report to spring training camps on April 2. The start of the regular season was delayed until April 25, when the Dodgers beat the Marlins at Miami's Joe Robbie Stadium.

(ROBERT WILLIAM VERDI)

Latin America. The 1995 Caribbean Series was held in San Juan, P.R., on February 4–9. The tournament, in which winners of the four major winter tournaments in Latin America compete against one another, was played in a round-robin format, with every team playing each rival twice. The host team, the San Juan Senators, swept the series easily with six straight victories before an enthusiastic home crowd. In the final game the Senators defeated the Sugar Growers from Este, of the Dominican Republic, by 9–3.

The Sugar Growers took second place with four wins and two defeats. Mexico's Orange Growers of Hermosillo and Venezuela's Caracas Lions, with identical records of one win and five losses, were relegated to last place.

Mexico's economic crisis affected Mexican League baseball, played during the summer. The season was shortened from 132 to 116 games by eliminating contests between teams from the southern and northern divisions during the regular season. Eventually the Monterrey Sultans won the northern division by virtue of a good performance during the play-offs; they had finished far behind the Reynosa Broncos during the regular season. The Sultans then easily defeated the Mexico City Red Devils, the champions of the southern zone, in four straight games during the best-of-seven championship series.

(SERGIO SARMIENTO)

Japan. The Yakult Swallows of the Central League, based in Tokyo, defeated the Pacific League's Orix Blue Wave of Kobe four games to one in the 1995 Japan Series. The Swallow pitchers gave up only 10 earned runs in the five games and had a combined ERA of 1.76, while the ERA for the Blue Wave pitching corps was 3.28. After the Swallows won the first game, the next three went into extra innings, and each was decided by a home run: in game two, by Swallow first baseman Thomas O'Malley; in game three, by Swallow shortstop Takahiro Ikeyama; and in game four, by Blue Wave first baseman Doug Jennings. The Swallows won the fifth game 3–1. O'Malley, who hit .529—including two home runs—was voted the Most Valuable Player of the series.

The Swallows, a preseason underdog, got off to a good start and by the end of April were in first place, where they remained for the rest of the season. O'Malley, with a batting average of .302, 31 home runs, and 87 runs batted in, was voted the Most Valuable Player of the Central League. Hiroshima Carp pitcher Yasuyuki Yamauchi won 14 games against 10 losses and got the Rookie of the Year award.

The Blue Wave floundered during April and May but in June overtook the then league-leading defending champions Seibu Lions and led for the rest of the season. Ichiro Suzuki, an outfielder for the Blue Wave who led the league in stolen bases (49) and in four batting categories—batting average (.342), runs batted in (80), hits (179), and on-base percentage (.432)—was named the Most Valuable Player of the year in the Pacific League. Pitcher Masafumi Hirai of the Blue Wave, with a 15–5 record and 27 saves, was voted the Rookie of the Year.

(TOSHIHIKO SUZUKI)

BASKETBALL

United States. Without Tyus Edney, it appeared that UCLA might not have one more big game left to cap a colossal 1994–95 season. But the Bruins did, even though the 1.8-m (5-ft 10-in) Edney made only a token appearance during their 89–78 victory over defending champion Arkansas in the finals of the National Collegiate Athletic Association (NCAA) basketball tournament. Sidelined by a sprained right wrist, sustained in UCLA's 74–61 NCAA semifinal victory over Oklahoma State, Edney could only watch and hope on the bench.

The senior guard had distinguished company a few rows behind in the crowd of 38,340 packing the Kingdome in Seattle, Wash., for this showdown. Legendary coach John Wooden, who had masterminded UCLA to an unprecedented string of 10 national championships, 7 of them in a row, also was there to see history recreated. The Bruins had not captured another NCAA title since Wooden retired 20 years earlier.

When all hope seemed lost in the West Regional quarterfinal, Edney saved the Bruins by taking the ball and the outcome into his hands. With Missouri on the verge of a stunning upset, leading 74–73 only 4.8 seconds before the end, Edney drove the length of the court to bank in a dramatic game-winning basket at the final horn.

Arkansas had been discovering all season that the road to a second straight NCAA crown would be more than twice as tough. Still, it survived some close calls to come within 40 minutes of joining Duke as the second repeat college basketball champion in 22 years.

The Razorbacks defeated their first four NCAA tournament foes by a total of 15 points and then regrouped to oust North Carolina 75–68 in the semifinal. Unfortunately for Arkansas, its path to the throne room was blocked by UCLA. Led by sophomore Cameron Dollar, the Bruins jumped ahead early, repulsed a second-half Arkansas surge, and eased away at the finish.

Ed O'Bannon led UCLA with a game-high 30 points and 17 rebounds. When he

JOHN MCDONOUGH—SPORTS ILLUSTRATED

Freshman Toby Bailey of UCLA drives up to the basket for a shot against Arkansas, the defending champion, in the NCAA finals. UCLA won the game 89–78 to take its first national basketball championship since the retirement of legendary coach John Wooden 20 years earlier.

was named Most Valuable Player of the tournament, he showed why the Bruins had racked up a 31–2 season record. Pulling Edney onto the platform, he declared, "Yo, yo, yo, that's the real MVP right there."

UCLA had won 10 of 11 previous NCAA finals with Wooden at the helm. This 11th triumph widened the Bruins' lead over Kentucky and Indiana, each with five championships, in the all-time tournament rankings.

In women's basketball, Connecticut completed a storybook season by winning a ferocious NCAA tournament final from Tennessee 70–64. The Huskies' courageous second-half comeback made them the second unbeaten national champion in women's NCAA basketball history.

Connecticut finished with a 35–0 record, one game better than the perfect slate turned in by Texas in 1986. In a dream matchup of the country's two top teams, Connecticut overcame a shaky start by all-American Rebecca Lobo (*see* BIOGRAPHIES) and Jennifer Rizzotti to repeat a regular-season victory over the Lady Vols (34–3).

Both teams peaked at the right moment. Connecticut routed Stanford 87–60, and Tennessee had little trouble beating Georgia 73–51 in the semifinals.

Only one player could overshadow the entire 1995 National Basketball Association (NBA) play-off picture, even after his team was eliminated in the second round of the Eastern Conference pairings. Because Michael Jordan elected to come out of retirement near the end of the regular season, a second straight NBA title for Hakeem Olajuwon and the Houston Rockets could not command full attention.

Nonetheless, it was still quite a show when the Rockets swept the best-of-seven final series from the Orlando Magic, providing a somewhat anticlimactic finish to some exciting battles in earlier play-off rounds. In the last act, the 2.13-m (7-ft) Olajuwon was so overpowering that he embarrassed 2.16-m (7-ft 1-in) Magic superstar Shaquille O'Neal and his visibly nervous teammates.

Adding a fourth crown to the trio that the Chicago Bulls had won in 1991–93 would have been tough enough for Jordan. But the 32-year-old guard, who went back to the Bulls after a fling in baseball's minor leagues, was not the same gravity-defying missile he had been. Jordan's shooting touch failed to come back with him, nor was he able to show fans the spectacular hang time that made him the most celebrated athlete of his generation.

Jennifer Rizzotti of Connecticut dribbles downcourt against a Tennessee defender in the final game of the NCAA tournament. Connecticut, which won the game 70–64, had a 35–0 season record, only the second time that a women's NCAA champion compiled a perfect record.
DAVID KLUTHO SPORTS ILLUSTRATED

Houston won only 47 games during the season and was not expected to be a strong play-off factor. However, a late-season trade that reunited Olajuwon with his former University of Houston teammate Clyde Drexler turned things around for the struggling club. The champions responded by beating the Utah Jazz, Phoenix Suns, and San Antonio Spurs in Western Conference preliminaries, advancing to the showdown with Orlando.

There Olajuwon and Drexler provided almost all of the magic there was to see. What was supposed to be a duel of superstar centres, pitting Olajuwon's experience against O'Neal's potential, turned out to be a mismatch. The Rockets won the first two games in Orlando and went home to Houston with a stranglehold on their championship defense.

National Basketball Association (NBA) Championship

Season	Winner	Runner-up	Results
1990–91	Chicago Bulls	Los Angeles Lakers	4–1
1991–92	Chicago Bulls	Portland Trail Blazers	4–2
1992–93	Chicago Bulls	Phoenix Suns	4–2
1993–94	Houston Rockets	New York Knicks	4–3
1994–95	**Houston Rockets**	**Orlando Magic**	**4–0**

NBA Final Standings, 1994–95

EASTERN CONFERENCE

Team	Won	Lost
Atlantic Division		
*Orlando	57	25
*New York	55	27
*Boston	35	47
Miami	32	50
New Jersey	30	52
Philadelphia	24	58
Washington	21	61

Team	Won	Lost
Central Division		
*Indiana	52	30
*Charlotte	50	32
*Chicago	47	35
*Cleveland	43	39
*Atlanta	42	40
Milwaukee	34	48
Detroit	28	54

WESTERN CONFERENCE

Team	Won	Lost
Midwest Division		
San Antonio	62	20
*Utah	60	22
Houston	47	35
*Denver	41	41
Dallas	36	46
Minnesota	21	61

Team	Won	Lost
Pacific Division		
*Phoenix	59	23
*Seattle	57	25
*L.A. Lakers	48	34
*Portland	44	38
Sacramento	39	43
Golden State	26	56
L.A. Clippers	17	65

*Gained play-off berth.

Division I National Collegiate Athletic Association (NCAA) Championship—Men

Year	Winner	Runner-up	Score
1991	Duke	Kansas	72–65
1992	Duke	Michigan	71–51
1993	North Carolina	Michigan	77–71
1994	Arkansas	Duke	76–72
1995	**UCLA**	**Arkansas**	**89–78**

Division I National Collegiate Athletic Association (NCAA) Championship—Women

Year	Winner	Runner-up	Score
1991	Tennessee	Virginia	70–67
1992	Stanford	Western Kentucky	78–62
1993	Texas Tech	Ohio State	84–82
1994	North Carolina	Louisiana Tech	60–59
1995	**Connecticut**	**Tennessee**	**70–64**

National Invitation Tournament (NIT) Championship

Year	Winner	Runner-up	Score
1991	Stanford	Oklahoma	78–72
1992	Virginia	Notre Dame	81–76
1993	Minnesota	Georgetown	62–61
1994	Villanova	Vanderbilt	80–73
1995	**Virginia Tech**	**Marquette**	**65–64**

Hakeem Olajuwon of the Houston Rockets shoots over Shaquille O'Neal of the Orlando Magic in the second game of the NBA finals. Houston swept the series in four games to take its second consecutive NBA title.

NATHANIEL S. BUTLER—NBA PHOTOS

Late in June seven NBA players, dissatisfied with the new labour agreement with the owners, filed a class action antitrust lawsuit against the NBA. They challenged the league's salary cap, draft, and free-agent system and invited their union to join them. The NBA responded on July 1 by locking out the players until a new collective bargaining agreement was reached. On September 13 the players voted to ratify the previous labour agreement. The dissident players did not challenge the vote, and the lockout was ended. (ROBERT G. LOGAN)

International. A number of championships throughout the Continent caused 1995 to be an exciting year for European basketball. Especially prominent were the European championships for men and women, held in Athens and Brno, Czech Rep., respectively. In Athens, Yugoslavia returned to prominence in world basketball by defeating Lithuania 96–90 in a final that was regarded by many as the most exciting in 20 years. In the women's tournament Ukraine won the championship for the first time, defeating Italy 77–66.

World Amateur Basketball Championship Men

Year	Winner	Runner-up
1986	United States	U.S.S.R.
1988	U.S.S.R.	Yugoslavia
1990	Yugoslavia	U.S.S.R.
1992	United States	Croatia
1994	United States	Russia

World Amateur Basketball Championship Women

Year	Winner	Runner-up
1986	United States	U.S.S.R.
1988	United States	Yugoslavia
1990	United States	Yugoslavia
1992	Unified Team	China
1994	Brazil	China

In Asia championships for men and women were held for the 18th and 16th time, respectively. At the men's tournament in Seoul, China was victorious, with Korea runner-up. In Shizuoka, Japan, the women's championship was also won by China, with Korea again placing second.

The European champions at Cadet (under 16) level were Croatia in the men's tournament and Russia in the women's competition. Runners-up were Spain and Italy.

The major club competition during the 1995–96 European season, the European Championship for Men's Clubs, was won by Real Madrid (Spain), which defeated Olympiakos (Greece) 73–61 in the final at Zaragoza, Spain. In other European tournaments Treviso (Italy) won the European Cup by beating Vitoria Álava (Spain); Alba Berlin (Germany) defeated Olimpia Stefanel Milan of Italy to take the European Korac Cup; Como (Italy) retained the Women's European Champions Cup with a victory over Dorna Valencia (Spain); and the Ronchetti Cup went to France, with Bourges defeating Parma (Italy).

The World Student Games (Universiade) finished a great year of basketball with its finals in Japan. The men's championship was won by the U.S., which completely overpowered the host nation 141–81.

(MARK HANNEN)

BILLIARD GAMES

Carom Billiards. The 1994 Billiard World Cup Association (BWA) three-cushion championship was won by Torbjorn Blomdahl of Sweden, despite his inability to finish first in any of the four international BWA Tour events used to determine the champion. But the accumulated point total from his strong and steady performances at all of the tour stops enabled Blomdahl to become the first man to win four career BWA world three-cushion titles (his previous championships were in 1988, 1991, and 1992).

Blomdahl's first-place finish was aided by the fact that no one else could muster more than a single title in the series. At the first meet, the Efes Pilsen World Cup in Istanbul, legendary Belgian star Raymond Ceulemans defeated Blomdahl in the semifinal round, relegating the Swede to third place. In Oosterhout, Neth., Blomdahl lost in the final of the Wetsteijn Dutch Open World Cup to emergency fill-in entrant Christoph Pilss of Austria. At the German Open World Cup in Halle, the runner-up spot again went to Blomdahl, with The Netherlands' Dick Jaspers the champion. Blomdahl's improbable "victory without a victory" was realized at the last tour event, the World Cup Final in Ghent, Belgium, where he was again second, this time to Semih Sayginer of Turkey.

Blomdahl's four-tournament PPI (points-per-inning average) was a fine 1.761, though overall runner-up Jaspers did post a slightly higher 1.770 PPI. Only Jaspers' 12th place at the Oosterhout event enabled Blomdahl to edge past him for the championship. Oosterhout was also the scene of new BWA records by Blomdahl: tied (with Jaspers) for best match PPI, 3.124, and best PPI for the tournament, 2.250 (breaking his own two-year-old record of 2.204).

The world championship in five-pins billiards was held in October in St. Vincent, Italy, where the top-ranked player in the world, 22-year-old Gustave Zito of Argentina, went undefeated to win the $61,000 first prize. He also won $64,000 in the four-tournament qualifying series.

World Three-Cushion Championship

Year	Winner
1991	R. Ceulemans (Belg.)
1992	T. Blomdahl (Swed.)
1993	T. Blomdahl (Swed.)
1994	Sang Lee (U.S.)
1995	**T. Blomdahl (Swed.)**

WPA World Nine-Ball Championships

Year	Men's champion
1992	J. Archer (U.S.)
1993	Chao Feng-pang (Taiwan)
1994	T. Okumura (Japan)
1995	**O. Ortmann (Ger.)**
Year	**Women's champion**
1992	F. Stark (Ger.)
1993	L.J. Jones (U.S.)
1994	E. Mataya-Laurance (U.S.)
1995	**G. Hofstatter (Austria)**

World Professional Snooker Championships

Year	Winner	Year	Winner
1991	J. Parrott	1994	S. Hendry
1992	S. Hendry	**1995**	**S. Hendry**
1993	S. Hendry		

As in 1994, Sang Chun Lee of New York City and Carlos Hallon of Miami, Fla., finished first and second, respectively, in the U.S. national three-cushion championship in New York City. It was the sixth time Lee had taken a U.S. national title.

Pocket Billiards. Nine-ball competitions dominated professional pocket billiards. The Professional Billiards Tour (PBT) Players' Championship in King of Prussia, Pa., was won by Jim Rempe of Scranton, Pa. Efren Reyes of the Philippines won the 19th annual U.S. Open 9-ball championships in Chesapeake, Va. In Reno, Nev., the Sands Regency Hotel was host to its usual two semiannual PBT events; Sands XX was won by Johnny Archer of Raleigh, N.C., and Sands XXI by Reyes. The Philippine star also won both the sixth and seventh Bicycle Club invitationals in Bell Gardens, Calif., raising him to the top of the PBT player rankings for the first time.

The PBT also held its first world 8-ball championship in Toledo, Ohio. Nick Varner of Owensboro, Ky., was the winner. Varner was also named 1994 Player of the Year by both *Billiards Digest* (third time) and *Pool & Billiard Magazine* (fourth award).

At the World Pool-Billiard Association (WPA) world women's nine-ball championship in Arlington Heights, Ill., Ewa Mataya-Laurance returned to the top spot. The 10th Women's Professional Billiard Association (WPBA) U.S. 9-Ball Open in Chesapeake, Va., was won by Jeanette Lee, who also won four WPBA tournaments and the 16th WPBA national championship in Sioux City, Iowa. That onslaught was enough to secure for her the number one WPBA tour ranking. Loree Jon Jones won $60,000 in prize money on the rich 1995 Gordon's Women's 9-Ball Series, held in Nashville, Tenn., Chicago, and San Francisco.

FIQ World Bowling Championships—Men

Year	Singles	Pairs	Triples	Team (fives)
1983	T. Cariello (U.S.)	Australia	Sweden	Finland
1987	P. Rolland (Fr.)	Sweden	United States	Sweden
1991	Ying Chieh Ma (Taiwan)	United States	United States	Taiwan
1995	**M. Doi (Can.)**	**Sweden**	**The Netherlands**	**The Netherlands**

FIQ World Bowling Championships—Women

Year	Singles	Pairs	Triples	Team (fives)
1983	L. Sulkanen (Swed.)	Denmark	West Germany	Sweden
1987	E. Piccini (Mex.)	United States	United States	United States
1991	M. Beckel (Ger.)	Japan	Canada	South Korea
1995	**D. Ship (Can.)**	**Thailand**	**Australia**	**Finland**

ABC Bowling Championships—Regular Division

Year	Singles	Score	All-events	Score
1991	E. Deines	826	T. Howery	2,216
1992	G. Blatchford, B. Youker (tie)	801	M. Tucker	2,158
1993	D. Bock	798	J. Nimke	2,254
1994	J. Weltzien	810	T. Holt	2,190
1995	**M. Surina**	**826**	**J. Kwiatkowski**	**2,191**

WIBC Bowling Championships—Open Division

Year	Singles	Score	All-events	Score
1991	D. Kuhn	773	D. Kuhn	2,036
1992	P. Ann	680	M. Tokimoto	1,928
1993	K. Collura, K. Murph (tie)	747	A.M. Duggan	1,990
1994	V. Fifield	716	W. Macpherson-Papanos	1,940
1995	**B. Owen**	**749**	**B. Owen**	**1,983**

International mixed-team nine-ball was featured in the inaugural Miller Pilsner Mosconi Cup in Romford, England, where the Billiard Congress of America (BCA) team defeated the European Pocket Billiard Federation squad 16–12. The BCA inducted Cisero Murphy, the first African-American to win a world pocket billiard championship (1965), to its Hall of Fame in ceremonies at its 12th International Trade Expo in Las Vegas, Nev.

The winners of the WPA world nine-ball championship, held in Taipei, Taiwan, in November, were Gerda Hofstatter of Austria and Oliver Ortmann of Germany. The junior champion was Kun-chang Huang of Taiwan. (BRUCE H. VENZKE)

Snooker. Stephen Hendry of Scotland maintained his mastery at snooker by winning the world professional title at Sheffield, England, in April 1995. His victory over Nigel Bond of England in the final by 18 frames to 9 enabled him to achieve his fourth successive triumph in the event and the fifth in all. He went on to defeat Peter Ebdon of England 9–5 in the Scottish Masters final at Motherwell, Scotland, in September and John Higgins of Scotland by the same score in the Grand Prix final at Sunderland, England, in October. At Preston, England, in December, he beat Ebdon again by 10–3 in the U.K. final. He had earlier won the European Open title at Antwerp, Belgium, in December 1994 by defeating John Parrott of England 9–3 in the final. Higgins gained the British Open title in April at Plymouth, England, with a 9–6 win in the final over Ronnie O'Sullivan of England to reverse the result of the English Masters final at Wembley in February, when O'Sullivan won 9–3.

(SYDNEY E. FRISKIN)

BOWLING

World Tenpins. The 13th world tenpin bowling championships took place July 9–15, 1995, in Reno, Nev. A record number of participants, 358 men and 253 women from 61 countries, bowled in a new five-story stadium with 80 lanes.

In men's singles Canada's Marc Doi (1,364) and Bill Rowe (1,356) won the gold and silver medals. In women's singles Debby Ship, also from Canada, won the world title (1,318). Second was Elizabeth Johnson of the U.S. (1,295).

The world champion in men's doubles was Sweden (2,702), and Thailand (2,489) won the women's doubles. In the trio event the young Dutch male team silenced the rest of the field with their double victory (3,954 and 3,889). Australia won the women's competition (3,626). In the five-player team event the Dutch men captured their second world title (6,282), and the Finnish women won the gold (5,974).

The total score of these four events decided the all-events champions. The men's winner was the tournament's youngest participant, 17-year-old Michael Sassen from The Netherlands, with a new world record of 5,496. Jaana Puhakka from Finland made bowling history as the first woman to win the world youth champion's title twice in a row and then in her first adult world championships the all-events (4,916).

The top 16 men and women continued bowling a one-game round-robin, after which the three on top bowled a step-ladder final for the Masters crown. Yang Cheng-ming of Taiwan was the men's champion, and Celia Flores of Mexico won the women's crown. (YRJÖ SARAHETE)

COURTESY OF WIBC

Sandy Postma watches her ball roll toward the pins in the WIBC Queens Tournament. The winner, Postma was a part-time professional who previously had never finished better than 11th in national competition.

Professional Bowlers Association (PBA) Tournament of Champions

Year	Champion	Year	Champion
1991	D. Ozio	1994	N. Duke
1992	M. McDowell	**1995**	**M. Aulby**
1993	G. Branham		

U.S. Tenpins. A long-shot contender for Bowler of the Year honours emerged in the summer of 1995 when 57-year-old John Handegard of Las Vegas, Nev., stunned the Professional Bowlers Association (PBA) by winning its Northwest Classic in Kennewick, Wash. He became the oldest bowler ever to win on the PBA regular tour. A few months later he captured the PBA Senior Championship in Jackson, Mich.

Handegard defeated Mark Williams of Beaumont, Texas, 278–247 in the Northwest final. In the title match of the Senior event, he scored a 246–185 victory over Avery LeBlanc of Houma, La.

The more likely Bowler of the Year for 1995, however, was Mike Aulby of Indianapolis, Ind., winner of the Brunswick World Tournament of Champions 237–232 over Bob Spaulding of Greenville, S.C., and the ABC Bud Light Masters 200–187 over Williams.

A record 91,059 individual entries in the American Bowling Congress Tournament helped the ABC celebrate its 100th anniversary. The winners in the five-month-long event were: team, Arden Lanes, of Seattle, Wash., 3,387; singles, Matt Surina, Mead, Wash., 826; doubles, Scott Kruppenbacher and Michael Wambold, Rochester, N.Y., 1,486; all-events, Jeff Kwiatkowski, Maumee, Ohio, 2,191.

In the Women's International Bowling Congress Queens Tournament in Tucson, Ariz., Sandy Postma, a 48-year-old grandmother from Lansing, Mich., was the unexpected winner. Postma, who previously had never finished better than 11th in national competition, topped Carolyn Dorin of North Richland Hills, Texas, 226–187 in the final.

Beth Owen, a Dallas, Texas, bowling instructor, won the singles event with 749 and the all-events title with 1,983 in the Classic Division of the WIBC Tournament. The Contour Power Grips of West Bloomfield, Mich., set a tournament record in the team competition with 3,125. The doubles winners were Carol Harsh and Debbie Villani of Las Vegas with 1,299.

(JOHN J. ARCHIBALD)

BOXING

The world heavyweight championship in 1995 lost further credibility in another disappointing year, leaving it in a more confused state than ever before. George Foreman (U.S.), who late in 1994—after 10 years of retirement—had sensationally regained the title he had lost 20 years earlier, ceased to be recognized by most of the many organizations that claimed to control the sport. The 47-year-old Foreman made only one unsatisfactory defense of his title in 1995, against Axel Schulz of Germany in Las Vegas, Nev., on April 22. Foreman won the bout, but the decision was hotly disputed. The World Boxing Association (WBA), which had refused to sanction the fight, had stripped Foreman of his title for refusing to fight the WBA top-ranked challenger, former champion Tony Tucker (U.S.). When Foreman declined to meet Schulz in a return contest in Germany, the International Boxing Federation (IBF) declared the title vacant and left Foreman without a championship belt. The WBA recognized Bruce Seldon (U.S.) as champion after he defeated Tucker. On December 9 Schulz fought Frans Botha (South Africa) in Stuttgart, Germany, for the IBF version of the title. When Botha was declared the winner in a split decision, angry German fans threw coins and bottles into the ring.

There was further devaluation of the World Boxing Council's (WBC's) heavyweight championship when Frank Bruno (England) outpointed Oliver McCall (U.S.) in London in September. In three previous attempts to win the title, the 33-year-old Bruno had been stopped by Tim Witherspoon (U.S.), Mike Tyson (U.S.), and Lennox Lewis (England).

Tyson's comeback contest after three years in prison—against the almost unknown Peter McNeeley—lasted 89 seconds before McNeeley was knocked helpless. In a widely ridiculed move, McNeeley's manager climbed into the ring and stopped the fight. Tyson's share of the gross purse was reported at approximately $35 million. Buster Mathis, Jr. (U.S.), was chosen as Tyson's next opponent, in November, but after disappointing advance sales, the fight was postponed when Tyson reported a damaged thumb. Finally, at a poorly attended fight on December 16, Tyson knocked out the overmatched Mathis in the third round.

Adding to the complications that left the heavyweight championship in confusion, Riddick Bowe (U.S.), a former champion who relinquished the WBC title, strengthened his claim to be the top-ranked heavyweight by battering to defeat in eight rounds another former champion, Evander Holyfield (U.S.), in Las Vegas in November.

Julio César Chávez (Mexico) carried on another year as a remarkable champion, successfully defending his WBC super lightweight title against David Kamau (Kenya) in September. Chávez was reported to have been paid $1 million for the fight, though at 33 the Mexican, who had fought in 19 world title bouts, seemed to be losing his old sparkle. Nonetheless, his record of 95 wins, 1 loss, and 1 tie made him the most outstanding boxer seen in years.

Two popular fighters relinquished newly won titles in 1995. WBC welterweight champion Pernell Whitaker (U.S.) defeated Julio César Vásquez of Argentina in March to win the WBA junior middleweight title and immediately abandoned it. In July Oscar De La Hoya, the only American to win gold at the 1992 Olympic Games, gave up the IBF lightweight belt, only two months after taking it from Rafael Ruelas (U.S.).

The most promising new champion in 1995 was Roy Jones (U.S.), the IBF super middleweight champion, who remained undefeated in 30 fights. His closest rival was Nigel Benn (England), the WBC super middleweight champion. Benn's greatest triumph during the year was overshadowed by tragedy. In a bout to retain his WBC crown, he knocked out the highly rated Gerald McClellan (U.S.) in 10 rounds in London in late February. McClellan collapsed and was rushed to the hospital for

World Heavyweight Champions No Weight Limit
WBA
Evander Holyfield (U.S.; 11/6/93)
Michael Moorer (U.S.; 4/22/94)
George Foreman (U.S.; 11/5/94) **stripped of title in 1995**
Bruce Seldon (U.S.; 4/8/95)
WBC
Riddick Bowe (U.S.; 11/13/92) stripped of title in 1992
Lennox Lewis (U.K.; 12/14/92)
Oliver McCall (U.S.; 9/24/94)
Frank Bruno (U.K.; 9/2/95)
IBF
Evander Holyfield (U.S.; 11/6/93)
Michael Moorer (U.S.; 4/22/94)
George Foreman (U.S.; 11/5/94) **gave up title in 1995**
Frans Botha (S.Af.; 12/9/95)

World Cruiserweight Champions Top Weight 195 Pounds
WBA
declared vacant in 1989
Robert Daniels (U.S.; 11/28/89)
Bobby Czyz (U.S.; 3/8/91) vacant
Orlin Norris (U.S.; 11/6/93)
Nate Miller (U.S.; 7/22/95)
WBC
Evander Holyfield (U.S.; 4/9/88) gave up title in 1988
Carlos de Léon (P.R.; 5/17/89)
Massimiliano Duran (Italy; 7/27/90)
Anaclet Wamba (Fr.; 7/20/91)
IBF
Glenn McCrory (U.K.; 6/3/89)
Jeff Lampkin (U.S.; 3/22/90) gave up title in 1991
James Warring (U.S.; 9/7/91)
Alfred Cole (U.S.; 7/30/92)

World Light Heavyweight Champions Top Weight 175 Pounds
WBA
Virgil Hill (U.S.; 9/5/87)
Thomas Hearns (U.S.; 6/3/91)
Iran Barkley (U.S.; 3/21/92) gave up title in 1992
Virgil Hill (U.S.; 9/92)
WBC
Jeff Harding (Australia; 6/24/89)
Dennis Andries (U.K.; 7/28/90)
Jeff Harding (Australia; 9/11/91)
Mike McCallum (Jam.; 7/23/94)
Fabrice Tiozzo (Fr.; 6/16/95)
IBF
Slobodan Kacar (Yugos.; 12/21/85)
Bobby Czyz (U.S.; 9/6/86)
Charles Williams (U.S.; 10/29/87)
Henry Maske (Ger.; 3/20/93)

World Super Middleweight Champions Top Weight 168 Pounds
WBA
Baek In-chul (S.Kor.; 5/27/89)
Christophe Tiozzo (Fr.; 3/30/90)
Victor Cordoba (Pan.; 4/5/91)
Michael Nunn (U.S.; 9/12/92)
Steve Little (U.S.; 2/26/94)
Frank Liles (U.S.; 8/12/94)
WBC
Sugar Ray Leonard (U.S.; 11/7/88) gave up title in 1990
Mauro Galvano (Italy; 12/15/90)
Nigel Benn (U.K.; 10/3/92)
IBF
Lindell Holmes (U.S.; 1/27/90)
Darrin Van Horn (U.S.; 5/18/91)
Iran Barkley (U.S.; 1/10/92)
James Toney (U.S.; 2/13/93)
Roy Jones (U.S.; 11/18/94)

World Middleweight Champions Top Weight 160 Pounds
WBA
Reggie Johnson (U.S.; 4/22/92)
John David Jackson (U.S.; 10/2/93) stripped of title in 1994
Jorge Castro (Arg.; 8/12/94)
Shinji Takehara (Japan; 12/19/95)
WBC
Julian Jackson (U.S.; 11/24/90)
Gerald McClellan (U.S.; 5/8/93) **vacant**
Julian Jackson (U.S.; 3/17/95)
Quincy Taylor (U.S.; 8/19/95)
IBF
James Toney (U.S.; 5/10/91) gave up title in 1993
Roy Jones (U.S.; 5/22/93) gave up title in 1994
Bernard Hopkins (U.S.; 4/29/95)

World Junior Middleweight Champions Top Weight 154 Pounds (also called super welterweight)
WBA
Pernell Whitaker (U.S.; 3/4/95) gave up title in 1995
Carl Daniels (U.S.; 6/16/95)
Julio César Vásquez (Arg.; 12/16/95)
WBC
John Mugabi (Uganda; 7/8/89)
Terry Norris (U.S.; 3/31/90)
Simon Brown (U.S.; 12/18/93)
Terry Norris (U.S.; 5/7/94)
Luis Santana (Dom.Rep.; 11/12/94)
Terry Norris (U.S.; 8/19/95)
IBF
Darrin Van Horn (U.S.; 2/4/89)
Gianfranco Rosi (Italy; 7/16/89)
Vincent Pettway (U.S.; 9/17/94)
Paul Vaden (U.S.; 8/12/95)
Terry Norris (U.S.; 12/16/95)

WBC super middleweight champion Nigel Benn of the U.K. lands a blow to Gerald McClellan of the U.S. in their match in February in which Benn successfully defended his title. Knocked out in the 10th round, McClellan subsequently underwent brain surgery and was forced to quit boxing.
JOHN GICHIGI—ALLSPORT

World Welterweight Champions
Top Weight 147 Pounds

WBA

Mark Breland (U.S.; 2/4/89)
Aaron Davis (U.S.; 7/8/90)
Meldrick Taylor (U.S.; 1/19/91)
Crisanto España (Venez.; 10/31/92)
Ike Quartey (Ghana; 6/4/94)

WBC

Marlon Starling (U.S.; 2/4/89)
Maurice Blocker (U.S.; 8/19/90)
Simon Brown (Jam.; 3/18/91)
James McGirt (U.S.; 11/29/91)
Pernell Whitaker (U.S.; 3/6/93)

IBF

Simon Brown (Jam.; 4/23/88)
gave up title in 1991
Maurice Blocker (U.S.; 10/4/91)
Felix Trinidad (P.R.; 6/19/93)

World Junior Welterweight Champions
Top Weight 140 Pounds
(also called super lightweight)

WBA

Edwin Rosario (P.R.; 6/15/91)
Akinobu Hiranaka (Japan; 4/10/92)
Morris East (Phil.; 9/9/92)
Juan Martin Coggi (Arg.; 1/12/93)
Frankie Randall (U.S.; 9/17/94)

WBC

René Arrendondo (Mex.; 7/22/87)
Roger Mayweather (U.S.; 11/12/87)
Julio César Chávez (Mex.; 5/13/89)
Frankie Randall (U.S.; 1/29/94)
Julio César Chávez (Mex.; 5/7/94)

IBF

Pernell Whitaker (U.S.; 7/18/92)
gave up title in 1993
Charles Murray (U.S.; 5/15/93)
Jake Rodriguez (P.R.; 2/13/94)
Kostya Tszyu (Austl.; 1/28/95)

World Lightweight Champions
Top Weight 135 Pounds

WBA

Pernell Whitaker (U.S.; 8/11/90)
gave up title in 1992
Joey Gamache (U.S.; 6/13/92)
Tony Lopez (U.S.; 10/24/92)
Dingaan Thobela (S.Af.; 6/26/93)
Orzubek Nazarov (Russia; 10/30/93)

WBC

Julio César Chávez (Mex.; 10/29/88)
gave up title in 1989
Pernell Whitaker (U.S.; 8/20/89)
gave up title in 1992
Miguel González (Mex.; 8/24/92)

IBF

Fred Pendleton (U.S.; 1/10/93)
Rafael Ruelas (U.S.; 2/19/94)
Oscar De La Hoya (U.S.; 5/6/95)
gave up title in [illegible]
Philip Holiday (S.Af.; 8/19/95)

World Junior Lightweight Champions
Top Weight 130 Pounds
(also called super featherweight)

WBA

Joey Gamache (U.S.; 6/28/91)
gave up title in 1991
Genaro Hernandez (U.S.; 11/22/91)
gave up title in 1995
Choi Yong Soo (S.Kor.; 10/21/95)

WBC

Azumah Nelson (Ghana; 2/29/88)
Jesse James Leija (U.S.; 5/7/94)
Gabriel Ruelas (U.S.; 9/17/94)
Azumah Nelson (Ghana; 12/1/95)

IBF

Brian Mitchell (S.Af.; 9/13/91)
gave up title in 1992
Juan Molina (P.R.; 2/22/92)
vacant
Eddie Hopson (U.S.; 4/22/95)
Tracy Patterson (U.S.; 7/9/95)

World Featherweight Champions
Top Weight 126 Pounds

WBA

Barry McGuigan (N.Ire.; 6/8/85)
Steve Cruz (U.S.; 6/23/86)
Antonio Esparragoza (Venez.; 3/6/87)
Park Yung Kyun (S.Kor.; 3/30/91)
Eloy Rojas (Venez.; 12/4/93)

WBC

Paul Hodkinson (U.K.; 11/13/91)
Gregorio Vargas (Mex.; 4/28/93)
Kevin Kelley (U.S.; 12/4/93)
Alejandro González (Mex.; 1/7/95)
Manuel Medina (Mex.; 9/23/95)
Luisito Espinosa (Phil.; 12/11/95)

IBF

Jorge Paez (Mex.; 8/4/88)
gave up title in 1991
Troy Dorsey (U.S.; 6/3/91)
Manuel Medina (Mex.; 8/12/91)
Tom Johnson (U.S.; 2/26/93)

World Junior Featherweight Champions
Top Weight 122 Pounds
(also called super bantamweight)

WBA

Luís Mendoza (Colom.; 9/11/90)
Raul Pérez (Mex.; 10/7/91)
Wilfredo Vásquez (P.R.; 3/27/92)
Antonio Cermeno (Venez.; 5/13/95)

WBC

Daniel Zaragoza (Mex.; 6/14/91)
Thierry Jacob (Fr.; 3/20/92)
Tracy Patterson (U.S.; 6/23/92)
Hector Acero-Sánchez (U.S.; 8/26/94)
Daniel Zaragoza (Mex.; 11/6/95)

IBF

José Sanabria (Venez.; 5/21/88)
Fabrice Benichou (Fr.; 3/10/89)
Welcome Ncita (S.Af.; 3/10/90)
Kennedy McKinney (U.S.; 12/2/92)
Vuyani Bungu (S.Af.; 8/20/94)

World Bantamweight Champions Top Weight 118 Pounds
WBA
Eliecer Julio (Colom.; 10/10/92)
Junior Jones (U.S.; 10/23/93)
John Michael Johnson (U.S.; 4/22/94)
Daorung Chuvatana (Thai.; 7/16/94)
Veeraphol Sahaprom (Thai; 9/17/95)
WBC
Joichiro Tatsuyoshi (Japan; 9/19/91) vacant
Victor Rabañales (Mex.; 3/30/92)
Byun Jong-Il (S.Kor.; 3/28/93)
Yasuei Yakushiji (Japan; 12/22/93)
Wayne McCullough (N.Ire.; 7/30/95)
IBF
Kelvin Seabrooks (U.S.; 5/16/87)
Orlando Canizales (U.S.; 7/9/88) gave up title in 1994
Harold Mestre (Colom.; 1/21/95)
Mbulelo Botile (S.Af.; 4/29/95)

World Junior Bantamweight Champions Top Weight 115 Pounds (also called super flyweight)
WBA
Khaosai Galaxy (Thai.; 11/21/84) gave up title in 1991
Katsuya Onizuka (Japan; 4/10/92)
Lee Hyung Chul (S.Kor.; 9/18/94)
Alima Goitia (Venez.; 7/22/95
WBC
Gilberto Román (Mex.; 4/8/88)
Nana Konadu (Ghana; 11/7/89)
Moon Sung Kil (S.Kor.; 1/20/90)
José Luis Bueno (Mex.; 11/13/93)
Hiroshi Kawashima (Japan; 5/4/94)
IBF
Juan Polo Pérez (Colom.; 10/14/89)
Robert Quiroga (U.S.; 4/21/90)
Julio Borboa (Mex.; 1/16/93)
Harold Grey (Colom.; 8/29/94)
Carlos Salazar (Arg.; 10/7/95)

World Flyweight Champions Top Weight 112 Pounds
WBA
Elvis Alvarez (Colom.; 3/14/91)
Kim Yong Kang (S.Kor.; 6/1/91)
Aquiles Guzmán (Venez.; 9/26/92)
David Griman (Venez.; 12/92)
San Sow Ploenchit (Thai.; 2/13/94)
WBC
Kim Young Kang (S.Kor.; 7/24/88)
Sot Chitalada (Thai.; 6/3/89)
Muangchai Kittlkasem (Thai.; 2/15/91)
Yury Arbachakov (Russia; 6/23/92)
IBF
Dave McAuley (U.K.; 6/7/89)
Rodolfo Blanco (Colom.; 6/11/92)
Phichit Sithbangprachan (Thai.; 11/29/92) **vacant**
Francisco Tejedor (Colom.; 2/95)
Danny Romero (U.S.; 4/22/95)

World Junior Flyweight Champions Top Weight 108 Pounds
WBA
Yuh Myung Woo (S.Kor.; 12/8/85)
Hiroki Ioka (Japan; 12/17/91)
Yuh Myung Woo (S.Kor.; 11/18/92) gave up title in 1993
Leo Gamez (Venez.; 10/21/93)
Choi Hi Yong (S.Kor.; 2/4/95)
WBC
Melchor Cob Castro (Mex.; 3/25/91)
Humberto González (Mex.; 6/4/91)
Michael Carbajal (U.S.; 3/13/93)
Chiquita Gonzalez (Mex.; 2/19/94)
Saman Sorjaturong (Thai.; 7/15/95)
IBF
Tacy Macalos (Phil.; 11/6/88)
Muangchai Kittikasem (Thai.; 5/2/89)
Michael Carbajal (U.S.; 7/29/90)
Chiquita Gonzalez (Mex.; 2/19/94)
Saman Sorjaturong (Thai.; 7/15/95)

World Mini-flyweight Champions Top Weight 105 Pounds (also called strawweight)
WBA
Kim Bong Jun (S.Kor.; 4/16/89)
Choi Hi Yong (S.Kor.; 2/2/91)
Ohashi Hideyuki (Japan; 10/14/92)
Chana Porpaoin (Thai.; 2/10/93)
Rosendo Alvarez (Nic.; 12/2/95)
WBC
Napa Kiatwanchai (Thai.; 11/13/88)
Choi Jum Hwan (S.Kor.; 11/12/89)
Ohashi Hideyuki (Japan; 2/7/90)
Ricardo López (Mex.; 10/25/90)
IBF
Nico Thomas (Indon.; 6/17/89)
Eric Chavez (Phil.; 9/21/89)
Falan Lookmingkwan (Thai.; 2/21/90)
Manny Melchor (Phil.; 9/6/92)
Ratanapol Vorapin (Thai.; 12/10/92)

brain surgery. Though he survived, his career was over and he remained disabled. Until he collapsed, McClellan had put up a spirited challenge in what was Benn's ninth title defense, and the British champion was all but knocked out in the first round.

After severe brain damage ended the career of another super middleweight, Michael Watson (England), when he was stopped in 12 rounds by Chris Eubank (England) in 1991, the British Boxing Board had ruled that an anesthetist, paramedics, and physicians had to be at ringside and that an ambulance had to be available so that a brain-damaged boxer could be rushed to a hospital with a neurosurgeon on duty. But tragedies continued to occur. James Murray (Scotland) died following brain surgery after being knocked out by Drew Docherty (Scotland) in a clash for the British bantamweight crown at Glasgow, Scotland, in October. In May Jimmy Garcia (Colombia) died 13 days after being knocked out in a world super featherweight championship in Las Vegas by Gabriel Ruelas (U.S.). Dong Choon Lee (South Korea) died after boxing in Japan, and two young Filipinos suffered fatal injuries in bouts in the Philippines.

The deaths and permanent injuries in Britain brought another call from the British Medical Association for boxing to be banned in the U.K. Pro-boxing people argued that if the sport was banned it would continue more dangerously underground, where bouts would be held without control or medical precautions. (FRANK BUTLER)

CHESS

The continuing power struggle between the world ruling body of chess, the Fédération Internationale des Échecs (FIDE), and the Professional Chess Association (PCA), founded in 1993, seemed no nearer resolution at the end of 1995, a year in which Garry Kasparov of Russia successfully defended his PCA title in New York City but also in which the FIDE world title match between Anatoly Karpov of Russia and Gata Kamsky of the U.S. did not come to fruition. As a result, the PCA-FIDE agreement made in Moscow in December 1994 was not endorsed, and the General Assembly of FIDE at Paris in November 1995 replaced FIDE Pres. Florencio Campomanes.

Campomanes had been a controversial figure since his election to the post in 1982. He had been successful in finding tournament sponsors over the years but was thought autocratic. During a meeting of FIDE in the autumn, widespread support for censuring recent FIDE policy forced Campomanes to resign. In a surprising move, his successor was 33-year-old Kirsan Ilyumdzhinov, a chess enthusiast who was president of the republic of Kalmykia in the south of the Russian Federation. The new appointee was endorsed by Russian Pres. Boris Yeltsin, which overcame objections from Kasparov and the president of the Russian Chess Federation, the two figures instrumental in cobbling together the Moscow agreement of 1994.

Ilyumdzhinov had been instrumental in having the last two Russian championships played at Elista, the capital of Kalmykia, and arranged for the 1998 World Chess Olympiad to be held at the same place. His election may have healed the split that threatened to cause Western countries such as the U.S. to leave the world ruling body and set up one of their own.

Meanwhile, Kasparov was in uncertain form throughout the year, fueling rumours that he might soon leave international chess to pursue a career in Russian business and politics. In the springtime Max Euwe Memorial International tournament in Amsterdam, he was beaten twice, by Joel Lautier of France and Jeroen Piket of The Netherlands. Final standings in the tournament were: (1) Lautier, 4 points of a possible 6; (2) Kasparov, 3.5; (3) Veselin Topalov of Bulgaria, 2.5; and (4) Piket, 2. Kasparov also failed badly in the Credit Suisse Masters tournament, held in Horgen, Switz., in October and November, placing fifth in an 11-player contest won by Vladimir Kramnik of Russia and Vasily Ivanchuk of Ukraine.

However, Kasparov was successful in the Mikhail Tal Memorial Tournament in Riga, Latvia, in April; the top three finishers were: (1) Kasparov, 7.5 points of a possible 10; (2) Viswanathan Anand of India, 7; and (3) Ivanchuk, 6.5. He also won at Novgorod, Russia (May 27–June 5), with 6.5 points of a possible 9 and in the PCA Grand Prix series of Quickplay knockouts.

The Intel World Chess Championship, a PCA match between Kasparov and Anand,

Queen's Gambit Accepted

White: Miguel Illescas — Black: Matthew Sadler

White	Black	White	Black
1 d4	d5	7 Nf3	Bd6
2 c4	dxc4	8 Qa4+	Bd7!
3 e4	Nc6	9 Qxa5	a6
4 Be3	Nf6	10 Nb1?*	Nxe4
5 Nc3	e5	11 Kd1	c3
6 d5	Na5	12 white resigns†	

*White should consider 10 Na4.
†In view of 12 b4 b6 13 Qa3 a5 etc.

World Chess Championships—Men

Year	Winner	Runner-up
1986	G. Kasparov (U.S.S.R.)	A. Karpov (U.S.S.R.)
1987	G. Kasparov (U.S.S.R.)	A. Karpov (U.S.S.R.)
1990	G. Kasparov (U.S.S.R.)	A. Karpov (U.S.S.R.)
1993	A. Karpov (Russia)	J. Timman (Neth.)

World Chess Championships—Women

Year	Winner	Runner-up
1986	M. Chiburdanidze (U.S.S.R.)	E. Akhmilovskaya (U.S.S.R.)
1988	M. Chiburdanidze (U.S.S.R.)	N. Ioseliani (U.S.S.R.)
1991	Xie Jun (China)	M. Chiburdanidze (U.S.S.R.)
1993	Xie Jun (China)	N. Ioseliani (Georgia)

Olympiads—Men

Year	Winner	Runner-up
1988	U.S.S.R.	United Kingdom
1989	U.S.S.R.	Yugoslavia
1992	Russia	Uzbekistan
1994	Russia	Bosnia

Olympiads—Women

Year	Winner	Runner-up
1986	U.S.S.R.	Hungary
1988	Hungary	U.S.S.R.
1992	Georgia	Ukraine
1994	Georgia	Hungary

Garry Kasparov (right) of Russia shakes hands with Viswanathan Anand of India after retaining his Professional Chess Association championship. The match, which was played in New York City in October, ended after Kasparov had built an insurmountable lead at the end of 18 games.
PETER MORGAN—REUTERS

was originally scheduled to be played at Cologne, Germany, but was transferred on short notice to New York City at the invitation of Mayor Rudolph Giuliani. The 20-game match, with prize money of $1,350,000, was played from September 11 to October 10. It began with eight fairly tame ties, which did not support Kasparov's aspiration to bring the game to the television screens of the U.S. Anand won the ninth game but then fell badly behind, and the match came to an end after 18 games with a score of 4 wins, 1 loss, and 13 draws in Kasparov's favour. The innovative time limit of seven hours for each game, with no adjournments, was designed to be media-friendly. It was regrettable that the microphone commentary for the audience in the World Trade Center in New York was often audible to the players in their supposedly soundproof booth.

Kramnik won the Dortmund (Germany) tournament (July 14–23), scoring 7 points of a possible 9. Karpov finished second with 6.5, and Peter Leko of Hungary and Ivanchuk tied for third with 5. Kramnik's victory added support to those who believed he would be Kasparov's main challenger in the next few years. In December Patrick Wolff won the U.S. championship in a speed chess tiebreaker over Nick DeFirmian and Alexander Ivanov. The three grandmasters had finished regular play with identical scores of 8½–4½.

Mikhail Botvinnik, longtime Soviet "patriarch of chess," died in May. (*See* OBITUARIES.) Other noteworthy deaths included British player Harry Golombek, a prolific journalist and book author (*see* OBITUARIES), and Lev Polugayevsky, a former Soviet grandmaster.

One of the year's curiosities was the ultrashort game played in the Western European zone of the 1995–97 world championship qualifying series. (*See* Table.) The series was won by Miguel Illescas despite this defeat at the hands of British champion Matthew Sadler, who failed to qualify for the next stage. (BERNARD CAFFERTY)

CONTRACT BRIDGE

The most successful contract bridge team of 1995 was from the U.S. In August, Nick Nickell, Dick Freeman, Bob Hamman, Bobby Wolff, Jeff Meckstroth, and Eric Rodwell won the Spingold Master Knockout Teams event for an unprecedented third consecutive time, and in October they won the Bermuda Bowl world team championship. Yet, to show how thin the dividing line between success and failure can be, during the qualifying rounds of the Bermuda Bowl a Brazilian declarer was in three no-trump doubled against Hamman and Wolff. He had taken eight tricks and was on lead holding the ace of spades. However, he thought he had won only seven tricks. So, instead of cashing his ninth trick, he tried for an endplay, lost the rest of the tricks, and finished one down. If the Brazilian player had taken his contract-fulfilling trick and all the other results had been the same in the rest of the qualifying matches, the U.S. team would not have advanced to the quarterfinals.

The Marlboro world bridge championships were held in Beijing. Sixteen teams competed in both the Bermuda Bowl, open to all, and the Venice Cup, for women only.

The best-played deal of the year, in the opinion of the International Bridge Press Association, was declared by Philippe Cronier of France, a European team champion in 1983.

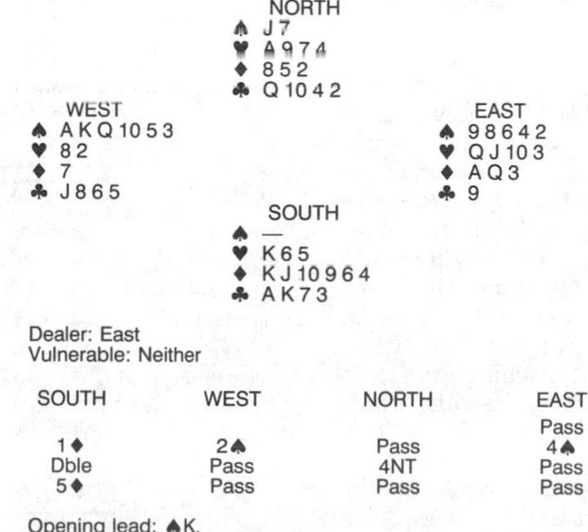
NORTH
♠ J 7
♥ A 9 7 4
♦ 8 5 2
♣ Q 10 4 2

WEST
♠ A K Q 10 5 3
♥ 8 2
♦ 7
♣ J 8 6 5

EAST
♠ 9 8 6 4 2
♥ Q J 10 3
♦ A Q 3
♣ 9

SOUTH
♠ —
♥ K 6 5
♦ K J 10 9 6 4
♣ A K 7 3

Dealer: East
Vulnerable: Neither

SOUTH	WEST	NORTH	EAST
			Pass
1♦	2♠	Pass	4♠
Dble	Pass	4NT	Pass
5♦	Pass	Pass	Pass

Opening lead: ♠K.

West's 2♠ was a rather strong weak jump overcall, the bid no doubt being influenced by his partner's original pass. South's double showed short spades and extra values, here more in terms of distribution than high cards. North's four no-trump suggested that South choose between the minors. Cronier went with his long suit.

Cronier ruffed the spade lead, played a heart to dummy's ace, and called for the ♦8. If East had played low, the eight would have won the trick. Then another trump from the dummy would have made everything easy for declarer. So East put up his ♦A. However, this marked him with the ♦Q too.

After East returned the ♥Q, Cronier won with his king and exited with his last heart, West discarding a spade. East played back the ♥J, and when West could not overruff South's ♦6, Cronier's reading of the trump position was confirmed.

In Cronier's assessment of the situation, East was four times more likely to have a low club than the singleton jack. Thus, Cronier played a club to dummy's 10, taking an immediate finesse against the jack despite having the three higher honours. When the 10 held, declarer played a diamond to his jack, cashed the ♦K, and thus made the contract.

World Contract Bridge Pair Championship			
Year	Open winners	Women's winners	Mixed winners
1990	Marcelo Branco, Gabriel Chagas (Braz.)	Kerri Shuman, Karen McCallum (U.S.)	Peter Weichsel, Juanita Chambers (U.S.)
1994	Marcin Lesniewski, Marek Szymanowski (Pol.)	Carla Arnolds, Bep Vriend (Neth.)	Danuta Hocheker, Apolinare Kowalski (Pol.)

World Team Olympiad				
Year	Open winner	Open runner-up	Women's winner	Women's runner-up
1988	United States	Austria	Denmark	United Kingdom
1992	France	United States	Austria	United Kingdom

Bermuda Bowl		
Year	Winner	Runner-up
1989	Brazil	United States
1991	Iceland	Poland
1993	Netherlands	Norway
1995	**United States**	**Canada**

The final of the Venice Cup was a repeat of the previous one, held in 1993 between Germany and the U.S. In 1993 the U.S. was victorious. This time Germany turned the tables, winning by 312–248 international match points. The new world champions were Sabine Auken, Daniela von Arnim, Beate ("Pony") Nehmert, and Andrea Rauscheid. Karen Caesar and Marianne Mögel were also on the team, but they did not play in the final. The nonplaying captain was Klaus Reps.

In the Bermuda Bowl final, the U.S. played against Canada. Early in the final session, the U.S. led by only 13 points, but they pulled away to win 338–295. For Nickell and Freeman it was their first world championship. Meckstroth and Rodwell gained their second Bermuda Bowl, and Hamman and Wolff their seventh. Edgar Kaplan was the nonplaying captain.

On June 15 the International Olympic Committee recognized bridge as an Olympic sport. At first, it was to be a demonstration sport in the Olympic Games.

Giorgio Belladonna died on May 12 at the age of 71. He was the only person to have played in all 16 world championship victories amassed by the Italian Blue Team. (*See* OBITUARIES.) (PHILLIP ALDER)

CRICKET

After nearly two decades of domination, the West Indies in 1994–95 finally had to cede its unofficial title of cricket's world champions to Australia, a 2–1 defeat on home soil being its first loss of a Test series since 1979–80 in New Zealand. The Australians, led by M.A. Taylor, fully deserved their historic victory. Outstanding batting by S.R. Waugh, who scored 429 runs at an average of 107.25 for the four Tests, and superb fielding and catching exposed a strangely lethargic West Indies side, which looked as though it had played one Test series too many. Not even the trenchant criticism of home supporters could lift the West Indies, which lost the deciding fourth Test by a humiliating innings and 53 runs in Jamaica after leveling the series on an underprepared pitch in Trinidad. For once, S.K. Warne, the Australian leg-spinner, did not contribute significantly to victory, largely because the pitches were made to suit the fast bowlers, but he still remained the most charismatic and influential bowler through the year. (*See* BIOGRAPHIES.) A hard-fought drawn series with England in the summer confirmed that the West Indians were in a period of transition.

A new controversy hit the game, though, when two Australian players, Warne and T. May, accused the Pakistan captain, Salim Malik, of offering them a bribe to lose a match during the Australian tour of Pakistan in late 1994. The accusations were investigated by Pakistan authorities, and Malik's innocence was confirmed, but many in the game felt that the matter had not been properly handled and that the International Cricket Council should have carried out its own inquiries, particularly as neither Warne nor May was called to give evidence to officials in Pakistan. The lingering bitterness did nothing to ease the relationships between the two sides, which had been strained to near the breaking point during a fluctuating and ultimately decisive first Test of a three-match series in Pakistan, when only a last-wicket partnership of 57 between Inzamam-ul-Haq and Mushtaq Ahmed brought the home side victory. Wasim Akram (8 for 139) and Waqar Younis (7 for 144) had set up victory, but Warne (8 for 150) had bowled Australia back into the match. In his first match as captain of Australia, Taylor had the unhappy distinction of making two noughts. The next two Tests were drawn, leaving Pakistan as the winner by 1–0. Malik was the leading run-scorer with 557, and Warne was the most successful bowler, with 18 wickets (at an average of 28.00).

With West Indies wicketkeeper Courtney Browne behind him, Australia's Steve Waugh bats his way to a double century during the third day of the fourth Test on May 1. Australia won by an innings and 53 runs.

ANDY CLARK—REUTERS

Australia's superiority over England was confirmed with a 3–1 victory in the Ashes series in Australia. After a promising summer this was a disappointing result for England, whose batsmen had no answer to the spin of Warne or the pace of C.J. McDermott, while in M.J. Slater, Australia had the most promising young batsman of the year. Slater scored 623 runs in five Tests against England at an average of 62.30 to confirm his promise. For England, D. Gough, a sturdy fast bowler from Yorkshire, enhanced his reputation by taking 6 for 49 in the third Test in Sydney before breaking down with an ankle injury, and G.P. Thorpe, a left-handed batsman from Surrey, showed style and determination in being top scorer for England with 444 runs. But England never recovered from the loss

World Cup				
Year	Result			
1975	West Indies	291–8	Australia	274
1979	West Indies	286–9	England	194
1983	India	183	West Indies	140
1987	Australia	253–5	England	246–8
1992	Pakistan	249–6	England	227

All-Time First-Class Test Cricket Standings (as of Sept. 30, 1995)

	England			Australia			South Africa			West Indies			New Zealand		
	Wins	Draws	Losses	W	D	L	W	D	L	W	D	L	W	D	L
England *v.*				90	81	108	47	39	19	27	40	48	34	37	4
Australia *v.*	108	81	90	—	—	—	31	15	13	32	22*	27	13	11	7
South Africa *v.*	19	39	47	13	15	31				0	0	1	22	6	3
West Indies *v.*	48	40	27	27	22*	32	1	0	0	—	—	—	9	13	4
New Zealand *v.*	4	37	34	7	11	13	3	6	22	4	13	9			
India *v.*	14	36	30	8	18*	24	0	3	1	7	31	27	12	14	6
Pakistan *v.*	7	31	14	10	15	12	0	0	1	7	12	12	16	16	4
Sri Lanka *v.*	1	1	3	0	3	4	0	2	1	0	1	0	2	7	4
Zimbabwe *v.*	†			†			†			†			0	1	1

	India			Pakistan			Sri Lanka			Zimbabwe		
	W	D	L	W	D	L	W	D	L	W	D	L
England *v.*	30	36	14	14	31	7	3	1	1	†		
Australia *v.*	24	18*	8	12	15	10	4	3	0	†		
South Africa *v.*	1	3	0	1	0	0	1	2	0	†		
West Indies *v.*	27	31	7	12	12	7	0	1	0	†		
New Zealand *v.*	6	14	12	4	16	16	4	7	2	1	1	0
India *v.*	—	—	—	4	33	7	8	4	1	1	1	0
Pakistan *v.*	7	33	4				9	5	3	4	1	1
Sri Lanka *v.*	1	4	8	3	5	9	—	—	—	0	3	0
Zimbabwe *v.*	0	1	1	1	1	4	0	3	0			

*Including one tie. †No matches.

of the first two Tests, in which McDermott and Warne took 31 wickets between them, the latter taking a hat trick at Melbourne in the second Test. England's solitary victory came in the fourth Test when D.E. Malcolm and C.C. Lewis took four wickets each in the second innings as Australia was bowled out for 156.

Perhaps the best series of the year was that between the West Indies and England, which ended in a 2–2 draw after a summer of changing fortune and unrelenting excitement. Twice the West Indies, led by R.B. Richardson, went ahead; twice England came back, until the two sides resembled exhausted heavyweight boxers. In D.G. Cork, England discovered an all-rounder with the spirit of I.T. Botham, while B.C. Lara ended a quiet period with three successive centuries, averaging 85 for his 765 runs in the six-Test series, his batting once again showing the certainty of judgment and execution that had brought him the individual Test and first-class batting records in the previous year. In full flow the little left-hander had no equal. Cork marked his Test debut by taking eight wickets as England recorded its first victory over the West Indies at Lord's in 38 years. At Manchester he also took a hat trick, the first by an Englishman in a Test match in 38 years, while in the final Test C.A. Walsh became only the third West Indian (after L. Gibbs and M. Marshall) to have taken 300 Test wickets.

Zimbabwe played host to Sri Lanka in a three-Test series that ended with three draws. Later in the season, however, Zimbabwe recorded its first victory in its 11th Test, at home against an erratic Pakistan, though it lost the next two Tests and the series 2–1. Pakistan was well beaten in the inaugural Test against South Africa, while the decline of New Zealand continued with defeats by Sri Lanka (the country's first series win on foreign soil) and South Africa. Sri Lanka continued to show signs of becoming a competitive force by defeating Pakistan 2–1 in a three-Test series in Pakistan. Meanwhile, India split a three-Test series (its only Test series of the season) against West Indies, with one win apiece and one draw. Much of the rest of international cricket play was marked more by quantity than quality, with a proliferation of spurious one-day tournaments, perhaps in anticipation of the World Cup scheduled to be held in India, Pakistan, and Sri Lanka in 1995–96.

In domestic cricket in England, Warwickshire, under the captaincy of D. Reeve, won the championship, for the second successive year, and the NatWest Trophy, the one title the county had not won the previous year. Kent won the one-day Sunday league title and Lancashire the one-day Benson and Hedges Cup. In Australia, Queensland won its first Sheffield Shield title, the nation's premier domestic trophy, after a 68-year drought. Barbados won the Red Stripe Cup in the West Indies, while Auckland won the Shell Trophy in New Zealand, and Natal the Castle Cup in South Africa.

In England a controversy triggered by an article in the *Wisden Cricket Monthly* spilled over into the general media and provoked widespread discussion of the issues of race and nationalism in sports. The article, an essay by Robert Henderson, allegedly questioned whether or not black cricketers could be fully committed to the England cause. Two black England players, P.A.J. DeFreitas and D.E. Malcolm threatened to file suit. (ANDREW LONGMORE)

Test Series Results, September 1994–September 1995

Test	Host country	Ground	Date	Scores	Result
1st	Pakistan	Karachi	Sept. 28–Oct. 2	Australia 337 and 232; Pakistan 256 and 315 for 9	Pakistan won by 1 wkt
2nd	Pakistan	Rawalpindi	Oct. 5–9	Australia 521 for 9 dec and 14 for 1; Pakistan 260 and 537	Match drawn
3rd	Pakistan	Lahore	Nov. 1–5	Pakistan 373 and 404; Australia 455	Match drawn
1st	Zimbabwe	Harare	Oct. 11–16	Sri Lanka 383; Zimbabwe 319 for 8	Match drawn
2nd	Zimbabwe	Bulawayo	Oct. 20–24	Zimbabwe 462 for 9 dec; Sri Lanka 218 and 193 for 4	Match drawn
3rd	Zimbabwe	Harare	Oct. 26–31	Sri Lanka 402 and 89 for 3; Zimbabwe 375	Match drawn
1st	India	Bombay	Nov. 18–22	India 272 and 333; West Indies 243 and 266	India won by 96 runs
2nd	India	Nagpur	Dec. 1–5	India 546 for 9 dec and 208 for 7 dec; West Indies 428 and 132 for 5	Match drawn
3rd	India	Chandigarh	Dec. 10–14	West Indies 443 and 301 for 3 dec; India 387 and 114	West Indies won by 243 runs
1st	Australia	Brisbane	Nov. 25–29	Australia 426 and 248 for 8 dec; England 167 and 323	Australia won by 184 runs
2nd	Australia	Melbourne	Dec. 24–29	Australia 279 and 320 for 7 dec; England 212 and 92	Australia won by 295 runs
3rd	Australia	Sydney	Jan. 1–5	England 309 and 255 for 2 dec; Australia 116 and 344 for 7	Match drawn
4th	Australia	Adelaide	Jan. 26–30	England 353 and 328; Australia 419 and 156	England won by 106 runs
5th	Australia	Perth	Feb. 3–7	Australia 402 and 345 for 8 dec; England 295 and 123	Australia won by 329 runs
1st	South Africa	Johannesburg	Nov. 25–29	New Zealand 411 and 194; South Africa 279 and 189	New Zealand won by 137 runs
2nd	South Africa	Durban	Dec. 26–30	New Zealand 185 and 192; South Africa 226 and 153 for 2	South Africa won by 8 wkt
3rd	South Africa	Cape Town	Jan. 2–6	New Zealand 288 and 239; South Africa 440 and 89 for 3	South Africa won by 7 wkt
1st	South Africa	Johannesburg	Jan. 19–23	South Africa 460 and [illegible] for 7 dec; Pakistan [illegible] and [illegible]	South Africa won by 324 runs
1st	Zimbabwe	Harare	Jan. 31–Feb. 4	Zimbabwe 544 for 4 dec; Pakistan 322 and 158	Zimbabwe won by an innings and 64 runs
2nd	Zimbabwe	Bulawayo	Feb. 7–9	Zimbabwe 174 and 146; Pakistan 260 and 61 for 2	Pakistan won by 8 wkt
3rd	Zimbabwe	Harare	Feb. 15–19	Pakistan 231 and 250; Zimbabwe 243 and 139	Pakistan won by 99 runs
1st	New Zealand	Christchurch	Feb. 3–7	New Zealand 341 for 8 dec and 61 for 2; West Indies 312	Match drawn
2nd	New Zealand	Wellington	Feb. 10–13	West Indies 660 for 5 dec; New Zealand 216 and 122	West Indies won by an innings and 322 runs
1st	New Zealand	Auckland	March 4–8	South Africa 294 and 308 for 6 dec; New Zealand 328 and 181	South Africa won by 93 runs
1st	New Zealand	Napier	March 11–15	Sri Lanka 183 and 352; New Zealand 109 and 185.	Sri Lanka won by 241 runs
2nd	New Zealand	Dunedin	March 18–22	Sri Lanka 233 and 411; New Zealand 307 and 0 for 0	Match drawn
1st	West Indies	Bridgetown	March 31–April 2	West Indies 195 and 189; Australia 346 and 39 for 0	Australia won by 10 wkt
2nd	West Indies	St. John's	April 8–13	Australia 216 and 300 for 7 dec; West Indies 260 and 80 for 2	Match drawn
3rd	West Indies	Port-of-Spain	April 21–23	Australia 128 and 105; West Indies 136 and 98 for 1	West Indies won by 9 wkt
4th	West Indies	Kingston	April 29–May 3	West Indies 265 and 213; Australia 531	Australia won by an innings and 53 runs
1st	England	Leeds	June 8–11	England 199 and 208; West Indies 282 and 129 for 1	West Indies won by 9 wkt
2nd	England	London (Lord's)	June 22–26	England 283 and 336; West Indies 324 and 223	England won by 72 runs
3rd	England	Birmingham	July 6–8	England 147 and 89; West Indies 300	West Indies won by an innings and 64 runs
4th	England	Manchester	July 27–30	West Indies 216 and 314; England 437 and 94 for 4	England won by 6 wkt
5th	England	Nottingham	Aug. 10–14	England 440 and 269 for 9 dec; West Indies 417 and 42 for 2	Match drawn
6th	England	London (Oval)	Aug. 24–28	England 454 and 223 for 4; West Indies 692 for 8 dec	Match drawn
1st	Pakistan	Peshawar	Sept. 8–11	Pakistan 459 for 9 dec; Sri Lanka 186 and 233	Pakistan won by an innings and 40 runs
2nd	Pakistan	Faisalabad	Sept. 15–19	Sri Lanka 223 and 361; Pakistan 333 and 209	Sri Lanka won by 42 runs
3rd	Pakistan	Sialkot	Sept. 22–26	Sri Lanka 232 and 338 for 9 dec; Pakistan 214 and 212	Sri Lanka won by 144 runs

CURLING

Canada dominated curling in 1995, winning two world titles, losing in the final of another, and finishing third in the men's junior championships. Kerry Burtnyk won the world men's title with a 4–2 victory over Scotland's Gordon Muirhead. Sweden's Elisabet Gustafson defeated Connie Laliberte of Canada 6–5 for the women's championship. The competitions were held simultaneously in Brandon, Man., close to Burtnyk's and Laliberte's hometown of Winnipeg.

The world junior women's crown was won by Kelly MacKenzie of Winnipeg, who defeated Sweden 6–5 at Perth, Scotland. Tom Brewster of Scotland won the men's junior crown with a 6–3 win over Germany.

The 1996 world championships were to be held in Hamilton, Ont., and the juniors at Red Deer, Alta. At the 1998 winter Olympic Games in Nagano, Japan, curling would for the first time be an official sport.

Since curling was first introduced as a demonstration sport at the 1988 Winter Games in Calgary, Alta., the World Curling Federation had grown from 19 countries to 31. (JAMES MORRIS)

World Curling Championship—Men

Year	Winner	Runner-up
1991	Scotland	Canada
1992	Switzerland	Scotland
1993	Canada	Scotland
1994	Canada	Sweden
1995	**Canada**	**Scotland**

World Curling Championship—Women

Year	Winner	Runner-up
1991	Norway	Canada
1992	Sweden	United States
1993	Canada	Germany
1994	Canada	Scotland
1995	**Sweden**	**Canada**

Kerry Burtnyk of Canada prepares to slide his stone across the ice in the men's world curling championships, which were held in Brandon, Man., in April. Burtnyk won the men's title 4–2 over Gordon Muirhead of Scotland as Canada dominated both men's and women's play.

ST. CLAIR GROUP; PHOTOGRAPH, MICHAEL BURNS

CYCLING

Miguel Indurain of Spain again dominated the professional cycling season in 1995, winning the Tour de France, the premier international event, for a record fifth successive year and later taking his first world title. Indurain showed his mastery against the clock by winning the eighth stage of the tour, an individual time trial of 54 km (1 km = 0.62 mi) between Huy and Seraing, Belgium, to take the overall lead, which he held for the next 14 days until the finish in Paris. Also winning the 46.5-km time trial at Lac de Vassiviere, France, Indurain finished with a victory margin of 4 min 35 sec over runner-up Alex Zülle of Switzerland after 21 stages and a total distance of 3,635 km. Indurain joined Jacques Anquetil (1957, 1961–64), Eddy Merckx (1969–72, 1974), and Bernard Hinault (1978–79, 1981–82, 1985) as the only riders to have won the tour on five occasions.

The race was marred by the death of Italian rider Fabio Casartelli following a crash on the 206-km stage between Saint-Girons and Cauterets, France, on July 18. Casartelli, the 1992 Olympic Games road-race champion, fell at high speed on the descent from the Col de Portet d'Aspet in the Pyrenees and died in Tarbes, France, from head injuries. As a mark of respect, the field rode the next day's stage together, without racing.

Tony Rominger of Switzerland won the Tour of Italy for the first time. The Tour of Spain, moved from its traditional date in May to September, was won by Laurent Jalabert of France, who ended the season as the world's top-ranked rider on the basis of points earned in each race.

The world road and track championships were held at high altitude in Colombia. Four world records fell in the track program on a new 333-m (1,092-ft) concrete track at the Luis Carlos Galan velodrome in Bogotá. Curtis Harnett of Canada became the first rider to break 10 seconds for 200 m with his time of 9.865, a speed of 72.985 km/h, in the qualifying round of the men's sprint. Harnett lost in the final to Darryn Hill of Australia. Other world records were set by Shane Kelly (1-km time trial, 1 min 0.613 sec), Felicia Ballanger (women's 500-m time trial, 34.017 sec), and Rebecca Twigg (women's 3,000-m pursuit, 3 min 36.081 sec). Twigg won the title 14 days after breaking her collarbone in a crash and rode with seven steel pins in her shoulder.

The professional road race at Duitama, Colombia, was won by Abraham Olano of Spain, his country's first champion since the series began in 1927. Indurain finished second after having taken the individual time

Tour de France

Year	Winner	Kilometres
1991	M. Indurain (Spain)	3,935
1992	M. Indurain (Spain)	3,983
1993	M. Indurain (Spain)	3,700
1994	M. Indurain (Spain)	3,978
1995	**M. Indurain (Spain)**	**3,635**

Cycling World Track Championships—Men

Year	Sprint (amateur)	Sprint (professional)	Pursuit (amateur)	Pursuit (professional)	Motor-paced (amateur)	Motor-paced (professional)
1992	not held	M. Hübner (Ger.)	not held	M. McCarthy (U.S.)	C. Podlesch (Ger.)	P. Steiger (Switz.)
1993*	G. Niewand (Austl.)		G. Obree (U.K.)		J. Veggerby (Den.)	
1994	M. Nothstein (U.S.)		C. Boardman (U.K.)		C. Podlesch (Ger.)	
1995	**D. Hill (Austl.)**		**G. Obree (U.K.)**		**not held**	

*From 1993 professionals and amateurs competed in the same event.

Cycling World Track Championships—Women (Amateur)

Year	Sprint	3-km pursuit
1991	I. Haringa (Neth.)	P. Rossner (Ger.)
1992	E. Salumae (Est.)	P. Rossner (Ger.)
1993	T. Dubnicoff (Can.)	R. Twigg (U.S.)
1994	G. Yenyukhina (Russia)	M. Clignet (Fr.)
1995	**F. Ballanger (Fr.)**	**R. Twigg (U.S.)**

Cycling World Road-Racing Championships

Year	Men (amateur)	Men (professional)	Women (amateur)
1991	V. Pjaksinski (U.S.S.R.)	G. Bugno (Italy)	L. van Moorsel (Neth.)
1992	F. Casartelli (Italy)	G. Bugno (Italy)	K. Watt (Austl.)
1993	J. Ullrich (Ger.)	L. Armstrong (U.S.)	L. van Moorsel (Neth.)
1994	A. Pedersen (Den.)	L. Leblanc (Fr.)	M. Valvik (Nor.)
1995	**D. Nelissen (Neth.)**	**A. Olano (Spain)**	**J. Longo (Fr.)**

1995 Cycling Champions

Event	Winner	Country
WORLD CHAMPIONS—TRACK		
Men		
Sprint	D. Hill	Australia
Individual pursuit	G. Obree	Britain
Kilometre time trial	S. Kelly	Australia
40-km points	S. Martinello	Italy
Team pursuit	B. McGee, R. McGee, S. O'Grady, T. O'Shannessy	Australia
Keirin	F. Magne	France
Olympic sprint	J. Fielder, M. Hubner, J. Van Eijden	Germany
50-km Madison	S. Martinello, M. Villa	Italy
Women		
Sprint	F. Ballanger	France
Individual pursuit	R. Twigg	U.S.
500-m time trial	F. Ballanger	France
25-km points	S. Samokhalova	Russia
WORLD CHAMPION—ROAD		
Individual time trial	M. Indurain	Spain
WORLD AMATEUR CHAMPIONS—ROAD		
Men		
Individual road race	D. Nelissen	Netherlands
Women		
Individual road race	J. Longo	France
Individual time trial	J. Longo	France
WORLD PROFESSIONAL CHAMPION—ROAD		
Individual road race	A. Olano	Spain
WORLD CHAMPION—CYCLO-CROSS		
	D. Runkel	Switzerland

Event	Winner	Country
WORLD CHAMPIONS—MOUNTAIN BIKES		
Men		
Individual cross-country	B. Brentjens	Netherlands
Individual downhill	N. Vouilloz	France
Women		
Individual cross-country	A. Sydor	Canada
Individual downhill	L. Donovan	U.S.
MAJOR PROFESSIONAL ROAD-RACE WINNERS		
Tour de France	M. Indurain	Spain
Tour of Italy	T. Rominger	Switzerland
Tour of Spain	L. Jalabert	France
Tour of Switzerland	P. Tonkov	Russia
Milan-San Remo	L. Jalabert	France
Tour of Flanders	J. Museeuw	Belgium
Paris-Roubaix	F. Ballerini	Italy
Liège-Bastogne-Liège	M. Gianetti	Switzerland
Amstel Gold	M. Gianetti	Switzerland
Leeds Classic	M. Sciandri	Britain
Championship of Zürich	J. Museeuw	Belgium
San Sebastian Classic	L. Armstrong	U.S.
Paris-Nice	L. Jalabert	France
Ghent-Wevelgem	L. Michaelsen	Denmark
Flèche Wallonne	L. Jalabert	France
Tour of Romandie	T. Rominger	Switzerland
Dauphiné Libéré	M. Indurain	Spain
Midi-Libre	M. Indurain	Spain
Dunkirk 4-Day	J. Museeuw	Belgium
Grand Prix of Frankfurt	F. Frattini	Italy
Tour DuPont	L. Armstrong	U.S.

Miguel Indurain of Spain holds up five fingers to indicate his fifth consecutive victory in the Tour de France. He was one of only four cyclists to have won the race five times and the only person to win it five times in a row.
PASCAL PAVANI—AFP

trial title four days earlier. French rider Jeannie Longo won both the women's time trial and road race, her 9th and 10th world titles. (JOHN R. WILKINSON)

EQUESTRIAN SPORTS

Thoroughbred Racing. Cigar, a five-year-old that had competed in relative obscurity as a colt, was revealed to be one of the finest thoroughbreds of all time in 1995 when he won all 10 of his starts to become racing's first undefeated male horse in an entire year of major competition since Spectacular Bid went 9-for-9 in 1980 and became the first thoroughbred to do so since the filly Personal Ensign won 13 in 1988.

Eight of Cigar's victories came in Grade I events, including four at the classic distance of 1¼ mi (1 mi = 0.62 km). His 1995 earnings of $4,819,800 established a North American single-season earnings record, surpassing the previous standard of $4,578,454 earned by Sunday Silence in 1989.

The powerful bay son of Palace Music captured the $3 million Breeders' Cup Classic in his final start of the year. In that race he sped to a stakes record of 1 min 59 sec over a muddy track to become the first horse since Secretariat to run 1¼ mi in less than two minutes. Secretariat won the 1973 Kentucky Derby in 1 min 59 sec.

The Breeders' Cup Classic, Cigar's 12th consecutive victory during a streak that began in the autumn of 1994, clinched Eclipse Awards for the horse as 1995 Horse of the Year and as Champion Older Male. Unraced as a two-year-old and winner of only one of 11 starts on grass during the next two years, Cigar was switched to running on dirt only as a last resort. At the end of 1995 he was the 13th richest thoroughbred of all time, with career earnings of $5,089,813.

Holy Bull, which had won the hearts and captured the imaginations of racing fans during his 1994 Horse of the Year campaign, dealt the sport a stunning blow on February 11 in the Donn Handicap at Gulfstream Park when he broke down during the running of the race and was subsequently retired. Ironically, the winner of the Donn was Cigar, which was making only his second start of the year.

Cigar's regular jockey, Jerry Bailey, may have clinched the Eclipse Award as the outstanding jockey of 1995. Bailey's victory with Cigar in the Breeders' Cup Classic was his third in a row in the prestigious event and his fourth in five years. Bailey was inducted into the National Racing Hall of Fame in Saratoga Springs, N.Y., in 1995. His earnings for the year totaled more than $15.2 million, tops among all riders in the U.S.

Earlier in the year trainer D. Wayne Lukas (*see* BIOGRAPHIES) made racing history when he sent Thunder Gulch postward to victory in the 127th Belmont Stakes. The win was Lukas' fifth straight in the Triple Crown classics. The veteran trainer won the 1995 Kentucky Derby with Thunder Gulch and the 1995 Preakness Stakes with Timber Country. His string of five began in 1994 with Tabasco Cat's triumphs in the Preakness and Belmont.

Thunder Gulch injured himself during the running of the Jockey Club Gold Cup Stakes on October 7 at Belmont Park and was retired to stud with a career record of 9 wins in 16 starts and earnings of $2,915,086. His 1995 earnings of $2,644,080 made him the leading money-winning three-year-old colt in 1995 and a favourite to win an Eclipse Award.

The outstanding three-year-old filly of 1995 was Serena's Song. Trained by Lukas, she was the first filly since Winning Colors in 1988 to compete against the colts in the Kentucky Derby. Unlike Winning Colors, which won the Derby, Serena's Song finished 16th in the field of 19. She then went on to a sensational season, however, winning 9 of 13 starts and earning more than $1.5 million with victories in such prestigious races for fillies as the Mother Goose and Beldame. She defeated colts in the Haskell Invitational and the Jim Beam and placed fifth against older fillies and mares in the Breeders' Cup Distaff.

Inside Information, trained by Shug McGaughey, won the Breeders' Cup Distaff by 13½ lengths, the largest victory margin in the 12-year history of the Breeders' Cup races. She was timed in 1 min 46 sec over the muddy track, a Breeders' Cup stakes record for 1⅛ mi. She was retired after making the Breeders' Cup her 14th win in 17 career starts. With career earnings of $1,641,806, she won the Eclipse Award as the best older female of 1995.

Earlier in the Breeders' Cup program, trainer McGaughey notched his first Cup victory with My Flag in the Juvenile Fillies. She charged from off the pace to a stakes record of 1 min 42.4 sec over 1$\frac{1}{16}$ mi. Among the fillies she vanquished was third-place finisher Golden Attraction, the leader of the two-year-old-filly division going into the race.

Ridgewood Pearl, a three-year-old bred in Great Britain, captured the Breeders' Cup Mile over soft turf in 1 min 43.6 sec. The filly, a prominent stakes winner in Europe with victories in the Irish One Thousand Guineas, Royal Ascot's Coronation Stakes, and the Prix du Moulin de Longchamp, was trained by John Oxx.

(JOHN G. BROKOPP)

Dubayy joined the world's leading racing nations in 1995 when it was announced that the first $4 million Dubayy World Cup, the world's richest race, would be run at the Nad ash-Sheba racetrack on March 27, 1996. The sport was introduced to the United Arab Emirates, of which Dubayy is one of seven members, in 1986, and the first race in Dubayy itself was not run until November 1991.

Dubayy was also becoming an important winter training centre. The first experiment was with Dayflower, which finished fifth in the 1993 One Thousand Guineas a few days after her return to Britain. In 1995 Red Bishop, which had left Dubayy in December 1994 to win in Hong Kong, added another valuable prize there in April and later that month won the San Juan Capistrano at Santa Anita, Calif.

When the Godolphin Racing team, organized in 1994 by Sheikh Muhammad al-Maktoum for the purpose of wintering horses in Dubayy, returned to Europe, Moonshell, Lammtarra, and Halling won Group One races in England, while Vettori scored at the top level in France and Flagbird in Italy. Lammtarra became only the second horse—his predecessor was Mill Reef in 1971—to have won the English Derby, King George VI and Queen Elizabeth Diamond Stakes, and Prix de l'Arc de Triomphe in the same season.

Sheikh Muhammad rejected a Japanese offer for Lammtarra. However, though Lammtarra was retired to stud at Newmarket, the sheikh did sell his 1994 Arc de Triomphe winner, Carnegie, to Japan.

Lammtarra, which raced in the name of the sheikh's nephew, Saʿīd ibn Maktoum al-Maktoum, ran only four times. None of his victories was easy. He beat Tamure by one length in the Derby, Pentire by a neck in the King George, and Freedom Cry by three-quarters of a length in the Arc de Triomphe. In between the last two, Pentire, which won six of his seven races in 1995, beat Freedom Cry by half a length in the Guinness Champion Stakes at Leopardstown, Ireland, to confirm that Lammtarra was only slightly superior to his rivals. Lammtarra, however, was not named Cartier Horse of the Year, that honour going to Ridgewood Pearl, which gained Group One success in Britain, France, and Ireland and then won the Breeders' Cup Mile.

Pennekamp, the champion two-year-old of 1994 in France, beat his British equivalent, Celtic Swing, by a head in the Two Thousand Guineas. But he suffered a fracture in his right foreleg when finishing 11th behind Lammtarra in the Derby and did not race again. Celtic Swing went on to win the Prix du Jockey-Club (French Derby) but injured himself in the Irish Derby and also vanished from the scene.

Andre Fabre was French champion trainer for the ninth consecutive year, and John Dunlop filled that position in Britain for the first time in a 30-year career. Earlier in the season Dunlop had trained his 2,000th winner in Britain. Henry Cecil was the only other active British trainer to have passed that mark.

Thierry Jarnet and Lanfranco Dettori retained their jockeys championships in France and Britain, respectively, as did Peter Schiergen in Germany. Schiergen had ridden 256 winners by November 19 and was on course to set a new European record for winners in a season.

British racing lost Lester Piggott, 11 times champion jockey between 1960 and 1982, who announced his retirement at the age of 59.

(BELOW) PETER MORGAN—REUTERS; (BOTTOM) PHIL COLE—ALLSPORT

(Below) Cigar, ridden by Jerry Bailey, crosses the finish line to win the Breeders' Cup Classic. The five-year-old had won 12 consecutive starts, the first male horse since 1980 to be undefeated in one season. (Bottom) Walter Swinburn rides Lammtarra to victory in the English Derby. Lammtarra was only the second horse ever to win the English Derby, King George VI and Queen Elizabeth Diamond Stakes, and Prix de l'Arc de Triomphe in the same season.

Major Thoroughbred Race Winners, 1995

Race	Won by	Jockey
United States		
Acorn	Cat's Cradle	C. Antley
Arlington Million	Awad	E. Maple
Beldame	Serena's Song	G. Stevens
Belmont	Thunder Gulch	G. Stevens
Breeders' Cup Juvenile	Unbridled's Song	M. Smith
Breeders' Cup Juvenile Fillies	My Flag	J. Bailey
Breeders' Cup Sprint	Desert Stormer	K. Desormeaux
Breeders' Cup Mile	Ridgewood Pearl	J. Murtagh
Breeders' Cup Distaff	Inside Information	M. Smith
Breeders' Cup Turf	Northern Spur	C. McCarron
Breeders' Cup Classic	Cigar	J. Bailey
Champagne	Maria's Mon	R. Davis
Charles H. Strub Stakes	Dare and Go	A. Solis
Coaching Club American Oaks	Golden Bri	J. Santos
Donn Handicap	Cigar	J. Bailey
Florida Derby	Thunder Gulch	M. Smith
Futurity	Maria's Mon	R. Davis
Gulfstream Park Handicap	Cigar	J. Bailey
Haskell Invitational	Serena's Song	G. Stevens
Hollywood Derby	Labeeb	E. Delahoussaye
Hollywood Futurity	Matty G.	A. Solis
Hollywood Gold Cup	Cigar	J. Bailey
Hollywood Turf Cup	Royal Chariot	A. Solis
Hollywood Turf Handicap	Earl of Barking	G. Almeida
International	Race discontinued	
Jockey Club Gold Cup	Cigar	J. Bailey
Kentucky Derby	Thunder Gulch	G. Stevens
Kentucky Oaks	Gal In A Ruckus	H. McCauley
Man o' War	Millkom	G. Stevens
Meadowlands Cup	Peaks and Valleys	J. Krone
Metropolitan	You And I	J. Chavez
Mother Goose	Serena's Song	G. Stevens
Oak Tree Invitational	Northern Spur	C. McCarron
Pacific Classic	Tinners Way	E. Delahoussaye
Philip H. Iselin	Schossberg	D. Penna
Pimlico Special	Cigar	J. Bailey
Preakness	Timber Country	P. Day
Santa Anita Derby	Larry The Legend	G. Stevens
Santa Anita Handicap	Urgent Request	G. Stevens
Spinster	Inside Information	M. Smith
Suburban	Key Contender	J. Bailey
Super Derby	Mecke	J. Bailey
Travers	Thunder Gulch	G. Stevens
Turf Classic	Turk Passer	J. Velazquez
Whitney	Unaccounted For	P. Day
Woodward	Cigar	J. Bailey
England		
One Thousand Guineas	Harayir	R. Hills
Two Thousand Guineas	Pennekamp	T. Jarnet
Derby	Lammtarra	W.R. Swinburn
Oaks	Moonshell	L. Dettori
St. Leger	Classic Cliche	L. Dettori
Coronation Cup	Sunshack	P. Eddery
Ascot Gold Cup	Double Trigger	J. Weaver
Eclipse Stakes	Halling	W.R. Swinburn
King George VI and Queen Elizabeth Diamond Stakes	Lammtarra	L. Dettori
Sussex Stakes	Sayyedati	B. Doyle
International Stakes	Halling	W.R. Swinburn
Dubayy Champion Stakes	Spectrum	J. Reid
France		
Poule d'Essai des Poulains	Vettori	L. Dettori
Poule d'Essai des Pouliches	Matiara	F. Head
Prix du Jockey-Club	Celtic Swing	K. Darley
Prix de Diane	Carling	T. Thulliez
Prix Royal-Oak	Sunshack	T. Jarnet
Prix Ganay	Pelder	L. Dettori
Prix Lupin	Flemensfirth	L. Dettori
Grand Prix de Paris	Valanour	G. Mosse
Grand Prix de Saint-Cloud	Carnegie	T. Jarnet
Prix Vermeille	Carling	T. Thulliez
Prix de l'Arc de Triomphe	Lammtarra	L. Dettori
Grand Critérium	Loup Solitaire	O. Peslier
Ireland		
Irish Two Thousand Guineas	Spectrum	J. Reid
Irish One Thousand Guineas	Ridgewood Pearl	C. Roche
Irish Derby	Winged Love	O. Peslier
Irish Oaks	Pure Grain	J. Reid
Irish St. Leger	Strategic Choice	T. Quinn
Irish Champion Stakes	Pentire	M. Hills
Italy		
Derby Italiano	Luso	M. Kinane
Gran Premio del Jockey-Club	Court of Honour	W. Ryan
Germany		
Deutsches Derby	All My Dreams	K. Woodburn
Grosser Preis von Baden	Germany	L. Dettori
Preis der Privatbankiers Merck, Finck & Co.	Lando	P. Schiergen
Europa Preis	Solon	P. Schiergen
Australia		
Melbourne Cup	Doriemus	D. Oliver

The Kentucky Derby

Year	Horse	Jockey
1991	Strike the Gold	C. Antley
1992	Lil E. Tee	P. Day
1993	Sea Hero	J. Bailey
1994	Go For Gin	C. McCarron
1995	**Thunder Gulch**	**G. Stevens**

The Preakness Stakes

Year	Horse	Jockey
1991	Hansel	J. Bailey
1992	Pine Bluff	C. McCarron
1993	Prairie Bayou	M. Smith
1994	Tabasco Cat	P. Day
1995	**Timber Country**	**P. Day**

The Belmont Stakes

Year	Horse	Jockey
1991	Hansel	J. Bailey
1992	A.P. Indy	E. Delahoussaye
1993	Colonial Affair	J. Krone
1994	Tabasco Cat	P. Day
1995	**Thunder Gulch**	**G. Stevens**

Triple Crown Champions—U.S.

Year	Horse
1946	Assault
1948	Citation
1973	Secretariat
1977	Seattle Slew
1978	Affirmed

2,000 Guineas

Year	Horse	Jockey
1991	Mystiko	M. Roberts
1992	Rodrigo de Triano	L. Piggott
1993	Zafonic	P. Eddery
1994	Mister Baileys	J. Weaver
1995	**Pennekamp**	**T. Jarnet**

The Derby

Year	Horse	Jockey
1991	Generous	A. Munro
1992	Dr Devious	J. Reid
1993	Commander in chief	M. Kinane
1994	Erhaab	W. Carson
1995	**Lammtarra**	**W.R. Swinburn**

The St. Leger

Year	Horse	Jockey
1991	Toulon	P. Eddery
1992	User Friendly	G. Duffield
1993	Bob's Return	P. Robinson
1994	Moonax	P. Eddery
1995	**Classic Cliche**	**L. Dettori**

Triple Crown Champions—British

Year	Winner
1915	Pommern
1917	Gay Crusader
1918	Gainsborough
1935	Bahram
1970	Nijinsky

Melbourne Cup

Year	Horse	Jockey
1991	Let's Elope	S. King
1992	Subzero	G. Hall
1993	Vintage Crop	M. Kinane
1994	Jeune	W. Harris
1995	**Doriemus**	**D. Oliver**

Doriemus, a five-year-old bred in New Zealand, became the ninth horse in the 20th century to have won both the Caulfield Cup and the Melbourne Cup in the same year. He gave trainer Lee Freedman his third Melbourne Cup victory in seven years when he beat the Victoria Derby winner, Nothin' Leica Dane, by four lengths. Lando, only 12th in the Breeders' Cup Turf, returned to top form in the Japan Cup in Tokyo on November 26. The German five-year-old ended his career with a 1½-length victory over Hishi Amazon in the richest race of 1995. (ROBERT W. CARTER)

Harness Racing. Helen Johansson of Sweden made Prix d'Amerique history in January at the Hippodrome de Vincennes near Paris, where she not only became the first woman to drive in the prestigious event for trotters but actually won it, guiding Ina Scot. At odds of 28 to 1, Ina Scot ran down the French favourite Vourasie (a half sister to the only four-time winner of the race, Orausie) in the final metres to beat her in a torrid finish. Ina Scot had become a star in Sweden, where she won 31 consecutive races from April 1992 through November 1993.

At Stockholm's Solvalla track in May, defending Swedish champion Copiad won the $462,962 Elitlopp. Driven by Erik Berglof for owner Stall Succe, the six-year-old trotter won his elimination heat in 1 min 54.7 sec and the final in 1 min 54.4 sec, earning $290,000 to push his career bankroll past $1.7 million.

David's Pass, driven by John Campbell, won the $1 million North American Cup at Toronto's Woodbine Raceway in June and then added the $1 million Meadowlands Pace at the Meadowlands in New Jersey in 1 min 50.8 sec. In August, also at the Meadowlands, David's Pass won the Adios Pace in 1 min 51.8 sec to boost his seasonal earnings to $1.4 million.

Tagliabue, whose sire Super Bowl won the 1972 Hambletonian, scored an upset victory in the $1 million 1995 Hambletonian at the Meadowlands in August. The heavy favourite in the premier race for three-year-old trotters, world record holder CR Kay Suzie, broke stride when challenging in the first of the two $100,000 elimination heats and failed to qualify. Tagliabue won that heat and the final, both in 1 min 54.8 sec. CR Kay Suzie's 1995 wins included the $585,000 World Trotting Derby at Du Quoin, Ill., in September, beating Tagliabue in straight heats in 1 min 53.4 sec and 1 min 52.8 sec. The same month, the Royal Troubador filly overpowered seven of the best older mares in the $300,000 Breeders Crown at Delaware, Ohio.

Nick's Fantasy, aided by a heady drive on the part of John Campbell, scored an upset win over favourite Village Connection in the final of the $512,830 50th running of the Little Brown Jug for three-year-old pacers at Delaware, Ohio, in September. Nick's Fantasy comfortably won his heat in 1 min 54.6 sec before easily taking the final in 1 min 51.4 sec—a world record for three-year-old geldings on a half-mile oval (1 mile = 1.61 km).

A Stud Named Sue, a two-year-old pacing colt, driven by little-known reinsman George Brennan, convincingly won the $585,500 Woodrow Wilson Pace at the Meadowlands in August in 1 min 52.8 sec. Ball And Chain, a five-year-old son of Albatross, broke the 1-min 50-sec barrier for the first time in Canadian harness racing history, winning his elimination heat in the Canadian Pacing Derby on the ⅞-mi (7 furlongs) Woodbine Raceway in August in 1 min 49.8 sec. In the $278,250 final, however, Pacific Rocket beat Ball And Chain by a nose in 1 min 50.2 sec.

The Hambletonian Trot

Year	Horse	Driver
1991	Giant Victory	J. Moiseyev
1992	Alf Palema	M. McNicholl
1993	American Winner	R. Pierce
1994	Victory Dream	M. Lachance
1995	**Tagliabue**	**J. Campbell**

His Majesty, one of the two Swedish horses that were the only European representatives in a nine-horse field for the $300,000 International Trot at Yonkers (N.Y.) Raceway in August, won easily. The $NZ 400,000 1995 Inter-Dominion Pacing Championship Grand Final at Addington, N.Z., in March was won handsomely by five-year-old Golden Reign. The $NZ 300,000 New Zealand Cup, run at Addington on November 7, was won by Il Vicolo. Only the fifth four-year-old to win the grueling test in 92 runnings, Il Vicolo paced the 3,200 m (3,500 yd) in a record-equaling 4 min 0.4 sec. (RONALD W. BISMAN)

Steeplechasing. Trainer Kim Bailey and jockey Norman Williamson were responsible for both of the big jumping winners at Cheltenham-Master Oats in the Gold Cup and Alderbrook in the Champion Hurdle. Royal Athlete, at 40–1, gave Jenny Pitman her second training success in the Grand National. Algan, trained in France by Francis Doumen, won the King George VI Chase in England, while his stablemates, Ubu III and Val d'Alene, filled the first two places in the Grand Steeple-Chase de Paris.

British racing lost one of its heroes when Red Rum died at the age of 30 on October 18. He won the Grand National in 1973, 1974, and 1977 and finished second in the two intervening years.

(ROBERT W. CARTER)

Show Jumping and Dressage. Peter Charles and Lucy Thompson, two British riders now representing Ireland, won individual gold medals at, respectively, the European show jumping championships at St. Gallen, Switz., and the Open European Three-Day Event championships at Pratoni del Vivaro, Italy. Charles, who rode La Ina, switched countries to gain more international opportunities; Thompson, who won on Welton Romance, represented Ireland because her husband was Irish.

Switzerland successfully defended the show jumping team championship it had won in 1993, and Britain gained a narrow victory over New Zealand in the three-day event. (ROBERT W. CARTER)

Polo. The Argentine Open, the climax of the Argentine high-handicap season, from October to December 1995, was won again by Indios Chapaleufú. Consisting of the four Heguy brothers—Bautista, Gonzalo, Horacio, Jr., and Marcos—the new champions defeated La Mariana (Mike Azzaro, Sebastian and Juan Ignacio Merlos, and Milo Fernández Araujo) 14–10 in the final. Ellerstina, the 1994 Open champion, had earlier scored triumphs in the Los Indios Tortugas and Hurlingham Open, defeating La Martina and Indios Chapaleufú, respectively, in the finals. But Kerry Packer's team lost its chance to repeat as Open champion when it was beaten by Indios Chapaleufú in the semifinals.

In July the International Polo Federation held the fourth world championship for teams with handicaps between 10 and 14 goals. The preliminary round was played in Düsseldorf, Germany, with six teams taking part: Switzerland (host nation), Argentina (defending champion), and qualifying zone winners England, Mexico, Brazil, and India. The teams then moved to Saint Moritz, Switz., for the final round. In the match for the championship, Brazil defeated favoured Argentina 11–10. Mexico beat England 11–10 in overtime in the consolation final.

In England, Labegorce won the Queen's Cup, played in Windsor, beating Alcatel in the final. Meanwhile, Packer's Ellerston White outclassed Urs Schwarzenbach's Black Bears to obtain the Gold Cup. Both champions then clashed in the Silver Jubilee Cup, which Labegorce won 12–11 after two extra chukkers. Argentina won the Coronation Cup 14–8 over England.

The U.S. Open in September featured as its two finalists Outback and White Birch. The winner was Outback, whose leader, Memo Gracida, had also been a member of the 1994 champion, Aspen. At Palm Beach, Fla., in January, the outstanding teams were Ellerston White, White Birch, and Calumet, which won the Challenge and World Cup, Gold Cup, and Sterling Cup, respectively. (JORGE ADRIÁN ANDRADES)

FENCING

Dominating international fencing during the 1994–95 season was the global limit of 220 fencing places for the 1996 Olympic Games in Atlanta, Ga. Operating under this constraint, the Fédération Internationale d'Escrime (FIE—the international governing body) was forced to devise a convoluted qualification process that gave a fair representation for each of fencing's world zones while at the same time maintaining high athletic standards. Most of the qualifications for the Olympics took place at the world championships in The Hague in July 1995 during the team competitions. Emerging from the championships was a strong team from China that seemed certain to challenge past European domination. Only Italy and Russia qualified directly in all disciplines.

At the start of the season, international rule changes, designed to make the sport more attractive to spectators and television viewers, were introduced. In the opinion of many, the most effective of these was the return to traditional foot and leg movements at sabre, which thus outlawed running and flèching. This forced fencers to pay greater attention to defense and substantially reduced the number of simultaneous hits, which had plagued the weapon in the past. Sabre was still the fastest of the three weapons (the other two being foil and épée) but with the new rule should be easier for the nonexpert to follow.

Other changes important to athletes included an increase in the size of sponsorship names allowed on clothing and the introduction of coloured clothing, although the latter was not generally adopted. Additionally, the strength of protective clothing was increased, and development of the trans-

World Fencing Championships—Men

Year	Individual			Team		
	Foil	Épée	Sabre	Foil	Épée	Sabre
1989	A. Koch (W.Ger.)	M. Pereira (Spain)	G. Kirienko (U.S.S.R.)	U.S.S.R.	Italy	U.S.S.R.
1990	P. Omnès (Fr.)	T. Gerull (W.Ger.)	G. Nebald (Hung.)	Italy	Italy	U.S.S.R.
1991	I. Weissenborn (Ger.)	A. Shuvalov (U.S.S.R.)	G. Kirienko (U.S.S.R.)	Cuba	U.S.S.R.	Hungary
1992	P. Omnès (Fr.)	E. Srecki (Fr.)	B. Szabo (Hung.)	Germany	Germany	Unified Team
1993	A. Koch (Ger.)	P. Kolobkov (Russia)	G. Kirienko (Russia)	Germany	Italy	Hungary
1994	R. Tucker (Cuba)	P. Kolobkov (Russia)	F. Becker (Ger.)	Germany	France	Russia
1995	**D. Chevtchenko (Russia)**	**E. Srecki (Fr.)**	**G. Kirienko (Russia)**	**Cuba**	**Germany**	**Italy**

World Fencing Championships—Women

Year	Individual foil	Team foil	Individual épée	Team épée
1990	A. Fichtel (W.Ger.)	Italy	T. Chappe (Cuba)	West Germany
1991	G. Trillini (Italy)	Italy	M. Horvath (Hung.)	Hungary
1992	G. Trillini (Italy)	Italy	M. Horvath (Hung.)	Hungary
1993	F. Bortolozzi (Italy)	Germany	O. Jermakova (Est.)	Hungary
1994	B. Szabo (Rom.)	Romania	L. Chiesa (Italy)	Spain
1995	**L. Badea (Rom.)**	**Italy**	**J. Jakimiuk (Pol.)**	**Hungary**

Team members throw Dmitry Chevtchenko in the air in celebration of his victory in the world fencing championships in The Hague. The Russian fencer won the men's title in the individual foil competition by defeating José Guerra of Spain 15–3 in the final on July 20.
PAUL VREEKER—AFP

parent mask continued. The FIE hoped that this mask would replace the traditional metal gauze-fronted head protection in order to render fencers identifiable.

(GRAHAM MORRISON)

FIELD HOCKEY

Germany won the two main prizes for men's field hockey in 1995, retaining the European Nations Cup in Dublin in August and regaining the Champions Trophy in Berlin in the autumn. The Dublin final was decided on penalty strokes after a 2–2 draw against The Netherlands. England finished third and Belgium fourth. In Berlin the Champions Trophy final was also settled on penalty strokes after the match against Australia was tied at 2–2. Pakistan, The Netherlands, India, and England filled the remaining places in that order.

Earlier in the year South Korea won the Indira Gandhi Gold Cup in New Delhi in February after defeating India 3–1 in the final. In third place was Australia, ahead of Kazakhstan, England, Malaysia, South Africa, and Poland. Argentina served as host for the Pan American Games at Mar del Plata in March and finished first, followed by Canada, the U.S., Cuba, Trinidad and Tobago, Chile, and Paraguay. Spain won a four-nation tournament at Lisburn, Northern Ireland, in June, with Ireland in second place, the U.S. third, and Scotland fourth. At a similar event in Atlanta, Ga., in September, Germany finished first, Australia second, India (A) third, and the U.S. fourth. Germany was later disqualified on a technical fault, and all other finishers moved up one place. In Sardinia, Italy, Australia won a tournament for six nations, finishing ahead of South Korea, Canada, India (B), Italy, and France. South Africa took the title at the African Games at Harare, Zimbabwe, where Egypt was second.

World Cup Field Hockey Championships Men

Year	Winner	Runner-up
1986	Australia	England
1990	The Netherlands	Pakistan
1994	Pakistan	The Netherlands

World Cup Field Hockey Championships Women

Year	Winner	Runner-up
1986	The Netherlands	West Germany
1990	The Netherlands	Australia
1994	Australia	Argentina

In women's competition, Australia won the Champions Trophy at Mar del Plata in September. South Korea was second, followed by the U.S., Germany, Spain, and Argentina. South Africa took first in the African Games tournament at Bulawayo, Zimbabwe, ahead of Zimbabwe, Kenya, Namibia, Nigeria, and Ghana. Australia won a tournament at Atlanta in August. Spain was second, the U.S. third, and South Africa fourth. The Netherlands regained the European Nations Cup at Amstelveen, Neth., in June with a victory over Spain on penalties after a 2–2 draw in the final. Germany finished third, followed by England, Russia, Scotland, France, Ireland, Italy, the Czech Republic, Belgium, and Sweden.

(SYDNEY E. FRISKIN)

FOOTBALL

Association Football (Soccer). The qualifying matches for the 1996 European championships included a record 48 countries. Spain became the first to qualify for the championship round of 16, while Sweden, the host nation in 1992, was eliminated along with Switzerland in its centenary year. France achieved a record score in beating Azerbaijan 10–0, with eight different players scoring goals. Croatia, despite the strain of the ongoing Balkan conflict, emerged as a likely finalist. (Yugoslavia was the only European country that did not enter the competition.) Other Eastern European countries to show prominence were Romania, Russia, and Bulgaria, which was led by European soccer's Player of the Year Hristo Stoichkov (*see* BIOGRAPHIES).

The Union des Associations Européenes de Football (UEFA) switched its Swiss headquarters to Nyon, on the shores of Lake Geneva, and made moves to challenge the previously unquestioned authority of the Fédération Internationale de Football Association (FIFA), the world governing body. UEFA was now responsible for 10 different competitions at the club and international levels. A record 170 clubs entered its three major tournaments.

In England attendance at matches increased for the ninth successive season, but a number of scandals flawed the image of the game: three players were charged with fixing the results of matches; George Graham, the Arsenal manager of nine years, was dismissed and banned for a year after accepting a gift of money from a player trade; serious outbreaks of hooliganism took place; and some players were found to be taking drugs. England's match against Ireland at Dublin on February 15 was aban-

Association Football National Champions

Nation	League winners	Cup winners
Albania	SK Tirana	Teuta Durres
Argentina	San Lorenzo	
Armenia	Shizak Gyunri	Ararat Yerevan
Austria	Casino Salzburg	Rapid Wien
Belarus	Dynamo Minsk	Dynamo 93
Belgium	Anderlecht	FC Brugge
Bolivia	Bolivar	
Brazil	Palmeiras	Corinthians
Bulgaria	Levski Sofia	Lokomotiv Sofia
Chile	Universidad de Chile	
Colombia	Atletico Nacional	
Costa Rica	Saprissa	
Croatia	Hajduk Split	Hajduk Split
Cyprus	Anorthosis	Apoel
Czech Republic	Sparta Prague	Hradec Kralove
Denmark	Aalborg	FC Copenhagen
Ecuador	Emelec	
El Salvador	FAS	
England	Blackburn Rovers	Everton
Estonia	Flora Tallinn	Lantana
Faroe Islands	GI Gotu	KI Klaksvik
Finland	TPV Tampere	HJK Helsinki
France	Nantes	Paris St. Germain
Georgia	Tbilisi Dynamo	Tbilisi Dynamo
Germany	Borussia Dortmund	Mönchengladbach
Greece	Panathinaikos	Panathinaikos
Guatemala	Comunicaciones	
Honduras	Victoria	
Hungary	Ferencvaros	Ferencvaros
Iceland	IA Akrànes	KR Reykjavik
Ireland	Dundalk	Derry City
Israel	Maccabi Tel Aviv	Maccabi Haifa
Italy	Juventus	Juventus
Japan	Verdy Kawasaki	
Latvia	Skonto Riga	Olympia Riga
Lithuania	Zalgiris Vilnius	Inkaras
Luxembourg	Jeunesse Esch	Grevenmacher
Malta	Hibernians	Valletta
Mexico	Necaxa	
Moldova	Zimbrul Chisinau	Tiligul
Netherlands, The	Ajax Amsterdam	Feyenoord
Northern Ireland	Crusaders	Linfield
Norway	Rosenborg	Molde
Paraguay	Certo Porteño	
Peru	Sporting Cristal	
Poland	Legia Warsaw	Legia Warsaw
Portugal	FC Porto	Sporting Lisbon
Romania	Steaua Bucharest	Petrolul Ploiesti
Russia	Spartak Moscow	Moscow Dynamo
San Marino	Tre Fiori	
Scotland	Rangers	Celtic
Slovakia	Slovan Bratislava	Inter Bratislava
Slovenia	Olimpija Ljubljana	Mura
Spain	Real Madrid	La Coruña
Sweden	IFK Gothenburg	Halmstad
Switzerland	Grasshopper	Sion
Turkey	Besiktas	Trabzonspor
Ukraine	Dynamo Kiev	Donetsk
Uruguay	Peñarol	
Venezuela	Caracas	
Wales	Bangor City	Wrexham
Yugoslavia (Serbia and Montenegro)	Red Star Belgrade	Red Star Belgrade

European Cup-Winners' Cup

Season	Result			
1990–91	Manchester United (Eng.)	2	Barcelona	1
1991–92	Werder Bremen (Ger.)	2	AS Monaco	0
1992–93	Parma (Italy)	3	Royal Antwerp	1
1993–94	Arsenal (Eng.)	1	Parma (Italy)	0
1994–95	**Real Zaragosa (Spain)**	**2**	**Arsenal (Eng.)**	**1**

The European Cup of Champion Clubs

Season	Result			
1990–91	Red Star Belgrade*	0	Marseille	0
1991–92	Barcelona	1	Sampdoria (Italy)	0
1992–93	Olympique Marseille	1	AC Milan	0
1993–94	AC Milan	4	Barcelona	0
1994–95	**Ajax Amsterdam**	**1**	**AC Milan**	**0**

*Won on penalty kicks.

FIFA World Cup

Year	Result			
1986	Argentina	3	West Germany	2
1990	West Germany	1	Argentina	0
1994	Brazil*	0	Italy	0

*Won on penalty kicks.

doned after 27 minutes because of rioting by some England supporters. Eric Cantona, who played for France and Manchester United, was found guilty of assaulting a spectator. He received a two-week jail sentence that on appeal was reduced to community service.

After a spectator was stabbed to death in Genoa, Italy, the match between the home team and AC Milan was abandoned at halftime. On the following Sunday Italian officials canceled all national sports events as a mark of respect as well as protest against the escalation of violence.

Average league attendances in Italy declined slightly to 29,215 per match but rose significantly to 29,271 for a record in Germany. The premier league in England reported final average figures of 24,271. In England the Blackburn Rovers achieved their first championship since 1914, assisted by the £60 million spent on players and ground improvements given by millionaire supporter Jack Walker. In Scotland the Rangers won their 45th championship, the seventh in succession.

In Spain, La Coruña's cup final against Valencia was interrupted by rain in the 79th minute with the score at 1–1. The remaining 11 minutes were played three days later, La Coruña scoring the winning goal in the first minute. Dynamo Kiev, the champion of Ukraine, was eliminated from the European Champions' Cup competition for bribing a referee.

Jean-Marc Bosman, a former player with FC Liège in Belgium, appeared before the European Court of Justice in Luxembourg claiming that the transfer (trade) and quota system on foreign players imposed by UEFA infringed community law. He was able to prove that transfer fees at the end of a player's contract were illegal; thus, the financial implications for the professional game were likely to be widespread.

Despite this expected outcome, the English premier league clubs spent a record of more than £100 million in transfer fees. Many of the transfers involved players from other nations, and their total increased to 66 at the start of the 1995–96 season. The English record was broken when Stan Collymore, a striker, moved from Nottingham Forest to Liverpool for £8.5 million.

AC Milan invested £12.9 million in Juventus forward Roberto Baggio and signed another striker, George Weah from Paris St. Germain, for £10 million. A record fee for a teenager brought 19-year-old midfield player Clarence Seedorf to the Italian club Sampdoria from Ajax Amsterdam in a £4.5 million transaction.

Ajax Amsterdam, undefeated in 34 domestic league games, completed its third victory of the season over the defending champion, AC Milan, in the European Champions' Cup final in Vienna on May 24. Ajax's previous two wins, both by a 2–0 margin, were achieved in the Champions League section of the competition. The third success came in a quiet, undistinguished match in which AC Milan was unable to re-create the enterprise and verve displayed a year earlier. Yet Milan might have scored first close to halftime. A volley from Marco Simone almost surprised Ajax goalkeeper Edwin Van der Sar. The chief threat from Milan came from the penetration of Demetrio Albertini into the heart of the Ajax defense. But the Dutch team coach, Louis Van Gaal, made an inspired substitution in the 65th minute, bringing on Patrick Kluivert for Jari Litmanen, a Finnish international. Twenty minutes later, with time running toward a possible extra period of play, Edgar Davids drifted in from the left flank of the Ajax attack and found Frank Rijkaard, who angled the ball into the centre and raced for a return pass, distracting the Milan defense enough for Kluivert to stab a shot past goalkeeper Sebastiano Rossi. The victory brought Ajax its first European Cup win since the early 1970s.

There had been fewer more dramatic goals than the one that enabled Real

Zaragoza of Spain to defeat the European Cup-Winners' Cup defending champion, Arsenal of England, 2–1 in the final at Paris on May 10. The seconds of extra time had almost ticked away when Nayim (Mohamed Ali Amar) tried a high lob from 40 yd out near the right touchline. The attempt caught the poorly positioned Arsenal goalkeeper, David Seaman, yards out of his goal, and despite a desperate leap, he was unable to prevent the ball from entering the net under the bar. Although Arsenal had more territorial advantage, Zaragoza was dangerous on the counterattack. It scored first in the 68th minute when Juan Esnaider spectacularly controlled the ball, turned, and shot left-footed in one concise movement. It took eight minutes for Arsenal to respond. Ray Parlour on the right found Paul Merson, who squared the ball for John Hartson to slide in for the tying goal from six yards out.

For the seventh successive season, at least one Italian team played in the final of the UEFA Cup. This time Parma defeated fellow Italian club Juventus 2–1 on aggregate scores, depriving its victim of a possible third honour; Juventus had already won the Italian League and Italian Cup. At Parma on May 3, a goal by Dino Baggio after five minutes settled the first game. From a Gianfranco Zola pass, he lobbed the ball in from the edge of the penalty area. Two weeks later, in the second leg, played in Milan, Gianluca Vialli tied the aggregate score with a volleyed goal after 33 minutes, but 20 minutes later Baggio, a former Juventus player, again rescued Parma. This time he headed in a cross from substitute Roberto Mussi. (JACK ROLLIN)

Uruguay used its home-field advantage to win the Copa America, a biennial contest of national teams traditionally from South America but since 1993 also including two North American squads, Mexico and the U.S. In the final game Uruguay tied Brazil 1–1 in regulation time and then edged its archrival 5–3 in a penalty shootout. Brazil had reached the semifinals after defeating Argentina in a controversial quarterfinal game in which Túlio, a Brazilian forward, scored a crucial goal after illegally handling the ball.

The U.S. was the surprising team of the tournament. After beating Chile 2–1 and Argentina 3–0 in the first round, it edged Mexico in a penalty shootout in the quarterfinals before finally being defeated 1–0 by Brazil in the semifinals. Colombia beat the U.S. in the game for third place. Mexico's Luis García and Argentina's Gabriel Batistuta were the leading scorers of the tournament, with four goals each.

Grêmio of Pôrto Alegre, Brazil, took the Libertadores de América Cup, South America's club championship. Among the teams it defeated were Olimpia of Paraguay, Palmeiras of Brazil, and, in the semifinal, Emelec of Ecuador. In the two-game final series, Grêmio gained a decisive advantage by beating Colombia's Atletico Nacional 3–1 in Pôrto Alegre. A 1–1 tie in Medellín, Colombia, was sufficient to give the Brazilians the coveted title. Grêmio later lost the Toyota Cup, the unofficial world club championship, however, after battling Ajax Amsterdam of The Netherlands to a 0–0 tie and then falling 4–3 in a penalty shootout.

In national play San Lorenzo was the winner of the spring Closing Tournament in Argentina, and Vélez Sarsfield took the autumn Opening Tournament. Rio de Janeiro's Botafogo became Brazil's national champion after beating Santos in a 3–2 penalty shootout after a 1–1 tie. Peñarol took Uruguay's opening national club championship, while Necaxa beat its Mexico City rival Cruz Azul in the final game to win Mexico's league championship.

Olimpia, winner of the second-round tournament, edged Cerro Porteño, winner of the first round, in Paraguay's national championship. Universidad de Chile won Chile's league championship by edging Universidad Católica by a single point. Nacional of Medellín won Colombia's national championship. Emelec of Guayaquil became Ecuador's champion, and Oruro took Bolivia's national title.

(SERGIO SARMIENTO)

U.S. Football. Nebraska won its second consecutive national championship of college football by defeating Florida 62–24 in the Fiesta Bowl at Tempe, Ariz., on Jan. 2, 1996. The victory gave the Big Eight champion a 12–0–0 record, 25 consecutive victories, and a 36–1 record for three seasons. The Fiesta Bowl, matching the only Division I-A teams with perfect regular-season records, was the Bowl Alliance's first national championship game. The alliance ensures that the top two teams play each other in a bowl game if they are not from the Big Ten or Pacific Ten conferences, which are committed to the Rose Bowl.

Florida, 12–1 and the Southeastern Conference champion, ranked second in the Associated Press writers' poll and third in the *USA Today*/CNN coaches' poll. The other team ranked second and third was Tennessee, 11–1, the Citrus Bowl winner 20–14 over Ohio State.

Florida State, Colorado, Ohio State, Kansas State, Northwestern, Kansas, and Virginia Tech, all with 10–2 records except Ohio State at 11–2, were ranked 4th through 10th by both polls, though not in the same order. Northwestern gained its first Big Ten championship in 59 years, first Rose Bowl appearance in 47 years, and first winning season in 24 years, earning Coach of the Year honours for Gary Barnett. (*See* BIOGRAPHIES.)

Florida State, the Atlantic Coast Conference cochampion with Virginia, defeated Notre Dame 31–26 in the Orange Bowl. Pac Ten champ Southern California (9–2–1) won the Rose Bowl 41–32 against Northwestern. Virginia Tech, the Big East cochampion with Miami (Florida), defeated Southwest Conference champion Texas 28–10 in the Sugar Bowl.

Ohio State's Eddie George won the Heisman Trophy and the Maxwell Award, both honouring the best player in Division I-A, and the Doak Walker Award for the best running back. He led the division with 144 points on 24 touchdowns. Also for Ohio State, Terry Glenn won the Fred Biletnikoff Award for the best wide receiver, and offensive tackle Orlando Pace won the Vince Lombardi Award for the best lineman. Glenn's 17 touchdown catches tied Chris Doering of Florida for the division lead.

Nebraska had Division I-A's dominant offense, leading it with 77 touchdowns and averages of 52.4 points per game, 399.8 yd rushing per game, and 7 yd per rushing attempt. Defensively, Nebraska ranked a close second in rushing defense to Virginia Tech, which allowed 77.4 yd per game.

Nevada ranked first in passing at 416.3 yd per game. Quarterback Mike Maxwell led the division with a .677 completion percentage and 402.6 yd per game of total offense, and teammate Alex Van Dyke set records with 129 catches and 1,854 yd in 11 regular-season games. With 569.4 total yards per game, Nevada ranked ahead of Nebraska, Florida State, Florida, Ohio State, and Colorado in that order.

Florida quarterback Danny Wuerffel set a record with 178.4 passing efficiency points and also led the Division I-A passers with 10.05 yd per attempt and 35 touchdowns. He won the Davey O'Brien Award for the best quarterback and was named National Football Foundation Player of the Year.

The leading defensive teams were Northwestern, Kansas State, and Miami (Ohio). Northwestern allowed the fewest points per game, 12.7, just ahead of Kansas State, which allowed the fewest yards, 250.8 per game. No one in the division allowed fewer rushing touchdowns than Miami and Kansas State (4), fewer passing touchdowns than Northwestern (5), or fewer offensive touchdowns than Miami and Northwestern (15). Northwestern linebacker Pat Fitzgerald won the Chuck Bednarik Award as the best defensive player.

UCLA offensive tackle Jonathan Ogden won the Outland Trophy as the best lineman; Colorado State's Greg Myers took the Scholar-Athlete Award and the Jim Thorpe Award as the best defensive back; Illinois' Kevin Hardy gained the Dick Butkus Award as the best linebacker; and Texas Christian's Michael Reeder won the Lou Groza Award as the best placekicker. Reeder led Division I-A with 23 field goals, and his .920 percentage on 25 attempts was just behind Chris Ferencik's .923 for Pittsburgh on 13 attempts. Troy Davis of Iowa State led Division I-A with 2,466 all-purpose yards and 2,010 yd rushing but was the first of the five 2,000-yd rushers in Division I-A history not to win the Heisman Trophy.

After winning a record fifth Super Bowl for the 1994 season, the San Francisco 49ers in 1995 missed their conference's championship game for only the second time in eight years. San Francisco defeated the San Diego Chargers 49–26 in Super Bowl XXIX on Jan. 29, 1995, at Miami, Fla., but lost their first play-off game, to Green Bay, in trying to defend their National Football League (NFL) championship.

The 49ers and the Dallas Cowboys were the only teams to win their fourth consecu-

Libertadores de América Cup

Year	Winner (country)	Runner-up (country)	Scores
1991	Colo Colo (Chile)	Olimpia (Paraguay)	0–0, 3–0
1992	São Paulo (Braz.)	Newell's Old Boys (Arg.)	0–1, 1–0, 3–2*
1993	São Paulo (Braz.)	Universidad Catolica (Chile)	5–1, 0–2
1994	Velez Sarsfield (Arg.)	São Paulo (Braz.)	1–0, 0–1, 5–3*
1995	**Grêmio (Braz.)**	**Atletico Nacional (Colom.)**	**3–1, 1–1**

*Winner determined in penalty shootout after tiebreaking game.

(Top) Northwestern running back Darnell Autry is surrounded by the Southern California defense in the Rose Bowl. USC won the game 41–32, dashing the hopes of Northwestern, which had won its first Big Ten title in 59 years. (Above) Quarterback Steve Young of the San Francisco 49ers eludes the defense of the San Diego Chargers in Super Bowl XXIX, played on Jan. 29, 1995. San Francisco defeated San Diego by a score of 49–26 to win a record fifth Super Bowl.

(TOP) JED JACOBSON—ALLSPORT; (BOTTOM) BRYAN YABLONSKY—DUOMO

tive division titles in 1995, San Francisco at 11–5 in the National Football Conference West and Dallas at 12–4 in the NFC East. The only other division champion to repeat was Pittsburgh in the American Football Conference (AFC) Central, but 8 of the 12 teams in the play-offs had been there a year earlier.

Buffalo returned to the top of the AFC East after a one-year absence, as did Kansas City in the AFC West with an NFL-leading 13–3 record. Green Bay won the NFC Central for the first time since 1972. Of the six wild-card teams, Miami, San Diego, and Detroit returned from the 1994 season play-offs; Philadelphia had been absent for two years, Atlanta for three years, and Indianapolis for seven years. Indianapolis won its first play-off game since 1971 by defeating San Diego 35–20 on December 31.

The Carolina Panthers, one of two new NFL teams, went 7–9, nearly doubling the previous record of four wins by an expansion team. The St. Louis Rams and Oakland Raiders changed cities during the off-season, leaving Los Angeles without an NFL team, and the Cleveland Browns and Houston Oilers announced plans to move to Baltimore and Nashville, respectively. The Browns' announcement, after they had consistently ranked in the NFL's top 10 in attendance and revenue, led to a congressional hearing and legal action to block the move. The Browns then slumped to 5–11, a six-game decline from 1994.

NFL average scoring of 43 points per game was the highest in 10 years. The NFL also had records of 21 overtime games and 21.3% of its games decided after the two-minute warning. With nine receivers catching at least 100 passes, the league exceeded its previous all-time total of 100-catch receivers by two.

Detroit became the first team with two 100-catch receivers, and Herman Moore's 123 set a league record. One catch behind him were previous record holder Cris Carter of Minnesota and Jerry Rice of San Francisco, whose 1,848 yd on receptions also set a record. Rice also set career records of 942 catches and 15,123 yd, and Arizona's Larry Centers set the season record for running backs with 101 catches. The other 100-catch receivers were St. Louis' Isaac Bruce, Dallas' Michael Irvin, Detroit's Brett Perriman, Atlanta's Eric Metcalf, and Green Bay's Robert Brooks.

The 49ers led the league with 288 passing yards per game, and AFC leader Miami

Rose Bowl

Season	Result			
1990–91	Washington	46	Iowa	34
1991–92	Washington	34	Michigan	14
1992–93	Michigan	38	Washington	31
1993–94	Wisconsin	21	UCLA	16
1994–95	Penn State	38	Oregon	20
1995–96	**Southern California**	**41**	**Northwestern**	**32**

Orange Bowl

Season	Result			
1990–91	Colorado	10	Notre Dame	9
1991–92	Miami (Fla.)	22	Nebraska	0
1992–93	Florida St.	27	Nebraska	14
1993–94	Florida St.	18	Nebraska	16
1994–95	Nebraska	24	Miami	17
1995–96	**Florida St.**	**31**	**Notre Dame**	**26**

Sugar Bowl

Season	Result			
1990–91	Tennessee	23	Virginia	22
1991–92	Notre Dame	39	Florida	28
1992–93	Alabama	34	Miami (Fla.)	13
1993–94	Florida	41	West Virginia	7
1994–95	Florida State	23	Florida	17
1995–96	**Virginia Tech**	**28**	**Texas**	**10**

Cotton Bowl

Season	Result			
1990–91	Miami (Fla.)	46	Texas	3
1991–92	Florida State	10	Texas A&M	2
1992–93	Notre Dame	28	Texas A&M	3
1993–94	Notre Dame	24	Texas A&M	21
1994–95	Southern California	55	Texas Tech	14
1995–96	**Colorado**	**38**	**Oregon**	**6**

U.S. College Football National Champion

Season	Champion
1990–91	Colorado*/Georgia Tech*
1991–92	Miami (Fla.)*/Washington*
1992–93	Alabama
1993–94	Florida St.
1994–95	Nebraska
1995–96	Nebraska

*Tied.

ranked fourth in quarterback Dan Marino's record-setting season. Marino established career passing records with 6,531 attempts, 3,913 completions, 48,841 yd, and 352 touchdowns.

The leading AFC passer, Jim Harbaugh of Indianapolis, had 100.7 rating points, 1.2 more than the league's Most Valuable Player, Brett Favre of Green Bay, the NFC leader. Harbaugh led NFL passers with 8.2 yd per attempt and five interceptions (1.6%), while Favre led with 38 touchdowns and 4,413 yd.

Kansas City had the league's best rushing offense with 138.9 yd per game, Detroit the best total offense with 382.1 yd per game, and San Francisco the most points with 28.6 per game. Emmitt Smith led the league with 1,773 yd rushing and 2,148 total yards from scrimmage for Dallas, the best NFC rushing team. He also set a league record with 25 touchdowns, all on runs, for an NFL-high 150 points. Detroit's Barry Sanders led the league with 4.8 yd per carry, and New England rookie Curtis Martin led AFC rushers with 1,487 yd. Denver had the AFC's best total offense, and Pittsburgh scored its most points.

San Francisco allowed the fewest yards (274.9) and rushing yards (66.3) per game and Kansas City the fewest points (15.1 per game). Buffalo's 49 sacks and San Francisco's 26 interceptions were the best team totals.

Placekicking leaders were Norm Johnson of Pittsburgh with 34 field goals and 141 points and Dallas' Chris Boniol with a .964 field-goal percentage on 27 for 28, the NFL's second best ever. Morten Andersen set two records with three field goals of more than 50 yd in one game and eight in the season, and Fuad Reveiz set another with 30 successful field-goal attempts in a row. Punting leader Rick Tuten averaged 45 yd for Seattle.

Canadian Football. By defeating the Calgary Stampeders 37–20 at Regina, Sask., on Nov. 19, 1995, the Baltimore Stallions became the first U.S. team to win the Grey Cup, the championship of the Canadian Football League (CFL). Quarterback Tracy Ham was the game's Most Valuable Player for Baltimore, which had won the South (U.S.) Division (SD) with a 15–3–0 won-lost-tied record. Calgary won the North Division (ND) with the same record.

Baltimore's Mike Pringle, named the league's Most Outstanding Player, led the CFL with 1,791 yd rushing and 2,067 yd from scrimmage, and the same team's Mike Withycombe was voted the Most Outstanding Offensive Lineman. Calgary had the league's best offense, with 35.1 points, 434.6 yd per game, and 356.4 passing yards per game. Saskatchewan's Don Narcisse had the most catches, with 123. Calgary had the CFL's best rushing defense and Baltimore the best rushing offense.

The passing leaders were San Antonio's David Archer with a 108.4 efficiency rating and 9.8 yd per attempt, Calgary's Doug Flutie with a .672 completion percentage, and Birmingham's Matt Dunigan with 4,911 yd and 34 touchdowns. Kicking leaders were Roman Anderson of San Antonio with 235 points, Bjorn Nittmo of Shreveport with an .868 field goal percentage, and Josh Miller of Baltimore with 47.7 yd per punt. Cory Philpot led the league with 22 touchdowns for British Columbia.

Defensively, Memphis allowed league lows of 282 yd and 220.2 passing yards per game, and Tim Cofield's league-high 24 sacks helped Memphis lead with 60. Edmonton allowed the fewest points per game, 19.9, and had commanding leads with 87 takeaways and a plus-38 turnover differential. Edmonton linebacker Willie Pless was Most Outstanding Defensive Player and CFL tackles leader with 100, while teammate and wide receiver Shalon Baker was Most Outstanding Rookie. Hamilton's Eric Carter led with 10 interceptions.

(KEVIN M. LAMB)

Australian Football. The Carlton Football Club emerged as the premier team in the Australian Football League (AFL) in 1995. This gave the club its 16th premiership—a record number. During the home and away season, Carlton established a league record of 20 wins and just 2 losses. Carlton then won a hollow grand final against Geelong, scoring 21.15 (141) to 11.14 (80). Geelong had to deal with the disappointment of losing its fourth grand final since 1989.

The AFL also had a record-breaking year, with more than five million spectators attending the home and away series for the first time. Television and radio ratings also reached record levels, and a record number of clubs competed—16. The new club was Fremantle in Western Australia.

The major award winners in 1995 were: Brownlow Medal (for the best and fairest player in the competition), Sydney captain Paul Kelly; Norm Smith Medal (best player in the grand final), Carlton's Greg Williams; Coleman Medal (leading goalkicker in the home and away rounds), Gary Ablett (Geelong), 118 goals.

(GREG HOBBS)

Rugby Football. The year 1995 would go down as one of the most momentous in the history of Rugby Union. The sport, which had been fiercely amateur since its inception in the 19th century, finally succumbed to the pressures of the 20th century and declared itself open to professionals. The previous few years had been blighted with allegations of payments to players, which breached the amateur laws. The game at the highest level in some countries was seen as sham amateur, with a situation akin to

Super Bowl

	Season	Result			
XXV	1990–91	New York Giants (NFC)	20	Buffalo Bills (AFC)	19
XXVI	1991–92	Washington Redskins (NFC)	37	Buffalo Bills (AFC)	24
XXVII	1992–93	Dallas Cowboys (NFC)	52	Buffalo Bills (AFC)	17
XXVIII	1993–94	Dallas Cowboys (NFC)	30	Buffalo Bills (AFC)	13
XXIX	**1994–95**	**San Francisco 49ers (NFC)**	**49**	**San Diego Chargers (AFC)**	**26**

NFL Final Standings, 1995

AMERICAN CONFERENCE

Eastern Division	W	L	T	Central Division	W	L	T	Western Division	W	L	T
*Buffalo	10	6	0	*Pittsburgh	11	5	0	*Kansas City	13	3	0
*Indianapolis	9	7	0	Cincinnati	7	9	0	*San Diego	9	7	0
*Miami	9	7	0	Houston	7	9	0	Denver	8	8	0
New England	6	10	0	Cleveland	5	11	0	Seattle	8	8	0
New York Jets	3	13	0	Jacksonville	4	12	0	Oakland	8	8	0

NATIONAL CONFERENCE

Eastern Division	W	L	T	Central Division	W	L	T	Western Division	W	L	T
*Dallas	12	4	0	*Green Bay	11	5	0	*San Francisco	11	5	0
*Philadelphia	10	6	0	*Detroit	10	6	0	*Atlanta	9	7	0
Washington	6	10	0	Chicago	9	7	0	St. Louis	7	9	0
New York Giants	5	11	0	Minnesota	8	8	0	Carolina	7	9	0
Arizona	4	12	0	Tampa Bay	7	9	0	New Orleans	7	9	0

*Qualified for play-offs.

AFL Final Standings, 1995

(League ladder after round 22)

Team*	W	L	D	Points
Carlton	20	2	0	80
Geelong	16	6	0	64
Richmond	15	6	1	62
Essendon	14	6	2	60
West Coast	14	8	0	56
North Melbourne	14	8	0	56
Footscray	11	10	1	46
Brisbane	10	12	0	40

*Teams that qualified for play-offs.

Grey Cup

Year	Result			
1990	Winnipeg Blue Bombers (EFC)	50	Edmonton Eskimos (WFC)	11
1991	Toronto Argonauts (EFC)	36	Calgary Stampeders (WFC)	21
1992	Calgary Stampeders (WFC)	24	Winnipeg Blue Bombers (EFC)	10
1993	Edmonton Eskimos (WFC)	33	Winnipeg Blue Bombers (EFC)	23
1994	British Columbia Lions (WFC)	26	Baltimore Stallions (EFC)	23
1995	**Baltimore Stallions (SD)**	**37**	**Calgary Stampeders (ND)**	**20**

Record of International Test matches 1871 to Aug. 31, 1995

	England Wins	Draws	Losses	Scotland Wins	Draws	Losses	Ireland Wins	Draws	Losses	Wales Wins	Draws	Losses	British Isles Wins	Draws	Losses
England *v.*				55	17	39	61	8	38	40	12	48			
Scotland *v.*	39	17	55	—			55	5	45	42	2	54	—		
Ireland *v.*	38	8	61	45	5	55				33	6	58			
Wales *v.*	48	12	40	54	2	42	58	6	33	—			—		
British Isles* *v.*															
South Africa *v.*	8	1	4	5	0	3	8	1	1	6	1	0	20	6	14
New Zealand *v.*	13	0	4	15	2	0	11	1	0	12	0	3	24	3	5
Australia *v.*	12	0	6	7	0	7	10	0	6	8	0	8	3	0	14
France *v.*	24	7	39	32	3	30	37	5	25	28	3	37			

	South Africa Wins	Draws	Losses	New Zealand Wins	Draws	Losses	Australia Wins	Draws	Losses	France Wins	Draws	Losses
England *v.*	4	1	8	4	0	13	6	0	12	39	7	24
Scotland *v.*	3	0	5	0	2	15	7	0	7	30	3	32
Ireland *v.*	1	1	8	0	1	11	6	0	10	25	5	37
Wales *v.*	0	1	6	3	0	12	8	0	8	37	3	28
British Isles* *v.*	14	6	20	5	3	24	14	0	3			
South Africa *v.*	—			20	3	18	22	0	10	13	5	5
New Zealand *v.*	18	3	20				66	5	27	24	0	8
Australia *v.*	10	0	22	27	5	66	—			10	2	13
France *v.*	5	5	13	8	0	24	13	2	10			

*The British Isles ("British Lions") is a combined team from the four "Home Unions" (England, Ireland, Scotland, and Wales).

Five Nations Championship

Year	Result
1991	England*
1992	England*
1993	France
1994	Wales
1995	**England***

*Grand Slam winner.

Rugby Union World Cup

Year	Result			
1987	New Zealand	29	France	9
1991	Australia	12	England	6
1995	**South Africa**	**15**	**New Zealand**	**12**

Rugby League World Cup

Year	Result			
1975*	Australia†			
1977*	Australia	13	Great Britain	12
1988	Australia	25	New Zealand	12
1992	Australia	10	Great Britain	6
1995	**Australia**	**16**	**England**	**8**

*Called International Championship from 1975 to 1977.
†Championships played without a grand final match; England was the runner-up.

such sports as tennis and track and field before they became professional.

An August meeting in Paris of the game's governing body, the International Rugby Football Board, was expected to allow some form of limited professionalism. When the delegates met, however, they found that payments were so rife within the game that they had no option but to declare Rugby Union an open sport. The decision came almost 100 years to the day after a group of clubs based in northern England rebelled over the amateurism issue and broke away to form a professional game that became known as Rugby League.

It was left to the individual unions that administered the sport in countries throughout the world to decide how they would proceed. Some, such as Argentina, declared that the sport in their country would remain amateur, but for most the decision heralded a new professional age.

PHILIP LITTLETON—AFP

New Zealand All Black fullback Glen Osborne is tackled by Mark Andrews of the South Africa Springboks in the Rugby Union World Cup final, held in Johannesburg on June 24. South Africa, serving as host of the event for the first time, defeated rival New Zealand 15–12.

The advent of professionalism was hastened by the growing success of the sport, and 1995 saw the third and most successful Rugby Union World Cup tournament. Held in South Africa, which was taking part in the competition for the first time, the tournament had a fairy-tale ending when the host country took first place.

The tournament had significant social and political implications, as it was the first such sporting event held in South Africa since that nation abolished apartheid.

The final itself proved a nail-biting affair, with old rivals New Zealand and South Africa locked at 9–9 after 80 highly charged minutes. New Zealand's Andrew Mehrtens and South Africa's Joel Stransky swapped penalty kicks in overtime before Stransky landed the winning dropkick goal to make the final score 15–12. Although disappointed, New Zealand had the consolation of having played some of the most exhilarating rugby of the competition and had the Player of the Tournament in Jonah Lomu (*see* BIOGRAPHIES), a man mountain who stood 1.95 m (6 ft 5 in), weighed 118 kg (260 lb), and ran the 100 m in 10.8 seconds.

At least in the new era, Lomu would not have to worry about getting a job. Despite million-dollar offers to join one of the big Rugby League clubs, the 20-year-old decided to pledge his immediate future to the newly open Rugby Union.

The Rugby League Centenary World Cup was held in England and Wales in the autumn, with the 11th World Cup final at Wembley stadium before a crowd of 66,540 on October 28. Australia, which had not lost the League tournament since 1972, once again defeated England in the final, this time by the score of 16–8.

(DAVID LAWRENSON)

GOLF

Nobody could accuse golf of following a familiar or predictable path in 1995. Even by the standards of a sport that deals in the unexpected more than most, it was an exceptional season. Two of the four major men's championships were decided only after play-offs, and the other two had memorable finishes as well; history was made in the women's game; and, by the smallest possible margin, Europe achieved its second victory on U.S. soil in the Ryder Cup.

As surprising as anything was the inability of Zimbabwe's Nick Price, the dominant figure at the beginning of the year, to make an impact. Not only did Price—winner in 1994 of both the British Open and the U.S. Professional Golfers' Association of America (PGA) championships—fail to add to his major titles, but he failed to register a single tour success.

His top spot, both in the U.S. and in the Sony world rankings, was taken by Greg Norman of Australia. Yet Norman would also look back on the 1995 season with some disappointment. The world tour he had hoped to see launched did not get off the ground and, as so often in the past, he came up just short on the big occasions, finishing in a tie for third in the Masters Tournament and second in the U.S. Open. His three victories helped him earn a record $1,654,959 for the season, however, and made him one of nine golfers to top the million-dollar mark.

A year that began, uniquely, with no U.S. golfer in possession of a major championship ended with Americans holding three of the four. Ben Crenshaw did not anticipate being the first of them, but after poor early season form, the 43-year-old won his second Masters title at the Augusta (Ga.) National Golf Club. Crenshaw, the 1984 champion, was overcome with emotion the moment he sank the short putt that gave him a 14-under-par total of 274 and a one-stroke victory over fellow American Davis Love III. Seven days earlier his 90-year-old coach, Harvey Penick, author of *Har-*

Ben Crenshaw of the U.S., the 1984 Masters champion, is comforted by his caddie after winning the title for the second time. The day before the tournament, Crenshaw had left practice to be a pallbearer at the funeral of Harvey Penick, the renowned golf teacher who had been his coach.
JOHN BIEVER—SPORTS ILLUSTRATED

British Open Tournament—Men

Year	Winner
1991	I. Baker-Finch (Austl.)
1992	N. Faldo (U.K.)
1993	G. Norman (Austl.)
1994	N. Price (Zimb.)
1995	**J. Daly (U.S.)**

United States Open Championship—Men

Year	Winner
1991	P. Stewart (U.S.)
1992	T. Kite (U.S.)
1993	L. Janzen (U.S.)
1994	E. Els (S.Af.)
1995	**C. Pavin (U.S.)**

Masters Tournament

Year	Winner
1991	I. Woosnam (U.K.)
1992	F. Couples (U.S.)
1993	B. Langer (Ger.)
1994	J. Olazábal (Spain)
1995	**B. Crenshaw (U.S.)**

U.S. Professional Golfers' Association (PGA) Championship

Year	Winner
1991	J. Daly (U.S.)
1992	N. Price (Zimb.)
1993	P. Azinger (U.S.)
1994	N. Price (Zimb.)
1995	**S. Elkington (Austl.)**

British Amateur Championship—Men

Year	Winner
1991	R. Willison (U.K.)
1992	S. Dundas (U.K.)
1993	I. Pyman (U.K.)
1994	L. James (U.K.)
1995	**G. Sherry (U.K.)**

United States Amateur Championship—Men

Year	Winner
1991	M. Voges (U.S.)
1992	J. Leonard (U.S.)
1993	J. Harris (U.S.)
1994	T. Woods (U.S.)
1995	**T. Woods (U.S.)**

Women's British Open Championship

Year	Winner
1991	P. Grice-Whittaker (U.K.)
1992	P. Sheehan (U.S.)
1993	K. Lunn (Austl.)
1994	L. Neumann (Swed.)
1995	**K. Webb (Austl.)**

Ladies' British Amateur Championship

Year	Winner
1991	J. Morley (U.K.)
1992	P. Pedersen (Den.)
1993	C. Lambert (U.K.)
1994	E. Duggleby (U.K.)
1995	**J. Hall (U.K.)**

United States Women's Open Champions

Year	Winner
1991	M. Mallon (U.S.)
1992	P. Sheehan (U.S.)
1993	L. Merten (U.S.)
1994	P. Sheehan (U.S.)
1995	**A. Sorenstam (Swed.)**

United States Women's Amateur Championship

Year	Winner
1991	A. Fruhwirth (U.S.)
1992	V. Goetze (U.S.)
1993	J. McGill (U.S.)
1994	W. Ward (U.S.)
1995	**K. Kuehne (U.S.)**

Ladies' Professional Golf Association (LPGA) Champions

Year	Winner
1991	M. Mallon (U.S.)
1992	B. King (U.S.)
1993	P. Sheehan (U.S.)
1994	L. Davies (U.K.)
1995	**K. Robbins (U.S.)**

Walker Cup—Men (Amateur)

Year	Result
1987	United States 16½, Britain and Ireland 7½
1989	Britain and Ireland 12½, United States 11½
1991	United States 14, Britain and Ireland 10
1993	United States 19, Britain and Ireland 5
1995	**Britain and Ireland 14, United States 10**

World Cup—Men (Professional)

Year	Winner
1991	Sweden (A. Forsbrand and P.-U. Johansson)
1992	United States (F. Couples and D. Love III)
1993	United States (F. Couples and D. Love III)
1994	United States (F. Couples and D. Love III)
1995	**United States (F. Couples and D. Love III)**

Ryder Cup—Men (Professional)

Year	Result
1987	Europe 15, United States 13
1989	Europe 14, United States 14
1991	United States 14½, Europe 13½
1993	United States 15, Europe 13
1995	**Europe 14½, United States 13½**

Curtis Cup—Women (Amateur)

Year	Result
1986	Britain and Ireland 13, United States 5
1988	Britain and Ireland 11, United States 7
1990	United States 14, Britain and Ireland 4
1992	Britain and Ireland 10, United States 8
1994	Britain and Ireland 9, United States 9

vey Penick's Little Red Book, which in 1992 became the best-selling sports book of all time, had died in Austin, Texas. The funeral was on the eve of the Masters, yet Crenshaw broke off his practice to be a pallbearer and after his victory said, "I had a 15th club in my bag—Harvey. It was like someone put their hand on my shoulder and guided me through."

At the centennial U.S. Open at Shinnecock Hills Golf Club in Southampton, N.Y., Corey Pavin won his first major title. While others struggled in a challenging wind, he compiled a closing 68 for an even-par total of 280. A marvelous 4-wood approach to within 1.5 m (1 m = 3.3 ft) of the final hole led to a two-stroke winning margin over Norman.

For a record 25th time, the British Open was staged at the course regarded as the home of golf, St. Andrews in Fife, Scotland. In wild weather the player known as the "Wild Thing," John Daly of the U.S., emerged triumphant, although only after a play-off with Costantino Rocca of Italy. Daly's total of 282, six under par, looked good enough to give him the title until Rocca, needing a birdie to tie, made dramatic amends for the poorest of chip shots by holing a 20-m putt. In the four-hole play-off, however, Rocca never recovered from three-putting the first green and eventually lost by four strokes.

The week marked the end of an era for the tournament as Arnold Palmer, who first played in the Open in 1960, announced that it would be his last. While his opening rounds of 83 and 75 prevented him from qualifying for the final two rounds, the reception the 65-year-old American received from the crowd and other players left nobody in any doubt about the special place he held in the sport's annals.

Annika Sorenstam of Sweden shoots out of a bunker at the U.S. Women's Open on her way to winning the tournament, her first major championship. Sorenstam was the leading money winner in both the U.S. and Europe, the first time any golfer had accomplished the feat.

JOHN BIEVER—SPORTS ILLUSTRATED

Senior Golf

One of sports' biggest recent success stories was the Professional Golfers' Association's (PGA's) Senior Tour. Beginning in 1980 with two tournaments and $250,000 in prize money, this competition for golfers over 50 years old had grown into a $33.3 million tour with 38 official stops in 1995. A record six seniors earned more than $1 million in 1994, and players on the regular PGA tour began to look forward to turning 50.

The foundation for the Senior Tour was laid in 1978 at the first Legends of Golf tournament. In January 1980 a meeting between PGA Commissioner Deane Beman and six of the tour's all-time leading money winners, all over 50 (Julius Boros, Gardner Dickinson, Don January, Bob Goalby, Dan Sikes, and Sam Snead), led to the official start of the Senior Tour. Vital to the tour's early survival was its professional-amateur (pro-am) component, which allowed fans to play a round with the pros for a fee. Initially, one of those rounds was part of the competition, but by 1987 the tour had established a standard format: a two-day pro-am followed by a three-day 54-hole competition.

As the year 2000 approached, the fastest-growing segment of the U.S. population was 45–54 years old. Many in this age group and above not only were fans of the senior players and could afford pro-am fees but also were in positions of power with potential corporate sponsors. Moreover, many who followed the senior game were part of the affluent target group that sponsors sought to reach. (Cadillac attributed $90 million in sales to tour sponsorship in one three-year period.)

Yet the tour's appeal was more than just nostalgic. Unlike "old-timers" baseball, senior golf was not a half-speed imitation of a game once played but the game itself (albeit with favourable tee and pin placements). Equipment innovations helped seniors to maintain the distance and accuracy of their games; however, their play had more in common with the golf played by the average fan than did the mechanical precision of the regular tour. Seniors had quirkier personalities than the businesslike "flat bellies" (Lee Trevino's name for regular tour players). They seemed to like each other and love what they were doing, and they knew how to play to the crowd. Each year the ranks of longtime favourites grew, and the participation of the PGA's Big Four (Trevino, Arnold Palmer, Jack Nicklaus, and Gary Player) lent a special magic.

Although career victories and position on the all-time money-winning list were the criteria for eligibility, eight players could also join the tour each year by way of a qualifying tournament. As a result, some of golf's biggest names, such as the 1995 senior championship winner Raymond Floyd, competed with late bloomers such as Jim Albus, winner of only $3,750 on the regular tour but more than $3 million as a senior. As the first generation of seniors contemplated retirement, fans looked forward to the approaching 50th birthdays of the likes of Johnny Miller and Tom Watson.

(JEFF WALLENFELDT)

The one major championship to have eluded Palmer during his career was the PGA, which in 1995 returned to the Riviera Country Club in Los Angeles. It produced another play-off, this time between Steve Elkington of Australia and Scotland's Colin Montgomerie. Elkington scored a final-round 64, but Montgomerie birdied the last three holes for a 65 and a matching 17-under-par total of 267. Unlike the Daly-Rocca play-off, Elkington and Montgomerie went into sudden death, and at the first hole Elkington, fifth in the Masters and sixth in the British Open, made a 7.6-m birdie putt, while Montgomerie, also seeking his first major, missed from 6.1 m.

Montgomerie, who also lost a play-off for the 1994 U.S. Open, did win another close affair, however, becoming the leading money winner on the European tour for the third successive season. He went into the final event, the Volvo Masters at Valderrama, Spain, just behind his fellow Scot Sam Torrance and holed a one-metre putt on the final green to take second place. It gave him record official earnings of £835,051 against Torrance's £755,706.

In the Ryder Cup competition at Oak Hill Country Club in Rochester, N.Y., the U.S. players built a 9–7 lead in the foursomes and fourballs, and as they had lost the singles only once since 1957, few foresaw that the final day would conclude as it did. Europe, however, produced a stirring comeback. With 3 of the 12 singles contests left, the U.S. still held the lead, but England's Nick Faldo came from one down with two to play to beat Curtis Strange, and then Philip Walton of Ireland defeated Jay Haas on the final green. In Pavin the U.S. had the most successful player, four points out of a possible five, but every one of the European players enjoyed at least one win, and their 14½–13½ victory was a personal triumph for captain Bernard Gallacher—after eight defeats as a player and two as captain.

The Toyota World Match Play championship at Wentworth, Surrey, England, was successfully defended by 1994 champion Ernie Els of South Africa. Another trophy to remain in the same hands was the Heineken World Cup. The event broke new ground for top-level golf by being held in China at the Mission Hills Club in Shenzhen, but the story remained the same. Fred Couples and Davis Love III won for the U.S. for the fourth time in a row and, as in Puerto Rico in 1994, they finished 14 shots ahead of their nearest challengers, this time Australians Robert Allenby and Brett Ogle.

The history maker in the women's competition was Sweden's Annika Sorenstam, who became the first player, male or female, to be the leading money winner in both the U.S. and Europe in the same season. Sorenstam won the U.S. Women's Open at the Broadmoor Golf Club in Colorado Springs, Colo., by one stroke from Meg Mallon of the U.S. with a two-under-par total of 278 and finished the Ladies' Professional Golf Association tour with $666,533. On the Women's Professional Golfers' European Tour, Sorenstam won two tournaments, was joint runner-up behind Karrie Webb of Australia in the Weetabix British Women's Open, and earned £130,324. Webb's victory was an extraordinary one. A professional for only 10 months, she had rounds of 69, 70, 69, and 70 on the par-73 Woburn course in Milton Keynes, England, to win by six shots.

Sorenstam's success overshadowed another superb season by England's Laura Davies. Four victories in Europe, including the Guardian Irish Holidays Open at St. Margaret's, Dublin, by a tour-record 16 strokes, and two in the U.S. left Davies in second place on both circuits, but she did remain at the top of the world rankings throughout the year.

The outstanding players at the amateur level were Eldrick ("Tiger") Woods of the U.S. and Scotland's Gordon Sherry. Woods, still only 19, retained his U.S. amateur title at the Newport (R.I.) Country Club, while the 21-year-old Sherry, runner-up in 1994, won the British Amateur at the Royal Liverpool club, Hoylake, England. The Walker Cup match at Royal Porthcawl in Wales brought the two together as leaders of their teams. Great Britain and Ireland won the tournament 14–10, only their fourth victory over the U.S. in a series dating back to 1922. (MARK GARROD)

GYMNASTICS

A record number of 56 nations participated in the gymnastics world championships in Sabae, Japan, on Oct. 1–10, 1995. China won the men's team title on the basis of strong performances in the optional exercises. It was the second straight team

ROBERT SULLIVAN—AFP

Members of the European Ryder Cup team celebrate their victory over the highly favoured U.S. team, which had won the cup in 1991 and 1993. Trailing 9–7 at the start of the final day of play, the Europeans made an impressive comeback to beat the U.S. by a score of 14½–13½.

(Left) Li Xiaoshuang of China, who won the men's all-around individual title, shows his form on the pommel horse during the world gymnastics championships, held in Sabae, Japan, in October. (Above) The women's all-around individual winner, Lilia Podkopayeva of Ukraine, performs a flip on the balance beam at the championships.

(LEFT) KAZUHIRO NOGI—AFP; (ABOVE) SUSUMI TAKAHASHI—REUTERS

World Gymnastics Championships—Men

Year	All-around Team	All-around Individual	Horizontal bar	Parallel bars
1992	not held	not held	G. Misutin (CIS)	Li Jing (China)* V. Voropayev (CIS)*
1993	not held	V. Sherbo (Bela.)	S. Charkov (Russia)	V. Sherbo (Bela.)
1994	China	I. Ivankov (Bela.)	V. Sherbo (Bela.)	Liping Huang (China)
1995	**China**	**Li Xiaoshuang (China)**	**A. Wecker (Ger.)**	**V. Sherbo (Bela.)**
Year	**Pommel horse**	**Rings**	**Vault**	**Floor exercise**
1992	Pae Gil Su (N.Kor.)* V. Sherbo (CIS)* Li Jing (China)*	V. Sherbo (CIS)	You Ok Youl (S.Kor.)	I. Korobchinsky (CIS)
1993	Pae Gil Su (N.Kor.)	Y. Chechi (Italy)	V. Sherbo (Bela.)	G. Misutin (Ukr.)
1994	M. Urzica (Rom.)	Y. Chechi (Italy)	V. Sherbo (Bela.)	V. Sherbo (Bela.)
1995	**Li Donghua (Switz.)**	**Y. Chechi (Italy)**	**A. Nemov (Russia)*** **G. Misutin (Ukr.)***	**V. Sherbo (Bela.)**

*Tied.

World Gymnastics Championships—Women

Year	All-around Team	All-around Individual	Balance beam
1992	not held	not held	K. Zmeskal (U.S.)
1993	not held	S. Miller (U.S.)	L. Milosovici (Rom.)
1994	Romania	S. Miller (U.S.)	S. Miller (U.S.)
1995	**Romania**	**L. Podkopayeva (Ukr.)**	**Mo Huilan (China)**
Year	**Uneven parallel bars**	**Vault**	**Floor exercise**
1992	L. Milosovici (Rom.)	H. Onodi (Hung.)	K. Zmeskal (U.S.)
1993	S. Miller (U.S.)	Y. Piskun (Bela.)	S. Miller (U.S.)
1994	Li Luo (China)	G. Gogean (Rom.)	D. Kochetkova (Russia)
1995	**S. Chorkina (Russia)**	**S. Amanar (Rom.)*** **L. Podkopayeva (Ukr.)***	**G. Gogean (Rom.)**

*Tied.

championship for China. In addition, Li Xiaoshuang of China won the men's all-around title by defeating Vitaly Sherbo of Belarus, the reigning Olympic champion and 1993 world champion, 57.998 to 57.499.

Romania won the women's team title, with China second and the United States third. In the all-around competition, Lilia Podkopayeva of Ukraine outscored Svetlana Chorkina of Russia 39.248 to 39.130. The best U.S. finishes in this event were by Dominique Moceanu, 5th, Kerri Strug, 7th, and former world champion Shannon Miller, 12th.

Both compulsory and optional exercises were part of the team competition. However, only optionals were used in the event finals.

China won 10 medals in the men's and women's competitions, including three golds. Romania and Ukraine also won a trio of gold medals. Sherbo had the best individual performances, winning gold medals in the floor exercise and the parallel bars and a bronze in the vault.

Other winners in the men's competition included Yuri Chechi of Italy on the rings, for the third straight year; Li Donghua, born in China but competing for Switzerland, on the pommel horse; and Andreas Wecker of Germany on the horizontal bar. Grigory Misutin of Ukraine and Russia's Aleksey Nemov shared the vaulting crown.

In addition to her all-around title, Podkopayeva tied for first in the vault with Simona Amanar of Romania. The most exciting routine was the original exercise presented by Chorkina on her way to the gold medal on the uneven bars. Other individual winners in the women's competition were Mo Huilan of China on the balance beam and Gina Gogean of Romania in the floor exercise. (CHARLES ROBERT PAUL, JR.)

ICE HOCKEY

North America. A 103-day lockout by club owners delayed the start of the National Hockey League's (NHL's) 1994–95 season and shortened the regular season, normally 84 games for each team, to 48 games each. When the season was over, the New Jersey Devils had won their first Stanley Cup.

The 1994–95 competition had loomed as a breakthrough season for major league hockey in the United States and Canada. There were new teams in the Sun Belt, more good European players, increased television coverage, and wider visibility because a New York team (the Rangers) had won the Stanley Cup during the previous season.

The 1994–95 competition was scheduled to start October 1. Because there was no collective bargaining agreement, the club owners feared the players would allow the season to start and then strike. The players promised they would not strike while negotiating. Still, on October 1, after collective bargaining had broken down, the owners locked them out.

The owners wanted a heavy payroll tax to control salaries, which averaged $560,000. They also sought a rookie salary cap and restrictions on arbitration and free agency.

On January 13 the owners and players agreed on a six-year contact and saved what had almost become the first entire professional sports season to be lost to a labour dispute. The players accepted the owners' demands except for a payroll tax and a team salary cap.

The season began January 20 and was extended to May 3. All games were played only against conference opponents, however, with the result that such traditional rivals as the Montreal Canadiens and the Toronto Maple Leafs did not meet. Still, the lockout had minimal impact on attendance. Eight of the 26 clubs sold out every game, and 11 others played to more than 90% of capacity.

The Detroit Red Wings won the Western Conference title with the league's best record—33 victories, 11 defeats, and 4 ties for 70 points. In the Eastern Conference, the Quebec Nordiques led with 65 points, and New Jersey finished fifth with 52. The Rangers barely won the last play-off berth in the East, and Montreal was shut out of the 16-team play-offs after its worst season in 47 years.

In the first three rounds of the play-offs, New Jersey eliminated the Boston Bruins (4 games to 1), the Pittsburgh Penguins (4–1), and the Philadelphia Flyers (4–2). Detroit overran the Dallas Stars (4–1), the San Jose Sharks (4–0), and the Chicago Blackhawks (4–1).

Detroit, with great offensive talent, was a strong favourite in the final. It had not won the cup in 40 years, and New Jersey had never won it. However, New Jersey had disrupted its first three play-off victims with a neutral-zone trap, a defense in the middle third of the rink that broke up plays before they formed. New Jersey did the same to Detroit and swept the best-of-seven finals in four games, 2–1, 4–2, 5–2, and 5–2. Forward Claude Lemieux of New Jersey won the Conn Smythe Trophy as the most valuable player in the play-offs.

Eric Lindros, Philadelphia's 22-year-old centre, was named the NHL's most valuable player in two separate polls. He won the Hart Trophy in a vote of writers and broadcasters and the Lester Pearson Award in a poll of players. Lindros and Jaromir Jagr, Pittsburgh's Czech-born forward, tied for the scoring title with 70 points each, but Jagr became the champion because he had more goals (32 to Lindros' 29). Lindros missed the last game of the season when an errant puck left him with a six-stitch cut under his left eye.

In voting by writers and broadcasters, Dominik Hasek of the Buffalo Sabres won his second consecutive Vezina Trophy for goaltending. He had allowed only 2.11 goals per game. For the third time in 11 years, Paul Coffey of Detroit won the Norris Trophy as the outstanding defenseman. Ron Francis of Pittsburgh won the Selke Trophy as the best defensive forward and the Lady Byng Trophy for sportsmanship. Peter Forsberg, a Quebec forward, earned the Calder Trophy as rookie of the year, and Marc Crawford of Quebec won the Jack Adams Award as coach of the year.

Mario Lemieux, the Pittsburgh centre, had been one of the NHL's best players when healthy. He was worn down from treatment for Hodgkin's disease and from a chronic back condition, and he took a one-year sabbatical. He returned for the 1995–96 season.

After the season New Jersey, Quebec, and the Winnipeg Jets seemed likely to

DAVID KLUTHO—SPORTS ILLUSTRATED

Neal Broten (9) of the New Jersey Devils scores a goal against the Detroit Red Wings in the fourth game of the Stanley Cup finals. The Devils won their first National Hockey League championship by sweeping the best-of-seven series with scores of 2–1, 4–2, 5–2, and 5–2.

NHL Final Standings, 1995

EASTERN CONFERENCE	Won	Lost	Tied	Points
Atlantic Division				
*Philadelphia	28	16	4	60
*New Jersey	22	18	8	52
*Washington	22	18	8	52
*New York Rangers	22	23	3	47
Florida	20	22	6	46
Tampa Bay	17	28	3	37
New York Islanders	15	28	5	35
Northeast Division				
*Quebec	30	13	5	65
*Pittsburgh	29	16	3	61
*Boston	27	18	3	57
*Buffalo	22	19	7	51
Hartford	19	24	5	43
Montreal	18	23	7	43
Ottawa	9	34	5	23

WESTERN CONFERENCE	Won	Lost	Tied	Points
Central Division				
*Detroit	33	11	4	70
*St. Louis	28	15	5	61
*Chicago	24	19	5	53
*Toronto	21	19	8	50
*Dallas	17	23	8	42
Winnipeg	16	25	7	39
Pacific Division				
*Calgary	24	17	7	55
*Vancouver	18	18	12	48
*San Jose	19	25	4	42
Los Angeles	16	23	9	41
Edmonton	17	27	4	38
Anaheim	16	27	5	37

*Qualified for play-offs.

The Stanley Cup

Season	Winner	Runner-up	Games
1990–91	Pittsburgh Penguins	Minnesota North Stars	4–2
1991–92	Pittsburgh Penguins	Chicago Blackhawks	4–0
1992–93	Montreal Canadiens	Los Angeles Kings	4–1
1993–94	New York Rangers	Vancouver Canucks	4–3
1994–95	**New Jersey Devils**	**Detroit Red Wings**	**4–0**

World Hockey Championships

Year	Winner
1991	Sweden
1992	Sweden
1993	Russia
1994	Canada
1995	**Finland**

move to new cities, but only Quebec did so. The corporation that owned the Denver Nuggets of the National Basketball Association bought the Nordiques for $75 million and moved them to Denver, where they were renamed the Avalanche.

Before its Stanley Cup victory, New Jersey received a stunning offer to relocate to Nashville, Tenn., a package that included a $20 million relocation fee. Instead, the Devils renegotiated their lease at Brendan Byrne Arena in East Rutherford, N.J., and stayed there. The Winnipeg owners sold their team, which seemed likely to move for the 1996–97 season. (FRANK LITSKY)

International. The 59th world championship was contested by a record 39 nations, three more than the previous year, requiring an enlarged two-section Pool C. The 12 title-contending nations in the elite Pool A, held in Stockholm and Gävle, Sweden, were divided into the customary two preliminary round-robin groups, each providing four of the quarterfinalists. Two teams, the United States and Russia, survived unbeaten from the qualifying groups, Russia winning all of its five games and the U.S. winning three and drawing two.

France gained its first-ever Pool A win against Canada 4–2, thanks mainly to two goals and an assist from Christian Pouget, but the Canadians, although not at full strength, shook off this upset to make the semifinals after knocking out the U.S. 4–1. Canada gave the host country a hard time in the first semifinal, eventually losing 3–2 in overtime in a match that revived memories of Sweden's penalty shoot-out victory over Canada in the previous year's Olympic final. The Czech Republic reached the second semifinal through a notable 2–0 quarterfinal triumph over Russia but, perhaps suffering from a letdown, then lost 3–0 to a dominant Finland.

After pressing close for several years, Finland at last won its first title with a convincing 4–1 success against Sweden before a capacity crowd of 13,850 in Stockholm in the electric atmosphere of an all-Scandinavian final. The hero was Ville Peltonen, who scored three goals and had an assist on the fourth. Jarmo Myllys, outstanding in the Finnish net, was denied a shutout in the third period.

Ironically, the victorious Finns were coached by a Swede, Curre Lindstrom, who had previously coached Sweden. The Americans, who ultimately placed sixth, gained the distinction in the preliminary stages of taking a point from each of the two finalists. Because the NHL started late, it coincided with the world championships; consequently, Canada and the U.S. were deprived of some star talent. However, there can be no doubt that the Finns were worthy winners, with the talent of their younger players suggesting more titles to come. Peltonen seemed likely to follow his teammates defender Marko Kiprusoff and centre Saku Koivu to the NHL.

Canada gained the bronze medal by comfortably defeating the Czech Republic 4–1. Canada's Andrew McKim led the Pool A tournament scorers with 13 points (6 goals and 7 assists), followed by Peltonen with 11 (6 goals and 5 assists).

After only one season in the top flight, the newly promoted Switzerland finished at the bottom of Pool A, to be replaced by Slovakia. With home-ice advantage, Slovakia won all its seven matches in the eight-team round-robin Pool B held in Bratislava. Only one year earlier Slovakia had topped Pool C. Runner-up Latvia, which lost only to the leaders, proved too strong for the other six Pool B competitors, of which Great Britain, demoted from Pool A the previous winter, narrowly avoided the humiliation of another demotion by finishing above last-place Romania.

Belarus decisively clinched promotion to Pool B from the nine-team group one of Pool C, contested in Sofia, Bulg. Kazakhstan, Ukraine, and Estonia filled the next three positions and suggested great potential. Yugoslavia and Bulgaria, eighth and ninth, respectively, were both demoted to group two of Pool C, to be replaced by Croatia, winner of the 10-team group two, contested in Johannesburg, South Africa. This group largely comprised nations relatively new to ice sports and apparently earmarked for a resurrected Pool D. The continuing emergence of such nations as Israel, South Africa, and Greece reflected the sport's worldwide expansion.

Jokerit Helsinki of Finland won the 18th European Cup, open to national club champions, by beating Lada Togliatti of Russia 4–2 in the final in Helsinki, Fin. TPS Turku, also of Finland and competing as defending champion, finished third by overwhelming HC Olomouc of Czechoslovakia 8–1.

(HOWARD BASS)

ICE SKATING

The worldwide expansion of ice skating continued in 1995 as Andorra, Cyprus, and Portugal increased the membership of the International Skating Union to 55 nations.

Figure Skating. More than 200 skaters from a record 42 nations contested the world championships in Birmingham, England, on March 5–12, the first for which England had served as host in 45 years. The retention of the men's title by Canada's Elvis Stojko was an inspiring achievement, the more noteworthy because he was suffering from torn ankle ligaments. Although failing an attempted quadruple toe loop jump, Stojko executed eight triple jumps and gained a maximum score of six for technical merit from the French judge. Todd Eldredge, the veteran United States national champion, who had led after the initial round, fell on a triple axel, which arguably cost him first place. Philippe Candeloro of France, not skating his best, finished third, ahead of Russia's Olympic gold medalist, Aleksey Urmanov.

Chen Lu won China's first world title in figure skating by gaining the women's crown in a close contest with Surya Bonaly of France. Making her seventh attempt for the gold medal, Bonaly finished second for the third consecutive time. She presented a free program of ferocious difficulty, accomplishing seven triples with entertaining, ostentatious athleticism; but they were not always well fitted to her music, and she received relatively poor marks for presentation.

Chen's skillful interpretation of music from the film *The Last Emperor* featured nine major jumps, all landed without a quiver. Nicole Bobek, the U.S. national champion, led going into the free skating, but two tumbles dropped her to third place just above her highly promising compatriot Michelle Kwan, only 14.

With superior overhead lifts and daring triple throws, Radka Kovarikova and Rene Novotny, of the Czech Republic, maintained the pairs lead that they had established early in the competition and deposed the Russian defending champions, Yevgeniya Shishkova and Vadim Naumov. Jenni Meno and Todd Sand won the bronze medal for the U.S.

The class of the Russian Olympic champions Oksana Grichuk and Yevgeny Platov successfully defended their ice dance title with an enterprising free-skating performance that simulated tap dancing. The fast-improving Susanna Rahkamo and Petri Kokko featured a popular emotional display to music of the Beatles to gain Finland its first silver medal in the event, marginally in front of the French couple Sophie Moniotte and Pascal Lavanchy.

Speed Skating. Rintje Ritsma of The Netherlands coped with hazardous weather conditions to claim the overall title in the men's world championships at the small Italian mountain resort of Baselga di Pinè on February 11–12. Keiji Shirahata of Japan finished second, and Roberto Sighel of Italy was third. Gunda Niemann of Germany captured the women's crown at Savalen, Norway, on March 4–5, ahead of Lyudmila Prokasheva from Kazakhstan and Annamarie Thomas of The Netherlands.

In the separate world sprint championships, at Milwaukee, Wis., on February 18–19, Kim Yoon Man of South Korea was a surprising men's winner. But his feat was somewhat eclipsed by a glorious women's title defense by the outstanding American Bonnie Blair, who—in her farewell appear-

(ABOVE) BOB MARTIN—SPORTS ILLUSTRATED; (LEFT) RICHARD MARTIN—VANDYSTADT/ALLSPORT

Elvis Stojko (above) of Canada demonstrates the form that helped him retain the men's title in the world figure skating championships, held in Birmingham, England, in March. Chen Lu (left), the first Chinese figure skater to win a world title, performs in the women's competition, in which she came from behind to defeat veteran Surya Bonaly of France.

World Figure Skating Champions—Men

Year	Winner
1991	K. Browning (Can.)
1992	V. Petrenko (UT)
1993	K. Browning (Can.)
1994	E. Stojko (Can.)
1995	**E. Stojko (Can.)**

World Figure Skating Champions—Women

Year	Winner
1991	K. Yamaguchi (U.S.)
1992	K. Yamaguchi (U.S.)
1993	O. Baiul (Ukr.)
1994	Y. Sato (Japan)
1995	**Chen Lu (China)**

World Figure Skating Champions—Pairs

Year	Winners
1991	N. Mishkutenok, A. Dmitriyev (U.S.S.R.)
1992	N. Mishkutenok, A. Dmitriyev (UT)
1993	I. Brasseur, L. Eisler (Can.)
1994	Ye. Shishkova, V. Naumov (Russia)
1995	**R. Kovarikova, R. Novotny (Cz.Rep.)**

World Ice Dancing Champions

Year	Winners
1991	I. Duchesnay, P. Duchesnay (Fr.)
1992	M. Klimova, S. Ponomarenko (UT)
1993	M. Usova, A. Zhulin (Russia)
1994	O. Grichuk, Ye. Platov (Russia)
1995	**O. Grichuk, Ye. Platov (Russia)**

World Ice Speed-Skating Records Set in 1995 on Major Tracks

Event	Name	Country	Time
	WOMEN		
500 m	Bonnie Blair	U.S.	38.69 sec

World Ice Speed-Skating Records Set in 1995 on Short Tracks

Event	Name	Country	Time
	MEN		
1,500 m	Marc Gagnon	Canada	2 min 18.61 sec
3,000 m	Chae Ji Hoon	S. Korea	4 min 56.29 sec
5,000-m relay	Marc Gagnon, Sylvain Gagnon, Frédéric Blackburn, Bryce Holbech	Canada	7 min 09.76 sec
	WOMEN		
500 m	Kim Yun Mi	S. Korea	45.53 sec
1,500 m	Chun Lee Kyung	S. Korea	2 min 27.38 sec
3,000 m	Chun Lee Kyung	S. Korea	5 min 02.18 sec
3,000-m relay	Wang Chunlu, Zhang Yanmei, Yang Jilin, Zhang Dongxiang	China	4 min 24.68 sec

World All-Around Speed-Skating Champions—Men

Year	Winner
1991	J.O. Koss (Nor.)
1992	R. Sighel (Italy)
1993	F. Zandstra (Neth.)
1994	J.O. Koss (Nor.)
1995	**R. Ritsma (Neth.)**

World All-Around Speed-Skating Champions—Women

Year	Winner
1991	G. Kleeman (Ger.)
1992	G. Niemann (Ger.)
1993	G. Niemann (Ger.)
1994	E. Hunyady (Austria)
1995	**G. Niemann (Ger.)**

World Speed-Skating Sprint Championships

Year	Men	Women
1991	I. Zhelezovsky (U.S.S.R.)	M. Garbrecht (Ger.)
1992	I. Zhelezovsky (UT)	Ye Qiaobo (China)
1993	I. Zhelezovsky (Bela.)	Ye Qiaobo (China)
1994	D. Jansen (U.S.)	B. Blair (U.S.)
1995	**Kim Yoon Man (S.Kor.)**	**B. Blair (U.S.)**

World Short-Track Speed-Skating Championships—Overall Winners

Year	Men	Women
1991	W. O'Reilly (U.K.)	N. Lambert (Can.)
1992	Ki Hoon Kim (S.Kor.)	So He Kim (S.Kor.)
1993	M. Gagnon (Can.)	N. Lambert (Can.)
1994	M. Gagnon (Can.)	N. Lambert (Can.)
1995	**Chae Ji Hoon (S.Kor.)**	**Chun Lee Kyung (S.Kor.)**

ance—won all four races just a week after she lowered the women's world 500-m record to 38.69 sec at Calgary, Alta.

Two women's world records were also set in short-track racing. Nathalie Lambert of Canada covered 1,000 m in 1 min 34.07 sec at Hamar, Norway, and Chun Lee Kyung of South Korea clocked the 1,500 m in 2 min 27.38 sec at Jaca, Spain. Marc Gagnon of Canada set a new men's 1,500-m world record of 2 min 18.61 sec at Guildford, England.

In the world short-track championships at Gjövik, Norway, on March 17–19, the South Korean Olympic champion Chae Ji Hoon took the men's title, and Chun gained the women's. The team relay events were won by Canada (men) and China (women).

(HOWARD BASS)

JUDO

The 1995 judo season got under way with the Paris International Tournament in February. The Japanese team led with six gold medals, while South Korea collected four, and France, Belgium, Poland, and Spain gained one each. Naoya Ogawa captured his sixth All-Japan Judo Championship on May 27 at the Nippon Budokan in Tokyo. In the World Student Games in Fukuoka, Japan, in August, Japan dominated the competition with eight gold, two silver, and four bronze medals.

The major judo event of the year, however, was the world championships at Makuhari, Japan, September 29–October 1. No one country monopolized the medals, but South Korea, Japan, Cuba, and The Netherlands excelled. Monique van der Lee of The Netherlands took the women's open title, and Japan's Ryoko Tamura won in the women's 48-kg (106-lb) event. Toshihiko Koga, the 1992 Olympic gold medalist in the 71-kg (156-lb) class, captured the men's 78-kg (172-lb) title; David Douillet of France successfully defended his world title in the over-95-kg (209-lb) class; and Poland's Pavel Nastula won the 95-kg category. South Korea's Cho Min Sun and Jung Sung Sook won the women's 66-kg (145-lb) and 61-kg (134-lb) categories, respectively, while Chun Ki Young, the 78-kg world champion in 1993 and also from South Korea, won the men's 86-kg (189-lb) class.

World champion Tamura extended her winning streak to 77 by taking the 48-kg title at the 13th Fukuoka international women's judo championships on December 10. Japan also won the 52-kg class when Noriko Sugawara pinned her Cuban opponent, but Jung Sun Yong of South Korea took the 56-kg title and Claudia Ziers of The Netherlands won the 66-kg class. Other winners were Noriko Anno of Japan in the over-72-kg class, Je Min Jung of South Korea in the 72-kg class, and Catherine Fleury of France in the 61-kg class.

(ANDY ADAMS)

LAWN BOWLS

During 1995 lawn bowls continued to expand worldwide. The establishment of a World Bowls Council and increased representation at the world bowls outdoor championships at Adelaide, Australia, in March 1996 seemed certain to further this progress.

Meanwhile, British players continued to dominate the sport. Andy Thomson, a Scot who had lived in and represented England since 1980, retained the world indoor singles championship at Preston, England, outbowling another Scotsman, Richard Corsie, in the final. Corsie, partnered by Alex Marshall, won the pairs title and a few weeks later had another notable success in Australia, winning the outdoor Mazda International Jack High singles competition in Sydney by defeating Australia's Cameron Curtis in the final.

Scottish women players also excelled. Joyce Lindores captured the women's world

World Judo Championships—Men

Year	Open weights	60 kg	65 kg	71 kg
1987	N. Ogawa (Japan)	Kim Jae Yup (S.Kor.)	Y. Yamamoto (Japan)	M. Swain (U.S.)
1989	N. Ogawa (Japan)	A. Totikashvili (U.S.S.R.)	D. Becanovic (Yugos.)	T. Koga (Japan)
1991	N. Ogawa (Japan)	T. Koshino (Japan)	G. Quellmalz (Ger.)	T. Koga (Japan)
1993	R. Kubacki (Poland)	R. Sonada (Japan)	Y. Nakamura (Japan)	Yung Chung Hoon (S.Kor.)
1995	**D. Douillet (Fr.)**	**N. Ojeguine (Russia)**	**U. Quellmalz (Ger.)**	**D. Hideshima (Japan)**
Year	**78 kg**	**86 kg**	**95 kg**	**+ 95 kg**
1987	H. Okada (Japan)	F. Canu (Fr.)	H. Sugai (Japan)	G. Verichev (U.S.S.R.)
1989	Kim Bying Ju (S.Kor.)	F. Canu (Fr.)	K. Kurtanidze (U.S.S.R.)	N. Ogawa (Japan)
1991	D. Lascau (Ger.)	H. Okada (Japan)	S. Traineau (Fr.)	S. Kosorotov (U.S.S.R.)
1993	Chun Ki Young (S.Kor.)	Y. Nakamura (Japan)	A. Kovacs (Hung.)	D. Douillet (Fr.)
1995	**T. Koga (Japan)**	**Chun Ki Young (S.Kor.)**	**P. Nastula (Pol.)**	**D. Douillet (Fr.)**

World Judo Championships—Women

Year	Open weights	48 kg	52 kg	56 kg
1987	Fengliang Gao (China)	Zhang Yun Li (China)	S. Rendle (U.K.)	C. Arnaud (Fr.)
1989	E. Rodriguez (Cuba)	K. Briggs (U.K.)	S. Rendle (U.K.)	C. Arnaud (Fr.)
1991	Zhuang Xiaoyan (China)	C. Nowak (Fr.)	A. Giungi (Italy)	M. Blasco (Spain)
1993	B. Maksymow (Poland)	R. Tamura (Japan)	R. Verdecia (Cuba)	N. Fairbrother (U.K.)
1995	**M. van der Lee (Neth.)**	**R. Tamura (Japan)**	**M. Restoux (Fr.)**	**D. Gonzalez (Cuba)**
Year	**61 kg**	**66 kg**	**72 kg**	**+72 kg**
1987	D. Bell (U.K.)	A. Schreiber (W.Ger.)	I. de Kok (Neth.)	Fengliang Gao (China)
1989	C. Fleury (Fr.)	E. Pierantozzi (Italy)	I. Berghmans (Belg.)	Fengliang Gao (China)
1991	F. Eickoff (Ger.)	E. Pierantozzi (Italy)	Kim Mi Jong (S.Kor.)	Moon Ji Yoon (S.Kor.)
1993	G. van de Cavaye (Belg.)	Cho Min Sun (S.Kor.)	Leng Chin Hui (China)	J. Hagn (Ger.)
1995	**Jung Sung Sook (S.Kor.)**	**Cho Min Sun (S.Kor.)**	**C. Luna (Cuba)**	**A. Seriese (Neth.)**

World Lawn Bowls Championships		
Year	Singles	Pairs
1984	P. Bellis (N.Z.)	United States
1988	D. Bryant (Eng.)	New Zealand
1992	T. Allcock (Eng.)	Scotland

Year	Triples	Fours	Team
1984	Ireland	England	Scotland
1988	New Zealand	Ireland	England
1992	Israel	Scotland	Scotland

indoor singles championship at Cumbernauld, Scotland, winning a best-of-five-sets encounter against Margaret Johnston, Ireland's world outdoor titleholder.

Twelve countries took part in the Atlantic Rim Outdoor Women's Games at Durban, South Africa. The South Africans captured the gold medal in singles, pairs, and triples, but Scotland deprived them of a clean sweep by taking the fours.

(DONALD J. NEWBY)

RODEO

In June 1995 Ty Murray, the six-time world all-around champion from Stephenville, Texas, tore the posterior cruciate ligament of his right knee at a Professional Bull Riding (PBR) competition in Rancho Murieta, Calif. Clint Branger of Roscoe, Mont., sustained a neck injury while riding a bull on September 30 at the New Mexico State Fair and Rodeo in Albuquerque. Neither Murray nor Branger was able to compete at the season-ending $3 million National Finals Rodeo (NFR), held December 1–10 in Las Vegas, Nev.

Bull rider Richard ("Tuff") Hedeman's comeback season came to an abrupt halt on October 15 when Bucking Bull of the Year Bodacious collided with the three-time world champion's face during the PBR Tour Finals in Las Vegas. Hedeman, of Morgan Mill, Texas, underwent reconstructive surgery to repair damaged facial bones and was able to return to competition in time for the NFR.

Men's World All-Around Rodeo Championship			
Year	Winner	Year	Winner
1990	T. Murray	1993	T. Murray
1991	T. Murray	1994	T. Murray
1992	T. Murray	**1995**	**J. Beaver**

At the NFR Hedeman again drew the fearsome bull but chose not to ride it. Scott Breding of Edgar, Mont., tried Bodacious in the ninth round, and the bull raised its massive head in mid jump and clobbered the rider with stunning force, knocking him unconscious. Sammy Andrews, the owner of Bodacious, decided to retire the bull from competition following the accident.

With Murray temporarily out of contention for the all-around title, Joe Beaver of Huntsville, Texas, won the coveted championship, which is awarded to the cowboy winning the most money in two or more standard rodeo events. Beaver, a five-time calf-roping world champion, won the 1995 all-around title with season earnings of $141,753.

World titles in seven standard professional rodeo events—bareback riding, steer wrestling, calf roping, saddle bronc riding, women's barrel racing, team roping, and bull riding—were also decided at the NFR. Marvin Garrett of Belle Fourche, S.D., scored 775 points on 10 horses to claim top honours among the field of 15 NFR bareback riders and finished the year with record earnings of $156,733. It was Garrett's fourth bareback riding world title.

Dan Mortensen of Manhattan, Mont., claimed his third straight world championship in the saddle bronc riding with earnings of $145,325. Calf roper Fred Whitfield of Hockley, Texas, was another repeat world champion, staving off the attack of Beaver by winning $58,183 at the NFR to finish the season with $146,760.

Other PRCA world titlists for 1995 were: Ote Berry, Checotah, Okla., $117,987, steer wrestling; Sherry Potter-Cervi, Marana, Ariz., $157,172, barrel racing; Allen Bach, Toltec, Ariz., and Bobby Hurley, Ceres, Calif., $81,658 each, team roping; and Jerome Davis, Archdale, N.C., $135,280, bull riding. (GAVIN FORBES EHRINGER)

ROWING

The United States and Italy were the most successful nations in world rowing in 1995, with each winning a total of five titles. Following with double successes each were Germany, Great Britain, Denmark, Canada, and Australia. The remaining winners were Switzerland, Austria, Slovenia, and Sweden.

In the world championships at Tampere, Fin., the standard was exceptionally high, with 22 countries sharing the medals. Eight of the reigning champions retained their titles in the 24 events. The margin of victory was less than two seconds in 15 races, and the biggest winning margin was little more than three seconds.

Italy took the honours in men's events with three wins. It narrowly defeated Great Britain by 0.61 sec to retain the coxless fours and successfully defended the quadruple sculls by 1.54 sec against Germany. Its third triumph, in coxed pairs, was achieved more comfortably, by 2.86 sec. The U.S. was 1.15 sec too fast for New Zealand in coxed fours but lost its eights title to Germany, with The Netherlands taking second place. Great Britain triumphed for the third consecutive year in coxless pairs, while Denmark and Germany foiled Norway's bid to retain the double sculls. In single sculls Iztok Cop (Slovenia) unexpectedly captured the title by the slender margin of 0.55 sec from the 1990 champion, Juri Jaanson (Estonia). Only seven weeks earlier Cop had lost to Jaanson by 1.14 sec in the World Cup final in Lucerne, Switz.

In the men's lightweight events, Italy won two more titles. It retained the coxless pairs and defeated Denmark, the defending champion, by 1.37 sec in coxless fours.

KAINULAINEN/LEHTIKUVA/SABA

Matthew Pinsent (left) and Steven Redgrave of Britain compete in the coxless pairs in the world rowing championships in Tampere, Fin., in August. They won the final by 1.76 sec to gain their 52nd consecutive victory since 1992, including five world championships and the 1992 Olympic Games.

World Rowing Championships—Men

Year	Single sculls	Min:s	Double sculls	Min:s	Coxed pairs	Min:s
1991	T. Lange (Ger.)	6:41.29	H.-J. Zwolle, N. Rienks (Neth.)	6:06.14	G. Abbagnale, C. Abbagnale (Italy)	7:34.39
1992	T. Lange (Ger.)	6:51.40	S. Hawkins, P. Antonie (Austl.)	6:17.32	J. Searle, G. Searle (U.K.)	6:49.83
1993	D. Porter (Can.)	6:59.03	Y. Lamarque, S. Barathay (Fr.)	6:24.69	J. Searle, G. Searle (U.K.)	7:01.50
1994	A. Willims (Ger.)	6:46.33	R. Thorsen, L. Bjoenness (Nor.)	6:08.33	T. Frankovic, I. Boraska (Croatia)	6:42.16
1995	**I. Cop (Slov.)**	**6:52.93**	**L. Christensen, M. Haldbo-Hansen (Den.)**	**6:17.01**	**L. Sartori, G. DeStabile (Italy)**	**7:35.11**

Year	Coxless pairs	Min:s	Coxed fours	Min:s	Coxless fours	Min:s	Eights	Min:s
1991	S. Redgrave, M. Pinsent (U.K.)	6:21.35	Germany	5:58.96	Australia	6:29.69	Germany	5:50.98
1992	S. Redgrave, M. Pinsent (U.K.)	6:27.72	Romania	5:59.37	Australia	5:55.04	Canada	5:29.53
1993	S. Redgrave, M. Pinsent (U.K.)	6:37.11	Romania	6:14.64	France	6:04.54	Germany	5:37.08
1994	S. Redgrave, M. Pinsent (U.K.)	6:18.65	Romania	6:06.69	Italy	5:48.44	United States	5:24.50
1995	**S. Redgrave, M. Pinsent (U.K.)**	**6:28.11**	**United States**	**6:37.50**	**Italy**	**5:58.28**	**Germany**	**5:53.40**

World Rowing Championships—Women

Year	Single sculls	Min:s	Double sculls	Min:s	Quadruple sculls	Min:s
1991	S. Laumann (Can.)	8:17.58	K. Boron, B. Schramm (Ger.)	6:44.71	Germany	6:55.85
1992	E. Lipa (Rom.)	7:25.54	K. Boron, K. Köppen (Ger.)	6:49.00	Germany	6:20.18
1993	J. Thieme (Ger.)	7:26.00	P. Baker, B. Lawson (N.Z.)	7:03.42	China	6:21.07
1994	T. Hansen (Den.)	7:23.96	P. Baker, B. Lawson (N.Z.)	6:45.30	Germany	6:11.73
1995	**M. Brandin (Swe.)**	**7:26.00**	**M. McBean, K. Heddle (Can.)**	**6:55.76**	**Germany**	**6:40.80**

Year	Coxless pairs	Min:s	Coxless fours	Min:s	Eights	Min:s
1991	M. McBean, K. Heddle (Can.)	6:57.42	Canada	6:25.43	Canada	6:28.20
1992	M. McBean, K. Heddle (Can.)	7:06.22	Canada	6:30.85	Canada	6:02.62
1993	C. Gosse, H. Cortin (Fr.)	7:24.74	China	6:42.06	Romania	6:18.88
1994	C. Gosse, H. Cortin (Fr.)	7:01.77	Netherlands	6:30.76	Germany	6:07.42
1995	**M. Still, K. Slatter (Aust.)**	**7:12.70**	**United States**	**7:03.53**	**United States**	**6:50.73**

The Diamond Challenge Sculls

Year	Winner	Min:s
1991	W. Van Belleghem (Belg.)	*
1992	R. Henderson (Leander R.C.)	7:44
1993	T. Lange (Ger.)	7:39
1994	X. Muller (Grasshopper, Switz.)	7:35
1995	**J. Jaanson (Parnu, Est.)**	**7:24**

*Not rowed out.

Grand Challenge Cup

Year	Winner	Min:s
1991	Leander and Star R.C.	6:22
1992	University of London	6:04
1993	Dortmund, Ger.	6:11
1994	Charles River and San Diego	6:13
1995	**San Diego Training Center**	**5:59**

Great Britain and Australia successfully defended their titles in the single and quadruple sculls, respectively, but Denmark foiled Great Britain's bid to retain the eights by 2.25 sec. Switzerland beat Sweden by 1.27 sec to become the first winner of the new double sculls event.

The U.S. was foremost in the women's events. It defeated Germany by 1.60 sec in coxless fours and Romania by 2.03 sec in eights but lost to Australia by 2.20 sec in coxless pairs. Canada narrowly defeated The Netherlands by 0.08 sec in double sculls, and the other winners were Germany (quadruple sculls) and Sweden (single sculls). In lightweight classes the U.S. won twice over Great Britain, by 1.26 sec in coxless fours and by more than 3 sec in coxless pairs. Australia took the single sculls, while Canada retained the double sculls by a margin of 0.83 sec over Denmark.

In the under-23 international championships in Groningen, Neth., nine nations shared the honours in 18 classes. Germany won three of the men's titles, Great Britain claimed two, and Australia, Denmark, Italy, Slovenia, Sweden, and Yugoslavia gained one apiece. Germany dominated the seven women's events with five wins, leaving Romania and Sweden to take the other titles.

Germany won 9 of the 14 gold medals in the world junior championships in Poznan, Poland. Australia took two titles, and France, Denmark, and Italy won one each. The minor medals were shared by 17 nations, including three each for Croatia and Spain.

At the Henley Royal Regatta in England, there were five overseas winners and 24 new records. In eights the Grand Challenge Cup went to San Diego (Calif.) Training Center, and there was a second success for the U.S. by Augusta (Ga.) Training Center in quadruple sculls. Australia triumphed in the double sculls, while Jaanson captured the Diamond Challenge Sculls. Oarsmen from seven countries rowed in the 141st University Boat Race, which Cambridge won by four lengths to lead Oxford 72–68 in the series. (K.L. OSBORNE)

SAILING (YACHTING)

At the start of 1995, the Sydney–Hobart classic was won by *Raptor,* a new Bashford-Howison 41 production boat launched just in time for the race. Owned and skippered by Andreas Eichenauer of Germany, *Raptor* was designed by Iain Murray and Associates. Second overall was the 1994 winner, *Ninety Seven,* a Farr 47, skippered by Andrew Strachan.

Also at the start of the year, Isabelle Autissier of France was being airlifted to safety from her stricken and sinking yacht *Ecureuil Poitou-Charentes 2* some 1,445 km (900 mi) southwest of Adelaide, Australia. Competing in the BOC Round-the-World Challenge, she had earlier won the first leg of this race by an amazing 5½ days. The winner of the race, for solo sailors, was Christophe Auguin of France in *Sceta Calberson.*

New Zealand first challenged for the America's Cup in 1987 and had competed vigorously ever since, clearly learning from each challenge. Led in 1995 by Peter Blake (*see* BIOGRAPHIES), with Russell Coutts as his handpicked skipper, Team New Zealand's *Black Magic* appeared to be a winner from the day she was launched in mid-1994. She swept to victory in the challenge selection series for the Louis Vuitton Cup, losing only one race on the water in 43 starts. The America's Cup series was a completely one-sided affair, as the New Zealand yacht was too good in almost every way for U.S. defender Dennis Conner and his team in *Young America.* The New Zealanders' 5–0 victory allowed them to celebrate one of

PETER READ MILLER—SPORTS ILLUSTRATED

New Zealand's *Black Magic* sails in a race in the America's Cup competition, which she won 5–0 over the U.S. defender, *Young America*. *Black Magic* had lost only once in 43 starts in earning the right to challenge for the Cup.

America's Cup

Year	Winning yacht	Owner	Skipper	Losing Yacht	Owner
1983	*Australia II* (Australia)	A. Bond and syndicate	J. Bertrand	*Liberty* (U.S.)	Maritime College at Fort Schuyler Foundation, Inc.
1987	*Stars & Stripes* (U.S.)	Sail America syndicate	D. Conner	*Kookaburra III* (Australia)	K. Parry and syndicate
1988	*Stars & Stripes* (U.S.)	Sail America syndicate	D. Conner	*New Zealand* (New Zealand)	M. Fay
1992	*America³* (U.S.)	America³ Foundation	B. Koch	*Il Moro di Venezia* (Italy)	Compagnia della Vela di Venezia
1995	***Black Magic* (N.Z.)**	**P. Blake and Team New Zealand**	**R. Coutts**	***Young America***	**Pact 95 syndicate**

Bermuda Race

Year	Winning yacht	Owner
1986	*Silver Star* and *Puritan*	D. Clarke D. Robinson
1988	*Congere*	B. Koeppel
1990	*Denali*	L. Huntington
1992	*Constellation*	U.S. Naval Academy
1994	Gaylark	K. Smith

Transpacific Race

Year	Winning yacht	Owner
1987	*Merlin*	D. Campion
1989	*Silver Bullet*	J. DeLaura
1991	*Chance*	R. McNulty
1993	*Silver Bullet*	J. DeLaura
1995	***Merlin***	**D. Sinclair**

Admiral's Cup

Year	Winning team
1987	New Zealand
1989	United Kingdom
1991	France
1993	Germany
1995	**Italy**

World Class Boat Champions, 1995

Class	Winner	Country
Cadet	Francisco Avermaete	Argentina
Dragon	Nick Rogers	Australia
Etchells	Colin Beashel	Australia
Flying Dutchman	Sabolcs Majthenyi	Hungary
Finn	Herbert Spitzauer	Austria
505	Jeremy Robinson	U.K.
Hornet	Rob Larke	U.K.
International 14	Ian Walker	U.K.
Laser	Robert Scheidt	Brazil
Mirror	Clive Goodwin	U.K.
Solo	Andy Bond	U.K.
Star	Mark Reynolds	U.S.
Wayfarer	Stu Rix	U.K.

their finest hours in sports. The match had been partially overshadowed by a variety of rule changes that many claimed to favour Conner, and in the aftermath of victory Blake revealed that he hoped to clarify the controversial cup rules before the next series, which probably would begin in March 2000 in Auckland, N.Z.

In the Admiral's Cup competition off the southern coast of the U.K., only eight teams entered. The Nordic countries were allowed to compete as one Scandinavian team, and the British home team only just made it to the starting line after a frantic last-ditch effort by Robin Aisher. The U.S. team set out in determined style, establishing a commanding lead over the Italians and Germans before the high-scoring last race, the 974-km (605-mi) Fastnet. In the first days of the race, during which conditions were tricky because of light winds, the Americans lost contact with their closest rivals, the Italians, who sailed their three yachts into top positions in each class. This won them the Admiral's Cup, with the U.S. second and Germany third.

After the Cup competition, the format of the event was being actively questioned. Many believed that the time had come for radical change. For example, with so few yachts entering the competition, it seemed that three divisions might be excessive. Other questions that arose concerned premium scoring for some races and the appropriateness of technically advanced, very expensive designs. The voting at the year's end seemed to indicate that the same formula would be used for at least the next series. (ADRIAN JARDINE)

SKIING

Belief in global warming seemed to become unavoidable in skiing circles in 1995, when exceptionally warm winter weather played havoc with both competitive and leisure skiing. The long history of the International Ski Federation probably had never seen a more catastrophic season. Television ratings confirmed that viewers were not put off, however, because organizers somehow managed to transmit competitions at the times advertised, even though the events may have been held at a changed venue or in a different discipline.

Alpine Skiing. For the first time the world championships, scheduled for Sierra Nevada, Spain, had to be postponed for a year because of insufficient snow. The 29th Alpine World Cup series overcame the problem by switching sites and by using artificially made snow. Interest in the series was heightened by the popularity of the men's and women's overall winners, each a slalom specialist of sufficient skill to thwart challenges from the more versatile all-rounders. In the men's competition Alberto Tomba of Italy at last gained the crystal trophy he had sought since he began competing in 1986. He finished comfortably ahead of Günther Mader of Austria, with Slovenia's Jure Kosir taking the bronze medal. Marc Girardelli of Luxembourg, seeking a record sixth success in 11 years, this time could manage only fourth place.

Tomba was a convincing leader in the slalom and won the giant slalom by five points, his 11 race victories comprising seven slaloms and four giant slaloms. He was the first slalom specialist to win the World Cup since Ingemar Stenmark of Sweden took the prize in 1978. Second in the slalom was Michael Tritscher of Austria. Kosir, third in the slalom, was giant slalom runner-up, ahead of Harald Strand-Nilsen of Norway. Luc Alphand of France narrowly outpointed Kristian Ghedina of Italy to win the downhill competition, with Patrick Ortlieb third for Austria. Peter Runggaldier of Italy took the supergiant slalom (super G), in front of Mader and another Italian, Werner Perathoner.

Switzerland's Vreni Schneider claimed her third women's World Cup trophy, edg-

Alpine World Cup

Year	Men	Women
1991	M. Girardelli (Lux.)	P. Kronberger (Austria)
1992	P. Accola (Switz.)	P. Kronberger (Austria)
1993	M. Girardelli (Lux.)	A. Wachter (Austria)
1994	K.A. Aamodt (Nor.)	V. Schneider (Switz.)
1995	**A. Tomba (Italy)**	**V. Schneider (Switz.)**

World Alpine Skiing Championships—Slalom

Year	Men's slalom	Men's giant slalom	Men's supergiant	Women's slalom	Women's giant slalom	Women's supergiant
1991	M. Girardelli (Lux.)	R. Nierlich (Austria)	S. Eberharter (Austria)	V. Schneider (Switz.)	P. Wiberg (Swed.)	U. Maier (Austria)
1992	F.C. Jagge (Nor.)	A. Tomba (Italy)	K.A. Aamodt (Nor.)	P. Kronberger (Austria)	P. Wiberg (Swed.)	D. Compagnoni (Italy)
1993	K.A. Aamodt (Nor.)	K.A. Aamodt (Nor.)	not held	K. Buder (Austria)	C. Merle (Fr.)	K. Seizinger (Ger.)
1994	T. Stangassinger (Austria)	M. Wasmeier (Ger.)	M. Wasmeier (Ger.)	V. Schneider (Switz.)	D. Compagnoni (Italy)	D. Roffe-Steinrotter (U.S.)
1995	**not held**					

World Alpine Skiing Championships—Downhill

Year	Men	Women
1991	F. Heinzer (Switz.)	P. Kronberger (Austria)
1992	P. Ortlieb (Austria)	K. Lee-Gartner (Can.)
1993	U. Lehmann (Switz.)	K. Pace (Can.)
1994	T. Moe (U.S.)	K. Seizinger (Ger.)
1995	**not held**	

World Alpine Skiing Championships—Combined

Year	Men	Women
1991	S. Eberharter (Austria)	C. Bournissen (Switz.)
1992	J. Polig (Italy)	P. Kronberger (Austria)
1993	L. Kjus (Nor.)	M. Vogt (Ger.)
1994	L. Kjus (Nor.)	P. Wiberg (Swed.)
1995	**not held**	

Alberto Tomba of Italy skis a World Cup slalom run at Garmisch-Partenkirchen, Germany, in January. Tomba won a total of seven slaloms and four giant slaloms in Alpine World Cup competition and captured the overall title.

ZOOM/VANDYSTADT/ALLSPORT

ing Katja Seizinger of Germany by only six points, the smallest-ever winning margin. Another Swiss, Heidi Zeller-Baehler, finished third. Schneider sealed her victory with a courageous run in the slalom, which she won during the final tournament at Bormio, Italy. She then announced her retirement after culminating a career that encompassed 55 cup race wins, 3 overall titles, and 3 Olympic gold medals. Like Tomba, she was top points scorer in both the slalom and the giant slalom. Sweden's Pernilla Wiberg placed second in the slalom, followed by Martina Ertl of Germany. Zeller-Baehler was giant slalom runner-up, with Spela Pretnar of Slovenia third. Seizinger and Zeller-Baehler finished first and second, respectively, in the super G, chased by Switzerland's Heidi Zurbriggen.

ZOOM/VANDYSTADT/ALLSPORT

Picabo Street of the United States races on her way to capturing the women's downhill title in the Alpine World Cup. Street, who dominated women's downhill skiing during the season, became the first American man or woman ever to win the World Cup downhill title.

In the downhill Picabo Street was so dominant that by mid season the American had all but sewn up the event, but her season nearly ended in tragedy when she crashed in the final race. There were fears she had been badly injured but, although airlifted off the slopes, she turned out to have suffered nothing more than severe bruises. Street was the first American, man or woman, to head the downhill rankings. Her compatriot Hilary Lindh was runner-up, with Seizinger third.

Nordic Skiing. Bjørn Dæhlie of Norway recaptured the men's overall title in the 16th Nordic World Cup. The women's crown was regained by Yelena Vyalbe of Russia, her third success in four years. The separate Nordic Combined World Cup was retained by Kenji Ogiwara of Japan, and the Jumping World Cup was taken by Andreas Goldberger of Austria.

Vladimir Smirnov of Kazakhstan was the outstanding man in the world championships at Thunder Bay, Ont., winning the 10 km, 15 km, and 30 km, while Silvio Fauner of Italy bagged the grueling 50 km, in which Smirnov finished third. Norway won the team relay. Larissa Lazhutina of Russia was dominant in the women's events, winning the 5 km, 10 km, and 15 km. Vyalbe claimed the 30 km and was also on the winning Russian relay team. The Nordic combination victor was Ogiwara.

World Nordic Skiing Championships—Men

Year	10-km	15-km	30-km	50-km	Relay
1991	T. Langli (Nor.)	B. Daehlie (Nor.)	G. Svan (Swed.)	T. Mogren (Swed.)	Norway
1992	V. Ulvang (Nor.)	B. Daehlie (Nor.)	V. Ulvang (Nor.)	B. Daehlie (Nor.)	Norway
1993	S. Sivertsen (Nor.)	B. Daehlie (Nor.)	B. Daehlie (Nor.)	T. Mogren (Swed.)	Norway
1994	B. Daehlie (Nor.)	B. Daehlie (Nor.)	T. Alsgaard (Nor.)	V. Smirnov (Kazakh.)	Italy
1995	**V. Smirnov (Kazakh.)**	**V. Smirnov (Kazakh.)**	**V. Smirnov (Kazakh.)**	**S. Fauner (Italy)**	**Norway**

World Nordic Skiing Championships—Women

Year	5-km	10-km	15-km	30-km	Relay
1991	T. Dybendahl (Nor.)	Ye. Vyalbe (U.S.S.R.)	Ye. Vyalbe (U.S.S.R.)	L. Yegorova (U.S.S.R.)	U.S.S.R.
1992	M. Lukkarinen (Fin.)	L. Yegorova (UT)	L. Yegorova (UT)	S. Belmondo (Italy)	Unified Team
1993	L. Lazhutina (Russia)	S. Belmondo (Italy)	Ye. Vyalbe (Russia)	S. Belmondo (Italy)	Russia
1994	L. Yegorova (Russia)	L. Yegorova (Russia)	M. Di Centa (Italy)	M. Di Centa (Italy)	Russia
1995	**L. Lazhutina (Russia)**	**L. Lazhutina (Russia)**	**L. Lazhutina (Russia)**	**Ye. Vyalbe (Russia)**	**Russia**

World Nordic Skiing Championships—Ski Jump

Year	70-m hill	90-m hill	120-m hill	Team jump	Combined	Team combined
1991	H. Kuttin (Austria)	F. Petek (Yugos.)		Austria	F.-B. Lundberg (Nor.)	Austria
1992		E. Vettori (Austria)	T. Nieminen (Fin.)	Finland	F. Guy (Fr.)	Japan
1993		M. Harada (Japan)	E. Bredeson (Nor.)	Norway	K. Ogiwara (Japan)	Japan
1994		E. Bredesen (Nor.)	J. Weissflog (Ger.)	Germany	F.-B. Lundberg (Nor.)	Japan
1995		**T. Okabe (Japan)**	**T. Ingebrigtsen (Nor.)**	**Finland**	**F.-B. Lundberg (Nor.)**	**Japan**

Nordic World Cup

Year	Men	Women
1991	V. Smirnov (U.S.S.R.)	Ye. Vyalbe (U.S.S.R.)
1992	B. Daehlie (Nor.)	Ye. Vyalbe (Russia)
1993	B. Daehlie (Nor.)	L. Yegorova (Russia)
1994	V. Smirnov (Kazakh.)	M. Di Centa (Italy)
1995	**B. Daehlie (Nor.)**	**Ye. Vyalbe (Russia)**

ZOOM/VANDYSTADT/ALLSPORT

Larissa Lazhutina of Russia skis in the Nordic world championships held at Thunder Bay, Ont., in March. Lazhutina dominated the women's events, winning gold in the 5 km, 10 km, 15 km, and mixed relay.

The 120-m jump went to Tommy Ingebrigtsen of Norway and the 90 m to Takanobu Okabe of Japan.

Freestyle Skiing. In the 16th Freestyle World Cup series, Jon Moseley of the U.S. clinched the men's title, with compatriot Trace Worthington placing second and David Belhumeur of Canada third. Another American, Kristean Porter, retained the women's trophy, ahead of Maja Schmid of Switzerland and Katherina Kubenk of Canada.

Worthington won the men's title in the biennial world championships at La Clusaz, France, followed by Darcy Downs from Canada and with Moseley third. Porter captured the women's prize from Schmid and Kubenk, the three ending in the same order as in the World Cup. (HOWARD BASS)

SQUASH

Jansher Khan of Pakistan and Michelle Martin of Australia won the major squash championships in 1995. Both retained the world titles they had gained the previous year.

Khan won a record-breaking seventh World Open title in November when he beat Del Harris of England in a tight final 15–10, 17–14, 16–17, 15–8 at Nicosia, Cyprus. It was not always easy for him, however, as he was handicapped by blisters on his feet and nearly withdrew, in pain, before the final. His foot problems forced him to sit out some matches in the men's world team championship, which immediately followed the World Open in Cairo. He returned, however, to lead Pakistan to an acrimonious semifinal win over Australia. They failed in the finals to retain their title, losing two matches to one to England. In June, Khan had announced he would no longer play in the British squash league.

Playing in his first world championship, Mark Chaloner beat experienced Mir Zaman Gul in the deciding match to enable England to win the title for the first time.

While Martin did acquire a third World Open title in Hong Kong in July, it was not a vintage year for the Australian. The world title match was itself a focus of controversy that arose over the quality of refereeing during Martin's semifinal match against Cassandra Jackman of England. During the summer Martin was beaten in Japan and South Korea by another Australian, Sarah FitzGerald, and bowed out of the semifinals of the Malaysian Open. Martin retained her top position in the world rankings, and FitzGerald moved far ahead of the rest of the contenders to take the second spot for the first time.

The world junior women's championship took place in Sydney, Australia, during July. The home team took the title, beating England two matches to one in the final. The individual champion was Jade Wilson of New Zealand, who beat Rachael Grinham of Australia 9–3, 9–4, 9–7 in a 32-minute final. (ANDREW SHELLEY)

World Open Championships—Men

Year	Winner
1991	R. Martin (Austl.)
1992	Jan. Khan (Pak.)
1993	Jan. Khan (Pak.)
1994	Jan. Khan (Pak.)
1995	**Jan. Khan (Pak.)**

World Open Championships—Women

Year	Winner
1991	not held
1992	S. Devoy (N.Z.)
1993	M. Martin (Austl.)
1994	M. Martin (Austl.)
1995	**M. Martin (Austl.)**

British Open Championships—Men

Year	Winner
1990–91	Jah. Khan (Pak.)
1991–92	Jan. Khan (Pak.)
1992–93	Jan. Khan (Pak.)
1993–94	Jan. Khan (Pak.)
1994–95	**Jan. Khan (Pak.)**

British Open Championships—Women

Year	Winner
1990–91	L. Opie (U.K.)
1991–92	S. Devoy (N.Z.)
1992–93	M. Martin (Austl.)
1993–94	M. Martin (Austl.)
1994–95	**M. Martin (Austl.)**

SWIMMING

In 1995, the year between the 1996 Olympic Games and the 1994 world championships, during which 10 world records were set, no one anticipated that there would be so few new records. Men swimmers could set only three in the 50-m Olympic-size pool, and women set none.

On June 14 at Canet, France, Denis Pankratov of Russia swam the 200-m butterfly in 1 min 55.22 sec, breaking the record of 1 min 55.69 sec set by Mel Stewart of the U.S. in the 1991 world championships. At the European championships in Vienna on August 23, Pankratov lowered the oldest existing world record, swimming the 100-m butterfly in 52.32 sec to better by 0.52 sec the previous record set by Pablo Morales in 1986. At the Pan Pacific Swimming Championships on August 12 in Atlanta, Ga., the U.S. 4 × 100-m freestyle relay of David Fox, Joseph Hudepohl, Jonathan Olsen, and Gary Hall, Jr., set a world record of 3 min 15.11 sec, shattering by 1.42 sec the previous record set by the U.S. national team in the 1988 Olympic Games.

The 1995 FINA (Fédération Internationale de Natation Amateur) Swimming World Cup for 25-m pools was contested in seven countries, beginning in Hong Kong January 3–4 and ending in Gelsenkirchen, Germany, on February 19. In the men's competition at Sheffield, England, three world records were set. On February 11 Danyon Loeder of New Zealand lowered the mark in the 400-m freestyle to 3 min 40.46 sec, and Mark Foster of Great Britain swam the 50-m butterfly in 23.55 sec, a record he broke in December with a time of 23.45 sec. On February 12 Jeff Rouse of the U.S. set a record of 24.37 sec in the 50-m backstroke. At Gelsenkirchen on February 18, Mark Warnecke of Germany established a new mark of 27.00 sec in the 50-m breaststroke. Amy Van Dyken of the U.S. set a record of 26.73 sec for the 50-m butterfly at Espoo, Fin., on February 1. This time was bettered by Angela Kennedy of Australia, who swam the distance in 26.56 sec on February 12 at Sheffield. At Gelsenkirchen on February 18, Kennedy also set a 100-m butterfly record of 58.77 sec.

U.S. swimmers dominated the Pan American Games at Mar del Plata, Arg., March 11–26, winning 22 gold, 15 silver, and 15 bronze medals and setting 10 Pan Am records. Canada followed with six gold, nine silver, and six bronze medals. Eight swimmers won two gold medals: Barbara Bedford, U.S., 100-m and 200-m backstroke (both new Pan Am records); Angel Martino, U.S., 50-m and 100-m freestyle; Trina Jackson, U.S., 800-m freestyle and 200-m butterfly; Joanne Malar, Canada, 200-m and 400-m individual medley; Lisa Flood, Canada, 100-m and 200-m breaststroke; Gustavo Borges, Brazil, 100-m (Pan Am record) and 200-m freestyle; Seth van Neerden, U.S., 100-m and 200-m breaststroke; and Curtis Myden, Canada, 200-m and 400-m individual medley. The U.S. won all six relays.

A record number of 24 countries competed in the Pan Pacific championships, now open to all countries outside of Europe. In 34 events the U.S. won 42 medals—15 golds, 16 silvers, and 11 bronzes. Australia placed second with 13 golds, 12 silvers, and 9 bronzes. China was barred from the tournament because of the 1994 doping scandal, in which seven Chinese swimmers tested positive in drug tests. Men's double individual championship winners included Gary Hall, Jr., U.S., 50-m and 100-m freestyle; Thomas Dolan, U.S., 200-m and 400-m individual medley; Scott Miller, Australia, 100-m and 200-m butterfly; and Daniel Kowalski, Australia, 400-m and 800-m freestyle. The women's double winners were Brooke Bennett, U.S., 400-m and 1,500-m freestyle, and Susan O'Neill, Australia, 100-m and 200-m butterfly. The U.S. won four of the six relays. Thirteen records were set.

World Swimming Records Set in 1995 in 50-m Pools

Event	Name	Country	Time
MEN			
100-m butterfly	Denis Pankratov	Russia	52.32 sec
200-m butterfly	Denis Pankratov	Russia	1 min 55.22 sec
4 × 100-m freestyle relay	U.S. national team (David Fox, Joseph Hudepohl, Jonathan Olsen, Gary Hall, Jr.)	U.S.	3 min 15.11 sec

World Swimming Records Set in 1995 in 25-m Pools

Event	Name	Country	Time
MEN			
400-m freestyle	Danyon Loeder	New Zealand	3 min 40.46 sec
50-m backstroke	Jeff Rouse	U.S.	24.37 sec
50-m breaststroke	Mark Warnecke	Germany	27.00 sec
50-m butterfly	Mark Foster	Great Britain	23.55 sec
50-m butterfly	Mark Foster	Great Britain	23.45 sec
WOMEN			
50-m butterfly	Amy Van Dyken	U.S.	26.73 sec
50-m butterfly	Angela Kennedy	Australia	26.56 sec
100-m butterfly	Angela Kennedy	Australia	58.77 sec

World Swimming Championships—Men

	Freestyle				
Year	50 m	100 m	200 m	400 m	1,500 m
1982		J. Woithe (E.Ger.)	M. Gross (W.Ger.)	V. Salnikov (U.S.S.R.)	V. Salnikov (U.S.S.R.)
1986	T. Jager (U.S.)	M. Biondi (U.S.)	M. Gross (W.Ger.)	R. Henkel (W.Ger.)	R. Henkel (W.Ger.)
1991	T. Jager (U.S.)	M. Biondi (U.S.)	G. Lamberti (Italy)	J. Hoffmann (Ger.)	J. Hoffmann (Ger.)
1994	A. Popov (Russia)	A. Popov (Russia)	A. Kasvio (Fin.)	K. Perkins (Austl.)	K. Perkins (Austl.)

	Backstroke		Breaststroke		Butterfly	
	100 m	200 m	100 m	200 m	100 m	200 m
1982	D. Richter (E.Ger.)	R. Carey (U.S.)	S. Lundquist (U.S.)	V. Davis (Can.)	M. Gribble (U.S.)	M. Gross (W.Ger.)
1986	I. Polyansky (U.S.S.R.)	I. Polyansky (U.S.S.R.)	V. Davis (Can.)	J. Szabo (Hung.)	P. Morales (U.S.)	M. Gross (W.Ger.)
1991	J. Rouse (U.S.)	M. López Zubero (Spain)	N. Rozsa (Hung.)	M. Barrowman (U.S.)	A. Nesty (Suriname)	M. Stewart (U.S.)
1994	M. López Zubero (Spain)	V. Selkov (Russia)	N. Rozsa (Hung.)	N. Rozsa (Hung.)	R. Szukala (Pol.)	D. Pankratov (Russia)

	Individual medley		Team relays		
	200 m	400 m	4 × 100-m freestyle	4 × 200-m freestyle	4 × 100-m medley
1982	A. Sidorenko (U.S.S.R.)	R. Prado (Braz.)	United States	United States	United States
1986	T. Darnyi (Hung.)	T. Darnyi (Hung.)	United States	East Germany	United States
1991	T. Darnyi (Hung.)	T. Darnyi (Hung.)	United States	Germany	United States
1994	J. Sievinen (Fin.)	T. Dolan (U.S.)	United States	Sweden	United States

	Diving		
	1-m springboard	3-m springboard	Platform
1982		G. Louganis (U.S.)	G. Louganis (U.S.)
1986		G. Louganis (U.S.)	G. Louganis (U.S.)
1991	E. Jongejans (Neth.)	K. Ferguson (U.S.)	Sun Shuwei (China)
1994	E. Stewart (Zimb.)	Yu Zhuocheng (China)	D. Sautin (Russia)

World Swimming Championships—Women

Year	Freestyle 50 m	100 m	200 m	400 m	800 m
1982		B. Meineke (E.Ger.)	A. Verstappen (Neth.)	C. Schmidt (E.Ger.)	K. Linehan (U.S.)
1986	T. Costache (Rom.)	K. Otto (E.Ger.)	H. Friedrich (E.Ger.)	H. Friedrich (E.Ger.)	A. Strauss (E.Ger.)
1991	Zhuang Yong (China)	N. Haislett (U.S.)	H. Lewis (Austl.)	J. Evans (U.S.)	J. Evans (U.S.)
1994	Le Jingyi (China)	Le Jingyi (China)	F. van Almsick (Ger.)	Yang Aihua (China)	J. Evans (U.S.)

Year	Backstroke 100 m	Backstroke 200 m	Breaststroke 100 m	Breaststroke 200 m	Butterfly 100 m	Butterfly 200 m
1982	K. Otto (E.Ger.)	C. Sirch (E.Ger.)	U. Geweniger (E.Ger.)	S. Varganova (U.S.S.R.)	M.T. Meagher (U.S.)	I. Geissler (E.Ger.)
1986	B. Mitchell (U.S.)	C. Sirch (E.Ger.)	S. Gerasch (E.Ger.)	S. Hörner (E.Ger.)	K. Gressler (E.Ger.)	M. Meagher (U.S.)
1991	K. Egerszegi (Hung.)	K. Egerszegi (Hung.)	L. Frame (Austl.)	E. Volkova (U.S.S.R.)	Qian Hong (China)	S. Sanders (U.S.)
1994	He Cihong (China)	He Cihong (China)	S. Riley (Austl.)	S. Riley (Austl.)	Liu Limin (China)	Liu Limin (China)

Year	Individual medley 200 m	Individual medley 400 m	Team relays 4 × 100-m freestyle	4 × 200-m freestyle	4 × 100-m medley
1982	P. Schneider (E.Ger.)	P. Schneider (E.Ger.)	East Germany		East Germany
1986	K. Otto (E.Ger.)	K. Nord (E.Ger.)	East Germany	East Germany	East Germany
1991	Lin Li (China)	Lin Li (China)	United States	Germany	United States
1994	Lu Bin (China)	Dai Guohong (China)	China	China	China

Year	Diving 1-m springboard	3-m springboard	platform
1982		M. Neyer (U.S.)	W. Wyland (U.S.)
1986		Gao Min (China)	Chen Lin (China)
1991	Gao Min (China)	Gao Min (China)	Fu Mingxia (China)
1994	Chen Lixia (China)	Tan Shuping (China)	Fu Mingxia (China)

The European championships in Vienna on August 22–27 were dominated by Germany (10 gold, 7 silver, and 7 bronze medals) and Russia (9 golds and 1 bronze). Franziska van Almsick, a 17-year-old from Germany, won five gold medals and one silver. She won the 400-m freestyle in 4 min 8.37 sec, the fastest time for 1995, and the 100-m freestyle in 55.34 sec. Germany, with van Almsick, won all three women's relays. Women double individual event winners were Kristina Egerszegi, Hungary, 200-m backstroke and 400-m individual medley; Brigitte Becue, Belgium, 100-m and 200-m breaststroke; Mette Jacobsen, Denmark, 100-m backstroke and 100-m butterfly; and Michelle Smith, Ireland, 200-m butterfly and 200-m individual medley. Smith's victories brought Ireland its first titles in the 69-year history of the championships. Pankratov was the outstanding male swimmer. In addition to his world record in the 100-m butterfly, he won the 200-m butterfly and joined teammates Vladimir Selkov, Andrey Korneyev, and Aleksandr Popov to win the 4 × 100 medley, setting a European record of 3 min 38.11 sec. Jani Sievinen of Finland

RICHARD MARTIN/VANDYSTADT/ALLSPORT

Denis Pankratov of Russia swims to a world record in the 100-m butterfly at the European championships, held in Vienna in August. His time of 52.32 sec broke the record that had been set by Pablo Morales of the U.S. in 1986 and that was the oldest existing world record in swimming.

Anne Pelletier of Canada waves after receiving her gold medal in the women's 3-m springboard at the Pan American Games, held in March in Mar del Plata, Arg. Pelletier also won a silver medal in the 1-m springboard.
TIMOTHY CLARY—AFP

Dean Panaro of the United States dives from the 1-m springboard during the men's diving finals of the Pan American Games. He won the gold medal in the event with a total of 404.82 points, while Mexico's Fernando Platas took the 3-m springboard and 10-m platform events.
VANDERLEI ALMEIDA—REUTERS

set a European record of 1 min 58.61 sec in the 200-m individual medley. Sievinen also won the 200-m freestyle and 400-m individual medley.

Diving. At the Pan American Games, Canada and Mexico each won two of the six events. Gold medal winners were Mayte Garbey of Cuba with 270.15 points, 0.81 more than Anne Pelletier of Canada in the 1-m springboard; Pelletier, 519.81 in the 3-m springboard; and Anne Montminy, Canada, 492.39 in the 10-m platform. The male gold medalists were Dean Panaro, U.S., 404.82 in the 1-m springboard; Fernando Platas, Mexico, 661.80 in the 3-m springboard; and Platas, 617.52 in the 10-m platform.

Twenty countries competed in the FINA/Alamo Diving Grand Prix on May 11–14 in Fort Lauderdale, Fla. Gold medal winners for women included Yuki Motobuchi of Japan, 268.41 in 1-m springboard; Tan Shuping, China, 522.03 in the 3-m springboard; and Svetlana Timoshinina, Russia, 475.20 in the 10-m platform. In men's competition the gold medal winners were David Pilcher, U.S., 386.61 in the 1-m springboard; Xiong Ni, China, 666.69 in the 3-m springboard; and Jan Hempel, Germany, 663.30 in the 10-m platform.

At the Diving World Cup on August 24–29 in Atlanta, 140 divers from 34 countries competed in the biggest international event leading up to the 1996 Olympics. Gold medal winners included Vera Ilyina, Russia, 287.49 in the 1-m springboard; Fu Mingxia, China, 540.63 in the 3-m springboard; and Chi Bin, China, 512.82 in the 10-m platform. The men's gold medal winners were Yu Zhoucheng, China, 418.50 in the 1-m springboard; Dmitry Sautin, Russia, 684.21 in the 3-m springboard; and Sun Shuwei, China, 681.48 in the 10-m platform. Chinese divers won 10 of the 18 medals. Added to the Diving World Cup for the first time were the synchronized 3-m springboard and synchronized 10-m platform. In this competition two divers attempt to complete their maneuvers in unison and enter the water simultaneously. Women gold medal winners were Guo Jingjing and Deng Ling, China, 278.37 in the 3-m springboard, and Guo Jingjing and Wang Rui, China, 321.42 in the 10-m platform. In men's competition Brian Earley and Kevin McMahon of the U.S. won the 3-m springboard with a score of 327.09, and Xiao Hailang and Tian Liang, China, scored 304.59 to win the 10-m platform.

At the European championships Russia won four of the six events. In women's competition the gold medal winners were Ilyina in the 1-m and 3-m springboard and Ute Wetzig of Germany in the 10-m platform. The men's gold medalists were Edwin Jongejans, The Netherlands, in the 1-m springboard; Sautin in the 3-m springboard; and Vladimir Timoshinin, Russia, in the 10-m platform.

Synchronized Swimming. The U.S. triumphed at the Pan American Games. Becky Dyroen-Lancer won the solo gold medal and, paired with Jill Sudduth, the duet. The U.S. took the team title.

In the Diving World Cup in Atlanta, 195 synchronized swimmers from 19 countries competed. The U.S. won all three championships. Dyroen-Lancer scored 197.163 and won the solo gold medal and teamed with Sudduth to win the duet with a score of 196.535. With 196.615 the U.S. won the team gold medal ahead of Canada, 195.539, and Russia, 194.899.

Russia dominated the European championships. Olga Sedakova won the gold medal in solo; Maria Kisselova and Elena Azarova won the gold in duet; and Russia won the gold in the team event ahead of France and Italy. (ALBERT SCHOENFIELD)

1995 Table Tennis World Rankings

Men	Women
1. Wang Tao (China)	1. Deng Yaping (China)
2. Kong Linghui (China)	2. Qiao Hong (China)
3. Jean-Michel Saive (Belgium)	3. Liu Wei (China)
4. Jorg Rosskopf (Germany)	4. Geng Lijuan (Canada)
5. Liu Gioliang (China)	5. Chai Po Wu (Hong Kong)

World Table Tennis Championships—Men

Year	St. Bride's Vase (singles)	Iran Cup (doubles)	Swaythling Cup (team)
1989	J.-O. Waldner (Swed.)	J. Rosskopf, S. Fetzner (W.Ger.)	Sweden
1991	J. Persson (Swed.)	P. Karlsson, T. Von Scheele (Swed.)	Sweden
1993	J.-P. Gatien (Fr.)	Wang Tao, Lu Lin (China)	Sweden
1995	**Kong Linghui (China)**	**Wang Tao, Lu Lin (China)**	**China**

World Table Tennis Championships—Mixed

Year	Heydusek Prize
1987	Hui Jun, Geng Lijuan (China)
1989	Yoo Nam Kyu, Hyung Jung Hwa (S.Kor.)
1991	Wang Tao, Liu Wei (China)
1993	Wang Tao, Liu Wei (China)
1995	**Wang Tao, Liu Wei (China)**

World Table Tennis Championships—Women

Year	G. Geist Prize (singles)	W.J. Pope Trophy (doubles)	Corbillon Cup (team)
1989	Qiao Hong (China)	Qiao Hong, Deng Yaping (China)	China
1991	Deng Yaping (China)	Gao Jun, Chen Zihe (China)	Korea
1993	Hyun Jung Hwa (S.Kor.)	Liu Wei, Qiao Yunping (China)	China
1995	**Deng Yaping (China)**	**Deng Yaping, Qiao Hong (China)**	**China**

Table Tennis World Cup

Year	Winner
1991	J. Persson (Swed.)
1992	Ma Wenge (China)
1993	Z. Primorac (Croatia)
1994	J.-P. Gatien (Fr.)
1995	**Kong Linghui (China)**

TABLE TENNIS

In 1995 the table tennis world championships returned to China in two senses: they took place in Tianjin, and all seven events were won by China, as they had been in 1981. Thus ended Sweden's domination of the men's team event (in 1989, 1991, and 1993) and the run of European triumphs in the men's singles over the same period. The world champions were: men's singles, Kong Linghui; women's singles, Deng Yaping; men's doubles, Wang Tao and Lu Lin; women's doubles, Deng Yaping and Qiao Hong; mixed doubles, Wang Tao and Liu Wei; men's team, China; and women's team, China.

Table tennis in the United States continued to advance as an increasing number of immigrants brought a new vitality to what had been more of a summer pastime for children than a serious sport. Half of the top 20 players in the United States had been born in China, and only one player on the men's national team, which finished third in the World Team Cup competition held in Atlanta, Ga., was born in the United States.

The use of toxic glues for attaching rubber to the rackets continued to cause controversy. In the world championships Kim Taek Soo of South Korea was disqualified after the men's singles quarterfinal for having used a previously banned solvent.

(TONY BROOKS)

Deng Yaping of China returns the ball during the finals of the women's table tennis championships, which were held on May 13 in Tianjin. Deng defeated her opponent, Qiao Hong, also of China, by scores of 14–21, 21–17, 21–17, 14–21, and 21–14 to take the title.

AFP

TENNIS

During a fascinating year on the courts, Pete Sampras and Steffi Graf were reaffirmed as the outstanding singles competitors at the major tennis championships. Sampras won the Wimbledon and U.S. Open titles, and Graf celebrated victories at the French Open, Wimbledon, and the U.S. Open. In addition, Mary Pierce, in Australia, and Thomas Muster (*see* BIOGRAPHIES), in France, added their names to the roll of Grand Slam singles champions. During the summer Monica Seles made a splendid return to the sport, demonstrating that she had lost none of the verve that had defined her performances as the world's top woman player before her career was interrupted when she was stabbed during a break in play in a match in April 1993.

Australian Open. The burgeoning rivalry between Sampras and his U.S. compatriot Andre Agassi at the top level of the men's game was a source of eager anticipation at the Australian Open in Melbourne in January. There was little reason to suppose, however, that the women's tournament would generate as much interest as it did. Graf, who had experienced mixed fortunes since losing a keenly contested Australian final to Seles in 1993, was unable to compete after straining a calf muscle while practicing, the penalty of overcompensating for a chronic back injury. In her absence Arantxa Sánchez Vicario of Spain was expected to justify her number one seeding.

Although Sánchez Vicario reached the final in six matches without losing a set, Pierce, the fourth seed, made similar progress, defeating Conchita Martínez, the 1994 Wimbledon champion, in the semifinals. Nonetheless, most judges considered that Sánchez Vicario had more to fear from the Yarra River, which had flooded the rubberized asphalt Centre Court during a freak storm the day before the women's final, than she did from Pierce.

In the final, however, Pierce, whose hit-or-miss style afforded little margin for error, enjoyed one of those days when the majority of the balls she struck landed within, or on, the lines, and there were only so many that the scurrying Sánchez Vicario was able to retrieve. Thus, Pierce, a Canadian-born resident of France, won 6–3, 6–2. It was of some consolation to Sánchez Vicario that shortly afterward she succeeded Graf temporarily as the world's top-ranked woman player.

Agassi was paying his first visit to the Australian Open, having previously been either indifferent or indisposed. This time he proved to be a cut above the rest, defeating a weary Sampras in the final 4–6, 6–1, 7–6, 6–4. Three months later Agassi would supplant Sampras as the top-ranked men's player.

The abiding memory of the tournament, however, was of Sampras' emotional quarterfinal win against Jim Courier. After losing the opening two sets in tiebreakers, Sampras won the next two. At that point he was reminded of his coach, Tim Gullikson, who had collapsed during the tournament and was later discovered to be suffering from a brain tumour. "Do it for your coach, Pete," a spectator called out. Sampras broke down and wept on the court, but even so he won the final set 6–3, conceding only two points on his serve.

French Open. Agassi was seeded number one ahead of Sampras for the French Open as the two Americans endeavoured to win the only Grand Slam singles title missing from their collection. It was not to be. Sampras barely had set foot on the slow clay courts of Paris when he was eliminated by Gilbert Schaller of Austria, who won their first-round match in five sets. Agassi advanced to the quarterfinals, to be defeated by a combination of a hip injury and the potent ground strokes of his Russian opponent, Yevgeny Kafelnikov.

Paris belonged to Muster, who verified his credentials as a master of the clay-court game by adding the premier championship played on that surface to a long list of accomplishments. Michael Chang of the U.S., the sixth seed, had ended the two-year reign of Spain's Sergi Bruguera in the semifinals but was overwhelmed in two hours by Muster's power and tenacity 7–5, 6–2, 6–4. It was the left-hander's 35th consecutive clay-court win since October 1994, elevating him to number three in the world and making him the first Austrian to win a Grand Slam singles title.

Graf's fourth French Open singles title came as a surprise to her. She did not believe that she had the form and physical conditioning to reach the final after her pretournament training had been disrupted when she came down with a virus. She was able to wear down Sánchez Vicario 7–5, 4–6, 6–0, however, allowing her opponent only six points in the final set and relieving her of both the title and the world number one ranking.

Wimbledon. A month later Graf and Sánchez Vicario produced a classic final at Wimbledon, the players a blur of activity as they drove or coaxed the balls to the corners of the court, barely clearing the net. One game, with the score at one set all and 5–5, lasted for 20 minutes and featured 32 points, 13 deuces, and 8 game points for Sánchez Vicario before Graf hit a winning cross-court forehand drive on her sixth break point. The German served out the match for a 4–6, 6–1, 7–5 victory, which gave her the title for a sixth time and made amends for her embarrassing performance in 1994, when she became the first defending women's champion not to advance beyond the opening round of the competition.

Steffi Graf of Germany hits a return against Monica Seles in the women's finals of the U.S. Open. Graf won her 18th Grand Slam title and became the first player to win each of the major championships at least four times.
PAUL J. SUTTON—DUOMO

The first week of Wimbledon would be remembered for a series of unusual disqualifications. A Briton, Tim Henman, had the dubious distinction of becoming the first player to be defaulted at Wimbledon since the championships began in 1877. He hit a ball in anger during a doubles match, and a ball girl was accidentally struck in the head.

Jeff Tarango, an American, then walked out of his match against Germany's Alexander Mronz after calling the French umpire, Bruno Rebeuh, "the most corrupt official in the game." Tarango's French wife, Benedicte, assaulted Rebeuh as he made his way to the referee's office, and Tarango, during his media conference, accused the umpire of showing favouritism to certain players in exchange for their friendship. Tarango was fined the equivalent of his prize money and banned from the 1996 Wimbledon championships and another Grand Slam tournament. These penalties were under appeal at the year's end.

Murphy Jensen, another American, was disqualified for failing to turn up for a mixed doubles match in which he was supposed to partner Brenda Schultz-McCarthy. Jensen had overslept.

The tournament gathered momentum at the quarterfinal stage, thanks to a stirring contest between Boris Becker and Cédric Pioline of France, with the German winning 9–7 in the fifth set. This guaranteed that for the first time since seedings began 68 years earlier, the top four men and women would advance to the semifinals.

Becker eliminated Agassi, the top seed, 2–6, 7–6, 6–4, 7–6 but was unable to keep pace with Sampras once the American recovered from losing a first set tiebreaker. In winning 6–7, 6–2, 6–4, 6–2, Sampras did not offer his opponent so much as a break point. He became the first man since Swe-

Australian Open Tennis Championships—Singles

Year	Men	Women
1991	B. Becker (Ger.)	M. Seles (Yugos.)
1992	J. Courier (U.S.)	M. Seles (Yugos.)
1993	J. Courier (U.S.)	M. Seles (Yugos.)
1994	P. Sampras (U.S.)	S. Graf (Ger.)
1995	**A. Agassi (U.S.)**	**M. Pierce (Fr.)**

French Open Tennis Championships—Singles

Year	Men	Women
1991	J. Courier (U.S.)	M. Seles (Yugos.)
1992	J. Courier (U.S.)	M. Seles (Yugos.)
1993	S. Bruguera (Spain)	S. Graf (Ger.)
1994	S. Bruguera (Spain)	A. Sánchez Vicario (Spain)
1995	**T. Muster (Austria)**	**S. Graf (Ger.)**

All-England (Wimbledon) Tennis Championships—Singles

Year	Men	Women
1991	M. Stich (Ger.)	S. Graf (Ger.)
1992	A. Agassi (U.S.)	S. Graf (Ger.)
1993	P. Sampras (U.S.)	S. Graf (Ger.)
1994	P. Sampras (U.S.)	C. Martínez (Spain)
1995	**P. Sampras (U.S.)**	**S. Graf (Ger.)**

United States Open Tennis Championships—Singles

Year	Men	Women
1991	S. Edberg (Swed.)	M. Seles (Yugos.)
1992	S. Edberg (Swed.)	M. Seles (Yugos.)
1993	P. Sampras (U.S.)	S. Graf (Ger.)
1994	A. Agassi (U.S.)	A. Sánchez Vicario (Spain)
1995	**P. Sampras (U.S.)**	**S. Graf (Ger.)**

Australian Open Tennis Championships—Doubles

Year	Men	Women
1991	S. Davis, D. Pate	P. Fendick, M.J. Fernandez
1992	T. Woodbridge, M. Woodforde	A. Sánchez Vicario, H. Sukova
1993	D. Visser, L. Warder	G. Fernandez, N. Zvereva
1994	P. Haarhuis, J. Eltingh	G. Fernandez, N. Zvereva
1995	**J. Palmer, R. Reneberg**	**A. Sánchez Vicario, J. Novotna**

French Open Tennis Championships—Doubles

Year	Men	Women
1991	J. Fitzgerald, A. Jarryd	G. Fernandez, J. Novotna
1992	J. Hlasek, M. Rosset	G. Fernandez, N. Zvereva
1993	L. Jensen, M. Jensen	G. Fernandez, N. Zvereva
1994	B. Black, J. Stark	G. Fernandez, N. Zvereva
1995	**P. Haarhuis, J. Eltingh**	**G. Fernandez, N. Zvereva**

All-England (Wimbledon) Tennis Championships—Doubles

Year	Men	Women
1991	J. Fitzgerald, A. Jarryd	L. Savchenko, N. Zvereva
1992	J. McEnroe, M. Stich	G. Fernandez, N. Zvereva
1993	T. Woodbridge, M. Woodforde	G. Fernandez, N. Zvereva
1994	T. Woodbridge, M. Woodforde	G. Fernandez, N. Zvereva
1995	**T. Woodbridge, M. Woodforde**	**A. Sánchez Vicario, J. Novotna**

United States Open Tennis Championships—Doubles

Year	Men	Women
1991	J. Fitzgerald, A. Jarryd	P. Shriver, N. Zvereva
1992	J. Grabb, R. Reneberg	G. Fernandez, N. Zvereva
1993	K. Flach, R. Leach	A. Sánchez Vicario, H. Sukova
1994	P. Haarhuis, J. Eltingh	A. Sánchez Vicario, J. Novotna
1995	**T. Woodbridge, M. Woodforde**	**G. Fernandez, N. Zvereva**

Davis Cup

Year	Winner	Runner-up	Results
1991	France	United States	3–1
1992	United States	Switzerland	3–1
1993	Germany	Australia	4–1
1994	Sweden	Russia	4–1
1995	**United States**	**Russia**	**3–2**

Federation Cup

Year	Winner	Runner-up	Results
1991	Spain	United States	2–1
1992	Germany	Spain	2–1
1993	Spain	Australia	3–0
1994	Spain	United States	3–0
1995	**Spain**	**United States**	**3–2**

den's Björn Borg to win three consecutive Wimbledon singles titles.

U.S. Open. On July 29 Seles returned to competition after an absence of 27 months. She eased her way back with a straight-sets win in an exhibition match against the semiretired Martina Navratilova in Atlantic City, N.J., before resuming her career two weeks later at the Canadian Open in Toronto. There she swept to victory without losing a set and conceded only 14 games in 5 matches, one of those to Gabriela Sabatini in the semifinals. In her first defeat of the year, Graf lost her opening match against Amanda Coetzer of South Africa. After a week's rest Seles challenged for the U.S. Open, which she had won in 1991 and 1992. She advanced to the final without dropping a set. Graf was waiting. She, too, was a victim of personal anguish, the worries about her back now secondary to concern about the welfare of her father-manager, Peter, who was in prison in Germany accused of evading taxes on her earnings. The strain was evident as she struggled through another first-round match against Coetzer, but in later rounds she regained her dominance.

GARY M. PRIOR—ALLSPORT

Pete Sampras of the U.S. concentrates on the ball in his match against Boris Becker in the men's finals of the Wimbledon championships. Sampras won his third straight Wimbledon title by scores of 6–7, 6–2, 6–4, 6–2.

When Günther Parche, an unemployed lathe operator, was charged with wounding Seles in 1993, he said he did it so that Graf would regain her top ranking in the world. Now, at last, the two women were able to renew their rivalry, Graf winning a magnificent, oscillating contest 7–6, 0–6, 6–3. It was the German's 18th Grand Slam singles title, and she became the first player to win each of the major championships at least four times.

The men's singles also produced a final to savour between the top seeds, Sampras, the number two, defeating number one Agassi 6–4, 6–3, 4–6, 7–5, with Sampras serving 24 aces, 142 for the tournament. The opening set was decided after a dazzling 22-shot rally on set point. The 24-year-old Sampras' third U.S. Open title raised his Grand Slam total to seven.

Davis Cup. Sampras also led the U.S. team to its 3–2 victory over Russia in Davis Cup final round play in Moscow, first defeating Andrey Chesnokov 3–6, 6–4, 6–3, 6–7 (7–5), 6–4 and later Yevgeny Kafelnikov 6–2, 6–4, 7–6 (7–4).

In December, Stefan Edberg, ranked number one in 1990, announced his retirement from play effective November 1996.

(JOHN ROBERTS)

TRACK AND FIELD SPORTS (ATHLETICS)

One year before the 1996 Olympic Games, track and field did not lack for championship-calibre competition. Foremost on the season's schedule was the outdoor world championships; the biennial event was staged in Göteborg, Sweden, in August. The other major tournament was the world indoor championships in Barcelona, Spain, in March.

World Outdoor Championships. Many of the world's best athletes convened in Göteborg on Sweden's west coast, and the pressure-cooker atmosphere helped produce four world records. One man set two marks; triple jumper Jonathan Edwards of Great Britain hopped, stepped, and jumped 18.16 m (59 ft 7 in) on his first leap to better the world record of 17.98 m (59 ft) he had set earlier in the summer. On his next leap, however, Edwards went one better, reaching 18.29 m (60 ft ¼ in) to break the event's long-sought 60-ft barrier. The new record highlighted Edwards' undefeated 14-meet season, in which he produced the four longest leaps in history.

The pair of women's records were established by Kim Batten of the U.S. in the 400-m hurdles (52.61 sec) and by triple jumper Inessa Kravets of Ukraine, who jumped 15.50 m (50 ft 10¼ in). In a thrilling finish Batten just edged U.S. teammate Tonja Buford, whose time of 52.62 sec also bettered the former mark of 52.74 sec set in 1993 by Sally Gunnell of the U.K. Kravets saved herself from possible elimination from the final by sailing to her record distance on her third jump in the preliminary round. Her first two attempts had been fouls.

The largest medal haul was claimed by U.S. sprint superstar Michael Johnson (*see* BIOGRAPHIES), who first defended his global crown at 400 m with the second fastest time in history, 43.39 sec. Next he sped 200 m in 19.79 sec to reclaim the title of that distance, which he had won at the 1991 championships in Tokyo but surrendered two years later in Stuttgart, Germany, when he concentrated on just the 400. Johnson capped his trying schedule of nine races in as many days by anchoring the United States' 4 × 400-m relay team to a comfortable victory in 2 min 57.32 sec.

Jonathan Edwards of Great Britain sets a new record of 18.29 m (60 ft ¼ in) in the men's triple jump at the world track and field championships. It was his third record in the event during the year.

MIKE POWELL—ALLSPORT

Men from Africa won every track race from 800 m through 10,000 m. Algeria's Noureddine Morceli easily won his third consecutive world championship at 1,500 m with a time of 3 min 33.73 sec. Moses Kiptanui of Kenya made it three consecutive wins in the 3,000-m steeplechase, his time of 8 min 4.16 sec the third fastest ever in this event.

The 1993 winners at 5,000 m and 10,000 m both defended their titles. Ismael Kirui of Kenya ran the shorter distance in 13 min 16.77 sec, while Ethiopian star Haile Gebrselassie sprinted home strongly to win the 10,000 m in 27 min 12.95 sec. The other African winner was Kenyan-born Wilson Kipketer, who won the 800 m in 1 min 45.08 sec for his newly adopted nation of Denmark, giving that nation its first-ever world champion.

In the pole vault Ukrainian superstar Sergey Bubka became the only athlete to have won his event in all five editions of the world championships. He reached a height of 5.92 m (19 ft 5 in) to claim gold medal number five.

Other U.S. men winners included hurdlers Allen Johnson (13.00 sec over the 110-m high barriers) and Derrick Adkins (47.98 sec in the 400-m event), shot putter John Godina (21.47 m [70 ft 5¼ in]), and Dan O'Brien (8,695 points for his third consecutive decathlon title). U.S. women to strike gold included 100-m hurdles defending champion Gail Devers (12.68 sec) and also the 4 × 100-m (42.12 sec) and 4 × 400-m (3 min 22.39 sec) relay teams.

1995 World Outdoor Records—Men

Event	Competitor and country	Performance
1,500 m	Noureddine Morceli (Algeria)	3 min. 27.37 sec
2,000 m	Noureddine Morceli (Algeria)	4 min 47.88 sec
3,000-m steeplechase	Moses Kiptanui (Kenya)	7 min 59.18 sec
2 mi*	Haile Gebrselassie (Ethiopia)	8 min 7.46 sec
5,000 m	Haile Gebrselassie (Ethiopia)	12 min 44.39 sec
10,000 m	Haile Gebrselassie (Ethiopia)	26 min 43.53 sec
200-m low hurdles*	Laurent Ottoz (Italy)	22.55 sec
Triple jump	Jonathan Edwards (Great Britain)	18.29 m (60 ft ¼ in)

1995 World Indoor Records—Men

Event	Competitor and country	Performance
200 m	Linford Christie (Great Britain)	20.25 sec
400 m	Michael Johnson (U.S.)	44.63 sec
3,000 m	Moses Kiptanui (Kenya)	7 min 35.15 sec
110-m hurdles*	Allen Johnson (U.S.)	13.34 sec
5,000-m walk	Mikhail Shchennikov (Russia)	18 min 7.08 sec
35-lb weight throw*	Lance Deal (U.S.)	25.86 m (84 ft 10¼ in)
Pentathlon*	Steve Fritz (U.S.)	4,478 points

*Not an officially ratified record event; best performance on record.

World Track and Field Championships—Men

Event	1993	1995
100 m	L. Christie (U.K.)	D. Bailey (Can.)
200 m	F. Fredericks (Namib.)	M. Johnson (U.S.)
400 m	M. Johnson (U.S.)	M. Johnson (U.S.)
800 m	P. Ruto (Kenya)	W. Kipketer (Den.)
1,500 m	N. Morceli (Alg.)	N. Morceli (Alg.)
5,000 m	I. Kirui (Kenya)	I. Kirui (Kenya)
10,000 m	H. Gebrselassie (Eth.)	H. Gebrselassie (Eth.)
steeplechase	M. Kiptanui (Kenya)	M. Kiptanui (Kenya)
110-m hurdles	C. Jackson (U.K.)	A. Johnson (U.S.)
400-m hurdles	K. Young (U.S.)	D. Adkins (U.S.)
marathon	M. Plaatjes (U.S.)	M. Fiz (Spain)
20-km walk	V. Massana (Spain)	M. Didoni (Italy)
50-km walk	J.A. Garcia (Spain)	V. Kononen (Fin.)
4 × 100-m relay	United States (J. Drummond, A. Cason, K. Mitchell, L. Burrell)	Canada (R. Esmie, G. Gilbert, B. Surin, D. Bailey)
4 × 400-m relay	United States (A. Valmon, Q. Watts, B. Reynolds, M. Johnson)	United States (M. Ramsey, D. Mills, B. Reynolds, M. Johnson)
high jump	J. Sotomayor (Cuba)	T. Kemp (Bahamas)
pole vault	S. Bubka (Ukr.)	S. Bubka (Ukr.)
long jump	M. Powell (U.S.)	I. Pedroso (Cuba)
triple jump	M. Conley (U.S.)	J. Edwards (U.K.)
shot put	W. Günthör (Switz.)	J. Godina (U.S.)
discus throw	L. Riedel (Ger.)	L. Riedel (Ger.)
hammer throw	A. Abduvaliyev (Tajik.)	A. Abduvaliyev (Tajik.)
javelin throw	J. Zelezny (Cz.Rep.)	J. Zelezny (Cz. Rep.)
decathlon	D. O'Brien (U.S.)	D. O'Brien (U.S.)

1995 World Outdoor Records—Women

Event	Competitor and country	Performance
1,000 m*	Maria Mutola (Mozambique)	2 min 29.34 sec
5,000 m*	Fernanda Ribeiro (Portugal)	14 min 36.45 sec
400-m hurdles	Kim Batten (U.S.)	52.61 sec
10-km walk†	Larisa Ramazanova (Russia)	41 min 29 sec
Pole vault	Daniela Bartova (Czech Republic)	4.21 m (13 ft 9¾ in)
Pole vault*	Daniela Bartova (Czech Republic)	4.22 m (13 ft 10 in)
Pole vault*	Sun Caiyun (China)	4.23 m (13 ft 10½ in)
Pole vault*	Emma George (Australia)	4.25 m (13 ft 11¼ in)
Pole vault*	Emma George (Australia)	4.28 m (14 ft ½ in)
Triple jump	Inessa Kravets (Ukraine)	15.50 m (50 ft 10¼ in)
Hammer throw	Olga Kuzenkova (Russia)	68.16 m (223 ft 7 in)

*Awaiting ratification.
†Road walking performance (officially ratified times must be set on track); best performance on record.

1995 World Indoor Records—Women

Event	Competitor and country	Performance
50 m	Irina Privalova (Russia)	5.96 sec
60 m	Irina Privalova (Russia)	6.92 sec
Pole vault	Sun Caiyun (China)	4.15 m (13 ft 7¼ in)
Triple jump	Yolanda Chen (Russia)	15.03 m (49 ft 3¾ in)

World Track and Field Championships—Women

Event	1993	1995
100 m	G. Devers (U.S.)	G. Torrence (U.S.)
200 m	M. Ottey (Jam.)	M. Ottey (Jam.)
400 m	J. Miles (U.S.)	M.-J. Pérec (Fr.)
800 m	M. Mutola (Mozam.)	A. Quirot (Cuba)
1,500 m	Liu Dong (China)	H. Boulmerka (Alg.)
3,000 m*	Qu Yunxia (China)	S. O'Sullivan (Ire.)
10,000 m	Wang Junxia (China)	F. Ribeiro (Port.)
100-m hurdles	G. Devers (U.S.)	G. Devers (U.S.)
400-m hurdles	S. Gunnell (U.K.)	K. Batten (U.S.)
marathon	Asari Junko (Japan)	M. Machado (Port.)
10-km walk	S. Essayeh (Fin.)	I. Stankina (Rus.)
4 × 100-m relay	Russia (O. Bogoslovskaya, G. Malchugina, N. Voronova, I. Privalova)	United States (C. Mondie-Milner, C. Guidry, C. Gaines, G. Torrence)
4 × 400-m relay	United States (G. Torrence, M. Malone, N. Kaiser-Brown, J. Miles)	United States (K. Graham, R. Stevens, C. Jones, J. Miles)
high jump	I. Quintero (Cuba)	S. Kostadinova (Bul.)
long jump	H. Drechsler (Ger.)	F. May (Italy)
triple jump		I. Kravets (Ukr.)
shot put	Huang Zhihong (China)	A. Kumbernuss (Ger.)
discus throw	O. Burova (Russia)	E. Zvereva (Bel.)
javelin throw	T. Hattestad (Nor.)	N. Shikolenko (Bel.)
heptathlon	J. Joyner-Kersee (U.S.)	G. Shouaa (Syria)

*5,000 m in 1995.

IAAF World Cup—Men

	100 metre	200 metre	400 metre	800 metre	1,500 metre
1989	L. Christie (Gr.Brit.)	R. Caetano da Silva (Amer.)	R. Hernandez (Amer.)	T. McKean (Gr.Brit.)	A. Bile (Africa)
1992	L. Christie (Gr.Brit.)	R. Caetano da Silva (Amer.)	S. Bada (Africa)	D. Sharpe (U.K.)	M. Suleiman (Asia)
1994	L. Christie (Gr.Brit.)	J. Regis (Gr.Brit.)	A. Pettigrew (U.S.)	M. Everett (U.S.)	N. Morceli (Africa)
	5,000 metre	**10,000 metre**	**Steeplechase**	**110-m hurdles**	**400-m hurdles**
1989	S. Aouita (Africa)	S. Antibo (Europe)	J. Kariuki (Africa)	R. Kingdom (U.S.)	D. Patrick (U.S.)
1992	F. Bayesa (Africa)	A. Abebe (Africa)	P. Barkutwo (Africa)	C. Jackson (U.K.)	S. Matete (Africa)
1994	B. Lahlafi (Africa)	K. Skah (Africa)	M. Kiptanui (Africa)	T. Jarrett (Gr.Brit.)	S. Matete (Africa)
	4 × 100-m relays	**4 × 400-m relays**	**Triple jump**	**High jump**	**Pole vault**
1989	United States	Americas	M. Conley (U.S.)	P. Sjoberg (Europe)	P. Collet (Europe)
1992	United States	Africa	J. Edwards (U.K.)	Y. Sergeyenko (UT)	I. Potapovich (UT)
1994	Great Britain	Great Britain	Y. Quesada (Amer.)	J. Sotomayor (Amer.)	O. Brits (Africa)
	Long jump	**Shot put**	**Discus throw**	**Hammer throw**	**Javelin throw**
1989	L. Myricks (U.S.)	U. Timmermann (E.Ger.)	J. Schult (E.Ger.)	H. Weis (Europe)	S. Backley (Gr.Brit.)
1992	I. Pedroso (Amer.)	M. Stulce (U.S.)	T. Washington (U.S.)	T. Gécsek (Europe)	J. Zelezny (Europe)
1994	F. Salle (Gr.Brit.)	C.J. Hunter (U.S.)	V. Dubrovshchik (Europe)	A. Abduvaliyev (Asia)	S. Backley (Gr.Brit.)
	Team				
1989	United States				
1992	Africa				
1994	Africa				

IAAF World Cup—Women					
	100 metre	200 metre	400 metre	800 metre	1,500 metre
1989	S. Echols (U.S.)	S. Moller (E.Ger.)	A. Quirot (Amer.)	A. Quirot (Amer.)	P. Ivan (Europe)
1992	N. Voronova (UT)	M.-J. Pérec (Europe)	J. Miles (U.S.)	M. Mutola (Africa)	Y. Podkopayeva (UT)
1994	I. Privalova (Europe)	M. Ottey (Amer.)	I. Privalova (Europe)	M. Mutola (Africa)	H. Boulmerka (Africa)
	3,000 metre	10,000 metre	100-m hurdles	400-m hurdles	4 × 100-m relays
1989	Y. Murray (Europe)	K. Ullrich (E.Ger.)	C. Oschkenat (E.Ger.)	S. Farmer-Patrick (U.S.)	East Germany
1992	D. Tulu (Africa)	D. Tulu (Africa)	A. López (Amer.)	S. Farmer-Patrick (U.S.)	Asia
1994	Y. Murray (Gr.Brit.)	E. Meyer (Africa)	A. López (Amer.)	S. Gunnell (Gr.Brit.)	Africa
	4 × 400-m relays	Triple Jump	High jump	Long jump	Shot put
1989	Americas		S. Costa (Amer.)	G. Chistyakova (U.S.S.R.)	Zhihong Huang (Asia)
1992	Americas		I. Quintero (Amer.)	H. Drechsler (Ger.)	B. Laza (Amer.)
1994	Great Britain	A. Biryukova (Europe)	B. Bilac (Europe)	I. Kravets (Europe)	Zhihong Huang (Asia)
	Discus throw	Javelin throw	Team		
1989	I. Wyludda (E.Ger.)	P. Felke (E.Ger.)	East Germany		
1992	M. Marten (Amer.)	T. Sanderson (U.K.)	Unified Team		
1994	I. Wyludda (Europe)	T. Hattestad (Europe)	Europe		

Stunning disqualifications eliminated two women after each ran several steps on the lane stripe. U.S. sprint star Gwen Torrence won the 100-m dash in 10.85 sec and crossed the finish line first in the 200-m event. But judges detected that she had stepped on the lane line around the turn. Similarly, Mozambique's Maria Mutola, heavily favoured to repeat as 800-m champion, stepped outside her lane in her semifinal race and was disqualified, ending her string of consecutive victories at 42.

World Indoor Championships. U.S. men to win at the indoor world championships included Darnell Hall at 400 m (46.17 sec), Allen Johnson in the 60-m hurdles (7.39 sec), and the 4 × 400-m relay team of Rod Tolbert, Calvin Davis, Tod Long, and Frankie Atwater (3 min 7.37 sec). The lone U.S. woman to score a victory was Regina Jacobs at 1,500 m (4 min 12.61 sec).

The women's triple jump again produced a world record as Russia's Yolanda Chen extended the mark to 15.03 m (49 ft 3¾ in). Russian sprint star Irina Privalova, who had set indoor records at 50 m and 60 m, stepped up to the 400 m and won easily in 50.23 sec.

Men's International Competition. The African trio of Morceli-Kiptanui-Gebrselassie all had set world records before the world tournament at Göteborg, and the latter pair also set records after the worlds. Gebrselassie began his season spectacularly in late May, running the seldom-contested two-mile distance in a record 8 min 7.46 sec to trim Kiptanui's two-year-old record of 8 min 9.01 sec. Gebrselassie termed the two-mile race as just a "warm-up" for an attempt on the 10,000-m record nine days later—and he made good in that attempt as he ran the distance in 26 min 43.53 to lower the mark by almost 10 full seconds. Kiptanui chimed in just three days later with a 5,000-m best of 12 min 55.30 sec, breaking Gebrselassie's 1994 record of 12 min 56.96.

Morceli got in his licks twice in a span of nine days, first in the 2,000 m with a clocking of 4 min 47.88 sec and then at his 1,500-m specialty. His 3 min 27.37 sec broke his own record of 3 min 28.86 sec.

At the prestigious Zürich (Switz.) invitational meet in August, both Kiptanui and Gebrselassie produced stunning performances. Kiptanui broke through the steeplechase's fabled barrier of eight min-

MIKE POWELL—ALLSPORT

Gail Devers of the U.S. won the 100-m hurdles for women in 12.68 sec at the world track and field championships, held in Göteborg, Sweden, in August. Devers was the defending champion in the 100-m hurdles, having won the event in the 1993 games.

World Cross Country Championship Men (12,000 m)

Year	Individual	Team
1991	K. Shah (Mor.)	Kenya
1992	J. Ngugi (Kenya)	Kenya
1993	W. Sigei (Kenya)	Kenya
1994	W. Sigei (Kenya)	Kenya
1995	**P. Tergat (Kenya)**	**Kenya**

World Cross Country Championship Women (5,000 m)

Year	Individual	Team
1991	L. Jennings (U.S.)	Kenya
1992	L. Jennings (U.S.)	Kenya
1993	A. Dias (Port.)	Kenya
1994	H. Chepngeno (Kenya)	Portugal
1995	**D. Tulu (Eth.)**	**Kenya**

World Marathon Cup

Year	Men	Women
1987	A. Salah (Djib.)	Z. Ivanova (U.S.S.R.)
1989	K. Metaferia (Eth.)	S. Marchiano (U.S.)
1991	Y. Tolstikov (U.S.S.R.)	R. Mota (Port.)
1993	R. Nerurkar (U.K.)	Wang Junxia (China)
1995	**D. Wakiihuri (Kenya)**	**A. Catuna (Rom.)**

Boston Marathon

Year	Men	h:min:s
1991	I. Hussein (Kenya)	2:11:06
1992	I. Hussein (Kenya)	2:08:14
1993	C. N'Deti (Kenya)	2:09:33
1994	C. N'Deti (Kenya)	2:07:15
1995	**C. N'Deti (Kenya)**	**2:09:22**
Year	**Women**	**h:min:s**
1991	W. Panfil (Pol.)	2:24:18
1992	O. Markova (Russia)	2:23:43
1993	O. Markova (Russia)	2:25:27
1994	U. Pippig (Ger.)	2:21:45
1995	**U. Pippig (Ger.)**	**2:25:11**

New York City Marathon

Year	Men	h:min:s
1991	S. Garcia (Mex.)	2:09:28
1992	W. Mtolo (S.Afr.)	2:09:29
1993	A. Espinosa (Mex.)	2:10:04
1994	G. Silva (Mex.)	2:11:21
1995	**G. Silva (Mex.)**	**2:11:00**
Year	**Women**	**h:min:s**
1991	L. McColgan (Scot.)	2:27:23
1992	L. Ondieki (Austl.)	2:24:40
1993	U. Pippig (Ger.)	2:26:24
1994	T. Loroupe (Kenya)	2:27:37
1995	**T. Loroupe (Kenya)**	**2:28:06**

utes as he ran virtually solo to a record 7 min 59.18 sec. Shortly afterward, however, Gebrselassie one-upped the Kenyan by regaining the 5,000-m record. His blistering 12 min 44.39 sec lowered Kiptanui's earlier mark by 10.91 sec, the widest margin by which the record had been broken in more than 50 years.

The pair met in a climactic 5,000-m race in Berlin at the beginning of September. They were together after four kilometres, but Gebrselassie's surge over the final 1,000 m was so strong that he came home almost 10 seconds ahead of Kiptanui with a time (12 min 53.19 sec) second only to his own record. Kiptanui finished in 13 min 0.90 sec. Kiptanui, however, scored $130,000 worth of revenge, gaining that amount as overall points winner in the Grand Prix circuit of top-level European invitational meets.

In the long jump Cuba's Ivan Pedroso appeared to have set a new world record when he leaped 8.96 m (29 ft 4¾ in) in the rarefied air of the Italian Alpine city of Sestriere, but videotapes showed that an official had inadvertently stood in front of the wind-measuring gauge on each of Pedroso's attempts, which negated any wind-speed measurement necessary for acceptance of a record. As a result, Pedroso's mark could not be eligible for record consideration.

Women's International Competition. Distance runners also starred in women's events. Portugal's Fernanda Ribeiro clocked a 5,000-m record of 14 min 36.45 sec, although she ended up losing that distance in Göteborg to Ireland's Sonia O'Sullivan. Ribeiro did claim the 10,000-m world crown, however. Maria Mutola atoned to some degree for her world championship disqualification at 800 m by clocking a record 2 min 29.34 sec for 1,000 m. Mutola was the women's overall Grand Prix champion and winner of the $130,000 prize.

Two new record events were contested in 1995, the best marks in the pole vault and hammer throw at the end of the season being recognized as world records. In the vault former gymnast Daniela Bartova of the Czech Republic achieved 4.21 m (13 ft 9¾ in). That mark was exceeded late in the season by four higher leaps. The highest was by Australia's Emma George at 4.28 m (14 ft ½ in), which awaited ratification. In the hammer Russia's Olga Kuzenkova set a mark of 68.16 m (223 ft 7 in).

Cross Country and Marathon Running. Kenya's Paul Tergat won the men's title at the world cross country championships in Durham, England, in March, while Ethiopia's Derartu Tulu took the women's crown. Kenya won all four team titles (seniors and juniors for both men and women).

The world championship marathon victories went to Spain's Martin Fiz (2 hr 11 min 41 sec) and Portugal's Manuela Machado (2 hr 25 min 39 sec). The women's race was 400 m short, as officials erroneously directed the runners out of the stadium after only three laps of the track, rather than the necessary four.

The world half-marathon championship was won by yet another Kenyan, Moses Tanui, who covered the 21.1-km (13.1-mi) distance on the road in 1 hr 1 min 46 sec. The women's title went to Russia's Valentina Yegorova, the 1992 Olympic marathon champion, in 1 hr 9 min 58 sec. Kenya's men and Romania's women successfully defended their team titles.

The men's and women's winners of other major marathons in 1995 were: Boston, Cosmas N'Deti (Kenya) 2 hr 9 min 22 sec, for his third consecutive victory, and Uta Pippig (Germany) 2 hr 25 min 11 sec; Rotterdam, Neth., Martin Fiz (Spain) 2 hr 8 min 57 sec and Monica Pont (Spain) 2 hr 30 min 34 sec; London, Dionicio Cerón (Mexico) 2 hr 8 min 30 sec and Malgorzata Sobanska (Poland) 2 hr 27 min 43 sec; Berlin, Sammy Lelei (Kenya) 2 hr 7 min 2 sec (second fastest time in history) and Pippig 2 hr 25 min 36 sec; and New York, German Silva (Mexico) 2 hr 11 min and Tecla Loroupe (Kenya) 2 hr 28 min 6 sec.

(JON HENDERSHOTT)

VOLLEYBALL

World Volleyball Championships

Year	Men	Women
1986	United States	China
1988	United States	U.S.S.R.
1990	Italy	U.S.S.R.
1992	Brazil	Cuba
1994	Italy	Cuba

The United States women's and men's volleyball teams reinforced their places among the world's elite following their impressive 1995 campaigns. The U.S. women posted more than 50 victories, including their first major international tournament championship in the $2 million World Grand Prix. Tara Cross-Battle of the U.S. won the Most Valuable Player honours during the five-week tournament, in which the U.S. triumphed in 14 of its 15 matches, including its final 12. Elaina Oden of the U.S. was named the best blocker during the competition.

The U.S. men posted several major victories during the campaign, including three wins over world power Cuba and triumphs over reigning Olympic champion Brazil and defending world champion Italy. They also won a silver medal at the Pan American Games but failed to reach the play-offs in the $6 million World League. The team was anchored by three players from the 1992 Olympic bronze medal team, Bob Ctvrtlik, Scott Fortune, and Bryan Ivie. The U.S. men were seeking to capture their fourth successive Olympic medal in 1996 (they took golds in 1984 and 1988 in addition to the 1992 bronze).

World Cup competition took place late in the year in Japan. At the men's tournament in Tokyo, Italy defeated the U.S. 15–8, 15–5, 15–4 to clinch the championship and become the first country to earn an invitation to compete in the sport in the 1996 Olympic Games. The women's tournament, held in Osaka, was won by Cuba.

Beach volleyball was to make its Olympic Games debut in Atlanta, Ga., in 1996. The U.S. and Brazil appeared to be the strongest teams. (RICHARD S. WANNINGER)

WEIGHT LIFTING

For the first time, China dominated both the men's and women's competition in the 1995 world weight lifting championships. The championships were held for the first time in Asia, at Guangzhou (Canton), China.

In the men's events China won two gold, one silver, and two bronze medals for total lifts and scored 359 points in the team competition, placing all 10 of its lifters in the top 15 for the snatch, clean and jerk, and total lifts. Greece won three gold medals; Russia won two; and Turkey, Cuba, and Ukraine gained one each. Both Greece and Russia earned five medals overall.

Naim Suleymanoglu of Turkey won his seventh world title. He tied with Valerios Leonidis of Greece in the 64-kg (141-lb) class but was awarded first place because of his lower body weight. Similarly, Kahki Kakhiasvillis of Greece won the 99-kg class over Russia's Sergey Syrtsov because of a lower body weight.

In the women's events China won five gold and three silver medals. The other gold medals went to Taiwan with two and to India and Hungary with one each. In addition to Suleymanoglu, the only other 1994 champions to repeat were Russia's

1995 World Weight Lifting Champions

MEN			WOMEN		
Weight	Winner and country	Performance	Weight	Winner and country	Performance
54 kg (119 lb)	Zhang Xiangsen, China	285 kg (628 lb)	46 kg (101 lb)	Guan Hong, China	180 kg (397 lb)
59 kg (130 lb)	Leonidas Sabonis, Greece	302.5 kg (666 lb)	50 kg (110 lb)	Liu Xiuhua, China	187.5 kg (413 lb)
64 kg (141 lb)	Naim Suleymanoglu, Turkey	327.5 kg (722 lb)	54 kg (119 lb)	Karnam Malleswari, India	202.5 kg (445.5 lb)
70 kg (154 lb)	Zhan Xugang, China	347.5 kg (766 lb)	59 kg (130 lb)	Chen Xiaomin, China	215 kg (473 lb)
76 kg (167.5 lb)	Pablo Lara, Cuba	367.5 kg (811 lb)	64 kg (141 lb)	Chen Jun-lien, Taiwan	212.5 kg (467.5 lb)
83 kg (183 lb)	Pyrros Dimas, Greece	385 kg (849 lb)	70 kg (154 lb)	Tang Weifang, China	225 kg (496 lb)
91 kg (200 lb)	Aleksei Petrov, Russia	410 kg (904 lb)	76 kg (167.5 lb)	Li Yan, China	227.5 kg (501.5 lb)
99 kg (217 lb)	Kahki Kakhiasvillis, Greece	410 kg (904 lb)	83 kg (183 lb)	Chen Shu-chi, Taiwan	240 kg (529 lb)
108 kg (237.5 lb)	Igor Razorenov, Ukraine	417.5 kg (920 lb)	+83 kg (+183 lb)	Erika Takacs, Hungary	232.5 kg (511.5 lb)
+108 kg (+238 lb)	Andrei Chemerkin, Russia	442.5 kg (975.5 lb)			

Aleksey Petrov in the 91-kg division and Cuba's Pablo Lara in the 76-kg class.

(CHARLES ROBERT PAUL, JR.)

WRESTLING

Freestyle and Greco-Roman. The United States served as host for the 1995 freestyle wrestling world championships, held in Atlanta, Ga., on August 10–13. The host country took first place with 71 points and four gold medals. Iran placed second with 59 points and one gold. Russia was third with 58 points, followed by Turkey with 35 points and Cuba with 34 points. Valentin Jordanov of Bulgaria won his seventh world championship.

The Greco-Roman world championships took place in Prague on October 12–15. Russia won with 75 points, and Germany followed with 39 points. Russian heavyweight Aleksandr Karelin won his seventh world championship.

The freestyle World Cup took place in Chattanooga, Tenn., on April 7–8. The U.S. won its third straight dual meet title by defeating Russia in the final match 20–19 and gained a total of 10 team points. Russia scored 8 points, Turkey 6, Iran 4, and Canada 2.

The 65th U.S. collegiate championships were held in Iowa City, Iowa, on March 16–18. Winning the team title was host school Iowa with 134 points and one champion. Winning his third collegiate title was North Carolina's T.J. Jaworsky at 60.8 kg (134 lb).

(JOHANNA SCHNEIDER)

Sumo. Sumo's new star, Takanohana, gained promotion to the top rank of *yokozuna* at the end of November 1994 and dominated 1995 by winning four of the six annual 15-day tournaments. His older brother, *ozeki* (the second highest rank) Wakanohana, and *yokozuna* Akebono, a Hawaiian-American, won the other two titles. Takanohana captured the Hatsu *basho* (New Year's tournament) with a strong 13–2 record, defeating *ozeki* Musashimaru, an American-Samoan from Hawaii, in a playoff. In the Haru *basho* in March, Akebono had a near-perfect 14–1 mark to win his eighth *yusho* (tournament title). But Takanohana won three consecutive *yusho,* in May, July, and September. In May's Natsu *basho,* he won by 14–1; in the Nagoya *basho* in July, he took the title with a 13–2 record; and finally in the Aki *basho* in September, he breezed to his third straight *yusho* with a perfect 15–0 mark, increasing his total *yusho* to 11. In the year's sixth and final *basho* in November—a historic encounter involving two brothers competing for the first time ever—*ozeki* Wakanohana defeated Takanohana in a play-off after they finished the Kyushu *basho* with identical 12–3 records.

(ANDY ADAMS)

1995 Sumo Tournament Champions

Tournament	Location	Winner	Winner's record
Hatsu *basho* (New Year's tournament)	Tokyo	Takanohana	13–2
Haru *basho* (spring tournament)	Osaka	Akebano	14–1
Natsu *basho* (summer tournament)	Tokyo	Takanohana	14–1
Nagoya *basho* (Nagoya tournament)	Nagoya	Takanohana	13–2
Aki *basho* (autumn tournament)	Tokyo	Takanohana	15–0
Kyushu *basho* (Kyushu tournament)	Fukuoka	Wakanohana	12–3

World Wrestling Championships—Freestyle

Year	48 kg	52 kg	57 kg	62 kg	68 kg
1990	A. Martínez (Cuba)	M. Torkan (Iran)	A. Puerto (Cuba)	J. Smith (U.S.)	A. Fadzaev (U.S.S.R.)
1991	V. Orudzhev (U.S.S.R.)	Z. Jones (U.S.)	S. Smal (U.S.S.R.)	J. Smith (U.S.)	A. Fadzaev (U.S.S.R.)
1992	Park Il (N.Kor.)	Li Hak (N.Kor.)	A. Puerto (Cuba)	J. Smith (U.S.)	A. Fadzaev (UT)
1993	A. Vila (Cuba)	V. Jordanov (Bulg.)	Terry Brands (U.S.)	Tom Brands (U.S.)	A.A. Fallah (Iran)
1994	A. Vila (Cuba)	V. Jordanov (Bulg.)	A. Puerto (Cuba)	M. Azizov (Russia)	A. Leipold (Ger.)
1995	**V. Orudzhev (Russia)**	**V. Jordanov (Bulg.)**	**Terry Brands (U.S.)**	**E. Tedeev (Ukr.)**	**A. Gevorkian (Arm.)**
Year	**74 kg**	**82 kg**	**90 kg**	**100 kg**	**130 kg**
1990	R. Sofiyadi (Bulg.)	J. Lohyna (Czech.)	M. Khadartsev (U.S.S.R.)	L. Khabelov (U.S.S.R.)	D. Gobedzhishvili (U.S.S.R.)
1991	A. Khadem (Iran)	K. Jackson (U.S.)	M. Khadartsev (U.S.S.R.)	L. Khabelov (U.S.S.R.)	A. Schroder (Ger.)
1992	Park Jang (S.Kor.)	K. Jackson (U.S.)	M. Khadartsev (UT)	L. Khabelov (UT)	B. Baumgartner (U.S.)
1993	Park Jang (S.Kor.)	S. Ozturk (Tur.)	A. Jadidi (Iran)	L. Khabelov (Russia)	B. Baumgartner (U.S.)
1994	T. Ceylan (Tur.)	L. Jabrailov (Moldova)	R. Khadem (Iran)	A. Sabejey (Ger.)	M. Demir (Tur.)
1995	**B. Saitiev (Russia)**	**K. Jackson (U.S.)**	**R. Khadem (Iran)**	**K. Angle (U.S.)**	**B. Baumgartner (U.S.)**

World Wrestling Championships—Greco-Roman Style

Year	48 kg	52 kg	57 kg	62 kg	68 kg
1990	O. Kucherenko (U.S.S.R.)	A. Ignatenko (U.S.S.R.)	R. Yildiz (Ger.)	M. Oliveras (Cuba)	I. Duguchiyev (U.S.S.R.)
1991	Duk Yong Gooun (S.Kor.)	R. Martínez (Cuba)	R. Yildiz (Ger.)	S. Martynov (U.S.S.R.)	I. Duguchiyev (U.S.S.R.)
1992	O. Kucherenko (UT)	J. Ronningen (Nor.)	An Han Bong (S.Kor.)	A. Pirim (Tur.)	A. Repka (Hung.)
1993	W. Sánchez (Cuba)	R. Martínez (Cuba)	A. Manukjan (Arm.)	S. Martynov (Russia)	I. Duguchiyev (Russia)
1994	W. Sánchez (Cuba)	A. Mkrtchyan (Ger.)	J. Melnichenko (Kazakh.)	S. Martynov (Russia)	I. Duguchiyev (Russia)
1995	**Sim Kwon Ho (S.Kor.)**	**S. Danielane (Russia)**	**D. Hall (U.S.)**	**S. Martynov (Russia)**	**R. Adzhy (Ukr.)**
Year	**74 kg**	**82 kg**	**90 kg**	**100 kg**	**130 kg**
1990	M. Iskandarian (U.S.S.R.)	P. Farcas (Hung.)	M. Bullmann (Ger.)	S. Demiaschkievish (U.S.S.R.)	A. Karelin (U.S.S.R.)
1991	M. Iskandarian (U.S.S.R.)	P. Farcas (Hung.)	M. Bullmann (Ger.)	H. Milian (Cuba)	A. Karelin (U.S.S.R.)
1992	M. Iskandarian (UT)	P. Farcas (Hung.)	M. Bullmann (Ger.)	H. Milian (Cuba)	A. Karelin (UT)
1993	N. Alamanza (Cuba)	M. Yerlikaya (Tur.)	G. Koguchavili (Russia)	M. Ljungberg (Swed.)	A. Karelin (Russia)
1994	M. Iskandarian (Russia)	T. Zander (Ger.)	G. Koguchavili (Russia)	A. Wronski (Pol.)	A. Karelin (Russia)
1995	**Y. Riemer (Fr.)**	**H. Yerlikaya (Tur.)**	**H. Baser (Tur.)**	**M. Ljungberg (Swed.)**	**A. Karelin (Russia)**

Transportation

As the world economy continued to lift slowly out of recession in 1995, transport issues focused on how to provide better and more efficient transport as a means of improving the quality of urban life. This focus reflected several underlying social concerns ranging from the environment to health and personal security. A drive continued for more affordable and cost-effective public transport services, with governments using approaches ranging from automation to privatization. Privatization continued to be a widespread means of raising necessary investment capital through private finance initiatives and served to sustain the renaissance in rail systems begun in the early 1990s. Rail transport operators, among others, desired a "level playing field" in the debate over efficiency for road and rail in both freight and passenger transport accompanied by a move away from road dominance. (JOHN H. EARP)

AVIATION

World airline traffic, both passenger and freight, took off in 1995 to such an extent that a few of the bigger carriers, while awaiting the arrival of a new generation of high-capacity aircraft, had to turn away some business. The first major airport to be completed in the U.S. in 21 years—Denver (Colo.) International Airport—opened in February, late and over budget. Macao's new airport was expected to open by year-end. The French authorities reopened Paris' Orly airport to additional international competition in January and announced that a site was being sought for a third airport in the Paris area.

According to the International Civil Aviation Organization (ICAO), the UN aviation body, total scheduled passenger traffic rose 6% in 1995 and was projected to go up by a further 7% in both 1996 and 1997. Airlines in the Asia-Pacific area, spurred by high economic growth, were expected to show the largest gains, although below the impressive 12% that they recorded in 1994.

Passenger traffic of African and North American airlines showed rising trends, but the total volume was expected to be below the world average throughout the forecast period. European airlines showed steadily improving growth as a result of increasingly competitive market conditions within the European Union and the stabilization of aviation markets in the Commonwealth of Independent States. The ICAO projected that Latin-American and Caribbean airlines would improve their traffic growth and approach the world average. Growth among airlines in the Middle East was expected to remain close to the world average. Estimates from the airlines' trade body, the International Air Transport Association, generally confirmed the ICAO's projections.

Boeing's new 400-plus-seat, twin-engine 777 airliner entered service during 1995. The 777, together with the wide-bodied A330 and A340, the newest models from the European Airbus Industrie consortium began to relieve some traffic pressure on airlines. As jet engines became increasingly reliable, flights became longer, with 12-hour sectors now commonplace between Europe and the Far East and between the east coast of North America and Asia.

The problem of how to occupy their customers (and how to expand revenues) on such lengthy flights came close to solution for the airlines with the advent of a new generation of electronic in-flight entertainment. Using small video screens in the seat backs, passengers were able to view (and pay for) movies, shop for items on display, or play gambling games such as poker, roulette, and dice. Vendors promised the airlines that income from each wide-bodied airliner so equipped could be as high as $2 million a year.

Looking beyond the new 400-seat aircraft, airlines continued to study the future economic, financial, and logistic implications of a proposed "super-jumbo" family of double-deck airliners with 600, 700, and even 1,000 seats. Such a project between the U.S. and four European nations was put on hold during 1995 on the grounds that although technically feasible, there was insufficient interest among the airlines. Nonetheless, Airbus Industrie continued with

JIM LEYNSE—SABA

The interior of the terminal building at the new Denver (Colo.) International Airport reflects the structure's striking design. The nation's largest airport, the first of consequence to be built in the U.S. in 21 years, opened 16 months late and subsequently over its construction budget.

designs for its 600-seat project, the A3XX. At the same time, the major world aircraft manufacturers were exploring the possibility of developing a 250-seat supersonic airliner to succeed the Concorde sometime in the first decade of the 21st century.

In other technological developments, the first operational use of navigation via satellite took place in the South Pacific in 1995. "Free flight," a concept that would allow crews of individual aircraft to select the most economic flight paths with minimal contact with air traffic control, was under intense review.

Increasing freedom in the air was not matched on the ground. The industry complained bitterly about skyrocketing ticket and airport taxes at 1,000 facilities—double the number in 1989. Total charges paid by airlines for using airports and navigation facilities increased to $9.9 billion—9% of operating costs—and constituted the second largest expense after fuel. (ARTHUR REED)

SHIPPING AND PORTS

The world shipping fleet continued to show a steady growth. In 1994 total size stood at 475.9 million gross tons (gt), an annual increase of 17.9 million gt—the largest in at least 10 years. Traffic increased as well, and in January 1995, partly because of an overhaul of the locks, Panama Canal officials reported the worst bottleneck in the canal's history, with delays in transit averaging a week. Normally 35 ships could pass through the facility in a day.

Much concern continued over the increasing age of the world fleet. At the start of 1995, about 58.4% (49.8% of total deadweight tons [dwt]) was over 14 years old, and the average age of the world fleet was 17.3 years. Important new measures from the UN's International Maritime Organization (IMO) to improve the safety of existing oil tankers came into operation on July 6. These included an enhanced program of inspections applying to all oil tankers aged five years and older and changes to the construction requirements of tankers aged 25 years and older, including mandatory fitting of double hulls or an equivalent design. The IMO also set up a panel of experts after the sinking of the "roll-on, roll-off" ferry *Estonia* in the Baltic Sea in September 1994, but the London-based organization received criticism from many quarters throughout 1995 for moving too timidly and too slowly on the issue of ferry safety. Following the June council meeting of the International Association of Classification Societies, details were released of a program to reinforce member societies' increasingly tough stance on safety compliance. The program included further tightening of the Transfer of Class Agreement, greater transparency of class and statutory information, and automatic suspension of class under specific circumstances.

The first ship bearing Green Award certification, the 254,000-dwt *Ambon,* owned by ICB Shipping of Sweden, called at the port of Rotterdam, Neth. The Green Award scheme was an initiative of the Rotterdam Municipal Port Management in conjunction with the Dutch Ministry of Transport to promote safe and environmentally friendly ship and crew management. Aimed at oil tankers larger than 50,000 dwt, the scheme rewarded certificated ships with a reduction in port fees.

In Russia a change of port-construction priorities halted plans to build three new ports on the Baltic until the port of St. Petersburg had been completely rebuilt. Handling capacity of the modernized port was planned to increase from 21 million to 40 million tons. The three new ports were to have been built on the Gulf of Finland at Ust-Luga, Batareynaya, and Primorsk. The Russians' goal was to have northwestern ports with an annual capacity of 70 million tons.

In The Bahamas an $80 million deal for a container transshipment facility in Freeport Harbour was signed between Grand Bahama Development Co. and Hutchinson International Holdings. It was the largest investment in Freeport since the building of an oil refinery in 1960. In August the government of Sri Lanka awarded a $720 million contract to a U.K.-Chinese consortium to build a new port at Galle, 112 km (70 mi) south of Colombo. In the same month, Vietnam approved in principle plans for a $560 million deep-sea port and industrial zone near Haiphong, in the north of the country. (EDWARD CROWLEY)

FREIGHT AND PIPELINES

Worldwide freight volumes, as reflected by container movements, showed modest rises in 1995, while the busiest activity continued to be in the Pacific Rim. Singapore, which began restructuring for outright privatization, and Hong Kong retained their status as the busiest ports. Both ports were above the level of 10 million TEU (20-ft equivalent units) per annum. Linked to this was growth in China of container crane and container manufacturing. Penang, Malaysia, embarked on a major capital expenditure to cope with an annual growth of 16% over the previous eight years, and Manila developed new intermodal freight services. Intermodalism, which was pioneered in Europe, continued to gather strength. A Pan-European Transport System initiative was promoted by the European Union to facilitate trade and economic development, with a focus on maintaining the balance of road, rail, and waterway traffic in Eastern Europe and avoiding domination by road transport. In the U.S., rapid growth in intermodal trade had put a great strain on service reliability. This led to plans for the development of new "mega terminals" in six U.S. West Coast ports and might prompt a decline in medium-sized container ports.

Pipeline construction was down by 5% in 1995. Decline in the U.S. was linked to the cost of meeting environmental, safety, and regulatory mandates, while Russian recession and political upheaval reduced activity. Nonetheless, in Europe and especially the Far East, new long-distance natural gas networks spurred ambitious new programs. In the U.S. natural gas schemes prevailed. Of significance were expansions in California, with 1,489 km (1 km = 0.62 mi) of pipeline laid, and a 604-km line from Malin, Ore., to Reno, Nev. In Europe the focus of gas-line construction was in the North Sea and Spain. Plans were made to lay dual 122 cm (40-in) pipes across the Baydarata Bay as part of the development of the Yamal Peninsula in Siberia. Oman planned a 1,135-km crossing of the Arabian Sea, while Australia went ahead with a 1,400-km 20.3-cm (8-in) ethane line from Moomba to Botany. Other major developments included a start on phase three of the 645-km line extension to Bukit Ketei, Malaysia, and major gas lines in South Korea, the Philippines, Taiwan, and China. In South America there were plans to link Bolivia with Brazil and to construct a 1,200-km main line from Argentina to Chile.

ROADS AND TRAFFIC

Priority for improvement and extension of road networks varied considerably around the world in 1995, depending largely upon degrees of motorization, urbanization, and economic development. Members of the Organisation for Economic Co-operation and Development were concerned with the dominance of road transport, which threatened environmental gains made by improved emission standards. The use of unleaded gasoline (petrol) in the European Union rose to 60% in 1994, with Austria, Finland, and Sweden recording 99%. Emissions from diesel engines were recognized as a health hazard.

In Stockholm 12 km of a 14-km ring road were constructed as a tunnel for environmental reasons, although urban tunneling projects were usually used to overcome key natural obstacles. The $500 million immersed tube linking Kobe, Japan, with Port Island, the $32 million Preveza-Aktio tunnel in Greece, and the $554 million Elbe Tunnel in Hamburg, Germany, all began construction during 1995. In the U.K. local authorities sought to provide a second crossing to the River Tyne, and authorities in Sydney, Australia, planned a $120 million double-decked tunnel in the downtown area. In Seoul, South Korea, the twin 1.8-km pilot tunnels for the Bukak road project were completed.

Development of key national links were typified by plans to build a 6.8-km tunnel to connect Magerøy, an island off of Norway, to the mainland. In the U.S. plans were in place to expand the Chesapeake Bay Bridge–Tunnel, which at 28 km was still one of the longest crossings in the world. Funding was in hand for the $67 million, 33-km Lakhdaria-Bouria section of the trans-Algerian motorway, while in Bolivia there were plans for a 50-km Cotapata–Santa Barbara road link to the Pacific. The most ambitious project was a 30-year, 35,000-km motorway network in China, which included a section of the "Silk Road" project that would connect the Middle East and Europe.

Authorities in Germany were reviewing plans to enhance urban pedestrian movement with the construction of a people mover system to link metro stations in Düsseldorf, Germany, while Singapore examined similar schemes for improving access to its metro.

INTERCITY RAIL

In addition to privatization initiatives, many of the world's railways underwent significant restructuring as part of a search for increased productivity in 1995. In the U.S. this took the form of cooperation between rail operators, while in Europe the movement was toward a divestment of responsibilities from governments to private operators and greater access to networks. Automation, BOT (build, own/operate, transfer) schemes, and privatization were thought to open the way for sustaining investment in railways. Some 30 countries had privatization programs, ranging from total sell-off (Brazil, Britain, the Czech Republic, and New Zealand) to more modest goals involving commercial operations (Austria, Finland) or maintenance services (Mexico). Overnight services were reintroduced, and security became an important issue with the derailment by sabotage of an Amtrak passenger train in Arizona. High speed trains (HST) remained the flagship service of many operators. Sweden introduced 250-km/h trains from Södertälje to Stockholm, and an extension of the European network was spearheaded by the new Thalys system linking Paris, Brussels, and Cologne, Germany. Italy started a Rome-to-Naples service, and both Russia and South Korea began studying high-speed systems with private investment. China opened two sections of a 1,300-km rail link from Beijing to Kowloon, Hong Kong, which was intended eventually to utilize HST units.

Increased speed was the main concern for both a new express diesel TGV (Train à Grande Vitesse) and a new 360 km/h prototype in France. Gas turbine vehicles were reconsidered in the U.S. in order for emissions standards to be met. Tilting trains, which provided enhanced performance, were introduced in New South Wales and Brisbane, Australia; Finland; and Switzerland. Extra capacity was provided by double-decked rolling stock in Russia, The Netherlands, and Italy. In the U.S., triple loading of containers was tested, while automation of train-control networks scaled new heights with a 37,350-route kilometre system controlled from Fort Worth, Texas.

Officials watch as an experimental 300X bullet train is prepared for a test run at Nagoya, in central Japan. Developed by Central Japan Railway, the new-generation train was designed to travel at a maximum speed of 350 km (220 mi) an hour.

KYODO—REUTERS

Iran opened the 635-km link from Bandar Abbas to Bafq, and the 248-km line for grain shipments in Brazil reached Cascavel. South Africa proposed a major rehabilitation of its Metro Rail system. The opening of the Sarnia Tunnel under the St. Clair River in Canada, the 6.5-km Karbube Kowkan tunnel in India, and the 6.3-km Grauholz Tunnel for Swiss Federal Railways were other noteworthy achievements during 1995.

URBAN MASS TRANSIT

Cities showed an ever-greater interest in efficient, affordable, and environmentally acceptable mass transit systems in 1995, which continued to open the way for profound changes in urban mobility. Many rail lines were converted to metros (as in Oslo, Norway), and metro networks were upgraded or extended in many areas. Almost without exception, new metros were more likely to be based on light rail transit (LRT) and to include elements of automation in train control or ticketing. Smartcard ticketing systems were on trial in London, Paris, and Sydney, Australia.

New metro systems opened during the year in Lima, Peru; Bilbao, Spain; Shanghai; Sheffield, England; and Mexico City, where the fastest-growing metro in the world opened a 10th line. Extensions to metros were opened in Madrid; San Diego, Calif.; and Prague. Many other cities were planning and building metro extensions, including Boston; Cairo; Istanbul; Nagoya, Japan; Nantes, France; Rio de Janeiro; and Toronto. The bulk of urban transit expansion was provided through LRT schemes in both less developed countries and traditional locations, however. Of note were the automated schemes proposed for Turin, Italy, a privatized system for Auckland, N.Z., and a dual-mode (heavy rail/LRT) system in Saarbrücken, Germany.

Urban transit connections to airports continued to proliferate, with structures either under construction or planned in Berlin; Bangkok, Thailand; Hong Kong; Madrid; Pusan, South Korea; Osaka, Japan; San Francisco; and Sydney. The Arlanda Airport at Stockholm was a BOM (build, operate, and maintain) project. Improvements in buses, which provided the backbone for most urban services, were mainly expansions of fleets to meet higher environmental standards or the restructuring of services to link existing lines to new LRT services. (JOHN H. EARP)

See also Architecture and Civil Engineering; Business and Industry Review: *Aerospace; Automobiles; Energy;* The Environment.
This article updates the *Macropædia* article TRANSPORTATION.

World Affairs

The crosscurrents of peace and war, of both agreement and conflict, were as much in appearance in 1995 as they had been in 1994, and it was impossible to say with certainty which of the two trends was prevailing in world politics. The agreement concluded in 1994 between the United States and North Korea concerning nuclear reactors was implemented during 1995. In May 1995, for the first time in 23 years, representatives of the British government met leaders of the Irish Republican Army in an attempt to find a solution to a conflict that had claimed thousands of victims over two decades. In March the Syrian government made it known that it would establish relations with Israel if the Golan Heights was restored to its sovereignty. More important, on September 28 in Washington, D.C., Palestinian and Israeli leaders signed an accord that scheduled an end to Israeli occupation of the main urban centres of the West Bank by March 1996. It was not clear what effect the assassination of Israel's prime minister, Yitzhak Rabin (*see* OBITUARIES), would have on the continuation of the peace process. Even in former Yugoslavia a cease-fire came into being in October that effectively split Bosnia and Herzegovina more or less equally between the existing Bosnian Serbs and the Bosnian government. The cease-fire followed intensification of the civil war, a Croatian offensive in the Slavonia region and in northern Bosnia, and, for the first time, NATO bombing of the Bosnian Serbs in an attempt to end their shelling of Sarajevo and to compel them to withdraw their heavy weapons from the area.

Encouraging as such developments were, there was universal agreement that the road to peace in all these conflicts was still long and that even the achievements already gained were not secure and could be undone by the enemies of peace. Particularly in former Yugoslavia there still was danger that ethnic conflicts could turn into war between states that might involve countries that had previously stayed out of the conflict. Furthermore, old conflicts continued, such as the fighting between Hutu and Tutsi in Rwanda and Burundi in February and March, which led to a new exodus and thousands of victims. Also in March Turkish forces crossed the Iraqi border and in the course of a two-month campaign battled the Kurdish separatists who had launched guerrilla attacks from bases there.

Worldwide attention was drawn to the Russian invasion of Chechnya in December 1994; fighting in the northern Caucasus lasted throughout 1995—despite a cease-fire ordered by Pres. Boris Yeltsin in June—and revealed surprising weaknesses in the morale, organization, and effectiveness of the Russian military units. The list of armed conflicts in 1995 was long; it included a war in January between Peru and Ecuador over the demarcation of their state borders, fighting between governments and nationalist separatists (as in Jammu and Kashmir), attacks by religious fanatics (in Algeria, Egypt, and Pakistan), and terrorist actions, both national and international, in the course of which sarin, a highly poisonous gas, was used by Japanese terrorists in an attack in the Tokyo subway in March.

The United Nations played no role in the settlement of any of these conflicts except for an ineffectual one in former Yugoslavia. There was no progress on the road toward the establishment of an armed intervention force there, as Boutros Boutros-Ghali, the UN secretary-general, had demanded since 1992. This failure to act decisively in the Balkans further deepened the crisis of the UN, perpetuating its status as an organization without teeth, incapable of taking decisive action.

A certain deterioration in the international climate was also felt in the relations between the great powers. China ignored appeals to improve its human rights record; it increased pressure on Taiwan and other neighbours, and relations with the United States were bedeviled by the Chinese reluctance to abide by copyright and other international trade conventions. The United States reacted by imposing temporary trade sanctions and, at the same time, practicing political appeasement. French nuclear tests in the South Pacific created worldwide protests, and anti-Western feelings in Russia spread markedly during the year. The latter development was connected in part with Western initiatives to expand NATO into Eastern Europe, a policy regarded in Moscow as a threat to Russian national security even though Russia had also been invited to join and, in any case, only a loose association had been envisaged. Generally speaking, a trend toward nationalism and populism could be observed in Russia as in Eastern Europe. The West was held responsible for the economic, social, and political failures of recent years, and there was even nostalgia for the past, in which order had prevailed and prices had been stable. The number of those who had materially benefited from reform was relatively small, which led to a backlash bound to manifest itself also in the field of foreign relations.

Further tension was generated by the willingness of major nations to supply the technology of arms of mass destruction to rogue countries building up their arsenals to attack or, at the very least, to threaten and blackmail their neighbours. As a result of the defection of two key members of Pres. Saddam Hussein's inner circle, it became known that Iraqi preparations in this direction had been much further advanced than had been anticipated even by confirmed pessimists, and the Iranian nuclear buildup continued with undiminished speed. In Europe and North America the preoccupation with domestic affairs took pride of place, on the basis of the assumption that with all the conflicts occurring, the danger to world peace was now less than in previous decades. The assumption was correct inasmuch as military spending had declined in all major nations. It was wrong, however, in the sense that the absence of international controls made the approach of an age of conflict fought with unconventional weapons even more certain. This view also overrated the extent of international, social, and economic stability. In fact, the world order remained highly vulnerable on all levels, from the disorder of money markets and the weaknesses of many currencies and central banks to growing mass unemployment, not only in countries where it had long been endemic, as in Africa and the Middle East, but also elsewhere. Unemployment among young persons under age 25 was, with few exceptions, in the 20–30% range even in Europe, a grave portent not just for social stability but, in the long run, also for the European political and social system and for international affairs.

A worldwide trend toward democratic systems or at least away from dictatorship had been noted in the late 1980s and early 1990s. By late 1995 this trend seemed to have come to a halt in various countries, including France, Italy, and Austria, as well as in Eastern Europe and the states of the former Soviet Union, where authoritarian parties polled more votes than before. In the Middle East religious fundamentalists preached that democracy was an abomination. There was no clear trend that could be defined as either left-wing or right-wing, rather only a feeling of discontent directed against the incumbents, be they conservatives in Britain or Socialists in France and Spain, to give but examples. The discontent was directed against a political system that provided neither economic nor political security; participation in grassroots politics and in elections declined in most parts of the world, and separatism, another frequent phenomenon in recent years, led to demands for strengthening central state power. These were primarily developments witnessed on the domestic scene, but they also were bound to affect relations between nations. The feeling of discontent led to a search for scapegoats, more likely than not to be found among minorities and foreigners. Aggressive nationalism was likely to trigger conflicts not only at home but also between states. At the very least, this negative mood was making cooperation between nations more difficult, and the movement toward greater unity, in Europe as elsewhere, came to a standstill. (WALTER LAQUEUR)

This article updates the *Macropædia* article 20th-Century INTERNATIONAL RELATIONS.

UNITED NATIONS

Anniversaries. Fiftieth-anniversary celebrations for the United Nations were somewhat muted. In San Francisco on June 26, only two heads of state (U.S. Pres. Bill Clinton and Poland's Pres. Lech Walesa) celebrated the signing of the UN Charter there in 1945. Clinton's address was anything but celebratory; he advised the UN to trim its "bloated" bureaucracy and refocus its missions lest "new isolationists" force the U.S. to withdraw from the organization. Others, too, considered the UN overstretched, lacking modern management practices and clear priorities. While developed countries recommended curtailing UN operations, however, less developed countries wanted them expanded.

Secretary-General Boutros Boutros-Ghali's message was not cheering either; he warned that the UN was going broke. By October 1995 member states owed the UN $3.7 billion; the U.S. was the most delinquent ($1,255,000,000 in arrears on October 20). Earlier, Canada's Prime Minister Jean Chrétien complained, "We are growing tired of UN-bashing, and it is especially irritating when it comes from those . . . not paying their bills." Britain's Foreign Secretary Malcolm Rifkind (*see* BIOGRAPHIES) on October 2 objected that the U.S. enjoyed "representation without taxation." International tribunals established to prosecute charges of genocide and war crimes in Rwanda and the Balkans were partially crippled by shortages of funds. Even efforts at reform slowed because the organization could not afford to bring experts together to recommend changes. The UN stayed afloat only by borrowing from peacekeeping budgets $125 million for general purposes.

On the other hand, on June 26 in London, Britain's Queen Elizabeth II called the UN "one of the most remarkable outcomes of the Second World War." Other UN defenders insisted that critics had lost all sense of proportion, given that the $2.5 billion UN budget for the whole world was less than Americans spend annually at barbershops, beauty parlours, and health clubs. UN expenses amounted to $2 per person, in contrast to the $150 per capita governments spent on their military machines. On October 26 Karl T. Paschke, undersecretary-general for UN internal oversight services, conceded that waste existed but that he had "not

Fourth World Conference on Women

Women from 185 countries convened in Beijing on Sept. 4, 1995, for the Fourth World Conference on Women. Among the prominent personalities in attendance were Pakistan's Prime Minister Benazir Bhutto and U.S. first lady Hillary Rodham Clinton, who delivered a stirring (and controversial) speech on September 5. The assembly agreed on a "platform for action" at the close of the conference on September 15.

The platform's preamble called for improvements in the economic circumstances of women, protection from increasing levels of violence, and improvements in the status of girls; it also urged states to take steps to achieve these goals. The document aimed at empowering women by ensuring that they enjoyed all human rights and fundamental freedoms.

The conferees sought to ensure "women's equal access to economic resources including land, credit, science and technology, vocational training, information, communication and markets" as ways of further advancing and empowering women and girls. The document asserted that women have the right to decide freely all matters relating to their sexuality and childbearing and condemned forced abortions and sterilizations. Abhorring "ethnic cleansing" in Rwanda and former Yugoslavia, it characterized the systematic rape of women in wartime as criminal and called for perpetrators to be tried as war criminals. It recognized domestic violence as a worldwide problem and censured domestic battering, sexual harassment at work, genital mutilation of girls, and attacks on women with small dowries.

The platform claimed that girls are discriminated against throughout the world, often before birth in cultures where more value is placed on boys, and it censured such practices. It called upon governments and international lending institutions to support banking services and credit facilities for low-income women. Governments were urged to guarantee women equal rights with men to inherit, even if they may not inherit the same amount as men.

The declaration called for strengthening, protecting, and supporting the family as the basic unit of society. Acknowledging various forms of family in different cultural, political, and social systems, it insisted that whatever the form, women must not suffer discrimination just because they are mothers. Efforts to bar discrimination based on "sexual orientation" failed to achieve a consensus because of objections by more than 30 national delegations. The conferees also failed to obtain sizable financial commitments from governments to pay for new programs for women, but they did elicit official pledges to redirect funds already appropriated. The document did not bind countries to action but gave the issues new visibility and served as a model for national policy makers. The conference asked the UN secretary-general to appoint an undersecretary-general for women's issues, but some feared that such a post might be politically vulnerable and face overpowering resistance from UN member nations.

China had intended to enjoy the prestige of being the conference host, but its heavy-handed and oppressive "security measures" against the delegates and the press and pro-democracy and human rights campaigners called attention to the least attractive aspects of Chinese society. Many delegates were offended by China's exiling nongovernmental organization representatives to an inadequate site about 50 km (30 mi) from the main conference. (RICHARD N. SWIFT) found the UN . . . more corrupt . . . than any other comparable public organization."

Celebrations in New York City marking the 50th anniversary of the Charter's taking effect (Oct. 24, 1945) were more festive. Before they began, Pope John Paul II on October 5 urged the UN to serve as a model "family of nations," with rich, strong countries looking after the interests of weaker, more vulnerable ones. Even some of the more than 140 heads of state and heads of government who attended the official celebrations spoke kind words. Clinton praised the UN on October 22 for nourishing once-starving children, immunizing them against diseases, educating students, sustaining the environment, saving refugees, and, in some areas, preserving peace and promoting human rights. Others noted that the UN was able to withdraw its Observer Mission in El Salvador on April 28 after having helped heal the violence and divisions of 12 years of civil war. Heads of state also hailed UN specialized agencies for having eliminated smallpox and acknowledged that the now inactive Trusteeship Council had speeded decolonization.

Former Yugoslavia. Much of the disillusion with the UN had arisen from the failure of the UN Protection Force (UNPROFOR) to "keep" a peace that never existed in former Yugoslavia. As Clinton emphasized in San Francisco, however, the fault lay in asking the "Blue Helmets" to "undertake missions they cannot be expected to handle [and] . . . to work miracles while [states were] denying them the military and political support required and the modern command-and-control systems they need."

In response to Croatia's demands, the Security Council reduced the number of UN forces there from over 13,000 on March 31 to 2,500 on November 15 and reconstituted them as the UN Confidence Restoration Operation in Croatia. It also restricted UNPROFOR to Bosnia and Herzegovina and restructured its units in the former Yugoslav Republic of Macedonia as the UN Preventive Deployment Force. Because UN forces never received the mandate, weapons, or political backing to contain the combatants, they were unable in May to prevent Bosnian Serbs from seizing over 300 peacekeepers to use as "human shields" against NATO air strikes near Pale; were incapable in July, despite NATO air strikes, to defend Srebrenica and Zepa, "safe areas" established to protect Muslim communities in Bosnia; failed to keep a steady movement of supplies into Sarajevo or to keep control of the heavy weapons around the city; and could not stop "ethnic cleansing." When Bosnian Serbs stormed Srebrenica on July 11, they allegedly perpetrated the worst war crimes in Europe since World War II, summarily killing 6,000 people, mostly Muslims. On July 27, to protest the failure to halt these atrocities and the international acceptance of the occupation of the safe areas, Tadeusz Mazowiecki resigned as UN chief investigator in former Yugoslavia. He accused the UN of hypocrisy in claiming to defend Bosnia while actually abandoning it.

Acknowledging UN failures, the secretary-general gradually disengaged the UN from Bosnia. In Vienna on March 2, he foresaw the need to "contract out" peacekeeping operations to regional organizations or to multinational forces led by states with special interests in the disputes, like the 1994 operations by France in Rwanda and by the U.S. in Haiti. (UN peacekeepers would remain in Haiti until February 1996, after the next Haitian president was scheduled to be inaugurated.) On May 31 Boutros-Ghali suggested that the Security Council replace UN troops with multinational military forces commanded by officers from nations contributing troops. On July 26 he relinquished his authority over NATO air attacks in Bosnia to ground commanders. On November 1 he replaced Yasushi Akashi, his special envoy in the region, with Undersecretary-General Kofi Annan, who also became special envoy to NATO. The UN began on October 5 to scale down its troops from 30,500 to 21,000, partly because of the fiscal crisis and as the first move to transfer authority to NATO. Russia charged that employing NATO illegally bypassed the Security Council.

On July 25 the International War Crimes Tribunal for the Former Yugoslavia, meeting at The Hague, indicted Radovan Karadzic, the Bosnian Serb leader, and Ratko Mladic, the Bosnian Serb military commander, as war criminals. On November 9 it indicted three senior officers in Serbia's army, suggesting that indictments were moving closer to the Serbian political leadership, perhaps even to Pres. Slobodan Milosevic himself. On November 13 the tribunal charged six Bosnian Croat leaders with war crimes and crimes against humanity in connection with scores of civilian deaths and the burning of whole villages in central Bosnia. The indictments subjected those named to arrest, prosecution, and punishment anywhere in the world. Only one Serbian alleged war criminal was in custody; the tribunal held preliminary hearings on his case on April 26.

Under UN and U.S. pressure, Balkan leaders began peace talks in Dayton, Ohio, on November 1 and signed a treaty in Paris on December 14. On November 12 secessionist Serbs in Croatia agreed to give up eastern Slavonia to Croatia over two years. The Security Council was to establish a "transitional administration" there and would deploy an international force to maintain peace and security. The Security Council officially transferred its peacekeeping authority to a NATO-led force on December 20. Judge Richard Goldstone, chief prosecutor for the Yugoslav War Crimes Tribunal, warned on November 14 against any peace deal that shielded suspected war criminals from trial. UN refugee authorities began planning to help some three million people displaced by the Yugoslav wars to return home.

Iraq. The Security Council extended trade sanctions against Iraq several times. On October 13 Rolf Ekeus, head of the Special Commission charged with eliminating Iraq's ballistic, chemical, and biological weapons, reported that Iraq was still withholding many details about its military programs. Former Iraqi weapons chief Lieut. Gen. Hussein Kamel Hassan, Iraqi Pres. Saddam Hussein's son-in-law, defected to Jordan in August and revealed that Iraq had an ambitious biological and nuclear weapons program, contradicting Hussein's claims in July that Iraq had abandoned the program. On July 16 Iraq pardoned and released two Americans jailed four months earlier (March 13) for having crossed illegally from Kuwait through a UN checkpoint into Iraq, and Hussein suggested relief from sanctions as a quid pro quo. Council members refused, however, insisting that Iraq first had to cooperate fully with UN weapons monitors.

Africa. In Rwanda, Burundi, Somalia, Liberia, and Angola, the UN continued trying to contain civil wars and to prevent genocide. Zaire found itself sheltering over one million refugees from the Rwandan and Burundian civil wars. In February its troops, at the UN's request, started restoring order in UN refugee camps, but on August 19 it began forcibly repatriating refugees to Rwanda. Zairean officials considered a Security Council resolution of August 17 lifting the arms embargo on Rwanda as a security threat; they also accused the refugees of being sources of pestilence and disease and devastators of the environment.

The UN High Commissioner for Refugees, Sadako Ogata, who originally had welcomed Zairean troops to the refugee camps, condemned the forcible repatriations for flouting Article 33 of the International Convention on the Status of Refugees and flew to Zaire on August 30 to try to restore voluntary repatriations. UN officials, attempting to count and document expelled refugees before taking them to Rwandan transit camps, said that 85,000 had fled into the bush and to the hills to escape possible repatriation. The Zairean government allowed the UN to continue voluntary repatriations but threatened on August 29 to resume expelling refugees in 1996 if UN efforts failed. After Rwanda assured the Security Council that it could protect its own citizens without the help of UN troops, the Council on June 9 decided to reduce the numbers of UN troops there in stages from 5,600 to 1,800 by year's end. Voluntary repatriation received a setback in mid-September, late October, and early November when Rwandan forces killed Hutu civilians and military forces, confirming some refugees' beliefs that they could not return safely. An agreement brokered by former U.S. president Jimmy Carter in November appeared to end the threat of further compulsory expulsions, and UN forces agreed to stay into early 1996 to assist with repatriations.

A Security Council mission to Burundi in February called the political and security situation there "potentially explosive." It recommended establishing an unbiased judicial system, training impartial civilian police and investigators, and establishing sound provincial governments. Its fears were confirmed when ethnic killings in March caused thousands to flee. The Security Council on March 29 warned that Burundi extremists could face war crimes trials.

UN peacekeepers completed their withdrawal from Somalia on March 2 protected by "United Shield" forces from seven countries, but more than 50 international staff members from UN agencies and other international aid groups remained to manage (along with more than 800 Somali staff members) operations in 14 regions of the country. The Security Council voted unanimously on February 8 to send 7,000 peacekeepers to Angola, the largest African operation since the one to Somalia in 1993. Their mission was to preserve the cease-fire there, improve access for humanitarian assistance, restore peace, and achieve national reconciliation. The UN Observer Mission in Liberia, established in 1993, continued monitoring Liberian attempts to constitute a Council of State as provided by the Accra Agreement of Dec. 21, 1994, but fighting once again broke out on Dec. 31, 1995.

Arms. UN efforts to halt the spread of land mines, which killed or maimed over 20,000 people annually, foundered in Vienna on October 12 on resistance from China, India, Iran, Pakistan, and Russia. These countries, which manufactured the weapons, refused to accept restrictions that were acceptable to nearly 40 other countries reviewing a 1980 convention on weapons deemed indiscriminate or excessively injurious. The UN estimated that 110 million land mines remained buried in 64 countries, and a three-day International Meeting on Mine Clearance, held on July 5–8 in Geneva, undertook to raise $75 million to begin removing them. The next day the Vienna conferees adopted a new protocol prohibiting laser weapons designed to blind the enemy. More than 170 nations agreed on May 11, after four weeks of often bitter debate in New York City, to extend in perpetuity the Nuclear Non-proliferation Treaty, which had limited the spread of nuclear weapons for 25 years.

Environment. The UN World Meteorological Organization warned on September 12 that the biggest hole (10 million sq km [3,860,000 sq mi], an area nearly the size of Europe) ever measured in the Earth's protective ozone layer had formed over Antarctica. The UN Intergovernmental Panel on Climate Change reported in September that climatic changes were likely to cause widespread economic, social, and environmental dislocations over the next century if the world did not reduce emissions of heat-trapping gases. A UN-sponsored fishing conference of 99 states on August 4 adopted by consensus an agreement regulating fishing for many threatened species. It would enter into force when ratified by 30 countries. (RICHARD N. SWIFT)

This article updates the *Macropædia* article UNITED NATIONS.

COMMONWEALTH OF NATIONS

One of the most dramatic Commonwealth Heads of Government Meetings (CHOGM) for many years was held in New Zealand on Nov. 10–13, 1995. During the meeting the leaders voted to suspend Nigeria from membership of the Commonwealth for gross abuse of human rights and violation of the principles set out in the Harare Declaration of 1991.

Within hours of the meeting's opening, the Nigerian military government headed by Gen. Sani Abacha executed nine men, including Ken Saro-Wiwa, an author, environmentalist, and champion of the Ogoni people in eastern Nigeria. (*See* OBITUARIES.) The Commonwealth leaders convening in Auckland immediately adopted rules that would mean the expulsion of Nigeria from the Commonwealth if it did not release political prisoners and return the country to civilian rule within two years.

Such rules were to be applied to other countries that flagrantly breached the Harare principles, under which members committed themselves to just and honest government, democracy, and protection of human rights. The Commonwealth thus became the first international organization to set out such a program of self-discipline. The adopted plan of action described steps to be taken in the event of an unconstitutional overthrow of a democratically elected government. A group of foreign ministers from eight countries—Britain, Canada, Ghana, Jamaica, Malaysia, New Zealand, South Africa, and Zimbabwe—was set up to deal with "serious or persistent violations" of the principles and to recommend collective Commonwealth action. Other measures would provide advice, training, and other technical assistance to governments on such matters as voter education and the promotion of the independence of the judiciary. It was agreed that the 1991 declaration had to be seen as more than mere rhetoric; the Auckland summit gave the Commonwealth the power to act.

For Nigeria suspension meant it could no longer attend intergovernmental meetings or receive documentation and technical assistance. Its flag would not fly on Commonwealth occasions. The Commonwealth secretary-general, Chief Emeka Anyaoku, who was himself a Nigerian, remained in place, having been elected to serve until 1999. During the year he spoke out against the Abacha regime several times and made efforts to secure the release of Nigerian political prisoners, to no avail.

The summit also condemned French nuclear testing in the South Pacific, which had angered most Commonwealth countries. British Prime Minister John Major dissociated himself from criticism of the French action. The Auckland summit was notable for the presence of South African Pres. Nelson Mandela, attending his first CHOGM.

In 1995 Commonwealth membership rose to 53 countries. On November 1, Cameroon became a member following the dispatch of a mission to assess whether it fulfilled the criteria laid down in the Harare Declaration. At the Auckland summit, in response to strong pressure from South Africa and all the other southern African Commonwealth states, the group agreed to accept Mozambique as a member. This move broke new ground because, unlike all other Commonwealth members, Mozambique, a former Portuguese colony, had no historic connection with the old British Empire. Cameroon, on the other hand, was partly made up of the former British Cameroon. CHOGM also set up an intergovernmental group to decide on criteria for assessing future applications for membership. There had been concern about the effect enlargement could have on the character of the Commonwealth. (DEREK INGRAM)

EUROPEAN UNION

For the European Union (EU), 1995 was a year marked by introspection and internal debate about both its future constitutional development and its role in international affairs. The year began with the formal accession of three new member states—Austria, Finland, and Sweden—bringing the number of EU member states to 15, but it ended on a note of uncertainty about the pace of further European integration and enlargement.

The declared objective of full monetary union and a single European currency by 1999 provided the focus for much of the discussion about future European integration. Uncertainty about the single-currency project was underscored with evidence of the economic difficulties facing a majority of EU member states during 1995. These suggested that several EU countries might not be able to fulfill the economic conditions laid down for participation in the single currency by the 1992 Maastricht Treaty on European union. At a special meeting of EU finance ministers in Valencia, Spain, in September, however, there was broad agreement on a detailed technical strategy for introducing a single currency in stages after January 1999. At the EU summit in Madrid in December, the single currency was formally given a name, the Euro, and the timetable for its introduction was extended to 2002. A final decision on which EU countries would be eligible to participate would be taken in January 1998.

There were disagreements within and between EU countries about the speed with which the EU should open its doors to new member states in Central and Eastern Europe. There was also little agreement about the extent to which any enlargement (to perhaps 30 member states over the next decade or so) should be preceded and balanced by steps toward closer political as well as monetary union.

Many of these issues were due to be resolved in a special conference of the 15 EU governments in 1996 to review the Maastricht Treaty—which laid down the shape of the EU's decision-making institutions and processes. At the summit meeting in Cannes, France, in June, EU heads of government set up a "reflection group" under the presidency of the senior Spanish diplomat, Carlos Westendorp, to prepare for the 1996 intergovernmental conference and to seek a consensus among the key EU governments.

By late summer it was clear that major differences still separated governments about any radical changes in the EU decision-making institutions. At one end of the spectrum, the German government pressed for the introduction of qualified majority voting instead of unanimity for almost all areas of policy, as well as a bigger lawmaking role for the EU Council of Ministers and the directly elected European Parliament. Germany and other supporters of closer integration argued that the EU itself should take more responsibility for some policy areas still being decided by national governments alone. These included foreign and security policy as well as some aspects of immigration, justice, and police cooperation.

At the other end of the spectrum, the British government continued at both summit and ministerial meetings during the year to resist any moves to closer political union. British Prime Minister John Major also repeated his government's refusal to commit itself to taking part in an eventual single European currency even if the U.K. met the economic conditions.

France and a number of other countries found themselves in the middle of the argument about closer European integration. French Pres. Jacques Chirac appeared closer to the British government in resisting stronger powers for the European Parliament, the European Commission, and the European Court of Justice. He also angered his more integration-minded European partners in June when he announced France's temporary withdrawal from a seven-nation agreement to abolish internal frontier controls.

Bilateral summit meetings between Chirac and German Chancellor Helmut Kohl in Strasbourg, France, at the end of June and in Bonn, Germany, during October showed significant French and German agreement about the need for more majority-vote decisions in the EU Council of Ministers and progress to a common European defense system. Meanwhile, in Germany itself Kohl faced increasing domestic opposition to monetary union from those who feared it might involve swapping the strong Deutsche Mark for a less-strong single European currency.

Apart from the 1996 intergovernmental conference, the political agenda of the EU during 1995 was dominated by two more immediate issues: the continuing war in Bosnia and Herzegovina and concern about unemployment and the competitiveness of the European economies. At year's end there was guarded optimism that the war in Bosnia was over as NATO troops began arriving to help carry out peace accords signed in Paris on December 14, but the future role of EU countries in the Balkans was far from clear.

The perceived failure of the EU member states to respond adequately to the challenge of the war in Bosnia was cited by those governments pressing for a stronger European common foreign and security policy. A discussion paper put forward by the European Commission in Brussels in June suggested that after 1996 the EU end its requirement that all decisions be taken only with the unanimous agreement of all 15 governments and take at least some foreign and security policy decisions by majority vote.

During the year there were calls from the Commission and a number of EU governments for European defense to be brought within the decision-making framework of the EU. European defense policy was discussed only in the Western European Union (WEU), the European pillar of NATO, to which not all EU countries belonged.

Disagreements between the United States and its European allies over security issues—most notably over the use of NATO airpower in Bosnia—also influenced the discussion about future European security and defense policy. As the year drew to a close, negotiations were continuing over an agreement under which NATO military resources might be used by the WEU in future European-run security missions.

During the first half of 1995, there was evidence of a sharp recovery in economic growth rates in most EU countries, but the fall in unemployment proved much slower than had been hoped. At the end of the year, there were signs that economic growth and the rate of decline in unemployment were also beginning to slow.

In October the European Commission issued a policy strategy that predicted that unemployment in the 15 EU countries could be halved by the end of the decade. The Commission stressed that this could be achieved only if member states maintained progress toward monetary union and introduced new measures to boost job creation and improve labour market flexibility, but with national governments facing serious difficulty in bringing their budget deficits under control, there were growing doubts about the speed of future reductions in the number of unemployed.

The economic problems of the EU were compounded by the political difficulties faced by many of its member state governments during the year. The fall of the right-wing coalition led by Silvio Berlusconi in Italy and the emergence of a technocratic administration led by Lamberto Dini did not answer all the questions about that country's long-term political future. There were fears that domestic political instability might adversely affect Italy's six-month tenure running the EU presidency during the first half of 1996.

When France took over the rotating EU presidency from Germany at the start of 1995, there were also concerns that the looming French presidential election would complicate the day-to-day running of EU affairs. Indeed, for the first five months of its six-month tenure, the French presidency was prevented from taking any significant political initiative. The flow of legislative business in Brussels, the site for the main EU institutions, almost ground to a halt.

In spite of the striking electoral victory of Chirac and his centre-right allies in May, there were continuing questions about the new French government's attitude to closer European integration. In contrast with his strongly pro-European predecessor, Pres. François Mitterrand, Chirac did not disguise his somewhat more skeptical attitude about closer European political union.

France's decision to launch a series of nuclear tests in the South Pacific led to conflict with other EU governments in the months that followed. These came to a head at informal EU heads of government summits in Cannes during June and in Majorca, Spain, during September in a series of bitter exchanges between Chirac and the prime ministers of Sweden, Denmark, Austria, and The Netherlands, who demanded an immediate end to the tests.

The French government's annual budget, introduced in July, was badly received on international currency markets, where there were renewed predictions that France would not be able to meet its single currency targets for reducing the public spending deficit. After Prime Minister Alain Juppé reshuffled his government in November, he reaffirmed France's intention of reducing its budget deficit to less than 3% of its gross production by the end of 1997, as called for in the Maastricht Treaty.

The Spanish Socialist government, led by Prime Minister Felipe González, which succeeded France in the EU presidency at the end of June, was hit by a series of internal financial and political scandals during the second half of the year. Once it became clear that the government would survive until it had to face a general election in March 1996, the Spanish presidency was able to complete its term with few major problems.

In spite of the internal difficulties facing the EU a growing number of countries announced their desire to join. At the end of October, Latvia followed Cyprus, Malta, Poland, Hungary, Slovakia, Bulgaria, and Romania in delivering its membership application. Slovenia, Estonia, and the Czech Republic were expected to follow suit.

At Cannes the European Council agreed on a development aid budget of some $6.7 billion to help countries in Central and Eastern Europe prepare for eventual EU membership. As the financial cost to the EU of a potential doubling in membership was assessed during 1995, some argued that enlargement might have to be tackled more slowly and in stages over a 10–15-year period. At the Madrid summit in December, however, EU leaders pledged to treat all applicants equally and said some talks could begin as early as 1997.

At the Cannes meeting EU leaders also agreed on an aid budget of about $4.7 billion to assist the EU's economically troubled and increasingly unstable neighbours in the Mediterranean region and elsewhere. A joint partnership for development and security cooperation was agreed to at a summit held in Barcelona, Spain, at the end of November, which brought together the 15 EU states and 11 countries from North Africa and the eastern Mediterranean.

The doubts about the future of the EU inevitably had an impact on the operation of its day-to-day executive—the European Commission. The European Parliament approved former Luxembourg prime minister Jacques Santer as the new Commission president in January, after a narrow vote in his favour. (JOHN PALMER)

COMMONWEALTH OF INDEPENDENT STATES

In 1995 Russia continued its efforts to integrate member states of the Commonwealth of Independent States (CIS). Its appeals were welcomed by Belarus and often by Kazakhstan but were resolutely rebuffed by Ukraine. At a summit meeting in Almaty, Kazakhstan, in February, little progress was made on creating common external borders to be guarded by CIS troops. Russian Pres. Boris Yeltsin expressed his frustration at the slow pace of CIS integration and criticized those states that signed agreements but were very lax in implementing them. He received support from Kazakh Pres. Nursultan Nazarbayev. At a meeting in Minsk, Belarus, in May, Russia and Ukraine clashed over closer ties. Ukraine headed a group of states (including Moldova, Azerbaijan, and Turkmenistan) that refused to sign accords on closer political and military integration. Relations improved somewhat in June after Russia and Ukraine reached an agreement on the division of the Black Sea Fleet. Russia and Belarus signed an agreement that removed all customs barriers. There was also agreement on a customs union between Russia and Kazakhstan, and the Central Asian states had expressed interest in a customs union.

After a meeting of foreign ministers in October to discuss peacekeeping operations, economic cooperation, and joint border security, Russian Foreign Minister Andrey Kozyrev stated that a whole packet of documents on a collective CIS security system had been adopted. The Georgian minister of defense, Varido Nadibaidze, was of the opinion that a CIS military bloc was "inevitable," but Pres. Leonid Kuchma of Ukraine made it clear that Ukraine opposed a "Europe split into two camps" and would not join a CIS bloc. In November, however, agreements were signed on the creation of a joint CIS air defense system and on the integration of certain nonmilitary activities. The rise in organized crime led Gen. Anatoly Kulikov, Russian minister of internal affairs, at a CIS conference in Yerevan, Armenia, in October to propose a CIS Council of Interior Ministers to coordinate the battle with organized crime.

Moscow was widely criticized, especially in the Muslim states, for its ongoing war in Chechnya. In Ankara, Turkey, in October, a conference of Muslim clergy from the CIS and the Balkan states ended with the signing of a declaration advocating the formation of a Eurasian Islamic Council.

After declining in 1992–94, Russia's trade within the CIS began to recover during the first half of 1995; exports rose by 10% and imports by 6%. Russian trade with non-CIS states rose faster, however, so that overall Russian trade with the CIS declined from 25% in 1994 to 23% during the first half of 1995. (MARTIN MCCAULEY)

MULTINATIONAL AND REGIONAL ORGANIZATIONS

The Association of Southeast Asian Nations (ASEAN) met July 24–28, 1995, in Brunei. On July 28 the members (Brunei, Indonesia, Malaysia, the Philippines, Singapore, and Thailand) admitted Vietnam, the first communist nation allowed to join, transforming ASEAN from its original (1967) role as a bulwark against the spread of communism into a more comprehensive cooperative regional organization. Cambodia and Laos attended as official observers, Myanmar (Burma) sat in unofficially. After July 10, when the Yangon government freed imprisoned opposition leader Daw Aung San Suu Kyi, ASEAN considered admitting Myanmar. Association leaders argued that Western tolerance of Bosnian human rights violations had undermined their authority to insist on improved human rights in Myanmar as a precondition for membership. They also believed that ASEAN's policy of "constructive engagement," using trade, investment, and political contacts, had opened Myanmar to outside influences. ASEAN was working to establish a common market by 2003 by phasing in tariff reductions and promoting growth around the region. (Vietnam would be allowed to phase in tariff reductions until 2006.)

On July 29–30 the ASEAN Regional Forum convened. Foreign ministers from the European Union (EU) and 17 Asia-Pacific countries, led by U.S. Secretary of State Warren Christopher, discussed regional security issues, including competing claims to the Spratly Islands in the South China Sea. China, which had occupied Mischief Reef in the Spratlys (*see* SPOTLIGHT: *The Spat over the Spratlys*), affirmed its willingness to negotiate separately with each of the other claimants and attempted to allay fears by offering more information about its defense program, but ASEAN maintained that multilateral claims could not be settled bilaterally. At the end of their meetings, ASEAN foreign ministers condemned nuclear testing in the Asia-Pacific region. ASEAN met again in Bangkok, Thailand, on August 21 to tackle the growing drug problem in the region and yet again in December to consider advancing the deadline for completing regional tariff cuts to the year 2000.

The Asia-Pacific Economic Cooperation summit meeting of 18 Pacific Rim countries, including China, Japan, and the U.S., convened in Osaka, Japan, on the weekend of November 17–19 to work toward establishing what could become the world's largest free-trade and investment zone. It could include the region's developed countries by the year 2010 and the less developed ones by 2020.

On January 1 the Southern Cone Common Market (Mercosur) put into effect the terms of the Protocol of Ouro Prêto (signed in December 1994) by abandoning tariffs on about 90% of goods traded between Argentina, Brazil, Paraguay, and Uruguay, establishing express passport lanes for nationals of its members, and erecting a common tariff averaging 12% for goods imported from elsewhere. On January 2 Brazilian Pres. Fernando Henrique Cardoso hailed the new "full customs union" and played host at a meeting of the presidents of the four Mercosur countries as well as those of Chile and Bolivia, neighbours moving close to free trade with the Mercosur countries. Mercosur members and their neighbours also planned to adopt a regional passport, the Andean Migration Card. Regional trade between the members had tripled by 1994, reaching $12 billion, and Brazil had become Argentina's largest trading partner, displacing the U.S. The new market embraced 190 million people and registered some $800 billion in economic activity. Other Latin-American states meanwhile intensified their efforts to associate with Mercosur by expanding their commercial relations through the Andean Group (Bolivia, Peru, Colombia, Venezuela, and Ecuador), and on December 7 Mercosur signed an agreement in Montevideo, Uruguay, looking to closer regional cooperation with Bolivia. On December 15, in Madrid, the EU agreed to gradually drop trade barriers between members of the two groups.

At a conference held in Barcelona, Spain, on November 27–28, members of the EU met for the first time with delegates from 11 North African and Middle Eastern states (Algeria, Cyprus, Egypt, Israel, Jordan, Lebanon, Malta, Morocco, Mauritania, Tunisia, and Turkey) as well as Palestinian representatives to discuss a Mediterranean regional pact. Agreement was reached on a framework for cooperation in such areas as trade, migration, economic development, drug trafficking, and environmental protection.

The Visegrad Group (the Czech Republic, Hungary, Poland, and Slovakia) seemed less relevant in 1995 as all the members competed to join the EU and NATO. The EU once regarded the four as leading candidates for membership but now bracketed them with other former communist states (Bulgaria, Estonia, Latvia, Lithuania, Romania, and Slovenia) and declined to negotiate with any of them until 1997, after an intergovernmental conference reviewed the Maastricht Treaty in 1996. Western states were seeking a more stable relationship with Russia, which opposed expanding NATO, a factor that also undermined cooperation between members of the Visegrad Group.

Environmentalists at the Regional Organization for the Protection of the Marine Environment, citing experts from the International Marine Organization in London, said on April 23 that a corroded Iraqi tanker sunk during the Persian Gulf War in 1991 could soon spill 100,000 tons of oil trapped inside it, polluting hundreds of kilometres of coast reaching to Qatar and Bahrain. The organization asked the UN to help countries in the region salvage the ship.

(RICHARD N. SWIFT)

DEPENDENT STATES

Europe and the Atlantic. In July 1995 the government of Gibraltar's chief minister, Joe Bossano, facing tight border controls by Spain and intense pressure from the U.K., approved legislation designed to end drug and cigarette smuggling in the territory. The legislation triggered demonstrations by both those who supported the crackdown and those who opposed it. Spain eased the border controls immediately, and by early September London and Madrid agreed that the smuggling problem had been resolved.

On September 27 the European Court of Human Rights narrowly ruled that the 1988 shooting of three Irish Republican Army terrorists by Special Air Service British commandos in Gibraltar had breached international conventions on the use of excessive force. The decision reversed a ruling by a Gibraltarian court. The families of the three killed, alleging that British authorities had engineered a cover-up, demanded an investigation by the UN.

Relations between Britain and Argentina improved in 1995 as the two signed an agreement for joint oil exploration and possible exploitation in the waters around the Falkland Islands/Islas Malvinas. It was also agreed that talks on regulating the local squid catch should resume.

In a general election in Greenland in March, the ruling centre-left coalition, led by Prime Minister Lars Emil Johansen, remained in power with 58.8% of the vote. After years of silence, Copenhagen admitted that a former Danish prime minister had broken official policy by allowing U.S. planes carrying atomic weapons to overfly Greenland during the Cold War. In October the Danish government said it would pay compensation to 1,500 Greenlanders (including the families of those who died) who had been exposed to nuclear debris after a plane carrying such material crashed near the Thule Air Base in 1968.

Faroese leaders expressed anger over Danish economic intervention after the collapse of the local fishing industry and the failure of Føroya Banken, the island's largest bank, had forced Thorshavn to turn to Copenhagen for a bailout. The Faroese government, which took control of Føroya Banken in 1992, claimed that the bank's finances were far worse than they had been led to believe. Outside observers noted that most of the islands' problems were the result of overfishing, overspending, and overborrowing in the 1980s. Negotiations with the U.K. over the boundary between the Faroes and the Shetland Islands continued.

Caribbean and Bermuda. Hurricanes in September severely disrupted the economies of several dependent states in the Caribbean and set back economic progress for some time to come. It was the worst Atlantic hurricane season in decades. The U.S. Virgin Islands were the hardest hit, with damage to property, utilities, and business installations put at a staggering $3 billion. Anguilla suffered damages of $28.8 million and lost 50% of its housing. In Sint Maarten, in the Netherlands Antilles, long regarded as the region's premier yacht haven, hundreds of yachts were sunk or damaged, and five deaths were reported. On the French side of the island, St. Martin, one person died and 80% of the buildings were affected. In Guadeloupe the key banana crop sustained damages estimated at F 735 million.

Montserrat spent much of the year living under a threat from the Chances Peak volcano in the south of the island, which seemed ready to erupt for the first time in 100 years. Half the population was evacuated to the north. In September the international scientific team monitoring the volcano declared an eruption unlikely in the near future.

In the Cayman Islands the opposition People's Democratic Movement defeated the Progressive National Party in the general election in January, winning 8 out of 10 legislative council seats. Derek Taylor became chief minister. One of his most pressing problems was the question of Cuban refugees. More than 1,000 Cubans landed on the islands during the year, an influx the Cayman economy and social services system were ill-equipped to handle. Under an agreement hammered out with the U.S., most refugees were transferred to the naval base at Guantánamo, Cuba. Only those who could prove political refugee status were allowed to stay.

Chief Minister H. Lavity Stoutt, the leading political figure in the British Virgin Islands for years, died in May, only three months after being returned to office in a general election. He was succeeded by his deputy, Ralph O'Neal.

The Antillean Restructuring Party (PAR) in the Netherlands Antilles consolidated its position in May by becoming the major partner in a coalition government formed following island council elections in Curaçao. This came on the heels of PAR's victory in the Netherlands Antilles federal elections in February 1994.

Dependent States[1]

Australia	**Portugal**
Christmas Island	Macau
Cocos (Keeling) Islands	**United Kingdom**
Norfolk Island	Anguilla
Denmark	Bermuda
Faroe Islands	British Virgin Islands
Greenland	Cayman Islands
France	Falkland Islands
French Guiana	Gibraltar
French Polynesia	Guernsey
Guadeloupe	Hong Kong
Martinique	Isle of Man
Mayotte	Jersey
New Caledonia	Montserrat
Réunion	Pitcairn Island
Saint Pierre and Miquelon	Saint Helena and Dependencies
Wallis and Futuna	Turks and Caicos Islands
Netherlands, The	**United States**
Aruba	American Samoa
Netherlands Antilles	Guam
New Zealand	Northern Mariana Islands
Cook Islands	Puerto Rico
Niue	Virgin Islands (of the U.S.)
Tokelau	
Norway	
Jan Mayen	
Svalbard	

[1]Excludes territories (1) to which Antarctic Treaty is applicable in whole or in part, (2) without permanent civilian population, (3) without internationally recognized civilian government (Western Sahara, Gaza Strip), or (4) representing unadjudicated unilateral or multilateral territorial claims.

In a referendum in Bermuda in August, 74% of the voters rejected the idea of independence from Britain, thus putting to rest a subject of long-standing controversy in the colony. Prime Minister Sir John Swan (*see* BIOGRAPHIES), who had supported independence, resigned and was succeeded by former finance minister David Saul.

Pacific. French Polynesia became the focus of world attention when France resumed nuclear testing at Mururoa atoll in September 1995. At the atoll itself, a peace flotilla of yachts from Australia and New Zealand challenged France's 12-mi exclusion zone, which resulted in the arrest of several demonstrators and the seizure of three Greenpeace vessels. In Papeete, Tahiti, antinuclear protest became closely linked to the pro-independence movement (supported by some 15% of the population), and large public demonstrations escalated into strikes and violence. After a second test in October, the South Pacific Forum suspended France as one of its dialogue partners.

In New Caledonia there were continuing differences over the future of the territory. The conservative Rally for Caledonia in the Republic (RPCR) wanted the 1998 referendum canceled and a 30-year agreement of cooperation and development with France. The Kanak Socialist National Liberation Front (FLNKS) demanded a negotiated independence and an early return of sovereignty. The administration's budget was attacked by the FLNKS because it would promote the capital, Nouméa, and the southern area, where European settlement dominated, and because low income tax, the absence of a tax on mining, and high indirect taxes discriminated against low-income Kanaks. In provincial elections in July, the RPCR was challenged by a new party—New Caledonia for All.

Allegations that New Zealand companies had avoided tax through the complicity of Cook Islands companies and tax-haven agencies were the subject of a commission of inquiry. The government of the Cook Islands also became embroiled in a scandal over letters of guarantee (signed by Prime Minister Sir Geoffrey Henry) that potentially exposed the government to losses of $NZ 1.1 billion. An inquiry concluded that the government had been the gullible victim of attempted fraud. In June the Cook Islands currency was virtually abandoned when the government faced a cash crisis. In replying to attacks on his government, Henry blamed the U.S. CIA and the international news media for attempting to undermine his administration.

In Niue the Niue People's Party, led by Premier Frank Lui, survived the year despite a deadlocked parliament. Lui refused to resign, and his opponents could not obtain a majority for a vote of no confidence. In October a compromise allowed the budget to proceed on the understanding that there would be an early general election.

American Samoa was forced to cut public services by 20% early in 1995. To that point 80% of government income was required for the payment of 4,000 public employees. The government carried a debt of $20 million to $30 million in an annual budget of $140 million, of which more than half was provided by the U.S. government. In September a U.S. court ordered the American Samoan government's insurer to pay out a further $29 million for damage incurred during Typhoon Val in 1991 and added $57 million in punitive damages. An appeal was expected.

East Asia. Events in 1995 clearly indicated that British authority in Hong Kong was on the wane. After long delays Sino-British negotiators finally agreed on the setup of the Court of Final Appeal, which was not to begin hearing cases until after the July 1, 1997, handover of the territory to China. Critics of the deal said that the British had capitulated to the Chinese, dropping their previous demand that

Citizens of Tahiti march to protest French nuclear tests on nearby Mururoa atoll in September. The decision by France to conduct the tests in French Polynesia angered the residents of the overseas territory and led to protests throughout the world.

GAEL KERBAOL—GAMMA LIAISON

the crucial court be established before the transition. After Britain and China signed an agreement on the financing for a new airport, the Hong Kong government announced that the facility, originally scheduled to open in 1997, would not be completed until 1998.

The year in Hong Kong was capped by Legislative Council (Legco) elections on September 17—the first time the chamber had been wholly elected. Twenty seats were determined by geographic area, while 30 were chosen by professions or "functional constituency" and the remaining 10 by district board electors. These were the first legislative polls held under electoral reforms introduced by Gov. Christopher Patten and, to China's dismay, approved by Legco in 1994. With just 35.8% of eligible voters turning out, "pro democracy" forces won 29 seats, nearly half of the 60 on offer. Two "pro-China" parties together took 17 seats, while a quarter of the posts went to independents. China promised to disband Legco after the handover and hold fresh polls.

While Beijing continued to snub Patten, his second-in-command, Chief Secretary Anson Chan Fang On Sang, revealed that she had met senior Chinese officials during a clandestine visit to the mainland. In October there were signs that London and Beijing were seeking to improve ties. Chinese Foreign Minister Qian Qichen visited Britain, and both sides agreed to work more closely as the transition approached. At year's end, however, Beijing announced that it would not permit Patten to attend the official handover ceremony in June 1997. China also released a list of 94 Hong Kong citizens named to the 150-member transition committee. None of the appointees represented the DP.

Economic growth moderated to about 5%, while inflation hovered above 8%. Unemployment hit a record-high 3.5% as more factories moved across the border to China.

Macau continued to enjoy smooth relations with China. In November the Portuguese-run territory's new international airport began operations. The facility was expected to lure traffic away from Hong Kong's congested airport once Macau's fledgling regional airline had begun unprecedented same-plane flights linking Taiwan and the mainland with a stopover in the enclave.

(BARRIE MACDONALD; DAVID RENWICK; ALEJANDRO REYES; MELINDA C. SHEPHERD)

This article updates the *Macropædia* articles HONG KONG; PACIFIC ISLANDS; The WEST INDIES.

ANTARCTICA

Antarctica, as defined by the 42-nation Antarctic Treaty that entered into effect in 1961, comprises all lands and waters south of latitude 60° S. The land area is about 14.2 million sq km (5.3 million sq mi), principally the Antarctic continent itself and adjoining islands. There is no capital or permanent human habitation; scientific and support personnel, housed in some 40 year-round scientific stations, number about 4,100 in summer and about 1,000 in winter. Antarctica is effectively internationalized by the Antarctic Treaty, which places the territorial claims of seven countries (Argentina, Australia, Chile, France, New Zealand, Norway, and the United Kingdom) in abeyance for the duration of the treaty. The treaty also provides managerial mechanisms for regulating international affairs, scientific activity, environmental protection, and formal inspections to verify compliance.

In September 1995 ice-core drillers at Russia's Vostok Station, atop the great ice sheet in the interior of East Antarctica, passed 3,100 m (10,170 ft)—the world's deepest ice core and a depth at which the ice is about 300,000 years old. The core would reveal greater ages than other deep ice cores, including that drilled from the Greenland ice sheet in 1992. Russian, U.S., and French analysis of the Vostok cores over a decade had yielded unique information about environmental and climatic changes over the last interglacial period. For example, air bubbles trapped in the ice confirmed that levels of carbon dioxide and methane were higher between glacial periods than during them. The coring was particularly gratifying for Vostok, which had had to be closed for the 1994 winter owing to the inability to deliver fuel there from a coastal depot. The 1994 closure had been the station's first since its establishment in 1957.

Fossils of a gigantic mollusk and an oversized relative of the armadillo were discovered on Seymour Island near the Antarctic Peninsula. The two creatures joined fossils of 800 different species collected from the island, a treasure trove of fossils that piled up almost continuously between 80 million and 37 million years ago. The new mollusk specimen resembles a fire hose curled back on itself like a giant paper clip; it became extinct about 65 million years ago. Called *Diplomoceras maximum,* it was the most complete example of this species known, according to William Zinsmeister, paleontologist at Purdue University, West Lafayette, Ind. The armadillo pieces were from an automobile-sized armoured creature that lived some 20 million years after the mollusk, when the Antarctic Peninsula had a temperate climate like that now in the U.S. Pacific Northwest. Remains had been found in North and South America, though never before this far south. Patagonia was connected to the Antarctic Peninsula at that time yet somehow cut off biologically from the rest of South America.

The ozone hole covered an area twice the size of Europe in the Antarctic spring of 1995, but research indicated that worldwide levels of an ozone-depleting chemical were falling. This was the first decrease ever measured of a substance restricted by the Montreal Protocol, an international treaty limiting the production of ozone depleters. Concentrations of methyl chloroform had decreased 2% a year since mid-1990. Until then levels had increased 4% a year since 1978. *Time* magazine in October credited the ozone hole with creating the sense of urgency that stimulated the 1987 Montreal accord and called the protocol a precedent that showed how quickly nations can act when they finally recognize a disaster. The World Meteorological Organization, a UN body, said the curb on harmful emissions should start recovery of the ozone layer by the mid-21st century.

British investigators dated ice back more than eight

million years in an area of the Transantarctic Mountains where earlier glaciologists had estimated the ice to be no more than three million years old. The glaciologists had contended that the ice formed immediately after warmer weather swept the prehistoric earth. While ice-sheet history remained controversial, the new research suggested that the risk of melting the polar caps through global warming might be less acute than previously thought. The discovery was made possible by the presence of a thin film of volcanic ash dating back 8.1 million years.

A Norwegian study warned, however, that sea ice around Antarctica and the Arctic was melting more quickly than in earlier decades. Data from microwave sensors on satellites were used to compare the extent of sea ice melt between 1978 and 1994 and showed a statistically significant decline in Antarctic sea ice of 1.4% per decade and accelerated melting of Arctic sea ice from 2.5% per decade to 4.3%. The report was important because sea ice change had been predicted to be one of the first signs of global warming.

Past and present Antarctic explorers met in January in Wellington, N.Z., to toast the centenary of the first Antarctic landing. Four New Zealanders had been among a Norwegian expedition that in 1895 was the first to set foot on Antarctica, at Cape Adare near the entrance to the Ross Sea. Another reminder of the newness of Antarctic exploration came in the form of new statistics on the length and proportions of coastline types and the total area of Antarctica. The refined measurements were possible because of improved mapping and completion of a digital database of Antarctic maps and satellite images. A particularly significant change was in the amount of ice-free ground, which was only about one-seventh of the 2–3% of Antarctica's total area often quoted from previous studies.

Four live broadcasts from Antarctica to U.S. public television stations marked the continent's first use of live TV for education and the first live broadcast ever from the geographic South Pole. The shows included on-the-air questions and answers between students at schools and studios in the U.S. and scientists in Antarctica. Although scientists routinely had Internet and telephone access to and from Antarctica, transmission of TV signals was made difficult by the region's high latitudes, because most communications satellites orbit Earth over the Equator.

Meanwhile, tourism remained the fastest-growing portion of the Antarctic economy, with nearly 8,000 visitors to the Antarctic in 1995. The number of tourists in a typical year exceeded the number of scientists and support staff, but the visits usually were short, and person-days spent by tourists still represented less than 1% of human activity in the Antarctic.

Astronomical and astrophysical projects continued to increase their role at the U.S. research station at the South Pole with the installation of a 1.7-m (5.5-ft) telescope for viewing celestial objects at submillimetre wavelengths. The telescope, which joined others at the site for different wavelengths, was surveying the southern galactic plane, giant molecular clouds, and the Large Magellanic Cloud. Astronomers valued the site because its clear, dry, dark atmosphere enabled detection, at some wavelengths, that rivaled the clarity of space. The South Pole also was the site of photosensors buried in the highly transparent ice sheet. The sensors were intended to record the presence of extremely high-energy particles called neutrinos that pass through the Earth before colliding, occasionally, with ice molecules to create a flash of light. The hoped-for result, finding the source of the neutrinos, would help to elucidate the early history of the universe. (GUY G. GUTHRIDGE)

This article updates the *Macropædia* article ANTARCTICA.

ARCTIC REGIONS

The Arctic regions may be defined in physical terms (astronomical [north of the Arctic Circle, latitude 66° 30′ N], climatic [above the 10° C (50° F) July isotherm], or vegetational [above the northern limit of the tree line]) or human (the territory inhabited by the circumpolar cultures—Inuit, or Eskimo, and Aleut in North America; Saami, or Lapp, in northern Scandinavia; and, west to east, Uralic, Paleosiberian, Middle Asian, and Arctic peoples in northern Russia). No single national sovereignty or treaty regime governs the region, which includes portions of seven countries: Canada, the United States, Russia, Finland, Sweden, Norway, and Greenland (part of Denmark). The Arctic Ocean, 14,090,000 sq km (5,440,000 sq mi) in area, constitutes about two-thirds of the region, the remaining land area consisting of permanent ice cap, tundra, or taiga. Population (1995 est.) of peoples belonging to the circumpolar cultures, 1,260,000. International organizations concerned with the Arctic include: Arctic Environmental Protection Strategy, Council of the Euro-Arctic Region, International Arctic Committee, International Arctic Science Committee, and the Inuit Circumpolar Conference.

In September 1995 U.S. Pres. Bill Clinton considered blocking development of the so-called 1002 lands in the energy-rich Arctic National Wildlife Refuge on the Alaska-Yukon border. The 1002 lands, 607,000 ha (1.5 million ac) of territory along the Beaufort Sea, were thought to contain one of the last great unexplored oil fields in the U.S. The move to declare the area a national monument was well received by the Canadian government, which had established the Ivavvik National Park on the Canadian side of the border in 1984 to prevent oil and gas developments. Development pressure from the energy industry had increased as production and revenues from the massive Prudhoe Bay oil fields to the west of the refuge dwindled. Recent studies, however, had concluded that the oil reserves might be only half of the previously estimated 3.2 billion gal of oil and that oil and gas development would be more disruptive to wildlife, vegetation, and the native communities of Alaska and Yukon than previously believed.

During 1995 further progress was made in the political development of Canada's Northwest Territories. The split of the territories into two separate regions—and the dividing of assets and the debt of the existing government—were major issues in the October election. The Northwest Territories were scheduled to be divided by April 1, 1999, into an eastern territory—Nunavut—and a new, yet-unnamed western territory. At the beginning of the year, Joe Clark, former prime minister of Canada, chaired a conference that attempted to forge a set of constitutional principles for the new western territory, with a population of about 35,000 people. The central question that was addressed at the conference was the division of power between communities and the regional and central governments. Meanwhile, the 23,000 residents of the eastern Arctic were engaged in planning for the eventual carrying out of self-government in Nunavut.

In February a native lands-claim settlement between Ottawa and the Yukon was proclaimed in which 8,000 Yukon Indians would receive Can$242.6 million over 15 years in income from some nonrenewable resources and also ownership of 41,439 sq km (16,000 sq mi) of land. The agreement also entrenched the rights of Indians to harvest wildlife and guaranteed them up to 50% representation on boards responsible for land-use, fish and wildlife management, and renewable resource developments.

In October the Quebec Cree and the Inuit populations held their own referenda to decide whether to remain in Canada, should Quebec decide to establish a separate country. The Cree and Inuit voted overwhelmingly to remain in Canada. Under the James Bay and Northern Quebec Agreement, the native populations had acquired defined rights to approximately 400,000 sq km (154,000 sq mi) of traditional lands in northern and Arctic Quebec. Earlier in the year the government of Quebec had declared that it would not respect the outcome of any native-run referendum that gave aboriginal communities a mandate to secede from an independent Quebec. In spite of these constitutional differences, Falconbridge in October signed a deal with the Quebec government to invest about Can$495 million in a mine in Nunavik, the Inuit territory in the north of the province.

In July the Inuit and Innu peoples of Labrador began negotiations on a partnership proposal with several giant mining companies to develop the Voisey Bay mineral discovery. The mine site was located on Labrador's remote northern coast, in a region that was the focus of overlapping land claims by Labrador's 4,000 Inuit and 1,500 Innu. In October new mineral discoveries by Diamond Fields Resources suggested that the area might become one of the world's major sources of nickel.

In February Greenland threatened to cut its ties to Denmark after Denmark reportedly proposed cutting the island's annual subsidy of about $700 million to just $17 million. The threat was seen more as a sign of frustration than intent because semi-independent Greenland was heavily dependent upon Danish aid and such administrative services as foreign policy, defense, and justice. According to Danish authorities, they sought to reduce the subsidy because Greenland's economy was in sound shape. In 1993, for example, the island had a surplus of $32 million.

In the face of concerns about the possible collapse of the fishing industry, it was reported in September that the Greenland government was looking at mining and tourism as alternative economic developments. Fishing, which had been the mainstay of Greenland since the island attained full self-government from Denmark in 1979, had helped the Greenlanders become the most industrially developed of the indigenous Arctic societies. More than 5,000 workers were involved in the fishing industry, which brought in about $625,000 annually to Greenland and accounted for almost all its exports. The decline in the industry was being blamed on changes in the environment, overfishing, and bad economic planning that had transferred small-scale fishing activities and people out of tiny settlements into the larger settlements.

In June participants in the International Arctic Social Science Conference, held in Finland, concluded that Arctic pollution and development were endangering the environment and the lifestyles of the indigenous peoples. It was proposed that "an umbrella organization . . . be created that would be responsible for . . . deciding claims of all parties relating to Arctic pollution." New procedures to analyze the impacts of Arctic pollution were required because existing agreements were not enforceable. The proposal emerged because of concerns about damage to the environment and to native peoples of Russia.

Time magazine reported that the complex of smelters in Russia's central Siberian city of Norilsk was perhaps the largest source of air pollution in the world, pumping two million tons of sulfur, along with other poisons, into the air each year. Industrial emissions from Siberia were thought to be contributing significantly to the threat of global warming.

(KENNETH DE LA BARRE)

This article updates the *Macropædia* article The ARCTIC.

BENOIT DECOUT—REA/SABA

Scientists prepare one of a number of helium balloons sent aloft to measure ozone levels over the Arctic. The European project, which was based in Sweden, confirmed that an ozone hole similar to the one already known to be present over the Antarctic was developing above the Arctic.

POLITICAL PARTIES

The following table is a general guide to the principal political parties and coalitions of the world. All countries that were independent on Dec. 31, 1995, are included, except the Vatican City State. In most instances parties are included only if represented in elected parliaments (in the lower house in bicameral legislatures). (Party names may be condensed or omitted for reasons of space or to more clearly indicate party groupings.) Figures in the column "Parliamentary representation" indicate the number of seats obtained in the most recent general election (figures in parentheses are those of the penultimate one) and exclude nonelective seats and seats still undecided. If only a portion of the seats were at stake in the last general election, the figure given indicates the total number of seats held by each party after the election. The date of the most recent election follows the name of the country.

The capital letters in the column "Affiliation" show the relative positions of the parties within the political spectrum of each country. The key chosen is as follows: F-fascist; ER-extreme right; R-right; CR-centre right; C-centre; CL-centre left; SD-social democratic; S-socialist; L-non-Marxist left; K-Communist; and EL-extreme left. In addition, within some countries there are political organizations that exist chiefly to advance a special interest as distinct from a political orientation. These are represented by lower-case letters as follows: x-parties that have repudiated former Communist affiliation; e-parties based on distinct regional, ethnic, or linguistic identity; r-religious fundamentalist; g-environmental, or Green; and p-parties based largely on personalities.

The numbers in the column "Voting strength" indicate proportions of the valid votes cast for the respective parties. (MELINDA C. SHEPHERD)

Political Parties

Country / Name of party	Affiliation	Voting strength (%)	Parliamentary representation	
Afghanistan				
Multifactional warfare from January 1993	—	—	—	
Albania (March 1992)				
Democratic Party	CR	62.1	92	(75)
Social Democratic Party	SD	4.4	7	—
Socialist Party	x	25.7	38	(169)
Other	—	7.8	3	(6)
Algeria				
Interim government since January 1992	—	—	—	
Andorra (December 1993)				
National Democratic Grouping and allies	...	...	15	
Others and independents	...	...	13	
Angola (September 1992)				
Popular Liberation Movement of Angola–Labour Party (MPLA–PT)	x	53.7	129	(203)
National Union for the Total Independence of Angola (UNITA)	—	34.1	70	—
Others	—	12.2	21	—
Antigua and Barbuda (March 1994)				
Antigua Labour Party	C	54.4	11	(15)
United Progressive Party	C	43.7	5	(1)
Barbuda People's Movement	e	1.4	1	(1)
Argentina (May 1995)				
Justicialist National Movement (Peronist)	CR–CL	...	136	(125)
Radical Civic Union	C	...	69	(83)
Front for a Country in Solidarity (Frepaso coalition)	CL	...	26	(13)
Others	—	...	26	(36)
Armenia (July 1995)				
Armenian National Movement and allies	—	42.7	119	
Women's organization	—	16.9	8	
Democratic Party	x	12.1	7	
Others and independents	—	28.3	56	
Australia (March 1993)				
National	R	7.5	16	(14)
Liberal	C	36.8	49	(55)
Labor	L	44.9	80	(78)
Others and independents	—	10.8	2	(1)
Austria (December 1995)				
Austrian Freedom Party	R	22.1	41	(42)
Austrian People's Party	C	28.3	53	(52)
Austrian Social Democratic Party	SD	38.3	72	(65)
Liberal Forum	—	5.3	9	(11)
Greens	Lg	4.6	8	(13)
Azerbaijan				
Interim parliament from May 1992	—	—	—	
Bahamas, The (August 1992)				
Progressive Liberal Party	C	44.7	15	(31)
Free National Movement	C	55.0	34	(16)
Others	—	0.3	0	(2)
Bahrain				
Consultative Council (advisory body)	—	—	—	
Bangladesh (February 1991)				
Bangladesh Nationalist Party	CR	31	166	(18)
National Party (coalition)	—	11	35	(251)
Awami League	SD	31	89	—
Islamic Assembly	r	12	21	(5)
Others	—	15	19	(25)
Barbados (September 1994)				
Democratic Labour Party	C	38.4	8	(18)
National Democratic Party	—	12.7	1	(0)
Barbados Labour Party	SD	48.3	19	(10)
Belarus (May–December 1995)				
Communist Party }	K	...	42	
Agrarian Party }		...	33	
Other parties	—	...	19	
Independents	—	...	96	
Belgium (May 1995)				
National Front (French)	ERe	2.3	2	(1)
Vlaams Blok (Flemish)	ERe	7.8	11	(12)
Volksunie (Flemish)	Re	4.7	5	(10)
Liberals { Flemish	CR	13.1	21	(26)
Liberals { French	CR	10.3	18	(20)
Social Christians { Flemish	C	17.2	29	(39)
Social Christians { French	C	7.7	12	(18)
Socialists { Flemish	SD	12.6	20	(28)
Socialists { French	SD	11.9	21	(35)
Greens { Flemish	g	4.4	5	(7)
Greens { French	g	4.0	6	(10)
Others	—	4.0	0	(6)
Belize (June 1993)				
United Democratic Party	R	48.8	16	(13)
People's United Party	C	51.2	13	(15)
Benin (March–May 1995)				
Government party and allies	—	...	28	
Opposition parties	—	...	55	
Bhutan				
National Assembly, no parties	—	—	105	
Bolivia (June 1993)				
Civic Solidarity Union	R	...	20	—
Nationalist Revolutionary Movement	CR	36	52	(40)
Patriotic Accord (coalition)	—	21	35	(71)
Conscience of the Fatherland	CL	...	13	(9)
Free Bolivia Movement	L	...	7	—
Others	—	...	3	(10)
Bosnia and Herzegovina				
normal legislative operations in abeyance from 1992				
Botswana (October 1994)				
Botswana Democratic Party	C	54.6	27	(31)
Botswana National Front	CL	37.1	13	(3)
Brazil (October 1994; preliminary results)				
Rightist parties	R	...	90 }	(243)
Social Democracy and allies	C	...	175 }	
Democratic Movement and allies	CL	...	105	(146)
Workers Party and allies	L	...	77	(95)
Others	—	...	66	(14)
Brunei				
Legislative Council (nonelected)	—	—	—	
Bulgaria (December 1994)				
People's Union	CR	6.6	18	—
Union of Democratic Forces	CL	24.5	69	(110)
Bulgarian Socialist Party	x	44.0	125	(106)
Movement for Rights and Freedoms (Turkish)	e	5.5	15	(24)
Bulgarian Business Bloc	—	4.8	13	—
Burkina Faso (May 1992)				
Government coalition	...	...	84	
Opposition parties	...	...	23	
Burundi (June 1993)				
Burundi Democratic Front	—	72.6	65	
Unity for National Progress	—	21.9	16	
Cambodia (May 1993)				
Funcinpec	CR	45.5	58	
Buddhist Liberal Democrats	L	3.8	10	
Cambodian People's Party	x	38.2	51	
Others	—	12.5	1	
Cameroon (March 1992)				
People's Democratic Movement and allied party	—	...	94	(180)
Opposition parties	—	...	86	—
Canada (October 1993)				
Reform	R	18.1	52	—
Progressive Conservative	CR	16.1	2	(170)
Liberal	C	41.6	177	(82)
New Democratic	SD	6.6	9	(43)
Bloc Québécois	e	13.9	54	—
Others and independents	—	3.7	1	(0)
Cape Verde (December 1995)				
Movement for Democracy	—	...	50	(56)
African Party for the Independence of Cape Verde	—	...	21	(23)
Democratic Convergence Party	—	...	1	—
Central African Republic (August–September 1993)				
Central African People's Liberation Movement	—	...	34	
Others	—	...	51	
Chad				
Transitional government since March 1991	—	—	—	
Chile (December 1993)				
Independent Democratic Union	ER	...	15	(11)
National Renovation and allied party	R	...	31	(29)
Centre-right independents	CR	...	4	(8)
Christian Democratic Party	C	...	37	(38)
Leftist parties and independent	CL–L	...	33	(34)
China (September 1992–March 1993)				
National People's Congress	K	...	2,978	
Colombia (March 1994)				
Social Conservative Party	R	...	56	(15)
Other rightist parties	R	...	2	(24)
Liberal Party	C	...	89	(86)
Democratic Alliance–April 19 Movement	L	...	2	(15)
Others	—	...	14	(21)
Comoros (December 1993)				
Government supporters	—	...	24	(17)
Opposition parties	—	...	18	(25)
Congo (May 1993–April 1995)				
Presidential Tendency	—	...	66	(69)
Opposition Coalition	—	...	57	(49)
Others	—	...	0	(7)
Costa Rica (February 1994)				
Social Christian Unity Party	CR	40.4	25	(29)
National Liberation Party	CL	44.6	28	(25)
Others	—	15.0	4	(3)
Côte d'Ivoire (November 1995)				
Democratic Party	—	...	147	(163)
Rally of Democratic Forces	—	...	14	—
Popular Front	SD	...	10	(9)
Others and independents	—	...	0	(3)
Croatia (October 1995)				
Croatian Party of Rights	ERe	5.0	4	(5)
Croatian Democratic Union	Re	45.2	75	(85)
Moderate opposition coalition	R–C	18.3	20	(6)
Croatian Social-Liberal Party	CL	11.6	11	(14)
Social Democratic Party	x	8.9	9	(11)
Others and independents	—	11.0	8	(17)
Cuba (February 1993)				
Communist Party	K	...	589	(499)
Cyprus				
Greek Zone (May 1991)				
Democratic Rally	R	35.8	20	(19)
Democratic Party (DIKO)	CR	19.5	11	(16)
Socialist Party (EDEK)	CL	10.9	7	(6)
Progressive Party of the Working People	K	30.6	18	(15)
Turkish Zone (December 1993)				
National Unity Party	CR	29.9	17	
Democrat Party	—	29.2	15	
Communal Liberation Party	CL	13.3	5	
Republican Turkish Party	S	24.2	13	
Czech Republic (June 1992)				
Association for the Republic–Czech Republican Party	ER	6.0	14	
Governing coalition	R–CR	41.9	105	
Czech Social Democratic Party	SD	6.5	16	
Liberal Social Union (coalition)	L	6.5	16	
Left Bloc	x	14.1	35	
Moravia/Silesia regional party	e	5.9	14	
Others	—	19.1	0	
Denmark (September 1994)				
Progress	ER	6.4	11	(12)
Liberal	R	23.3	42	(29)
Conservative People's	R	15.0	27	(30)
Christian People's	CR	1.8	0	(4)
Centre Democrats	C	2.8	5	(9)
Radical Liberal	C	4.6	8	(7)
Social Democrats	SD	34.6	62	(69)
Socialist People's	S	7.3	13	(15)
Unity List	EL	3.1	6	(0)
Faroe Islands and Greenland	—	—	4	(4)
Independents	—	1.0	1	(0)
Djibouti (December 1992)				
Popular Rally for Progress	—	74.6	65	(65)
New Democratic Party	—	25.4	0	—

Political Parties

Country Name of party	Affiliation	Voting strength (%)	Parliamentary representation	
Dominica (June 1995)				
Dominica Freedom Party	CR	...	5	(11)
Dominica United Workers' Party	CL	...	11	(6)
Labour Party	L	...	5	(4)
Independents	—	...	0	(1)
Dominican Republic (May 1994)				
Social Christian Reformist Party	CR	...	50	(40)
Dominican Revolutionary Party and allies	L	...	57	(36)
Dominican Liberation Party	L	...	13	(44)
Ecuador (May 1994)				
Conservative Party	R	...	6	(6)
Republican Unity Party	CR	...	3	(12)
Social Christian Party	CR	...	26	(21)
Popular Democracy	C	...	4	(5)
Roldosist Party	—	...	11	(13)
Democratic Left	SD	...	8	(7)
Democratic Popular Movement	EL	...	8	(4)
Others	—	...	11	(9)
Egypt (November–December 1995)				
New Wafd Party	R	...	6	—
National Democratic Party	CR	...	331	(348)
National Progressive Unionist	L	...	5	(6)
Other parties	—	...	2	—
Independents	—	...	100	(83)
El Salvador (March 1994)				
Nationalist Republican Alliance (Arena)	R	45	39	(39)
National Conciliation Party	R	...	4	(9)
Christian Democratic Party	CR	16	18	(26)
Democratic Convergence	L	...	1	(8)
Farabundo Martí National Liberation Front	L	29	21	—
Others	—	...	1	(2)
Equatorial Guinea (November 1993)				
Democratic Party	—	...	68	(41)
Principal opposition parties	—	(Boycotted)		—
Others	—	...	12	—
Eritrea				
Transitional government from May 1993	—	—	—	
Estonia (March 1995)				
Republican and Conservative People's Party	R	5.0	5	—
Pro Patria ("Fatherland") Coalition	CR	7.9	8	(29)
Estonian Reform Party	CR	16.2	19	—
Estonian Centre Party	CL	14.2	16	—
Coalition and Rural People's Union	CL/x	32.2	41	(17)
Moderates	SD	6.0	6	(12)
Our Home is Estonia (pro-Russian alliance)	c	5.9	6	—
Others	—	12.6	0	(43)
Ethiopia (May–June 1995)				
Ethiopian People's Revolutionary Democratic Front	...	...	493	
Major opposition parties		(Boycotted)		
Others and independents	—	...	54	
Fiji (February 1994)				
Ethnic Fijian seats	e	...	37	(37)
Ethnic Indian seats	e	...	27	(27)
Chinese/European seats	e	...	4	(4)
Multiracial seat	e	...	1	(1)
Rotuma Island	e	...	1	(1)
Finland (March 1995)				
Finnish Christian Union	R	3.0	7	(8)
National Coalition	CR	17.9	39	(40)
Swedish People's Party	c	5.1	12	(12)
Finnish Centre	C	19.9	44	(55)
Social Democratic Party	S	28.3	63	(48)
Left-Wing Alliance	L–K	11.2	22	(19)
Green Union	g	6.5	9	(10)
Others	—	8.1	4	(8)
France (March 1993; 1st round %s)				
National Front	ER	12.4	0	(1)
Rally for the Republic (RPR)	R	20.4	247	(127)
Other right-wing parties	R	4.7	24	(16)
Union for French Democracy (UDF)	CR	19.1	213	(129)
Socialist Party	S	17.6	54	(260)
Other left-wing parties	L	4.5	16	(16)
Communist Party	K	9.2	23	(27)
Others	—	12.1	0	(1)
Gabon (September 1990–March 1991)				
Gabonese Democratic Party	—	...	66	(111)
Progress Party	—	...	19	—
Rally of Woodcutters	—	...	17	—
Others	—	...	18	—
Gambia, The				
Military government since July 1994	—	—	—	
Georgia (November 1995; partial results)				
All Georgian Union of Revival	CR	6.8 }	59	—
National Democratic Party	CR	7.9 }		(12)
Citizens of Georgia Union	—	23.7	91	—
Others and independents	—	61.6	...	(228)
Germany (October 1994)				
Christian Social Union	R	7.3	50	(51)
Christian Democratic Union	CR	34.2	244	(268)
Free Democratic Party	C	6.9	47	(79)
Social Democratic Party	SD	36.4	252	(239)
Party of Democratic Socialism	x	4.4	30	(17)
Greens/Alliance '90	g	7.3	49	(8)
Others	—	3.5	0	(0)
Ghana (December 1992)				
National Democratic Congress	—	...	189	
Others	—	...	11	
Greece (October 1993)				
Political Spring	CR	4.9	10	—
New Democracy	CR	39.3	111	(152)
Panhellenic Socialist Movement (Pasok)	S	46.9	170	(124)
Progressive Left Coalition	L–K	2.9 }	0	(21)
Communist Party	K	4.5 }	9	
Others	—	1.5	0	(3)
Grenada (June 1995)				
Grenada United Labour Party	R	...	2	(4)
National Democratic Congress	C	...	5	(7)
National Party	C	...	0	(2)
New National Party	C	...	8	(2)
Guatemala (August 1994)				
National Advancement Party	R	25.3	24	(12)
Guatemalan Republican Front	R	32.2	32	(...)
Solidarity Action Movement	CR	3.2	0	(18)
Christian Democratic Party	C	12.1	13	(28)
National Centre Union	C	8.9	8	(41)
Others and independents	—	18.3	3	(17)
Guinea (June 1995)				
Presidential party and allies	—	...	76	
Opposition parties	—	...	38	
Guinea-Bissau (July 1994)				
African Party for the Independence of Guinea and Cape Verde	—	46.0	62	(150)
Resistance Party	—	19.2	19	
Other opposition parties	—	34.8	19	—
Guyana (October 1992)				
United Force	CR	1.2	1	(2)
People's National Congress	Se	43.6	31	(42)
People's Progressive Party	Se	52.3	32	(8)
Working Peoples Alliance	L	1.7	1	(1)
Haiti (June–September 1995)				
Lavalas movement	L	...	68	
Others	—	...	15	
Honduras (November 1993)				
National Party	R	43.0	55	(71)
Liberal Party	CR	53.0	71	(55)
Others	—	4.0	2	(2)
Hungary (May 1994)				
Independent Smallholders	R	8.8	26	(43)
Hungarian Democratic Forum	CR	11.7	37	(165)
Christian Democratic People's Party	CR	7.1	22	(21)
Alliance of Free Democrats	CL	19.8	70	(92)
Federation of Young Democrats	L	7.0	20	(21)
Hungarian Socialist Party	x	33.0	209	(33)
Others and independents	—	12.6	2	(11)
Iceland (April 1995)				
Independence Party	R	37.1	25	(26)
Progressive Party	C	23.3	15	(13)
Women's Alliance	CL	4.9	3	(5)
People's Movement	CL	7.1	4 }	(10)
Social Democratic Party	SD	11.4	7 }	
People's Alliance	I	14.3	9	(0)
India (May 1991–February 1992)				
Bharatiya Janata	Rr	...	121	(88)
Congress (I)	C	...	245	(192)
Janata Dal	CL	...	58	(141)
Communist parties	K	...	49	(43)
Others	—	...	72	(59)
Indonesia (June 1992)				
Golkar (Functional Groups)	—	68	281	(299)
United Development Party	r	17	63	(61)
Indonesian Democratic Party	—	15	56	(40)
Iran (April–May 1992)				
Consultative Assembly, no parties	—	...	270	
Iraq (April 1989)				
Ba'th Party	—	64 }	250	
Others	—	36 }		
Ireland (November 1992)				
Progressive Democrats	R	4.7	10	(5)
Fianna Fail (Republican)	C	39.1	68	(77)
Fine Gael (United Ireland)	C	24.5	45	(55)
Labour Party	SD	19.3	33	(16)
Democratic Left	S	2.8	4	(7)
Green Alliance	g	1.4	1	(1)
Others	—	8.2	5	(5)
Israel (June 1992)				
Moledet	ER	2.4	3	(2)
Tzomet	R	6.4	8	(2)
United Torah Judaism	r	3.3	4	(7)
Shas	Rr	4.9	6	(6)
Likud	R	24.9	32	(40)
National Religious (Mafdal)	CRr	5.0	6	(5)
Labour	SD	34.6	44	(39)
Meretz	SD	9.6	12	(10)
Arab (Democracy)	e	1.6	2	(1)
Hadash	K	2.4	3	(4)
Others	—	4.9	0	(4)
Italy (March 1994)				
National Alliance	F	13.5	109	(34)
Northern League	Re	8.4	113	(55)
Forza Italia	R	21.0	112	—
Other rightists	R	3.5	32	—
Centrist parties (formerly Christian Democratic Party)	C	15.7	46	(206)
Democratic Alliance/Italian Socialists	SD/L	3.4	33	(119)
The Network (anti-Mafia)	L	1.9	8	(12)
Democratic Party of the Left	x	20.4	114	(107)
Communist Refoundation Party	K	6.0	41	(35)
Green List	g	2.7	11	(16)
Others	—	7.0	11	(46)
Jamaica (March 1993)				
Jamaica Labour Party	CL	39	8	(15)
People's National Party	L	61	52	(45)
Japan (July 1993)				
Liberal-Democratic Party	R	36.7	225	(275)
Shinseito (Japan Renewal)	R	10.1	55	—
Japan New Party	R	8.1	36	—
New Party Sakigake	R	2.6	13	—
Komeito (Clean Government)	C	8.1	52	(45)
Democratic Socialist Party	SD	3.5	15	(14)
United Social Democratic Party	SD	0.7	4	(4)
Social Democratic Party	S	15.4	70	(136)
Japan Communist Party	L	7.7	15	(16)
Others and Independents	—	7.1	27	(22)
Jordan (November 1993)				
Islamic Action Front	r	...	16	(20)
Independent Islamic fundamentalists	r	...	5	(12)
Tribal/traditional candidates	C	...	49 }	(17)
Independent centrists	C	...	3 }	
Leftists	L	...	7	(11)
Kazakhstan				
Parliament dissolved March 1995				
Kenya (December 1992)				
Kenya African National Union	—	...	100	(188)
Forum for Restoration of Democracy (2 wings)	—	...	62	—
Democratic Party	—	...	23	—
Others	—	...	3	—
Kiribati (July 1994)				
House of Assembly	p	...	39	
Korea, North (April 1990)				
Korean Workers' Party	K	99.8	687	
Korea, South (March 1992)				
United People's Party	R	17.3	31	
Democratic Liberal Party	—	38.5	149	
Democratic Party	CL	29.2	97	
Others and independents	—	15.0	22	
Kuwait (October 1992)				
Government supporters	—	...	19	
Fundamental opposition	r	...	19	
Liberal opposition	—	...	12	
Kyrgyzstan (February–April 1995)				
Legislative Assembly	—	—	35	
Laos (December 1992)				
Government party	K	...	85	(79)
Latvia (October 1995)				
People's Movement for Latvia	FRn	15.1	16	
Fatherland and Freedom	ERe	11.6	14	(6)
National Conservative Party	Re	6.2	8	(15)
Farmer's Union and allies	CR	6.1	8	(18)
Latvia's Way	C	14.7	17	(36)
Saimnieks ("In Charge")	CL	15.3	18	—
National Harmony Party (pro-Russian)	CL	5.6	6	(13)
Unity Party	K	7.2	8	—
Others	—	5.7	5	(12)
Lebanon (August–October 1992)				
Christian members	—	...	64	
Muslim/Druze members	—	...	64	
Lesotho (March 1993)				
Basotho Congress Party	—	74.8	65	
Basotho National Party	—	22.7	0	
Liberia				
Transitional government from September 1995	—	—	—	
Libya				
General People's Congress	—	—	750	
Liechtenstein (October 1993)				
Progressive Citizens' Party	CR	41.3	11	(12)
Fatherland Union	C	50.1	13	(11)
The Free List	g	8.5	1	(2)
Lithuania (October–November 1992)				
Christian Democrats and allies	R	12.9	18	
Reform Movement (Sajudis)	CR	21.7	29	
Social Democratic Party	SD	6.2	8	
Democratic Labour Party	x	45.1	74	
Others and independents	—	14.1	14	
Luxembourg (June 1994)				
Christian Social People's Party	CR	29.3	21	(22)
Democratic Party	C	11.6	12	(11)
Socialist Workers' Party	S	33.5	17	(18)

Political Parties

Country / Name of party	Affiliation	Voting strength (%)	Parliamentary representation	
Communist Party	K	2.8	0	(1)
Action Committee for Democracy and Justice	—	7.1	5	(4)
Green Alternative	g	10.2	5	(4)
Macedonia (October–November 1994)				
Alliance of Macedonia	x	...	95	
Party for Democratic Prosperity (Albanian)	e	...	10	
Others and independents	—	...	15	
Madagascar (June 1993)				
Living Forces coalition	—	...	75	
Others	—	...	59	
Malawi (May 1994)				
United Democratic Front	—	46.4	84	—
Malawi Congress Party	—	33.6	55	(136)
Alliance for Democracy	—	18.9	36	—
Malaysia (April 1995)				
Islamic parties	CR	...	13	(15)
National Front coalition	e	64.0	162	(127)
Democratic Action Party	—	...	9	(20)
Others and independents	—	...	8	(118)
Maldives (December 1994)				
People's Council	—	...	40	
Mali (February–March 1992)				
Alliance for Democracy in Mali	—	48.4	76	
Others	—	51.6	40	
Malta (February 1992)				
Nationalist Party	R	51.8	34	(35)
Labour Party	SD	46.5	31	(34)
Marshall Islands (November 1995)				
House of Representatives	—	—	33	
Mauritania (March 1992)				
Democratic and Social Republican Party	R	85	67	
Others and independents	—	15	12	
Mauritius (December 1995)				
Mauritian Socialist Movement and allied parties	—	19.7	0	(59)
Mauritian Militant Movement }				
Mauritian Labour Party and allied parties }	—	65.2	62	(3)
Others	—	15.1	0	—
Mexico (August 1994)				
National Action Party (PAN)	CR	...	119	(89)
Institutional Revolutionary Party (PRI)	C	...	300	(320)
Democratic Revolutionary Party	CL	...	69	(41)
Labour Party	L	...	12	(0)
Others	—	...	0	(50)
Micronesia (March 1995)				
Congress, no parties	—	...	14	
Moldova (February 1994)				
Popular Front alliance	Re	7.5	9	
Peasants/Intellectuals bloc	Ce	9.2	11	
Agrarian Democratic Party	C–x	43.2	56	
Socialist/Unity bloc (Russian)	xe	22.0	28	
Others	—	18.1	0	
Monaco (January 1993)				
Campora list	p	...	15	
Others	p	...	3	
Mongolia (June 1992)				
People's Revolutionary Party	x	56.9	71	(33)
Others	—	43.1	5	(20)
Morocco (June–September 1993)				
Constitutional Union	CR	...	54	(83)
National Democratic Party	CR	...	24	(24)
Berber parties	CRe	...	76	(47)
National Assembly of Independents	C	...	41	(61)
Democratic Bloc	CL–EL	...	120	(85)
Others and independents	—	...	18	(6)
Mozambique (October 1994)				
Mozambique Liberation Front (Frelimo)	x	44.3	129	(250)
Mozambique National Resistance (Renamo)	—	37.8	112	
Democratic Union	—	5.2	9	
Myanmar				
Military government since September 1988	—	—	—	
Namibia (December 1994)				
Democratic Turnhalle Alliance	C	20.8	15	(21)
South West Africa People's Organization (SWAPO)	L	73.9	53	(41)
Others	—	5.3	4	(10)
Nauru (November 1995)				
Parliament	p	—	18	(18)
Nepal (November 1994)				
National Democratic Party	R	17.9	20	(4)
Nepali Congress Party	C	33.4	83	(110)
Communist parties	K	30.9	88	(82)
Others and independents	—	17.8	14	(9)
Netherlands, The (May 1994)				
Christian Democratic Appeal	CR	22.2	34	(54)
People's Party for Freedom and Democracy	CR	19.9	31	(22)
Democrats 66	CL	15.5	24	(12)
Labour Party	SD	24.0	37	(49)
Green Left	Lg	3.5	5	(6)
General Union of the Elderly	—	4.5	6	—
Others	—	10.4	13	(7)
New Zealand (November 1993)				
New Zealand First	—	8.4	2	—
National Party	CR	35.0	50	(67)
Labour Party	CL	34.7	45	(29)
The Alliance (coalition)	CL	18.2	2	(1)
Nicaragua (February 1990)				
National Opposition Union	CR	54.7	51	
Sandinista National Liberation Front	L	40.8	39	
Others	—	4.5	2	
Niger (January 1995)				
Government Coalition	—	...	40	(50)
National Movement for a Developing Society (former single party)	—	...	29	(29)
Others	—	...	14	(4)
Nigeria				
Military government since 1993	—	—	—	
Norway (September 1993)				
Progress Party	R	6.3	10	(22)
Conservative Party	R	16.9	28	(37)
Christian People's Party	CR	7.9	13	(14)
Centre Party	CR	16.8	32	(11)
Labour Party	SD	37.0	67	(63)
Socialist Left	S	7.9	13	(17)
Others	—	7.2	2	(1)
Oman				
Consultative Council (advisory body)	—	—	—	
Pakistan (October 1993)				
Religious parties	Rr	...	10	(6)
Pakistan Muslim League (Nawaz)	—	41.0	73	(105)
Pakistan Muslim League (Junejo)	—	...	6	
Pakistan People's Party	CL	38.0	86	(45)
Mohajir Qaumi Movement	e	(Boycotted)		(15)
Other and independents	—	...	26	(30)
Palau (November 1992)				
House of Delegates	—	—	14	
Panama (May 1994)				
Democratic Revolutionary Party and allies	—	...	31	(12)
Others	—	...	41	(55)
Papua New Guinea (June 1992)				
United Party (Pangu Pati)	p	...	22	(26)
People's Democratic Movement	p	...	15	(18)
Others	p	...	40	(41)
Independents	—	...	31	(21)
Paraguay (May 1993)				
Colorado Party	R	43.0	38	(48)
Authentic Radical Liberal Party	CL	35.1	33	(19)
National Encounter coalition	—	17.1	9	—
Others	—	4.8	0	(5)
Peru (April 1995)				
Popular Christian Party	R	...	3	(8)
Popular Action	CR	...	4	—
Change 90-New Majority (coalition of independents)	—	...	67	(44)
Union for Peru	—	...	17	—
Independent Moralizing Front	—	...	6	(7)
American Popular Revolutionary Alliance	CL	...	8	—
Others	—	...	15	(21)
Philippines (May 1995)				
Government coalition	...	...	170	
Others	...	...	31	
Poland (September 1993)				
Confederation for an Independent Poland	R	5.8	22	(46)
Non-Party Bloc to Support Reform	R	5.4	16	—
Democratic Union	CL	10.6	74	(62)
Labour Union	L	7.3	41	(4)
Democratic Left Alliance	x	20.4	171	(60)
Polish Peasant Party	x	15.4	132	(48)
German minority organizations	e	0.5	4	(7)
Others	—	34.6	0	(233)
Portugal (October 1995)				
Popular Party	R	9.1	15	(5)
Social Democratic Party	CR	34.0	88	(135)
Socialist Party	CL	43.9	112	(72)
Unified Democratic Coalition	L–K	8.6	15	(17)
Others	—	4.4	0	(1)
Qatar				
Consultative Council (advisory body)	—	—	—	
Romania (September 1992)				
Romanian National Unity Party	ERe	7.7	30	
Greater Romania	e	3.9	16	
Democratic Convention of Romania	CR	20.0	82	
Democratic National Salvation Front	x	27.7	117	
National Salvation Front	x	10.2	43	
Hungarian Democratic Union	e	7.5	27	
Others	—	23.0	13	
Russia (December 1995)				
Liberal Democratic Party	ERe	11.2	51	(64)
Congress of Russian Communities	R/CLe	4.3	5	—
Our Home is Russia	CR	10.1	55	—
Forward Russia!	C	4.0	1	—
Russia's Democratic Choice	CL	3.9	9	(76)
Yabloko (Bloc of Three)	CL	6.9	45	(28)
Women of Russia	CL	4.6	3	(24)
Communist Party	L	22.3	157	(45)
Agrarian Party	L	3.8	20	(55)
Power to the People	Le	1.6	9	—
Workers' Russia	EL	4.5	1	(0)
Other parties	—	...	17	(137)
Independents	—	...	77	(21)
Rwanda				
Transitional government from July 1994	—	—	—	
Saint Kitts and Nevis (July 1995)				
People's Action Movement	CL	...	1	(4)
Nevis Reformation Party	CL	...	1	(1)
St. Kitts-Nevis Labour Party	L	...	7	(4)
Concerned Citizens' Movement	—	...	2	(2)
Saint Lucia (April 1992)				
United Workers' Party	C	54.9	11	(9)
St. Lucia Labour Party	CL	41.9	6	(8)
Saint Vincent and the Grenadines (February 1994)				
New Democratic Party	C	54.6	12	(15)
St. Vincent Labour Party	SD	26.0	2	(0)
Movement for National Unity	L	17.3	1	(0)
San Marino (May 1993)				
Christian Democrats	CR	41.4	26	(27)
Socialist Party	S	23.7	14	(7)
Progressive Democratic Party	x	18.6	11	(18)
Popular Democratic Alliance	—	7.7	4	—
Other parties	—	8.6	5	(8)
São Tomé and Príncipe (October 1994)				
Party of Democratic Convergence	C	17	14	(33)
Movement for the Liberation of São Tomé and Príncipe	L	43	27	(21)
Independent Democratic Action	—	26	14	—
Others	—	4	0	(1)
Saudi Arabia				
Consultative Council (advisory body)	—	—	—	
Senegal (May 1993)				
Socialist Party	SD	56.6	84	(103)
Senegalese Democratic Party	—	30.2	27	(17)
Let Us Unite Senegal	EL	4.9	3	—
Other parties	—	8.3	6	—
Seychelles (July 1993)				
People's Progressive Front	L	57.5	28	(23)
Others	—	42.5	5	—
Sierra Leone				
Military government since May 1992	—	—	—	
Singapore (August 1991)				
People's Action Party	CR	61	77	(80)
Democratic Party	CL	12	3	(1)
Workers' Party	L	14	1	(0)
Slovakia (September–October 1994)				
Slovak National Party	Re	5.4	9	(15)
Movement for a Democratic Slovakia	CR	35.0	61	(74)
Democratic Union	C	8.6	15	—
Christian Democratic Movement	CL	10.1	17	(18)
Party of the Democratic Left	x	10.4	18	(29)
Hungarian minority coalition	e	10.2	17	(14)
Others	—	20.3	13	(0)
Slovenia (December 1992)				
Slovenian National Party	ER	10.2	12	
Slovenian People's Party	R	8.7	10	
Christian Democrats	CR	14.5	15	
Associated List coalition	—	13.6	14	
Democratic Party	C	5.1	6	
Liberal Democratic Party	CL	23.5	22	
Social Democratic Party	SD	3.3	4	
Greens of Slovenia	g	3.7	5	
Others	—	17.4	0	
Solomon Islands (May 1993)				
Government Alliance	p	...	24	
Opposition party	p	...	23	
Somalia				
No government since 1991	—	—	—	
South Africa (April 1994)				
Freedom Front	ER	2.2	9	
National Party	CR	20.4	82	
Inkatha Freedom Party	e	10.5	43	
Democratic Party	C	1.7	7	
African National Congress	CL	62.7	252	
Pan-Africanist Congress	EL	1.2	5	
Others	—	1.3	2	
Spain (June 1993)				
Popular Party	R	34.8	141	(107)
Democratic and Social Centre	C	1.7	0	(14)
Basque Nationalist Party	Ce	1.2	5	(5)
Canary Islands coalition	Ce	0.9	4	—
Convergence and Union (Catalan)	CLe	5.0	17	(18)
Socialist Workers' Party	S	38.7	159	(175)
United Left	L–K	9.6	18	(17)
Herri Batasuna (Basque radicals)	ELe	0.9	2	(4)
Others	—	7.2	4	(10)

Political Parties

Country Name of party	Affiliation	Voting strength (%)	Parliamentary representation
Sri Lanka (August 1994)			
United National Party	CR	44.0	94 (125)
People's Alliance	CL	48.9	105 } (86)
Others and independents	—	3.6	14 }
Sri Lanka Muslim Congress	r	1.8	7 (4)
Tamil United Liberation Front	e	1.7	5 (10)
Sudan, The			
Transitional government since February 1992	—	—	—
Suriname (May 1991)			
National Democratic Party	—	21.8	12 (3)
Front for Democracy and Development (four-party coalition)	—	54.2	30 (42)
Democratic Alternative '91	—	16.7	9 —
Swaziland (September–October 1993)			
House of Assembly, no parties	—	—	55
Sweden (September 1994)			
New Democracy	R	1.2	0 (24)
Christian Democrats	R	4.1	15 (27)
Moderate Coalition Party	CR	22.4	80 (80)
Centre Party	CR	7.7	27 (31)
Liberal People's Party	C	7.2	26 (33)
Social Democrats	S	45.3	161 (138)
Left Party	x	6.2	22 (16)
Greens	g	5.0	18 (0)
Switzerland (October 1995)			
Swiss People's Party	R	14.9	29 (25)
Christian Democrats	CR	17.0	34 (36)
Liberal Party	CR	2.7	7 (10)
Radical Democrats	C	20.2	45 (44)
Social Democrats	SD	21.8	54 (42)
Green Party	g	5.0	9 (14)
Freedom Party	—	4.0	7 (8)
Others	—	14.4	15 (21)
Syria (August 1994)			
Ba'th Party and allies	—	...	167 (166)
Independents	—	...	83 (84)
Taiwan (December 1995)			
New Party (pro-unification)	R	12.9	21 —
Nationalist (Kuomintang)	—	46.1	85 (96)
Democratic Progressive Party (pro-independence)	—	33.2	54 (50)
Others and independents	—	7.8	4 (15)
Tajikistan (February–March 1995)			
Communist Party	K	...	60
Others and independents	—	...	119
Western/Islamic parties		(Banned)	
Tanzania (October–November 1995)			
Revolutionary Party of Tanzania (CCM)	—	...	182 (216)
Others	—	...	45 —
Thailand (July 1995)			
Government coalition:			
Thai Nation	—	...	92 (77)
New Aspiration Party	—	...	57 (51)
Righteous Force	—	...	23 (47)
Social Action Party	—	...	22 (22)
Others	—	...	39 (7)
Opposition:			
Democrat Party	—	...	86 (79)
National Development Party	—	...	53 (60)
Others	—	...	19 (17)
Togo (February 1994)			
Rally of the Togolese People (former single party)	—	...	35
Action Committee for Renewal	—	...	34
Union for Democracy	—	...	6
Others	—	...	3
Tonga (February 1993)			
Pro-Democracy Movement	—	...	6 (6)
Others	—	...	3 (3)
Trinidad and Tobago (November 1995)			
People's National Movement	C	50	17 (21)
National Alliance for Reconstruction	C	...	2 (2)
United National Congress	—	45	17 (13)
Tunisia (March 1994)			
Government party	CL	97.7	144 (141)
Others	—	2.3	19 (0)
Turkey (December 1995)			
Nationalist Action Party	ER	8.2	0 } (62)
Welfare (Refah) Party	Rr	21.4	158 }
True Path Party	CR	19.3	135 (178)
Motherland Party	CR	19.8	132 (115)
Democratic Left Party	CL	14.7	75 (7)
Republican People's Party	CL	10.8	50 —
Other leftist	CL–L	...	0 (88)
Turkmenistan (December 1994)			
Democratic Party of Turkmenistan	x	...	50
Tuvalu (November 1993)			
Parliament, no parties	—	—	12
Uganda			
Military regime from July 1985	—	—	—
Ukraine (March–November 1994)			
Extreme nationalist parties	ERe	...	5
Less extreme nationalist parties	CRe	...	15
Ukrainian Popular Movement (Rukh)	Ce	...	20
Centrist parties	C	...	17
Communist Party and allies	K–EL	...	123
Independents	—	...	225
United Arab Emirates			
Federal National Council (advisory body)	—	—	—
United Kingdom (April 1992)			
Democratic Unionists	Re	0.3	3 (3)
Conservative Party	CR	41.9	336 (375)
Liberal Democrats	CL	17.9	20 (22)
Labour Party	L	34.4	271 (229)
Scottish National Party	o	1.9	3 (3)
Plaid Cymru (Welsh Nationalists)	e	0.5	4 (3)
Ulster Unionists	—	0.8	9 (9)
Social Democratic and Labour Party (Northern Ireland)	CLe	0.6	4 (3)
Sinn Fein (Northern Ireland)	ELe	0.2	0 (1)
Other	—	1.5	1 (2)
United States (November 1994)			
Republican	CR	...	230 (175)
Democratic	C	...	204 (259)
Other	—	...	1 (1)
Uruguay (November 1994)			
National (Blanco) Party	C	31.4	31 (39)
Colorado Party	C	32.5	32 (30)
New Space	CL	5.1	5 (9)
Progressive Encounter	L	30.8	31 —
Broad Front	L	...	— (21)
Uzbekistan (December 1994–January 1995)			
People's Democratic Party and allies	x	100.0	250
Opposition parties		(Banned)	
Vanuatu (November 1995)			
Union of Moderate Parties	CR	...	17 (19)
Vanuatu National United Party	CR	...	9 (10)
Unity Front coalition	—	...	20 (16)
Others and independents	—	...	4 (1)
Venezuela (December 1993)			
COPEI (Social Christians)	CR–CL	...	54 (67)
Democratic Action	SD	...	55 (97)
National Convergence }	L	...	50 —
Movement to Socialism }			(18)
The Radical Cause	EL	...	40 (3)
Others	—	...	0 (16)
Vietnam (July 1992)			
Vietnam Fatherland Front	—	...	395
Western Samoa (April 1991)			
Human Rights Protection Party	—	...	30 (27)
National Development Party	—	...	14 (19)
Independents		...	3 (1)
Yemen (April 1993)			
Yemeni Alliance for Reform	Rr	...	62
General People's Congress	—	...	123
Yemeni Socialist Party	K	...	56
Others and independents	—	...	60
Yugoslavia (December 1992)			
Serbian Radical Party	Fe	24.4	34 (33)
Serbian Democratic Movement	C	18.7	20 —
Democratic Party	C	6.5	5 —
Socialist Party of Serbia	xe	34.2	47 (73)
Democratic Party of Socialists of Montenegro	xe	3.0	17 (23)
Democratic Community (Hungarian)	e	2.4	3 (2)
Others	—	10.8	12 (6)
Zaire			
Transitional government from April 1994	—	—	—
Zambia (October 1991)			
Movement for Multiparty Democracy	—	75.8	125 —
United National Independence	—	24.2	25 (125)
Zimbabwe (April 1995)			
Zimbabwe African National Union-Patriotic Front	—	82.3	118 (117)
Others and independents	—	17.7	2 (3)

Changes to Flags of the World

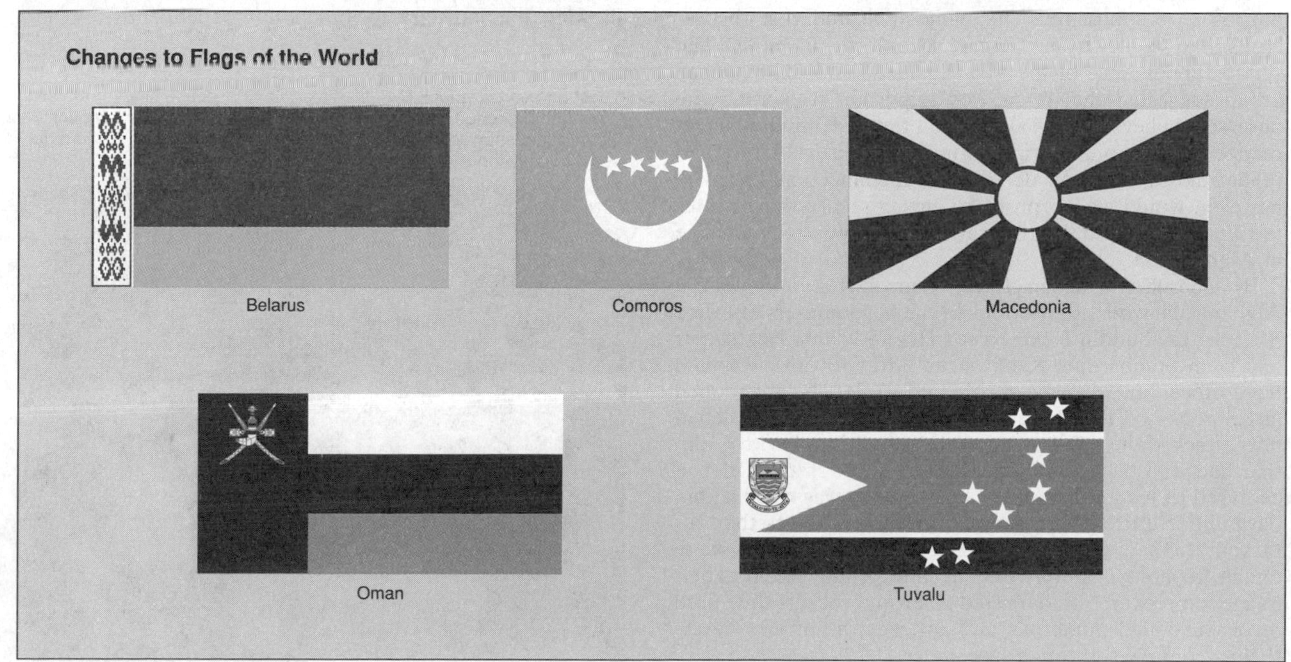

Belarus

Comoros

Macedonia

Oman

Tuvalu

AFGHANISTAN

Afghanistan is a landlocked Islamic state in central Asia. Area: 652,225 sq km (251,825 sq mi). Pop. (1995 est.): 18,129,000 (excluding Afghan refugees estimated to number about 1.6 million in Pakistan and about 1.6 million in Iran). Cap.: Kabul. Monetary unit: afghani, with (Oct. 6, 1995) a free rate of 4,442 afghanis to U.S. $1 (7,022 afghanis = £1 sterling). President in 1995, Burhanuddin Rabbani; prime minister, Gulbuddin Hekmatyar.

A new national force that called itself Taleban (Persian for "students") brought a degree of calm to parts of Afghanistan in 1995, in part by neutralizing several powerful leaders and their supporters. The dispute over control of Kabul was not resolved, however, and regions of the country remained divided.

Early in the year, Pres. Burhanuddin Rabbani, whose extended term had expired, offered to relinquish power if an acceptable replacement could be found. Efforts by Mahmoud Mestiri and other UN mediators to bring the contending factions together and select a successor to Rabbani came to naught. The military-political situation was so unstable that serious negotiations were impossible.

The armed group Taleban had appeared in southern Afghanistan in late 1994. The group's first accomplishment was the defeat of local commanders who had hijacked a truck convoy traveling from Pakistan to Central Asia. These mainly Pashtun students secured the release of the convoy and within days took control of Kandahar; later they extended their control to neighbouring provinces. While maintaining a low profile in a council in Kandahar, the Taleban declared that their goal was to disarm all factions and create a united, Islamic government in Afghanistan.

Most ordinary Afghans, particularly in traditionally Pashtun areas of the country, welcomed the sudden and effective success of the Taleban. Drug trafficking and lawlessness were targeted, and religious conformity was enforced. The latter included severe restrictions on women's appearance in public and especially on their access to education and employment. Public executions and amputations were used to enforce Islamic behaviour.

The origin of Taleban, as well as its organization and purpose, were obscure. The name indicated that the recruits had come from Islamic schools in Pakistan. The sudden appearance of the well-organized and well-financed group suggested that it enjoyed important backing. Some observers believed that Taleban had ties to Pakistan's secret service, even though Prime Minister Benazir Bhutto and other Pakistani officials denied such a connection. Pakistan, however, would clearly profit by having secure trade routes to Central Asia and the restoration of Pashtun preeminence in Afghanistan.

By February Taleban forces had moved into central Afghanistan, where they occupied the headquarters of Prime Minister Gulbuddin Hekmatyar's Hezb-i-Islami. Hekmatyar had been bombarding Kabul in an effort to drive Rabbani from office, but when he was forced to flee, he abandoned large stocks of heavy weapons and aircraft. The Taleban next attacked the pro-Iranian Wahdat militia, a Shi'ite group that had also been attacking Kabul. In March the Taleban captured its leader, Abdul Ali Mazari, who was killed within days under unclear circumstances. Taleban forces then attacked Rabbani's troops, but this time the students were unable to hold positions directly threatening Kabul. Their image, moreover, was damaged when the rockets they fired on Kabul killed numerous civilians, but the attacks nevertheless continued through December.

In northwestern Afghanistan Gen. 'Abd ar-Rashid Dostam continued to strengthen his independent position in Mazar-i-Sharif. With the destruction of Kabul, almost two-thirds of Afghanistan's total population was living in territory controlled by the Uzbek general. With a well-equipped army of 60,000, he continued to build economic and diplomatic relations with Afghanistan's neighbours. For Pakistan and Iran, Dostam's authority promised stable trade links to Central Asia, where he was seen as insurance against the threat of Islamic fundamentalism.

Ismail Khan, a close ally of Rabbani, had achieved a degree of normality in Herat until early September, when Taleban militias overran the area and Ismail escaped to Iran. Although the Pashtun population was a minority in the area, the new Taleban administration undertook the Islamization of society amid tension and suspicion. In Kabul an angry crowd stormed the embassy of Pakistan as relations between Kabul and Islamabad degenerated.

(STEVE SEGO)

ALBANIA

A republic in the western Balkan Peninsula of southeastern Europe, Albania is situated on the Adriatic Sea. Area: 28,748 sq km (11,100 sq mi). Pop. (1995 est.): 3,412,000. Cap.: Tirana. Monetary unit: lek, with (Oct. 6, 1995) a free rate of 93.65 leks to U.S. $1 (148.05 leks = £1 sterling). President in 1995, Sali Berisha; prime minister, Aleksander Meksi.

Pres. Sali Berisha's ruling Democratic Party (PDS) withstood the damaging effects of defeat in the November 1994 constitutional referendum but still faced formidable political, economic, and social problems in 1995. Following the referendum defeat, the PDS replaced incompetent and corrupt personnel at all party levels. The leading opposition Socialist Party (the former communist party) threatened the PDS's hold on power, while the PDS cited notable successes in economic and foreign affairs and predicted victory in the parliamentary elections scheduled for March 1996.

Albania's admission as the 36th member to the Council of Europe was a huge political success and came after the country proved it had made substantial progress in implementing economic, political, and social reforms. At the same time, the administration came under sharp criticism for not allowing the judiciary to function independently. A new

CATHERINE KARNOW—MATERIAL WORLD WOMEN'S PROJECT

A husband and wife look over flour for sale at a local market in Albania. A number of economic indicators, including gross domestic product and inflation, showed significant improvement during 1995, but in other areas, notably industry and exports, there were declines.

A housing complex for police families in Algiers stands in rubble after being bombed in March by an Islamist group. Vicious fighting between Islamic fundamentalists and the military-backed government of Algiers continued throughout 1995, with scores of people being killed and wounded.

ABBAS—MAGNUM

penal code and penal procedure came into force, however, enhancing the country's commitment to upholding human rights. Among the 49 new legislative decisions approved by the People's Assembly in 1995 were land and property laws that positively affected the flow of domestic and foreign investments, especially in the field of agriculture. The process of privatization continued, with some 1,400 small-sized enterprises privatized (only some middle- and large-sized companies awaited privatization). Albania's $700 million foreign debt was substantially reduced. As a result of an agreement between Albania and 41 Western banks, the country's debt owed to those institutions dropped from $500 million to $100 million on September 1.

On the domestic front gross domestic product grew by an estimated 6%, and the budget deficit was expected to be reduced to 7%. Inflation dropped to about 10%; the national currency, the lek, stabilized ($1 to 90 leks); and unemployment hovered at 260,000 (about 18%), despite the fact that an estimated 500,000 workers were employed abroad. The agricultural, construction, and private-service sectors registered high rates of growth—15%, 90%, and 25%, respectively. The industrial sector remained the weakest economic link, with continued production losses. Exports also lagged.

Continued progress was made in foreign affairs, with the exception of an impasse between Tirana and Belgrade. A slight improvement in Greek-Albanian relations was evidenced, and a first-ever meeting between U.S. and Albanian heads of state occurred in September. U.S.-Albanian military cooperation developed quickly. Joint projects in 1995 included U.S. intelligence-gathering flights to Bosnia and Herzegovina from bases in Albania, exchanges of high-level military delegations, medical and military exercises, and the construction of Albania's only military hospital.

(LOUIS ZANGA)

This article updates the *Macropædia* article BALKAN STATES: *Albania.*

ALGERIA

Algeria is a republic of North Africa on the Mediterranean Sea. Area: 2,381,741 sq km (919,595 sq mi). Pop. (1995 est.): 27,939,000. Cap.: Algiers. Monetary unit: Algerian dinar, with (Oct. 6, 1995) a controlled rate of 50.51 dinars to U.S. $1 (79.85 dinars = £1 sterling). President in 1995, Liamine Zeroual; prime ministers, Mokdad Sifi and, from December 31, Ahmen Ouyahia.

During 1995 the Algerian government was unable to end its severe domestic crisis. As many as 40,000 persons had lost their lives in fierce fighting that began in January 1992 when the government canceled the second round of legislative elections and banned the Islamic Salvation Front (FIS). The government oscillated between all-out repression of antigovernment factions and sporadic efforts to seek peace through negotiations. At the same time, Islamic groups became increasingly divided between the uncompromising extremism represented by the Armed Islamic Group (GIA) and the more moderate policies of the FIS.

In January the FIS, the National Liberation Front, the Socialist Forces Front, the Hamas Party (unrelated to the Palestinian organization called Hamas), and several other legally recognized political institutions met in Rome. They agreed on the need to end violence, release prisoners, and form a government of national unity that could oversee new multiparty elections. The government rejected that proposal, even though it had the backing of France, Italy, Spain, the U.S., and most antigovernment groups. The GIA also accepted the proposal, but its demand that Algeria's current leaders be punished was unrealistic.

The government riposted with a proposal that a presidential election be held in November. Only four persons were able to gather the required total of 75,000 signatures of support from at least 25 of Algeria's 48 provinces to qualify as candidates. Two who did were the respective

(continued on page 369)

SPOTLIGHT: THE BERBERS OF NORTH AFRICA

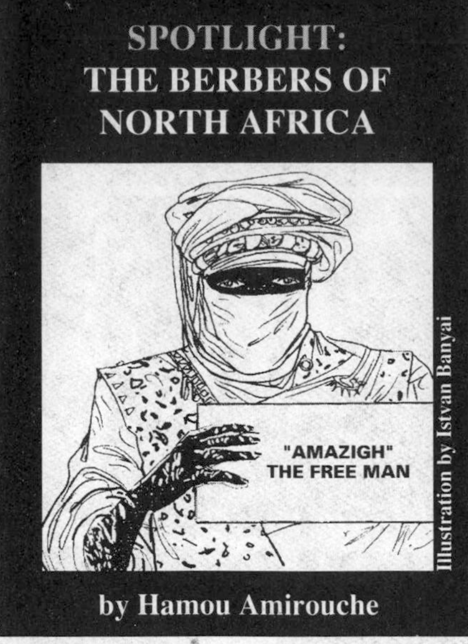

by Hamou Amirouche

The Berber revival and reassertion of cultural identity are integral parts of a larger quest for justice and political inclusion. Berbers scored a victory in Algeria in 1995 that is likely to have a far-reaching impact on the future of their communities.

Berbers Today. Berbers are descended from the aboriginal inhabitants of North Africa. Their earliest kingdoms go back to the 5th and 4th centuries BC. Their writing system, *tifinagh,* is derived from ancient Libyan, and their tongue belongs to the Afro-Asiatic language group. In isolated areas their language, art, and way of life have resisted the changes of time. Today they shun the use of the alien name Berber, favouring instead Amazigh (plural: Imazighen, "free men"), derived from Maxyes, their historic name.

The largest populations of Berbers are found in Morocco (30–35% of the population) and Algeria (about 15%). (The numbers used here are census and scholarly figures; some estimates are higher.) Morocco's nine million Berber speakers are located primarily in the Rif and Atlas mountain regions. In Algeria two-thirds of the nearly five million Berbers live in the Kabylie, particularly in the Djurdjura Mountains. Other significant Algerian groups include the Shawia in the Aurès Mountains and the M'zabites in the northern Sahara.

Another important Berber group is the Tuaregs, who straddle several states in the Sahara-Sahel region, particularly Niger (some 950,000) and Mali (about 660,000). Significant numbers also inhabit southern Algeria, Libya, and other countries.

The Plight of the Tuaregs. Since 1990 Tuareg uprisings and government massacres in Niger and Mali have sent thousands of refugees to Burkina Faso, Algeria, Mauritania, and Libya. The violence has been fueled by traditional disputes over land, compounded by what Berbers feel is political exclusion and economic discrimination. The signing of a pact between the Mali government and the Unified Movements and Fronts of Azawad in mid-1994 granted limited autonomy to the Tuaregs and provided for development of their regions. In June 1995 the Arab Islamic Front of Azawad, one of the last armed groups still holding out, joined the peace process.

The conflict in Niger was brought to a halt in April 1995 by a peace accord signed by the Organization of the Armed Resistance and the central government. The agreement provided for greater autonomy and economic development of the Tuareg region in the north. Although sporadic violence continued to plague the area, a fragile peace prevailed, easing the return of some refugees in December 1995.

Maghreb Berbers. In North Africa failures in nation building, along with social and cultural fragmentation, served as catalysts for violence and agitation. In Morocco the issue of Berber identity has not had the same vigour and political overtones as in Algeria. In May 1994, however, a demonstration called for the acceptance of Berber as an official language, and several leaders were subsequently put in jail. King Hassan II defused the crisis in 1995 when he allowed the introduction of news broadcasts and school programs in Berber.

In Algeria the Berbers scored a victory in May 1995 when the government instituted a council to rehabilitate and promote the Amazigh language. The Mouvement Culturel Berbere and two political parties headed by Berbers—the Socialist Forces Front (FFS) and the Rally for Culture and Democracy—were behind the accomplishment. The FFS was one of the opposition parties that signed the Rome covenant in early 1995 calling for a return to the democratic process. In the Rome meeting the FFS negotiated to include in the covenant the Amazighity, along with the Arabo-Islamic, as one of the elements defining the Algerian state.

The geographic dispersal of the people helps explain why there is no such entity as a Berber state or a clearly voiced aspiration to establish one. This might change, however, if Berbers' aspirations for political inclusion and for minority rights are thwarted. Transnational self-awareness is growing, as exemplified by the Berber festival held in August 1994 in Douarnenez, France, at which it was agreed to hold the first international Amazigh congress in 1996.

Hamou Amirouche is a freelance author who has written extensively on North African affairs and published articles on democracy in North Africa.

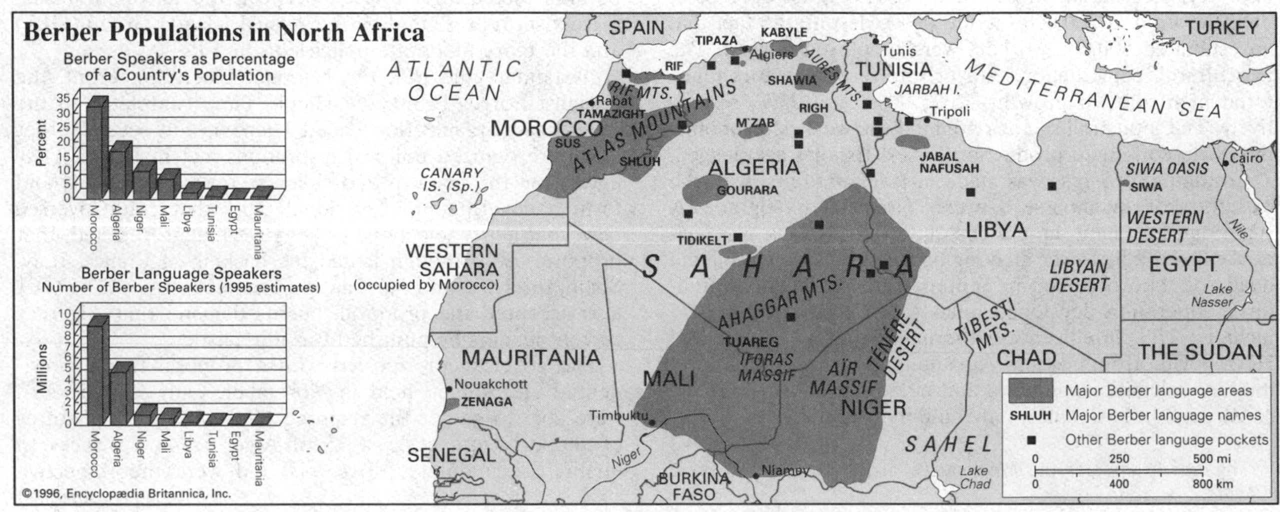

(continued from page 367)
leaders of the moderate Hamas Party and of the Rally for Culture and Democracy, which represented Berber interests and advocated a secular government. As expected, Pres. Liamine Zeroual was easily reelected. He later named as prime minister a man who had earlier negotiated a peace accord with guerrillas.

From the president's point of view, the major advantage of the election was that it allowed him to escape from extremists in his own party and to renew the process of negotiating a settlement to the Algerian crisis. That, after all, had been the basis for choosing him to lead the country in late January 1994. A further attempt at negotiations with the imprisoned leaders of the FIS collapsed in July when the FIS said it could not agree to the terms the government set down as a condition for restoring the legal status of a renamed FIS. International complaints about the human rights situation in Algeria continued with Amnesty International's criticism of the government for the deaths of 96 inmates during a riot in Serkadji prison in Algiers early in the year and for its permission of extrajudicial killings by the security forces.

The economy remained weak despite a new $1.8 billion extended fund facility with the International Monetary Fund in February. Agreement had first been reached on a new economic structural adjustment program. This enabled further rescheduling of Algeria's massive foreign debt ($29.6 billion at the end of 1994 and $32.3 billion at the end of 1995). In June the commercial debt was rescheduled, and in July $7.5 billion of the official debt was rescheduled. The first such rescheduling, which involved $5.3 billion, had taken place in June 1994. All in all, the economic situation still looked grim. (GEORGE JOFFÉ)

This article updates the *Macropædia* article NORTH AFRICA: *Algeria.*

ANDORRA

A landlocked parliamentary coprincipality of Europe, Andorra is in the Pyrenees Mountains between Spain and France. Area: 468 sq km (181 sq mi). Pop. (1995 est.): 62,900. Cap.: Andorra la Vella. Monetary units: French franc and Spanish peseta. Coprinces: the president of France and the bishop of Urgell, Spain; head of the government in 1995, Marc Forné Molné.

Andorra began 1995 with a new government led by Marc Forné Molné, who replaced Oscar Ribas Reig as president of the Executive Council. Ribas Reig, who had led the country out of more than 700 years of feudalism to independence, announced his government's resignation after losing a vote of confidence in the General Council of the Valleys (parliament) on Nov. 25, 1994. On Dec. 21, 1994, Molné, of the Liberal Union Party (Unió Liberal, UL), was sworn in at the head of a minority government. The political parties in coalition with the UL were the Liberal Group (Grup Liberal), the National Andorran Coalition (Coalició Nacional Andorrana), and the Canillo-La Massana Grouping (Agrupació Canillo-La Massana).

Andorra's clean mountain air, lack of income tax, and discreet banking industry continued to attract foreigners and tax exiles. In 1995 the population remained three-quarters foreign; in addition, some 12 million people visited annually, drawn by the duty-free shopping. The country looked forward to expanding its banking services in hopes of becoming a major European financial services centre.

In international affairs Andorra became a member of the Council of Europe on Nov. 10, 1994. It had been admitted to the UN as a full member in 1993. (ANNE ROBY)

This article updates the *Micropædia* article ANDORRA.

ANGOLA

A republic, Angola is located on the Atlantic coast in southwestern Africa. The small exclave of Cabinda is separated from Angola by a strip of Zaire. Area: 1,246,700 sq km (481,354 sq mi). Pop. (1995 est.): 11,558,000. Cap.: Luanda. Monetary unit: readjusted kwanza, with (Oct. 6, 1995) a controlled rate of 5,692 readjusted kwanzas to U.S. $1 (8,998 readjusted kwanzas = £1 sterling). President in 1995, José Eduardo dos Santos; prime minister, Marcolino Moco.

To the relief of the UN negotiators who had orchestrated the deal, the accord signed by the government of Angola and representatives of the rebel National Union for the Total Independence of Angola (UNITA) in Lusaka, Zambia, on Nov. 20, 1994, seemed still to be in force as 1995 began, in spite of mutual accusations of default by the signatories. Pressure from Presidents Robert Mugabe of Zimbabwe and Nelson Mandela of South Africa had helped to curb Pres. José Eduardo dos Santos' impulse to follow up the government's run of military successes against the rebels, and the guarantee of a role in the government of Angola encouraged UNITA to adopt a more cooperative attitude.

Aid agencies were faced with a formidable task even if the cease-fire persisted. The World Food Programme alone earmarked $65 million to help 1.2 million displaced persons, refugees, demobilized soldiers, and others in areas where there was an acute shortage of food. On February 8 the UN Security Council resolved to send a 7,000-strong peacekeeping force to monitor developments, a far more substantial and consequently more effective presence than had been provided by the 700 observers sent in 1992 when elections were held in Angola. One of the less pleasant tasks to be undertaken by the force was helping to clear up the land mines, numbering 26 million at the highest estimate, laid during the civil war.

Encouraged by a letter from the French prime minister, Édouard Balladur, UNITA leader Jonas Savimbi agreed to meet dos Santos. His decision was approved by the eighth ordinary congress of UNITA, which also endorsed the accord of November 20. In these more promising circumstances the two former opponents met in Lusaka on May 6 for the first time since 1992. Their discussions resulted in a vote by the National Assembly in July to amend the constitution to provide for the creation of two vice presidential posts, one of which would be filled by Savimbi after he had demobilized his army. UNITA would then become simply a political party and would be offered ministerial posts in a power-sharing government, but there would be no presidential election until the expiration of dos Santos' present term. Savimbi declared himself willing to act as vice president and said his party would accept the ministerial appointments offered. This cleared the way for the deployment of the peacekeeping force, though the process was delayed until the roads were made passable.

UNITA nevertheless experienced continuing unease, which was reflected in a call to the international community to refrain from sending arms to the government and in the citing of Russia and Portugal as being among those countries that were still doing so. The Portuguese parliamentary opposition had made similar charges against the government in January. In August, too, UNITA claimed that the new national army was behaving with an unduly heavy hand in regions that it had formerly controlled. A more positive response to the peace accord had been made by South Africa, which entered into an agreement with Angola to undertake joint explorations for oil and diamonds. As early as April South African companies were reported to be prospecting in Angola. Portugal agreed to train a national police force.

With the threat of military action by UNITA receding, the government began to contemplate the transfer of troops to Cabinda, where they hoped to be able to abandon their mainly defensive role in favour of a more aggressive policy toward the rebel forces that were posing a threat to any plans for increasing the region's oil production and processing. Fortunately, offshore production had increased steadily in spite of the civil war, and the facilities for offshore processing and for loading the petroleum into tankers prevented exports from being hindered by rebel activity.

(KENNETH INGHAM)

This article updates the *Macropædia* article SOUTHERN AFRICA: *Angola.*

ANTIGUA AND BARBUDA

A constitutional monarchy and member of the Commonwealth, Antigua and Barbuda comprises the islands of Antigua, Barbuda, and Redonda in the eastern Caribbean Sea. Area: 442 sq km (171 sq mi). Pop. (1995 est.): 63,900. Cap.: Saint John's. Monetary unit: Eastern Caribbean dollar, with (Oct. 6, 1995) a par value of EC$2.70 to U.S. $1 (free rate of EC$4.26 = £1 sterling). Queen, Elizabeth II; governor-general in 1995, James Carlisle; prime minister, Lester Bird.

Antiguans marked the opening of the new year with a spirited demonstration in January against new taxes. First mooted in 1994 but delayed until 1995, the taxes included higher fees for public services and a levy on incomes to finance education. One-day token strikes followed in February and March, but the government refused to budge, its only concession being not to impose any new taxes in the 1995 budget.

The island's first political family, the Birds, were in trouble again in May when Prime Minister Lester Bird's younger brother, Ivor, was found guilty of being in possession of cocaine and fined EC$200,000. The leniency of the sentence surprised most Antiguans. The fine was paid by his father, former prime minister Vere Bird.

An increasing number of crimes against tourists forced the government to institute joint police and army patrols in tourist areas.

Antigua received a heavy blow in September from Hurricane Luis, which left in its wake destruction estimated at U.S. $300 million. Sixty percent of the building stock was damaged, including leading hotels, which would affect the tourist industry's performance in 1995. The U.S. joined other nations in sending relief supplies to the island.

(DAVID RENWICK)

This article updates the *Macropædia* article THE WEST INDIES: *Antigua and Barbuda.*

ARGENTINA

The federal republic of Argentina occupies the eastern section of the Southern Cone of South America, along the Atlantic Ocean. Area: 2,780,400 sq km (1,073,518 sq mi). Pop. (1995 est.): 34,587,000. Cap.: Buenos Aires. Monetary unit: peso, with (Oct. 6, 1995) an official (pegged) rate of A1 to U.S. $1 (A1.58 = £1 sterling). President in 1995, Carlos Saúl Menem.

The year 1995 began inauspiciously, with Argentina in the shadow of Mexico's currency crisis, which had erupted in December 1994. With presidential, gubernatorial, and some congressional elections scheduled for May 14 and Pres. Carlos Menem running for reelection, prompt action was taken by Economy Minister Domingo Cavallo to ensure that the country did not succumb to the so-called tequila effect of Mexico's crisis and also to reduce the chances of the opposition Radical Civic Union (UCR) and the Frepaso grouping, which had emerged from the former Broad Front (Frente Grande), gaining victories in the election.

Cavallo's strategy included budget spending cuts announced in early January, subsequently reinforced by a package of austerity measures in early March. The country's extended financing facility program with the International Monetary Fund (IMF), which had been allowed to lapse in September 1994, was resumed. The program, under which the authorities originally had agreed to achieve a fiscal surplus of $4.4 billion (reduced in September) and growth of 3% (down from 7.1% in 1994), was approved on April 6. This helped rekindle business confidence and tempt back some of the estimated $8.2 billion of capital that had left the country early in the year.

Against this backdrop, and with signs of unrest as the economy slowed sharply, the election campaign was fought. In his May 1 Labour Day address, Menem pledged his commitment to cut by 50% the unemployment rate (then thought to be slightly above the 12.2% registered in October 1994 but later shown to have been 18.6%) by means of a five-year public works program that would create 300,000 jobs.

In fact, the economic slowdown did assist the opposition to some degree, with José Octavio Bordón—a senator and former member of the ruling Justicialist National Movement (Peronist) party, who defected in late 1994 to become the presidential candidate of the Frepaso grouping—appearing to make significant headway in the race for the presidency. But the election proved to be a resounding victory for Menem, who received about 50% of the vote, followed by Bordón with 29% and the UCR's Horacio Massaccesi with 17%. Of the 14 governorships contested on the same date, Peronist candidates won 10 and the UCR the remaining 4. The ruling party's position was also strengthened in the Chamber of Deputies, where it gained sufficient additional members to give it a quorum (136 of 257 seats).

Menem officially began his second term of office—to run for four years (reduced from six as part of the 1994 constitutional revision)—on July 8. His Cabinet was unchanged, except that the new post of coordinating minister—a virtual prime minister—came into effect in September as specified in the revised constitution. The appointment, made by the president, went to Menem's former chief of staff, Eduardo Bauzá. However, a bill submitted to the national legislature in late September proposed the creation of several new ministries in line with the increased emphasis being placed by Menem in his second term on social and environmental matters.

On the economic front, despite the relative success of measures to avert a Mexico-style financial crisis in Argentina, there were casualties among small banks and finance houses as liquidity was reduced. Some 50 banks had disappeared by year's end. The slowdown in activity also resulted in a significant reduction in tax revenues, which compromised the IMF target of achieving a fiscal surplus. The IMF program was thus renegotiated in late August, and revised terms were agreed upon by early September. Growth also turned negative, with a 3.7% contraction in the second quarter; this resulted in a first-half decline of 0.4% and official downward revision (in late September) of the annual growth forecast from 3% to 1%. Inflation remained at a stable low level, with the annual rate expected to be 3.6%.

Given the high rate of unemployment (18.6% in May) and the impact of budget cuts, there was disquiet among the labour unions. This was partly demonstrated in a half-day general strike by the main labour confederation on September 6 and by provincial unrest on repeated occasions,

An Armenian boy stands at the door of his family's "container" home, fashioned from a storage tank. Thousands of families were forced to move into such facilities, thought to be temporary, when their homes were destroyed by the severe earthquakes that struck Armenia in 1987 and 1988.

DAVID TURNLEY—DETROIT FREE PRESS/BLACK STAR

including riots in Córdoba in June, San Juan in late July, and Santa Fe in September.

The nation's trade position improved markedly in the first half of 1995 under the impact of the reduction of domestic consumption and strong demand from neighbouring Brazil. A quarrel with Brazil, its chief partner in the Southern Cone Common Market (Mercosur), over that country's plans to restrict automobile imports was largely defused in top-level meetings in June and July. At the end of June there was a six-month surplus of $883 million based on exports of $10,590,000,000 and imports of $9.7 billion. This contributed to a stronger current account position. After a first-quarter deficit of $1.8 billion, there was a surplus in the second quarter of $857 million; thus, the deficit at midyear was $951 million, down from $4,980,000,000 at the same time in 1994. In the international arena a pact signed with Britain on September 27 covered future arrangements for oil exploration and revenue sharing in the Falkland Islands/Islas Malvinas, and relations with Cuba were reported to be improving. (SUSAN M. CUNNINGHAM)

ARMENIA

A landlocked republic of Transcaucasia, Armenia borders Georgia to the north, Azerbaijan to the east, Iran to the south, the Azerbaijani exclave of Nakhichevan to the southwest, and Turkey to the west. Area: 29,800 sq km (11,500 sq mi). Pop. (1995 est.) 3,548,000. Cap.: Yerevan. Armenia claims the predominantly Armenian-populated Nagorno-Karabakh region, which has been part of Azerbaijan since 1923. Monetary unit: dram, with (Oct. 6, 1995) an official rate of 400 dram = U.S. $1 (632.36 dram = £1 sterling). President in 1995, Levon Ter-Petrosyan; prime minister, Hrant Bagratyan.

The ruling Armenian National Movement (ANM) consolidated its grip on power in 1995. In January, despite Western expressions of concern, the Armenian Supreme Court upheld a six-month suspension of the activities of the Armenian Revolutionary Federation (ARF)—the country's main opposition party, which was thus prevented from fielding candidates in the July 5 parliamentary elections. Several other small opposition parties were similarly barred from participating in the elections, which were subsequently designated by international observers as "free but not fair." The ANM won some 70% of the 190 seats. In a simultaneous referendum, voters endorsed a new constitution that bestowed broad powers on Pres. Levon Ter-Petrosyan. After the elections the Armenian security service threatened a permanent ban on the ARF, accusing it of planning terrorist activities; four of its members went on trial on charges of terrorism, and several more were arrested.

The incipient economic upswing of 1994 gathered momentum in 1995. Gross domestic product for the first seven months of the year was up 9.4% from 1994, and industrial production was up 9%. The inflation rate for the first 10 months was 20%. Privatization made steady progress, and the World Bank granted Armenia a credit of $60 million to underpin economic stabilization. In late October the controversial Medzamor nuclear power station, mothballed in 1989, was reactivated in order to circumvent the energy shortage that had paralyzed industry for the past four years.

Armenia's special relationship with Russia was further underscored by the signing in March of a 25-year agreement allowing Russia to maintain two military bases in Armenia. In September, Iranian Foreign Minister Ali Akbar Velayati visited Yerevan to sign agreements on political and economic cooperation. Armenian leaders continued to seek improved relations with Turkey. (ELIZABETH FULLER)

This article updates the *Macropædia* article TRANSCAUCASIA: *Armenia.*

AUSTRALIA

A federal parliamentary state (formally a constitutional monarchy) and member of the Commonwealth, Australia occupies the smallest continent and includes the island state of Tasmania. Area: 7,682,300 sq km (2,966,200 sq mi). Pop. (1995 est.): 18,025,000. Cap.: Canberra. Monetary unit: Australian dollar, with (Oct. 6, 1995) a free rate of $A 1.31 to U.S. $1 ($A 2.08 = £1 sterling). Queen, Elizabeth II; governor-general in 1995, Bill Hayden; prime minister, Paul Keating.

Domestic Affairs. The debate in Australia over republicanism intensified in 1995 when Prime Minister Paul Keating announced that Sir William Deane, a High Court judge, would replace Bill Hayden as Australia's 42nd governor-general. Deane's appointment, which came as a complete surprise, was set to run from Feb. 16, 1996, to Dec. 31, 2000, fitting in with Keating's agenda to replace the post of governor-general with the first Australian president no later than 2001.

Uncertainty about the timing of the next general election distracted both the government and the opposition during the year. Keating held the initiative, but he was unable to find a window of opportunity when public opinion was sufficiently on his side to make the risk of calling an early election worth it. In January, Alexander Downer resigned after only eight months as head of the Liberal Party of Australia. He was replaced by former party leader John Howard. Polls later showed much support in the main cities for Howard and the Liberal coalition in preference to Keating's governing Australian Labor Party (ALP).

In the electorate, women and minorities were disenchanted by the ALP's failure to live up to its rhetoric on preference for underrepresented gender and ethnic groups. These two issues came to a head when the ALP's national hierarchy took away from a local branch the right to select a candidate for the safe Labor seat of Batman in Melbourne's western suburbs. The local branch wanted either Theo Theophanous or Jenny Mikakos, but Keating intervened, with the help of the ALP national secretary, and installed the outgoing president of the Australian Council of Trade Unions (ACTU), Martin Ferguson, as the ALP's candidate. ACTU Assistant Secretary Jennie George was groomed to replace Ferguson as chief of the trade union movement. The first woman to hold this job, George faced a rapid downturn in union membership, with less than 40% of the workforce paid-up union members.

Two cases on Aboriginal rights were before the High Court early in the year. In March the High Court ruled against Western Australia's challenge to the 1993 Native Title Act, thereby reinstating Aboriginal property claims in that state. Less than a month later, a group of Aborigines who had been taken from their families as children under a 1918–53 law in the Northern Territory filed suit in the High Court.

Health Minister Carmen Lawrence (*see* BIOGRAPHIES) saw herself as the target of a royal commission. This view was endorsed by the prime minister, who used all the resources at the government's disposal to protect Lawrence's reputation. For his part, Howard was severely embarrassed by his inability to control a power broker in the west, Sen. Noel Crichton-Browne, who was eventually expelled from the party.

The Australian literary and artistic world was rocked in 1995 by three events. Helen Garner published a controversial book, *The First Stone,* in which she provoked a feminist backlash for her assertion that women should grow up where sexual politics are concerned. *The First Stone* was

AFP

Australian citizens march in Sydney on August 6 to commemorate the 50th anniversary of the dropping of the atomic bomb on Hiroshima, Japan. Throughout the year the Australian government strongly protested the decision by France to conduct nuclear tests in the South Pacific.

overshadowed by the furor over *The Hand That Signed the Paper,* which won the Miles Franklin Literary Award only to land its author in hot water for misrepresentation of her ancestry. The author, Helen Demidenko, claimed that her tale of Ukrainian complicity in the Holocaust was based on her Ukrainian father's family history. She was later unmasked as Helen Darville, the daughter of middle-class British immigrants. Subsequent arguments over the propriety of writers' using misleading noms de plume were overshadowed by a controversy about the book's main theme, anti-Semitism.

Hilary McPhee, the general manager of the Australia Council, ruffled literary feathers by describing Australian artists and intellectuals as malcontents who "deep in their bones seem to me to wish each other ill." McPhee's Australia Council distributed $A 60 million each year and was often criticized because its funding procedures were deemed unfair by some. McPhee responded by saying that the Australian artistic community was unique in its lack of generosity, which had "more in common with a provincial town than a serious nation." There was a literary bright spot during the year when Western Australian novelist Tim Winton (*see* BIOGRAPHIES) was short-listed for the Booker Prize.

A best-forgotten chapter in Australian aviation history closed in 1995 when the government finally bowed to pressure from its military pilots and withdrew the Nomad aircraft from service. Crashes killed 56 people before Sen. Robert Ray, the defense minister, axed the Nomad after a joint army and navy report found that the aircraft was not capable of carrying out its assigned tasks. Originally designed 20 years earlier in the hope that its short take-off and landing capacity would lead to a new export industry, the Nomad was soon found to have a basic design fault in the tail, which, Ray admitted, did not provide an acceptable margin of safety for military operations. The Australian Broadcasting Corporation followed up with a hard-hitting television exposé that lamented the prospect of the Nomad's still being on sale for civilian purposes.

The Economy. Opinions varied on the strength of the Australian economy during 1995. The World Bank rated Australia as the world's richest country by measuring national net worth, including natural resources, and concluding that each Australian had a net worth of $A 1.9 million. With an election due in early 1996, the government and opposition disputed the meaning of economic indicators. The Australian treasurer declared that Australians were living "in very good economic times," pointing to growth in gross domestic product. There were 16 consecutive quarters of positive growth, the best record in 25 years. By August 1995 annual growth stood at 3.7%, which indicated that the economy had broken free of the boom-bust cycle and had slowed to sustainable levels. Howard dismissed the good news as transitory, saying that it amounted only to "five minutes of economic sunshine." The opposition shadow treasurer, Peter Costello, commented that growth levels of less than 4% would not send anyone reaching for the suntan cream and criticized the ALP for hardening the Australian electorate to accepting bad news with equanimity. The Australian current account deficit, said Costello, was unacceptable when compared with those of Australia's trading partners.

In May the deficit reached $A 3.1 billion a month, easing slightly in June and July to $A 2.5 billion and $A 2.1 billion. The small improvement was caused by the increase in exports of sugar, gold, coal, petroleum, and gas and brought the deficit into line with the budget forecast of $A 427 billion. Economists and politicians alike agreed that the key question was whether the huge balance of payments deficit and foreign debt would lead to a rise in domestic interest rates, something that would enormously damage the Keating government's chances of reelection. Howard's criticism was dismissed by the governor of the reserve bank, Bernie Fraser. Fraser was himself criticized by Costello for becoming involved in party politics while a civil servant.

Privatization remained a major weapon in the government's economic arsenal. The national airline, Qantas, was privatized in 1995 in a relatively successful return of capital to the government. Although foreign buyers snapped up 53.2% of the stock (exceeding the government's 49% limit), investors were happy with the market price.

Maximizing the sale price proved possible in the case of Qantas but very hard when it came to selling the national shipping company. The Australian National Line (ANL) had an annual history of high debt and financial loss, but maritime unions and waterfront stevedores resisted privatization. On May 22 the Peninsular and Oriental Steam Navigation Co. (P&O) line emerged as the only bidder. Three months later the auditor general revealed that the ANL had cost taxpayers $A 53.7 million since 1991. At the end of August, the Cabinet agreed to sell 100% of the ANL to P&O, despite the opposition of the Maritime Union of Australia and the ACTU. P&O guaranteed that the ANL would remain under the Australian flag with Australian-only crews on Australian award conditions. The prime minister warned the unions that jobs would be slashed if the ANL remained in government hands and urged the unions to accept the P&O bid. Keating made it clear that restructuring rather than privatizing the ANL would lead to massive job losses, with five of the company's six vessels in international trade scrapped and lost. P&O, on the other hand, promised to keep at least four of the six vessels and to consider replacements for the other two.

The management of Australia's largest retailer, Coles Myer Ltd., was subject to intense scrutiny in September 1995 as the company lost its second internal auditor in a month and sacked its finance director. Coles Myer's most vocal activist shareholder, Laurence Gruzman, argued that the firing was an indication of wider problems within Coles Myer. Gruzman identified as the most important matter the transfer of the purchasing power of Coles Myer—one of the largest corporations in Australia—to small private companies. In response, Mark Leibler, a nonexecutive director of Coles Myer, pointed out that more had been written about the company in a week than about any other corporation in recent history and that every column inch had caused the company immense damage.

Foreign Affairs. The decision by Pres. Jacques Chirac (*see* BIOGRAPHIES) of France to hold a series of nuclear weapon tests in the South Pacific at Mururoa atoll seriously damaged relations with Australia. Demonstrations against the French tests were overwhelmingly peaceful except in Perth, where the French consulate was firebombed. Keating took a full-page advertisement in the Paris newspaper *Le Monde* on June 28 to explain to the French people why Australia said "no" to French nuclear tests, saying that if France had to test atomic weapons, why not test them in metropolitan France. The Australian government, said Keating, was deeply concerned about the possibility of accidents, as no one could foresee the long-term changes associated with possible leakage from the fragile atoll.

Another newspaper, *Le Figaro,* accused the Australian government of a "fetishist hatred of France," claiming that Australia was attacking the French in order to dominate Oceania. Chirac repeated the claim that Australia was behind the anticolonialist movement in the Pacific, accused Australian members of Parliament and journalists of being responsible for the destruction of the airport at Tahiti, and threatened to cut off importation of Australian uranium. Ambassadors were withdrawn by both countries as an expression of serious displeasure. France recalled its ambassador to Australia in August, denouncing Australia for breaking international law by stopping mail to the French embassy, delaying diplomatic bags, permitting demonstrators to attack the embassy, and holding French ships in Australian ports.

Significant political fallout from the Mururoa tests also affected foreign relations with the U.K. A delegation of senior Australian political figures, including the minister for Pacific Island affairs, Gordon Bilney, and the shadow foreign minister, former Liberal leader Downer, was snubbed by the British government. Bilney's group traveled to Europe to protest against the French tests and to seek support from their European allies. While Finland, Denmark, and Sweden were sympathetic and helpful to the Australian cause, in London the delegation was able to see only a junior minister in the Foreign Office who refused to criticize France. The *Weekend Australian* pointed out that the conclusion Australia should draw from this was that the constitutional link between Australia and Britain was obsolete. In a lengthy editorial the newspaper explained that the divergence of interests between the British and Australian people was too great to allow the constitutional status quo to remain.

Australia's growing emphasis on its relations with other nations in the Asia-Pacific region was apparent during the year. Keating had talks with Indonesian President Suharto in Bali in September and afterward testified to the warmth and strength of the relationship. Australian Foreign Minister Gareth Evans had earlier turned a very difficult situation around when Suharto nominated Lieut. Gen. Herman Mantiri as Indonesian ambassador to Australia. Some segments of the Australian press and the public complained that in 1992 Mantiri had made inappropriate comments on the Dili massacre in East Timor. Evans, through the careful handling of his relationship with his Indonesian counterpart, Ali Alatas, was able to persuade the Indonesians to withdraw Mantiri's nomination. The incident was typical of Evans' skillful handling of Indonesian relations, which were further improved when Indonesian ground troops took part in military exercises on Australian soil. Defense Minister Ray was keen to use every opportunity to conduct joint maneuvers and break down barriers between the armies of the two neighbours. Ray even threatened to outlaw flag burning when East Timor refugees marked the 50th anniversary of Indonesian independence by setting fire to the Indonesian flag in Darwin.

China was more difficult for Australian foreign policy makers. The poor treatment by Chinese police of Australian delegates to the UN Fourth World Conference on Women in Beijing received front-page status when the Australian ambassador to China, Michael Lightowler, became involved in a fracas while defending women under Australian consular protection from assault. (A.R.G. GRIFFITHS)

See also *Dependent States.*

AUSTRIA

The federal republic of Austria is a landlocked state of Central Europe. Area: 83,858 sq km (32,378 sq mi). Pop. (1995 est.): 8,063,000. Cap.: Vienna. Monetary unit: Austrian Schilling, with (Oct. 6, 1995) a free rate of 10.04 Schillings to U.S. $1 (15.87 Schillings = £1 sterling). President in 1995, Thomas Klestil; chancellor, Franz Vranitzky.

The year 1995 was an eventful one in Austria. On January 1 the country became a member of the European Union (EU). Vienna was allowed to remain neutral for the time being but would cooperate in the construction of a future European Security System. Austria, which had already joined the "Partnership for Peace," aspired to membership in the coming European economic and currency union. Although the country had a hard currency and was the third wealthiest country in the EU, as measured in purchasing power, it might not meet the EU's stringent criteria for economic stability. Franz Fischler, the Austrian minister of agriculture, became commissioner of agriculture and rural development for the EU.

After the October 1994 national parliamentary election, in which both the Social Democrats (SPÖ) and the Austrian People's Party (ÖVP) lost seats, the parties concluded a coalition agreement that November. Erhard Busek subsequently lost his positions as vice-chancellor and as chairman of the ÖVP. He was replaced in both offices by Wolfgang Schüssel, who also took over the Foreign Ministry from Alois Mock.

In spite of a favourable business cycle, economic growth, higher employment, and a rate of inflation finally lowered to 2–3%, the gap between state revenues and expenditures had been wide for quite some time, and the budget deficit and state indebtedness became even greater in 1995. In order to hold the value of the schilling and to meet the EC criteria, it would be necessary to bring the budget deficit to 2.7% and state expenditures to 65% of gross domestic product by 1998.

Disagreements over how to achieve this soon arose, however. The SPÖ, which supported higher taxes, and the ÖVP, which sought greater spending cuts, failed to reach a compromise. The coalition collapsed on October 12, and Chancellor Franz Vranitzky scheduled new elections for December 17. When the elections were held, Austrians rejected the sharp turn to the right many had predicted and gave the SPÖ 38.3% of the vote. Schüssel, leader of the ÖVP, lost his chance to form a rightist coalition government when his party garnered only 28.3%, and Jörg Haider's right-wing Freedom Party—third, with 22.1%—suffered its first electoral setback since 1986.

The unsolved murders of four Gypsies and a series of letter-bomb attacks caused anxiety among the populace and revealed differences of opinion on the relative importance of safety and civil liberties—for example, on the question of wiretapping. One leader of a neo-Nazi radical-right group was sentenced to a prison term. Meanwhile, an Austrian national fund for the victims of the Nazis in World War II was set up, with an initial capitalization of 500 million Schillings.

Accusations of sexual abuse of seminarians at the hands of the nation's highest Roman Catholic dignitary, Hans Hermann Cardinal Groer, caused a wave of revolt among the laity, many of whom had been unhappy with the leadership of the church for some time. The consequences were a massive flight from the churches, financial disaster, and a popular initiative signed by more than 400,000 people. Groer's successor as archbishop of Vienna, Christoph Schönborn, sought a way to mediate between the unpopular conservative leaders and the reformers, who demanded, among other things, more consultation on appointments, relaxation of celibacy requirements, admission of women to the priesthood, and less interference by the church in sexual matters.

The number and severity of commercial insolvencies in 1994–95 reached heights heretofore unknown. The loss for 1995 was reckoned to be between 50 and 60 billion Schillings. In the foreground was the bankruptcy of Konsum, the flagship of the Social Democrats and the unions. (ELFRIEDE DIRNBACHER)

AZERBAIJAN

A republic of Transcaucasia, Azerbaijan borders Russia on the north, the Caspian Sea on the east, Iran on the south, Armenia on the west, and Georgia on the northwest. The 5,500-sq km exclave of Nakhichevan to the southwest is separated from Azerbaijan proper by a strip of Armenia. Area (including Nakhichevan): 86,600 sq km (33,400 sq mi). Pop. (1995 est.): 7,525,000. Cap.: Baku (Azerbaijani: Bakı). Monetary unit: manat, with (Oct. 6, 1995) a free rate of 4,440 manat to U.S. $1 (7,019 manat = £1 sterling). President in 1995, Heydar Aliyev; prime minister, Fuad Guliyev.

Azerbaijan's Pres. Heydar Aliyev maintained his hold on power in 1995 by continuing his policy of heavy-handed repression of any political unrest. Some 70 people were killed in March when a purported uprising by the head of the security police was forcibly suppressed. Procuracy officials implicated the opposition Azerbaijan Popular Front and arrested some 200 people, including former interior minister Iskander Hamidov, who in September was sentenced to 14 years' imprisonment for embezzlement and abuse of his official position. The March incident was subsequently offered as the rationale for the arrest in October of former foreign minister and prominent opposition leader Tofik Gasymov. In August several high-ranking military officials were accused of planning to assassinate Aliyev.

Despite Western protests, the influential Musavat Party was banned from contesting the November 12 parliamentary elections, as were the Communist and Islamic parties. Widespread procedural violations led international observers to condemn the voting as undemocratic. Aliyev's New Azerbaijan party won a clear majority in the new 125-member parliament; the names of over half the new deputies figured on a list of the composition of the new parliament leaked to the press prior to the actual voting. Also on November 12, a new constitution increasing the powers of the president was adopted by referendum. Five young journalists jailed in October for publishing materials allegedly satirizing the president were formally pardoned by Aliyev on the eve of the elections, but censorship remained in force.

Economic decline continued in 1995: gross domestic product for the period January–August fell by 19% and industrial output by 26.6% compared with 1994; inflation for the same period was 790%. A short-term privatization program adopted by the parliament in July was not systematically implemented.

Hopes for an economic upswing continued to be predicated on Western investment in the oil sector. A decision reached in late 1994 to cede to Iran one-quarter of Azerbaijan's 20% stake in a multinational consortium to develop three offshore Caspian oil fields was reversed in March under pressure from the U.S. As a result of energetic Western lobbying, and to Russia's displeasure, the consortium opted in October to export the first oil from these fields through two pipelines, one through Russia and a second through Georgia. In November a second major agreement was signed with Russian, U.S., and Italian companies on joint exploitation of a fourth Caspian oil field.

Relations with Russia remained strained for much of the year, partly as a result of Moscow's closure of the Russian-Azerbaijan frontier in December 1994, allegedly in order to preclude the clandestine transport of arms and mercenaries from Azerbaijan to Chechnya. Tensions were exacerbated in August when a senior Azerbaijani foreign policy adviser gave a talk in Washington in which he characterized Russia as the single most serious threat to Azerbaijan's independence. The coolness in relations with Iran that resulted from the Azerbaijani leadership's backtracking on the oil deal was compounded by Iranian expressions of displeasure over Azerbaijan's increased cooperation with Israel and by the article in the new constitution stipulating that Azerbaijan is a secular state.

The cease-fire in Nagorno-Karabakh mediated by Russia in May 1994 remained in force, with sporadic minor exchanges of fire, throughout 1995. Virtually no progress was made, however, toward a political solution of the conflict despite seven separate rounds of talks chaired jointly by Russia and the Organization for Security and Cooperation in Europe. (ELIZABETH FULLER)

This article updates the *Macropædia* article TRANSCAUCASIA: *Azerbaijan.*

BAHAMAS, THE

A constitutional monarchy and member of the Commonwealth, The Bahamas comprises an archipelago of about 700 islands in the North Atlantic Ocean just southeast of the United States. Area: 13,939 sq km (5,382 sq mi). Pop. (1995 est.): 276,000. Cap.: Nassau. Monetary unit: Bahamian dollar, with (Oct. 6, 1995) a par value of B$1 to U.S. $1 (free rate of B$1.58 = £1 sterling). Queen, Elizabeth II; governor-general in 1995, Clifford Darling; prime minister, Hubert Ingraham.

The Bahamian government was preoccupied for much of the year with the twin problems of refugees from Haiti and, to a lesser extent, those from Cuba. It reached an agreement with Haiti on a program of planned repatriation of several thousand Haitians. The Cubans were a more difficult matter since they refused to go home and wanted instead to immigrate to the United States.

While a commission of inquiry continued looking into the way the state-owned Bahamas Hotel Corporation had conducted its affairs during the regime of former prime minister Sir Lynden Pindling, the government was completing the sale of the hotels within the corporation's portfolio. Jamaican hotelier Gordon ("Butch") Stewart was one of the buyers, paying $8.5 million for the 170-room Royal Bahamian Hotel in Nassau.

Meanwhile, the commission of inquiry was unable to complete its report into the hotel corporation because Pindling challenged its right to inspect his bank accounts. But it did present its findings in the affairs of the national airline, Bahamasair. It found evidence that two former Bahamasair chairmen, Philip Bethel and Darrell Rolle, had taken bribes to facilitate the purchase of aircraft and recommended that they be prosecuted. Both were serving as opposition members of the parliament. (DAVID RENWICK)

This article updates the *Macropædia* article The WEST INDIES: *The Bahamas.*

BAHRAIN

The monarchy (emirate) of Bahrain consists of a group of islands in the Persian Gulf between the peninsula of Qatar and Saudi Arabia. Area: 694 sq km (268 sq mi). Pop. (1995 est.): 579,000. Cap.: Manama. Monetary unit: Bahrain dinar, with (Oct. 6, 1995) an official rate of 0.38 dinar to U.S. $1 (0.60 dinar = £1 sterling). Emir in 1995, Isa ibn Sulman al-Khalifah; prime minister, Khalifah ibn Sulman al-Khalifah.

Sheikh Ali Salman Ahmad Salman, a Bahraini cleric, was arrested on Dec. 5, 1994, after signing a petition calling for the restoration of the constitution and the National Assembly, which had been dissolved in 1975. The arrest sparked the worst riots in Bahrain in decades. The country was put under martial law, and security forces arrested an estimated 2,000 protesters and exiled others. On Jan. 15, 1995, Sheikh Salman was deported to the United Arab Emirates, whence he flew to London seeking political asylum. Throughout the spring more arrests and deportations of Shi'ite clerics, as well as raids on Shi'ite mosques, took place. On April 1 another leading signatory of the petition, Sheikh 'Abd al-Amir al-Jamri, was arrested, which provoked more violent clashes with the security forces.

On April 2 Emir Isa ibn Sulman al-Khalifah met for the first time with about 20 leading religious and opposition figures to start a dialogue aimed at ending the ongoing violence. In June the government resigned, and a new Cabinet was appointed. An agreement was reached at the end of August whereby Sheikh al-Jamri and 40 other political prisoners were released in September. A total of 250 prisoners were released between August and September.

(MARY-JANE DEEB)

This article updates the *Macropædia* article ARABIA: *Bahrain.*

BANGLADESH

A republic and member of the Commonwealth, Bangladesh is in the northeastern part of the Indian subcontinent, on the Bay of Bengal. Area: 147,570 sq km (56,977 sq mi). Pop. (1995 est.): 120,093,000. Cap.: Dhaka. Monetary unit: taka, with (Oct. 6, 1995) an official rate of Tk 40.20 to U.S. $1 (Tk 63.55 = £1 sterling). President in 1995, Abdur Rahman Biswas; prime minister, Khaleda Zia.

Prime Minister Khaleda Zia's government continued to come under virulent attack from the Awami League-led opposition in 1995, as it had in the previous year. Accusing the Zia government of mismanagement, the opposition continued to demand the immediate resignation of the ruling Bangladesh Nationalist Party (BNP) and the holding of fresh elections under a neutral caretaker government. A compromise proposal by Commonwealth mediators, led by former Australian governor-general Sir Ninian Stephen, had brought hope of a breakthrough, but the plan was rejected by the opposition in October 1994. The proposal called for the formation of an 11-member Cabinet headed by Zia, to include five opposition leaders and one technocrat acceptable to both sides. In December 1994 all opposition members resigned from Parliament. In late November 1995 Pres. Abdur Rahman Biswas dissolved Parliament, with elections likely to be held in January 1996. The opposition rejected Zia's offer to step down one month before the voting and threatened to boycott the elections unless a caretaker government was installed before the polling began.

Meanwhile, the violent antigovernment protests and strikes that plagued the country in 1994 persisted throughout 1995. A three-day general strike that began on January 2 paralyzed the capital, Dhaka, and led to demonstrations in which at least 50 people were injured. Later that month two people died when police clashed with jute and cotton workers in the country's second largest city, Chittagong. Violent strikes by jute and textile workers in Dhaka and the southern city of Khulna in February resulted in the deaths of seven people and injuries to more than 100 others. In mid-March the opposition organized a two-week program of agitation in Dhaka and other major cities. It culminated in an eight-hour siege of the prime minister's office by over 5,000 demonstrators. In that incident more than 250 people were injured in clashes between security forces and protesters. The political violence continued into December.

Zia was confronted with another political crisis in March when farmers staged violent protests against the government for having caused a severe fertilizer shortage. According to a government-commissioned study, the shortage was caused by excessive exports of urea, which depleted local buffer stocks, even though there already was a shortage of fertilizer. This crisis added further grist to the opposition's accusation of government mismanagement. Zia quickly dismissed Industry Minister Zahiruddin Khan on April 4 and forced into early retirement the chairman of the Bangladesh Chemical Industries Corp., which operated the fertilizer factories owned by six states. Although Zia accused the opposition of creating "an artificial fertilizer crisis for political gain," the crisis was sure to cost the BNP at the next elections.

Bangladesh was once again battered by natural disasters. May rainstorms devastated coastal areas, killing more than 100 people and leaving at least one million homeless. These same storms caused an outbreak of malaria and diarrhea that subsequently claimed the lives of an estimated 1,100 people. Monsoon storms in June and July caused further massive flooding, adding more than 200 additional names to the year's death toll from natural disasters.

(CLAUDE RAKISITS)

BARBADOS

The constitutional monarchy of Barbados, a member of the Commonwealth, occupies the most easterly island in the southern Caribbean Sea. Area: 430 sq km (166 sq mi). Pop. (1995 est.): 265,000. Cap.: Bridgetown. Monetary unit: Barbados dollar, with (Oct. 6, 1995) a par value of BDS$2 to U.S. $1 (free rate of BDS$3.16 = £1 sterling). Queen, Elizabeth II; governor-general in 1995, Dame Nita Barrow; prime minister, Owen Arthur.

Prime Minister Owen Arthur signaled early in the year that the economy of Barbados was now strong enough for the government to be able to surrender its right to reduce salaries in the public sector. The previous Democratic Labour Party (DLP) administration had used wage cuts as an instrument of fiscal policy, but Arthur said that civil servants' salaries, like those of judges, should be protected by statute. A bill to this effect was passed by the House of Assembly in February.

Arthur again showed his faith in the underlying strength of the economy when he rejected the advice of the International Monetary Fund (IMF) and introduced a deficit budget in April. The IMF had urged prudence, but the prime minister insisted that deficit spending was necessary to reduce unemployment, which stood at 21.2% at the end of 1994. To demonstrate that the government would not sanction fiscal laxity, Arthur announced at the end of April that the state-owned Barbados Development Bank, which had accumulated losses of BDS$65 million in its 25 years of existence, would be closed down and two new agencies formed to take over its business, with the involvement of the private sector. Dame Nita Barrow, the popular and respected governor-general, died on December 19. (*See* OBITUARIES.)

(DAVID RENWICK)

This article updates the *Macropædia* article The WEST INDIES: *Barbados.*

BELARUS

A landlocked republic of Eastern Europe, Belarus borders Latvia on the north, Russia on the north and east, Ukraine on the south, Poland on the west, and Lithuania on the northwest. Area: 207,595 sq km (80,153 sq mi). Pop. (1995 est.): 10,332,000. Cap.: Minsk. Monetary unit: Belarusian rubel, with (Oct. 6, 1995) an official rate of 11,500 rubli = U.S. $1 (18,180 rubli = £1 sterling). Chairman of the Supreme Soviet in 1995, Myachaslau Hryb; president, Alyaksandr Lukashenka; prime minister, Mikhail Chyhir.

In Belarus 1995 was dominated by a power struggle between Pres. Alyaksandr Lukashenka and the Supreme Soviet, in which the former was successful in virtually every sphere. Belarus moved closer toward full integration with Russia while becoming an authoritarian state ruled increasingly by presidential decree.

On January 6–24 a customs union was created between Belarus and Russia, and an agreement on economic cooperation in 1995 was signed. On February 21 Belarus and Russia signed a treaty of friendship and cooperation, permitting Russia to continue to deploy strategic and military forces on Belarusian territory, promising Russian aid in combating the effects of the 1986 Chernobyl disaster, and regulating the supply of Russian energy resources to Belarus.

In February the president proposed a national referendum on the state flag, symbols, and languages, to be held on the same day as the new parliamentary elections, May 14. On April 11–12, 18 Belarusian Popular Front (BPF) deputies held a hunger strike within the Supreme Soviet to protest the referendum. The strike ended violently when the deputies were physically removed from the building and beaten by presidential troops.

The parliament subsequently agreed to four referendum questions: on the elevation of Russian to state-language status, the establishment of a new state flag and state symbols, economic integration with the Russian Federation, and amendments to the constitution permitting the president to dissolve the parliament in cases of violations of the constitution. Large majorities supported each of these proposals.

The two rounds of elections were characterized by low voter turnout (especially in Minsk, with 32.4% and 38.5%) and presidential pressure against opponents, especially the BPF, which lost all its seats in the parliament. Because a minimum voter turnout of 50% was required, the new parliament contained only 119 deputies (well below the 174 needed for a quorum in the 260-seat assembly), including 44 Independents, 25 Agrarians, and 23 Communists. A constitutional crisis resulted when the president refused to accept the right of the old parliament to amend the election laws. A new round of elections on November 29 raised the number of deputies to 139, still short of a quorum.

The economy remained in a critical state. Although inflation was reduced to less than 5% per month and the Belarusian rubel was stabilized at a rate of 11,600 rubli to the U.S. dollar, prices outpaced wages, bankrupt factories continued to operate, and privatization was minimal.

On September 15 Stanislau Bahdankevich, chairman of the National Bank of Belarus and one of the few proponents of monetarism and economic reform within the Belarusian hierarchy, resigned from office. Two days earlier he had negotiated an agreement with the International Monetary Fund allocating Belarus a credit of $300 million in five stages. Unfavourable international attention was attracted in September when a Belarusian helicopter gunship shot down a hydrogen racing balloon and killed the two U.S. pilots.

(DAVID R. MARPLES)

BELGIUM

A federal constitutional monarchy, Belgium is situated on the North Sea coast of northwestern Europe. Area: 30,528 sq km (11,787 sq mi). Pop. (1995 est.): 10,064,000. Cap.: Brussels. Monetary unit: Belgian franc, with (Oct. 6, 1995) a free rate of BF 29.39 to U.S. $1 (BF 46.46 = £1 sterling). King, Albert II; prime minister in 1995, Jean-Luc Dehaene.

On May 21 Belgium held its first federal elections to the Chamber of Representatives and the country's three regional assemblies of Flanders, Wallonia, and Brussels. The event was a triumph for Prime Minister Jean-Luc Dehaene and his Flemish Christian People's Party (CVP). Dehaene quickly reshaped his coalition government with the same four political parties as before—CVP, French-speaking Social Christians, French-speaking Socialists (PS), and Flemish Socialists. Expected gains by extreme right-wing parties did not materialize. Under the new federal structure, the size of the national Chamber of Representatives fell from 212 to 150 members and that of the Senate from 184 to 71. The regional assemblies in Brussels and Wallonia had 75 deputies each and in Flanders 118.

The key challenge facing the new government was preparation of the country's 1996 budget, which would have to reduce Belgium's budget deficit to 3% to ensure that it would join other European Union (EU) countries in introducing a single currency in 1999. Workers protested the austerity measures proposed by the government, and the issue was unresolved at the end of December.

Speculation over two of Belgium's longest-running political scandals continued to dog the country's leading politicians. The Agusta affair, with its investigation into an alleged BF 50 million bribe in 1988 to secure the contract for the purchase of Agusta S.p.A. helicopters, involved two of Belgium's most prominent politicians. Karel Van Miert continued untroubled as Belgium's EU commissioner, but Willy Claes, former foreign minister, was forced to resign as NATO secretary-general.

The affair claimed other victims. In March the retired chief of staff of the Belgian air force, Lieut. Gen. Jacques Lefebvre, committed suicide after his house had been searched and he had been questioned about the Agusta affair, and on March 22 Frank Vandenbroucke resigned as foreign minister after just five months in the post.

Investigators also tried to determine, but without success, whether there were any links between the Agusta contract and the second scandal, the murder in July 1991 of André Cools, the former leader of the PS.

Also in March Belgium became one of seven EU countries to abolish passport and customs border checks on EU nationals and legally resident third-country citizens traveling within the seven-member group. The removal of controls was not totally achieved, partly for technical problems and partly because of an upsurge in terrorist attacks in France.

Several changes took place in Belgium's economic landscape in 1995. The Leuven-based brewing company, Interbrew, took over Canada's John Labatt at the end of July and became the fourth largest brewing company in the world.

The year also saw an alliance between Belgium's national airline, Sabena, and Swissair. The deal, whereby the Swiss carrier took a 49% stake in the Belgian company, was a welcome source of cash for Sabena. The agreement also liquidated the 25% stake that Air France had earlier held in Sabena.

Pope John Paul II made a brief visit to Belgium in June after having canceled a trip a year earlier because of injury. The purpose was to beatify Joseph De Veuster, better known as Father Damien, who died in 1889 after caring for lepers in Hawaii.

(RORY WATSON)

BELIZE

A constitutional monarchy and member of the Commonwealth, Belize is on the Caribbean coast of Central America. Area: 22,965 sq km (8,867 sq mi). Pop. (1995 est.): 216,000. Cap.: Belmopan. Monetary unit: Belize dollar, with (Oct. 6, 1995) a par value of BZ$2 to U.S. $1 (free rate of BZ$3.16 = £1 sterling). Queen, Elizabeth II; governor-general in 1995, Colville Young; prime minister, Manuel Esquivel.

In January 1995 Prime Minister Manuel Esquivel of the United Democratic Party (UDP) restructured responsibilities in the Cabinet in an effort to deal with such problems as the recession-hit economy and an escalating crime rate.

Deputy Prime Minister Dean Barrow was appointed to the Ministry of National Security in addition to his responsibilities as minster of foreign affairs and attorney general. Elito Urbina assumed responsibility for the Ministries of Labour and Local Government, and Joseph Cayetano's Ministry of Energy and Communications was renamed Ministry of Science, Technology and Transportation. Prime Minister Esquivel added Economic Development to his portfolio. Elodio Aragón and Hubert Elrington lost their Labour and Local Government portfolios, respectively.

A seven-member committee, under the Ministry of Finance, was responsible for an economic citizenship program aimed at raising $30 million. An "economic citizen" would pay $25,000 to the government for registration and $50,000 to a special investment fund. The economic citizen would not have to live in Belize. A portion of the money would be used to finance Belize's foreign debt. Revenues from this program were included in the year's budget. Early in the year, Esquivel imposed a public-sector wage freeze for fiscal 1995–96 to help reduce the budget deficit.

Relations with Canada went less smoothly during the year when Fisheries Minister Brian Tobin sent notice to Belize in April that two trawlers flying Belizean flags of convenience had been illegally fishing off the Grand Banks. "If necessary," Tobin said, "we'll take the measures required to put an end to that flag-of-convenience presence." A spokeswoman for the Fisheries Department announced later that one of the ships was believed to be Spanish-operated.

On a visit to Cuba during the year by Deputy Prime Minister Barrow, diplomatic relations with Cuba were upgraded to full ambassador level. (INES PARKER)

This article updates the *Macropædia* article CENTRAL AMERICA: *Belize.*

BENIN

The republic of Benin is on the southern coast of West Africa, on the Gulf of Guinea. Area: 112,680 sq km (43,500 sq mi). Pop. (1995 est.): 5,409,000. Cap.: Porto-Novo (executive offices remain in Cotonou). Monetary unit: CFA franc, with (from Jan. 12, 1995) a par value of CFAF 100 to the French franc and (as of Oct. 6, 1995) a free rate of CFAF 501.49 to U.S. $1 (CFAF 792.78 = £1 sterling). President in 1995, Nicéphore Soglo.

In the March 28, 1995, elections for 83 National Assembly seats, there were 5,580 candidates representing 31 parties. Adrien Houngbedji's Democratic Renewal Party (PRD) and other opposition parties won an absolute majority of the 83 seats over Pres. Nicéphore Soglo's Benin Renaissance Party (PRB) and its allies. In April the Constitutional Court invalidated the results of 13 contests because of voting irregularities. Nevertheless, the opposition still held 43 of the 70 decided seats and dominated the new National Assembly, which was convened in April. On May 28 new elections for the 13 annulled districts gave the PRB five seats, the PRD two, and other opposition parties six. Benin's four-year-old democratic system thus faced a new challenge, with the opposition gaining control of the National Assembly.

Inflation continued to weaken the economy, and in May food exports were banned in an attempt to halt the soaring increases in prices of basic necessities. Labour union leaders demanded higher salaries to offset the spiraling cost of living. The government, already under pressure from international donors to reduce expenditures, and with revenues down, refused. One bright spot was a record cotton crop.

In April Benin responded to a UN request to dispatch soldiers to help keep order in Rwandan refugee camps in Zaire. Internally the refugee problem had eased considerably since 1993, when more than 150,000 people fleeing unrest in Chad, Togo, and Zaire traveled to Benin. In May the UN estimated that of the original number of refugees, some 44,000, mostly Togolese, still remained in the country.

The biennial summit meeting of the Francophone states, held in Cotonou in December, called upon Nigeria, Benin's neighbour to the east, to return to democratic principles and the rule of law. (NANCY ELLEN LAWLER)

This article updates the *Macropædia* article WESTERN AFRICA: *Benin.*

BHUTAN

The monarchy of Bhutan is a landlocked state situated in the eastern Himalayas between China and India. Area: 47,000 sq km (18,150 sq mi). Pop. (1995 est.): 816,000 (excluding Nepalese residents declared stateless by the Bhutanese government in late 1990, more than 100,000 of whom are now refugees in Nepal or India). Cap.: Thimphu. Monetary unit: ngultrum, at par with the Indian rupee (which is also in use), with (Oct. 6, 1995) a free rate of 33.90 ngultrums to U.S. $1 (53.59 ngultrums = £1 sterling). Druk gyalpo (king) in 1995, Jigme Singye Wangchuk.

A 16-year-old girl studies in a school run by the government of Bhutan. Although King Jigme Singye Wangchuk approved the establishment of the Asian country's first television station, other measures to protect the people against Western influences continued.
JOANNA PINNEO—MATERIAL WORLD WOMEN'S PROJECT

In April 1995 Bhutan and Nepal held their sixth round of ministerial talks, begun in 1991, in an attempt to resolve the status of approximately 85,000 Bhutanese refugees of Nepalese origin (called Lhotsampas) who had taken shelter in eight UN-run refugee camps located in eastern Nepal. The participants failed to reach an agreement, however. Nepal wanted to repatriate all the refugees who claimed to be Bhutanese, while the representatives of Bhutan insisted on joint verification of the refugees' nationality before allowing them back into the country.

The refugee problem developed after the Bhutanese government, fearing a threat to the monarchy, the religion, and the laws of Bhutan from the Hindu Lhotsampas, tightened its immigration laws and demanded that the Lhotsampas accept the Bhutanese Buddhist traditions. Discrimination against Lhotsampas reportedly was increasing in the army and in public service.

Bhutan rejected claims by the banned Bhutan People's Party (BPP), that evictions were state-sponsored. The BPP's campaign of terror was directed against the government and loyal Lhotsampas from across the Bhutan-India border. It severely disrupted trade and industry in the vibrant economic zone of southern Bhutan, where most Lhotsampas resided. (CLAUDE RAKISITS)

BOLIVIA

Bolivia is a landlocked republic in central South America. Area: 1,098,581 sq km (424,164 sq mi). Pop. (1995 est.): 7,414,000. Administrative cap., La Paz; judicial cap., Sucre. Monetary unit: boliviano, with (Oct. 6, 1995) a free rate of Bs4.87 to U.S. $1 (Bs7.69 = £1 sterling). President in 1995, Gonzalo Sánchez de Lozada Bustamente.

During 1995 the government pressed ahead with its Capitalization Program, aiming to transfer state enterprises to private control. Those on the list were electricity (ENDE), telecommunications (ENTEL), railways (ENFE), the airline (LAB), steel (ENAF), and the oil and gas corporation (YPFB), whose output alone accounted for 9% of Bolivia's gross domestic product. The scheme was innovative, with 50% of the shares in the enterprises being transferred to all Bolivian citizens in the form of pension fund contributions. The other half was to be sold to private investors.

YPFB, which produced 75% of the country's gas and 81% of its oil, was expected to be auctioned in December after first having been divided into five operating companies. Its value was increased by the agreement signed in July by the presidents of Bolivia and Brazil to build a $2 billion gas pipeline linking Santa Cruz de la Sierra and Potosí in Bolivia with São Paulo in Brazil. Negotiations were difficult, but World Bank and Inter-American Development Bank funding was expected, as well as export credit agency financing from around the world.

Despite the purported benefits to the population, the Capitalization Program was deeply unpopular among workers, who feared job losses. Labour unrest and civil disturbances were widespread throughout the year and brought fears that investors would be discouraged. April was a month of civil unrest as teachers, hospital workers, and some state miners went on strike, demanding higher wages and protesting educational and economic reforms. A state of emergency was declared; nighttime curfew was imposed, security forces were given sweeping powers of arrest, and all public meetings were banned. More than 100 unionists were imprisoned in remote Andean villages. The teachers ended their 50-day strike in May after the government agreed to reconsider pay cuts.

Social unrest flared up again in July with strikes and violent clashes. There were battles between police and coca growers in the Chapare region following the arrest of representatives of 53 coca farmers. The U.S. administration required Bolivia to destroy 1,750 ha (4,323 ac) of coca plantations by the end of June or have aid cut and sanctions imposed. The target was achieved, but at the price of much resentment. A second 90-day state of emergency was imposed on July 18, when the earlier one expired. The Bolivian Labour Confederation organized a 24-hour general strike in protest. (SARAH CAMERON)

BOSNIA AND HERZEGOVINA

A republic of the western Balkans, Bosnia and Herzegovina borders Croatia on the north, southwest, and south, the Adriatic Sea on the south (via a narrow extension), and Yugoslavia on the east. Area: 51,129 sq km (19,741 sq mi). Pop. (1995 est.): 3,459,000 (excluding about 800,000 refugees in adjacent countries and Western Europe). Monetary unit: Bosnia & Herzegovina dinar, with (Oct. 1, 1995) a free rate of 147 dinars to U.S. $1 (233.33 dinars = £1 sterling). President in 1995, Alija Izetbegovic; prime minister, Haris Silajdzic.

The four-month cease-fire in Bosnia and Herzegovina negotiated by former U.S. president Jimmy Carter, which had come into force on Jan. 1, 1995, failed to stick. Following a military agreement on February 20 on closer cooperation between Bosnian and Croatian Serbs, combined Serb forces tightened their blockade of the Bihac enclave in northwestern Bosnia, one of the UN-designated "safe areas." On March 6 the governments of Croatia and Bosnia and Herzegovina concluded a military alliance. On March 19 Bosnian government forces started successful offensives against Serb positions on strategic Mt. Vlasic near Travnik in central Bosnia, as well as north and east of Tuzla.

Heavy shelling of Sarajevo was resumed by Serb forces in April. The offensive by Bosnian government forces in May aimed at breaking the siege of Sarajevo failed after heavy government losses. On May 24 the UN forces commander in Bosnia, Lieut. Gen. Rupert Smith, issued an ultimatum to the Bosnian Serbs and the Bosnian government to pull back their heavy weapons from a 32-km (20-mi) exclusion zone around Sarajevo. The next day Smith ordered bombing raids by NATO aircraft against Serb arms dumps near their headquarters at Pale, whereupon the Serbs took over 300 UN soldiers hostage. The last of the hostages were all released by June 18 following mediation by Pres. Slobodan Milosevic of Serbia. In early June defense ministers from NATO and other countries decided to create a 14,000-strong rapid deployment force consisting of British, French, and Dutch troops to support UN units and to protect the remaining safe areas. A U.S. F-16 plane flown by Capt. Scott O'Grady was shot down by Serb fire over Bosnia on June 2. The pilot bailed out and was found and rescued in a U.S. operation after six nights.

The Serbs captured the safe area of Srebrenica in July, having previously disarmed the Dutch UN battalion stationed there. The safe area of Zepa, also in eastern Bosnia, fell to the Serbs that same month. Tadeusz Mazowiecki, former prime minister of Poland and since 1992 UN rapporteur on humanitarian affairs in former Yugoslavia, accused the world of "inactivity" and "hypocrisy" and resigned. On July 25 the International War Crimes Tribunal for the Former Yugoslavia at The Hague indicted Radovan Karadzic, leader of the so-called Republika Srpska in Bosnia, and his military commander, Gen. Ratko Mladic, on charges of genocide and crimes against humanity.

On July 22 an agreement on political, diplomatic, and military cooperation was signed by Pres. Franjo Tudjman of Croatia and Alija Izetbegovic of Bosnia and Herzegovina. Just days later Croatian army forces entered western Bosnia from Croatia to relieve Bihac in a combined operation with Bosnian Croat forces. In August Serb forces suffered a series of military defeats at the hands of Croatian and Bosnian government forces in western and central Bosnia and lost a significant amount of territory. A mortar bomb fired into a Sarajevo market on August 28 killed 37 people and injured many others. NATO ordered a number of large-scale attacks against strategic Serb targets throughout Bosnia.

A new U.S. peace initiative in former Yugoslavia led by U.S. Assistant Secretary of State Richard Holbrooke, which had begun on August 9, allowed U.S. Pres. Bill Clinton to announce a cease-fire on October 5. U.S.-sponsored peace talks held in Dayton, Ohio, resulted in a detailed agreement officially signed in Paris on December 14. It provided for a Bosnian and Herzegovinian state consisting of two entities: the Muslim-Croatian federation (approximately 51% of the territory, including the whole of Sarajevo) and the Serb Republic (Republika Srpska) with about 49%. People indicted as war criminals would not be allowed to hold public office in either of the two entities. Bosnia and Herzegovina was to have a constitution and central institutions. Free elections were to be held within a specified period, and all refugees

A Bosnian government soldier passes dead Serbs lying along the road. In August Croatian forces went on the offensive, successfully attacking Serb positions in Krajina and in western Bosnia and Herzegovina and forcing the Serbs to give up several areas that had been under their control.
GILLES PERESS—MAGNUM

were to be allowed to return to their homes or—if this was not possible—awarded proper compensation. The agreement provided for the presence of 60,000 NATO troops (including 20,000 from the United States) for one year to supervise the implementation of the agreement. NATO, whose forces were deployed immediately after the signing of the Dayton agreements on December 14, took over officially from the UN in Bosnia on December 20. The International Monetary Fund admitted Bosnia and Herzegovina on the same day and approved a $45 million emergency loan. As provided in the Dayton accords, the IMF would nominate the head of a new central bank for the country.

(K.F. CVIIC)

This article updates the *Macropædia* article BALKAN STATES: *Bosnia and Herzegovina.*

BOTSWANA

A landlocked republic of southern Africa, Botswana is a member of the Commonwealth. Area: 581,730 sq km (224,607 sq mi). Pop. (1995 est.): 1,549,000. Cap.: Gaborone. Monetary unit: pula, with (Oct. 6, 1995) a free rate of 2.80 pula to U.S. $1 (4.42 pula = £1 sterling). President in 1995, Sir Ketumile Masire.

In February 1995 Botswana was shocked by a level of rioting that had not previously occurred in its history. The cause was the release without charge of three people accused of the ritual murder of a girl at Mochudi, where the unrest started in January. Disturbances broke out in Gaborone when students and unemployed youths stormed the parliament buildings and demanded the arrest of the three; in subsequent police action to restore order, one youth was killed. The government blamed the opposition Botswana National Front (BNF) for the violence, but the BNF said it arose out of frustration with social conditions and unemployment.

Festus Mogae, vice president and finance and development planning minister, presented the 1995–96 budget on February 14 and claimed the economy had improved over that of the previous year. For the period 1992–93 to 1993–94, he estimated a 4.1% rise in gross domestic product and a 2.3% growth in formal employment from 226,275 to 231,324. Total income for 1995–96 was estimated at 5,162,000,000 pula, with mineral revenues contributing 47.6% of this figure; expenditure at 5,391,000,000 pula would result in a deficit for the year of 229 million pula.

On April 6 Pres. Ketumile Masire reduced the voting age from 21 to 18.

(GUY ARNOLD)

This article updates the *Macropædia* article SOUTHERN AFRICA: *Botswana*.

BRAZIL

Brazil is a federal republic in eastern South America on the Atlantic Ocean. Area: 8,547,404 sq km (3,300,171 sq mi). Pop. (1995 est.): 155,822,000. Cap.: Brasília. Monetary unit: real, with (Oct. 6, 1995) a controlled rate of 0.96 real to U.S. $1 (1.52 reais = £1 sterling). President in 1995, Fernando Henrique Cardoso.

The year 1995 began on an optimistic note as Pres. Fernando Henrique Cardoso took office on January 1, having been elected with 54% of the vote in a single round in the elections held on Oct. 3, 1994. Most state governors were also inaugurated at the beginning of 1995, but new members of the national legislature took their seats on February 1, with business beginning in earnest in mid-March.

In common with the previous administration—first under Pres. Fernando Collor de Mello (1990–92) and then Itamar Franco (1992–94)—Cardoso lacked a majority in the legislature. His Party of Brazilian Social Democracy (PSDB) needed to forge a core alliance with the conservative Liberal Front Party (PFL), the Brazilian Labour Party (PTB), and minor parties and enlist support from the Party of the Brazilian Democratic Movement (PMDB) and the Progressive Reform Party (PPR) to win approval for constitutional amendments, which required a three-fifths majority in two rounds of voting in both houses of the legislature.

The first group of economic-reform proposals were presented to the legislature as amendments to the constitution on February 22. These consisted of four main items: permitting private-sector participation in the distribution of natural gas by pipeline; opening coastal shipping to foreign lines; redefining what constitutes a Brazilian enterprise; and breaking down monopolies conferred upon the state telecommunications concern, Telebras, and the oil concern, Petrobrás (each requiring a separate amendment). All secured approval in the Chamber of Deputies during May and June, with the first three also having cleared the Senate by June 28 and the telecommunications amendment in early July. The Senate voted on October 18 by 58–17 to end the government's monopoly of oil exploration, refining, and importing by allowing private investment in Petrobrás. Final passage of the bill came on November 8 by a vote of 60–15.

Plans launched in March to reform the Social Security system had to be shelved temporarily owing to opposition in the legislature. They were resubmitted in August, together with proposals for fiscal and administrative reform. Along with the fiscal package, the government sought to extend until 1999 the Emergency Social Fund (FSE), which was due to expire in December 1995, in order to achieve greater flexibility for its budgeting plans.

Legislative deliberations on the reforms were complicated by the souring of relations between the government and the PFL following the central bank's intervention in the Banco Economico, a private-sector bank in the state of Bahia that ran into difficulty in August. The former Bahia state governor and current PFL senator Antônio Carlos Magalhães sought to retain the bank in private hands, but the government's demand for a substantial injection of funds could not be met.

In early October the president of the Chamber of Deputies, Luis Eduardo Magalhães, indicated that an extension of the FSE for the full period was unlikely, but the Congress finally agreed in October to extend the FSE for another 18 months. There were doubts whether the other reforms would be fully approved before the end of the year. Also evident was opposition to plans to privatize the Rio Doce mining concern during 1996.

On the economic front, the Cardoso administration during 1995 was able to sustain the stability engendered by the "Real Plan" that began with the plan's inception in 1994, when Cardoso was still finance minister, and continued after the launch of the new currency on July 1, 1994. Monthly inflation averaged about 2% in the first nine months of 1995, with the University of São Paulo index down to 0.74% in September. During the first quarter of the year, gross domestic product (GDP) grew 10.5%, which signaled that the economy was overheating despite continuing high real interest rates (high rates also had the adverse effect of pushing up federal public debt from 61.8 billion reais at the end of 1994 to 92 billion reais at the end of September 1995). The authorities took action at the end of March to tighten credit and restrict imports, especially of automobiles and approximately 100 consumer durables, on which import tariffs were increased to 70%.

During the second quarter the growth rate briefly turned negative but came out at about 8%, and there was some easing of credit in the third quarter as output fell and unemployment rose. By midyear there was a continuing deficit on the trade account—which had begun in November 1994. Between January and the end of June 1995, the trade deficit reached some $4.2 billion. Ostensibly in a further attempt to reverse this trend, quotas for automobile imports were introduced in June; this caused a furor with neighbouring Argentina, Brazil's major partner in the Southern Cone Common Market (Mercosur) and an exporter of automobiles to Brazil. The row was defused after meetings between Cardoso and Pres. Carlos Menem of Argentina. Following other protests to the World Trade Organization, it was announced in the second week of October that the remaining quota restrictions would be lifted.

Having allowed the real to become overvalued against the U.S. dollar by some 30% between July 1994 and March 1995, the authorities formally established a floating trading band of 0.88–0.93 real per dollar for the currency in early March 1995, widening the band to 0.91–0.99 per dollar from June 23. In subsequent months central bank management resulted in an orderly downward adjustment that brought the real to 0.958 per U.S. dollar by October 10.

The improved competitiveness of the real and continued slowing of GDP growth (5.7% was projected for the year) began to help reverse the trade position during the third quarter, with modest monthly surpluses returning (by the end of August the deficit stood at about $3.9 billion). In October the central bank was projecting a current account deficit for 1995 of some $16 billion–$17 billion, about 3% of GDP. With the country's international reserves having rebuilt to $45.8 billion (on a cash basis) by the end of August from a low of $29.9 billion in April, the authorities were in a comfortable position to meet payments obligations.

(SUSAN M. CUNNINGHAM)

BRUNEI

The sultanate of Brunei is located on the northern coast of the island of Borneo, on the South China Sea. Area: 5,765 sq km (2,226 sq mi). Pop. (1995 est.): 291,000. Cap.: Bandar Seri Begawan. Monetary unit: Brunei dollar, with (Oct. 6, 1995) a free rate of B$1.43 to U.S. $1 (B$2.26 = £1 sterling). Sultan and prime minister in 1995, Sir Muda Hassanal Bolkiah Mu'izzadin Waddaulah.

In February 1995 the Brunei Solidarity National Party, the sultanate's only political party, held its inaugural assembly after having lain dormant for close to a decade. Its members declared their full support for Sultan Hassanal Bolkiah. Referring to a royal decree in 1984, leader Abdul Latif Chuchu endorsed Brunei nation building based on the principle of a democratic Malay Islamic monarchy.

As a sign of the changing political climate, the sultan, for the first time, publicized his decision to extend emergency rule. The rule had been renewed every two years since the British crushed an armed revolt in 1962. A government committee recommended revisions to the 1959 constitution, which called for an elected parliament. The last time elections were held was in 1968, a year after the sultan ascended the throne, though grassroots polls for village chiefs had been permitted in recent years.

In October Brunei joined the World Bank and International Monetary Fund to help reduce its reliance on oil and gas earnings, which in 1993 accounted for 60% of gross domestic product. The sultan agreed to keep on a battalion of 500 Gurkha troops from the British army for a further five years after their tour of duty in Brunei ended in 1998.

(MATTHEW FLETCHER)

This article updates the *Macropædia* article SOUTHEAST ASIA: *Brunei.*

BULGARIA

The republic of Bulgaria is on the eastern Balkan Peninsula of southeastern Europe, along the Black Sea. Area: 110,994 sq km (42,855 sq mi). Pop. (1995 est.): 8,406,000. Cap.: Sofia. Monetary unit: lev, with (Oct. 6, 1995) a free rate of 68.17 leva to U.S. $1 (107.77 leva = £1 sterling). President in 1995, Zhelyu Zhelev; prime ministers, Reneta Indzhova and, from January 25, Zhan Videnov.

Following its victory in the December 1994 election, the Bulgarian Socialist Party (BSP) formed a government on January 25–26, 1995, under its youthful party leader, Zhan Videnov. The Cabinet included some members of the Bulgarian Agrarian National Union and a representative of the Ecoglasnost Political Club. It was the first government in postcommunist Bulgaria to enjoy an absolute majority in the National Assembly.

The domestic political scene was dominated by a confrontation between the government and Pres. Zhelyu Zhelev. The president rejected bills readmitting former communists to senior academic posts and allowing economic development without reference to environmental considerations. He also vetoed an amendment to the land law that provided that those wishing to sell land had to offer it first to their neighbours and to the state; only if these parties should not wish to buy could the property be placed on the open market. This was one of a number of proposed amendments that were intended to encourage cooperative land ownership.

The Assembly overruled the presidential veto on May 10, in response to which Zhelev referred the issue to the Constitutional Court. On June 19 the court endorsed the president's view. In July Zhelev criticized the government for lack of progress on economic reform and in the battle against crime; the latter failure, he suggested, was because the BSP was "genetically connected" with criminal circles.

Videnov hit back during the BSP party conference at the end of July, accusing Zhelev of behaving like a candidate for opposition leader. Videnov also attacked the Constitutional Court. In August the government, invoking an alleged lack of space, ordered the court to leave its offices in the government building. The court appealed successfully to the Supreme Court. In September the Constitutional Court ruled a new local government law illegal because, it said, a clause forbidding reporters in state-controlled media to express their opinions was an infringement of the constitutional right to free speech.

In external affairs both the prime minister and the president remained committed to taking Bulgaria into the European Union. A new feature of Bulgarian foreign policy was the reassertion of the country's close ties with Russia. These included a deal under which $100 million of Russian debt would be paid to Bulgaria in the form of spare parts for military aircraft, an agreement to inherit outdated Russian tanks to replace even older ones in the Bulgarian army, the reintroduction of compulsory Russian-language lessons in Bulgarian schools, and plans to construct pipelines to transport Russian gas via Burgas to Greece and Italy.

(RICHARD J. CRAMPTON)

This article updates the *Macropædia* article BALKAN STATES: *Bulgaria.*

BURKINA FASO

Burkina Faso is a landlocked country of West Africa. Area: 274,400 sq km (105,946 sq mi). Pop. (1995 est.): 10,324,000. Cap.: Ouagadougou. Monetary unit: CFA franc, with a par value of CFAF 100 to the French franc and (as of Oct. 6, 1995) a free rate of CFAF 501.49 to U.S. $1 (CFAF 792.78 = £1 sterling). President (chairman) of the Popular Front in 1995, Capt. Blaise Compaoré; prime minister, Marc-Christian Kaboré.

The presidential party, the Organization for Popular Democracy-Labour Movement, won control of 26 of Burkina Faso's 33 major towns in municipal elections on Feb. 12, 1995. The opposition parties called for a boycott of the election because there was no independent electoral commission.

The death of two students during demonstrations on May 9 resulted in a 48-hour strike at the University of Ouagadougou. In August former Cabinet minister Ernest Ouédraogo, leader of the Burkinabe Socialist Party (PSB), was sentenced to six months in prison for insulting Pres. Blaise Compaoré in a newspaper.

The devaluation in 1994 of the CFA franc caused a 30% jump in the cost of living between January and June. Sharp increases in the value of livestock exports reduced domestic supply by 11%. Consequently, meat prices rose 40%; there was also a 25% increase in the price of rice. To encourage production, government payments to cotton growers were increased and prices of pesticides and fertilizers cut. In June Burkina Faso formally joined the World Trade Organization. Railroad employees struck after the management of the now privatized rail firm implemented plans to lay off 500 workers. In August the stoppage ended when the company agreed to provide severance pay and salary arrears.

(NANCY ELLEN LAWLER)

This article updates the *Macropædia* article WESTERN AFRICA: *Burkina Faso.*

BURUNDI

Burundi is a landlocked republic of central Africa. Area: 27,816 sq km (10,740 sq mi). Pop. (1995 est.): 5,936,000. Cap.: Bujumbura. Monetary unit: Burundi franc, with (Oct. 6, 1995) a free rate of FBu 247.40 to U.S. $1 (FBu 391.12 = £1 sterling). President in 1995, Sylvestre Ntibantunganya; prime ministers, Anatole Kanyenkiko until February 15 and, from February 22, Antoine Nduwayo.

The year 1995 was dominated by fears that Burundi would descend into ethnic violence. In January the Unity for National Progress (UPRONA) withdrew from the government and called for the dismissal of the prime minister, Anatole Kanyenkiko, who was expelled from UPRONA. Pressures continued through February to force Kanyenkiko to resign, with UPRONA disowning him for "disloyalty" and calling an indefinite general strike; he finally stepped down on February 15, when activity in Bujumbura had come to a standstill as a result of the strike. Antoine Nduwayo, a Tutsi member of UPRONA, was nominated as prime minister and, after obtaining the support of the majority Burundi Democratic Front, assumed the office on February 22. These political uncertainties resulted in a new exodus of refugees; on February 21 Tanzania reported that 25,000 had arrived there since the beginning of the month.

Growing international fears that Burundi might collapse into chaos prompted the UN to send a mission to assess the situation. During March fighting between dissident Tutsi from the army and Hutu extremists led to 500 deaths, and on March 26 the UN High Commissioner for Refugees reported that 24,000 people had fled to Zaire over two days.

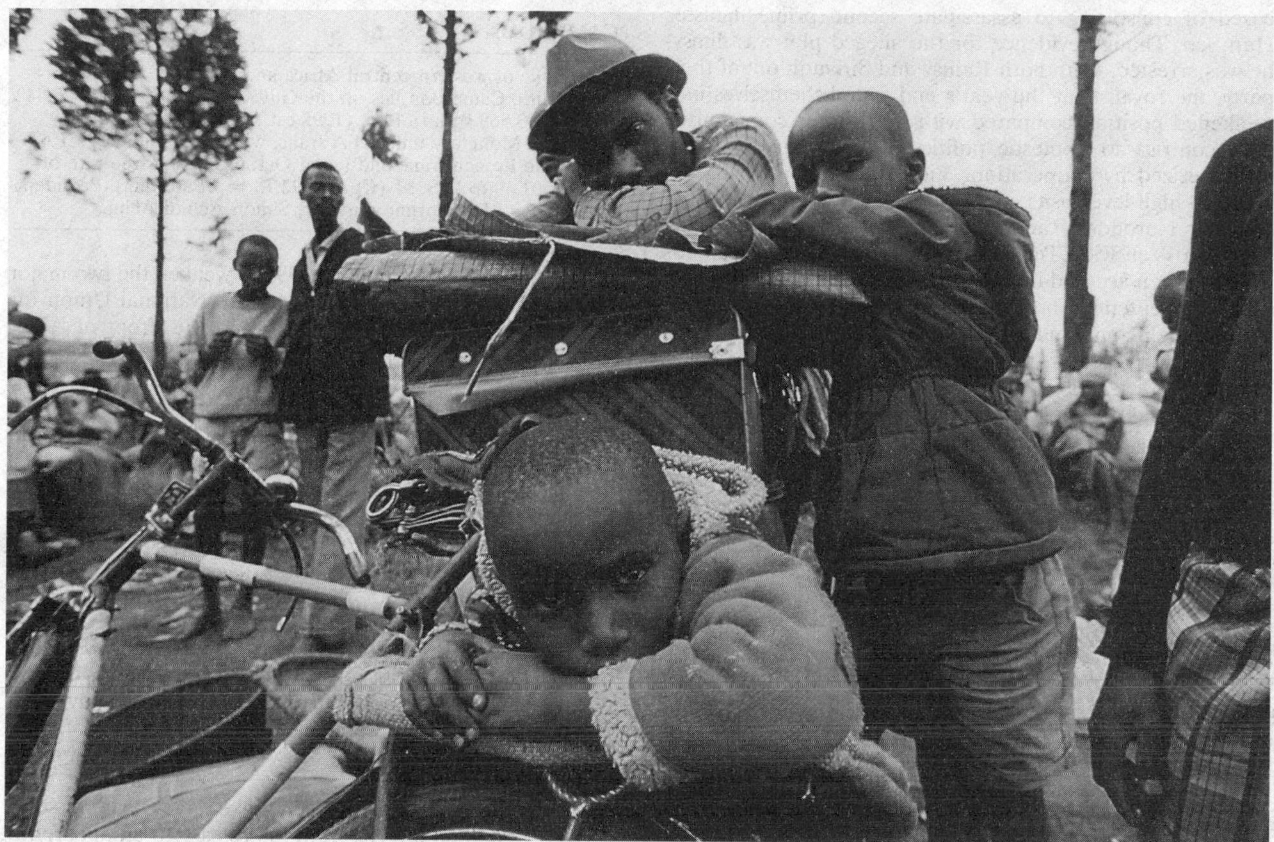

Hutu refugees flee ethnic violence in Burundi. Sporadic fighting between the Tutsi, who are in a minority but nonetheless dominate the country's government, and the Hutu continued throughout the year, with many thousands on both sides killed, wounded, or displaced from their homes.
MARIELLA FURRER—REA/SABA

At the end of March more than 300 European expatriates left the country, most by airlift, following the murder of three Belgians.

In early April 400 Hutu were massacred by Tutsi in the Gasorwe region, fueling fears of ever-higher levels of killing; in mid-April the extreme Hutu group, the National Council for the Defense of Democracy, announced that it was forming an army, and by late April hundreds were reported to be fleeing from Hutu in the Gasorwe region. The secretary-general of the Organization of African Unity (OAU), Salim Ahmed Salim, visited Burundi, and the OAU observer mission was increased from 47 to 67.

The violence escalated throughout the rest of the year. In July Amnesty International accused the Burundi Security Forces of having collaborated with Tutsi extremists to kill thousands of Hutu since 1993, and by late summer both the OAU and the UN were discussing the possibility of military intervention if the violence worsened. (GUY ARNOLD)

This article updates the *Macropædia* article CENTRAL AFRICA: *Burundi*.

CAMBODIA

A constitutional monarchy of Southeast Asia, Cambodia occupies the southwestern part of the Indochinese Peninsula, on the Gulf of Thailand. Area: 181,916 sq km (70,238 sq mi). Pop. (1995 est.): 9,608,000. Cap.: Phnom Penh. Monetary unit: riel, with (Oct. 6, 1995) an official rate of CR 2,300 to U.S. $1 (CR 3,636 = £1 sterling). King, Norodom Sihanouk; first prime minister in 1995, Norodom Ranariddh, and second prime minister, Hun Sen.

Soon after 1995 began, the Khmer Rouge made headlines when an American tourist and her Cambodian guide were murdered near Angkor. Through the year the rebels fought the army in the north, northwest, and southwest, with the heaviest fighting in Batdambang province. Neither force was strong enough to hold captured territory. In July the army took, then lost, a guerrilla base 20 km (12.5 mi) from the main rebel command at Phnom Malai, while the insurgents twice overran Treng, a heavily defended village some 40 km (25 mi) from Batdambang, the country's second largest city. The government, pointing out that thousands of insurgents had defected and gained amnesty, claimed that the Khmer Rouge no longer posed a threat.

Political maneuvers in Phnom Penh earned more attention than military campaigns. While King Sihanouk spent much of the year receiving medical treatment abroad, the coalition government of the royalist Funcinpec party and the Cambodian People's Party took steps some viewed as limiting opposition. In January the National Assembly started debate on a press law requiring jail sentences for those publishing material considered harmful to national stability and security. After the law was passed by the Assembly in July, at least one newspaper was shut down and three others charged. Even before the law's passage, one journalist was jailed and at least two others fined for printing material deemed critical of government leaders.

In May Funcinpec expelled a prominent government critic, former finance minister Sam Rainsy, for planning to create an opposition group and argued that Rainsy could not represent Funcinpec in the National Assembly because he had lost his party credentials. He was stripped of his seat and announced he would form a reform party.

In November another critic, Funcinpec Secretary-General Prince Norodom Sirivudh, the king's half-brother, was accused of conspiring to assassinate second prime minister Hun Sen. Though evidence for the alleged plot was flimsy, he was arrested. With both Rainsy and Sirivudh out of their party, the royalists at the year's end found themselves in a weakened position compared with the former communists.

In contrast to domestic politics, foreign relations were characterized by cooperation. Vietnam and Cambodia exchanged high-level visits, including a July trip by First Prime Minister Norodom Ranariddh for private talks with Vietnam's Vo Van Kiet. Tensions with Thailand, which Cambodia had often accused of supporting the Khmer Rouge, also eased. In September both countries formed a commission to oversee their common land border, though competing claims over territorial waters in the Gulf of Thailand remained unsettled. On April 5 Vietnam, Thailand, Cambodia, and Laos founded the Mekong River Commission, charged with

A Cambodian cyclist rides past a sign warning of land mines. Heavily mined after some 20 years of warfare that involved both domestic factions and external forces, Cambodia was host to an international conference in 1995 that called for a ban on the weapons.
ALAN DEJECACION—GAMMA LIAISON

developing and protecting the waterway. But perhaps most important for Cambodia's integration into the region was its admission to observer status in the Association of Southeast Asian Nations in July.

Though the country depended largely on foreign aid (some $1.3 billion was promised by donors for 1995–96), investments continued to flow in. Singapore was the top foreign investor in the first half of the year, pledging some $46 million of a total of $410 million worth of projects. In late December 1994 a Malaysian aviation company had assumed a 40% stake in the regenerated flag carrier, Royal Air Cambodge. Multilateral aid agencies, such as the International Monetary Fund and the Asian Development Bank, expressed confidence in the health of the economy. Government officials forecast a 7% growth rate in gross domestic product, despite a complete ban on timber and rubber exports.

But after one bank's license was revoked in May owing to inadequate capitalization, confidence in the financial regulatory system was shaken. In July the Interior Ministry claimed that over half of the country's 30 banks were involved in money laundering. Lawlessness and crime in the capital also became significant concerns for both investors and Cambodians. (JOSE MANUEL TESORO)

This article updates the *Macropædia* article SOUTHEAST ASIA: *Cambodia.*

CAMEROON

A republic of western central Africa and member of the Commonwealth, Cameroon lies on the Gulf of Guinea. Area: 475,442 sq km (183,569 sq mi). Pop. (1995 est.): 13,233,000. Cap.: Yaoundé. Monetary unit: CFA franc, with a par value of CFAF 100 to the French franc and (as of Oct. 6, 1995) a free rate of CFAF 501.49 to U.S. $1 (CFAF 792.78 = £1 sterling). President in 1995, Paul Biya; prime minister, Simon Achidi Achu.

Internal disputes continued in 1995 to weaken the two major opposition coalitions in Cameroon, the National Union for Democracy and Progress (UNDP) and the Front of Allies for Change (FAC). In February the UNDP expelled two of its members who had been serving in Pres. Paul Biya's Cabinet. As a result, a new breakaway party, still unnamed, was announced. In late May the Social Democratic Front of John Fru Ndi, part of the FAC, was split after seven members of the executive committee were denied entrance to the SDF's congress in Maroua. One of these, former SDF secretary-general Siga Assanga, then formed the Social Democratic Movement.

After a meeting with the French ambassador, Ndi announced that the opposition-led boycott of French products would end on May 26, stating that this would give France's new president, Jacques Chirac (*see* BIOGRAPHIES), the opportunity to review policies toward Africa. In July most independent newspapers suspended publication for four days to protest government censorship and intimidation of journalists.

Attempts continued to clear Lake Nyos, where some 1,700 people died in 1986 from the release of an apparently naturally occurring toxic gas. Cameroon's application to join the Commonwealth was accepted in November.

The economy was expected to grow by 5% in 1995. In June Biya announced plans to speed up the privatization of public utilities and other state-owned enterprises. Initial steps were taken to create a stock exchange. After having settled its arrears with the World Bank, Cameroon continued to receive assistance from that agency.

(NANCY ELLEN LAWLER)

This article updates the *Macropædia* article WESTERN AFRICA: *Cameroon.*

CANADA

Canada is a federal parliamentary state and member of the Commonwealth covering North America north of conterminous United States and east of Alaska. Area: 9,970,610 sq km (3,849,674 sq mi). Pop. (1995 est.): 29,463,000. Cap.: Ottawa. Monetary unit: Canadian dollar, with (Oct. 6, 1995) a free rate of Can$1.33 to U.S. $1 (Can$2.11 = £1 sterling). Queen, Elizabeth II; governors-general in 1995, Ramon Hnatyshyn and, from February 8, Roméo LeBlanc; prime minister, Jean Chrétien.

Domestic Affairs. Canada faced a great crisis in 1995 when the voters of Quebec only narrowly rejected secession. With about 93% of eligible voters—almost five million Quebeckers—voting, the plan was rejected by a margin just over 1%, but about 60% of French-speaking residents voted "yes" on the October 30 referendum. The forces urging secession, emboldened by their near victory, vowed to raise the question again, which posed a serious challenge to the national government led by Prime Minister Jean Chrétien.

Separatists had received a boost from the election of the Parti Québécois (PQ) to form the government of Quebec in September 1994. The party was committed to Quebec's "sovereignty," and this was the second occasion on which the issue had been placed before the electorate. Quebeckers had rejected independence by a 60–40% margin in 1980, but the party was resolved to try again.

In February the PQ government led by Premier Jacques Parizeau conducted hearings all over the province to take the sovereignty option before the people. The opposition Liberal Party, led by former premier Daniel Johnson, had boycotted the hearings, and a report based on the public consultations was released in April recommending that sovereignty be declared after it had been endorsed in a popular referendum. The government then would enter into negotiations with the rest of Canada to work out a new political and economic partnership. The three groups in the province advocating sovereignty came together in a common front on June 12. Premier Parizeau, leading the PQ, was named head of the coalition. He was joined by Lucien Bouchard, leader of the Bloc Québécois (BQ) and the Partie de l'Action Démocratique, under Mario Dumont, who put forward a more moderate version of Quebec nationalism.

Following the summer recess the Quebec legislature, dominated by the PQ, began preparations for a referendum on the question. Furthermore, a bill was passed that looked to the drafting of a constitution for an independent Quebec. It stated that Quebec would continue to use the Canadian dollar and sought to reassure both the aboriginal population of the province and the English-speaking minority that their rights would be respected.

The campaign got off to a slow start in early October but began to generate excitement when Parizeau named Bouchard, a fiery and widely popular speaker, to be the chief negotiator with Canada following a referendum victory. He placed less emphasis on sovereignty than Parizeau had done, dwelling on the advantages of a new partnership with Canada. His model was a European-style economic union, which he stated the rest of Canada would be forced to enter because of economic realities, and he used his considerable oratorical skills to appeal to the self-esteem of the Quebec people and their pride in their language and culture. The present federal system had nothing to offer Quebec, Bouchard claimed; it was time for a *virage,* a turning.

Bouchard's activities galvanized pro-sovereignty sentiment, and Daniel Johnson countered by pointing out the dangerous economic risks that would arise from Quebec's sovereignty; there could be no guarantee that Canada would enter into a partnership with Quebec, and sovereignty could lead to a mounting Quebec deficit as the new state took on its share of Canada's national debt and lost the federal transfer payments it received for social services.

Chrétien had always expressed the view that the separation of Quebec would never receive a popular mandate, but late in the campaign, worried about the impact of Bouchard's message upon Quebec voters, he took a more active role, speaking several times in Quebec and addressing a massive outdoor rally in Montreal three days before the vote. Chrétien also began talking of constitutional change, holding out the prospect of "distinct society" status for Quebec and a constitutional veto for the province.

In the end, 2,361,526 voters (50.6%) voted "no" to the sovereignty proposal, and 2,308,028 (49.4%) voted "yes." Only 53,498 votes divided the two sides. Although "yes" votes were more numerous in 80 of Quebec's 125 voting districts, a number of regions returned large majorities for "no." One was the island of Montreal, home to most English-speaking Quebeckers and virtually all the immigrants living in the province; another was western Quebec north of the Ottawa River, where the national capital is the principal city; and a third was communities in the Eastern Townships along the United States border. In the far north the Cree Indians and the Inuit voted to stay with Canada.

After the results became known, Parizeau launched an angry tirade against Quebec's ethnic minorities and the power of big business, and he announced his retirement from public life. The way was now open for Bouchard to succeed him as premier of Quebec and carry on the sovereignty struggle. Bouchard announced he would stand for the PQ leadership in November, a position he was expected to win easily.

The result of the referendum was a blow to Prime Minister Chrétien, who had seriously misjudged the nationalist mood in his native province. His new task was to offer constitutional and administrative reforms that would meet Quebec's demands for distinct status while satisfying those who viewed Canada as a union of equal parts. If Chrétien's position in Quebec was weak, he nevertheless had a good grasp of political conditions in the rest of Canada and was trusted there as its spokesman in the debate over Canadian unity that was bound to continue.

The federal government had pursued a careful course in 1995, avoiding steps that might antagonize Quebec voters before the October referendum on independence while reassuring the rest of Canada that it was not being soft toward Quebec's demands. Thus, a major reform of the social welfare system, promised by the Liberal Party when it assumed office in 1993, was shelved until after the referendum.

The most controversial piece of legislation was a gun-control bill that would ban the sale of some handguns and require registration of all firearms. Although there was broad public support for the bill, Western and rural MPs attacked its provisions as an ineffective and costly way to combat violent crime. The bill was passed in the House of Commons on June 13 by a majority of 192–63. It was then sent on to the Senate, where it passed on November 22.

The Liberal Party's comfortable majority in the federal House of Commons was not shaken during the year. It won three by-elections on February 13. Two seats in Ottawa and Montreal were easily retained, while a third one in Quebec's Eastern Townships was wrested from the separatist BQ. Party standings after the by-elections were: Liberals 177; BQ 53; Reform Party 52; New Democratic Party (NDP) 9; Progressive Conservatives 2; independents 2. There was only one Cabinet change during the year. Lucienne Robillard, elected in the Montreal by-election, was named minister of labour on February 22. A former minister of health and education in the Quebec provincial government, she led the federal government forces in the referendum on separation.

Canada gained its first governor-general of Acadian extraction when Roméo LeBlanc, a former teacher, journalist, and Liberal Cabinet minister, was installed in the largely ceremonial post on February 8. The Acadians, French-speaking residents of the Maritime Provinces, saw themselves as quite distinct from the citizens of Quebec.

Four of Canada's 10 provinces held elections in 1995. Only in the most populous, Ontario, did the government change hands. On June 8 the Progressive Conservative Party, vowing to cut public spending, decrease the deficit, and reduce personal income taxes, swept into power. The Tories captured 82 seats in the 130-seat legislature, defeating the NDP administration that had been in office since 1990. Michael Harris was sworn in as Ontario's 22nd premier on June 26. In Manitoba the Progressive Conservatives under Gary Filmon won a third term on April 25. Next door, in Saskatchewan, the NDP under Roy Romanow easily won a second majority government on June 21. Romanow's record as a responsible manager of the province's budget had been a major factor in his victory. In the Atlantic province of New Brunswick, the Liberals under Frank McKenna won a third term, capturing 47 of the 54 seats in the legislature. The victory on September 11 reflected voter satisfaction with McKenna's efforts to attract high-technology industries to the province.

The Northwest Territories elected a new Assembly on October 16. A form of consensus government is followed in the Territories, and the 24 members of the new legislature elected a speaker and a leader of the government from their number. It was the final election scheduled before the eastern portion of the Territories became the self-governing region of Nunavut in 1999.

The Economy. In 1995 Canada experienced modest economic growth. The annual rate of increase in the economy was expected to reach 2.5%. Gross domestic product (GDP), seasonally adjusted at market prices, was estimated at Can$777.2 billion at midyear. A slowdown in the U.S. economy led to weak exports, although buoyant prices in the pulp, paper, and metal industries offered prospects for growth. Capital investment was heavy in these industries. A national rail strike in March slowed the economy, and consumers remained cautious in the face of the debate over Quebec's future. Interest rates fluctuated little during the summer, and the consumer price index stood at 2.1% in November. There was virtually no change in employment from the end of 1994, with the unemployment rate in November standing at 9.4%. The Canadian dollar, battered in foreign money markets by the uncertainty over Quebec, fluctuated from U.S. 70 cents in January, its lowest level since 1986, to U.S. 74 cents in September.

Finance Minister Paul Martin drastically reduced federal government expenditures in his second budget, introduced on February 27. Spending for government programs was slated to decrease by $10.4 billion, or 8.8% for fiscal year 1996–97. This was expected to bring the federal deficit down from $37.9 billion in 1994–95 to $24.3 billion two years later. The new figure represented the equivalent of 3% of Canada's GDP, a goal set by the Liberal government when it assumed office in 1993.

Martin's financial plan hit the federal public service industry especially hard. Forty-five thousand jobs, 14% of the total, were to be eliminated over the next three years in the largest workforce reduction ever made by an employer in Canada. The Department of National Defence saw its expenditures cut by 14% over two years with six military facilities and three service command headquarters to be closed.

CANAPRESS

Fellow Chippewa protest the death of a man killed by police at Ipperwash Provincial Park in southwestern Ontario. The government agreed to turn over to the Chippewa band nearby land that had been seized in 1942 for establishment of a government military base.

Transportation subsidies of $560 million to assist Canadian farmers in marketing their wheat were terminated.

Martin introduced few new taxes, claiming that his budget contained $4 in expenditure cuts for each $1 raised in new taxes. The excise tax on gasoline was raised 1.5 cents a litre; corporate taxes were increased, but there were no changes in personal income tax. A number of new fees were introduced, such as a fee of $975 imposed on new immigrants to Canada. The government announced that it would sell its stake in state enterprises such as Petro-Canada and the Canadian National Railways.

In response, the U.S. bond-rating service Moody's Investors Service, which was skeptical about the Liberal government's commitment to a long-range deficit-cutting program, announced on April 12 that it was downgrading the country's Canadian dollar bonds from their triple A credit rating to double A-1 standing.

Foreign Affairs. Canada played host for the third time to the summit meeting of the Group of Seven countries in June. At Prime Minister Chrétien's urging, the meeting discussed new operating rules for the World Bank and an early-warning system for the International Monetary Fund. Credits for emergency financing were doubled to U.S. $58 billion in an attempt to prepare in advance for financial crises such as had occurred in Mexico earlier in the year.

Canada announced in August that it would withdraw a battalion of ground troops from Croatia, with the remaining soldiers removed from Bosnia and Herzegovina in November. In October, though, the Chrétien government had to reconsider its plan when NATO called for fresh troops for a proposed force led by the U.S.

The problem of overfishing by foreigners, which had led to vanishing stocks of cod in Canada's Atlantic coastal waters, led to a confrontation with Spain in March. The problem arose with fish that live in waters on either side of the 200-nautical-mile fishing zone over which coastal states have jurisdiction. Canada passed legislation in 1994 to enforce regulations beyond the 200-mi limit.

A clash occurred on March 9 when Canadian patrol vessels intercepted a Spanish fishing boat engaged in what Canada claimed were illegal fishing practices. The boat was taken to St. John's, Newfoundland, where its captain was charged with taking undersized turbot. The European Union (EU), on behalf of Spain, formally protested the seizure, and Spain sent patrol boats to the area to protect its fishermen. Negotiations between Canada and the EU led to a resolution of the issue on April 16. The result was an agreement on the management of turbot stocks outside Canada's 200-mi fisheries protection zone. At the same time, a UN convention negotiated in New York laid down stricter international controls on high-seas fishing. Turbot stocks in the North Atlantic were not expected to recover until after the year 2000, but 1995 had seen the first steps toward conservation of a historic resource.

Overfishing became a problem on the northern Pacific coast of Canada and the United States as well. Commercial fishermen using long lines and gill nets, together with native Indians and sport fishermen, competed to catch the several species of Pacific salmon in those waters.

International cooperation to conserve the northern Pacific salmon proved difficult. British Columbia cut its total allowable catch by 50%, while Washington and Oregon took comparable measures. But Alaska refused to cut its limit by more than 5%, arguing that it had protected the habitat around its rivers and that its harvest was sustainable. British Columbia responded by pointing out that 60% of the salmon caught in Alaskan waters originated in British Columbian rivers, with only 10% coming from Alaskan streams. Alaska's decision had been taken outside the bilateral procedures set forth in the Pacific Salmon Treaty, and the issue went before the courts in August when native fishermen from Washington and Oregon, supported by the government of Canada, applied for an injunction to close down the southeastern Alaska chinook fishery until the future of the resource could be fully studied. On September 7 a United States district court judge in Washington state confirmed an earlier temporary closure, halting the Alaska chinook fishery until September 30, by which time the commercial fishing season would be over in Alaska.

In an effort to find a long-term solution to the impasse, Canada and the United States agreed to send the dispute to an independent mediator. A report was issued in December calling for a one-third reduction in the fishing fleet. Some groups claimed this would not be enough, and it seemed that much bargaining lay ahead before an effective management regime could be established for the valuable Pacific salmon.

(D.M.L. FARR)

CAPE VERDE

The republic of Cape Verde occupies an island group in the Atlantic Ocean about 620 km (385 mi) off the west coast of Africa. Area: 4,033 sq km (1,557 sq mi). Pop. (1995 est.): 392,000. Cap.: Praia. Monetary unit: Cape Verde escudo, with (Oct. 6, 1995) a free rate of 82.97 escudos to U.S. $1 (131.17 escudos = £1 sterling). President in 1995, Antonio Mascarenhas Monteiro; prime minister, Carlos Veiga.

In January, Prime Minister Carlos Veiga carried out a major reshuffle of his Cabinet. His object, he claimed, was to facilitate the country's shift from a state-run to a market-oriented economy. The most important change was to combine the Ministries of Finance, of Economic Coordination, and of Tourism, Industry and Commerce into a single Ministry of Economic Coordination. A new Ministry of the Sea was also established to deal with fisheries, marine affairs, and ports.

A volcano erupted on the island of Fogo in early April. After apparently quieting down, it then began to erupt more violently, sending lava in streams toward populated areas at a rate of five to seven metres per hour.

The Cape Verde economy remained substantially dependent upon foreign aid, and in this respect the European Union (EU) was an important donor. EU aid projects included the electrification of rural Praia, the improvement of living conditions in the centre of Praia, and the development of a road infrastructure program in São Tiago, São Nicolau, and Maio islands. Cape Verde was also included in an EU regional solar energy program. Inflation during the year was 6%.

(GUY ARNOLD)

This article updates the *Macropædia* article WESTERN AFRICA: *Cape Verde*.

CENTRAL AFRICAN REPUBLIC

The Central African Republic is a landlocked state in central Africa. Area: 622,436 sq km (240,324 sq mi). Pop. (1995 est.): 3,141,000. Cap.: Bangui. Monetary unit: CFA franc, with (Oct. 6, 1995) a par value of CFAF 100 to the French franc and a free rate of CFAF 501.49 to U.S. $1 (CFAF 792.78 = £1 sterling). President in 1995, Ange-Félix Patassé; prime ministers, Jean-Luc Mandaba and, from April 12, Gabriel Koyambounou.

A new constitution was approved by 83% of the voters in a referendum on Dec. 28, 1994. Opposition parties, however, called it a defeat for Pres. Ange-Félix Patassé, as only 46% of the electorate voted. Prime Minister Jean-Luc Mandaba resigned in April when deputies of the majority Central African People's Liberation Party called for a vote of no-confidence. He was replaced by former inspector general Gabriel Koyambounou, who promised to launch an all-out campaign against corruption.

The government banned a May 1 protest organized by the opposition Democratic Movement for the Rebirth and Evolution of the Central African Republic (MDRERC). Its leader, Joseph Bendounga, had called the march to demand that President Patassé convene the national conference promised before his April 1993 election. A presidential decree of July 8, announcing the formation of a special anti-corruption squad with powers of arrest, also drew opposition fire. The MDRERC claimed that the squad would be dominated by the government and could be used to silence political protest.

Thousands of Chadian refugees who had fled to the Central African Republic during the years of civil war in their nation began returning home on April 22 in accordance with a 1994 repatriation agreement signed in Bangui. In May the Central African Republic lodged an official protest with Zaire over several border incidents in the Ubangi River, which separates the two countries.

Sharp increases in cotton and diamond production fueled an improvement in the economy. A real growth rate of 7% was anticipated, although consumers were continuing to feel the inflationary effects of the devaluation of the CFA franc.

(NANCY ELLEN LAWLER)

This article updates the *Macropædia* article CENTRAL AFRICA: *Central African Republic*.

CHAD

Chad is a landlocked republic of central Africa. Area: 1,284,000 sq km (495,755 sq mi). Pop. (1995 est.): 6,361,000. Cap.: N'Djamena. Monetary unit: CFA franc, with a par value of CFAF 100 to the French franc and (as of Oct. 6, 1995) a free rate of CFAF 501.49 to U.S. $1 (CFAF 792.78 = £1 sterling). President in 1995, Col. Idriss Déby; prime ministers, Delwa Kassire Koumakoye and from April 8, Koibla Djimasta.

The 1995–96 national budget presented in January, estimated an expenditure of CFAF 61 billion against revenues of only CFAF 41 billion. On March 31, 1995, the Higher Transitional Council (CST; the transitional legislature) extended the transition period (for a return to full democracy), which was due to end on April 9, for an additional 12 months (it had already been extended once since it began in 1993). The CST claimed the government had failed to discharge its commitments and had not taken adequate action to cushion the impact of the devaluation of the CFA franc. On April 8, after dismissing Prime Minister Delwa Kassire Koumakoye, the CST elected Koibla Djimasta in his place. The new prime minister said he expected to bring the final stage of the transition period to a close. In November the independent national election commission rescheduled the election timetable: a constitutional referendum to be held on March 31, 1996; presidential elections in June 1996; and legislative elections on December 22–24, 1996.

In August the deposed prime minister, Koumakoye, announced that he would run as a presidential candidate in 1996. Also that month the opposition National Liberation Front (Frolinat) called for a conference of all Chad's politico-military groups to be held in a neutral country such as Nigeria. Following a corruption scandal the CST Bureau resigned, and a new CST chairman, Abbas Ali, was elected to replace Abderamane Hagar, who had stepped down because of the corruption charges.

(GUY ARNOLD)

This article updates the *Macropædia* article WESTERN AFRICA: *Chad*.

CHILE

The republic of Chile extends along the Pacific coast of the Southern Cone of South America. Area: 756,626 sq km (292,135 sq mi), not including Chile's Antarctic claim. Pop. (1995 est.): 14,210,000. Cap.: Santiago (national); Valparaíso (legislative). Monetary unit: Chilean peso, with (Oct. 6, 1995) a free rate of 401.10 pesos to U.S. $1 (634.08 pesos = £1 sterling). President in 1995, Eduardo Frei.

The dictatorship of Gen. Augusto Pinochet (1973–90) cast a shadow over Chilean politics in 1995. In May the Supreme Court upheld the convictions of Gen. Manuel Contreras, head of the secret police from 1973 to 1977, and his former deputy, Brig. Gen. Pedro Espinoza, on charges of involvement in the 1976 car-bomb murder in Washington, D.C., of Orlando Letelier, a leading Socialist and former ambassador to the United States. Pinochet, still commander in chief of the army, castigated the Supreme Court judgment as "shameful . . . unjust and political" and "unconstitutional." The army then hindered Contreras' imprisonment, but he nevertheless handed himself in to begin his prison sentence in October. Espinoza was imprisoned in Punta Pueco, a new prison purposely built for military officers. On July 22 some 300 officers and their families, led by the commander of the Santiago garrison, demonstrated outside the prison. In a later speech Pinochet asked officers to remain calm and respect the civil authorities and the rule of law. When the government subsequently intervened to stop investigations into corruption charges against Pinochet's son, some observers suspected that a deal had been struck.

JEFFREY AARONSON—NETWORK/ASPEN

Men work in a winery in Santiago. Despite a number of unresolved political and social problems, the Chilean economy continued to grow strongly during 1995, with the rate of inflation slightly lower than in the previous year and with exports dramatically higher.

In August Pres. Eduardo Frei announced a package of proposals to the legislature: a bill to clarify the fate of some 1,000 people who disappeared during the dictatorship and reforms to Pinochet's 1980 constitution to allow the president to appoint and dismiss top military commanders and to abolish the nine nonelected seats in the Senate. The current nonelected senators, appointed by Pinochet, enabled the right-wing opposition to block constitutional reforms. Because their terms were to expire in 1998 and Frei would appoint their successors, the opposition might be tempted to accept the constitutional reforms in return for an end to investigations into human rights violations.

In March, in a speech marking his first year in office, Frei stressed concern over the widespread poverty that persisted in Chile despite the economic growth of the past decade. In May the minimum wage was increased by 12.9%. The government also introduced a new tax on cigarettes and cars to fund a 10% rise in the lowest pensions and a 5% increase in education spending.

Negotiations opened for Chilean membership in the Southern Cone Common Market (Mercosur) and the North American Free Trade Agreement (NAFTA). Prospects for rapid success in the NAFTA talks faltered when the U.S. Congress failed to approve the use of "fast-track" authority (under which it would merely vote on the final treaty); without this, Chilean entry was likely to be delayed until after the 1996 presidential election. The major opposition to associate membership in Mercosur (which included Argentina, Brazil, Paraguay, and Uruguay) came from Chilean farmers, worried about cheaper imported produce. The government also pursued a trade pact with the European Union; Frei visited Europe in March to press Chile's case, which was accepted in principle in August.

In August LAN-Chile announced the purchase of 57% of the rival airline Ladeco, which made the LAN-Chile/Ladeco group the third largest airline in Latin America. The two carriers retained their separate identities.

The effect of the Mexican economic crisis was limited. Chile's annual growth rate in 1995 was 7%, and inflation was 8% (8.9% in 1994). Chilean exports were very strong, resulting in a first-half trade surplus of $1.3 billion, compared with $344.6 million for the corresponding period in 1994. Fruit exports increased 15.8% by volume, and copper earnings rose owing to increased exports and high world prices. By July the peso had risen 20% against its year-end rate of 403 to the dollar, though a cut in interest rates and other measures brought it down to 391 (Sept. 25, 1995).

(CHARLIE NURSE)

CHINA

The People's Republic of China is situated in eastern Asia, with coastlines on the Yellow Sea and the East and South China seas. Area: 9,572,900 sq km (3,696,100 sq mi), including Tibet and excluding Taiwan. (See *Taiwan,* below.) Pop. (1995 est., excluding Taiwan): 1,206,600,000. Cap.: Beijing. Monetary unit: renminbi yuan, with (Oct. 6, 1995) a free rate of 8.32 yuan to U.S. $1 (13.15 yuan = £1 sterling). President in 1995, Jiang Zemin; premier, Li Peng.

In the midnight hour of Deng Xiaoping's reign, the political contours of the era that would follow the 91-year-old patriarch's passing began to emerge a little more clearly during 1995. Displaying an unwonted boldness, Pres. Jiang Zemin decisively strengthened his political position. China pursued an assertive foreign policy that could presage its global role in the 21st century. The economy continued to grow by nearly 9%, benefiting the urban middle and upper classes in particular, but none of the basic economic and social problems that a decade and a half of rapid growth had created seemed any closer to solution. Until Deng's successor was firmly in charge, those favouring liberalization would be challenged by those attempting to restore a quasi-centralized authoritarianism. Underlying China's continuing preparation for the post-Deng era was a peculiar generational division of labour between the young and the old. While the dynamic nonstate sector of the economy rocked to the beat of young entrepreneurs and workers, the shuffle step of superannuated politicians sounded in the corridors of power. The ancient would be replaced by the elderly.

Domestic Affairs. When Deng's youngest daughter acknowledged in January that her father was fading, official media were quick to contradict her. Nevertheless, Deng's capacity to intervene in politics was severely diminished, though even his occasional word still resonated. In April Deng's long-time rival Chen Yun, an opponent of radical reform and patron of conservative Premier Li Peng, died at the age of 89. Deng and 87-year-old Yang Shangkun were the only survivors among the top first-generation communist revolutionaries.

The major political development of the year was the purge of Chen Xitong, a powerful member of the Political Bureau and Beijing first party secretary. A major corruption scandal that implicated top officials of the municipally owned Capital Iron and Steel Corp. and dozens of Beijing city officials precipitated Chen's fall from grace. In April Vice-Mayor Wang Baosen, who reportedly embezzled $37 million in government funds, committed suicide, and shortly thereafter Chen was forced to resign. At the 14th Central Committee's Fifth Plenum in September, Chen was officially ousted from the Political Bureau and placed under house arrest while undergoing investigation. By engineering the purge of Chen, despised by many Chinese for his role in the bloody June 4, 1989, Tiananmen Square massacre of democracy activists, Jiang not only eliminated a potential rival but also demonstrated his commitment to the faltering anticorruption campaign. The elevation of Defense Minister Chi Haotian and chief of staff Zhang Wannian to vice-chairmen of the Communist Party of China's (CPC's) Central Military Commission, a key organ of power, demonstrated Jiang's success in garnering support from the People's Liberation Army (PLA). That success, however, depended upon his acquiescence to an ever-growing political role for the military, which was dominated by conservative nationalists.

Nevertheless, Jiang's position was still not impregnable, one indication being his inability to appoint one of his own stalwarts as Beijing's new party boss, a position filled by Wei Jianxing, a follower of Qiao Shi, head of the National People's Congress (NPC). An uncharismatic figure who lacked his own political compass, the president frequently tacked in the direction of China's neoconservatives such as Xiao Gongqin, Wang Huning, and Chen Yuan. Decrying the liberalizing and centrifugal effects of the reform era, they argued that Dengist rule had brought China perilously close to the brink of social anarchy and political disintegration. They yearned for a new strongman to rebuild centralized state authority.

If Jiang relied on the party apparatus and the PLA, his rivals possessed their own bases of support. At the March meeting of the national congress, more than one-third of the representatives abstained or openly voted against the nomination of Jiang's choice for two vice-premiers. Qiao Shi, former chief of China's intelligence services turned legal and institutional reformer, continued to boost the lawmaking role of the NPC, the foundation of his authority. Although the NPC was still far from being an effective parliament, it had the potential to become one. Meanwhile, the increasing number of contested local elections in which voters exercised genuine if limited choice suggested that ordinary citizens possessed a political capacity that elitist neoconservative theorists were reluctant to acknowledge. Be that as it may, the perhaps temporary ascendancy of Jiang and his allies had dimmed the once bright political prospects of economic reformer Zhu Rongji, who, like Li, was at least partially overshadowed.

Christian worshipers pray in a cathedral in Beijing. Despite the government's continuing clampdown on political dissent, many Chinese citizens were finding some opportunities for free expression in other areas of their lives, including religion.
PETER TURNLEY—BLACK STAR

In February and March the first major stirrings of political dissent since the Tiananmen democracy movement emerged. A dozen leading intellectuals called on the NPC to investigate official corruption and halt the abuse of police power. On May 15, just three weeks before the sixth anniversary of the Tiananmen affair, 45 leading intellectuals and scientists addressed a political petition drafted by venerable physicist Xu Liangying to Jiang and Qiao. Counterposing the Western legacy of freedom to China's heritage of repression, the petitioners called upon party leaders to adopt "a spirit of tolerance" toward ideology, political thought, and religious belief; to release prisoners of conscience; and to end China's "ignominious tradition of literary inquisitions." In so doing, the petitioners politely but boldly challenged the foundations of CPC rule.

These daring initiatives elicited only hostile responses. Signers of the petitions were called in for questioning and otherwise harassed. In June Beijing arrested U.S. citizen Harry Wu (*see* BIOGRAPHIES), a human rights activist, on trumped-up charges of espionage. A 19-year veteran of China's political prisons, Wu had infuriated Beijing authorities with his widely publicized exposés of human rights abuses in China. After sentencing Wu to 15 years in prison, China immediately expelled him to relieve enormous international pressure. Wei Jingsheng, China's leading democracy activist, was released from prison in September 1993 after having served 14½ years for challenging Deng Xiaoping's authority. He resumed his peaceful political activity but was rearrested on April 1, 1994. After a closed trial he was sentenced to 14 years in prison. This harsh warning against political dissent evoked condemnation around the world. A host of lesser-known dissidents and democrats, including Tibetan supporters of the Dalai Lama, continued to languish in Chinese prisons. Seeking to undermine the Dalai Lama's authority, Beijing compelled leading Tibetan clerics to reject the exiled leader's designation of a new Panchen Lama, Tibet's second most important religious leader, in favour of China's own choice.

The Economy. Underlying the political dynamics of contemporary China and posing difficult policy choices for the country's leaders were the immense economic and social changes that the Dengist era had produced. Many changes had been for the better. Even though the political system stifled open dissent, most Chinese enjoyed an unprecedented degree of personal mobility and freedom. The standard of living of most Chinese had improved substantially. The number of rural poor had declined from 200 million to 80 million in a decade. Fifteen years of rapid economic growth had transformed the face of urban and rural China, creating unprecedented prosperity for many while widening the gap between rich and poor. The continuing influx of tens of millions of rural Chinese into coastal and interior boom towns in search of employment and a better life followed the pattern of other less developed countries. Such migrants overburdened municipal services, drove up the crime rate, and contributed to a growing sense of social disorder that had translated into support for leaders who promised stability at any price. Among other negative phenomena was the growing illegal drug problem. A burgeoning trade in heroin, manufactured from opium poppies in Myanmar (Burma), had entered the world market via southwestern China. Rising rates of addiction plagued Yunnan and Guizhou provinces. Drug use was growing among young urban sophisticates. As elsewhere, violent crime accompanied the drug trade. A commodity culture heavily influenced by the West, Taiwan, Hong Kong, and Japan was supplanting values associated with communitarian socialism.

China's economy remained a hybrid in which thriving capitalist limbs had been grafted onto an anemic state socialist body. At its Fifth Plenum in September, the party's Central Committee ratified the Ninth Five-Year Plan (1996–2000), which envisioned an 8–9% growth rate. In recent years China's growth, most of it outside the state sector, had exceeded government estimates, although the five-year projection was almost identical with the 8.9% rate achieved during the first three quarters of 1995. Viewing balanced growth as the key to achieving social and political stability, the CPC endorsed economic reform and underscored the importance of the electronics, petrochemical, motor vehicle, machinery, and building materials industries. Again no solution was offered to the perennial problem of heavily subsidized and debt-ridden state enterprises that continued to employ the majority of China's industrial workers. China's state-dominated banking industry had to absorb the annual loss of billions of yuan in bad loans to insolvent state-owned enterprises, which were kept afloat for essentially political reasons. Understandably, no one in power was willing to risk the serious social instability that mass layoffs might entail. Moreover, because state-owned enterprises constituted the economic essence of state socialism, they also embodied the CPC's resolve to prevent the final victory of a market economy with its concomitant threat to party rule.

Since gaining power in 1949, the CPC had had to face the nightmare of inflation, which had accelerated the downfall of its Nationalist predecessors. In 1995 inflation was cut nearly in half to just over 13% as China slowed the growth of its money supply. Now one of the world's top trading nations, China enjoyed a $20.3 billion trade surplus through September, and its foreign-exchange reserves nearly doubled to $64.2 billion, the sixth highest in the world. Nevertheless, a number of economic problems continued to plague China's relations with the industrialized world. In late February, after the U.S. and China had initiated trade sanctions against each other, China finally acceded to U.S. pressure by pledging to curb the rampant pirating of U.S. software and audio- and videocassettes. The ballooning of the U.S. trade deficit with China, projected to reach $38 billion in 1995 (according to U.S. statistics), further soured Sino-American relations, already strained by political factors. At the annual Asia-Pacific Economic Cooperation forum in November, Beijing promised to slash import tariffs in 1996 by 30% on more than 4,000 kinds of imported goods as one concrete step toward the 25-year goal of an Asia-Pacific free-trade zone. The U.S.-led Organisation for Economic Co-operation and Development stipulated further changes that China would have to undertake to secure admission to the World Trade Organization.

Rapid sustained economic growth had been the key to China's coming of age as a global power. China continued to attract substantial foreign investment in 1995, with particular interest being shown in such massive infrastructural projects as energy, telecommunications, and highways. The U.S.-based auto giant General Motors received the coveted partnership it sought to develop a mass-produced people's car. As work progressed on the approximately $30 billion Three Gorges Dam, the administration of U.S. Pres. Bill Clinton directed the U.S. Export-Import Bank to withhold financing for U.S. companies engaging in the project, widely criticized by Chinese as well as foreign environmentalists. On the whole, however, Chinese leaders were able to rely on their country's enormous potential for investment, trade, and economic cooperation as an effective buffer against unwelcome intervention by foreign governments.

Foreign Affairs. The terms on which China related to the world had been in flux for more than a century and a half. China's rapidly growing economic achievements and military muscle lent a new urgency to this question. A cooperative China integrated into global and regional economic and security institutions would be a major force for stability and progress. An uncooperative or even obstreperous China could sabotage international agreements, bully its neighbours, and threaten regional security. Resurgent nationalism, expressing pride in Chinese identity and recent accomplishments, was encouraged by government leaders, who saw in nationalism an effective substitute for moribund Marxism-Leninism.

China's growing assertiveness expressed itself in 1995 in several ways. Most important was a prolonged contretemps with the U.S. over the issue of Taiwan. Yielding to overwhelming congressional pressure, the Clinton administration granted Lee Teng-hui, president of the Republic of China in Taiwan, permission for a private visit in June to give a speech at his alma mater, Cornell University, Ithaca, N.Y. Beijing hardliners, already convinced of U.S. hostility toward China, treated the visit as a major provocation requiring a firm response. Claiming that Washington had reneged on its promise to deny Lee a visa, Beijing discerned a U.S. plot to bolster Taiwan's international status notwithstanding Washington's assurances, first given by Pres. Richard Nixon in 1972, that it viewed Taiwan as a Chinese province. Beijing recalled its ambassador, backed out of arms control talks, arrested Harry Wu, and denounced the U.S. for perfidy.

In a crude attempt at military intimidation, China carried out two series of missile and naval artillery tests in the East China Sea just north of Taiwan and practiced joint combat exercises involving air and naval forces. Beijing's message about Taiwan's vulnerability was unmistakable. PLA leaders also publicly discussed the circumstances under which

China might seize Taiwan by force. Although Taiwan's stock market temporarily dipped, Beijing failed to erode political support for Lee, whom it accused of covertly supporting Taiwanese independence.

This latest in a series of bumpy stretches in Sino-American relations smoothed out after Beijing's expulsion of Harry Wu, which cleared the way for Hillary Rodham Clinton to attend the UN Fourth World Conference on Women in Beijing. In her address, however, she blasted China for human rights abuses with undiplomatic forthrightness. Meanwhile, the Chinese government had angered many of those taking part in a concurrent nongovernmental women's forum by severely limiting contact between foreign participants and Chinese women. (*See* UNITED NATIONS *Sidebar.*) The resumption in the fall of U.S.-China military exchanges and a brief October meeting in New York between Jiang and Clinton signaled the end of the contretemps. Washington stopped just short of categorically promising it would never again grant Lee permission to visit the U.S., but the price of risking Chinese ire was now clearly marked on the ticket. In the final analysis, Beijing again demonstrated its willingness to speak its mind.

For more than two decades, China had been systematically pursuing its territorial claims in the South China Sea through a strategy that wrapped incremental military encroachment in a cloak of diplomatic flexibility. In February the Chinese navy established a presence on Mischief Reef, one of the Spratly Islands claimed by the Philippines, whose minuscule navy retaliated by dismantling Chinese territorial markers and structures and detaining Chinese fishing vessels in adjacent waters. (*See* SPOTLIGHT: *The Spat over the Spratlys.*) Chinese actions risked antagonizing the Association of Southeast Asian Nations (ASEAN), four of whose members—the Philippines, Malaysia, Brunei, and Vietnam—asserted claims in the Spratlys along with China and Taiwan. At the ASEAN foreign ministers' meeting in July, China reiterated both its own claim to sovereignty over the entire South China Sea and its willingness to seek a peaceful resolution of competing claims while engaging in joint development of maritime resources in the area. Throughout Asia there was a growing awareness shading into anxiety about the implications for regional security of China's growing military strength, and quiet discussions about how to counterbalance it took place. China took another step toward control of Hong Kong by naming in December the committee that would oversee the transition.

At the Nuclear Non-proliferation Treaty review conference in April–May, China, a nuclear weapons state, echoed Third World criticism of the treaty but nonetheless endorsed its indefinite extension. Seeking to deflect criticism of its own nuclear weapons tests, Beijing condemned the other nuclear weapons states, and especially the U.S., for developing high-tech missile defense systems and promoting overseas arms sales.

The 50th anniversary of the end of World War II provided an opportunity for China to join fellow victims in condemning Japanese wartime aggression and chastising Tokyo for its reluctance to accept full responsibility for its transgressions. This theme was sounded again by Jiang during his November visit to Seoul, the first state visit to South Korea by China's president. Relations with India and Russia continued to improve, although in the long term strong elements of rivalry overshadowed the cooperative dimension, particularly with respect to Sino-Indian relations.

China's future remained impossible to forecast with confidence even for the relatively near term. In part this was attributable to its size and complexity, but it also reflected the political uncertainties of a transition period and the unresolved choices in domestic and foreign affairs that awaited either the consolidation of Jiang's power in a post-Deng era or his replacement at the apex of power by one or another of his rivals. Although unlikely, the fragmentation of the country or even the collapse of the regime could not be ruled out entirely. Whatever scenario one envisioned, the problem of governing this huge, unwieldy country undergoing rapid economic and social transformation was a challenge of staggering proportions. But governing China had never been a simple matter. (STEVEN I. LEVINE)

PETER TURNLEY—NEWSWEEK/BLACK STAR

Chinese youth enjoy the scene at one of Beijing's discos. Even as the government maintained a strong measure of control over political events, the private economy was booming in China, and there seemed to be little if any letup in the cultural changes that were taking place.

SPOTLIGHT: THE SPAT OVER THE SPRATLYS

Illustration by Istvan Banyai

by Ricardo Saludo

Scattered over 388,000 sq km (150,000 sq mi) of the South China Sea midway between Vietnam and the Philippines, the 500–600 largely uninhabited islets, reefs, and shoals of the Spratly Islands seem a curious prize in Southeast Asia's most contentious territorial dispute. China, Vietnam, and Taiwan lay claim to the entire archipelago, and Brunei, Malaysia, and the Philippines to islands close to their shores.

At the annual Association of Southeast Asian Nations (ASEAN) regional forum on security in Brunei in July, ASEAN, bolstered by seventh member Vietnam, pressed China to abide by a 1992 ASEAN declaration to settle the Spratly dispute through negotiations. Over Chinese opposition to U.S. involvement, Washington said that it wanted freedom of navigation maintained. Some 200 vessels ply the South China Sea at any one time, conveying nearly half of Asia's commerce, including 70% of Japan's oil.

While asserting its sovereignty over the Spratlys, Beijing agreed in Brunei to resolve claims according to international law, softening its past insistence on historical title. In talks lasting until August, China and the Philippines adopted measures to avoid military conflict. Beijing allowed the Filipinos to destroy its stone markers and small structures on islets around Mischief Reef (but not the main facilities, which China contended were for fishermen). The Philippines detained 62 Chinese fishing in a nearby area but later released all except four captains. Analysts believed Beijing was conciliatory in order to preserve relations with ASEAN and to forestall any regional alliance to "contain" China.

While the Mischief Reef problem was smoothed over, a general Spratlys resolution remained remote. At a workshop on the issue at which Indonesia served as host in October, the sixth since 1990, participants from the six claimants endorsed a call to set aside sovereignty questions and undertake joint development. Besides abundant fish, the area may contain oil, tin, manganese, and other minerals, judging by what is found in surrounding waters. The workshop in Borneo agreed on low-level programs, and Indonesia hoped joint projects would create an atmosphere for tackling weightier matters, but some participants opposed discussing such measures in the next meeting.

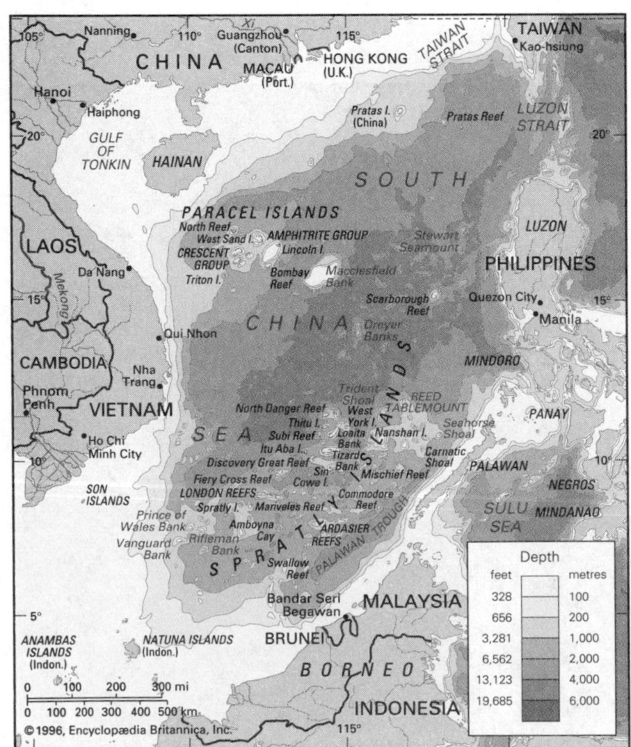

Seeds of the dispute were planted 50 years ago. In 1945 the Allies took the Spratlys from Japanese control. The Nationalist Chinese occupied Spratly Island but withdrew in 1950. After Tokyo formally relinquished the islands in its 1951 peace treaty with the Allies, other countries began staking claims. In 1956 South Vietnam occupied Spratly Island and the Paracels group farther north. That same year, by Manila's account, Filipino mariner Tomas Cloma claimed a group of 53 islands, reefs, and shoals, which he named Freedomland. In 1962 Taiwan drove Filipino settlers from Itu Aba, the largest Spratly island at 43 ha (106 ac). In 1968 the Philippines occupied three islets. In the 1970s, when China took the Paracels, unified Vietnam took more islands. In 1995 Vietnam held 25 islands, China 12, the Philippines 8, Malaysia 4, and Taiwan 1.

In 1988 Vietnam lost three vessels and 77 seamen in a half-hour battle with China. Hanoi said Chinese troops also took over a reef it had held and six unoccupied islands. That same year Malaysian gunboats detained 49 Filipino fishermen near Commodore Reef, also claimed by Manila. In 1992 China passed legislation formally claiming—by force, if necessary—the Spratlys, the Paracels, the East China Sea's Senkaku islands (claimed by Japan), and most of the South China Sea. Beijing then gave Crestone, a U.S. oil firm, a concession in waters within Vietnam's claimed exclusive economic zone. In 1994 Vietnam drove Crestone away, which prompted a temporary Chinese blockade of a Russo-Vietnamese oil rig. The Philippines also awarded oil concessions, while Malaysia developed one island into a diving resort. In recent years the addition of new warplanes and vessels to their forces has augmented the ability of most claimants to intervene in the area.

While accepting international law, China still preferred bilateral, not multilateral, talks with rival claimants. Legal experts, though, believe that all six claims are weak. Spratly references in Chinese and Vietnamese historical records are intermittent, which suggests no lasting claim, occupation, or settlement. No nation has administered the area anywhere near the 50 years normally conferring title. Under the UN Law of the Sea, none of the claimants seemed qualified to claim 200-nautical-mile economic zones around the Spratlys, and zones based on the continental shelves of Malaysia and Vietnam probably carry greater legal weight. So despite tough talk and some military buildup, claimants are unlikely to wage war over the Spratlys and torpedo lucrative relations among themselves—unless national pride overcomes pragmatism.

Ricardo Saludo is a senior editor at *Asiaweek* magazine and is based in Hong Kong.

COLOMBIA

A republic in northwestern South America, Colombia has coastlines on the Caribbean Sea and the Pacific Ocean. Area: 1,141,568 sq km (440,762 sq mi). Pop. (1995 est.): 35,099,000. Cap.: Santafé de Bogotá, D.C. Monetary unit: Colombian peso, with (Oct. 6, 1995) a free rate of 979 pesos to U.S. $1 (1,547.65 pesos = £1 sterling). President in 1995, Ernesto Samper Pizano.

The position of Pres. Ernesto Samper Pizano was steadily eroded during 1995 by revelations that money from the drug cartels assisted his election in June 1994. Santiago Medina, the Liberal Party campaign treasurer, was arrested in July and in August admitted receiving about $6 million from the Cali cartel. He implicated Fernando Botero Zea, the minister of defense, who was forced to resign and later was charged with illicit enrichment and falsifying documents. The investigation was led by Colombia's chief prosecutor, Alfonso Valdivieso. (*See* BIOGRAPHIES.) By the end of August, Samper had declared a state of emergency because of the wave of violence and kidnappings in the country, though it was widely believed that this was also an attempt to protect himself from the drug-money scandals. The assassination of a prominent critic of the government, coupled with a decision not to investigate Samper, fortified this impression.

In fact, a dramatic weakening of the largest of the Colombian drug cartels took place in 1995. After the death of Pablo Escobar at the end of 1993, the Medellín drug cartel dwindled in favour of the Cali cartel, which by 1995 was believed to control up to 70% of the world's trade in cocaine. Pressure on the Colombian government led to a concerted effort to neutralize the leadership of the Cali cartel. Between June and August seven of the cartel's principal figures were arrested or voluntarily surrendered, including Gilberto Rodríguez Orejuela and his brother Miguel, acknowledged as the leaders.

FABIO SERRANO—GAMMA LIAISON

Police in Bogotá escort Miguel Rodríguez Orejuela, second in command in the Cali drug cartel, after his arrest on August 6. In its crackdown on the group, the Colombian government had earlier taken into custody his brother Gilberto (the cartel head) and other leaders.

Efforts continued in the eradication of the coca and poppy plantations in the hope of replacing them with other crops. There were army operations against airfields and transit points used by the cartels, such as the island of San Andrés, where the army took control of aircraft movements.

Though those events slowed down the Colombian drug traffic, the outlook remained pessimistic. There were rumours that other drug-trafficking groups in Colombia were becoming more active and that some operations were moving to neighbouring countries. One suspected reason for the many arrests was that sentences given by Colombian courts could enable even the worst offenders to be freed within relatively few years. Indeed, the Ochoa brothers of the former Medellín cartel were scheduled to leave jail at the end of 1995 after only four-year sentences.

Meanwhile, the level of violence and kidnapping in Colombia remained high. Two left-wing groups, the Colombia Revolutionary Armed Forces (FARC) and the National Liberation Army (ELN), were active in many parts of the country, damaging power lines and oil pipelines and attacking police and military installations. Sporadic urban violence included a bomb that exploded in the centre of Medellín in June, killing at least 29 and injuring more than 200. The explosion destroyed a monument crowned with a dove of peace by the sculptor Fernando Botero, father of the minister of defense.

Strong reaction to the FARC and the ELN on the part of the armed forces substantially added to the high level of violent deaths, estimated to be eight times the U.S. rate. Human rights organizations continued to highlight Colombia's poor record, and President Samper dismissed Gen. Alvaro Velandia Hurtado in September after a tribunal found that he had approved human rights violations as commander of Colombia's Third Army.

Inflation in Colombia in 1995 was forecast at 18% (22.5% in 1994), and the economy was expected to grow 4.5%, a little below 1994. Privatization of such state-owned enterprises as Banco Popular progressed slowly. British Petroleum reported significant new oil and gas finds in the north of the country and expected a substantial increase in production during the next three years. There was disarray in the emerald trade, with violence affecting the world's richest mines in the department of Boyacá. Production of bananas was also disrupted by strikes linked to ELN guerrilla activity.

(PETER POLLARD)

COMOROS

The Islamic republic of the Comoros is an island state in the Indian Ocean off the east coast of Africa. Area: 1,862 sq km (719 sq mi), excluding the island of Mayotte, which continued to be a de facto dependency of France. Pop. (1995 est.; excluding Mayotte): 545,000. Cap.: Moroni. Monetary unit: Comorian franc, with a par value of CF 75 to the French franc and (as of Oct. 6, 1995) a free rate of CF 371.60 to U.S. $1 (CF 587.47 = £1 sterling). President in 1995, Said Mohamed Djohar; prime ministers, Halifa Houmadi and, from April 29, Caabi el Yachroutou Mohamed. From October 4 the constitutional president and prime minister were unclear.

Prime Minister Halifa Houmadi resigned at the end of April 1995 as a result of growing tensions in the ruling Rally for Democracy and Renewal. Pres. Said Mohamed Djohar then asked the former finance minister, Caabi el Yachroutou Mohamed, to form a government; it was the 14th administration in five years. The new prime minister kept only five members of the outgoing Cabinet and demoted Said Mohamed Sagaf (the president's son-in-law) from Foreign Affairs to Posts and Telecommunications, Information, Culture, Youth and Sports in an effort to reduce his influence.

A coup against the government was mounted at the end of September by French mercenary Bob Denard and a number of followers who were joined by between 300 and 700 Comorans. Prime Minister Yachroutou took refuge in the French embassy and appealed for help; a week later French special forces arrived from Mayotte to reverse the coup. Denard and his mercenaries negotiated their surrender and were flown off the island. Opposition groups demanded an early election, claiming Djohar was corrupt and incompetent. The octogenarian president flew to Réunion for medical treatment on October 4. Yachroutou then declared himself "interim president" and appointed a government. Thereupon Djohar announced his intentions to return and on October 31 faxed a statement appointing his own government. The Organization of African Unity sent a delegation, but the political situation in the Comoros was still confused at year's end. (GUY ARNOLD)

This article updates the *Micropædia* article COMOROS.

CONGO

A republic, Congo is in central Africa on the Atlantic Ocean. Area: 342,000 sq km (132,047 sq mi). Pop. (1995 est.): 2,590,000. Cap.: Brazzaville. Monetary unit: CFA franc, with (Oct. 6, 1995) a par value of CFAF 100 to the French franc and a free rate of CFAF 501.49 to U.S. $1 (CFAF 792.78 = £1 sterling). President in 1995, Pascal Lissouba; prime minister, Jacques Yhombi-Opango.

Despite the peace accord between the government and opposition parties reached in August 1994, the problem of disarming the urban militias and restructuring the army dominated the political arena in 1995. In January the defense minister announced that only 2,000 of the estimated 3,000 militia members would be integrated into the army. In September the government announced that the army would become more representative of the population and was to be reorganized along ethnic and regional lines. The opposition charged that the plan was designed to give Pres. Pascal Lissouba control of the army.

A general strike was called on February 19 by labour unions demanding the payment of months of salary arrears. Although an agreement was reached on March 1, civil servants refused to return to work, rejecting the agreement's provision of lower pay in exchange for shorter hours. Most of the discontent arose from the government's attempts to comply with the International Monetary Fund-imposed structural adjustment program, which had already reduced the civil service from 80,000 to 55,000. A student strike over unpaid grants led to escalating violence in June, while soldiers, demanding payment of food subsidies already 17 months in arrears, staged a three-day sit-down after the student strike ended.

Despite cuts in civil service salaries, intensified exploitation of offshore oil reserves, and the sale of its share of the oil firm Elf-Congo, the government was virtually without cash. The economy's overall weak performance continued, and Congo remained one of the world's poorest and most debt-ridden countries. (NANCY ELLEN LAWLER)

This article updates the *Macropædia* article CENTRAL AFRICA: *Congo.*

COSTA RICA

The Central American republic of Costa Rica has coastlines on the Caribbean Sea and the Pacific Ocean. Area: 51,100 sq km (19,730 sq mi). Pop. (1995 est.): 3,344,000. Cap.: San José. Monetary unit: Costa Rican colón, with (Oct. 6, 1995) a free rate of ₡187.50 to U.S. $1 (₡296.42 = £1 sterling). President in 1995, José María Figueres Olsen.

The year 1995 began with Costa Rica's government struggling to cope with a deteriorating economy, high inflation, and a budget deficit of 8% of gross domestic product. In February Pres. José María Figueres announced a plan to reduce the deficit with spending cuts and increased taxes, which was widely unpopular. Instead of increasing taxes to raise revenue, the opposition Social Christian Unity Party (PUSC) proposed an accelerated privatization program.

The nation's economic team failed to convince the International Monetary Fund that the government was taking the necessary steps to meet its economic targets. As a result, the World Bank refused to grant Costa Rica $100 million earmarked to finance the implementation of the country's structural adjustment program. Divisions within the Cabinet and the ruling National Liberation Party (PLN) led to a Cabinet reshuffle in March in which the president of the central bank was replaced.

On April 28 President Figueres and the leader of the PUSC, Rafael Angel Calderón, signed an accord that was followed the next day by approval of part of the fiscal reform package at a special session of the Legislative Assembly. As a result of the accord, the PLN agreed to vote in favour of a law to liberalize the banking system, support privatization, and end state monopolies in insurance, hydrocarbons, and telecommunications. Labour unions continued to organize strikes in protest against the economic measures, however, especially the tax increase and the planned layoff of 8,000 public-sector workers. Teachers went on strike in July and did not return until the government agreed in August to review its economic plan with labour union leaders.

(SARAH CAMERON)

This article updates the *Macropædia* article CENTRAL AMERICA: *Costa Rica.*

CÔTE D'IVOIRE

A republic of West Africa, Côte d'Ivoire lies on the Gulf of Guinea. Area: 322,463 sq km (124,504 sq mi). Pop. (1995 est.): 14,253,000. Cap.: Abidjan; capital designate, Yamoussoukro. Monetary unit: CFA franc, with (Oct. 6, 1995) a par value of CFAF 100 to the French franc and a free rate of CFAF 501.49 to U.S. $1 (CFAF 792.78 = £1 sterling). President in 1995, Henri Konan Bédié; prime minister, Daniel Kablan Duncan.

A fierce struggle against a new electoral code dominated politics as all parties prepared for the presidential election on Oct. 22, 1995. For the first time since independence, no foreigners were allowed to vote, and all candidates had to have resided in the country for five consecutive years prior to the election and to have been born of Ivorian parents. Opposition parties charged that this last provision was designed specifically to exclude the candidacy of former prime minister Alassane Ouattara, whose father was Burkinabe. Three mass demonstrations against the code took place in May, July, and September; 50,000 backers of Pres. Henri Bédié and the ruling Democratic Party of Côte d'Ivoire (PDCI) marched in Abidjan on May 27 to support the new code. Bédié refused to withdraw the code but did announce the creation of an independent electoral commission. This was rejected by the opposition on the grounds that it would be dominated by government appointees. The election, plagued by violence and an opposition boycott, resulted in Bédié's reelection.

When the results of the November 26 parliamentary election were announced, the ruling PDCI had won 147 seats, and opposition parties took a total of 24. (One seat was suspended, and elections for three seats were postponed until 1996 for security reasons.) Though voting was orderly, turnout was below the 50% mark.

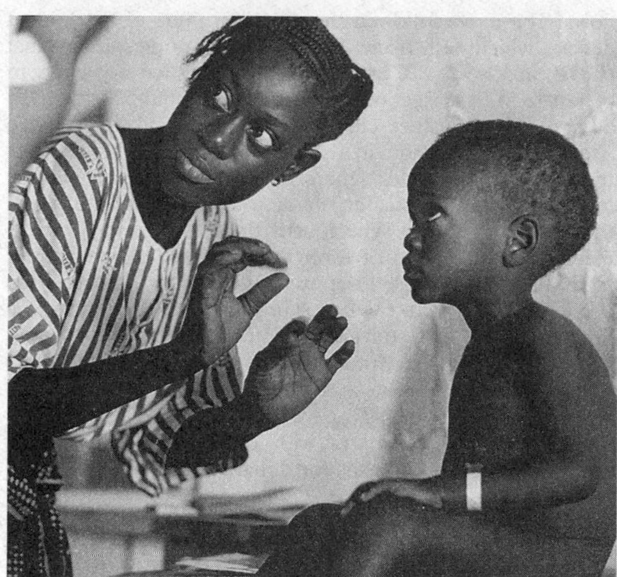

Liberian refugees receive care in Côte d'Ivoire at a facility set up by Médecins sans Frontières. As thousands continued to flee the bloody civil war in Liberia, many of them were being cared for in neighbouring Côte d'Ivoire by international relief organizations.
LEONARD FREED—MAGNUM

A border raid by Liberian rebels killed 32 people, including 10 Ivorians, on June 13. In reprisal, Liberians living in Abidjan were attacked, despite an appeal by the government for calm.

The economy continued its strong recovery, posting the first trade surplus with France in 10 years. Privatization of major state-owned industries was ahead of schedule.

(NANCY ELLEN LAWLER)

This article updates the *Macropædia* article WESTERN AFRICA: *Côte d'Ivoire.*

CROATIA

A republic lying at the southeastern end of central Europe, Croatia is an elongated crescent-shaped country to the north, west, and southwest of Bosnia and Herzegovina. In the north it borders on Hungary and in the northwest on Slovenia. Its extensive Adriatic coastal region on the southwest includes nearly 1,200 islands and islets. Area: 56,691 sq km (21,889 sq mi). Pop.: (1995 est.): 4,495,000. Cap.: Zagreb. Monetary unit: kuna, with (Oct. 6, 1995) a free rate of 5.33 kune to U.S. $1 (8.43 kune = £1 sterling). President in 1995, Franjo Tudjman; prime ministers Nikica Valentic and, from November 4, Zlatko Matesa.

In 1995 Croatia achieved significant military victories both against rebel Serbs who had occupied nearly a third of Croatia since 1991 and against Serb forces in Bosnia and Herzegovina. On January 12 Croatia gave notice that the existing mandate of the United Nations Protection Force (UNPROFOR) in Croatia would not be renewed beyond March 31. Under a new UN Security Council resolution, the number of UN forces in Croatia was to be reduced and the name of the unit was changed to United Nations Confidence Restoration Operation in Croatia (UNCRO). On April 11 Russian Maj. Gen. Aleksandr Perelyakin, who headed UNCRO in eastern Croatia (UN Sector East), was dismissed after being accused of incompetence and corruption, including trading arms with the Serbs.

On April 13 Serb forces shelled the airport in Dubrovnik, and Zagreb, the capital, was shelled on May 2 and 3, with casualties in both cities. On April 24 rebel Serbs in western Slavonia (UN Sector West), one of the three regions controlled by the Serbs since 1991, blocked the recently reopened Zagreb-Belgrade highway running through territory they controlled. In a 36-hour operation on May 1–2, western Slavonia was retaken by the Croatian army, and on August 4–7, in a similar blitz, the whole of the second Serb-held region, the Krajina, in central Croatia (UN Sectors North and South), including the town of Knin, was retaken. In both areas virtually the entire Serb population, many from families who had settled there centuries ago, left with the Serb forces. Widespread looting by Croatian and Bosnian Croat troops as well as returning Croat civilians was reported, as was harassment of the mainly elderly Serbs who had stayed behind. UN monitors reported that some 120 bodies of elderly residents had been found by early October.

On October 3 representatives of the Croatian government and the leaders of the rebel Serbs in eastern Slavonia reached an agreement on the principles of peaceful reintegration of this region, the last major Serb-held area, into Croatia. Croatia was disappointed that the U.S.-brokered agreement negotiated at Dayton, Ohio, in November failed to provide a clear timetable for its return to Zagreb's control. The U.S. ambassador to Croatia noted that for this first time in the current conflict, an issue had been resolved "by a signature and not by a bullet." A further hitch occurred at the signing of the Balkan agreements in Paris when Yugoslavia refused to extend diplomatic recognition to Croatia unless it ceded Prevlaka, a strategic promontory dominating the entry to the Yugoslav naval base on the Gulf of Kotor.

In elections on October 29 for the 127-seat lower house of Parliament, the ruling Croatian Democratic Union (HDZ) of Pres. Franjo Tudjman obtained 45.23% of all votes cast and 75 seats but failed to win the two-thirds majority Tudj-

GAMMA LIAISON

A soldier raises the Croatian flag over the city of Knin, capital of Krajina, which had been a Serb enclave for 500 years. Croatian troops went on the offensive in August, retaking control of the region in just five days and driving out tens of thousands of Serbs.

man sought in order to change the constitution to give more powers to the president. (For a detailed breakdown of the vote, see *Political Parties,* above.) The HDZ also lost its majority in several big cities, including Zagreb, where, despite its loss, the HDZ refused to hand over power to the opposition.

Monetary stability was maintained in 1995, with inflation running at an annual rate of 3.7%. In the January–September period, exports were 21% higher than in the corresponding period in 1994, but imports were 74% higher. Tourist income was sharply reduced because of the impact of military operations in May and August. Industrial output in January–September 1995 was up 1.2% from 1994, but overall growth stagnated. Under an agreement signed on December 14 by INA, the Croatian oil company, and Jugopetrol, its counterpart in Yugoslavia, oil supplies to Yugoslavia were to be restored in the near future. Croatia signed a major ships-for-oil deal with Iran on November 29. (K.F. CVIIC)

This article updates the *Macropædia* article BALKAN STATES: *Croatia.*

CUBA

The socialist republic of Cuba comprises the island of Cuba and more than 1,600 smaller islands and cays in the Caribbean Sea. Area: 110,861 sq km (42,804 sq mi). Pop. (1995 est.): 11,068,000. Cap.: Havana. Monetary unit: Cuban peso, with an official rate of 1 CUP to U.S. $1 (1.58 CUP = £1 sterling); a truer value of the peso was on the black market, where about 20–25 CUP = U.S. $1 (about 32–40 CUP = £1 sterling). President of the Councils of State and Ministers in 1995, Fidel Castro Ruz.

In 1995 the Cuban government concentrated on implementing economic reforms to increase private-sector investment in the economy and generate greater foreign exchange inflows. The move followed the severe pruning of the budget deficit, which fell from 33% of gross domestic product (GDP) in 1993 to 8% in 1994. The 1995 deficit was likely to be less than the target of 1 billion pesos (about 5% of GDP) as a result of further cuts in government subsidies, price rises, and a reduction in the public-sector workforce. For the first time since 1989, there was in 1994 a slight increase in GDP, of 0.7%, which accelerated to an annualized 2% in the first half of 1995. The tourist trade and foreign investment brought inflows of foreign currency, and the greater supply of dollars caused the exchange rate to improve from a low of 150 pesos to the dollar in 1994 to about 25 pesos in September 1995. A convertible peso was introduced at par with the U.S. dollar, with the aim of eventually withdrawing dollars from circulation and replacing them with the convertible peso. About 44% of the population had access to foreign exchange, compared with 21% in 1994. In October the legal exchange of pesos for dollars at the rate of 30 to 1 quietly began.

In September the National Assembly passed a new investment law allowing 100% foreign ownership of enterprises in Cuba. Investment was to be allowed in real estate and in free-trade and export-manufacturing zones but not in education, health, and defense. Investment proposals would continue to be considered on a discretionary basis, but Cuban exiles were assured that they would not be discriminated against if they wished to invest in their homeland.

Negotiations also were proceeding on reform of the banking system in order to cope with the increasing numbers of Cubans using foreign exchange but having to operate with cash. The lack of international credit arrangements also affected large businesses and the export sector. It was proposed that the National Bank of Cuba become a central bank and that its commercial and other banking activities be spun off. A broader domestic financial services sector

AD VAN DENDEREN

In a Havana hospital for foreigners, surgeons perform an operation to remove a brain tumour. Offering medical care to patients from Latin America and elsewhere was one of the ways the Cuban government was attempting to increase the flow of foreign currency into the economy.

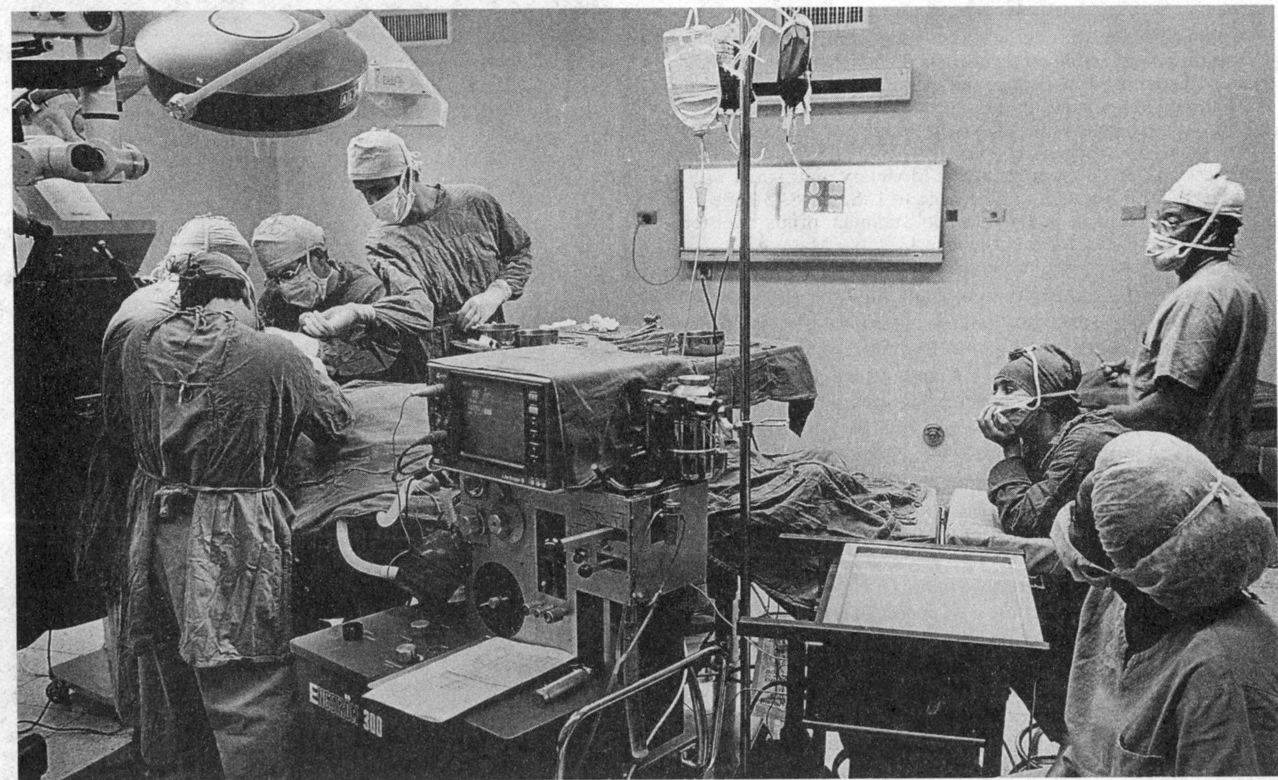

would be created, including trade finance specialists and an investment bank. In September Cuban banks for the first time advertised dollar accounts paying market rates to allow Cubans to accumulate capital in hard currency.

Despite the gradual opening of the Cuban economy and the increasing frustration of many U.S. companies wanting to do business with Cuba, the U.S. House of Representatives voted in September to tighten the U.S. embargo. A controversial bill, introduced in February by Sen. Jesse Helms, sought to penalize those doing business with Cuba through third countries. It generated widespread international opposition; the European Union said that its application to third countries would be in breach of World Trade Organization rules and 1994 General Agreement on Tariffs and Trade (GATT) agreements. Canada and Caribbean countries also opposed the bill. Nevertheless, the House voted in its favour by 294 to 130.

The action of the House contrasted with the softer attitude of the U.S. administration toward Cuba. In May a joint U.S.-Cuban declaration was issued in which Cuba agreed on the admission to the U.S. of most of the 21,000 Cubans still held at the U.S. base at Guantánamo since the 1994 mass emigration. The U.S. agreed that future migrants intercepted at sea would be repatriated, a move that sparked demonstrations among Cuban exiles in Miami, Fla. Cuba ratified the international convention against torture and other degrading treatment, bringing to 16 the number of human rights agreements it had signed. Several political prisoners were released as a result of official requests from abroad, and Pres. Fidel Castro held a cordial meeting in Havana with a Cuban exile who headed Cambio Cubano, which advocated a peaceful transition to democracy in Cuba.

Though there was improvement in the tourism, nickel, and seafood exchange earning sectors, Cuba's main export, sugar, remained in crisis. The 1994–95 harvest was at its lowest level in 50 years, at about 3.3 million metric tons. The 1995–96 crop was expected to increase slightly for the first time in three years as a result of purchases of fertilizers and weed killers, but most of the export earnings were allocated to cover debt payments. (SARAH CAMERON)

This article updates the *Macropædia* article The WEST INDIES: *Cuba*.

CYPRUS

An island republic and member of the Commonwealth, Cyprus is in the eastern Mediterranean Sea. Island area: 9,251 sq km (3,572 sq mi). Island pop. (1995 est.): 806,000. Area of the Turkish Republic of Northern Cyprus (TRNC), proclaimed unilaterally (1983) in the occupied northern third of the island (controlled by Turkish Cypriots since 1974): 3,355 sq km (1,295 sq mi); pop. (1995 est.): 155,000. Cap.: Nicosia. Monetary unit: Cyprus pound, with (Oct. 6, 1995) a free rate of £C 0.46 to U.S. $1 (£C 0.72 = £1 sterling). President in 1995, Glafcos Clerides. President of TRNC in 1995, Rauf Denktash.

Events in Cyprus in 1995 continued the trends of the past: partition, intercommunal distrust, intervention by outside powers, and economic prosperity. The island's division into Greek and Turkish republics plus the British Sovereign Base Areas remained. The United Nations continued as peacekeepers. The major protagonists were occupied with other problems—Greece with former Yugoslavia, and Turkey with its dissident Kurdish minority. A serious forest fire in Turkish Cyprus was thought to have been set by Kurdish sympathizers.

A move toward resolving the island's political impasse came with a proposal to integrate Cyprus into the European Union. The complex plan called for negotiations to begin in 1996 and included economic incentives for Turkey, with the expectation that only a reunified Cyprus could realistically be integrated into the EU. The project was still under consideration at year's end.

The island's economy continued to prosper. Its geographic situation and the growth of capitalism in Eastern Europe brought opportunities. Much of the world's merchant shipping sailed under the Cypriot flag, and more than 19,000 overseas corporations, many of them Russian, were chartered in Cyprus. The island provided a centre for corporate regional offices, broadcast monitoring, and support of diplomatic missions in the area. Prosperity also brought problems. Eastern European investment led to occasional allegations of the use of the island's banks and warehouses for laundering money and diverting restricted materials such as zirconium.

Tourism, Cyprus' major industry, employed about a fourth of the workforce and generated about the same percentage of gross national product in the Greek area. The island was host to well over two million tourists in 1995, including a million from Britain and 75,000 from Russia. Like the island's economic prosperity as a whole, the tourist boom had a down side, with tourist-related crime and incidents that raised occasional diplomatic concern about the legal rights of tourists. The tourist industry was looking at expanding its base through such diverse enterprises as eco- and agrotourism and casinos. (GEORGE H. KELLING)

CZECH REPUBLIC

The Czech Republic is a landlocked state of central Europe. Area: 78,864 sq km (30,450 sq mi). Pop. (1995 est.): 10,346,000. Cap.: Prague. Monetary unit: koruna, with (Oct. 6, 1995) a free rate of 26.31 koruny to U.S. $1 (41.60 koruny = £1 sterling). President in 1995, Vaclav Havel; prime minister, Vaclav Klaus.

For the Czech Republic, 1995 passed relatively uneventfully, and the patterns established in the years since the separation from Slovakia were maintained. Prime Minister Vaclav Klaus's Civic Democratic Party (ODS) recovered much of the popular support it had lost. While in the summer the gap between the ODS and the opposition Social Democrats was negligible, by the autumn the ODS had reestablished a commanding lead of around 12% and kept it. This augured well for the stability of the political scene before the 1996 general elections.

The few political setbacks suffered by Klaus, however, could be seen as symptomatic of a certain impatience with the need for compromise that all democratic systems demand. Thus, Klaus sought to introduce fees for university students, a move that was eventually thrown out by Parliament. More significant than anything else was that this initiative was announced without much attempt to build a political consensus. The popular protests against this move could be interpreted as evidence of the survival of a dependency culture inherited from communism that was incompatible with the individualism that underpins democracy.

Something similar to this was the decision—finally—to make provision for the election of a Senate, a second chamber. The Czech constitution had intended for there to be a Senate, but the Klaus government had simply ignored this requirement. In the end, the law to elect a Senate—after three drafts had been rejected—was enacted in the autumn, but even then there was conflict. Klaus wanted the Senate elected at the same time as the Chamber of Deputies, but no one else did. This crisis simmered on, and in December he finally gave in.

There were a few more troublesome problems. The country's banking system was at one stage flooded by so much money, more than a little of it from very dubious sources, that it was threatening the stability of the currency, not to mention prompting raised eyebrows elsewhere about what the Czechs were up to. In October the government took action and announced legislation that would require the notification of all deposits of sums in excess of $20,000. This was intended as a way of cutting back on illegal transfers. In addition, there was the trial of the former head of the privatization agency, Jaroslav Lizner, who had been arrested in 1994 on charges of having accepted bribes in complicated share deals; indeed, he was carrying 8.3 million koruny in cash when he was picked up. He was given a seven-year prison sentence.

Far more disturbing was the persistence of very powerful anti-Roma (anti-Gypsy) sentiment. This expressed itself in constant attacks on individual Roma, agitation, discrimination—the mayor of one town was obliged to deny that he had banned Roma from using the local public baths on the grounds that they were "dirty"—and the occasional pogrom. The minister of the interior warned that attacks on Roma were becoming more violent and that the public generally sympathized with the attackers; on the other hand, the number of such attacks was still comparatively small. At a deeper level, however, dislike of Roma could be interpreted as evidence of something else—the difficulty the populace had in coming to terms with diversity.

Coming to terms with the communist past was another problem area. First, the leaders of the Communist Party who had invited the Soviet intervention in 1968 were charged with treason and, second, the screening law that banned from public office anyone who had worked for the secret police or held senior party office was extended by Parliament to 2000, despite a veto by Pres. Vaclav Havel. The veto was overridden by a second vote.

The economy, as in previous years, performed well, with an increase in gross domestic product of around 4–4.5%; unemployment was low, though it would rise in the future; the Czech koruna became convertible; and the country was accepted as the first postcommunist member of the Organisation for Economic Co-operation and Development. This solid economic performance was the key to Klaus's popularity and to the stability of the country.

(GEORGE SCHÖPFLIN)

This article updates the *Macropædia* article CZECH AND SLOVAK REPUBLICS: *Czech Republic.*

DENMARK

A constitutional monarchy of north-central Europe, Denmark lies between the North and Baltic seas. Area: 43,094 sq km (16,639 sq m), excluding the Faroe Islands and Greenland. Pop. (1995 est.): 5,223,000. Cap.: Copenhagen. Monetary unit: Danish krone (crown), with (Oct. 6, 1995) a free rate of 5.55 kroner to U.S. $1 (8.77 kroner = £1 sterling). Queen, Margrethe II; prime minister in 1995, Poul Nyrup Rasmussen.

Political debate in Denmark in 1995 centred on the survival and upholding of one of the world's most sophisticated cradle-to-grave social welfare systems, in a country that levied more tax in relation to gross domestic product (GDP)—51.2%—than any other European Union (EU) member state. At the opening of the new session of the Folketing (parliament) in October, Prime Minister Poul Nyrup Rasmussen announced plans to tighten the generous welfare benefits that many blamed for the country's chronic unemployment. "The welfare state should not just be a safety net," he said. "It should also be a springboard of opportunity." A poll indicated that most Danes had misgivings about their role in the EU, however.

In November Denmark's Social Democrat-led government reached an accord with the opposition Conservative People's Party on a 1996 budget that modestly tightened fiscal policy to ensure a soft landing after a powerful economic upswing. The budget forecast GDP growth falling to 2.9% in 1996 from 3.9% in 1995 and 4.4% in 1994, when fiscal policy was eased to increase private consumption and promote growth after a long recession. The budget was designed to tighten government spending, with cuts corresponding to 0.5% of GDP in a move aimed at countering financial market fears that the economy might overheat and cause inflation to rise. It called for a deficit of 29 billion kroner for 1996, a tightening of unemployment benefits, and small cuts in military spending. The target date for a balanced budget was set at 1997. Denmark's impressive economic recovery continued in 1995, with inflation at a low rate of just over 2%, solid trade and balance of payments surpluses, and unemployment—the government's chief concern—falling to just over 10% from 12.5%, thanks to government job-activation schemes.

In Denmark's first impeachment trial in 85 years, former justice minister Erik Ninn-Hansen was found guilty of having violated refugee legislation and sentenced to a provisional four months in prison by a special 20-judge tribunal. Ninn-Hansen stood accused of having broken the law in 1987 when as justice minister he ordered a halt to family reunifications for Tamil refugees from Sri Lanka. Meanwhile, Denmark's Supreme Court upheld an eight-year prison sentence on a Bosnian Muslim refugee found guilty by a lower court of having tortured other Muslims to death at a Croatian-run prisoner-of-war camp in Bosnia and Herzegovina; the verdict was the first delivered in a series of war crime trials being held outside former Yugoslavia.

In March Copenhagen served as host to one of the major global gatherings of the year, the weeklong UN World Summit for Social Development, a forum that assembled to address goals of eradicating poverty, creating jobs, and ensuring the well-being and security of peoples in the post-Cold War era. It was attended by approximately 20,000 participants from some 180 nations. Copenhagen was also to be European City of Culture in 1996, the 12th host for this yearlong, 1 billion kroner, 600-event arts jamboree.

(CHRISTOPHER FOLLETT)

DJIBOUTI

The republic of Djibouti is in the Horn of northeastern Africa on the Gulf of Aden. Area: 23,200 sq km (8,950 sq mi). Pop. (1995 est.): 586,000. Cap.: Djibouti. Monetary unit: Djibouti franc, with (Oct. 6, 1995) a par value of DF 177.72 to U.S. $1 (free rate of DF 280.96 = £1 sterling). President in 1995, Hassan Gouled Aptidon; prime minister, Barkat Gourad Hamadou.

Divisions in the Afar Front for the Restoration of Unity and Democracy (FRUD) that had surfaced in March 1994 became open in October 1994 when the FRUD congress banned Ahmad Dini Ahmad and Muhammad Adoyta Yussuf from exercising any "activity or responsibility" in FRUD for opposing peace negotiations with the government. Following a peace and reconciliation agreement on Dec. 26, 1994, between the government and the principal FRUD faction led by Ahmad Ougoureh Kible and Ali Muhammad Daoud, it was expected that former FRUD rebel troops would be integrated into the national army. A cease-fire was followed by a revision of the constitution and by an alliance between the FRUD faction and the government party, the Popular Rally for Progress, for "the management of affairs," which suggested that FRUD would later be included in the government. Ahmad Dini Ahmad (of the expelled faction) condemned these agreements as a betrayal. In a Cabinet reshuffle on June 8, Kible and Daoud joined the government, as did five other FRUD leaders.

On May 1, following an extended Cabinet meeting, the government cut expenditure by DF 27 million. This was done under pressure from the International Monetary Fund, which had called for measures to stabilize the country's finances. Other measures taken would increase government revenues. (GUY ARNOLD)

This article updates the *Macropædia* article EASTERN AFRICA: *Djibouti.*

DOMINICA

An island republic within the Commonwealth, Dominica is in the eastern Caribbean Sea. Area: 750 sq km (290 sq mi). Pop. (1995 est.): 72,100. Cap.: Roseau. Monetary unit: Eastern Caribbean dollar, with (Oct. 6, 1995) a par value of EC$2.70 to U.S. $1 (free rate of EC$4.27 = £1 sterling). President in 1995, Crispin Sorhaindo; prime ministers, Eugenia Charles and, from June 14, Edison James.

The Dominica Freedom Party's (DFP's) desire for a fourth term in office was frustrated in June 1995 when the Dominica United Workers' Party (UWP) narrowly won the general election, capturing 11 of the 21 parliamentary seats. The DFP and the Dominica Labour Party (DLP) won five seats each.

The new prime minister was Edison James, a former general manager of the Dominica Banana Growers Association. He pledged to reenergize the crucial banana industry as one of his government's initial priorities. The DFP's defeat was partly attributable to the leadership wrangle that accompanied the departure of its venerable leader, Dame Eugenia Charles, prior to the election.

In early August the new government presented its first budget, providing for EC$259 million in spending for 1995–96. The emphasis was on fiscal restraint and the creation of surpluses for future investment. The UWP also decided to sell a number of government enterprises in order to raise money for improving the social infrastructure.

But in August and September the government's development ambitions received a severe setback when Dominica was hit in quick succession by Tropical Storm Iris and Hurricanes Luis and Marilyn. The banana industry was all but devastated, and all export prospects were curtailed for the foreseeable future. Overall, hurricane damage was estimated at EC$150 million. This included the loss of the banana crop plus destruction of bridges, roads, homes, hotels, and public utility installations. (DAVID RENWICK)

This article updates the *Macropædia* article The WEST INDIES: *Dominica.*

DOMINICAN REPUBLIC

The Dominican Republic covers the eastern two-thirds of the Caribbean island of Hispaniola, which it shares with Haiti. Area: 48,443 sq km (18,704 sq mi). Pop. (1995 est.): 7,823,000. Cap.: Santo Domingo. Monetary unit: Dominican peso, with (Oct. 6, 1995) a free rate of RD$13.74 to U.S. $1 (RD$21.72 = £1 sterling). President in 1995, Joaquín Balaguer.

Campaigning for the May 1996 presidential elections dominated the activities of the political parties in 1995 as they prepared for the first real opportunity in decades to replace 88-year-old Pres. Joaquín Balaguer. At a Dominican Liberation Party conference, Leonel Fernández, a lawyer, won 93.2% of his party's vote for the candidacy. José Francisco Peña Gómez, recovered from cancer surgery, retained the candidacy for the Dominican Revolutionary Party. There were six contenders (later five) and much infighting for the nomination of the ruling Social Christian Reformist Party. Vice Pres. Jacinto Peynado won the primary election on October 1 with 57% of the vote. He announced his intention to unite the party and heal the rifts that had emerged during the campaign.

The nation's economic performance was affected by ongoing electricity shortages as the two-year-old drought continued. The government-owned Corporación Dominicana de Electricidad was able to produce only about 700 MW, compared with a demand of 1,050 MW; about a quarter of the production was regularly lost through technical failures. A report stated that about 40% of the electricity used was not paid for.

The country's growth and inflation targets were jeopardized by the power crisis. Public transport companies raised bus fares by 50% in March, which sparked demonstrations and violent riots. The increases were declared illegal by the government, but in June it allowed fares to rise again, which led to further clashes between demonstrators and police that resulted in several deaths. On May 9 there was a one-day general strike against higher food prices and the deteriorating electricity and transport services.

(SARAH CAMERON)

This article updates the *Macropædia* article The WEST INDIES: *Dominican Republic.*

ECUADOR

The republic of Ecuador is in western South America, on the Pacific Ocean. Area: 272,045 sq km (105,037 sq mi), including the Galápagos Islands. Pop. (1995 est.): 11,460,000. Cap.: Quito. Monetary unit: sucre, with (Oct. 6, 1995) a free rate of 2,626 sucres to U.S. $1 (4,151 sucres = £1 sterling). President in 1995, Sixto Durán Ballén.

The year 1995 started badly for Ecuador. The border dispute with Peru flared up again in January with skirmishes in dense jungle between the Santiago and Zamora rivers in the Cordillera del Cóndor, where the border had never been properly defined. Ecuador declared a state of emergency and called up its reserves. Fighting caused dozens of casualties, although Ecuadorean forces suffered fewer fatalities than did the Peruvians, principally because they had better access to the area, had better antiaircraft weapons, controlled the higher ground, and had laid minefields that caught the Peruvian troops unawares.

The dispute dated back to Ecuadorean independence from Spain in 1830 but more recently to a 10-day war in 1941, when Peru invaded Ecuador. At that time peace was achieved with the signing (1942) of the Rio de Janeiro Protocol, which defined the border; the U.S., Brazil, Chile, and Argentina agreed to act as guarantors of the peace treaty. Although the U.S. Air Force had completed mapping and marking most of the border by 1947, a 78-km (48-mi) stretch in the Cordillera del Cóndor remained unmarked. Skirmishes occurred several times in this area, usually around the January anniversary of the signing of the protocol. There were believed to be deposits of gold, uranium, and oil in the disputed region.

The four guarantor countries organized peace negotiations, but the first cease-fire, the Itamaraty Declaration, signed in Rio de Janeiro in February, was not respected. A second accord, the Montevideo Declaration, was signed two weeks later after tense negotiations. It called for an "immediate and effective cease-fire."

The war had a severe impact on Ecuador's budget, with direct costs initially estimated at $340 million, or about 2% of gross domestic product (GDP). Capital outflows put pressure on the sucre, and foreign exchange reserves declined sharply. The government was forced to introduce an emergency financial package, cutting subsidies and raising prices and taxes, while reducing capital spending in order to bring the deficit down to under 1% of GDP. Although this did not meet the International Monetary Fund target of a budget surplus in 1995, confidence was restored, and by the end of April foreign exchange reserves had been rebuilt to their previous level of $1.7 billion.

Ecuadoreans rejected in November a set of constitutional proposals offered by the government. Opponents charged that the changes would have strengthened the executive at the expense of other branches of government, while proponents saw the package as necessary to the state's modernization.

Politics took on a more combative tone late in the year when several government ministers were attacked by members of Congress. The culmination of the struggle was the flight of Vice Pres. Alberto Dahik and the arrest of other ministers for misuse of government funds.

After much opposition and debate, in August the National Congress approved a bill allowing the sale of 35% of the government-owned telecommunications company, EMETEL, with a possible market value of $2.2 billion. The government wanted to complete this first major privatization before its term of office expired in August 1996. Proceeds were to go to an investment fund for social spending.

(SARAH CAMERON)

EGYPT

A republic of North Africa, Egypt has coastlines on the Mediterranean and Red seas. Area: 997,739 sq km (385,229 sq mi). Pop. (1995 est.): 59,695,000. Cap.: Cairo. Monetary unit: Egyptian pound, with (Oct. 6, 1995) a free rate of LE 3.40 to U.S. $1 (LE 5.37 = £1 sterling). President in 1995, Hosni Mubarak; prime minister, Atef Sedki.

There were four major developments in Egypt during 1995: Pres. Hosni Mubarak continued his active support of Palestinian-Israeli negotiations; he made an official visit to the U.S. in April; the militants of al-Jama'a al-Islamiya (Islamic Group) and the al-Jihad organization continued their violent challenge of Egyptian authorities, and the government linked the mainstream Muslim Brotherhood movement to these radical groups by imprisoning the movement's leaders; and there was an attempt on Mubarak's life while he was visiting Ethiopia to attend the Organization of African Unity (OAU) summit.

The year began with the euphoria that accompanied the convening of the tripartite summit of the leaders of Egypt, Saudi Arabia, and Syria in Alexandria, Egypt, on Dec. 28–29, 1994. It was hailed by the Egyptian press as the revival of Egypt's historic leadership role in the Arab world. President Mubarak followed this meeting with a summit with King Hussein I of Jordan, on January 21, his first visit to Jordan since the Iraqi invasion of Kuwait in August 1990. To save the peace process and show that Egypt had regained its pivotal role in the region, but without being at loggerheads with Israel, a summit was convened in Cairo on February 2 that included Mubarak, Hussein, Israeli Prime Minister Yitzhak Rabin, and Palestine Liberation Organization (PLO) leader Yasir Arafat.

In his meetings with members of Congress and with President Clinton, President Mubarak explained how Egypt had been the pioneer of peace in the Middle East by taking the first steps in that direction. Mubarak pointed to the continued Egyptian role of mediating between the PLO and Israel whenever problems arose and also to the frequent contacts between Egypt and Syria. On September 28 Mubarak attended the White House ceremony of signing the peace accord between the PLO and Israel and was praised by Arafat for his tireless mediating efforts that enabled the two sides to reach an agreement. Later, on November 5, Mubarak made his first visit to Israel since he came to power in 1981, to attend the funeral of the Prime Minister Rabin. (*See* OBITUARIES.)

The challenge to the government by the Islamic Group in Upper (southern) Egypt continued unabated. The Islamic Group's main battleground with Egyptian authorities during the year was in al-Minya, where it enjoyed support from the local population. A new head of security for al-Minya province was appointed in January, an indication that the government's campaign against the Islamic Group had not been successful. The lull since January in attacking foreign tourists ended in November when trains carrying tourists were attacked in Qina province.

Minister of Interior Hasan al-Alfi continued to accuse the mainstream Muslim Brotherhood of playing "a very clear role in supporting the terrorist groups," whose ultimate objective was to overthrow the existing regime. On January 23, 28 prominent members of the Muslim Brotherhood were arrested and charged with forming a secret organization that maintained cells within the various government organizations, infiltrated political parties and professional associations, and obstructed the law and constitutional principles.

Documents written by ʿIsam al-ʿUryan, the assistant secretary-general of the Physicians Association and a leading member of the Muslim Brotherhood, revealed an alliance between the Brotherhood and the Islamic Group and al-Jihad in confronting and ultimately overthrowing the present Egyptian regime. On March 30 the Egyptian government arrested four prominent members of the Muslim Brotherhood, accusing them of exploiting the Physicians Association's Humanitarian Relief Committee to send young members of the Muslim Brotherhood and of the Islamic Group abroad, under the cover of working for relief projects, to receive military training on the use of weapons and explosives. Interior Minister al-Alfi attended a meeting of Arab ministers of the interior in Tunis, Tunisia, in January to coordinate efforts with other Arab countries in the fight against militants of the various Islamic organizations that had resorted to violence.

The Egyptian authorities in February accused members of al-Jihad, the group that assassinated Pres. Anwar as-Sadat in 1981, of having reactivated their organization under the name Tala'i' al-Fath (Vanguard of the Conquest) and of plotting to kill President Mubarak. On June 26 there was an unsuccessful attempt to assassinate Mubarak on his arrival in Addis Ababa to attend the meeting of the OAU. Investigations carried out by the Ethiopian government revealed that leading members of the Islamic Group who were living in exile in The Sudan planned the attack in coordination with the real power behind the Sudanese regime, Hasan at-Turabi.

Elections for the People's Assembly were held on November 29. All legally recognized political parties participated. Shortly before the polling, however, Mubarak again cracked down on the Muslim Brotherhood. Its headquarters in Cairo was closed, and a military court sentenced 54 members of the group, mostly middle-class professionals, to prison terms.

The government won an overwhelming victory. When the results were tallied, the National Democratic Party effectively held 416 of the 444 seats. The opposition parties won 13 seats, and independents held the remainder. Violence marred the elections, and there were charges of widespread electoral fraud.

(MARIUS K. DEEB)

EL SALVADOR

The republic of El Salvador is situated on the Pacific coast of Central America. Area: 21,041 sq km (8,124 sq mi). Pop. (1995 est.): 5,768,000. Cap.: San Salvador. Monetary unit: Salvadoran colón, with (Oct. 6, 1995) a free rate of ₡8.75 to U.S. $1 (₡13.83 = £1 sterling). President in 1995, Armando Calderón Sol.

On April 30, 1995, the United Nations Observer Mission in El Salvador ended its job of monitoring the 1992 peace accords between the government and the guerrillas. A small UN office was to remain until October 31 to verify the last parts of the accords to be implemented, principally the land-transference program and compensation for ex-combatants. A newly appointed human rights commissioner was to be primarily responsible for monitoring the human rights situation.

The National Civilian Police (PNC) proved unable to cope with the wave of crime sweeping El Salvador. Youth gangs, allegedly from inner-city Los Angeles, gained a foothold, and it was reported in the newspapers that there was a death every hour as a result of crime. The government sent 5,000 soldiers to support police patrols on highways and rural areas. Also emerging during the year were death squads whose targets were criminal rather than political, and there were attacks on the young gang members. By July there had been 17 killings attributed to the Black Shadow death squad and another 20 to other groups. A raid on 14 suspected members of the Black Shadow group revealed three of them to be members of the PNC. In San Salvador in June, authorities discovered an arsenal of sophisticated weapons that belonged to a criminal gang called Los Benedictos, notorious for assassinations, kidnappings, and car thefts. The group, whose leader was captured, was linked to arms trafficking and a network of organized crime in Central America.

In May the value-added tax was raised from 10% to 13% in a congressional pact between the ruling Nationalist Republican Alliance party and the Democratic Party, a newly created offshoot of the former guerrilla party, the Farabundo Martí National Liberation Front. The tax increase was one of several elements in a program designed to pay for land transfers, electoral and judicial reforms, and the repair of infrastructure damaged during the civil war. The slow pace of implementation of the reintegration and compensation programs of the 1992 accords led to demonstrations by former combatants of both sides. In July a former guerrilla was killed in clashes between police and 600 protesters traveling to the capital. In August former combatants took to the streets and occupied public buildings to demand the fulfillment of the 1992 accords. The government claimed it was doing everything possible. (SARAH CAMERON)

This article updates the *Macropædia* article CENTRAL AMERICA: *El Salvador.*

EQUATORIAL GUINEA

The republic of Equatorial Guinea consists of Río Muni, on the Atlantic coast of West Africa, and the offshore islands of Bioko and Annobon. Area: 28,051 sq km (10,831 sq mi). Pop. (1995 est.): 396,000. Cap.: Malabo. Monetary unit: CFA franc, with a par value of CFAF 100 to the French franc and (as of Oct. 6, 1995) a free rate of CFAF 501.49 to U.S. $1 (CFAF 792.78 = £1 sterling). President in 1995, Brig. Gen. Teodoro Obiang Nguema Mbasogo; prime minister, Silvestre Siale Bileka.

In March 1995 Severo Moto, the leader of the opposition Progress Party of Equatorial Guinea (PPGE), was sentenced to 2½ years in prison and fined CFAF 50 million after

Former Los Angeles gang members who had been deported from the United States write graffiti on a wall in El Salvador. The government was hard pressed to deal with the great increase of crime occurring in El Salvador, much of it allegedly by gang members.

DONNA DECESARE—IMPACT VISUALS

being found guilty of collusion in bribing a police officer and harming the reputation of the head of state. Spain protested his treatment, and there were fears for his safety when the deputy leader of the PPGE, Armengol Engonga, warned that the government was planning a treason trial accusing Moto of complicity in a coup attempt. On April 24 Moto was sentenced to 28 years in prison on treason and conspiracy charges with 12 others. Western governments, especially Spain, condemned the sentences as excessive.

On August 3, the anniversary of the coup that had brought him to power in 1979, Pres. Teodoro Obiang Nguema Mbasogo pardoned Moto for his part in the coup plot.

In July the government arrested members of the Movement for the Self-Determination of Bioko, composed mainly of Bubi tribesmen. Bioko, formerly known as Fernando Po, is an offshore island of Equatorial Guinea. (GUY ARNOLD)

This article updates the *Macropædia* article WESTERN AFRICA: *Equatorial Guinea.*

ERITREA

Eritrea is in the Horn of Africa, on the Red Sea. Area: 117,400 sq km (45,300 sq mi). Pop. (1995 est.): 3,531,000 (including nearly 400,000 refugees in The Sudan). Cap.: Asmara. Monetary unit: Ethiopian birr, with (Oct. 6, 1995) a free rate of 5.80 birr to U.S. $1 (free rate of 9.17 birr = £1 sterling). President in 1995, Isaias Afwerki.

The year 1995 was one of consolidation in Eritrea. The Constitutional Commission established in November 1994 held consultative meetings concerning the form of the new constitution. Work proceeded during 1995 on a first draft, and the final text was expected to be ready by June 1996; there was strong opposition within the ruling People's Front for Democracy and Justice (formerly the Eritrean People's Liberation Front, or EPLF) to the legalization of parties based on ethnicity or religion. The National Assembly in May approved a resolution that would divide Eritrea into six administrative regions. A drastic cut in civil service staffing, from about 30,000 to 20,000, was announced in May; the Ministry of Defense was not affected, but some soldiers were demobilized or transferred to other posts. A compulsory youth national service scheme, which got under way in January, was intended to promote the process of national integration and to provide youth in peacetime Eritrea with some equivalent to the formative experience of EPLF fighters during the long war for independence. Jehovah's Witnesses, a Christian fundamentalist group whose members refused to participate in national service or otherwise recognize the authority of the state, were deprived of their citizenship rights in March.

Good relations with Ethiopia were maintained, and an agreement between the two countries in April removed customs duties on trade in agricultural and industrial goods and fees on commercial services; it was expected to lead to a full customs and monetary union. Relations with Eritrea's other neighbour, The Sudan, continued to deteriorate after the breach in diplomatic relations initiated by Eritrea in December 1994. Eritrea took the lead in coordinating opposition to the Islamist military regime in Khartoum by serving as host for a major meeting of Sudanese opposition movements in June. In October Pres. Isaias Afwerki offered to provide weapons to any group attempting to overthrow the Khartoum regime. These problems complicated the return to Eritrea of up to half a million refugees from The Sudan, but an increased rate of return was reported. Relations with Israel and the United States remained close.

(CHRISTOPHER S. CLAPHAM)

This article updates the *Micropædia* article ERITREA.

ESTONIA

A republic of northern Europe, Estonia borders the Baltic Sea on the west and north. Area: 45,227 sq km (17,462 sq mi). Pop. (1995 est.): 1,487,000. Cap.: Tallinn. Monetary unit: kroon, with (Oct. 6, 1995) a par value of EEK 8 to DM 1 (free rates of EEK 11.41 = U.S. $1 and EEK 18.04 = £1 sterling). President in 1995, Lennart Meri; prime ministers, Andres Tarand and, from March 23, Tiit Vahi.

After two and a half years in power, the coalition that had steered Estonia away from its Soviet legacy was soundly defeated in the elections of March 1995. The new prime minister, Tiit Vahi (Coalition Party), successfully rebuffed charges of a possible turn leftward due to the disproportionate number of former communists currently in power. His government collapsed in October, however, because of a scandal involving Minister of the Interior Edgar Savisaar over illegal surveillance. A realigned coalition with the Reform Party enabled Vahi to continue as prime minister.

An associate membership agreement was signed with the European Union in June, and an official application was signed in November. Estonia continued to lead the Baltic countries in attracting Western investments. The major public worries remained crime, rural underdevelopment, and the status of the elderly.

Active participation in NATO programs continued, and Estonian soldiers served in UN peacekeeping operations in Croatia during the year. Although the former Soviet nuclear training facility in Paldiski was turned over to Estonia in September, Estonian-Russian relations remain strained because of the dispute over borders. Pres. Lennart Meri undertook landmark visits to Sweden in September and to the U.S. and Mexico in October. U.S. Vice Pres. Al Gore visited Tallinn in March.

(TÕNU PARMING)

This article updates the *Macropædia* article BALTIC STATES: *Estonia*.

ETHIOPIA

The landlocked republic of Ethiopia is in the Horn of northeastern Africa. Area: 1,133,882 sq km (437,794 sq mi). Pop. (1995 est.): 55,053,000. Cap.: Addis Ababa. Monetary unit: birr, with (Oct. 6, 1995) a free rate of 5.80 birr to U.S. $1 (9.17 birr = £1 sterling). Presidents in 1995, Meles Zenawi (interim) and, from August 22, Negasso Gidada; prime ministers, Tamirat Layne (acting) and, from August 22, Meles Zenawi.

The new constitution approved in December 1994 retained the key features of the draft presented earlier in 1994 to the Constituent Assembly, including the right of all peoples within Ethiopia to self-determination, including secession from the country. Uniquely among African constitutions, it

MELISSA FARLOW—MATERIAL WORLD WOMEN'S PROJECT

An Ethiopian man plows, and his wife follows to weed, as they prepare their field for planting. With Ethiopian agriculture unable to supply the country's needs, the government continued to depend heavily on food aid and, to a lesser extent, purchases from abroad.

instituted a largely ceremonial presidency, vesting executive power in the prime minister elected by the National Assembly. Assembly elections were held in May in most of the country but were postponed to June in the east. They were, however, boycotted by the four major opposition groupings and contested by only three small opposition parties. The conduct of the elections was reported by foreign observers to have been fair, but there was little challenge to the ruling Ethiopian People's Revolutionary Democratic Front (EPRDF), a multiethnic grouping whose constituent parties won 493 of the 548 seats. Only in Addis Ababa, where 10 of the 23 seats were won by independents, was government control seriously contested.

The new Federal Democratic Republic of Ethiopia was formally established on August 22. The new president, Negasso Gidada, was a Christian Oromo from the Welega region of western Ethiopia who had served as minister of information in the outgoing transitional government. The outgoing president, Meles Zenawi, became prime minister and head of government. The 17-member Council of Ministers was carefully selected to reflect the ethnic balance of the country, with four each for Oromo and Amhara, two each for Tigray (including the prime minister) and Gurage, and one each for five smaller groups.

New regional assemblies were also elected in May and June and were likewise controlled by the EPRDF. The transfer of powers from the central government to the regions increasingly became a reality. For example, in the large Oromo region surrounding Addis Ababa, Oromifa increasingly replaced Amharic as the language of administration. A number of leading members of Meles Zenawi's Tigray People's Liberation Front were posted back to Tigray.

The trials of members of the former regime charged with serious human rights abuses, which had been adjourned until May 1995 to allow both sides to prepare their cases, were further postponed until later in the year. Attempts to secure the extradition of the ousted dictator Mengistu Haile Mariam from his refuge in Zimbabwe were unsuccessful. At the same time, alleged human rights abuses by the new regime, though not remotely approaching those committed by the old one, continued to attract international attention. There was some harassment of journalists, though the press continued to be more independent than under previous governments, and Amnesty International condemned the arrest in June of five opposition politicians on what it described as "slender and dubious evidence of conspiracy."

The government's standing in Africa was reflected in the election of Meles Zenawi as chairman of the Organization of African Unity in June. Relations with Eritrea, which had separated from Ethiopia in 1993, continued to be close, but those with the Islamist military regime in The Sudan deteriorated rapidly. Ethiopia accused The Sudan of complicity in the attempted assassination of Pres. Hosni Mubarak of Egypt in Addis Ababa in June; it subsequently ordered the reduction of the Sudanese diplomatic staff from 15 to 4, denied Sudan Airways landing rights in Addis Ababa, and closed the Sudanese consulate at Gambela in southwestern Ethiopia.

The economy grew by about 5.4% in 1994, supported by continuing aid inflows and a boom in world coffee prices. Progress was made on privatizing 144 state-owned businesses, half of those being transferred to their employees. Following the 1994 harvest, an overall food deficit of one million tons of grain was estimated for 1995, 85% of this being met from food aid and the remainder from commercial purchases. (CHRISTOPHER S. CLAPHAM)

This article updates the *Macropædia* article EASTERN AFRICA: *Ethiopia.*

FIJI

The republic of Fiji occupies an island group in the South Pacific Ocean. Area: 18,272 sq km (7,055 sq mi). Pop. (1995 est.): 791,000. Cap.: Suva. Monetary unit: Fiji dollar, with (Oct. 6, 1995) a free rate of F$1.41 to U.S. $1 (F$2.22 = £1 sterling). President in 1995, Ratu Sir Kamisese Mara; prime minister, Sitiveni Rabuka.

In November 1994 the government initiated a review of Fiji's racially biased constitution, but early submissions indicated little willingness to compromise. Prime Minister Sitiveni Rabuka reconstituted his government on several occasions in 1995 to cope with divisions within the coalition. Rabuka also initiated court action to overturn the findings of a commission that implicated him in improper government dealings. It was alleged that the National Bank of Fiji had issued unauthorized and unsecured loans, had failed to insure secured assets, had not been properly audited, and had a shortfall in funds of F$80 million.

The 1995 government budget projected a deficit of F$62 million (2.5% of gross domestic product) from revenue of F$694 million. Income tax on those with low incomes was decreased, but indirect taxes on alcohol, tobacco, and motor vehicles increased. In 1994 a record amount of sugar (516,589 metric tons) was exported. Economic growth for 1995 was projected at 2.7%.

A government plan to allow the immigration of 28,000 Hong Kong Chinese who could pay U.S.$130,000 aroused strong criticism. Fiji also protested Japan's proposed shipment of plutonium through the region and the renewal of French nuclear testing. (BARRIE MACDONALD)

This article updates the *Macropædia* article PACIFIC ISLANDS: *Fiji.*

FINLAND

The republic of Finland is in northern Europe, on the Gulf of Bothnia and the Gulf of Finland. Area: 338,145 sq km (130,559 sq mi). Pop. (1995 est.): 5,101,000. Cap.: Helsinki. Monetary unit: Finnish markka, with (Oct. 6, 1995) a free rate of 4.31 markkaa to U.S. $1 (6.81 markkaa = £1 sterling). President in 1995, Martti Ahtisaari; prime ministers, Esko Aho and, from April 13, Paavo Lipponen.

Finland joined the European Union (EU) at the start of 1995. The impact of its entry into the EU's single market was softened by special subsidies for Finland's cold-climate farming. Finland was also allowed, on the grounds of public health, to retain part of its state monopoly on the sale of alcoholic beverages, a lucrative source of government revenue.

Pres. Martti Ahtisaari said that Finland, despite accession to the EU, would retain its observer status on the Western European Union and would not assume WEU full membership, a move that might imply eventual membership in NATO. He also warned the West against isolating Russia, saying that democracy there would not take root unless given time. In a departure from his country's former practice of avoiding open criticism of its powerful neighbour, however, he also pointed to the environmental risks to Europe of Russia's polluting industries and possibly unsafe atomic power stations, several of which lay close to the border between Russia and Finland.

Parliament moved toward accepting a proposal by Ahtisaari and Prime Minister Paavo Lipponen that Finland set up a rapid deployment force that could be made available for crisis situations involving the UN or the Organization for Cooperation and Security in Europe. Finland had traditionally provided the UN with troops meant only for police duties. Lipponen also announced that Finland would be among the first countries in the EU to accede to its economic and monetary union, a scheme that was intended, among other things, to lead to a single EU currency.

In general elections in March, the Social Democratic Party, led by Lipponen, displaced the rural-based Centre Party as the biggest group in Parliament. Lipponen formed and headed a majority coalition government excluding the centrists but retaining the conservative National Coalition and Swedish People's parties and bringing into office the Green Union and the Left-Wing Alliance, an organization of former communists. The Centre Party had been a part of almost all governments since World War II, including a lengthy period when it was largely responsible for maintaining relations with the Soviet Union.

In October the government proposed a plan to reduce unemployment, which was about 17%. Inflation fell to about 1% according to the central bank. The two big Finnish commercial banks, Kansallis-Osake-Pankki and Union Bank of Finland, merged during the year to form the Merita Bank. They announced a recovery from losses accumulated in recent years, during which they were forced to accept a still-outstanding loan from the government. Mergers also took place in the forestry industry, a key export sector that reported big profits. (EDWARD M. SUMMERHILL)

FRANCE

A republic of western Europe, France includes the island of Corsica in the Mediterranean Sea and has coastlines on the English Channel, the Mediterranean, and the Atlantic Ocean. Area: 543,965 sq km (210,026 sq mi). Pop. (1995 est.): 58,172,000. Cap.: Paris. Monetary unit: franc, with (Oct. 6, 1995) a free rate of F 5.01 to U.S. $1 (F 7.93 = £1 sterling). Presidents in 1995, François Mitterrand and, from May 17, Jacques Chirac; prime ministers, Édouard Balladur and, from May 17, Alain Juppé.

The year 1995 was a time of mixed hope and bewilderment in France as the election of the candidate for the neo-Gaullist Rally for the Republic (RPR), Jacques Chirac (*see* BIOGRAPHIES), to the presidency drew hundreds of thousands of rejoicing well-wishers into the streets on the night of May 7. Six months later his perceived failure to make good on campaign promises to reduce unemployment and homelessness sent many of the same voters marching again—demonstrating against welfare cuts during the three-week transport, public utilities, and mail strike that paralyzed the country in November and December.

Chirac's first 100 days began well with his forceful call for action to bring peace to war-torn Bosnia and Herzegovina at the European Union's (EU's) June summit in Cannes. This laid the groundwork for the U.S.-led NATO intervention later in the year. Chirac's initiative, as well as the fact that for the past four years France had contributed the largest military contingent to the UN forces in former Yugoslavia (70% of troops on the ground), was acknowledged with the choice of Paris for the signing of the Bosnia peace agreement on December 14. Part of the international goodwill the new French president had earned swiftly vanished, however, when he announced that France would resume nuclear testing in the South Pacific. There was little real opposition in France to the tests, as opposed to massive protests throughout the world.

The civil war that for three years had been tearing apart Algeria, France's former colony, traveled across the Mediterranean as Algerian Islamic fundamentalist terrorism hit Paris and several provincial towns with a series of bloody bombings in 1995, causing scores of casualties.

France Elects a President

In January 1995 conservative Prime Minister Édouard Balladur felt fairly confident that he could easily win the forthcoming presidential election and succeed François Mitterrand, the ailing Socialist who had held the job for two consecutive seven-year terms. Jacques Delors, the outgoing Socialist president of the European Commission, who had been tipped as the most popular candidate, had decided not to run, which left the Socialist Party (PS) in disarray. Former prime minister Jacques Chirac (*see* BIOGRAPHIES), now the mayor of Paris and head of the neo-Gaullist Rally for the Republic, the party to which Balladur belonged, had pushed Balladur forward for prime minister in 1993 in order to devote himself to preparations for this election. At the start of 1995, however, Chirac, making his third run for the presidency, was seen as yesterday's man, barely polling 17% against Balladur's 55%.

Balladur's high popularity ratings had survived a series of crises in 1994, and he looked set to weather new student strikes over a proposed university reform announced on Dec. 29, 1994, and suspended on Feb. 10, 1995. On January 18 Balladur declared his candidacy, and on February 13 he formally launched his campaign. This final confirmation that he was running against his old political mentor Chirac gave rise to calls of "treason" among many Gaullists and, as it turned out, voters. Within days Balladur's high standing in the polls started an inexorable slide, harmed by the loss of his image as a "selfless servant of the state" who had vowed that he would not run.

Meanwhile, Chirac's relentless campaigning throughout France started bearing fruit. He spoke on social themes, such as unemployment and homelessness, and appeared as the opponent of the establishment embodied by Balladur. By early March, Chirac's political image had been transformed from old tired politico to new people's advocate.

On February 3 a nationwide vote among PS members gave Lionel Jospin a 65.8% majority over the party's first secretary, Henri Emmanuelli, making Jospin the main opposition candidate. The Communist candidate, the relatively unknown Robert Hue, had declared as early as September 1994. The rest of the field included National Front leader Jean-Marie Le Pen, the anti-European Union and pro-life campaigner Philippe de Villiers, the unknown retired businessman Jacques Cheminade, the Green candidate Dominique Voynet, and the Trotskyist candidate Arlette Laguiller, who was running for the fourth time since 1974. Laguiller's obvious sincerity and loyalty to her lifelong ideals earned her respect and sympathy far beyond party lines; ultimately she polled 5.3% of the vote in the first round, more than either Villiers or Voynet.

Balladur's progressive fall from grace was hastened by a political scandal involving Interior Minister Charles Pasqua. The division of the conservative vote between Chirac and Balladur caused Jospin to come in first in the first round on April 23, polling 23.3% of the vote, while Chirac scored 20.84% and Balladur won 18.58%. Balladur immediately called on his supporters to vote for Chirac, who was elected president in the runoff on May 7 with 52.64% of the vote against 47.36% for Jospin. (ANNE-ELISABETH MOUTET)

Even though the recession had ended two years before and economic growth was stable at 2% of gross domestic product, the country's mood remained pessimistic. Consumer spending lagged for most of the year, then dropped by more than half in the key pre-Christmas period. This was mostly as a result of public-sector strikes triggered by Prime Minister Alain Juppé's announcement of a series of structural reforms to overhaul the heavily indebted and extremely generous social security, health, and welfare system.

Domestic Affairs. Édouard Balladur had been the darling of the polls for his entire two-year stint as prime minister, and he remained well ahead until February 13, when he formally launched his presidential campaign. In the event, he came in third in the first round and threw his support to his mentor and rival, Chirac. (*See* Sidebar.)

On February 10 the flight from France of Didier Schuller, a corrupt official in charge of social housing in Interior Minister Charles Pasqua's constituency, revealed a covert operation to wrongly accuse of blackmail the father-in-law of a judge investigating major misappropriation of funds by some of Pasqua's closest political allies, so that the judge, Eric Halphen, would be taken off the case. Regular disclosure of financial scandals also contributed to the growing atmosphere of public exasperation.

Bernard Tapie, the embattled tycoon and former minister for inner cities, was declared bankrupt by the commercial tribunal of Paris on March 31 and was sentenced to two years in jail (14 months suspended) on November 28 for fixing a game of his former football club, Olympique Marseille, against the Valenciennes team. At year's end he still faced four different indictments for financial misdeeds.

After Chirac's election the emphasis of the scandals seemed to switch from the old guard to the new president's associates, especially to Juppé. On June 28 the well-informed satirical weekly *Le Canard Enchaîné* reported that both Juppé and his elder son, Laurent, rented City of Paris-owned apartments in the best part of town at about 40% below market price. On July 5 the paper revealed that Juppés' daughter, half-brother, and first wife enjoyed similar housing. Dogged by polemic and a court case brought against him by a taxpayers association (it was dropped in October), the prime minister saw his popularity ratings fall to 12% in November, an all-time low for any Cabinet minister of the Fifth Republic. On July 3 Judge Halphen held for interrogation the treasurer of the RPR in connection with alleged misappropriation of RPR social housing money to fund the president's campaign.

In June municipal elections saw for the first time the victory of extreme-right National Front candidates in three major southeastern towns—Toulon, Marignane, and Orange—elected on a xenophobic law-and-order platform. In Toulon the new mayor, Jean-Marie Le Chevallier, vowed that the city's social services and subsidies would go only to French-born residents. The election results confirmed the weakening of the traditional parties, while the Communists confirmed their progress at close to 10% of the vote nationally.

On July 16 in a speech commemorating the rounding up of Jews by French police during the World War II Nazi occupation of France, Chirac formally acknowledged the "faults" of France and its role in the extermination of Jews, something his predecessor, Pres. François Mitterrand (who had served at Vichy and been decorated by Marshal Philippe Pétain), had always refused to do.

On July 25 a bomb exploded in the Métro at Saint Michel station in the afternoon rush hour, killing seven and injuring more than 80 people. This was the beginning of a bloody bombing campaign by terrorists allegedly from the fundamentalist Armed Islamic Group (GIA), based in Algeria. On August 17 another bomb exploded on the Champs-Élysées, injuring 17 people. Bombs were discovered before they could explode on a high-speed-railroad track near Lyon on August 26 and in a public toilet near a marketplace in Paris on September 4. More bombs were detonated, usually on public transport, bringing the total toll of the terrorism wave to as many as 10 dead and some 170 injured. The new interior minister, Jean-Louis Debre, instituted a series of stiff security measures under the name "Plan Vigipirate," and France unilaterally decided to delay by six months the enforcement of the Schengen agreement to lift all border controls between 14 countries of the EU.

October 10 was a day of a general strike in the civil services in protest against a pay freeze decreed by Juppé. The strike was also supported by students at Rouen University, who were demanding additional scholarship loan credits and more professors. They were soon joined by 22 other universities in France. The government finally granted F 9 million extra credits on October 30, together with the promise of an overhaul of the overcrowded state university system. On November 7, trying to jolt the country by a sign of purposeful change, Juppé called a Cabinet reshuffle; of the 12 women ministers he initially appointed, only 4 remained.

Hardly had the students started trickling back to their classrooms than the prime minister announced his projected reform of the money-hemorrhaging social security and national health system, as well as across-the-board budget cuts, including lower pension benefits for state employees and an austerity plan for the loss-making SNCF, the state railways, with job cuts and line closures. On November 24 the railway workers went on strike, followed by other public transport employees. The post office, utilities, schools, banks, and social security employees followed suit, paralyzing the country until mid-December. Juppé gave up on the railways and pension reform but held fast on the social security overhaul.

The Economy. The year was one of moderate growth (about 2%) and low consumer spending and ended in disarray, with the cost of the three-week December strikes estimated at F 20 billion in lost tax revenue and input in the economy. Figures published on January 20 showed that inflation had been only 1.6% in 1994. On March 17 Balladur's economy and finance minister, Edmond Alphandery, announced a second plan to save the state-owned Crédit Lyonnais and write off some F 50 billion in bad debts over five years with state funds. On March 22 France's other two

A. GYORI—SYGMA

A victim of the bombing of a commuter train in central Paris on July 25 receives emergency treatment. The bombing was only the first of a number of similar incidents, attributed to Algerian terrorists, that occurred throughout France during the summer and fall.

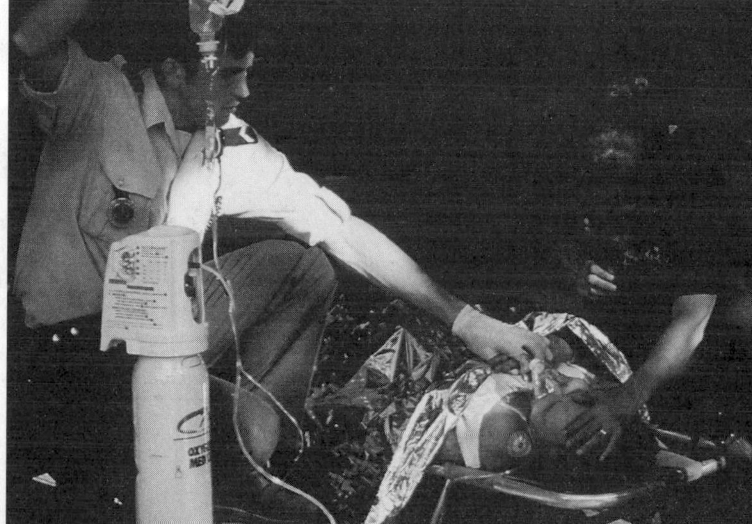

major banks, the privatized Société Générale and Banque Nationale de Paris, formally protested the plan at the Competition and Fair Trade Office of the European Commission in Brussels.

During the presidential campaign, some of Chirac's partisans accused the Balladur-appointed Banque de France governor, Jean-Claude Trichet, of causing high unemployment through his use of strict monetary policies (the *franc fort*). The franc fell against the Deutsche Mark on April 18 to a low of F 3.54. Chirac's election sent the franc back up again, to F 3.43, a sign of confidence from international markets. On August 25 Juppé ousted his avowedly free-trading economy and finance minister, Alain Madelin, for criticizing "privileges" (job security and higher pensions) enjoyed by four million employees of the state. The franc dropped as low as F 3.58 for a few days, then slowly rose again as the new minister, Jean Arthuis, made it clear that he too was committed to budget cuts.

Foreign Affairs. On September 5 France proceeded to set off the first of a series of five nuclear weapons tests at Mururoa atoll in the South Pacific. The international outcry was great. Anti-French demonstrations took place in Australia, New Zealand, the U.S., Japan, and many of the Pacific islands. New Zealand and Chile recalled their ambassadors. This was the culmination of a reprobation campaign that had started when the newly elected Chirac announced on June 13 that the tests, which had been interrupted by Mitterrand in 1992, were needed for technical reasons before France could sign the nuclear nonproliferation treaty of 1996. Following the second test, held on October 2, the 16-nation South Pacific Forum suspended official links with Paris.

French commitment to continued involvement in Bosnia and Herzegovina changed radically after the election of Chirac. After two French soldiers were killed by snipers in Sarajevo in April, Balladur stated that "the question of French withdrawal from Bosnia was now in order." In early June at a meeting in Paris of EU and NATO defense ministers, Chirac and British Prime Minister John Major pushed through the creation of a multinational Rapid Reaction Force to be made up of crack troops and equipment from NATO and EU armies. At the EU summit that began June 26 at Cannes (the last of the six-month French EU presidency), Chirac pressed for a five-point European initiative to get the siege of Sarajevo lifted and for a partition of Bosnia to be negotiated on the basis of allotting 51% of the area to Muslims and Croats and 49% to Serbs, all points that eventually were covered at the peace talks in Dayton, Ohio.

France's other major foreign policy concern was Algeria, where presidential elections with universal suffrage were to be held for the first time ever in November. On October 22 Chirac was to meet with Algerian Pres. Liamine Zeroual (who was reelected) in New York City on the occasion of the UN's 50th-anniversary celebrations. The announcement of what could be seen as an "endorsement" by France caused an uproar in the Algerian opposition—and more terrorist threats on French soil from the GIA. The meeting was eventually canceled. (ANNE-ELISABETH MOUTET)

See also *Dependent States.*

GABON

Gabon is a republic of central Africa, on the Atlantic Ocean. Area: 267,667 sq km (103,347 sq mi). Pop.: (1995 est.): 1,156,000. Cap.: Libreville. Monetary unit: CFA franc, with (Oct. 6, 1995) a par value of CFAF 100 to the French franc and a free rate of CFAF 501.49 to U.S. $1 (CFAF 792.78 = £1 sterling). President in 1995, Omar Bongo; prime minister, Paulin Obame-Nguema.

After the violent protests that nearly paralyzed the government in 1994, 1995 proved to be one of compromise and cooperation between Pres. Omar Bongo's Gabonese Democratic Party (PDG) and the opposition parties. A new electoral code requiring a complete revision of the voters list was agreed upon. All parties urged their members to back the new constitution in a referendum on July 23. Approximately 63.5% of the electorate voted in the referendum, 96.5% of whom approved the constitution. New presidential and legislative elections were scheduled for early 1997.

The government stepped up its campaign to control immigration, setting a deadline of February 15 for illegal aliens to regularize their status. Few were able to do so since the cost of a residence permit had risen to CFAF 1 million. A new marriage bill proposed by the government that would make polygamy easier drew fierce protests from women's groups.

Television and radio journalists staged a series of strikes beginning in March. Protesting the government's placement of patronage workers in their ranks, the strikers threatened to block publicity for the constitutional referendum. Broadcasts resumed on June 30 after the government agreed to integrate the patronage employees into the journalists association and to establish a new job classification rating system.

In April President Bongo threatened to withdraw from OPEC unless Gabon's production quota, the cartel's smallest, was increased. Neither his visit to Kuwait for talks on the matter nor the September visit to Gabon of OPEC's secretary-general resolved the issue. The introduction of a value-added tax on April 1 resulted in a huge leap in the price of consumer goods, forcing the government in August to impose price controls on basic foodstuffs.

(NANCY ELLEN LAWLER)

This article updates the *Macropædia* article CENTRAL AFRICA: *Gabon.*

GAMBIA, THE

A republic and member of the Commonwealth, The Gambia extends from the Atlantic Ocean along the lower Gambia River in West Africa; it is surrounded by Senegal. Area: 10,689 sq km (4,127 sq mi). Pop. (1995 est.): 1,115,000. Cap.: Banjul. Monetary unit: dalasi, with (Oct. 6, 1995) a free rate of 9.65 dalasis to U.S. $1 (15.26 dalasis = £1 sterling). Chairman of the Armed Forces Provisional Ruling Council in 1995, Capt. Yahya Jammeh.

Two members of the Armed Forces Provisional Ruling Council who had opposed plans to hand power back to civilian rule earlier than originally intended led an attempt to overthrow the government in January 1995. The two, Capt. Sana Sabally (vice-chairman of the Council) and Capt. Sadibu Hydara, minister of the interior, failed in their attempt, and they were arrested by the head of the government, Capt. Yahya Jammeh.

Donor countries exerted pressure throughout the year to persuade The Gambia to return to civilian rule, and on March 20 Jammeh announced a Cabinet reshuffle in an exercise to convince outsiders that he would soon restore such a government. But the following day Fafa Idrissa M'baye, who had just been dismissed as minister of justice and attorney general, was arrested for advocating an early return to civilian rule.

In November the junta reportedly extended the power of the security forces to detain suspected opponents without charge for up to three months. As many as 40 people had been detained for a week in October. (GUY ARNOLD)

This article updates the *Macropædia* article WESTERN AFRICA: *The Gambia.*

GEORGIA

A republic of Transcaucasia, Georgia borders Russia on the north and northeast, Azerbaijan on the southeast, Armenia and Turkey on the south, and the Black Sea on the west. Area: 69,492 sq km (26,831 sq mi). Pop. (1995 est.): 5,514,000. Cap.: T'bilisi. Monetary unit: lari, with (Oct. 4, 1995) a free rate of 1.30 lari = U.S. $1 (2.07 lari = £1 sterling); the lari replaced the Georgian coupon (a transitional currency) from September 25 at a rate of 1 lari = 1 million coupons. Head of state in 1995 (chairman of Parliament, and from November 26, president), Eduard A. Shevardnadze; prime minister to October 5, Otar Patsatsia, and secretary of state from December 8, Niko Lekishvili.

After three years of civil war, rampant crime, and economic collapse, in 1995 the situation in Georgia began to stabilize. Parliament Chairman Eduard Shevardnadze escaped an assassination attempt and finally succeeded in neutralizing those political figures who helped his return to Georgia in 1992 but had since become rivals. Two of these, former prime minister Tengiz Sigua and former defense minister Tengiz Kitovani, were arrested in January after making a symbolic march on the breakaway western region of Abkhazia with the aim of forcing the region back under central government control.

The series of political assassinations that began in 1993 continued during the first half of the year. Shevardnadze himself suffered only minor injuries in late August when a car bomb exploded as his motorcade was leaving the Parliament building in T'bilisi. The Georgian security service chief, Igor Giorgadze, was held responsible for this and several previous terrorist incidents and fled to Russia.

In August Parliament finally endorsed a new constitution that defined Georgia as a presidential republic. Presidential and parliamentary elections were scheduled for November 5. Shevardnadze was elected president with about 73% of the vote, defeating five rival candidates, including his successor as Georgian Communist Party first secretary, Dzhumber Patiashvili, and hard-line communist Panteleimon Giorgadze (Igor's father). Similarly, Shevardnadze's Union of Citizens of Georgia gained a 124-seat majority in the new 235-seat Parliament. Paramilitary leader Dzhaba Ioseliani, who failed in his bid for reelection, was arrested in mid-November on charges of involvement in the August car bomb attack on Shevardnadze.

In late November Shevardnadze implemented changes in the structure of executive power, replacing the post of prime minister with that of secretary of state. He then formed a new government, retaining the former ministers for economics and defense but appointing as foreign minister former deputy prime minister Irakli Menagharishvili.

The stringent fiscal and monetary policy adopted in December 1994 brought hyperinflation under control, and by late February the interim currency, the coupon, had gained in value against the dollar. A new currency, the lari, was introduced in September and maintained its value, thanks in part to a second International Monetary Fund loan. Greater political stability stimulated an increase in industrial output of 20% during the first 11 months of the year. The decision in October to export some oil from Azerbaijan via Georgia engendered hopes of an economic upswing.

The standoff between the central government in T'bilisi and the breakaway regions of Abkhazia and South Ossetia continued. The apparent inability of the Russian peacekeeping force stationed in Abkhazia to prevent reprisals against the Georgian population there in the early part of the year induced Georgian politicians to demand their withdrawal. Angered by the Abkhazian leadership's expressions of support for Chechnya and their repeated refusal to

A Georgian soldier registers his weapon near the border with Abkhazia. Despite the 1993 cease-fire between the breakaway province and the Georgian government and despite the presence of Russian troops and UN observers, sporadic and vicious fighting continued to break out.
DAVID TURNLEY—DETROIT FREE PRESS/BLACK STAR

discuss a Russian draft settlement giving Abkhazia federal status within Georgia, Moscow imposed a naval blockade on the Abkhazian port of Sukhumi in October. Peacekeepers from the Organization for Security and Cooperation in Europe prevented violence in South Ossetia, but only minimal progress was made toward a political settlement there.

In March an agreement was signed giving Russia the right to maintain three military bases in Georgia; a further bilateral agreement on economic cooperation was signed in September. At the same time, Georgia sought to expand economic ties with neighbouring Turkey and Iran.

(ELIZABETH FULLER)

This article updates the *Macropædia* article TRANSCAUCASIA: *Georgia*.

GERMANY

Germany is in central Europe, on the North and Baltic seas. Area: 356,974 sq km (137,828 sq mi). Pop. (1995 est.): 81,912,000. Cap. designate, Berlin, seat of government, Bonn. Monetary unit: Deutsche Mark, with (Oct. 6, 1995) a free rate of DM 1.43 to U.S. $1 (DM 2.26 = £1 sterling). President in 1995, Roman Herzog; chancellor, Helmut Kohl.

For the Federal Republic of Germany the year 1995 brought the 50th anniversary of the end of World War II and a long moment of contemplation and reflection about its identity as a democratic nation. Was May 8 the day of unconditional surrender or the day of liberation? Was the so-called zero hour of the year 1945 really a fresh start in every respect? And what now was the balance in Germany between a self-restraint imposed by its history and the growing creative impulses of a country that had such size and influence?

The days of remembrance of the concentration camps and of the victory over the Nazi regime started with the commemoration of the anniversary of the liberation of Auschwitz on January 27. At these ceremonies, in Germany as well as elsewhere, many believed that the Germany that came into being after 1945 was prepared to remember its past and never to forget. January 27 was henceforth to be an official day of remembrance in Germany.

The 50th anniversary of the end of the war was given greater resonance by the 100th birthday of Ernst Jünger, a militarist who won the medal Pour le Mérite in 1918 but later broke with the Nazis. The celebration, which was attended by Pres. Roman Herzog and Chancellor Helmut Kohl, was seen to poignantly reflect the breaks and continuities of a full century as well as the most recent 50 years of German history.

Domestic Affairs. Germany skidded into 1995 on unusually heavy rainfall that had begun in December, continued into January, and led to the so-called floods of the century. Numerous rivers—among them the Rhine, the Moselle, the Main, the Danube, the Fulda, and the Saar—overflowed their banks and flooded vast regions containing many villages and cities. Even the federal capital of Bonn was partly underwater, but the political life of Parliament and government agencies continued unimpeded. There were some significant developments in the structure of the political parties that could have considerable short- and long-term consequences. For the Free Democratic Party (FDP), the centrist coalition partner of the ruling conservative Christian Democratic Union/Christian Social Union (CDU/CSU), the downturn that began in 1994 continued. At the state elections in Bremen and North Rhine–Westphalia (both on May 14) as well as in Berlin (October 22), the loss of votes was so severe that the party did not reach the 5% threshold needed to send members to the parliaments. Only in Hessen on February 19 did they qualify for parliamentary representation. Thus, to a great extent the party lost its parliamentary basis on both the federal and the state levels. This shock was accompanied by major shake-ups in the party. The leader of the FDP, Foreign Minister Klaus Kinkel, had to resign because of these repeated failures, and Wolfgang Gerhardt from Hessen was chosen leader at the party conference in June. The FDP lost its status as the third strongest political force in Germany to the Greens/Alliance '90, the party of the environmental movement.

A further shock to the ruling coalition came in December when the minister of justice, Sabine Leutheusser-Schnarrenberger, resigned after her party, the FDP, abandoned its opposition to proposed legislation that would have allowed electronic surveillance of suspected criminals. As she would probably be replaced by another FDP member, the coalition was expected to survive.

Under the leadership of figures like Joschka Fischer (*see* BIOGRAPHIES), the Greens were able to improve their results in every election, and in North Rhine–Westphalia, the most populous federal state, they became the coalition partner of the Social Democratic Party (SPD), which had lost its overall majority. Nevertheless, conflicts and clashes among the leadership weakened the SPD more than the loss of their majority in North Rhine–Westphalia. The internal criticism of Rudolf Scharping's style of leadership began early in January and escalated over the summer into a power struggle between Scharping, the party leader, and Gerhard Schröder, the prime minister of Lower Saxony, who also was the SPD's official spokesman for economic affairs. The differences of opinion were aired publicly and raised questions not only about party leadership but also about the SPD's economic positions. Schröder had for the time being been stripped of his political power in the national party, but the conflict that had reached so deeply into the SPD had by no means come to an end. On November 16 Oskar Lafontaine was chosen SPD leader at the party conference in Mannheim. Scharping remained leader of the parliamentary delegation.

The ruling CDU/CSU benefited from these quarrels within the opposition, which tended to cover up Kohl's weaknesses.

The Party of Democratic Socialism (PDS), the successor party to the communists in the former East Germany, had also won representation in the Bundestag (lower house of Parliament) because of its continuing strength in the new federal states. But the PDS broke with Stalinist ideas and structures in its party conference in late January; the reformist wing of the party gained a clear majority, and the communist minority in the party could not win a single seat on the party's executive committee.

There was an unusual consensus evident among the parties in the Bundestag when a bill was passed in June with an overwhelming majority—more than two-thirds voted for a joint motion—that after decades of confrontations settled the question of the legality of abortion. Abortion within the first 12 weeks of pregnancy was no longer a crime, but the woman had to undergo counseling at an appropriate centre before an abortion could be performed. The asylum laws were once again a significant political issue. Turkish actions against the Kurdish minority in Turkey resulted in a growing criticism among Germans of the practice of too quickly deporting asylum seekers to their native countries. The protest against the asylum policy of the government led more and more church groups to give sanctuary to people whose petitions for asylum had been rejected. A judgment of the Federal Constitutional Court on the constitutionality of the asylum laws was expected in the spring of 1996.

Dissatisfaction on the part of foreigners resident in Germany, most of whom were Turkish, led to the formation of the Democratic Party of Germany in the fall of 1995. The party intended to campaign for changes in the country's electoral system and citizenship law.

Two decisions by the Constitutional Court caused a great deal of public discussion for many weeks. On May 23 it ruled that former East German spies and their bosses generally cannot be prosecuted for treason—only some clearly defined exceptions to this ruling were possible. Then, in August, on the grounds that education and cultural affairs lie within the responsibility of the federal government, the court declared unconstitutional a requirement of the Bavarian state government that a crucifix had to be displayed in every classroom in Bavarian elementary schools. Especially in conservative, heavily Roman Catholic, and traditional Bavaria, the court order provoked excited debates over whether Christianity itself would disappear from public life along with its symbol.

On December 13 the Bavarian state Parliament, in response to the ruling, passed a law requiring that crucifixes be displayed in all classrooms in the state as a reflection of "the historical and cultural character of Bavaria." The law, which was open to constitutional challenge, required school principals to reach an "amicable agreement" with parents who objected to the new law.

Another symbol, this one of German history, disappeared from public view at least temporarily: the Reichstag building. This building, which was built under Kaiser Wilhelm II and burned shortly after the Nazis gained power, was wrapped in silver polypropylene fabric by installation artist Christo and his wife, Jeanne-Claude. (*See* BIOGRAPHIES.) The Bundestag had finally approved the action after it had been planned for years. Contrary to all skepticism about public acceptance of the work, the project became an immense success. More than two million visitors went to view the wrapped building.

The annual award of the peace prize of the German book trade at the Frankfurt Book Fair led to fierce criticism soon after the recipient was named in May. The prize was awarded to 73-year-old Annemarie Schimmel, a professor emeritus of Oriental studies at the University of Bonn, on the grounds that she had fostered understanding between the Islamic and the Christian worlds through her extensive academic and journalistic writings. Critics accused her of showing too much understanding for Islamic fundamentalism and of endorsing the death sentence passed on novelist Salman Rushdie by the Iranian ayatollahs. Although the candidate repeatedly denied these accusations, in early September 100 distinguished writers and scientists—among them Günter Grass (*see* BIOGRAPHIES) and Jürgen Habermas—wrote in protest against the award.

The Economy. The economic recovery, which had already progressed markedly in 1994, continued in 1995. Gross domestic product grew by 2.8% in 1994, and the annual economic report issued by the government on January 27 forecast a growth of 3% for 1995 and a noticeable increase in exports based on a strengthened competitiveness. Labour demanded a share of the profits of the thriving economy, which led to long and tough wage negotiations. IG Metall, Germany's largest trade union, demanded a pay increase of 6% in addition to the 35-hour workweek that in 1990 had been agreed on for 1995. The employers rejected these demands without making a concrete counteroffer. Numerous warning strikes and demonstrations followed, and 88.36% of the trade union membership eventually voted in favour of industrial action. In early March the two parties reached agreement on a contract that would be valid for the next two years. Wages would increase by nearly 4% over the life of the contract, and the workweek in the steel and engineering industries was reduced to 35 hours beginning in October 1995. These pay increases set a guideline for the wage negotiations in most other industrial sectors. For example, the wage settlement for the public sector signed in May was 3.2% plus a one-time payment of DM 140, and in September the huge Volkswagen company agreed to an increase of 4% as of January 1996. The demands of the unions for a reduction in working hours were aimed at reducing the persistent unemployment rate. The employers, on the other hand, had called for flexibility in setting work time. In the automobile industry, as in other sectors, settlements were reached in which job security was to be maintained through such flexible arrangements. Unemployment was somewhat lower in January, at 3.8 million, than in the previous year, but the unemployment rate was still about 10% and fell during the year by only a few tenths of a percent.

At the end of January, Chancellor Kohl met with representatives of the industry and the unions to discuss unemployment and employment policies. The participants agreed to raise DM 3 billion to provide jobs to 180,000 of the long-term unemployed over the next four years. In connection with this concern over long-term unemployment, various charitable organizations and the Catholic and Protestant churches also called for action against the increasing poverty within affluent German society. The fall in unemployment was greater in the new federal states in the east than in the west, though the unemployment rate in the east was much higher, as was the rate of economic growth.

Despite notable gains of their economies, the new federal states were still dependent on capital transfer from the former West Germany. The audit office of the European Union caused quite a stir in February when it charged that the enormous funds were not always being spent wisely but were sometimes wasted.

Growth in important sectors of the economy came under pressure from the appreciation of the Deutsche Mark. At the same time, the Deutsche Mark increased in value against other hard currencies and became increasingly important as a reserve currency and more attractive to foreign investors. This international strength coupled with a decline in inflation and positive developments in the money supply led the Deutsche Bundesbank to lower the discount rate and the repurchase rate in March. These, and the Lombard rate, were lowered in August. In December the Lombard rate and the discount rate were lowered again, to 5% and 3%, respectively. The principal economic discussion of the year was over the means to secure and improve Germany's economic condition. Topics revolved around modernization, taxation, the public sector, and working hours. The key items were simplification of the tax system and tax relief, consolidation of the federal and state budgets, the welfare state, a lean public sector, and flexible work time.

Foreign Affairs. Relations with Russia, and especially the personal relationship between Chancellor Kohl and Russian Pres. Boris Yeltsin, were strained by the deployment of Russian troops in Chechnya. Despite the fact that Kohl avoided serious criticism of the Russian policy, he nevertheless distanced himself several times from the Russian actions. In a unanimous resolution of the Bundestag on January 20,

A foreigner works in the pouring of concrete at a construction project in Germany. It was estimated that in Berlin alone there were as many as 50,000 Gastarbeiter ("guest workers") in construction, while many native Germans, particularly manual labourers, remained unemployed.

AD VAN DENDEREN

all parties joined in passing a resolution holding that Russia's right to territorial integrity could be maintained only within the framework of the Russian constitution and the principles of international law and human rights. With its partners in the European Union, the government in Bonn agreed that sanctions should not be imposed on Russia because of its actions in Chechnya. Russian Defense Minister Pavel Grachev, who had planned to visit Germany for political talks, was disinvited by his German counterpart, Volker Rühe, because of Grachev's remarks about human rights abuses in Chechnya.

In an official state ceremony in Berlin on May 8, Germany commemorated the end of the Nazi regime. Representatives only of the four former allied nations had been invited as foreign guests: French Pres. François Mitterrand, U.S. Vice Pres. Al Gore, British Prime Minister John Major, and Russian Prime Minister Viktor Chernomyrdin. Vehement protests issued from Poland, where World War II had begun with the German invasion in 1939, because it had not been invited. In compensation, the Polish foreign minister, Wladyslaw Bartoszewski, was invited as the only foreigner,

Flooding threatens the buildings in Cologne's old city at the end of January. Germany, The Netherlands, Belgium, and France all suffered from severe flooding early in the year, blamed partly on changes in land use and partly on the failure to strengthen Holland's dikes.
JORN SACKERMANN—DAS FOTOARCHIVE/BLACK STAR

to address a joint meeting of the Bundestag and the Bundesrat (the second chamber of the Parliament). U.S. Pres. Bill Clinton, President Mitterrand, Prime Minister Major, and Chancellor Kohl were all invited by President Yeltsin to a ceremony in Moscow that marked the same occasion.

The principles of future German foreign policy were set out on March 13 by Pres. Roman Herzog in an address to the German Society for Foreign Affairs. He held that within the framework of a strengthened partnership with the U.S. and the completion of European unity, Germany must be not only an object but a subject of international politics. The "Berlin Republic," as he called the new and larger Germany that resulted from unification, must be prepared to articulate its own economic and security interests, and it must also be prepared to use military power in concert with other democracies. The principles, which mirrored the attitude of the ruling coalition, were put into action for the first time on June 30, when the Bundestag voted to deploy German troops in Bosnia and Herzegovina under NATO command. For the first time since the Bundeswehr (the German armed forces) was founded 40 years earlier, German soldiers were active in battle conditions outside the territory of NATO members. Some members of the SPD and Green deputies voted in favour of this decision, despite the fact that these parties disapproved of an operational mission in former Yugoslavia and wanted to accept a mission only under UN auspices. The question of using Bundeswehr troops outside the territory of NATO member states had provoked wide discussion within the SPD ever since the Federal Constitutional Court judged that German troops could take part in international peacekeeping missions without restrictions, as long as Parliament voted in favour of them. The question could now be considered resolved.

An unresolved question was touched upon when Kohl warned the other members of the EU on November 24 that they would be expected to bear much of the cost of rebuilding former Yugoslavia.

The events in connection with the planned sinking of the oil rig *Brent Spar* in June and the protests against the French underground nuclear tests on Mururoa atoll showed that German foreign policy, and foreign policy generally, was no longer a matter only of parliaments and governments. The protests and appeals for a boycott against the Royal Dutch/Shell Group led by the international environmental group Greenpeace, which had an especially strong backing in Germany, met with such an enthusiastic response that important politicians of all parties, including Chancellor Kohl, joined in. Kohl's appeal not to sink the rig in deep water was opposed by British Prime Minister Major. Shell abandoned the sinking because of the pressure and opted for disposal ashore. Greenpeace also started a campaign against the resumption of French nuclear testing, and numerous politicians again joined the protests. The federal government tried not to take sides too openly and took care—in spite of its support for the protests—not to annoy the French government, particularly after Jacques Chirac became president. The desire of both sides was to avoid friction in the special relationship between France and Germany.

Kohl's visit to South Africa and Namibia in mid-September awakened memories of a time long earlier when Germany was a colonial power in present-day Namibia, where there still was a strong German presence and influence. The chancellor promised both countries a privileged place on the list of recipients of German aid to less developed countries. Kohl, who was accompanied by the minister for economic cooperation and development, Carl-Dieter Spranger, emphasized that Germany would help not only with financial aid but also with assistance in the development of a system of education, particularly vocational training on the German model. (ROBERT SIGEL)

GHANA

A republic of West Africa and member of the Commonwealth, Ghana lies on the Gulf of Guinea. Area: 238,533 sq km (92,098 sq mi). Pop. (1995 est.): 16,472,000. Cap.: Accra. Monetary unit: cedi, with (Oct. 6, 1995) a free rate of 1,315 cedis to U.S. $1 (2,079 cedis = £1 sterling). Chairman of the Provisional National Defense Council and president in 1995, Jerry John Rawlings.

Kwesi Botchwey, Ghana's minister of finance, presented the 1995 budget at the beginning of February; he set a growth target of 5% for the year and sought to reduce the rate of inflation by 25%. The 1994 budget had yielded an $80 million surplus (after two deficit years). The prices of gasoline and kerosene were increased by 25%, and the minimum wage was increased from 790 cedis a month to 1,200 as of February 1.

During the first 11 days of May, the government was shaken by demonstrations against the 17.5% value-added tax that had been introduced as part of the 1995 budget. The violence led to five deaths and forced Botchwey to scrap the new measures in June and replace them with the former sales tax. After 13 years as finance minister, Botchwey resigned in July.

On February 8 Pres. Jerry Rawlings granted an amnesty to a number of prisoners to mark the second anniversary of Ghana's Fourth Republic. There was a renewal of ethnic violence in the north during March between the Konkomba and an alliance of the Namumba, Dagomba, and Gonja, and about 100 people were killed; the situation was potentially more dangerous than in 1994 because both sides had acquired automatic weapons. Peace moves were supervised by the minister of defense, Mahama Iddrissu, and a joint committee of Konkomba and Namumba was formed. The government set aside $1.2 million to aid an estimated 200,000 people who had been displaced in the conflict since it began in 1994.

In July Rawlings made an official and successful state visit to Britain, and later that month, prior to serving as host of the annual Economic Community of West African States meeting in Accra, he also made a surprise visit to Togo for talks with Pres. Gnassingbé Eyadéma. Relations between the two countries had not been good. By late September the various opposition parties were beginning to prepare for the presidential and parliamentary elections scheduled for 1996. (GUY ARNOLD)

This article updates the *Macropædia* article WESTERN AFRICA: *Ghana.*

GREECE

The republic of Greece occupies the southern part of the Balkan Peninsula and several adjoining island groups in southeastern Europe, in and between the Ionian and Aegean seas. Area: 131,957 sq km (50,949 sq mi). Pop. (1995 est.): 10,493,000. Cap.: Athens. Monetary unit: drachma, with (Oct. 6, 1995) a free rate of 234.67 drachmas to U.S. $1 (370.97 drachmas = £1 sterling). Presidents in 1995, Konstantinos Karamanlis and, from March 10, Kostis Stefanopoulos; prime minister, Andreas Papandreou.

Despite some bold moves by the socialist government of Andreas Papandreou to rectify the course of the economy and mend fences in the Balkans, political uncertainty prevailed throughout 1995 as a result of the prime minister's weakening physical condition.

Papandreou, who publicly thanked his wife, Dimitra, for helping him recover from critical heart surgery in 1988, shrugged off outraged protests over the construction of a luxury villa for her, the so-called pink villa scandal. Criticism came mainly from within Papandreou's own party, the Panhellenic Socialist Movement (Pasok). In February the minister of justice resigned, accusing the prime minister's entourage of unwarranted interference; in August a Pasok deputy was ousted from the party for publicly deploring the role of the prime minister's wife, which led Pasok cadres to openly urge a change of leadership. In September, Industry Minister Kostas Simitis resigned, stating that he refused to be a yes-man. His departure prompted a Cabinet reshuffle on September 15 that purged those of doubtful loyalty to Papandreou.

When the second five-year term of Pres. Konstantinos Karamanlis was due to expire in May, Papandreou decided to support the candidate proposed by the small Political Spring party, Kostis Stefanopoulos, a respected former politician. The post was largely ceremonial.

Papandreou had been hospitalized for pneumonia in November, and his health continued to deteriorate during the rest of 1995. He underwent dialysis treatments as his kidneys began to fail, and by late December his breathing was being continually assisted by a respirator. Because he had not named a successor, political uncertainty was widespread throughout Greece and all of Europe.

Political uncertainty was all the more unwelcome in a year when the finance minister, Alexandros Papadopoulos, pushed through unpopular fiscal reforms and enforced a tight budgetary discipline. By April year-on-year inflation had dropped to single digits for the first time in 23 years; by the end of September it stood at 8.4%. The parity of the drachma remained remarkably stable, and interest rates on state bonds fell by 3.25 points to 14.25% in October. Nonetheless, the basic structure of the economy remained weak. The public debt stood at 115% of gross domestic product, the trade balance sagged, and there were delays in privatization. The government wavered between pledges of social justice and the need to abide by the European Union's convergence program in order to bring Greece's economy in line with the rest of the EU by 1999. This required massive layoffs to make ailing state enterprises solvent enough to attract private investors. The prospect of early elections, which would tempt parties to forsake austerity in favour of votes, discouraged serious buyers. Major infrastructure projects that would have lowered the unemployment rate, which had soared above 10%, suffered further delays during the year. The $2.5 billion contract for a major international airport for Athens was signed in August, though, and was promptly ratified by Parliament.

The United States government actively intervened to ease tensions between Greece and its neighbours. Following pressure from Washington, in February the Albanian regime released five leaders of the Greek minority party Omonia who had been convicted of subversion. Greek police later arrested a band of seven armed extremists and charged them with conspiring to disrupt relations with Albania. A joint committee prepared a draft friendship and cooperation treaty, but when the Albanian foreign minister, Alfred Sereki, paid a return visit to Athens early in September, the talks broke down over a Greek proposal regarding Greek minority schools in Albania.

An interim agreement with the former Yugoslav republic of Macedonia was signed in New York on September 13, thanks to American mediation. The accord did not resolve the conflict over the name Macedonia, which the Greeks said implied territorial claims on the adjacent Greek province of the same name. Both sides eventually pledged to respect each other's frontiers and territorial integrity. The former Yugoslav republic formally declared that nothing in its constitution should be construed as implying revanchism against Greece or any intention to interfere in Greece's internal affairs. It further agreed to replace on its national flag the image of the so-called Star of Vergina, an ancient Macedonian emblem associated with Philip II, father of Alexander the Great. In return, Greece agreed to lift its trade embargo imposed 19 months earlier. An assassination attempt against Macedonian Pres. Kiro Gligorov on October 3 came just as delegations from the two countries were meeting in Athens to implement the interim agreement. Any motives for the attempt were unknown, and both sides expressed hope that the outrage would not hamper their efforts to restore relations.

Tensions with Turkey, the main foreign policy problem for Greece, persisted despite U.S. efforts to assist in resolving them. A meeting between Foreign Minister Karolos Papoulias and his Turkish counterpart, Erdal Inonu, in New York at the end of September simply underlined the sharp differences that divided the two countries. Those differences had been intensified by Greece's ratification of the Law of the Sea convention, which prompted the Turkish National Assembly to give the Ankara government authorization to use force if Greece extended its territorial waters in the Aegean Sea from 6 to 12 mi. The Greeks dismissed Turkey's calls for a diplomatic dialogue as a ploy to placate the European Parliament, which refused to ratify a EU-Turkey customs union unless Turkey drastically improved its human rights record. (MARIO MODIANO)

GRENADA

A constitutional monarchy within the Commonwealth, Grenada (with its dependency, the Southern Grenadines) is in the eastern Caribbean Sea. Area: 344 sq km (133 sq mi). Pop. (1995 est.): 92,000. Cap.: Saint George's. Monetary unit: Eastern Caribbean dollar, with (Oct. 6, 1995) a par value of EC$2.70 to U.S. $1 (free rate of EC$4.27 = £1 sterling). Queen, Elizabeth II; governor-general in 1995, Reginald Palmer; prime ministers, Nicholas Brathwaite, George Brizan from February 1, and, from June 22, Keith Mitchell.

In June 1995 the incumbent National Democratic Congress (NDC) government lost the general election to the New National Party (NNP), and Keith Mitchell, a 47-year-old former mathematics lecturer at Howard University, Washington, D.C., became the new prime minister. The NNP won 8 of the 15 parliamentary seats. Five were retained by the NDC, and two went to the Grenada United Labour Party, led by Sir Eric Gairy, who was prime minister of Grenada in 1979, when the left-wing New Jewel Movement, headed by Maurice Bishop, overthrew the government.

The NNP's victory no doubt owed something to its promise to abolish the income tax. The tax had been dropped in 1986 but was reintroduced by the NDC in 1994.

Grenada stepped up its fight against drug trafficking in February when it signed an assistance treaty with Britain that provided for the tracing, freezing, and confiscation of the assets of drug pushers. A series of strikes in key foreign exchange-earning industries, including hotels, sugar, and cocoa, took place in March and April.

A more serious threat was posed to the nutmeg industry by the sustained fall in prices on world markets. Grenada and Indonesia were the world's main nutmeg suppliers, and the two got together in May to continue efforts begun in 1994 to stabilize the price and encourage greater use of nutmeg. World demand had fallen to 9,000 metric tons in 1994, compared with production of 14,000 metric tons. (DAVID RENWICK)

This article updates the *Macropædia* article The WEST INDIES: *Grenada.*

GUATEMALA

A republic of Central America, Guatemala has coastlines on the Caribbean Sea and the Pacific Ocean. Area: 108,889 sq km (42,042 sq mi). Pop. (1995 est.): 10,621,000. Cap.: Guatemala City. Monetary unit: quetzal, with (Oct. 6, 1995) a free rate of 5.92 quetzales to U.S. $1 (9.36 quetzales = £1 sterling). President in 1995, Ramiro de León Carpio.

Guatemalans went to the polls in November 1995 to vote for a new president. Alvaro Arzú, candidate of the conservative National Advancement Party and former mayor of Guatemala City, finished first with about 42% of the votes, nearly twice as many as his nearest rival, Alfonso Portillo of the right-wing Guatemalan Republican Front (FRG). Because no candidate received a majority of the votes, a runoff between Arzú and Portillo was scheduled for Jan. 7, 1996. Economist Jorge Luis González del Valle, the candidate of a new left-wing coalition, the New Guatemala Democratic Front, finished a surprising fourth in the field of 19.

Col. Julio Roberto Alpírez, accused of being a paid informant for the CIA and of involvement in two murders, answers questions at a news conference. In September a Guatemalan military tribunal acquitted Alpírez of one of the murders.
MOISES CASTILLO—LATIN FOCUS

As in 1990, retired general Efraín Ríos Montt's bid to be the candidate of the FRG was blocked by the Supreme Electoral Tribunal because his previous presidency, in 1982–83, had been achieved as a result of a military coup. The FRG had been victorious in the 1994 congressional elections, and in January 1995 Ríos Montt was named president of the Congress. Later in the year, however, the party's popularity plummeted, and several key members deserted it. In August the Supreme Court stripped Ríos Montt and three other FRG congressmen of their immunity from prosecution so that they could be tried on charges of wiretapping, document forgery, and usurpation of powers.

Peace negotiations between the government and the Guatemalan National Revolutionary Unity failed to keep to the schedule agreed upon at the beginning of the year. The talks were affected by the elections and the perceived weakness of the government, combined with reluctance to pursue them on the part of the army and entrenched interests such as large landowners. The United Nations Mission for Guatemala reported that the lack of punishment continued to be the most serious obstacle to achieving respect for human rights in Guatemala and described specific cases of torture, illegal detention, extrajudicial killings, and obstruction of justice, based on the 570 human rights cases reported to it in the three months ended May 21.

(SARAH CAMERON)

This article updates the *Macropædia* article CENTRAL AMERICA: *Guatemala.*

GUINEA

The republic of Guinea is located in West Africa, on the Atlantic Ocean. Area: 245,857 sq km (94,926 sq mi). Pop. (1995 est.): 6.7 million (excluding 500,000–600,000 refugees from Liberia and Sierra Leone). Cap.: Conakry. Monetary unit: Guinean franc, with (Oct. 6, 1995) a free rate of GF 992.70 to U.S. $1 (GF 1,569 = £1 sterling). President in 1995, Gen. Lansana Conté.

Preparations for the often-postponed legislative elections dominated 1995. The Democratic Party of Guinea–African Democratic Rally, which finished last in the 1993 elections, suffered a further setback when a breakaway faction formed the Democratic Party of Guinea–Ahmed Sékou Touré (PDG-AST) in January. Subsequently, the opposition parties regrouped. Most important, three opposition parties formed an alliance in April with the Rally of the Guinean People, led by Alpha Condé. That same month, after the government published its new electoral code banning Guineans living abroad from voting, various opposition groups organized demonstrations and threatened to boycott the elections. In May the opposition National Democratic Union of Guinea agreed to cooperate with the PDG-AST. Each of the opposition coalitions agreed to present one candidate list for each district. Despite these maneuvers, however, Pres. Lansana Conté's Party for Unity and Progress (PUP) won 71 of the 114 seats on June 11, and 5 additional seats were taken by other parties allied with the PUP.

On July 6, opposition parties formed the Coordination of the Democratic Opposition (CODEM) and, charging the government with widespread vote fraud, announced that they would not take their 37 seats. Conté refused to negotiate with CODEM, insisting that such matters were the concern of the legislature and the judiciary. In September CODEM ended its boycott, and the opposition deputies took their seats.

Real gross domestic product was expected to grow by 4.9% in 1995, although the inflation rate was likely to be higher than the government's target of 4%. In recognition of Guinea's improved economic performance, the Paris Club canceled $85 million of the nation's external debt and rescheduled repayments of another $85 million.

(NANCY ELLEN LAWLER)

This article updates the *Macropædia* article WESTERN AFRICA: *Guinea.*

GUINEA-BISSAU

A republic of West Africa, Guinea-Bissau lies on the Atlantic Ocean. Area: 36,125 sq km (13,948 sq mi). Pop. (1995 est.): 1,073,000. Cap.: Bissau. Monetary unit: Guinea-Bissau peso, with (Oct. 6, 1995) a free rate of 16,036 pesos to U.S. $1 (28,513 pesos = £1 sterling). President in 1995, João Bernardo Vieira; prime minister, Manuel Saturnino da Costa.

In mid-January 1995 the International Monetary Fund approved a number of loans equivalent to $14 million to Guinea-Bissau to extend over a three-year period in support of the government's economic reform program. The first loan of $5 million was to be disbursed in semiannual installments. On October 10 negotiations between the government and the country's principal trade union resulted in a 50% increase in the minimum salary for the public sector.

On June 12 Pres. Abdou Diouf of Senegal visited Guinea-Bissau to bring to an end a period of mutual hostility between the two countries. Pres. João Bernardo Vieira and Diouf issued a statement promising better economic relations between the two countries and signed an accord to share equally the offshore mineral and energy resources on their joint continental shelf. The two nations agreed to joint exploitation of an offshore oilfield that straddles their territorial waters. They also reaffirmed a 20-year agreement that committed them to joint management and exploitation of their maritime zones.

In August, Kumba Iala, the defeated candidate in the 1994 presidential elections, denounced the government for entering into preferential relations with France. He also accused the government of causing an increase in prices, especially for rice, and denounced its record on human rights.

(GUY ARNOLD)

This article updates the *Macropædia* article WESTERN AFRICA: *Guinea-Bissau.*

GUYANA

A republic and member of the Commonwealth, Guyana is situated in northeastern South America, on the Atlantic Ocean. Area: 215,083 sq km (83,044 sq mi). Pop. (1995 est.): 770,000. Cap.: Georgetown. Monetary unit: Guyana dollar, with (Oct. 6, 1995) an official rate of G$143.80 to U.S. $1 (G$227.33 = £1 sterling). President in 1995, Cheddi Jagan; prime minister, Sam Hinds.

The government agreed in March 1995 to set up an official inquiry into the death in 1980 of the opposition political activist Walter Rodney, a historian of international repute. Rodney was blown up by a bomb concealed in a radio transmitter, and it was widely believed at the time that the government, headed by Forbes Burnham, was involved. The inquiry was to be conducted by an international commission.

As part of its anticorruption drive, the government decided in April that it would require all public employees, including Pres. Cheddi Jagan, to declare their assets and liabilities to an independent tribunal.

In July it was announced that six privatization deals would be completed by the end of the year. Entities to be sold included a government-owned pharmaceutical company and a mortgage bank. The Canadian company Alcan announced it would purchase as much as 300,000 metric tons of bauxite over the next three years. The contract was scheduled to take effect in March 1996 so that the company would have time to procure the spare parts needed for production.

Guyana's worst environmental disaster took place in August when a retaining wall for a storage pond at the giant Omai gold mine collapsed and allowed 2.3 million cu m (3 million cu yd) of cyanide waste to contaminate parts of the Essequibo River, a major source of water and fish for tens of thousands of people. A commission of inquiry was set up, and the Canadian company that owned the mine offered compensation to those affected. (DAVID RENWICK)

HAITI

The republic of Haiti occupies the western one-third of the Caribbean island of Hispaniola, which it shares with the Dominican Republic. Area: 27,700 sq km (10,695 sq mi). Pop. (1995 est.): 6,589,000. Cap.: Port-au-Prince. Monetary unit: gourde, with (Oct. 6, 1995) a free rate of 19 gourdes to U.S. $1 (30.04 gourdes = £1 sterling). President in 1995, Jean-Bertrand Aristide; prime ministers, Smarck Michel and, from November 7, Claudette Werleigh.

Haitian children carry water from a water hole to their home, a 15-minute walk away. In 1995 a number of international and regional agencies approved economic development programs for Haiti, where the living standards of most of the people remained extremely low.
MAGGIE STEBER—MATERIAL WORLD WOMEN'S PROJECT

In January 1995 U.S. commanders certified that a secure and stable environment had been achieved in Haiti since the military occupation of the nation began in September 1994, which thus allowed the 6,000 U.S. troops to be replaced by a UN force of the same size. Security was nevertheless fragile. In the absence of a trained police force and a working justice system, robberies and shootings were frequent, and there were several murders daily. People continued to flee the country by boat, but most were repatriated by U.S. authorities. In August more than 100 Haitian migrants were thrown overboard and drowned when an overcrowded boat began to sink on its way to The Bahamas.

At the end of January a $1 billion aid package was approved in Paris, but the money was slow in reaching Haiti, which led to resentment at the delay. The International Finance Corporation agreed to oversee the unpopular privatization of 9 of Haiti's 33 state enterprises, with the proceeds to be used for improving rural roads, hospitals, pension funds, and education. The International Monetary Fund offered a $31 million standby facility, with economic targets including annual inflation of 15%, growth of gross domestic product of 4.5%, and an increase in foreign reserves of $45 million during the year. The Inter-American Development Bank disbursed loans of $30 million for balance of payments support and $5.8 million for infrastructural development and a grant of $600,000 for the implementation of government projects. In May the Paris Club of creditor countries agreed to cancel $75 million of bilateral debt, with the remainder to be rescheduled over 23 years.

In February Pres. Jean-Bertrand Aristide weakened the Haitian army's power by retiring all 43 of its officers who held a rank above major. The president said in April that he would ask the legislature to amend the constitution in order to abolish the army.

The Provisional Electoral Council announced that elections would be held in two rounds, on June 4 and June 25, for the 83-member Chamber of Deputies, for 18 of the 27 Senate seats, and for about 2,000 local council posts and 100 mayoralties. However, amid rising political dissension both within the government and in the opposition, the first round was delayed until June 25, with a second round on July 23 (for those seats that did not receive a majority in the first round). Many of the opposition parties threatened to boycott the elections and claimed that the president's Lavalas movement had taken control of the electoral machinery.

In the first round of the elections, contested by 10,500 candidates, supporters of Lavalas swept the board. Voter turnout was low, less than 50%, although 90% of the 3.7 million electorate had registered to vote. Charging that the vote had been marked by fraud and a heavy pro-Aristide bias in the Provisional Electoral Council, the major opposition parties and many of the smaller groups decided to boycott the second round of the elections. President Aristide admitted that the elections could have been administered better and, after talks with the opposition parties, dismissed the president of the Provisional Electoral Council. It was decided that there would be reruns of the first round in many areas, with the second round not held until September. Reruns took place on August 13 and were orderly, although voter turnout was less than 33%. Most opposition candidates ignored the boycott order of their parties, but the Lavalas coalition again swept the board, winning all 34 of the seats theretofore decided.

After the second round, on September 17, Lavalas candidates held 68 of the 83 seats in the Chamber of Deputies and 17 of the 27 seats in the Senate. His party's victory notwithstanding, Aristide insisted that he would retire from office in 1996 despite calls for his term to be extended. Two candidates were announced for the presidential elections, scheduled to be held by the end of the year: Ernst Verdieu, the former social affairs minister and head of the Haitian branch of the Caritas aid agency, and Leon Jeune, the former deputy justice minister.

Though an official tally of the December election was not immediately available, Aristide's handpicked successor, René Préval, was the winner by a landslide. High U.S. officials met with Préval after the balloting to discuss extending the stay of UN troops in Haiti. (SARAH CAMERON)

This article updates the *Macropædia* article The WEST INDIES: *Haiti.*

HONDURAS

A republic of Central America, Honduras has coastlines on the Caribbean Sea and the Pacific Ocean. Area: 112,492 sq km (43,433 sq mi). Pop. (1995 est.): 5,512,000. Cap.: Tegucigalpa. Monetary unit: lempira, with (Oct. 6, 1995) a free rate of 9.47 lempiras to U.S. $1 (15.40 lempiras = £1 sterling). President in 1995, Carlos Roberto Reina.

In January 1995 the civilian-run Criminal Investigations Unit began operations, replacing the secret police, the National Investigation Unit, which was disbanded in 1994. The new force, initially of 1,500 agents, was trained by the Israeli police and the FBI of the U.S. Though the military remained involved in police work, the Legislative Assembly began the constitutional reform process to change control of the Public Security Forces from military to civilian hands. The police and the armed forces discussed ways in which they could combat the rising crime wave, which was claiming about 50 lives a day, as well as stem the trafficking of arms and drugs through Honduran territory. The constitutional reform to abolish obligatory military service, approved by the previous Congress in 1994, was ratified by the new Congress in April by 125 votes to 3.

Pres. Carlos Roberto Reina's election campaign promise of a "moral revolution" and an anticorruption drive was put into effect by the courts with several notable investigations. In January the sister of the foreign minister was arrested for selling official passports; in April the minister, Ernesto Paz

Aguilar, a close friend of Reina, resigned from the Cabinet, and in August he and six other government officials were detained in prison on fraud charges related to the sale of official passports. The Supreme Court of Justice revoked the immunity granted to former president Rafael Leonardo Callejas so that he could answer charges relating to the falsification of documents and misappropriation of funds. President Reina himself was investigated over the inappropriate use of state funds to resolve a private labour dispute.

(SARAH CAMERON)

This article updates the *Macropædia* article CENTRAL AMERICA: *Honduras.*

HUNGARY

A republic, Hungary is a landlocked state in central Europe. Area: 93,030 sq km (35,919 sq mi). Pop. (1995 est.): 10,231,000. Cap.: Budapest. Monetary unit: forint, with (Oct. 6, 1995) a free rate of 131.49 forints to U.S. $1 (207.86 forints = £1 sterling). President in 1995, Arpad Goncz; prime minister, Gyula Horn.

Three areas dominated the Hungarian scene in 1995—the economy, the stability of the coalition, and foreign relations. To the credit of the coalition, made up of the communist successors—the Hungarian Socialist Party (HSP) and the left-liberal Alliance of Free Democrats—in March the prime minister, Gyula Horn, finally decided to grasp the nettle and to introduce a far-reaching austerity package.

The package was brought in by the new minister of finance, Lajos Bokros, and came to be known as the Bokros package. It was profoundly unpopular. Essentially, it was aimed at trimming the budget deficit by cutting back on government expenditure through introducing new taxes, scrapping allowances, and charging fees in certain circumstances. Furthermore, the Hungarian currency, the forint, would undergo creeping monthly devaluation, aimed at reducing its value against the Deutsche Mark by up to 20% over a year. The central problem was that Hungary had been living beyond its means for many years and subsidizing this through foreign credits. In 1995 the day of reckoning had arrived, not least because the country's deficit had reached about $3 billion, giving Hungary the highest per capita debt in Europe.

The popularity of the government plummeted; the main beneficiary was the right wing Independent Smallholders' Party. It was generally estimated, however, that eventually the coalition would regain its standing, though this would take time. It was notable that the government, not least the prime minister, had not been particularly successful in attempting to sell the Bokros package to the public. If anything, it was imposed with hardly any explanation.

The austerity package was a bitter pill to swallow for the left of the HSP as well. The HSP regarded itself as a socialist party, and cutting welfare benefits was painful indeed. Several ministers resigned, and the left of the party spent a good deal of time grumbling. According to some estimates, anything up to a quarter of the HSP parliamentary caucus could not be relied on to vote for austerity measures. It was to placate the left that Horn sought to promote the trade union leader, Sandor Nagy, to a senior position in the government in August.

But this move, which had not been coordinated with the Free Democrats, nearly destroyed the coalition entirely. The role of the Free Democrats was to provide Horn with the necessary votes to get the austerity package through against his own left wing, but otherwise he had little time for them; he had, after all, been raised as a communist politician, and the subtleties of coalition politics did not figure high in communist politicking.

The attempt to impose a trade union leader on the coalition had the Free Democrats up in arms, and they made the rescinding of the appointment an issue of confidence. Eventually Horn retreated, having thereby lost face with both his left wing and his coalition partner. The general feeling, however, was that the coalition would struggle on, despite the near-constant friction.

Matters were made worse for the coalition by intervention from an unexpected quarter—the Constitutional Court. Under Hungary's improvised constitution—the old communist document as amended—the court had extraordinarily wide powers of supervision and revision. By the end of the year, it had brought in well over 10 decisions striking down as unconstitutional various parts of the measures put forward in the Bokros package. Bokros tendered his resignation, but he was persuaded to stay on. When all was said and done, the government seemed determined to continue its policies, despite their unpopularity. Whatever the political fallout from the austerity package, early figures indicated that its economic effect was beginning to show positive results, with the Hungarian economy very slowly coming out of the doldrums.

In foreign policy Hungary pursued the options that it had elaborated since the fall of communism—closer integration with the West and attempts to find ways of improving conditions for the Hungarian minorities in the neighbouring states. Unlike the centre-right coalition that lost power in 1994, the present coalition was determined to bring home major successes in both areas. In the event, it did not manage to do so. Its difficulty with Western integration was that the terms, pace, and date were under the West's control, and Western leaders, despite verbal declarations to the contrary, gave the integration of the postcommunist states a low priority. Horn made a number of statements in which he argued that early membership of the Central European states in NATO and the European Union would be beneficial to the security of Europe as a whole; this met with polite indifference.

There was an equal lack of success with the neighbouring states. The coalition prided itself on its professionalism and sold itself to the Hungarian electorate as being better placed to solve the minority issue than its nationalist-minded predecessor. Unfortunately, it was unable to find negotiating partners in either Slovakia or Romania, where the presence of the ethnic Hungarians was seen as a major threat.

(GEORGE SHÖPFLIN)

ICELAND

Iceland is an island republic in the North Atlantic Ocean, near the Arctic Circle. Area: 102,819 sq km (39,699 sq mi). Pop. (1995 est.): 269,000. Cap.: Reykjavík. Monetary unit: Icelandic króna, with (Oct. 6, 1995) a free rate of 64.78 krónur to U.S. $1 (102.38 krónur = £1 sterling). President in 1995, Vigdís Finnbogadóttir; prime minister, Davíd Oddsson.

Pres. Vigdís Finnbogadóttir announced at the initial session of the Althing, Iceland's national legislature, that she would not run for the presidency again when her term expired in mid-1996. She took office in 1980, the fourth president of the republic since its establishment in 1944.

Elections to the Althing took place on April 8. Of the 63 seats being contested, the Independence Party won 25, one fewer than in the 1991 election; the Progressive Party won 15, a gain of two. The People's Alliance won nine seats, the same as in 1991, and the Social Democratic Party won seven, a loss of three. The Women's Alliance returned three, two fewer than in 1991, and a new party, the People's Movement, won four seats. As a result of the election, the government coalition of the past four years, composed of the Independence Party and the Social Democratic Party, had a majority of only one vote in the new Althing. This was too small for the Independence Party, which therefore switched coalition partners and took in the farmer-backed Progressive Party. The new coalition consisted of 40 members out of the total of 63 in the Althing.

The Icelandic economy picked up in 1995 after having grown very slowly in recent years. Gross domestic product was estimated to have increased by 3%, primarily because of a 3% growth in exports and a rise in domestic demand. Inflation was estimated to be below 2%, remarkable for Iceland after its long history of high inflation. Unemployment was about 5%.

Iceland's dispute with Norway and Russia over fishing rights in the Barents Sea continued without solution in 1995. Icelandic vessels continued to fish in a small area between the 200-mi exclusive economic zones of Norway, Svalbard, and Russia, taking advantage of fish stocks that, after being depleted several years earlier, had been carefully husbanded back to health by Norway and Russia. Toward the end of the year, there were indications that the matter could be solved through diplomatic negotiations.

Heavy snows in the early months of 1995 hit the northern part of the country, particularly the northwestern peninsula. On January 16 an avalanche fell on the village of Sudavik, killing 14 persons. On October 26 another avalanche killed 20 persons in the fishing village of Flateyri.

(BJÖRN MATTHIASSON)

INDIA

A federal republic of southern Asia and member of the Commonwealth, India is situated on a peninsula extending into the Indian Ocean, with the Arabian Sea to the west and the Bay of Bengal to the east. Area: 3,165,596 sq km (1,222,243 sq mi), including the Indian-administered portion of Jammu and Kashmir. Pop. (1995 est): 935.7 million, including Indian-administered Jammu and Kashmir. Cap.: New Delhi. Monetary unit: Indian rupee, with (Oct. 6, 1995) a free rate of Rs 33.90 to U.S. $1 (Rs 53.59 = £1 sterling). President in 1995, Shankar Dayal Sharma; prime minister, P.V. Narasimha Rao.

Domestic Affairs. In 1995, with elections to the Lok Sabha (House of the People) due early in 1996, the major political parties did not appear to be in fighting trim. The Indian National Congress (I) underwent another split, with former minister Arjun Singh, who was expelled, being joined by Narain Dutt Tiwari to form a rival Congress party in May. The Bharatiya Janata Party (BJP), reputed for discipline, was also riven by dissension. The National Front–Left Front alliance was badly damaged with the breakup of the Telugu Desam Party in Andhra Pradesh and squabbles in the Communist Party of India (Marxist). In June a new political party for members of the lower castes was launched by Phoolan Devi, "the Bandit Queen." (*See* BIOGRAPHIES.)

The outlook for the non-Congress parties had been brighter in March–April when, in elections to assemblies in five states, Congress (I) lost power in two major states, Maharashtra and Gujarat, and fared poorly in another big state, Bihar. The BJP won 121 out of 182 seats in the Gujarat Assembly and formed a government under Keshubhai Patel. In Maharashtra it teamed up with another Hindu chauvinist party, the Shiv Sena, and the coalition won 138 out of 288 seats, compared with 81 by Congress (I), and formed a government led by Manohar Joshi of the Shiv Sena. Among the first acts of the new government were the renaming of Bombay as Mumbai and the abolition of the state minorities commission. Within five months it had also canceled the agreement with the U.S. company Enron Corp. to build a $2.8 billion power project on grounds of overpricing. The deal was renegotiated, and Enron agreed to reduce the cost of the second phase by $300 million.

In Bihar the Janata Dal under Laloo Prasad Yadav was swept back to power. Congress (I) had the satisfaction of wresting the Orissa Assembly from the Janata Dal, winning 80 out of 147 seats and forming a ministry led by Janki Ballabh Patnaik. It also retained power in Arunachal Pradesh, where Geegong Apang remained chief minister. In Manipur, Rishang Keishing of Congress (I) was sworn in as chief minister for a sixth time.

There was also a change of government in Uttar Pradesh. The Bahujan Samaj Party broke away from the Samajwadi Party and formed a government under Mayawati with the support of the BJP. The government lasted just over four months. The BJP withdrew, and presidential rule was promulgated. In Andhra Pradesh, N.T. Rama Rao's ministry was toppled in a family revolt, and his son-in-law, M. Chandrababu Naidu, took away the majority in the Telugu Desam Party to form the government on September 1. The BJP had problems in its stronghold in Gujarat when Shankersinh Vaghela and 46 legislators rebelled against Keshubhai Patel and a new BJP Cabinet was sworn in under Suresh Mehta.

In Kerala, Congress (I), bowing to the pressure of its partners in the United Democratic Front, replaced K. Karunakaran with A.K. Antony as chief minister in March. The Punjab chief minister, Beant Singh, was assassinated in a bomb explosion on August 31, shattering the belief that terrorist activity had been put down in the state. Harcharan Singh Brar was the new chief minister.

Separatist activity continued in Jammu and Kashmir, and the government's plans to hold elections in the state were negated by the Election Commission because of a fear of violence. The 535-year-old shrine of Nooruddin Noorani at Charar-i-Sharif was burned down by militants on May 11 after a prolonged engagement with security forces.

Prime Minister P.V. Narasimha Rao reshuffled his Council of Ministers three times during the year, in February, June, and September. Pranab Kumar Mukherjee was given the External Affairs portfolio. Among those inducted into the Cabinet were A.R. Antulay (Health), Madhav Rao Scindia (Human Resource Development) and K. Karunakaran (Industry). P. Chidambaram returned as minister of state for commerce.

Three major welfare schemes were launched from mid-August: a national social assistance scheme for persons over age 65, a school meal plan to benefit 110 million children, and a group insurance scheme, together costing Rs 39 billion annually. The prime minister also announced a plan to build 10 million rural houses.

The Indian constitution was amended through the 78th amendment to give protection to certain land laws of states. The Terrorist and Disruptive Activities (Prevention) Act lapsed, and the government introduced a bill to amend the criminal law to deal more effectively with terrorism.

The chief election commissioner, T.N. Seshan, continued to be in the news. His petition challenging the appointment of two more members to the election commission was rejected by the Supreme Court, which advised him to mend his ways and reach decisions in the commission by consensus or majority. In another judgment, the court directed the government to appoint an independent authority for allocating airwaves. The court also ruled that the conversion of a Hindu to another religion (*e.g.,* Islam) to contract a second marriage was illegal. The court asked the government to consider the feasibility of a uniform civil code but

(continued on page 418)

SPOTLIGHT: SECULARISM IN SOUTH ASIA

by Akeel Bilgrami

The ideals of secularism have always been important, though precarious, in South Asia. Because of its diverse population, the region has long been a theatre of conflict between religious communities. Even when the threat of conflict has been centred around ethnicity or caste, political parties and governments have sometimes appealed to religious considerations to distract attention from these other forms of conflict. In all such circumstances it is secularism that has been eroded.

In 1993 conflict between Hindus and Muslims in northern India came to a head with the destruction of the mosque at Ayodhya and took on a scale and significance not witnessed since the communal troubles during the partition period that culminated in the creation of Pakistan in 1947. The partition left India with a sizable Muslim population (10–12% of the whole) who did not become citizens of the new state of Pakistan, and this population has recently come under an attack from a Hindu nationalist majoritarian movement known as Hindutva. The parliamentary party explicitly committed to a policy of opposition to the Muslim minorities is the Bharatiya Janata Party (BJP), but it has important extraparliamentary support from bodies that propagandize for Hindu dominance. This group of organizations, known as the *sangh parivar,* has a distinctive ideology that claims India is a Hindu nation and that minorities in it, particularly the Muslims, may live in India only if they acknowledge these claims. This means, among other things, that Muslims would not be allowed to live as they do now, under their own code of personal laws. (India, though a secular state, allows Muslims and Hindus to live according to a code of personal laws based on their religion.) This has made the Muslim community particularly defensive on the matter of this code, which many Muslims now believe is the only thing that can preserve their cultural identity. This attitude gives popular currency to the Hindutva claim that Muslims were pampered during the years of British rule and by the "pseudosecular" state of postindependence India.

Perhaps the most significant event relevant to secularism in the past year was the election of the BJP to power in India's most prosperous state, Maharashtra, in alliance with a militant regional party called Shiv Sena. This newly elected government has already proposed legislation to abolish a separate civil code for Muslims, a move that Muslims resist on the grounds that this federal matter is not subject to state legislation. At the federal level, however, the Supreme Court ruled earlier that conversion by Hindu men to Islam as a means of marrying more than one women was prohibited.

In Uttar Pradesh, the state with the largest Muslim population after Kashmir, the government led by Mulyalam Singh Yadav fell when a party of the Untouchable community called the Bahujan Samaj Party withdrew its support and formed an alliance with the BJP. This shows how the condition of secularism in India is influenced by the question of caste. Singh's government had assumed that Hindutva was a movement of upper-caste Hindus with no support among the Untouchables, but the defection of the BSP indicates that some groups will put aside economic concerns when jockeying for immediate political power.

Secularism in Pakistan is an issue of the extent to which the official religion, Islam, will be allowed to dominate the state, and the chief problem in Pakistan at present is threats to the government of Prime Minister Benazir Bhutto from an increasingly Islamic and conservative army.

In Bangladesh there was an Islamist outcry against Taslima Nasrin's feminist novel *Lajja,* which expressed sympathy for the plight of the Hindu minority in the country. A similar situation surfaced in India with the publication of Salman Rushdie's new novel, *The Moor's Last Sigh,* which satirizes a leader of the Shiv Sena in Maharashtra.

The ongoing civil war in Sri Lanka between the Sinhalese majority, mostly Bhuddist, and the Hindu Tamil separatists in the north seems no closer to resolution, but in Nepal most people prefer making the new multiparty democracy work, and there are few who wish for a return to the absolutist Hindu monarchy.

In spite of such groups as the "guru busters" of Calcutta, which agitate against religious influence in India, and groups that want to preserve a multireligious state, the secular commitment to free expression of religious dissent will no doubt continue to be under some attack and strain in the countries of southern Asia in the near future.

RELIGIOUS CONFLICTS IN SOUTH ASIA

AFGHANISTAN
PAKISTAN
JAMMU AND KASHMIR
CHINA
NEPAL
UTTAR PRADESH
BHUTAN
BANGL.
Karachi
ARABIAN SEA
INDIA
MAHARASHTRA
MYANMAR (BURMA)
BAY OF BENGAL
KARNATAKA
INDIAN OCEAN
SRI LANKA
JAMMU AND KASHMIR
Data unavailable
Srinagar
Charar-i Sharif
International boundaries
Disputed boundaries
Line of control
UTTAR PRADESH STATE, India
Moradabad
Aligarh
Agra
Ayodhya
Bombay (Mumbai)
MAHARASHTRA STATE, India
KARNATAKA STATE, India
Hubli-Dharwad
Jaffna
SRI LANKA
TAMILS
Trincomalee
SINHALESE
BUDDHISTS HINDUS MUSLIMS SIKHS
Religious majorities
Religious minorities
Political subdivision boundaries
Centers of conflict

Akeel Bilgrami is professor of philosophy at Columbia University, New York City and the author of the forthcoming *Postcolonial Politics and Cultural Identity.*

(continued from page 416)
later clarified that this was not advice but rather a passing observation.

A special judge in New Delhi convicted 43 persons of offenses committed during the anti-Sikh riots following Indira Gandhi's assassination in 1984. A judge in Baroda awarded life sentences to 13 Shiv Sena members, and a Bombay judge held 166 persons guilty for their part in the Hindu-Muslim riots of 1993. (*See* SPECIAL REPORT: *Secularism in South Asia.*)

Former prime minister Morarji Desai died in April, a few weeks after his 99th birthday. (*See* OBITUARIES.) In August, Sonia Gandhi (*see* BIOGRAPHIES), Rajiv Gandhi's widow, expressed regret over the government's slowness in investigating her husband's assassination in 1991. It was the Italian-born Gandhi's first public statement since the event.

The Economy. An official estimate placed the growth rate in 1994–95 at 5.3% and the increase in exports at 27%. Several state-owned industries made public equity offerings, but the government's plan to award contracts for different telecommunications services met political and legal obstacles. The value of the rupee fell sharply in October, but the reserve bank was able to stabilize exchange rates. The stock market plunged in November.

Presenting the federal budget on March 15, Finance Minister Manmohan Singh announced increases of 12% and 14.6%, respectively, in the allocations for education and agriculture. Import duties were cut, especially on metals, electrical parts, paper, chemicals, and drugs. Revenue receipts for 1995–96 were placed at Rs 1,007,870,000,000, capital receipts at Rs 663,640,000,000, and expenditure at Rs 1,721,510,000,000, leaving a budgetary deficit of Rs 50 billion. The provision for defense was Rs 255 billion, a rise of Rs 25 billion over the previous year. The annual inflation rate stood at 8.23% during the week ended November 11.

BARTOLOMEW—GAMMA LIAISON

Kashmiri separatists demand freedom from Indian rule after fire destroyed much of the town of Charar-i-Sharif in May. In the second of two fires in one week, a 15th-century Muslim shrine dedicated to the patron saint of Kashmir burned to the ground.

Foreign Affairs. Relations with Pakistan remained uneasy, with India continuing to accuse Pakistan of aiding and abetting Kashmiri and Punjabi separatists and Pakistan alleging Indian help to antigovernment elements in Sind. The move in the U.S. Congress in September to resume arms supplies to Pakistan was viewed in India as encouraging an arms race in the subcontinent. By an agreement reached with China, both countries began withdrawing troops along the border in August. The South Asia Association for Regional Cooperation, at a meeting held in New Delhi in May, decided to launch a South Asia Preferential Trade Arrangement from December 8.

Prime Minister Rao participated in the World Social Summit in Denmark in March and the 50th anniversary of the UN in New York City in October. He also made trips to Maldives, France, Malaysia, Turkmenistan, Kyrgyzstan, Egypt, Burkina Faso, and Ghana. Pres. Shankar Dayal Sharma paid visits to Trinidad and Tobago, Chile, Namibia, and Zimbabwe. Among important visitors to India were Pres. Nelson Mandela of South Africa; Pres. Hashemi Rafsanjani of Iran; the presidents of Turkey, Italy, Pakistan, Maldives, Sri Lanka, and Mali; the prime ministers of Bangladesh, Nepal, and Denmark; and the king of Bhutan. During Rafsanjani's visit a tripartite agreement was signed between Iran, Turkmenistan, and India to provide road-and-rail access for Indian trade with Central Asia through Iran.

India rejected the call to sign the Nuclear Non-proliferation Treaty after 174 nations resolved at a conference in New York City in May to extend the treaty indefinitely. The government maintained that the extension perpetuated the discriminatory aspects of the treaty and provided legitimacy to the nuclear arsenals of nuclear weapons states. It reiterated its resolve to work for elimination of all nuclear weapons. India also staked a claim for a permanent seat in the enlarged UN Security Council.

(H.Y. SHARADA PRASAD)

INDONESIA

A republic of Southeast Asia, Indonesia consists of the major islands of Sumatra, Java, Kalimantan (Indonesian Borneo), Celebes (Indonesian: Sulawesi), and Irian Jaya (West New Guinea) and more than 13,000 smaller islands and islets. Area: 1,919,317 sq km (741,052 sq mi). Pop. (1995 est.): 195,283,000. Cap.: Jakarta. Monetary unit: rupiah, with (Oct. 6, 1995) a free rate of 2,268 rupiah to U.S. $1 (3,585 rupiah = £1 sterling). President in 1995, Suharto.

Speculation about a successor to President Suharto subsided in 1995, but grumbling from an increasingly well-educated and well-off middle class that wanted more openness in government grew louder. Suharto, whose 28-year rule made him one of the world's most resilient leaders, still had a firm grip on the levers of power. Most expected him to seek and win another five-year term in 1998. At celebrations for the country's 50th anniversary of independence on August 17, Suharto said, "This is a time for more transparency." The government's actions, however, did not always live up to his promises.

Just before Independence Day, Suharto ordered the release of three political prisoners who had been jailed nearly 30 years earlier for their roles in the 1965 upheaval that eventually led to Sukarno's ouster and brought Suharto to power. The government also promised to remove a stigma from the national identification cards of some 1.3 million former detainees. In May the president announced a plan to reduce the parliamentary seats allotted to the military from 100 to 75 beginning in 1997. This reduction seemed symbolic to some and did not end the armed forces' constitutionally guaranteed role in political and social affairs, however. Government supporters contended that the military's diminished presence in the parliament was a sign that democracy was being broadened.

With an eye toward the mid-1997 national elections for the 500-member legislature, information minister and Suharto loyalist Harmoko traversed the country to boost the standing of Golkar, the nation's most potent political organization. Members of the other two legal political parties, the Indonesian Democratic Party (PDI) and the Muslim-based United Development Party (PPP), asked the government in June to explain Harmoko's early rush to the hustings, implicitly questioning the fairness of the government's practices. Critics contended that Jakarta made life tough for the opposition in other ways as well. One vocal parliamentarian was disowned by Golkar in February, and the PPP expelled one of its members in March. PDI officials said that the government was attempting to block the rise of their party, which was led by Sukarno's daughter Megawati Sukarnoputri.

Amid the electioneering, Indonesia's justice system delivered three rulings that led some civil liberties advocates to suggest that the courts might be asserting their independence. Harmoko said he would appeal one of the lower court's verdicts. In March Harmoko had ordered the arrest of three members of the Alliance of Independent Journalists, a group formed after the 1994 banning of three popular publications. In September the government banned the published memoires of Oei Tjoe Tat, the former assistant to President Sukarno. The list of those forbidden to speak in public included Abdurrahman Wahid (*see* BIOGRAPHIES), leader of the nation's largest Islamic organization.

The Supreme Court in May exonerated six persons imprisoned for the 1993 killing of labour activist Marsinah. Critics had long viewed the convicts as scapegoats forced to confess to a crime that many blamed on the military. Another prominent labour activist, Muchtar Pakpahan, was released from a four-year jail term in May. Strikes organized in April 1994 by his independent labour group in Medan, Sumatra, had led to rioting in which one person died.

Dissidents claimed that the military had stepped up its campaign to crush the popular separatist movement in the former Portuguese colony of East Timor. After an army inquiry into the killing of six civilians there in January, two soldiers were court-martialed. The army was also checking claims that troops murdered 17 independence activists in Irian Jaya, an island province in the far eastern part of the Indonesian archipelago.

Political tension had little effect on economic growth. Boom conditions and strong investment continued to drive the economy, which grew at about 8% in 1995, though inflation rose to nearly 10%. Approved foreign investment for the first five months totaled $33.5 billion, 40% more than was approved in all of 1994. The current account for the first quarter of the year jumped 29% owing to greater imports of services. In May the government reduced tariffs on a range of goods and set a timetable for further reductions. Just a week before independence celebrations, Indonesia's first domestically produced aircraft successfully completed its maiden flight; it was vindication for B.J. Habibie, minister for research and technology, whose high-tech development plans had been criticized as wasteful and misguided.

(SUSAN BERFIELD)

IRAN

The Islamic Republic of Iran is in southwestern Asia on the Caspian and Arabian seas and the Persian Gulf. Area: 1,638,057 sq km (632,457 sq mi). Pop. (est., excluding about 1.6 million Afghan refugees): 61,271,000. Cap.: Tehran. Monetary unit: Iranian rial, with (Oct. 6, 1995) a fixed rate of 3,000 rials to U.S. $1 (4,742 rials = £1 sterling). *Rahbar* (spiritual leader) in 1995, Ayatollah Sayyed Ali Khamenei; president, Hojatolislam Ali Akbar Hashemi Rafsanjani.

In 1995 the Islamic regime in Iran endured a year of economic hardship but domestic political quiescence. On January 20 Iran's outstanding nonclerical political figure, Mehdi Bazargan, died. (*See* OBITUARIES.) He was the country's first prime minister following the 1979 revolution and the only surviving secular leader accepted by the Islamic regime. His death left a marked gap in the ranks of the opposition, since few other Iranians had been permitted publicly to attack the regime with impunity. Ahmad Khomeini, son of the late Ayatollah Ruhollah Khomeini, died on March 17. He represented an uncompromising face of the Islamic revolution, but his departure was not expected to significantly weaken the hard-line wing of the regime.

A major challenge to the authority of the government came in June when the trial began of officials accused of embezzling funds from the state-owned Bank Saderat. One of the defendants was Morteza Rafiqdoust, brother of Mohsen Rafiqdoust, the powerful head of the Foundation of the Oppressed (Bonyad Mostazafin & Janbazan). The trial added to public disquiet over allegations that officials in the Islamic Republic had consistently taken illicit pecuniary advantage of their positions. In July a senior mullah, Ayatollah Mahdavi Kani, resigned as secretary-general of the Society of Combatant Clerics, which suggested a trend toward a weakening of the direct role of senior religious leaders in political life. In August two bomb attacks occurred in Tehran, and in Ahvaz an oil pipeline was damaged in a separate incident. These bombings indicated that terrorism against the regime had not been entirely suppressed.

In foreign affairs the country remained a pariah state. Relations with the U.S. worsened as a result of an executive order by Pres. Bill Clinton in May that placed a ban on U.S. trade with Iran. Although allies of the U.S. did not adopt similar trade sanctions, other issues, such as the death sentence levied against novelist Salman Rushdie, gave cause for concern. An initiative by the European Union (EU) in June to get this death threat revoked failed, but the Iranian authorities noticeably played down the matter during the year. Nonetheless, the Norwegian ambassador was withdrawn from Tehran because of differences with Iran on the Rushdie affair. Commercial relations between the EU states and Iran improved.

In the Middle Eastern arena Iran continued to be regarded with suspicion. Tehran was entirely opposed to the Israeli-Palestinian peace settlement and maintained its moral and material support for Islamic fundamentalist causes across the region. Iran kept up a strong backing for the territorial integrity of Iraq despite its reservations concerning Iraqi leader Saddam Hussein. The defection from Iraq of two of Hussein's politically powerful sons-in-law and their families to Jordan was not welcomed in Iran. It was seen as a prelude to greater U.S. intervention in Iraq and possibly the unwelcome emergence there of a pro-U.S. government.

The domestic economy fared badly in 1995. Oil production ran at some 3.6 million bbl per day. The annual budget forecast oil revenues for the fiscal year from March 1995 to March 1996 at approximately $15 billion, with actual re-

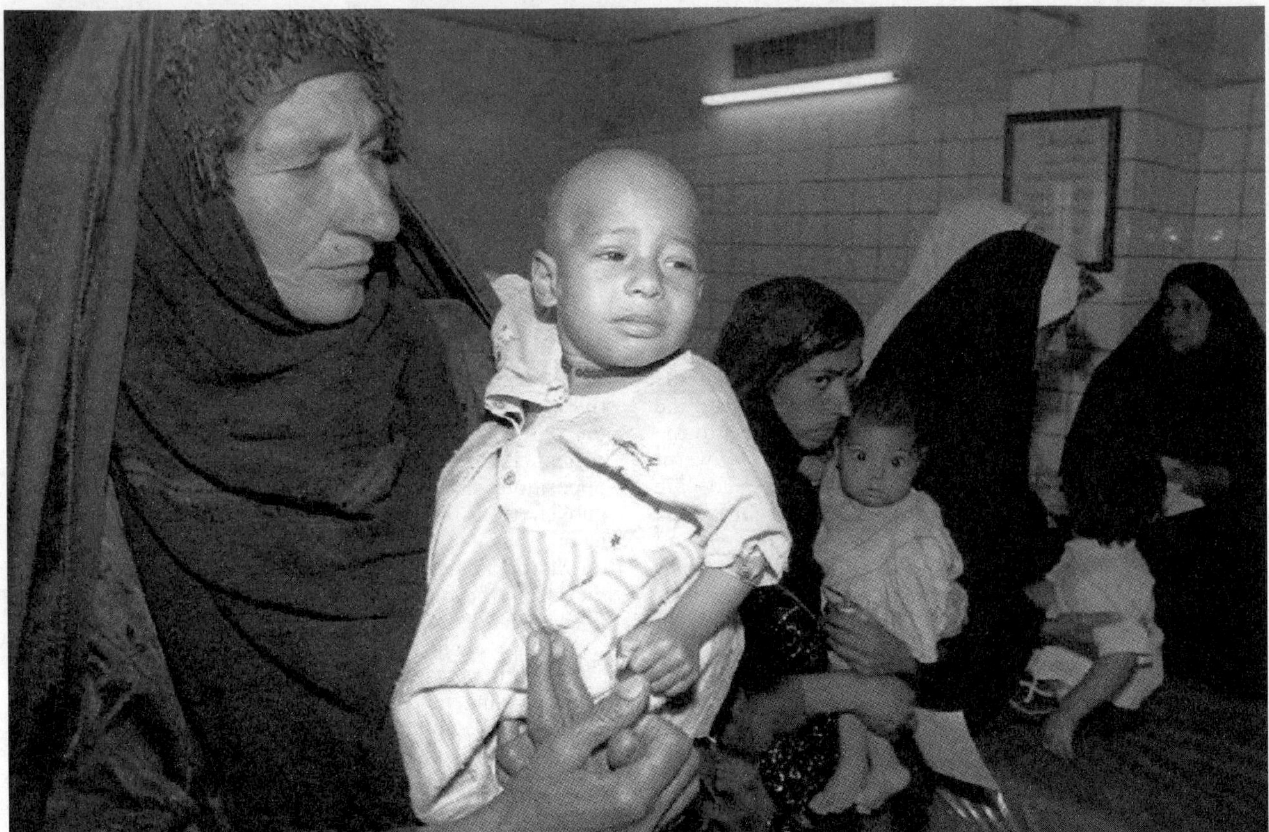

Iraqi mothers wait with their children, suffering from leukemia, in the hope of being able to get medicine and treatment at a Baghdad hospital. UN economic sanctions against Iraq, in force since 1990, continued to produce shortages and to make life difficult for many Iraqis.
AFP

ceipts in the first half of that period meeting the budgetary target. Other economic indicators were less promising. The currency came under great stress, partly as a result of the U.S. trade sanctions, and there was a marked fall in the value of the rial on the black market, which dropped at one stage to 6,000 rials to the U.S. dollar, against the official rate of 1,750 rials, used for the import of essential commodities. (The fixed rate of 3,000 rials was used for all other foreign transactions.) Attempts to ban private-sector dealings in foreign currency and to fix the rial at a stable rate were largely ineffectual and triggered a reshuffle of Pres. Hojatolislam Rafsanjani's Cabinet in August. Inflation rose to 58.8%, according to the central bank, and even higher in practice. Iran's foreign borrowing was at last brought under control but in total stood at more than $30 billion, according to British banking sources. Despite some improvement in exports of non-oil goods to $4 billion a year, the overall foreign exchange position was risky, and the government remained unable to initiate economic recovery for a population increasingly disillusioned with rising prices and deteriorating living standards. (KEITH S. MCLACHLAN)

IRAQ

A republic of southwestern Asia, Iraq has a short coastline on the Persian Gulf. Area: 435,052 sq km (167,975 sq mi). Pop. (1995 est.): 20,413,000. Cap.: Baghdad. Monetary unit: Iraqi dinar, with (Oct. 12, 1995) a black-market rate of 2,600 dinars to U.S. $1 (4,095 dinars = £1 sterling). President and prime minister in 1995, Saddam Hussein.

UN sanctions continued to take a heavy toll on the Iraqi people in 1995. Agricultural production suffered, despite an increase in the purchase price of agricultural commodities. Sporadic food shortages were reported, and the ration allotment for the population was lowered. The government raised interest rates and introduced another bond issue in an attempt to reduce soaring inflation, estimated at a rate of 250% a year. The World Health Organization reported that health care and water-treatment systems had collapsed, with some resulting spread of disease.

On May 17 a violent rebellion against the regime by the Sunni Muslim tribes of Dulaim took place in and around the city of ar-Ramadi. Sparked by the execution of a Dulaimi air force general for conspiracy, the unsuccessful revolt left thousands killed, wounded, or imprisoned. It was the first time that important elements in the country's Sunni centre, considered the regime's strongest base of support, had challenged the Baghdad government in such a direct and bloody way.

Relations with Iran improved, but a number of issues stood in the way of better ties. Iraq claimed that Iran held several thousand Iraqi prisoners of war, while Iran was dissatisfied with the refuge Iraq gave to a major group opposing the regime in Tehran.

In March some 35,000 Turkish army units with heavy armaments and air support crossed the Iraqi border and penetrated deep into northern Iraq. Their objective was to halt attacks across the frontier by the Kurdish Workers' Party (PKK) from their bases inside northern Iraq. The Turks subsequently declared the operation a success and withdrew their forces, but some attacks continued.

Fighting continued between Kurdish factions in northern Iraq in a zone uncontrolled by the Baghdad government but under air protection by U.S., U.K., and French forces under UN mandate. The two main Kurdish parties, the Kurdish Democratic Party and the Patriotic Union of Kurdistan, feuded over leadership in the north and control over land and customs revenues collected from truck traffic passing from Turkey through northern Iraq to Baghdad or Iran. The U.S., attempting to mediate the dispute, met twice in Ireland with representatives of the parties, Turkish representatives, and the Iraq National Congress, an umbrella opposition group to which the Kurdish parties belonged. On August 11 the parties reached an agreement to share the revenues and to reconvene the previously elected Kurdish congress. Fresh fighting was reported between the two parties after that. A second meeting on September 12–15 ended without any additional progress.

On August 8 Jordan announced that two of Saddam Hussein's sons-in-law and their wives had been granted political asylum in Amman. The defection of Lieut. Gen. Hussein Kamel Hasan al-Majid was a particularly serious blow to the regime. Kamel had been minister of industry and minerals, head of the military industrial organization, and the man responsible for the development of Iraq's chemical, biological, and nuclear weapons program. Baghdad tried to deflect the damage by accusing Kamel of being a CIA agent, responsible for withholding sensitive information on these programs from the UN. Kamel's defection prompted Baghdad to invite Rolf Ekeus, head of the UN Special Commission (Unscom), to Baghdad, where he was given a huge cache of documents supposedly hidden by Kamel. Ekeus announced it would take months to study the documents, which might delay the time when Unscom could declare Iraq in compliance with UN resolutions.

The defections gave rise to a flurry of intense diplomatic activity. King Hussein of Jordan distanced himself from Saddam Hussein, and both Kuwait and Saudi Arabia, encouraged by the U.S., made some efforts to mend ties with Jordan, broken when that country sympathized with Iraq during the Persian Gulf War.

On October 15 Saddam Hussein held a national referendum in which he was confirmed as president for seven more years with 99.96% of the vote. There were reports late in the year that Iraqi troops were massing on the Kuwaiti border.

(LOUAY BAHRI)

IRELAND

The republic of Ireland, separated from Great Britain by the North Channel, the Irish Sea, and St. George's Channel, shares its island with Northern Ireland to the northeast. Area: 70,285 sq km (27,137 sq mi). Pop. (1995 est.): 3,590,000. Cap.: Dublin. Monetary unit: Irish pound (punt), with (Oct. 6, 1995) a free rate of £Ir 0.62 to U.S. $1 (£Ir 0.98 = £1 sterling). President in 1995, Mary Robinson; prime minister, John Bruton.

Despite gloomy predictions at the beginning of the year, Ireland enjoyed political and economic stability in 1995 as the three-party coalition government, consisting of Fine Gael, Labour, and Democratic Left, held together well. The budget, introduced in February, benefited employers, small firms, and low-paid workers and set the rate of economic growth at 5.25%. In June the minister for finance announced that public service recruitment was to be severely curtailed in order to hold spending growth below the 2% ceiling. This decision was reinforced by better-than-expected Exchequer figures for the third quarter of the year, indicating that the government was on course to stay below its borrowing target and improve the outlook for the 1996 budget. Forecasts made at the beginning of the year that an investment boom, helped by the impending European recovery, would increase employment by more than 100,000 over the next five years were not borne out by end-of-year figures, which showed unemployment largely unchanged at 279,100.

It was feared that the new government, under the leadership of Prime Minister John Bruton, would not sustain the Northern Ireland peace process. His political views were markedly different from those of his predecessor, Albert Reynolds; Bruton was more sympathetic to the Unionists (those favouring the continued unification of Northern Ireland and Great Britain). He established an excellent working relationship with the British prime minister, John Major, but also maintained and strengthened ties with John Hume and Gerry Adams, leaders in Northern Ireland of the movement to reunify with Ireland.

Bruton also showed foresight in canceling a late summer summit meeting with Major because, in his judgment, there was an unbridgeable gap between the expectations by Republicans (those advocating the union of Northern Ireland with Ireland) of early all-party talks and the Unionist opposition to all-party talks without the decommissioning of arms by paramilitary organizations (chiefly the Irish Republican Army). The continuing difficulties of the peace process revolved around the issue of decommissioning arms as a precondition of such talks. The visit of U.S. Pres. Bill Clinton in late November and early December acted as an incentive for all parties to find a formula that would resolve the arms issue. But progress was slow and difficult, and few expected the pace to quicken dramatically, in spite of the optimism generated by the president's visit.

The benefits of the peace were real enough, however. They were felt in many areas, especially tourism. During his historic official visit to Dublin in late May and early June, Prince Charles emphasized the need to enforce the links and friendships between Britain and Ireland. His visit marked a step forward in Anglo-Irish relations, and its success prompted hopes for an official visit by Queen Elizabeth II in the near future. Opposition to Prince Charles was limited to a small and peaceful demonstration in the city centre.

During the year the Roman Catholic Church was rocked by several serious allegations of sexual abuse of children by priests. It was revealed that in more than one case, large sums of money had been paid to the alleged victim by the abuser. In one case in the Dublin diocese, there was a cover-up of both the abuse and the fact that money had been lent to the priest to pay off his victim. The archbishop, Desmond Connell, in a public broadcast, explained that he had taken the money from diocesan funds to lend to the priest. This caused widespread dismay and outrage. It also prompted calls for priests who were alleged sexual abusers to be reported to the police in the same way as were members of the public and not to be dealt with by church authorities, as had been the case in the past.

In May the Supreme Court ruled that controversial legislation allowing physicians and clinics to provide women with the names and addresses of foreign abortion clinics was constitutional. This was a major victory for the government and a severe blow to the antiabortion groups, which had mounted a strong campaign against it. It also strengthened the government's hand as it prepared for the Referendum on Divorce on November 24. Requiring an amendment to the constitution, it would allow for divorce if the spouses had lived apart for a period of four years and if there was no reasonable prospect of a reconciliation. The referendum was passed by a majority of 50.28% to 49.72%. Antidivorce groups subsequently threatened to initiate a court challenge of the referendum's constitutionality.

The 1995 Nobel Prize for Literature was awarded to the Irish poet Seamus Heaney. (*See* NOBEL PRIZES.)

(MAVIS ARNOLD)

See also *United Kingdom.*

ISRAEL

A republic of southwestern Asia, Israel is situated on the Mediterranean Sea. Area: 20,400 sq km (7,876 sq mi), not including territory occupied in the June 1967 war. Pop. (1995 est.): 5,385,000. Cap.: Jerusalem (but *see* Israel table in *World Data* section). Monetary unit: New (Israeli) sheqel, with (Oct. 6, 1995) a free rate of 3.01 sheqalim to U.S. $1 (4.76 sheqalim = £1 sterling). President in 1995, Ezer Weizman; prime ministers, Yitzhak Rabin and, from November 4 (acting), Shimon Peres.

The year 1995 saw great strides in peacemaking overshadowed by the most radical act of political violence in Israel's history. The assassination of Prime Minister Yitzhak Rabin (*see* OBITUARIES) by a Jewish religious fanatic on November 4 shocked the nation to the core and made a mockery of the widely believed axiom that a Jew would never kill another Jew over politics. The confessed assassin, 25-year-old Yigal Amir, shot the prime minister as he walked to his car after a peace rally in Tel Aviv. Amir said his motive was to destroy a peace process that violated religious law. Extremist rabbis had reportedly ruled that the prime minister deserved to die because the Israeli-Palestinian accords entailed giving up parts of the sacred land of Israel and allegedly put Jewish lives at risk. Within days a state commission of inquiry was set up to look into the security lapse that enabled the killer to get within centimetres of his target. Several leading members of Israel's much-vaunted General Security Service, the Shin Bet, resigned.

The assassination followed months of religious and right-wing incitement against Rabin and his peace policies and reflected a deep divide within Israeli society. The immediate effect was a closing of ranks and a moderation of the tone of political debate. Tensions persisted, however, as the left accused the right of having helped create a climate of violence and the right charged that the left was using the assassination for political gain.

The assassination was followed by a spontaneous outpouring of grief as over a million Israelis filed past the slain prime minister's coffin. The funeral was attended by world leaders from over 80 countries, including Pres. Hosni Mubarak of Egypt, King Hussein of Jordan, and representatives from four other Arab states. For days tens of thousands of young Israelis gathered at the graveside, outside the family home, and in the square where the prime minister was killed, lighting candles in his memory and singing peace songs.

Rabin's partner in peacemaking, Foreign Minister Shimon Peres, took over as acting prime minister and pledged to do all he could to accelerate the peace process. Differences of emphasis and style quickly emerged, most importantly in the negotiations with Syria. Where Rabin had insisted on focusing on security arrangements for the strategic Golan Heights after an Israeli withdrawal, Peres proposed tackling all outstanding problems simultaneously.

The security focus had spawned a Washington meeting on June 27–29 between the Israeli and Syrian army chiefs of staff, which ended in deadlock over Israel's insistence on a land-based early warning system on the Golan. Syrian

AD VAN DENDEREN

Palestinian labourers from the Gaza Strip pass a checkpoint on their way to work in Israel. Because of suicide bombings, the Israeli government dramatically reduced the number of Palestinians allowed to work in Israel, which increased the already high rate of unemployment in Gaza.

Pres. Hafez al-Assad refused to renew the talks until Israel withdrew its demand.

The assassination changed fundamental attitudes and seemed to convince the Syrians of the genuineness of Israel's peacemaking overtures. Peres proposed a "grand peace" based on Israeli withdrawal from the Golan Heights in return for full normalization of relations with Syria and the rest of the Arab world. On December 11 Peres spelled out his new ideas at a summit with U.S. Pres. Bill Clinton. After receiving a positive response from Assad, Clinton pledged intensified U.S. involvement in the peacemaking process.

The major breakthrough in 1995 was with the Palestinians. On September 28, two years and two weeks after their historic handshake on the White House lawn, Rabin and Palestine Liberation Organization leader Yasir Arafat signed an agreement to extend Palestinian self-rule from the Gaza Strip and Jericho to the rest of the West Bank.

This second interim agreement provided for Israeli withdrawal from seven West Bank towns, prepared the way for Palestinian elections, and set in motion the machinery for ending Israel's 28-year-long military occupation. Negotiations were extremely complex because of the need to guarantee the security of roughly 140,000 Jewish settlers in the areas being handed over to Palestinian control. The solution was to divide the territory into three categories—towns under Palestinian control, villages under joint control, and Jewish settlements and all other territory under Israeli control—and to build a system of roads enabling Jewish settlers to bypass major Palestinian population centres.

The accord took well over a year to negotiate and was finalized only on September 24 after an intensive week-long session between Peres and Arafat at Taba, Egypt. On October 6 the Israeli Knesset (parliament) approved the agreement 61–59. Implementation began almost immediately with the handover of the civil administration building in Salfit and the release of about 900 Palestinian prisoners on October 10. In November the Israeli army withdrew from Janin and then in December from Tulkarm, Nabulus, Qalqilyah, Ram Allah, and Bethlehem. Hebron was due to be evacuated in March 1996.

The interim agreement was made possible by the deferment of negotiations on the sensitive issues of final borders, Palestinian refugees, Jewish settlements, and Jerusalem. "Final status" talks were scheduled to begin in May 1996.

On April 27 the Israeli government approved the expropriation of about 53 ha (130 ac) of mainly Arab land in Jerusalem. The Palestinians complained to the Arab League and the UN, where the U.S. found itself having to veto a Security Council resolution against Israel. On May 22, its survival threatened by a no-confidence motion introduced by two mainly Arab left-wing parties and somewhat idiosyncratically supported by the right-wing opposition, the Israeli government suspended its expropriation plans.

In October the U.S. Congress endorsed Israel's position on Jerusalem as its capital and passed a bill obligating the administration to move the U.S. embassy from Tel Aviv to Jerusalem by May 1999, the target date for completion of final status negotiations with the Palestinians.

In 1995 Israel and Jordan built on the peace treaty they had signed the previous October. Over 80,000 Israeli tourists visited Jordan, and significant steps were taken to solve the common water shortage. On June 5 King Hussein, Rabin, and German Chancellor Helmut Kohl met on the border at Naharayim, Israel, to expedite plans for dams, desalination plants, and new water pipelines the Germans had agreed to help finance. In December, after a Peres-Hussein summit in Amman, Jordan, it was announced that Israel would upgrade Jordanian frontline F-16 fighter planes.

As Israel and Jordan moved closer, Israel and Egypt embarked on a subtle competition for regional hegemony, clashing over the Nuclear Non-proliferation Treaty (NPT), due for renewal in April. Mubarak persistently criticized Israel's undeclared and unmonitored nuclear potential and threatened to block ratification of the NPT unless Israel signed. Israel argued it would do so only after reaching bilateral agreements on nuclear arms limitation with all Middle Eastern countries. Under intense U.S. pressure, the Egyptians backed down, and the treaty was renewed for an indefinite period without Israel's signing.

Israel demonstrated further military potential when it launched its first spy satellite, Ofek 3, on April 5. Apart from the contribution to intelligence gathering, the launch indicated a high level of ground-to-ground missile technology. In a dramatic accentuation of shifting regional and global relations, Israel and Russia established low-level military ties. December saw the first visit to Israel by a Russian defense minister and the signing of a military memorandum of understanding.

Throughout the year military clashes between Israeli forces and the Iranian-backed Hezbollah Islamic fundamentalists in southern Lebanon were an almost daily occurrence. On several occasions the Hezbollah responded to Israeli military pressure by firing rockets at civilians across the border in northern Israel. An attack in late November stopped abruptly after the U.S. urged Syria to rein the Hezbollah in, which indicated that in the context of a peace agreement with Syria and Lebanon, the Syrians would be able to guarantee quiet on Israel's northern border.

Inside Israel and the occupied territories, the fundamentalist Hamas and Islamic Jihad kept up a campaign of terror designed to torpedo the peace process with the Palestinians. Suicide bombings at Bayt Lid in January, Kefar Darom and Netzarim in April, Ramat Gan in July, and Jerusalem in August claimed 40 lives and fueled Israeli opposition arguments and demonstrations.

To stop would-be bombers, Rabin imposed periodic closures on Gaza and the West Bank, denying thousands of Palestinian workers access to their jobs in Israel. But where previously the Palestinians had tended to blame Israel for the economic hardship caused by the closures, they began to blame the bombers, and the radicals lost ground. The Islamic Jihad suffered a further setback when its Damascus-based leader, Fathi Shiqaqi, was assassinated in Malta on October 26.

The peace process and the continuing immigration from Russia and the former Soviet republics had a major impact on the economy, which grew for a second successive year by nearly 7%. Business production was up by 8%, personal spending rose by 4%, and inflation was down from 14.5% to about 8.5%. The major economic problem the country faced was a spiraling trade deficit, up to $10 billion and nearly double the figure four years earlier. Most of that deficit was in trade with Europe, expected to grow both ways after Israel became an associate member of the European Union in mid-November. In June the government allocated $560 million for a new terminal at Ben-Gurion International Airport. The construction was part of a $1.9 billion package for developing trade infrastructure and transforming Israel into a major axis for regional trade and transportation.

In late October Israel and nearly all the other Middle Eastern countries convened in Amman for a follow-up to the 1994 economic conference in Casablanca, Morocco. It was decided to set up a Middle East investment bank in Cairo, and Israel concluded a major natural gas deal with Qatar. (LESLIE D. SUSSER)

ITALY

A republic of southern Europe, Italy occupies the Apennine Peninsula, Sicily, Sardinia, and a number of smaller islands in the Mediterranean Sea. Area: 301,309 sq km (116,336 sq mi). Pop. (1995 est.): 57,386,000. Cap.: Rome. Monetary unit: Italian lira, with (Oct. 6, 1995) a free rate of 1,617 lire to U.S. $1 (2,557 lire = £1 sterling). President in 1995, Oscar Luigi Scalfaro; prime ministers, Silvio Berlusconi and, from January 17, Lamberto Dini.

Three well-known former prime ministers were called upon to answer to alleged criminal offenses in Italy in 1995, a year in which the country was ruled by an unelected government. Scandal also left its mark during the year.

One of the accused was Silvio Berlusconi, business tycoon and Italy's biggest media magnate, who resigned as prime minister in December 1994 after the defection of a coalition partner but stayed on in a caretaker capacity until mid-January. Unable to find a successor able to command a parliamentary majority, Pres. Oscar Luigi Scalfaro swore in a stopgap government of nonpoliticians to replace him. It was led by Lamberto Dini, a former director-general of the Bank of Italy and international economist, of known rightist leanings.

On January 25 Dini presented a compact government of 20 technocrats, not one of whom was an elected deputy. (Neither was Dini.) His team immediately won a parliamentary vote of confidence by 302 votes to 39, mainly thanks to the support of the communist Democratic Party of the Left (PDS) and smaller centre groups. A total of 270 deputies who abstained belonged to Berlusconi's rightist Freedom Alliance, the big winner of the March 1994 national elections. Dini's Cabinet continued to be supported by the losers of those elections throughout the year. Critics branded the curious situation "undemocratic" and accused Dini of being "the president's man."

Hounded by Berlusconi and partners crying for quick new elections, Dini pledged to bow out after the completion of a four-point program: a cure to slim Italy's massive deficit, pension reform, a new regional election system, and measures to ensure fair play during electoral campaigns through the media. Regional elections in April strengthened Dini's hand since his PDS and centrist allies seized 9 of the 15 councils at stake. This led Scalfaro to put off any idea of early elections. Returns from a second round of municipal and provincial elections in May confirmed the shift.

In June a referendum sponsored by Berlusconi's left-wing enemies in the hope of destroying his near monopoly of commercial television in Italy backfired. Some 57% of the voters rejected a proposal to prevent anyone from owning more than one TV channel. (Berlusconi owned three.) More than 55% also vetoed a suggested ban on advertisements during the showing of films on television, while some 56% saw nothing wrong in one advertising agency (such as Berlusconi's) being allowed to sell screen time for three channels. The chastened PDS complained that its opponent had won through manipulating the media he controlled.

Many predicted that the most lasting change engineered by Dini would be his scheme for dismantling Italy's lavish, antiquated pensions system, a generator of debts estimated at $44 billion a year. Pension reform had defied governments for two decades. Worked out in conjunction with the trade unions and adopted by Parliament in August, the revamp was a promised cornerstone of an undertaking to repair Italy's financial credibility abroad. It was due to come into effect gradually by the year 2012. The basic idea was to abolish pensions as state handouts tagged to wage levels and replace them with funds built up through individual contributions. Leaders of industry criticized the extended time frame as ineffectual. They thought the same of the draft of Dini's budget unveiled in September, which aimed at cutting the public-sector deficit through spending cuts and by raising extra revenue, partly through yet another clampdown on rampant tax evasion.

Spectacular moves by the judiciary began in July when judges in Milan issued an international arrest warrant for Bettino Craxi, a former Socialist prime minister living stylishly in self-imposed exile in Tunisia and already declared a fugitive from justice. The warrant was issued by a court trying Craxi and others for having taken bribes during work on Milan's underground railway, one of a score of corruption charges laid against him. Other warrants followed, but Craxi's lawyers argued he was a political refugee and thus protected under the extradition treaty between Italy and Tunisia. Tunisia remained silent.

Next, Giulio Andreotti, seven times a Christian Democratic prime minister and a perennial symbol of Italian politics for more than 40 years, was put on trial in Palermo, Sicily, in September, accused of criminal association with the Mafia. The trial was expected to last at least two years, with 90,000 pages of written testimony and some 400 witnesses. The prosecution declared in court it would prove that for 24 years Andreotti had stood by a pact with the Mafia, protecting and abetting its criminal activities and expansion; in return, the Mafia had boosted Andreotti's personal political clout by "arranging" electoral support in Sicily for his own clan within the (later dissolved) Christian Democratic Party. The prosecutors added that they would show that a key go-between used by Andreotti was a former mayor of Palermo, named Salvatore Lima, who was assassinated by the Mafia in 1992. Andreotti stated his innocence, denying the existence of any real evidence against him. He dismissed with contempt most of the testimony as based on the word of unreliable *pentiti,* former Mafia henchmen turned police informers. A much-publicized claim by one of them was that in 1987 he had watched Andreotti at a secret meeting plant a ritual Mafia-style kiss on the cheek of Salvatore ("Toto") Riina, the Mafia boss of bosses, who was arrested in 1993.

OLYMPIA—GAMMA LIAISON

Giulio Andreotti (right), who had been prime minister of Italy seven times, confers with lawyers at his trial in Palermo, Sicily, on charges of criminal association with the Mafia. The trial was the most spectacular development in the effort to rid Italian politics of corruption.

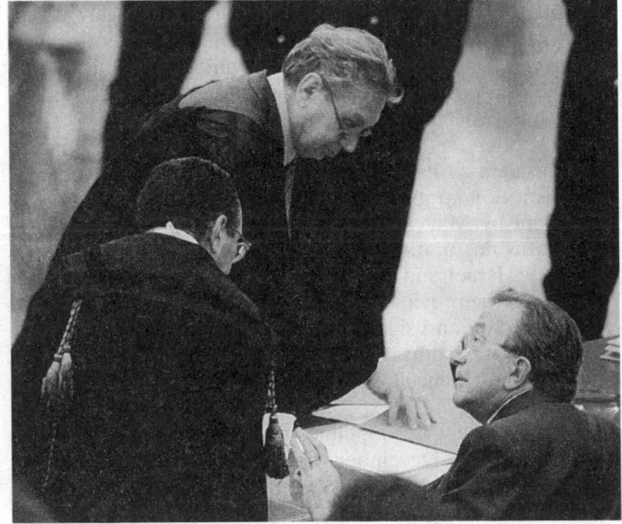

In the state's otherwise lacklustre contest with the Mafia itself in 1995, its main success was the capture on June 24 of Leoluca Bagarella, Riina's successor and brother-in-law. Bagarella was the convicted killer of the chief of the Palermo Flying Squad, Boris Giuliano, in 1979 and the presumed master-executioner of Giovanni Falcone, a pugnacious judge who led a fruitful fight against the Mafia until 1992, when a segment of highway exploded beneath his car. Police were stupefied to discover that Bagarella's hideout was a luxury apartment overlooking the heavily guarded home of two anti-Mafia judges who had helped set the trap that caught him. Picked up soon afterward was Natale D'Emanuele, the alleged financial wizard behind the Mafia in Catania. He was in lucrative control of all local funeral rites, and police said he used hearses and coffins to traffic in arms throughout Italy. Serafino Fama, a lawyer who had defended local Mafia figures, was gunned down in Catania in November.

Judges again snatched headlines in October when they ordered Berlusconi himself to stand trial for corruption, along with his brother Paolo and nine others. The charge, arising from a matter first aired a year previously, was that he tacitly sanctioned bribes of some $2 million to state finance police to buy their indulgence over the bookkeeping of four companies within his huge business conglomerate, Fininvest. Berlusconi claimed he was unaware of the payoffs, already acknowledged by his brother, and wrote off the trial, set for January 1996, as the outcome of a campaign of persecution against him and Fininvest waged by Milanese judges as a political vendetta. The judges firmly rejected Berlusconi's accusations, while the latter vowed that no trial would deter him from fighting to lead the country again.

Berlusconi's indictment came against the murky background of a year marked by repeated investigations into the past conduct of the "pool" of Milan judges who had probed Berlusconi's affairs, the same men who three years previously had launched the resounding Operation Clean Hands anticorruption campaign that brought down the old, post-World War II order in Italy. The judges were grilled by inspectors dispatched by Dini's justice minister, Filippo Mancuso, who in October was stripped of his post by Scalfaro after a Senate vote of no confidence in the minister, moved by the left wing, for undue interference in the judiciary. Berlusconi and his Freedom Alliance retaliated with a vote of no confidence in Dini's government, which survived the challenge on October 26 by a margin of 19 votes (310 to 291), thanks to a pledge by the prime minister that he would resign before year's end. The pledge prompted a group of 24 orthodox communist deputies to withdraw a threat to vote against Dini. In early December Dini successfully argued that his government's mandate should be extended beyond Jan. 1, 1996, when Italy would assume the presidency of the European Union.

By then the Milan judges had come under scrutiny by the Supreme Council of the Magistracy in Rome, and a fellow judge from Brescia, Fabio Salamone, had interrogated the most flamboyant member of the Milan "pool," Antonio Di Pietro, on the circumstances of his unexplained resignation in December 1994. Salamone later warned Cesare Previti, defense minister under Berlusconi, that he and two others were under suspicion for having forced Di Pietro to quit. Most Italians came to believe in an attempt to eliminate the "inconvenient" Milan pool.

Other magistrates examined renewed scandals brought on by the end of summer. First, there was an uproar over a discovery that many prominent political and other figures had paid only token rents for years in spacious housing owned by state or local bodies. A cleanup was ordered, and the PDS leader, Massimo D'Alema, announced a change of address.

Next, it transpired that out of seven million Italians drawing disability pensions, many were doing so illegally. In the Post Office, where the racket first came officially to light, 94 out of 100 employees taken on as "invalids" were found to be healthy. Computer checks on a larger scale quickly brought an army of some 28,000 "invalids" into the sights of the judiciary. Many more were suspected of being in hiding. Main cogs in the fraud included bribed officials or doctors, some of whom participated by resuscitating the medical records of the dead.

In Rome a significant event was the inauguration—after a 21-year delay—of the first mosque in the capital of Christendom, designed by the noted Italian architect Paolo Portoghesi and funded mainly by Saudi Arabia. It became a beacon for an estimated 700,000 Muslims in Italy. By 1995 Muslims constituted the second biggest religious community in the country, after Roman Catholics.

During the year Italy served as the springboard for NATO land-based air operations over Bosnia and Herzegovina, with some 300 planes making sorties from 17 airfields. Italy tardily contributed 14 fighters and 5 transport planes to the effort, which prompted Scalfaro to inquire of military chiefs about the apparently inadequate state of Italy's military readiness. (DEREK WILSON)

JAMAICA

A constitutional monarchy within the Commonwealth, Jamaica occupies an island in the Caribbean Sea. Area: 10,991 sq km (4,244 sq mi). Pop. (1995 est.): 2,520,000. Cap.: Kingston. Monetary unit: Jamaica dollar, with (Oct. 6, 1995) a free rate of J$35.75 to U.S. $1 (J$56.52 = £1 sterling). Queen, Elizabeth II; governor-general in 1995, Howard Cooke; prime minister, Percival J. Patterson.

Prime Minister Percival Patterson began the year by reducing the size of his Cabinet from 17 to 15 members. The changes were designed to strengthen the People's National Party government as it prepared for the next general election. In March former prime minister Edward Seaga, leader of the Jamaica Labour Party (JLP), survived an attempt by party dissidents to have him step down and make way for someone who, they felt, would increase their chance of regaining control of the government. In a special poll Seaga won 78.8% of the votes cast by representatives of JLP party groups. Seaga had said that he would relinquish the party leadership if his support fell below 70%. He had been at the helm of the JLP since 1974.

The two main political parties agreed in principle in August to a new voter-registration system recommended by the Electoral Advisory Committee.

A third political party, the National Democratic Movement, was formed on October 29 by Bruce Golding, who had resigned as JLP chairman in February so that he could align himself with the anti-Seaga forces. Opinion polls suggest that a third party could seriously challenge the JLP in the next election.

In a bid to maintain investor confidence in the country's financial system, one of the fastest-growing sectors of the economy, the government agreed in June to bail out depositors of the failed Blaise Building Society and merchant banking group. Following a slip in the value of the Jamaica dollar to J$41 = U.S. $1 in November, Patterson announced stabilization measures, including intervention by the Bank of Jamaica. (DAVID RENWICK)

This article updates the *Macropædia* article The WEST INDIES: *Jamaica.*

JAPAN

A constitutional monarchy in the northwestern Pacific Ocean, Japan comprises an archipelago with four main islands (Hokkaido, Honshu, Kyushu, and Shikoku), the Ryukyus (including Okinawa), and lesser adjacent islands. Area: 377,800 sq km (145,869 sq mi). Pop. (1995 est.): 125,362,000. Cap.: Tokyo. Monetary unit: yen, with (Oct. 12, 1995) a free rate of 100 yen to U.S. $1 (160 yen = £1 sterling). Emperor, Akihito; prime minister in 1995, Tomiichi Murayama.

In 1995 Japanese confidence was shaken by two disasters, one natural and the other of human origin. The Great Hanshin Earthquake (named after the Kobe-Osaka region) claimed about 6,000 lives and caused extensive damage to buildings and infrastructure. Later the nation was frightened by a series of gas attacks, mounted by a fringe religious sect, on subway and rail lines.

Domestic Affairs. Early on the morning of January 17, an earthquake centred on Awaji Island, 20 km (12.4 mi) southwest of Kobe, devastated the Hanshin region. Highways and rail lines were severely damaged, at least 100,000 buildings were destroyed, and 900,000 homes were without electricity. Early estimates of damage in Hyogo prefecture ranged from $95 billion to $150 billion (about 13–21% of the national budget for fiscal year 1994). The government's slow response to the crisis was widely criticized. On January 23 Prime Minister Tomiichi Murayama acknowledged "shortcomings" in the government's emergency management system.

Within six months after the quake, about 40,000 temporary houses had been built for more than 300,000 homeless people. Reconstruction, expected to take up to four years, continued to dominate budget discussions. Some economists, however, noted that construction work might provide a stimulus to the lagging economy.

Two months after the earthquake, Japanese morale suffered another blow. On March 15 three briefcases containing a strange liquid and small fans were discovered in a Tokyo subway station before the devices could be activated. Five days later, at the height of the morning rush hour, fumes were detected at Tsukiji Station in the centre of Tokyo and in 15 stations on the busy Hibiya, Marunouchi, and Chiyoda subway lines. Twelve passengers were killed and 5,500 sickened, many of whom had to be hospitalized. In June 1994 a similar attack had killed 7 and injured 200 in Matsumoto. Investigation centred on a "new religion," whose members denied involvement. The group called itself Aum Shinrikyo (Supreme Truth) and was officially recognized in 1989. It was founded by Chizuo Matsumoto, who had assumed the name Shoko Asahara (*see* BIOGRAPHIES), a legally blind former yoga instructor and pharmacist. Aum Shinrikyo had an estimated 10,000 followers in Japan and branch chapters abroad.

Within days of the Tokyo gas incidents, more than 2,000 police officers raided Aum offices in Tokyo and its laboratory headquarters at Kamikuishiki, Yamanashi prefecture. They seized numerous canisters of toxic chemicals used to manufacture sarin, the nerve gas that had been identified as the substance used in the subway attacks. Lethal chemical devices were also found in Yokohama rail stations and at Shinjuku, the busiest rail and subway transfer point in Tokyo.

On May 16 Asahara and 16 other cult leaders were arrested in nationwide raids. Although Asahara denied that his sect had been involved in the gas attacks, five followers later confessed to participation in the Matsumoto incident and implicated the sect in the prior abduction and killing of a lawyer who had represented families attempting to recover their children from the cult. Ashara's trial began on October 26, and on December 14, on the basis of an antisubversion law, the government outlawed Aum Shinrikyo.

Public dissatisfaction with established parties became clear on April 9, when local elections were held to choose prefectural governors and assemblies. In assembly elections Murayama's Social Democratic Party of Japan (SDPJ) suffered the most stinging defeat in its history. Yukio Aoshima, an author tied to no party, became governor of Tokyo by defeating the candidate backed by most of the major parties. Fulfilling a campaign promise, he promptly announced cancellation of the World City Expo Tokyo '96, even though the city had already spent $250 million on the project. After comedian "Knock" Yokoyama rode a tidal wave of dissent to score an upset in Osaka, he announced that as governor he would generally use his real name, Isamu Yamada. On May 27 the SDPJ approved plans to disband and reorganize as a "democratic-liberal" group, pledged to support a "mature society."

In an election held in July for half (126) the seats in the (upper) House of Councillors, the socialists absorbed additional losses. They won only 16 seats, giving them, with carryovers, a total of 38. The coalition, however, retained a majority because the LDP held 110 seats and New Party Sakigake controlled 3. The opposition Shinshinto increased its total to 56 seats.

On August 8 Murayama reshuffled the Cabinet to reflect the new balance of power within his coalition. The LDP was given 13 portfolios, the SDPJ 5, and Sakigake 2. No woman was appointed to the Cabinet. A newspaper poll in September indicated that the Cabinet's public approval rating had fallen to a record low of 22%. On September 25 Ryutaro Hashimoto, well known to U.S. trade negotiators, was formally elected president of the LDP. Many expected him to become Japan's next prime minister. At year's end Shinshinto chose Ichiro Ozawa as party leader, a move that seemed likely to be welcomed by Japanese businessmen as well as Japan's foreign partners.

Throughout 1995 the country's leaders agonized over how to mark the 50th anniversary of the end of World War II in the Pacific. They seemed not to know how to respond when victim nations revived memories of the sufferings they endured as a result of Japanese aggression. On April 7 the Cabinet announced the establishment of a private-sector Asian Peace and Friendship Fund for Women. With a government subsidy of $23.5 million, it was designed to express "remorse" to non-Japanese "comfort women," who had been forced to serve as prostitutes for Japan's military during the war.

In May Sakigake threatened to withdraw from the coalition if the LDP continued to oppose a clear apology and a no-war resolution in the Diet. Former prime minister Yasuhiro Nakasone declared that such a statement would be "inappropriate." On June 9 the lower house, with 70 members absent, passed a resolution expressing "deep remorse" for "acts of aggression," particularly in Asia, and pledging adherence to Japan's no-war constitution. The upper house took no action. On August 15 Murayama became the first prime minister to use the word *owabi* (unambiguously, "apology") in a statement made before, and separated from, Emperor Akihito's presiding over the annual memorial to the war dead.

The Economy. In December 1994 the Cabinet had proposed an austere budget of $709.9 billion for fiscal 1995, a reflection of sluggish tax revenues. The sum was 2.9% lower than that of 1994, the first decline in 40 years. Only official development assistance (ODA, up 4% to $11 billion)

Investigators wear gas masks as they sort through chemicals removed from a laboratory maintained by Aum Shinrikyo in Yamanashi prefecture in Japan. The religious cult was charged with having used the nerve gas sarin in attacks in the Tokyo subway on March 20.
KYODO NEWS SERVICE

and defense (up 1% to $47.2 billion) showed increases. On February 27 the House of Representatives approved the budget in record time and added a supplementary $10.2 billion package to expedite restoration in the Hanshin area. The House of Councillors concurred on March 22.

In April the value of the U.S. dollar had fallen to 80.75 yen in Tokyo, the lowest level since modern exchange rates were established. The yen's sharp rise foreshadowed a deepening recession in Japan because its exports would become more costly. On April 14 the government announced that it was taking the "maximum measures possible" to stem the yen's rise. These included an early supplemental budget for fiscal 1995 and increased expenditures on public works. The Diet approved the extra $32 billion budget on May 19, including funds for reconstruction in the quake areas ($16.8 billion) and for additional security ($400 million) in the wake of the rail and subway gas attacks. Meanwhile, the Bank of Japan had cut the official discount rate to a historic low of 1%, but the impact was minimal.

The government announced a further stimulus on June 27, front-loading public works expenditures. Yet another followed on September 20 and provided $142 billion, the largest stimulus package ever. On September 8 the Bank of Japan again lowered the discount rate, to a record low of 0.5%, to prevent further deflationary conditions.

Mindful of the fraud and scandal surrounding the New York branch of Daiwa Bank Ltd. earlier in the year (*see* ECONOMIC AFFAIRS: *Banking*), on December 26 Finance Minister Masayoshi Takemura announced tighter controls on banks. Three days later Kyosuke Shinozawa, Takemura's top deputy and Japan's chief financial officer, resigned in order to draw fire away from his boss and to improve morale in the ministry.

Foreign Affairs. Despite the domestic recession, which had begun in 1991, Japan retained its position as the world's eminent creditor nation. The Ministry of Finance announced that at the end of 1994, net overseas assets (government and business holdings abroad, minus debts) totaled a record $689 billion. A swelling current account surplus, which reached $125 billion in the fiscal year ended March 31, added to the credits. Ryutaro Hahsimoto, head of the Ministry of International Trade and Industry (MITI), outlined a plan to reduce the surplus to 1% of GDP by 1998.

During 1994 Japan had disbursed $13.3 billion in ODA (up 7.2% from 1993 in yen terms). It remained the largest foreign aid provider for the fourth year in a row. China received $1,480,000,000, and in September MITI announced that for fiscal 1996 it would seek $33 million for the Asia-Pacific Economic Cooperation (APEC) forum. APEC, a new grouping of 18 Pacific Basin nations, met in November in Osaka. Although ties with the U.S. remained the core of Japan's foreign policy, Asia had top priority in the realm of aid.

Japan and the U.S. continued to experience friction in trade relations. On January 11 Murayama attended a summit meeting in Washington. His call for a "creative partnership" was countered by Pres. Bill Clinton's emphasis on the need to reduce Japan's trade surplus. He singled out the automobile industry, which, according to the U.S. Department of Commerce, made up 59% of the $62.7 billion American trade deficit with Japan. On May 8 Hashimoto informed Murayama that talks with U.S. trade representative Mickey Kantor had failed. On May 16, when Kantor announced a plan to impose tariffs totaling $5.9 billion on 13 Japanese luxury-car imports, Hashimoto promptly threatened to file complaints with the new World Trade Organization (WTO).

The trade dispute dominated discussion among lobbyists at the Group of Seven summit meeting held in mid-June in Halifax, Nova Scotia, even though the formal meetings took no account of details. Japanese officials appeared satisfied with the outcome. Although they failed to win condemnation of "unilateralism" (their code word for sanctions), the communiqué supported the WTO and opposed "protectionism." Japan and the U.S. reached an 11th-hour agreement on June 28, thereby avoiding the imposition of U.S. tariffs. Clinton immediately claimed victory, predicting that Japan's purchase of auto parts would reach $9 billion in three years. Hashimoto also declared victory because the Japanese government had no responsibility to meet specific numerical targets.

Trade friction with the U.S. also affected aviation. On June 19 the U.S. Department of Transportation threatened sanctions after Tokyo denied requests by Federal Express to carry its cargoes to other Asian airports via Japan. The dispute involved "beyond rights" of both nations. On July 20, after Japan broke off the talks, a last-minute accord was reached.

A different kind of tension arose from the stationing of some 29,000 U.S. military personnel on the island of Okinawa. Local residents were critical of both the U.S. and their own government in Tokyo for agreeing to base 75% of the U.S. forces in Japan on their island, which accounted for only 1% of Japan's land area.

On September 29 three U.S. servicemen were indicted in the prefectural capital of Naha for the abduction and rape of a young Okinawan girl. Gen. Charles C. Krulak, commandant of the U.S. Marine Corps, flew out from Washington to lead a "day of reflection" with troops, and U.S. Secretary of Defense William Perry formally apologized for the incident on November 1. The governor of Okinawa continued to press for revisions to the Status of Forces Agreement governing U.S. servicemen, particularly those off duty, but in late November Murayama pledged to seek renewal of the leases on property for the U.S. bases.

In May Murayama became the first Japanese leader to visit the Marco Polo Bridge (outside Beijing), the site of the 1937 clash that triggered the Sino-Japanese War. On May 3, in a meeting with Chinese Premier Li Peng, Murayama reiterated his remorse over "aggression and colonial rule," which caused "unbearable suffering" in Asia. He urged a more active Chinese role in the U.S.-North Korea talks on nuclear weapons but received no clear answer to a request for Beijing's suspension of its own weapons experiments. Shortly after the visit, China carried out another nuclear test, the 42nd in a series. Japan's foreign minister summoned China's ambassador to protest another test in August. A few days later he called on the U.S., Russia, and Great Britain to continue their moratorium on nuclear trials, even though the Chinese and French were determined to test nuclear devices. On August 29 Tokyo cut grants to China from $80.4 million in fiscal 1994 to $5.2 million in 1995. Loans and humanitarian aid, however, would be continued. The Chinese Foreign Ministry promptly responded by reviving demands for war reparations, which they had renounced in the normalization declaration of 1972.

During the year, remarks by officials in Tokyo damaged Japan's image in both Koreas. On June 3 former foreign minister Michio Watanabe declared that Korea had "harmoniously" become a Japanese colony by accepting the 1910 treaty. South Korean Prime Minister Lee Hong Koo promptly protested. Koreans were of one mind that their country was subjugated by superior military force. Japan had relinquished control over Korea at the end of World War II, and the Tokyo-Seoul normalization agreement of 1965 had invalidated the 1910 treaty. Watanabe retracted his statement a few months before his death on September 15. (*See* OBITUARIES.) On October 5, however, Murayama elaborated on the theme. When he stated in the Diet that the 1910 treaty had been signed in a "legally valid" way, he was bitterly criticized in both North and South Korea. Cabinet minister Takami Eto resigned on November 13 for a similarly ill-considered remark he had made.

Meanwhile, North Korea continued to be the only Asian country without formal ties to Japan. On March 30 in Pyongyang, a delegation representing Japan's governing coalition parties and leaders of the Korean Workers' Party signed a document calling for resumption of normalization talks. On May 29 Japan pledged aid in the form of rice shipments, so long as the dialogue between the two sides continued. On April 17 Do Muoi, general secretary of Vietnam's Communist Party, arrived in Tokyo, where he received pledges of a $700 million loan and a $36 million grant.

A peace treaty with Russia still awaited settlement of the persistent Kuril Islands territorial dispute. In a two-day meeting in Tokyo in March, the foreign ministers of the two countries discussed but did not resolve the issue. Significantly, Japan's relations with the new state of Ukraine were more fruitful. On March 23 in Tokyo, Murayama greeted Pres. Leonid Kuchma and pledged $200 million to help Ukraine develop a market-oriented economy.

(ARDATH W. BURKS)

PHILLIP JONES GRIFFITHS—MAGNUM

Citizens of Hiroshima burn incense in Peace Memorial Park as part of their commemoration of the dropping of the atomic bomb on Aug. 6, 1945. Ceremonies in the Japanese city and elsewhere in many nations in 1995 helped mark the 50th anniversary of the end of World War II.

JORDAN

A constitutional monarchy, Jordan is located in southwestern Asia and has a short coastline on the Gulf of Aqaba. Area: 89,-246 sq km (34,458 sq mi). Pop. (1995 est.): 4,187,000 (including Palestinian refugees estimated to number nearly 1.2 million). Cap.: Amman. Monetary unit: Jordan dinar, with (Oct. 6, 1995) an official rate of 0.70 dinar to U.S. $1 (1.11 dinars = £1 sterling). King, Hussein I; prime ministers in 1995, ʿAbd as-Salam al-Majali and, from January 8, Sharif Zaid ibn Shaker.

Jordan faced a year of critical adjustment in 1995. In the wake of its peace agreement with Israel in October 1994, Amman resumed its former warm relationship with the U.S. and restored ambassadorial ties with Saudi Arabia after four years of alienation. There was a rapprochement with Qatar, and even relations with Kuwait were thawing. On the other hand, Jordan distanced itself from Iraq; in August King Hussein granted asylum to two top-level Iraqi defectors, both sons-in-law of Iraqi Pres. Saddam Hussein, and their wives and children. At the end of November, King Hussein's envoy met with Sunni, Shiʿite, and Kurdish Iraqi opposition leaders in London and urged them to form a united front. Despite a controversy at the end of 1994 over the proposed Jordanian guardianship of Islamic holy places in Jerusalem, Jordan and the Palestine National Authority signed a formal cooperation agreement in January. On November 6 King Hussein arrived in Jerusalem for the first time since the city came under Israeli control in 1967 in order to deliver a personal eulogy at the funeral of slain Israeli Prime Minister Yitzhak Rabin (*see* OBITUARIES), with whom he reportedly had shared a longtime private friendship.

The Jordanian public was disoriented by the abruptness with which the peace agreement had come about and was disappointed as few of the expected economic benefits of the treaty materialized quickly. The Islamic movement (the single strongest bloc in the parliament) opposed the peace treaty, and the government resorted to allegedly high-handed tactics in securing the parliament's endorsement of the agreement and of subsequent economic cooperation accords with Israel, which were perceived to be unilaterally concessionary on Jordan's part. The newly formed Cabinet of Prime Minister Sharif Zaid ibn Shaker, who was recalled to office in January, lost its liberal credentials after the banning in May of an opposition conference organized by the Islamic Action Front, which prompted the resignation of one Cabinet minister. The electoral strength of the Islamists appeared to weaken in nationwide municipal elections in July, and in December, Leith Shubailat, a maverick Islamist and vocal critic of the peace accord, was arrested.

The government proceeded cautiously with plans for privatization, tax reform, foreign debt reduction, lower tariffs, and increased foreign investment. Gross domestic product in 1995 was estimated at 4.5 billion dinars, reflecting a 6% growth rate. Inflation was under control as a result of tight monetary and fiscal policy. Merchandise exports rose an estimated 12.3% to $1.6 billion, but the trade gap was set to expand to $2.1 billion, and the current account deficit was expected to rise to $560 million.

The Middle East and North Africa Economic Summit was held in Amman at the end of October. Jordan's main goals for the conference were to secure financing for a variety of industrial, tourist, telecommunications, and transport projects. Perhaps the most important achievement of the conference, however, was the declaration of intent to establish a Bank for Economic Co-operation and Development in the Middle East and North Africa.

(JENAB TUTUNJI)

Palestinian children, part of a group expelled from Libya, wait on a bus in Jordan for permission to travel to the Gaza Strip. The expulsion of Palestinians by Libyan leader Muammar al-Qaddafi was seen as a reaction to Arab-Israeli agreements in the Middle East.
AFP

KAZAKHSTAN

A republic of Central Asia, Kazakhstan borders Russia on the west and north, China on the east, Kyrgyzstan on the southeast, Uzbekistan and the Aral Sea on the south, and Turkmenistan and the Caspian Sea on the southwest. Area: 2,717,300 sq km (1,049,200 sq mi). Pop. (1995 est.): 16,669,000. Cap.: Almaty (formerly Alma-Ata); capital-designate: Aqmola (formerly Tselinograd). Monetary unit: tenge, with (Oct. 6, 1995) a free rate of 61.37 tenge = U.S. $1 (97.01 tenge = £1 sterling). President in 1995, Nursultan Nazarbayev; prime minister, Akezhan Kazhegeldin.

In 1995 Kazakhstan took major steps in the direction of authoritarianism that disappointed those who hoped Western-style democracy and a civil society would develop in the largest country in Central Asia. Foreign investors still saw Kazakhstan as one of the most promising areas in the Commonwealth of Independent States, largely on the strength of its rich endowment of natural resources and the government's commitment to rapid introduction of a market economy. The government was reportedly considering selling a stake in the development of the Tengiz oil field to the Mobil Corp., and in November the huge state-owned Karmet steelworks was sold to a British-based company, Ispat International.

The country's first constitutional crisis began in March when Kazakhstan's Constitutional Court declared the 1994 parliamentary elections illegal. The parliament was forced to resign, and Pres. Nursultan Nazarbayev announced that he would rule by decree until new elections could be held. Shortly after the dissolution of the parliament, a consultative Assembly of the Peoples of Kazakhstan that had been handpicked by the president called for a nationwide referendum on the extension of Nazarbayev's term in office to the end of December 2000. Some critics saw this as an attempt by Nazarbayev to avoid standing for reelection in 1996 and facing possible defeat at the hands of citizens angered over the effects his economic reforms had on their standard of living. Others attributed it to the president's already-demonstrated taste for running the country without interference.

Official results of the referendum that was held on April 29 indicated near-unanimous support for the extension of Nazarbayev's term. Two months later he introduced a draft constitution that would greatly expand the powers of the president. It was immediately attacked by the Constitutional Court, the trade unions, and various opposition groups as being undemocratic and inimical to the creation of a civil society. Leaders of Kazakhstan's large Russian community asserted that Nazarbayev's proposed constitution gave unfair advantages to ethnic Kazakhs. In late December Nazarbayev decreed that he had the right on his own initiative to remove any minister or replace the entire government.

The leadership's response was to revise the draft, abolishing the Constitutional Court, which had earned a solid reputation for its commitment to establishing the rule of law. Among the first decrees issued by the president after the dissolution of the parliament was a restriction on demonstrations and rallies. Nazarbayev defended his growing authoritarianism by citing the need to counter the increase in criminality that had accompanied the advent of a market economy. Nazarbayev likened his rule to that of former French president Charles de Gaulle, arguing that greater presidential powers would be the key to a democratic society. Despite the protests, 89% of those who voted in the August 30 referendum approved the new constitution. Elections for a new Senate were held on December 5, and a second round of voting for the lower house took place on December 23. (BESS BROWN)

This article updates the *Macropædia* article CENTRAL ASIA: *Kazakhstan.*

KENYA

A republic and member of the Commonwealth, Kenya is in eastern Africa, on the Indian Ocean. Area: 582,646 sq km (224,961 sq mi), including 11,230 sq km of inland water. Pop. (1995 est.): 28,626,000. Cap.: Nairobi. Monetary unit: Kenya shilling, with (Oct. 6, 1995) a free rate of 55.58 shillings to U.S. $1 (87.86 shillings = £1 sterling). President in 1995, Daniel arap Moi.

The government faced 1995 with cautious optimism after donor countries, meeting on Dec. 8, 1994, had praised its economic reforms, its introduction of multiparty democracy, and its promotion of human rights. A promise of financial assistance amounting to $800 million demonstrated their goodwill. Pres. Daniel arap Moi's new year address echoed this progressive note with the announcement that he would invite experts from the West to help him in assessing the views of the people regarding a new constitution. The Finance Ministry also declared that the sale of the government's share in a number of unprofitable companies was among its main priorities. At the same time, the Nairobi stock exchange was opened to foreign investors for the first time in 30 years. The chief executives of the railway corporations of Kenya, Tanzania, and Uganda further announced that in pursuance of the agreements reached at a meeting of the heads of state of their three countries in Kampala, Uganda, in 1994, they would adopt common fares and harmonize staff training.

The optimism generated by these policies soon began to fade. Foreign investors did not pour their money into the country, because they were permitted to invest only in Kenyan-owned companies and even there only to a maximum of 20% of share capital. Tribal clashes again threatened the peace of the country after 2,000 Kikuyu farmers were forcibly relocated from the Rift Valley at the end of 1994, and in January scores of people were injured when police broke up a meeting to mark the first anniversary of the death of the longtime critic of the government Oginga Odinga. Riots broke out between Nubian and Luo tribesmen in Kibera, a large Nairobi slum, in October. There was loud protest, too, in March when the public accounts committee announced the result of its inquiries into the scandal surrounding the payment by the government of vast sums of compensation to a jewelry export company to encourage what had proved to be nonexistent exports. Far from owing money to the government, they had concluded, the company's owner was actually owed 2.1 billion shillings in arrears of compensation. As a result, the chairman of the committee, Kijana Wamalwa, leader of the Forum for Restoration of Democracy-Kenya opposition party, found his party deeply divided and himself challenged for the leadership by Raila Odinga, son of Oginga Odinga, who had undertaken private suits against some of those he believed responsible for the scandal. Would-be foreign importers were also disturbed by a six-month ban imposed on imported cereals that were deemed to threaten home production.

Street children meet to sniff glue in a park in downtown Nairobi, capital of Kenya. It was estimated that as many as 50,000 children lived on the streets of the capital city, only one of the serious economic and social problems faced by the African nation.

AFP

Dismayed by what they saw as a resurgence of corruption and human rights abuse and a reluctance on the part of the government to implement promised economic reforms, donor countries called an emergency meeting for July 24. In an attempt to calm their fears, the finance minister, Musalia Mudavadi, published conciliatory proposals in his budget on June 15. They included the immediate rescinding of the ban on foreign cereal imports, the raising of the ceiling on the purchase of shares by foreign investors to 40%, the privatization of Kenya Airways by the end of the year, and the targeting of other important companies for privatization in the near future. His efforts proved successful. The donor countries commended his endeavour to stabilize the economy. They were less pleased by reports of delays in the implementation of multiparty government, reflected in President Moi's attacks upon Richard Leakey for trying to set up a new opposition party. These events, together with Amnesty International's attack upon the government's recent human rights record, delivered on the eve of the donors meeting, led the donor countries to express their particular concern.

The government did not relish these criticisms, regarding them as an unwarranted intrusion into the affairs of a sovereign state. The adverse comments of a British minister, Baroness Chalker, during a visit to Kenya in July brought a brusque rejoinder from the Kenyan authorities. (KENNETH INGHAM)

This article updates the *Macropædia* article EASTERN AFRICA: *Kenya.*

KIRIBATI

A republic in the western Pacific Ocean and member of the Commonwealth, Kiribati comprises the Gilbert Islands, Banaba (Ocean Island), the Line Islands, and the Phoenix Islands. Area: 811 sq km (313 sq mi). Pop. (1995 est.): 80,400. Cap.: Bairiki, on Tarawa. Monetary unit: Australian dollar, with (Oct. 6, 1995) a free rate of $A 1.31 to U.S. $1 ($A 2.08 = £1 sterling). President (*beretitenti*) in 1995, Teburoro Tito.

In 1995 Pres. Teburoro Tito's new administration committed itself to the abolition of school fees for junior-high-school students, a significant increase in the price paid to producers for copra, and a substantial raise in public-sector salaries. Tito also rejected the privatization policies of his predecessors. The new government faced a constitutional crisis when the performance of the chief justice was publicly criticized and he was suspended from office by the president. Further court action saw the issue resolved, and the chief justice resigned.

In March the leaders of a subregional grouping comprising Kiribati, the Marshall Islands, Nauru, and Tuvalu met for the first time to consider matters of common concern—especially the expansion of a regional air service, cooperation over fisheries, and the marketing of copra. Tito indicated that Kiribati wanted a larger share and higher returns from the tuna treaty between the U.S. and South Pacific countries. His government expressed concern to Japan over the shipment of plutonium through the region and severed diplomatic relations with France over the resumption of nuclear testing. (BARRIE MACDONALD)

This article updates the *Macropædia* article PACIFIC ISLANDS: *Kiribati*.

KOREA, DEMOCRATIC PEOPLE'S REPUBLIC OF

A socialist republic of northeastern Asia on the northern half of the peninsula of Korea, the Democratic People's Republic of Korea (North Korea) borders the Sea of Japan, the Yellow Sea, and the Republic of Korea at roughly the 38th parallel. Area: 122,762 sq km (47,399 sq mi). Pop. (1995 est.): 23,487,000. Cap.: Pyongyang. Monetary unit: won, with (Oct. 6, 1995) a free rate of 2.15 won to U.S. $1 (3.40 won = £1 sterling). President in 1995, Kim Jong Il (designated); chairman of the Council of Ministers (premier), Kang Song San.

Severe flooding aggravated North Korea's food shortages in 1995. Heavy rains and a typhoon during the summer reportedly affected five million people, nearly a quarter of the population. The government made a rare appeal for foreign assistance, asking for food and clothing. A UN team visiting the North reported that 1.9 million tons of crops had been lost and that many irrigation systems had been damaged.

Pyongyang had earlier asked for emergency food aid to cover a projected harvest shortfall. Japan contributed 300,000 tons of rice and South Korea 150,000 tons. For several years defectors and visitors had spoken of shortages, of official exhortations to eat only twice a day, and even of food riots. In December the UN World Food Programme warned of the possibility of widespread famine.

In January the U.S. sent 50,000 tons of fuel oil to help generate electricity, part of a 1994 agreement to end an international dispute over North Korea's suspected nuclear weapons program. Pyongyang pledged to freeze all its projects, which involved operation of a five-megawatt nuclear plant and construction of two others. In exchange, the U.S. promised to arrange for North Korea to acquire two modern nuclear power reactors worth over $4 billion. Throughout the year the two sides haggled over details implementing the agreement, with the North periodically threatening to restart its nuclear program if concessions were not granted. The main sticking point seemed to be U.S. insistence that the reactors come from South Korea. An agreement calling for contributions from Japan, South Korea, and the U.S. was finally signed on December 15.

During the year North Korea and the U.S. made cautious moves toward ending their long enmity. The U.S. lifted its trade embargo, and the first investment mission visited the country in February. As part of the October 1994 accord, the two sides agreed to move toward establishing some kind of informal relationship, probably in the form of liaison-level offices in each other's capital.

Pyongyang had reportedly even dropped its opposition to the stationing of U.S. troops in South Korea. This was seen as part of a yearlong effort by North Korea to undo the Panmunjon peace arrangements and sign a formal peace treaty with the U.S. Washington insisted that Pyongyang first make peace with the south.

The status of Kim Jong Il, son and successor of the late dictator Kim Il Sung, continued to cast a cloud over North Korean affairs. Several auspicious dates passed without the younger Kim's assuming the vacant titles of president and secretary-general of the Korean Workers' (communist) Party. He was seen in public only rarely. Most analysts, however, believed that Kim Jong Il was in charge and was slowly but carefully consolidating his power. In October he promoted army Chief of Staff Gen. Choe Gwang to defense minister. He replaced Marshal O Jin U, an influential Kim supporter who had died in February. Also in October, a 10.7-m (35-ft) granite monument of Kim Jong Il was unveiled in Pyongyang. (GEORGE T. CROWELL)

This article updates the *Macropædia* article KOREA: *North Korea*.

Workers in South Korea load rice for shipment to North Korea. With the country experiencing what apparently were serious food shortages, the North Korean government signed an agreement on June 21 to accept emergency shipments of food from South Korea.
REUTERS

KOREA, REPUBLIC OF

A republic of northeastern Asia on the southern half of the peninsula of Korea, the Republic of Korea (South Korea) borders the Sea of Japan, the Korea Strait, the Yellow Sea, and the Democratic People's Republic of Korea at roughly the 38th parallel. Area: 99,392 sq km (38,375 sq mi). Pop. (1995 est.): 44,834,000. Cap.: Seoul. Monetary unit: won, with (Oct. 6, 1995) a free rate of 768.60 won to U.S. $1 (1,215 won = £1 sterling). President in 1995, Kim Young Sam; prime ministers, Lee Hong Koo and, from December 18, Lee Soo Song.

In 1995 South Koreans confronted the dark side of their recent past. Two former presidents, Chun Doo Hwan (1980–88) and Roh Tae Woo (1988–93), were arrested and indicted for insurrection for their part in the Dec. 12, 1979, coup that brought Chun to power. Both were then senior army generals. Roh provided the troops that tipped the balance toward Chun. Eight years later Roh narrowly won the presidency himself in South Korea's first modern democratic election. Roh stunned the nation when on October 27 he went on television and tearfully confessed to having amassed a political slush fund of approximately $650 million. Most Koreans had assumed that "donations" were a normal part of politics. They were nevertheless shocked at the sheer size of the fund and the fact that Roh admitted that he had kept more than $200 million of it for his own use.

Prosecutors later accused Roh of having taken $369 million in bribes from the large business conglomerates called *chaebols*. Roh admitted taking the payments but denied that they were bribes. If convicted of the several charges, both former presidents technically could receive the death penalty, although that was considered unlikely. Eight leaders of some of South Korea's biggest business ventures, including the chairmen of Daewoo, Samsung, and Hanbo, were also indicted for having given Roh money or laundered it for him. The unfolding scandal was another blow to Pres. Kim Young Sam, who was already suffering from falling popularity and electoral reverses. His main political rival, the veteran campaigner Kim Dae Jung, quickly acknowledged that he had received about $2.5 million from Roh's fund, implying that the other Kim, being a member of Roh's own party, must have received much more. The president denied it.

On June 27, 1995, South Koreans went to the polls in a historic election. For the first time since Park Chung Hee seized power in 1961, local and provincial government officials were elected rather than appointed. Some 5,700 politicians, including 15 governors or mayors of major cities, were chosen in what was considered a fair election.

The outcome was a disaster for Pres. Kim Young Sam's Democratic Liberal Party (DLP), which won only 5 of the top 15 posts. The main opposition, the centre-left Democratic Party, took over control of Seoul, the capital, by winning not only the mayor's office but 23 of the city's 25 wards as well. Even the new right-wing United Liberal Democrats, formed after Kim Jong Pil quit as chairman of the DLP, managed to win three governorships.

The election results significantly altered the nation's political landscape. When Kim was elected in 1992—the first president in three decades not to come from the ranks of the military—it seemed to permanently relegate to the sidelines two of the country's most prominent politicians: Kim Jong Pil, who opted to join the ruling coalition, and Kim Dae Jung, who retired from politics to form a foundation dedicated to reunifying Korea.

Within months of taking office, Kim Young Sam saw his popularity soar to 90%, the highest mark ever recorded for a South Korean president. In 1995, however, halfway through his five-year term, Kim no longer had the same appeal. His reform initiatives appeared to be more cosmetic than real, and corruption was as deeply rooted as ever. With Kim's rating at about 30%, political analysts interpreted the June 27 election as an implicit affirmation by voters that Kim Dae Jung was not far off target when he made reference to "two and a half years of misrule and blunders."

After the June election Kim Dae Jung came out of retirement and in September launched a new party, the National Congress for New Politics. Most assemblymen from the Democratic Party promptly joined its ranks. Kim Dae Jung remarked that he had not made up his mind about running for president for the fourth time in 1997. A decision could depend on how well his candidates did in the National Assembly elections in April 1996. If voters once again rejected the DLP, as many believed they would, especially in the wake of the scandal, pressure could mount to change South Korea's presidential form of government to a parliamentary system. Trying to distance itself from the scandal, the ruling party in December changed its name to the New Korea Party.

Kim's popularity also suffered from a series of man-made disasters, which seemed to call attention to a seamy side of South Korea's rush toward economic development. The worst was the collapse of the Sampoong Department Store in Seoul on June 29, which took the lives of more than 500 shoppers and store clerks. This, however, was only the worst of a number of recent accidents that killed more than 1,000 people and caused billions of dollars in damage. On April 28 a gas explosion tore through the heart of Taegu, South Korea's third largest city, killing more than 100 people. In October 1994 the Songsu Bridge spanning the Han River in Seoul had collapsed.

Corruption appeared to be the root cause of many of these disasters. Five builders were arrested and charged with direct or indirect responsibility for the Taegu disaster. Korean authorities also arrested the founder of Sampoong after evidence emerged that local bureaucrats had been bribed to approve the addition of an unplanned fifth story, which caused the collapse of the entire structure. Ironically, the accident occurred only two days after voters ousted the mayor of Seoul and 23 of the 25 ward administrators.

Many of Korea's world-class construction corporations concentrated on prestige projects in other countries and were therefore unable to handle all of the country's infrastructure needs. With millions of people pouring into the cities and their sprawling industrial suburbs, the demand for new construction was often met by small and medium-sized firms. The tragedy that occurred at the Sampoong building confirmed the seriousness of the problem.

Labour troubles surfaced in the wake of efforts to privatize Korea Telecom (KT), the telephone company that was 80% owned by the state. When 64 union leaders were fired or demoted for encouraging unrest, 13 took refuge in a Roman Catholic cathedral and a Buddhist temple. Nevertheless, after a two-week standoff, police raided the premises in an unprecedented violation of church sanctuary.

South Korea made little progress toward reconciliation with North Korea during the year. The highly touted summit meeting between the presidents of the two Koreas was postponed indefinitely after the death of Kim II Sung in 1994. In May Seoul approved two pilot investment projects in North Korea. Daewoo Corp. planned to spend $5 million making shirts, jackets, and travel bags, and Kohap Ltd., a trading company, was also prepared to invest millions producing plastic bottles, textiles, and garments. South Korea had lifted a ban on direct trade with an investment in the North in November 1994.

Relations with Japan took on an acrimonious air because 1995 marked the 50th anniversary of the end of World War II. It was a reminder of the years during which Korea had been occupied by Japan. Michio Watanabe (*see* OBITUARIES), a former Japanese Cabinet minister, sparked a riot in Seoul when he remarked that the Koreans had "harmoniously" signed the treaty annexing the country to Japan in 1910. As if to exorcise the memories associated with 35 years of occupation, South Korea began demolishing an imposing building in downtown Seoul that had been erected by Japan as a palace for its then governor-general.

(GEORGE T. CROWELL)

This article updates the *Macropædia* article KOREA: *South Korea*.

KUWAIT

A constitutional monarchy (emirate), Kuwait is in the northeastern Arabian Peninsula, on the Persian Gulf. Area: 17,818 sq km (6,880 sq mi). Pop. (1995 est.): 1,691,000. Cap.: Kuwait City. Monetary unit: Kuwaiti dinar, with (Oct. 6, 1995) a controlled rate of 0.30 dinar to U.S. $1 (0.47 dinar = £1 sterling). Emir, Sheikh Jabir al-Ahmad al-Jabir as-Sabah; prime minister in 1995, Crown Prince Sheikh Saad al-Abdullah as-Salim as-Sabah.

During 1995 Kuwait avoided acute new problems and made progress toward resolving some of its chronic difficulties. Others remained to trouble citizens and policy makers in the future. The October 1994 Iraqi military buildup provoked the U.S. and Great Britain to hold military exercises in Kuwait and urge the UN not to lift the sanctions it had imposed on Iraq. These rapid responses to Iraqi provocations eased Kuwaitis' fears, but efforts by Russia and France to lift the UN sanctions highlighted Kuwait's dependence on extraregional military intervention. Arms purchases from Western allies weakened Kuwait's economy without enabling the country to defend itself. As the clock ran down on Kuwait's military treaties with former coalition partners, its strategic vulnerability remained unchanged.

The domestic economy showed strength, but the lack of clear policies hampered growth. The drain on the treasury from arms purchases and the September compromise between the government and the National Assembly on the most recent plan to resolve the nation's lingering debt crisis compounded the problem. The compromise received the endorsement of the crown prince, reputed to be among the largest debtors.

The construction industry and the stock market enjoyed minibooms. Privatization measures were greeted enthusiastically by Kuwaiti investors, although knowledgeable observers were concerned about the lack of planning and hints of insider trading. Oil industry recovery continued, with production averaging two million barrels per day. Repayment of Kuwait's $5.5 billion foreign loan to finance postwar reconstruction proceeded on schedule.

Little progress was made on the resolution of structural deficits. The 1995–96 budget included no new taxes. A "defense tax" might have been feasible following the 1994 Iraqi scare, but no action was taken. Strategic insecurity and persistent polarization between the head of government and the national legislature foreshadowed continuing conflicts and an acrimonious election year in 1996.

(MARY ANN TÉTREAULT)

This article updates the *Macropædia* article ARABIA: *Kuwait.*

KYRGYZSTAN

A landlocked republic of Central Asia, Kyrgyzstan borders Kazakhstan to the north, China to the southeast, Tajikistan to the south and west, and Uzbekistan to the west. Area: 198,500 sq km (76,600 sq mi). Pop. (1995 est.): 4,483,000. Cap.: Bishkek. Monetary unit: som, with (Oct. 4, 1995) a free rate of 10.86 som = U.S. $1 (17.26 som = £1 sterling). President in 1995, Askar Akayev; prime minister, Apas Djumagulov.

Kyrgyzstan approached the end of 1995 with a currency that was one of the most stable in the Commonwealth of Independent States (CIS); the economic decline that had characterized its first years of independence had almost stopped. A report from the International Monetary Fund issued in May stated that Kyrgyzstan led the states of the CIS in market reforms. This assessment led to a pledge by international donors of $680 million in credits in 1995 and 1996.

Parliamentary elections on February 5 resulted in only 13 seats being filled in the new 105-seat bicameral parliament because there were so many candidates registered in most constituencies. A runoff on February 19 filled most of the rest of the seats, with 8 of Kyrgyzstan's 13 registered parties represented in the legislature. By mid-April relations between Pres. Askar Akayev and the parliament were strained, as the legislature sought to establish its authority by refusing to confirm some of Akayev's ministerial appointments and defying the president's wishes in other ways.

The issue of a referendum on extending Akayev's term in office resurfaced throughout the year and was finally squelched in September when the Legislative Assembly, the house of parliament that remained in permanent session, set December 24 as the date for a presidential election. Opposition parties called on Akayev to step down during the electoral campaign, as his incumbency was seen as giving him an unfair advantage. His chief rival for the presidency, former parliament chairman Medetkan Sherimkulov, challenged the election date and referred the question to the courts. Turnout was high (82%), and Akayev won a convincing 60% of the votes.

In September heads of state from six countries, including Pakistan and Turkey, gathered in Kyrgyzstan to celebrate the millennium of the Kyrgyz national epic, the *Manas.*

(BESS BROWN)

This article updates the *Macropædia* article CENTRAL ASIA: *Kyrgyzstan.*

LAOS

A landlocked republic, Laos is in the northern part of the Indochinese Peninsula. Area: 236,800 sq km (91,429 sq mi). Pop. (1995 est.): 4,882,000. Cap.: Vientiane (Viangchan). Monetary unit: kip, with (Oct. 6, 1995) a controlled rate of 920 kip to U.S. $1 (1,454 kip = £1 sterling). President in 1995, Nouhak Phoumsavan; prime minister, Gen. Khamtai Siphandon.

Laotian Foreign Minister Somsavat Lengsavat surprised delegates at the ministerial meeting of the Association of Southeast Asian Nations (ASEAN) held in Brunei in late July and early August when he announced that Laos would seek full membership within two years. It was recognized that financial and logistic assistance would have to be extended to Laos, which would otherwise be unable to attend some 200 ASEAN meetings each year or to employ translators. Later in the year, Laotian diplomats began attending training seminars at the ASEAN secretariat in Jakarta, Indon.

A visit by Pres. Nouhak Phoumsavan to Myanmar (Burma) in May continued to improve relations between the neighbouring states, both of which were turning away from socialism. Agreements were reached on trade, transport, and agricultural cooperation. A border demarcation pact signed the previous year was ratified. The following week Winston Lord, U.S. assistant secretary of state for East Asian and Pacific affairs, arrived in Vientiane, where he announced the lifting of a ban on U.S. aid. It had been in place since the Vietnam War.

In April Laos joined Thailand, Cambodia, and Vietnam in setting up a commission to manage the resources of the Mekong River. Because China and Myanmar did not attend the first meeting in Phnom Penh, no effective policies could be implemented. Laos announced that it would join the 128 other nations supporting the Convention on International Trade in Endangered Species. Eighteen areas of natural forest totaling 2.5 million ha (6.2 million ac) were designated protected areas. It was acknowledged that Laos lacked both the funds and the trained personnel to implement the program effectively, however. Both Vietnam and Thailand pressed Laos to give priority to building Road 9, which would connect Thailand's Savanakhet province to the city of Quang Tri in Vietnam. Laos, however, favoured Road 8, which led to the Vietnamese port of Vinh.

Laos's economy was troubled by the progressive weakness of the kip. This accentuated the trade deficit and caused rising prices of imported goods, especially oil products. Because the government was reluctant to allow retail prices to climb, higher inflation and a larger budget deficit resulted, which thus made Laos less attractive to foreign investors. Some confidence was restored in August when the Asian Development Bank granted an interest-free loan of $20 million for urban infrastructure. (ROBERT WOODROW)

This article updates the *Macropædia* article SOUTHEAST ASIA: *Laos.*

LATVIA

A republic of northern Europe, Latvia is on the eastern shore of the Baltic Sea. Area: 64,610 sq km (24,946 sq mi). Pop. (1995 est.): 2,515,000. Cap.: Riga. Monetary unit: lats, with (Oct. 6, 1995) a free rate of 0.54 lats to U.S. $1 (0.85 lats = £1 sterling). President in 1995, Guntis Ulmanis; chairman of the Saeima (parliament), Anatolijs Gorbunovs; prime ministers, Maris Gailis and, from December 21, Andris Skele.

Latvia was beset by serious economic problems and internal political disarray in 1995 but made progress in achieving some of its important foreign policy goals. The lack of proper control over commercial banks resulted in the issuance of bad loans that led to the bankruptcies of many commercial banks, including the country's largest, Banka Baltija. The government's failure to collect projected tax revenues resulted in a growing budget deficit that threatened to surpass the limit agreed to with the International Monetary Fund. Compounding the problem, the government issued state treasury bills whose very high interest rates made them overly attractive to banks, which led to a credit shortage for local industries. The privatization of apartment buildings had to be put off until 1996.

The parliamentary elections on September 30–October 1 did not result in a clear winner; nine parties received between 5% and 16% of the vote. The National Conciliation Bloc (NIB), formed by three leftist parties and a right extremist party, elected the parliament leadership on November 7. The formation of a government was more difficult, for neither the rightist National Bloc (NB) nor the NIB was able to get the majority vote needed to form a Cabinet. To avoid new elections, two leftist parties then joined forces with the NB to elect the nonparty businessman Andris Skele prime minister on December 21.

After having been admitted to the Council of Europe in February, on June 12 Latvia signed an associate membership agreement with the European Union, and four months later it submitted a formal membership application. Latvian units participated in both naval and ground exercises of NATO's Partnership for Peace program. (SAULIUS A. GIRNIUS)

This article updates the *Macropædia* article BALTIC STATES: *Latvia.*

LEBANON

A republic of southwestern Asia, Lebanon is situated on the Mediterranean Sea. Area: 10,230 sq km (3,950 sq mi). Pop. (1995 est.): 3,009,000 (including Palestinian refugees estimated to number nearly 340,000). Cap.: Beirut. Monetary unit: Lebanese pound, with (Oct. 6, 1995) a free rate of LL 1,609 to U.S. $1 (LL 2,544 = £1 sterling). President in 1995, Elias Hrawi; prime minister, Rafiq al-Hariri.

As the region moved toward a more comprehensive solution to the Middle East conflict in 1995, the Lebanese government was concerned with continued violence in southern Lebanon, the appointment of a new Cabinet, and renewed efforts in the reconstruction of Beirut.

On January 30 the UN Security Council adopted a resolution to extend the mandate of the United Nations Interim Force in Lebanon (UNIFIL). In the wake of the negotiations between Israel and Palestine in Oslo, Norway, violence resumed in southern Lebanon between pro-Iranian Hezbollah forces and Israeli troops and militia from the South Lebanese Army (SLA) in Israel's "security zone." Though the sporadic conflict in southern Lebanon was fought according to rules agreed to in 1993 between Syria and the U.S., the war had taken many Lebanese and Israeli lives. Several incidents, including an Israeli blockade of the southern Lebanese coast from February 8 through March 9, attacks by Hezbollah guerrillas on Israel, and Israeli retaliatory raids, left the 150,000 residents of the region insecure. Similarly, the goals of the Hezbollah continued to be the removal of Israeli troops from southern Lebanon and the postponement of any Israeli negotiations with Syria. Anticipating the possibility of an Israeli-Syrian agreement in 1992, the Hezbollah became a bona fide participant in Lebanese politics, with eight members still in the National Assembly in 1995. Syria remained a dominant force, with 35,000 troops stationed in Lebanon.

The future of the Palestinians in Lebanon was unsure. The UN Relief and Works Agency estimated that some 338,000 Palestinians were denied civil rights by the Lebanese authorities, encouraged to move, and denied work permits in Lebanon. Of the hundreds of Palestinians deported by Libya in September who attempted a return to Lebanon, only those few who held Lebanese residence permits were allowed reentry.

On June 24 former Maronite Christian leader Samir Geagea was sentenced to life imprisonment for the murder of his rival, Dany Chamoun, and Chamoun's wife and two sons. The verdict underscored the Maronite defeat in the civil war that had beset Lebanon since 1975. The balance of political power now shifted to the Muslims. Maronite political leadership had all but disappeared; the former commander of the Lebanese army, Michel Aoun, was in exile in France, and the Maronite patriarch, Nasrallah Sfeir, did not take an active political role. Christians seemed to fear that the elections in 1996 would reflect a shift in Lebanon's power structure.

Prime Minister Rafiq al-Hariri resigned on May 19 only to be reappointed by Pres. Elias Hrawi on May 21. Hariri, prime mover of the "Horizon 2000" project of Beirut urban renewal, requested a new Cabinet and advocated an amendment to the constitution that would allow the president to extend his six-year term for three additional years in the hope of providing the stability necessary for a massive reconstruction of Beirut. Although discussion of the new amendment was opposed by Nabih Berri, the Shiʿite speaker of the National Assembly, a compromise was reached in mid-May, and the amendment passed on October 19.

Hariri was able to appoint a new Cabinet on May 25. Most of the posts remained unchanged, including Fares Bouez (minister of foreign and expatriate affairs), Michel Murr (minister of the interior), and Mohsen Dalloul (minister of national defense). New appointments included the former head of the Council for Development and Reconstruction, al-Fadl Chalaq (minister of posts and telecommunications).

Prime Minister Hariri's goal to reestablish Lebanon as the financial market centre of the Middle East moved a step

Archaeologists excavate a 2,500-year-old Phoenician town in the centre of Beirut. The discovery of Canaanite, Phoenician, Byzantine, and Roman remains, which some people demanded be preserved, was making attempts to rebuild the Lebanese capital more difficult.
AFP

forward with the reopening of the stock market on September 19. A program to rebuild the central business and residential district of Beirut was aided by $1.8 billion raised from domestic and Arab sources, including a contribution of $125 million from the prime minister. Unfortunately, the project hit an "archaeological" impasse in 1995. Canaanite, Phoenician, Byzantine, and Roman artifacts, mosaics, and temples were uncovered, all of which were to be preserved as archaeological monuments or retrieved for museums. Because preservation is expensive, controversy abounded over whether to charge private developers for the excavations and risk threatening a predicted 8% economic rate of growth or to sacrifice archaeology in the name of urban renewal.

(REEVA S. SIMON)

LESOTHO

A constitutional monarchy of southern Africa and member of the Commonwealth, Lesotho forms a landlocked enclave within South Africa. Area: 30,355 sq km (11,720 sq mi). Pop. (1995 est.): 2,050,000. Cap.: Maseru. Monetary unit: loti (plural: maloti), at par with the South African rand, with (Oct. 6, 1995) a free rate of 3.66 maloti to U.S. $1 (5.79 maloti = £1 sterling). Kings in 1995, Letsie III and, from January 25, Moshoeshoe II; prime minister, Ntsu Mokhehle.

King Moshoeshoe II was formally restored to the throne of Lesotho on Jan. 25, 1995. A bill had been presented to the National Assembly the previous November that provided for the abdication of his son Letsie III and the reversion of the crown to Moshoeshoe while Letsie went back to his former role as crown prince. Addressing a crowd of 10,000 at a ceremony to mark the occasion, King Moshoeshoe II promised reconciliation and peace. A new era had dawned, it was hoped, after a deeply troubled political phase in the country's life. During February the prime minister, Ntsu Mokhehle, announced a number of Cabinet changes, which included the promotion of the minister of education, Pakalitha Mosisili, to the post of deputy prime minister. Also in February, Lesotho concluded an extradition treaty with South Africa. There was concern in both countries about the level of smuggling across the borders.

Enormous machines completed drilling on the 82-km (51-mi) Lesotho Highlands Tunnel in March. The Lesotho Highlands Water Project was scheduled to deliver water to the arid Vaal River basin in South Africa beginning in 1997.

At the end of March, the minister of finance and economic planning, Moeketsi Senaona, presented the budget for 1995–96. Revenue and grants were expected to amount to 1,790,300,000 maloti, 13% above the figure for 1994, while expenditure would be 1,608,800,000 maloti. Education, at 335.6 million maloti, was the biggest single item of expenditure.

In March members of the National Security Services kidnapped several senior officers, including Maj. Gen. Leaboa Seoane and Col. Simon Thaha, and held them for 14 days. The kidnappers demanded their immediate retirement and accused them of attempted murder, corruption, and breach of security laws.

(GUY ARNOLD)

This article updates the *Macropædia* article SOUTHERN AFRICA: *Lesotho.*

LIBERIA

The republic of Liberia is located in West Africa, on the Atlantic Ocean. Area: 99,067 sq km (38,250 sq mi). Pop. (1995 est.): 2,380,000 (including Liberian refugees temporarily residing in surrounding countries estimated to number about 750,000). Cap.: Monrovia. Monetary unit: Liberian dollar, with (Oct. 6, 1995) an official par value of L$1 to U.S. $1 (free rate of L$1.58 = £1 sterling); a truer value of the L$ was on the free market, where (August 28) L$42 = U.S. $1 (L$65 = £1 sterling). Chairmen of the Council of State in 1995, David Kpormakor and, from September 1, Wilton Sankawulo.

Liberia made slow progress toward a cease-fire and the formation of a new government in 1995. Negotiations held in Accra, Ghana, during January ended without the six main warring factions' agreeing on the composition of a Council of State. But the cease-fire held. In February Charles Taylor of the National Patriotic Front of Liberia (NPFL) proposed a new plan that included the appointment of an old traditional leader, Chief Tamba Tailor, as chairman of the Council and Taylor himself as first vice-chairman, but this was rejected. Fighting then broke out between Taylor's NPFL and the Liberian Peace Council, forcing 35,000 people to flee their homes and seek refuge in the port of Buchanan. Further fighting between the two factions in April led to a massacre of 62 people, mainly women and children, in Yosi in the south, though it was not clear who was responsible.

Talks continued through the year in both Accra and Abuja, Nigeria, under the auspices of the Economic Community of West African States committee on Liberia. The UN renewed the mandate of its Observer Mission, but Tanzania withdrew its 300 peacekeeping troops in frustration at the lack of progress. In July accusations were leveled at Taylor's NPFL for importing arms and for conducting raids across the border into Guinea. Also in July all the warring factions met in Monrovia for the first time since the civil war erupted in 1989, and by the end of August an agreement had been reached upon the composition of the Council of State; it was to include two neutral members and a neutral chairman, Wilton Sankawulo. A new Cabinet of 16 members was then sworn in, and Charles Taylor became one of six members of the Council of State. Renewed fighting was reported north of Monrovia at year's end, however.

(GUY ARNOLD)

This article updates the *Macropædia* article WESTERN AFRICA: *Liberia.*

LIBYA

A socialist country of North Africa, Libya lies on the Mediterranean Sea. Area: 1,757,000 sq km (678,400 sq mi). Pop. (1995 est.): 5,407,000. Cap.: Tripoli (policy-making body meets in Surt). Monetary unit: Libyan dinar, with (Oct. 6, 1995) an official rate of 0.36 dinar to U.S. $1 (0.56 dinar = £1 sterling) and a private-import rate of 1.02 dinar to U.S. $1 (1.61 dinar to £1 sterling). De facto chief of state in 1995, Col. Muammar al-Qaddafi; secretary of the General People's Congress (nominal chief of state), Zanati Muhammad az-Zanati; secretary of the General People's Committee (premier), ʿAbd al-Majid al-Qaʾud.

Libya remained isolated during 1995 despite continued overtures to the Western governments responsible for its status. Their investigations of the December 1988 sabotage of Pan Am Flight 103 over Lockerbie, Scotland, and of a French flight over the Sahara discovered evidence of Libyan

CHRIS BROWN—SABA

A contingent of the National Patriotic Front of Liberia (NPFL), the faction headed by Charles Taylor, patrols the countryside. After outbreaks of fighting between the NPFL and the Liberian Peace Council during the year, an agreement was reached at the end of August on a new Council of State.

involvement, and the U.S., the U.K., and France subsequently used their influence to have the UN impose a trade and international flight embargo on Libya. In regard to the Lockerbie issue, Libya offered that Libyan suspects be tried at the International Court of Justice by a Scottish judge.

The U.K. government was also particularly insistent that Libya provide details of its involvement in arming the Irish Republican Army during 1984–87. In October it appeared that Egyptian mediation had contributed to a promise by Libya to provide sufficient detail.

The Libyan leader, Col. Muammar al-Qaddafi, had been unusually reticent during the major Middle East peace talks and agreements during 1992–95. Previously his position on the Palestinian issue had been uncompromising and confrontational. With the unfolding of Palestinian-Israeli peace negotiations, however, Qaddafi began to reverse his position, and at the beginning of September he initiated a campaign to expel Palestinians from Libya. In early October it was estimated that 10,000 would be deported. A camp was set up close to the Egyptian border, and the international media were invited to record the visit of the Libyan leader to the site when he argued that Palestinians should now return to their own homelands.

The embargo continued to make it difficult for Libyans to travel and for overseas visitors to reach Libya. It also severely restricted the Libyan economy, which was already in poor shape after the difficult 1980s. As an oil economy, Libya endured that decade's reduction in world demand for oil as well as the fall in the value of the dollar, in which the international oil trade is denominated.

At home the trend toward the reduction of the role of the public sector continued. The international restrictions on trade provided an additional impetus for local enterprises, and the agricultural sector, which had never been nationalized, was stimulated to meet the national demand for food. The capacity to produce sufficient staple foods for the growing national economy remained an impossible challenge, however, because of the limited water resources of the country. The remarkable Great Man Made River brought new water from the highlands to the coast but at a cost that was too high for agricultural purposes. Despite current problems, the future appeared to be brighter, as a number of international companies were looking closely at the possibility of playing a role in a new phase of oil exploration and development.

Qaddafi announced in the autumn that workers and their families from Palestine and neighbouring North African countries had to leave Libya. The Libyan leader doubted the loyalty of these people to his regime and sought by this move to reduce Libyan dependence on overseas workers.

(J.A. ALLAN)

This article updates the *Macropædia* article NORTH AFRICA: *Libya.*

LIECHTENSTEIN

A landlocked constitutional monarchy of central Europe, Liechtenstein is united with Switzerland by a customs and monetary union. Area: 160 sq km (62 sq mi). Pop. (1995 est.): 30,900. Cap.: Vaduz. Monetary unit: Swiss franc, with (Oct. 6, 1995) a free rate of Sw F 1.15 to U.S. $1 (Sw F 1.82 = £1 sterling). Sovereign prince, Hans Adam II; head of government in 1995, Mario Frick.

In a referendum held on April 9, 1995, Liechtenstein's voters approved the country's participation in the European Economic Area (EEA). The revised terms of the treaty had been negotiated over the previous two years and successfully concluded in October 1994. The renegotiation and a second referendum became necessary when Switzerland, with which Liechtenstein had customs and currency unions dating from 1923, voted against joining the EEA. Although opposition to the treaty was strong—with arguments that the country would be surrendering its sovereignty, opening its doors to a flood of immigrants, and risking its status as a tax haven—in a high turnout of 82% of the electorate, 6,411 votes (55.9%) were cast in favour of membership. The treaty did not cover banking and tax issues, and Liechtenstein won a special concession limiting immigration.

An art collection from Liechtenstein was part of Luxembourg's festival of the arts during its reign as European City of Culture, 1995. The exhibition "Treasures from Collections of the Prince of Liechtenstein" was on display from July 8 to September 3.

(ANNE ROBY)

This article updates the *Micropædia* article LIECHTENSTEIN.

LITHUANIA

A republic of northern Europe, Lithuania is on the southeastern shore of the Baltic Sea. Area: 65,301 sq km (25,213 sq mi). Pop. (1995 est.): 3.7 million. Cap.: Vilnius. Monetary unit: litas, with (Oct. 6, 1995) a par value of 4 litai to U.S. $1 (6.32 litai = £1 sterling). President in 1995, Algirdas Brazauskas; prime minister, Adolfas Slezevicius.

The ruling Lithuanian Democratic Labor Party retained firm control of the parliament and government in 1995 but gathered less than 20% of the vote in local elections on March 25. Right-of-centre parties won more than half the votes, with the conservatives gaining almost 30%. Only 45% of eligible voters participated in the elections, an indication of a general disillusionment with politics. The central authorities continued to reduce the already limited powers of local government by introducing an intermediary level of regional governors, appointed directly by the prime minister.

Surveys indicated a growing disenchantment with all government institutions, including the parliament, the Cabinet, the presidency, and the courts; only the media and the church had positive ratings. The lack of trust was caused in part by the impoverishment of the population; 80% of Lithuanians were considered poor, 15% middle class, and 5% rich. The government seemed unable or unwilling to stamp out corruption. The decline in the republic's gross national product was halted, but it was expected to regain the level of 1989 only in the next century. Agricultural production continued to decrease, and many large industrial enterprises avoided bankruptcy only by being allowed to delay tax payments.

Lithuania was a very active participant in NATO's Partnership for Peace program, and on June 12 it became an associate member of the European Union. Trade was being reoriented toward the West; Lithuania was transacting the same amount of business with the EU as with the Commonwealth of Independent States. Relations with Russia improved after a compromise was found to the problem of military transit regulations between Russia and Kaliningrad.

(SAULIUS A. GIRNIUS)

This article updates the *Macropædia* article BALTIC STATES: *Lithuania.*

LUXEMBOURG

Luxembourg is a landlocked constitutional monarchy in western Europe. Area: 2,586 sq km (999 sq mi). Pop. (1995 est.): 409,000. Cap.: Luxembourg. Monetary unit: Luxembourg franc, at par with the Belgian franc, with (Oct. 6, 1995) a free rate of Lux F 29.39 to U.S. $1 (Lux F 46.46 = £1 sterling). Grand duke, Jean; prime ministers in 1995, Jacques Santer and, from January 20, Jean-Claude Juncker.

For this tiny country situated in the heart of Western Europe, 1995 was a banner year. Highlights included the appointment of its former prime minister, Jacques Santer, as president of the European Commission, its selection as European City of Culture 1995, and its growing prosperity as a financial services center.

As the European City of Culture, Luxembourg served as host for a yearlong series of exhibitions, concerts, and entertainments for visitors. The celebrations were launched January 13 with a concert by the Symphonic Orchestra of Radio Television Luxembourg and a landmark exhibition featuring the works of such artists as Paul Cézanne, Paul Gauguin, Vincent van Gogh, Henri Matisse, Pierre-August Renoir, and Henri de Toulouse-Lautrec. The festival included three exhibitions of the work of the Luxembourg-born U.S. photographer Edward Steichen. An especially notable concert was Benjamin Britten's *War Requiem* on April 22 in the Diekirch Historical Museum, also known as the Museum of the Battle of the Bulge. The closing ceremonies for the cultural year took place on December 21.

Luxembourg continued to build on its success as a leader in the financial services industry in banking. The country was also a leader in the mutual funds industry, with some $356 billion under Luxembourg management. Insurers had flocked to Luxembourg as well. According to insurance commissioner Victor Rod, the country offered an infrastructure of banking and fund-management skills, a strategic location, and highly skilled personnel. (ANNE ROBY)

MACEDONIA

A landlocked republic of the central Balkans, Macedonia borders Yugoslavia to the north, Bulgaria to the east, Greece to the south, and Albania to the west. Area: 25,713 sq km (9,928 sq mi). Pop. (1995 est.): 2,104,000. Cap.: Skopje. Monetary unit: denar, with (Oct. 6, 1995) a free rate of 39.30 denars to U.S. $1 (62.13 denars = £1 sterling). President in 1995, Kiro Gligorov; prime minister, Branko Crvenkovski.

The most dramatic event in Macedonia in 1995 was the October 3 attempted assassination by car bomb of Pres. Kiro Gligorov, who had just returned to Skopje from a visit to Belgrade, Yugos. Although severely injured, Gligorov survived and was recovering well at year's end, but the running of the country was temporarily taken over by Stojan Andov, speaker of the Sobranje (parliament). Ljubomir Frckovski, the interior minister, resigned his post on October 26, assuming responsibility for security lapses. He claimed that international criminal interests were behind the attempt, but no arrests had been made by the end of the year. If the assassination attempt was intended to destabilize the country, it was largely unsuccessful.

Macedonia's domestic situation remained volatile, with the Albanian minority continuing to demand a greater role for itself in the country's educational system. An independent ethnic Albanian university was established on February 15 at Mala Recica, a village near the town of Tetovo. The government had called the project "illegal." On April 22 the Party for Democratic Prosperity, which had members in the Cabinet, changed its name to the Party for Democratic Prosperity of Albanians in Macedonia.

Macedonia's external position strengthened significantly in 1995. On September 13 Stevo Crvenkovski, the foreign minister, initialed an agreement in New York with Karolos Papoulias, his Greek counterpart, under which Greece would lift its trade embargo against Macedonia, which it had instituted in February 1994, in return for Macedonia's renouncing the use of the star of Vergina as its national symbol. The issue of the republic's name was left to be settled later. On October 15 Greece lifted its trade blockade. In the same month, Macedonia was admitted into the Organization for Security and Cooperation in Europe. A month earlier, on September 27, it had been received into the Council of Europe under the name of The Former Yugoslav Republic of Macedonia. On April 13 an agreement was signed with Turkey on cooperation in the technical and military spheres.

In 1995 Macedonia's industrial output stagnated, with unemployment at an average of 28%. The annual inflation rate was around 18%, and average per capita income stood at $700. (K.F. CVIIC)

This article updates the *Macropædia* article BALKAN STATES: *Macedonia.*

MADAGASCAR

The republic of Madagascar occupies the island of the same name and minor adjacent islands in the Indian Ocean off the southeastern coast of Africa. Area: 587,041 sq km (226,658 sq mi). Pop. (1995 est.): 14,763,000. Cap.: Antananarivo. Monetary unit: Malagasy franc, with (Oct. 6, 1995) a free rate of FMG 3,300 to U.S. $1 (FMG 5,217 = £1 sterling). President in 1995, Albert Zafy; prime ministers, Francisque Ravony and, from October 30, Emmanuel Rakotovahiny.

The need to reach an agreement with the International Monetary Fund (IMF) so that the government could carry out its promise to tackle the economy led to demonstrations against Pres. Albert Zafy at the end of 1994. The opposition Movement for Proletarian Power called for the dismissal of Zafy as well as of the National Assembly president and the prime minister. The National Assembly president, Richard Andriamanjato, was accused of making "shady financial agreements" with the president, while Zafy himself was accused of overstepping his "constitutional powers."

WOLFGANG KAEHLER

A farmer clears land in the highlands of Madagascar, southwest of the capital of Antananarivo. Because of slash-and-burn farming, many of the country's forested areas, along with unique flora and fauna, had disappeared, and erosion had become a serious problem.

On January 11 the governor of the central bank was dismissed following demands for his departure by the IMF and the World Bank, which accused him of various questionable financial deals. The minister of finance, José Yvon Raserijaona, also resigned. Prime Minister Francisque Ravony took over the Finance portfolio and stated his belief that negotiations with the IMF and World Bank could continue.

In August, following six weeks of political deadlock after the failure of a no-confidence motion against the prime minister by supporters of the president, an agreement between Zafy and Ravony was reached. Zafy accepted a new government in which his opponents would be in a majority. A referendum in September increased the president's powers, notably to dismiss and appoint the prime minister. Ravony resigned on October 13, and Zafy appointed the agriculture minister, Emmanuel Rakotovahiny, on October 30. Rakotovahiny named his new government on November 10.

The death in January of British environmentalist Andrew Lees, who was campaigning to prevent the multinational mining firm RTZ from opening up the southern coastline near Tolanaro to mine titanium dioxide, highlighted the conflict between environmental preservation and mining development, since the operation would lead to the destruction of unique fauna and flora. (GUY ARNOLD)

MALAWI

A republic and member of the Commonwealth, Malawi is a landlocked state in eastern Africa. Area: 118,484 sq km (45,747 sq mi). Pop. (1995 est.): 9,939,000. Cap.: Lilongwe. Monetary unit: Malawi kwacha, with (Oct. 6, 1995) a free rate of 15.26 kwacha to U.S. $1 (24.13 kwacha = £1 sterling). President in 1995, Bakili Muluzi.

For its recognition of the need for a strong and comprehensive adjustment program to arrest the country's economic and financial deterioration, Malawi received a vote of confidence by the International Monetary Fund at the end of 1994. Finance Minister Aleke Banda promised in his budget on March 24, 1995, that there would be cuts in government spending and a review of civil service staffing levels, together with additional taxes on electricity, cars, and luxury imports, but the government also stressed that responsibility for economic recovery rested upon the whole population.

For the public in general, however, concern for economic regeneration was overshadowed by the arrest early in January of former president Hastings Kamuzu Banda, his chief aide, John Tembo, and three senior policemen on charges of murdering three former Cabinet ministers and a member of the National Assembly in 1983. Related charges brought against Tembo's niece and Banda's "official hostess," Cecilia Kadzamira, who was arrested on March 31, were later dropped on technical grounds. Pending trial, the former president was held under house arrest because of his age and poor health, and the trial itself was postponed on a number of occasions when Banda's lawyers pleaded that he was unfit to appear in court. In May the trial judge accepted medical advice to that effect but ruled that the trial should go ahead in Banda's absence.

Talk of an attempted coup, following the fatal shooting in April of Gen. Manken Chigawa, the Army commander, was dismissed as speculation by Pres. Bakili Muluzi. The general's death, he said, was the work of armed robbers.

The reputation of the government for upholding the freedom of the press, recently reinforced by a commendation from Johann P. Fritz, director of the International Press Institute, was challenged by local journalists. In August they accused the authorities of censoring the state-controlled radio and intimidating journalists working for independent newspapers. The government did not immediately respond to the charges. (KENNETH INGHAM)

This article updates the *Macropædia* article SOUTHERN AFRICA: *Malawi.*

MALAYSIA

A federal constitutional monarchy of Southeast Asia and member of the Commonwealth, Malaysia consists of the former Federation of Malaya at the southern end of the Malay Peninsula (excluding Singapore) and Sabah and Sarawak on the northern part of the island of Borneo. Area: 330,442 sq km (127,584 sq mi). Pop. (1995 est.): 19,948,000. Cap.: Kuala Lumpur. Monetary unit: ringgit, with (Oct. 6, 1995) a free rate of 2.54 ringgit to U.S. $1 (4.01 ringgit = £1 sterling). Paramount ruler in 1995, with the title of *yang di-pertuan agong,* Tuanku Ja'afar ibni al-Marhum Tuanku Abdul Rahman; prime minister, Datuk Seri Mahathir bin Mohamad.

Malaysians gave Prime Minister Datuk Seri Mahathir bin Mohamad an even bigger parliamentary victory in 1995 than the 71% majority his ruling National Front coalition had won in the 1990 general election. Members of the United Malays National Organization (UMNO) who were elected to Parliament, together with others belonging to five allied parties, totaled 162 and represented a majority of 84% in the expanded 192-seat House of Representatives. In state elections the coalition strengthened its grip on the Chinese-majority state of Penang, which the opposition Democratic Action Party (DAP) had hoped to control. The Malaysian Chinese Association, a Front partner, won 29 of 33 seats in the state legislature.

The DAP lost 11 of the 20 seats it had won in 1990, and the Sabah United Party (PBS), another opposition group, lost 6 of the 14 seats it had previously occupied. UMNO had wrested control of the Borneo state of Sabah from the PBS in 1994. The conservative Pan-Malaysian Islamic Party (Pas) did better, not only keeping all the 7 parliamentary seats it had won five years earlier but also gaining 24 of 43 state seats. Pas ally Spirit of '46 (Semangat '46), a splinter group of UMNO, won 11 seats, making Kelantan the nation's only opposition-ruled state. In August a Kelantan court stripped Spirit of '46 leader Tengku Razaleigh Hamzah of his state seat because of a nomination technicality, but Razaleigh easily regained it in a by-election.

In the ensuing Cabinet reshuffle, Mahathir reappointed most of his loyalists or moved them to new posts. Those close to his designated successor, Deputy Prime Minister Anwar Ibrahim, were given minor portfolios. Mahathir encountered a few setbacks later in the year, however. Several of his high-profile allies, among them former finance minister Daim Zainuddin and former agriculture minister Sanusi Junid, were eased out as UMNO division chiefs. Party members voted in many Anwar backers instead, fueling speculation that Anwar might challenge Mahathir for the presidency of UMNO (which brings with it the premiership) the following year.

In announcing his Cabinet appointments, Mahathir said that government officials would be bound by a new code of conduct that, among other regulations, limited their involvement in business and regulated sexual conduct. Rahim Tamby Chik had been forced to resign as chief minister of Malacca state over allegations that he had had an affair with a minor. Rafidah Aziz, minister of industry and international trade, was accused of conflict of interest, but she was cleared by the anticorruption agency. She was present when a committee in her ministry allocated a large number of stocks to her son-in-law. Minister of Youth and Sports Muhyiddin Yassin was taken to court for alleged improper involvement in land acquisition when he was chief minister of Johore state.

The government came under attack for reviving a plan to build the Bakun hydroelectric dam in Sarawak state at a cost of $6 billion. Dismissing an environmental-impact report that warned of serious ecological damage, the government awarded a contract in February to build the dam. With construction scheduled to begin in January 1996, some 80,000 ha (200,000 ac) of rain forest would eventually be submerged and nearly 10,000 people, most from tribal communities, displaced.

The economy expanded at more than 9% in 1995, continuing the economic growth rates of 8% or better of the previous eight years. There were worries about a ballooning current-account deficit, which topped $5 billion in October. Mahathir also voiced concern about the 3.5% inflation rate, saying prices should not rise at all. In an address to the UN General Assembly in September, Mahathir said that the world body had become the preserve of rich nations and had to be reformed. (CESAR BACANI)

This article updates the *Macropædia* article SOUTHEAST ASIA: *Malaysia.*

MALDIVES

A republic and member of the Commonwealth in the Indian Ocean, Maldives consists of about 1,200 small islands southwest of the southern tip of India. Area: 298 sq km (115 sq mi). Pop. (1995 est.): 253,000. Cap.: Male. Monetary unit: rufiyaa, with (Oct. 6, 1995) a free rate of 11.77 rufiyaa to U.S. $1 (18.60 rufiyaa = £1 sterling). President in 1995, Maumoon Abdul Gayoom.

With government revenues of 991,100,000 rufiyaa and expenditures of 1,524,000,000 rufiyaa, Maldives was in deficit in 1994; as in past years, the shortfall was to be made up by regular injections of foreign aid. Of the population of some 250,000, just over one-fifth were economically active, with a quarter of this number involved in agriculture and fisheries. Fishing was the mainstay of the economy, with canned tuna accounting for 40% of all exports, dried skipjack tuna for 18%, and frozen skipjack tuna for another 8.9%. The other major export was apparel and clothing (21%).

Despite its limited economic base, Maldives was relatively successful in maintaining a high level of employment; industries included boatbuilding, the production of coir yarn, mat weaving, coconut and fish processing, lacquerwork, and garment manufacturing. Tourism was becoming increasingly important, and income from this source in 1994 totaled approximately $113 million.

Maldives continued to have no political parties or organized opposition. Nonetheless, there were signs of growing opposition to the presidential system among foreign-educated younger Maldivians as well as some government concern about the growth of religious extremism on the islands. (GUY ARNOLD)

This article updates the *Micropædia* article MALDIVES.

MALI

Mali is a landlocked republic of West Africa. Area: 1,248,574 sq km (482,077 sq mi). Pop. (1995 est.): 9,008,000. Cap.: Bamako. Monetary unit: CFA franc, with (Oct. 6, 1995) a par value of CFAF 100 to the French franc and a free rate of CFAF 501.49 to U.S. $1 (CFAF 792.78 = £1 sterling). President in 1995, Alpha Oumar Konaré; prime minister, Ibrahima Boubacar Keita.

Substantial progress was made in 1995 in reconciling dissident groups to the peace agreement signed in June 1994 between the government and representatives of the main

A man's two wives prepare food and care for their children in the courtyard of the family home in Mali. The polygynous marriage, in which the wives shared many of the duties of feeding and caring for the family, was a typical arrangement in contemporary Malian society.
MELISSA FARLOW—MATERIAL WORLD WOMEN'S PROJECT

Tuareg coalition, the Unified Movements and Fronts of Azawad. On January 13 Ghanda Koi and the Popular Front for the Liberation of the Azawad agreed to end the fighting in the north. In June, for the first time, the government entered into negotiations with other unreconciled Tuareg groups. Sedentary and nomadic communities in the northern district of Bamba, the site of numerous conflicts over the past four years, met in July and agreed to disarm and to guarantee free movement throughout the region for all. International donors estimated that it would take at least $400 million to restart economic development in the north and to resettle the estimated 120,000 Tuareg refugees living in camps in Algeria, Burkina Faso, Mauritania, and Niger. A three-year refugee-repatriation program began in October.

More splits appeared in the National Committee for a Democratic Initiative, the main opposition coalition. Ten of its leaders were suspended from the party's governing committee on March 26, and on September 18 they formed the National Renaissance Party (PRN). The PRN became Mali's 57th political party.

Following Mali's good economic performance in 1994, the International Monetary Fund approved the nation's third annual structural adjustment loan, $46 million for 1995. Reconstruction of Bamako's renowned central market, destroyed by fire in August 1994, began in February, financed mainly by the French Development Fund. The discovery of new gold deposits in the south, combined with the doubling of production at the existing operations at Siama, sparked further international interest in Mali's mineral resources. (NANCY ELLEN LAWLER)

This article updates the *Macropædia* article WESTERN AFRICA: *Mali.*

MALTA

The republic of Malta, a member of the Commonwealth, comprises the islands of Malta, Gozo, and Comino in the Mediterranean Sea between Sicily and Tunisia. Area: 316 sq km (122 sq mi). Pop. (1995 est.): 370,000. Cap.: Valletta. Monetary unit: Maltese lira, with (Oct. 6, 1995) a free rate of 0.35 lira to U.S. $1 (0.56 lira = £1 sterling). President in 1995, Ugo Mifsud Bonnici; prime minister, Eddie Fenech Adami.

It was announced in March 1995 that according to a report of the European Commission, negotiations on Malta's application to join the European Union (EU) would start six months after the conclusion of the 1996 Inter-Governmental Conference. In June a financial protocol was signed for ECU 45 million in EU funds to help Malta achieve economic reforms. Malta's House of Representatives in April approved a motion to join the Partnership for Peace movement on a NATO initiative addressed to all member countries of the Organization for Security and Cooperation in Europe (OSCE). Later, in a ministerial reshuffle, four ministers were replaced.

In October the first-ever Mediterranean Crans-Montana Forum, organized by the Swiss-based Foundation du Forum Universale, was held in Malta. Over a four-day period, more than 500 delegates, including heads of state and prime ministers, discussed the formation of a Euro-Mediterranean area to bring about a systematic development of mechanisms of cooperation in all fields. An especially large delegation from Libya comprising government officials, financial experts, and businessmen was present to take advantage of a small chink in the international isolation imposed on that country in the wake of the Lockerbie incident. Awards were conferred on Yasir Arafat for his "exceptional contribution to peace" and Janez Drnovsek, prime minister of Slovenia, for his work in his country's smooth transition from communism to democracy. Immediately afterward, Li Peng, premier of China, led a high-level trade delegation to Malta. He voiced plans about a Malta-China air services agreement. Two ships built in Malta for China were officially named.

(ALBERT GANADO)

MARSHALL ISLANDS

A republic in the central Pacific Ocean, the Marshall Islands comprises two 1,300-km (800-mi)-long parallel chains of coral atolls. Area: 181 sq km (70 sq mi). Pop. (1995 est.): 56,200. Cap.: Majuro. Monetary unit: U.S. dollar, with (Oct. 6, 1995) a free rate of U.S. $1.59 to £1 sterling. President in 1995, Amata Kabua.

Nuclear issues continued to be the focus of controversy in the Marshall Islands in 1995, especially after Foreign Minister Phillip Muller announced a preliminary feasibility study for nuclear waste storage at Bikini atoll during his address to the UN General Assembly at the end of 1994. The proposal was rejected by the Bikini Council in May 1995. The proposal would have placed a nuclear waste dump on Bikini, which had been totally contaminated by the 23 nuclear tests conducted by the United States in the 1940s and 1950s. Most of the residents of Bikini atoll, numbering about 200, had been evacuated before the tests in 1948 and were currently living on the small southerly atoll of Kili.

The nuclear waste proposal had been seen as one option for future revenue when the Marshall Islands' Compact of Free Association with the U.S. ended in 2001. At that time the 75% of the nation's $85 million budget that the U.S. provided in direct aid and federal programs would cease. In anticipation of the compact's termination, the International Monetary Fund urged measures to reduce the size of the public service, reduce subsidies to public agencies, and privatize government services. Because of public opposition, a 10% wage cut for government workers, approved by the Nitijela (parliament) in October 1994, was not implemented.

In March the Marshall Islands served as host for the inaugural summit of a new subregional grouping consisting of Kiribati, Nauru, Tuvalu, and the Marshall Islands. Leaders of those countries discussed issues of common concern, including economic cooperation and civil aviation.

(BARRIE MACDONALD)

This article updates the *Macropædia* article PACIFIC ISLANDS: *Marshall Islands.*

MAURITANIA

The republic of Mauritania is on the Atlantic coast of West Africa. Area: 1,030,700 sq km (398,000 sq mi). Pop. (1995 est.): 2,274,000. Cap.: Nouakchott. Monetary unit: ouguiya, with (Oct. 6, 1995) a free rate of 132.56 ouguiya to U.S. $1 (209.56 ouguiya = £1 sterling). President in 1995, Col. Maaouya Ould Sidi Ahmad Taya; prime minister, Sidi Mohamed Ould Boubacar.

Massive demonstrations erupted in Nouakchott on Jan. 21, 1995, when crowds protested the huge increases in the costs of basic commodities as a result of the imposition of a value-added tax. For three days the capital was virtually shut down as students and unemployed young men burned cars and looted shops. The government accused the opposition of instigating the riots and arrested eight prominent leaders, including Ahmad Ould Daddah of the coalition Union of Democratic Forces–New Era (UFD-EN), and Hamdi Ould Mouknass of the Union for Democracy and Progress (UDP). Although all were released within a few weeks, opposition groups in turn accused the government of mistreating the detainees.

In March the Movement of Independent Democrats withdrew from the UFD-EN in March, and aligned itself with Pres. Maaouya Taya's ruling Democratic and Social Republican Party. In July six opposition parties, including the UFD-EN and the UDP, formed a new coalition to achieve a transition to democracy and to press for a new electoral code and an accurate electoral roll. Cracks in the opposition appeared, however, when UFD-EN dissidents, apparently representing black Mauritanians, announced the formation of a new party on August 29.

Mauritania's international creditors agreed on June 30 to reschedule the government's public debt. Part of the debt was annulled, and payments on the remainder were to be spread over 23 years. Late rains and a plague of locusts delayed the normal July start of the planting season. As a result, agricultural production was likely to suffer. All offshore fishing in Mauritanian waters, except for tuna, was suspended in September in order to allow sharply diminished stocks to recover.

(NANCY ELLEN LAWLER)

This article updates the *Macropædia* article WESTERN AFRICA: *Mauritania.*

MAURITIUS

The republic of Mauritius, a member of the Commonwealth, occupies an island in the Indian Ocean about 800 km (500 mi) east of Madagascar and includes the island dependencies of Rodrigues, Agalega, and Cargados Carajos Shoals. Area: 2,040 sq km (788 sq mi). Pop. (1995 est.): 1,128,000. Cap.: Port Louis. Monetary unit: Mauritian rupee, with (Oct. 6, 1995) a free rate of Mau Rs 17.99 to U.S. $1 (Mau Rs 28.43 = £1 sterling). President in 1995, Cassam Uteem; prime ministers, Sir Anerood Jugnauth and, from December 22, Nuvin Ramgoolam.

Prime Minister Sir Anerood Jugnauth carried out Cabinet changes at the end of 1994; Ramduthsing Jaddoo, the minister of manpower resources and vocational and technical training, was promoted to become minister of external affairs, and one minister, Mahyendrah Utchanah, was dismissed for corruption, having shown bias in the awarding of a gas contract. The government suffered an election defeat at the end of January 1995 when the Mauritian Militant Renaissance (RMM), one of the coalition partners, lost a seat. In subsequent maneuvering with the next elections in mind, Jugnauth expanded his Cabinet in order to accommodate members of the right-wing Mauritian Social Democratic Party (PMSD), which had joined the coalition. Jugnauth's preparations went for naught, however. In the December 20 elections the opposition alliance led by Nuvin Ramgoolam and Paul Berenger won nearly two-thirds of the vote and all the seats in the Legislative Assembly, cleanly sweeping Jugnauth's coalition out of power.

Clothing and textiles became the leading export earners for Mauritius, accounting for more than 52% of all exports. Sugar, the former staple of the economy, was in second place at 28%. (GUY ARNOLD)

This article updates the *Micropædia* article MAURITIUS.

MEXICO

A federal republic of North America, Mexico has coastlines on the Pacific Ocean, the Gulf of Mexico, and the Caribbean Sea. Area: 1,958,201 sq km (756,066 sq mi). Pop. (1995 est.): 91,145,-000. Cap.: Mexico City. Monetary unit: Mexican new peso, with (Oct. 6, 1995) a free rate of 6.54 new pesos to U.S. $1 (10.33 new pesos = £1 sterling). President in 1995, Ernesto Zedillo Ponce de León.

Mexico began 1995 amid a deepening financial crisis that had been unleashed in late December 1994 following the mishandled devaluation of the currency and rising tensions on the political front. An initial effort to stem the continuing run on the peso by means of an international aid package in early January failed. A more successful result occurred in early March after the administration of Pres. Ernesto Zedillo Ponce de León inaugurated an austerity program that helped qualify the country for substantial support from the U.S. and the International Monetary Fund; they made available up to $20 billion and nearly $17.8 billion (as a standby loan), respectively. This enabled Mexico to underwrite the repayment of most of the $28 billion of short-term, dollar-denominated debt that matured during the year. An additional $10 billion of credits was granted via the Bank for International Settlements.

The terms for Mexico's receiving the international financial support were hard and were expected to result in the onset of a severe recession in the country's economy as part of an adjustment process in which the large 1994 deficits on trade ($18.5 billion) and current accounts ($28.7 billion) were to be sharply reduced. The austerity plan announced on March 9 set out the key targets for 1995. They included a decline of about 2% in gross domestic product (GDP), which contrasted sharply with the 4% increase President Zedillo had envisioned during his 1994 election campaign. The target for annual inflation rose to 42%, compared with the 7.05% registered for 1994. Even more dramatic was the projected reduction in the current account deficit to no more than $2.4 billion, which would result in a major improvement in the trade account to a surplus of $5.4 billion.

In fact, however, it became clear by September that the recession was more severe than initially thought, with a projected annual decline in GDP of 5%. Government spending was to be reduced by 10% during the year, with only about 35% being spent in the first half. Having peaked at 8% in April as a result of an increase in sales taxes, monthly inflation was cut to about 2% in the third quarter of the year; the annual rate, however, was expected to rise to perhaps 46%. By the end of September, the annual target for the trade surplus had been achieved, with positive monthly balances being registered from February onward. Still, the peso began falling again in November, bottoming at 7.80 to the dollar before the central bank intervened to stabilize it.

There were some measures to help offset the austerity program for the poorest Mexicans. On April 1 the minimum wage was increased 10%, and all other wages were to be freely negotiated; subsidies for many staple items were temporarily retained; a rural employment program was set up to provide minimum incomes to rural workers; income tax rebates were to be made available to those earning up to four times the minimum wage; and health benefits for the unemployed would run for six months instead of two. The Alliance for Economic Recuperation, an agreement worked out on October 29 between the government, labour, and business, foresaw minimum wage raises of 20% to keep pace with projected inflation, and steps were taken to reduce consumption and restrain inflation.

As 1995 progressed, millions of Mexicans joined spontaneous protest movements, of which "El Barzón" ("The Yoke") was probably the largest. These sprang up to demand government action in regard to mounting personal debts alleged to have been incurred as a result of official mismanagement. This especially applied to the middle sectors of society and to small businesses that had taken on increased financial commitments in the belief (promoted by the former administration of Carlos Salinas de Gortari) that the country was headed for sustained prosperity.

Zedillo responded on August 22 by announcing a debt-relief plan. This aimed to ease the debt burdens of some 7.5 million borrowers, 6 million of whom owed banks and other financial institutions up to 200,000 new pesos and the remainder of whom owed sums greater than that. The bad loan portfolios of the country's banks, which were estimated at $15.2 billion—15% of total loans—were also expected to be reduced under the plan.

On the political front, President Zedillo was beleaguered by the backlog of adverse developments inherited from the previous administration. Local elections late in the year suggested that the hold of the ruling Institutional Revolutionary Party (PRI) was slipping. In January he tried to achieve a rapid and peaceful resolution of the conflict with the Zapatista National Liberation Army (EZLN) in the southern state of Chiapas, which had begun a year earlier. When this failed, he launched in February a brief military offensive against the EZLN, issuing an arrest warrant for the most prominent member of its leadership (Subcomandante Marcos; *see* BIOGRAPHIES) and other key figures. The unpopularity of this led Zedillo to reverse the policy again, with a series of negotiations taking place in April. During subsequent months progress was slow, and late in the year negotiations were still ongoing. Fernando Yáñez Muñoz, known as "Comandante Germán," a founder of the EZLN, was arrested on weapons charges in October but was quickly released when the government realized that the incident was undermining the talks with the Chiapas rebels. Official inquiries continued into the assassinations of the PRI's original presidential candidate, Luis Donaldo Colosio, on March 23, 1994, and of its secretary-general, José Francisco Ruiz Massieu, on Sept. 28, 1994. While neither of these murders was satisfactorily explained, it was widely suspected that senior members of the PRI were involved, perhaps in collaboration with the drug mafia.

The decision to arrest Raúl Salinas de Gortari, the brother of the former president, on February 28 on the grounds that he masterminded the murder of Ruiz Massieu was heralded as a bold move that temporarily helped to restore Zedillo's credibility. This came along with moves to extradite the former deputy attorney general, Mario Ruiz Massieu, from the U.S. to face charges that he obstructed the investigation into his brother's murder; he was denied release on bail in late December. Paulina Castañón, the wife of Raúl Salinas, was arrested in Switzerland in November for using false documents to withdraw funds, thought to be laundered drug money, from her husband's bank account.

(continued on page 444)

SPOTLIGHT: ACCELERATING CHANGES IN MEXICO

Illustration by Istvan Banyai

by Sergio Sarmiento

Rarely had a country turned from a showcase into a basket case in such a short period of time. At the end of 1993, after signing the North American Free Trade Agreement (NAFTA), Mexico seemed strong, stable, and poised to enter the developed world. By the end of 1995, the country was suffering the deepest recession in its history, and its political system appeared to be in shambles. What happened over those 24 months was important not only for Mexico, which was paying dearly for any errors it may have committed, but also for the U.S., which as a neighbour bore the immediate consequences of any Mexican crisis.

There were no agreed-upon answers about what actually caused the Mexican downfall. Ernesto Zedillo Ponce de León, who took over as president on Dec. 1, 1994, claimed that his administration inherited an overvalued peso, which produced an unaffordable current-account deficit of almost $29 billion in 1994. It was this that led to the peso's devaluation, he argued, and to the ensuing economic crisis.

Former finance minister Pedro Aspe disagreed, however. The peso was not overvalued, he claimed, as was proved by the fact that exports rose 23% in 1994. Capital did not flee because of economic circumstances. At first, capital left as a response to political events and crimes—most notably the assassination of Luis Donaldo Colosio, presidential candidate of the ruling Institutional Revolutionary Party (PRI), on March 23, 1994. The real collapse, said Aspe, was provoked by the devaluation of the peso ordered in December 1994 by President Zedillo.

Mexico's powerful leftist groups disagreed with both views. They argued that the economic crisis was provoked by the economic liberalization engineered by Pres. Carlos Salinas de Gortari from 1988 to 1994. Privatizing state companies and opening the borders to trade were the crucial decisions that weakened Mexico. NAFTA, in their opinion, was the straw that broke the camel's back.

It would be hard to argue against the view that the current-account deficit was at least part of the problem. It was true that Mexico's exports were rising in 1994, but the current-account deficit made the country excessively dependent on short-term foreign money. Maintaining this capital flow was not a problem when the country was hailed as a showcase, but the flow reversed when the Colosio assassination generated doubts about Mexico's political future.

Aspe was right, however, when he claimed that devaluation had aggravated the problem. The drastic drop in the peso's value, only days after the government had vowed not to devalue, shattered the confidence of investors and savers. It took four weeks for the country to lose $10 billion in reserves after the Colosio assassination—but only two days for the same amount to move from pesos into dollars after the devaluation.

Mexico's privatizations and trade opening were probably necessary. During the 1980s Mexico had carried an unsustainable budget deficit, which peaked at 16% of gross domestic product (GDP). The privatizations were a crucial part of a strategy that eliminated this deficit and brought the public sector's debt from 68% of GDP in 1988 to 32% in 1994. A highly protected domestic economy had been maintained for decades, so the trade opening sharply increased imports, but it also generated competition benefiting consumers and promoted exports. Mexico's foreign sales stood at $21 billion in 1988; by 1995 they were forecast to rise to $80 billion.

There was no indication that NAFTA, which went into effect on Jan. 1, 1994, either precipitated or accelerated the economic collapse. In October of that year, when the peso was allegedly overvalued, Mexico was already chalking up a trade surplus with its North American partners, the U.S. and Canada. Mexico's deficit was a consequence of trade with East Asia and Europe, where protectionist practices allegedly prevented the importation of Mexican products.

On the contrary, a dearth of domestic savings was a major factor in the crisis. During the Salinas administration, improved expectations and the privatization of the nation's banks boosted credit to private companies and individuals. Consumption and investment rose more than income, while savings declined, generating demand for foreign money. In 1995 President Zedillo increased the value-added tax to reduce consumption and reformed the country's pensions system to boost savings. This was expected to reduce dependence on foreign capital and to provide stability to Mexico's volatile financial markets. It would take years, however, for accumulated pensions to provide the kind of long-term capital Mexico needed.

This was why political reform became so urgent. The assassination of presidential candidate Colosio sparked the initial bout of capital flight in 1994 because investors saw the country as lacking adequate political institutions. Mexico's traditionally benign authoritarianism, built upon an extremely powerful presidency, had provided stability for decades, but it made the country's entire political structure dependent on the president—and his successor. Reform negotiations involving the three major political parties began in early 1995 and sought to generate a new and more balanced political structure, giving greater power to the legislative and judicial branches of government as well as to municipal and state administrations. The reforms, said to be nearly agreed upon at the end of 1995, were set to change electoral rules that had allowed the PRI to remain in power since 1929 and thus be one of the longest-ruling parties in the world.

President Zedillo did not wait for political reform to try to clean the country's fraud-marred elections. In 1995, the first year of his administration, there were five elections involving state governorships. The PRI lost three of them. Traditionalists in Mexico claimed that these defeats demonstrated the weakness of the president, but Zedillo argued that in a true democracy it was normal for a ruling party to lose elections during a recession.

It was not easy for a country to change from a closed to an open economy and from an authoritarian to a democratic system at the same time. Every change generates turbulence, of course, and this turbulence was what was seen in Mexico in 1994 and 1995. Liberalizing the economy and democratizing political life would not turn Mexico into a showcase again any time soon, but at least they could generate more solid foundations for building a better future.

Sergio Sarmiento, a syndicated newspaper columnist in Mexico, is also vice president for news operations at Televisión Azteca, Mexico's second largest TV network.

(continued from page 442)
Meanwhile, Carlos Salinas, whose whereabouts in exile were not known, expressed his "amazement" that his brother had amassed $84 million and deposited it in a Swiss account under a false name.

The arrest of Raúl Salinas and the judicial order on March 6 that he stand trial for the Ruiz Massieu murder apparently ended the long-standing tradition that former presidents and their kin are immune from the law after leaving office. Allegations that former president Salinas was personally involved in a cover-up after the Colosio murder were withdrawn, however, after he staged a hunger strike.

The assassination on May 10 of the former attorney general in the state of Jalisco, Leobardo Larios Guzmán, who had been investigating the murder (in 1993) of Juan Jesús Cardinal Posadas Ocampo, focused attention back on the role of the drug mafia and contributed to pressure on Zedillo to produce results in the following months. Little real progress was made, however.

Zedillo announced in September that the government planned to carry out an electoral reform within the next 12 months aimed at putting an end to disputes over election results. The PRI and the two main opposition parties were reported to have reached an agreement on December 15 that made provision for independent candidates, an election commission outside government control, and limits on election spending by candidates.

Several significant Cabinet changes took place during the year. On June 28 it was announced that the interior minister, Estebán Moctezuma Barragán, was being replaced by Emilio Chuayffet Chemor, a former governor of Mexico state. The new appointee was a member of the PRI's hard-line "political" wing of the party, which had for some years been subordinate to the "technocrats" (of whom Zedillo was one). During the weekend of August 19–20, the resignations of PRI leader Mario de Los Angeles Moreno and Secretary-General Pedro Joaquin Coldwell were announced. These were followed by the appointment of Labour Minister Santiago Oñate Laborde, an economist, to head the party and of Juan Sigfrido Millan, a senator and top-ranking official within the Mexican Labour Confederation (CTM), to be secretary-general. Oñate's post at the Labour Ministry went to the veteran labour official Javier Bonilla Garciá. A serious blow was dealt Zedillo and the PRI with the resignation from the party on October 13 of Manuel Camacho Solis, a top party leader and former Mexico City mayor.

(SUSAN M. CUNNINGHAM)

MICRONESIA, FEDERATED STATES OF

A republic in the western Pacific Ocean, the Federated States of Micronesia comprises more than 600 islands and islets in the Caroline Islands archipelago. Area: 701 sq km (271 sq mi). Pop. (1995 est.): 105,000. Cap.: Palikir, on Pohnpei. Monetary unit: U.S. dollar, with (Oct. 6, 1995) a free rate of U.S. $1.59 to £1 sterling. President in 1995, Bailey Olter.

At national elections in March, there were 28 candidates for 14 seats in Congress. Pres. Bailey Olter and Vice Pres. Jacob Nena were both returned in their constituencies. Despite some pressure to introduce the principle of the rotation of high office among representatives from the various regions, Olter and Nena were reelected to office unanimously by Congress. The speaker, Jack Fritz, was also reelected.

An Asian Development Bank report published in June drew attention to deficiencies in government management that were explained by the rapid expansion of government

JAVIER BAULUZ

Farmers supporting the government hold a demonstration in front of the cathedral in San Cristóbal de Las Casas to protest the role of the bishop of Chiapas in supporting the Zapatista National Liberation Army. Talks between the government and the revolutionaries continued throughout the year.

and the economy in recent years and a consequential shortage of qualified staff. The $87 million received from the U.S. under the Compact of Free Association with the United States was the major component in the government's budget. The next largest source of income was the sale of international fishing licenses, which had contributed an annual average of $14 million in recent years.

In April the government expressed concern to Japan over planned plutonium shipments through the region.

(BARRIE MACDONALD)

This article updates the *Macropædia* article PACIFIC ISLANDS: *Micronesia.*

MOLDOVA

A landlocked republic of the extreme northeastern Balkans, Moldova borders Ukraine on the north, northeast, and southeast and Romania on the west. Area: 33,700 sq km (13,000 sq mi). Pop. (1995 est.) 4,346,000. Cap.: Chisinau. Monetary unit: Moldovan leu, with (Oct. 6, 1995) a free rate of 4.55 lei = U.S. $1 (7.19 lei = £1 sterling). President in 1995, Mircea Snegur; prime minister, Andrei Sangheli.

The prospects of stability for the republic were greatly enhanced by the announcement on April 19 of the staged withdrawal from Transdniester of the Russian 14th Army and the resignation in June of its commander, Lieut. Gen. Aleksandr Lebed. Without the underpinning of this army, the authorities in the breakaway province of Transdniester became more conciliatory, and in July the Moldovan government granted political amnesty to those charged with crimes relating to the conflict. Transdniester's constitutional status, however, remained unresolved. By year's end the results of the December 24 elections in Transdniester were not clear, although the pro-Russian party was thought to have dominated. In a referendum on the same date, some 81.8% of voters approved the region's separatist constitution. After elections in Gagauzia, the second autonomous region, the Moldovan prime minister declared that the dispute between that area and Moldova was at an end.

Encouraging results over the summer in the economy fueled hopes that a recovery was on the horizon. Tight monetary policy produced a dramatic fall in inflation, down to a December-to-December rate of 10%, compared with 800% in 1993 and 108% in 1994. The government's privatization program, relying partly on a voucher method in which at least 90% of Moldovans had participated by November 30, was accelerated and 800 companies earmarked. Foreign involvement in privatization was also encouraged, with the result that foreigners could purchase up to 60% of the shares in 39 companies. In July the Moldova stock exchange was opened, and on July 13 Moldova was admitted to the Council of Europe.

(DENNIS J. DELETANT)

This article updates the *Macropædia* article BALKAN STATES: *Moldova.*

MONACO

A sovereign principality on the northern Mediterranean coast, Monaco is bounded on land by the French département of Alpes-Maritimes. Area: 1.95 sq km (0.75 sq mi). Pop. (1995 est.): 30,400. Monetary unit: French franc, with (Oct. 6, 1995) a free rate of F 5.01 to U.S. $1 (F 7.93 = £1 sterling). Chief of state, Prince Rainier III; ministers of state in 1995, Jacques Dupont and, from November 24, Paul Dijoud.

The tiny principality of Monaco sustained its serenity and its prosperity during 1995. Amid speculation that he would abdicate in favour of his son, Prince Albert, Prince Rainier reigned on, and the economy remained buoyant. Imminent abdication was reported by the French magazine *Paris Match* shortly after Prince Rainier's heart-bypass surgery in November 1994. Prince Albert was unmarried, which raised questions about the succession. Under a 1918 treaty, France can annex the principality if there is no male Grimaldi heir. There were also rumours that Prince Rainier might name Princess Caroline's eldest son as his heir. Outside Monaco, speculation abounded even after the rumours were denounced as "sheer fantasy." Meanwhile, Princess Stephanie married Daniel Ducruet, her former bodyguard, in July.

The move to diversify Monaco's economy continued. A country once funded by the proceeds of gambling in the casinos was now estimated to receive only 4% of its income from that source. Tourism continued to drive the economy, especially the lucrative business-conference sector. Construction cranes were everywhere as building continued for new housing, a conference and cultural centre, a railroad station, a new jetty, and other projects.

(ANNE ROBY)

This article updates the *Micropædia* article MONACO.

MONGOLIA

A landlocked republic between Russia and China in eastern Asia, Mongolia was formerly known as Outer Mongolia. Area: 1,566,500 sq km (604,800 sq mi). Pop. (1995 est.): 2,307,000. Cap.: Ulaanbaatar (Ulan Bator). Monetary unit: tugrik, with (Oct. 6, 1995) a free rate of Tug 449.10 to U.S. $1 (Tug 709.98 = £1 sterling). President in 1995, Punsalmaagiyn Ochirbat; prime minister, Puntsagiyn Jasray.

For the first time since the ruling Mongolian People's Revolutionary Party (MPRP) won the 1992 general elections with a massive majority, a real possibility of cooperation between the parliamentary political parties emerged in 1995. Pres. Punsalmaagiyn Ochirbat cobbled together a pact between the MPRP and the opposition National Democrats and Social Democrats under which 24 of the 76 members of the Great Hural (national assembly) would be chosen by proportional representation at the June 1996 general elections; the other 52 would be elected as before, by simple majority vote. If the Great Hural adopted the necessary amendment to the Law on Elections, opposition parties were likely to be more fairly represented.

It was unclear whether the 70 MPRP members who dominated the Great Hural would approve the amendment. The parties differed fundamentally in their attitudes toward the country's communist past and its democratic revolution of 1990. To distract attention from Mongolia's 1992 constitution, the MPRP inaugurated a November public holiday to celebrate the anniversary of Mongolia's 1924 constitution. Ochirbat called the 1924 constitution socially divisive and ruinous to Mongolia's independence and appealed to all Mongols "to give a correct assessment to history and work harder and with greater unity to build a new democratic society in keeping with the new constitution."

The MPRP raised new doubts about its claim to have given up Marxism by rehabilitating (posthumously) the "Mongolian Brezhnev," former MPRP general secretary Yumjaagiyn Tsedenbal, who was ousted in August 1984. The MPRP combined nostalgia for the communist past with the search for a new national ideology based on state monopoly to satisfy the government model of an "economy with state regulation and a social orientation."

Such a model was already coming into conflict with the bodies that funded Mongolia's debts. The UN Development Programme noted that many "privatized" enterprises were still partly state-owned, while the government was not promoting new private-sector businesses. The International Monetary Fund was critical of state interference in the allocation of bank credits, which tended to crowd out private-sector activity. Despite these concerns, grants and credits for Mongolia in 1995 amounted to $210 million.

The U.S. Congress issued a statement in May supporting Mongolia, and the president authorized U.S. military assistance. (ALAN J.K. SANDERS)

MOROCCO

A constitutional monarchy of North Africa, Morocco has coastlines on the Atlantic Ocean and the Mediterranean Sea. Area: 458,730 sq km (177,117 sq mi). Pop. (1995 est.): 26,980,000. (Area and population figures refer to Morocco as constituted prior to the purported division of Western Sahara between Morocco and Mauritania and the subsequent Moroccan occupation of the Mauritanian zone in 1979.) Cap.: Rabat. Monetary unit: dirham, with (Oct. 6, 1995) a free rate of 8.45 dirhams to U.S. $1 (13.36 dirhams = £1 sterling). King, Hassan II; prime minister, ʿAbd al-Latif Filali.

The conflict between Morocco and the Polisario Front over the control of Western Sahara continued to drag on throughout 1995, with new difficulties emerging over the registration process for voters in the planned self-determination referendum. As a result of the disputes, the referendum was postponed again until mid-1996 at the earliest, despite objections from the Polisario Front. Tensions in the Western Sahara were highlighted in midyear when eight Saharans were condemned to long periods of imprisonment (later reduced to one year each by King Hassan) for anti-Moroccan demonstrations in El Aaiun.

The most important problems facing Morocco during 1995 were, however, economic in nature. Negotiations for a new association agreement with the European Union (EU) were finally concluded in November; indeed, because the concept of the industrial free-trade area had been developed with Morocco specifically in mind, it was expected to be the first nation to sign such an agreement. During the negotiations, however, many problems emerged, not least the question of what would happen to Morocco's developing industrial sector if the transitional terms were not carefully set. Some reports suggested that up to 60% of the sector would be destroyed by competition with European producers.

Difficulties over agriculture and fishing also delayed signature of the association agreement. In midyear Morocco demanded the renegotiation of its fishing agreement with the EU, proposing a reduction of between 35% and 65% in catches, depending on the species, in order to preserve fishing stocks. It also insisted that 35% of all fishing crews be Moroccan and that landings take place in Morocco. Spain, which operated 650 of the 730 licensed EU fishing boats, was adamant that it could not agree to such terms.

Quite apart from these external problems, however, Morocco faced a domestic crisis as a lack of rainfall caused the harvest to fall to an estimated 1.6 million metric tons, compared with 9.4 million metric tons the year before. Gross domestic product was expected to fall by about 4%, compared with an increase of some 12% in 1994, which thus underlined the continuing dependence of the Moroccan economy on rainfall and the agricultural sector, despite a decade of economic restructuring. A confidential report prepared for the Moroccan government underlined the consequences of this dependence, warning that Morocco faced losing all the gains it had made since 1983 unless further restructuring was undertaken without delay. Foreign direct investment figures emphasized the plight the country faced; despite the ambitious privatization program, investment continued to fall—by 7.3% in 1994. (GEORGE JOFFÉ)

This article updates the *Macropædia* article NORTH AFRICA: *Morocco.*

MOZAMBIQUE

A republic and member of the Commonwealth, Mozambique is located in eastern Africa, on the Indian Ocean. Area: 812,379 sq km (313,661 sq mi). Pop. (1995 est.): 17,889,000. Cap.: Maputo. Monetary unit: metical, with (Oct. 6, 1995) a free rate of 9,974 meticais to U.S. $1 (15,768 meticais = £1 sterling). President in 1995, Joaquim Chissano; prime minister, Pascoal Mocumbi.

Although Afonso Dhlakama, leader of the Mozambique National Resistance party (Renamo), had accepted the results of the elections in October 1994 while protesting that they had been unfair, relations between Renamo and the governing Mozambique Liberation Front (Frelimo) were conducted with considerable caution. The fact that the two parties had won virtually all the 250 seats in the national legislature, and that Frelimo had gained fewer than 20 seats more than its rival, led Renamo to expect an audible voice in the government of the country. The tension was already present in December 1994 when Renamo refused to take part in the election of a new chairman of the legislature because the vote was not taken in secret. Again, in February, Dhlakama said he would not join a presidential consultation forum because it was not provided for in the constitution. But he insisted that he had no intention of reviving the armed struggle, a statement made all the more credible by his admission that he himself hoped to be elected president in due course.

By the end of March, Renamo for the first time had taken part in a vote in the national legislature. In May, however, Pres. Joaquim Chissano said that Dhlakama would not be accorded the title of leader of the opposition because he was not an elected member of the legislature. Nevertheless, he would receive a salary of 10 million meticais a month and various other benefits because he had finished second in the previous October's presidential election.

In March the Paris Club of donor countries and financial institutions pledged $780 million in loans and grants, and the government hoped for a further $350 million in debt relief. The finance minister, Tomas Salomao, estimated that the budget deficit for 1995 would amount to $1.1 billion. On March 30, acting on the advice of the World Bank, the government announced details of measures to eradicate poverty and to increase the growth rate of gross domestic product. In response to labour union pressure, the minimum wage, including that of the armed forces, was raised 35%. Another financial windfall was announced in May when the European Union High Commissioner for Africa signed an agreement to provide aid amounting to $65 million to assist, among other projects, in the rehabilitation of the Cabora Bassa Dam and the Beira Corridor.

On May 31 Yusuf Hassan, speaking for the UN High Commissioner for Refugees, reported that the last of 100,000 Mozambican refugees had been repatriated from Zimbabwe and that all the 1.7 million people who had taken refuge in southern African countries would have returned home when the remaining 39,000 had been repatriated from Malawi. In August, however, there were disturbing rumours that former Renamo guerrillas in the western provinces, the onetime power base of Renamo, were growing disgruntled by the fact that their party appeared able to wield little influence in spite of holding nearly half the seats in the legislature. Renamo officials insisted, however, there was no intention of resorting to violence. In November Mozambique became the first non-former British dependency to be admitted to the Commonwealth of Nations. (KENNETH INGHAM)

This article updates the *Macropædia* article SOUTHERN AFRICA: *Mozambique.*

MYANMAR (BURMA)

Myanmar is a republic of Southeast Asia with coastlines on the Bay of Bengal and the Andaman Sea. Area: 676,577 sq km (261,228 sq mi). Pop. (1995 est.): 46,527,000. Cap.: Yangon (Rangoon). Monetary unit: kyat, with (Oct. 6, 1995) a free rate of 5.66 kyats to U.S. $1 (8.94 kyats = £1 sterling). Chairman of the State Law and Order Restoration Council in 1995, Gen. Than Shwe.

On July 10, 1995, Myanmar's military junta, the State Law and Order Restoration Council (SLORC), released Daw Aung San Suu Kyi, the leader of the National League for Democracy (NLD), who had been under house arrest since July 1989. Suu Kyi's unconditional release, however, did not change the SLORC's tough stance on political dissent. It rejected Suu Kyi's call for talks, kept in place all martial law regulations banning political debate, and continued to hold hundreds of political dissidents in jail. Even though Suu Kyi's house arrest had prevented her from leading the NLD in the 1990 campaign, her party won the 1990 legislative elections by a landslide. The SLORC subsequently annulled the results and jailed many of the NLD politicians who had been elected.

The SLORC-controlled National Convention continued its work on a new constitution. The military ensured itself a leading role in the country's political affairs with a clause allowing it to appoint a quarter of all future parliamentarians. In December the SLORC expelled the NLD from the convention after the NLD had walked out in protest over SLORC's opposition to political reform. The draft of the new constitution stipulated that anyone who had not lived in Myanmar for 20 consecutive years, was married to a foreigner, or had children who held foreign citizenship could not run for the presidency. This disqualified Suu Kyi, who was married to a Briton, had lived abroad most of her life, and had two children who held British citizenship.

The SLORC overran the Karen minority rebel headquarters in Manerplaw in January. The fall of Manerplaw was a major defeat for government opponents because it was also the base for several umbrella organizations comprising rebel ethnic armies and pro-democracy activists. The Mong Tai Army was the only remaining significant insurgent group.

D. AUBERT—SYGMA

A child works in a brick factory in Myanmar. Cheap labour, including some children, attracted investment by a number of Asian and Western companies during the 1990s even though human rights groups had urged a boycott of the country's military government.

Because the Association of Southeast Asian Nations (ASEAN) was concerned that China was using Myanmar as a springboard to extend its influence in the region, ASEAN adopted a policy of "constructive engagement" with the SLORC government. In January the Thai foreign minister visited Yangon, and SLORC chairman Gen. Than Shwe, who visited Indonesia and Singapore, attended the ASEAN summit in Bangkok, Thailand, in December. In July Myanmar acceded to the ASEAN Treaty of Amity and Cooperation, a step toward full membership in the organization.

(CLAUDE RAKISITS)

This article updates the *Macropædia* article SOUTHEAST ASIA: *Myanmar.*

NAMIBIA

A republic and member of the Commonwealth, Namibia is in southern Africa, on the Atlantic Ocean. Area: 825,118 sq km (318,580 sq mi). Pop. (1995 est.): 1,651,000. Cap.: Windhoek. Monetary unit: Namibian dollar, at par with the South African rand (also legal currency), with (Oct. 6, 1995) a free rate of Nam$3.66 to U.S. $1 (Nam$5.79 = £1 sterling). President in 1995, Sam Nujoma; prime minister, Hage Geingob.

In the wake of his sweeping victory in the December 1994 elections, Pres. Sam Nujoma promised that any amendments to the constitution would be submitted to a referendum. In May dissidents within his South West Africa People's Organization (SWAPO) left to form a new party called SWAPO for Justice. Misheke Muyongo, leader of the Democratic Turnhalle Alliance, labeled Namibia an "ethnic democracy" because, he said, SWAPO's support came overwhelmingly from the Ovambo.

The economy, which grew by about 5% in 1994, was expected to grow by 3% in 1995 even though foreign investors had shown little interest in the country. About 38% of the workforce was unemployed, and the rate of inflation approached 11%. When a severe drought cut agricultural harvests in half, the government appealed for Nam$100 million in aid. The request was ignored because earlier aid had been misused.

The government authorized an Export Processing Zone (EPZ) in the port of Walvis Bay, aimed at creating 10,000 jobs over a period of five years. The trade unions and the Namibian Council of Churches objected to the proposed suspension of the 1992 Labour Act in the EPZ. A compromise kept the act in place but prohibited strikes and lockouts.

In December 1994 a new diamond-mining company, Namdeb, was established. De Beers, an equal partner with the government, acquired a 25-year right to mine diamonds on payment of 4% of income. The feasibility of opening a large new copper mine at Haib was studied, as was also the construction, with Scandinavian assistance, of a hydroelectric dam on the Kunene River. Construction of the trans-Caprivi Highway linking Namibia to Zambia and Zimbabwe was expected to be completed at the end of 1996.

The inquest into the 1989 assassination of SWAPO activist Anton Lubowski by a South African "hit squad" was reopened. Four agents of the South African Civil Cooperation Bureau had been subpoenaed to testify. Environmentalists continued to protest Namibia's seal culling, even though the quotas had been cut from preceding years. In May Namibia became the first African nation to act as host of the Miss Universe contest.

(MARTIN LEGASSICK)

This article updates the *Macropædia* article SOUTHERN AFRICA: *Namibia.*

NAURU

An island republic within the Commonwealth, Nauru lies in the Pacific Ocean about 1,900 km (1,200 mi) east of New Guinea. Area: 21 sq km (8 sq mi). Pop. (1995 est.): 10,400. Cap.: Government offices in Yaren district. Monetary unit: Australian dollar, with (Oct. 6, 1995) a free rate of $A 1.31 to U.S. $1 ($A 2.08 = £1 sterling). President in 1995, Bernard Dowiyogo.

In 1995 Nauruan Pres. Bernard Dowiyogo took a major role in leading Pacific opposition to the resumption of French nuclear bomb testing in French Polynesia. He declared that the tests were a blatant example of the arrogance of the French government and its unbridled colonial attitudes "from which we in the Pacific and all the world wish to escape." Nauru suspended diplomatic relations with France as a protest against the explosion of the first bomb of the planned series on Mururoa atoll on September 5. Nauru also boycotted the South Pacific Games in French Tahiti, and Dowiyogo traveled to France to express his opposition. At the South Pacific Forum meeting, held in Papua New Guinea soon after the first French nuclear test, Dowiyogo urged—unsuccessfully—the 16 members of the Forum to prevent the French minister for economic development and cooperation, Jacques Godfrain, from attending a post-Forum dialogue meeting.

Amid allegations that his government had long been squandering revenue from Nauru's rich but now nearly depleted phosphate reserves, Dowiyogo lost a bid for re-election as president on November 22 to Lagumot Harris by a vote of 9–7 in Parliament, which had been elected on November 18. (A.R.G. GRIFFITHS)

This article updates the *Macropædia* article PACIFIC ISLANDS: *Nauru.*

NEPAL

A constitutional monarchy, Nepal is a landlocked country in the Himalayas between India and the Tibetan Autonomous Region of China. Area: 147,181 sq km (56,827 sq mi). Pop. (1995 est.): 20,093,000. Cap.: Kathmandu. Monetary unit: Nepalese rupee, with (Oct. 6, 1995) a free rate of NRs 50.39 to U.S. $1 (NRs 79.67 = £1 sterling). King, Birendra Bir Bikram Shah Dev; prime ministers in 1995, Man Mohan Adhikari and, from September 12, Sher Bahadur Deuba.

Prime Minister Man Mohan Adhikari's minority communist government (United Communist Party of Nepal [UCPN]), which had been installed on Nov. 30, 1994, had never had more than a precarious hold on power because its survival depended on the royalist National Democratic Party (NDP). Although it favoured a liberal market economy, the government's plans for a modest land reform were not well received by opposition parties. On June 13, 1995, King Birendra, on the advice of Adhikari, who claimed that talks with the opposition parties on the government's economic policies had broken down, dissolved the legislature and ordered new elections.

The largest opposition party, the Nepali Congress Party (NCP), supported by the NDP, contested the king's decision to dissolve Parliament and argued before the Supreme Court that it had the right to try to form a new government. On August 28 the court concurred that Adhikari had acted unconstitutionally when he persuaded the king to dismiss the legislature. Accordingly, on September 12, after losing a vote of confidence (88–107), Adhikari was compelled to yield the prime ministership to Sher Bahadur Deuba, leader of the NCP, who then formed a coalition government with the NDP. The UCPN's image was tarnished when some of its members, unhappy with the new state of affairs, staged several anti-Supreme Court marches.

In early February Adhikari's foreign minister held talks with his Indian counterpart in New Delhi. The security provisions of the 1950 Indo-Nepalese Friendship Treaty were among the items Nepal wanted to discuss. Adhikari brought the matter up again when he visited India and China in April. (CLAUDE RAKISITS)

NETHERLANDS, THE

A constitutional monarchy of northwestern Europe, The Netherlands, a Benelux country, is on the North Sea. Area: 41,526 sq km (16,033 sq mi). Pop. (1995 est.): 15,487,000. Cap., Amsterdam; seat of government, The Hague. Monetary unit: Netherlands guilder, with (Oct. 6, 1995) a free rate of 1.60 guilders to U.S. $1 (2.53 guilders = £1 sterling). Queen, Beatrix; prime minister in 1995, Wim Kok.

During the period Jan. 23–Feb. 6, 1995, people living near the Meuse, Rhine, Waal, and IJssel rivers in The Netherlands suffered from heavy flooding. At the same time, large areas in the southern and central regions of the nation were threatened by the bursting of dikes. Almost a quarter of a million people had to leave their homes and were evacuated to safer parts of the country. Severe breaches in the dikes were prevented, however. It was the second year in a row that The Netherlands had experienced problems with its elaborate hydraulic system.

One of the causes of the flooding was that the riverbeds in Germany, Belgium, and France had been canalized. Another was that urbanization in the surrounding countries prevented the regions near the rivers from functioning naturally as a sponge for the rainwater. Thus, in those countries the buffer capacity for rainwater was decreased, and The Netherlands consequently had to deal with faster and higher streams of water during the winter. Risks were also increased because the dikes were in a bad state of repair. In February a plan to restore and strengthen 685 km (425 mi) of the dike system at an estimated cost of 1.3 billion guilders was announced. The efforts were to be concluded at the end of 1996.

Elections in the 12 provinces of The Netherlands took place on March 8. The centre-right People's Party for Freedom and Democracy (VVD) was the big winner, increasing its representation in the provincial legislatures from 116 to 208 seats. The major loser was the centre-right Christian Democratic Appeal, which declined from 257 to 185 seats, thus continuing the fall that began in the national election in 1994. Generally, the success of the VVD was ascribed to the independent role that its leader, Frits Bolkestein, played in the States-General.

In July Srebrenica, one of the so-called safe areas in Bosnia and Herzegovina, was conquered by Serb troops. Dutchbat, a lightly armed contingent of 300 Dutch troops that had a peacekeeping task in that area on behalf of the United Nations, was taken hostage. One Dutch soldier was killed. At home a vigorous public debate began concerning the extent to which Dutchbat had been confronted with a "mission impossible" in trying to keep peace where none had existed since before the unit arrived.

Queen Beatrix paid an official visit to Indonesia, a former Dutch colony, in August. It was an emotional occasion because 50 years earlier, on Aug. 17, 1945, Indonesia had proclaimed its independence from Dutch rule. The Dutch government did not recognize the proclamation until 1949. On September 19 the queen delivered her traditional speech to open the new parliamentary year. It was an optimistic address foreseeing a period of economic growth.

The island of St. Martin in the Caribbean Sea, the southern third of which is controlled by The Netherlands, was severely hit in September by Hurricane Luis. Wind speeds of more than 190 km/h (120 mph) were measured. At least nine people died, and between 7,000 and 10,000 people lost their homes. (KLAAS J. HOEKSEMA)

See also *Dependent States.*

NEW ZEALAND

New Zealand, a constitutional monarchy and member of the Commonwealth in the South Pacific Ocean, consists of North and South islands and Stewart, Chatham, and other minor islands. Area: 270,534 sq km (104,454 sq mi). Pop. (1995 est.): 3,568,000. Cap.: Wellington. Monetary unit: New Zealand dollar, with (Oct. 6, 1995) a free rate of $NZ 1.51 to U.S. $1 ($NZ 2.39 = £1 sterling). Queen, Elizabeth II; governor-general in 1995, Dame Catherine Tizard; prime minister, Jim Bolger.

After being elected with a single-seat majority in the November 1993 general elections, the mildly conservative National Party (NP) government of the farmer-politician prime minister, Jim Bolger, consolidated its hold in 1995. This was done mainly through a more thoughtful threading of alliances required in a proportional representation system, which was to replace New Zealand's first-past-the-post electoral tradition in 1996. The NP needed alliances in the short term, too, and shed so many of its own members to splinter groupings in Parliament that it could look forward to some of these becoming the basis for coalitions of the future.

The traditionally socialist opposition Labour Party, so close to power after the elections, had been unable since to settle under its new leader, former health minister Helen Clark. It was also unable to live with the only political factions that could have given it crucial numbers. The various opposition parties that developed as the session wore on worked up more suspicion of each other than they directed at the government, so a potentially powerful force hardly challenged on any substantive issue. The NP was able to round out some of the privatization and deregulatory programs it had on hand and began to repair frayed relations with the U.S. over joint naval armament in the nuclear age.

Bolger had brought the NP through without personal public support in popularity polls until mid-August, when he caught the public mood against French nuclear testing in the South Pacific. He did this with a controlled anger that sent him, for the first time, to the top of the popularity charts. By the second week in October, when the tests drew to a close, a tough-sounding government had a majority in the polls, with the numbers to go it alone in any government forming under the upcoming mixed member proportional formula.

The choice of a New Zealand-born Court of Appeal judge, Michael Hardie Boys, to succeed Dame Catherine Tizard as governor-general in 1996 was seen as a precaution. If this was insurance against a hung Parliament or other situation requiring judicial initiative, however, that seemed unlikely as the government hit a 10-year peak with the economy, projected a $NZ 3,280,000,000 surplus in the June budget, and began to detail plans for tax cuts in 1996.

Indigenous Maori New Zealanders remained in focus during the year, with sit-ins on disputed lands, violent demonstrations, and demands for sovereignty highlighting compensation claims for old confiscations. In October Parliament approved a bill worth $NZ 170 million to help settle claims by the Tainui Federation of Tribes on North Island. The agreement included cash compensation and some 15,400 ha (38,000 ac) of land. Maori representatives had approved the deal in May.

A landmark and symbol of racial cooperation, the Rangiatea Anglican Church at Otaki, north Wellington, also known as the Maori Cathedral, was burned to the ground in

ARTHUR PENGELLY—AFP

Mt. Ruapehu, located in a resort area halfway between Auckland and Wellington on North Island, erupts with ash and boulders. New Zealand officials declared an alert within a 100-km (62-mi) radius when the volcano began erupting in late September, but the damage turned out not to be great.

October, apparently by an arsonist. In light of the growing unrest, the government canceled the Waitangi Day celebrations, an annual holiday commemorating the signing in 1840 of the Treaty of Waitangi. On November 2 Queen Elizabeth II, visiting New Zealand to attend the Commonwealth Conference, signed the Tainui agreement, which contained a statement of "profound regret and apologies" from the Crown for the loss of lives because of past hostilities.

In 1994 New Zealand had emerged from several years of concern over high unemployment. A 4.9% rise in employment was the most impressive since a household labour force survey began in 1986. Unemployment had not been so low for nine years. The improvement was fueled by economic growth rates of more than 6%, which were expected to moderate to 3–4% under anti-inflationary restraints on spending. The unemployment rate was lower than Australia's 8.4%.

Beginning September 23, eruptions in the crater of Mt. Ruapehu, which crowns a ski resort on North Island, provided a spectacular ongoing news story and a novelty: it could be monitored live internationally by computer on the Internet. A knighthood for yachting team skipper Peter Blake (*see* BIOGRAPHIES) crowned New Zealand's successful challenge for the America's Cup. (JOHN A. KELLEHER)

See also *Dependent States.*

NICARAGUA

A republic of Central America, Nicaragua has coastlines on the Caribbean Sea and the Pacific Ocean. Area: 131,670 sq km (50,838 sq mi). Pop. (1995 est.): 4,340,000. Cap.: Managua. Monetary unit: córdoba oro, with (Oct. 6, 1995) an official rate of 7.75 córdobas oro to U.S. $1 (12.25 córdobas oro = £1 sterling). President in 1995, Violeta Barrios de Chamorro.

Constitutional reform dominated politics in 1995. On February 7 the National Assembly sent Pres. Violeta Barrios de Chamorro a partial reform bill for her signature. Many of the 67 reforms were generally accepted, such as the change in the name of the army, the prohibition of obligatory military service, and guarantees of private property rights. However, there were others that radically altered the balance of power from the executive to the legislature, such as the right to levy taxes, and President Chamorro and her government strongly objected to many of these. Despite a deadline of 15 days for acting on the bill, she refused to sign and publish it, requesting further negotiation. The National Assembly unilaterally published the reforms on February 24 and began to implement them. One of these concerned the Supreme Court of Justice, which was to be expanded from 9 to 12 members. The National Assembly elected the three new judges, but the president refused to recognize them.

On June 15, after several rounds of negotiations, the president and representatives of the National Assembly signed a political accord to help solve the constitutional crisis. The pact required that a framework law to implement constitutional reforms be passed by a 60% majority in the Assembly before President Chamorro would sign the reforms, and this duly occurred on July 4. The National Assembly then reaffirmed its selection of judges for the Supreme Court of Justice, and a new Supreme Electoral Tribunal was also sworn in. The Nepotism Law was postponed until 1996. This would have prevented the president's close relations from serving in the Cabinet or running for president. President Chamorro's son-in-law, Antonio Lacayo, was therefore able to remain in the government, although he announced his intention to resign anyway in order to campaign for the presidency in the November 1996 elections.

The government reaffirmed its commitment to the International Monetary Fund's Economic Structural Adjustment Facility (ESAF) while renegotiating its debt to the Paris Club of creditor nations. The terms of the ESAF included the controversial privatization of the telephone company, TELCOR, which was stalled by the constitutional crisis.

(SARAH CAMERON)

This article updates the *Macropædia* article CENTRAL AMERICA: *Nicaragua.*

NIGER

Niger is a landlocked republic of West Africa. Area: 1,287,000 sq km (497,000 sq mi). Pop. (1995 est.): 9,151,000. Cap.: Niamey. Monetary unit: CFA franc, with (Oct. 6, 1995) a par value of CFAF 100 to the French franc and a free rate of CFAF 501.49 to U.S. $1 (CFAF 792.78 = £1 sterling). President in 1995, Mahamane Ousmane; prime ministers, Souley Abdoulaye, Boubacar Cissé Amadou from February 8, and, from February 21, Hama Amadou.

Opposition parties won an absolute majority of National Assembly seats in Niger's legislative elections on Jan. 12, 1995. Their coalition, led by the National Movement for the Developing Society–Victory, used a motion of censure to oust Prime Minister Boubacar Cissé Amadou and selected Hama Amadou as his replacement. Hama announced an austerity program that would curtail the travel and housing allowances of deputies. In March agreement was finally reached between the civil service union and the government over payment of salary arrears.

Pres. Mahamane Ousmane refused to preside at the April 6 Council of Ministers meeting, precipitating a political crisis between the legislative and executive branches. In retaliation, Hama dismissed 19 heads of state-owned corporations, all of whom were presidential appointees. They were soon after reinstated. Mediation attempts, including one in July by Lieut. Col. Amadou Touré, who had led Niger's transition to democracy, failed. Finally, after the National Trade Union Association threatened to organize public demonstrations if the two men did not achieve a compromise, Mahamane agreed to attend a Cabinet meeting on August 16. In September the Supreme Court supported the prime minister and ordered Mahamane to enforce laws passed by the parliament.

On April 24 the government and representatives of the Tuareg coalition entered into a peace agreement to end their three-year conflict. In June the National Assembly passed a full amnesty bill for former rebels, and on July 24 all jailed Tuaregs were released. (NANCY ELLEN LAWLER)

This article updates the *Macropædia* article WESTERN AFRICA: *Niger.*

NIGERIA

A republic and suspended member of the Commonwealth, Nigeria is located in West Africa, on the Gulf of Guinea. Area: 923,768 sq km (356,669 sq mi). Pop. (1995 est.): 95,434,000. Cap.: Abuja. Monetary unit: naira, with (Oct. 6, 1995) an official par value of 22 naira to U.S. $1 (free rate of 34.78 naira = £1 sterling); a truer value of the naira was on the free market, where 86.10 naira = U.S. $1 (136.11 naira = £1 sterling). Chairman of the Provisional Ruling Council in 1995, Gen. Sani Abacha.

On Nov. 10, 1995, nine members of the minority Ogoni ethnic group, including playwright Ken Saro-Wiwa (*see* OBITUARIES), were hanged in Port Harcourt. Saro-Wiwa had been convicted by a secret tribunal on October 31 of ordering the murders of four political rivals at a 1994 political rally. He maintained that he was framed and that he and the other eight men were being executed because of their opposition to the nation's ruler, Gen. Sani Abacha, and to the policies of Nigeria's oil industry; most of the nation's oil came from the Ogoni region, and the impoverished Ogonis claimed that they were denied rights to oil revenues and that the area was suffering from high levels of pollution because of the oil operations.

After the executions many countries, including the United States, recalled their ambassadors from Nigeria or otherwise expressed their displeasure—but stopped short of boycotting Nigerian oil. The Commonwealth of Nations suspended Nigeria's membership and said that the nation would be expelled from the organization if it did not end its military dictatorship and restore democracy within two years.

In April the National Constitutional Conference (NCC) adopted a draft constitution. Among its provisions were a presidency that would rotate between north and south, the lifting of the ban on politics, and the formation of new political parties. The NCC, however, reneged on an earlier proposal that Nigeria revert to civilian rule in 1996; instead, it gave Abacha an open-ended term of office. In June Abacha lifted the ban on political activity but did not specify a timetable for the return to civilian rule. When pro-democracy groups demonstrated in June, the government met their activities with repression and many arrests. On June 18 a group of leading Nigerian intellectuals, including Nobel Prize winner Wole Soyinka, announced the formation of a 17-member National Liberation Council to create a government-in-exile.

On March 6, amid rumours of a coup attempt, the government announced that numbers of officers and civilians had been arrested, but only on March 10 did the government report that there had been a plot and that 29 people, including the former vice president, retired brigadier general Shehu Yar'Adua, had been arrested. Four days later the former head of state, retired general Olusegun Obasanjo, was also arrested. Both had been campaigning openly for a return to civilian rule. Many observers believed that there had not been any coup attempt and that it had been invented as an excuse to eliminate opposition to the government. A report in *The Observer* (London) of April 16 claimed that 60 members of the armed forces had been shot in the wake of the alleged coup, though this was denied by the government. International concern over the fate of Obasanjo and Yar'Adua was expressed by the U.K., the European Union, and the U.S. In July South African Pres. Nelson Mandela sent his first vice president, Thabo Mbeki, to Nigeria to protest against Obasanjo's treatment.

In April, Archbishop Desmond Tutu of South Africa, representing President Mandela, visited Nigeria to plead for the release of Moshood ("MKO") Abiola, who had been in detention since June 1994. Abiola, however, remained in detention, despite telling Tutu that he would accept the bail terms that he had refused in August 1994, which would have included acceptance of the government decision to annul the presidential election of June 1993, in which he received the most votes. The government refused his offer.

In a speech on the 35th anniversary of Nigeria's independence (October 1), General Abacha said that he would not permit a return to democracy for three years and that Abiola was to remain in prison. In deference to international appeals, however, he commuted sentences on 40 people charged with having plotted the alleged March coup. He announced that the Provisional Ruling Council would step down in 1998 following legislative and presidential elections.

(GUY ARNOLD)

This article updates the *Macropædia* article WESTERN AFRICA: *Nigeria.*

An oil derrick rises behind a village in the Niger River delta area of Nigeria. The writer Ken Saro-Wiwa and other Ogoni activists who had protested what they considered to be the exploitation of their homeland were tried for murder and executed in 1995 by the military government.
SARA LEIGH LEWIS—PANOS

NORWAY

A constitutional monarchy of northern Europe, Norway occupies the western part of the Scandinavian Peninsula, with coastlines on the Skagerrak, the North Sea, the Norwegian Sea, and the Arctic Ocean. Area: 323,878 sq km (125,050 sq mi), excluding the Svalbard Archipelago and Jan Mayen Island. Pop. (1995 est.): 4,360,000. Cap.: Oslo. Monetary unit: Norwegian krone, with (Oct. 6, 1995) a free rate of 6.31 kroner to U.S. $1 (9.97 kroner = £1 sterling). King, Harald V; prime minister in 1995, Gro Harlem Brundtland.

The economy was the main highlight of 1995 in Norway, bounding from strength to strength and buoyed by exports of bulk commodities—crude oil, light metals, and pulp and paper—and a 30% increase in investment in industries other than petroleum. The robust economy also proved wrong skeptics' doomsday forecasts of the disastrous effects of remaining outside the European Union (EU), a decision made by Norwegians in an advisory referendum on Nov. 28, 1994, in sharp contrast to Nordic neighbours Finland and Sweden. Economic growth accelerated to a 20-year high of 5% in 1994 and was forecast to expand by more than 4% in 1995 and 1996. Excluding petroleum, the annual growth rate was 3%.

The government budget deficit and net foreign debt were expected to be eliminated in 1996 as unemployment was forecast to decline from 4.8% of the workforce in 1995 to 3.5% by the end of the decade. Norway's petroleum bonanza disguised the continued relative decline of the non-oil economy, however, with the manufacturing sector accounting for less than 15% of gross domestic product (GDP), well below levels in other industrialized countries.

New petroleum production capacity boosted Norway's GDP in 1995, with crude-oil output surging by more than 12% to well over three million barrels a day as investments hit a peak of 56 billion kroner, 7% of GDP. Western Europe's largest crude-oil producer, Norway in 1995 became the world's second largest net oil exporter, after Saudi Arabia. The government pledged to establish a petroleum fund to be managed by the Bank of Norway and into which budget surpluses would flow for foreign investments and as a buffer for the oil-dependent economy during cycles of depressed oil prices.

Norway's 500 largest companies paid 1994 dividends of 1 billion kroner, a 40% increase over the previous year. The top 212 companies boosted 1994 profits by 26%, and higher full-year profits were forecast for 1995. Reprivatization of the country's largest banks began with Fokus Bank, in which the government sold its 97.8% share to foreign and domestic investors.

Politically the year was insignificant, as no party harnessed the energy or backing to threaten to unseat the ruling minority Labour Party government, led by Prime Minister Gro Harlem Brundtland. In local elections held in September, however, the right-wing Progress Party, led by Carl Hagen, was surprisingly propelled to the rank of second largest party as Norwegians lodged a protest vote against the country's liberal immigration policy.

Relations between Norway and Iran broke down over a diplomatic dispute centring on the *fatwa* (death edict) imposed in 1989 by Iran's late revolutionary leader Ayatollah Ruhollah Khomeini on the author Salman Rushdie. Rushdie's Norwegian publisher was seriously wounded in a 1993 shooting, but Iran denied any involvement in the incident. Both countries recalled their respective ambassadors and downgraded diplomatic relations in 1995.

Norway continued whaling and resumed the killing of baby seals for "scientific research" despite international bans on these activities. Errors were discovered in the software Norway used to provide estimates of the North Atlantic minke whale population, however, which weakened its arguments justifying whaling. (KAREN L. FOSSLI)

See also *Dependent States.*

OMAN

The sultanate of Oman occupies the southeastern part of the Arabian Peninsula, facing the Persian Gulf, the Gulf of Oman, and the Arabian Sea. A small part of the country lies to the north and is separated from the rest of Oman by the United Arab Emirates. Area: 306,000 sq km (118,150 sq mi). Pop. (1995 est.): 2,163,000. Cap.: Muscat. Monetary unit: rial Omani, with (Oct. 6, 1995) a par value of 0.38 rial to U.S. $1 (free rate of 0.61 rial = £1 sterling). Sultan and prime minister in 1995, Qabus ibn Sa'id.

The Omani government enjoyed good relations with neighbouring countries and focused greater attention on internal economic concerns in 1995. Oman had recorded government deficits since 1981, and its oil output was expected to level off at about one million barrels a day by the end of the decade. A 1994 World Bank report warned that the government's current expenditure trends were "unsustainable."

Reacting in part to the report, the government during 1995 announced a comprehensive program for reform, including cuts in government spending to reduce the budget deficit, privatization of state-owned infrastructure projects, and steps to encourage foreign investment. Meeting the most important of these targets, a reduction of government spending, had proved difficult, however. Government spending in 1995 was projected to reach $5.6 billion, a 6.2% increase over 1994, with a deficit of $811 million, a figure that even Omani officials acknowledged as much too high. Once again defense and security services spending was the main reason for the overrun.

Oman continued plans to develop its natural gas resources, with exports projected to begin in the year 2000. In January Oman announced that it had taken a 50% share in the project to build a 102-cm (40-in)-diameter pipeline from oilfields in Kazakhstan to the Russian port of Novorossiysk on the Black Sea. Engineering studies for a proposed 1,135-km (705-mi) undersea gas pipeline to India were completed in July.

In foreign policy, Oman continued to take the lead among Gulf countries in support of the Arab-Israeli peace process. It served as host to a visit by Israeli Prime Minister Yitzhak Rabin in December 1994, and in October 1995 Oman and Israel announced a trade agreement that would result in the opening of trade offices in both countries. (MICHAEL STERNER)

This article updates the *Macropædia* article ARABIA: *Oman.*

PAKISTAN

A federal republic and member of the Commonwealth, Pakistan is in the northwestern part of the Indian subcontinent, on the Arabian Sea. Area: 796,095 sq km (307,374 sq mi), excluding the 83,716-sq km Pakistani-controlled section of Jammu and Kashmir. Pop. (1995 est., including 1.6 million Afghan refugees and 4 million residents of Pakistani-controlled Jammu and Kashmir): 140,497,000. Cap.: Islamabad. Monetary unit: Pakistan rupee, with (Oct. 6, 1995) a free rate of PRs 31.59 to U.S. $1 (PRs 49.94 = £1 sterling). President in 1995, Farooq Ahmed Leghari; prime minister, Benazir Bhutto.

For much of 1995, the government of Prime Minister Benazir Bhutto remained under siege as ethnic violence in Karachi escalated and sectarian violence nationwide took its toll. It was the bloodiest year in Pakistan's history since the 1971 separation of the country's eastern province, which became Bangladesh. (*See* SPOTLIGHT: *Secularism in South Asia.*)

The main battleground was Karachi, Pakistan's largest city and the capital of southern Sindh province. Bhutto's nemesis was the Mohajir Qaumi Movement (MQM), the national movement for Mohajir people (Muslim immigrants from India who fled to Pakistan after the 1947 partition and their descendants), which represented nearly two-thirds of the city's people. MQM, which had won every election it had contested in Karachi since 1986, was lobbying for greater autonomy for Karachi and more say in running Sindh province than native Sindhis have. That was unacceptable to Bhutto, herself a native Sindhi. Violence in Karachi alone left over 2,500 people dead by late October—more than 150 of whom were police officers or members of the security forces. Several hundred others died in clashes in other Sindh cities, as well as in sectarian clashes in Punjab.

Government security forces battled for much of the year with heavily armed militia supporting the MQM. Even within the nine million-strong Mohajir community in Sindh province, MQM extremists fought pitched battles with the moderate Haqiqi faction. In July Bhutto, under pressure from army commanders, began peace talks with the MQM. The talks foundered, then restarted, only to reach another deadlock. At year's end the two sides were still hurling accusations at each other, but they were still talking. On November 19, 15 people died in a suicide car-bombing attack on the Egyptian embassy in Islamabad; the militant Islamic Group and two other groups that opposed the Egyptian government claimed responsibility.

Despite the violence in Karachi, sectarian clashes between Sunni and Shi'ite Muslim sects, and attacks by religious fanatics on minority Christians and Ahmedis, Bhutto continued to enjoy the backing of Gen. Abdul Waheed Kakar, the chief of army staff. In October the government foiled an attempted coup by a group of senior Islamic fundamentalist military officials. One general, several brigadiers, and other

Members of a group agitating for the union of Jammu and Kashmir with Pakistan maintain their headquarters in Rawalpindi, Pak. Throughout the year the government of Pakistan denied charges by India that it supported terrorist incidents in the disputed territory.
CHRIS STOWERS—PANOS PICTURES

senior officials were among the 36 military men arrested, and scores of other top military officials were questioned. The arrested officers were reportedly disgusted at Waheed Kakar's backing of Bhutto.

In April Bhutto visited Washington, D.C., where she passionately argued for lifting the embargo on military and economic aid to Pakistan, which was imposed in 1990 owing to U.S. concerns about Pakistan's nuclear program. A cornerstone of the trip was the issue of the sale of 28 U.S. F-16 jet fighters to Pakistan. Islamabad had paid $1.4 billion for the planes and other military hardware and for four years had lobbied for either the delivery of the planes or return of the money. In late October the U.S. Congress voted to restore partial military and economic aid, supply some military hardware, and refund the money by selling the jets to a third country. One reason for Washington's dramatic turnaround just three years after branding Pakistan a terrorist state was Islamabad's cooperation in the capture and extradition of Ramzi Ahmed Yousef, an Arab terrorist accused of having masterminded the bombing of the World Trade Center in New York City in 1993.

In September the Bhutto government reluctantly hammered out a deal with the International Monetary Fund, just three months after the IMF had canceled a $300 million loan—part of a $1.5 billion economic stabilization package—because Islamabad had failed to keep its promise to liberalize the economy by implementing structural reforms. Pakistan's economy continued to improve, despite work stoppages and strikes in Karachi that repeatedly paralyzed the port. The healthy growth was primarily due to a bumper cotton crop of 13 million bales—a record high in spite of serious floods. Gross domestic product (GDP) grew 4.5% in the fiscal year ended June 1995, and a bigger cotton crop was likely to boost production of textiles and garments in the second half of 1995. The strikes and work stoppages in Karachi shaved off an estimated 0.5% of GDP growth.

(ASSIF A. SHAMEEN)

PALAU

A republic in the Caroline Islands of the western Pacific Ocean, Palau comprises a 640-km (400-mi)-long chain of some 340 volcanic and coralline islands. The main islands of Babelthuap and Koror are situated about 900 km east of the Philippines. Area: 488 sq km (188 sq mi). Pop. (1995 est.): 16,900. Provisional cap.: Koror, on Koror; a site on Babelthuap was designated to be the eventual permanent capital. Monetary unit: U.S. dollar, with (Oct. 6, 1995) a free rate of $1.58 to £1 sterling. President in 1995, Kuniwo Nakamura.

In 1995 the new nation opened diplomatic talks with the U.S. and Japan, which had ruled the archipelago from 1914 until its capture by U.S. marines in 1944. Palauan Pres. Kuniwo Nakamura, who was of second-generation Japanese ancestry, visited Japan in April 1995. His top priorities were the increase of trade and tourism between the two nations and, if possible, the establishment of direct airlinks to facilitate fish exports to Tokyo.

Earlier he had visited Taiwan, with a view to opening up diplomatic relations and soliciting business aid. In Taipei Nakamura met with Taiwan's foreign minister, Frederick Chien, hoping to build on existing links under which Taiwanese agriculturalists and technicians had helped with economic development. The Australian minister for Pacific affairs, Gordon Bilney, joined the independence celebrations by declaring that Australia would give Palau a Pacific-class naval patrol boat, the kind of boat Canberra had given to almost all the other member states of the Pacific Island Forum. (A.R.G. GRIFFITHS)

This article updates the *Macropædia* article PACIFIC ISLANDS: *Palau.*

PANAMA

A republic of Central America, Panama lies between the Caribbean Sea and the Pacific Ocean on the Isthmus of Panama. Area: 75,517 sq km (29,157 sq mi). Pop. (1995 est.): 2,631,000. Cap.: Panama City. Monetary unit: balboa, at par with the U.S. dollar, with a free rate (Oct. 6, 1995) of 1.58 balboas to £1 sterling. President in 1995, Ernesto Pérez Balladares.

An alleged plot to assassinate Pres. Ernesto Pérez Balladares and several members of his Cabinet was uncovered on Jan. 11, 1995. Ten members of the National Police were arrested for conspiracy to overthrow the government and install a civilian-military junta. The investigation into the alleged plot was closed one month later, however, owing to lack of evidence.

Panama's location on the arms- and drugs-trafficking routes was emphasized in February. When port officials at Cristóbal opened a crate for drug inspection, it exploded, killing 3 and wounding 25. The contents—explosives, grenades, and ammunition—were being sent to Ecuador and were believed to be destined for South American guerrillas. Two caches of arms were also discovered in Panama City on property belonging to a Colombian. There was evidence that Colombian drug traffickers were using Panama's financial system and business sector for illicit operations.

Labour stoppages and unrest erupted into violence during the year because of the government's controversial labour-code reform. Trade unions were worried that the reforms, designed to attract foreign investment, would reduce job security, end wage guarantees, and restrict collective bargaining and the freedom to organize. Clashes between striking workers, students, and police on August 4 left 4 people dead, an estimated 86 wounded, and up to 300 in prison. However, the reform package was approved by the Legislative Assembly on August 12 and signed into law by President Balladares two days later. The defeated workers returned to work.

Panama and the U.S. held exploratory talks on the future U.S. military role in Panama after the transfer of the canal to Panamanian sovereignty in 1999. It was agreed that Howard Air Force Base and the naval base should remain. This would provide an economic cushion for Panama, as the U.S. military injected about $400 million a year into the economy and provided 18,000 jobs. (SARAH CAMERON)

This article updates the *Macropædia* article CENTRAL AMERICA: *Panama.*

PAPUA NEW GUINEA

A constitutional monarchy and Commonwealth member, Papua New Guinea is situated in the southwestern Pacific Ocean and comprises the eastern part of the island of New Guinea, the islands of the Bismarck, Kiriwina (Trobriand), Louisiade, and D'Entrecasteaux groups, Muyua (Woodlark) Island, and parts of the Solomon Islands group, including Bougainville. Area: 462,840 sq km (178,704 sq mi). Pop. (1995 est.): 4,302,000. Cap.: Port Moresby. Monetary unit: kina, with (Oct. 6, 1995) a free rate of 1.32 kinas to U.S. $1 (2.09 kinas = £1 sterling). Queen, Elizabeth II; governor-general in 1995, Wiwa Korowi; prime minister, Sir Julius Chan.

French nuclear bomb tests in the South Pacific, continuing unrest in Bougainville, and problems with mining companies overshadowed Papua New Guinea's celebrations of 20 years of independence in 1995. Nine Papua New Guinea soldiers were killed in Bougainville fighting guerrillas of the secessionist Bougainville Revolutionary Army (BRA). A spokesman for the BRA and three other rebel representatives began talks on a cease-fire at a meeting in Cairns, Australia, but Prime Minister Sir Julius Chan announced on November 10 that the talks were being abandoned.

At the heart of the disputes was the closure of one of the world's biggest copper mines. Fearing a similar fate for operations at the Ok Tedi and Fly mines, the government moved to restrict compensation for environmental damage. While Prime Minister Chan warned against villagers' being given unrealistic expectations, the Australian mining resources company BHP was criticized by the minister for mining and petroleum, John Giheno, for extraordinary and blatant interference in Papua New Guinea affairs. BHP denied the charge that it helped draft legislation aimed at outlawing individual claims for compensation against mining firms. Chan took a leading role as chairman of the South Pacific Forum, setting trade, tourism, and transportation as the main discussion points for the September meeting. He showed poise and sangfroid in condemning France and putting a stop to post-Forum dialogue with France after the detonation of the second nuclear test explosion on October 2. (A.R.G. GRIFFITHS)

This article updates the *Macropædia* article PACIFIC ISLANDS: *Papua New Guinea.*

PARAGUAY

Paraguay is a landlocked republic of central South America. Area: 406,752 sq km (157,048 sq mi). Pop. (1995 est.): 4,828,000. Cap.: Asunción. Monetary unit: guaraní, with (Oct. 6, 1995) a free rate of 1,963 guaranies to U.S. $1 (3,103 guaranies = £1 sterling). President in 1995, Juan Carlos Wasmosy.

The transition to civilian rule after the 40-year dictatorship of Gen. Alfredo Stroessner continued to cause difficulties in 1995. In January a report by the National Human Rights Commission described Paraguay as a "controlled democracy," adding that many crimes committed under Stroessner had not been punished and that assassinations of peasant activists still occurred.

In February Pres. Juan Carlos Wasmosy retired eight senior military officers, including two who had publicly questioned his authority, and reshuffled the High Command. The new promotions were seen as strengthening the position of Gen. Lino Oviedo, who had commanded the troops that overthrew Stroessner. Some observers suspected that Oviedo had ambitions for the presidency in 1999.

In May the ruling Colorado Party and the opposition parties finally agreed on legislation to break the Colorado link with the armed forces by banning members of the military from joining political parties or participating in politics. Relations between the military and the national legislature, which was controlled by the opposition, continued to present problems. In July the inauguration of an army parade ground by Wasmosy was marked by scuffles as members of the Authentic Radical Liberal Party protested against its cost. In August a group of senior officers wrote to the newspapers demanding that the legislature honour Wasmosy's 1994 pledge to double army salaries in 1995–96.

The Paraguayan economy was generally sheltered from the direct effects of the Mexican financial crisis. Inflation was about 17% (18.3% in 1994). There were record harvests for soybeans (up 17%), corn (maize; up 80%), and wheat (up 40%). The trade deficit was projected to remain at its 1994 level of $1 billion (exports $2 billion, imports $3 billion). (CHARLIE NURSE)

PERU

The republic of Peru is located in western South America, on the Pacific Ocean. Area: 1,285,216 sq km (496,225 sq mi). Pop. (1995 est.): 23,489,000. Cap.: Lima. Monetary unit: nuevo sol, with (Oct. 6, 1995) a free rate of 2.25 nuevos soles to U.S. $1 (3.56 nuevos soles = £1 sterling). President in 1995, Alberto Fujimori; prime ministers, Efraín Godenberg Schreiber and, from July 28, Danté Cordova.

In late January and February 1995 Peru and its northern neighbour, Ecuador, engaged in serious fighting over their shared border. Despite the Rio de Janeiro Protocol of 1942, which resolved earlier battles over Peruvian-Ecuadorean territory, one area in the Cordillera del Cóndor remained ill-defined. Skirmishes periodically occurred, but the 1995 military operations were the fiercest since 1981. Late in the year negotiations were in progress under the auspices of the Rio Protocol guarantors, Argentina, Brazil, Chile, and the U.S.

On April 9 Pres. Alberto Fujimori won a resounding victory in the presidential elections. His chief rival was Javier Pérez de Cuéllar, former secretary-general of the United Nations, whose campaign at the head of the Union for Peru alliance failed to attract sufficient support even to force a second ballot. Having secured the right in 1994 to run for a second term, Fujimori capitalized on his successes in reducing terrorism, engineering a return to economic growth, and ridding Peru of hyperinflation. In the 120-seat Congress, Fujimori's party, Change 90–New Majority, won an overall majority, while traditional political parties gained few seats. Fujimori's wife, Susana Higuchi, failed to win the right to campaign as a presidential candidate, despite a hunger strike. Her party, Harmony 21st Century, also failed to contest congressional seats, owing to irregularities in the party's candidate list. Relations between the president and his wife deteriorated, and they agreed in July to divorce.

ANNIBAL SOLIMANO—GAMMA LIAISON

Alberto Fujimori celebrates his election in April to a second term as president of Peru. Campaigning on his success in controlling terrorism and promoting economic growth, Fujimori defeated rival Javier Pérez de Cuéllar, former secretary-general of the UN, on the first ballot.

The electorate's confidence in Fujimori did not prompt a less autocratic style of government. Between his reelection and reinauguration (July 28), the autonomy of the San Marcos and La Cantuta universities was removed, the national electoral board was reorganized, and amnesty was granted to military and police personnel convicted of illegal actions undertaken during antiguerrilla operations since 1980. This applied to opponents as well as supporters of the administration, but critics at home and abroad expressed concerns about the law's implications for the respect of human rights.

Though the operations of the Sendero Luminoso (Shining Path) terrorist group were restricted mainly to the Upper Huallaga valley, the María Angola Hotel and Casino in Miraflores, a suburb of Lima, was bombed in May, reviving fears of a renewal of urban terrorism. The policy of trying terrorists in courts where judges' faces were hidden had by the end of 1995 led to over 2,000 convictions since 1992.

The decline in terrorist activity was a major spur to tourism; the number of foreign visitors had, by October, returned to the levels prior to the years of heaviest Sendero Luminoso attacks and the cholera epidemic of 1991. Tourism mirrored the buoyancy of the economy as a whole. Gross domestic product was forecast to grow by 8% in 1995, compared with more than 12% in 1994. Inflation was predicted to fall to between 10% and 12% for the year, compared with over 15% in 1994. A consequence of the expanding economy was an increase in both consumer debt and, as a result of consumer demand, rapidly growing imports. Their value outstripped receipts from exports, which caused an increase of approximately $300 million in the trade deficit, which totaled $1.1 billion in 1994. (BEN BOX)

PHILIPPINES

Situated in the western Pacific Ocean off the southeast coast of Asia, the republic of the Philippines consists of an archipelago of about 7,100 islands. Area: 300,076 sq km (115,860 sq mi). Pop. (1995 est.): 70,011,000. Cap.: Manila (lower house of the legislature meets in Quezon City). Monetary unit: Philippine peso, with (Oct. 6, 1995) a free rate of 25.89 pesos to U.S. $1 (40.92 pesos = £1 sterling). President in 1995, Fidel V. Ramos.

Even though many supporters of Philippine Pres. Fidel V. Ramos won their congressional elections on May 8, 1995, the political scene continued to be agitated. Amid speculation that he favoured changing the constitution so that he could seek a second term, Ramos announced on September 6 that he would step down at the end of his term on June 30, 1998. Discussions about switching to a parliamentary system of government, however, raised the possibility that Ramos could remain in power as prime minister.

In the national legislative elections, the ruling coalition won 9 of 12 seats contested for the 24-member Senate and a two-thirds majority in voting for all 204 seats of the House of Representatives. On August 29 the Senate ousted its president, Edgardo Angara, the leader of a coalition party; his demotion dimmed whatever hopes he entertained of becoming Ramos' successor. Ramos had earlier removed Vice Pres. Joseph Estrada from leadership of a faltering anticrime campaign, thus damaging the former movie star's presidential prospects. In several high-profile cases, the government filed criminal charges against members of the country's elite, who had long seemed above the law.

Imelda Marcos won a disputed election to the House of Representatives while appealing a 1993 conviction for graft and awaiting the outcome of other criminal charges. Swiss banks turned over to the Philippines $475 million looted by Ferdinand Marcos during his dictatorial presidency, but the government believed that somewhere there were billions more in hidden accounts.

In January the Philippines discovered a Chinese garrison on Mischief Reef in the South China Sea, 233 km (145 mi) west of Palawan Island. The reef was part of the disputed Spratly Islands. (*See* SPOTLIGHT: *The Spat over the Spratlys.*) After angry exchanges with China, the Philippines made plans to update its armed forces, which had been trained to fight internal guerrilla wars. In February Congress approved $1.9 billion to cover the first five years of a 15-year modernization program.

The main guerrilla threat during 1995 came from offshoots of the Moro National Liberation Front. While the MNLF accepted negotiations as a road leading to regional autonomy for Muslims, the radical Moro Islamic Liberation Front built up a jungle army of some 30,000. In April an even more radical splinter group, Abu Sayyaf (Sword of the Father), attacked Ipil, a mostly Christian town on Mindanao Island. Its foreign-trained fighters killed at least 47, looted banks, and burned buildings before escaping into the jungle. The MNLF said the attack was intended to disrupt ongoing peace negotiations. The communist New People's Army continued to weaken.

Ramos' efforts to reduce business restrictions, break up monopolies, and encourage foreign investment were credited with stimulating economic growth of some 6%. Exports of electronics, textiles, and other industrial products increased. Agricultural output remained low, however, as the country's population continued to grow. As a result, widespread poverty, malnutrition, and underemployment persisted. About 4.2 million Filipinos worked abroad—half of them as domestic servants—and sent some $2 billion a year back to their families.

Problems of overseas workers focused on two cases. On March 17 Singapore hanged a 42-year-old woman who worked there as a maid to support an unemployed husband and four children in the Philippines. She had been convicted of two murders, but protesters in Manila questioned her guilt. This caused months of tension between the two countries until U.S. forensic experts confirmed the evidence set forth by Singaporean authorities. On September 16 the United Arab Emirates sentenced to death a 16-year-old Filipino maid, who claimed that she had stabbed her employer to death after he raped her. The sentence was later reduced to imprisonment.

Typhoon Angela, the most powerful to hit the Philippines in over a decade, killed more than 700 people in early November. (HENRY S. BRADSHER)

POLAND

A republic of eastern Europe, Poland is on the Baltic Sea. Area: 312,685 sq km (120,728 sq mi). Pop. (1995 est.): 38,641,000. Cap.: Warsaw. Monetary unit: zloty, with (Oct. 6, 1995) a free rate of 2.44 zlotys to U.S. $1 (3.86 zlotys = £1 sterling); the zloty was devalued on Jan. 1, 1995, at a rate of 1 (new) zloty to 10,000 (old) zlotys. Presidents in 1995, Lech Walesa and, from December 23, Aleksander Kwasniewski; prime ministers, Waldemar Pawlak and, from March 6, Jozef Oleksy.

November 1995 marked the end of an era in Polish politics and the beginning of another phase in the country's economic transformation. The stage was set for change when Lech Walesa faced 16 challengers in the presidential election on November 5. No candidate received 50% of the popular vote, a requirement for outright victory, so a runoff election was held on November 19. Walesa, who had won the presidency in 1990 on the strength of the popularity he had won as leader of Solidarity, the federation of trade unions that had defied the communist regime, won only 48.3% of the 18 million votes cast. He was defeated by Aleksander Kwasniewski (*see* BIOGRAPHIES), leader of the ex-communist Democratic Left Alliance, which formed the ruling coalition government with Walesa's Polish Peasant Party. An immediate change occurred with the resignation of the ministers of foreign affairs, defense, and internal affairs, who were Walesa appointees.

Kwasniewski immediately resigned from the Democratic Left Alliance (SLD), the communist successor party of which he had been leader, in order to better depict himself as representing the interest of the whole of society. This reconciliation would be difficult to achieve, given the evident polarization of opinion observed during the campaign. The Roman Catholic Church, despite a vigorous endorsement of Walesa in the latter stages of the electoral battle, found itself unable to turn the tide of popular opinion, especially among youth who appeared ready to accept Kwasniewski's vision of a common future that relegated past differences to history.

During the coming year there would probably be attempts to reconstruct a coalition around the Walesa constituency in time for the Sejm (parliament) elections in 1997. It remained to be seen whether the poor first-round showing of Waldemar Pawlak, the leader of the Polish Peasant Party (PSL) and prime minister until his ouster by Walesa in February, would put pressure on the SLD-PSL coalition and precipitate premature elections. The parliamentary opposition, led by the Freedom Union and its newly elected leader, Leszek Balcerowicz, had few issues over which to confront a government that had considerable popular support. Outside the Sejm the Solidarity trade union appeared to feel less hampered in its activities on behalf of an increasingly restive membership, as demonstrated by the Silesian rail strike in October. The ratification of the concordat between Poland and the Vatican City State and the referendum over the constitution remained unfinished business that could further divide society.

Economic results indicated just how far Poland lagged behind the European Union (EU) countries, even the poorest among them. Having partially floated the zloty at the beginning of the year and allowed creeping devaluation to continue alongside high domestic interest rates, Poland found itself with an embarrassingly large surplus of foreign currency reserves, as well as a 40% increase in exports over the first half of the year, most of which was generated by the vibrant private sector. The budget deficit rose slightly to 3.1% of gross domestic product (GDP), and economic growth was in the region of 6.5%. Inflation figures were variously projected at 23–30%, while unemployment dropped slightly to about 14.5%, albeit with a worrying rate of 37% for those 18–24 years of age. The informal economy produced as much as one-third of GDP, employed one in three adults, and provided extra income to over one million of the 2.6 million unemployed. The "brain drain" of educated professionals to the West (one in five doctors, one in three mathematicians) was accompanied by an enormous influx of casual labour.

The government of Prime Minister Jozef Oleksy and his ruling SLD was committed to reforming the tax and pension structure, although both bills were vetoed by the outgoing president. Poland, in common with other reforming countries, faced the difficult task of reshaping its welfare state at a time when some 50% of the population was living below the social minimum, life expectancy and infant mortality were unacceptably high, employment in agriculture

Aleksander Kwasniewski and his wife acknowledge the cheers of supporters after his election as president of Poland in runoffs in November. Kwasniewski, a member of what had been the communist party, narrowly defeated incumbent Lech Walesa for the post.
JANEK SKARZNSKI—EPA/AFP

and in the raw materials and energy sector was inordinately high at 27% and 7%, respectively, and its educational levels were still too low by European standards.

It was hoped that privatization of the tobacco and other sectors, such as petroleum, could provide an important impulse to reform. In November citizens over 18 years of age could collect privatization certificates exchangeable for shares in the 514 enterprises that made up the 15 National Investment Funds. Although they originally sold for a nominal 20 new zlotys, a secondary market was already offering a 50% markup.

In its desire to join both the EU and NATO, Poland was about to allow British forces to use Polish territory for tank maneuvers. Russian objections to NATO enlargement were, nevertheless, not jeopardizing plans to build a continuation of the Russian Yamal gas pipeline across the country, which would allow the first supplies to flow by 1997. Trade with Russia and the Central European Free Trade Agreement partners was the major growth area during the year, pointing to a reassessment of Eastern European foreign policy, which was likely to continue under the new president.

(GEORGE KOLANKIEWICZ)

PORTUGAL

A republic of southwestern Europe, metropolitan Portugal is on the Atlantic coast of the Iberian Peninsula, which it shares with Spain. Area: 92,135 sq km (35,574 sq mi), including the Azores and Madeira Islands groups/archipelagoes in the Atlantic. Pop. (1995 est.): 9,906,000. Cap.: Lisbon. Monetary unit: Portuguese escudo, with (Oct. 6, 1995) a free rate of 150.13 escudos to U.S. $1 (237.33 escudos = £1 sterling). President in 1995, Mário Soares; prime ministers, Aníbal Cavaco Silva and, from October 30, António Guterres.

Portugal set sail into a new political era late in 1995 as the left-wing Socialist Party swept to victory in general elections in October. The Socialists fell just short of an absolute majority in the 230-seat Assembly of the Republic but were able to win more seats than the outgoing centre-right Social Democratic Party (PSD) and the right-leaning Popular Party combined, which indicated that the Socialists would not have to rely on support from the Communist alliance to govern. (For detailed election results, see *Political Parties,* above.) By the end of October the Socialists' leader, António Guterres, had been officially named prime minister, replacing Aníbal Cavaco Silva after a decade in power.

Cavaco Silva had started the political ball rolling when he announced in January that he would step down when his term expired in the fall. That set off a battle for control of the PSD, eventually won by former defense minister Joaquim Fernando Nogueira but causing deep rifts in the once-mighty political machine. Cavaco Silva, meanwhile, kept the country on tenterhooks throughout the summer, maintaining silence as to whether he would run for the presidency in 1996. Following the Socialists' victory, Cavaco Silva threw his hat into the ring to challenge Lisbon mayor and Socialist Jorge Sampaio in the race for president.

The presidential vote, scheduled for early 1996, would mark yet another milestone in Portugal's political history: the exit of revolutionary icon, former prime minister, and Socialist éminence gris Mário Soares, who had held the prestigious yet largely ceremonial position for two straight terms.

The Socialists' return to power after 10 years in opposition followed on the heels of a slower-than-expected economic recovery after the European recession and a growing popular sense that the PSD's Europe-oriented, modernizing, free-market policies had ignored growing problems at home. Guterres ran on a platform of renewed attention to critical social issues, such as education and health care, promising to boost spending in those areas without raising taxes. The Socialist leader also made a particular effort to calm financial markets by stressing his party's commitment to European economic and monetary union (EMU) and his intention to meet the monetary targets set out in the Maastricht Treaty, including lower interest rates and a smaller budget deficit as a percentage of gross domestic product (GDP). Guterres also pledged to continue with the PSD's ambitious privatization program and said he would not interfere with the operations of the Bank of Portugal, noting that his party was also in favour of low inflation and a stable escudo.

Other significant events during the year included the massive 304 billion escudo hostile takeover of Banco Português do Atlântico SA by Banco Comercial Português and its partner, insurer Companhia de Seguros Imperio SA, and the 153 billion escudo purchase of a contested 50% stake of Banco Totta e Açores by exiled financier António Champalimaud. Both buyouts pointed to the growing need for consolidation in the banking sector as European competition intensified and the relatively small Portuguese banks started feeling the pressure of smaller profit margins.

The PSD was able to undertake two more privatizations before leaving office. In June some 52 million shares, or 28%, of telecommunications giant Portugal Telecom SA were sold to private investors; this was followed in August by the sale of 34.8 million shares, or 40%, of pulp producer Portucel Industrial SA. The government said that privatizations in the first half of 1995 brought in a total of 282 billion escudos, more than 2% of estimated GDP for 1995, and made a significant contribution toward reducing the budget deficit.

(ERIK BURNS)

See also *Dependent States.*

QATAR

A monarchy (emirate) on the Arabian Peninsula, Qatar occupies a desert peninsula and the nearby small Hawar Islands (also claimed by Bahrain) on the west coast of the Persian Gulf. Area (including Hawar Islands): 11,427 sq km (4,412 sq mi). Pop. (1995 est.): 579,000. Cap.: Doha. Monetary unit: Qatar riyal, with (Oct. 6, 1995) an official rate of 3.64 riyals to U.S. $1 (5.76 riyals = £1 sterling). Emirs and prime ministers in 1995, Sheikh Khalifah ibn Hamad ath-Thani and, from June 27, Sheikh Hamad ibn Khalifah ath-Thani.

On June 27, 1995, in a nonviolent palace coup, Crown Prince Hamad ibn Khalifah ath-Thani ousted his father as emir of Qatar while the latter was traveling abroad. Sheikh Hamad's assumption of power received broad support within the ruling family as well as prompt recognition from neighbouring states. Sheikh Hamad had already been running the country's day-to-day affairs for three years. His move was reportedly motivated mainly by differences with his father's more conservative approach to the pace of economic development and by indications that his father was planning to reassert his authority. Sheikh Hamad promised to intensify efforts to resolve Qatar's border disputes with Saudi Arabia and Bahrain. Negotiations continued with Saudi Arabia. In the case of the dispute with Bahrain over the Hawar Islands, Qatar was prepared to accept adjudication by the International Court of Justice, but Bahrain refused. Qatar surprised its neighbours by walking out of a Gulf Cooperation Council meeting in December on a procedural point and announcing it was "reviewing" its membership.

Qatar pressed ahead with development of its huge gas resources. In September the first phase of Qatargas' North Field project, producing four million tons per year of liquefied natural gas, was inaugurated. (MICHAEL STERNER)

This article updates the *Macropædia* article ARABIA: *Qatar.*

ROMANIA

A republic on the Balkan Peninsula in southeastern Europe, Romania has a coastline on the Black Sea. Area: 237,500 sq km (91,699 sq mi). Pop. (1995 est.): 22,693,000. Cap.: Bucharest. Monetary unit: leu, with (Oct. 6, 1995) a free rate of 2,192 lei to U.S. $1 (3,466 lei = £1 sterling). President in 1995, Ion Iliescu; prime minister, Nicolae Vacaroiu.

Romania's domestic and foreign policy in 1995 was marked by its efforts to meet the conditions for greater convergence with the structures of the European Union (EU) and of NATO. Military units from nine countries, including Romania, took part in the first-ever NATO exercise in Romania between September 11 and 14 under the Partnership for Peace program. On June 22 Romania applied for full membership in the EU, which it hoped to achieve by about the year 2000. EU norms were the starting point for much of the new legislation introduced into the Romanian parliament, and in March special "European Union" departments were set up in each ministry to ensure that existing laws met EU practice. In June a parliamentary committee for European integration was set up.

Western governments, however, continued to be concerned that the government of Nicolae Vacaroiu, a coalition of the left that also included some ultranationalists, was encouraging unrealistic expectations in the population and that while proclaiming support for European integration, it was dragging its feet over reform. Romania was behind other countries in the region in complying with some of the conditions of the association agreement signed with the EU on Feb. 1, 1993. No antimonopoly laws had been introduced, for example, and laws identifying and authorizing state subsidies had yet to be framed. A competition law, drafted in 1993, had been blocked in the parliament since December 1994. A bankruptcy law apparently was passed by the parliament and promulgated by the president, but no details of it were immediately made public.

The most graphic sign of this legislative lethargy was the belated passage of the law on the privatization of commercial enterprises, which came into force on June 19 after two years in gestation. Privatization coupons were distributed to all persons over the age of 18. Under the scheme, Romanians could swap the coupons and previously distributed preshare vouchers for up to 60% of some 2,500 enterprises. The remainder would then be sold for cash to Romanian or foreign investors. The value of the coupon was set in June at 875,000 lei.

Despite the slow pace of reform, a major part of the basic legislation necessary for a market economy was in place and prompted the appearance of a dynamic private sector. The government continued to achieve notable success in reducing inflation, bringing it down from 62% in 1994 to a year-on-year average in April of 34%. Total industrial output in the first five months of the year showed a 10% increase over the same period in 1994, although much of this remained in factory warehouses. State-sector wages were increased in spring by 8%, but unemployment continued to rise at a rate of 11%.

An Amnesty International report in May accused Romania of failing to uphold its international human rights obligations, particularly in respect to the Roma (Gypsy) minority. The status of the Hungarian minority in Transylvania remained the major obstacle in concluding a Romanian-Hungarian treaty. Pres. Ion Iliescu attempted to dispel suspicions that Romania was the reluctant party by calling for a "historic reconciliation" between Hungary and Romania in a speech delivered in Vienna on August 30. He appealed to the Hungarian government to sign a document based on reciprocal support for each country's efforts to join the EU and NATO and for relations to be based on principles set out in the UN Charter and in the Organization for Security and Cooperation in Europe documents. The Hungarian prime minister gave a cautious welcome to Iliescu's proposals. Doubts about Iliescu's ability to deliver reconciliation were fueled, however, by a statement of Gheorghe Funar, leader of the ultranationalist Romanian National Unity Party (PUNR), a government coalition partner. In a speech in late June, Funar sought to exploit nationalist sensibilities among the mixed population in the Transylvanian capital of Cluj by calling for the removal from the city of a statue to a Hungarian king. (DENNIS J. DELETANT)

This article updates the *Macropædia* article BALKAN STATES: *Romania.*

RUSSIA

Russia is a federal republic occupying eastern and northeastern Europe and all of northern Asia. Area: 17,075,400 sq km (6,592,800 sq mi). Pop. (1995 est.): 147,168,000. Cap.: Moscow. Monetary unit: ruble, with (Oct. 6, 1995) a free rate of 4,496 rubles = U.S. $1 (7,107 rubles = £1 sterling). President in 1995, Boris Yeltsin; prime minister, Viktor Chernomyrdin.

In the tumultuous year of 1995, Pres. Boris Yeltsin's hold on power was challenged on many occasions. He was hospitalized in July with heart trouble and again in October, after returning from New York. The victory of the Communists in the December elections was widely seen as a rejection of the government's reform policies. All this created the impression that the Yeltsin era was coming to an end and that the president could not stand for reelection in June 1996.

Domestic Affairs. An intense struggle for influence took place during the year among Yeltsin's aides and ministers. Two main centres of power emerged, the government and its central ministries on the one side and the president and his administration on the other, but many administrative functions overlapped, which promoted inefficient decision making as officials fought for the president's ear. Another conflict also was raging throughout the country, this one between the pro- and antireform lobbies. Communists and nationalists opposed the government's commitment to the

A man takes a short break from his job in a metallurgical plant in Novokuznetsk that has been privatized. Virtually all Russian companies in ferrous metallurgy had been privatized by 1995, but in the machine tool industry and a number of other sectors, the process was much less advanced.
VLADMIR VYATKIN—MIR

market economy and democracy and its essentially pro-Western foreign policy stance.

The disastrous war in Chechnya, launched in December 1994, dragged on, and by year's end no binding peace agreement had been negotiated with the forces of the rebellious Chechen president, Dzhokhar Dudayev. Militarily defeated, the rebels took to the southern hills of Chechnya and launched daring attacks on the occupying Russian forces. In June Chechen rebels penetrated southern Russia and attacked Budennovsk, killing over 100. The rebels had bribed Russian guards to pass through the border. They later took hostages and used them to negotiate their safe return to Chechnya. The Chechen terrorists took their campaign to the heart of Moscow in November by placing a radioactive parcel in a public park and causing great anxiety.

The president and the government were savaged in the State Duma (lower house of the parliament) for their handling of the affair and the Chechen war in general. On June 30 Yeltsin made concessions on the eve of the State Duma's no-confidence motion in the government by sacking Minister of the Interior Viktor Yerin; Sergey Stepashin, head of the Federal Counterintelligence Service; and Nikolay Yegorov, deputy prime minister responsible for nationality affairs. In the no-confidence vote on July 1, only 193 deputies voted against the government, far short of the 226 needed to carry the motion. This was the most dangerous confrontation with the parliament since the bloody events of October 1993.

On several occasions during the early part of the year, Yeltsin stated that Russian bombardment of Grozny and Russian attacks on stated targets had ceased. Local observers refuted these claims, however, and revealed that the war was continuing. Some commentators took this to mean that the president was not in control of his own armed forces, but the more likely explanation was that the "war party" in Moscow, centred in the Security Council, had a mandate to defeat the Chechens militarily as quickly as possible. Yeltsin maintained that Russia would never negotiate with the "bandit" Dudayev, but his assurances seemed to be for international consumption only. While noting Yeltsin's erratic behaviour, commentators praised Prime Minister Viktor Chernomyrdin for his flexibility and willingness to compromise.

The war in Chechnya weakened ties between the centre and the non-Russian republics and polarized Russians and non-Russians (about 19% of the population) in a way not seen since 1991. A summit meeting of various republican leaders from the Volga and Urals regions held in Cheboksary, Chuvash Republic, in early January revealed the depth of opposition to the war, especially among Muslims. The meeting condemned the war, demanded its immediate cessation, and criticized Yeltsin, notably for his disinclination to consult with republican leaders. The meeting called for the convening of a "congress of the peoples of Russia" to debate, draft, and take action on national issues. Although the congress had not come into being by the end of the year, the implicit warning that another centre of power, rivaling Moscow and speaking for the regions, could emerge in the future was not lost. The president of the Ingush Republic, which borders Chechnya and was home to many refugees, strongly criticized Russia's use of force and warned that it could lead in turn to the use of force against Russians throughout the Caucasus. The president of the North Ossetian Republic, on the other hand, welcomed Moscow's

(continued on page 461)

SPOTLIGHT: POLLUTION IN EASTERN EUROPE

Illustration by Istvan Banyai

by Norman Myers

In 1995 Eastern Europe pondered ways to clean itself up. Well it might, since it is arguably the most polluted region on Earth. From Poland to Romania and from the Czech Republic to Moldova, its skies are dirty, its rivers and lakes contaminated, and its soils so poisoned that in some places the crops are inedible. Shortly before the Soviet Union's demise in 1991, the Kremlin admitted that 3.5 million sq km (1.35 million sq mi), 16% of the nation's territory, were so polluted as to be a risk to human health. They were a risk to political health as well; some of the 45 million people who were worst affected joined other protesters in making environmental degradation a catalyst for ending communist mismanagement.

Poland serves well as an example of how bad things can get. The Polish Academy of Sciences has described the country as the most polluted in the world. Few of its coal-burning industrial facilities and power plants have effective pollution-control systems, yet coal is crucial since it supplies about 80% of the country's energy. Air pollution in nearly every major city is 50 times the legal limit; it also has reduced yields of barley, beans, and potatoes by 10–55%.

About half of Poland's cities have no wastewater-treatment systems. Even in Warsaw only half of the sewage is treated, the rest being dumped raw into the Vistula River, which carries it to the Baltic Sea. Water along most of the lengths of the country's monitored rivers is too polluted to drink even after disinfection. A fourth of the country's soil is believed to be so contaminated that it cannot grow food that is safe for people or livestock, and in the Katowice region 90% of fruit and vegetables are thought to be toxic to humans.

Fortunately, Poland is now working to reduce pollution. In 1992 the government shut down 18 of the dirtiest industrial plants. In 1995 it tried—with only moderate success—to implement the antipollution standards laid down in the comprehensive National Environmental Policy of 1990, the first such plan in Eastern Europe.

Other countries of the region face similar problems. In the former East Germany, average levels of sulfur dioxide and particulates are many times those found in the U.S. The town of Boxberg, with its lignite-burning power plant, emits more sulfur dioxide annually than the total emissions of Denmark and Norway combined. Acid rain has damaged 35% of Hungary's forests, 50% of the former East Germany's, 73% of the former Czechoslovakia's, 78% of Bulgaria's, and 82% of Poland's. A third of the rivers in the Czech Republic and half of those in Slovakia no longer support aquatic life. As much as 80% of Romania's river water is unfit for drinking. The Black Sea receives so much chemical pollution, large amounts of it via the Danube and Dnieper rivers, that 90% of the sea is biologically dead.

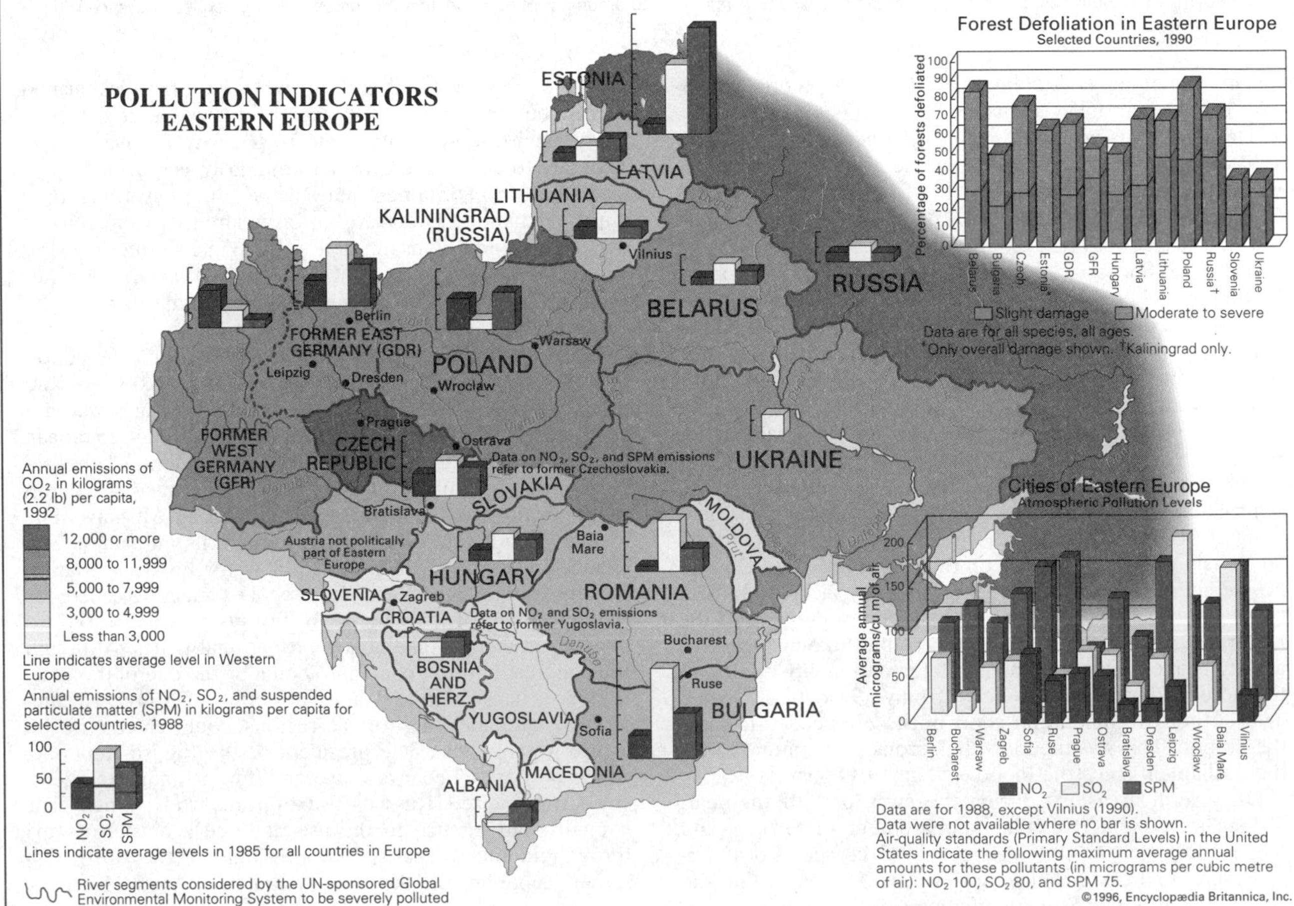

All this environmental damage levies sizable economic costs. In the Czech Republic and Slovakia, annual crop losses from sulfur dioxide alone cost the economy almost $200 million. In the Czech Republic, air pollution of all kinds accounts for losses totaling the equivalent of 1.3 million metric tons of wheat, or about 125 kg (275 lb) per person—half of a Czech citizen's grain needs for a year.

Then there are health costs. In the dirtiest parts of Eastern Europe, life expectancy is several years lower than in cleaner areas, and the incidence of cancer, reproductive problems, and other ailments is far higher. In Hungary one in 17 deaths is thought to be due to pollution. Lack of environmental safeguards and poor health care have combined to reduce the average life expectancy in the former Soviet Union to less than 64 years. In several high-pollution areas of western Russia, 10–20% of children are born with environmentally related birth defects.

The worst environmental debacle centres on the Chernobyl nuclear power station accident in the Soviet Union in 1986. The explosions and fire, which produced more fallout than the atomic bombing of Hiroshima and Nagasaki, Japan, and irradiated an area of 200,000 sq km (77,000 sq mi), caused the evacuation of a quarter of a million people in Ukraine, Russia, and Belarus. Belarusian officials believe that as much as one-fifth of their country's farmlands has been rendered unusable by Chernobyl radiation, and it is expected that more than two million people eventually will be moved from contaminated areas. Another 16 Chernobyl-type power stations exist in western Russia and Eastern Europe, some of them notoriously unsafe.

Amid the gloom there nonetheless are rays of hope. Eastern Europeans are realizing that environmental degradation accounts for losses of 5–10% in their countries' gross national products. They are outraged and are saying so. A poll in Russia found that almost one in two citizens considers pollution to be the nation's most urgent problem, ahead of housing shortages and poor medical services. In the former Czechoslovakia four people out of five believe the top priority should be environmental rehabilitation. The Romanian Ecological Movement has 112 local groups and more than 100,000 members, plus a good number of small "green" organizations. These are encouraging signs, but it remains to be seen whether Eastern Europe's newfound environmental awareness can be exercised in time to reverse the decades of gross neglect.

Norman Myers is a consultant scientist in environment and development, a visiting fellow of Green College, Oxford, and a senior fellow of the World Wildlife Fund.

TOMAS MUSCIONICO—CONTACT PRESS IMAGES

A power plant pollutes the town of Bedzin in Poland.

(continued from page 459)

intervention—apparently the only republican leader to do so. The imams everywhere criticized Russia's military action and attempted to increase feelings of solidarity among Muslims (about 12% of Russia's population). The leaders of several ethnically Russian oblasts, including Moscow, as well as of Stavropol Kray, criticized the anti-interventionist stance of the Cheboksary summit. Opinion polls in Russia revealed little enthusiasm for the war, and by the summer there was a clear majority in favour of letting Chechnya secede. This paralleled the isolationist feeling in Russia that Chechnya, as well as the now independent republics of Ukraine and Belarus, were millstones around Russia's neck. There was little sympathy for the 22 million Russians living outside Russia. All this was related to declining living standards in Russia and the belief that Russian policy should concentrate on its domestic agenda.

The political climax of the year was the December 17 elections, which, if only an early act in the much more important drama of the presidential election in the summer of 1996, revealed the depth of popular disenchantment with the reform policies of the government and the erratic performance of President Yeltsin. In the event, the Communists came out on top with 22.3% of the vote, while the ultranationalists of Vladimir Zhirinovsky's Liberal Democratic Party (LDP) were in second place with 11.2%; moderate and reformist parties generally fared poorly. Taken together, three radical parties—the Communists, their Agrarian Party allies, and the LDP—would control over half the seats in the State Duma. (For a detailed breakdown, see *Political Parties,* above.) The December elections threw the spotlight on likely challengers to Yeltsin for the presidency; Communist Party leader Gennady Zyuganov, Zhirinovsky, reformist Grigory Yavlinsky (of Yabloko, which won 6.9%), and Prime Minister Chernomyrdin (of the Our Home Is Russia party, 10.1%) were in, as was Lieut. Gen. Aleksandr I. Lebed, the nationalist veteran of the Afghanistan war, who threw his hat in the ring at year's end even though his party in the elections failed to win seating in the State Duma.

The Economy. The major government objectives—increasing budget revenue, restricting expenditure, and reining in inflation—were, on the whole, achieved. In the first half of the year, the federal budget deficit was only 3.2% of gross domestic product (GDP), below the target agreed with the International Monetary Fund when it made available a $6.5 billion standby loan to Russia. The small deficit was due to increased revenue and lower expenditure than in 1994. In turn, the monthly rate of inflation fell from about 18% in January to 4.5% in October.

On the downside, however, the government was tardy in paying its bills, and there were many strikes resulting from the nonpayment of wages. Cuts in federal subsidies hurt poorer regions, especially those in the north. After falling almost continuously for three years against the dollar, the ruble began to appreciate in May, and from May 4 to August 7 it rose 16%. In July the government and the central bank announced that the ruble would be held within a corridor of 4,300–4,900 to the dollar until October 1, and that date was later extended to the end of the year. Gross foreign exchange reserves reached $10 billion in June, the highest amount since the beginning of reforms. The ruble also appreciated against the currencies of other members of the Commonwealth of Independent States (CIS). Total credits provided by Russia to the CIS climbed to $5.6 billion in mid-1995, and these states were proving quite unable to service the debt. Total CIS and Baltic states shortfall for Russia's energy supplies was $3.1 billion by July 1.

Wealth was spread unevenly over the country. The Far

East, with 5% of the population, reported 8% of national income; the Central region, including Moscow, increased its share in 1995 (20% of the population and 29% of national income), while the Volga region and the North Caucasus had the lowest income figures.

Federal provision for health, social security, and education was proving inadequate. Unemployment climbed to 7.6% of the labour force in July. Benefits were kept low in order to encourage the unemployed to seek new employment rapidly. There was a great increase in the number of Russians with second jobs. In July about 28% of the population was living below the poverty line, compared with 25% in July 1994. The old and the very young were the most seriously affected. Real consumption declined by 6% in the first half of the year compared with the previous year; retail trade was 8% less over the same period. Russia's GDP fell an estimated 5% in 1995, compared with 15% in 1994.

Agriculture turned in a dismal performance, recording a harvest of about 65 million metric tons of grain and necessitating imports of at least 10 million metric tons. Production figures for meat, poultry, milk, and eggs were significantly down during the first half of the year compared with the same period in 1994, following a steady trend since 1991. Only about 2% of food output came from private farms, which demonstrated that privatization in the countryside was only just beginning.

Privatization of Russia's state-owned industries encountered some difficulties in early 1995, but in April the government published a list of some 7,000 companies in which it planned to sell its remaining shares. The sales took place between September and December and boosted the second stage of privatization, which involved large companies. Selloffs were slow during the first half of the year because the government feared that its assets would move at excessively low prices, given the depressed state of the Russian stock market. Initially the government expected revenue of some 9.1 trillion rubles, with 3.6 trillion rubles coming in the first half of the year, but the actual total was 100 billion rubles, partly because over 3,000 of the most attractive Russian companies were excluded from privatization.

Given the need to boost budget revenue, however, the government had second thoughts. In October it announced it would sell 25% of Svyazinvest, a state-owned telecommunications holding company, to an Italian investor for $1.2 billion. The deal fell through on December 25, however. Privatization nevertheless had changed the face of the Russian economy. By April 1995, 73% of industrial enterprises responsible for 85% of total industrial production were in the private sector. In some industries the advance was more spectacular. Practically all companies in ferrous metallurgy were private, and in the fuel industry the figure stood at over 90%.

In housing only 33%, or 11 million, apartments designated for privatization had been sold. Renters were wary of buying, fearing high taxes and repair bills. An increasingly popular method of restructuring enterprises was the formation of financial industrial groups, clusters of enterprises and commercial banks. In July there were 18 such groups in Russia, notably in the metals and automobile sectors.

In July Russia's first hostile takeover attempt occurred. The bid for the Red October chocolate factory failed, but the suitor, a company controlled by Menatep Bank, was granted two seats on Red October's board.

In 1995 just over 2,500 commercial banks traded, and 770 possessed licenses to engage in foreign-currency transactions. Bad debts jumped to 20% of total loans in January, however, and this contributed to the first banking crisis in Russia. Panic spread in August as 10 banks acknowledged that they could not repay their loans, and overnight interbank rates reached 1,000%. The crisis was overcome when the Russian central bank bought government bonds to provide liquidity. It seemed clear that some banks would have to be closed, if only because only 20% of the 1,000 joint stock banks met the central bank's requirement of charter capital over 6 billion rubles. Western banking authorities mentioned these figures as one reason why they would not be granting any Russian bank a banking license in the near future.

Foreign Affairs. Publicly President Yeltsin and U.S. Pres. Bill Clinton got on famously; they met in Moscow in May and in New York in October and enjoyed many telephone conversations as well. Behind the smiles, however, there were several points of friction in the relationship; Russia insisted that it would supply nuclear reactors to Iran, was resolutely opposed to the expansion of NATO into Eastern Europe, and made clear that its troops would not serve under a NATO general in Bosnia and Herzegovina—much to the U.S.'s chagrin. Russia also went its own way over Cuba, signing an oil-for-sugar deal and promising to finish building a Soviet-era nuclear reactor. Two undiplomatic comments late in the year, in turn, roused Russia's ire. First, a senior political officer at the U.S. embassy in Moscow published an unflattering article in a Moscow newspaper about the level of democracy in the forthcoming elections. Then, on December 8, Ambassador Thomas R. Pickering told journalists on Sakhalin Island that the U.S. supported Japanese claims in the sensitive Kuril Islands dispute with Russia.

Yeltsin also lacked faith in his own foreign minister, Andrey Kozyrev, for not prosecuting Russia's interests vigorously enough abroad and went so far as to talk about sacking him in October.

Within the CIS the war in Chechnya sowed distrust of Russia among most states, which resisted entering into a close security arrangement with Moscow; the exception was Kazakhstan. Russian trade with CIS states increased, and Russia obtained stakes in some companies in Ukraine and elsewhere in a debt-for-equity swap. Gazprom, the Russian monopoly gas producer, attempted to gain control over pipelines in Ukraine, Belarus, and Moldova.

(MARTIN MCCAULEY)

RWANDA

The landlocked republic of Rwanda is situated in central Africa. Area: 26,338 sq km (10,169 sq mi). Pop. (1995 est.): 6.7 million, including 2 million refugees, of whom 1.1 million are in Zaire and 600,000 are in Tanzania. Cap.: Kigali. Monetary unit: Rwanda franc, with (Oct. 6, 1995) a free rate of RF 302.21 to U.S. $1 (RF 477.76 = £1 sterling). President in 1995, Pasteur Bizimungu; prime ministers, Faustin Twagiramungu and, from August 31, Pierre Celestin Rwigema.

In January 1995, Médecins sans Frontières (Doctors Without Borders) called for the UN International Criminal Tribunal for Rwanda to act to find those responsible for the massacres that had occurred during the Rwandan civil war. The group called upon other agencies to abandon the "aid only" approach and, instead, link aid to justice in Rwanda and elsewhere. On January 7 Pres. Pasteur Bizimungu met heads of state and senior ministers of Burundi, Kenya, Tanzania, Uganda, Zaire, and Zambia in Nairobi, Kenya, in an attempt to reconcile supporters of the defeated Hutu regime with the new government, which was dominated by the Tutsi-led Rwandan Patriotic Front. At the beginning of 1995, there were some 1.1 million refugees in Zaire and another 800,000 in Burundi and Tanzania. By the end of January, the UN had abandoned its attempt to create a

A young Rwandan student shows her work in arithmetic on a chalkboard donated by UNESCO. The education of children had been badly affected by the turmoil taking place in Rwanda, but with outside aid from the UN and other sources some schools were beginning to reopen.
BETTY PRESS—PANOS

peacekeeping force for the camps in Zaire; instead, it was obliged to place Zairean troops under UN auspices.

Fresh evidence of massacres was uncovered in February when 4,500 bodies were unearthed on the grounds of the Kigali central hospital, including leading political figures identified by their identity cards. The UN Security Council unanimously approved Resolution 977, which named Arusha, Tanzania, as the venue for the International Criminal Tribunal for Rwanda. There was growing fear in the refugee camps that Interahamwe (the extremist Hutu group responsible for the massacres in Rwanda) was establishing its control. In April 2,000 Hutu refugees were massacred in the Kibeho camp inside Rwanda by elements of the Rwandan Patriotic Army. At the genocide trial beginning in April, one defendant admitted to having killed 900 people. A Human Rights Watch report claimed that Zaire, France, and South Africa were assisting the former Hutu government with arms and training. Meanwhile, Rwanda's prisons were overcrowded with vast numbers of people (47,000) accused of genocide and awaiting processing by the courts. Navanethem Pillay, a member of the International Criminal Tribunal for Rwanda, said in December that a lack of cooperation from African nations was delaying the work of the tribunal.

At the end of August, the president dismissed Prime Minister Faustin Twagiramungu, the most senior non-Tutsi in the government. The new government contained a number of Hutu, including Prime Minister Pierre Celestin Rwigema. At year's end fighting continued between Tutsi government forces and Hutu rebels. (GUY ARNOLD)

This article updates the *Macropædia* article CENTRAL AFRICA: *Rwanda.*

SAINT KITTS AND NEVIS

A constitutional monarchy and member of the Commonwealth, St. Kitts and Nevis comprises the islands of St. Kitts and Nevis in the eastern Caribbean Sea. Area: 269 sq km (104 sq mi). Pop. (1995 est.): 39,400. Cap.: Basseterre. Monetary unit: Eastern Caribbean dollar, with (Oct. 6, 1995) a par value of EC$2.70 to U.S. $1 (free rate of EC$4.27 = £1 sterling). Queen, Elizabeth II; governor-general in 1995, Sir Clement Arrindell; prime ministers, Kennedy Alphonse Simmonds and, from July 7, Denzil Douglas.

In the general election in July 1995, the People's Action Movement (PAM), after 15 years in power, found itself decisively defeated by the St. Kitts–Nevis Labour Party (SKNLP), led by Denzil Douglas. SKNLP won 7 of the 11 seats, PAM retained only one seat, and two smaller parties picked up the rest. Even Prime Minister Kennedy Simmonds lost his seat. The election had been called only 20 months after the previous election in November 1993, which had produced an inconclusive result and sparked social unrest.

The government called in British police advisers during the year to help reorganize the local police force, following an upsurge in drug-related crime. St. Kitts and Nevis, like other Caribbean countries, had found itself becoming a transit point in the illegal drug trade.

In September, St. Kitts and Nevis suffered the same fate as many other Caribbean territories when it was battered by Hurricanes Luis and Marilyn. Damage to industrial installations, utilities, homes, and public institutions like hospitals was estimated at U.S. $70 million. (DAVID RENWICK)

This article updates the *Macropædia* article The WEST INDIES: *Saint Kitts and Nevis.*

SAINT LUCIA

A constitutional monarchy and member of the Commonwealth, St. Lucia is the second largest of the Windward Islands in the eastern Caribbean Sea. Area: 617 sq km (238 sq mi). Pop. (1995 est.): 143,000. Cap.: Castries. Monetary unit: Eastern Caribbean dollar, with (Oct. 6, 1995) a par value of EC$2.70 to U.S. $1 (free rate of EC$4.27 = £1 sterling). Queen, Elizabeth II; governor-general in 1995, Stanislaus A. James; prime minister, John Compton.

Strikes in the banana industry were a feature of the industrial scene in early 1995 as a farmers group, the Banana Salvation Committee, tried to pressure the government into reforming the St. Lucia Banana Growers' Association. The work stoppage affected production, which only added to the industry's woes, following the damage to the banana crop by Tropical Storm Debby in late 1994.

In March, Prime Minister John Compton's government reacted to the industrial unrest by threatening to strengthen the law relating to incitement and to amend the Public Order Act to allow the police to ban demonstrations.

Public-sector workers struck in June over a deadlocked pay dispute. The seven unions involved demanded a 30% increase, while the government offered 6%. The strike caused shortages of imported goods and kept some tourists away. It was called off in July, without the main issues' having been resolved.

In August the commission of inquiry into the misappropriation of U.S. $110,800 in UN funds found that the government was not implicated and the fraud had been perpetrated solely by former UN ambassador Charles Flemming.

A new political party, the Citizens' Democratic Party, was announced in September by a group of businessmen. The head of the party, which was to be publicly launched the following month, was expected to be Calixte George, managing director of the Saint Lucia Banana Growers' Association. He had announced his resignation from that position in August. (DAVID RENWICK)

This article updates the *Macropædia* article The WEST INDIES: *Saint Lucia.*

SAINT VINCENT AND THE GRENADINES

A constitutional monarchy within the Commonwealth, St. Vincent and the Grenadines comprises the islands of St. Vincent and the northern Grenadines in the eastern Caribbean Sea. Area: 389 sq km (150 sq mi). Pop. (1995 est.): 112,000. Cap.: Kingstown. Monetary unit: Eastern Caribbean dollar, with (Oct. 6, 1995) a par value of EC$2.70 to U.S. $1 (free rate of EC$4.27 = £1 sterling). Queen, Elizabeth II; governor-general in 1995, David Jack; prime minister, Sir James Fitz-Allen Mitchell.

Hanging of convicted murderers was resumed in St. Vincent when three men went to the gallows in February 1995. An unofficial moratorium on hanging had been maintained for many years. Amnesty International condemned the move.

In late February the government appointed a three-member commission to review the pay and working conditions of its 4,000 public employees. The union expressed unhappiness over the use of a tribunal to determine wages, rather than the normal collective bargaining process.

The deputy prime minister and attorney general, Parnell Campbell, resigned from the government in September after being accused of "financial impropriety" by the opposition Unity Labour Party. Campbell admitted borrowing U.S. $83,591 from an offshore bank operating in St. Vincent and experiencing difficulty in repaying the loan. He remained in the House of Assembly as a backbencher.

Prime Minister James Mitchell, who was knighted in January, declared in October that his plans for retirement from politics before the next election had been shelved in the "national" interest. (DAVID RENWICK)

This article updates the *Macropædia* article The WEST INDIES: *Saint Vincent and the Grenadines.*

SAN MARINO

The republic of San Marino is a landlocked enclave in northeastern Italy. Area: 61 sq km (24 sq mi). Pop. (1995 est.): 24,900. Cap.: San Marino. Monetary unit: Italian lira, with (Oct. 6, 1995) a free rate of 1,617 lire to U.S. $1 (2,557 lire = £1 sterling). The republic is governed by two *capitani reggenti,* or coregents, appointed every six months by a popularly elected Great and General Council. Executive power rests with the Congress of State, headed by the coregents and composed of three secretaries of state and seven ministers.

The year 1995 was an eventful one for Europe's smallest republic. San Marino, which the Italian press liked to term a fiscal paradise, attracted major foreign investors interested in the neighbouring Italian economy. Such activities helped contribute not only to the wealth of this tiny nation but also to its troubles as high-ranking financial officials from Italy visited the country to investigate allegations that bribes paid in Italy's notorious illegal trading scandal had passed through some of San Marino's financial institutions. Domestic industry fared well, though, and one of San Marino's oldest manufacturing companies launched a new line of construction machinery into European markets.

The year was also significant for its cultural activities, including an art exhibition that displayed spectacular findings from an Ostrogoth tomb. They provided an impressive view of life on the San Marino hills more than a thousand years ago. In October two new heads of state were sworn into office for their six-month term in a ceremony as old as modern Europe. (GREGORY O. SMITH)

This article updates the *Micropædia* article SAN MARINO.

SÃO TOMÉ AND PRÍNCIPE

The republic of São Tomé and Príncipe comprises two main islands and several smaller islets that straddle the Equator in the Gulf of Guinea, off the west coast of Africa. Area: 1,001 sq km (386 sq mi). Pop. (1995 est.): 131,000. Cap.: São Tomé. Monetary unit: dobra, with (Oct. 6, 1995) a free rate of 1,446 dobras to U.S. $1 (2,286 dobras = £1 sterling). President in 1995, Miguel Trovoada; prime minister, Carlos da Graça.

On Feb. 13, 1995, the government of São Tomé and Príncipe, in response to the rising cost of living, agreed to a general salary increase for both public- and private-sector workers. The increases were to range between 64% and 90% and become effective at the end of the month. The action was then followed by a number of austerity measures, however, including a rise in fuel prices, the dismissal of 300 civil servants, and an increase in the central bank reference interest rate from 32% to 50%. The measures were designed to persuade the World Bank to release funds that had already been committed.

In March local elections were held on the island of Príncipe, and on April 29 the island became autonomous, with a five-member regional government.

A five-member group of young army officers seized control of the government on August 15 in a coup attempt. Pres. Miguel Trovoada and Prime Minister Carlos da Graça and others were placed in custody, but there was no bloodshed. The leader of this self-styled national salvation junta, Lieut. Manuel Quintas de Almeida, claimed they wished to "recover the dignity of the country." On August 18 mediators arrived from Angola, and by August 21 the government had been restored, while the rebels were guaranteed immunity from prosecution.

On December 30 Graça announced an agreement between his administration and two opposition parties to form a new multiparty government. Deputy Prime Minister Armindo Vaz d'Almeida was expected to take over as prime minister in January 1996 in preparation for presidential elections in March. (GUY ARNOLD)

This article updates the *Macropædia* article CENTRAL AFRICA: *São Tomé and Príncipe.*

SAUDI ARABIA

The kingdom of Saudi Arabia occupies four-fifths of the Arabian Peninsula, with coastlines on the Red Sea and the Persian Gulf. Area: 2,240,000 sq km (865,000 sq mi). Pop. (1995 est.): 17,880,000. Cap.: Riyadh. Monetary unit: Saudi Arabian riyal, with (Oct. 6, 1995) an official rate of 3.75 riyals to U.S. $1 (5.93 riyals = £1 sterling). King and prime minister in 1995, Fahd.

Economic issues, political reform, the royal succession, religious dissension, and the border dispute with Yemen occupied the Saudi leadership in 1995. Heeding calls by the International Monetary Fund for financial restraint due to declining cash reserves and the anticipation of lower prices for oil, the government in January announced an austerity budget calling for reduced government expenditure. A slight rise in oil prices during the summer, however, from the $14-per-barrel budget projection to $16.25, increased Saudi income by an additional $6 billion–$7 billion over the estimate of $42 billion. That was enough to offset the immediate threat of financial crisis. Consequently, by mid-1995 instead of the anticipated 20% budget cut that King Fahd had threatened, the government decreed a reduction of only 6.2%, which included a 20% decline in funds for education. Fees for water, electricity, gasoline, and domestic air fares were raised, and other subsidies were canceled.

Spending on defense, more than one-third of the budget, was not affected. Responding to Iran's purchase of two submarines from Russia and its expected future purchases of additional ships and surface-to-surface missiles, the Saudis began to negotiate to buy several $1 billion Aegis-class warships from the U.S. for delivery by the end of the decade.

The important question of whether the austerity measures would affect some 4,000 princes who derived their income directly from government largesse remained a continuing point of dissension. This was emphasized by the increasing economic inequality in the country; salaries for civil servants had not been raised for more than a decade, and more and more educated commoners were unemployed. Middle-class Saudis were beginning to feel the financial pinch.

Fifteen members of the Consultative Council (*majlis ash-shura*) were assigned Cabinet posts in August. This change brought Western-educated technocrats, including 18 Ph.D.'s, to new posts, some of importance. In a government dominated by princes of the royal family, this change gave the impression of political reform. Key positions in the Cabinet—Defense, Foreign Affairs, and Interior—remained in the hands of Saudi princes, however. Also, the heads of the armed forces and security services, as well as the senior officials in the royal court, had their terms renewed and remained in power.

The retention of power bases by the various princes reflected the continuous jockeying for power by members of the royal family over the succession to the throne as King Fahd approached his mid-70s. Fahd's half brother Prince Abdullah, whose support was chiefly tribal, was next in line for the throne, followed by Fahd's full brother Prince Sultan, who had begun to increase his responsibilities in recent months. Both men, however, were also in their 70s, a situation that could open up succession to the next generation. The question assumed somewhat more urgency in late November when King Fahd, who was reportedly a chain smoker and a diabetic, suffered a minor stroke.

Because its leaders were no longer in Saudi Arabia, the Committee for the Defense of Legitimate Rights (CDLR), which moved its headquarters to London in 1994, was not seen as a major threat to Saudi stability. Led by a former physics professor, Muhammad ibn al-Masa'ari, the CDLR had become the focus of opposition to the royal family and considered itself a pressure group for peaceful reform and the improvement of human rights in Saudi Arabia. A car bomb on November 13 devastated a building in Riyadh used by U.S. advisers to the Saudi National Guard, and at least 6 persons were killed and more than 60 were injured. The U.S. embassy said afterward that it had received threats earlier in the year from the Islamic Movement for Change.

The government continued to crack down on local Islamists but allowed the religious police (*mutuwwa*) to operate freely in an attempt to appease the extremists. Amnesty International reported serious concern over the sharp increase in executions; there were more beheadings during the first quarter of 1995 than in all of 1994. Of the 90 people executed for crimes that included drug trafficking, possession of alcohol, and blasphemy, 5 were women. Most of the condemned were foreigners.

Though women were relegated to less active pursuits in Saudi Arabia, and were segregated in public and at work, an increasing number of them had received higher education. More and more were working in the professions, where they outnumbered men in some fields. The number of women investing in private businesses had increased in recent years to the extent that as much as 40% of the private wealth in Saudi Arabia was in the hands of women. In 1995 more than 2,000 women were registered with the Riyadh Chamber of Commerce. They were purchasing real estate and operating shops in Riyadh and Jiddah.

Saudi Arabia during the year began to settle its border dispute with Yemen. The declaration of principles signed in February included mutual pledges of nonaggression and a pledge to negotiate the demarcation of the entire frontier. The Treaty of At-Ta'if in 1934 concerned primarily urban areas in southwestern Arabia and recognized Saudi sovereignty over the former Yemeni provinces of Najran and Asir. The 1,500-km (950-mi) border area of desert and undemarcated oil fields was now the subject of discussion as the committees consulted records, patterns of tribal movements, and historical documents in order to come to some resolution of the border. On December 13 Prince Khalid ibn Sultan, a prominent member of the royal family, called for ending the sanctions against Iraq imposed after the 1991 Persian Gulf War. (REEVA S. SIMON)

This article updates the *Macropædia* article ARABIA: *Saudi Arabia.*

SENEGAL

The republic of Senegal is located in West Africa, on the Atlantic Ocean; it surrounds the country of The Gambia. Area: 196,712 sq km (75,951 sq mi). Pop. (1995 est.): 8,312,000. Cap.: Dakar. Monetary unit: CFA franc, with (Oct. 6, 1995) a par value of CFAF 100 to the French franc and a free rate of CFAF 501.49 to U.S. $1 (CFAF 792.78 = £1 sterling). President in 1995, Abdou Diouf; prime minister, Habib Thiam.

In February 1995 local elections were postponed owing to difficulties in achieving complete voter registration. They were rescheduled for early 1996 to coincide with regional elections. After months of negotiations Abdoulaye Wade, secretary-general of the opposition Senegalese Democratic Party, agreed to join the government of Pres. Abdou Diouf as a minister of state, and on March 15 he became a member of the new 33-member coalition Cabinet.

Clashes between the Senegalese armed forces and separatists from the Casamance region escalated during the year. The Movement of Democratic Forces of Casamance (MFDC) split in January when dissident elements rejected the July 1993 cease-fire, broke with the MFDC, and launched a series of attacks on government soldiers. In retaliation, government forces bombed several separatist strongholds in Guinea-Bissau. On July 25, ignoring an MFDC call for a new cease-fire, southern separatists ambushed a military convoy near Babonda, killing 23 soldiers and wounding 14. After fierce fighting the army recaptured the village on August 11, driving the rebels into the forest.

The introduction of a new investment code designed to encourage foreign ventures, combined with President Diouf's decision to speed up privatization of state-owned industries, won favour with international donors. The World Bank and the International Development Association authorized a series of new loans and grants for economic and educational reform. One unexpected bright spot was a 15% rise in tourism over 1994, despite the increase in separatist violence. (NANCY ELLEN LAWLER)

This article updates the *Macropædia* article WESTERN AFRICA: *Senegal.*

SEYCHELLES

A republic and member of the Commonwealth, the Seychelles consists of about 100 islands widely scattered over the western Indian Ocean. The main island of Mahé is 1,800 km (1,100 mi) from the east coast of the African continent. Area: 455 sq km (176 sq mi). Pop. (1995 est.): 75,000. Cap.: Victoria. Monetary unit: Seychelles rupee, with (Oct. 6, 1995) a free rate of SR 4.84 to U.S. $1 (SR 7.65 = £1 sterling). President in 1995, France-Albert René.

Seychelles sustained a reasonable rate of growth during 1995, although unemployment, at more than 22%, appeared to be relatively permanent. International debts, at $147.2 million, were less than half the gross national product ($376 million), while per capita income at $5,450 placed the islands well into the middle-income group of countries. Petroleum products accounted for more than 55% of export earnings, with tuna as the second source of export income. Tourism, however, was more important as a source of income than either petroleum or tuna. Britain was Seychelles' principal trading partner for both imports and exports.

Seychelles continued its attempt to establish the archipelago as an international business centre. New laws were passed that provided tax breaks and reductions in offshore licensing fees. A law passed in November granting immunity from prosecution in criminal proceedings—including extradition—in exchange for a $10 million investment in the Seychelles drew the attention of world law-enforcement agencies. The government also announced plans to move away from a welfare state by requiring payment for services that were once free. During 1994 Seychelles had implemented similar measures to improve the economy. Taxes on luxury goods were increased to discourage imports, and the port of Mahé was privatized, which resulted in the replacement of the state-owned Union Lighterage Co. by four firms specializing in separate activities—ship engineering, ship handling, and cargo handling. (GUY ARNOLD)

This article updates the *Micropædia* article SEYCHELLES.

SIERRA LEONE

A republic of West Africa and member of the Commonwealth, Sierra Leone lies on the Atlantic Ocean. Area: 71,740 sq km (27,699 sq mi). Pop. (1995 est.): 4,509,000. Cap.: Freetown. Monetary unit: leone, with (Oct. 6, 1995) a free rate of 756 leones to U.S. $1 (1,195 leones = £1 sterling). Chairman of the Supreme Council of State in 1995, Capt. Valentine E.M. Strasser; vice chairman (and head of government), Lieut. Julius Maada Bio.

After a year of fighting and uncertainty, the possibility of a return to civilian rule appeared nearer by late 1995 than at any previous time. In January there was widespread fighting throughout most of the country outside Freetown, and thousands of people fled their homes to become refugees, many moving into neighbouring Guinea. The violence was attributed to the rebel Revolutionary United Front (RUF), although there was both argument and uncertainty as to why the outbreak had occurred. The government of Capt. Valentine Strasser claimed that the RUF was a pawn of the National Patriotic Front of Liberia (NPFL), which was trying to undermine the Sierra Leone government because it had supported intervention in the Liberian civil war. In February government forces recaptured the Sierra Rutile titanium mine from the rebels; the mine earned more than 50% of the country's foreign exchange and was its largest employer.

On April 27 Captain Strasser lifted the ban on political parties and promised to relinquish power to a democratically elected president in January 1996. He also sought a settlement with the RUF. Rebel raids continued through September, and in mid-December the RUF attacked a village just 65 km (38 mi) from the capital, Freetown. Despite the expansion of the army to about 13,000 and the expenditure of 75% of budget revenue on the war, the government appeared unable to contain the RUF. By the deadline of August 14, a total of 17 political parties had registered for the elections, which were originally scheduled for late 1995 but were put off until 1996. An attempted officers' coup on October 3 was put down by the government, and seven officers were arrested. (GUY ARNOLD)

This article updates the *Macropædia* article WESTERN AFRICA: *Sierra Leone.*

CHRIS BROWN—SABA

Women in a displaced persons camp in Sierra Leone take their children with them to the fields. Fighting between a rebel group and the military government in 1995 had an especially severe effect on civilians, with tens of thousands killed and hundreds of thousands made homeless.

SINGAPORE

Singapore, a republic of Southeast Asia and member of the Commonwealth, consists of the island of Singapore and 58 nearby islets, at the southern extremity of the Malay Peninsula. Area: 641 sq km (247 sq mi). Pop. (1995 est.): 2,989,000. Monetary unit: Singapore dollar, with (Oct. 6, 1995) a free rate of S$1.43 to U.S. $1 (S$2.26 = £1 sterling). President in 1995, Ong Teng Cheong; prime minister, Goh Chok Tong.

In late February 1995 Britain's 233-year-old Barings PLC collapsed after running up losses of over $1 billion in futures trading on the Singapore International Monetary Exchange. Barings trader Nicholas Leeson fled Singapore and was later arrested in Frankfurt, Germany. (*see* ECONOMIC AFFAIRS: *Banking*.)

Relations with the Philippines were strained in March when Filipino maid Flor Contemplacion was executed for the 1991 murders of fellow domestic Delia Maga and a local boy under Maga's care. Many in the Philippines contended that Contemplacion was innocent, but Singapore denied Manila's request to postpone the hanging pending further investigation. As anti-Singapore protests raged, the Philippines recalled its ambassador. After U.S. forensic experts performed an autopsy on the exhumed remains of Maga and confirmed Singapore's medical report that Maga had died by strangulation, Philippine Pres. Fidel V. Ramos accepted the findings and declared the matter closed.

In his newspaper column, U.S. commentator William Safire berated Williams College, Williamstown, Mass., for awarding an honorary degree to Prime Minister Goh Chok Tong. Condemning what he said was Singapore's lack of freedom of expression, Safire challenged Goh to participate in a forum that would feature Singaporean opposition figures. Singapore responded with an invitation for Safire to debate Goh on the prime minister's home turf. The columnist refused, suggesting instead that Goh take on exiled opposition politician Francis Seow, while Safire would meet Senior Minister Lee Kuan Yew in Switzerland.

With new polls required by April 1997, the question of the prime minister's political future resurfaced when former Cabinet minister Tony Tan returned to government in August as his deputy. Lee, whose decision to step aside in 1990 had led to Goh's appointment as prime minister, had indicated that he preferred Tan to succeed him. In October, Pres. Ong Teng Cheong flew to the U.S. for medical consultations after cancer, previously diagnosed in 1992, recurred.

The economy continued to perform strongly, with growth above 8% and inflation dropping below 2%. Strong demand for electronics kept export growth in double digits. The government continued to encourage businessmen to venture abroad. (ALEJANDRO REYES)

This article updates the *Macropædia* article SOUTHEAST ASIA: *Singapore*.

SLOVAKIA

Slovakia is a landlocked state in central Europe. Area: 49,036 sq km (18,933 sq mi). Pop. (1995 est.): 5,355,000. Cap.: Bratislava. Monetary unit: Slovak koruna, with (Oct. 6, 1995) a free rate of 29.60 koruny to U.S. $1 (46.80 koruny = £1 sterling). President in 1995, Michal Kovac; prime minister, Vladimir Meciar.

Three domestic sources of power were not under Prime Minister Vladimir Meciar's control in 1995, and his policies appeared designed to minimize their significance. The first of these was the parliamentary opposition, possibly the easiest target because it had never fully recovered from having lost the 1994 elections. Meciar's second target was the president, Michal Kovac. Kovac had played a very active role in engineering Meciar's removal in 1994, and Meciar was implacable in his determination to oust him. There were votes in the National Council criticizing Kovac, he was snubbed, and then additional pressure was put on him through his son. The younger Kovac was wanted by the German authorities in connection with a corruption investigation, and in the autumn he was kidnapped, almost certainly by the Slovak intelligence service, forced into a car, and driven over the border into Austria, where the Austrian authorities released him on bail while he awaited possible extradition to Germany. Kovac held out, but the pressure was taking its toll.

The third target, and in this Meciar had the full-throated backing of the opposition Slovak Nationalist Party as well as of many members of his own party, was the Hungarian minority. The government moved on several occasions to curtail the rights of the Hungarians—in education, for example, and in the legality of bilingualism in local government—which the minority viewed with considerable distress.

Under some Western pressure, Slovakia and Hungary signed a bilateral security treaty, which provided for minority rights. Bratislava had still to ratify it at the end of the year and, indeed, signing it earned Meciar significant attacks from the nationalists. Then, as a concession to the nationalists, Meciar agreed to introduce a new law on the Slovak language, overtly nationalist in intent. By promoting Slovak as the unique language of the state, the law upset the Hungarians greatly, but their campaign against the law found no echo even among democratic-minded Slovaks, who ended up voting for the law.

The growing encroachment on the freedom of civil society was attracting the attention of the West. Both the European Union and the United States protested in the autumn, warning the Slovak government that it was running the risk of being excluded from the West. The Slovak authorities' response was to opt for isolation and, equally, for intensified, if pointless, relationships with Ukraine and Russia.

(GEORGE SCHÖPFLIN)

This article updates the *Macropædia* article CZECH AND SLOVAK REPUBLICS: *Slovakia*.

SLOVENIA

A republic of the extreme northwestern Balkans, Slovenia borders Austria to the north, Hungary to the east, Croatia to the southeast and south, the Adriatic Sea to the southwest, and Italy to the west. Area: 20,255 sq km (7,820 sq mi). Pop. (1995 est.): 1,971,000. Cap.: Ljubljana. Monetary unit: tolar, with (Oct. 6, 1995) a free rate of 122.93 tolarji to U.S. $1 (194.34 tolarji = £1 sterling). President in 1995, Milan Kucan; prime minister, Janez Drnovsek.

Although Slovenia's aspirations to join the European Union (EU) continued to be frustrated in 1995 by Italy's opposition, the country maintained a steady rate of economic progress. There was hope for progress on EU membership in March, after Italy lifted its veto on talks, and on May 19 the European Commission approved the terms of Slovenia's associate membership. Then Italy called for further changes to the 1975 Osimo Treaty and the 1983 Rome Agreement between Italy and Yugoslavia (of which Slovenia was then a part) and insisted on material compensation for Italians displaced in the 1945 border adjustments as preconditions for agreeing to further EU talks. Italy further demanded that Italian citizens have the right to buy property in Slovenia. Pres. Milan Kucan visited Brussels on November 30, but Italy continued to insist on its preconditions, and talks on Slovenia's association with the EU made no further progress.

A woman tends a field near Celje planted in hops. The privatization of Slovenia's extensive agricultural industry—which was diversified among field crops, livestock, and fruits and was the most productive of those of the republics of the former Yugoslavia—began in 1992.

CHRIS ANDERSON—AURORA

On December 6 Prime Minister Janez Drnovsek acknowledged that the talks had reached an impasse. Nonetheless, Slovenia was voted a full member of the Central European Free Trade Agreement in September, and relations with NATO continued to develop within the Partnership for Peace program. U.S. Defense Secretary William Perry visited Slovenia on September 16.

In June Slovenia agreed with a consortium of nearly 300 banks to assume responsibility for 18% of the total debt of $4.7 billion owed to the banks by former Yugoslavia. Relations with Croatia remained tense mainly because of the continuing dispute over the territorial waters of the Bay of Piran. On November 30 Slovenia recognized Yugoslavia.

Relations between the government and the country's Roman Catholic Church deteriorated sharply in 1995. The church demanded the return of property nationalized under the communist regime.

Slovenia registered 5% growth in gross domestic product in 1995. The annual inflation rate was 11%. Its exports, at $6,180,000,000 for the January–September 1995 period increased by 26.1% over the corresponding period in 1994. In the same period, Slovene imports, at $7 billion, were 35.2% higher than in 1994. For January–September Slovenia's trade deficit was $804 million, compared with $266 million in the first nine months of 1994. The tolar became fully convertible on Sept. 1, 1995. (K.F. CVIIC)

This article updates the *Macropædia* article BALKAN STATES: *Slovenia*.

SOLOMON ISLANDS

A constitutional monarchy and member of the Commonwealth, the Solomon Islands comprises a 1,450-km (900-mi) chain of islands and atolls in the western Pacific Ocean. Area: 28,370 sq km (10,954 sq mi). Pop. (1995 est.): 382,000. Cap.: Honiara. Monetary unit: Solomon Islands dollar, with (Oct. 6, 1995) a free rate of SI$3.40 to U.S. $1 (SI$5.38 = £1 sterling). Queen, Elizabeth II; governor-general in 1995, Moses Pitakaka; prime minister, Solomon Mamaloni.

After Prime Minister Francis Billy Hilly was forced to resign in October 1994, Solomon Mamaloni was recalled to office for his third term as prime minister, with a majority of 29 to 18 over former governor-general Sir Baddeley Devesi. Mamaloni's coalition, the Group for National Unity and Reconciliation, promised to increase the size of Parliament and to extend its term to five years.

The new government vowed to place renewed emphasis on investment in production, to encourage the privatization of the public sector, and to increase trade. It also effectively halved taxes on the export of round logs and persisted with logging projects. On April 3, 1995, the government announced that Pavuvu Island would be cleared of timber, despite the objections of residents, who would be relocated. These policies amounted to a reversal of Hilly's attempt to control the logging industry, which he had seen as a source of corruption and improper influence in government. The government faced significant economic difficulties. In August the central bank accused the government of defaulting on debt-servicing obligations. (BARRIE MACDONALD)

This article updates the *Macropædia* article PACIFIC ISLANDS: *Solomon Islands.*

SOMALIA

Situated in the Horn of northeastern Africa, Somalia lies on the Gulf of Aden and the Indian Ocean. Area: 637,000 sq km (246,000 sq mi). Pop. (1995 est.): 6,734,000 (excluding Somali refugees in neighbouring countries estimated to number about 500,000). Cap.: Mogadishu. Monetary unit: Somali shilling, with (Oct. 6, 1995) a free rate of 2,620 Somali shillings to U.S. $1 (4,142 Somali shillings = £1 sterling). Somalia had no functioning government in 1995.

On Jan. 2, 1995, Somalia's former dictator Muhammad Siad Barre (*see* OBITUARIES) died in exile in Nigeria. In the country that he left in fragments, the last of the United Nations intervention force UNOSOM II (UN Operation in Somalia) was evacuated in March, covered by an international flotilla led by 1,800 U.S. marines. Fears that the withdrawal would lead to the widespread renewal of civil war were not realized, though local conflicts continued; trade and economic life appeared to be recovering.

Nevertheless, the country remained divided; besides the breakaway "Republic of Somaliland" in the north, there were several de facto independent areas. Mogadishu, the capital and port, and its hinterland remained split between the factions of Gen. Muhammad Farah Aydid and his rival, the nominal national president, Ali Mahdi Muhammad. Each was attempting to unite the whole country through his own alliance of clan and faction groupings: Aydid with the Somali National Alliance (SNA) and Ali Mahdi with the Somali Salvation Alliance (SSA). Northeastern Somalia and the port of Boosaaso were controlled by the Somali Salvation Democratic Front (SSDF). In the far south the valley of the Jubba River with its plantations remained divided between the forces of Gen. Muhammad Said Hersi ("Morgan") in the port of Kismaayo and those of Col. Ahmad Omar Jess in the hinterland, while in the fertile plain between the Jubba and Shebeli rivers, the Rahanwayn group of clans set up a supreme council in the town of Baydhabo to administer the region. Aydid's position was threatened by a split with his former right-hand man, the millionaire businessman Osman Hassan Ali ("Ato"), who became an ally of Ali Mahdi.

In June Aydid's United Somali Congress voted to replace him as SNA chairman with Ato. In response, a meeting of Aydid's supporters elected him president of all of Somalia (in direct rivalry to Ali Mahdi). Following this, Aydid attempted to consolidate his power throughout the south. In mid-September his forces took Baydhabo; Rahanwayn forces counterattacked, and fighting continued into December.

In the breakaway Somaliland the government of Pres. Muhammad Ibrahim Egal repelled attacks by the opposition led by his predecessor ʿAbd ar-Rahman Ahmad Ali "Tur," who favoured reunion with Somalia and joined forces with Aydid's SNA; by March Egal appeared to be in control. In January Somaliland introduced its own currency.

In September representatives from all parties met in Jiddah, Saudi Arabia, at the latest of many peace conferences and resolved to set up a national government. Aydid, though invited, did not attend. (VIRGINIA R. LULING)

This article updates the *Macropædia* article EASTERN AFRICA: *Somalia.*

SOUTH AFRICA

South Africa, a member of the Commonwealth, occupies the southern tip of Africa, with the Atlantic Ocean to the west and the Indian Ocean to the east. Area: 1,219,080 sq km (470,689 sq mi). Pop. (1995 est.): 41,465,000. Executive cap., Pretoria; judicial cap., Bloemfontein; legislative cap., Cape Town. Monetary unit: South African rand, with (Oct. 6, 1995) a free rate of R 3.66 to U.S. $1 (R 5.79 = £1 sterling); the dual exchange rate system introduced in 1979 was abolished on March 13, 1995. State president in 1995, Nelson Mandela.

Domestic Affairs. Opening Parliament in February 1995, Pres. Nelson Mandela threatened battle against the "forces of anarchy and chaos." He called for the country to become "investor-friendly," warning that freedom did not mean license and that the government did not have the means to meet the demands on it. People must rid themselves, he said, of the "culture of entitlement." A campaign was instituted to try to break the boycott of rent and service payments, estimated to involve 80% of black township residents. Mandela also continued his policy of racial reconciliation, holding a lunch for the wives of former presidents and prime ministers together with those of liberation movement leaders and taking tea with Betsie Verwoerd, widow of a leading architect of apartheid, Hendrik Verwoerd. Mandela expressed his sympathy for the Freedom Front's idea of an Afrikaner *volkstaat* because "compromise is something very important" in nation building.

Implementation of the government's reconstruction and development program proceeded slowly, owing to limited financial resources, bureaucratic inertia, and delayed transference of powers to provincial and local governments. Plans were, however, proposed for a publicly funded and universally accessible primary health care system, and a program of state subsidies for housing for the poor was initiated. A new framework for national education was legislated. In October it was reported that more than 300 rural water projects, benefiting 3.5 million people, and improvements of more than 600 municipal services were completed or would be within the next 18 months.

The year was punctuated by tensions between the parties constituting the government of national unity, particularly as local elections approached in November. The issues revolved particularly around the relative powers of central government and provinces. The National Party (NP) became torn by conflict over how to carve an independent profile as a party of opposition to the dominant African National Congress (ANC) while continuing to serve in the government, conflict that was resolved only by the authority of its leader, Deputy Pres. F.W. de Klerk.

In January, to the anger of the NP, the ANC denied the validity of the indemnity granted just before the April 1994 election by the NP government in secret to 3,500 policemen and two former Cabinet ministers. It said that their cases had to be considered by the Truth and Conciliation Commission, which was established during the year. In the same month, in an atmosphere of wildcat strikes by black police and accusations of white racism in the police, police chief Johan van der Merwe resigned and was replaced by George Fivaz, who pledged himself to reform in the police force, including the demilitarization of ranks. Concern about the nation's rising crime rate mounted during the year, and the government imposed tougher bail conditions on criminals. The newly established Constitutional Court controversially abolished the death penalty on June 6.

The trial of former security policeman Col. Eugene de Kock on 121 charges of murder, kidnapping, fraud, and theft produced further evidence of past police involvement in assassinations and the fomenting of political violence. Prominent Inkatha Freedom Party (IFP) leaders were alleged to have been in the pay of the security police. A secret report of the Goldstone Commission to President de Klerk in 1994 was published that alleged the security police had been "involved for many years in the most serious criminal conduct including murder, fraud, blackmail, and a huge operation of dishonest political disinformation." Prominent former policemen criticized the report for a lack of facts.

In pursuit of the goal of maximum autonomy for the KwaZulu/Natal province, Chief Mangosuthu Buthelezi, IFP leader and home affairs minister, was elected chairman of the KwaZulu/Natal House of Traditional Leaders in January against the opposition of King Goodwill Zwelithini, who—to the consternation of other traditional leaders in KwaZulu/Natal—had distanced himself from the IFP. Both the ANC and King Goodwill declared this House unconstitutionally established. The IFP walked out of Parliament in February, alleging that the ANC had broken its 1994 pledge to international mediation regarding the form of the South African state and restoration of the Zulu kingdom. The ANC claimed that these were matters for decision by the Constitutional Assembly (both houses of Parliament meeting to draw up a final constitution). The IFP returned to Parliament but withdrew in April from participation in the Constitutional Assembly and later from an intergovernmental forum of regional premiers. Buthelezi accused the ANC of attempting to establish a "one-party hegemony" in the country; the ANC in response accused the IFP of advocating secession of KwaZulu/Natal.

In response to calls by Buthelezi for the Zulu people to "rise and resist" central government, President Mandela in May threatened to cut government funds to KwaZulu/Natal and stepped up the army and police presence in the province. Mandela claimed Buthelezi was fomenting violence, while Buthelezi claimed he was calling for peaceful mass resistance. In June Mandela admitted that in March 1994 he had given guards at the ANC headquarters in Johannesburg "shoot to kill" orders in self-defense against an IFP demonstration, which had resulted in deaths. To the anger of the IFP, Parliament passed legislation authorizing payment of the salaries of traditional leaders by the central government rather than the provinces. In the KwaZulu/Natal legislature, the IFP tried to secure the passage of a provincial constitution described as "highly confederal," including provision for an army and sovereignty over territorial waters, but could not secure the necessary two-thirds majority for this. There was evidence of tension between hard-liners and moderates in the IFP, the latter favouring greater cooperation with the ANC in government.

In the months prior to the April 1994 election, death tolls of 300 persons a month due to political violence were being recorded in Natal. They declined in the months following the election to a low of 57 in March 1995 but began to increase again thereafter, to about 70 a month. There were nearly 80 deaths in one week in July and 55 in one week in

August. Accusations were made by the ANC of a "culture of immunity" in KwaZulu/Natal and of failure to prosecute perpetrators of violence. In June a special investigative unit secured the arrest of the IFP's deputy secretary-general, Zakhele Khumalo, and two police officers on 13 counts of murder committed in 1987.

Local elections held on November 1, except in certain parts of the Western Cape and Natal, resulted in substantial gains for the ANC. In the NP-governed Western Cape, the elections were delayed because of a dispute with the government over whether the populous African township Khayelitsha should be included in the Tygerberg area or with central Cape Town. The controversy was taken to the Constitutional Court, where it escalated into a dispute over the relative powers of central and provincial governments. A draft constitution presented by Cyril Ramaphosa, the chairman of the Constitutional Assembly, on November 22 would give the regional governments more power in the South African federal structure through a new upper chamber of Parliament.

A Labour Relations Act guaranteeing the right to strike was passed. It contained the innovative idea of workplace forums as arenas of management-worker cooperation. The Congress of South African Trade Unions (COSATU), the National Congress of Trade Unions, and the Federation of South African Labour Unions engaged in demonstrations and a half-day general strike in June to secure more favourable terms for workers in the act. The final version of the act was described by COSATU's general secretary, Sam Shilowa, as a "quantum leap for workers." Workdays lost in industrial strikes in 1995 were the lowest in many years. There were, however, wildcat strikes by nurses and a strike in four provinces by municipal workers demanding higher pay.

Winnie Mandela, the estranged wife of President Mandela, criticized the ANC for overindulgence in racial reconciliation at the expense of the masses. In February, 11 leaders of the ANC Women's League resigned in protest against her conduct as president of the League. In March, while Mandela was absent in West Africa, her home was raided by police looking for evidence of financial misdealing. She was dismissed on March 27 as deputy minister of arts, culture, science, and technology. Though the dismissal was reversed in court on a technicality, she resigned on April 17. During the year President Mandela instituted divorce proceedings against her.

The Rev. Allan Boesak, former leader of the Western Cape ANC and ambassador-designate to the United Nations in Geneva, was accused by donors to DanChurch Aid of unlawfully enriching himself at the expense of the Foundation for Peace and Justice, which he headed. He resigned his appointment as ambassador in February. Amid similar cases of alleged corruption, the ANC drew up a code of financial conduct for its parliamentarians, requiring them to reveal their own and their families' business interests.

At a conference in April, the South African Communist Party (SACP) reported 50,000 members, 50 of them serving as ANC members of Parliament or government ministers and three as provincial premiers of the nine provinces. Two prominent SACP leaders, Joe Slovo and Harry Gwala, died during the year. (*See* OBITUARIES.)

In one of the country's worst-ever mining disasters, more than 100 miners died at Vaal Reefs gold mine in May when a runaway underground locomotive fell on top of an elevator carrying them down a shaft. The Rugby Union World Cup was staged in the country in May and June and was won by the South African team, the Springboks.

South African schoolchildren receive a government-subsidized lunch, consisting of a sandwich and a drink of milk or orange juice. Providing education for black South Africans, millions of whom lived in poverty, remained one of the country's most pressing problems.

LOUISE GUBB—JB PICTURES

The Economy. The economic upswing that began in May 1993 continued, strongly in the second half of 1994 and more weakly in the first half of 1995. Gross domestic product (GDP) grew by 2.3% in 1994—the first year since 1988 that it had exceeded population growth—and by 1.5% in the first quarter of 1995 and 0.8% in the second, pulled down by poor performances in agriculture and mining. GDP growth for 1995 was predicted at 2.8–3%. The upswing was fueled by gross domestic fixed investment (GDFI), which grew by 7% in 1994 (the first year of growth since 1989) and by 5% in the first quarter and 8% in the second quarter of 1995. GDFI was expected to grow by more than 10% in 1995 overall. In 1994 this represented a few big investments by private companies, but in 1995 it was becoming more widely distributed.

Official estimates put unemployment at about 4.7 million, one-third of the economically active population. Between 1990 and 1994 formal-sector employment shrank by 8%. Despite the upswing, it declined by 0.5% in 1994 to 7,410,000 jobs, but growth was anticipated in 1995.

The upswing continued to stimulate imports of capital goods. A surplus on the current account of the balance of payments of R 500 million in the first half of 1994 was transformed into a deficit of R 2.1 billion for the year overall. During the first half of 1995, the deficit was R 5.6 billion, which led to estimates of an annualized deficit of R 8 billion–R 10 billion. Net capital inflows of R 8.8 billion in the second half of 1994 (compared with an outflow of R 3.8 billion in the first half) and of R 9.8 billion in the first half of 1995 allowed this deficit to be sustainable. At the end of June, gross foreign exchange reserves were

R 15.2 billion, about six weeks of exports. The governor of the reserve bank expressed concern that much of the capital inflow was short-term and warned that the upswing was exposing the insufficiency of domestic savings and the nation's low labour productivity.

The dual rand (financial and commercial), an exchange control measure, was abolished in March without substantially affecting the value of the currency. In June a series of measures liberalizing trade were introduced, with phased major reductions in tariff protection barriers and the scrapping of the local content requirements in the automobile industry.

The first budget wholly drawn up by the government of national unity allocated 46.7% of spending to social services (compared with 44% in 1994–95). Education received 26%, the largest amount, and the allocation for housing and urban upgrading, at 2.7%, was more than doubled from 1994–95. Interest payments on debt accounted for 18.6% of spending, the second largest amount. Military spending was cut by 11.7% to R 9.8 billion, which represented a continuing decline since 1989. A decision on whether to purchase four new corvettes for the navy was postponed by the Cabinet. The budget's deficit before borrowing was projected at 5.8% of GDP, compared with 6.4% in 1994–95.

Consumer price inflation reached a low of 7.1% in April 1994, averaged 9% for 1994 as a whole (the lowest since 1972), increased to 11% by June 1995, and fell to 6.4% in September, the lowest rate in 23 years. The money supply increased at rates deemed excessive by the reserve bank, which increased its interest charges to other banks from 13% in September 1994 to 15% at the end of June 1995.

Foreign Affairs. South Africa had planned during the year to place more emphasis on "south-south" relations: with countries in southern Africa and Asia. Criticism, however, emerged concerning the lacklustre qualities of Foreign Affairs Minister Alfred Nzo and the failure to provide the moral leadership expected of the Mandela presidency and to replace staff of the former government. This criticism focused particularly on the failure to criticize the human rights records of such governments as Indonesia, Nigeria, Kenya, and The Sudan and on the decision to store oil for the Iranian government.

Despite urging by the Organization of African Unity to commit its army to peacekeeping forces in Africa, the new government insisted that its priorities were domestic. In Angola it offered to provide demolition specialists to detect mines laid in that nation's long civil war. South Africa was criticized for its support for the "Big Five" nuclear powers at the UN nuclear nonproliferation summit in April but responded that its package of proposals for strengthening the operation of the Nuclear Non-proliferation Treaty had been accepted by the conference.

The Cameron Commission investigated the clandestine sales of weapons to other nations by the government-owned Armscor, which had occurred under the former government. It recommended that arms sales be based on the country's "commitment to democracy, human rights, and international peace and security," and a list of countries to which arms sales were permissible was prepared. Control over such sales was transferred from Armscor to a Cabinet committee. Armscor obtained contracts to supply arms to UN forces in Rwanda and Bosnia and Herzegovina.

The European Union on March 29 agreed to reduce trade tariffs on South African goods during the next 10 years. South Africa would also receive ECU 500 million in aid over the next four years. (MARTIN LEGASSICK)

This article updates the *Macropædia* article SOUTHERN AFRICA: *South Africa.*

SPAIN

A constitutional monarchy of southwestern Europe with coastlines on the Bay of Biscay, the Atlantic Ocean, and the Mediterranean Sea, Spain shares the Iberian Peninsula with Portugal; it includes the Balearic and Canary island groups, in the Mediterranean and the Atlantic, respectively, and enclaves in northern Morocco. Area: 504,783 sq km (194,898 sq mi). Pop. (1995 est.): 39,188,000. Cap.: Madrid. Monetary unit: Spanish peseta, with (Oct. 6, 1995) a free rate of 123.75 pesetas to U.S. $1 (195.63 pesetas = £1 sterling). King, Juan Carlos I; prime minister in 1995, Felipe González Márquez.

Expectations that after 13 years Prime Minister Felipe González Márquez was rapidly nearing the end of his tenure in office dominated politics in 1995 as an increasingly wobbly Socialist government lost key parliamentary support amid growing scandals. González, Europe's second longest governing leader, after Helmut Kohl of Germany, pledged to call elections on March 3, 1996, a year ahead of schedule, while steadfastly defending his record and that of his government. González agreed to lead the party again himself.

The widely shared perception that the Socialist era would soon give way to a government led by the conservative Popular Party had a major impact on the lingering conflict in Spain's three northeastern Basque provinces. The armed Basque separatist group, Euskadi Ta Askatasuna (ETA), showed signs of changing strategy with the assassination on January 23 of Gregorio Ordóñez, a leader of the Popular Party in Guipúzcoa province. Of the roughly 800 deaths during ETA's 27-year-old independence campaign, all but a handful had been military or police officers. ETA's failed assassination attempt on April 19 against José María Aznar, the Popular Party's intended candidate for prime minister, was followed by ETA demands to negotiate Basque self-determination. Violence flared up anew in December as bombings attributed to ETA killed six civilian naval employees in Madrid on December 11, a shopper in a department store in Valencia on December 16, and an army major in León on December 22.

While both the government and the opposition roundly rejected talks with ETA, the country's fight against the separatists gave rise to continuing scandal. A former Socialist official in the Basque country, Ricardo García Damborenea, and a former chief of state security, Rafael Vera, were jailed and questioned on February 17 in connection with the shadowy Anti-Terrorist Liberation Group (GAL), which judicial investigations tied to Spanish security forces. Damborenea later told a court that González himself had been responsible for GAL, which killed 27 people in southern France between 1983 and 1987 in the so-called dirty war against ETA. The newspaper *El Mundo* published documents in October indicating that French border officials had been paid by the Spanish Ministry of the Interior to help track down ETA guerrilla squads across the border. In late November the Cortes (parliament) lifted the immunity of José Barrionuevo, a former minister of the interior, so he could be questioned about GAL.

Spaniards' attention was shifted abroad when Canadian authorities seized the Spanish trawler *Estai* on March 9 on the high seas off Newfoundland, claiming to be defending stocks from overfishing to the point of depletion. After Spanish warships had been sent to defend the fishing fleet, weeks of bitter dispute between Canada and the European Union (EU) ended in an agreement to lower the Spanish fishermen's halibut catch in the Grand Banks.

On March 18 Spain's first royal wedding in 89 years, the marriage in Seville of the Infanta Elena to banker Jaime de Marichalar, captivated the country and highlighted the popularity of the restored Bourbon monarchy. King Juan Carlos and Queen Sofia welcomed the heir to the throne, Prince Felipe, back from two years of graduate study in the United States to assume an increasingly prominent role in the family's official engagements.

Benefiting from the Socialists' troubles, the Popular Party comfortably won regional and municipal elections on May 28, taking charge of 10 of 13 regional governments and winning a plurality in 42 of 52 provincial capitals. An increase of 10% in the PP's results over the previous election (1991) put the conservatives five points ahead of the Socialists and in the lead for the first time.

Long-standing efforts to direct more of Europe's attention southward reached their zenith during Spain's six-month presidency of the EU that began July 1. Throughout the spring and summer, unrest hit Spanish ports as some 600 fishing boats were idled because of stalled negotiations on an EU fishing treaty with Morocco. In Madrid a political rather than economic decision was made to accept Rabat's demands for severe cuts in the EU's catch in Moroccan waters. Concessions were also made on granting Morocco access to EU agricultural markets, which thereby would put it in competition with Europe's home-grown fruit and vegetables, in order to help strengthen ties between North Africa and southern Europe.

Spain's most ambitious initiative under its EU presidency was the Mediterranean Conference held November 28–29 in Barcelona, in which 12 North African and Middle Eastern countries met with the 15 EU nations to discuss aid, trade, and cultural and political relations. González' principal political passion had always been foreign affairs, and the prime minister repeatedly cited Spain's incumbency in the EU presidency as a key reason why the country should not schedule early elections during 1995. He was willing to hold the elections, he said, following an EU-U.S. summit in December to redefine transatlantic relations and the final EU summit in Madrid that month, in which Spain hoped to influence the future course of the union.

Opposition parties, however, saw Spain's prospects differently, particularly its economic ones. Though the economy had been recovering strongly since late 1994, investors remained doubtful about Spain's ability to meet criteria for the EU's single currency by 1997, as government spending and inflation remained wide of its targets. Market pressure on the peseta forced a 7% devaluation on March 6. Unemployment barely declined from a European high of over 21%, and inflation seemed unlikely to come in within the government's 3.5% target.

By the time the Socialists came to sound out other parties about the upcoming budget in the summer, pressure on González from the GAL case, as well as other scandals, was leading even his allies to conclude there was little to gain from supporting him. The Catalan nationalist grouping Convergence and Union, which had provided the minority Socialists with a working parliamentary majority since González' party won 159 of 350 seats in the most recent national election in June 1993, withdrew its support from the government in July. Rather than lend their votes to a no-confidence motion that would bring down the government, the Catalans decided in October to join with the Popular Party in defeating the government's proposed 1996 budget. It was the Socialists' first parliamentary defeat since taking office in 1982 and the first time a budget had been rejected under Spain's post-Franco democracy.

In December Foreign Minister Javier Solana Madariaga was appointed NATO secretary-general; he was replaced by Carlos Westendorp, a career diplomat.

(GARY ABRAMSON)

Oil-storage tanks near Colombo burn out of control after being set on fire by Tamil guerrillas on October 20. The guerrillas struck the oil facility in Sri Lanka at the same time government troops were launching an attack to take control of the Tamil stronghold of Jaffna.

AFP

SRI LANKA

A republic and member of the Commonwealth, Sri Lanka occupies an island in the Indian Ocean off the southeast coast of peninsular India. Area: 65,610 sq km (25,332 sq mi). Pop. (1995 est.): 18,090,000. Legislative cap., Sri Jayawardenepura Kotte; administrative cap., Colombo. Monetary unit: Sri Lanka rupee, with (Oct. 6, 1995) a free rate of SL Rs 52.10 to U.S. $1 (SL Rs 82.36 = £1 sterling). President in 1995, Chandrika Kumaratunga; prime minister, Sirimavo Bandaranaike.

The 12-year-old civil conflict between the Sri Lankan government and the Liberation Tigers of Tamil Eelam (LTTE), who demanded an independent state for the two million Tamils, continued to be a major preoccupation for Pres. Chandrika Kumaratunga in 1995. Upon her election in 1994, Kumaratunga had pledged that she would seek a peaceful solution to the civil war, which by late 1995 had already claimed close to 50,000 lives.

In January 1995 the government and the LTTE agreed to a truce, the first one in five years, opening the way for talks. Expectations were high as Canada, The Netherlands, and Norway sent monitors to supervise the cease-fire. The Colombo government sweetened the truce with a SL Rs 40 billion rehabilitation plan for the northern region, where the Tamils were concentrated. Public opinion, including that of Tamils living in LTTE-controlled areas, supported the talks.

The LTTE unilaterally ended the truce on April 19, accusing the government of having failed to meet its demands, which included dismantling the Sri Lankan army camp at Pooneryn (located southwest of the LTTE's Jaffna stronghold) and a complete lifting of the government's trade embargo with the Tamil north. In a series of bold guerrilla attacks in April and May, the LTTE dealt severe military blows against the government armed forces.

With the aim of regaining the initiative, the military launched its biggest offensive in eight years in July. Operation Leap Forward ran into serious trouble after a week, however, when it was confronted with daring LTTE counterattacks.

On August 3 Kumaratunga unveiled a plan that would turn Sri Lanka into a federation of eight regions, each with considerable powers. The central government would be left with control over defense, foreign affairs, and international economic relations. To be accepted the plan would require the support of two-thirds of Parliament and a favourable vote in a national referendum. The Tamils in Parliament supported the plan, but the opposition United National Party was lukewarm to it. The LTTE responded by vowing to pursue a "protracted conflict." Undaunted, the government approved a $100 million weapons purchase, determined to deal the LTTE a military blow before resuming talks.

In October the government launched another offensive, causing both sides hundreds of casualties and forcing up to 300,000 people to flee the fighting. As government forces closed in on Jaffna, the LTTE forcefully depopulated the entire city of 140,000, using the Tamil refugees as a shield against government artillery fire. Government forces captured a deserted Jaffna on December 5, with the remaining inhabitants, numbering only 400, sheltering in the Catholic church. The LTTE rejected a government amnesty offer, emphasizing their determination to carry on with sporadic attacks throughout the month. On December 31, however, the LTTE offered to resume peace talks, in the presence of foreign mediators, if government troops would leave Jaffna.

(CLAUDE RAKISITS)

SUDAN, THE

A republic of North Africa, The Sudan has a coastline on the Red Sea. Area: 2,503,890 sq km (966,757 sq mi). Pop. (1995 est.): 28,098,000. Executive cap., Khartoum; legislative cap., Omdurman. Monetary units: Sudanese dinar, with (Oct. 6, 1995) a free rate of Sd 75 to U.S. $1 (Sd 118.57 = £1 sterling), and the Sudanese pound (the former sole unit of currency circulating in parallel with the Sudanese dinar at a rate of 10 pounds = Sd 1). President of the Revolutionary Command Council for National Salvation, president, and prime minister in 1995, Lieut. Gen. Omar Hassan Ahmad al Bashir.

At the beginning of January 1995, The Sudan opened its first stock exchange in an attempt to attract much-needed investment. With the country having a public debt in the region of $16 billion and few donors willing to continue their support, however, its economic and financial problems remained acute. Already formally suspended from the International Monetary Fund (IMF), The Sudan was on the verge of complete expulsion when it saved the day by resuming payment of arrears on its debts. The Sudan's minister of finance, Abdalla Hassan Ahmad, was concerned that the burden of finding $7 million a month to service the country's debt was unsustainable and sought emergency talks with the IMF in August. The IMF was unsympathetic, declaring that it would review the position in the light of future progress.

In July, Canada's Arakis Energy Corp. introduced a ray of hope when it announced that it had arranged the financing of an oil project in the centre of the country. It was estimated that the project, from which the government would receive 50% of all profits, would make The Sudan a net exporter of oil within two years.

The Sudan's reputation among Western nations was not enhanced by the arrest on May 16 of former prime minister Sadiq al-Mahdi, overthrown in 1989 by the present military government. He was released toward the end of August. Meanwhile, in June relations with Egypt, never very good, were further strained when Egyptian Pres. Hosni Mubarak accused The Sudan of involvement in an attempt to assassinate him when he was arriving at an Organization of African Unity conference in Addis Ababa, Eth. Although some investigators claimed that the assassination squad was composed of Egyptian extremists, the charges of Sudanese complicity led to skirmishes along the disputed Egypt-Sudan border near the Red Sea. There was further bad news in July when the London-based human rights group African Rights charged the government with having undertaken a campaign of genocide against the Nuba people in southern Kordofan; in September riot police were called upon to quell unrest in Khartoum.

(KENNETH INGHAM)

SEBASTIÃO SALGADO

People wait for their food allotment in return for dirt they transported for construction of a hospital at a refugee camp in the southern part of The Sudan. In 1995 the animist and Christian south continued to suffer at the hands of the country's oppressive Muslim military government.

SURINAME

The republic of Suriname is in northern South America, on the Atlantic Ocean. Area: 163,820 sq km (63,251 sq mi), not including a 17,635-sq km area disputed with Guyana. Pop. (1995 est.): 430,000. Cap.: Paramaribo. Monetary unit: Suriname guilder, with (Oct. 6, 1995) a free rate of 492 guilders to U.S. $1 (777.80 guilders = £1 sterling). President in 1995, Ronald Venetiaan; prime minister, Jules Adjodhia.

On Jan. 10, 1995, information was leaked that Dési Bouterse, former military leader and president of Suriname, had shared in the bribes from Dutch trade companies that in 1993 had cost several high-ranking officials their jobs. Despite these charges, Bouterse announced in February that he was preparing for a political comeback in the presidential elections of 1996.

For the first time after a long period of recession, signs of economic recovery were seen in June. The new president of the central bank, Andre Telting, received much of the credit for this. By ending inflationary financing, he succeeded in reducing the inflation rate, which in the previous year had reached a record 470%.

A meeting of Amerindian and Bush Negro leaders took place in August; both groups lived in the interior of Suriname. Two items were on the agenda: the disturbance of the environment by a Canadian gold-mining company and by an Indonesian logging firm and the lack of a welfare policy for the two generally impoverished groups. During the meeting a new organization, the Higher Authority in the Rural territories (HGB), was formed. The HGB demanded that no more concessions for gold mining and logging be granted in the interior region.

On November 25, Suriname celebrated 20 years of independence from The Netherlands. (KLAAS J. HOEKSEMA)

SWAZILAND

Swaziland is a landlocked monarchy of southern Africa and a member of the Commonwealth. Area: 17,364 sq km (6,704 sq mi). Pop. (1995 est.): 913,000. Administrative cap., Mbabane; royal and legislative cap., Lobamba. Monetary unit: lilangeni (plural: emalangeni), at par with the South African rand, with (Oct. 6, 1995) a free rate of 3.66 emalangeni to U.S. $1 (5.79 emalangeni = £1 sterling). King, Mswati III; prime minister in 1995, Prince Jameson Mbilini Dlamini.

On Feb. 6, 1995, a fire swept through the national House of Assembly; the Swaziland Youth Congress claimed responsibility for the incident, which followed other fires at the homes of the deputy prime minister and the vice-chancellor of the University of Swaziland. A magistrate's court and government vehicles had also been targets of arson. These attacks coincided with hunger strikes by students protesting the election procedures for the students' council.

On March 2 the finance minister, Isaac Shabangu (later dismissed by King Mswati III), presented his budget for 1995–96. This assumed revenues and grants totaling about 1,430,000,000 emalangeni, as opposed to predicted expenditure, excluding redemption of loans, of 1,515,000,000 emalangeni.

A two-day general strike was called in March by the Swaziland Federation of Trade Unions (SFTU) to force the government to act upon a list of 27 demands, including the reemployment of dismissed workers. As a result, Mbabane and other towns were shut down on March 13–14. At Manzini approximately 40,000 people attended a rally to support the strike action. Industrial unrest continued, and the SFTU called for another strike on July 17 but then abandoned it when the government strengthened its power against the unions by establishing penalties on trade union federations and officers should they call meetings that lead to work stoppages. Unions were also obliged to consult the government before applying for membership in international bodies, a measure that implied that the SFTU was under foreign influence. (GUY ARNOLD)

This article updates the *Macropædia* article SOUTHERN AFRICA: *Swaziland*.

SWEDEN

A constitutional monarchy of northern Europe, Sweden occupies the eastern side of the Scandinavian Peninsula, with coastlines on the North and Baltic seas and the Gulf of Bothnia. Area: 449,964 sq km (173,732 sq mi). Pop. (1995 est.): 8,826,000. Cap.: Stockholm. Monetary unit: Swedish krona, with (Oct. 6, 1995) a free rate of 7.03 kronor to U.S. $1 (11.11 kronor = £1 sterling). King, Carl XVI Gustaf; prime minister in 1995, Ingvar Carlsson.

Sweden entered the European Union (EU) on Jan. 1, 1995, in a significant break with its traditionally aloof and neutral stance in foreign affairs. It joined the EU alongside its Nordic neighbour Finland as well as Austria, expanding the union from 12 to 15 members. Although a net contributor to EU budgets, Sweden hoped to enhance the country's influence in Europe and increase inward investment.

One early Swedish initiative was a move to get employment targets included in EU economic strategy at the 1996 Intergovernmental Conference on the union's future. Relations with France went sour, however, after Sweden vociferously opposed the French decision to carry out nuclear tests in the South Pacific.

For many Swedes the first months in the EU were a disappointment. They did not see any early visible benefits from membership, such as lower food prices or big regional aid programs. A backlash made itself felt in elections for the country's 22 seats in the European Parliament in September. The anti-EU left and environment parties gained 30.1% of the vote—almost triple their support in the country's 1994 general election. By contrast, the three parties that unequivocally supported the EU polled only 32%, and the ruling Social Democrats, whose party was split on the issue, gained just 28.1% in its worst election result since 1911. At just 41.3% of the electorate, the turnout was the lowest ever recorded in a Swedish election.

It was a difficult year for the Social Democrats, who had formed a minority government after winning elections in September 1994. In the early months of the year, the party announced a series of spending cuts and tax increases to restore the health of the state's deficit-ridden finances. A number of the measures, including a cut in unemployment benefits, were deeply unpopular with the rank and file as well as with the party's traditional allies in the strong trade union movement. Business leaders objected to the higher taxes. In April the Social Democrats began to cooperate with the Centre Party to gain a parliamentary majority. This was an informal pact rather than a coalition.

In August Ingvar Carlsson said he would step down as leader of the Social Democrats and prime minister in March 1996. The party leadership had hoped for a smooth succession, with the mantle of power passing to Mona Sahlin, Carlsson's 38-year-old deputy. Sahlin's candidacy ran into serious trouble in October, however, when she admitted using a government credit card for private purposes. The public prosecutor launched a preliminary inquiry into the matter to see if breach of trust or fraud had occurred. The name of another possible candidate for prime minister, Finance Minister Göran Persson, emerged in December.

There was better news on the economy as the recovery that began in 1994 continued into 1995. Gross domestic product (GDP) rose more than 3% during the year, mainly because of a strong performance by the country's big exporters. Inflation peaked above 3% at midyear but then began to ease.

The country also regained the confidence of international financial markets. At the start of the year, the krona sank sharply and bond yields rose as Sweden became caught up in the turbulence that followed the crisis over the Mexican peso. From April onward, however, market analysts became convinced that the country was doing enough to tackle its debt, which climbed above 80% of GDP, and cut its budget deficit. The krona gained strength, and bond yields dropped sharply. In October Carlsson said economic growth was stronger than expected and the country would stabilize its debt as a proportion of GDP in 1995, a year ahead of an earlier forecast. Unemployment remained a serious blight; around 12% of the workforce was affected, including those in training schemes.

Carl Bildt, former prime minister and leader of the Moderate (conservative) Party, stepped into the international limelight in June when he became the EU's peace mediator in former Yugoslavia. In August the country staged the world track and field championships in Göteborg, the biggest global sporting event of the year.

(CHRISTOPHER BROWN-HUMES)

SWITZERLAND

A landlocked federal state in west central Europe, Switzerland consists of a confederation of 26 cantons (6 of which are demicantons). Area: 41,285 sq km (15,940 sq mi). Pop. (1995 est.): 7,039,000. Administrative cap., Bern; judicial cap., Lausanne. Monetary unit: Swiss franc, with (Oct. 6, 1995) a free rate of Sw F 1.15 to U.S. $1 (Sw F 1.82 = £1 sterling). President in 1995, Kaspar Villiger.

Although voter turnout was only 42%, the outcome of the general elections—held once every four years—on Oct. 22, 1995, showed a wind of change, or at very least a breeze, in Switzerland. Chief beneficiaries were the Social Democrats, who gained a dozen additional parliamentary seats, putting them on top with 54. On the right the Swiss People's Party took four more seats, giving it 29. If poles apart on major issues, such as social services and unemployment, financial policies, and possible membership in the European Union (EU), the two parties in the coalition government had stated their aims more clearly, and with more verve, than the two other coalition parties, the Radicals (45 seats, up one) and the Christian Democrats (34, down 2). Most of the eight minority parties found themselves deprived of one or more seats, the hardest hit being the Green Party, which lost five seats, leaving it with nine. A group of 31 parliamentarians—Socialists, Radicals, Christian Democrats, and Greens—which had been meeting discreetly for two and a half years, called for political renewal within the new parliament in helping the coalition government formulate policies, including association with the EU.

Late in the year a Max Schmidheiny Foundation "White Paper" said bluntly that revitalizing the Swiss economy necessitated more work for less money in facing up to Asian competition in export markets. The analysis opposed the concept of increased productivity ensuring shorter working hours and more leisure, as well as the idea of job sharing to reduce unemployment. In calling for privatization of postal, telecommunications, and railway services, it also supported the principle of free movement of persons across frontiers within the EU.

The unemployment rate, well under half the European average, decreased over the year to about 4%. It was still a nagging worry, however, especially in French-speaking Swiss Romande, where it was around 5.5%, more than double the level in German-speaking Switzerland. With many enterprises restructuring in their drive for improved competitiveness, sizable layoffs were commonplace. Forecasts for 1996 held little prospect of a brisk economic upturn. According to an official study, the total of 150,000 unemployed—compared with 180,000 at the trough of the recent depression and a mere 17,500 in 1989—could be reduced to a hard-core 60,000 by the year 2000 if the gross national product growth rate could be kept at no less than 2.25%. This was regarded as a realistic projection, provided exports were not further disadvantaged by the soaring Swiss franc in its function as a safe-haven currency. With the high franc hitting tourism, hoteliers reported their worst year in decades; some even began to quote firm prices in French francs or dollars for advance bookings.

Switzerland's collective labour contracts, which incorporate no-strike clauses and periodic renegotiation of wage levels, came under strain as well. Scope for concessions was extremely narrow, the parties were increasingly intractable, and some employees accepted reduced pay to keep their jobs. The construction industry, emerging from the doldrums, heard its main trade union observe, "We have the funds to afford it," and assert that 1996 could see "a real strike"—as compared with the occasional tentative examples of recent years.

After calling repeatedly for brakes on excessive government spending induced by the "euphoric years" of boom, Finance Minister Otto Stich, in office for more then a decade, resigned. He handed over his portfolio on November 1 to Kaspar Villiger. As defense minister since 1989, Villiger had adroitly presided over introducing the "Army 95" plan, which trimmed the ranks of the militia-type citizen army from 600,000 to 400,000 men and restricted liability for service to ages 20–42. The family and friends of Paul Grüninger, police chief at St. Gallen who was dismissed from his post in 1940, finally succeeded in having the original verdict quashed. Grüninger, who died in 1972 at age 81, had been pronounced guilty of disobeying a government order in 1938 not to allow more Jewish refugees to enter Switzerland. His disobedience saved the lives of some 3,000 people who would otherwise have been sent to Nazi extermination camps.

(ALAN MCGREGOR)

SYRIA

A republic of southwestern Asia, Syria is on the Mediterranean Sea. Area: 185,180 sq km (71,498 sq mi). Pop. (1995 est.): 14,313,000. Cap.: Damascus. Monetary unit: Syrian pound, with (Oct. 6, 1995) a par value (official rate) of LS 11.22 to U.S. $1 (LS 17.74 = £1 sterling) and a "primary trade" rate of LS 41.95 to U.S. $1 (LS 66.32 = £1 sterling). President in 1995, Gen. Hafez al-Assad; prime minister, Mahmoud Zuabi.

Despite persistent speculation that Syria and Israel were on the verge of concluding an agreement regarding the future of the Golan Heights, Syria remained adamant throughout 1995 that Israel had to promise to return not only all of the territory it occupied in June 1967 but also several disputed enclaves around Lake Tiberias before it would normalize relations with the Jewish state. At the beginning of April, Syrian officials proposed that demilitarized zones of equal size be established on both sides of the pre-1967 border. An Israeli spokesperson dismissed the proposal on the grounds that the western zone would stretch "halfway to Haifa." When the United States in mid-May vetoed a United Nations Security Council resolution condemning Israel for confiscating Palestinian lands outside Jerusalem, Syrian Foreign Minister Farouk ash-Shara told reporters that the U.S. had abandoned its role as an honest broker and thus could not be expected to police any agreement concerning the Golan.

Syria and Israel came closest to compromise at the end of June, when the Syrian chief of staff, Lieut. Gen. Hikmat ash-Shihabi, met his Israeli counterpart in Washington, D.C., to discuss mutually acceptable security arrangements along the Golan front. The generals provisionally agreed that Israel would dismantle its network of forward listening posts and depend instead upon surveillance aircraft to provide the Israel Defense Forces (IDF) with tactical intelligence. As soon as the two chiefs of staff returned home, however, Israel announced that it planned to maintain a military presence inside the Golan indefinitely. The Israeli government's outright rejection of the bargain that had been hammered out by its own senior military commander convinced Syria that there was little to be gained from continuing negotiations. As a result, Syrian officials adopted a much less flexible posture toward both Israeli representatives and U.S. mediators.

Relations between Syria and Israel deteriorated further when in mid-October Hezbollah guerrillas ambushed an Israeli armoured column in southern Lebanon, killing six Israeli soldiers, and then raided a fortified outpost garrisoned by the Israeli-sponsored South Lebanon Army. Israel's foreign minister, Shimon Peres, quickly blamed Syrian forces for allowing such operations to take place. Peres told a radio audience on October 15 that Syria had an obligation to prevent the conflict in Lebanon from escalating. These sentiments were echoed by Israeli Prime Minister Yitzhak Rabin (*see* OBITUARIES), while other Israeli officials warned that the IDF would retaliate against both Hezbollah and its supporters at times and places of their own choosing. For its part, Syria denied that forces under Syrian control had anything to do with the attacks and suggested that festering resentment over the prolongation of Israel's "aggressive policy" toward Lebanon led inhabitants of southern villages to take up arms against the IDF and its Lebanese clients. Following the assassination of Rabin in November, Syrian Pres. Hafez al-Assad continued the hard-line stance toward Israel. Still, Syria was feeling somewhat isolated among the Arab states, and there was a perception that now was the time for talks with the Israelis. Assad agreed to resume the dialogue, and Syrian officials began a week of preparatory meetings with Israel in the U.S. on December 31.

Meanwhile, the Syrian leadership moved to consolidate ties to Egypt and the Arab Gulf states. In April Syria joined Egypt in arguing that the Nuclear Non-proliferation Treaty should not be renewed until Israel agreed to sign the pact. When Hussein Kamil al-Majid, a high-ranking Iraqi official, defected to Jordan at the beginning of August, Assad flew to Cairo to confer personally with Egyptian Pres. Hosni Mubarak. Assad told reporters following the meeting that the defector was not "as big as the media have made him out to be," and there was virtually no chance that the Iraqi regime would collapse anytime soon. The two presidents took the occasion to reiterate their common opposition to outside interference in the domestic politics of Iraq.

Inside Syria itself, officials promulgated measures designed to encourage the expansion of private enterprise. Such key industries as electricity generation, cotton ginning, sugar refining, cement production, and pharmaceuticals manufacturing were opened to private investors. The government at the beginning of April rescinded its longstanding ban on the possession and use of credit cards issued by overseas banks. (FRED H. LAWSON)

TAIWAN

Taiwan, which consists of the island of Taiwan and surrounding islands off the coast of China, is the seat of the Republic of China (Nationalist China). Area: 36,179 sq km (13,969 sq mi), including the island of Taiwan and its 86 outlying islands, 22 in the Taiwan group and 64 in the Pescadores group. Pop. (1995 est.): 21,268,000. (Area and population figures include the Quemoy and Matsu groups, which are administered as an occupied part of Fujian [Fukien] province.) Cap.: Taipei. Monetary unit: New Taiwan dollar, with (Oct. 6, 1995) a free rate of NT$26.90 to U.S. $1 (NT$42.52 = £1 sterling). President in 1995, Lee Teng-hui; president of the Executive Yuan (premier), Lien Chan.

During Taiwan's past decade of democratic development, its once frigid relationship with the People's Republic of China improved significantly even though tension persisted. By 1995 thousands of businesses on Taiwan had invested an estimated $22 billion in mainland enterprises, making Taiwan the second largest investor, after Hong Kong.

In 1995 China also cast a long shadow on the future of Taiwan itself. Enraged by Lee Teng-hui's unofficial June visit to the U.S. to attend an alumni reunion at Cornell University, Ithaca, N.Y., Beijing denounced Washington for permitting the visit and threatened military action against Taiwan. It charged that Lee, the president of the Republic of China on Taiwan, was covertly guiding the island toward independence. In July and August, attempting to frighten Lee's supporters, China conducted a series of long-range-missile tests in waters 140 km (90 mi) north of Taiwan and suspended the cross-strait talks. This sabre rattling caused Taiwan's stock market to plunge, but Lee's political stock was hardly affected. Taiwan raised its defense budget by 20% to acquire more advanced defensive aircraft and missiles and paraded its own military might in October.

Public attention, in any case, had already shifted to the December elections for the Legislative Yuan. As in past years, the dominant issues were domestic and local, including alleged government mismanagement of state-funded development projects, official corruption, and government favouritism toward big business. The elections marked a further decline in the fortunes of the ruling Kuomintang (KMT), marginal gains by the chief opposition Democratic Progressive Party (DPP), and a surprising surge of support for the New Party, which was competing for the first time in Legislative Yuan elections. The KMT's popular vote slipped from 53% to 46%; the DPP's inched upward from 31% to 33%, and the New Party, which had broken off from the KMT in 1993, received almost 13%. This translated into 85 KMT seats in the new Legislative Yuan, a decline of 11 from 1992, 54 DPP seats (+4), and 21 New Party seats (+7).

In August Lee announced his decision to run for reelection in March 1996, when Taiwan voters would directly elect a president for the first time. Lee chose Premier Lien Chan as his vice presidential running mate. Law professor Peng Ming-min, a veteran of the democracy movement, was selected by the DPP to carry its banner; his running mate would be Frank Hsieh. By December the presidential race had generated unexpected excitement. The team of Lin Yang-kang and former premier Hau Pei-tsun—both KMT vice-chairmen—announced that they would enter the presidential race as independents, a move that prompted the KMT to revoke their party memberships. The New Party, for its part, announced that it would support the Lin-Hau ticket. Others who declared their intention to run as independents included Chen Li-an, a former president of the Control Yuan, who teamed up with Wang Ching-feng.

Taiwan's economy in 1995 grew 6.4%, a shade better than the previous year. In the first three quarters, exports and

A Taiwanese soldier stands guard over an array of loudspeakers that were once used to broadcast to the mainland from Quemoy Island. In 1958 the Chinese shelled the island, 2.3 km (1.4 mi) offshore, and despite the fact that it was later opened to tourists, it remained heavily fortified.
CHRIS STOWERS—PANOS PICTURES

imports surged by 22.8% and 27.5% respectively. Taiwan enjoyed a positive trade balance of $6.9 billion through November. The nation's trade and investment increasingly turned toward Southeast Asian countries such as Vietnam, the Philippines, Malaysia, and Indonesia. Taiwan's per capita gross national product exceeded $12,000 per annum, unemployment was virtually nonexistent, and consumer prices were stable, with inflation a low 2.5%.

Taiwan accelerated its efforts to rejoin the United Nations, but China's stubborn opposition again stopped this effort well short of success. The long-term problem of how to reconcile Taiwan's de facto independence with China's determination to reestablish control over the island was thrown into sharper relief in 1995, but no viable solution to this problem presented itself. (STEVEN I. LEVINE)

TAJIKISTAN

A landlocked republic of Central Asia, Tajikistan borders Kyrgyzstan on the north, Uzbekistan on the north and west, Afghanistan on the south, and China on the east. Area: 143,100 sq km (55,300 sq mi). Pop. (1995 est.): 5,832,000. Cap.: Dushanbe. Monetary unit: Tajik ruble (new currency introduced May 10, 1995, to replace the at par value [interim] Tajik ruble and Russian ruble at a rate of 1 Tajik ruble to 100 Russian rubles; on May 15 the Tajik ruble became sole legal tender), with (Oct. 4, 1995) a free rate of 44.90 Tajik rubles to U.S. $1 (71.35 Tajik rubles = £1 sterling). Chief of state in 1995 (president of the National Assembly), Imomali Rakhmonov; prime minister, Jamshed Karimov.

Sporadic fighting continued in Tajikistan throughout 1995 despite efforts by the United Nations and individual states alike to obtain a settlement of the three-year-old civil war. Increasingly, clashes between government troops and the forces of the Islamic opposition occurred in the interior of the country rather than on the border between Tajikistan and Afghanistan, where the opposition had its headquarters.

On February 26 the first post-Soviet parliamentary elections were held in Tajikistan. Voter turnout was high, even in regions that had been opposition strongholds. The Islamic opposition in exile rejected the election results on the grounds that not all parties could take part and that the opposition had been denied freedom of the press. Among the first actions of the new parliament was a vote for a new currency, the Tajik ruble, to replace the Russian ruble. Tajikistan had hoped for a monetary union with Russia, but Russian financial officials were reluctant to link their country's economy so closely with that of war-ravaged Tajikistan.

Despite the extension of a fragile cease-fire arranged in late 1994 between government and opposition troops, the level of fighting on the Tajik-Afghan border increased sharply in April, shortly before UN-sponsored talks began in Moscow between Tajik government and opposition representatives to set a date for a fourth round of peace negotiations. The Moscow talks were nearly derailed at the start by Russian Foreign Minister Andrey Kozyrev, who warned the opposition that Russia would not tolerate further attacks on its peacekeeping troops in Tajikistan. The opposition, deeply offended, condemned his remarks as interference in internal Tajik affairs.

At the Moscow talks a date was set in May for the fourth round of negotiations, which were preceded by a meeting between Tajik Pres. Imomali Rakhmonov and Islamic opposition chief Said Abdullo Nuri in Kabul, Afghanistan, the first face-to-face meeting of the leaders of the two sides

A man is led away blindfolded after having been caught trying to cross the Afghani-Tajik border illegally. Russian troops continued to help patrol Tajikistan's border with Afghanistan, where Islamic rebels opposed to the Tajik government maintained their headquarters.
MORKOVIN—WOSTOK PRESS/MIR

in the Tajik conflict. Despite this encouraging prologue, the negotiations, held in Almaty, Kazakhstan, resulted in little progress on the constitutional issues dividing the two sides. Uzbekistan and Kazakhstan, two of the states that contributed troops to the Commonwealth of Independent States (CIS) peacekeeping contingent in Tajikistan, let it be known that they were considering withdrawing their forces if no solution to the conflict was found.

A fifth round of peace negotiations between the government and opposition was scheduled to begin on September 18, but it was postponed indefinitely when the two sides were unable to agree on a venue for the talks. In August Islamic opposition chief Nuri agreed to extend the cease-fire until mid-November, but sporadic fighting continued between opposition troops and Russian peacekeepers on the Tajik-Afghan border, with the commander of the CIS troops accusing the opposition of "terrorist" activities.

(BESS BROWN)

This article updates the *Macropædia* article CENTRAL ASIA: *Tajikistan.*

TANZANIA

The republic of Tanzania, a member of the Commonwealth, consists of Tanganyika, on the east coast of Africa, and Zanzibar, just off the coast in the Indian Ocean, which includes Zanzibar Island, Pemba Island, and small islets. Area: 942,799 sq km (364,017 sq mi). Pop. (1995 est.): 28,072,000. Cap.: government in process of being transferred from Dar es Salaam; legislature meets in Dodoma, the new capital. Monetary unit: Tanzania shilling, with (Oct. 6, 1995) a free rate of 600 shillings to U.S. $1 (948.54 shillings = £1 sterling). Presidents in 1995, Ali Hassan Mwinyi and, from November 23, Benjamin William Mkapa; prime ministers, Cleopa Msuya and, from November 28, Frederick Tulway Sumaye.

For Tanzania, 1995 opened on a gloomy economic note. After the nation's chief donor countries had decided in November 1994 to suspend aid because of serious fraud over the noncollection of customs duties, the governor of the central bank informed the National Assembly in January that inflation was being made more severe by heavy expenditure and borrowing. He stated that unless government borrowing from commercial banks was curtailed, it would gravely damage the economic recovery program. In June, however, Finance Minister Jakaya Kikwete introduced a budget that won praise from the International Monetary Fund. Particular commendation was accorded to proposals for narrowing the budget deficit and for cutting company taxes.

On March 31, with thousands of Rwandan refugees threatening to pour into the country and join those in already overcrowded camps, it became necessary to close the northwestern border.

For most politicians the main focus of attention was the first multiparty election since independence for members of the National Assembly and for president. This took place in October. Former president Julius Nyerere threw the weight of his reputation behind the ruling Revolutionary Party of Tanzania (CCM), arguing that the other contenders needed more political experience.

Elections in Zanzibar and Pemba were held on October 22, a week before those on the mainland. The opposition Civic United Front (CCW) campaigned for greater autonomy for the islands, but even before the results were known, the CCW brought charges of vote rigging and called for a recount. The contest was expected to be close and proved to be so. In the legislative elections the CCM won 25 seats against 23 for the CCW, while the CCM candidate for the presidency, the incumbent, Salmin Amour, triumphed by less than 0.5% of the votes cast.

The opposition National Convention for Construction and Reform–Mageuzi party threatened briefly to boycott the mainland elections unless a recount took place in Zanzibar, but it was maladministration rather than malpractice that brought chaos on October 29. Polling stations did not open at the appointed time; there were delays in supplying voting papers; and would-be voters were left waiting in the rain. The chairman of the national electoral commission, Lewis Makame, concluded that the voting in Dar es Salaam had to be declared null and void and that the elections should be repeated during the following week. To avoid a similar situation in the rest of the country, he decided to extend the voting period for an additional two days. The CCM was declared victorious, Benjamin Mkapa was elected president, and Frederick Sumaye became prime minister.

(KENNETH INGHAM)

This article updates the *Macropædia* article EASTERN AFRICA: *Tanzania.*

THAILAND

Thailand is a constitutional monarchy in Southeast Asia, on the Andaman Sea and the Gulf of Thailand. Area: 513,115 sq km (198,115 sq mi). Pop. (1995 est.): 58,791,000. Cap.: Bangkok. Monetary unit: baht, with (Oct. 6, 1995) a free rate of 25.12 baht to U.S. $1 (39.70 baht = £1 sterling). King, Bhumibol Adulyadej; prime ministers in 1995, Chuan Leekpai and, from July 13, Banharn Silpa-archa.

During the first parliamentary session of 1995, the Democrat Party, leading component in the ruling five-party coalition, found itself embroiled in scandal over the granting, to some of its members, of land reserved for the poor. Opposition parliamentarians, many of whom were also accused of illicit dealings, focused on the issue to the point of paralyzing the legislative process. The Righteous Force Party's exit from the government in May deprived the coalition of its majority. Facing a certain vote of no confidence, Prime Minister Chuan Leekpai, himself untainted by the scandals, called a general election for July 2. Twelve parties contested 391 multiple-member constituencies. When the opposition Thai Nation Party gained 25% of the seats, 3% more than the Democrats, its leader, Banharn Silpa-archa, claimed the right to try to form a government. His seven-party, 233-member coalition included Chart Thai, New Aspiration, Righteous Force, and smaller parties.

Within hours of victory, Banharn was engulfed in crisis. The U.S. State Department warned that relations with Washington would deteriorate if two leading Chart Thai members, whom the U.S. had accused of links to the drug trade, were included in the Cabinet. As a result, deputy leader Vatana Asavahame, who had expected to be named to the powerful post of interior minister, and Narong Wongwan, whose appointment as prime minister had been blocked for similar reasons in 1992, were left out of the Cabinet presented to King Bhumibol Adulyadej. In October former foreign minister Thanat Khoman, appointed to inquire into the issue, called the U.S. accusations "unwarranted and dishonourable." The exclusion of the two men accentuated bitter factional rivalries and prevented Banharn, a rural magnate famed for his mastery of political patronage, from exercising firm control.

The press and public opinion polls expressed strong disapproval of the Cabinet, which contained ministers investigated for corruption after the 1991 army coup. In an ominous development that upset the stock market, an army radio program in August declared that the nation looked forward to the day when it had a brave leader. Banharn retorted that coups were "obsolete."

In an address on August 17, even Thailand's revered king appeared to be critical when he warned that politicians should concentrate on the needs of the country. Chaovalit Yongchaiyuth, deputy prime minister, defense minister, and a former army commander, was a major figure on the political scene. His New Aspiration Party, wrenched by dissension before the election, emerged as a cohesive force. Chaovalit exerted unprecedented sway over military appointments in the traditionally self-regulating army. In the always sensitive annual promotions list, he replaced military leaders with men close to himself. Gen. Pramon Phalasin became army commander and assured the nation that he would keep out of politics. Respected statesman and politician Kukrit Pramoj died on October 9. (*See* OBITUARIES.)

FUMINOHI SATO—IMPACT VISUALS

A Myanmar (Burmese) rebel weaves a basket in a temporary camp set up in Thailand by the All Burma Students' Democratic Front. After Myanmar government forces captured their jungle stronghold of Manerplaw in January, many rebels fled to the neighbouring country.

By October months of flooding in 66 of Thailand's 76 provinces had claimed more than 200 lives, damaged the rice crop, and caused weeks of traffic disruption in Bangkok. Banharn's economic program, while retaining many budgetary and monetary policies of the Chuan government, called for very large expenditure on rural roads. Despite signs of a slowdown in the last quarter, the economy maintained its vigour. As a result of continued overseas investor confidence, foreign reserves in November stood at an impressive $36 billion, notwithstanding a current account deficit that was running at $8.5 billion. Inflation was edging up to 6.5%, but central bank officials considered this level manageable. Expected gross national product growth of 8.3% looked set to put the country once again among the best performers in the world.

In September Chaovalit strengthened neighbourly ties with visits to both Myanmar (Burma) and Cambodia.

(ROBERT WOODROW)

This article updates the *Macropædia* article SOUTHEAST ASIA: *Thailand.*

TOGO

A republic of West Africa, Togo is situated on the Bight of Benin. Area: 56,785 sq km (21,925 sq mi). Pop. (1995 est.): 4,138,000. Cap.: Lomé. Monetary unit: CFA franc, with (Oct. 6, 1995) a par value of CFAF 100 to the French franc and a free rate of CFAF 501.49 to U.S. $1 (CFAF 792.78 = £1 sterling). President in 1995, Gen. Gnassingbé Eyadéma; prime minister, Edem Kodjo.

In 1994 Yao Agboyibo, leader of the opposition Action Committee for Renewal (CAR), had announced a boycott of the legislature to protest voting irregularities in the February elections of that year. As a result, Togo's government remained virtually paralyzed for the first eight months of 1995. On April 26, the eve of Togo's independence day celebrations, Pres. Gnassingbé Eyadéma's call for reconciliation was ignored. The protracted boycott finally ended in late August, after the CAR received assurances from Eyadéma and Prime Minister Edem Kodjo that an independent electoral commission would be established for all future elections.

Meeting with representatives of Amnesty International in March, Kodjo expressed regret over violations of human rights that had occurred during the turbulent years (1991–93) of Togo's transition to democracy. Full diplomatic relations with Ghana were restored in July, and Togo's first ambassador since 1982 was appointed.

Citing improved political conditions, the European Union, after a three-year suspension, renewed aid to Togo in March. In July severe flooding in Lomé left an estimated 150,000 people homeless. Three weeks of heavy rains during September brought massive destruction to entire villages, roads, and bridges, especially in the northern and central regions. At least 21,000 more people lost their homes. Despite these disasters, the economy showed overall improvement during the year. Agricultural production grew, Lomé's port traffic revived, government revenues rose by 96%, and civil service salaries were paid regularly.

(NANCY ELLEN LAWLER)

This article updates the *Macropædia* article WESTERN AFRICA: *Togo.*

TONGA

A constitutional monarchy and member of the Commonwealth, Tonga comprises about 170 islands split into three main groups in the Pacific Ocean east of Fiji. Area: 750 sq km (290 sq mi). Pop. (1995 est.): 100,000. Cap.: Nuku'alofa. Monetary unit: pa'anga, with (Oct. 6, 1995) a free rate of 1.31 pa'anga (T$) to U.S. $1 (2.08 pa'anga = £1 sterling). King, Taufa'ahau Tupou IV; prime minister in 1995, Baron Vaea.

There was continuing political controversy in 1995 over commoner challenges to the power of King Taufa'ahau Tupou IV and his nominees in Tongan politics. The king's statement that he thought Western-style democracy or some form of power sharing between the monarch and the people was inevitable was subsequently modified. In May Cecil Cocker, the minister of finance, was forced to resign over alleged sexual harassment incidents at an Asian Development Bank conference in Auckland, N.Z.

The cultivation of squash for export remained a major focus of economic interest, with the government setting a quota of 17,000 tons for export to Japan, Tonga's major market for squash. Discontented growers who had planted for a U.S. order that subsequently collapsed unsuccessfully petitioned the king for an increase of 3,000 tons. In 1994 tourism grew by 11.3%, with most of the growth coming from Tonga's traditional tourist markets—Australia, New Zealand, and the U.S. Tonga rejected an application from Japanese interests for the revival of whaling in Tongan waters and, with other members of the South Pacific Forum, condemned the resumption of French nuclear testing.

(BARRIE MACDONALD)

This article updates the *Macropædia* article PACIFIC ISLANDS: *Tonga.*

TRINIDAD AND TOBAGO

A republic and member of the Commonwealth, Trinidad and Tobago consists of two islands in the Caribbean Sea off the coast of Venezuela. Area: 5,128 sq km (1,980 sq mi). Pop. (1995 est.): 1,265,000. Cap.: Port of Spain. Monetary unit: Trinidad and Tobago dollar, with (Oct. 6, 1995) a free rate of TT$5.70 to U.S. $1 (TT$9.02 = £1 sterling). President in 1995, Noor Mohammed Hassanali; prime ministers, Patrick Manning and, from November 9, Basdeo Panday.

The illicit-drug-related criminal activity that bedeviled Trinidad and Tobago for most of 1995 took a particularly vicious turn in June when unknown gunmen assassinated Selwyn Richardson, who had established a reputation as an anticorruption fighter while serving as attorney general from 1981 to 1991.

In July and August the country came close to a constitutional crisis when the speaker of the House of Representatives, Occah Seapaul, refused to resign at the request of Prime Minister Patrick Manning after she gave questionable testimony in a court matter. Instead, she chose a confrontational approach and began suspending government members, thus endangering its parliamentary majority. Manning invoked a state of emergency and put the speaker under house arrest; the government then introduced a bill in the legislature providing for the removal of a speaker.

With the economic situation improving, Manning decided to call a general election in early November, one year ahead of time. His gamble did not pay off, however. His People's National Movement retained only 17 of the 21 seats it had won in the previous election, and the United National Congress (UNC), led by Basdeo Panday, also won 17. Manning said that he would not enter a coalition, and the UNC teamed up with the National Alliance for Reconstruction, which had held on to the two Tobago seats, to form a government. Panday, the first Trinidadian of Indian descent to hold the office, was sworn in as prime minister on November 9.

(DAVID RENWICK)

This article updates the *Macropædia* article THE WEST INDIES: *Trinidad and Tobago.*

TUNISIA

A republic of North Africa, Tunisia lies on the Mediterranean Sea. Area: 164,150 sq km (63,378 sq mi). Pop. (1995 est.): 8,896,000. Cap.: Tunis. Monetary unit: Tunisian dinar, with (Oct. 6, 1995) a free rate of 0.95 dinar to U.S. $1 (1.49 dinars = £1 sterling). President in 1995, Gen. Zine al-Abidine Ben Ali; prime minister, Hamed Karoui.

Tunisia's foreign relations during 1995 were dominated by the negotiations for and the implications of the new Association Agreement signed with the European Union (EU), the first of a new generation of such agreements designed to create a multilateral industrial and financial free-trade area in the Mediterranean basin. The agreement, which was signed on July 17, provided for a 12-year transition period before Tunisia would be fully integrated into the European Economic Area in regard to industrial goods and for future negotiations to bring agricultural products and services into the agreement.

Although Tunisian officials were enthusiastic about the potential of the new agreement to transform the Tunisian economy, there were acute anxieties over the medium-term consequences. An EU report suggested that without substantial transitional help, as many as 4,000 Tunisian companies either would be forced into bankruptcy or would face severe difficulties. The Tunisian government was seeking 2.2 billion dinars over the next five years to cover such costs and was looking toward Europe for up to 80% of these funds.

On the domestic front, the Tunisian government continued to feel threatened by dissident and opposition movements. Although the influence of the exiled Nahda movement was diminishing, the authorities continued to perceive it to be a real threat and complained repeatedly to the British government over the status of the movement's leader, Rachid Ghannouchi, as a political refugee in London. The French government uncovered a new clandestine group, the Tunisian Islamic Front, during arrests of Algerian Islamist supporters in Paris in June. The movement, allegedly operating from London, was accused of collusion with the Armed Islamic Group (GIA), Algeria's feared Islamist terrorist movement; the GIA attacked Tunisian border patrols in February, killing at least six Tunisian soldiers, in a move designed to warn Tunisia against supporting the Algerian government in its campaign against the Islamists.

The Tunisian government's intolerance of opposition was demonstrated again in October with the arrest of Mohamed Mouada, the leader of the Democratic Socialist Movement, Tunisia's most respected opposition party, on the grounds that he had been in contact with a foreign power (Libya) but in reality because he had complained about repression in an open letter to Pres. Zine al-Abidine Ben Ali. His objections arose from the conduct of the municipal elections in May, in which his party failed to obtain control of municipalities where it had expected to do well and saw, as a result, government manipulation of the vote. In reality, the Ben Ali regime had little to fear from the opposition, as its economic record continued to be good.

(GEORGE JOFFÉ)

This article updates the *Macropædia* article NORTH AFRICA: *Tunisia.*

TURKEY

A republic of Asia Minor and southeastern Europe, Turkey has coastlines on the Aegean, Black, and Mediterranean seas. Area: 779,452 sq km (300,948 sq mi), including 23,764 sq km in Europe. Pop. (1995 est.): 62,526,000. Cap.: Ankara. Monetary unit: Turkish lira, with (Oct. 6, 1995) a free rate of 50,093 liras to U.S. $1 (79,189 liras = £1 sterling). President in 1995, Suleyman Demirel; prime minister, Tansu Ciller.

Prime Minister Tansu Ciller survived a succession of political crises in 1995, but in December parliamentary elections (due originally in October 1996) left the pro-Islamic Welfare Party as the single largest bloc, with 158 of the 550 seats. The leader of the Welfare Party, Necmettin Erbakan, had based the election campaign on opposition to secularism in Turkish political life. He had decried "the yoke of the West" and promised to create Islamic counterparts to NATO and the European Union. Ciller remained at the head of a caretaker government as her centre-right True Path Party (DYP) negotiated with its archrival centre-right Motherland Party to prevent the Islamists from taking power.

The ruling coalition of Ciller's DYP and the centre-left social democratic parties had been threatened repeatedly by the attempts of the social democrats to assert themselves and regain some of the popular support lost by their acquiescence in unpopular government decisions. On February 18 the Social Democratic Populist Party (SHP) and the smaller Republican People's Party (CHP) voted to merge, adopting the latter's name. Hikmet Cetin, a former foreign minister, was elected to the leadership of the united party, replacing Murat Karayalcin, while the former SHP leader, Erdal Inonu, became foreign minister when the CHP team of ministers was reshuffled on March 27. At a party convention on September 10, Cetin lost the leadership to Deniz Baykal, the leader of the CHP before the merger. Ten days later Baykal withdrew his support from the coalition. Ciller formed a minority administration, relying on, among others, Alpaslan Turkes, leader of the extreme right-wing Nationalist Action Party, and Bulent Ecevit, leader of the left-wing nationalist Democratic Left Party. Ecevit withdrew his support when Ciller failed to resolve a strike of public-sector workers, and the minority government, which took office on October 5, was defeated in a vote of confidence on October 15. The following day the prime minister patched up her differences with Baykal and agreed to revive the DYP-CHP coalition. The new government took office on October 30, after parliament had scheduled elections on December 24 and passed an electoral law accommodating changes in the constitution, which lowered the voting age from 21 to 18, gave the vote to Turks living abroad, and increased the size of the parliament from 450 to 550 members.

The constitutional amendments, which also increased trade-union rights and widened political participation, sought to meet the demands for democratic reforms voiced by European Union foreign ministers on March 6 when they agreed to implement a customs union with Turkey on Jan. 1, 1996. The decision was approved by the European Parliament at its meeting on December 13.

On October 26 four of the imprisoned deputies of the dissolved Democracy Party, which championed the views of radical Kurdish nationalists, were freed on appeal, but the court confirmed the sentences of 15 years' imprisonment passed on four others convicted of involvement in the armed campaign waged by the Kurdish Workers' Party (PKK). The death toll since the start of the insurgency in 1984 exceeded

RICHARD WAYMAN

A resident of the ancient town of Hasankeyf, in the mountains of eastern Turkey, mounts his mule for a trip to the local market. Archaeologists were attempting to save the historic site from flooding that would result from an irrigation and hydroelectric project along the Tigris and Euphrates rivers.

20,000 by the end of 1995. On March 20 Turkish forces launched a major incursion into Kurdish areas of northern Iraq and destroyed PKK camps before withdrawing two months later. They returned in smaller numbers in the autumn in an effort to end the fighting between rival militias and establish some security in the area.

The decision by the Azerbaijani oil consortium to export early production through both Russia and Georgia was hailed as a victory by Turkey, which intended to link the Georgian route to the existing pipeline from Iraq to the Gulf of Iskenderun. U.S.-Turkish cooperation, which made this decision possible, was further reinforced when, at U.S. prompting, NATO launched air strikes against Bosnian Serbs, a course long advocated by Turkey. Pres. Suleyman Demirel, who visited the Turkish contingent in Bosnia and Herzegovina in March, reached agreements with Bosnia and Croatia when he attended a UN meeting in October. Both Demirel and Ciller cultivated relations with the Turkic Central Asian countries. Visits to all these republics, as well as to Tajikistan and Mongolia, led up to the Turkic summit in Bishkek, Kyrgyzstan, in August.

Before leaving the scene, the minority government settled the public-sector strike, at the cost of $1.3 billion in wage increases. Civil service salaries and pensions also were raised. Living standards had dropped sharply as a result of the austerity program introduced in April 1994, which had led to a record drop of 6% in the gross national product (GNP) in 1994. After stagnating in the first quarter of 1995, however, the GNP jumped by 12% in the second quarter. The foreign trade deficit doubled to over $6 billion in the first seven months of the year, while consumer prices rose by 52% by the end of September. The government imposed a levy on foreign supplier credits while negotiating new performance targets with the International Monetary Fund, which had backed the austerity program.

(ANDREW MANGO)

TURKMENISTAN

A republic of Central Asia, Turkmenistan borders Uzbekistan on the northeast, Kazakhstan on the northwest, the Caspian Sea on the west, Iran on the southwest, and Afghanistan on the southeast. Area: 488,100 sq km (188,500 sq mi). Pop. (1995 est.): 4,081,000. Cap.: Ashgabat (formerly Ashkhabad). Monetary unit: manat, with (Oct. 4, 1995) an official rate of 200 manat to U.S. $1 (316.18 manat = £1 sterling). President in 1995, Saparmurad Niyazov.

In January 1995 Turkmenistan, Turkey, Iran, Kazakhstan, and Russia agreed on the financing of a pipeline to enable Turkmenistan to export its natural gas to Western Europe via Iran and Turkey. A separate agreement with Iran provided for the construction of a pipeline to furnish Turkmen gas to Iran. Turkmenistan's neighbours were concerned over the closeness of its ties to Iran but were unable to persuade Pres. Saparmurad Niyazov to reorient his foreign policy.

In October the U.S. company Unocal and Delta Oil Co. of Saudi Arabia announced plans to build a $3 billion pipeline to Pakistan via Afghanistan, while an Argentine company, Bridas, reported the discovery of a major natural gas field at Yashiar, east of Ashgabat.

Niyazov continued to ignore foreign attempts to pressure him into changing his human rights policies at home. In May he asserted that his stewardship of the country had resulted in no budget deficit despite social guarantees such as free water, gas, and electricity for citizens. He did not mention that these things were not widely available.

On July 12 a crowd of 300–500 people staged a demonstration—the first since independence—in Ashgabat protesting Niyazov's dictatorial rule—he was the first Central Asian head of state to have his term of office extended into the next century—and calling for new presidential elections. The Turkmen opposition headquartered in Moscow denied involvement, and some Russian observers speculated that the protest may have been organized with the help of Russian officials annoyed at Niyazov's pro-Iranian bent.

(BESS BROWN)

This article updates the *Macropædia* article CENTRAL ASIA: *Turkmenistan.*

TUVALU

A constitutional monarchy within the Commonwealth, Tuvalu comprises nine main islands and their associated islets and reefs in the western Pacific Ocean. Area: 24.4 sq km (9.4 sq mi). Pop. (1995 est.): 9,400. Cap.: Fongafale, on Funafuti Atoll. Monetary unit: Australian dollar, with (Oct. 6, 1995) a free rate of $A 1.31 to U.S. $1 ($A 2.08 = £1 sterling). Queen, Elizabeth II; governor-general in 1995, Tulaga Manuella; prime minister, Kamuta Laatasi.

At the annual Independence Day celebrations in October 1995, a new flag, which deleted the Union Jack, was flown publicly for the first time. Suggestions of a republican future for Tuvalu, which would involve severing links with the British crown, met with little enthusiasm, however.

Tuvalu's capacity to patrol its large exclusive economic zone was improved with the gift of a patrol vessel from Australia and with the related construction of a national coordinating centre and support workshop. The gift would be supported by a detachment of Australian naval personnel and a guaranteed future refit to extend the life of the vessel. Prime Minister Kamuta Laatasi visited Tokyo for talks on overseas development assistance and attended meetings of the Pacific Islands Development Program in Honolulu. A major urban-planning project for Funafuti and for Vaitupu had been initiated by the Asian Development Bank.

In March Laatasi attended the inaugural meeting of a new regional subgrouping of Kiribati, the Marshall Islands, Nauru, and Tuvalu, which was intended to foster cooperation in economic development, civil aviation, and other matters. Tuvalu joined other South Pacific Forum states in condemning French nuclear testing. (BARRIE MACDONALD)

This article updates the *Macropædia* article PACIFIC ISLANDS: *Tuvalu.*

UGANDA

A landlocked republic and member of the Commonwealth, Uganda is located in eastern Africa. Area: 241,040 sq km (93,070 sq mi), including 44,000 sq km of inland water. Pop. (1995 est.): 18,659,000. Cap.: Kampala. Monetary unit: Uganda shilling, with (Oct. 6, 1995) a priority rate of 995 shillings to U.S. $1 (1,573 shillings = £1 sterling). President in 1995, Yoweri Museveni; prime minister, Kintu Musoke.

In October 1995 the International Monetary Fund granted $175 million to Uganda to assist in implementing the country's program of economic reform over the next three years. The offer reflected the growing confidence of donor countries and institutions in the government's ability to maintain its economic stability. Earlier in the year donor countries canceled 67% of Uganda's official bilateral debt and rescheduled the remaining 33%. In July creditor countries meeting in Paris agreed to further increases in funding.

This favourable climate of opinion was due to a number of factors. Inflation had fallen during the previous 12 months from 16% to 5%, largely as a result of a decline in food prices after the ending of a period of drought. Moreover, although the income from coffee, the country's main export earner, was less than expected because of the collapse of world prices in July, gross domestic product was expected to grow by 5%. The government had also shown its determination to reduce unnecessary expenditure by making cuts in the civil service and the armed forces. Encouraged by these indicators, foreign investors brought new capital to the country, and there was a marked increase in business activity. Tourism, too, was beginning to revive, at least in the south and west, and three new hotels opened in 1995; also, Entebbe airport was being rehabilitated in an effort to attract more international airlines.

These developments could not disguise the fact that a country generously endowed with natural resources remained one of the poorest, dependent for the foreseeable future on external aid and with no immediate prospect of reducing the poverty of the majority of the population. The U.S. also had misgivings about the way in which Pres. Yoweri Museveni had set his face against reintroducing multiparty democracy, but other Western nations, which had pressed for multiparty elections elsewhere in Africa, appeared to accept the president's claim that a multiplicity of political parties would encourage tribal divisions.

Support for Museveni's stand on that issue came from Uganda's Constituent Assembly in June when it voted 199 to 68 to prolong the existing system for an additional five years. The 68 votes came primarily from representatives of the eastern and northern parts of the country. The new constitution announced by the Constituent Assembly on October 8 legalized the ban on parties but called for nonparty parliamentary and presidential elections in 1996. Among those opposed to a multiparty system were some, particularly among the inhabitants of the kingdoms of the south and west, who preferred a federal form of government.

More extreme opposition to the government persisted in the north, particularly from a group calling itself the Lord's Resistance Army, which, the government maintained, was aided and abetted by The Sudan. In April a Sudanese diplomat's house in Kampala was searched for weapons, and although nothing of significance was found, it was announced that diplomatic relations with The Sudan would be severed. Museveni further promised to pursue relentlessly any rebels attempting to prolong their armed struggle in the north. He later also affirmed that there would be no pardon for the former dictator, Idi Amin, still living in exile in Saudi Arabia. Under Amin, the president said, hundreds of thousands of Ugandans had lost their lives.

(KENNETH INGHAM)

This article updates the *Macropædia* article EASTERN AFRICA: *Uganda.*

UKRAINE

A republic in eastern Europe, Ukraine borders Russia to the north and east, the Black Sea to the south, Romania and Moldova to the southwest, and Hungary, Slovakia, and Poland to the west. Area: 603,700 sq km (233,100 sq mi). Pop. (1995 est.): 52,003,000. Cap.: Kiev. Monetary unit: karbovanets (Ukrainian coupon), with (Oct. 6, 1995) a free rate of 172,000 karbovantsy = U.S. $1 (271,915 karbovantsy = £1 sterling). President in 1995, Leonid Kuchma; prime ministers, Vitaly Masol and, acting from March 1 and official from June 8, Yevhen Marchuk.

The year 1995 could be described as a year of stabilizing trends in Ukraine. The country improved its international profile as a result of its acceptance on October 18 into the Council of Europe and because of its decision, late in the year, to close the Chernobyl nuclear power plant. Relations with the United States also remained warm. U.S. Pres. Bill Clinton's visit to Kiev in May was followed by Prime Minister Yevhen Marchuk's trip to Washington in September.

A Tatar man works at building a house for his family in Ukraine's Crimean Peninsula. Thousands of Crimean Tatars, many of them recently returned from Russia or Central Asia to their ancestral homeland, were living without official authorization and in substandard conditions.

MORKOVKIN—WOSTOK PRESS/MIR

At the same time, Ukraine limited its commitment to the Commonwealth of Independent States, noting at a meeting in Tbilisi in mid-October that it firmly opposed the division of Europe into two blocs and rejected the notion of Ukraine as a buffer state between NATO and the CIS. Earlier in the year, Ukraine had asserted that the role of the CIS should be to decide matters of mutual economic concern rather than political and military issues. During a visit of Belarusian Pres. Alyaksandr Lukashenka to Kiev on September 23–24, Ukraine refused to accept the idea of a three-way customs union and implicitly rebuffed the Belarusian president's support for a "Slavic triangle."

On February 8 Ukraine and Russia initialed the Treaty of Friendship and Cooperation, but the final signatures were never provided. First, in February, the two sides differed on the issue of dual citizenship, and later they disagreed over the Russian desire to maintain the city of Sevastopol as the home base exclusively of the Russian part of the Black Sea Fleet. The latter issue was ostensibly resolved at a meeting of the respective presidents, Leonid Kuchma and Boris Yeltsin, at Sochi, Russia, on June 8–9. Sevastopol was designated as the Russian base, and the two sides agreed to divide the fleet, with Russia receiving 82% of the ships. Nonetheless, other issues, including Yeltsin's illness and disagreements over the Crimea, served to delay the signing of the treaty indefinitely.

Ukraine firmly asserted its authority over the recalcitrant Crimean Peninsula on March 17, abolishing the post of the separatist Crimean president, Yury Meshkov. The Ukrainian parliament also annulled the Crimean constitution and instituted direct rule from Kiev. The Crimea responded defiantly at first, resolving to hold a referendum on autonomy in June, but subsequently gave in to pressure from Kiev. The summer in Crimea was marred by violence in which four Crimean Tatars were killed, evidently by organized crime elements. The Tatars were also the subject of a major Organization for Security and Cooperation in Europe conference that noted that 100,000 out of 250,000 on the peninsula were living in extreme conditions, without adequate shelter, and with very high rates of infant mortality. Some 70,000 Tatars who returned to their ancestral homeland after November 1991 were not yet eligible for Ukrainian citizenship and were effectively disenfranchised until 1996.

The key event in Ukrainian domestic politics was a compromise reached between the president and the legislature over the division of powers (the so-called Power Bill). Following a vote of no confidence by the parliament on April 3, and strong opposition from the parliamentary left faction, the two sides reached an unexpected compromise on June 7. The agreement canceled President Kuchma's plans for a plebiscite on the Power Bill but implemented a Law on State Power that omitted both the parliament's right to impeach the president and the latter's right to dissolve the legislature.

A new government was appointed on July 3 with 27 new officials. Marchuk, who was named prime minister on June 8, was the dominant figure. On October 11 the parliament issued a new government program aimed at gradual economic reform, an anticipated 0.6% rise in industrial output in 1996, and a state budget deficit to be limited to 6%.

Economic performance in 1995 was mixed. Inflation stood at 21.2% in January, dropped to 4.6% in May, and then rose to 14% in September. The karbovanets appeared more stable than it had been (giving rise to speculation that the hryvnya currency would at last be introduced), but then it collapsed against the dollar in August, from 152,000 to 167,700 (and to 179,400 at year's end) and over 200,000 on the black market. Plans to close 19 unprofitable mines led to a brief coal strike in the Donbass region in October, while unemployment in real figures (including hidden unemployment) was estimated at almost four million, or about 15% of the workforce. Progress toward economic reform was, however, sufficient for the International Monetary Fund to provide three standby loans during the course of the year.

The protracted discussions with the Group of Seven (G-7) major industrial countries over the closure of the Chernobyl nuclear power plant were finally resolved on December 20. In April President Kuchma had declared that the station would be closed by the year 2000, but Ukraine's decision was based on the premise that the West would assist with the construction of a thermal power station in the region. A figure of approximately $4 billion was cited by Ukraine to cover these developments. On September 25–27, G-7 experts suggested a figure of $1,440,000,000 and rejected the notion of a thermal station in favour of modernization of Ukraine's entire energy structure. The final agreement was signed in Ottawa by Yury Kostenko, the Ukrainian minister of the environment, and Sheila Copps, Canadian deputy prime minister. (Canada held the rotating chairmanship of the G-7 in 1995.) It called for $2.3 billion in assistance to close the Chernobyl station by the year 2000, construct two safer nuclear power stations, and assist Ukraine in developing its energy sector.

Ukraine's economic decline in recent years exacerbated the health situation within the country. On July 19, 256 cases of cholera were reported in Mykolayiv region, while in October hepatitis B infection killed 8 people and afflicted nearly 1,000 in Dnepropetrovsk and surrounding areas. Thyroid cancer rates rose fivefold in children in the wake of the Chernobyl disaster of 1986, while infant mortality in Ukraine was among the highest in Europe. The country was plagued by social problems, including a notable expansion of organized crime, while living standards continued to fall, albeit less catastrophically than in recent years. Gross domestic product fell by 12% between January and June, compared with 24% in the first six months of 1994.

(DAVID R. MARPLES)

UNITED ARAB EMIRATES

Consisting of Abu Dhabi, Ajman, Dubayy, al-Fujayrah, Ra's al-Khaymah, ash-Shariqah, and Umm al-Qaywayn, the United Arab Emirates is a federation of seven largely autonomous emirates located on the eastern Arabian Peninsula. Area: 83,600 sq km (32,280 sq mi). Pop. (1995 est.): 2,925,000. Cap.: Abu Dhabi. Monetary unit: United Arab Emirates dirham, with (Oct. 6, 1995) an official rate of 3.67 dirhams to U.S. $1 (5.81 dirhams = £1 sterling). President in 1995, Sheikh Zaid ibn Sultan an-Nahayan; prime minister, Sheikh Maktum ibn Rashid al-Maktum.

In January 1995 the ruler of Dubayy, Sheikh Maktum ibn Rashid al-Maktum, appointed his younger brother, Sheikh Muhammad, as crown prince of Dubayy and Sheikh Muhammad's older brother, Sheikh Hamdan, as deputy ruler. Also in January, the Supreme Petroleum Council in Abu Dhabi approved a plan by the Abu Dhabi National Oil Company for a major expansion of the Ruwais Refinery that would increase its capacity to 400,000 bbl per day. In addition, a petrochemical plant (300,000 tons per year) was being considered in the same locale.

The United Arab Emirates (U.A.E.) adopted a budget of $4.9 billion for 1995. Oil production continued at close to the quota of 2,161,000 bbl per day set by OPEC. U.A.E banks continued to show profits in 1995. On January 31 a Luxembourg court approved terms of a settlement in the Bank of Credit and Commerce International case whereby bank creditors would receive from Abu Dhabi the $1.8 billion settlement first agreed upon in 1994.

No progress was achieved in the dispute with Iran over the islands of Greater and Lesser Tunbs and Abu Musa, which remained under Iranian occupation. Military ties with the U.S. continued to develop after the signing in July 1994 of a defense cooperation agreement. A defense agreement with France was signed in January 1995. Saudi Arabian plans to develop a major oil field near the U.A.E. border led to high-level discussions between the two nations. The Saudi-U.A.E. Border Agreement concluded in August 1974 was deposited with the United Nations. (JAMAL A. SA'D)

This article updates the *Macropædia* article ARABIA: *United Arab Emirates.*

UNITED KINGDOM

A constitutional monarchy in northwestern Europe and member of the Commonwealth, the United Kingdom comprises the island of Great Britain (England, Scotland, and Wales) and Northern Ireland, together with many small islands. Area: 244,110 sq km (94,251 sq mi), including 3,218 sq km of inland water but excluding the crown dependencies of the Channel Islands and Isle of Man. Pop. (1995 est.): 58,586,000. Cap.: London. Monetary unit: pound sterling, with (Oct. 6, 1995) a free rate of £0.63 to U.S. $1 (U.S. $1.58 = £1 sterling). Queen, Elizabeth II; prime minister in 1995, John Major.

Domestic Affairs. Despite presiding over a growing economy with low inflation and falling unemployment, a reduction in reported crime, and sustained peace in Northern Ireland, the Conservative government of Prime Minister John Major remained deeply unpopular throughout 1995. Mounting speculation about Major's own position prompted him to call a special parliamentary party election in which he was duly reelected as leader of the Conservative Party, although more than one in four Tory MPs voted against him.

Evidence of public dissatisfaction with the government was everywhere. Most opinion polls through the year showed that the main opposition Labour Party commanded twice as much support as the Conservatives. In May support for the Conservatives in elections to district and city councils slipped to 25%—the party's lowest ever in a nationwide election. The scale of Conservative losses was so great that the party emerged from these local elections with fewer councillors, and controlling fewer councils, in British local government than either Labour or the Liberal Democrats.

The Conservatives also lost two by-elections heavily, falling from first to third place both at Perth and Kinross in Scotland (in May; won by the separatist Scottish National Party) and at Littleborough and Saddleworth in northern England (in July; won by the Liberal Democrats). These losses reduced the Conservatives' majority to nine in the 651-member House of Commons. In October, Alan Howarth, a former government minister, resigned from the Conservative Party and joined Labour—the first MP ever to transfer directly from Conservative to Labour. In December Emma Nicholson, a former vice-chairman of the Conservative Party, also switched sides; she joined the Liberal Democrats. These defections reduced the government's majority to five.

On June 22 Major responded to mounting criticism of his leadership by resigning as leader of the Conservative Party—and announcing his intention to stand in the consequent election. He challenged his opponents to "put up or shut up." His aim was to demonstrate that his critics inside the party were in a small minority and thereby to reassert his authority. On June 26 John Redwood, the secretary of state for Wales, resigned from Major's Cabinet and announced his candidacy. Redwood was a right-wing enthusiast of free competition, low taxes, and reduced government spending; a critic of European integration; and an opponent of plans for a single currency for Europe. He sought to appeal to other Conservative MPs—the electorate in the party's leadership elections—by claiming that the party could not win the next general election under Major. Redwood's campaign slogan was "No change means no chance." In the event, Major won the support of 218 MPs to Redwood's 89; 22 other MPs abstained or spoiled their ballot papers.

Major's victory put an end to speculation about the Conservative leadership, at least for the time being, even though his margin of victory was not as decisive as his campaign team had hoped. On the day following his victory, Major reshaped his Cabinet. His most significant appointment was that of Michael Heseltine as deputy prime minister. Heseltine was one of his party's most flamboyant MPs and arguably its most effective orator. He had long harboured his own ambitions to lead the party; his challenge to Prime Minister Margaret Thatcher in November 1990 had led directly to her downfall and Major's elevation. During the leadership election, Heseltine had urged his own followers to back Major; his appointment as deputy prime minister was his reward. It also meant that should Major stand down for any reason before the next election, Heseltine would be well placed to grasp the prize he had always sought.

Foreign Secretary Douglas Hurd decided to retire from the government during the July reshuffle. Major replaced Hurd with Malcolm Rifkind, formerly defense secretary. (*See* BIOGRAPHIES.) The new defense secretary, Michael Portillo, shared Redwood's outlook on Europe, taxation, and government spending, but he had remained in Major's Cabinet during the leadership contest rather than resign. Jonathan Aitken also resigned from the Cabinet following allegations that during the 1980s he had been a director of a company, BMARC, that circumvented the U.K.'s embargo on the sale of arms to Iran. Aitken denied that he had knowledge of any illegality by BMARC, but his presence in Major's Cabinet impeded the Conservatives' attempts to fend off charges that the government turned a blind eye to "sleaze" (dubious personal behaviour) by ministers.

Following his confirmation as party leader and the Cabinet reshuffle, Major's public popularity rose slightly, but Labour retained its commanding poll lead throughout the second half of 1995.

Meanwhile, Labour itself had continued to shed its left-wing image in an attempt to convince voters of its more centrist credentials. Tony Blair, who had been elected Labour's new leader in July 1994, persuaded a special conference of his party on April 29 to adopt a new statement of aims and values. By a margin of 65% to 35%, the conference agreed to discard the old Clause 4 of the party's constitution, which committed Labour to seeking "the common ownership of the means of production, distribution and exchange." That commitment, which dated from 1918, was replaced by an ambition to create a society "in which power, wealth and opportunity are in the hands of the many, not the few," and where "the enterprise of the market and rigour of competition are joined with the forces of partnership and co-operation." This explicit embrace of the market system, combined with Blair's repudiation of ideological socialism, represented a significant moment in the evolution of the Labour Party—or, as Blair increasingly described it, "New Labour."

On May 11 a government-appointed committee, chaired by Lord Nolan, published its first report on standards of conduct in public life. The committee had been established in October 1994 following a series of financial scandals, mostly minor but mainly involving Conservative MPs. The Nolan committee recommended that MPs (other than ministers) continue to be allowed to earn money outside Parliament but that these earnings be regulated by a new code of conduct and that details of all contracts, consultancies, and payments be published. Nolan also recommended changes to the way in which ministers appointed members to non-governmental public bodies ("quangos"), and to the rules under which civil servants were allowed to accept work in the private sector after leaving government service. The government accepted most of Nolan's recommendations but advised MPs to reject disclosure of the details and amounts of outside earnings. Twenty-three Conservative MPs joined the opposition and voted for full disclosure, however, and the government was defeated by a majority of 51.

One continuing problem for the government through 1995 concerned prison security. In January three dangerous prisoners escaped from Parkhurst Prison on the Isle of Wight, off the coast of southern England. They had managed to obtain a copy of the master key to make their escape. Although the prisoners were caught after five days, their escape—coming just four months after a breakout by five Irish terrorist prisoners from a top security prison in Cambridgeshire—provoked widespread concern about the management of Britain's prisons. This concern was intensified in February by a report by the government's chief inspector of prisons, Judge Stephen Tumim, who described conditions in Leeds Prison, one of the largest in the country, as an "affront to dignity."

In October a report of an official inquiry by a retired army general, Sir John Learmont, into the Parkhurst breakout criticized the management of the Prison Service in forthright terms. Michael Howard, the home secretary, responded by dismissing the service's director-general, Derek Lewis. Lewis responded by suing Howard for unfair dismissal and accusing the home secretary of intervening improperly in the day-to-day running of the service, thus making it impossible for him to do his job properly. Howard rejected this charge and resisted loud demands from the opposition parties for his resignation.

A major confrontation between the environmental group

Greenpeace and the Royal Dutch/Shell Group occurred during the year when Shell sought to dispose of its *Brent Spar* North Sea oil-storage platform. Germany's Chancellor Helmut Kohl also criticized the British government's support for Shell. (*See* ENVIRONMENT: *Sidebar.*)

The continuing drama of the royal family's personal troubles took a new twist as the marriage of Prince Charles and Diana, Princess of Wales, finally collapsed in full public view. On November 20, just under three years after the couple's formal separation, Diana gave an hour-long interview on BBC television during which she admitted adultery (with a former guards officer, James Hewitt) and cast doubts on the fitness of Prince Charles to become king. The public debate that followed the interview brought to a head the issue of whether the prince and princess should formally seek a divorce, which would, among other things, have the effect of preventing Diana from becoming queen upon Charles's ascent to the throne. On December 20 Buckingham Palace announced that Queen Elizabeth II had advised the prince to begin divorce proceedings. The following day Charles made clear his intention to become king in due course and not to remarry for the foreseeable future. This dampened speculation that Charles intended to take the controversial step of marrying Camilla Parker-Bowles, with whom he had previously admitted having an affair.

During 1995 the British people set a new record as the world's keenest lottery players. Each week an estimated 75% of all adults bought at least one of the £1 lottery tickets or scratch cards. During its first 12 months the national lottery, which began in November 1994, exceeded all expectations by raising more than £4 billion. Half of this money went in prizes, with the jackpot reaching £20 million in some weeks. The other half was divided between administration and taxes (22%) and money for good causes (28%).

The Economy. The U.K. achieved its third consecutive year of steady economic growth and low inflation in 1995. Gross domestic product rose by 2.5%—slightly less than in 1994 but at a rate that was deemed less likely to cause inflationary pressure. Retail prices rose by 3.5%—inside, although toward the top end of, the government's target range of 1–4%. Unemployment fell by 300,000 to 2.2 million.

These achievements, however, produced few political rewards for the Conservative government. Tax increases announced in 1993 and 1994 were still being implemented in early 1995; many large companies continued to cut back on their workforce, especially white-collar and management staff. The result was persistent middle-class insecurity. This helped to prevent the stagnant housing market from recovering. Average house prices across the U.K. remained 20% lower than their peak in 1989. By late 1995 more than one million homeowners suffered from "negative equity"; that is, their mortgage debt exceeded the value of their home.

The smooth running of the economy was not helped by a dispute during the early months of the year between Eddie George, the governor of the Bank of England (*see* BIOGRAPHIES), and Kenneth Clarke, the chancellor of the Exchequer. George wanted to put the fight against inflation above everything else and sought to raise interest rates to prevent the economy from overheating. Clarke did not want to discourage borrowing, investment, or the fragile housing market and resisted any increase in the base rate above the 6.75% agreed in February (itself a 0.5% increase on the rate at the end of 1994). In the end, Clarke had to use his formal authority as chancellor to overrule George. Clarke was subsequently seen by most economists to have been right—growth slowed anyway, but the spectacle of the governor being directly overruled on monetary policy did nothing to soothe frayed nerves in the financial markets.

There were other signs of economic weakness. Government borrowing had been projected to fall from £35 billion in 1994–95 to £23 billion in 1995–96. At the end of 1995, however, borrowing was persisting at the same rate as a year earlier, mainly because the slowdown in economic growth caused tax revenues to fall short of their expected levels. Moreover, as the year progressed, there was mounting evidence of a rise in Britain's balance of payments deficit.

MARTIN MCCULLOUGH—PRESS ASSOCIATION

A truck burns during disturbances that broke out in Belfast on July 3 after the release of a British soldier who had served four years of a life sentence for killing a teenage girl in 1990. Overall, however, violence in Northern Ireland in 1995 was much below the levels of previous years.

Against this background, Clarke sought to fashion his annual budget, presented on November 28, in a manner that would appeal to both voters and the financial markets. He reduced public spending (although protecting the health and education budgets) and also reduced the standard rate of income tax by 1% to 24%. He reinforced his policy with a quarter-point cut in interest rates in December—the first reduction in almost two years. By taking no economic risks, Clarke achieved no immediate political benefits; the Conservatives remained as far behind Labour directly after the budget as they had been before.

On February 26 one of Britain's oldest banks, Barings PLC, collapsed following massive losses incurred on the futures market in Singapore. (*See* SPECIAL REPORT: *Economic Affairs.*) The government blamed the collapse on the activities of a single "rogue" trader on Barings' Singapore staff, Nicholas Leeson, who was subsequently detained in Germany. In a report on July 18, the Board of Banking Supervision concluded that Barings had suffered from serious failures of internal management, but opposition parties called for tougher external regulation in order to protect the wider reputation of the City of London in the future. In November the government announced it would not seek the extradition of Leeson, who was then returned to Singapore to face criminal charges and was subsequently sentenced to a prison term of 6½ years.

Foreign Affairs. The United Kingdom's relations with the rest of the European Union (EU) remained tense throughout 1995, although Major believed that events were gradually moving his way on monetary union. At a meeting of EU heads of government in Formentor, Málaga, Spain, in September, Major said that "few, perhaps very few" EU states would meet the Maastricht Treaty's economic convergence conditions by 1999; as a result, Britain—if it exercised its opt-out and decided not to join a single currency—would not be alone. Major said that if an inner group of EU states insisted on introducing a single currency, a two-speed Europe would be inevitable and should be planned for. Major also repeated his intention to resist any widening of the powers of the EU at the intergovernmental conference, due to start in 1996. Major warned that the EU would lose the respect of people throughout Europe if it leaped too far ahead of public opinion.

In May the government announced its intention to send a further 6,700 troops to Bosnia and Herzegovina, to add to the 4,400 already taking part in the 25,000-strong United Nations peacekeeping force. Major announced that Britain's forces had two objectives: to distribute humanitarian aid and to prevent a wider conflagration across the Balkans. His announcement attracted all-party support in the House of Commons, although both Labour and the Liberal Democrats urged tougher action against the Bosnian Serb forces. Following the peace agreement in November, Major announced that British troops would play a significant role in peacekeeping efforts in Bosnia and Herzegovina.

In Hong Kong, Britain negotiated its first substantive agreement with China on the future of the colony after control passed to China in 1997. On June 9 the two countries agreed to establish a new Court of Final Appeal with limited powers. Sensitive "acts of state" issues, such as those concerning defense and foreign affairs, would be referred to Beijing. Britain and China also reached agreement on the financing of a new airport for Hong Kong, to be opened in 1998. Meanwhile, a new Legislative Council was elected on September 17, but only about 35% of Hong Kong's electors took part in the election. (See *Dependent States,* above.)

Northern Ireland. Following the cease-fires in 1994, Northern Ireland remained at peace throughout 1995, although only slow progress was made toward a lasting political settlement. On February 22 the British and Irish governments presented a framework document setting out some agreed proposals for the future of the province. These included the establishment of a new assembly for Northern Ireland with 90 members elected by proportional representation; a directly elected three-member panel to oversee the work of the assembly; a new cross-border body of members of the Irish Dail (parliament) and Northern Ireland assembly to deal with issues of shared concern; an end to Ireland's claim, in art. 2 of the constitution, to regard Northern Ireland as part of its "national territory"; and confirmation by the United Kingdom government that any change in the constitutional position of Northern Ireland would require the consent of a majority of its people.

Gerry Adams, president of Sinn Fein, the political wing of the Irish Republican Army (IRA), welcomed the framework document, saying, "Its ethos is for one Ireland and an all-Ireland arrangement." The two main unionist parties shared this analysis and, consequently, rejected the document. They announced their intention to boycott any talks based on the document's provisions.

Separately, the British government said that Sinn Fein could take part in roundtable talks only if it started to decommission its weapons. Sinn Fein said that it would be willing to discuss handing in its weapons as part of an overall peace agreement, but not before. Nevertheless, a number of bilateral meetings were held between the Sinn Fein leadership and government officials. On May 24 Adams met Sir Patrick Mayhew, Britain's Northern Ireland secretary, in Washington, D.C., when both attended an Irish-U.S. investment conference.

Nevertheless, with the unionists refusing to join roundtable talks and Sinn Fein barred from them, no substantive progress was made during the rest of 1995. Apart from a few isolated incidents, however, the cease-fire continued to hold. One consequence was a sharp increase in confidence, investment, and employment in the province as it benefited from a substantial "peace dividend." The British government also sought to reduce tension by withdrawing two army battalions from Northern Ireland and gradually releasing convicted terrorists from prison.

On August 28 James Molyneaux announced his resignation after 16 years as leader of the Ulster Unionist Party. On September 8 the party elected David Trimble as his successor. Trimble, a former law lecturer, was regarded as the most hard-line of the main candidates. In his early weeks as leader, however, Trimble went to some lengths to open up a dialogue with both London and Dublin.

On November 28 Major and John Bruton, Ireland's prime minister, announced a new agreement between the two governments on the next stage of the peace process. On the most contentious issue, the decommissioning of the IRA arsenal, they agreed to establish a three-member international commission, chaired by former U.S. senator George Mitchell, to consult and deliberate on ways of breaking the deadlock. Major and Bruton agreed that if the commission found that the IRA and Protestant paramilitary bodies had "a clear commitment" to disarm as part of the peace process, then they would be able to take part in preparatory talks in early 1996 aimed at clearing the ground for full all-party negotiations. Two days later U.S. Pres. Bill Clinton visited Northern Ireland, where he was given an immense ovation from both the nationalist and unionist communities for his contribution to the peace process. In return, Clinton said that the people of Northern Ireland were "making a miracle." (PETER KELLNER)

See also *Commonwealth of Nations; Dependent States.*

UNITED STATES

The United States of America is a federal republic composed of 50 states. Area: 9,372,571 sq km (3,618,770 sq mi), including 205,856 sq km of inland water but excluding the 156,492 sq km of the Great Lakes that lie within U.S. boundaries. Pop. (1995 est.): 263,057,000. Cap.: Washington, D.C. Monetary unit: U.S. dollar, with (Oct. 6, 1995) a free rate of U.S. $1.58 to £1 sterling. President in 1995, Bill Clinton.

By all rights 1995 should have marked a political nadir for U.S. Pres. Bill Clinton. As a result of the 1994 congressional elections, he had become chief executive in what amounted, in U.S. terms, to a minority government. Control of the legislative agenda shifted to Congress, dominated, for the first time in 40 years, by Republicans, and especially to the combative speaker of the House of Representatives, Newt Gingrich. (*See* BIOGRAPHIES.) A massive rollback of welfare legislation and federal dominance was set in motion as the Republicans moved to fulfill the conservative "Contract with America" within their first 100 days in office. (*See* Special Report.) The president seemed reduced to the role of a bystander. Defections from the Democratic Party continued apace; in all, five Democrats switched parties after the elections. Nonetheless, by the end of the year, the president, while giving considerable ground, had managed to achieve more of a stalemate with Congress than many had believed possible.

In November the president's veto of the Republican budget led to a standoff that idled 800,000 employees and shut down so-called nonessential functions of the federal government for six days. Treasury Secretary Robert Rubin nimbly raided selected federal pension funds in the interim to forestall default on the government's obligations, while the two sides reached accommodation on such issues as the target of balancing the budget in seven years, as Republicans demanded.

The president and the Congress remained far apart on the specifics of how to achieve that aim, however, with Republicans looking for more than $1 trillion in spending cuts, largely from social welfare programs, along with $245 billion in tax relief, spearheaded by a $500-per-child tax credit. Along with the tax issue, one of the central disagreements was over controlling Medicare and Medicaid costs. The Republicans wanted to save $270 billion over seven years by cutting back increases in Medicare spending from 10% to 7% annually. Clinton deemed that unacceptable and proposed savings of $124 billion. On Medicaid, Congress was determined to make cutbacks in spending, convert the remainder into block grants to the states, and allow each state to set eligibility requirements. The president was determined to keep Medicaid as an entitlement. When agreement was not reached by mid-December, those parts of the government not yet funded were again forced to shut down while the president and congressional leaders attempted to work out a compromise. This time some 280,000 government employees were furloughed, and thousands who did government work on a contract basis also were not paid. In spite of a series of meetings between Clinton and top congressional leaders, no solution to the impasse had been reached by the time the year ended. Bipartisan attempts by senate leaders to reach a compromise failed to gain backing from hard-line Republicans in the House of Representatives.

American Disaffection. While the budget dominated headlines, the forces swirling in the American political cauldron in 1995 were more dramatically epitomized in an event far from Washington, D.C. The country was stunned on April 19 when a rented truck parked outside the Alfred P. Murrah Federal Building in Oklahoma City, Okla., erupted shortly after 9 AM, tearing the front off the nine-story structure and leaving 168 people dead, including 19 children. In addition, a nurse was killed during rescue efforts. The truck had contained homemade explosives, a mixture of diesel fuel and ammonium nitrate. The man who was allegedly responsible for the bomb was a former member of the U.S. Army and a veteran of the Persian Gulf War, Timothy J. McVeigh, a fringe member of a heavily armed American subculture of "militia" that espoused antigovernment views. His alleged coconspirator was Terry Lynn Nichols, a farmer from Herington, Kan. Both men were charged with offenses that carried the death penalty.

The Oklahoma bombing drew attention to a radical degree of disaffection with the government in general and a number of federal agencies in particular. In its most extreme form, the disaffected militia movement claimed about 100,000 members who expressed hostility to the federal government, believed in foreign conspiracies to erode the sovereignty or even the territory of the nation, and often stored food and arms and practiced military training in anticipation of either invasion or some form of federal police state. All such groups disclaimed anything to do with the Oklahoma City bombing.

Like McVeigh, however, almost all militia members were virulently opposed to gun-control laws, like the 1994 federal assault weapons ban, and many saw the antigun actions of the FBI and the Bureau of Alcohol, Tobacco and Firearms as being, in the words of a National Rifle Association official, the work of "jack-booted government thugs" intent on tearing down what they saw as the Second Amendment's guarantee of the right to bear arms. In particular, they saw the 1993 siege in Waco, Texas, of the Branch Davidian compound, in which 82 cult members died, as being evidence of a sinister and cold-blooded federal government attitude toward like-minded dissidents. Authorities investigating the Oklahoma tragedy were convinced that the date of the crime—the anniversary of the federal raid at Waco—was no coincidence.

At a series of congressional hearings, Attorney General Janet Reno justified her endorsement of the assault on Waco, but she did not convince many skeptics. The FBI, however, took a more self-critical view in another case that had aroused a similar furor: the 1992 attempt to arrest a heavily armed Idaho man named Randall Weaver, a believer in white racial separatism, at his mountain cabin. After Weaver's 14-year-old son was killed in the clash, an FBI sharpshooter killed Weaver's wife as she stood behind a door with their 10-month-old daughter in her arms. Three years after the firefight, the agency paid Weaver and his surviving children $3.1 million in a civil settlement. FBI Director Louis Freeh also suspended his close friend and the number two man at the FBI, Larry Potts, while probing Potts's involvement in a change of the rules of engagement at the shoot-out.

The militias were only the most highly charged manifestation of a deep-rooted anger with the encroachments of the federal government that also showed itself in hostility to those wearing its civil uniforms, from the FBI to the Bureau of Land Management and the Forestry Service. The anger led to a sense of siege among many members of the federal bureaucracy. In some parts of the country—notably the West, where feelings ran high against federal control of as much as 80% of the land in certain jurisdictions—some federal officials refused to be seen in their work clothes for fear of attracting sniper fire. Others faced lawsuits and even disobedience from state officials, who claimed that they, rather than federal authorities, should claim ownership of such public property.

Much like the fringe anti-Vietnam War radicalism of the 1970s, the antigovernment terrorism and civil disobedience of 1995 represented the overheated froth of a much broader and more moderate consensus—that government, particularly the federal government, had taken more than its share of resources and political space and had to be reduced. The consensus, however, was coupled with a continuing sense of disquiet and uncertainty about the future that gave a sharp edge to the national debate in many arenas, including the jostling leading up to the 1996 elections. Anti-Washington sentiment and a desire for leadership outside the traditional mold powered a deep groundswell of support for the idea of a presidential candidacy by Gen. Colin Powell, a black man who had retired as chairman of the Joint Chiefs of Staff. Powell, who declared himself a Republican, eventually declined to run, however, leaving Senate Majority Leader Robert Dole as the Republican front-runner, but it also fueled renewed candidacies by Texas billionaire H. Ross Perot, who announced the Independence Party as his political vehicle, and by the nativist conservative Patrick Buchanan, a combative orator with a strong anti-immigrant and anti-free-trade platform. Both of the dissident candidates reflected an isolationist uncertainty about the U.S. political and economic role in the world that paralleled the domestic uncertainty.

The Economy. There was considerable uncertainty on the economic front. For the first time since 1992, in July the Federal Reserve Board (Fed) announced a cut in short-term interest rates, from 6% to 5.75%. Chairman Alan Greenspan and the Fed's Open Market Committee then made another, year-end rate cut, to 5.5%. The Fed actions signaled that the economy, in Greenspan's view, had achieved the so-called soft landing that he had tried to manage through seven previous interest-rate hikes. Growth for 1995 appeared to be headed for the 2.5% level that Greenspan deemed optimal. The unemployment rate was hovering in the range of 5.4%, and inflation seemed likely to be no more than 2.5% for the year. Flat retail sales and weakness in a number of leading indicators, however, gave some warning of slightly lower growth in early 1996.

Meanwhile, in the midst of the budget battle, the Dow Jones industrial average rose past 5,000 after having pushed through 4,000 early in the year. Low interest rates, the prospect of reduced government spending, and a welter of high-performing high-tech issues had a lot to do with the performance, as did a continuing wave of mergers and acquisitions. Hikes in stock prices and merger mania went hand in hand with economies of scale, however, and the continuing globalization of the U.S. economy produced pink slips and fear alongside the bullishness. Typical of the paradox was the behaviour of AT&T, a profitable $75 billion megalith, which announced that it would break itself into three separate companies and shed 78,000 jobs.

In the atmosphere of uncertainty amid fast-changing economic forces, many Americans found it easy to believe that stability was indeed eroding and that their government was not doing enough to stem the advantages wielded by foreign countries that "gained" the jobs lost at home. Mindful of the sentiment, the Clinton administration used the threat of 100% tariffs on luxury-car imports to pressure the Japanese into expanding their North American auto production and buying more U.S.-made parts and also threatened China with $1 billion in tariffs to force the government into policing the rights of U.S. manufacturers of such often-pirated goods as computer software.

One of Clinton's earlier international economic initiatives came back to haunt him, however. When the Mexican peso collapsed in December 1994, the U.S. had rushed to bail

A migrant worker in the Imperial Valley of California protects her face from the sun and dust. With the collapse of the peso and the Mexican economy, the numbers of Mexicans entering the U.S. increased, which produced renewed demands for tighter restrictions on immigration.
JIMMY DORANTES

out its partner in the hard-won North American Free Trade Agreement (NAFTA). The administration helped to cobble together a $50 billion international credit arrangement that included $20 billion worth of U.S. guarantees, and Congress grudgingly went along with the fiscal legerdemain. By international standards the bailout was a considerable success in stemming a financial hemorrhage from Mexico and in restoring investment confidence. The country's living standards, currency values, and labour costs swooned, however. Purchases of foreign-made goods, especially from the U.S., collapsed, while exports, boosted by a cheap peso, took off. The result was that after years of enjoying trade surpluses with Mexico, the U.S. suddenly found itself running a deficit, and a number of U.S. companies announced that they would forsake the U.S. for the cheaper labour available there. At the same time, the number of Mexicans entering the U.S. illegally in search of work took a strong upward hike.

One effect of the Mexican crisis was a likely halt to further expansion of NAFTA. A more dramatic effect was the boost that Mexico's plight gave to opponents of immigration to the U.S., both nationally and in states like California that were particularly hard hit by the influx. In the 1994 elections California residents had already given approval to Proposition 187, a measure that would deny schooling and other benefits to the children of illegal immigrants. The proposition was endorsed by Gov. Pete Wilson, but parts of the measure, notably the schooling ban, were declared unconstitutional by a federal judge. Meanwhile, the U.S. Congress also seemed intent on cutting back benefits to legal immigrants as part of its budget tightening. In a bow to the same anti-immigrant sentiments, the Clinton administration announced that it would end the policy of giving Cuban boat people special status as political refugees and would instead return them to their homeland.

Developments in Government. President Clinton had long been notorious in his critics' eyes for trimming sails to suit whatever political breezes were blowing, but the new Republican majority in Congress made that tendency a sometimes helpful tool of statecraft. While it caused considerable anguish in left-wing Democratic circles, the president, who was the native of a region where states' rights were still a shibboleth, found it easier to accept many of the decentralizing initiatives of the Republican legislators. On the other hand, the president also seemed capable of taking advantage of splits in his opponents' ranks. He was able, for example, to head off some cutbacks in the Environmental Protection Agency, long a demon of many Republicans, after a number of more moderate Senate Republicans reconsidered the measure.

In the midst of the new federal diffidence toward expanding or defending its reach, more initiatives emerged from the states. Some were nothing less than reactionary, like the decision of Alabama to restore prison road gangs and bring back leg irons (though other states concurred with the notion of a tougher prison regimen less aimed at catering to prisoner comfort). On issues of broader import, however, many states had shown the way in endorsing programs of voucher-driven education and "workfare" for welfare recipients, but many also began to tackle other areas. One of the touchiest and most explosive issues was race-based preferment. In California, Governor Wilson signed an executive order that abolished almost all affirmative action policies. (President Clinton ordered a review of federal affirmative action policies but then declared that most should continue.)

The issue of race, perhaps the most sensitive tissue in the body politic, seemed to be undergoing a different kind of examination on each side of the black-white divide. While whites debated affirmative action, the largest black demonstration in Washington, D.C.'s history—larger than the 1963 march led by Martin Luther King, Jr.—took place under the auspices of the black separatist Louis Farrakhan, head of the Nation of Islam. The "Million Man March" was a powerful demonstration of the concerns of black males about family disintegration and personal responsibility and endorsed personal and spiritual, rather than governmental, solutions to such ills. The demonstration also gave a powerful boost to the standing of Farrakhan, hitherto considered a mesmerizing but marginal racial demagogue.

Race also played an underlying role in the trial of O.J. Simpson, a black television pitchman and former football star, for the slaying of his white former wife, Nicole Brown Simpson, and her acquaintance Ronald Goldman. Simpson was acquitted after less than four hours of jury deliberation. The trial's turning points were the fiery, racially tinged address of Simpson defense counsel Johnnie Cochran and the discrediting of the Los Angeles police detective Mark Fuhrman, an investigator of the slaying who had, long before the trial, boasted to an interviewer of his racial prejudice and his planting of evidence to convict other alleged criminals. Enthusiasm or dismay at the trial outcome seemed to split largely along racial lines, which reinforced the notion that blacks and whites had entirely different views about the nature of the justice system.

In looking anew at affirmative action, both federal and state governments were following the lead of the Supreme Court. In 1995 the court agreed that affirmative action programs had to meet tests of strict judicial scrutiny to be constitutional. By a 5–4 vote the justices also struck down a Georgia statute that allowed the gerrymandering of electoral districts to compensate for past racial segregation. In a setback for homosexual activists, the court ruled that private parades such as Boston's St. Patrick's Day celebration could exclude those it did not want to participate.

In a decision that could prove to be one of the more far-reaching of its term, the court set a limit on the federal government's ability to use the interstate commerce clause of the U.S. Constitution to impinge on matters otherwise outside its jurisdiction. The clause, which became a cornerstone of federal activism in the era of Franklin D. Roosevelt, had been used to justify everything from food standards to civil rights investigations. In overturning the federal Gun-Free School Zones Act of 1990, which used the clause to declare the possession of firearms around education sites to be a federal crime, the justices ended its infinite elasticity. On the other hand, the court agreed that no limits could be set on reelection to Congress without a constitutional amendment, a blow to the term-limits movement.

In another development relating to interstate commerce, the Interstate Commerce Commission (ICC), once the most powerful bureaucracy in Washington, closed its doors at the end of the year. As of the first day of 1996, it would be no longer in existence. Established in 1887 to curb the power of the railroad "robber barons," the commission at one time had the power to regulate almost everything that moved across state lines. The deregulation of transportation in the 1980s had deprived the ICC of most of its reason for existing, but it had survived several attempts to close it. The remaining employees and commissioners were transferred to the Department of Transportation.

The House of Representatives passed a nearly total ban on gifts from lobbyists, following in the wake of a less stringent Senate ban. The measure did little, however, to stem the most questionable source of money for influence, donations to political action committees, and other devices that congressmen used to finance their political survival. House Speaker Gingrich, who had earlier given up a multimillion-dollar book advance from communications mogul Rupert Murdoch, whose vast holdings were much affected by federal oversight, drew a House ethics investigation after questions were raised about his alleged use of GOPAC, a not-for-profit organization, to funnel money to Republican causes. Congress proved itself tough on matters of legislators' sexual behaviour. Sen. Robert Packwood, a Republican who headed the Finance Committee, resigned after the Senate Ethics Committee voted for his expulsion. Packwood had been charged with sexual harassment by 19 women, including a 17-year-old.

On the most high-profile ethics issue, the turgid Whitewater scandal, little insight was gleaned. Much of the focus of congressional concern had long since shifted from the original property deal, which took place long before the Clintons reached Washington, to the behaviour of administration officials after the July 1993 suicide of Vincent Foster, the White House counsel and overseer of the Clintons' personal finances. Deputy Attorney General Philip Hyman told a Senate investigating committee that his department had been forced to stand by while White House Counselor Bernard Nussbaum entered Foster's office and took files related to the Clinton family's personal affairs. The senators were intrigued by telephone logs that showed long conversations between Hillary Rodham Clinton and two of the intruders immediately after the entry. After initially balking, President Clinton agreed at the end of the year to turn over to Senate investigators notes from meetings on the matter.

Foreign Affairs. Nothing a president does is likely to affect the feelings of the American people as much as his decision to send U.S. troops into harm's way. In this, Clinton crossed the Rubicon with his Bosnian policy. The war in the Balkans between Serbs, Croats, and Muslims had been a frustration and a challenge to U.S. diplomacy since its inception. A Vietnam-era protester who had not served in the military, Clinton was sensitive to the difficulty, frequently underlined by his military advisers, in becoming involved in a civil war in a country where American high-tech superiority might count for little and the possibility of casualties was high. The scale of the Balkan atrocities—perhaps 250,000 killed and 3 million displaced in "ethnic cleansing"—and the inability of European allies in NATO to find a solution prompted Clinton to act, however.

Members of a militia organization in Michigan salute the American flag. A man with ties to such a group was charged with the bombing of a federal building in Oklahoma, which directed attention to the militia movement and its conspiracy theories and hostility toward the government.
MARK PETERSON—SABA

At first Clinton did so rhetorically, urging a relatively safe bombing campaign against the Bosnian Serbs—considered the chief aggressors—as a way of halting the war. This did not suit American allies, who pointed out that the U.S. had no UN peacekeeping troops on the ground to worry about. Eventually, however, when the Bosnian Serbs began overrunning protected "safe areas" and killing or expelling Muslim inhabitants, Clinton acted, with unhappy results. As NATO aircraft bombed Bosnian Serb artillery positions, the Serbs took over 300 UN peacekeepers hostage and threatened to kill them if the bombing did not stop.

In August a sudden Croatian military offensive regained territory previously taken by the Serbs. The offensive, it turned out, was the result of a covert U.S. retraining and reorganizing of the army of Croatian Pres. Franjo Tudjman, part of a policy advocated by Assistant Secretary of State Richard Holbrooke, who had emerged as the maestro of Balkan realpolitik. The next important stage was to bring together Tudjman with Serbian Pres. Slobodan Milosevic and Bosnian Pres. Alija Izetbegovic at Wright-Patterson Air Force Base near Dayton, Ohio, for talks in November that ended after three weeks with a fragile treaty. The agreement was to be overseen by a 60,000-member NATO force that would keep the enemies apart along 4-km (2.5-m) cease-fire zones. In the long run, the U.S. would train the weaker Muslim army to underpin the peace with a credible balance of power.

The peace accord was a dramatic vindication of the U.S.'s role as the only remaining superpower and a huge political risk for Clinton as he entered an election year. Despite assurances that the troops would depart from Bosnia and Herzegovina within a year and would be able to respond with maximum force if attacked, the likelihood of at least some U.S. casualties seemed high, and no vital U.S. interest appeared to be served. Public opinion polls registered a great deal of opposition, but Clinton received support for his initiative from his likely presidential rival, Senator Dole. Other prominent Republicans attacked him for the risky venture.

Twenty years after the end of the Vietnam War, Clinton extended diplomatic recognition to Hanoi. The action was greeted with protest by disaffected U.S. military veterans, but it was hailed by American business, which rushed in to make deals long available to European and Asian competitors. Skeptics also growled as the U.S. and North Korea signed a deal in which the U.S. provided two nuclear reactors in exchange for an agreement by the economically battered regime of Kim Jong Il that it would dismantle its nuclear enrichment program, widely seen as a prelude to acquiring nuclear weapons.

Under congressional pressure, Clinton reversed a decade-old policy that had kept Taiwan's head of state, Pres. Lee Teng-hui, from setting foot on U.S. soil, a bow to China's claim to be the sole legitimate government. The administration decided to allow Lee to visit his alma mater, Cornell University, Ithaca, N.Y., to receive an honorary degree. The action led to strong statements from China about subversive American intentions, the punitive awarding of lucrative automotive contracts to non-American firms, and a tougher stance toward selected dissidents. China's continuing desire to gain entry to the world trading community, however, made it unlikely that the U.S. gesture would permanently mar relations with the world's most populous nation.

(GEORGE RUSSELL)

See also *Dependent States.*

Special Report

The "Contract" with America

BY NINA MASSEN

Fortified with a significant electoral victory on Election Day 1994, Republican leader Newt Gingrich, the new speaker of the U.S. House of Representatives, initiated a 10-point legislative program called the "Contract with America," a mix of promises to repeal existing statutes and promises to enact new legislation that was based on a document signed the previous September by many Republican candidates. The agenda targeted a vast array of areas in which government action was to be enhanced, redirected, or eliminated. The scope of the mandate was equaled only by the speed with which the speaker and his House colleagues promised that the package would be enacted: a mere 100 days.

The Contract was headline news for much of the first 100 days of the new Congress. There was debate over the substantive merits of the individual pieces of the legislative package as well as discussion of whether the 10 planks, taken as a whole, would create a fundamentally new relationship between the federal government, the states, and the electorate. Proponents and opponents of the Contract recognized that even if the House passed each of the 10 planks, the ultimate success of the Contract lay with the Senate, the president, and ultimately the voters, all of whom would have to approve of the measures.

What was absent from the debate, however, was any discussion of whether the Contract was in fact a legal contract. Was the title selected to fit neatly into the nine-second-sound-bite style of 20th-century American politics, or was it a throwback to Jean-Jacques Rousseau's 18th-century social contract? If the term *contract* was to be taken literally, then a routine application of traditional contract principles raised the possibility that the Contract, regardless of any substantive merit, did not embody a meeting of the minds between the governing and the governed.

The 10 parts of the Contract with America were variously titled to try to capture the essence of the legislation—the Fiscal Responsibility Act, for example. As the 10 parts wound their way through the legislative process, fulfillment of each basic plank required passage of a group of splinter bills. In the end, however, all but one of the 10 initial measures—the Citizen Legislature Act—was approved by the House in 100 days, by April 13, 1995.

The Fiscal Responsibility Act contained two budgetary reforms: a constitutional amendment requiring a balanced budget and a permanent line-item veto. As initially posed, the balanced budget bill (H.J. Res. 1) would be an amendment to the Constitution to require that the federal budget be balanced by the year 2002 or two years after enactment of the amendment, whichever was later. The bill passed the House but failed in the Senate. The line-item veto bill (H.R. 2) would give the president the authority to veto specific portions of appropriations acts, unless overridden by Congress. The House version passed, but owing to the substantively different configuration of the Senate bill, the bills were sent to conference in June 1995.

The Taking Back Our Streets Act was the House Republicans' crime-fighting measure (H.R. 3). It shifted federal spending from crime-prevention programs to prison construction, called for hiring more police officers, and limited the appeal rights of death-row inmates. The House Judiciary Committee divided H.R. 3 into smaller bills, all of which passed. The Senate began hearings on its bill (S. 3) on July 27, 1995.

The Personal Responsibility Act was a welfare-reform bill aimed at capping welfare spending, encouraging a reduction in illegitimacy by prohibiting welfare benefits to mothers under 18, and creating several large block grants for the states for items such as child care, school meals, and nutrition for young children. Additions to the bill allowed for child-support enforcement and a capped food-stamp-entitlement program. The House bill (H.R. 4) passed on March 24, 1995. A watered-down version of the bill was passed by the Senate after nearly 100 hours of debate on Sept. 19, 1995.

The Family Reinforcement Act was drafted to provide tax breaks for child adoption and elder care, toughen penalties for child pornographers, and protect the privacy rights of minors and their parents. Bills encompassing this legislation passed the House on April 4, 1995, followed by Senate passage two days later.

The American Dream Restoration Act was intended to provide tax relief for middle-income families by providing a $500-per-child tax credit, reform the so-called marriage penalty, and authorize more flexible individual retirement accounts (IRAs). The House passed H.R. 6 in early April 1995, whereas the Senate bill entered hearings on June 19, 1995.

The main goals of the National Security Restoration Act were twofold: to prohibit further cuts in defense spending to finance social-spending programs and to prohibit the use of American troops in UN operations under foreign control. The bill (H.R. 7) passed the House on Feb. 16, 1995. The Senate Foreign Relations Committee began hearings on the Senate bill on March 21, 1995.

The Senior Citizens' Fairness Act was intended to relieve the financial burdens of the American elderly by permitting them to earn up to $30,000 per year without losing Social Security benefits, repealing the 1993 law that made 85% of Social Security benefits subject to income tax for middle- and upper-income persons, and granting a tax incentive to encourage the purchase of long-term-care insurance. The House passed the bill, and the Senate version went into hearings on June 19, 1995.

The Job Creation and Wage Enhancement Act was actually several bills that sought to reduce the capital-gains tax, strengthen individuals' property rights, reduce governmental red tape, and overhaul the governmental regulatory process. Four bills, not including the capital-gains reduction, were passed as H.R. 9 and were referred to the Senate on March 9, 1995. (H.R. 1215, which included a decrease in capital-gains taxes, passed the House on April 5.)

The Common Sense Legal Reforms Act (H.R. 10) encompassed a number of legal reforms, including limiting punitive damages, instituting a modified "loser pays" rule to discourage litigation, and limiting product manufacturers' liability. Portions of the bill, which was split into several provisions, were passed by both the House and the Senate, whereas other provisions were calendared in the Senate.

The final bill, the Citizen Legislature Act, was a House joint resolution that would have limited the number of terms of House and Senate members. The measure failed in

---

Nina Massen is an attorney and author who lives in Westchester, N.Y.

both chambers. Thus, only two contract proposals actually received congressional approval before the 100 days were up: a bill curtailing the ability of Congress to impose "unfunded mandates" on the states and legislation making the House and Senate subject to health, safety, labour, and civil rights laws.

At the end of the 100 days, the House Republicans celebrated the fulfillment of their part of the bargain while House Democrats challenged that appraisal or warned that Republican successes did not bode well for the country. Polls indicated that most of "the country" did not know that they were parties to a contract. A *New York Times*/CBS News poll of 1,089 adults conducted April 1–4, 1995, found that only 38% had read or heard anything about it. In a *USA Today*–CNN–Gallup poll of 1,015 adults on March 27–29, 1995, 47% of those polled said that they were unaware of proposals contained in the Contract with America. This raised the question of whether a contract existed at all.

A contract is a legally enforceable agreement in which the parties manifest an intention to contract, commonly referred to as a "meeting of the minds." There are two basic types of contracts: bilateral and unilateral, and most contracts are bilateral, which requires an exchange of mutual promises between the promisor and the promisee. (A unilateral contract, on the other hand, is one in which the offer anticipates performance rather than a reciprocal promise.) Formation of a contract requires mutual assent, consideration, and the absence of any legal or factual bar to the creation of the contract.

Mutual assent consists of an offer—which can be manifested by a promise, an undertaking, or a commitment—and acceptance. There must be certainty in its essential terms, and the offer must be communicated to the offeree. Acceptance is the manifestation of assent to the terms of the offer. It follows that knowledge of the offer is required before there can be a valid acceptance, and silence is rarely an acceptance. In a bilateral contract, acceptance is manifested by the exchange of a counterpromise. (In a unilateral contract an offer can be accepted by undertaking the desired performance.)

Moreover, there must be consideration, or something of value exchanged for the other party's promise, for a contract to be enforceable. For example, consideration can be doing something, or promising to do something, one is otherwise not legally obligated to do. It follows that past consideration—that is, the performance of an already existing duty—does not suffice, on the theory that one cannot bargain for something that is already accomplished. Thus, the performance of a preexisting duty is not consideration.

When these basic principles are applied to the Contract with America, it is questionable whether a legal contract exists at all. If the Contract is a unilateral one, then there must have been an offer and acceptance by means of performance of the desired act. The difficulty is that the House Republicans appear to have made the offer to the American public to enact the 10-point platform but then performed it themselves. The promisor and the promisee were the same entity. On the other hand, it is conceivable that it was the electorate that made the unilateral offer to the Republican candidates for House seats, to the effect that "we promise to elect you in exchange for your performance of the Contract." This scenario is legally plausible but unrealistic, given that more than half of the citizens questioned could not identify or situate the Contract with America, an essential term of any contract.

The Contract with America goes a little farther as a bilateral contract. The exchange of mutual promises could be that the Republican candidates for election to the House promised that they would usher through the House a legislative platform that reflected the issues of most concern to the electorate if the American public promised to elect them to those seats in November. The first difficulty, though, is in determining whether the offer was definite as to the essential terms and whether it was communicated to the offerees, the voting public. The lack of communication is best evidenced by the poll results referred to above, which indicate that most voters did not know what they had contracted for. More important from a legal perspective, there is a question of whether there was consideration supporting the Contract—that is, an exchange of something of value for a promise of performance. Arguably, the voters gave up the right to elect another candidate on the promise that the House Republicans candidates would come through with their promise, but it is not clear what consideration supported the House Republican promise in the first instance. Furthermore, as the Contract with America was presented in its final form after the election, it is arguable that, at best, there was only past consideration supporting the Contract, because once the House Republicans were elected, they had a preexisting duty to heed the mandate of their constituencies. In the absence of consideration, there is not a contract but a gift.

As for a legal or factual bar, one might question whether the parties had legal capacity to contract, particularly given the fact that most Americans subsequently stated that they either did not know they were party to a contract or did not know its contents. It is also arguable that the Contract is unenforceable because the American public made a "unilateral mistake" (a mistake or misunderstanding as to the terms or effect of a contract, made by one of the parties to it but not by the other) in accepting the offer. Although unilateral mistake is usually insufficient to prevent formation of a contract, there is an exception that could apply here. When the unmistaken party (the House Republicans) knows or has reason to know of the mistake made by the other party (the electorate), the unmistaken party would not be permitted to take advantage of the offer.

The media spectacle surrounding the announcement of the Contract and its completion by the House, as promised, in 100 days has faded. To be sure, the close of 1995 provided two opportunities for the resuscitation of the Contract with America—the budget debate, with its partial shutdowns of the government, and the upcoming 1996 presidential election—and the Contract played its part. In the budget debate, polls indicated that voters were not willing to sacrifice Medicare, on top of the pullback of federal entitlements, to achieve a balanced budget or substantial tax reductions. On the election front, the Contract was now a litmus test against which declared and undeclared candidates were to be measured. Even here, though, a candidate's adherence to the 10 planks of the original Contract might turn out to be less important than his or her stand on such issues as abortion or school prayer.

Thus, the Contract with America has become much more, and much less, than it was when first announced. As a legislative agenda comprising 10 specific planks, it has all but disappeared from the landscape. On the other hand, the Contract with America has become a code word defining adherence to Republican ideological orthodoxy.

From a legal perspective, however, one has reason to doubt the legitimacy and enforceability of the undertaking, owing to the absence of a meeting of the minds. History will show whether the Contract with America was a revolution or a media ploy, but the law does not need to wait that long—whatever it is, or will become, in a legal sense the Contract with America is not a contract at all.

SPOTLIGHT: NATIVE AMERICAN CULTURAL FERMENT

Illustration by Istvan Banyai

by Ron McCoy

In the United States and Canada, tribal cultures exist in a delicate, somewhat precarious balance relative to the power and interests of the dominant European cultures. Now, however, national policy in both countries seems to be moving in a direction that favours—or at least accommodates—the promotion of Native American heritage. During 1995, for example, several museums agreed to repatriate culturally sensitive objects to tribes. The Navajo Nation Museum in Window Rock, Ariz., stipulated that a wooden False Face mask in its possession was in fact the rightful property of the Oneida Nation in New York. The Field Museum of Natural History in Chicago responded similarly to the Oneidas' claim to a shell bead wampum belt and recognized the right of the Pawnee tribe in Oklahoma to possess two other significant pieces in its collection, the Little Elk Standing Village Bundle and the Big Black Meteorite Bundle. Such transfers of culturally significant materials represent a dramatic change in public policy.

For many years the American Indian peoples of both the United States and Canada were perceived as a vanishing race—unfortunate, but inevitable, victims of Western civilization's march toward perfection. Today these tribes are not usually depicted as teetering on the brink of cultural or physical extinction. In fact, many members of U.S. Indian tribes and Canada's First Nations actively engage in cultural nurturing and revitalization, including new emphasis on tribal government, identification of stable sources for group economic well-being, and encouragement of the use of indigenous languages. There is also increased concern about the preservation of sacred sites and the repatriation of sacred objects.

The Indian policies of the U.S. and Canada have long developed in tandem. In 1883, for example, the U.S. government's Indian Religious Crimes Code virtually outlawed tribal religions and established Courts of Indian Offenses, staffed by cooperative "progressive" tribe members, to aid Indians in "adopting and following civilized habits and pursuits." The following year the Canadian Indian Act banned communal potlatch giveaway ceremonies among Northwest Pacific Coast tribes because the practice was deemed deleterious to instilling respect for private, as opposed to common, property.

Ultimately, both U.S. and Canadian efforts to eradicate or control tribal religions proved unsuccessful. Although those religions often bent to the winds of change, the old belief systems did not break. Today organized religions such as the Native American Church enjoy broad, intertribal support. Other forms of worship, linked to the land and a belief in myriad spiritual forces, also thrive. The legal battles surrounding the preservation of sacred sites and repatriation of sacred objects have so far largely taken place in the U.S., though developments are keenly watched by the tribal peoples of Canada as well.

Religions throughout the world hold certain geographic locations sacred to their systems of belief. Many among the Hopi, a Puebloan people who have lived in northeastern Arizona since prehistoric times, think of the San Francisco Peaks near Flagstaff as the home of the kachinas, supernatural beings who help bring rain to their arid fields. Likewise, Hopi make pilgrimages to the *sipapu,* a site near the confluence of the Colorado and Little Colorado rivers in the Grand Canyon, believing their ancestors emerged at that spot after escaping from a flood that inundated their previous home below the earth's crust. Some American Indian sacred sites are located on tribal land, some on government land, and still others on private property. No matter where a site is lo-

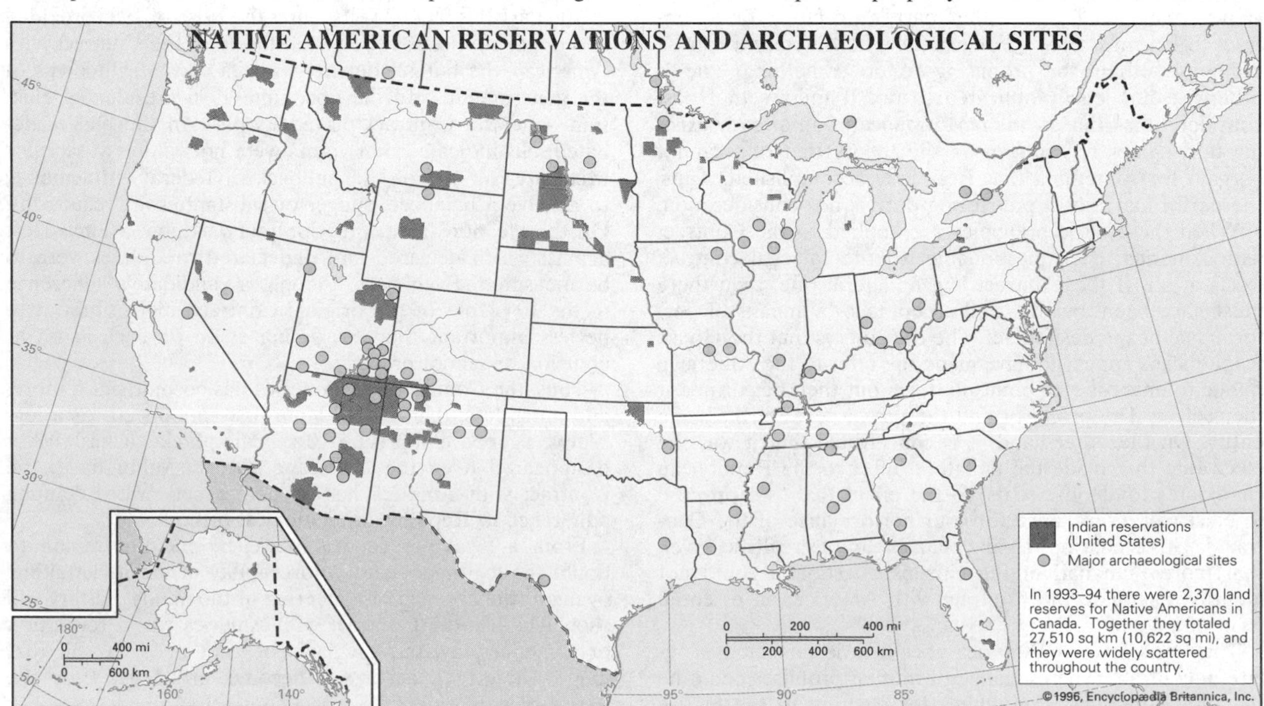

cated, however, its care and condition remain of paramount concern to believers. Understandably, many Hopi resent the presence of ski operations on the San Francisco Peaks.

Likewise, the vitality of a tribal religion depends on its control of the objects it holds sacred. Basically, repatriation involves the return to tribal control of such culturally sensitive items as human remains that may have been recovered during archaeological investigations and physical paraphernalia intimately entwined in the tapestry of indigenous religion. Examples include the Lakota's White Buffalo Calf Woman pipe, the Arapaho's flat pipe, and the Cheyenne's sacred arrows—all currently under tribal control.

Although museums and governmental institutions in North America have sometimes dealt with Indians' concern about sacred sites and objects in a casual and ad hoc fashion, the U.S. legal code is undergoing fundamental changes in response to mounting pressures from tribal peoples. In 1978, reversing the long-standing policy of persecuting, or at best ignoring, tribal religions, the U.S. Congress passed the American Indian Religious Freedom Act. AIRFA commits the federal government to protecting and preserving "for American Indians their inherent right of freedom to believe, express, and exercise the traditional religions . . . including but not limited to access to sites, use and possession of sacred objects, and the freedom to worship through ceremonials and traditional rites." The Archaeological Resources Protection Act of 1979 restricts the removal of "archaeological resources on public lands and Indian lands," categorizing such materials as "an accessible and irreplaceable part of the Nation's heritage." In some jurisdictions the legal protection now has been extended to cover artifacts on private land as well. This may be leading in the direction of Roman law, which held that recovered objects of antiquity were the property of the entire nation. Although this is not yet the position of the U.S. or Canadian government, the concept appears to be gaining some currency in both nations.

Through the Native American Graves Protection and Repatriation Act (NAGPRA) of 1990, U.S. law addresses not only human remains (also covered in the National Museum of the American Indian Act of 1989, which focuses on the return of remains housed at the Smithsonian Institution) but "sacred objects" as well, defined as "ceremonial objects which are needed by traditional Native American religious leaders for the practice of traditional Native American religions by their present day adherents." NAGPRA also defines "cultural patrimony" as "an object having ongoing historical, traditional, or cultural importance central to the Native American group or culture itself, rather than property owned by an individual Native American, and which, therefore, cannot be alienated, appropriated, or conveyed by any individual regardless of whether or not the individual is a member of the Indian tribe." Because ownership is communal, an object of cultural patrimony is "considered inalienable by such Native American group at the time the object was separated from such group."

NAGPRA allows tribes to press claims for the repatriation of certain categories of objects from any institution receiving federal funds. There is no statute of limitations. Some of the objects returned to tribal control under NAGPRA include: a Hopi Koyemsi (Mudhead) mask, a bandolier used in the Navajo Enemyway ceremony, several Zuni war god carvings, the Elk Tongue Beaver Bundle of the Blackfeet, and 31,651 funerary objects sacred to the Pawnee.

The repatriation of objects under NAGPRA remains controversial, but sacred sites issues are perhaps even more difficult to resolve, especially when the sites in question are no longer under tribal control. In *United States* v. *Sioux Nation of Indians* (1980), for example, the U.S. Supreme Court ruled that the government's 1877 acquisition of the Black Hills region of South Dakota from the seven Lakota tribes was extralegal. Although the Lakota were offered substantial monetary compensation, all seven tribal governments refused to accept payment, insisting upon the return of the land they regard as a holy place. As far as the Lakota are concerned, the issue remains unresolved.

A young Nez Perce woman stands on ancestral land in Idaho and gazes toward the sky. Like other American Indian peoples, the Nez Percé have begun to nurture their traditional culture, which includes speaking indigenous languages and preserving sacred sites.
PHIL BORGES

Conflicts over sites of religious significance can occur between tribes as well—or even divide a single tribe. Some Navajo in northern Arizona, for example, revere sites in the Chuska Mountains, while others work for the tribe's logging company that harvests timber in the Chuskas. Strip mining of coal on Black Mesa, another site of spiritual significance, is offensive to some Navajo despite support for the mining corporation by the Navajo tribal government.

One might expect the First Amendment to the U.S. Constitution to provide some protection to sacred places, but this has not been the case to date. In *Lyng* v. *Northwest Indian Cemetery Protective Association* (1987), the Supreme Court announced that the government's use of federal land thought of as sacred by an Indian tribe does not impose an onerous burden on the free exercise of religion, even if that use results in the physical destruction of the site. Still, the freedom of religion issue lies at the core of tribal perceptions about sacred sites. As the *Lyng* case implies, this is something of an ambiguous area in U.S. law, a condition almost certainly attributable to the fact that Indian religions were long grouped with superstitions. This view seems to be losing favour, although Euro-American conceptions of property rights will require considerable adjustment to accommodate the spiritual needs and claims of the continent's oldest inhabitants.

Ron McCoy is director of the Center for Great Plains Studies at Emporia (Kansas) State University and is the author of *Kiowa Memories: Images from Indian Territory, 1880.*

State and Local Affairs

The U.S. states were at the epicentre of national policy debates during 1995. The Republican Congress attempted to transfer responsibility back to state and local levels. Although budget disagreements at year-end prevented any substantial transfer of federal funding to states via block grants, the trend toward increased state powers during the year was unmistakable.

The states continued their leadership role in devising innovative answers to social concerns, from welfare to corrections to health care. The crackdown on crime continued to have repercussions, with state prison populations topping the one million mark for the first time. A strong national economy and conservative-trending politics led to record state tax cuts during the year. Affirmative action was challenged in California, the nation's most populous state, and measures allowing the carrying of concealed weapons were approved in several states, but the enthusiasm for limiting the terms of public officials stalled.

Party Strengths. After two consecutive years of substantial advances, Republicans failed to make additional major gains in 1995 state elections. Persistent party switching, particularly in the South, however, gave the Republicans control of more state legislative chambers at year-end than at any other time since the early 1930s. In November gubernatorial balloting Republicans wrested away one additional governorship, in Louisiana, boosting their total to 31. Democrats had 18 governorships at year-end, with one (Maine) held by an independent.

Democrats gained an edge in limited off-year legislative elections. In the most closely watched balloting, Democrats thwarted a Republican assault on both of Virginia's legislative chambers, although Republicans did manage a tie in the state Senate. Going into 1995, Republicans controlled both houses in 20 legislatures, with Democrats having two-house majorities in 19. Party switches during the year reduced the Democrats' control to 17 states. Following the November balloting, Republicans had control of legislatures in 19 states and Democrats in 16, with 14 states split. (Nebraska had a unicameral, nonpartisan legislature.)

Government Structures and Powers. Federalism—the distribution of power between Washington, D.C., and the states—enjoyed a resurgence in 1995. Governors, state legislators, the Republican Congress, and the nation's courts all participated. The United States Supreme Court gave states victories in such areas as health care spending, welfare, school desegregation, prisoner lawsuits, and parole policy. For its part, Congress moved toward giving back the responsibility and funding, via block grants, to states in areas such as welfare, Medicaid, and job training.

Early in the year, Congress overwhelmingly approved a law curbing "unfunded mandates," federal laws imposed on states without funds for their enforcement. State officials lobbied Washington virtually nonstop during the year for fewer strings on federally assisted programs. Governors were particularly active in seeking a compromise on Medicaid grants, the health program for low-income citizens. Both congressional and state Republicans generally favoured block grants for such programs. Democrats were less enthusiastic, worrying that states would abandon support for the poor. No significant changes were instituted, however, largely because of unresolved disagreements with Pres. Bill Clinton.

The states were affected by the two partial federal shutdowns over the budget late in the year. Fearing the loss of revenue from tourism, Arizona Gov. Fife Symington, for example, sent National Guard troops to the Grand Canyon in November in an attempt to reopen the national park, shuttered in the budget fight. A month later Arizona and New Mexico averted a second lockout by using state funds to keep furloughed federal park workers on the job at the Grand Canyon and Carlsbad Caverns.

In a startling 5–4 ruling, the U.S. Supreme Court struck down the Gun-Free School Zone Act of 1990 as an unconstitutional federal infringement on state powers. It was the first time since 1935 that the high court had thrown out a federal law on the grounds that the Congress had exceeded its authority under the commerce clause. Even when the states lost, however, the Supreme Court's reasoning heartened advocates of federalism. In another 5–4 decision invalidating 23 state laws setting term limits for Congress, a solid minority maintained that states must be allowed to exercise all powers not specifically withheld from them by the Constitution.

The trend toward federalism produced a number of developments with major influences on everyday lives. After Congress repealed the speed-limit mandate on states in November, for example, only five (Connecticut, Delaware, Hawaii, New Jersey, and Rhode Island) opted to retain the 55-mph limit in nonurban areas. Most states went to 65 or 70 mph as a new limit, but Nevada and Wyoming immediately allowed 75 mph. Montana abolished daytime speed limits entirely but kept a 65-mph limit at night.

At year-end, Congress banned states from taxing the pension income of former residents living in other states.

The five-year trend toward imposing term limits on public officials seemed to stall during 1995. Not only did the Supreme Court invalidate state attempts to cap congressional terms, but no new state legislatures joined the 23 states that previously had imposed limits. In the only general balloting on the idea, Mississippi voters in November rejected a proposal to limit the terms of most state officials. North Carolina joined the other 49 states in granting veto authority to its governor. The constitutional amendment was subject to ratification by state voters in 1996.

Oregon enacted a law requiring special elections to be held via mail balloting. At year-end, filling an open U.S. Senate seat, Oregon staged the nation's first congressional election conducted entirely by mail. Although critics worried about possible electioneering misconduct, no serious fraud complaints were reported.

Maryland legislators rebelled after Gov. Parris Glendening promised professional football team owners substantial concessions for relocating teams to Maryland. After the governor offered to pay $78 million for road improvements in Prince Georges county for the Washington Redskins and to build a $200 million stadium in Baltimore rent-free for the Cleveland Browns, legislators ordered renegotiations.

Finances. Buoyed by an expanding economy and spurred by Republican political advances, the states cut taxes by $1.1 billion during 1995, the biggest aggregate state tax cut in a decade. Combined with previously enacted cuts, the overall tax liability of residents fell by $3.1 billion during the year, a record drop. The reduction in taxes would have been even greater, analysts said, except for fears about the effects of federal deficit reduction and of the devolution of greater responsibilities to the states.

Personal income levies were the source of the bulk of state tax cuts. Arizona, Delaware, and New Jersey cut personal income rates, while the top rates in California and New York fell under previous

BRIAN PLONKA—COPLEY NEWS SERVICE

A patient receives care at home, one of the ways medical providers were trying to cut costs. Proposals to slow the growth of Medicare and to convert Medicaid into a state block-grant program met with strong resistance from groups advocating for the elderly and the poor.

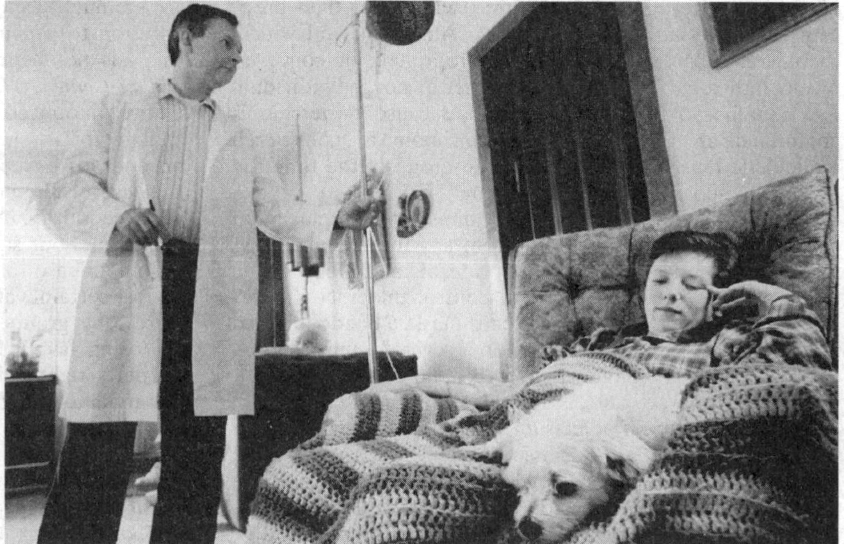

legislation. A number of states—including Arizona, Delaware, Iowa, Michigan, North Carolina, and Ohio—increased personal exemptions and standard deductions. Connecticut also granted a personal credit for property taxes, while Iowa and Virginia increased their pension exclusions for retirees, and New York expanded its earned income credit for low-income workers.

Montana and Oregon authorized large personal income tax rebates during the year. Business taxes were reduced in three states; Michigan and Pennsylvania trimmed major corporate taxes, while Oregon also provided business tax rebates. Only three states—Hawaii, South Dakota, and Vermont—authorized significant overall tax increases, and some of their levies were offset by local tax reductions.

Although several states extended health care provider taxes that were due to expire, three states—Illinois, New Hampshire, and Rhode Island—reduced levies on Medicaid providers. Sales tax changes were minor, with Kansas and Washington providing additional exemptions and South Dakota broadening its sales tax base in order to provide property tax relief.

Among excise tax actions, cigarette taxes were raised in Arizona (by voter initiative), Rhode Island, South Dakota, Vermont, Washington, and Wisconsin. Washington's cigarette tax rose to 81.5 cents per pack on July 1, the highest in the U.S. New Mexico and New York reduced motor fuels taxes, and Oregon reduced trucker taxes, while Connecticut boosted its gas levy.

North Carolina repealed its intangibles tax. Utah and Washington reduced statewide property taxes. Idaho, South Carolina, and Wisconsin provided local property tax relief by putting more state funds into schools. Pennsylvania repealed an inheritance tax on surviving spouses, and Kentucky began a four-year phaseout of its inheritance tax.

Education. In December a coalition of 21 western state governors announced plans for developing a "virtual university" over the next decade. Students would have access to classroom and teaching materials via computers, television, the Internet, and other high-tech devices, making long distance learning a reality. Alabama approved a new education law specifically allowing educators to impose corporal punishment.

Health and Welfare. As the U.S. Congress deliberated over reform of the welfare system, widely judged a failure nationwide, states continued to create innovative solutions on their own. Massachusetts, Connecticut, and New Hampshire joined Indiana and Wisconsin in tough new legislation requiring the poor to work. The new laws typically required all able-bodied welfare recipients with no children under age six to work, granted credits to businesses hiring them, and assigned public service duties if jobs were not available.

Arkansas, Maryland, New Jersey, New York, Oregon, and Wyoming moved to combat excessive managed-care cost-saving techniques by approving "patient protection acts" to preserve the choice of doctors. The Arkansas law was particularly tough, allowing any person under managed-care to go to "any willing provider" of medical services. Statutes in Maryland and New Jersey required health insurers to provide new mothers and their children with specified minimum hospital care. The new laws mandated the provision of at least 48 hours of hospital care following a normal birth and 96 hours following a cesarean section. Similar laws were pending in eight other states.

Montana, New Mexico, Utah, and West Virginia joined nine other states approving medical savings accounts. The accounts were designed to reduce health care consumption by making consumers responsible for their own health payments.

A federal court invalidated a state law allowing Oregon doctors to prescribe lethal doses of medication for dying patients. The judge declared that the law, approved by state voters in 1994, violated the U.S. Constitution's equal protection clause.

Reversing a 20-year national trend, Washington became the first state to toughen its law on runaway youngsters. The new measure allowed police to pick up runaways and return them to their parents, required schools to report all truancies, and permitted parents to commit their children for drug or mental health care. Most states had previously decriminalized running away, leaving parents without legal recourse.

Massachusetts began putting the names and pictures of individuals in arrears on child-support payments on the Internet. The state's revenue department had previously sponsored a successful "Ten Most Wanted" poster campaign.

Maryland joined California, Utah, Vermont, and Washington in banning smoking in most workplaces. Massachusetts joined Florida, Minnesota, Mississippi, and West Virginia in suing the tobacco industry to recover $1 billion in state-paid health costs. A federal appeals court overturned a Colorado constitutional amendment that prohibited the state from funding abortions except in cases where the mother's life was at risk. The state had to pay for abortions as long as it accepted federal Medicaid money, the court ruled.

Laws and Justice. Washington state's sexual predator law, the first in the nation to keep sex criminals in confinement after they had served their sentences, was invalidated by a federal court on the grounds that it punished an offender twice for a single crime. Ohio voters approved a measure requiring the governor to consult with parole authorities before cutting any prison sentences. Pennsylvania voters allowed children to testify via videotape or television in highly charged cases. Alabama legislators repealed a unique law requiring rape victims to pay up to $200 for a forensic examination.

States continued to ease restrictions on concealed weapons. Following action in a dozen states, only eight states—Illinois, Kansas, Kentucky, Missouri, Nebraska, New Mexico, Ohio, and Wisconsin—now generally prohibited private citizens from carrying concealed guns for self-protection. Florida had led the trend with a 1987 law, and gun enthusiasts noted that the state's homicide rate had dropped significantly in the ensuing eight years.

After 18 consecutive years of legislative approval followed by gubernatorial vetoes, New York in March became the 38th state to provide for capital punishment. States executed 56 convicts during 1995, the highest total since capital punishment was reinstated by the U.S. Supreme Court in 1976. Nearly 200 individuals were sentenced to death over the same period, however, which left some 3,100 inmates on death row at year-end.

Ethics. Arkansas Gov. Jim Guy Tucker was indicted on June 7 by a federal grand jury on three felony counts alleging conspiracy to defraud the Internal Revenue Service and Small Business Administration over cable television contracts. Tucker was charged again on August 17 on an additional fraud count alleging loan laundering to deceive state and federal authorities. The charges were pressed by an independent counsel investigating the role of present and former Arkansas officials and bankers in the so-called Whitewater affair.

Joseph Salema, chief of staff to former New Jersey governor James Florio, pleaded guilty on February 23 to one count in a kickback payment scheme to direct municipal bond business. In Florida, a former Escambia county commissioner was among those pleading guilty on March 3 to bribery in a similar case. Former Pennsylvania attorney general Ernie Preate was sentenced to 14 months in prison on December 15 after pleading guilty to felony mail fraud. Preate was accused of having failed to report $20,000 in campaign contributions from video poker operators.

Minnesota's Democrat-Farmer-Labor Party was jolted during the fall when six state representatives and two state senators were arrested on various unrelated charges ranging from domestic assault and shoplifting to felony drunk driving and fraud. One defendant, charged with 24 counts of conspiracy, bribery, mail fraud, and theft, offered a novel defense; Sen. Harold ("Skip") Finn claimed that the federal government could not legally prosecute him because he was a Native American. A federal judge rejected the argument.

A new ethics law in Alabama required all public employees making $50,000 or more to publicly report all outside income, debts, and assets. When critics noted that college coaches were specifically exempted, Alabama's governor promised remedial legislation in 1996.

Prisons. Accelerated state prison construction continued to open new beds. According to the U.S. Department of Justice, the number of state prisoners surged by 9.1% during the year to reach 1,004,608 at midyear. The jump, the largest annual increase in the nation's history, meant that the U.S. was locking up a larger percentage of its residents than any other nation.

Inmate growth was attributed to stiff mandatory sentences for violent and drug crimes, toughened parole rules, and an increased likelihood of being imprisoned once arrested. A 1995 Department of Justice study showed that 104 of every 1,000 persons arrested for drug offenses went to prison, compared with only 19 of every 1,000 in 1980.

In part because federal and state sentencing guidelines mandated stiffer sentences for crack cocaine, used mainly by blacks, than for powder cocaine, used mostly by whites, civil rights groups charged racial discrimination in the faster growth of minority inmates. Only 13% of the U.S. population was black, but blacks accounted for nearly half of the nation's prisoner population. Some 6.8% of all black male adults were in prison or jail at midyear, compared with less than 1% of white male adults.

Prisoners in Alabama have their leg irons adjusted before beginning work on a chain gang along a highway. Not since the 1980s had a U.S. state shackled prisoners with leg irons, but Alabama officials pledged to crack down on criminals and problem prisoners and also wanted to cut costs.
DONNA BINDER—IMPACT VISUALS

Another study showed that at midyear a record 2.9 million adults were on probation and another 690,000 on parole following a prison sentence. Probation and parole populations nationwide had tripled since 1980.

The beginnings of a backlash against spiraling convict populations were evident during the year, however. New York's newly elected Republican Gov. George Pataki successfully proposed repealing a mandatory prison law for drug convictions. Seventeen other states enacted presumptive sentencing rules designed to ensure that prison beds went first to violent offenders.

Another trend involved making prison life as unpleasant as possible. Arizona, Florida, and Mississippi joined Alabama in reinstituting high-profile, well-publicized chain gangs for inmate work. More than a dozen states approved regulations restricting prisoner access to amenities such as weight-lifting equipment, television, and telephones. California became the first state to prohibit inmates from being interviewed by journalists. Five states restricted tobacco use by prisoners, and Kansas, Oregon, Texas, and Utah banned smoking altogether.

Reacting to what was perceived as escalating abuse of the legal process, the U.S. Supreme Court ruled that most state prisoner lawsuits complaining about the "ordinary incidents of prison life" should be dismissed. The ruling promised to reduce the more than 30,000 federal suits filed annually by state prisoners, most of which were considered a costly nuisance by administrators.

A nationwide trend toward contracting out correctional facility construction and operation to private firms continued during the year. Thirty-two states had established statutory authority to contract for private corrections by year-end, and nearly 50,000 prisoners were being held in 88 secure adult facilities run by private companies. Advocates said that privatization, growing by an estimated 25% per year, was already saving taxpayers at least $150 million annually.

Gambling. Proponents of state-sanctioned games of chance had mixed luck during the year. Legislators in Florida and New York approved proposals to set up casino gambling in selected areas, subject to voter approval in 1996.

Several problems arose in gambling, however. Prominent Louisiana legislators were subpoenaed in a federal probe of alleged payoffs to protect gambling interests, and in Mississippi eight persons were indicted on charges of fixing blackjack games. Casino gambling bills were rejected in Alabama and Pennsylvania, and the proposed expansion of riverboat gambling to the Chicago area stalled in the Illinois legislature. Governors in Michigan and Texas rejected the expansion of gambling in their states.

Backers of a Washington state initiative to allow video poker and slot machines in American Indian casinos came up with a unique selling point; they offered to share 10% of all profits with everyone who voted in the November election, or an estimated $100 per voter every year. In a resulting backlash, critics charged gaming proponents with trying to buy votes, and the measure was defeated.

The Alaska legislature allowed organizers of the Iditarod sled dog race to stage a fund-raising sweepstakes. Sponsors of the $2 million annual race were fewer in recent years because of protests from animal rights activists.

The Environment. California put the brakes on antismog regulations that would have required automakers to sell more than 20,000 electric-powered cars per year in the state starting in 1998. The reversal came after both domestic and foreign manufacturers complained that the best available battery technology did not allow sufficient range.

Several states tangled with the federal government over a tough new centralized emissions testing regulation imposed under the 1990 Clean Air Act. Connecticut, Maine, New Jersey, New York, and Texas rebelled, forcing the Environmental Protection Agency to allow simpler, less burdensome testing that put the states into compliance.

Civil Rights. Federal courts continued to wrestle with the constitutionality of black-majority congressional districts drawn to ensure minority representation, but no clear guidelines emerged. Judges threw out black-majority districts in Georgia, North Carolina, and Texas on the grounds that they were drawn primarily for racial reasons. The U.S. Supreme Court heard two new cases in the fall, however, and experts awaited more definitive rulings in 1996.

For the first time, substantial opposition to the concept of affirmative action emerged in the states. Several states joined President Clinton in initiating research on the effectiveness of affirmative action programs.

California Gov. Pete Wilson banned most affirmative action hiring and contracting by state agencies, pushed the University of California to drop admissions policies that favoured applicants according to race, and even sued his own state government to rid it of racial preferences, goals, and set-asides. Wilson acted while running as a Republican presidential candidate, and critics accused him of pandering to conservatives. Even so, complaints by whites and a more conservative political climate put affirmative action on the defensive during much of the year.

The ban on taking race or sex into account in hiring, promotions, or admissions at the University of California was particularly controversial. Some academics charged that the number of black and Hispanic students at the university's Los Angeles and Berkeley campuses would drop significantly, while Asians would increase.

Michigan approved a law requiring that state education and employment forms include "multiracial" as a classification for people having parents of different races. "Other" was no longer to be used.

A federal appeals court ordered South Carolina to establish a comparable, separate collegiate program for women or else to enroll a woman at the Citadel, a state-supported military school. The woman was admitted, but after encountering difficulty with the rigorous physical drills, she dropped out. California became the first state prohibiting employers from refusing to allow employees to wear pants solely on the basis of their sex.

By a 53–47% margin, Maine voters rejected a ballot initiative prohibiting state laws that protected homosexuals as a group. The bill's sponsors said that they were outspent 12–1 by out-of-state gay rights groups, but the winners hailed the result as a rejection of right-wing discrimination.

Consumer Protection. Massachusetts joined Maryland and Vermont in requiring that consumers receive free access to their credit reports. The new Massachusetts law held providers of credit information legally liable for mistakes on a report. About 20 states now had some type of credit-reporting regulation.

In a 5–4 decision, the U.S. Supreme Court upheld a Florida law prohibiting lawyers from sending sales letters to accident victims or their relatives within 30 days of the mishap. Justice Sandra Day O'Connor, writing for the majority, justified the law as preventing lawyers from "engaging in conduct that . . . is universally regarded as deplorable." Hawaii became the 25th state to require that home sellers disclose the details of defects in property.

(DAVID C. BECKWITH)

URUGUAY

A republic of eastern South America, Uruguay lies on the Atlantic Ocean. Area: 176,215 sq km (68,037 sq mi). Pop. (1995 est.): 3,186,000. Cap.: Montevideo. Monetary unit: peso uruguayo, with (Oct. 6, 1995) a free rate of 6.60 pesos uruguayos to U.S. $1 (10.43 pesos uruguayos = £1 sterling). Presidents in 1995, Luis Alberto Lacalle and, from March 1, Julio María Sanguinetti.

Having won the November 1994 elections with a majority of less than 1%, Julio María Sanguinetti of the centre-right Colorado Party took office as president of Uruguay on March 1, 1995. In one of his first acts as president, Sanguinetti proposed sweeping constitutional and economic reforms. The *ley de lemas,* a long-established electoral system that allows any number of candidates to run for president, was to be replaced by a party-based system of primary and national elections. Sanguinetti, along with the left-wing Broad Front and the Social Democratic New Space parties, believed that the change would reduce the legislative factionalism that had thwarted previous moves to tackle the country's trade gap and its social security burden.

In June the minister of economy and finance, Luis Mosca, announced a five-year austerity budget aimed at reducing inflation, which was 45% in 1994, and cutting government spending from 35% of gross domestic product (GDP) to 30%. His policies, many of which had been unsuccessfully attempted by the outgoing National (Blanco) Party government, centred on tax increases and pension reforms since the cost of pensions had risen from 10% of GDP in 1990 to an estimated 15% in 1995. The general workers confederation staged a 24-hour strike protesting a bill that would postpone the retirement age and introduce a pension system based on personal savings. Further cuts included a reduction in public-sector employment and a privatization program.

Mosca hoped to reduce Uruguay's trade deficit of $600 million by means of exports to Argentina and Brazil. Despite Uruguay's objections, the Southern Cone Common Market (Mercosur), consisting of Argentina, Brazil, Paraguay, and Uruguay, became operational on Jan. 1, 1995.

(CHERRY AUSTIN)

UZBEKISTAN

A republic of Central Asia, Uzbekistan borders the Aral Sea to the north, Kazakhstan to the north and west, Turkmenistan to the southwest, Afghanistan to the south, and Tajikistan and Kyrgyzstan to the east. Area: 447,400 sq km (172,700 sq mi). Pop. (1995 est.): 22,886,000. Cap.: Tashkent (Uzbek: Toshkent). Monetary unit: sum, with (Oct. 4, 1995) a free rate of 33.80 sumy to U.S. $1 (53.72 sumy = £1 sterling). President in 1995, Islam Karimov; prime minister, Abdulhashim Mutalov.

Throughout 1995 Uzbekistan's diplomatic representatives in the West made notable efforts to overcome the negative impression created in earlier years by their country's poor human rights record and the slow pace of market reform. Fearful of increasingly close Iranian ties with neighbouring Tajikistan and Turkmenistan, Uzbekistan actively supported the U.S. trade embargo against Iran.

In January Uzbekistan received a $74 million loan to help the country stabilize its currency and accelerate privatization. The International Monetary Fund noted that the inflation rate had been halved and the budget deficit cut to 3.5% of the gross national product, with a significant reduction in the unemployment rate. One of the major foreign deals of the year was an agreement on Japanese credits for the development of the Kokdumalak oil and gas field.

A woman stands on the balcony of a palace, next to a mosaic-covered wall, in the Uzbek town of Khiva. Like the cities of Samarkand and Bukhara, Khiva was in danger of losing many of its historic buildings unless the money to restore them properly could be found.
HECTOR MATA—AFP

Uzbekistan's new parliament, the Olii Majlis (Supreme Assembly), elected in December 1994 and January 1995, proposed a referendum on extending Pres. Islam Karimov's term in office until 2000 in order to maintain political stability. The referendum, on March 26, produced an overwhelming vote in favour of the president.

A few days after the referendum, the Supreme Court sentenced several activists of the banned opposition Erk (Freedom) Democratic Party to jail terms ranging from 5 to 12 years on charges of seeking to overthrow the existing order. Protests by foreign human rights groups against the sentences and other human rights violations by the Uzbek authorities had little effect.

Karimov refused to endorse Kazakh Pres. Nursultan Nazarbaev's scheme for a Eurasian Union comprising the successor states to the U.S.S.R. Although relations with Russia remained cordial, in May the Uzbek leader called for the creation of a "common Turkestan," a union of Central Asian states, to counter outside pressure on Central Asia, warning that unnamed powers could "conquer us one by one." Foreign observers concluded that his chief concern was the rise of imperialist sentiment in Russia. This concern did not prevent Karimov from expressing an interest in joining the customs union of Russia, Belarus, and Kazakhstan that went into force in 1995.

Uzbekistan remained the main provider of foreign aid to civil-war-torn Tajikistan after the Russian Federation, but persistent reports throughout the year indicated that the Uzbek leadership was increasingly nervous at the presence of some 25,000 Russian troops on Tajik soil as part of the Commonwealth of Independent States (CIS) peacekeeping contingent stationed in that country. In early April Karimov infuriated the neocommunist government of Tajikistan when he failed to notify them that he planned to meet with the deputy head of the Tajik Islamic opposition prior to the start of talks between opposition and government representatives in Moscow. For Karimov this was a major reversal of policy, as he had been one of the chief supporters of armed CIS resistance to Islamic forces in Tajikistan since the beginning of the civil war in 1992. (BESS BROWN)

This article updates the *Macropædia* article CENTRAL ASIA: *Uzbekistan.*

VANUATU

The republic of Vanuatu, a member of the Commonwealth, comprises 12 main islands and some 60 smaller ones in the southwestern Pacific Ocean. Area: 12,190 sq km (4,707 sq mi). Pop. (1995 est.): 168,000. Cap.: Vila. Monetary unit: vatu, with (Oct. 6, 1995) a free rate of 112.30 vatu to U.S. $1 (172.53 vatu = £1 sterling). President in 1995, Jean-Marie Leye; prime minister, Maxime Carlot Korman.

Late in 1994 the government sought a Supreme Court ruling on controversial uses of the president's judicial power. In mid-1995 Supreme Court Judge Robert Kent resigned, claiming that the chief justice was too closely linked to the government and was acting in its interest.

In 1994 the government had restructured the provincial councils, and after subsequent elections two councils each were controlled by the Unity Front (UF), the Vanuatu National United Party (VNUP), and the Union of Moderate Parties (UMP). The November elections gave no party a majority. The UF took 20 of the 50 seats, the UMP 17, and the VNUP 9.

Tax issues were the subject of debate in 1995, with local businesses seeking the same tax advantages that applied to offshore companies. A 4% turnover tax went into effect on import, export, and retail businesses on April 1.

When French nuclear testing resumed in September, Vanuatu refused to join the other members of the South Pacific Forum in their condemnation, on the grounds that it was France's domestic matter. (BARRIE MACDONALD)

This article updates the *Macropædia* article PACIFIC ISLANDS: *Vanuatu.*

VATICAN CITY STATE

The independent sovereignty of Vatican City State is surrounded by but is not part of Rome. As a state with territorial limits, it is properly distinguished from the Holy See, which constitutes the worldwide administrative and legislative body for the Roman Catholic Church. Area: 44 ha (109 ac). Pop. (1995 est.): 1,000. As sovereign pontiff, John Paul II is the chief of state. Vatican City is administered by a pontifical commission of five cardinals headed by the secretary of state, in 1995 Angelo Cardinal Sodano.

The year 1995 began with a powerful expression of support for Pope John Paul II during his visit to the Philippines, where half a million faithful gathered for mass with the Holy Father. This titanic display of sympathy belied troubled relations with Asia's largest Roman Catholic country, which had implemented family-planning methods that were in contrast with the teachings of the Roman Catholic hierarchy.

Concern for moral issues punctuated the entire year, and even at home the Holy See felt compelled to require that its 1,350 lay employees endorse a code allowing them to be sacked for such moral lapses as abortion and divorce. Another doctrinal issue was the ordination of women, on which the pope's ban was reasserted.

The Vatican maintained a high profile in world affairs, including visits by the pope to the U.S., Sri Lanka, Slovakia, and a host of other countries. After the slaying of Israeli Prime Minister Yitzhak Rabin (*see* OBITUARIES) in November, the pontiff received Rabin's widow, as well as the representative of the Palestine Liberation Organization, in order to discuss problems for peace in the Middle East.

It was another positive financial year for the Holy See, which continued the recent trend of operating in the black after years of budgetary worries. (GREGORY O. SMITH)

See also RELIGION: *Roman Catholic Church.*

This article updates the *Micropædia* article VATICAN CITY.

VENEZUELA

A republic of northern South America, Venezuela lies on the Caribbean Sea. Area: 912,050 sq km (352,144 sq mi). Pop. (1995 est.): 21,844,000. Cap.: Caracas. Monetary unit: bolívar, with (Oct. 6, 1995) an official (fixed) rate of 170 bolivares to U.S. $1 (268.75 bolivares = £1 sterling). President in 1995 Rafael Caldera.

The year 1995 began as 1994 had ended; following the collapse of a major financial group, Grupo Latino Americano, in December, January saw the failure of three more banks, leading to state intervention in Banco Italo-Venezolano, Banco Profesional, and Banco Principal. Two other banks, Banco Unión and Banco Federal, almost collapsed at the same time but were rescued by private bailout packages. By the end of August, 18 of the 41 private banks that had existed at the beginning of 1994 had been taken over by the government, and an estimated 70% of commercial bank deposits were under government control.

In early February, Finance Minister Julio Sosa Rodríguez resigned, and Pres. Rafael Caldera appointed Luis Raúl Matos Azócar as his replacement. Although a recent political opponent of Caldera, Azócar supported the president in the face of growing Cabinet divisions over economic policy. Not only did the president win support for the retention of government controls, but he also won greater-than-normal powers from Congress with three new bills. The new exchange regime bill imposed severe penalties for breaking exchange controls; the consumer protection law established price controls and state intervention in the affairs of private business; and the finance emergency law allowed direct control of the banking system. These laws also allowed Caldera to restore the constitutional rights that had been suspended at the end of June 1994 in an attempt to prevent capital flight and seize assets from fugitive bankers.

Although inflation figures for the first seven months of 1995 were an improvement on the previous year—25.5% compared with 37.6%—inflationary pressure remained high owing to price controls. The government's target of 40% annual inflation looked increasingly unrealistic, and by September the annual figure had been set at 57%. An anti-inflation pact agreed to between government, unions, and the main employers confederation fell apart when it became apparent that the government's revised budget proposals would prove inadequate to reduce the growing deficit. Ocepre, the government's budget office, forecast a 1995 deficit of $5.4 billion, or 6.9% of gross domestic product (GDP), but only $3.8 billion was allocated for debt servicing in the 1995 budget plan. Some efforts were made to cut government expenditure, namely, by not increasing public-sector wages in line with inflation. Two weeks before unions were asked to accept a pay freeze, however, Congress voted itself a 46% pay increase, which only encouraged unions to demand a doubling of the minimum wage.

Labour tensions grew steadily throughout the year. A strike by air traffic controllers was ended by military intervention, and court employees paralyzed the entire judicial system for weeks during an industrial action that ended in August. Social unrest grew, and disturbances became a frequent occurrence in all major cities as a consequence of rising food prices and shortages of basic goods. On September 10 the government risked further public disquiet when it raised gasoline prices. The average cost more than doubled but was still below production cost of 10.5 bolívares per litre (26 cents per gallon).

Revenue from the state-owned oil company, Petróleos de Venezuela (PDVSA), fell sharply as a percentage of GDP despite stronger-than-expected world oil prices and output volumes. This was due to the fact that most of PDVSA's income was in U.S. dollars and the bolívar had appreciated in real terms because of the fixed exchange rate.

The government's efforts to attract foreign investments through privatization continued to prove unsuccessful. Then, in July, Venezuela allowed foreign equity and investment in oil exploration and production for the first time since the nationalization of the petroleum industry in 1976. Congress approved a model profit-sharing contract under which PDVSA would be able to call for international tenders on exploring and developing 10 areas containing light and medium crude reserves. This agreement would allow the establishment of joint ventures with private companies to develop and produce from these areas.

The December 3 elections reflected the unpopularity of the Caldera government, with 13 of the 22 governorships and half the mayoralties at stake going to the opposition party, Democratic Action. The government responded by devaluing the bolívar by 41%, from 170 to the dollar to 290. Finance Minister Azócar said he hoped this action would help Venezuela secure $3 billion in financial support from the International Monetary Fund. (ALAN MURPHY)

VIETNAM

The socialist republic of Vietnam occupies the eastern part of the Indochinese Peninsula in Southeast Asia and is bounded on the south and east by the South China Sea. Area: 331,041 sq km (127,816 sq mi). Pop. (1995 est.): 74,545,000. Cap.: Hanoi. Monetary unit: dong, with (Oct. 6, 1995) a free rate of 11,014 dong to U.S. $1 (17,412 dong = £1 sterling). President in 1995, Le Duc Anh; prime minister, Vo Van Kiet.

A series of milestones made 1995 a pivotal year for Vietnam as it continued to undo its decades of isolation. On January 28 Vietnam and the U.S. opened liaison offices in each other's capital, and on August 5 they formally established diplomatic relations. Warren Christopher, the first U.S. secretary of state to visit Hanoi, attended the opening of the U.S. embassy. This was a clear sign that the former adversaries were putting some 40 years of animosity behind them. Pres. Bill Clinton, however, reiterated the U.S. concern that about 2,200 American soldiers still considered missing in action in Southeast Asia had not yet been accounted for.

Perhaps of greater immediate significance to the nation was Vietnam's admission as a full member into the Association of Southeast Asian Nations (ASEAN) on July 28. Ironically, the all-capitalist grouping of Brunei, Indonesia, Malaysia, the Philippines, Singapore, and Thailand was formed in 1967 partly to counter what were perceived to be expansionist threats posed by the communist nation. Vietnam was expected to have enhanced opportunities for investment and trade with ASEAN, which already accounted for about a quarter of its trade. Vietnam also signed a historic multilateral pact on the management of the Mekong River. Vietnam, Cambodia, Laos, and Thailand—with China and Myanmar (Burma) as observers—signed the Agreement on Cooperation for the Sustainable Development of the Mekong River Basin in April. Among other things, the 42-clause accord outlined mechanisms for settling disputes on how to develop and share the resources of the strategically located river.

Vietnam marked two important anniversaries. The country looked back to April 30, 1975, when communist forces from the north marched into Saigon, effectively ending the Vietnam War, in which millions of Vietnamese died. Former U.S. defense secretary Robert McNamara said in his 1995 memoirs that he and other U.S. officials had been "terribly wrong" in key decisions affecting the war. The Vietnamese government, however, placed far greater emphasis on the nation's 50th anniversary of independence. On September 2 the country commemorated nationalist leader Ho Chi Minh's 1945 declaration of independence. During the celebration Pres. Le Duc Anh remarked, "All of our great victories in the wars of resistance and all important achievements of the reform process demonstrate that our way is right and our future is bright."

The economy continued on its expansionist path, growing at a 9.5% annual rate. Among new joint ventures, the largest was a $1.2 billion pledge by the South Korean conglomerate

HANS KEMP—ASIAWEEK

Workers make repairs by hand on Vietnam's main north south road. With the establishment of full diplomatic relations with the U.S. and the entry of Vietnam into ASEAN in 1995, it was expected that outside investment in the country, accompanied by modernization, would accelerate.

Vietnam Reemerges

On April 30, 1995, amid colourful billboards, bustling cafes, and roaring motorbikes, the Vietnamese people celebrated the 20th anniversary of the end of a war that had both devastated and unified their nation. As Communist Party members and invited guests watched a grand parade move through Ho Chi Minh City, once known as Saigon, they had reason to feel both thrilled and uneasy. These conflicting sentiments were visible everywhere as Vietnamese sought to release their pent-up energy and realize their potential while not forgetting that the freedom they enjoyed had been secured by communist soldiers.

Since the institution of *doi moi* (economic renovation) in 1986, Vietnam's economy had thrived. While it was still among the poorest of the less developed nations (its gross national product per capita was $220), it had had more than 8% annual growth for the previous four years. Inflation had fallen from 700% in 1986 to 14.4% in 1995. Land reforms that gave more control and greater profits to farmers had been a tremendous success. A nation that once could barely feed itself was now the world's third largest exporter of rice. Vietnam's liberal investment laws, moreover, had triggered an enormous influx of money from neighbouring nations. With the end of the U.S. trade embargo in 1994 and the restoration of normal diplomatic relations between the U.S. and Vietnam in 1995, there was great promise of even more foreign investment. Chrysler planned to build cars there, Mobil Oil was searching for petroleum offshore, and Coca-Cola was the country's trendiest drink. Finally, with financial incentives from both Vietnam and developed nations, many boat people who fled the country had returned home.

All this positive growth, however, carried with it a deep concern about unintended and undesirable consequences. Within the government there was heated debate about privatizing the economy and opening markets to outsiders. Many hard-line communists feared that the power and autonomy that they fought so hard for would be lost with the emergence of free markets. Such fears had already led to several setbacks for Vietnam's new economy. The conversion of agricultural land for industrial use had been stopped, and so had borrowing against land values. The government's uncertain long-term commitment to open trade had scared off many potential investors. The progress of the past decade had also deeply affected the culture of Vietnam. There was an unrestrained mania for all things Western, and the prospect of growing wealthy had, for example, tempted both students and teachers to seek well-paying jobs in the business sector. Vietnam's future would largely depend on who succeeded Communist Party leader Do Muoi and Prime Minister Vo Van Kiet. Perhaps the most important development in Vietnam during the year was its admission into the Association of Southeast Asian Nations in July. By linking its own economic strategies with those of non-communist Thailand, Malaysia, Singapore, Indonesia, the Philippines, and Brunei and pursuing peaceful relations with other nations, it had shown that, as popular T-shirts in Ho Chi Minh City declared, "Vietnam is a country, not a war." (JAMES HENNELLY)

Daewoo to build an industrial park near Hanoi. Still, business complaints about official corruption and complicated bureaucracy became so widespread they were reported to have scared potential investors away. In one typical case in September, Total SA of France said it would pull out of a proposed oil-refinery project north of Ho Chi Minh City, formerly called Saigon. Businessmen, however, saw the adoption of a landmark civil code as an indication that Vietnam was moving away from government by decree and toward the rule of law. The code was due to come into effect on July 1, 1996.

Though the country had taken huge strides toward liberalizing its central-command economy since it began the *doi moi* (economic renovation) process in 1986, there was no complementary movement toward political reform. The Communist Party, which remained the only legal political entity, continued to crack down on individuals who openly supported political or religious pluralism. While calling for more openness, President Anh remarked that "hostile forces" compelled the party to strengthen its leadership over the "government, over the entire political system, and over the renovation process." One of the high-profile instances in which the government demonstrated its iron grip was the case of Thich Quang Do, a leader of the outlawed United Buddhist Church of Vietnam. He and five others were arrested in January and later sentenced to as much as five years in prison for "sabotaging religious solidarity" by organizing a flood-relief mission without government permission. (STEVEN FRANK)

This article updates the *Macropædia* article SOUTHEAST ASIA: *Vietnam.*

WESTERN SAMOA

A constitutional monarchy and member of the Commonwealth, Western Samoa occupies an island group in the South Pacific Ocean. Area: 2,831 sq km (1,093 sq mi). Pop. (1995 est.): 166,000. Cap.: Apia. Monetary unit: Western Samoa tala, with (Oct. 6, 1995) a free rate of 2.50 tala to U.S. $1 (3.95 tala = £1 sterling). Head of state (*O le Ao o le Malo*) in 1995, Malietoa Tanumafili II; prime minister, Tofilau Eti Alesana.

In February 1995, after a petition (with some 80,000 signatures) opposing the new value-added goods and services tax was submitted to Parliament, the government laid sedition charges against two leaders of Tumua ma Pule, an organization of traditional chiefs and orators. The case was dismissed by the Supreme Court in June. An Audit Office report, severely critical of the government and alleging mismanagement and corruption, led to the dismissal of the auditor-general.

After a 6% contraction in 1994, the government anticipated 5% economic growth in 1995 and 1996. Inflation, 18.4% in 1994, was expected to be less than 10% in 1995. The government took control of Polynesian Airlines and injected $30 million to keep the company afloat. Two-thirds of aircraft leases were terminated, and route sharing with Air New Zealand was introduced as part of a recovery plan.

Western Samoa joined other South Pacific Forum nations in protesting against the resumption of French nuclear testing in the region. (BARRIE MACDONALD)

This article updates the *Macropædia* article PACIFIC ISLANDS: *Western Samoa.*

YEMEN

A republic of the southwestern Arabian Peninsula, Yemen has coastlines on the Red Sea, the Gulf of Aden, and the Arabian Sea. Area: 527,970 sq km (203,850 sq mi), including 55,871 sq km of undemarcated area bordered by Saudi Arabia and claimed by the former Yemen Arab Republic (North Yemen). Pop. (1995 est.): 13,058,000. Cap.: San'a'. Monetary unit: Yemen Rial, with (Oct. 6, 1995) an official par value of YRls 50 to U.S. $1 (YRls 79.04 = £1 sterling) and a free market rate of YRls 140 to U.S. $1 (YRls 221.32 = £1 sterling). President in 1995, Maj. Gen. Ali Abdallah Salih; prime minister, 'Abd al-Aziz 'Abd al-Ghani.

Despite tensions, Yemen retained its national unity throughout 1995. Eleven parties agreed in February to a document establishing a new alliance, the Opposition Democratic Coalition. In March the minister of defense declared that the integration of the northern and southern armed forces had been "successfully completed." In June a Cabinet reshuffle further consolidated the power of the president, Maj. Gen. Ali Abdallah Salih, by tipping the balance of the coalition government in favour of his General People's Congress over the Yemeni Alliance for Reform.

Border tensions with Saudi Arabia, which had heated up in December 1994 and January 1995, led to the signing in February of a memorandum of understanding. The parties renewed their commitment to the agreement signed in at-Ta'if, Saudi Arabia, in 1934 and established joint committees to arrive at definitive boundaries and promote bilateral ties. There were subsequent talks, and in June President Salih met with King Fahd. Later in the year, however, there were further border clashes. Agreement was reached defining the boundaries with Oman. In December Yemen accused Eritrea of "armed aggression" for landing forces on the Hanish Islands in the Red Sea. After fighting in the area was followed by a cease-fire, the Eritreans continued to hold one of the islands at year-end.

Estimated daily oil production averaged 340,000 bbl in 1995. The World Bank granted an economic recovery credit of $80 million in December as various free-market reforms began to get under way. (JAMAL A. SA'D)

This article updates the *Macropædia* article ARABIA: *Yemen.*

YUGOSLAVIA

A federal republic comprising the republics of Serbia and Montenegro, Yugoslavia borders Hungary to the north, Romania to the northeast, Bulgaria to the southeast, Macedonia and Albania to the south, the Adriatic Sea to the southwest, and Croatia and Bosnia and Herzegovina to the west. Area: 102,173 sq km (39,449 sq mi). Pop. (1995 est.): 10,555,000. Cap.: Belgrade. Monetary unit: new dinar (second), with (Oct. 6, 1995) a par value equal to the Deutsche Mark (free rates of 1.42 new dinars [second] = U.S. $1 and 2.25 new dinars [second] = £1 sterling). President in 1995, Zoran Lilic; prime minister, Radoje Kontic.

Serbia's president, Slobodan Milosevic, regarded by many as the principal instigator of the war in former Yugoslavia, continued to play a key role in the peace process in Bosnia and Herzegovina in 1995. As before, his main concern seemed to be the lifting of UN sanctions imposed on Yugoslavia in May 1992 because of its involvement in the Bosnian war. Meanwhile, Milosevic continued to maintain a firm grip on power at home in Serbia and, to lesser degree, in Montenegro.

During the first half of 1995, Yugoslavia continued to supply military aid and personnel to the Serbs of western Slavonia and the self-declared "Serb Republic of Krajina" in Croatia. In response to appeals from Croatian Serbs for more soldiers, the Yugoslav authorities rounded up able-bodied Serbs from Croatia living in Serbia and sent them to the Serb-controlled regions of Croatia. Politically, however, Yugoslavia continued to distance itself from the Croatian Serbs and their policy of close cooperation with the Bosnian Serb leaders, Radovan Karadzic and Ratko Mladic. Yugoslavia made no attempt to go to the aid of Serbs of western Slavonia in May or the Serbs of the Krajina in August when Croatia recaptured these areas in lightning military actions. Some Serb refugees were allowed to enter Yugoslavia and were typically sent either to Kosovo province, largely populated by the Albanian minority, or to Vojvodina, where they were given the homes of Croats and Hungarians who had fled or been expelled.

In June Milosevic played a key role in the release of UN hostages who had been captured by Bosnian Serbs following NATO raids on arms dumps near Pale, the Bosnian Serb headquarters near Sarajevo. Milosevic sent Jovica Stanisic, his chief of secret police, to put pressure on Karadzic and Mladic to release the hostages. They were all released by June 18. On November 28 Milosevic carried out a purge of pro-Karadzic members of his own party, including the party's vice president, Borislav Jovic, his close ally from the last days of former Yugoslavia, and Mihailo Markovic, Milosevic's chief ideologue in the Socialist Party of Serbia (SPS), the recycled League of Communists of Serbia. Jovic published a diary late in the year that was extremely unflattering of the Serbian president and suggested that he deliberately began the war in Yugoslavia. A similar purge had been carried out earlier in the organs of the mass media, where heads of radio and television as well as of some of the most important newspapers, such as the daily *Politika,* were replaced by people more attuned to Milosevic's policy in Bosnia.

The Bosnian Serbs' military actions in July, the bloody conquest of Srebrenica and Zepa, the threat to Gorazde, and the military push in the Bihac area all contributed to the marginalization of the Serbian political opposition. Meanwhile, Milosevic seemed to be attempting, with the aid of his wife, Mirjana Markovic, who led a small party called the United Yugoslav Left, to take Serbia away from a policy of overt nationalism. Often by precipitating scandals or using other means of pressure, pro-government people were slowly taking over constituencies where the opposition had won in 1993. The most radical nationalist opponent of Milosevic's, Vojislav Seselj, an erstwhile ally, had been imprisoned following an incident engineered by the secret police. His parliamentary immunity was lifted during a nocturnal session of the parliament, and he was quickly packed off to prison. Opinion polls, even in the small independent Belgrade press, showed Milosevic by far the most popular politician in the country.

His popularity in Serbia increased still further in the wake of the U.S.-brokered negotiations at Dayton, Ohio, in November at which he was seen to be playing a key role, negotiating on behalf of the Bosnian Serbs. Milosevic's greatest triumph in the eyes of war-weary Serbs was the lifting of sanctions by the United States after the signing of the Balkan accords in Paris on December 14. Throughout the year the constituent republic of Montenegro demonstrated irritation with Serbian policies. It refused to cooperate in the roundup of Serb troops to fight in Croatian territories, and it viewed Serbia's refusal to recognize Croatia unless it ceded the strategic Prevlaka promontory (at the entrance to the Yugoslav Gulf of Kotor naval base) as a potential threat to Montenegro's postwar relations with Croatia. In October Montenegro withheld payment of customs duties and taxes to the federal government as a protest against its nonpayment of Montenegrin pensions and disability benefits. One of the most prominent figures from the Tito era, Milovan

Djilas, a dissident and writer hailing from Montenegro, died on April 20 at the age of 83.

Industrial production in Yugoslavia in January–November 1995 was 4.6% higher than in the corresponding period of 1994 but 48.5% lower than in 1991. Inflation was running at an annual rate of 114%. (K.F. CVIIC)

This article updates the *Macropædia* article BALKAN STATES: *Yugoslavia.*

ZAIRE

The republic of Zaire is located in central Africa with a short coastline on the Atlantic Ocean. Area: 2,344,858 sq km (905,354 sq mi). Pop. (1995 est.): 43,901,000 (excluding 1.1 million Rwandan refugees). Cap.: Kinshasa. Monetary unit: new zaïre, with (Oct. 6, 1995) a free rate of 5,422 new zaïres to U.S. $1 (8,572 new zaïres = £1 sterling). President in 1995, Mobutu Sese Seko; first state commissioner (prime minister), Joseph Kengo Wa Dondo.

In his 1995 New Year message, Pres. Mobutu Sese Seko said that the future prosperity of the country depended upon putting an end to political confusion. Soon afterward direct talks began between government representatives and members of the Sacred Union of the Radical Opposition and Allies (USORAS), which led to an announcement of cooperation by opposition leader and former prime minister Étienne Tshisekedi on January 7. The press was more skeptical, accusing members of the national legislature of devoting more time to political squabbles than to legislative business, and by January 27 USORAS was demanding that the Supreme Court annul the appointment of Kengo Wa Dondo as prime minister. Yet it was Kengo's appointment that encouraged foreign governments, including the U.S., to look more favourably on relations with Zaire. Meanwhile, none appeared capable of halting or even of slowing down the galloping inflation that had driven the majority of people to rely on barter. The prime minister's efforts to bring the banks back into operation were foundering owing to a shortage of cash.

Concern for the political stability of the country was briefly pushed aside in May by news of deaths from the Ebola virus in Kikwit, 500 km (310 mi) east of Kinshasa. The outbreak, the origin of which remained obscure, was quickly contained, and fewer than 300 people died from the disease. The speed with which the infection overwhelmed its victims and the dreadful nature of its progress caused widespread disquiet, however.

The announcement that the transitional government would continue in office for an additional two years because it was impossible to arrange elections in time to meet the deadline previously set gave rise to another wave of unrest. Clashes on July 29 between security forces and demonstrators loyal to the memory of assassinated former prime minister Patrice Lumumba resulted in the deaths of nine civilians and one police officer. Leaders of USORAS, while dissociating themselves from the Lumumbist cause, insisted that the clashes would not deter them from conducting a campaign to oust Kengo Wa Dondo and to reinstate Tshisekedi as prime minister. A rally called to launch the campaign on August 6 took place peacefully.

Later in August attention became focused on the more than one million refugees from Rwanda and Burundi who were living in camps just inside the country's eastern border. The local population had for some time complained of food shortages in the region and said that the refugees were cutting down vast numbers of trees to use for firewood and as building materials. In June and July more than 100 Zaireans were reported to have been killed in clashes with the refugees, which prompted the prime minister to ask the refugees to return home. The government was gravely concerned about the security problems created by the existence of the camps and was dissatisfied with the inadequate provisions made for the refugees by the international community. When the UN Security Council resolved on August 16 to end its embargo on the sale of arms to Rwanda, the government protested. It argued that this could only lead to attacks on the camps by Rwandan soldiers seeking reprisals against those responsible for the massacres in Rwanda that had led to the revolution there.

Zaire's response was to begin the forcible repatriation of refugees on August 19. This caused an international outcry, but representatives of aid agencies in the camps recognized that the government's action had encouraged many of the refugees who wanted to go home to say so openly. Previously, they had been afraid to act because of rumours that they would be arrested or killed if they did so. As a result, the UN High Commissioner for Refugees offered on August 24 to transform the expulsion program into a scheme for voluntary repatriation, an offer that the government readily accepted. (KENNETH INGHAM)

This article updates the *Macropædia* article CENTRAL AFRICA: *Zaire*.

ZAMBIA

A landlocked republic and member of the Commonwealth, Zambia is in eastern Africa. Area: 752,614 sq km (290,586 sq mi). Pop. (1995 est.): 9,456,000. Cap.: Lusaka. Monetary unit: kwacha, with (Oct. 6, 1995) a free rate of 941 kwacha to U.S. $1 (1,489 kwacha = £1 sterling). President in 1995, Frederick Chiluba.

With yet another prolonged period of drought causing acute shortages of food in the southern half of the country and with the output of copper continuing to fall—though the effect of this was partially offset by the increase in world prices—Zambia started 1995 in a beleaguered condition. The decline in copper production, coupled with the reopening of trade with South Africa and peace in Mozambique, also resulted in a serious reduction in traffic on the Tanzam railway and led to proposals to reduce the workforce from 6,600 to 4,000. By the admission of Minister of Commerce Dipak Patel in July, 5.5 million of Zambia's 9.5 million people were living in abject poverty.

Accusations that after 40 months in office his government still had not formulated a policy for agriculture, together with charges of corruption leveled against his administration, led Pres. Frederick Chiluba to take drastic action. On February 9 he ordered all his ministers and members of the National Assembly to declare their assets within 48 hours. He had already dismissed his minister of lands, Chuulu Kalima, for gross indiscipline and irresponsibility. He followed this, a few weeks later, by sacking the governor of the Bank of Zambia, Dominic Mulaisho, when the value of the kwacha suddenly and inexplicably fell by more than 20% and after criticism that the bank had failed to foresee and forestall the crisis that led to the failure of Meridien BIAO, Zambia's fourth largest commercial bank. Chiluba also pointed out that economic recovery could not be expected as long as the country was burdened with a crushing international debt, the servicing of which cost 40% of the gross national product.

The president's actions did not put an end to sniping by the opposition, including the charge (firmly denied) that he was born in Zaire and therefore not entitled to hold office in Zambia. When on June 28 former president Kenneth Kaunda was again elected leader of the opposition United

(continued on page 506)

SPOTLIGHT: SUB-SAHARAN AFRICA IN A NEW ERA

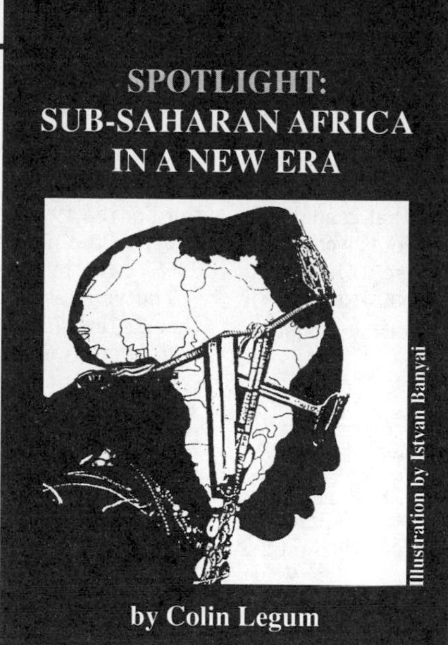
Illustration by Istvan Banyai

by Colin Legum

The momentum for democratization continued to sweep sub-Saharan Africa, but with varying degrees of success. The outlook for economic recovery, however, remained unpromising.

Although 41 of the 48 governments in the region had committed themselves to establishing multiparty parliamentary systems, by year's end only 9 could be judged to have met the criteria for pluralism in an open society; another 21 qualified as "semidemocratic" or transitional democracies. The number of single-party or military regimes shrank to 9 from about 36 in the previous year. With the end of the civil wars in Angola and Mozambique, the number of serious armed conflicts had dropped to just five—Sudan, Somalia, Sierra Leone, Rwanda, and, again, Liberia, where the civil war seemed to be finding renewed vigour at year's end. There was also a significant decline in the number of successful military coups—only one (The Gambia). The mass killings of Tutsi in Rwanda in 1994 were the most horrific in the continent's postcolonial experience. South Africa continued to be the flagship of the region's democratic transformation.

The prolonged civil war in The Sudan between the Islamic fundamentalist military regime and rebel groups in the non-Muslim southern region spilled across the borders. Four of The Sudan's neighbours—Eritrea, Ethiopia, Uganda, and Kenya—agreed on a strategy to bring down the government in Khartoum. The two precipitating causes of this unprecedented decision were the abortive attempt to assassinate the Egyptian president, Hosni Mubarak, when he went to attend the summit meeting of the Organization of African Unity (OAU) in Addis Ababa, Eth., and allegations that the Sudanese National Islamic Front was engaged in spreading Islamic fundamentalism to Eritrea and Ethiopia. The defeated Rwandan government accused Uganda of arming the successful Rwandan Patriotic Front.

The collapse of the Soviet Union and the end of the Cold War opened up a new chapter in black Africa's relations with Western Europe and North America. In the absence of Cold War politics, African concerns were what came to be described as the "marginalization" of the continent—*i.e.,* that Western interest in the continent would decline and, at the same time, economic aid would dwindle as more economic support was provided to Russia and Eastern Europe. Regional governments, with the exception of South Africa, had entered into agreements with the World Bank and the International Monetary Fund in support of structural adjustment programs. Despite some criticism, many prominent Africans—especially those opposed to their governments—welcomed the terms imposed by donor countries, making the provision of aid conditional upon good governance and respect for human rights. Fears that the European Union would not renew the favourable terms under the Lomé Convention proved to be unjustified when a new agreement was signed in November.

The peace process in the Middle East also contributed to ending the difficult choice between siding with Israel or the Arab world. By year's end almost all regional governments had restored their diplomatic and economic ties with Israel. Moreover, almost all the governments in the region maintained close links with the Commonwealth of Nations, the Francophone community, or a Lusophone (Portuguese) grouping. Japan became one of the largest aid-donor countries and, with the two Koreas, substantially expanded trade relations.

The OAU, revivified by its secretary-general, Salim Ahmed Salim, was beginning to play a more active role in mediation and peacekeeping operations. At its 1995 summit in Addis Ababa, a decision was made to set up specialized military units in member countries to be available for either UN or OAU operations in dealing with conflicts in the continent. The summit also diluted its previous policy of nonintervention in the internal conflicts of member states. A proposal submitted by the United Kingdom and Nigeria, reflecting the consensus of 15 United Nations members, outlined the kind of help the international community should offer to strengthen the OAU's capability for peacekeeping.

The outbreak of an Ebola epidemic in Zaire early in the year caused widespread concern because of the mystery of its cause and the high fatality rate among its victims. The virus claimed 244 lives out of 315 reported cases. The outbreak ended as suddenly as it began, with little more known about the virus than was known before its latest occurrence. Both the Ebola virus and HIV helped focus attention on the paucity of health services in Zaire and other African countries. Between 1985 and 1995, the number of persons infected with HIV rose from 1.5 million to more than 10 million; more than 1% of the 15–49-year age group was HIV-positive, and an estimated one million more were expected to contract the virus in each of the years following 1995. More than half the region's population of about 560 million had no access to public health services, and almost two-thirds had no safe drinking water.

Sub-Saharan Africa's population constituted 10% of the world's total, but the region produced only slightly more than 1% of the world's gross domestic product. In the region's 24 better-off countries, average income in 1989 was less than $400 per person, while in the remaining 23 countries the average was even lower. The level of poverty continued to decline, with average incomes falling by 15% in the 1980s. Despite the support of international finance institutions, a survey of its impact showed little evidence of improvement in the first half of the decade. According to the United Nations, economic growth remained blocked despite considerable improvements in a few of the better-off countries. The World Bank forecast that sub-Saharan Africa's exports would grow only 3% a year to the year 2000, which was below the growth of population. The Organisation for Economic Co-operation and Development estimated that in the coming years the average annual growth in aid funds was unlikely to exceed the modest performance of 2%, whereas the World Bank warned that unless this figure was doubled, the financial gap in the region was set to widen even further. Foreign debt in sub-Saharan Africa tripled from $56 billion to $173 billion between 1980 and 1990, and although debt relief for some of the poorest countries eased their debt-repayment burden to some extent, the total debt in fact increased to $176 billion by 1991 and was still increasing.

Colin Legum is the editor of *Third World Reports* and consulting editor of the *Africa Contemporary Record*.

(continued from page 504)
National Independence Party, he, too, was accused of having been president of the country for five years before renouncing his Malawian citizenship. A threat to deport him from Zambia was dropped, although a clause in the country's proposed new constitution, stating that candidates for the presidency must be citizens whose parents were both Zambians by birth, presented a further obstacle to Kaunda's hoped-for comeback. (KENNETH INGHAM)

This article updates the *Macropædia* article SOUTHERN AFRICA: *Zambia.*

ZIMBABWE

A republic and member of the Commonwealth, Zimbabwe is a landlocked state in eastern Africa. Area: 390,757 sq km (150,872 sq mi). Pop. (1995 est.): 11,261,000. Cap.: Harare. Monetary unit: Zimbabwe dollar, with (Oct. 6, 1995) a free rate of Z$8.85 to U.S. $1 (Z$14 = £1 sterling). President in 1995, Robert Mugabe.

A meeting of Zimbabwe's donor countries, scheduled to take place in Paris in February 1995, was postponed until March to give the government time to "put its books in order." Although there were fears that donors were becoming impatient at the slow rate at which the country was implementing the financial reforms required by the International Monetary Fund (IMF) and the World Bank, the latter agreed on March 10 to ratify disbursements to Zimbabwe of $792 million, an increase of $175 million over the amount already committed. The donor countries praised the government for its efforts to carry out the reforms.

Those efforts had not met with uniform approval inside Zimbabwe. New excise taxes and the threat of a new surcharge on profits and income aroused considerable criticism, which led Pres. Robert Mugabe to express his anger at the severity of the measures his government was having to take to meet the requirements of the IMF and the World Bank.

The situation was not helped by the lengthy illness of the finance minister, Bernard Chidzero. In his absence there had been some mismanagement of public spending. Other factors that adversely affected the country's economic prospects were not easily dealt with. Continuing drought led to food shortages and to a wheat crop that was barely a third of the 1994 harvest. Also, the national debt was almost equal to the annual gross domestic product, which caused 23% of the budget to be earmarked for interest payments.

The general election, held in April, did not appreciably change the situation. Owing in part to a boycott by several opposition parties, which claimed that the electoral system was unfairly weighted against them, the governing Zimbabwe African National Union-Patriotic Front (ZANU-PF) won all but two seats in the House of Assembly. The new minister of finance, Ariston Chambati, recognized that the credibility of his July budget would depend upon "a high degree of political commitment and fiscal discipline." Though he died of meningitis in October, Chambati had imposed a virtual standstill on public spending, increased taxes on a number of consumer goods, and reduced import duties on spare parts and industrial components.

Increases in the tobacco crop and in the output of gold—the two main foreign currency earners—provided grounds for optimism. Also encouraging was a deal in April involving three of the world's largest mining companies, which opened the way for Zimbabwe to become the second biggest producer of platinum.

In October Ndabaningi Sithole, leader of the ZANU-Ndonga and one of the only two non-ZANU-PF members of the House of Assembly was arrested in connection with an alleged plot to assassinate President Mugabe. Critics of Mugabe believed that the arrest was the result of Sithole's announcement that he would be a candidate in the presidential election in 1996 and was, consequently, a further manifestation of Mugabe's refusal to allow any opposition. (KENNETH INGHAM)

This article updates the *Macropædia* article SOUTHERN AFRICA: *Zimbabwe.*

ALEXANDER JOE—AFP

A farmer in Zimbabwe stands in a field amid crops that have dried up. Shortages of food in the east African country were made worse in 1995 because of continuing drought, and famine threatened to be added to Zimbabwe's many economic problems.

Major New Revisions from the Encyclopædia Britannica

This section of the *Britannica Book of the Year* consists of articles or parts of articles that have recently been revised or rewritten for the Britannica database and have been incorporated in *Britannica Online*™, an electronic version of *Encyclopædia Britannica.* These materials may appear in future print editions of the encyclopaedia as well. The articles appearing here have been chosen by the yearbook editors for their general interest or their timeliness.

The selection from the article BALKAN STATES: *Bosnia and Herzegovina: History* has been revised to include recent developments in that region. The revision of ITALY: *History, Italy Since 1870,* covers the period up to the end of World War II. The selection *Cultural Life* from RUSSIA has been revised to treat the topic in a manner somewhat more historical than previously, and the article TOKYO-YOKOHAMA METROPOLITAN AREA is included here in its entirety.

Subscribers desiring update sheets to put in their encyclopaedia to indicate that an article has been revised or added and owners of older sets wishing information about the exact articles being replaced by the reprints should address their requests to Britannica Home Library Service, Encyclopædia Britannica, Inc., 310 South Michigan Avenue, Chicago IL 60604. There is no charge for the article update sheets.

Balkan States

Bosnia and Herzegovina

HISTORY

Ancient and medieval periods. When the Romans extended their conquests into the territory of modern Bosnia during the 2nd and 1st centuries BC, the people they encountered there belonged mainly to Illyrian tribes. During the 4th and 5th centuries AD, Roman armies suffered heavy defeats in this region at the hands of invading Goths. When the Goths were eventually driven out of the Balkans by the Byzantine emperor Justinian I in the early 6th century, the Bosnian territory became, notionally at least, part of the Byzantine Empire.

Slavs began to settle in this territory during the 6th century. A second wave of Slavs in the 7th century included two powerful tribes, the Croats and the Serbs; Croats probably covered most of central, western, and northern Bosnia, while Serbs extended into the Drina River valley and modern Herzegovina.

During the 11th and 12th centuries Bosnia experienced rule by Byzantium through Croatian or Serb intermediaries, incorporation into a Serb kingdom, rule by Hungary, and a brief period of renewed Byzantine rule. After the death of the emperor Manuel I Comnenus in 1180, Byzantine rule fell away but government by Croatia or Hungary was not restored: a Bosnian territory thus became, for the first time, an independent entity.

A Bosnian state of some kind existed during most of the period from 1180 to 1463, despite periodic aggression from the neighbouring kingdom of Hungary, which maintained a theoretical claim to sovereignty over Bosnia. Bosnia enjoyed periods of power and independence, especially under three prominent rulers: Ban Kulin (1180–1204), Ban Stjepan Kotromanić (1322–53), and King Tvrtko I (1353–91). Under Kotromanić, Bosnia expanded southward, incorporating the principality of Hum (modern Herzegovina). During the reign of Tvrtko I, Bosnia expanded farther south and acquired a portion of the Dalmatian coast. However, for most of the medieval period, Bosnia was mainly a landlocked state, isolated and protected by its impenetrable terrain.

The Bosnian church

One consequence of this isolation was the development of a distinctive Bosnian church. After the division between Roman and Eastern Orthodox Christianity, most of the Bosnian territory had been Roman Catholic, but during the long period of isolation from Rome the Bosnian church fell into de facto schism, electing its own leaders from among the heads of the monastic houses. A combination of poor theological training, lax observances, and Eastern Orthodox practices led to frequent complaints from neighbouring areas, beginning in the 1190s, that the Bosnian church was infected with heresy. In 1203 a papal legate was sent to investigate these charges, and Ban Kulin gathered a special council at Bolino Polje (near modern Zenica), where the church leaders signed a declaration undertaking a series of reforms. The extent to which these reforms were observed is very uncertain, since over the following century the church in Bosnia became increasingly isolated. By 1340 the official view from Rome was that the entire Bosnian church had fallen into heresy, from which its members needed to be converted. Although many historians have argued that the Bosnian church adopted the extreme dualist heresy of the Bulgarian Bogomils, modern scholarship has indicated that the Bosnian church should be considered an essentially nonheretical branch of the Catholic church, based in monastic houses in which some Eastern Orthodox practices also were observed. During the 14th century the Franciscans established a network of friaries in Bosnia and spent more than a century trying to convert members of the Bosnian church to mainstream Catholicism. In 1459 this campaign received the full support of the Bosnian king, Stjepan Tomaš, who summoned the clergy of the Bosnian church and ordered them to convert to Catholicism or leave the kingdom. When most of the clergy converted, the back of the Bosnian church was broken.

The final decades of the medieval Bosnian state were troubled by civil war, Hungarian interference, and the threat of Turkish invasion. The nobleman Stefan Vukčić engaged in tactical alliances against the Bosnian rulers, establishing his own rule over the territory of Hum and giving himself the title *herceg* (duke), from which the name Herzegovina is derived. Turkish forces captured an important part of central Bosnia in 1448, centred on the settlement of Vrhbosna, which they developed into the city of Sarajevo. In 1463 they conquered most of the rest of Bosnia proper.

Ottoman Bosnia. Bosnia was rapidly absorbed into the Ottoman Empire and was divided into military-administrative districts, or sanjaks (from Turkish *sancàk,* "banner"). In 1580 a broad area covering modern Bosnia and some surrounding areas of Croatia and Serbia was given the full status of an *eyalet,* or constituent province of the empire. Bosnia enjoyed this status as a distinct entity throughout the rest of the Ottoman period. The Bosnian *eyalet* was governed by a vizier and administered through a network of junior pashas and local judges. Land was distributed according to the Ottoman feudal system, in which the holder of a timar (estate) had to report for military duty, bringing and supporting other soldiers. A wide range of taxes was imposed, including the *harač,* a graduated poll tax on non-Muslims. The notorious system called *devşirme* was also introduced, under which Christian children were taken off for training in the imperial administration and the Janissary corps, an elite army division. In all these respects, conditions in Bosnia were similar to those in the other conquered areas of Europe.

Conversion to Islām

In one crucial way, however, Bosnia differed from the other Balkan lands (except, later, Albania): a large part of the native population converted to Islām. This was a gradual development; it took more than a hundred years for Muslims to become an absolute majority. The lack of a strong, unified Christian church in Bosnia enabled Islām to spread. The motives that inclined Bosnians to adopt Islām were partly economic: the prosperous cities of Sarajevo and Mostar were mainly Muslim, and it was not possible to lead a full civic life there without converting to Islām. Other motives included the privileged legal status enjoyed by Muslims and, possibly, a desire to avoid the *harač,* though Muslims were subject, unlike Christians, both to the alms tax and to the duties of general military service. During the period of Islamicization, the Ottomans encouraged settlement in northern and western Bosnia; many of the settlers were Vlachs, members of a largely Serbian Orthodox Balkan population.

Major wars affecting Bosnia took place almost every two generations throughout the Ottoman period. In the Habsburg-Ottoman war of 1683–99, Austria reconquered Ottoman Hungary and Slavonia, sending a flood of Muslim refugees into Bosnia. In 1697 a small Austrian army under Prince Eugene of Savoy marched into the heart of Bosnia, put Sarajevo to the torch, and hurried back to Austrian territory, taking thousands of Catholic Bosnians. In the next major war (1714–18) Austria joined forces with Venice; at the Treaty of Passarowitz (Požarevac) in 1718, Venetian-ruled Dalmatia was allowed to extend its territory inland, reaching a line that since then has formed part of the southwestern border of Bosnia. Austria invaded Bosnia again in 1736 but was repelled by local forces; at the subsequent peace settlement, Austria gave up its claim to the territory south of the Sava River. This settlement formed the basis of the northern border of modern Bosnia.

The chronic fighting weakened Bosnia. War necessitated increased taxation, causing tax revolts. Forced conscription and frequent plague epidemics led to a relative reduction in the Muslim population, which contributed its manpower to Ottoman campaigns throughout the empire and may have suffered disproportionately from the effects of plague in the cities. Nevertheless, Ottoman Bosnia was not permanently sunk in misery. Descriptions of Sarajevo by visiting travelers portray it as one of the wonders of the Balkans, with fountains, bridges, schools, libraries, and mosques. Fine mosques were also built in towns such as Foča and Banja Luka. (Many of these buildings were systematically demolished by Serb forces in 1992–93.) Numerous works of poetry, philosophy, and theology were written. The cities of Sarajevo and Mostar, where such urban culture flourished, enjoyed a large degree of autonomy under elected officials. Real local power passed increasingly into the hands of a type of hereditary official (unique to the Bosnian *eyalet*) known as a *kapetan.*

Ottoman reforms

The existence of these powerful local institutions meant that Bosnia was well equipped to resist the reforming measures that the Ottoman sultans began to issue in the early 19th century. When Sultan Mahmud II reformed the military in 1826 and abolished the Janissary corps, the reform was fiercely resisted by local Janissaries in Bosnia. In 1831 a charismatic young *kapetan* called Husein seized power in Bosnia, imprisoning the vizier in Travnik. With an army of 25,000 men, Husein then marched into Kosovo to negotiate with the Ottoman grand vizier, demanding local autonomy for Bosnia and an end to the reform process there. During these final decades of Ottoman rule, Muslims were violently expelled from Serbia; the rise of Serbia as a quasi-autonomous Christian province made Bosnian Muslims feel more isolated and vulnerable, and the increasing role of foreign powers (especially Austria and Russia) as "protectors" of the interests of Christians in the Balkans also raised their suspicions. Bosnian landowners, feeling that they could no longer trust the Ottoman authorities in Constantinople (now Istanbul) to maintain their power, frequently turned to more repressive measures against their Christian subjects.

However, two Bosnian governors succeeded in forcing through some of the sultan's reforms and curbing local resistance. The first of these, Omer-paša Latas, crushed a major rebellion in 1850–51 and revoked the separate status of Herzegovina. The second, Topal Osman-paša, introduced a new method of military conscription in 1865 and a completely new administrative system in 1866, dividing Bosnia into seven sanjaks and establishing a consultative assembly. Tax demands on Bosnian peasants continued to grow. In 1875 a revolt against the state tax collectors began among Christian peasants in the Nevesinje region of Herzegovina; unrest soon spread. Serbia and Montenegro declared war on the Ottoman Empire in 1876, and Russia came into the war on their behalf in the following year. When the Serbo-Turkish War ended in 1878, the other great powers of Europe intervened at the Congress of Berlin to counterbalance Russia's new influence in the Balkans. The congress decided that Bosnia and Herzegovina, while remaining notionally under Turkish sovereignty, would be occupied and governed by Austria-Hungary. In 1878 Austro-Hungarian troops took control of Bosnia, overcoming vigorous resistance from local Bosnian forces; they also occupied the neighbouring sanjak of Novi Pazar, which had been one of the seven Bosnian sanjaks in the late Ottoman period.

Bosnia under Austro-Hungarian rule. Bosnia was governed by a special joint commission under the Common Ministry of Finance. The Ottoman administrative division of Bosnia was preserved, and Ottoman laws were only gradually replaced or supplemented. This policy of gradualism was the most striking aspect of Austro-Hungarian rule in Bosnia under the Common Finance Minister Benjamin Kállay, who directed Bosnian policy from 1882 to

1903. Kállay's rule was extremely active. A public works program was initiated, and by 1907 Bosnia had a well-developed infrastructure, including an extensive railway and road network.

However, Kállay failed in his central political project: developing a Bosnian national consciousness to insulate the people of Bosnia from the growing movements of Croatian, Serbian, and Yugoslav ("South Slav") nationalism. Catholic and Orthodox people of Bosnia had begun by the mid-19th century to identify themselves as "Croats" and "Serbs." During the first decade of the 20th century, "national organizations" of Muslims, Serbs, and Croats were set up that functioned as embryonic political parties. In response, Kállay's successor, István, Baron von Burián, granted a degree of autonomy in religious affairs to both the Muslims and the Serbs.

In October 1908 nationalist feeling was strongly aroused by the sudden announcement that Bosnia would be fully annexed by Austria-Hungary. Inside Bosnia, one effect of this change was beneficial: Burián felt able to promote democratic institutions, introducing a parliament there (with limited powers) in 1910. But the bitter resentment that the annexation caused among Serb and South Slav nationalists led to the growth of revolutionary groups and secret societies dedicated to the overthrow of Habsburg rule. One of these, Mlada Bosna ("Young Bosnia"), was especially active in Bosnian schools and universities. Tension was heightened by the First Balkan War of 1912–13, in which Serbia expanded southward, driving Turkish forces out of Kosovo, Novi Pazar, and Macedonia. In May 1913 the military governor of Bosnia, General Oskar Potiorek, declared a state of emergency, dissolving the parliament, closing down Serb cultural associations, and suspending the civil courts. The heir to the Habsburg throne, Archduke Francis Ferdinand, traveled to Bosnia to review a military exercise. He entered Sarajevo and was killed there on June 28, 1914, by a young assassin from the Mlada Bosna organization, Gavrilo Princip, who had received some assistance from inside Serbia. Austria-Hungary declared war on Serbia one month later, precipitating World War I.

Assassination of Francis Ferdinand

Bosnia was under military rule throughout World War I, and repressive measures were applied to those Bosnian Serbs whose loyalty was suspect. At the end of the war, Bosnian politicians from each of the three main communities followed the political leaders of Croatia and Slovenia in throwing off Habsburg rule and joining in the creation of a new South Slav state, the Kingdom of Serbs, Croats, and Slovenes.

Bosnia in the Yugoslav kingdom. When the constitution of this new state was finally settled in June 1921, Bosnia retained no formal status of its own; however, its outline was preserved on the map, in the form of six *oblasti* (provinces) corresponding to the sanjaks (excluding that of Novi Pazar) of the late Ottoman period. Serfdom was abolished, though Bosnia remained something of a social and political backwater in the Yugoslav kingdom. In the territorial division of 1929, Bosnia was divided between four other administrative districts and thus was wiped off the map. Further adjustments were made in 1939, with the creation of a special Croatian territory within Yugoslavia that included portions of Bosnian territory. Two years later, after the Axis invasion of Yugoslavia, the entire Bosnian territory was absorbed into the puppet state known as the Independent State of Croatia.

The killing that took place in Bosnia between 1941 and 1945 was terrible in both scale and complexity. The Ustaša, the fascist movement that ruled Croatia during the war, exterminated most of Bosnia's 14,000 Jews and massacred Serbs on a large scale: more than 100,000 Serbs from Bosnia died in this way, roughly half in death camps. Two organized resistance movements emerged, a Serb royalist force known as the Chetniks, led by Draža Mihailović, and a communist Partisan force (including Serbs, Croats, and Muslims) led by Josip Broz Tito. The sharply divergent aims of the two movements resulted in a civil war. Royalist forces turned increasingly to German and Italian forces for assistance and committed atrocities against Bosnian Muslims; some Bosnian Muslims joined an SS division that operated in northern and eastern Bosnia for six months during 1944, exacting reprisals against the local Serb population. The Partisans liberated Sarajevo in April 1945 and declared a "people's government" for Bosnia later that month. It is estimated that the total number of deaths in Bosnia during the war was 164,000 Serbs, 75,000 Muslims, and 64,000 Croats.

Bosnia in communist Yugoslavia. In 1946 the Socialist Republic of Bosnia and Herzegovina became one of the constituent republics of the Federal People's Republic of Yugoslavia. Life in Bosnia underwent all the social, economic, and political changes that were imposed on the whole of Yugoslavia by its new communist government, but Bosnia was particularly affected by the abolition of many traditional Muslim institutions. However, a change of official policy in the 1960s led to the acceptance of "Muslim" as a term denoting a national identity. By 1971 Muslims formed the largest single component of the Bosnian population. During the next 20 years the Serb and Croat populations fell in absolute terms as the relative backwardness of the Bosnian economy led many Serbs and Croats to emigrate.

During the 1980s the rapid decline of the Yugoslav economy led to widespread public dissatisfaction with the political system. This attitude, together with the manipulation of nationalist feelings by politicians, destabilized Yugoslav politics. Independent political parties began to appear in 1988; multiparty elections were held in Slovenia and Croatia in early 1990. When elections were held in Bosnia in December 1990, new parties representing the three national communities gained seats in rough proportion to their populations. A tripartite coalition government was formed, with the Muslim politician Alija Izetbegović leading a joint presidency. Growing tensions both inside and outside Bosnia, however, made cooperation with the Serb party, led by Radovan Karadžić, increasingly difficult.

The breakup of Yugoslavia

In 1991 several self-styled "Serb Autonomous Regions" were declared in areas of Bosnia with large Serb populations. In August the Serb party began boycotting the Bosnian presidency meetings; in October it removed its deputies from the Bosnian assembly and set up a "Serb National Assembly" in Banja Luka. By then full-scale war had broken out in Croatia, and the breakup of Yugoslavia was under way. When the European Community (EC) recognized the independence of Croatia and Slovenia in December, it invited Bosnia to apply for recognition also. A referendum on independence was held on Feb. 29–March 1, 1992, although Karadžić's party obstructed voting in many Serb-populated areas. Nearly two-thirds of the electorate cast a vote; almost all voted for independence.

Independence and war. Attempts by EC negotiators to promote a new division of Bosnia into ethnic "cantons" during February and March 1992 failed. When Bosnia's independence was recognized by the United States and the EC on April 7, Serb paramilitary forces immediately began firing on Sarajevo, and the bombardment of the city by heavy artillery began soon thereafter. During April many of the towns in eastern Bosnia with large Muslim populations were attacked by a combination of paramilitary forces and Yugoslav army units. Most of the local Muslim population was expelled from these areas, the first victims in Bosnia of a process described as "ethnic cleansing." Within six weeks, a coordinated offensive by the Yugoslav army, Serbian paramilitary groups, and local Bosnian Serb forces left roughly two-thirds of Bosnian territory under Serb control.

From the summer of 1992, the military situation remained fairly static. A hastily assembled Bosnian government army, together with some better-prepared Croat forces, held the front lines for the rest of that year, though its power was gradually eroded in parts of eastern Bosnia. The Bosnian government was weakened militarily by an international arms embargo and by a conflict with Croat forces, which broke out on a large scale in February 1993. The United Nations (UN) refused to intervene militarily in the war but sent troops to facilitate the delivery of humanitarian aid; this mandate was later extended to the protection of a number of UN-declared "safe areas." Meanwhile, the international community continued, without success, to encourage the combatants to reach a negotiated settlement. A series of peace proposals based on a division of Bosnia along ethnic lines failed, largely because of the Serbs' refusal to accept territorial concessions. An agreement signed in March 1994, which ended the conflict between the Bosnian government and Bosnian Croats, created a Croat-Muslim federation within Bosnia and a confederal arrangement between that federation and the Republic of Croatia. Throughout 1994 a so-called contact group (representing Britain, France, Germany, Russia, and the United States) tried to arrange a settlement on the basis of a Bosnia divided between the Croat-Muslim federation, which would control 51 percent of the land, and the Serbs, who would hold the remainder. This proposal was accepted with reluctance by the Bosnian government but rejected by the Serbs, who controlled more than 70 percent of Bosnian territory. It was estimated that by the end of 1994 at least 200,000 people had died and more than 2,000,000 had been driven from their homes.

(NOEL R. MALCOLM)

Italy

Italy since 1870

DEVELOPMENTS FROM 1870 TO 1914

Politics and the political system, 1870–87. After the conquest of Rome in 1870, Italian politicians settled down to manage the economy, to build up the country's military power, and—in the telling phrase of the Piedmontese author and statesman Massimo d'Azeglio—to "make Italians." Popular disaffection remained high, especially because of the grist tax that had been introduced in 1869. Governments of the "right" remained in office, first under Giovanni Lanza (to 1873) and then under Marco Minghetti (1873–76). The "right" was not an organized party but a group of patriotic, mostly northern, landowners committed to a strong currency and free trade. Under both prime ministers the main domestic task was to balance the budget. Minghetti eventually managed this, but raising taxes and squeezing expenditure had made the "right" unpopular, and its candidates did badly in the 1874 elections. In March 1876 the Minghetti government fell when its Tuscan supporters refused to support a state takeover of the railways.

The end of government by the "right"

Italy was then ruled for many years by governments of the "left," which were usually led by Agostino Depretis (until his death in 1887). The deputies of the "left," heirs of the Risorgimento's democratic tradition, were more anticlerical, more frequently members of the middle class (many of them were lawyers), more often from the south, and less concerned about the value of money than the rentier "right" had been. They were, however, splintered into various groups, and factional disputes soon became endemic. "Left" governments abolished the grist tax (1883) and made two years' primary education compulsory (1877).

A main achievement of the "left" government was the widening of the suffrage in 1882. The voting age was reduced to 21 (from 25); the requirement to pay 40 lire in direct taxes per annum was halved and abolished altogether for those with two years' schooling. The electorate thus increased from approximately 500,000 to 2,000,000 men, including now many urban artisans, especially in the north where schools were more common. Within a few years modern political parties were founded and won seats in northern Italy, but southern constituencies remained dominated by elite groups of lawyers and local notables, often linked to prominent landowners.

Local government was also very significant, and there were often bitter disputes among local factions. The 8,300-odd local municipalities (*comuni*) were in charge of primary schools and most welfare services, raised much of their own revenue, and appointed their own staff. The central government tried to control them by appointing the mayors and also by giving veto powers over municipal decisions to provincial bodies that were strongly influenced by the provincial prefect, a government official. The prefect frequently dissolved councils for alleged financial or legal abuses and replaced them with a government "commissioner" until new elections were held. This power was often used when local council leaders opposed government candidates at parliamentary elections. However, government attempts to control local government were never really successful. The prefects had to make sure government candidates would win the next parliamentary elections, and so they had to conciliate, not bully, local elites, including the mayors and municipal councillors. Corruption was therefore often left unchecked. National governments became remarkably dependent on local power-holders. Depretis himself won over ("transformed") deputies and kept his governments in office by distributing patronage and favours to local notables. *Trasformismo* soon became the normal way of conducting parliamentary business, for there were few serious disputes between the leading politicians. The constitutional settlement of 1861 was accepted by virtually all of them; foreign and colonial policy was not contentious and, in any case, was conducted by foreign ministers and prime ministers without much reference to Parliament. In 1881 the government was greatly annoyed by the French occupation of Tunisia, and in the following year, in order to avoid diplomatic isolation, Italy joined the Triple Alliance with Germany and Austria-Hungary. This was essentially a defensive alliance guaranteeing German and Austrian support against any attack by France, Italy's main rival in the Mediterranean. However, it encouraged Italy's first real colonial venture, the takeover of the Red Sea port of Massawa (Mitsiwa) in 1885. Southern politicians favoured colonial expansion as an outlet for surplus population and agricultural produce; northern ones wanted Italy to be a great power, saw the army as an essential guarantor of public order, and supported high military spending—the army and navy ministries spent more than all other ministries combined between 1862 and 1913.

Joining the Triple Alliance

Forces of opposition. The political elite may have agreed on most issues, but there was plenty of opposition in the country. Most men owned guns, and violent crime was common: there were 3,000 murders a year, many of them a result of vendettas or blood feuds. Brigands were still active in parts of the southern mainland in the 1870s, and banditry was still common in the mountainous zones of Sardinia. In the towns, rioting was frequent; more than 250 people were killed in riots against the grist tax in 1869, and similar riots against local taxes or for land and jobs continued well into the 20th century. The strikes of the 1880s—especially by agricultural labourers in Mantua province—much alarmed respectable opinion. Anarchists were active in the Romagna and parts of the south and occasionally attempted to carry out insurrections, as at Matese in 1877, or to kill the king, as Giovanni Passanante attempted to do in 1878.

However, the anarchist leader in the Romagna, Andrea Costa, soon converted to socialist ideas. In 1881 he founded the Revolutionary Socialist Party of Romagna (later the Italian Revolutionary Socialist Party), which preached eventual revolution but also agitated for such issues as universal suffrage and labour and welfare legislation; in 1882, on the new suffrage, Costa became Italy's first socialist deputy. In Lombardy a moderate, labour-oriented Italian Workers' Party was founded in 1885, which helped to organize the Po Valley peasantry into "leagues" and labour cooperatives. The northern labour movement—unions, mutual aid societies, and cooperatives—became infused with either revolutionary or reformist socialist ideas.

Republican opposition also survived, particularly in central Italy, long after Mazzini's death in 1872. Republicans ran many of the mutual aid societies and cooperatives. They opposed strikes, nationalizations, and the class struggle but strongly favoured social protective legislation and civil rights. Some of them, including Matteo Renato Imbriani, also advocated an active "irredentist" foreign policy—that is, a policy that aimed to liberate Italians living in Habsburg territory; in particular they wanted to wrest Trento and Trieste from Austrian control. They regarded the Triple Alliance and colonial expansionism as inimical to Italian interests and as expressions of Italy's monarchical and conservative political institutions.

Perhaps the most serious opposition force in the country was the Roman Catholic church. The Risorgimento had deprived the church of the Papal States, including Rome itself, and of much of its income. Its previous virtual monopoly of education and welfare had been overthrown, and compulsory state education was deliberately secular. Many religious orders had been disbanded; monasteries and convents had become public buildings, used by the state. In the south, particularly, ecclesiastical organization had relied heavily on monks and friars and could barely continue to function. Bishops were not allowed to receive their revenues and take up their posts without royal approval, which was often refused. The pope himself was permitted, by the state's "Law of Guarantees" of 1871, to retain only the Vatican and Lateran palaces as well as Castelgandolfo. Pius IX denounced the new usurping state, forbade Catholics to vote at parliamentary elections or to become candidates, and appointed a new generation of "intransigent" bishops. New laymen's organizations were founded; the Opera dei Congressi, with committees at parish level, became the focus of Catholic resistance to the new state. It organized cooperatives, welfare insurance, credit banks and mutual aid societies, as well as a host of local journals and campaigns against Liberal "lay" proposals (such as a divorce law). Church and state remained mutually suspicious, particularly in the Veneto region, where "regionalist" opposition to centralizing government and peasant hostility to landlords and free trade were both mobilized effectively by the Catholic social movement.

The "Law of Guarantees"

Land reform. The main issue of political debate in late 19th-century Italy was land. Liberal governments insisted that the municipalities should sell off most of the common land to private owners—at least 740,000 acres (about 300,000 hectares) were sold by 1880 in southern Italy alone, and more was occupied illegally. Another 1,250,000 acres of ecclesiastical estates were similarly sold, often at extremely low prices. Overall, at least 5,000,000 acres were transferred. In some regions, including Piedmont, Liguria, and Sardinia, the sales did set up a "property-owning democracy"—that is, a large number of rural people became small landowners, albeit with scattered strips that made improvement unprofitable. The sales also introduced people to the market economy, as they had to repay their mortgages in cash as well as find money for high land taxes. Small ownership did not become widespread in most other regions, despite the land sales; peasants who did acquire land were often forced to sell it again to meet tax debts or interest payments. However, land transfers did often create a nonnoble rural middle class that owned an adequate amount of land or extensive flocks and could dominate local politics; this was particularly true in the former Papal States of central Italy.

Privatization of the commons

Privatization of the commons also had serious environmental and social consequences. Much common land was woodland, bought up and felled by speculators who could sell timber to railway companies (for sleepers) or to mines (for roof support). Deforestation became widespread: Sardinia, for example, lost four-fifths of its trees in the 19th century. The results included soil erosion, landslides, stagnant water in valley bottoms, and increased malaria—the greatest scourge of rural Italy, which in turn prevented much fertile low-lying land from being cultivated. Furthermore, the state also abolished traditional rights such as grazing and wood-gathering on the remaining unsold common land. Millions of households that had relied on access to this land to provide fuel for heating and cooking or pasture for their pigs were suddenly forced either to suffer real poverty or to break the law.

Protectionism. Most agricultural land in Italy was used to grow grain, especially wheat. In the early 1880s world wheat prices fell by one-third, and the incomes of the larger and more prosperous farmers (who grew for the market rather than for their own consumption) collapsed. As landowners were the most powerful pressure group in the country and were strongly represented in Parliament, their demands for protectionism became irresistible.

Tariff protection was also favoured by the most prominent wool and cotton manufacturers of northern Italy, and these industries were second only to the silk industry in importance and numbers employed. Some tariff protection (up to 40 percent) had, in fact, already been given to textiles and other light industries in 1878, but employers naturally wanted more, particularly after the restoration of gold convertibility in 1883 in effect revalued the lira. Moreover, in the 1880s Italy also acquired a steel industry (Terni Steelworks, founded 1886), which was designed to build warships and railways but sold to subsidized industries and was itself unable to survive without protection. All this meant the rise of a strong protectionist lobby, based on large landowners and textile manufacturers and linked to powerful steel and naval interests.

Social changes. In 1871 there were 26.8 million Italians. Both birth and death rates were high, and almost half the children born alive died before the age of five. As time went on, both rates gradually declined—the first because of later marriages, the second because of improved housing, sanitation, and diet. Most people worked in agriculture but often lived in hill towns to avoid malaria or bandits; however, living in the countryside began to be more common later in the 19th century. Large-scale transatlantic emigration began in the 1880s; in 1888 more than 200,000 Italians went to the Americas in search of jobs, 10 times as many as a decade previously. Most emigrants, whether bound for the Americas or for other parts of Europe, were northerners, often seasonal migrants from hill areas of peasant ownership, where jobs were scarce and where younger sons who stayed behind had little prospect of marriage. But even in 1888 more than a quarter of the emigrants were southerners, and the great exodus of southern emigrants to both North and South America was just about to begin. Most people (68.8 percent in 1871) were illiterate and usually spoke only dialect. Illiteracy was particularly common among women, peasants, and southerners. The compulsory schooling law of 1877 was widely ignored in practice; in any case, it provided for only two years of schooling, not enough to guarantee the ability to read and count. Conscripts were likely to be taught to read during military service, but only one-quarter of the age group was actually called up into the army. Italian education was more successful at the secondary level in the towns: the "technical schools" and "technical institutes" taught science, engineering, and accounting and had high prestige among urban parents. As for the universities, they essentially trained lawyers and doctors, both professions in which supply considerably exceeded demand.

The Crispi era, 1887–1900. *Domestic policies.* On the death of Depretis in 1887 the Sicilian and former Mazzinian Francesco Crispi became prime minister and pursued a policy of administrative reforms at home and expansion abroad. His main domestic achievement was to extend the suffrage at local elections to all males over the age of 21 who paid five lire per annum in local taxes—that is, to 3.5 million people. This was a real blow to the local "notables" who had previously controlled local government. The larger councils (after 1896, all councils) were also permitted to choose their own mayors and were required to meet in public. The Crispi government also brought in a reasonably effective system of administrative law for the first time, through the provincial councils (*giuntas*) and the Council of State. The charities were reformed; the clergy was excluded from running them, and the funds were often diverted to more secular purposes. The minister of justice, Giuseppe Zanardelli, promulgated a new code of criminal law that abolished the death penalty and legalized strikes unless violence or intimidation occurred.

The tariff of 1887

However, the most important act of Crispi's first government was the new tariff of 1887. It was a response to demands from northern steel and textile interests, from farmers (also mainly from the north) faced with imports of cheap American grain or Asian rice, and from social reformers eager to secure legislative measures that employers could afford. A duty of 50 lire per ton was placed on imported wheat by 1888, and later it went higher still; food prices rose sharply, provoking considerable unrest. Similar measures protected steel, shipbuilding, and textiles. Italy's largest trading partner was France, and the French retaliated against Italian goods. A "tariff war" began between the two countries and continued until 1898. Franco-Italian trade was more than halved, and entire sectors of Italian agriculture, including wine, silk, cattle, and olive oil, collapsed overnight as their markets were cut off. When excess food supplies drove all agricultural prices down, even grain growers failed to benefit from the new tariff. Moreover, the crisis helped to drag down many of Italy's banks, including one of the largest, the Banca Romana. Resulting inquiries revealed that the bank had made interest-free loans to leading politicians, including Crispi himself and former treasury minister Giovanni Giolitti, who was prime minister from May 1892 to November 1893. Politicians needed the money to finance their election expenses and to run or bribe newspapers. The Banca Romana scandal was the first of many famous Italian corruption scandals, and, like the others, it discredited the whole political system.

Colonialism. Crispi's colonial policy brought additional blows. The Italian settlement at Massawa soon led to conflict with the neighbouring Ethiopians, who in 1887 killed 500 Italian troops at Dogali. Peace was made at Wichale in 1889, and Crispi expanded the Italian possessions along the Red Sea to include most of present-day Eritrea and southern Somalia. In 1895 the Italians annexed a large portion of the province of Tigray, and war with Ethiopia began again. In March 1896 the Italian army was overwhelmed at the Battle of Adwa: about 5,000 Italian troops were killed. This disaster forced Crispi to resign and ended any further colonial adventures for some years. It was widely seen in Italy as a disgrace to the whole political system and to Italy's aspirations to great-power status; it would have to be avenged in the future.

The Sicilian *fasci*

Years of crisis. Economic hardship and political corruption at home, together with military failure abroad, provoked riots and uprisings throughout the country. In the early 1890s the "Sicilian *fasci*" (normally peasant leagues organized by urban socialists) led successful strikes and land occupations until Crispi, in January 1894, used the army to restore order. The *fasci*'s leaders were imprisoned, and the movement soon collapsed. At the same time, an anarchist insurrection in Lunigiana was also suppressed by martial law. Further riots occurred in 1898, mainly in towns, over the high price of bread and over civil liberties. At least 80 people were killed in Milan by the troops, whose commander was shortly afterward decorated by the king. Government repression also took the form of attempting to govern without Parliament (as Crispi did in 1895), of dissolving opposition associations and unions (as the government of Antonio Starabba, Marquis di Rudinì, did in 1897), and of attempting to push through restrictions on civil liberties by royal decree, without parliamentary approval (as both the di Rudinì and the Luigi Pelloux governments tried to do in 1898–99).

Repression soon led to a constitutional crisis. Conservative politicians, notably Baron Sidney Sonnino in 1897, argued that the Italian Parliament was corrupt and unfit to govern and that the king should provide strong executive rule, according to the letter of the 1848 Statuto (Statute). Most moderate Liberals rejected this argument. The campaign for constitutional government was led by Felice Cavallotti and the "Radical" group in Parliament, who in the 1890s strongly denounced bank scandals, tariff protectionism, colonial wars, and the Triple Alliance. The Radicals were a northern, anticlerical, moralistic group that denounced the corruption of the south (Crispi was the first southern prime minister), of the monarchy, and of the Roman establishment and strongly favoured wider civil liberties and army reform. In 1900, after months of bitter parliamentary dispute and obstructionism, Pelloux called a general election to resolve the constitutional issue; the Left triumphed; the Radicals won 34 seats, and their allies, the Republicans, won a further 28 out of a total of 557. (The two groups had had 51 seats between them in the previous Parliament.)

Furthermore, in 1892 a young Milanese lawyer, Filippo Turati, had helped to found the Italian Socialist Party among the various socialist and labour groups of northern and central Italy and Sicily. The new party was mainly social democratic, heavily influenced by the German model: it preached the class struggle and aspired to parliamentary representation and state socialism. Formally Marxist, it envisaged a long period of "evolution" before an eventual "revolutionary" transformation of society. Crispi dissolved the party in 1894, but it revived in the late 1890s and won 32 seats in 1900. While its deputies worked closely with the Radicals to secure constitutional liberties and social reforms, ordinary party members were often much more revolutionary in their aims. Other socialist organizations, such as trade unions and cooperatives, also grew in the 1890s and by 1900 were significant in the newly industrializing economy of northern Italy. They campaigned for concrete short-term gains on wages and working conditions and were usually more "reformist" than the party.

The Giolitti era, 1900–14. The elections of June 1900 marked the defeat of the Pelloux government and of attempts to impose illiberal laws. The following month King Umberto I was assassinated by an anarchist. The new king, Victor Emmanuel III, favoured a return to constitutional government, as did the governments led by Pelloux's successors, Giuseppe Saracco, Giuseppe Zanardelli, and Giovanni Giolitti, the last-named most often holding the office of prime minister between 1903 and 1914. His policy was to defuse popular discontent by social reforms and public works and to conciliate the major organized opposition groups in the country, the Socialists and the Roman Catholics.

Domestic policies. The social reforms passed in these years included laws prohibiting child labour, establishing a compulsory maternity fund and compulsory rest days, and limiting the working day of women to 11 hours. Central governments also subsidized municipal welfare schemes such as orphanages and old people's homes and encouraged municipal transport, housing, and water and sewage schemes—especially in northern Italy, where the municipalities could afford such innovations. Often these schemes were pioneered by Catholic- or Socialist-dominated local councils which entrusted the management to their "own" cooperatives; government approval of "municipal socialism" was much resented by local businessmen and taxpayers. Moreover, Giolitti's governments allowed trade unions to operate freely and generally avoided interfering in private-sector labour disputes—another source of middle-class resentment.

Giolitti enjoyed Radical support, and his governments often included Radical deputies. He also received the tacit support of moderate Socialist deputies and union leaders. Trade unionism grew rapidly in the new atmosphere after 1900, not only in industry but among the agricultural labourers of the Po Valley and Puglia; the various Socialist-led unions formed a General Confederation of Labour in 1906. Some unions depended heavily on public works schemes subsidized by government; others, such as the Federation of Agricultural Labourers (Federterra), relied on Giolitti's reform legislation favouring cooperatives and on contracts provided by Socialist councils. All the major Socialist institutions became reliant on government willingness not to repress them; in turn, they gave up any attempt to overthrow the government. However, the Socialist Party in the country was dominated by revolutionary views from 1904 to 1908 and was always more militant than its leaders. Moreover, there was also a pow-

General Confederation of Labour

erful group of revolutionary syndicalists, who broke away from the Socialist Party in 1907 but still controlled many unions, especially in Liguria. This popular militancy ensured that Socialist deputies could not compromise too openly with Giolitti or accept posts in his governments.

The Catholics, too, had founded trade unions and workers' cooperatives, as well as mutual aid societies and rural banks, throughout northern Italy in the 1890s. These associations were particularly strong among the peasantry of Lombardy and Piedmont and among the largely female textile workers, and they, too, controlled many local councils. In 1897–98 most Catholic associations were dissolved by the di Rudinì government, but later governments permitted them to be refounded in return for tacit support against socialism. This support even became overt at parliamentary elections—in 1904 and 1909 the papal prohibition on Catholics voting (*non expedit*) was lifted in many constituencies, and Catholics were permitted to vote for Liberal candidates in order to keep Socialists out. The old "intransigents" of the Opera dei Congressi, deeply hostile to a united Italy, were replaced early in the century by a new generation of "clerico-moderate" leaders favoured by Pius X, who even dissolved the Opera dei Congressi in 1904 and brought the Catholic lay movement under the bishops. The clerico-moderates gave Giolitti their support, but they too could not enter government or even operate as a lay party independent of the bishops or the Vatican.

Economic developments. Giolitti's political dominance had rested on Italy's rapid economic growth after the mid-1890s. Industrial production probably doubled between 1896 and 1913. The tariff dispute with France was settled in 1898. Cotton remained the largest industry, but by 1914 Italy had also acquired—for military reasons—a large, protected steel industry, together with extensive shipbuilding yards in Liguria. The railways were nationalized in 1905, and this stimulated demand for rolling stock and engines. Hydroelectricity from the Alps provided cheap, renewable energy for the factories of the northern "industrial triangle" (Lombardy, Liguria, and Piedmont). Moreover, a major new industry—automobile production—developed, in which Italy did not have to compete against established interests elsewhere. Fiat, founded in Turin in 1899 by Giovanni Agnelli, soon became one of Europe's largest producers and exporters of automobiles and also made buses, trucks, airplanes, and military vehicles. The state finances were healthy, and the balance of payments was boosted by remittances from the enormous numbers of emigrants in Europe and the Americas.

Fiat

Agriculture was still the dominant sector of the economy, providing jobs for almost 60 percent of employed adults in 1911. It, too, enjoyed a boom, partly because of state-subsidized land reclamation and irrigation schemes (particularly in the Po Valley) and partly because of continued high tariff protection on grains, which gave ample incentive to produce more food on suitable land. Wheat production rose by about one-third in these years. In central Italy, sugar beet production, another heavily protected sector, stimulated a new refining industry.

Economic growth, however, was heavily concentrated in the north. The south languished, and income there was less than half that in the north. The southern economy was arguably linked more closely to northern Europe and South America (to which it exported wine, olive oil, fruit, and labour) than to northern Italy. Southern produce needed markets abroad, and the south was very badly hit by the tariff war with France. Moreover, the southerners were widely held, by the positivist school of anthropology fashionable in the 1890s and later, to be more criminal than northerners and even racially degenerate—an argument that lent racial overtones to the debate on "southern backwardness."

Southern politicians soon began demanding, and when in office securing, tax relief and development schemes, which provided, among other things, roads, schools, and irrigation. In 1897 the first "special law" provided Italy's poorest region, Sardinia, with cheaper credit and some funds for irrigation and reforestation; Sardinia's leading politician, Francesco Cocco Ortu, was minister of agriculture. Later laws extended similar or greater benefits to other regions and in 1906 to the entire south. In practice, the legislation had little impact, as World War I interrupted any progress. However, it was the first time that funds derived from taxes paid by the prosperous north were used by central government agencies to stimulate economic activity in the south—or, at least, to win votes for supporters of central politicians.

Emigration

Continuing southern poverty stimulated mass emigration from Sicily and the southern mainland, averaging more than 500,000 people per year from about 1901 onward and rising to 900,000 in 1913, mainly to North and South America. About half of the migrants to the New World returned later, bringing new values as well as new money. Some southerners crossed the Atlantic twice a year, moving to seasonal agricultural work in Argentina. In the north most emigration was seasonal, to other European countries; but many rural dwellers migrated within Italy to jobs in the expanding industrial cities. Migrants were usually young, male, unskilled, and illiterate. They tended to come from areas of small farms and peasant landownership, where there were no trade unions able to protect the rural poor and where people married late.

Health and education. The other major social changes in these years, apart from emigration, were those brought about by the decline in serious illnesses and in illiteracy. Improved water supplies and sewerage meant fewer cholera epidemics—though these still occurred at times, as at Barletta in 1910–12. Malaria, a major scourge of the rural south, declined sharply as quinine became widely available after 1900. Pellagra, a vitamin-deficiency disease endemic among the northern peasantry, rapidly declined as diets improved. By 1901, for the first time, a majority (51.3 percent) of Italians could read and write. Emigrants needed to be able to write home, and so they had an incentive to learn. In 1911 the primary schools were removed from municipal control—poor communes had not been able to build schools or to enforce attendance—and were henceforth run and financed by the central government. Millions of people now spoke Italian, having learned it in school or in the army or needing to use it as a lingua franca in the cities. A common language, common education, and common experience of military service had begun, by 1914, to "make Italians"—but religion, social class, and local loyalties still greatly divided them.

WORLD WAR I AND FASCISM

War and its aftermath. *Conduct of the war.* On Giolitti's resignation in March 1914 a new government was formed by the more conservative Antonio Salandra. In June came "Red Week," a period of widespread rioting throughout Romagna and the Marche, which was precipitated by the killing of three antimilitarist demonstrators at Ancona. When World War I broke out in August, the Salandra government stayed neutral and began to negotiate with both sides—a policy described by Foreign Minister Sidney Sonnino as "sacred egoism." The Austrians eventually agreed to grant Trentino to Italy, but the Entente (France, Britain, and Russia) made a more generous offer, promising Italy not only Trentino but also South Tyrol, Trieste, Gorizia, Istria, and northern Dalmatia. The Italians accepted this offer at the secret Treaty of London (April 1915) and joined the war against Austria-Hungary a month later, hoping for major territorial gains.

The negotiations, conducted by the foreign and prime ministers and a handful of diplomats, had been kept secret. The majority of deputies, meanwhile, favoured neutrality, as did former prime minister Giolitti, the major opposition groups (Catholics and Socialists), and most of the population. War, therefore, was supported only by the conservatives in government, by the Nationalist Association, a group formed in 1910 by Enrico Corradini and others to support Italian expansionism, by some Liberals who saw it as the culmination of the Risorgimento's fight for national unity, by Republicans and reformist Socialists who thought they were fighting for national liberation, and by some syndicalists and extremist Socialists—including Benito Mussolini, editor of the Socialist Party newspaper—who thought the war would bring about the overthrow of capitalism. Mussolini was soon expelled from the Socialist

Supporters of the war

Party, but with help from the Entente he managed to found his own alternative, pro-war newspaper, *Il popolo d'Italia.* In April–May 1915 the government, helped by noisy demonstrations by pro-war activists, pushed through its war policy despite the opposition of the majority in Parliament and in the country. Neither Giolitti nor any other "neutralist" could form a government without renouncing the Treaty of London, betraying Italy's new allies, and compromising the king.

In June 1916, after a series of military failures, the Salandra government resigned. The new prime minister was Paolo Boselli, who in turn resigned after a military disaster at Caporetto in October 1917, which enabled the Austrians to occupy much of the Veneto in 1917–18. The war was deeply unpopular both among the troops—mostly conscript peasants, who were undernourished and fighting for a cause few could understand—and among the civilian population back home, which included almost one million workers in arms factories who were also subject to military discipline. Serious bread riots took place among the industrial workers of Turin in August 1917, and the defeat at Caporetto was widely attributed to poor morale and "defeatism." After November 1917 a more "democratic" government under Vittorio Emanuele Orlando rallied the country to defend its frontiers and appointed a new army commander, Armando Diaz. Diaz made welfare concessions to the troops and fought a far more defensive campaign until October 1918, when, in the closing stages of the war, the Italians won a final, decisive victory at the Battle of Vittorio Veneto.

The cost of victory. Italy won the war, therefore, but at a huge cost: 600,000 dead and a legacy of bitterness and division. The victorious patriots and Nationalists now detested Parliament, where the Giolittian majority had never supported the war; the returning veterans also regarded Catholics and Socialists as defeatists and most industrial workers as "shirkers" (*imboscati*). These divisions greatly weakened the postwar political regime. Furthermore, the pro-war groups were themselves bitterly divided when the war ended. Should Italy, at the Paris Peace Conference (1919–20), try to secure the terms of the Treaty of London, as Foreign Minister Sonnino urged, or should it support U.S. President Woodrow Wilson and adhere to the "principle of nationality"—that is, be willing to accept less territory in the Adriatic region, as the Left Liberals and Republicans advocated? In the Treaty of Saint-Germain (1919), Italy was granted Trentino, Trieste, (the German-speaking) South Tyrol, and Istria. But Dalmatia was excluded, despite the Treaty of London, as was Fiume (now Rijeka), a Croatian port largely inhabited by Italian speakers, which Sonnino had also decided to claim; so, too, were any colonial territories in Africa or Asia and any claim on Albania. Nationalists therefore argued that Italy had been robbed of its rightful gains ("a mutilated victory"). Orlando resigned in June 1919. When the new government of the Radical leader Francesco Saverio Nitti was also unsuccessful in foreign affairs, the flamboyant poet Gabriele D'Annunzio led a group of volunteer "legionaries" to Fiume in September and captured the city himself. Fiume became a centre of nationalist agitation for more than a year, and D'Annunzio was dislodged only in December 1920, when Fiume became, briefly, an independent republic.

D'Annunzio's capture of Fiume

Economic and political crisis. Italy was faced with serious postwar economic problems. Wartime governments had printed money to pay for arms, and inflation became deep-rooted: by the end of 1920 the lira was worth only one-sixth of its 1913 value. Savings became worthless, and landowners found themselves receiving insignificant rents. Meanwhile the major arms and shipbuilding firms went bankrupt after the war for lack of government orders. Unemployment rose to two million, as returning soldiers searched for work. Peasants, organized by ex-servicemen's groups or Catholic leagues, seized land for themselves; agricultural labourers went on strike at harvest time. Trade unions, now operating again, pressed for higher wages, and strikes became routine, including those in the public services. Throughout September 1920 most of the northern Italian factories were occupied by workers staging sit-down strikes. The Socialist Party, dominated by its "maximalist" wing, proclaimed the need for immediate revolution, as had recently occurred in Russia. The postwar governments of Nitti (1919–20) and his successors Giolitti (1920–21), Ivanoe Bonomi (1921–22), and Luigi Facta (February–October 1922) were weak and could do little except urge industrialists and landowners to make concessions not only on pay but even on "control" of the workplace.

Diplomatic and economic failures soon undermined middle-class confidence in government, especially as Giolitti also imposed taxes on war profits. In 1919 proportional representation was introduced for parliamentary elections. The result, in the new Parliament elected in November 1919, was that the Socialists, with 30 percent of the vote, won 156 seats and the new (Catholic) Italian Popular Party, with more than 20 percent of the vote, 100 seats; these two parties dominated northern and central Italy. Giolitti had to bring the Popular Party into his government in 1920 and make many concessions to peasant interests, including giving guarantees to squatters and giving the Ministry of Agriculture to the Catholics. Furthermore, the two "subversive" parties won control of almost half the municipalities in the autumn of 1920, ensuring that Socialist or Catholic cooperatives would be given all local public works contracts. And in January 1921 the left wing of the Socialists split away to found the Italian Communist Party, which increased middle-class alarm.

The Fascist era. *The rise of Mussolini.* The political crisis of the postwar years provided an opportunity for militant, patriotic movements, including those of ex-servicemen and former assault troops, radical students, ex-syndicalists, and former pro-war agitators. D'Annunzio in Fiume led one such movement, but the ex-Socialist journalist Benito Mussolini soon became even more prominent, founding his Fasci di Combattimento ("Fighting Leagues") in Milan in March 1919. It was initially unsuccessful, but local Fascist groups were soon founded in Emilia and Tuscany and by autumn 1920 were busy not only breaking up strikes but also dismantling Socialist and Catholic labour unions and peasants' cooperatives and overthrowing newly elected local councils. Within a few months paramilitary Fascist squad leaders controlled most of the rural areas of central Italy. The Fascists had become a major political force, backed not only by landowners but also by many members of the urban middle class, including students, shopkeepers, and clerical workers. In May 1921, when Prime Minister Giolitti called new elections, 35 Fascists were elected to Parliament as part of a government "block" of 275 deputies. In October Mussolini abandoned republicanism, and in November he formed his movement into a proper political party, the National Fascist Party (PNF), which by this time was well-financed if ill-disciplined and extremely disparate: local bosses remained paramount in their areas. The Fascists also organized their own trade unions, the Fascist "syndicates," in order to replace Socialist or Catholic organizations, to provide mass membership, and to control labour.

Mussolini maneuvered brilliantly in the next few months, and the Liberal political establishment sought to conciliate him and the Fascist thugs. The police, the army, and much of the middle class sympathized with Fascist disruption of Socialist unions. Mussolini, as "duce" (leader) of fascism, gradually made himself indispensable in Rome. A major anti-Fascist protest strike, called by the Socialist-led Confederation of Labour in August 1922, soon collapsed, strengthening Mussolini's bargaining position even further. In October 1922 he organized a "March on Rome" by Fascist supporters. Prime Minister Facta asked the king to declare martial law, but Victor Emmanuel III eventually refused in order to avoid possible army disloyalty or even a possible civil war. Instead, he asked Mussolini to form a government, hoping to tame him by constitutional means.

Mussolini's March on Rome

Mussolini became prime minister, therefore, in a more or less constitutional manner. He was appointed by the king, and he headed a coalition government that included Nationalists, Liberals, and even (until April 1923) two Catholic ministers from the Popular Party. For 18 months he ruled through the usual government machinery and pursued a policy of "normalization." The squads were incorporated into an official Voluntary Militia for National Security. Ordinary middle-class job seekers flooded into the Fascist Party, making it more respectable and amenable; the Nationalists also merged their organization into it, bringing with them much respectable backing in the south. In 1923 the electoral law was changed once more, so that a group of parties with the largest vote—even if only 25 percent of the total—would receive an absolute majority of the seats. This enabled the Fascists to attract most of the old Liberal deputies into a "national alliance." In April 1924 elections were held under this system; the Fascist-dominated bloc won 64 percent of the votes and 374 seats, doing particularly well in the south. The opposition parties—by now including the Popular Party—remained divided but won a majority of the votes in northern Italy. The Socialists, indeed, had by this time split into three rival parties: the Communists, the Socialists, and the reformist Socialists. None of them had much influence. The Popular Party was being disowned by the Vatican, and its leader, Luigi Sturzo, resigned at the Vatican's request.

The end of constitutional rule. Mussolini's success as leader of a "normalizing" constitutional government with widespread support did not last long. When the new Parliament met, Giacomo Matteotti, leader of the reformist Socialists, denounced the recent elections as a sham and claimed there had been widespread intimidation of opposition voters. On June 10, 1924, Matteotti disappeared. He was later found to have been murdered by Fascist thugs led by the assistant to Mussolini's press office, Amerigo Dumini. A great crisis of confidence ensued. Mussolini was suspected of personal complicity and of having ordered the murder in order to eliminate a troublesome opponent. The press denounced the government, and the opposition parties walked out of Parliament. However, Mussolini still had a majority in Parliament, and the king backed him. But by autumn his Liberal supporters were drifting away, and in any case the "normalization" policy infuriated Fascist extremists in the country. They demanded a showdown, and Mussolini—who was too weak by this time to rule by constitutional means—had to agree. On Jan. 3, 1925, he made a famous speech in the Chamber of Deputies accepting responsibility for fascism and promising a tough crackdown on dissenters. The king made no move.

Mussolini's speech in the Chamber of Deputies

During the next two years Mussolini disbanded most of Italy's constitutional and conventional safeguards against government autocracy. Free speech and free association disappeared; opposition parties and unions were dissolved and their leaders forced into exile. At the local level, appointed podestas replaced elected mayors and councils. Freemasonry was outlawed—a real blow to most non-Catholic anti-Fascists. A Special Tribunal for the Defense of the State, run by militia and army officers, was set up to try anti-Fascist "subversives"; it imprisoned or sent to exile on remote islands thousands of political opponents, including the Communist leader Antonio Gramsci, and it imposed 31 death penalties. However, the repression was carried out essentially by the old state institutions, such as the police and army, not by Fascist bodies. The prefects—mostly still career civil servants—retained their traditional dominance over local government, and the new podesta was nearly always a landowner or retired army officer rather than a Fascist enthusiast. The Fascist party itself was soon swamped by more than a million job seekers and clerical workers, and thousands of the original Fascists were purged. The party, and the militia, soon had little to do except engage in propaganda and parades. The Fascist regime was mostly run by the traditional elites in the military and civilian bureaucracy, which were linked, as previously, to landowners and the court. That said, it was much more authoritarian and also much more nationalistic and interventionist than the Liberal governments had been.

Fascist indoctrination was never really successful, but the press was tightly censored, cinema newsreels were largely government propaganda, and the regime controlled the new radio broadcasting. It also ran semicompulsory Fascist youth movements, and new textbooks were imposed on the schools. The government also provided mass leisure activities, such as sports, concerts, and seaside holidays, which were genuinely popular.

Anti-Fascist movements. For a long time organized anti-Fascist movements remained weak, divided, and illegal and had no access to press or radio. The Communists were soon the most significant of these movements, as they had an underground organization and some Russian support and finance, but even they had 7,000 members at most and had great difficulty in spreading their propaganda in Italy. New anti-Fascist groups were founded occasionally, but the secret police soon cracked down on them. Apart from the Communists, only Justice and Liberty, an alliance of Republicans, Democrats, and reformist Socialists founded by Carlo Rosselli and others in 1929, managed to build up a clandestine organization in Italy. Most prominent anti-Fascists were in prison, in "confinement" on remote islands, or in exile and had little contact with Italian reality.

The only strong non-Fascist organization in the country was the Roman Catholic church. The Vatican implicitly supported Mussolini in the early years and was rewarded in February 1929 by the Lateran Treaty, which settled the "Roman question" at last. Vatican City became an independent state, Italy paid a large financial indemnity to the pope for taking over his pre-1870 lands, and a concordat granted the church many privileges in Italy, including recognition of church weddings as valid in civil law, religious education in secondary—as well as in primary—schools, and freedom for the lay Catholic organizations in Catholic Action. However, the government soon began curbing Catholic Action, seeing it as a front for anti-Fascist activity by former members of the Popular Party. The Catholic youth organizations were closed for a time in 1931. When they reopened, they had to avoid sports, but, even so, they grew considerably in the 1930s. They were a serious rival to the Fascist youth bodies and trained a new generation that often managed to avoid Fascist indoctrination. The 1929 concordat remained in force until the 1980s and was the legal basis for church dominance of Italian society after World War II. Anti-Fascist feeling became more widespread after the mid-1930s. Italy sent "volunteer" militiamen to fight on Francisco Franco's side in the Spanish Civil War (1936–39), but they were defeated in 1937 at the Battle of Guadalajara. Italy's increasingly close alliance with Adolf Hitler's Germany was also resented and feared, even by many Fascists. So, too, was the sudden decision to impose anti-Semitic laws in 1938: Jews were condemned as unpatriotic, excluded from government jobs, and forbidden to marry "Aryans." It had become clear that the Fascist government was likely to involve Italy in a disastrous European war, as indeed it did in 1940.

The Lateran Treaty

Economic policy. Fascist intervention in the economy was designed for prestige and to boost military strength. In the early years the Fascists compromised with the business establishment and rescued failing banks. However, in 1926 the lira was suddenly revalued for political reasons, and Italy suffered all the usual consequences of an overvalued currency. Exports fell sharply, unemployment rose, wages were frozen or even cut, and prices fell. The steel, electricity, and chemical industries expanded, for their markets were domestic, and they were helped by cheaper raw material imports; industries producing textiles, food, and vehicles, which were reliant on foreign markets, declined.

When the Great Depression came after 1929, these deflationary processes were accentuated. The leading banks, which had lent heavily to industry, had to be rescued in the early 1930s, as did many large industrial companies. Two new state-run holding companies, the Italian Industrial Finance Institute (Istituto Mobiliare Italiano; IMI) and the Institute for Industrial Reconstruction (Istituto per la Ricostruzione Industriale; IRI), were set up to bail out failing firms and to provide capital for new industrial investment; they also provided trained managers and effective financial supervision. Italy thus acquired a huge, state-owned industrial sector, which was especially important in banking, steel, shipping, armaments, and the supply of hydroelectricity. However, these firms were not nationalized; they operated in the market as private companies and still had many private shareholders. In the long term they gave Italy a modern infrastructure—including roads and cheap energy—a sounder financial sector, and some efficient modern industries in expanding sectors such as chemicals and synthetic fibres. Most industrial development, and most workers, remained in northern Italy, although by this time large steelmaking and shipbuilding plants had been started at Naples and Taranto.

The Fascist syndicates

After October 1925 the Fascist syndicates, or trade unions, were the sole recognized negotiators for workers' interests. Strikes and lockouts became illegal, and wages fell between 1927 and 1934, but the syndicates had considerable political influence. They secured a shorter working week (40 hours in November 1934), higher welfare benefits (such as family allowances, also introduced in 1934), and public works schemes, and they also helped run leisure and social activities. Most industrial jobs were protected throughout the depression, and the syndicates remained fairly popular until World War II. In 1934 the Fascists also set up "corporations"—mixed bodies of syndicalists and employers—to decide labour disputes and supervise wage settlements. Despite much rhetoric and propaganda about them, they had little impact in practice and virtually none on industrial management or economic policy making.

In agricultural policy the government aimed at self-sufficiency by encouraging grain production ("the battle for wheat"). A high tariff was reimposed on imported wheat, and grain prices were kept artificially high. Production rose sharply as northern farmers used more chemical fertilizers. In much of the south the climate was unsuitable for growing wheat, but vineyards and olive groves were nonetheless plowed up. The real beneficiaries of this policy were the large farmers of the Po Valley and of the southern latifundia. These men also benefited most from the government's land-reclamation schemes, forming their own consortia and receiving government money to drain or irrigate their own land. Moreover, during the depression they could buy land cheaply from the smaller landowners because many of the peasants who had acquired land during and after World War I were forced to sell after 1926.

After Italy's invasion of Ethiopia in 1935–36, the Italian economy was subjected to sanctions by the League of Nations. This led to a more extensive drive for self-sufficiency ("autarchy"); imports were replaced where possible by native products, and most exports were diverted to Germany and Switzerland or to Africa. Ethiopia, once conquered, became a vast drain on resources. Government intervention and licensing became more marked, with official cartels and quasi-monopolies encouraged; resources were shifted, from above, to heavy industry and armaments. All this led to budget deficits, big tax increases, and capital levies, which were hugely resented because they were mainly needed to pay for wars in Africa and Spain. Resented, too, was the obvious corruption of the Fascist governing clique, without whose permits—available at a price—nothing could be done. The various conservative groups, including those in the army, the civil service, the law, and the church, which in the mid-1920s had looked to Fascism to protect their interests, realized by the late 1930s that Fascism was unreliable and withdrew their support.

Declining emigration

American restrictions, European recession, and Fascist economic nationalism combined to curtail emigration drastically in the 1930s, from more than 600,000 people per annum before 1914 to fewer than 50,000 per annum. The closing of emigration outlets hit the south particularly badly. As they could not go abroad, rural Italians moved to the cities: Rome doubled in size between 1921 and 1940, and northern cities became full of southern immigrants. Moreover, government policy encouraged population growth by providing tax incentives to have children and excluding the childless from public jobs. Admittedly, all this had little effect before 1937: Italians married later than ever and had fewer children than previously, so much so that in several northern and central regions the birth rate dropped below replacement level in the 1930s.

Foreign policy. Fascist foreign policy became more expansionist as time went on. In particular, Mussolini aimed at acquiring territory in Africa and in the Mediterranean, which he termed "mare nostrum" ("our sea"). Even in 1923, in his first year in office, he briefly invaded the Greek island of Corfu to avenge the murder of four Italian nationals forming part of an international boundary delegation. During the next decade he played the European statesman, and in 1924 he reached an agreement with Yugoslavia that gave Fiume to Italy. He also continued to strengthen the Italian hold on Libya, to build up the armed forces, and to plan further expansion in Africa—particularly in Ethiopia, where the defeat at Adwa in 1896 still needed to be avenged. In October 1935 Italy finally invaded Ethiopia and by May 1936 had conquered the country. However, the war antagonized the British and French governments, led to sanctions by the League of Nations, and isolated Italy diplomatically. Mussolini moved into Hitler's orbit, hoping that German backing would frighten the British and French into granting further concessions to Italy. The policy was unsuccessful: no more territory was acquired in Africa. Furthermore, Italy became a junior partner in the "Rome-Berlin Axis," and in 1938 Mussolini had to accept Hitler's annexation of Austria, bringing the German Reich right up to the Italian border. In May 1939 Mussolini entered a formal military alliance with Hitler, the "Pact of Steel," which further reduced his scope for maneuvering. Even so, when the Germans unexpectedly invaded Poland in September 1939, Mussolini insisted on remaining neutral.

World War II. *Military disaster.* Only in June 1940, when France was about to fall and the war seemed virtually over, did Italy join the war on Germany's side, still hoping for territorial spoils. Italy's initial attack on the French Alps in June 1940 was soon cut short by the Franco-German armistice. The real war for Italy began only in October, when Mussolini attacked Greece in a disastrous campaign that obliged the Germans, in 1941, to rescue the Italian forces and take over Greece themselves. The Germans also had to lend support in the hard-fought campaigns of North Africa, where eventually the decisive second battle of el-Alamein (October 1942) destroyed the Italian position and led to the surrender of the whole of Italy's North African forces in May 1943. Meanwhile, the Italians had lost their extensive empire in eastern Africa, including Ethiopia, early in 1941; and their 250,000 troops in Russia, sent to help the German invaders, suffered untold hardships. In short, the war was an almost unrelieved succession of military disasters. The main reason was poor equipment. Italy had few tanks or antitank guns; clothing, food, vehicles, and fuel were all scarce; and supplies could not safely be taken to North Africa or Russia. Italian factories could not produce weapons without steel, coal, or oil, and, even when raw materials were available, production was limited because the northern Italian factories were subject to heavy Allied bombing, especially in 1942–43.

Mounting opposition to the war

Bombing, indeed, was one of the causes of the first major strikes since 1925. In March 1943 the leading factories in Milan and Turin stopped work in order to secure evacuation allowances for workers' families. By this time civilian morale was clearly very low, food shortages were endemic, and hundreds of thousands of people had fled to the countryside. Government propaganda was ineffective, and Italians could easily hear more accurate news on Radio Vatican or even Radio London. In Friuli–Venezia Giulia, as in Italian-occupied Slovenia and Croatia, the local Slav population supported armed resistance movements, and anti-Italian terrorism was widespread. The anti-Fascist movements cautiously revived in 1942–43. The Communists helped to organize strikes, the leading Roman Catholics formed a Christian Democratic Party in 1943, and a new Party of Action was founded in January 1943, mainly by republicans and Radicals. By this time most of the leading clandestine parties were more willing to work together to overthrow fascism; in April 1943 they signed an agreement to do so.

By the summer of 1943 the Italian position was hopeless. Northern and eastern Africa had been lost, the northern Italian cities were being regularly bombed, war production was minimal, and morale had collapsed. Court circles began sounding out Allied terms, which of course included the ouster of Mussolini. In July 1943 the Allies invaded Sicily, and within a few weeks they controlled the island. On July 24–25 the Fascist Grand Council met in Rome and passed a motion asking the king to resume his full constitutional powers—that is, to dismiss Mussolini. The king did so the same day and installed Marshal Pietro Badoglio as prime minister. The army took over the key positions in Rome, the duce was arrested, and the main Fascist institutions were dissolved.

End of the regime. Badoglio assured the Germans that the war would continue, but he also attempted, rather feebly, to reach armistice terms with the Allies. An armistice was eventually agreed on, and U.S. General Dwight D. Eisenhower, the Allied commander in chief in the Mediterranean, announced it on Sept. 8, 1943. The Germans immediately took over Rome; they had already, in the previous few weeks, taken over most of central and northern Italy. The Italian army, left without orders even to defend Rome, disintegrated. The king and his government fled south to Brindisi, leaving Rome to the Germans. Italy became a war zone: for 18 months the Allies and Germans fought each other up the peninsula, wreaking untold devastation throughout the land. The Allies took Naples in October 1943 but reached Rome only in June 1944, Florence in August, and the northern cities in April 1945.

The south was ruled by the Allies, and Badoglio's government, although it declared war on Germany in October 1943, had very little influence on events. The anti-Fascist parties, who detested Badoglio and wanted the king to abdicate, refused to join the government until April 1944, when the Communist Party leader Palmiro Togliatti agreed to do so. When Rome was liberated, Victor Emmanuel was replaced by his son, Umberto, as "lieutenant general of the realm," and the leading anti-Fascist parties formed a "government" led by the reformist Socialist Ivanoe Bonomi, who had been prime minister in 1921–22. In the meantime the Germans had rescued Mussolini from his mountain prison and restored him in the north as puppet ruler of the "Italian Social Republic," a last-ditch Fascist regime based in Salò on Lake Garda. He, too, had little influence on events or even on his own police forces and army. He spent his last months railing against the king for dismissing him and protesting against German dominance. At the end of April 1945 he fled toward Switzerland but was captured by Communist partisans at Dongo and shot; his body was then brought back for public display in Milan.

Mussolini and the Italian Social Republic

The partisans. After September 1943 partisan groups were active throughout northern and much of central Italy. Often they were former soldiers cut off from home and still in possession of their weapons; many were young men fleeing from Mussolini's attempts to conscript them; others were urban evacuees or released prisoners of war. They were most active in summer in the hills, where they were usually supported by the peasants, and they tied down thousands of German troops. There were also terrorist groups in the cities and major strikes in industrial areas sabotaging war production. The Communist Party, although still very small in 1943 (around 5,000 members), led the largest group of partisans (at least 50,000 by summer 1944). Success in the Resistance transformed the Communists into a major force in postwar Italian politics. The new Party of Action was also very active in the Resistance, with about a quarter of all partisan units; it had a strong commitment to radical political change (including the change to a republic and a purge of officials) as well as to military victory. The Christian Democrats had roughly 20,000 partisans, and both Socialists and Liberals had significant armed bands in some areas. Partisans of different political persuasions normally worked together in local Committees of National Liberation (CLNs), which coordinated strategy, administered liberated areas, and appointed new officials. Above all, they organized the uprisings in the northern cities, including Milan in April 1945, which fell to the partisans before Allied troops arrived. They thus laid the basis for postwar political collaboration.

(MARTIN CLARK)

Russia

Cultural life

THE DEVELOPMENT OF RUSSIAN CULTURE

Slavic and borrowed elements

Russia's unique and vibrant culture developed, as did the country itself, from a complicated interplay of native Slavic cultural material and borrowings from a wide variety of foreign cultures. In the Kievan period (*c.* 10th–13th century) the borrowings were primarily from Eastern Orthodox Byzantine culture. During the Muscovite period (*c.* 14th–17th century) the Slavic and Byzantine cultural substrates were enriched and modified by Asiatic influences carried by the Mongol hordes. Finally, in the modern period (since the 18th century) the cultural heritage of western Europe was added to the Russian melting pot.

The Kievan period. Although many traces of the Slavic culture that existed in the territories of Kievan Rus survived beyond its Christianization (which occurred, according to the Russian Primary Chronicle, in AD 988), the cultural system that organized the lives of the early Slavs is far from being understood. From the 10th century on, however, enough material has survived to give a reasonable portrait of Old Russian cultural life. High culture in Kievan Rus was primarily ecclesiastical. The level of literacy was low, and artistic composition was undertaken almost exclusively by monks. The earliest literary works to have circulated were translations from Greek into Old Church Slavonic (a South Slavic dialect that was, in this period, close enough to Old Russian to be understandable). By the 11th century, however, Russian monks were producing original works (on Byzantine models), primarily in the genres of saints' lives, historical chronicles, and homilies. At least one great secular work was produced as well; the epic *The Song of Igor's Campaign,* which dates from the late 12th century and describes a failed Russian military expedition against the neighbouring Polovtsy. Evidence also exists (primarily in the form of church records of suppression) of a thriving popular culture based on pre-Christian traditions centring around harvest, marriage, birth, and death rituals. The most important aspects of Kievan culture for the development of modern Russian culture, however, were not literary or folkloric but rather artistic and architectural. The early Slavic rulers expressed their religious piety and displayed their wealth through the construction of stone churches, at first in Byzantine style (like the 11th-century Cathedral of St. Sophia that still stands in Kiev, Ukraine) and later in a distinctive Russian style (best preserved today in churches in and around the city of Vladimir, to the east of Moscow). The interiors of many of these churches were ornately decorated with frescoes and icons.

The Muscovite period. The Mongol (Tatar) invasions of the 1230s decimated Kievan Rus. By the time Russian political and cultural life began to recover in the 14th century, a new centre had arisen: Muscovy (Moscow). Continuity with Kiev was provided by the Orthodox church, which had acted as a beacon of national life during the period of Tatar domination and which continued to play the central role in Russian cultural life into the 17th century. As a result, Russian cultural development in the Muscovite period was quite different from that of western Europe, which at this time was experiencing the secularization of society and the rediscovery of the classical cultural heritage that characterized the Renaissance. At first, the literary genres employed by Muscovite writers were the same as those that had dominated in Kiev. The most remarkable literary monuments of the Muscovite period, however, are unlike anything that came before. Most noteworthy is the correspondence between Tsar Ivan IV the Terrible and Prince Andrey Kurbsky during the 1560s and '70s. Kurbsky, a former general in Ivan's army, defected to Poland, from where he sent a letter critical of the tsar's regime. Ivan's diatribes in response are both wonderful expressions of outraged pride and literary tours de force, combining the highest style of Muscovite hagiographic writing with pithy and vulgar attacks on his enemy. Similarly vigorous in style is the first full-scale autobiography in Russian literature, *The Life of the Archpriest Avvakum, by Himself* (*c.* 1672–75).

As in the Kievan period, however, the most significant cultural achievements of Muscovy were not in literature but rather in the visual arts and architecture. The Moscow school of icon painting produced great masters, among them Andrey Rublyov (whose "Old Testament Trinity," now in Moscow's State Tretyakov Gallery, is among the most beautiful icons ever painted). Russian architects continued to design and build impressive churches, including the celebrated Cathedral of St. Basil the Blessed on Moscow's Red Square. St. Basil's is a perfect example of the confluence of Byzantine and Asiatic cultural streams that characterizes Muscovite culture.

Icon painting

The emergence of modern Russian culture. The gradual turn of Russia toward western Europe that began in the 17th century led to an almost total reorientation of Russian interests during the reign of Peter I the Great (1694–1725). Although Peter was not particularly interested in cultural questions, the influx of Western ideas and the weakening of the Orthodox church led to a cultural renaissance in the reigns of his successors. In the late 1730s the poets Mikhail Lomonosov and Vasily Trediakovsky carried out reforms as far-reaching as those of Peter. They adapted German syllabo-tonic versification to Russian, developing the system of "classical" metres that prevails in Russian poetry to this day. In the 1740s, in imitation of French Neoclassicism, Aleksandr Sumarokov wrote the first Russian stage tragedies. In the course of the century, Russian writers assimilated all the European genres; much of their work was derivative, but the comedies of Denis Fonvizin and the powerful solemn odes of Gavrila Derzhavin were original and have remained part of the active Russian cultural heritage. Prose fiction made its appearance at the end of the century in the works of the sentimentalist Nikolay Karamzin. By the beginning of the 19th century, after a 75-year European cultural apprenticeship, Russia was ready to produce fully original cultural work.

THE ARTS

Literature. *The 19th century.* The first quarter of the 19th century was dominated by romantic poetry. Vasily Zhukovsky's 1802 translation of Thomas Gray's *An Elegy Written in a Country Church Yard* ushered in a vogue for the personal, elegiac mode that was soon amplified in the work of Konstantin Batyushkov, Prince Pyotr Vyazemsky, and the young Aleksandr Pushkin. Although there was a call for civic-oriented poetry in the late 1810s and early '20s, most of the strongest poets followed Zhukovsky's lyrical path. The mature Pushkin of the 1820s, however, went his own way, producing a series of masterpieces that laid the foundation for his eventual recognition as Russia's national poet (Pushkin, for Russians, is the equivalent of Shakespeare for English readers or Dante for Italians); these works include the "Byronic" long poems *The Prisoner of the Caucasus* (1820–21) and *The Gypsies* (1824), the "novel in verse" *Yevgeny Onegin* (published 1833), and the "Shakespearean" tragedy *Boris Godunov* (1825), as well as exquisite lyrical verse.

The rise of prose

During the 1830s there was a gradual decline in poetry and a rise of prose. This shift coincided with a change in literary institutions: the aristocratic salon, which had been the seedbed for Russian literature, was gradually supplanted by the monthly "thick journals," the editors and critics of which became Russia's tastemakers. The turn to prose was signaled in the work of Pushkin, whose *Tales of the Late Ivan Petrovich Belkin* (1831), *The Queen of Spades* (1834), and *The Captain's Daughter* (1836) all appeared before his death in 1837. Also in the 1830s the first publications appeared by Nikolay Gogol, a comic writer of Ukrainian origin, whose grotesquely hilarious oeuvre includes the story "The Nose," the play *The Government Inspector* (both 1836), and the epic novel *Dead Souls* (1842). Although Gogol was known in his own day primarily as a satirist, he now is appreciated as a verbal magician, whose works seem akin to the absurdists of the 20th century. One final burst of poetic energy appeared in the late 1830s in the verse of Mikhail Lermontov, known also as the author of the first Russian psychological novel, *A Hero of Our Time* (1840).

In the 1840s the axis of Russian literature shifted decisively from the personal and Romantic to the civic and realistic, a shift presided over by the great Russian literary critic Vissarion Belinsky. Belinsky called for a literature concerned with current social problems, although he never expected it to give up the aesthetic function entirely. By the end of the 1840s, Belinsky's ideas had triumphed. Early works of Russian realism include Ivan Goncharov's antiromantic novel *A Common Story* (1847) and Fyodor Dostoyevsky's *Poor Folk* (1846).

From the 1840s until the turn of the 20th century, the realist novel was the dominant genre in Russian literature. Realism was not, however, a monolithic movement. In the early period, the favoured method was the "physiological sketch," often depicting a typical member of the downtrodden classes: quintessential examples are found in Ivan Turgenev's 1852 collection *A Sportsman's Sketches.* In these beautifully crafted stories, Turgenev describes the life of Russian serfs as seen through the eyes of a Turgenev-like narrator. The power of Turgenev's artistic depiction was credited with convincing Tsar Alexander II of the need to emancipate the serfs. Turgenev followed *Sketches* with a series of novels, each of which was felt by contemporaries to have captured the essence of Russian society at the time it appeared. The most celebrated is *Fathers and Sons* (1862), in which generational and class conflict in the period of Alexander II's reforms is described through the interactions of the Kirsanov family (father, son, and uncle) with the young "nihilist" Bazarov.

Dostoyevsky and Tolstoy

The two other great realists of the 19th century were Fyodor Dostoyevsky and Leo Tolstoy. Dostoyevsky, who was arrested in 1849 for his involvement in a socialist reading group, reentered the literary scene in the late 1850s. While in prison, he experienced a religious conversion, and his novels of the 1860s and '70s are suffused with messianic Orthodox ideas. Dostoyevsky's major novels—*Crime and Punishment* (1866), *The Idiot* (1868–69), *The Possessed* (1872), and *The Brothers Karamazov* (1879–80)—are filled with riveting, often unstable characters and dramatic scenes. While Dostoyevsky delves into the psychology of men and women at the edge, Tolstoy's novels treat the everyday existence of normal people. In both *War and Peace* (1865–69) and *Anna Karenina* (1875–77) Tolstoy draws beautifully nuanced portraits filled with deep psychological and sociological insight.

By the early 1880s, the hegemony of the realist novel was waning. What was to replace the novel, however, was unclear. Russian poetry, notwithstanding the civic verse of Nikolay Nekrasov and the subtle lyrics of Afanasy Fet, had not played a central role in the literary process since the 1830s, and drama, despite the able work of Aleksandr Ostrovsky, was a marginal literary activity for most writers. The only major prose writer to appear in the 1880s and '90s was Anton Chekhov, whose specialty was the short story. In his greatest stories—including "The Man in a Case" (1898), "The Lady with a Lapdog" (1899), "The Darling" (1899), and "In the Ravine" (1900)—Chekhov manages to attain all the power of his great predecessors in a remarkably compact form. Toward the end of his career, Chekhov also became known for his dramatic work, including such pillars of the world theatrical repertoire as *Uncle Vanya* (1897) and *The Cherry Orchard* (1903). Chekhov's heirs in the area of short fiction were the lower-class writer Maksim Gorky (who later would become the dean of Soviet letters) and the aristocrat Ivan Bunin (who emigrated after the Russian Revolution of 1917 and received the Nobel Prize for Literature in 1933).

The 20th century. The turn of the century ushered in a new renaissance in Russian poetry and drama, a "Silver Age" that rivaled, and in some respects surpassed, the Pushkinian "Golden Age." The civic orientation that had dominated Russian literature since the 1840s was, for the moment, abandoned. The avant-garde's new cry was "art for art's sake," and the new idols were the French Symbolists. The first, "decadent" generation of Russian Symbolists included the poets Valery Bryusov, Konstantin Balmont, and Zinaida Gippius. The second, more mystically and apocalyptically oriented generation included Aleksandr Blok (perhaps the most talented lyric poet Russia ever produced), the poet and theoretician Vyacheslav Ivanov, and the poet and prose writer Andrey Bely. The Symbolists remained ascendant until 1910, when internal dissension led to the collapse of the movement.

Poetry of the 1917 Revolution period

The period just before and immediately following the 1917 Revolution was marked by the work of six spectacularly talented, difficult poets. Anna Akhmatova's brief, finely chiseled lyrics brought her fame at the outset of her career, but later in life she produced such longer works as *Requiem,* her memorial to the victims of Joseph Stalin's purges. The Futurists Velimir Khlebnikov and Vladimir Mayakovsky engaged in innovative experiments to free poetic discourse from the fetters of tradition. Marina Tsvetayeva was a great poetic experimenter as well. She produced much of her major work as an émigré but returned to the Soviet Union in 1939, only to commit suicide there in 1941. Boris Pasternak, who won the Nobel Prize for Literature in 1958, produced lyrics of great depth and power in this period, and Osip Mandelshtam brought his great erudition to the creation of some of the most beautiful and haunting lyric poems in the Russian language.

Many of the writers who began to publish immediately after the Revolution turned to prose, particularly the short story and the novella. Some were inspired by the recent Revolution and Russian Civil War, including Boris Pilnyak (*The Naked Year* [1922]), Isaak Babel (*Red Cavalry* [1926]), and Mikhail Sholokhov, who won the Nobel Prize in 1965 for his writings. Others described life in the new Soviet Union with varying degrees of mordant sarcasm; the short stories of Mikhail Zoshchenko, the comic novels of Ilya Ilf and Yevgeny Petrov, and the short novel *Envy* (1927) by Yury Olesha fall into this category.

The first decade after the Revolution also was a time of significant advances in literary theory and criticism, which changed methods of literary study throughout the world. Members of the Moscow Linguistic Circle and of the Society for the Study of Poetic Language (OPOYAZ) in Petrograd (now St. Petersburg) combined to create Formalist literary criticism, a movement that concentrated on analyzing the internal structure of literary texts. At the same time, the theorist Mikhail Bakhtin began to develop a sophisticated criticism concerned with ethical problems and ways of representing them, especially in his favorite genre, the novel.

By the late 1920s the period of Soviet experimentation had ended. Censorship became much stricter, and many of the best writers were silenced. During the late 1920s and the '30s there appeared what became known as the classics of Socialist Realism, a literary method that in 1934 was declared to be the only acceptable one for Soviet writers. A few among these classics—Fyodor Gladkov's *Cement* (1925), Nikolay Ostrovsky's *How the Steel Was Tempered* (1932–34), and Valentin Katayev's *Time, Forward!* (1932)—have retained some literary interest. The masterpieces of this period, however, did not fit the canons of Socialist Realism and were not published until many years later. They include Mikhail Bulgakov's grotesquely funny *The Master and Margarita* (1966–67) and Andrey Platonov's dark pictures of rural and semi-urban Russia, *The Foundation Pit* (1973) and *Chevengur* (1972).

New writers and trends appeared during the "thaw" period of the 1950s and early 1960s. The vibrant young poetic voices of Joseph Brodsky, Yevgeny Yevtushenko, and Andrey Voznesensky were heard. Aleksandr Solzhenitsyn emerged from a Soviet prison camp to shock the U.S.S.R. and the world with his story *One Day in the Life of Ivan Denisovich* (1962). "Youth" prose on the model of J.D. Salinger appeared as well, in the work of Vasily Aksyonov and Vladimir Voynovich. By the late 1960s, however, most of these writers had again been silenced. Brodsky, Aksyonov, Voynovich, and Solzhenitsyn were forced to leave the country by 1980, and the best writing was again unpublishable. Practically the only decent writing acceptable for publication from the late 1960s through the mid-1980s came from the "village prose" writers (the best include the novelist Valentin Rasputin and the short-story writer Vasily Shukshin), who treated the clash of rural traditions with modern life in a realistic idiom. Somewhat apart stands the morally complex fiction of Yury Trifonov (*The House on the Embankment* [1976]). Nevertheless, as with the 1930s and '40s, the most important literature of this period first appeared outside the Soviet Union. Notable writers include Varlam Shalamov, author of exquisitely artistic stories that chronicled the horrors of the Gulag; Andrey Sinyavsky, whose complex novel *Goodnight!* appeared in Europe in 1984, long after he had been forced to emigrate from the U.S.S.R.; and Venedikt Yerofeyev, whose grotesque latter-day picaresque *Moscow-Petushki*—published in a clandestine (samizdat) edition in 1968—is a minor classic.

"Village prose"

The literature that first appeared in the 1980s has yet to stand the test of time, but it appears that most of the best work published was in poetry—as in the work of conceptualists like Dmitry Prigov and in the meta-metaphoric poetry of Aleksey Parshchikov, Olga Sedakova, Ilya Kutik, and others.

Music. *The 19th century.* Secular music on a Western model appeared later than did Westernized literature in Russia. Although a few works of interest have survived from the 18th century, the "father" of modern Russian classical music, Mikhail Glinka, worked in the second quarter of the 19th century. Glinka created a Russian national music by grafting Russian melodies onto European harmonies. His patriotic *A Life for the Tsar* (1836) and his Pushkin-inspired *Ruslan and Lyudmila* (1842) are the oldest Russian operas that remain in the standard repertoire.

By the second half of the 19th century, an active Russian musical life was in place. Like so many other areas of Russian culture, music was split into Westernizer and Slavophile (nationalist) camps. The principal composer of the former was Peter Ilich Tchaikovsky, whose symphonies, overtures, ballets, and operas combined a careful European craftsmanship with a judicious use of native melodies. The Slavophile camp called for a more national music that would be based not merely on native melodies but also on the harmonic system of the Russian folk song. Although to the musical Westernizers' ears the work of the nationalists sounded barbaric, the major compositions of the Slavophile composers Aleksandr Borodin, Modest Mussorgsky, and Nikolay Rimsky-Korsakov have become staples of the international repertoire, just as have those of Tchaikovsky.

The 20th century. In the immediate pre-Revolutionary period, three major Russian composers emerged: Aleksandr Scriabin, Sergey Rachmaninoff, and Igor Stravinsky. Scriabin was a piano virtuoso and mystic whose compositions were close in spirit to Symbolist literature. Rachmaninoff, also a major pianist, is known primarily for his lyrical piano works. Stravinsky, who began as a student of Rimsky-Korsakov, quickly outgrew his teacher and, in the course of the century, produced a dazzling string of groundbreaking works in a wide variety of styles, including the ballets *Petrushka* (1911) and *The Rite of Spring* (1913). Stravinsky emigrated in 1914, Rachmaninoff following after the Revolution.

Shostakovich and Prokofiev

Soviet music was dominated by two major composers: Dmitry Shostakovich and Sergey Prokofiev. Both composed in a wide variety of styles and genres, and (even though Shostakovich in particular had serious problems with the artistic authorities) both were able to remain productive even during the worst years of Stalinism. Shostakovich is known primarily for his 15 symphonies, although he also produced masterpieces of chamber music, opera, and ballet. Prokofiev's best-known works are his ballet music for *Romeo and Juliet* (1935–36) and his score for Sergey Eisenstein's film *Alexander Nevsky* (1938), although he, too, wrote a wide variety of chamber music, orchestral music, and opera. Among contemporary composers, the complex work of Alfred Schnittke is highly valued and frequently perfomed.

Popular culture also produced many renowned performers. Particularly notable is the legacy of two balladeers—composers who perform their own songs to guitar accompaniment. The raspy-voiced actor and musician Vladimir Vysotsky, whose songs circulated on thousands of bootleg cassettes throughout the 1960s and '70s, was perhaps the best-known performer in the U.S.S.R. until his death in 1980. The Georgian Bulat Okudzhava has an almost equally loyal following. The pop singer Alla Pugacheva drew large audiences in the 1970s, and the rock bands Aquarium (Akvarium) and Kino became quite popular in the 1980s.

In the area of classical musical performance, Soviet conservatories turned out generations of world-renowned soloists. Among the best-known were the violinists David Oistrakh and Gidon Kremer, the cellist Mstislav Rostropovich, the pianists Svyatoslav Richter and Emil Gilels, and the vocalist Galina Vishnevskaya.

The visual arts. *The 19th century.* Like music, the visual arts were slower to develop along European lines than was literature in Russia. The 18th and early 19th centuries did not produce any great Russian painters, with the exception of the portraitist Dmitry Levitsky. In the 1830s the Russian Academy of Arts (which had been founded in 1757) began sending Russian painters abroad for training. Among the most gifted of these were Aleksandr Ivanov and Karl Bryullov: both are known for Romantic historical canvases. A truly national tradition did not begin, however, until the 1870s with the appearance of the "Itinerants." Although their work is not well known outside Russia, the serene landscapes of Isaac Levitan, the expressive portraits of Ivan Kramskoy and Ilya Repin, and the socially oriented genre paintings of Vladimir Makovsky, Vasily Perov, and Repin deserve an international reputation.

The 20th century. As was the case with literature, there was a burst of creativity in the visual arts in the years just before the 1917 Revolution. Russian painters interacted frequently with their European counterparts and played a major role in the European art scene. This period was marked by a turning away from realism to primitivism, symbolism, and abstract painting. The careers of such major artists as Wassily Kandinsky, Marc Chagall, Natalya Goncharova, Mikhail Larionov, Kazimir Malevich, and Vladimir Tatlin all began in the immediate pre-Revolutionary years.

As in literature, the 1920s were a period of continued experimentation. Perhaps the most noteworthy movement was Constructivism. Led by El Lissitzky and Aleksandr Rodchenko, the Constructivists favoured strict geometrical forms and crisp graphic design. Many also became actively involved in the task of creating living spaces and forms of daily life, working in such fields as furniture, ceramic, and clothing design and architecture. Non-Constructivist artists, including Pavel Filonov and Mariya Ender, also produced major works in this period.

Constructivism

By the end of the 1920s, however, the same pressures that confronted experimental writing were brought to bear on the visual arts. A return to the classics of realism was decreed, and the great painters of the early 1920s found themselves increasingly isolated. Eventually their works were removed from museums, and in many cases the artists themselves were almost completely forgotten. It was not until the late 1980s that the greatest works of Russian art of the 20th century were again made available to the public. Experimental art was replaced by countless pictures of Lenin, as, for example, Isaak Brodsky's "Lenin at the Smolny" (1930), and by a seemingly unending string of rose-tinted Socialist Realist depictions of everyday life bearing titles like "The Tractor Drivers' Supper" (1951).

The visual arts took longer to recover from the Stalinist years than did literature. It was not until the 1960s and '70s that a new group of artists, all of whom worked "underground," appeared. Major artists included Ernst Neizvestny, Ilya Kabakov, Mikhail Shemyakin, and Erik Bulatov. They employed techniques as varied as primitivism, hyperrealism, grotesque, and abstraction, but they shared a common distaste for the canons of Socialist Realism. By the late 1980s a large number of them had emigrated.

The performing arts. *The 19th century.* The dramatic and ballet theatres were entirely under government control until the end of the 19th century. Actors and dancers were government employees and often were treated badly. Nevertheless, theatrical life was quite active throughout the century. From an international perspective, however, the greatest success of the Russian theatre was in the area of classical ballet. Since the 1820s, Russian dancers have reigned supreme on the ballet stage. Many great choreographers, even those of non-Russian origin, worked for the Russian Imperial Theatres, including Marius Petipa, who choreographed Tchaikovsky's ballets *Swan Lake* and *The Sleeping Beauty.*

The 20th century. Two directors and one producer dominated Russian theatrical life in the first decades of the 20th century: the producer was Sergey Diaghilev, and the directors were Konstantin Stanislavsky and Vsevolod Meyerhold. Together with Vladimir Nemirovich-Danchenko, Stanislavsky founded the Moscow Art Theatre (later called the Moscow Academic Art Theatre) in 1898. Stanislavsky's insistence on historical accuracy, exact realism, and intense psychological preparation by his actors led to a string of successful productions from the beginning of the century into the 1930s. The theatre was known particularly for its productions of the plays of Anton Chekhov, whose *The Seagull* (1896) was the hit of the theatre's inaugural season.

Moscow Art Theatre

Meyerhold was one of Stanislavsky's students, but he broke with his master's insistence on realism. He welcomed the Revolution and put his considerable talent and energy into creating a new theatre for the new state. Throughout the 1920s and into the '30s he staged brilliant, inventive productions, both of contemporary drama and of the classics. However, his iconoclastic style fell out of favour in the 1930s, and he was arrested and executed in 1940.

Diaghilev was a brilliant organizer and impresario whose innovative Ballets Russes premiered many of the most significant ballets of the first quarter of the century. Although the company was based primarily in Paris, Diaghilev employed major Russian composers (particularly Stravinsky), artists (*e.g.,* Alexandre Benois, Goncharova, and Larionov), and dancers (including Vaslav Nijinsky and Tamara Karsavina) in his legendary company.

Ballet was one of the great successes of the Soviet period as well, not because of any innovations but because the great troupes of the Bolshoi Theatre in Moscow and the Kirov Theatre in Leningrad were able to preserve the traditions of classical dance that had been perfected in pre-Revolutionary Russia. The Soviet Union's choreography schools produced one internationally famous star after another, including the incomparable Maya Plisetskaya, Rudolf Nureyev, and Mikhail Baryshnikov.

Another extremely successful area of theatrical performance was puppet theatre. The State Central Puppet Theater founded by Sergey Obraztsov in Moscow continues to give delightful performances for patrons of all ages. The same can be said for the spectacular presentations of the Moscow State Circus.

Motion pictures. The Soviet cinema, too, was a hotbed of invention in the immediate post-Revolutionary period. Its most celebrated director was Sergey Eisenstein (a student of Meyerhold), whose great films include *Battleship Potemkin* (1925) and *Alexander Nevsky* (1938). Film did not escape the strictures of Socialist Realism, but a few post-World War II films in this style were artistically successful, including *The Cranes are Flying* (1957; directed by Mikhail Kalatozov) and *Ballad of a Soldier* (1959; directed by Grigory Chukhrai). A number of successful film versions of classic texts were made in the 1950s and

'60s, particularly Grigory Kozintsev's spectacular versions of *Hamlet* (1964) and *King Lear* (1971). The 1960s and '70s produced a few great directors and artistically successful films. Two standouts were Andrey Tarkovsky (*Andrey Rublev* [1966] and *Mirror* [1974]) and the Georgian-born Armenian Sergey Paradzhanov (*Shadows of Forgotten Ancestors* [1964] and *The Colour of Pomegranates* [1969]).

CULTURAL AND EDUCATIONAL INSTITUTIONS

The press and media. Russian 19th-century journalism was extremely vigorous, with newspapers and monthly "fat" journals being the most important forums. Daily newspapers and monthly journals of all political and artistic stripes continued to appear in the immediate aftermath of the Revolution. However, most independent newspapers were eliminated by the early 1920s. What remained were the ubiquitous daily duo of *Pravda* ("Truth") and *Izvestiya* ("News"). Journals were in a somewhat better position, especially those that published mostly works of literature. Periodicals like *Krasnaya nov* ("Red Virgin Soil") and *LEF* ("The Left Front of Art") published much significant literature in the 1920s. In the 1960s the journal *Novy mir* revived this tradition. In the 1980s it was joined by a revitalized *Ogonyok* ("Spark").

State control of news media

Radio and television from the time of their appearance in the Soviet Union were heavily dominated by the party apparatus and were seen as primary tools for propaganda. Until the mid-1980s most television programming consisted of either direct or indirect propaganda spiced with high art (*e.g.,* filmed concerts and plays) and occasional grade-B thrillers. In the period of *glasnost,* television was a leader in innovative programming, helping to create the situation in which the Soviet state was destroyed.

Museums. Some of the greatest museums in the world can be found in the cities of Moscow and St. Petersburg. In Moscow the Pushkin Fine Arts Museum houses treasures of western European art, while the Tretyakov Gallery has a strong collection of Russian art. In St. Petersburg the Hermitage is one of the great art museums of the world, and the Russian Museum has wonderful examples of Russian art. In addition, in the suburbs outside St. Petersburg, the former tsarist palaces at Pavlovsk, Pushkin, and Petrodvorets have been restored as museums.

Universities. Russia's oldest university, in Moscow, was founded in 1755. Throughout the 19th century and into the 20th, Russian universities in Moscow, St. Petersburg, and Kazan produced world-class scholars, notably the mathematician Nikolay Lobachevsky and the chemist Dmitry Mendeleyev. Although universities suffered severely during the Stalinist purges, a number of universities have continued to provide high-quality education, particularly in the sciences. The most important include Moscow M.V. Lomonosov State University, St. Petersburg State University, and Novosibirsk State University.

SPORTS AND RECREATION

Sports played a major role in the Soviet state in the post-World War II period. The achievements of Soviet athletes in the international arena, particularly in the Olympic Games, were a source of great national pride. Although athletes were technically amateurs, they were well supported by the Sports State Committee. In team sports the U.S.S.R. was especially successful in ice hockey—winning numerous world championships and Olympic gold medals—volleyball, and later basketball. Soviet gymnasts and track-and-field athletes (male and female), weight lifters, wrestlers, and boxers were consistently among the best in the world. Even after the collapse of the Soviet empire, Russian athletes have continued to dominate international competition in these areas.

Olympic participation

On the amateur level, the lack of facilities and equipment have prevented many average Russian citizens from participating in sporting activities, but jogging, soccer, and fishing have been popular. Finally, many Russians are avid chess players, and the country has produced most of the greatest players of the 20th century.

(ANDREW B. WACHTEL)

For statistical data on the land and people of Russia, see the *Britannica World Data* section in the BRITANNICA BOOK OF THE YEAR.

Tokyo-Yokohama Metropolitan Area

The Tokyo-Yokohama metropolitan area—commonly called Greater Tokyo—is a huge metropolitan complex along the northern and western shores of Tokyo Bay, on the Pacific coast of the island of Honshu, central Japan. At its centre is the metropolitan prefecture, or metropolis (*to*), of Tokyo. The three prefectures (*ken*) bordering it—Saitama on the north, Chiba on the east, and Kanagawa on the south—may be said to make up the remainder of the complex, but there is more than one definition of Greater Tokyo, and large numbers of people live beyond the four prefectures and commute to work in the region.

The expression "city of Tokyo" usually refers to the 23 wards (*ku*) that constitute the city proper. In 1943, however, this city ceased to exist as an administrative unit and was subsumed within the larger Tokyo metropolis, which includes rural and mountainous regions west of the city and the Izu Islands stretching southward from the mouth of Tokyo Bay and Bonin (Ogasawara) Islands some 500 miles (800 kilometres) to the southeast in the Pacific Ocean. There are three other major cities within the complex. Yokohama, about 20 miles southwest of Tokyo, is the second largest city in Japan. The industrial city of Kawasaki lies between Tokyo and Yokohama. Both Yokohama and Kawasaki are in Kanagawa prefecture. Chiba, in Chiba prefecture east of Tokyo on the northeast coast of the bay, is also heavily industrialized.

Tokyo (Japanese: Tōkyō), meaning "Eastern Capital," was the name given to the city of Edo when the seat of the imperial family was moved there from Kyōto ("Capital City") in 1868.

This article is divided into the following sections:

Physical and human geography

THE LANDSCAPE

Site. The old city of Edo occupied alluvial and reclaimed lands along and to the east of the Sumida River (which flows just east of central Tokyo) and hills to the west of the river. The site was chosen for strategic reasons. It commands the southern approaches to the Kantō Plain, the largest in Japan. Saitama is mostly flat, and in Kanagawa hills prevail, though both prefectures give way to mountains along their inland extremities, as also does Tokyo. Much of the mercantile centre of Edo was reclaimed from the Sumida estuary, which reached to the grounds of the premodern castle (now the imperial palace).

Two other rivers of note in the region are the Tama, the lower reaches of which form the eastern boundary between Tokyo and Kanagawa prefectures; and the Tone, the main course of which lies some distance north of Tokyo. The Tone is the second longest river in Japan, and its drainage basin is the largest. Before the 17th century it flowed through what is now Tokyo and into the bay, but for flood control the Tokugawa shogunate diverted it. The main mouth of the Tone is now at the northeastern corner of Chiba prefecture, although a minor branch, the Edo River, continues to flow into the bay and forms the boundary between Tokyo and Chiba prefectures. The Sumida, of different origins, continued to flood the city until the Arakawa Drainage Channel, roughly parallel to the Sumida and a short distance to the east of it, was put through in the years before the 1923 earthquake.

The eastern districts, because they lie on unconsolidated, geologically unstable land and because they have been the more crowded and less affluent parts of the city, have been prone to disaster. They were almost completely destroyed by the earthquake of 1923 and the aerial bombings of 1945. The palace lies at the boundary between the flatlands and the more prosperous and geologically stable hilly regions. The flatlands—the Downtown, or Low City—dominated the mercantile culture of Edo. The hilly Uptown, or High City, has been increasingly dominant in the 20th century.

The Low City and High City

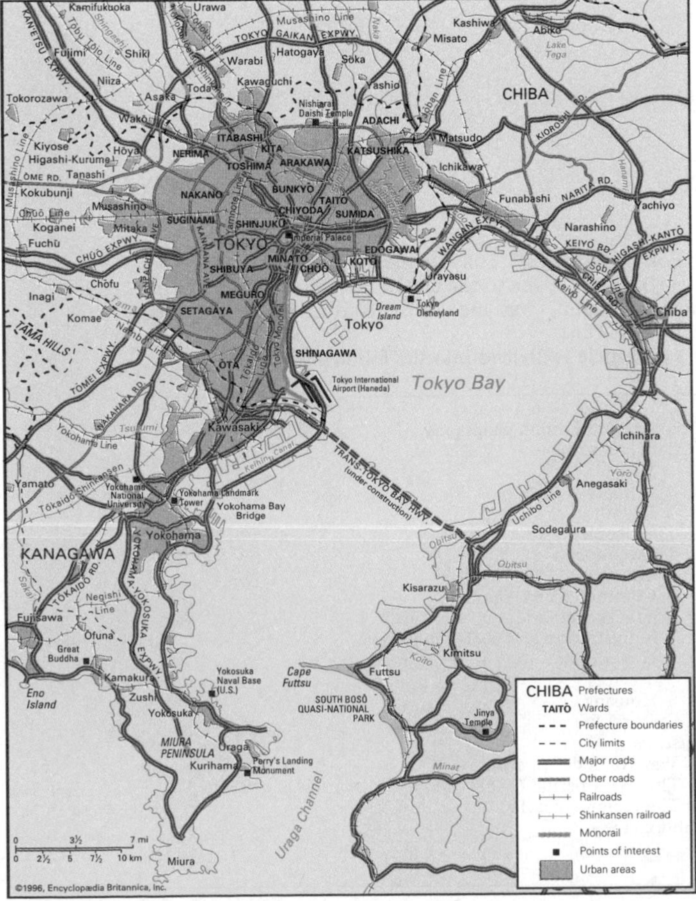

The shift may be taken as a concise summary of what has transpired since Edo became Tokyo.

From its origins along the Sumida estuary, the city has spread in all directions, even into the bay. Reclamation has been continuous and since 1950 has been so extensive that the reclaimed lands are the centre of highly imaginative, perhaps somewhat dreamy, schemes for the future. This is inevitable, since most of the rest of Tokyo metropolitan prefecture is now full of people and since vast tracts of suburbia lie beyond the authority of the prefectural government. The general direction of movement for this constantly moving city has been westward. Until 1991 City Hall, which might more properly be called the Prefectural Office, was near the old centre of the city, just east of the palace and within the outer moat of Edo Castle. In 1991 it moved to a part of Shinjuku, a western "satellite centre" that was not fully within the city limits until 1932. The new site is nearer the population centre of the prefecture than the old.

By 1932 the city limits were no longer realistic. Twenty new wards were added around the old 15, and Tokyo suddenly became the second (or perhaps third) largest city in the world. It does not matter so much now that the 23 wards, to which the 35 were reduced in 1947, no longer contain the city, because the "ward part" has no administrative significance. A popular saying had it that Edo ended at what is now the campus of the University of Tokyo, to the north of the palace. It would not take an hour for a good walker to go the distance from the old mercantile centre, east of the palace and castle, to the university. A walk today to the farthest northern suburbs would take the best of walkers many hours.

Climate. Although Tokyo lies somewhat farther south than Washington, D.C., the two cities have similar climates. In both the one really uncomfortable season is the summer, when humidity is extreme, and the temperature may rise to above 100° F (38° C). On most August days in Tokyo it rises to near 90° F (32° C), and it is not the heat but the humidity, near saturation, that matters. The winters are brisk but not savagely cold. Heavy snowstorms usually come in early spring and quickly melt away. The temperature sometimes drops below freezing but only slightly. Winter is the sunniest season of the year and has the cleanest air. It is the only season when one would not be startled to see Mount Fuji from a high building near the centre of the city.

Spring and autumn are delightful, though the weather tends to be more turbulent than in Washington. There are rainy periods in early summer and early autumn. The latter is associated with typhoons, the Pacific equivalent of the hurricane. It is a rare year in which one or more does not strike the region. The flowers of spring and the leaves of autumn have been endlessly and justly celebrated in Japanese poetry. May, with its peonies, azaleas, wisteria, and dogwood, is the most flowery month, although the more famous cherry blossoms come early in April. Plums, camellias, and witch hazel bloom yet earlier. At no time of the year, even the "dead" of winter, is the city without outdoor blossoms.

Typhoons

Layout. *Centre and satellites.* Western visitors of the 19th century described Edo and Tokyo as not so much a city as a collection of villages. This characterization is found, for instance, in one of the most detailed of these early accounts, by an American who accompanied Ulysses S. Grant on his visit to the city in 1879. Doubtless it was accurate a century and some decades ago, and it still obtains today, though "cities" might now be a more appropriate word than "villages."

Most people would probably still put the centre of Tokyo much where the centre of Edo was, immediately to the east of the palace. Marunouchi, inside the outer castle moat (now filled in), is the entrepreneurial hub of the city and of Japan; it is where the prefectural offices were until 1991. Farther east, immediately beyond the avenue built on the filled-in moat, there has been a shift. Nihombashi, the "Japan Bridge" that was (and still is) considered the starting point for roads to the provinces, was the unchallenged mercantile centre of Edo. Today Ginza, farther south, is more important, even though it is not the largest retail district in the city. Kasumigaseki, immediately to the south of the palace, has been the bureaucratic centre of the city since shortly after it became the imperial capital. Located there and in neighbouring districts to the west are the main offices of the national government, including the National Diet Building and the prime minister's residence.

For the rest of Tokyo, there has been a huge proliferation of what are called "satellite centres," the largest of them every bit as deserving of the name city as are Kawasaki and Chiba. Shinjuku is the largest and is the main retail and entertainment district in the city and in the land. More people pass through Shinjuku railway station, on their way from and to home in the sprawling western suburbs, than through any other station in Japan and, quite possibly, in the world. Second—and perhaps catching up because of its popularity among teenagers—is Shibuya, to the south; and third is Ikebukuro, to the north. All three lie along the western arc of the Yamanote Line, the railway that circles much of the main part of the city. They bespeak the general tendency of the city to move westward.

Yokohama

There are others, such as Ueno, a short distance west of the Sumida, and Nakano, west of Shinjuku; and to the number might be added central Yokohama, even though Yokohama is a separate city and not a satellite centre. Its traditional role as the port for greater Tokyo having declined, it is asserting its independence as a hub for shopping, conventions, and the like. The beautification of the nondescript waterfront has been a conspicuous success. Though Chinese are numerous in such Tokyo centres as Shinjuku, Yokohama is alone among them in having a genuine and vibrant Chinatown.

Street patterns. Despite disasters and modernization, the street pattern of central Tokyo resembles that of Edo. Old streets have been widened and new streets cut through, but after both of its great modern disasters, in 1923 and 1945, the city pulled itself together in much the same shape that it had had before. The old centre of the city is essentially a cobweb, with the palace grounds at its centre, reflecting the defensive arrangement of the castle town. The old flatlands to the east are in a grid pattern, with the grids not ideally joining one another.

One might expect the plan of a city to become more rational as it expands and planners start exerting themselves. This has not been true of Tokyo, and still less is it true of the suburbs that lie beyond the prefectural boundaries. There really is no plan and no pattern, except, in a rudimentary sense, the old cobweb. Streets wander along valleys and ridges, and one can often sense in them what the disorder of the old paddy fields must have been.

The cobweb survives in main arteries that radiate out from the centre, leaving the old city through post stations called the Five Mouths. The most important of these was Shinagawa, to the south, first of the 53 stages on the Tōkaidō (the main coastal road to Kyōto) celebrated in the woodblock prints of Hiroshige and others. It is still situated on the oldest and most important highway to Yokohama and beyond. The old highway to the mountainous province of Kai (modern Yamanashi prefecture) passes through Shinjuku, directly west of the palace. To the northwest, not as important as it once was, is Itabashi, through which passes the old inland road to Kyōto. More than one highway departed for the north through Senjū, which had two of the Five Mouths.

Most of Yokohama is like the western part of Tokyo, which is to say, confusing—more consistently confusing, even, than Tokyo. Motorists, defeated by its random streets, have been known to descend from their automobiles and look for the North Star, though the air is seldom clear enough to reveal it. The city is for the most part hilly, and, confronted with a hill, a Japanese road or street tends to wander off in search of a detour. Only a limited band to the south and west of the original Yokohama railway terminus (now Sakuragi-chō station) and the harbour area are in something like a grid pattern.

One looks in vain for traces of the old Kanagawa post station in Yokohama and is similarly frustrated with regard to the one that was in Kawasaki, farther north toward Tokyo. Probably because it lost its castle some centuries ago, Chiba wears the aspect of a medieval castle town less than does Tokyo: a visitor to the city has to be told where the castle was.

Green space. Mists, natural and man-made, so pile upon one another in the Tokyo skies that the view from one of the Shinjuku skyscrapers is not likely, on an average day, to go very far. When it does, one may be surprised at the amount of greenery. Ōsaka is an ashen city by comparison, and even Kyōto, the ancient capital, is wanting in the wide and beautiful parks that are scattered throughout Tokyo. The cemeteries are also wide, verdant, and beautiful. Grave viewing can be a satisfying pastime.

Blossom viewing

The traditional pattern for viewing the flowers and grasses of the seasons has shown remarkable powers of survival. The famous places of Edo were mostly in the northern and eastern districts, and they are so situated in Tokyo as well. In spite of disasters and crowding, the flatlands and the hills along their immediate fringes are still where the blossom-viewing crowds gather. In this phenomenon may be found, indeed, the only regard in which the old Low City has held its own against the growing cultural hegemony of the High City.

There are famous new places, to be sure, such as the iris gardens of the Meiji Shrine, said to have been designed by the Meiji emperor himself; and such blossoms as the camellia and the chrysanthemum are to be seen everywhere. For the first in the annual procession of important blossoms, the plum, most people go to the Yushima Shrine, near Ueno Park. Ueno Park itself, along with the Sumida embankment, was the most famous place in Edo for cherry blossoms. It remains the most famous of Tokyo as well. Ueno also contains a renowned peony garden. Probably the most famous of peony gardens is at Nishiarai Daishi temple, north of the Ara River. The best-known azalea garden is at the Nezu Shrine, just north of the University of Tokyo. For wisteria one can do no better than the Kameido shrine, in the eastern suburbs until 1932. As beautiful as the iris garden at the Meiji Shrine are those at Horikiri and Mizumoto, in the eastern part of the city. For the lotuses of full summer it is Ueno again. Then come chrysanthemums and autumn foliage, the latter best viewed in the mountains.

The parks of Yokohama are newer than those of Tokyo, but there are fine ones. The most popular, Yamashita, is on land reclaimed from the bay with debris from the 1923 earthquake. The Sankei Garden, some distance south of the city centre, was built and presented to the city by a 19th-century silk merchant. The park once reposed by the bay, but reclamation has put it inland some distance and in some measure lessened its beauty. It contains a collection of fine old buildings moved from elsewhere. The lands between Sakuragi-cho and the harbour were once grim docks and warehouses. Now they are like a field of densely blooming wildflowers, the impression of wildness being carefully cultivated.

Building styles. Tamed nature in parks, gardens, temples, and cemeteries aside, it cannot be said that Tokyo is a beautiful city. Physically, it is among the newest cities in the world: almost nothing is as much as a century old. Disaster helps explain this fact, but it is not the only reason. Traditionally, the Japanese have not built for durability. Buildings are torn down at a rate that would be remarkable in most places and is next to unbelievable in a country that thinks itself strapped for resources. So almost everything is new, and rebuilding seems to result inevitably in something less distinguished than what was replaced. The view from a moderately high window will most commonly look out on several dozens of buildings, all of which are in unimaginative modern styles.

Skyscrapers

Skyscrapers are a relatively recent phenomenon, dating only from the completion (1968) of the 36-story Kasumigaseki Building just south of the government ministries. Until then, aesthetic and engineering considerations had kept buildings to a maximum of about 10 stories, but there soon blossomed a number of high-rise structures, all purported by their builders to be earthquake-resistant. The largest cluster of skyscrapers rises to the west of Shinjuku station, although Yokohama boasts the tallest building in Japan: the 70-story Landmark Tower, completed in 1993.

Surviving pockets of wooden structures from perhaps the

turn of the 20th century, as well as the xylographic art of Edo, tell us that Tokyo must once have been a very pleasing city—in the severe, monochrome manner held by many to be peculiarly Japanese. The pockets will soon go, to be replaced by cheaper, perhaps more comfortable, certainly uglier modern things. The city still contains a scattering of buildings in premodern European styles, including a rather fine Queen Anne building in the Kasumigaseki bureaucratic quarter; but cracker-box modern has been overwhelmingly favoured since World War II. To let these facts prey on one's mind is to overlook a very important point: that an ugly face can also be a very animated and endearing face.

THE PEOPLE

The most striking fact about the population of Greater Tokyo is that it is so large. The four prefectures of the metropolitan area contain one-fourth of all the people in Japan. The population of the 23 wards of Tokyo is stabilized at roughly eight million, while that of outlying regions continues to grow rapidly. Two other cities within the complex, Yokohama and Kawasaki, have populations of more than a million.

The average age for Tokyoites is well under that for the rest of the nation. It is a city of young people, and they flood the streets. Though the very young are a little afraid of Shinjuku and its gangs, the streets on the whole are safe. So, Tokyo is filled with young people nudging past one another not in automobiles but on sidewalks; in this regard, not many cities can be its equal. It conveys a sense of irresistible vitality. It may be quiet and unpeopled in the hours before and after dawn, but at other hours none of the bustling centres is without its crowds. Ordinary neighbourhoods are quieter than they once were, because more people are indoors watching television—notably baseball (the national sport) during the season. Nonetheless, the pedestrian crowds continue to be far more widely diffused than in any American city.

The origins of the Tokyo populace are mostly in the northern and eastern parts of the country. Japan's other great megalopolis, centred upon Ōsaka, draws from the south and west. It is reasonable to ask why masses of people continue to pour in who know full well how crowded it already is and how trying it can be, especially for the newcomer. It is dangerous to generalize about national traits, but one may hazard a simple answer: the Japanese love to be where everyone is, and there are nearly as many people in one conurbation or the other as everywhere else in Japan put together.

The attraction of Tokyo

Although Yokohama has passed Ōsaka in population, the latter is still considered Japan's "second" city. Ōsaka is the focal point of its conurbation, while Yokohama is largely a bedroom town for Tokyo. Yokohama retains its international flavour from the days when it was Japan's chief entrepôt with the West, even though its foreign community is much smaller than it once was. Tokyo, in spite of a substantial foreign population and its world-class status, has considerably less of a cosmopolitan feel than a city such as New York.

THE ECONOMY

Industry. Since the war Tokyo has taken over from Ōsaka the role of leading industrial centre in the country. The region has a highly diversified manufacturing base. Heavy industries—such as metals, chemicals, machinery, transportation equipment, and oil refining—are concentrated in Chiba, Kawasaki, and Yokohama. Tokyo proper is strongly inclined toward light industry. Most of Japan's books and much of its electronic equipment, for instance, are produced there.

Commerce and finance. More noteworthy than the concentration of industry is the concentration of management and finance in and near Tokyo. Even companies with factories elsewhere maintain large offices in Tokyo, and the proper corporate location is Marunouchi. There is a good reason for keeping a Tokyo office—proximity to government offices—although a chumminess between managers and bureaucrats is thought by many to be not entirely healthy.

Finance has been more conservative geographically than has management, with Nihombashi, the commercial and financial centre of Edo, as its main seat. Located there are the Bank of Japan and the Tokyo Stock Exchange, Japan's two most important financial institutions. The latter is much busier than the Ōsaka Stock Exchange, but this may be somewhat misleading: a very large proportion of stocks are in intercompany holdings that do not go on the market. This arrangement is a defense against hostile takeovers and also a continuing assurance of cooperation among the members of the giant conglomerates; but it makes the stock market easily manipulatable and less than ideally subject to market forces.

During the 1980s, as Japan was emerging as an economic superpower, Tokyo suddenly found itself a global financial centre. This remarkable growth rate came to be called the "bubble economy." The expression refers to speculation in general, but most particularly to land speculation and to Tokyo, where land prices have been the most outrageously exorbitant in the country. By the early 1990s, however, overinflated stock and land prices led to a "bursting" of the bubble, so curious a phenomenon that the Japanese grasp of the word "bubble" seems in doubt. The English word is most commonly used, and when it is put into Japanese (*awa*) the rendition is "foam" rather than "bubble." What has happened does seem more like a subsidence of foam than a thorough burst of a bubble.

The "bubble economy"

Transportation. The emergence of modern Tokyo came at the beginning of the transportation revolution of the late 19th century. The first railroad in Japan was put through from Tokyo to Yokohama in 1872. The city continues to be the most important transportation centre in the country. The busiest rail stations are those accommodating commuters to the western suburbs, but the traveler who wishes to go considerable distances by rail usually leaves from Tokyo station, in Marunouchi, or Ueno station, a couple of miles to the north. Only since 1991 has it been possible to take a Shinkansen express train to northern Japan from Tokyo station, as Ueno was the traditional terminus for northbound travel.

Most international travel is through the highly inconvenient airport at Narita, in Chiba prefecture, at least an hour by rail from central Tokyo. Opened in 1978, the facility has been at the centre of controversy since its inception, mainly because of opposition by landowners to the appropriation of their property. The older, smaller, and rather more convenient airport at Haneda, near the Tama River, accommodates domestic travel and a few international flights. Yokohama still is the most important port in the region, the other major ports being Chiba, Kawasaki, and Tokyo.

Tokyo's streets are flooded not only with people but also with vehicles, and traffic can become almost gridlocked at busy times and in busy places. There is a good system of roads and express highways in the city and region, but it is woefully inadequate for the crush of traffic. A splendid network of subways and commuter rail lines provides an alternative to the automobile.

ADMINISTRATION AND SOCIAL CONDITIONS

Government. The two most populous prefectures of Japan, Tokyo and Ōsaka, are the two smallest in area. Though somewhat larger than Ōsaka, Tokyo occupies roughly a third of the premodern province of Musashi, the remainder of which is in Saitama prefecture. Tokyo and Ōsaka were two of the three urban prefectures (*fu*) established in 1872, the third being Kyōto. The thinking seems to have been that the two should be just that, metropolitan complexes—each essentially a city and its suburbs—and the smaller they were, the more easily they could be controlled. Kyōto, which was not expected to grow like the other two and did not, was not so treated.

Expansion of the city

The expansion of the city in 1932 made the city limits coincide with the prefectural boundaries in all directions but the west, where lay the "county part" of the prefecture, as distinguished from the "ward part." The amalgamation of city and prefecture and establishment of the metropolitan prefecture in 1943 made the largest municipality in the land the only one without a mayor. The county part now consists largely of incorporated cities, all of which have mayors.

Legislative authority in the metropolis rests with the Tokyo Metropolitan Assembly, consisting of 127 members elected to 4-year terms. The principal elected official is the prefectural governor, who has authority over a number of administrative commissions and commissioners, including the fire department and those for public works. Each of the 23 wards has a popularly elected council and ward head, with limited authority over local matters.

Services. Edo had a sophisticated, though inadequate, system of aqueducts. Three principal ones brought water from the highlands to the west of the city. Many houses and clusters of houses had wells, which could turn brackish, especially in the low flatlands. (Some districts east of the Sumida lay below sea level. Subsidence, from drawing underground water, made them sink yet lower.) Thus, the purveying of fresh water was a thriving business.

Most of the water for the city now comes from the Tama and, increasingly, the Tone rivers. Tokyo would like to go yet farther afield, bringing water that now flows into the Sea of Japan across the mountains by tunnel to the Tone. It cannot do this by itself, and there is opposition in the rural prefecture chiefly affected. Yokohama and Kawasaki draw their water from the Sagami River, which rises near the base of Mount Fuji and empties into the ocean a short distance southwest of Yokohama.

Sewers did not exist in Edo. The common means of waste disposal was the sewage cart, sometimes called the "honey-bucket" wagon. A seller's market, with the carter paying for sewage, gradually became a buyer's market as the city grew and the fields to which the carts traveled got farther away. During the years after World War I, Shinjuku was known as the "anus of Tokyo." The principal route to the fields ran through it, and every afternoon and evening carts would be backed up along the main street. Even in the years after World War II, Tokyo was a most malodorous city. The goal of sewers accommodating all the built-up regions is in sight. They probably will never get to remote mountain and island regions.

Refuse disposal

Tens of thousands of tons of garbage must be disposed of each day. The mass grows more rapidly than the population, for affluence brings less careful and efficient habits of consumption than in the past. In the years after the Olympic Games of 1964, the city was on the verge of civil war over the problem of what to do about the huge accumulation. The poorer eastern wards were called upon to dispose of it, and the affluent western wards produced most of it. The prefectural government agreed that disposal arrangements were unfair. Today there are garbage plants throughout the city that incinerate what they can. The remainder goes into fills in the bay that are at the heart of the grandest development schemes of the city. Though pretty parks are situated on them, for the most part they remain eyesores. From one of these fills, named with great though probably unintended irony "Dream Island" (Yume no shima), originated in 1965 a huge plague of flies that spread over the eastern part of the city. The site has been under better control since but continues to be a not very dreamlike place.

Electricity and gas are provided by private companies. The electric company has plants, including nuclear ones, as far afield as the coast of the Sea of Japan. Most of the gas is produced at a plant along the bay in Yokohama that is widely held to be a marvel of advanced technology.

Housing. Inflated land prices have been among the most serious and intractable problems facing Tokyo. Almost no one who does not inherit land can hope to own it in the old city, and estate taxes can take away even family land. Those who can afford to live closer in typically inhabit relatively small condominium apartments in buildings with the Japanese-English name *manshon* ("mansions"); those of lesser means may be fortunate enough to rent a cramped apartment in the rather dreary public-housing structures called *danchi.* The typical office worker, however, must commute cruel distances, for as many as four and five hours a day round-trip. Land prices have fallen since the early 1990s, but not enough to make land near the several centres affordable to the middle class.

CULTURAL LIFE

Tokyo dominates Japanese culture as no American city dominates American culture. Perhaps France and its Paris are a similar instance, but there cannot be many such in the world. Greater Tokyo contains a third of the universities in the country. In addition, the majority of important learned societies, research institutes, and libraries and most of the publishing houses are found there. Most writers, journalists, and "opinion makers" live in Greater Tokyo. Museums may not be as grand as those of New York City, but they are far grander than those of any other Japanese city. So, too, are the theatres and concert halls. The most important cultural institutions (*e.g.,* the Tokyo National Museum, National Diet Library, National Theatre, and Tokyo Metropolitan Art Museum) are found near national government offices or in Ueno.

It is arguable that Tokyo is culturally the most varied city in the world. Certainly it is a city in which one has little excuse for being bored. One with time to kill has a choice of doing it in several cities, each different from the others, and a choice between the present and the past and between East and West as well. It may be that at any one time Tokyo has a more limited choice in the Western arts than a great American or European city, but everything comes if one but waits, and no Occidental city is a competitor in offering the arts of the Orient, modern or traditional.

History

THE PREMODERN PERIOD

Tokyo celebrated its 500th anniversary in 1957. The calculation was from the most likely date for the initial fortification of Edo. The structure cannot have been elaborate, probably little more than a house upon a low eminence with log ramparts. There must have been a village on the site from much earlier. The ancient Sensō Temple (popularly called the Asakusa Kannon), east of Ueno station and near the Sumida, dates from perhaps the late 7th century (although nearly all its structures are postwar). The name Edo means something like "estuary" or "inlet." The clan in possession of the area bore the name Edo, taken from the name of the village.

Establishment of Edo

Edo did not amount to much until the 17th century. The first Tokugawa shogun, Ieyasu, took possession of Edo in 1590 and in 1603 made it the seat of his government, which effectively controlled the country and left only ceremonial functions with the imperial court and Kyōto. The marshy estuary was largely filled in during the course of the century, and Nihombashi became the heart of the mercantile city. The military aristocracy did not disdain the flatlands, but they quite dominated the hilly regions to the west. The court aristocracy remained in Kyōto.

Growth was rapid through the 17th and 18th centuries. Early in the Tokugawa period (1603–1867) Kyōto maintained its old cultural preeminence. Cultural hegemony then moved to Ōsaka, Japan's other great mercantile city. By the end of the 18th century it had moved to Edo, where it reposed in 1868, when the emperor moved from Kyōto and the name was changed to Tokyo. The Edo century, as it may be called, was not among Japan's finer periods for the graphic and literary arts, but it was very good for the theatre. The kabuki, the great love of the Edo townspeople, reached remarkable heights of subtlety and sophistication.

Edo may well have become the largest city in the world in the 18th century. It passed a million people before London and Paris did and probably was larger than the capitals of the Ottoman and Chinese empires. At the end of the Tokugawa period the regions east of the castle were much more important than those to the west, where only a thin residential band lay. The districts immediately east of the castle and on beyond the Sumida River had become the most important cultural centre in the land. This changed utterly during the 20th century. Today the east has scarcely anything to offer in cultural terms, while the west has everything.

Throughout its history the city has been prone to disaster. There were severe earthquakes between the arrival of the first shogun and the end of the Tokugawa regime, but the commonest disaster was fire, known as "the flower of Edo." Though there were fires of great magnitude in 1923 and 1945, the flower gradually has been extirpated. The most considerable Edo fire occurred in 1657, which happened to have been the city's bicentennial (though no one seems to have noticed). About two-thirds of the city was destroyed, including much of the castle, and upwards of 100,000 people died.

Kawasaki was, during the Tokugawa centuries, the second stage from Nihombashi on the Tōkaidō, the main coastal road to Kyōto. Yokohama was an isolated fishing village that did not really emerge into history until after the visit of Commodore Matthew Perry and his "black ships" in 1853. Though it is not known exactly what stood on the Sumida estuary before 1457, Chiba may be called an older city than Edo-Tokyo: it had a castle from the 12th century.

THE MEIJI PERIOD (1868–1912)

Edo becomes Tokyo

The population of the city plummeted during the disturbances that made it the capital. By the middle of the Meiji period it had returned to the highest Edo figure, and by the end of the reign it had passed two million. The city limits reached to the Shinagawa post stage on the south but fell short of Shinjuku on the west. On the north they passed a short distance beyond Tokyo Imperial University (now the University of Tokyo), and on the east they stretched a short distance beyond the Sumida. At no point did they reach as far as the boundaries of the urban prefecture.

Ginza, which had not amounted to much during the Tokugawa centuries, was thrust to the fore of "civilization and enlightenment"—by which was meant, essentially, Westernization—by an accident: the great fire of 1872. The rebuilding was in brick, a material not before used by the Japanese. Sometime later the Mitsubishi enterprises set about turning their "meadow," vacant land within the outer castle moat, into a business centre. This became the Marunouchi district, also largely built of brick. Only fragments of the Ginza "bricktown" and of what came to be called the Mitsubishi "Londontown" survive. Monumental architecture in those years tended toward decorated European styles, though sometimes, as in the Bank of Japan building, Grecian austerity prevailed. Most of the city continued to be wooden, low, and of small units. No specimens of an earlier hybrid style, Western in many of its details but Japanese in its general aspect, survive in the city, but examples may still be found in the provinces.

These were the years of the great national effort—presided over, of course, from Tokyo—to catch up with the world. It was a huge success. By the end of the Meiji period, Japan was an ally of England and had won wars with China and Russia.

The history of Yokohama begins just before Meiji. The Harris Treaty of 1858 provided that Kanagawa was to be among the ports opened to foreign trade. The Japanese quickly began having second thoughts. Kanagawa was a well-trodden place, the third stage from Nihombashi on the Tōkaidō. This seemed to invite trouble, the situation being one in which Japanese and foreigners could not easily be kept in their places. So Yokohama, a more isolated and easily policed spot, was opened instead. A fishing village, it lay some distance from the Tōkaidō road, beyond the inlet that was to become Yokohama Harbour. By the end of the Meiji it was numbered, along with Tokyo, Ōsaka, Kōbe, Nagoya, and Kyōto, among the large cities of the nation. Japanese demography in those days was somewhat peculiar. There were the six cities just mentioned, no mid-size cities, and a multitude of small cities.

Kawasaki was by the end of the Meiji period already a growing industrial centre. Chiba remained a sleepy country town. Kanagawa is now a part of Yokohama, near the central railway station.

THE REGION SINCE 1912

Neither the earthquake of Sept. 1, 1923, nor the firebombing of March 9–10, 1945, much the most damaging, destroyed as large a part of the city or killed as many people as the fire of 1657. Both were huge disasters all the same, and in both cases the worst damage was in the crowded, flimsily built eastern flatlands. In 1930 a festival was held celebrating complete recovery from the earthquake. It was in a way prophetic, for the dark years of military adventuring lay ahead, and further development of the capital was not a matter of central concern. There was no similar festival after 1945, nor has rebuilding and new building ever come to a halt. The metropolitan region has relentlessly grown and developed.

The Olympic Games

The Olympic Games of 1964 have been given exaggerated importance as one of the great events in the history of the city and as the equivalent of the 1930 festival. In fact, profits from the Korean War (1950–53) had been put to good use in rebuilding city and country, and, as with the earthquake, recovery from the disaster of 1945 might be put at about a decade after its occurrence. Yet the Olympics without doubt did great things for the morale of city and country. They were the first Asian Olympics, and they marked the return of Japan to international respectability. If much has been built since the war, much has also been destroyed. The last of the Mitsubishi Londontown disappeared. So, too, did Frank Lloyd Wright's Imperial Hotel, finished just in time to survive the earthquake but not the wrecking ball some four decades later.

Among other notable events since Meiji times have been the expansion of the city in 1932 and the amalgamation of city and prefecture in 1943. The eastern Low City still had some life as recently as the 1930s. Asakusa, by the Sumida, was the busiest of centres for popular entertainment. Now it languishes, and there is no such centre in the flatlands—unless one wishes to count the enormously successful Tokyo Disneyland, built on landfill just inside Chiba prefecture at the Edo River mouth.

Yokohama, being nearer the epicentre of the earthquake, was more grievously damaged than was Tokyo; it was badly damaged again by the bombings. Its past, however, is more of a presence than that of Tokyo. Relics of Meiji, when its history began, are still prominent in the central parts of the city. Coastal Kawasaki continues to be industrial. Both Yokohama and Kawasaki stretch far inland from their coastal origins. The inland parts are residential and largely suburban in character. Efforts by Yokohama since the 1970s to renovate the waterfront area and take on an identity of its own have been more successful than many would have thought possible. The industrialization of Chiba has occurred only since the war. A person dropped off by abductors along the industrial coast of Kanagawa or Chiba prefecture might have trouble knowing which area was which. These coasts may become even more indistinguishable when Kawasaki and Kisarazu (in Chiba prefecture) are linked by the Trans-Tokyo Bay Highway (under construction since 1989).

BIBLIOGRAPHY. R.P. DORE, *City Life in Japan* (1958, reissued 1973), is a sociological study of a district near the borderline between the plebeian Low City and the moneyed High City. GARY D. ALLINSON, *Suburban Tokyo: A Comparative Study in Politics and Social Change* (1979), is a similar study concerning the fringes of the metropolis. PETER POPHAM, *Tokyo: The City at the End of the World* (1985); and PAUL WALEY, *Tokyo Now & Then* (1984), are lively accounts that convey in ample measure the modern feel of the city. KATHARINE SANSOM, *Living in Tokyo* (1936), performs the same service for an earlier day. CHARLES A. BEARD, *The Administration and Politics of Tokyo: A Survey and Opinions* (1923), is a still-relevant survey of the governance of the city.

The closest thing to an exhaustive history of the city from its origins down to the recent past is in Japanese: *Tōkyō hyakunenshi,* 7 vol. (1972–73), published by the prefectural office; the work of several hands, it is uneven but indispensable. KATO YUZO (YUZO KATO) (ed.), *Yokohama, Past and Present* (1990; originally published in Japanese, 1990), is interesting and helpful, if somewhat diffuse. EDWARD SEIDENSTICKER, *Low City, High City* (1983, reprinted 1991), is a cultural history of Tokyo from the Meiji Restoration of 1867–68 to the great earthquake of 1923, and his *Tokyo Rising* (1990), takes the story from the earthquake to the date of publication.

(EDWARD GEORGE SEIDENSTICKER)

Bibliography: Recent Books

The following list encompasses more than 150 recent books in English that have been judged significant contributions to learning in their respective fields. Each citation includes a few lines of commentary to indicate the tenor of the work. The citations are organized by broad subject area, using the 10 parts of the *Propædia* as an outline.

Matter and Energy

Gordon Kane, *The Particle Garden: Our Universe as Understood by Particle Physicists* (1995), a historical survey that reveals how the subatomic "universe" and the origins of the cosmos are related.

P.W. Atkins, *The Periodic Kingdom: A Journey into the Land of the Chemical Elements* (1995), a treatment of the chemical elements that likens them to letters of the alphabet to explain their properties and functions.

Jim Baggott, *Perfect Symmetry: The Accidental Discovery of Buckminsterfullerene* (1994), an account of the fortuitous discovery of a new carbon molecule whose name reflects its structural resemblance to Fuller's geodesic dome.

Roald Hoffmann, *The Same and Not the Same* (1995), a study of chemistry as both philosophy and science, panacea and poison, looking at what chemists do.

Albert-László Barabási and H. Eugene Stanley, *Fractal Concepts in Surface Growth* (1995), a technical discussion of the disorderly surface growth of molecular structures in such natural fields as biochemistry, geology, and astronomy.

Paul Teller, *An Interpretive Introduction to Quantum Field Theory* (1995), an attempt to make quantum field theory accessible to philosophers and students by raising questions about its philosophical implications.

Ignazio Ciufolini and John Archibald Wheeler, *Gravitation and Inertia* (1995), an account of current thinking on the connection between gravitation and inertia in Einstein's theory of general relativity.

Alan Dressler, *Voyage to the Great Attractor: Exploring Intergalactic Space* (1995), a history of cosmology since Galileo's time, with a characterization of the dimensions and composition of the universe.

Joseph Silk, *A Short History of the Universe* (1994), an accessible description of the big bang theory, extrapolating from visible relics of Earth's past an explanation of the universe's origins.

Ken Croswell, *The Alchemy of the Heavens: Searching for Meaning in the Milky Way* (1995), recent thinking on the structure, origin, and evolution of the Milky Way Galaxy and its attraction as a source of study and speculation throughout the ages.

The Earth

Shawna Vogel, *Naked Earth: The New Geophysics* (1995), an account of the way contemporary geophysicists work, their description of both Earth's geologic past and its composition from core to mantle.

Kenneth J. Hsü, *The Geology of Switzerland: An Introduction to Tectonic Facies* (1995), a history of the geologic formation of the Swiss Alps as an illustration of the theory of plate tectonics.

Bill Green, *Water, Ice & Stone: Science and Memory on the Antarctic Lakes* (1995), a biography of Earth revealed through the geochemistry of Antarctic water and rocks.

Michael L. Weber and Judith A. Gradwohl, *The Wealth of Oceans: Environment and Development on Our Ocean Planet* (1995), a description of the symbiotic relationship between land and ocean, warning that their respective inhabitants are showing the effects of the disruption brought about by human activity.

J. Alan Holman, *Ancient Life of the Great Lakes Basin, Precambrian to Pleistocene* (1995), an account of life in the Great Lakes area 12,000 years ago and an analysis of the principles that govern the study of fossil remains.

David Brez Carlisle, *Dinosaurs, Diamonds, and Things from Outer Space: The Great Extinction* (1995), a hypothesis to account for recurring mass extinctions on Earth, using the Cretaceous-Tertiary boundary event 65 million years ago as an example.

Stephen J. Pyne, *World Fire: The Culture of Fire on Earth* (1995), a survey of the "energizing geography of global fire," noting the pros and cons of human-fire interaction.

Gregg Easterbrook, *A Moment on the Earth: The Coming Age of Environmental Optimism* (1995), a claim that antipollution methods currently in use mean an end to predation by humans and other animals as Earth's bounty is finally made available to all.

Ernst Frankel, *Ocean Environmental Management: A Primer on the Role of Oceans and How to Maintain Their Contribution to Life on Earth* (1995), an account of the present state of the ocean environment, with a warning about future degradation and suggestions for preventing further damage.

Life on Earth

Christian de Duve, *Vital Dust: Life as a Cosmic Imperative* (1995), the most recent theories on the origin of life and on its increasing complexity and biodiversity, based on seven key defining events.

Michael Rosenzweig, *Species Diversity in Space and Time* (1995), a study of the where, how, and why of biodiversity: where maximum diversity occurs (near the Equator) and how and why species have spread.

Lynn Margulis and Dorion Sagan, *What Is Life?* (1995), a history of thought on the question and an attempt at an answer that displays the dazzling diversity of life in both words and illustrations.

James H. Brown, *Macroecology* (1995), a broadscale statistical approach to the impact of human technology and population on environmental quality and biodiversity.

Niles Eldridge, *Reinventing Darwin: The Great Debate at the High Table of Evolutionary Theory* (1995), an account of the differences between Darwinians and naturalists highlighted by current developments in molecular biology.

Ed Regis, *Nano: The Emerging Science of Nanotechnology: Remaking the World—Molecule by Molecule* (1995), a futuristic vision of a molecular industry that can transform grass into prime sirloin or can manufacture monsters and machines of unimaginable destructiveness.

Stuart Kauffman, *At Home in the Universe: The Search for the Laws of Self-Organization and Complexity* (1995), reflections on the thrust toward spontaneous order within complexity, which may be as significant as natural selection in the formation of life on Earth and possibly elsewhere.

Roger Payne, *Among Whales* (1995), a biologist's account of his numerous excursions into the whales' world, including informed speculations and observations.

Delta Willis, *The Sand Dollar and the Slide Rule: Drawing Blueprints from Nature* (1995), a tribute to design engineering in nature, using such examples as the "gearshifts" in a fly's wing as models of adaptive technology.

Glenn Searfoss, *Skulls and Bones: A Guide to the Skeletal Structures and Behavior of North American Mammals* (1995), an approach to the classification of mammals based on the identification of bones and the reciprocal relationship of skeletal structure, behaviour, and environmental lifestyle.

John L. Hoogland, *The Black-Tailed Prairie Dog: Social Life of a Burrowing Mammal* (1995), a detailed study of the behavioral ecology of this most colonial of animals.

Ron Larson, *Swamp Song: A Natural History of Florida's Swamps* (1995), a naturalist's catalog and history of Florida's varied swamps and wetlands, emphasizing the value to the entire planet of these endangered biosystems.

John A. Long, *The Rise of Fishes: 500 Million Years of Evolution* (1995), an evolutionary history of fishes based on the discovery and interpretation of fossil remains in the Western Hemisphere, Europe and Africa, and Asia.

Richard E. Michod, *Eros and Evolution: A Natural Philosophy of Sex* (1995), a hypothesis that justifies sexual reproduction as an effective way to repair and overcome genetic errors; an answer to the question, Why does sex exist?

Jacob Höglund and Rauno V. Alatalo, *Leks* (1995), an account of the mating behaviour of certain species of male animals in arenas, or leks, and description of the evolution of the lek and its genetic advantages.

Human Life

Ian Tattersall, *The Fossil Trail: How We Know What We Think We Know About Human Evolution* (1995), a view of *Homo sapiens* as one species among many, suggesting that future research should investigate diversity among species rather than comparative anatomy within a single species.

Paul Churchland, *The Engine of Reason, the Seat of the Soul: A Philosophical Journey into the Brain* (1995), a description—and an appreciation—of the animal brain's cognitive capabilities and its neural, chemical, and biological activity.

Sander L. Gilman, *Picturing Health and Illness: Images of Identity and Difference* (1995), a history of illustrated histories of medicine and their message that illness is ugly and health beautiful.

Tony Gould, *A Summer Plague: Polio and Its Survivors* (1995), a history of epidemic polio in England and the United States in the 20th century, emphasizing the significant political and social impact of the disease.

Wayne Riddle, *A Field Guide to Germs* (1995), a concise guide to diseases new and ancient that are visited on humans by viruses, bacteria, and parasites.

Arno Karlen, *Man and Microbes: Disease and Plagues in History and Modern Times* (1995), a suggestion that the current proliferation of "new" diseases can be understood through a study of changes in the environment and behaviour of both diseases and their victims.

Bernard Asbell, *The Pill: A Biography of the Drug That Changed the World* (1995), a history of the oral contraceptive, and of the social, economic, political, and emotional fallout as it catapulted the planet into "the age of biointervention."

Benson Bobrick, *Knotted Tongues: Stuttering in History and the Quest for a Cure* (1995), an account of a mystifying dysfunction, its social and psychological effects on some prominent sufferers, and information on current treatments.

Jeff Lyon and Peter Gorner, *Altered Fates: Gene Therapy and the Retooling of Human Life* (1995), an account of the first 60 gene therapy experiments, with speculation on the effect of gene therapy on the practice of medicine.

Robert Ornstein, *The Roots of the Self: Unraveling the Mystery of Who We Are* (1995), a survey of what constitutes the human temperament, mind, and brain, discussing evolutionary biology, brain physiology, and personality development in nontechnical terms.

Jean-Pierre Changeux and Alain Connes, *Conversations on Mind, Matter, and Mathematics,* ed. and trans. by M.B. De Bevoise (1995), dialogues between a neurobiologist and a mathematician on human cognition, the nature of mathematical objects, and the relation of science to ethics.

Human Society

Joe Starita, *The Dull Knifes of Pine Ridge: A Lakota Odyssey* (1995), the history of a Sioux family and of the Sioux nation, drawn from the narratives of the ancients, archival materials, and the recollections of the oldest living Native American World War I veteran.

Diane Singerman, *Avenues of Participation: Family, Politics, and Networks in Urban Quarters of Cairo* (1995), an account of the way Cairo's "popular classes" (excluded groups) manipulate the bureaucracy to obtain political, economic, and social advantages.

James L. Newman, *The Peopling of Africa: A Geographic Interpretation* (1995), a history of the cultural origins of the peoples of Africa from earliest times to the beginnings of the colonial era, analyzed by region.

Ronald Segal, *The Black Diaspora: Five Centuries of the Black Experience Outside Africa* (1995), a history of the dispersion of Africans as slaves both within Africa and in Europe and the New World and their rich contributions to their own and their masters' cultures.

Richard Critchfield, *The Villagers: Changed Values, Altered Lives, the Closing of the Urban-Rural Gap* (1994), a plea for the conservation of village culture worldwide, with descriptions of villages portraying both their common characteristics and their exquisite individuality.

John H. Kagel and Alvin E. Roth (eds.), *The Handbook of Experimental Economics* (1995), a survey of current experimental thinking in such topics as game theory, industrial organization, investment and public policy, and auctions.

Kenichi Ohmae, *The End of the Nation State: The Rise of Regional Economics* (1995), an argument that the end of the Cold War has rendered the traditional nation-state obsolete as an economic unit and that globalization of markets should—and will—follow.

Robert H. Frank and Philip J. Cook, *The Winner-Take-All Society: How More and More Americans Compete for Ever Fewer and Bigger Prizes, Encouraging Economic Waste, Income Inequality, and an Impoverished Cultural Life* (1995), an argument in favour of realigning the system of economic rewards that gives disproportionate wealth to a handful of "stars" at the top while depriving others of motivation, the incentive to compete, and a reasonable income.

Desmond King, *Actively Seeking Work? The Politics of Unemployment and Welfare Policy in the United States and Great Britain* (1995), a history of the three principal British and U.S. work-welfare programs, analyzing them in relation to each country's political and social policy framework.

I. Bernard Cohen, *Science and the Founding Fathers* (1995), a survey of the influence of scientific principles on the politics of the newly created United States—for example, viewing Newtonian equilibrium as a metaphor for the checks and balances of the Constitution.

David L. Shapiro, *Federalism: A Dialogue* (1995), a presentation of early writings on the Nationalist-Federalist debate that seeks to establish a 20th-century position favouring multistate and regional political jurisdictions.

Neil Duxbury, *Patterns of American Jurisprudence* (1995), a history and analysis of U.S. law and the intellectual and political traditions that have influenced the way courts and judges function in the U.S.

George Anastaplo, *The Amendments to the Constitution: A Commentary* (1995), an analysis of the historical, philosophical, and ethical and legal significance of each of the Constitution's 27 amendments.

Paul Goldstein, *Copyright's Highway: The Law and Lore of Copyright from Gutenberg to the Celestial Jukebox* (1994), an account of the history of copyright and of its social, cultural, and economic implications, with observations on challenges presented by the "celestial jukebox"—that is, digital and satellite-enhanced technology.

Jere R. Behrman, Robert A. Pollak, and Paul Taubman, *From Parent to Child: Intrahousehold Allocations and Intergenerational Relations in the United States* (1995), a series of discussions on the economic approach to family decision making about children's higher education.

Morris Shamos, *The Myth of Scientific Literacy* (1995), an argument that the "scientific literacy" laymen can acquire is not as useful to society as is understanding what can be expected of science and of scientific experts.

Deborah Meier, *The Power of Their Ideas: Lessons for America from a Small School in Harlem* (1995), a defense of public education by a teacher who emphasizes the importance of exploiting children's innate inventiveness and curiosity in order to establish a lifelong love of learning.

William J. Reese, *The Origins of the American High School* (1995), a portrait of the high school in the 19th century as a promoter of republican values, provider of educational opportunity for an emerging middle class, and cornerstone of the American free public-school system.

Art

Nicholas Mirzoeff, *Silent Poetry: Deafness, Sign, and Visual Culture in Modern France* (1995), a study of the visual culture of the deaf, relating it to the group of 19th-century deaf painters in France who helped to banish the notion of deafness as pathology.

Peter Brook, *Thoughts on Acting and Theatre* (1995), musings, observations, and reminiscences of an eminent British director and teacher on the intimate yet public experience of acting.

Ashish Rajadhyaksha and Paul Willemen, *Encyclopaedia of Indian Cinema* (1994), an exhaustive reference source for Indian film that reflects the political and social development of the subcontinent and offers an in-depth view of the world's largest national film industry.

Roger Bray (ed.), *The Blackwell History of Music in Britain: The Sixteenth Century* (1995), a history of music and musicians in Tudor England, including theory of composition, sacred and secular music, and observations on the changing role of music from 1485 to about 1625.

Charles Rosen, *The Romantic Generation* (1995), a view of 19th-century music and its interaction with literary fragments and landscape painting, with a 75-minute compact disc of selections from Chopin, Liszt, and Schumann keyed to the text and performed by the author.

Francis Sparshott, *A Measured Pace: Toward a Philosophical Understanding of the Arts of Dance* (1995), a survey of dance from theory to performance, illustrating its relation to music, narrative, and theatre and its pervasive influence in human life.

Francis D.K. Ching, *A Visual Dictionary of Architecture* (1995), a practicing architect's novel way of defining architectural terms, arranging them under simple subject headings ("door," "load") and using drawings to group the related components.

Steve Yates (ed.), *Poetics of Space: A Critical Photographic Anthology* (1995), a selection of essays by theorists and artists who reflect on the uses of space and perspective in the context of the art and technology of the photograph.

Aileen Ribeiro, *The Art of Dress: Fashion in England and France, 1750–1820* (1995), a study that relates social and political conditions to fashion and dress, using portraits and caricatures of the period as sources and showing how France became the centre for women's fashions, while England captured the market for male attire.

Claire Richter Sherman, *Imaging Aristotle: Verbal and Visual Representations in Fourteenth-Century France* (1995), an examination of the interrelationship between text and image in Nicole Oresme's vernacular translation of Aristotle's works on ethics and politics, emphasizing the associative and mnemonic value of calligraphy and decoration to a medieval lay readership.

Technology

Martin Bauer (ed.), *Resistance to New Technology: Nuclear Power, Information Technology, and Biotechnology* (1995), a history of post-World War II resistance to three major technological fields, discussing responses to the "acute pain of technological progress."

Jeremy Rifkin, *The End of Work: The Decline of the Global Labor Force and the Dawn of the Post-Market Era* (1995), an evaluation of the "third industrial revolution," a workerless future in which computers supplant both the human brain and human labour.

Edward Wenk, Jr., *Making Waves: Engineering, Politics, and the Social Management of Technology* (1995), a call for a more informed public to oversee the future management of technology, from space exploration to environmental protection.

Alan M. MacEachren, *How Maps Work: Representation, Visualization, and Design* (1995), an account of mapmaking, with suggestions for improving map representation and design by using the unique visualizing properties of the computer.

David Woodward and J.B. Harley (eds.), *The History of Cartography,* vol. 2, bk. 2: *Cartography in the Traditional East and Southeast Asian Societies* (1994), a survey of the mapping traditions of Asia, in which not only the geographic but also the spiritual space of the entire cosmos is brought under cartographic scrutiny.

J. Barry DuVall, *Contemporary Manufacturing Processes* (1996), a survey of methods of transforming industrial stock into consumable products, analyzed by "material families": metallics, ceramics, composites, and polymerics.

Paul Raeburn, *The Last Harvest: The Genetic Gamble That Threatens to Destroy American Agriculture* (1995), a warning that increased susceptibility to catastrophic crop failure from diseases and pests might result from genetic manipulation that sacrifices biodiversity to achieve higher yields.

Council on Tall Buildings and Urban Habitat, *Architecture of Tall Buildings* (1995), a definition of the tall building, its political and urban influence, its design and engineering, and its past and future in the United States, Europe, and Asia.

Arne Petter Eggen and Bjørn Normann Sandaker, *Steel, Structure, and Architecture: A Survey of the Material and Its Application* (1995), a discussion by an engineer and an architect of the uses of steel in architecture in combination with glass, masonry, wood, and fabric.

Alan Black, *Urban Mass Transportation Planning* (1995), the historical and political background of urban mass transit and the issues it raises: land use, crime, urban development, and energy consumption.

Ian Friel, *The Good Ship: Ships, Shipbuilding, and Technology in England, 1200–1520* (1995), a history of shipbuilding and maritime technology, embracing war, commerce, and discovery from the Middle Ages to the dawn of the age of global exploration.

Joel D. Howell, *Technology in the Hospital: Transforming Patient Care in the Early Twentieth Century* (1995), a study of the relation between technology and medical care in the United States between 1908 and 1925, using three clinical technologies to illustrate the changes that took place in doctor-patient-hospital transactions during those years.

Edward Barrett and Marie Redmond (eds.), *Contextual Media: Multimedia and Interpretation* (1995), a look at future applications of multimedia technology, mentioning the Shakespeare Interactive Archive as an example of the new electronic approach to scholarship on text and performance.

Nicholas Negroponte, *Being Digital* (1995), an explanation of digitalized information comprehensible to the nonscientist.

Richard Rhodes, *Dark Sun: The Making of the Hydrogen Bomb* (1995), the history of thermonuclear weapons technology, describing the international research and development race and emphasizing the necessity of becoming a world without war.

Charles Beveridge and Paul Rocheleau, *Frederick Law Olmstead: Designing the American Landscape* (1995), a recounting, documented with numerous photographs, of Olmstead's accomplishments as a designer of American park systems and his contributions to urban culture through a reverence for nature and for the dignity of all humankind.

Alan C. Tribble, *The Space Environment: Implications for Spacecraft Design* (1995), an analysis of the interaction between the environment in space and the design and function of man-made orbiting spacecraft, listing factors that threaten the performance capability of the vehicles.

Religion

Simon Coleman and John Elsner, *Pilgrimage: Past and Present in World Religions* (1995), a study of the phenomenon of pilgrimage, sacred travel based on the canonical texts of Christianity, Buddhism, Hinduism, and Islam, and of 20th-century pilgrimages to such secular destinations as Lenin's tomb and Elvis Presley's Graceland.

Jeffrey J. Kripal, *Kālī's Child: The Mystical and the Erotic in the Life and Teachings of Ramakrishna* (1995), a study of the 19th-century Bengali mystic and Hindu saint that illustrates how erotic, mystical, and ecstatic revelation became for him and his followers a single, profound religious experience.

Lawrence A. Babb and Susan S. Wadley (eds.), *Media and the Transformation of Religion in South Asia* (1995), essays discussing the changes wrought by 20th-century media images (comic books, videotapes) on traditional sacred symbols and practices in India.

Donald S. Lopez, Jr., *Curators of the Buddha: The Study of Buddhism under Colonialism* (1995), a cultural analysis of Buddhist studies in the West over the past century.

David S. Ariel, *What Do Jews Believe? The Spiritual Foundations of Judaism* (1995), a study of the fundamental tenets of Judaism as they are grounded in both the historical past and the writings of Jewish thinkers.

Jack Miles, *God: A Biography* (1995), an examination of human spiritual and ethical values in light of the ways God has interacted with his children—from action to speech to silence—as portrayed in the Hebrew Bible.

Elaine Pagels, *The Origin of Satan* (1995), a "social history of Satan," who first appeared in the New Testament as the heretic son of darkness who contended with the angelic son of light.

Caroline Walker Bynum, *The Resurrection of the Body in Western Christianity, 200–1336* (1995), observations on the analogy to rebirth of burying a seed, reflecting historical concerns about the disposition of human remains and about conceptions of the body.

Elizabeth Isichei, *A History of Christianity in Africa from Antiquity to the Present* (1995), a study of African Christianity from 700 BC to the 20th century, which has been called the fourth great age of Christian expansion.

Hans Küng, *Christianity: Essence, History, and Future* (1995), a historical survey of the three major Christian religious traditions, Roman, Orthodox, and Protestant, that, by exploring how Christianity became what it is today, asks how and what it will be in the future.

Patrick Collinson, Nigel Ramsay, and Margaret Sparks (eds.), *A History of Canterbury Cathedral* (1995), a collection of essays on the community that created, surrounded, and has helped sustain Canterbury cathedral since its Anglo-Saxon origins in 597.

M A Salahi, *Muhammad: Man and Prophet, a Complete Study of the Life of the Prophet of Islam* (1995), a description by a practicing Muslim of the Prophet, his personality, his mission, the state he established, and the Qur'an, Allah's word as it was revealed to Muhammad over a 23-year period.

The History of Mankind

Robert Ruby, *Jericho: Dreams, Ruins, Phantoms* (1995), the 11,000-year history of the settlement, describing its geologic past, with profiles of some of its scientific investigators and a correlation of biblical with archaeological accounts.

Prudence Jones and Nigel Pennick, *A History of Pagan Europe* (1995), a study of pagan history from its first written records in Crete in 2800 BC to its contemporary resurgence in the part of the ecological movement that views nature as a manifestation of the female divinity principle.

John Ash, *A Byzantine Journey* (1995), a history of the Byzantine Empire and Anatolia that brings to life the turbulent society of a thousand years ago while also drawing unmistakable parallels to contemporary bloodshed in Bosnia and Herzegovina.

Felipe Fernández-Armesto, *Millennium: A History of the Last Thousand Years* (1995), a survey of the explorations, societies, religious and geographic influences, and revolutions that have shaped the world and that may provide insights into the future.

B. Netanyahu, *The Origins of the Inquisition in Fifteenth-Century Spain* (1995), a study of the origins and causes of the Inquisition, asserting that it was primarily anti-Jewish rather than an institution designed to eradicate heresy generally.

Nicholas Orme and Margaret Webster, *The English Hospital, 1070–1570* (1995), a history of the origin and mission, patient population, and resources of English hospitals in the later Middle Ages and the Reformation.

Alison Weir, *The Wars of the Roses* (1995), an account of the personalities whose strong and often bloody imprints mark the period that led up to and included the first of the wars between the houses of Lancaster and York.

Cemal Kafadar, *Between Two Worlds: The Construction of the Ottoman State* (1995), a study of the Ottoman Empire, outlining the contributions of modern scholarship to its history and historiography.

Valerie Hansen, *Negotiating Daily Life in China: How Ordinary People Used Contracts, 600–1400* (1995), an account of life in early China seen through the contracts that covered the purchase, sale, and rental of goods and properties.

Linda Cooke Johnson, *Shanghai: From Market Town to Treaty Port, 1074–1858* (1995), a portrait of the growth and development of what had been a commercial centre long before the arrival of the British in the 19th century.

Georg Feuerstein, Subash Kak, and David Frawley, *In Search of the Cradle of Civilization: New Light on Ancient India* (1995), a history of ancient India, suggesting the Indus-Sarasvati civilization as one of the earliest, with archaeological evidence from *c.* 6000 BC of Vedic cities and a seafaring society.

Robert B. Edgerton, *The Fall of the Asante Empire: The 100-Year War for Africa's Gold Coast* (1995), an account of the fierce resistance Asante warriors mounted against British efforts in the 19th century to dominate what is present-day Ghana.

Robin Law (ed.), *From Slave Trade to "Legitimate" Commerce: The Commercial Transition in Nineteenth-Century West Africa* (1995), a group of 10 case studies considering the impact on African economy, society, and culture of the decline of the slave trade in the 19th century, when agriculture and other "legitimate" commercial undertakings supplanted it.

Malyn Newitt, *A History of Mozambique* (1995), an account of the interaction between cycles of drought and efforts by Afro-Portuguese ruling monarchies to achieve political control in Mozambique from the 15th century to the present.

Thor Heyerdahl, Daniel H. Sandweiss, and Alfredo Narváez, *Pyramids of Túcume: The Quest for Peru's Forgotten City* (1995), the story of excavations of a 900-year-old Peruvian pyramid city suggesting that long-distance sea trade might account for the presence of nonnative materials in the structures.

Robert M. Kingdon, *Adultery and Divorce in Calvin's Geneva* (1995), a study of divorce after the Protestant Reformation, illustrating the operation of the consistory, an institution urged by Calvin to monitor the public's behaviour.

Thomas DaCosta Kaufmann, *Court, Cloister, & City: The Art and Culture of Central Europe, 1450–1800* (1995), a study of 300 years of painting, sculpture, and architecture in what is now Central and Eastern Europe, exploring the relationship of monumental and domestic objects to the indigenous cultures of which they remain a lasting expression.

Helmut Walser Smith, *German Nationalism and Religious Conflict: Culture, Ideology, Politics, 1870–1914* (1995), an analysis of the forces, especially the Catholic-Protestant schism, that profoundly influenced German national identity during the period of the German Empire.

James Tertius de Kay, *Chronicles of the Frigate Macedonian, 1809–1922* (1995), a biography of the most important prize ever taken by the U.S. Navy, from its initial fitting out to its transformation into, and loss by fire as, a Bronx hotel, with accounts of the ship's seafaring exploits and flamboyant skippers.

Hans Schmidt, *The United States Occupation of Haiti: 1915–1934* (1995; originally published in 1971), a history of an earlier hapless occupation of Haiti, which remains a timely cautionary tale.

Robert F. Rogers, *Destiny's Landfall: A History of Guam* (1995), an account of the island of Guam from the time of Magellan's landing through successive occupations to the present, when political control has been restored to the resident population.

W.G. Beasley, *Japan Encounters the Barbarian: Japanese Travellers in America and Europe* (1995), adventures of the first Japanese tourists to the West in the 19th century, their motives for studying Western ways, and the effect on Japanese culture of what they learned.

Peter Duus, *The Abacus and the Sword: The Japanese Penetration of Korea, 1895–1910* (1995), a history of the Meiji economic and military incursion into Korea.

Richard Crockatt, *The Fifty Years War: The United States and the Soviet Union in World Politics, 1941–1991* (1995), a political history of the Cold War, pointing out the need to replace that "long peace" with the kind of global coordination that is responsive to regional and national interests.

Philip Zelikow and Condoleeza Rice, *Germany United and Europe Transformed: A Study in Statecraft* (1995), a diplomatic history of the events that culminated in German reunification during 1989–90.

William Clarke, *The Lost Fortunes of the Tsars* (1995), an attempt to learn the whereabouts of the Romanov gems and gold still in private hands by examining Moscow's recently opened Central State Archives.

Susan L. Woodward, *Balkan Tragedy: Chaos and Dissolution After the Cold War* (1995), an effort to explain what happened to Yugoslavia and to urge greater attention to the connection between the internal affairs of countries and the international environment.

Michael Lind, *The Next American Nation: The New Nationalism and the Fourth American Revolution* (1995), a descriptive history of the first three American republics, the Anglo-American, the Euro-American, and the multicultural American, with a call to embark on a fourth, called the trans-American melting pot.

Page Smith, *Democracy on Trial: The Japanese-American Evacuation and Relocation in World War II* (1995), an account, based on interviews and archival research, of the forced relocation of more than 100,000 Japanese, three-quarters of whom were U.S. citizens, and their lives in the internment camps during a three-year period of World War II.

Joseph A. Page, *The Brazilians* (1995), a detailed history and character study of Brazil and its multiracial, multiethnic population, an effort to ferret out "Brazilianness."

Richard Wilson, *Maya Resurgence in Guatemala: Q'eqchi' Experience* (1995), a study of the Maya of central Guatemala, describing their traditional ways and the Maya's efforts to recover them.

David Bonavia, *China's Warlords* (1995), a chronology of the bloody period of the warlords from 1912 to the beginning of World War II, organized by geographic region and including biographies of some of the principals.

Chalmers Johnson, *Japan Who Governs: The Rise of the Developmental State* (1995), an account of how the best and brightest who entered the bureaucracy have influenced the history, politics, and foreign relations of Japan.

Diego Cordovez and Selig S. Harrison, *Out of Afghanistan: The Inside Story of the Soviet Withdrawal* (1995), a narrative chronology of the developments leading up to and facilitating the Soviet withdrawal from Afghanistan that credits six years of negotiation rather than the U.S.-backed military presence.

Parvin Paidar, *Women and the Political Process in Twentieth-Century Iran* (1995), an inquiry into the effect on Iranian women of the impetus toward establishing modern nation-states in the Middle East.

The Branches of Knowledge

John Allen Paulos, *A Mathematician Reads the Newspaper* (1995), examples of skeptical mathematical thinking applied to everyday newspaper stories that illustrate the author's injunction "Always be smart; seldom be certain."

S. Chandrasekhar, *Newton's* Principia *for the Common Reader* (1995), a Nobel laureate's scholarly re-creation, in the language of equations, of Isaac Newton's mathematical writings that led to his universal law of gravitation and an appreciation of Newton's creative intelligence.

Theodore M. Porter, *Trust in Numbers: The Pursuit of Objectivity in Science and Public Life* (1995), an attempt to explain the 20th-century propensity to imbue quantitative methods with the prestige of scientific objectivity.

Ian Stewart, *Nature's Numbers: The Unreal Reality of Mathematics* (1995), an overview of mathematics, what it is and how it is used, and its presence in the patterns of nature and the cosmos.

John Cornwell (ed.), *Nature's Imagination: The Frontiers of Scientific Vision* (1995), a series of essays reexamining the nature and uses of science, defining it as an art form rather than a philosophical method and reevaluating the relationship of parts to the whole in scientific thinking.

M.R. Wright, *Cosmology in Antiquity* (1995), a history of cosmology, its main themes and its texts, based on the most significant surviving evidence from Mesopotamia, Egyptian and Semitic cultures, and the early Greeks.

Paul Davies, *About Time: Einstein's Unfinished Revolution* (1995), the riddle of time explored and seen as cosmic force, will-o'-the-wisp, the foundation of quantum physics, a product of Einstein's legerdemain, and more.

Evelyn Fox Keller, *Refiguring Life: Metaphors of Twentieth-Century Biology* (1995), three essays dealing with the "border crossings" between genetics and embryology, physics and biology, and cyberscience and molecular biology.

Jonathan Sawday, *The Body Emblazoned: Dissection and the Human Body in Renaissance Culture* (1995), a history of the beginnings of the Western science of the body in Renaissance dissection practices, in which the knowledge gained about the structure and function of the body became part of literature, art, and religion.

Donald N. Levine, *Visions of the Sociological Tradition* (1995), a study of sociology and its present status and direction, examining its Hellenic, French, German, Italian, British, Marxian, and American traditions.

Timur Kuran, *Private Truths, Public Lies: The Social Consequences of Preference Falsification* (1995), analysis by an economist of the cost to society of the willful distortion of public opinion, which can confer a false image of stability on weak or vulnerable institutions.

Catherine Wilson, *Early Modern Philosophy and the Invention of the Microscope* (1995), a discussion of the effect of the invention of the microscope on the scientific revolution and the philosophy of science in the 17th century and after.

Louis L. Bucciarelli, *Designing Engineers* (1994), a study of engineers at work, describing how the need for a specific product—for example, a baggage-inspection system for airports—becomes transformed into a design project and finally into the object itself.

Thomas L. Hankins and Robert J. Silverman, *Instruments and the Imagination* (1995), a study of seemingly marginal instruments and machines, invented between the 16th and the 19th century, viewing them as philosophical experiments rather than discredited novelties.

Howard Bloom, *The Lucifer Principle: A Scientific Expedition into the Forces of History* (1995), reflections on the human propensity for dominance and suggestions for neutralizing it in human life through "competition without carnage."

Josep Fontana, *The Distorted Past: A Reinterpretation of Europe*, trans. by Colin Smith (1995), a critique of traditional historiography, whose linear approach trumpeting European "superiority" provides neither an accurate nor a balanced picture of the past.

Simon Schama, *Landscape and Memory* (1995), a chronicle of humankind's symbiotic relationship to landscape as history, art, and politics and as a continuing source of both nurturance and peril.

Joseph Cropsey, *Plato's World: Man's Place in the Cosmos* (1995), a study of Plato's worldview examined through seven of his dialogues that constitute a dramatic chronology of the life and death of Socrates.

Ramon M. Lemos, *The Nature of Value: Axiological Investigations* (1995), a study of value theory based on the tradition of rational objectivity, asserting that value is not a matter of liking or disliking and noting that a philosophy of value is among the goals of higher education.

Carol Duncan, *Civilizing Rituals: Inside Public Art Museums* (1995), a sociopolitical history of the art museum, viewing it as a ritual space akin to the theatre, the medieval church, or the floor of a stock exchange.

Armando Petrucci, *Writers and Readers in Medieval Italy: Studies in the History of Written Culture*, ed. and trans. by Charles M. Radding (1995), an account of the uses of literacy, with observations on the reciprocal influence of books, ideas, and the preservation of culture from 400 to 1400 CE.

(JEAN S. GOTTLIEB)

CONTRIBUTORS

Abramson, Gary. Reporter on Spain for *Business Week,* the *Chicago Tribune,* and the Associated Press. • WORLD AFFAIRS: *Spain*

Adams, Andy. Editor and Publisher, *Sumo World.* Author of *Sumo* and *Sumo World Record Book.* • SPORTS AND GAMES: *Judo; Wrestling:* Sumo

Alder, Phillip. Syndicated Bridge Columnist. Author of *Get Smarter at Bridge;* Contributor to the *Daily Bridge Calendar.* • SPORTS AND GAMES: *Contract Bridge*

Allaby, Michael. Writer and Lecturer. Author of *Ecology Facts; A Guide to Gaia; Facing the Future.* • THE ENVIRONMENT: *Environmental Issues; International Environmental Activities;* Sidebar

Allan, J.A. Professor of Geography, School of Oriental and African Studies, University of London. Coauthor of *The Nile: Sharing a Scarce Resource.* • WORLD AFFAIRS: *Libya*

Amirouche, Hamou. Former Consultant, the Algerian Institute for Strategic Studies. • WORLD AFFAIRS: *Spotlight:* The Berbers of North Africa

Andrades, Jorge Adrián. • SPORTS AND GAMES: *Equestrian Sports:* Polo

Archibald, John J. Retired Feature Writer, *St. Louis* (Mo.) *Post Dispatch;* Adjunct Professor, Washington University, St. Louis. Member of the American Bowling Congress Hall of Fame. • SPORTS AND GAMES: *Bowling:* U.S. Tenpins

Arnold, Guy. Freelance Writer. Author of *Modern Nigeria; Aid in Africa;* and others. • WORLD AFFAIRS: *Botswana; Burundi; Cape Verde; Chad; Comoros; Djibouti; Equatorial Guinea; Gambia, The; Ghana; Guinea-Bissau; Lesotho; Liberia; Madagascar; Maldives; Mauritius; Nigeria; Rwanda; São Tomé and Príncipe; Seychelles; Sierra Leone; Swaziland*

Arnold, Mavis. Freelance Journalist, Dublin. • WORLD AFFAIRS: *Ireland*

Arrington, Leonard J. Formerly Church Historian, Church of Jesus Christ of Latter-day Saints. • RELIGION: *Church of Jesus Christ of Latter-day Saints*

Atkinson, Peter J. Conservation Information Officer. • THE ENVIRONMENT: *Botanical Gardens*

Austin, Cherry. Associate Editor, *The Brazil Handbook; South American Handbook.* • WORLD AFFAIRS: *Uruguay*

Bacani, Cesar. Senior Editor, *Asiaweek* magazine. • WORLD AFFAIRS: *Malaysia*

Bahry, Louay. Adjunct Professor of Political Science. • WORLD AFFAIRS: *Iraq*

Bakker, Martinus A. Professor of Germanic Languages, Calvin College, Grand Rapids, Mich. Editor of *Studies in Netherlandic Culture and Literature.* • LITERATURE: *Netherlandic*

Balaban, Avraham. Professor of Modern Hebrew Literature, University of Florida. Author of *Between God and Beast: An Examination of Amos Oz's Prose.* • LITERATURE: *Jewish:* Hebrew

Ballentine, Jane Coyle. Director of Public Affairs, American Zoo and Aquarium Association. • THE ENVIRONMENT: *Zoos*

Barford, Michael F. Editor and Director, *Tabacosmos.* • BUSINESS AND INDUSTRY REVIEW: *Tobacco*

Barlow, Margaret. Freelance Writer. Associate Editor, *Woman's Art Journal;* Editor, *Florida Architect.* • NOBEL PRIZES *(in part)*

Barrett, David B. Research Professor of Missiometrics, Regent University, Virginia Beach, Va. Author of *World Christian Encyclopedia; Schism and Renewal in Africa.* • RELIGION: *Tables*

Barrett, John C.A. Headmaster, the Leys School; Secretary, British Committee, World Methodist Council. Author of *Family Worship in Theory and Practice.* • RELIGION: *Methodist Churches*

Bass, Howard. Journalist and Author; formerly Editor, *Winter Sports;* Ice Hockey Correspondent, *Daily Telegraph;* Skiing and Skating Correspondent, *Daily Mail.* Author of 17 books on winter sports. • BIOGRAPHIES *(in part);* SPORTS AND GAMES: *Ice Hockey:* International; *Ice Skating; Skiing*

Beckwith, David C. Director, Government Affairs, EDS Corp. • WORLD AFFAIRS: *United States:* State and Local Affairs

Belaski, Ann M. Copy Editor, Encyclopædia Britannica. • BIOGRAPHIES *(in part)*

Berfield, Susan. Staff Writer, *Asiaweek* magazine. • WORLD AFFAIRS: *Indonesia*

Bernstein, Barton J. Professor of History, Stanford University. • LIBRARIES AND MUSEUMS: *Sidebar*

Bickelhaupt, David L. Professor Emeritus, Fisher College of Business, Ohio State University. • BUSINESS AND INDUSTRY REVIEW: *Insurance*

Bilgrami, Akeel. Professor of Philosophy, Columbia University. Author of *Belief and Meaning.* • WORLD AFFAIRS: *Spotlight:* Secularism in South Asia

Binczewski, George J. Principal Technical Adviser, S.C. Systems, Moraga, Calif. • BUSINESS AND INDUSTRY REVIEW: *Materials and Metals:* Light Metals

Bird, Thomas E. Director, Council for the Study of Ethics and Public Policy, Queens College, City University of New York. • LITERATURE: *Jewish:* Yiddish

Bisman, Ronald W. North Island Editor, *New Zealand Harness Racing Weekly.* Author of *Cardigan Bay; Salute to Trotting.* • SPORTS AND GAMES: *Equestrian Sports:* Harness Racing

Bleibtreu, Hermann K. Professor of Anthropology, University of Arizona. • ANTHROPOLOGY AND ARCHAEOLOGY: *Anthropology:* Physical

Boddy, William C. Founder and Editor, *Motor Sport.* Full Member, Guild of Motoring Writers. • SPORTS AND GAMES: *Automobile Racing:* Grand Prix Racing

Boden, Edward. Publications Adviser, British Veterinary Association; formerly Editor, *Veterinary Record.* • HEALTH AND DISEASE: *Veterinary Medicine*

Booth, John Nicholls. Lecturer and Writer. Author of *The Quest for Preaching Power; Psychic Paradoxes.* • RELIGION: *Unitarian (Universalist) Churches*

Boswall, Jeffery. Senior Lecturer in Biological Imaging, University of Derby, Delaware. • LIFE SCIENCES: *Ornithology*

Box, Ben. Editor, Trade and Travel Handbooks (*South American Handbook* and others). • WORLD AFFAIRS: *Peru*

Boye, Roger. Formerly Coin Columnist, *Chicago Tribune.* • ART, ANTIQUES, AND COLLECTIONS: *Numismatics*

Boylan, Patrick J. Professor and Head, Department of Arts Policy and Management, City University, London. Author of *Museums 2000: Politics, People, Professionals and Profit* and others. • LIBRARIES AND MUSEUMS: *Museums* (international)

Bradsher, Henry S. Foreign Affairs Writer. • WORLD AFFAIRS: *Philippines*

Braidwood, Robert J. Professor Emeritus of Old World Prehistory, Oriental Institute and Department of Anthropology, University of Chicago. Author of *Prehistoric Men.* • ANTHROPOLOGY AND ARCHAEOLOGY: *Archaeology:* Eastern Hemisphere

Brant, Sara N. Yearbooks Assistant, Encyclopædia Britannica. • BIOGRAPHIES *(in part);* BUSINESS AND INDUSTRY REVIEW: *Games and Toys:* Sidebar

Brazee, Rutlage J. Geophysical Consultant. • EARTH AND SPACE SCIENCES: *Geophysics*

Brecher, Kenneth. Professor of Astronomy and Physics, Boston University. Coauthor and coeditor of *Astronomy of the Ancients.* • EARTH AND SPACE SCIENCES: *Astronomy*

Brokopp, John G. Specialist in publicity, public relations, and writing about equestrian racing. • SPORTS AND GAMES: *Equestrian Sports:* Thoroughbred Racing (U.S. and Canada)

Brooks, Tony. Retired Secretary-General, International Table Tennis Federation. • SPORTS AND GAMES: *Table Tennis*

Brown, Bess. Journalist; Formerly Senior Research Analyst, Radio Free Europe/Radio Liberty Research Institute. • WORLD AFFAIRS: *Kazakhstan; Kyrgyzstan; Tajikistan; Turkmenistan; Uzbekistan*

Brown, Maggie. Media Editor, the Independent Newspapers. • MEDIA AND PUBLISHING: *Magazines* (international); *Newspapers* (international)

Brown-Humes, Christopher. Stockholm Correspondent, *Financial Times.* • WORLD AFFAIRS: *Sweden*

Burdin, Joel L. Director, Florida Institute of Education. Author of *Diversity and Leadership in Education.* • EDUCATION (U.S.)

Burks, Ardath W. Professor Emeritus of Asian Studies, Rutgers University, New Brunswick, N.J. Author of *Japan: A Postindustrial Power.* • WORLD AFFAIRS: *Japan*

Burns, Erik. Freelance Writer; Correspondent. • WORLD AFFAIRS: *Portugal*

Butler, Frank. Formerly Sports Editor, *News of the World.* Author of *The Good, the Bad and the Ugly: A Story of Boxing.* • SPORTS AND GAMES: *Boxing*

Cafferty, Bernard. Associate Editor, *British Chess Magazine;* Chess Columnist, the *Sunday Times.* • SPORTS AND GAMES: *Chess*

Cameron, Sarah. Freelance Writer and Editor, Trade and Travel Handbooks. • WORLD AFFAIRS: *Bolivia; Costa Rica; Cuba; Dominican Republic; Ecuador; El Salvador; Guatemala; Haiti; Honduras; Nicaragua; Panama*

Campbell, Robert. Architect and Architecture Critic. Author of *Cityscapes of Boston;* Coauthor of *American Architecture of the 1980s.* • ARCHITECTURE AND CIVIL ENGINEERING: *Architecture*

Carter, Robert W. Journalist, London. • SPORTS AND GAMES: *Equestrian Sports:* Show Jumping and Dressage; Steeplechasing; Thoroughbred Racing (Europe and Australia)

Chapman, Kenneth F. Formerly Editor, *Stamp Collecting* and *Philatelic Magazine.* • ART, ANTIQUES, AND COLLECTIONS: *Philately*

Chappell, Duncan. Research Fellow, United Nations Interregional Crime and Justice Research Institute. • LAW, CRIME, AND LAW ENFORCEMENT: *Crime; Law Enforcement*

Chapple, Abby. Writer and Consultant, Consumer Communications (Largent, W.Va.) • BUSINESS AND INDUSTRY REVIEW: *Home Furnishings:* Furniture

Cheuse, Alan. Writing Faculty, English Department, George Mason University, Fairfax, Va.; Book Commentator, National Public Radio. Author of *The Light Possessed* and others. • LITERATURE: *English:* United States

Chinnery, John. Supervising Copy Editor, Springer International, Berlin. • BIOGRAPHIES *(in part)*

Clapham, Christopher S. Professor of Politics and International Relations, University of Lancaster, England. Author of *Transformation and Continuity in Revolutionary Ethiopia.* • WORLD AFFAIRS: *Eritrea; Ethiopia*

Clark, David D. Managing Editor, *World Literature Today.* • LITERATURE: *English:* Other Literature in English

Clark, Martin. Reader in Politics, University of Edinburgh. Author of *Modern Italy, 1871–1982* and others. • MACROPÆDIA: *Italy:* History, Italy Since 1870

Clarke, Douglas L. Captain, U.S. Navy (ret.). Military Analyst. Author of *The Missing Man: Politics and the MIA.* • MILITARY AFFAIRS

Clarke, R.O. Lecturer and Consultant on Industrial Relations, London. • ECONOMIC AFFAIRS: *Labour-Management Relations*

Coates, James. Computer Writer, *Chicago Tribune.* Author of *Armed and Dangerous.* • COMPUTERS AND INFORMATION SYSTEMS

Cogle, T.C.J. Consultant, *Electrical Review.* • BUSINESS AND INDUSTRY REVIEW: *Electrical*

Cooper, Melanie Anne. Senior Editorial Assistant, *Newsweek.* • MEDIA AND PUBLISHING: *Newspapers* (U.S.)

Corzine, Robert. Oil and Gas Correspondent, the *Financial Times.* • BUSINESS AND INDUSTRY REVIEW: *Energy:* Alternative Energy; Natural Gas; Petroleum

Cosgrave, Bronwyn. Freelance Fashion Writer; Fashion Editor, *The European.* • FASHIONS

Coveney, Michael. Theatre Critic, *The Observer.* Author of *The Aisle Is Full of Noises* and others. • PERFORMING ARTS: *Theatre:* Great Britain and Ireland

Craine, Anthony G. Researcher, Encyclopædia Britannica. • BIOGRAPHIES *(in part)*

Crampton, Richard J. Fellow, St. Edmund Hall, Oxford; formerly Professor of East European History, University of Kent at Canterbury, England. Author of *Eastern Europe in the Twentieth Century* and others. • WORLD AFFAIRS: *Bulgaria*

Crisp, Jeff. Senior Research Officer, UNHCR, Geneva. Author of *The State of the World's Refugees: In Search of Solutions.* • POPULATIONS AND HUMAN RELATIONS: *International Migration*

Crowell, George T. Senior Writer. • WORLD AFFAIRS: *Korea, Democratic People's Republic of; Korea, Republic of*

Crowley, Edward. Journalist, Director, Technical Writing Services. • BUSINESS AND INDUSTRY REVIEW: *Shipbuilding;* TRANSPORTATION: *Shipping and Ports*

Cunningham, Susan M. Economic and Political Analyst; Freelance Writer. Author of *Latin America Since 1945* (in preparation). • WORLD AFFAIRS: *Argentina; Brazil; Mexico*

Curwen, Peter J. Reader in Business Policy, Sheffield (England) Business School. Author of *The U.K. Publishing Industry* and others. • MEDIA AND PUBLISHING: *Book Publishing* (international)

Cviic, K.F. East European Specialist, Royal Institute of International Affairs, London. • WORLD AFFAIRS: *Bosnia and Herzegovina; Croatia; Macedonia; Slovenia; Yugoslavia*

Czerwinski, Edward J. Professor Emeritus of Slavic and Comparative Literature, State University of New York at Stony Brook. Author of *A Dictionary of Polish Literature* and others. Area Editor, *Theater Companies of the World.* • LITERATURE: *Eastern European (in part); Russian (in part)*

Deeb, Marius K. Professor, George Washington University, Washington, D.C. Author of *Political Parties and Democracy in Egypt.* • WORLD AFFAIRS: *Egypt*

Deeb, Mary-Jane. Editor, *The Middle East Journal.* Author of *Libya's Foreign Policy.* • WORLD AFFAIRS: *Bahrain*

Deam, John B. Retired Technical Director, AMT—The Association for Manufacturing Technology, McLean, Va. • BUSINESS AND INDUSTRY REVIEW: *Machinery and Machine Tools*

de la Barre, Kenneth. Director, the Bridge Group. • WORLD AFFAIRS: *Arctic Regions*

Deletant, Dennis J. Senior Lecturer in Romanian Studies, University of London. Author of *Studies in Romanian History; Colloquial Romanian;* and others. • WORLD AFFAIRS: *Moldova; Romania*

Denselow, Robin. Rock Music Critic, *The Guardian;* Current Affairs Reporter, BBC Television. Author of *When the Music's Over: The Politics of Pop.* • PERFORMING ARTS: *Music:* Popular (international)

de Puy, Norman R. Minister, American Baptist Churches; Editor and Publisher, *Cabbages and Kings* newsletter. • BIOGRAPHIES *(in part);* RELIGION: *Baptist Churches*

Dicks, Geoffrey R. U.K. Economist, NatWest Markets. Author of *Sources of World Financial and Banking Information.* • BUSINESS AND INDUSTRY REVIEW: *Introduction*

Dirnbacher, Elfriede. Austrian Civil Servant. • WORLD AFFAIRS: *Austria*

Dixon, Bernard. Science Writer; Consultant. European Editor, *Bio/Technology;* Editor, *Medical Science Research.* Author of *Health and the Human Body* and others. • HEALTH AND DISEASE: *Medicine* (international); *Mental Health;* HEALTH AND DISEASE: Sidebar

Dizard, John W. Columnist, *National Review.* • ECONOMIC AFFAIRS: *Banking (in part)*

Dooling, Dave. Consultant and Writer, D^2 Associates. • EARTH AND SPACE SCIENCES: *Space Exploration*

Earp, John H. Director, Halcrow Fox and Associates. • TRANSPORTATION: *Introduction; Freight and Pipelines; Intercity Rail; Roads and Traffic; Urban Mass Transit*

Ehringer, Gavin Forbes. Rodeo Columnist, *Western Horseman.* • SPORTS AND GAMES: *Rodeo*

Ellis, Roger. Editor, *Mining Journal,* London. • BUSINESS AND INDUSTRY REVIEW: *Mining*

Everett-Green, Robert. Senior Features Writer, the *Globe and Mail.* • SPECIAL REPORT: *Cyberspace*

Fagan, Brian. Professor of Anthropology, University of California, Santa Barbara. Author of *Time Detectives.* • ANTHROPOLOGY AND ARCHAEOLOGY: *Archaeology:* Western Hemisphere

Farr, D.M.L. Professor Emeritus of History, Carleton University, Ottawa. • WORLD AFFAIRS: *Canada*

Fendell, Robert J. Columnist, *Sport Scene Florida.* Author of *How to Make Your Car Last and others.* • SPORTS AND GAMES: *Automobile Racing:* U.S. Racing

Finkelstein, Ellen. Copy Supervisor, Electronic Products, Encyclopædia Britannica. • BIOGRAPHIES *(in part)*

Flagg, Gordon. Senior Editor, *American Libraries.* • LIBRARIES AND MUSEUMS: *Libraries* (U.S.)

Flanders, Douglas L. Director of Education and Information, the United Church of Canada. • RELIGION: *The United Church of Canada*

Fletcher, Charmaine. Media and Press Officer, the Salvation Army. • RELIGION: *Salvation Army*

Fletcher, Matthew. Staff Writer, *Asiaweek* magazine. • WORLD AFFAIRS: *Brunei*

Flores, Ramona Monette S. Professor, University of the Philippines; Editorial Consultant, *Masks and Voices.* • MEDIA AND PUBLISHING: *Radio* (international); *Television* (international)

Follett, Christopher. Denmark Correspondent, *The Times;* Danish Correspondent, Radio Sweden; Newscaster, Radio Denmark; Freelance Correspondent, Reuters. Author of *Fodspor paa Cypern.* • WORLD AFFAIRS: *Denmark*

Forsås-Scott, Helena. Lecturer in Swedish, University College, London. Editor of *Textual Liberation.* • LITERATURE: *Swedish*

Fossli, Karen L. Oslo Correspondent, *Financial Times.* • WORLD AFFAIRS: *Norway*

Foye, Stephen. Project Coordinator, Center for Strategic and International Studies. • BIOGRAPHIES *(in part)*

Frank, Steven. General Editor, *Asiaweek* magazine. • WORLD AFFAIRS: *Vietnam*

Freeman, Laurie. Freelance Writer and Editor. • BUSINESS AND INDUSTRY REVIEW: *Advertising*

Friday, Elbert W., Jr. Assistant Administrator for Weather Services, National Oceanic and Atmospheric Administration. • EARTH AND SPACE SCIENCES: *Meteorology and Climate*

Fridovich, Irwin. James B. Duke Professor of Biochemistry, Duke University Medical Center, Durham, N.C. • LIFE SCIENCES: *Molecular Biology (in part)*

Fridovich-Keil, Judith L. Assistant Professor, Department of Genetics and Molecular Medicine, Emory University School of Medicine. • LIFE SCIENCES: *Molecular Biology (in part)*

Friedrich, Mary Jane. Associate Editor, Encyclopædia Britannica. • BIOGRAPHIES *(in part)*

Friskin, Sydney E. Hockey Correspondent, *The Times.* • SPORTS AND GAMES: *Billiard Games:* Snooker; *Field Hockey*

Fuller, Amanda E. Assistant Editor, *The Great Ideas Today,* Encyclopædia Britannica. • BIOGRAPHIES *(in part);* BUSINESS AND INDUSTRY REVIEW: *Advertising:* Sidebar

Fuller, Elizabeth. Senior Research Analyst, Open Media Research Institute. • WORLD AFFAIRS: *Armenia; Azerbaijan; Georgia*

Gaddum, Anthony H. Chairman, H.T. Gaddum and Co.; Deputy Vice President, International Silk Association. • BUSINESS AND INDUSTRY REVIEW: *Textiles:* Silk

Galbraith, John Kenneth. Emeritus Paul M. Warburg Professor of Economics, Harvard University. Author of *Journey Through Economic Time;* and others. • COMMENTARY: *The Outlines of an Emerging World*

Ganado, Albert. Lawyer. Coauthor of *Malta in British and French Caricature 1798–1815.* • WORLD AFFAIRS: *Malta*

Garrod, Mark. Golf Correspondent, PA Sport, Britain. Contributor to *Golf World* and *Amateur Golf* magazines. • SPORTS AND GAMES: *Golf*

Gaughan, Thomas. Former Editor, *American Libraries.* • LIBRARIES AND MUSEUMS: *Libraries* (international)

Gibbons, Anne R. Freelance Writer. • LIFE SCIENCES: *Entomology*

Gibbons, J. Whitfield. Professor of Zoology, Savannah River Ecology Laboratory, University of Georgia. Author of *Keeping All the Pieces.* • LIFE SCIENCES: *Zoology*

Gill, Martin J. Editor, *World Fishing* magazine. • AGRICULTURE AND FOOD SUPPLIES: *Fisheries*

Girnius, Saulius A. Senior Research Analyst, Open Media Research Institute. • WORLD AFFAIRS: *Latvia; Lithuania*

Glickman, Harvey. Professor of Political Science, Haverford (Pa.) College. • POPULATION AND HUMAN RELATIONS: *Race and Ethnic Relations*

Goldsmith, Arthur. Contributing Editor, *National Geographic Traveler.* • ART, ANTIQUES, AND COLLECTIONS: *Photography;* BUSINESS AND INDUSTRY REVIEW: *Photography*

Gottlieb, Jean S. Freelance Editor; Historian of Science. Author of *A Checklist of the Newberry Library's Printed Books in Science, Medicine, Technology, and the Pseudosciences, ca. 1460–1750.* • BIBLIOGRAPHY

Gould, Kira. Metro Editor, *Metropolis.* • BUSINESS AND INDUSTRY REVIEW: *Home Furnishings:* Housewares

Greeman, Adrian Lee. Editor, *Civil Engineer International.* • ARCHITECTURE AND CIVIL ENGINEERING: *Bridges*

Green, Anthony L. Senior Copy Editor, Encyclopædia Britannica. • BIOGRAPHIES *(in part);* MEDIA AND PUBLISHING: *Magazines:* Sidebar

Green, Theresa. Information Officer. • BUSINESS AND INDUSTRY REVIEW: *Materials and Metals:* Glass

Greskovic, Robert J. Dance Reviewer, *Arts & Entertainment Monthly;* Freelance Writer. • PERFORMING ARTS: *Dance:* North America

Gribbin, John. Visiting Fellow in Astronomy, University of Sussex, Brighton, England. Author of *In the Beginning: The Birth of the Living Universe; In Search of the Edge of Time;* and others. • MATHEMATICS AND PHYSICAL SCIENCES: *Physics*

Griffiths, A.R.G. Senior Lecturer in History, Flinders University of South Australia. Author of *Contemporary Australia; Beautiful Lies.* • BIOGRAPHIES *(in part);* WORLD AFFAIRS: *Australia; Nauru; Palau; Papua New Guinea*

Grumet, Robert S. Anthropologist, New Hope, Pa. Author of *Northeastern Indian Lives* and others. • ANTHROPOLOGY AND ARCHAEOLOGY: *Anthropology:* Cultural

Guthridge, Guy G. Manager, Polar Information Program, U.S. National Science Foundation. • WORLD AFFAIRS: *Antarctica*

Hafez, Sabry. Professor of Modern Arabic, School of Oriental and African Studies, University of London. Author of *The Genesis of Arabic Narrative Discourse; Arabic Cinema.* • LITERATURE: *Arabic*

Halman, Talat S. Research Professor; Chairman, Department of Near Eastern Languages and Literatures, New York University. • LITERATURE: *Turkish*

Hanlon, John. Art Marketing Consultant. • ART, ANTIQUES, AND COLLECTIONS: *Antiquarian Books; Art Auctions and Sales*

Hannen, Mark. Competitions Officer, English Basket Ball Association. • SPORTS AND GAMES: *Basketball* (international)

Harakas, Stanley S. Emeritus Archbishop Iakovos Professor of Orthodox Theology, Holy Cross Greek Orthodox School of Theology. Author of *Health and Medicine in the Eastern Orthodox Tradition* and others. • RELIGION: *Oriental Orthodox Church; The Orthodox Church*

Haub, Carl V. Demographer, Population Reference Bureau. Author of *Population Change in the Former Soviet Union* and others. • POPULATION AND HUMAN RELATIONS: *Demography*

Haufler, Daniel A. Journalist, *Die Zeit.* • LITERATURE: *German*

Hawkland, William D. Chancellor Emeritus of Law and Boyd Professor, Louisiana State University. • LAW, CRIME, AND LAW ENFORCEMENT: *Court Decisions*

Heiderstadt, Donna. Editor, *Footwear News.* • BUSINESS AND INDUSTRY REVIEW: *Apparel:* Footwear

Heinzl, John. Business Reporter, the *Globe and Mail.* • BUSINESS AND INDUSTRY REVIEW: *Retailing*

Hendershott, Jon. Associate Editor, *Track & Field News.* Author of *Track's Greatest Women.* • SPORTS AND GAMES: *Track and Field Sports*

Hendershott, Myrl C. Professor of Oceanography, Scripps Institution of Oceanography, La Jolla, Calif. • EARTH AND SPACE SCIENCES: *Oceanography*

Hennelly, James. Researcher, Encyclopædia Britannica. • BIOGRAPHIES *(in part);* WORLD AFFAIRS: *Vietnam:* Sidebar

Henschel, Milton. President, Watchtower Bible and Tract Society. • RELIGION: *Jehovah's Witnesses*

Hering, Howard. Administrative Manager, Frederick Wildman and Sons. • BUSINESS AND INDUSTRY REVIEW: *Beverages:* Wine

Hobbs, Greg. Editor, *The Football Record.* Author of 12 books on Australian Football. • SPORTS AND GAMES: *Football:* Australian

Hoeksema, Klaas J. Staff Member, Institute for Polytechnics, Amsterdam. • WORLD AFFAIRS: *Netherlands, The; Suriname*

Hollar, Sherman. Researcher, Encyclopædia Britannica. • BIOGRAPHIES *(in part)*

Hope, Thomas W. Chairman/CEO, Hope Reports, Inc. • PERFORMING ARTS: *Motion Pictures:* Nontheatrical Films

Hunnings, Neville March. Editor, *Encyclopedia of European Union Laws—Constitutional Texts.* • LAW, CRIME, AND LAW ENFORCEMENT (international)

IEIS. International Economic Information Services. • ECONOMIC AFFAIRS: *World Economy; Stock Exchanges* (international)

Ingham, Kenneth. Professor Emeritus of History, University of Bristol, England. Author of *Politics in Modern Africa: The Uneven Tribal Dimension* and others. • WORLD AFFAIRS: *Angola; Kenya; Malawi; Mozambique; Sudan, The; Tanzania; Uganda; Zaire; Zambia; Zimbabwe*

Ingram, Derek. Consultant Editor, Gemini News Service. Author of *Commonwealth for a Colour-Blind World; The Imperfect Commonwealth.* • WORLD AFFAIRS: *Commonwealth of Nations*

Jardine, Adrian. Member, Guild of Yachting Writers. • SPORTS AND GAMES: *Sailing*

Jessell, Harry A. Executive Editor, *Broadcasting and Cable.* • MEDIA AND PUBLISHING: *Radio:* (U.S., *in part*); *Radio:* Amateur Radio *(in part); Television* (U.S., *in part*)

Joffé, George. Journalist and Writer on North African and Middle Eastern Affairs. • WORLD AFFAIRS: *Algeria; Morocco; Tunisia*

Johnsson, William G. Editor, *Adventist Review.* Author of *Behold His Glory* and others. • RELIGION: *Seventh-day Adventist Church*

Jones, D.A.N. Novelist and Critic. Author of *Parade in Pairs; Never Had It So Good.* • LITERATURE: *Introduction; English:* United Kingdom

Jones, W. Glyn. Professor Emeritus of Scandinavian Studies, University of East Anglia, Norwich, England. Author of *Colloquial Danish* and others. • LITERATURE: *Danish*

Jotischky, Helma. Principal Research Officer, Paint Research Association. • BUSINESS AND INDUSTRY REVIEW: *Paints and Varnishes*

Kang, Suk-kyu. President of Hoseo University, Chonan City, South Korea. • BIOGRAPHIES *(in part)*

Karimi-Hakkak, Ahmad. Associate Professor of Persian Languages and Literature, University of Washington. Author of *Recasting Persian Poetry: Scenarios of Poetic Modernity in Iran.* • LITERATURE: *Persian*

Katz, William A. Professor, School of Information Science and Policy, State University of New York at Albany. • MEDIA AND PUBLISHING: *Magazines* (U.S.)

Kelleher, John A. Journalist, New Zealand. Formerly Editor, the *Dominion* and *Dominion Sunday Times* (Wellington). • BIOGRAPHIES *(in part);* WORLD AFFAIRS: *New Zealand*

Kelling, George H. Historian and Media Relations Officer, Wilford Hall Air Force Medical Center. Author of *Countdown to Rebellion: British Policy in Cyprus 1939–1955.* • WORLD AFFAIRS: *Cyprus*

Kellner, Peter. Political Commentator, BBC Television; Columnist, the *Sunday Times,* London. Author of *The Civil Servants: An Inquiry into Britain's Ruling Class* and others. • BIOGRAPHIES *(in part);* WORLD AFFAIRS: *United Kingdom*

Kind, Joshua B. Professor of Art History, Northern Illinois University. Author of *Rouault; Geometry as Abstract Art;* and others. • LIBRARIES AND MUSEUMS: *Museums* (U.S.)

Kitts, David B. Professor Emeritus of the History of Science, University of Oklahoma. • LIFE SCIENCES: *Paleontology*

Knapp, Rebecca. Senior Editor, *Art and Antiques.* • ART, ANTIQUES, AND COLLECTIONS: *Introduction*

Knox, Richard A. Editor, *Power Technology International* • BUSINESS AND INDUSTRY REVIEW: *Energy:* Nuclear

Koberstein, Wayne. Editor, *Pharmaceutical Executive* magazine. • BUSINESS AND INDUSTRY REVIEW: *Pharmaceuticals*

Kolankiewicz, George. Lecturer in Sociology, University of Essex, Colchester, England; Research Director, Research Programme on East-West Studies, U.K. Economic and Social Research Council. Coauthor of *Social Groups in Polish Society* and others. • WORLD AFFAIRS: *Poland*

Kovel, Ralph and Terry. Authors; Publishers. Authors of *Kovels' Antiques & Collectibles Price List 1995.* • ART, ANTIQUES, AND COLLECTIONS: *Collectibles*

Kroll, Thomas E. Lecturer, Roosevelt University and Northwestern University, Chicago; President, Thomas Kroll Associates. Author of *Introduction to Data Processing; C Language Programming.* • BUSINESS AND INDUSTRY REVIEW: *Microelectronics; Telecommunications*

Kuhn, Howard A. Vice President; Chief Technical Officer, Concurrent Technologies Corp. Author of *Powder Forging; Powder Processing.* • BUSINESS AND INDUSTRY REVIEW: *Materials and Metals:* Metalworking

Kuiper, Kathleen. Associate Editor, Encyclopædia Britannica; Editor, Merriam-Webster's *Encyclopedia of Literature.* • BIOGRAPHIES *(in part)*

Kuptsch, Christiane. Research Officer, ISSA. • POPULATION AND HUMAN RELATIONS: *Social Protection* (international)

Lamb, Kevin M. Special Projects Writer, *Dayton* (Ohio) *Daily News.* Author of *Quarterbacks, Nickelbacks & Other Loose Change.* • SPORTS AND GAMES: *Football:* Canadian, U.S.

Lambert, Philip. Associate Professor of Music, Baruch College, City University of New York. Author of *The Music of Charles Ives.* • PERFORMING ARTS: *Music:* Classical

Laqueur, Walter. Chairman, International Research Council, Center for Strategic and International Studies, Washington, D.C. Author of *Europe in Our Time* and others. • WORLD AFFAIRS: *Introduction*

Larsson, Gerd. Japan Correspondent, *Dagens Industri.* • BIOGRAPHIES *(in part)*

Latham, Daniel. Freelance Writer. • BIOGRAPHIES *(in part)*

Latham, Arthur. Associate Editor, Encyclopædia Britannica. • CHRONICLE OF 1995

Lau, Joseph S.M. Dean of Arts Faculty; Professor of Translation, the University of Wisconsin at Madison. Coeditor, *The Columbia Anthology of Modern Chinese Literature.* • LITERATURE: *Chinese*

Lavallée, H.-Claude. Director, Pulp and Paper Research Centre, University of Quebec at Trois-Rivières. • BUSINESS AND INDUSTRY REVIEW: *Wood Products:* Paper and Pulp

Lawler, Nancy Ellen. Professor of Economics, Oakton Community College, Des Plaines, Ill. Author of *Soldiers of Misfortune* and others. • WORLD AFFAIRS: *Benin; Burkina Faso; Cameroon; Central African Republic; Congo; Côte d'Ivoire; Gabon; Guinea; Mali; Mauritania; Niger; Senegal; Togo*

Lawrenson, David. Deputy Editor, *Rugby World* magazine. Author of *Blaze of Glory.* • BIOGRAPHIES *(in part);* SPORTS AND GAMES: *Football:* Rugby

Lawson, Fred H. James Irvine Professor of Government, Mills College, Oakland, Calif. • WORLD AFFAIRS: *Syria*

Legassick, Martin. Professor, History Department, University of Western Cape, Bellville, South Africa. • BIOGRAPHIES *(in part);* WORLD AFFAIRS: *Namibia; South Africa*

Legum, Colin. Consulting Editor, *Africa Contemporary Record;* Editor, *Third World Reports.* Author of more than 20 books, mainly on Africa. • WORLD AFFAIRS: *Spotlight:* Sub-Saharan Africa in a New Era

Lennox-Kerr, Peter. Editor, *High Performance Textiles* and *OE Report & Fibre News;* European Editor, *Textile World.* Author of *World Fibres Book.* • BUSINESS AND INDUSTRY REVIEW: *Textiles:* Introduction; Cotton; Man-Made Fibres

Levine, Beth S. Freelance Writer. Author of *Divorce: Young People Caught in the Middle* and others. • MEDIA AND PUBLISHING: *Book Publishing* (U.S.)

Levine, Steven I. Director, Center for Slavic, Eurasian, and East European Studies, University of North Carolina. Author of *Anvil of Victory: The Communist Revolution in Manchuria* and others. • WORLD AFFAIRS: *China; Taiwan*

Litsky, Frank. Sportswriter, *New York Times.* • SPORTS AND GAMES: *Ice Hockey:* North America

Litweiler, John. Jazz Critic; Contributor to *Down Beat, Chicago Tribune,* and others. Author of *Ornette Coleman: A Harmolodic Life.* • BIOGRAPHIES *(in part);* PERFORMING ARTS: *Music:* Jazz

Logan, Robert G. Sportswriter, *Daily Herald* (Arlington Heights, Ill.). Author of *Cubs Win!* and others. • SPORTS AND GAMES: *Basketball* (U.S.)

Longmore, Andrew. Freelance Sportswriter, *The Times;* formerly Assistant Editor, *The Cricketer.* • BIOGRAPHIES *(in part);* SPORTS AND GAMES: *Introduction; Cricket;* Sidebar

Luling, Virginia R. Social Anthropologist. • WORLD AFFAIRS: *Somalia*

McCauley, Martin. Senior Lecturer in Politics, School of Slavonic and East European Studies, University of London. • WORLD AFFAIRS: *Commonwealth of Independent States; Russia*

McCoy, Ron. Director, Center for Great Plains Studies, Emporia (Kan.) State University.

• WORLD AFFAIRS: *Spotlight:* Native American Cultural Ferment

Macdonald, Barrie. Professor of History, Massey University, Palmerston, N.Z. • WORLD AFFAIRS: *Dependent States* (Pacific); *Fiji; Kiribati; Marshall Islands; Micronesia, Federated States of; Solomon Islands; Tonga; Tuvalu; Vanuatu; Western Samoa*

McElroy, John. Editorial Director, *Automotive Industries.* • BUSINESS AND INDUSTRY REVIEW: *Automobiles*

McGregor, Alan. Freelance Contributor, *The Times; The Lancet;* Swiss Radio International; CBS Radio. • WORLD AFFAIRS: *Switzerland*

McLachlan, Keith S. Professor, School of Oriental and African Studies, University of London. Author of *Boundaries of Modern Iran.* • WORLD AFFAIRS: *Iran*

Malcolm, Noel R. Historian and Writer. Author of *Bosnia: A Short History.* • MACROPÆDIA: *Balkan States:* Bosnia and Herzegovina: History

Mallett, H.M.F. Editor, *Wool Record Weekly Market Report.* • BUSINESS AND INDUSTRY REVIEW: *Textiles:* Wool

Mango, Andrew. Foreign Affairs Analyst. Author of *Turkey: The Challenge of a New Role.* • WORLD AFFAIRS: *Turkey*

Marples, David R. Professor of History, University of Alberta. Author of *Stalinism in Ukraine* and others. • WORLD AFFAIRS: *Belarus; Ukraine*

Massen, Nina. Attorney and Author. • SPECIAL REPORT: *The "Contract" with America*

Mathews, John H. Copy Editor, Encyclopædia Britannica. • BIOGRAPHIES *(in part);* ART, ANTIQUES, AND COLLECTIONS: Sidebar

Matthíasson, Björn. Economist, Ministry of Finance, Iceland. • WORLD AFFAIRS: *Iceland*

Mazie, David M. Staff Writer, *Reader's Digest;* Freelance Writer. • POPULATION AND HUMAN RELATIONS: *Social Protection* (U.S.)

Mermel, T.W. Consulting Engineer; formerly Chairman, Committee on World Register of Dams, International Commission on Large Dams. • ARCHITECTURE AND CIVIL ENGINEERING: *Dams*

Michael, Tom. Assistant Editor, Encyclopædia Britannica. • BIOGRAPHIES *(in part)*

Millikin, Sandra. Architectural Historian. • ART, ANTIQUES, AND COLLECTIONS: *Art Exhibitions*

Modiano, Mario. Formerly Athens Correspondent, *The Times.* • WORLD AFFAIRS: *Greece*

Morris, Jacqui M. Editor, *Oryx.* • THE ENVIRONMENT: *Wildlife Conservation*

Morris, James. Calgary (Alta.) Staff Correspondent, *The Canadian Press.* • SPORTS AND GAMES: *Curling*

Morrison, Graham. Press Officer, British Fencing Federation; Correspondent, the *Daily Telegraph.* • SPORTS AND GAMES: *Fencing*

Moutet, Anne-Elisabeth. Journalist, *The European.* • WORLD AFFAIRS: *France;* Sidebar

Munns, Thomas E. Senior Program Officer, National Materials Advisory Board, National Research Council. • BUSINESS AND INDUSTRY REVIEW: *Materials and Metals:* Advanced Composites *(in part)*

Murphy, Alan. Associate Editor, Trade and Travel Handbooks. • WORLD AFFAIRS: *Venezuela*

Myers, Norman. Science Consultant; Visiting Fellow, the University of Oxford. • WORLD AFFAIRS: *Spotlight:* Pollution in Eastern Europe

Naylor, Ernest. Lloyd Roberts Professor of Marine Zoology, University College of North Wales. • LIFE SCIENCES: *Marine Biology*

Neher, Stephen. Assistant Editor, Encyclopædia Britannica. • WORLD AFFAIRS: *Political Parties (in part)*

Newby, Donald J. Bowls Correspondent, *Daily Telegraph;* formerly Editor, *World Bowls.* Author of various bowls publications. • SPORTS AND GAMES: *Lawn Bowls*

Nicol, Patrick. Professor, College de Sherbrooke, Que. • LITERATURE: *French:* Canada

Niesz, Dale E. Director, Center for Ceramic Research, Rutgers University, New Brunswick, N.J. • BUSINESS AND INDUSTRY REVIEW: *Materials and Metals:* Ceramics

Noble, Thomas F.X. Associate Professor of History, University of Virginia. Author of *Soldiers of Christ: Saints and Saints' Lives.* • RELIGION: *Roman Catholic Church*

Nugent, Ann. Editor, *Dance Theatre Journal.* Dance Critic, *The Stage.* Author of *Swan Lake: Stories of the Ballets.* • PERFORMING ARTS: *Dance:* Europe

Nurse, Charlie. Associate Editor, Trade and Travel Handbooks. • WORLD AFFAIRS: *Chile; Paraguay*

O'Donoghue, Michael. Lecturer in Gemmology, London Guildhall University. • BUSINESS AND INDUSTRY REVIEW: *Gemstones*

Ogden, Shepherd. President, the Cook's Garden. Author of *Step by Step Organic Vegetable Gardening* and others. • THE ENVIRONMENT: *Gardening* (international)

Olson, Kay Melchisedech. Executive Editor, *Flower & Garden.* • THE ENVIRONMENT: *Gardening* (U.S.)

O'Quinn, Jim. Editor in Chief, *American Theatre* magazine. • PERFORMING ARTS: *Theatre:* U.S. and Canada

Orr, Jay. Entertainment Writer, *Nashville* (Tenn.) *Banner.* • PERFORMING ARTS: *Music:* Popular (U.S.)

Osborne, K.L. Editor, *British Rowing Almanack.* Author of *Boat Racing in Britain, 1715–1975.* • SPORTS AND GAMES: *Rowing*

Palmer, John. European Editor, *The Guardian.* Author of *Europe Without America?* • WORLD AFFAIRS: *European Union*

Parker, Ines. Freelance Writer. • WORLD AFFAIRS: *Belize*

Parker, Sandy. Publisher, newsletter on fur industry; Copublisher, *Fur World.* • BUSINESS AND INDUSTRY REVIEW: *Apparel:* Furs

Parming, Tõnu. President, Estonian Publishing Co. Author of *A Case Study of a Soviet Republic: The Estonian SSR.* • WORLD AFFAIRS: *Estonia*

Paul, Charles Robert, Jr. Consultant, U.S. Olympic Committee. • SPORTS AND GAMES: *Gymnastics; Weight Lifting*

Pawlaczyk, Paul. Communications Director, United States Badminton Association. • SPORTS AND GAMES: *Badminton*

Penfold, Robin C. Freelance Writer on industrial topics. • BUSINESS AND INDUSTRY REVIEW: *Materials and Metals:* Plastics

Perlinska, Agnieszka. Adjunct Professor, Norwich University, Northfield, Vt. • LITERATURE: *Eastern European (in part); Russian (in part)*

Pertile, Lino. Professor of Romance Languages and Literature, Harvard University. • LITERATURE: *Italian*

Pfeffer, Irving. Attorney. Author of *The Financing of Small Business.* • ECONOMIC AFFAIRS: *Stock Exchanges* (North America)

Pinfold, Geoffrey M. Director, NCL Stewart Scott. Author of *Reinforced Concrete Chimneys and Towers.* • ARCHITECTURE AND CIVIL ENGINEERING: *Buildings*

Poirié, François. Writer and Critic. Author of *La Passade légendaire; Ils dansent.* • LITERATURE: *French:* France

Pollard, Peter. Associate Editor, Trade and Travel Handbooks. • WORLD AFFAIRS: *Colombia*

Prasad, H.Y. Sharada. Formerly Information Adviser to the Prime Minister of India. • WORLD AFFAIRS: *India*

Prince, Greg W. Senior Editor, *Beverage World.* • BUSINESS AND INDUSTRY REVIEW: *Beverages:* Beer; Soft Drinks; Spirits

Rakisits, Claude. International Affairs Consultant. • WORLD AFFAIRS: *Bangladesh; Bhutan; Myanmar (Burma); Nepal; Sri Lanka*

Rauch, Robert. Editor; Writer. • BIOGRAPHIES *(in part)*

Réamonn, Páraic. Communications Director, World Alliance of Reformed Churches. • RELIGION: *Reformed, Presbyterian, and Congregational Churches*

Rebelo, L.S. Reader Emeritus; Visiting Professor, Department of Portuguese Studies, King's College, University of London. • LITERATURE: *Portuguese:* Portugal

Reed, Arthur. Senior Editor, Europe, *Air Transport World.* Author of *Britain's Aircraft Industry;* coauthor of *RAE Farnborough.* • TRANSPORTATION: *Aviation*

Reid, Philip D. Louise C. Harrington Professor of Biological Sciences, Smith College, Northampton, Mass. • LIFE SCIENCES: *Botany*

Rengers, Maria Ottolino. Copy Editor, Encyclopædia Britannica. • BIOGRAPHIES *(in part)*

Renwick, David. Editorial Director, *Daily News* (Trinidad). • WORLD AFFAIRS: *Antigua and Barbuda; Bahamas, The; Barbados; Dependent States* (Caribbean and Bermuda); *Dominica; Grenada; Guyana; Jamaica; Saint Kitts and Nevis; Saint Lucia; Saint Vincent and the Grenadines; Trinidad and Tobago*

Reyes, Alejandro. Correspondent. • WORLD AFFAIRS: *Dependent States* (East Asia); *Singapore*

Roberts, John. Tennis Correspondent, the *Independent.* Author of *The Team That Wouldn't Die.* • SPORTS AND GAMES: *Tennis*

Robinson, David. Film Critic and Historian. Author of *A History of World Cinema; Chaplin: His Life and Art.* • MOTION PICTURES

Roby, Anne. Freelance Writer and Editor. • WORLD AFFAIRS: *Andorra; Liechtenstein; Luxembourg; Monaco*

Rollin, Jack. Association Football Columnist, *Sunday Telegraph.* Editor, *Rothmans Football Yearbook.* Author of *World Cup 1930–1990* and others. • SPORTS AND GAMES: *Football:* Association (Soccer)

Romano, Frank J. Professor. Author of *Pocket Guide to Digital Prepress.* • BUSINESS AND INDUSTRY REVIEW: *Printing*

Rusch, William G. Director, Department for Ecumenical Affairs, ELCA. Author of *Reception: An Ecumenical Opportunity.* • RELIGION: *Lutheran Communion*

Russell, Cristine. Freelance Science Writer and Special Health Correspondent, the *Washington Post.* • HEALTH AND DISEASE: *Medicine* (U.S.)

Russell, George. Senior Editor, *Time International.* Author of *Eyewitness: A History of Photojournalism.* • WORLD AFFAIRS: *United States*

Rutherford, Andrew. Professor, University of Southampton, England. Author of *Criminal Justice and the Pursuit of Decency* and others. • LAW, CRIME, AND LAW ENFORCEMENT: *Prisons and Penology*

Sa'd Jamal A. Visiting Professor, Arabian Peninsula and Gulf Studies, University of Virginia. • WORLD AFFAIRS: *United Arab Emirates; Yemen*

Saeki, Shoichi. Professor Emeritus, Tokyo University. Author of *Japanese Autobiographies.* • LITERATURE: *Japanese*

Salisbury, Jonathan M. Publisher, *World Toy News.* • BUSINESS AND INDUSTRY REVIEW: *Games and Toys*

Saludo, Ricardo L. Senior Editor, *Asiaweek* magazine. • BIOGRAPHIES *(in part);* WORLD AFFAIRS: *Spotlight:* The Spat over the Spratleys

Sanders, Alan J.K. Lecturer in Mongolian Studies, School of Oriental and African Studies, University of London. Author of *Mongolia: Politics, Economics and Society.* • WORLD AFFAIRS: *Mongolia*

Sarahete, Yrjö. General Secretary, Fédération Internationale des Quilleurs. • SPORTS AND GAMES: *Bowling:* World Tenpins

Sarmiento, Sergio. Newspaper Columnist; Vice President for News Operations at Televisión Azteca, Mexico. • SPORTS AND GAMES: *Baseball:* Latin America; *Football:* Association (Soccer): Latin America; WORLD AFFAIRS: *Spotlight:* Accelerating Changes in Mexico

Schafrik, Robert E. Director, National Materials Advisory Board, National Research Council. • BUSINESS AND INDUSTRY REVIEW: *Materials and Metals:* Advanced Composites *(in part)*

Schneider, Johanna. Assistant Editor, *Amateur Wrestling News.* • SPORTS AND GAMES: *Wrestling*

Schoenfield, Albert. Formerly Member, U.S. Swimming Olympic International Committee. Formerly Publisher, *Swimming World.* Honouree, International Swimming Hall of Fame.

Author of *The Saga of the Exterminators Squadron.* • SPORTS AND GAMES: *Swimming*

Schöpflin, George. Lecturer in East European Political Institutions, London School of Economics and School of Slavonic and East European Studies, University of London. • WORLD AFFAIRS: *Czech Republic; Hungary; Slovakia*

Sego, Steven. Formerly Director, Radio Free Afghanistan; Freelance Writer. • WORLD AFFAIRS: *Afghanistan*

Seidensticker, Edward George. Emeritus Professor of Japanese, Columbia University, New York City. Author of *Tokyo Rising: The City Since the Great Earthquake* and many others. • MACROPÆDIA: *Tokyo-Yokohama Metropolitan Area*

Shackleford, Peter. Chief of Environment, Planning, and Finance, World Tourism Organization. • BUSINESS AND INDUSTRY REVIEW: *Tourism*

Shameen, Assif A. Correspondent for *Asiaweek* magazine. • WORLD AFFAIRS: *Pakistan*

Sharples, Jerry A. Visiting Professor, Ohio State University. • AGRICULTURE AND FOOD SUPPLIES: *International Issues; Agricultural Commodities*

Shelley, Andrew. Chairman, JSM, London. • SPORTS AND GAMES: *Squash Rackets*

Shepherd, Melinda C. Associate Editor, Encyclopædia Britannica. • ECONOMIC AFFAIRS: *Banking (in part);* OBITUARIES *(in part);* WORLD AFFAIRS: *Dependent States* (Europe and the Atlantic); *Political Parties (in part)*

Sherry, Paul H. President, United Church of Christ. • RELIGION: *United Church of Christ*

Sigel, Robert. Author of several books in German. • WORLD AFFAIRS: *Germany*

Simon, Reeva S. Assistant Director, Middle East Institute, Columbia University, New York City. Author of *The Middle East in Crime Fiction.* • WORLD AFFAIRS: *Lebanon; Saudi Arabia*

Smith, Donald. Editor, *Rubber World.* • BUSINESS AND INDUSTRY REVIEW: *Materials and Metals:* Rubber

Smith, Gregory O. Dean of Academic Affairs, American University of Rome. • WORLD AFFAIRS: *San Marino; Vatican City State*

Smith, Reuben W. Emeritus Professor of History, University of the Pacific, Stockton, Calif. • RELIGION: *Islam*

Solomon, Norman. Fellow, Oxford Centre for Hebrew and Jewish Studies. Author of *The Analytic Movement.* • RELIGION: *Judaism*

Spangenberg, N. Earl. Professor, College of Natural Resources, University of Wisconsin at Stevens Point. Editor, *HYDATA—News and Views.* • EARTH AND SPACE SCIENCES: *Hydrology*

Sparks, Karen J. Senior Editor, Encyclopædia Britannica. • DISASTERS; OBITUARIES *(in part);* POPULATION AND HUMAN RELATIONS: *Social Protection:* Sidebar

Spencer, Peter L. Editor, *Consumers' Research.* • ECONOMIC AFFAIRS: *Consumer Affairs* (U.S.)

Stern, Irwin. Senior Lecturer in Portuguese, Columbia University, New York City. • LITERATURE: *Portuguese:* Brazil

Sterner, Michael. Partner, the IRC Group, Inc. • WORLD AFFAIRS: *Oman; Qatar*

Stewart, Ian. Professor of Mathematics, University of Warwick, Coventry, England. Author of *Does God Play Dice?; The Collapse of Chaos.* • MATHEMATICS AND PHYSICAL SCIENCES: *Mathematics*

Støverud, Torbjørn. Honorary Research Fellow, University College, London. • LITERATURE: *Germanic:* Norwegian

Suh, Ji-moon. Professor of English, Korea University, Seoul. Author of *Faces in the Well.* • BIOGRAPHIES *(in part)*

Sullivan, H. Patrick. Dean Emeritus of the College and Professor of Religion, Vassar College, Poughkeepsie, N.Y. • RELIGION: *Hinduism*

Summerhill, Edward M. Part-Time Staff Member, Reuters; Freelance Writer, Finnish News Agency. • WORLD AFFAIRS: *Finland*

Sumner, David E. Journalism Professor; Contributor to Episcopal Church periodicals. Author of *The Episcopal Church's History: 1945–1985.* • RELIGION: *Anglican Communion*

Susser, Leslie D. Diplomatic Correspondent, *The Jerusalem Report.* • WORLD AFFAIRS: *Israel*

Suzuki, Toshihiko. Communication Officer, the Delegation of the European Commission, Japan. • SPORTS AND GAMES: *Baseball:* Japan

Swan, Russ. Editor, *World Highways.* • ARCHITECTURE AND CIVIL ENGINEERING: *Roads*

Swift, Richard N. Professor Emeritus of Politics, New York University. • WORLD AFFAIRS: *Multinational and Regional Organizations; United Nations; United Nations:* Sidebar

Synan, Vinson. Dean, School of Divinity, Regent University, Virginia Beach, Va. Author of *In the Latter Days; Pentecostal Churches.* • RELIGION: *Pentecostal Churches*

Taishoff, Lawrence B. Chairman, *Broadcasting and Cable;* Adviser, Cahners Consumer/ Entertainment Publishing Division. • MEDIA AND PUBLISHING: *Radio* (U.S., *in part*); *Radio:* Amateur Radio *(in part); Television* (U.S., *in part*)

Tateishi, Kay K. Freelance Writer and Translator, Tokyo. • BIOGRAPHIES *(in part)*

Taylor, Thomas F. General Secretary, Friends World Committee for Consultation. Formerly Editor, *Friends World News.* • RELIGION: *Religious Society of Friends*

Tehan, Patricia. Banking Correspondent, *The Times.* • ECONOMIC AFFAIRS: *Special Report:* The Concern over Derivatives

Tesoro, Jose Manuel. Staff Writer, *Asiaweek* magazine. • WORLD AFFAIRS: *Cambodia*

Tétreault, Mary Ann. Professor of Political Science, Iowa State University. • WORLD AFFAIRS: *Kuwait*

Thomas, Robert Murray. Professor Emeritus of Education and Head, Program in International Education, University of California, Santa Barbara. Author of *International Comparative Education* and others. • EDUCATION (international)

Tobis, David. Director of Social Welfare Research and Planning, Center for Study of Family Policy, Hunter College, City University of New York. Consultant, UNICEF and The World Bank. • SOCIAL PROTECTION: *Special Report:* Child Welfare Crisis

Trenberth, Kevin E. Head, Climate Analysis Section, National Center for Atmospheric Research. Editor of *Climate System Modeling.* • EARTH AND SPACE SCIENCES: Sidebar

Trickett, Anthony. General Manager, Economic Affairs, International Iron and Steel Institute. Author of *Indirect Trade in Steel.* • BUSINESS AND INDUSTRY REVIEW: *Materials and Metals:* Iron and Steel

Tugend, Alina. Press Officer, Consumers International. • ECONOMIC AFFAIRS: *Consumer Affairs* (international)

Turner, Darrell J. Religion Writer, *Journal Gazette,* (Fort Wayne, Ind). • RELIGION: *Introduction*

Tutunji, Jenab. Assistant Professorial Lecturer, Political Science, George Washington University, Washington, D.C. • WORLD AFFAIRS: *Jordan*

UNHCR. The Office of the United Nations High Commissioner for Refugees. • POPULATION AND HUMAN RELATIONS: *Refugees*

Utt, Roger L. Editor, *Puerta del Sol;* formerly Assistant Professor of Spanish, Department of Romance Languages and Literatures, University of Chicago. • LITERATURE: *Spanish:* Spain

Venzke, Bruce H. Associate Editor, *Pool & Billiard Magazine;* Past President, Billiard Congress of Wisconsin. • SPORTS AND GAMES: *Billiard Games:* Carom Billiards; Pocket Billiards

Verdi, Robert William. Sports Columnist, *Chicago Tribune.* Author of *Once a Dodger, Always a Bum* and others. • SPORTS AND GAMES: *Baseball:* U.S.

Wachtel, Andrew B. Associate Professor of Slavic Languages and Literatures, Northwestern University, Evanston, Ill. Author of *The Battle for Childhood: Creation of a Russian Myth.* • MACROPÆDIA: *Russia:* Cultural Life

Wallenfeldt, Jeff. Assistant Editor, Encyclopædia Britannica. • BIOGRAPHIES *(in part);* SPORTS AND GAMES: *Golf:* Sidebar

Wallis, Shani. Independent Technical Journalist. • ARCHITECTURE AND CIVIL ENGINEERING: *Tunnels*

Walters, Jonathan S. Assistant Professor of Religion, Whitman College, Walla Walla, Wash. • RELIGION: *Buddhism*

Wanninger, Richard S. • SPORTS AND GAMES: *Volleyball*

Warren, J. Robert. Editor, Asia-Pacific Report, *Chemical Marketing Reporter.* • BUSINESS AND INDUSTRY REVIEW: *Chemicals*

Watson, Rory. Deputy Editor, *European Voice.* • WORLD AFFAIRS: *Belgium*

Way, Diane Lois. Historical Researcher. • BIOGRAPHIES *(in part)*

Westberg, M. Victor. Manager of Committees on Publication, the First Church of Christ, Scientist, Boston. • RELIGION: *Church of Christ, Scientist*

Whitney, Barbara. Copy Supervisor, Encyclopædia Britannica. • BIOGRAPHIES *(in part);* OBITUARIES *(in part)*

Wilkinson, John R. Sportswriter, Coventry Newspapers. • SPORTS AND GAMES: *Cycling*

Williams, Raymond Leslie. Professor of Spanish, University of Colorado. Author of *The Colombian Novel, 1844–1987.* • LITERATURE: *Spanish:* Latin America; *Special Report:* Postmodern Literature in Latin America

Willis, Clifford L. Director of News and Information, Office of Communication, Christian Church (Disciples of Christ). • RELIGION: *Christian Church (Disciples of Christ)*

Wilson, Derek. Correspondent, BBC, Rome. • WORLD AFFAIRS: *Italy*

Wilson, Michael. Freelance Aviation Writer and Consultant; Managing Editor, *Testimony.* • BUSINESS AND INDUSTRY REVIEW: *Aerospace*

Wise, Larry. Tournament Staff Director, Indian Industries. • SPORTS AND GAMES: *Archery*

Wolf, Allison Wheeler. Director of Communications, American Apparel Manufacturers Association. • BUSINESS AND INDUSTRY REVIEW: *Apparel:* Clothing

Wolff, Anita. Managing Editor, Print, Encyclopædia Britannica. • BIOGRAPHIES *(in part)*

Woodrow, Robert. Former Assistant Managing Editor, *Asiaweek* magazine. • WORLD AFFAIRS: *Laos; Thailand*

Woods, Elizabeth. Writer. Author of *If Only Things Were Different (I): A Model for a Sustainable Society; Bird Salad;* and others. • LITERATURE: *English:* Canada

Woods, Michael. Science Editor, *Toledo* (Ohio) *Blade.* Author of *Science in Antarctica.* • MATHEMATICS AND PHYSICAL SCIENCES: *Chemistry;* NOBEL PRIZES *(in part)*

Woollen, Anthony. Former Editor, *Food Manufacture.* Former Editor, *Food Industries Manual.* • AGRICULTURE AND FOOD SUPPLIES: *Food Processing*

World Forest Institute. Information Specialists. • BUSINESS AND INDUSTRY REVIEW: *Wood Products:* Wood

Wright, Andrew G. Associate Editor, *Engineering News-Record.* • BUSINESS AND INDUSTRY REVIEW: *Building and Construction*

Wyllie, Peter John. Professor, Division of Geological and Planetary Sciences, California Institute of Technology. Author of *The Dynamic Earth; The Way the Earth Works.* • EARTH AND SPACE SCIENCES: *Geology and Geochemistry*

Wyllie, Robert J.M. Editor, *Engineering & Mining Journal.* • BUSINESS AND INDUSTRY REVIEW: *Energy:* Coal

Young, M. Norvel. Chancellor Emeritus, Pepperdine University, Malibu, Calif. Author of *Preachers of Today.* • RELIGION: *Churches of Christ*

Zanga, Louis. Freelance Journalist. • WORLD AFFAIRS: *Albania*

1996 Britannica World Data

Encyclopædia Britannica, Inc.
Chicago
Auckland/London/Madrid/Manila/Paris/Rome
Seoul/Sydney/Tokyo/Toronto

CONTENTS

INTRODUCTION

Britannica World Data provides a statistical portrait of some 217 countries and dependencies of the world, at a level appropriate to the size and importance of each. It contains 194 country statements (the "Nations of the World" section), ranging in length from one to four pages, and permits, in the 24 major thematic tables (the "Comparative National Statistics" section), simultaneous comparisons among all of these larger countries and 23 additional smaller dependent states.

Updated annually, *Britannica World Data* can be consulted as a separate work of reference, but it is particularly intended as direct, structured support for many of Britannica's other reference works—encyclopaedias, yearbooks, atlases—at a level of detail that their editorial style or design do not permit.

Like the textual, graphic, or cartographic modes of expression of these other products, statistics possess their own inherent editorial virtues and weaknesses. Two principal goals in the creation of *Britannica World Data* were up-to-dateness and comparability, each possible to maximize separately, but not always possible to combine. If, for example, research on some subject is completed during a particular year (x), figures may be available for 100 countries for the preceding year ($x - 1$), for 140 countries for the year before that ($x - 2$), and for 180 countries for the year before that ($x - 3$).

Which year should be the basis of a thematic compilation for 220 countries so as to give the best combination of up-to-dateness and comparability? And, should $x - 1$ be adopted for the thematic table, ought up-to-dateness in the country table (for which year x is already available) be sacrificed for agreement with the thematic table? In general, the editors have opted for maximum up-to-dateness in the country statistical boxes and maximum comparability in the thematic tables, so as to take the best advantage of recent information.

Comparability, however, also resides in the meaning of the numbers compiled, which may differ greatly from country to country. The headnotes to the thematic tables explain many of these definitional problems; the Glossary serves the same purpose for the country statistical pages. Published data do not always provide the researcher or editor with a neat, unambiguous choice between a datum compiled on two different bases (say, railroad track length, or route length), one of which is wanted and the other not. More often a choice must be made among a variety of official, private, and external intergovernmental (UN, FAO, IMF) sources, each reporting its best data but each representing a set of problems: (1) of methodological variance from (or among) international conventions; (2) of analytical completeness (data for a single year may, successively, be projected [based on 10 months' data], preliminary [for 12 months], final, revised or adjusted, etc.); (3) of time frame, or accounting interval (data may represent a full Gregorian calendar year [preferred], a fiscal year, an Islamic or other national or religious year, a multiyear period or average [when a one-year statement would contain unrepresentative results]); (4) of continuity with previous data; and the like. Finally, published data on a particular subject may be complete and final but impossible to summarize in a simple manner. The education system of a single country may include, for example, public and private sectors; local, state, or national systems; varying grades, tracks, or forms within a single system; or opportunities for double-counting or fractional counting of a student, teacher, or institution. When no recent official data exist, the tables may show unofficial estimates, a range (of published opinion), analogous data, or no data at all. For certain subjects, especially population, the editors have prepared their own estimates.

The published basis of the information compiled is the statistical collections of Encyclopædia Britannica, Inc., some of the principal elements of which are enumerated in the Bibliography. Usual holdings for a country with a well-developed statistical program may include any of the following kinds of documents: the national statistical abstract; the constitution; the most recent censuses of population; periodic or occasional reports on vital statistics, social indicators, agriculture, mining, labour, manufacturing, domestic and foreign trade, finance and banking, transportation, and communications. Those works are supplemented by data received in correspondence. Further information is received in a variety of formats—telephone communications, fax, microfilm and microfiche, and most recently, in electronic formats such as computer disks, CD-ROMs, and the on-line resources of the Internet. Though the primary sources remain print documents, the balance is changing rapidly and with it standards as to what constitutes the research process itself. Fewer than a score of national statistical offices were publishing on the Internet at this writing, but more will surely follow, as will other ministries and departments, intergovernmental and nongovernmental organizations, and institutional and commercial providers. The challenge of balancing the editorial goals and readers' expectations of the distinctly different print and on-line versions of *World Data, Book of the Year,* and the *Britannica* itself against the panoply of sources and media now available will provide a daunting editorial challenge for the coming years.

The great majority of the social, economic, and financial data contained in this work should not be interpreted in isolation. Interpretive text of long perspective, such as that of the *Encyclopædia Britannica* itself; political, geographic, and topical maps, such as those in the *Britannica Atlas;* and recent analysis of political events and economic trends, such as that contained in the articles of the *Book of the Year,* will all help to supply balance, physical framework, and analytic focus that numbers alone cannot provide. By the same token, study of those sources will be made more concrete by use of *Britannica World Data* to supply up-to-date geographic, demographic, and economic detail.

GLOSSARY

A number of terms that are used to classify and report data in the "Nations of the World" section require some explanation.

Those italicized terms that are used regularly in the country compilations to introduce specific categories of information (*e.g., birth rate, budget*) appear in this glossary in italic boldface type, followed by a description of the precise kind of information being offered and how it has been edited and presented.

All other terms are printed here in roman boldface type. Many terms have quite specific meanings in statistical reporting, and they are so defined here. Other terms have less specific application as they are used by different countries or organizations. Data in the country compilations based on definitions markedly different from those below will usually be footnoted.

Terms that appear in small capitals in certain definitions are themselves defined at their respective alphabetical locations.

Terms whose definitions are marked by an asterisk (*) refer to data supplied only in the larger two- to four-page country compilations.

access to services, a group of measures indicating a population's level of access to public services, including electrical power, treated public drinking water, sewage removal, and fire protection.*

activity rate, *see* participation/activity rates.

age breakdown, the distribution of a given population by age, usually reported here as percentages of total population in 15-year age brackets. When substantial numbers of persons do not know, or state, their exact age, distributions may not total 100.0%.

area, the total surface area of a country or its administrative subdivisions, including both land and inland (nontidal) water area. Land area is usually calculated from "mean low water" on a "plane table," or flat, basis.

area and population, a tabulation usually including the first-order administrative subdivisions of the country (such as the states of the United States), with capital (headquarters, or administrative seat), area, and population. When these subdivisions are especially numerous or, occasionally, nonexistent, a planning, electoral, census, or other nonadministrative scheme of regional subdivisions has been substituted.

associated state, *see* state.

atheist, in statements of religious affiliation, one who professes active opposition to religion; "nonreligious" refers to those professing only no religion, nonbelief, or doubt.

balance of payments, a financial statement for a country for a given period showing the balance among: (1) transactions in goods, services, and income between that country and the rest of the world, (2) changes in ownership or valuation of that country's monetary gold, SPECIAL DRAWING RIGHTS, and claims on and liabilities to the rest of the world, and (3) unrequited transfers and counterpart entries needed (in an accounting sense) to balance transactions and changes among any of the foregoing types of exchange that are not mutually offsetting. Detail of national law as to what constitutes a transaction, the basis of its valuation, and the size of a transaction visible to fiscal authorities all result in differences in the meaning of a particular national statement.*

balance of trade, the net value of all international goods trade of a country, usually excluding reexports (goods received only for transshipment), and the percentage that this net represents of total trade.

Balance of trade refers only to the "visible" international trade of goods as recorded by customs authorities and is thus a segment of a country's BALANCE OF PAYMENTS, which takes all visible and invisible trade with other countries into account. (Invisible trade refers to imports and exports of money, financial instruments, and services such as transport, tourism, and insurance.) A country has a favourable, or positive (+), balance of trade when the value of exports exceeds that of imports and negative (−) when imports exceed exports.

barrel (bbl), a unit of liquid measure. The barrel conventionally used for reporting crude petroleum and petroleum products is equal to 42 U.S. gallons, or 159 litres. The number of barrels of crude petroleum per metric ton, ranging typically from 6.20 to 8.13, depends upon the specific gravity of the petroleum. The world average is roughly 7.33 barrels per ton.

birth rate, the number of live births annually per 1,000 of midyear population. Birth rates for individual countries may be compared with the estimated world annual average of 25.0 births per 1,000 population between 1990 and 1995.

budget, the annual receipts and expenditures—of a central government for its activities only; does not include state, provincial, or local governments or semipublic (parastatal, quasi-nongovernmental) corporations unless otherwise specified. Figures for budgets are limited

Abbreviations

Measurements

cu m	cubic metre(s)
kg	kilogram(s)
km	kilometre(s)
kW	kilowatt(s)
kW-hr	kilowatt-hour(s)
metric ton-km	metric ton-kilometre(s)
mi	mile(s)
passenger-km	passenger-kilometre(s)
passenger-mi	passenger-mile(s)
short ton-mi	short ton-mile(s)
sq km	square kilometre(s)
sq m	square metre(s)
sq mi	square mile(s)
troy oz	troy ounce(s)
yr	year(s)

Political Units and International Organizations

CACM	Central American Common Market
Caricom	Caribbean Community and Common Market
CFA	Communauté Financière Africaine
CFP	Comptoirs Françaises du Pacifique
CIS	Commonwealth of Independent States
CUSA	Customs Union of Southern Africa
E.Ger.	East Germany
EC	European Communities
EU	European Union
FAO	United Nations Food and Agriculture Organization
IMF	International Monetary Fund
OECS	Organization of Eastern Caribbean States
U.A.E.	United Arab Emirates
U.K.	United Kingdom
U.S.	United States
U.S.S.R.	Union of Soviet Socialist Republics
W.Ger.	West Germany

Months

Jan.	January	Oct.	October
Feb.	February	Nov.	November
Aug.	August	Dec.	December
Sept.	September		

Miscellaneous

AIDS	Acquired Immune Deficiency Syndrome
avg.	average
c.i.f.	cost, insurance, and freight
commun.	communications
CPI	consumer price index
est.	estimate(d)
excl.	excluding
f.o.b.	free on board
GDP	gross domestic product
GNP	gross national product
govt.	government
incl.	including
mo.	month(s)
n.a.	not available (in text)
n.e.s.	not elsewhere specified
NMP	net material product
no.	number
pl.	plural
pos.	position
pub. admin.	public administration
PVC	Polyvinyl Chloride
SDR	Special Drawing Right
SITC	Standard International Trade Classification
svcs.	services
teacher tr.	teacher training
transp.	transportation
voc.	vocational
$	dollar (of any currency area)
£	pound (of any currency area)
...	not available (in tables)
—	none, less than half the smallest unit shown, or not applicable (in tables)

to ordinary (recurrent) receipts and expenditures, wherever possible, and exclude capital expenditures—*i.e.,* funds for development and other special projects originating as foreign-aid grants or loans.

When both a recurrent and a capital budget exist for a single country, the former is the budget funded entirely from national resources (taxes, duties, excises, etc.) that would recur (be generated by economic activity) every year. It funds the most basic governmental services, those least able to suffer interruption. The capital budget is usually funded by external aid and may change its size considerably from year to year.

capital, usually, the actual seat of government and administration of a state. When more than one capital exists, each is identified by kind; when interim arrangements exist during the creation or movement of a national capital, the de facto situation is described.

Anomalous cases are annotated, such as those in which (1) the de jure designation under the country's laws differs from actual local practice (*e.g.,* Benin's designation of one capital in constitutional law, but another in actual practice), (2) international recognition does not validate a country's claim (as with the proclamation by Israel of a capital on territory not fully recognized as part of Israel), or (3) both a state and a capital have been proclaimed on territory recognized as part of another state (as with the Turkish Republic of Northern Cyprus).

capital budget, *see* budget.

causes of death, as defined by the World Health Organization, "the disease or injury which initiated the train of morbid events leading directly to death, or the circumstances of accident or violence which produced the fatal injury." This principle, the "underlying cause of death," is the basis of the medical judgment as to cause; the statistical classification system according to which these causes are grouped and named is the *International List of Causes of Death,* the latest revision of which is the Tenth. Reporting is usually in terms of events per 100,000 population. When data on actual causes of death are unavailable, information on morbidity, or illness rate, usually given as reported cases per 100,000 of infectious diseases (notifiable to WHO as a matter of international agreement), may be substituted.

chief of state/head of government, paramount national governmental officer(s) exercising the highest executive and/or ceremonial roles of a country's government. In general usage, the chief of state is the formal head of a national state. The primary responsibilities of the chief of state may range from the purely ceremonial—convening legislatures and greeting foreign officials—to the exercise of complete national executive authority. The head of government, when this function exists separately, is the officer nominally charged (by the constitution) with the majority of actual executive powers, though they may not in practice be exercised, especially in military or single-party regimes in which effective power may reside entirely outside the executive governmental machinery provided by the constitution. A prime minister, for example, usually the actual head of government, may in practice exercise only cabinet-level authority.

In communist countries an official identified as the chief of state may be the chairman of the policy-making organ, and the official given as the head of government the chairman of the nominal administrative/executive organ.

c.i.f. (trade valuation): *see* imports.

colony, an area annexed to, or controlled by, an independent state but not an integral part of it; a non-self-governing territory. A colony has a charter and may have a degree of self-government. A crown colony is a colony originally chartered by the British government.

commonwealth (U.K. and U.S.), a self-governing political entity that has regard to the common weal, or good; usually associated with the United Kingdom or United States. Examples include the Commonwealth of Nations (composed of independent states [from 1931 onward]), Puerto Rico since 1952, and the Northern Marianas since 1979.

communications, collectively, the means available for the public transmission of information within a country. Data are provided for daily newspapers, their number and total circulation, and the per capita rate of circulation implied by that total; for radio, television, and telephone receivers, total numbers and rates of availability are supplied. Telephone data refer to "main lines," or the number of subscriber lines (not the number of receivers) having access to the public switched network.

constant prices, an adjustment to the members of a financial time series to eliminate the effect of inflation year by year. It consists of referring all data in the series to a single year so that "real" change may be seen.

constitutional monarchy, *see* monarchy.

consumer price index (CPI), also known as the retail price index, or the cost-of-living index, a series of index numbers assigned to the price of a selected "basket," or assortment, of basic consumer goods and services in a country, region, city, or type of household in order to measure changes over time in prices paid by a typical household for those goods and services. Items included in the CPI are ordinarily determined by governmental surveys of typical household expenditures and are assigned weights relative to their proportion of those expenditures. Index values are period averages unless otherwise noted.

coprincipality, *see* monarchy.

current prices, the valuation of a financial aggregate as of the year reported.

daily per capita caloric intake (supply), the calories equivalent to the known average daily supply of foodstuffs for human consumption in a given country divided by the population of the country (and the proportion of that supply provided, respectively, by vegetable and animal sources). The daily per capita caloric intake of a country may be compared with the corresponding recommended minimum daily requirement. The latter is calculated by the Food and Agriculture Organization of the United Nations from the age and sex distributions, average body weights, and environmental temperatures in a given region to determine the calories needed to sustain a person there at normal levels of activity and health. The daily per capita caloric requirement ranges from 2,200 to 2,500.

de facto population, for a given area, the population composed of those actually present at a particular time, including temporary residents and visitors (such as immigrants not yet granted permanent status, "guest" or expatriate workers, refugees, or tourists), but excluding legal residents temporarily absent.

de jure population, for a given area, the population composed only of those legally resident at a particular time, excluding temporary residents and visitors (such as "guest" or expatriate workers, refugees, or tourists), but including legal residents temporarily absent.

deadweight tonnage, the maximum weight of cargo, fuel, fresh water, stores, and persons that may safely be carried by a ship. It is customarily measured in long tons of 2,240 pounds each, equivalent to 1.016 metric tons. Deadweight tonnage is the difference between the tonnage of a fully loaded ship and the fully unloaded tonnage of that ship.

See also gross ton.

death rate, the number of deaths annually per 1,000 of midyear population. Death rates for individual countries may be compared with the estimated world annual average of 9.3 deaths per 1,000 population between 1990 and 1995.

density (of population), usually, the DE FACTO POPULATION of a country divided by its total area. Special adjustment is made for large areas of inland water, desert, or other uninhabitable areas—*e.g.,* excluding the ice cap of Greenland.

department, a first-order civil administrative subdivision. The *overseas department* (France) is an overseas subdivision of the French Republic, almost equivalent to a department of metropolitan France, with elected representation in the French Parliament.

dependent state, constitutionally or statutorily organized political entity outside of and under the jurisdiction of an independent state (or a

Dependent states[1]

Australia
- Christmas Island
- Cocos (Keeling) Islands
- Norfolk Island

Denmark
- Faroe Islands
- Greenland

France
- French Guiana
- French Polynesia
- Guadeloupe
- Martinique
- Mayotte
- New Caledonia
- Réunion
- Saint Pierre and Miquelon
- Wallis and Futuna

Netherlands, The
- Aruba
- Netherlands Antilles

New Zealand
- Cook Islands
- Niue
- Tokelau

Norway
- Jan Mayen
- Svalbard

Portugal
- Macau

United Kingdom
- Anguilla
- Bermuda
- British Virgin Islands
- Cayman Islands
- Falkland Islands
- Gibraltar
- Guernsey
- Hong Kong
- Isle of Man
- Jersey
- Montserrat
- Pitcairn Island
- Saint Helena and Dependencies
- Turks and Caicos Islands

United States
- American Samoa
- Guam
- Northern Mariana Islands
- Puerto Rico
- Virgin Islands (of the U.S.)

[1]Excludes territories (1) to which Antarctic Treaty is applicable in whole or in part, (2) without permanent civilian population, (3) without internationally recognized civilian government (Western Sahara, Gaza Strip), or (4) representing unadjudicated unilateral or multilateral territorial claims.

federal element of such a state) but not formally annexed to it (*see* Table).

direct taxes, taxes levied directly on firms and individuals, such as taxes on income, profits, and capital gains. The *immediate* incidence, or burden, of direct taxes is on the firms and individuals thus taxed; direct taxes on firms may, however, be passed on to consumers and other economic units in the form of higher prices for goods and services, blurring the distinction between direct and indirect taxation.

distribution of income/wealth, the portion of personal income or wealth accruing to households or individuals constituting each respective decile (tenth) or quintile (fifth) of a country's households or individuals.*

divorce rate, the number of legal, civilly recognized divorces annually per 1,000 population.

doubling time, the number of complete years required for a country to double its population at its current rate of natural increase.

earnings index, a series of index numbers comparing average wages in a collective industrial sample for a country or region with the same industries at a previous period to measure changes over time in those wages. It is most commonly reported for wages paid on a daily, weekly, or monthly basis; annual figures represent averages of these shorter periods. The scope of the earnings index varies from country to country; the index is often limited to earnings in manufacturing industries. The index for each country applies to all wage earners in a designated group and ordinarily takes into account basic wages (overtime is normally distinguished), bonuses, cost-of-living allowances, and contributions toward social security. Some countries include payments in kind. Contributions toward social security by employers are usually excluded, as are social security benefits received by wage earners.

economically active population, *see* population economically active.

education, tabulation of the principal elements of a country's educational establishment, classified as far as possible according to the country's own system of primary, secondary, and higher levels (the usual age limits for these levels being identified in parentheses), with total number of schools (physical facilities) and of teachers and students (whether full- or part-time). The student-teacher ratio is calculated whenever available data permit.

educational attainment, the distribution of the population age 25 and over with completed educations by the highest level of formal education attained or completed; it must sometimes be reported, however, for age groups still in school or for the economically active only.

emirate, empire, *see* monarchy.

enterprise, a legal entity formed to conduct a business, which it may do from more than one establishment (place of business or service point).

ethnic/linguistic composition, ethnic, racial, or linguistic composition of a national population, reported here according to the most reliable breakdown available, whether published in official sources (such as a census) or in external analysis (when the subject is not addressed in national sources).

exchange rate, the value of one currency compared with another, or with a standardized unit of account such as the SPECIAL DRAWING RIGHT, or as mandated by local statute when one currency is "tied" by a par value to another. Rates given usually refer to free market values when the currency has no, or very limited, restrictions on its convertibility into other currencies.

exports, material goods legally leaving a country (or customs area) and subject to customs regulations. The total value and distribution by percentage of the major items (in preference to groups of goods) exported are given, together with the distribution of trade among major trading partners (usually single countries or trading blocs). Valuation of goods exported is free on board (f.o.b.) unless otherwise specified. The value of goods exported and imported f.o.b. is calculated from the cost of production and excludes the cost of transport.

external debt, public and publicly guaranteed debt with a maturity of more than one year owed to nonnationals of a country and repayable in foreign currency, goods, or services. The debt may be an obligation of a national or subnational governmental body (or an agency of either), of an autonomous public body, or of a private debtor that is guaranteed by a public entity. The debt is usually either outstanding (contracted) or disbursed (drawn).

external territory (Australia), *see* territory.

federal, consisting of first-order political subdivisions that are prior to and independent of the central government in certain functions.

federal republic, *see* republic.

federation, union of coequal, preexisting political entities that retain some degree of autonomy and (usually) right of secession within the union.

fertility rate, *see* total fertility rate.

financial aggregates, tabulation of seven-year time series, providing principal measures of the financial condition of a country, including: (1) the exchange rate of the national currency against the U.S. dollar, the pound sterling, and the International Monetary Fund's SPECIAL DRAWING RIGHT (SDR), (2) the amount and kind of international reserves (holdings of SDRs, gold, and foreign currencies) and reserve position of the country in the IMF, and (3) principal economic rates and prices (central bank discount rate, government bond yields, and industrial stock [share] prices). For BALANCE OF PAYMENTS, the origin in terms of component balance of trade items and balance of invisibles (net) is given.*

fish catch, the live-weight equivalent of the aquatic animals (including fish, crustaceans, mollusks, etc., but excluding whales, seals, and other aquatic mammals) caught in freshwater or marine areas by national fleets and landed in domestic or foreign harbours for commercial, industrial, or subsistence purposes.

f.o.b. (trade valuation): *see* exports.

food, *see* daily per capita caloric intake.

form of government/political status, the type of administration provided for by a country's constitution—whether or not suspended by extralegal military or civil action, although such de facto administrations are identified—together with the number of members (elected, appointed, and ex officio) for each legislative house, named according to its English rendering. Dependent states (*see* Table) are classified according to the status of their political association with the administering country.

global social product, *see* material product.

gross domestic product (GDP), the total value of the final goods and services produced by residents and nonresidents within a given country during a given accounting period, usually a year. Unless otherwise noted, the value is given in current prices of the year indicated. The *System of National Accounts* (SNA, published under the joint auspices of the UN, IMF, OECD, EC, and World Bank) provides a framework for international comparability in classifying domestic accounting aggregates and international transactions comprising "net factor income from abroad," the measure that distinguishes GDP and GNP.

gross national product (GNP), the total value of final goods and services produced both from within a given country *and* from external (foreign) transactions in a given accounting period, usually a year. Unless otherwise noted, the value is given in current prices of the year indicated. GNP is equal to GROSS DOMESTIC PRODUCT (*q.v.*) adjusted by net factor income from abroad, which is the income residents receive from abroad for factor services (labour, investment, and interest) less similar payments made to nonresidents who contribute to the domestic economy.

gross ton, volumetric unit of measure (equaling 100 cubic feet [2.83 cu m]) of the permanently enclosed volume of a ship, above and below decks available for cargo, stores, or passenger accommodation. Net, or register, tonnage exempts certain nonrevenue spaces—such as those devoted to machinery, bunkers, crew accommodations, and ballast—from the gross tonnage. *See also* deadweight tonnage.

head of government, *see* chief of state/head of government.

health, a group of measures including number of accredited physicians currently practicing or employed and their ratio to the total population; total hospital beds and their ratio; and INFANT MORTALITY RATE.

household, economically autonomous individual or group of individuals living in a single dwelling unit. A family household is one composed principally of individuals related by blood or marriage.

household income and expenditure, data for average size of a HOUSEHOLD (by number of individuals) and median household income. Sources of income and expenditures for major items of consumption are given as percentages.

In general, household income is the amount of funds, usually measured in monetary units, received by the members (generally those 14 years old and over) of a household in a given time period. The income can be derived from (1) wages or salaries, (2) nonfarm or farm SELF-EMPLOYMENT, (3) transfer payments, such as pensions, public assistance, unemployment benefits, etc., and (4) other income, including interest and dividends, rent, royalties, etc. The income of a household is expressed as a gross amount before deductions for taxes. Data on expenditure refer to consumption of personal or household goods and services; they normally exclude savings, taxes, and insurance; practice with regard to inclusion of credit purchases differs markedly.

immigration, usually, the number and origin of those immigrants admitted to a nation in a legal status that would eventually permit the granting of the right to settle permanently or to acquire citizenship.*

imports, material goods legally entering a country (or customs area) and subject to customs regulations; excludes financial movements. The total value and distribution by percentage of the major items (in preference to groups of goods) imported are given, together with the direction of trade among major trading partners (usually single countries), trading blocs (such as the European Union), or customs areas (such as Belgium-Luxembourg). The value of goods imported is given free on board (f.o.b.) unless otherwise specified; f.o.b. is defined above under EXPORTS.

The principal alternate basis for valuation of goods in international trade is that of cost, insurance, and freight (c.i.f.); its use is restricted to imports, as it comprises the principal charges needed to bring the goods to the customs house in the country of destination. Because it inflates the value of imports relative to exports, more countries have, latterly, been estimating imports on an f.o.b. basis as well.

incorporated territory (U.S.), *see* territory.

independent, of a state, autonomous and controlling both its internal and external affairs. Its date usually refers to the date from which the country was in effective control of these affairs within its present boundaries, rather than the date independence was proclaimed or the date recognized as a de jure act by the former administering power.

indirect taxes, taxes levied on sales or transfers of selected intermediate goods and services, including excises, value-added taxes, and tariffs, that are ordinarily passed on to the ultimate consumers of the goods and services. Figures given for individual countries are limited to indirect taxes levied by their respective central governments unless otherwise specified.

infant mortality rate, the number of children per 1,000 live births who die before their first birthday. Total infant mortality includes neonatal mortality, which is deaths of children within one month of birth.

invisibles (invisible trade), *see* balance of trade.

kingdom, *see* monarchy.

labour force, portion of the POPULATION ECONOMICALLY ACTIVE (PEA) comprising those most fully employed or attached to the labour market (the unemployed are considered to be "attached" in that they usually represent persons previously employed seeking to be re-employed), particularly as viewed from a short-term perspective. It normally includes those who are self-employed, employed by others (whether full-time, part-time, seasonally, or on some other less than full-time basis), and, as noted above, the unemployed (both those previously employed and those seeking work for the first time). In the "gross domestic product and labour force" table, the majority of the labour data provided refer to population economically active, since PEA represents the longer-term view of working population and, thus, subsumes more of the marginal workers who are often missed by shorter-term surveys.

land use, distribution by classes of vegetational cover or economic use of the land area only (excluding inland water, for example, but not marshland), reported as percentages.

leisure, the principal monetary expenditures, uses, or reported preferences in the use of the individual's free time for recreation, rest, or self-improvement.*

life expectancy, the number of years a person born within a particular population group (age cohort) would be expected to live, based on actuarial calculations.

literacy, the ability to read and write a language with some degree of competence; the precise degree constituting the basis of a particular national statement is usually defined by the national census and is often tested by the census enumerator. Elsewhere, particularly where much adult literacy may be the result of literacy campaigns rather than passage through a formal educational system, definition and testing of literacy may be better standardized.

major cities, usually the five largest cities proper whose population is at least one-tenth that of the primate (largest) city; fewer will be listed if the size disparity is very great or there are fewer urban localities in the country. For multipage tables, 10 or more will be listed without regard for the size of the primate city.* Populations for cities will usually refer to the city proper—*i.e.,* the legally bounded corporate entity, or the most compact, contiguous, demographically urban portion of the entity defined by the local authorities. Occasionally figures for METROPOLITAN AREAS are cited when the relevant civil entity at the core of a major agglomeration had an unrepresentatively small population.

manufacturing, mining, and construction enterprises/retail sales and service enterprises, a detailed tabulation of the principal industries in these sectors, showing for each industry the number of enterprises and employees, wages in that industry as a percentage of the general average wage, and the value of that industry's output in terms of value added or turnover.*

marriage rate, the number of legal, civilly recognized marriages annually per 1,000 population.

material (or social) product, in the national accounting systems of the socialist countries, the aggregate (sometimes "global") value of all "productive" economic activity, generally omitting personal (nonpublic) services, financial activities, and the like that in conventional Western national accounts would contribute to the GROSS DOMESTIC PRODUCT, a more comprehensive measure that includes not only material output but also every identifiable service element of a national economy. Socialist countries that are members of the International Monetary Fund have begun, however, to report gross domestic, and national, product according to the *System of National Accounts* that forms the basis of international standardization of national accounts.

material well-being, a group of measures indicating the percentage of households or dwellings possessing certain goods or appliances, including automobiles, telephones, television receivers, refrigerators, air conditioners, and washing machines.*

merchant marine, the privately or publicly owned ships registered with the maritime authority of a nation (limited to those in Lloyd's of London statistical reporting of 100 or more GROSS TONS) that are employed in commerce, whether or not owned or operated by nationals of the country.

metropolitan area, a city and the region of dense, predominantly urban, settlement around the city; the population of the whole usually has strong economic and cultural affinities with the central city.

military expenditure, the apparent value of all identifiable military expenditure by the central government on hardware, personnel, pensions, research and development, etc., reported here both as a percentage of the GNP, with a comparison to the world average, and as a per capita value in U.S. dollars.

military personnel, *see* total active duty personnel.

mobility, the rate at which individuals or households change dwellings, usually measured between censuses and including international as well as domestic migration.*

monarchy, a government in which the CHIEF OF STATE holds office, usually hereditarily and for life, but sometimes electively for a term. The state may be a coprincipality, emirate, empire, kingdom, principality, sheikhdom, or sultanate. The powers of the monarch may range from absolute (*i.e.,* the monarch both reigns and rules) through various degrees of limitation of authority to nominal, as in a constitutional monarchy, in which the titular monarch reigns but others, as elected officials, effectively rule.

monetary unit, currency of issue, or that in official use in a given country; name, spelling, and abbreviation in English according to International Monetary Fund recommendations or local practice; name of the lesser, usually decimal, monetary unit constituting the main currency; and valuation in U.S. dollars and U.K. pounds sterling, usually according to free-market or commercial rates.

See also exchange rate.

natural increase, also called natural growth, or the balance of births and deaths, the excess of births over deaths in a population; the rate of natural increase is the difference between the BIRTH RATE and the DEATH RATE of a given population. The estimated world average during 1990–95 was 15.7 per 1,000 population, or 1.57% annually. Natural increase is added to the balance of migration to calculate the total growth of that population.

net material product, *see* material product.

nonreligious, *see* atheist.

official language(s), that (or those) prescribed by the national constitution for day-to-day conduct and publication of a country's official business or, when no explicit constitutional provision exists, that of the constitution itself, the national gazette (record of legislative activity), or like official documents. Other languages may have local protection, may be permitted in parliamentary debate or legal action (such as a trial), or may be "national languages," for the protection of which special provisions have been made, but these are not deemed official. The United States, for example, does not yet formally identify English as "official," though it uses it for virtually all official purposes.

official name, the local official form(s), short or long, of a country's legal name(s) taken from the country's constitution or from other official documents. The English-language form is usually the protocol form in use by the country, the U.S. Department of State, and the United Nations.

official religion, generally, any religion prescribed or given special status or protection by the constitution or legal system of a country. Identification as such is not confined to constitutional documents utilizing the term explicitly.

organized territory (U.S.), *see* territory.

overseas department (France), *see* department.

overseas territory (France), *see* territory.

parliamentary state, *see* state.

part of a realm, a dependent Dutch political entity with some degree of self-government and having a special status above that of a colony (*e.g.,* the prerogative of rejecting for local application any law enacted by The Netherlands).

participation/activity rates, measures defining differential rates of economic activity within a population. Participation rate refers to the percentage of those employed or economically active who possess a particular characteristic (sex, age, etc.); activity rate refers to the fraction of the total population who *are* economically active.

passenger-miles, or **passenger-kilometres,** aggregate measure of passenger carriage by a specified means of transportation, equal to the number of passengers carried multiplied by the number of miles (or kilometres) each is transported. Figures given for countries are often calculated from ticket sales and ordinarily exclude passengers carried free of charge.

people's republic, *see* republic.

place of birth/national origin, if the former, numbers of native- and foreign-born population of a country by actual place of birth; if the latter, any of several classifications, including those based on origin of passport at original admission to country, on cultural heritage of family name, on self-designated (often multiple) origin of (some) ancestors, and on other systems for assigning national origin.*

political status, *see* form of government/political status.

population, the number of persons present within a country, city, or other civil entity at the date of a census of population, survey, cumulation of a civil register, or other enumeration. Unless otherwise specified, populations given are DE FACTO, referring to those actually present, rather than DE JURE, those legally resident but not necessarily present on the referent date. If a time series, noncensus year, or per capita ratio referring to a country's total population is cited, it will usually refer to midyear of the calendar year indicated.

population economically active, the total number of persons (above a set age for economic labour, usually 10–15 years) in all employment statuses—self-employed, wage- or salary-earning, part-time, seasonal, unemployed, etc. The International Labour Organisation defines the economically active as "all persons of either sex who furnish the supply of labour for the production of economic goods and services." National practices vary as regards the treatment of such groups as armed forces, inmates of institutions, persons seeking their first job, unpaid family workers, seasonal workers and persons engaged in part-time economic activities. In some countries, all or part of these groups may be included among the economically active, while in other countries the same groups may be treated as inactive. In general, however, the data on economically active population do not include students, persons occupied solely in family or household work, retired persons, persons living entirely on their own means, and persons wholly dependent upon others.

See also labour force.

population projection, the expected population in the years 2000 and 2010, embodying the country's own projections wherever possible. Estimates of the future size of a population are usually based on assumed levels of fertility, mortality, and migration. Projections in the tables, unless otherwise specified, are medium (*i.e.,* most likely) variants, whether based on external estimates by the United Nations, World Bank, or U.S. Department of Commerce or on those of the country itself.

price and earnings indexes, tabulation comparing the change in the CONSUMER PRICE INDEX over a period of seven years with the change in the general labour force's EARNINGS INDEX for the same period.

principality, *see* monarchy.

production, the physical quantity or monetary value of the output of an industry, usually tabulated here as the most important items or groups of items (depending on the available detail) of primary (extractive) and secondary (manufactured) production, including construction. When a single consistent measure of value, such as VALUE ADDED, can be obtained, this is given, ranked by value; otherwise, and more usually, quantity of production is given.

public debt, the current outstanding debt of all periods of maturity for which the central government and its organs are obligated. Publicly guaranteed private debt is excluded. For countries that report debt under the World Bank Debtor Reporting System (DRS), figures for outstanding, long-term EXTERNAL DEBT are given.

quality of working life, a group of measures including weekly hours of work (including overtime); rates per 100,000 for job-connected injury, illness, and mortality; coverage of labour force by insurance for injury, permanent disability, and death; workdays lost to labour strikes and stoppages; and commuting patterns (length of journey to work in minutes and usual method of transportation).*

railroads, mode of transportation by self-driven or locomotive-drawn cars over fixed rails. Length-of-track figures include all mainline and spurline running track but exclude switching sidings and yard track. Route length, when given, does not compound multiple running tracks laid on the same trackbed.

recurrent budget, *see* budget.

religious affiliation, distribution of nominal religionists, whether practicing or not, as a percentage of total population. This usually assigns to children the religion of their parents.

republic, a state with elected leaders and a centralized presidential form of government, local subdivisions being subordinate to the national government. A *federal republic* (as distinguished from a unitary republic) is a republic in which power is divided between the central government and the constituent subnational administrative divisions (*e.g.,* states, provinces, or cantons) in whom the central government itself is held to originate, the division of power being defined in a written constitution and jurisdictional disputes usually being settled in a court; sovereignty usually rests with the authority that has the power to amend the constitution. A *unitary republic* (as distinguished from a federal republic) is a republic in which power originates in a central authority and is not derived from constituent subdivisions. A *people's republic,* in the dialectics of Communism, is the first stage of development toward a communist state, the second stage being a *socialist republic.* An *Islamic republic* is structured around social, ethical, legal, and religious precepts central to the Islamic faith.

retail price index, *see* consumer price index.

retail sales and service enterprises, *see* manufacturing, mining, and construction enterprises/retail sales and service enterprises.

roundwood, wood obtained from removals from forests, felled or harvested (with or without bark), in all forms.

rural, *see* urban-rural.

self-employment, work in which income derives from direct employment in one's own business, trade, or profession, as opposed to work in which salary or wages are earned from an employer.

self-governing, of a state, in control of its internal affairs in degrees ranging from control of most internal affairs (though perhaps not of public order or of internal security) to complete control of all internal affairs (*i.e.,* the state is autonomous) but having no control of external affairs or defense. In this work the term self-governing refers to the final stage in the successive stages of increasing self-government that generally precede independence.

service/trade enterprises, *see* manufacturing, mining, and construction enterprises/retail sales and service enterprises.

sex distribution, ratios, calculated as percentages, of male and female population to total population.

sheikhdom, *see* monarchy.

social deviance, a group of measures, usually reported as rates per 100,000, for principal categories of socially deviant behaviour, including specified crimes, alcoholism, drug abuse, and suicide.*

social participation, a group of measures indicative of the degree of social engagement displayed by a particular population, including rates of participation in such activities as elections, voluntary work or memberships, trade unions, and religion.*

social security, public programs designed to protect individuals and families from loss of income owing to unemployment, old age, sickness or disability, or death and to provide other services such as medical care, health and welfare programs, or income maintenance.

socialist republic, *see* republic.

sources of income, *see* household income and expenditure.

Special Drawing Right (SDR), a unit of account utilized by the International Monetary Fund (IMF) to denominate monetary reserves available under a quota system to IMF members to maintain the value of their national currency unit in international transactions.*

state, in international law, a political entity possessing the attributes of: territory, permanent civilian population, government, and the capacity to conduct relations with other states. Though the term is sometimes limited in meaning to fully independent and internationally recognized states, the more general sense of an entity possessing a *preponderance* of these characteristics is intended here. It is, thus, also a first-order civil administrative subdivision, especially of a federated union. An *associated state* is an autonomous state in free association with another that conducts its external affairs and defense; the association may be terminated in full independence at the instance of the autonomous state in consultation with the administering power. A *parliamentary state* is an independent state of the Commonwealth that is governed by a parliament and that may recognize the British monarch as its titular head.

structure of gross domestic product and labour force, tabulation of the principal elements of the national economy, according to standard industrial categories, together with the corresponding distribution of the labour force (when possible POPULATION ECONOMICALLY ACTIVE) that generates the GROSS DOMESTIC PRODUCT.

sultanate, *see* monarchy.

territory, a noncategorized political dependency; a first-order administrative subdivision; a dependent political entity with some degree of self-government, but with fewer rights and less autonomy than a colony because there is no charter. An *external territory* (Australia) is a territory situated outside the area of the country. An *organized territory* (U.S.) is a territory for which a system of laws and a settled government have been provided by an act of the United States Congress. An *overseas territory* (France) is an overseas subdivision of the French Republic with elected representation in the French Parliament, having individual statutes, laws, and internal organization adapted to local conditions.

ton-miles, or **ton-kilometres,** aggregate measure of freight hauled by a specified means of transportation, equal to tons of freight multiplied by the miles (or kilometres) each ton is transported. Figures are compiled from waybills (nationally) and ordinarily exclude mail, specie, passengers' baggage, the fuel and stores of the conveyance, and goods carried free.

total active duty personnel, full-time active duty military personnel (excluding militias and part-time, informal, or other paramilitary elements), with their distribution by percentages among the major services.

total fertility rate, the sum of the current age-specific birth rates for each of the child-bearing years (usually 15–49). It is the probable number of births, given present fertility data, that would occur during the lifetime of each woman should she live to the end of her child-bearing years.

tourism, service industry comprising activities connected with domestic and international travel for pleasure or recreation; confined here to international travel and reported as expenditures in U.S.$ by tourists of all nationalities visiting a particular country and, conversely, the estimated expenditures of that country's nationals in all countries of destination.

transfer payments, *see* household income and expenditure.

transport, all mechanical methods of moving persons or goods. Data reported for national establishments include: for railroads, length of track and volume of traffic for passengers and cargo (but excluding mail, etc.); for roads, length of network and numbers of passenger cars and of commercial vehicles (*i.e.,* trucks and buses); for merchant marine, the number of vessels of more than 100 gross tons and their total deadweight tonnage; for air transport, traffic data for passengers and cargo and the number of airports with scheduled flights.

unincorporated territory (U.S.), *see* territory.

unitary republic, *see* republic.

urban-rural, social characteristic of local or national populations, defined by predominant economic activities, "urban" referring to a group of largely nonagricultural pursuits, "rural" to agriculturally oriented employment patterns. The distinction is usually based on the country's own definition of urban, which may depend only upon the size (population) of a place or upon factors like employment, administrative status, density of housing, etc.

value added, also called value added by manufacture, the gross output value of a firm or industry minus the cost of inputs—raw materials, supplies, and payments to other firms—required to produce it. Value added is the portion of the sales value or gross output value that is actually created by the firm or industry. Value added generally includes labour costs, administrative costs, and operating profits.

The Nations of the World

Afghanistan

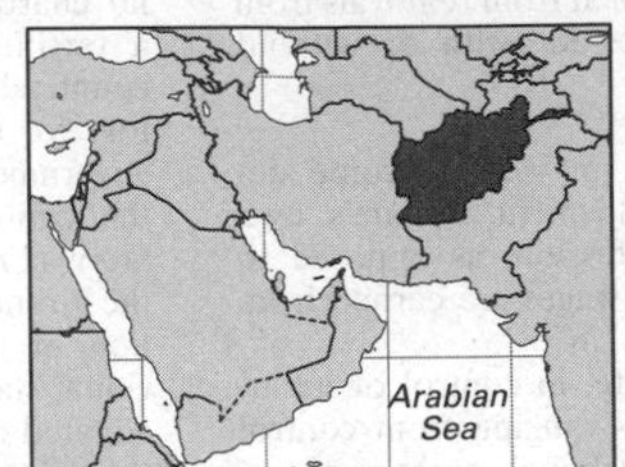

Official name: Islamic State of Afghanistan (Dowlat-e Eslāmī-ye Afghānestān [Persian]; Pashtu long-form name, n.a.).
Form of government[1]: Islamic state with an interim parliament[2] (250).
Chief of state: President.
Head of government: Prime Minister[3].
Capital: Kabul.
Official languages: Pashto; Dari (Persian).
Official religion: Islam.
Monetary unit: 1 afghani (Af) = 100 puls (puli); valuation (Oct. 6, 1995) 1 U.S.$ = Af 4,442; 1 £ = Af 7,022.

Area and population[4]	area		population
	sq mi	sq km	1988 estimate
Regions			
Eastern	28,664	74,240	2,050,400
North-central	20,461	52,994	2,584,400
North-east	29,911	77,468	1,478,400
North-west	50,581	131,005	2,157,100
South-central	32,963	85,375	1,215,700
South-east	12,546	32,494	4,252,000
Western	76,699	198,649	1,666,400
TOTAL	251,825	652,225	15,404,400

Demography

Population (1995): 18,129,000[5].
Density (1995): persons per sq mi 72.0, persons per sq km 27.8.
Urban-rural (1995): urban 20.0%; rural 80.0%.
Sex distribution (1995): male 51.30%; female 48.70%.
Age breakdown (1995): under 15, 40.7%; 15–29, 28.4%; 30–44, 16.1%; 45–59, 10.0%; 60–74, 4.1%; 75 and over, 0.6%.
Population projection: (2000) 25,725,000; (2010) 32,889,000.
Doubling time: 25 years.
Ethnic composition (early 1990s): Pashtun 38%; Tadzhik 25%; Ḥazāra 19%; Uzbek 6%; Chahar Aimak, Turkmen, Baluchi, and other 12%.
Religious affiliation (1990): Sunnī Muslim 84%; Shīʿī Muslim 15%; other 1%.
Major cities (1988): Kabul 700,000[6]; Kandahār (Qandahār) 225,500; Herāt 177,300; Mazār-e Sharīf 130,600.

Vital statistics

Birth rate per 1,000 population (1995): 42.7 (world avg. 25.0).
Death rate per 1,000 population (1995): 18.5 (world avg. 9.3).
Natural increase rate per 1,000 population (1995): 24.2 (world avg. 15.7).
Total fertility rate (avg. births per childbearing woman; 1995): 6.2.
Life expectancy at birth (1995): male 46.0 years; female 44.7 years.
Major causes of death per 100,000 population: n.a.; however, in the early 1990s, injuries and poisoning, infectious and parasitic diseases, and diseases of the respiratory system were the leading causes of death reported in hospitals.

National economy

Budget (1987–88). Revenue: Af 79,800,000,000 (1984–85; tax revenue 45.4%, nontax revenue 54.6%). Expenditures: Af 105,800,000,000 (1981–82; governmental ministries 50.0%, developmental budget 31.9%, debt service 13.9%).
Production (metric tons except as noted). Agriculture, forestry, fishing (1994): wheat 1,750,000, corn (maize) 360,000, rice 350,000, grapes 330,000, potatoes 228,000, barley 180,000; livestock (number of live animals) 14,200,000 sheep, 2,150,000 goats, 1,500,000 cattle, 1,160,000 asses, 300,000 horses, 265,000 camels, 7,000,000 chickens; roundwood (1993) 7,817,000 cu m; fish catch (1993) 1,200. Mining and quarrying (1993): salt 13,000; copper 5,000; gypsum 3,000; barite 2,000. Manufacturing (by production value in Af '000,000; 1988–89): food products 4,019; leather and fur products 2,678; textiles 1,760; printing and publishing 1,070; industrial chemicals (including fertilizers) 1,053; footwear 999; plastic products 452. Construction (Af '000,000; 1985): 1,094. Energy production (consumption): electricity (kW-hr; 1992) 703,000,000 (834,000,000); coal (metric tons; 1992) 8,000 (8,000); petroleum products (metric tons; 1992) none (302,000); natural gas (cu m; 1992) 188,947,000 (188,947,000).
Population economically active (1994)[7]: total 5,557,000; activity rate of total population 29.4% (participation rates: female 9.0%; unemployed [1990] 3.4%).

Price index (1990 = 100)	1988	1989	1990	1991	1992	1993	1994
Consumer price index	64.3	83.1	100.0	266.0	420.8	563.9	676.7

Public debt (external, outstanding; 1993): U.S.$5,381,000,000.
Tourism: receipts (1989) U.S.$1,000,000; expenditures (1987) U.S.$1,000,000.
Gross national product (1988): U.S.$3,100,000,000 (U.S.$220 per capita).

Structure of gross domestic product and labour force	1990–91		1990–92	
	in value Af '000,000[8]	% of total value	labour force	% of labour force
Agriculture	59,600	51.9	2,777,300	61.0
Manufacturing, mining, and public utilities	30,400	26.5	637,400	14.0
Construction	7,500	6.5		
Transp. and commun.	4,700	4.1		
Trade	10,500	9.1	1,138,200	25.0
Public administration				
Public services	2,100	1.8		
Other				
TOTAL	114,800	100.0[9]	4,552,900	100.0

Land use (1993): forested 2.9%; meadows and pastures 46.0%; agricultural and under permanent cultivation 12.4%; other 38.7%.

Foreign trade[10]

Balance of trade (current prices)	1989	1990	1991	1992	1993	1994
U.S.$'000,000	−249	−351	−265	−236	+234	−306
% of total	29.1%	38.7%	27.4%	24.7%	15.5%	34.1%

Imports (1994): U.S.$602,000,000 (1989–90; machinery 37.7%, basic manufactures 18.3%, minerals and fuels 10.9%). *Major import sources* (1994): Japan 14.8%; European Union 10.6%; China 5.0%; Pakistan 4.6%.
Exports (1994): U.S.$296,000,000 (1991; dried fruits and nuts 49.6%, carpets and rugs 23.6%, karakul wool and hides 6.7%, cotton 1.3%). *Major export destinations* (1994): European Union 9.5%; China 3.7%.

Transport and communications

Transport. Railroads (1995): length 25 km. Roads (1988): total length 19,200 km (paved 47%). Vehicles (1993): passenger cars 31,000; trucks and buses 25,000. Merchant marine: none. Air transport (1992): passenger-km 265,000,000; metric ton-km cargo 11,000,000; airports (1995) 3.
Communications. Daily newspapers (1992): total number 16; total circulation 206,000; circulation per 1,000 population 12.8. Radio (1994): 1,670,000 receivers (1 per 10 persons). Television (1994): 100,000 receivers (1 per 169 persons). Telephones (main lines; 1993): 29,000 (1 per 769 persons).

Education and health

Education (1988–89)	schools	teachers	students	student/ teacher ratio
Primary	553	16,756	586,014	35.0
Secondary	819	5,715	271,000	47.4
Voc., teacher tr.	33	556	8,537	15.4
Higher	5	198	1,491	7.5

Educational attainment (1980). Percentage of population age 25 and over having: no formal schooling 88.5%; some primary education 6.8%; complete primary 0.3%; some secondary 1.2%; postsecondary 3.2%. *Literacy* (1990): percentage of total population age 15 and over literate 29.4%; males 44.1%; females 13.9%.
Health (1988–93): physicians 2,347 (1 per 6,690 persons); hospital beds 5,331 (1 per 2,945 persons); infant mortality rate (1995) 152.8.
Food (1992): daily per capita caloric intake 1,523 (vegetable products 89%, animal products 11%); 62% of FAO recommended minimum requirement.

Military

Total active duty personnel (1995): no identifiable military units appear to represent the central government. *Military expenditure as percentage of GNP* (1990): 15.0% (world 4.4%); per capita expenditure U.S.$29.

[1]Central government in Kabul unites a number of Sunnī mujahedin guerrilla groups who, following traditional deliberative and legislative models, have established a state, a parliament, and a draft constitution (January 1995), though none is fully established in all of Afghanistan. But as of October 1995, there was no effective central authority. [2]Consisting of a nonelective body (named by the previous Shura, or constituent assembly), having the purpose of approving a draft constitution and restoring civilian government. [3]Office vacant from June 1994. [4]In the early 1990s an administrative reorganization created 31 provinces (*wilayāh*), but detailed breakdown of area and population is unavailable. [5]Excluding Afghan refugees estimated to number about 1.6 million in Pakistan and less than a million in Iran. [6]1993 estimate. [7]Based on settled population only. [8]At prices of 1978–79. [9]Detail does not add to total given because of rounding. [10]Exports are f.o.b. and imports are c.i.f.

Albania

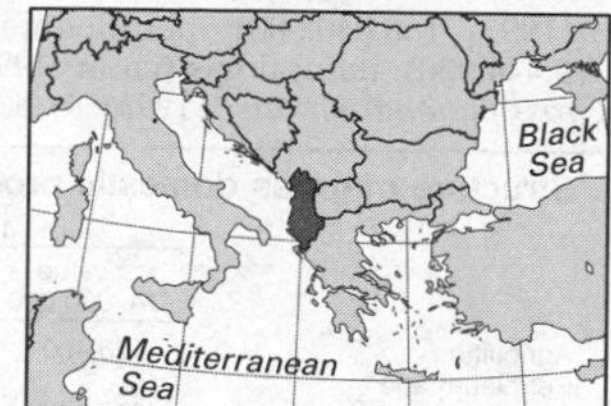

Official name: Republika e Shqipërisë (Republic of Albania).
Form of government: unitary multiparty republic with one legislative house (People's Assembly [140])[1].
Chief of state: President.
Head of government: Prime Minister.
Capital: Tiranë.
Official language: Albanian.
Official religion: none.
Monetary unit: 1 lek = 100 qindars; valuation (Oct. 6, 1995) 1 U.S.$ = 93.65 leks; 1 £ = 148.05 leks.

Area and population

Provinces	Capitals	area sq mi	area sq km	population 1990 estimate
Berat	Berat	396	1,027	180,489
Dibër	Peshkopi	605	1,568	153,775
Durrës	Durrës	327	848	251,029
Elbasan	Elbasan	572	1,481	248,676
Fier	Fier	454	1,175	251,115
Gjirokastër	Gjirokastër	439	1,137	67,392
Gramsh	Gramsh	268	695	44,791
Kolonjë	Ersekë	311	805	25,291
Korçë	Korçë	842	2,181	218,219
Krujë	Krujë	234	607	109,876
Kukës	Kukës	514	1,330	104,731
Lezhë	Lezhë	185	479	63,505
Librazhd	Librazhd	391	1,013	73,871
Lushnjë	Lushnjë	275	712	137,830
Mat	Burrel	397	1,028	78,754
Mirditë	Rrëshen	335	867	51,701
Përmet	Përmet	359	929	40,419
Pogradec	Pogradec	280	725	73,333
Pukë	Pukë	399	1,031	50,200
Sarandë	Sarandë	424	1,097	89,459
Shkodër	Shkodër	976	2,528	241,549
Skrapar	Çorovoda	299	775	47,605
Tepelenë	Tepelenë	315	817	51,022
Tiranë	Tiranë	478	1,238	374,483
Tropojë	Bajram	403	1,043	45,965
Vlorë	Vlorë	621	1,609	180,725
TOTAL		11,100[2]	28,748	3,255,091

Demography

Population (1995): 3,412,000[3].
Density (1995): persons per sq mi 307.4, persons per sq km 118.7.
Urban-rural (1990): urban 36.1%; rural 63.9%.
Sex distribution (1990): male 51.40%; female 48.60%.
Age breakdown (1990): under 15, 33.0%; 15–29, 28.9%; 30–44, 18.5%; 45–59, 11.7%; 60–74, 5.9%; 75 and over, 2.0%.
Population projection: (2000) 3,610,000; (2010) 4,016,000.
Doubling time: 37 years.
Ethnic composition (1989): Albanian 98.0%; Greek 1.8%; Macedonian 0.1%; other 0.1%.
Religious affiliation (1992): a significant portion of the population are nonreligious; believers identify themselves as Muslim 65%, Orthodox 20%, Roman Catholic 13%, other 2%.
Major cities (1990): Tiranë 243,000; Durres 85,400; Elbasan 83,300; Shkodër 81,800; Vlorë 73,800.

Vital statistics

Birth rate per 1,000 population (1991): 23.8 (world avg. 25.0).
Death rate per 1,000 population (1991): 5.4 (world avg. 9.3).
Natural increase rate per 1,000 population (1991): 18.4 (world avg. 15.7).
Total fertility rate (avg. births per childbearing woman; 1993): 2.9.
Marriage rate per 1,000 population (1990): 8.9.
Divorce rate per 1,000 population (1990): 0.8.
Life expectancy at birth (1993): male 70.0 years; female 76.2 years.
Major causes of death per 100,000 population: n.a.; however, principal health problems in the mid-1990s included malnutrition (especially of children), perinatal and child health care, environmental pollution, and lack of funding for medical supplies.

National economy

Budget (1994). Revenue: 46,049,000,000 leks (taxes 78.1%, of which excise taxes 20.6%, social-security contributions 13.9%, import duties and export taxes 13.6%, income taxes 9.0%; nontax revenue 21.9%). Expenditures: 68,259,000,000 leks (current expenditure 76.4%, of which personnel costs 22.6%, social security 15.9%, government operations and maintenance 15.4%, service of public debt 6.5%; capital expenditure 17.2%).
Public debt (1993): U.S.$861,000,000.
Tourism (1990): number of tourist arrivals 30,000; receipts from visitors, n.a.
Production (metric tons except as noted). Agriculture, forestry, fishing (1994): total cereals 692,000, of which wheat 470,000, maize (corn) 180,000; vegetables and melons 352,000, mainly beans, peas, onions, tomatoes, cabbage, eggplants, and carrots; potatoes 100,000; tree fruits 97,000, of which apples 45,000, oranges 14,000; grapes 40,000; sugar beets 26,000; olives 20,000; livestock (number of live animals) 1,900,000 sheep, 1,280,000 goats, 630,000 cattle, 138,000 mules and asses, poultry 3,600,000; roundwood (1993) 2,556,000 cu m; fish catch (1993) 3,500. Mining and quarrying (value in '000,000 leks; 1994): chromium ore 2,547; copper ore 1,030. Manufacturing (value of production in '000 leks; 1993)[4]: food products 824,000; textiles 263,000; clothing 139,000; consumer products 93,000; tobacco 70,000; building materials 64,000; leather 63,000. Construction (1990): 12,428 units. Energy production (consumption): electricity (kW-hr; 1993) 3,450,000,000 (2,880,000,000); coal (metric tons; 1993) 430,000 (630,000); crude petroleum (barrels; 1993) 3,627,000 (5,275,000); petroleum products (metric tons; 1993) 410,000 (430,000); natural gas (cu m; 1993) 90,000,000 (90,000,000).
Gross national product (1993): U.S.$1,163,000,000 (U.S.$340 per capita).

Structure of gross domestic product and labour force

	1994 value '000,000 leks	1994 % of total value	1991 labour force[3]	1991 % of labour force[3]
Agriculture	92,254	55.5	662,000	49.0
Manufacturing, mining, public utilities	20,966	12.6	300,000	22.2
Construction	15,732	9.5	99,000	7.3
Transp. and commun.	5,546	3.3	29,000	2.1
Trade }			25,000	1.9
Pub. admin., defense }	31,799	19.1	...	...
Services }			236,000	17.5
Other	—	—	...	...
TOTAL	166,297	100.0	1,351,000	100.0

Population economically active (1993): total 1,540,000[3]; activity rate of total population 49.4% (participation rates: ages 15–64, 90.2%; female 49.0%; unemployed 17.5%).

Price and earnings indexes (1990 = 100)

	1988	1989	1990	1991	1992	1993	1994
Consumer price index	...	97.6	100.0	136.2	442.3	818.2	c. 950
Annual earnings index	96.4	97.2	100.0	117.1	...	...	...

Household income and expenditure. Average household size (1989) 4.7; annual income per rural household 80,835 leks (U.S.$ value, n.a.); sources of income: wages 53.0%, transfers from relatives abroad 21.5%, social insurance 11.4%; expenditure: n.a.
Land use (1993): forested 36.5%; meadows and pastures 14.7%; agricultural and under permanent cultivation 24.4%; other 24.4%.

Foreign trade

Balance of trade (current prices)

	1989	1990	1991	1992	1993	1994
'000,000 leks	−83	−150	−308	−454	−490	−460
% of total	12.1%	24.5%	60.3%	76.4%	68.6%	62.0%

Imports (1994): U.S.$601,000,000 (machinery and transport equipment 31.8%; food, beverages, live animals, and tobacco 25.5%; manufactured goods 18.9%; mineral fuels 10.9%, of which crude petroleum 8.2%; chemicals 6.5%). *Major import sources:* Italy 35.0%; Greece 24.0%; Bulgaria 8.2%; Germany 5.5%; Turkey 4.6%; states of the former Yugoslavia 4.5%.
Exports (1994): U.S.$141,300,000 (manufactured goods 45.3%; mineral fuels 26.7%; food, beverages, live animals, and tobacco 14.3%). *Major export destinations:* Italy 52.1%; United States 11.1%; Greece 10.4%; states of the former Yugoslavia 6.0%.

Transport and communications

Transport. Railroads (1990): length 720 km; passenger km 779,200,000, metric ton-km cargo 584,000,000. Roads (1990): total length 7,450 km (paved 38%). Vehicles (1994): passenger cars 67,959; trucks and buses 50,420. Merchant marine (1992): vessels (100 gross tons and over) 24; total deadweight tonnage 80,954. Air transport: n.a.; airports (1995) with scheduled flights 1.
Communications. Daily newspapers (1992): total number 4; total circulation 165,000; circulation per 1,000 population 50. Radio (1994): 550,000 receivers (1 per 6.1 persons). Television (1989): 324,905[5] receivers (1 per 9.8 persons). Telephones (main lines; 1993): 49,000 (1 per 70 persons).

Education and health

Education (1990)

	schools	teachers	students	student/teacher ratio
Primary (age 6–13)	1,726	28,798	557,000	19.3
Secondary (age 14–17)	47	2,318	68,000	29.3
Voc., teacher tr.	466	7,390	138,000	18.7
Higher	8	1,806	27,000	15.0

Educational attainment (1989). Population age 10 and over having: primary education 65.3%; secondary 29.1%; higher 5.6%. *Literacy* (1989): total population age 10 and over literate 91.8%; males 95.5%; females 88.0%.
Health (1990): physicians 5,566[6] (1 per 585 persons); hospital beds 19,000 (1 per 173 persons); infant mortality rate per 1,000 live births (1991) 32.9.
Food (1992): daily per capita caloric intake 2,605 (vegetable products 83%, animal products 17%); 108% of FAO recommended minimum requirement.

Military

Total active duty personnel (1995): 73,000 (army 82.2%, navy 3.4%, air force 13.7%). *Military expenditure as percentage of GNP* (1993): 8.2% (world 3.3%); per capita expenditure U.S.$28.

[1]A transitional constitution was adopted on April 29, 1991. The proposed text of a permanent constitution was rejected in a referendum on Nov. 6, 1994. [2]Detail does not add to total given because of rounding. [3]At mid-year 1995, approximately 500,000 Albanians were believed to be working in neighbouring countries. [4]Value of production in constant prices of 1990. [5]Families that had a television receiver. [6]Includes dentists.

Algeria

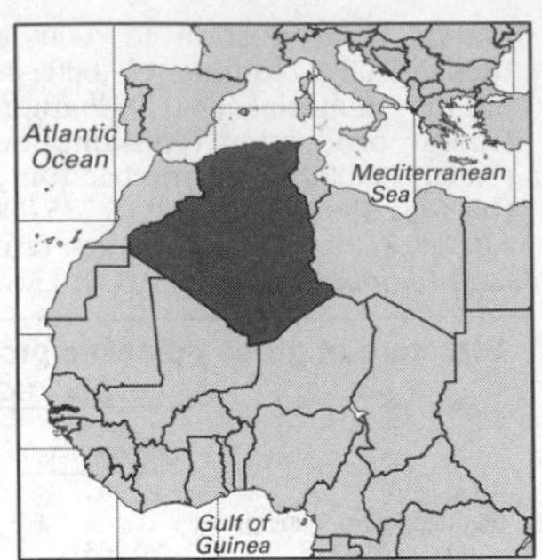

Official name: al-Jumhūrīyah al-Jazā'irīyah ad-Dīmuqrāṭīyah ash-Sha'bīyah (Arabic) (Democratic and Popular Republic of Algeria).
Form of government: military-backed regime with one interim legislative body (National Transition Council [200]).
Chief of state: President.
Head of government: Prime Minister.
Capital: Algiers.
Official language: Arabic.
Official religion: Islam.
Monetary unit: 1 Algerian dinar (DA) = 100 centimes; valuation (Oct. 6, 1995) 1 U.S.$ = DA 50.51; 1 £ = DA 79.85.

Population (1987 census)

Wilāyat	population	Wilāyat	population
Adrar	217,678	Médéa	652,863
Aïn Defla	537,256	Mila	511,605
Aïn Temouchent	274,990	Mostaganem	505,932
Alger	1,690,191	M'Sila	604,693
Annaba	455,888	Naâma	113,700
Batna	752,617	Oran	932,473
el-Bayadh	153,254	Ouargla	284,454
Béchar	185,346	el-Oued	376,909
Bejaïa	700,952	Oum el-Bouaghi	403,936
Biskra	430,202	Relizane	544,877
Blida	702,188	Saïda	235,494
Bordj Bou Arreridj	424,828	Sétif	1,000,694
Bouira	526,900	Sidi bel-Abbès	446,277
Boumerdes	650,975	Skikda	622,510
ech-Chleff	684,192	Souk Ahras	296,077
Constantine	664,303	Tamanrasset	95,822
Djelfa	494,494	et-Tarf	275,315
Ghardaïa	216,140	Tébessa	410,233
Guelma	353,309	Tiaret	575,794
Illizi	18,930	Tindouf	16,428
Jijel	472,312	Tipaza	620,151
Khenchela	246,541	Tissemsilt	228,120
Laghouat	212,388	Tizi Ouzou	936,948
Mascara	566,901	Tlemcen	714,862
		TOTAL	23,038,942[1]

Demography

Area: 919,595 sq mi, 2,381,741 sq km.
Population (1995): 27,939,000[2].
Density (1995): persons per sq mi 30.4, persons per sq km 11.7.
Urban-rural (1995): urban 55.8%; rural 44.2%.
Sex distribution (1995): male 50.60%; female 49.40%.
Age breakdown (1995): under 15, 38.7%; 15–29, 29.7%; 30–44, 17.8%; 45–59, 8.1%; 60–74, 4.6%; 75 and over, 1.1%.
Population projection: (2000) 31,158,000; (2010) 37,489,000.
Doubling time: 31 years.
Ethnic composition (1992): Arab *c.* 80%; Berber *c.* 20%, of which Kabyle *c.* 13%, Shawia *c.* 6%.
Religious affiliation (1990): Muslim 99.9%, of which Sunnī 99.5%, Ibāḍīyah 0.4%; Roman Catholic 0.1%.
Major cities (1987): Algiers 1,507,241; Oran 609,823; Constantine 440,842; Annaba 222,518; Batna 181,601.

Vital statistics

Birth rate per 1,000 population (1993): 28.9 (world avg. 25.0).
Death rate per 1,000 population (1993): 6.2 (world avg. 9.3).
Natural increase rate per 1,000 population (1993): 22.7 (world avg. 15.7).
Total fertility rate (avg. births per childbearing woman; 1994): 3.8.
Marriage rate per 1,000 population (1993): 5.7.
Divorce rate per 1,000 population (1985): 2.1.
Life expectancy at birth (1994): male 67.0 years; female 69.0 years.
Notified cases of infectious diseases per 100,000 population (1990): hepatitis 15.1; typhoid fever 11.3; measles 7.2; cholera 5.2; tuberculosis 4.8.

National economy

Budget (1994). Revenue: DA 410,000,000,000 (petroleum taxes 45.6%, turnover taxes 19.0%, direct taxes 11.6%). Expenditures: DA 535,300,000,000 (current expenditure 60.4%, development expenditure 39.6%).
Public debt (external, outstanding; 1993): U.S.$24,587,000,000.
Tourism: (1993) receipts from visitors U.S.$55,000,000; (1992) expenditures by nationals abroad U.S.$163,000,000.
Production (metric tons except as noted). Agriculture, forestry, fishing (1994): wheat 1,350,000, potatoes 1,200,000, barley 800,000, tomatoes 515,000, oranges 270,000, dates 265,000, onions 260,000, grapes 250,000, olives 130,000; livestock (number of live animals) 17,850,000 sheep, 1,370,000 cattle; roundwood (1993) 2,367,000 cu m; fish catch (1993) 90,460. Mining and quarrying (1993): iron ore (gross weight) 2,311,000; phosphate rock (gross weight) 718,000; mercury 545,000 kg. Manufacturing (1992): cement 6,940,000[3]; flour and semolina 2,540,000; bricks 1,776,000; crude steel 1,400,000[3]; pig iron 1,300,000[3]; edible oils 277,000; refined sugar 192,000; phosphate fertilizer 154,000; methanol 95,000. Construction: n.a. Energy production (consumption): electricity (kW-hr; 1993) 19,415,000,000 (18,174,000,000); coal (metric tons; 1993) 20,000 (1,420,000); crude petroleum (barrels; 1994) 283,300,000 ([1993] 168,640,000); petroleum products (metric tons; 1993) 39,628,000 (9,444,000); natural gas (cu m; 1993) 53,117,000,000 (18,546,000,000).
Gross national product (1993): U.S.$44,347,000,000 (U.S.$1,650 per capita).

Structure of gross domestic product and labour force

	1993		1990	
	in value DA '000,000	% of total value	labour force	% of labour force
Agriculture	126,400	10.9	907,490	15.9
Petroleum and natural gas	250,100[4]	21.5[4]	55,000	1.0
Other mining	2,100	0.2	...	...
Manufacturing	125,700[4]	10.8[4]	646,390	11.3
Public utilities	13,100	1.1	651,370	11.4
Construction	133,200	11.5		
Pub. admin., defense	158,100	13.6	1,318,370	23.1
Transp. and commun.	353,100[5]	30.4[5]	252,230	4.4
Trade			444,970	7.8
Other			1,435,180[6]	25.1[6]
TOTAL	1,161,800	100.0	5,711,000	100.0

Population economically active (1990): total 5,711,000; activity rate of population 22.8% (participation rates [1987]: ages 15–64, 44.3%; female 9.2%; unemployed [1994] 27.3%).

Price and earnings indexes (1990 = 100)

	1989	1990	1991	1992	1993	1994	1995
Consumer price index	85.7	100.0	125.9	165.8	199.8	257.8	314.3[7]
Earnings index[8]	...	100.0	131.1	170.2	199.1	203.7	...

Household income and expenditure. Average household size (1987) 6.9; income per household: n.a.; sources of income (1994): wages and salaries 44.9%, self-employment 35.3%, transfers 19.8%; expenditure (1988): food and beverages 52.3%, transportation and communications 12.0%, clothing and footwear 8.6%, housing and energy 6.7%, other 20.4%.
Land use (1993): forested 1.7%; meadows and pastures 12.9%; agricultural and under permanent cultivation 3.3%; other (mostly desert) 82.1%.

Foreign trade[9]

Balance of trade (current prices)

	1989	1990	1991	1992	1993	1994
U.S.$'000,000	+360	+3,215	+5,032	+2,557	+2,460	−260
% of total	1.9%	14.2%	25.0%	13.0%	13.7%	1.4%

Imports (1993): U.S.$7,770,000,000 (1992[10]; agricultural products 24.5%, nonelectrical machinery 18.3%, iron and steel 9.5%). *Major import sources:* France 29.1%; U.S. 12.4%; Italy 11.7%; Spain 10.8%; Germany 5.1%.
Exports (1993): U.S.$10,230,000,000 (crude petroleum 44.3%, natural gas 30.3%, refined petroleum 17.6%, dates 0.5%). *Major export destinations:* Italy 17.6%; U.S. 15.5%; Germany 12.8%; France 12.3%; The Netherlands 7.5%.

Transport and communications

Transport. Railroads (1993): route length 2,965 mi, 4,772 km; passenger-km 2,768,000,000; metric ton-km cargo 2,291,000,000. Roads (1992): total length 95,576 km (paved 66%). Vehicles (1993): passenger cars 725,000; trucks and buses 480,000. Merchant marine (1992): vessels (100 gross tons and over) 149; total deadweight tonnage 1,093,363. Air transport (1992)[11]: passenger-km 3,234,000,000; metric ton-km cargo 20,223,000; airports (1995) 28.
Communications. Daily newspapers (1992): total number 5; total circulation 1,000,000; circulation per 1,000 population 38. Radio (1994): 3,500,000 receivers (1 per 7.8 persons). Television (1994): 2,000,000 receivers (1 per 14 persons). Telephones (main lines; 1993): 1,068,100 (1 per 25 persons).

Education and health

Education (1992–93)

	schools	teachers	students	student/teacher ratio
Primary (age 6–11)	13,970	153,793	4,436,363	28.8
Secondary (age 12–17) / Voc., teacher tr.	3,402	135,730	2,305,198	17.0
Higher	...	14,379	243,397	16.9

Educational attainment (1989). Percentage of economically active population age 16 and over having: no formal schooling 38.2%; Qur'ānic education 0.9%; primary education 20.8%; secondary education 11.1%; vocational 19.7%; higher 9.3%. *Literacy* (1990): total population age 15 and over literate 8,090,000 (57.4%); males literate 4,840,000 (69.8%); females literate 3,250,000 (45.5%).
Health (1992): physicians 25,304 (1 per 1,041 persons); hospital beds 57,879 (1 per 455 persons); infant mortality rate per 1,000 live births (1994) 52.0.
Food (1992): daily per capita caloric intake 2,897 (vegetable products 89%, animal products 11%); 121% of FAO recommended minimum requirement.

Military

Total active duty personnel (1995): 121,700 (army 86.3%, navy 5.5%, air force 8.2%). *Military expenditure as percentage of GNP* (1993): 3.0% (world 3.3%); per capita expenditure U.S.$51.

[1]De facto population. [2]Excludes about 1,800,000 Algerians abroad. [3]1993. [4]Petroleum and natural gas includes (and Manufacturing excludes) refined petroleum and manufacture of hydrocarbons. [5]Includes import duties of DA 86,300,000,000. [6]Includes 1,141,278 unemployed. [7]February. [8]Public workers only; all data based on January averages of gross income. [9]Imports c.i.f., exports f.o.b. [10]Imports (1992): U.S.$8,648,000,000. [11]Air Algérie.

Andorra

Official name: Principat d'Andorra; (Principality of Andorra).
Form of government: parliamentary coprincipality with one legislative house (General Council [28]).
Chiefs of state: President of France; Bishop of Urgell, Spain.
Head of government: Head of the Government.
Capital: Andorra la Vella.
Official language: Catalan.
Official religion: none[1].
Monetary unit: There is no local currency of issue; the French franc and Spanish peseta are both in circulation. 1 franc (F) = 100 centimes; 1 peseta (Pta) = 100 céntimos. Valuation (Oct. 6, 1995) 1 U.S.$ = F 5.02, 1 £ = F 7.93; 1 U.S.$ = Ptas 123.75, 1 £ = Ptas 195.63.

Area and population

		area		population
Parishes	Capitals	sq mi	sq km	1993[2] estimate
Andorra la Vella	Andorra la Vella	49[3]	127[3]	22,387
Canillo	Canillo }	74	191	2,193
Encamp	Encamp }			9,654
La Massana	La Massana	25	65	5,302
Les Escaldes-Engordany	—	[3]	[3]	13,177
Ordino	Ordino	33	85	1,652
Sant Julià de Lòria	Sant Julià de Lòria	[3]	[3]	7,234
TOTAL		181	468	61,599

Demography

Population (1995): 62,900.
Density (1995): persons per sq mi 347.5, persons per sq km 134.4.
Urban-rural (1994): urban 62.5%; rural 37.5%.
Sex distribution (1993): male 53.14%; female 46.86%.
Age breakdown (1993): under 15, 16.3%; 15–29, 27.7%; 30–44, 27.2%; 45–59, 15.1%; 60–74, 9.9%; 75 and over, 3.8%.
Population projection: (2000) 66,000; (2010) 71,000.
Doubling time: 82 years.
Ethnic composition (by nationality; 1993): Spanish 46.4%; Andorran 28.3%; Portuguese 11.1%; French 7.6%; British 1.8%; German 0.5%; other 4.3%.
Religious affiliation (1992): Roman Catholic 92.0%; Protestant 0.5%; Jewish 0.4%; other 7.1%.
Major cities (1993): Andorra la Vella 22,387; Les Escaldes 13,177; Encamp 9,654.

Vital statistics

Birth rate per 1,000 population (1994): 10.9[4] (world avg. 25.0).
Death rate per 1,000 population (1994): 2.8[4] (world avg. 9.3).
Natural increase rate per 1,000 population (1993): 8.1 (world avg. 15.7).
Total fertility rate (avg. births per childbearing woman; 1994): 1.7.
Marriage rate per 1,000 population (1992): 2.2.
Divorce rate per 1,000 population: n.a.
Life expectancy at birth (1994): male 76.0 years; female 82.0 years.
Major causes of death per 100,000 population: n.a.; however, health problems are those of a developed country—cardiovascular disease, hypertension, malignant neoplasms (cancers).

National economy

Budget (1993). Revenue: Ptas 18,165,000,000 (excise taxes on imported consumer goods and gasoline 75.6%; nonspecific taxes 11.2%; concessions 3.7%). Expenditures: Ptas 23,220,000,000 (public services 26.9%; administration 26.7%; education and culture 12.4%; tourism and exports 7.5%; health, labour, and welfare 5.9%).
Public debt (1992): U.S.$132,000,000.
Production (value of recorded exported products in Ptas '000 except as noted). Agriculture (1992): important crops include tobacco, hay, and grapes; livestock (number of live animals) 9,000 sheep[5], 1,100 cattle. Quarrying (1992): marble 11,800. Manufacturing (1992): wearing apparel (primarily woolen goods and leather goods) 1,045,700; motor vehicles and parts 816,100; mineral water 343,100; furniture 213,300; newspapers and periodicals 204,700; electrical machinery and apparatus for industry 167,600; other products include cigars and cigarettes and liqueurs. Construction: n.a. Energy production (consumption): electricity (kW-hr; 1991) 140,000,000 ([1992] 316,000,000); coal, none (n.a.); crude petroleum, none (n.a.); petroleum products, none (n.a.); natural gas, none (n.a.).
Population economically active (1989): total 24,734; activity rate of total population 55.1% (participation rates: ages 15–64, 74.3%; female 45.6%; unemployed, n.a.[6]).

Price and earnings indexes (1990 = 100)[7]

	1989	1990	1991	1992	1993	1994	1995[8]
Consumer price index	97.9	100.0	105.9	112.2	117.3	122.9	126.4
Earnings index	...	...	...	...	...	...	...

Gross national product (at current market prices; 1992): U.S.$1,231,000,000 (U.S.$19,990 per capita)[9].

Structure of labour force

	1989	
	labour force	% of labour force
Agriculture	291	1.2
Mining	...	...
Manufacturing	2,719	11.0
Construction	2,914	11.8
Public utilities	...	...
Transportation and communications	...	...
Trade	5,984	24.2
Restaurants, hotels	4,698	18.9
Finance, real estate, insurance	1,331	5.4
Pub. admin., defense	2,553	10.3
Other	4,127	16.7
Unknown	117	0.5
TOTAL	24,734	100.0

Land use (1993): forested 22.0%; meadows and pastures 56.0%; agricultural and under permanent cultivation 2.0%; other 20.0%.
Household income and expenditure. Average household size: n.a.; income per household: n.a.; sources of income: n.a.; expenditure: n.a.
Tourism: n.a.

Foreign trade

Balance of trade (current prices)

	1987	1988	1989	1990	1991	1992
Ptas '000,000	−73,200	−78,988	−89,007	−117,280	...	−112,177
% of total	93.8%	93.4%	94.2%	95.5%	...	93.0%

Imports (1992): Ptas 116,385,000,000 (wearing apparel 10.3%, electrical and electronic equipment 10.2%, transport equipment 8.8%, perfumes and cosmetics 5.5%, alcoholic beverages 5.3%, milk and related products 5.0%, nonelectrical machinery and equipment 4.7%). *Major import sources:* Spain 35.8%; France 35.1%; Japan 6.7%; Germany 5.6%; Italy 3.6%.
Exports (1992): Ptas 4,208,000,000 (wearing apparel 24.8%, motor vehicles and parts 19.4%, mineral water 8.2%, furniture 5.1%, newspapers and periodicals 4.9%). *Major export destinations:* Spain 59.3%; France 35.3%; Germany 1.9%; Italy 1.5%.

Transport and communications

Transport. Railroads: none; however, both French and Spanish railways stop near the border. Roads (1991): total length 167 mi, 269 km (paved 74%). Vehicles (1993): passenger cars 36,660; trucks and buses 4,362. Merchant marine: vessels (100 gross tons and over) none. Airports (1995) with scheduled flights: none.
Communications. Daily newspapers (1992): total number 3; circulation 4,000; circulation per 1,000 population 66. Radio (1994): total number of receivers 10,000 (1 per 6.5 persons). Television (1993): total number of receivers 4,000 (1 per 15 persons). Telephones (main lines; 1993): 26,800 (1 per 2.3 persons).

Education and health

Education (1992–93)

	schools	teachers	students	student/teacher ratio
Primary/Lower secondary (age 7–15)	12	...	5,519	...
Upper secondary	6		1,659	...
Higher	—	—	—	—

Educational attainment (mid-1980s). Percentage of population age 15 and over having: no formal schooling 5.5%; primary education 47.3%; secondary education 21.6%; postsecondary education 24.9%; unknown 0.7%. *Literacy:* resident population is virtually 100% literate.
Health (1992): physicians 110 (1 per 548 persons); hospital beds 121 (1 per 500 persons); infant mortality rate per 1,000 live births (1991–92 avg.) 6.4.
Food (1992)[10]: daily per capita caloric intake 3,670 (vegetable products 64%, animal products 36%); 147% of FAO recommended minimum requirement.

Military

Total active duty personnel (1994): none. France and Spain are responsible for Andorra's external security; a 100-person police force maintains domestic security.

[1]Roman Catholicism enjoys special recognition in accordance with Andorran tradition. [2]January 1. [3]Andorra la Vella includes Les Escaldes–Engordany and Sant Julià de Lòria. [4]Data may be incomplete. [5]Large herds of sheep and goats from Spain and France feed in Andorra in the summer. [6]The restricted size of the indigenous labour force necessitates high levels of immigration to serve the tourist trade. [7]In Spanish pesetas. [8]January. [9]Tourism (including winter-season sports, fairs, festivals, and income earned from low-duty imported manufactured items), and the banking system (of some importance as a tax haven for foreign financial investment and transactions) are the primary sources of GNP. [10]Composite values derived from Spanish and French food data.

Angola

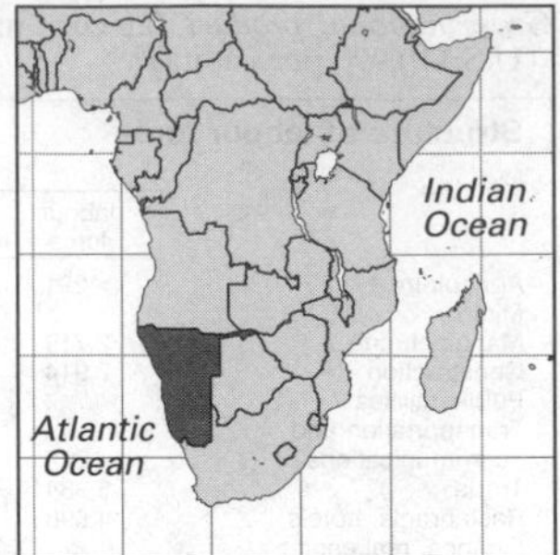

Official name: República de Angola (Republic of Angola).
Form of government: multiparty republic with one legislative house (National Assembly [220[1]]).
Head of state and government: President[2].
Capital: Luanda.
Official language: Portuguese.
Official religion: none.
Monetary unit: 1 readjusted kwanza (NKz) = 100 lwei; valuation (Oct. 6, 1995) 1 U.S.$ = NKz 5,692; 1 £ = NKz 8,998.

Area and population		area		population
				1995
Provinces	Capitals	sq mi	sq km	estimate[3]
Bengo	Caxito	12,112	31,371	184,000
Benguela	Benguela	12,273	31,788	702,000
Bié	Kuito	27,148	70,314	1,246,000
Cabinda	Cabinda	2,807	7,270	185,000
Cunene	N'Giva	34,495	89,342	245,000
Huambo	Huambo	13,233	34,274	1,687,000
Huíla	Lubango	28,958	75,002	948,000
Kuando Kubango	Menongue	76,853	199,049	137,000
Kuanza Norte	N'Dalatando	9,340	24,190	412,000
Kuanza Sul	Sumbe	21,490	55,660	688,000
Luanda	Luanda	934	2,418	2,002,000
Lunda Norte	Lucapa	39,685	102,783	311,000
Lunda Sul	Saurimo	17,625	45,649	160,000
Malanje	Malanje	37,684	97,602	953,000
Moxico	Lwena	86,110	223,023	349,000
Namibe	Namibe	22,447	58,137	135,000
Uíge	Uíge	22,663	58,698	948,000
Zaire	M'Banza Kongo	15,494	40,130	247,000
TOTAL		481,354[4]	1,246,700	11,558,000[4]

Demography

Population (1995): 11,558,000.
Density (1995): persons per sq mi 24.0, persons per sq km 9.3.
Urban-rural (1990): urban 28.3%; rural 71.7%.
Sex distribution (1991): male 48.80%; female 51.20%.
Age breakdown (1995): under 15, 45.0%; 15–29, 25.5%; 30–44, 15.1%; 45–59, 8.9%; 60 and over, 5.5%.
Population projection: (2000) 13,400,000; (2010) 18,082,000.
Doubling time: 22 years.
Ethnic composition (1983): Ovimbundu 37.2%; Mbundu 21.6%; Kongo 13.2%; Luimbe-Nganguela 5.4%; Nyaneka-Humbe 5.4%; Chokwe 4.2%; Luvale (Luena) 3.4%; Luchazi 2.4%; Ambo (Ovambo) 2.4%; Lunda 1.2%; Mbunda 1.2%; Portuguese 0.5%; mestizo 0.5%; other 0.4%.
Religious affiliation (1980): Christian 90.0%, of which Roman Catholic 68.7%, Protestant 19.8%; traditional beliefs 9.5%; other 0.5%.
Major cities (1988): Luanda 1,134,000; Huambo 203,000[5]; Benguela 155,000[5]; Lobito 150,000[5]; Lubango 105,000[6].

Vital statistics

Birth rate per 1,000 population (1990–95): 51.3 (world avg. 25.0).
Death rate per 1,000 population (1990–95): 19.2 (world avg. 9.3).
Natural increase rate per 1,000 population (1990–95): 32.1 (world avg. 15.7).
Total fertility rate (avg. births per childbearing woman; 1990–95): 7.2.
Marriage rate per 1,000 population (1972): 4.5.
Divorce rate per 1,000 population: n.a.
Life expectancy at birth (1990–95): male 44.9 years; female 48.1 years.
Major causes of death (percentage of total deaths; 1990): diarrheal diseases 25.8%; malaria 19.4%; cholera 7.3%; acute respiratory infections 6.8%; measles 6.2%.

National economy

Budget (1991). Revenue: NKz 186,383,000,000 (1989; tax revenue 82.8%, of which petroleum taxes 53.1%, income and property taxes 11.6%, domestic production taxes 9.5%, import duties 6.3%; nontax revenue 17.2%). Expenditures: NKz 275,468,000,000 (defense and internal security 36.9%; administration 23.9%; education 17.5%; health 7.5%; energy 3.6%; other 10.6%).
Public debt (external, outstanding; 1993): U.S.$7,727,000,000.
Tourism: receipts from visitors (1993) U.S.$20,000,000; expenditures by nationals abroad (1992) U.S.$75,000,000.
Production (metric tons except as noted). Agriculture, forestry, fishing (1994): cassava 986,000, bananas 275,000, sugarcane 220,000, corn (maize) 201,000, sweet potatoes 182,000, millet 53,000, palm oil 50,000, dry beans 34,000, peanuts (groundnuts) 17,000, coffee 5,000; livestock (number of live animals) 3,280,000 cattle, 1,570,000 goats, 820,000 pigs, 255,000 sheep, 6,000,000 chickens; roundwood (1993) 6,583,000 cu m; fish catch (1993) 80,723. Mining and quarrying (1994): diamonds 1,350,000 carats. Manufacturing (1990): fresh meat 93,000; bread 45,000; corn flour 35,000; wheat flour 22,000; laundry soap 7,556; sugar 3,190[7]; pasta 3,190[7]; leather shoes 132,000 pairs[7]; beer 410,000 hectolitres; soft drinks 69,050 hectolitres[7]; matches 6,357,000 boxes[7]. Construction (value in NKz '000,000; 1986): residential 608; nonresidential 1,977. Energy production (consumption): electricity (kW-hr; 1992) 1,855,000,000 (1,855,000,000); coal, none (none); crude petroleum (barrels; 1992) 192,634,000 (10,373,000); petroleum products (metric tons; 1992) 1,317,000 (346,000); natural gas (cu m; 1992) 166,576,000 (166,576,000).

Gross national product (at current market prices; 1989): U.S.$6,010,000,000 (U.S. $620 per capita).

Structure of gross domestic product and labour force	1991			
	in value NKz '000,000[8]	% of total value	labour force	% of labour force
Agriculture	28,558	10.3	2,892,000	69.4
Mining	160,750	58.2		
Manufacturing	6,935	2.5		
Construction	5,235	1.9		
Finance	2,360	0.9	438,000	10.5
Trade	16,803	6.1		
Public utilities	818	0.3		
Transportation and communications	6,255	2.3		
Pub. admin., defense; Services	48,391	17.5	836,000	20.1
Other	...	...		
TOTAL	276,105	100.0	4,166,000	100.0

Population economically active (1991): total 4,166,000; activity rate of total population 40.3% (participation rates over age 10, 60.1%; female 38.4%; unemployed, n.a.).
Price and earnings indexes: n.a.
Household income and expenditure. Average household size (1980) 4.8; annual income per household: n.a.; sources of income: n.a.; expenditure: n.a.
Land use (1993): forested 41.6%; meadows and pastures 23.3%; agricultural and under permanent cultivation 2.8%; other 32.3%.

Foreign trade

Balance of trade (current prices)	1989	1990	1991	1992	1993	1994
U.S.$'000,000	+1,191	+1,276	+2,080	+1,160	+1,551	+1,565
% of total	25.1%	25.1%	43.6%	19.0%	35.2%	37.6%

Imports (1991): U.S.$1,347,000,000 (current consumption goods 50.2%, capital goods 20.2%, intermediate consumption goods 18.9%, transport equipment 6.8%). *Major import sources:* Portugal 29.8%; United States 10.5%; France 9.7%; Japan 7.8%; Brazil 7.3%.
Exports (1991): U.S.$3,427,000,000 (mineral fuels 89.8%, diamonds 5.5%). *Major export destinations:* United States 56.6%; Germany 5.6%; Brazil 4.9%; The Netherlands 4.2%; United Kingdom 3.4%; Belgium-Luxembourg 3.3%.

Transport and communications

Transport. Railroads (1988): route length 1,739 mi, 2,798 km; passenger-mi 203,000,000, passenger-km 326,000,000; short ton-mi cargo 1,178,000,000, metric ton-km cargo 1,720,000,000. Roads (1992): total length 45,128 mi, 72,626 km (paved 25%). Vehicles (1992): passenger cars 122,000; trucks and buses 42,200. Merchant marine (1992): vessels (100 gross tons and over) 113; total deadweight tonnage 123,479. Air transport (1991)[9]: passenger-mi 771,000,000, passenger-km 1,241,000,000; short ton-mi cargo 28,000,000, metric ton-km cargo 42,000,000; airports (1995) with scheduled flights 17.
Communications. Daily newspapers (1994): total number 4; total circulation 84,500[10]; circulation per 1,000 population 7.5[10]. Radio (1994): total number of receivers 450,000 (1 per 25 persons). Television (1994): total number of receivers 50,500 (1 per 222 persons). Telephones (main lines; 1993): 53,300 (1 per 204 persons).

Education and health

Education (1990–91)	schools	teachers	students	student/ teacher ratio
Primary (age 7–10)	6,308[11]	31,062	990,155	31.9
Secondary (age 11–16)	5,276[11]	5,138[12]	166,812	...
Voc., teacher tr.	...	566[12]	19,687	...
Higher	1[11]	439	6,534	14.9

Educational attainment: n.a. *Literacy* (1990): percentage of population age 15 and over literate 41.7%; males literate 55.6%; females literate 28.5%.
Health (1990): physicians 662 (1 per 15,136 persons); hospital beds 11,857 (1 per 845 persons); infant mortality rate per 1,000 live births (1990–95) 124.0.
Food (1992): daily per capita caloric intake 1,839 (vegetable products 90%, animal products 10%); (1984) 84% of FAO recommended minimum requirement.

Military

Total active duty personnel (1995): 82,000 (army 91.5%, navy 1.8%, air force 6.7%). *Military expenditure as percentage of GNP* (1986): 23.9% (world 5.4%); per capita expenditure U.S.$173.

[1]Excludes 3 seats for Angolans abroad not filled at October 1992 elections. [2]President to be assisted by two vice presidents pending implementation of the November 1994 Lusaka Protocol. [3]Unified national estimates and projections based on sample surveys, partial censuses, and analysis of provincial vital statistics. [4]Detail does not add to total given because of rounding. [5]1983. [6]1984. [7]1989. [8]At official prices of 1980. [9]TAAG Airline only. [10]Circulation for three newspapers only. [11]1985–86. [12]1989–90.

Antigua and Barbuda

Official name: Antigua and Barbuda.
Form of government: constitutional monarchy with two legislative houses (Senate [17]; House of Representatives [17]).
Chief of state: British Monarch represented by Governor-General.
Head of government: Prime Minister.
Capital: Saint John's.
Official language: English.
Official religion: none.
Monetary unit: 1 Eastern Caribbean dollar (EC$) = 100 cents; valuation (Oct. 6, 1995) 1 U.S.$ = EC$2.70; 1 £ = EC$4.26.

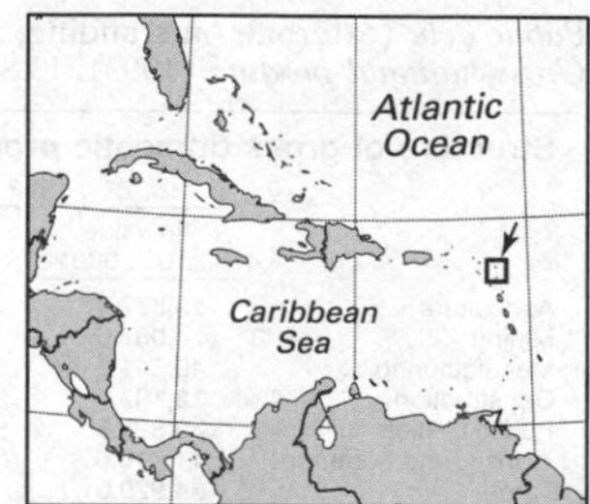

Area and population	area		population
			1991
	sq mi	sq km	census
Parishes[1]			
Saint George	9.3	24.1	4,473
Saint John's	28.5	73.8	35,635
Saint Mary	22.0	57.0	5,303
Saint Paul	18.5	47.9	6,117
Saint Peter	12.7	32.9	3,622
Saint Phillip	17.0	44.0	2,964
Islands[1]			
Barbuda	62.0	160.6	1,241
Redonda	0.5	1.3	[2]
TOTAL	170.5	441.6	59,355[3]

Demography

Population (1995): 63,900.
Density (1995): persons per sq mi 374.8, persons per sq km 144.7.
Urban-rural (1991)[4]: urban 36.2%; rural 63.8%.
Sex distribution (1991): male 48.20%; female 51.80%.
Age breakdown (1991): under 15, 30.4%; 15–29, 27.8%; 30–44, 20.5%; 45–59, 10.2%; 60–74, 7.7%; 75 and over, 3.4%.
Population projection: (2000) 64,000; (2010) 64,000.
Doubling time: 58 years.
Ethnic composition (1991): black 91.3%; mixed 3.7%; white 2.4%; Syrian/Lebanese 0.6%; Indo-Pakistani 0.4%; Amerindian 0.3%; other 1.3%.
Religious affiliation (1991): Protestant 73.7%, of which Anglican 32.1%, Moravian 12.0%, Methodist 9.1%, Seventh-day Adventist 8.8%; Roman Catholic 10.8%; Jehovah's Witness 1.2%; Rastafarian 0.8%; other religion/no religion/not stated 13.5%.
Major cities (1991)[5]: Saint John's 21,514.

Vital statistics

Birth rate per 1,000 population (1994): 17.3 (world avg. 25.0); (1988) legitimate 23.4%; illegitimate 76.6%.
Death rate per 1,000 population (1994): 5.4 (world avg. 9.3).
Natural increase rate per 1,000 population (1994): 11.9 (world avg. 15.7).
Total fertility rate (avg. births per childbearing woman; 1994): 1.7.
Marriage rate per 1,000 population (1988): 4.9.
Divorce rate per 1,000 population (1988): 0.2.
Life expectancy at birth (1994): male 71.1 years; female 75.3 years.
Major causes of death per 100,000 population (1988): diseases of the circulatory system 237.5; malignant neoplasms (cancers) 44.5; diseases of the respiratory system 44.5; endocrine and metabolic disorders 25.4; ill-defined conditions 68.6.

National economy

Budget (1993). Revenue: EC$277,900,000 (current revenue 91.4%, of which consumption taxes 25.5%, taxes on goods and services 16.6%, import duties 15.8%, nontax revenue 15.3%; development revenue 5.0%; grants 3.6%). Expenditures: EC$299,700,000 (current expenditures 89.1%; development expenditures 10.9%).
Production (metric tons except as noted). Agriculture, forestry, fishing (1994): vegetables 3,000, mangoes 2,000, cantaloupes and other melons 1,000, limes 249[6], sweet potatoes 219[6], "Antiguan Black" pineapples 126[6]; livestock (number of live animals) 16,000 cattle, 13,000 sheep; roundwood, n.a.; fish catch (1993) 2,400 (of which spiny lobster 300). Mining and quarrying: crushed stone for local use. Manufacturing (1988): rum 4,000 hectolitres; wine and vodka 2,000 hectolitres; other manufactures include beer, garments, paints, and furniture. Construction (1993): gross value of building applications EC$151,600,000. Energy production (consumption): electricity (kW-hr; 1992) 95,000,000 (95,000,000); coal, none (none); crude petroleum, none (none); petroleum products (metric tons; 1992) negligible (94,000); natural gas, none (none).
Population economically active (1991): total 26,753; activity rate of total population 45.1% (participation rates: ages 15–64, 69.7%; female 45.6%; unemployed, n.a.[7]).

Price and earnings indexes (1990 = 100)	1988	1989	1990	1991	1992	1993
GDP deflator[8]	94.0	97.6	100.0	103.1	104.5	105.8
Weekly earnings index	...	...	...	...	...	...

Household income and expenditure. Average household size (1991) 3.2; income per household: n.a.; sources of income: n.a.; expenditure (1974)[9]: food and nonalcoholic beverages 42.9%, housing 23.3%, transportation 10.0%, clothing and footwear 7.5%, energy 5.5%, alcoholic beverages and tobacco 3.6%, other 7.2%.
Gross national product (at current market prices; 1993): U.S.$425,000,000 (U.S.$6,390 per capita).

Structure of gross domestic product and labour force	1992		1991	
	in value EC$'000,000[10]	% of total value	labour force	% of labour force
Agriculture, fishing	41.2	4.1	1,040	3.9
Quarrying	17.2	1.7	64	0.2
Manufacturing	26.8	2.7	1,444	5.4
Construction	104.4	10.5	3,109	11.6
Public utilities	43.2	4.3	435	1.6
Transportation and communications	198.6	19.9	2,395	9.0
Trade, restaurants, and hotels	227.8	22.8	8,524	31.9
Finance, real estate	151.3	15.1	1,454	5.4
Pub. admin., defense	166.3	16.6	2,572	9.6
Services	68.8	6.9	5,207	19.5
Other	−46.3[11]	−4.6[11]	509	1.9
TOTAL	999.4[12]	100.0	26,753	100.0

Land use (1993): forested 11.0%; meadows and pastures 9.0%; agricultural and under permanent cultivation 18.0%; other 62.0%.
Public debt (external, outstanding; end of 1994): U.S.$327,000,000.
Tourism (1993): receipts from visitors U.S.$277,000,000; expenditures by nationals abroad U.S.$23,000,000.

Foreign trade[13]

Balance of trade (current prices)	1988	1989	1990	1991	1992	1993
U.S.$'000,000	−280	−316	−325	−347	−346	−385
% of total	80.5%	83.4%	83.0%	80.0%	70.7%	77.8%

Imports (1992): U.S.$398,000,000 ([14]agricultural products 11.0%, unspecified 89.0%). *Major import sources* (1989)[14]: United States 27.0%; United Kingdom 16.0%; Canada 4.0%; OECS 3.0%; Italy 3.0%.
Exports (1992): U.S.$34,000,000 ([14]reexports [significantly, petroleum products] 82.0%, domestic exports 18.0%). *Major export destinations* (1989)[14]: United States 41.0%; United Kingdom 19.0%; Germany 19.0%.

Transport and communications

Transport. Railroads[15]. Roads (1993): total length 721 mi, 1,161 km (paved 33%). Vehicles (1993): passenger cars 14,300; trucks and buses 3,800. Merchant marine (1992): vessels (100 gross tons and over) 292; total deadweight tonnage 997,381. Air transport (1991): passenger-mi 121,000,000, passenger-km 195,000,000; short ton-mi cargo 137,000, metric ton-km cargo 200,000; airports (1995) with scheduled flights 2.
Communications. Daily newspapers: none[16]. Radio (1994): total number of receivers 75,000 (1 per 0.9 persons). Television (1994): total number of receivers 28,000 (1 per 2.3 persons). Telephones (main lines; 1993): 19,200 (1 per 3.3 persons).

Education and health

Education (1991–92)	schools	teachers	students	student/ teacher ratio
Primary (age 5–10)	43	549	10,770	19.6
Secondary (age 11–16)	12	353	4,373	12.5
Higher	1	45	590	13.1

Educational attainment (1991). Percentage of population age 25 and over having: no formal schooling 1.1%; primary education 50.5%; secondary 33.4%; higher (not university) 5.4%; university 6.2%; other/unknown 3.4%.
Literacy (1990): total population age 15 and over literate 40,000 (90.0%).
Health (1991): physicians 59 (1 per 1,085 persons); hospital beds 226[17] (1 per 283 persons); infant mortality rate per 1,000 live births (1994) 18.5.
Food (1992): daily per capita caloric intake 2,458 (vegetable products 69%, animal products 31%); 105% of FAO recommended minimum requirement.

Military

Total active duty personnel (1992): a 90-member defense force is part of the Eastern Caribbean regional security system.

[1]Community councils on Antigua and the local government council on Barbuda are the organs of local government. [2]Uninhabited. [3]Unadjusted de jure population excluding institutionalized population; de jure population adjusted for undercount (including institutionalized population) is 63,896; de facto population adjusted for undercount (de jure population plus visitors) is 65,978. [4]Urban defined as city of Saint John's. [5]Large settlements include (1991): All Saints 2,230; Liberta 1,473; Codrington 814. [6]1988. [7]In 1993 unemployment probably decreased in the government sector and increased in the construction and manufacturing sectors. [8]The consumer price index is unavailable after 1991; the GDP deflator is a broad measure of price trends in the overall economy. [9]Weights of consumer price index components. [10]At factor cost. [11]Less imputed bank service charges. [12]Detail does not add to total given because of rounding. [13]Exports f.o.b.; imports c.i.f. [14]Estimated percentages. [15]Privately owned tracks are mostly nonoperative. [16]Three weekly newspapers and one twice-weekly newspaper had a total circulation of 12,200 in 1990. [17]Number of beds in public general hospital.

Argentina

Official name: República Argentina (Argentine Republic).
Form of government: federal republic with two legislative houses (Senate [72]; Chamber of Deputies [257]).
Head of state and government: President.
Capital: Buenos Aires.
Official language: Spanish.
Official religion: Roman Catholicism.
Monetary unit: 1 peso (pl. pesos)[1] (Ps) = 100 centavos; valuation (Oct. 6, 1995) 1 U.S.$ = Ps 1.00; 1 £ = Ps 1.58.

Area and population

		area		population
				1991
Provinces	Capitals	sq mi	sq km	census
Buenos Aires	La Plata	118,754	307,571	12,594,974
Catamarca	Catamarca	39,615	102,602	264,234
Chaco	Resistencia	38,469	99,633	839,677
Chubut	Rawson	86,752	224,686	357,189
Córdoba	Córdoba	63,831	165,321	2,766,683
Corrientes	Corrientes	34,054	88,199	795,594
Entre Ríos	Paraná	30,418	78,781	1,020,257
Formosa	Formosa	27,825	72,066	398,413
Jujuy	San Salvador de Jujuy	20,548	53,219	512,329
La Pampa	Santa Rosa	55,382	143,440	259,996
La Rioja	La Rioja	34,626	89,680	220,729
Mendoza	Mendoza	57,462	148,827	1,412,481
Misiones	Posadas	11,506	29,801	788,915
Neuquén	Neuquén	36,324	94,078	388,833
Río Negro	Viedma	78,384	203,013	506,772
Salta	Salta	60,034	155,488	866,153
San Juan	San Juan	34,614	89,651	528,715
San Luis	San Luis	29,633	76,748	286,458
Santa Cruz	Río Gallegos	94,187	243,943	159,839
Santa Fe	Santa Fe	51,354	133,007	2,798,422
Santiago del Estero	Santiago del Estero	52,645	136,351	671,988
Tierra del Fuego[2]	Ushuaia	8,329	21,571	69,369
Tucumán	San Miguel de Tucumán	8,697	22,524	1,142,105
Other federal entity				
Distrito Federal	Buenos Aires	77	200	2,965,403
TOTAL		1,073,518[3]	2,780,400	32,615,528

Demography

Population (1995): 34,587,000.
Density (1995): persons per sq mi 32.2, persons per sq km 12.4.
Urban-rural (1991): urban 86.9%; rural 13.1%.
Sex distribution (1991): male 48.90%; female 51.10%.
Age breakdown (1991): under 15, 30.6%; 15–29, 23.3%; 30–44, 19.3%; 45–59, 13.9%; 60–74, 9.6%; 75 and over, 3.3%.
Population projection: (2000) 36,648,000; (2010) 40,755,000.
Doubling time: 63 years.
Ethnic composition (1986): European 85%; mestizo, Amerindian, and other 15%.
Religious affiliation (1992): Roman Catholic 91.6%; other 8.4%.
Major cities (1991): Buenos Aires 2,960,976 (Greater Buenos Aires 12,582,-321); Córdoba 1,179,067; Rosario 1,078,374[4]; La Plata 542,567.

Vital statistics

Birth rate per 1,000 population (1995): 19.5 (world avg. 25.0); (1982) legitimate 67.5%; illegitimate 29.8%; unknown 2.7%.
Death rate per 1,000 population (1995): 8.6 (world avg. 9.3).
Natural increase rate per 1,000 population (1995): 8.6 (world avg. 15.7).
Total fertility rate (avg. births per childbearing woman; 1995): 2.7.
Marriage rate per 1,000 population (1990): 5.8.
Life expectancy at birth (1995): male 68.2 years; female 71.5 years.
Major causes of death per 100,000 population (1991): circulatory diseases 337.3; neoplasms (cancers) 143.0; accidents 51.6; respiratory diseases 49.0.

National economy

Budget (1993). Revenue: U.S.$51,885,200,000 (current revenue 97.2%, of which tax revenue 90.5%, nontax revenue 6.1%, other 0.6%; captial revenue 2.8%). Expenditure: U.S.$52,151,000,000 (1989; social security 35.3%; economic services 16.0%; education 9.9%; defense 9.9%; transportation and communications 8.8%; debt service 7.4%).
Land use (1993): forested 18.6%; meadows and pastures 51.9%; agricultural and under permanent cultivation 9.9%; other 19.6%.
Production (metric tons except as noted). Agriculture, forestry, fishing (1994): sugarcane 17,500,000, soybeans 11,318,000, corn (maize) 10,246,000, wheat 10,680,000, sunflower seeds 3,903,000, grapes 2,900,000, sorghum 2,160,000, potatoes 2,100,000, tomatoes 750,000; livestock (number of live animals) 50,000,000 cattle, 20,000,000 sheep; roundwood (1993) 11,865,000 cu m; fish catch (1993) 930,592. Mining and quarrying (1993): silver 2,674,938 troy oz; gold 49,833 troy oz. Manufacturing (1992): processed meat 8,785,000; wheat flour 3,113,000; vegetable 3,068,000; sugar 1,282,000; paper 977,000; sulfuric acid 218,000; soda 19,545,000 hectolitres; wine 16,193,000 hectolitres; beer 9,505,000 hectolitres. Construction (authorized; 1990): 7,750,600 sq m. Energy production (consumption): electricity (kW-hr; 1993) 63,038,000,-000 (64,280,000,000); coal (metric tons; 1993) 167,000 (1,133,000); crude petroleum (barrels; 1993) 216,836,000 (186,053,000); petroleum products (metric tons; 1993) 22,134,000 (19,430,000); natural gas (cu m; 1993) 26,614,-000,000 (28,602,000,000).

Public debt (external, outstanding; 1993): U.S.$61,534,000,000.
Gross national product (1993): U.S.$244,013,000,000 (U.S.$7,290 per capita).

Structure of gross domestic product and labour force

	1992		1980	
	in value A'000,000[1]	% of total value	labour force	% of labour force
Agriculture	13,577.4	6.0	1,200,992	12.0
Mining	4,067.0	1.8	47,171	0.5
Manufacturing	49,541.1	21.9	1,985,995	19.9
Construction	12,107.4	5.3	1,003,175	10.1
Public utilities	3,825.8	1.7	103,256	1.0
Transp. and commun.	11,718.6	5.2	460,476	4.6
Trade	34,929.0	15.4	1,702,080	17.0
Finance	38,132.6	16.8	395,704	4.0
Pub. admin., defense; Services	59,021.5	26.0	2,399,039	24.0
Other	−282.9[5]	−0.1[5]	691,302	6.9
TOTAL	226,637.6[3]	100.0	9,989,190	100.0

Population economically active (1990): total 12,305,346; activity rate of total population 38.1% (participation rates: ages 15–64, 59.6%; female 28.2%; unemployed [1989] 7.3%).

Price and earnings indexes (1990 = 100)[1]

	1990	1991	1992	1993	1994
Consumer price index	100.0	272	339	375	391
Hourly earnings index	100.0	194.3	238.4	...	...

Household size and expenditure. Average household size (1991) 3.8; expenditure (1985–86): food 38.2%, transportation 11.6%, housing 9.3%, energy 9.0%, clothing and footwear 8.0%, health 7.9%, recreation and culture 7.5%, education 2.6%, other 5.9%.
Tourism (1993): receipts U.S.$3,614,000,000; expenditures U.S.$2,445,000,000.

Foreign trade[6]

Balance of trade (current prices)

	1989	1990	1991	1992	1993	1994
U.S.$'000,000	+5,706	+8,627	+4,572	−1,388	−1,576	−4,002
% of total	42.5%	53.7%	23.6%	5.4%	5.7%	11.3%

Imports (1993): U.S.$16,651,400,000 (machinery and transport equipment 47.1%, chemical products 13.8%, manufactured products 13.7%, food products and live animals 4.8%, petroleum and petroleum products 2.5%). *Major import sources:* U.S. 23.2%; Brazil 21.4%; Germany 6.1%; Italy 5.9%; France 4.4%; Chile 4.2%; Japan 4.0%.
Exports (1993): U.S.$12,869,100,000 (food products and live animals 40.7%, manufactured products 13.7%, machinery and transport equipment 11.0%, petroleum and petroleum products 9.5%, vegetable and animal oils 8.1%, chemical products 5.3%). *Major export destinations:* Brazil 21.5%; U.S. 9.7%; The Netherlands 9.7%; Germany 4.8%; Chile 4.5%; Italy 3.9%; Spain 3.8%; Japan 3.8%.

Transport and communications

Transport. Railroads (1992): route length (1990) 34,059 km; passenger-km 6,705,059,000; metric ton-km cargo 3,707,489,000. Roads (1992): total length 133,954 mi, 215,578 km (paved 29%). Vehicles (1993): passenger cars 4,856,-000; commercial vehicles and buses 1,664,000. Merchant marine (1992): vessels (100 gross tons and over) 423; total deadweight tonnage 1,173,-105. Air transport (1993): passenger-km 9,380,188,000; metric ton-km cargo 1,118,323,000; airports (1995) with scheduled flights 42.
Communications. Daily newspapers (1992): total number 190; total circulation 4,780,000; circulation per 1,000 population 143. Radio (1994): 21,500,000 receivers (1 per 1.6 persons). Television (1994): 7,165,000 receivers (1 per 4.8 persons). Telephones (main lines; 1993): 4,114,500 (1 per 8.2 persons).

Education and health

Education (1991–92)

	schools	teachers	students	student/ teacher ratio
Primary (age 6–12)	24,511	306,372	5,041,090	16.5
Secondary (age 13–17)[7]	7,224[8]	283,583	2,262,378	8.0
Higher	1,540[9]	89,609	1,077,212	12.0

Educational attainment (1991). Percentage of population age 25 and over having: no formal schooling 5.7%; less than primary education 22.3%; primary 34.6%; incomplete secondary 12.5%; complete secondary 12.8%; higher 12.0%. *Literacy* (1995): percentage of total population age 15 and over literate 96.2%; males literate 96.2%; females literate 96.2%.
Health (1992): physicians 88,800 (1 per 376 persons); hospital beds 147,000 (1 per 227 persons); infant mortality rate 34.0.
Food (1992): daily per capita caloric intake 2,880 (vegetable products 66%; animal products 34%); 109% of FAO recommended minimum requirement.

Military

Total active duty personnel (1995): 67,300 (army 60.0%, navy 26.8%, air force 13.2%). *Military expenditure as percentage of GNP* (1993): 1.7% (world 3.3%); per capita expenditure: U.S.$127.

[1]On Jan. 1, 1992, the austral was replaced by the peso at a ratio of 10,000 to 1. [2]Area of Tierra del Fuego (province since 1991) excludes claims to British-held islands in the South Atlantic Ocean. [3]Detail does not add to total given because of rounding. [4]*Municipio.* [5]Import duties. [6]Import figures are f.o.b. in balance of trade and c.i.f. in commodities and trading partners. [7]Secondary includes vocational and teacher training. [8]1988–89. [9]1987.

Armenia

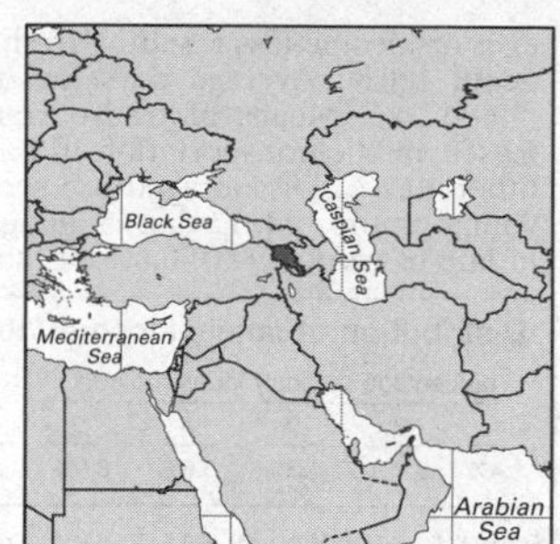

Official name: Hayastani Hanrapetut'yun (Republic of Armenia).
Form of government: unitary multiparty republic with a single legislative body (Supreme Council [190]).
Head of state: President.
Head of government: Prime Minister.
Capital: Yerevan.
Official language: Armenian.
Official religion: none.
Monetary unit[1]: 1 dram = 100 lumas; valuation (Oct. 6, 1995) official, 1 U.S.$ = 400.00 drams; 1 £ = 632.36 drams.

Area and population

Administrative subdivisions	Capitals	area sq mi	area sq km	population 1987 estimate
Cities[2]				
Gyumri	—	...	...	228,400
Kirovakan	—	...	...	169,400
Yerevan	—	...	...	1,184,500
Rural districts				
Akhuryani	Akhuryan	223	577	39,500
Amasiayi	Amasia	235	609	19,300
Anii	Maralik	166	429	19,700
Aparani	Aparan	228	591	19,900
Aragatsi	Tsaghkahovit	148	382	14,100
Ararati	Vedi	540	1,399	85,100
Artashati	Artashat	200	517	95,500
Art'iki	Art'ik	187	484	44,800
Ashotski	Ghukasyan	211	547	9,800
Ashtaraki	Ashtarak	267	692	36,400
Baghramyani	Baghramyan	175	453	16,100
Ejmiatsini	Ejmiatsin	141	366	121,000
Ghap'ani	Ghap'an	529	1,371	61,600
Gorisi	Goris	290	752	38,000
Gugark'i	Gugark'	297	770	31,000
Hoktemberyani	Hoktemberyan	163	423	109,900
Hrazdan	Hrazdan	366	948	78,600
Ijevani	Ijevan	516	1,336	46,600
Kamoyi	Kamo	269	697	56,400
Kotayki	Kotayk	313	810	108,200
Krasnoselski	Krasnoselsk	269	697	27,900
Martunu	Martuni	458	1,185	67,900
Masisi	Masis	70	182	64,400
Meghru	Meghri	256	664	15,100
Nairii	Yeghvard	133	344	47,200
Noyemberyani	Noyemberyan	208	538	29,700
Sevani	Sevan	152	393	42,700
Sisiani	Sisian	664	1,719	34,600
Spitaki	Spitak	212	549	46,300
Step'anavani	Step'anavan	246	637	36,500
T'alini	T'alin	421	1,091	35,100
Tashiri	Tashir	266	690	39,100
Taushi	Berd	318	824	34,200
T'umanyani	Alaverdi	433	1,121	58,200
Vardenisi	Vardenis	444	1,151	60,200
Vayki	Vayk	453	1,172	17,000
Yeghegnadzori	Yeghegnadzor	438	1,134	35,400
TOTAL		11,500[3]	29,800[3]	3,411,900[3]

Demography

Population (1995): 3,548,000.
Density (1995): persons per sq mi 308.5, persons per sq km 119.1.
Urban-rural (1993): urban 67.7%; rural 32.3%.
Sex distribution (1993): male 48.45%; female 51.55%.
Age breakdown (1993): under 15, 30.1%; 15–29, 24.4%; 30–44, 22.4%; 45–59, 12.3%; 60–74, 8.6%; 75 and over, 2.2%.
Population projection: (2000) 3,685,000; (2010) 3,854,000.
Doubling time: 87 years.
Ethnic composition (1989): Armenian 93.3%; Azerbaijani 2.6%; other 4.1%.
Religious affiliation: believers are predominantly Armenian Apostolic.
Major cities (1991): Yerevan 1,283,000; Gyumri 163,000[4]; Kirovakan 76,000[4].

Vital statistics

Birth rate per 1,000 population (1994): 13.5 (world avg. 25.0); (1992) legitimate 87.7%; illegitimate 12.3%.
Death rate per 1,000 population (1994): 6.5 (world avg. 9.3).
Natural increase rate per 1,000 population (1994): 7.0 (world avg. 15.7).
Total fertility rate (avg. births per childbearing woman; 1993): 3.3.
Marriage rate per 1,000 population (1994): 4.6.
Divorce rate per 1,000 population (1994): 0.9.
Life expectancy at birth (1993): male 68.4 years; female 75.4 years.
Major causes of death per 100,000 population (1993): circulatory diseases 369.7; cancers 93.8; accidents and violence 62.8; respiratory diseases 51.4.

National economy

Budget (1993). Revenue: 293,800,000,000 rubles (tax revenue 74.3%, of which value-added tax 29.0%, enterprise profits tax 25.4%, income tax 8.9%, excise taxes 6.6%). Expenditures: 303,400,000,000 rubles (national economy 23.9%; education 8.3%; health 6.3%).
Production (metric tons except as noted). Agriculture, forestry, fishing (1994): vegetables (except potatoes) 424,000, potatoes 400,000, milk 270,000, cereals 240,000, wheat 174,000, grapes 130,000; livestock (number of live animals) 736,000 sheep and goats, 502,000 cattle, 115,000 pigs, 3,000,000 poultry; roundwood (1991) 44,100 cu m; fish catch (1993) 4,300. Mining and quarrying (1993): copper ore 500,000; limestone 500,000; gold 16,100 troy oz. Manufacturing (value in drams; 1993): mechanical equipment 105,465; food products 69,004; textiles 28,620; leather products 21,981; fabricated metal products 19,800; chemical products 16,097. Construction (value in '000,000 Russian rubles; 1993): residential 21,729; nonresidential 28,404. Energy production (consumption): electricity (kW-hr; 1992) 9,000,000,000 (9,000,000,000); coal (metric tons; 1992) none (141,000); petroleum products (metric tons; 1990) 292,000 (4,346,000); natural gas (cu m; 1992) none (1,860,000,000).
Gross national product (1993): U.S.$2,462,000,000 (U.S.$660 per capita).

Structure of gross domestic product and labour force

	1993 in value '000,000 rubles	% of total value	labour force	% of labour force
Agriculture	412,137	56.7	493,000	30.2
Manufacturing, mining }	221,993	30.5	380,000	23.2
Public utilities }			46,000	2.8
Construction	33,016	4.5	122,000	7.5
Transp. and commun.	5,241	0.7	57,000	3.5
Trade	16,662	2.3	69,000	4.2
Finance	—	—	8,000	0.5
Pub. admin., defense	—	—	29,000	1.8
Services	—	—	302,000	18.5
Other	38,312	5.3	127,000[5]	7.8[5]
TOTAL	727,361	100.0	1,633,000	100.0

Land use (1993): forest 14.1%; pasture 23.1%; agriculture 19.2%; other 43.6%.
Population economically active (1994): total 1,591,700; activity rate of total population 42.4% (participation rates: ages 16–59 [male], 16–54 [female] 75.4%; female [1990] 49.4%; unemployed 5.6%).

Price and earnings indexes (1990 = 100)

	1988	1989	1990	1991	1992	1993	1994
Consumer price index	103.0	104.0	100.0	200.3	1,852	70,956	3,779,686
Monthly earnings index	81.7	91.2	100.0	142.8	581.4	1,615.7	...

Household income and expenditure. Average household size (1989) 4.7; income per household (1990) 11,100 rubles; sources of income (1992): salaries and wages 55.8%, social benefits 31.9%, agricultural income 12.3%; expenditure (1992): retail goods 70.5%, taxes 6.2%, services 16.2%.

Foreign trade

Balance of trade (current prices)

	1990	1991	1992	1993
'000,000 drams	−869	−2,279	5,499	−134,811
% of total	11.1%	18.8%	6.2%	30.2%

Imports (1993): 290,477,000,000 drams (food products 51.2%, machinery 10.2%, light-industrial products 2.5%, chemical products 1.9%). *Major import sources:* Russia 64.4%; Georgia 16.2%; Turkmenistan 12.9%; Ukraine 3.3%.
Exports (1993): 155,666,000,000 drams (machinery 26.5%, light-industrial products 15.5%, chemical products 6.0%, nonferrous metals 6.0%). *Major export destinations:* Russia 74.4%; Turkmenistan 11.2%; Ukraine 5.2%; Georgia 4.0%; Belarus 2.4%.

Transport and communications

Transport. Railroads (1991): length 823 km; (1990) passenger-km 316,000,000; metric ton-km cargo 4,884,000,000. Roads (1991): length 7,700 km (paved 99%). Vehicles (1988): passenger cars 230,100. Air transport (1990): passenger km 5,556,900,000; metric ton-km cargo 49,000,000; airports (1995) 2.
Communications. Daily newspapers (1992): total number 7; total circulation 84,000; circulation per 1,000 population 23. Radio (1993): 642,000 receivers (1 per 5.6 persons). Television (1993): 722,000 receivers (1 per 5.0 persons). Telephones (main lines; 1993): 583,500 (1 per 6.4 persons).

Education and health

Education (1993–94)

	schools	teachers[6]	students	student/teacher ratio[6]
Primary (age 6–13) }	1,374	54,000	574,500	11.0
Secondary (age 14–17) }				
Voc., teacher tr.	69	...	25,200	...
Higher	14	...	46,500	...

Educational attainment (1989). Percentage of population age 25 and over having: primary education or no formal schooling 7.4%; some secondary 18.6%; completed secondary and some postsecondary 57.7%; higher 13.8%.
Health (1993): physicians 14,300 (1 per 262 persons); hospital beds 31,000 (1 per 121 persons); infant mortality rate 17.1.

Military

Total active duty personnel (1994)[7]: *c.* 32,700 (army 100%). About 9,000 Russian troops remained in Armenia in late 1994. *Military expenditure as percentage of GNP* (1992): 2.3%; per capita expenditure (1992): U.S.$20.

[1]The Armenian dram was introduced Nov. 22, 1993, to replace the Russian ruble, at a rate of 200 Russian rubles to 1 dram. [2]18 additional cities of republic jurisdiction exist. [3]Estimated total includes areas of Lake Sevan and cities and 86,700 persons not distributed by administrative subdivision. [4]1989; reduced in population by evacuation following Dec. 7, 1988, earthquake. [5]Includes self-employed and unemployed. [6]1991–92. [7]Total mobilization for war with Azerbaijan is not available; however, total reserve strength is 300,000.

Australia

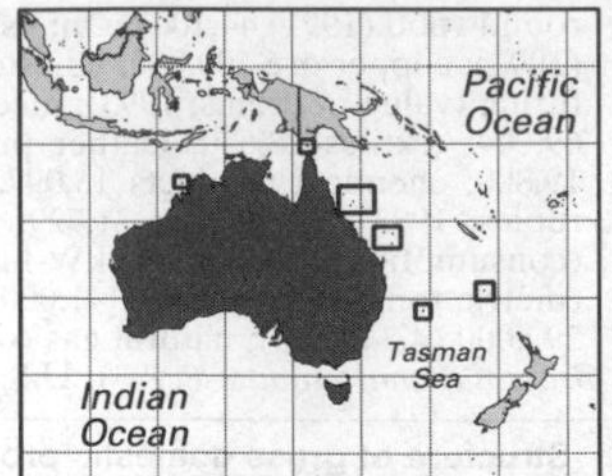

Official name: Commonwealth of Australia.
Form of government: federal parliamentary state (formally a constitutional monarchy) with two legislative houses (Senate [76]; House of Representatives [147]).
Chief of state: British Monarch represented by Governor-General.
Head of government: Prime Minister.
Capital: Canberra.
Official language: English.
Official religion: none.
Monetary unit: 1 Australian dollar ($A) = 100 cents; valuation (Oct. 6, 1995) 1 U.S.$ = $A 1.31; 1 £ = $A 2.08.

Area and population

		area		population
				1995[1]
States	Capitals	sq mi	sq km	estimate
New South Wales	Sydney	309,500	801,600	6,097,600
Queensland	Brisbane	666,900	1,727,200	3,256,000
South Australia	Adelaide	379,900	984,000	1,473,000
Tasmania	Hobart	26,200	67,800	473,200
Victoria	Melbourne	87,900	227,600	4,496,300
Western Australia	Perth	975,100	2,525,500	1,724,200
Territories				
Australian Capital Territory	Canberra	900	2,400	303,900
Northern Territory	Darwin	519,800	1,346,200	173,500
TOTAL		2,966,200	7,682,300	17,997,700

Demography

Population (1995): 18,025,000.
Density (1995): persons per sq mi 6.1, persons per sq km 2.4.
Urban-rural (1991): urban 85.3%; rural 14.7%.
Sex distribution (1994): male 49.81%; female 50.19%.
Age breakdown (1994): under 15, 21.5%; 15–29, 22.9%; 30–44, 23.4%; 45–59, 16.4%; 60–74, 11.1%; 75 and over, 4.7%.
Population projection: (2000) 18,974,000; (2010) 20,778,000.
Doubling time: 99 years.
Ethnic composition (1986): white 95.2%; aboriginal 1.5%; Asian 1.3%; other 2.0%.
Religious affiliation (1991): Christian 74.0%, of which Roman Catholic 27.3%, Anglican Church of Australia 23.8%, other Protestant 20.1% (Uniting Church and Methodist 8.2%, Presbyterian 4.3%), Orthodox 2.8%; Muslim 0.9%; Buddhist 0.8%; Jewish 0.4%; no religion 12.9%; other 11.0%.
Major cities (1994): Sydney 3,738,500; Melbourne 3,198,200; Brisbane 1,454,800; Perth 1,239,400; Adelaide 1,076,400; Newcastle 460,200; Canberra-Queanbeyan 328,000; Gold Coast–Tweed 314,000; Wollongong 251,400; Hobart 194,200.
Place of birth (1991): 77.3% native-born; 22.7% foreign-born, of which Europe 13.9% (United Kingdom 7.1%[2], Italy 1.5%, Yugoslavia 1.0%, Greece 0.8%, East and West Germany 0.7%, other Europe 1.9%), Asia and Middle East 4.8%, New Zealand 1.7%, Africa and the Americas 1.5%, other 0.8%.
Mobility (1988). Population age 15 and over living in the same residence as in 1987: 84.1%; different residence, same state 14.4%; different state or territory 1.5%.
Households (1993–94). Total number of households 6,616,800. Average household size 2.6; (1986) 1 person 19.5%, 2–3 persons 47.1%, 4–5 persons 28.2%, 6 or more persons 5.2%. Family households (1993): 4,638,000 (70.1%); nonfamily 1,978,800 (29.9%).
Immigration (1994): permanent immigrants admitted 77,940, from United Kingdom and Ireland 12.3%, New Zealand 11.5%, Vietnam 6.9%, Philippines 5.2%, Hong Kong 4.7%, India 4.0%, China 3.8%, Malaysia 1.5%, Lebanon 1.5%. Refugee arrivals (1992–93): 10,939.

Vital statistics

Birth rate per 1,000 population (1994): 14.5 (world avg. 25.0); (1993) legitimate 75.0%; illegitimate 25.0%.
Death rate per 1,000 population (1994): 7.1 (world avg. 9.3).
Natural increase rate per 1,000 population (1994): 7.4 (world avg. 15.7).
Total fertility rate (avg. births per childbearing woman; 1994): 1.85.
Marriage rate per 1,000 population (1994): 6.2.
Divorce rate per 1,000 population (1994): 2.7.
Life expectancy at birth (1994): male 74.5 years; female 80.8 years.
Major causes of death per 100,000 population (1992): diseases of the circulatory system 312.4; cancers 182.4; respiratory diseases 57.7; accidents, poisoning, and violence 26.2; digestive system diseases 22.5; nervous system diseases 15.3; endocrine, nutritional, and metabolic diseases 13.8.

Social indicators

Educational attainment (1992). Percentage of population age 15 to 69 having: no formal schooling 0.3%; incomplete secondary education 41.3%; completed secondary 14.8%[3]; postsecondary, technical, or other certificate/diploma 34.0%; university 9.6%.
Quality of working life (1992–93). Average workweek: 40.3 hours (18% overtime). Annual rate per 100,000 workers for: accidental injury and industrial disease, 3,200; death, n.a. Proportion of employed persons insured for damages or income loss resulting from: injury 100%; permanent disability 100%; death 100%. Average days lost to labour stoppages per 1,000 workdays (1993): 0.6. Means of transportation to work (1986): private automobile 69.4%; public transportation 10.1%; motorcycle and bicycle 3.2%; foot 6.6%; other 10.7%. Discouraged job seekers (considered by employers to be too young or too old, having language or training limitations, or no vacancies in line of work; 1993): 0.6% of labour force.

Distribution of family income (1990[4])

percentage of family income by decile

1	2	3	4	5	6	7	8	9	10 (highest)
1.4%	3.1%	4.2%	5.5%	6.9%	8.6%	10.6%	13.3%	17.2%	29.2%

Access to services (1976). Proportion of dwellings having access to: electricity 99.5%; bathroom 96.0%; flush toilet 92.2%; kitchen 97.9%; public sewer 73.4%.
Social participation. Eligible voters participating in last national election (1993): 95.3%; voting is compulsory. Population age 16 and over participating in voluntary work: n.a. Trade union membership in total workforce (1993): 34.7%.
Social deviance (1993). Offense rate per 100,000 population for: murder and attempted murder 4.5; sexual assault 70.2; assault (1989) 401.9; auto theft 637.0; burglary and housebreaking 2,160.7; fraud and forgery (1989) 760.4. Incidence per 100,000 in general population of: alcoholism, n.a.; drug offenses (1985) 388.2; suicide (1992) 13.1.
Material well-being (1983). Households possessing: automobile 86.0%; telephone 85.0%; refrigerator 99.6%; air conditioner 32.3%; washing machine 91.7%; hot water 98.7%; central heating 3.9%; swimming pool 10.1%.

National economy

Gross national product (1993): U.S.$310,050,000,000 (U.S.$17,510 per capita).

Structure of gross domestic product and labour force

	1992–93			
	in value $A '000,000	% of total value	labour force	% of labour force
Agriculture	12,869	3.2	398,000	4.6
Mining	17,315	4.3	91,600	1.1
Manufacturing	59,771	14.7	1,106,200	12.9
Construction	28,177	6.9	526,900	6.1
Public utilities	14,076	3.5	105,400	1.2
Transportation and communications	30,384	7.5	490,600	5.7
Trade	70,707	17.4	1,594,700	18.6
Finance	95,432	23.5	898,800	10.5
Pub. admin., defense	16,355	4.0	346,200	4.0
Services	70,735	17.4	2,120,900	24.7
Other	−9,961[5]	−2.4[5]	906,400[6]	10.6[6]
TOTAL	405,860	100.0	8,585,700	100.0

Budget (1993–94). Revenue: $A 99,100,000,000 (1991–92; income tax 68.9%, of which individual 51.1%, corporate 17.8%; excise duties and sales tax 23.5%). Expenditures: $A 115,100,000,000 (1991–92; social security and welfare 34.2%; transfers to state governments 25.2%; transfers to the nonbudget sector 9.1%; interest on public debt 5.6%).
Public debt (1993): $A 80,948,000,000.
Tourism (1993): receipts from visitors U.S.$4,655,000,000; expenditures by nationals abroad U.S.$4,100,000,000.

Manufacturing, mining, and construction enterprises (1991–92)[7]

	no. of estab-lishments	no. of employees	Avg. annual wages[8] as a % of all wages	annual turnover ($A '000,000)
Manufacturing				
Food, beverages, and tobacco	4,228	166,000	91.7	35,768
Basic metal products	889	62,100	133.5	20,521
Machinery and equipment-	5,910	114,200	99.3	15,902
Transport equipment	2,099	81,600	103.3	14,153
Chemical, petroleum, and coal products	1,213	50,500	126.8	23,462
Paper, printing, and publishing	4,913	100,300	106.0	14,332
Fabricated metal products	6,528	88,800	89.9	11,555
Miscellaneous manufacturing	3,843	58,200	92.0	8,402
Wood, wood products, and furniture	6,590	71,700	77.7	7,638
Nonmetallic mineral products	1,757	37,600	107.6	7,319
Clothing and footwear	2,574	49,800	74.8	4,847
Textiles	936	26,200	93.6	4,121
Mining[9]				
Coal, oil, and gas	257	34,111	191.8	16,901
Metallic minerals	269	31,667	163.9	11,985
Nonmetallic minerals	699	8,799	116.0	2,240
Construction	98,100	518,200	104.0[10]	34,407

Production (gross value in $A '000 except as noted). Agriculture, forestry, fishing (1992–93): livestock slaughtered 6,074,700 (cattle 3,860,400, poultry 827,900, sheep and lambs 674,600, pigs 672,900); wool 2,604,400, wheat 2,139,900, sugarcane 803,200, cotton 744,400, barley 703,900, grapes 355,800, potatoes 314,400, tomatoes 274,600, bananas 233,100, apples 168,700, oats 166,900, oranges 148,200, rice 137,200, pears 80,800, sorghum 71,500, carrots 65,700, tobacco 63,600, onions 54,100, pineapples 36,900, peaches 36,700, cauliflower 33,700, corn (maize) 31,300; livestock (number of live animals; 1994) 138,102,000 sheep, 24,062,000 cattle, 2,646,000 pigs, 63,722,000 poultry; roundwood (1993) 20,531,000 cu m; fish catch (1993) 218,339 metric tons. Mining and quarrying (metric tons [tons of contained metal]; 1993–94): iron ore 123,892,000; bauxite 41,646,000; zinc 1,025,000; lead 540,000; copper 432,000; tin 7,948; gold 255,698 kg; diamonds 39,909,000 carats. Manufacturing (metric tons except as noted; 1994–95): pig iron 7,449,000; cement 7,124,000; beef and veal 1,779,600; lamb and mutton 588,800; pork 349,300; woven cotton cloth 51,154,000 sq m; textile floor coverings 47,257,000 sq m; woven woolen cloth 8,624,000 sq m; beer 17,890,000 hectolitres; electric motors 3,101,000 units; motor vehicles 301,100 units; colour television receivers 191,800 units. Construction (buildings completed, by value in $A '000; 1994–95): new dwellings 15,509,200; alterations and additions to dwellings 2,433,300; nonresidential 9,627,100.

Retail and service enterprises (1991–92)

	no. of establishments	no. of employees	total wages and salaries ($A '000,000)	annual turnover ($A '000,000)
Retail				
Motor vehicle dealers, gasoline and tire dealers	37,305	220,661	2,572[11]	44,954
Food stores	53,166	406,299	2,461[11]	40,811
Department and general stores	459	87,148	1,175[11]	9,880
Clothing, fabrics, and furniture stores	21,688	91,138	965[11]	8,495
Household appliances and hardware stores	14,268	75,355	629	12,012
Services[12]				
Real estate agents	5,741	42,196	835	2,201
Architectural services	4,534	17,717	354	1,030
Surveying services	1,104	6,872	116	309
Engineering and technical services	5,190	28,326	682	1,716
Legal services	6,459	55,363	500	3,069
Accounting services	6,048	49,479	503	2,334
Computing services	3,691	24,067	585	1,628
Advertising services	2,390	16,048	423	4,675
Debt collecting and credit reporting services	234	2,658	52	142
Pest control services	565	2,902	44	135
Cleaning services	4,181	44,322	330	622
Security/protection and business services	1,087	25,483	365	839

Energy production (consumption): electricity (kW-hr; 1993) 155,300,000,000 (155,300,000,000); coal (metric tons; 1993) 183,230,000 (94,030,000); crude petroleum (barrels; 1993) 200,750,000 (2,774,000,000); petroleum products (metric tons; 1992) 31,226,000 (33,085,000); natural gas (cu m; 1993) 24,352,000,000 (17,783,000,000).

Population economically active (1994–95): total 9,003,100; activity rate of total population 49.5% (participation rates: ages 15–64, 63.7%; female 44.0%; unemployed 7.9%).

Price and earnings indexes (1990 = 100)

	1989	1990	1991	1992	1993	1994	1995[13]
Consumer price index	93.2	100.0	103.2	104.2	106.1	108.1	112.6
Weekly earnings index	92.1	100.0	105.1	109.3	111.3	115.0	120.3

Household income and expenditure (1993–94). Average household size 2.7; average annual income per household $A 37,700 (U.S.$27,585); sources of income: wages and salaries 72.7%, transfer payments 13.0%, self-employment 7.5%, other 6.8%; expenditure: food and beverages 18.7%, transportation and communications 15.3%, housing 13.9%, recreation 13.3%, household durable goods 6.6%, clothing and footwear 5.7%, health 4.6%, energy 2.8%, other 19.1%.

Financial aggregates

	1989	1990	1991	1992	1993	1994	1995[14]
Exchange rate, $A 1.00 per:							
U.S. dollar	0.70	0.70	0.78	0.69	0.68	0.78	0.76
£	0.48	0.44	0.44	0.45	0.46	0.50	0.48
SDR	0.60	0.54	0.53	0.50	0.49	0.53	0.50
International reserves (U.S.$)							
Total (excl. gold; '000,000)	13,780	16,264	16,534	11,208	11,102	11,285	11,055
SDRs ('000,000)	307	311	290	96	82	73	60
Reserve pos. in IMF ('000,000)	322	349	351	420	550	506	510
Foreign exchange ('000,000)	13,150	15,605	15,894	10,536	10,470	10,706	10,485
Gold ('000,000 fine troy oz)	7.93	7.93	7.93	7.93	7.90	7.90	7.9
% world reserves	0.8	0.8	0.8	0.8	0.9	0.9	0.9
Interest and prices							
Central bank discount (%)	17.23	15.24	11.0	6.25	5.83	5.75	5.75[13]
Govt. bond yield (%)	15.14	13.46	9.94	7.00	5.63	7.65	7.70[13]
Industrial share prices (1990 = 100)	97.6	100.0	96.4	100.3	104.9	113.1	115.6[13]
Balance of payments (U.S.$'000,000)							
Balance of visible trade	−3,436	+366	+3,511	+1,554	+12	−3,199	−1,564[15]
Imports, f.o.b.	40,329	38,966	38,494	40,820	42,362	50,272	13,635[15]
Exports, f.o.b.	36,893	39,332	42,005	42,374	42,374	47,073	12,071[15]
Balance of invisibles	−14,231	−15,465	−13,782	−12,499	−10,792	−12,025	−3,102[15]
Balance of payments, current account	−17,667	−15,099	−10,271	−10,945	−10,780	−15,224	−4,666[15]

Land use (1993): meadows and pastures 53.6%; agricultural and under permanent cultivation 6.0%; other 40.4%[16].

Foreign trade

Balance of trade (current prices)

	1989	1990	1991	1992	1993	1994
$A '000,000	−4,100	1,194	4,141	2,898	−2,302	−5,021
% of total	4.1%	1.2%	4.0%	2.6%	2.0%	2.9%

Imports (1993–94): $A 66,910,000,000 (machinery 29.6%, of which office machines and automatic data-processing equipment 7.2%; basic manufactures 14.4%, of which textile yarn and fabrics 3.5%, paper and paper products 2.4%, nonferrous metals 0.7%; transport equipment 13.2%, of which road motor vehicles 10.4%; chemicals and related products 10.2%; mineral fuels and lubricants 6.1%; food and live animals 3.7%; crude materials [inedible] excluding fuels 2.4%; beverages and tobacco 0.7%). *Major import sources:* U.S. 21.5%; Japan 18.9%; Germany 5.8%; U.K. 5.7%; China 4.7%; New Zealand 4.6%; South Korea 3.1%; Singapore 2.6%; France 2.2%; Italy 2.2%.

Exports (1993–94): $A 62,839,000,000 (mineral fuels and lubricants 18.6%, of which coal, coke, and briquettes 13.0%, petroleum, petroleum products, and natural gas 5.6%; crude materials excluding fuels 17.0%, of which textile fibres and their waste 7.8%, metalliferous ores and metal scrap 7.6%; food and live animals 16.8%, of which meat 6.5%, cereals 3.9%; machinery and transport equipment 7.2%; chemicals 2.6%). *Major export destinations:* Japan 24.5%; U.S. 8.0%; South Korea 6.8%; New Zealand 5.8%; Singapore 5.2%; U.K. 4.5%; Taiwan 4.4%; Hong Kong 4.3%; Indonesia 2.8%.

Trade by commodity group (1992–93)

SITC Group		imports U.S.$'000,000	imports %	exports U.S.$'000,000	exports %
00	Food and live animals	1,563	3.8	6,968	15.5
01	Beverages and tobacco	304	0.7	238	0.6
02	Crude materials, excluding fuels	1,035	2.4	7,052	15.7
03	Mineral fuels, lubricants, and related materials	2,392	5.6	7,674	17.0
04	Animal and vegetable oils, fat, and waxes	—	—	—	—
05	Chemicals and related products, n.e.s.	3,867	9.0	1,205	2.7
06	Basic manufactures	6,120	14.2	4,970	11.0
07	Machinery and transport equipment	16,997	39.7	4,146	9.2
08	Miscellaneous manufactured articles	6,247	14.6	1,271	2.8
09	Goods not classified by kind	4,296	10.0	11,504	25.5
TOTAL		42,821	100.0	45,028	100.0

Direction of trade (1992–93)

	imports U.S.$'000,000	imports %	exports U.S.$'000,000	exports %
Africa	171	0.4	675	1.5
Asia	16,230	37.9	24,270	53.9
Japan	7,536	17.6	11,122	24.7
South America	428	1.0	450	1.0
North and Central America	10,620	24.8	5,854	13.0
United States	9,892	23.1	4,908	10.9
Europe	11,133	26.0	7,024	15.6
EEC	9,078	21.2	6,259	13.9
former U.S.S.R.	...	...	...	...
Other Europe	2,055	4.8	765	1.7
Oceania	2,098	4.9	3,917	8.7
New Zealand	1,799	4.2	2,567	5.7
Other	2,141	5.0	2,838	6.3
TOTAL	42,821	100.0	45,028	100.0

Transport and communications

Transport. Railroads (1993)[17]: route length 22,774 mi, 36,652 km; passenger-mi 1,359,051,000[18], passenger-km 2,187,120,000[18]; short ton-mi cargo 63,235,000,000, metric ton-km cargo 92,322,000,000. Roads (1993): total length 507,316 mi, 816,447 km (paved 36%). Vehicles (1993): passenger cars 8,280,200; trucks and buses 1,936,100. Merchant marine (1992): vessels (100 gross tons and over) 695; total deadweight tonnage 3,857,271. Air transport (1992–93): passenger-mi 32,426,400,000, passenger-km 52,185,362,000; short ton-mi cargo 2,157,600,000, metric ton-km cargo 3,150,036,000, airports (1991) with scheduled flights 428.

Communications. Daily newspapers (1992): total number 69; total circulation 4,600,000; circulation per 1,000 population 261. Radio (1994): 20,000,000 receivers (1 per 0.9 persons). Television (1994): 8,000,000 receivers (1 per 2.2 persons). Telephones (main lines; 1993): 8,540,000 (1 per 2.1 persons).

Education and health

Education (1993)

	schools	teachers	students	student/ teacher ratio
Primary (age 6–12)	9,865	98,526	1,816,066	18.4
Secondary (age 13–17)		103,385	1,282,309	12.4
Vocational[19]	234[20]	52,587[20]	985,942[21]	...
Higher[22]	95	25,916	420,640	16.2

Literacy (1980): percentage of total population age 15 and over literate 99.5%.

Health: physicians (1991) 39,984 (1 per 434 persons); hospital beds (1992) 86,036 (1 per 199 persons); infant mortality rate (1994) 5.8.

Food (1992): daily per capita caloric intake 3,179 (vegetable products 62%, animal products 38%); 120% of FAO recommended minimum requirement.

Military

Total active duty personnel (1995): 56,100 (army 42.2%, navy 26.7%, air force 31.1%). *Military expenditure as percentage of GNP* (1993): 2.4% (world 3.3); per capita expenditure U.S.$410.

[1]March 31. [2]Includes both Northern Ireland and Republic of Ireland. [3]Completed highest level of secondary school available. [4]December. [5]Less imputed bank service charges. [6]Mostly unemployed. [7]Excludes operations of single-establishment enterprises employing fewer than four persons. [8]Excludes the drawings of working proprietors. [9]1990–91. [10]1985. [11]1985–86. [12]1987–88. [13]Second quarter. [14]September. [15]June 30. [16]Urban areas, state forests and mining leases, unoccupied land (mainly desert). [17]Government railways only. [18]1978–79. [19]Includes special education. [20]1986. [21]1992. [22]1989.

Austria

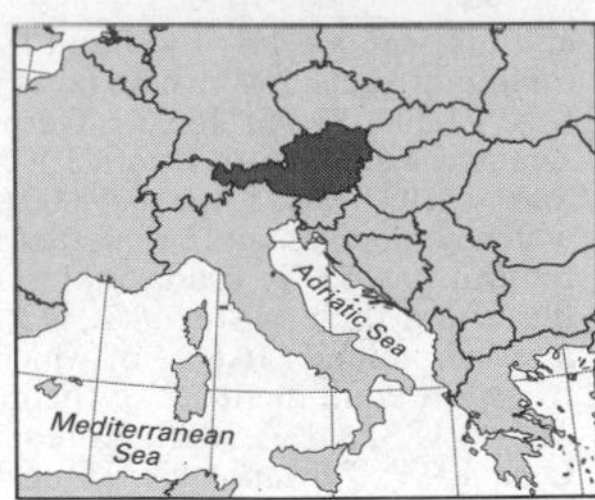

Official name: Republik Österreich (Republic of Austria).
Form of government: federal multiparty republic with two legislative houses (Federal Council [63]; National Council [183]).
Chief of state: President.
Head of government: Chancellor.
Capital: Vienna.
Official language: German.
Official religion: none.
Monetary unit: 1 Austrian Schilling (S) = 100 Groschen; valuation (Oct. 6, 1995) 1 U.S.$ = S 10.04; 1 £ = S 15.87.

Area and population

		area		population
States	Capitals	sq mi	sq km	1993 estimate
Burgenland	Eisenstadt	1,531	3,965	273,000
Kärnten	Klagenfurt	3,681	9,533	559,000
Niederösterreich	Sankt Pölten	7,403	19,174	1,507,000
Oberösterreich	Linz	4,626	11,980	1,373,000
Salzburg	Salzburg	2,762	7,154	501,000
Steiermark	Graz	6,327	16,388	1,203,000
Tirol	Innsbruck	4,883	12,648	649,000
Vorarlberg	Bregenz	1,004	2,601	341,000
Wien (Vienna)	—	160	415	1,583,000
TOTAL		32,378[1]	83,858	7,988,000[1]

Demography

Population (1995): 8,063,000.
Density (1995): persons per sq mi 249.0, persons per sq km 96.2.
Urban-rural (1991): urban 64.5%; rural 35.5%.
Sex distribution (1995): male 48.83%; female 51.17%.
Age breakdown (1995): under 15, 17.8%; 15–29, 21.1%; 30–44, 23.5%; 45–59, 18.2%; 60–74, 13.3%; 75 and over, 6.1%.
Population projection: (2000) 8,245,000; (2010) 8,350,000.
Doubling time: not applicable; population is stable.
Ethnic composition (national origin; 1991): Austrian 93.4%; citizens of former Yugoslavia 2.5%; Turkish 1.5%; German 0.7%; other 1.9%.
Religious affiliation (1991): Roman Catholic 78.0%; nonreligious and atheist 8.6%; Lutheran 4.8%; Muslim 2.0%; Jewish 0.2%; other (mostly Christian) 2.7%; unknown 3.7%.
Major cities (1991): Vienna 1,539,848; Graz 237,810; Linz 203,044; Salzburg 143,978; Innsbruck 118,112.

Vital statistics

Birth rate per 1,000 population (1994): 11.6 (world avg. 25.0); (1993) legitimate 73.7%; illegitimate 26.3%.
Death rate per 1,000 population (1994): 10.1 (world avg. 9.3).
Natural increase rate per 1,000 population (1994): 1.5 (world avg. 15.7).
Total fertility rate (avg. births per childbearing woman; 1994): 1.5.
Marriage rate per 1,000 population (1993): 5.6.
Divorce rate per 1,000 population (1993): 2.0.
Life expectancy at birth (1993): male 72.9 years; female 79.4 years.
Major causes of death per 100,000 population (1993): diseases of the circulatory system 544.5, of which ischemic heart diseases 207.9, diseases of pulmonary circulation and other forms of heart disease 148.8; malignant neoplasms (cancers) 244.3.

National economy

Budget (1992). Revenue: S 750,100,000,000 (tax revenue 90.5%, of which social-security contributions 36.4%, value-added taxes 16.1%, individual income taxes 15.7%; nontax revenue 8.8%). Expenditures: S 808,500,000,000 (social security and welfare 44.7%; health 13.4%; education 9.4%; general administration 5.4%; defense 2.3%).
National debt (end of year 1992): U.S.$88,149,000,000.
Production (metric tons except as noted). Agriculture, forestry, fishing (1994): sugar beets 2,800,000, corn (maize) 1,476,000, barley 1,368,000, wheat 1,265,000, potatoes 750,000, grapes 410,000, apples 334,000, rye 292,000, rapeseed 131,000, sunflower seed 95,000; livestock (number of live animals) 3,800,000 pigs, 2,430,000 cattle, 13,000,000 chickens; roundwood (1993) 12,857,000 cu m; fish catch (1993) 4,605. Mining and quarrying (1993): iron ore 1,500,000; magnesite 1,000,000; high-grade graphite 19,500. Manufacturing (value added in S '000,000,000; 1991): electrical machinery and apparatus 46.4; nonelectrical machinery and apparatus 40.1; fabricated metal products 29.0; food products 28.2; transport equipment 21.2; iron and steel 21.1; cement, bricks, and tile 18.8. Construction (completed; 1991): residential 3,981,000 sq m; nonresidential, n.a. Energy production (consumption): electricity (kW-hr; 1993) 52,656,000,000 ([1992] 51,734,000,000); coal (metric tons; 1993) 1,788,000 ([1992] 5,000,000); crude petroleum (barrels; 1994) 7,819,000 ([1992] 63,838,000); petroleum products (metric tons; 1992) 8,321,000 (10,086,000); natural gas (cu m; 1994) 1,343,000,000 ([1992] 6,868,000,000).
Land use (1993): forested 39.2%; meadows and pastures 23.6%; agricultural and under permanent cultivation 18.1%; other 19.1%.
Tourism (1993): receipts from visitors U.S.$13,400,000,000; expenditures by nationals abroad U.S.$8,200,000,000.
Population economically active (1992): total 3,679,100; activity rate of total population 46.7% (participation rates: ages 15–64, 69.1%; female 41.6%; unemployed [July 1994–June 1995] 6.5%).

Price and earnings indexes (1990 = 100)

	1989	1990	1991	1992	1993	1994	1995[2]
Consumer price index	96.8	100.0	103.3	107.5	111.4	114.7	116.5
Monthly earnings index	93.3	100.0	105.2	110.3	116.1	120.7	106.4

Gross national product (at current market prices; 1993): U.S.$183,530,000,000 (U.S.$23,120 per capita).

Structure of gross domestic product and labour force

	1993		1992	
	in value S '000,000	% of total value	labour force	% of labour force
Agriculture	47,400	2.2	252,500	6.9
Mining	508,600	24.1	13,000	0.4
Manufacturing			959,500	26.1
Construction	157,200	7.5	303,900	8.3
Public utilities	59,100	2.8	38,600	1.0
Transportation and communications	139,200	6.6	237,900	6.5
Trade, restaurants	341,400	16.2	694,100	18.9
Finance, real estate	394,300	18.7	268,900	7.3
Pub. admin., defense	308,000	14.6	862,200	23.4
Services	95,300	4.5		
Other	59,200[3]	2.8[3]	48,500	1.3
TOTAL	2,109,700	100.0	3,679,100	100.0[1]

Household income and expenditure. Average household size (1993) 2.6; net income per household[4] (1991) S 262,080 (U.S.$21,930); sources of income (1992): wages and salaries 55.7%, transfer payments 24.4%, other 19.9%; expenditure (1992): food and beverages 18.8%, transportation 18.5%, housing 11.8%, cafe and hotel expenditures 9.7%, clothing and footwear 8.5%.

Foreign trade[5]

Balance of trade (current prices)

	1989	1990	1991	1992	1993	1994
S '000,000	−62,180	−65,190	−86,300	−79,700	−72,500	−89,300
% of total	6.8%	6.5%	8.3%	7.6%	7.2%	8.0%

Imports (1993): S 593,900,000,000 (machinery and transport equipment 39.5%, of which road vehicles 12.7%, electrical machinery and apparatus 6.3%; chemicals and related products 9.8%; clothing 4.8%; food products 4.5%).
Major import sources (1994): Germany 40.0%; Italy 8.8%; France 4.7%; United States 4.4%; Japan 4.3%; Switzerland 4.1%.
Exports (1993): S 487,600,000,000 (machinery and transport equipment 38.9%, of which electrical machinery and apparatus 6.7%, road vehicles 6.5%, machine tools 5.9%; paper and paper products 5.9%; iron and steel 5.3%).
Major export destinations (1994): Germany 38.1%; Italy 8.1%; Switzerland 6.4%; France 4.5%; Hungary 3.9%; United States 3.5%.

Transport and communications

Transport. Railroads (1994)[6]: length (1993) 3,480 mi, 5,600 km; passenger-mi 5,988,000,000, passenger-km 9,636,000,000; short ton-mi cargo 8,934,000,000, metric ton-km cargo 13,044,000,000. Roads (1992): total length 68,400 mi[7], 110,000 km[7] (paved 100%[8]). Vehicles (1993): passenger cars 3,367,626; trucks and buses 745,987. Merchant marine (1992): vessels (100 gross tons and over) 26; total deadweight tonnage 208,504. Air transport[9] (1994): passenger-mi 4,552,000,000, passenger-km 7,325,000,000; short ton-mi cargo 94,567,000, metric ton-km cargo 138,065,000; airports (1995) with scheduled flights 6.
Communications. Daily newspapers (1992): total number 27; total circulation 3,108,357; circulation per 1,000 population 394. Radio (1994): total receivers 4,710,000 (1 per 1.7 persons). Television (1994): total receivers 2,706,000 (1 per 3.0 persons). Telephones (main lines; 1993): 3,579,200 (1 per 2.2 persons).

Education and health

Education (1993–94)

	schools	teachers	students	student/ teacher ratio
Primary (age 6–10)	3,684	36,208	401,147	11.1
Secondary (age 11–18)	1,899	54,822	457,970	8.4
Voc., teacher tr.	1,028	24,752	299,323	12.1
Higher	44	15,576	219,204	14.1

Educational attainment (1993). Percentage of population age 25 and over having: lower-secondary education 37.5%; vocational education ending at secondary level 44.6%; completed upper secondary 6.1%; higher vocational 5.5%; higher 6.3%. *Literacy:* virtually 100%.
Health (1993): physicians 26,121 (1 per 307 persons); hospital beds 73,239 (1 per 109 persons); infant mortality rate per 1,000 live births (1994) 6.1.
Food (1992): daily per capita caloric intake 3,497 (vegetable products 64%, animal products 36%); 133% of FAO recommended minimum requirement.

Military

Total active duty personnel (1994): 51,250 (army 85.9%; navy, none; air force 14.1%). *Military expenditure as percentage of GNP* (1993): 1.0% (world 3.3%); per capita expenditure U.S.$216.

[1]Detail does not add to total given because of rounding. [2]February. [3]Value-added tax plus import duties (S 194,400,000,000) less imputed bank service charges (S 135,200,000,000). [4]Two-person households without children only. [5]Import figures are f.o.b. in balance of trade and c.i.f. in commodities and trading partners. [6]Federal railways only. [7]Excludes 62,100 mi (100,000 km) of private roads. [8]Includes macadamized roads. [9]Austrian Airlines, Lauda Air, and Tyrolean Airways.

Azerbaijan

Official name: Azärbayjan Respublikasi (Azerbaijani Republic).
Form of government: federal multiparty republic with a single legislative body (National Assembly [50]).
Head of state: President.
Head of government: Prime Minister.
Capital: Baku (Azerbaijani: Bakı).
Official language: Azerbaijani.
Official religion: none.
Monetary unit: 1 manat[1] = 100 gopik; valuation (Oct. 6, 1995) free rate, 1 U.S.$ = 4,440 manat; 1 £ = 7,019 manat.

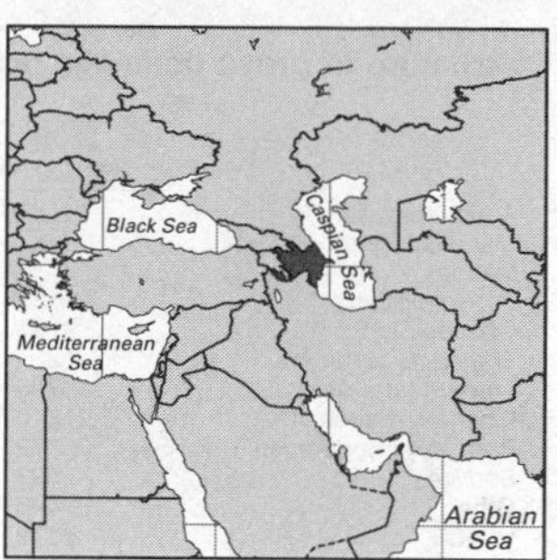

Area and population

Republics	Capitals	area sq mi	area sq km	population 1991 estimate
Naxçıvan (Nakhichevan)	Naxçıvan (Nakhichevan)	2,100	5,500	305,700
Qarabağ[2] (Nagorno Karabakh)	Xankändi (Stepanakert)	1,700	4,400	193,300
Regions under republican jurisdiction	—	29,600	76,700	4,924,300
Cities				
Baku (Bakı)	—	...	...	1,713,300
TOTAL		33,400	86,600	7,136,600

Demography

Population (1995): 7,525,000.
Density (1995): persons per sq mi 225.3, persons per sq km 86.9.
Urban-rural (1993): urban 53.2%; rural 46.8%.
Sex distribution (1992): male 49.31%; female 50.69%.
Age breakdown (1989): under 15, 32.8%; 15–29, 29.7%; 30–44, 16.8%; 45–59, 12.8%; 60–74, 5.7%; 75 and over, 2.2%.
Population projection: (2000) 7,937,000; (2010) 8,832,000.
Doubling time: 50 years.
Ethnic composition (1989): Azerbaijani 82.7%; Russian 5.7%; Armenian 5.6%; Lezgin 2.4%; Avar 0.6%; Ukrainian 0.5%; Tatar 0.4%; other 2.1%.
Religious affiliation (1991): Shīʿī Muslim 70%; Sunnī Muslim 30%.
Major cities (1991): Baku 1,080,500; Gäncä (formerly Kirovabad) 282,200; Sumqayıt (Sumgait) 236,200; Mingacevir (Mingechaur) 90,900; Naxçıvan (Nakhichevan) 61,700.

Vital statistics

Birth rate per 1,000 population (1994): 21.6 (world avg. 25.0); (1992) legitimate 95.6%; illegitimate 4.4%.
Death rate per 1,000 population (1994): 7.4 (world avg. 9.3).
Natural increase rate per 1,000 population (1994): 14.2 (world avg. 15.7).
Total fertility rate (avg. births per childbearing woman; 1993): 2.8.
Marriage rate per 1,000 population (1993): 8.3.
Divorce rate per 1,000 population (1993): 0.9.
Life expectancy at birth (1993): male 66.7 years; female 74.6 years.
Major causes of death per 100,000 population (1993): diseases of the circulatory system 347.1; diseases of the respiratory system 100.3; accidents, poisoning, and violence 81.9; malignant neoplasms (cancers) 68.2; infectious and parasitic diseases 26.4; diseases of the digestive system (1989) 25.6; diseases of the nervous system (1989) 9.7; endocrine and metabolic disorders (1989) 8.6.

National economy

Budget (1993). Revenue: 61,549,000,000 manat (tax revenue 96.0%, of which value-added tax 23.1%, excise tax 21.0%, enterprise profits tax 19.7%, individual income tax 5.8%; nontax revenue 4.0%). Expenditures: 74,601,000,000 manat (1992; social welfare and culture 82.1%, of which education 27.3%, pensions 14.1%, health 11.2%, defense 10.5%; national economy 17.9%).
Public debt (external, outstanding): n.a.
Production (metric tons except as noted). Agriculture, forestry, fishing (1994): fruit (except grapes) 1,282,000, cereals 1,012,000, grapes 860,000, vegetables (except potatoes) 813,000, wheat 760,000, cotton 340,000, potatoes 150,000, tobacco 68,000, tea 4,000; livestock (number of live animals) 4,539,000 sheep and goats, 1,621,000 cattle, 115,000 pigs, 30,000 horses, 23,000,000 poultry; roundwood (1993) 17,000 cu m; fish catch (1993) 36,000. Mining and quarrying (1992): iron ore 300,000. Manufacturing (value of production in '000,000 rubles; 1992): fuel and energy 68,547; food products 36,248; textiles 31,217; machine-building equipment 29,757; ferrous and nonferrous metals 16,297; chemical products 13,234; construction materials 4,116; wood products 1,609. Construction (1991): 2,600,000 sq m. Energy production (consumption): electricity (kW-hr; 1992) 20,000,000,000 (20,000,000,000); coal (metric tons; 1992) none (27,000); crude petroleum (barrels; 1992) 77,698,000 (91,273,000); petroleum products (metric tons; 1992) 400,000 (400,000); natural gas (cu m; 1992) 7,800,000,000 (11,553,000,000).
Household income and expenditure. Average household size (1989) 4.8; income per household: n.a.; sources of income (1992): salaries and wages 70.2%, social benefits 19.0%, agricultural income 10.8%; expenditure: retail goods 73.7%, services 7.4%, taxes 10.2%.
Gross national product (at current market prices; 1993): U.S.$5,428,000,000 (U.S.$730 per capita)[3].

Structure of net material product and labour force

	1993 in value '000,000 manat	1993 % of total value	1992 labour force	1992 % of labour force
Agriculture	34,802	29.4	958,000	33.4
Mining }				
Manufacturing }	53,985	45.6	456,000	15.9
Public utilities }			110,000	3.8
Construction	16,247	13.7	250,000	8.7
Transportation and communications	9,111	7.7	74,000	2.6
Trade	2,595	2.2	...	...
Finance	—	—	10,000	0.4
Pub. admin., defense	—	—	52,000	1.8
Services	—	—	582,000	20.3
Other	1,655	1.4	377,000	13.1
TOTAL	118,395	100.0	2,869,000	100.0

Population economically active (1992): total 2,869,000; activity rate of total population 39.7% (participation rates: ages 16–59 [male], 16–54 [female] 71.5%; female [1989] 42.6%; unemployed [1991] 3.7%).

Price and earnings indexes (1990 = 100)

	1988	1989	1990	1991	1992	1993	1994
Consumer price index	...	...	100.0	205.6	2,082	25,602	451,722
Monthly earnings index	87.7	91.8	100.0	177.3	1,406	10,642	74,563

Tourism: receipts from visitors, n.a.; expenditures by nationals abroad, n.a.
Land use (1993): forest 21.9%; pasture 25.4%; agriculture 11.0%; other 41.7%.

Foreign trade

Balance of trade (current prices)

	1987	1988	1989	1990	1991	1992	1993
'000,000 rubles	1,209	1,110	1,933	678	2,502	78,818	3,838
% of total	...	...	...	...	12.3%	18.9%	1.7%

Imports (1993): 117,427,000,000 rubles (petroleum products 39.0%, ferrous metals 30.0%, textiles 10.6%, nonferrous metals 5.9%, chemical products 3.0%). *Major import sources:* Russia 24.7%; Turkey 12.8%; Turkmenistan 10.6%; Ukraine 10.4%; Iran 8.5%; Kazakhstan 6.8%.
Exports (1993): 113,589,000,000 rubles (food products 33.2%, machinery 20.1%, chemical products 16.1%, consumer products 16.0%, textiles 7.2%). *Major export destinations:* Iran 29.1%; Russia 26.9%; Turkey 9.1%; Ukraine 7.0%; Georgia 4.5%; Kazakhstan 4.4%.

Transport and communications

Transport. Railroads (1991): length 1,299 mi, 2,090 km; passenger-mi 3,025,400,000, passenger-km 4,868,900,000; cargo traffic, n.a. Roads (1991): total length 22,800 mi, 36,700 km (paved 87%). Vehicles (1988): passenger cars 235,600; trucks and buses, n.a. Merchant marine: vessels (100 gross tons and over) n.a.; total deadweight tonnage, n.a. Air transport (1990): passenger-mi 3,025,400,000, passenger-km 4,868,900,000; cargo traffic, n.a.; airports (1995) with scheduled flights 1.
Communications. Daily newspapers (1992): total number 6; total circulation 427,000; circulation per 1,000 population 58. Radio (1992): total number of receivers 1,174,000 (1 per 6.1 persons). Television (1992): total number of receivers 1,522,000 (1 per 4.8 persons). Telephones (main lines; 1993): 647,000 (1 per 11.0 persons).

Education and health

Education (1994–95)

	schools	teachers	students	student/teacher ratio
Primary (age 6–13) } Secondary (age 14–17) }	4,500	139,000[4]	1,462,000	9.9[4]
Voc., teacher tr.	78	...	30,400	...
Higher	23	...	89,100	...

Educational attainment (1989). Percentage of population age 25 and over having: primary education or no formal schooling 12.2%; some secondary 19.2%; completed secondary and some postsecondary 58.1%; higher 10.5%.
Literacy (1989): percentage of total population 15 and over literate 97.3%; males literate 98.9%; females 95.9%.
Health (1994): physicians 29,000 (1 per 251 persons); hospital beds 79,000 (1 per 98 persons); infant mortality rate per 1,000 live births 26.9.

Military

Total active duty personnel (1995): 86,700[5] (army 84.5%, navy[6] 2.6%, air force 12.9%). *Military expenditure as percentage of GNP* (1993): *c.* 5.6% (world 3.3%); per capita expenditure (1993) U.S.$40.

[1]The manat was introduced Aug. 15, 1992, at a 10 to 1 ratio with the Russian ruble and circulated parallel with it; on June 20, 1993, the manat became the sole legal tender. [2]In November 1991 the Azerbaijan Supreme Soviet abolished Nagorno Karabakh's autonomous status. [3]Ruble-area GNP and exchange-rate data are very speculative. [4]1991–92. [5]Total mobilization data for war with Armenia is not available; however, total reserve strength is 560,000. [6]Azerbaijan shares a portion of the Caspian Flotilla.

Bahamas, The

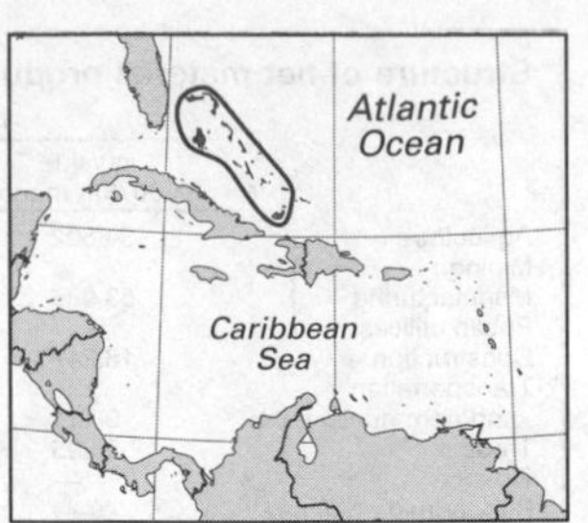

Official name: Commonwealth of The Bahamas.
Form of government: constitutional monarchy with two legislative houses (Senate [16]; House of Assembly [49]).
Chief of state: British Monarch represented by Governor-General.
Head of government: Prime Minister.
Capital: Nassau.
Official language: English.
Official religion: none.
Monetary unit: 1 Bahamian dollar (B$) = 100 cents; valuation (Oct. 6, 1995) 1 U.S.$ = B$1.00; 1 £ = B$1.58.

Area and population

	area[1]		population
Islands and Island Groups[2]	sq mi	sq km	1990 census
Abaco, Great and Little	649	1,681	10,034
Acklins	192	497	405
Andros	2,300	5,957	8,187
Berry Islands	12	31	628
Bimini Islands	9	23	1,639
Cat Island	150	388	1,698
Crooked and Long Cay	93	241	412
Eleuthera	187	484	7,993
Exuma, Great, and Exuma Cays	112	290	3,556
Grand Bahama	530	1,373	40,898
Harbour Island	3	8	1,219
Inagua, Great and Little	599	1,551	985
Long Island	230	596	2,954
Mayaguana	110	285	312
New Providence	80	207	172,196
Ragged Island	14	36	89
Rum Cay	30	78	53
San Salvador	63	163	465
Spanish Wells	10	26	1,372
Other uninhabited cays and rocks	9	23	—
TOTAL	5,382	13,939[3]	255,095

Demography

Population (1995): 276,000.
Density (1995)[4]: persons per sq mi 71.0, persons per sq km 27.4.
Urban-rural (1995): urban 86.0%; rural 14.0%.
Sex distribution (1995): male 48.91%; female 51.09%.
Age breakdown (1995): under 15, 29.3%; 15–29, 28.6%; 30–44, 23.2%; 45–59, 11.6%; 60–74, 5.1%; 75 and over, 2.2%.
Population projection: (2000) 295,000; (2010) 332,000.
Doubling time: 52 years.
Ethnic composition (1993): black 85.0%; white 12.0%; Asian or Hispanic 3.0%.
Religious affiliation (1980): non-Anglican Protestant 55.2%, of which Baptist 32.1%, Methodist 6.1%, Church of God (Anderson Ind.) 5.7%; Anglican 20.1%; Roman Catholic 18.8%; other 5.9%.
Major cities (1990): Nassau 172,196[5]; Freeport/Lucaya 26,574; Marsh Harbour 3,611; Bailey Town 1,490; Dunmore Town (Harbour Island) 1,219.

Vital statistics

Birth rate per 1,000 population (1994): 18.9 (world avg. 25.0); (1990) legitimate 42.8%, illegitimate 57.2%.
Death rate per 1,000 population (1994): 5.4 (world avg. 9.3).
Natural increase rate per 1,000 population (1994): 13.5 (world avg. 15.7).
Total fertility rate (avg. births per childbearing woman; 1994): 1.9.
Marriage rate per 1,000 population (1992): 9.1.
Divorce rate per 1,000 population (1992): 1.2.
Life expectancy at birth (1994): male 67.7 years; female 75.5 years.
Major causes of death per 100,000 population (1991): ischemic heart diseases 95.0; malignant neoplasms (cancers) 79.2; cerebrovascular disease 28.6; pneumonia 23.2.

National economy

Budget (1994). Revenue: B$613,700,000[6] (import taxes 49.5%, stamp taxes 16.9%, departure taxes 9.3%, fines and forfeits 6.5%, business and professional licenses 3.9%). Expenditures: B$597,800,000[7] (education 18.7%, health 14.9%, interest on public debt 12.3%, general administration 11.2%, public order 10.9%, public works and water supply 9.0%, defense 3.4%).
National debt (December 1994): U.S.$1,463,000,000.
Production (value of production in B$'000 except as noted). Agriculture, forestry, fishing (1994): crayfish 57,700, other marine products (mostly sponges, groupers, conchs) 4,800, fruits and vegetables 22,800[8], poultry products (1993) 20,200; roundwood (1993) 117,000 cu m. Mining and quarrying (value of export production; 1994): salt 15,100; aragonite 3,300. Manufacturing (value of export production; 1994): pharmaceuticals and other chemical products 54,700; rum 10,900. Construction (gross value of buildings completed in B$'000,000; 1994)[9]: residential 83; nonresidential 36. Energy production (consumption): electricity (kW-hr; 1992) 975,000,000 (975,000,000); coal, none (none); crude petroleum, none (none); petroleum products (metric tons; 1992) negligible (592,000); natural gas, none (none).
Tourism: receipts from visitors (1994) U.S.$1,333,000,000; expenditures by nationals abroad (1993) U.S.$195,000,000.
Gross national product (1993): U.S.$3,059,000,000 (U.S.$11,500 per capita).

Structure of gross domestic product and labour force

	1992		1993	
	in value B$'000,000	% of total value	labour force	% of labour force
Agriculture, fishing	89	2.9	6,435	4.7
Manufacturing }	105	3.4	4,935	3.6
Mining }		}	1,785	1.3
Public utilities	88	2.9 }		
Construction	91	3.0	7,730	5.6
Transp. and commun.	227	7.4	9,093	6.6
Trade, restaurants	705	23.0	36,711	26.8
Finance, real estate	610	19.9	11,201	8.2
Pub. admin., defense	179	5.8 }	40,543	29.6
Services	523	17.1 }		
Other	443[10]	14.5[10]	18,467[11]	13.5[11]
TOTAL	3,059[3]	100.0[3]	136,900	100.0[3]

Population economically active (1993): total 136,900; activity rate of total population 51.5% (participation rates: ages 15–64, n.a.; female 47.5%; unemployed [1994] unofficially exceeds 20%).

Price and earnings indexes (1991 = 100)

	1989	1990	1991	1992	1993	1994	1995
Consumer price index	89.2	93.3	100.0	105.7	108.5	110.2	111.9[12]
Annual earnings index[13]	99.7	...	100.0	112.8	116.8[14]	...	

Household income and expenditure. Average household size (1993) 3.7; income per household (1993) B$26,373 (U.S.$26,373); sources of income: n.a.; expenditure (1988)[15]: food and beverages 19.8%, housing 19.2%, transportation and communications 18.9%, household furnishings 10.2%, education 7.8%.
Land use (1993): forested 32.4%; meadows and pastures 0.2%; agricultural and under permanent cultivation 1.0%; other 66.4%.

Foreign trade[16]

Balance of trade (current prices)

	1988	1989	1990	1991	1992	1993
B$'000,000	−99	−534	−327	−284	−380	−600
% of total	2.4%	9.4%	5.9%	8.1%	11.4%	18.7%

Imports (1991): B$1,801,000,000 (petroleum for storage 34.3%, machinery and transport equipment 14.5%, food products 11.3%, chemicals and chemical products 9.1%). *Major import sources* (1990): Saudi Arabia 36.9%; United States 35.6%; United Kingdom 3.7%; Nigeria 3.1%; Iraq 2.8%.
Exports (1991): B$1,517,000,000 (chemicals [mostly pharmaceuticals] 50.8%, distillate fuels 24.4%, hormones 4.3%, crayfish 3.0%, rum 2.2%). *Major export destinations* (1990): United States 76.5%; Puerto Rico 17.3%; Belgium 1.0%; Canada 0.9%; United Kingdom 0.8%.

Transport and communications

Transport. Railroads: none. Roads (1993): total length 1,491 mi, 2,400 km (paved 56%). Vehicles (1993): passenger cars 69,000; trucks and buses 14,000. Merchant marine (1992): vessels (100 gross tons and over) 1,061; total deadweight tonnage 33,081,652. Air transport (1991): passenger-mi 215,000,000, passenger-km 346,000,000; short ton-mi cargo 205,000, metric ton-km cargo 300,000; airports (1995) with scheduled flights 24.
Communications. Daily newspapers (1992): total number 3; total circulation 35,000; circulation per 1,000 population 133. Radio (1994): total receivers 134,000 (1 per 2.0 persons). Television (1994): total receivers 60,000 (1 per 4.5 persons). Telephones (main lines; 1993): 79,500 (1 per 3.4 persons).

Education and health

Education (1992–93)

	schools	teachers	students	student/ teacher ratio
Primary/Secondary (age 5–16)	227[17]	3,161[17]	61,464	19.0[17]
Higher[18]	1	300	3,201	10.7

Educational attainment: n.a. *Literacy:* total population age 15 and over literate, n.a.
Health (1992): physicians 357 (1 per 714 persons); hospital beds 1,020 (1 per 250 persons); infant mortality rate per 1,000 live births (1994) 33.5.
Food (1992): daily per capita caloric intake 2,624 (vegetable products 71%, animal products 29%); 108% of FAO recommended minimum requirement.

Military

Total active duty personnel (1994): 850 (all paramilitary coast guard). *Military expenditure as percentage of GNP* (1993)[19]: 0.5% (world 3.3%); per capita expenditure U.S.$68.

[1]Includes areas of lakes and ponds, as well as lagoons and sounds almost entirely surrounded by land; area of land only is about 3,890 sq mi (10,070 sq km). [2]Family (Out) Islands (all islands other than New Providence) are administered by commissioners assigned by the central government. Extent of commissioner districts varies from part of an island to island groups. [3]Detail does not add to total given because of rounding. [4]Land area only. [5]Population cited is for New Providence Island. [6]Current revenue only. [7]Of which current expenditure 91.1%, development expenditure 8.9%. [8]1990. [9]New Providence and Grand Bahama islands only. [10]Includes net indirect taxes (B$430,000,000) and statistical discrepancy (B$13,000,000). [11]Includes 517 not adequately defined and 17,950 unemployed. [12]March. [13]Annual mean household income. [14]May. [15]Domestic purchases by resident households only; data for expenditures in restaurants and hotels are not available. [16]Imports c.i.f.; exports f.o.b. [17]1991–92. [18]College of The Bahamas only. [19]Includes police.

Bahrain

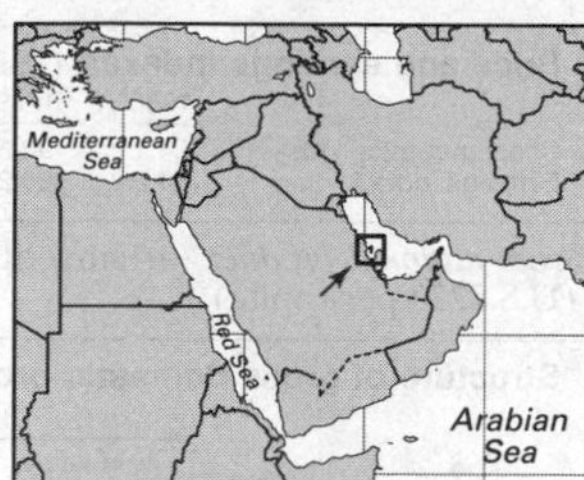

Official name: Dawlat al-Baḥrayn (State of Bahrain).
Form of government: monarchy (emirate) with an advisory Consultative Council (30).
Chief of state: Emir.
Head of government: Prime Minister.
Capital: Manama.
Official language: Arabic.
Official religion: Islam.
Monetary unit: 1 Bahrain dinar (BD) = 1,000 fils; valuation (Oct. 6, 1995) 1 BD = U.S.$2.63 = £1.67.

Area and population

	area		population
Regions[1]	sq mi	sq km	1991 census
al-Gharbīyah (Western)	60.3	156.1	22,034
al-Ḥadd	2.3	6.0	8,610
Jidd (Judd) Ḥafṣ	8.3	21.6	44,769
al-Manāmah (Manama)	10.0	25.8	136,999
al-Muḥarraq	6.2	16.0	74,245
ar-Rifā'	112.6	291.6	49,752
ash-Shamālīyah (Northern)	14.2	36.8	33,763
ash-Sharqīyah (Eastern)	...	...	3,242[2]
Sitrah	11.1	28.8	36,755
al-Wusṭā (Central)	13.6	35.2	34,304
Towns with special status			
Ḥammād	5.1	13.1	29,055
Madīnat 'Īsā	4.8	12.4	34,509
Islands			
Ḥawār[3] and other	19.5	50.6	[2]
TOTAL	268.0	694.2[4]	508,037

Demography

Population (1995): 579,000.
Density (1995): persons per sq mi 2,160.4, persons per sq km 834.0.
Urban-rural (1995): urban 90.3%; rural 9.7%.
Sex distribution (1995): male 57.27%; female 42.73%.
Age breakdown (1995): under 15, 32.3%; 15–29, 22.7%; 30–44, 30.6%; 45–59, 10.1%; 60–74, 3.6%; 75 and over, 0.7%.
Population projection: (2000) 650,000; (2010) 778,000.
Doubling time: 29 years.
Ethnic composition (1991): Bahraini Arab 63.6%; Persian, Indian, Pakistani, and other Asians 30.3%; other Arab 3.5%; European 1.2%; other 1.4%.
Religious affiliation (1995): Muslim 81.8%, of which Shī'ī 57.2%, Sunnī 24.5%; Christian 8.5%; other 9.7%.
Major cities (1991): Manama (1992) 140,401; ar-Rifā' 45,956; al-Muḥarraq 45,337; Madīnat 'Īsā 34,509.

Vital statistics

Birth rate per 1,000 population (1994): 27.0 (world avg. 25.0); legitimate 100%.
Death rate per 1,000 population (1994): 4.0 (world avg. 9.3).
Natural increase rate per 1,000 population (1994): 23.0 (world avg. 15.7).
Total fertility rate (avg. births per childbearing woman; 1995): 3.9.
Marriage rate per 1,000 population (1991): 6.8.
Divorce rate per 1,000 population (1991): 1.3.
Life expectancy at birth (1994): male 71.0 years; female 76.0 years.
Major causes of death per 100,000 population (1991): diseases of the circulatory system 100.4; malignant neoplasms (cancers) 34.1; diseases of the respiratory system 29.7; accidents and violence 28.5; endocrine, nutritional, and metabolic diseases 17.4; congenital anomalies 13.8; diseases of the genitourinary system 13.4; diseases of the digestive system 10.7.

National economy

Budget (1993). Revenue: BD 580,000,000 (1991; petroleum company dividends and oil field receipts 59.8%, non-oil revenue including grants and loans 40.2%). Expenditures: BD 643,000,000 (1991; government services 30.7%, defense 17.8%, education 15.5%, transport and communication 11.8%, health 9.2%).
Public debt (external, outstanding; 1991): U.S.$1,810,000,000[5].
Population economically active (1991): total 226,448; activity rate of total population 44.6% (participation rates: ages 15–64, 66.1%; female 17.5%; unemployed 6.3%).

Price and earnings indexes (1990 = 100)

	1988	1989	1990	1991	1992	1993	1994
Consumer price index	97.6	99.1	100.0	100.8	100.6	103.1	104.0
Earnings index	...	...	...	...	...	...	...

Production (metric tons except as noted). Agriculture, forestry, fishing (1994): fruit (excluding melons) 24,000, cow's milk 20,000, dates 19,000, tomatoes 8,000, hen's eggs 3,400, onions 1,000, cucumbers 1,000; livestock (number of live animals) 29,000 sheep, 17,000 goats, 16,000 cattle, 1,000 camels, 1,000,000 chickens; fish catch (1993) 8,958. Manufacturing (barrels; 1993): gas oil 29,360,000; fuel oil 22,188,000; kerosene 12,282,000; gasoline 9,228,000; jet fuel 4,410,000; heavy lubricant distillate 2,613,000[6]; naphtha 1,800,000; petroleum bitumen 523,000; aluminum 447,514 metric tons; other manufactures include methanol, ammonia, plastics, and paper products. Construction (permits issued; 1991): residential 5,931; nonresidential 718. Energy production (consumption): electricity (kW-hr; 1993) 4,330,000,000 (4,330,000,000); coal, none (none); crude petroleum (barrels; 1993) 14,852,000 (90,254,000); petroleum products (metric tons; 1993) 10,428,000 (500,000); natural gas (cu m; 1993) 6,517,000,000 (6,517,000,000).
Gross national product (at current market prices; 1993): U.S.$4,283,000,000 (U.S.$7,870 per capita).

Structure of gross domestic product and labour force

	1992		1991	
	value in BD '000,000[7]	% of total value	labour force	% of labour force
Agriculture	15.1	0.9	5,108	2.3
Mining	293.2	17.9	3,638	1.6
Manufacturing	270.9	16.5	26,618	11.8
Construction	92.5	5.6	26,738	11.6
Public utilities	26.5	1.6	2,898	1.3
Transp. and commun.	211.0	12.9	13,789	6.1
Trade	173.4	10.6	29,961	13.2
Finance	280.0	17.1	17,256	7.6
Pub. admin., defense	330.0	20.1	83,944	37.1
Services	84.0	5.1		
Other	−135.7	−8.3	16,498	7.3
TOTAL	1,640.9	100.0	226,448	100.0[3]

Household income and expenditure. Average household size (1991) 5.8; income per household: n.a.; sources of income: n.a.; expenditure (1984): food and tobacco 33.3%, housing 21.2%, household durable goods 9.8%, transportation and communications 8.5%, recreation 6.4%, clothing and footwear 5.9%, education 2.7%, health 2.3%, energy and water 2.2%.
Land use (1993): meadows and pastures 5.9%; agricultural and under permanent cultivation 2.9%; built-on and wasteland (mostly sand plains and salt marshes) 91.2%.
Tourism (1992): receipts from visitors U.S.$177,000,000; expenditures by nationals abroad U.S.$141,000,000.

Foreign trade[8]

Balance of trade (current prices)

	1989	1990	1991	1992	1993	1994
BD '000,000	+3.1	+156.7	−73.1	−138.2	+88.2	+33.0
% of total	1.4%	5.9%	2.7%	5.1%	3.3%	1.3%

Imports (1992): BD 1,559,000,000 (crude petroleum products 36.5%, transport equipment and machines 26.0%, chemicals 7.0%, food and live animals 6.5%). *Major import sources:* United States 8.3%; United Kingdom 6.9%; Japan 6.6%; Germany 6.5%; Australia 3.9%; Saudi Arabia 3.6%; not specified 42.9%.
Exports (1992): BD 1,285,000,000 (petroleum products 76.2%, basic manufactured goods 16.0%). *Major export destinations:* Saudi Arabia 4.2%; South Korea 2.9%; Japan 2.2%; United States 2.0%; not specified 79.9%.

Transport and communications

Transport. Railroads: none. Roads (1993): total length 1,719 mi, 2,767 km (paved 79%). Vehicles (1993): passenger cars 114,045; trucks and buses 26,771. Merchant marine (1992): vessels (100 gross tons and over) 87; total deadweight tonnage 192,487. Air transport (1994)[9]: passenger-mi 1,515,000,000, passenger-km 2,438,000,000; short ton-mi cargo 73,360,000, metric ton-km cargo 107,104,000; airports (1995) with scheduled flights 1.
Communications. Daily newspapers (1992): total number 3; total circulation 43,000; circulation per 1,000 population 60. Radio (1994): total number of receivers 320,000 (1 per 1.7 persons). Television (1994): total number of receivers 270,000 (1 per 2.0 persons). Telephones (main lines; 1993): 124,400 (1 per 4.4 persons).

Education and health

Education (1992–93)

	schools	teachers	students	student/ teacher ratio
Primary (age 6–11)	114	3,312	68,808	20.0
Secondary (age 12–17)	35[10]	2,309	45,020	19.5
Voc., teacher tr.	9[10]	823	6,393	7.8
Higher	4[10]	582	7,763	13.3

Educational attainment (1991). Percentage of population age 25 and over having: no formal education 38.4%; primary education 26.2%; secondary 25.1%; higher 10.3%. *Literacy* (1991): percentage of population age 15 and over literate 69.7%; males literate 76.5%; females literate 58.6%.
Health (1991): physicians 542 (1 per 953 persons); hospital beds 1,187 (1 per 435 persons); infant mortality rate per 1,000 live births (1994) 19.0.
Food: n.a.

Military

Total active duty personnel (1995): 10,700 (army 79.4%, navy 6.5%, air force 14.1%). *Military expenditure as percentage of GNP* (1994): 5.5% (world 2.6%); per capita expenditure U.S.$439.

[1]Regions have no administrative function; the six major cities of Bahrain are administered by a single municipal council. [2]Ash-Sharqīyah includes population of Ḥawār and other islands. [3]Also claimed by Qatar. [4]Detail does not add to total given because of rounding. [5]Includes long-term private debt not guaranteed by the government. [6]1991. [7]In purchasers' value at current prices. [8]Import figures are f.o.b. in balance of trade and c.i.f. for commodities and trading partners. [9]One-fourth apportionment of international flights of Gulf Air (jointly administered by the governments of Bahrain, Oman, Qatar, and the United Arab Emirates). [10]1987–88.

Bangladesh

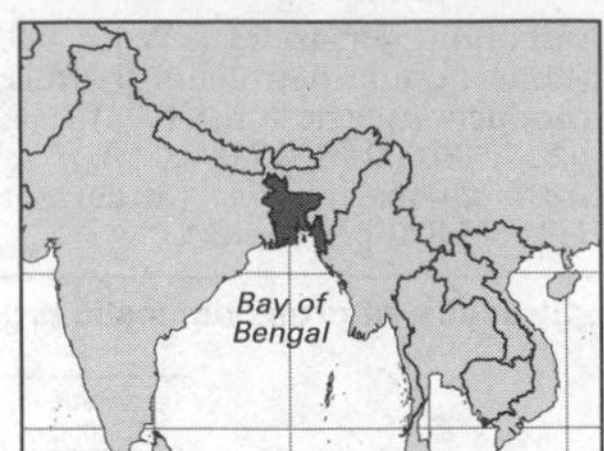

Official name: Gana Prajātantrī Bangladesh (People's Republic of Bangladesh).
Form of government: unitary multiparty republic with one legislative house (Parliament [330[1]]).
Chief of state: President.
Head of government: Prime Minister.
Capital: Dhākā.
Official language: Bengali.
Official religion: Islam.
Monetary unit: 1 Bangladesh taka (Tk) = 100 paisa; valuation (Oct. 6, 1995) 1 U.S.$ = Tk 40.20; 1 £ = Tk 63.55.

Area and population

		area		population
Divisions[2]	Administrative centres	sq mi	sq km	1991 census[3]
Barisal	Barisal	5,134	13,297	7,757,334
Chittagong	Chittagong	17,902	46,367	29,015,222
Dhākā	Dhākā	12,015	31,119	33,939,848
Khulna	Khulna	8,600	22,274	13,243,054
Rājshāhi	Rājshāhi	13,326	34,513	27,499,727
TOTAL		56,977	147,570	111,455,185

Demography

Population (1995): 120,093,000.
Density (1995): persons per sq mi 2,107.7, persons per sq km 813.8.
Urban-rural (1991): urban 20.2%; rural 79.8%.
Sex distribution (1991): male 51.47%; female 48.53%.
Age breakdown (1991): under 15, 45.1%; 15–29, 25.2%; 30–44, 16.2%; 45–59, 8.1%; 60–74, 4.3%; 75 and over, 1.1%.
Population projection: (2000) 133,324,000; (2010) 158,162,000.
Doubling time: 30 years.
Ethnic composition (1991): Bengali 98.8%; tribal (Chakmā, Gāro, Khāsi, Santāl, etc.) 1.1%; other 0.1%.
Religious affiliation (1991): Muslim 88.3%; Hindu 10.5%; Buddhist 0.6%; Christian 0.3%; other 0.3%.
Major cities (1991)[4]: Dhākā 6,105,160; Chittagong 2,040,663; Khulna 877,388; Rājshāhi 517,136; Mymensingh 185,517[5].

Vital statistics

Birth rate per 1,000 population (1995): 34.0 (world avg. 25.0).
Death rate per 1,000 population (1995): 11.0 (world avg. 9.3).
Natural increase rate per 1,000 population (1995): 23.0 (world avg. 15.7).
Total fertility rate (avg. births per childbearing woman; 1995): 4.1.
Marriage rate per 1,000 population (1992): 10.7.
Divorce rate per 1,000 population (1981): 3.6.
Life expectancy at birth (1995): male 57.0 years; female 57.0 years.
Major causes of death (1990; percentage of recorded deaths): typhoid fever 19.8%; old age 14.8%; tetanus 10.1%; tuberculosis and other respiratory diseases 8.7%; diarrhea 6.4%; suicide, accidents, and poisoning 5.1%; high blood pressure and heart diseases 5.0%.

National economy

Budget (1992–93). Revenue: Tk 110,040,000,000 (sales tax 30.2%, customs duties 29.7%, business tax 10.8%, dividends and profits from public enterprises 8.2%, income taxes 3.9%, interest receipts 2.7%). Expenditures: Tk 86,554,000,000 (employee compensation 39.4%, transfer payments 34.9%, goods and services 21.9%, capital formation 3.8%).
Public debt (external, outstanding; 1993): U.S.$13,048,000,000.
Production (metric tons except as noted). Agriculture, forestry, fishing (1994): paddy rice 27,537,000, sugarcane 7,111,000, wheat 1,131,000, jute 790,000, bananas 630,000, pulses 517,000, oilseeds 462,000[6], condiments and spices 322,000[6], jackfruit 255,000[6], mangoes 184,000, pineapples 150,000, tea 51,000; livestock (number of live animals) 28,050,000 goats, 24,130,000 cattle, 1,070,000 sheep, 874,000 buffalo, 116,000,000 chickens, 15,000,000 ducks; roundwood (1993) 32,513,000 cu m; fish catch (1993) 1,047,170. Mining and quarrying (1993): marine salt 340,000; industrial limestone 50,000. Manufacturing (1993–94): chemical fertilizers 2,366,120; jute manufactures 428,100; sugar 220,178; food products 60,466; newsprint 47,423; paper 44,391; iron and steel 28,394; glass sheet 1,002,000 sq m; cotton yarn 282,000 bales; matches 13,090,000 gross boxes. Construction: n.a. Energy production (consumption): electricity (kW-hr; 1993) 9,685,000,000 (9,685,000,000); coal (metric tons; 1993) none (380,000); crude petroleum (barrels; 1993) 224,000 (8,198,000); petroleum products (metric tons; 1993) 1,004,000 (2,182,000); natural gas (cu m; 1993) 5,960,000,000 (5,960,000,000).
Household income. Average household size (1991) 5.5; average annual income per household (1991–92) Tk 40,092 (U.S.$1,061); sources of income (1988–89): self-employment 48.3%, wages and salaries 18.7%, transfer payments 7.5%, other 25.5%; expenditure (1991–92): food and drink 66.6%, housing and rent 10.4%, fuel and light 5.6%, clothing and footwear 4.7%, other 12.7%.
Land use (1993): forested 14.6%; meadows and pastures 4.6%; agricultural and under permanent cultivation 74.5%; other 6.3%.
Population economically active (1990): total 51,200,000; activity rate of total population 46.9% (participation rates: over age 10, 69.7%; female 39.3%; unemployed 1.0%[7]).

Price and earnings indexes (1990 = 100)

	1988	1989	1990	1991	1992	1993	1994
Consumer price index	84.1	92.5	100.0	107.2	111.8	111.8	115.8
Earnings index[8]	81.2	88.2	100.0	104.9	109.3	...	...

Gross national product (at current market prices; 1993): U.S.$25,882,000,000 (U.S.$220 per capita).

Structure of gross domestic product and labour force

	1993–94		1990	
	in value Tk '000,000	% of total value	labour force	% of labour force
Agriculture	314,945	30.4	33,303,000	65.0
Mining	103,012	9.9	15,000	—
Manufacturing			5,925,000	11.6
Construction	60,134	5.8	525,000	1.0
Public utilities	20,607	2.0	40,000	0.1
Transp. and commun.	129,221	12.5	1,611,000	3.1
Trade	82,213	7.9	4,285,000	8.4
Finance	21,395	2.1	296,000	0.6
Public admin., defense	55,148	5.3	5,200,000	10.2
Services and other	248,789	24.0		
TOTAL	1,035,464	100.0[9]	51,200,000	100.0

Tourism (1993): receipts from visitors U.S.$15,000,000; expenditures by nationals abroad U.S.$153,000,000.

Foreign trade

Balance of trade (current prices)

	1989	1990	1991	1992	1993	1994
Tk '000,000	−63,910	−55,550	−48,564	−55,276	−52,113	−59,665
% of total	43.1%	32.4%	28.2%	25.3%	22.5%	21.9%

Imports (1993–94): Tk 160,450,000,000 (textile yarn, fabrics, and made-up articles 25.1%; machinery and transport equipment 10.6%; petroleum and petroleum products 7.3%; chemicals 5.7%; iron and steel 3.2%; cereals and cereal preparations 1.0%). *Major import sources* (1991–92): South Korea 8.9%; Hong Kong 7.4%; Singapore 7.4%; China 7.3%; Japan 7.2%; United States 6.3%; Taiwan 4.8%; Germany 3.5%; India 3.3%; Pakistan 3.3%.
Exports (1993–94): Tk 93,870,000,000 (ready-made garments 60.2%; fish and prawns 10.8%; jute manufactures 10.2%; hides, skins, and leather 6.7%; raw jute 2.7%; tea 1.9%). *Major export destinations* (1991–92): United States 34.0%; Germany 8.2%; Italy 6.0%; United Kingdom 5.9%; France 5.6%; Belgium 4.1%; Singapore 4.1%; The Netherlands 3.1%; Japan 2.8%.

Transport and communications

Transport. Railroads (1991–92): route length 1,706 mi, 2,746 km; passenger-mi 3,323,000,000, passenger-km 5,348,000,000; short ton-mi cargo 492,000,000, metric ton-km cargo 718,000,000. Roads (1990): total length 120,100 mi, 193,283 km (paved 4%). Vehicles (1992): passenger cars 75,409; trucks and buses 96,853. Merchant marine (1992): vessels (100 gross tons and over) 301; total deadweight tonnage 566,775. Air transport (1993)[10]: passenger-mi 1,588,000,000, passenger-km 2,556,000,000; short ton-mi cargo 190,238,000, metric ton-km cargo 277,743,000; airports with scheduled flights (1995) 8.
Communications. Daily newspapers (1992): total number 51; total circulation 710,000; circulation per 1,000 population 6. Radio (1994): 4,650,000 receivers (1 per 25 persons). Television (1994): 350,000 receivers (1 per 336 persons). Telephones (main lines; 1993): 268,400 (1 per 435 persons).

Education and health

Education (1991–92)

	schools	teachers	students	student/ teacher ratio
Primary (age 6–10)	49,964	208,271	13,717,000	65.9
Secondary (age 11–17)	9,892	116,336	4,009,000	34.5
Voc., teacher tr.	153	1,722	31,275	18.2
Higher	1,046	25,195	853,343	33.9

Educational attainment (1991). Percentage of population age 5 and over having: no formal schooling 58.6%; primary education 25.0%; secondary 15.3%; postsecondary 1.1%. *Literacy* (1991): total population age 15 and over literate 34.8%; males literate 45.2%; females literate 23.7%.
Health (1992): physicians 21,749 (1 per 5,264 persons); hospital beds 34,603 (1 per 3,218 persons); infant mortality rate (1993) 109.2.
Food (1992): daily per capita caloric intake 2,019 (vegetable products 97%, animal products 3%); 87% of FAO recommended minimum requirement.

Military

Total active duty personnel (1995): 115,500 (army 87.5%, navy 6.9%, air force 5.6%). *Military expenditure as percentage of GNP* (1993): 1.5% (world 3.3%); per capita expenditure U.S.$3.

[1]Includes 30 seats reserved for women. [2]Geographic reorganization at the district level took place in 1993; each division is now divided into the following number of new districts: Barisal 6, Chittagong 15, Dhākā 17, Khulna 10, and Rājshāhi 16. [3]Adjusted for underenumeration. [4]Metropolitan population. [5]Municipal population. [6]1991–92. [7]Excluding underemployment. [8]Wage earnings in manufacturing. [9]Detail does not add to total given because of rounding. [10]Bangladesh Biman only.

Barbados

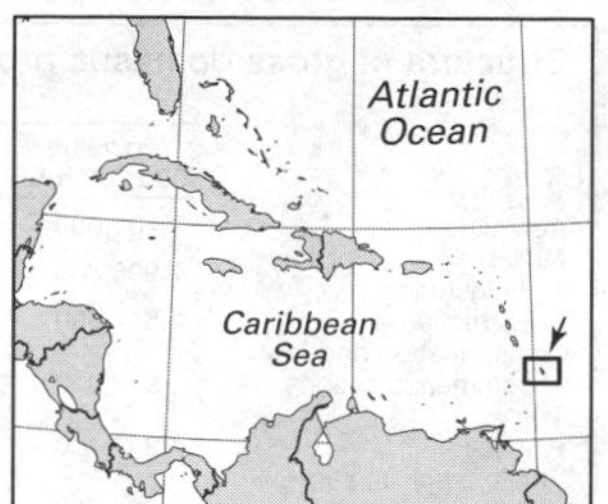

Official name: Barbados.
Form of government: constitutional monarchy with two legislative houses (Senate [21]; House of Assembly [28]).
Chief of state: British Monarch represented by Governor-General.
Head of government: Prime Minister.
Capital: Bridgetown.
Official language: English.
Official religion: none.
Monetary unit: 1 Barbados dollar (BDS$) = 100 cents; valuation (Oct. 6, 1995) 1 U.S.$ = BDS$2.00; 1 £ = BDS$3.16.

Area and population	area		population
			1990
Parishes[1]	sq mi	sq km	census
Christ Church	22	57	44,993
St. Andrew	14	36	6,426
St. George	17	44	18,390
St. James	12	31	20,827
St. John	13	34	10,206
St. Joseph	10	26	7,619
St. Lucy	14	36	9,454
St. Michael[2]	15	39	97,517
St. Peter	13	34	10,388
St. Philip	23	60	19,755
St. Thomas	13	34	11,508
TOTAL	166	430[3]	257,083

Demography

Population (1995): 265,000.
Density (1995): persons per sq mi 1,595, persons per sq km 616.
Urban-rural (1990): urban 37.9%; rural 62.1%.
Sex distribution (1994): male 47.88%; female 52.12%.
Age breakdown (1990): under 15, 24.1%; 15–29, 27.0%; 30–44, 22.1%; 45–59, 11.4%; 60 and over, 15.4%.
Population projection: (2000) 269,000; (2010) 278,000.
Doubling time: n.a.; doubling time exceeds 100 years.
Ethnic composition (1988): black 80.0%; mixed 16.0%; white 4.0%.
Religious affiliation (1980): Anglican 39.7%; other Protestant 25.6%, of which Pentecostal 7.6%, Methodist 7.1%; nonreligious 17.5%; Roman Catholic 4.4%; not stated 2.7%; other 10.1%.
Major cities (1990): Bridgetown 6,070 (urban area 85,000); Speightstown, c. 3,500.

Vital statistics

Birth rate per 1,000 population (1994): 13.4 (world avg. 25.0); (1979) legitimate 26.9%; illegitimate 73.1%.
Death rate per 1,000 population (1994): 8.7 (world avg. 9.3).
Natural increase rate per 1,000 population (1994): 4.7 (world avg. 15.7).
Total fertility rate (avg. births per childbearing woman; 1992): 1.8.
Marriage rate per 1,000 population (1993): 8.5.
Divorce rate per 1,000 population (1993): 16.7.
Life expectancy at birth (1989–91): male 72.9 years, female 77.4 years.
Major causes of death per 100,000 population (1992): diseases of the circulatory system 366.8; malignant neoplasms (cancers) 178.5; endocrine and metabolic disorders 120.2; accidents, poisonings, and violence 40.3; diseases of the respiratory system 40.0; diseases of the digestive system 28.9; infectious and parasitic diseases 19.0; diseases of the nervous system 17.1.

National economy

Budget (1994–95). Revenue: BDS$1,054,700,000[4] (tax revenue 91.9%, of which goods and services taxes 39.1%, personal income and company taxes 28.5%, import duties 7.9%; nontax revenue 8.1%). Expenditures: BDS$1,192,800,000 (1993–94; current expenditure 89.7%, of which education 22.1%, general public services 15.1%, health 13.1%, economic services 10.9%; development expenditure 10.3%).
Production (metric tons except as noted). Agriculture, forestry, fishing (1994): raw sugar 50,700, sweet potatoes 1,254, yams 1,173, onions 726, pumpkins 596, tomatoes 565, cucumbers 367, carrots 330; livestock (number of live animals; 1993) 66,000 sheep, 45,000 pigs, 38,000 goats, 33,000 cattle; roundwood, n.a.; fish catch (1992) 2,852. Manufacturing (value added in BDS$'000; 1994): food, beverages, and tobacco (mostly sugar, molasses, rum, beer, and cigarettes) 106,200; paper products, printing, and publishing 28,400; metal products and assembly-type goods (mostly electronic components) 37,800; textiles and wearing apparel 10,300. Construction (value added in BDS$; 1994): 133,800,000. Energy production (consumption): electricity (kW-hr; 1993) 511,900,000 (511,900,000); coal, none (none); crude petroleum (barrels; 1993) 462,450 (1,803,000); petroleum products (metric tons; 1990) 266,000 (265,000); natural gas (cu m; 1993) 28,000,000 (26,000,000).
Household income and expenditure. Average household size (1980) 3.7; income per household (1988) BDS$13,455 (U.S.$6,690); sources of income: n.a.; expenditure (1978–79): food 43.2%, housing 13.1%, household operations 9.6%, alcohol and tobacco 8.4%, fuel and light 6.2%, clothing and footwear 5.1%, transportation 4.6%, other 9.8%.
Population economically active (1994): total 129,000; activity rate of total population 48.8% (participation rates: ages 15 and over, 67.4%; female 61.0%; unemployed 21.9%).

Price and earnings indexes (1990 = 100)	1988	1989	1990	1991	1992	1993	1994
Consumer price index	91.4	97.0	100.0	106.3	112.7	114.0	114.1
Hourly earnings index	92.7	95.3	100.0	...	...	...	...

Gross national product (at current market prices; 1993): U.S.$1,620,000,000 (U.S.$6,240 per capita).

Structure of gross domestic product and labour force	1994			
	in value BDS$'000,000	% of total value	labour force	% of labour force
Agriculture, fishing	149.5	4.3	5,900	4.6
Mining	17.9[5]	0.5[5]	...	...
Manufacturing	208.0	6.0	10,000	7.7
Construction	133.8	3.8	7,800	6.0
Public utilities	104.6[5]	3.0[5]	1,200	0.9
Transportation and communications	270.0	7.8	4,200	3.3
Trade, restaurants	923.9	26.6	25,700	19.9
Finance, real estate	471.5	13.6	6,300	4.9
Pub. admin., defense	522.8	15.0	39,700	30.8
Services	122.0	3.5		
Other	553.2[6]	15.9[6]	28,200[7]	21.9[7]
TOTAL	3,477.2	100.0	129,000	100.0

Public debt (1993): U.S.$346,500,000.
Tourism: receipts from visitors (1993) U.S.$502,000,000; expenditures by nationals abroad (1992) U.S.$41,000,000.
Land use (1993): forested 11.6%; meadows and pastures 4.7%; agricultural and under permanent cultivation 37.2%; other 46.5%.

Foreign trade[8]

Balance of trade (current prices)	1988	1989	1990	1991	1992	1993
BDS$'000,000	−703.9	−856.7	−858.8	−984.6	−568.8	−689.3
% of total	49.8%	53.4%	50.5%	53.6%	42.6%	48.9%

Imports (1994): BDS$1,234,814,000 (retained imports 92.5%, of which food and beverages 18.4%, machinery 15.1%, construction materials 7.3%, chemicals 6.5%, fuels 4.0%; reexported imports 7.5%). *Major import sources* (1993): United States 31.4%; Trinidad and Tobago 15.5%; United Kingdom 9.2%; Netherlands Antilles 6.1%; Venezuela 4.5%; Canada 3.7%; The Netherlands 3.7%; Germany 3.1%.
Exports (1994): BDS$363,036,000 (domestic exports 74.4%, of which sugar 17.3%, electrical components 14.0%, chemicals 11.3%, rum 2.3%, clothing 1.7%; reexports 25.6%). *Major export destinations* (1993): United Kingdom 16.7%; United States 15.2%; Trinidad and Tobago 7.6%; St. Lucia 3.8%; Canada 3.3%; Dominica 2.4%; Jamaica 1.9%.

Transport and communications

Transport. Railroads: none. Roads (1989): total length 977 mi, 1,573 km (paved 95%). Vehicles (1993): passenger cars 43,077; trucks and buses 8,479[9]. Merchant marine (1992): vessels (100 gross tons and over) 37; total deadweight tonnage 84,000. Air transport (1994): passenger arrivals 649,700, passenger departures 650,200; cargo unloaded 8,584 metric tons, cargo loaded 5,052 metric tons; airports (1995) with scheduled flights 1.
Communications. Daily newspapers (1994): total number 2; total circulation 41,405; circulation per 1,000 population 157. Radio (1994): total number of receivers 224,000 (1 per 1.2 persons). Television (1994): total number of receivers 69,350 (1 per 3.8 persons). Telephones (1992): 110,960 (1 per 2.4 persons).

Education and health

Education (1989–90)	schools	teachers	students	student/ teacher ratio
Primary (age 3–11)[10]	106	1,553	26,662	17.2
Secondary (age 12–16)	33	1,406	21,259	15.1
Vocational[11]	8	79	996	12.6
Higher[12]	1	153	1,314	8.6

Educational attainment (1980). Percentage of population age 25 and over having: no formal schooling 0.8%; primary education 63.5%; secondary 32.3%; higher 3.3%. *Literacy* (1985): total population age 15 and over literate[13] 180,000 (98.0%).
Health (1992): physicians 312 (1 per 842 persons); hospital beds 1,966 (1 per 134 persons); infant mortality rate per 1,000 live births (1994) 8.5.
Food (1988–90): daily per capita caloric intake 3,217 (vegetable products 73%, animal products 27%); 133% of FAO recommended minimum requirement.

Military

Total active duty personnel (1989): 154 (paramilitary marine and coast guard components only). *Military expenditure as percentage of GNP* (1992): 0.6% (world 3.7%); per capita expenditure U.S.$34.

[1]Parishes and city of Bridgetown have no local administrative function. [2]Includes city of Bridgetown. [3]Detail does not add to total given because of rounding. [4]Current revenue only. [5]Mining excludes natural gas; Public utilities includes natural gas. [6]Net indirect taxes. [7]Unemployed. [8]Import figures are f.o.b. in balance of trade and c.i.f. in commodities and trading partners. [9]Includes taxis. [10]1991–92. [11]1987–88. [12]University of the West Indies, Cave Hill campus. [13]National literacy standard based solely on school attendance. Functional literacy may be appreciably lower.

Belarus

Official name: Respublika Belarus (Republic of Belarus).
Form of government: unitary multiparty republic with a single legislative body (Supreme Soviet[1] [260]).
Head of state and government: President.
Capital: Minsk.
Official language: Belarusian.
Official religion: none.
Monetary unit[2]: Belarusian rubel (plural rubli) valuation (Oct. 6, 1995) free rate, 1 U.S.$ = 11,500 rubli; 1 £ = 18,180 rubli.

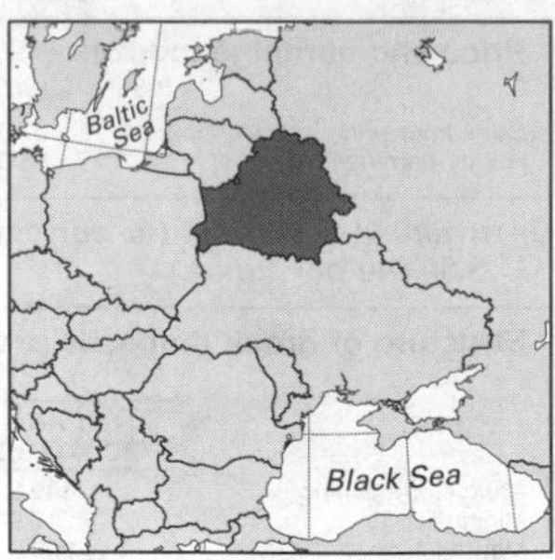

Area and population

Provinces	Capitals	area sq mi	area sq km	population 1992[3] estimate
Brest	Brest	12,500	32,300	1,494,000
Homel (Gomel)	Homel	15,600	40,400	1,611,000
Hrodno (Grodno)	Hrodno	9,700	25,000	1,199,000
Mahilyoŭ (Mogilyov)	Mahilyoŭ	11,200	29,000	1,267,000
Minsk (Mensk)	Minsk	15,700	40,800	3,272,000
Vitebsk	Vitebsk	15,500	40,100	1,438,000
TOTAL		80,200[4]	207,600[4]	10,281,000

Demography

Population (1995): 10,332,000.
Density (1995): persons per sq mi 128.8, persons per sq km 49.8.
Urban-rural (1992): urban 67.9%; rural 32.1%.
Sex distribution (1992): male 46.97%; female 53.02%.
Age breakdown (1991): under 15, 23.2%; 15–29, 21.5%; 30–44, 22.1%; 45–59, 16.5%; 60–69, 10.1%; 70 and over, 6.6%.
Population projection: (2000) 10,239,000; (2010) 10,056,000.
Doubling time: not applicable; doubling time exceeds 100 years.
Ethnic composition (1991): Belarusian 77.9%; Russian 13.5%; Ukrainian 3.0%; Jewish 0.7%; other 4.9%.
Religious affiliation: believers are predominantly Belarusian Orthodox; there is a Roman Catholic minority.
Major cities (1992): Minsk 1,671,000; Homel 517,000; Vitebsk 373,000; Mahilyoŭ 364,000; Hrodno 291,000.

Vital Statistics

Birth rate per 1,000 population (1993): 11.3 (world avg. 25.0); (1992) legitimate 90.2%; illegitimate 9.8%.
Death rate per 1,000 population (1993): 12.4 (world avg. 9.3).
Natural increase rate per 1,000 population (1993): −1.1 (world avg. 15.7).
Total fertility rate (avg. births per childbearing woman; 1993): 1.9.
Marriage rate per 1,000 population (1993): 7.9
Divorce rate per 1,000 population (1993): 4.3.
Life expectancy at birth (1993): male 66.0 years; female 75.7 years.
Major causes of death per 100,000 population (1992): diseases of the circulatory system 614.5; malignant neoplasms (cancers) 181.5; accidents and violence 130.5; diseases of the respiratory system 68.6; diseases of the digestive system 25.1.

National economy

Budget (1995). Revenue: 58,602,000,000,000 rubli[2] (social-security contributions 28.2%, taxes on goods and services 27.5%, income and profit taxes 26.0%). Expenditures: 62,603,000,000,000 rubli[2] (administration and defense 35.3%, social security and welfare 28.5%, education 11.3%, health 10.7%).
Tourism: receipts from visitors, n.a.; expenditures by nationals abroad, n.a.
Land use (1993): forested 33.7%; meadows and pastures 15.1%; agricultural and under permanent cultivation 30.1%; other 21.1%.
Production (metric tons except as noted). Agriculture, forestry, fishing (1994): potatoes 8,241,000, grain 5,675,000, sugar beets 1,078,000, other vegetables 981,000, fruit 298,000, wheat 255,000; livestock (number of live animals) 5,851,000 cattle, 4,175,000 pigs, 403,000 sheep and goats, 215,000 horses, 45,000,000 poultry; roundwood (1993) 10,031,000 cu m; fish catch (1993) 14,000. Mining and quarrying (1993): potash 1,900,000; salt 300,000. Manufacturing (value of production in Russian rubles '000,000; 1993): machine-building equipment 1,228,901; food products 584,372; chemical products 559,408; petroleum products 396,263; textiles 353,153; wood products 197,990; construction materials 197,527; clothing 122,079; leather products 117,069. Construction (1991): 5,395,000 sq m. Energy production (consumption): electricity (kW-hr; 1993) 33,369,000,000 (39,374,000,000); coal (1993) none (1,608,000); crude petroleum (barrels; 1993) 14,697,000 (104,687,000); petroleum products (1993) 13,358,000 (13,379,000); natural gas (cu m; 1993) 259,200,000 (15,124,000,000).
Population economically active (1993): 4,826,000; activity rate of total population 46.9% (participation rate: ages 16–59 [male], 16–54 [female] 83.5%; female [1991] 53.3%; unemployed [1992] 7.5%).

Price and earnings indexes (1990 = 100)

	1989	1990	1991	1992	1993	1994
Consumer price index	95.6	100.0	183.5	1,962	25,265	*c.* 586,148
Monthly earnings index	86.2	100.0	300.0	3,150	40,950	*c.* 696,150

Gross national product (at current market prices; 1993): U.S.$29,306,000,000 (U.S.$2,840 per capita).

Structure of gross domestic product and labour force

	1994 in value '000,000 rubli[2]	1994 % of total value	1994 labour force	1994 % of labour force
Agriculture	2,781,000	15.9	882,000	19.1
Mining / Manufacturing	7,906,200	45.1	1,294,000	28.0
Construction	1,517,300	8.7	336,000	7.3
Transportation and communununications	912,900	5.2	297,000	6.4
Trade	[5]	[5]	253,000	5.5
Finance	1,347,100	7.7	37,000	0.8
Public administration, defense	264,300	1.5	174,000	3.8
Services	1,211,800	6.9	727,000	15.7
Other	1,576,900[5]	9.0	625,000	13.5
TOTAL	17,517,500	100.0	4,625,000	100.0[6]

Public debt (external, outstanding; 1994): U.S.$1,489,400,000.
Household income and expenditure. Average household size (1989) 3.2; income per household (1991) 8,000 Russian rubles[2]; sources of income (1992): wages and salaries 66.5%, transfers 23.6%, agricultural income 9.9%; expenditure (1992): retail goods 76.0%, taxes 6.4%, services 5.6%, housing 1.1%, other 10.9%.

Foreign trade

Balance of trade (current prices)

	1992	1993	1994
U.S.$'000,000	+377	−276	−542
% of total	5.6%	4.5%	7.9%

Imports (1994): U.S.$3,038,000,000 (former Soviet Union [FSU] 81.3%, mainly petroleum, natural gas, rolled metal; non-FSU 18.7%, mainly intermediate inputs [rolled metal, rubber, paint] and consumer goods [shoes, cotton textiles]). *Major import sources:* Russia and Ukraine constitute 96% of FSU-area trade; Europe, mainly Germany, the majority of non-FSU imports.
Exports (1994): U.S.$3,680,000,000 (FSU 66.4%, mainly trucks, diesel fuel, gasoline, polyethylene, refrigerators, rolled metal, tractors, television sets; non-FSU commodities 33.6%, mainly tractors, potassium and nitric fertilizers, consumer durables). *Major export destinations:* Russia and Ukraine constitute 95% of FSU-area trade; Europe, mainly Germany, the majority of non-FSU exports.

Transport and communications

Transport. Railroads (1993): length 3,459 mi, 5,567 km; passenger-mi 11,195,000,000, passenger-km 18,017,000,000; short ton-mi cargo 38,659,000,000, metric ton-km cargo 56,441,000,000. Roads (1992): total length 30,600 mi, 49,300 km (paved 96%). Vehicles (1993): passenger cars 773,582; trucks and buses 10,279. Merchant marine (1992): vessels (100 gross tons and over) n.a.; total deadweight tonnage 18,373,000,000. Air transport (1992): passenger-mi 3,487,000,000, passenger-km 5,611,000,000; short ton-mi cargo 23,200,000, metric ton-km cargo 34,000,000; airports (1995) with scheduled flights 1.
Communications. Daily newspapers (1992): total number 10; total circulation 1,899,000; circulation per 1,000 population 181. Radio (1993): 3,185,000 receivers (1 per 3.3 persons). Television (1993): 2,775,000 receivers (1 per 3.7 persons). Telephones (main lines; 1993): 1,814,400 (1 per 5.7 persons).

Education and health

Education (1993–94)

	schools	teachers	students	student/ teacher ratio
Primary (age 6–13) / Secondary (age 14–17)	4,900	122,700	1,628,500	13.3
Voc., teacher tr.	147	...	126,400	...
Higher	38	16,900	178,016	10.5

Educational attainment (1989). Percentage of population age 25 and over having: primary education or no formal schooling 23.0%; some secondary 16.8%; completed secondary and some postsecondary 49.4%; higher 10.8%.
Literacy (1989): total population age 15 and over literate 7,690,000 (97.9%); males literate 3,661,000 (99.4%); females literate 4,029,000 (96.6%).
Health (1994): physicians 45,000 (1 per 230 persons); hospital beds 126,000 (1 per 82 persons); infant mortality rate per 1,000 live births 12.5.
Food: daily per capita caloric intake, n.a.

Military

Total active duty personnel (1995): 98,400 (army 51.3%, air force and air defense 27.4%, CIS-controlled and other 21.3%); about 21,000 Russian troops remained in Belarus in late 1995. *Military expenditure as percentage of GNP* (1993): 1.8% (world 3.3%); per capita expenditure U.S.$50.

[1]Though the Belarusian Supreme Soviet's five-year term formally expired May 15, 1995, four rounds of parliamentary elections were necessary before a quorum was achieved (198 seats; December 11) permitting the new Parliament to be convened; during the interval the Supreme Soviet remained a legal organ. [2]The Belarusian rubel was introduced May 25, 1992, at a rate of 1 rubel to 10 Russian rubles and circulated parallel with the Russian ruble; the fixed rates to the Russian ruble were adjusted on Aug. 15, 1993 (2 Belarusian rubli to 1 Russian ruble), and on Oct. 14, 1993 (3 Belarusian rubli to 1 Russian ruble). An April 12, 1994, agreement on monetary union between Belarus and Russia never went into effect. The Belarusian rubel was declared the sole legal tender in October 1994; it is unofficially known as the zaichik, or "hare." [3]January 1. [4]Rounded area figures; exact area figures are 80,153 sq mi (207,595 sq km). [5]Other includes trade. [6]Detail does not add to total given because of rounding.

Belgium

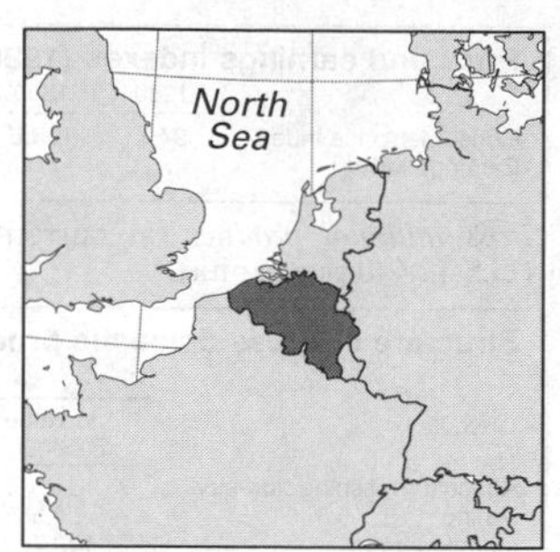

Official name: Koninkrijk België (Dutch); Royaume de Belgique (French) (Kingdom of Belgium).
Form of government: federal constitutional monarchy with two legislative houses (Senate [71[1]]; House of Representatives [150]).
Chief of state: Monarch.
Head of government: Prime Minister.
Capital: Brussels.
Official languages: Dutch; French; German.
Official religion: none.
Monetary unit: 1 Belgian franc (BF) = 100 centimes; valuation (Oct. 6, 1995) 1 U.S.$ = BF 29.39; 1 £ = BF 46.46.

Area and population

Regions[3] / Provinces	Capitals	area sq mi	area sq km	population 1993[2] estimate
Brussels	—	62	161	950,339
Flanders	—	5,221[4]	13,522	5,824,628
Antwerp	Antwerp	1,107	2,867	1,619,613
Brabant[5]	—	813	2,106	982,943
East Flanders	Ghent	1,151	2,982	1,344,263
Limburg	Hasselt	935	2,422	761,565
West Flanders	Brugge	1,214	3,145	1,116,244
Wallonia	—	6,504[4]	16,844	3,293,352
Brabant[6]	—	421	1,091	329,614
Hainaut	Mons	1,462	3,786	1,285,934
Liège	Liège	1,491	3,862	1,011,368
Luxembourg	Arlon	1,714	4,440	236,850
Namur	Namur	1,415	3,666	429,586
TOTAL		11,707	30,528[4]	10,068,319

Demography

Population (1995): 10,064,000.
Density (1995): persons per sq mi 853.8, persons per sq km 329.7.
Urban-rural (1992): urban 96.5%; rural 3.5%.
Sex distribution (1993[2]): male 48.90%; female 51.10%.
Age breakdown (1991): under 15, 18.1%; 15–29, 21.8%; 30–44, 22.5%; 45–59, 16.9%; 60–74, 14.1%; 75 and over, 6.6%.
Population projection: (2000) 10,058,000; (2010) 10,048,000.
Doubling time: not applicable; doubling time exceeds 100 years.
Nationality (1992): Belgian 91.0%; Italian 2.4%; Moroccan 1.4%; French 0.9%; Turkish 0.8%; Dutch 0.6%; other 2.9%.
Religious affiliation (1980): Roman Catholic 90.0%; Muslim 1.1%; Protestant 0.4%; nonreligious and atheist 7.5%; other 1.0%.
Major cities (1994[2]): Brussels 136,424[7] (949,070[8]); Antwerp 462,880; Ghent 228,490; Charleroi 206,898; Liège 195,389.

Vital statistics

Birth rate per 1,000 population (1993): 11.9 (world avg. 25.0); (1988) legitimate 89.3%; illegitimate 10.7%.
Death rate per 1,000 population (1993): 10.6 (world avg. 9.3).
Natural increase rate per 1,000 population (1993): 1.3 (world avg. 15.7).
Total fertility rate (avg. births per childbearing woman; 1990–95): 1.6.
Marriage rate per 1,000 population (1993): 5.4.
Divorce rate per 1,000 population (1992): 2.2.
Life expectancy at birth (1988–90): male 72.4 years; female 79.1 years.
Major causes of death per 100,000 population (1989): diseases of the circulatory system 412.8; malignant neoplasms (cancers) 274.6.

National economy

Budget (1993). Revenue: BF 2,090,371,000,000 (direct taxes 35.5%; value-added, stamp, and similar duties 10.5%; customs and excise duties 8.2%). Expenditures: BF 2,531,970,000,000 (public debt 27.4%; government departments 23.6%; pension 10.3%; defense 3.8%).
Production (metric tons except as noted). Agriculture, forestry, fishing (1993): sugar beets 6,264,200, potatoes 2,155,100, wheat 1,392,100, apples 536,000[9], barley 354,600, tomatoes 345,000[9], carrots 105,000[9], corn (maize) 76,600, oats 54,000; livestock (number of live animals) 6,876,100 pigs, 3,084,200 cattle, 127,300 sheep, 21,800 horses; roundwood (1992) 4,730,000 cu m; fish catch (1992) 37,356, of which European plaice (flounder) 14,828, common sole 4,505, Atlantic cod 4,246. Mining and quarrying (1993): quartz 500,000; barite 30,000; granite (Belgium bluestone) 1,200,000 cu m; marble 358 cu m. Manufacturing (value added in BF '000,000; 1990): metal products and machinery 422,238; chemical and plastic products 344,743; food, beverages, and tobacco 198,942; pig iron, steel, and nonferrous metals 136,244; paper, printing, and publishing 96,623; textiles 94,861; furniture and fixtures 61,626. Construction (1992): residential 31,316,000 cu m; nonresidential 45,639,000 cu m. Energy production (consumption): electricity (kW-hr; 1992) 72,259,000,000 (72,387,000,000); coal (metric tons; 1992) 1,197,000 (14,387,000); crude petroleum (barrels; 1992) none (211,646,000); petroleum products (metric tons; 1992) 26,311,000 (17,165,000); natural gas (cu m; 1992) 6,945,000 (13,230,000,000).
Household income and expenditure. Avg. household size (1991) 2.7; sources of income (1992): wages 49.6%, transfer payments 20.7%, property income 18.8%, self-employment 10.9%; expenditure (1992): food 18.0%, housing 17.0%, transp. 13.3%, health 11.8%, durable goods 10.7%, clothing 7.7%.
Gross national product (1993): U.S.$213,435,000,000 (U.S.$21,210 per capita).

Structure of gross domestic product and labour force

	1993 in value BF '000,000	1993 % of total value	1992 labour force	1992 % of labour force
Agriculture	120,000	1.8	109,200	2.7
Mining	15,500	0.2	872,800	21.4
Manufacturing	1,563,000	23.2		
Construction	362,800	5.4	246,600	6.0
Public utilities	179,800	2.7	44,300	1.1
Transp. and commun.	544,100	8.1	269,100	6.6
Trade	946,200	14.1	670,800	16.4
Finance	1,322,500	19.7	327,500	8.0
Pub. admin., defense	1,139,700	16.9	1,232,300	30.1
Services	681,200	10.1		
Other	−149,100[10]	−2.2[10]	316,000[11]	7.7[11]
TOTAL	6,725,700	100.0	4,088,600	100.0

Public debt (1995[2]): U.S.$250,900,000,000.
Population economically active (1992): total 4,088,600; activity rate of total population 40.6% (participation rates: ages 14–64, 61.1%; female 40.7%; unemployed 7.7%).

Price and earnings indexes (1990 = 100)

	1988	1989	1990	1991	1992	1993	1994
Consumer price index	93.8	96.7	100.0	103.2	105.7	108.6	111.2
Hourly earnings index	90.7	95.8	100.0	105.1	110.1	112.4	114.7

Land use (1992)[9]: forested 21.3%; meadows and pastures 20.9%; agricultural and under permanent cultivation 23.9%; other 33.9%.
Tourism (1993): receipts from visitors U.S.$4,071,000,000; expenditures by nationals abroad U.S.$6,363,000,000.

Foreign trade[9]

Balance of trade (current prices)

	1987	1988	1989	1990	1991	1992
BF '000,000	+124,300	+96,400	+177,300	+61,200	+21,700	+65,200
% of total	2.0%	1.4%	2.3%	0.8%	0.3%	0.8%

Imports (1993): BF 3,791,874,000,000 (machinery and transport equipment 25.0%; chemicals and chemical products 12.7%; food and live animals 8.9%; mineral fuels and lubricants 7.5%, of which petroleum and petroleum products 5.1%; nonindustrial [gem] diamonds 5.1%). *Major import sources:* Germany 21.5%; The Netherlands 17.9%; France 16.1%; U.K. 9.4%; U.S. 5.4%; Italy 4.4%.
Exports (1993): BF 4,158,382,000,000 (machinery and transport equipment 27.4%, chemicals 15.4%, of which plastics 5.0%; food and live animals 9.5%; nonindustrial [gem] diamonds 7.0%; iron and steel 5.6%; textiles 5.1%; petroleum and petroleum products 3.1%). *Major export destinations:* Germany 21.0%; France 19.0%; The Netherlands 13.1%; U.K. 8.4%; Italy 5.4%; U.S. 4.7%.

Transport and communications

Transport. Railroads (1993): route length 2,119 mi, 3,410 km; passenger-mi 4,159,000,000, passenger-km 6,694,000,000; short ton-mi cargo 5,184,000,000, metric ton-km cargo 7,568,000,000. Roads (1990[2]): total length 85,672 mi, 137,876 km (paved 97%). Vehicles (1993): passenger cars 4,109,601; trucks and buses 389,812. Merchant marine (1992): vessels (100 gross tons and over) 232; total deadweight tonnage 218,506. Air transport (1993): passenger-mi 4,026,000,000, passenger-km 6,480,000,000; short ton-mi cargo 287,440,000, metric ton-km cargo 419,650,000; airports (1995) with scheduled flights 2.
Communications. Daily newspapers (1994): total number 46; total circulation 3,186,700[12]; circulation per 1,000 population 315[12]. Radio (1994): 7,640,000 receivers (1 per 1.3 persons). Television (1994): 4,200,000 receivers (1 per 2.4 persons). Telephones (main lines; 1993): 4,395,700 (1 per 2.3 persons).

Education and health

Education (1992–93)

	schools	teachers	students	student/ teacher ratio
Primary (age 6–12)	4,450	72,589[13]	735,670	...
Secondary (age 12–18)	1,962	110,599	790,377	6.9
Voc., teacher tr.	304	14,548[14]	155,192	...
Higher	21	10,517[14]	123,320	...

Educational attainment (1981). Percentage of population age 15 and over having: less than secondary education 44.4%; lower secondary 26.5%; upper secondary 17.0%; vocational 2.9%; teacher's college 0.6%; university 3.5%. *Literacy* (1991): virtually 100% literate.
Health (1993): physicians 36,178 (1 per 278 persons); hospital beds (1991) 80,549 (1 per 124 persons); infant mortality rate per 1,000 live births 8.0.
Food (1988–90): daily per capita caloric intake 3,925 (vegetable products 60%, animal products 40%); 149% of FAO recommended minimum requirement.

Military

Total active duty personnel (1994): 63,000 (army 76.2%, navy 4.6%, air force 19.2%). *Military expenditure as percentage of GNP* (1993): 1.8% (world 3.3%); per capita expenditure U.S.$373.

[1]Includes 40 directly and 31 indirectly elected members. [2]January 1. [3]On May 8, 1993, the legislature approved constitutional establishment of federal regions. [4]Detail does not add to total given because of rounding. [5]Composed of Brabant districts Hal-Vilvorde and Louvaine. [6]Composed of Brabant district Nivelles. [7]1991. [8]Région Bruxelloise. [9]Includes Luxembourg. [10]Includes imputed bank service charges and statistical adjustments. [11]Unemployed. [12]For 31 newspapers only. [13]Includes preschool teachers. [14]1987–88.

Belize

Official name: Belize.
Form of government: constitutional monarchy with two legislative houses (Senate [9]; House of Representatives [29[1]]).
Chief of state: British Monarch represented by Governor-General.
Head of government: Prime Minister.
Capital: Belmopan.
Official language: English.
Official religion: none.
Monetary unit: 1 Belize dollar (BZ$) = 100 cents; valuation (Oct. 6, 1995) 1 U.S.$ = BZ$2.00[2]; 1 £ = BZ$3.16.

Area and population

		area		population
Districts	Capitals	sq mi	sq km	1993 estimate
Belize	Belize City	1,663	4,307	61,732
Cayo	San Ignacio	2,006	5,196	40,800
Corozal	Corozal	718	1,860	30,809
Orange Walk	Orange Walk	1,790	4,636	33,207
Stann Creek	Dangriga	986	2,554	19,575
Toledo	Punta Gorda	1,704	4,413	18,877
TOTAL		8,867[3]	22,965[3, 4]	205,000

Demography

Population (1995): 216,000.
Density (1995): persons per sq mi 24.4, persons per sq km 9.4.
Urban-rural (1993): urban 47.5%; rural 52.5%.
Sex distribution (1993): male 50.73%; female 49.27%.
Age breakdown (1993): under 15, 43.9%; 15–29, 27.9%; 30–44, 14.9%; 45–59, 7.2%; 60–74, 4.5%; 75 and over, 1.6%.
Population projection: (2000) 245,000; (2010) 304,000.
Doubling time: 23 years.
Ethnic composition (1991): mestizo (Spanish-Indian) 43.6%; Creole (predominantly black) 29.8%; Mayan Indian 11.0%; Garifuna (black-Carib Indian) 6.7%; white 3.9%; East Indian 3.5%; other or not stated 1.5%.
Religious affiliation (1991): Roman Catholic 57.7%; Protestant 34.3%, of which Anglican 7.0%, Pentecostal 6.3%, Methodist 4.2%, Seventh-day Adventist 4.1%, Mennonite 4.0%; other Christian 1.7%; other 0.3%; none or not stated 6.0%.
Major cities (1993): Belize City 47,723; Orange Walk 11,922; San Ignacio/Santa Elena 9,702; Corozal 7,644; Belmopan 3,852.

Vital statistics

Birth rate per 1,000 population (1993): 35.7 (world avg. 25.0); (1992) legitimate 43.5%; illegitimate 56.5%.
Death rate per 1,000 population (1993): 6.1 (world avg. 9.3).
Natural increase rate per 1,000 population (1993): 29.6 (world avg. 15.7).
Total fertility rate (avg. births per childbearing woman; 1992): 4.1.
Marriage rate per 1,000 population (1992): 6.2.
Divorce rate per 1,000 population (1992): 0.6.
Life expectancy at birth (1994): male 66.0 years; female 70.0 years.
Major causes of death per 100,000 population (1990): accidents 92.6; heart diseases 84.7; diseases of the respiratory system 57.1; malignant neoplasms (cancers) 52.4; cerebrovascular disease 47.6; diabetes mellitus 37.0.

National economy

Budget (1994–95). Revenue: BZ$308,800,000 (current revenue 88.4%, of which taxes on international trade 43.4%, taxes on income and profits 22.7%, nontax revenue 9.9%, excise taxes 9.9%; grants 10.8%). Expenditures: BZ$429,100,000 (current expenditures 56.4%; development expenditures 43.6%, of which from foreign sources 31.9%).
Public debt (external, outstanding; 1994): U.S.$180,300,000.
Production (metric tons except as noted). Agriculture, forestry, fishing (1994): sugarcane 1,210,000, oranges 82,500, grapefruits 30,200, corn (maize) 23,300, bananas 21,800, rice 6,500, red kidney beans 3,200, coconuts 3,000, cocoa (1993) 72, honey 72; livestock (number of live animals) 59,000 cattle, 26,000 pigs, 1,000,000 chickens; roundwood (1993) 188,000 cu m; fish catch (1993) 2,129, of which shrimp 1,060, lobsters 442, freshwater and marine fish 390, conchs 232. Mining and quarrying (1992): limestone 300,000; sand and gravel 300,000. Manufacturing (1994): sugar 107,100; molasses 57,400; fertilizer 24,900; flour 12,100; orange concentrate 59,300 hectolitres; beer (1992) 36,000 hectolitres; grapefruit concentrate 25,900 hectolitres; cigarettes (1992) 114,000,000 units; garments 4,276,000 units. Construction (publicly financed buildings under construction; 1991): residential 180 units; nonresidential, n.a. Energy production (consumption): electricity (kW-hr; 1992–93) 145,400,000 (120,900,000); coal, none (none); crude petroleum, none (none); petroleum products (metric tons; 1992) none (86,000); natural gas, none (none).
Household income and expenditure. Average household size (1991) 4.9; average annual income of employed head of household (1993) BZ$6,450[5] (U.S.$3,225[5]); sources of income: n.a.; expenditure (1990): food, beverages, and tobacco 34.0%, transportation 13.7%, energy and water 9.1%, housing 9.0%, clothing and footwear 8.8%, household furnishings 8.0%, recreation 4.1%.
Population economically active (1993): total 66,060[6]; activity rate of total population, 33.1% (participation rates: over age 13, 55.7%; female 30.8%; unemployed [1994] 13.1%).

Price and earnings indexes (1990 = 100)

	1989	1990	1991	1992	1993	1994	1995
Consumer price index	97.1	100.0	102.3	104.7	106.2	108.7	111.5[7]
Earnings index	...	...	...	...	...	...	...

Gross national product (at current market prices; 1993): U.S.$499,000,000 (U.S.$2,440 per capita).

Structure of gross domestic product and labour force

	1994		1991	
	in value BZ$'000[8]	% of total value	labour force[9]	% of labour force[9]
Agriculture, fishing, forestry	181,513	19.3	18,256	17.6
Mining	4,565	0.5	326	0.3
Manufacturing	132,794	14.1	5,951	5.7
Construction	69,267	7.4	4,059	3.9
Public utilities	37,189	4.0	721	0.7
Transportation and communications	107,505	11.4	2,925	2.8
Trade, restaurants	161,565	17.2	10,013	9.7
Finance, real estate, insurance	104,976	11.2	1,771	1.7
Pub. admin., defense	123,689	13.2	5,352	5.2
Services	55,544	5.9	5,967	5.8
Other	–38,375[10]	–4.1[10]	48,226[11]	46.6[11]
TOTAL	940,232	100.0[4]	103,567	100.0

Land use (1993): forested 92.1%; meadows and pastures 2.1%; agricultural and under permanent cultivation 2.5%; other 3.3%.
Tourism (1993): receipts from visitors U.S.$73,000,000; expenditures by nationals abroad U.S.$20,500,000.

Foreign trade[12]

Balance of trade (current prices)

	1989	1990	1991	1992	1993	1994
BZ$'000,000	–143.1	–118.2	–203.9	–217.2	–237.8	–170.6
% of total	22.3%	18.2%	28.8%	27.9%	30.3%	22.0%

Imports (1993): BZ$561,600,000 ([13]machinery and transport 27.0%; manufactured goods 19.8%; food and live animals 14.4%; chemicals and chemical products 11.8%). *Major import sources:* United States 56.0%; Mexico 10.0%; United Kingdom 7.0%; Japan 5.0%; Guatemala 3.0%.
Exports (1993)[14]: BZ$263,100,000 (domestic exports 86.9%, of which sugar 31.5%, garments 15.4%, bananas 9.2%, orange concentrate 6.7%, shrimp 4.7%; reexports 13.1%). *Major export destinations:* United States 45.0%; United Kingdom 36.0%; Canada 7.0%; Caricom countries 5.0%.

Transport and communications

Transport. Railroads: none. Roads (1991): total length 1,684 mi, 2,710 km (paved 18%). Vehicles (1992): passenger cars 9,989; trucks and buses 6,294. Merchant marine (1992): vessels (100 gross tons and over) 32; total deadweight tonnage 45,706. Air transport (1993)[15]: passenger arrivals 115,346, passenger departures 121,878; cargo loaded 489 metric tons, cargo unloaded 2,887 metric tons. Airports (1995) with scheduled flights 9.
Communications. Daily newspapers: none[16]. Radio (1994): total number of receivers 106,000 (1 per 2.0 persons). Television (1994): total number of receivers 27,048 (1 per 7.8 persons). Telephones (main lines; 1993): 28,600 (1 per 7.2 persons).

Education and health

Education (1992–93)

	schools	teachers	students	student/teacher ratio
Primary (age 5–12)[17]	237	1,804	48,612[18]	26.2
Secondary (age 13–16)	30	643[18]	9,457	11.4
Voc., teacher tr. / Higher	8[19]	...	1,191[19]	...

Educational attainment (1991). Percentage of population age 25 and over having: no formal schooling 12.8%; primary education 63.3%; secondary 14.7%; higher 9.2%. *Literacy* (1991): total population age 15 and over literate 99,000 (93%).
Health (1992): physicians 110 (1 per 1,809 persons); hospital beds 585 (1 per 340 persons); infant mortality rate per 1,000 live births (1994) 36.0.
Food (1992): daily per capita caloric intake 2,662 (vegetable products 75%, animal products 25%); 118% of FAO recommended minimum requirement.

Military

Total active duty personnel (1994): 950 (army 94.7%, maritime wing 3.7%, air wing 1.6%); British troops 600[20]. *Military expenditure as percentage of GNP* (1990): 2.6% (world 4.5%); per capita expenditure U.S.$51.

[1]Excludes speaker of the House of Representatives, who may be elected by the House from outside its elected membership. [2]The Belize dollar is officially pegged to the U.S. dollar. [3]Includes offshore cays totaling 266 sq mi (689 sq km). [4]Detail does not add to total given because of rounding. [5]Estimated figure for about 33,000 employed heads of household. [6]Population economically active over age 13. [7]Average of 2nd quarter. [8]At factor cost. [9]Data based on total population over age 15. [10]Less imputed bank service charges. [11]Includes not available and not stated for 45,452 persons. [12]Import figures are f.o.b. in balance of trade and c.i.f. in commodities and trading partners. [13]Based on imports through September only, totaling BZ$426,600,000. [14]*Exports* (1994): BZ$285,900,000 (domestic exports 83.5%, of which sugar 28.2%, garments 12.8%, orange and grapefruit concentrate 11.7%, bananas 10.4%, marine products 9.2%; reexports 16.5%). [15]Belize international airport only. [16]Four weekly newspapers in 1994. [17]Includes preprimary. [18]1993–94. [19]1991–92. [20]Most British troops were scheduled to withdraw in 1995.

Benin

Official name: République du Bénin (Republic of Benin).
Form of government: multiparty republic with one legislative house (National Assembly [82[1]]).
Head of state and government: President.
Capital[2]: Porto-Novo.
Official language: French.
Official religion: none.
Monetary unit: 1 CFA franc (CFAF) = 100 centimes; valuation (Oct. 6, 1995) 1 U.S.$ = CFAF 501.49; 1 £ = CFAF 792.78.

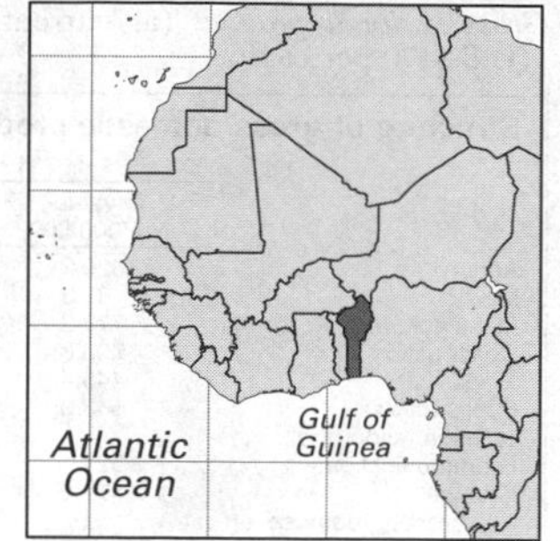

Area and population		area		population
				1992
Provinces	Capitals	sq mi	sq km	census
Atacora	Natitingou	12,050	31,200	648,330
Atlantique	Cotonou	1,250	3,200	1,060,310
Borgou	Parakou	19,700	51,000	816,278
Mono	Lokossa	1,500	3,880	646,954
Ouémé	Porto-Novo	1,800	4,700	869,492
Zou	Abomey	7,200	18,700	813,985
TOTAL		43,500	112,680	4,855,349

Demography

Population (1995): 5,409,000.
Density (1995): persons per sq mi 124.3, persons per sq km 48.0.
Urban-rural (1992): urban 39.6%; rural 60.4%.
Sex distribution (1992): male 48.72%; female 51.28%.
Age breakdown (1995): under 15, 47.4%; 15–29, 25.5%; 30–44, 14.4%; 45–59, 8.1%; 60–74, 3.7%; 75 and over, 0.8%.
Population projection: (2000) 6,266,000; (2010) 8,300,000.
Doubling time: 24 years.
Ethnic composition (1982): Fon 25.0%; Yoruba (Nago) 13.5%; Goun 11.8%; Bariba 11.8%; Adjara 10.7%; Somba (Otomary) 7.0%; Aizo 4.4%; Mina 2.9%; Dendi 2.0%; other 10.9%.
Religious affiliation (1991): traditional beliefs 62.0%; Christian 23.3%, of which Roman Catholic 21.0%, Protestant 2.3%; Muslim 12.0%; other 2.7%.
Major cities (1992): Cotonou 533,212; Porto-Novo 177,660; Djougou 132,192; Abomey-Calavi 125,565; Parakou 106,708.

Vital statistics

Birth rate per 1,000 population (1992): 44.0 (world avg. 25.0).
Death rate per 1,000 population (1992): 15.0 (world avg. 9.3).
Natural increase rate per 1,000 population (1992): 29.0 (world avg. 15.7).
Total fertility rate (avg. births per childbearing woman; 1992): 6.2.
Marriage rate per 1,000 population (1980–85): 12.8.
Divorce rate per 1,000 population (1980–85): 0.8.
Life expectancy at birth (1992): male 49.0 years; female 52.0 years.
Major causes of death per 100,000 population (1986): n.a.; however, of the 184,310 reported cases of infectious diseases (notifiable to the World Health Organization), 82.0% were malaria, 4.2% dysentery, 4.0% measles, 2.6% pneumonia, 2.2% chicken pox, 1.4% mumps, 1.3% schistosomiasis.

National economy

Budget (1994). Revenue: CFAF 127,100,000,000 (current receipts 83.1%, of which nonpetroleum fiscal receipts and customs duties 71.7%, other current receipts 11.4%; foreign aid 16.9%). Expenditures: CFAF 161,800,000,000 (current expenditures 67.0%, of which debt service 16.2%; public-investment program 33.0%).
Production (metric tons except as noted). Agriculture, forestry, fishing (1994): yams 1,287,000, cassava 1,169,000, corn (maize) 490,000, seed cotton 260,000, sorghum 113,000, tomatoes 85,000, peanuts (groundnuts) 83,000, dry beans 63,000, sweet potatoes 50,000, millet 25,000, coconuts 20,000, paddy rice 14,000, bananas 13,000, mangoes 12,000, oranges 12,000, karité (a butter from the nut of the shea tree) 11,410[3], pineapples 3,000, palm kernels 2,155, tobacco 1,000; livestock (number of live animals) 1,223,000 cattle, 1,198,000 goats, 940,000 sheep, 555,000 pigs, 20,000,000 chickens; roundwood (1993) 5,538,000 cu m; fish catch (1993) 39,000. Mining and quarrying (1993): limestone 500,000, marine salt 100. Manufacturing (1994): cement 380,000[4]; cotton fibre 103,000; meat 68,000; wheat flour 11,515; palm oil 9,432. Construction: n.a. Energy production (consumption): electricity (kW-hr; 1993) 5,000,000 (245,000,000); coal, none (none); crude petroleum (barrels; 1993) 2,214,000 (negligible); petroleum products (metric tons; 1993) none (136,000); natural gas, none (none).
Land use (1993): forested 30.7%; meadows and pastures 4.0%; agricultural and under permanent cultivation 17.0%; other 48.3%.
Tourism (1993): receipts from visitors U.S.$38,000,000; expenditures by nationals abroad U.S.$11,000,000.
Population economically active (1991): total 2,195,000; activity rate of total population 46.0% (participation rates: ages 15–64, 60.2%[5]; female 46.0%; unemployed, n.a.).

Price and earnings indexes (1990 = 100)	1988	1989	1990	1991	1992	1993	1994
Consumer price index[6]	...	...	100.0	102.1	108.1	108.7	150.6
Hourly earnings index[7]	100.0	100.0	100.0	100.0	100.0	100.0	144.1

Gross national product (at current market prices; 1993): U.S.$2,182,000,000 (U.S.$420 per capita).

Structure of gross domestic product and labour force	1994		1991	
	in value CFAF '000,000,000	% of total value	labour force	% of labour force
Agriculture	281.8	33.4	1,333,000	60.7
Mining and manufacturing	71.4	8.4	194,000	8.8
Public utilities	6.2	0.7		
Construction	37.6	4.5		
Trade and finance	169.0	20.0	668,000	30.4
Transportation and communications	70.3	8.3		
Pub. admin., defense	72.4	8.6		
Services	93.6	11.1		
Other	42.3	5.0		
TOTAL	844.5[8]	100.0	2,195,000	100.0[8]

Public debt (external, outstanding; 1993): U.S.$1,409,000,000.
Household income and expenditure. Average household size (1979) 5.4; income per household (1983) U.S.$240; sources of income: self-employment 73.7%, wages and salaries 26.3%; expenditure: n.a.

Foreign trade

Balance of trade (current prices)	1990	1991	1992	1993	1994
CFAF '000,000,000	−38.3	−41.1	−50.1	−56.1	−36.1
% of total	19.7%	17.8%	20.3%	22.5%	9.7%

Imports (1994): CFAF 203,200,000,000 (1989; manufactured goods 30.7%, of which cotton yarn and fabric 16.9%; food products 19.4%, of which cereals 10.3%; machinery and transport equipment 14.5%, of which transport equipment 5.8%, nonelectrical equipment 5.3%, electrical equipment 3.4%; chemical products 7.1%; beverages and tobacco 7.1%). *Major import sources* (1989): India 23.4%; France 15.9%; The Netherlands 5.0%, Côte d'Ivoire 4.6%; Thailand 4.6%; United States 3.7%; West Germany 3.4%; Italy 3.2%; Taiwan 2.9%; Korea 2.7%.
Exports (1994): CFAF 167,100,000,000 (1993; reexports 67.2%; domestic exports 32.8%, of which cotton lint 21.6%, crude petroleum 4.7%, seed cotton 2.6%). *Major export destinations* (1989): Portugal 15.2%; Italy 9.9%; Tailand 9.6%; Taiwan 9.0%; United States 7.4%; Niger 6.2%; France 6.1%.

Transport and communications

Transport. Railroads (1994): length 359 mi, 578 km; passenger-mi 66,500,000, passenger-km 107,000,000; short ton-mi cargo 172,000,000, metric ton-km cargo 253,000,000. Roads (1992): total length 3,770 mi, 6,070 km (paved 20.0%). Vehicles (1991): passenger cars 25,000; trucks and buses 13,000. Merchant marine (1992): vessels (100 gross tons and over) 12; total deadweight tonnage 210. Air transport (1994)[9]: passenger-mi 133,440,000, passenger-km 214,745,000; short ton-mi cargo 9,892,000, metric ton-km cargo 14,442,000; airports (1995) with scheduled flights 1.
Communications. Daily newspapers (1990): total number 1; total circulation 12,000; circulation per 1,000 population 2.6. Radio (1994): total number of receivers 400,000 (1 per 13 persons). Television (1994): total number of receivers 20,000 (1 per 262 persons). Telephones (main lines; 1993): 20,410 (1 per 260 persons).

Education and health

Education (1991)	schools	teachers	students	student/ teacher ratio
Primary	2,904	13,422	534,810	39.8
Secondary	151[10]	2,178	76,672	35.2
Voc., teacher tr.[10]	13	687	6,879	10.0
Higher[11]	13[10]	956	10,873	11.4

Educational attainment (1979). Percentage of population age 25 and over having: no formal schooling 89.2%; primary education 8.3%; some secondary 1.4%; secondary 0.8%; postsecondary 0.3%. *Literacy* (1995): total percentage of population age 15 and over literate 37.0%; males literate 48.7%; females literate 25.8%.
Health: physicians (1989) 323 (1 per 13,879 persons); hospital beds (1982) 4,902 (1 per 749 persons); infant mortality rate per 1,000 live births (1991) 119.0.
Food (1992): daily per capita caloric intake 2,532 (vegetable products 96%, animal products 4%); 110% of FAO recommended minimum requirement.

Military

Total active duty personnel (1995): 4,800 (army 93.8%, navy 3.1%, air force 3.1%). *Military expenditure as percentage of GNP* (1992): 1.3% (world 3.7%); per capita expenditure U.S.$5.

[1]83rd seat, provided for by Constitution, vacated by constitutional court. [2]Porto-Novo, the official capital established under the constitution, is the seat of the legislature, but the president and most government ministers reside in Cotonou. [3]1992. [4]1993. [5]1986. [6]October 1990 = 100. [7]Minimum hourly industrial wage; January 1. [8]Detail does not add to total given because of rounding. [9]Represents 1/11 of the traffic of Air Afrique, which is operated by 11 West African states. [10]1987–88. [11]1990.

Bhutan

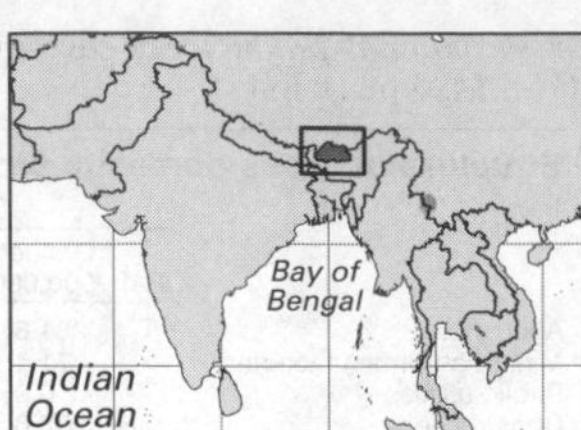

Official name: Druk-Yul (Kingdom of Bhutan).
Form of government: constitutional[1] monarchy with one legislative house (National Assembly [152[2]]).
Head of state and government: Monarch (*druk gyalpo*).
Capital: Thimphu.
Official language: Dzongkha (a Tibetan dialect).
Official religion: Mahāyāna Buddhism.
Monetary unit: 1 ngultrum[3] (Nu) = 100 chetrum; valuation (Oct. 6, 1995) 1 U.S.$ = Nu 33.90; 1 £ = Nu 53.59.

Area and population

Districts	Capitals	area sq mi	area sq km	population 1994 estimate
Bumthang	Jakar	1,150	2,990	...
Chirang	Damphu	310	800	...
Chhukha	Chhukha	...	...	...
Dagana	Dagana	540	1,400	...
Gaylegphug	Gaylegphug	1,020	2,640	...
Ha	Ha	830	2,140	...
Lhuntshi	Lhuntshi	1,120	2,910	...
Mongar	Mongar	710	1,830	...
Paro	Paro	580	1,500	...
Pema Gatsel	Pema Gatsel	150	380	...
Punakha	Punakha	2,330	6,040	...
Samchi	Samchi	830	2,140	...
Samdrup Jongkhar	Samdrup Jongkhar	900	2,340	...
Shemgang	Shemgang	980	2,540	...
Tashigang	Tashigang	1,640	4,260	...
Thimphu	Thimphu	630	1,620	...
Tongsa	Tongsa	570	1,470	...
Wangdi Phodrang	Wangdi Phodrang	1,160	3,000	...
TOTAL		18,150[4, 5]	47,000[4, 5]	800,000[6]

Demography

Population (1995): 816,000[6].
Density (1995): persons per sq mi 45.0, persons per sq km 17.4.
Urban-rural (1985): urban 13.1%; rural 86.9%.
Sex distribution (1988): male 50.97%; female 49.03%.
Age breakdown (1988): under 15, 40.3%; 15–29, 26.4%; 30–44, 16.5%; 45–59, 10.5%; 60–74, 5.2%; 75 and over, 1.1%.
Population projection: (2000) 900,000; (2010) 1,100,000.
Doubling time: 30 years.
Ethnic composition (1993): Bhutiā (Ngalops) 50.0%; Nepalese (Gurung) 35.0%; Sharchops 15.0%.
Religious affiliation (1980): Buddhist 69.6%; Hindu 24.6%; Muslim 5.0%; other 0.8%.
Major cities (1993): Thimphu 30,340; Phuntsholing 10,000[7].

Vital statistics

Birth rate per 1,000 population (1994): 39.3 (world avg. 25.0); legitimate, n.a.; illegitimate, n.a.
Death rate per 1,000 population (1994): 15.9 (world avg. 9.3).
Natural increase rate per 1,000 population (1994): 23.4 (world avg. 15.7).
Total fertility rate (avg. births per childbearing woman; 1994): 5.4.
Marital status of population 15 years and over (1985): married 71.2%; single 19.7%; widowed 7.5%; divorced 1.6%.
Divorce rate per 1,000 population: n.a.
Life expectancy at birth (1994): male 51.2 years; female 50.0 years.
Major causes of death (percentage distribution; 1989): respiratory tract infections 19.5%; diarrhea/dysentery 15.2%; skin infections 12.2%; parasitic worm infestations 10.0%; malaria 9.4%.

National economy

Budget (1994–95). Revenue: Nu 4,396,000,000 (grants from UN and other international agencies 41.6%, internal revenue 37.2%, grants from government of India 21.2%). Expenditures: Nu 4,708,000,000 (capital expenditures 63.5%, current expenditures 36.5%).
Public debt (external, outstanding; 1993): U.S.$83,300,000.
Production (metric tons except as noted). Agriculture, forestry, fishing (1994): oranges 58,000, rice 43,000, corn (maize) 40,000, potatoes 34,000, sugarcane 13,000, green peppers and chilies 9,000, millet 7,000, apples 6,000, wheat 5,000, barley 4,000, pulses 2,000; livestock (number of live animals) 435,000 cattle, 75,000 pigs, 59,000 sheep, 42,000 goats; roundwood (1993) 1,491,000 cu m; fish catch (1993) 350. Mining and quarrying (1993): limestone 198,000; dolomite 90,000; gypsum 20,000. Manufacturing (value in Nu; 1980–81): distillery products 47,000,000; cement 36,000,000; chemical products 19,000,000; processed food 14,000,000; forest products 3,000,000. Construction (number of buildings completed; 1977–78): residential 10; nonresidential (guest house) 1. Energy production (consumption): electricity (kW-hr; 1992) 1,627,000,000 (185,000,000); coal (metric tons; 1992) 2,000 (18,000); crude petroleum, none (n.a.); petroleum products (metric tons; 1992) none (27,000); natural gas, none (n.a.).
Household income and expenditure. Average household size (1980) 5.4[6]; income per household: n.a.; sources of income: n.a.; expenditure (1979): food 72.3%, clothing 21.2%, energy 3.7%, household durable goods 0.7%, personal effects and other 2.1%.

Gross national product (at current market prices; 1993): U.S.$253,000,000 (U.S.$170 per capita).

Structure of gross domestic product and labour force

	1993 in value Nu '000,000	1993 % of total value	1984 labour force	1984 % of labour force
Agriculture	2,820.2	40.7	303,000[8]	87.2
Mining	88.3	1.3		
Manufacturing	773.2	11.1		
Construction	703.8	10.1		
Trade	448.4	6.5	3,000[8]	0.9
Public utilities	543.0	7.8		
Transportation and communications	521.1	7.5		
Finance	472.2	6.8		
Pub. admin., defense	633.9	9.1	12,000[8]	3.4
Services			30,000[8]	8.5[9]
Other	−68.0[10]	−0.9[10]	...	...
TOTAL	6,936.1	100.0	348,000	100.0

Population economically active (1984)[6]: total 348,000; activity rate of total population 53.4% (participation rates: ages 15–64, 94.8%; female 55.0%; unemployed 6.5%).

Price and earnings indexes (1990 = 100)

	1986	1987	1988	1989	1990	1991	1992
Consumer price index	71.4	74.8	83.6	90.9	100.0	112.3	126.6
Earnings index	...	...	...	...	...	...	...

Land use (1993): forested 66.0%; meadows and pastures 5.8%; agricultural and under permanent cultivation 2.9%; other 25.3%.
Tourism (1993): receipts from visitors U.S.$3,000,000; expenditures by nationals abroad, n.a.

Foreign trade[11]

Balance of trade (current prices)

	1988–89	1989–90	1990–91	1991–92	1992–93	1993–94
Nu '000,000	−833.8	−481.6	−583.5	−687.9	−1,633.6	−966.2
% of total	28.6%	17.5%	18.3%	17.4%	30.8%	18.7%

Imports (1993–94): Nu 3,064,100,000 (1992–93[12]; petroleum products 5.9%, motor vehicles and parts 5.0%, rice 3.5%, iron and steel products 1.8%, fabrics 1.4%, machinery parts 0.5%). *Major import source:* India 60.1%.
Exports (1993–94): Nu 2,097,900,000 (1992–93[12]; electricity 29.4%, timber and wood manufactures 17.0%, fruit and vegetables 11.1%, cement 10.4%). *Major export destination:* India 87.0%.

Transport and communications

Transport. Railroads: none. Roads (1991): total length 1,502 mi, 2,418 km (paved 79%). Vehicles (1988): passenger cars 2,590; trucks and buses 1,367. Merchant marine: none. Air transport (1986): passenger-mi 2,722,000, passenger-km 4,381,000; metric ton-km cargo, n.a.; airports (1995) with scheduled flights 1.
Communications. Daily newspapers: none[13]. Radio (1994): total number of receivers 23,000 (1 per 35 persons). Television (1983): total number of receivers 200 (1 per 6,180 persons). Telephones (main lines; 1993): 3,800 (1 per 400 persons).

Education and health

Education (1990)

	schools	teachers	students	student/teacher ratio
Primary (age 7–11)	156	1,757	52,029	29.6
Secondary (age 12–16)	31	662	15,984	24.1
Voc., teacher tr.	8	149	1,822	12.2
Higher	2	57	519	9.1

Educational attainment: n.a. *Literacy* (1977): total population age 15 and over literate 124,000 (18.0%); males literate 98,000 (31.0%); females literate 26,000 (9.0%).
Health (1991): physicians 141 (1 per 5,335 persons); hospital beds 922 (1 per 816 persons); infant mortality rate per 1,000 live births (1994) 121.0.
Food (1975–77): daily per capita caloric intake 2,058 (vegetable products 98%, animal products 2%); 89% of FAO recommended minimum requirement.

Military

Total active duty personnel (1993): about 7,000 (army 100%).

[1]There is no formal constitution, but a form of constitutional monarchy is in place. [2]Includes 47 nonelective seats occupied by representatives of the King and religious groups. [3]Indian currency is also accepted legal tender; the ngultrum is at par with the Indian rupee. [4]2,700 sq mi (7,000 sq km) are not included in the district area totals. [5]Includes Chhukha area. [6]The figure stated is an estimate based on recent reported figures resulting from the repudiation of the 1980 census by the King and from the existence of a large number of Nepalese refugees; as such the actual population could range from 800,000 to 1,600,000. [7]1982. [8]Derived value. [9]Includes 6.5% with no occupation. [10]Imputed bank service charges. [11]Import figures are c.i.f. in balance of trade, commodities, and trading partners. [12]Trade data with India only. [13]A weekly newspaper is published from Thimphu in Dzongkha, Nepalese, and English, circulation (1995) 10,000.

Bolivia

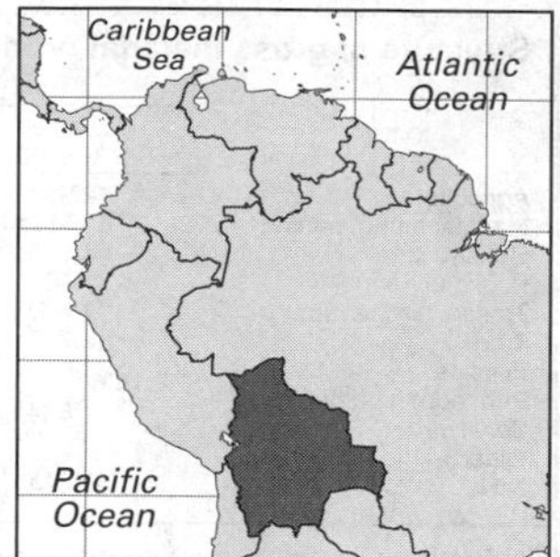

Official name: República de Bolivia (Republic of Bolivia).
Form of government: unitary multiparty republic with two legislative houses (Chamber of Senators [27]; Chamber of Deputies [130]).
Head of state and government: President.
Capitals: La Paz (administrative); Sucre (judicial).
Official languages: Spanish, Aymara, Quechua.
Official religion: Roman Catholicism.
Monetary unit: 1 boliviano (Bs) = 100 centavos; valuation (Oct. 6, 1995) 1 U.S.$ = Bs 4.87; 1 £ = Bs 7.69.

Area and population

		area		population
Departments	Capitals	sq mi	sq km	1996 estimate[1]
Beni	Trinidad	82,458	213,564	312,772
Chuquisaca	Sucre	19,893	51,524	481,600
Cochabamba	Cochabamba	21,479	55,631	1,237,458
La Paz	La Paz	51,732	133,985	2,030,176
Oruro	Oruro	20,690	53,588	348,074
Pando	Cobija	24,644	63,827	39,041
Potosí	Potosí	45,644	118,218	642,794
Santa Cruz	Santa Cruz	143,098	370,621	1,605,987
Tarija	Tarija	14,526	37,623	325,694
TOTAL		424,164	1,098,581	7,023,596

Demography

Population (1995): 7,414,000.
Density (1995): persons per sq mi 17.5, persons per sq km 6.7.
Urban-rural (1992): urban 57.7%; rural 42.3%.
Sex distribution (1995): male 49.64%; female 50.36%.
Age breakdown (1995): under 15, 40.6%; 15–29, 27.5%; 30–44, 16.3%; 45–59, 9.6%; 60–74, 5.0%; 75 and over, 1.0%.
Population projection: (2000) 8,329,000; (2010) 10,229,000.
Doubling time: 29 years.
Ethnic composition (1982): mestizo 31.2%; Quechua 25.4%; Aymara 16.9%; white 14.5%; other 12.0%.
Religious affiliation (1992): Roman Catholic 85.0%; Protestant 11.0%; other 4.0%.
Major cities (1992): La Paz 711,036; Santa Cruz 694,616; El Alto 404,367; Cochabamba 404,102; Oruro 183,194; Sucre 130,952.

Vital statistics

Birth rate per 1,000 population (1994): 32.2 (world avg. 25.0).
Death rate per 1,000 population (1994): 8.4 (world avg. 9.3).
Natural increase rate per 1,000 population (1994): 23.8 (world avg. 15.7).
Total fertility rate (avg. births per childbearing woman; 1994): 4.2.
Marriage rate per 1,000 population (1980): 4.8.
Divorce rate per 1,000 population: n.a.
Life expectancy at birth (1994): male 60.9 years; female 65.9 years.
Major causes of death (percentage of total registered deaths; 1980–81): infectious and parasitic diseases 23.9%; diseases of the circulatory system 19.5%; diseases of the respiratory system 14.0%; accidents, homicides, and violence 9.8%; diseases of the digestive system 8.6%.

National economy

Budget (1993). Revenue: Bs 3,479,700,000 (taxes on goods and services 38.2%, income of government enterprises 11.9%, property taxes 9.6%, social-security contributions 8.2%, taxes on international trade 7.0%, income taxes 5.9%). Expenditures: Bs 5,876,500,000 (transportation and communications 22.4%, public services 14.2%, social security 12.0%, education 11.0%, defense 8.2%, health 6.6%, public order and safety 3.2%).
Production (metric tons except as noted). Agriculture, forestry, fishing (1994): sugarcane 3,164,000, potatoes 810,000, soybeans 709,000, corn (maize) 521,000, bananas and plantains 521,000, cassava 447,000, rice 259,000, wheat 88,000, coffee 31,000; livestock (number of live animals) 7,789,000 sheep, 6,012,000 cattle, 2,331,000 pigs, 1,517,000 goats, 636,000 asses, 324,000 horses; roundwood (1993) 1,555,000 cu m; fish catch (1993) 6,167. Mining and quarrying (metric tons of pure metal; 1993): zinc 122,640; lead 21,240; tin 18,624; silver 46,344 kg; gold 6,563 kg. Manufacturing (value added in Bs '000; 1992): food products 1,459,318; petroleum products 856,675; wood products 517,201; textiles 299,955; beverages 288,796; nonferrous metals 210,903. Construction (1985)[2]: residential dwellings 226. Energy production (consumption): electricity (kW-hr; 1992) 2,412,000,000 (2,424,000,000); coal, none (none); crude petroleum (barrels; 1992) 8,110,000 (8,149,000); petroleum products (metric tons; 1992) 1,135,000 (1,167,000); natural gas (cu m; 1992) 2,895,000,000 (674,000,000).
Population economically active (1992): total 2,530,409; activity rate of total population 33.6% (participation rates: ages 15–64, 63.6%; female 39.0%; unemployed 2.5%).

Price and earnings indexes (1990 = 100)

	1988	1989	1990	1991	1992	1993	1994
Consumer price index	74.1	85.4	100.0	121.4	136.1	147.7	159.3
Monthly earnings index[3]	68.2	82.0	100.0	113.8	131.8	152.6	178.2

Public debt (external, outstanding; 1993): U.S.$3,687,000,000.
Gross national product (at current market prices; 1993): U.S.$5,472,000,000 (U.S.$770 per capita).

Structure of gross domestic product and labour force

	1993		1992	
	in value Bs '000[4]	% of total value	labour force[5]	% of labour force[5]
Agriculture	2,400,446	17.0	984,407	38.9
Mining	1,092,737	7.7	52,623	2.1
Manufacturing	2,262,772	16.0	222,485	8.8
Construction	726,208	5.1	129,409	5.1
Public utilities	183,251	1.3	6,086	0.2
Transportation and communications	1,588,580	11.2	116,800	4.6
Trade	1,425,021	10.1	232,429	9.2
Finance	1,322,761	9.4	54,711	2.2
Pub. admin., defense; Services	2,323,929	16.4	406,928	16.1
Other	821,699[6]	5.8[6]	324,531	12.8
TOTAL	14,147,404	100.0	2,530,409	100.0

Household income and expenditure. Average household size (1992): 3.8; average annual income per household: n.a.; sources of income: n.a.; expenditure (1988): food 35.5%, transportation and communications 17.7%, housing 14.8%, household durable goods 7.3%, clothing and footwear 5.1%, beverages and tobacco 4.5%, recreation 2.7%, health 2.1%, education 0.3%.
Tourism (1993): receipts from visitors U.S.$115,000,000; expenditures by nationals abroad U.S.$151,000,000.
Land use (1993): forested 53.5%; meadows and pastures 24.4%; agricultural and under permanent cultivation 2.2%; other 19.9%.

Foreign trade[7]

Balance of trade (current prices)

	1989	1990	1991	1992	1993	1994
U.S.$'000,000	+301.8	+326.6	+59.0	−294.4	−384.1	−89.3
% of total	22.5%	21.4%	3.6%	17.2%	20.9%	4.1%

Imports (1993): U.S.$1,205,900,000 (capital goods 43.0%, of which capital goods for industry 25.7%, transport equipment 15.6%; raw materials 35.1%, of which raw materials for industry 28.8%; consumer goods 20.1%, of which durable consumer goods 11.0%, nondurable consumer goods 9.1%). *Major import sources:* United States 23.5%; Argentina 12.0%; Brazil 10.5%; Japan 10.4%; Chile 7.4%; United Kingdom 5.4%; Germany 4.9%.
Exports (1993): U.S.$754,500,000 (zinc 15.8%; natural gas 12.0%; tin 11.1%; gold 10.1%; soybeans 9.1%; silver 7.4%; timber 6.9%; sugar 2.5%; hides and skins 1.6%). *Major export destinations:* United States 22.6%; United Kingdom 21.1%; Argentina 16.6%; Peru 9.9%; Belgium 6.5%; Colombia 4.7%; Germany 4.3%; Brazil 2.8%.

Transport and communications

Transport. Railroads (1993): route length 2,295 mi, 3,694 km; passenger-mi 216,800,000, passenger-km 348,900,000; short ton-mi cargo 521,900,000, metric ton-km cargo 761,900,000. Roads (1993): total length 26,370 mi, 42,438 km (paved 4%). Vehicles (1993): passenger cars 340,365; trucks and buses 185,922. Merchant marine (1992): vessels (100 gross tons and over) 1; total deadweight tonnage 15,765. Air transport (1993): passenger-mi 729,000,000, passenger-km 1,173,000,000; short ton-mi cargo 108,491,000, metric ton-km cargo 158,394,000; airports (1995) with scheduled flights 21.
Communications. Daily newspapers (1992): total number 16; total circulation 390,000, circulation per 1,000 population 52. Radio (1994): total number of receivers 4,250,000 (1 per 1.9 persons). Television (1992): total number of receivers 775,000 (1 per 8.9 persons). Telephones (main lines; 1993): 234,400 (1 per 33 persons).

Education and health

Education (1990–91)

	schools[8]	teachers	students	student/ teacher ratio
Primary (age 6–13)	9,758	51,763	1,278,775	24.7
Secondary (age 14–17); Voc., teacher tr.	724; 47	12,434	219,232	17.6
Higher[9]	10	4,261	109,503	25.7

Educational attainment (1992). Percentage of population age 25 and over having: no formal schooling 23.3%; some primary 20.3%; primary education 21.7%; some secondary 9.0%; secondary 6.5%; some higher 5.0%; higher 4.8%; not specified 9.4%. *Literacy* (1992): total population age 15 and over literate 79.5%; males literate 87.7%; females literate 71.8%.
Health (1993): physicians 2,008 (1 per 3,518 persons); hospital beds 7,203 (1 per 981 persons); infant mortality rate per 1,000 live births (1990–95) 75.1.
Food (1992): daily per capita caloric intake 2,094 (vegetable products 84%, animal products 16%); 88% of FAO recommended minimum requirement.

Military

Total active duty personnel (1994): 33,500 (army 74.6%, navy 13.4%, air force 12.0%). *Military expenditure as percentage of GNP* (1993): 2.4% (world 3.3%); per capita expenditure U.S.$18.

[1]Based on unadjusted 1992 census results. [2]National government sponsored only. [3]Private sector earnings in La Paz. [4]In 1988 prices. [5]Population 7 years and over. [6]Net import duties. [7]Import figures are f.o.b. in balance of trade and c.i.f. for commodities and trading partners. [8]1986–87. [9]1991–92.

Bosnia and Herzegovina[1]

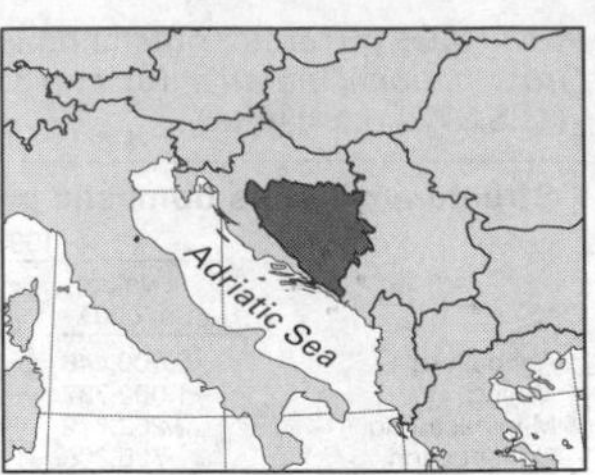

Official name: Republika Bosna i Hercegovina (Republic of Bosnia and Herzegovina).
Form of government: unitary multiparty republic with bicameral legislature (National Assembly [240[2]]).
Chief of state: President[3].
Head of government: Prime Minister[3].
Capital: Sarajevo.
Official language: Serbo-Croatian.
Official religion: none.
Monetary unit: [4].

Area and population (1991 census)

Districts	area sq km	population	Districts	area sq km	population
Banja Luka	1,232	195,139	Livno	994	39,526
Banovići	176	26,507	Ljubinje	326	4,162
Bihać	689	70,896	Ljubuški	289	27,182
Bijeljina	734	96,796	Lopare	429	32,400
Bileća	633	13,269	Lukavac	350	56,830
Bosanska Dubica	499	31,577	Maglaj	384	43,294
Bosanska Gradiška	762	60,062	Modriča	297	35,413
Bosanska Krupa	780	58,212	Mostar	1,300	126,067
Bosanski Brod	234	33,962	Mrkonjič Grad	679	27,379
Bosanski Novi	554	41,541	Neum	230	4,268
Bosanski Petrovac	853	15,552	Nevesinje	923	14,421
Bosanski Šamac	219	32,835	Odžak	205	30,651
Bosansko Grahovo	780	8,303	Olovo	408	16,901
Bratunac	793	33,575	Orašje	166	28,201
Brčko	493	87,332	Posušje	372	16,659
Breza	83	17,266	Prijedor	834	112,470
Bugojno	366	46,843	Prnjavor	631	46,894
Busovača	145	18,883	Prozor	477	19,601
Čajniče	275	8,919	Pucarevo	232	30,624
Capljina	249	27,852	Rogatica	664	21,812
Çazin	381	63,406	Rudo	344	11,572
Çelinac	365	18,666	Sanski Most	984	60,119
Čitluk	181	14,709	Şarajevo	2,049	525,980
Derventa	516	56,328	Şekovići	195	9,639
Doboj	684	102,546	Šipovo	470	15,553
Donji Vakuf	338	24,232	Skender Vakuf	360	19,416
Foča	1,270	40,513	Sokolac	723	14,833
Fojnica	308	16,227	Srbac	447	21,660
Gacko	736	10,844	Srebrenica	527	37,211
Glamoč	1,096	12,421	Srebrenik	249	40,769
Goražde	383	37,505	Stolac	541	18,845
Gornji Vakuf	402	25,130	Tešanj	223	48,390
Graćanica	387	59,050	Teslič	846	59,632
Gradačac	405	56,378	Titov Drvar	950	17,079
Grude	218	15,976	Tomislavgrad	967	29,261
Han Pijesak	342	6,346	Travnik	563	70,402
Jablanica	289	12,664	Trebinje	1,205	30,879
Jajce	398	44,903	Tuzla	307	131,861
Kakanj	462	55,857	Ugljevik	199	25,641
Kalesija	272	41,795	Vareš	356	22,114
Kalinovik	732	4,657	Velika Kladuša	304	52,921
Kiseljak	165	24,081	Višegrad	448	21,202
Kladanj	325	16,028	Visoko	242	46,130
Ključ	850	37,233	Vitez	156	27,728
Konjic	1,101	43,636	Vlasenica	532	33,817
Kotor Varoš	574	36,670	Zavidovići	540	57,153
Kreševo	149	6,699	Zenica	500	145,577
Kupres	622	10,728	Žepče	210	22,840
Laktaši	387	29,910	Živinice	281	54,653
Lištica	388	26,437	Zvornik	500	81,111
			TOTAL	51,129[5]	4,365,639

Demography

Population (1995): 3,459,000.
Density (1995): persons per sq mi 175.2, persons per sq km 67.6.
Urban-rural (1981): urban 36.2%; rural 63.8%.
Sex distribution (1991): male 49.79%; female 50.21%.
Age breakdown (1991): under 15, 23.4%; 15–29, 26.5%; 30–44, 22.8%; 45–64, 16.0%; 65 and over, 11.3%.
Population projection: (2000) 4,330,000; (2010) 4,420,000.
Doubling time: 99 years.
Ethnic composition (1991): Muslim 49.2%; Serb 31.3%; Croat 17.3%.
Religious affiliation (1992): Muslim 40%; Serbian Orthodox 31%; Roman Catholic 15%; Protestant 4%; other 10%.
Major cities (1991): Sarajevo 415,631; Banja Luka 142,634; Zenica 96,238.

Vital statistics

Birth rate per 1,000 population (1993): 13.5 (world avg. 25.0); legitimate 92.6%; illegitimate 7.4%.
Death rate per 1,000 population (1993): 6.4 (world avg. 9.3).
Natural increase rate per 1,000 population (1993): 7.7 (world avg. 15.7).
Total fertility rate (avg. births per childbearing woman; 1993): 1.6.
Marriage rate per 1,000 population (1991): 6.0.
Divorce rate per 1,000 population (1991): 0.3.
Life expectancy at birth (1993): male 72.1 years; female 77.7 years.
Major causes of death per 100,000 population (1989): circulatory diseases 344.1; malignant neoplasms (cancers) 122.6; accidents, violence, and poisoning 47.1; digestive system diseases 29.2.; respiratory diseases 29.0.

National economy

Gross national product (1990): U.S.$10,667,000,000 (U.S.$2,454 per capita).

Structure of gross material product and labour force

	1989		1990	
	in value Din '000,000	% of total value	labour force[6]	% of labour force[6]
Agriculture	2,963	10.9	39,053	3.8
Manufacturing, mining	15,589	57.6	496,190	48.3
Construction	1,918	7.1	74,861	7.3
Public utilities	403	1.5	22,345	2.2
Transp. and commun.	1,600	5.9	68,798	6.7
Trade	3,777	13.9	130,914	12.8
Finance			38,686	3.8
Pub. admin., defense	834	3.1		
Services			155,411	15.1
Other				
TOTAL	27,084	100.0	1,026,258	100.0

Production (metric tons except as noted). Agriculture, forestry, fishing (1994): wheat 340,000, potatoes 134,000, corn (maize) 133,000: livestock (head) 600,000 sheep, 390,000 cattle, 223,000 pigs, 7,000,000 poultry; roundwood (1990) 5,379,000 cu m; fish catch (1993) 2,500. Mining (1993): lead-zinc ore 10,000; iron ore 250,000; bauxite 100,000. Manufacturing (1990): crude steel 1,421,000; pig iron 1,284,000; cement 797,000, alumina 735,000; paper 281,000. Construction (residential units constructed; 1990): 26,568. Energy production (consumption): electricity (kW-hr; 1993) 11,000,000,000 (11,075,000,000); coal (metric tons; 1992) 15,000,000 (15,000,000); crude petroleum (barrels; 1992) none (14,836,000); petroleum products (metric tons; 1992) 1,590,000 (1,590,000); natural gas (cu m; 1993) none (380,000,000).
Population economically active (1991): total 992,000; activity rate of total population 22.7% (participation rates: ages 15–64, 35.6%; female [1990] 37.7%).

Price and earnings indexes (1985 = 100)

	1984	1985	1986	1987	1988	1989	1990[7]
Consumer price index	58	100	188	400	1,188	16,169	109,000
Monthly earnings index[8]	99	100	106	99	86	109	87

Land use (1993): forest 39.1%; pasture 19.6%; agricultural 18.4%.
Tourism (1991): total tourist nights 2,360,000.
Household income and expenditure. Average household size (1991) 3.4; income per household (1990) Din 72,850 (U.S.$6,437); sources of income (1990): wages 53.2%, transfers 18.2%, self-employment 12.0%, other 16.6%; expenditure (1988): food 41.3%, clothing 8.3%, fuel and lighting 7.8%, housing 7.8%, transportation 6.0%, beverages and tobacco 5.7%.

Foreign trade

Balance of trade (current prices)

	1985	1986	1987	1988	1989	1990
Din '000,000	–4	2	15	77	962	2,141
% of total	4.5%	1.2%	6.2%	9.2%	7.4%	4.8%

Imports (1990): Din 21,130,000,000 (fuels 31.6%; raw materials and semifinished goods 26.8%; basic manufactures 17.5%; consumer goods 13.3%).
Exports (1990): Din 23,271,000,000 (machinery 20.8%; chemicals 9.4%; clothing 9.2%; furniture 5.0%).

Transport and communications

Transport. Railroads (1990): length 646 mi, 1,039 km; passenger-mi 883,000,000, passenger-km 1,421,000,000; short ton-mi cargo 3,205,000,000, metric ton-km cargo 4,679,000,000. Roads (1991): total length 13,153 mi, 21,168 km (paved 54%). Vehicles (1990): passenger cars 438,080; trucks and buses 50,578. Airports (1995) with scheduled flights 1.
Communications. Daily newspapers (1992): total number 2; circulation 518,000; circulation per 1,000 population 131. Radio (1990): number of receivers 733,000 (1 per 5.9 persons). Television (1990): number of receivers 629,000 (1 per 6.9 persons). Telephones (main lines; 1993): 600,000 (1 per 7.3 persons).

Education and health

Education (1990–91)

	schools	teachers	students	student/ teacher ratio
Primary (age 7–14)	2,205	23,369	539,875	23.1
Secondary (age 15–18)	238	9,030	172,063	19.1
Higher	44	2,802	37,541	13.4

Educational attainment (1981). Percentage of population age 15 and over having: less than full primary education 49.5%; primary 24.2%; secondary 21.7%; postsecondary and higher 4.3%. *Literacy* (1981): total population age 10 and over literate 2,962,400 (85.5%); males 96.5%; females 76.6%.
Health: physicians (1989) 6,929 (1 per 624 persons); hospital beds (1990) 19,858 (1 per 219 persons); infant mortality rate per 1,000 live births (1993) 13.2.

Military

Total active duty personnel (1995)[9]: 92,000 (army 100%).

[1]Facts given refer to conditions prior to the formal signing of the peace accord on Dec. 14, 1995. The formal signing ended the war begun in early 1992 and established two political entities within Bosnia and Herzegovina (a Bosnian-Muslim–Bosnian-Croat federation and a Bosnian-Serb republic). [2]159 seats occupied as of early December 1995. [3]Executive leadership of Bosnian-Muslim–Bosnian-Croat federation as of Dec. 14, 1995. [4]No national currency of issue exists. The principal currency in de facto use is the Yugoslav new dinar (Din), for which no exchange rate is offered. [5]Detail adds to 554 sq km more than total given; the reason for the discrepancy is unknown. [6]Excludes 28,000 workers in the private sector. [7]On Jan. 1, 1990, the new dinar, equal to 10,000 old dinars, was introduced. [8]Based on worker real net personal income. [9]Excludes 150,000 foreign combatants and a 31,000-member UN protection force.

Botswana

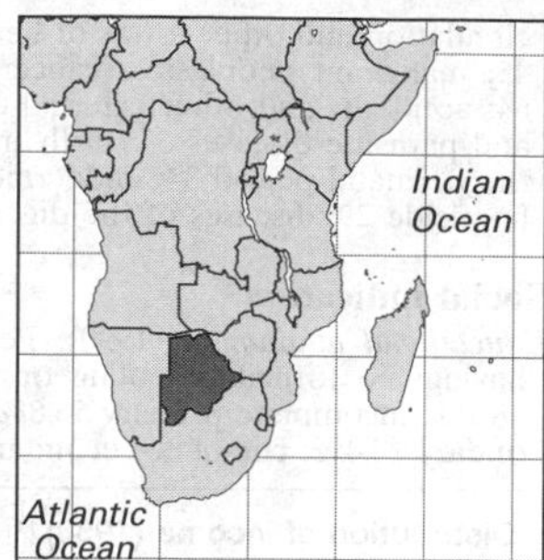

Official name: Republic of Botswana.
Form of government: multiparty republic with one legislative body[1] (National Assembly [46[2]]).
Head of state and government: President.
Capital: Gaborone.
Official language: English[3].
Official religion: none.
Monetary unit: 1 pula (P) = 100 thebe; valuation (Oct. 6, 1995) 1 U.S.$ = P 2.80; 1 £ = P 4.42.

Area and population

Districts	Capitals	area sq mi	area sq km	population 1991 census[4]
Barolong	...	425	1,100	18,365
Central	Serowe	57,039[5]	147,730[5]	284,264
Ghanzi	Ghanzi	45,525	117,910	24,695
Kgalagadi	Tsabong	41,290	106,940	30,873
Kgatleng	Mochudi	3,073	7,960	57,168
Kweneng	Molepolole	13,857	35,890	169,835
Ngwaketse	Kanye	10,568	27,370	129,474
North East	Masunga	1,977	5,120	43,361
North West				
Chobe	Kasane	8,031	20,800	14,186
Ngamiland	Maun	42,135	109,130	94,322
Serowe/Palapye	...	5	5	111,300
South East	Ramotswa	687[5]	1,780[5]	31,101
Towns[6]				
Francistown	—	31	79	65,026
Gaborone	—	37	97	133,791
Jwaneng	—	39	100	11,199
Lobatse	—	12	30	25,992
Orapa	—	4	10	8,853
Palapye	—	8	21	17,131
Selebi-Pikwe	—	19	50	39,769
Sowa		...	...	2,220
Tlokweng	—	10	26	12,366
TOTAL		224,607	581,730	1,325,291

Demography

Population (1995): 1,549,000.
Density (1995): persons per sq mi 6.9, persons per sq km 2.7.
Urban-rural (1993): urban 26.1%; rural 73.9%.
Sex distribution (1995): male 48.96%; female 51.04%.
Age breakdown (1995): under 15, 43.2%; 15–29, 28.5%; 30–44, 16.5%; 45–59, 7.9%; 60–74, 3.2%; 75 and over, 0.7%.
Population projection: (2000) 1,789,000; (2010) 2,318,000.
Doubling time: 23 years.
Ethnic composition (1983): Tswana 75.5%; Shona 12.4%; San (Bushman) 3.4%; Khoikhoin (Hottentot) 2.5%; Ndebele 1.3%; other 4.9%.
Religious affiliation (1980): traditional beliefs 49.2%; Protestant 29.0%; African Christian 11.8%; Roman Catholic 9.4%; other 0.6%.
Major cities (1991): Gaborone 133,791; Francistown 65,026; Selebi-Pikwe 39,-769; Molepolole 36,928; Kanye 31,341.

Vital statistics

Birth rate per 1,000 population (1992): 37.1 (world avg. 25.0); (1986) legitimate 28.8%[7]; illegitimate 71.2%[7].
Death rate per 1,000 population (1992): 6.6 (world avg. 9.3).
Natural increase rate per 1,000 population (1992): 30.5 (world avg. 15.7).
Total fertility rate (avg. births per childbearing woman; 1993): 4.8.
Marriage rate per 1,000 population (1987): 1.6.
Life expectancy at birth (1993): male 59.5 years; female 65.6 years.
Major causes of death (as percentage of total registered deaths; 1986): diseases of the circulatory system 17.3%; infectious and parasitic diseases 16.6%; malignant neoplasms (cancers) 13.4%; diseases of the respiratory system 12.2%; endocrine, nutritional, and metabolic diseases 6.1%.

National economy

Budget (1993–94). Revenue: P 5,127,000,000 (mineral royalties 44.8%, nontax revenue 28.0%, customs and excise taxes 16.0%, other [nonmineral] income taxes 8.2%). Expenditures: P 4,049,000,000 (economic services 21.4%, education 20.1%, regional and urban development 8.9%, health 4.8%, social welfare 3.7%).
Population economically active (1991): total 443,455; activity rate of total population 33.4% (participation rates: ages 15–64, 59.6%; female 38.4%; unemployed 13.9%).

Price and earnings indexes (1990 = 100)

	1988	1989	1990	1991	1992	1993	1994
Consumer price index	80.5	89.8	100.0	111.8	129.8	148.4	164.1
Monthly earnings index	77.0	90.4	100.0	114.4	137.8	...	...

Production (metric tons except as noted). Agriculture, forestry, fishing (1994): cereals 51,000 (of which sorghum 38,000, corn [maize] 8,000, millet 3,000), vegetables and melons 16,000, pulses 13,000, fruits 11,000, roots and tubers 9,000, seed cotton 3,000, cottonseed 2,000; livestock (number of live animals) 2,800,000 cattle, 2,475,000 goats, 344,000 sheep, 158,000 mules and asses, 35,000 horses; roundwood (1993) 1,440,000 cu m; fish catch (1993) 2,000. Mining and quarrying (1994): diamonds 15,547,000 carats; copper 21,563; nickel 17,468; cobalt 223. Manufacturing (value added in P '000,000; 1987–88): food products 295.4; textiles 93.5; chemicals 68.6; paper and paper products 35.3; wood products 22.5. Construction (1985): residential 70,200 sq m; nonresidential 80,700 sq m. Energy production (consumption): electricity (kW-hr; 1991) 929,000,000 (929,000,000); coal (metric tons; 1992) 901,452 (n.a.); crude petroleum, none (n.a.).
Public debt (external, outstanding; 1992): U.S.$537,500,000.
Tourism (1991): receipts U.S.$79,000,000; expenditures U.S.$40,000,000.
Gross national product (1993): U.S.$3,631,000,000 (U.S.$2,590 per capita).

Structure of gross domestic product and labour force

	1992–93 in value P '000,000[8]	1992–93 % of total value	1991 labour force	1991 % of labour force
Agriculture	217.8	5.1	100,446	22.7
Mining	1,472.5	34.8	13,287	3.0
Manufacturing	235.8	5.5	26,635	6.0
Construction	179.5	4.2	57,001	12.9
Public utilities	112.0	2.6	6,425	1.4
Transp. and commun.	163.6	3.8	10,094	2.3
Trade	642.5	15.1	34,322	7.7
Finance and business services	234.4	5.5	13,392	3.0
Pub. admin., defense	877.7	20.6 }	103,045	23.2
Services	120.5	2.8 }		
Other	...	...	78,808[9]	17.8[9]
TOTAL	4,256.3	100.0	443,455	100.0

Household income and expenditure (1985–86). Average household size 5.0; average annual income per household P 3,910 (U.S.$2,080); sources of income (1987): wages and salaries 73.3%, self-employment 15.9%, transfers 10.8%; expenditure: food, beverages, and tobacco 39.4%, household durable goods 14.0%, rent and services 13.3%, transportation 13.1%, clothing 5.6%, health 2.3%.
Land use (1993): forested 46.8%; meadows and pastures 45.2%; agricultural and under permanent cultivation 0.7%; other 7.3%.

Foreign trade[10]

Balance of trade (current prices)

	1988	1989	1990	1991	1992	1993
P '000,000	831.2	1,174.9	231.1	492.1	518.2	526.7
% of total	18.4%	18.6%	3.6%	5.0%	5.5%	6.7%

Imports (1992): P 3,970,062,000 (machinery and electrical goods 18.8%; food, beverages, and tobacco 18.7%; metal and metal products 10.8%; transport equipment 10.0%; chemical and rubber products 9.4%; textiles and footwear 7.0%; wood and paper 5.7%; mineral fuels 5.5%). *Major import sources:* Customs Union of Southern Africa 85.0%; European countries 7.1%, of which U.K. 2.6%; U.S. 1.0%.
Exports (1992): P 3,674,991,000 (diamonds 78.8%; copper-nickel matte 7.2%; meat products 3.5%). *Major export destinations:* European countries 86.7%, of which U.K. 1.6%; Customs Union of Southern Africa 6.9%; U.S. 0.3%.

Transport and communications

Transport. Railroads (1993): length 551 mi, 887 km; passenger-km 257,000,-000[11]; metric ton-km cargo 1,266,000,000. Roads (1991): total length 11,933 mi, 19,204 km (paved 13%). Vehicles (1992): passenger cars 20,785; trucks and buses 42,136. Merchant marine: none. Air transport (1992)[12]: passenger-km 84,000,000; metric ton-km cargo 648,000; airports (1995) 4.
Communications. Daily newspapers (1993): total number 2; total circulation 49,700, circulation per 1,000 population 34.6. Radio (1994): total receivers 1,400,000 (1 per 1.1 persons). Television (1994): total receivers 13,800 (1 per 108 persons). Telephones (main lines; 1993): 43,500 (1 per 33 persons).

Education and health

Education (1994)

	schools	teachers	students	student/ teacher ratio
Primary (age 6–13)	781	9,552	301,370	31.6
Secondary (age 14–18)	199	5,192	99,560	19.2
Voc., teacher tr.	45	856	9,570	11.2
Higher	1	475	4,533	9.5

Educational attainment (1991). Percentage of population age 25 and over having: no formal schooling 42.9%; primary education 17.3%; some secondary 32.3%; complete secondary 3.9%; postsecondary 3.7%. *Literacy* (1990): total population over age 15 literate 486,500 (73.6%); males literate 253,300 (83.7%); females literate 233,200 (65.1%).
Health (1990): physicians 240 (1 per 5,417 persons); hospital beds 3,212 (1 per 395 persons); infant mortality rate (1994) 39.0.
Food (1992): daily per capita caloric intake 2,266 (vegetable products 79%, animal products 21%); 98% of FAO recommended minimum requirement.

Military

Total active duty personnel (1994): 7,500 (army 93.3%, navy, none [landlocked], air force 6.7%). *Military expenditure as percentage of GNP* (1993): 5.9% (world 3.3%); per capita expenditure U.S.$148.

[1]In addition, the House of Chiefs, a 15-member body consisting of chiefs, subchiefs, and associated members, serves in an advisory capacity to the government. [2]Including four specially elected members and two nonelective seats. [3]Tswana is the national language. [4]Preliminary. [5]Areas for Central district and South East district include the area for Serowe/Palapye. [6]Areas are included with respective district totals; population figures are not included with district totals. [7]Registered births only. [8]At 1985–86 prices. [9]Includes 61,638 unemployed. [10]Import figures are f.o.b. in balance of trade and c.i.f. in commodities and trading partners. [11]1986–87. [12]Air Botswana only.

Brazil

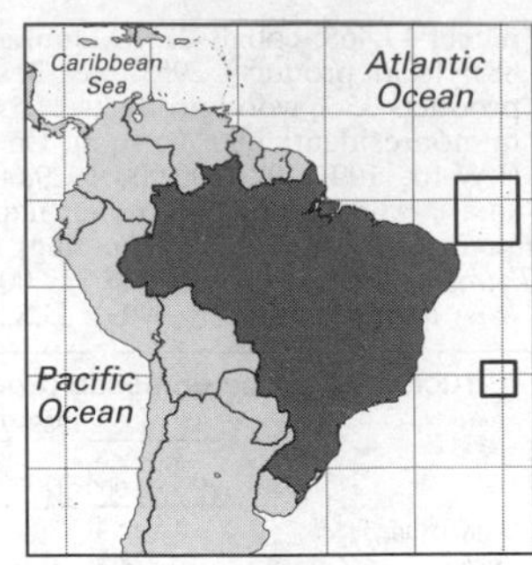

Official name: República Federativa do Brasil (Federative Republic of Brazil).
Form of government: multiparty federal republic with 2 legislative houses (Senate [81]; Chamber of Deputies [513]).
Chief of state and government: President.
Capital: Brasília.
Official language: Portuguese.
Official religion: none.
Monetary unit: 1 real[1] = 100 centavos; valuation (Oct. 6, 1995) 1 U.S.$ = 0.96 real; 1 £ = 1.52 reais.

Area and population

		area		population
States	**Capitals**	sq mi	sq km	1995 estimate[2]
Acre	Rio Branco	59,132	153,150	455,200
Alagoas	Maceió	10,785	27,933	2,685,400
Amapá	Macapá	55,388	143,454	326,200
Amazonas	Manaus	609,200	1,577,820	2,320,200
Bahia	Salvador	219,034	567,295	12,646,000
Ceará	Fortaleza	56,505	146,348	6,714,200
Espírito Santo	Vitória	17,836	46,194	2,786,700
Goiás	Goiânia	131,772	341,289	4,308,400
Maranhão	São Luís	128,713	333,366	5,231,300
Mato Grosso	Cuiabá	350,120	906,807	2,313,600
Mato Grosso do Sul	Campo Grande	138,286	358,159	1,912,800
Minas Gerais	Belo Horizonte	227,176	588,384	16,505,300
Pará	Belém	483,850	1,253,165	5,448,600
Paraíba	João Pessoa	21,848	56,585	3,340,000
Paraná	Curitiba	77,108	199,709	8,712,800
Pernambuco	Recife	38,200	98,938	7,445,200
Piauí	Teresina	97,444	252,379	2,725,000
Rio de Janeiro	Rio de Janeiro	16,954	43,910	13,296,400
Rio Grande do Norte	Natal	20,582	53,307	2,582,300
Rio Grande do Sul	Pôrto Alegre	108,905	282,062	9,578,600
Rondônia	Pôrto Velho	92,090	238,513	1,339,500
Roraima	Boa Vista	86,918	225,116	262,200
Santa Catarina	Florianópolis	36,851	95,443	4,836,600
São Paulo	São Paulo	96,066	248,809	33,699,600
Sergipe	Aracaju	8,514	22,050	1,605,300
Tocantins	Palmas	107,499	278,421	1,007,000
Federal District				
Distrito Federal	Brasília	2,248	5,822	1,737,800
Disputed areas[3]		1,149	2,977	—
TOTAL		3,300,171[4, 5]	8,547,404[4, 5]	155,822,400[4]

Demography

Population (1995): 155,822,000.
Density (1995): persons per sq mi 47.2, persons per sq km 18.2.
Urban-rural (1993): urban 70.8%; rural 29.2%.
Sex distribution (1995): male 49.38%; female 50.62%.
Age breakdown (1995): under 15, 31.8%; 15–29, 28.5%; 30–44, 21.2%; 45–59, 11.4%; 60–74, 5.7%; 75 and over, 1.4%.
Population projection: (2000) 165,715,000; (2010) 184,157,000.
Doubling time: 58 years.
Ethnic composition (1990): white 54.0%; mulatto and mestizo 39.0%; black and black/Amerindian 5.9%; Asian 0.9%; Amerindian 0.2%.
Religious affiliation (1995): Roman Catholic *c.* 70%[6]; evangelical Protestant *c.* 19%; other *c.* 11%.
Major cities and metropolitan areas (1991)[2]: São Paulo 9,393,753 (15,416,416); Rio de Janeiro 5,473,909 (9,796,498); Salvador 2,070,296 (2,493,224); Belo Horizonte 1,529,566 (3,431,755); Brasília[7] 1,492,542 (1,598,415[8]); Recife 1,296,995 (2,871,261); Pôrto Alegre 1,237,223 (3,026,029); Manaus[7] 1,005,634; Goiânia[7] 912,136; Curitiba 841,882 (1,998,807); Belém 765,476 (1,332,723); Campinas[7] 748,076; Fortaleza 743,335 (2,303,645).

Other principal cities (1991)[2]

	population		population		population
Aracaju	401,676	Natal	459,827	São Bernardo do Campo	550,030[10]
Campo Grande	516,403	Niterói	400,586[9]	São Jose dos Campos	385,879
Guarulhos	544,698[10]	Nova Iguaçu	562,062[9]	Sorocaba	348,952
João Pessoa	497,306	Osasco	566,949[10]	Teresina	556,073
Juiz de Fora	377,538	Ribeirão Preto	416,186	Uberlândia	354,710
Londrina	355,062	Santo André	518,272[10]		
Maceió	554,727	Santos	415,554		

Place of birth/national origin: n.a.
Mobility: n.a.
Families (1990)[11]. Average family size 3.9; 1–2 persons 26.2%, 3 persons 21.3%, 4 persons 21.5%, 5–6 persons 22.3%, 7 or more persons 8.7%.
Immigration: n.a.

Vital statistics

Birth rate per 1,000 population (1994): 21.0 (world avg. 25.0).
Death rate per 1,000 population (1994): 9.0 (world avg. 9.3).
Natural increase rate per 1,000 population (1994): 12.0 (world avg. 15.7).
Total fertility rate (avg. births per childbearing woman; 1994): 2.4.
Marriage rate per 1,000 population (1991): 4.9.
Divorce rate per 1,000 population (1991): 0.5.
Life expectancy at birth (1994): male 57.0 years; female 67.0 years.
Major causes of death per 100,000 population (1990)[12]: diseases of the circulatory system 206, of which cerebrovascular disease 70, diseases of pulmonary circulation and other forms of heart disease 51, acute myocardial infarction 45; malignant neoplasms (cancers) 75; diseases of the respiratory system 64; accidents and other external causes (excluding homicide) 62; infectious and parasitic diseases 37; birth trauma and other conditions originating in the perinatal period 34; endocrine, metabolic, and nutritional disorders 31; homicide 29; diseases of the digestive system 28; ill-defined conditions 133.

Social indicators

Educational attainment (1990). Percentage of population age 10 and over having: no formal schooling or less than one year of primary education 18.1%; incomplete primary 56.8%; complete primary 6.9%; incomplete secondary 12.4%; complete secondary or higher 5.7%; unknown 0.1%.

Distribution of income (1988)[11, 13]

percentage of national income by decile

1	2	3	4	5	6	7	8	9	10 (highest)
0.7	1.7	2.2	3.4	3.9	5.0	6.8	9.9	15.9	50.5

Quality of working life. Annual estimated rate per 100,000 insured workers (1990) for: on-the-job injury 2,032; industrial illness 17; death 4. Proportion of labour force participating in national social insurance system (1990): 50.1%. Proportion of formally employed population receiving minimum wage (1993): 25.0%.
Access to services. Proportion of households having access to: electricity (1990) 87.8%, of which urban households having access (1989) 97.2%, rural households having access (1989) 53.2%; safe public (piped) water supply (1990) 73.3%, of which urban households having access (1986) 88.7%, rural households having access (1986) 11.6%; public refuse collection (1990) 64.5%; public sewage collection (1990) *c.* 33%.
Social participation. Voting is mandatory for national elections; in the October 1994 elections blank or otherwise invalid ballots accounted for as many as 15% of all votes cast. Trade union membership in total workforce (1991): 16,748,155. Practicing Roman Catholic population in total affiliated Roman Catholic population (1990): 25%.
Social deviance (1990). The incidence of crime is not accurately reported. Crimes resulting in imprisonment: 159,071, of which murder 7.3%, assault 11.0%, theft, burglary, and housebreaking 26.6%, robbery and extortion 12.2%, narcotics trafficking 6.3%, narcotics usage 4.5%. Suicide: 5,142.
Leisure. Favourite leisure activities include: playing soccer, rehearsing all year in neighbourhood samba groups for celebrations of Carnival, and competing in water sports, volleyball, and basketball.
Material well-being (1990)[11]. Households possessing: radio receiver 84.3%; television receiver 73.7%; refrigerator 71.1%; stove 96.4%.

National economy

Gross national product (at current market prices; 1993): U.S.$471,978,000,000 (U.S.$3,020 per capita).

Structure of gross domestic product and labour force

	1993		1990	
	in value Cr$'000,000,000,000[1, 14]	% of total value	labour force[11]	% of labour force
Agriculture	4,206	12.4	14,180,519	22.0
Mining	608	1.8	860,453	1.3
Public utilities	1,403	4.2		
Manufacturing	8,399	24.9	9,410,712	14.6
Construction	2,490	7.4	3,823,154	5.9
Transportation and communications	2,090	6.2	2,439,920	3.8
Trade	2,550[15]	7.5[15]	7,975,670[15]	12.4[15]
Finance, real estate	5,626[16]	16.7[16]	1,715,598	2.7
Pub. admin., defense	3,707	11.0	3,117,005	4.8
Services	6,091[17]	18.0[17]	18,577,468[17]	28.8[17]
Other	−3,395[18]	−10.1[18]	2,367,482[19]	3.7[19]
TOTAL	33,775	100.0	64,467,981	100.0

Budget. Revenue (1993): CR$13,896,006,000,000[1] (current receipts 32.1%, of which social contributions 13.4% [including social security 7.6%], taxes 12.1%; development receipts 67.9%, of which credits 60.8%). Expenditures (1994): R$214,827,000,000[1] (current expenditures 33.9%; development expenditures 65.6%, of which amortization of domestic debt 40.5%; contingency reserve 0.5%).
Public debt (external, outstanding; 1993): U.S.$86,650,000,000.
Production ('000 metric tons except as noted; 1994). Agriculture, forestry, fishing: sugarcane 279,822, corn (maize) 32,217, soybeans 24,855, cassava 24,058, oranges 17,978[20], rice 10,644, bananas 5,593[20], dry beans 3,334, coffee 2,613, tomatoes 2,519, potatoes 2,426, wheat 2,372, papayas 1,750[20], seed cotton 1,139, onions 910[20], coconuts 826[20], pineapples 820[20], grapes 782[20], cottonseed 717[20], apples 698[20], tangerines 668[20], tobacco 542, cacao 346, peanuts (groundnuts) 151[20], avocados 112[20], cashews 62[20]; livestock (number of live animals; 1993) 153,350,000 cattle, 31,050,000 pigs, 19,710,000 sheep, 6,310,000 horses; roundwood (1993) 272,078,000 cu m; fish catch (1993) 780, of which freshwater fishes 208. Mining and quarrying (value of production in Cr$'000,000,000; 1992): iron ore 7,456; gold 4,331; crushed stone 2,633; calcites 2,075; bauxite 987; copper 916; sea salt 825; natural phosphate fertilizers 704; zinc ore 684; kaolin (clay) 585; diamonds 569; tin 557; manganese 535. Manufacturing (value added in CR$'000,000,000; 1993): industrial chemicals 1,050; food products 1,040; nonelectrical machinery 994; basic and fabricated metals 923; transport equipment 784; electrical machinery 591; textiles 379; nonmetallic mineral products 369; paper and paper products 296; clothing and footwear 272; printing and publishing 226. Construction (authorized[21]; 1987): residential 20,090,000 sq m; nonresidential 8,180,000 sq m.
Land use (1993): forested 57.7%; meadows and pastures 21.9%; agricultural and under permanent cultivation 5.8%; other 14.6%.

Manufacturing enterprises (1985)	no. of enter-prises	number of labourers	wages of labourers as a % of avg. of all mfg. wages	value added in producer's prices (in CR$'000,000,000[1])[20]
Chemical products (excl. pharmaceuticals)	5,066	287,742	191.7	1,134
Food products	43,034	733,199	68.4	1,040
Nonelectrical machinery	11,088	552,163	146.5	994
Fabricated metals, iron and steel, and nonferrous metals	18,964	565,036	117.1	923
Transport equipment	4,184	341,621	154.8	784
Electrical machinery	4,573	315,767	138.5	591
Textiles	5,570	351,360	75.1	379
Nonmetallic mineral products	28,974	365,643	65.7	369
Paper and paper products	2,107	132,948	120.7	296
Clothing and footwear	23,200	655,234	49.6	272
Publishing and printing	9,053	164,523	100.1	226
Pharmaceuticals	930	49,048	173.7	217
Plastics	2,975	146,151	85.1	193
Beverages	2,798	77,167	...	178
Rubber products	1,421	71,656	136.3	91
Wood and wood products (excl. furniture)	17,129	218,059	48.4	91
Furniture	13,759	186,467	...	86

Population economically active (1990)[11]: total 64,467,981; activity rate of total population 43.8% (participation rates: ages 15–59, 68.5%; female 35.5%; unemployed [1994] 6.0%).

Price and earnings indexes (1990 = 100)	1990	1991	1992	1993	1994	1995[22]
Consumer price index	100.0	541.3	6,002	134,800	3,733,100	6,541,500
Monthly earnings index[23]	100.0	515.0	5,859	97,000	...	...

Tourism (1993): receipts U.S.$1,449,000,000; expenditures U.S.$1,842,000,000.

Retail trade enterprises (1990)	no. of enterprises	total no. of employees	annual wage as a % of all trade wages	annual value of sales in Cr$'000,000
Vehicles, new and used; parts	45,385	406,568	152.1	1,685
General merchandise stores (including food products)	10,180	368,590	116.7	1,324
Clothing, footwear, and apparel	147,671	634,713	94.7	1,124
Gas stations	24,881	211,689	106.0	1,067
Food, beverages, and tobacco	228,922	606,341	53.1	1,059
Hardware, appliances, and construction materials	57,577	338,519	99.1	775
Domestic goods, equipment, kitchenware, and antiques	28,636	202,146	115.3	567
Pharmaceutical and cosmetic products	49,435	213,118	79.9	377
Agricultural and industrial equipment and machinery	9,897	90,900	154.1	289
Books, magazines, newspapers	14,383	69,771	81.8	110

Family income and expenditure. Average family size (1987–88)[24] 4.0; annual income per family (1987–88)[24] Cz$516,528[1] (U.S.$1,233); sources of income (1987–88)[24]: wages and salaries 54.3%, self-employed 27.3%, transfers 7.8%, other 10.6%; expenditure (early 1980s): food 35%, clothing and footwear 10%, housing 9%, transportation and communications 8%, household furnishings 8%.

Financial aggregates[25]	1990	1991	1992	1993	1994	1995[26]
Exchange rate, reais[1] per:						
U.S. dollar	—	—	.002	.049	.846	.906
£	—	—	.003	.073	1.322	1.453
SDR	—	.001	.006	.163	1.235	1.428
International reserves (U.S.$)						
Total (excl. gold; '000,000)	7,441	8,033	22,521	30,604	37,070	31,772
SDRs ('000,000)	11	13	1	2	—	2
Reserve pos. in IMF ('000,000)	—	—	—	—	—	—
Foreign exchange ('000,000)	7,430	8,020	22,520	30,602	37,069	31,770
Gold ('000,000 fine troy oz)	4.57	2.02	2.23	2.93	3.71	4.16
% world reserves	0.49	0.21	0.24	0.32	0.37	0.46
Interest and prices						
Central bank discount (%)	1,083	2,494	1,489	5,757	56	65
Govt. bond yield (%)	...	...	...	...	...	...
Industrial share prices	...	...	...	...	...	...
Balance of payments (U.S.$'000,000)						
Balance of visible trade	+10,747	+10,578	+15,239	+13,072	...	...
Imports, f.o.b.	20,661	21,041	20,554	25,711	...	..
Exports, f.o.b.	31,408	31,619	35,793	38,783	...	...
Balance of invisibles	−14,535	−11,986	−9,096	−13,709	...	...
Balance of payments, current account	−3,788	−1,408	+6,143	−637	...	...

Energy production (consumption): electricity (kW-hr; 1993) 251,508,000,000 (227,044,000,000); coal (metric tons; 1993) 4,596,000 (15,811,000); crude petroleum (barrels; 1994) 240,629,000 ([1993] 437,229,000); petroleum products (metric tons; 1993) 52,081,000 (54,477,000); natural gas (cu m; 1994) 7,728,000,000 ([1993] 3,958,000,000); carburant alcohol (cu m; 1992) 11,530,000 (8,052,000).

Foreign trade

Balance of trade (current prices)	1989	1990	1991	1992	1993	1994
U.S.$'000,000	+16,112	+10,747	+10,578	+15,239	+13,072	+10,391
% of total	30.6%	20.6%	20.1%	27.4%	20.3%	13.6%

Imports (1993): U.S.$25,711,000,000 (machinery and apparatus 24.8%, chemicals and chemical products 15.1%, transport equipment 9.3%, refined petroleum 8.7%, crude petroleum 8.3%). *Major import sources:* United States 21.9%; Argentina 9.5%; Germany 8.2%; Japan 5.5%; Saudi Arabia 5.3%; Italy 3.6%; France 2.5%; Canada 2.4%; Switzerland 2.0%; United Kingdom 1.9%.

Exports (1993): U.S.$38,783,000,000 (machinery and equipment 11.9%, iron and steel fabricated products 10.3%, transport equipment 8.7%, iron ore 5.8%, footwear 5.0%, soy products 4.7%, textiles 3.6%, coffee beans 3.3%, crude aluminum 2.3%, wood and wood products 2.2%, orange juice 2.1%). *Major export destinations:* United States 20.3%; Argentina 9.4%; The Netherlands 6.4%; Japan 6.0%; Germany 4.7%; Italy 3.4%; Belgium-Luxembourg 3.0%; United Kingdom 2.9%; Chile 2.9%; Mexico 2.6%.

Transport and communications

Transport. Railroads: route length (1993) 18,877 mi, 30,379 km; passenger-mi 8,723,000,000, passenger-km 14,038,000,000; short ton-mi cargo 85,439,000,000, metric ton-km cargo 124,738,000,000. Roads (1993): total length 1,031,693 mi, 1,660,352 km (paved 9%). Vehicles (1992): passenger cars 12,974,991; trucks and buses 1,371,127. Merchant marine (1992): vessels (100 gross tons and over) 635; total deadweight tonnage 9,348,339. Air transport (1994)[27]: passenger-mi 20,264,000,000, passenger-km 32,612,000,000; short ton-mi cargo 1,452,000,000, metric ton-km cargo 2,120,000,000; airports (1995) with scheduled flights 139.

Communications. Daily newspapers (1992): total number 373; total circulation 8,500,000; circulation per 1,000 population 55. Radio (1994): total number of receivers 55,000,000 (1 per 2.9 persons). Television (1994): total number of receivers 30,000,000 (1 per 5.3 persons). Telephones (main lines; 1993): 11,752,831 (1 per 13 persons).

Education and health

Education (1993)	schools	teachers	students	student/teacher ratio
Primary (age 7–14)	195,544	1,346,285	30,520,748	22.7
Secondary (age 15–18)	12,603	275,845	4,208,766	15.3
Higher	873	150,823	1,504,668	10.0

Literacy (1995)[28]: total population age 15 and over literate 91,100,000 (83.3%); males literate 45,200,000 (83.3%); females literate 45,900,000 (83.2%).

Health: physicians (1992) 208,966 (1 per 715 persons); hospital beds (1990) 533,558 (1 per 271 persons); infant mortality rate per 1,000 live births (1994) 60.0.

Food (1992): daily per capita caloric intake 2,824 (vegetable products 83%, animal products 17%); 118% of FAO recommended minimum requirement.

Military

Total active duty personnel (1995): 295,000 (army 66.0%, navy 17.0%, air force 17.0%). *Military expenditure as percentage of GNP* (1991): 1.3% (world 4.2%); per capita expenditure U.S.$35.

[1]The real (R$) replaced the cruzeiro real (CR$) on July 1, 1994, at a rate of 2,750 cruzeiros reais to 1 real (a rate par to the U.S.$ on that date). Previously, the cruzeiro real replaced the cruzeiro (Cr$) at a rate of 1,000 cruzeiros to 1 cruzeiro real on Aug. 2, 1993; the cruzeiro replaced the new cruzado (NCz$) at a rate of 1 to 1 on March 16, 1990; and the new cruzado replaced the (old) cruzado (Cz$) at a rate of 1,000 (old) to 1 new on Jan. 15, 1989. [2]Projection based on 1991 census. [3]Area in dispute between Ceará and Piauí. [4]Detail does not add to total given because of rounding. [5]Land area excluding inland water is 3,265,076 sq mi (8,456,508 sq km). [6]Includes syncretic Afro-Catholic cults having Spiritist beliefs and rituals. [7]City has no officially designated metropolitan area. [8]Population of federal district. [9]Within Rio de Janeiro metropolitan area. [10]Within São Paulo metropolitan area. [11]Excludes rural economically active population of Acre, Amapá, Amazonas, Pará, Rondônia, and Roraima states. [12]Projected rates based on about 75% of total deaths. [13]As of 1992, 33,000,000 Brazilians lived in extreme poverty (more than half of whom lived in the nine states of the northeast). [14]At factor cost. [15]Excludes restaurants and hotels. [16]Excludes business services. [17]Includes restaurants and hotels. [18]Less imputed bank service charges. [19]Unemployed. [20]1993. [21]Urban construction only for 74 cities. [22]April. [23]Minimum wages. [24]Based on 3,888,185 families in São Paulo metropolitan area. [25]End-of-period figures. [26]May. [27]Brasil Central, Transbrasil, VARIG, and VASP airlines only. [28]By official estimate; functional literacy, however, may be as low as 42% of total population over age 15.

Brunei

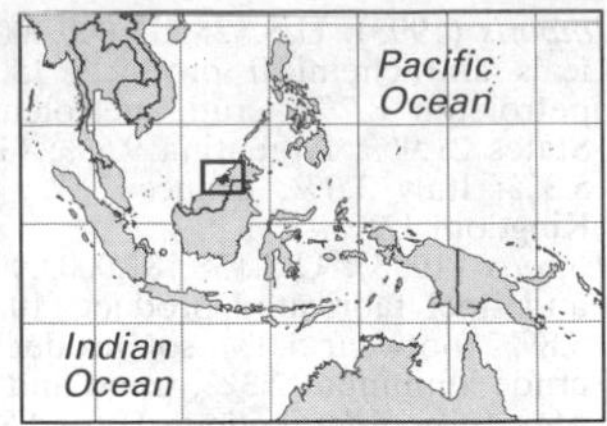

Official name: Negara Brunei Darussalam (State of Brunei, Abode of Peace).
Form of government: monarchy (sultanate)[1].
Head of state and government: Sultan.
Capital: Bandar Seri Begawan.
Official language: Malay[2].
Official religion: Islam.
Monetary unit: 1 Brunei dollar (B$) = 100 cents; valuation (Oct. 6, 1995) 1 U.S.$ = B$1.43; 1 £ = B$2.26.

Area and population

		area		population
Districts	Capitals	sq mi	sq km	1992 estimate
Belait	Kuala Belait	1,052	2,724	54,300
Brunei and Muara	Bandar Seri Begawan	220	571	175,800
Temburong	Bangar	504	1,304	7,900
Tutong	Tutong	450	1,166	29,800
TOTAL		2,226	5,765	267,800

Demography

Population (1995): 291,000.
Density (1995): persons per sq mi 130.7, persons per sq km 50.5.
Urban-rural (1993): urban 90.0%; rural 10.0%.
Sex distribution (1992): male 52.76%; female 47.24%.
Age breakdown (1992): under 15, 34.5%; 15–29, 28.3%; 30–44, 24.7%; 45–59, 8.2%; 60–74, 3.2%; 75 and over, 1.1%.
Population projection: (2000) 334,000; (2010) 432,000.
Doubling time: 29 years.
Ethnic composition (1992): Malay 67.1%; Chinese 15.4%; other indigenous 6.0%; Indian and other 11.5%.
Religious affiliation (1991): Muslim 67.2%; Buddhist 12.8%; Christian 10.0%; other religions and nonreligious 10.0%.
Major cities (1991): Bandar Seri Begawan 45,867[3]; Kuala Belait 21,163; Seria 21,082; Tutong 13,049.

Vital statistics

Birth rate per 1,000 population (1994): 26.2 (world avg. 25.0); (1982) legitimate 99.6%; illegitimate 0.4%.
Death rate per 1,000 population (1994): 5.0 (world avg. 9.3).
Natural increase rate per 1,000 population (1994): 21.2 (world avg. 15.7).
Total fertility rate (avg. births per childbearing woman; 1995): 3.1.
Marriage rate per 1,000 population (1992): 6.7.
Divorce rate per 1,000 population (1989): 0.8.
Life expectancy at birth (1994): male 69.5 years; female 72.8 years.
Major causes of death per 100,000 population (1992): cardiovascular disease 55.3; malignant neoplasms (cancers) 37.3; accidents, poisoning, and violence 30.6; cerebrovascular diseases 19.0; pneumonia 12.3; hypertensive diseases 9.7; congenital anomalies 9.7.

National economy

Budget (1992). Revenue: B$2,729,570,000 (indirect taxes 47.3%; government property 43.6%[4]; commercial receipts 8.9%). Expenditures: B$3,057,190,000 (current expenditure 69.9%, of which finance 15.5%, defense 13.4%, education 9.1%; development expenditure 15.1%; charged expenditure 15.0%).
Public debt (external, outstanding): none.
Tourism (1990): receipts from visitors U.S.$35,000,000; expenditures by nationals abroad, n.a.
Production (metric tons except as noted). Agriculture, forestry, fishing (1994): vegetables and melons 8,000, fruits (excluding melons) 5,000, eggs 3,300, rice 1,000, cassava 1,000, pineapples 1,000; livestock (number of live animals) 14,000 pigs, 10,000 buffalo, 1,000 cattle, 2,000,000 chickens; roundwood (1993) 295,000 cu m; fish catch (1993) 1,768. Mining and quarrying (1992): other than petroleum and natural gas (see below), none except sand and gravel for construction. Manufacturing (1992): gasoline 147,000; diesel oils 128,000; jet fuels 50,000; naphtha 45,000; kerosene 4,000. Construction (number of buildings completed; 1984): residential 195; nonresidential 5. Energy production (consumption): electricity (kW-hr; 1993) 1,285,000,000 (1,285,000,000); coal, none (none); crude petroleum (barrels; 1993) 57,758,000 (1,732,000); petroleum products (metric tons; 1993) 836,000 (832,000); natural gas (cu m; 1993) 8,548,000,000 (1,867,000,000).
Population economically active (1991): total 111,955; activity rate of total population 43.0% (participation rates: ages 15–64, 67.6%; female 32.9%; unemployed 4.7%).

Price and earnings indexes (1990 = 100)

	1986	1987	1988	1989	1990	1991	1992
Consumer price index	94.3	95.6	96.7	98.0	100.0	101.6	102.9
Monthly earnings index[5]	87.9	88.8	87.5	...	...	76.9	87.5

Household income and expenditure. Average household size (1991) 5.8; income per household: n.a.; sources of income: n.a.; expenditure (1990): food 38.7%, transportation and communications 19.9%, housing 18.6%, clothing 6.4%, other 16.4%.

Gross national product (at current market prices; 1993)[6]: U.S.$4,001,000,000 (U.S.$14,530 per capita).

Structure of gross domestic product and labour force

	1992		1991	
	in value B$'000,000	% of total value	labour force	% of labour force
Agriculture	191.5	3.0	2,162	1.9
Mining, Manufacturing	2,654.4	41.7	9,397	8.4
Construction	311.7	4.9	14,145	12.6
Public utilities	64.1	1.0	2,223	2.0
Transportation and communications	309.5	4.9	5,392	4.8
Trade	782.4	12.3	15,404	13.8
Finance	459.8	7.2	5,807	5.2
Services	1,754.8	27.5	52,121	46.6
Other	−156.2	−2.5	5,304[7]	4.7[7]
TOTAL	6,372.0	100.0	111,955	100.0

Land use (1993): forested 85.4%; meadows and pastures 1.1%; agricultural and under permanent cultivation 1.3%; other 12.2%.

Foreign trade

Balance of trade (current prices)

	1987	1988	1989	1990	1991	1992
B$'000,000	+2,655	+1,939	+1,998	+2,197	+2,417	+1,946
% of total	49.6%	39.3%	37.4%	37.7%	39.2%	33.7%

Imports (1992): B$2,280,700,000 (1990; machinery and transport equipment 34.4%, manufactured goods 27.0%, food and live animals 15.3%, miscellaneous manufactured articles 10.2%, chemicals 6.7%, beverages and tobacco 3.5%, crude materials 1.3%, mineral fuels 0.9%). *Major import sources:* ASEAN 38.6%, of which Singapore 29.3%, Malaysia 7.2%; EEC 27.5%; United States 21.9%; Japan 7.7%.
Exports (1992): B$3,630,200,000 (crude petroleum 56.1%, natural gas 43.0%, other 0.9%). *Major export destinations:* Japan 52.1%; ASEAN 20.2%, of which Thailand 8.4%, Singapore 7.8%, Philippines 3.9%; South Korea 12.1%.

Transport and communications

Transport. Railroads (1993)[8]: length 12 mi, 19 km. Roads (1992): total length 1,502 mi, 2,417 km (paved 51%). Vehicles (1992): passenger cars 122,104; trucks and buses 13,658. Merchant marine (1992): vessels (100 gross tons and over) 51; total deadweight tonnage 349,718. Marine transport (1992): cargo loaded 20,411,000 metric tons, cargo unloaded 1,377,000 metric tons. Air transport (1994): passenger-mi 1,261,000,000, passenger-km 2,029,000,000; short ton-mi cargo 64,662,000, metric ton-km cargo 94,405,000; airports (1995) with scheduled flights 1.
Communications. Daily newspapers (1993): total number 1; total circulation 30,000; circulation per 1,000 population 9.2. Radio (1994): total number of receivers 60,000 (1 per 4.7 persons). Television (1994): total number of receivers 70,000 (1 per 4.0 persons). Telephones (main lines; 1993): 55,200 (1 per 5.1 persons).

Education and health

Education (1992)

	schools	teachers	students	student/ teacher ratio
Primary (age 5–11)	161	3,047	50,434	16.6
Secondary (age 12–20)	23	1,939	25,309	13.1
Voc., teacher tr.	6	340	1,756	5.2
Higher	4	289	1,372	4.7

Educational attainment (1991). Percentage of population age 25 and over having: no formal schooling 17.0%; primary education 43.3%; secondary 26.3%; postsecondary and higher 12.9%; not stated 0.5%. *Literacy* (1991): total population age 15 and over literate 149,901 (87.8%); males literate 84,425 (92.5%); females literate 65,476 (82.5%).
Health (1993): physicians 197 (1 per 1,398 persons); hospital beds 967 (1 per 285 persons); infant mortality rate per 1,000 live births (1994) 25.2.
Food (1992): daily per capita caloric intake 2,745 (vegetable products 80%, animal products 20%); 123% of FAO recommended minimum requirement.

Military

Total active duty personnel (1995): 4,900[9] (army 79.6%, navy 14.3%, air force 6.1%). *Military expenditure as percentage of GNP* (1990): 8.4% (world 4.4%); per capita expenditure U.S.$1,190.

[1]A nonelective 21-member body advises the sultan on legislative matters. [2]All official documents that must be published by law in Malay are, however, also required to be issued in an official English version as well. [3]1988 metropolitan area population estimate. [4]In 1983 more than 98% of state revenue was derived from exports of oil and gas. [5]Nonagricultural sectors only; 1985 = 100. [6]GDP data. [7]Mostly unemployed. [8]Privately owned. [9]All services form part of the army.

Bulgaria

Official name: Republika Bŭlgaria (Republic of Bulgaria).
Form of government: unitary multiparty republic with one legislative body (Parliament [240]).
Chief of state: President.
Head of government: Prime Minister.
Capital: Sofia.
Official language: Bulgarian.
Official religion: none[1].
Monetary unit: 1 lev (leva) = 100 stotinki; valuation (Oct. 6, 1995) 1 U.S.$ = 68.17 leva; 1 £ = 107.77 leva.

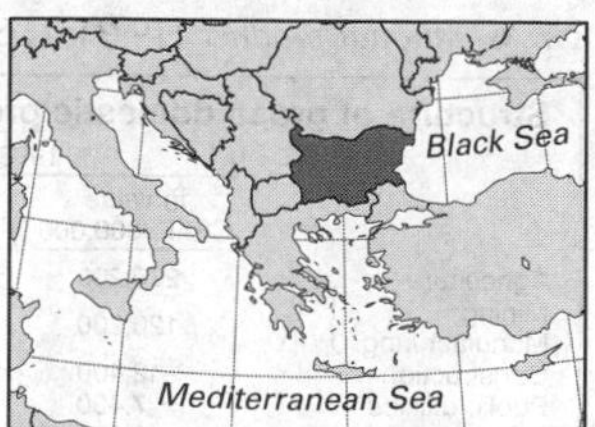

Area and population

Regions	Capitals	area sq mi	area sq km	population 1994 estimate
Burgas	Burgas	5,659	14,657	850,003
Khaskovo	Khaskovo	5,364	13,892	903,928
Lovech	Lovech	5,849	15,150	1,009,196
Montana	Mikhaylovgrad	4,095	10,607	626,205
Plovdiv	Plovdiv	5,262	13,628	1,221,449
Ruse	Ruse	4,186	10,842	765,719
Sofiya	Sofia (Sofiya)	7,328	18,978	980,588
Varna	Varna	4,606	11,929	914,079
City Commune				
Sofiya	Sofia (Sofiya)	506	1,311	1,188,556
TOTAL		42,855	110,994	8,459,723

Demography

Population (1995): 8,351,000.
Density (1995): persons per sq mi 194.9, persons per sq km 75.2.
Urban-rural (1994): urban 67.8%; rural 32.2%.
Sex distribution (1994): male 49.01%; female 50.99%.
Age breakdown (1994): under 15, 18.1%; 15–29, 21.2%; 30–44, 20.7%; 45–59, 18.9%; 60–74, 16.5%; 75 and over, 4.6%.
Population projection: (2000) 8,168,000; (2010) 7,849,000.
Doubling time: not applicable; population is declining.
Ethnic composition (1992): Bulgarian 85.8%; Turkish 9.7%; Gypsy 3.4%; other 1.1%.
Religious affiliation (1992)[2]: Eastern Orthodox 87.0%; Muslim 12.7%; other 0.3%.
Major cities (1993): Sofia 1,113,674; Plovdiv 345,205; Varna 307,200; Burgas 198,439; Ruse 170,209.

Vital statistics

Birth rate per 1,000 population (1994): 9.4 (world avg. 25.0); (1990) legitimate 77.8%; illegitimate 22.2%.
Death rate per 1,000 population (1994): 13.2 (world avg. 9.3).
Natural increase rate per 1,000 population (1994): −3.8 (world avg. 15.7).
Total fertility rate (avg. births per childbearing woman; 1993): 1.5.
Marriage rate per 1,000 population (1994): 4.5.
Divorce rate per 1,000 population (1993): 0.9.
Life expectancy at birth (1995): male 68.9 years; female 75.3 years.
Major causes of death per 100,000 population (1993): diseases of the circulatory system 814.7; malignant neoplasms (cancers) 185.5; accidents, poisoning, and violence 65.7; diseases of the respiratory system 63.7; diseases of the digestive system 38.3; endocrine and metabolic disorders 20.9.

National economy

Budget (1993). Revenue: 71,350,000,000 leva (1991; national economy 69.1%, taxes 29.9%). Expenditures: 98,933,000,000 leva (1991; social security 28.2%, education and health 18.8%, economy 11.8%, administration and other 34.1%).
Public debt (external, outstanding; 1991): U.S.$11,923,000,000.
Tourism (1993): receipts from visitors U.S.$307,000,000; expenditures by nationals abroad U.S.$257,000,000.
Production (metric tons except as noted). Agriculture, forestry, fishing (1994): wheat 3,788,000, corn (maize) 1,362,000, barley 1,146,000, sunflower seeds 596,000, grapes 498,000, potatoes 476,000, tomatoes 443,000, apples 76,000; livestock (number of live animals; 1994) 4,293,000 sheep, 1,998,000 pigs, 673,000 cattle; roundwood (1993) 3,565,000 cu m; fish catch (1993) 21,585. Mining and quarrying (1993): iron ore 266,000; manganese 4,000. Manufacturing (value of production in '000,000 leva; 1993): food products 60,855; chemical products 44,737; machine-building products 28,304; energy 27,887; electronics 13,436; ferrous metals 10,814; textiles 9,893. Construction (1994): residential 727,000 sq m. Energy production (consumption): electricity (kW-hr; 1993) 37,998,000,000 (39,628,000,000); coal (metric tons; 1993) 29,032,000 (33,958,000); crude petroleum (barrels; 1993) 366,600 (64,522,000); petroleum products (metric tons; 1993) 6,758 (7,443); natural gas (cu m; 1993) 6,499,000 (4,532,000,000).
Household income and expenditure (1992). Average household size (1992) 2.8; income per household (1994) 39,560 leva (U.S.$599); sources of income (1994): wages and salaries 38.2%, self-employment in agriculture 25.9%, transfer payments 18.4%; expenditure (1994): food 45.0%, transportation 7.7%, housing and energy 7.5%, clothing 7.4%, household durable goods 3.7%, health care 3.7%, education and culture 2.7%.
Gross national product (1993): U.S.$9,812,000,000 (U.S.$1,160 per capita).

Structure of gross domestic product and labour force

	1993 in value '000,000 leva[3]	% of total value[3]	labour force	% of labour force
Agriculture	61,117	12.6	698,100	19.2
Manufacturing, mining	137,655	28.5	934,900	25.6
Construction	24,622	5.1	185,700	5.1
Transp. and commun.	34,433	7.1	230,800	6.3
Trade	53,902	11.2	369,000	10.1
Public utilities, housing	161,602	33.4	65,900	1.8
Pub. admin., defense			67,800	1.9
Services			570,300	15.6
Other	10,267	2.1	523,842	14.4
TOTAL	483,598	100.0	3,646,342	100.0

Population economically active (1994): total 3,646,342; activity rate of total population 43.2% (participation rates: ages 16–59 [male], 16–54 [female] 76.9%; female [1993] 47.4%; unemployed 13.4%).

Price and earnings indexes (1990 = 100)

	1988	1989	1990	1991	1992	1993	1994
Consumer price index	78.8	80.8	100.0	438.5	786.6	1,228	2,296
Monthly earnings index	70.0	75.9	100.0	265.8	567.5	895.7	1,337

Land use (1993): forested 35.0%; meadows and pastures 16.5%; agricultural and under permanent cultivation 39.2%; other 9.3%.

Foreign trade

Balance of trade (current prices)

	1989	1990	1991	1992	1993	1994
'000,000 leva	+877.1	+244.6	+12,235.9	+1,049.1	−20,245	−8,652
% of total	3.3%	1.2%	11.9%	0.6%	9.3%	1.8%

Imports (1994): 234,120,000,000 leva (1993; fuels, mineral raw materials, and metals 35.1%; machinery and equipment 18.8%; chemical products and rubber 9.5%; food products 5.9%). *Major import sources* (1994): C.I.S. 31.4%; Germany 13.2%; Italy 5.7%; Greece 4.8%; Austria 2.9%.
Exports (1994): 225,468,000,000 leva (1993; machinery and equipment 17.0%; chemicals and rubber 14.6%; consumer goods 9.4%; fuels, minerals, and metals 8.6%; food and beverages 8.5%). *Major export destinations* (1994): C.I.S. 17.0%; Germany 8.4%; Greece 7.1%; Italy 7.0%.

Transport and communications

Transport. Railroads (1994): track length 4,044 mi, 6,508 km; passenger-mi 3,144,000,000, passenger km 5,059,000,000; short ton-mi cargo 5,325,000,000, metric ton-km cargo 7,774,000,000. Roads (1994): length 22,943 mi, 36,922 km (paved 92%). Vehicles (1993): cars 1,358,976; trucks and buses 130,000. Merchant marine (1992): vessels (100 gross tons and over) 222; deadweight tonnage 1,962,345. Air transport (1994): passenger-mi 2,239,000,000, passenger-km 3,604,000,000; short ton-mi cargo 32,200,000, metric ton-km cargo 47,000,000; airports (1995) with scheduled flights 3[4].
Communications. Daily newspapers (1992): total number 46; total circulation 1,464,000; circulation per 1,000 population 164. Radio (1994): 3,920,000 receivers (1 per 2.2 persons). Television (1994): 3,127,000 receivers (1 per 2.7 persons). Telephones (main lines; 1993): 2,300,000 (1 per 3.8 persons).

Education and health

Education (1994–95)

	schools	teachers	students	student/ teacher ratio
Primary (age 6–14) / Secondary (age 15–17)	3,359	70,487	980,491	13.9
Voc., teacher tr.	513	18,885	212,401	11.2
Higher	88	24,185	221,207	9.2

Educational attainment (1992). Percentage of population age 7 and over having: incomplete primary education 24.6%; primary 30.4%; secondary 37.0%; higher 8.0%. *Literacy* (1980): total population age 15 and over literate 95.5%.
Health (1994): physicians 28,362 (1 per 298 persons); hospital beds 87,316 (1 per 97 persons); infant mortality rate per 1,000 live births 16.3.
Food (1992): daily per capita caloric intake 2,831 (vegetable products 74%, animal products 26%); 113% of FAO recommended minimum requirement.

Military

Total active duty personnel (1995): 101,900 (army 75.9%, navy 2.9%, air force 21.2%). *Military expenditure as percentage of GNP* (1993): 6.0% (world 3.3%); per capita expenditure U.S.$70.

[1]Bulgaria has no official religion; the 1991 constitution, however, refers to Eastern Orthodoxy as the "traditional" religion. [2]Census data reflect the traditional religious identity of Bulgaria but apparently disregard the nonreligious, who may exceed half the adult population. [3]Data are based on estimates. [4]International only; the number of domestic airports is not available.

Burkina Faso

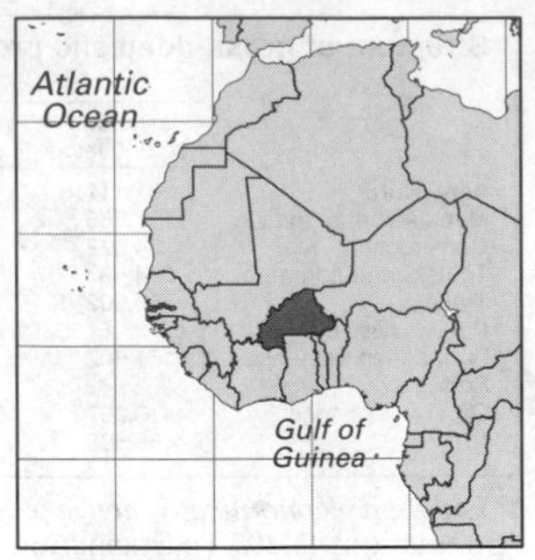

Official name: Burkina Faso (Burkina Faso).
Form of government: multiparty republic with one legislative house (Assembly of People's Deputies [107]).
Chief of state: President.
Head of government: Prime Minister.
Capital: Ouagadougou.
Official language: French.
Official religion: none.
Monetary unit: 1 CFA franc (CFAF) = 100 centimes; valuation (Oct. 6, 1995) 1 U.S.$ = CFAF 501.49; 1 £ = CFAF 792.78.

Area and population

		area		population
Provinces	Capitals	sq mi	sq km	1991 estimate
Bam	Kongoussi	1,551	4,017	173,516
Bazéga	Kombissiri	2,051	5,313	352,104
Bougouriba	Diébougou	2,736	7,087	242,986
Boulgou	Tenkodogo	3,488	9,033	465,845
Boulkiemde	Koudougou	1,598	4,138	393,900
Comoé	Banfora	7,102	18,393	296,083
Ganzourgou	Zorgho	1,578	4,087	223,555
Gnagna	Bogandé	3,320	8,600	272,203
Gourma	Fada N'Gourma	10,275	26,613	350,336
Houet	Bobo-Dioulasso	6,438	16,672	724,803
Kadiogo	Ouagadougou	451	1,169	652,377
Kénédougou	Orodara	3,207	8,307	162,010
Kossi	Nouna	5,088	13,177	389,360
Kouritenga	Koupéla	628	1,627	227,060
Mouhoun	Dédougou	4,032	10,442	329,115
Nahouri	Pô	1,484	3,843	119,144
Namentenga	Boulsa	2,994	7,755	214,564
Oubritenga	Ziniaré	1,812	4,693	328,682
Oudalan	Gorom Gorom	3,879	10,046	123,495
Passoré	Yako	1,575	4,078	232,278
Poni	Gaoua	4,000	10,361	258,647
Sanguie	Réo	1,994	5,165	234,079
Sanmatenga	Kaya	3,557	9,213	404,563
Sèno	Dori	5,202	13,473	269,892
Sissili	Léo	5,303	13,736	297,598
Soum	Djibo	5,154	13,350	217,972
Sourou	Tougan	3,663	9,487	313,355
Tapoa	Diapaga	5,707	14,780	187,785
Yatenga	Ouahigouya	4,746	12,292	558,318
Zoundwéogo	Manga	1,333	3,453	175,166
TOTAL		105,946	274,400	9,190,791

Demography

Population (1995): 10,324,000.
Density (1995): persons per sq mi 97.4, persons per sq km 37.6.
Urban-rural (1991): urban 14.0%; rural 86.0%.
Sex distribution (1995): male 49.54%; female 50.46%.
Age breakdown (1995): under 15, 44.9%; 15–29, 25.8%; 30–44, 15.2%; 45–59, 9.1%; 60–74, 4.2%; 75 and over, 0.8%.
Population projection: (2000) 11,884,000; (2010) 15,549,000.
Doubling time: 24 years.
Ethnic composition (1983): Mossi 47.9%; Mande 8.8%; Fulani 8.3%; Lobi 6.9%; Bobo 6.8%; Senufo 5.3%; Grosi 5.1%; Gurma 4.8%; Tuareg 3.3%; other 2.8%.
Religious affiliation (1980): traditional beliefs 44.8%; Muslim 43.0%; Christian 12.2%, of which Roman Catholic 9.8%, Protestant 2.4%.
Major cities (1985): Ouagadougou 441,514; Bobo-Dioulasso 228,668; Koudougou 51,926; Ouahigouya 38,902; Banfora 35,319.

Vital statistics

Birth rate per 1,000 population (1990–95): 46.8 (world avg. 25.0).
Death rate per 1,000 population (1990–95): 18.2 (world avg. 9.2).
Natural increase rate per 1,000 population (1990–95): 28.6 (world avg. 15.7).
Total fertility rate (avg. births per childbearing woman; 1990–95): 6.5.
Life expectancy at birth (1990–95): male 45.8 years; female 49.0 years.
Major causes of death (ages 15 and under; 1991): malaria, respiratory diseases, intestinal infectious diseases, meningitis.

National economy

Budget (1994). Revenue: CFAF 199,797,000,000 (1993; import duties 23.4%, personal income taxes 18.8%, sales taxes 14.7%, export duties 11.6%). Expenditures: CFAF 234,866,000,000 (1993; wages and salaries 28.8%, goods and services 10.6%, debt service 6.8%).
Production (metric tons except as noted). Agriculture, forestry, fishing (1994): sorghum 1,200,000, millet 800,000, corn (maize) 420,000, sugarcane 411,000, seed cotton 171,000, peanuts (groundnuts) 113,000, rice 70,000, pulses 63,000, sweet potatoes 20,000, sesame 8,000, cassava 5,000; livestock (number of live animals) 7,400,000 goats, 5,686,000 sheep, 4,261,000 cattle, 19,000,000 chickens; roundwood (1993) 9,520,000 cu m; fish catch (1993) 7,000. Mining and quarrying (1993): gold 851 kg[1]; silver 100 kg[2]. Manufacturing (value added in CFAF '000,000; 1991): cotton 6,095; beer and soft drinks 5,438; sugar 4,892; cigarettes 2,095[3]; soap 1,433; textiles and clothing 1,408; flour 1,257; batteries 924; bicycles and mopeds 869. Construction (value added in CFAF; 1993): 42,400,000,000. Energy production (consumption): electricity (kW-hr; 1993) 196,000,000 (196,000,000); crude petroleum, none (n.a.); petroleum products (metric tons; 1993) none (188,000).

Gross national product (1993): U.S.$2,928,000,000 (U.S.$300 per capita).

Structure of gross domestic product and labour force

	1993		1991	
	in value CFAF '000,000	% of total value	labour force	% of labour force
Agriculture	270,200	33.9	4,068,000	84.1
Mining / Manufacturing	120,200	15.1	251,000	5.2
Construction	42,400	5.3		
Public utilities	7,400	0.9		
Transp. and commun.	33,500	4.2	517,000	10.7
Trade	102,800	12.9		
Finance	...	...		
Pub. admin., defense / Services	195,700	24.6		
Other	22,100[4]	2.8[4]	...	...
TOTAL	796,000[5]	100.0[5]	4,836,000	100.0

Tourism (1993): receipts U.S.$8,000,000; expenditures U.S.$35,000,000.
Public debt (external, outstanding; 1993): U.S.$1,093,000,000.
Population economically active (1991): total 4,836,000; activity rate 52.2% (participation rates [1985]: over age 15, 83.0%; female 49.1%; unemployed 0.9%).

Price and earnings indexes (1990 = 100)

	1988	1989	1990	1991	1992	1993	1994
Consumer price index	101.1	100.8	100.0	102.5	100.5	101.1	126.5
Hourly earnings index[6]	93.5	100.0	100.0	100.0	100.0	...	...

Household income and expenditure. Average household size (1985) 6.2; average annual income per household CFAF 303,000 (U.S.$640); sources of income: n.a.; expenditure (1985)[7]: food 38.7%; transportation 18.6%; electricity and fuel 13.7%; beverages 9.0%; health 5.2%; housing 5.1%.
Land use (1993): forested 50.5%; meadows and pastures 21.9%; agricultural and under permanent cultivation 13.0%; other 14.6%.

Foreign trade

Balance of trade (current prices)

	1989	1990	1991	1992	1993	1994
CFAF '000,000	−91.40	−78.70	−94.02	−93.9	−105.2	−104.6
% of total	39.9%	32.2%	61.1%	37.8%	42.7%	28.8%

Imports (1993): CFAF 182,200,000,000 (machinery and transport equipment 41.5%, food products 16.1%, petroleum products 7.6%, raw materials 5.9%). *Major import sources* (1991): France 24.4%; Côte d'Ivoire 19.4%; United States 4.9%; Japan 4.2%; The Netherlands 4.0%; Nigeria 2.8%.
Exports (1993): CFAF 76,500,000,000 (raw cotton 23.8%, gold 13.3%, live animals 5.4%, hides and skins 4.1%). *Major export destinations* (1991): Japan 20.3%; France 13.4%; Côte d'Ivoire 11.2%; Thailand 8.3%; Taiwan 6.2%; Togo 2.9%.

Transport and communications

Transport. Railroads (1984)[8]: route length[9] 308 mi, 495 km; passenger-km 679,790,000; metric ton-km cargo 469,675,000. Roads (1992): total length 8,151 mi, 13,117 km (paved 12%[10]). Vehicles (1993): passenger cars 11,000; trucks and buses 13,300. Merchant marine: none. Air transport (1993): passenger-km 217,154,000; metric ton-mi cargo 34,204,000; airports (1995) 2.
Communications. Daily newspapers (1994): total number 4; total circulation 17,000[11]; circulation per 1,000 population 1.7[11]. Radio (1994): 225,000 receivers (1 per 45 persons). Television (1994): 45,500 receivers (1 per 221 persons). Telephones (main lines; 1993): 21,900 (1 per 447 persons).

Education and health

Education (1992–93)

	schools	teachers	students	student/ teacher ratio
Primary	2,741	9,412	562,644	59.7
Secondary	173[12]	2,419[12]	107,024	25.1[12]
Vocational	22[12]	493	8,329	16.9
Higher[12]	9	437	7,387	16.9

Educational attainment (1985). Percentage of population age 10 and over having: no formal schooling 86.1%; some primary 7.3%; general secondary 2.2%; specialized secondary and postsecondary 3.8%; other 0.6%. *Literacy* (1995): percentage of total population age 15 and over literate 18.2%; males 29.5%; females 9.2%.
Health (1991): physicians 341 (1 per 27,158 persons); hospital beds 5,041 (1 per 1,837 persons); infant mortality rate (1990–95) 130.0.
Food (1992): daily per capita caloric intake 2,387 (vegetable products 96%, animal products 4%); 101% of FAO recommended minimum requirement.

Military

Total active duty personnel (1995): 5,800 (army 96.6%, air force 3.4%). *Military expenditure as percentage of GNP* (1993): 2.2% (world 3.3%); per capita expenditure U.S.$6.

[1]Officially marketed gold only; does not include substantial illegal production. [2]1992. [3]1990. [4]Includes indirect taxes less imputed bank service charges and subsidies. [5]Detail does not add to total given because of rounding. [6]January 1; index refers to the *S.M.I.G.* (*salaire minimum interprofessionnel guaranti*), a form of minimum professional wage. [7]Weights of consumer price index components; Ouagadougou only. [8]Passenger-km and metric ton-km cargo figures are based on traffic between Abidjan, Côte d'Ivoire, and Ouagadougou. [9]1989. [10]1986. [11]Circulation for 3 newspapers only. [12]1991–92.

Burundi

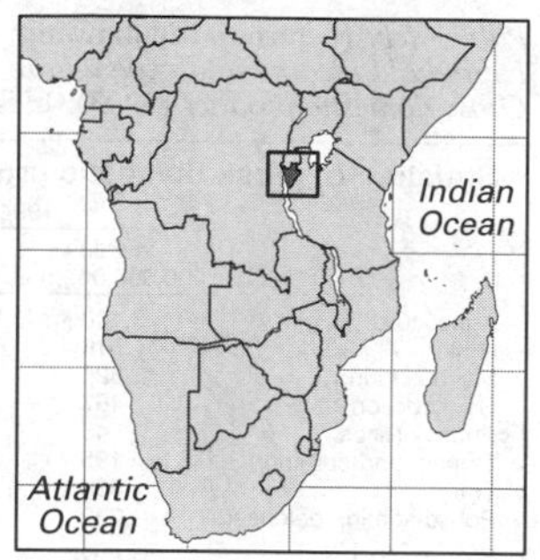

Official name: Republika y'u Burundi (Rundi); République du Burundi (French) (Republic of Burundi).
Form of government: transitional government[1] with one legislative house (National Assembly [81]).
Head of state and government: President, assisted by Prime Minister.
Capital: Bujumbura.
Official languages: Rundi; French.
Official religion: none.
Monetary unit: 1 Burundi franc (FBu) = 100 centimes; valuation (Oct. 6, 1995) 1 U.S.$ = FBu 247.40; 1 £ = FBu 391.12.

Area and population

		area		population
Provinces	Capitals	sq mi	sq km	1990 census
Bubanza	Bubanza	420	1,089	222,953
Bujumbura	Bujumbura	509	1,319	608,931
Bururi	Bururi	952	2,465	385,490
Cankuzo	Cankuzo	759	1,965	142,707
Cibitoke	Cibitoke	631	1,636	279,843
Gitega	Gitega	764	1,979	565,174
Karuzi	Karuzi	563	1,457	287,905
Kayanza	Kayanza	476	1,233	443,116
Kirundo	Kirundo	658	1,703	401,103
Makamba	Makamba	757	1,960	223,799
Muramvya	Muramvya	593	1,535	441,653
Muyinga	Muyinga	709	1,836	373,382
Ngozi	Ngozi	569	1,474	482,246
Rutana	Rutana	750	1,959	195,834
Ruyigi	Ruyigi	903	2,339	238,567
TOTAL LAND AREA		10,019	25,949	
INLAND WATER		721	1,867	
TOTAL		10,740	27,816	5,292,793[2]

Demography

Population (1995): 5,936,000[3].
Density (1995)[4]: persons per sq mi 592.5, persons per sq km 228.8.
Urban-rural (1990): urban 6.3%; rural 93.7%.
Sex distribution (1990): male 48.63%; female 51.37%.
Age breakdown (1990): under 15, 46.4%; 15–29, 25.3%; 30–44, 15.4%; 45–59, 7.0%; 60–74, 4.0%; 75 and over, 1.7%; not determined 0.2%.
Population projection: (2000) 6,674,000; (2010) 8,437,000.
Doubling time: 22 years.
Ethnic composition (1983): Rundi 97.4%, of which Hutu 81.9%, Tutsi 13.5%; Twa Pygmy 1.0%; other 1.6%.
Religious affiliation (1990): Roman Catholic 65.1%; nonreligious 18.6%; Protestant 13.8%; Muslim 1.6%; traditional beliefs 0.3%; other 0.6%.
Major cities (1990): Bujumbura 236,334; Gitega 20,708; Bururi 15,816; Ngozi 14,511; Cibitoke 8,280.

Vital statistics

Birth rate per 1,000 population (1991): 47.0 (world avg. 25.0).
Death rate per 1,000 population (1991): 15.0 (world avg. 9.3).
Natural increase rate per 1,000 population (1991): 32.0 (world avg. 15.7).
Total fertility rate (avg. births per childbearing woman; 1991): 6.9.
Marriage rate per 1,000 population: n.a.
Divorce rate per 1,000 population: n.a.
Life expectancy at birth (1991): male 50.0 years; female 54.0 years.
Major causes of death: n.a.; however, major health problems include malaria, influenza, diarrheal diseases, measles, and AIDS.

National economy

Budget (1994). Revenue: FBu 41,654,600,000 (excise duties 25.6%, customs duties 22.9%, taxes on goods and services 16.0%, income tax 10.2%, property tax 9.9%, administrative receipts 1.3%). Expenditures: FBu 42,065,900,000 (goods and services 59.2%, subsidies and transfers 23.5%, public debt 17.3%).
Tourism (1993): receipts from visitors U.S.$3,000,000; expenditures by nationals abroad U.S.$20,000,000.
Production (metric tons except as noted). Agriculture, forestry, fishing (1993): bananas 1,269,000, sweet potatoes 507,000, cassavas 471,000, dry beans 258,000, sugarcane 128,000, corn (maize) 116,000, yams and taros 111,000, sorghum 50,000, potatoes 37,000, coffee 33,000, rice 30,000, peanuts (groundnuts) 11,000, millet 10,000, wheat 7,000; livestock (number of live animals) 850,000 goats, 380,000 cattle, 350,000 sheep, 4,000,000 chickens; roundwood (1992) 4,483,000 cu m; fish catch (1992) 23,033. Mining and quarrying (1991): peat 10,026; kaolin clay 6,682; lime 86; gold 804 troy oz. Manufacturing (1994): beer 1,382,670 hectolitres; carbonated beverages 201,400 hectolitres; cigarettes 584,580,000 units; blankets 248,438 units; footwear 74,890 pairs. Construction: n.a. Energy production (consumption): electricity (kW-hr; 1993) 117,000,000 (141,000,000); coal, none (n.a.); crude petroleum, none (n.a.); petroleum products (metric tons; 1993) none (65,000); natural gas, none (n.a.); peat (metric tons; 1993) 12,000 (12,000).
Land use (1993): forested 3.3%; meadows and pastures 35.6%; agricultural and under permanent cultivation 53.0%; other 8.1%.
Gross national product (at current market prices; 1993): U.S.$1,102,000,000 (U.S.$180 per capita).

Structure of gross domestic product and labour force

	1991		1990	
	in value FBu '000,000[5]	% of total value	labour force	% of labour force
Agriculture	105,535.5	48.5	2,574,443	93.1
Mining	2,217.5 (Mining and Public utilities combined)	1.0 (Mining and Public utilities combined)	1,419	—
Public utilities			1,672	0.1
Manufacturing	26,160.5	12.0	33,867	1.2
Construction	8,922.5	4.1	19,737	0.7
Transportation and communications	6,650.8	3.1	8,504	0.3
Trade	19,770.6	9.1	25,822	0.9
Finance	...	...	2,005	0.1
Pub. admin., defense	24,084.6	11.1	85,191 (Pub. admin., defense and Services combined)	3.1 (Pub. admin., defense and Services combined)
Services	3,844.4	1.8		
Other	20,362.4	9.3	13,270	0.5
TOTAL	217,548.8	100.0	2,765,945[2]	100.0

Public debt (external, outstanding; 1993): U.S.$999,000,000.
Population economically active (1991): total 2,779,777; activity rate of total population 52.9% (participation rates: ages 15–64, 91.4%; female 52.6%; unemployed, n.a.).

Price and earnings indexes (1990 = 100)

	1988	1989	1990	1991	1992	1993	1994
Consumer price index	83.7	93.5	100.0	109.0	113.9	124.9	143.5
Earnings index	...	...	...	...	...	...	...

Household income and expenditure. Average household size (1990) 4.6; income per household: n.a.; sources of income: n.a.; expenditure[6]: food 59.6%, clothing and footwear 11.1%, furniture and household goods 6.0%, energy and water 5.8%, housing 4.4%, other 13.1%.

Foreign trade[7]

Balance of trade (current prices)

	1989	1990	1991	1992	1993	1994
FBu '000,000	−13,719	−26,583	−28,144	−30,751	−26,417	−22,603
% of total	35.8%	51.0%	45.8%	50.0%	44.0%	29.9%

Imports (1994): FBu 56,467,600,000 (machinery and transport equipment 21.3%, food and food products 17.9%, petroleum products 8.2%, pharmaceutical products 6.4%). *Major import sources* (1993): Belgium-Luxembourg 13.9%; France 11.4%; Japan 7.9%; Iran 7.2%; Germany 5.2%; The Netherlands 4.8%; Kenya 4.4%; China 4.1%.
Exports (1994): FBu 26,499,300,000 (coffee 76.1%, tea 10.2%, cotton 3.3%, animal hides and skins 2.4%). *Major export destinations* (1992): Germany 15.5%; United States 7.6%; Rwanda 7.6%; United Kingdom 5.8%; Kenya 4.9%; Zaire 3.4%; Switzerland 3.4%; France 2.8%, Zimbabwe 2.5%.

Transport and communications

Transport. Railroads: none. Roads (1992): total length 8,993 mi, 14,473 km (paved 7%). Vehicles (1992): passenger cars 14,483; trucks and other vehicles 14,914. Merchant marine (1979): vessels (100 gross tons and over) 1; total gross tonnage 385. Air transport (1994)[8]: passenger arrivals 28,762, departures 33,750; cargo loaded 1,760 short tons (1,597 metric tons), unloaded 14,841 short tons (13,463 metric tons); airports (1995) with scheduled flights 1.
Communications. Daily newspapers (1994): total number 1; total circulation 20,000, circulation per 1,000 population 3.4. Radio (1994): total number of receivers 300,000 (1 per 19 persons). Television (1994): total number of receivers 4,500 (1 per 1,289 persons). Telephones (main lines; 1993): 15,600 (1 per 363 persons).

Education and health

Education (1992–93)

	schools	teachers	students	student/teacher ratio
Primary (age 6–11)	1,418	10,400	651,086	62.6
Secondary (age 12–18)	113[9]	2,562	55,713	21.7
Higher	8[9]	556	4,256	7.6

Educational attainment: n.a. *Literacy* (1995): percentage of total population age 15 and over literate 35.3%; males literate 49.7%; females literate 22.5%.
Health (1990): physicians 168 (1 per 31,777 persons); hospital beds 10,370 (1 per 515 persons); infant mortality rate per 1,000 live births 111.0.
Food (1992): daily per capita caloric intake 1,941 (vegetable products 97%, animal products 3%); 83% of FAO recommended minimum requirement.

Military

Total active duty personnel (1995): 12,600 (army 99.2%, air force 0.8%). *Military expenditure as percentage of GNP* (1991): 2.4% (world 4.2%); per capita expenditure U.S.$5.

[1]A multiparty agreement signed in September 1994 stipulated the terms of a power-sharing government and a four-year (October 1994 to October 1998) transitional period. [2]Detail does not add to total given because of rounding. [3]Population is not adjusted for casualties or refugees of the recent civil war. [4]Based on land area. [5]Estimate. [6]Weights of consumer price index components. [7]Import figures are f.o.b. in balance of trade and c.i.f. in commodities and trading partners. [8]Figures for Bujumbura airport only. [9]1990–91.

Cambodia

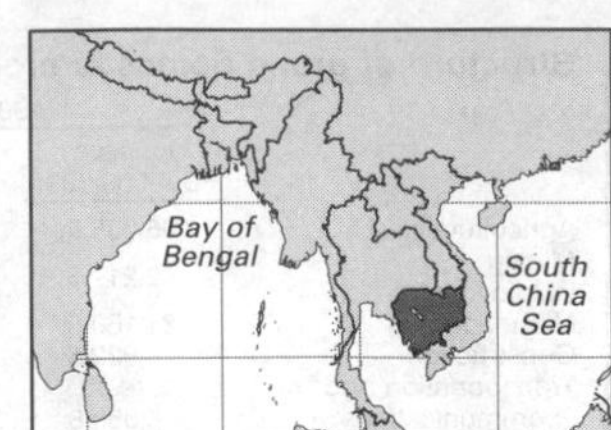

Official name: Preah Reach Ana Pak Kampuchea (Kingdom of Cambodia)[1].
Form of government: constitutional monarchy with one legislative house (National Assembly [120]).
Chief of state: King.
Heads of government: First Prime Minister assisted by Second Prime Minister.
Capital: Phnom Penh.
Official language: Khmer.
Official religion: Buddhism.
Monetary unit: 1 riel = 100 sen; valuation (Oct. 6, 1995) 1 U.S.$ = 2,300 riels; 1 £ = 3,636 riels.

Area and population

Provinces	Capitals	area sq mi	area sq km	population 1987 estimate
Bântéay Méanchey	...	[2]	[2]	[2]
Bătdâmbâng	Bătdâmbâng	7,353[2]	19,044[2]	837,000[2]
Kâmpóng Cham	Kâmpóng Cham	4,053	10,498	1,244,000
Kâmpóng Chhnăng	Kâmpóng Chhnăng	2,131	5,520	257,000
Kâmpóng Saôm	Kâmpóng Saôm	27	69	61,000
Kâmpóng Spoe	Kâmpóng Spoe	2,709	7,016	396,000
Kâmpóng Thum	Kâmpóng Thum	4,730	12,251	441,000
Kâmpôt	Kâmpôt	3,808	9,862	412,000
Kândal	...	1,472	3,813	838,000
Kaôh Kŏng	Krŏng Kaôh Kŏng	4,301	11,140	30,000
Krâchéh	Krâchéh	4,283	11,094	182,000
Môndól Kiri	Senmonorom	5,517	14,288	18,000
Phnom Penh	Phnom Penh	18	46	564,000
Poŭthĭsăt	Poŭthĭsăt	4,900	12,692	204,000
Preăh Vihéar	Phnum Tbéng Meanchey	5,541	14,350	80,000
Prey Vêng	Prey Vêng	1,885	4,883	782,000
Rôtânôkiri	Lumphăt	4,163	10,782	52,000
Siĕmréab–Ŏtdâr Méanchey[3]	Siĕmréab	4,207	10,897	555,000
Stŏeng Trêng	Stŏeng Trêng	4,328	11,209	46,000
Svay Riĕng	Svay Riĕng	1,145	2,966	340,000
Takêv	Takêv	1,474	3,818	618,000
TOTAL LAND AREA		68,045	176,238	
INLAND WATER		2,192	5,678	
TOTAL		70,238[4]	181,916	7,957,000

Demography

Population (1995): 9,610,000.
Density (1995)[5]: persons per sq mi 136.8, persons per sq km 52.8.
Urban-rural (1995): urban 21%; rural 79%.
Sex distribution (1995): male 48.17%; female 51.83%.
Age breakdown (1995): under 15, 44.9%; 15–29, 26.1%; 30–44, 16.6%; 45–59, 8.1%; 60–74, 3.5%; 75 and over, 0.7%.
Population projection: (2000) 10,910,000; (2010) 13,690,000.
Ethnic composition (1994): Khmer 88.6%; Vietnamese 5.5%; Chinese 3.1%; Cham 2.3%; other (Thai, Lao, and Kola) 0.5%.
Religious affiliation (1994): Buddhist 95%; Muslim 2%; other 3%.
Major cities (1987): Phnom Penh 920,000[6]; Bătdâmbâng 45,000; Kâmpóng Cham 33,000; Pursat 16,000; Kâmpóng Chhnăng 15,000.

Vital statistics

Birth rate per 1,000 population (1995): 40 (world avg. 25.0).
Death rate per 1,000 population (1995): 13 (world avg. 9.3).
Natural increase rate per 1,000 population (1995): 27 (world avg. 15.7).
Total fertility rate (avg. births per childbearing woman; 1995): 5.1.
Marriage rate per 1,000 population: n.a.
Divorce rate per 1,000 population: n.a.
Life expectancy at birth (1995): male 51 years; female 54 years.
Major causes of death per 100,000 population: n.a.; however, major health problems include tuberculosis, malaria, and pneumonia. Violence, acts of war, and military ordnance (especially unexploded mines) remain hazards.

National economy

Budget (1994). Revenue: 590,400,000,000 riels (customs duties 47.6%; timber removal fees paid by state enterprises 17.1%; consumption taxes 7.9%). Expenditures: 1,019,200,000,000 riels (current expenditure 67.1%, of which defense 34.1%, police 8.2%, education 5.9%, public health 2.9%; development expenditure 32.9%).
Tourism (1994): total number of tourist arrivals 178,000.
Production (metric tons except as noted). Agriculture, forestry, fishing (1994): rice 1,800,000, roots and tubers 233,000 (of which cassava 152,000, sweet potatoes 63,000), sugarcane 160,000, bananas 129,000, corn (maize) 64,000, oranges 49,000, rubber 43,000, soybeans 40,000, mangoes 26,000, tobacco leaves 10,000; livestock (number of live animals) 2,589,000 cattle, 2,154,000 pigs, 829,000 buffalo, 15,000,000 poultry; roundwood (1993) 7,025,000 cu m (the Khmer Rouge market additional quantities to Thailand); fish catch 103,200. Mining and quarrying (1994): legal mining is confined to fertilizers, salt, and construction materials; smuggling of gemstones from Khmer Rouge-controlled areas is believed to be extensive. Manufacturing (value of production in '000,000 riels; 1988): cigarettes 1,064.5; food 116.9; chemical products (including rubber) 83.5; light industries (including textiles) 63.2; mechanical equipment and parts 46.8; building materials 4.5. Construction: n.a. Energy production (consumption): electricity (kW-hr; 1992) 150,000,000 (150,000,000); petroleum products (metric tons; 1992) none (155,000).
Public debt (external, outstanding; 1993): U.S.$239,400,000.
Household income and expenditure. Average household size (1980) 5.6.
Gross domestic product (1993): U.S.$1,580,000,000 (U.S.$170 per capita).

Structure of gross domestic product and labour force

	1994 in value '000,000,000 riels	1994 % of total value	1992 labour force	1992 % of labour force
Agriculture	3,140	51.2	2,495,000	69.4
Mining	18	0.3		
Manufacturing	325	5.3		
Construction	467	7.6		
Public utilities	43	0.7		
Transp. and commun.	195	3.2	1,100,000	30.6
Trade	909	14.8		
Public admin., defense	232	3.8		
Services / Other	802	13.1		
TOTAL	6,131	100.0	3,595,000	100.0

Population economically active (1992): total 3,964,000; activity rate of total population 43.1% (participation rates: ages 16–60, 91.2%; female 55.7%).

Price and earnings indexes (1992 = 100)

	1990	1991	1992	1993	1994	1995
Consumer price index	19.2	57.1	100.0	214.4	213.3	229.6[7]
Earnings index	...	...	...	...	...	...

Land use (1993): forested 65.7%; meadows and pastures 11.3%; agricultural and under permanent cultivation 13.6%; other 9.4%.

Foreign trade[8]

Balance of trade (current prices)

	1989	1990	1991	1992	1993	1994
U.S.$'000,000	−97	−78	−33	−86	−203	−230
% of total	37.9%	31.2%	7.1%	14.0%	31.7%	18.7%

Imports (1994): U.S.$668,000,000 (cigarettes 14.4%; gold 11.7%; fabric 5.4%; diesel oil 4.5%; motorcycles 4.3%). *Major import sources* (1993[9]): Singapore 24.3%; Vietnam 17.5%; Japan 8.2%; Australia 5.1%.
Exports (1994): U.S.$458,000,000 (domestic exports 50.2%, of which logs 27.1%, sawn timber 15.9%, rubber 5.9%; reexports 49.8%). *Major export destinations* (1993)[10]: Singapore 65.8%; Japan 10.6%; Hong Kong 5.0%.

Transport and communications

Transport. Railroads (1995): length 380 mi, 612 km; passengers transported (1994) 500,000; cargo transported (1994) 100,000 metric tons. Roads (1994): total length 8,296 mi, 13,351 km (paved 20%). Vehicles (1993): passenger cars 28,919; trucks and buses 9,247. Merchant marine (1992): vessels (100 gross tons and over) 3; total deadweight tonnage 3,839. Air transport (1977): passenger-mi 26,098,800, passenger-km 42,000,000; short ton-mi cargo 274,000, metric ton-km cargo 400,000; airports (1995) with scheduled flights 6.
Communications. Daily newspapers (1991): total number 1. Radio (1994): 860,000 receivers (1 per 11 persons). Television (1994): 70,000 receivers (1 per 136 persons). Telephones (main lines; 1993): 5,900 (1 per 1,667 persons).

Education and health

Education (1992–93)

	schools	teachers	students	student/teacher ratio
Primary (age 6–10)	4,539	42,405	1,465,958	34.6
Secondary (age 11–16)	440	19,540	239,363	12.2
Voc., teacher tr.	65	2,618	15,537	5.9
Higher	9	268	22,182	82.8

Educational attainment: n.a. *Literacy* (1987): total population age 15 and over literate 3,778,042 (74.3%); males literate 2,001,084 (85.0%); females literate 1,776,958 (65.0%).
Health: physicians (1990) 600 (1 per 14,300 persons); hospital beds (1988) 12,953[11] (1 per 632[11] persons); infant mortality rate per 1,000 live births (1995) 109.
Food (1992): daily per capita caloric intake 2,021 (vegetable products 94%, animal products 6%); 91% of FAO recommended minimum requirement.

Military

Total active duty personnel (1994)[12]: 88,500 (army 40.7%, navy 2.3%, air force 0.6%, provincial 56.4%). Armed Khmer Rouge guerrillas may number 10,000–12,000. About 22,000 UNTAC[1] troops were withdrawn after civilian government was reestablished in 1993.

[1]The United Nations Transitional Authority in Cambodia (UNTAC) assumed administrative responsibility for Cambodia in March 1992. Cambodian sovereignty, however, was retained by a Supreme National Council (SNC) until UN-supervised elections were held May 23–29, 1993. The Kingdom of Cambodia was proclaimed from Sept. 24, 1993. [2]Bântéay Méanchey included in Bătdâmbâng. [3]The province of Ŏtdâr Méanchey has been combined with Siĕmréab, and area and population figures reflect the change. [4]Detail does not add to total given because of rounding. [5]Based on land area. [6]1994 estimate. [7]Average of June–July. [8]Trade statistics do not indicate whether imports are c.i.f. or f.o.b.; illegal or undeclared trade is not accounted for in the foreign-trade figures shown here. [9]Estimated figures. [10]Domestic exports only (U.S.$37,700,000). [11]Public hospitals only. [12]Figures include provincial, and exclude paramilitary, forces.

Cameroon

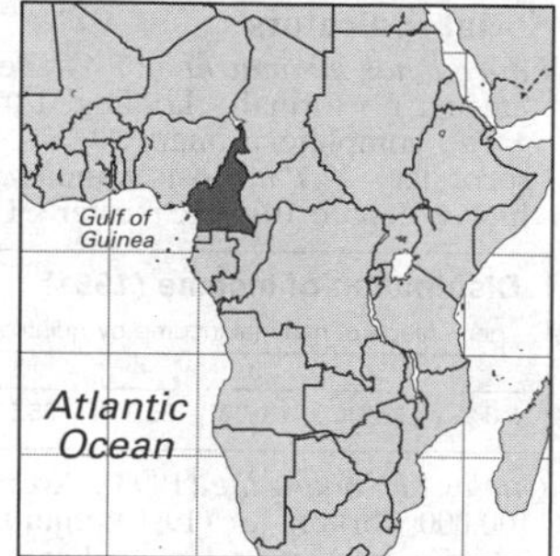

Official name: République du Cameroun (French); Republic of Cameroon (English).
Form of government: unitary multiparty republic with one legislative house (National Assembly [180]).
Chief of state: President.
Head of government: Prime Minister.
Capital: Yaoundé.
Official languages: French; English.
Official religion: none.
Monetary unit: 1 CFA franc (CFAF) = 100 centimes; valuation (Oct. 6, 1995) 1 U.S.$ = CFAF 501.49; 1 £ = CFAF 792.78.

Area and population

		area		population
Provinces	Capitals	sq mi	sq km	1987 census
Adamoua	Ngaoundéré	24,591	63,691	495,200
Centre	Yaoundé	26,613	68,926	1,651,600
Est	Bertoua	42,089	109,011	517,200
Extrême-Nord	Maroua	13,223	34,246	1,855,700
Littoral	Douala	7,814	20,239	1,354,800
Nord	Garoua	25,319	65,576	832,200
Nord-Ouest	Bamenda	6,877	17,810	1,237,400
Ouest	Bafoussam	5,356	13,872	1,339,800
Sud	Ebolowa	18,189	47,110	373,800
Sud-Ouest	Buea	9,448	24,471	838,000
LAND AREA		179,519	464,952	
INLAND WATER		4,051	10,492	
TOTAL		183,569[1]	475,442[1]	10,495,700

Demography

Population (1995): 13,233,000.
Density (1995)[2]: persons per sq mi 73.7, persons per sq km 28.5.
Urban-rural (1991): urban 41.2%; rural 58.8%.
Sex distribution (1991): male 49.88%; female 50.12%.
Age breakdown (1991): under 15, 46.4%; 15–29, 24.4%; 30–44, 15.1%; 45–59, 8.6%; 60 and over, 5.5%.
Population projection: (2000) 15,245,000; (2010) 20,163,000.
Doubling time: 25 years.
Ethnic composition (1983): Fang 19.6%; Bamileke and Bamum 18.5%; Duala, Luanda, and Basa 14.7%; Fulani 9.6%; Tikar 7.4%; Mandara 5.7%; Maka 4.9%; Chamba 2.4%; Mbum 1.3%; Hausa 1.2%; French 0.2%; other 14.5%.
Religious affiliation (1990): Roman Catholic 34.7%; animist 26.0%; Muslim 21.8%; Protestant 17.5%.
Major cities (1987): Douala 810,000; Yaoundé 649,000; Garoua 142,000; Maroua 123,000; Bafoussam 113,000.

Vital statistics

Birth rate per 1,000 population (1990–95): 40.7 (world avg. 25.0).
Death rate per 1,000 population (1990–95): 12.2 (world avg. 9.3).
Natural increase rate per 1,000 population (1990–95): 28.5 (world avg. 15.7).
Total fertility rate (avg. births per childbearing woman; 1990–95): 5.7.
Life expectancy at birth (1990–95): male 54.5 years; female 57.5 years.
Major causes of death per 100,000 population: n.a.; however, major health problems include measles, malaria, tuberculosis of respiratory system, anemias, meningitis, and intestinal obstruction and hernia.

National economy

Budget (1992–93). Revenue: CFAF 431,000,000,000 (sales tax 26.7%; petroleum royalties 25.9%; customs duties 19.1%). Expenditures: CFAF 632,000,000,000 (current expenditure 86.2%, of which wages and salaries 43.5%, debt service 24.3%, goods and services 10.7%).
Public debt (external, outstanding; 1993): U.S.$5,683,000,000.
Gross national product (at current market prices; 1993): U.S.$9,663,000,000 (U.S.$770 per capita).

Structure of gross domestic product and labour force

	1991		1985	
	in value CFAF '000,000	% of total value	labour force	% of labour force
Agriculture	749	23.9	2,900,871	74.0
Mining	406	12.9	1,793	0.1
Manufacturing	424	13.5	174,498	4.5
Construction	165	5.3	66,684	1.7
Public utilities	38	1.2	3,522	0.1
Transp. and commun.	195	6.2	51,688	1.3
Trade	368	11.7	154,014	3.9
Finance	417	13.3	8,009	0.2
Public admin., defense	310	9.9 }	292,922	7.5
Services	66	2.1 }		
Other	...	...	263,634	6.7
TOTAL	3,138	100.0	3,917,635	100.0

Household income and expenditure. Average household size (1980) 5.2; average annual income per household (1983)[3] U.S.$420; sources of income: n.a.; expenditure (1993)[3]: food 49.1%, housing 18.0%, transportation and communications 13.0%, health 8.6%, clothing 7.6%, recreation 2.4%.
Tourism (1993): receipts from visitors U.S.$47,000,000; expenditures by nationals abroad U.S.$225,000,000.

Population economically active (1991): total 4,740,000; activity rate of total population 40.0% (participation rates [1985]: ages 15–69, 66.3%; female 38.5%; unemployed, n.a.).

Price and earnings indexes (1990 = 100)

	1987	1988	1989	1990	1991	1992
Consumer price index	98.7	93.2	98.3	100.0	101.9	103.3
Earnings index	...	...	...	...	...	...

Production (metric tons except as noted). Agriculture, forestry, fishing (1994): sugarcane 1,350,000, cassava 1,300,000, plantains 860,000, vegetables and melons 466,000, corn (maize) 430,000, sweet potatoes 170,000, palm oil 120,000, bananas 100,000, peanuts (groundnuts) 100,000, cacao 100,000, yams 95,000, rice 95,000, millet 60,000, palm kernels 54,000; livestock (number of live animals) 4,867,000 cattle, 3,770,000 sheep, 3,767,000 goats, 1,380,000 pigs; roundwood (1993) 14,741,000 cu m; fish catch (1993) 80,000. Mining and quarrying (1994): marble 200,000; pozzolana 130,000; aluminum 85,000; limestone 57,000; tin ore and concentrate 4. Manufacturing (1990): cement 781,000; wheat flour 49,000[4]; soap 31,000; footwear 1,567,000 pairs; sawn wood 489,000 cu m; beer 6,815,000 hectolitres; soft drinks 1,172,000 hectolitres[4]. Construction (1983): residential 230,400 sq m; nonresidential 51,100 sq m. Energy production (consumption): electricity (kW-hr; 1992) 2,720,000,000 (2,720,000,000); coal (metric tons; 1992) 1,000 (1,000); crude petroleum (barrels; 1992) 50,565,000 (5,007,000); petroleum products (metric tons; 1992) 618,000 (609,000); natural gas, none (n.a.).
Land use (1993): forested 77.1%; meadows and pastures 4.3%; agricultural and under permanent cultivation 15.1%; other 3.5%.

Foreign trade[5]

Balance of trade (current prices)

	1988	1989	1990	1991	1992	1993
CFAF '000,000,000	−68.8	+40.3	+141.5	+198.6	+197.6	+249.7
% of total	11.1%	5.2%	14.8%	22.3%	25.0%	30.0%

Imports (1991): CFAF 650,610,000,000 (machinery and transport equipment 27.2%, of which road vehicles 5.5%; chemical products 14.7%; food and live animals 13.6%; iron and steel 4.6%; paper and paper products 3.5%; textiles 3.5%; nonmetallic minerals 3.0%). *Major import sources* (1993): France 37.3%; Belgium-Luxembourg 8.3%; Japan 5.3%; United States 5.0%; Germany 4.8%; Italy 3.8%; Spain 3.8%.
Exports (1993–94): CFAF 788,300,000,000 (crude petroleum 29.3%; coffee 13.2%; lumber 11.3%; cocoa 9.8%; cotton 4.8%). *Major export destinations* (1993): France 19.4%; Spain 16.4%; Italy 11.3%; The Netherlands 7.3%; United States 5.7%; Germany 5.6%; Morocco 5.0%; Nigeria 3.5%.

Transport and communications

Transport. Railroads (1992–93): route length 686 mi, 1,104 km; passenger-mi 247,000,000, passenger-km 398,000,000; short ton-mi cargo 405,000,000, metric ton-km cargo 592,000,000. Roads (1991): total length 30,074 mi, 48,400 km (paved 8%). Vehicles (1993): passenger cars 90,000; trucks and buses 79,000. Merchant marine (1992): vessels (100 gross tons and over) 47; total deadweight tonnage 39,797. Air transport (1991): passenger-mi 187,000,000, passenger-km 301,000,000; short ton-mi cargo 6,800,000, metric ton-km cargo 10,000,000; airports (1995) with scheduled flights 5.
Communications. Daily newspapers (1994): 2; total circulation 35,000[6]; circulation per 1,000 population 1.6[6]. Radio (1994): total number of receivers 1,500,000 (1 per 8.6 persons). Television (1994): total number of receivers 15,000 (1 per 858 persons). Telephones (main lines; 1993): 57,200 (1 per 219 persons).

Education and health

Education (1990–91)

	schools	teachers	students	student/ teacher ratio
Primary (age 6–14)	6,709	38,430	1,964,146	51.1
Secondary (age 15–24)	388[7]	11,400[8]	409,729	32.2[8]
Voc., teacher tr.	220[7]	6,267[8]	90,543	14.5[8]
Higher	5[7]	1,086	33,177	30.5

Educational attainment (1976). Percentage of population age 15 and over having: no schooling 51.1%; primary education 41.7%; some postprimary 0.2%; secondary 5.7%; some postsecondary 0.3%; higher 0.2%; other 0.8%.
Literacy (1990): percentage of total population age 15 and over literate 54.1%; males literate 66.3%; females literate 42.6%.
Health: physicians (1989) 945 (1 per 11,848 persons); hospital beds (1988) 29,285 (1 per 371 persons); infant mortality rate (1990–95) 63.0.
Food (1992): daily per capita caloric intake 1,981 (vegetable products 93%, animal products 7%); 85% of FAO recommended minimum requirement.

Military

Total active duty personnel (1995): 14,600 (army 89.0%, navy 8.9%, air force 2.1%). *Military expenditure as percentage of GNP* (1993): 2.1% (world 3.3%); per capita expenditure U.S.$14.

[1]Detail does not add to total given because of rounding. [2]Based on land area. [3]Weights of consumer price index components. [4]1988. [5]Import figures are f.o.b. in balance of trade and c.i.f. for commodities and trading partners. [6]Circulation for one newspaper only. [7]1986–87. [8]1989–90.

Canada

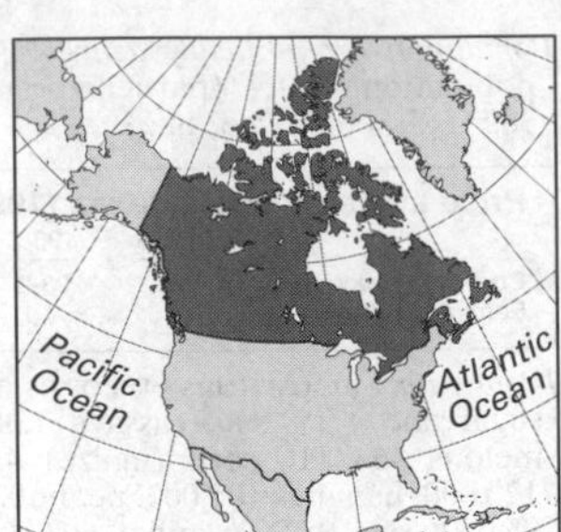

Official name: Canada.
Form of government: federal multiparty parliamentary state with two legislative houses (Senate [104]; House of Commons [295]).
Chief of state: Queen of Canada (British Monarch).
Representative of chief of state: Governor-General.
Head of government: Prime Minister.
Capital: Ottawa.
Official languages: English; French.
Official religion: none.
Monetary unit: 1 Canadian dollar (Can$) = 100 cents; valuation (Oct. 6, 1995) 1 U.S.$ = Can$1.33; 1 £ = Can$2.11.

Area and population

		area		population
				1993
Provinces	Capitals	sq mi	sq km	estimate
Alberta	Edmonton	255,287	661,190	2,662,000
British Columbia	Victoria	365,948	947,800	3,535,000
Manitoba	Winnipeg	250,947	649,950	1,116,000
New Brunswick	Fredericton	28,355	73,440	751,000
Newfoundland	St. John's	156,649	405,720	581,000
Nova Scotia	Halifax	21,425	55,490	923,000
Ontario	Toronto	412,581	1,068,580	10,746,000
Prince Edward Island	Charlottetown	2,185	5,660	132,000
Quebec	Quebec	594,860	1,540,680	7,209,000
Saskatchewan	Regina	251,866	652,330	1,003,000
Territories				
Northwest Territories[1]	Yellowknife	1,322,910	3,426,320	63,000
Yukon Territory	Whitehorse	186,661	483,450	32,000
TOTAL		3,849,674	9,970,610	28,753,000

Demography

Population (1995): 29,463,000.
Density (1995)[2]: persons per sq mi 8.3, persons per sq km 3.2.
Urban-rural (1993): urban 76.7%; rural 23.3%.
Sex distribution (1993): male 49.54%; female 50.46%.
Age breakdown (1993): under 15, 20.7%; 15–29, 22.1%; 30–44, 25.3%; 45–59, 15.9%; 60–74, 11.2%; 75 and over, 4.8%.
Population projection: (2000) 31,029,000; (2010) 33,946,000.
Doubling time: not applicable; doubling time exceeds 100 years.
Ethnic origin (1991): French 22.8%; British 20.8%; German 3.4%; Italian 2.8%; Chinese 2.2%; Amerindian and Inuktitut (Eskimo) 1.7%; Ukrainian 1.5%; Dutch 1.3%; multiple origin and other 43.5%[3].
Religious affiliation (1991): Roman Catholic 45.7%; Protestant 36.3%; Eastern Orthodox 1.5%; Jewish 1.2%; Muslim 1.0%; Buddhist 0.7%; Hindu 0.6%; nonreligious 12.4%; other 0.6%.
Major metropolitan areas (1991): Toronto 3,893,046; Montreal 3,127,242; Vancouver 1,602,502; Ottawa-Hull 920,857; Edmonton 839,924; Calgary 754,033; Winnipeg 652,354; Quebec 645,550; Hamilton 599,760; London 381,522.

Other metropolitan areas (1991)

	population		population		population
Chicoutimi-Jonquière	160,928	Regina	191,692	Sherbrooke	139,194
Halifax	320,501	St. Catharines–Niagara	364,552	Sudbury	157,613
Kitchener	356,421	St. John's	171,859	Trois Rivières	136,303
Oshawa	240,104	Saskatoon	210,023	Victoria	287,897
				Windsor	262,075

Place of birth (1986): 84.2% native-born; 15.8% foreign-born, of which United Kingdom 3.2%, other European 6.6%, Asian countries 3.2%, other 2.8%.
Mobility (1991). Population living in the same residence as in 1986: 53.3%; different residence, same municipality 23.2%; same province, different municipality 15.9%; different province 3.9%; different country 3.7%.
Households (1991). Total number of households 10,018,267. Average household size 2.7; (1985) 1 person 22.9%, 2 persons 31.4%, 3 persons 17.4%, 4 persons 17.6%, 5 persons 7.3%, 6 or more persons 3.4%. Family households (1991): 7,356,168 (73.4%), nonfamily 2,662,099 (26.6%, of which 1 person 22.9%).
Immigration (1992): permanent immigrants admitted 248,200, from Hong Kong 15.2%, Indonesia 5.2%, India 5.1%, Poland 4.7%, China 4.1%, Vietnam 3.1%; United States 2.9%; refugee arrivals 28,699.

Vital statistics

Birth rate per 1,000 population (1994): 13.1 (world avg. 25.0); (1985) legitimate 83.8%; illegitimate 16.2%.
Death rate per 1,000 population (1994): 7.2 (world avg. 9.3).
Natural increase rate per 1,000 population (1994): 5.9 (world avg. 15.7).
Total fertility rate (avg. births per childbearing woman; 1993): 1.9.
Marriage rate per 1,000 population (1992–93): 4.5.
Divorce rate per 1,000 population (1992–93): 1.7.
Life expectancy at birth (1994): male 74.7 years; female 81.7 years.
Major causes of death per 100,000 population (1992): diseases of the circulatory system 268.0; malignant neoplasms (cancers) 192.8; diseases of the respiratory system 58.2; accidents and violence 46.2 (including suicide 13.0).

Social indicators

Educational attainment (1991). Percentage of population age 25 and over having: no formal schooling, 1.0%; less than complete primary education 4.0%; complete primary 11.7%; lower-level secondary 34.3%; upper-level secondary 27.7%; postsecondary 21.4%; graduates by level (1987): 4-year higher degree 101,960, master's 15,790, doctorate 2,385.

Distribution of income (1991)

percentage of national income by quintile

1	2	3	4	5 (highest)
5.3%	13.6%	19.7%	25.9%	35.5%

Quality of working life (1993). Average workweek: 38.6 hours. Annual rate per 100,000 workers for (1990): injury, accident, or industrial illness 3,320; death 5.1[4]. Average days lost to labour stoppages per 1,000 employee-workdays (1993): 0.3. Average duration of journey to work (1983): 23 minutes[5] (72.8% automobile, 17.3% public transportation, 9.9% other). Rate per 1,000 workers of discouraged (unemployed no longer seeking work; 1983): 10.5.
Access to services (1990). Proportion of households having access to: electricity 100.0%; public water supply 99.8%; public sewage collection 99.3%.
Social participation. Eligible voters participating in last national election (October 1993): 69.7%. Population over 18 years of age participating in voluntary work (1987): 27.0%. Union membership in total workforce (1992): 29.7%. Practicing religious population in total affiliated population (1991): 87.6%.
Social deviance (1993). Offense rate per 100,000 population for: violent crime 1,079, of which assault 8.8[6], sexual assault 111.0[6], homicide 2.2; property crime 5,562, of which auto theft 510[6], burglary and housebreaking 1,589[6]. Incidence per 100,000 in general population of: alcoholism 2,285; drug abuse 258.
Leisure (1992). Favourite leisure activities (hours weekly): television 15.3; social time 12.7; reading 3.5; sports and entertainment 0.9.
Material well-being (1988). Households possessing: automobile 88.3%, of which two or more 25.1%; telephone 98.5%[7]; radio 99.1%[5]; television 99.0%[7]; refrigerator 99.6%; central air conditioner 24.6%[8]; cable television 69.0%; video recorder 58.8%[8]; microwave oven 63.4%[8].

National economy

Gross national product (1993): U.S.$574,936,000,000 (U.S.$20,670 per capita).

Structure of gross domestic product and labour force

	1993		1994	
	in value Can$'000,000[9]	% of total value	labour force	% of labour force
Agriculture	16,165	3.1	419,000	3.0
Mining	21,614	4.2	255,000	1.8
Manufacturing	92,431	17.9	1,820,000	12.9
Construction	27,624	5.3	655,000	4.7
Public utilities	16,316	3.2	928,000	6.6
Transportation and communications	44,087	8.5		
Trade	62,735	12.1	2,196,000	15.6
Finance	87,145	16.8	764,000	5.4
Pub. admin., defense	33,785	6.5	840,000	6.0
Services	115,494	22.3	4,620,000	32.9
Other	—	—	1,559,000[10]	11.1[10]
TOTAL	517,396[11]	100.0[12]	14,056,000	100.0

Budget (1992–93). Revenue: Can$140,981,000,000 (income taxes 54.3%, sales tax 21.0%, import duties 2.6%). Expenditures: Can$170,019,000,000 (public debt interest 23.3%, defense 7.0%, health 4.5%, education 2.6%, foreign assistance 2.2%).
National debt (1990–91): Can$443,278,000,000.
Tourism (1993): receipts from visitors U.S.$5,897,000,000; expenditures by nationals abroad U.S.$10,629,000,000.

Manufacturing, mining, and construction enterprises (1990)

	no. of establishments	no. of employees	hourly wages as a % of avg. of all mfg. wages	annual value added (Can$'000,000)
Manufacturing				
Food and beverages	3,657	222,000	91.3	18,260
Transport equipment	1,469	204,000	120.1	16,480
Chemicals and related products	1,629	101,000	115.0	12,910
Paper and related products	715	114,000	133.0	10,210
Printing, publishing, and related products	5,522	142,000	110.4	8,950
Machinery	4,694	148,000	96.0	8,840
Electrical and electronics products	1,378	123,000	97.2	8,710
Primary metals	493	97,000	150.8	7,530
Metal fabricating	3,913	135,000	94.1	7,530
Wood	2,672	104,000	100.9	5,210
Rubber and plastic	1,547	87,000	86.0	5,010
Clothing	2,994	110,000	59.2	3,880
Textiles	1,337	72,000	76.2	3,470
Nonmetallic mineral products	1,447	41,000	103.3	3,270
Furniture and fixtures	2,607	66,000	73.1	2,620
Petroleum and coal products	154	18,000	150.2	2,990
Tobacco products industries	18	5,000	...	1,140
Mining	1,232	113,000	149.3[13, 14]	29,650
Construction[15]	...	800,000	112.3[14]	28,182

Production (metric tons except as noted). Agriculture, forestry, fishing (1994): wheat 23,350,000, barley 11,690,000, rapeseed 7,187,000, corn (maize) 7,043,000, oats 3,699,000, potatoes 3,518,000, soybeans 2,251,000, vegetables 2,251,000 (of which tomatoes 600,000, carrots 305,000, onions 148,000, cabbage 135,000), dry peas 1,441,000, sugar beets 1,090,000, linseed 964,000, rye 677,000, apples 500,000, hops 490,000, lentils 450,000, pelts (1992) 1,919,025 units; livestock (number of live animals) 12,306,000 cattle, 11,200,000 pigs, 691,000 sheep, 425,000 horses; roundwood (1993) 179,967,000 cu m; fish catch (1993) 1,171,614. Mining and quarrying (1994): iron ore 36,854,000; zinc 961,405; copper 583,271; lead 166,420; nickel 144,323; uranium 11,174; molybdenum 9,723; silver 708; gold 4,667,300 troy oz.; platinum group metals 457,300 troy oz. Manufacturing (value in Can$'000,000; 1992): transportation equipment 54,049; food and beverages 44,124; chemical products 21,963; paper products 20,797; electrical products 17,567; petroleum and coal products 16,995; metal products 14,976; printing and publishing 12,631; rubber and plastic products 8,467; clothing 5,993; textiles 5,693; furniture 3,937; tobacco products 2,251; leather products 912. Construction (value of building permits; 1993): residential Can$16,405,000,000; nonresidential Can$9,150,000,000.

Service enterprises (1988)

	no. of enterprises	no. of employees[16]	weekly wages as a % of all wages	annual sales (Can$'000,000)
Retail trade				
Motor vehicle dealers	...	79,800	...	35,917
Food stores	...	213,400	...	35,187
Service stations	...	63,700	...	14,612
Department stores	...	[15]	...	13,271
Clothing stores	...	50,200	...	7,486
Pharmacies	...	52,400	...	7,459
Furniture and appliance stores	...	62,100	...	4,447
Automotive stores	...	31,500	...	3,767
General merchandise	...	231,700[17]	...	3,109
Sporting goods	...	...	...	2,669
General stores	...	[15]	...	2,415
Hardware stores	...	17,300	...	1,824
Shoe stores	...	18,400	...	1,599
Jewelry stores	...	14,000	...	1,215
Variety stores	...	45,100	...	1,057

Energy production (consumption): electricity (kW-hr; 1993) 527,316,000,000 (499,900,000,000); coal (metric tons; 1993) 69,016,000 (49,675,000); crude petroleum (barrels; 1993) 612,525,000 (516,448,000); petroleum products (metric tons; 1993) 84,738,000 (74,491,000); natural gas (cu m; 1993) 135,197,000,000 (74,077,000,000).

Population economically active (1994): total 14,056,000; activity rate of total population 48.3% (participation rates: ages 15–64, 74.9%[18]; female 45.0%; unemployed 11.1%).

Price and earnings indexes (1990 = 100)

	1988	1989	1990	1991	1992	1993	1994
Consumer price index	90.9	95.5	100.0	105.6	107.2	109.2	109.4
Hourly earnings index[19]	89.7	94.6	100.0	105.5	108.2	110.5	111.5

Household income and expenditure (1991). Average household size 2.8; average annual income per family Can$51,856 (U.S.$45,261); sources of income (1992): wages and salaries 63.9%, transfer payments 17.6%, property and entrepreneurial income 11.8%, profits 6.6%; expenditure (1992): housing 24.7%[20], food 15.5%, transp. and commun. 15.3%, household durable goods 9.1%, recreation 8.4%, clothing 5.1%, health 4.3%, education 3.0%.

Financial aggregates

	1990	1991	1992	1993	1994	1995[21]
Exchange rate, Can$ per:						
U.S. dollar	1.17	1.14	1.21	1.29	1.36	1.35
£	2.08	2.03	2.14	1.94	2.09	2.10
SDR	1.65	1.65	1.75	1.82	2.05	2.02
International reserves (U.S.$)						
Total (excl. gold; '000,000)	17,845	16,252	11,431	12,481	12,286	16,002
SDRs ('000,000)	1,526	1,581	1,038	1,062	1,148	1,186
Reserve pos. in IMF ('000,000)	517	592	1,011	948	919	1,225
Foreign exchange ('000,000)	15,802	14,079	9,382	10,471	10,219	13,591
Gold ('000,000 fine troy oz)	14.76	12.96	9.94	6.05	3.89	3.67
% world reserves	1.56	1.38	1.07	0.65	0.43	0.41
Interest and prices						
Central bank discount (%)	11.78	7.67	7.36	4.11	7.00	7.00[22]
Govt. bond yield (%)	10.85	9.76	8.77	7.85	8.63	8.24[22]
Industrial share prices (1990 = 100)	100.0	101.4	99.5	114.1	125.2	134.9[23]
Balance of payments (U.S.$'000,000)						
Balance of visible trade, of which:	8,330	3,695	5,981	7,612	12,202	...
Imports, f.o.b.	−120,108	−122,308	−126,370	−136,418	−151,290	...
Exports, f.o.b.	128,438	126,003	132,351	144,030	163,492	...
Balance of invisibles	−29,878	−27,747	−27,951	−31,481	−29,590	...
Balance of payments, current account	−21,548	−24,052	−22,060	−23,869	−17,388	...

Land use (1993): forested 53.6%; meadows and pastures 3.0%; agricultural and under permanent cultivation 4.9%; built-on, wasteland, and other 38.5%.

Foreign trade

Balance of trade (current prices)

	1989	1990	1991	1992	1993	1994
Can$'000,000,000	6.0	8.8	5.2	8.2	12.1	19.3
% of total	2.5%	3.5%	2.1%	3.2%	3.4%	4.5%

Imports (1993): Can$169,316,000,000 (machinery and transport equipment 54.9%, of which motor vehicles 23.5%; food, feed, beverages, and tobacco 6.5%; petroleum and energy products 4.1%; forestry products 0.9%). *Major import sources:* United States 65.0%; Japan 6.1%; United Kingdom 2.6%; Mexico 2.2%; Germany 2.0%; China 1.8%; France 1.3%; Italy 1.1%; South Korea 0.9%; Norway 0.6%.

Exports (1993): Can$181,026,000,000 (machinery and transport equipment 39.4%, of which motor vehicles 26.2%; mineral fuels 10.5%, of which crude petroleum 3.7%; food 6.4%, of which wheat 1.5%; lumber 5.0%; newsprint 3.2%; wood pulp 2.5%; office equipment 2.5%; aluminum 2.0%; refined petroleum products 1.4%). *Major export destinations:* United States 81.3%; Japan 4.6%; United Kingdom 1.5%; Germany 1.3%; China 0.9%; South Korea 0.9%; The Netherlands 0.7%; Italy 0.7%; France 0.6%; Mexico 0.4%.

Trade by commodities (1993)

	imports		exports	
SITC Group	U.S.$'000,000	%	U.S.$'000,000	%
00 Food and live animals	7,274.3	5.5	9,284.2	6.4
01 Beverages and tobacco	614.1	0.5	1,318.5	0.9
02 Crude materials, excluding fuels	4,116.7	3.1	16,397.1	11.3
03 Mineral fuels, lubricants, and related materials	5,288.3	4.0	15,197.4	10.5
04 Animal and vegetable oils, fats, and waxes	...	...	...	...
05 Chemicals and related products, n.e.s.	9,775.5	7.4	7,279.2	5.0
06 Basic manufactures	16,724.3	12.7	22,618.7	15.6
07 Machinery and transport equipment	66,581.1	50.6	57,082.4	39.4
08 Miscellaneous manufactured articles	16,302.8	12.4	6,680.4	4.6
09 Goods not classified by kind	4,638.5	3.5	8,550.7	5.9
TOTAL	131,478.9[24]	100.0[24]	144,730.5[24]	100.0[24]

Direction of trade (1994)

	imports		exports	
	U.S.$'000,000	%	U.S.$'000,000	%
Africa	1,130	0.0	000	0.5
Asia	20,332	13.4	13,979	8.7
Americas	105,686	69.7	136,129	84.4
United States	99,628	65.7	133,112	82.5
Mexico	3,438	2.3	715	0.4
South America	2,186	1.4	1,879	1.2
Other Americas	434	0.3	423	0.3
Europe	16,637	11.0	9,281	5.8
EU	14,307	9.4	7,749	4.8
Russia	274	0.2	121	0.1
Other Europe	2,056	1.4	1,411	0.9
Oceania	1,078	0.7	720	0.5
TOTAL	151,523[25]	100.0[25]	161,269[24]	100.0[24]

Transport and communications

Transport. Railroads (1992): length 44,182 mi, 71,104 km; passenger-mi 851,900,000, passenger-km 1,371,000,000; short ton mi cargo 166,057,000,000, metric ton-km cargo 242,439,000,000. Roads (1992): total length 527,794 mi, 849,404 km (paved 37%). Vehicles (1994): passenger cars 13,478,000; trucks and buses 3,773,523. Merchant marine (1992): vessels (100 gross tons and over) 1,185; total deadweight tonnage 2,896,830. Air transport (1994): passenger-mi 27,023,300,000, passenger-km 43,489,900,000; short ton-mi cargo 1,324,300,000, metric ton-km cargo 1,933,500,000; airports (1995) with scheduled flights 252.

Communications. Daily newspapers (1993): 108; total circulation 5,500,000; circulation per 1,000 population 195. Radio (1994): 26,878,000 receivers (1 per 1.1 persons). Television (1994): 17,400,000 receivers (1 per 1.7 persons). Telephones (main lines; 1993): 16,470,900 (1 per 1.7 persons).

Education and health

Education (1993–94)

	schools	teachers	students	student/teacher ratio
Primary (age 6–14)[26]	16,231	300,797	5,360,900	17.8
Secondary (age 14–18)[26]	...	...	...	...
Postsecondary and higher	272	64,100	921,300	14.4

Literacy (1986): total population age 15 and over literate 18,745,000 (96.6%); males literate (1975) 8,003,000 (95.6%); females literate (1975) 8,182,000 (95.7%).

Health: physicians (1991) 60,559 (1 per 464 persons); hospital beds (1992) 165,907 (1 per 171 persons); infant mortality rate per 1,000 live births (1994) 6.2.

Food (1992): daily per capita caloric intake 3,094 (vegetable products 68%, animal products 32%); 116% of FAO recommended minimum requirement.

Military

Total active duty personnel (1995): 70,500 (army 28.8%, navy 14.2%, air force 24.3%, not identified by service 32.7%). *Military expenditure as percentage of GNP* (1993): 2.0% (world 3.3%); per capita expenditure U.S.$371.

[1]On May 25, 1993, the Prime Minister and Inuit representatives signed an agreement (following a number of territory-wide referendums), officially establishing Nunavut as a territory in 1999. It would comprise 2,201,400 sq km (844,960 sq mi) of the eastern part of Northwest Territories, with a population of 22,000 (17,500 Inuit). [2]Based on land area of 3,558,096 sq mi (9,215,430 sq km). [3]Includes 4.0% who are of both French and British origin. [4]1992. [5]Urban areas. [6]1991. [7]1990. [8]1989. [9]At prices of 1986. [10]Unemployed. [11]GDP at current values in 1993 is Can$744,570,000,000. [12]Detail does not add to total given because of rounding. [13]1986. [14]Percentage of all wages. [15]1988. [16]1984. [17]Department and General stores included with General merchandise. [18]1993. [19]Manufacturing only. [20]Includes energy and utilities. [21]September. [22]August. [23]July. [24]Detail does not add to total because of discrepencies in estimates. [25]Total for imports includes U.S$6,651,000,000 (4.4% of total imports; mostly special transactions) not distributable by region. [26]Primary includes Secondary.

Cape Verde

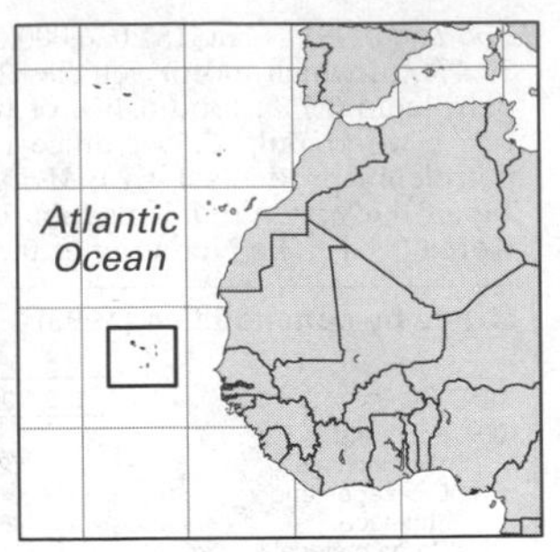

Official name: República de Cabo Verde (Republic of Cape Verde).
Form of government: multiparty[1] republic with one legislative house (National People's Assembly [79]).
Chief of state: President.
Head of government: Prime Minister.
Capital: Praia.
Official language: Portuguese.
Official religion: none.
Monetary unit: 1 escudo (C.V.Esc.) = 100 centavos; valuation (Oct. 6, 1995) 1 U.S.$ = C.V.Esc. 82.97; 1 £ = C.V.Esc. 131.17.

Area and population

Island Groups / Islands/Counties[2] / Counties	Capitals	area sq mi	area sq km	population 1990 census
Leeward Islands		696[3]	1,803	221,537
Brava	Nova Sintra	26	67	6,975
Fogo	São Filipe	184	476	33,902
Maio	Porto Inglês	104	269	4,969
Santiago		383	991	175,691
Praia	Praia	153	396	82,802
Santa Catarina	Assomada	94	243	41,584
Santa Cruz	Pedra Badejo	58	149	25,892
Tarrafal	Tarrafal	78	203	25,413
Windward Islands		861[3]	2,230	119,954
Boa Vista	Sal Rei	239	620	3,452
Sal	Santa Maria	83	216	7,715
Santo Antão		300	779	43,845
Paúl	Pombas	21	54	8,121
Porto Novo	Porto Novo	215	558	14,873
Ribeira Grande	Ponta do Sol	64	167	20,851
São Nicolau	Ribeira Brava	150	388	13,665
São Vicente	Mindelo	88	227	51,277
TOTAL		1,557	4,033	341,491

Demography

Population (1995): 392,000.
Density (1995): persons per sq mi 251.8, persons per sq km 97.2.
Urban-rural (1990): urban 29.7%; rural 70.3%.
Sex distribution (1990): male 47.29%; female 52.71%.
Age breakdown (1990): under 15, 45.0%; 15–29, 27.3%; 30–44, 11.4%; 45–59, 7.9%; 60 and over, 8.4%.
Population projection: (2000) 448,000; (2010) 565,000.
Doubling time: 19 years.
Ethnic composition (1986): mixed 71%; black 28%; white 1%.
Religious affiliation (1991): Roman Catholic 93.2%; Protestant and other 6.8%.
Major cities (1990): Praia 61,644; Mindelo 47,109; São Filipe 5,616.

Vital statistics

Birth rate per 1,000 population (1994): 46.2 (world avg. 25.0); (1975) legitimate 55.2%; illegitimate 44.8%.
Death rate per 1,000 population (1994): 9.0 (world avg. 9.3).
Natural increase rate per 1,000 population (1994): 37.2 (world avg. 15.7).
Total fertility rate (avg. births per childbearing woman; 1994): 6.3.
Marriage rate per 1,000 population (1990): 4.5.
Divorce rate per 1,000 population: n.a.
Life expectancy at birth (1994): male 60.7 years; female 64.6 years.
Major causes of death per 100,000 population (1987): enteritis and other diarrheal diseases 97.4; heart disease 77.9; malignant neoplasms (cancers) 47.9; pneumonia 46.4; accidents, poisoning, and violence 44.0.

National economy

Budget (1994). Revenue: C.V.Esc. 6,929,000,000 (import duties 43.2%; income taxes 19.6%; property income taxes 7.4%; transfers 7.1%; municipal taxes 1.8%). Expenditures: C.V.Esc. 19,037,000,000 (capital expenditure 63.5%; current expenditure 36.5%, of which wages and salaries 19.5%, transfers 6.7%, goods and services 2.0%, public debt 1.7%).
Public debt (external, outstanding; 1993): U.S.$148,000,000.
Tourism: n.a.
Land use (1993): forested 0.2%; meadows and pastures 6.2%; agricultural and under permanent cultivation 11.2%; other 82.4%.
Production (metric tons except as noted). Agriculture, forestry, fishing (1994): sugarcane 20,000, fruits (except melons) 16,000, coconuts 10,000, vegetables (including melons) 9,000, bananas 7,000, sweet potatoes 4,000, potatoes 3,000, cassava 2,000; livestock (number of live animals) 137,000 goats, 111,000 pigs, 18,000 cattle; roundwood, n.a.; fish catch (1993) 7,130. Mining and quarrying (1992): salt 4,000. Manufacturing (1991): bread 3,926; canned tuna 337; cigarettes 94; soft drinks 796,999 litres; rum 238,682 litres; other items also manufactured are beer and flour. Construction (1982): residential C.V.Esc. 365,800,000; nonresidential C.V.Esc. 1,700,000. Energy production (consumption): electricity (kW-hr; 1994) 59,527,000 (46,570,000); coal, none (none); crude petroleum, none (none); petroleum products (metric tons; 1993) none (65,383); natural gas, none (none).
Gross national product (at current market prices; 1993): U.S.$347,000,000 (U.S.$870 per capita).

Structure of gross domestic product and labour force

	1991 in value C.V.Esc. '000,000[4]	1991 % of total value	1990 labour force	1990 % of labour force
Agriculture	31	20.7	29,876	24.7
Manufacturing	9	6.0	5,520	4.6
Public utilities	4	2.7	883	0.7
Mining	...	...	410	0.3
Construction	30	20.0	22,722	18.9
Transportation and communications	18	12.0	6,138	5.1
Trade	42	28.0	12,747	10.6
Finance	5	5	821	0.7
Pub. admin., defense	13	8.7	17,358	14.4
Services	1[5]	0.7[5]		
Other	...	...	24,090	20.0
TOTAL	150[3]	100.0[3]	120,565	100.0

Population economically active (1990): total 120,565; activity rate of total population 35.3% (participation rates: ages 15–64, 64.3%; female 38.0%; unemployed, 25.8%).

Price and earnings indexes (1990 = 100)

	1989	1990	1991	1992	1993	1994[6]
Consumer price index	90.0	100.0	110.0	113.0	120.0	123.0
Earnings index	...	...	...	...	...	...

Household income and expenditure. Average household size (1990) 5.1; income per household: n.a.; sources of income: n.a.; expenditure (1988): food 51.1%, housing, fuel and power 13.5%, beverages and tobacco 11.8%, transportation and communications 8.8%, household durable goods 6.9%, other 7.9%.

Foreign trade[7]

Balance of trade (current prices)

	1988	1989	1990	1991	1992	1993
C.V.Esc. '000,000	−7,416	−8,179	−9,097	−10,031	−11,907	−12,075
% of total	93.8%	88.6%	92.0%	92.0%	94.8%	95.1%

Imports (1993): C.V.Esc. 12,387,000,000 (foodstuffs and beverages 34.6%, transport equipment 13.3%, machinery and apparatus 11.4%, nonmetallic mineral products 10.3%, metal products 7.3%). *Major import sources:* Portugal 33.6%; The Netherlands 8.5%; Germany 4.9%; France 4.4%; United States 3.5%.
Exports (1993): C.V.Esc. 312,200,000 (fish and fish preparations 62.6%, bananas 11.7%). *Major export destinations:* Portugal 48.8%; Angola 16.0%; The Netherlands 3.4%.

Transport and communications

Transport. Railroads: none. Roads (1987): total length 3,489 mi, 5,615 km (paved 29%). Vehicles (1992): passenger cars 10,000; trucks and buses 5,000. Merchant marine (1992): vessels (100 gross tons and over) 42; total deadweight tonnage 30,921. Air transport (1994)[8]: passenger-mi 106,000,000, passenger-km 171,000,000; short ton-mi cargo 13,156,000, metric ton-km cargo 19,207,000; airports (1995) with scheduled flights 9.
Communications. Daily newspapers: none. Radio (1994): total number of receivers 57,000 (1 per 6.7 persons). Television (1987): total number of receivers 5,000 (1 per 65 persons). Telephones (1994): 15,000 (1 per 25 persons).

Education and health

Education (1989–90)

	schools	teachers	students	student/teacher ratio
Primary (age 7–12)	367	2,028	67,761	33.4
Secondary (age 13–17)	16[9]	238	7,114	29.9
Voc., teacher tr.	3[9]	56[10]	752	...
Higher	...	...	...	...

Educational attainment (1990). Percentage of population age 25 and over having: no formal schooling 47.9%; primary 40.9%; incomplete secondary 3.9%; complete secondary 1.4%; higher 1.5%; unknown 4.4%. *Literacy* (1990): total population age 15 and over literate 122,806 (65.3%); males literate 64,698 (52.7%); females literate 58,108 (47.3%).
Health (1987): physicians 77 (1 per 4,208 persons); hospital beds 625 (1 per 550 persons); infant mortality rate per 1,000 live births (1995) 55.9.
Food (1992): daily per capita caloric intake 2,805 (vegetable products 88%, animal products 12%); 119% of FAO recommended minimum requirement.

Military

Total active duty personnel (1994): 1,100 (army 90.9%, air force 9.1%). *Military expenditure as percentage of GNP* (1992): 1.0% (world 3.3%); per capita expenditure U.S.$8.

[1]Constitution revised Sept. 28, 1990, to adopt a multiparty system; first multiparty elections took place on Jan. 13, 1991. [2]Island/county areas are coterminous except Santiago and Santo Antão islands. [3]Detail does not add to total given because of rounding. [4]At current factor cost. [5]Finance included in Services. [6]2nd quarter. [7]Imports are c.i.f. [8]TACV airline only. [9]1986–87. [10]Vocational teachers only.

Central African Republic

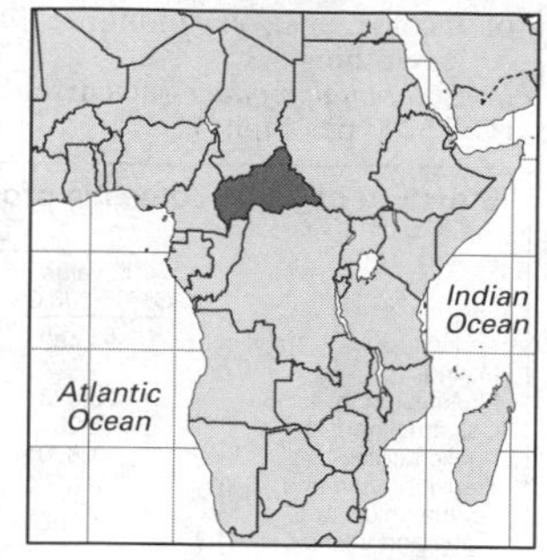

Official name: République Centrafricaine (Central African Republic).
Form of government: republic with one legislative body (National Assembly [85])[1].
Chief of state: President.
Head of government: Prime Minister.
Capital: Bangui.
Official languages: French; Sango.
Official religion: none.
Monetary unit: 1 CFA franc (CFAF) = 100 centimes; valuation (Oct. 6, 1995) 1 U.S.$ = CFAF 501.49; 1 £ = CFAF 792.78.

Area and population

Prefectures	Capitals	area sq mi	area sq km	population 1988 census
Bamingui-Bangoran	Ndélé	22,471	58,200	28,643
Basse-Kotto	Mobaye	6,797	17,604	194,750
Haut-Mbomou	Obo	21,440	55,530	27,113
Haute-Kotto	Bria	33,456	86,650	58,838
Kemo	Sibut	6,642	17,204	82,884
Lobaye	Mbaïki	7,427	19,235	169,554
Mambéré-Kadéï	Berbérati	11,661	30,203	230,364
Mbomou	Bangassou	23,610	61,150	119,252
Nana-Gribizi	Kaga-Bandoro	7,721	19,996	95,497
Nana-Mambéré	Bouar	10,270	26,600	191,970
Ombella-M'poko	Boali	12,292	31,835	180,857
Ouaka	Bambari	19,266	49,900	208,332
Ouham	Bossangoa	19,402	50,250	262,950
Ouham-Pendé	Bozoum	12,394	32,100	287,653
Sangha-Mbaéré	Nola	7,495	19,412	65,961
Vakaga	Birao	17,954	46,500	32,118
Autonomous commune				
Bangui	Bangui	26	67	451,690
TOTAL		240,324	622,436	2,688,426

Demography

Population (1995): 3,141,000.
Density (1995): persons per sq mi 13.1, persons per sq km 5.0.
Urban-rural (1992): urban 48.3%; rural 51.7%.
Sex distribution (1988): male 49.14%; female 50.86%.
Age breakdown (1988): under 15, 43.2%; 15–29, 27.5%; 30–44, 15.0%; 45–59, 9.2%; 60–74, 4.1%; 75 and over, 0.8%; unknown, 0.2%.
Population projection: (2000) 3,528,000; (2010) 4,449,000.
Doubling time: 32 years.
Ethnolinguistic composition (1988): Baya (Gbaya) 23.7%; Banda 23.4%; Mandjia 14.7%; Sara 6.5%; Mbum 6.3%; Mbaka 4.3%; Kare 2.4%; French 0.1%; other 18.6%.
Religious affiliation (1985): Protestant 40.0%; Roman Catholic 28.0%; traditional 24.0%; Muslim 8.0%.
Major cities (1988): Bangui 451,690; Berbérati 41,891; Bouar 39,676; Bambari 38,633; Bossangoa 31,502.

Vital statistics

Birth rate per 1,000 population (1994): 42.3 (world avg. 25.0); legitimate, n.a.; illegitimate, n.a.
Death rate per 1,000 population (1994): 20.7 (world avg. 9.3).
Natural increase rate per 1,000 population (1994): 21.6 (world avg. 15.7).
Total fertility rate (avg. births per childbearing woman; 1992): 5.8.
Marriage rate per 1,000 population: n.a.
Divorce rate per 1,000 population: n.a.
Life expectancy at birth (1990–95): male 44.7 years; female 49.4 years.
Mortality: n.a.; however, principal causes of death in the mid-1990s included respiratory infections (especially tuberculosis and pneumonia), diseases of the digestive system, meningitis, diarrheal diseases, malnutrition, cardiovascular diseases, malaria, viral hepatitis, and AIDS.

National economy

Budget (1994). Revenue: CFAF 35,400,000,000 (taxes 86.2%, nontax receipts 13.8%). Expenditures: CFAF 108,600,000,000 (current expenditure 55.1%, capital expenditure 44.9%).
Public debt (external, outstanding; 1993): U.S.$797,200,000.
Production (metric tons except as noted). Agriculture, forestry, fishing (1994): cassava 620,000, yams 235,000, bananas 96,000, plantains 73,000, peanuts (groundnuts) 72,000, corn (maize) 60,000, seed cotton 17,000, oranges 17,000, pulses 16,000, sorghum 15,000, coffee 15,000, cottonseed 10,000, cotton lint 7,000, paddy rice 7,000; livestock (number of live animals) 2,800,000 cattle, 1,340,000 goats, 480,000 pigs, 3,000,000 chickens; roundwood (1993) 3,701,000 cu m; fish catch (1993) 13,501. Mining and quarrying (1994): gold 138 kg, diamonds 532,000 carats[2]. Manufacturing (value added in CFAF '000,000; 1992): food, beverages, and tobacco 9,085; wood products 1,271; chemical products 964; textiles, wearing apparel, and leather products 344; metal products 321. Construction (1992)[3]: residential 10,052 sq m; nonresidential 82,411 sq m. Energy production (consumption): electricity (kW-hr; 1993) 97,000,000 (97,000,000); coal, none (none); crude petroleum, none (none); petroleum products (metric tons; 1993) none (73,000); natural gas, none (none).
Land use (1993): forested 75.0%; meadows and pastures 4.8%; agricultural and under permanent cultivation 3.2%; other 17.0%.
Gross national product (at current market prices; 1993): U.S.$1,267,000,000 (U.S.$390 per capita).

Structure of gross domestic product and labour force

	1994 in value[4] CFAF '000,000	1994 % of total value	1988 labour force	1988 % of labour force
Agriculture	246,900	53.4	1,113,900	80.4
Mining	26,700	5.8	15,400	1.1
Manufacturing	32,200	7.0	22,400	1.6
Construction	18,800	4.1	7,000	0.5
Public utilities	1,900	0.4	1,500	0.1
Transp. and commun.	13,000	2.8	1,500	0.1
Trade	53,600	11.6	118,000	8.5
Other services	23,200	5.0	15,600	1.1
Pub. admin., defense	45,700	9.9	91,700	6.6
TOTAL	462,000	100.0	1,387,000	100.0

Tourism (1991): receipts U.S.$8,000,000; expenditures U.S.$42,000,000.
Population economically active (1988): total 1,186,972; activity rate of total population 44.2% (participation rates: ages 15–64, 81.6%[5]; female 48.5%; unemployed 7.5%).

Price and earnings indexes (1990 = 100)

	1988	1989	1990	1991	1992	1993	1994
Consumer price index	99.3	100.1	100.0	97.3	96.2	93.4	116.4
Earnings index	...	...	...	...	...	...	...

Household income and expenditure. Average household size (1988) 4.7; average annual income per household CFAF 91,985 (U.S.$435); sources of income: n.a.; expenditure (1991)[6]: food 70.5%, clothing 8.5%, other manufactured products 7.6%, energy 7.3%, services (including transportation and communications, recreation, and health) 6.1%.

Foreign trade

Balance of trade (current prices)

	1989	1990	1991	1992	1993	1994
CFAF '000,000,000	−1.2	−24.8	−15.0	−19.4	−7.3	+9,3
% of total	1.4%	23.2%	17.5%	24.0%	8.9%	5.8%

Imports (1994): CFAF 76,100,000,000 (1992; food products 22.2%, transportation equipment 16.6%, chemical products 13.7%, energy products 11.0%). *Major import sources* (1992): Europe 62.4%, of which France 50.6%; Africa 13.1%, of which Cameroon 6.8%; Asia 7.9%, of which Japan 6.6%.
Exports (1994): CFAF 85,300,000,000 (diamonds 52.5%, wood products 27.0%, coffee 6.6%, cotton 6.3%). *Major export destinations* (1992): Belgium-Luxembourg 57.0%; France 9.8%; The Sudan 3.6%; Zaire 3.4%; Germany 0.6%.

Transport and communications

Transport. Railroads: none. Roads (1993): total length 14,750 mi, 23,738 km (paved 2%). Vehicles (1991): passenger cars 8,221; trucks and buses 8,541. Merchant marine: vessels (100 gross tons and over) none. Air transport (1993)[7]: passenger-mi 128,564,000, passenger-km 206,898,000; short ton-mi cargo 9,739,000, metric ton-km cargo 14,218,000; airports[8] (1995) with scheduled flights 1.
Communications. Daily newspapers (1990): total number 1, total circulation 2,000; circulation per 1,000 population 0.7. Radio (1994). 180,000 receivers (1 per 17.1 persons). Television (1994): 7,500 receivers (1 per 409 persons). Telephones (main lines; 1993): 6,800 (1 per 431 persons).

Education and health

Education (1990–91)

	schools	teachers	students	student/teacher ratio
Primary (age 6–11)	930	4,004	308,409	77.0
Secondary (age 12–18) / Vocational	46	845	46,989	55.6
Higher[9]	1	139	3,783	27.2

Educational attainment (1988). Percentage of population age 10 and over having: no formal schooling 59.3%; primary education 29.6%; lower secondary 7.5%; upper secondary 2.3%; higher 1.3%. *Literacy* (1995): total population age 15 and over literate 60.0%; males literate 68.5%; females literate 52.4%.
Health (1991): physicians (1992) 157 (1 per 18,660 persons); hospital beds 4,258 (1 per 672 persons); infant mortality rate per 1,000 live births 219.0.
Food (1992): daily per capita caloric intake 1,690 (vegetable products 88%, animal products 12%); 75% of FAO recommended minimum requirement.

Military

Total active duty personnel (1995): 2,650 (army 94.3%; navy, none; air force 5.7%). *Military expenditure as percentage of GNP* (1992): 2.1% (world 3.7%); per capita expenditure (1992) U.S.$9.

[1]New constitution promulgated on Jan. 14, 1995. [2]An unknown but substantial amount is believed to be smuggled out of the country annually. [3]Bangui only. [4]At factor cost. [5]January 1985. [6]Weights of consumer price index components. [7]Air Afrique traffic, an airline shared by 10 West African countries. [8]International air service only. [9]University of Bangui only.

Chad

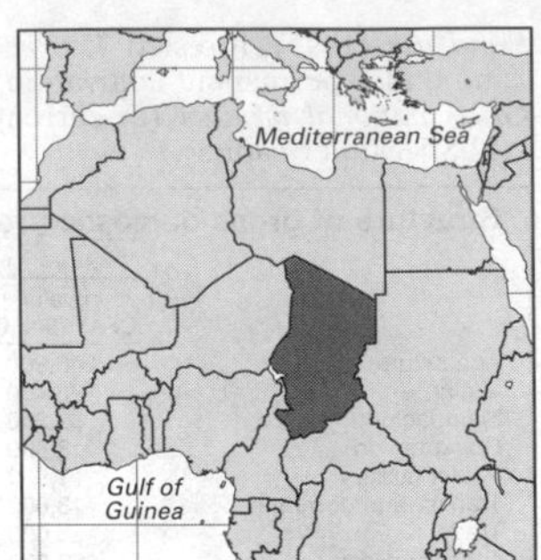

Official name: Jumhūrīyah Tshad (Arabic); République du Tchad (French) (Republic of Chad).
Form of government: transitional regime with one legislative house (Higher Transitional Council [57])[1].
Chief of state: President.
Head of government: Prime Minister.
Capital: N'Djamena.
Official languages: Arabic; French.
Official religion: none.
Monetary unit: 1 CFA franc (CFAF) = 100 centimes; valuation (Oct. 6, 1995) 1 U.S.$ = CFAF 501.49; 1 £ = CFAF 792.78.

Area and population

Préfectures	Capitals	area sq mi	area sq km	population 1993 census
Batha	Ati	34,285	88,800	288,458
Biltine	Biltine	18,090	46,850	184,807
Borkou-Ennedi-Tibesti	Faya Largeau	231,795	600,350	73,185
Chari-Baguirmi	N'Djamena	32,010	82,910	1,251,906
Guéra	Mongo	22,760	58,950	306,253
Kanem	Mao	44,215	114,520	279,927
Lac	Bol	8,620	22,320	252,932
Logone Occidental	Moundou	3,357	8,695	455,489
Logone Oriental	Doba	10,825	28,035	441,064
Mayo-Kebbi	Bongor	11,625	30,105	825,158
Moyen-Chari	Sarh	17,445	45,180	738,595
Ouaddaï	Abéché	29,436	76,240	543,900
Salamat	Am Timan	24,325	63,000	184,403
Tandjilé	Laï	6,965	18,045	453,854
TOTAL		495,755[2]	1,284,000	6,279,931

Demography

Population (1995): 6,361,000.
Density (1995): persons per sq mi 12.8, persons per sq km 5.0.
Urban-rural (1993): urban 21.4%; rural 78.6%.
Sex distribution (1993): male 48.46%; female 51.54%.
Age breakdown (1995): under 15, 43.4%; 15–29, 26.1%; 30–44, 15.7%; 45–59, 9.1%; 60–74, 4.7%; 75 and over, 1.0%.
Population projection: (2000) 7,307,000; (2010) 9,319,000.
Doubling time: 27 years.
Ethnolinguistic composition (1993): Sara 27.7%; Sudanic Arab 12.3%; Mayo-Kebbi 11.5%; Kanem-Bornu 9.0%; Ouaddaï 8.7%; Hadjeray (Hadjaraï) 6.7%; Tangale (Tandjilé) 6.5%; Gorane 6.3%; Fitri-Batha 4.7%; Fulani (Peul) 2.4%; Bagirmi 1.5%; other 2.7%.
Religious affiliation (1993): Muslim 53.9%; Christian 34.7% of which Roman Catholic 20.3%, Protestant 14.4%; traditional beliefs 11.4%.
Major cities (1993): N'Djamena 529,555; Moundou 281,477; Sarh 198,113; Abéché 187,757; Doba 185,477.

Vital statistics

Birth rate per 1,000 population (1990–95): 43.7 (world avg. 25.0); legitimate, n.a.; illegitimate, n.a.
Death rate per 1,000 population (1990–95): 18.0 (world avg. 9.3).
Natural increase rate per 1,000 population (1990–95): 25.7 (world avg. 15.7).
Total fertility rate (avg. births per childbearing woman; 1990–95): 5.9.
Marriage rate per 1,000 population: n.a.
Divorce rate per 1,000 population: n.a.
Life expectancy at birth (1990–95): male 45.9 years; female 49.1 years.
Major causes of death per 100,000 population: n.a.; however, major diseases include nutritional deficiencies, malaria, diseases of pregnancy and the neonatal period, sleeping sickness, leprosy, AIDS, venereal diseases, and respiratory diseases, especially tuberculosis.

National economy

Budget (1995). Revenue: CFAF 42,704,000,000 (taxes 43.6%, customs duties 22.3%, petroleum revenues 15.4%, other 18.7%). Expenditures: CFAF 61,652,000,000 (government salaries 39.3%, government operations 19.6%, debt service 11.9%, transfer payments 8.3%, other 20.9%).
Public debt (external, outstanding; 1993): U.S.$704,600,000.
Tourism (1993): receipts from visitors U.S.$23,000,000; expenditures by nationals abroad U.S.$12,000,000.
Production (metric tons except as noted). Agriculture, forestry, fishing (1994): sorghum 379,000, sugarcane 308,000, millet 307,000, yams 245,000, peanuts (groundnuts) 207,000, cassava 195,000, seed cotton 134,000, corn (maize) 94,000, rice 90,000, sweet potatoes 48,000, pulses 34,000, mangoes 32,000, dates 18,000, onions 14,000, sesame seeds 13,000, potatoes 8,000; livestock (number of live animals) 4,621,000 cattle, 3,178,000 goats, 2,152,000 sheep, 593,000 camels, 4,000,000 chickens; roundwood (1993) 4,283,000 cu m; fish catch (1993) 80,000. Mining and quarrying: clay, natron, tungsten, bauxite, and gold. Manufacturing (1995): cotton fibre 52,100; refined sugar 25,900; salted, dried, or smoked fish 19,000[3]; soap 3,781; woven cotton fabrics 166,000 metres; beer 118,700 hectolitres; edible oil 73,028 hectolitres; cigarettes 22,944,000 packets; bicycles 1,481 units. Construction: n.a. Energy production (consumption): electricity (kW-hr; 1992) 85,000,000 (85,000,000); coal, none (n.a.); crude petroleum, none (n.a.); petroleum products (metric tons; 1992) none (83,000); natural gas, none (n.a.).
Household income and expenditure (1993). Average household size *c.* 5.1; average annual income per household CFAF 96,806 (U.S.$458); sources of income: n.a.; expenditure (1983)[4]: food 45.3%, health 11.9%, energy 5.8%, clothing 3.3%.
Gross national product (at current market prices; 1993): U.S.$1,248,000,000 (U.S.$200 per capita).

Structure of gross domestic product and labour force

	1994		1993	
	in value CFAF '000,000	% of total value	labour force	% of labour force
Agriculture	94,482	21.1	1,903,492	83.0
Mining	[5]	[5]	756	—
Manufacturing	25,023	5.6	33,670	1.5
Construction	2,256	0.5	10,885	0.5
Public utilities	1,800[5]	0.4[5]	2,026	0.1
Transportation and communications	54,620	12.2	13,252	0.6
Trade and finance			179,169	7.8
Pub. admin., defense	21,249	4.8	61,875	2.7
Services			79,167	3.4
Other	248,000[6]	55.4[6]	9,311	0.4
TOTAL	447,430	100.0	2,293,603	100.0

Population economically active (1993): total 2,719,497; activity rate of total population 43.3% (participation rates: over age 15, 63.7%; female 48.4%; unemployed, n.a.).

Price and earnings indexes (1990 = 100)

	1988	1989	1990	1991	1992	1993	1994
Consumer price index	104.3	100.2	100.0	104.2	100.9	93.8	132.0
Earnings index	...	...	...	...	...	...	...

Land use (1993): forested 25.7%; meadows and pastures 35.7%; agricultural and under permanent cultivation 2.6%; other 36.0%.

Foreign trade

Balance of trade (current prices)

	1988	1989	1990	1991	1992	1993
CFAF '000,000	−7,470	−6,060	+364	−7,268	+606	−4,826
% of total	8.0%	5.8%	0.3%	6.2%	0.6%	6.1%

Imports (1994): CFAF 102,820,000,000 (1983; petroleum products 16.8%; cereal products 16.8%; pharmaceutical products and chemicals 11.5%; machinery and transport equipment 8.5%, of which transport equipment 7.3%; electrical equipment 5.7%; textiles 2.9%; raw and refined sugar 2.3%). *Major import sources* (1989): France 36.2%; United States 20.4%; Cameroon 18.4%; Italy 5.6%; West Germany 3.7%.
Exports (1994): CFAF 86,870,000,000 (raw cotton 33.2%; live cattle 17.8%; traditionally, other products have included frozen bovine meat and hides and skins). *Major export destinations* (1989): Portugal 21.0%; West Germany 16.9%; Japan 13.3%; France 9.9%; Spain 8.4%.

Transport and communications

Transport. Railroads: none. Roads (1991): total length 19,500 mi, 31,300 km (paved 1%). Vehicles (1992): passenger cars 9,000; trucks and buses 7,000. Merchant marine: vessels (100 gross tons and over) none. Air transport (1994)[7]: passenger-mi 133,436,000, passenger-km 214,745,000; short ton-mi cargo 13,642,000, metric ton-km cargo 19,917,000; airports (1995) with scheduled flights 4.
Communications. Daily newspapers (1992): total number 1; total circulation 2,000; circulation per 1,000 population 0.3. Radio (1994): total number of receivers 1,310,000 (1 per 4.7 persons). Television (1987): total number of receivers 5,000 (1 per 1,050 persons). Telephones (main lines; 1993): 4,600 (1 per 1,310 persons).

Education and health

Education (1991)

	schools	teachers	students	student/ teacher ratio
Primary (age 6–12)	2,544	9,238	591,417	64.0
Secondary (age 13–19)	66[8]	2,062	72,641	35.2
Voc., teacher tr.	25[9]	285[8]	3,819[3]	15.1[8]
Higher[3]	4	59	2,969	50.3

Educational attainment: n.a. *Literacy* (1990): percentage of total population age 15 and over literate 29.8%; males literate 42.2%; females literate 17.9%.
Health (1993): physicians 217 (1 per 27,765 persons); hospital beds 3,962 (1 per 1,521 persons); infant mortality rate per 1,000 live births (1990–95) 122.
Food (1992): daily per capita caloric intake 1,989 (vegetable products 93%, animal products 7%); 84% of FAO recommended minimum requirement.

Military

Total active duty personnel (1995): 25,350 (army 98.6%, navy, none, air force 1.4%). *Military expenditure as percentage of GNP* (1992): 2.7% (world 3.7%); per capita expenditure U.S.$6.

[1]A 30-month national charter (transitional constitution) was adopted in February 1991. A new transitional charter extending into 1996 was adopted in April 1993 by a broadly representative National Council. The Council also elected a 57-member interim legislature, the Higher Transitional Council. [2]Detail does not add to total given because of rounding. [3]1989. [4]Capital city only. [5]Mining included with public utilities. [6]Includes indirect taxes. [7]Chad's portion of total air transport of Air Afrique. [8]1988–89. [9]1987.

Chile

Official name: República de Chile (Republic of Chile).
Form of government: multiparty republic with two legislative houses (Senate [47[1]]; Chamber of Deputies [120]).
Head of state and government: President.
Capital: Santiago[2].
Official language: Spanish.
Official religion: none.
Monetary unit: 1 peso (Ch$) = 100 centavos; valuation (Oct. 6, 1995) 1 U.S.$ = Ch$401.10; 1 £ = Ch$634.08.

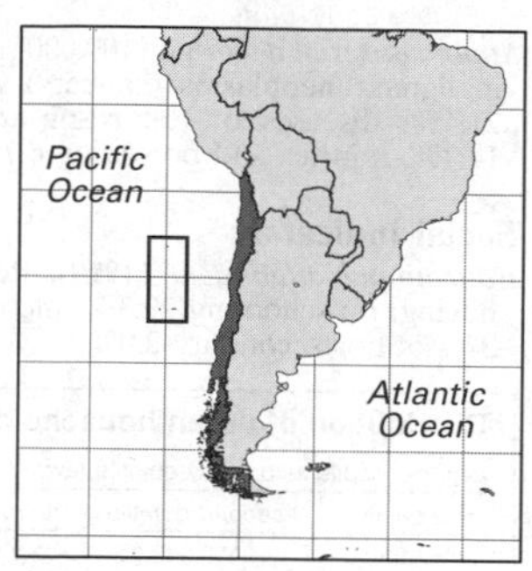

Area and population[3]

Regions	Capitals	area sq mi	area sq km	population 1994 estimate
Aisén del General Carlos Ibáñez del Campo	Coihaique	42,095	109,025	86,814
Antofagasta	Antofagasta	48,820	126,444	408,076
Araucanía	Temuco	12,300	31,858	839,046
Atacama	Copiapó	29,179	75,573	202,259
Bío-Bío	Concepción	14,258	36,929	1,737,323
Coquimbo	La Serena	15,697	40,656	516,171
Libertador General Bernardo O'Higgins	Rancagua	6,319	16,365	675,532
Los Lagos	Puerto Montt	25,868	66,997	949,894
Magallanes y la Antártica Chilena	Punta Arenas	50,979	132,034	176,598
Maule	Talca	11,700	30,302	890,195
Santiago, Región Metropolitana de	Santiago	5,926	15,349	5,680,520
Tarapacá	Iquique	22,663	58,698	398,654
Valparaíso	Valparaíso	6,331	16,396	1,465,084
TOTAL		292,135[4]	756,626[4]	14,026,116[5, 6]

Demography

Population (1995): 14,210,000.
Density (1995): persons per sq mi 48.6, persons per sq km 18.8.
Urban-rural (1994): urban 85.5%; rural 14.5%.
Sex distribution (1994): male 49.39%; female 50.61%.
Age breakdown (1994): under 15, 30.5%; 15–29, 25.9%; 30–44, 21.9%; 45–59, 12.5%; 60–74, 6.9%; 75 and over, 2.3%.
Population projection: (2000) 15,211,000; (2010) 17,010,000.
Doubling time: 44 years.
Ethnic composition (1992): European and mestizo 89.7%; Araucanian (Mapuche) 9.6%; Aymara 0.5%; Rapa Nui Polynesian 0.2%.
Religious affiliation (1992): Roman Catholic 76.7%; Protestant 13.2%; atheist and nonreligious 5.8%; other 4.3%.
Major cities (1993): Greater Santiago 4,628,320; Viña del Mar 319,440; Concepción 318,140; Valparaíso 301,677; Temuco 262,624; Talcahuano 257,767.

Vital statistics

Birth rate per 1,000 population (1992): 21.6 (world avg. 25.0); (1990): legitimate 65.7%, illegitimate 34.3%.
Death rate per 1,000 population (1992): 5.4 (world avg. 9.3).
Natural increase rate per 1,000 population (1993): 16.2 (world avg. 15.7).
Total fertility rate (avg. births per childbearing woman; 1990): 2.6.
Marriage rate per 1,000 population (1992): 6.6.
Divorce rate per 1,000 population (1987): 0.4.
Life expectancy at birth (1990–95): male 70.4 years; female 76.0 years.
Major causes of death per 100,000 population (1992): diseases of the circulatory system 158.5; malignant neoplasms (cancers) 109.4; diseases of the respiratory system 60.5; accidents and adverse effects 11.4.

National economy

Budget (1993). Revenue: Ch$4,177,500,000,000 (income from taxes 84.4%, nontax revenue 15.6%). Expenditures: Ch$3,842,730,000,000 (social security and welfare 33.6%, economic affairs and services 14.6%, education 13.4%, health 11.5%, housing 5.6%).
Public debt (external, outstanding; 1993): U.S.$16,031,000.
Production (metric tons except as noted). Agriculture, forestry, fishing (1994): sugar beets 3,547,000, wheat 1,271,000, grapes 1,200,000, tomatoes 1,151,000, corn (maize) 937,000, potatoes 900,000, apples 810,000, onions (dry) 305,000, oats 176,000, rice 133,000, barley 100,000; livestock (number of live animals) 4,649,000 sheep, 3,692,000 cattle, 1,407,000 pigs; roundwood (1993) 32,241,000 cu m; fish catch (1993) 6,190,600. Mining (1993): iron 5,809,000; copper 2,065,219; zinc 29,435; molybdenum 14,899; silver 967,551 kg; gold 33,502 kg. Manufacturing (1993): cement 3,024,300; cellulose 1,123,600; refined sugar 408,992; newsprint 185,100; noodles 55,200[7]; carbonated drinks 7,197,000 hectolitres[7]; tires 2,197,000 units; pressed-fibre panels 9,082,900 sq m[7]; flat glass 7,068,700 sq m. Construction (1993)[8]: residential 7,054,453 sq m; nonresidential 2,919,710 sq m. Energy production (consumption): electricity (kW-hr; 1992) 22,146,000,000 (22,362,000,000); coal (metric tons; 1991) 1,626,000 (2,643,000); crude petroleum (barrels; 1992) 5,502,000 (45,937,000); petroleum products (metric tons; 1992) 6,306,000 (7,010,000); natural gas (cu m; 1992) 2,093,000,000 (2,093,000,000).
Land use (1993): forested 22.0%; meadows and pastures 18.2%; agricultural and under permanent cultivation 5.7%; other 54.1%.
Gross national product (1993): U.S.$42,454,000,000 (U.S.$3,070 per capita).

Structure of gross domestic product and labour force

	1993 in value Ch$'000,000[9]	% of total value	labour force	% of labour force
Agriculture	448,649	8.0	825,300	15.8
Mining	458,665	8.2	92,100	1.8
Manufacturing	975,604	17.4	835,300	16.0
Construction	316,800	5.6	402,900	7.7
Public utilities	153,614	2.7	26,900	0.5
Transp. and commun.	418,308	7.5	354,800	6.8
Trade	956,597	17.0	925,600	17.7
Finance	932,766	16.6	288,900	5.5
Pub. admin., defense / Services	543,569	9.7	1,233,800	23.6
Other	411.842[10]	7.3[10]	233,600[11]	4.5[11]
TOTAL	5,616,414	100.0	5,219,300[6]	100.0[6]

Population economically active (1993): total 5,219,300; activity rate of total population 38.6% (participation rates: ages 15–64, 59.8%; female 32.9%; unemployed 4.6%).

Price and earnings indexes (1990 = 100)

	1988	1989	1990	1991	1992	1993	1994
Consumer price index	68.0	79.0	100.0	122.0	141.0	158.0	177.0
Monthly earnings index	62.0	73.9	100.0	121.2	146.2	...	...

Household income and expenditure. Average household size (1992) 4.1; average annual income per family (household; 1985)[12] Ch$440,738 at June prices (U.S.$2,840); sources of income (1990): wages and salaries 75.1%, transfer payments 12.0%, other 12.9%; expenditure (1989): food 27.9%, clothing 22.5%, housing 15.2%, transportation 6.4%.
Tourism (1993): receipts U.S.$824,000,000; expenditures U.S.$568,000,000.

Foreign trade[13]

Balance of trade (current prices)

	1989	1990	1991	1992	1993	1994
U.S.$'000,000	+1,578	+1,273	+1,575	+749	−979	+660
% of total	10.8%	8.3%	9.7%	3.9%	5.1%	2.9%

Imports (1993): U.S.$11,125,400,000 (intermediate goods 52.4%; capital goods 29.0%; consumer goods 18.6%). *Major import sources:* U.S. 23.5%; Brazil 10.1%; Japan 8.4%; Germany 5.9%; Argentina 5.5%; France 3.3%.
Exports (1993): U.S.$9,416,200,000 (industrial products 44.3%, of which paper and paper products 6.6%, chemical and petroleum products 5.6%; mining 42.9%; fruits and vegetables 9.3%). *Major export destinations:* U.S. 17.6%; Japan 16.0%; Argentina 6.3%; U.K. 5.9%; Germany 5.2%; Brazil 4.3%; France 4.0%.

Transport and communications

Transport. Railroads (1993): length 4,076 mi, 6,560 km; passenger-km 937,000,000; metric ton-km cargo 2,528,000,000. Roads (1993): total length 49,270 mi, 79,293 km (paved 16%). Vehicles (1992): passenger cars 826,794; trucks and buses 437,520. Merchant marine (1992): vessels (100 gross tons and over) 392; total deadweight tonnage 854,850. Air transport (1993): passenger-km 4,425,000,000; metric ton-km cargo 616,200,000; airports (1995) with scheduled flights 18.
Communications. Daily newspapers (1994): total number 33; total circulation 887,200[14]; circulation per 1,000 population 63[14]. Radio (1994): 4,100,000 receivers (1 per 3.2 persons). Television (1994): 2,000,000 receivers (1 per 7.0 persons). Telephones (main lines; 1993): 1,520,300 (1 per 9.1 persons).

Education and health

Education (1991)

	schools	teachers	students	student/teacher ratio
Primary (age 6–13)	8,626	81,742	2,033,982	36.0
Secondary (age 14–17)	1,694[15]	...	436,892	...
Vocational	1,262[15]	...	262,563	...
Higher	201[15]	15,131[16]	286,962	...

Educational attainment (1992). Percentage of population age 25 and over having: no formal schooling 5.7%; primary education 44.2%; secondary 42.2%; higher 7.9%. *Literacy* (1992): total population age 15 and over literate 81.1%; males 81.3%; females 80.9%.
Health (1992): physicians 15,062 (1 per 889 persons); hospital beds 42,895 (1 per 312 persons); infant mortality rate per 1,000 live births 14.3.
Food (1992): daily per capita caloric intake 2,582 (vegetable products 81%, animal products 19%); 106% of FAO recommended minimum requirement.

Military

Total active duty personnel (1994): 93,000 (army 58.1%, navy 26.9%, air force 15.0%). *Military expenditure as percentage of GNP* (1993): 2.4% (world 3.3%); per capita expenditure U.S.$73.

[1]Includes 8 nonelective seats. [2]Legislative bodies meet in Valparaíso. [3]Excludes the 480,000-sq mi (1,250,000-sq km) section of Antarctica claimed by Chile (and administered as part of Magallanes y la Antártica Chilena region) and "inland" (actually tidal) water areas. The 1992 census population of Chilean-claimed Antarctica was 126. [4]Includes 205 sq mi (530 sq km) of waters, known as Laguna del Desierto, lost in a border dispute with Argentina, resolved on Oct. 21, 1994. [5]Population projection based on 1992 census. [6]Detail does not add to total given because of rounding. [7]1991. [8]Construction approved and already begun only. [9]In constant prices of 1986. [10]Less imputed bank service charges. [11]Unemployed persons. [12]Greater Santiago area. [13]Import figures are f.o.b. in balance of trade and c.i.f. for commodities and trading partners. [14]Circulation for 31 newspapers only. [15]1988. [16]1984.

China

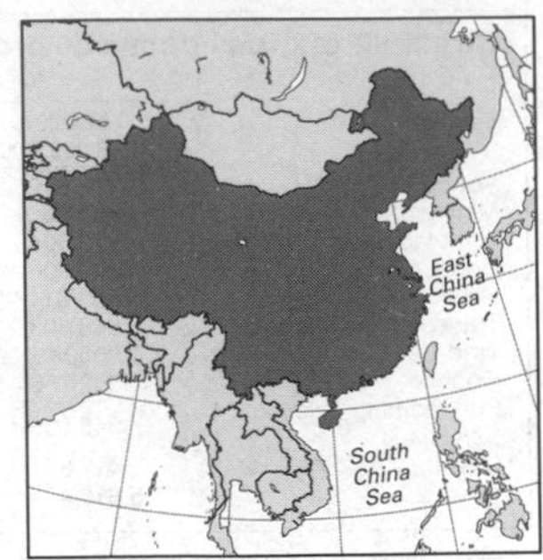

Official name: Chung-hua Jen-min Kung-ho-kuo (People's Republic of China).
Form of government: single-party people's republic with one legislative house (National People's Congress [2,978]).
Chief of state: President.
Head of government: Premier.
Capital: Peking (Beijing).
Official language: Mandarin Chinese.
Official religion: none.
Monetary unit: 1 Renminbi (yuan) (Y) = 10 jiao = 100 fen; valuation (Oct. 6, 1995) 1 U.S.$ = Y 8.32; 1 £ = Y 13.15.

Area and population[1, 2]

		area		population
Provinces	Capitals	sq mi	sq km	1994[3] estimate
Anhwei (Anhui)	Ho-fei (Hefei)	54,000	139,900	58,970,000
Chekiang (Zhejiang)	Hang-chou (Hangzhou)	39,300	101,800	42,660,000
Fukien (Fujian)	Fu-chou (Fuzhou)	47,500	123,100	31,500,000
Hainan (Hainan)	Hai-k'ou (Haikou)	13,200	34,300	7,010,000
Heilungkiang (Heilongjiang)	Harbin	179,000	463,600	36,400,000
Honan (Henan)	Cheng-chou (Zhengzhou)	64,500	167,000	89,490,000
Hopeh (Hebei)	Shih-chia-chuang (Shijiazhuang)	78,200	202,700	63,340,000
Hunan (Hunan)	Ch'ang-sha (Changsha)	81,300	210,500	63,110,000
Hupeh (Hubei)	Wu-han (Wuhan)	72,400	187,500	56,530,000
Kansu (Gansu)	Lan-chou (Lanzhou)	141,500	366,500	23,450,000
Kiangsi (Jiangxi)	Nan-ch'ang (Nanchang)	63,600	164,800	39,660,000
Kiangsu (Jiangsu)	Nanking (Nanjing)	39,600	102,600	69,670,000
Kirin (Jilin)	Ch'ang-ch'un (Changchun)	72,200	187,000	25,550,000
Kwangtung (Guangdong)	Canton (Guangzhou)	76,100	197,100	66,070,000
Kweichow (Guizhou)	Kuei-yang (Guiyang)	67,200	174,000	34,090,000
Liaoning (Liaoning)	Shen-yang (Shenyang)	58,300	151,000	40,420,000
Shansi (Shanxi)	T'ai-yüan (Taiyuan)	60,700	157,100	30,120,000
Shantung (Shandong)	Chi-nan (Jinan)	59,200	153,300	86,420,000
Shensi (Shaanxi)	Sian (Xi'an)	75,600	195,800	34,430,000
Szechwan (Sichuan)	Ch'eng-tu (Chengdu)	219,700	569,000	111,040,000
Tsinghai (Qinghai)	Hsi-ning (Xining)	278,400	721,000	4,670,000
Yunnan (Yunnan)	K'un-ming (Kunming)	168,400	436,200	38,850,000
Autonomous regions				
Inner Mongolia (Nei Monggol)	Hu-ho-hao-t'e (Hohhot)	454,600	1,177,500	22,320,000
Kwangsi Chuang (Guangxi Zhuang)	Nan-ning (Nanning)	85,100	220,400	44,380,000
Ningsia Hui (Ningxia Hui)	Yin-ch'uan (Yinchuan)	25,600	66,400	4,950,000
Sinkiang Uighur (Xinjiang Uygur)	Wu-lu-mu-c'hi (Urumqi)	635,900	1,646,900	16,050,000
Tibet (Xizang)	Lhasa	471,700	1,221,600	2,320,000
Municipalities				
Peking (Beijing)	—	6,500	16,800	11,120,000
Shanghai (Shanghai)	—	2,400	6,200	13,490,000
Tientsin (Tianjin)	—	4,400	11,300	9,280,000
TOTAL		3,696,100[4]	9,572,900[4]	1,185,170,000[5]

Demography

Population (1995): 1,206,600,000.
Density (1995): persons per sq mi 326.5, persons per sq km 126.0.
Urban-rural (1993): urban 28.1%; rural 71.9%.
Sex distribution (1993): male 51.02%; female 48.98%.
Age breakdown (1990): under 15, 27.7%; 15–29, 31.0%; 30–44, 20.7%; 45–59, 12.0%; 60–74, 6.9%; 75 and over, 1.7%.
Population projection: (2000) 1,268,970,000; (2010) 1,371,580,000.
Doubling time: 63 years.
Ethnic composition (1990): Han (Chinese) 91.96%; Chuang 1.37%; Manchu 0.87%; Hui 0.76%; Miao 0.65%; Uighur 0.64%; Yi 0.58%; Tuchia 0.50%; Mongolian 0.42%; Tibetan 0.41%; Puyi 0.23%; Tung 0.22%; Yao 0.18%; Korean 0.17%; Pai 0.14%; Hani 0.11%; Kazakh 0.10%; Tai 0.09%; Li 0.09%; other 0.51%.
Religious affiliation (1980): nonreligious 59.2%; Chinese folk-religionist 20.1%; atheist 12.0%; Buddhist 6.0%; Muslim 2.4%; Christian 0.2%; other 0.1%.
Major cities (1990): Shanghai 7,496,509; Peking 5,769,607; Tientsin 4,574,689; Shen-yang 3,603,712; Wu-han 3,284,229; Canton 2,914,281; Harbin 2,443,398; Chungking (Chongqing) 2,266,772; Nanking 2,090,204; Sian 1,959,044; Ta-lien (Dalian) 1,723,302; Ch'eng-tu 1,713,255; Ch'ang-ch'un 1,679,270; T'ai-yüan 1,533,884; Tsinan 1,480,915; Ch'ing-tao (Qingdao) 1,459,195; An-shan (Anshan) 1,203,986; Fu-shun 1,202,388; Lan-chou 1,194,640; Cheng-chou 1,159,679; Tzu-po (Zibo) 1,138,074; K'un-ming 1,127,411.
Households (1993). Average rural household size 4.6; urban household size 3.4. Family households (1990): 277,390,000 (99.4%); collective 1,671,000 (0.6%).

Vital statistics

Birth rate per 1,000 population (1994): 17.7 (world avg. 25.0).
Death rate per 1,000 population (1994): 6.5 (world avg. 9.3).
Natural increase rate per 1,000 population (1994): 11.2 (world avg. 15.7).
Total fertility rate (avg. births per childbearing woman; 1995): 2.0.
Marriage rate per 1,000 population (1993): 7.7.
Divorce rate per 1,000 population (1993): 0.8.
Life expectancy at birth (1992): male 69.1 years; female 72.4 years.
Major causes of death per 100,000 population (percentage distribution; 1993)[6]: malignant neoplasms (cancers) 21.8%; diseases of the circulatory system 21.4%; diseases of the respiratory system 17.1%; diseases of the heart 14.7%; injuries and poisoning 6.7%; digestive diseases 3.7%.

Social indicators

Educational attainment (1990). Percentage of population age 25 and over having: no schooling 29.3%; incomplete primary 34.3%; completed primary 34.4%; postsecondary 2.0%.

Distribution of urban household income (1993)

avg. per capita income by quintile (avg. Y 2,583)

first quintile	second quintile	third quintile	fourth quintile	fifth quintile
Y 1,539	Y 2,042	Y 2,454	Y 2,986	Y 4,266

Quality of working life (1991). Average workweek: 48 hours. Annual rate per 100,000 workers for: injury or accident, n.a.; industrial illness, n.a.; death, n.a. Funds for pensions and social welfare relief (1993): Y 91,370,000,000. Average days lost to labour stoppages per 1,000 workdays: n.a. Average duration of journey to work: n.a. Method of transport: n.a. Rate per 1,000 workers of discouraged (unemployed no longer seeking work): n.a.
Access to services. Proportion of communes having access to electricity (1979) 87.1%. Percentage of urban population with: safe public water supply (1993) 93.1%; public sewage collection, n.a.; public fire protection, n.a.
Social participation. Eligible voters participating in last national election: n.a. Population participating in voluntary work: n.a. Trade union membership in total labour force (1991): 17.9%. Practicing religious population in total affiliated population: n.a.
Social deviance. Annual reported arrest rate per 100,000 population (1986) for: property violation 20.7; infringing personal rights 7.2; disruption of social administration 3.3; endangering public security[7] 1.0.
Leisure. Favourite leisure activities: n.a.
Material well-being (1993). Urban families possessing (number per family): bicycles 2.0; televisions 1.2; washing machines 0.9; sewing machines 0.7; cameras 0.3. Rural families possessing (number per family): bicycles 1.3; televisions 0.7.; sewing machines 0.6; cameras 0.1; washing machines 0.1.

National economy

Gross national product (at current market prices; 1993): U.S.$581,109,000,000 (U.S.$490 per capita).

Structure of gross national product and labour force

	1993			
	in value Y '000,000,000	% of total value	labour force ('000)[8]	% of labour force[8]
Agriculture	665.00	21.2	339,660	56.4
Mining	...	...	10,760	1.8
Manufacturing	1,414.00	45.1	92,950	15.4
Construction	210.49	6.7	30,500	5.1
Public utilities	...	...	2,400	0.4
Transp. and commun.	190.10	6.1	16,880	2.8
Trade	178.24	5.7	34,590	5.7
Finance	...	...	3,360	0.6
Pub. admin.	...	...	10,300	1.7
Services	480.20	15.3	23,420	3.9
Other	−3.80	−0.1	37,400	6.2
TOTAL	3,134.23	100.0	602,220	100.0

Budget (1995). Revenue: Y 652,300,000,000 (taxes 81.8%; funds collected for energy and transport projects 6.9%). Expenditures: Y 806,100,000,000 (culture, education, and public health 12.0%; debt service 10.8%; capital construction 9.2%; defense 7.8%; government administration 6.2%; enterprise development 5.8%).
Public debt (external, outstanding; 1993): U.S.$70,024,000,000.
Tourism: receipts from visitors (1994) U.S.$7,323,000,000; expenditures by nationals abroad U.S.$812,000,000.

Retail and service enterprises (1992)

	no. of enter-prises	no. of employees	annual wage as a % of all wages	annual gross output value (Y '000,000)
Retail trade	10,063,000	24,345,000	...	...
Grocery stores	171,000	1,213,000	...	...
Department stores	174,000	2,120,000	...	...
Other food shops	120,000	824,000	...	...
Agricultural supplies stores	100,000	508,000	...	...
Electrical appliances stores	96,000	930,000	...	...
Household supplies stores	71,000	377,000	...	...
Grain and oil shops	81,000	783,000	...	...
Textile stores	40,000	288,000	...	...
Drugstores	32,000	251,000	...	...
Bookstores	28,000	151,000	...	...
Coal stores	16,000	200,000	...	...
Service trade	1,842,000	4,522,000	...	...
Repair shops	742,000	1,110,000	...	...
Barbershops	508,000	779,000	...	...
Hotels	189,000	1,427,000	...	...
Photo studios	98,000	225,000	...	...

Production (metric tons except as noted). Agriculture, forestry, fishing (1993): grains—rice 187,211,000, wheat 105,005,000, corn (maize) 103,380,000, sorghum 5,605,000, millet 3,961,000, barley 3,700,000; oilseeds—soybeans 13,007,000, peanuts (groundnuts) 8,086,000, rapeseed 6,950,000, sunflower seeds 1,150,000; fruits and nuts—watermelons 6,570,000, apples 5,018,000, oranges 4,685,000, cantaloupes 3,384,000, walnuts 175,000; other—sweet potatoes 105,185,000, sugarcane 68,419,000, potatoes 35,050,000, sugar beets 12,100,000, seed cotton 11,280,000, cabbage 9,705,000, tomatoes 8,665,000, cucumbers 7,850,000, eggplants 5,220,000, garlic 4,783,000, onions 4,432,000, tobacco leaves 3,438,000, tea 619,000; livestock (number of live animals) 393,965,000 pigs, 109,720,000 sheep, 97,812,000 goats, 82,641,000 cattle, 22,217,000 water buffalo, 10,983,000 asses, 10,018,000 horses, 2,688,000,000 chickens, 430,000,000 ducks; roundwood (1992) 296,557,000 cu m; fish catch (1992) 15,007,450. Mining and quarrying (1993): metal concentrates—zinc 838,000, copper 690,000, lead 387,000, tin 43,000, tungsten 20,000; metal ores—iron ore 234,660,000, manganese ore 5,400,000, bauxite 2,900,000, silver 200, gold 160; nonmetals—salt 29,530,000, gypsum 11,500,000, phosphates 7,000,000, talc 2,700,000, fluorite 2,400,000, barite 1,800,000, graphite 310,000, asbestos 240,000. Manufacturing (1994): cement 405,000,000; rolled steel 80,036,000; chemical fertilizer 22,760,000; paper and paperboard 20,000,000; sulfuric acid 14,947,000; sugar 5,819,000; cotton yarn 4,700,000; cotton fabrics 20,000,000,000 m; cigarettes 34,213,000 cases; colour television sets 16,895,000 units; household washing machines 10,964,000 units; household refrigerators 7,645,000 units; motor vehicles 1,402,000 units. Construction (1993): residential 807,790,000 sq m; nonresidential 412,420,000 sq m. Distribution of industrial production (percentage of total value of output by sector; 1978 [1993]): state-operated enterprises 80.6% (43.1%); collectives 19.2% (38.4%); privately operated enterprises 0.2% (18.5%). Retail sales (percentage of total sales by sector; 1978 [1993]): state-operated enterprises 90.5% (39.7%); collectives 7.4% (26.3%); privately operated enterprises 2.1% (34.0%).

Manufacturing and mining enterprises (1993)

	no. of enter- prises	no. of employees[9]	annual wages as a % of avg. of all wages[10]	annual gross output value (Y '000,000)
Manufacturing				
Machinery, transport equipment, and metal manufactures, of which,	133,699	18,870,000	96.7	1,146,310
Metal products	28,427	...	...	130,205
Industrial equipment	25,211	4,190,000	...	196,555
Transport equipment	15,439	3,380,000	...	259,928
Electronic goods	6,313	1,510,000	...	120,912
Measuring equipment	4,975	860,000	...	36,574
Textiles	24,613	6,840,000	95.5	352,074
Garments	17,921	1,640,000	...	99,358
Foodstuffs, of which,	56,553	4,550,000	87.5	390,016
Food processing	27,015	1,870,000	...	172,683
Beverages	12,705	1,130,000	...	76,734
Tobacco manufactures	391	290,000	...	77,610
Chemicals, of which,	49,268	7,000,000	92.1	468,058
Pharmaceuticals	4,198	910,000	...	68,983
Plastics	16,274	1,010,000	...	71,200
Secondary forest products (including paper and stationery)	32,364	2,320,000	96.1	104,347
Primary forest products	1,110	1,120,000	114.3	15,192
Mining				
Nonferrous and ferrous metals	4,704	730,000	107.6	27,679
Crude petroleum	74	1,230,000	...	96,809
Coal	10,116	5,100,000	119.8	83,019

Energy production (consumption): electricity (kW-hr; 1992) 753,940,000,000 (758,920,000,000); coal (metric tons; 1992) 1,116,369,000 (1,090,809,000); crude petroleum (barrels; 1992) 1,040,150,000 (963,056,000); petroleum products (metric tons; 1992) 102,090,000 (106,770,000); natural gas (cu m; 1992) 15,753,000,000 (15,753,000,000).

Financial aggregates[11]

	1988	1989	1990	1991	1992	1993	1994
Exchange rate, Y per:							
U.S. dollar	3.72	4.72	5.22	5.43	5.75	5.80	8.45
£	6.73	7.58	10.06	10.16	8.70	8.59	13.18
SDR	5.01	6.21	7.43	7.77	7.91	7.97	12.33
International reserves (U.S.$)							
Total (excl. gold; '000,000)	18,541	17,960	29,586	43,674	20,620	22,387	52,914
SDRs ('000,000)	586	540	562	577	419	484	539
Reserve pos. in IMF ('000,000)	407	398	430	433	758	704	755
Foreign exchange	17,548	17,022	28,594	42,664	19,443	21,199	51,620
Gold ('000,000 fine troy oz)	12.7	12.7	12.7	12.7	12.7	12.7	12.7
% world reserves	1.3	1.4	1.4	1.4	1.4	1.4	1.4
Interest and prices							
Central bank discount (%)	...	...	...	...	...	...	...
Govt. bond yield (%)	...	...	...	...	...	...	...
Industrial share prices	...	...	...	...	...	...	...
Balance of payments (U.S.$'000,000)							
Balance of visible trade, of which:	−5,315	−5,620	+9,165	+8,743	+5,183	−10,654	...
Imports, f.o.b.	−46,369	−48,840	−42,354	−50,176	−64,385	−86,313	...
Exports, f.o.b.	41,054	43,220	51,519	58,919	69,568	75,659	...
Balance of invisibles	+1,513	+1,303	+2,833	+5,022	+1,218	−955	...
Balance of payments, current account	−3,802	−4,317	+11,998	+13,765	+6,401	−11,609	...

Household income and expenditure. Average household size (1993) 4.2; rural household 4.6, urban household 3.3. Average annual income per household Y 6,805; rural household Y 6,122, urban household Y 8,550. Sources of income: rural household (1993)—income from household businesses 81.2%, wages 14.6%, other 4.2%; urban household (1993)—wages 78.0%, business income 18.6%, other 3.4%. Expenditure (1993): rural household—food 58.1%, housing 13.9%, cultural activities 7.6%, clothing 7.2%, household materials 5.8%, health 3.5%, transportation 2.3%; urban household—food 50.1%, clothing 14.2%, cultural activities 9.2%, household materials 8.8%, transportation 3.8%, health 2.7%, utilities 2.2%.
Population economically active (1987): total 584,569,200; activity rate of total population 54.7% (participation rates: over age 15, 76.8%; female 49.7%; unemployed 2.0%[12]). Urban workforce by sector of employment, 1978 (1993): state-run enterprises 74,500,000 (109,201,000); collectives 20,000,000 (33,930,000); self-employment or privately run enterprises 150,000 (53,570,000).

Price and earnings indexes (1990 = 100)

	1987	1988	1989	1990	1991	1992	1993
Consumer price index	70.2	84.8	98.6	100.0	105.1	114.1	133.5
Annual earnings index[13]	68.2	81.6	90.4	100.0	109.3	...	...

Land use (1992): forested 14.0%; meadows and pastures 42.9%; agricultural and under permanent cultivation 10.3%; other 32.8%.

Foreign trade[14]

Balance of trade (current prices)

	1989	1990	1991	1992	1993	1994
Y '000,000	−6,600	+62,570	+69,470	+57,730	−20,780	+126,800
% of total	1.7%	12.0%	10.2%	7.0%	1.9%	6.5%

Imports (1993): U.S.$103,950,000,000 (machinery and transport equipment 43.3%; products of textile industries, rubber and metal products 27.5%; chemical and related products 9.3%; mineral fuels and lubricants 5.6%; inedible raw materials 5.2%; food and live animals 2.1%). *Major import sources:* Japan 22.4%; Taiwan 12.4%; United States 10.3%; Hong Kong 10.1%; Germany 5.8%; South Korea 5.2%; Russia 4.8%; Italy 2.6%; Singapore 2.5%; Australia 1.9%; United Kingdom 1.6%.
Exports (1993): U.S.$91,763,000,000 (products of textile industries, rubber and metal products 17.9%; machinery and transport equipment 16.7%; food and live animals 9.2%; chemicals and allied products 5.0%; mineral fuels and lubricants 4.5%; inedible raw materials 3.3%). *Major export destinations:* Hong Kong 24.0%; United States 18.5%; Japan 17.2%; Germany 4.3%; South Korea 3.1%; Russia 2.9%; Singapore 2.4%; United Kingdom 2.1%; The Netherlands 1.8%; Taiwan 1.6%; Italy 1.4%.

Transport and communications

Transport. Railroads (1993): length 43,131 mi, 69,412 km; (1994) passenger-mi 225,990,000,000, passenger-km 363,700,000,000; short ton-mi cargo 853,576,000,000, metric ton-km cargo 1,246,200,000,000. Roads (1993): total length 673,239 mi, 1,083,476 km (paved 89%). Vehicles (1993): passenger cars 2,859,800; trucks and buses 5,010,000. Merchant marine (1992): vessels (100 gross tons and over) 2,390; total deadweight tonnage 20,657,996. Air transport (1994): passenger-mi 33,100,000,000, passenger-km 53,300,000,000; short ton-mi cargo 1,336,000,000, metric ton-km cargo 1,950,000,000; airports (1995) with scheduled flights 108.
Communications. Daily newspapers (1988): total number (1992) 74; total circulation 39,597,000[15]; circulation per 1,000 population 37[15]. Radio (1994): total number of receivers 206,000,000 (1 per 5.8 persons). Television (1994): total number of receivers 227,880,000 (1 per 5.2 persons). Telephones (1992): 18,888,200 (1 per 62 persons).

Education and health

Education (1993)

	schools	teachers	students	student/ teacher ratio
Primary (age 7–13)	861,878	6,388,000	140,737,000	23.4
Secondary (age 13–17)	82,795	3,167,000	47,391,000	15.0
Secondary specialized	13,945	501,000	6,446,000	12.9
Higher	1,065	388,000	2,536,000	6.6

Literacy (1990): total population age 15 and over literate 636,112,000 (77.7%); males literate 364,687,000 (87.0%); females literate 271,425,000 (68.0%).
Health (1993): physicians 1,832,000 (1 per 647 persons); hospital beds 3,099,000 (1 per 382 persons); infant mortality rate per 1,000 live births 26.
Food (1988–90): daily per capita caloric intake 2,641 (vegetable products 89%, animal products 11%); 112% of FAO recommended minimum requirement.

Military

Total active duty personnel (1994): 2,930,000 (army 75.1%, navy 8.9%, air force 16.0%). *Military expenditure as percentage of GNP* (1993): 2.7% (world 3.3%); per capita expenditure U.S.$47.

[1]Names of the provinces, autonomous regions, and municipalities are stated in conventional form, followed by Pinyin transliteration; names of capitals are stated in conventional form or Wade-Giles transliteration, followed by Pinyin transliteration. [2]Data for Taiwan, Quemoy, and Matsu are excluded. [3]January 1. [4]Includes 4,600 sq mi (11,900 sq km) not shown separately. [5]Total includes servicemen not assigned to any political division. [6]Based on urban sample population. [7]Excludes arrests for anti-Communist activities. [8]Social labour force. [9]In state-owned and collective-owned industries only. [10]1979. [11]Exchange rates and international reserves are end-of-year figures. [12]Rate of waiting for employment in cities and towns. [13]Average annual wage in industrial establishments in urban areas. [14]Imports and exports f.o.b. [15]Circulation data based on 58 dailies.

Colombia

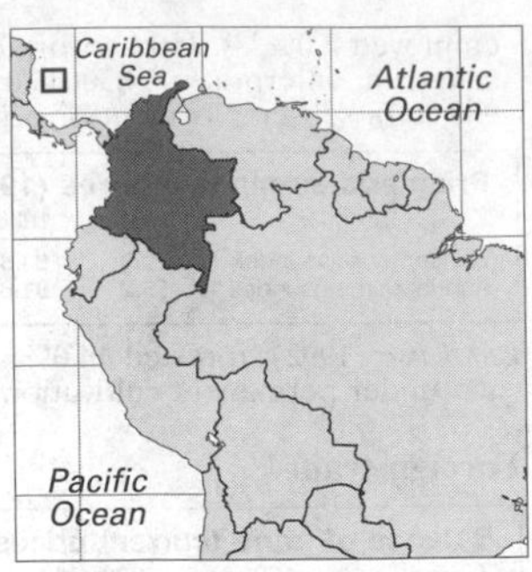

Official name: República de Colombia (Republic of Colombia).
Form of government: unitary, multiparty republic with two legislative houses (Senate [102]; House of Representatives [163]).
Head of state and government: President.
Capital: Santafé de Bogotá, D.C.
Official language: Spanish.
Official religion: none.
Monetary unit: 1 peso (Col$) = 100 centavos; valuation (Oct. 6, 1995) 1 U.S.$ = Col$979.00; 1 £ = Col$1,548.

Area and population

Departments	Capitals	area sq mi	area sq km	population 1995 estimate
Amazonas	Leticia	42,342	109,665	59,378
Antioquia	Medellín	24,445	63,312	4,672,545
Arauca	Arauca	9,196	23,818	100,061
Atlántico	Barranquilla	1,308	3,388	1,818,367
Bolívar	Cartagena	10,030	25,978	1,534,820
Boyacá	Tunja	8,953	23,189	1,311,433
Caldas	Manizales	3,046	7,888	925,746
Caquetá	Florencia	34,349	88,965	332,948
Casanare	Yopal	17,236	44,640	191,502
Cauca	Popayán	11,316	29,308	972,846
Cesar	Valledupar	8,844	22,905	851,701
Chocó	Quibdó	17,965	46,530	370,140
Córdoba	Montería	9,660	25,020	1,167,353
Cundinamarca	Santafé de Bogotá, D.C.	8,735	22,623	1,756,135
Guainía	Puerto Inírida	27,891	72,238	13,389
Guaviare	Guaviare	16,342	42,327	72,592
Huila	Neiva	7,680	19,890	820,149
La Guajira	Riohacha	8,049	20,848	371,613
Magdalena	Santa Marta	8,953	23,188	1,025,536
Meta	Villavicencio	33,064	85,635	608,995
Nariño	Pasto	12,845	33,268	1,207,787
Norte de Santander	Cúcuta	8,362	21,658	1,057,482
Putumayo	Mocoa	9,608	24,885	245,564
Quindío	Armenia	712	1,845	425,799
Risaralda	Pereira	1,598	4,140	776,894
San Andrés y Providencia	San Andrés	17	44	44,088
Santander	Bucaramanga	11,790	30,537	1,715,423
Sucre	Sincelejo	4,215	10,917	637,369
Tolima	Ibagué	9,097	23,562	1,221,759
Valle	Cali	8,548	22,140	3,493,287
Vaupés	Mitú	25,200	65,268	38,760
Vichada	Puerto Carreño	38,703	100,242	19,673
Capital District				
Santafé de Bogotá, D.C.		613[1]	1,587[1]	5,237,635
TOTAL		440,762	1,141,568	35,098,736[1]

Demography

Population (1995): 35,099,000.
Density (1995): persons per sq mi 79.6, persons per sq km 30.7.
Urban-rural (1990): urban 70.3%; rural 29.7%.
Sex distribution (1993): male 49.59%; female 50.41%.
Age breakdown (1993): under 15, 33.9%; 15–29, 29.6%; 30–44, 20.4%; 45–59, 9.7%; 60–74, 4.9%; 75 and over, 1.5%.
Population projection: (2000) 37,822,000; (2010) 42,959,000.
Doubling time: 39 years.
Ethnic composition (1985): mestizo 58.0%; white 20.0%; mulatto 14.0%; black 4.0%; mixed black-Indian 3.0%; Amerindian 1.0%.
Religious affiliation (1993): Roman Catholic 93.1%; other 6.9%.
Major cities (1995): Santafé de Bogotá, D.C., 5,237,635; Cali 1,718,871; Medellín 1,621,356; Barranquilla 1,064,255; Cartagena 745,689.

Vital statistics

Birth rate per 1,000 population (1990–95): 24.0 (world avg. 25.0).
Death rate per 1,000 population (1990–95): 6.0 (world avg. 9.3).
Natural increase rate per 1,000 population (1990–95): 18.0 (world avg. 15.7).
Total fertility rate (avg. births per childbearing woman; 1990–95): 2.7.
Life expectancy at birth (1990–95): male 69.3 years; female 72.3 years.
Major causes of death per 100,000 population (1990)[2]: homicide with firearms 101.0; malignant neoplasms (cancers) 82.6; ischemic heart disease 70.4; accidents 49.0; infectious and parasitic diseases 25.5.

National economy

Budget (1992). Revenue: Col$7,349,538,000,000 (indirect taxes 26.1%, credit resources 24.1%, direct taxes 22.8%). Expenditures: Col$5,869,789,000,000 (finance and public credit 39.4%, education 18.9%, defense 8.8%, public works and transportation 6.1%, police 4.6%, health 4.5%).
Public debt (external, outstanding; 1993): U.S.$12,861,000,000.
Tourism (1992): receipts U.S.$705,000,000; expenditures U.S.$641,000,000.
Production (metric tons except as noted). Agriculture (1994): sugarcane 29,000,000, potatoes 3,095,000, plantains 2,970,000, bananas 2,000,000, rice 1,679,000, corn (maize) 1,185,000, coffee (green) 684,000, sorghum 680,000; livestock (number of live animals) 25,700,000 cattle, 3,708,000 vicuña[3], 2,635,000 pigs, 2,540,000 sheep; roundwood (1993) 20,903,000 cu m; fish catch (1993) 146,407. Mining and quarrying (1994): iron ore 609,615; gold 667,448 troy oz; silver 189,625 troy oz; emeralds 7,201,703 carats. Manufacturing (value added in Col$'000,000; 1991): processed food 1,361,583; beverages 763,978; textiles and clothing 407,683; machinery and electrical apparatus 256,286; transport equipment 193,554; pharmaceutical products 172,083; basic steel 168,330. Construction (1992)[4]: residential 9,436,277 sq m; nonresidential 2,180,763 sq m. Energy production (consumption): electricity (kW-hr; 1992) 35,993,000,000 (36,331,000,000); coal (metric tons; 1992) 23,776,000 (6,049,000); crude petroleum (barrels; 1992) 157,052,000 (93,119,000); petroleum products (metric tons; 1992) 11,772,000 (10,300,000); natural gas (cu m; 1992) 4,307,212,000 (4,307,212,000).
Gross national product (1993): U.S.$50,119,000,000 (U.S.$1,350 per capita).

Structure of gross domestic product and labour force

	1993 in value Col$'000,000	1993 % of total value	1980 labour force	1980 % of labour force
Agriculture	5,888,857	14.0	2,412,413	28.5
Mining	2,473,002	5.9	49,740	0.6
Manufacturing	7,782,930	18.6	1,136,735	13.4
Construction	2,535,781	6.0	242,191	2.9
Public utilities	1,341,870	3.2	44,233	0.5
Transp. and commun.	4,544,936	10.8	352,623	4.2
Trade	6,711,380	16.0	1,261,633	14.9
Finance	4,925,290	11.8	278,210	3.2
Pub. admin., defense	6,059,533	14.5	1,998,460	23.6
Services	...	...		
Other	−331,938[5]	−0.8[5]	690,762[6]	8.2[6]
TOTAL	41,931,641	100.0	8,467,000	100.0

Population economically active (1985): total 9,558,000; activity rate 34.3% (participation rates: over age 12, 49.4%; female 32.8%; unemployed 4.3%).

Price and earnings indexes (1990 = 100)

	1988	1989	1990	1991	1992	1993	1994
Consumer price index	61.5	77.4	100.0	130.4	165.6	203.1	251.5
Monthly earnings index[7]	62.5	79.4	100.0	126.1	158.9	198.7	...

Household income and expenditure. Average household size (1985) 4.7; sources of income (1992): wages 45.1%, self-employment 35.4%, transfer payments 14.2%; expenditure (1992): food 34.2%, transportation 18.5%, housing 7.8%, health care 6.4%, household durable goods 5.7%, clothing 4.5%.
Land use (1993): forest 48.1%; pasture 39.1%; agriculture 5.3%; other 7.5%.

Foreign trade[8]

Balance of trade (current prices)

	1989	1990	1991	1992	1993	1994
U.S.$'000,000	+729.9	+1,621.0	+2,720.1	+920.1	−1,970.0	−2,640.7
% of total	6.8%	13.6%	23.2%	7.1%	12.2%	13.6%

Imports (1992)[9]: U.S.$6,485,200,000 (machinery and transport equipment 34.6%, chemicals 24.4%, vegetable products 7.4%, metals 7.0%, petroleum 5.6%, textiles and leather products 4.3%). *Major import sources:* U.S. 38.4%; Japan 7.5%; Venezuela 6.7%; Germany 6.3%; Brazil 4.1%; France 3.0%.
Exports (1992)[9]: U.S.$7,263,200,000 (forestry and fisheries 32.4%, petroleum products 19.2%, coffee 17.3%, textiles and apparel 12.5%, chemicals 5.4%, food and tobacco 4.8%, paper and publishing 2.5%). *Major export destinations:* U.S. 39.2%; Germany 8.6%; Venezuela 8.5%; The Netherlands 4.0%.

Transport and communications

Transport. Railroads (1992): route length (1994) 3,230 km; passenger-km 15,524,000; metric ton-km cargo 242,917,000. Roads (1991): total length 107,377 km (paved 12%). Vehicles (1992): cars 854,160; trucks and buses 430,611. Merchant marine (1992): vessels (100 gross tons and over) 101; deadweight tonnage 403,047. Air transport (1993): passenger-km 5,278,143,000; metric ton-km cargo 903,890,000; airports (1995) 70.
Communications. Daily newspapers (1994): 45; circulation 1,910,020[10]; circulation per 1,000 population 55[10]. Radio (1994): 5,400,000 receivers (1 per 6.4 persons). Television (1994): 5,500,000 receivers (1 per 6.3 persons). Telephones (main lines; 1993): 3,827,900 (1 per 8.9 persons).

Education and health

Education (1992)

	schools	teachers	students	student/ teacher ratio
Primary (6–10)	44,139	162,445	4,525,929	27.9
Secondary (11–16)[11]	6,134[12]	130,514	2,686,515	20.6
Higher	235[13]	54,164	510,649	9.4

Educational attainment (1985). Percentage of population age 25 and over having: no schooling 15.3%; primary education 50.1%; secondary 25.4%; higher 6.8%; not stated 2.4%. *Literacy* (1990): population age 15 and over literate 86.7%; males literate 87.5%; females literate 85.9%.
Health: physicians (1992) 33,498 (1 per 1,078 persons); hospital beds (1989) 45,888 (1 per 693 persons); infant mortality rate (1990–95) 37.0.
Food (1992): daily per capita caloric intake 2,677 (vegetable products 84%, animal products 16%); 115% of FAO recommended minimum requirement.

Military

Total active duty personnel (1994): 146,400 (army 82.6%, navy 12.4%, air force 5.0%). *Military expenditure as percentage of GNP* (1993): 2.6% (world 3.3%); per capita expenditure U.S.$35.

[1]Detail does not add to total given because of rounding. [2]Estimates based on about 75% of total deaths. [3]1991. [4]Construction permits issued for 11 urban centres. [5]Less imputed bank service charges. [6]Includes unemployed. [7]Minimum legal wages revised annually January 2. [8]Import figures are f.o.b. in balance of trade and c.i.f. in commodities and trading partners. [9]Estimate. [10]Circulation for 26 newspapers only. [11]Secondary includes vocational and teacher training. [12]1988. [13]1987.

Comoros[1]

Official name: Jumhurīyat al-Qumur al-Ittihādīyah al-Islāmīyah (Arabic); République Fédérale Islamique des Comores (French) (Federal Islamic Republic of the Comoros).
Form of government: federal Islamic republic with one legislative house (Federal Assembly [42]).
Chief of state: President.
Head of government: Prime Minister.
Capital: Moroni.
Official languages: Comorian; Arabic; French.
Official religion: Islam.
Monetary unit: 1 Comorian franc (CF) = 100 centimes; valuation (Oct. 6, 1995) 1 U.S.$ = CF 371.60; 1 £ = CF 587.47.

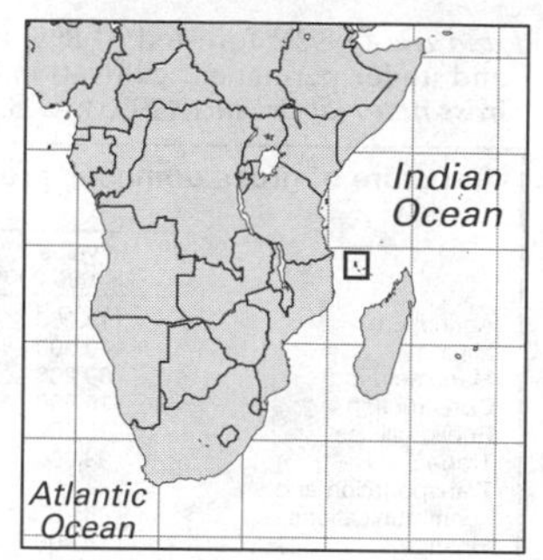

Area and population

Islands[2, 3]	Capitals	area sq mi	area sq km	population 1991 census[4]
Mwali (Mohéli)	Fomboni	112	290	24,331
Ndzuwani (Anjouan)	Mutsamudu	164	424	188,953
Ngazidja (Grande-Comore)	Moroni	443	1,148	233,533
TOTAL		719	1,862	446,817

Demography

Population (1995): 545,000.
Density (1995): persons per sq mi 758.0, persons per sq km 292.7.
Urban-rural (1992)[5]: urban 28.9%; rural 71.1%.
Sex distribution (1995)[5]: male 50.69%; female 49.31%.
Age breakdown (1995)[5]: under 15, 48.5%; 15–29, 26.4%; 30–44, 13.8%; 45–59, 7.3%; 60–74, 3.4%; 75 and over, 0.6%.
Population projection: (2000) 640,000; (2010) 883,000.
Doubling time: 20 years.
Ethnic composition (1995): nearly all Comorian (a mixture of Bantu, Arab, Malay, and Malagasy peoples).
Religious affiliation (1990): Sunnī Muslim 99.4%; Roman Catholic 0.6%.
Major cities (1990): Moroni 24,000; Mutsamudu 15,000; Domoni 8,000; Fomboni 5,600; Mitsamiouli 4,200.

Vital statistics

Birth rate per 1,000 population (1994): 46.0 (world avg. 25.0).
Death rate per 1,000 population (1994): 11.0 (world avg. 9.3).
Natural increase rate per 1,000 population (1994): 35.0 (world avg. 15.7).
Total fertility rate (avg. births per childbearing woman; 1994): 6.8.
Marriage rate per 1,000 population: n.a.[6]
Divorce rate per 1,000 population: n.a.
Life expectancy at birth (1994): male 56.0 years; female 60.0 years.
Major causes of death per 100,000 population: n.a.; however, major diseases include malaria (afflicts 80% of the adult population), tuberculosis, leprosy, and kwashiorkor (a nutritional deficiency disease).

National economy

Budget (1994). Revenue: CF 27,085,000,000 (grants 47.4%, tax revenue 36.4%, loans 11.9%, nontax revenue 4.3%). Expenditures: CF 33,740,000,000 (current expenditures 60.9%, development expenditures 39.1%).
Production (metric tons except as noted). Agriculture, forestry, fishing (1994): bananas 56,500, coconuts 51,000[5], cassava 48,250, pulses 7,600, copra 6,000[5], corn (maize) 3,650, rice 2,980, cloves 2,754[7], vanilla 131[7], ylang-ylang essence 45[7], other export crops grown in small quantities include coffee, cinnamon, and tuberoses; livestock (number of live animals) 125,600 goats, 50,000 cattle, 18,600 sheep; roundwood, n.a.; fish catch (1993) 7,000[5], of which tuna 4,280[5]. Mining and quarrying (1993): sand, gravel, and crushed stone from coral mining for local construction. Manufacturing: products of small-scale industries include processed vanilla and ylang-ylang, cement, handicrafts, soaps, soft drinks, woodwork, and clothing. Construction: n.a. Energy production (consumption): electricity (kW-hr; 1994) 30,300,000 ([1993] 20,000,-000); coal, none (none); crude petroleum, none (none); petroleum products (metric tons; 1992) none (21,000); natural gas, none (none).
Population economically active (1991): total 126,500; activity rate of total population 28.3% (participation rates: ages 15–64 [1985] 53.1%; female [1985] 26.2%; unemployed [1994]: unofficially more than 75%).

Price and earnings indexes (1985 = 100)

	1987	1988	1989	1990	1991	1992	1993
Consumer price index[8]	111.1	114.0	117.6	122.3	...	9	10
Earnings index	...	...	...	...	...	...	...

Tourism (1994): receipts from visitors U.S.$15,700,000; expenditures by nationals abroad U.S.$5,900,000.
Public debt (external, outstanding; 1993): U.S.$169,400,000.
Household income and expenditure. Average household size (1985) 5.6; income per household: n.a.; sources of income: n.a.; expenditure (1986)[11]: food and beverages 67.3%, clothing and footwear 11.6%, tobacco and cigarettes 4.1%, energy 3.8%, health care 3.2%, household furnishings 3.0%, other 7.0%.
Gross national product (at current market prices; 1993): U.S.$272,000,000 (U.S.$520 per capita).

Structure of gross domestic product and labour force

	1993 in value CF '000,000	1993 % of total value	1980 labour force[12]	1980 % of labour force
Agriculture, fishing	27,550	39.2	53,063	53.3
Mining	...	...	62	0.1
Manufacturing	3,161	4.5	3,946	4.0
Construction	3,897	5.6	3,267	3.3
Public utilities	995	1.4	129	0.1
Transportation and communications	3,197	4.6	2,118	2.1
Trade, restaurants, hotels	19,647	28.0	1,873	1.9
Finance, insurance }	9,669	13.8	237	0.2
Public admin., defense }			2,435	2.5
Services	2,093	3.0	4,646	4.7
Other	—	—	27,687[13]	27.8[13]
TOTAL	70,209	100.0[14]	99,463	100.0

Land use (1993)[5]: forested 17.9%; meadows and pastures 6.7%; agricultural and under permanent cultivation 44.9%; other 30.5%.

Foreign trade[15]

Balance of trade (current prices)

	1989	1990	1991	1992	1993	1994
CF '000,000,000	−7.8	−9.2	−9.4	−12.3	−10.6	−17.2
% of total	40.1%	48.4%	40.0%	50.4%	46.2%	64.8%

Imports (1994): CF 21,900,000,000 (rice 11.9%, petroleum products 11.6%, cement 7.6%, vehicles 7.4%, meat and fish 5.9%, milk products 3.9%, unspecified commodities 38.8%). *Major import sources* (1993): France 40.9%; Kenya 10.5%; South Africa 8.3%; Réunion 4.0%.
Exports (1994): CF 4,700,000,000 (vanilla 59.0%, ylang-ylang 19.8%, cloves 11.1%). *Major export destinations* (1993): United States 46.0%; France 41.7%; Germany 8.4%.

Transport and communications

Transport. Railroads: none. Roads (1992): total length 466 mi, 750 km (paved 28%). Vehicles (1991)[5]: passenger cars, 2,000; trucks and buses, 5,000. Merchant marine (1992): vessels (100 gross tons and over) 6; total deadweight tonnage 3,579. Air transport (1990): passenger-mi 1,900,000, passenger-km 3,000,000; short ton-mi cargo, n.a., metric ton-mi cargo, n.a.; airports (1995) with scheduled flights 4.
Communications. Daily newspapers: none[16]. Radio (1994): total number of receivers 61,000 (1 per 8.6 persons). Television: no local television broadcasting in 1992. Telephones (main lines; 1994): 4,510 (1 per 117 persons).

Education and health

Education (1991–92)

	schools	teachers	students	student/ teacher ratio
Primary (age 7–12)	255	1,894	75,577	39.9
Secondary (age 13–19)	...	613	15,647	25.5
Teacher training	...	11	129	11.7
Higher	...	...	223	...

Educational attainment (1980). Percentage of population age 25 and over having: no formal schooling 56.7%; Qur'anic school education 8.3%; primary 3.6%; secondary 2.0%; higher 0.2%; not specified 29.2%. *Literacy* (1990): total population age 15 and over literate, about 125,000 (slightly more than 50%).
Health (1990): physicians 57 (1 per 8,135 persons); hospital beds 649 (1 per 715 persons); infant mortality rate per 1,000 live births (1994) 80.0.
Food (1992): daily per capita caloric intake 1,897 (vegetable products 95%, animal products 5%); 81% of FAO recommended minimum requirement.

Military

Total active duty personnel (1995): 520. *Military expenditure as percentage of GNP:* n.a.

[1]Excludes Mayotte, a *collectivité territoriale* ("territorial collectivity") of France, unless otherwise indicated. [2]Island names in Comorian (French), respectively. [3]Each island is administered locally by a governor and island council. [4]Preliminary figure. [5]Includes Mayotte. [6]In the early 1990s, 20% of adult men had more than one wife. [7]Exported production only. [8]GDP price deflator. [9]0.4% decrease compared with 1991. [10]0.4% increase compared with 1992. [11]Weights of consumer price index components for Moroni. [12]The wage labour force was very small in 1993; total of 8,800 including government employees, and less than 2,000 excluding them. [13]Not adequately defined. [14]Detail does not add to total given because of rounding. [15]Imports c.i.f.; exports f.o.b. [16]Weekly newspapers (1992): 2.

Congo

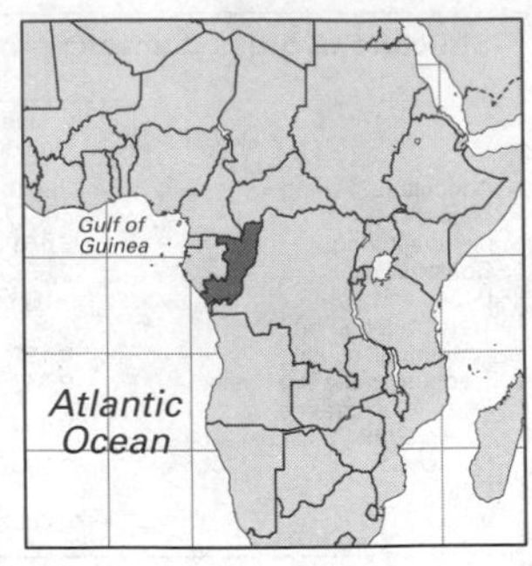

Official name: République du Congo (Republic of the Congo).
Form of government: multiparty republic with two legislative houses (Senate [60]; National Assembly [125]).
Chief of state: President.
Head of government: Prime Minister.
Capital: Brazzaville.
Official language: French[1].
Official religion: none.
Monetary unit: 1 CFA franc (CFAF) = 100 centimes; valuation (Oct. 6, 1995) 1 U.S.$ = CFAF 501.49; 1 £ = CFAF 792.78.

Area and population

		area		population
				1992
Regions	Capitals	sq mi	sq km	estimate
Bouenza	Madingou	4,733	12,258	177,357
Cuvette	Owando	28,900	74,850	151,839
Kouilou	Pointe-Noire	5,270	13,650	89,296
Lékoumou	Sibiti	8,089	20,950	74,420
Likouala	Impfondo	25,500	66,044	70,675
Niari	Loubomo	10,007	25,918	120,077
Plateaux	Djambala	14,826	38,400	119,722
Pool	Kinkala	13,110	33,955	182,671
Sangha	Ouesso	21,542	55,795	35,961
Communes				
Brazzaville	—	39	100	937,579
Loubomo	—	7	18	83,605
Mossendjo	—	2	5	16,405
Nkayi	—	3	8	42,465
Ouesso	—	2	5	16,171
Pointe-Noire	—	17	44	576,206
TOTAL		132,047	342,000	2,694,449

Demography

Population (1995): 2,590,000.
Density (1995): persons per sq mi 19.6, persons per sq km 7.6.
Urban-rural (1991): urban 41.1%; rural 58.9%.
Sex distribution (1995): male 48.92%; female 51.08%.
Age breakdown (1995): under 15, 45.6%; 15–29, 26.4%; 30–44, 14.6%; 45–59, 8.1%; 60–74, 4.2%; 75 and over, 1.0%.
Population projection: (2000) 2,970,000; (2010) 3,853,000.
Doubling time: 23 years.
Ethnic composition (1983): Kongo 51.5%; Teke 17.3%; Mboshi 11.5%; Mbete 4.8%; Punu 3.0%; Sango 2.7%; Maka 1.8%; Pygmy 1.5%; other 5.9%.
Religious affiliation (1980): Roman Catholic 53.9%; Protestant 24.9%; African Christian 14.2%; traditional beliefs 4.8%; other 2.2%.
Major cities (1992): Brazzaville 937,579; Pointe-Noire 576,206; Loubomo 83,605; Nkayi 42,465; Mossendjo 16,405.

Vital statistics

Birth rate per 1,000 population (1990–95): 44.7 (world avg. 25.0); legitimate, n.a.; illegitimate, n.a.
Death rate per 1,000 population (1990–95): 14.9 (world avg. 9.3).
Natural increase rate per 1,000 population (1990–95): 29.8 (world avg. 15.7).
Total fertility rate (avg. births per childbearing woman; 1990–95): 6.3.
Marriage rate per 1,000 population: n.a.
Divorce rate per 1,000 population: n.a.
Life expectancy at birth (1990–95): male 48.9 years; female 53.8 years.
Major causes of morbidity and mortality in the early 1990s included malaria, acute respiratory infections, diarrhea, trauma, helminthiasis[2], and sexually transmitted diseases; major causes of death among adults included AIDS as well.

National economy

Budget (1994). Revenue: CFAF 227,000,000,000 (petroleum revenue 58.7%; nonpetroleum receipts 40.3%; aid 1.0%). Expenditures: CFAF 339,300,000,000 (current expenditure 91.2%, of which salaries 38.5%, interest 31.0%, transfers, subsidies, goods, and services 11.2%; capital expenditure 8.4%).
Public debt (external, outstanding; 1993): U.S.$4,097,000,000.
Tourism (1993): receipts U.S.$2,000,000; expenditures U.S.$81,000,000.
Production (metric tons except as noted). Agriculture, forestry, fishing (1994): cassava 630,000, sugarcane 370,000, plantains 85,000, bananas 44,000, corn (maize) 26,000, peanuts (groundnuts) 25,000, avocados 25,000, palm oil 14,500, yams 13,000, pineapples 12,000, cacao beans 1,000, coffee 1,000; livestock (number of live animals) 305,000 goats, 111,000 sheep, 68,000 cattle; roundwood (1993) 3,561,000 cu m; fish catch (1993) 41,503. Mining and quarrying (1993): gold 5 kg. Manufacturing (1992): residual fuel oil 267,000; cement 115,854; distillate fuel oils 90,000; gasoline 53,000; aviation gas 50,000; kerosene 49,000; raw sugar 36,000[3]; wheat flour 12,000[4]; dried, cured, or salted fish 4,000; soap 3,200; cigarettes 431,000,000 units; mechanical cultivators 294,404 units; beer 708,000 hectolitres; soft drinks 294,000 hectolitres; cotton textiles 5,100,000 m; veneer sheets 60,000 cu m; footwear 300,000 pairs[4]. Construction: n.a. Energy production (consumption): electricity (kW-hr; 1993) 431,000,000 (541,000,000); coal (metric tons; 1993) none (none); crude petroleum (barrels; 1993) 65,115,000 (4,800,000); petroleum products (metric tons; 1993) 542,000 (521,000); natural gas (cu m; 1993) 4,410,000 (4,410,000).

Land use (1993): forested 61.8%; meadows and pastures 29.3%; agricultural and under permanent cultivation 0.5%; other 8.4%.
Gross national product (1993): U.S.$2,307,000,000 (U.S.$920 per capita).

Structure of gross domestic product and labour force

	1991			
	in value CFAF '000,000[5]	% of total value	labour force	% of labour force
Agriculture	113,000	14.8	471,000	59.1
Mining	160,300	21.0	101,000	12.7
Manufacturing	69,200	9.1		
Construction	10,900	1.4		
Public utilities	15,500	2.0	225,000	28.2
Trade	93,800	12.3		
Transportation and communications	86,700	11.4		
Finance	6,400	0.8		
Pub. admin., defense	133,000	17.5		
Services	73,200	9.6		
TOTAL	762,000	100.0[6]	797,000	100.0

Population economically active (1992): total 886,000; activity rate of total population 37.4% (participation rates [1984]: ages 15–64, 54.0%; female 45.6%; unemployed[7] 2.3%).

Price and earnings indexes (1990 = 100)

	1988	1989	1990	1991	1992	1993	1994
Consumer price index	100.9	105.0	100.0	109.2	111.3	113.6	159.4
Earnings index	...	...	...	...	...	...	...

Household income and expenditure. Average household size (1984) 5.2; income per household: n.a.; sources of income: n.a.; expenditure (1977)[8]: food, beverages, and tobacco 62.0%, housing 10.1%; transportation and recreation 8.6%, clothing and footwear 6.9%, fuel, energy, and water 5.7%, health and medical care 3.8%.

Foreign trade

Balance of trade (current prices)

	1989	1990	1991	1992	1993	1994
CFAF '000,000,000	+210.4	+238.4	+173.0	+196.0	+175.3	+272.7
% of total	39.7%	46.0%	38.3%	45.8%	38.2%	34.2%

Imports (1994): CFAF 262,100,000,000 (1991[9]; machinery and transport equipment 38.0%, basic manufactures 27.4%, food and live animals 11.2%, chemicals and chemical products 8.4%, mineral fuels 3.2%, beverages and tobacco 2.3%). *Major import sources* (1990)[9]: France 48.1%; Cameroon 6.4%; Italy 6.1%; West Germany 4.2%; Zaire 4.1%; The Netherlands 3.9%.
Exports (1994): CFAF 534,800,000,000 (petroleum and petroleum products 85.0%, wood and wood products 11.1%, other 3.9%). *Major export destinations* (1990)[9]: United States 42.9%; France 16.1%; Belgium-Luxembourg 8.3%; Italy 7.8%; The Netherlands 7.2%; Spain 6.2%.

Transport and communications

Transport. Railroads (1991): length 494 mi, 795 km; passenger-mi 340,000,000, passenger-km 547,000,000; short ton-mi cargo 273,000,000, metric ton-km cargo 399,000,000. Roads (1993): total length 7,920 mi, 12,745 km (paved 10%). Vehicles (1993): passenger cars 28,999; trucks and buses 16,617. Merchant marine (1992): vessels (100 gross tons and over) 22; total deadweight tonnage 10,840. Air transport (1994)[10]: passenger-mi 133,440,000, passenger-km 214,745,000; short ton-mi cargo 9,892,000, metric ton-km cargo 14,442,000; airports (1995) with scheduled flights 5.
Communications. Daily newspapers (1992): total number 6; total circulation 19,000; circulation per 1,000 population 8.0. Radio (1994): 240,000 receivers (1 per 11 persons). Television (1994): 8,500 receivers (1 per 326 persons). Telephones (main lines; 1993): 19,200 (1 per 132 persons).

Education and health

Education (1993)

	schools	teachers	students	student/ teacher ratio
Primary (age 6–13)	1,623	6,891	505,921	73.4
Secondary (age 14–18)	238[11]	6,048	192,229	31.8
Voc., teacher tr.	60[11]	1,813	20,621	11.4
Higher	12[11]	656[12]	13,806[12]	21.0

Educational attainment (1984). Percentage of population age 25 and over having: no formal schooling 58.7%; some primary education 21.4%; secondary education 16.9%; postsecondary 3.0%. *Literacy* (1995): total population age 15 and over literate 74.9%; males literate 83.1%; females literate 67.2%.
Health (1989): physicians 567 (1 per 3,873 persons); hospital beds 4,817 (1 per 456 persons); infant mortality rate per 1,000 live births (1990–95) 84.
Food (1992): daily per capita caloric intake 2,296 (vegetable products 92%, animal products 8%); 99% of FAO recommended minimum requirement.

Military

Total active duty personnel (1995): 10,000 (army 80.0%, navy 8.0%, air force 12.0%). *Military expenditure as percentage of GNP* (1992): 5.8% (world 3.7%); per capita expenditure U.S.$54.0.

[1]"Functional" national languages are Lingata and Monokotuba. [2]Parasitic infestation by helminthic worms. [3]1993. [4]1990. [5]At current factor cost. [6]Detail does not add to total given because of rounding. [7]Previously employed only. [8]Cost-of-living components for Brazzaville, African households only. [9]Based on c.i.f. valuation. [10]Represents 1/11 of the traffic of Air Afrique, which is operated by 11 African states. [11]1989. [12]1992.

Costa Rica

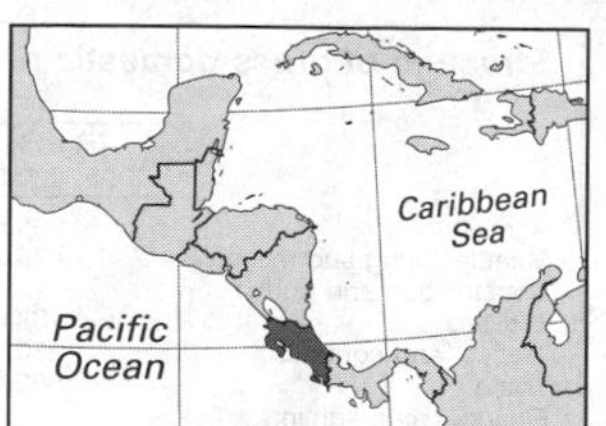

Official name: República de Costa Rica (Republic of Costa Rica).
Form of government: unitary multiparty republic with one legislative house (Legislative Assembly [57]).
Head of state and government: President.
Capital: San José.
Official language: Spanish.
Official religion: Roman Catholicism.
Monetary unit: 1 Costa Rican colón (₡) = 100 céntimos; valuation (Oct. 6, 1995) 1 U.S.$ = ₡187.50; 1 £ = ₡296.42.

Area and population

		area		population
Provinces	**Capitals**	sq mi	sq km	1994[1] estimate
Alajuela	Alajuela	3,766	9,753	576,441
Cartago	Cartago	1,207	3,125	363,790
Guanacaste	Liberia	3,915	10,141	256,963
Heredia	Heredia	1,026	2,657	259,495
Limón	Limón	3,548	9,188	241,012
Puntarenas	Puntarenas	4,354	11,277	360,781
San José	San José	1,915	4,959	1,175,651
TOTAL		19,730[2]	51,100	3,234,133

Demography

Population (1995): 3,344,000.
Density (1995): persons per sq mi 169.5, persons per sq km 65.4.
Urban-rural (1993): urban 44.1%; rural 55.9%.
Sex distribution (1993): male 50.55%; female 49.45%.
Age breakdown (1993): under 15, 35.2%; 15–29, 27.5%; 30–44, 20.6%; 45–59, 10.0%; 60–74, 5.2%; 75 and over, 1.5%.
Population projection: (2000) 3,709,000; (2010) 4,428,000.
Doubling time: 32 years.
Ethnic composition (1993): white 87.0%; mestizo 7.0%; black/mulatto 3.0%; East Asian (mostly Chinese) 2.0%; Amerindian 1.0%.
Religious affiliation (1992): Roman Catholic 80.0%; Evangelical Protestant 15.0%; other 5.0%.
Major cities (1992): San José 280,613[3, 4] (metropolitan area 921,726[4]); Desamparados 54,668[5]; Limón 50,939[6]; Alajuela 45,442; Puntarenas 38,274.

Vital statistics

Birth rate per 1,000 population (1993): 25.7 (world avg. 25.0); (1984) legitimate 62.8%; illegitimate 37.2%.
Death rate per 1,000 population (1993): 4.2 (world avg. 9.3).
Natural increase rate per 1,000 population (1993): 21.5 (world avg. 15.7).
Total fertility rate (avg. births per childbearing woman; 1993): 3.1.
Marriage rate per 1,000 population (1993): 6.8.
Divorce rate per 1,000 population (1990): 1.1.
Life expectancy at birth (1990–95): male 71.9 years; female 77.5 years.
Major causes of death per 100,000 population (1991): diseases of the circulatory system 111.3; malignant neoplasms (cancers) 74.6; accidents, poisoning, and violence 39.7; diseases of the respiratory system 38.5; diseases of the digestive system 19.9.

National economy

Budget (1993). Revenue: ₡277,910,000,000 (tax revenue 86.6%, of which social-security contributions 27.6%, sales tax 21.0%, import duties 12.4%; nontax revenue 13.2%). Expenditures: ₡279,960,000,000 (health 28.7%, education 22.5%, social-security and welfare 10.6%, general public services 10.1%, public order 5.8%).
Public debt (external, outstanding; 1993): U.S.$3,139,000,000.
Gross national product (at current market prices; 1993): U.S.$7,041,000,000 (U.S.$2,160 per capita).

Structure of gross domestic product and labour force

	1993			
	in value ₡'000,000,000	% of total value	labour force	% of labour force
Agriculture, forestry, fishing	169.3	15.8	256,816	22.5
Mining }	211.6	19.7	1,789	0.2
Manufacturing }			204,943	17.9
Construction	29.9	2.8	70,814	6.2
Public utilities	39.6	3.7	15,954	1.4
Transp. and commun.	60.2	5.6	53,257	4.7
Trade, restaurants	222.7	20.7	204,078	17.8
Finance, real estate	120.1	11.2	47,488	4.2
Public administration	144.8	13.5 }	267,604	23.4
Services	76.2	7.1 }		
Other	—	—	20,581	1.8
TOTAL	1,074.4	100.0[2]	1,143,324	100.0[2]

Production (metric tons except as noted). Agriculture, forestry, fishing (1993): sugarcane 2,987,000, bananas 1,827,000, pineapples 190,000, rice 170,000, oranges 160,000, coffee 148,000, plantains 101,000, palm oil 84,000, potatoes 53,000, corn (maize) 34,000, other products include other tropical fruits, cut flowers, and ornamental plants grown for export; livestock (number of live animals) 2,122,000 cattle, 244,000 pigs, 14,000,000 chickens; roundwood (1992) 4,306,000 cu m; fish catch (1992) 18,096, of which shrimp 3,994. Mining and quarrying (1992): limestone 1,300,000, gold 17,700 troy oz. Manufacturing (value added in ₡'000,000; 1992): food products 44,484, of which bakery products 10,348; malt liquors and malt 11,172; soft drinks and carbonated waters 8,978; paper and paper products 6,495; plastic products 5,835; fertilizers and pesticides 5,797. Construction (completed; 1989): 1,914,000 sq m. Energy production (consumption): electricity (kW-hr; 1993) 4,385,000,000 (3,890,000,000); coal, none (none); crude petroleum (barrels; 1992) none (3,936,000); petroleum products (metric tons; 1992) 501,000 (1,116,000); natural gas, none (none).
Population economically active (1993): total 1,143,324; activity rate of total population 38.1% (participation rates: ages 15–69, 59.1%; female 29.9%; unemployed [February 1995] 4.2%).

Price and earnings indexes (1990 = 100)

	1989	1990	1991	1992	1993	1994	1995[7]
Consumer price index	84.0	100.0	128.7	156.8	172.1	195.4	227.3
Monthly earnings index[8]	84.9	100.0	122.6	150.7	183.5	...	...

Tourism (1993): receipts from visitors U.S.$577,000,000; expenditures by nationals abroad U.S.$266,000,000.
Family income and expenditure. Average household size (1993) 4.2; (1983) income per urban family ₡181,416 (U.S.$4,415), income per rural family ₡98,328 (U.S.$2,393); sources of income: n.a.; expenditure (1980–85): food and beverages 33.0%, household furnishings 9.0%, housing 8.0%, clothing and footwear 8.0%, education 8.0%, transportation 8.0%, other 26.0%.
Land use (1992): forested 32.1%; meadows and pastures 45.8%; agricultural and under permanent cultivation 10.4%; other 11.7%.

Foreign trade[9]

Balance of trade (current prices)

	1989	1990	1991	1992	1993	1994
U.S.$'000,000	−136.4	−349.2	−97.5	−375.2	−556.4	−558.2
% of total	4.6%	10.8%	3.0%	9.3%	12.0%	11.1%

Imports (1993): U.S.$2,900,700,000 (raw materials for industry 31.1%; capital goods for industry 17.7%; nondurable consumer goods 17.0%; durable consumer goods 11.4%). *Major import sources:* United States 43.2%; Japan 7.6%; Venezuela 5.0%; Mexico 4.0%; Germany 3.6%.
Exports (1993): U.S.$1,944,600,000 (bananas 29.6%; coffee 10.4%; textiles, clothing, and footwear 5.7%; fish and shrimp 4.7%; ornamental plants, leaves, and flowers 4.6%). *Major export destinations:* United States 41.6%; Germany 8.9%; Italy 4.5%; Guatemala 4.5%. Nicaragua 3.9%.

Transport and communications

Transport. Railroads (1993): route length 590 mi, 950 km; passenger-mi 3,700,000, passenger-km 5,900,000; short ton mi cargo 45,800,000, metric ton-km cargo 66,800,000. Roads (1993): total length 22,084 mi, 35,541 km (paved 17%). Vehicles (1993): passenger cars 220,142; trucks and buses 114,911. Merchant marine (1992): vessels (100 gross tons and over) 24; total deadweight tonnage 8,368. Air transport (1993)[10]: passenger-mi 885,000,000, passenger-km 1,425,000,000; short-ton mi cargo 25,946,000, metric ton-km cargo 37,881,000; airports (1995) with scheduled flights 13.
Communications. Daily newspapers (1992): total number 4; total circulation 322,000; circulation per 1,000 population 103. Radio (1994): total number of receivers 760,000 (1 per 4.3 persons). Television (1994): total number of receivers 340,000 (1 per 9.6 persons). Telephones (main lines; 1993): 364,100 (1 per 8.8 persons).

Education and health

Education (1993)

	schools	teachers	students	student/ teacher ratio
Primary (age 7–12)	3,442	15,107	484,958	32.1
Secondary (age 13–17)	179[11]	5,281[12]	117,975[12]	22.3[12]
Vocational	77[11]	2,360[12]	33,538[12]	14.2[12]
Higher[13]	6	7,969	65,625	8.2

Educational attainment (1984). Percentage of economically active population age 25 and over having: no formal schooling 8.3%; incomplete primary education 28.6%; complete primary 26.3%; secondary 22.6%; postsecondary and higher 14.2%. *Literacy* (1990): total population age 15 and over literate 1,798,000 (92.8%); males literate 913,000 (92.6%); females literate 885,000 (93.1%).
Health (1993): physicians 3,327 (1 per 962 persons); hospital beds 6,126 (1 per 528 persons); infant mortality rate per 1,000 live births 13.7.
Food (1988–90): daily per capita caloric intake 2,711 (vegetable products 83%, animal products 17%); 121% of FAO recommended minimum requirement.

Military

Military expenditure as percentage of GNP (1991): 0.4% (world 4.1%); per capita expenditure U.S.$7. The army was officially abolished in 1948. Paramilitary and police forces had 7,500 members in 1994.

[1]January 1. [2]Detail does not add to total given because of rounding. [3]Population of San José canton. [4]1993. [5]Within San José metropolitan area. [6]1991. [7]February. [8]Data for June average of each year. [9]Import figures are f.o.b. in balance of trade and c.i.f. for commodities and trading partners. [10]Lacsa (Costa Rican Airlines) only. [11]1990. [12]1992. [13]Universities only.

Côte d'Ivoire

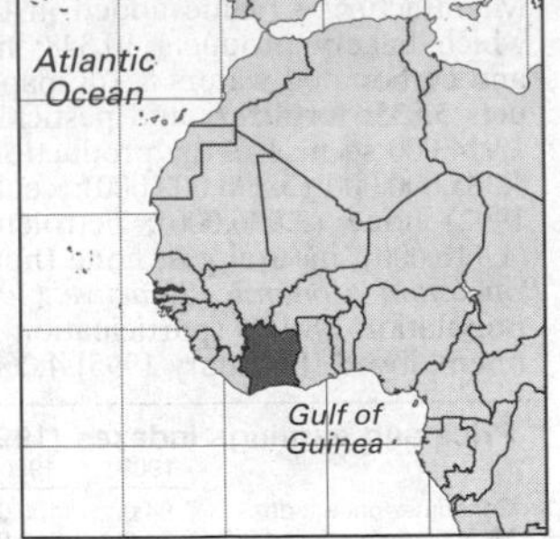

Official name: République de Côte d'Ivoire (Republic of Côte d'Ivoire [Ivory Coast][1]).
Form of government: multiparty republic with one legislative house (National Assembly [175]).
Chief of state: President.
Head of government: Prime Minister.
Capital: Abidjan (de facto; legislative).
Capital designate: Yamoussoukro (de jure; administrative).
Official language: French.
Official religion: none.
Monetary unit: 1 CFA franc (CFAF) = 100 centimes; valuation (Oct. 6, 1995) 1 U.S.$ = CFAF 501.49; 1 £ = CFAF 792.78.

Area and population (1988 census)

Department	area sq km	population	Department	area sq km	population
Abengourou	5,200	216,058	Guiglo	11,220	170,321
Abidjan	8,550	2,485,847	Issia	3,590	195,663
Aboisso	6,250	225,895	Katiola	9,420	130,635
Adzopé	5,230	237,870	Korhogo	12,500	390,229
Agboville	3,850	203,493	Lakota	2,730	116,771
Agnibilékrou	1,700	84,349	Man	4,990	294,724
Bangolo	2,060	79,979	Mankono	10,660	123,362
Béoumi	2,820	90,327	M'bahiakro	5,460	102,531
Biankouma	4,950	98,236	Odiénné	20,600	169,764
Bondoukou	10,040	174,251	Oumé	2,400	141,268
Bongouanou	5,570	224,958	Sakassou	1,880	59,362
Bouaflé	3,980	165,822	San-Pédro	6,900	170,669
Bouaké	4,700	450,594	Sassandra	5,190	108,090
Bouna	21,470	135,813	Séguéla	11,240	121,235
Boundiali	7,895	127,847	Sinfra	1,690	121,903
Dabakala	9,670	81,820	Soubré	8,270	310,790
Daloa	5,450	359,753	Tabou	5,440	58,147
Danané	4,600	222,839	Tanda	6,490	204,070
Daoukro	3,610	86,494	Tengréla	2,200	54,847
Dimbokro	4,920	141,968	Tiassalé	3,370	133,708
Divo	7,920	387,106	Touba	8,720	107,886
Duékoué	2,930	102,168	Toumodi	2,780	80,802
Ferkessedougou	17,728	172,893	Vavoua	6,160	168,292
Gagnoa	4,500	276,217	Yamoussoukro	6,160	281,442
Grand-Lahou	2,280	52,559	Zuénoula	2,830	114,027
			TOTAL	320,763[2]	10,815,694

Demography

Population (1995): 14,253,000.
Density (1995): persons per sq mi 115.1, persons per sq km 44.4.
Urban-rural (1992): urban 42.0%; rural 58.0%.
Sex distribution (1988): male 51.10%; female 48.90%.
Age breakdown (1988): under 15, 46.8%; 15–29, 27.3%; 30–44, 15.0%; 45–59, 7.5%; 60–74, 2.8%; 75 and over, 0.6%.
Population projection: (2000) 16,761,000; (2010) 23,058,000.
Ethnolinguistic composition (1988)[3]: Akan 41.8%; Voltaic 16.3%; Malinke 15.9%; Kru 14.6%; Southern Mande 10.7%; other 0.7%.
Religious affiliation (1988): Muslim 38.7%; Catholic 20.8%; animist 17.0%; atheist 13.4%; Protestant 5.3%, excluding Harrism (1.4%); other 3.4%.
Major cities (1988): Abidjan (1990) 2,168,000; Bouaké 329,850; Daloa 121,842; Korhogo 109,445; Yamoussoukro 106,786.

Vital statistics

Birth rate per 1,000 population (1990–95): 49.9 (world avg. 25.0).
Death rate per 1,000 population (1990–95): 15.1 (world avg. 9.3).
Natural increase rate per 1,000 population (1990–95): 34.8 (world avg. 15.7).
Total fertility rate (avg. births per childbearing woman; 1990–95): 7.4.
Life expectancy at birth (1988): male 53.6 years; female 57.2 years.
Major causes of death per 100,000 population: n.a.; however, AIDS was a major cause of both morbidity and mortality among adults in the mid-1990s; other endemic diseases included yellow fever, trypanosomiasis, dracunculiasis, childhood diseases, yaws, and tuberculosis.

National economy

Budget (1994). Revenue: CFAF 840,100,000,000 (current revenues 81.7%, of which duties 28.1%, taxes on income, goods, and services 16.8%). Expenditures: CFAF 789,800,000,000 (current expenses 79.1%; investments 20.9%).
Public debt (external, outstanding; 1993): U.S.$10,551,000,000.
Production (metric tons except as noted). Agriculture, forestry, fishing (1994): yams 2,824,000, cassava 1,564,000, sugarcane 1,469,000, plantains 1,300,000, cacao beans 809,000, paddy rice 701,000, corn (maize) 536,000, coconuts 213,000, coffee 148,000; livestock (number of live animals) 1,251,000 sheep, 1,232,000 cattle, 976,000 goats; roundwood (1993) 13,694,000 cu m; fish catch (1993) 70,174. Mining and quarrying (1993)[4]: gold 1,500 kg; diamonds 20,000 carats. Manufacturing (value added in CFAF '000,000,000; 1991): food products 168, refined petroleum products 93, textiles 58, transport equipment 41, industrial chemicals 32, wood products 30, fabricated metal products 24. Construction (in CFAF; 1984): 62,000,000,000. Energy production (consumption): electricity (kW-hr; 1993) 1,910,000,000 (1,910,000,000); coal, none (n.a.); crude petroleum (barrels; 1993) 2,380,000 (23,900,000); petroleum products (metric tons; 1993) 2,471,000 (2,453,000).
Land use (1993): forest 22.3%; pasture 40.9%; agricultural 11.7%.
Gross national product (1993): U.S.$8,416,000,000 (U.S.$630 per capita).

Structure of gross domestic product and labour force

	1991		1988	
	in value CFAF '000,000,000	% of total value	labour force	% of labour force
Agriculture	985.6	33.3	2,723,900	63.9
Manufacturing and mining	474.1	16.0	149,200	3.5
Construction and public utilities	138.5	4.7	89,500	2.1
Transp. and commun.	230.6	7.8	123,600	2.9
Trade	602.4	20.3	558,400	13.1
Finance, pub. admin., defense, and services	383.0	12.9	618,100	14.5
Other (customs receipts)	145.8	5.0	...	...
TOTAL	2,960.0	100.0	4,262,700	100.0

Population economically active (1992): total 4,826,000; activity rate of total population 37.4% (participation rates [1988]: ages 15–54, 66.4%; female 33.9%; unemployed 0.6%).

Price and earnings indexes (1990 = 100)

	1988	1989	1990	1991	1992	1993	1994
Consumer price index	99.8	100.8	100.0	101.7	106.0	108.3	136.5
Hourly earnings index[5]	100.0	100.0	100.0	100.0	100.0	...	...

Household income and expenditure. Average household size (1988) 5.4; average annual income per household (1980) CFAF 500,000; sources of income: self-employment 49.9%, wages 44.9%, transfers and other resources 5.2%; expenditure (1992)[6]: food 48.0%, clothing 10.1%, energy and water 8.5%, housing 7.8%, transportation 6.8%.
Tourism (1993): receipts U.S.$64,000,000; expenditures U.S.$111,000,000.

Foreign trade

Balance of trade (current prices)

	1989	1990	1991	1992	1993	1994
U.S.$'000,000	+919.7	+1,093.8	+923.4	+994.7	+850.8	+1,308.5
% of total	20.6%	23.1%	20.6%	20.3%	19.1%	29.5%

Imports (1993): CFAF 452,600,000,000 (1992; crude and refined petroleum 22.5%; machinery and transport equipment 21.2%; food and food products 16.6%; pharmaceuticals 5.7%; plastics 3.3%; paper and paper products 2.9%; chemicals 2.6%; iron 2.5%). *Major import sources* (1992): France 34.2%; Nigeria 18.7%; Japan 4.2%; Germany 3.9%; The Netherlands 3.9%.
Exports (1993): CFAF 755,600,000,000 (1992; food products 53.1%, of which cocoa beans and products 33.8%, coffee and coffee products 7.3%, fish products 3.4%; petroleum products 11.2%; wood and wood products 9.7%; cotton and cotton cloth 5.2%). *Major export destinations* (1992): France 15.0%; The Netherlands 11.5%; Germany 5.8%; Italy 5.6%; Burkina Faso 5.3%; Mali 4.5%; Nigeria 4.3%; Belgium-Luxembourg 4.3%; U.S. 4.2%.

Transport and communications

Transport. Railroads (1991): route length 660 km; passenger-km 199,000,000; metric ton-km cargo 274,000,000. Roads (1995): total length 43,500 mi, 70,000 km (paved 8%). Vehicles (1992): passenger cars 175,000; trucks and buses 95,000. Merchant marine (1992): vessels (100 gross tons and over) 51; total deadweight tonnage 98,618. Air transport (1994)[7]: passenger-km 201,718,000; metric ton-km cargo 15,256,000; airports (1995) 10.
Communications. Daily newspapers (1990): total number 1; total circulation 90,000; circulation per 1,000 population 8. Radio (1994): 1,600,000 receivers (1 per 8.9 persons). Television (1994): 810,000 receivers (1 per 18 persons). Telephones (main lines; 1993): 93,880 (1 per 140 persons).

Education and health

Education (1993)

	schools	teachers	students	student/ teacher ratio
Primary (age 7–12)	7,249	39,691	1,553,540	39.1
Secondary (age 13–19)[8]	147	9,644	445,505	46.2
Voc., teacher tr.	15[9]	1,947[10]	3,094[9]	...
Higher	1	...	*c.* 40,000	...

Educational attainment (1988). Percentage of population age 6 and over having: no formal schooling 60.0%; Koranic school 3.6%; primary education 24.8%; secondary 10.7%; higher 0.9%. *Literacy* (1995): percentage of population age 15 and over literate 40.1%; males 49.9%; females 30.0%.
Health: physicians (1990) 1,020 (1 per 11,745 persons); hospital beds (1993) 7,928 (1 per 1,698 persons); infant mortality rate (1990–95) 92.0.
Food (1992): daily per capita caloric intake 2,491 (vegetable products 96%, animal products 4%); 107% of FAO recommended minimum requirement.

Military

Total active duty personnel (1995): 8,400[11] (army 81.0%, navy 10.7%, air force 8.3%). *Military expenditure as percentage of GNP* (1992): 1.7% (world avg. 3.7%); per capita expenditure U.S.$10.

[1]Since 1986, Côte d'Ivoire has requested that the French form of the country's name be used as the official protocol version in all languages. [2]Total area per more recent survey is 322,463 sq km; area breakdown by department is not available. [3]"Ivoirian" nationals only, representing about 65% of the de facto population. [4]Excludes production smuggled out of country. [5]January 1; index refers to the S.M.I.G. (*salaire minimum interprofessionel garanti*), a form of minimum professional wage. [6]Weights of consumer price index components for a worker's family living in the capital city. [7]Represents 1/11 share of traffic of Air Afrique, which is operated by 11 West African states. [8]Data exclude 208 private schools, with (1992) 107,096 students. [9]1992. [10]1991. [11]Excluding about 700 French military personnel stationed in Côte d'Ivoire.

Croatia

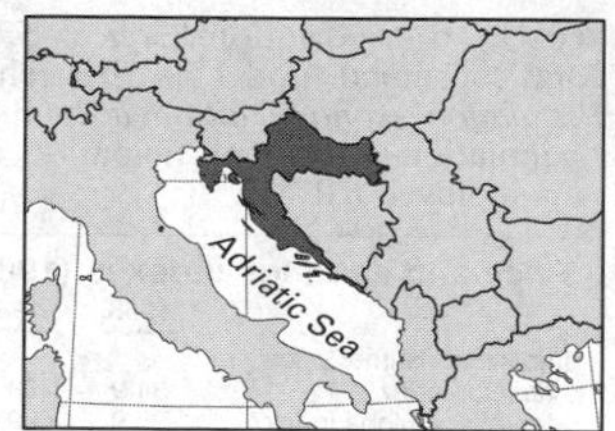

Official name: Republika Hrvatska (Republic of Croatia).
Form of government: multiparty republic with a two-chambered legislature (House of Counties [68[1]]; House of Representatives [127[2]]).
Head of state: President.
Head of government: Prime Minister.
Capital: Zagreb.
Official language: Croatian.
Official religion: none.
Monetary unit: 1 kuna (plural kune)[3] = 100 lipa; valuation (Oct. 6, 1995) 1 U.S.$ = 5.33 kune; 1 £ = 8.43 kune.

Area and population (1991 census)

City	Capitals	area sq mi	area sq km	population 1991 census
Zagreb	—	495	1,282	867,717
County				
Bjelovar-Bilogora	Bjelovar	1,022	2,647	144,042
Dubrovnik-Neretva	Dubrovnikvn	689	1,784	126,329
Istra	Pazin	1,087	2,815	204,346
Karlovac	Karlovac	1,276	3,306	174,105
Koprivnica-Križevci	Koprimica	684	1,772	129,907
Krapina-Zagorje	Krapina	472	1,222	149,534
Lika-Senj	Gospić	1,440	3,729	71,215
Međimurje	Čakovec	282	730	119,866
Osijek-Baranja	Osijek	1,393	3,608	331,979
Požega-Slavonija	Požega	918	2,377	134,548
Primorje-Gorski Kotar	Rijeka	1,388	3,594	323,130
Šibenik	Šibenik	746	1,932	109,171
Sisak-Moslavina	Sisak	1,984	5,138	207,002
Slavonski Brod-Posavina	Slavonski Brod	785	2,034	174,998
Split-Dalmatia	Split	1,747	4,526	474,019
Varaždin	Varaždin	402	1,248	187,343
Virovitica-Podravina	Virovitica	798	2,068	104,625
Vukovar-Srijem	Vukovar	943	2,442	231,241
Zadar-Knin	Zadar	2,451	6,347	272,003
Zagreb	Zagreb	807	2,090	167,145
TOTAL		21,889	56,601	4,784,265

Demography

Population (1995): 4,495,000.
Density (1995): persons per sq mi 205.9, persons per sq km 79.5.
Urban-rural (1991): urban 50.8%; rural 49.2%.
Sex distribution (1991): male 48.46%, female 51.54%.
Age breakdown (1991): under 15, 19.4%; 15–29, 20.7%; 30–44, 22.7%; 45–59, 18.3%, 60–74, 12.9%; 75 and over, 4.5%; not stated 1.5%.
Population projection: (2000) 4,433,000; (2010) 4,373,000.
Doubling time: not applicable; population is declining.
Ethnic composition (1991): Croat 78.1%; Serb 12.2%; Bosnian 0.9%; Magyar 0.5%; Slovene 0.5%; other 7.8%.
Religious affiliation (1991): Roman Catholic 76.5%; Eastern Orthodox 11.1%; Muslim 1.2%; other 11.2%[4].
Major cities (1991): Zagreb 706,770; Split 189,388; Rijeka 167,964; Osijek 104,761; Zadar 76,343.

Vital statistics

Birth rate per 1,000 population (1993): 10.8 (world avg. 25.0); legitimate 92.2%; illegitimate 7.8%.
Death rate per 1,000 population (1993): 11.4 (world avg. 9.3).
Natural increase rate per 1,000 population (1993): −0.6 (world avg. 15.7).
Total fertility rate (avg. births per childbearing woman; 1992): 1.4.
Marriage rate per 1,000 population (1993): 5.1.
Divorce rate per 1,000 population (1993): 1.0.
Life expectancy at birth (1991): male 65.6 years; female 75.0 years.
Major causes of death per 100,000 population (1992): diseases of the circulatory system 518.0; malignant neoplasms (cancers) 213.1; accidents, violence, and poisoning 132.6; diseases of the digestive system 49.4; diseases of the respiratory system 47.0.

National economy

Budget (1993). Revenue: HrD 10,002,000,000[3] (sales tax 57.5%, income tax 15.1%, import duties 12.3%). Expenditures: HrD 9,969,000,000[3] (national economy 18.6%, social services 9.5%, education 2.4%, health 0.5%, defense 0.2%).
Production (metric tons except as noted). Agriculture, forestry, fishing (1994): corn (maize) 1,685,000, wheat 750,000, sugar beets 592,000, potatoes 563,000, grapes 363,000, barley 108,000, plums 36,000; livestock (number of live animals) 1,347,000 pigs, 519,000 cattle, 444,000 sheep, 14,000,000 poultry; roundwood (1993) 3,136,000 cu m; fish catch (1993) 25,862, of which freshwater 5,339. Mining and quarrying (1993): lime 156,451; bauxite 1,690. Manufacturing (1993): ammonia 344,812; crude steel 73,815; detergents 43,278; aluminum 25,956; cotton fibre 10,301. Construction (value in HrD '000,000; 1993): residential 1,255; nonresidential 2,059. Energy production (consumption): electricity (kW-hr; 1993) 9,359,000,000 (11,797,000,000); coal (metric tons; 1993) 116,000 (1,012,000); crude petroleum (barrels; 1993) 13,890,000 (36,474,000); petroleum products (metric tons; 1993) 4,632,000 (3,084,000); natural gas (cu m; 1993) 1,785,000,000 (2,116,000,000).
Gross domestic product (1993): U.S.$14,614,900,000 (U.S.$3,058 per capita).

Structure of gross domestic product and labour force

	1993 in value Din '000,000[3]	% of total value	labour force	% of labour force
Agriculture	6,881,186	13.1	57,400	4.3
Mining, Manufacturing	16,045,057	30.6	384,700	28.8
Construction	1,768,714	3.4	66,300	5.0
Public utilities	1,370,135	2.6	23,300	1.7
Transp. and commun.	4,904,057	9.4	90,000	6.7
Trade	1,243,866	2.3	175,700	13.1
Finance	6,237,164	11.9	51,500	3.9
Pub. admin., defense	2,810,963	5.4	48,200	3.6
Services	11,175,156 (Services and Other)	21.3 (Services and Other)	187,500	14.0
Other			250,800[5]	18.9[5]
TOTAL	52,436,298	100.0	1,335,400	100.0

Population economically active (1993): total 1,335,400; activity rate of total population 27.9% (participation rates [1991]: ages 15–64, 57.1%; female 42.9%; unemployed 18.8%).

Price and earnings indexes (1990 = 100)

	1990	1991	1992	1993	1994
Consumer price index	100	224	1,647	26,127	54,122
Annual earnings index[6]	100	168	697	11,187	26,089

Household income and expenditure. Average household size (1991) 3.1; income per household (1990) Din 165,813[3] (U.S.$14,650); sources (1990): self-employment 40.8%, wages 40.2%, transfers 12.1%, other 6.9%; expenditure (1988): food 34.2%, transportation 9.3%, clothing 8.6%, housing 8.3%, energy 7.6%, drink and tobacco 5.1%, durable goods 4.5%, health care 4.3%.
Land use (1993): forest 37.1%; pasture 19.3%; agricultural 23.2%; other 20.4%.

Foreign trade

Balance of trade (current prices)

	1988	1989	1990	1991	1992	1993
HrD '000,000[3]	−329	−603	−871	−472	199	−439
% of total	7.3%	11.5%	12.7%	7.8%	2.2%	5.4%

Imports (1993): HrD 4,221,000,000[3] (machinery 23.1%, basic manufactures 17.4%, consumer goods 16.1%, chemicals 14.2%, food 8.7%). *Major import sources:* Germany 21.2%; Italy 20.0%; Austria 6.6%; former U.S.S.R. 5.5%.
Exports (1993): HrD 3,782,000,000[3] (consumer goods 27.6%, basic manufactures 14.5%, chemicals 14.2%, machinery 13.6%, food 12.0%). *Major export destinations:* Germany 23.5%; Italy 21.1%; Slovenia 18.3%; former U.S.S.R. 4.9%; Austria 3.6%.

Transport and communications

Transport. Railroads (1993): length 1,676 mi, 2,699 km; passenger-km 951,000,000; metric ton-km cargo 1,592,000,000. Roads (1993): total length 26,928 km (paved 81%). Vehicles (1993): passenger cars 646,210; trucks and buses 39,203. Merchant marine (1993): fishing vessels 314. Air transport (1993): passenger-km 316,000; metric ton-km cargo 2,620,000; airports (1995) with scheduled flights 4.
Communications. Daily newspapers (1990): 9; total circulation 715,000; circulation per 1,000 population 150. Radio (1992): 1,090,000 receivers (1 per 4.4 persons). Television (1992): 1,045,000 receivers (1 per 4.6 persons). Telephones (main lines; 1993): 1,027,400 (1 per 4.7 persons).

Education and health

Education (1991–92)[7]

	schools	teachers	students	student/ teacher ratio
Primary (age 7–14)	1,930	23,873	446,621	18.7
Secondary (age 15–18)	504	12,886	188,466	14.6
Voc., teacher tr.[8]	3	101	3,362	33.3
Higher[8]	57	5,875	76,307	13.0

Educational attainment (1991). Percentage of population age 15 and over having: no schooling or unknown 10.1%; less than full primary education 21.2%; primary 23.4%; secondary 40.0%; postsecondary and higher 5.3%.
Literacy (1991): total population age 10 and over literate 3,734,000 (97.0%); males 98.8%; females 95.3%.
Health (1993): physicians 9,280 (1 per 515 persons); hospital beds 28,462 (1 per 168 persons); infant mortality rate per 1,000 live births 9.9.

Military

Total active duty personnel (1995): 105,000 (army 97.9%, navy 1.1%, air force and air defense 1.0%). *Military expenditure as percentage of GNP:* n.a.

[1]Includes 5 nonelective seats. [2]Includes 12 seats reserved for Croatians abroad. [3]On Jan. 1, 1990, the Yugoslav new dinar (Din), equal to 10,000 Yugoslav old dinars (Din), was introduced. On Dec. 23, 1991, the Croatian dinar (HrD) was introduced at parity with the Yugoslav new dinar, which it replaced as Croatia's official currency. On May 30, 1994, the kuna, equal to 1,000 Croatian dinars, was introduced. [4]Includes a significant minority of adherents of the Croatian Old Catholic Church, as well as small communities of Protestant Christians and Jews. [5]Includes unemployed and private sector. [6]Based on worker real net personal income. [7]Data exclude private (combined) primary and secondary schools. [8]1992–1993.

Cuba

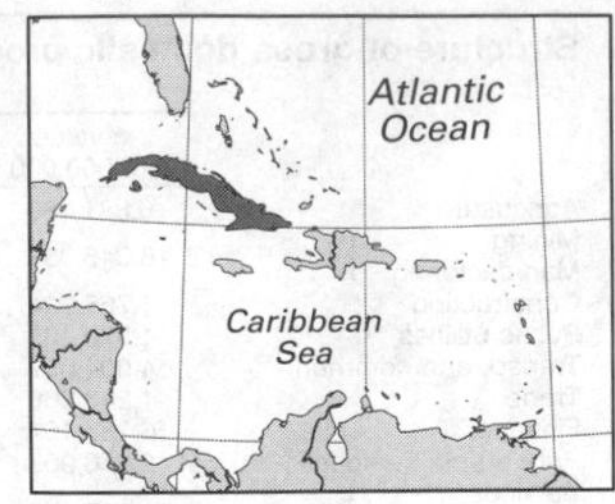

Official name: República de Cuba (Republic of Cuba).
Form of government: unitary socialist republic with one legislative house (National Assembly of the People's Power [589]).
Head of state and government: President.
Capital: Havana.
Official language: Spanish.
Official religion: none.
Monetary unit: 1 Cuban peso (CUP) = 100 centavos; valuation (Oct. 6, 1995) 1 U.S.$ = 1.00 CUP[1]; 1 £ = 1.58 CUP.

Area and population

Provinces	Capitals	area sq mi	area sq km	population 1990[2] estimate
Camagüey	Camagüey	6,174	15,990	744,744
Ciego de Avila	Ciego de Avila	2,668	6,910	367,489
Cienfuegos	Cienfuegos	1,613	4,178	366,531
Ciudad de la Habana[3]	—	281	727	2,107,557
Granma	Bayamo	3,232	8,372	793,868
Guantánamo	Guantánamo	2,388	6,186	499,182
Holguín	Holguín	3,591	9,301	997,735
La Habana[4]	Havana	2,213	5,731	647,280
Las Tunas	Las Tunas	2,544	6,589	495,133
Matanzas	Matanzas	4,625	11,978	612,268
Pinar del Río	Pinar del Río	4,218	10,925	694,306
Sancti Spíritus	Sancti Spíritus	2,604	6,744	430,662
Santiago de Cuba	Santiago de Cuba	2,382	6,170	995,370
Villa Clara	Santa Clara	3,345	8,662	810,249
Special municipality				
Isla de la Juventud	Nueva Gerona	926	2,398	73,319
TOTAL		42,804	110,861	10,635,693[5]

Demography

Population (1995): 11,068,000.
Density (1995): persons per sq mi 258.6, persons per sq km 99.8.
Urban-rural (1990): urban 72.8%; rural 27.2%.
Sex distribution (1994): male 50.20%; female 49.80%.
Age breakdown (1994): under 15, 22.8%; 15–29, 28.0%; 30–44, 21.8%; 45–59, 15.2%; 60–74, 8.4%; 75 and over, 3.8%.
Population projection: (2000) 11,502,000; (2010) 12,181,000.
Doubling time: over 100 years.
Ethnic composition (1994): mixed 51.0%; white 37.0%; black 11.0%; other 1.0%.
Religious affiliation (1980): nonreligious 48.7%; Roman Catholic 39.6%; atheist 6.4%; Protestant 3.3%; Afro-Cuban syncretist 1.6%; other 0.4%.
Major cities (1993): Havana 2,175,995; Santiago de Cuba 440,084; Camagüey 293,961; Holguín 242,085; Guantánamo 207,796.

Vital statistics

Birth rate per 1,000 population (1993): 14.0 (world avg. 25.0).
Death rate per 1,000 population (1993): 7.2 (world avg. 9.3).
Natural increase rate per 1,000 population (1993): 6.8 (world avg. 15.7).
Total fertility rate (avg. births per childbearing woman; 1990–95): 1.9.
Marriage rate per 1,000 population (1992): 17.7.
Divorce rate per 1,000 population (1992): 4.2.
Life expectancy at birth (1990–95): male 73.9 years; female 77.6 years.
Major causes of death per 100,000 population (1992): heart disease 173.4; malignant neoplasms (cancers) 115.5; cerebrovascular disease 60.9%; accidents 45.8; diseases of the blood vessels 23.5; influenza and pneumonia 22.7.

National economy

Budget (1990). Revenue: CUP 12,463,200,000. Expenditures: CUP 14,448,400,000 (capital investment 37.7%; education and public health 20.4%; social, cultural, and scientific activities 17.3%; defense, internal security 9.5%; housing, community services 6.0%).
Production (metric tons except as noted). Agriculture, forestry, fishing (1994): sugarcane 39,000,000, oranges and tangerines 448,000, grapefruit 317,000, bananas and plantains 295,000, cassava 290,000, potatoes 216,000, tomatoes 200,000, sweet potatoes 200,000, rice 186,000, tobacco leaves 44,000, coffee beans 21,000; livestock (number of live animals) 4,500,000 cattle, 1,503,000 pigs, 25,000,000 chickens; roundwood (1993) 3,146,000 cu m; fish catch (1993) 93,435. Mining and quarrying (1994): chromite (1993) 50,000; nickel (metal content of ores) 26,000[6]. Manufacturing (value added in U.S.$'000,000; 1990): tobacco products 2,629; food products 1,033; beverages 358; chemical products 354; transport equipment 225; nonelectrical machinery 176; textiles (excluding ready-made clothing) 109; wearing apparel 88; rubber products 83. Construction (gross value of construction in CUP '000,000; 1989): residential 227; nonresidential 872. Energy production (consumption): electricity (kW-hr; 1993) 11,054,000,000 (11,054,000,000); coal (metric tons; 1993) none (152,000); crude petroleum (barrels; 1993) 6,288,000 (36,766,000); petroleum products (metric tons; 1993) 4,434,000 (7,962,000); natural gas (cu m; 1993) 38,005,000 (38,005,000).
Public debt (hard currency to the West; 1989): U.S.$6,800,000,000.
Household income and expenditure. Average household size (1990) 3.7; average annual income per household (1982) CUP 3,680 (U.S.$4,330); sources of income (1982): wages and salaries 57.3%, bonuses and other payments 42.7%; personal consumption (1989): food 26.7%, other retail purchases 60.5%, transportation services 5.4%, energy 2.7%, value of self-produced and consumed food 1.5%, household repairs 1.3%, other 1.9%.
Population economically active (1988): total 4,570,236; activity rate of total population 43.7% (participation rates: over age 15, 56.9%; female 36.1%; unemployed 6.0%).

Price and earnings indexes (1985 = 100)

	1983	1984	1985	1986	1987	1988	1989
Implicit consumer price deflator index	94.9	98.0	100.0	101.4	102.8	103.1	...
Monthly earnings index[7]	95.9	99.0	100.0	100.1	98.1	99.6	100.0

Tourism: receipts from visitors (1993) U.S.$216,000,000; expenditures by nationals abroad (1990) U.S.$48,000,000.
Gross national product (1991): U.S.$17,000,000,000 (U.S.$1,580 per capita).

Structure of global social product and labour force

	1989 in value CUP '000,000	% of total value	labour force[7]	% of labour force
Agriculture	4,273	15.9	721,100	20.4
Mining[8]	1,039	3.9		
Manufacturing	10,617	39.4	767,500	21.8
Public utilities	733	2.7		
Construction	2,510	9.3	344,300	9.8
Transp. and commun.	2,151	8.0	235,900	6.7
Finance, insurance	—	—	21,700	0.6
Trade	5,401	20.1	395,300	11.2
Public administration	—	—	151,700	4.3
Services	—	—	835,700	23.7
Other	191	0.7	53,400	1.5
TOTAL	26,915	100.0	3,526,600	100.0

Land use (1993): forested 23.7%; meadows and pastures 27.0%; agricultural and under permanent cultivation 30.4%; other 18.9%.

Foreign trade[9]

Balance of trade (current prices)

	1989	1990	1991	1992	1993	1994
U.S.$'000,000	−1,576	−1,599	−1,332	−412	−551	−797
% of total	32.1%	37.1%	38.4%	15.1%	19.2%	24.4%

Imports (1994): U.S.$2,032,000,000 (1992; mineral fuels and lubricants 39.4%, food and live animals 25.4%, machinery and transport equipment 15.8%, chemicals 6.9%, basic manufactures 6.6%, inedible crude materials 3.2%). *Major import sources:* Spain 15.7%; Russia 13.4%; China 8.0%; France 7.3%; Mexico 7.0%; Venezuela 6.7%; Netherlands Antilles 5.1%.
Exports (1994): U.S.$1,235,000,000 (1992; sugar 63.4%, minerals and concentrates 10.6%, fish products 5.9%, raw tobacco and tobacco products 4.6%, citrus and other agricultural products 3.4%). *Major export destinations:* Russia 22.1%; Canada 11.5%; China 8.9%; The Netherlands 7.1%; Spain 5.7%; Algeria 4.7%; Japan 4.6%.

Transport and communications

Transport. Railroads (1991): length 3,033 mi, 4,881 km; passenger-km 3,025,000,000; metric ton-km cargo 1,368,000,000. Roads (1986): total length 28,928 mi, 46,555 km (paved 27%). Vehicles (1988): passenger cars 241,300; trucks and buses 208,400. Merchant marine (1992): vessels (100 gross tons and over) 393; total deadweight tonnage 924,591. Air transport (1993): passenger-km 2,393,000,000; metric ton-km cargo 240,161; airports with scheduled flights (1995) 14.
Communications. Daily newspapers (1992): total number 17; total circulation 1,315,000; circulation per 1,000 population 122. Radio (1994): 3,608,000 receivers (1 per 3.0 persons). Television (1994): 2,500,000 receivers (1 per 4.4 persons). Telephones (main lines; 1993): 344,200 (1 per 31 persons).

Education and health

Education (1993–94)

	schools	teachers	students	student/teacher ratio
Primary (age 6–11)	9,440	76,193	983,459	12.9
Secondary (age 12–17)	2,175[10]	53,423	459,140	8.6
Voc., teacher tr.	618[10]	31,671	266,660	8.4
Higher	35[10]	25,264[11]	198,474[11]	7.9[11]

Educational attainment (1981). Percentage of population age 25 and over having: no formal schooling or some primary education 39.6%; completed primary 26.6%; secondary 29.6%; higher 4.2%. *Literacy* (1995 est.): total population age 15 and over literate 95.7%; males literate 96.2%; females literate 95.3%.
Health (1992): physicians 46,860 (1 per 231 persons); hospital beds 80,684 (1 per 134 persons); infant mortality rate per 1,000 live births (1994) 9.4.
Food (1992): daily per capita caloric intake 2,833 (vegetable products 84%, animal products 16%); 123% of FAO recommended minimum requirement.

Military

Total active duty personnel (1995): 105,000 (army 80.9%, navy 4.8%, air force 14.3%). *Military expenditure as percentage of GDP* (1994): 2.7% (world 2.6%); per capita expenditure: U.S.$27.

[1]Official rate; the black-market rate is about 20–25 pesos (CUP) to U.S.$1. [2]January 1. [3]Province coextensive with the city of Havana. [4]Province bordering the city of Havana on the east, south, and west. [5]The 1993 census total was 10,900,000; detail, n.a. [6]Includes cobalt. [7]State sector only; excludes military and unemployed. [8]Mining includes metallurgy and refined petroleum products. [9]Imports c.i.f.; exports f.o.b. [10]1989–90. [11]1992–93.

Cyprus

Island of Cyprus

Area: 3,572 sq mi, 9,251 sq km.
Population (1995): 806,000[1].

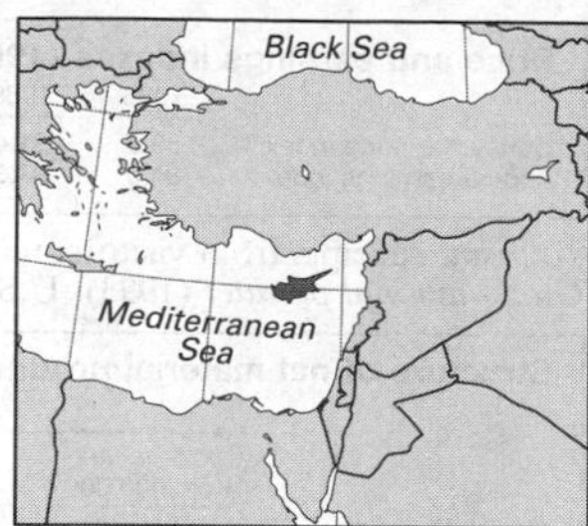

Two de facto states currently exist on the island of Cyprus: the Republic of Cyprus (ROC), predominantly Greek in character, occupying the southern two-thirds of the island, which is the original and still the internationally recognized de jure government of the whole island; and the Turkish Republic of Northern Cyprus (TRNC), proclaimed unilaterally Nov. 15, 1983, on territory originally secured for the Turkish Cypriot population by the July 20, 1974, intervention of Turkey. Only Turkey recognizes the TRNC, and the two ethnic communities have failed to reestablish a single state. Provision of separate data below does not imply recognition of either state's claims but is necessitated by the continuing lack of unified data.

Republic of Cyprus

Official name: Kipriakí Dimokratía (Greek); Kıbrıs Cumhuriyeti (Turkish) (Republic of Cyprus).
Form of government: unitary multiparty republic with a unicameral legislature (House of Representatives [80[2]]).
Head of state and government: President.
Capital: Lefkosia (Nicosia).
Official languages: Greek; Turkish.
Monetary unit: 1 Cyprus pound (£C) = 100 cents; valuation (Oct. 6, 1995) 1 £C = U.S.$2.17 = £1.39.

Area and population

Census districts	Main towns	area: sq mi	area: sq km	population[3]: 1992 census
Ammochostos	Paralimni	...	...	30,798
Larnaca	Larnaca	433	1,121	100,242
Lefkosia	Lefkosia	...	...	244,779
Limassol	Limassol	538	1,393	173,634
Paphos	Paphos	539	1,396	52,572
TOTAL		2,276[4]	5,090[4]	602,025[5]

Demography

Population (1995): 651,000[3].
Urban-rural (1992): urban 67.7%; rural 32.3%.
Age breakdown (1992): under 15, 25.4%; 15–29, 22.0%; 30–44, 22.3%; 45–59, 15.4%; 60–74, 10.2%; 75 and over, 4.7%.
Ethnic composition (1992): Greek Cypriot 95.1%; British 0.8%; other 4.1%.
Religious affiliation (1990): Cypriot Orthodox 82.0%; Maronite 1.5%; other 16.5%.
Urban areas (1992): Lefkosia 177,451[6]; Limassol 136,741, Larnaca 60,337.

Vital statistics

Birth rate per 1,000 population (1993): 16.8 (world avg. 25.0).
Death rate per 1,000 population (1993): 7.7 (world avg. 9.3).
Natural increase rate per 1,000 population (1993): 9.1 (world avg. 15.7).
Life expectancy at birth (1992–93): male 74.6 years; female 79.1 years.

National economy

Budget (1993). Revenue: £C 991,800,000 (indirect taxes 36.9%, direct taxes 24.7%, social-security contributions 21.1%). Expenditures: £C 1,068,900,000 (current expenditures 88.5%, development expenditures 10.2%).
Tourism (1993): receipts U.S.$1,396,000,000; expenditures U.S.$133,000,000.
Household expenditure (1992): food and beverages 22.7%, transportation and communications 15.6%, expenditures in cafes and hotels 13.6%.
Gross national product (1993): U.S.$6,616,000,000 (U.S.$10,480 per capita).

Structure of gross domestic product and labour force

	1994: in value £C '000,000	% of total value	labour force	% of labour force
Agriculture	185.0	5.2	34,000	11.5
Mining	11.1	0.3	800	0.3
Manufacturing	443.5	12.6	45,300	15.4
Construction	322.6	9.1	22,900	7.8
Public utilities	70.7	2.0	1,500	0.5
Transp. and commun.	282.5	8.0	17,000	5.8
Trade	685.7	19.4	69,500	23.6
Finance, insurance	570.1	16.1	20,500	7.0
Pub. admin., defense	459.1	13.0 }	60,500	20.6
Services	259.4	7.4 }		
Other	243.6	6.9	22,100[7]	7.5[7]
TOTAL	3,533.3	100.0	294,100	100.0

Production. Agriculture (value of production in £C '000,000; 1992): milk 25.6, potatoes 23.1, poultry 21.2, pork 19.8, barley 19.3, grapes 14.5. Manufacturing (value added in £C '000,000; 1992): wearing apparel 56.5; food 56.2; cement, bricks, and tiles 34.7; alcoholic beverages 27.5; fabricated metals 27.1. Energy production: electricity (kW-hr; 1993) 2,592,000,000.

Foreign trade[8]

Imports (1994): £C 1,482,200,000 (consumer goods 27.2%; capital goods 11.6%; transport equipment 10.5%; mineral fuels 8.4%). *Major import sources:* U.K. 11.4%; U.S. 10.3%; Italy 9.9%; Germany 8.2%; Greece 6.8%.
Exports (1994): £C 476,000,000 (reexports 46.5%; domestic exports 44.4%, of which clothing 9.3%, potatoes 5.0%; ships' stores 9.1%). *Major export destinations:* U.K. 14.8%; CIS 11.7%; Lebanon 8.6%; Greece 7.6%.

Transport and communications

Transport. Roads (1993): total length 10,857 km (paved 54%). Vehicles (1993): cars 203,610; trucks and buses 90,209. Merchant marine (1992): vessels 1,416; deadweight tonnage 36,198,083. Air transport (1994)[9]: passenger-km 3,063,000,000; metric ton-km cargo 35,767,000; airports (1995) 2.
Communications. Daily newspapers (1993): 9; total circulation 84,600; circulation per 1,000 population 135. Television (1994): 234,500 receivers (1 per 2.7 persons). Telephones (main lines; 1993): 311,000 (1 per 2.5 persons).

Education and health

Education (1993–94)

	schools	teachers	students	student/teacher ratio
Primary (age 6–11)	381	3,424	64,907	19.0
Secondary (age 12–17)	103	3,714	50,870	13.7
Vocational	11	501	3,867	7.7
Higher	30	568	6,732	11.9

Educational attainment (1992). Percentage of population age 25 and over having: no formal schooling 5.1%; higher education 17.0%. *Literacy* (1992): population age 15 and over literate 95.2%; male 97.8%; female 92.8%.
Health (1992): physicians 1,428 (1 per 428 persons); hospital beds 3,479 (1 per 176 persons); infant mortality rate per 1,000 live births (1993) 8.7.

Turkish Republic of Northern Cyprus

Official name: Kuzey Kıbrıs Türk Cumhuriyeti (Turkish) (Turkish Republic of Northern Cyprus).
Capital: Lefkoşa (Nicosia).
Official language: Turkish.
Monetary unit: 1 Turkish lira (LT) = 100 kurush; valuation (Oct. 6, 1995) 1 U.S.$ = LT 50,093; 1 £ = LT 79,189.

Area and population

Districts	Administrative centres	area: sq mi	area: sq km	population[1]: 1992 estimate
Lefkoşa	Lefkoşa	...	...	81,492
Gazimağusa (Famagusta)	Gazimağusa	...	...	66,408
Girne (Kyrenia)	Girne	247	640	27,218
TOTAL		1,295	3,355	175,118

Population (1995): 155,000 (Lefkoşa 41,815[10]; Gazimağusa 21,722[10]).
Ethnic composition (1985): Turkish 98.7%; other 1.3%.

Structure of gross domestic product and labour force

	1993: in value LT '000,000,000	% of total value	labour force	% of labour force
Agriculture and fishing	735	10.8	18,100	23.8
Mining and manufacturing	635	9.3	8,198	10.8
Construction	443	6.5 }	9,584	12.6
Public utilities	115	1.7 }		
Transp. and commun.	588	8.6	6,144	8.1
Trade, restaurants	1,420	20.8	7,889	10.4
Pub. admin.	1,280	18.7	16,365	21.5
Finance, real estate } Services	993	14.5	9,098	12.0
Other	619[11]	9.1[11]	569[12]	0.8[12]
TOTAL	6,828	100.0	75,947	100.0

Budget (1993). Revenue: LT 2,504,000,000 (domestic sources 67.5%, loans 20.7%, aid from Turkey 11.7%). Expenditures: LT 2,504,000,000.
Imports (1993): U.S.$363,900,000 (machinery and equipment 32.1%, food 11.7%). *Major import sources:* Turkey 41.5%; U.K. 18.0%; other EC 15.5%.
Exports (1993): U.S.$54,500,000 (industrial products 55.0%, citrus fruits 30.5%). *Major export destinations:* U.K. 49.0%; Turkey 22.9%.

Education (1993–94)

	schools	teachers	students	student/teacher ratio
Primary[13]	354	1,834	29,126	15.9
Secondary (age 15–17)	15	429	5,751	13.4
Vocational	10	308	2,297	7.5
Higher	7	...	12,333	...

Health (1992): physicians 243 (1 per 680 persons); hospital beds 1,073 (1 per 154 persons); infant mortality rate per 1,000 live births 8.0.

[1]Includes "settlers" from Turkey in the TRNC; excludes 35,000 Turkish military in the TRNC, 3,900 British military in the Sovereign Base Areas in the ROC, and 1,200 UN peacekeeping forces. [2]Twenty-four seats reserved for Turkish Cypriots are not occupied. [3]Population excludes British and UN military forces. [4]Area includes 99 sq mi (256 sq km) of British military Sovereign Base Areas and *c.* 107 sq mi (*c.* 278 sq km) of the UN Buffer Zone. [5]Preliminary figure; final figure equals 615,013. [6]ROC only. [7]Includes 8,000 unemployed. [8]Imports c.i.f.; exports f.o.b. [9]Cyprus Airways. [10]1994. [11]Customs duties. [12]Unemployed. [13]Includes preprimary.

Czech Republic

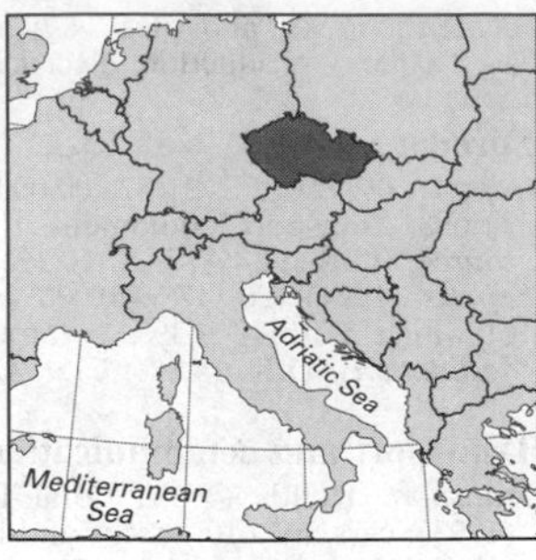

Official name: Česká Republika.
Form of government: unitary multiparty republic with two legislative houses (Senate [81[1]]; Chamber of Deputies [200]).
Chief of state: President.
Head of government: Prime Minister.
Capital: Prague.
Official language: Czech.
Official religion: none.
Monetary unit[2]: 1 koruna (Kc) = 100 halura; valuation (Oct. 6, 1995) 1 U.S.$ = 26.31 Kc; 1 £ = 41.60 Kc.

Area and population

		area		population
Regions	Capitals	sq mi	sq km	1993[3] estimate
Jižní Čechy	České Budějovice	4,380	11,345	699,329
Jižní Morava	Brno	5,802	15,027	2,055,674
Severní Čechy	Ustí nad Labem	3,003	7,777	1,176,707
Severní Morava	Ostrava	4,273	11,068	1,969,366
Střední Čechy	Prague	4,262	11,038	1,110,114
Východní Čechy	Hradec Králové	4,340	11,240	1,236,368
Zapadní Čechy	Plzeň	4,198	10,873	860,824
Capital city				
Prague	—	192	496	1,217,315
TOTAL		30,450	78,864	10,325,697

Demography

Population (1995): 10,345,644.
Density (1995): persons per sq mi 339.8, persons per sq km 131.2.
Urban-rural: n.a.
Sex distribution (1993): male 48.55%; female 51.45%.
Age breakdown (1993): under 15, 20.0%; 15–29, 22.7%; 30–44, 21.7%; 45–59, 17.7%; 60–74, 13.3%; 75 and over, 4.6%.
Population projection: (2000) 10,393,000; (2010) 10,488,930.
Doubling time: not applicable; population growth is negligible.
Ethnic composition (1991): Czech 81.2%; Moravian 13.2%; Slovak 3.1%; Polish 0.6%; German 0.5%; Silesian 0.4%; Gypsy 0.3%; Hungarian 0.2%; Ukrainian 0.1%; other 0.4%.
Religious affiliation (1991): Roman Catholic 39.0%; Protestant 4.3%, of which Czechoslovak Brethren Reformed 2.0%, Czechoslovak Hussite 1.7%, Silesian Evangelical 0.3%; Eastern Orthodox 0.2%; Greek Catholic 0.1%; other Christian 0.3%; undenominational 39.9%; other 16.2%.
Major cities (1994): Prague 1,217,000; Brno 390,100; Ostrava 326,200; Plzeň 172,300; Olomouc 105,900.

Vital statistics

Birth rate per 1,000 population (1993): 11.7 (world avg. 25.0); (1992) legitimate 89.3%; illegitimate 10.7%.
Death rate per 1,000 population (1993): 11.4 (world avg. 9.3).
Natural increase rate per 1,000 population (1993): 0.3 (world avg. 15.7).
Total fertility rate (avg. births per childbearing woman; 1992): 1.8.
Marriage rate per 1,000 population (1993): 6.4.
Divorce rate per 1,000 population (1993): 2.9.
Life expectancy at birth (1993): male 68.9 years; female 76.6 years.
Major causes of death per 100,000 population (1992): diseases of the circulatory system 649.9; malignant neoplasms (cancers) 271.5; accidents, poisoning, and violence 84.2; diseases of the respiratory system 49.4; diseases of the digestive system 43.0; diseases of the genitourinary system 19.2; endocrine and metabolic disorders 16.0.

National economy

Budget (1994). Revenue: Kc 381,800,000[2] (taxes 62.2%, of which value-added taxes 39.8%, income taxes 32.6%, sales taxes 17.7%, other taxes 9.9%; other revenue 37.8%). Expenditures: Kc 381,800,000[2] (current expenditures 88.6%; capital expenditures 9.5%).
Public debt (external, outstanding; 1993): U.S.$6,580,000,000.
Production (metric tons except as noted). Agriculture, forestry, fishing (1994): cereals 6,777,000 (of which wheat 3,713,000, barley 2,419,000, rye 276,000, corn [maize] 91,000), sugar beets 3,240,000, potatoes 1,231,000; livestock (number of live animals; 1994) 4,071,000 pigs, 2,113,000 cattle, 24,000,000 poultry; roundwood (1993) 10,306,000 cu m; fish catch (1993) 24,388. Mining and quarrying (1993): lead-zinc 180,000; iron ore 153,000. Manufacturing (value of production in Kc '000,000[2]; 1993): machinery and transport equipment 60,766; metal products 48,151; textiles 19,330; chemical products 18,484; food products 16,638. Construction (value in Kc '000,000[2]; 1993): residential 19,496; nonresidential 236,611. Energy production (consumption): electricity (kW-hr; 1992) 59,132,000,000 (41,263,000,000); coal (1992) 68,084,000 (n.a.); crude petroleum (barrels; 1992) 549,000 (n.a.); petroleum products, n.a. (n.a.); natural gas (cu m; 1992) 1,552,000,000 (n.a.).
Household income and expenditure. Average household size (1993) 2.7; income per household (1993) Kčs 137,408[2] (U.S.$4,774); sources of income (1993): wages and salaries 84.6%, transfer payments 10.0%, other 5.4%; expenditure (1993): food and beverages 25.0%, clothing and footwear 8.3%, housing and utilities 8.0%, household durable goods 4.8%, other 53.9%.
Population economically active (1993): total 5,197,242; activity rate of total population 50.3% (participation rates: [1992] ages 15–59 [male], 15–54 [female] 86.3%; female 44.4%; unemployed 3.5%).

Price and earnings indexes (1990 = 100)

	1988	1989	1990	1991	1992	1993	1994
Consumer price index	89.9	91.4	100.0	170.0	174.0	210.3	231.6
Annual earnings index	94.0	97.3	100.0	116.6	127.3	177.7	209.9

Tourism: receipts from visitors, n.a.; expenditures by nationals abroad, n.a.
Gross national product (1993): U.S.$28,182,000,000 (U.S.$2,730 per capita).

Structure of net material product and labour force

	1993			
	in value Kčs '000,000[2]	% of total value	labour force	% of labour force
Agriculture	47,900	5.2	306,486	5.9
Mining and manufacturing	260,000	28.1	1,576,658	30.3
Construction	33,000	3.6	446,389	8.6
Public utilities	56,200	6.1	87,770	1.7
Transportation and communications	60,000	6.5	377,215	7.3
Trade	76,400	8.3	725,125	13.9
Finance	} 265,100	} 28.7	69,077	1.3
Pub. admin., defense			144,078	2.8
Services			1,043,852	20.1
Other	124,500	13.5	420,592[4]	8.1[4]
TOTAL	923,100	100.0	5,197,242	100.0

Land use (1993): forested 33.3%; meadows and pastures 11.1%; agricultural and under permanent cultivation 41.8%; other 13.8%.

Foreign trade

Balance of trade (current prices)

	1989	1990	1991	1992	1993	1994
Kc '000,000[2]	+13,460	−14,410	+41,680	−60,368	+28,600	−12,507
% of total	2.8%	2.8%	5.9%	6.8%	2.8%	1.5%

Imports (1994): Kc 423,964,000,000[2] (machinery and transport equipment 34.9%, manufactured goods 16.4%, chemicals 13.1%, fuels and lubricants 10.1%). *Major import sources:* Germany 25.3%; Russia 18.5%; Slovakia 14.2%; Austria 8.1%; Italy 5.3%.
Exports (1994): Kc 411,457,000,000[2] (manufactured goods 30.5%, machinery and transport equipment 26.1%, chemicals 9.9%, fuels and lubricants 5.7%, food and live animals 5.2%). *Major export destinations:* Germany 29.3%; Slovakia 16.3%; Austria 7.2%; Italy 4.9%; Russia 4.2%.

Transport and communications

Transport. Railroads (1993): length 5,866 mi, 9,441 km; passenger-mi 5,311,000,000, passenger-km 8,548,000,000; short ton-mi cargo 17,520,000,000, metric ton-km cargo 25,579,000,000. Roads (1993): total length 34,734 mi, 55,912 km (paved, n.a.). Vehicles (1993): passenger cars 2,693,905; trucks and buses 354,690. Merchant marine (1993): vessels (oceangoing) 18; total deadweight tonnage 514,126. Air transport (1993): passenger-mi 1,588,000, passenger-km 2,555,062; short ton-mi 46,695,000, metric ton-km 68,174,000; airports (1995) with scheduled flights 4.
Communications. Daily newspapers (1992): total number 55; total circulation 6,000,000; circulation per 1,000 population 582. Radio (1993): total number of receivers 2,732,000 (1 per 3.8 persons). Television (1993): total number of receivers 3,180,000 (1 per 3.3 persons). Telephones (main lines; 1993): 1,961,100 (1 per 5.2 persons).

Education and health

Education (1993–94)

	schools	teachers	students	student/ teacher ratio
Primary (age 6–14)	4,199	63,767	1,061,396	16.6
Secondary (age 15–18)	324	8,456	122,171	14.4
Voc., teacher tr.	821	16,854	219,249	13.0
Higher	23	13,463	127,137	9.4

Educational attainment (1991). Percentage of adult population having: primary and incomplete secondary 33.1%; complete secondary 22.8%; higher 7.2%. *Literacy* (1990): total population age 15 and over literate 8,170,442 (100%); males literate 3,914,080 (100%); females literate 4,256,362 (100%).
Health (1993): physicians 37,068 (1 per 272 persons); hospital beds 103,556 (1 per 79 persons); infant mortality rate per 1,000 live births 8.5.
Food (1992): daily per capita caloric intake 3,303 (vegetable products 70%, animal products 30%); 128% of FAO recommended minimum requirement.

Military

Total active duty personnel (1994): 92,900 (army 73.1%, air force 26.9%). *Military expenditure as percentage of GNP* (1993): 2.8% (world 3.3%). Per capita expenditure (1993): U.S.$77.

[1]Seats not yet occupied as of October 1995. [2]The koruna (Kc) was introduced Feb. 8, 1993, at par with the former Czechoslovak koruna (Kčs), which it replaced. For settlement of obligations existing prior to February 8 between the Czech and Slovak republics, an interim currency, the clearing koruna (XCS) was introduced. [3]January 1. [4]Includes 183,972 unemployed and 225,484 women on maternity leave.

Denmark

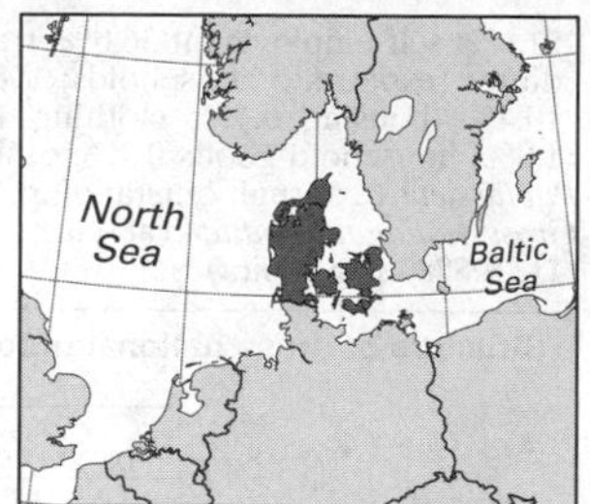

Official name: Kongeriget Danmark (Kingdom of Denmark).
Form of government: parliamentary state and constitutional monarchy with one legislative house (Folketing [179]).
Chief of state: Danish Monarch.
Head of government: Prime Minister.
Capital: Copenhagen.
Official language: Danish.
Official religion: Evangelical Lutheran.
Monetary unit: 1 Danish krone (Dkr; plural kroner) = 100 øre; valuation (Oct. 6, 1995) 1 U.S.$ = Dkr 5.55; 1 £ = Dkr 8.77.

Area and population[1]

Counties	Capitals	area sq mi	area sq km	population 1994[2] estimate
Århus	Århus	1,761	4,561	614,223
Bornholm	Rønne	227	588	45,067
Frederiksborg	Hillerød	520	1,347	348,491
Fyn	Odense	1,346	3,486	466,567
København	—	203	526	604,762
Nordjylland	Ålborg	2,383	6,173	487,757
Ribe	Ribe	1,209	3,131	221,368
Ringkøbing	Ringkøbing	1,874	4,853	269,448
Roskilde	Roskilde	344	891	222,704
Sønderjylland	Åbenrå	1,520	3,938	251,663
Storstrøm	Nykøbing Falster	1,312	3,398	257,148
Vejle	Vejle	1,157	2,997	335,266
Vestsjælland	Sorø	1,152	2,984	287,266
Viborg	Viborg	1,592	4,122	230,193
Communes				
Copenhagen (København)	—	34	88	467,253
Frederiksberg	—	3	9	87,466
TOTAL		16,639[3]	43,094[3]	5,196,642

Demography

Population (1995): 5,223,000.
Density (1995): persons per sq mi 313.9, persons per sq km 121.2.
Urban-rural (1992): urban 84.9%; rural 15.1%.
Sex distribution (1994): male 49.33%; female 50.67%.
Age breakdown (1994): under 15, 17.1%; 15–29, 21.7%; 30–44, 21.8%; 45–59, 19.4%; 60–74, 13.0%; 75 and over, 7.0%.
Population projection: (2000) 5,278,000; (2010) 5,320,000.
Doubling time: not applicable; population is stable.
Ethnic composition (1994): Danish 96.4%; Asian 1.5%, of which Turkish 0.7%; other Scandinavian 0.5%; residents of former Yugoslavia 0.2%; British 0.2%; other 1.2%.
Religious affiliation (1993): Evangelical Lutheran 87.7%; other Christian 1.6%; Muslim 1.4%; other/nonreligious 9.3%.
Major cities (1992): Greater Copenhagen 1,342,679[4]; Århus 204,139; Odense 140,886; Ålborg 114,970; Frederiksberg 87,466[5, 6].

Vital statistics

Birth rate per 1,000 population (1994): 13.4 (world avg. 25.0); (1993) legitimate 53.2%; illegitimate 46.8%.
Death rate per 1,000 population (1994): 11.8 (world avg. 9.3).
Natural increase rate per 1,000 population (1994): 1.6 (world avg. 15.7).
Total fertility rate (avg. births per childbearing woman; 1993): 1.7.
Marriage rate per 1,000 population (1993): 6.1.
Divorce rate per 1,000 population (1993): 2.5.
Life expectancy at birth (1992–93): male 72.5 years; female 77.8 years.
Major causes of death per 100,000 population (1993): malignant neoplasms (cancers) 298.5; ischemic heart disease 277.3; cerebrovascular disease 114.1.

National economy

Budget (1993). Revenue: Dkr 366,819,000,000 (tax revenue 82.1%, of which individual income taxes 28.2%, value-added taxes 23.5%; nontax revenue 15.6%). Expenditures: Dkr 387,411,000,000 (current expenditure 95.9%; development expenditure 4.1%).
National debt (end of year; 1993): Dkr 628,370,000,000.
Tourism (1993): receipts from visitors U.S.$3,052,000,000; expenditures by nationals abroad U.S.$3,214,000,000.
Population economically active (1993): total 2,910,325; activity rate of total population 56.2% (participation rates: ages 16–66, 79.6%; female 46.5%; unemployed [June 1994–May 1995] 11.2%).

Price and earnings indexes (1990 = 100)

	1989	1990	1991	1992	1993	1994	1995[7]
Consumer price index	97.4	100.0	102.4	104.5	105.9	108.0	110.4
Hourly earnings index	96.2	100.0	103.9	106.9	109.9	113.4	...

Household income and expenditure. Average household size (1994) 2.2; income per household (1988) Dkr 199,354 (U.S.$29,613); principal sources of income (1992): wages and salaries 63.3%, transfers 25.9%, self-employment 14.6%, other −3.8%; expenditure (1992): housing 22.7%, food and beverages 18.4%, transportation and communications 15.3%, recreation 8.0%, household furnishings 6.2%, cafe and hotel expenditures 6.1%.
Production (in Dkr '000,000 except as noted). Agriculture, forestry, fishing (value added; 1993): pork 14,577, milk 11,625, beef 4,060, wheat 3,864, flowers and plants 2,476, barley 2,390, furs 1,485, poultry 1,172; roundwood 2,192,000 cu m; fish catch 1,534,058 metric tons. Mining and quarrying (1993): sand and gravel 25,000,000 cu m; chalk 400,000 metric tons. Manufacturing (value added; 1992): food products 28,174; nonelectrical machinery and apparatus 19,609; chemicals and chemical products 17,300; metal products 12,210; printing and publishing 9,919; transport equipment 7,831; electrical machinery and apparatus 7,638. Construction (completed; 1993): residential 1,202,000 sq m; nonresidential 3,190,000 sq m. Energy production (consumption): electricity (kW-hr; 1994) 37,640,000,000 ([1992] 34,595,000,000); coal (metric tons; 1992) none (11,044,000); crude petroleum (barrels; 1993) 64,632,000 ([1992] 64,272,000); petroleum products (metric tons; 1992) 8,310,000 (7,365,000); natural gas (cu m; 1992) 4,025,000,000 (2,284,000,000).
Gross national product (at current market prices; 1993): U.S.$137,610,000,000 (U.S.$26,510 per capita).

Structure of gross domestic product and labour force

	1993 in value Dkr '000,000[8]	% of total value	labour force[2]	% of labour force[2]
Agriculture, fishing	28,576	3.7	140,087	4.8
Mining	6,331	0.8	[9]	[9]
Manufacturing	144,232	18.9	481,179	16.5
Construction	39,680	5.2	147,966	5.1
Public utilities	15,145	2.0	21,054[9]	0.7[9]
Transp. and commun.	71,567	9.4	186,876	6.4
Trade, restaurants	110,386	14.5	432,696	14.9
Finance, real estate	143,597	18.8	233,297	8.0
Pub. admin., defense	172,487	22.6	944,729	32.5
Services	41,870	5.5		
Other	−11,443[10]	−1.5[10]	322,441[11]	11.1[11]
TOTAL	762,425[3]	100.0[3]	2,910,325	100.0

Land use (1993): forested 10.5%; meadows and pastures 4.6%; agricultural and under permanent cultivation 59.9%; other 25.0%.

Foreign trade[12]

Balance of trade (current prices)

	1989	1990	1991	1992	1993	1994
Dkr '000,000	+18,764	+26,404	+32,060	+53,178	+49,973	+120,497
% of total	4.8%	6.5%	7.5%	12.0%	12.0%	29.8%

Imports (1993): Dkr 191,325,000,000 (food products 9.1%, nonelectrical machinery 8.1%, fuels and lubricants 6.2%, transport equipment 6.0%). *Major import sources:* Germany 22.7%; Sweden 10.9%; United Kingdom 7.5%; The Netherlands 6.4%; France 5.3%; Norway 5.2%.
Exports (1993): Dkr 232,884,000,000 (nonelectrical and electrical machinery 23.1%, fresh or frozen swine meat 6.0%, textiles and clothing 4.6%, furniture 4.4%, pharmaceuticals 4.1%). *Major export destinations:* Germany 23.8%; Sweden 10.0%; United Kingdom 8.7%; Norway 6.9%; France 5.4%; United States 5.3%.

Transport and communications

Transport. Railroads (1993): length 1,763 mi, 2,838 km; passenger-mi 2,793,000,000, passenger-km 4,495,000,000[13]; short ton-mi cargo 1,231,000,000, metric ton-km cargo 1,797,000,000[13]. Roads (1993): total length 44,186 mi, 71,111 km (paved 100%). Vehicles (1993): passenger cars 1,674,939; trucks and buses 260,833. Merchant marine (1992): vessels (100 gross tons and over) 456; total deadweight tonnage 7,569,069. Air transport (1993)[14]: passenger-mi 2,714,000,000, passenger-km 4,368,000,000, short ton-mi cargo 91,243,000, metric ton-km cargo 133,212,000, airports (1995) with scheduled flights 13.
Communications. Daily newspapers (1993): total number 42; total circulation 1,668,000; circulation per 1,000 population 321. Radio (1994): 5,200,000 receivers (1 per 1.0 persons). Television (1994): 2,700,200 receivers (1 per 1.9 persons). Telephones (main lines; 1993): 3,059,800 (1 per 1.7 persons).

Education and health

Education (1992–93)

	schools	teachers	students	student/ teacher ratio
Primary/lower secondary (age 7–15)	2,668	56,323	589,123	10.5
Upper secondary (age 16–18)	153	7,500[15]	72,704	9.9[15]
Vocational	204[15]	...	153,987	...
Higher	235[15]	...	165,559	...

Educational attainment (1990). Percentage of population age 25–69 having: primary education 3.0%; completed lower secondary 23.4%; completed upper secondary or vocational 48.0%; advanced vocational 5.0%; undergraduate 7.4%; graduate 3.9%; unknown 9.3%. *Literacy:* virtually 100%.
Health: physicians (1994) 14,497 (1 per 358 persons); hospital beds (1992) 26,764 (1 per 193 persons); infant mortality rate per 1,000 live births (1993) 5.6.
Food (1992): daily per capita caloric intake 3,664 (vegetable products 56%, animal products 44%); 136% of FAO recommended minimum requirement.

Military

Total active duty personnel (1994): 27,000 (army 60.4%, navy 17.0%, air force 22.6%). *Military expenditure as percentage of GNP* (1993): 2.0% (world 3.3%); per capita expenditure U.S.$517.

[1]Excludes the Faroe Islands and Greenland. [2]January 1. [3]Detail does not add to total given because of rounding. [4]1993. [5]Within Greater Copenhagen. [6]1994. [7]June. [8]At factor cost. [9]Public utilities includes Mining. [10]Imputed bank service charges less other producers. [11]Includes 21,795 not adequately defined and 300,646 unemployed. [12]Import figures are f.o.b. in balance of trade and c.i.f. in commodities and trading partners. [13]Danish State Railways only. [14]Danish share of Scandinavian Airlines System; scheduled air service only. [15]1991–92.

Djibouti

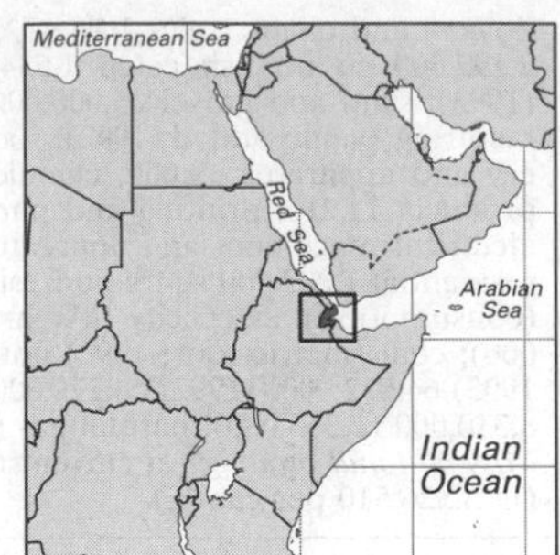

Official name: Jumhūrīyah Jībūtī (Arabic); République de Djibouti (French) (Republic of Djibouti).
Form of government: multiparty republic with one legislative house (National Assembly [65]).
Head of state and government: President.
Capital: Djibouti.
Official languages: Arabic; French.
Official religion: none.
Monetary unit: 1 Djibouti franc (DF) = 100 centimes; valuation (Oct. 6, 1995) 1 U.S.$ = DF 177.72; 1 £ = DF 280.96.

Area and population

		area[1]		population
Districts	Capitals	sq mi	sq km	1982 estimate
ʿAlī Sabīḥ (Ali-Sabieh)	ʿAlī Sabīḥ	925	2,400	15,000
Dikhil	Dikhil	2,775	7,200	30,000
Djibouti	Djibouti	225	600	200,000
Obock	Obock	2,200	5,700	15,000
Tadjoura (Tadjourah)	Tadjoura	2,825	7,300	30,000
TOTAL		8,950	23,200	335,000[2]

Demography

Population (1995): 586,000[3].
Density (1995): persons per sq mi 65.4, persons per sq km 25.3.
Urban-rural (1991): urban 81.1%; rural 18.9%.
Sex distribution (1995): male 49.39%; female 50.61%.
Age breakdown (1995): under 15, 41.8%; 15–29, 27.2%; 30–44, 15.9%; 45–59, 9.9%; 60–74, 4.3%; 75 and over, 0.7%.
Population projection: (2000) 680,000; (2010) 916,000.
Doubling time: 32 years.
Ethnic composition (1983): Somali 61.7%, of which Issa 33.4%, Gadaboursi 15.0%, Issaq 13.3%; Afar 20.0%; Arab (mostly Yemeni) 6.0%; European 4.0%; other (refugees) 8.3%.
Religious affiliation (1988): Sunnī Muslim 96%; Christian 4%, of which Roman Catholic 2%, Protestant 1%, Orthodox 1%.
Major city and towns (1989): Djibouti 450,000[4]; ʿAlī Sabīḥ 4,000; Tadjoura 3,500; Dikhil 3,000.

Vital statistics

Birth rate per 1,000 population (1990–95): 38.1 (world avg. 25.0).
Death rate per 1,000 population (1990–95): 16.1 (world avg. 9.3).
Natural increase rate per 1,000 population (1990–95): 22.0 (world avg. 15.7).
Total fertility rate (avg. births per childbearing woman; 1990–95): 5.8.
Marriage rate per 1,000 population (1982): 6.7.
Divorce rate per 1,000 population (1982): 1.9.
Life expectancy at birth (1990–95): male 46.7 years; female 50.0 years.
Major causes of death (percentage of total deaths [infants and children to age 10, district of Djibouti only]; 1984): diarrhea and acute dehydration 16.0%; malnutrition 16.0%; poisoning 11.0%; tuberculosis 6.0%; acute respiratory disease 6.0%; malaria 6.0%; anemia 6.0%; heart disease 2.0%; kidney disease 1.0%; other ailments 19.0%; no diagnosis 11.0%.

National economy

Budget (1993). Revenue: DF 29,011,000,000 (1990; current receipts 80.2%, of which indirect and direct taxes 72.9%, nontax revenue 7.3%; external development receipts 19.8%). Expenditures: DF 28,990,000,000 (defense 17.5%; education 9.4%; health 7.2%; debt service 5.2%; agriculture 1.6%; commerce 0.4%; industry 0.2%).
Tourism: receipts from visitors (1993) U.S.$13,000,000; expenditures by nationals abroad U.S.$15,000,000.
Production (metric tons except as noted). Agriculture, forestry, fishing (1994): vegetables and melons 22,000, of which tomatoes 1,000, eggplant (1985–86) 66; livestock (number of live animals) 507,000 goats, 470,000 sheep, 190,000 cattle, 62,000 camels, 8,000 asses; fish catch (1993) 300. Mining and quarrying: mineral production limited to locally used construction materials and evaporated salt. Manufacturing (1991): structural detail, n.a.; main items produced include furniture, nonalcoholic beverages, meat and hides, light electromechanical goods, and mineral water. Construction (1989): 53,900 sq m. Energy production (consumption): electricity (kW-hr; 1993) 182,000,000 (182,000,000); firewood and charcoal, n.a. (n.a.)[5]; coal, none (n.a.); crude petroleum, none (n.a.); petroleum products (metric tons; 1993) none (428,000); natural gas, none (n.a.); geothermal, wind, and solar resources are substantial but largely undeveloped.
Population economically active (1991): total 282,000; activity rate of total population 54.2% (participation rates [1988]: over age 10, 67.0%; female 40.0%; unemployed [1987] *c.* 40–50%).

Price and earnings indexes (1990 = 100)

	1988	1989	1990	1991	1992	1993	1994
Consumer price index	90.1	92.8	100.0	106.8	112.1	118.6	120.7
Earnings index	...	...	...	...	...	...	...

Household income and expenditure. Average household size (1985)[6] 7.2; income per household: n.a.; sources of income (1976): wages and salaries 51.6%, self-employment 36.0%, transfer payments 10.5%, other 1.9%; expenditure (expatriate households; 1984): food 50.3%, energy 13.1%, recreation 10.4%, housing 6.4%, clothing 1.7%, personal effects 1.4%, health care 1.0%, household goods 0.3%, other 15.4%.
Public debt (external, outstanding; 1993): U.S.$192,600,000.
Gross national product (at current market prices; 1993): U.S.$448,000,000 (U.S.$780 per capita).

Structure of gross national product and labour force

	1991			
	in value DF '000,000	% of total value	labour force	% of labour force
Agriculture	1,281	2.4	212,000	75.2
Mining	—	—	31,000	11.0
Manufacturing	1,911	3.6		
Construction	2,588	4.8		
Public utilities	5,117	9.5		
Transportation and communications	10,896	20.3	39,000	13.8
Trade	8,718	16.3		
Finance	3,574	6.7		
Pub. admin., defense	17,620	32.9		
Services	1,903	3.5		
TOTAL	53,608	100.0	282,000	100.0

Land use (1993): forested 0.3%; meadows and pastures 8.6%; agricultural and under permanent cultivation[7]; built-on, wasteland, and other 91.1%.

Foreign trade[8]

Balance of trade (current prices)

	1989	1990	1991	1992	1993
DF '000,000	−27,624	−29,735	−31,509	−31,188	−30,669
% of total	35.0%	32.0%	32.9%	35.7%	34.1%

Imports (1991): DF 38,103,000,000 (food, beverages, and tobacco 32.7%; textiles and footwear 11.7%; fossil fuels 9.2%; machinery and electrical machinery 8.5%; transport equipment 7.1%; chemical products 6.2%; base metals and base metal products 6.2%). *Major import sources:* France 26.1%; Ethiopia 8.3%; Japan 7.2%; Italy 6.5%; Saudi Arabia 5.0%; United States 3.7%.
Exports (1991): DF 3,083,000,000 (unspecified special transactions 71.7%; live animals [including camels] 15.5%; food and food products 12.8%). *Major export destinations:* France 57.1%; Yemen 16.0%; Saudi Arabia 5.5%; Somalia 4.1%; Italy 3.2%.

Transport and communications

Transport. Railroads (1989): length 66 mi, 106 km; passenger-mi 182,000,000, passenger-km 293,000,000; short ton-mile cargo 81,700,000[9], metric ton-km cargo 119,300,000[9]. Roads (1991): total length 1,789 mi, 2,879 km (paved 13%). Vehicles (1992): passenger cars 13,000; trucks and buses 3,000. Merchant marine (1992): vessels (100 gross tons and over) 10; total deadweight tonnage 4,090. Air transport (1990)[10]: passenger arrivals 61,700, passenger departures 62,500; cargo loaded 1,145 metric tons, cargo unloaded 6,381 metric tons; airports (1995) with scheduled flights 1.
Communications. Weekly newspapers (1990): total number 1; total circulation 4,000; circulation per 1,000 population 7.6. Radio (1994): total number of receivers 35,000 (1 per 16 persons). Television (1994): total number of receivers 17,000 (1 per 34 persons). Telephones (main lines; 1993): total number of receivers 7,350 (1 per 78 persons).

Education and health

Education (1993)

	schools	teachers	students	student/teacher ratio
Primary (age 6–11)	56	787	33,005	41.9
Secondary (age 12–18)[11] / Voc., teacher tr.	26	362	9,363	28.6
Higher[11]	1	13	108	8.3

Educational attainment: n.a. *Literacy* (1995): percentage of population age 15 and over literate 46.2%; males literate 60.3%; females literate 32.7%.
Health (1989): physicians 97 (1 per 5,258 persons); hospital beds[12] 1,383 (1 per 369 persons); infant mortality rate per 1,000 live births (1990–95) 112.
Food: daily per capita caloric intake 2,338 (vegetable products 89%, animal products 11%); 101% of FAO recommended minimum requirement.

Military

Total active duty personnel (1995): 8,400[13] (army 95.2%, navy 2.4%, air force 2.4%). *Military expenditure as percentage of GNP* (1993): 6.0% (world 3.3%); per capita expenditure U.S.$69.

[1]Original figures are those given in sq km; sq mi equivalent is rounded to appropriate level of generality. [2]Includes 45,000 persons not distributed by district. [3]Excludes about 40,000 Somali and 20,000 Ethiopian refugees. [4]Excludes 20,000 transients. [5]Represents about 15% of total energy consumption. [6]City of Djibouti only. [7]In 1988–89 only 1,005 acres (407 hectares) of land were cultivated. [8]Import figures are c.i.f. [9]Based on total weight of Ethiopian exports and imports transported to and from the port of Djibouti. [10]Djibouti International Airport only. [11]1991. [12]Public health facilities only. [13]Excludes 3,900 French troops.

Dominica

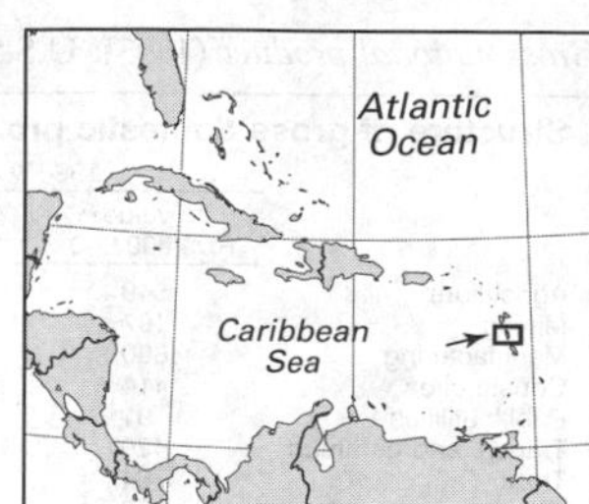

Official name: Commonwealth of Dominica.
Form of government: multiparty republic with one legislative house (House of Assembly [31[1]]).
Chief of state: President.
Head of government: Prime Minister.
Capital: Roseau.
Official language: English.
Official religion: none.
Monetary unit: 1 East Caribbean dollar (EC$) = 100 cents; valuation (Oct. 6, 1995) 1 U.S.$ = EC$2.70; 1 £ = EC$4.27.

Area and population

	area		population
			1991
Parishes	sq mi	sq km	census
St. Andrew	69.3	179.6	11,106
St. David	49.0	126.8	6,977
St. George	20.7	53.5	20,365
St. John	22.5	58.5	4,990
St. Joseph	46.4	120.1	6,183
St. Luke	4.3	11.1	1,552
St. Mark	3.8	9.9	1,943
St. Patrick	32.6	84.4	8,929
St. Paul	26.0	67.4	7,495
St. Peter	10.7	27.7	1,643
TOTAL	285.3[2]	739.0[2]	71,183[3]

Demography

Population (1995). 72,100.
Density (1995): persons per sq mi 248.6, persons per sq km 96.1.
Urban-rural: n.a.
Sex distribution (1991): male 49.78%; female 50.22%.
Age breakdown (1991): under 15, 33.3%; 15–29, 28.3%; 30–44, 16.3%; 45–59, 9.7%; 60 and over, 11.8%; unknown, 0.6%.
Population projection: (2000) 73,000; (2010) 74,000.
Doubling time: 45 years.
Ethnic composition (1991): black 89.1%; mixed race 7.2%; Amerindian/Carib 2.4%; white 0.4%; other 0.7%; not stated 0.2%.
Religious affiliation (1991): Roman Catholic 70.1%; six largest Protestant groups 17.2%, of which Seventh-day Adventist 4.6%, Pentecostal 4.3%, Methodist 4.2%; other 8.9%; nonreligious 2.9%; unknown 0.9%.
Major towns (1991): Roseau 15,853; Portsmouth 3,621; Marigot 2,919; Atkinson 2,518; Mahaut 2,372.

Vital statistics

Birth rate per 1,000 population (1994): 20.5 (world avg. 25.0); (1991) legitimate 24.1%; illegitimate 75.9%.
Death rate per 1,000 population (1994): 5.0 (world avg. 9.3).
Natural increase rate per 1,000 population (1994): 15.5 (world avg. 15.7).
Total fertility rate (avg. births per childbearing woman; 1994): 2.0.
Marriage rate per 1,000 population (1990): 3.2.
Divorce rate per 1,000 population (1990): 0.4.
Life expectancy at birth (1994): male 74.1 years; female 79.9 years.
Major causes of death per 100,000 population (1990): diseases of the circulatory system 273.5, of which ischemic heart diseases 120.8, hypertensive disease 88.8; malignant neoplasms (cancers) 116.6; endocrine, metabolic, and nutritional disorders 51.4; diseases of the respiratory system 43.0; infectious and parasitic diseases 37.5.

National economy

Budget (1994–95). Revenue: EC$286,500,000 (current revenue 58.7%, external loans and sales of securities 22.9%, grants 15.1%, other 3.3%). Expenditures: EC$286,500,000 (current expenditures 54.7%, development expenditures 38.7%, debt repayment 3.5%, other 3.1%).
Public debt (external, outstanding; 1993): U.S.$85,500,000.
Tourism: receipts from visitors (1994) U.S.$34,800,000; expenditures by nationals abroad (1993) U.S.$5,000,000.
Gross national product (at current market prices; 1993): U.S.$193,000,000 (U.S.$2,680 per capita).

Structure of gross domestic product and labour force

	1994		1991	
	in value EC$'000,000	% of total value	labour force[4]	% of labour force[4]
Agriculture	97.5	17.5	7,344	30.8
Mining	3.7	0.7	65	0.3
Manufacturing	35.3	6.3	1,947	8.2
Construction	37.2	6.7	2,819	11.8
Public utilities	20.5	3.7	304	1.3
Transportation and communications	82.7	14.8	1,202	5.0
Trade, hotels, restaurants	67.6	12.1	3,658	15.4
Finance, real estate, insurance	68.5	12.3	810	3.4
Pub. admin., defense	87.7	15.7	1,520	6.4
Services	4.6	0.8	3,446	14.5
Other	52.4[5]	9.4[5]	699	2.9
TOTAL	557.7	100.0	23,814	100.0

Population economically active (1991): total 26,364; activity rate of total population 38.0% (participation rates: ages 15–64, 62.4%; female 34.5%; unemployed [1994] 23%).

Price and earnings indexes (1990 = 100)

	1988	1989	1990	1991	1992	1993	1994
Consumer price index	91.2	96.9	100.0	105.6	111.3	113.1	114.8
Earnings index	...	...	...	...	...	...	...

Household income and expenditure. Average household size (1991) 3.6; income per household: n.a.; expenditure (1984)[7]: food and nonalcoholic beverages 43.1%, housing and utilities 16.1%, transportation 11.6%, clothing and footwear 6.5%, household furnishings 6.0%.
Production (metric tons except as noted). Agriculture, forestry, fishing (1993): bananas 69,000[8], root crops 28,057 (of which dasheens 11,390, yams 7,985, tanias 6,176), coconuts 23,213, grapefruit 12,212, plantains 8,097, oranges 3,157, cacao 842, bay oil 46, cinnamon 39; livestock (number of live animals; 1994) 10,000 goats, 9,000 cattle, 8,000 sheep; roundwood, n.a.; fish catch 795 metric tons. Mining and quarrying: pumice, limestone, and sand and gravel are quarried primarily for local consumption. Manufacturing (value of production in EC$'000; 1994): laundry soap 15,661; toilet soap 13,382; crude coconut oil 3,281; copra 2,525; bottled spring water 323,000 cases[9]; other products include fruit juices, rum, garments, furniture, paint, and cardboard boxes. Construction (value of starts; 1993): U.S.$12,100,000. Energy production (consumption): electricity (kW-hr; 1994) 52,400,000 (43,500,000); coal, none (none); crude petroleum, none (none); petroleum products (metric tons; 1992) none (19,000); natural gas, none (none).
Land use (1993): forested 67.0%; meadows and pastures 3.0%; agricultural and under permanent cultivation 23.0%; other 7.0%.

Foreign trade[10]

Balance of trade (current prices)

	1989	1990	1991	1992	1993
EC$'000,000	−159.9	−129.3	−110.5	−115.9	−131.2
% of total	34.2%	29.9%	26.9%	28.3%	32.6%

Imports (1992): EC$299,200,000 (machinery and transport equipment 28.5%; basic manufactures 25.1%; food 18.4%; chemicals and chemical products 12.8%). *Major import sources:* United States 27.0%; Caricom countries 24.2%; United Kingdom 15.3%; Japan 4.4%; Canada 3.8%.
Exports (1992): EC$151,400,000 (domestic exports 97.1%, of which bananas 55.7%, coconut-based laundry and toilet soaps 20.7%, fresh vegetables and roots and tubers 2.5%, plantains 2.1%, bay oil 1.5%; reexports 2.9%). *Major export destinations*[11]: United Kingdom 47.6%; Caricom countries 27.9%; Italy 9.3%.

Transport and communications

Transport. Railroads: none. Roads (1993): total length 466 mi, 750 km (paved 66%). Vehicles (1992): passenger cars 4,700; trucks and buses 5,500. Merchant marine (1992): vessels (100 gross tons and over) 7; total deadweight tonnage 3,153. Air transport (1991): passenger arrivals 43,312, passenger departures, n.a.; cargo unloaded 259 metric tons, cargo loaded 415 metric tons; airports (1995) with scheduled flights 2.
Communications. Daily newspapers: none[12]. Radio (1994): 45,000 receivers (1 per 1.6 persons). Television (1994): 5,200 receivers (1 per 14 persons). Telephones (main lines; 1994): 15,791 (1 per 4.6 persons).

Education and health

Education (1992–93)

	schools[13]	teachers	students	student/ teacher ratio
Primary	65 }	608	12,795 }	31.2
Secondary	13 }		6,179 }	
Higher	2	40[14]	658[14]	16.5[14]

Educational attainment (1991). Percentage of population age 25 and over having: no formal schooling 4.2%; primary education 78.4%; secondary 11.0%; higher vocational 2.3%; university 2.8%; other/unknown 1.3%. *Literacy* (1990): total population age 15 and over literate, *c.* 42,000 (90.0%).
Health (1994): physicians 23 (1 per 3,130 persons); hospital beds 312 (1 per 231 persons); infant mortality rate per 1,000 live births 10.3.
Food (1992): daily per capita caloric intake 2,778 (vegetable products 83%, animal products 17%); 115% of FAO recommended minimum requirement.

Military

Total active duty personnel (1990): none[15].

[1]Includes 10 nonelective seats. Nine of the 10 nonelective seats are potentially elective according to the constitution. [2]Area breakdown by parish is based on 1961 survey. Total area of Dominica per more recent survey is 290 sq mi (750 sq km). [3]Includes institutionalized population of 1,717. [4]Employed persons only. [5]Net of indirect taxes less imputed banking service charge. [6]Detail does not add to total given because of rounding. [7]Weights of consumer price index components. [8]1994. [9]1990. [10]Imports f.o.b. in balance of trade and c.i.f. in commodities and trading partners. [11]Excludes reexports. [12]Weekly newspapers (1991): total number 2; total circulation 5,050; circulation per 1,000 population 14. [13]1993–94. [14]1991–92. [15]300-member police force includes a coast guard unit.

Dominican Republic

Official name: República Dominicana (Dominican Republic).
Form of government: multiparty republic with two legislative houses (Senate [30]; Chamber of Deputies [120]).
Head of state and government: President.
Capital: Santo Domingo.
Official language: Spanish.
Official religion: none[1].
Monetary unit: 1 Dominican peso (RD$) = 100 centavos; valuation (Oct. 6, 1995) 1 U.S.$ = RD$13.74; 1 £ = RD$21.72.

Area and population

Provinces	Capitals	area sq mi	area sq km	population 1990 estimate
Azua	Azua	938	2,430	195,420
Bahoruco (Baoruco)	Neiba	531	1,376	87,376
Barahona	Barahona	976	2,528	152,405
Dajabón	Dajabón	344	890	64,123
Duarte	San Francisco de Macorís	499	1,292	261,725
El Seíbo	El Seíbo	641	1,659	97,590
Espaillat	Moca	386	1,000	182,248
Hato Mayor	Hato Mayor	514	1,330	77,823
Independencia	Jimaní	719	1,861	43,077
La Altagracia	Higüey	1,191	3,084	111,241
La Estrelleta	Elías Piña	690	1,788	72,651
La Romana	La Romana	209	541	169,223
La Vega	La Vega	916	2,373	303,047
María Trinidad Sánchez	Nagua	506	1,310	125,148
Monseñor Nouel	Bonao	388	1,004	124,794
Monte Cristi	Monte Cristi	768	1,989	92,678
Monte Plata	Monte Plata	841	2,179	174,799
Pedernales	Pedernales	373	967	18,896
Peravia	Baní	626	1,622	186,810
Puerto Plata	Puerto Plata	726	1,881	229,738
Salcedo	Salcedo	206	533	110,216
Samaná	Samaná	382	989	73,002
San Cristóbal	San Cristóbal	604	1,564	320,921
San Juan	San Juan	1,375	3,561	266,628
San Pedro de Macorís	San Pedro de Macorís	450	1,166	197,862
Sánchez Ramírez	Cotuí	453	1,174	140,635
Santiago	Santiago de los Caballeros	1,205	3,122	704,835
Santiago Rodríguez	Sabaneta	394	1,020	61,570
Santo Domingo[2]	—	570	1,477	2,411,895
Valverde	Mao	220	570	111,470
TOTAL		18,704[3]	48,443[3]	7,169,846[4]

Demography

Population (1995): 7,823,000.
Density (1995): persons per sq mi 418.3, persons per sq km 161.5.
Urban-rural (1995): urban 64.6%; rural 35.4%.
Sex distribution (1995): male 50.82%; female 49.18%.
Age breakdown (1995): under 15, 35.1%; 15–29, 29.0%; 30–44, 19.8%; 45–59, 9.9%; 60–74, 4.9%; 75 and over, 1.3%.
Population projection: (2000) 8,495,000; (2010) 9,708,000.
Doubling time: 32 years.
Ethnic composition (1990): mixed 70%; white 15%; black 15%.
Religious affiliation (1992): Roman Catholic 91.2%; other 8.8%.
Major urban centres (1993): Santo Domingo 2,100,000; Santiago de los Caballeros 690,000; La Vega 189,000[5]; San Pedro de Macorís 137,000[5].

Vital statistics

Birth rate per 1,000 population (1993): 30.0 (world avg. 25.0).
Death rate per 1,000 population (1993): 8.0 (world avg. 9.3).
Natural increase rate per 1,000 population (1993): 22.0 (world avg. 15.7).
Total fertility rate (avg. births per childbearing woman; 1994): 2.8.
Marriage rate per 1,000 population (1987): 2.3.
Life expectancy at birth (1993): male 60.0 years; female 64.0 years.
Major causes of death per 100,000 population (1985)[6]: diseases of the circulatory system 165; infectious and parasitic diseases 85; malignant neoplasms (cancers) 45; diseases of the respiratory system 41.

National economy

Budget (1994). Revenue: RD$22,498,000,000 (tax revenue 85.4%, of which taxes on goods and services 43.1%, import duties 26.9%, income taxes 14.3%; grants and loans 8.5%; nontax revenue 6.1%). Expenditures: RD$22,933,000,000 (development expenditure 59.5%; current expenditure 40.5%).
Public debt (external, outstanding; 1993): U.S.$3,763,000,000.
Production (metric tons except as noted). Agriculture, forestry, fishing (value of production in RD$'000,000; 1994): sugarcane 2,034, chicken meat 1,879, rice 1,742, coffee 1,470, milk 1,391, plantains 1,301, beef 1,090, beans 859, cacao beans 659, bananas 545, eggs 517, cassava 474, fish 120; roundwood (1993) 982,000 cu m. Mining (1994): nickel 30,757; gold 51,400 troy oz[7]. Manufacturing (1994)[8]: cement 1,276,000; refined sugar 100,600; beer 2,200,000 hectolitres; rum 437,000 hectolitres; cigarettes 222,300,000 20-unit packs; cigars 65,000,000 units[9]. Construction (value of authorized construction in RD$'000,000; 1987): residential 352; nonresidential 253. Energy production (consumption): electricity (kW-hr; 1994) 5,734,000,000 (3,427,000,000); coal (metric tons; 1993) none (120,000); crude petroleum (barrels; 1993) none (14,286,000); petroleum products (metric tons; 1993) 1,907,000 (3,236,000); natural gas, none (none).

Gross national product (1993): U.S.$8,039,000,000 (U.S.$1,080 per capita).

Structure of gross domestic product and labour force

	1994[10] in value RD$'000,000	1994[10] % of total value	1981 labour force	1981 % of labour force
Agriculture	549	12.6	420,463	22.0
Mining	107	2.4	4,743	0.2
Manufacturing	800	18.4	224,437	11.7
Construction	414	9.5	80,850	4.3
Public utilities	91	2.1	13,891	0.7
Transp. and commun.	420	9.6	40,470	2.1
Trade	764	17.5	192,181	10.0
Finance, real estate	457	10.5	22,369	1.2
Pub. admin., defense	386	8.9	363,125	18.9
Services	370	8.5		
Other	—	—	552,859[11]	28.9[11]
TOTAL	4,358	100.0	1,915,388	100.0

Tourism (1994): receipts U.S.$1,148,000,000; expenditures U.S.$171,000,000.
Population economically active (1991)[12]: total 2,758,000; activity rate of total population 37.6% (participation rates: age 10 and over, 50.3%; female 29.0%; unemployed [1994] 28.0%).

Price and earnings indexes (1990 = 100)

	1989	1990	1991	1992	1993	1994	1995
Consumer price index	62.7	100.0	153.9	160.9	169.4	183.4	205.3[13]
Monthly earnings index	64.1	100.0	125.3	150.8	...	...	...

Household income and expenditure. Average household size (1981) 5.1; average income: n.a.; sources of income: n.a.; expenditure (1980–85): food and beverages 46.0%, housing 10.0%, household goods 8.0%.
Land use (1993): forested 12.4%; meadows and pastures 43.2%; agricultural and under permanent cultivation 30.0%; other 14.4%.

Foreign trade[14]

Balance of trade (current prices)

	1989	1990	1991	1992	1993	1994
U.S.$'000,000	−1,039	−1,058	−1,071	−1,613	−1,607	−1,631
% of total	36.0%	41.9%	44.8%	58.9%	61.1%	55.9%

Imports (1993): U.S.$2,118,000,000 (crude petroleum and petroleum products 21.4%; agricultural products 19.2%, of which cereals 6.2%; forest products 3.9%). *Major import sources* (1994)[12]: U.S. 41%; Venezuela 7%; Mexico 7%; Japan 6%; Netherlands Antilles 4%.
Exports (1994): U.S.$644,000,000[15] (ferronickel 28.4%; raw sugar 18.2%; raw coffee 9.7%; cacao 8.1%; tobacco and cigarettes 3.5%). *Major export destinations:* U.S. 52.3%; The Netherlands 12.9%; Puerto Rico 6.3%; South Korea 5.8%; Belgium 5.1%.

Transport and communications

Transport. Railroads (1991)[16]: length 1,028 mi, 1,655 km. Roads (1991): total length 11,400 km (paved 51%). Vehicles (1993): passenger cars 117,800; trucks and buses 78,900. Merchant marine (1992): vessels (100 gross tons and over) 28; total deadweight tonnage 10,369. Air transport (1992): passenger-km 1,431,000,000; metric ton-km cargo 75,000,000; airports (1995) 5.
Communications. Daily newspapers (1992): total number 11; total circulation 265,000; circulation per 1,000 population 35. Radio (1994): 1,180,000 receivers (1 per 6.6 persons). Television (1994): 728,000 receivers (1 per 11 persons). Telephones (main lines; 1993): 552,400 (1 per 14 persons).

Education and health

Education (1993–94)

	schools	teachers	students	student/teacher ratio
Primary (age 7–14)	6,207	39,464	1,336,211	33.9
Secondary (age 15–18)	...	11,605	232,999	20.1
Higher[17, 18]	7	5,041	68,301	13.5

Educational attainment (1981). Percentage of population age 25 and over having: no formal schooling 48.0%; incomplete primary education 31.7%; complete primary 4.0%; secondary 14.0%; higher 2.3%. *Literacy* (1995): total population age 15 and over literate, *c.* 4,164,000 (82.1%); males literate, *c.* 2,118,000 (82.0%); females literate, *c.* 2,046,000 (82.2%).
Health (1993): physicians[19] 3,056 (1 per 2,511 persons); hospital beds[19] 12,618 (1 per 608 persons); infant mortality rate (1993) 66.0.
Food (1992): daily per capita caloric intake 2,286 (vegetable products 86%, animal products 14%); 101% of FAO recommended minimum.

Military

Total active duty personnel (1995): 24,500 (army 61.2%, navy 16.3%, air force 22.5%). *Military expenditure as percentage of GNP* (1993): 1.4% (world 3.3%); per capita expenditure U.S.$14.

[1]Roman Catholicism is the state religion per concordat with Vatican City. [2]National district. [3]Total includes 63 sq mi (163 sq km) of area not accounted for by province. [4]Preliminary 1993 census total released in late 1994 was 7,089,000. [5]1989. [6]Projected rates based on about 60% of total deaths. [7]Gold production resumed in May 1994. [8]Excludes free-zone sector for reexport (mostly ready-made garments) employing (1994) 164,000; 1992 value added of free-zone sector equaled RD$3,800,000,000. [9]Export production for 1992. [10]At prices of 1970. [11]Not adequately defined (421,628) and those seeking work for first time (131,231). [12]Estimated figures. [13]July. [14]Excludes free zones. [15]1992 reexports of free zones were estimated to equal U.S.$1,191,000,000. [16]Most track serves the sugar industry only. [17]1992–93. [18]Universities only. [19]Public sector only.

Ecuador

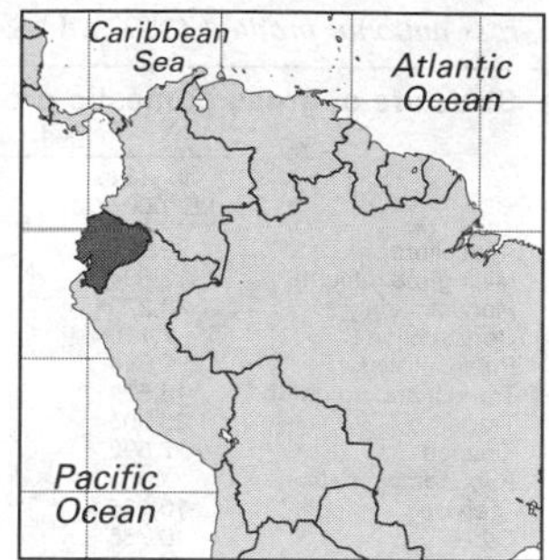

Official name: República del Ecuador (Republic of Ecuador).
Form of government: unitary multiparty republic with one legislative house (National Congress [77]).
Head of state and government: President.
Capital: Quito.
Official language: Spanish.
Official religion: none.
Monetary unit: 1 Sucre (S/.) = 100 centavos; valuation (Oct. 6, 1995) 1 U.S.$ = S/. 2,626; 1 £ = S/. 4,151.

Area and population

Regions / Provinces	Capitals	area sq mi	area sq km	population 1990 census
Amazonica				
Morona-Santiago	Macas	13,100	33,930	84,216
Napo	Tena	9,918	25,690	103,387
Pastaza	Puyo	11,496	29,774	41,811
Sucumbíos	Nueva Loja	7,076	18,327	76,952
Zamora-Chinchipe	Zamora	8,923	23,111	66,167
Costa				
El Oro	Machala	2,259	5,850	412,572
Esmeraldas	Esmeraldas	5,884	15,239	306,628
Guayas	Guayaquil	7,916	20,503	2,515,146
Los Ríos	Babahoyo	2,770	7,175	527,559
Manabí	Portoviejo	7,289	18,879	1,031,927
Insular				
Galápagos	Puerto Baquerizo Moreno	3,093	8,010	9,785
Sierra				
Azuay	Cuenca	3,137	8,125	506,090
Bolívar	Guaranda	1,521	3,940	155,088
Cañar	Azogues	1,205	3,122	189,347
Carchi	Tulcán	1,392	3,605	141,482
Chimborazo	Riobamba	2,536	6,569	364,682
Cotopaxi	Latacunga	2,344	6,072	276,324
Imbabura	Ibarra	1,760	4,559	265,499
Loja	Loja	4,257	11,026	384,698
Pichincha	Quito	4,987	12,915	1,756,228
Tungurahua	Ambato	1,288	3,335	361,980
TOTAL		105,037[1,2]	272,045[2]	9,648,189[3]

Demography

Population (1995): 11,460,000.
Density (1995): persons per sq mi 109.1, persons per sq km 42.1.
Urban-rural (1994): urban 59.9%; rural 40.1%.
Sex distribution (1994): male 50.25%; female 49.75%.
Age breakdown (1995): under 15, 36.4%; 15–29, 29.0%; 30–44, 18.5%; 45–59, 9.6%; 60–74, 5.0%; 75 and over, 1.5%.
Population projection: (2000) 12,646,000; (2010) 14,899,000.
Doubling time: 34 years.
Ethnic composition (1989): Amerindian 40.0%; mestizo 40.0%; white 15.0%; black 5.0%.
Religious affiliation (1992): Roman Catholic 93.0%; other 7.0%.
Major cities (1990): Guayaquil 1,508,844; Quito 1,100,847; Cuenca 194,981; Machala 144,197; Portoviejo 132,937.

Vital statistics

Birth rate per 1,000 population (1993): 26.5[4] (world avg. 25.0); (1982) legitimate 67.9%; illegitimate 32.1%.
Death rate per 1,000 population (1993): 5.8[4] (world avg. 9.3).
Natural increase rate per 1,000 population (1993): 20.7[4] (world avg. 15.7).
Total fertility rate (avg. births per childbearing woman; 1994): 3.1.
Marriage rate per 1,000 population (1992): 6.4[4,5].
Divorce rate per 1,000 population (1992): 0.6[4,5].
Life expectancy at birth (1994): male 67.5 years; female 72.6 years.
Major causes of death per 100,000 population (1992): circulatory diseases 93.1; accidents, poisoning, and violence 66.7; infectious and parasitic diseases 52.0; neoplasms (cancers) 50.0; respiratory diseases 40.6.

National economy

Budget (1992). Revenue: S/. 3,008,560,000,000 (income from petroleum 51.1%, production and sales tax 22.7%, import duties 9.1%, income taxes 6.5%). Expenditures: S/. 3,102,440,000,000 (debt service 33.1%, public services 23.7%, education 19.5%, health 6.4%, transport and communications 4.1%).
Production (metric tons except as noted). Agriculture, forestry, fishing (1994): sugarcane 7,110,000, bananas 4,715,000, rice 1,366,000, plantains 978,000, corn (maize) 495,000, potatoes 425,000, soybeans 158,000, cacao 84,000; livestock (number of live animals) 4,963,000 cattle, 2,540,000 pigs, 1,728,000 sheep, 59,000,000 chickens; roundwood (1993) 7,499,000 cu m; fish catch (1993) 330,720. Mining and quarrying (1992): limestone 3,078,000; gold 12,000 kg. Manufacturing (value added in S/. '000,000; 1990): food products 175,126, of which beverages (including liquors) 25,606; textiles 72,554; chemical products 71,241; metal products 33,686. Construction (in S/.; 1992)[6]: residential 93,166,704,000; nonresidential 58,102,274,000. Energy production (consumption): electricity (kW-hr; 1992) 7,165,000,000 (7,165,000,000); crude petroleum (barrels; 1992) 119,470,000 (44,418,000); petroleum products (metric tons; 1992) 6,230,000 (5,277,000); natural gas (cu m; 1992) 100,000,000 (100,000,000).
Tourism (1993): receipts U.S.$230,000,000; expenditures U.S.$190,000,000.
Public debt (external, outstanding; 1993): U.S.$9,935,000,000.

Gross national product (1993): U.S.$13,217,000,000 (U.S.$1,170 per capita).

Structure of gross domestic product and labour force

	1993 in value S/. '000,000[7]	1993 % of total value	1990 labour force	1990 % of labour force
Agriculture	34,555	17.2	1,035,712	30.8
Mining	35,866	17.8	20,870	0.6
Manufacturing	22,163	11.0	370,338	11.0
Construction	5,032	2.5	196,716	5.9
Public utilities	2,980	1.5	12,660	0.4
Transp. and commun.	17,992	8.9	131,084	3.9
Trade	29,919	14.9	476,730	14.2
Finance	33,269	16.5	81,357	2.4
Pub. admin., defense	15,754	7.8	838,129	24.9
Services	27,899	13.8		
Other	−23,982[8]	−11.9[8]	196,171[9]	5.8[9]
TOTAL	201,447	100.0	3,359,767	100.0[1]

Population economically active (1990): total 3,359,767; activity rate of total population 34.8% (participation rates: ages 8 and over, 44.0%; female 26.4%; unemployed 1.3%).

Price and earnings indexes (1990 = 100)

	1988	1989	1990	1991	1992	1993	1994
Consumer price index	38.3	67.3	100.0	148.7	229.9	333.3	424.3
Hourly earnings index[10]	68.7	100.0	100.0	125.0	187.5	...	...

Household income and expenditure. Average household size (1990) 4.1; average annual income per household (1982) S/. 28,747 (U.S.$956); sources of income (1993): self-employment 76.9%, wages 17.4%, transfer payments 3.6%, other 2.1%; expenditure (1991): food and tobacco 38.2%, transportation and communications 12.4%, clothing 10.4%, household furnishings 7.7%, housing and utilities 5.3%, health care 4.1%.
Land use (1993): forested 56.4%; meadows and pastures 17.9%; agricultural and under permanent cultivation 10.9%; other 14.8%.

Foreign trade[11]

Balance of trade (current prices)

	1989	1990	1991	1992	1993	1994
U.S.$'000,000	+719.7	+1,077.7	+736.0	+1,031.9	+680.7	+508.0
% of total	18.0%	24.7%	14.1%	20.7%	13.3%	7.3%

Imports (1993): U.S.$2,552,700,000 (1992; industrial raw materials 33.4%, industrial capital goods 21.9%, transport equipment 13.9%, nondurable consumer goods 9.5%, durable consumer goods 9.2%). *Major import sources* (1992): U.S. 32.5%; EEC 21.4%; Latin American Integration Association 19.3%; Japan 13.0%.
Exports (1993): U.S.$2,960,600,000 (crude petroleum 42.3%, bananas 18.5%, shrimp 15.5%, petroleum products 3.3%, coffee 2.7%, prepared fish 2.3%). *Major export destinations* (1992): U.S. 46.8%; EEC 15.5%; Latin American Integration Association 13.4%; Andean Group 5.8%; Taiwan 2.1%.

Transport and communications

Transport. Railroads (1993): route length 956 km; passenger-km 48,200,000; metric ton-km cargo 5,300,000. Roads (1993): total length 45,400 km (paved 14%). Vehicles (1993): passenger cars 191,746; trucks and buses 292,830. Merchant marine (1992): vessels (100 gross tons and over) 154; deadweight tonnage 504,127. Air transport (1993): passenger-km 1,255,000,000; metric ton-km cargo 64,200,000; airports (1995) 14.
Communications. Daily newspapers (1992): total number 36; total circulation 688,000; circulation per 1,000 population 62. Radio (1994): 3,240,000 receivers (1 per 3.5 persons). Television (1994): 900,000 receivers (1 per 12 persons). Telephones (main lines; 1993): 598,300 (1 per 19 persons).

Education and health

Education (1990–91)

	schools[12]	teachers	students	student/teacher ratio
Primary (age 4–12)	16,146	61,039	1,846,338	30.2
Secondary (age 12–18) / Vocational	2,207	60,126	785,844	13.1
Higher	21	12,856[13]	206,541[13]	16.1[13]

Educational attainment (1990). Percentage of population age 25 and over having: no formal schooling 2.2%; incomplete primary 54.3%; primary 28.0%; postsecondary 15.5%. *Literacy* (1990): total population age 15 and over literate 5,217,543 (88.3%); males 2,616,192 (90.5%); females 2,601,351 (86.2%).
Health (1992): physicians 12,853 (1 per 836 persons); hospital beds 17,253 (1 per 623 persons); infant mortality rate per 1,000 live births (1994) 39.3.
Food (1992): daily per capita caloric intake 2,583 (vegetable products 86%, animal products 14%); 113% of FAO minimum requirement.

Military

Total active duty personnel (1994): 57,500 (army 87.0%, navy 7.8%, air force 5.2%). *Military expenditure as percentage of GNP* (1993): 1.1% (world 3.3%); per capita expenditure U.S.$14.

[1]Detail does not add to total given because of rounding. [2]Includes 884 sq mi (2,289 sq km) in nondelimited areas. [3]Total includes 70,621 persons in nondelimited areas. [4]Excluding nomadic Indian tribes. [5]Based on incomplete registration. [6]Authorized construction in Cuenca, Guayaquil, and Quito only. [7]At constant 1975 prices. [8]Statistical discrepancy. [9]Includes unemployed persons not previously employed. [10]General minimum wage. [11]Import figures are f.o.b. in balance of trade and c.i.f. for commodities and trading partners. [12]1986–87. [13]1989–90.

Egypt

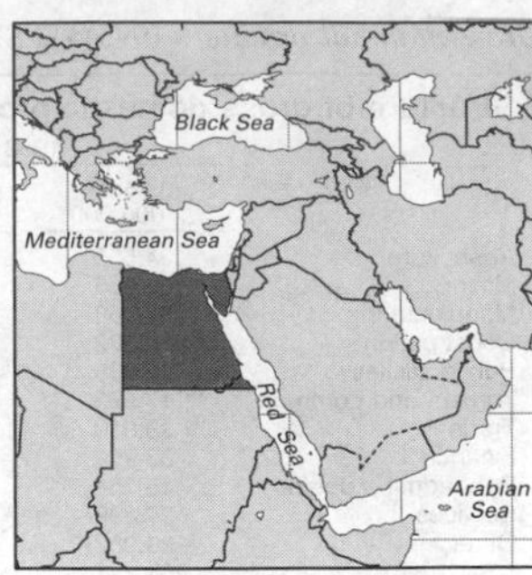

Official name: Jumhūrīyah Miṣr al-ʿArabīyah (Arab Republic of Egypt).
Form of government: republic with one legislative house (People's Assembly [454[1]]).
Chief of state: President.
Head of government: Prime Minister.
Capital: Cairo.
Official language: Arabic.
Official religion: Islam.
Monetary unit: 1 Egyptian pound (LE) = 100 piastres; valuation (Oct. 6, 1995) 1 U.S.$ = LE 3.40; 1 £ = LE 5.37.

Area and population

Regions / Governorates	Capitals	area sq mi	area sq km	population 1994[2] estimate
Frontier				
al-Baḥr al-Aḥmar	al-Ghurdaqah	78,643	203,685	111,000
Maṭrūḥ	Marsā Maṭrūḥ	81,897	212,112	179,000
Janūb Sīnāʾ	aṭ-Ṭūr	12,796	33,140	34,000
Shamāl Sīnāʾ	al-ʿArish	10,646	27,574	213,000
al-Wādī al-Jadīd	al-Kharijah	145,369	376,505	134,000
Lower Egypt				
al-Buḥayrah	Damanhūr	3,911	10,130	3,895,000
ad-Daqahlīyah	al-Manṣūrah	1,340	3,471	4,144,000
Dumyāṭ	Dumyāṭ	227	589	879,000
al-Gharbīyah	Ṭanṭā	750	1,942	3,373,000
al-Ismāʿīlīyah (Ismailia)	—	557	1,442	665,000
Kafr ash-Shaykh	Kafr ash-Shaykh	1,327	3,437	2,209,000
al-Minūfīyah	Shibīn al-Kawm	592	1,532	2,619,000
al-Qalyūbīyah	Banhā	387	1,001	2,983,000
ash-Sharqīyah	az-Zaqāzīq	1,614	4,180	4,125,000
Upper Egypt				
Aswān	Aswān	262	679	1,017,000
Asyūṭ	Asyūṭ	600	1,553	2,762,000
Banī Suwayf	Banī Suwayf	510	1,322	1,785,000
al-Fayyūm	al-Fayyūm	705	1,827	1,943,000
al-Jīzah	al-Jīzah	32,878	85,153	4,400,000
al-Minyā	al-Minyā	873	2,262	3,288,000
Qinā	Qinā	715[3]	1,851[3]	2,694,000
Sawhāj	Sawhāj	597	1,547	2,982,000
Urban				
Būr Saʿīd (Port Said)	—	28	72	460,000
al-Iskandarīyah (Alexandria)	—	1,034	2,679	3,382,000
al-Qāhirah (Cairo)	—	83	214	6,849,000
al-Uqṣur (Luxor)	—	...[3]	...[3]	155,000
as-Suways (Suez)	—	6,888	17,840	393,000
TOTAL		385,229	997,739	57,673,000

Demography

Population (1995): 59,690,000.
Density (1995): persons per sq mi 155.0, persons per sq km 55.8.
Urban-rural (1995): urban 44.8%; rural 55.2%.
Sex distribution (1993): male 51.06%; female 48.94%.
Age breakdown (1995): under 15, 38.0%; 15–29, 26.4%; 30–44, 19.3%; 45–59, 9.8%; 60–74, 5.3%; 75 and over, 1.2%.
Population projection: (2000) 66,091,000; (2010) 75,751,000.
Doubling time: 29 years.
Ethnic composition (1986): Egyptian 99.9%; other 0.1%.
Religious affiliation (1990): Sunnī Muslim *c.* 90%; Christian *c.* 10%[4].
Major cities (1994): Cairo 6,849,000; Alexandria 3,382,000; al-Jīzah 2,144,000[5].

Vital statistics

Birth rate per 1,000 population (1993): 28.2 (world avg. 25.0).
Death rate per 1,000 population (1993): 6.9 (world avg. 9.3).
Natural increase rate per 1,000 population (1993): 21.3 (world avg. 15.7).
Total fertility rate (avg. births per childbearing woman; 1995): 3.9.
Life expectancy at birth (1992): male 65.0 years; female 69.3 years.
Major causes of death per 100,000 population (1987): diseases of the circulatory system 314.4; diseases of the respiratory system 140.7; infectious and parasitic diseases 98.9; malignant neoplasms (cancers) 22.0.

National economy

Budget (1995–96). Revenue: LE 66,195,000,000 (1993–94; general taxes 60.3%, of which sales taxes 15.7%, customs duties 11.7%; oil revenue 8.9%; Suez Canal fees 5.0%). Expenditures: LE 71,492,000,000 (1993–94; debt servicing 29.7%; wages and salaries 19.9%; defense 10.6%; pensions 7.0%).
Public debt (external, outstanding; 1993): U.S.$36,603,000,000.
Production (metric tons except as noted). Agriculture, forestry, fishing (1994): sugarcane 11,900,000, corn (maize) 4,883,000, tomatoes 4,600,000, rice 4,582,000, wheat 4,437,000, oranges 1,300,000, sorghum 717,000, cotton (lint) 314,000; livestock (number of live animals) 3,382,000 sheep, 3,210,000 goats, 3,200,000 buffalo, 3,070,000 cattle, 38,000,000 chickens, 10,380,000 pigeons[6]; roundwood (1993) 2,404,000 cu m; fish catch (1993) 302,829. Mining and quarrying (1993): iron ore 2,190,000; salt 972,000; clay 593,000. Manufacturing (1993–94): cement 17,430,000; nitrate fertilizers 5,437,000[7]; reinforcing iron 1,681,000; sugar 1,311,000; phosphate fertilizers 970,000[7]; cotton yarn 336,000[7]; refrigerators 373,000 units[7]; automobiles 6,800 units[7]. Construction (1992–93): urban residential units 123,098. Energy production (consumption): electricity (kW-hr; 1993) 47,500,000,000 (39,320,000,000); coal (metric tons; 1992) n.a. (1,155,000); crude petroleum (barrels; 1993) 333,200,000 (178,300,000); petroleum products (metric tons; 1993) 24,209,000 (19,269,000); natural gas (cu m; 1993) 11,620,000,000 (11,620,000,000).

Gross national product (1993): U.S.$36,679,000,000 (U.S.$660 per capita).

Structure of gross domestic product and labour force

	1993–94[8] in value LE '000,000	1993–94[8] % of total value	1989 labour force	1989 % of labour force
Agriculture	22,975	16.5	6,335,200	39.5
Mining (petroleum)	13,694	9.8	43,300	0.3
Manufacturing	23,275[9]	16.7[9]	1,958,700	12.2
Construction	7,110	5.1	990,200	6.2
Public utilities	2,844	2.0	99,900	0.6
Transp. and commun.	15,504[10]	11.1[10]	780,200	4.9
Trade	25,305	18.2	1,340,000	8.4
Finance	7,592	5.5	255,300	1.6
Pub. admin., defense, services	10,125	7.3	3,115,500	19.4
Other	10,756	7.7	1,107,900[11]	6.9[11]
TOTAL	139,180	100.0[12]	16,033,600[13]	100.0[13]

Population economically active (1993–94): total 16,013,000; activity rate 27.8% (participation rates: ages 15–64, 48.9%; unemployed 9.8%).

Price and earnings indexes (1990 = 100)

	1989	1990	1991	1992	1993	1994	1995[14]
Consumer price index	85.6	100.0	119.7	136.1	152.5	165.0	176.7
Annual earnings index[15]	95.3	100.0	119.9	133.9	155.4	...	...

Household income and expenditure. Average household size (1986) 4.9; expenditure (1986–87)[16]: food 55.7%, clothing 10.9%, housing 10.5%.
Tourism (1993): receipts U.S.$1,332,000,000; expenditures U.S.$1,048,000,000.
Land use (1993): agricultural 2.8%; other 97.2%.

Foreign trade

Balance of trade (current prices)[17]

	1989	1990	1991	1992	1993	1994
U.S.$'000,000	−5,933	−6,699	−5,975	−5,501	−7,315	−7,651
% of total	50.5%	48.2%	43.6%	44.7%	51.7%	55.5%

Imports (1993–94)[18]: U.S.$10,715,600,000 (machinery and transport equipment 27.5%; foodstuffs 18.1%; chemical products 10.9%; base metals 9.4%). *Major import sources:* EU 36.3%; U.S. 17.7%; other western European countries 13.0%; Russia and eastern Europe 2.3%.
Exports (1993–94): U.S.$3,064,800,000 (petroleum and petroleum products 48.9%; cotton yarn, textiles, and fabrics 16.2%; engineering and metallurgical goods 10.7%). *Major export destinations:* EU 40.6%; U.S. 16.1%.

Transport and communications

Transport. Railroads (1992–93): length 8,487 km; passenger-km 47,992,000,000; metric ton-km cargo 2,332,000,000. Roads (1993): length 47,387 km (paved 73%). Vehicles (1993): passenger cars 1,119,727; trucks and buses 466,650. Merchant marine (1992): vessels (100 gross tons and over) 444; total deadweight tonnage 1,685,245. Inland water (1993): Suez Canal, number of transits 16,946; metric ton cargo 380,800,000. Air transport (1994)[19]: passenger-km 5,531,000,000; metric ton-km cargo 100,476,000; airports (1995) 14.
Communications. Daily newspapers (1992): total number 16; total circulation 2,426,000[20]; circulation per 1,000 population 44[20]. Radio (1994): 16,450,000 receivers (1 per 3.5 persons). Television (1994): 5,000,000 receivers (1 per 11.7 persons). Telephones (main lines; 1993): 2,374,800 (1 per 23.5 persons).

Education and health

Education (1992–93)

	schools	teachers[21]	students	student/ teacher ratio
Primary (age 6–11)[22]	14,654	273,055	6,333,703	...
Secondary (age 12–17)[22]	7,307	201,040	4,071,936	...
Vocational	1,351	77,951	1,464,836	...
Teacher training	56	...	2,664	...
Higher	12[23]	36,609[24]	542,602	...

Educational attainment (1986). Percentage of population age 25 and over having: no formal education 64.1%; some primary education 16.5%; primary and secondary 14.8%; higher 4.6%. *Literacy* (1990): total population age 15 and over literate 15,470,000 (48.4%); males 62.9%; females 33.8%.
Health: physicians (1990) 31,312 (1 per 1,698 persons); hospital beds (1993) 108,006 (1 per 529 persons); infant mortality rate (1994) 76.0.
Food (1992): daily per capita caloric intake 3,335 (vegetable products 94%, animal products 6%); 125% of FAO recommended minimum requirement.

Military

Total active duty personnel (1995): 436,000 (army 71.1%, navy 3.7%, air force [including air defense] 25.2%). *Military expenditure as percentage of GNP* (1993): 4.3% (world 3.7%); per capita expenditure U.S.$28.

[1]Includes 10 nonelective seats. [2]January 1. [3]The area of al-Uqṣur (Luxor) is included with Qinā governorate. [4]According to the 1986 census, the Christian population of Egypt was 5.9% of the total; this figure is considered by some external authorities to understate the Christian population by as much as 60%. [5]1992. [6]1991. [7]1992–93. [8]At factor cost. [9]Manufacturing includes mining but excludes petroleum. [10]Transportation includes earnings from traffic on the Suez Canal. [11]Unemployed and those seeking work for the first time. [12]Detail does not add to total given because of rounding. [13]Total includes 7,400 persons not classifiable by sector. [14]June. [15]Average nominal wages for each fiscal year (*e.g.,* 1990–91). [16]Weight of consumer price components; urban households only. [17]Import figures are f.o.b. except for 1994. [18]Figures are c.i.f. [19]Egypt Air only. [20]Partial circulation only. [21]1991–92. [22]Data exclude 1,770 primary and 1,449 secondary schools in the al-Azhar education system. [23]Universities only. [24]Excludes al-Azhar University.

El Salvador

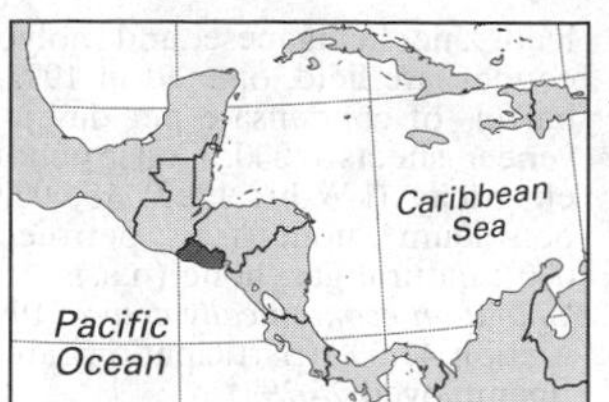

Official name: República de El Salvador (Republic of El Salvador).
Form of government: republic with one legislative house (Legislative Assembly [84]).
Chief of state and government: President.
Capital: San Salvador.
Official language: Spanish.
Official religion: none[1].
Monetary unit: 1 colón (₡) = 100 centavos; valuation (Oct. 6, 1995) 1 U.S.$ = ₡8.75; 1 £ = ₡13.83.

Area and population

Departments	Capitals	area sq mi	area sq km	population 1992 census[2]
Ahuachapán	Ahuachapán	479	1,240	260,563
Cabañas	Sensuntepeque	426	1,104	136,293
Chalatenango	Chalatenango	779	2,017	180,627
Cuscatlán	Cojutepeque	292	756	167,290
La Libertad	Nueva San Salvador	638	1,653	522,071
La Paz	Zacatecoluca	473	1,224	246,147
La Unión	La Unión	801	2,074	251,143
Morazán	San Francisco	559	1,447	166,772
San Miguel	San Miguel	802	2,077	380,442
San Salvador	San Salvador	342	886	1,477,766
San Vicente	San Vicente	457	1,184	135,471
Santa Ana	Santa Ana	781	2,023	451,620
Sonsonate	Sonsonate	473	1,226	354,641
Usulután	Usulután	822	2,130	317,079
TOTAL		8,124	21,041	5,047,025

Demography

Population (1995): 5,768,000.
Density (1995): persons per sq mi 710.0, persons per sq km 274.1.
Urban-rural (1993): urban 44.6%; rural 55.4%.
Sex distribution (1992): male 47.97%; female 52.03%.
Age breakdown (1995): under 15, 40.7%; 15–29, 30.2%; 30–44, 14.0%; 45–59, 8.9%; 60–74, 4.9%; 75 and over, 1.3%.
Population projection: (2000) 6,425,000; (2010) 7,772,000.
Doubling time: 26 years.
Ethnic composition (1993): mestizo (white and Indian) 89.0%; Amerindian 10.0%; white 1.0%.
Religious affiliation (1993): Roman Catholic 75.0%; other (mostly fundamentalist Protestant, Mormon, or Jehovah's Witness) 25.0%.
Major cities (1992)[3]: San Salvador 422,570 (metropolitan area 1,522,126); Soyapango 251,811[4]; Santa Ana 202,337; San Miguel 182,817; Mejicanos 145,000[4].

Vital statistics

Birth rate per 1,000 population (1994): 33.0 (world avg. 25.0); (1990) legitimate 30.6%; illegitimate 69.3%.
Death rate per 1,000 population (1994): 6.0 (world avg. 9.3).
Natural increase rate per 1,000 population (1994): 27.0 (world avg. 15.7).
Total fertility rate (avg. births per childbearing woman; 1994): 3.8.
Marriage rate per 1,000 population (1991): 4.3.
Divorce rate per 1,000 population (1991): 0.5.
Life expectancy at birth (1994): male 64.0 years; female 70.0 years.
Major causes of death per 100,000 population (1990)[5]: diseases of the circulatory system 120; violence 73; accidents 63; infectious and parasitic diseases 52; diseases of the respiratory system 49; ill-defined conditions 93.

National economy

Budget (1993). Revenue: ₡8,128,900,000 (current revenue 80.6%, of which value-added taxes 35.4%, income taxes 15.5%, import duties 12.1%, consumption taxes 7.1%; other revenue 19.4%). Expenditures: ₡8,492,900,000 (current expenditure 76.4%; development expenditure 23.6%).
Public debt (external, outstanding; 1993): U.S.$1,897,000,000.
Production (value added in ₡'000,000 except as noted). Agriculture, forestry, fishing (1993): coffee 1,492, corn (maize) 592, sugarcane 423, beans 418, aviculture 409, fish catch 261, *maicillo* (variety of millet) 202, forest products 96, rice 87, tobacco 61, oranges 126,000 metric tons[6], bananas 71,000 metric tons[6]; livestock (number of live animals; 1994) 1,256,000 cattle, 325,000 pigs. Mining and quarrying (1992): limestone 1,900,000 metric tons. Manufacturing (1993): food products 4,764; beverages 1,847; petroleum products 783; textiles 759; chemical products 691; nonmetallic mineral products 657; clothing and footwear 549; tobacco products 529. Construction (1993): private residential 858; private nonresidential 363; total public 853. Energy production (consumption): electricity (kW-hr; 1993) 2,718,000,000 (2,431,000,000); coal, none (none); crude petroleum (barrels; 1992) none (5,937,000); petroleum products (metric tons; 1992) 762,000 (1,017,000); natural gas, none (none).
Household income and expenditure (1990–91)[7]. Average household size 4.5; average income per household: ₡25,830 (U.S.$3,212); sources of income: n.a.; expenditure: food and beverages 37.0%, housing 12.1%, transportation and communications 10.2%, clothing and footwear 6.7%, household furnishings 5.7%.
Population economically active (1992): total 1,762,002; activity rate of total population 34.4% (participation rates: ages 15–64, 53.5%; female 28.3%; urban unemployed [1993] 8.1%).

Price and earnings indexes (1990 = 100)

	1989	1990	1991	1992	1993	1994	1995[8]
Consumer price index	80.7	100.0	114.4	127.2	150.9	166.8	177.4
Annual earnings index[9]	85.7	100.0	111.9	128.6	...	...	...

Gross national product (at current market prices; 1993): U.S.$7,233,000,000 (U.S.$1,320 per capita).

Structure of gross domestic product and labour force

	1993 in value ₡'000,000	1993 % of total value	1992 labour force	1992 % of labour force
Agriculture	5,690	8.6	598,738	34.0
Mining	125	0.2	967	0.1
Manufacturing	12,639	19.0	245,800	13.9
Construction	2,073	3.1	82,664	4.7
Public utilities	1,734	2.6	9,984	0.6
Transportation and communications	3,298	5.0	62,209	3.5
Trade	24,299	36.6	275,518	15.6
Finance, real estate	5,364	8.1	51,544	2.9
Public admin., defense	4,330	6.5	100,800	5.7
Services	6,804	10.3	195,411	11.1
Other	—	—	138,367[10]	7.9[10]
TOTAL	66,356	100.0	1,762,002	100.0

Tourism (1993): receipts U.S.$121,000,000; expenditures U.S.$61,000,000.
Land use (1993): forested 5.0%; meadows and pastures 29.5%; agricultural and under permanent cultivation 35.2%; other 30.3%.

Foreign trade[11]

Balance of trade (current prices)

	1989	1990	1991	1992	1993	1994
₡'000,000	−3,324	−3,585	−6,374	−9,069	−10,270	−12,254
% of total	40.1%	30.6%	40.8%	47.1%	44.6%	45.4%

Imports (1993): ₡16,636,000,000 (machinery and equipment 17.8%, chemicals and chemical products 14.3%, food and beverages 13.2%, transport equipment 12.6%). *Major import sources:* United States 44.2%; Guatemala 10.8%; Mexico 5.9%; Japan 5.1%, Venezuela 5.0%.
Exports (1993): ₡6,366,000,000 (coffee 31.1%, clothing 4.7%, pharmaceuticals 4.6%, raw sugar 4.3%, paper and paperboard 4.0%). *Major export destinations:* United States 29.9%; Guatemala 22.0%; Costa Rica 9.0%; Germany 7.2%; Honduras 6.5%.

Transport and communications

Transport. Railroads (1992): route length 374 mi, 602 km; (1993) passenger-mi 3,771,000, passenger-km 6,074,000, short ton-mi cargo 24,215,000, metric ton-km cargo 35,353,000. Roads (1993): total length 7,791 mi, 12,539 km (paved 16%). Vehicles (1992): passenger cars 95,670; trucks and buses 150,385. Merchant marine (1992): vessels (100 gross tons and over) 15; total deadweight tonnage, n.a. Air transport (1992)[12]: passenger-mi 801,000,000, passenger-km 1,289,000,000; short ton-mi cargo 4,800,000, metric ton-km cargo 7,000,000; airports (1995) with scheduled flights 1.
Communications. Daily newspapers (1992): total number 8; total circulation 485,000; circulation per 1,000 population 90. Radio (1994): total number of receivers 2,080,000 (1 per 2.7 persons). Television (1994): total number of receivers 500,700 (1 per 11 persons). Telephones (main lines; 1993): 173,500 (1 per 32 persons).

Education and health

Education (1992)

	schools	teachers	students	student/teacher ratio
Primary (age 7–15)	3,806	23,339[13]	1,028,877	38.0[13]
Secondary (age 16–18)	...	...	28,032	...
Voc. teacher tr.	...	...	77,061	...
Higher[14, 15]	6	2,850	56,868	20.0

Educational attainment (1992): Percentage of population over age 25 having: no formal schooling 34.7%; incomplete primary education 37.6%; complete primary[16] 10.8%; secondary 9.4%; higher technical 2.4%; incomplete undergraduate 1.1%; complete undergraduate 2.9%; other/unknown 1.1%.
Literacy (1992): total population age 15 and over literate, 2,326,800 (74.1%); males literate, 1,141,007 (77.4%); females literate, 1,185,793 (71.3%).
Health (1991): physicians 2,483 (1 per 2,126 persons); hospital beds 5,726 (1 per 922 persons); infant mortality rate per 1,000 live births (1994) 41.0.
Food (1992): daily per capita caloric intake 2,663 (vegetable products 90%, animal products 10%); 116% of FAO recommended minimum requirement.

Military

Total active duty personnel (1994): 30,700 (army 91.2%, navy 2.3%, air force 6.5%). *Military expenditure as percentage of GNP* (1993): 1.3% (world 3.3%); per capita expenditure U.S.$18.

[1]Roman Catholicism, although not official, enjoys special recognition in the constitution. [2]Preliminary figure. [3]Population of *municipios* (second-order administrative units). [4]Within San Salvador metropolitan area. [5]Projected rates based on about 75% of total deaths. [6]1994. [7]536,628 urban households only. [8]March. [9]Minimum wages in manufacturing and services in San Salvador metropolitan area. [10]Includes 35,043 activities not defined and 103,324 unemployed. [11]Imports c.i.f., exports f.o.b. [12]TACA International Airlines. [13]Public schools only. [14]Universities only. [15]1993. [16]Education completed through ninth grade.

Equatorial Guinea

Official name: República de Guinea Ecuatorial (Republic of Equatorial Guinea).
Form of government: republic with one legislative house (Chamber of People's Representatives [80[1]]).
Chief of state: President.
Head of government: Prime Minister.
Capital: Malabo.
Official language: Spanish.
Official religion: none.
Monetary unit[2]: 1 CFA franc (CFAF) = 100 centimes; valuation (Oct. 6, 1995) 1 U.S.$ = CFAF 501.49; 1 £ = CFAF 792.78.

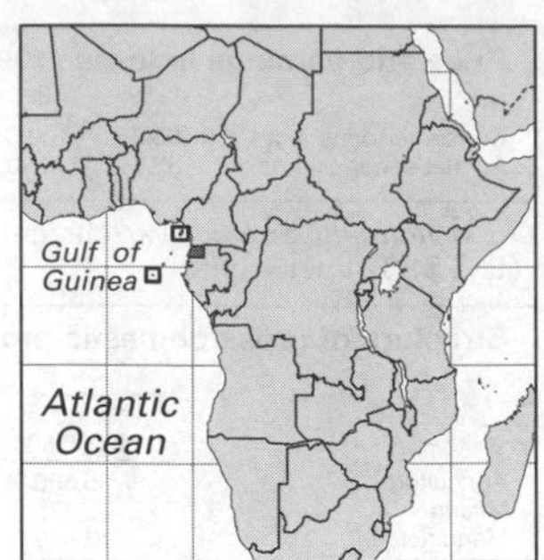

Area and population

Regions		area		population
Provinces	Capitals	sq mi	sq km	1987 estimate
Insular		785[3]	2,034	70,280
Annobón	Palé	7	17	2,360
Bioko Norte	Malabo	300	776	56,600
Bioko Sur	Luba	479	1,241	11,320
Continental		10,045[3]	26,017	259,950
Centro-Sur	Evinayong	3,834	9,931	55,970
Kie-Ntem	Ebebiyin	1,522	3,943	74,050
Litoral	Bata	2,573	6,665	75,640
Wele-Nzas	Mongomo	2,115	5,478	54,290
TOTAL		10,831[3]	28,051	330,230

Demography

Population (1995): 396,000.
Density (1995): persons per sq mi 36.6, persons per sq km 14.1.
Urban-rural (1992): urban 29.4%; rural 70.6%.
Sex distribution (1995): male 49.25%; female 50.75%.
Age breakdown (1995): under 15, 43.2%; 15–29, 25.5%; 30–44, 15.6%; 45–59, 9.3%; 60–74, 5.3%; 75 and over, 1.1%.
Population projection: (2000) 448,000; (2010) 573,000.
Doubling time: 27 years.
Ethnic composition (1983): Fang 82.9%; Bubi 9.6%; Ndowe 3.8%; Annobonés 1.5%; Bujeba 1.4%; other 0.8%.
Religious affiliation (1980): Christian (mostly Roman Catholic) 88.8%; traditional beliefs 4.6%; atheist 1.4%; Muslim 0.5%; other 0.2%; none 4.5%.
Major cities (1983): Malabo 30,418; Bata 24,308; Ela-Nguema 6,179; Campo Yaunde 5,199; Los Angeles 4,079.

Vital statistics

Birth rate per 1,000 population (1994): 40.7 (world avg. 25.0); legitimate, n.a.; illegitimate, n.a.
Death rate per 1,000 population (1994): 14.7 (world avg. 9.3).
Natural increase rate per 1,000 population (1994): 26.0 (world avg. 15.7).
Total fertility rate (avg. births per childbearing woman; 1994): 5.3.
Marriage rate per 1,000 population: n.a.
Divorce rate per 1,000 population: n.a.
Life expectancy at birth (1994): male 50.0 years; female 54.3 years.
Major causes of death per 100,000 population: n.a.; however, major diseases include malaria (about 24% of total mortality), respiratory infections (12% of mortality), cholera, leprosy, trypanosomiasis (sleeping sickness), and waterborne (especially gastrointestinal) diseases.

National economy

Budget (1994). Revenue: CFAF 19,600,000,000 (fiscal receipts 57.1%; other receipts 42.9%). Expenditures: CFAF 26,200,000,000 (capital expenditure 52.7%; current expenditure 47.3%, of which interest 19.5%, salaries 11.8%).
Public debt (external, outstanding; 1993): U.S.$218,700,000.
Gross national product (at current market prices; 1994): U.S.$142,500,000 (U.S.$373 per capita).

Structure of gross domestic product and labour force

	1991		1983	
	in value CFAF '000,000	% of total value	labour force	% of labour force
Agriculture, forestry	23,328	50.2	59,390	57.9
Manufacturing, mining	597	1.3	1,616	1.6
Construction	1,299	2.8	1,929	1.9
Public utilities	1,358	2.9	224	0.2
Transportation and communications	855	1.8	1,752	1.7
Trade	3,319	7.1	3,059	3.0
Finance	1,005	2.2	409	0.4
Pub. admin., defense	6,354	13.7	8,377	8.2
Services	5,817	12.5		
Other	2,497	5.4	25,809	25.2
TOTAL	46,429	100.0[3]	102,565	100.0[3]

Production (metric tons except as noted). Agriculture, forestry, fishing (1994): roots and tubers 84,000 (of which cassava 48,000, sweet potatoes 36,000), bananas 17,000, coconuts 8,000, coffee 7,000, cacao beans 5,000, palm oil 5,000, palm kernels 3,000; livestock (number of live animals) 36,000 sheep, 8,000 goats, 5,000 pigs, 5,000 cattle; roundwood (1993) 638,000 cu m; fish catch (1993) 3,800. Mining and quarrying: details, n.a.; however, in addition to quarrying for construction materials, unexploited deposits of iron ore, lead, zinc, manganese, and molybdenum are present; the offshore Alba gas-condensate field, opened in 1992, achieved commercial production of 7,000 barrels of condensate per day in 1994 (11 months). Manufacturing (1993): veneer sheets 8,000. Construction: n.a. Energy production (consumption): electricity (kW-hr; 1992) 19,000,000 (19,000,000); coal, none (n.a.); crude petroleum[4], none (n.a.); petroleum products (metric tons; 1992) none (38,000); natural gas, none (n.a.).
Population economically active (1991): total 148,000; activity rate of total population 41.0% (participation rates [1983]: ages 15–64, 66.7%; female 35.7%; unemployed 24.2%).

Price and earnings indexes (1990 = 100)

	1987	1988	1989	1990	1991	1992	1993
Consumer price index	92.3	93.4	98.9	100.0	96.8	89.9	93.5
Earnings index	...	...	...	...	...	...	...

Household income and expenditure. Average household size (1980) 4.5; income per household: n.a.; sources of income (1988): wages and salaries 57.0%, business income 42.0%, other 1.0%; expenditure (1988): food and beverages 62.0%, clothing and footwear 10.0%, medical care 6.0%.
Tourism: tourism is a government priority but remains undeveloped.
Land use (1993): forested 46.3%; meadows and pastures 3.7%; agricultural and under permanent cultivation 8.2%; built-on, wasteland, and other 41.8%.

Foreign trade

Balance of trade (current prices)

	1988	1989	1990	1991	1992	1993
CFAF '000,000	−2,949	−4,083	−8,522	−6,017	−10,932	+2,537
% of total	9.5%	12.1%	29.7%	11.4%	33.5%	7.7%

Imports (1994): CFAF 21,900,000,000 (capital equipment 21.0%; petroleum products 12.3%; other 66.7%). *Major import sources* (1991): United States 29.4%; Cameroon 25.7%; Liberia 19.4%; Spain 10.3%; France 5.2%; Italy 2.6%; Japan 0.8%; Gabon 0.7%.
Exports (1994): CFAF 32,900,000,000 (petroleum products 50.5%; wood 35.6%; food products 4.6%, of which cocoa 4.3%). *Major export destinations* (1991): Cameroon 54.8%; Spain 13.5%; Nigeria 10.4%; Gabon 2.8%; The Netherlands 2.4%; São Tomé and Príncipe 2.3%; Italy 1.9%; France 1.7%.

Transport and communications

Transport. Railroads: none. Roads (1993): total length 1,667 mi, 2,682 km (paved 19%). Vehicles (1993): passenger cars 6,200; trucks and buses 4,100. Merchant marine (1992): vessels (100 gross tons and over) 3; total deadweight tonnage 6,699. Air transport (1985): passenger-mi 4,000,000, passenger-km 7,000,000; short ton-mi cargo 700,000, metric ton-km cargo 1,000,000; airports (1995) with scheduled flights 2.
Communications. Daily newspapers (1992): total number 1; total circulation 1,000; circulation per 1,000 population 3.0. Radio (1994): total number of receivers 128,000 (1 per 3.0 persons). Television (1994): total number of receivers 2,500 (1 per 154 persons). Telephones (main lines; 1993): 1,300 (1 per 333 persons).

Education and health

Education (1987–88)

	schools	teachers	students	student/ teacher ratio
Primary (age 6–11)	703	1,065	61,009	57.3
Secondary (age 12–17)	9	319	9,226	28.9
Voc., teacher tr.[5]	1	52	882	17.0
Higher	4	81	660	8.1

Educational attainment (1983). Percentage of population age 15 and over having: no schooling 35.4%; some primary education 46.6%; primary 13.0%; secondary 2.3%; postsecondary 1.1%; not specified 1.6%. *Literacy* (1983): percentage of total population age 15 and over literate 62.2%; males literate 77.8%; females literate 48.6%.
Health: physicians (1990) 99 (1 per 3,532 persons); hospital beds (1990) 992 (1 per 350 persons); infant mortality rate per 1,000 live births (1994) 102.6.
Food (latest): daily per capita caloric intake 2,230; 68% of FAO recommended minimum requirement.

Military

Total active duty personnel (1995): 1,320 (army 83.3%, navy 9.1%, air force 7.6%). *Military expenditure as percentage of GNP* (1994): 1.4% (world c. 3.0%); per capita expenditure U.S.$6.

[1]Conduct of November 1993 legislative elections was unacceptable to international observers. [2]As of Jan. 1, 1985, Equatorial Guinea became a member of the franc zone, substituting the CFA franc for the previous monetary unit, the ekwele; the CFA franc has a par value of 100 CFA francs to the French franc. [3]Detail does not add to total given because of rounding. [4]Equatorial Guinea announced an oil strike off Bioko in 1995 having an estimated production capacity of 10,000 barrels per day. [5]Efforts are being undertaken to provide the training necessary to qualify nondegree teachers for service. Also, teacher-training schools are to be expanded in order to increase the number of primary-school teachers.

Eritrea

Official name: State of Eritrea.
Form of government: transitional regime[1] with one legislative house (National Assembly [150][2]).
Head of state and government: President.
Capital: Asmara.
Official language: none.
Official religion: none.
Monetary unit: Ethiopian birr (Br) = 100 cents; valuation (Oct. 6, 1995) 1 U.S.$ = Br 5.80; 1 £ = Br 9.17.

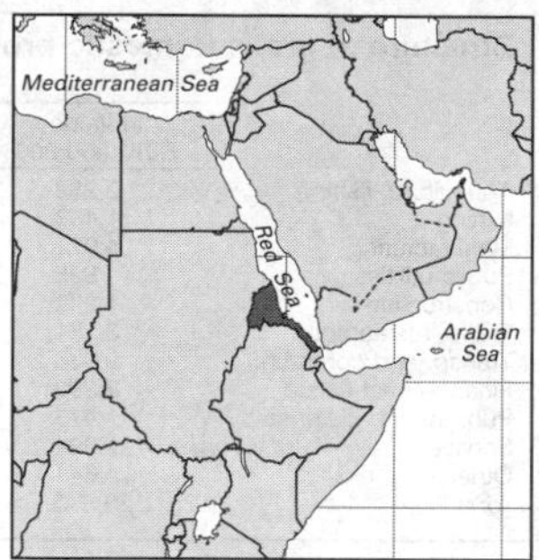

Area and population

		area[3]		population
				1995
Provinces[4]	Capitals	sq mi	sq km	estimate
Akele Guzai	Adi Qayeh	3,200	8,400	...
Asmara	Asmara (Asmera)	100	200	...
Barka	Agordat (Akordat)	10,700	27,800	...
Dankalia	Asseb (Aseb)	9,400	24,300	...
Gash and Setit	Barentu	7,200	18,600	...
Hamasien	...	1,000	2,700	...
Sahel	Nakfa	6,300	16,400	...
Semhar	Massawa (Mitsiwa)	2,400	6,300	...
Senhit	Keren	2,300	5,900	...
Seraye	Mendefera	2,600	6,800	...
TOTAL		45,300[5]	117,400	3,531,000

Demography

Population (1995): 3,531,000.
Density (1995): persons per sq mi 77.9, persons per sq km 30.1.
Urban-rural (1989): urban 15.4%; rural 84.6%.
Sex distribution (1993): male 49.62%; female 50.38%.
Age breakdown (1995): under 15, 44.3%; 15–29, 26.4%; 30–44, 15.5%; 45–59, 9.1%; 60–74, 4.0%; 75 and over, 0.7%.
Population projection: (2000) 4,025,000; (2010) 5,153,000.
Doubling time: 24 years.
Linguistic composition (1976): Tigrinya 47.9%; Tigré 31.0%; Afar 4.2%; Hedareb 3.9%; Bilen 3.1%; Saho 3.0%; Kunama 2.7%; Nara 2.1%; Amharic 1.7%; Rashaida 0.4%.
Religious affiliation (1993): believers are *c.* 50% Christian and *c.* 50% Muslim; there are also a few animists.
Major cities (1992): Asmara 400,000; Asseb 50,000; Keren 40,000; Massawa 40,000; Mendefera 14,833[6].

Vital statistics

Birth rate per 1,000 population (1992): 47.0 (world avg. 25.0).
Death rate per 1,000 population (1992): 18.0 (world avg. 9.3).
Natural increase rate per 1,000 population (1992): 29.0 (world avg. 15.7).
Total fertility rate (avg. births per childbearing woman; 1992): 6.8.
Marriage rate per 1,000 population (1992): 6.8.
Divorce rate per 1,000 population: n.a.
Life expectancy at birth (1994): 46 years.
Major causes of death per 100,000 population: n.a.; morbidity (principal causes of illness) arises mainly in malaria and other infectious diseases, parasitic infections, malnutrition, diarrheal diseases, and dysenteries.

National economy

Budget (1993). Revenue: Br 898,800,000 (taxes 57.4%, of which import duties 20.7%, direct taxes 19.2%, indirect taxes 16.0%, export duties 1.6%; nontax revenue 42.6%). Expenditures: Br 1,507,400,000 (capital expenditure 69.8%, of which materials 47.4%, wages and salaries 15.5%; capital 30.2%).
Public debt: n.a.
Tourism (1993): 12 major hotels.
Production (metric tons except as noted). Agriculture, forestry, fishing (1994): roots and tubers 109,000, cereals 72,000, sorghum 50,000, vegetables and melons 25,000, pulses 13,000, millet 8,000, corn (maize) 5,000, barley 4,000, wheat 3,000; livestock (number of live animals) 1,550,000 cattle, 1,510,000 sheep, 1,400,000 goats, 69,000 camels; fish catch (1994) 4,581, of which sharks 2,600. Mining and quarrying: detail, n.a.; salt and sand and aggregate for construction are the principal minerals exploited; deposits of copper, zinc, mica, gold, iron, manganese, nickel, and lead exist but remain unexploited. Manufacturing (value added in Br '000; 1983–84): petroleum products 120,513; beverages 60,868, of which beer 54,275; food products 53,480; textiles 23,699, of which spinning and weaving 14,404, knitting products 5,816, rope and twine 3,479; chemical products 9,641; plastic products 9,423; tobacco products 6,262; nonmetallic mineral products 5,057; footwear 4,249; metal products 3,830; glass and glass products 3,258. Construction: reconstruction, after some 30 years of civil war, is a principal concern of the government. Energy production: energy resources include hydroelectricity, fossil fuels, geothermal power, coal, biogas, solar power, and wind; commercial electricity production for 1986–87 was 148,664,000 kW-hr.
Persons economically active: n.a.

Price and earnings indexes (1990 = 100)

	1987	1988	1989	1990	1991	1992	1993
Consumer price index[7]	82.4	88.2	95.1	100.0	135.7	150.0	155.3
Earnings index	...	...	...	...	...	...	...

Gross national product (at current market prices; 1993): *c.* U.S.$393,415,000 (U.S.$115 per capita).

Structure of gross domestic product and labour force

	1994			
	in value Br '000,000	% of total value	labour force	% of labour force
Agriculture	499.4	17.9	...	...
Manufacturing	322.3	11.6	...	...
Mining	1.1	—	...	...
Public utilities	33.7	1.2	...	...
Construction	119.7	4.3	...	...
Transp. and commun.	353.4	12.7	...	...
Trade	790.1	28.3	...	...
Finance	100.8	3.6	...	...
Public admin., defense	283.0	10.1	...	...
Services	82.9	3.0	...	...
Other	204.6[8]	7.3[8]	...	...
TOTAL	2,791.0	100.0	15,310	100.0[5]

Household income and expenditure. Average household size (1984) 4.5; average annual income per household: n.a.; sources of income: n.a.; expenditure: n.a.
Land use (1993): forested 0.5%; woodland and scrubland 5.5%; agricultural and under permanent cultivation 3.5%; meadows and pastures 57.2%; other (predominantly barren land) 33.3%.

Foreign trade

Balance of trade (current prices)

	1992	1993
U.S.$'000,000	–316.1	–276.1
% of total	91.2%	79.3%

Imports (1993): Br 1,022,800,000 (machinery and transport equipment 37.3%, manufactured goods 21.7%, food products 16.3%, chemical products 5.5%, beverages and tobacco 3.5%, raw materials 3.1%, animal and vegetable oils 1.0%). *Major import sources:* Saudi Arabia 31.4%[9]; Italy 15.2%; United Arab Emirates 10.7%; Germany 8.8%; Ethiopia 7.4%; Sudan 5.9%.
Exports (1993): Br 209,200,000 (raw materials 36.6%, manufactured goods 25.3%, food products 13.3%, beverages and tobacco 4.2%, chemical products 3.0%, machinery and transport equipment 1.7%). *Major export destinations:* Ethiopia 68.7%; Sudan 24.5%; Italy 2.9%; Saudi Arabia 1.9%; Germany 0.7%.

Transport and communications

Transport. Railroads (1994): none; a 217-mi (350-km) rail line that formerly connected Massawa and Agordat is under reconstruction. A rail line of 3 mi (5 km) inside Massawa was in service by late 1994. Roads (1994): total length 621 mi, 1,000 km (paved, n.a.). Vehicles: n.a. Merchant marine: vessels (100 gross tons and over) n.a. Air transport (1993)[10]: passenger arrivals 47,645[11], passenger departures 42,548[11], short ton cargo handled 25,907[12], metric ton cargo handled 28,557[12]; airports (1995) with scheduled flights 2.
Communications. Daily newspapers: none; (1994) 2 biweekly newspapers published; circulation *c.* 26,000[13]; circulation per 1,000 population 7.8[13]. Radio (1994): the government operates a station in Asmara. Television (1994): the government operates a station in Asmara. Telephones (main lines; 1993): 20,000 (1 per 167 persons).

Education and health

Education (1993–94)

	schools	teachers	students	student/ teacher ratio
Primary (age 7–12)	491	5,272	207,099	39.3
Secondary (age 13–18)	86[14]	1,993	65,537	32.9
Voc., teacher tr.	4[14]	102	987	9.7
Higher[15]	1	144	2,032	14.1

Literacy (1993): total population literate *c.* 20%.
Health (1993): physicians 69 (1 per 36,000 persons); hospital beds (1986–87): 2,449 (1 per 1,100 persons); infant mortality rate per 1,000 live births 135.
Food (1993): daily per capita caloric intake 1,750 (vegetable and animal products, n.a.); 93% of FAO recommended minimum requirement.

Military

Total active duty personnel (1995): estimated strength of Eritrean armed forces (predominantly former guerrillas) is some 55,000 to be reduced to 35,000.

[1]Transitional regime (independent May 24, 1993) to govern for up to four years pending the drafting of a constitution and holding of multiparty elections. [2]Still in the process of being created as of late 1995. [3]Approximate figures. [4]On May 20, 1995, a resolution was approved dividing the country into six administrative regions, which would then be divided into region, sub-region, and village categories. A parliamentary committee to oversee implementation has been formed. [5]Detail does not add to total given because of rounding. [6]1989. [7]Ethiopian CPI; no separate data available as yet. [8]Including indirect taxes less subsidies. [9]Saudi Arabia is a transshipment point; not all goods included here are of Saudi Arabian origin. [10]Asmara airport only. [11]January to June only. [12]1987–88. [13]1992. [14]1992–93. [15]1993–94; full-time students only.

Estonia

Official name: Eesti Vabariik (Republic of Estonia).
Form of government: unitary multiparty republic with a single legislative body (Riigikogu[1] [101]).
Chief of state: President.
Head of government: Prime Minister.
Capital: Tallinn.
Official language: Estonian.
Official religion: none.
Monetary unit: 1 kroon (EEK) = 100 senti; valuation (Oct. 6, 1995) 1 U.S.$ = EEK 11.41; 1 £ = EEK 18.04.

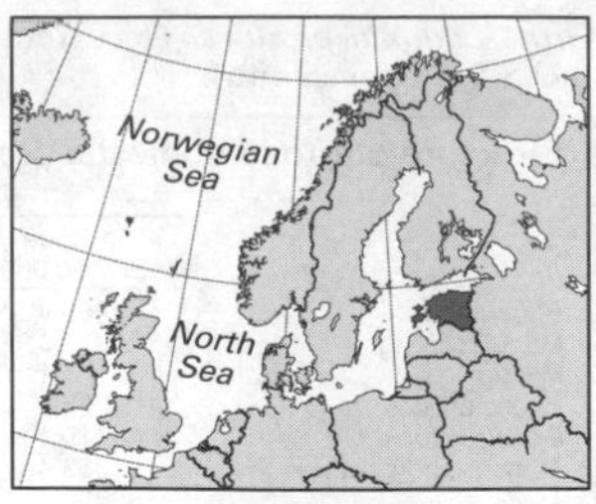

Area and population

		area		population
		sq mi	sq km	1994[2] estimate
Counties	**Capitals**			
Harju	Tallinn	1,673	4,333	566,853
Hiiu	Kärdla	395	1,023	11,986
Ida-Viru	Jõhvi	1,299	3,364	209,827
Järva	Paide	1,013	2,623	43,746
Jõgeva	Jõgeva	1,005	2,604	42,549
Lääne	Haapsalu	920	2,383	32,756
Lääne-Viru	Rakvere	1,337	3,464	76,099
Pärnu	Pärnu	1,856	4,806	99,869
Põlva	Põlva	836	2,165	36,544
Rapla	Rapla	1,151	2,980	40,111
Saare	Kuressaare	1,128	2,922	40,822
Tartu	Tartu	1,193	3,090	155,568
Valga	Valga	790	2,047	40,342
Viljandi	Viljandi	1,386	3,589	64,793
Võru	Võru	890	2,305	45,062
TOTAL		17,462[3, 4]	45,227[3, 4]	1,506,927

Demography

Population (1995): 1,487,000.
Density (1995)[5]: persons per sq mi 90.8, persons per sq km 35.1.
Urban-rural (1994): urban 70.3%; rural 29.7%.
Sex distribution (1994): male 46.69%; female 53.31%.
Age breakdown (1994): under 15, 21.1%; 15–29, 20.9%; 30–44, 21.8%; 45–59, 17.8%; 60–74, 13.6%; 75 and over, 4.8%.
Population projection: (2000) 1,441,000; (2010) 1,352,000.
Ethnic composition (1989): Estonian 61.5%; Russian 30.3%; Ukrainian 3.1%; Belorussian 1.8%; Finnish 1.1%; other 2.2%.
Religious affiliation: believers are predominantly Evangelical Lutheran, with Orthodox and Baptist minorities.
Major cities (1994): Tallinn 442,679; Tartu 105,844; Narva 79,094; Kohtla-Järve 72,659; Pärnu 51,963.

Vital statistics

Birth rate per 1,000 population (1994): 9.5 (world avg. 25.0); (1993) legitimate 61.8%; illegitimate 38.2%.
Death rate per 1,000 population (1994): 14.7 (world avg. 9.3).
Natural increase rate per 1,000 population (1993): −5.2 (world avg. 15.7).
Total fertility rate (avg. births per childbearing woman; 1993): 1.4.
Marriage rate per 1,000 population (1993): 5.1.
Divorce rate per 1,000 population (1993): 3.8.
Life expectancy at birth (1994): male 65.0 years; female 75.0 years.
Major causes of death per 100,000 population (1993): diseases of the circulatory system, 792.9, of which ischemic heart diseases 485.6, cerebrovascular disease 255.6; malignant neoplasms (cancers) 225.3; accidents 110.5; suicide 38.2.

National economy

Budget (1995). Revenue: EEK 15,952,000,000 (payments for social security and welfare 31.7%, value-added taxes 27.0%, personal income taxes 24.5%, corporate taxes 7.3%). Expenditures: EEK 15,498,000,000 (current expenditure 94.8%, capital expenditure 5.2%).
Production (metric tons except as noted). Agriculture, forestry, fishing (1994): potatoes 700,000, hay 472,000[6], barley 430,000, wheat 80,000, rye 56,000, carrots 15,000[6], plums 11,000[6], strawberries 8,000[6]; livestock (number of live animals) 463,000 cattle, 424,000 pigs; roundwood (1991) 2,439,000 cu m; fish catch 132,700. Mining and quarrying (value of production in EEK '000,000; 1993): oil shale 588; peat 54. Manufacturing (value of production in EEK '000,000; 1993): meat and meat products 1,382; dairy products 1,195; chemicals and chemical products 976; beverages 890; textiles 664; furniture 652; fish and fish products 627; transport equipment 579. Construction (completed; 1993): residential 180,500 sq m; nonresidential, n.a. Energy production (consumption): electricity (kW-hr; 1993) 9,117,000,000 (4,927,000,000); oil shale (metric tons; 1993) 14,915,000 (16,465,000); coal and coke (metric tons; 1993) none (136,000); crude petroleum, none (n.a.); natural gas (cu m; 1993) none (441,000,000).
Household income and expenditure. Average household size (1994) 3.1[7]; average net income per household (1994) EEK 46,303 (U.S.$3,681)[7]; sources of income (1994)[7]: wages and salaries 66.4%, social security 8.8%, other 24.8%; expenditure (1993)[8]: food and beverages 43.1%, transportation 9.2%, clothing and footwear 8.0%, energy 7.2%.
Gross national product (at current market prices; 1993): U.S.$1,663,000,000 (U.S.$1,100 per capita).

Structure of gross domestic product and labour force

	1993			
	in value EEK '000,000	% of total value	labour force	% of labour force
Agriculture, fishing	2,252	10.9	58,500[9]	7.8[9]
Mining	468	2.3	13,400	1.8
Manufacturing	4,971	24.0	127,300	17.0
Public utilities	895	4.3	11,700	1.6
Construction	1,202	5.8	33,200	4.4
Trade, restaurants	3,251	15.7	66,500	8.9
Transp. and commun.	2,936	14.2	47,400	6.4
Finance, real estate	2,290	11.1	29,100	3.9
Pub. admin., defense	473	2.3	27,800	3.7
Services	1,294	6.3	101,700	13.6
Other	641	3.1	230,500[9]	30.9[9]
TOTAL	20,673	100.0	747,100	100.0

Public debt (external, outstanding; 1993): U.S.$85,800,000.
Population economically active (1989): total 856,000; activity rate of total population 54.7% (participation rates: ages 15–64, 79.7%; female 50.0%; unemployed [1994] 8.1%).

Price and earnings indexes (1992 = 100)

	1988	1989	1990	1991	1992	1993	1994[10]
Consumer price index	2.1	2.2	2.7	8.3	100.0	186.4	286.1
Monthly earnings index	...	...	...	...	100.0	194.1	325.9

Tourism (1993): receipts from visitors U.S.$51,000,000; expenditures by nationals abroad U.S.$26,000,000.
Land use (1993): forested 47.8%; meadows and pastures 7.4%; agricultural and under permanent cultivation 27.1%; other 17.7%.

Foreign trade[11]

Balance of trade (current prices)

	1991	1992	1993	1994
EEK '000,000	+65	+79	−1,309	−5,176
% of total	6.8%	0.8%	5.8%	13.0%

Imports (1994): EEK 22,553,000,000 (nonelectrical and electrical machinery 20.8%, mineral fuels 13.2%, transport equipment 9.9%, textiles and clothing 9.9%, food products 9.5%). *Major import sources:* Finland 37.3%; Russia 15.7%; Sweden 10.1%; Germany 8.8%; The Netherlands 3.4%.
Exports (1994): EEK 17,377,000,000 (food products 20.8%, textiles and clothing 13.4%, nonelectrical and electrical machinery 10.5%, wood and wood products 9.4%, transport equipment 8.5%). *Major export destinations:* Russia 18.7%; Finland 15.5%; Sweden 8.5%; Latvia 6.3%; Germany 5.5%; Lithuania 4.3%.

Transport and communications

Transport. Railroads (1993): route length 636 mi, 1,024 km; passenger-mi 449,000,000, passenger-km 722,000,000; short ton-mi cargo 2,844,000,000, metric ton-km cargo 4,152,000,000. Roads (1993): total length 9,178 mi, 14,771 km (paved 55%). Vehicles (1993): passenger cars 317,400; trucks and buses 82,800. Merchant marine (1992): vessels (1,000 gross tons and over) 234; total deadweight tonnage 680,367. Air transport (1993): passenger-mi 141,800,000, passenger-km 228,200,000; short ton-mi cargo 270,000, metric ton-km cargo 400,000; airports (1995) with scheduled flights 2.
Communications. Daily newspapers: total number (1992) 7; total circulation 239,000; circulation per 1,000 population 155. Radio: n.a. Television (1993): total number of receivers 600,000 (1 per 2.5 persons). Telephones (main lines; 1993): 358,300 (1 per 4.2 persons).

Education and health

Education (1993–94)

	schools	teachers	students	student/ teacher ratio
Primary } Secondary }	724	15,298	215,400	14.1
Vocational	83	1,073	28,200	26.3
Higher	22	...	23,214	9.6[12]

Educational attainment (1989). Percentage of persons age 25 and over having: no formal schooling 2.2%; primary education 39.7%; secondary 45.1%; higher 13.7%. *Literacy* (1989): 99.7%.
Health (1993): physicians 5,117 (1 per 296 persons); hospital beds 14,377 (1 per 105 persons); infant mortality rate per 1,000 live births (1994) 14.5.
Food: daily per capita caloric intake, n.a.

Military

Total active duty personnel (1994): 2,500[13] (army 100%). *Military expenditure as a percentage of GNP* (1993): 0.8% (world 3.3%); per capita expenditure U.S.$9.

[1]Official legislation bans translation of parliament's name. [2]January 1. [3]Total includes 1,092 sq mi (2,827 sq km) of inland water, of which the Estonian portion of Lake Peipus (590 sq mi [1,529 sq km]) is not distributed by county. [4]Total includes 1,596 sq mi (4,133 sq km) of Baltic Sea islands. [5]Based on land area only. [6]1993. [7]Monthly average for December. [8]Annual average. [9]Agriculture, fishing excludes small farmers and Other includes 164,800 self-employed, small farmers, and others and 65,700 unemployed. [10]Average of 3rd quarter. [11]Exports f.o.b.; imports c.i.f. [12]Tallinn Technical University and University of Tartu only. [13]The last Russian military personnel left Estonia in August 1994.

Ethiopia

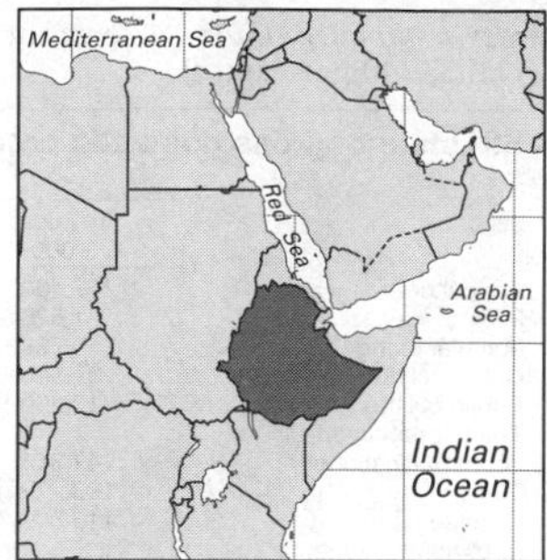

Official name: Federal Democratic Republic of Ethiopia.
Form of government: federal republic[1] with two legislative houses (Federal Council [117]; Council of People's Representatives [548]).
Chief of state: President.
Head of government: Prime Minister.
Capital: Addis Ababa.
Official language: none[2].
Official religion: none.
Monetary unit: 1 birr (Br) = 100 cents; valuation (Oct. 6, 1995) 1 U.S.$ = Br 5.80; 1 £ = Br 9.17.

Area and population

		area		population
				1993
Regions[3]	**Capitals**	sq mi	sq km	estimate
Addis Ababa	...	2,003	5,188	2,657,559
Arsi	Asela	9,155	23,710	2,157,227
Asosa	...	8,906	23,067	570,910
Bale	Goba	25,996	67,330	1,063,382
Borena	...	36,301	94,018	723,746
Eastern Gojam	...	5,381	13,936	1,699,460
Eastern Harerge	...	34,981	90,600	2,774,346
Eastern Shewa	...	4,924	12,754	1,026,180
Gambela	...	10,064	26,065	195,023
Ilubabor	Mefa	12,905	35,059	3,117,220
Kefa	Jima	15,476	40,083	1,148,596
Metekel	...	11,768	30,481	416,380
Northern Gonder	...	23,946	62,020	2,038,164
Northern Omo	...	11,553	29,923	3,046,859
Northern Shewa	...	10,436	27,030	2,570,128
Northern Welo	...	11,906	30,835	1,621,520
Sidamo	Awasa	8,009	20,742	2,980,044
Southern Gonder	...	6,594	17,079	1,867,766
Southern Omo	...	8,494	22,000	269,197
Southern Shewa	...	6,486	16,799	3,235,768
Southern Welo	...	7,993	20,702	2,675,995
Welega	Nekemte	16,460	42,632	2,673,652
Western Gojam	...	6,675	17,289	2,210,466
Western Harerge	...	12,814	33,188	1,482,628
Western Shewa	...	8,964	23,218	2,934,434
Autonomous regions				
Aseb[4]	...	17,786	46,065	246,373
Dire Dawa	...	11,291	29,244	521,691
Ogaden	...	69,239	179,327	906,632
Tigray	Mekele	20,656	53,498	2,999,948
TOTAL		437,794[5]	1,133,882	51,831,290

Demography

Population (1995): 55,053,000.
Density (1995): persons per sq mi 125.8, persons per sq km 48.6.
Urban-rural (1995): urban 11.5%; rural 88.5%.
Sex distribution (1995): male 49.93%; female 50.07%.
Age breakdown (1993): under 15, 46.5%; 15–29, 22.8%; 30–44, 15.6%; 45–59, 8.9%; 60–74, 4.5%; 75 and over, 1.7%.
Population projection: (2000) 63,785,000; (2010) 85,078,000.
Ethnolinguistic composition (1983)[6]: Amhara 37.7%; Galla (Oromo) 35.3%; Tigrinya 8.6%; Gurage 3.3%, Ometo (Omotic) 2.7%; Sidamo 2.4%.
Religious affiliation (1980)[6]: Ethiopian Orthodox 52.5%; Muslim 31.4%; traditional beliefs 11.4%; other Christian 4.5%; other 0.2%.
Major cities (1988): Addis Ababa 1,673,060; Dire Dawa 117,734; Gonder 95,000; Nazret 90,975.

Vital statistics

Birth rate per 1,000 population (1990–95): 48.5 (world avg. 25.0).
Death rate per 1,000 population (1990–95): 18.0 (world avg. 9.3).
Natural increase rate per 1,000 population (1990–95): 30.5 (world avg. 15.7).
Total fertility rate (avg. births per childbearing woman; 1990–95): 7.0.
Life expectancy at birth (1990–95): male 45.9 years; female 49.1 years.
Major causes of death (1987–88)[6, 7]: infectious and parasitic diseases 33.1%; respiratory diseases 15.7%; digestive system diseases 10.7%.

National economy[6]

Budget (1993–94). Revenue: Br 3,780,300,000 (taxes 79.1%, of which import duties 31.8%, income and profit tax 23.3%, sales tax 9.5%, export duties 1.3%; nontax revenue 20.9%). Expenditures: Br 4,474,900,000 (general services 32.5%; social services 27.4%, of which education 16.6%, public health 6.2%; debt payment 21.3%).
Public debt (external, outstanding; 1993): U.S.$4,530,000,000.
Tourism: receipts (1993) U.S.$20,000,000; expenditures (1992) U.S.$10,000,000.
Production (metric tons except as noted). Agriculture, forestry, fishing (1994): corn (maize) 1,711,000, sugarcane 1,700,000, barley 1,236,000, wheat 1,180,000, sorghum 1,109,000, pulses 800,000, potatoes 350,000, yams 236,000, millet 233,000, coffee 198,000, seed cotton 42,000; livestock (number of live animals) 29,450,000 cattle, 21,700,000 sheep, 16,700,000 goats, 8,580,000 horses, mules, and asses, 1,000,000 camels; roundwood (1993) 46,969,000 cu m; fish catch (1993) 4,200. Mining and quarrying (1994): cement 400,000; limestone 200,000; salt 165,000; gold 128,603 troy oz; platinum 48 troy oz. Manufacturing (gross value in Br '000[8]; 1991–92): food and beverages 555,800; textiles 251,400; leather and shoes 162,300; cigarettes 106,000; chemicals 53,400. Construction (authorized; 1987–88)[9]: residential 260,251 sq m; nonresidential 63,346 sq m, of which commercial 16,994 sq m. Energy production (consumption): electricity (kW-hr; 1993) 1,386,956,000 (1,386,956,000); coal, none (n.a.); crude petroleum (barrels; 1993) n.a. (5,424,000); petroleum products (metric tons; 1993) 739,000 (907,000); natural gas, n.a. (n.a.).
Land use (1993): forest 25.0%; pasture 40.0%; agriculture 12.7%; other 22.3%.
Gross national product (1993): U.S.$5,329,000,000 (U.S.$100 per capita).

Structure of gross domestic product and labour force

	1993–94		1991	
	in value Br '000,000	% of total value	labour force	% of labour force
Agriculture	13,754.1	54.4	14,900,000	74.2
Manufacturing, mining	1,932.3	7.6		
Construction	736.0	2.9	2,065,000	10.3
Public utilities	254.8	1.0		
Transp. and commun.	1,163.5	4.6		
Trade	2,551.3	10.1		
Finance	2,035.2	8.0		
Pub. admin., defense	1,792.7	7.1	3,103,000	15.5
Services	1,008.2	4.0		
Other	66.6[10]	0.3[10]		
TOTAL	25,294.7	100.0	20,068,000	100.0

Population economically active (1992): total 23,518,000; activity rate of total population 41.3% (participation rates: ages 15–64, 70.1%; female 41.1%; unemployed [1990] 44.2%).

Price index (1990 = 100)

	1987	1988	1989	1990	1991	1992	1993
Consumer price index	82.4	88.2	95.1	100.0	135.7	150.0	155.3

Household income and expenditure. Average household size (1984) 4.5; income per household (1981–82) Br 1,728 (U.S.$835); sources of income (1981–82): self-employment 79.5%, wages and salaries 0.2%, other 20.3%; expenditure (1988): food 66.7%, fuel and power 15.9%, clothing and footwear 6.8%, health care 3.1%, education 2.5%, household goods 2.1%.

Foreign trade[6]

Balance of trade (current prices)

	1988	1989	1990	1991	1992	1993
Br '000,000	−1,081.2	−747.6	−1,271.6	−433.1	−1,360.5	−2,325.1
% of total	60.8%	29.1%	50.8%	55.5%	60.3%	53.9%

Imports (1992–93): Br 3,618,718,000 (petroleum products 22.7%, machinery [including aircraft] 19.3%, food and live animals 13.7%, motor vehicles 11.1%, metal wares 4.7%, chemicals 3.7%, pharmaceuticals 3.6%, textiles 3.6%). *Major import sources* (1993): Saudi Arabia 18.8%; Germany 10.6%; Italy 10.3%; U.S. 9.5%; Djibouti 4.5%; U.K. 3.9%.
Exports (1992–93): Br 800,814,000 (coffee 67.1%, hides 16.8%, petroleum products 3.8%). *Major export destinations* (1993): Germany 19.7%; Japan 19.0%; Djibouti 12.1%; Saudi Arabia 9.9%; U.S. 9.1%; Italy 7.6%.

Transport and communications[6]

Transport. Railroads (1990–91)[11]: length 782 km; passenger-km 277,000,000; metric ton-km cargo 126,000,000. Roads (1991): total length 27,972 km (paved 15%). Vehicles (1993): passenger cars 40,000; trucks and buses 18,800. Merchant marine (1992): vessels (100 gross tons and over) 27; total deadweight tonnage 84,326. Air transport (1993): passenger-km 829,380,000; metric ton-km cargo 127,100,000; airports (1995) 25.
Communications. Daily newspapers (1994): 3; circulation 107,000; circulation per 1,000 population 2.0. Radio (1994): 9,000,000 receivers (1 per 5.9 persons). Television (1994): 100,000 receivers (1 per 534 persons). Telephones (main lines; 1993): 132,500 (1 per 391 persons).

Education and health

Education (1992)

	schools	teachers	students	student/ teacher ratio
Primary (age 7–12)	8,120	69,743	1,855,894	26.6
Secondary (age 13–18)	1,209[12]	21,970	712,489	32.4
Voc., teacher tr.	...	602	8,290	13.8
Higher[13]	11[14]	1,697	26,218	15.4

Educational attainment: n.a. *Literacy* (1995): total population age 15 and over literate 35.5%; males 45.5%; females 25.3%.
Health: physicians (1988) 1,466 (1 per 30,195 persons); hospital beds (1986–87) 11,745 (1 per 3,873 persons); infant mortality rate (1990–95) 119.0.
Food (1992): daily per capita caloric intake 1,610 (vegetable products 93%, animal products 7%); 69% of FAO recommended minimum.

Military

Total active duty personnel (1995): the estimated strength of Ethiopian armed forces was some 120,000. *Military expenditure as percentage of GNP* (1993): 4.4% (world 3.3%); per capita expenditure U.S.$3.

[1]New republic formally established on Aug. 22, 1995. [2]Amharic is the "working" language of the Federal Democratic Republic of Ethiopia. [3]In December 1991 the Council of Representatives established a regional administrative system comprising 14 ethnically based "national local administrations" and a single region made up of the towns of Addis Ababa and Harare. [4]Estimates adjusted to exclude the Eritrean portion of Aseb area. [5]Detail does not add to total given because of rounding. [6]Includes Eritrea. [7]Percentage of illnesses in a sample population of hospital outpatients. [8]At constant prices of 1978–79. [9]Addis Ababa only. [10]Less imputed bank service charges. [11]Includes 62 mi (100 km) of the Chemin de Fer Djibouti-Ethiopiën (CDE) in Djibouti; excludes 190 mi (306 km) of Northern Ethiopia Railway, not in use since 1978. [12]1985–86. [13]1991. [14]1983–84.

Fiji

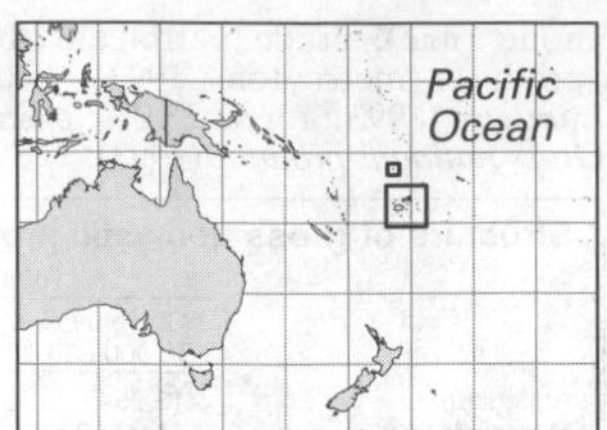

Official name: Sovereign Democratic Republic of Fiji.
Form of government: republic with two legislative houses (Senate [34[1]]; House of Representatives [70]).
Chief of state: President.
Head of government: Prime Minister.
Capital: Suva.
Official language: English.
Official religion: none.
Monetary unit: 1 Fiji dollar (F$) = 100 cents; valuation (Oct. 6, 1995) 1 U.S.$ = F$1.41; 1 £ = F$2.22.

Area and population

Divisions Provinces	Capitals	area sq mi	area sq km	population 1986 census
Central	Suva			
Naitasiri	—	643	1,666	100,227
Namosi	—	220	570	4,836
Rewa	—	105	272	97,442
Serua	—	320	830	13,356
Tailevu	—	369	955	44,249
Eastern	Levuka			
Kadavu	—	185	478	9,805
Lau	—	188	487	14,203
Lomaiviti	—	159	411	16,066
Rotuma	—	18	46	2,688
Northern	Labasa			
Bua	—	532	1,379	13,986
Cakaudrove	—	1,087	2,816	40,433
Macuata	—	774	2,004	74,735
Western	Lautoka			
Ba	—	1,017	2,634	197,633
Nadroga-Navosa	—	921	2,385	54,431
Ra	—	518	1,341	31,285
TOTAL	—	7,055[2]	18,272[2]	715,375

Demography

Population (1995): 791,000.
Density (1995): persons per sq mi 112.1, persons per sq km 42.3.
Urban-rural (1987): urban 38.7%; rural 61.3%.
Sex distribution (1990): male 50.65%; female 49.35%.
Age breakdown (1990): under 15, 37.3%; 15–29, 28.5%; 30–44, 18.7%; 45–59, 10.0%; 60–74, 4.1%; 75 and over, 1.4%.
Population projection: (2000) 855,218; (2010) 999,178.
Doubling time: 32 years.
Ethnic composition (1994): Fijian 50.4%; Indian 44.2%[3]; other 5.4%.
Religious affiliation (1986): Christian 52.9%; Hindu 38.1%; Muslim 7.8%; Sikh 0.7%; other 0.5%.
Major cities (1986): Suva 69,665; Lautoka 28,728; Lami 8,601; Nadi 7,679; Ba 6,518.

Vital statistics

Birth rate per 1,000 population (1994): 24.9 (world avg. 25.0); (1978) legitimate 82.7%; illegitimate 17.3%.
Death rate per 1,000 population (1994): 5.4 (world avg. 9.3).
Natural increase rate per 1,000 population (1994): 19.5 (world avg. 15.7).
Total fertility rate (avg. births per childbearing woman; 1995): 2.9.
Marriage rate per 1,000 population (1988): 9.6.
Divorce rate per 1,000 population (1979): 0.7.
Life expectancy at birth (1995): male 70.0 years; female 74.0 years.
Major causes of death per 100,000 population (1987): diseases of the circulatory system 153.4; malignant neoplasms (cancers) 35.5; accidents, poisoning, and violence 32.2; diseases of the respiratory system 31.7; diabetes mellitus 27.3; infectious and parasitic diseases 18.2; birth trauma 16.5.

National economy

Budget (1994). Revenue: F$685,732,000 (income taxes, estate taxes, and gift duties 53.9%; customs duties and port dues 27.8%; fees, royalties, and sales 7.0%). Expenditures: F$650,288,000 (departmental expenditure 73.9%; public-debt charges 21.7%; pensions and gratuities 4.4%).
Public debt (external, outstanding; 1993): U.S.$283,400,000.
Production (metric tons except as noted). Agriculture, forestry, fishing (1994): sugarcane 4,064,000, paddy rice 18,019, copra 8,407, ginger 4,627; livestock (number of live animals) 334,000 cattle, 205,000 goats, 115,000 pigs; roundwood (1993) 501,542 cu m; fish catch (1993) 31,399. Mining and quarrying (1994): gold 3,440 kg; silver 1,386 kg. Manufacturing (1994): refined sugar 517,000; cement 94,000; flour 37,581; stock feed 29,402; soap 7,248; coconut oil 6,486; beer 160,000 hectolitres; paint 26,260 hectolitres. Construction (1994): residential 104,000 sq m; nonresidential 57,000 sq m. Energy production (consumption): electricity (kW-hr; 1992) 477,000,000 (477,000,000); coal (metric tons; 1992) none (20,000); crude petroleum, none (n.a.); petroleum products (metric tons; 1992) none (200,000); natural gas, none (n.a.).
Population economically active (1986): total 241,160; activity rate of total population 33.7% (participation rates: ages 15–64, 56.0%; female 21.2%; unemployed [1990] 6.4%).

Price and earnings indexes (1990 = 100)

	1988	1989	1990	1991	1992	1993	1994
Consumer price index	87.0	92.4	100.0	106.5	111.7	117.5	118.2
Earnings index	...	...	...	...	...	...	...

Gross national product (at current market prices; 1993): U.S.$1,626,000,000 (U.S.$2,140 per capita).

Structure of gross domestic product and labour force

	1994 in value F$'000[4]	1994 % of total value	1986 labour force	1986 % of labour force
Agriculture	207,468	22.0	106,305	44.1
Mining	1,528	0.2	1,345	0.5
Manufacturing	116,739	12.4	18,106	7.5
Construction	31,518	3.3	11,786	4.9
Public utilities	13,290	1.4	2,154	0.9
Transportation and communications	142,346	15.1	13,151	5.4
Trade	193,472	20.5	26,010	10.8
Finance	115,800	12.3	6,016	2.5
Pub. admin., defense Services	151,165	16.0	36,619	15.2
Other	−29,957[5]	−3.2[5]	19,668[6]	8.2[6]
TOTAL	943,369	100.0	241,160	100.0

Household income and expenditure. Average household size (1986) 5.7; income per household (1980) F$2,837 (U.S.$3,546); sources of income (1973): wages and salaries 81.5%, self-employment 9.1%, other 9.4%; expenditure (1991): food, beverages, and tobacco 41.5%, housing and energy 21.4%, transportation and communications 12.9%, household durable goods 6.5%, clothing and footwear 5.4%.
Tourism (1993): receipts from visitors U.S.$236,000,000; expenditures by nationals abroad U.S.$39,000,000.
Land use (1993): forested 64.9%; agricultural and under permanent cultivation 14.2%; meadows and pastures 9.6%; other 11.3%.

Foreign trade

Balance of trade (current prices)

	1989	1990	1991	1992	1993	1994
F$'000,000	−253.87	−251.32	−279.57	−275.53	−521.42	−409.36
% of total	18.7%	14.1%	20.1%	20.9%	30.7%	20.4%

Imports (1994): F$1,209,852,000 (machinery and transport equipment 31.2%; durable manufactures 23.1%; food, beverages, and tobacco 13.7%; mineral fuels 11.3%; miscellaneous manufactured consumer articles 9.8%; chemicals 7.4%). *Major import sources:* Australia 33.0%; New Zealand 16.9%; United States 14.8%; Japan 8.1%; Singapore 7.4%; China 3.2%; Taiwan 2.4%; Hong Kong 2.1%; United Kingdom 1.7%.
Exports (1994)[7]: F$657,041,000 (sugar 38.4%; gold 9.5%; fish 6.0%; timber 4.7%; molasses 2.1%; coconut oil 0.6%). *Major export destinations*[8]: Australia 26.5%; United Kingdom 23.7%; United States 21.8%; Japan 8.3%; New Zealand 6.4%; Canada 5.6%.

Transport and communications

Transport. Railroads (1994)[9]: length 370 mi, 595 km. Roads (1991): total length 2,996 mi, 4,821 km (paved 13%). Vehicles (1993): passenger cars 45,309; trucks and buses 31,711. Merchant marine (1992): vessels (100 gross tons and over) 64; total deadweight tonnage 60,444. Air transport (1993)[10]: passenger-mi 671,050,000, passenger-km 1,079,953,000; short ton-mi cargo 38,237,000, metric ton-km cargo 55,826,000; airports (1995) with scheduled flights 13.
Communications. Daily newspapers (1992): total number 1; total circulation 27,000; circulation per 1,000 population 36. Radio (1994): total number of receivers 450,000 (1 per 1.7 persons). Television (1992): total number of receivers 12,000 (1 per 63 persons). Telephones (main lines; 1993): 53,997 (1 per 14.2 persons).

Education and health

Education (1992)

	schools	teachers	students	student/ teacher ratio
Primary (age 5–15)	693	4,644	145,630	31.4
Secondary (age 16–19)	142	3,045	60,237	19.8
Voc., teacher tr.	45	625	7,283	11.6
Higher[11]	5[12]	277	7,908	28.5

Educational attainment (1986). Percentage of population age 25 and over having: no formal schooling 28.3%; primary only 19.1%; some secondary 44.1%; secondary 4.1%; postsecondary 3.3%; other 1.1%. *Literacy* (1986): total population age 15 and over literate 87.0%; males literate 90.0%; females literate 84.0%.
Health (1993): physicians 354 (1 per 2,161 persons); hospital beds 1,747 (1 per 438 persons); infant mortality rate per 1,000 live births (1995) 22.0.
Food (1992): daily per capita caloric intake 3,089 (vegetable products 80%, animal products 20%); 116% of FAO recommended minimum requirement.

Military

Total active duty personnel (1993): 3,900 (army 92.3%, navy 7.7%, air force, none). *Military expenditure as percentage of GNP* (1993): 1.6% (world 3.3%); per capita expenditure U.S.$34.

[1]All seats are appointed. [2]Detail does not add to total given because of rounding. [3]The emigration of Indian population after the coup in 1987 has resulted in the reemergence of a Fijian majority. [4]Constant 1977 prices. [5]Less imputed bank service charges. [6]Not stated and unemployed. [7]Excludes reexports, valued at F$143,454,000. [8]Based on exports of local products only. [9]Owned by the Fiji Sugar Corporation. [10]Air Pacific only. [11]1991. [12]1983.

Finland

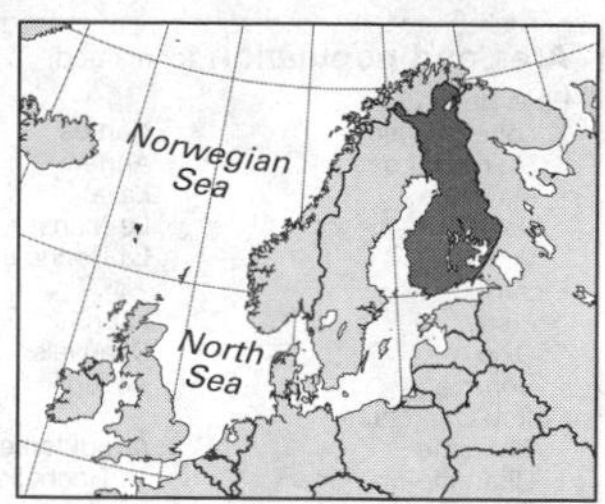

Official name: Suomen Tasavalta (Finnish); Republiken Finland (Swedish) (Republic of Finland).
Form of government: multiparty republic with one legislative house (Parliament [200]).
Chief of state: President.
Head of government: Prime Minister.
Capital: Helsinki.
Official languages: Finnish; Swedish.
Official religion: none[1].
Monetary unit: 1 markka (Fmk) = 100 penniä; valuation (Oct. 6, 1995) 1 U.S.$ = Fmk 4.31; 1 £ = Fmk 6.81.

Area and population

		land area		population
Provinces	**Capitals**	sq mi	sq km	1995[2] estimate
Häme	Hämeenlinna	7,423	19,226	727,418
Keski-Suomi	Jyväskylä	6,274	16,249	257,716
Kuopio	Kuopio	6,375	16,510	258,800
Kymi	Kouvola	4,163	10,783	333,411
Lappi	Rovaniemi	35,930	93,057	202,325
Mikkeli	Mikkeli	6,302	16,323	206,682
Oulu	Oulu	21,957	56,868	449,709
Pohjois-Karjala	Joensuu	6,866	17,782	177,917
Turku ja Pori	Turku	7,704	19,954	700,703
Uusimaa	Helsinki	3,822	9,898	1,309,549
Vaasa	Vaasa	10,200	26,418	449,366
Autonomous Province				
Åland (Ahvenanmaa)	Mariehamn (Maarianhamina)	590	1,527	25,158
TOTAL LAND AREA		117,605[3]	304,595	
INLAND WATER		12,954	33,551	
TOTAL		130,559	338,145[3]	5,098,754

Demography

Population (1995): 5,101,000.
Density (1995)[4]: persons per sq mi 43.4, persons per sq km 16.7.
Urban-rural (1994): urban 64.1%; rural 35.9%.
Sex distribution (1995): male 48.67%; female 51.33%.
Age breakdown (1995): under 15, 19.1%; 15–29, 19.4%; 30–44, 23.1%; 45–59, 19.5%; 60–74, 13.2%; 75 and over, 5.7%.
Population projection: (2000) 5,160,000; (2010) 5,226,000.
Doubling time: not applicable; population is stable.
Linguistic composition (1995): Finnish 93.0%; Swedish 5.8%; other 1.2%.
Religious affiliation (1995): Evangelical Lutheran 85.9%; Finnish (Greek) Orthodox 1.1%; nonreligious 12.0%; other 1.0%.
Major cities (1994): Helsinki 515,765 (metro area 874,953); Espoo 186,507[5]; Tampere 179,251; Vantaa 164,376[5]; Turku 162,370.

Vital statistics

Birth rate per 1,000 population (1994): 13.0 (world avg. 25.0); (1992) legitimate 71.1%; illegitimate 28.9%.
Death rate per 1,000 population (1994): 9.4 (world avg. 9.3).
Natural increase rate per 1,000 population (1994): 3.6 (world avg. 15.7).
Total fertility rate (avg. births per childbearing woman; 1994): 1.8.
Marriage rate per 1,000 population (1993): 4.7.
Divorce rate per 1,000 population (1993): 2.4.
Life expectancy at birth (1992): male 71.7 years; female 79.4 years.
Major causes of death per 100,000 population (1993): ischemic heart diseases 280.4; malignant neoplasms (cancers) 198.4; cerebrovascular disease 124.4; diseases of the respiratory system 85.4; accidents 50.7.

National economy

Budget (1994). Revenue: Fmk 187,998,000,000 (tax revenue 53.7%, of which sales taxes 18.0%, income and property taxes 17.9%, excise duties 11.2%; loans 34.6%). Expenditures: Fmk 187,998,000,000 (social security and health 27.3%; education 12.3%; state debt 11.6%; credit institutions for industry 6.5%; pensions 6.3%; defense 4.4%; agriculture 4.1%).
Tourism (1993): receipts from visitors U.S.$1,239,000,000; expenditures by nationals abroad U.S.$1,617,000,000.
Production (metric tons except as noted). Agriculture, forestry, fishing (1994): silage 5,337,000[6], barley 1,858,000, sugar beets 1,097,000, oats 1,050,000, potatoes 726,000, peas 30,000[6]; livestock (number of live animals) 1,300,000 pigs, 1,230,000 cattle, 215,000 reindeer[6]; roundwood (1993) 39,644,000 cu m; fish catch (1993) 152,491. Mining and quarrying (1993): chromite concentrate 511,000; talc 399,000. Manufacturing (value added in Fmk '000,000; 1992): wood pulp, paper, and paperboard 13,360; nonelectrical machinery 9,679; food products 9,324; electrical machinery 8,959; printing and publishing 6,846; chemicals and chemical products 6,785; wood and wood products 4,544. Construction (completed; 1993): residential 11,540,000 cu m; nonresidential 17,100,000 cu m. Energy production (consumption): electricity (kW-hr; 1993–94) 60,406,000 ([1993] 62,856,000,000); coal (metric tons; 1992) none (4,980,000); crude petroleum (barrels; 1992) none (68,308,000); petroleum products (metric tons; 1992) 9,993,000 (8,072,000); natural gas (cu m; 1992) none (2,990,000,000).
Household income and expenditure (1992). Average household size 2.3; disposable income per household Fmk 128,100 (U.S.$28,598); sources of gross income: wages and salaries 56.5%, transfer payments 27.1%, self-employment 10.0%, other 6.4%; expenditure: food 21.5%, housing 18.3%, transportation and communications 14.3%, recreation and education 9.5%.

Gross national product (at current market prices; 1993): U.S.$96,220,000,000 (U.S.$16,840 per capita).

Structure of gross domestic product and labour force

	1993			
	in value Fmk '000,000	% of total value	labour force	% of labour force
Agriculture, fishing	12,514	3.0	193,000	7.7
Forestry	8,821	2.1		
Mining	1,743	0.4	5,000	0.2
Manufacturing	101,962	24.4	472,000	18.8
Public utilities	11,106	2.7	25,000	1.0
Construction	19,766	4.7	193,000	7.7
Transp. and commun.	37,556	9.0	176,000	7.0
Trade, restaurants	47,518	11.4	356,000	14.2
Finance, real estate	82,988	19.9	203,000	8.1
Pub. admin., defense	85,458	20.5	798,000	31.8
Services	12,950	3.1		
Other	−4,784	−1.1	87,000[7]	3.5[7]
TOTAL	417,598	100.0[3]	2,508,000	100.0

Population economically active (1993): total 2,508,000; activity rate of total population 49.5% (participation rates: ages 15–64, 73.5%; female 46.9%; unemployed [May 1994–April 1995] 17.8%).

Price and earnings indexes (1990 = 100)

	1989	1990	1991	1992	1993	1994	1995[8]
Consumer price index	94.3	100.0	104.3	107.4	109.7	110.9	111.9
Annual earnings index	91.6	100.0	106.4	108.4	109.2	111.5	...

National debt (1992): Fmk 171,920,000,000.
Land use (1993): forested 75.9%; meadows and pastures 0.3%; agricultural and under permanent cultivation 8.5%; other 15.3%.

Foreign trade[9]

Balance of trade (current prices)

	1989	1990	1991	1992	1993	1994
Fmk '000,000	−5,732	−1,700	+5,098	+12,516	+30,849	+33,659
% of total	2.8%	0.8%	2.8%	6.2%	13.0%	12.3%

Imports (1994): Fmk 120,200,000,000 (raw materials 54.8%; consumer goods 20.5%; mineral fuels 9.7%). *Major import sources:* Germany 14.7%; Sweden 10.4%; Russia 8.9%; United Kingdom 8.3%; United States 7.6%; Japan 6.5%; Norway 4.8%.
Exports (1994): Fmk 153,859,000,000 (metal products and machinery 36.1%; paper, paper products, and publishing 26.8%; chemicals and chemical products 10.2%). *Major export destinations:* Germany 13.4%; Sweden 10.9%; United Kingdom 10.3%; United States 7.2%; Russia 5.2%; The Netherlands 5.1%; France 5.1%.

Transport and communications

Transport. Railroads: route length (1993) 3,657 mi, 5,885 km; passenger-mi 1,514,000,000, passenger-km 2,436,000,000; short ton-mi cargo 6,345,000,000, metric ton-km cargo 9,264,000,000. Roads (1994): total length[10] 47,763 mi, 76,868 km (paved 63%). Vehicles (1993): passenger cars 1,872,933; trucks and buses 261,364. Merchant marine (1992): vessels (100 gross tons and over) 263; total deadweight tonnage 989,270. Air transport (1993)[11]: passenger-mi 5,142,000,000, passenger km 8,275,000,000; short ton-mi cargo 115,384,000, metric ton-km cargo 168,458,000; airports (1995) 25.
Communications. Daily newspapers (1992): total number 60; total circulation 2,640,381, circulation per 1,000 population 524. Radio (1993): 4,950,000 receivers (1 per 1.0 person). Television (1993): 1,900,000 receivers (1 per 2.7 persons). Telephones (main lines; 1993): 2,760,700 (1 per 1.8 persons).

Education and health

Education (1992–93)

	schools	teachers	students	student/teacher ratio
Primary (age 7–15)[12]	4,734	41,222	584,749	14.2
Secondary (age 16–18)[13]	448	6,322	121,516	19.2
Voc. (incl. higher)	570	...	197,894	...
Higher	20	7,917	121,736	15.4

Educational attainment (1993). Percentage of population age 15 and over having: incomplete upper-secondary education 44.4%; complete upper secondary or vocational 35.0%; some postsecondary 8.3%; undergraduate 3.9%; graduate 7.5%; postgraduate 0.8%. *Literacy:* virtually 100%.
Health (1993): physicians 13,344[14] (1 per 380 persons); hospital beds 53,890[15] (1 per 94 persons); infant mortality rate per 1,000 live births 4.4.
Food (1992): daily per capita caloric intake 3,018 (vegetable products 60%, animal products 40%); 111% of FAO recommended minimum requirement.

Military

Total active duty personnel (1994): 31,200 (army 82.4%, navy 8.0%, air force 9.6%). *Military expenditure as percentage of GNP* (1993): 2.2% (world 3.3%); per capita expenditure U.S.$338.

[1]The Evangelical Lutheran and Finnish (Greek) Orthodox churches have special recognition. [2]January 1. [3]Detail does not add to total given because of rounding. [4]Based on land area only. [5]Within Helsinki urban area. [6]1993. [7]Includes 77,000 unemployed persons not previously employed and 10,000 not adequately defined. [8]April. [9]Imports c.i.f., exports f.o.b. [10]Excludes Åland Islands. [11]Finnair. [12]Includes lower secondary. [13]Excludes lower secondary. [14]Registered professionals of working age. [15]Excludes beds in hospitals operated by specialized institutions.

France

Official name: République Française (French Republic).
Form of government: republic with two legislative houses (Parliament; Senate [321], National Assembly [577]).
Chief of state: President.
Head of government: Prime Minister.
Capital: Paris.
Official language: French.
Official religion: none.
Monetary unit: 1 franc (F) = 100 centimes; valuation (Oct. 6, 1995) 1 U.S.$ = F 5.01; 1 £ = F 7.93.

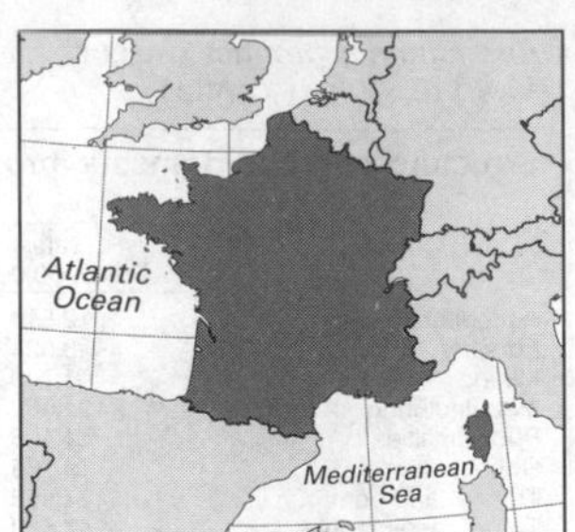

Area and population

Regions Departments	Capitals	area sq mi	area sq km	population 1993[1] estimate
Alsace				
Bas-Rhin	Strasbourg	1,836	4,755	969,200
Haut-Rhin	Colmar	1,361	3,525	680,100
Aquitaine				
Dordogne	Périgueux	3,498	9,060	388,200
Gironde	Bordeaux	3,861	10,000	1,236,900
Landes	Mont-de-Marsan	3,569	9,243	316,500
Lot-et-Garonne	Agen	2,070	5,361	306,600
Pyrénées-Atlantiques	Pau	2,952	7,645	593,200
Auvergne				
Allier	Moulins	2,834	7,340	353,600
Cantal	Aurillac	2,211	5,726	156,900
Haute-Loire	Le Puy	1,922	4,977	206,100
Puy-de-Dôme	Clermont-Ferrand	3,077	7,970	598,500
Basse-Normandie				
Calvados	Caen	2,142	5,548	627,200
Manche	Saint-Lô	2,293	5,938	483,600
Orne	Alençon	2,356	6,103	294,100
Bretagne				
Côtes-d'Armor	Saint-Brieuc	2,656	6,878	539,700
Finistère	Quimper	2,600	6,733	840,500
Ille-et-Vilaine	Rennes	2,616	6,775	818,000
Morbihan	Vannes	2,634	6,823	629,300
Bourgogne				
Côte-d'Or	Dijon	3,383	8,763	500,600
Nièvre	Nevers	2,632	6,817	230,800
Saône-et-Loire	Mâcon	3,311	8,575	554,900
Yonne	Auxerre	2,868	7,427	327,200
Centre				
Cher	Bourges	2,793	7,235	322,000
Eure-et-Loir	Chartres	2,270	5,880	404,200
Indre	Châteauroux	2,622	6,791	236,000
Indre-et-Loire	Tours	2,366	6,127	538,600
Loiret	Orléans	2,616	6,775	595,000
Loir-et-Cher	Blois	2,449	6,343	308,600
Champagne-Ardenne				
Ardennes	Charleville-Mézières	2,019	5,229	295,600
Aube	Troyes	2,318	6,004	292,000
Haute-Marne	Chaumont	2,398	6,211	202,500
Marne	Châlons-sur-Marne	3,151	8,162	561,100
Corse[2]				
Corse-du-Sud	Ajaccio	1,550	4,014	120,100
Haute-Corse	Bastia	1,802	4,666	133,100
Franche-Comté				
Doubs	Besançon	2,021	5,234	489,400
Haute-Saône	Vesoul	2,070	5,360	231,100
Jura	Lons-le-Saunier	1,930	4,999	250,700
Territoire de Belfort	Belfort	235	609	136,000
Haute-Normandie				
Eure	Évreux	2,332	6,040	529,200
Seine-Maritime	Rouen	2,424	6,278	1,230,900
Île-de-France				
Essonne	Évry	696	1,804	1,124,800
Hauts-de-Seine	Nanterre	68	176	1,405,400
Paris	Paris	40	105	2,155,700
Seine-et-Marne	Melun	2,284	5,915	1,141,800
Seine-Saint-Denis	Bobigny	91	236	1,409,400
Val-de-Marne	Créteil	95	245	1,235,800
Val-d'Oise	Pontoise	481	1,246	1,088,100
Yvelines	Versailles	882	2,284	1,347,100
Languedoc-Roussillon				
Aude	Carcassonne	2,370	6,139	304,400
Gard	Nîmes	2,260	5,853	601,200
Hérault	Montpellier	2,356	6,101	830,800
Lozère	Mende	1,995	5,167	72,500
Pyrénées-Orientales	Perpignan	1,589	4,116	374,000
Limousin				
Corrèze	Tulle	2,261	5,857	236,800
Creuse	Guéret	2,149	5,565	128,600
Haute-Vienne	Limoges	2,131	5,520	353,100
Lorraine				
Meurthe-et-Moselle	Nancy	2,024	5,241	709,200
Meuse	Bar-le-Duc	2,400	6,216	194,400
Moselle	Metz	2,400	6,216	1,009,600
Vosges	Épinal	2,268	5,874	383,000
Midi-Pyrénées				
Ariège	Foix	1,888	4,890	138,500
Aveyron	Rodez	3,373	8,736	268,400
Gers	Auch	2,416	6,257	174,400
Haute-Garonne	Toulouse	2,436	6,309	963,300
Haute-Pyrénées	Tarbes	1,724	4,464	225,300
Lot	Cahors	2,014	5,217	157,800
Tarn	Albi	2,223	5,758	340,900
Tarn-et-Garonne	Montauban	1,435	3,718	203,300
Nord-Pas-de-Calais				
Nord	Lille	2,217	5,742	2,542,600
Pas-de-Calais	Arras	2,576	6,671	1,440,000
Pays de la Loire				
Loire-Atlantique	Nantes	2,631	6,815	1,074,800
Maine-et Loire	Angers	2,767	7,166	716,300
Mayenne	Laval	1,998	5,175	281,600
Sarthe	Le Mans	2,396	6,206	518,800
Vendée	La Roche-sur-Yon	2,595	6,720	521,200
Picardie				
Aisne	Laon	2,845	7,369	540,500
Oise	Beauvais	2,263	5,860	753,400
Somme	Amiens	2,382	6,170	554,100
Poitou-Charentes				
Charente	Angoulême	2,300	5,956	342,500
Charente-Maritime	La Rochelle	2,650	6,864	539,700
Deux-Sèvres	Niort	2,316	5,999	346,400
Vienne	Poitiers	2,699	6,990	388,600
Provence-Alpes-Côte d'Azur				
Alpes-de-Haute-Provence	Digne	2,674	6,925	135,300
Alpes-Maritimes	Nice	1,660	4,299	996,800
Bouches-du-Rhône	Marseille	1,964	5,087	1,791,100
Hautes-Alpes	Gap	2,142	5,549	116,600
Var	Toulon	2,306	5,973	855,000
Vaucluse	Avignon	1,377	3,567	480,400
Rhône-Alpes				
Ain	Bourg-en-Bresse	2,225	5,762	492,600
Ardèche	Privas	2,135	5,529	280,300
Drôme	Valence	2,521	6,530	423,900
Haute-Savoie	Annecy	1,694	4,388	600,700
Isère	Grenoble	2,869	7,431	1,045,400
Loire	Saint-Étienne	1,846	4,781	748,700
Rhône	Lyon	1,254	3,249	1,531,200
Savoie	Chambéry	2,327	6,028	365,800
TOTAL		210,026	543,965	57,529,700

Demography

Population (1995): 58,172,000.
Density (1995): persons per sq mi 277.0, persons per sq km 106.9.
Urban-rural (1993): urban 72.8%; rural 27.2%.
Sex distribution (1994[1]): male 48.71%; female 51.29%.
Age breakdown (1994[1]): under 15, 19.8%; 15–29, 21.7%; 30–44, 22.4%; 45–59, 16.4%; 60–74, 13.6%; 75 and over, 6.1%.
Population projection: (2000) 59,628,000; (2010) 62,648,000.
Doubling time: not applicable; doubling time exceeds 100 years.
Ethnolinguistic composition (1990): French (mother tongue) 93.6%, of which fully or substantially bilingual in Occitan 2.7%, German (mostly Alsatian) 2.3%, Breton 1.0%, Catalan 0.4%; Arabic 2.5%; other 3.9%.
Religious affiliation (1980): Roman Catholic 76.4%; other Christian 3.7%; atheist 3.4%; Muslim 3.0%; other 13.5%.
Major cities (1990): Paris 2,152,423 (metropolitan area 9,060,257); Marseille 800,550 (1,231,082); Lyon 415,487 (1,262,223); Toulouse 358,688 (608,430); Nice 342,439 (475,507); Strasbourg 252,338 (338,483); Nantes 244,995 (492,-255); Bordeaux 210,336 (685,456); Montpellier 207,996 (236,788).
National origin (1990): French 93.6%, of which Martiniquais 0.2%, Guadeloupian 0.2%, Réunionese 0.2%; Portuguese 1.1%; Algerian 1.1%; Moroccan 1.0%; Italian 0.4%; Spanish 0.4%; Turkish 0.3%; other 2.1%.
Mobility (1990). Population living in same residence as in 1982: 51.4%; same region 89.0%; different region 8.8%; different country 2.2%.
Households (1993). Average household size 2.6; 1 person 27.7%, 2 persons 32.0%, 3 persons 17.4%, 4 persons 14.7%, 5 persons or more 8.2%. Family households (1990): 14,118,940 (72.1%); nonfamily 5,471,460 (27.9%, of which 1-person 24.6%).
Immigration (1992): permanent immigrants admitted 110,669 (Morocco 14.6%, Algeria 10.3%, Turkey 8.4%, Tunisia 3.5%, Sri Lanka 2.7%, Lebanon 1.5%, Vietnam 1.2%).

Vital statistics

Birth rate per 1,000 population (1994): 12.3 (world avg. 25.0); (1992) legitimate 66.8%; illegitimate 33.2%.
Death rate per 1,000 population (1994): 9.0 (world avg. 9.3).
Natural increase rate per 1,000 population (1994): 3.3 (world avg. 15.7).
Total fertility rate (avg. births per childbearing woman; 1993): 1.6.
Marriage rate per 1,000 population (1994): 4.4.
Divorce rate per 1,000 population (1992): 1.9.
Life expectancy at birth (1991–93): male 73.1 years; female 81.3 years.
Major causes of death per 100,000 population (1993): heart disease and other circulatory diseases 301.5; malignant neoplasms (cancers) 253.3; accidents and violence 80.5; respiratory diseases 69.9; digestive-tract diseases 45.2.

Social indicators

Educational attainment (1990). Percentage of population age 25 and over having: primary 22.1%; lower secondary 7.8%; higher secondary and vocational 29.4%; postsecondary 11.6%; undeclared attainment 29.1%.

Distribution of income (1984)

percentage of household income by quintile

1	2	3	4	5 (highest)
7.1%	12.3%	17.1%	23.2%	40.3%

Quality of working life. Average workweek (1994): 38.9 hours. Annual rate per 100,000 workers (1992) for: injury or accident 3,386 (deaths 4.6); accidents in transit to work 847 (deaths 40.1); industrial illness 16.6[3]; death 4.8[3]. Proportion of labour force insured for damages or income loss resulting from: injury, permanent disability, or death, n.a. Average days lost to labour stoppages per 1,000 workers (1993): 23.0. Average length of journey to work (1990): 8.7 mi (14 km).
Access to services (1992). Proportion of dwellings having: central heating 86.0%; piped water 97.0%; indoor plumbing 95.8%.

Social deviance. Offense rate per 100,000 population (1992) for: murder 0.8; rape 9.6; other assault 96.5; theft (including burglary and housebreaking) 4,558.6. Incidence per 100,000 in general population of: alcoholism, n.a. (deaths related to alcoholism; 1991) 5.0; suicide (1993) 21.1.
Social participation. Eligible voters participating in last (May 1995) national election: 79.7%. Population over 15 years of age participating in voluntary associations: 28.0%.
Leisure (1987–88). Participation rate for favourite leisure activities: watching television 82%; reading magazines 79%; listening to radio 75%; entertaining relatives 64%; visiting relatives 61%; attending fairs/expositions 56%.
Material well-being (1991). Households possessing: automobile 76.8%; television receiver 94.7%, of which colour 89.1%; videocassette recorder 37.1%; refrigerator 97.9%; washing machine 88.4%.

National economy

Gross national product (1994): U.S.$1,317,950,000,000 (U.S.$22,760 per capita).

Structure of gross domestic product and labour force

	1994			
	in value F '000,000	% of total value	labour force	% of labour force
Agriculture	177,196	2.6	1,055,200	4.1
Mining	50,992	0.8	118,700	0.4
Manufacturing	1,395,678	20.4	3,997,800	15.7
Construction	335,104	4.9	1,471,800	5.8
Public utilities	176,232	2.6	161,100	0.6
Transp. and commun.	427,520	6.3	1,267,500	5.0
Trade[4]	973,816	14.3	3,468,500	13.6
Finance	385,334	5.6	599,100	2.4
Pub. admin., defense	1,270,319	18.6	6,148,000	24.1
Services	1,209,835	17.7	3,839,600	15.1
Other	420,691[5]	6.2[5]	3,358,200[6]	13.2[6]
TOTAL	6,822,717	100.0	25,485,500	100.0

Budget (1995). Revenue: F 1,448,500,000,000 (value-added taxes 46.5%; direct taxes 39.1%; customs taxes 11.0%). Expenditure (1995): F 1,470,400,000,000 (current expenditures 88.0%, of which education 17.8%, defense 16.5%, health 4.2%; capital expenditure 12.0%).

Manufacturing enterprises (1994)

	no. of enter-prises[7]	no. of employees	annual salaries as a % of avg. of all salaries[7]	annual value added (F '000,000)
Food products	55,197	551,300	87	198,717
Electrical machinery	15,620	420,100	118	143,298
Petroleum refineries	180	47,000	174	112,653
Transport equipment	4,293	509,700	108	117,555
Mechanical equipment	32,134	385,300	104	114,856
Iron and steel	27,847	403,400	96	124,628
Printing, publishing	30,359	236,000	125	84,338
Rubber products	5,875	200,200	94	65,039
Textiles and wearing apparel	29,701	285,800	78	65,011
Chemical products	1,442	101,600	128	46,070
Paper and paper products	1,916	100,100	102	32,387
Metal products	442	44,100	103	26,787
Glass products	1,536	53,500	104	15,401
Footwear	4,236	57,300	75	12,848

Production (metric tons except as noted). Agriculture, forestry, fishing (1994): wheat 30,652,000, sugar beets 28,997,000, corn (maize) 13,040,000, barley 7,637,000, grapes 6,933,000, potatoes 5,456,000, apples 2,157,000, sunflower seeds 2,056,000, rapeseed 1,771,000, tomatoes 788,000, oats 685,000, cauliflower 553,000, peaches 531,000, pears 459,000, sorghum 266,000, soybeans 262,000, rye 176,000; livestock (number of live animals) 20,112,000 cattle, 13,383,000 pigs, 10,452,000 sheep, 1,055,000 goats; roundwood (1993) 44,069,000 cu m; fish catch (1993) 830,000. Mining and quarrying (1994): iron ore 710,000[8]; potash salts 950,000; uranium 1,275[8]; gold 122,200 troy oz[8]; silver 19,300 troy oz[8]. Manufacturing (1993): cement 19,320,000; crude steel 17,112,000; pig iron 13,056,000[9]; sulfuric acid 3,627,000[7]; aluminum 628,800[9]; rubber products 486,360, of which tires 62,520,000 units; automobiles 3,103,200 units. Construction (dwelling units completed; 1993) 299,000.

Retail trade enterprises (1992)

	no. of enter-prises	no. of employees	weekly wages as a % of all wages	annual turnover (F '000,000)
Large food stores	4,777	396,986	...	627,770
Clothing stores	73,840	233,602	...	139,596
Small food stores	80,400	210,235	...	132,028
butcher shops	38,411	110,658	...	65,447
Pharmacies	21,836	120,605	...	107,900
Department stores	1,419	63,776	...	71,858
Furniture stores	7,423	52,046	...	51,128
Electrical and electronics stores	9,673	53,174	...	48,295
Publishing and paper	20,010	54,899	...	30,729
Gas, coal, and other energy products	2,737	11,503	...	23,556

Energy production (consumption)[10]: electricity (kW-hr; 1992) 462,263,000,000 (408,467,000,000); coal (metric tons; 1992) 11,056,000 (28,565,000); crude petroleum (barrels; 1992) 21,014,000 (543,301,000); petroleum products (metric tons; 1992) 69,773,000 (77,165,000); natural gas (cu m; 1992) 2,385,630,000 (33,750,289,000).
Household income and expenditure. Average household size (1994) 2.6; average annual income per household (1994) F 300,960 (U.S.$53,140). Sources of income (1992): wages and salaries 51.1%, social security 27.5%, self-employment 21.4%; expenditure (1994): housing 21.3%, food 18.3%, transportation 16.4%, health 10.2%, recreation 7.4%, clothing 5.7%.
Tourism (1993): receipts from visitors U.S.$23,410,000,000; expenditures by nationals abroad U.S.$12,800,000,000.

Population economically active (1994): total 25,485,500; activity rate of total population 44.1% (participation rates: ages 15–64, 67.6%[11]; female 44.5%; unemployed 12.4%).

Price and earnings indexes (1990 = 100)

	1988	1989	1990	1991	1992	1993	1994
Consumer price index	93.5	96.7	100.0	103.2	105.7	107.9	109.7
Earnings index	94.1	98.5	100.0	104.4	108.4	111.7	115.0

Public debt (1994): F 2,246,000,000,000 (U.S.$420,100,000,000).

Financial aggregates	1990	1991	1992	1993	1994	1995[12]
Exchange rate, F per:						
U.S. dollar	5.13	5.18	5.51	5.90	5.35	4.91[13]
£	9.89	9.67	9.37	8.73	8.35	7.76[13]
SDR	7.30	7.41	7.57	8.10	7.80	7.40[13]
International reserves (U.S.$)						
Total (excl. gold; '000,000)	36,778	31,284	27,028	22,649	26,257	27,181
SDRs ('000,000)	1,283	1,326	163	331	362	978
Reserve pos. in IMF ('000,000)	1,428	1,666	2,482	2,310	2,375	2,765
Foreign exchange	21,868	28,292	24,384	20,008	23,520	23,438
Gold ('000,000 fine troy oz)	81.85	81.85	81.85	81.85	81.85	81.85
% world reserves	8.7	8.7	8.7	8.7	8.7	9.1
Interest and prices						
Central bank discount (%)	9.50	9.50	9.50	9.50	9.50	...
Govt. bond yield (%)	9.96	9.05	8.60	6.91	8.52	7.45
Industrial share prices (1990 = 100)	100.0	97.5	107.8	116.2	...	...
Balance of payments (U.S.$'000,000)						
Balance of visible trade	−13,667	−10,139	1,661	8,418	7,868	...
Imports, f.o.b.	220,339	217,233	223,561	187,873	215,593	...
Exports, f.o.b.	206,672	207,084	225,222	196,291	223,461	...
Balance of invisibles	−105	3,991	1,819	3,503	263	...
Balance of payments, current account	−13,772	−6,148	3,480	11,921	8,128	...

Land use (1993): forested 27.1%; meadows and pastures 19.6%; agricultural and under permanent cultivation 35.3%; other 18.0%.

Foreign trade

Balance of trade (current prices)

	1989	1990	1991	1992	1993	1994
F '000,000,000	−43.9	−49.6	−29.6	+31.0	+101.7	+87.8
% of total	1.9%	3.1%	1.2%	1.3%	4.5%	3.5%

Imports (1994): F 1,279,663,000,000 (machinery and transport equipment 41.2%, of which transport equipment 14.3%, electrical equipment 11.4%; agricultural products 12.3%; chemical products 8.1%; fuels 7.7%). *Major import sources:* Germany 17.8%; U.S. 10.1%; Italy 10.1%; Belgium-Luxembourg 9.2%; U.K. 8.0%; Spain 6.1%; The Netherlands 5.0%; Japan 4.4%.
Exports (1994): F 1,311,798,000,000 (machinery and transport equipment 45.4%, of which transport equipment 18.3%, electrical equipment 10.6%; agricultural products 15.5%; chemical products 8.1%; pharmaceuticals 6.2%). *Major export destinations:* Germany 17.1%; U.K. 9.9%; Italy 9.4%; Belgium-Luxembourg 8.8%; U.S. 8.4%; Spain 7.1%; The Netherlands 4.6%.

Transport and communications

Transport. Railroads (1993): route length 34,074 km; passenger-km 58,380,000,000; metric ton-km cargo 45,864,000,000. Roads (1993): total length 829,400 km (paved [1985] 92%). Vehicles (1993): passenger cars 24,385,000; trucks and buses 4,890,000. Merchant marine (1992): vessels (100 gross tons and over) 729; total deadweight tonnage 4,981,027. Air transport (1993): passenger-km 59,200,000,000; metric ton-km cargo 3,700,000,000; airports (1995) with scheduled flights 66.
Communications. Daily newspapers (1993): number 116; circulation 10,096,000[14]; circulation per 1,000 population 175[14]. Radio (1993): 49,000,000 receivers (1 per 1.2 persons). Television (1993): 29,300,000 receivers (1 per 2.0 persons). Telephones (1994): 31,600,000 (1 per 1.8 persons).

Education and health

Education (1993–94)	schools	teachers	students	student/teacher ratio
Primary (age 6–10)	41,656	218,100[15]	4,060,607	18.6
Secondary (age 11–18) } Voc., teacher tr. }	11,325[16]	454,000	4,486,063 } 1,251,295 }	12.6
Higher	1,062[17]	57,429[18]	1,700,800[18]	29.6[18]

Literacy (1980): total population literate 41,112,000 (98.8%); males literate 19,933,000 (98.9%); females literate 21,179,000 (98.7%).
Health: physicians (1994) 160,235 (1 per 361 persons); hospital beds (1993) 680,840 (1 per 85 persons); infant mortality rate (1994) 5.6.
Food (1992): daily per capita caloric intake 3,633 (vegetable products 60%, animal products 40%); 144% of FAO recommended minimum requirement.

Military

Total active duty personnel (1995): 409,000 (army 59.0%, navy 15.7%, air force 21.8%, other 3.5%). *Military expenditure as percentage of GNP* (1993): 3.4% (world 3.3%); per capita expenditure U.S.$740.

[1]January 1. [2]In May 1992, Corse was granted local autonomy (with its own directly elected assembly), changing its regional status to "territorial collective." [3]1989. [4]Includes hotels. [5]Imputed rents and imputed bank service charges. [6]Includes 3,164,700 unemployed. [7]1991. [8]Metal content of ores. [9]1992. [10]All energy statistics include Monaco. [11]1993. [12]July, unless otherwise noted. [13]September. [14]For 90 newspapers only. [15]Includes preprimary teachers. [16]1990–91. [17]1988–89. [18]1991–92.

Gabon

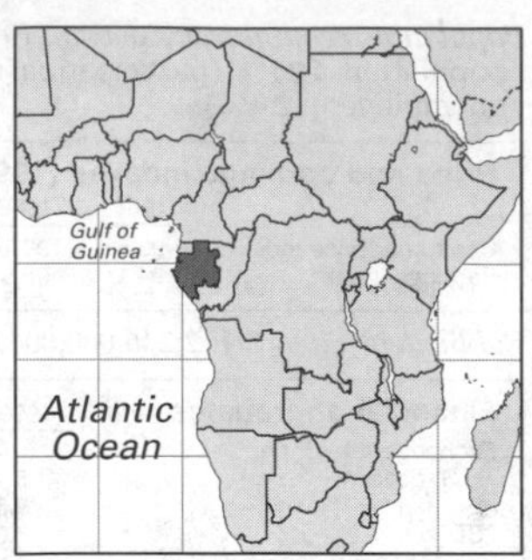

Official name: République Gabonaise (Gabonese Republic).
Form of government: unitary multiparty republic with one legislative house (National Assembly [120]).
Chief of state: President.
Head of government: Prime Minister.
Capital: Libreville.
Official language: French.
Official religion: none.
Monetary unit: 1 CFA franc (CFAF) = 100 centimes; valuation (Oct. 6, 1995) 1 U.S.$ = CFAF 501.49; 1 £ = CFAF 792.78.

Area and population

		area		population
Provinces	Capitals	sq mi	sq km	1993 census[1]
Estuaire	Libreville	8,008	20,740	462,086
Haut-Ogooué	Franceville	14,111	36,547	102,387
Moyen-Ogooué	Lambaréné	7,156	18,535	41,827
Ngounié	Mouila	14,575	37,750	77,871
Nyanga	Tchibanga	8,218	21,285	39,826
Ogooué-Ivindo	Makokou	17,790	46,075	48,847
Ogooué-Lolo	Koulamoutou	9,799	25,380	42,783
Ogooué-Maritime	Port-Gentil	8,838	22,890	98,299
Woleu-Ntem	Oyem	14,851	38,465	97,739
TOTAL		103,347[2]	267,667	1,011,710[3]

Demography

Population (1995): 1,156,000.
Density (1995): persons per sq mi 11.2, persons per sq km 4.3.
Urban-rural (1993): urban 73.2%; rural 26.8%.
Sex distribution (1995): male 49.32%; female 50.68%.
Age breakdown (1995): under 15, 39.1%; 15–29, 22.3%; 30–44, 17.2%; 45–59, 12.4%; 60–74, 7.2%; 75 and over, 1.7%.
Population projection: (2000) 1,244,000; (2010) 1,445,000.
Doubling time: 32 years.
Ethnic composition (1983): Fang 35.5%; Mpongwe 15.1%; Mbete 14.2%; Punu 11.5%; other 23.7%.
Religious affiliation (1980): Christian 96.2%, of which Roman Catholic 65.2%, Protestant 18.8%, African indigenous 12.1%; traditional religion 2.9%; Muslim 0.8%; other 0.1%.
Major cities (1993): Libreville 419,596; Port-Gentil 78,225; Franceville (1988) 75,000.

Vital statistics

Birth rate per 1,000 population (1990–95): 37.3 (world avg. 25.0).
Death rate per 1,000 population (1990–95): 15.5 (world avg. 9.3).
Natural increase rate per 1,000 population (1990–95): 21.8 (world avg. 15.7).
Total fertility rate (avg. births per childbearing woman; 1990–95): 5.3.
Marriage rate per 1,000 population: n.a.
Divorce rate per 1,000 population: n.a.
Life expectancy at birth (1990–95): male 51.9 years; female 55.2 years.
Major causes of death per 100,000 population: n.a.; however, in the early 1990s major causes of morbidity and mortality included malaria, shigellosis (infection with dysentery), tetanus, cardiovascular diseases, trypanosomiasis, and tuberculosis.

National economy

Budget (1994). Revenue: CFAF 524,000,000,000 (oil revenues 61.3%; customs duties and other current revenues 38.7%). Expenditures: CFAF 615,200,000,000 (current expenditure 82.9%, of which service on public debt 33.4%, wages and salaries 26.8%; capital expenditure 17.1%).
Public debt (external, outstanding; 1993): U.S.$2,889,000,000.
Tourism (1993): receipts from visitors U.S.$5,000,000; expenditures by nationals abroad U.S.$132,000,000.
Production (metric tons except as noted). Agriculture, forestry, fishing (1994): roots and tubers 374,000 (of which cassava 200,000, yams 110,000), plantains 246,000, sugarcane 220,000, corn (maize) 26,000, peanuts (groundnuts) 15,000, bananas 9,000, palm oil 2,600, cacao beans 2,000; livestock (number of live animals) 170,000 sheep, 165,000 pigs, 83,000 goats, 38,000 cattle, 3,000,000 chickens; roundwood (1993) 4,436,000 cu m; fish catch (1993) 28,289. Mining and quarrying (1993): manganese 1,460,000; uranium 509. Manufacturing (1992): cement 138,381; wheat flour 31,000; refined sugar 15,000; beer 785,000 hectolitres; soft drinks 410,000 hectolitres; cigarettes 399,000,000 units; textiles are also significant. Construction: n.a. Energy production (consumption): electricity (kW-hr; 1993) 922,000,000 (922,000,000); crude petroleum (barrels; 1993) 110,072,000 (6,903,000); petroleum products (metric tons; 1993) 761,000 (616,000); natural gas (cu m; 1993) 50,700,000 (50,700,000); fuelwood (cu m; 1992) 2,711,000 (2,711,000).
Population economically active (1993): total 376,000; activity rate of total population 37.0% (participation rates [1985]: ages 15–64, 68.2%; female 38.4%; unemployed, n.a.).

Price and earnings indexes (1985 = 100)

	1988	1989	1990	1991	1992	1993	1994
Consumer price index	109.7	103.2	111.1	118.7	100.8	91.3	123.4
Earnings index	...	...	...	...	...	...	...

Land use (1993): forested 77.2%; meadows and pastures 18.2%; agricultural and under permanent cultivation 1.8%; other 2.8%.
Gross national product (at current market prices; 1993): U.S.$5,002,000,000 (U.S.$4,050 per capita).

Structure of gross domestic product and labour force

	1991		1993	
	in value CFAF '000,000	% of total value	labour force	% of labour force
Agriculture, forestry, fishing	85,920	8.8	156,000[4]	41.6
Mining	297,880	30.6		
Manufacturing	71,730	7.4	43,000[4]	11.5
Construction	90,410	9.3		
Public utilities	27,410	2.8		
Transportation and communications	61,500	6.3		
Trade	93,430	9.6		
Finance	73,900	7.6	115,000[4]	30.7
Services, Other	15,530	1.6		
Pub. admin., defense	156,770	16.1	61,000[4]	16.2
TOTAL	974,470[2]	100.0[2]	376,000[2]	100.0

Household income and expenditure. Average household size (1980) 4.0; income per household: n.a.; sources of income (1983): private sector 73.4%, public sector 26.6%; expenditure (1969)[5]: food and tobacco 54.7%, clothing and footwear 17.5%, housing 13.0%, transportation and communications 6.3%.

Foreign trade

Balance of trade (current prices)

	1989	1990	1991	1992	1993	1994
CFAF '000,000	+279,000	+466,000	+397,000	+373,000	+410,600	+877,000
% of total	37.0%	52.6%	45.7%	44.3%	46.2%	51.7%

Imports (1992): CFAF 230,000,000,000 (1989; machinery and mechanical equipment 29.2%, food and agricultural products 14.6%, transport equipment 12.5%, manufactured products 12.1%, metal and metal products 11.2%, chemical products 5.4%, mining products 1.6%). *Major import sources:* France 50.0%; other EEC 22.0%; United States 9.0%; Japan 7.0%; Africa 5.0%.
Exports (1992): CFAF 614,000,000,000 (crude petroleum and petroleum products 80.0%, wood 9.0%, manganese ore and concentrate 7.0%, uranium ore and concentrate 2.0%). *Major export destinations* (1989): France 36.2%; United States 26.1%; The Netherlands 6.2%; Japan 3.3%; Côte d'Ivoire 2.9%; Italy 2.3%.

Transport and communications

Transport. Railroads (1993): length 414 mi, 668 km; passenger-mi 21,000,000[6], passenger-km 34,000,000[6]; short ton-mi cargo 126,000,000[6], metric ton-km cargo 184,000,000[6]. Roads (1993): total length 4,671 mi, 7,518 km (paved 8%). Vehicles (1992): passenger cars 23,000; trucks and buses 17,000. Merchant marine (1992): vessels (100 gross tons and over) 29; total deadweight tonnage 30,186. Air transport (1993): passenger-mi 354,000,000, passenger-km 570,000,000; short ton-mi cargo 56,000,000, metric ton-km cargo 82,000,000; airports (1995) with scheduled flights 6.
Communications. Daily newspapers (1992): total number 1; total circulation 20,000; circulation per 1,000 population 16. Radio (1994): total number of receivers 155,000 (1 per 4.5 persons). Television (1994): total number of receivers 40,000 (1 per 28 persons). Telephones (main lines; 1993): 29,800 (1 per 41 persons).

Education and health

Education (1991)

	schools	teachers	students	student/ teacher ratio
Primary	1,024	4,782	210,000	43.9
Secondary	51[7]	1,356[7]	42,871	...
Voc., teacher tr.	29[7]	476	8,477	11.8
Higher[8]	2	299	3,000	10.0

Educational attainment: n.a. *Literacy* (1995): total population age 15 and over literate 63.2%; males literate 73.7%; females literate 53.3%.
Health: physicians (1989) 448 (1 per 2,337 persons); hospital beds (1984) 10,980 (1 per 103 persons); infant mortality rate per 1,000 live births (1990–95) 94.
Food (1992): daily per capita caloric intake 2,500 (vegetable products 88%, animal products 12%); 108% of FAO recommended minimum requirement.

Military

Total active duty personnel (1995): 4,700 (army 68.1%, navy 10.6%, air force 21.3%), excluding 600 French troops. *Military expenditure as percentage of GNP* (1990): 3.4% (world 4.4%); per capita expenditure U.S.$144.

[1]De jure; excludes an estimated 100,000 to 150,000 nonnationals. [2]Detail does not add to total given because of rounding. [3]Includes 45 persons not distributed by province. [4]Derived values. [5]Libreville only. [6]1987. [7]1984–85. [8]Universities only.

Gambia, The

Official name: Republic of The Gambia.
Form of government: military regime[1].
Head of state and government: Chairman of Armed Forces Provisional Ruling Council.
Capital: Banjul.
Official language: English.
Official religion: none.
Monetary unit: 1 dalasi (D) = 100 butut; valuation (Oct. 6, 1995) 1 U.S.$ = D 9.65; 1 £ = D 15.26.

Area and population

Divisions	Capitals	area sq mi	area sq km	population 1993 census[2]
Kombo St. Mary[3, 4]	Kanifing	29	76	228,214
Lower River	Mansakonko	625	1,618	65,146
MacCarthy Island	Kuntaur/Georgetown	1,117	2,894	156,021
North Bank	Kerewan	871	2,256	156,462
Upper River	Basse	799	2,069	155,059
Western	Brikama	681	1,764	234,917
City				
Banjul[4]	—	5	12	42,326
TOTAL		4,127[5]	10,689[5]	1,038,145

Demography

Population (1995): 1,115,000.
Density (1995)[6]: persons per sq mi 335.3, persons per sq km 129.5.
Urban-rural (1993): urban 36.7%; rural 63.3%.
Sex distribution (1993): male 50.08%; female 49.92%.
Age breakdown (1993): under 15, 43.8%; 15–29, 27.7%; 30–44, 15.1%; 45–59, 6.8%; 60–74, 3.5%; 75 and over, 1.4%; not stated 1.7%.
Population projection: (2000) 1,288,000; (2010) 1,607,000.
Doubling time: 28 years.
Ethnic composition (1993): Malinke 34.1%; Fulani 16.2%; Wolof 12.6%; Dyola 9.2%; Soninke 7.7%; other 20.2%.
Religious affiliation (1993): Muslim 95.0%; Christian 4.0%; traditional beliefs and other 1.0%.
Major cities/urban areas (1986): Serekunda 102,600[3]; Banjul 42,326 (Greater Banjul 270,540[4, 7]); Brikama 24,300; Bakau 23,600[3]; Farafenni 10,168[8].

Vital statistics

Birth rate per 1,000 population (1990–95): 44.1 (world avg. 25.0); legitimate, n.a.; illegitimate, n.a.
Death rate per 1,000 population (1990–95): 19.4 (world avg. 9.3).
Natural increase rate per 1,000 population (1990–95): 24.7 (world avg. 15.7).
Total fertility rate (avg. births per childbearing woman; 1990–95): 6.1.
Marriage rate per 1,000 population: n.a.
Divorce rate per 1,000 population: n.a.
Life expectancy at birth (1990–95): male 43.4 years; female 46.6 years.
Major causes of death per 100,000 population: n.a.; however, major infectious diseases include malaria, gastroenteritis and dysentery, pneumonia and bronchitis, measles, schistosomiasis, and whooping cough.

National economy

Budget (1992–93). Revenue: D 890,500,000 (tax revenue 78.9%, of which import duties and excises 37.4%, sales tax 27.8%, income taxes 13.7%; nontax revenue and grants 21.1%). Expenditures: D 847,800,000 (administrative expenses 19.0%; interest payments 15.6%; goods and services 14.6%; transportation and communications 13.2%; education and culture 5.4%; agriculture 3.2%; public services 2.6%).
Production (metric tons except as noted). Agriculture, forestry, fishing (1994): peanuts (groundnuts) 85,000, millet 54,000, corn (maize) 22,000, paddy rice 21,000, seed cotton 10,000, cassava 6,000, pulses (mostly beans) 4,000, palm oil 2,500, palm kernels 2,000; livestock (number of live animals) 414,000 cattle, 150,000 goats, 121,000 sheep; roundwood (1993) 958,000 cu m; fish catch (1993) 20,479, of which Atlantic Ocean 18,079, inland water 2,400. Mining and quarrying: sand and gravel are excavated for local use. Manufacturing (value of production in D '000; 1982): processed food, including peanut and palm-kernel oil 62,878; beverages 10,546; textiles 3,253; chemicals and related products 1,031; nonmetals 922; printing and publishing 358; leather 150. Construction: n.a. Energy production (consumption): electricity (kW-hr; 1992) 71,000,000 (71,000,000); coal, none (none); crude petroleum, none (none); petroleum products (metric tons; 1992) none (64,000); natural gas, none (none).
Population economically active (1992): total 412,000; activity rate of total population 47.2% (participation rates: [1983] ages 15–64, 78.2%; female 46.3%; unemployed, n.a.).

Price and earnings indexes (1990 = 100)

	1988	1989	1990	1991	1992	1993	1994
Consumer price index	82.3	89.1	100.0	108.6	118.9	126.6	128.7
Earnings index	...	...	...	...	...	...	...

Tourism: receipts from visitors (1993) U.S.$26,000,000; expenditures by nationals abroad (1992) U.S.$13,000,000.
Household income and expenditure. Average household size (1983) 8.3; income per household: n.a.; sources of income: n.a.; expenditure (1986)[9]: food and beverages 58.0%, clothing and footwear 17.5%, energy and water 5.4%, housing 5.1%, education, health, transportation and communications, recreation, and other 14.0%.
Public debt (external, outstanding; 1993): U.S.$348,800,000.
Gross national product (at current market prices; 1993): U.S.$372,000,000 (U.S.$360 per capita).

Structure of gross domestic product and labour force

	1992–93 in value D'000,000[10]	1992–93 % of total value	1983 labour force	1983 % of labour force
Agriculture	108.4	18.9	239,940	73.7
Mining	—	—	66	0.0
Manufacturing	33.3	5.8	8,144	2.5
Construction	34.4	6.0	4,373	1.3
Public utilities	3.5	0.6	1,233	0.4
Transportation and communications	93.7	16.4	8,014	2.5
Trade	111.5	19.5	16,551	5.1
Finance	34.2	6.0	4,577	1.4
Public administration	58.8	10.3	8,295	2.5
Services	18.0	3.1	9,381	2.9
Other	76.7[11]	13.4[11]	25,049[12]	7.7[12]
TOTAL	572.5	100.0	325,623	100.0

Land use (1993): forested 28.0%; meadows and pastures 9.0%; agricultural and under permanent cultivation 18.0%; built-on area, wasteland, and other 45.0%.

Foreign trade[13]

Balance of trade (current prices)

	1987	1988	1989	1990	1991	1992
D '000,000	−615.9	−530.7	−1,023.0	−1,195.3	−1,561.4	−1,675.9
% of total	52.3%	40.6%	72.1%	61.2%	67.8%	59.7%

Imports (1992–93). D 2,363,486,000 (food 29.1%; machinery and transport equipment 23.2%; basic manufactures 19.8%; mineral fuels and lubricants 5.9%; chemicals and related products 5.2%). *Major import sources* (1993): China 20.3%; Hong Kong 11.1%; United Kingdom 10.3%; France 7.9%; Belgium-Luxembourg 7.9%; Italy 3.2%.
Exports (1992–93): D 543,751,000 (domestic exports 53.5%, of which fish and fish preparations 4.4%; reexports 46.5%[14]). *Major export destinations* (1993): Belgium-Luxembourg 50.9%; Japan 22.0%; Guinea 5.7%; United Kingdom 5.0%; Hong Kong 2.5%; Thailand 1.9%; Spain 1.3%.

Transport and communications

Transport. Railroads: none. Roads (1990): total length 1,483 mi, 2,386 km (paved 32%). Vehicles (1993): passenger cars 7,300; trucks and buses 3,100. Merchant marine (1992): vessels (100 gross tons and over) 11; total deadweight tonnage 2,029. Air transport (1991): passenger arrivals and departures 128,000, cargo 1,603 metric tons; airports (1995) with scheduled flights 1.
Communications. Daily newspapers (1992): total number 2; total circulation 2,000; circulation per 1,000 population 2.2. Radio (1994): total number of receivers 140,000 (1 per 7.7 persons). Television: none. Telephones (main lines; 1993): 16,300 (1 per 64 persons).

Education and health

Education (1992)

	schools	teachers	students	student/teacher ratio
Primary (age 8–14)	245	3,193	97,262	30.5
Secondary (age 15–21)[15]	32	1,054	25,929	24.6
Postsecondary[16]	9	177	1,489	8.4

Educational attainment (1973). Percentage of population age 20 and over having: no formal schooling 90.8%; primary education 6.2%; secondary 2.6%; higher 0.4%. *Literacy* (1990): total population age 15 and over literate 27.2%; males literate 39.0%; females literate 16.0%.
Health (1990–91): physicians 61 (1 per 14,536 persons); hospital beds 601 (1 per 1,475 persons); infant mortality rate per 1,000 live births (1990–95) 132.
Food (1992): daily per capita caloric intake 2,360 (vegetable products 94%, animal products 6%); 103% of FAO recommended minimum requirement.

Military

Total active duty personnel (1994): 800. *Military expenditure as percentage of GNP* (1993): 0.8% (world 3.3%); per capita expenditure U.S.$3.

[1]Constitutional government overthrown July 22, 1994. [2]Preliminary. [3]Kombo St. Mary includes the urban areas of Serekunda and Bakau. [4]Kombo St. Mary and Banjul city make up Greater Banjul. [5]Includes inland water area of 2,077 sq km (802 sq mi). [6]Based on land area only. [7]1993. [8]1983. [9]Low-income population in Banjul and Kombo St. Mary only; weights of consumer price index components. [10]At constant prices of 1976–77. [11]Indirect taxes. [12]Not adequately defined. [13]Imports c.i.f.; exports f.o.b. [14]Mostly unofficial trade with Senegal. [15]Includes teacher training and vocational. [16]1984–85.

Georgia

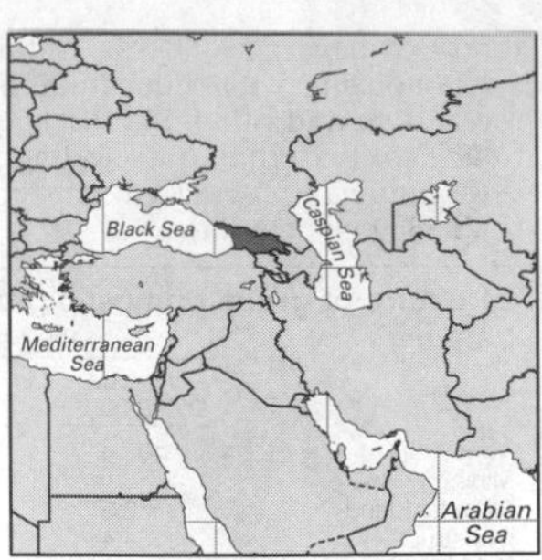

Official name: Sakartvelos Respublika (Republic of Georgia).
Form of government: unitary multiparty republic with a single legislative body (Parliament [223]).
Head of state: Chairman of Parliament.
Head of government: Prime Minister.
Capital: T'bilisi.
Official language: Georgian.
Official religion: none.
Monetary unit: lari[1] (decimal unit, 100 tetri); valuation (Oct. 4, 1995), 1 U.S.$ = 1.30 lari; 1 £ = 2.07 lari.

Area and population

		area		population
Autonomous republics	**Capitals**	sq mi	sq km	1993[2] estimate
Abkhazia[3]	Sokhumi (Sukhumi)	3,343	8,660	516,600
Ajaria (Adzharia)	Bat'umi	1,120	2,900	386,700
Regions under republican jurisdiction				
Guria	...	785	2,033	160,800
Imereti	...	2,452	6,349	788,900
Kakheti	...	4,717	12,217	464,000
Kvemo Kartli	...	2,615	6,772	601,500
Racha-Lechkumi	...	1,245	3,224	45,400
Samegrelo	...	1,697	4,395	418,000
Samtskhe-Javakheti	...	2,017	5,224	198,800
Shida Kartli	...	3,043	7,882	485,900
Svaneti	...	1,694	4,389	23,200
Tianeti	...	1,569	4,063	43,800
Region under the authority of urban council				
T'bilisi	...	534	1,384	1,271,800
TOTAL		26,831	69,492	5,405,400

Demography

Population (1995): 5,514,000.
Density (1995): persons per sq mi 205.5, persons per sq km 79.3.
Urban-rural (1993): urban 55.7%; rural 44.3%.
Sex distribution (1992): male 47.6%; female 52.4%.
Age breakdown (1989): under 15, 24.8%; 15–29, 24.1%; 30–44, 19.2%; 45–59, 17.5%; 60–74, 10.8%; 75 and over, 3.6%.
Population projection: (2000) 5,569,000; (2010) 5,680,000.
Doubling time: 77 years.
Ethnic composition (1989): Georgian 70.1%; Armenian 8.1%; Russian 6.3%; Azerbaijani 5.7%; Ossetian 3.0%; Greek 1.9%; Abkhazian 1.8%; other 3.1%.
Religious affiliation: believers are predominantly Georgian Orthodox (65%); minorities include Muslims (11%), Russian Orthodox (10%), and Armenian Orthodox (8%).
Major cities (1993): T'bilisi 1,270,000; K'ut'aisi 240,000; Rust'avi 158,000; Bat'umi 137,000; Sokhumi (Sukhumi) 112,000.

Vital statistics

Birth rate per 1,000 population (1993): 12.6 (world avg. 25.0); (1989) legitimate 82.3%; illegitimate 17.7%.
Death rate per 1,000 population (1990): 10.1 (world avg. 9.3).
Natural increase rate per 1,000 population (1993): 8.6 (world avg. 15.7).
Total fertility rate (avg. births per childbearing woman; 1993): 2.5.
Marriage rate per 1,000 population (1993): 4.9.
Divorce rate per 1,000 population (1993): 0.7.
Life expectancy at birth (1991): male 68.9 years; female 76.5 years.
Major causes of death per 100,000 population (1992): diseases of the circulatory system 676.3; malignant neoplasms (cancers) 97.3; accidents, poisoning, and violence 63.5; diseases of the digestive system 34.7; diseases of the respiratory system 28.4; infectious and parasitic diseases 13.5.

National economy

Budget (1995). Revenue: 243,828,000,000,000 coupons (1992; profit tax 37.6%, value-added tax 26.3%, individual income tax 10.5%, turnover tax 4.5%). Expenditures: 243,828,000,000,000 (defense 29.7%, debt financing 13.2%, government administration 4.8%, education 3.2%, health care 2.0%).
Public debt (external; 1994): U.S.$1,000,000,000.
Land use (1993): forest 38.7%; pasture 28.7%; agriculture 14.3%; other 18.3%.
Production (metric tons except as noted). Agriculture, forestry, fishing (1994): fruit (other than grapes) 1,265,000, vegetables (other than potatoes) 1,130,000, grapes 480,000, milk 465,000, potatoes 229,000, corn (maize) 200,000, wheat 110,000, barley 38,000, sugarbeets 26,000, sunflower seeds 10,000, soybeans 6,000; livestock (number of live animals) 1,385,000 sheep and goats, 1,050,000 cattle, 650,000 pigs, 17,000,000 poultry; roundwood, n.a.; fish catch (1993) 37,000. Mining and quarrying (1993): manganese ore 250,000. Manufacturing (value of production in '000,000 rubles; 1992): food products 4,145; textiles 1,473; machinery 688; clothing 581; metallurgy 439; chemical products 339; construction materials 336; fuel and energy 330; wood and paper products 235; leather products 103. Construction (1990): 1,313,000,000,000 rubles. Energy production (consumption): electricity (kW-hr; 1992) 9,300,000,000 (9,300,000,000); coal (metric tons; 1992) 500,000 (736,000); crude petroleum (barrels; 1992) 733,000 (5,658,000); petroleum products (metric tons; 1991) 2,215,400 (n.a.); natural gas (cu m; 1992) none (4,856,000,000).
Gross national product (1993): U.S.$3,055,000,000 (U.S.$560 per capita)[4].

Structure of gross domestic product and labour force

	1992		1993	
	in value '000,000 rubles	% of total value	labour force	% of labour force
Agriculture	78,065	52.3	645,000	32.9
Mining, Manufacturing	26,057	17.5	355,000	18.1
Public utilities	2,927	2.0	70,000	3.6
Construction	9,282	6.2	126,000	6.4
Transportation and communications	5,702	3.8	72,000	3.7
Trade	4,014	2.7	152,000	7.8
Finance	9.155	6.1	12,000	0.6
Public administration, defense	4,361	2.9	35,000	1.8
Services	7,879	5.3	431,000	22.0
Other	1,774	1.2	61,000	3.1
TOTAL	149,216	100.0	1,959,000	100.0

Population economically active (1993): total 1,959,000; activity rate of total population 36.3% (participation rates [1992]: ages 16–59 [male], 16–54 [female] 72.9%; female [1989] 45.9%; unemployed [1989] 3.5%).

Price and earnings indexes (1990 = 100)

	1988	1989	1990	1991	1992	1993
Consumer price index	...	...	100.0	178.7	1,706	214,303
Monthly earnings index	77.1	87.5	100.0	126.3	709.3	106,485

Household income and expenditure. Average household size (1989) 4.1; income per household: n.a.; sources of income (1993): wages and salaries 65.0%, benefits 23.5%, agricultural income 11.5%; expenditure (1993): retail goods 67.3%, savings 12.5%, taxes 8.6%, transportation 4.1%, housing 4.0%, health care 3.5%.

Foreign trade

Balance of trade (current prices)

	1988	1989	1990	1991	1992
'000,000 rubles	−592	−385	−855	−1,154	−18,627
% of total	4.8%	3.1%	6.7%	8.6%	35.7%

Imports (1992): 35,389,000,000 rubles (oil and gas 52.9%, food 14.1%, energy 11.0%, light-industrial products 8.9%, machinery 4.3%). *Major import sources:* Turkmenistan 50.3%; Russia 32.0%; Azerbaijan 11.1%; Ukraine 7.7%; Estonia 2.3%.
Exports (1992): 16,762,000,000 rubles (ferrous metals 48.4%, food products 19.1%, machinery 16.9%, light-industrial products 7.6%, chemicals 3.4%). *Major export destinations:* Russia 56.3%; Ukraine 13.2%; Turkmenistan 10.6%; Sweden 6.7%; Georgia 5.7%; Kazakhstan 4.6%.

Transport and communications

Transport. Railroads (1990): length 976 mi, 1,570 km; (1989) passenger-mi 10,600,000, passenger-km 17,000,000; cargo traffic, n.a. Roads (1989): length 21,000 mi, 33,900 km (paved 87%). Vehicles (1988): passenger cars 427,400; trucks and buses, n.a. Merchant marine: vessels (1,000 gross tons and over) 54; total deadweight tonnage 1,108,068. Air transport (1989): passenger-mi 3,290,500,000, passenger-km 5,295,600,000; short ton-mi cargo, n.a., metric ton-km cargo, n.a.; airports (1995) with scheduled flights 1.
Communications. Daily newspapers (1989): total number 147; total circulation 3,677,000; circulation per 1,000 population 671. Radio and television (1990): total number of receivers 3,760,000 (1 per 1.5 persons). Telephones (main lines; 1993): 1,002,000 (1 per 5.5 persons).

Education and health

Education (1989–90)

	schools	teachers	students	student/ teacher ratio
Primary (age 6–13), Secondary (age 14–17)	3,788	...	924,700	...
Voc., teacher tr.	...	...	...	...
Higher	19	...	93,100	...

Educational attainment (1989). Percentage of population age 25 and over having: primary education or no formal schooling 12.3%; some secondary 15.2%; completed secondary and some postsecondary 57.4%; higher 15.1%.
Literacy (1989): percentage of total population age 15 and over literate 99.0%; males literate 99.5%; females literate 98.5%.
Health (1990): physicians 32,100 (1 per 170 persons); hospital beds 60,000 (1 per 90 persons); infant mortality rate per 1,000 live births 15.9.
Food: daily per capita caloric intake, n.a.

Military

Total active duty personnel (1994): 4,500 (army 95.5%, navy[5], air force 4.5%). About 22,000 Russian troops remained in Georgia in late 1995. *Military expenditure as percentage of GNP* (1993): 3.1% (world 3.3%) per capita expenditure U.S.$17.

[1]The Georgian lari, introduced Sept. 25, 1995, replaced the Georgian coupon, at a rate of 1,000,000 coupons to 1 lari; on the same date, the Georgian lari became the sole legal tender, floating against all currencies. The Georgian coupon was introduced April 5, 1993, at par with the Russian ruble and circulated parallel with it; on Aug. 20, 1993, the coupon became sole legal tender, floating against all currencies. [2]January 1. [3]Abkhazia adopted a constitution declaring it an independent state on Nov. 26, 1994; on Feb. 9, 1995, it was granted wider autonomy. [4]Ruble-area GNP and exchange-rate data are very speculative. [5]A portion of the former U.S.S.R. Black Sea Fleet has been allocated to Georgia.

Germany

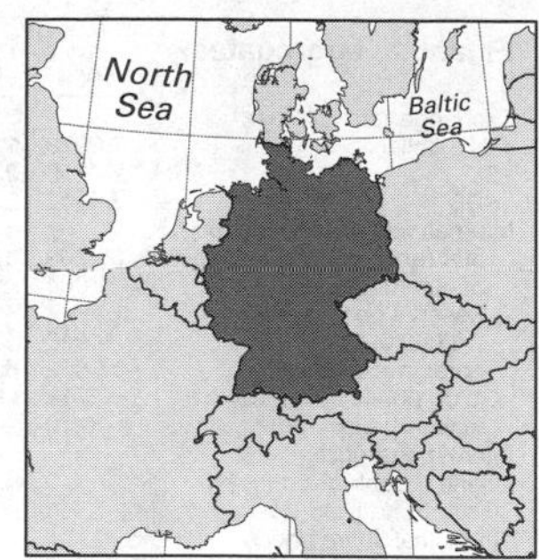

Official name: Bundesrepublik Deutschland (Federal Republic of Germany).
Form of government: federal multiparty republic with two legislative houses (Federal Council [68]; Federal Diet [672]).
Chief of state: President.
Head of government: Chancellor.
Seat of government: Bonn (Berlin is capital-designate).
Official language: German.
Official religion: none.
Monetary unit: 1 Deutsche Mark (DM) = 100 Pfennige; valuation (Oct. 6, 1995) 1 U.S.$ = DM 1.43; 1 £ = DM 2.26.

Area and population

States Administrative districts	Capitals	area sq mi	area sq km	population 1993 estimate
Baden-Württemberg	Stuttgart	13,804[1]	35,751[1]	10,233,900
Freiburg	Freiburg	3,613	9,357	2,058,600
Karlsruhe	Karlsruhe	2,671	6,919	2,636,900
Stuttgart	Stuttgart	4,076	10,558	3,832,100
Tübingen	Tübingen	3,443	8,918	1,706,300
Bayern	Munich	27,239	70,548	11,863,300
Mittelfranken	Ansbach	2,798	7,246	1,652,200
Niederbayern	Landshut	3,987	10,326	1,120,900
Oberbayern	Munich	6,768	17,529	3,948,200
Oberfranken	Bayreuth	2,792	7,231	1,100,200
Oberpfalz	Regensburg	3,741	9,690	1,040,600
Schwaben	Augsburg	3,859	9,994	1,701,300
Unterfranken	Würzburg	3,294	8,532	1,299,900
Berlin	—	343	889	3,475,400
Brandenburg	Potsdam	11,383	29,481	2,537,700
Bremen	Bremen	156	404	683,100
Hamburg	Hamburg	292	755	1,702,900
Hessen	Wiesbaden	8,152[1]	21,114	5,967,300
Darmstadt	Darmstadt	2,875	7,445	3,671,000
Giessen	Giessen	2,078	5,381	1,042,500
Kassel	Kassel	3,200	8,288	1,253,800
Mecklenburg-Vorpommern	Schwerin	8,946	23,169	1,843,500
Niedersachsen	Hannover	18,381[1]	47,606[1]	7,648,000
Braunschweig	Braunschweig	3,126	8,097	1,674,700
Hannover	Hannover	3,493	9,048	2,120,500
Lüneburg	Lüneburg	5,891	15,260	1,560,500
Weser-Ems	Oldenburg	5,775	14,958	2,292,300
Nordrhein-Westfalen	Düsseldorf	13,155[1]	34,072	17,759,300
Arnsberg	Arnsberg	3,088	7,999	3,806,600
Detmold	Detmold	2,517	6,518	1,975,100
Düsseldorf	Düsseldorf	2,042	5,288	5,289,000
Köln	Köln	2,844	7,365	4,141,600
Münster	Münster	2,665	6,902	2,547,000
Rheinland-Pfalz	Mainz	7,662	19,845	3,925,900
Koblenz	Koblenz	3,116	8,071	1,463,600
Rheinhessen-Pfalz	Mainz	2,646	6,852	1,963,300
Trier	Trier	1,900	4,922	499,000
Saarland	Saarbrücken	992	2,570	1,084,500
Sachsen	Dresden	7,108	18,409	4,607,700
Sachsen-Anhalt	Magdeburg	7,894	20,446	2,777,900
Dessau	Dessau	1,643	4,256	576,600
Halle	Halle/Saale	1,880	4,870	987,600
Magdeburg	Magdeburg	4,371	11,320	1,213,700
Schleswig-Holstein	Kiel	6,077	15,739	2,694,900
Thüringen	Erfurt	6,245	16,175	2,532,800
TOTAL		137,828[1]	356,973[1]	81,338,100

Demography

Population (1995): 81,912,000.
Major cities (1992): Berlin 3,471,000; Hamburg 1,706,000; Munich 1,256,300; Cologne 961,600; Frankfurt am Main 663,600; Essen 624,600; Dortmund 602,400; Stuttgart 598,000; Düsseldorf 577,600; Bremen 552,700; Duisburg 538,100; Hannover 525,300; Leipzig 494,200.

Other principal cities (1993)

	population		population		population
Aachen	246,100	Heilbronn	122,600	Oberhausen	226,300
Augsburg	265,000	Herne	180,500	Offenbach am	
Bergisch		Hildesheim	106,500	Main	117,100
Gladbach	105,000	Ingolstadt	109,200	Oldenburg	147,300
Bielefeld	324,400	Jena	100,400	Osnabrück	167,500
Bochum	400,700	Kaiserslautern	102,100	Paderborn	129,500
Bonn	297,900	Karlsruhe	278,500	Pforzheim	117,500
Bottrop	119,400	Kassel	201,200	Potsdam	139,500
Braunschweig	257,800	Kiel	249,100	Recklingshausen	127,100
Bremerhaven	131,700	Koblenz	109,900	Regensburg	125,000
Chemnitz	282,000	Krefeld	249,200	Remscheid	124,000
Cottbus	129,100	Leverkusen	161,900	Reutlingen	107,600
Darmstadt	140,900	Lübeck	217,100	Rostock	239,700
Dresden	480,500	Ludwigshafen		Saarbrücken	191,300
Erfurt	202,200	am Rhein	168,200	Salzgitter	117,100
Erlangen	102,700	Magdeburg	272,400	Schwerin	123,500
Freiburg		Mainz	185,200	Siegen	111,800
im Breisgau	196,700	Mannheim	318,800	Solingen	166,200
Furth	107,800	Moers	106,400	Ulm	114,700
Gelsenkirchen	294,800	Mönchenglad-		Wiesbaden	269,600
Gera	124,100	bach	265,100	Witten	105,700
Göttingen	128,400	Mülheim		Wolfsburg	128,500
Hagen	215,000	an der Ruhr	177,400	Wuppertal	387,700
Halle an der Saale	298,100	Münster	267,000	Würzburg	129,200
Hamm	183,200	Neuss	148,600	Zwickau	109,400
Heidelberg	139,900	Nürnberg	499,800		

Density (1995): persons per sq mi 594.3, persons per sq km 229.5.
Urban-rural (1990): urban 85.3%; rural 14.7%.
Population projection: (2000) 84,468,000; (2010) 89,822,000.
Sex distribution (1994): male 48.59%; female 51.41%.
Age breakdown (1994): under 15, 16.4%; 15–29, 20.6%; 30–44, 23.0%; 45–59, 19.7%; 60–74, 14.1%; 75 and over, 6.2%.
Doubling time: not applicable; doubling time exceeds 100 years.
Ethnic composition (by nationality; 1990): German 93.4%; Turkish 2.1%, of which Kurdish 0.5%; Yugoslav 0.8%; Italian 0.7%; Greek 0.4%; Polish 0.4%; Spanish 0.2%; other 2.0%.
Religious affiliation: (former West Germany; 1987) Roman Catholic 42.9%, Lutheran-Reformed and Lutheran traditions 41.6%, Muslim 2.7%, Reformed tradition 0.6%, Jewish 0.1%, other 12.1%; (former East Germany; 1990) Protestant 47.0%, Roman Catholic 7.0%, unaffiliated and other 46.0%.
Households (1992). Number of households 35,700,000; average household size 2.3; 1 person 33.7%, 2 persons 31.3%, 3 persons 16.9%, 4 persons 13.2%, 5 or more persons 4.9%.

Vital statistics

Birth rate per 1,000 population (1993): 9.8 (world avg. 25.0); legitimate 85.2%; illegitimate 14.8%.
Death rate per 1,000 population (1993): 11.1 (world avg. 9.3).
Natural increase rate per 1,000 population (1993): −1.2 (world avg. 15.7).
Total fertility rate (avg. births per childbearing woman; 1994): 1.5.
Marriage rate per 1,000 population (1993): 5.5.
Divorce rate per 1,000 population (1993): 1.9.
Life expectancy at birth (1994): male 73.20 years; female 79.80 years.
Major causes of death per 100,000 population (1993): diseases of the circulatory system 510.9; malignant neoplasms (cancers) 257.4, of which stomach, colon, and rectum 56.1, bronchial, lung, and tracheal 43.2; diseases of the respiratory system 62.1, of which pneumonia 19.0, chronic bronchitis 14.7; chronic liver disease and cirrhosis 23.6.

Social indicators

Educational attainment (1989)[2]. Percentage of population age 25 and over having: less than full primary education 0.9%; primary and lower (junior) secondary 67.2%; primary and intermediate secondary 17.7%; vocational postsecondary and certification for higher education 14.2%, of which post-secondary vocational degree 6.6%, university graduates (all levels) 5.7%.
Quality of working life. Average workweek (1994)[2]: 38.6 hours. Annual rate per 100,000 workers (1993) for: injuries or accidents at work 4,808; deaths, including commuting accidents, 6.7. Proportion of labour force insured for damages or income loss resulting from: injury, virtually 100%; permanent disability, virtually 100%; death, virtually 100%. Average days lost to labour stoppages per 1,000 workers (1993): 3.1.

Distribution of income (1984)[2]

percentage of household income by quintile

1	2	3	4	5 (highest)
6.8	12.7	17.8	24.0	38.7

Access to services. Proportion of dwellings (1994) having: electricity, virtually 100%; piped water supply, virtually 100%; flush sewage disposal (1992) 98.5%; public fire protection, virtually 100%.
Social participation. Eligible voters participating in last (October 1994) national election 79.1%. Trade union membership in total workforce (1994): 30.0%. Practicing religious population (1993): 7% of Protestants and 20% of Roman Catholics "regularly" attend religious services.
Social deviance (1993). Offense rate per 100,000 population for: murder and manslaughter 5; sexual abuse 55, of which child molestation 19, rape and forcible sexual assault 14; robbery 76; assault and battery 108; larceny 5,126. Incidence per 100,000 in general population (late 1970s) of: alcoholism 2,500–3,000; drug and substance abuse 650; suicide 16.5.
Material well-being (1994; median income)[2]. Households possessing: automobile 95.8%; telephone 98.5%; colour television receiver 96.3%; refrigerator 77.8%; washing machine 99.0%; home freezer 80.2%.

Recreational and leisure activities[2]

(Monthly household expenditures, 1994; median income)

Activity	DM	percentage
Vacations	189	24.9
Expenditures for motor vehicles	104	13.7
Sporting and camping equipment and sporting events	112	14.7
Televisions, radios, and their fees	85	11.2
Books, newspapers, and magazines	60	7.9
Gardening and pets	51	6.7
Games and toys	36	4.7
Photographic and moviemaking equipment and film	18	2.4
Visits to theatre and cinema	18	2.4
Tools	7	0.9
Other activities	80	10.5
TOTAL	761	100.0

National economy

Budget (1994). Revenue: DM 1,553,085,000,000 (taxes 84.6%). Expenditures: DM 1,684,881,000,000 (1991; consumption 43.5%, current transfers 40.1%, debt interest payments 6.1%).
Total national debt (1993[3]): DM 651,180,000,000.
Production (value of production in DM except as noted; 1993–94). Agriculture, forestry, fishing: cereal grains 5,631,000,000, fruits 2,990,000,000, sugar beets 2,698,000,000, flowers and ornamental plants 2,665,000,000, grapes for wine 1,928,000,000, vegetables 1,805,000,000, nurseries 1,580,000,000, pota-

toes 1,504,000,000, oilseed crops 1,005,000,000; livestock (number of live animals) 26,007,000 pigs, 21,259,000 cattle, 1,732,000,000 chicken eggs, 46,-008,000 poultry; roundwood (1993) 36,156,000 cu m; fish catch (metric tons; 1993) 316,373. Mining and quarrying (metric tons; 1993): potash 30,434,000; iron ore 180,000; zinc 14,300; lead 2,100. Manufacturing (value added at factor cost in DM; 1992): capital equipment 319,988,000,000, of which electrical equipment 85,418,000,000, machinery 81,338,000,000, transport equipment 79,522,000,000; chemicals (including pharmaceuticals) 57,581,000,000; food and beverages 39,411,000,000; calculators and computers 25,274,000,000; plastics and other synthetic products 20,029,000,000; furniture and other wood products 15,506,000,000; stone and ceramic products 14,370,000,000; printing and copy machines 12,811,000,000; iron founding 11,903,000,000; textiles 11,409,000,000; precision instruments 10,280,000,000; paper and cardboard products 8,919,000,000; office equipment 8,317,000,000; clothing 7,433,000,000; musical instruments and toys 3,578,000,000; fine pottery and ceramic products 2,549,000,000. Construction (value of construction in DM '000; 1993): residential 108,589,000; nonresidential 67,179,000.

Service enterprises (1991)

	no. of enter-prises	no. of employees	weekly wage as a % of all wages	annual turnover (DM '000,000)
Gas	151	37,000	...	42,228
Water	183	40,000	...	3,443
Electrical power	462	296,000	...	147,076
Transport				
air	133	57,390	...	20,270
buses	6,054	192,869	...	12,586
rail	1	416,199	...	14,697
shipping	1,449	9,076	...	...
Communications				
press	2,452	240,075	...	31,096
film[4]	615	3,000	...	836
Postal services	17,616[5]	652,573	...	68,346
Hotels and restaurants	135,141	652,251	...	60,257
Wholesale trade	36,605[5]	1,214,000	...	1,015,984
Retail trade	152,629	2,241,000	...	605,755

Energy production (consumption): electricity (kW-hr; 1993) 525,721,000,-000 (526,591,000,000); hard coal (metric tons; 1993) 64,174,000 (77,884,-000); lignite (metric tons; 1993) 221,802,000 (226,086,000); crude petroleum (barrels; 1992) 22,205,000 (745,970,000); petroleum products (metric tons; 1993) 97,932,000 (119,631,000); natural gas (cu m; 1993) 20,603,000,000 (90,957,000,000).

Manufacturing, mining, and construction enterprises (1993)

	no. of enter-prises	no. of tradesmen and professionals	wages as a % of avg. of all wages[2]	annual gross production value (DM '000,000)
Manufacturing	43,261	7,353,000	101.1	1,894,801
of which				
Road motor vehicles	2,225	836,000	110.9	247,026
Machinery (nonelectric)	6,359	1,183,000	101.2	226,305
Machinery and appliances (electric)	3,555	1,074,000	91.9	231,594
Chemical	1,441	614,000	109.8	197,013
Food and beverages	4,603	587,000	95.1	245,918
Petroleum and natural gas	59	[6]	138.2	[6]
Calculators, computers	2,631	416,000	95.4	92,647
Plastics	2,674	380,000	96.2	80,005
Iron and steel	119	167,000	101.5	40,706
Textiles	1,253	187,000	81.0	36,144
Wood and wood products	5,607	520,000	91.7	107,709
Mining and quarrying	2,459	382,000	105.1	85,724
Construction	22,667	1,438,000	105.5	220,202

Gross national product (at current market prices; 1993): U.S.$1,908,570,000,-000 (U.S.$23,630 per capita).

Structure of gross domestic product and labour force

	1994		1993	
	in value DM '000,000	% of total value	labour force	% of labour force
Agriculture	30,000	0.9	1,255,000	3.1
Public utilities, mining	74,050	2.2	655,000	1.6
Manufacturing	770,430	23.2	10,423,000	26.0
Construction	168,940	5.1	3,053,000	7.6
Transp. and commun.	161,010	4.8	2,219,000	5.5
Trade	251,880	7.6	4,352,000	10.8
Finance, real estate	420,450	12.7	1,300,000	3.2
Services	614,680	18.5	8,903,000	22.2
Pub. admin., defense	302,160	9.1	3,405,000	8.5
Other (productive)	415,010	12.5	4,614,000	11.5
Other (accounting)	112,490	3.4	—	—
TOTAL	3,321,100	100.0	40,179,000	100.0

Population economically active (1993): total 40,179,000; activity rate of total population 49.5% (participation rates: ages 15–64, 78.1%; female 41.0%; unemployed 8.7%).

Price and earnings indexes (1990 = 100)

	1988	1989	1990	1991	1992	1993	1994
Consumer price index	94.8	97.4	100.0	103.5	107.6	112.0	115.4
Hourly earnings index	91.0	94.9	100.0	107.2	114.8	121.7	123.6

Household income and expenditure. Average household size (1993) 2.3; average annual income per household (1994) DM 75,984 (U.S.$46,823); sources of take-home income (1994): wages 81.5%, self-employment 11.3%, transfer payments 7.2%; expenditure (1994): rent 18.0%, food 13.3%, transportation 10.0%, entertainment and education 7.2%, household operations and maintenance 4.7%, clothing and footwear 4.4%.

Land use (1993): forest 30.0%; pasture 14.7%; agriculture 33.9%; other 21.4%.

Financial aggregates[7]

	1989	1990	1991	1992	1993	1994	1995 (Aug.)
Exchange rate, DM per:							
U.S. dollar	1.6978	1.4940	1.5160	1.6140	1.7263	1.5488	1.4665
£	2.7258	2.8804	2.8360	2.4404	2.1988	2.4207	2.2682
SDR	2.2312	2.1255	2.1685	2.2193	2.3712	2.2610	2.1887
International reserves (U.S.$)							
Total (excl. gold; '000,000)	60,709	67,902	63,001	90,967	77,640	77,363	81,832
SDRs ('000,000)	1,804	1,880	1,917	841	962	1,114	1,335
Reserve pos. in IMF ('000,000)	3,043	3,056	3,567	4,239	3,951	4,030	5,005
Foreign exchange	55,862	62,967	57,517	85,877	72,727	72,219	74,834
Gold ('000,000 fine troy oz)	95.18	95.18	95.18	95.18	95.18	95.18	95.18
% world reserves	10.10	10.12	10.13	10.24	10.43	10.46	10.55
Interest and prices							
Central bank discount (%)	6.0	6.0	8.0	8.3	4.8	4.5	3.5[8]
Govt. bond yield (%)	7.1	8.9	8.6	8.0	6.3	6.7	6.4[8]
Industrial share prices (1990 = 100)[9]	87.3	100.0	89.1	86.2	87.8	105.9	104.6
Balance of payments (U.S.$'000,000,000)							
Balance of visible trade	75.04	68.62	18.51	26.94	39.68	50.47	19.10[8]
Imports, f.o.b.	265.90	343.43	385.20	403.75	343.00	379.83	112.41
Exports, f.o.b.	340.94	412.04	403.71	430.69	382.68	430.30	131.51
Balance of invisibles	−17.85	−20.29	−37.24	−48.66	−55.24	−72.15	−19.94[8]
Balance of payments, current account	57.19	48.33	−18.73	−21.72	−15.56	−21.68	−0.84[8]

Tourism (1994): receipts U.S.$10,587,000,000; expenditures U.S.$41,424,000,-000.

Foreign trade

Balance of trade (current prices)[2]

	1988	1989	1990	1991	1992	1993	1994
DM '000,000,000	+139.23	+147.85	+118.90	+15.31	+29.46	+59.13	+72.16
% of total	13.9%	13.0%	9.9%	1.2%	2.7%	5.2%	5.7%

Imports (1994): DM 600,966,000,000 (machinery and transport equipment 33.7%, of which transport equipment 9.1%, electrical machinery other than office equipment 6.6%, office equipment 4.7%; chemicals and chemical products 8.8%, of which organic chemical products 2.1%, unfabricated plastics 1.7%; food and beverages 8.2%, of which fruits and vegetables 2.8%, meat and meat products 1.3%, milk and milk products 0.8%; clothing and wearing apparel 7.2%; mineral fuels 7.0%, of which crude petroleum and petroleum products 5.0%, natural gas 1.5%; iron and steel 2.9%; thread, yarn, and finished spinning goods 2.8%). *Major import sources:* France 11.1%; Italy 8.4%; The Netherlands 8.2%; United States 7.3%; United Kingdom 6.2%; Belgium-Luxembourg 6.1%; Japan 5.7%; Austria 4.8%; Switzerland 4.4%.

Exports (1994): DM 673,121,000,000 (machinery and transport equipment 49.1%, of which transport equipment 16.1%, electrical machinery other than office equipment 7.7%, office equipment 2.3%; chemicals and chemical products 13.5%, of which organic chemical products 2.8%, unfabricated plastics 2.3%, medical and pharmaceutical products 2.1%). *Major export destinations:* France 12.0%; United Kingdom 8.0%; United States 7.9%; The Netherlands 7.5%; Italy 7.5%; Belgium-Luxembourg 7.0%; Austria 6.2%; Switzerland 5.4%; Japan 5.0%; Spain 3.2%; Sweden 2.2%.

Transport and communications

Transport. Railroads (1993): length 54,994 mi, 88,504 km; passengers carried 1,579,000,000; passenger-mi 36,041,000, passenger-km 58,003,000,000; short ton-mi cargo 45,649,000,000, metric ton-km cargo 66,646,000,000. Roads (1993): total length 395,367 mi, 636,282 km (paved 99%). Vehicles (1994): passenger cars 39,917,600; trucks and buses 2,167,900. Merchant marine (1993): vessels (100 gross tons and over) 1,527; total deadweight tonnage 5,278,000. Air transport (1992)[10]: passengers carried 71,000,000; passenger-mi 12,633,000,000, passenger-km 20,331,000,000; short ton-mi cargo 260,-000,000, metric ton-km cargo 379,000,000; airports (1995) with scheduled flights 40.

Communications. Daily newspapers (1991): total number 355; total circulation 26,425,000; circulation per 1,000 population 331. Radio (1994): 36,186,000 receivers (1 per 2.3 persons). Television (1994): 32,314,000 receivers[11] (1 per 2.5 persons[11]). Telephones (main lines; 1993): 36,899,800 (1 per 2.2 persons).

Education and health

Education (1994–95)

	schools	teachers	students	student/ teacher ratio
Primary (age 6–10) Secondary (age 10–19)	43,238	659,738	9,558,455	14.5
Voc., teacher tr.	9,069	105,363	2,449,083	23.2
Higher	325	171,025[2, 12]	1,856,542	10.7[2, 12]

Health (1994): physicians 267,186 (1 per 304 persons); dentists 59,211 (1 per 1,366 persons); hospital beds 628,658 (1 per 130 persons); infant mortality rate per 1,000 live births 5.8.

Food (1992): daily per capita caloric intake 3,344 (vegetable products 65%, animal products 35%); 126% of FAO recommended minimum requirement.

Military

Total active duty personnel (1995): 339,900 (army 68.8%, navy 8.4%, air force 22.8%). *Military expenditure as percentage of GNP* (1993): 1.6% (world 3.3%); per capita expenditure U.S.$375.

[1]Detail does not add to total given because of rounding. [2]Former West Germany only. [3]August. [4]1984. [5]1990. [6]Data withheld for reasons of confidentiality. [7]End-of-period figures unless footnoted otherwise. [8]Through June. [9]Period averages. [10]Domestic service only. [11]Data include officially registered sets only. [12]1991.

Ghana

Official name: Republic of Ghana.
Form of government: unitary multiparty republic with one legislative house (House of Parliament [200]).
Head of state and government: President.
Capital: Accra.
Official language: English.
Official religion: none.
Monetary unit: 1 cedi (₵) = 100 pesewas; valuation (Oct. 6, 1995) 1 U.S.$ = ₵1,315; 1 £ = ₵2,079.

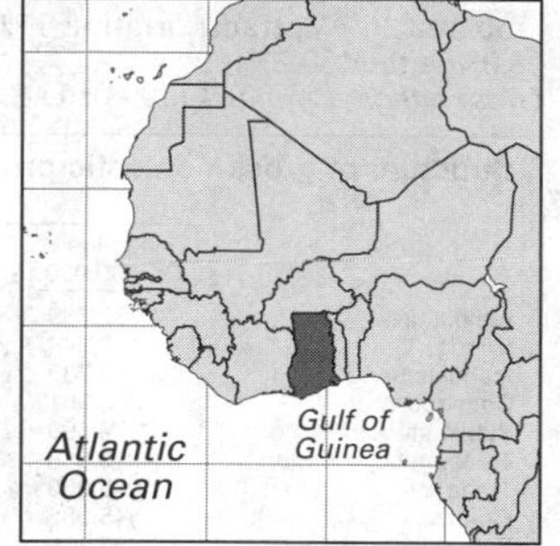

Area and population

Regions[2]	Capitals	area sq mi	area sq km	population 1991[1] estimate
Ashanti	Kumasi	9,417	24,389	2,485,766
Brong-Ahafo	Sunyani	15,273	39,557	1,432,971
Central	Cape Coast	3,794	9,826	1,359,861
Eastern	Koforidua	7,461	19,323	2,003,235
Greater Accra	Accra	1,253	3,245	1,696,170
Northern	Tamale	27,175	70,384	1,389,105
Upper East	Bolgatanga	3,414	8,842	921,196
Upper West	Wa	7,134	18,476	526,398
Volta	Ho	7,942	20,570	1,432,971
Western	Sekondi-Takoradi	9,236	23,921	1,374,483
TOTAL		92,098[3]	238,533	14,622,156

Demography

Population (1995): 16,472,000.
Density (1995): persons per sq mi 178.8, persons per sq km 69.1.
Urban-rural (1993): urban 35.4%; rural 64.6%.
Sex distribution (1990): male 49.64%; female 50.36%.
Age breakdown (1990): under 15, 46.8%; 15–29, 26.2%; 30–44, 14.4%; 45–59, 8.0%; 60–74, 3.8%; 75 and over, 0.8%.
Population projection: (2000) 18,749,000; (2010) 24,293,000.
Doubling time: 23 years.
Ethnolinguistic composition (1983): Akan 52.4%; Mossi 15.8%; Ewe 11.9%; Ga-Adangme 7.8%; Gurma 3.3%; Yoruba 1.3%; other 7.5%.
Religious affiliation (1980): Christian 62.6%, of which Protestant 27.9%, Roman Catholic 18.7%, African indigenous 16.0%; traditional beliefs 21.4%; Muslim 15.7%, of which Ahmadīyah 7.9%; other 0.3%.
Major cities (1988[1]): Accra 949,100; Kumasi 385,200; Tamale 151,100; Tema 110,000; Sekondi-Takoradi 103,600.

Vital statistics

Birth rate per 1,000 population (1990–95): 41.7 (world avg. 25.0); legitimate, n.a.; illegitimate, n.a.
Death rate per 1,000 population (1990–95): 11.7 (world avg. 9.3).
Natural increase rate per 1,000 population (1990–95): 30.0 (world avg. 15.7).
Total fertility rate (avg. births per childbearing woman; 1993): 5.9.
Life expectancy at birth (1993): male 53.3 years; female 57.2 years.
Major causes of death per 100,000 population: n.a.; however, major infectious diseases as a percentage of outpatients (1989): malaria 43.8%, respiratory infections (including tuberculosis) 8.0%, diarrheal diseases 6.7%, intestinal worms 3.1%.

National economy

Budget (1994). Revenue: ₵1,270,555,000,000 (import-export duties 28.5%, of which cocoa export duty 11.5%; excise and value-added taxes 24.3%, of which petroleum tax 15.9%; divestiture of government assets 20.6%; income taxes 13.4%). Expenditures: ₵896,851,000,000 (education 22.3%; debt service 20.1%; health 6.9%; transportation and communications 3.8%; social security and welfare 3.6%; defense 2.9%).
Production (metric tons except as noted). Agriculture, forestry, fishing (1994): roots and tubers 6,650,000 (of which cassava 4,378,000, taro 1,272,000, yams 1,000,000), cereals 1,450,000 (of which corn [maize] 900,000, sorghum 260,000, millet 150,000, rice 140,000), bananas and plantains 1,326,000, cacao 270,000, coconuts 220,000, green peppers 185,000, tomatoes 115,000, sugarcane 112,000, peanuts (groundnuts) 100,000, oranges 50,000, palm kernels 34,000, lemons and limes 30,000, pulses 20,000; livestock (number of live animals) 3,337,000 goats, 3,288,000 sheep, 1,680,000 cattle, 595,000 pigs, 12,000,000 chickens; roundwood (1993) 17,192,000 cu m; fish catch (1993) 371,227 (of which anchovies 81,350). Mining and quarrying (1994): bauxite 451,802; manganese ore 238,429; gold 44,505 kg; diamonds 739,969 carats. Manufacturing (1992): cement 1,023,900; kerosene, gasoline, and diesel fuel 806,600; wheat flour 121,000; soap 37,400; iron rods 26,200; cocoa cake, cocoa butter, and cocoa liquor 21,300; edible fats and oils 19,000; toothpaste 556; textiles 19,000,000 m; soft drinks 3,300,000 hectolitres; beer 649,000 hectolitres; evaporated milk 231,000 hectolitres; ice cream 10,540 hectolitres; cigarettes 1,687,000,000 units. Construction (value added in ₵; 1992): 105,216,500,000. Energy production (consumption): electricity (kW-hr; 1993) 6,154,000,000 (5,870,000,000); coal (metric tons; 1993) none (3,000); crude petroleum (barrels; 1993) none (7,245,000); petroleum products (metric tons; 1993) 910,000 (1,082,000); natural gas, none (n.a.).
Household income and expenditure. Average household size (1984) 4.9; average annual income per household (1978) ₵9,600 (U.S.$[4]); sources of income: n.a.; expenditure (1978): food and beverages 57.4%, clothing and footwear 14.3%, housing and energy 11.5%, transportation and communications 3.3%, health care 1.3%.

Gross national product (1993): U.S.$6,992,000,000 (U.S.$430 per capita).

Structure of gross domestic product and labour force

	1993 in value ₵'000,000	1993 % of total value	1984 labour force	1984 % of labour force
Agriculture	1,879,676.4	47.8	3,310,967	59.4
Mining	74,715.2	1.9	26,828	0.5
Manufacturing	357,846.3	9.1	588,418	10.5
Construction	125,836.1	3.2	64,686	1.2
Public utilities	70,782.8	1.8	15,437	0.3
Transp. and commun.	169,092.2	4.3	122,806	2.2
Trade	747,151.7	19.0	792,147	14.2
Finance	149,430.3	3.8	27,475	0.5
Pub. admin., defense	294,928.3	7.5	97,548	1.7
Services	43,256.2	1.1	376,168	6.7
Other	19,661.8[5]	0.5[5]	157,624[6]	2.8[6]
TOTAL	3,932,377.3	100.0	5,580,104	100.0

Tourism (1992): receipts from visitors U.S.$167,000,000; expenditures by nationals abroad U.S.$17,000,000.
Population economically active (1984): total 5,580,104; activity rate of total population 45.4% (participation rates: over age 15, 82.5%; female 51.2%; unemployed 2.8%).

Price and earnings indexes (1989 = 100)

	1988	1989	1990	1991	1992	1993	1994
Consumer price index	58.2	72.9	100.0	118.0	129.9	162.3	202.7
Monthly earnings index	45.9	80.7	100.0	117.2	...	...	...

Public debt (external, outstanding; 1994): U.S.$3,542,500,000.
Land use (1993): forested 34.7%; meadows and pastures 22.0%; agricultural and under permanent cultivation 19.0%; other 24.3%.

Foreign trade

Balance of trade (current prices)

	1989	1990	1991	1992	1993	1994
U.S.$'000,000	−197.8	−308.2	−320.7	−470.2	−664.3	−353.1
% of total	10.9%	14.7%	13.8%	19.2%	23.8%	12.6%

Imports (1994): U.S.$1,579,900,000 (1987; machinery and transport equipment 28.1%; mineral fuels and lubricants 14.0%; chemicals 12.0%; food and live animals 5.2%; beverages and tobacco 0.4%). *Major import sources* (1993): United Kingdom 18.1%; United States 12.0%; Germany 6.0%; France 5.0%; Japan 4.2%.
Exports (1994): U.S.$1,226,800,000 (gold 44.7%; food and live animals 26.3%, of which cocoa 26.1%; logs and sawn timber 13.5%; electricity 4.6%; diamonds 1.7%). *Major export destinations* (1993): United States 19.3%; Germany 17.3%; United Kingdom 9.5%; France 5.6%; Japan 5.1%; The Netherlands 4.1%.

Transport and communications

Transport. Railroads (1993): route length 592 mi, 953 km; passenger-mi 731,400,000, passenger-km 117,700,000; short ton-mi cargo 93,906,000, metric ton-km cargo 137,100,000. Roads (1992): total length 22,800 mi, 36,700 km (paved 32%). Vehicles (1993): passenger cars 90,000; trucks and buses 44,200. Merchant marine (1992): vessels (100 gross tons and over) 155; total deadweight tonnage 130,977. Air transport (1991): passenger-mi 206,000,000, passenger-km 331,000,000; short ton-mi cargo 13,000,000, metric ton-km cargo 19,000,000; airports (1995) with scheduled flights 1.
Communications. Daily newspapers (1993): total number 4; total circulation 1,060,000; circulation per 1,000 population 68. Radio (1994): 4,300,000 receivers (1 per 3.7 persons). Television (1994): 250,000 receivers (1 per 64 persons). Telephones (main lines; 1993): 48,700 (1 per 321 persons).

Education and health

Education (1991–92)

	schools	teachers	students	student/teacher ratio
Primary (6–12)	11,056	66,068	1,796,490	27.2
Secondary (13–20)	5,513[7]	43,367	816,578	18.8
Voc., teacher tr.[7]	57	422	13,232	31.4
Higher[7]	16	700	9,274	13.2

Educational attainment (1984). Percentage of population age 25 and over having: no formal schooling 60.4%; primary education 7.1%; middle school 25.4%; secondary 3.5%; vocational and other postsecondary 2.9%; higher 0.6%. *Literacy* (1990): total population age 15 and over literate 4,960,000 (60.4%); males literate 2,835,000 (70.0%); females literate 2,125,000 (50.9%).
Health: physicians (1989) 628 (1 per 22,452 persons); hospital beds (1991) 18,477 (1 per 791 persons); infant mortality rate per 1,000 live births (1994) 83.
Food (1992): daily per capita caloric intake 2,199 (vegetable products 95%, animal products 5%); 96% of FAO minimum recommended requirement.

Military

Total active duty personnel (1995): 7,000 (army 71.4%, navy 14.3%, air force 14.3%). *Military expenditure as percentage of GNP* (1992): 0.7% (world 3.7%); per capita expenditure U.S.$2.

[1]January 1. [2]Government administration has been decentralized to the local level of 103 district assemblies, 4 municipal assemblies, and 3 metropolitan assemblies. [3]Detail does not add to total given because of rounding. [4]Unofficial 1978 exchange rate (7.5 to 9.9 times the official rate) does not permit meaningful conversion into other currencies. [5]Import duties and statistical adjustments less imputed bank service charges. [6]Unemployed only. [7]1989–90.

Greece

Official name: Ellinikí Dhimokratía (Hellenic Republic).
Form of government: unitary multiparty republic with one legislative house (Greek Chamber of Deputies [300]).
Chief of state: President.
Head of government: Prime Minister.
Capital: Athens.
Official language: Greek.
Official religion: Eastern Orthodox.
Monetary unit: 1 drachma (Dr) = 100 lepta; valuation (Oct. 6, 1995) 1 U.S.$ = Dr 234.67; 1 £ = Dr 370.97.

Area and population

Regions		area sq mi	area sq km	population 1991 census
Anatolikí Makedhonía kaí Thráki	(Eastern Macedonia and Thrace)	5,466	14,157	570,496
Attikí	(Attica)	1,470	3,808	3,523,407
Dhytikí Ellás	(Western Greece)	4,382	11,350	707,687
Dhytikí Makedhonía	(Western Macedonia)	3,649	9,451	293,015
Iónioi Nísoi	(Ionian Islands)	891	2,307	193,734
Ípiros	(Epirus)	3,553	9,203	339,728
Kedrikí Makedhonía[1]	(Central Macedonia)	7,393	19,147	1,710,513
Kríti	(Crete)	3,218	8,336	540,054
Nótion Aiyaíon	(Southern Aegean)	2,041	5,286	257,481
Pelopónnisos	(Peloponnesos)	5,981	15,490	607,428
Stereá Ellás	(Central Greece)	6,004	15,549	582,280
Thessalía	(Thessaly)	5,420	14,037	734,846
Vóreion Aiyaíon	(Northern Aegean)	1,481	3,836	199,231
TOTAL		50,949	131,957	10,259,900

Demography

Population (1995): 10,493,000.
Density (1995): persons per sq mi 206.0, persons per sq km 79.5.
Urban-rural (1991): Urban 71.7%; rural 28.3%.
Sex distribution (1993): male 49.36%; female 50.64%.
Age breakdown (1993): under 15, 17.8%; 15–29, 22.5%; 30–44, 20.5%; 45–59, 18.2%; 60–74, 14.9%; 75 and over, 6.1%.
Population projection: (2000) 10,616,000; (2010) 10,500,000.
Doubling time: not applicable; doubling time exceeds 100 years.
Ethnic composition (1983): Greek 95.5%; Macedonian 1.5%; Turkish 0.9%; Albanian 0.6%; other 1.5%.
Religious affiliation (1980): Christian 98.1%, of which Eastern Orthodox 97.6%, Roman Catholic 0.4%, Protestant 0.1%; Muslim 1.5%; other 0.4%.
Major cities (1991): Athens 772,072; Thessaloníki 383,967; Piraeus (Piraiévs) 182,671; Pátrai 152,570; Peristérion 137,288.

Vital statistics

Birth rate per 1,000 population (1994): 9.8 (world avg. 25.0); (1993) legitimate 97.1%; illegitimate 2.9%.
Death rate per 1,000 population (1994): 9.3 (world avg. 9.3).
Natural increase rate per 1,000 population (1994): 0.5 (world avg. 15.7).
Total fertility rate (avg. births per childbearing woman; 1993): 1.4.
Marriage rate per 1,000 population (1992): 5.1.
Divorce rate per 1,000 population (1990): 0.6.
Life expectancy at birth (1990): male 74.6 years; female 79.8 years.
Major causes of death per 100,000 population (1993): malignant neoplasms (cancers) 201.5; cerebrovascular disease 169.6; diseases of pulmonary circulation and other forms of heart disease 146.8; ischemic heart disease 117.2.

National economy

Budget (1995). Revenue: Dr 12,792,300,000,000[2] (indirect and excise taxes 30.8%, direct taxes 17.4%, European Community 3.5%). Expenditures: Dr 12,801,276,000,000 (1993; health and social insurance 13.7%, defense 7.9%, education and culture 6.6%, police and other sectors 2.1%).
Public debt (1993): U.S.$16,193,000,000.
Tourism (1993): receipts from visitors U.S.$3,293,000,000; expenditures by nationals abroad U.S.$1,003,000,000.
Production (metric tons except as noted). Agriculture, forestry, fishing (1994): sugar beets 2,600,000, wheat 2,387,000, tomatoes 1,810,000, olives 1,612,000, grapes 1,400,000, potatoes 1,000,000, oranges 900,000, barley 434,000, cotton 345,000, tobacco 130,000, rice 120,000, onions 141,000; livestock (number of live animals) 9,604,000 sheep, 5,557,000 goats, 1,143,000 pigs, 608,000 cattle, 110,000 asses, 27,000,000 chickens; roundwood (1993) 2,779,000 cu m; fish catch (1993) 199,607. Mining and quarrying (1994): bauxite 2,200,000; nickel ore 2,000,000; zinc 33,200[3]; lead 28,400[3]; chromium ore 5,650[3]. Manufacturing (value added in Dr; 1992): food, beverages, and tobacco 492,276,000,000; chemicals 274,191,000,000; textiles 227,507,000,000; paper and printing 147,484,000,000; transport equipment 141,563,000,000; clothing and footwear 129,732,000,000. Construction (authorized; 1990): residential 46,434,236 cu m; nonresidential 12,535,570 cu m. Energy production (consumption): electricity (kW-hr; 1992) 37,410,000,000 (38,015,000,000); coal (metric tons; 1992) 55,051,000 (56,424,000); crude petroleum (barrels; 1992) 4,687,000 (98,390,000); petroleum products (metric tons; 1992) 14,949,000 (14,352,000); natural gas (cu m; 1992) 147,714,000 (147,714,000).
Household income and expenditure. Average household size (1991) 3.0; income per household (1982) Dr 252,300 (U.S.$3,777); sources of income (1992): property and entrepreneurial income 45.7%, wages and salaries 37.6%, transfer payments 16.7%; expenditure (1992): food, beverages, and tobacco 36.7%, transportation 15.0%, housing 10.1%, clothing and footwear 8.0%, other 30.2%.
Gross national product (1993): U.S.$76,679,000,000 (U.S.$7,390 per capita).

Structure of gross domestic product and labour force

1993	in value Dr '000,000	% of total value	labour force	% of labour force
Agriculture	1,982,789	13.7	793,900	19.3
Mining	172,944	1.2	19,300	0.5
Manufacturing	2,219,730	15.4	579,500	14.1
Construction	945,501	6.6	261,400	6.4
Public utilities	376,599	2.6	39,600	1.0
Transp. and commun.	1,015,958	7.0	249,000	6.0
Trade	1,975,000	13.7	791,500	19.0
Finance	445,935	3.1	220,800	5.4
Pub. admin., defense	2,756,279	19.1	765,200	18.6
Services	1,352,782	9.4		
Other	1,179,016[4]	8.2[4]	398,200[5]	9.7[5]
TOTAL	14,422,533	100.0	4,118,400	100.0

Population economically active (1993): total 4,118,400; activity rate of total population 39.7% (participation rates: ages 15–64, 55.6%[6]; female 37.3%; unemployed 9.7%).

Price and earnings indexes (1990 = 100)

	1988	1989	1990	1991	1992	1993	1994
Consumer price index	73.0	83.1	100.0	119.5	138.4	158.4	175.7
Hourly earnings index	69.5	83.8	100.0	116.7	132.8	146.7	165.9

Land use (1993): forested 20.3%; meadows and pastures 40.7%; agricultural and under permanent cultivation 27.1%; other 11.9%.

Foreign trade

Balance of trade (current prices)

	1987	1988	1989	1990	1991	1992
Dr '000,000,000	−688.4	−861.4	−1,199.2	−1,613.3	−1,886.1	−2,113.5
% of total	28.1%	33.8%	30.8%	44.3%	37.3%	36.8%

Imports (1993): Dr 5,050,531,000,000 (machinery and transport equipment 35.2%, of which transport equipment 18.4%; food, beverages, and tobacco 11.2%, of which meat products 3.5%, dairy products 2.5%; chemical products 11.0%, of which plastic products 2.3%; crude petroleum 7.6%). *Major import sources:* Germany 16.9%; Italy 14.0%; France 7.9%; Japan 6.8%; The Netherlands 6.6%; United Kingdom 6.1%; United States 3.7%; Belgium-Luxembourg 3.3%.
Exports (1993): Dr 1,933,432,000,000 (food, beverages, and tobacco 29.6%, of which tobacco 6.3%, olive oil 3.6%; clothing 21.0%; petroleum products 7.7%; textiles 5.1%; iron and steel 2.8%). *Major export destinations:* Germany 23.7%; Italy 13.2%; France 6.2%; United Kingdom 5.7%; United States 4.5%; Bulgaria 3.6%.

Transport and communications

Transport. Railroads (1993): route length 1,552 mi, 2,497 km; passenger-mi 1,072,000,000, passenger-km 1,726,000,000; short ton-mi cargo 358,000,000, metric ton-km cargo 523,000,000. Roads (1992): total length 72,170 mi, 116,150 km (paved 92%). Vehicles (1993): passenger cars 2,807,447; trucks and buses 848,903. Merchant marine (1994): vessels (100 gross tons and over) 2,149; total deadweight tonnage 30,536,000. Air transport (1993): passenger-mi 4,908,023,000, passenger-km 7,898,713,000; short ton-mi cargo 86,995,000, metric ton-km cargo 127,010,000; airports (1995) with scheduled flights 31.
Communications. Daily newspapers (1993): total number 144; total circulation, n.a. Radio (1993): 4,085,492 receivers (1 per 2.5 persons). Television (1993): 2,300,000 receivers (1 per 4.5 persons). Telephones (1993): 5,571,293 (1 per 1.9 persons).

Education and health

Education (1992–93)

	schools	teachers	students	student/ teacher ratio
Primary (age 6–12)	7,634	37,549	745,666	19.9
Secondary (age 12–18)	2,988	45,794	700,488	15.3
Voc., teacher tr.	695	14,319	190,443	13.3
Higher[7]	17	9,124	115,464	12.6

Educational attainment (1991). Percentage of population age 25 and over having: no formal schooling (illiterate) 6.8%; some primary education 10.6%; completed primary 39.7%; lower secondary 10.8%; higher secondary 20.6%; some postsecondary 4.9%; a degree from institution of higher education 6.6%. *Literacy* (1991): total population age 15 and over literate 7,870,000 (95.2%); males literate 3,900,000 (97.7%); females literate 3,970,000 (93.0%).
Health: physicians (1993) 40,116 (1 per 259 persons); hospital beds (1992) 34,610 (1 per 298 persons); infant mortality rate per 1,000 live births (1994) 8.3.
Food (1992): daily per capita caloric intake 3,815 (vegetable products 75%, animal products 25%); 153% of FAO recommended minimum requirement.

Military

Total active duty personnel (1994): 159,300 (army 70.9%, navy 12.3%, air force 16.8%). *Military expenditure as percentage of GNP* (1993): 5.5% (world 3.3%); per capita expenditure U.S.$389.

[1]Includes Mount Athos (Áyion Óros), an autonomous, self-governing monastic region; 1991 population 1,557. [2]Includes Dr 4,772,500,000,000 of domestic borrowing. [3]Metal content of ore. [4]Income from ownership of buildings. [5]Unemployed. [6]1991. [7]1991–92.

Grenada

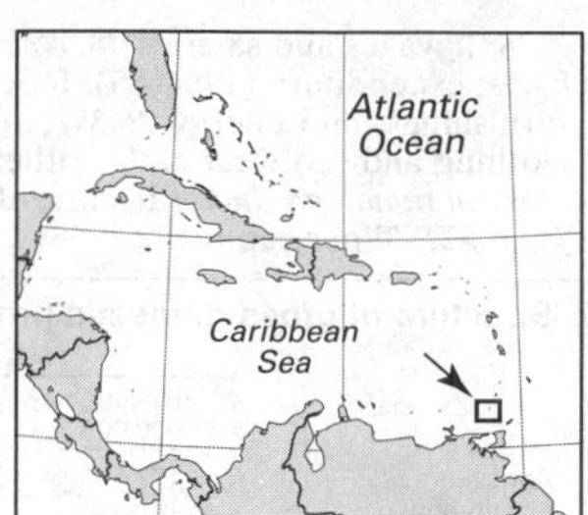

Official name: Grenada.
Form of government: constitutional monarchy with two legislative houses (Senate [13]; House of Representatives [15[1]]).
Chief of state: British Monarch represented by Governor-General.
Head of government: Prime Minister.
Capital: St. George's.
Official language: English.
Official religion: none.
Monetary unit: 1 East Caribbean dollar (EC$) = 100 cents; valuation (Oct. 6, 1995) 1 U.S.$ = EC$2.70; 1 £ = EC$4.27.

Area and population

Local Councils	Principal towns	area sq mi	area sq km	population 1991 census[2]
Carriacou	Hillsborough	10	26	4,595
Petite Martinique	...	3	8	720
St. Andrew	Grenville	38	99	23,531
St. David	...	17	44	10,703
St. George	...	25[3]	65[3]	24,719
St. John	Gouyave	14	35	8,547
St. Mark	Victoria	10	25	3,785
St. Patrick	Sauteurs	16	42	9,652
Town				
St. George's	—	3	3	4,439
TOTAL		133	344	90,691

Demography

Population (1995): 92,000.
Density (1995): persons per sq mi 691.7, persons per sq km 267.4.
Urban-rural (1991)[4]: urban 32.2%; rural 67.8%.
Sex distribution (1991): male 49.35%; female 50.65%.
Age breakdown (1988): under 15, 35.9%; 15–29, 28.5%; 30–44, 14.2%; 45–59, 8.5%; 60 and over, 11.3%; not stated, 1.6%.
Population projection: (2000) 93,000; (2010) 95,000.
Doubling time: 29 years.
Ethnic composition (1991): black 84.9%; mixed 11.0%; Indo-Pakistani 3.0%; other 1.1%.
Religious affiliation (1991): Roman Catholic 53.0%; Anglican 14.0%; Seventh-day Adventist 8.5%; Pentecostal 7.2%; other 17.3%.
Major localities (1991): St. George's 4,439; Gouyave 3,000[5]; Grenville 2,000[5].

Vital statistics

Birth rate per 1,000 population (1994): 30.0 (world avg. 25.0).
Death rate per 1,000 population (1994): 6.0 (world avg. 9.3).
Natural increase rate per 1,000 population (1994): 24.0 (world avg. 15.7).
Total fertility rate (avg. births per childbearing woman; 1994): 3.9.
Marriage rate per 1,000 population: n.a.
Divorce rate per 1,000 population: n.a.
Life expectancy at birth (1994): male 68.0 years; female 73.0 years.
Major causes of death per 100,000 population (1984): diseases of the circulatory system 290.3; malignant neoplasms (cancers) 90.5; endocrine and metabolic diseases 62.9; diseases of the respiratory system 54.1; accidents and violence 47.9; diseases of the digestive system 39.5.

National economy

Budget (1995). Revenue[6]: EC$779,300,000 (taxes on international trade 50.2%, personal income taxes 10.8%, corporate income taxes 8.4%). Expenditures[7]: EC$294,000,000 (public works 15.3%, education 12.9%, health 8.8%, agriculture and fisheries 7.1%).
Public debt (external, outstanding; 1993): U.S.$96,200,000.
Tourism: receipts from visitors (1994) U.S.$58,700,000; expenditures by nationals abroad (1992) U.S.$4,000,000.
Gross national product (at current market prices; 1993): U.S.$219,000,000 (U.S.$2,410 per capita).

Structure of gross domestic product and labour force

	1993 in value EC$'000,000[8]	1993 % of total value	1988 labour force	1988 % of labour force
Agriculture	58.7	11.6	5,560	14.3
Quarrying	2.4	0.5	111	0.3
Manufacturing	35.1	6.9	2,835	7.3
Construction	34.1	6.7	3,531	9.1
Public utilities	21.0	4.2	389	1.0
Transportation and communications	111.2	22.0	1,696	4.4
Trade, restaurants	100.1	19.8	5,421	13.9
Finance, real estate	64.8	12.8	778	2.0
Pub. admin., defense	95.9	19.0 }	5,949	15.3
Services	14.9	2.9 }		
Other	−32.3[9]	−6.4[9]	12,650[10]	32.5[10]
TOTAL	505.7[11]	100.0	38,920	100.0[11]

Production (metric tons except as noted). Agriculture, forestry, fishing (1994): coconuts 7,000, sugarcane 7,000, bananas 4,553, roots and tubers 4,000, mangoes 2,000, avocados 2,000, grapefruit 2,000, nutmeg 1,794, cacao 1,131, mace 93, other crops include cotton, limes, cinnamon, cloves, and pimiento; livestock (number of live animals) 12,000 sheep, 11,000 goats, 4,000 cattle; roundwood, n.a.; fish catch (1993) 2,093. Mining and quarrying: excavation of gravel for local use. Manufacturing (value of production in EC$'000; 1993): wheat flour 9,240; soft drinks 8,922; beer 5,343; rum 5,131; animal feed 4,412; other products include clothing, edible coconut oil, paints, pharmaceutical products, and cigarettes. Construction: n.a. Energy production (consumption): electricity (kW-hr; 1992) 62,000,000 (62,000,000); coal, none (none); crude petroleum, none (none); petroleum products (metric tons; 1992) none (39,000); natural gas, none (none).
Household income and expenditure. Average household size (1991) 3.7; income per household (1988) EC$7,097 (U.S.$2,629); sources of income: n.a.; expenditure (1987): food, beverages, and tobacco 40.7%, household furnishings and operations 13.7%, housing 11.9%, transportation 9.1%, personal effects and medical care 8.6%.
Population economically active (1988): total 38,920; activity rate of total population 39.9% (participation rates: ages 15–65, 72.7%; female 48.6%; unemployed [1994] 16.7%).

Price and earnings indexes (1990 = 100)

	1988	1989	1990	1991	1992	1993	1994
Consumer price index	92.2	97.3	100.0	102.7	106.5	109.5	112.8[12]
Annual earnings index[13]	...	...	100.0	108.0	118.8	124.1	...

Land use (1993): forested 9.0%; meadows and pastures 3.0%; agricultural and under permanent cultivation 32.0%; other 56.0%.

Foreign trade[14]

Balance of trade (current prices)

	1988	1989	1990	1991	1992	1993
U.S.$'000,000	−59.2	−72.5	−82.6	−93.9	−86.6	−94.4
% of total	47.2%	56.2%	61.2%	66.9%	68.4%	70.0%

Imports (1993): U.S.$114,600,000 ([15]food 25.8%; machinery and transport equipment 22.7%; basic manufactures 19.1%; chemicals and chemical products 9.4%). *Major import sources*[16]: Trinidad and Tobago 27%; United States 22%; United Kingdom 9%; Italy 7%; Japan 3%.
Exports (1993): U.S.$20,200,000 (cocoa beans 15.4%; nutmeg 11.2%; fish 11.0%[16]; bananas 10.5%; mace 2.9%; other exports include fresh fruit, vegetables, spices, electronic components, and pharmaceuticals). *Major export destinations*[16]: United States 25%; Venezuela 25%; United Kingdom 16%; St. Lucia 6%.

Transport and communications

Transport. Railroads: none. Roads (1993): total length 650 mi, 1,046 km (paved 66%). Vehicles: n.a. Merchant marine (1992): vessels (100 gross tons and over) 3; total deadweight tonnage 484. Air transport (1993)[17]: passenger arrivals and departures 277,000; cargo loaded and unloaded 2,300 metric tons; airports (1995) with scheduled flights 2.
Communications. Daily newspapers: none[18]. Radio (1994): total number of receivers 53,000 (1 per 1.7 persons). Television (1994): total number of receivers 30,000 (1 per 3.1 persons). Telephones (main lines; 1993): 20,100 (1 per 4.6 persons).

Education and health

Education (1993–94)

	schools	teachers	students	student/teacher ratio
Primary (age 5–11)	57	781	21,311	27.3
Secondary (age 12–16)	19	352	6,030	19.7
Vocational	...	...	...	...
Higher	1	66	651	9.9

Educational attainment (1981). Percentage of population age 25 and over having: no formal schooling 2.2%; primary education 87.8%; secondary 8.5%; higher 1.5%. *Literacy* (1992): total population age 15 and over literate 50,000 (85.0%).
Health: physicians (1991) 63 (1 per 1,445 persons); hospital beds (1992) 401 (1 per 228 persons); infant mortality rate per 1,000 live births (1994) 12.0.
Food (1992): daily per capita caloric intake 2,402 (vegetable products 79%, animal products 21%); 99% of FAO recommended minimum requirement.

Military

Total active duty personnel (1993): [19]. *Military expenditure as percentage of GNP:* n.a.; per capita expenditure, n.a.

[1]Excludes the speaker, who may be elected from outside its elected membership. [2]Preliminary; excludes 434 institutionalized residents and 33 Grenadians in foreign service. [3]St. George local council includes St. George's town. [4]Urban defined as St. George's town and St. George local council. [5]1987. [6]Current revenue only. [7]Current and development expenditures. [8]At factor cost in 1990 prices. [9]Less imputed bank service charges. [10]Includes 1,752 persons in activities not adequately defined and 10,898 unemployed. [11]Detail does not add to total given because of rounding. [12]August. [13]Private sector only. [14]Imports c.i.f.; exports f.o.b. [15]Based on imports for 1992 equaling U.S.$106,600,000. [16]Estimated figure(s). [17]Point Salines airport. [18]Weekly newspapers (1993): 5. [19]The 650-member police force includes an 80-member paramilitary unit and a 30-member coast guard unit.

Guadeloupe

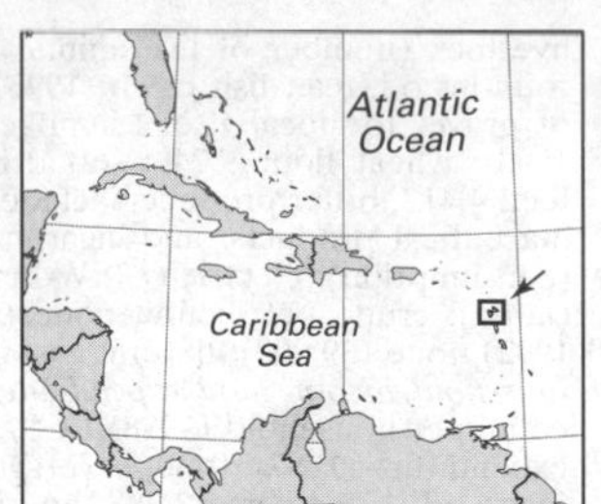

Official name: Département de la Guadeloupe (Department of Guadeloupe).
Political status: overseas department (France[1]) with two legislative houses (General Council [43]; Regional Council [41]).
Chief of state: President of France.
Heads of government: Commissioner of the Republic (for France); President of the General Council (for Guadeloupe); President of the Regional Council (for Guadeloupe).
Capital: Basse-Terre.
Official language: French.
Official religion: none.
Monetary unit: 1 French franc (F) = 100 centimes; valuation (Oct. 6, 1995) 1 U.S.$ = F 5.01; 1 £ = F 7.93.

Area and population

		area		population
Arrondissements	**Capitals**	sq mi	sq km	1990 census
Basse-Terre[2]	Basse-Terre	332	861	151,979
Pointe-à-Pitre[3]	Pointe-à-Pitre	297	769	192,643
Saint-Martin–Saint-Barthélemy[4]	Marigot	29	75	33,556
TOTAL		687[5]	1,780[5]	378,178[6]

Demography

Population (1995): 434,000.
Density (1995): persons per sq mi 631.7, persons per sq km 243.8.
Urban-rural (1995[7]): urban 99.4%; rural 0.6%.
Sex distribution (1991): male 48.88%; female 51.12%.
Age breakdown (1991): under 15, 24.8%; 15–29, 29.5%; 30–44, 21.4%; 45–59, 12.5%; 60–74, 8.3%; 75 and over, 3.5%.
Population projection: (2000) 473,000; (2010) 541,000.
Doubling time: 58 years.
Ethnic composition (1991): Creole (mulatto) 77.0%; black 10.0%; Guadeloupe mestizo (French–East Asian) 10.0%; white 2.0%; other 1.0%.
Religious affiliation (1992[8]): Roman Catholic 85.9%; other 14.1%.
Major communes (1990): Les Abymes 62,605; Saint-Martin 28,518; Pointe-à-Pitre 26,029 (141,000[9, 10]); Le Gosier 20,708; Basse-Terre 14,000 (53,000[9]).

Vital statistics

Birth rate per 1,000 population (1994): 17.4 (world avg. 25.0); legitimate 38.7%; illegitimate 61.3%.
Death rate per 1,000 population (1994): 5.6 (world avg. 9.3).
Natural increase rate per 1,000 population (1994): 11.8 (world avg. 15.7).
Total fertility rate (avg. births per childbearing woman; 1990–95): 2.2.
Marriage rate per 1,000 population (1994): 4.6.
Divorce rate per 1,000 population (1994): 1.3.
Life expectancy at birth (1990–95): male 71.1 years; female 78.0 years.
Major causes of death per 100,000 population (1990): diseases of the circulatory system 186.8; malignant neoplasms (cancers) 121.2; accidents and violence 72.9; diseases of the respiratory system 30.5; diseases of the digestive system 29.7.

National economy

Budget (1994). Revenue: F 2,971,000,000 (tax revenues 64.8%, of which direct taxes 33.7%; advances, loans, and transfers 29.8%; nontax revenues 4.6%). Expenditures: F 6,199,000,000 (current expenditures 65.6%; capital [development] expenditures 17.2%; advances and loans 17.1%).
Public debt (external, outstanding; 1990[11]): U.S.$58,000,000.
Tourism (1993): receipts from visitors U.S.$370,000,000; expenditures by nationals abroad, n.a.
Production (metric tons except as noted). Agriculture, forestry, fishing (1994): sugarcane (1995) 376,000, bananas 150,000, plantains 7,000, pineapples 5,000, tomatoes 4,000, melons 4,000, cucumbers 3,000; livestock (number of live animals) 56,000 cattle, 54,000 goats, 30,000 pigs; roundwood (1993) 22,000 cu m; fish catch (1993) 7,990. Mining and quarrying (1993): pumice 210,000. Manufacturing (1994): cement 282,943; raw sugar (1995) 32,560; rum 36,673 hectolitres; other products include clothing, wooden furniture and posts, and metalware. Construction (buildings authorized; 1992): residential 358,474 sq m; nonresidential 160,084 sq m. Energy production (consumption): electricity (kW-hr; 1994) 1,004,000,000 (914,200,000); coal, none (none); crude petroleum, none (none); petroleum products (metric tons; 1992) none (341,000); natural gas, none (none).
Population economically active (1992): total 181,000; activity rate of total population 44.0% (participation rates [1990]: ages 15–64, 68.0%; female 45.5%; unemployed [1993] 26.1%).

Price and earnings indexes (1990 = 100)[12]

	1989	1990	1991	1992	1993	1994	1995[13]
Consumer price index	96.4	100.0	102.0	104.5	106.7	108.4	109.6
Monthly earnings index[14]	95.4	100.0	102.0	104.7	105.0	106.5	108.7

Household income and expenditure. Average household size (1991) 3.4; income per household (1988) F 105,400 (U.S.$17,700); sources of income (1988): wages and salaries 78.9%, self employment 12.7%, transfer payments 8.4%; expenditure (1984–85): food and beverages 29.8%, housing, household furnishings, and energy 26.3%, transportation and communications 13.3%, clothing and footwear 8.2%, other 22.4%.
Gross national product (at current market prices; 1990): U.S.$1,160,000,000 (U.S.$2,970 per capita).

Structure of gross domestic product and labour force

	1989		1993	
	in value F '000,000	% of total value	labour force	% of labour force
Agriculture	1,177.4	9.2	9,079	5.2
Mining and manufacturing	758.4	5.9	10,376	5.9
Construction	949.3	7.4	15,564	8.9
Public utilities	38.7	0.3	...	...
Transportation and communications	773.3	6.1	54,474	31.0
Trade	2,499.6	19.6		
Finance, real estate	848.8	6.6		
Pub. admin., defense	4,242.4	33.2	40,207	22.9
Services	2,056.6	16.1		
Other	−563.3	−4.4[15]	45,800[16]	26.1[16]
TOTAL	12,781.2	100.0	175,500	100.0

Land use (1993): forested 39.1%; meadows and pastures 13.6%; agricultural and under permanent cultivation 17.7%; other 29.6%.

Foreign trade

Balance of trade (current prices)

	1989	1990	1991	1992	1993	1994
F '000,000	−6,995	−8,439	−8,209	−7,505	−7,309	−7,693
% of total	83.8%	86.3%	79.8%	83.8%	83.2%	82.0%

Imports (1994): F 8,539,962,000 (consumer goods 27.8%; food and agriculture products 22.9%; machinery and equipment 17.8%; transport vehicles and parts 11.9%). *Major import sources:* France 66.7%; other EEC 14.2%; United States 3.1%; Martinique 2.6%; Japan 2.4%.
Exports (1994): F 847,130,000 (agricultural products 61.4%, of which bananas 21.8%, sugar 13.1%, wheat flour 6.5%; consumer goods 20.7%; machinery and equipment 10.3%). *Major export destinations:* France 75.5%; Martinique 13.4%; other EEC 4.4%; French Guiana 2.4%.

Transport and communications

Transport. Railroads: none. Roads (1992): total length 1,480 mi, 2,384 km (paved [1986] 80%). Vehicles (1992): passenger cars 94,700; trucks and buses 36,000. Merchant marine (1992): vessels (100 gross tons and over) 20; deadweight tonnage 4,430. Air transport (1994): passenger arrivals and departures 1,551,464; cargo loaded 9,322 metric tons, cargo unloaded 5,548 metric tons; airports (1995) with scheduled flights 6.
Communications. Daily newspapers (1993): total number 1; total circulation 25,000; circulation per 1,000 population 60. Radio (1993): total number of receivers 100,000 (1 per 4.2 persons). Television (1993): total number of receivers 150,000 (1 per 2.8 persons). Telephones (main lines; 1993): 148,700 (1 per 2.7 persons).

Education and health

Education (1992–93)

	schools	teachers	students	student/ teacher ratio
Primary (age 6–10)	340	3,135	39,075	12.5
Secondary (age 11–17) Vocational	78	3,813	49,295	12.9
Higher[17]	1	310	4,296	13.9

Educational attainment (1982). Percentage of population age 25 and over having: no formal schooling 10.7%; primary education 54.6%; secondary 29.5%; higher 5.2%. *Literacy* (1982): total population age 15 and over literate 225,400 (90.1%); males literate 108,700 (89.7%); females literate 116,700 (90.5%).
Health (1991): physicians 590 (1 per 680 persons); hospital beds 3,230 (1 per 122 persons); infant mortality rate per 1,000 live births (1994) 7.9.
Food (1992): daily per capita caloric intake 2,682 (vegetable products 77%, animal products 23%); 111% of FAO recommended minimum requirement.

Military

Total active duty personnel (1994): 535 French troops.

[1]Guadeloupe elects 4 deputies and 2 senators to French parliament. [2]Comprises Basse-Terre 327 sq mi (848 sq km), pop. 149,943, and Îles des Saintes 5 sq mi (13 sq km), pop. 2,036. [3]Comprises Grande-Terre 228 sq mi (590 sq km), pop. 177,570; Marie-Galante 61 sq mi (158 sq km), pop. 13,463; La Désirade 8 sq mi (20 sq km), pop. 1,610; and the uninhabited Îles de la Petite-Terre. [4]Comprises the French part of Saint-Martin 20 sq mi (52 sq km), pop. 28,518; Saint-Barthélemy 8 sq mi (21 sq km), pop. 5,038; and the small, uninhabited island of Tintamarre. [5]Total area includes 29 sq mi (75 sq km) not allocated by arrondissement. [6]Preliminary; final 1990 census total was 386,987. [7]Urban defined as locality with 2,000 or more inhabitants. [8]January 1. [9]Urban agglomeration. [10]Includes Les Abymes. [11]Includes external long-term private debt not guaranteed by the government. [12]Base and indexes are end of year unless footnoted. [13]June. [14]Based on minimum-level wage of public employees. [15]Less imputed bank service charges. [16]Unemployed. [17]University of Antilles–French Guiana, Guadeloupe campus.

Guatemala

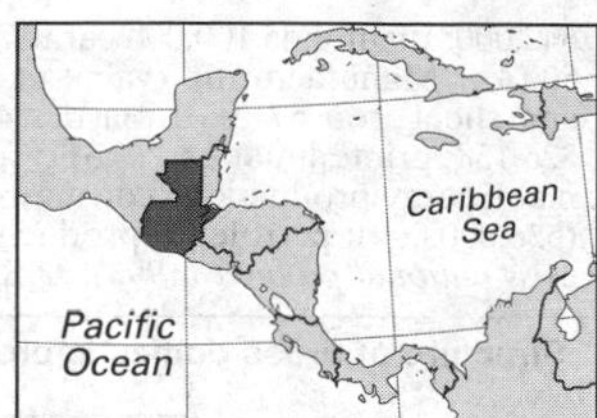

Official name: República de Guatemala (Republic of Guatemala).
Form of government: republic with one legislative house (Congress of the Republic [80]).
Head of state and government: President.
Capital: Guatemala City.
Official language: Spanish.
Official religion: none.
Monetary unit: 1 Guatemalan quetzal (Q) = 100 centavos; valuation (Oct. 6, 1995) 1 U.S.$ = Q 5.92; 1 £ = Q 9.36.

Area and population

		area		population
Departments	Capitals	sq mi	sq km	1995 estimate[1]
Alta Verapaz	Cobán	3,354	8,686	670,815
Baja Verapaz	Salamá	1,206	3,124	205,481
Chimaltenango	Chimaltenango	764	1,979	385,856
Chiquimula	Chiquimula	917	2,376	274,091
El Progreso	Guastatoya (Progreso)	742	1,922	117,943
Escuintla	Escuintla	1,693	4,384	610,322
Guatemala	Guatemala City	821	2,126	2,246,170
Huehuetenango	Huehuetenango	2,857	7,400	816,376
Izabal	Puerto Barrios	3,490	9,038	370,538
Jalapa	Jalapa	797	2,063	211,830
Jutiapa	Jutiapa	1,243	3,219	387,177
Petén	Flores	13,843	35,854	310,008
Quetzaltenango	Quetzaltenango	753	1,951	623,571
Quiché	Santa Cruz del Quiché	3,235	8,378	652,022
Retalhuleu	Retalhuleu	717	1,856	268,996
Sacatepéquez	Antigua Guatemala	180	465	202,243
San Marcos	San Marcos	1,464	3,791	790,118
Santa Rosa	Cuilapa	1,141	2,955	291,611
Sololá	Sololá	410	1,061	274,356
Suchitepéquez	Mazatenango	969	2,510	403,618
Totonicapán	Totonicapán	410	1,061	333,634
Zacapa	Zacapa	1,039	2,690	174,450
TOTAL		42,042[2]	108,889	10,621,226

Demography

Population (1995): 10,621,000.
Density (1995): persons per sq mi 252.6, persons per sq km 97.5.
Urban-rural (1995): urban 38.7%; rural 61.3%.
Sex distribution (1990): male 50.52%; female 49.48%.
Age breakdown (1990): under 15, 45.4%; 15–29, 26.7%; 30–44, 14.6%; 45–59, 8.2%; 60–74, 4.1%; 75 and over, 1.0%.
Population projection: (2000) 12,222,000; (2010) 15,827,000.
Doubling time: 24 years.
Ethnic composition (1987): Amerindian 45%; Ladino (Hispanic/Amerindian) 45%; white 5%; black 2%; other mixed race and Chinese 3%.
Religious affiliation (1986): Roman Catholic *c.* 75%, of which Catholic/traditional syncretist *c.* 25%; Protestant (mostly fundamentalist) *c.* 25%.
Major cities (1995): Guatemala City 1,167,495; Mixco 436,668; Villa Nueva 165,567; Chinautla 61,335; Amatitlan 40,229.

Vital statistics

Birth rate per 1,000 population (1994): 35.4 (world avg. 25.0).
Death rate per 1,000 population (1994): 7.5 (world avg. 9.3).
Natural increase rate per 1,000 population (1994): 27.9 (world avg. 15.7).
Total fertility rate (avg. births per childbearing woman; 1994): 4.8.
Marriage rate per 1,000 population (1988): 5.4.
Divorce rate per 1,000 population (1988): 0.2.
Life expectancy at birth (1994): male 61.9 years; female 67.1 years.
Major causes of death per 100,000 population (1988): infectious and parasitic diseases 121.6; diseases of the respiratory system 110.8; perinatal causes 58.7; malnutrition 50.2; dehydration 18.5.

National economy

Budget (1994). Revenue: Q 5,712,300,000 (tax revenue 89.3%, of which taxes on goods and services 48.4%, customs duties 22.6%, income taxes 15.1%; nontax revenue 10.7%). Expenditures: Q 6,592,300,000 (current expenditures 78.3%, of which disbursements for goods and services 46.2%, transfer payments 22.0%; capital expenditures 21.7%).
Tourism (1993): receipts from visitors U.S.$265,000,000; expenditures by nationals abroad U.S.$116,000,000.
Land use (1993): forested 53.6%; meadows and pastures 24.0%; agricultural and under permanent cultivation 17.3%; other 5.1%.
Production (metric tons except as noted). Agriculture, forestry, fishing (1994): sugarcane 11,900,000, corn (maize) 1,350,000, bananas 484,000, coffee 168,000, tomatoes 135,000, dry beans 100,000, sorghum 85,000, plantains 50,000, seed cotton 22,000, cottonseed 13,000; livestock (number of live animals) 2,210,000 cattle, 720,000 pigs, 440,000 sheep; roundwood (1993) 11,263,000 cu m; fish catch (1993) 8,147. Mining and quarrying (1993): gypsum 60,000; iron ore 3,300; antimony ore 600. Manufacturing (value added in Q '000,000; 1989[3]): food products 138.0; beverages 66.2; clothing and footwear 47.6; textiles 43.2; metal products 30.2. Construction (value of buildings authorized in Q '000,000; 1991)[4]: residential 170.2; nonresidential 127.5. Energy production (consumption): electricity (kW-hr; 1992) 2,340,000,000 (2,340,000,000); crude petroleum (barrels; 1992) 2,206,000 (6,035,000); petroleum products (metric tons; 1992) 727,000 (1,583,000).

Gross national product (1993): U.S.$11,123,000,000 (U.S.$1,110 per capita).

Structure of gross domestic product and labour force

	1994		1990	
	in value Q '000[3]	% of total value	labour force	% of labour force
Agriculture	969,678	24.3	1,625,125	58.1
Mining	13,986	0.3	2,797	0.1
Manufacturing	569,065	14.3	380,408	13.6
Construction	82,456	2.1	114,682	4.1
Public utilities	119,121	3.0	8,391	0.3
Transp. and commun.	342,001	8.6	69,928	2.5
Trade	966,854	24.3	204,190	7.3
Finance, real estate	376,765	9.5	} 335,654	} 12.0
Pub. admin., defense	306,035	7.7		
Services	233,974	5.9		
Other	—	—	55,942[5]	2.0[5]
TOTAL	3,979,935	100.0	2,797,117	100.0

Public debt (external, outstanding; 1993): U.S.$2,301,000,000.
Population economically active (1990): total 2,797,117; activity rate of total population 31.4% (participation rates: ages 15–64, 46.5%; female [1989] 25.5%; unemployed 2.9%[6]).

Price and earnings indexes (1990 = 100)

	1988	1989	1990	1991	1992	1993	1994
Consumer price index	63.6	70.8	100.0	133.2	146.5	163.9	...
Annual earnings index[7]	73.3	86.9	100.0	126.6	162.3	203.8	232.4

Household income and expenditure. Average household size (1989) 5.4; income per household (1989) Q 4,306 (U.S.$1,529); sources of income: n.a.; expenditure (1981): food 64.4%, housing and energy 16.0%, transportation and communications 7.0%, household furnishings 5.0%, clothing 3.1%.

Foreign trade[8]

Balance of trade (current prices)

	1989	1990	1991	1992	1993	1994
U.S.$'000,000	−389.2	−207.4	107.3	−1,190.0	−1,096.2	−755.3
% of total	14.9%	8.0%	7.5%	35.7%	29.0%	19.9%

Imports (1994): U.S.$2,647,629,800 (machinery 16.4%, chemical products 14.9%, transport equipment 14.8%, mineral products 12.2%, metal products 8.4%, plastic products 5.5%). *Major import sources:* United States 43.0%; Mexico 7.0%; El Salvador 6.2%; Venezuela 5.2%; Germany 4.0%; Japan 3.8%.
Exports (1994): U.S.$1,502,610,400 (coffee 21.2%, sugar 10.7%, bananas 7.6%, fish and other seafoods 4.0%, vegetable seeds 3.4%). *Major export destinations:* United States 31.9%; El Salvador 15.2%; Costa Rica 6.5%; Honduras 5.8%; Mexico 4.5%; Germany 4.3%.

Transport and communications

Transport. Railroads (1993)[9]: route length 708 mi, 1,139 km; passenger-km (1990) 10,099,000; metric ton-km cargo 135,100,000. Roads (1993): total length 7,363 mi, 11,849 km (paved 26%). Vehicles (1993): passenger cars 98,700; trucks and buses 95,000. Merchant marine (1992): vessels (100 gross tons and over) 8; total deadweight tonnage 353. Air transport (1993)[10]: passenger-km 384,000,000; metric ton-km cargo 21,000,000; airports (1995) with scheduled flights 2.
Communications. Daily newspapers (1992): total number 5; total circulation 180,000; circulation per 1,000 population 18. Radio (1994): 570,000 receivers (1 per 18 persons). Television (1994): 475,000 receivers (1 per 22 persons). Telephones (main lines; 1993): 231,100 (1 per 43 persons).

Education and health

Education (1991)

	schools	teachers	students	student/ teacher ratio
Primary (age 7–12)	9,362	36,757	1,249,413	34.0
Secondary (age 13–18)	1,274	13,588	207,935	15.3
Voc., teacher tr.	626	7,129	94,485	13.3
Higher[11]	5	4,346	69,532	16.0

Educational attainment (1989). Percentage of population age 25 and over having: no formal schooling 50.0%; incomplete primary education 21.6%; complete primary 16.2%; secondary 9.2%; higher 3.0%. *Literacy* (1989): total population age 15 and over literate 2,809,000 (60.3%); males literate 1,544,000 (69.7%); females literate 1,265,000 (51.7%).
Health (1987): physicians 3,579 (1 per 2,356 persons); hospital beds 13,667 (1 per 602 persons); infant mortality rate per 1,000 live births (1994) 53.9.
Food (1992): daily per capita caloric intake 2,255 (vegetable products 93%, animal products 7%); 103% of FAO recommended minimum requirement.

Military

Total active duty personnel (1994): 44,200 (army 95.0%, navy 3.4%, air force 1.6%). *Military expenditure as percentage of GNP* (1993): 1.0% (world 3.3%); per capita expenditure U.S.$11.

[1]Population of departments and cities taken from official projections based on 1973–81 intercensal growth rates and subsequent vital (birth and death) rates. [2]Detail does not add to total given because of rounding. [3]At prices of 1958. [4]Private construction in Guatemala City metropolitan area only. [5]Persons in activities not adequately defined. [6]Officially unemployed; 63% of economically active population is estimated to be underemployed. [7]Based on employees entitled to social security. [8]Import figures are f.o.b. in balance of trade and c.i.f. for commodities and trading partners. [9]Guatemala Railways only. [10]Aviateca Airlines only. [11]1989.

Guinea

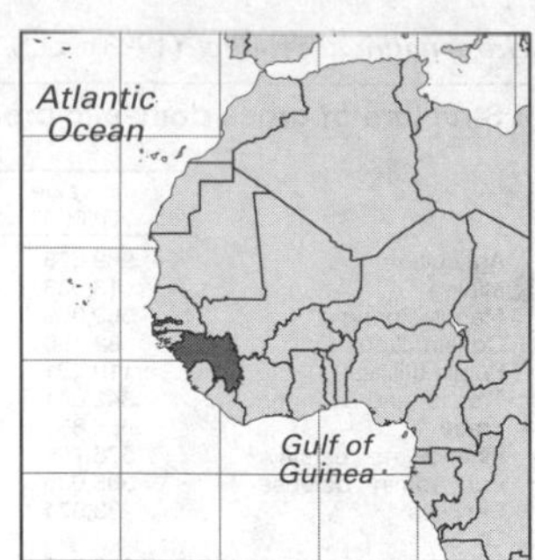

Official name: République de Guinée (Republic of Guinea).
Form of government: multiparty republic with one legislative house (National Assembly [114 seats][1].
Head of state and government: President.
Capital: Conakry.
Official language: French.
Official religion: none.
Monetary unit: 1 Guinean franc (GF) = 100 cauris; valuation (Oct. 6, 1995) 1 U.S.$ = GF 993; 1 £ = GF 1,569.

Area and population

Regions	Capitals	area sq mi	area sq km	population 1983 census
Beyla	Beyla	6,738	17,452	161,347
Boffa	Boffa	1,932	5,003	141,719
Boké[2]	Boké	3,881	10,053	225,207
Conakry	Conakry	119	308	705,280
Coyah (Dubréka)	Coyah	2,153	5,576	134,190
Dabola	Dabola	2,317	6,000	97,986
Dalaba	Dalaba	1,313	3,400	132,802
Dinguiraye	Dinguiraye	4,247	11,000	133,502
Faranah[2]	Faranah	4,788	12,400	142,923
Forécariah	Forécariah	1,647	4,265	116,464
Fria	Fria	840	2,175	70,413
Gaoual	Gaoual	4,440	11,500	135,657
Guéckédou	Guéckédou	1,605	4,157	204,757
Kankan	Kankan	7,104	18,400	229,861
Kérouané	Kérouané	3,070	7,950	106,872
Kindia	Kindia	3,409	8,828	216,052
Kissidougou	Kissidougou	3,425	8,872	183,236
Koubia	Koubia	571	1,480	98,053
Koundara	Koundara	2,124	5,500	94,216
Kouroussa	Kouroussa	4,647	12,035	136,926
Labé	Labé	973	2,520	253,214
Lélouma	Lélouma	830	2,150	138,467
Lola	Lola	1,629	4,219	106,654
Macenta	Macenta	3,363	8,710	193,109
Mali	Mali	3,398	8,800	210,889
Mamou	Mamou	2,378	6,160	190,525
Mandiana	Mandiana	5,000	12,950	136,317
Nzérékoré	Nzérékoré	1,460	3,781	216,355
Pita	Pita	1,544	4,000	227,912
Siguiri	Siguiri	7,626	19,750	209,164
Télimélé	Télimélé	3,119	8,080	243,256
Tougué	Tougué	2,394	6,200	113,272
Yomou	Yomou	843	2,183	74,417
TOTAL		94,926[3]	245,857	5,781,014

Demography

Population (1995): 6,700,000.
Density (1995): persons per sq mi 70.6, persons per sq km 27.3.
Urban-rural (1990): urban 25.6%; rural 74.4%.
Sex distribution (1995): male 50.23%; female 49.77%.
Age breakdown (1995): under 15, 47.1%; 15–29, 25.9%; 30–44, 15.0%; 45–59, 7.8%; 60–74, 3.6%; 75 and over, 0.6%.
Population projection: (2000) 7,759,000; (2010) 10,301,000.
Doubling time: 27 years.
Ethnic composition (1990): Fulani 40.3%; Malinke 25.8%; Susu 11.0%; Kissi 6.5%; Kpelle 4.8%; other 11.6%.
Religious affiliation (1988): Muslim 85.0%; traditional beliefs 5.0%; Christian 1.5%; other 8.5%.
Major cities (1983): Conakry 650,000; Kankan 55,010; N'zérekoré 44,598; Kindia 39,121; Kissidougou 30,724.

Vital statistics

Birth rate per 1,000 population (1991): 47.0 (world avg. 25.0).
Death rate per 1,000 population (1991): 21.0 (world avg. 9.3).
Natural increase rate per 1,000 population (1991): 26.0 (world avg. 15.7).
Total fertility rate (avg. births per childbearing woman; 1990): 6.5.
Life expectancy at birth (1990–95): male 44.0 years; female 45.0 years.
Major causes of death per 100,000 population: n.a.; however, in the mid-1990s, the major causes of illness were (in order): malaria, acute respiratory infections, intestinal parasitic diseases, gastroenteritis, and malnutrition.

National economy

Budget (1993). Revenue: GF 464,300,000,000,000 (current revenues 75.7%, of which mining sector 29.6%, other 46.1%; foreign aid 24.3%). Expenditures: GF 579,600,000,000,000 (capital spending 49.4%; current expenditure 50.6%, of which personnel 24.2%, other goods and services 13.9%).
Public debt (external, outstanding; 1993): U.S.$2,675,000,000.
Tourism (1993): receipts U.S.$6,000,000; expenditures U.S.$21,000,000.
Production (metric tons except as noted). Agriculture, forestry, fishing (1994): roots and tubers 1,203,000 (of which cassava 945,000, yams 75,000), fruits 1,054,000 (of which plantains 441,000, bananas 151,000, pineapples 94,000), paddy rice 916,000, vegetables and melons 420,000, sugarcane 220,000, corn (maize) 114,000, peanuts (groundnuts) 112,000, pulses 60,000, palm kernels 40,000, palm oil 40,000, coffee 29,000, coconuts 18,000, eggs 14,910; livestock (number of live animals) 1,658,000 cattle, 460,000 goats, 435,000 sheep, 33,000 pigs, 14,000,000 chickens; roundwood (1993) 4,549,000 cu m; fish catch (1993) 40,000. Mining and quarrying (1993): bauxite 16,259,000; alumina 642,000; diamonds 100,000 carats (the Banankoro mine closed in 1994); gold 500 kg. Manufacturing (value of production in GF '000; 1985): corrugated and sheet iron 571,081; plastics 462,242; tobacco products 375,154; cement 326,138; printed matter 216,511; fruit juice 75,763; beer 69,934. Construction: n.a. Energy production (consumption): electricity (kW-hr; 1993) 536,000,000 (536,000,000); petroleum products (metric tons; 1993) none (344,000).
Gross national product (1993): U.S.$3,260,000,000 (U.S.$520 per capita).

Structure of gross domestic product and labour force

	1993		1983	
	in value[4] GF '000,000,000	% of total value	labour force	% of labour force
Agriculture	395.7	23.9	1,423,615	78.2
Mining	322.2	19.5	12,241	0.7
Manufacturing	75.4	4.6	11,215	0.6
Construction	113.8	6.9	9,115	0.5
Public utilities	3.6	0.2	3,205	0.2
Transp. and commun.	85.0	5.1	29,496	1.6
Trade, finance	423.1	25.6	40,865	2.0
Pub. admin., defense	92.9	5.6	137,600	7.5
Services	103.4	6.3		
Other	39.0	2.3	155,679	8.5
TOTAL	1,654.1	100.0	1,823,031	100.0

Population economically active (1992): total 2,590,000; activity rate of total population 42.3% (participation rates [1983]: ages 15–64, 63.5%; female 39.4%; unemployed, n.a.).

Price index (1990 = 100)

	1988	1989	1990	1991	1992	1993	1994
Consumer price index	65.3	83.8	100.0	119.6	139.5	149.4	155.5

Household income and expenditure. Average household size (1983) 6.7; average annual income per capita (1984) GS 7,660 (U.S.$305); sources of income: n.a.; expenditure (1985): food 61.5%, health care 11.2%, clothing and footwear 7.9%, housing and energy 7.3%, transportation 5.1%.
Land use (1993): forest 58.8%; pasture 22.4%; agricultural 3.0%; other 15.8%.

Foreign trade[5]

Balance of trade (current prices)

	1988	1989	1990	1991	1992	1993	1994
U.S.$'000,000	+1.3	+64.0	+85.5	−7.8	−91.2	−21.6	−169.6
% of total	0.1%	5.7%	6.8%	0.6%	8.1%	1.9%	14.1%

Imports (1993): U.S.$730,000,000 (1992; goods for mining companies 29.8%; goods for public sector 19.9%; other private sector 50.2%, of which petroleum products 4.4%). *Major import sources* (1992): France 28.7%; Côte d'Ivoire 11.8%; U.S. 8.6%; Hong Kong 8.2%; Belgium-Luxembourg 6.0%; The Netherlands 4.6%; China 4.4%; Italy 4.4%.
Exports (1993): U.S.$607,100,000 (bauxite 53.3%; alumina 17.9%; diamonds 11.5%; coffee 6.0%; fish 2.7%). *Major export destinations:* U.S. 19.3%; Belgium-Luxembourg 15.2%; Ireland 12.1%; Spain 10.9%; France 7.9%.

Transport and communications

Transport. Railroads (1993): route length 411 mi, 662 km; (latest) passenger-mi 25,800,000, passenger-km 41,500,000; short ton-mi cargo 5,000,000, metric ton-km cargo 7,300,000. Roads (1992): total length 9,974 mi, 16,051 km (paved 9%). Vehicles (1992): passenger cars 23,155; trucks and buses 13,000. Merchant marine (1992): vessels (100 gross tons and over) 23; total deadweight tonnage 1,749. Air transport (1992): passenger-mi 20,804,000, passenger-km 33,480,000; short ton-mi cargo 622,000, metric ton-km cargo 686,000; airports (1995) with scheduled flights 2.
Communications. Daily newspapers (1988): 1; total circulation 13,000; circulation per 1,000 population 2.0. Radio (1994): 230,000 receivers (1 per 28 persons). Television (1994): 65,000 receivers (1 per 100 persons). Telephones (main lines; 1993): 11,580 (1 per 560 persons).

Education and health

Education (1993)

	schools	teachers	students	student/ teacher ratio
Primary (age 7–12)	2,849	9,718	471,792	48.5
Secondary (age 13–18)	225[6]	3,417	97,533	28.5
Voc., teacher tr.	35[6]	1,302	9,278	7.1
Higher	10[6]	805[7]	6,245[7]	7.8[7]

Educational attainment of those age six and over having attended school (1983): primary 55.2%; secondary 32.7%; vocational 3.4%; higher 8.7%. *Literacy* (1995): percentage of total population age 15 and over literate 35.9%; males 49.9%; females 21.9%.
Health: physicians (1990) 773 (1 per 7,445 persons); hospital beds (1988) 3,382 (1 per 1,934 persons); infant mortality rate (1990–95) 134.
Food (1992): daily per capita caloric intake 2,389 (vegetable products 96%, animal products 4%); 103% of FAO recommended minimum requirement.

Military

Total active duty personnel (1995): 9,700 (army 87.6%, navy 4.1%, air force 8.2%). *Military expenditure as percentage of GNP* (1992): 1.5% (world 3.7%); per capita expenditure U.S.$7.

[1]Met for first session Oct. 5, 1995. [2]The provinces of Boké and Faranah were abolished by presidential decree in January 1988. [3]Detail does not add to total given because of rounding. [4]Constant prices of 1989. [5]Imports c.i.f.; exports f.o.b. in commodities and direction of trade. [6]1987–88. [7]Universities only.

Guinea-Bissau

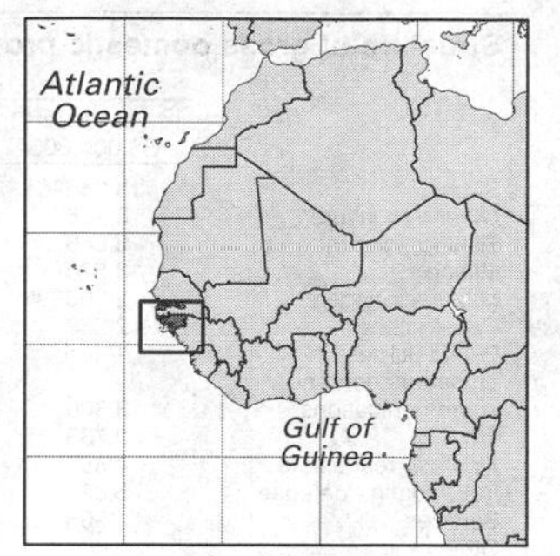

Official name: República da Guiné-Bissau (Republic of Guinea-Bissau).
Form of government: multiparty republic with one legislative house (National Popular Assembly [100]).
Chief of state: President.
Head of government: Prime Minister.
Capital: Bissau.
Official language: Portuguese.
Official religion: none.
Monetary unit: 1 Guinea-Bissau peso (PG) = 100 centavos; valuation (Oct. 6, 1995) 1 U.S.$ = PG 16,036; 1 £ = PG 28,513.

Area and population

Regions	Capitals	area sq mi	area sq km	population 1979 census[1]
Bafatá	Bafatá	2,309	5,981	115,656
Biombo[2]	Bissau	324	840	51,796
Bolama	Bolama	1,013	2,624	25,449
Cacheu	Cacheu	1,998	5,175	127,514
Gabú	Gabú	3,533	9,150	103,683
Oio	Farim	2,086	5,403	131,271
Quinara	Fulacunda	1,212	3,138	35,567
Tombali	Catió	1,443	3,736	55,088
Autonomous Sector				
Bissau[2]	—	30	78	107,281
TOTAL		13,948	36,125	753,305

Demography

Population (1995): 1,073,000.
Density (1995): persons per sq mi 76.9, persons per sq km 29.7.
Urban-rural (1991): urban 20.3%; rural 79.7%.
Sex distribution (1995): male 49.21%; female 50.79%.
Age breakdown (1995): under 15, 41.7%; 15–29, 25.1%; 30–44, 16.2%; 45–59, 10.5%; 60–74, 5.4%; 75 and over, 1.1%.
Population projection: (2000) 1,192,000; (2010) 1,473,000.
Doubling time: 33 years.
Ethnic composition (1979): Balante 27.2%; Fulani 22.9%; Malinke 12.2%; Mandyako 10.6%; Pepel 10.0%; other 17.1%.
Religious affiliation (1992): traditional beliefs 54%; Muslim 38%; Christian 8%.
Major cities (1979): Bissau 125,000[3]; Bafatá 13,429; Gabú 7,803; Mansôa 5,390; Catió 5,179.

Vital statistics

Birth rate per 1,000 population (1990–95): 42.7 (world avg. 25.0); legitimate, n.a.; illegitimate, n.a.
Death rate per 1,000 population (1990–95): 21.3 (world avg. 9.3).
Natural increase rate per 1,000 population (1990–95): 21.4 (world avg. 15.7).
Total fertility rate (avg. births per childbearing woman; 1995): 5.0.
Marriage rate per 1,000 population (1981): 0.1.
Divorce rate per 1,000 population: n.a.
Life expectancy at birth (1990–95): male 41.9 years; female 45.1 years.
Major causes of death per 100,000 population: n.a.; however, major diseases include tuberculosis of the respiratory system, whooping cough, typhoid fever, cholera, bacillary dysentery and amebiasis, malaria, pneumonia, and meningococcal infections; malnutrition is widespread.

National economy

Budget (1989). Revenue: PG 148,167,000,000 (grants from abroad 71.2%, nontax revenue 18.4%, tax revenue 10.4%). Expenditures (1989): PG 201,725,000,000 (capital expenditures 58.0%, current expenditures 36.4%).
Public debt (external, outstanding; 1993): U.S.$633,600,000.
Tourism: n.a.
Production (metric tons except as noted). Agriculture, forestry, fishing (1994): rice 130,000, fruits 67,000, roots and tubers (sweet potatoes and cassava) 65,000, millet 40,000, cashews 35,000, plantains 34,000, coconuts 25,000, vegetables 20,000, peanuts (groundnuts) 18,000, sorghum 15,000, corn (maize) 14,000, palm kernels 8,000, sugarcane 6,000, palm oil 5,100, bananas 5,000, copra 5,000, seed cotton 2,000; livestock (number of live animals) 494,000 cattle, 312,000 pigs, 276,000 goats, 263,000 sheep, 1,000,000 chickens; roundwood (1993) 574,000 cu m; fish catch (1993) 5,350. Mining and quarrying: extraction of construction materials only. Manufacturing (1993): fresh pork 9,000; palm oil 5,000; copra 5,000; fresh beef 4,000; animal hides 1,227, of which cattle 875, goat 194, sheep 158; sawlogs 40,000 cu m; brewing of beer is also important. Construction: n.a. Energy production (consumption): electricity (kW-hr; 1993) 42,000,000 (42,000,000); coal, none (none); crude petroleum, none (none); petroleum products (metric tons; 1993) none (74,000); natural gas, none (none).
Population economically active (1992): total 461,000; activity rate of total population 45.8% (participation rates: ages 15–64 [1979] 41.0%; female 3.6%; unemployed, n.a.).

Price and earnings indexes (1990 = 100)

	1988	1989	1990	1991	1992	1993	1994
Consumer price index	41.6	75.2	100.0	157.6	267.3	395.8	455.9
Earnings index	...	...	...	...	...	...	...

Gross national product (at current market prices; 1993): U.S.$241,700,000 (U.S.$233 per capita).

Structure of gross domestic product and labour force

	1991 in value PG '000,000	% of total value	labour force	% of labour force
Agriculture	382,400	44.7	362,000	78.0
Mining / Manufacturing / Public utilities	72,556	8.5	21,000	4.5
Construction	71,874	8.4		
Transportation and communications	33,364	3.9	81,000	17.5
Trade	220,356	25.8		
Finance, Services	27,914	3.3		
Pub. admin., defense	46,522	5.4		
TOTAL	854.986	100.0	464,000	100.0

Land use (1993): forested 38.1%; meadows and pastures 38.4%; agricultural and under permanent cultivation 12.1%; other 11.4%.
Household income and expenditure. Average household size (1981) 4.1; income per household: n.a.; sources of income: n.a.; expenditure: n.a.

Foreign trade

Balance of trade (current prices)

	1989	1990	1991	1992	1993	1994
PG'000,000	−96,304	−120,821	−166,698	−530,592	−378,141	−293,146
% of total	65.2%	58.9%	52.7%	85.5%	54.0%	26.0%

Imports (1991): U.S.$90,000,000 (1988; transport equipment 28.7%, building materials 17.9%, foodstuffs 8.6%, fuel and lubricants 8.6%, other 36.2%). *Major import sources* (1989): Italy 27.3%; Portugal 23.0%; Thailand 7.6%; The Netherlands 7.2%; France 4.3%; Senegal 4.2%; U.S.S.R. 3.0%.
Exports (1991): U.S.$23,000,000 (1988; cashews 52.8%, peanuts [groundnuts] 11.3%, frozen fish 3.1%). *Major export destinations* (1989): Portugal 34.4%; Spain 19.2%; France 18.1%; Japan 6.7%; The Netherlands 6.1%; Italy 6.0%; Belgium-Luxembourg 4.5%.

Transport and communications

Transport. Railroads: none. Roads (1991): total length 2,579 mi, 4,150 km (paved 9%). Vehicles (1992): passenger cars 3,500; trucks and buses 2,500. Merchant marine (1992): vessels (100 gross tons and over) 19; total deadweight tonnage 1,846. Air transport (1993): passenger-mi 3,700,000, passenger-km 6,000,000; short ton-mi cargo 700,000, metric ton-km cargo 1,000,000; airports (1995) with scheduled flights 2.
Communications. Daily newspapers (1992): total number 1; total circulation 6,000; circulation per 1,000 population 6. Radio (1994): total number of receivers 40,000 (1 per 26 persons). Television: n.a. Telephones (main lines; 1993): 8,600 (1 per 122 persons).

Education and health

Education (1988)

	schools	teachers	students	student/ teacher ratio
Primary (age 7–13)	632[4]	3,065[4]	79,035	24.6[4]
Secondary (age 13–18)	12[5]	824[5]	5,505	7.8[5]
Voc., teacher tr.	4[4]	107	825	7.7

Educational attainment (1979). Percentage of population age 7 and over having: no formal schooling or knowledge of reading and writing 90.4%; primary education 7.9%; secondary 1.0%; technical 0.5%; higher 0.2%. *Literacy* (1995): total population age 15 and over literate 54.9%; males literate 68.0%; females literate 42.5%.
Health (1986): physicians 274 (1 per 3,263 persons); hospital beds 2,430 (1 per 368 persons); infant mortality rate per 1,000 live births (1990–95) 140.
Food (1992): daily per capita caloric intake 2,556 (vegetable products 93%, animal products 7%); 110% of FAO recommended minimum requirement.

Military

Total active duty personnel (1995): 7,250 (army 93.8%, navy 4.8%, air force 1.4%). *Military expenditure as percentage of GNP* (1992): 3.3% (world 3.7%); per capita expenditure U.S.$7.0.

[1]Preliminary. [2]Biombo region excludes Bissau city. [3]1988. [4]1987. [5]1986.

Guyana

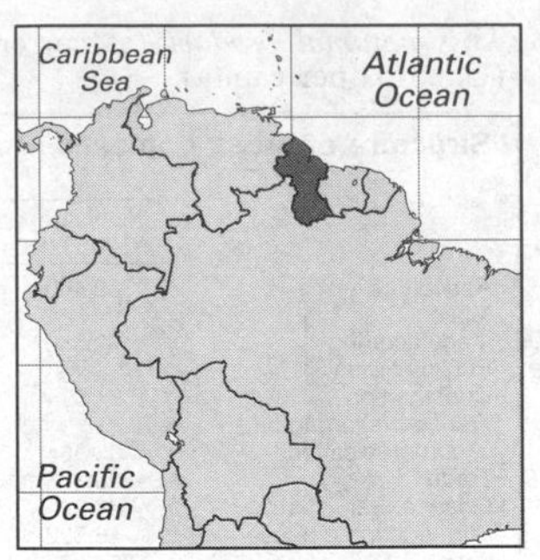

Official name: Co-operative Republic of Guyana.
Form of government: unitary multiparty republic with one legislative house (National Assembly [65[1]]).
Head of state and government: President.
Capital: Georgetown.
Official language: English.
Official religion: none.
Monetary unit: 1 Guyana dollar (G$) = 100 cents; valuation (Oct. 6, 1995) 1 U.S.$ = G$143.80; 1 £ = G$227.33.

Area and population

Administrative Regions	Capitals	area sq mi	area sq km	population 1986 estimate
Region 1 (Barima/Waini)	Mabaruma	7,853	20,339	18,516
Region 2 (Pomeroon/Supenaam)	Anna Regina	2,392	6,195	41,966
Region 3 (Essequibo Islands/West Demerara)	Vreed-en-Hoop	1,450	3,755	102,760
Region 4 (Demerara/Mahaica)	Paradise	862	2,233	310,758
Region 5 (Mahaica/Berbice)	Fort Wellington	1,610	4,170	55,556
Region 6 (East Berbice/Corentyne)	New Amsterdam	13,998	36,255	148,967
Region 7 (Cuyuni/Mazaruni)	Bartica	18,229	47,213	17,941
Region 8 (Potaro/Siparuni)	Mahdia	7,742	20,052	5,672
Region 9 (Upper Takutu/Upper Essequibo)	Lethem	22,313	57,790	15,338
Region 10 (Upper Demerara/Berbice)	Linden	6,595	17,081	38,598
TOTAL		83,044[2]	215,083[2]	756,072

Demography

Population (1995): 770,000.
Density (1995)[3]: persons per sq mi 10.1, persons per sq km 3.9.
Urban-rural (1992–93): urban 31.0%; rural 69.0%.
Sex distribution (1995): male 49.46%; female 50.54%.
Age breakdown (1995): under 15, 32.2%; 15–29, 30.1%; 30–44, 22.2%; 45–59, 9.5%; 60–74, 4.8%; 75 and over, 1.2%.
Population projection: (2000) 788,000; (2010) 823,000.
Doubling time: 54 years.
Ethnic composition (1992–93): East Indian 49.4%; black (African Negro and Bush Negro) 35.6%; mixed 7.1%; Amerindian 6.8%; Portuguese 0.7%; Chinese 0.4%.
Religious affiliation (1990): Christian 52.0%, of which Protestant 34.0% (including Anglican 17.0%), Roman Catholic 18.0%; Hindu 34.0%; Muslim 9.0%; other 5.0%.
Major cities (1992): Georgetown 248,500; Linden 27,200; New Amsterdam 17,700.

Vital statistics

Birth rate per 1,000 population (1994): 20.0 (world avg. 25.0).
Death rate per 1,000 population (1994): 7.0 (world avg. 9.3).
Natural increase rate per 1,000 population (1994): 13.0 (world avg. 15.7).
Total fertility rate (avg. births per childbearing woman; 1994): 2.3.
Marriage rate per 1,000 population: n.a.
Divorce rate per 1,000 population: n.a.
Life expectancy at birth (1994): male 62.0 years; female 68.0 years.
Major causes of death per 100,000 population (1984): diseases of the circulatory system 202.5, of which cerebrovascular disease 79.0; diseases of the digestive system 74.0; accidents and violence 56.5; diseases of the respiratory system 39.8; malignant neoplasms (cancers) 37.1.

National economy

Budget (1994). Revenue: G$32,418,000,000 (current revenue 83.0%, of which consumption taxes 23.9%, income taxes on companies 13.9%, personal income taxes 9.8%, import duties 8.8%; development revenue 17.0%, of which external grants 3.2%). Expenditures: G$36,983,000,000 (current expenditure 73.5%, of which interest payments on debt 33.0%, personal emoluments 12.5%; development expenditure 26.5%).
Production (metric tons except as noted). Agriculture, forestry, fishing (1994): raw sugar 256,700, rice 233,400, coconuts 49,000, roots and tubers 32,000, plantains 24,000, bananas 22,000, oranges 15,000; livestock (number of live animals) 190,000 cattle, 131,000 sheep, 79,000 goats; roundwood (1994) 469,600 cu m; fish catch (1994) 38,200, of which shrimps and prawns 8,200. Mining and quarrying (1994): bauxite 1,991,100; gold 375,500 troy oz; diamonds 14,141 carats[4]. Manufacturing (1994): flour 35,600; rum 258,000 hectolitres; beer and stout 96,600 hectolitres; cigarettes 314,000,000 units; soft drinks 3,449,000 cases; pharmaceuticals 12,200,000 tablets; other products include cotton cloth and dyed and printed fabrics. Construction: n.a. Energy production (consumption): electricity (kW-hr; 1994) 290,800,000 (210,200,000); coal, none (none); crude petroleum, none (none); petroleum products (metric tons; 1993) none (344,000); natural gas, none (none).
Tourism: receipts from visitors (1993) U.S.$36,000,000; expenditures by nationals abroad, n.a.
Public debt (external, outstanding; 1993): U.S.$1,727,000,000.
Household income and expenditure. Average household size (1980) 5.1; income per household: n.a.; sources of income: n.a.; expenditure: n.a.
Gross national product (at current market prices; 1993): U.S.$285,000,000 (U.S.$350 per capita).

Structure of gross domestic product and labour force

	1994		1980	
	in value G$'000,000[5]	% of total value	labour force	% of labour force
Sugar	13,246[6]	21.2[6]	50,316	20.4
Other agriculture	8,466[7]	13.5[7]		
Fishing, forestry	5,860	9.4		
Mining	13,570	21.7	9,669	3.9
Manufacturing	2,296[8, 9]	3.7[8, 9]	28,980	11.8
Construction	2,253	3.6	7,024	2.8
Public utilities	[9]	[9]	2,850	1.2
Transportation and communications	3,300	5.3	9,412	3.8
Trade	2,733	4.4	15,231	6.2
Finance, real estate	4,567	7.3	2,944	1.2
Pub. admin., defense	5,323	8.5	29,948	12.1
Services	906	1.4	29,295	11.9
Other	—	—	61,002[10]	24.7[10]
TOTAL	62,520	100.0	246,671	100.0

Population economically active (1987): total 270,074; activity rate of total population 35.7% (participation rates: ages 15–64, 60.4%; female 29.9%; unemployed [1992] 12.9%).

Price and earnings indexes (1990 = 100)

	1988	1989	1990	1991	1992	1993	1994
Consumer price index[11]	92.7	96.4	100.0	183.1	208.4	224.4	260.5
Earnings index	...	...	...	...	...	...	...

Land use (1993): forested 83.8%; meadows and pastures 6.3%; agricultural and under permanent cultivation 2.5%; other 7.4%.

Foreign trade[12]

Balance of trade (current prices)

	1989	1990	1991	1992	1993	1994
U.S.$'000,000	−32.7	−52.6	−15.5	+15.9	−29.0	+19.0
% of total	6.8%	11.3%	3.1%	2.6%	4.1%	2.6%

Imports (1994): U.S.$350,000,000 (capital goods 28.8%; consumer goods 25.9%; fuels and lubricants 17.7%). *Major import sources* (1993): Caricom countries 27.8%, of which Trinidad and Tobago 12.7%; United States 26.4%; Japan 17.2%; United Kingdom 11.1%.
Exports (1994): U.S.$369,000,000 (domestic exports 95.7%, of which sugar 31.3%, gold 15.8%, rice 15.0%, bauxite 14.1%, shrimps 3.3%, rum 2.7%; reexports 4.3%). *Major export destinations* (1993)[13]: Canada 27.9%; United Kingdom 24.3%; United States 23.6%; Caricom countries 6.2%; Germany 5.0%.

Transport and communications

Transport. Railroads: length (1992) 116 mi, 187 km. Roads (1993): total length 4,474 mi, 7,200 km (paved 10%). Vehicles (1993): passenger cars 24,000; trucks and buses 9,000. Merchant marine (1992): vessels (100 gross tons and over) 82; total deadweight tonnage 13,509. Air transport (1994): passenger-mi 200,000,000, passenger-km 322,000,000; short ton-mi cargo 1,900,000[14], metric ton-km cargo 2,800,000[14]; airports (1994) with scheduled flights 1[15].
Communications. Daily newspapers (1992): total number 2; total circulation 80,000; circulation per 1,000 population 109. Radio (1994): total number of receivers 386,000 (1 per 1.9 persons). Television (1994): total number of receivers 15,000 (1 per 49 persons). Telephones (main lines; 1993): 41,000 (1 per 18 persons).

Education and health

Education (1989–90)

	schools	teachers	students	student/ teacher ratio
Primary (age 6–11)	423	4,010[16]	118,015[16]	...
Secondary (age 12–17)	93	...	72,096[16]	...
Voc., teacher tr.	8	176	5,388	30.6
Higher[17, 18]	1	220	3,607	16.4

Educational attainment (1980). Percentage of population age 25 and over having: no formal schooling 8.1%; primary education 72.8%; secondary 17.3%; higher 1.8%. *Literacy* (1995): total population age 15 and over literate, *c.* 511,000 (98.1%); males literate, *c.* 254,000 (98.6%); females literate, *c.* 257,000 (97.5%).
Health: physicians (1992) 138 (1 per 5,314 persons); hospital beds (1989) 2,488 (1 per 300 persons); infant mortality rate per 1,000 live births (1994) 49.0.
Food (1992): daily per capita caloric intake 2,384 (vegetable products 86%, animal products 14%); 105% of FAO recommended minimum requirement.

Military

Total active duty personnel (1995): 1,600 (army 86.6%, navy 7.2%, air force 6.2%). *Military expenditure as percentage of GNP* (1992): 2.0% (world 3.7%); per capita expenditure U.S.$7.

[1]Includes 12 indirectly elected seats. [2]Includes inland water area equaling *c.* 7,000 sq mi (*c.* 18,000 sq km). [3]Based on land area only. [4]Declared output. [5]At factor cost. [6]Includes sugar manufacturing. [7]Includes rice manufacturing. [8]Excludes sugar and rice manufacturing. [9]Manufacturing includes Public utilities. [10]Represents "not stated." [11]Weights of consumer price index components for Georgetown, Linden, and New Amsterdam only. [12]Imports c.i.f.; exports f.o.b. [13]Excludes reexports. [14]1991. [15]International only; domestic air service is provided on a charter basis. [16]1988–89. [17]University of Guyana only. [18]1993–94.

Haiti

Official name: Repiblik Dayti (Haitian Creole); République d'Haïti (French) (Republic of Haiti).
Form of government: multiparty republic with two legislative houses (Senate [27]; Chamber of Deputies [83]).
Chief of state: President.
Head of government: Prime Minister.
Capital: Port-au-Prince.
Official languages: Haitian Creole; French.
Official religion: none[1].
Monetary unit: 1 gourde (G) = 100 centimes; valuation (Oct. 6, 1995) 1 U.S.$ = G 19.00; 1 £ = G 30.04.

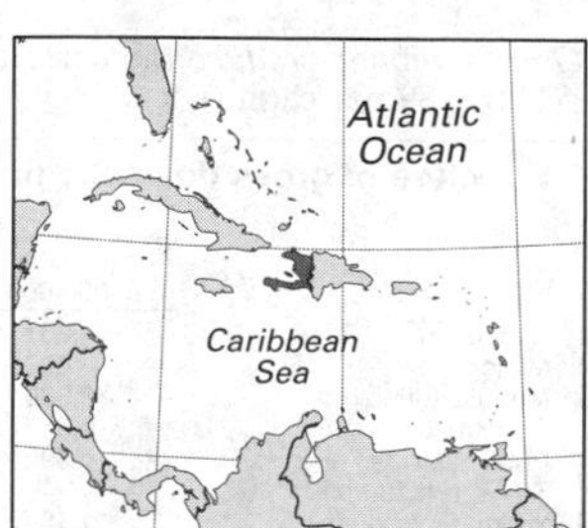

Area and population

		area[2]		population
Departements	**Capitals**	sq mi	sq km	1992 estimate
Artibonite	Gonaïves	1,924	4,984	961,447
Centre	Hinche	1,419	3,675	467,514
Grande Anse	Jérémie	1,278	3,310	616,151
Nord	Cap-Haïtien	813	2,106	724,084
Nord-Est	Fort-Liberté	697	1,805	239,734
Nord-Ouest	Port-de-Paix	840	2,176	395,442
Ouest	Port-au-Prince	1,864	4,827	2,285,044
Sud	Les Cayes	1,079	2,794	630,007
Sud-Est	Jacmel	781	2,023	444,323
TOTAL		10,695	27,700	6,763,746[3]

Demography

Population (1995): 6,589,000.
Density (1995): persons per sq mi 616.1, persons per sq km 237.9.
Urban-rural (1994): urban 30.7%; rural 69.3%.
Sex distribution (1995): male 49.03%; female 50.97%.
Age breakdown (1995): under 15, 40.2%; 15–29, 27.3%; 30–44, 17.0%; 45–59, 9.5%; 60–74, 4.8%; 75 and over, 1.2%.
Population projection: (2000) 7,102,000; (2010) 8,121,000.
Doubling time: 33 years.
Ethnic composition (1993): black 95.0%; mulatto/other 5.0%.
Religious affiliation (1982). Roman Catholic 80.3%[4]; Protestant 15.8%, of which Baptist 9.7%, Pentecostal 3.6%; nonreligious 1.2%; other 2.7%.
Major cities (1992): Port-au-Prince 752,600 (metropolitan area 1,255,078); Carrefour 241,223[5]; Delmas 200,251[5]; Cap-Haïtien 92,122; Gonaïves 63,291.

Vital statistics

Birth rate per 1,000 population (1994): 40.0 (world avg. 26.0).
Death rate per 1,000 population (1994): 19.0 (world avg. 9.2).
Natural increase rate per 1,000 population (1994): 21.0 (world avg. 16.8).
Total fertility rate (avg. births per childbearing woman; 1992): 4.7.
Marriage rate per 1,000 population: n.a.
Divorce rate per 1,000 population: n.a.
Life expectancy at birth (1994): male 43.0 years; female 47.0 years.
Major causes of death per 100,000 population (1982)[6]: infectious and parasitic diseases 46.0; diseases of the circulatory system 11.9; diseases associated with malnutrition 8.5; diseases of the respiratory system 8.3; endocrine and metabolic disorders 8.0; ill-defined conditions 115.2.

National economy

Budget (1993–94). Revenue: G 816,400,000 (excises 24.1%, of which petroleum taxes 13.6%; escrow accounts 18.3%; income taxes 17.4%; customs duties 11.7%). Expenditures: G 2,091,300,000 (current expenditures 96.0%; development expenditure 4.0%).
Tourism: receipts from visitors (1993) U.S.$46,000,000; expenditures by nationals abroad (1991–92) U.S.$21,000,000.
Production (metric tons except as noted). Agriculture, forestry, fishing (1994): sugarcane 2,250,000, plantains 272,000, mangoes 230,000, bananas 230,000, corn (maize) 210,000, sweet potatoes 190,000, rice 90,000, sorghum 80,000, dry beans 51,000, coffee 34,000, oranges 26,000, lemons and limes 22,000, sisal 8,000, cacao 3,000; livestock (number of live animals) 910,000 goats, 800,000 cattle, 200,000 pigs; roundwood (1993) 6,171,000 cu m; fish catch (1993) 5,600. Mining and quarrying (1992): limestone 220,000; marble 500 cu m. Manufacturing (1993–94): cement 84,000[7]; essential oils (mostly amyris, neroli, and vetiver) 227[7]; cigarettes 408,000,000 units; malt liquor 2,300,000 bottles; beer 1,000,000 bottles; articles assembled for reexport (export value in U.S.$'000,000) 105.7, of which garments 80.5, sports equipment and toys 9.2, electronic components 7.2, luggage and handbags 2.8. Construction: n.a. Energy production (consumption): electricity (kW-hr; 1992–93) 422,500,000 (229,200,000); coal, none (none); crude petroleum, none (none); petroleum products (metric tons; 1992) none (223,000); natural gas, none (none).
Population economically active (1990): total 2,679,140; activity rate of total population 41.1% (participation rates: ages 15–64, 64.8%; female 40.0%; unemployed [1994] unofficially more than 50.0%).

Price and earnings indexes (1990 = 100)

	1989	1990	1991	1992	1993	1994	1995[8]
Consumer price index	82.5	100.0	115.4	137.8	168.8	240.7	280.6
Annual earnings index[9]	100.0	100.0	100.0	100.0	100.0	...	...

Household income and expenditure. Average household size (1982) 4.4; average annual income of wage earners (1984): urban (G 1,545 [U.S.$309]), rural (G 629 [U.S.$126]); expenditure (1986–87)[10]: food, beverages, and tobacco 51.1%, household furnishings 9.2%, clothing and footwear 8.7%, transportation and communications 7.6%.
Gross national product (1992): U.S.$2,479,000,000 (U.S.$370 per capita).

Structure of gross domestic product and labour force

	1992–93		1990	
	in value G '000,000[11]	% of total value	labour force	% of labour force
Agriculture	1,593	38.6	1,535,444	57.3
Mining	3	0.1	24,012	0.9
Manufacturing	534	12.9	151,387	5.6
Construction	141	3.4	28,001	1.0
Public utilities	34	0.8	2,577	0.1
Transp. and commun.	87	2.1	20,691	0.8
Trade, restaurants	427	10.4	352,970	13.2
Finance, real estate }	508	12.3 }	5,057	0.2
Services }			155,347	5.8
Pub. admin., defense	695	16.9 }		
Other	104[12]	2.5[12]	403,654[13]	15.1[13]
TOTAL	4,126	100.0	2,679,140	100.0

Public debt (external, outstanding; 1993): U.S.$617,600,000.
Land use (1993): forested 5.1%; meadows and pastures 18.0%; agricultural and under permanent cultivation 33.0%; other 43.9%.

Foreign trade[14, 15]

Balance of trade (current prices)

	1988–89	1989–90	1990–91	1991–92	1992–93	1993–94
U.S.$'000,000	−162.9	−172.4	−156.1	−221.1	−233.5	−204.4
% of total	34.8%	33.8%	35.9%	43.9%	46.0%	55.8%

Imports (1993–94): U.S.$285,300,000 (food and live animals 20.7%, mineral fuels 17.1%, basic manufactures 16.3%, chemicals and chemical products 12.9%). *Major import sources* (1991–92): United States 45.7%; Japan 6.4%; France 6.2%, Canada 3.3%; Germany 3.6%.
Exports (1993–94): U.S.$80,900,000 (local manufactures—mostly processed foods, electrical equipment, textiles, and clothing—68.5%, coffee 9.0%, handicrafts [primarily wood carvings and masks and woven sisal products] 7.4%, essential oils 4.9%, sisal and twine 2.7%). *Major export destinations* (1991–92): United States 53.1%; Italy 11.6%; France 8.2%; Belgium 8.0%.

Transport and communications

Transport. Railroad (1994): none. Roads (1991): total length 2,485 mi, 4,000 km (paved 15%). Vehicles (1993): passenger cars 32,000; trucks and buses 21,000. Merchant marine (1992): vessels (100 gross tons and over) 4; total deadweight tonnage 429. Air transport (1993)[16]: passenger arrivals and departures 497,000; cargo unloaded and loaded 32,900 metric tons; airports (1995) with scheduled flights 2.
Communications. Daily newspapers (1993): total number 4; total circulation 17,500; circulation per 1,000 population 2.7. Radio (1994): total number of receivers 270,000 (1 per 24 persons). Television (1994): total number of receivers 25,000 (1 per 260 persons). Telephones (1993): 39,000[17] (1 per 164 persons).

Education and health

Education (1992–93)

	schools	teachers	students	student/ teacher ratio
Primary (age 6–12)	7,306[18]	27,607	787,553	28.5
Secondary (age 13–18) } Voc., teacher tr. }	...	10,174	193,624	19.0
Higher[19]	2	554	6,678	12.1

Educational attainment (1986–87). Percentage of population age 25 and over having: no formal schooling 59.5%; primary education 30.5%; secondary 8.6%; vocational and teacher training 0.7%; higher 0.7%. *Literacy* (1990): total population age 15 and over literate 2,096,900 (53.0%); males literate 1,128,000 (59.1%); females literate 968,000 (47.4%).
Health: physicians (1992) 623 (1 per 10,060 persons); hospital beds (1993) 5,312 (1 per 1,201 persons); infant mortality rate per 1,000 live births (1994) 109.0.
Food (1992): daily per capita caloric intake 1,706 (vegetable products 95%, animal products 5%); 75% of FAO recommended minimum requirement.

Military

Total active duty personnel:[20].

[1]Roman Catholicism has special recognition. [2]Estimated. [3]Official population projection based on 1982 census. [4]About 80% of all Roman Catholics also practice voodoo. [5]Within Port-au-Prince metropolitan area. [6]Public health facilities only. [7]1992–93. [8]February. [9]Standard minimum wage. [10]Based on nationwide sample survey of 3,120 households. [11]At prices of 1975–76. [12]Import duties. [13]Includes 63,975 not adequately defined and 339,679 officially unemployed. [14]The import and export value of preassembled and assembled U.S.-made components is excluded. Virtually all components used in the export assembly plants are imported. [15]Import figures c.i.f., export figures f.o.b. for fiscal year ending March 31. [16]Port-au-Prince Airport only. [17]Number of operating lines. [18]1990–91. [19]Port-au-Prince universities only. [20]Future status of Haitian army/police force was under review in July 1995. A 7,000-member UN force was to provide security between April 1995 and February 1996.

Honduras

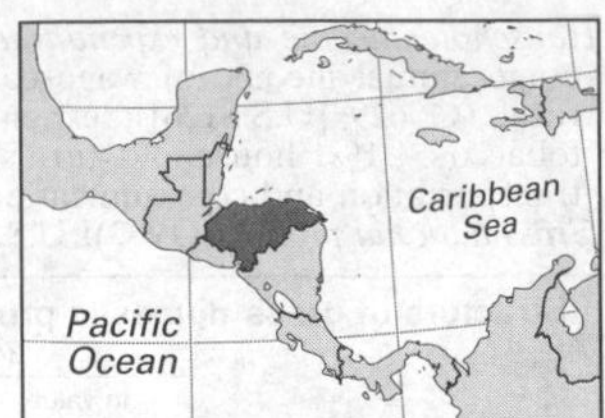

Official name: República de Honduras (Republic of Honduras).
Form of government: multiparty republic with one legislative house (Congress [128]).
Head of state and government: President.
Capital: Tegucigalpa[1].
Official language: Spanish.
Official religion: none.
Monetary unit: 1 Honduran lempira (L) = 100 centavos; valuation (Oct. 6, 1995) 1 U.S.$ = L 9.47; 1 £ = L 15.40.

Area and population

		area		population
Departments	Administrative centres	sq mi	sq km	1991 estimate
Atlántida	La Ceiba	1,641	4,251	255,000
Choluteca	Choluteca	1,626	4,211	309,000
Colón	Trujillo	3,427	8,875	164,000
Comayagua	Comayagua	2,006	5,196	257,000
Copán	Santa Rosa de Copán	1,237	3,203	226,000
Cortés	San Pedro Sula	1,527	3,954	706,000
El Paraíso	Yuscarán	2,787	7,218	277,000
Francisco Morazán	Tegucigalpa	3,068	7,946	878,000
Gracias a Dios	Puerto Lempira	6,421	16,630	37,000
Intibucá	La Esperanza	1,186	3,072	130,000
Islas de la Bahía	Roatán	100	261	24,000
La Paz	La Paz	900	2,331	112,000
Lempira	Gracias	1,656	4,290	180,000
Ocotepeque	Nueva Ocotepeque	649	1,680	77,000
Olancho	Juticalpa	9,402	24,351	309,000
Santa Bárbara	Santa Bárbara	1,975	5,115	291,000
Valle	Nacaome	604	1,565	121,000
Yoro	Yoro	3,065	7,939	355,000
TOTAL		43,277[2]	112,088[2]	4,708,000

Demography

Population (1995): 5,512,000.
Density (1995)[3]: persons per sq mi 126.9, persons per sq km 49.0.
Urban-rural (1993): urban 42.3%; rural 57.7%.
Sex distribution (1990): male 50.07%; female 49.93%.
Age breakdown (1990): under 15, 44.6%; 15–29, 28.3%; 30–44, 14.4%; 45–59, 7.8%; 60–74, 3.9%; 75 and over, 1.0%.
Population projection: (2000) 6,323,000; (2010) 7,998,000.
Doubling time: 24 years.
Ethnic composition (1987): mestizo 89.9%; Amerindian 6.7%; black (including Black Carib) 2.1%; white 1.3%.
Religious affiliation (1986): Roman Catholic 85.0%; Protestant (mostly fundamentalist, Moravian, and Methodist) 10.0%; other 5.0%.
Major cities (1993): Tegucigalpa 738,500[4]; San Pedro Sula 353,800; La Ceiba 82,900; El Progreso 77,300; Choluteca 69,400.

Vital statistics

Birth rate per 1,000 population (1993): 35.8 (world avg. 25.0); legitimate, n.a.; illegitimate, n.a.
Death rate per 1,000 population (1993): 6.4 (world avg. 9.3).
Natural increase rate per 1,000 population (1993): 29.4 (world avg. 15.7).
Total fertility rate (avg. births per childbearing woman; 1993): 4.9.
Marriage rate per 1,000 population (1983): 4.9.
Divorce rate per 1,000 population (1983): 0.4.
Life expectancy at birth (1993): male 64.8 years; female 69.2 years.
Major causes of death per 100,000 population (1983): diseases of the circulatory system 48.4; infectious and parasitic diseases 46.6; accidents and violence 42.2; diseases of the respiratory system 26.3.

National economy

Budget (1993). Revenue: L 6,488,700,000 (current revenue 96.6%, of which taxes on production and consumption 18.9%, import duties 15.2%, income taxes 14.8%; capital revenue 3.4%). Expenditures: L 8,756,400,000 (current expenditure 61.5%; capital expenditure 25.7%; public-debt service 12.8%).
Public debt (external, outstanding; 1993): U.S.$3,479,000,000.
Production (metric tons except as noted). Agriculture, forestry, fishing (1994): sugarcane 3,069,000, bananas 930,000, corn (maize) 518,000, plantains 142,000, coffee 128,000, sorghum 87,000, palm oil 75,600, dry beans 41,000, rice 33,000; livestock (number of live animals) 2,286,000 cattle, 603,000 pigs, 12,000,000 chickens; roundwood (1993) 6,454,000 cu m; fish catch (1993) 24,401. Mining and quarrying (1992): zinc concentrate 32,000; lead (metal content) 9,000; copper 1,600. Manufacturing (1993): cement 933,000; raw sugar 393,000; wheat flour 228,000; beer 6,684,000 hectolitres; milk 700,000 hectolitres; cigarettes 2,193,000,000 units. Construction (value of private construction in L '000,000; 1993)[5]: residential 231.7; nonresidential 250.3. Energy production (consumption): electricity (kW-hr; 1992) 2,313,000,000 (2,508,000,000); coal, none (none); crude petroleum (barrels; 1992) none (3,064,000); petroleum products (metric tons; 1992) 352,000 (825,000); natural gas, none (none).
Household income and expenditure. Average household size (1988) 5.4; income per household: n.a.; sources of income (1985): wages and salaries 58.8%, transfer payments 1.8%, other 39.4%; expenditure (1986): food 44.4%, utilities and housing 22.4%, clothing and footwear 9.0%, household furnishings 8.3%, health care 7.0%, transportation and communications 3.0%, other 5.9%.

Gross national product (at current market prices; 1993): U.S.$3,220,000,000 (U.S.$580 per capita).

Structure of gross domestic product and labour force

	1993			
	in value L '000,000[6]	% of total value	labour force	% of labour force
Agriculture	3,661	19.7	733,800	44.4
Mining	380	2.0	4,200	0.3
Manufacturing	3,300	17.8	194,900	11.8
Construction	1,257	6.8	102,500	6.2
Public utilities	695	3.8	12,200	0.7
Transportation and communications	1,134	6.1	46,300	2.8
Trade	2,083	11.2	174,200	10.6
Finance, real estate	2,698	14.6	32,000	1.9
Public admin., defense	1,375	7.4	352,700	21.3
Services	1,971	10.6		
TOTAL	18,554	100.0	1,652,800	100.0

Population economically active (1993): total 1,652,800; activity rate of total population 31.5% (participation rates: over age 15 [1992] 58.3%; female 31.7%; unemployed [1990] 40.0%).

Price and earnings indexes (1990 = 100)

	1988	1989	1990	1991	1992	1993	1994
Consumer price index	73.8	81.1	100.0	134.0	145.7	161.4	196.4
Weekly earnings index[7]	100.0	100.0	100.0	132.9	151.1	...	...

Land use (1993): forested 53.6%; meadows and pastures 13.7%; agricultural and under permanent cultivation 18.0%; other 14.7%.
Tourism (1993): receipts U.S.$32,000,000; expenditures U.S.$39,000,000.

Foreign trade[8]

Balance of trade (current prices)

	1989	1990	1991	1992	1993	1994
L '000,000	+5.4	−29.8	+11.9	−129.3	−208.6	−113.1
% of total	0.1%	0.8%	0.7%	7.5%	11.4%	6.3%

Imports (1993): U.S.$1,130,000,000 (industrial chemicals 16.5%, electrical machinery 15.9%, mineral fuels 15.7%, transport equipment 10.4%, metal products 7.6%, plastics and resins 7.4%). *Major import sources:* United States 49.8%; Mexico 8.4%; Guatemala 6.3%; El Salvador 3.8%; Japan 3.6%; Costa Rica 3.1%.
Exports (1993): U.S.$814,000,000 (bananas 28.3%, shrimp and lobsters 16.5%, coffee 15.3%, frozen meats 4.8%, lead and zinc 3.4%). *Major export destinations:* United States 53.2%; Germany 11.2%; Belgium 8.2%; United Kingdom 4.7%; Italy 3.8%; Japan 2.4%.

Transport and communications

Transport. Railroads (1989): length (1993) 614 mi, 988 km; passenger-km 7,700,000; metric ton-km cargo 30,200,000. Roads (1993): total length 8,825 mi, 14,203 km (paved 18%). Vehicles (1993): passenger cars 67,777; trucks and buses 128,264. Merchant marine (1992): vessels (100 gross tons and over) 966; total deadweight tonnage 1,437,321. Air transport (1990): passenger-mi 321,000,000, passenger-km 516,000,000; short ton-mi cargo 2,000,000, metric ton-km cargo 3,000,000; airports (1995) with scheduled flights 8.
Communications. Daily newspapers (1992): total number 4; total circulation 159,000; circulation per 1,000 population 29. Radio (1994): total number of receivers 1,910,000 (1 per 2.8 persons). Television (1994): total number of receivers 160,000 (1 per 33 persons). Telephones (main lines; 1993): 117,100 (1 per 48 persons).

Education and health

Education (1993)

	schools	teachers	students	student/ teacher ratio
Primary (age 7–13)	8,054	27,056	990,352	36.6
Secondary (age 14–19)	661	10,303	151,196	14.7
Voc., teacher tr.	5[9]	581[9]	65,539	13.7[9]
Higher	10	3,758	48,468	12.9

Educational attainment (1988). Percentage of population age 10 and over having: no formal schooling 33.4%; primary education 50.1%; secondary education 13.4%; higher 3.1%. *Literacy* (1990): total population age 15 and over literate 2,082,000 (73.1%); males literate 1,078,000 (75.5%); females literate 1,004,000 (70.6%).
Health (1993): physicians (1990) 2,900 (1 per 1,586 persons); hospital beds 5,739 (1 per 900 persons); infant mortality rate per 1,000 live births 47.2.
Food (1992): daily per capita caloric intake 2,305 (vegetable products 88%, animal products 12%); 102% of FAO recommended minimum.

Military

Total active duty personnel (1994): 16,800 (army 83.3%, navy 6.0%, air force 10.7%). *Military expenditure as percentage of GNP* (1993): 1.4% (world 3.3%); per capita expenditure U.S.$9.

[1]Tegucigalpa and adjacent city of Comayagüela jointly form the capital according to the constitution. [2]The 1993 area is 43,433 sq mi (112,492 sq km); breakdown by department is not available. [3]Based on the revised area. [4]Population cited is for Central District (Tegucigalpa and Comayagüela). [5]Tegucigalpa, San Pedro Sula, and 10 other urban centres. [6]At factor cost. [7]Official minimum wages in all sectors. Minimum wages were fixed from June 1981 to Jan. 1, 1990, when new minimum wages were introduced. [8]Import figures are f.o.b. in balance of trade and c.i.f. for commodities and trading partners. [9]1989.

Hong Kong

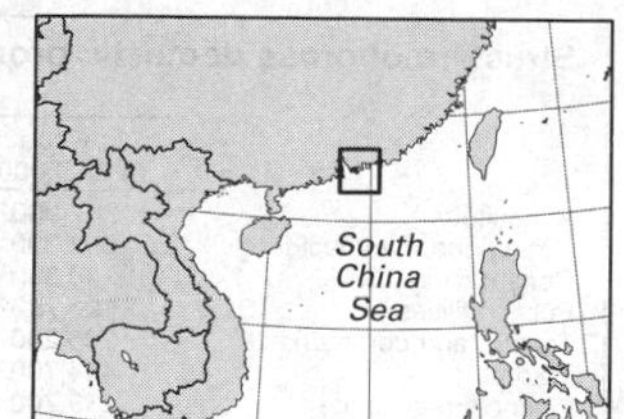

Official name: Hsiang Kang (Chinese); Hong Kong (English).
Political status: Crown Colony (United Kingdom)[1] with one legislative house (Legislative Council [60[2]]).
Chief of state: British Monarch.
Head of government: Governor.
Capital: none[3].
Official languages: Chinese; English.
Official religion: none.
Monetary unit: 1 Hong Kong dollar (HK$) = 100 cents; valuation (Oct. 6, 1995) 1 U.S.$ = HK$7.73; 1 £ = HK$12.22.

Area and population	area[4]		population
			1991
Area	sq mi	sq km	census
Hong Kong Island	30.8	79.9	1,214,253
Kowloon and New Kowloon	16.5	42.7	1,975,265
New Territories	368.0	953.1	2,321,661
Marine	—	—	11,102
TOTAL	415.3	1,075.7	5,609,951[5]

Demography

Population (1995): 6,205,000.
Density (1995): persons per sq mi 14,941.7, persons per sq km 5,768.6.
Urban-rural (1994): urban 100.0%.
Sex distribution (1994): male 50.95%; female 49.05%.
Age breakdown (1994)[6]: under 15, 19.4%; 15–29, 23.7%; 30–44, 29.4%; 45–59, 14.1%; 60–74, 10.1%; 75 and over, 3.3%.
Population projection: (2000) 6,796,000; (2010) 8,152,000.
Doubling time: 99 years.
Linguistic composition (1991)[7]: Chinese 96.8%, of which Cantonese 88.7%; English 2.2%; other 1.0%.
Religious affiliation (1994): predominantly Buddhist and Taoist; however, there are about 260,000 Protestants, 254,100 Roman Catholics, 50,000 Muslims, and 12,000 Hindus.
Major cities: no bounded localities exist within Hong Kong.

Vital statistics

Birth rate per 1,000 population (1994): 11.9 (world avg. 25.0); legitimate (1985) 94.5%; illegitimate 5.5%.
Death rate per 1,000 population (1994): 4.9 (world avg. 9.3).
Natural increase rate per 1,000 population (1994): 7.0 (world avg. 15.7).
Total fertility rate (avg. births per childbearing woman; 1990): 1.2.
Marriage rate per 1,000 population (1993): 6.3.
Divorce rate per 1,000 population (1993): 1.3.
Life expectancy at birth (1994): male 75.4 years; female 81.0 years.
Major causes of death per 100,000 population (1994): malignant neoplasms (cancers) 154.8; diseases of the circulatory system 139.7; diseases of the respiratory system 88.9; accidents and poisoning 28.0; diseases of the digestive system 22.1; infectious and parasitic diseases 18.4; diseases of the genitourinary system 17.7.

National economy

Budget (1994–95). Revenue: HK$173,561,000,000 (earnings and profit taxes 43.0%; indirect taxes 24.2%, of which entertainment and stamp duties 13.2%, duties 4.5%; capital revenue 15.4%). Expenditures: HK$170,852,000,000 (education 17.1%; transportation and public works 16.1%; housing 12.2%; health 11.1%; law and order 9.1%; social welfare 6.5%; culture and recreation 4.9%).
Public debt: n.a.
Gross domestic product (at current market prices; 1993): U.S.$104,731,000,000 (U.S.$17,860 per capita).

Structure of gross domestic product and labour force	1993			
	in value HK$'000,000	% of total value	labour force	% of labour force
Agriculture	1,612	0.2	17,600	0.6
Mining	198	—	300	—
Manufacturing	94,294	10.7	615,400	21.4
Construction	41,534	4.7	230,400	8.0
Public utilities	17,588	2.0	19,300	0.7
Transp. and commun.	81,805	9.3	321,400	11.2
Trade	219,115	24.9	816,200	28.4
Finance, insurance, and real estate	212,681	24.2	272,400	9.5
Pub. admin., defense, and services	126,649	14.4	572,000	19.9
Other	84,188[8]	9.6[8]	8,000	0.3
TOTAL	879,664	100.0	2,873,000	100.0

Production (metric tons except as noted). Agriculture, forestry, fishing (1994): vegetables 89,000, fruits and nuts 5,340, field crops 710, milk 370, eggs 35,400,000 units; livestock (number of live animals) 186,000 pigs[9], 180 cattle, 4,000,000 chickens; roundwood (1993) 193,000 cu m; fish catch 189,970. Mining and quarrying (1990): clay and kaolin 16,587; feldspar 3,820. Manufacturing (value added in HK$; 1992): wearing apparel 19,540,000,000; textiles 14,800,000,000; electrical and electronic products 12,396,000,000; publishing and printed material 7,815,000,000; basic metals and fabricated metal products 6,137,000,000; plastic products 4,824,000,000. Construction (1992): residential 714,000 sq m; nonresidential 1,578,000 sq m. Energy production (consumption): electricity (kW-hr; 1992) 34,914,000,000 (29,951,000,000); coal (metric tons; 1992) none (10,214,000); petroleum products (metric tons; 1992) none (4,157,000); natural gas (cu m; 1990) none (385,800,000).
Population economically active (1993): total 2,873,000; activity rate of total population 48.5% (participation rates: over age 15, 62.5%; female 46.5%; unemployed 2.0%).

Price and earnings indexes (1990 = 100)	1988	1989	1990	1991	1992	1993	1994
Consumer price index	82.8	91.2	100.0	111.6	122.0	132.5	143.2
Daily earnings index[10]	79.7	89.0	100.0	110.4	121.4	133.2	143.6

Household income and expenditure. Average household size (1994) 3.5; monthly income per household (1991) HK$9,964 (U.S.$1,282); sources of income: n.a.; expenditure (1989–90): food 34.2%, housing 25.6%, transportation and vehicles 7.6%, clothing and footwear 7.5%, durable goods 3.8%.
Tourism (1994): receipts from visitors U.S.$8,318,000,000; expenditures by nationals abroad, n.a.
Land use (1994): forested 20.3%; agricultural and under permanent cultivation 5.9%; fishponds 1.5%; built-on, scrublands, and other 72.3%.

Foreign trade

Balance of trade (current prices)	1989	1990	1991	1992	1993	1994
HK$'000,000	+7,728	−2,656	−13,096	−30,342	−26,347	−80,695
% of total	0.7%	0.2%	0.1%	1.6%	1.2%	3.3%

Imports (1994): HK$1,250,709,000,000 (machinery and transport equipment 34.6%, of which electrical machinery 10.8%, telecommunications equipment 9.4%; textile yarn and fabrics 9.2%; apparel and accessories 7.5%; chemicals and related products 6.6%; photographic apparatus, watches, and clocks 4.2%; food and live animals 4.0%). *Major import sources:* China 37.6%; Japan 15.6%; Taiwan 8.6%; United States 7.1%; Singapore 5.0%; South Korea 4.6%; Germany 2.3%; United Kingdom 2.0%.
Exports (1994): HK$222,092,000,000[11] (clothing accessories and apparel 32.9%; electrical machinery 11.2%; office and automatic data-processing machines 7.9%; watches and clocks 7.3%; textile fabrics 6.8%; telecommunications equipment 5.2%; metal products 3.2%; articles of artificial resins and plastics 2.2%; paper and paper products 1.3%). *Major export destinations:* United States 27.7%; China 27.5%; Germany 5.8%; Singapore 5.5%; Japan 4.7%; United Kingdom 4.6%; Taiwan 2.7%.

Transport and communications

Transport. Railroads (1993): route length 21 mi, 34 km; passenger-mi 1,971,000,000, passenger-km 3,172,000,000; short ton-mi cargo 75,000,000, metric ton-km cargo 109,000,000. Roads (1993): total length 1,010 mi, 1,625 km (paved 100%). Vehicles (1994): passenger cars 311,929; trucks and buses 158,107. Merchant marine (1992): vessels (100 gross tons and over) 387; total deadweight tonnage 11,688,605. Air transport (1994): passenger arrivals 9,889,567, passenger departures 10,027,849; airports (1995) with scheduled flights 1.
Communications. Daily newspapers (1993): total number 77; total circulation 2,951,000[12]; circulation per 1,000 population 498[12]. Radio (1994): total number of receivers 3,700,000 (1 per 1.6 persons). Television (1994): total number of receivers 1,749,000 (1 per 3.5 persons). Telephones (main lines; 1994): 3,111,000 (1 per 1.9 persons).

Education and health

Education (1994–95)	schools	teachers[13]	students	student/ teacher ratio[13]
Primary (age 6–11)	884	19,122	476,847	25.4
Secondary (age 12–18)	488	21,391	471,121	22.1
Vocational	9	2,488[14]	47,900	18.5[14]
Higher	10	1,422[14]	73,167	32.4[14]

Educational attainment (1991). Percentage of population age 15 and over having: no formal schooling 12.8%; primary education 25.2%; secondary 45.8%; matriculation 4.9%; nondegree higher 5.4%; higher degree 5.9%.
Literacy (1985): total population age 15 and over literate 3,668,000 (88.1%); males literate 2,040,000 (94.7%); females literate 1,628,000 (80.9%).
Health (1994): physicians 7,670[15] (1 per 790 persons); hospital beds 27,506 (1 per 220 persons); infant mortality rate per 1,000 live births 4.8.
Food (1992): daily per capita caloric intake 3,129 (vegetable products 70%, animal products 30%); 137% of FAO recommended minimum requirement.

Military

Total active duty personnel (1994): 1,900[16] (army 73.7%, navy 13.2%, air force 13.1%). *Military expenditure as percentage of GNP* (1984): 0.6% (world 5.9%); per capita expenditure U.S.$39.

[1]On July 1, 1997, Hong Kong will revert to China as a Special Administrative Region in which the existing socioeconomic system would remain unchanged for a period of 50 years. [2]Includes 21 nonelective seats. [3]Victoria, for some time, had been regarded as the capital because it is the seat of the British administration of the Crown Colony. [4]Excludes the surface areas of reservoirs. [5]Includes 35,823 transients and 51,847 Vietnamese migrants not enumerated by area. [6]Excludes transients and Vietnamese refugees. [7]Excludes about 59,900 Vietnamese refugees, about 1% of the population. [8]Indirect taxes less subsidies. [9]Excludes local pigs not slaughtered in abattoirs. [10]September. [11]Excludes reexports valued at HK$947,921,000,000. [12]Thirty-two newspapers only. [13]1993–94. [14]1987–88. [15]Registered personnel; all may not be present and working in the country. [16]British forces with a few locally enlisted personnel.

Hungary

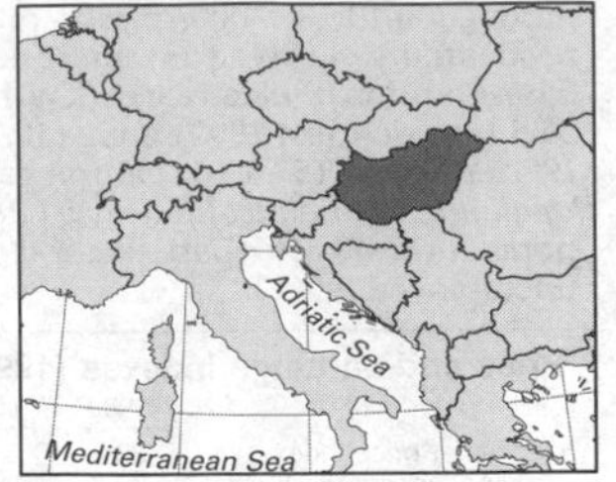

Official name: Magyar Köztársaság (Republic of Hungary).
Form of government: unitary multiparty republic with one legislative house (National Assembly [394[1]]).
Chief of state: President.
Head of government: Prime Minister.
Capital: Budapest.
Official language: Hungarian.
Official religion: none.
Monetary unit: 1 forint (Ft) = 100 filler; valuation (Oct. 6, 1995) 1 U.S.$ = Ft 131.49; 1 £ = Ft 207.86.

Area and population

		area		population
Counties	Capitals	sq mi	sq km	1994[2] estimate
Bács-Kiskun	Kecskemét	3,229	8,362	539,000
Baranya	Pécs	1,732	4,487	416,000
Békés	Bekéscsaba	2,175	5,632	401,000
Borsod-Abaúj-Zemplén	Miskolc	2,798	7,247	744,000
Csongrád	Szeged	1,646	4,263	437,000
Fejér	Székesfehérvár	1,688	4,373	422,000
Győr-Moson-Sopron	Győr	1,568	4,062	427,000
Hajdú-Bihar	Debrecen	2,398	6,211	549,000
Heves	Eger	1,404	3,637	329,000
Jász-Nagykun-Szolnok	Szolnok	2,165	5,607	419,000
Komárom-Esztergom	Tatabánya	869	2,251	312,000
Nógrád	Salgótarján	982	2,544	221,000
Pest	Budapest[3]	2,469	6,394	965,000
Somogy	Kaposvár	2,331	6,036	338,000
Szabolcs-Szatmár-Bereg	Nyíregyháza	2,292	5,937	561,000
Tolna	Szekszárd	1,430	3,704	250,000
Vas	Szombathely	1,288	3,336	273,000
Veszprém	Veszprém	1,791	4,639	378,000
Zala	Zalaegerszeg	1,461	3,784	301,000
Capital City				
Budapest[3]		203	525	1,996,000
TOTAL		35,919	93,030[4]	10,277,000[4]

Demography

Population (1995): 10,231,000.
Density (1995): persons per sq mi 284.8, persons per sq km 110.0.
Urban-rural (1994): urban 63.2%; rural 36.8%.
Sex distribution (1994): male 47.90%; female 52.10%.
Age breakdown (1994): under 15, 18.6%; 15–29, 22.0%; 30–44, 21.9%; 45–59, 18.2%; 60–74, 14.6%; 75 and over, 4.7%.
Population projection: (2000) 10,170,000; (2010) 9,951,000. The population has declined at an average annual rate of 0.3% since 1980.
Ethnic composition (1993): Magyar 92%; Gypsy 3%; German 1%; Slovak 1%; Jewish 1%; Southern Slav 1%; other 1%.
Religious affiliation (1992): Christian 92.9%, of which Roman Catholic 67.8%, Protestant 25.1%; atheist and nonreligious 4.8%; other 2.3%.
Major cities (1994[2]): Budapest 1,995,696; Debrecen 217,706; Miskolc 189,655; Szeged 178,878; Pécs 172,177.

Vital statistics

Birth rate per 1,000 population (1994): 11.3 (world avg. 25.0); (1993) legitimate 82.4%; illegitimate 17.6%.
Death rate per 1,000 population (1994): 14.3 (world avg. 9.3).
Natural increase rate per 1,000 population (1994): −3.0 (world avg. 15.7).
Total fertility rate (avg. births per childbearing woman; 1993): 1.7.
Marriage rate per 1,000 population (1994): 5.3.
Divorce rate per 1,000 population (1993): 2.2.
Life expectancy at birth (1993): male 64.5 years; female 73.8 years.
Major causes of death per 100,000 population (1993): diseases of the circulatory system 751.7; malignant neoplasms (cancers) 312.8; accidents and self-inflicted injuries 119.5.

National economy

Budget (1994). Revenue: Ft 1,191,356,000,000 (value-added tax 28.2%, payments by enterprises 21.7%, income tax 20.4%, excise duties 13.8%). Expenditures: Ft 1,430,257,000,000 (debt service 20.4%, health 15.9%[5], education 15.7%[5], social security 14.7%, defense 11.3%).
Production (metric tons except as noted). Agriculture, forestry, fishing (1994): corn (maize) 4,920,000, wheat 4,900,000, sugar beets 3,600,000, barley 1,580,000, potatoes 823,000, apples 700,000, sunflower seeds 650,000, grapes 600,000, rye 193,000; livestock (number of live animals) 5,002,000 pigs, 1,280,000 sheep, 1,002,000 cattle; roundwood (1994) 3,564,000 cu m; fish catch (1993) 23,404. Mining and quarrying (1994): limestone 3,922,000[5]; bauxite 900,000; manganese ore 40,000. Manufacturing (1994): cement 2,813,000; rolled steel 2,076,000; crude steel 1,937,000; pig iron 1,595,000; fertilizers 267,767; aluminum 29,617; cotton fabrics 71,698,000 sq m; leather footwear 11,474,000 pairs; refrigerators 540,911 units; buses 1,576 units. Construction (in Ft '000,000; 1993): residential 2,429[6]; nonresidential 20,393. Energy production (consumption): electricity (kW-hr; 1993) 32,784,000,000 (35,258,000,000); coal (metric tons; 1993) 14,616,000 (16,765,000); crude petroleum (barrels; 1993) 11,065,000 (51,660,000); petroleum products (metric tons; 1993) 6,787,000 (6,862,000); natural gas (cu m; 1993) 4,491,000,000 (9,650,000,000).
Tourism (1993): receipts U.S.$1,181,000,000; expenditures U.S.$741,000,000.
Public debt (external, outstanding; 1993): U.S.$21,535,000,000.
Gross national product (1993): U.S.$34,254,000,000 (U.S.$3,330 per capita).

Structure of gross domestic product and labour force

	1992			
	in value Ft '000,000	% of total value	labour force[2]	% of labour force[2]
Agriculture	207,900	7.4	588,900	12.7
Mining and manufacturing	653,300	23.3	1,286,200[7]	27.7[7]
Construction	149,300	5.3	272,800	5.9
Public utilities	121,700	4.3	[7]	[7]
Transp. and commun.	205,200	7.3	372,900	8.0
Trade	444,700	15.9	564,200	12.1
Finance, real estate	239,700	8.6		
Services	429,300	15.3	1,156,800	24.9
Other	354,000[8]	12.6[8]	406,100[9]	8.7[9]
TOTAL	2,805,100	100.0	4,647,900	100.0

Population economically active (1995[2]): total 4,433,500; activity rate of total population 43.3% (participation rates: working age 90.3%; female [1994] 47.4%; unemployed 9.7%).

Price and earnings indexes (1990 = 100)

	1988	1989	1990	1991	1992	1993	1994
Consumer price index	66.3	77.6	100	135.1	166.1	203.4	241.6
Monthly earnings index	66.7	78.6	100	133.4	165.8	201.6	170.5

Household income and expenditure. Average household size (1991) 2.8; income per household (1990) Ft 376,195 (U.S.$5,900); sources of income (1992): wages 46.1%, social income 22.4%, self-employment 11.9%; expenditure (1992): food and beverages 38.5%, transportation and communications 15.1%, housing 10.5%, culture and recreation 9.4%, household durable goods 8.3%, clothing 7.1%.
Land use (1993): forested 19.1%; meadows and pastures 12.5%; agricultural and under permanent cultivation 53.9%; other 14.5%.

Foreign trade[10]

Balance of trade (current prices)

	1989	1990	1991	1992	1993	1994
Ft '000,000,000	+47.8	+58.7	−91.4	−34.9	−342.6	−317.7
% of total	4.4%	5.1%	5.6%	2.0%	17.3%	16.2%

Imports (1994): Ft 1,537,000,000,000 (1993; intermediate industrial goods 33.4%, machinery and transport equipment 26.9%, industrial consumer goods 21.2%, fuels and electrical energy 12.6%, food and live animals 5.9%).
Major import sources: former U.S.S.R. 22.2%; Germany 21.6%; Austria 11.6%; Italy 6.0%; Czech and Slovak republics 4.0%.
Exports (1994): Ft 1,128,700,000,000 (1993; intermediate industrial goods 36.4%, industrial consumer goods 25.2%, food and live animals 21.4%, machinery and transport equipment 13.9%, fuels and electrical energy 3.4%).
Major export destinations: Germany 26.6%; former U.S.S.R. 15.3%; Austria 10.1%; Italy 8.0%; U.S. 4.2%.

Transport and communications

Transport. Railroads (1993): length 8,300 mi, 13,300 km; passenger-mi 6,355,000,000, passenger-km 10,227,000,000; short ton-mi cargo 5,279,000,000, metric ton-km cargo 7,708,200,000. Roads (1993): total length 18,618 mi, 29,963 km (paved 99%). Vehicles (1994[2]): passenger cars 2,091,623; trucks and buses 259,367. Merchant marine (1992): vessels (100 gross tons and over) 15; total deadweight tonnage 93,204. Air transport (1993): passenger-mi 1,013,000,000, passenger-km 1,631,000,000; short ton-mi cargo 7,600,000, metric ton-km cargo 11,100,000; airports (1995) with scheduled flights 1.
Communications. Daily newspapers (1992): total number 28; total circulation 2,896,000; circulation per 1,000 population 275. Radio (1993): 6,250,000 (1 per 1.6 persons). Television (1993): 4,261,600 (1 per 2.4 persons). Telephones (main lines; 1993): 1,497,600 (1 per 6.9 persons).

Education and health

Education (1992–93)

	schools	teachers	students	student/ teacher ratio
Primary (age 6–13)	3,959	96,223	1,092,563	11.4
Secondary (age 14–17)	876	26,335	335,153	12.7
Vocational	343	6,624	212,932	32.2
Higher	91	17,743	119,828	6.8

Educational attainment (1990). Population age 10 and over having: no formal schooling 1.2%; primary education 78.1%; secondary 29.2%; higher 10.1%.
Literacy (1984): population age 15 and over literate 8,269,850 (98.9%); males literate 3,934,250 (99.2%); females literate 4,335,600 (98.6%).
Health (1993): physicians 41,397 (1 per 249 persons); hospital beds 100,438 (1 per 102 persons); infant mortality rate per 1,000 live births (1994) 11.5.
Food (1992): daily per capita caloric intake 3,503 (vegetable products 64%; animal products 36%); 133% of FAO recommended minimum.

Military

Total active duty personnel (1995): 70,500 (army 76.2%, air force 23.8%).
Military expenditure as percentage of GNP (1993): 2.0% (world 3.3%); per capita expenditure U.S.$122.

[1]Includes 8 nonelective seats. [2]January 1. [3]Budapest has separate county status. The area and population of the city are excluded from the larger county (Pest), which it administers. [4]Detail does not add to total given because of rounding. [5]1993. [6]Includes hotel construction. [7]Mining and manufacturing includes Public utilities. [8]Taxes on products. [9]Unemployed. [10]Import figures are f.o.b. in balance of trade and c.i.f. for commodities and trading partners.

Iceland

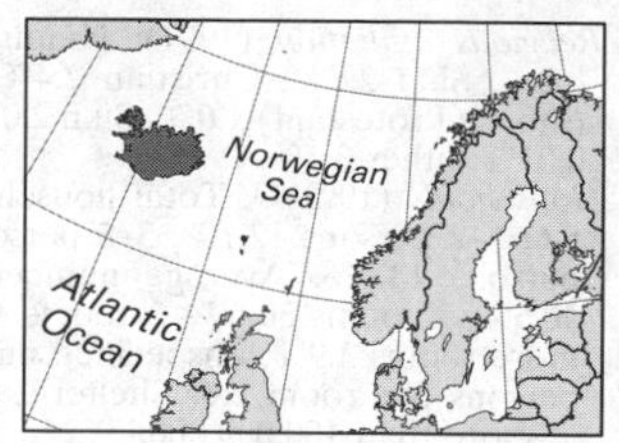

Official name: Lýdhveldidh Ísland (Republic of Iceland).
Form of government: unitary multiparty republic with one legislative house (Althing [63]).
Chief of state: President.
Head of government: Prime Minister.
Capital: Reykjavík.
Official language: Icelandic.
Official religion: Evangelical Lutheran.
Monetary unit: 1 króna (ISK) = 100 aurar; valuation (Oct. 6, 1995) 1 U.S.$ = ISK 64.78; 1 £ = ISK 102.38.

Area and population

Administrative units	Administrative centres	area sq mi	area sq km	population 1994[1] estimate
Austurland	Egilsstadhir	8,491	21,991	12,909
Nordhurland eystra	Akureyri	8,636	22,368	26,783
Nordhurland vestra	Saudhárkrókur	5,055	13,093	10,294
Reykjanes	...	765[2]	1,982[2]	69,162
Reykjavík	Reykjavík	[2]	[2]	103,036
Sudhurland	Selfoss	9,735	25,214	20,876
Vestfirdhir	Ísafjördhur	3,657	9,470	9,448
Vesturland	Borgarnes	3,360	8,701	14,278
TOTAL		39,699	102,819	266,786

Demography

Population (1995): 269,000.
Density (1994)[3]: persons per sq mi 29.3, persons per sq km 11.3.
Urban-rural (1993): urban 91.4%; rural 8.6%.
Sex distribution (1994): male 50.16%; female 49.84%.
Age breakdown (1994): under 15, 24.8%; 15–29, 23.7%; 30–44, 22.7%; 45–59, 13.9%; 60–74, 10.2%; 75 and over, 4.7%.
Population projection: (2000) 282,000; (2010) 307,000.
Doubling time: 68 years.
Ethnic composition (1993)[4]: Icelandic 96.1%; Danish 0.8%; Swedish 0.5%; persons born in the United States 0.5%; German 0.3%; other 1.8%.
Religious affiliation (1994): Protestant 95.7%, of which Evangelical Lutheran 91.8%, other Lutheran 3.2%; Roman Catholic 1.0%; nonreligious 1.4%, other 1.9%.
Major cities (1994): Reykjavík 103,036 (urban area [1993] 154,268); Kópavogur 17,431[5]; Hafnarfjördhur 17,238[5]; Akureyri 14,914; Sudhurnesjabær 10,347.

Vital statistics

Birth rate per 1,000 population (1994): 16.7 (world avg. 25.0); (1993) legitimate 41.7%; illegitimate 58.3%.
Death rate per 1,000 population (1994): 6.5 (world avg. 9.3).
Natural increase rate per 1,000 population (1994): 10.2 (world avg. 15.7).
Total fertility rate (avg. births per childbearing woman; 1993): 2.2.
Marriage rate per 1,000 population (1993): 4.6.
Divorce rate per 1,000 population (1993): 2.0.
Life expectancy at birth (1992–93): male 76.8 years; female 80.7 years.
Major causes of death per 100,000 population (1993): diseases of the circulatory system 294.3, of which ischemic heart diseases 177.7, cerebrovascular disease 67.0; malignant neoplasms (cancers) 170.8; diseases of the respiratory system 88.6.

National economy

Budget (1994). Revenue: ISK 109,602,000,000 (value-added tax 37.3%, income tax 20.7%, import duties 7.2%, taxes on alcohol and tobacco 6.0%). Expenditures: ISK 116,986,000,000 (health and welfare 47.6%, education 15.2%, general services 10.7%, communications 7.9%, agriculture 6.0%).
Production (metric tons except as noted). Agriculture, forestry, fishing (1993): potatoes 3,900, dried hay 1,788,000 cu m, silage 1,069,000 cu m; livestock (number of live animals) 488,800 sheep, 76,700 horses, 73,900 cattle; fish catch (value in ISK '000,000) cod 16,489, redfish 6,877, shrimp 5,617, Greenland halibut 4,730. Mining and quarrying (1993): diatomite 19,000. Manufacturing (value added in ISK '000,000; 1991): preserved and processed fish 17,341; printing and publishing 5,652; wood furniture 2,679; nonmetallic mineral products 2,261; bakery products 1,863. Construction (completed; 1992): residential 742,000 cu m; nonresidential 992,000 cu m. Energy production (consumption): electricity (kW-hr; 1993) 4,728,000,000 (4,721,000,000); coal (metric tons; 1992) none (50,000); crude petroleum, none (none); petroleum products (metric tons; 1992) none (510,000); natural gas, none (none).
Land use (1993): forested 1.2%; meadows and pastures 22.7%; agricultural and under permanent cultivation 0.1%; other 76.0%.
Population economically active (November 1994): total 145,600; activity rate of total population 54.6% (participation rates: ages 16–69, 84.3%; female 47.3%; unemployed [April 1994–March 1995] 4.7%).

Price and earnings indexes (1990 = 100)

	1989	1990	1991	1992	1993	1994	1995[6]
Consumer price index	87.2	100.0	107.0	111.4	116.9	118.9	119.8
Hourly wages index[7]	92.8	100.0	108.7	112.9	115.2	115.1	114.2

Tourism (1994): receipts from visitors U.S.$137,800,000; expenditures by nationals abroad U.S.$250,400,000.
Gross national product (at current market prices; 1993): U.S.$6,236,000,000 (U.S.$23,620 per capita).

Structure of gross national product and labour force

	1993 in value ISK '000,000[8]	1993 % of total value[8]	1994 labour force[9]	1994 % of labour force[9]
Agriculture	10,000	2.5	5,800	4.0
Fishing	43,200	10.8	6,400	4.4
Fish processing	23,600	5.9	9,700	6.7
Manufacturing	43,500	10.9	14,600	10.0
Construction	30,000	7.5	11,100	7.6
Public utilities	16,800	4.2	1,500	1.0
Transportation and communications	29,600	7.4	8,600	5.9
Trade	48,700	12.2	22,800	15.7
Finance, real estate	75,900	19.0	12,400	8.5
Public administration	70,700	17.7	6,000	4.1
Health, education, other services	22,000	5.5	39,800	27.3
Other	−14,400[10]	−3.6[10]	6,900[11]	4.8[11]
TOTAL	399,600[12]	100.0	145,600	100.0

Public debt (external, outstanding; September 1994): U.S.$2,406,000,000.
Household income and expenditure. Average household size (1990)[13] 3.6; annual income per household (1990)[13] ISK 2,605,563 (U.S.$44,712); sources of income (1993): wages and salaries 72.9%, pension 9.9%, self-employment 2.4%, other 14.8%; expenditure (1992): food and beverages 24.2%, transportation and communications 15.3%, housing 13.4%, recreation 10.3%, household furnishings 8.2%, clothing and footwear 8.0%, expenditures in restaurants and hotels 7.3%.

Foreign trade

Balance of trade (current prices)

	1989	1990	1991	1992	1993	1994
ISK '000,000	+6,943	+4,540	−3,253	−392	+12,082	+20,311
% of total	4.5%	2.5%	1.7%	0.2%	6.8%	9.8%

Imports (1994): ISK 93,243,000,000 (nonelectrical machinery and apparatus 12.1%; transport equipment 10.3%; food products 9.4%; electrical machinery and apparatus 9.2%; crude petroleum and petroleum products 7.6%). *Major import sources*[14]: Norway 14.3%; Germany 11.2%; United Kingdom 9.9%; Denmark 9.0%; United States 8.9%; Sweden 7.0%; The Netherlands 6.3%.
Exports (1994): ISK 113,554,000,000 (marine products 75.5%, of which frozen fish 35.2%, frozen shrimp, lobster, and scallops 12.5%, salted fish 9.3%, fresh fish on ice 6.5%; aluminum 9.5%; ferrosilicon 2.4%). *Major export destinations:* United Kingdom 20.3%; United States 14.5%; Japan 14.1%; Germany 12.8%; France 7.2%; Denmark 6.4%.

Transport and communications

Transport. Railroads: none. Roads (1994): total length 7,008 mi, 11,279 km (paved 24%). Vehicles (1993): passenger cars 116,195; trucks and buses 15,644. Merchant marine (1992): vessels (100 gross tons and over) 394; total deadweight tonnage 114,851. Air transport (1994)[15]: passenger-mi 1,474,000,000, passenger-km 2,372,000,000; short ton-mi cargo 28,786,000, metric ton-km cargo 42,026,000; airports (1995) with scheduled flights 24.
Communications. Daily newspapers (1992): total number 5; total circulation 135,000; circulation per 1,000 population 517. Radio (1994): total number of receivers 197,000 (1 per 1.4 persons). Television (1994): total number of receivers 76,250 (1 per 3.5 persons). Telephones (main lines; 1993): 143,597 (1 per 1.8 persons).

Education and health

Education (1992–93)

	schools	teachers	students	student/ teacher ratio
Primary/lower secondary (age 7–14)	...	...	27,500	...
Upper secondary/vocational (ages 15 and over)	...	...	17,888	...
Higher	...	...	5,672[16]	...

Educational attainment: n.a. *Literacy:* virtually 100%.
Health: physicians (1990) 726 (1 per 353 persons); hospital beds (1991) 2,878[17] (1 per 90 persons); infant mortality rate per 1,000 live births (1994) 3.2.
Food (1992): daily per capita caloric intake 3,058 (vegetable products 60%, animal products 40%); 115% of FAO recommended minimum requirement.

Military

Total active duty personnel (1994): 130 coast guard personnel; NATO-sponsored U.S.-manned Iceland Defense Force (1994): 2,200 (navy 81.8%, air force 18.2%). *Military expenditure as percentage of GNP* (1993): none (world average 3.3%).

[1]December 1. [2]Reykjanes includes Reykjavík. [3]Population density calculated with reference to 9,191 sq mi (23,805 sq km) area free of glaciers, lava fields, and lakes. [4]By country of birth. [5]Within Reykjavík urban area. [6]February. [7]Based on weighted average of skilled and unskilled nonclerical workers. [8]Data estimated from percentage distribution of sectors. [9]November. [10]Net of imputed bank service charges and income not classified elsewhere. [11]Unemployed. [12]GDP (1993) equals ISK 411,700,000,000. [13]Based on sample survey. [14]Import sources based on a c.i.f. total of ISK 102,541,000,000. [15]Icelandair only. [16]Excludes 1,970 studying abroad. [17]Excludes nursing wards in old-age homes.

India

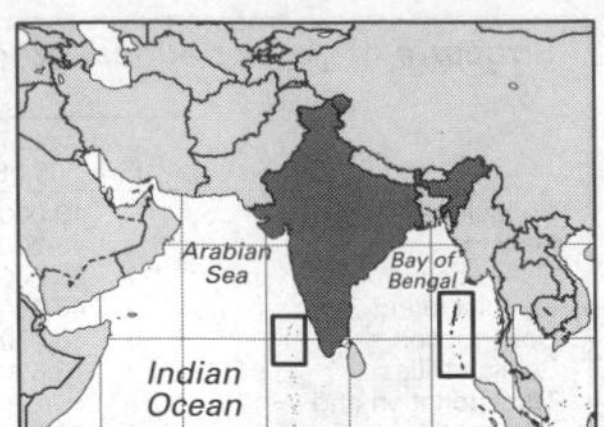

Official name: Bhārat (Hindī); Republic of India (English).
Form of government: multiparty federal republic with two legislative houses (Council of States [245][1], House of the People [545][2]).
Chief of state: President.
Head of government: Prime Minister.
Capital: New Delhi.
Official languages: Hindī; English.
Official religion: none.
Monetary unit: 1 Indian rupee (Re, plural Rs) = 100 paise; valuation (Oct. 6, 1995) 1 U.S.$ = Rs 33.90; 1 £ = Rs 53.59.

Area and population

		area		population
States	**Capitals**	sq mi	sq km	1991 census
Andhra Pradesh	Hyderābād	106,204	275,068	66,508,008
Arunāchal Pradesh	Itānagar	32,333	83,743	864,558
Assam	Dispur	30,285	78,438	22,414,322
Bihār	Patna	67,134	173,877	86,374,465
Goa	Panaji	1,429	3,702	1,169,793
Gujarāt	Gāndhīnagar	75,685	196,024	41,309,582
Haryāna	Chandīgarh	17,070	44,212	16,463,648
Himāchal Pradesh	Shimla	21,495	55,673	5,170,877
Jammu and Kashmir	Srīnagar	38,830	100,569	7,718,700[3]
Karnātaka	Bangalore	74,051	191,791	44,977,201
Kerala	Trivandrum	15,005	38,863	29,098,518
Madhya Pradesh	Bhopāl	171,215	443,446	66,181,170
Mahārāshtra	Bombay (Mumbai)	118,800	307,690	78,937,187
Manipur	Imphāl	8,621	22,327	1,837,149
Meghālaya	Shillong	8,660	22,429	1,774,778
Mizoram	Āīzawl	8,140	21,081	689,756
Nāgāland	Kohīma	6,401	16,579	1,209,546
Orissa	Bhubaneshwar	60,119	155,707	31,659,736
Punjab	Chandīgarh	19,445	50,362	20,281,969
Rājasthān	Jaipur	132,140	342,239	44,005,990
Sikkim	Gangtok	2,740	7,096	406,457
Tamil Nādu	Madras	50,216	130,058	55,858,946
Tripura	Agartala	4,049	10,486	2,757,205
Uttar Pradesh	Lucknow	113,673	294,411	139,112,287
West Bengal	Calcutta	34,267	88,752	68,077,965
Union Territories				
Andaman and Nicobar Islands	Port Blair	3,185	8,249	280,661
Chandīgarh	Chandīgarh	44	114	642,015
Dādra and Nagar Haveli	Silvassa	190	491	138,477
Damān and Diu	Damān	43	112	101,586
Delhi	Delhi	572	1,483	9,420,644
Lakshadweep	Kavaratti	12	32	51,707
Pondicherry	Pondicherry	190	492	807,785
TOTAL		1,222,243[4]	3,165,596[4]	846,302,688[5]

Demography

Population (1995): 935,744,000.
Density (1995)[4]: persons per sq mi 765.6, persons per sq km 295.6.
Urban-rural (1995): urban 26.8%; rural 73.2%.
Sex distribution (1991): male 51.90%; female 48.10%.
Age breakdown (1995): under 15, 35.2%; 15–29, 27.2%; 30–44, 19.1%; 45–59, 11.2%; 60–74, 5.9%; 75 and over, 1.4%.
Population projection: (2000) 1,022,021,000; (2010) 1,189,082,000.
Doubling time: 37 years.
Linguistic composition (1981)[6]: Hindī (lingua franca) 45.00%; Hindī (including associated languages and dialects) 38.77%; Telugu 7.96%; Bengalī 7.56%; Marāṭhī 7.28%; Tamil 6.56%; Urdū 5.18%; Gujarātī 4.87%; Kannaḍa 3.95%; Malayālam 3.81%; Oṛiyā 3.36%; Punjābī 2.73%; English (lingua franca) 2.50%; Assamese 1.64%[7]; Bhīlī/Bhilodī 0.65%; Santhālī 0.62%; Kashmirī 0.47%; Goṇḍī 0.29%; Sindhī 0.29%; Konkaṇī 0.23%; Dogrī 0.22%; Tulu 0.20%; Kurukh 0.19%; Nepālī 0.18%; Khandeshī 0.17%; Manipurī 0.13%; other 2.69%.
Place of birth (foreign born; 1981): other Asia 7,875,399, of which Bangladesh 4,170,524, Pakistan 2,736,038, Nepal 501,292, Sri Lanka 211,514, Myanmar 134,783; Africa 42,726; Europe 13,046; United States and Canada 5,923.
Major cities (urban agglomerations; 1991): Greater Bombay (Greater Mumbai) 9,925,891 (12,596,243); Delhi 7,206,704 (8,419,084); Calcutta 4,399,819 (11,021,915); Madras 3,841,396 (5,421,985); Bangalore 3,302,296 (4,130,288); Hyderābād 3,145,939 (4,253,759); Ahmadābād 2,954,526 (3,312,216); Kānpur 1,879,420 (2,029,889); Nāgpur 1,624,752 (1,664,006); Lucknow 1,619,115 (1,669,204); Pune 1,566,651 (2,493,987); New Delhi[8] 301,297.

Other principal cities (1991)

	population		population		population
Āgra	891,790	Indore	1,091,674	Rājkot	612,458
Allahābād	806,486	Jabalpur	764,586	Rānchi	599,306
Amritsar	708,835	Jaipur	1,458,183	Sholāpur	
Aurangābād	573,272	Jalandhar (Jullundur)	509,510	(Solāpur)	604,215
Bareilly	590,661	Jodhpur	666,279	Srīnagar	594,775[12]
Bhopāl	1,062,771	Kalyān[10]	1,014,557	Sūrat	1,505,872
Chandīgarh	510,565	Kota	537,371	Thāne (Thāna)[10]	803,389
Cochin (Kochi)	582,588	Ludhiāna	1,042,740	Trivandrum	699,872
Coimbatore	816,321	Madurai	940,989	Vadodara	
Farīdābād	617,717	Meerut	753,778	(Baroda)	1,061,598
Guwāhāti	584,342	Mysore	606,755	Vārānasi	
Gwalior	690,765	Nāshik (Nāsik)	656,925	(Benares)	932,399
Howrah (Hāora)[9]	950,435	Patna	917,243	Vijayawāda	701,827
Hubli-Dhārwād	648,298	Pimpri-Chinchwad[11]	517,083	Vishākhapatnam	752,037

Religious affiliation (1991): Hindu 80.3%; Muslim 11.0%, of which Sunnī 8.2%, Shīʿī 2.8%; Christian 2.4%, of which Roman Catholic 1.4%, other (mostly Protestant) 1.0%; Sikh 2.0%; Buddhist 0.7%; Jain 0.5%; Zoroastrian 0.01%; other 3.1%.
Households (1991)[13]. Total households 151,032,898. Average household size 5.6; 1–2 persons 12.1%, 3–5 persons 44.4%, 6–8 persons 30.5%, 9 or more persons 13.0%. Average number of rooms per household 2.2; 1 room 40.5%, 2 rooms 30.6%, 3 rooms 13.8%, 4 rooms 7.1%, 5 rooms 3.2%, 6 or more rooms 3.9%, unspecified number of rooms 0.9%. Average number of persons per room 2.6. Shelterless (homeless) population estimated (1987) at more than 100,000,000.
Emigration (1987 estimation): persons living abroad 12,697,000 (accepting foreign citizenship 8,200,000), of which in Nepal (1980) 3,800,000 (2,388,000); Malaysia 1,170,000 (1,029,000); Middle Eastern countries 1,064,000 (102,000); Sri Lanka 1,028,000 (457,000); South Africa 850,000 (850,000); United Kingdom 789,000 (395,000); Mauritius 701,000 (700,000); United States 500,000 (287,000); Trinidad and Tobago 430,000 (430,000); Fiji 339,000 (339,000); Myanmar 330,000 (50,000); Canada 229,000 (129,000).

Vital statistics

Birth rate per 1,000 population (1992): 29.0 (world avg. 25.0).
Death rate per 1,000 population (1992): 10.0 (world avg. 9.3).
Natural increase rate per 1,000 population (1992): 19.0 (world avg. 15.7).
Total fertility rate (avg. births per childbearing woman; 1994): 3.5.
Marital status of male (female) population age 25 and over (1981): single 6.4% (1.1%); married 87.4% (79.4%); widowed 5.7% (18.8%); divorced or separated 0.5% (0.7%).
Life expectancy at birth (1992–93): male 60.4 years; female 61.2 years.
Major causes of death per 100,000 population (1987)[14]: diseases of the circulatory system 227; infectious and parasitic diseases 215; diseases of the respiratory system 108; certain conditions originating in the perinatal period 108; accidents, homicide, and other violence 102; diseases of the digestive system 48; diseases of the nervous system 43; malignant neoplasms (cancers) 41; endocrine, metabolic, and nutritional disorders 30; diseases of the blood and blood-forming organs 25; ill-defined conditions 129.

Social indicators

Educational attainment (1981)[15]. Percentage of population age 25 and over having: no formal schooling (illiterate) 64.8%; no formal schooling (literate) 1.0%; some primary education 7.1%; completed primary 10.9%; some secondary 6.2%; completed secondary 7.1%; higher vocational 0.4%; completed undergraduate degree 2.5%.

Distribution of expenditure (1989–90)

percentage of household expenditure by quintile				
1	2	3	4	5 (highest)
8.8%	12.5%	16.2%	21.3%	41.2%

Quality of working life[16]. Average workweek (1989): 42 hours. Rate of fatal (nonfatal) injuries per 100,000 workers: industrial workers (1989) 17 (3,625); miners (1990) 32 (172); railway workers (1989) 15 (1,059). Employees covered under Employee's State Insurance Scheme (1991) 6,070,000; number of beneficiaries 26,749,000. Average days lost to labour stoppages per 1,000 workdays (1991): 6.
Access to services (1991). Percentage of total (urban, rural) households having access to: electricity for lighting purposes 42.4% (75.8%, 30.5%); attached toilet or nearby latrine 23.7% (63.9%, 9.5%). Source of drinking water: piped water 32.3%, well 32.2%, hand pump or tube well 30.0%, river or canal 2.0%, public tank 1.3%; other 2.2%.
Social participation. Eligible voters participating in last (May/June 1991) national election: 53%. Trade union membership (1989): 9,295,000.
Social deviance (1986)[17]. Offense rate per 100,000 population for: murder 3.5; dacoity (gang robbery) 1.3; theft and housebreaking 57.9; riots 12.0. Rate of suicide per 100,000 population (1990): 6.9.
Material well-being (1994). Households possessing: black and white television receivers 18.8%, colour television receivers 6.3%, videocassette recorders 1.3%, refrigerators 6.9%, washing machines 2.3%.

National economy

Public debt (external, outstanding; 1993): U.S.$80,985,000,000.
Gross national product (1993): U.S.$262,810,000,000 (U.S.$290 per capita).

Structure of gross domestic product and labour force

	1993–94		1991	
	in value Rs '000,000,000[18]	% of total value	labour force[19]	% of labour force
Agriculture, forestry	2,144	30.3	191,340,829	60.9
Mining	170	2.4	1,751,275	0.6
Manufacturing	1,223	17.3	28,671,479	9.1
Construction	398	5.6	5,543,205	1.8
Public utilities	200	2.8	...	...
Transp. and commun.	575	8.1	8,017,746	2.5
Trade, restaurants	920	13.0	21,296,337	6.8
Finance, real estate	598	8.5	...	...
Pub. admin., defense	406	5.8	29,311,622	9.3
Services	437	6.2		
Other	—	—	28,198,877[20]	9.0[20]
TOTAL	7,071	100.0	314,131,370	100.0

Budget (1994–95). Revenue: Rs 1,445,700,000,000 (tax revenue 56.2%, of which excise taxes 25.5%, customs duties 18.3%, corporation taxes 9.2%; nontax revenue 43.8%, of which economic services 22.1%, interest receipts 11.2%). Expenditures: Rs 1,787,000,000,000 (interest payments and debt servicing 24.6%; transportation 12.1%; grants to state governments 11.3%; defense

9.8%; communications 5.3%; agriculture 4.9%; industry and minerals 3.3%; social services 2.9%).

Production. Agriculture, forestry, fishing (value of production in Rs '000,000 except as noted; 1989–90): rice 239,120, wheat 115,270, sugarcane 78,760, peanuts (groundnuts) 53,950, kapoks 42,320, rapeseed and mustard 31,350, chick-peas 31,020, sorghum 27,140, corn (maize) 19,180, potatoes 19,140, coconuts 18,790, pigeon peas 18,210, bananas 13,230, pearl millet 12,330, tea 11,080, urd beans 10,670, mung beans 10,560, chilies 9,320, soybeans 8,470, tobacco 6,890, sesame seeds 6,740, finger millet 5,810, jute 5,790, rubber 4,650, betel nuts 4,420, red lentils 4,390, sunflower seeds 4,340, onions 4,270, tapioca 4,160, guar seeds 3,670, cashews 3,600, turmeric 3,600, coffee 3,600, safflower seeds 3,170, barley 3,110; livestock (number of live animals; 1994) 192,980,000 cattle, 118,347,000 goats, 78,825,000 water buffalo, 44,809,000 sheep; roundwood (1992) 282,359,000 cu m; fish catch (metric tons; 1993) 4,324,231, of which freshwater fish 1,791,910. Mining and quarrying (in '000 metric tons except as noted; 1993–94): limestone 83,900; iron ore 56,400; bauxite 5,029; manganese 1,781; chromite 1,094; zinc ore 144; copper (metal content) 45[21]; lead (primary metal) 39[21]; gold 62,300 troy oz; gem diamonds 19,707 carats. Manufacturing (in '000 metric tons except as noted; 1992–93): cement 54,300; finished steel 15,200; steel ingots 13,250; refined sugar 10,589; nitrogenous fertilizers 7,407; paper and paperboard 2,152; soda ash 1,391; jute manufactures 1,310; aluminum 483; nylon and polyester yarns 278; bicycles 6,963,000 units; motorcycles and scooters 1,496,000 units; power-driven pumps 525,000 units; passenger cars and jeeps 198,100 units; passenger buses and trucks 132,600 units; cotton cloth 13,054,000,000 metres; other important manufactured products include drugs and pharmaceuticals, computer software, gold jewelry, and silk goods. Construction (value of new construction in Rs; 1989–90): 563,670,000,000.

Manufacturing enterprises (1989–90)[22, 23]

	no. of factories	no. of persons engaged	avg. wages as a % of avg. of all wages[24]	annual value added (Rs '000,000)
Chemicals and chemical products,	6,631	568,196	148.6	52,320
of which drugs and medicine	1,009	139,184	170.0	11,948
fertilizers and pesticides	556	94,394	207.7	9,689
industrial chemicals	1,264	86,470	166.7	9,350
paints, soaps, and cosmetics	1,607	96,652	92.7	9,204
Textiles (excl. clothing),	12,450	1,438,208	87.8	48,305
of which cotton	7,021	865,134	...	25,588
synthetic fibres	2,280	228,443	...	12,915
Food products,	19,342	1,111,243	56.7	39,749
of which sugar	361	234,533	...	12,834
tea	1,014	116,713	...	7,853
Electrical machinery/apparatus,	4,790	385,811	149.1	32,845
of which radios and televisions	812	93,912	130.8	8,336
Iron and steel	3,116	420,981	131.0	29,886
Nonelectrical machinery/apparatus	7,753	445,800	129.1	28,183
Transport equipment,	3,637	476,925	147.9	27,373
of which motor vehicles	1,569	182,489	171.4	15,819
Refined petroleum	140	23,621	243.7	10,227
Bricks, cement, plaster products	4,881	227,900	67.0	11,750
Fabricated metal products	6,683	224,182	100.2	9,854
Paper and paper products	1,967	136,310	100.0	8,134

Energy production (consumption): electricity (kW-hr; 1993–94) 323,500,000,000 ([1993] 357,759,000,000); coal (metric tons; 1993–94) 246,000,000 ([1993] 250,564,000); crude petroleum (barrels; 1993–94) 225,700,000 ([1993] 420,000,000); petroleum products (metric tons; 1993) 42,379,000 (53,346,000); natural gas (cu m; 1993–94) 14,728,000,000 ([1993] 12,214,000,000).

Financial aggregates[25]

	1989	1990	1991	1992	1993	1994	1995[26]
Exchange rate, Rs per:							
U.S. dollar	17.03	18.07	25.83	26.20	31.38	31.38	31.40
£	27.35	34.84	48.33	39.61	46.48	49.03	50.32
SDR	22.39	25.71	36.95	36.02	43.10	45.81	48.97
International reserves (U.S.$)							
Total (excl. gold; '000,000)	3,859	1,521	3,627	5,757	10,199	19,698	20,234
SDRs ('000,000)	113	316	46	4	100	2	20
Reserve pos. in IMF ('000,000)	640	—	—	292	292	310	332
Foreign exchange ('000,000)	3,105	1,205	3,580	5,461	9,807	19,386	19,882
Gold ('000,000 fine troy oz)	10.449	10.692	11.282	11.348	11.457	11.800	12.782
% world reserves	1.1	1.1	1.2	1.2	1.3	1.3	1.4
Interest and prices							
Central bank discount (%)	10.0	10.0	12.0	12.0	12.0	12.0	...
Advance (prime) rate (%)	16.5	16.5	17.9	18.9	16.3	...	...
Industrial share prices (1990 = 100)[27]	72.1	100.0	134.8	247.3	202.9	322.1	...
Balance of payments (U.S.$'000,000)							
Balance of visible trade	−6,110	−5,151	...	...	...	...	...
Imports, f.o.b.	22,254	23,437	...	...	...	...	...
Exports, f.o.b.	16,144	18,286	...	...	...	...	...
Balance of invisibles	−716	−1,886	...	...	...	...	...
Balance of payments, current account	−6,826	−7,037	...	...	...	...	...

Land use (1993): forested 23.0%; meadows and pastures 3.8%; agricultural and under permanent cultivation 57.1%; other 16.1%.

Population economically active (1991): total 314,131,370; activity rate of total population 37.5% (participation rates: over age 15 [1981] 60.7%; female 28.6%; unemployed[28].

Price and earnings indexes (1990 = 100)

	1989	1990	1991	1992	1993	1994	1995[29]
Consumer price index	91.8	100.0	113.9	127.3	135.4	149.2	164.3
Earnings index	...	...	...	...	...	...	...

Household income and expenditure. Average household size (1991)[13] 5.6; income per household: n.a.; sources of income (1984–85): salaries and wages 42.2%, self-employed 39.7%, interest 8.6%, profits and dividends 6.0%, rent 3.5%; expenditure (1991–92): food and beverages 52.0%, transportation and communications 11.5%, clothing and footwear 10.0%, housing 5.8%.

Service enterprises (net value added at factor cost in Rs '000,000; 1989–90): wholesale and retail trade 468,450; community, social, and personal services 226,320; construction 211,520; finance and insurance 172,770; transport and storage 169,630; real estate and business services 115,140; communication 30,780; electricity, gas, and water 29,050; restaurants and hotels 25,390.

Tourism: receipts from visitors (1993) U.S.$1,487,000,000; expenditures by nationals abroad (1990) U.S.$393,000,000.

Foreign trade[30, 31]

Balance of trade (current prices)

	1988–89	1989–90	1990–91	1991–92	1992–93	1993–94
Rs '000,000	−49,417	−40,249	−61,163	+12,031	−30,841	+38,134
% of total	10.9%	6.8%	8.6%	1.4%	2.8%	2.6%

Imports (1993–94): Rs 728,060,000,000 (machinery, transport equipment, and fabricated metals 26.0%; mineral fuels and lubricants 24.8%; pearls and precious and semiprecious stones [mostly diamonds] 11.4%; industrial chemicals 6.0%; fertilizers 3.6%). *Major import sources* (1994): U.S. 9.5%; Germany 7.8%; Japan 7.8%; U.K. 7.0%; Saudi Arabia 5.8%; Belgium 5.8%; United Arab Emirates 4.8%; Kuwait 3.7%; South Korea 3.1%; Australia 3.0%.

Exports (1993–94): Rs 695,470,000,000 (cut and polished diamonds and jewelry 18.0%; machinery, transport equipment, metal products, iron and steel, and electronic components 13.6%; ready-made garments 11.8%; cotton yarn, fabrics, and thread 7.0%; chemicals and chemical products 6.7%; leather and leather manufactures 6.0%; fish products 3.6%; oil cakes 3.3%). *Major export destinations* (1994): U.S. 19.8%; Japan 8.4%; Germany 7.2%; U.K. 6.7%; Hong Kong 5.6%; United Arab Emirates 4.1%; Belgium 3.7%; Italy 3.4%; France 2.5%; The Netherlands 2.1%.

Transport and communications

Transport. Railroads (1993–94): route length 38,189 mi, 61,459 km; (1994–95) passenger-mi 195,926,000,000, passenger-km 315,313,000,000; short ton-mi cargo 171,213,000,000, metric ton-km cargo 249,966,000,000. Roads (1991–92): total length 1,342,000 mi, 2,160,000 km (paved 46%). Vehicles (1993): passenger cars 3,330,000; trucks and buses 1,980,000. Merchant marine (1992): vessels (100 gross tons and over) 888; total deadweight tonnage 10,365,939. Air transport (1994)[32]: passenger-mi 10,878,000,000, passenger-km 17,506,000,000; short ton-mi cargo 379,651,000, metric ton-km cargo 554,281,000; airports (1995) with scheduled flights 66.

Communications. Daily newspapers (1993): total number 3,805; total circulation 18,800,000; circulation per 1,000 population 21. Radio (1994): 65,000,000 receivers (1 per 14 persons). Television (1994): 20,000,000 receivers (1 per 47 persons). Telephones (main lines; 1993): 8,037,400 (1 per 112 persons).

Education and health

Education (1993–94)

	schools	teachers	students	student/ teacher ratio
Primary (age 6–10)	572,923	1,703,164	108,200,539	63.5
Secondary (age 11–17)	241,129	2,485,160	60,817,397	24.5
Higher[33]	7,958	215,234	4,804,773	22.3

Literacy (1991): total population age 7 and over literate 359,016,000 (52.6%); males literate 229,192,000 (64.1%); females literate 129,824,000 (39.3%).

Health: physicians (1991) 394,068 (1 per 2,211 persons); hospital beds (1992) 642,103 (1 per 1,357 persons); infant mortality rate (1994) 78.4.

Food (1992): daily per capita caloric intake 2,395 (vegetable products 93%, animal products 7%); 108% of FAO recommended minimum requirement.

Military

Total active duty personnel (1995): 1,145,000 (army 85.6%, navy 4.8%, air force 9.6%); personnel in paramilitary forces for border security 282,000. *Military expenditure as percentage of GNP* (1993): 3.3% (world 3.3%); per capita expenditure U.S.$9.

[1]Council of States can have a maximum of 250 members; a maximum of 12 of these members may be nominated by the president. [2]Includes 2 nonelective seats. [3]Census not conducted; population based on projection of 1989 official estimate. [4]Excludes 46,976 sq mi (121,667 sq km) of territory claimed by India as part of Jammu and Kashmir but occupied by Pakistan or China; inland water constitutes 9.0% of total area of India (including all of Indian-claimed Jammu and Kashmir). [5]Unadjusted for undercount; census total adjusted for undercount was officially estimated to be 858,997,000. [6]Mother tongue unless otherwise noted. [7]Percentage based on 1971 census. [8]Within Delhi urban agglomeration. [9]Within Calcutta urban agglomeration. [10]Within Greater Bombay urban agglomeration. [11]Within Pune urban agglomeration. [12]1981 census. [13]Excludes Jammu and Kashmir. [14]Projected rates based on about 3.5% of total deaths (317,392 registered deaths out of an estimated total of nearly 9,000,000 deaths). [15]Excludes Assam. [16]Data apply to the workers employed in the "organized sector" only (28 million in 1994, of which 20 million are employed in the public sector and 8 million are employed in the private sector); few legal protections exist for the other 348 million workers in the "unorganized sector." [17]Crimes reported to National Crime Records Bureau by police authorities of state governments. [18]At factor cost. [19]All persons aged 5 years or older designated "workers" per 1991 census. [20]Not adequately defined. [21]1992–93. [22]Establishments with 10 or more workers using electrical power or 20 or more workers not using electrical power. [23]Excludes Arunāchal Pradesh, Mizoram, Sikkim, and Lakshadweep. [24]1987–88. [25]End-of-period unless otherwise noted. [26]July. [27]Annual average. [28]36,040,000 persons were registered at government unemployment offices in March 1994. [29]June. [30]Import figures are f.o.b. in balance of trade and c.i.f. in commodities and trading partners. [31]Fiscal year beginning April 1. [32]Air-India, Indian Airlines, Jet Airways, and Modiluft only. [33]Excludes teacher training.

Indonesia

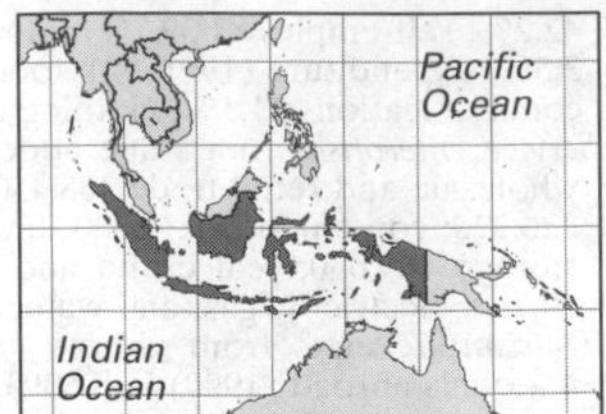

Official name: Republik Indonesia (Republic of Indonesia).
Form of government: unitary multiparty republic with two legislative houses (House of People's Representatives [500[1]]; People's Consultative Assembly [1,000[2]]).
Head of state and government: President.
Capital: Jakarta.
Official language: Bahasa Indonesia.
Official religion: monotheism.
Monetary unit: 1 Indonesian rupiah (Rp) = 100 sen; valuation (Oct. 6, 1995) 1 U.S.$ = Rp 2,268; 1 £ = Rp 3,585.

Area and population

		area		population
Metropolitan district	**Capitals**	sq mi	sq km	1995 estimate
Jakarta Raya	Jakarta	228	590	9,160,500
Provinces				
Bali	Denpasar	2,147	5,561	2,902,200
Bengkulu	Bengkulu	8,173	21,168	1,415,000
Irian Jaya	Jayapura	162,928	421,981	1,956,300
Jambi	Jambi	17,297	44,800	2,383,400
Jawa Barat	Bandung	17,877	46,300	39,336,500
Jawa Tengah	Semarang	13,207	34,206	29,688,100
Jawa Timur	Surabaya	18,502	47,921	33,885,900
Kalimantan Barat	Pontianak	56,664	146,760	3,651,800
Kalimantan Selatan	Banjarmasin	14,541	37,660	2,900,400
Kalimantan Tengah	Palangkaraya	58,919	152,600	1,637,300
Kalimantan Timur	Samarinda	78,162	202,440	2,331,000
Lampung	Tanjung Karang	12,860	33,307	6,680,300
Maluku	Ambon	28,767	74,505	2,094,700
Nusa Tenggara Barat	Mataram	7,790	20,177	3,654,800
Nusa Tenggara Timur	Kupang	18,485	47,876	3,582,800
Riau	Pakanbaru	36,510	94,561	3,924,600
Sulawesi Selatan	Ujung Pandang	28,101	72,781	7,577,800
Sulawesi Tengah	Palu	26,921	69,726	1,947,500
Sulawesi Tenggara	Kendari	10,690	27,686	1,594,000
Sulawesi Utara	Menado	7,345	19,023	2,652,300
Sumatera Barat	Padang	19,219	49,778	4,328,200
Sumatera Selatan	Palembang	40,034	103,688	7,232,700
Sumatera Utara	Medan	27,331	70,787	11,145,300
Timor Timur[3]	Dili	5,743	14,874	843,100
Special autonomous districts				
Aceh	Banda Aceh	21,387	55,392	3,860,000
Yogyakarta	Yogyakarta	1,224	3,169	2,916,700
TOTAL		741,052	1,919,317	195,283,200

Demography

Population (1995): 195,283,000.
Density (1995): persons per sq mi 263.5, persons per sq km 101.7.
Urban-rural (1995): urban 35.0%; rural 65.0%.
Sex distribution (1990): male 49.88%; female 50.12%.
Age breakdown (1990): under 15, 36.5%; 15–29, 28.3%; 30–44, 18.1%; 45–59, 10.7%; 60–74, 5.3%; 75 and over, 1.1%.
Population projection: (2000) 210,249,000; (2010) 236,806,000.
Doubling time: 47 years.
Ethnolinguistic composition (1990): Javanese 39.4%; Sundanese 15.8%; Indonesian (Malay) 12.1%; Madurese 4.3%; Minang 2.4%; other 26.0%.
Religious affiliation (1990): Muslim 87.2%; Christian 9.6%, of which Roman Catholic 3.6%; Hindu 1.8%; Buddhist 1.0%; other 0.4%.
Major cities (1990): Jakarta 8,259,266; Surabaya 2,421,016; Bandung 2,026,893; Medan 1,685,972; Semarang 1,005,316.

Vital statistics

Birth rate per 1,000 population (1995): 23.0 (world avg. 25.0).
Death rate per 1,000 population (1995): 8.0 (world avg. 9.3).
Natural increase rate per 1,000 population (1995): 15.0 (world avg. 15.7).
Total fertility rate (avg. births per childbearing woman; 1995): 2.7.
Marriage rate per 1,000 population (1991–92): 7.4[4].
Divorce rate per 1,000 population (1991–92): 0.8[4].
Life expectancy at birth (1995): male 62.0 years; female 65.0 years.
Major causes of death (percent distribution, 1986): infectious and parasitic diseases 43.5%; diseases of the respiratory system 21.9%; cardiovascular diseases 9.7%; diseases of the nervous system 6.0%.

National economy

Budget (1993–94). Revenue: Rp 56,318,000,000,000 (corporate income tax 38.9%, value-added tax 21.8%, nontax revenue 15.9%, individual income tax 8.2%, import duties 5.1%). Expenditures: Rp 54,983,000,000,000 (general public services 28.1%, education 10.0%, transportation and communications 9.7%, agriculture 6.7%, defense 6.2%, fuel and energy 5.9%, health 2.7%).
Public debt (external, outstanding; 1993): U.S.$52,451,000,000.
Tourism (1993): receipts U.S.$3,988,000,000; expenditures U.S.$1,539,000,000.
Production (metric tons except as noted). Agriculture, forestry, fishing (1994): rice 46,245,000, sugarcane 31,500,000, cassava 15,000,000, corn (maize) 6,617,-000, palm oil 3,890,000, copra 1,365,000, rubber 1,312,000; livestock (number of live animals) 12,281,000 goats, 11,595,000 cattle, 6,411,000 sheep, 3,512,000 buffalo; roundwood (1993) 188,118,000 cu m; fish catch (1993) 3,637,700. Mining and quarrying (1994): nickel ore 2,300,000; bauxite 1,360,000; copper concentrate 1,065,468; iron sand 334,895; tin concentrate 33,980; silver 111,-064 kg. Manufacturing (1993): cement 18,990,000; fertilizer 6,406,000; paper 2,489,300; plywood 9,227,000 cu m[5]. Energy production (consumption): electricity (kW-hr; 1992) 45,760,000,000 (45,760,000,000); coal (metric tons; 1992) 21,146,000 (5,520,000); crude petroleum (barrels; 1992) 557,266,000 (312,546,000); petroleum products (metric tons; 1992) 33,173,000 (26,684,-000); natural gas (cu m; 1992) 51,809,000,000 (20,623,000,000).
Gross national product (1993): U.S.$136,620,000,000 (U.S.$730 per capita).

Structure of gross domestic product and labour force

	1993		1994	
	in value Rp '000,000,000	% of total value	labour force	% of labour force
Agriculture	55,745.5	18.4	37,857,499	46.2
Mining	30,749.5	10.2	741,283	0.9
Manufacturing	67,441.4	22.3	10,840,195	13.2
Construction	18,139.9	6.0	3,558,344	4.3
Public utilities	2,714.3	0.9	182,845	0.2
Transp. and commun.	20,728.2	6.9	3,376,711	4.1
Trade	49,789.4	16.5	13,967,234	17.0
Finance, real estate	22,867.2	7.6	623,899	0.8
Pub. admin., defense	22,458.0	7.4 }	10,755,020	13.1
Services	11,384.4	3.8 }		
Other	...	...	135,079	0.2
TOTAL	302,017.8	100.0	82,038,109	100.0

Population economically active: total (1994) 82,038,109; activity rate 43.2% (participation rates: ages 15–64 [1992] 57.3%; female [1990] 38.2%; unemployed [1993] 2.8%).

Price and earnings indexes (1990 = 100)

	1988	1989	1990	1991	1992	1993	1994
Consumer price index	87.2	92.8	100.0	109.9	115.5	127.2	134.6
Earnings index[6]	85.4	92.5	100.0	109.6	...	...	...

Household income and expenditure. Average household size (1990) 4.5; income per household: n.a.; sources of income (1976): wages 42.1%, self-employment 41.5%, transfer payments 2.5%; expenditure (1990): food 51.4%, housing and utilities 20.1%, clothing 5.5%, durable goods 2.9%.
Land use (1993): forested 61.7%; meadows and pastures 6.5%; agricultural and under permanent cultivation 17.1%; other 14.7%.

Foreign trade

Balance of trade (current prices)

	1989	1990	1991	1992	1993	1994
U.S.$'000,000	+7,229	+6,240	+6,075	+4,937	+8,872	+11,496
% of total	19.6%	13.8%	11.6%	9.2%	13.4%	16.8%

Imports (1993): U.S.$28,327,800,000 (machinery and transport equipment 42.9%, chemicals 14.3%, crude materials 8.6%, mineral fuels 7.6%). *Major import sources:* Japan 22.1%; U.S. 11.5%; Germany 7.3%.
Exports (1993): U.S.$36,823,000,000 (crude petroleum 13.0%, plywood 11.6%, natural gas 11.0%, garments 9.5%, preparation rubber 2.9%). *Major export destinations:* Japan 30.3%; U.S. 14.2%; Singapore 9.2%.

Transport and communications

Transport. Railroads (1993): route length 6,583 km; passenger-km 12,376,000,-000; metric ton-km cargo 4,092,000,000. Roads (1991): length 315,458 km (paved 43%). Vehicles (1993): passenger cars 1,676,781; trucks and buses 1,554,582. Merchant marine (1992): vessels (100 gross tons and over) 2,014; deadweight tonnage 3,130,175. Air transport (1994): passenger-km 19,751,-000,000; metric ton-km cargo 669,284,000; airports (1995) 122.
Communications. Daily newspapers (1992): total number 68; total circulation 4,591,000; circulation per 1,000 population 24. Radio (1994): 26,000,000 receivers (1 per 7.3 persons). Television (1994): 11,000,000 receivers (1 per 17 persons). Telephones (main lines; 1993): 1,713,000 (1 per 109 persons).

Education and health

Education (1992–93)

	schools[5]	teachers	students	student/ teacher ratio
Primary (age 7–12)	147,683	1,276,217	29,598,790	23.2
Secondary (age 13–18)	27,664	594,000[5]	9,433,778	13.6[5]
Voc., teacher tr.	3,557	103,000[5]	1,429,657	13.1[5]
Higher	1,000	135,462	1,973,094	11.6

Educational attainment (1990). Percentage of population age 25 and over having: no schooling 34.6%; less than complete primary 28.2%; primary 23.3%; some secondary and secondary 12.5%; higher 1.4%. *Literacy* (1990): total population age 15 and over literate 59,134,871 (77.0%); males literate 31,716,520 (84.5%); females literate 27,418,351 (69.8%).
Health: physicians (1989–90) 25,752 (1 per 6,861 persons); hospital beds (1991–92) 111,160 (1 per 1,660 persons); infant mortality rate (1993) 53.
Food (1992): daily per capita caloric intake 2,752 (vegetable products 96%, animal products 4%); 127% of FAO recommended minimum.

Military

Total active duty personnel (1994): 276,000 (army 77.5%, navy 15.2%, air force 7.3%). *Military expenditure as percentage of GNP* (1993): 1.5% (world 3.3%); per capita expenditure U.S.$11.

[1]Includes 100 nonelective seats reserved for the military. [2]Includes the 500 members of the House of People's Representatives plus 500 other delegates. [3]The legality of Indonesian administration of this province is disputed by the United Nations. [4]Muslim population only. [5]1991. [6]Based on daily wage rate of production workers in manufacturing.

Iran

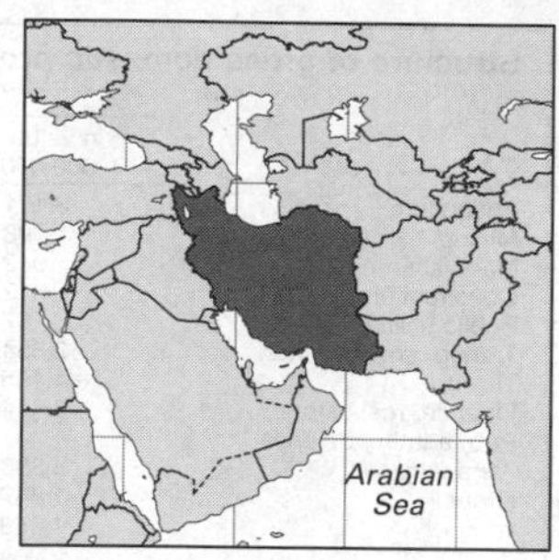

Official name: Jomhūrī-ye Eslāmī-ye Irān (Islamic Republic of Iran).
Form of government: unitary Islamic republic with one legislative house (Islamic Consultative Assembly [270]).
Supreme political/religious authority: Leader[1].
Head of state and government: President.
Capital: Tehrān.
Official language: Farsī (Persian).
Official religion: Islam.
Monetary unit: 1 rial (Rls); valuation (Oct. 6, 1995) 1 U.S.$ = Rls 3,000[2]; 1 £ = Rls 4,742[2].

Area and population

		area		population
Provinces	Capitals	sq mi	sq km	1991 census
Āzārbāyjān-e Gharbī	Orūmīyeh	14,517	37,599	2,283,707
Āzārbāyjān-e Sharqī[3]	Tabrīz	25,421	65,842	4,390,303
Bākhtarān	Bākhtarān	9,121	23,622	1,600,568
Būshehr	Būshehr	9,792	25,360	692,211
Chahār Maḥāll va Bakhtīārī	Shahr Kord	5,722	14,820	722,504
Eṣfahān	Eṣfahān	40,852	105,805	3,657,040
Fārs	Shīrāz	46,334	120,005	3,480,112
Gīlān	Rasht	5,722	14,820	2,203,560
Hamadān	Hamadān	7,508	19,445	1,649,269
Hormozgān	Bandar ʿAbbās	25,243	65,379	923,965
Īlām	Īlām	7,369	19,086	425,336
Kermān	Kermān	71,690	185,675	1,789,992
Khorāsān	Mashhad	121,887	315,687	5,997,468
Khūzestān	Ahvāz	25,688	66,532	3,155,453
Kohkīlūyeh va Būyer Aḥmadī	Yāsūj	5,289	13,699	476,564
Kordestān	Sanandaj	10,756	27,858	1,233,264
Lorestān	Khorramābād	11,027	28,560	1,470,524
Markazī	Arāk	11,402	29,530	1,182,611
Māzandarān	Sārī	18,010	46,645	3,792,772
Semnān	Semnān	35,345	91,544	458,125
Sīstān va Balūchestān	Zāhedān	70,066	181,471	1,440,251
Tehrān	Tehrān	10,896	28,221	9,981,878
Yazd	Yazd	26,875	69,605	691,067
Zanjān	Zanjān	14,047	36,382	1,774,645
TOTAL LAND AREA		630,578[4]	1,633,189[4]	
INLAND WATER		1,880[5]	4,868[5]	
TOTAL		632,457[4]	1,638,057	55,473,189[6]

Demography

Population (1995): 61,271,000[7].
Density (1995): persons per sq mi 97.2, persons per sq km 37.4.
Urban-rural (1991): urban 57.3%; rural 42.7%.
Sex distribution (1991): male 51.52%; female 48.48%.
Age breakdown (1991): under 15, 44.3%; 15–29, 26.6%; 30–44, 15.1%; 45–59, 8.2%; 60–74, 4.8%; 75 and over, 0.8%; unknown 0.2%.
Population projection: (2000) 67,304,000; (2010) 84,005,000.
Doubling time: 21 years.
Ethnic composition (1983): Persian 45.6%; Azerbaijani 16.8%; Kurdish 9.1%; Gīlakī 5.3%; Luri 4.3%; Māzandarānī 3.6%; Baluchi 2.3%; Arab 2.2%; Bakhtiari 1.7%; Turkmen 1.5%; Armenian 0.5%; other 7.1%.
Religious affiliation (1994): Muslim 99.1% (Shīʿī 93.4%, Sunnī 5.7%); Bahāʾī 0.6%; Christian 0.1%; Zoroastrian 0.1%; Jewish 0.1%.
Major cities (1991): Tehrān 6,475,527; Mashhad 1,759,155; Eṣfahān 1,127,030; Tabriz 1,088,985; Shīrāz 965,117; Ahvāz 724,653; Qom 681,253.

Vital statistics

Birth rate per 1,000 population (1994): 42.0 (world avg. 25.0).
Death rate per 1,000 population (1994): 8.0 (world avg. 9.3).
Total fertility rate (avg. births per childbearing woman; 1992): 5.5.
Marriage rate per 1,000 population (1991): 8.1.
Life expectancy at birth (1994): male 65.0 years; female 67.0 years.
Major causes of death per 100,000 population (1990)[8]: diseases of the circulatory system 304; accidents and violence 108; malignant neoplasms (cancers) 61; diseases of the respiratory system 48; infectious diseases 34.

National economy

Budget (1994–95). Revenue: Rls 33,592,000,000,000 (oil revenue 65.8%, taxes 19.1%, other 15.1%). Expenditures: Rls 33,768,000,000,000 (current expenditure 62.6%, development expenditure 37.4%).
Production (metric tons except as noted). Agriculture, forestry, fishing (1994): wheat 11,500,000, sugar beets 5,900,000, barley 3,100,000, rice 2,700,000, grapes 1,875,000, apples 1,690,000, oranges 1,485,000, dates 630,000, seed cotton 310,000, pistachios 210,000; livestock (head) 45,400,000 sheep, 7,100,000 cattle; roundwood 7,467,000 cu m; fish catch 343,888. Mining and quarrying (1993): copper ore (concentrate) 12,106,000; iron ore (concentrate) 8,690,000. Manufacturing (value added, in Rls '000,000; 1989–90): textiles (excl. wearing apparel) 375,200; food products 235,700; bricks, tiles, and cement 211,500; nonelectrical machinery 160,000; iron and steel 133,200; nonindustrial chemical products 131,500. Energy production (consumption): electricity (kW-hr; 1993–94) 76,014,000 (53,200,000[9]); coal (metric tons; 1992) 1,500,000 (2,000,000); crude petroleum (barrels; 1993–94) 1,426,800,000 (340,500,000[9]); petroleum products (metric tons; 1992) 42,246,000 (46,135,000); natural gas (cu m; 1993–94) 35,600,000,000 (35,100,000,000).
Gross national product (1992–93): U.S.$111,008,000,000 (U.S.$1,940 per capita).

Structure of gross domestic product and labour force

	1993–94		1991	
	in value Rls '000,000,000[10]	% of total value	labour force	% of labour force
Agriculture	19,446	20.8	3,205,430	21.8
Petroleum, natural gas	16,495	17.6	100,545	0.7
Other mining	495	0.5		
Manufacturing	12,873	13.7	2,013,724	13.7
Construction	3,134	3.3	1,372,437	9.3
Public utilities	1,079	1.2	129,000	0.9
Transp. and commun.	6,582	7.0	762,178	5.2
Trade, restaurants	14,536	15.5	1,238,305	8.4
Finance, real estate	9,698	10.3	194,686	1.3
Pub. admin., defense	8,576	9.2	3,517,897	23.9
Services	1,754	1.9		
Other	−959[11]	−1.0[11]	2,202,505[12]	14.9[12]
TOTAL	93,709	100.0[4]	14,736,707	100.0[4]

Public debt (external, outstanding; 1993): U.S.$8,880,000,000.
Tourism (1993–94): receipts U.S.$70,000,000; expenditures U.S.$493,000,000.
Population economically active (1986): total 12,854,702; activity rate 26.0% (participation rates: ages 15–64, 46.8%; female 10.3%; unemployed [1994] 30%).

Price and earnings indexes (1990–91 = 100)

	1989–90	1990–91	1991–92	1992–93	1993–94	1994–95
Consumer price index	91.8	100.0	120.7	150.2	184.5	249.5
Daily earnings index[13]	91.5	100.0	113.6	136.9	161.4	...

Household income and expenditure. Average household size (1991): 5.1; income per urban household (1988) Rls 1,339,970 (U.S.$19,536); sources of urban income (1988): wages 37.4%, self-employment 30.5%, other 32.1%; expenditure (1990–91): food and hotels 42.9%, housing and energy 24.9%.
Land use (1993): forested 7.0%; meadows and pastures 26.9%; agricultural and under permanent cultivation 11.1%; other 55.0%.

Foreign trade

Balance of trade (current prices)

	1988–89	1989–90	1990–91	1991–92	1992–93	1993–94
U.S.$'000,000	−810	−367	+975	−6,529	−3,406	−1,207
% of total	3.6%	1.4%	2.6%	14.9%	7.9%	3.2%

Imports (1993–94): U.S.$19,287,000,000 ([14]nonelectrical machinery 28.9%, iron and steel 13.5%, transportation equipment 12.9%). *Major import sources* (1993)[15]: Germany 18.0%; Japan 10.0%; Italy 9.0%; U.A.E. 7.0%; U.K. 5.0%.
Exports (1993–94): U.S.$18,080,000,000 (petroleum and natural gas 79.3%, carpets 7.7%, pistachios 2.4%, iron and steel 2.2%, copper bars and sheets 0.8%). *Major export destinations* (1993)[15]: Japan 15.0%; France 9.0%; Italy 8.0%; The Netherlands 8.0%; South Korea 7.0%.

Transport and communications

Transport. Railroads (1993): route length 3,014 mi, 4,851 km; (1991) passenger-km 4,584,000,000; metric ton-km cargo 7,704,000,000. Roads (1991): length 94,130 mi, 151,488 km (paved [1989] 34%). Vehicles (1993): passenger cars 1,557,000; trucks and buses 584,100. Merchant marine (1992): vessels (100 gross tons and over) 403; total deadweight tonnage 8,345,269. Air transport (1994)[16]: passenger-km 5,023,000,000; metric ton-km cargo 78,811,000; airports (1995) with scheduled flights 20.
Communications. Daily newspapers (1992): 13; circulation 1,250,000, circulation per 1,000 population 22. Radio (1994): 13,000,000 receivers (1 per 4.6 persons). Television (1994): 7,000,000 receivers (1 per 8.5 persons). Telephones (main lines; 1993–94): 3,598,000 (1 per 16 persons).

Education and health

Education (1992–93)

	schools	teachers	students	student/teacher ratio
Primary (age 7–11)	61,323	311,839	9,937,309	31.9
Secondary (age 12–18)	...	211,711	5,995,051	28.3
Voc., teacher tr.	...	20,947	327,937	15.7
Higher	...	25,208[17]	724,000	25.2[17]

Educational attainment (1986). Percentage of population age 25 and over having: no formal schooling 12.8%; secondary education 38.0%; higher 7.8%.
Literacy (1990): total population age 15 and over literate 18,200,000 (54.0%); males literate 11,600,000 (64.5%); females literate 6,600,000 (43.3%).
Health (1994): physicians 37,000 (1 per 1,600 persons); hospital beds (1995) 93,000 (1 per 650 persons); infant mortality rate 60.0.
Food (1992): daily per capita caloric intake 2,860 (vegetable products 91%, animal products 9%); 119% of FAO recommended minimum requirement.

Military

Total active duty personnel (1994): 513,000 (revolutionary guard corps 23.4%, army 67.3%, navy 3.5%, air force 5.8%). *Military expenditure as percentage of GNP* (1993): 3.5% (world 3.3%); per capita expenditure U.S.$83.

[1]Not required to be a supreme theological authority. [2]Fixed rate. [3]The former province of Āzārbāyjān-e Sharqī (East Azerbaijan) was divided into Ardabīl and Āzārbāyjān-e Markazī (Central Azerbaijan) provinces in 1993. [4]Detail does not add to total given because of rounding. [5]Area of Lake Urmia. [6]Excludes nomadic population of 363,974. [7]De jure estimate excluding refugees. [8]Projected rates based on about 20% of total deaths. [9]1992. [10]At factor cost. [11]Less imputed bank service charge. [12]Includes 1,640,092 unemployed. [13]Construction sector only. [14]Based on 1991–92 imports equaling U.S.$29,677,000,000. [15]Estimated figures. [16]Iran Air. [17]1991–92.

Iraq

Official name: al-Jumhūrīyah al-ʿIrāqīyah (Republic of Iraq).
Form of government: unitary multiparty[1] republic with one legislative house (National Assembly [250]).
Head of state and government: President.
Capital: Baghdad.
Official language: Arabic[2].
Official religion: Islam.
Monetary unit: 1 Iraqi dinar (ID) = 20 dirhams = 1,000 fils; valuation (Oct. 12, 1995) 1 U.S.$ = 2,600 ID[3]; 1 £ = 4,095 ID[3].

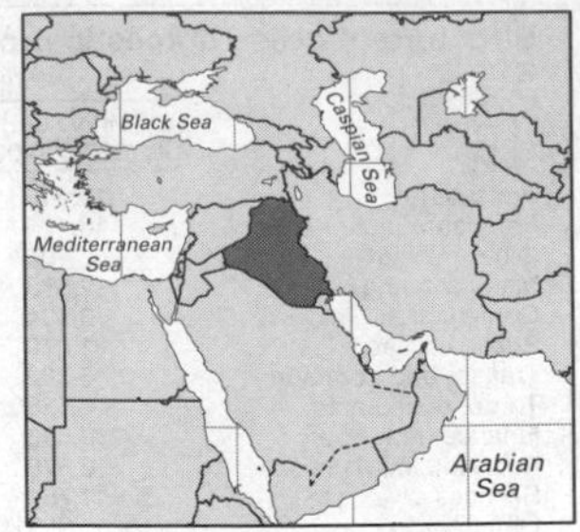

Area and population

Governorates	Capitals	area[4] sq mi	area[4] sq km	population 1991 estimate
al-Anbār	ar-Ramādī	53,208	137,808	865,500
Bābil	al-Ḥillah	2,163	5,603	1,221,100
Baghdād	Baghdad	1,572	4,071	3,910,900
al-Baṣrah[4]	Basra	7,363	19,070	1,168,800
Dhī Qār	an-Nāṣirīyah	4,981	12,900	1,030,900
Diyālā	Baʿqūbah	6,828	17,685	1,037,600
Karbalāʾ	Karbalāʾ	1,944	5,034	567,600
Maysān	al-ʿAmārah	6,205	16,072	524,200
al-Muthannā	as-Samāwah	19,977	51,740	350,000
an-Najaf	an-Najaf	11,129	28,824	666,400
Nīnawā	Mosul	14,410	37,323	1,618,700
al-Qādisīyah	ad-Dīwānīyah	3,148	8,153	595,600
Ṣalāḥ ad-Dīn	Tikrīt	9,407	24,363	772,200
at-Taʾmīm	Kirkūk	3,737	9,679	605,900
Wāsiṭ	al-Kūt	6,623	17,153	605,700
Kurdish Autonomous Region[5]				
Dahūk	Dahūk	2,530	6,553	309,300
Irbīl	Irbīl	5,820	15,074	928,400
as-Sulaymānīyah	as-Sulaymānīyah	6,573	17,023	1,124,200
LAND AREA		167,618	434,128	
OTHER[6]		357	924	
TOTAL		167,975	435,052	17,903,000

Demography

Population (1995): 20,413,000[7].
Density (1995): persons per sq mi 121.7, persons per sq km 47.0.
Urban-rural (1991): urban 70.4%; rural 29.6%.
Sex distribution (1992): male 50.59%; female 49.41%.
Age breakdown (1992): under 15, 44.6%; 15–29, 29.3%; 30–44, 14.0%; 45–59, 7.0%; 60–74, 3.8%; 75 and over, 1.3%.
Population projection: (2000) 23,631,000; (2010) 30,565,000.
Doubling time: 19 years.
Ethnic composition (1983): Arab 77.1%; Kurd 19.0%; Azerbaijani 1.7%; Assyrian 0.8%; other 1.4%.
Religious affiliation (1994): Shīʿī Muslim 62.5%; Sunnī Muslim 34.5%; Christian (primarily Chaldean rite and Syrian rite Roman Catholic and Nestorian) 2.7%; other (primarily Yazīdī syncretist) 0.3%.
Major cities (1987): Baghdad (1990; urban agglomeration) 4,044,000; Diyālā 961,073; as-Sulaymānīyah 951,723; Irbīl 770,439; Mosul 664,221.

Vital statistics

Birth rate per 1,000 population (1994): 44.0 (world avg. 26.0).
Death rate per 1,000 population (1994)[8]: 7.0 (world avg. 9.2).
Natural increase rate per 1,000 population (1994): 37.0 (world avg. 16.8).
Total fertility rate (avg. births per childbearing woman; 1994): 6.7.
Marriage rate per 1,000 population (1990): 8.1.
Life expectancy at birth (1991)[9]: male 46.0 years; female 57.0 years.
Major causes of death (1994). Deprivation of medical care (because of acute medical supply shortages) and malnutrition.

National economy

Budget (1992). Revenue: ID 13,935,000,000. Expenditures: ID 13,935,000,000. Details of more recent proposed budgets were not released. Special emphasis was to be placed on the reconstruction of the infrastructure.
Tourism (1989): receipts U.S.$59,000,000; expenditures, n.a.
Public debt (external, outstanding; 1994): U.S.$20,000,000,000.
Production (metric tons except as noted). Agriculture, forestry, fishing (1994): wheat 1,008,000, barley 1,002,000, tomatoes 750,000, dates 600,000, watermelons 460,000, grapes 410,000, cucumbers 340,000, oranges 310,000, corn (maize) 285,000, rice 220,000; livestock (number of live animals) 6,320,000 sheep, 1,100,000 cattle; roundwood (1993) 155,000 cu m; fish catch (1993) 23,500. Mining and quarrying (1993): phosphate rock 1,000,000; sulfur 1,000,000; gypsum 450,000. Manufacturing (value added in ID '000,000; 1990): petroleum products and chemical products 668; nonmetal mineral products 152; food 114; textiles 91; paper products, printing, and publishing 78; beverages 56; footwear 56; electrical machinery 54; nonelectrical machinery 53; tobacco products 53. Construction (authorized; 1991): residential 4,558,000 sq m; nonresidential 410,000 sq m. Energy production (consumption): electricity (kW-hr; 1992) 25,300,000,000 (25,300,000,000); coal, none (none); crude petroleum (barrels; 1993) 175,000,000 ([1992] 156,000,000); petroleum products (metric tons; 1992) 16,020,000 (13,755,000); natural gas (cu m; 1993) 1,892,000,000 ([1992] 3,010,000,000).
Gross national product (1991): U.S.$12,640,000,000 (U.S.$710 per capita).

Structure of gross domestic product and labour force

	1991 in value ID '000,000[10]	1991 % of total value	1988 labour force	1988 % of labour force
Agriculture	6,171	28.1	477,264	11.6
Mining	98	0.4	60,701	1.5
Manufacturing	912	4.2	337,293	8.2
Construction	612	2.8	460,788	11.2
Public utilities	67	0.3	41,200	1.0
Transp. and commun.	2,854	13.0	266,233	6.4
Trade	4,465	20.3	281,877	6.8
Finance, real estate	3,414	15.6	41,532	1.0
Pub. admin., defense, and services	5,333	24.3	2,160,406	52.3
Other	−1,967	−9.0		
TOTAL	21,959[11]	100.0	4,127,294	100.0

Population economically active (1988): total 4,127,294; activity rate of total population 24.7% (participation rates: ages 15–64, 45.3%; female 12.0%).

Price and earnings indexes (1990 = 100)

	1990	1991	1992	1993	1994
Consumer price index	100.0	287	860[12]	2,600[12]	10,000[12]
Earnings index	...	...	...	...	...

Household income and expenditure (1988). Average household size 8.9; sources of income: self-employment 33.9%, wages and salaries 23.9%, transfers 23.0%, rent 18.6%; expenditure: food and beverages 50.2%, housing and energy 19.9%, clothing and footwear 10.6%.
Land use (1993): forested 0.4%; meadows and pastures 9.1%; agricultural and under permanent cultivation 12.5%; built-on, wasteland, and other 78.0%.

Foreign trade[13, 14]

Balance of trade (current prices)

	1989	1990[12]	1991[12]	1992[12]	1993[12]
U.S.$'000,000	+7,644	+6,686	+3,900	+6,920	+4,400
% of total	35.5%	40.9%	21.4%	31.1%	30.2%

Imports (1993): U.S.$5,100,000,000[12] (agricultural products 18.6%, of which cereals 6.3%; fish and forestry products 2.3%; unspecified 79.1%). *Major import sources* (1992)[15]: Australia 19.0%; Jordan 17.0%; Turkey 14.0%; United Kingdom 10.0%; Indonesia 7.0%.
Exports (1993): U.S.$9,500,000,000[12] (mostly crude petroleum and petroleum products). *Major export destinations* (1992)[16]: Jordan 71.0%; Portugal 15.0%; Greece 13.0%.

Transport and communications

Transport. Railroads (1992): route length 1,493 mi, 2,403 km; passenger-mi 572,000,000, passenger-km 920,000,000; short ton-mi cargo 79,000,000, metric ton-km cargo 115,000,000. Roads (1989): total length 28,305 mi, 45,554 km (paved 84%). Vehicles (1993): passenger cars 672,000; trucks and buses 368,000. Merchant marine (1992): vessels (100 gross tons and over) 131; total deadweight tonnage 1,578,822. Air transport: [17].
Communications. Daily newspapers (1992): total number 6; total circulation 660,000; circulation per 1,000 population 35. Radio (1994): 3,700,000 receivers (1 per 5.4 persons). Television (1994): 1,000,000 receivers (1 per 20 persons). Telephones (main lines; 1993): 675,000 (1 per 29 persons).

Education and health

Education (1992–93)

	schools	teachers	students	student/ teacher ratio
Primary (age 6–11)	8,003	131,271	2,857,467	21.8
Secondary (age 12–17)	2,746[18]	48,496	992,617	20.5
Voc., teacher tr.	296[18]	10,621	152,321	14.3
Higher[18]	20	10,520	197,786	18.8

Educational attainment (1987). Percentage of population age 10 and over having: no formal schooling 52.8%; primary education 21.5%; secondary 11.6%; higher 4.1%; unknown 10.0%. *Literacy* (1990): total population age 15 and over literate 6,030,000 (59.7%); males literate 3,570,000 (69.8%); females literate 2,460,000 (49.3%).
Health: physicians (1991) 9,366 (1 per 1,922 persons); hospital beds (1990) 31,227 (1 per 568 persons); infant mortality rate per 1,000 live births (1994) 67.
Food (1992): daily per capita caloric intake 2,121 (vegetable products 94%, animal products 6%); 88% of FAO recommended minimum requirement.

Military

Total active duty personnel (1985)[12]: 382,500 (army 91.5%, navy 0.7%, air force 7.8%). *Military expenditure as percentage of GNP* (1991): 74.9% (world 4.1%); per capita expenditure U.S.$528.

[1]Multipartyism authorized by a September 1991 law, but political power is in fact concentrated in a single-party apparatus. [2]Kurdish is official in the Kurdish Autonomous Region only. [3]Black market rate. [4]Includes territory ceded to Kuwait as of Jan. 15, 1993, per UN resolution of May 1992. [5]De facto self-government as of May 1992 elections. [6]Territorial water at the mouth of the Shaṭṭ al-ʿArab. [7]UN estimate; war deaths, deaths caused by the UN trade sanctions begun August 1990, and campaigns against ethnic groups may have reduced the population to 17,000,000 in 1994. [8]Excludes deaths caused by UN sanctions; death rate may be about 20 per 1,000 population. [9]Postwar estimate. [10]At factor cost. [11]Estimated gross domestic product (1994): U.S.$15,000,000,000. [12]Estimated figure(s). [13]Imports c.i.f.; exports f.o.b. [14]UN-imposed trade sanctions in place from August 1990 through October 1995. [15]Based on estimated imports equaling U.S.$647,000,000. [16]Based on estimated exports equaling U.S.$557,000,000. [17]No scheduled air service since June 1992. [18]1991–92.

Ireland

Official name: Éire (Irish); Ireland[1] (English).
Form of government: unitary multiparty republic with two legislative houses (Senate [60[2]]; House of Representatives [166]).
Chief of state: President.
Head of government: Prime Minister.
Capital: Dublin.
Official languages: Irish; English.
Official religion: none.
Monetary unit: 1 Irish pound (£Ir) = 100 new pence; valuation (Oct. 6, 1995) 1 £Ir = U.S.$1.61 = £1.02.

Area and population

Provinces Counties	area sq mi	area sq km	population 1991 census
Connacht	6,611	17,122	423,031
Galway[3]	2,293	5,940	180,364
Leitrim	581	1,525	25,301
Mayo	2,084	5,398	110,713
Roscommon	951	2,463	51,897
Sligo	693	1,796	54,756
Leinster	7,580	19,633	1,860,949
Carlow	346	896	40,942
Dublin[3]	356	922	1,025,304
Kildare	654	1,694	122,656
Kilkenny	796	2,062	73,635
Laoighis	664	1,719	52,314
Longford	403	1,044	30,296
Louth	318	823	90,724
Meath	902	2,336	105,370
Offaly	771	1,998	58,494
Westmeath	681	1,703	61,880
Wexford	908	2,351	102,069
Wicklow	782	2,025	97,265
Munster	9,315	24,127	1,009,533
Clare	1,231	3,188	90,918
Cork[3]	2,880	7,460	410,369
Kerry	1,815	4,701	121,894
Limerick[3]	1,037	2,686	161,956
Tipperary North Riding	771	1,996	57,854
Tipperary South Riding	872	2,258	74,918
Waterford[3]	710	1,838	91,624
Ulster (part of)	3,093	8,012	232,206
Cavan	730	1,891	52,796
Donegal	1,865	4,830	128,117
Monaghan	498	1,291	51,293
TOTAL LAND AREA	26,600	68,895[4]	
INLAND WATER	537	1,390	
TOTAL	27,137	70,285	3,525,719

Demography

Population (1995): 3,590,000.
Density (1995): persons per sq mi 132.3, persons per sq km 51.1.
Urban-rural (1991): urban 57.0%; rural 43.0%.
Sex distribution (1991): male 49.74%; female 50.26%.
Age breakdown (1991): under 15, 26.7%; 15–29, 24.1%; 30–44, 20.2%; 45–59, 13.8%; 60–74, 10.6%; 75 and over, 4.6%.
Population projection: (2000) 3,672,000; (2010) 3,841,000.
Doubling time: not applicable; doubling time exceeds 100 years.
Place of birth (1986): native born 93.7%; Eng. and Wales 3.6%; N.Ire. 1.0%.
Religious affiliation (1991). Roman Catholic 91.6%; Church of Ireland (Anglican) 2.3%; Presbyterian 0.4%; other 5.7%.
Major cities (1991)[5]: Dublin 477,675; Cork 127,024; Limerick 52,040; Galway 50,842; Waterford 40,345.

Vital statistics

Birth rate per 1,000 population (1993): 13.9 (world avg. 26.0); legitimate 80.5%; illegitimate 19.5%.
Death rate per 1,000 population (1993): 8.9 (world avg. 9.2).
Natural increase rate per 1,000 population (1993): 5.0 (world avg. 16.8).
Total fertility rate (avg. births per childbearing woman; 1990–95): 2.1.
Life expectancy at birth (1985–87): male 71.0 years; female 76.7 years.
Major causes of death per 100,000 population (1993): heart and circulatory diseases 399.2, of which ischemic heart disease 218.7; malignant neoplasms (cancers) 211.5; respiratory disease 66.7, of which pneumonia 52.0.

National economy

Budget (1995). Revenue: £Ir 11,542,000,000 (income taxes 34.1%, value-added tax 24.6%, excise taxes 18.3%). Expenditures: £Ir 11,686,000,000 (social welfare 34.2%, debt service 20.6%, health 18.5%, education 16.9%).
Public debt (1993): U.S.$41,603,000,000.
Tourism (1993): receipts U.S.$1,639,000,000; expenditures U.S.$1,256,000,000.
Production (metric tons except as noted). Agriculture, forestry, fishing (1993): sugar beets 1,380,000, barley 952,000, potatoes 650,000, wheat 520,000, oats 134,000, milk 52,270,000 hectolitres; livestock (number of live animals) 6,265,000 cattle, 6,125,000 sheep, 1,423,000 pigs; roundwood (1992) 1,834,000 cu m; fish catch (1992) 275,418. Mining and quarrying (1993): gypsum 317,600; zinc ore 194,100[6]; lead ore 48,300[6]. Manufacturing (value added in £Ir; 1990): metals and engineering goods 3,237,500,000; food products 1,828,300,000; chemical products 1,492,600,000; paper, printing, and publishing 452,900,000; nonmetallic mineral products 441,400,000. Construction (1992): residential 2,499,000 sq m; nonresidential 2,067,000 sq m. Energy production (consumption): electricity (kW-hr; 1992) 16,011,000,000 (16,011,000,000); coal (metric tons; 1992) 1,000 (3,060,000); crude petroleum (barrels; 1992) none (14,975,000); petroleum products (metric tons; 1992) 1,919,000 (4,172,000); natural gas (cu m; 1992) 2,220,000,000 (2,220,000,000).
Gross national product (1992): U.S.$44,906,000,000 (U.S.$12,580 per capita).

Structure of gross domestic product and labour force

	1993			
	in value £Ir '000,000[7]	% of total value	labour force	% of labour force
Agriculture	2,570	8.8	144,000	10.5
Mining			5,000	0.4
Manufacturing	10,828	37.2	224,000	16.3
Construction			71,000	5.1
Public utilities			12,000	0.9
Transp. and commun.	4,986	17.2	70,000	5.1
Trade			245,000[8]	17.8[8]
Pub. admin., defense	1,714	5.9	66,000	4.8
Services			309,000	22.4
Finance	8,999	30.9	[8]	[8]
Other			230,000[9]	16.7[9]
TOTAL	29,097	100.0	1,376,000	100.0

Population economically active (1993): total 1,376,000; activity rate of total population 39.1% (participation rates: ages 15–64, 59.2%[10]; female 30.5%[10]; unemployed 15.5%[11]).

Price and earnings indexes (1990 = 100)

	1988	1989	1990	1991	1992	1993	1994
Consumer price index	93.0	96.8	100.0	103.2	106.4	107.9	110.4
Weekly earnings index	92.6	96.3	100.0	104.4	108.6	114.4	117.9[12]

Household income and expenditure. Average household size (1983) 3.9; income per household: n.a.; sources of income (1987): wages and salaries 58.6%, self-employment 13.3%, interest and dividends 8.2%; expenditure (1993): food 26.9%, rent and household goods 11.5%, transportation 10.0%.
Land use (1992): forest 4.6%; pasture 68.1%; agricultural 13.4%; other 13.9%.

Foreign trade[13]

Balance of trade (current prices)

	1988	1989	1990	1991	1992	1993
£Ir '000,000	2,574	2,880	2,458	2,784	4,062	5,563
% of total	11.7%	11.0%	9.4%	10.2%	13.9%	16.5%

Imports (1993): £Ir 14,795,700,000 (machinery and transport equipment 36.9%, chemicals 12.3%, manufactured goods 11.6%, food 8.3%, petroleum and petroleum products 4.8%, crude materials [inedible] 2.2%, beverages and tobacco 1.3%). *Major import sources:* U.K. 33.4%; U.S. 17.1%; Germany 7.2%; Japan 6.5%; France 3.9%; The Netherlands 3.1%.
Exports (1993): £Ir 19,671,000,000 (machinery and transport equipment 28.9%, food 19.6%, chemical products 19.2%, manufactured goods 5.8%). *Major export destinations:* U.K. 24.9%; Germany 13.2%; France 9.1%; U.S. 9.1%.

Transport and communications

Transport. Railroads (1993): route length 1,947 km; passenger-km 1,070,900,000; metric ton-km cargo 574,600,000. Roads (1992): length 92,327 km (paved 94%). Vehicles (1993): passenger cars 891,027; trucks and buses 146,204. Merchant marine (1992): vessels (100 gross tons and over) 189; total deadweight tonnage 208,573. Air transport (1990): passenger-km 3,804,000,000; metric ton-km cargo 431,618,000; airports (1995) 10.
Communications. Daily newspapers (1992): 8; total circulation 652,350; circulation per 1,000 population 186. Radio (1994): 2,150,000 receivers (1 per 1.6 persons). Television (1993): 1,000,000 receivers (1 per 3.5 persons). Telephones (main lines; 1993): 1,170,000 (1 per 3.1 persons).

Education and health

Education (1992–93)[14]

	schools	teachers	students	student/ teacher ratio
Primary (age 6–11)	3,405	20,761	521,531	25.1
Secondary (age 12–18)	467	12,250	221,167	18.1
Voc., teacher tr.	323	7,630	138,022	18.1
Higher	26	4,535	80,322	17.7

Educational attainment (1981). Percentage of population age 25 and over having: primary education 52.3%; secondary 23.3%; some postsecondary 16.5%; university or like institution 7.9%. *Literacy* (1987): virtually 100% literate.
Health (1993): physicians (1984) 5,180 (1 per 681 persons); hospital beds 13,806[15] (1 per 255 persons); infant mortality rate 6.0.
Food (1988–90): daily per capita caloric intake 3,952 (vegetable products 62%, animal products 38%); 157% of FAO recommended minimum requirement.

Military

Total active duty personnel (1994): 13,000 (army 86.1%, navy 7.7%, air force 6.2%). *Military expenditure as percentage of GNP* (1993): 1.3% (world 3.3%); per capita expenditure U.S.$146.

[1]As provided by the constitution; the 1948 Republic of Ireland Act provides precedent for this longer formulation of the official name but, per official sources, "has not changed the usage *Ireland* as the name of the state in the English language." [2]Includes 11 nonelective seats. [3]Includes county borough(s). [4]Detail does not add to total given because of rounding. [5]County boroughs. [6]Metal content of ores. [7]At factor cost. [8]Trade includes Finance. [9]Unemployed. [10]1988. [11]1991. [12]First quarter. [13]Import figures are f.o.b. in balance of trade and c.i.f. for commodities and trading partners. [14]National schools only. [15]Acute-care public hospitals only.

Israel

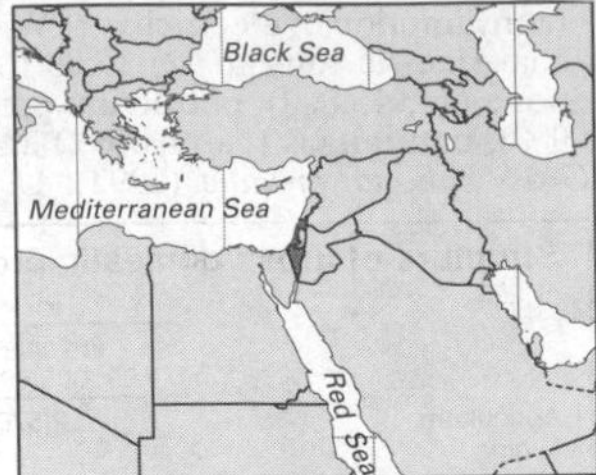

Official name: Medinat Yisra'el (Hebrew); Isrā'īl (Arabic) (State of Israel).
Form of government: multiparty republic with one legislative house (Knesset [120]).
Chief of state: President.
Head of government: Prime Minister.
Capital: Jerusalem is the proclaimed capital of Israel (since Jan. 23, 1950) and the actual seat of government, but recognition of its status as capital by the international community has largely been withheld pending final settlement of territorial and other issues through peace talks between Israel and the Arab parties concerned.
Official languages: Hebrew; Arabic.
Official religion: none.
Monetary unit: 1 New (Israeli) sheqel (NIS) = 100 agorot; valuation (Oct. 6, 1995) 1 U.S.$ = NIS 3.01; 1 £ = NIS 4.76.

Area and population

		area[1]		population
				1994[2]
Districts	Capitals	sq mi	sq km	estimate
Central (Ha Merkaz)	Ramla	479	1,242	1,138,200
Haifa (Ḥefa)	Haifa	330	854	705,200
Jerusalem (Yerushalayim)	Jerusalem	215	557	630,400
Northern (Ha Ẓafon)	Tiberias	1,347	3,490	901,600
Southern (Ha Darom)	Beersheba	5,439	14,087	695,200
Tel Aviv	Tel Aviv–Yafo	66	170	1,140,700
TOTAL		7,876	20,400	5,211,300[3, 4]

Demography

Population (1995): 5,386,000[3, 5].
Density (1995)[5, 6]: persons per sq mi 673.9, persons per sq km 260.2.
Urban-rural (1994)[2]: urban 90.5%; rural 9.5%.
Sex distribution (1993): male 49.6%; female 50.4%.
Age breakdown (1993): under 15, 30.0%; 15–29, 25.0%; 30–44, 20.0%; 45–59, 12.3%; 60–74, 8.9%; 75 and over, 3.8%.
Population projection: (2000) 5,881,000; (2010) 6,713,000.
Doubling time: 44 years.
Ethnic composition (1994): Jewish 81.4%; Arab and other 18.6%.
Religious affiliation (1994): Jewish 81.4%; Muslim (mostly Sunnī) 13.9%; Christian 2.7%; Druze and other 2.0%.
Major cities (1991): Jerusalem 567,100; Tel Aviv–Yafo 357,400; Haifa 246,500; Ḥolon 162,800; Petah Tiqwa 151,100; Bat Yam 143,200.

Vital statistics

Birth rate per 1,000 population (1994): 21.2 (world avg. 25.0); (1990)[7] legitimate 98.5%; illegitimate 1.5%.
Death rate per 1,000 population (1994): 6.2 (world avg. 9.3).
Natural increase rate per 1,000 population (1994): 15.0 (world avg. 15.7).
Total fertility rate (avg. births per childbearing woman; 1993): 2.9.
Marriage rate per 1,000 population (1994): 6.4.
Divorce rate per 1,000 population (1994): 1.4.
Life expectancy at birth (1992): male 75.1 years; female 78.5 years.
Major causes of death per 100,000 population (1991): diseases of the circulatory system 263.8; malignant neoplasms (cancers) 127.9; diseases of the respiratory system 42.0; accidents 32.9.

National economy

Budget (1994). Revenue: NIS 115,944,000,000 (1993; income tax and property tax 25.2%, value-added tax 18.1%, internal loans 18.0%, external loans 12.8%). Expenditures: NIS 118,101,000,000 (1993; defense 17.5%, debt 16.4%, interest on loans 13.2%, labour and social welfare 10.2%, education and culture 8.8%).
Public debt (1992): U.S.$54,742,000,000.
Production (metric tons except as noted). Agriculture, forestry, fishing (1994): grapefruit 370,000, tomatoes 365,000, potatoes 235,000, wheat 145,000, watermelons 125,000, seed cotton 90,000; livestock (number of live animals) 362,000 cattle, 330,000 sheep, 100,000 goats, 23,000,000 chickens; roundwood (1993) 113,000 cu m; fish catch (1993) 18,661. Mining and quarrying (1993): phosphate rock 5,787,000; potash 1,309,000; lime 210,000; bromine 130,000; bromine compounds 121,000. Manufacturing (1993): cement 3,500,000; polyethylene 144,147; sulfuric acid 130,000; paper 95,872; cardboard 95,108; chlorine 35,241; ammonium sulfate 11,817; wine 12,733,000 litres. Construction (1993): residential 3,696,000 sq m; nonresidential 1,872,000 sq m. Energy production (consumption): electricity (kW-hr; 1994) 28,300,000 (28,300,000); coal (metric tons; 1993) none (5,180,000); crude petroleum (barrels; 1993) 55,800 (74,825,000); petroleum products (metric tons; 1992) 8,958,000 (8,178,000); natural gas (cu m; 1993) 23,920,000 (23,920,000).
Land use (1993): forested 6.0%; meadows and pastures 6.9%; agricultural and under permanent cultivation 20.7%; other 66.4%.
Population economically active (1994)[8]: total 2,019,200; activity rate of total population 37.1% (participation rates: over age 15, 53.6%; female 42.8%; unemployed 7.8%).

Price and earnings indexes (1990 = 100)

	1988	1989	1990	1991	1992	1993	1994
Consumer price index	71	85	100	119	133	138	149
Monthly earnings index	70	85	100	116	130	148	166

Tourism (1993): receipts from visitors U.S.$2,110,000,000; expenditures by nationals abroad U.S.$2,313,000,000.
Gross national product (1993): U.S.$72,667,000,000 (U.S.$13,760 per capita).

Structure of gross domestic product and labour force

	1991		1994	
	in value NIS '000,000	% of total value	labour force	% of labour force
Agriculture	2,398	2.3	62,100	3.1
Manufacturing, mining	21,488	20.9	396,200	19.6
Construction	7,777	7.6	118,000	5.8
Public utilities	2,299	2.2	20,300	1.0
Transp. and commun.	7,560	7.4	108,900	5.4
Trade	9,665	9.4	280,900	13.9
Finance	24,065	23.4	206,300	10.2
Public and community services	4,110	4.0	524,300	26.0
Services }	23,481	22.8	143,200	7.1
Other }			159,000[9]	7.9[9]
TOTAL	102,843	100.0	2,019,200[8]	100.0[8]

Household income and expenditure (1993). Average household size 3.5; monthly income per household[10] NIS 6,125 (U.S.$2,034); sources of income (1993)[10]: salaries and wages 63.4%, allowances and assistance 18.9%, self-employment 14.6%, other 3.1%; expenditure (1993): housing 19.5%, food, beverages, and tobacco 16.6%, transportation 12.8%, clothing 4.9%, household durable goods 4.5%, energy 2.5%.

Foreign trade

Balance of trade (current prices)

	1989	1990	1991	1992	1993	1994
U.S.$'000,000	−2,358.1	−3,504.0	−5,473.3	−6,135.0	−5,692.1	−6,695.4
% of total	10.0%	13.1%	19.6%	19.8%	16.1%	16.5%

Imports (1994): U.S.$23,701,100,000 (investment goods 17.9%; diamonds 16.6%; consumer goods 13.0%; fuel and lubricants 7.1%). *Major import sources:* U.S. 18.0%; Belgium 12.8%; Germany 10.4%; U.K. 8.7%; Italy 7.8%; Switzerland 6.5%; France 4.5%; Japan 4.1%.
Exports (1994): U.S.$17,005,700 (machinery 30.8%; worked diamonds 22.1%; chemicals 14.4%; textiles 6.2%; food, beverages, and tobacco 5.0%; rubber and plastic 3.2%). *Major export destinations:* U.S. 31.0%; Japan 5.4%; Belgium 5.3%; U.K. 5.0%; Germany 5.0%; Hong Kong 5.0%; The Netherlands 3.7%; France 3.4%; Italy 3.0%.

Transport and communications

Transport. Railroads (1993): route length 356 mi, 573 km; passenger-mi 132,800,000, passenger-km 213,700,000; short ton-mi cargo 734,000,000, metric ton-km cargo 1,072,000,000. Roads (1993): total length 8,620 mi, 13,872 km (paved 100%). Vehicles (1993): passenger cars 978,652; trucks and buses 222,108. Merchant marine (1992): vessels (100 gross tons and over) 58; total deadweight tonnage 723,418. Air transport (1992)[11]: passenger-mi 5,332,000,000, passenger-km 8,581,000,000; short ton-mi cargo 534,832,000, metric ton-km cargo 860,731,000; airports (1995) with scheduled flights 7.
Communications. Daily newspapers (1992): total number 31; total circulation 1,240,000; circulation per 1,000 population 242. Radio (1991): 2,250,000 receivers (1 per 2.2 persons). Television (1991): 1,200,000 receivers (1 per 4.1 persons). Telephones (main lines; 1993): 1,958,100 (1 per 2.7 persons).

Education and health

Education (1993–94)

	schools	teachers	students	student/teacher ratio
Primary (age 6–13)	1,844	52,135	677,404	12.8
Secondary (age 14–17)	838	34,956	341,929	9.8
Vocational	383	19,479	122,721	6.3
Higher	7	6,150[12]	91,480	...

Educational attainment (1991). Percentage of population age 25 and over having: no formal schooling 6.7%; primary education 22.5%; secondary 39.6%; postsecondary, vocational, and higher 31.2%. *Literacy* (1992): total population age 15 and over literate 3,390,027 (94.8%); males literate 1,698,696 (97.1%); females literate 1,692,331 (92.7%).
Health (1993): physicians (1987) 11,895 (1 per 345 persons); hospital beds 31,992 (1 per 177 persons); infant mortality rate per 1,000 live births 7.5.
Food (1992): daily per capita caloric intake 3,050 (vegetable products 80%, animal products 20%); 119% of FAO recommended minimum.

Military

Total active duty personnel (1995): 172,000 (army 77.9%, navy 3.5%, air force 18.6%). *Military expenditure as percentage of GNP* (1993): 9.4% (world 3.3%); per capita expenditure U.S.$1,226.

[1]Excluding West Bank (2,270 sq mi [5,879 sq km]), Gaza Strip (146 sq mi [378 sq km]), Golan Heights (444 sq mi [1,150 sq km]), and East Jerusalem (27 sq mi [70 sq km]). [2]January 1. [3]Includes population of Golan Heights (29,000) and East Jerusalem. [4]Excludes Israelis in Jewish localities (pop. 116,300) in the West Bank and Gaza Strip. [5]Includes Israelis in Jewish localities in the West Bank and Gaza Strip. [6]Includes area and population of East Jerusalem and Golan Heights. [7]Jewish population only. [8]Excludes armed forces; includes Israelis in occupied territories. [9]Mostly unemployed. [10]Urban population only. [11]El Al only. [12]1991–92.

Italy

Official name: Repubblica Italiana (Italian Republic).
Form of government: republic with two legislative houses (Senate [326[1]]; Chamber of Deputies [630]).
Chief of state: President.
Head of government: Prime Minister.
Capital: Rome.
Official language: Italian.
Official religion: none.
Monetary unit: 1 lira (Lit, plural lire) = 100 centesimi; valuation (Oct. 6, 1995) 1 U.S.$ = Lit 1,617; 1 £ = Lit 2,557.

Area and population

Regions / Provinces[3]	Capitals	area sq mi	area sq km	population 1993[2] estimate[4]
Abruzzi	L'Aquila	4,168	10,794	1,255,549
Chieti	Chieti	999	2,587	384,364
L'Aquila	L'Aquila	1,944	5,034	298,786
Pescara	Pescara	473	1,225	290,585
Teramo	Teramo	752	1,948	281,814
Basilicata	Potenza	3,858	9,992	610,821
Matera	Matera	1,331	3,447	208,934
Potenza	Potenza	2,527	6,545	401,887
Calabria	Catanzaro	5,823	15,080	2,074,763
Catanzaro	Catanzaro	924	2,392	743,717[5]
Cosenza	Cosenza	2,568	6,650	753,159
Crotone	Crotone	662	1,716	[5]
Reggio di Calabria	Reggio di Calabria	1,229	3,183	577,887
Vibo Valentia	Vibo Valentia	440	1,139	[5]
Campania	Naples	5,249	13,595	5,668,895
Avellino	Avellino	1,078	2,792	441,632
Benevento	Benevento	800	2,071	293,600
Caserta	Caserta	1,019	2,639	823,646
Napoli	Naples	452	1,171	3,037,837
Salerno	Salerno	1,900	4,922	1,072,180
Emilia-Romagna	Bologna	8,542	22,123	3,920,223
Bologna	Bologna	1,429	3,702	908,926
Ferrara	Ferrara	1,016	2,632	359,079
Forlì	Forlì	969	2,510	611,548[6]
Modena	Modena	1,039	2,690	606,828
Parma	Parma	1,332	3,449	392,232
Piacenza	Piacenza	1,000	2,589	268,209
Ravenna	Ravenna	718	1,859	350,282
Reggio nell'Emilia	Reggio nell'Emilia	885	2,292	423,119
Rimini	Rimini	154	400	[6]
Friuli-Venezia Giulia	Trieste	3,029	7,845	1,195,055
Gorizia	Gorizia	180	467	138,120
Pordenone	Pordenone	878	2,273	275,660
Trieste	Trieste	82	212	259,172
Udine	Udine	1,889	4,893	522,104
Lazio	Rome	6,642	17,203	5,102,073
Frosinone	Frosinone	1,251	3,239	482,327
Latina	Latina	869	2,251	481,178
Rieti	Rieti	1,061	2,749	147,167
Roma	Rome	2,066	5,352	3,770,157
Viterbo	Viterbo	1,395	3,612	281,244
Liguria	Genoa	2,092	5,418	1,668,896
Genova	Genoa	709	1,836	940,470
Imperia	Imperia	446	1,155	216,788
La Spezia	La Spezia	341	882	226,450
Savona	Savona	596	1,545	285,182
Lombardia	Milan	9,211	23,857	8,882,408
Bergamo	Bergamo	1,051	2,722	939,870[7]
Brescia	Brescia	1,846	4,782	1,050,405
Como	Como	497	1,288	800,770[7]
Cremona	Cremona	684	1,771	328,867
Lecco	Lecco	315	816	[7]
Lodi	Lodi	302	783	[8]
Mantova	Mantova	903	2,339	369,410
Milano	Milan	765	1,980	3,926,161[8]
Pavia	Pavia	1,145	2,965	490,619
Sondrio	Sondrio	1,240	3,212	176,015
Varese	Varese	463	1,199	800,291
Marche	Ancona	3,743	9,693	1,433,994
Ancona	Ancona	749	1,940	438,138
Ascoli Piceno	Ascoli Piceno	806	2,087	363,127
Macerata	Macerata	1,071	2,774	296,250
Pesaro e Urbino	Pesaro	1,117	2,892	336,479
Molise	Campobasso	1,713	4,438	331,494
Campobasso	Campobasso	1,123	2,909	239,473
Isernia	Isernia	590	1,529	92,021
Piemonte	Turin	9,807[9]	25,399	4,303,830
Alessandria	Alessandria	1,375	3,560	437,476
Asti	Asti	583	1,511	208,376
Biella	Biella	352	913	[10]
Cuneo	Cuneo	2,665	6,903	548,354
Novara	Novara	530	1,373	498,673[11]
Torino	Turin	2,637	6,830	2,236,422
Verbano-Cusio-Ossola	Verbania	858	2,221	[11]
Vercelli	Vercelli	806	2,088	374,529[10]
Puglia	Bari	7,470	19,348	4,049,972
Bari	Bari	1,980	5,129	1,540,319
Brindisi	Brindisi	710	1,838	412,619
Foggia	Foggia	2,774	7,185	697,321
Lecce	Lecce	1,065	2,759	809,261
Taranto	Taranto	941	2,437	590,452
Sardegna	Cagliari	9,301	24,090	1,651,902
Cagliari	Cagliari	2,662	6,895	764,907
Nuoro	Nuoro	2,720	7,044	273,105
Oristano	Oristano	1,016	2,631	157,344
Sassari	Sassari	2,903	7,520	456,546
Sicilia (Sicily)	Palermo	9,926	25,709	4,997,705
Agrigento	Agrigento	1,175	3,042	478,352
Caltanissetta	Caltanissetta	822	2,128	278,696
Catania	Catania	1,371	3,552	1,045,545
Enna	Enna	989	2,562	186,597
Messina	Messina	1,254	3,248	651,465
Palermo	Palermo	1,927	4,992	1,231,733
Ragusa	Ragusa	623	1,614	291,617
Siracusa	Siracusa	814	2,109	404,667
Trapani	Trapani	951	2,462	429,033
Toscana	Florence	8,877	22,992[9]	3,528,735
Arezzo	Arezzo	1,248	3,232	314,907
Firenze	Florence	1,365	3,536	1,180,689[12]
Grosseto	Grosseto	1,739	4,504	217,769
Livorno	Livorno	468	1,213	337,176
Lucca	Lucca	684	1,773	376,875
Massa-Carrara	Massa-Carrara	447	1,157	200,079
Pisa	Pisa	945	2,448	385,061
Pistoia	Pistoia	373	965	265,191
Prato	Prato	133	344	[12]
Siena	Siena	1,475	3,821	250,988
Trentino-Alto Adige	Bolzano	5,258	13,618	896,722
Bolzano-Bozen	Bolzano	2,857	7,400	444,243
Trento	Trento	2,401	6,218	452,479
Umbria	Perugia	3,265	8,456	814,796
Perugia	Perugia	2,446	6,334	591,811
Terni	Terni	819	2,122	222,985
Valle d'Aosta	Aosta	1,259	3,262	117,204
Veneto	Venice	7,090	18,364	4,395,263
Belluno	Belluno	1,420	3,678	212,033
Padova	Padova	827	2,142	823,890
Rovigo	Rovigo	691	1,789	247,322
Treviso	Treviso	956	2,477	747,960
Venezia	Venice	950	2,460	819,530
Verona	Verona	1,195	3,096	791,977
Vicenza	Vicenza	1,051	2,722	752,551
TOTAL		116,324[13]	301,277[13]	56,960,300

Demography

Population (1995): 57,386,000.
Density (1995): persons per sq mi 493.3, persons per sq km 190.5.
Urban-rural (1993[2]): urban 66.9%; rural 33.1%.
Sex distribution (1991): male 48.61%; female 51.39%.
Age breakdown (1991): under 15, 16.4%; 15–29, 23.9%; 30–44, 20.9%; 45–59, 18.2%; 60–74, 14.1%; 75 and over, 6.5%.
Population projection: (2000) 57,453,000; (2010) 56,180,000.
Doubling time: not applicable; population stable.
Ethnolinguistic composition (1983): Italian 94.1%; Sardinian 2.7%; Rhaetian 1.3%; other 1.9%.
Religious affiliation (1980): Roman Catholic 83.2%; nonreligious 13.6%; atheist 2.6%; other 0.6%.
Major cities (1993[2, 4]): Rome 2,723,327; Milan 1,358,627; Naples 1,071,744; Turin 952,736; Palermo 696,735; Genoa 667,563; Bologna 401,308; Florence 397,434; Bari 342,129; Catania 329,898; Venice 305,617.
National origin (1980): Italian 98.8%; foreign-born 1.2%, of which Austrian 0.4%, French 0.2%, Slovene 0.2%, Albanian 0.1%, other 0.3%.
Mobility (1981). Population living in the same residence as in 1976: 92.4%.
Households. Average household size (1991) 2.8; composition of households: 1 person 20.6%, 2 persons 24.7%, 3 persons 22.2%, 4 persons 21.2%, 5 or more persons 11.3%. Family households (1983): 15,205,000 (85.3%); nonfamily 2,617,000 (14.7%), of which 1-person 13.0%.
Immigration (1991): immigrants admitted 126,935, from Europe 42.0%, of which EC countries 18.4%; Africa 25.3%; Western Hemisphere 20.7%; Asia 11.1%.

Vital statistics

Birth rate per 1,000 population (1994): 9.3 (world avg. 25.0); (1992) legitimate 93.3%; illegitimate 6.7%.
Death rate per 1,000 population (1994): 9.5 (world avg. 9.3).
Natural increase rate per 1,000 population (1994): −0.2 (world avg. 15.7).
Total fertility rate (avg. births per childbearing woman; 1992): 1.3.
Marriage rate per 1,000 population (1993): 5.1.
Divorce rate per 1,000 population: (1992): 0.5.
Life expectancy at birth (1990): male 73.6 years; female 80.2 years.
Major causes of death per 100,000 population (1991): diseases of the circulatory system 425.3; malignant neoplasms (cancers) 260.6; diseases of the respiratory system 59.6; accidents and violence 53.2; diseases of the digestive system 50.1.

Social indicators

Educational attainment (1989–90). Percentage of population age 14 and over having: no formal schooling 9.1%; primary education 60.7%; lower secondary 6.5%; upper secondary 18.8%; higher 4.9%.
Quality of working life. Average workweek (1985): 36.6 hours. Annual rate per 100,000 workers (1988) for: injury or accident 3,697; industrial illness 405[14]; death 5.7. Percentage of labour force insured for damages or income loss (1992) resulting from: injury 100%; permanent disability 100%; death 100%. Number of working days lost to labour stoppages per 1,000 workers (1993): 389. Average duration of journey to work: n.a. Rate per 1,000 workers of discouraged (unemployed no longer seeking work; 1990): 1.1.
Material well-being. Rate per 1,000 of population possessing (1991): telephone 579; automobile 494; television 299 (colour[15] 188).
Social participation. Eligible voters participating in last national election (1994): 73.0%. Trade union membership in total workforce (1990): *c.* 28%.
Social deviance (1993). Offense rate per 100,000 population for: murder 2.5; rape 3.0; assault 203.3; theft, including burglary and housebreaking 2,918.
Access to services (1981). Proportion of dwellings having access to: electricity 99.5%; safe water supply 98.7%; toilet facilities 98.5%; bath facilities 86.4%.
Leisure (1992). Favourite leisure activities (as percentage of household spending on culture): sporting events 17.8%; cinema 16.3%; theatre 14.0%.

National economy

Gross national product (1993): U.S.$1,134,800,000,000 (U.S.$19,620 per capita).

Structure of gross domestic product and labour force

	1993			
	in value (Lit '000,000,000)	% of total value	labour force	% of labour force
Agriculture	45,459	2.9	1,984,100	8.8
Mining	314,939	20.2	457,300	2.0
Manufacturing			4,162,100	18.4
Construction	86,824	5.6	1,664,500	7.4
Public utilities	89,086	5.7	184,400	0.8
Transp. and commun.	98,649	6.3	1,456,500	6.4
Trade	284,534	18.2	4,915,000	21.7
Finance	210,883	13.5	439,600	1.9
Pub. admin., defense	200,201	12.8	3,649,500	16.1
Services	215,499	13.8	3,708,800	16.4
Other	14,040[16]	0.9[16]	...	...
TOTAL	1,560,114	100.0[9]	22,621,800	100.0[9]

Budget (1993). Revenue: Lit 430,573,000,000,000 (income taxes 43.4%, of which individual 34.3%, corporate 5.3%; value-added and excise taxes 31.3%). Expenditures: Lit 634,690,000,000,000 (1992; social security and welfare 24.4%; debt service 23.7%; education and culture 9.9%; transportation 5.4%; defense 3.1%).

Public debt (1993): U.S.$1,038,200,000,000.

Tourism (1993): receipts U.S.$20,521,000,000; expenditures U.S.$13,053,000,000.

Manufacturing, mining, and construction enterprises (1991)

	no. of enterprises[17]	no. of employees[18]	hourly wages as a % of avg. of all wages[19]	annual value added (Lit '000,000,000)
Manufacturing				
Electrical machinery	2,300	340,057	112.1	24,343
Machinery (nonelectrical)	4,017	357,654	98.0	23,939
Industrial chemicals	1,076	193,527	119.7	17,947
Transport equipment	932	316,404	117.7	16,745
Printing, publishing[20]	1,749	148,807	103.2	12,837
Textiles	2,964	229,829	84.4	12,549
Pottery, ceramics, and glass	2,054	161,592	...	12,089
Wearing apparel	4,808	254,781	75.0	10,794
Iron and steel[21]	1,027	151,000	122.6	10,706
Food products	1,404	122,784	92.2	9,187
Rubber and plastic products	1,753	138,054	84.4	8,969
Metal products	535	118,578	86.7	7,509
Paper and paper products[20]	...	...	...	...
Petroleum and gas	16	7,781	136.6	2,843
Mining and quarrying	343[21]	18,000[21]	...	931
Construction	326,000[22]	1,849,000[23]	...	53,465[23]

Production (metric tons except as noted). Agriculture, forestry, fishing (1994): sugar beets 12,400,000, grapes 9,372,000, wheat 7,805,000, corn (maize) 7,661,000, tomatoes 5,295,000, olives 2,779,000, apples 2,103,000, potatoes 1,967,000, peaches and nectarines 1,679,000, barley 1,507,000, pears 946,000, soybeans 740,000; livestock (number of live animals) 10,370,000 sheep, 8,200,000 pigs, 7,683,000 cattle, 137,000,000 chickens; roundwood (1993) 9,860,000 cu m; fish catch (1993) 552,024. Mining and quarrying (1993): rock salt 3,021,427; feldspar 1,534,421; potash 1,438,850; zinc 62,558; barite 51,097; lead 23,160[24]. Manufacturing (1993): cement 33,770,601; crude steel 25,352,672; pig iron 11,188,311; plastics 3,212,363; sulfuric acid 2,287,762; caustic soda 934,157; textiles 423,850; wine 62,618,000 hectolitres; beer 10,488,900 hectolitres[24]; olive oil 6,290,000 hectolitres; 5,132,500 washing machines[24]; 4,010,600 refrigerators[24]; 2,051,556 motorized road vehicles, of which 1,115,782 automobiles, 745,194 motorcycles, scooters, and mopeds, 150,580 trucks and buses; 2,434,484 televisions[25], of which 2,433,067 colour[25]. Construction (1992): residential 95,781,826 cu m; commercial, industrial, and other 88,078,352 cu m.

Service enterprises (1993)

	no. of enterprises[19]	no. of employees[26]	hourly wage as a % of all wages	annual value added (Lit '000,000,000)
Public utilities	1,398	230,000[15]	...	89,086
Transportation, Communications	132,164	1,146,000	...	98,649
Finance	89,092	895,000	...	210,883
Wholesale and retail trade	1,495,702	4,537,000	...	284,534
Pub. admin., services	...	5,986,000	...	200,201

Energy production (consumption): electricity (kW-hr; 1992) 226,243,000,000 (261,543,000,000); coal (metric tons; 1992) 825,000 (18,389,000); crude petroleum (barrels; 1992) 30,694,000 (598,165,000); petroleum products (metric tons; 1992) 85,102,000 (92,982,000); natural gas (cu m; 1992) 17,996,000,000 (50,216,000,000).

Population economically active (1993): total 22,621,800; activity rate of total population 40.6% (participation rates: ages 14–64, 59.3%[26]; female 37.0%; unemployed 10.4%).

Price and earnings indexes (1990 = 100)

	1988	1989	1990	1990	1992	1993	1994
Consumer price index	88.4	93.9	100.0	106.3	111.8	116.8	121.5
Earnings index	87.9	93.2	100.0	109.8	115.4	119.8	...

Household income and expenditure (1992). Average household size 2.7; average annual income per household (1984) Lit 19,692,000 (U.S.$11,208); sources of income (1991): salaries and wages 41.7%, property income and self-employment 38.0%, transfer payments 20.3%; expenditure: food and beverages 20.5%, housing 13.8%, transportation and communications 13.2%, recreation and education 9.1%.

Financial aggregates

	1990	1991	1992	1993	1994	1995[27]
Exchange rate, Lit per:						
U.S. dollar	1,198.1	1,240.6	1,232.4	1,573.7	1,612.4	1,609.7
£	2,138.1	2,195.1	2,175.8	2,363.7	2,469.6	2,567.0
SDR	1,607.8	1,646.5	2,022.4	2,340.5	2,379.2	2,471.1
International reserves (U.S.$)						
Total (excl. gold; '000,000)	62,927	48,679	27,643	27,545	32,265	37,783
SDRs ('000,000)	1,037	930	238	241	125	92
Reserve pos. in IMF ('000,000)	1,714	2,255	2,439	2,164	2,033	2,089
Foreign exchange ('000,000)	60,176	45,495	24,966	25,140	30,107	35,602
Gold ('000,000 fine troy oz)	66.67	66.67	66.67	66.67	66.67	66.67
% world reserves	7.1	7.1	7.1	7.3	7.3	7.3
Interest and prices						
Central bank discount (%)	12.50	12.00	12.00	8.00	7.50	9.00[28]
Govt. bond yield (%)	11.87	11.37	13.67	11.21	10.57	12.06[28]
Industrial share prices (1990 = 100)	100.0	84.7	70.5	83.5	104.1	99.1[28]
Balance of payments (U.S.$'000,000)						
Balance of visible trade	724	−895	3,088	32,825	35,497	...
Imports, f.o.b.	−169,216	−169,701	−175,067	−136,328	−154,308	...
Exports, f.o.b.	169,940	168,806	178,155	169,153	189,805	...
Balance of invisibles	−14,946	−20,556	−31,082	−21,763	−19,875	...
Balance of payments, current account	−14,222	−21,451	−27,994	11,062	15,622	...

Land use (1993): forested 23.0%; meadows and pastures 14.6%; agricultural and under permanent cultivation 40.3%; other 22.1%.

Foreign trade

Balance of trade (current prices)

	1988	1989	1990	1991	1992	1993
Lit '000,000,000	−1,012	−3,358	+724	−1,913	2,229	50,789
% of total	0.3%	0.8%	0.2%	0.4%	0.5%	10.6%

Imports (1993): Lit 232,187,445,000,000 (machinery and transport equipment 30.3%, of which transport equipment 11.7%, precision machinery 6.1%; chemicals 16.2%; metal and semiprocessed metal 8.1%; food and live animals 6.9%; crude petroleum 6.0%; textiles 3.9%). *Major import sources:* Germany 19.4%; France 13.6%; U.K. 5.8%; The Netherlands 5.7%; U.S. 5.3%; Switzerland 5.1%.

Exports (1993): Lit 265,092,306,000,000 (machinery and transport equipment 41.0%, of which transport equipment 10.3%, electrical machinery 4.9%, precision machinery 4.0%; chemicals 10.4%; textiles 8.5%; wearing apparel 7.5%, of which shoes 3.5%; metal and processed metal 7.0%). *Major export destinations:* Germany 19.5%; France 13.1%; U.S. 7.8%; U.K. 6.4%.

Transport and communications

Transport. Railroads (1992): length 12,176 mi, 19,595 km; passenger-mi 30,050,000,000, passenger-km 48,361,000,000; short ton-mi cargo 15,091,000,000, metric ton-km cargo 22,033,000,000. Roads (1991): total length 188,597 mi, 303,518 km (paved 100%). Vehicles (1991): passenger cars 28,200,000; trucks and buses 2,521,000. Merchant marine (1992): vessels (100 gross tons and over) 1,636; total deadweight tonnage 10,940,065. Air transport (1993): passenger-mi 18,429,000,000, passenger-km 29,658,600,000; short ton-mi cargo 914,300,000, metric ton-km cargo 1,334,900,000; airports (1995) 32.

Communications. Daily newspapers (1993): total number 111; total circulation 9,048,700; circulation per 1,000 population 157. Radio (1994): 45,350,000 receivers (1 per 1.3 persons). Television (1994): 17,000,500 receivers (1 per 3.4 persons). Telephones (1992[2]): 32,945,122 (1 per 1.7 persons).

Education and health

Education (1993–94)

	schools	teachers	students	student/teacher ratio
Primary (age 6–10)	21,378	172,777	2,863,003	16.6
Secondary (age 11–18)	9,721	101,800	1,996,677	19.6
Voc., teacher tr.	7,774	129,821	2,718,958	20.9
Higher[29, 30]	50	56,723	1,538,606	27.1

Literacy (1990): total population age 15 and over literate 47,507,000 (97.1%); males literate 22,832,000 (97.8%); females literate 24,675,000 (96.4%).

Health (1992): physicians 296,385 (1 per 193 persons); hospital beds 389,432 (1 per 147 persons); infant mortality rate per 1,000 live births (1994) 6.7.

Food (1992): daily per capita caloric intake 3,561 (vegetable products 75%, animal products 25%); 141% of FAO recommended minimum requirement.

Military

Total active duty personnel (1994): 322,300 (army 63.6%, navy 13.7%, air force 22.7%). *Military expenditure as percentage of GNP* (1991): 2.1% (world 4.2%); per capita expenditure U.S.$421.

[1]Includes 11 nonelective seats. [2]January 1. [3]Six provinces were created in 1992. [4]Resident population only. [5]Catanzaro includes Crotone and Vibo Valentia. [6]Forlì includes Rimini. [7]Lecco is included partly in Bergamo and partly in Como. [8]Milano includes Lodi. [9]Detail does not add to total given because of rounding. [10]Vercelli includes Biella. [11]Novara includes Verbano-Cusio-Ossola. [12]Firenze includes Prato. [13]The total area for Italy, per the latest survey, is 301,309 sq km (116,336 sq mi). [14]1978. [15]1988. [16]Imputed bank charges less duties on imports. [17]Enterprises with 20 or more persons engaged. [18]Total number of persons engaged. [19]1981. [20]Printing, publishing includes Paper products. [21]1989. [22]All enterprises (1982). [23]1987. [24]1992. [25]1991. [26]1990. [27]July. [28]May. [29]Universities only. [30]1992–93.

Jamaica

Official name: Jamaica.
Form of government: constitutional monarchy with two legislative houses (Senate [21]; House of Representatives [60]).
Chief of state: British Monarch represented by governor-general.
Head of government: Prime Minister.
Capital: Kingston.
Official language: English.
Official religion: none.
Monetary unit: 1 Jamaica dollar (J$) = 100 cents; valuation (Oct. 6, 1995) 1 U.S.$ = J$35.75; 1 £ = J$56.52.

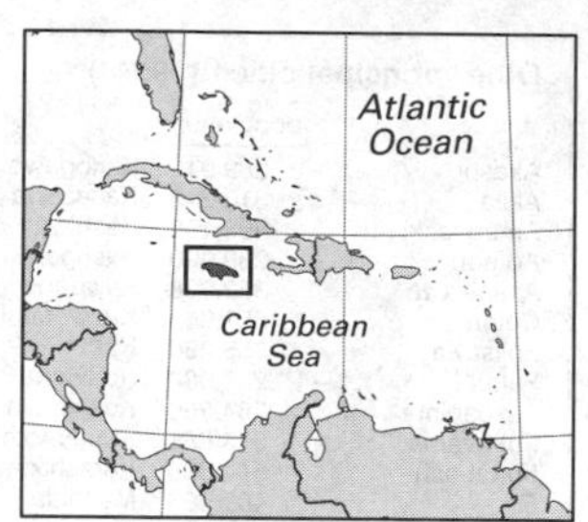

Area and population

Parishes	Capitals	area sq mi	area sq km	population 1994[1] estimate
Clarendon	May Pen	462	1,196	222,500
Hanover	Lucea	174	450	66,600
Kingston	[2]	8	22	[3]
Manchester	Mandeville	321	830	173,100
Portland	Port Antonio	314	814	78,500
Saint Andrew	[2]	166	431	697,000
Saint Ann	Saint Ann's Bay	468	1,213	154,500
Saint Catherine	Spanish Town	460	1,192	370,600
Saint Elizabeth	Black River	468	1,212	146,600
Saint James	Montego Bay	230	595	166,000
Saint Mary	Port Maria	236	611	113,700
Saint Thomas	Morant Bay	287	743	88,900
Trelawny	Falmouth	338	875	74,100
Westmoreland	Savanna-la-Mar	312	807	130,500
TOTAL		4,244	10,991	2,482,600

Demography

Population (1995): 2,520,000.
Density (1995): persons per sq mi 593.8, persons per sq km 229.3.
Urban-rural (1991): urban 50.2%; rural 49.8%.
Sex distribution (1994): male 49.96%; female 50.04%.
Age breakdown (1994): under 15, 31.6%; 15–29, 29.8%; 30–44, 18.7%; 45–59, 9.7%; 60 and over, 10.2%.
Population projection: (2000) 2,619,000; (2010) 2,925,000.
Doubling time: 38 years.
Ethnic composition (1982): black 74.7%; mixed black 12.8%; East Indian 1.3%; other 11.2%, of which not stated 9.5%.
Religious affiliation (1982): Protestant 55.9%, of which Church of God 18.4%, Baptist 10.0%, Anglican 7.1%, Seventh-day Adventist 6.9%, Pentecostal 5.2%; Roman Catholic 5.0%; nonreligious or atheist 17.7%; not stated 11.2%; other 10.2%, of which Rastafarian c. 5.0%.
Major cities (1991): Kingston 103,771[4] (metropolitan area 587,798); Spanish Town 92,383; Portmore 90,138; Montego Bay 83,446; May Pen 46,785.

Vital statistics

Birth rate per 1,000 population (1994): 23.7 (world avg. 25.0); (1987) legitimate 14.9%, illegitimate 85.1%.
Death rate per 1,000 population (1994): 5.4 (world avg. 9.3).
Natural increase rate per 1,000 population (1994): 18.3 (world avg. 15.7).
Total fertility rate (avg. births per childbearing woman; 1992): 2.6.
Marriage rate per 1,000 population (1993): 6.6.
Divorce rate per 1,000 population (1993): 0.6.
Life expectancy at birth (1990–95): male 71.4 years; female 75.8 years.
Major causes of death per 100,000 population (1991): diseases of the circulatory system 189.4; malignant neoplasms (cancers) 84.1; endocrine and metabolic disorders 51.3; diseases of the respiratory system 30.1.

National economy

Budget (1994–95). Revenue J$43,636,000,000 (tax revenue 87.1%, of which income taxes 32.0%, consumption taxes 30.9%, stamp duties 4.7%; nontax revenue 12.9%). Expenditures: J$68,384,000,000 (current expenditure 56.6%, of which debt interest 22.7%).
Production (metric tons except as noted). Agriculture, forestry, fishing (1994): sugarcane 2,450,000, yams 233,907, vegetables 171,821, bananas 78,577, citrus fruits 52,634, plantains 35,372, legumes 11,512, coffee 10,035, cacao beans 6,150, pimientos 1,500; livestock (number of live animals; 1993) 440,000 goats, 330,000 cattle, 180,000 pigs; roundwood (1992) 169,000 cu m; fish catch (1992) 10,717. Mining and quarrying (1994): crude bauxite 3,628,800; alumina 3,221,200; gypsum 203,700. Manufacturing (1994): sugar 223,041; flour 147,793; molasses 94,485; beer and stout 709,660 hectolitres; rum 210,730 hectolitres; cigarettes 1,273,260,000 units. Construction (1992): residential units completed 7,820[5]; factory space completed 6,989 sq m[6]. Energy production (consumption): electricity (kW-hr; 1992) 2,735,000,000 (2,735,000,000); coal, none (none); crude petroleum (barrels; 1992) none (8,708,000); petroleum products (metric tons; 1992) 1,206,000 (1,028,000); natural gas, none (none).
Household income and expenditure. Average household size (1991) 4.2; average annual income per household (1988) J$8,356 (U.S.$1,525); sources of income (1989): wages and salaries 66.1%, self-employment 19.3%, transfers 14.6%; expenditure (1988)[7]: food and beverages 55.6%, housing 7.9%, fuel and other household supplies 7.4%, health care 7.0%, transportation 6.4%, clothing and footwear 5.1%, household furnishings 2.8%, other 7.8%.
Gross national product (at current market prices; 1993): U.S.$3,927,000,000 (U.S.$1,190 per capita).

Structure of gross domestic product and labour force

	1994 in value J$'000,000	% of total value	labour force	% of labour force
Agriculture	11,912.1	9.7	218,100	20.0
Mining	9,434.7	7.7	6,800	0.6
Manufacturing	24,263.3	19.7	95,100	8.7
Construction	15,554.8	12.6	66,300	6.1
Public utilities	2,839.2	2.3	5,000	0.5
Transp. and commun.	11,300.6	9.2	40,100	3.7
Trade	30,290.4	24.6	195,500	17.9
Pub. admin., defense	4,960.0	4.0		
Finance, real estate	17,668.4	14.4	284,000	26.0
Services	5,769.2	4.7		
Other	−10,946.2[8]	−8.9	179,800[9]	16.5[9]
TOTAL	123,046.5	100.0	1,090,700	100.0

Population economically active (1994): total 1,090,500; activity rate of total population 43.4% (participation rates: ages 14–64 [1990] 71.6%; female 48.0%; unemployed [1993] 15.4%).

Price and earnings indexes (1990 = 100)

	1988	1989	1990	1991	1992	1993	1994[10]
Consumer price index	71.7	82.0	100.0	151.1	267.8	327.0	427.9
Earnings index	...	...	...	...	...	...	...

Public debt (external, outstanding; 1993): U.S.$3,604,000,000.
Tourism: receipts from visitors (1994) U.S.$915,000,000; expenditures by nationals abroad (1993) U.S.$64,000,000.
Land use (1992): forested 17.0%; meadows and pastures 23.7%; agricultural and under permanent cultivation 20.2%; other 39.1%.

Foreign trade[11]

Balance of trade (current prices)

	1989	1990	1991	1992	1993	1994
U.S.$'000,000	−873	−785	−654	−636	−1,121	−957.7
% of total	30.4%	25.3%	22.2%	23.2%	34.9%	20.7%

Imports (1994): U.S.$2,177,200,000 (raw materials 62.6%, of which fuels 15.1%; capital goods 16.6%, of which machinery and apparatus 8.2%; consumer goods 20.8%). *Major import sources* (1993): United States 54.1%; Mexico 5.9%; Japan 5.8%; United Kingdom 4.1%; Venezuela 3.4%; Trinidad and Tobago 3.4%; Netherlands Antilles 3.1%; Canada 3.0%.
Exports (1994): U.S.$1,219,500,000 (alumina 44.1%; bauxite 5.9%; raw sugar 5.6%; bananas 3.7%; rum 1.7%; coffee 1.3%). *Major export destinations* (1993): United States 47.0%; United Kingdom 11.2%; Canada 9.4%; Norway 6.5%; France 4.3%; Ghana 3.6%.

Transport and communications

Transport. Railroads (1991): route length 129 mi, 208 km; passenger-mi 12,127,000[6], passenger-km 19,516,000[6]; short ton-mi cargo 1,700,000, metric ton-km cargo 2,482,000. Roads (1991): total length 10,212 mi, 16,435 km (paved 29%). Vehicles (1992–93): passenger cars 73,015; trucks and buses 30,548. Merchant marine (1992): vessels (100 gross tons and over) 12; total deadweight tonnage 16,207. Air transport (1993)[12]: passenger-mi 934,814,000, passenger-km 1,504,440,000; short ton-mi cargo 107,242,000, metric ton-km cargo 156,570,000; airports (1995) with scheduled flights 4.
Communications. Daily newspapers (1993): total number 3; total circulation 130,400[13], circulation per 1,000 population 53[13]. Radio (1994): 995,000 receivers (1 per 2.5 persons). Television (1994): 484,000 receivers (1 per 5.2 persons). Telephones (main lines; 1993): 255,200 (1 per 9.5 persons).

Education and health

Education (1993–94)[14]

	schools	teachers	students	student/ teacher ratio
Primary (age 6–11)[15]	788[16]	10,417	311,146	29.9
Secondary (age 12–16)	126	7,848	216,285	27.6
Voc., teacher tr.	18	897	15,776	17.6
Higher	15[17]	1,047[18]	23,834	17.9[18]

Educational attainment (1982). Percentage of population age 25 and over having: no formal schooling 3.2%; some primary education 79.8%; some secondary 15.0%; complete secondary and higher 2.0%. *Literacy* (1990): total population age 15 and over literate 1,630,000 (98.4%); males literate 800,000 (98.2%); females literate 830,000 (98.6%).
Health: physicians[19] (1994) 394 (1 per 6,335 persons); hospital beds (1993) 5,023 (1 per 492 persons); infant mortality rate per 1,000 live births (1989) 27.0.
Food (1988–90): daily per capita caloric intake 2,558 (vegetable products 83%, animal products 17%); 114% of FAO recommended minimum requirement.

Military

Total active duty personnel (1994): 3,320 (army 90.4%; coast guard 4.5%; air force 5.1%). *Military expenditure as percentage of GNP* (1993): 1.1% (world 3.3%); per capita expenditure U.S.$16.

[1]January 1. [2]The parishes of Kingston and Saint Andrew are jointly administered from the Half Way Tree section of Saint Andrew. [3]Kingston included with Saint Andrew. [4]City of Kingston is coextensive with Kingston parish. [5]51% public sector. [6]1990. [7]Weights of consumer price index components. [8]Less imputed service charges. [9]Includes 167,400 unemployed. [10]Second quarter. [11]Import figures are c.i.f. [12]Air Jamaica only. [13]Circulation for 2 newspapers only. [14]Public schools only. [15]Includes lower-secondary students at all-age schools. [16]1991–92. [17]1988–89. [18]1987–88. [19]Public health only.

Japan

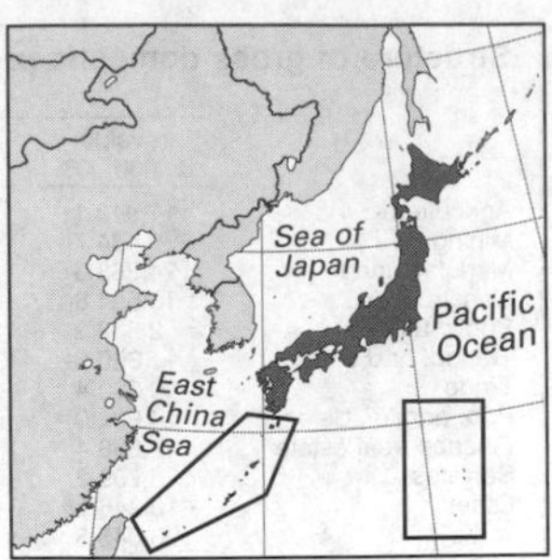

Official name: Nihon (Japan).
Form of government: constitutional monarchy with a National Diet consisting of two legislative houses (House of Councillors [252]; House of Representatives [511]).
Chief of state: Emperor.
Head of government: Prime Minister.
Capital: Tokyo.
Official language: Japanese.
Official religion: none.
Monetary unit: 1 yen (¥) = 100 sen; valuation (Oct. 6, 1995) 1 U.S.$ = ¥100.75; 1 £ = ¥159.27.

Area and population

Regions / Prefectures	Capitals	area sq mi	area sq km	population 1994[1] estimate
Chūbu				
Aichi	Nagoya	1,984	5,139	6,819,000
Fukui	Fukui	1,619	4,192	827,000
Gifu	Gifu	4,091	10,596	2,090,000
Ishikawa	Kanazawa	1,621	4,198	1,173,000
Nagano	Nagano	5,245	13,585	2,177,000
Niigata	Niigata	4,857	12,579	2,482,000
Shizuoka	Shizuoka	3,001	7,773	3,723,000
Toyama	Toyama	1,642	4,252	1,122,000
Yamanashi	Kōfu	1,723	4,463	869,000
Chūgoku				
Hiroshima	Hiroshima	3,269	8,467	2,876,000
Okayama	Okayama	2,738	7,092	1,939,000
Shimane	Matsue	2,559[2]	6,629[2]	770,000
Tottori	Tottori	1,349[2]	3,494[2]	615,000
Yamaguchi	Yamaguchi	2,358	6,107	1,560,000
Hokkaidō				
Hokkaidō (Territory)	Sapporo	32,247	83,520	5,677,000
Kantō				
Chiba	Chiba	1,989	5,151	5,754,000
Gumma	Maebashi	2,454	6,356	1,993,000
Ibaraki	Mito	2,353	6,094	2,935,000
Kanagawa	Yokohama	928	2,403	8,184,000
Saitama	Urawa	1,467	3,799	6,692,000
Tochigi	Utsunomiya	2,476	6,414	1,973,000
Kinki				
Hyōgo	Kōbe	3,236	8,381	5,514,000
Mie	Tsu	2,231	5,778	1,827,000
Nara	Nara	1,425	3,692	1,422,000
Shiga	Ōtsu	1,551	4,016	1,269,000
Wakayama	Wakayama	1,824	4,725	1,082,000
Kyūshū				
Fukuoka	Fukuoka	1,916	4,963	4,896,000
Kagoshima	Kagoshima	3,539	9,167	1,787,000
Kumamoto	Kumamoto	2,860	7,408	1,851,000
Miyazaki	Miyazaki	2,986	7,735	1,173,000
Nagasaki	Nagasaki	1,588	4,113	1,549,000
Ōita	Ōita	2,447	6,338	1,232,000
Saga	Saga	942	2,440	880,000
Ryukyu				
Okinawa	Naha	871	2,255	1,259,000
Shikoku				
Ehime	Matsuyama	2,190	5,672	1,508,000
Kagawa	Takamatsu	727	1,883	1,026,000
Kōchi	Kōchi	2,744	7,107	814,000
Tokushima	Tokushima	1,601	4,146	829,000
Tohoku				
Akita	Akita	4,484[3]	11,613[3]	1,215,000
Aomori	Aomori	3,714[3]	9,619[3]	1,471,000
Fukushima	Fukushima	5,322	13,784	2,126,000
Iwate	Morioka	5,898	15,277	1,416,000
Miyagi	Sendai	2,815	7,292	2,301,000
Yamagata	Yamagata	3,601	9,327	1,253,000
Metropolis				
Tōkyō[4]	Tokyo	836	2,166	11,771,000
Urban prefectures				
Kyōto[5]	Kyōto	1,781	4,613	2,604,000
Ōsaka[5]	Ōsaka	722	1,869	8,708,000
TOTAL		145,883[6, 7]	377,835[6, 7]	125,034,000[7]

Demography

Population (1995): 125,362,000.
Density (1995): persons per sq mi 859.3, persons per sq km 331.8.
Urban-rural:(1993): urban 77.4%; rural 22.6%.
Sex distribution (1994[1]): male 49.05%; female 50.95%.
Age breakdown (1994[1]): under 15, 16.4%; 15–29, 22.0%; 30–44, 20.2%; 45–59, 21.5%; 60–74, 14.4%; 75 and over, 5.5%.
Population projection: (2000) 127,287,000; (2010) 130,344,000.
Doubling time: not applicable; doubling time exceeds 100 years.
Composition by nationality (1993): Japanese 98.9%; Korean 0.5%; Chinese 0.2%; Brazilian 0.1%; other 0.3%.
Place of birth (1994): 99.2% native-born; 0.8% foreign-born (mainly Korean).
Immigration (1993): permanent immigrants/registered aliens admitted 1,320,748, from North and South Korea 51.7%, Taiwan, Hong Kong, and China 15.9%, Brazil 11.7%, Philippines 5.5%, United States 3.2%, Peru 2.5%, United Kingdom 0.9%, Thailand 0.9%, Vietnam 0.6%, Canada 0.5%, Australia 0.5%, other 6.1%.
Major cities (1994[1]): Tokyo 8,021,943; Yokohama 3,300,513; Ōsaka 2,575,042; Nagoya 2,153,293; Sapporo 1,744,806; Kōbe 1,518,982; Kyōto 1,448,377; Fukuoka 1,275,165; Kawasaki 1,202,069; Hiroshima 1,106,367; Kita-Kyūshū 1,019,372.

Other principal cities (1994[1])

	population		population		population
Akashi	282,912	Kakogawa	251,735	Okayama	608,115
Akita	310,219	Kanazawa	447,733	Okazaki	322,162
Amagasaki	493,158	Kashiwa	319,321	Ōmiya	427,519
Aomori	289,920	Kasugai	275,728	Ōtsu	272,668
Asahikawa	362,908	Kawagoe	320,639	Sagamihara	567,058
Chiba	853,853	Kawaguchi	452,381	Sakai	803,640
Fujisawa	365,250	Kōchi	320,498	Sendai	958,705
Fukui	255,084	Koriyama	324,321	Shimonoseki	259,581
Fukushima	284,250	Koshigaya	297,131	Shizuoka	473,859
Fukuyama	373,685	Kumamoto	642,847	Suita	338,079
Funabashi	540,306	Kurashiki	419,528	Takamatsu	330,707
Gifu	409,063	Machida	360,200	Takatsuki	361,494
Hachiōji	495,053	Maebashi	287,145	Tokorozawa	318,714
Hakodate	302,135	Matsudo	463,973	Tokushima	265,670
Hamamatsu	562,156	Matsuyama	457,497	Toyama	324,638
Higashi-Ōsaka	513,876	Miyazaki	296,201	Toyohashi	351,702
Himeji	465,941	Morioka	284,906	Toyonaka	399,988
Hirakata	397,183	Nagano	354,532	Toyota	342,968
Hiratsuka	253,485	Nagasaki	439,471	Urawa	447,281
Ibaraki	255,586	Naha	299,898	Utsunomiya	434,860
Ichihara	275,129	Nara	357,728	Wakayama	395,491
Ichikawa	444,468	Neyagawa	257,521	Yamagata	252,716
Ichinomiya	267,136	Niigata	492,009	Yao	275,865
Iwaki	360,111	Nishinomiya	424,328	Yokkaichi	284,052
Kagoshima	542,932	Ōita	424,453	Yokosuka	435,158

Religious affiliation (1992): Shintō and related religions 51.3%; Buddhism 38.3%; Christian 1.2%; other 8.9%.
Households (1990). Total households 40,670,000; average household size 3.0; composition of households 1 person 23.1%, 2 persons 20.6%, 3 persons 18.1%, 4 persons 21.7%, 5 persons 9.3%, 6 or more persons 7.2%. Family households 31,204,000 (76.7%); nonfamily 9,466,000 (23.3%), of which 1 person 9,390,000 (23.1%).

Type of household (1993)

Total number of occupied dwelling units: 40,835,000

	number of dwellings	percentage of total
by kind of dwelling		
exclusively for living	38,518,000	94.3
mixed use	169,000	0.4
combined with nondwelling	2,148,000	5.3
detached house	24,183,000	59.2
apartment building	14,253,000	34.9
tenement (substandard or overcrowded building)	2,205,000	5.4
other	194,000	0.5
by legal tenure of householder		
owned	24,410,000	59.8
rented	15,721,000	38.5
other	704,000	1.7
by kind of amenities		
flush toilet	30,524,000	74.7
bathroom	38,196,000	93.5
by year of construction		
prior to 1945	2,146,000	5.4
1945–70	9,700,000	24.3
1971–80	12,548,000	31.5
1981–88	9,258,000	23.2
1988–93	6,224,000	15.6

Mobility (October 1990). Population living in same residence as in October 1985, 74.7%; different residence, same town 9.5%; same prefecture 7.9%; different prefecture 7.6%; different country 0.3%.

Vital statistics

Birth rate per 1,000 population (1994): 10.0 (world avg. 25.0); (1985) legitimate 99.0%; illegitimate 1.0%.
Death rate per 1,000 population (1994): 7.1 (world avg. 9.3).
Natural increase rate per 1,000 population (1994): 2.9 (world avg. 15.7).
Total fertility rate (avg. births per childbearing woman; 1994): 1.5.
Marriage rate per 1,000 population (1993): 6.4; median age at first marriage (1992) men 29.7 years, women 27.0 years.
Divorce rate per 1,000 population (1993): 1.5.
Life expectancy at birth (1994): male 76.6 years; female 83.0 years.
Major causes of death per 100,000 population (1993): malignant neoplasms (cancers) 189.1; heart diseases 144.6; cerebrovascular diseases 95.3; pneumonia and bronchitis 70.1; accidents and adverse effects 27.8; senility without mention of psychosis 18.5; suicide 16.4; nephritis, nephrotic syndrome, and nephrosis 14.8; cirrhosis of the liver 13.6; diabetes mellitus 8.2.

Social indicators

Educational attainment (1990). Percentage of population age 25 years and over having: primary 34.3%; secondary education 44.5%; postsecondary 21.2%.

Distribution of income (1993)

percentage of average household income by quintile				
1	2	3	4	5 (highest)
11.3	15.6	19.0	23.0	31.1

Quality of working life. Average workweek (1993): 38.2 hours. Annual rate of industrial deaths per 100,000 workers (1992): 2.8. Proportion of labour force insured for damages or income loss resulting from injury, permanent disability, and death (1991): 50.1%. Average man-days lost to labour stoppages per 1,000,000 workdays (1993): 4.2. Average duration of journey to work (1988)[8]: 26.8 minutes (1983; 26.7% private automobile, 67.4% public

transportation, 5.5% taxi, 0.4% other). Rate per 1,000 workers of discouraged (unemployed no longer seeking work; 1993): 87.8.
Access to services (1989). Proportion of households having access to: gas supply 64.6%; safe public water supply 94.0%; public sewage collection 89.4%.
Social participation. Eligible voters participating in last national election (1993): 67.3%. Population 15 years and over participating in social-service activities on a voluntary basis (1987): 25.2%. Trade union membership in total workforce (1993): 24.2%.
Social deviance (1992). Offense rate per 100,000 population for: homicide 1.0; rape 1.2; robbery 1.8; larceny and theft 1,227.3. Incidence in general population of: alcoholism, n.a.; drug and substance abuse, n.a. Rate of suicide per 100,000 population: 16.8.

Leisure/use of personal time

Discretionary daily activities (1991)
(Population age 15 years and over)

	weekly average hrs./min.
Total discretionary daily time	5:56[7]
of which	
Hobbies and amusements	0:36
Sports	0:11
Learning (except schoolwork)	0:12
Social activities	0:05
Associations	0:29
Radio, television, newspapers, and magazines	2:23
Rest and relaxation	1:21
Other activities	0:21

Major leisure activities (1991)
(Population age 15 years and over)

	percentage of participation		
	male	female	total
Hobbies and amusements	93.0	90.8	91.9
Sports	84.2	72.1	78.0
Light exercises	30.8	34.1	32.0
Swimming	27.1	20.8	23.8
Bowling	33.0	23.1	27.9
Learning (except schoolwork)	36.3	37.0	36.7
Travel			
Domestic	72.7	68.3	70.4
Foreign	10.4	7.6	9.0

Material well-being (1994). Households possessing: automobile 79.7%; telephone, virtually 100%; colour television receiver 99.3%; refrigerator 98.9%; air conditioner 72.3%; washing machine 99.4%; vacuum cleaner 98.7%; videocassette recorder 82.8%; camera 86.8%; microwave oven 84.3%; compact disc player 53.8%.

National economy

Gross national product (at current market prices; 1994): U.S.$4,693,200,000,000 (U.S.$37,560 per capita).

Structure of gross domestic product and labour force

	1993		1994	
	in value ¥'000,000,000[9]	% of total value	labour force	% of labour force
Agriculture, fishing	9,360.9	2.2	3,730,000	5.6
Mining	1,030.3	0.3	60,000	0.1
Manufacturing	127,509.7	30.4	14,960,000	22.5
Construction	37,137.9	8.8	6,550,000	9.9
Public utilities	15,710.2	3.7	390,000	0.6
Transportation and communications	26,820.7	0.4	3,920,000	5.9
Trade	59,059.8	14.1	14,430,000	21.7
Finance	65,266.2	15.5	2,620,000	3.9
Pub. admin., defense	14,853.7	3.5	2,150,000	3.2
Services	77,961.0	18.6	15,420,000	23.2
Other	−14,954.4[10]	−3.6[10]	2,200,000[11]	3.3
TOTAL	419,765.1[7, 12]	100.0[7]	66,430,000	100.0[7]

Budget (1994). Revenue: ¥59,384,700,000,000 (income tax 34.2%; corporation tax 20.6%; value-added tax 9.6%; liquor and tobacco tax 5.3%; fuel taxes 4.1%; stamp duties 2.7%; customs duties 1.5%). Expenditures: ¥73,081,700,000,000 (debt service 19.6%; social security 18.4%; transfer to local governments 17.4%; public works 15.2%; culture, education, and science promotion 8.2%; national defense 6.4%; pensions 2.4%).
Public debt (1994): U.S.$2,166,400,000,000.
Population economically active (1994): total 66,430,000; activity rate of total population 53.2% (participation rates: age 15 and over, 63.6%; female 40.5%; unemployed 2.9%).

Price and earnings indexes (1990 = 100)

	1989	1990	1991	1992	1993	1994	1995[13]
Consumer price index	97.0	100.0	103.3	105.1	106.4	107.1	107.3
Monthly earnings index	96.3	100.0	103.4	105.6	107.8	110.6	113.4

Household income and expenditure (1992). Average household size 3.7; average annual income per household ¥6,766,300 (U.S.$53,420); sources of income: wages and salaries 59.3%, transfer payments 19.5%, self-employment 10.1%, other 11.1%; expenditure: food 24.3%, reading and recreation 10.0%, transportation 9.9%, clothing and footwear 6.6%, fuel, light, and water charges 5.7%, housing 5.6%, education 4.5%, furniture and household utensils 3.7%, medical care 2.9%.
Tourism (1993): receipts from visitors U.S.$3,557,000,000; expenditures by nationals abroad U.S.$26,860,000,000.
Land use (1993): forested 66.7%; meadows and pastures 1.8%; agricultural and under permanent cultivation 11.8%; other 19.7%.

Manufacturing and mining enterprises (1992)

	no. of establishments	avg. no. of persons engaged	monthly wages as a % of avg. of all mfg. wages	annual value added (¥'000,000,000)
Electrical machinery	35,091	1,927,000	97.8	19,093
Nonelectrical machinery	44,472	1,197,000	108.9	13,304
Transport equipment	15,177	974,000	114.6	12,359
Food, beverages, and tobacco	48,403	1,244,000	75.5	11,965
Chemical products	5,340	415,000	132.1	11,826
Fabricated metal products	49,413	850,000	102.7	8,781
Printing and publishing	28,107	566,000	118.3	6,658
Iron and steel	6,205	331,000	125.6	5,842
Ceramic, stone, and clay	20,225	454,000	102.2	5,159
Plastic products	19,695	447,000	91.1	4,315
Paper and paper products	10,882	281,000	101.1	3,103
Textiles	28,154	496,000	73.3	3,093
Apparel products	30,386	567,000	51.2	2,344
Precision instruments	6,612	236,000	95.7	1,938
Nonferrous metal products	3,966	170,000	111.6	1,933
Furniture and fixtures	16,403	221,000	86.2	1,715
Rubber products	5,566	171,000	98.6	1,704
Lumber and wood products	18,611	237,000	85.2	1,623
Petroleum and coal products	1,092	34,000	162.8	1,345
Leather products	5,701	77,000	74.7	485
Mining and quarrying	651	13,216	115.1	107

Energy production (consumption): electricity (kW-hr; 1992) 895,336,000,000 (895,336,000,000); coal (metric tons; 1992) 7,613,000 (116,813,000); crude petroleum (barrels; 1992) 6,243,000 (1,541,000,000); petroleum products (metric tons; 1992) 172,668,000, of which (by volume) diesel 29.7%, heavy fuel oil 22.6%, gasoline 18.1%, kerosene and jet fuel 13.8% (187,570,000); natural gas (cu m; 1992) 2,243,000,000 (56,363,000,000). Composition of energy supply by source (1992): crude oil and petroleum products 58.2%, coal 16.1%, natural gas 10.6%, nuclear power 10.0%, hydroelectric power 3.8%, other 1.3%. Domestic energy demand by end use (1992): mining and manufacturing 47.6%, residential and commercial 25.8%, transportation 23.8%, other 2.8%.

Financial aggregates

	1989	1990	1991	1992	1993	1994	1995[14]
Exchange rate[15], ¥ per:							
U.S. dollar	143.45	134.40	125.20	124.75	111.85	99.74	98.30
£	226.21	258.41	234.21	188.62	172.27	157.59	156.01
SDR	188.52	191.21	179.09	171.53	153.63	145.61	148.07
International reserves (U.S.$)							
Total (excl. gold; '000,000)	83,957	78,501	72,059	71,623	98,524	125,860	180,735
SDRs ('000,000)	2,447	3,042	2,579	1,094	1,543	2,083	2,909
Reserve pos. in IMF ('000,000)	3,518	5,971	7,722	8,641	8,261	8,631	7,985
Foreign exchange ('000,000)	77,992	69,487	61,758	61,888	88,720	115,146	169,841
Gold ('000,000 fine troy oz)	24.23	24.23	24.23	24.23	24.23	24.23	24.23
% world reserves	2.6	2.6	2.6	2.6	2.6	2.7	2.7
Interest and prices							
Central bank discount (%)[15]	4.25	6.00	4.50	3.25	1.75	1.75	1.00[16]
Govt. bond yield (%)	5.05	7.36	6.53	4.94	3.69	3.71	2.14[13]
Industrial share prices (1990 = 100)	117.8	100.0	84.5	62.6	76.5	73.3	59.5[16]
Balance of payments (U.S.$'000,000,000)							
Balance of visible trade	76.9	63.6	103.1	132.4	141.6	145.9	...
Imports, f.o.b.	192.7	216.8	203.5	198.5	209.7	238.2	...
Exports, f.o.b.	269.6	280.4	306.6	330.9	351.3	384.2	...
Balance of invisibles	−15.6	−22.2	−17.7	−14.8	−10.1	16.7	...
Balance of payments, current account	79.6	57.0	35.9	72.9	131.5	129.2	...

Retail and wholesale trade and services (1991)

	no. of establishments	avg. no. of employees	annual sales (¥'000,000,000)
Retail trade	1,519,186	6,936,000	140,634
Food and beverages	622,751	2,542,000	41,453
Grocery	68,913	643,000	16,404
Liquors	106,650	315,000	6,323
General merchandise	4,347	440,000	19,898
Department stores	2,004	427,000	19,574
Motor vehicles and bicycles	93,230	566,000	18,934
Apparel and accessories	240,989	809,000	14,844
Furniture and home furnishings	158,104	587,000	11,987
Gasoline service stations	72,807	385,000	11,234
Books and stationery	76,730	600,000	4,722
Wholesale trade	475,967	4,773,000	572,982
Machinery and equipment	111,046	1,286,000	130,512
General machinery except electrical	54,612	577,000	47,910
Motor vehicles and parts	17,318	222,000	32,019
General merchandise	705	51,000	98,548
Minerals and metals	22,657	264,000	61,300
Farm, livestock, and fishery products	43,331	416,000	60,273
Food and beverages	56,656	561,000	47,677
Textiles, apparel, and accessories	44,748	506,000	38,517
Building materials	63,885	444,000	35,698
Chemicals	18,140	179,000	24,457
Drugs and toilet goods	21,319	291,000	19,783
Medical services[17]	171,986	2,026,000	...
Educational services[17]	84,512	2,065,000	...

Production (metric tons except as noted). Agriculture, forestry, fishing (1994): rice 14,976,000, sugar beets 3,853,000, potatoes 3,400,000, cabbages 2,700,000, sugarcane 1,670,000, mandarin oranges 1,512,000, onions 1,400,000, sweet potatoes 1,264,000, apples 1,048,000, raw sugar 887,000, cucumbers 800,000, tomatoes 750,000, carrots 720,000, watermelons 710,000, wheat 565,000, pears 431,000, eggplants 430,000, pumpkins 285,000, grapes 246,000, barley 225,000, strawberries 207,000, peaches 174,000, oranges 139,000, dry beans 110,000, soybeans 99,000, tea 86,000, green beans 75,000, tobacco leaves

74,000, green peas 50,000, cow's milk 8,365,000, hen's eggs 2,562,000; livestock (number of live animals) 10,621,000 pigs, 4,989,000 cattle (of which dairy cows 28%), 31,000 goats, 28,000 horses, 25,000 sheep, 324,000,000 chickens; roundwood (1993) 32,570,000 cu m; fish catch (1993) 8,707,000, of which sardines 1,714,000, mackerel 665,000, Alaska pollack 382,000, squid 316,000, oysters 236,000, crabs 56,000, river eels 34,000, carp 13,000. Mining and quarrying (1994): limestone 202,488,000; silica stone 18,479,000; silica sand 3,944,000; dolomite 3,831,000; pyrophyllite 662,000; pyrophyllite clay 274,000; zinc 100,653; lead 9,946; copper 6,043; tungsten 578[18]; silver 133,410 kg; gold 9,550 kg. Manufacturing (1993): crude steel 99,623,000; semifinished steel 102,727,000[19]; cement 88,044,000; hot-rolled steel products 87,982,000[19]; pig iron 73,738,000; sulfuric acid 6,937,000; fertilizers 6,091,000; plastic products 4,742,000; newsprint 2,917,000; spun yarn 729,000; synthetic fabrics 2,265,000,000 sq m; cotton fabrics 1,205,000,000 sq m; finished products (in number of units) 447,693,000 watches and clocks, 41,576,000 electronic desk calculators, 21,615,000 air conditioners, 19,986,000 videocassette recorders, 12,428,000 cameras, 10,717,000 colour television receivers, 8,494,000 passenger cars, 7,699,000 video cameras, 6,858,000 bicycles, 5,163,000 automatic washing machines, 5,109,000 facsimile machines, 4,351,000 electric refrigerators, 3,459,000 microwave ovens, 3,282,000 computers, 3,023,000 motorcycles, 2,207,000 photocopy machines. Construction (value in ¥ '000,000; 1993): residential 25,789,000; nonresidential 59,239,000.

Foreign trade[20]

Balance of trade (current prices)

	1989	1990	1991	1992	1993	1994
¥'000,000,000	+11,235	+10,398	+13,093	+15,922	+15,591	+14,736
% of total	17.4%	14.3%	18.3%	22.7%	24.1%	22.2%

Imports (1994): ¥28,100,000,000,000 (machinery and transport equipment 24.6%, food products 15.2%, petroleum and petroleum products 10.1%, textiles 8.1%, chemicals and chemical products 7.4%). *Major import sources:* United States 22.8%; China 10.0%; Australia 5.0%; South Korea 4.9%; Indonesia 4.7%; Germany 4.1%; Taiwan 3.9%; Canada 3.3%; Saudi Arabia 3.1%; Malaysia 3.0%.

Exports (1994): ¥40,500,000,000,000 (electrical machinery 24.6%, motor vehicles 14.4%, chemicals 6.0%, scientific and optical equipment 4.6%, iron and steel products 3.8%, textiles and allied products 2.1%). *Major export destinations:* United States 29.7%; Hong Kong 6.5%; South Korea 6.2%; Taiwan 6.0%; Singapore 5.0%; China 4.7%; Germany 4.5%; Thailand 3.7%; United Kingdom 3.2%; Malaysia 3.1%.

Trade by commodity group (1993)

	imports		exports	
SITC group	U.S.$'000,000	%	U.S.$'000,000	%
00 Food and live animals; 01 Beverages and tobacco	39,140	16.2	1,643	0.5
02 Crude materials, excluding fuels	28,255[21]	11.7[21]	2,237[21]	0.6[21]
03 Mineral fuels, lubricants, and related materials	49,384	20.5	2,149	0.6
04 Animal and vegetable oils, fats, and waxes	[21]	[21]	[21]	[21]
05 Chemicals and related products, n.e.s.	17,523	7.2	19,534	5.4
06 Basic manufactures	27,005	11.2	40,142	11.0
07 Machinery and transport equipment	40,859	16.9	259,583	71.6
08 Miscellaneous manufactured articles	32,942	13.6	29,080	8.0
09 Goods not classified by kind	6,492	2.7	8,355	2.3
TOTAL	241,600	100.0	362,723	100.0

Direction of trade (1993)

	imports		exports	
	U.S.$'000,000	%	U.S.$'000,000	%
Africa	3,794	1.6	7,333	2.0
Asia	110,187	45.6	149,895	41.3
South America	6,377	2.7	5,717	1.6
North America and Central America	66,024	27.3	123,712	34.1
United States	55,943	23.1	106,898	29.5
other North and Central Am.	10,081	4.2	16,814	4.6
Europe	40,205	16.6	66,614	18.4
EEC	30,403	12.6	56,917	15.7
Russia	2,777	1.1	1,508	0.4
other Europe	7,025	2.9	8,189	2.3
Oceania	15,014	6.2	9,447	2.6
TOTAL	241,601	100.0	362,718	100.0

Transport and communications

Transport. Railroads (1993): length 23,690 mi[19], 38,125 km[19]; rolling stock—locomotives 5,879, passenger cars 43,753, freight cars 46,661; passengers carried 22,759,000,000; passenger-mi 250,242,000,000, passenger-km 402,727,000,000; short ton-mi cargo 17,420,000,000, metric ton-km cargo 25,433,000,000. Roads (1993): total length 702,702 mi, 1,130,892 km (paved 72%). Vehicles (1993): passenger cars 40,772,407; trucks 22,493,773; buses 247,000. Merchant marine (1993): vessels (100 gross tons and over) 7,323; total deadweight tonnage 23,600,000. Air transport (1993): passengers carried 69,580,000; passenger-mi 69,346,000,000, passenger-km 111,602,000,000; short ton-mi cargo 3,697,000,000, metric ton-km cargo 5,398,000,000; airports (1995) with scheduled flights 74.

Distribution of traffic (1993)

	cargo carried ('000,000 tons)	% of national total	passengers carried ('000,000)	% of national total
Road	5,822.0	90.5	59,285.0	72.1
Rail (intercity)	79.0	1.2	22,759.0	27.7
Urban transport	—	—	17,445.0[18]	...
road	—	—	8,445.0[18]	...
rail	—	—	9,000.0[18]	...
Inland water	529.0	8.2	157.0	0.2
Air	0.9	0.0	70.0	0.1
TOTAL	6,430.9	100.0[7]	82,271.0[22]	100.0[7, 22]

Communications. Daily newspapers (1994): total number 121; total circulation 71,924,000; circulation per 1,000 population 576. Radio (1994): 110,000,000 receivers (1 per 1.1 persons). Television (1994): 100,000,000 receivers (1 per 1.2 persons). Telephones (main lines; 1993): 58,459,000 (1 per 2.1 persons).

Other communications media (1993)

	titles		traffic ('000)
Print		**Electronic**	
Books (new)	48,053	Telegram	45,327
of which		Domestic	44,997
Social sciences	10,614	International	330
Fiction	9,633	Telex	11,120[18]
Arts	5,612		
Natural sciences	3,799		
Engineering	3,749		
History	3,157	**Post**	
Philosophy	2,312	Mail	24,284,000
Magazines/journals	3,895	Domestic	23,950,000
Weekly	107	International	334,000
Monthly	2,690	Parcels	406,700
		Domestic	401,000
Cinema		International	5,700
Feature films	590		
Domestic	238		
Foreign	352		

Radio and television broadcasting (1993): total radio stations 1,324, of which commercial 464; total television stations 14,475, of which commercial 7,553. Commercial broadcasting hours (by percentage of programs; 1992): reports—radio 13.0%, television 20.0%; education—radio 4.3%, television 12.2%; culture—radio 15.4%, television 24.2%; entertainment—radio 66.5%, television 41.5%. Advertisements (daily average; 1992): radio 158, television 291.

Education and health

Education (1994)

	schools	teachers	students	student/teacher ratio
Primary (age 6–11)	24,635	435,000	8,583,000	19.7
Secondary (age 12–17)	16,786	556,000	9,544,000	17.2
Higher	1,207	160,000	3,059,000	19.1

Literacy: total population age 15 and over literate, virtually 100%.

Health (1992): physicians 219,704 (1 per 566 persons); dentists 77,416 (1 per 1,606 persons); nurses 795,810 (1 per 156 persons); pharmacists 162,021 (1 per 767 persons); midwives 22,690 (1 per 5,476 persons); hospital beds 1,686,696 (1 per 74 persons), of which general 75.0%, mental 21.5%, tuberculosis 2.3%, other 1.2%; infant mortality rate per 1,000 live births (1994) 4.2.

Food (1992): daily per capita caloric intake 2,903 (vegetable products 78%, animal products 22%); 124% of FAO recommended minimum.

Military

Total active duty personnel (1995): 239,500 (army 63.1%, navy 18.3%, air force 18.6%). *Military expenditure as percentage of GNP* (1993): 1.0% (world 3.3%); per capita expenditure U.S.$335.

[1]October 1; preliminary. [2]Excludes Lake Naka (38 sq mi [98 sq km]), which is part of both Shimane and Tottori prefectures. [3]Excludes Lake Towada (23 sq mi [60 sq km]), which is part of both Akita and Aomori prefectures. [4]Part of Kantō geographic region. [5]Part of Kinki geographic region. [6]1987 survey; includes Lake Naka and Lake Towada. [7]Detail does not add to total given because of rounding. [8]Applies to passengers carried within metropolitan areas only. [9]At prices of 1985. [10]Import duties and statistical discrepancy less imputed bank service charge. [11]Includes 1,900,000 unemployed. [12]GDP in current values for 1993 is ¥465,972,400,000,000. [13]June. [14]September. [15]End of period. [16]July. [17]1985. [18]1992. [19]1991. [20]Import figures are f.o.b. in balance of trade and c.i.f. in commodities and trading partners. [21]Crude materials includes Animal and vegetable oils, fats, and waxes. [22]Totals refer to intercity traffic only.

Jordan

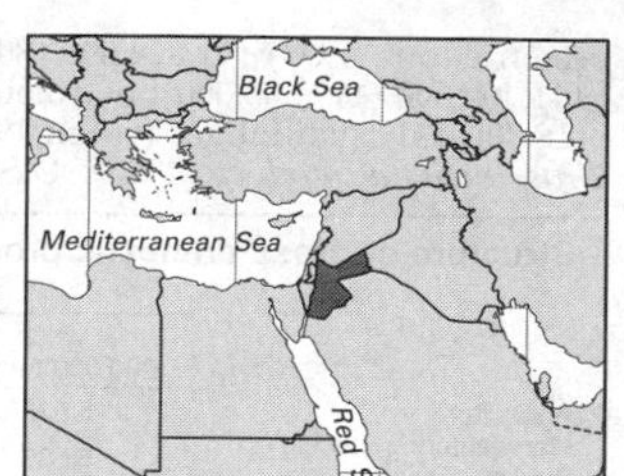

Official name: al-Mamlakah al-Urdunnīyah al-Hāshimīyah (al-Urdun) (Hashemite Kingdom of Jordan).
Form of government: constitutional monarchy[1] with a National Assembly comprising two legislative houses (Senate [40 appointed by king]; House of Deputies [80]).
Head of state and government: King assisted by Prime Minister.
Capital: Amman.
Official language: Arabic.
Official religion: Islam.
Monetary unit: 1 Jordan dinar (JD) = 1,000 fils; valuation (Oct. 6, 1995) JD 1.00 = U.S.$1.43 = £0.90.

Area and population

Governorates	Capitals	area sq mi	area sq km	population 1994 census[2]
ʿAjlūn	ʿAjlun	...[3]	...[3]	94,205
ʿAmman	Amman	4,097[4]	10,612[4]	1,567,908
al-ʿAqabah	al-ʿAqabah	...[5]	...[5]	79,745
al-Balqāʾ	aṣ-Ṣalt	425	1,100	273,489
Irbid	Irbid	985[3]	2,551[3]	745,774
Jarash	Jarash	...[3]	...[3]	123,195
al-Karak	al-Karak	1,548	4,010	169,552
Maʿān	Maʿān	13,954[5]	36,141[5]	79,401
Mādabā	Mādabā	...[4]	...[4]	106,308
al-Mafraq	al-Mafraq	10,475	27,129	170,903
aṭ-Ṭafīlah	aṭ-Ṭafīlah	850	2,202	61,156
az-Zarqāʾ	az-Zarqāʾ	2,008	5,201	623,943
TOTAL		34,342	88,946	4,095,579

Demography

Population (1995): 4,187,000.
Density (1995): persons per sq mi 121.9, persons per sq km 47.1.
Urban-rural (1995): urban 71.5%; rural 28.5%.
Sex distribution (1994): male 52.15%; female 47.85%.
Age breakdown (1995): under 15, 43.2%; 15–29, 29.8%; 30–44, 14.9%; 45–59, 7.6%; 60–74, 3.6%; 75 and over, 0.9%.
Population projection: (2000) 4,932,000; (2010) 6,590,000.
Doubling time: 20 years.
Ethnic composition (1983): Arab 99.2%, of which Palestinian *c.* 50.0%; Circassian 0.5%; Armenian 0.1%; Turk 0.1%; Kurd 0.1%.
Religious affiliation (1980): Sunnī Muslim 93.0%; Christian 4.9%; other 2.1%.
Major cities (1994): Amman 963,490; az-Zarqāʾ 344,524; Irbid 208,201; aṣ-Ṣalt 187,014; ar-Ruṣayfah 131,130; al-Mafraq 109,841.

Vital statistics

Birth rate per 1,000 population (1993): 38.8 (world avg. 25.0).
Death rate per 1,000 population (1993): 3.1 (world avg. 9.3).
Natural increase rate per 1,000 population (1993): 35.7 (world avg. 15.7).
Total fertility rate (avg. births per childbearing woman; 1993): 5.8.
Marriage rate per 1,000 population (1993): 9.3.
Divorce rate per 1,000 population (1993): 1.4.
Life expectancy at birth (1991): male 70.0 years, female 73.0 years.
Major causes of death per 100,000 population: n.a.; however, major diseases include tuberculosis, typhoid, paratyphoid fevers, salmonella, hepatitis, and dysentery; nonvenereal syphilis is widespread in the southern desert region.

National economy

Budget (1994). Revenue: JD 1,270,000,000 (direct and indirect taxes 55.6%, of which custom duties 34.1%; fees from telecommunication 14.9%). Expenditures: JD 1,669,000,000 (administration 43.2%; defense and security 22.6%; social welfare 14.7%; economic development 13.1%; transportation and communications 3.0%).
Production (metric tons except as noted). Agriculture, forestry, fishing (1994): tomatoes 550,000, oranges and tangerines 114,000, melons 78,000, olives 70,000, lemons and lime 68,000, barley 65,000, wheat 50,000, grapes 50,000, eggplants 50,000, cucumbers 35,000, cauliflower and cabbage 32,000, bananas 12,000; livestock (number of live animals) 2,100,000 sheep, 555,000 goats, 42,000 cattle, 18,000 camels, 77,000,000 chickens; roundwood (1993) 11,000 cu m; fish catch (1993) 62. Mining and quarrying (1994): phosphate ore 4,218,000; potash 1,550,000. Manufacturing (value added in JD '000; 1992): nonmetallic mineral products, pottery, and china 205,064; chemicals 91,384; food products 79,416; fabricated metal products, except machinery 38,159; plastic and plastic products 26,620; petroleum refining 26,199; furniture and wood products 25,192; printing and publishing 19,676; textiles 18,142; paper and paper products 17,310; beverages 15,755; basic metal products 13,155; nonelectrical machinery 11,412; clothing 7,178; electrical machinery 6,579. Construction (1994): 4,875,100 sq m. Energy production (consumption): electricity (kW-hr; 1993) 4,761,000,000 (4,761,000,000); coal, none (n.a.); crude petroleum (barrels; 1993) none (20,908,000); petroleum products (metric tons; 1993) 2,929,000 (3,455,000); natural gas, none (n.a.).
Tourism (1993): receipts from visitors U.S.$563,000,000; expenditures by nationals abroad U.S.$345,000,000.
Population economically active (1992): total 706,000; activity rate of total population 19.3% (participation rates: over age 15 [1986] 39.0%; female [1988] 10.9%; unemployed [1992] 15.0%).

Price and earnings indexes (1990 = 100)

	1989	1990	1991	1992	1993	1994	1995[6]
Consumer price index	86.1	100.0	108.2	112.5	117.8	122.0	123.2
Daily earnings index	98.1	100.0	100.0	...	...	...	...

Household income and expenditure. Average household size (1994) 6.0; income per household (1979) JD 1,820 (U.S.$6,055); sources of income: n.a.; expenditure (1992): food and beverages 40.6%; housing and energy 26.9%; transportation 11.2%; clothing and footwear 8.2%; education 3.5%; health care 2.2%; other goods and services 7.4%.
Public debt (external, outstanding; 1993): U.S.$6,825,000,000.
Gross national product (1993): U.S.$4,881,000,000 (U.S.$1,190 per capita).

Structure of gross domestic product and labour force

	1994 in value JD '000,000[7]	1994 % of total value	1993 labour force	1993 % of labour force
Agriculture	288.1	7.9	54,995	6.4
Mining	112.4	3.1	91,086	10.6
Manufacturing	520.0	14.4		
Construction	269.6	7.4	60,151	7.0
Public utilities	77.5	2.1	6,015	0.7
Transp. and commun.	569.3	15.7	57,573	6.7
Trade	352.7	9.7	129,754[8]	15.1[8]
Finance	631.8	17.4	24,920	2.9
Pub. admin., defense	694.9	19.2	434,806	50.6
Services[9]	154.2	4.3		
Other	−48.4[10]	−1.2[10]		
TOTAL	3,622.1	100.0	859,300	100.0

Land use (1993): forested 0.8%; meadows and pastures 8.9%; agricultural and under permanent cultivation 4.5%; other 85.8%.

Foreign trade

Balance of trade (current prices)

	1990	1991	1992	1993	1994	1995[11]
JD '000,000	−1,009	−994	−1,462	−1,585	−1,362	−338
% of total	43.1%	43.0%	51.3%	50.4%	43.2%	43.1%

Imports (1994): JD 2,362,600,000 (food and live animals 17.3%, of which cereals 2.9%; machinery and appliances 15.3%; mineral fuels 12.7%; transport [mainly equipment and parts] 10.1%; iron and steel 5.5%; clothing, textiles, and footwear 5.2%; pharmaceuticals 2.8%; plastics 2.4%). *Major import sources:* Iraq 12.3%; United States 9.9%; Germany 7.8%; Italy 5.9%; United Kingdom 5.1%; France 4.7%; Japan 4.0%; The Netherlands 3.8%.
Exports (1994): JD 793,900,000 (phosphate fertilizers 12.6%; potash 11.7%; pharmaceuticals 11.5%; fertilizers 11.2%; fruits, vegetables, and nuts 8.2%; machinery and transport equipment 5.0%). *Major export destinations:* Iraq 13.3%; India 11.1%; Saudi Arabia 9.1%; United Arab Emirates 4.9%; Indonesia 3.5%, Syria 3.4%; Lebanon 2.2%; Pakistan 2.1%.

Transport and communications

Transport. Railroads (1992): route length 490 mi, 789 km; passengers carried (1988) 31,304; short ton-mi cargo 542,000,000, metric ton-km cargo 791,000,000. Roads (1992): total length 3,958 mi, 6,370 km (paved 100%). Vehicles (1993): passenger cars 162,000; trucks and buses 91,600. Merchant marine (1992): vessels (100 gross tons and over) 5; total deadweight tonnage 113,557. Air transport (1994)[12]: passenger-mi 1,455,000,000, passenger-km 2,342,000,000, short ton-mi cargo 81,882,000, metric ton-km cargo 119,546,000; airports (1995) with scheduled flights 2.
Communications. Daily newspapers (1992): total number 4; total circulation 250,000; circulation per 1,000 population 58. Radio (1994): 980,000 receivers (1 per 4.3 persons). Television (1994): 250,000 receivers (1 per 16.9 persons). Telephones (main lines; 1993): 288,100 (1 per 14.2 persons).

Education and health

Education (1992–93)

	schools	teachers	students	student/ teacher ratio
Primary (age 6–14)	2,441	45,871	1,014,295	22.1
Secondary (age 15–17)	662	6,915	86,475	12.5
Voc., teacher tr.	49	2,107	27,435	13.0
Higher	55[13]	4,014[14]	88,506[14]	22.0

Educational attainment (1979). Percentage of population age 14 and over having: no formal schooling 47.9%; primary education 19.8%; secondary 26.4%; higher 5.9%. *Literacy* (1991): percentage of population age 15 and over literate 83.2%; males literate 90.8%; females literate 75.1%.
Health (1992): physicians (1991) 6,395 (1 per 574 persons); hospital beds 4,291 (1 per 920 persons); infant mortality rate per 1,000 live births 33.8.
Food (1988–90): daily per capita caloric intake 2,710 (vegetable products 89%, animal products 11%); 110% of FAO recommended minimum requirement.

Military

Total active duty personnel (1994): 98,600 (army 91.3%, navy 0.6%, air force 8.1%). *Military expenditure as percentage of GDP* (1994): 7.1% (world 2.6%); per capita expenditure U.S.$96.

[1]Political parties legalized July 1992; November 1993 legislative elections were multiparty. [2]Preliminary. [3]Irbid includes area of ʿAjlūn and Jarash governorates. [4]ʿAmman includes area of Mādabā governorate. [5]Maʿān includes area of al-ʿAqabah governorate. [6]May only. [7]At factor cost. [8]Includes restaurants and hotels. [9]Includes domestic help employed in households. [10]Less imputed bank service charges. [11]First quarter only. [12]Royal Jordanian airlines only. [13]1988–89. [14]Includes community colleges.

Kazakhstan

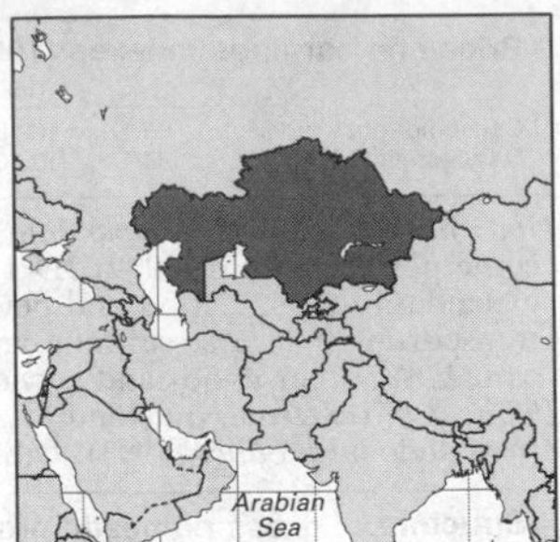

Official name: Qazaqstan Respublikasï (Republic of Kazakhstan).
Form of government[1]: unitary republic with a Parliament consisting of two chambers (Senate [40[2]] and Assembly [67]).
Head of state and government[1]: President assisted by Prime Minister.
Capital: Almaty (formerly Alma-Ata); Aqmola (formerly Tselinograd) is the capital-designate[3].
Official language: Kazakh.
Official religion: none.
Monetary unit: tenge[4] (T; decimal unit, n.a.); valuation (Oct. 6, 1995) free rate, 1 U.S.$ = 61.37; 1 £ = 97.01 tenge.

Area and population

		area		population
		sq mi	sq km	1991 estimate
Provinces	**Capitals**			
Almaty (Alma-Alta)	Almaty (Alma-Alta)	40,600	105,100	2,153,700
Aqmola	Aqmola	35,600	92,100	885,400
Aqtöbe	Aqtöbe	115,300	298,700	752,900
Atyraū	Atyraū	43,800	113,500	447,100
Batys Qazaqstan	Oral	58,400	151,200	648,000
Kökchetaū	Kökchetaū	30,200	78,100	669,400
Mangghystaū	Aqtaū	63,800	165,100	331,700
Ongtüstik Qazaqstan	Shymkent	44,900	116,300	1,879,200
Pavlodar	Pavlodar	49,200	127,500	956,900
Qaraghandy	Qaraghandy	45,500	117,900	1,339,900
Qostanay	Qostanay	44,200	114,500	1,074,400
Qyzylorda	Qyzylorda	88,100	228,100	664,900
Semey	Semey	69,300	179,600	841,900
Shyghys Qazaqstan	Shyghys Qazaqstan	37,600	97,300	949,000
Soltüstik Qazaqstan	Petropavl	17,100	44,300	610,400
Taldyqorghan	Taldyqorghan	45,700	118,500	731,000
Torghay	Arqalyq	43,200	111,900	304,600
Zhambyl	Zhambyl (Aullye-Alta)	55,700	144,200	1,056,400
Zhezkazghan	Zhezkazghan	121,000	313,400	496,200
TOTAL		1,049,200	2,717,300	16,793,100[5]

Demography

Population (1995): 16,669,000.
Density (1995): persons per sq mi 15.9, persons per sq km 6.1.
Urban-rural (1993): urban 56.6%; rural 43.4%.
Sex distribution (1992): male 48.60%; female 51.40%.
Age breakdown (1991): under 15, 31.4%; 15–29, 25.1%; 30–44, 21.3%; 45–59, 12.2%; 60–69, 6.1%; 70 and over, 3.9%.
Population projection: (2000) 17,237,000; (2010) 18,828,000.
Doubling time: 58 years.
Ethnic composition (1991): Kazakh 41.1%; Russian 37.3%; Ukrainian 5.3%; German 5.0%; Uzbek 2.1%; Tatar 2.0%; other 7.2%.
Religious affiliation: believers are predominantly Sunnī Muslims (Ḥanafīyah); there is a Christian minority (mainly Russian Orthodox and Baptist).
Major cities (1991): Almaty (Alma-Ata) 1,156,200; Qaraghandy (Karaganda) 608,600; Shymkent (Chimkent) 438,800; Semey (Semipalatinsk) 344,700; Pavlodar 342,500.

Vital statistics

Birth rate per 1,000 population (1993): 18.6 (world avg. 25.0); (1992) legitimate 86.6%; illegitimate 13.4%.
Death rate per 1,000 population (1993): 9.2 (world avg. 9.2).
Natural increase rate per 1,000 population (1993): 12.4 (world avg. 15.7).
Total fertility rate (avg. births per childbearing woman; 1993): 2.5.
Marriage rate per 1,000 population (1993): 8.6.
Divorce rate per 1,000 population (1993): 2.7.
Life expectancy at birth (1993): male 63.2 years; female 72.7 years.
Major causes of death per 100,000 population (1993): diseases of the circulatory system 426.0; malignant neoplasms (cancers) 135.5; accidents, poisoning, and violence 133.3; diseases of the respiratory system 85.7; diseases of the digestive system 29.4; infectious and parasitic diseases 26.6.

National economy

Budget (1994). Revenue: 90,962,000,000 tenge (current revenue 86.8%, of which income and capital-gains taxes 24.7%, taxes on goods and services 19.3%, taxes on international trade 12.2%, other tax revenue 11.5%, nontax revenue 19.1%; capital revenue 9.0%; grants and aid 4.2%). Expenditures: 119,009,000,000 tenge (national economy 19.0%; defense and public safety 13.1%; education 11.2%; foreign economic activity 9.2%; health care 9.2%; social security 5.0%).
Public debt (external, outstanding; 1994): 2,291,000,000.
Production (metric tons except as noted). Agriculture, forestry, fishing (1994): wheat 9,052,000, grain 7,060,000, potatoes 1,950,000, oats 822,000, sugar beets 469,000, rice 283,000, rye 264,000, corn (maize) 233,000, seed cotton 207,000, fruit 177,000, sunflower seeds 120,000, grapes 37,000; livestock (number of live animals) 34,208,000 sheep and goats, 9,347,000 cattle, 2,445,000 pigs, 1,400,000 horses, 55,000 camels; roundwood (1991) 1,974,000 cu m; fish catch (1993) 75,000. Mining and quarrying (1993): iron ore 17,000,000; chrome 2,900,000; copper 250,000; manganese 200,000. Manufacturing (value of production in '000,000 tenge; 1993): metallurgy 5,485; petroleum products 3,664; food products 3,058; machinery 1,669; chemical products 925; textiles 857. Construction (1994): residential 2,300,000 sq m. Energy production (consumption): electricity (kW-hr; 1993) 77,444,000,000 (77,444,000,000); coal (metric tons; 1993) 111,874,000 (80,526,000); crude petroleum (barrels; 1993) 141,400,000 (117,300,000); petroleum products (metric tons; 1993) 16,744,000 (18,808,000); natural gas (cu m; 1993) 6,712,000,000 (13,718,000,000).
Gross national product (1993): U.S.$26,440,000,000 (U.S.$1,540 per capita)[6].

Structure of gross domestic product and labour force

	1993		1992	
	in value '000,000 tenge	% of total value	labour force	% of labour force
Agriculture	5,578	28.6	1,794,000	24.3
Manufacturing, mining }	5,637	28.9	1,490,000	20.2
Public utilities }			283,000	3.8
Construction	2,417	12.4	740,000	10.0
Transp. and commun.	1,629	8.4	664,000	9.0
Trade	974	5.0	533,000	7.3
Finance	496	2.5	46,000	0.6
Public administration, defense	51	0.3	184,000	2.4
Services	2,446	12.5	1,476,000	20.0
Other	281	1.4	180,000	2.4
TOTAL	19,509	100.0	7,390,000	100.0

Population economically active (1992): total 7,390,000; activity rate of total population 43.8% (participation rates: ages 16–59 [male], 16–54 [female] 80.1%; female [1991] 60.0%; unemployed [1993] 4.9%).

Price and earnings indexes (1990 = 100)

	1988	1989	1990	1991	1992	1993	1994
Consumer price index	84.0	84.4	100.0	191.0	2,829	49,850	986,984
Monthly earnings index	80.8	88.1	100.0	166.0	1,743	2,374	3,297

Land use (1993): forested 3.5%; meadows and pastures 68.7%; agricultural and under permanent cultivation 12.8%; other 15.0%.
Household income and expenditure. Average household size (1989) 4.0; income per household (1991) 5,290 rubles; sources of income (1993): salaries and wages 75.9%, social benefits 17.7%, agricultural income 2.3%, other 4.1%; expenditure (1993): retail goods 59.3%, taxes 27.5%, services 8.8%, other 4.4%.

Foreign trade

Balance of trade (current prices)

	1990	1991	1992	1993
U.S.$'000,000	−10,280	−3,160	−1,670	−414
% of total	26.5%	13.4%	10.2%	4.2%

Imports (1993): U.S.$5,183,000,000 (1991; machinery and transport equipment 37.6%, food 10.8%, textiles 9.8%, minerals 9.1%, manufactured items 5.8%). *Major import sources:* China 16.8%; Germany 15.1%; U.S. 6.6%; Austria 5.8%; Hungary 5.5%.
Exports (1993): U.S.$4,769,000,000 (1991; semifabricated metal 27.5%, chemical products 22.3%, manufactured items 16.9%, clothing 3.9%, textiles 2.0%). *Major export destinations* (1993): Switzerland 12.8%; China 11.5%; U.S. 10.3%; Germany 9.6%; Sweden 6.9%.

Transport and communications

Transport. Railroads (1991): length 13,173 mi, 21,200 km; passenger-km 19,400,000,000; metric ton-km cargo 374,200,000. Roads (1992): total length 102,464 mi, 164,900 km (paved 69%). Vehicles (1988): passenger cars 734,800; trucks and buses, n.a. Air transport (1992): passenger-mi 7,800,000,000, passenger-km 12,600,000,000; metric ton-km cargo 70,000,000; airports (1995) with scheduled flights 6[7].
Communications. Newspapers (1989): total number 450; total circulation 6,700,000; circulation per 1,000 population 405. Radio (1992): total number of receivers 4,188,000 (1 per 4.1 persons). Television (1992): total number of receivers 4,795,000 (1 per 3.6 persons). Telephones (main lines; 1993): 1,559,300 (1 per 11.0 persons).

Education and health

Education (1991–92)

	schools	teachers	students	student/teacher ratio
Primary (age 7–13) }	8,841	262,600	3,226,400	12.3
Secondary (age 14–17) }				
Voc., teacher tr.	3,115	...	1,091,600	...
Higher	61	...	288,000	...

Educational attainment (1989). Percentage of population age 25 and over having: primary education or no formal schooling 16.2%; some secondary 19.8%; completed secondary and some postsecondary 54.1%; higher 9.9%.
Health (1994): physicians[8] 66,000 (1 per 253 persons); hospital beds 223,000 (1 per 75 persons); infant mortality rate per 1,000 live births 27.4.

Military

Total active duty personnel (1995): about 40,000 (army 62.5%, air force 37.5%). *Military expenditure as percentage of GNP* (1993): 2.6% (world avg. 3.3%); per capita expenditure U.S.$41.

[1]According to a presidential edict of Oct. 16, 1995, implementing the new constitution approved by referendum Aug. 30, 1995. [2]Elected seats only. [3]Government offices are to be moved to Aqmola in 1997. [4]The Kazakh tenge was introduced Nov. 18, 1993, to replace the Russian ruble, at a rate of 500 Russian rubles to 1 tenge; on Nov. 25, 1993, the Kazakh tenge became the sole legal tender. [5]Detail does not add to total given because of rounding. [6]Ruble-area GNP and exchange-rate data are very speculative. [7]International only; the number of domestic airports is not available. [8]Data include dentists.

Kenya

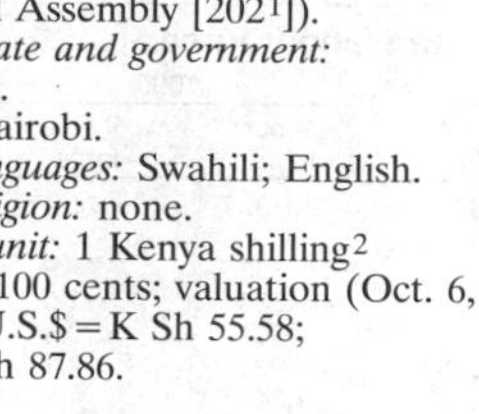

Official name: Jamhuri ya Kenya (Swahili); Republic of Kenya (English).
Form of government: unitary multiparty republic with one legislative house (National Assembly [202[1]]).
Head of state and government: President.
Capital: Nairobi.
Official languages: Swahili; English.
Official religion: none.
Monetary unit: 1 Kenya shilling[2] (K Sh) = 100 cents; valuation (Oct. 6, 1995) 1 U.S.$ = K Sh 55.58; 1 £ = K Sh 87.86.

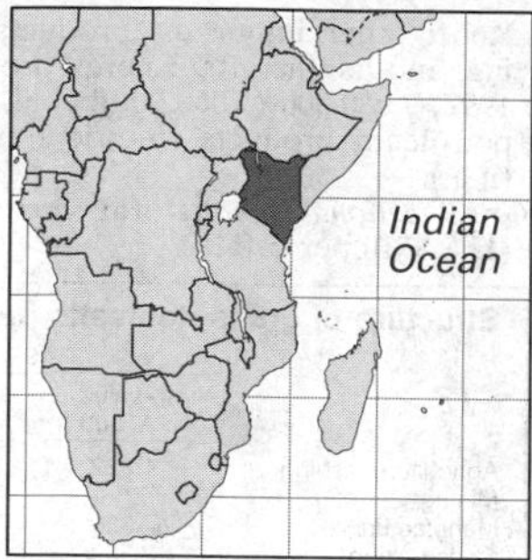

Area and population

		area		population
				1993
Provinces	Provincial headquarters	sq mi	sq km	estimate
Central	Nyeri	5,087	13,176	3,626,000
Coast	Mombasa	32,279	83,603	2,155,000
Eastern	Embu	61,734	159,891	4,334,000
North Eastern	Garissa	48,997	126,902	408,000
Nyanza	Kisumu	6,240	16,162	4,041,000
Rift Valley	Nakuru	67,131	173,868	5,690,000
Western	Kakamega	3,228	8,360	3,035,000
Special area				
Nairobi	—	264	684	1,678,000
TOTAL		224,961[3]	582,646	24,967,000

Demography

Population (1995): 28,626,000.
Density (1995): persons per sq mi 127.2, persons per sq km 49.1.
Urban-rural (1995): urban 20.4%; rural 79.6%.
Sex distribution (1995): male 49.98%; female 50.02%.
Age breakdown (1995): under 15, 51.2%; 15–29, 26.6%; 30–44, 12.6%; 45–59, 6.4%; 60–74, 2.7%; 75 and over, 0.5%.
Population projection: (2000) 32,997,300; (2010) 44,114,000.
Doubling time: 21 years.
Ethnic composition (1989): Kikuyu 17.7%; Luhya 12.4%; Luo 10.6%; Kalenjin 9.8%; Kamba 9.8%; other 39.7%.
Religious affiliation (1987): Christian 73.0%, of which Roman Catholic 27.0%, Protestant 19.0%, other Christian (mostly African Indigenous, Anglican, and Eastern Orthodox) 27.0%; traditional beliefs 19.0%; Muslim 6.0%; other 2.0%.
Major cities (1989): Nairobi 1,504,900[4]; Mombasa 465,000; Kisumu 185,100; Nakuru 162,800; Machakos 92,300[5].

Vital statistics

Birth rate per 1,000 population (1990–95): 44.5 (world avg. 25.0).
Death rate per 1,000 population (1990–95): 11.7 (world avg. 9.3).
Natural increase rate per 1,000 population (1990–95): 32.8 (world avg. 15.7).
Total fertility rate (avg. births per childbearing woman; 1990–95): 6.3.
Life expectancy at birth (1990–95): male 54.2 years; female 57.3 years.
Major causes of death per 100,000 population: n.a.; however, major infectious diseases include AIDS, malaria, gastroenteritis, venereal diseases, diarrhea and dysentery, trachoma, amebiasis, and schistosomiasis.

National economy

Budget (1993–94). Revenue: K£4,551,140,000[2] (indirect taxes 61.5%, of which sales tax 31.2%, custom and excise duties 28.2%; direct taxes 27.3%; other 11.2%). Expenditures: K£7,763,450,000[2] (recurrent expenditure 84.9%; development expenditure 15.1%).
Production (metric tons except as noted). Agriculture, forestry, fishing (1994): sugarcane 3,470,000, corn (maize) 2,970,000, cassava 842,000, sweet potatoes 650,000, plantains 360,000, pineapple 270,000, potatoes 250,000, wheat 230,000, bananas 220,000, tea 209,000, pulses 200,000, sorghum 130,000, millet 130,000, coffee 74,000, coconuts 43,000, barley 37,000, sisal 34,000, tomatoes 32,000, cashew nuts 15,000, sunflower seeds 15,000, seed cotton 12,000, cotton seeds 8,000, copra 7,000; livestock (number of live animals) 11,000,000 cattle, 7,438,000 goats, 5,500,000 sheep; roundwood (1993) 38,554,000 cu m; fish catch (1995) 241,064, of which freshwater fish 95.3%. Mining and quarrying (1993): soda ash 216,890; fluorite 78,725; salt 74,669. Manufacturing (1992): cement 1,507,000; sugar 427,000; wheat flour 186,000; beer 3,686,000 hectolitres; mineral water 1,323,000 hectolitres[4]; paint 47,000 hectolitres[4]; alcoholic beverages 22,591 hectolitres[4]. Construction (1990): residential 411,000 sq m; nonresidential 182,000 sq m. Energy production (consumption): electricity (kW-hr; 1993) 3,396,000,000 (3,074,000,000); coal (metric tons; 1992) none (110,000); crude petroleum (barrels; 1993) none (16,668,000); petroleum products (metric tons; 1993) 1,975,000 (1,507,000).
Public debt (external, outstanding; 1993): U.S.$5,121,000,000.
Household income and expenditure. Average household size (1980) 6.2; average annual income per household: n.a.; sources of income: n.a.; expenditure (1980): food 46.5%, housing 10.0%, furniture and utensils 9.4%, transportation 8.4%, clothing and footwear 7.7%, energy 2.6%, health 2.2%, education 1.0%.
Population economically active (1992): total 10,633,000; activity rate of total population 41.1% (participation rates [1985]: ages 15–64, 76.2%; female 40.9%; unemployed, n.a.).

Price and earnings indexes (1990 = 100)

	1988	1989	1990	1991	1992	1993	1994
Consumer price index	76.6	86.5	100.0	119.8	155.2	226.3	292.0
Monthly earnings index	86.3	91.7	100.0	109.3	...	...	...

Gross national product (at current market prices; 1993): U.S.$6,743,000,000 (U.S.$270 per capita).

Structure of gross domestic product and labour force

	1993			
	in value K£'000,000[2]	% of total value	labour force[6]	% of labour force[6]
Agriculture	3,934.0	28.9	274,300	18.6
Mining	35.2	0.3	4,500	0.3
Manufacturing	1,419.7	10.4	193,600	13.1
Construction	759.2	5.6	72,600	4.9
Public utilities	174.8	1.3	22,100	1.5
Transp. and commun.	1,117.7	8.2	77,300	5.3
Trade	1,920.7	14.1	121,100	8.2
Finance	2,260.4	16.6	72,600	4.9
Pub. admin., defense	2,051.3	15.1 }	636,800	43.2
Services	177.3	1.3 }		
Other	−247.6[7]	−1.8[7]	—	—
TOTAL	13,602.7	100.0	1,474,900	100.0

Tourism (1993): receipts from visitors U.S.$413,000,000; expenditures by nationals abroad U.S.$48,000,000.
Land use (1993): forested 29.5%; meadows and pastures 37.4%; agricultural and under permanent cultivation 8.0%; other 25.1%.

Foreign trade[8]

Balance of trade (current prices)

	1989	1990	1991	1992	1993	1994
K Sh '000,000	−18,131	−18,164	−11,890	−5,923	−5,938	−16,738
% of total	31.3%	27.7%	16.4%	0.2%	3.7%	0.8%

Imports (1993): K£5,056,420,000[2] (machinery and transport equipment 19.5%, crude petroleum 18.7%, iron and steel products 6.0%, pharmaceuticals 5.4%, plastics and plastic products 3.9%). *Major import sources:* United Arab Emirates 15.0%; United Kingdom 11.9%; Japan 7.6%; Germany 7.1%; U.S. 5.8%; Saudi Arabia 4.6%; Italy 4.5%; France 4.2%; India 2.7%.
Exports (1993): K£3,678,250,000[2, 9] (tea 26.2%, coffee [not roasted] 15.5%, fruits and vegetables 11.0%, petroleum products 9.4%, cement 1.8%, soda ash 1.7%). *Major export destinations:* United Kingdom 16.0%; Uganda 8.7%; Tanzania 7.4%; Germany 7.3%; The Netherlands 4.0%; U.S. 3.7%.

Transport and communications

Transport. Railroads (1993): route length 1,885 mi, 3,034 km; passenger-mi 288,000,000, passenger-km 464,000,000; short ton-mi cargo 898,600,000, metric ton-km cargo 1,312,000,000. Roads (1994): total length 39,400 mi, 63,400 km (paved 14%). Vehicles (1992): passenger cars 157,166; trucks and buses 133,968. Merchant marine (1992): vessels (100 gross tons and over) 29; total deadweight tonnage 11,649. Air transport (1994)[10]: passenger-mi 1,079,400,000, passenger-km 1,737,130,000; short ton-mi cargo 39,183,000, metric ton-km cargo 57,206,000; airports (1995) with scheduled flights 14.
Communications. Daily newspapers: total number (1993) 5; total circulation 324,000[11]; circulation per 1,000 population 12[11]. Radio (1994): 2,200,000 receivers (1 per 13 persons). Television (1994): 260,000 receivers (1 per 106 persons). Telephones (main lines; 1993): 214,000 (1 per 124 persons).

Education and health

Education (1993)

	schools	teachers	students	student/ teacher ratio
Primary (age 5–11)	15,804	173,002	5,428,600	31.4
Secondary (age 12–17)	2,639	31,657	517,577	16.3
Voc., teacher tr.	63	1,332[12]	29,593	13.4[12]
Higher	14	4,392[13]	88,180	8.1[13]

Educational attainment (1979). Percentage of population over age 25 having: no formal schooling 58.6%; primary education 32.2%; some secondary 7.9%; complete secondary and higher 1.3%. *Literacy* (1990): total population over age 15 literate 69.0%; males literate 79.8%; females literate 58.5%.
Health (1993): physicians 3,794 (1 per 7,410 persons); hospital beds 38,137 (1 per 737 persons); infant mortality rate per 1,000 live births (1990–95): 69.0.
Food (1992): daily per capita caloric intake 2,075 (vegetable products 88%, animal products 12%); 89% of FAO recommended minimum requirement.

Military

Total active duty personnel (1995): 24,200 (army 84.7%, navy 5.0%, air force 10.3%). *Military expenditure as percentage of GNP* (1993): 3.5% (world 3.3%); per capita expenditure U.S.$7.

[1]Includes 14 nonelective seats. [2]Kenya pound (K£) as a unit of account equals 20 K Sh. [3]Detail does not add to total given because of rounding. [4]1990. [5]1983. [6]Employed persons only. [7]Indirect taxes less subsidies and imputed bank service charges. [8]Import figures are f.o.b. in balance of trade and c.i.f. in commodities and trading partners. [9]Includes K£53,040,000 in reexports. [10]Kenya Airways only. [11]Circulation for four newspapers only. [12]1987–88; teacher training only. [13]1990–91; universities only.

Kiribati

Official name: Republic of Kiribati.
Form of government: unitary republic with a unicameral legislature (House of Assembly [41[1]]).
Head of state and government: President.
Capital: Bairiki, on Tarawa Atoll.
Official language: English.
Official religion: none.
Monetary unit: 1 Australian Dollar ($A) = 100 cents; valuation (Oct. 6, 1995) 1 U.S.$ = $A 1.31; 1 £ = $A 2.08.

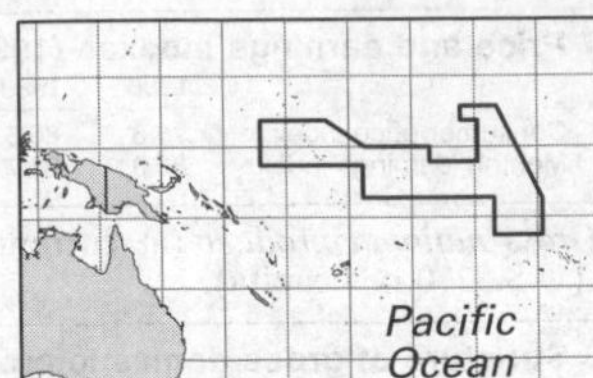

Area and population

Island Groups / Islands	Capitals	area[2] sq mi	area[2] sq km	population 1990 census
Gilberts Group	Bairiki Islet	110	286[3]	67,508
Abaiang	Tuarabu	7	18	5,233
Abemama	Kariatebike	11	27	3,218
Aranuka	Takaeang	5	12	1,002
Arorae	Roreti	3	9	1,440
Banaba	Anteeren	2	6	284
Beru	Taubukinberu	7	18	2,909
Butaritari	Butaritari	5	13	3,774
Kuria	Tabontebike	6	16	990
Maiana	Tebangetua	6	17	2,180
Makin	Makin	3	8	1,762
Marakei	Rawannawi	5	14	2,863
Nikunau	Rungata	7	19	1,994
Nonouti	Teuabu	8	20	2,814
Onotoa	Buariki	6	16	2,100
Tabiteuea North	Utiroa	10	26	3,201
Tabiteuea South	Buariki	5	12	1,331
Tamana	Bakaka	2	5	1,385
Tarawa North	Abaokoro	6	15	3,648
Tarawa South	Bairiki	6	16	25,380
Line Group	Kiritimati	192	496	4,782
Northern		167	432	—
Kiritimati (Christmas)	London	150	388	2,537
Tabuaeran (Fanning)	Paelau	13	34	1,309
Teraina (Washington)	Washington	4	10	936
Southern (Caroline, Flint, Malden, Starbuck, Vostok)		25	64	—
Phoenix Group (Birnie, Enderbury, Kanton [Canton], McKean, Manra [Sydney], Nikumaroro [Gardner], Orona [Hull], Rawaki [Phoenix])	Kanton	11	29	45
TOTAL		313	811	72,335

Demography

Population (1995): 80,400.
Density (1995)[4]: persons per sq mi 287.1, persons per sq km 110.7.
Urban-rural (1995): urban 36.0%; rural 64.0%.
Sex distribution (1990): male 49.45%; female 50.55%.
Age breakdown (1990): under 15, 40.3%; 15–29, 27.5%; 30–44, 17.3%; 45–59, 9.2%; 60–74, 4.8%; 75 and over, 0.9%.
Population projection: (2000) 88,000; (2010) 106,000.
Doubling time: 36 years.
Ethnic composition (1990): I-Kiribati 97.4%; mixed (part I-Kiribati and other) 1.5%; Tuvaluan 0.5%; European 0.2%; other 0.4%.
Religious affiliation (1990): Roman Catholic 53.4%; Kiribati Protestant (Congregational) 39.2%; Bahā'ī 2.4%; Seventh-day Adventist 1.9%; Mormon 1.6%; other 1.5%.
Major cities (1990): urban Tarawa 25,154.

Vital statistics

Birth rate per 1,000 population (1994): 31.6 (world avg. 25.0); legitimate, n.a.; illegitimate, n.a.
Death rate per 1,000 population (1994): 12.3 (world avg. 9.3).
Natural increase rate per 1,000 population (1994): 19.3 (world avg. 15.7).
Total fertility rate (avg. births per childbearing woman; 1994): 3.8.
Marriage rate per 1,000 population (1988): 5.2.
Divorce rate per 1,000 population: n.a.
Life expectancy at birth (1994): male 52.6 years; female 55.8 years.
Major causes of death per 100,000 population (1993): senility without mention of psychosis 61.2; stroke 39.1; diarrhea 37.8; hepatitis 32.5; diabetes mellitus 28.6; malnutrition 23.4; meningitis 18.2.

National economy

Budget (1991). Revenue: $A 22,800,000 (1988; nontax revenue 46.0%, of which reserve fund drawdown 32.1%, fishing licenses 9.8%; tax revenue 28.4%, of which import duties 9.4%, income tax 4.9%; development revenue 25.6%). Expenditures: $A 22,800,000 (1988; education 16.1%; development 15.9%; health 13.0%; natural resources 7.3%; communications 7.0%; public works 6.6%).
Production (metric tons except as noted). Agriculture, forestry, fishing (1994): coconuts 65,000, roots and tubers 8,000 (of which taro 1,000), copra 8,000, vegetables and melons 5,000, bananas 4,000, seaweed 1,200; livestock (number of live animals) 9,000 pigs, 191,000 chickens[5]; fish catch (1993) 29,295. Mining and quarrying: none. Manufacturing (1991): processed copra 8,661; other important products are processed fish, baked goods, clothing, and handicrafts. Energy production (consumption): electricity (kW-hr; 1992) 7,000,000 (7,000,000); coal, none (n.a.); crude petroleum, none (n.a.); petroleum products (metric tons; 1992) none (7,000); natural gas, none (n.a.).
Gross national product (at current market prices; 1993): U.S.$54,000,000 (U.S.$710 per capita).

Structure of gross domestic product and labour force

	1992 in value $A '000	1992 % of total value	1990 labour force	1990 % of labour force
Agriculture, fishing	11,022	23.8	23,137[6]	71.0[6]
Mining	—	—	—	—
Manufacturing	920	2.0	622	1.9
Construction	2,300	5.0	339	1.0
Public utilities	800	1.7	301	0.9
Transp. and commun.	7,130	15.4	921	2.8
Trade	6,530	14.1	1,341	4.1
Finance	3,210	6.9	441	1.4
Pub. admin., defense	11,935	25.8	2,123	6.5
Services			2,286	7.0
Other	2,413	5.2	1,099[7]	3.4[7]
TOTAL	46,260	100.0[3]	32,610	100.0

Public debt (external, outstanding; 1992): U.S.$18,000,000.
Population economically active (1990): total 32,610; activity rate of total population 45.1% (participation rates: over age 15, 75.6%; female 46.4%; unemployed 2.8%).

Price and earnings indexes (1985 = 100)

	1988	1989	1990	1991	1992	1993	1994
Consumer price index	113.8	120.8	126.9	131.7	138.3	146.7	151.0
Earnings index	...	...	...	...	...	...	...

Household income and expenditure. Average household size (1990) 6.6; income per household: n.a.; sources of income (1978): wages 69.7%, self-employment 21.4%, transfer payments 6.0%, other 2.9%; expenditure (1982): food 50.0%, tobacco and alcohol 14.0%, clothing 8.0%, transportation 8.0%, housing, energy, and household operation 7.5%.
Tourism (1993): receipts from visitors U.S.$1,000,000; expenditures by nationals abroad, n.a.
Land use (1993): forested 2.7%; agricultural and under permanent cultivation 50.7%; other 46.6%.

Foreign trade

Balance of trade (current prices)

	1988	1989	1990	1991	1992	1993
$A '000	−21,515	−22,161	−30,765	−29,529	−44,017	−29,478
% of total	61.7%	63.3%	80.7%	80.0%	77.2%	73.8%

Imports (1992): $A 50,530,000 (machinery and transport equipment 47.3%; food 21.1%; manufactured goods 8.0%; mineral fuels 7.8%; beverages and tobacco 5.0%; chemicals 3.5%; crude materials 1.2%). *Major import sources:* Australia 38.4%; Japan 22.7%; Fiji 11.3%; New Zealand 5.4%; China 3.3%; United States 2.9%; Hong Kong 1.0%.
Exports (1992): $A 6,513,000 (domestic exports 86.7%, of which copra 66.8%, fish and fish preparations 11.3%; reexports 13.3%). *Major export destinations:* United States 12.3%; Australia 4.8%; Denmark 4.5%; Fiji 4.1%; New Zealand 1.6%; United Kingdom 0.9%.

Transport and communications

Transport. Roads (1991): total length 398 mi, 640 km (paved 5%). Vehicles (1982): passenger cars 307; trucks and buses 130. Merchant marine (1992): vessels (100 gross tons and over) 7; total deadweight tonnage 2,685. Air transport (1990): passenger-mi 5,331,000, passenger-km 8,579,000; short ton-mi cargo 514,000, metric ton-km cargo 750,000; airports (1994) with scheduled flights 18.
Communications. Daily newspapers: none. Radio (1994): total number of receivers 15,000 (1 per 5.2 persons). Television: none. Telephones (main lines; 1993): 1,800 (1 per 43 persons).

Education and health

Education (1993)

	schools	teachers	students	student/teacher ratio
Primary (age 6–13)	92	537	16,316	30.4
Secondary (age 14–18)	9[8]	179	3,152	17.6
Voc., teacher tr.	6[8]	43[9]	288[9]	6.7[9]
Higher[10]	—	—	—	—

Educational attainment (1990)[11]. Percentage of population age 15 and over having: no schooling 6.9%; primary 67.8%; secondary 24.5%; higher 0.6%; not stated 0.2%. *Literacy* (1985): total population age 15 and over literate 90%.
Health: physicians (1993) 10 (1 per 7,687 persons); hospital beds (1990) 283 (1 per 253 persons); infant mortality rate per 1,000 live births (1994) 98.4.
Food (1992): daily per capita caloric intake 2,651 (vegetable products 88%, animal products 12%); 116% of FAO recommended minimum requirement.

[1]Includes two nonelective members. [2]Includes uninhabited islands. [3]Detail does not add to total given because of rounding. [4]Based on inhabited island areas (280 sq mi, 726 sq km) only. [5]1982. [6]Includes 20,568 persons engaged in "village work" (subsistence agriculture or fishing). [7]Includes 900 unemployed. [8]1990. [9]1992. [10]54 students overseas. [11]For indigenous population.

Korea, North

Official name: Chosŏn Minjujuŭi In'min Konghwaguk (Democratic People's Republic of Korea).
Form of government: unitary single-party republic with one legislative house (Supreme People's Assembly [687]).
Chief of state:[1].
Head of government: Premier.
Capital: P'yŏngyang.
Official language: Korean.
Official religion: none.
Monetary unit: 1 won = 100 chŏn; valuation (Oct. 6, 1995) 1 U.S.$ = 2.15 won; 1 £ = 3.40 won.

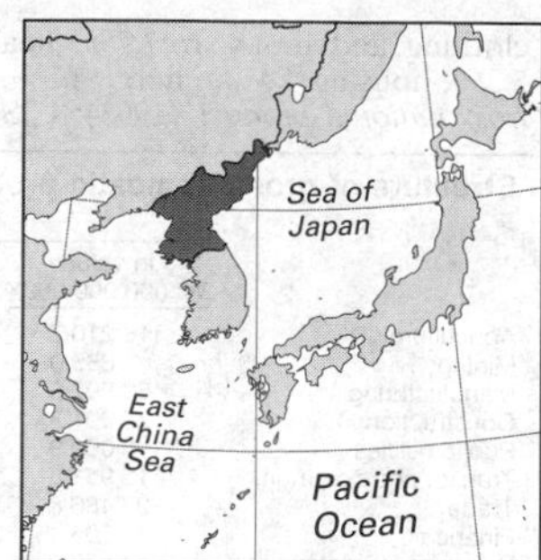

Area and population

		area		population[2]
Provinces	**Capitals**	sq mi	sq km	1987 estimate
Chagang-do	Kanggye	6,551	16,968	1,156,000
Hamgyŏng-namdo	Hamhŭng	7,324	18,970	2,547,000
Hamgyŏng-pukto	Ch'ŏngjin	6,784	17,570	2,003,000
Hwanghae-namdo	Haeju	3,090	8,002	1,914,000
Hwanghae-pukto	Sariwŏn	3,092	8,007	1,409,000
Kangwŏn-do	Wŏnsan	4,306	11,152	1,227,000
P'yŏngan-namdo	P'yŏngsan	4,470	11,577	2,653,000
P'yŏngan-pukto	Sinŭiju	4,707[3]	12,191[3]	2,380,000
Yanggang-do	Hyesan	5,528	14,317	628,000
Special cities				
Kaesŏng	—	485	1,255	331,000
Namp'o	—	291	753	715,000
P'yŏngyang	—	772	2,000	2,355,000
Special district				
Hyangsan-chigu	—	[3]	[3]	28,000
TOTAL		47,399[4]	122,762	19,346,000

Demography

Population (1995): 23,487,000.
Density (1995): persons per sq mi 495.5, persons per sq km 191.3.
Urban-rural (1995): urban 61.3%; rural 38.7%.
Sex distribution (1995): male 49.28%; female 50.72%.
Age breakdown (1995): under 15, 29.1%; 15–29, 30.9%; 30–44, 21.9%; 45–59, 11.2%; 60–74, 5.5%; 75 and over, 1.5%.
Population projection: (2000) 25,491,000; (2010) 28,491,000.
Doubling time: 39 years.
Ethnic composition (1989): Korean 99.8%; Chinese 0.2%.
Religious affiliation (1980): atheist or nonreligious 67.9%; traditional beliefs 15.6%; Ch'ŏndogyo 13.9%; Buddhist 1.7%; Christian 0.9%.
Major cities (1987): P'yŏngyang 2,355,000; Hamhŭng 701,000; Ch'ŏngjin 520,000; Namp'o 370,000; Sunch'ŏn 356,000.

Vital statistics

Birth rate per 1,000 population (1995): 23.3 (world avg. 25.0).
Death rate per 1,000 population (1995): 5.5 (world avg. 9.3).
Natural increase rate per 1,000 population (1995): 17.8 (world avg. 15.7).
Total fertility rate (avg. births per childbearing woman; 1995): 2.3.
Marriage rate per 1,000 population (1987): 9.3.
Divorce rate per 1,000 population (1987): 0.2.
Life expectancy at birth (1995): male 67.0 years; female 73.3 years.
Major causes of death per 100,000 population (1986): diseases of the circulatory system 224.9; malignant neoplasms (cancers) 69.0; diseases of the digestive system 51.6; diseases of the respiratory system 46.7; injuries and poisoning 38.2; infectious and parasitic diseases 19.4.

National economy

Budget (1994). Revenue: 41,525,200,000 won (1984; turnover tax 55.0%, payments by state enterprises 30.0%). Expenditures: 41,525,200,000 won (national economy 67.8%, social and cultural affairs 19.8%, defense 11.6%, administration 0.8%).
Public debt (external, outstanding; 1992): U.S.$8,000,000,000.
Tourism (1986): total number of tourist arrivals 85,000.
Population economically active (1994)[5]: total 12,486,000; activity rate of total population 53.2% (participation rates [1988–93]: ages 15–64, 49.5%; female 46.0%; unemployed, n.a.).
Price and earnings indexes: n.a.
Production (metric tons except as noted). Agriculture, forestry, fishing (1994): corn (maize) 2,140,000, rice 2,104,000, potatoes 1,762,000, cabbages 865,000, sweet potatoes 504,000, soybeans 400,000, pears 126,000, watermelons 112,000, barley 110,000, peaches 108,000, wheat 100,000, cucumbers and gherkins 74,000, tomatoes 73,000, tobacco leaves 65,000, millet 30,000, oats 30,000; livestock (number of live animals) 3,300,000 pigs, 1,300,000 cattle, 390,000 sheep, 300,000 goats, 46,000,000 chickens; roundwood (1993) 4,830,000 cu m; fish catch (1993) 1,780,000. Mining and quarrying (1993): iron ore 13,000,000; magnesite (metal content) 1,800,000; phosphate rock 510,000; sulfur 240,000; zinc 200,000; lead (metal content) 80,000; graphite 50,000; fluorspar 41,000; copper 16,000; gold 5,000 kg; silver 50 kg. Manufacturing (1993): cement 17,000,000; crude steel 8,100,000; pig iron 6,600,000; coke 3,000,000; chemical fertilizers 3,000,000[6]; steel semimanufactures 1,790,000; meat 230,000[7]; gasoline 8,600,000 barrels; textile fabrics 190,000,000 sq m. Construction: n.a. Energy production (consumption): electricity (kW-hr; 1992) 38,000,000 (38,000,000); coal (metric tons; 1992) 70,000,000 (72,050,000); crude petroleum (barrels; 1992) none (18,325,000); petroleum products (metric tons; 1992) 2,965,000 (4,505,000); natural gas, none (n.a.).
Household income and expenditure. Average household size (1987) 4.8; average annual income per household (1980) 3,677 won (U.S.$4,275); sources of income: n.a.; expenditure (1984)[8]: food 46.5%, clothing 29.9%, furniture 3.8%, energy 3.3%, housing 0.6%.
Gross national product (1992): U.S.$22,000,000,000 (U.S.$990 per capita).

Structure of gross domestic product and labour force

	1982		1990–92	
	in value '000,000 won	% of total value	labour force	% of labour force
Agriculture	...	...	4,987,000	43.0
Mining and manufacturing	...	...		
Construction	...	...	3,479,000	30.0
Public utilities	...	...		
Transportation and communications	...	...		
Trade	...	...		
Finance	...	...	3,131,000	27.0
Pub. admin., defense	...	...		
Services	...	...		
Other	...	...		
TOTAL	11,800	100.0	11,597,000	100.0

Land use (1993): forested 61.2%; meadows and pastures 0.4%; agricultural and under permanent cultivation 16.6%; other 21.8%.

Foreign trade[9]

Balance of trade (current prices)

	1987	1988	1989	1990	1991	1992
U.S.$'000,000	−391.7	−315.2	−433.9	−420.6	764.7	−600.0
% of total	20.0%	14.1%	21.0%	21.0%	35.6%	18.8%

Imports (1992): U.S.$1,900,000,000 (crude petroleum, coal and coke, industrial machinery and transport equipment [including trucks], industrial chemicals, textile yarn and fabrics, and grain are among the major imports). *Major import sources:* Russia 37.6%; China 23.0%; Japan 9.8%; Hong Kong 5.4%.
Exports (1992): U.S.$1,300,000,000 (minerals [including lead, magnesite, zinc], metallurgical products [iron and steel, nonferrous metals], cement, agricultural products [including fish, grain, fruit and vegetables, tobacco], and manufactured goods [textile fabrics, clothing] are among the major exports). *Major export destinations:* Russia 45.4%; Japan 22.9%; China 6.8%; Germany 5.8%; Hong Kong 3.2%.

Transport and communications

Transport. Railroads (1990): length 5,302 mi, 8,533 km; (latest) passenger-mi 2,100,000,000, passenger-km 3,400,000,000; (latest) short ton-mi cargo 5,100,000,000, metric ton-km cargo 9,100,000,000. Roads (1992): total length 18,600 mi, 30,000 km (paved 6.2%). Vehicles (1990): passenger cars 248,000. Merchant marine (1992): vessels (100 gross tons and over) 100; total deadweight tonnage 951,222. Air transport (1994): passenger-mi 52,200,000, passenger-km 84,000,000; short ton-mi cargo 1,370,000, metric ton-km cargo 2,000,000; airports (1995) with scheduled flights 1.
Communications. Daily newspapers (1992): total number 11; total circulation 5,000,000; circulation per 1,000 population 221. Radio (1994): total number of receivers 2,500,000 (1 per 9.2 persons). Television (1994): total number of receivers 2,000,000 (1 per 11.5 persons). Telephones (main lines; 1994): 1,089,300 (1 per 20.7 persons).

Education and health

Education (1987)

	schools	teachers	students	student/ teacher ratio
Primary (age 6–9)	6,122	138,945	1,543,000	11.1
Secondary (age 10–15)	...	111,000	2,468,000	22.2
Voc., teacher tr.	473[10]		220,000	...
Higher	281	27,000	390,000	14.4

Educational attainment (1987–88). Percentage of population age 16 and over having attended or graduated from postsecondary-level school: 13.7%. *Literacy* (1992): 95%.
Health (1989): physicians 57,690 (1 per 370 persons); hospital beds 290,590 (1 per 74 persons); infant mortality rate per 1,000 live births (1995) 26.8.
Food (1992): daily per capita caloric intake 2,833 (vegetable products 93%, animal products 7%); 121% of FAO recommended minimum requirement.

Military

Total active duty personnel (1995): 1,128,000 (army 88.6%, navy 4.1%, air force 7.3%). *Military expenditure as percentage of GNP* (1994): 26.6% (world [1993] 3.3%); per capita expenditure U.S.$234.

[1]Kim Jong Il (son of the previous president Kim Il Sung, who died on July 8, 1994) had not assumed the title of president as of mid-October 1995. [2]Civilian population only. [3]P'yŏngan-pukto includes special district of Hyangsan-chigu. [4]Detail does not add to total given because of rounding. [5]The Democratic People's Republic of Korea categorizes economically active as including students in higher education, retirees, and heads of households, as well as those in the civilian labour force. [6]1991. [7]1994. [8]Workers and clerical workers only. [9]Imports are f.o.b. [10]1986.

Korea, South

Official name: Taehan Min'guk (Republic of Korea).
Form of government: unitary multiparty republic with one legislative house (National Assembly [299]).
Chief of state: President.
Head of government: Prime Minister.
Capital: Seoul.
Official language: Korean.
Official religion: none.
Monetary unit: 1 won (W) = 100 chon; valuation (Oct. 6, 1995) 1 U.S.$ = W 798; 1 £ = W 1,215.

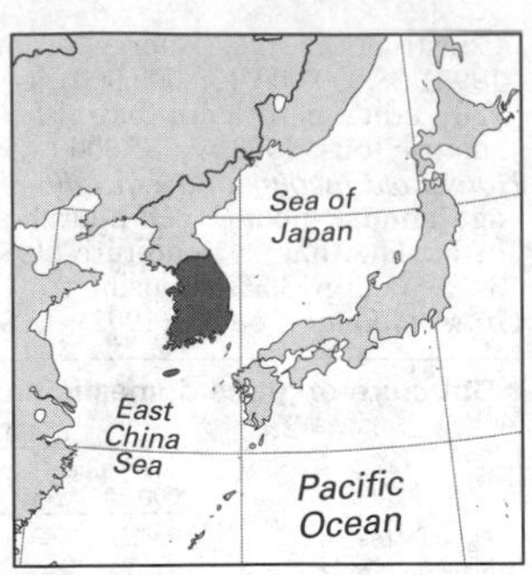

Area and population

Provinces	Capitals	area sq mi	area sq km	population 1990 census
Cheju-do	Cheju	705	1,827	514,605
Chŏlla-namdo	Kwangju	4,578	11,858	2,507,439
Chŏlla-pukto	Chŏnju	3,106	8,043	2,069,960
Ch'ungch'ŏng-namdo	Taejŏn	3,225	8,352	2,013,926
Ch'ungch'ŏng-pukto	Ch'ŏngju	2,871	7,436	1,389,686
Kangwŏn-do	Ch'unch'ŏn	6,524	16,897	1,580,430
Kyŏnggi-do	Suwŏn	4,162	10,780	6,155,632
Kyŏngsang-namdo	Masan	4,548	11,779	3,672,396
Kyŏngsang-pukto	Taegu	7,510	19,451	2,860,595
Special cities				
Inch'ŏn-si	Inch'ŏn	131	339	1,817,919
Kwangju-si	Kwangju	193	501	1,139,003
Pusan-si	Pusan	205	531	3,798,113
Sŏul-t'ŭkpyŏlsi	Seoul	234	605	10,612,577
Taegu-si	Taegu	176	456	2,229,040
Taejŏn-si	Taejŏn	207	537	1,049,578
TOTAL		38,375	99,392	43,410,899

Demography

Population (1995): 44,834,000.
Density (1995): persons per sq mi 1,168.3, persons per sq km 451.1.
Urban-rural (1995): urban 81.0%; rural 19.0%.
Sex distribution (1995): male 50.34%; female 49.66%.
Age breakdown (1995): under 15, 23.2%; 15–29, 28.2%; 30–44, 25.1%; 45–59, 14.5%; 60–74, 7.3%; 75 and over, 1.7%.
Population projection: (2000) 46,789,000; (2010) 49,683,000.
Doubling time: 70 years.
Ethnic composition (1990): Korean 99.9%; other 0.1%.
Religious affiliation (1991): religious[1] 54.0%, of which Buddhist 27.6%, Protestant 18.6%, Roman Catholic 5.7%, Confucian 1.0%, Wonbulgyo 0.3%, Ch'ondogyo 0.2%, other 0.6%; nonreligious 46.0%.
Major cities (1990): Seoul 10,612,577; Pusan 3,798,113; Taegu 2,229,040; Inch'ŏn 1,817,919; Kwangju 1,139,003.

Vital statistics

Birth rate per 1,000 population (1995): 16.0 (world avg. 25.0).
Death rate per 1,000 population (1995): 6.0 (world avg. 9.3).
Natural increase rate per 1,000 population (1995): 10.0 (world avg. 15.7).
Total fertility rate (avg. births per childbearing woman; 1995): 1.8.
Marriage rate per 1,000 population (1993): 7.0.
Divorce rate per 1,000 population (1993): 1.1.
Life expectancy at birth (1995): male 68.0 years; female 76.0 years.
Major causes of death per 100,000 population (1993): diseases of the circulatory system 149.0; malignant neoplasms (cancers) 105.9; accidents, poisoning, and violence 73.0; diseases of the digestive system 40.5; diseases of the respiratory system 24.1.

National economy

Budget (1994). Revenue: W 58,824,000,000,000 (taxes on goods and services 35.5%, income taxes 29.9%, nontax revenue 11.5%, social security contributions 7.8%, taxes on international trade 4.8%). Expenditures: W 53,952,000,000,000 (defense 19.3%, education 15.5%, general public services 10.6%, social security and welfare 10.2%, agriculture 8.5%, transportation and communications 7.7%).
Public debt (external, outstanding; 1993): U.S.$24,567,000,000.
Production (metric tons except as noted). Agriculture, forestry, fishing (1994): rice 7,056,000, cabbages 2,600,000, dry onions 1,051,000, apples 631,000, tangerines 555,000, garlic 476,000, barley 443,000, soybeans 160,000; livestock (number of live animals) 6,300,000 pigs, 3,200,000 cattle, 74,000,000 chickens; roundwood (1993) 6,485,000 cu m; fish catch (1993) 2,648,977. Mining and quarrying (1994): copper ore 224,000; iron ore 191,313; zinc concentrate 14,243; lead concentrate 4,345. Manufacturing (1993): cement 47,313,000; pig iron 21,870,000; urea fertilizers 831,066; newsprint 742,327; caustic soda 506,794; synthetic fabrics 2,459,299,000 sq m; television receivers 15,956,000 units; passenger cars 1,527;753 units. Construction (1994): residential 63,576,000 sq m; nonresidential 52,908,000 sq m. Energy production (consumption): electricity (kW-hr; 1993) 163,449,000,000 (163,449,000,000); coal (metric tons; 1993) 9,443,000 (42,419,000); crude petroleum (barrels; 1993) none (544,714,000); petroleum products (metric tons; 1993) 64,566,000 (59,079,000); natural gas (cu m; 1993) none (6,140,000,000).
Household income and expenditure (1993)[2]. Average household size (1990) 3.8; income per household W 27,470,000 (U.S.$34,223); sources of income: wages 55.7%, other 44.3%; expenditure: food and beverages 29.3%, education and recreation 13.5%, transportation and communications 10.2%, clothing and footwear 7.7%, health care 5.4%, household durable goods 5.2%, housing 4.4%, energy 4.3%, other 20.0%.
Gross national product (1993): U.S.$337,910,000,000 (U.S.$7,670 per capita).

Structure of gross domestic product and labour force

	1993			
	in value W '000,000,000[3]	% of total value	labour force	% of labour force
Agriculture	16,210.7	7.5	2,845,000	14.4
Mining	885.0	0.4	54,000	0.3
Manufacturing	62,997.3	29.0	4,584,000	23.2
Construction	24,901.7	11.5	1,680,000	8.5
Public utilities	5,069.9	2.3	65,000	0.3
Transp. and commun.	15,961.8	7.3	1,008,000	5.1
Trade	27,486.8	12.7	4,831,000	24.5
Finance	37,505.1	17.3	1,355,000	6.9
Pub. admin., defense	14,458.0	6.7	2,784,000	14.1
Services	12,860.2	5.9		
Other	−1,097.3[4]	−0.5[4]	551,000[5]	2.8[5]
TOTAL	217,239.2	100.0[6]	19,754,000[6]	100.0[6]

Population economically active (1993): total 19,754,000; activity rate 44.8% (participation rates: ages 15 and over, 61.0%; female 39.9%; unemployed 2.8%).

Price and earnings indexes (1990 = 100)

	1988	1989	1990	1991	1992	1993	1994
Consumer price index	87.1	92.1	100.0	109.3	116.1	121.7	129.3
Monthly earnings index	66.5	83.2	100.0	116.9	135.2	149.9	173.1

Tourism (1993): receipts from visitors U.S.$3,510,000,000; expenditures by nationals abroad U.S.$4,105,000,000.
Land use (1993): forested 65.4%; meadows and pastureland 0.9%; agricultural and under permanent cultivation 20.8%; other 12.9%.

Foreign trade

Balance of trade (current prices)

	1989	1990	1991	1992	1993	1994
U.S.$'000,000	+2,875	−701	−3,968	−588	+2,880	−729
% of total	3.6%	0.8%	3.6%	0.4%	1.8%	0.5%

Imports (1993): U.S.$83,800,100,000 (machinery and transport equipment 33.9%, mineral fuels and lubricants 18.0%, manufactured goods 14.4%, inedible crude materials 10.6%, chemicals 9.8%). *Major import sources:* Japan 23.9%; United States 21.4%; Germany 4.7%; Saudi Arabia 4.5%; Australia 4.0%; Indonesia 3.1%; Malaysia 2.3%; Canada 2.0%; Singapore 1.8%.
Exports (1993): U.S.$82,235,900,000 (machinery and transport equipment 44.9%, manufactured goods 25.2%, chemicals 6.0%, food and live animals 2.5%, mineral fuels 2.2%). *Major export destinations:* United States 22.1%; Japan 14.1%; Hong Kong 7.8%; Germany 4.4%; Singapore 3.8%; Taiwan 2.8%; Indonesia 2.5%; India 2.2%.

Transport and communications

Transport. Railroads (1994): length 4,049 mi, 6,517 km; passenger-km 30,216,000,000; metric ton-km cargo 14,064,000,000. Roads (1993): total length 38,087 mi, 61,296 km (paved 85%). Vehicles (1993): passenger cars 4,271,253; trucks and buses 2,002,755. Merchant marine (1992): vessels (100 gross tons and over) 2,138; total deadweight tonnage 11,724,942. Air transport (1994): passenger-km 39,260,000,000; metric ton-km cargo 4,825,626,000; airports (1995) with scheduled flights 14.
Communications. Daily newspapers (1993): total number 63; total circulation 9,736,000[7]; circulation per 1,000 population 221[7]. Radio (1994): 42,570,000 receivers (1 per 1.0 persons). Television (1994): 10,430,000 receivers (1 per 4.3 persons). Telephones (main lines; 1993): 16,632,600 (1 per 2.6 persons).

Education and health

Education (1994)

	schools	teachers	students	student/ teacher ratio
Primary (age 6–13)	5,900	139,096	4,099,395	29.5
Secondary (age 14–19)	3,691	155,528	3,717,987	23.9
Vocational	738	41,311	851,495	20.6
Higher	645	51,696	1,767,517	34.2

Educational attainment (1990). Percentage of population age 25 and over having: no formal schooling 11.0%; primary education or less 21.7%; some secondary and secondary 53.9%; postsecondary 13.4%. *Literacy* (1990): total population age 15 and over literate 96.3%; males literate 99.1%; females literate 93.5%.
Health (1993): physicians 51,518 (1 per 855 persons); hospital beds 164,588 (1 per 268 persons); infant mortality rate per 1,000 live births (1995) 10.0.
Food (1992): daily per capita caloric intake 3,285 (vegetable products 86%, animal products 14%); 140% of FAO recommended minimum requirement.

Military

Total active duty personnel (1995): 633,000 (army 82.1%, navy 9.5%, air force 8.4%). *Military expenditure as percentage of GNP* (1993): 3.6% (world 3.3%); per capita expenditure U.S.$271.

[1]Refers to persons who have received commandments, accepted baptism, or entered a faith and who participate in a religious function regularly or put the religious idea into practice. [2]Excludes farm households. [3]At 1990 constant prices. [4]Import duties less imputed bank service charges. [5]Unemployed. [6]Detail does not add to total given because of rounding. [7]Circulation for 20 newspapers only.

Kuwait

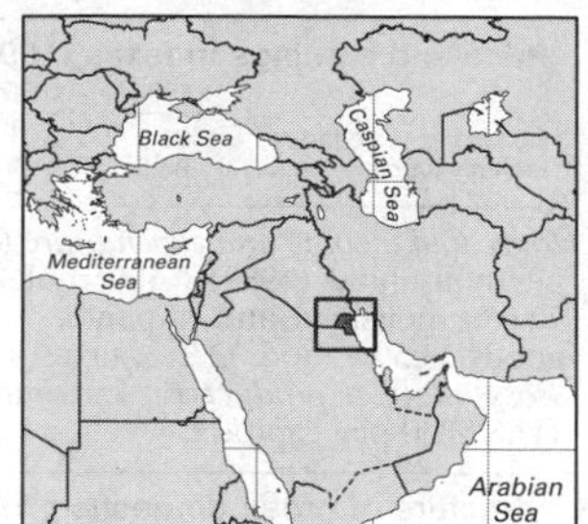

Official name: Dawlat al-Kuwayt (State of Kuwait).
Form of government: Constitutional monarchy with one legislative body (National Assembly [50[1]]).
Head of state and government: Emir[2].
Capital: Kuwait City.
Official language: Arabic.
Official religion: Islam.
Monetary unit: 1 Kuwaiti dinar (KD) = 1,000 fils; valuation (Oct. 6, 1995) 1 KD = U.S.$3.33 = £2.13.

Area and population[3]

		area		population
Governorates[4]	**Capitals**	sq mi	sq km	1995 estimate
al-Aḥmadī	al-Aḥmadī	1,984	5,138	283,902
al-Farwānīyah	al-Farwānīyah	...	...	451,707
al-Jahrā'	al-Jahrā'	4,372	11,324	228,457
Capital	Kuwait City	38	98	276,915
Ḥawallī	Ḥawallī	138	358	449,554
Islands[5]	—	347	900	...
TOTAL		6,880[6]	17,818	1,690,535

Demography

Population (1995): 1,691,000.
Density (1995): persons per sq mi 245.8, persons per sq km 94.9.
Urban-rural (1995): urban 96.6%; rural 3.4%.
Sex distribution (1995): male 61.45%; female 38.55%.
Age breakdown (1995): under 15, 40.4%; 15–29, 25.7%; 30–44, 22.5%; 45–59, 8.6%; 60–74, 2.2%; 75 and over, 0.6%.
Population projection: (2000) 1,987,000; (2010) 2,494,000.
Doubling time: 30 years.
Ethnic composition (by nationality; 1995): Kuwaiti 41.1%; non-Kuwaiti (including other Arab, South Asian, Palestinian, and Badoun [stateless immigrants]) 58.9%.
Religious affiliation (1995): Muslim 85%, of which Sunnī 45%, Shī'ah 30%; other Muslim 10%; other (mostly Christian and Hindu) 15.0%.
Major cities (1993): al-Jahrā' 139,476; as-Sālimīyah 116,104; Ḥawallī 84,478; al-Farwānīyah 47,106; Kuwait City 31,241.

Vital statistics

Birth rate per 1,000 population (1993): 25.6 (world avg. 25.0); legitimate, n.a.; illegitimate, n.a.
Death rate per 1,000 population (1993): 2.4 (world avg. 9.3).
Natural increase rate per 1,000 population (1993): 23.2 (world avg. 15.7).
Total fertility rate (avg. births per childbearing woman; 1995): 3.9.
Marriage rate per 1,000 population (1989): 5.4.
Divorce rate per 1,000 population (1989): 1.5.
Life expectancy at birth (1994): male 73.0 years; female 77.0 years.
Major causes of death per 100,000 population (1992): circulatory diseases 79.8; accidents, poisoning, and violence 40.3; malignant neoplasms (cancers) 22.6; respiratory diseases 17.1; congenital anomalies 9.2; endocrine, nutritional, and metabolic diseases 8.4; diseases of the nervous system 7.4; infectious and parasitic diseases 5.7; diseases of the digestive system 4.4.

National economy

Budget (1994–95). Revenue: KD 2,637,200,000 (oil revenue 84.7%). Expenditures[7]: KD 4,140,000,000 (defense 27.1%; education 10.5%; health 9.2%; administrative services 5.7%; electricity, water, and public utilities 4.8%; transportation and communications 2.3%).
Public debt (external, outstanding; 1991): U.S.$792,000,000[8].
Tourism (1993): receipts from visitors U.S.$83,000,000; expenditures by nationals abroad U.S.$1,888,000,000.
Gross national product (at current market prices; 1993): U.S.$34,120,000,000 (U.S.$23,350 per capita).

Structure of gross domestic product and labour force

	1994			
	in value KD '000,000[9]	% of total value	labour force[10]	% of labour force[10]
Agriculture	31.4	0.4	15,985	1.6
Mining (oil sector)	2,830.2	39.2	7,071	0.7
Manufacturing	766.3	10.6	70,659	7.1
Construction	244.6	3.4	128,813	13.0
Public utilities	−21.5	−0.3	7,017	0.7
Transportation and communications	288.7	4.0	38,706	3.9
Trade[11]	476.6	6.6	184,284	18.6
Finance and business services	886.3	12.3	35,341	3.6
Pub. admin., defense / Services	1,810.3	25.1	469,432	47.4
Other	−98.0[12]	−1.4[12]	33,210	3.4
TOTAL	7,214.9	100.0[6]	990,518	100.0

Production (metric tons except as noted). Agriculture, forestry, fishing (1994): tomatoes 35,000, cucumbers and gherkins 17,000, onions 16,000, eggplants 2,000, garlic 1,000; livestock (number of live animals) 150,000 sheep, 15,000 goats, 12,000 cattle, 1,000 camels, 14,000,000 chickens; fish catch (1993) 8,561. Mining and quarrying (1993): sulfur 175,000; lime 35,000. Manufacturing (1993): cement 533,500; ammonia (urea) 300,000; flour 127,000; concrete pipes 82,100; bread 70,000; bran 38,000; liquefied caustic soda 15,500; chlorine gas 13,700; biscuits 2,000; detergents 700; hydrochloric acid 1,427,900 gallons[13]; concrete 134,800 cu m; sodium hydrochloride 7,560 cu m[13]. Construction (floor area approved for construction; 1989): residential 2,563,000 sq m; nonresidential 416,000 sq m. Energy production (consumption): electricity (kW-hr; 1992) 16,885,000,000 (14,209,000,000); coal, none (none); crude petroleum (barrels; 1992) 388,700,000 (117,400,000); petroleum products (metric tons; 1992) 16,059,000 (3,064,000); natural gas (cu m; 1992) 2,619,800,000 (2,619,800,000).
Population economically active (1990): total 722,495; activity rate of total population 37.2% (participation rates [1988]: ages 15–64, 56.1%; female 18.8%; unemployed 1.9%).

Price and earnings indexes (1990 = 100)

	1987	1988	1989	1990	1991	1992	1993[14]
Consumer price index	93.5	94.8	98.1	100.0	116.9	116.9	110.8
Earnings index	...	...	...	...	...	...	...

Household income and expenditure. Average household size (1986) 7.4; annual income per household (1973)[15] KD 4,246 (U.S.$12,907); sources of income: wages and salaries 53.8%, self-employment 20.8%, other 25.4%; expenditure (1992): food, beverages, and tobacco 37.0%, housing and energy 18.7%, transportation 15.3%, household appliances and services 11.1%, clothing and footwear 10.0%, education and health 2.5%.
Land use (1993): forested 0.1%; meadows and pastures 7.7%; agricultural and under permanent cultivation 0.3%; other, built-up, and wasteland 91.9%.

Foreign trade[16]

Balance of trade (current prices)

	1989	1990	1991	1992	1993	1994
KD '000,000	+1,465	+917	−1,135	−202	+969	+1,331
% of total	28.0%	29.4%	64.9%	5.0%	18.7%	25.2%

Imports (1994): KD 1,988,200,000 (machinery and transport equipment 38.1%, manufactured goods 19.2%, miscellaneous manufactured articles 15.5%, food and live animals 14.9%, chemical products 7.6%, beverages and tobacco 1.6%). *Major import sources:* U.S. 14.5%; Japan 11.7%; Germany 8.2%; U.K. 6.9%; France 6.3%; Italy 6.0%; Saudi Arabia 5.7%; India 2.9%.
Exports (1994)[17]: KD 3,311,000,000 (crude petroleum and petroleum products 93.1%). *Major export destinations:* France 15.7%; Saudi Arabia 14.5%; United Arab Emirates 13.8%; India 13.5%; Hong Kong 8.2%; China 3.3%; Pakistan 2.8%; Egypt 2.1%; Italy 2.0%.

Transport and communications

Transport. Railroads: none. Roads (1990): total length 2,655 mi, 4,273 km (paved 100%). Vehicles (1993): passenger cars 530,000; trucks and buses 144,300. Merchant marine (1992): vessels (100 gross tons and over) 209; total deadweight tonnage 3,188,526. Air transport (1993)[18]: passenger mi 2,518,801,000, passenger-km 4,053,626,000; short ton-mi cargo 174,042,000, metric ton-km cargo 254,097,000; airports (1995) with scheduled flights 1.
Communications. Daily newspapers (1992): total number 9; total circulation 480,000; circulation per 1,000 population 244. Radio (1994): total number of receivers 1,000,000 (1 per 1.6 persons). Television (1994): total number of receivers 800,000 (1 per 2.0 persons). Telephones (main lines; 1993): 358,000 (1 per 4.1 persons).

Education and health

Education (1994–95)

	schools	teachers	students	student/ teacher ratio
Primary (age 6–9)	246	8,815	132,204	15.0
Secondary (age 10–17)	391	18,072	200,828	11.1
Voc., teacher tr.	34	683	2,936	4.3
Higher[19]	1	927[20]	11,284	...

Educational attainment (1988). Percentage of population age 25 and over having: no formal schooling 44.8%; primary education 8.6%; some secondary 15.1%; complete secondary 15.1%; higher 16.4%. *Literacy* (1988): total population age 15 and over literate 961,880 (79.7%); males literate 574,739 (83.3%); females literate 387,141 (74.9%).
Health (1993): physicians 2,403 (1 per 608 persons); hospital beds 4,093[21] (1 per 357 persons); infant mortality rate per 1,000 live births (1994) 13.0.
Food (1992): daily per capita caloric intake 2,523 (vegetable products 79%, animal products 21%); 104% of FAO recommended minimum requirement.

Military

Total active duty personnel (1995): 16,600 (army [including central staff] 69.8%, navy 15.1%, air force 15.1%). *Military expenditure as percentage of GNP* (1994): 12.2% (world 2.6%); per capita expenditure U.S.$2,019.

[1]Excludes ministers who were not elected as deputies and who sit as ex officio members. [2]Assisted by prime minister. [3]Area of governorates reflects situation prior to Amiri Decree No. 156 of 1988, which established al-Farwānīyah governorate; but population estimate accounts for the reorganization. [4]Governorates have no administrative function. [5]Bubian Island 333 sq mi (863 sq km) and Warba Island 14 sq mi (37 sq km). [6]Detail does not add to total given because of rounding. [7]Total includes current and capital expenditure, but 1993–94 breakdown is derived from current expenditure. [8]Includes external long-term debt not guaranteed by the government. [9]At purchaser's value. [10]Year-end. [11]Trade includes restaurants and hotels. [12]Includes import duties of KD 99,800,000 and imputed bank service charges of KD −197,800,000. [13]1992. [14]Third quarter. [15]Kuwaiti households only. [16]Imports are f.o.b. in balance of trade and c.i.f. in commodities and trading partners. [17]Total exports and reexports include oil and non-oil, but breakdown by destination is derived from non-oil exports. [18]Kuwait Airways only. [19]1992–93. [20]1989–90. [21]Public hospitals only.

Kyrgyzstan

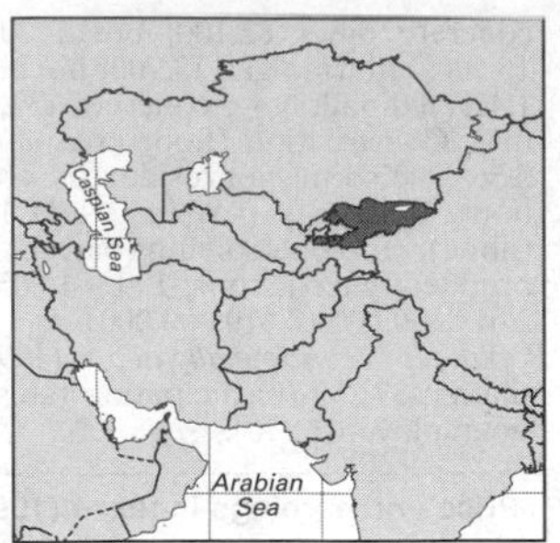

Official name: Kyrgyz Respublikasy (Kyrgyz Republic).
Form of government: unitary multiparty republic with a bicameral legislative body (Supreme Council, comprising a Legislative Assembly [35] and an Assembly of People's Representatives [70]).
Head of state: President.
Head of government: Prime Minister.
Capital: Bishkek (formerly Frunze).
Official languages: Kyrgyz; Russian.
Official religion: none.
Monetary unit: 1 som = 100 tyiyn; valuation (Oct. 4, 1995) free rate, 1 U.S.$ = 10.86 som; 1 £ = 17.26 som.

Area and population

Provinces	Capitals	area sq mi	area sq km	population 1993[1] estimate
Chüy (Chu)	Kara-Balta	7,200	18,700	774,000
Jalal-Abad (Dzhalal-Abad)	Jalal-Abad (Dzhalal-Abad)	15,200	39,500	812,800
Naryn	Naryn	18,300	47,300	267,900
Osh	Osh	14,700	38,100	1,360,900
Talas	Talas	4,400	11,400	203,000
Ysyk-Köl (Issyk-Kul)	Ysyk-Köl (Issyk-Kul)	16,800	43,500	429,300
City of republic subordination				
Bishkek (Frunze)	—	...	...	634,100
TOTAL		76,600	198,500	4,482,000

Demography

Population (1995): 4,483,000.
Density (1995): persons per sq mi 58.5, persons per sq km 22.6.
Urban-rural (1993): urban 37.2%; rural 62.8%.
Sex distribution (1993): male 49.16%; female 50.84%.
Age breakdown (1989): under 15, 37.5%; 15–29, 27.0%; 30–44, 16.3%; 45–59, 10.9%; 60–74, 6.2%; 75 and over, 2.1%.
Population projection: (2000) 4,551,000; (2010) 4,691,000.
Doubling time: 39 years.
Ethnic composition (1989): Kyrgyz 52.4%; Russian 21.5%; Uzbek 12.9%; Ukrainian 2.5%; German 2.4%; Tatar 1.6%; other 6.7%.
Religious affiliation: believers are predominantly Sunnī Muslim (Ḥanafīyah).
Major cities (1991): Bishkek (Frunze) 631,300; Osh 218,700; Jalal-Abad 74,200; Tokmok 71,200; Kara-Köl 64,300.

Vital statistics

Birth rate per 1,000 population (1994): 24.6 (world avg. 25.0); legitimate 83.2%; illegitimate 16.8%.
Death rate per 1,000 population (1994): 8.3 (world avg. 9.3).
Natural increase rate per 1,000 population (1994): 16.3 (world avg. 15.7).
Total fertility rate (avg. births per childbearing woman; 1994): 3.1.
Marriage rate per 1,000 population (1994): 5.8.
Divorce rate per 1,000 population (1994): 1.2.
Life expectancy at birth (1994): male 63.9 years; female 72.6 years.
Major causes of death per 100,000 population (1993): diseases of the circulatory system 291.1; diseases of the respiratory system 125.1; accidents, poisoning, and violence 91.6; malignant neoplasms (cancers) 67.6; infectious and parasitic diseases 30.3; diseases of the digestive system 29.9.

National economy

Budget (1994). Revenue: 2,606,700,000 som (tax revenue 63.8%, of which value-added tax 19.9%, enterprise profits tax 16.4%, personal income tax 8.6%, excise taxes 6.6%; nontax revenue 22.6%; recurrent development grants 11.6%). Expenditures: 3,514,000,000 som (education 18.0%; health 11.0%; social security 10.4%; government services 7.4%; industrial development 6.3%; public safety 4.8%; defense 3.0%).
Tourism: receipts from visitors, n.a.; expenditures by nationals abroad, n.a.
Production (metric tons except as noted). Agriculture, forestry, fishing (1994): grain 1,044,000, potatoes 290,000, vegetables (other than potatoes) 258,000, fruit (other than grapes) 56,000, seed cotton 54,000, grapes 17,000; livestock (number of live animals) 7,296,000 sheep and goats, 1,061,000 cattle, 300,000 horses, 165,000 pigs; roundwood (1990) 6,000 cu m; fish catch (1993) 1,100. Mining and quarrying (1993): antimony 1,600; mercury 650; gold 3,000 kg. Manufacturing (value of production in '000,000 som; 1994[2]): textiles 3,792; machinery and metalwork 1,472; ferrous and nonferrous metals 1,023; processed fish 786; other processed food 768; clothing 646; construction materials 269; footwear and leather goods 208. Construction (1992): residential 1,232,000 sq m. Energy production (consumption): electricity (kW-hr; 1994) 12,900,000,000 (10,400,000,000); coal (metric tons; 1993) 1,721,000 (2,136,000); crude petroleum (barrels; 1993) 645,000 (198,000); petroleum products (metric tons; 1993) none (815,000); natural gas (cu m; 1993) 36,200,000 (12,063,000,000).
Public debt (external, outstanding; 1994): U.S.$418,000,000.
Population economically active (1993): total 1,836,000; activity rate of total population 48.7% (participation rates: ages 16–59 [male], 16–54 [female] 81.1%; female [1990] 49.5%; unemployed 8.3%).

Price and earnings indexes (1990 = 100)

	1988	1989	1990	1991	1992	1993	1994
Consumer price index	95.2	97.1	100.0	185.0	1,766	23,122	89,534
Monthly earnings index	84.5	90.9	100.0	166.9	1,179	12,559	...

Household income and expenditure (1990). Average household size 4.7; income per household (1989) 6,100 rubles[3]; sources of income: wages and salaries 72.0%, pensions and stipends 7.5%, other 20.5%; expenditure: consumer goods 33.5%, food 32.9%, taxes 8.2%, alcohol 2.8%, housing 2.0%.
Gross national product (at current market prices; 1993): U.S.$3,745,000,000 (U.S.$830 per capita)[4].

Structure of gross domestic product and labour force

	1992 in value '000,000 rubles[3]	1992 % of total value	1993 labour force[5]	1993 % of labour force[5]
Agriculture	57,280	37.2	701,000	38.2
Mining, Manufacturing, Public utilities	53,020	34.4	300,000	16.3
Construction	4,920	3.2	114,000	6.2
Transportation and communications	5,320	3.5	94,000	5.1
Trade	6,600	4.3	107,000	5.8
Finance	6,380	4.1	50,000	2.7
Public administration, defense	2,400	1.6	54,000	2.9
Services	11,420	7.4	376,000	20.0
Other	6,660	4.3	40,000	2.8
TOTAL	154,000	100.0	1,836,000	100.0

Land use (1993): forested 3.5%; meadows and pastures 43.8%; agricultural and under permanent cultivation 7.2%; other 45.5%.

Foreign trade

Balance of trade (current prices)

	1988	1989	1990	1991	1992	1993
'000,000 rubles	−435	−813	−417	−958	−17,800	−89,896
% of total	7.9%	13.8%	7.9%	8.2%	14.4%	14.5%

Imports (1993): 354,618,000,000 rubles[3] (oil and gas 27.8%, machine-building equipment 24.1%, chemicals 11.0%, light industrial products 7.3%, ferrous metals 6.1%, food products 6.0%). *Major import sources:* Russian Federation 49.0%; Kazakhstan 23.2%; Uzbekistan 9.1%; Ukraine 8.1%; Turkmenistan 6.1%.
Exports (1993): 264,722,000,000 rubles[3] (machine-building equipment 40.7%, light industrial products 24.1%, nonferrous metals 10.7%, food products 7.1%, electricity 5.8%). *Major export destinations:* Russian Federation 39.1%; Kazakhstan 22.4%; Ukraine 17.3%; Uzbekistan 10.4%; Belarus 3.0%.

Transport and communications

Transport. Railroads (1992): length 230 mi, 370 km; passenger-mi 81,500,000, passenger-km 131,200,000; short ton-mi cargo 987,000,000, metric ton-km 1,588,900,000. Roads (1992): total length 17,650 mi, 28,400 km (paved 79%). Vehicles (1988): passenger cars 173,800; trucks and buses, n.a. Merchant marine: vessels (100 gross tons and over) none; landlocked state. Air transport (1992): passenger-mi 1,601,800,000, passenger-km 2,577,800,000; short ton-mi cargo 144,100,000; metric ton-km cargo 231,900,000; airports (1995) with scheduled flights 2.
Communications. Daily newspapers (1993): total number 128; total circulation 1,129,000; circulation per 1,000 population 250. Radio (1991): 825,000 receivers (1 per 18.5 persons). Television (1991): 875,000 receivers (1 per 19.6 persons). Telephones (main lines; 1993): 367,400 (1 per 12.3 persons).

Education and health

Education (1993–94)

	schools	teachers	students	student/teacher ratio
Primary (age 6–13)	1,832	77,000	2,130,000	27.7
Secondary (age 14–17)	1,474			
Voc., teacher tr.	53	...	32,800	...
Higher	23	...	55,200	...

Educational attainment (1989). Percentage of population age 19 and over having: primary education 4.7%; some secondary 20.9%; completed secondary 44.4%; some postsecondary 19.3%; higher 10.7%. *Literacy* (1989): total population age 15 and over literate 4,130,022 (97.0%); males literate 2,048,536 (98.6%); females literate 2,082,026 (95.5%).
Health (1994): physicians 14,000 (1 per 319 persons); hospital beds 47,000 (1 per 95 persons); infant mortality rate per 1,000 live births 29.1.
Food: daily per capita caloric intake, n.a.

Military

Total active duty personnel (1995): 7,000 (army 100%). *Military expenditure as percentage of GNP* (1993): 1.4% (world 3.3); per capita expenditure U.S.$11.

[1]January. [2]Prices of 1989. [3]Published values of the ruble during 1989–92 ranged from an official 1.61 rubles to more than 300 rubles per 1 U.S.$. [4]Ruble-area GNP and exchange-rate data are very speculative.

Laos

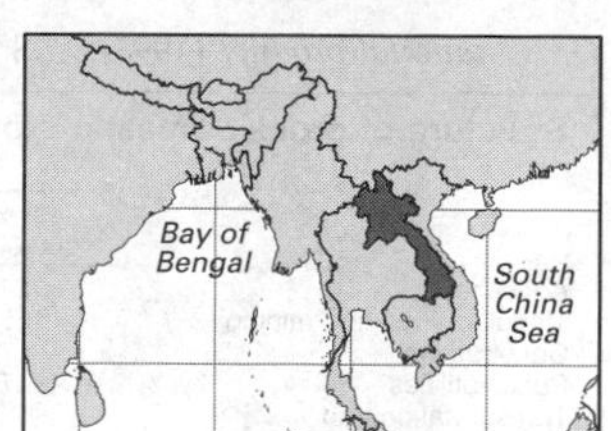

Official name: Sathalanalat Paxathipatai Paxaxôn Lao (Lao People's Democratic Republic).
Form of government: unitary single-party people's republic with one legislative house (National Assembly[1] [85]).
Chief of state: President.
Head of government: Prime Minister.
Capital: Vientiane (Viangchan).
Official language: Lao.
Official religion: none.
Monetary unit: 1 kip (KN) = 100 at; valuation (Oct. 6, 1995) 1 U.S.$ = KN 920; 1 £ = KN 1,454.

Area and population

		area		population
Provinces	**Capitals**	sq mi	sq km	1990 estimate
Attapu	Attapu	3,985	10,320	80,000
Bokèo	Houayxay	1,919	4,970	64,000
Bolikhamxai	Pakxan	6,359	16,470	145,000
Champasak	Pakxé	5,952	15,415	469,000
Houaphan	Xam Nua	6,371	16,500	243,000
Khammouan	Thakhek	6,299	16,315	249,000
Louangnamtha	Louangnamtha	3,600	9,325	114,000
Louangphrabang	Louangphrabang	6,515	16,875	339,000
Oudomxay	Xay	8,182	21,190	291,000
Phôngsali	Phôngsali	6,282	16,270	142,000
Salavan	Salavan	4,010	10,385	211,000
Savannakhét	Savannakhét	8,525	22,080	640,000
Viangchan	Muang Phôn-Hông	7,718	19,990	312,000
Xaignabouli	Xaignabouli	4,554	11,795	182,000
Xekong	Thong	2,959	7,665	58,000
Xiangkhoang	Phônsavan	6,685	17,315	189,000
Municipalities				
Viangchan	Vientiane (Viangchan)	1,514	3,920	442,000
TOTAL		91,429	236,800	4,170,000

Demography

Population (1995): 4,882,000.
Density (1995): persons per sq mi 53.4, persons per sq km 20.6.
Urban-rural (1995): urban 22.0%; rural 78.0%.
Sex distribution (1990): male 50.25%; female 49.75%.
Age breakdown (1990): under 15, 43.7%; 15–29, 26.0%; 30–44, 16.2%; 45–59, 9.2%; 60–74, 4.2%; 75 and over, 0.7%.
Population projection: (2000) 5,602,000; (2010) 7,188,000.
Doubling time: 24 years.
Ethnic composition (1983): Lao-Lum (Lao) 67.0%; Lao-Theung (Mon-Khmer) 16.5%; Lao-Tai (Tai) 7.8%; Lao-Soung (Miao [Hmong] and Man [Yao]) 5.2%; other 3.5%.
Religious affiliation (1980): Buddhist 57.8%; tribal religionist 33.6%; Christian 1.8%, of which Roman Catholic 0.8%, Protestant 0.2%; Muslim 1.0%; atheist 1.0%; Chinese folk-religionist 0.9%; none 3.8%; other 0.1%.
Major cities (1985): Vientiane (Viangchan) 178,203; Savannakhét 96,652; Louangphrabang 68,399; Pakxé 47,323.

Vital statistics

Birth rate per 1,000 population (1995): 43.0 (world avg. 25.0).
Death rate per 1,000 population (1995): 14.0 (world avg. 9.3).
Natural increase rate per 1,000 population (1995): 29.0 (world avg. 15.7).
Total fertility rate (avg. births per childbearing woman; 1995): 6.4.
Marriage rate per 1,000 population: n.a.
Divorce rate per 1,000 population: n.a.
Life expectancy at birth (1995): male 51.0 years; female 54.0 years.
Major causes of death per 100,000 population (incomplete, 1990): malaria 7.6; pneumonia 3.0; meningitis 1.5; diarrhea 1.2; tuberculosis 0.8.

National economy

Budget (1993). Revenue: KN 144,526,000,000 (taxes 59.5%, foreign grants 21.6%, nontax revenue 18.9%). Expenditures: KN 170,514,000,000 (current expenditure 61.5%, capital expenditure 38.5%).
Public debt (external, outstanding; 1993): U.S.$1,948,000,000.
Tourism (1991): total number of tourist arrivals 20,614.
Population economically active (1989): total 1,888,000; activity rate of total population 49.0% (participation rates [1985]: ages 15–64, 84.2%; female 45.3%; unemployed 3.0%).

Price and earnings indexes (1990 = 100)

	1988	1989	1990	1991	1992	1993	1994
Consumer price index	46.2	73.7	100.0	113.4	124.5	133.2	142.1
Earnings index	...	...	...	...	...	...	...

Production (metric tons except as noted). Agriculture, forestry, fishing (1994): rice 1,653,000, sugarcane 141,000, sweet potatoes 119,000, corn (maize) 77,000, cassava 68,000, pulses 43,000, potatoes 34,000, pineapples 34,000, melons 34,000, oranges 22,000, bananas 21,000; livestock (number of live animals) 1,605,000 pigs, 1,308,000 water buffalo, 1,137,000 cattle, 153,000 goats, 29,000 horses, 9,000,000 chickens; roundwood (1993) 4,906,000 cu m; fish catch (1993) 30,500. Mining and quarrying (1993): gypsum 80,000; rock salt 8,000; tin (metal content) 300; gemstones (mainly sapphires) 35,000 carats. Manufacturing (1991): detergent 566,000; soap 481,300; plastic products 85,000; nails 55,000; clothing 882,500 pieces; cigarettes 29,600,000 packets; plywood 346,600 sheets; electrical wire 101,000 metres; soft drinks 59,800 hectolitres; beer 68,900 bottles. Construction: n.a. Energy production (consumption): electricity (kW-hr; 1992) 910,000,000 (298,000,000); coal (metric tons; 1992) 1,000 (1,000); crude petroleum, n.a. (n.a.); petroleum products (metric tons; 1992) none (88,000); natural gas, n.a. (n.a.).
Gross national product (at current market prices; 1993): U.S.$1,308,000,000 (U.S.$290 per capita).

Structure of gross domestic product and labour force

	1993		1989	
	in value KN '000,000[2]	% of total value	labour force	% of labour force
Agriculture	406,233	56.3	1,359,000	72.0
Manufacturing	92,358	12.8		
Mining	1,272	0.2		
Construction	22,129	3.1		
Public utilities	9,499	1.3		
Transportation and communications	35,409	4.9	58,533	8.1
Trade	58,553	8.1		
Finance	65,399	9.1		
Pub. admin., defense; Services; Other	30,967	4.3		
TOTAL	721,819	100.0[3]	1,888,000	100.0

Household income and expenditure. Average household size (1985) 6.0; average annual income per household KN 3,710 (U.S.$371); sources of income: n.a.; expenditure: n.a.
Land use (1993): forested 54.2%; meadows and pastures 3.5%; agricultural and under permanent cultivation 3.5%; other 38.8%.

Foreign trade[4]

Balance of trade (current prices)

	1988	1989	1990	1991	1992	1993
U.S.$'000,000	−125.0	−162.0	−127.8	−131.7	−133.0	170.0
% of total	49.8%	58.7%	46.4%	45.8%	33.3%	27.8%

Imports (1993): U.S.$411,000,000 (1989; major imports include cereals, other food products, petroleum products, agricultural and general machinery, and transport equipment). *Major import sources* (1992): Thailand 56.7%; Japan 13.1%; China 13.0%; Hong Kong 1.7%; France 1.4%.
Exports (1993): U.S.$232,000,000 (1989; wood 33.3%, electricity 23.8%, coffee 14.3%, tin 3.2%). *Major export destinations* (1992): Thailand 38.9%, France 12.6%; Japan 11.4%; United States 6.0%; The Netherlands 5.9%.

Transport and communications

Transport. Railroads: none. Roads (1992): total length 8,780 mi, 14,130 km (paved 16%). Vehicles (1992): passenger cars 20,233; trucks and buses 12,987. Merchant marine (1992): vessels (100 gross tons and over) 1; total deadweight tonnage 1,469. Air transport (1989): passenger-mi 27,000,000, passenger-km 44,000,000; short ton-mi cargo 3,000,000, metric ton-km cargo 5,000,000; airports (1995) with scheduled flights 11.
Communications. Daily newspapers (1992): total number 3; total circulation 14,000; circulation per 1,000 population 3.0. Radio (1994): total number of receivers 500,000 (1 per 9.5 persons). Television (1994): total number of receivers 80,000 (1 per 59 persons). Telephones (main lines; 1993): 8,600 (1 per 526 persons).

Education and health

Education (1991–92)

	schools	teachers	students	student/ teacher ratio
Primary (age 6–10)	7,140	21,036	580,792	27.6
Secondary (age 11–16)	750[5]	8,936	117,504	13.1
Voc., teacher tr.	139[6]	1,262	8,198	6.5
Higher[5]	9	698	4,730	6.8

Educational attainment (1985). Percentage of population age 6 and over having: no schooling 49.3%; primary 41.2%; secondary 9.1%; higher 0.4%.
Literacy (1985): total population age 15 and over literate 83.9%; males literate 92.0%; females literate 75.8%.
Health (1990): physicians 1,173 (1 per 3,555 persons); hospital beds 10,364 (1 per 402 persons); infant mortality rate per 1,000 live births (1995) 92.0.
Food (1992): daily per capita caloric intake 2,259 (vegetable products 89%, animal products 11%); 102% of FAO recommended minimum requirement.

Military

Total active duty personnel (1994): 37,000 (army 89.2%, navy 1.4%, air force 9.4%). *Military expenditure as percent of GNP* (1993): 7.9% (world 3.3%); per capita expenditure U.S.$23.

[1]Formerly known as the Supreme People's Assembly. [2]At constant 1990 prices. [3]Detail does not add to total given because of rounding. [4]Import figures are c.i.f. in balance of trade and commodities. [5]1989–90. [6]1988–89.

Latvia

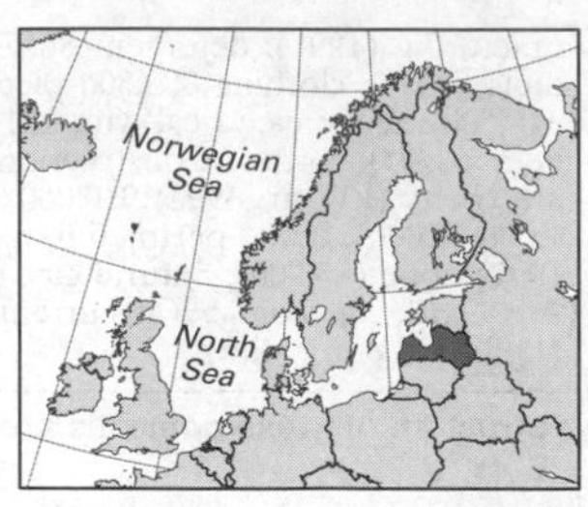

Official name: Latvijas Republika (Republic of Latvia).
Form of government: unitary multiparty republic with a single legislative body (Saeima, or Parliament [100]).
Chief of state: President.
Head of government: Prime Minister.
Capital: Rīga.
Official language: Latvian.
Official religion: none.
Monetary unit: 1 lats[1] (plural lati) = 10 santimi; valuation (Oct. 6, 1995) 1 U.S.$ = 0.54 lats; 1 £ = 0.85 lats.

Area and population

	area sq km[3]	population 1992[2] estimate
Cities of republic jurisdiction		
Daugavpils	72	127,279
Jelgava	60	73,917
Jūrmala	100	60,901
Liepāja	60	113,815
Rēzekne	17	43,073
Rīga	295	897,078
Ventspils	46	50,435
Rural districts		
Aizkraukle	2,558	45,093
Alūksne	2,246	28,631
Balvi	2,384	33,576
Bauska	1,884	55,612
Cēsis	3,062	63,820
Daugavpils	2,526	46,329
Dobele	1,680	44,749
Gulbene	1,876	30,243
Jēkabpils	2,998	61,435
Jelgava	1,613	39,137
Krāslava	2,288	41,019
Kuldīga	2,503	41,361
Liepāja	3,589	54,475
Limbaži	2,602	41,436
Ludza	2,566	41,747
Madona	3,348	49,953
Ogre	1,816	66,040
Preiļi	2,042	45,342
Rēzekne	2,654	42,899
Rīga	3,094	152,070
Saldus	2,134	40,235
Talsi	2,748	50,603
Tukums	2,457	59,069
Valka	2,444	37,119
Valmiera	2,377	63,067
Ventspils	2,471	15,400
TOTAL	64,610	2,656,958

Demography

Population (1995): 2,515,000.
Density (1995): persons per sq mi 100.8, persons per sq km 38.9.
Urban-rural (1993): urban 69.2%; rural 30.8%.
Sex distribution (1993): male 46.42%; female 53.58%.
Age breakdown (1993): under 15, 21.0%; 15–29, 20.3%; 30–44, 21.6%; 45–59, 18.4%; 60–74, 13.9%; 75 and over, 4.8%.
Population projection: (2000) 2,356,000; (2010) 2,068,000.
Ethnic composition (1994): Latvian 57.8%; Russian 31.0%; Belarusian 4.4%; Ukrainian 2.8%; Polish 2.6%; Lithuanian 1.4%.
Religious affiliation: believers are predominantly Evangelical Lutheran, Russian Orthodox, or Roman Catholic.
Major cities (1993): Rīga 803,952; Daugavpils 120,917; Liepāja 95,046; Jelgava 69,411; Jūrmala 55,256.

Vital statistics

Birth rate per 1,000 population (1993): 10.3 (world avg. 25.0); (1991) legitimate 81.6%; illegitimate 18.4%.
Death rate per 1,000 population (1993): 15.2 (world avg. 9.3).
Natural increase rate per 1,000 population (1993): −4.9 (world avg. 15.7).
Total fertility rate (avg. births per childbearing woman; 1993): 2.2.
Marriage rate per 1,000 population (1993): 7.2.
Divorce rate per 1,000 population (1993): 5.6.
Life expectancy at birth (1993): male 64.2 years; female 74.6 years.
Major causes of death per 100,000 population (1990): diseases of the circulatory system 756.5; malignant neoplasms (cancers) 204.9; accidents, poisoning, and violence 138.9; diseases of the respiratory system 49.6.

National economy

Budget (1995). Revenue: 475,000,000 Lats (1994; social-security taxes 35.2%, value-added taxes 32.1%, profit tax 13.2%, income tax 5.3%, customs duties 4.0%). Expenditures: 515,000,000 Lats (1994; social affairs 56.6%, economic affairs 34.0%).
Production (metric tons except as noted). Agriculture, forestry, fishing (1994): potatoes 994,000, barley 458,000, sugar beets 274,000, vegetables 232,000, wheat 124,000, fruits and berries 85,000; livestock (number of live animals) 995,000 cattle, 737,000 pigs, 133,000 sheep, 4,000,000 poultry; roundwood (1993) 4,558,000 cu m; fish catch (1993) 140,000. Mining and quarrying (1992): peat 3,500,000; gypsum 350,000. Manufacturing (1993): steel 584,000; processed meats 189,000; cement 114,000; synthetic fibre 28,000; telephones 310,000 units; diesel engines 17,000 units; buses 10,600 units; rail passenger cars 123 units; beer 900,000 hectolitres[4]; vodka 220,000 hectolitres[4]; textiles 16,000,000 sq m. Construction (1993): new residential 266,000 sq m. Energy production (consumption): electricity (kW-hr; 1993) 3,924,000,000 (6,426,000,000); coal (1993) none (599,000); crude petroleum, none (n.a.); petroleum products (1993) none (2,426,000); natural gas (1993) none (1,219,000,000).
Population economically active (1993): total 1,358,400; activity rate of total population 52.9% (participation rates [1992]: ages 16–59/55[5], 90.7%; female 53.9%[6]; unemployed [1994] 7.3%).

Price and earnings indexes (1990 = 100)

	1988	1989	1990	1991	1992	1993	1994
Consumer price index	71.4	74.7	100.0	272.0	2,861	5,986	8,136
Monthly earnings index	71.8	78.4	100.0	186.0	1,335	2,981	4,748

Gross national product (1993): U.S.$5,254,000,000 (U.S.$2,030 per capita).

Structure of gross domestic product and labour force

	1993 in value '000,000 lats[1]	1993 % of total value	1991 labour force	1991 % of labour force
Agriculture	244	15.3	83,000	5.7
Manufacturing and mining	350	22.0	351,400	24.0
Construction	70	4.4	82,200	5.6
Public utilities	77	4.8	...	...
Transportation and communications	}	}	103,700	7.1
Trade	}	}	119,600	8.2
Finance	853	53.5	}	}
Pub. admin., defense	}	}	194,000	13.3
Services	}	}	}	}
Other	}		528,000[7]	36.1[7]
TOTAL	1,594	100.0	1,461,900	100.0

Household income and expenditure. Average household size (1989) 3.1; average annual income per household: n.a.; sources of income (1991): wages and salaries 63.2%, pensions and transfers 16.6%, self-employment 5.3%, other 14.9%; expenditure (1991): food and alcohol 45.2%, consumer goods 34.8%, rent and social services 7.1%.
Land use (1993): forested 44.0%; meadows and pastures 12.5%; agricultural and permanent cultivation 26.5%; other 17.0%.

Foreign trade

Balance of trade (current prices)

	1992	1993	1994
U.S.$'000,000	−215	−59	−71
% of total	11.5%	2.9%	15.1%

Imports (1993): U.S.$1,058,000,000 (mineral products 45.6%, machinery and equipment 9.9%, transport equipment 9.3%, chemical products 7.1%, food and agricultural products 6.4%). *Major import sources:* Russia 25.6%; Africa and Middle East 9.8%; Lithuania 8.6%; Germany 6.6%; Sweden 3.7%; Belarus 3.7%.
Exports (1993): U.S.$998,000,000 (food and agricultural products 15.0%, mineral products 14.3%, textiles 12.7%, transport equipment 12.6%, forestry products 9.6%). *Major export destinations:* Russia 29.8%; The Netherlands 8.3%; Germany 6.6%; Sweden 6.3%; Ukraine 5.9%.

Transport and communications

Transport. Railroads (1993): length 2,413 km; passenger-km 2,388,000,000; metric-km cargo 9,828,000,000. Roads (1991): total length 60,224 km (paved 55%). Vehicles (1993): passenger cars 351,000; trucks and buses 85,000. Merchant marine (1992): cargo vessels 261; total deadweight tonnage 1,436,899. Air transport (1991): passenger-km 2,999,000,000; metric ton-km cargo 22,000,000; airports with scheduled flights (1995) 1.
Communications. Total newspapers (1991): total number 188; total circulation 3,676,000; circulation per 1,000 population 1,377. Radio (1991): 1,396,000 receivers (1 per 1.9 persons). Television (1991): 1,126,000 receivers (1 per 2.4 persons). Telephones (main lines; 1993): 694,300 (1 per 3.7 persons).

Education and health

Education (1992–93)

	schools	teachers	students	student/ teacher ratio
Primary	921	12,758	133,846	10.5
Secondary	...	18,344	187,332	10.2
Voc., teacher tr.	57	6,691	55,312	8.3
Higher	14	4,478	41,138	9.2

Educational attainment (1989). Percentage of persons age 25 and over having: primary or less 21.2%; complete secondary 46.3%; some higher 13.4%. *Literacy* (1989): percentage of total population age 15 and over literate 99.5%; males literate 99.8%; females literate 99.2%.
Health (1993): physicians 9,300 (1 per 275.9 persons); hospital beds 31,300 (1 per 81.9 persons); infant mortality rate per 1,000 live births (1992) 17.4.

Military

Total active duty personnel (1995): 2,650 (army 56.6%, navy 37.7%, air force 5.7%). *Military expenditure as percentage of GNP:* 0.9%; per capita expenditure U.S.$18.

[1]The lats (pre-World War II Latvian currency), reintroduced in parallel with the Latvian ruble (LR; at 200 LR per lats) on March 5, 1993, became the sole official currency Oct. 18, 1993. From May 7, 1992, LR circulated in parallel at par with the Soviet ruble, serving temporarily as the sole legal tender until introduction of the lats on March 5, 1993. [2]January 1. [3]One sq km is equal to approximately 0.3861 sq mi. [4]1991. [5]Males retire at age 59, females at 55. [6]Percentage of females employed in state sector. [7]Includes 313,600 employed outside the state sector, 65,000 unemployed, and 149,300 not allocated by sector.

Lebanon

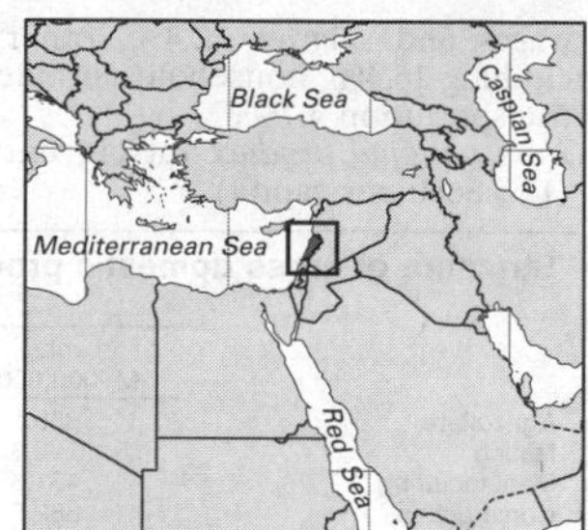

Official name: al-Jumhūrīyah al-Lubnānīyah (Republic of Lebanon).
Form of government: unitary multiparty republic with one legislative house (National Assembly [128])[1].
Chief of state: President.
Head of government: Prime Minister.
Capital: Beirut.
Official language: Arabic.
Official religion: none.
Monetary unit: 1 Lebanese pound (LL) = 100 piastres; valuation (Oct. 6, 1995) 1 U.S.$ = LL 1,609; 1 £ = LL 2,544.

Area and population

		area		population
Governorates	Capitals	sq mi	sq km	1970 estimate
Bayrūt	Beirut (Bayrūt)	7	18	474,870
al-Biqā'	Zaḥlah	1,653	4,280	203,520
Jabal Lubnān	B'abdā	753	1,950	833,055
al-Janūb	Sidon (Ṣaydā)	772	2,001	249,945
ash-Shamāl	Tripoli (Ṭarābulus)	765	1,981	364,935
TOTAL		3,950	10,230	2,126,325

Demography

Population (1995): 3,009,000.
Density (1995): persons per sq mi 761.8, persons per sq km 294.1.
Urban-rural (1995): urban 87.2%; rural 12.8%.
Sex distribution (1995): male 48.75%; female 51.25%.
Age breakdown (1995): under 15, 34.2%; 15–29, 29.9%; 30–44, 18.3%; 45–59, 9.3%; 60–74, 6.7%; 75 and over, 1.6%.
Population projection: (2000) 3,289,000; (2010) 3,742,000.
Doubling time: during the 1970–75 prewar period the average growth rate was 2.6%; however, the dislocation of the population by the civil war between 1976 and 1991 rendered both the absolute size and principal components of population change (births, deaths, migration) highly problematic.
Ethnic composition (1993): Lebanese, *c.* 80%; Palestinian 12%; Armenian 5%; Syrian, Kurd, and other 3%.
Religious affiliation: no official data exist subsequent to the 1932 census, when Christians (predominantly Maronite Roman Catholic) were a slight majority; it is thought that Muslims today constitute the majority, but by what margin is highly uncertain. Unofficial and CIA estimates (1984/1986) indicated the main religious groups as follows: Shī'ī Muslim 32/41%; Maronite Christian 24.5/16%; Sunnī Muslim 21/27%; Druze 7/7%; Greek Orthodox 6.5/5%; Greek Catholic 4/3%; Armenian Christian 4%/n.a.; other 1/1%.
Major cities (1991): Beirut 1,100,000; Tripoli 240,000; Jūniyah 100,000; Zaḥlah 45,000[2]; Sidon (Ṣaydā) 38,000[2]; Tyre 14,000[2].

Vital statistics

Birth rate per 1,000 population (1995): 27.9 (world avg. 25.0).
Death rate per 1,000 population (1995): 6.4 (world avg. 9.3).
Natural increase rate per 1,000 population (1995): 21.5 (world avg. 15.7).
Total fertility rate (avg. births per childbearing woman; 1995): 3.3.
Life expectancy at birth (1992): male 72.5 years; female 77.9 years.
Major causes of death: normally, cardiovascular and gastrointestinal diseases, including typhoid fever and dysentery; but violence and acts of war were also among the principal causes of mortality between 1975 and 1991.

National economy

Budget (1994). Revenue: LL 2,195,795,000,000 (almost entirely taxation, direct and indirect). Expenditures: LL 4,206,705,000,000 (debt service 35%, government salaries 32%, defense 22%, education 10%).
Production (metric tons except as noted). Agriculture, forestry, fishing (1994): grapes 391,000, potatoes 294,000, oranges 276,000, tomatoes 246,000, cucumbers 167,000, apples 165,000, lemons and limes 101,000, onions 72,000, olives 53,000; opium poppies and marijuana were important cash crops in the late 1980s and early '90s but were reportedly eradicated in 1993; livestock (number of live animals) 456,000 goats, 258,000 sheep, 80,000 cattle, 24,000,000 chickens; roundwood (1993) 496,000 cu m; fish catch (1993) 2,200. Mining and quarrying (1993): lime 15,000; salt 3,000; gypsum 2,000. Manufacturing (1993): cement 1,000,000; distillate fuel 85,000; gasoline 70,000; kerosene and jet fuel 5,000; dairying, curing of leather, meat cutting, and milling of flour are also significant. Construction (1995): 2,418,132 sq m[3]. Energy production (consumption): electricity (kW-hr; 1993) 3,950,000,000 (4,000,000,000); coal, n.a. (none); crude petroleum (barrels; 1993) none (2,602,000); petroleum products (metric tons; 1993) 323,000 (2,787,000).
Public debt (external, outstanding; 1995[4]): U.S.$1,169,200,000.
Household income and expenditure. Average household size (1987) 5.0; average annual income per household (1985) LL 120,000 (U.S.$6,630; in constant prices, about 75% of 1966 income levels); sources of income (1974): wages and salaries 27.9%, transfers 3.0%, other 69.1%; expenditure (1966)[5]: food 42.8%, housing 16.8%, clothing 8.6%, health care 7.2%.
Land use (1993): forested 7.8%; meadows and pastures 1.0%; agricultural and under permanent cultivation 29.9%; wasteland and other areas 61.3%.
Population economically active (1994): total 938,000; activity rate of total population 32.2% (participation rates: over age 15 [1988] 44%; female [1993] 27.8%; unemployed [1993] reported by the national trade union at 35% but perhaps as low as 7–8% according to a 1987 study of 60,000 households).

Consumer price index (1990 = 100)

	1988	1989	1990	1991	1992	1993	1994
Consumer price index	22.7	57.9	100.0	151.5	333.3	430.3	475.6

Gross national product (1994): U.S.$15,800,000,000 (U.S.$4,360 per capita).

Structure of gross domestic product and labour force

	1992		1986	
	in value[6] LL '000,000[7]	% of total value	labour force	% of labour force
Agriculture	575,800	8.8	132,211	19.1
Mining	—	—	694	0.1
Manufacturing	823,700	12.6	123,647	17.8
Construction	216,300	3.3	43,357	6.2
Public utilities	343,600	5.3	6,668	1.0
Transp. and commun.	246,000	3.8	48,242	7.0
Trade	1,853,200	28.4	114,706	16.5
Finance	503,600	7.7	24,224	3.5
Real estate and business services	583,500	9.0	} 200,063	} 28.8
Services	703,900	10.8	}	}
Pub. admin., defense	667,400	10.2	}	}
TOTAL	6,517,000	100.0[8]	693,812	100.0

Tourism (1980): number of tourist arrivals 135,548[9].

Foreign trade[10]

Balance of trade (current prices)

	1989	1990	1991	1992	1993	1994
U.S.$'000,000	−1,806	−2,073	−3,200	−3,633	−4,554	−5,364
% of total	65.5%	69.5%	74.5%	76.0%	77.0%	78.4%

Imports (1994): U.S.$6,101,000,000 (1982; consumer goods 40.0%, machinery and transport equipment 35.0%, petroleum products 20.0%). *Major import sources:* Italy 13.9%; France 9.2%; Germany 8.3%; U.S. 8.0%.
Exports (1994): U.S.$737,000,000 (1993; food and beverages 21%, machinery and appliances 18%, textiles 17%, metal products 10%). *Major export destinations:* Saudi Arabia 12.7%; Switzerland 12.2%; U.A.E. 11.1%.

Transport and communications

Transport. Railroads (1995)[11]: length 222 km; passenger-km (1982) 8,570,000; metric ton-km cargo 42,010,000. Roads (1987): total length 7,370 km (paved 85%). Vehicles (1985): passenger cars 300,000; trucks and buses 49,560. Merchant marine (1992): vessels (100 gross tons and over) 163; total deadweight tonnage 438,165. Air transport (1994)[12]: passenger-km 1,587,942,000; metric ton-km cargo 38,398,000; airports (1995) with scheduled flights 1.
Communications. Daily newspapers (1992): total number 16; total circulation 500,000; circulation per 1,000 population 176. Radio (1994): 2,247,000 receivers (1 per 1.3 persons). Television (1994): 1,100,000 receivers (1 per 2.6 persons). Telephones (main lines; 1993): 350,000 (1 per 10.8 persons).

Education and health

Education (1993–94)

	schools	teachers	students	student/ teacher ratio
Primary (age 5–9)	2,100[13]	22,810[14]	360,858	...
Secondary (age 10–16)	1,405[14]	21,344[14]	261,341	...
Voc., teacher tr.	181[14]	3,866	39,933	10.3
Higher	18[14]	5,400[13]	85,495[13]	15.8

Educational attainment (1970). Percentage of population age 25 and over having: no formal schooling 45.6%, of which, ability to read and write 35.6%; incomplete primary education 28.5%; complete primary 10.8%; incomplete secondary 7.1%; complete secondary 4.9%; higher 3.1%. *Literacy* (1995): total population age 15 and over literate 1,829,000 (92.4%); males literate 94.7%; females literate 90.3%.
Health: physicians (1989–91) 6,638 (1 per 407 persons); hospital beds (1993) 14,500 (1 per 200 persons); infant mortality rate (1995) 38.0.
Food (1992): daily per capita caloric intake 3,317 (vegetable products 88%, animal products 12%); 134% of FAO recommended minimum requirement.

Military

Total active duty personnel (1995): Lebanese national armed forces 44,300 (army 97.1%, navy 1.1%, air force 1.8%). External regular military forces include: UN peacekeeping force in Lebanon 4,963; Syrian army 30,000. Most civilian militias were progressively disbanded after the civil war ended in 1991. However, only two factions were still active in 1995, though on a much-reduced scale[15]: Shī'ī Muslim (pro-Iran Hezbollah [Party of God]) 3,000; predominantly Maronite Christian and some Shī'ī and Druze (South Lebanese Army) 2,500. *Military expenditure as percentage of GDP* (1994): 4.4% (world 2.6%); per capita expenditure: U.S.$75.

[1]The current legislature was elected between August and October 1992; one-half of its membership is Christian and one-half Muslim/Druze. [2]1988 estimate. [3]Permits authorized in July 1995. [4]July. [5]Weights based on consumer price index components. For capital city only. [6]In purchasers' value at current prices. [7]Although the Lebanese pound continues to be the official currency, most financial transactions are done in U.S. dollars. Since the mid-1980s, foreign currency in circulation and foreign deposits in the domestic banking system were increasingly "dollarized." In the mid-1990s, about two-thirds of bank deposits in Lebanon were transacted in U.S. dollars. By 1993, however, the pound had once again stabilized against the dollar. [8]Detail does not add to total given because of rounding. [9]Approximately one-fourth the annual prewar rates of the early 1970s. [10]Imports are f.o.b. [11]Apart from a 14-mi (23-km) section delivering oil from the Zahrani refinery to a thermal power station serving Beirut, no passenger or general cargo track is currently in use. [12]MEA-Airliban international flights only. [13]1991–92. [14]1981–82. [15]Active personnel.

Lesotho

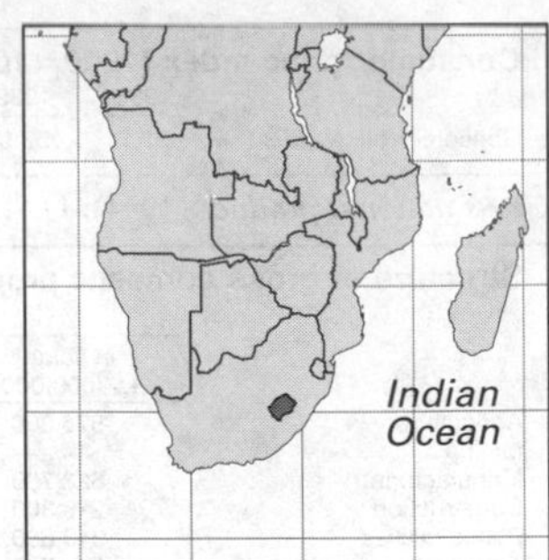

Official name: Lesotho (Sotho); Kingdom of Lesotho (English).
Form of government: multiparty republic[1] with 2 legislative houses (National Assembly [65]; Senate [33[2]]).
Chief of state: King.
Head of government: Prime Minister.
Capital: Maseru.
Official languages: Sotho; English.
Official religion: Christianity.
Monetary unit: 1 loti (plural maloti [M]) = 100 lisente; valuation (Oct. 6, 1995) 1 U.S.$ = M 3.66; 1 £ = M 5.79.

Area and population

Districts	Capitals	area sq mi	area sq km	population 1995 estimate
Berea	Teyateyaneng	858	2,222	206,200
Butha-Buthe	Butha-Buthe	682	1,767	135,400
Leribe	Hlotse	1,092	2,828	349,500
Mafeteng	Mafeteng	818	2,119	259,000
Maseru	Maseru	1,652	4,279	400,200
Mohale's Hoek	Mohale's Hoek	1,363	3,530	231,300
Mokhotlong	Mokhotlong	1,573	4,075	100,300
Qacha's Nek	Qacha's Nek	907	2,349	86,800
Quthing	Quthing	1,126	2,916	151,900
Thaba-Tseka	Thaba-Tseka	1,649	4,270	136,200
TOTAL		11,720	30,355	2,056,800

Demography

Population (1995): 2,057,000.
Density (1995): persons per sq mi 174.9, persons per sq km 67.5.
Urban-rural (1992): urban 20.9%; rural 79.1%.
Sex distribution (1995): male 49.23%; female 50.77%.
Age breakdown (1995): under 15, 41.3%; 15–29, 27.0%; 30–44, 16.0%; 45–59, 9.1%; 60–74, 5.0%; 75 and over, 1.6%.
Population projection: (2000) 2,338,000; (2010) 3,012,000.
Doubling time: 28 years.
Ethnic composition (1986): Sotho 85.0%; Zulu 15.0%.
Religious affiliation (1992): Christian 93.0%, of which Roman Catholic 42.8%, Protestant (mostly Lesotho Evangelical) 29.1%, other Christian 21.1%; other (mostly traditional beliefs) 7.0%.
Major urban centres (1986): Maseru 109,382; Maputsoe 20,000; Teyateyaneng 14,251; Mafeteng 12,667; Hlotse 9,595.

Vital statistics

Birth rate per 1,000 population (1990–95): 36.9 (world avg. 25.0); legitimate, n.a.; illegitimate, n.a.
Death rate per 1,000 population (1990–95): 10.0 (world avg. 9.3).
Natural increase rate per 1,000 population (1990–95): 26.9 (world avg. 15.7).
Total fertility rate (avg. births per childbearing woman; 1990–95): 5.2.
Marriage rate per 1,000 population: n.a.
Divorce rate per 1,000 population: n.a.
Life expectancy at birth (1990–95): male 58.0 years; female 63.0 years.
Major causes of death per 100,000 population: n.a.; however, major diseases include malaria, typhoid fever, and infectious and parasitic diseases.

National economy

Budget (1995–96). Revenue: M 1,790,300,000 (1993–94; tax revenue 78.8%, of which customs receipts 53.5%, sales tax 10.1%, income tax 7.3%, company tax 4.6%; grants and nontax revenue 21.2%). Expenditures: M 1,608,800,000 (recurrent expenditure 67.5%, of which education 20.9%, public works [1994–95] 12.8%, health 6.7%, defense 6.4%; capital expenditure 32.5%).
Production (metric tons except as noted). Agriculture, forestry, fishing (1994): corn (maize) 175,000, sorghum 60,000, fruit 18,000, roots and tubers 8,000, peas 2,000, beans 1,000; livestock (number of live animals) 1,691,000 sheep, 1,010,000 goats, 663,000 cattle, 168,000 asses, 123,000 horses, 78,000 pigs, 1,000,000 chickens; roundwood (1993) 651,000 cu m; fish catch (1993) 35. Mining and quarrying (1988): sand and gravel 50,000 cu m. Manufacturing (total value added; 1992): M 246,200,000, of which textiles, apparel, and leather 49.9%, food and beverages 39.5%, nonmetal products 2.9%, chemical products 1.9%, printing and publishing 1.7%, furniture and fixtures 1.6%, iron and steel products 1.1%. Construction (total value added; 1991): M 310,500. Energy production (consumption): electricity (kW-hr; 1988) 1,000,000 (n.a.); coal, none (n.a.); petroleum, none (n.a.); natural gas, none (n.a.).
Public debt (external, outstanding; 1993): U.S.$471,900,000.
Tourism (1993): receipts from visitors U.S.$17,000,000; expenditures by nationals abroad U.S.$7,000,000.
Population economically active (1993): total 617,871; activity rate of total population 45.1% (participation rates: ages 15–64 [1986], 79.8%; female 23.7%; unemployed [1992] 35%).

Price and earnings indexes (1990 = 100)

	1988	1989	1990	1991	1992	1993	1994
Consumer price index	78.1	89.6	100.0	117.7	137.9	156.0	168.9
Earnings index[3]	75.5	86.2	100.0	112.7	123.5	132.7	...

Household income and expenditure. Average household size (1986) 4.8; average annual income per household (1986–87) M 2,832 (U.S.$1,297); sources of income (1986–87): transfer payments 44.7%, self-employment 27.8%, wages and salaries 22.4%, other 5.1%; expenditure (1989): food 48.0%, clothing 16.4%, household durable goods 11.9%, housing and energy 10.1%, transportation 4.7%.
Gross national product (at current market prices; 1993): U.S.$1,254,000,000 (U.S.$660 per capita).

Structure of gross domestic product and labour force

	1994 in value M '000,000	1994 % of total value	1986 labour force	1986 % of labour force
Agriculture	335.1	11.3	474,171	66.2
Mining	2.7	0.1	6,446	0.9
Manufacturing	431.5	13.7	19,339	2.7
Construction	689.5	21.9	31,516	4.4
Public utilities	65.3	2.1	1,433	0.2
Transp. and commun.	88.5	2.8	5,014	0.7
Trade	269.9	8.6	22,204	3.1
Finance	361.9	11.5	3,581	0.5
Pub. admin., defense	359.5	11.4	17,907	2.5
Services	82.3	2.6	126,780	17.7
Other	439.2[4]	14.0[4]	7,879	1.1
TOTAL	3,145.4	100.0	716,270[5]	100.0[5]

Land use (1993): meadows and pastures 65.9%; agricultural and under permanent cultivation 10.5%; other 23.6%.

Foreign trade[6]

Balance of trade (current prices)

	1988	1989	1990	1991	1992	1993
M '000,000	−1,135.2	−1,323.6	−1,523.0	−1,976.0	−2,374.7	−2,435.9
% of total	79.7%	79.3%	83.3%	84.2%	79.3%	73.8%

Imports (1994): M 2,992,700,000 (1990; manufactured goods [excluding chemicals, machinery, and transport equipment] 42.5%; food and live animals 19.1%; machinery and transport equipment 15.3%; petroleum products 8.6%). *Major import sources:* Customs Union of Southern Africa 82.4%; Asia 12.6%; Europe 2.7%, of which European Economic Community 2.6%; the Americas 1.5%.
Exports (1994): M 509,300,000 (manufactured goods 87.5%, of which clothing 54.8%, furniture 8.0%, footwear 6.9%, machinery and transport equipment 2.0%; food and live animals 5.5%, of which cereals 1.5%, cattle 1.2%, vegetables 0.7%; crude materials 6.3%, of which wool 4.5%, mohair 1.7%; chemicals 0.5%; diamonds 0.2%). *Major export destinations:* Customs Union of Southern Africa 50.8%; Europe 10.5%, of which European Economic Community 10.1%; the Americas 37.8%; Asia 0.3%.

Transport and communications

Transport. Railroads (1993): length 1.6 mi, 2.6 km. Roads (1994): total length 3,308 mi, 5,324 km (paved 15%). Vehicles (1994): passenger cars 5,944; trucks and buses 17,785. Merchant marine: vessels (100 gross tons and over) none. Air transport (1995): passenger-mi 14,900,000, passenger-km 24,000,000; ton-mi cargo 144,000, metric ton-km cargo 210,000; airports (1995) with scheduled flights 1.
Communications. Daily newspapers (1993): total number 6; total circulation 36,000; circulation per 1,000 population 19. Radio (1994): total number of receivers 118,000 (1 per 16.9 persons). Television (1994): total number of receivers 50,000 (1 per 40 persons). Telephones (main lines; 1993): 10,500 (1 per 190 persons).

Education and health

Education (1993–94)

	schools	teachers	students	student/ teacher ratio
Primary (age 6–12)	1,201	7,292	354,275	48.6
Secondary (age 13–17)	187	2,526	55,312	21.9
Voc., teacher tr.	9	225	2,326	10.3
Higher	1	492	4,001	8.1

Educational attainment (1986–87). Percentage of population age 10 and over having: no formal education 22.9%; primary 52.8%; secondary 23.2%; higher 0.6%. *Literacy* (1995): total population age 15 and over literate 849,700 (71.3%); males literate 468,000 (81.1%); females literate 381,700 (62.3%).
Health (1993): physicians 136 (1 per 14,306 persons); hospital beds (1992) 2,400 (1 per 765 persons); infant mortality rate per 1,000 live births 71.5.
Food (1992): daily per capita caloric intake 2,201 (vegetable products 94%, animal products 6%); 97% of FAO recommended minimum requirement.

Military

Total active duty personnel (1995): 2,000[7]. *Military expenditure as percentage of GNP* (1992): 3.3% (world 3.7%); per capita expenditure U.S.$20.

[1]New constitution, effective April 1993, ended seven years of military rule. [2]Composed of 22 chiefs and 11 nominated members. [3]Based on average annual wages, including overtime, of mine workers. [4]Indirect taxes less imputed bank service charges. [5]Approximately 117,600 persons (*c.* 40% of Lesotho's adult male labour force) were employed as mine workers in South Africa in 1993. [6]Import figures are f.o.b. in balance of trade and c.i.f. in commodities and trading partners. [7]Royal Lesotho Defence Force.

Liberia

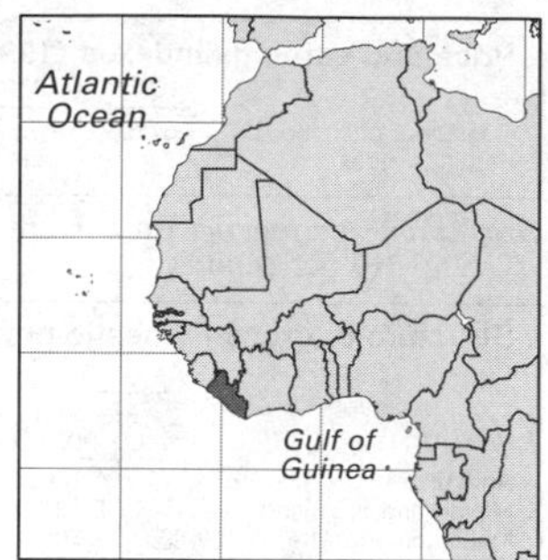

Official name: Republic of Liberia.
Form of government: transitional regime with one legislative body (Transitional Legislative Assembly [35][1]).
Head of state and government: President assisted by Council of State[1].
Capital: Monrovia.
Official language: English.
Official religion: none.
Monetary unit: 1 Liberian dollar (L$) = 100 cents; valuation (Oct. 6, 1995) 1 U.S.$ = L$1.00[2]; 1 £ = L$1.58.

Area and population

		area		population
Counties	Capitals	sq mi	sq km	1986 estimate
Bomi	Tubmanburg	755	1,955	67,300
Bong	Gbarnga	3,127	8,099	268,100
Grand Bassa	Buchanan	3,382	8,759	166,900
Grand Cape Mount	Robertsport	2,250	5,827	83,900
Grand Gedeh	Zwedru	6,575	17,029	109,000
Grand Kru	Barclayville	3	3	3
Lofa	Voinjama	7,475	19,360	261,000
Margibi	Kakata	1,260	3,263	104,000
Maryland	Harper	2,066[3]	5,351[3]	137,700[3]
Montserrado	Bensonville	1,058	2,740	582,400
Nimba	Sanniquellie	4,650	12,043	325,700
Rivercess	Rivercess City	1,693	4,385	39,900
Sinoe	Greenville	3,959	10,254	65,400
TOTAL		38,250	99,067[4]	2,221,300[5]

Demography

Population (1995): 2,380,000[6].
Density (1995): persons per sq mi 62.2[6], persons per sq km 24.0[6].
Urban-rural (1995): urban 44.9%; rural 55.1%.
Sex distribution (1995): male 50.54%; female 49.46%.
Age breakdown (1995): under 15, 46.0%; 15–29, 25.6%; 30–44, 14.5%; 45–59, 8.5%; 60–74, 4.0%; 75 and over, 1.4%.
Population projection: (2000) 2,760,000; (2010) 3,660,000.
Doubling time: 23 years.
Ethnic composition (1984): Kpelle 19.4%; Bassa 13.8%; Grebo 9.0%; Gio 7.8%; Kru 7.3%; Mano 7.1%; other 35.6%.
Religious affiliation (1984): Christian 67.7%; Muslim 13.8%[7]; traditional beliefs and other 18.5%.
Major cities (1985): Monrovia 400,000[8]; Harbel 60,000; Gbarnga 30,000[9]; Buchanan 25,000; Yekepa 16,000.

Vital statistics

Birth rate per 1,000 population (1994): 43.0 (world avg. 25.0).
Death rate per 1,000 population (1994): 12.0 (world avg. 9.3).
Natural increase rate per 1,000 population (1994): 31.0 (world avg. 15.7).
Total fertility rate (avg. births per childbearing woman; 1995): 6.3.
Marriage rate per 1,000 population: n.a.
Divorce rate per 1,000 population: n.a.
Life expectancy at birth (1990–95): male 54.0 years; female 57.0 years.
Major causes of death per 100,000 population (1985)[10]: complications during pregnancy 632.6[11]; malaria 79.8; pneumonia 64.2; anemia 50.2; malnutrition 23.4; measles 12.7. Violence and acts of war were major causes of both morbidity and mortality from 1990 onward.

National economy

Budget (1993). Revenue: L$249,825,000 (1989; income and profits taxes 33.9%; import duties and consular fees 29.6%; excise tax 12.7%; property taxes 1.9%). Expenditures: L$273,930,000 (1988; current expenditure 91.1%, of which wages and salaries 34.1%, interest on public debt 13.1%, goods and services 7.8%, subsidies and grants 5.1%; development expenditure 8.9%).
Tourism: receipts from visitors (1986) U.S.$6,000,000; expenditures by nationals abroad, n.a.
Population economically active (1984): total 704,321; activity rate 33.5% (participation rates: ages 15–64, 56.3%; female 41.0%; unemployed 12.5%).

Price and earnings indexes (1985 = 100)

	1984	1985	1986	1987	1988	1989	1990[12]
Consumer price index	100.6	100.0	103.6	108.8	119.3	130.6	139.4
Earnings index	...	...	...	...	...	...	...

Production (metric tons except as noted). Agriculture, forestry, fishing (1994): cassava 390,000, sugarcane 241,000, bananas 80,000, rice 50,000, plantains 33,000, sweet potatoes 18,000, pulses 18,000 (of which soybeans 2,000), yams 15,000, natural rubber 10,000, oranges 7,000, pineapples 7,000, peanuts (groundnuts) 3,000, cacao beans 2,000; livestock (number of live animals) 220,000 goats, 210,000 sheep, 120,000 pigs, 36,000 cattle, 4,000,000 chickens; roundwood (1993) 6,183,000 cu m; fish catch (1993) 7,782. Mining and quarrying (1993): iron ore[13]; diamonds 150,000 carats; gold 22,500 troy oz. Manufacturing (1990): cement 8,300[14]; palm oil 30,000; cigarettes 22,000,000 units; soft drinks 171,000 hectolitres[15]; beer 158,000 hectolitres[15]. Construction: n.a. Energy production (consumption): electricity (kW-hr; 1993) 480,000,000 (480,000,000); coal, none (n.a.); crude petroleum, none (n.a.); petroleum products (metric tons; 1993) none (101,000); natural gas, none (n.a.).

Public debt (external, outstanding; 1993): U.S.$1,070,000,000.
Household income and expenditure. Average household size (1983) 4.3; income per household: n.a.; sources of income: n.a.; expenditure: n.a.
Gross national product (1990): U.S.$1,178,000,000 (U.S.$498 per capita).

Structure of gross domestic product and labour force

	1989		1984	
	in value L$'000,000	% of total value	labour force	% of labour force
Agriculture	410.7	34.4	481,177	68.3
Mining	122.3	10.2	17,500	2.5
Manufacturing	81.6	6.8	10,699	1.5
Construction	26.3	2.2	4,072	0.6
Public utilities	19.0	1.6	2,878	0.4
Transp. and commun.	79.1	6.6	13,986	2.0
Trade	63.3	5.3	46,850	6.6
Finance	141.8	11.9	2,117	0.3
Pub. admin., defense	139.4	11.7	61,168	8.7
Services	35.5	3.0		
Other	74.8[16]	6.3[16]	63,874[17]	9.1[17]
TOTAL	1,193.6[4]	100.0	704,321	100.0

Land use (1993): forested 17.6%; meadows and pastures 58.9%; agricultural and under permanent cultivation 3.9%; other 19.6%.

Foreign trade

Balance of trade (current prices)

	1983	1984	1985	1986	1987	1988
L$'000,000	+73.8	+137.6	+189.4	+184.1	+115.9	+160.6
% of total	9.4%	17.1%	27.8%	29.1%	17.9%	25.4%

Imports (1991): L$4,081,200,000 (1990; machinery and transport equipment 26.9%, petroleum and petroleum products 23.5%, food and live animals 21.1%, basic manufactures 13.9%, chemicals 5.8%). *Major import sources:* South Korea 45.5%; Germany 4.2%; Japan 17.4%; Singapore 5.1%; Spain 3.8%.
Exports (1991): L$556,500,000 (1988; iron ore 55.1%, rubber 28.0%, logs and timber 8.4%, diamonds 2.1%, gold 1.8%, coffee 1.5%). *Major export destinations:* Norway 34.2%; Belgium-Luxembourg 28.8%; Spain 9.3%; France 8.5%; Malaysia 5.2%.

Transport and communications

Transport. Railroads (1991)[13, 18]: route length 306 mi, 493 km; short ton-mi cargo 1,746,000,000[15], metric ton-km cargo 2,549,000,000[15]. Roads (1991): total length 3,787 mi, 6,095 km (paved 39%). Vehicles (1993): passenger cars 8,000; trucks and buses 3,100. Merchant marine (1992): vessels (100 gross tons and over) 1,672; total deadweight tonnage 97,373,965. Air transport (1980): passenger-mi 10,600,000, passenger-km 17,000,000; short ton mi cargo 68,000, metric ton-km cargo 100,000; airports (1995) with scheduled flights 1.
Communications. Daily newspapers (1992): total number 8; total circulation 35,000; circulation per 1,000 population 14.8. Radio (1993): 600,000 receivers (1 per 3.9 persons). Television (1993): 45,000 receivers (1 per 53 persons). Telephones (main lines; 1993): 4,500 (1 per 528 persons).

Education and health

Education (1980)

	schools	teachers	students	student/ teacher ratio
Primary (age 6–12)	1,651	9,099	227,131	25.0
Secondary (age 13–18)	419	1,129	51,666	45.8
Voc., teacher tr.	6	63	2,322	36.9
Higher	3	472[19]	5,095[19]	10.8[19]

Educational attainment (1974). Percentage of population age 25 and over having: no grade completed 87.1%; some primary education 4.8%; complete primary 1.5%; some secondary 5.1%; higher 1.5%. *Literacy* (1995): total population age 15 and over literate 705,000 (38.3%); males literate 523,000 (56.9%); females literate 182,000 (22.4%).
Health: physicians (1985) 227 (1 per 9,687 persons); hospital beds (1981) 3,000 (1 per 653 persons); infant mortality rate (1993) 115.9.
Food (1992): daily per capita caloric intake 1,640 (vegetable products 96%, animal products 4%); 71% of FAO recommended minimum requirement.

Military

Total active duty personnel (1995): as a result of the civil war, the Armed Forces of Liberia (AFL), with a force of about 3,000, is confined to the capital city of Monrovia. *Military expenditure as percentage of GNP* (1988): 3.8% (world 4.9%); per capita expenditure U.S.$27.

[1]Five years of multifactional warfare officially ended with the swearing in of the transitional government on Sept. 2, 1995. [2]Officially at par with the U.S.$; the unofficial parallel exchange rate (a truer value of the L$) was roughly L$50 = U.S.$1. [3]Figures for Grand Kru included in Maryland. [4]Detail does not add to total given because of rounding. [5]Includes 10,000 persons not allocated by county. [6]Includes about 750,000 Liberian refugees in surrounding countries. [7]Some external sources estimate the Muslim population to exceed 30%. [8]The 1995 population is estimated to be more than 1,000,000 (including many persons displaced because of war). [9]1986. [10]Hospital inpatient morbidity rates. [11]1984. [12]July 1. [13]Mining ceased in late 1992. [14]1993. [15]1988. [16]Import duties less imputed bank service charges. [17]Includes 34,991 unemployed. [18]For iron-ore transport only. [19]1987.

Libya

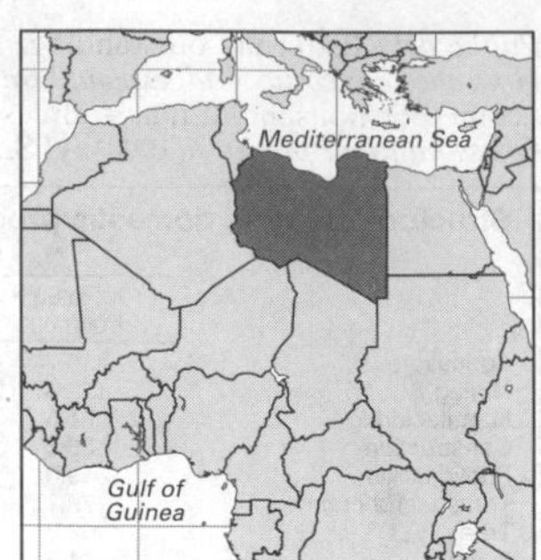

Official name: al-Jamāhīrīyah al-ʿArabīyah al-Lībīyah ash-Shaʿbīyah al-Ishtirākīyah (Socialist People's Libyan Arab Jamahiriya).
Form of government: socialist state with one policy-making body (General People's Congress [750]).
Chief of state: Muammar al-Qaddafi (de facto)[1]; Secretary of General People's Congress (de jure).
Head of government: Secretary of the General People's Committee (prime minister).
Capital: Tripoli[2].
Official language: Arabic.
Official religion: Islam.
Monetary unit: 1 Libyan dinar (LD) = 1,000 dirhams; valuation[3] (Oct. 6, 1995) 1 Libyan dinar = U.S.$2.78 = £1.79.

Area and population

		area		population
Baladīyāt	Capitals	sq mi	sq km	1988 estimate
Banghāzī	Banghāzī	5,800	15,000	512,200
al-Jabal al-Akhḍar	al-Bayḍā'	14,300	37,000	308,300
al-Jabal al-Gharbī	Gharyān	33,600	87,000	204,300
Khalīj Surt	Surt	145,200	376,000	382,100
al-Kufrah	al-Kufrah	186,900	484,000	23,800
Margib	al-Khums	11,200	29,000	408,900
Marzūq	Marzūq	135,100	350,000	45,200
Nikāt al-Khums	Zuwārah	39,000	101,000	196,000
Sabhā	Sabhā	31,700	82,000	121,700
Ṭarābulus	Tripoli (Ṭarābulus)	1,200	3,000	1,083,100
Ṭubruq	Ṭubruq	32,400	84,000	110,900
Wādī al-Ḥa'iṭ	Awbārī	40,500	105,000	49,600
az-Zāwiyah	az-Zāwiyah	1,500	4,000	326,500
TOTAL		678,400	1,757,000	3,772,600

Demography

Population (1995): 5,407,000.
Density (1995): persons per sq mi 8.0, persons per sq km 3.1.
Urban-rural (1995): urban 86.0%; rural 14.0%.
Sex distribution (1995): male 52.10%; female 47.90%.
Age breakdown (1995): under 15, 45.4%; 15–29, 26.4%; 30–44, 14.7%; 45–59, 9.1%; 60–74, 3.7%; 75 and over, 0.6%.
Population projection: (2000) 6,387,000; (2010) 8,724,000.
Doubling time: 21 years.
Ethnic composition (1984): Libyan Arab and Berber 89.0%; other 11.0%.
Religious affiliation (1992): Sunnī Muslim 97.0%; other 3.0%.
Major cities (1988): Tripoli 591,100; Banghāzī 446,250; Miṣrātah 121,700; az-Zāwiyah 89,338.

Vital statistics

Birth rate per 1,000 population (1995): 44.9 (world avg. 25.0).
Death rate per 1,000 population (1995): 7.9 (world avg. 9.3).
Natural increase rate per 1,000 population (1995): 37.0 (world avg. 15.7).
Total fertility rate (avg. births per childbearing woman; 1995): 6.3.
Marriage rate per 1,000 population (1988): 4.5[4].
Divorce rate per 1,000 population (1988): 0.6[4].
Life expectancy at birth (1995): male 62.1 years; female 66.6 years.
Major causes of death per 100,000 population: n.a.; however, the major causes of death in the early 1990s were pneumonia, dysentery and diarrhea, cardiovascular disease, accidents, and malignant neoplasms (cancers).

National economy

Budget (1991–92). Revenue: LD 2,655,000,000 (1990–91; current revenue 55.7%, of which oil revenues 17.7%, income taxes 13.7%, customs duties 9.7%, stamp duties 2.4%; capital revenue 44.3%). Expenditures: LD 2,846,000,000 (1990–91; current expenditures 55.7%, of which allocations to municipal people's committees 39.4%, education and scientific research 4.3%, health 2.7%; capital expenditures 44.3%, of which agriculture and land reclamation 13.6%, industry 5.3%).
Public debt (long-term debt; 1992): U.S.$2,592,000,000.
Production (metric tons except as noted). Agriculture, forestry, fishing (1994): watermelons 175,000, tomatoes 135,000, barley 130,000, potatoes 130,000, wheat 130,000, oranges 80,000, onions 70,000, dates 65,000, olives 50,000, almonds 31,000, lemons and limes 3,000; livestock (number of live animals) 3,500,000 sheep, 600,000 goats, 120,000 camels, 50,000 cattle, 15,000,000 chickens; roundwood (1993) 648,000 cu m; fish catch (1993) 8,800. Mining and quarrying (1993): lime 260,000; gypsum 180,000; salt 12,000. Manufacturing (1993): distillate fuel 4,470,000; cement 2,300,000; gasoline 1,995,000; jet fuel 1,664,000; crude steel 920,000; meat 95,000. Construction (gross value in LD; 1982): residential 127,051,000; nonresidential 200,877,000. Energy production (consumption): electricity (kW-hr; 1992) 16,950,000,000 (16,950,000,000); coal (metric tons; 1992) none (5,000); crude petroleum (barrels; 1992) 519,400,000 (113,500,000); petroleum products (metric tons; 1992) 13,002,000 (6,555,000); natural gas (cu m; 1992) 6,770,000,000 (5,470,000,000).
Population economically active (1992): total 1,210,000; activity rate of total population 24.8% (participation rates: ages 10 and over, n.a.; female 9.6%; unemployed, n.a.).

Price and earnings indexes (1990 = 100)

	1988	1989	1990	1991	1992	1993	1994
Consumer price index	67.5	88.5	100.0	111.7	128.5	154.1	200.4
Earnings index	...	...	...	...	...	...	...

Gross domestic product (at current market prices; 1994): U.S.$32,900,000,000 (U.S.$6,510 per capita).

Structure of gross domestic product and labour force

	1991		1992	
	in value LD '000,000	% of total value	labour force	% of labour force
Agriculture	768	7.5	191,600	19.2
Mining and quarrying	2,681	26.3	23,700	2.4
Manufacturing	809	7.9	92,200	9.3
Construction	1,209	11.8	156,300	15.7
Public utilities	231	2.3	28,500	2.9
Transportation and communications	644	6.3	78,500	7.9
Trade	896	8.8	52,800	5.3
Finance, insurance	1,162	11.4	15,000	1.5
Pub. admin., defense	1,079	10.6	308,000	31.0
Services	724	7.1	48,300	4.8
TOTAL	10,203	100.0	994,900	100.0

Household income and expenditure. Average household size (1980) 5.1; income per household: n.a.; sources of income: n.a.; expenditure (1977): food 37.2%, housing and energy 32.2%, transportation 9.4%, education and recreation 8.5%, clothing 6.9%, health care 3.3%.
Land use (1993): forested 0.5%; meadows and pastures 7.6%; agricultural and under permanent cultivation 1.2%; desert and built-up areas 90.7%.
Tourism: receipts from visitors (1993) U.S.$5,000,000; expenditures by nationals abroad (1992) U.S.$154,000,000.

Foreign trade[5, 6]

Balance of trade (current prices)

	1989	1990	1991	1992	1993	1994
U.S.$'000,000	+4,224	+8,215	+5,873	+4,768	+2,293	+3,440
% of total	32.5%	42.0%	35.5%	31.6%	17.5%	28.2%

Imports (1994): U.S.$4,386,000,000 (1991; manufactured goods 78.3%, agricultural goods 20.3%). *Major import sources:* Italy 18.9%; Germany 16.0%; United Kingdom 7.5%; France 6.3%; Turkey 5.1%.
Exports (1994): U.S.$7,826,000,000 (1991; crude petroleum 99.8%). *Major export destinations:* Italy 39.0%; Germany 17.7%; Spain 11.7%; France 4.8%; Turkey 3.3%; Switzerland 2.8%; United Kingdom 2.6%.

Transport and communications

Transport. Railroads: none. Roads (1992): total length 12,000 mi, 19,300 km (paved 56%). Vehicles (1993): passenger cars 448,000; trucks and buses 322,000. Merchant marine (1992): vessels (100 gross tons and over) 150; total deadweight tonnage 1,223,589. Air transport (1994)[7]: passenger-mi 264,180,000, passenger-km 425,157,000; short ton-mi cargo 229,500, metric ton-km cargo 335,000; airports (1995) with scheduled flights 12.
Communications. Daily newspapers (1992): total number 4; circulation 71,000; circulation per 1,000 population 14.6. Radio (1994): total number of receivers 1,000,000 (1 per 5.2 persons). Television (1994): total number of receivers 500,000 (1 per 10.5 persons). Telephones (main lines; 1993): 240,000 (1 per 21.0 persons).

Education and health

Education (1991–92)

	schools	teachers	students	student/ teacher ratio
Primary (age 6–12)	2,744[8]	99,623	1,238,986	12.4
Secondary (age 13–18)	1,555[8]	11,429	138,860	12.1
Voc., teacher tr.	195[8]	7,072	76,648	10.8
Higher	10[9]	...	72,899	...

Educational attainment (1984). Percentage of population age 25 and over having: no formal schooling (illiterate) 59.7%; incomplete primary education 15.4%; complete primary 8.5%; some secondary 5.2%; secondary 8.5%; higher 2.7%. *Literacy* (1990): percentage of total population age 15 and over literate 63.8%; males literate 75.4%; females literate 50.4%.
Health: physicians (1989–91) 4,749 (1 per 948 persons); hospital beds (1990) 18,503[10] (1 per 246 persons); infant mortality rate per 1,000 live births (1995) 61.4.
Food (1992): daily per capita caloric intake 3,308 (vegetable products 88%, animal products 12%); 140% of FAO recommended minimum requirement.

Military

Total active duty personnel (1995): 80,000 (army 62.5%, navy 10.0%, air force 27.5%). *Military expenditure as percentage of GNP* (1993): 5.1% (world 3.3%); per capita expenditure U.S.$328.

[1]No formal titled office exists. [2]Policy-making body (General People's Congress) meets in Surt. [3]Official exchange rate. [4]Registered events; incomplete to some degree. [5]Dollar values based on IMF Direction of Trade Statistics (DOTS), which are compiled from available reports of trading partners (not the subject country's reports) and may, thus, be substantially incomplete. [6]Import figures are f.o.b. [7]Jamahiriya Libyan Arab Airlines. [8]1982–83. [9]1988–89. [10]Includes beds in clinics.

Liechtenstein

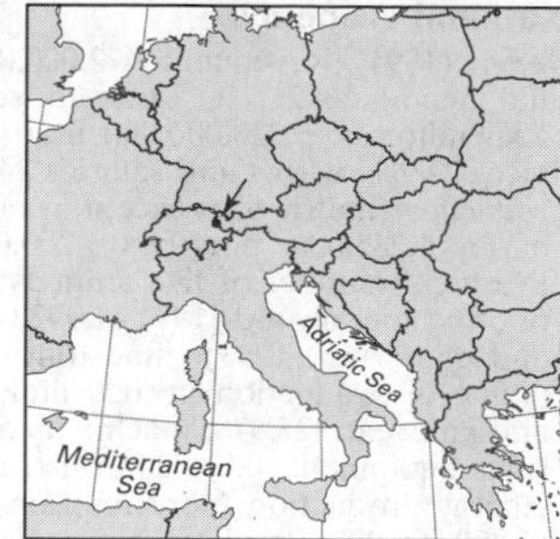

Official name: Fürstentum Liechtenstein (Principality of Liechtenstein).
Form of government: constitutional monarchy with one legislative house (Diet [25]).
Chief of state: Prince.
Head of government: Head of the Government.
Capital: Vaduz.
Official language: German.
Official religion: none.
Monetary unit: 1 Swiss franc (Sw F) = 100 centimes; valuation (Oct. 6, 1995) 1 U.S.$ = Sw F 1.15; 1 £ = Sw F 1.82.

Area and population

	area		population
Communes	sq mi	sq km	1995[1] estimate
Balzers	7.6	19.6	3,917
Eschen	4.0	10.3	3,443
Gamprin	2.4	6.1	1,092
Mauren	2.9	7.5	2,963
Planken	2.0	5.3	316
Ruggell	2.9	7.4	1,550
Schaan	10.3	26.8	5,143
Schellenberg	1.4	3.5	889
Triesen	10.2	26.4	3,789
Triesenberg	11.5	29.8	2,460
Vaduz	6.7	17.3	5,067
TOTAL	61.8[2]	160.0	30,629

Demography

Population (1995): 30,900.
Density (1995): persons per sq mi 500.0, persons per sq km 193.1.
Urban-rural: n.a.
Sex distribution (1994): male 48.64%; female 51.36%.
Age breakdown (1994): under 15, 19.1%; 15–29, 22.9%; 30–44, 24.9%; 45–59, 18.3%; 60–74, 10.0%; 75 and over, 4.8%.
Population projection: (2000) 33,300; (2010) 38,500.
Doubling time: n.a.; doubling time exceeds 100 years.
National composition (1994): Liechtensteiner 61.6%; Swiss 15.6%; Austrian 7.2%; German 3.6%; other 12.0%.
Religious affiliation (1994): Roman Catholic 80.3%; Protestant 7.1%; other 4.7%; not stated 7.9%.
Major cities (1995[1]): Schaan 5,143; Vaduz 5,067.

Vital statistics

Birth rate per 1,000 population (1994): 11.7 (world avg. 25.0); legitimate 92.3%; illegitimate 7.7%.
Death rate per 1,000 population (1994): 6.7 (world avg. 9.3).
Natural increase rate per 1,000 population (1994): 5.0 (world avg. 15.7).
Total fertility rate (avg. births per childbearing woman; 1994): 1.5.
Marriage rate per 1,000 population (1994): 13.1.
Divorce rate per 1,000 population (1994): 1.3.
Life expectancy at birth (1994): male 66.5 years; female 79.5 years.
Major causes of death per 100,000 population (1994): diseases of the circulatory system 326.4; malignant neoplasms (cancers) 133.9; diseases of the respiratory system 35.9; accidents, poisoning, and acts of violence 35.9.

National economy

Budget (1993). Revenue: Sw F 488,378,000 (taxes and interest 69.4%; post, telephone, and telegraph 15.5%; other revenue sources include real estate capital-gains taxes and death and estate taxes). Expenditures: Sw F 462,-465,000 (financial affairs 35.8%; education 15.8%; social affairs 15.7%; post, telephone, and telegraph 13.0%).
Public debt: none.
Tourism (1994): 134,280 tourist arrivals; receipts from visitors, n.a.; expenditures by nationals abroad, n.a.
Population economically active (1994[3]): total 15,109; activity rate of total population 49.3% (participation rates: ages 15–64, 65.7%; female 38.1%; unemployed 2.3%).

Price and earnings indexes (1990 = 100)

	1988	1989	1990	1991	1992	1993	1994
Consumer price index[4]	91.9	94.9	100.0	105.8	110.2	113.7	114.7
Earnings index	...	...	...	...	...	...	...

Household income and expenditure. Average household size (1990) 2.7; income per household: n.a.; sources of earned income (1987): wages and salaries 92.9%, self-employment 7.1%; expenditure (1990)[5]: rent 20.9%, food 17.7%, transportation 11.0%, education and self-improvement 9.7%, clothing 7.0%, health 4.7%.
Production (metric tons except as noted). Agriculture, forestry, fishing (1993): silo corn (maize) 27,880[6], milk 12,590, potatoes 1,040[6], wheat 460[6], barley 416[6]; livestock (number of live animals) 5,675 cattle, 3,236 pigs, 2,641 sheep; commercial timber 14,759 cu m. Mining and quarrying: n.a. Manufacturing (1993): whipped cream 1,462; yogurt 87; cheese 4; wine 635.2 hectolitres; small-scale precision manufacturing includes optical lenses, electron microscopes, electronic equipment, and high-vacuum pumps; metal manufacturing, construction machinery, and ceramics are also important. Construction (1993): residential 304,884 cu m; nonresidential 306,265 cu m. Energy production (consumption): electricity (kW-hr; 1993) 64,880,000 (235,000,000); coal (metric tons; 1993) none (38); petroleum products (metric tons; 1993) none (56,926); natural gas (cu m; 1993) none (19,348,000).
Gross national product (at current market prices; 1991): *c.* U.S.$978,000,000 (U.S.$33,510 per capita).

Structure of gross domestic product and labour force

	1988		1994	
	in value Sw F '000	% of total value	labour force	% of labour force
Agriculture	...	...	329	2.2
Mining	...	...	4	—
Manufacturing	...	...	4,682	31.0
Construction	...	...	1,158	7.7
Public utilities	...	...	157	1.0
Transportation and communications	...	...	476	3.2
Trade	...	...	2,089	13.8
Finance, insurance, real estate	...	...	1,119	7.4
Pub. admin., defense	...	...	909	6.0
Services	...	...	3,659	24.2
Other	...	...	527[7]	3.5[7]
TOTAL	1,700,000	100.0	15,109	100.0

Land use (latest): forested 34.8%; meadows and pastures 15.7%; agricultural and under permanent cultivation 24.3%; other 25.2%.

Foreign trade

Balance of trade (current prices)

	1988	1989	1990	1991	1992	1993
Sw F '000,000	+745.2	+742.8	+757.1	+822.8	+947.1	+1,024.2
% of total	37.3%	29.8%	27.8%	31.4%	30.6%	33.8%

Imports (1993): Sw F 1,002,735 (machinery and transport equipment 31.5%; other finished goods 30.0%; limestone, cement, and other building materials 11.8%; metal products 11.2%; chemical products 6.3%; unrefined and semifabricated metal 5.5%). *Major import sources:* n.a.
Exports (1993): Sw F 2,026,959 (machinery and transport equipment 44.6%; metal products 16.6%; other finished goods 14.6%; chemical products 10.7%; limestone, cement, and other building materials 8.5%). *Major export destinations:* European Economic Community countries 41.6%; Switzerland 13.8%; other European Free Trade Association countries 6.2%.

Transport and communications

Transport. Railroads (1993): length 11.5 mi, 18.5 km; passenger and cargo traffic, n.a. Roads (1993): total length 201 mi, 323 km. Vehicles (1993): passenger cars 17,767; trucks and buses 1,817. Merchant marine: none. Air transport: none.
Communications. Daily newspapers (1992): total number 2; total circulation 17,739; circulation per 1,000 population 611. Radio (1993): total number of receivers 11,000 (1 per 2.8 persons). Television (1993): total number of receivers 10,620 (1 per 2.9 persons). Telephones (main lines; 1993): 18,916 (1 per 1.6 persons).

Education and health

Education (1993–94)

	schools	teachers[8]	students	student/ teacher ratio
Primary (age 7–12)	14	122	1,986	16.3
Secondary (age 13–19)	8	124	1,587	12.8
Vocational	1	40	197	4.9

Educational attainment (1980). Percentage of population age 25 and over having: no formal schooling 0.2%; primary and lower secondary education 47.6%; higher secondary and vocational 41.0%; some postsecondary 6.6%; university 4.6%. *Literacy:* virtually 100%.
Health: physicians (1993) 32 (1 per 957 persons); hospital beds[9] (1985) 100 (1 per 269 persons); infant mortality rate per 1,000 live births (1994) 5.3.
Food (1992)[10]: daily per capita caloric intake 3,440 (vegetable products 64%, animal products 36%); 129% of FAO recommended minimum requirement.

Military

Total active duty personnel: none. *Military expenditure as percentage of GNP:* none.

[1]January 1. [2]Detail does not add to total given because of rounding. [3]December 31. [4]The index is for Switzerland, which is united with Liechtenstein in a customs and monetary union. [5]Household expenditures are taken from a 1986 Swiss sample survey; a similarity of consumption patterns is assumed. [6]1987. [7]Includes 177 unclassifiable and 350 unemployed persons. [8]Full-time teachers only. [9]Liechtenstein has one hospital. Agreements with the Swiss cantons of St. Gallen and Graubünden and the Austrian Federal State of Vorarlberg allow use of certain hospitals. [10]Figures are derived from statistics for Switzerland and Austria.

Lithuania

Official name: Lietuvos Respublika (Republic of Lithuania).
Form of government: unitary multiparty republic with a single legislative body, the Seimas (141).
Head of state: President.
Head of government: Prime Minister.
Capital: Vilnius.
Official language: Lithuanian.
Official religion: none.
Monetary unit[1]: 1 litas (plural litai) = 100 centai; valuation (Oct. 6, 1995) 1 U.S.$ = 4.00 litai; 1 £ = 6.32 litai.

Area and population

Cities of republic jurisdiction	Capitals	area sq mi	area sq km	population 1989 estimate
Alytus	—	1	3	73,100
Birštonas	—	5	12	4,100
Druskininkai	—	8	22	22,500
Kaunas	—	46	120	422,600
Klaipėda	—	27	71	204,000
Marijampolė	—	8	20	50,500
Neringa	—	35	90	2,500
Palanga	—	27	69	19,400
Panevėžys	—	12	30	126,500
Šiauliai	—	27	69	145,000
Vilnius	—	110	286	582,400
Regions				
Akmenė	Naujoji Akmenė	407	1,055	37,800
Alytus	Alytus	545	1,411	32,700
Anykščiai	Anykščiai	681	1,765	38,300
Biržai	Biržai	570	1,476	38,600
Ignalina	Ignalina	581	1,505	59,000
Jonava	Jonava	364	944	54,000
Joniškis	Joniškis	445	1,152	32,900
Jurbarkas	Jurbarkas	582	1,507	40,200
Kaišiadorys	Kaišiadorys	451	1,169	40,200
Kaunas	Kaunas	588	1,522	85,500
Kėdainiai	Kėdainiai	647	1,677	69,400
Kelmė	Kelmė	660	1,710	42,900
Klaipėda	Gargždai	527	1,366	45,000
Kretinga	Kretinga	385	997	44,100
Kupiškis	Kupiškis	417	1,080	25,900
Lazdijai	Lazdijai	595	1,542	33,400
Marijampolė	Marijampolė	599	1,551	49,200
Mažeikiai	Mažeikiai	390	1,009	61,200
Molėtai	Molėtai	528	1,368	27,300
Pakruojis	Pakruojis	508	1,316	30,700
Panevėžys	Panevėžys	849	2,199	41,900
Pasvalys	Pasvalys	498	1,289	36,800
Plungė	Plungė	653	1,691	53,900
Prienai	Prienai	443	1,148	39,500
Radviliškis	Radviliškis	631	1,635	54,800
Raseiniai	Raseiniai	607	1,573	46,100
Rokiškis	Rokiškis	697	1,806	47,800
Šakiai	Šakiai	623	1,613	41,600
Šalčininkai	Šalčininkai	578	1,498	41,500
Šiauliai	Šiauliai	701	1,815	49,900
Šilalė	Šilalė	459	1,188	31,700
Šilutė	Šilutė	866	2,243	69,000
Širvintos	Širvintos	350	906	21,500
Skuodas	Skuodas	352	911	26,600
Švenčionys	Švenčionys	653	1,692	37,800
Tauragė	Tauragė	455	1,179	52,600
Telšiai	Telšiai	556	1,439	59,200
Trakai	Trakai	640	1,657	81,700
Ukmergė	Ukmergė	539	1,395	52,500
Utena	Utena	475	1,229	52,300
Varėna	Varėna	933	2,416	38,500
Vilkaviškis	Vilkaviškis	497	1,286	52,200
Vilnius	Vilnius	855	2,215	93,800
Zarasai	Zarasai	515	1,334	25,900
TOTAL		25,213[2]	65,301[2]	3,690,000

Demography

Population (1995): 3,700,000.
Density (1995): persons per sq mi 146.7, persons per sq km 56.7.
Urban-rural (1994): urban 68.3%; rural 31.7%.
Sex distribution (1994): male 47.29%; female 52.71%.
Age breakdown (1994): under 15, 22.2%; 15–29, 22.4%; 30–44, 21.7%; 45–59, 16.9%; 60–74, 12.3%; 75 and over, 4.5%.
Population projection: (2000) 3,692,000; (2010) 3,736,000.
Doubling time: not applicable.
Ethnic composition (1994): Lithuanian 81.1%; Russian 8.5%; Polish 7.0%; Belorussian 1.5%; Ukrainian 1.0%; other 0.9%.
Religious affiliation (1990): Roman Catholic, about 80%; Russian Orthodox, Old Believer, Evangelical Lutheran, and nonreligious minorities.
Major cities (1994): Vilnius 584,400; Kaunas 423,900; Klaipėda 204,600.

Vital statistics

Birth rate per 1,000 population (1994): 11.5 (world avg. 25.0).
Death rate per 1,000 population (1994): 12.5 (world avg. 9.3).
Natural increase rate per 1,000 population (1994): −1.0 (world avg. 15.7).
Total fertility rate (avg. births per childbearing woman; 1989): 2.0.
Marriage rate per 1,000 population (1993): 6.3.
Divorce rate per 1,000 population (1993): 3.7.
Life expectancy at birth (1993): male 63.3 years; female 75.0 years.
Major causes of death per 100,000 population (1993): circulatory diseases 674; cancers 201; accidents 168; respiratory diseases 48.

National economy

Budget (1994). Revenue: 5,472,000,000 litai (social-security tax 27.1%, individual income tax 21.7%, value-added tax 21.0%, enterprise profits tax 10.1%). Expenditures: 5,920,000,000 litai (transfer payments 30.9%, good and services 27.9%, wages and salaries 24.8%, capital expenditures 11.3%).
Production (metric tons except as noted). Agriculture, forestry, fishing (1994): barley 1,285,000, potatoes 1,200,000, sugar beets 800,000, wheat 650,000; livestock (number of live animals) 1,650,000 cattle, 1,200,000 pigs, 8,000,000 poultry; roundwood (1991) 1,443,000 cu m; fish catch (1993) 119,852. Mining and quarrying (1993): limestone 4,000,000; peat 1,500,000. Manufacturing (value of production in '000 litai; 1993): processed foods 2,822,879; textile and knitwear 822,678; machinery 523,858; radio, television, and communications equipment 480,405. Construction (1993): residential 245,000,000 litai. Energy production (consumption): electricity (kW-hr; 1994) 10,020,000,000 (7,409,000,000); coal (metric tons; 1992) none (657,000); crude petroleum (barrels; 1992) 469,000 (30,000,000); petroleum products (metric tons; 1992) 3,591,000 (3,825,000); natural gas (cu m; 1992) none (3,437,000,000).
Public debt (external, outstanding; 1993): U.S.$163,500,000.
Gross national product (1993): U.S.$4,891,000,000 (U.S.$1,310 per capita).

Structure of gross national product and labour force

	1993 in value '000,000 litai	% of total value	labour force[3]	% of labour force
Agriculture, forestry	1,219.3	14.6	400,800	21.6
Manufacturing, mining	2,188.9	26.2	423,600	22.8
Construction	560.5	6.7	126,800	6.8
Public utilities	410.3	4.9	33,400	1.8
Transp. and commun.	677.4	8.1	99,900	5.4
Trade	1,437.4	17.2	190,900	10.3
Finance	518.8	6.2	60,800	3.3
Pub admin., defense	559.5	6.7	56,600	3.0
Services	393.5	4.7	385,400	20.7
Other	385.1	4.6	81,100	4.4
TOTAL	8,350.7	100.0[4]	1,859,300	100.0[4]

Population economically active (1994): total 1,741,000; activity rate of total population 46.8% (participation rates: ages 16–60/55[5], 82.9%; female [1993] 48.5%; unemployed 3.8%).

Price and earnings indexes (1990 = 100)

	1988	1989	1990	1991	1992	1993	1994
Consumer price index	...	...	100.0	216.4	2,207	9,054	13,125
Monthly earnings index	78.7	86.1	100.0	259.9	2,008	2,226	3,798

Household income and expenditure (1993). Avg. household size (1989) 3.2; sources of income: wages 65.2%, pensions and grants 15.9%, self-employment in agriculture 10.4%, other 8.5%; expenditures: food 50.9%, nonfood goods 18.6%, services 11.3%, taxes 10.8%, agricultural expenses 5.1%.
Land use (1993): forest 30.7%; pasture 7.1%; agricultural 46.1%; other 16.1%.

Foreign trade

Imports (1994): U.S.$2,210,000,000 (petroleum and gas 32.8%, machinery 16.5%, chemicals 8.8%, textiles 7.4%, base metals 6.5%). *Major import sources:* CIS countries 62.7%; market economies 31.9%; Baltic states 5.4%.
Exports (1994): U.S.$1,892,000,000 (mineral products 16.7%, textiles 12.3%, machinery 12.0%, food products 11.9%). *Major export destinations:* market economies 45.7%; CIS countries 35.3%; Baltic states 19.0%.

Transport and communications

Transport. Railroads (1993): length 2,996 km; passenger-km 880,000,000; metric ton-km cargo 11,030,000,000. Roads (1993): total length 55,603 km (paved 76%). Vehicles (1993): passenger cars 597,735; trucks and buses 93,920. Merchant marine (1992): vessels (100 gross tons and over) 52; total deadweight tonnage 373,911. Air transport (1994): passenger-km 217,500,000; metric ton-km cargo 1,086,000; airports (1995) 3.
Communications. Daily newspapers (1992): 18; circulation 836,000; circulation per 1,000 population 223. Radio (1994): 1,420,000 receivers (1 per 2.6 persons). Television (1994): 1,400,000 receivers (1 per 2.7 persons). Telephones (main lines; 1993): 858,500 (1 per 4.4 persons).

Education and health

Education (1993–94)

	schools	teachers	students	student/ teacher ratio
Primary and secondary	2,317	41,052	511,000	12.4
Voc., teacher tr.	168	5,035	69,000	13.7
Higher	14	9,003[6]	53,000	7.3[6]

Educational attainment (1989). Percentage of population age 25 and over having: no schooling 9.1%; complete primary 21.3%; incomplete secondary 57.0%; postsecondary 12.6%. *Literacy* (1989): total population age 15 and over literate 98.4%; males literate 99.2%; females literate 97.8%.
Health (1993): physicians 16,622 (1 per 225 persons); hospital beds 43,600 (1 per 86 persons); infant mortality rate (1994) 14.1.

Military

Total active duty personnel (1995): 8,900 (army 93.3%, navy 3.9%, air force 2.8%).

[1]The litas was established as the official currency on July 20, 1993, and pegged to the U.S. dollar at a rate of 4 to 1 on April 1, 1994. [2]Total includes 12 sq mi (30 sq km) not distributed by administrative subdivision. [3]Derived values, except total. [4]Detail does not add to total given because of rounding. [5]Males retire at age 60, females at 55. [6]1987–88.

Luxembourg

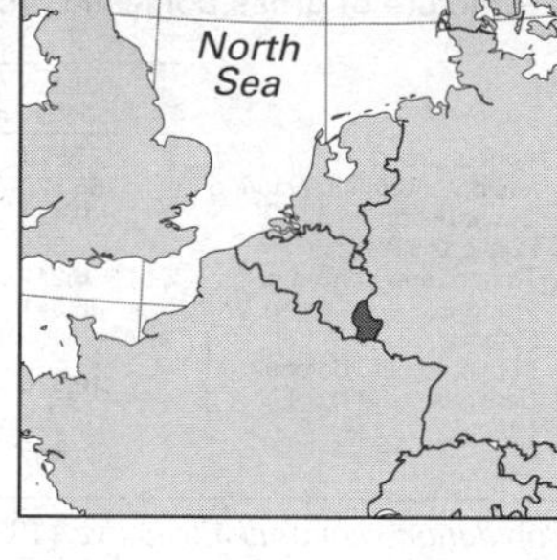

Official name: Groussherzogtum Lëtzebuerg (Luxemburgian); Grand-Duché de Luxembourg (French); Grossherzogtum Luxemburg (German) (Grand Duchy of Luxembourg).
Form of government: constitutional monarchy with two legislative houses (Council of State [21][1]; Chamber of Deputies [60]).
Chief of state: Grand Duke.
Head of government: Prime Minister.
Capital: Luxembourg.
Official language: none: Luxemburgian (national); French (used for most official purposes); German (lingua franca).
Official religion: none.
Monetary unit: 1 Luxembourg franc (Lux F) = 100 centimes; valuation (Oct. 6, 1995) 1 U.S.$ = Lux F 29.39; 1 £ = Lux F 46.46.

Area and population

Districts / Cantons	area sq mi	area sq km	population 1991 census
Diekirch	447	1,157	56,896
Clervaux	128	332	10,263
Diekirch	92	239	23,258
Redange	103	267	11,073
Vianden	21	54	2,720
Wiltz	102	265	9,582
Grevenmacher	203	525	42,837
Echternach	72	186	11,726
Grevenmacher	82	211	18,113
Remich	49	128	12,998
Luxembourg	349	904	284,329
Capellen	77	199	31,817
Esch	94	243	116,389
Luxembourg (Ville et Campagne)	92	238	116,900
Mersch	86	224	19,135
TOTAL	999	2,586	384,062

Demography

Population (1995): 409,000.
Density (1995): persons per sq mi 409.4, persons per sq km 158.2.
Urban-rural (1993): urban 88.0%; rural 12.0%.
Sex distribution (1994[2]): male 49.11%; female 50.89%.
Age breakdown (1991): under 15, 17.3%; 15–29, 21.5%; 30–44, 23.8%; 45–59, 17.5%; 60–74, 12.8%; 75 and over, 7.1%.
Population projection: (2000) 428,000; (2010) 443,000.
Doubling time: not applicable; population stable.
Ethnic composition (nationality; 1993): Luxemburger 69.7%; Portuguese 10.8%; Italian 5.0%; French 3.4%; Belgian 2.5%; German 2.2%; other 6.4%.
Religious affiliation (1990): Roman Catholic 94.9%; Protestant 1.1%; other 4.0%.
Major cities (1991): Luxembourg 75,833; Esch-sur-Alzette 24,018; Dudelange 14,674; Differdange 8,520; Schifflange 6,870.

Vital statistics

Birth rate per 1,000 population (1993): 13.4 (world avg. 25.0); legitimate 87.1%; illegitimate 12.9%.
Death rate per 1,000 population (1993): 9.8 (world avg. 9.3).
Natural increase rate per 1,000 population (1993): 3.6 (world avg. 15.7).
Total fertility rate (avg. births per childbearing woman; 1993): 1.7.
Marriage rate per 1,000 population (1993): 6.0.
Divorce rate per 1,000 population (1993): 1.9.
Life expectancy at birth (1990–92): male 72.6 years; female 79.1 years.
Major causes of death per 100,000 population (1992): circulatory diseases 432.3, of which cerebrovascular disease 140.0, ischemic heart disease and myocardial infarction 131.8; malignant neoplasms (cancers) 255.4; accidents and suicide 69.2, of which suicide 15.1.

National economy

Budget (1995). Revenue: Lux F 145,150,800,000 (income and excise taxes 55.5%, customs taxes 16.8%). Expenditures: Lux F 146,433,000,000 (social security 20.9%, education 12.1%, transportation 9.2%, administration 7.4%, defense 2.6%, debt service 1.3%).
Public debt (1993): U.S.$291,120,000.
Production (metric tons except as noted). Agriculture, forestry, fishing (1993): barley 68,000, wheat 48,600, potatoes 23,000, rye 19,100, oats 17,500, sugar beets 13,000, apples 5,300; livestock (number of live animals; 1994) 208,744 cattle, 68,854 pigs; roundwood (1991) 598,800 cu m. Mining and quarrying (1987): metal ores, none; sand and gravel 956,810; gypsum 420,000; crushed stone 344,841. Manufacturing (1993): steel ingots and castings 3,292,942; pig iron 2,412,000; milk 263,200; beef and pork 23,772; wine 169,268 hectolitres. Construction (1993): residential and semiresidential 618,754 sq m; nonresidential 181,997 sq m. Energy production (consumption): electricity (kW-hr; 1992) 1,198,000,000 (5,176,000,000); coal (metric tons; 1992) none (288,000); crude petroleum, none (n.a.); petroleum products (metric tons; 1992) none (1,806,000); natural gas (cu m; 1992) none (555,316,000).
Gross national product (at current market prices; 1993): U.S.$14,233,000,000 (U.S.$35,850 per capita).

Structure of gross domestic product and labour force

	1991 in value Lux F '000,000	% of total value	labour force	% of labour force
Agriculture	4,477	1.4	5,631	3.4
Mining	997	0.3	34	0.1
Manufacturing	77,303	24.3	29,711	18.0
Construction	23,905	7.5	15,347	9.3
Public utilities	5,264	1.6	1,876	1.1
Transp. and commun.	22,139	6.9	11,319	6.9
Trade	52,285	16.4	32,462	19.7
Finance	44,236	13.9	21,137	12.8
Pub. admin., defense	46,800	14.7	44,756	27.2
Services	48,656	15.3		
Other	−7,258[3]	−2.3[3]	2,441[4]	1.5[4]
TOTAL	318,804	100.0	164,713[5]	100.0

Population economically active (1991): total 164,713; activity rate of total population 42.8% (participation rates: ages 15–64, 61.6%; female 35.9%; unemployed 1.5%).

Price and earnings indexes (1990 = 100)

	1989	1990	1991	1992	1993	1994
Consumer price index	96.4	100.0	103.1	106.4	110.2	112.6
Hourly earnings index	96.8	100.0	105.3	112.0	116.5	...

Household income and expenditure. Average household size (1991) 2.6; income per household (1987) Lux F 1,113,000 (U.S.$29,800); sources of income (1987): wages and salaries 88.6%, self-employment 9.1%, transfer payments 2.3%; expenditure (1991): transportation and communications 19.1%, housing 13.7%, food and beverages 12.9%, household goods and furniture 10.8%, health 7.3%, clothing and footwear 5.9%.
Tourism (1989): receipts from visitors U.S.$286,000,000.
Land use (1992): forested 34.2%; meadows and pastures 25.6%; agricultural and under permanent cultivation 23.2%; other 17.0%.

Foreign trade

Balance of trade (current prices)

	1988	1989	1990	1991	1992	1993
Lux F '000,000	−27,300	−31,900	−43,100	−60,500	−56,300	−55,400
% of total	6.8%	6.8%	9.3%	12.4%	11.9%	11.9%

Imports (1993): Lux F 261,033,000,000 (metal products, machinery, and transport equipment 46.8%, of which transport equipment 14.0%; mineral products 12.3%; food, beverages, and tobacco 11.0%; chemical products 8.2%). *Major import sources:* Belgium 38.1%; Germany 28.5%; France 11.0%, U.S. 6.6%; The Netherlands 4.2%; Italy 2.1%.
Exports (1993). Lux F 205,588,000,000 (metal products, machinery, and transport equipment 56.6%, of which transport equipment 5.1%; plastic materials and rubber manufactures 13.2%; textile yarn, fabrics, and related products 8.1%; food, beverages, and tobacco 7.2%; chemical products 5.1%). *Major export destinations:* Germany 28.2%; France 17.8%; Belgium 15.0%; U.K. 6.5%; The Netherlands 5.4%; Italy 4.7%; U.S. 4.1%.

Transport and communications

Transport. Railroads (1993): route length 171 mi, 275 km; passenger-mi 176,000,000[6], passenger-km 284,000,000[6], short ton-mi cargo 443,156,000, metric ton-km cargo 646,997,000. Roads (1994): total length 3,190 mi, 5,134 km (paved 99%). Vehicles (1994): passenger cars 217,754; trucks and buses 25,050. Merchant marine (1992): vessels (100 gross tons and over) 54; total deadweight tonnage 2,603,611. Air transport (1993): passenger arrivals 539,029, departures 544,537; short ton-mi cargo 606,902,000[7], metric ton-km cargo 886,062,000[7]; airports (1995) with scheduled flights 1.
Communications. Daily newspapers (1993): total number 5; total circulation 152,600; circulation per 1,000 population 383. Radio (1994): 240,000 receivers (1 per 1.7 persons). Television (1991): 134,845 receivers (1 per 2.9 persons). Telephones (main lines; 1993): 214,821 (1 per 1.8 persons).

Education and health

Education (1993–94)

	schools	teachers	students	student/teacher ratio
Primary (age 6–11)[8]	...	1,911	27,595	14.4
Secondary (age 12–18)	...	1,948	8,712[9]	...
Voc., teacher tr.	...		12,662	6.5
Higher	...		4,957[10]	...

Educational attainment: n.a. *Literacy* (1995): virtually 100% literate.
Health (1994[2]): physicians 848 (1 per 469 persons); hospital beds (1993) 4,560 (1 per 87 persons); infant mortality rate per 1,000 live births (1993) 6.0.
Food (1992): daily per capita caloric intake 3,681 (vegetable products 65%, animal products 35%); 139% of FAO recommended minimum.

Military

Total active duty personnel (1994): 800 (army 100.0%). *Military expenditure as percentage of GNP* (1993): 0.8% (world 3.3%); per capita expenditure U.S.$271.

[1]Has limited legislative authority. [2]January 1. [3]Imputed bank service charges. [4]Unemployed. [5]Detail does not add to total given because of rounding. [6]1992. [7]1987. [8]Public schools only. [9]1992–93. [10]1990–91.

Macedonia

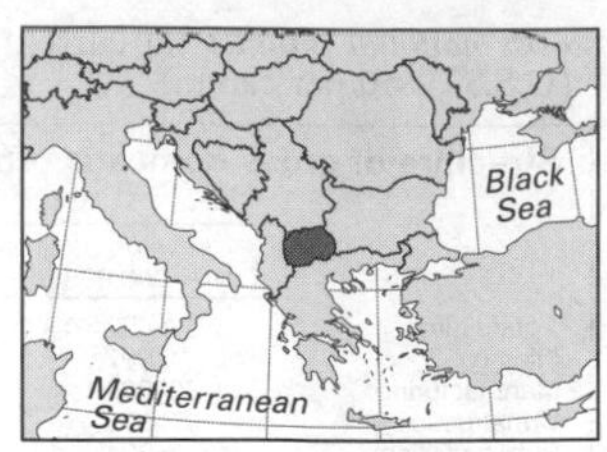

Official name[1]: Republika Makedonija (Republic of Macedonia).
Form of government: unitary multiparty republic with a unicameral legislature (Assembly [120]).
Head of state: President.
Head of government: Prime Minister.
Capital: Skopje.
Official language: Macedonian.
Official religion: none.
Monetary unit[2]: denar; valuation (Oct. 6, 1995) 1 U.S.$ = 39.30 denar; 1 £ = 62.13 denar.

Area and population (1994 census)

Districts	area sq km[3]	population	Districts	area sq km[3]	population
Berovo	806	19,737	Negotino	734	23,094
Bitolj	1,798	106,012	Ohrid	1,069	60,841
Brod	924	10,912	Prilep	1,675	93,248
Debar	274	26,449	Probištip	326	16,373
Delčevo	589	25,052	Radoviš	735	30,378
Demir Hisar	443	10,321	Resen	739	17,467
Gevgelija	757	34,767	Skopje	1,818	541,280
Gostivar	1,341	108,189	Štip	815	50,531
Kavadarci	1,132	41,801	Struga	507	62,305
Kičevo	854	53,044	Strumica	952	89,759
Kočani	570	48,105	Sveti Nikole	649	21,391
Kratovo	376	10,855	Tetovo	1,080	174,748
Kriva Palanka	720	25,112	Titov Veles	1,536	65,523
Kruševo	239	11,981	Valandovo	331	12,049
Kumanovo	1,212	126,543	Vinica	432	19,010
			TOTAL	25,713[4]	1,936,877

Demography

Population (1995): 2,104,000.
Density (1995): persons per sq mi 211.9, persons per sq km 81.8.
Urban-rural (1994): urban 58.7%; rural 41.3%.
Sex distribution (1994): male 50.39%; female 49.61%.
Age breakdown (1994): under 15, 21.8%; 15–29, 22.2%; 30–44, 23.7%; 45–59, 17.4%; 60–74, 12.1%; 75 and over, 2.8%.
Population projection: (2000) 2,185,000; (2010) 2,356,000.
Doubling time: 70 years.
Ethnic composition (1994): Macedonian 66.5%; Albanian 22.9%; Turkish 4.0%; Gypsy 2.3%; Serb 2.0%; other 2.3%.
Religious affiliation (1991): most believers are Christians, predominantly of the Eastern Orthodox church; other Christians include members of the Macedonian Orthodox church and the Roman Catholic church; there are also a substantial Islamic community and a small Jewish community.
Major cities (1994): Skopje 440,577; Bitolj (Bitola) 75,386; Prilep 67,371; Kumanovo 66,237; Tetovo 50,376.

Vital statistics

Birth rate per 1,000 population (1993): 15.7 (world avg. 25.0).
Death rate per 1,000 population (1993): 7.5 (world avg. 9.3).
Natural increase rate per 1,000 population (1993): 8.2 (world avg. 15.7).
Total fertility rate (avg. births per childbearing woman; 1993): 2.2.
Marriage rate per 1,000 population (1993): 7.3.
Divorce rate per 1,000 population (1993): 0.3.
Life expectancy at birth (1993): male 70.1 years; female 74.4 years.
Major causes of death per 100,000 population (1993): diseases of the circulatory system 385.8; accidents, violence, and poisoning 35.3; diseases of the respiratory system 34.5; diseases of the digestive system 14.8; infectious and parasitic diseases 12.9%; malignant neoplasms (cancers) 6.2.

National economy

Budget (1994). Revenue: 63,157,000,000 denar[2] (excise tax 31.6%, income tax 25.8%, sales tax 19.6%, import duties 16.3%, enterprise profit tax 6.6%). Expenditure: 67,061,000,000 denar[2] (national economy 52.3%, transfers 23.8%, debt service 14.0%).
Tourism (1994): receipts from visitors U.S.$21,000,000; expenditures by nationals abroad U.S.$23,000,000.
External debt (1994): U.S.$866,000,000.
Production (metric tons except as noted). Agriculture, forestry, fishing (1994): wheat 340,000, grapes 205,000, potatoes 134,000, corn (maize) 133,000, plums 25,000; livestock (number of live animals) 2,444,000 sheep, 276,000 cattle, 181,000 pigs, 4,000,000 poultry; roundwood (1993) 830,362 cu m; fish catch (1993) 1,384 (all freshwater). Mining and quarrying (1993): copper ore 2,500,000; lead-zinc ore 400,000; gypsum 30,000; lime 20,000; iron ore 20,000; refined silver 10,000. Manufacturing (1994): cement 486,500; steel sheets 73,045; sulfuric acid 72,100; crude steel 25,000; cotton yarn 7,600; woolen yarn 4,856; cotton fabric 27,548,000 sq m; upper-shoe leather 1,510,000 sq m; wine 811,300 hectolitres; refrigerators 95,192 units; buses 222 units. Construction (residential units constructed; 1992): 6,583. Energy production (consumption): electricity (kW-hr; 1993) 5,980,000,000 (6,230,000,000); coal (metric tons; 1993) 7,300,000 (7,450,000); crude petroleum (barrels; 1993) none (8,063,000); petroleum products (metric tons; 1993) 898,000 (949,000); natural gas (cu m; 1993) none (269,100,000).
Land use (1993): forested 38.9%; meadows and pastures 24.7%; agricultural and under permanent cultivation 25.8%; other 10.6%.
Gross national product (1993): U.S.$1,709,000,000 (U.S.$780 per capita).

Structure of gross domestic product and labour force

	1994		1993	
	in value '000,000 denar[2]	% of total value	labour force	% of labour force
Agriculture	27,973	18.9	214,900	22.9
Mining and manufacturing	56,572	38.3	167,500	17.9
Construction	9,473	6.4	36,500	3.9
Public utilities	361	0.4	8,000	0.8
Transp. and commun.	6,241	4.2	21,200	2.3
Trade	36,541	24.7	54,300	5.8
Finance			12,400	1.3
Public admin., defense	10,576	7.1	15,200	1.6
Services			84,200	9.0
Other			322,800	34.5
TOTAL	147,737	100.0	937,000	100.0

Population economically active (1994): total 937,000; activity rate 48.4% (participation rates: ages 15–64, 99%; female [1993] 37.5%; unemployed 27.6%).

Price and earnings indexes (1990 = 100)

	1990	1991	1992	1993	1994
Consumer price index	100.0	210.8	3,397	15,692	35,826
Earnings index[5]	100.0	184.3	1,993	11,863	24,520

Household income and expenditure. Average household size (1991) 3.9; income per household (1990) Din 75,556[2] (U.S.$6,676); sources of income (1992): wages and salaries 60.2%, transfer payments 18.7%, transfers from abroad 13.4%, other 7.7%; expenditure (1992): food 43.7%, clothing and footwear 7.9%, drink and tobacco 6.8%, transportation and communications 6.6%, fuel and lighting 6.3%, health care 4.8%, education and entertainment 2.8%.

Foreign trade

Balance of trade (current prices)

	1990	1991	1992	1993	1994
U.S.$'000,000	−418	−225	−7	−172	−433
% of total	15.8%	8.9%	0.3%	7.5%	17.1%

Imports (1994): U.S.$1,483,000,000 (machinery and transport equipment 19.0%, food products 19.0%, chemical products 14.0%, manufactured products 14.0%, petroleum products 12.0%). *Major import sources:* former Yugoslavia 23.0%; Bulgaria 17.0%; Germany 17.0%; Italy 6.0%; Austria 3.0%; former U.S.S.R. 3.0%.
Exports (1994): U.S.$1,050,000,000 (manufactured products 58.0%, food products 17.0%, machinery and transport equipment 13.0%, raw materials 6.0%, chemical products 5.0%). *Major export destinations:* Bulgaria 20.0%; Germany 13.0%; former Yugoslavia 13.0%; Italy 10.0%; former U.S.S.R 7.0%.

Transport and communications

Transport. Railroads (1992): length 922 km; passengers transported 1,804,000; cargo transported 3,995,000 tons. Roads (1993): total length 8,406 km (paved 60%). Vehicles (1992): passenger cars 279,861; trucks and buses 25,574. Merchant marine: n.a. Air transport (1993)[6]: passenger-km 292,372,000; metric tons cargo transported 625; airports (1995) with scheduled flights 1.
Communications. Daily newspapers (1992): total number 2; total circulation 55,000; circulation per 1,000 population 26. Radio (1992): 369,000 receivers (1 per 5.6 persons). Television (1992): 338,000 receivers (1 per 6.1 persons). Telephones (main lines; 1993): 324,300 (1 per 6.7 persons).

Education and health

Education (1994–95)

	schools	teachers[7]	students	student/ teacher ratio[7]
Primary (age 7–14)	1,050	13,102	258,955	19.9
Secondary (age 15–18)	95	4,520	77,754	16.5
Higher	44	2,320	27,340	11.8

Educational attainment (1981). Percentage of population age 15 and over having: less than full primary education 45.3%; primary 28.1%; secondary 21.2%; postsecondary and higher 5.1%; unknown 0.3%. *Literacy* (1981): total population age 10 and over literate 1,365,000 (89.1%); males literate 729,000 (94.2%); females literate 636,000 (83.8%).
Health (1993): physicians 4,528 (1 per 458 persons); hospital beds 10,438 (1 per 199 persons); infant mortality rate per 1,000 live births 24.1.

Military

Total active duty personnel (1995): 10,400 (army 100%). *Military expenditure as percentage of GNP* (1993): 1.8% (world 3.3%) per capita expenditure U.S.$14.

[1]Member of the United Nations under the name Former Yugoslav Republic of Macedonia. [2]Macedonia, as part of Yugoslavia, utilized the Yugoslav (old) dinar (Din) until Jan. 1, 1990, when it was replaced by the Yugoslav (new) dinar (Din) at a rate of 10,000 old for 1 new. Macedonia left the Yugoslav currency area in September 1991, utilizing a local coupon alone until May 1992, when a transitional local currency, the denar, was introduced. The denar (valued initially at denar 255 = 1 U.S.$) was established at par with the Yugoslav (new) dinar but circulated in parallel with the coupon until May 1993, when a differently defined denar was introduced, replacing both the transitional denar and the coupon. [3]One sq km is equal to approximately 0.3861 sq mi. [4]Total includes 280 sq km of inland water not distributed by district. [5]Based on nominal net wages per worker. [6]Palair Macedonian airline only. [7]1993–1994.

Madagascar

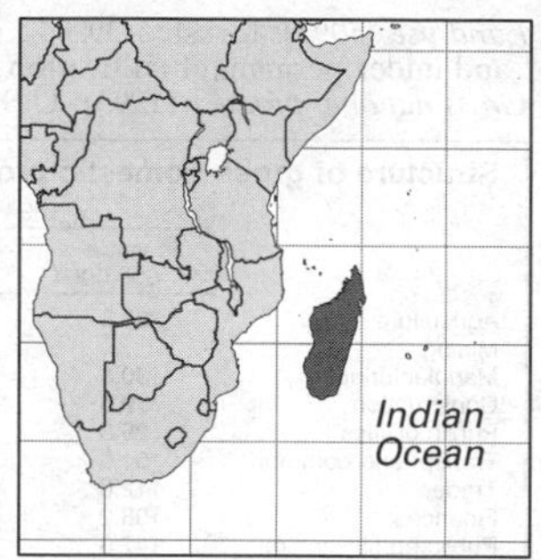

Official name: Repoblikan'i Madagasikara (Malagasy); République de Madagascar (French) (Republic of Madagascar).
Form of government: unitary multiparty republic with one legislative house (National Assembly [138]).
Chief of state: President.
Head of government: Prime Minister.
Capital: Antananarivo.
Official languages:[1].
Official religion: none.
Monetary unit: 1 Malagasy franc (FMG) = 100 centimes; valuation (Oct. 6, 1995) 1 U.S.$ = FMG 3,300; 1 £ = FMG 5,217.

Area and population

		area		population
				1993
Provinces	**Capitals**	sq mi	sq km	census[2]
Antananarivo	Antananarivo	22,503	58,283	3,483,236
Antsirañana	Antsirañana	16,620	43,046	942,410
Fianarantsoa	Fianarantsoa	39,526	102,373	2,671,150
Mahajanga	Mahajanga	57,924	150,023	1,330,612
Toamasina	Toamasina	27,765	71,911	1,935,330
Toliary	Toliary	62,319	161,405	1,729,419
TOTAL		226,658	587,041	12,092,157

Demography

Population (1995): 14,763,000.
Density (1995): persons per sq mi 65.1, persons per sq km 25.1.
Urban-rural (1991): urban 24.4%; rural 75.6%.
Sex distribution (1993): male 49.55%; female 50.45%.
Age breakdown (1995): under 15, 46.1%; 15–29, 26.2%; 30–44, 15.2%; 45–59, 8.0%; 60–74, 3.8%; 75 and over, 0.7%.
Population projection: (2000) 17,529,000; (2010) 23,326,000.
Doubling time: 22 years.
Ethnic composition (1983): Malagasy 98.9%, of which Merina 26.6%, Betsimisaraka 14.9%, Betsileo 11.7%, Tsimihety 7.4%, Sakalava 6.4%, Antandroy 5.3%; Comorian 0.3%; Indian and Pakistani 0.2%; French 0.2%; Chinese 0.1%; other 0.3%.
Religious affiliation (1980): Christian 51.0%, of which Roman Catholic 26.0%, Protestant 22.8%; traditional beliefs 47.0%; Muslim 1.7%; other 0.3%.
Major cities (1993): Antananarivo 1,052,835; Toamasina 127,441; Antsirabe 120,239; Mahajanga 100,807; Fianarantsoa 99,005.

Vital statistics

Birth rate per 1,000 population (1990–95): 43.9 (world avg. 25.0); legitimate, n.a.; illegitimate, n.a.
Death rate per 1,000 population (1990–95): 11.8 (world avg. 9.3).
Natural increase rate per 1,000 population (1990–95): 32.1 (world avg. 15.7).
Total fertility rate (avg. births per childbearing woman; 1993): 6.1.
Marriage rate per 1,000 population: n.a.
Divorce rate per 1,000 population: n.a.
Life expectancy at birth (1990–93): male 55.0 years; female 58.0 years.
Major causes of death per 100,000 population: n.a.; however, major causes of death in the early 1990s included maternal and perinatal diseases, malaria, infectious and parasitic diseases, malnutrition, diarrhea, and respiratory diseases.

National economy

Budget (1994). Revenue: FMG 976,300,000,000 (taxes 67.7%, of which import duties 28.4%, value-added tax 20.5%, income tax 14.4%; other receipts 26.3%). Expenditures: FMG 1,807,000,000,000 (1993; current expenditure 65.2%, of which education 7.2%, defense 4.0%, health 2.6%, agriculture 1.4%, public works 0.3%; capital expenditure 34.8%).
Tourism: receipts from visitors (1993) U.S.$41,000,000; expenditures by nationals abroad (1992) U.S.$22,000,000.
Production (metric tons except as noted). Agriculture, forestry, fishing (1994): paddy rice 2,360,000, cassava 2,260,000, sugarcane 1,980,000, sweet potatoes 560,000, potatoes 270,000, bananas 210,000, mangoes 200,000, corn (maize) 160,000, taro 120,000, oranges 80,000, coconuts 80,000, coffee 79,000, dry beans 60,000, pineapples 48,000, peanuts (groundnuts) 32,000, seed cotton 28,000; livestock (number of live animals) 10,288,000 cattle, 1,558,000 pigs, 1,300,000 goats, 740,000 sheep, 23,000,000 chickens; roundwood (1993) 8,858,000 cu m; fish catch (1993) 115,029. Mining and quarrying (1994): chromite ore 128,000; salt 62,000; graphite 14,100; mica 1,000; gold 200 kg; in addition, a wide variety of semiprecious stones and gemstones are produced. Manufacturing (1994): cotton cloth 38,683,000, refined sugar 79,280, rag paper 66,611, cement 22,400, soap 15,000, tobacco products 5,407, beer 218,976 hectolitres, fuel oil 60,981 cu m, gas oil 35,440 cu m, gasoline 31,536 cu m, kerosene 23,395 cu m, shoes 783,000 pairs. Construction (1986)[3]: residential 19,700 sq m; nonresidential 5,700 sq m. Energy production (consumption): electricity (kW-hr; 1993) 599,000,000 (599,000,000); coal (metric tons; 1993) none (14,000); crude petroleum (barrels; 1993) none (1,230,000); petroleum products (metric tons; 1993) 183,000 (305,000); natural gas, none (n.a.).
Household income and expenditure. Average household size (1993) 4.6[3]; average annual income per household: n.a.; sources of income (1975)[4]: wages and salaries 58.8%, self-employment 14.1%, other 27.1%; expenditure (1983)[5]: food 60.4%, fuel and light 9.1%, clothing and footwear 8.6%, household goods and utensils 2.4%.
Gross national product (1993): U.S.$3,055,000,000 (U.S.$240 per capita).

Structure of gross domestic product and labour force

	1991		1993	
	in value FMG '000,000[6]	% of total value	labour force	% of labour force
Agriculture	1,488,350	32.6	5,100,000	86.2
Manufacturing	530,560	11.6	86,000	1.5
Mining	14,800	0.3		
Construction	52,600	1.2	46,000	0.8
Public utilities	86,950	1.9		
Transportation and communications	747,920	16.4	42,000	0.7
Trade	497,990	10.9	149,000	2.5
Finance	70,020	1.5		
Services[7]	791,890	17.4	243,000	4.1
Pub. admin., defense	284,430	6.2	208,000	3.5
Other	...	...	40,000	0.7
TOTAL	4,565,510	100.0	5,914,000	100.0

Population economically active (1993): total 5,914,000; activity rate of total population 48.9% (participation rates [1985]: ages 15–64, 74.9%; female 39.3%; unemployed [1982] 0.6%).

Price and earnings indexes (1990 = 100)

	1988	1989	1990	1991	1992	1993	1994
Consumer price index	82.1	89.5	100.0	108.6	124.4	136.8	190.1
Monthly earnings index[8]	82.2	92.2	100.0	115.6	115.6	115.6	180.8

Public debt (external, outstanding; 1993): U.S.$3,920,000,000.
Land use (1993): forested 39.9%; meadows and pastures 41.3%; agricultural and under permanent cultivation 5.3%; other 13.5%.

Foreign trade

Balance of trade

	1989	1990	1991	1992	1993	1994
FMG '000,000,000	−20.4	−327.9	−93.0	−175.1	−244.3	−300.8
% of total	2.0%	25.6%	7.7%	14.5%	19.6%	15.0%

Imports (1994): FMG 1,150,780,000,000 (capital equipment 20.2%; food 16.8%, of which rice 6.9%; raw materials and spare parts 15.8%; nonfood consumer goods 15.3%; crude petroleum 11.4%). *Major import sources* (1992): France 30.3%; Germany 6.1%; U.S. 5.9%; Japan 5.8%; U.K. 5.0%; Italy 2.9%; The Netherlands 2.2%.
Exports (1994): FMG 849,960,000,000 (coffee 18.0%; vanilla 16.7%; shrimp 13.2%; cotton fabrics 2.9%; cloves and clove oil 2.6%; sugar 2.2%). *Major export destinations* (1992): France 26.6%; U.S. 15.5%; Germany 9.9%; Japan 8.6%; Belgium-Luxembourg 3.3%; Italy 3.1%; U.K. 2.6%; The Netherlands 2.2%.

Transport and communications

Transport. Railroads (1991): route length 640 mi, 1,030 km; passenger-mi 152,000,000, passenger-km 245,000,000; short ton-mi cargo 90,000,000, metric ton-km cargo 132,000,000. Roads (1992): total length 21,586 mi, 34,739 km (paved 15%). Vehicles (1992): passenger cars 47,711; trucks and buses 34,341. Merchant marine (1992): vessels (100 gross tons and over) 85; total deadweight tonnage 82,077. Air transport (1993): passenger-mi 310,137,000, passenger-km 499,104,000; short ton-mi cargo 18,556,000, metric ton-km cargo 27,091,000; airports (1995) with scheduled flights 18.
Communications. Daily newspapers (1992): total number 7; total circulation 48,000; circulation per 1,000 population 4. Radio (1994): total number of receivers 2,300,000 (1 per 6.2 persons). Television (1994): total number of receivers 130,000 (1 per 110 persons). Telephones (main lines; 1993): 34,810 (1 per 370 persons).

Education and health

Education (1993)

	schools	teachers	students	student/ teacher ratio
Primary (age 6–13)	13,624	37,676	1,504,668	39.9
Secondary (14–18)	1,142[9]	15,118	298,241	19.7
Voc., teacher tr.	61[10]	1,484[11]	17,419[11]	11.7[11]
Higher	5[9]	855[12]	42,681[12]	49.9[12]

Educational attainment: n.a. *Literacy* (1990): percentage of total population age 15 and over literate 80.2%; males literate 87.7%; females literate 72.9%.
Health: physicians (1990) 1,392 (1 per 8,628 persons); hospital beds (1989) 10,900 (1 per 1,067 persons); infant mortality rate per 1,000 live births (1990–95) 110.
Food (1992): daily per capita caloric intake 2,135 (vegetable products 89%, animal products 11%); 95% of FAO recommended minimum requirement.

Military

Total active duty personnel (1995): 21,000 (army 95.2%, navy 2.4%, air force 2.4%). *Military expenditure as percentage of GNP* (1993): 1.1% (world 3.3%); per capita expenditure U.S.$3.

[1]The 1992 constitution identifies Malagasy as the "national" language, although neither Malagasy nor French, the languages of the two official texts of the constitution, is itself "official." [2]Preliminary. [3]Antananarivo only. [4]Malagasy households only. [5]Weights of consumer price index components in Antananarivo only; housing not included. [6]At factor cost. [7]Includes artisans. [8]Minimum statutory nonagricultural wage as of July 1. [9]1988–89. [10]1987–88. [11]1990–91. [12]1992.

Malaŵi

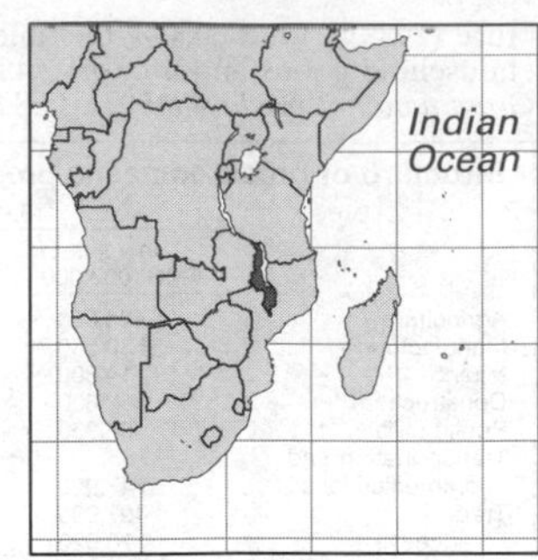

Official name: Republic of Malaŵi.
Form of government: multiparty republic with one legislative house (National Assembly [177]).
Head of state and government: President.
Capital: Lilongwe.
Official language: Chewa.
Official religion: none.
Monetary unit: 1 Malaŵi kwacha (MK) = 100 tambala; valuation (Oct. 6, 1995) 1 U.S.$ = MK 15.26; 1 £ = MK 24.13.

Area and population

Regions / Districts	Capitals	area sq mi	area sq km	population 1987 census
Central	Lilongwe	13,742	35,592	3,110,986
Dedza	Dedza	1,399	3,624	411,787
Dowa	Dowa	1,174	3,041	322,432
Kasungu	Kasungu	3,042	7,878	323,453
Lilongwe	Lilongwe	2,378	6,159	976,627
Mchinji	Mchinji	1,296	3,356	249,843
Nkhotakota	Nkhotakota	1,644	4,259	158,044
Ntcheu	Ntcheu	1,322	3,424	358,767
Ntchisi	Ntchisi	639	1,655	120,860
Salima	Salima	848	2,196	189,173
Northern	Mzuzu	10,398	26,931	911,787
Chitipa	Chitipa	1,353	3,504	96,794
Karonga	Karonga	1,141	2,955	148,014
Mzimba	Mzimba	4,027	10,430	433,696
Nkhata Bay	Nkhata Bay	1,579	4,090	138,381
Rumphi	Rumphi	2,298	5,952	94,902
Southern	Blantyre	12,260	31,753	3,965,734
Blantyre	Blantyre	777	2,012	589,525
Chikwawa	Chikwawa	1,836	4,755	316,733
Chiradzulu	Chiradzulu	296	767	210,912
Machinga	Machinga	2,303	5,964	515,265
Mangochi	Mangochi	2,422	6,272	496,578
Mulanje	Mulanje	1,332	3,450	638,062
Mwanza	Mwanza	886	2,295	121,513
Nsanje	Nsanje	750	1,942	204,374
Thyolo	Thyolo	662	1,715	431,157
Zomba	Zomba	996	2,580	441,615
TOTAL LAND AREA		36,400	94,276[1]	
INLAND WATER		9,347	24,208	
TOTAL		45,747	118,484	7,988,507

Demography

Population (1995): 9,939,000.
Density (1995)[2]: persons per sq mi 273.1, persons per sq km 105.4.
Urban-rural (1987): urban 10.7%; rural 89.3%.
Sex distribution (1987): male 48.40%; female 51.60%.
Age breakdown (1987): under 15, 46.0%; 15–29, 25.4%; 30–44, 14.5%; 45–59, 8.1%; 60 and over, 6.0%.
Population projection: (2000) 11,045,000; (2010) 13,233,000.
Doubling time: 23 years.
Ethnic composition (1983): Maravi (including Nyanja, Chewa, Tonga, and Tumbuka) 58.3%; Lomwe 18.4%; Yao 13.2%; Ngoni 6.7%; other 3.4%.
Religious affiliation (1980): Christian 64.5%, of which Protestant 33.7%, Roman Catholic 27.6%; traditional beliefs 19.0%; Muslim 16.2%; other 0.3%.
Major cities (1994): Blantyre 446,800[3]; Lilongwe 395,500; Mzuzu 62,700.

Vital statistics

Birth rate per 1,000 population (1990–95): 50.5 (world avg. 25.0).
Death rate per 1,000 population (1990–95): 20.0 (world avg. 9.3).
Natural increase rate per 1,000 population (1990–95): 30.5 (world avg. 15.7).
Total fertility rate (avg. births per childbearing woman; 1990–95): 7.2.
Marriage rate per 1,000 population (1987): 4.4.
Divorce rate per 1,000 population (1977): 1.4.
Life expectancy at birth (1990–95): male 45.0 years; female 46.2 years.
Major causes of death per 100,000 population (1986)[4]: infectious and parasitic diseases 711, of which malaria 270, diarrheal diseases 148, measles 128; malnutrition 267; diseases of the respiratory system 265.

National economy

Budget (1994–95). Revenue: MK 2,329,200,000 (tax revenue 84.2%, nontax revenue 8.2%, corn sales 7.6%). Expenditures: MK 5,940,700,000 (wages and salaries 17.2%, debt service 12.4%).
Public debt (external, outstanding; 1993): U.S.$1,724,000,000.
Production (metric tons except as noted). Agriculture (1993): sugarcane 2,000,000, corn (maize) 1,040,000, potatoes 350,000, cassava 200,000, plantains 200,000, tobacco 99,000, bananas 91,000, dry beans 81,000, tea 42,000, peanuts (groundnuts) 31,000, sorghum 17,000; livestock (number of live animals) 980,000 cattle, 890,000 goats, 245,000 pigs, 196,000 sheep; roundwood (1993) 10,075,000 cu m; fish catch (1993) 65,000. Mining and quarrying (1993): limestone 126,483; rubies and sapphires 123.7 kg. Manufacturing (value added in MK '000; 1986): chemicals 30,805; textiles 19,630; food products 11,988; beverages 11,988; tobacco 9,480; printing and publishing 9,250. Construction (value in MK; 1994): 41,700,000[5]. Energy production (consumption): electricity (kW-hr; 1993) 795,000,000 (795,000,000); coal (metric tons; 1993) none (15,000); petroleum products (metric tons; 1993) none (189,000).
Tourism: receipts (1991) U.S.$13,000,000; expenditures (1990) U.S.$13,000,000.

Land use (1993): forested 39.3%; meadows and pastures 19.6%; agricultural and under permanent cultivation 18.1%; other 23.0%.
Gross national product (1993): U.S.$2,034,000,000 (U.S.$230 per capita).

Structure of gross domestic product and labour force

	1994		1987	
	in value MK '000,000[6]	% of total value	labour force	% of labour force
Agriculture	295.8	31.3	2,967,933	85.8
Mining	...	...	7,164	0.2
Manufacturing	130.8	13.9	97,776	2.8
Construction	39.8	4.2	46,875	1.4
Public utilities	29.3	3.1	8,833	0.2
Transp. and commun.	51.8	5.5	24,863	0.7
Trade	112.6	11.9	94,445	2.7
Finance	108.2	11.5	5,590	0.3
Public administration	147.3	15.6	147,039	4.3
Services	46.4	4.9		
Other	−18.0[7]	−1.9[7]	57,235	1.6
TOTAL	944.0	100.0	3,457,753	100.0

Population economically active (1987): total 3,457,753; activity rate 43.3% (participation rates: ages 15–64, 84.6%; female 51.5%; unemployed 5.4%).

Price and earnings indexes (1990 = 100)

	1988	1989	1990	1991	1992	1993	1994
Consumer price index	79.5	89.4	100.0	112.6	138.2	163.7	222.6
Monthly earnings index	70.1	81.6	100.0	106.4	102.8	...	...

Household income and expenditure (1979–80). Average household size (1987) 4.3; income per household MK 1,934 (U.S.$2,419); sources of income: wages 83.3%, household enterprise 6.0%; expenditure (1990)[8]: food 55.5%, clothing and footwear 11.7%, housing 9.6%, household durable goods 8.4%, transportation 6.5%.

Foreign trade[9]

Balance of trade (current prices)

	1988	1989	1990	1991	1992	1993
MK '000,000	+139.4	−96.1	+180.1	+140.9	−103.4	−29.0
% of total	10.1%	6.1%	8.7%	5.6%	3.4%	1.0%

Imports (1994): MK 3,295,700,000 (1990; transport equipment 9.2%, petroleum products 8.3%, clothing 3.8%, pharmaceutical products 2.2%). *Major import sources* (1990): South Africa 30.7%; U.K. 22.9%; Japan 7.5%; W.Ger. 6.0%.
Exports (1994): MK 3,098,460,000 (tobacco 70.5%, tea 7.5%, sugar 7.4%, cotton 0.5%). *Major export destinations* (1990): W.Ger. 16.2%; U.K. 15.6%; Japan 13.5%; U.S. 12.0%; South Africa 7.2%.

Transport and communications

Transport. Railroads (1993): route length 490 mi, 789 km; passenger-km 45,547,000; metric ton-km cargo 42,264,000. Roads (1990): total length 16,960 mi, 27,294 km (paved 22%[10]). Vehicles (1992): passenger cars 13,898; trucks and buses 12,113. Merchant marine (1991): vessels (100 gross tons and over) 1; total deadweight tonnage 300. Air transport (1993)[11]: passenger-km 265,913,000; metric ton-km cargo 14,768,000; airports (1995) 6.
Communications. Daily newspapers (1994): total number 1; total circulation 22,000; circulation per 1,000 population 2.3. Radio (1994): total number of receivers 2,000,000 (1 per 4.9 persons). Television (1994): total number of receivers, n.a. Telephones (main lines; 1993): 32,800 (1 per 326 persons).

Education and health

Education (1989–90)

	schools	teachers	students	student/teacher ratio
Primary (age 6–13)[12]	3,118	26,333	1,795,451	68.2
Secondary (age 14–18)	94	1,096	29,326	26.8
Teacher tr., voc.	13	250	3,679	14.7
Higher	4	235	2,685	11.4

Educational attainment (1987). Percentage of population age 25 and over having: no formal education 55.0%; primary education 39.8%; secondary and higher 5.2%. *Literacy* (1995): total population age 15 and over literate 56.4%; males literate 71.9%; females literate 41.8%.
Health: physicians (1989) 186 (1 per 47,634 persons); hospital beds (1987) 12,617 (1 per 627 persons); infant mortality rate per 1,000 live births (1990–95) 143.0.
Food (1992): daily per capita caloric intake 1,825 (vegetable products 97%, animal products 3%); 79% of FAO recommended minimum requirement.

Military

Total active duty personnel (1995): 8,000 (army 97.5%, marines 2.5%, air force, none). *Military expenditure as percentage of GNP* (1993): 1.0% (world 3.3%); per capita expenditure U.S.$2.

[1]Detail does not add to total given because of rounding. [2]Based on land area. [3]Includes Limbe. [4]Estimates based on reported inpatient deaths in hospitals, constituting an estimated 8% of total deaths. [5]Cities of Blantyre, Lilongwe, and Mzuzu only. [6]At constant prices of 1978. [7]Less imputed bank service charges. [8]Weights of consumer price index components, cities of Blantyre and Lilongwe only. [9]Import figures are f.o.b. in balance of trade and c.i.f. in commodities and trading partners. Reexports included in balance of trade, excluded from commodities and trading partners. [10]1989. [11]Air Malaŵi only. [12]1992.

Malaysia

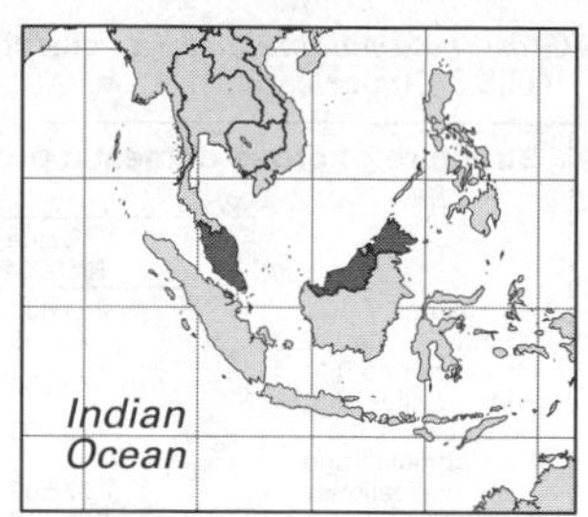

Official name: Malaysia.
Form of government: federal constitutional monarchy with two legislative houses (Senate [69[1]]; House of Representatives [192]).
Chief of state: Yang di-Pertuan Agong (Paramount Ruler).
Head of government: Prime Minister.
Capital: Kuala Lumpur.
Official language: Malay.
Official religion: Islam.
Monetary unit: 1 ringgit, or Malaysian dollar (M$) = 100 cents; valuation (Oct. 6, 1995) 1 U.S.$ = M$2.54; 1 £ = M$4.01.

Area and population

Regions States	Capitals	area sq mi	area sq km	population 1991 census[2]
East Malaysia				
Sabah	Kota Kinabalu	28,425	73,620	1,736,902
Sarawak	Kuching	48,050	124,449	1,648,217
West Malaysia				
Johor	Johor Baharu	7,331	18,986	2,074,297
Kedah	Alor Setar	3,639	9,426	1,304,800
Kelantan	Kota Baharu	5,769	14,943	1,181,680
Melaka	Melaka	637	1,650	504,502
Negeri Sembilan	Seremban	2,565	6,643	691,150
Pahang	Kuantan	13,886	35,965	1,036,724
Perak	Ipoh	8,110	21,005	1,880,016
Perlis	Kangar	307	795	184,070
Pulau Pinang	George Town	398	1,031	1,065,075
Selangor	Shah Alam	3,072	7,956	2,289,236
Terengganu	Kuala Terengganu	5,002	12,955	770,931
Federal Territories				
Kuala Lumpur	—	94	243	1,145,075
Labuan	—	35	91	54,307
TOTAL LAND AREA		127,320	329,758	
INLAND WATER		264	684	
TOTAL		127,584	330,442	17,566,982

Demography

Population (1995): 19,948,000.
Density (1995): persons per sq mi 156.4, persons per sq km 60.4.
Urban-rural (1995): urban 54.0%; rural 46.0%.
Sex distribution (1995): male 50.36%; female 49.64%.
Age breakdown (1995): under 15, 35.8%; 15–29, 27.4%; 30–44, 19.9%; 45–59, 10.6%; 60–74, 5.1%; 75 and over, 1.2%.
Population projection: (2000) 22,087,000; (2010) 25,989,000.
Doubling time. 30 years.
Ethnic composition (1995): Malay and other indigenous (Orang Asli, or Bumiputera) 59.9%; Chinese 29.9%; Indian 9.5%; other nonindigenous 0.7%.
Religious affiliation (1980): Muslim 52.9%; Buddhist 17.3%; Chinese folk-religionist 11.6%; Hindu 7.0%; Christian 6.4%; other 4.8%.
Major cities (1991): Kuala Lumpur 1,145,075; Ipoh 382,633; Johor Baharu 328,646; Melaka 295,999; Petaling Jaya 254,849.

Vital statistics

Birth rate per 1,000 population (1994): 28.0 (world avg. 25.0).
Death rate per 1,000 population (1994): 5.0 (world avg. 9.3).
Natural increase rate per 1,000 population (1994): 23.0 (world avg. 15.7).
Total fertility rate (avg. births per childbearing woman; 1995): 3.4.
Marriage rate per 1,000 population: n.a.
Divorce rate per 1,000 population: n.a.
Life expectancy at birth (1994): male 69.0 years; female 73.0 years.
Major causes of death per 100,000 population (1992): diseases of the circulatory system 54.1; malignant neoplasms (cancers) 32.8; accidents, homicide, and other violence 28.5; infectious and parasitic diseases 13.2; diseases of the respiratory system 7.5; endocrine and metabolic disorders 6.2; diseases of the digestive system 2.4.

National economy

Budget (1994). Revenue: M$44,730,000,000 (income tax 43.0%, nontax revenue 21.6%, import duties 12.1%, sales taxes 8.5%). Expenditures: M$33,285,000,000 (social services 33.9%, security 15.2%, administration 10.5%, economic services 8.4%).
Tourism (1993): receipts from visitors U.S.$1,876,000,000; expenditures by nationals abroad U.S.$1,960,000,000.
Production (metric tons except as noted). Agriculture, forestry, fishing (1994): palm oil 7,220,410, rice 2,040,000, rubber 1,074,000, bananas 526,000, pineapples 270,000, cacao beans 230,000; livestock (number of live animals) 3,098,000 pigs, 686,000 cattle, 356,000 goats, 336,000 sheep, 186,000 buffalo, 98,000,000 chickens; roundwood (1993) 54,332,000 cu m; fish catch (1993) 680,000. Mining and quarrying (1994): iron ore 202,682; bauxite 161,919; copper concentrates 106,468; tin concentrates 6,458. Manufacturing (1993): cement 8,797,000; refined sugar 957,000; wheat flour 621,000; fertilizer (1992) 325,000; plywood 2,491,000 cu m; radio receivers 34,537,000 units; automotive tires 9,486,000 units. Construction (completed; 1986)[3]: residential 8,809,100 sq m; nonresidential 959,900 sq m. Energy production (consumption): electricity (kW-hr; 1993) 35,579,000,000 (35,554,000,000); coal (metric tons; 1993) 260,000 (2,081,000); crude petroleum (barrels; 1993) 233,685,000 (82,477,000); petroleum products (metric tons; 1993) 11,089,000 (15,732,000); natural gas (cu m; 1993) 21,399,000,000 (6,150,000,000).

Gross national product (1993): U.S.$60,141,000,000 (U.S.$3,160 per capita).

Structure of gross domestic product and labour force

	1994 in value M$'000,000[4]	1994 % of total value	1993 labour force	1993 % of labour force
Agriculture	16,337	14.9	1,580,000	20.7
Mining	8,142	7.4	35,000	0.4
Manufacturing	34,293	31.4	1,766,000	23.1
Construction	4,514	4.1	550,000	7.2
Public utilities	2,467	2.3	...	...
Transp. and commun.	7,820	7.1	342,000	4.5
Trade	13,551	12.4	...	...
Finance	11,898	10.9	315,000	4.1
Pub. admin., defense	10,395	9.5	862,000	11.3
Services	2,274	2.1	1,920,000[5]	25.1[5]
Other	−2,310[6]	−2.1[6]	276,000	3.6
TOTAL	109,381	100.0	7,646,000	100.0

Public debt (external, outstanding; 1993): U.S.$13,863,000,000.
Population economically active (1993): total 7,646,000; activity rate 40.1% (participation rates: ages 15–64 [1990] 66.5%; female [1990] 35.5%; unemployed 3.6%).

Price index (1990 = 100)

	1988	1989	1990	1991	1992	1993	1994
Consumer price index	94.8	97.4	100.0	104.4	109.3	113.2	117.4

Household income and expenditure. Average household size (1991) 4.9; annual income per household (1987) M$12,890 (U.S.$5,120); sources of income: n.a.; expenditure (1983): food 28.7%, transportation 20.9%, recreation and education 11.0%, housing 10.2%, household durable goods 7.7%, clothing and footwear 4.3%, health 2.5%.
Land use (1993): forested 67.9%; meadows and pastures 0.1%; agricultural and under permanent cultivation 14.9%; other 17.1%.

Foreign trade[7]

Balance of trade (current prices)

	1989	1990	1991	1992	1993	1994
M$'000,000	+12,725	+7,947	+3,165	+11,446	+15,095	+12,628
% of total	10.3%	5.3%	1.7%	5.9%	6.6%	4.3%

Imports (1993): M$117,423,000,000 (machinery and transport equipment 55.6%; basic manufactured goods 15.1%; chemicals 7.6%; food 5.0%; mineral fuels 3.6%; inedible crude materials 2.7%). *Major import sources:* Japan 27.4%; U.S. 16.9%; Singapore 15.2%; Taiwan 5.4%; Germany 3.8%; U.K. 3.1%; South Korea 3.0%; Australia 2.8%.
Exports (1993): M$121,214,000,000 (machinery and transport equipment 48.5%; mineral fuels 10.3%; basic manufactures 9.6%; inedible crude materials 9.1%; animal and vegetable oils 6.0%; food, beverages, and tobacco 3.1%). *Major export destinations:* Singapore 21.7%; U.S. 20.3%; Japan 13.0%; U.K. 4.2%; Hong Kong 4.1%; Germany 3.7%; Thailand 3.6%.

Transport and communications

Transport. Railroads (1993): track length 2,222 km; passenger-km 1,848,000,000[8]; metric ton-km cargo 1,380,000,000[8]. Roads (1994): total length 92,443 km (paved 75%). Vehicles (1994): passenger cars 2,291,199; trucks and buses 501,096. Merchant marine (1992): vessels (100 gross tons and over) 552; total deadweight tonnage 2,916,315. Air transport (1994): passenger-km 17,466,000,000; metric ton-km cargo 765,920,000; airports (1995) 38.
Communications. Daily newspapers (1992): total number 39; circulation 2,200,000; circulation per 1,000 population 117. Radio (1994): 7,460,000 receivers (1 per 2.6 persons). Television (1994): 2,000,000 receivers (1 per 9.7 persons). Telephones (main lines; 1993): 2,410,700 (1 per 7.9 persons).

Education and health

Education (1993)

	schools	teachers	students	student/ teacher ratio
Primary (age 7–12)	6,968	134,579	2,718,906	20.2
Secondary (age 13–19)	1,336[9]	77,149[9]	1,531,893	18.1[9]
Voc., teacher tr.	75[9]	3,489[9]	40,944	9.5[9]
Higher	54[9]	11,471[10]	136,000[10]	11.9[10]

Educational attainment (1980). Percentage of population age 25 and over having: no formal schooling 36.6%; primary education 42.1%; secondary 19.4%; higher 1.9%. *Literacy* (1995 est.): total population age 15 and over literate 83.5%; males literate 89.1%; females literate 78.1%.
Health: physicians (1992) 7,719 (1 per 2,412 persons); hospital beds (1993) 38,982 (1 per 489 persons); infant mortality rate per 1,000 live births (1994) 14.
Food (1992): daily per capita caloric intake 2,888 (vegetable products 84%, animal products 16%); 130% of FAO recommended minimum.

Military

Total active duty personnel (1995): 114,500 (army 78.6%, navy 10.5%, air force 10.9%). *Military expenditure as percentage of GDP* (1994): 3.9% (world 2.6%); per capita expenditure U.S.$135.

[1]Includes 43 appointees of the paramount ruler; the remaining 26 are indirectly elected at different times. [2]Preliminary results. [3]Results of the Central Bank Survey of four major towns: Kuala Lumpur, Shah Alam, Kelang, and Seberang Prai. [4]At constant prices of 1978. [5]Includes data for Public utilities and Trade. [6]Net bank service charges. [7]Import figures are f.o.b. in balance of trade. [8]Peninsular Malaysia and Singapore. [9]1992. [10]1991.

Maldives

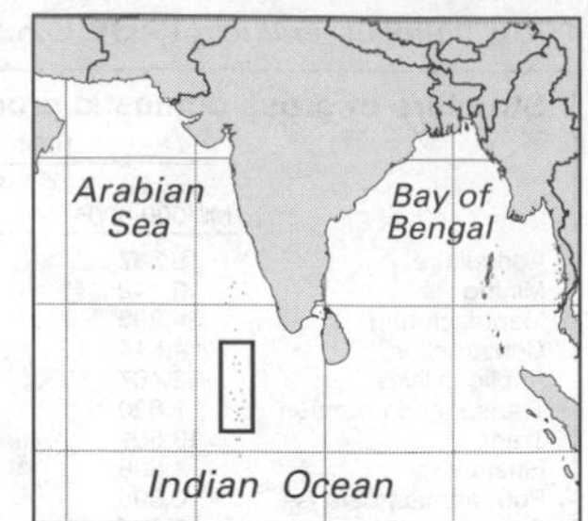

Official name: Divehi Jumhuriyya (Republic of Maldives).
Form of government: republic with one legislative house (People's Council [48[1]]).
Head of state and government: President.
Capital: Male'.
Official language: Divehi.
Official religion: Islam.
Monetary unit: 1 Maldivian rufiyaa (Rf) = 100 laari; valuation (Oct. 6, 1995) 1 U.S.$ = Rf 11.77; 1 £ = Rf 18.60.

Area and population[2]

Administrative atolls	Capitals	area sq mi	area sq km	population 1990 census
North Thiladhunmathi (Haa-Alifu)	Dhidhdhoo	...	...	12,031
South Thiladhunmathi (Haa-Dhaalu)	Nolhivaranfaru	...	...	12,890
North Miladhunmadulu (Shaviyani)	Farukolhu-funadhoo	...	...	9,022
South Miladhunmadulu (Noonu)	Manadhoo	...	...	8,437
North Maalhosmadulu (Raa)	Ugoofaaru	...	...	11,303
South Maalhosmadulu (Baa)	Eydhafushi	...	...	7,716
Faadhippolhu (Lhaviyani)	Naifaru	...	...	7,224
Male' (Kaafu)	Thulusdhoo	...	...	6,726
Ari Atoll Uthuru Gofi (Alifu)	Rasdhoo	...	...	3,998
Ari Atoll Dhekunu Gofi (Alifu)	Mahibadhoo	...	...	5,029
Felidhu Atoll (Vaavu)	Felidhoo	...	...	1,579
Mulakatholhu (Meemu)	Muli	...	...	4,186
North Nilandhe Atoll (Faafu)	Magoodhoo	...	...	2,614
South Nilandhe Atoll (Dhaalu)	Kudahuvadhoo	...	...	4,199
Kolhumadulu (Thaa)	Veymandoo	...	...	8,189
Hadhdhunmathi (Laamu)	Hithadhoo	...	...	9,101
North Huvadhu Atoll (Gaafu-Alifu)	Viligili	...	...	7,295
South Huvadhu Atoll (Gaafu-Dhaalu)	Thinadhoo	...	...	10,417
Foammulah (Gnyaviyani)	Foahmulah	...	...	6,160
Addu Atoll (Seenu)	Hithadhoo	...	...	15,177
Male'		...	...	55,130
TOTAL		115	298	213,215[3]

Demography

Population (1995): 253,000.
Density (1995): persons per sq mi 2,200, persons per sq km 849.
Urban-rural (1993): urban 30.0%; rural 70.0%.
Sex distribution (1995): male 51.16%; female 48.84%.
Age breakdown (1995): under 15, 46.5%; 15–29, 26.8%; 30–44, 14.2%; 45–59, 7.6%; 60–74, 4.2%; 75 and over, 0.7%.
Population projection: (2000) 286,000; (2010) 345,000.
Doubling time: 26 years.
Ethnic composition: the majority is principally of Sinhalese and Dravidian extraction; Arab, African, and Negrito influences are also present.
Religious affiliation: virtually 100% Sunnī Muslim.
Major cities (1990): Male' 55,130.

Vital statistics

Birth rate per 1,000 population (1993): 32.6 (world avg. 25.0); legitimate, n.a.; illegitimate, n.a.
Death rate per 1,000 population (1993): 5.5 (world avg. 9.3).
Natural increase rate per 1,000 population (1993): 27.1 (world avg. 15.7).
Total fertility rate (avg. births per childbearing woman; 1993): 6.1.
Marriage rate per 1,000 population (1993): 11.7.
Divorce rate per 1,000 population (1993): 6.8.
Life expectancy at birth (1993): male 65.0 years; female 62.0 years.
Major causes of death per 100,000 population (1988): rheumatic fever 106.0; ischemic heart diseases 65.0; bronchitis, emphysema, and asthma 61.0; tetanus 23.5; tuberculosis 13.0; accidents and suicide 10.0.

National economy

Budget (1994). Revenue: Rf 991,100,000 (nontax revenue 33.3%, import duties 32.0%, foreign grants 15.7%, tourism tax 14.4%). Expenditures: Rf 1,524,000,000 (fisheries and agriculture 22.3%, general administration 22.2%, education 15.8%, public order and safety 11.6%, health 7.2%, transportation 5.9%, interest on public debt 4.9%).
Public debt (external, outstanding; 1993): U.S.$111,600,000.
Production (metric tons except as noted). Agriculture, forestry, fishing (1994): vegetables and melons 19,000, coconuts 13,000, fruits (excluding melons) 10,000, roots and tubers (including cassava, sweet potatoes, and yams) 8,000, copra 2,000; fish catch (1993) 89,938. Mining and quarrying: coral for construction materials. Manufacturing: details, n.a.; however, major industries include boat building and repairing, coir yarn and mat weaving, coconut and fish processing, lacquerwork, garment manufacturing, and handicrafts. Construction: n.a. Energy production (consumption): electricity (kW-hr; 1992) 30,000,000 (30,000,000); coal, none (n.a.); petroleum products (metric tons; 1992) none (32,000); natural gas, none (n.a.).
Tourism (1993): receipts from visitors U.S.$146,000,000; expenditures by nationals abroad U.S.$29,000,000.
Household income and expenditure (1990). Average household size 7.1; annual income per household Rf 2,616 (U.S.$274); sources of income: n.a.; expenditure (1981)[4]: food and beverages 61.8%, housing equipment 17.0%, clothing 8.0%, recreation and education 5.9%, transportation 2.6%, health 2.5%, rent 1.6%.

Gross national product (at current market prices; 1993): U.S.$194,000,000 (U.S.$820 per capita).

Structure of gross domestic product and labour force

	1993 in value Rf '000[5]	1993 % of total value	1990 labour force	1990 % of labour force
Agriculture[6]	244,800	20.6	14,117	25.0
Mining	21,300	1.8	496	0.9
Manufacturing } Public utilities }	72,800	6.1	8,441 / 445	15.0 / 0.8
Construction	110,200	9.3	3,151	5.6
Transportation and communications	77,500	6.5	5,321	9.4
Trade	226,800	19.0	8,884	15.7
Finance	...	...	1,058	1.9
Public administration, defense	109,300	9.2 }	11,848 }	21.0 }
Services	327,500	27.5 }		
Other	...	...	2,674	4.7
TOTAL	1,190,200	100.0	56,435	100.0

Population economically active (1990): total 56,435; activity rate of total population 26.5% (participation rates: ages 15–64, 50.2%; female 19.9%; unemployed 0.9%).
Land use (1993): forested 3.3%; meadows and pastures 3.3%; agricultural and under permanent cultivation 10.0%; built-on, wasteland, and other 83.4%.

Foreign trade[7]

Balance of trade (current prices)

	1987	1988	1989	1990	1991	1992	1993
U.S.$'000,000	−42.9	−41.7	−51.0	−65.0	−83.3	−126.6	−133.7
% of total	41.1%	34.2%	36.3%	38.4%	43.7%	61.3%	65.9%

Imports (1993): Rf 2,096,704,000 (consumer products 50.4%, intermediate and capital goods 36.8%, petroleum products 12.8%). *Major import sources:* Singapore 51.8%; India 8.6%; Sri Lanka 6.7%; United Arab Emirates 6.5%; Japan 3.9%; Thailand 3.3%.
Exports (1993): Rf 377,397,000 (canned tuna 26.9%, frozen skipjack tuna 21.4%, apparel and clothing 15.9%, fish meal 3.4%). *Major export destinations:* Sri Lanka 30.3%; United Kingdom 24.5%; Thailand 13.9%; United States 11.3%; Germany 5.9%; Japan 4.1%.

Transport and communications

Transport. Railroads: none. Roads: total length, n.a. Vehicles (1993): passenger cars 823; trucks and buses 869. Merchant marine (1992): vessels (100 gross tons and over) 44; total deadweight tonnage 78,994. Air transport (1993): passenger arrivals 348,853, passenger departures 344,061; cargo loaded 2,756 metric tons, cargo unloaded 7,216 metric tons; airports (1995) with scheduled flights 1.
Communications. Daily newspapers (1993): total number 2; total circulation 4,300; circulation per 1,000 population 18. Radio (1994): total number of receivers 25,000 (1 per 9.8 persons). Television (1994): total number of receivers 4,750 (1 per 52 persons). Telephones (1992): 8,523 (1 per 27 persons).

Education and health

Education (1986)

	schools	teachers	students	student/teacher ratio
Primary (age 6–11)	243	1,138	41,812	36.7
Secondary (age 11–18)	9	291	3,581	12.3
Voc., teacher tr.	10	52	462	8.9
Higher	—	—	—	—

Educational attainment (1990). Percentage of population age 15 and over having: no standard passed 25.6%; primary standard 37.2%; middle standard 25.9%; secondary standard 6.3%; preuniversity 3.4%; higher 0.4%; not stated 1.2%. *Literacy* (1985): total population age 15 and over literate 90,189 (90.4%); males literate 47,412 (90.6%); females literate 42,777 (90.1%).
Health (1993): physicians 45 (1 per 5,297 persons); hospital beds 200 (1 per 1,192 persons); infant mortality rate per 1,000 live births 34.
Food (1992): daily per capita caloric intake 2,580 (vegetable products 80%, animal products 20%); 117% of FAO recommended minimum requirement.

Military

Total active duty personnel: Maldives maintains a single security force numbering about 700–1,000; it performs both army and police functions.

[1]Includes 8 nonelective seats. [2]Maldives is divided into 20 administrative districts corresponding to atoll groups; arrangement shown here is from north to south. Total area excludes 34,634 sq mi (89,702 sq km) of tidal waters. [3]Includes 4,792 people in resort and industrial islands. [4]Weights of consumer price index components. [5]At 1985 prices. [6]Primarily fishing. [7]Import figures are f.o.b. in balance of trade and c.i.f. for commodities and trading partners.

Mali

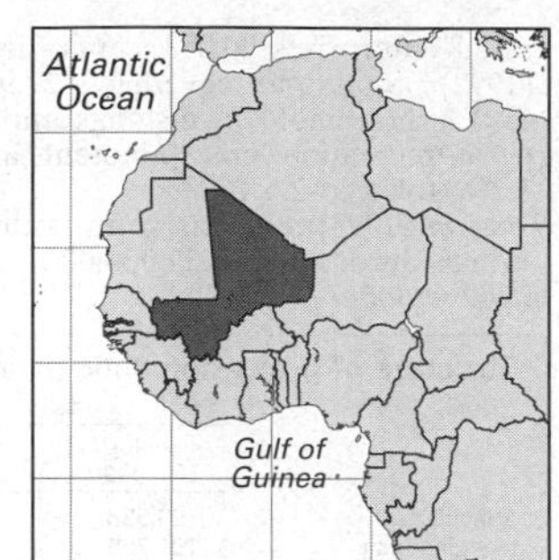

Official name: République du Mali (Republic of Mali).
Form of government: multiparty[1] republic with one legislative house (National Assembly [116]).
Chief of state: President.
Head of government: Prime Minister.
Capital: Bamako.
Official language: French.
Official religion: none.
Monetary unit: 1 CFA franc (CFAF) = 100 centimes; valuation (Oct. 6, 1995) 1 U.S.$ = CFAF 501.49; 1 £ = CFAF 792.78.

Area and population

		area		population
Regions[2]	Capitals	sq mi	sq km	1994 estimate
Gao	Gao	124,326	322,002	399,000
Kayes	Kayes	46,233	119,743	1,219,000
Koulikoro	Koulikoro	37,007	95,848	1,432,000
Mopti	Mopti	30,508	79,017	1,394,000
Ségou	Ségou	25,028	64,821	1,546,000
Sikasso	Sikasso	27,135	70,280	1,489,000
Tombouctou	Timbuktu (Tombouctou)	191,743	496,611	452,000
District				
Bamako	Bamako	97	252	894,000
TOTAL		482,077	1,248,574	8,825,000

Demography

Population (1995): 9,008,000.
Density (1995): persons per sq mi 18.7, persons per sq km 7.2.
Urban-rural (1994): urban 26.1%, rural 73.9%.
Sex distribution (1994): male 48.87%; female 51.13%.
Age breakdown (1991): under 15, 48.3%; 15–29, 22.5%; 30–44, 14.3%; 45–59, 8.8%; 60–74, 4.9%; 75 and over, 1.2%.
Population projection: (2000) 9,980,000; (2010) 12,252,000.
Doubling time: 22 years.
Linguistic composition (1987): Bambara-Malinké-Dyula (-Dioula) 50.3%; Fulani (Peulh-Foulfoulbe) 10.7%; Dogon-Kado 6.9%; Songhaï-Djerma 6.3%; Soninké-Marka 6.3%; Tamashek-Bella (Berber) 4.2%; Minianka 3.9%; Senufo 2.4%; Bwa- (Bobo-) Dafing 2.3%; Bozo-Somono 2.0%; other 4.7%.
Religious affiliation (1983): Muslim 90%; traditional beliefs 9%; Christian 1%.
Major cities (1987): Bamako 646,163; Ségou 88,877; Mopti 73,979; Sikasso 73,050; Gao 54,874.

Vital statistics

Birth rate per 1,000 population (1995): 51.9 (world avg. 25.0); legitimate, n.a.; illegitimate, n.a.
Death rate per 1,000 population (1995): 19.9 (world avg. 9.3).
Natural increase rate per 1,000 population (1995): 32.0 (world avg. 15.7).
Total fertility rate (avg. births per childbearing woman; 1995): 7.3.
Marriage rate per 1,000 population (1990)[3]: 0.4.
Divorce rate per 1,000 population: n.a.
Life expectancy at birth (1995): male 44.7 years; female 48.1 years.
Major causes of death per 100,000 population: n.a.; morbidity ([notified cases of illness] by cause as a percentage of all reported infectious disease; 1985): malaria 62.1%; measles 10.3%; amebiasis 10.3%; syphilis and gonococcal infections 6.0%; influenza 4.9%; other principal causes in 1989 included polio and conditions originating in the perinatal period.

National economy

Budget (1994). Revenue: CFAF 291,300,000,000 (fiscal receipts 45.2%, nonfiscal receipts 3.8%). Expenditures: CFAF 361,700,000,000 (current expenditure 44.1%; capital expenditure 36.1%).
Public debt (external, outstanding; 1993): U.S.$2,506,000,000.
Tourism (1993): receipts from visitors U.S.$11,000,000; expenditures by nationals abroad U.S.$61,000,000.
Population economically active (1987): total 3,437,489; activity rate of total population 44.7% (participation rates: ages 15–64, 67.4%; female 37.4%; unemployed 0.8%).

Price and earnings indexes (1990 = 100)

	1988	1989	1990	1991	1992	1993	1994
Consumer price index	99.5	99.4	100.0	101.8	95.4	95.2	117.2
Hourly earnings index[4]	100.0	100.0	100.0	100.0	127.9	...	...

Production (metric tons except as noted). Agriculture, forestry, fishing (1994): millet 905,000, sorghum 903,000, rice 548,000, seed cotton 354,000, corn (maize) 315,000, peanuts (groundnuts) 146,000, cassava 73,000, sweet potatoes 55,000; livestock (number of live animals) 12,553,000 goats and sheep, 5,542,000 cattle, 611,000 asses, 260,000 camels, 101,000 horses, 63,000 pigs; roundwood (1993) 6,145,000 cu m; fish catch (1993) 64,354. Mining and quarrying (1994): limestone 10,000[5]; gypsum 700; gold 5,700 kg; silver 200 kg. Manufacturing (1991): cotton fibre 46,396; sugar 29,040; cement 10,953; soft drinks 64,750 hectolitres; beer 37,754 hectolitres; shoes 127,000 pairs; cigarettes 141,757 cartons. Construction: n.a. Energy production (consumption): electricity (kW-hr; 1992) 313,000,000 (313,000,000); coal, none (n.a.); crude petroleum, none (n.a.); petroleum products (metric tons; 1992) none (141,000); natural gas, none (n.a.).
Gross national product (at current market prices; 1993): U.S.$2,744,000,000 (U.S.$300 per capita).

Structure of gross domestic product and labour force

	1993		1987	
	in value CFAF '000,000	% of total value	labour force	% of labour force
Agriculture	319,500	42.4	2,802,722	82.2
Mining	16,300	2.2	1,524	—
Manufacturing	66,900	8.9	186,243	5.5
Construction }	32,600	4.3	13,065	0.4
Public utilities }			3,157	0.1
Transp. and commun.	37,500	5.0	6,174	0.2
Trade	131,700	17.5	158,892	4.7
Finance	...	...	320	—
Pub. admin., defense	59,000	7.8	158,704	4.6
Services	52,900	7.0	...	...
Other	37,500[6]	5.0[6]	78,470	2.3
TOTAL	753,800[7]	100.0[7]	3,409,271	100.0

Household income and expenditure. Average household size (1987) 5.6; average annual income per household: n.a.; sources of income: n.a.; expenditure (1986–87)[3, 8]: food 54.6%, clothing 14.2%, transportation and communications 11.9%, housing and energy 8.7%, household durable goods 4.2%.
Land use (1993): forested 5.7%; meadows and pastures 24.6%; agricultural and under permanent cultivation 2.0%; other 67.7%.

Foreign trade[9]

Balance of trade (current prices)

	1989	1990	1991	1992	1993
CFAF '000,000,000	−24.9	−25.6	−26.1	−39.3	−32.1
% of total	12.6%	12.2%	11.5%	18.4%	14.3%

Imports (1993): CFAF 179,900,000,000 (machinery, appliances, and transport equipment 28.7%; food products 12.8%; petroleum products 11.6%; construction products 10.3%; chemicals 9.7%). *Major import sources:* Norway 28.1%; Côte d'Ivoire 18.3%; France 8.4%; Senegal 4.4%; Hong Kong 2.1%; Belgium-Luxembourg 2.1%; United States 1.7%; United Kingdom 1.4%; Germany 1.3%; Japan 1.2%; Italy 0.8%; The Netherlands 0.7%; Morocco 0.6%.
Exports (1993): CFAF 96,700,000,000 (raw cotton and cotton products 42.9%; live animals 30.5%; gold 18.0%). *Major export destinations:* Norway 28.8%; Thailand 18.3%; Brazil 13.7%; Ireland 9.6%; Belgium-Luxembourg 5.8%; China 2.2%; France 1.9%; Tunisia 1.4%; Côte d'Ivoire 1.1%; Spain 1.1%; Germany 1.1%; Japan 1.1%; United States 1.1%.

Transport and communications

Transport. Railroads (1994): route length 399 mi, 642 km; passenger-mi 304,155,000, passenger km 489,491,000; short ton-mi cargo 187,176,000, metric ton-km cargo 273,273,000. Roads (1994): total length 9,321 mi, 15,000 km (paved 17%). Vehicles (1993): passenger cars 21,000; trucks and buses 8,400. Merchant marine: vessels (100 gross tons and over) none. Air transport (1993): passenger-mi 134,932,000, passenger-km 217,154,000; short ton-mi cargo 23,428,000, metric ton-km cargo 34,204,000; airports (1995) with scheduled flights 1.
Communications. Daily newspapers (1994): total number 1; total circulation 40,000; circulation per 1,000 population 4.5. Radio (1994): total number of receivers 350,000 (1 per 25 persons). Television (1994): total number of receivers 10,000 (1 per 883 persons). Telephones (main lines; 1993): 13,800 (1 per 639 persons).

Education and health

Education (1991–92)

	schools	teachers	students	student/ teacher ratio
Primary (age 6–14)	1,514	7,963	375,131	47.1
Secondary (age 15–17)	307[11]	5,883[12]	88,529	...
Higher	7[12]	701	6,703	9.6

Educational attainment (1987). Percentage of population age 6 and over having: no formal schooling 86.0%; primary education 12.5%; secondary 1.2%; postsecondary and higher 0.3%. *Literacy* (1987): percentage of total population age 6 and over literate 1,116,019 (18.8%); males literate 767,981 (26.7%); females literate 348,038 (11.4%).
Health: physicians (1988) 435 (1 per 18,046 persons); hospital beds (1987) 3,430 (1 per 2,253 persons); infant mortality rate per 1,000 live births (1995) 105.
Food (1992): daily per capita caloric intake 2,278 (vegetable products 91%, animal products 9%); 97% of FAO recommended minimum requirement.

Military

Total active duty personnel (1995): 7,350 (army 93.9%, navy 0.7%, air force 5.4%). *Military expenditure as percentage of GNP* (1993): 2.2% (world 3.3%); per capita expenditure U.S.$6.

[1]Multiparty legislative elections of February–March 1992 were boycotted by most opposition parties. [2]Kidal region established on May 15, 1991. Separate data not available. [3]Bamako only. [4]Minimum hourly wages of industrial workers. [5]1990. [6]Less imputed bank service charges. [7]Detail does not add to total given because of rounding. [8]Weights of consumer price index components. [9]Import figures are f.o.b. in balance of trade and c.i.f. in commodities and trading partners. [10]Air Afrique only. [11]Excludes vocational. [12]1990–91.

Malta

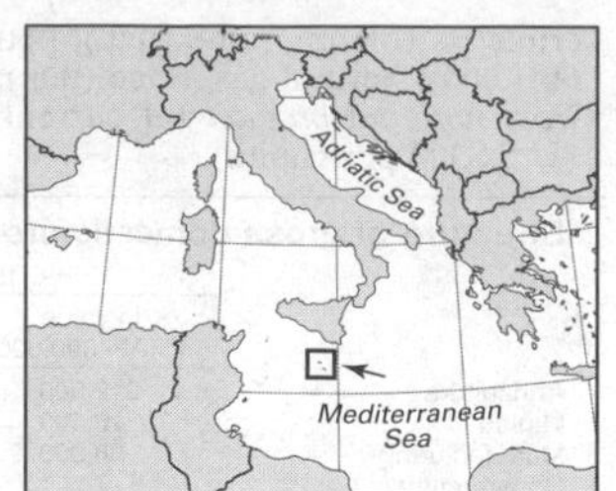

Official name: Malta (Maltese); Malta (English).
Form of government: unitary multiparty republic with one legislative house (House of Representatives [65]).
Chief of state: President.
Head of government: Prime Minister.
Capital: Valletta.
Official languages: Maltese; English.
Official religion: Roman Catholicism.
Monetary unit: 1 Maltese lira (Lm) = 100 cents = 1,000 mils; valuation[1] (Oct. 6, 1995) 1 U.S.$ = Lm 0.35; 1 £ = Lm 0.56.

Area and population

	area		population
Census regions[2]	sq mi	sq km	1994[3] estimate
Gozo and Comino	27	70	27,258
Inner Harbour	6	15	102,394
Northern	30	78	35,787
Outer Harbour	12	32	106,312
South Eastern	20	53	46,884
Western	27	69	47,796
TOTAL	122	316[4]	366,431

Demography

Population (1995): 370,000.
Density (1995): persons per sq mi 3,033, persons per sq km 1,171.
Urban-rural (1993): urban 88.6%; rural 11.4%.
Sex distribution (1994[3]): male 49.46%; female 50.54%.
Age breakdown (1994[3]): under 15, 22.4%; 15–29, 21.2%; 30–44, 23.4%; 45–59, 17.8%; 60–74, 11.4%; 75 and over, 3.8%.
Population projection: (2000) 378,000; (2010) 394,000.
Doubling time: 93 years.
Ethnic composition (by nationality; 1990): Maltese 95.7%; British 2.1%; other 2.2%.
Religious affiliation (1992): Roman Catholic 98.6%; other 1.4%.
Major cities (1994[3]): Birkirkara 21,770; Qormi 19,904; Hamrun 13,654; Sliema 13,514; Valletta 9,144.

Vital statistics

Birth rate per 1,000 population (1993): 14.8 (world avg. 25.0); legitimate 97.7%; illegitimate 2.3%.
Death rate per 1,000 population (1993): 7.3 (world avg. 9.3).
Natural increase rate per 1,000 population (1993): 7.5 (world avg. 15.7).
Total fertility rate (avg. births per childbearing woman; 1993): 2.1.
Marriage rate per 1,000 population (1993): 6.8.
Divorce rate per 1,000 population: n.a.
Life expectancy at birth (1992): male 73.0 years; female 77.8 years.
Major causes of death per 100,000 population (1993): diseases of the circulatory system 354.5; malignant neoplasms (cancers) 173.8; diseases of the respiratory system 58.4; accidents, poisoning, and violence 37.6; endocrine, nutritional, and metabolic diseases of the blood and blood-forming organs 32.3; diseases of the digestive system 26.9.

National economy

Budget (1995). Revenue: Lm 423,312,000 (1992; customs and excise taxes 19.5%, national insurance and Central Bank contributions 20.6%, income tax 19.2%, Central Bank profits 5.1%). Expenditures: Lm 397,009,000 (1992; national insurance benefits 41.1%, education 12.3%, health 9.8%, debt service 4.7%).
Public debt (1994): U.S.$921,700,000.
Production (wholesale value in Lm except where noted). Agriculture, forestry, fishing (1993): vegetables 5,578,155 (of which tomatoes 896,588, melons 828,205, cauliflower 338,829, onions 330,018, carrots 307,118), fruits 906,245 (of which peaches 249,611, strawberries 166,294, grapes 116,122), potatoes 657,760; livestock (number of live animals; 1992) 107,000 pigs, 23,000 cattle, 6,000 sheep, 5,000 goats, 1,000,000 chickens; fish catch 1,065,821. Quarrying (1991): 4,305,000. Manufacturing (value of sales in Lm; 1994): machinery and transport equipment 341,065,000, of which transport equipment 4,286,000; food and beverages 103,349,000; textiles and wearing apparel 76,990,000; paper and printing 39,784,000; chemicals 27,899,000; metal manufacture 12,437,000. Construction (buildings completed; 1994): residential 3,426[5]; nonresidential 3,079. Energy production (consumption): electricity (kW-hr; 1992) 1,418,656,000 (1,032,339,000); coal (metric tons; 1992) none (300,000); crude petroleum, none (n.a.); petroleum products (metric tons; 1992) none (320,000); natural gas, none (n.a.).
Population economically active (1993): total 139,868; activity rate of total population 38.2% (participation rates: ages 15–64 [1985] 45.9%; female 32.7%; unemployed 4.2%).

Price and earnings indexes (1990 = 100)

	1988	1989	1990	1991	1992	1993	1994
Consumer price index	96.3	97.1	100.0	102.5	104.2	108.5	113.0
Annual earnings index	95.5	98.4	100.0	108.5	111.8	...	...

Household income and expenditure. Average household size (1985) 3.3; average annual income per household (1982) Lm 4,736 (U.S.$11,399); sources of income (1992): wages and salaries 61.8%, professional and unincorporated enterprises 20.0%, rents, dividends, and interest 18.2%; expenditure (1992): food and beverages 27.9%, transportation and communications 17.0%, household furnishings and operations 9.5%, clothing and footwear 6.6%, recreation, entertainment, and education 6.9%, housing 5.7%, health 3.3%, tobacco 2.6%.
Tourism (1993): receipts from visitors U.S.$653,000,000; expenditures by nationals abroad U.S.$211,000,000.
Gross national product (1992): U.S.$2,606,000,000 (U.S.$7,210 per capita).

Structure of gross domestic product and labour force

	1992		1994	
	in value Lm '000	% of total value	labour force	% of labour force
Agriculture	23,528	3.0	2,755	2.0
Manufacturing	191,758	24.9	34,411	24.6
Mining / Construction	25,278	3.3	5,348	3.8
Public utilities	6	6	6	6
Transportation and communications	52,214	6.8	11,114	8.0
Trade	109,963	14.3	14,344	10.3
Finance	114,651[7]	14.9[7]	3,520	2.5
Pub. admin., defense	178,742[6]	23.2[6]	41,652[6]	29.8[6]
Services	73,504	9.6	16,469	11.8
Other	...	...	9,976[8]	7.2[8]
TOTAL	769,638	100.0	139,589	100.0

Land use (1993): agricultural and under permanent cultivation 40.6%; other (infertile clay soil with underlying limestone) 59.4%.

Foreign trade[9]

Balance of trade (current prices)

	1989	1990	1991	1992	1993	1994
Lm '000,000	−169.0	−172.8	−214.5	−182.9	−229.5	−226.9
% of total	22.3%	18.3%	21.1%	15.7%	18.2%	16.2%

Imports (1993): Lm 830,920,000 (machinery and transport equipment 50.1%, semimanufactured goods 15.7%, food and live animals 8.5%, chemicals and chemical products 6.8%, mineral fuels 4.7%, nonfuel materials 1.7%, beverages and tobacco 1.1%). *Major import sources:* Italy 27.6%; Germany 14.2%; U.K. 13.4%; U.S. 8.7%; France 8.4%.
Exports (1993): Lm 518,326,000 (machinery and transport equipment 54.1%, clothing and footwear 11.5%, reexports 8.0%, semimanufactured goods 6.4%, chemicals 2.0%, food and live animals 1.8%, beverages and tobacco 0.3%). *Major export destinations:* Italy 32.2%; Germany 15.6%; France 10.4%; U.K. 8.1%; U.S. 7.5%; Libya 4.8%; The Netherlands 2.4%.

Transport and communications

Transport. Railroads: none. Roads (1992): total length 988 mi, 1,588 km (paved 92%). Vehicles (1992): passenger cars 120,320; trucks and buses 27,978. Merchant marine (1992): vessels (100 gross tons and over) 889; total deadweight tonnage 17,073,207. Air transport (1993): passenger-mi 776,940,000, passenger-km 1,250,370,000; short ton-mi cargo 5,006,000, metric ton-km cargo 7,308,000; airports (1995) with scheduled flights 1.
Communications. Daily newspapers (1992): total number 3; total circulation 68,000; circulation per 1,000 population 192. Radio (1994): 90,000 receivers (1 per 4.1 persons). Television (1993): 146,107 receivers (1 per 2.5 persons). Telephones (main lines; 1993): 157,500 (1 per 2.3 persons).

Education and health

Education (1992–93)

	schools	teachers	students	student/ teacher ratio
Primary (age 5–10)	168[10]	1,478	35,488	24.0
Secondary (age 11–17)	46[10]	1,746	23,528	13.5
Voc., teacher tr.	31[10]	690	6,200	9.0
Higher	1	284	3,679	13.0

Educational attainment (1967). Percentage of economically active population having: no formal schooling 10.8%; primary education 60.4%; lower secondary 3.4%; upper secondary 17.6%; technical secondary 3.9%; post-secondary and higher 3.9%. *Literacy* (1985): total population age 15 and over literate 250,419 (96.0%); males literate 121,899 (96.2%); females literate 128,520 (95.9%).
Health (1995): physicians 900 (1 per 409 persons); hospital beds 2,131 (1 per 173 persons); infant mortality rate per 1,000 live births (1993) 7.8.
Food (1992): daily per capita caloric intake 3,468 (vegetable products 75%, animal products 25%); 140% of FAO recommended minimum requirement.

Military

Total active duty personnel (1995): 1,850 (army 100%). *Military expenditure as percentage of GNP* (1992): 0.9% (world 3.7%); per capita expenditure U.S.$63.

[1]The Maltese lira is tied to the currencies of several principal trading partners. [2]Data are reported according to census regions as of January 1993; in late 1993 new administrative districts (Local Councils) were created. [3]January 1. [4]Detail does not add to total given because of rounding. [5]Dwellings completed. [6]Pub. admin., defense includes Public utilities. [7]Finance includes income from property. [8]Includes 5,574 unemployed. [9]Import figures are f.o.b. in balance of trade and c.i.f. for commodities and trading partners. [10]1991–92.

Marshall Islands

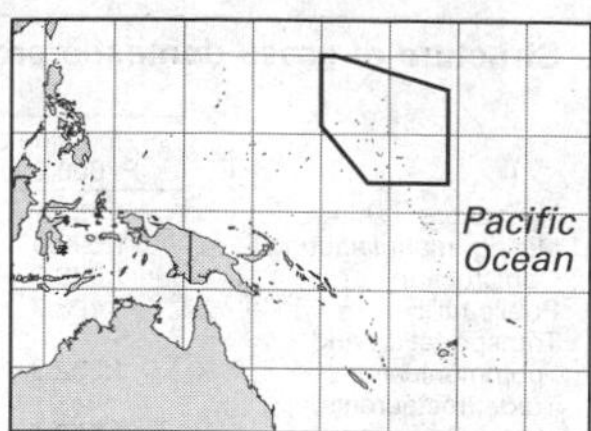

Official name: Majōl (Marshallese); Republic of the Marshall Islands (English).
Form of government: unitary republic with two legislative houses (Council of Iroij [12][1]; Nitijela [33]).
Head of state and government: President.
Capital: Majuro (Dalap-Uliga-Darrit).
Official languages: Marshallese (Kajin-Majōl); English.
Official religion: none.
Monetary unit: 1 U.S. dollar (U.S.$) = 100 cents; valuation (Oct. 6, 1995) 1 £ = U.S.$1.59.

Area and population

Election districts	area sq mi	area sq km	population 1988 census
Ailinglaplap	5.67	14.68	1,715
Ailuk	2.07	5.36	488
Arno	5.00	12.95	1,656
Aur	2.17	5.62	438
Bikini	2.32	6.01	10
Ebon	2.22	5.75	741
Enewetak	2.26	5.85	715
Jabat	0.22	0.57	112
Jaluit	4.38	11.34	1,709
Kili	0.36	0.93	602
Kwajalein	6.33	16.39	9,311
Lae	0.56	1.45	319
Lib	0.36	0.93	115
Likiep	3.96	10.26	482
Majuro	3.75	9.71	19,664
Maloelap	0.75	9.71	796
Mejit	0.72	1.86	445
Mili	6.15	15.93	854
Namorik	1.07	2.77	814
Namu	2.42	6.27	801
Rongelap	3.07	7.95	0
Ujae	0.72	1.86	448
Ujelang	0.67	1.74	0
Utrik	0.94	2.43	409
Wotho	1.67	4.32	90
Wotje	3.16	8.18	646
Other atolls	4.10	10.62	0
TOTAL	70.07	181.48[2]	43,380

Demography

Population (1995): 56,200.
Density (1995): persons per sq mi 802.0, persons per sq km 309.7.
Urban-rural (1988): urban 64.5%; rural 35.5%.
Sex distribution (1995): male 50.98%; female 49.02%.
Age breakdown (1995): under 15, 50.4%; 15–29, 25.6%; 30–44, 14.0%; 45–59, 6.3%; 60–74, 2.9%; 75 and over, 0.8%.
Population projection: (2000) 68,400; (2010) 100,000.
Doubling time: 18 years.
Ethnic composition (nationality; 1988): Marshallese 96.9%; other Pacific islanders 1.7%; Filipino 0.5%, all other 0.9%.
Religious affiliation (1973): Protestant 90.1%; Roman Catholic 8.5%; other 1.4%.
Major cities (1988): Majuro (Dalap-Uliga-Darrit) 14,649; Ebeye 8,324; no other urban localities.

Vital statistics

Birth rate per 1,000 population (1993): 46.6 (world avg. 25.0).
Death rate per 1,000 population (1993): 7.9 (world avg. 9.3).
Natural increase rate per 1,000 population (1993): 38.7 (world avg. 15.7).
Total fertility rate (avg. births per childbearing woman; 1993): 7.0.
Marriage rate per 1,000 population: n.a.
Divorce rate per 1,000 population: n.a.
Life expectancy at birth (1995): male 61.9 years; female 65.0 years.
Major causes of death per 100,000 population (1990–93)[3]: infectious and parasitic diseases 169.9; circulatory diseases 155.1; respiratory diseases 105.1; malignant neoplasms (cancers) 68.4; digestive diseases 63.3; accidents, injuries, and violence 36.7.

National economy

Budget (1994–95). Revenue: U.S.$67,200,000 (U.S. government grants 50.4%, income tax 11.6%, import tax 10.0%, value-added and excise taxes 7.4%, fishing rights 4.5%, fuel taxes 1.8%). Expenditures: U.S.$79,600,000 (1993–94; education 13.2%, debt service 10.2%, health services 10.2%, public works and social programs 9.2%, internal security 3.4%).
Production (metric tons except as noted). Agriculture, forestry, fishing (1991): copra 5,545, fruits 1,809 (of which pandanus 836, breadfruit 645, bananas 264, papaya 64), tubers 1,500 (of which taro 1,300, sweet potatoes 182), vegetables 136 (of which cabbage 36, pumpkins 36); livestock (number of live animals; 1994) 12,352 pigs, 59,086 chickens; roundwood, n.a.; fish catch (1993) 106,809[4]. Mining and quarrying: high-grade phosphate mining on Ailinglaplap Atoll, quarrying of sand and aggregate for local construction only. Manufacturing (1994): copra 4,387; coconut oil and processed (chilled or frozen) fish are important products; the manufacture of handicrafts and personal items (clothing, mats, boats, etc.) by individuals is also significant. Construction (1994): value added U.S.$9,300,000. Energy production (consumption): electricity (kW-hr; 1994) 57,891,000 (57,891,000); coal, none (n.a.); gasoline, oil, and lubricants (barrels; 1988)[5] n.a. (84,588).
Public debt (external, outstanding; 1994): U.S.$169,000,000.
Gross domestic product (1994): U.S.$88,800,000 (U.S.$1,640 per capita).

Structure of gross domestic product and labour force

	1994		1988	
	in value U.S.$'000	% of total value	labour force	% of labour force
Agriculture	14,614.3	16.4	2,150	18.7
Mining	248.0	0.3	2	—
Manufacturing	1,067.2	1.2	945	8.2
Public utilities	2,082.3	2.3	82	0.7
Construction	9,295.0	10.4	1,076	9.4
Transp. and commun.	4,209.7	4.7	537	4.7
Trade, restaurants, hotels	17,189.8	19.2	1,394	12.1
Finance, insurance, real estate	14,969.0	16.7	833	7.3
Public administration, Services	23,907.0	26.8	3,035	26.4
Other	1,790.9[6]	2.0[6]	1,434[7]	12.5[7]
TOTAL	89,373.2	100.0	11,488	100.0

Land use (1989)[8]: forested 22.5%; meadows and pastures 13.5%; agricultural and under permanent cultivation 33.1%; other 30.9%.
Household income and expenditure. Average household size (1988) 8.7; income per household (1979) U.S.$3,366; sources of income: n.a.; expenditure (1982): food 57.7%, housing 15.6%, clothing 12.0%, personal effects and other 14.7%.
Population economically active (1988): total 11,488; activity rate of total population 26.5% (participation rates: over age 14, 54.1%; female 30.1%; unemployed 12.5%).

Price and earnings indexes (1990 = 100)

	1988	1989	1990	1991	1992	1993	1994
Consumer price index	97.1	99.4	100.0	103.4	116.8	119.5	125.6
Earnings index	...	...	...	...	...	...	...

Tourism (1993): receipts from visitors U.S.$3,000,000; expenditures by nationals abroad, n.a.

Foreign trade

Balance of trade (current prices)

	1989	1990	1991	1992	1993	1994
U.S.$'000,000	−41.9	−53.9	−53.5	−52.6	−53.4	−49.3
% of total	89.4%	94.0%	90.3%	74.1%	77.7%	52.6%

Imports (1994): U.S.$71,433,000 (food and live animals 27.8%, mineral fuels and lubricants 22.9%, machinery and transport equipment 12.2%, manufactured goods 11.0%, beverages and tobacco 5.7%). *Major import sources:* United States 60.1%; Guam 25.2%; Japan 5.8%; Australia 1.9%.
Exports (1994): U.S.$22,170,000 (chilled fish 46.9%, frozen fish 21.1%, crude coconut oil 8.8%, pet fish 1.3%). *Major export destinations* (1983): United States 79.4%; other 20.6%.

Transport and communications

Transport. Railroads: none. Roads: n.a. Vehicles (1994): passenger cars 1,418; trucks and buses 193. Merchant marine (1992): vessels (100 gross tons and over) 35; total deadweight tonnage 4,182,356. Air transport (1994): passenger-km 52,000,000[9]; metric ton-km cargo 30,433; airports (1995) with scheduled flights 23.
Communications. Daily newspapers (1993): there are no dailies, only weeklies, of which there are two with a total circulation of over 10,000. Radio (1990): receivers, n.a.; but there are two radio stations. Television (1990): n.a.; but there are two television stations. Telephones (main lines; 1993): 2,300 (1 per 23 persons).

Education and health

Education (1993–94)

	schools	teachers	students	student/ teacher ratio
Primary (age 6–14)	104	833	13,565	16.3
Secondary (age 15–18)	11	138	2,483	18.0
Voc., teacher tr.	...	...	...	...
Higher	...	...	...	...

Educational attainment (1988). Percentage of population age 25 and over having: no grade completed 5.1%; elementary education 43.2%; secondary 39.7%; higher 11.4%; not stated 0.6%. *Literacy* (latest): total population age 15 and over literate 19,377 (91.2%); males literate 9,993 (92.4%); females literate 9,384 (90.0%).
Health (1991): physicians 20 (1 per 2,309 persons); hospital beds (1985) 54 (1 per 698 persons); infant mortality rate per 1,000 live births 53.0.
Food: daily per capita caloric intake, n.a.

Military

Under the 1984 Compact of Free Association, the United States provides for the defense of the Republic of the Marshall Islands.

[1]Council of Iroij is an advisory body only. [2]Detail does not add to total given because of rounding. [3]Registered deaths only. [4]Total for foreign vessels only. [5]Imports only. [6]Import duties less imputed bank service charges. [7] Includes 1,432 unemployed. [8]Data are for the former Trust Territory of the Pacific Islands. [9]1990.

Martinique

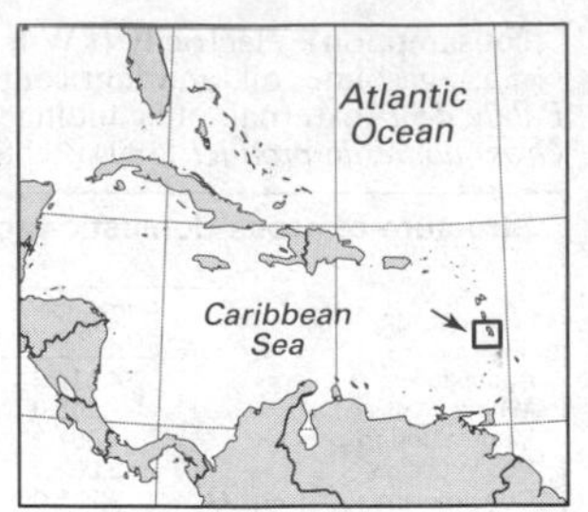

Official name: Département de la Martinique (Department of Martinique).
Political status: overseas department (France) with two legislative houses (General Council [45]; Regional Council [41]).
Chief of state: President of France.
Heads of government: Prefect (for France); President of the General Council (for Martinique); President of the Regional Council (for Martinique).
Capital: Fort-de-France.
Official language: French.
Official religion: none.
Monetary unit: 1 French franc (F) = 100 centimes; valuation (Oct. 6, 1995) 1 U.S.$ = F 5.01; 1 £ = F 7.93.

Area and population

Arrondissements	Capitals	area sq mi	area sq km	population 1990 census
Fort-de-France	Fort-de-France	147	381	187,275
Le Marin	Le Marin	158	409	93,411
La Trinité	La Trinité	131	338	78,893
TOTAL		436	1,128	359,579

Demography

Population (1995): 388,000.
Density (1995): persons per sq mi 889.9, persons per sq km 344.0.
Urban-rural (1990): urban 80.5%; rural 19.5%.
Sex distribution (1990): male 48.36%; female 51.64%.
Age breakdown (1990): under 15, 23.1%; 15–29, 28.9%; 30–44, 20.5%; 45–59, 13.5%; 60–74, 9.7%; 75 and over, 4.3%.
Population projection: (2000) 415,000; (2010) 458,000.
Doubling time: 77 years.
Ethnic composition (1983): mulatto 93.7%; French (metropolitan and Martinique white) 2.6%; East Indian 1.7%; other 2.0%.
Religious affiliation (1993): Roman Catholic 84.6%; other (mostly Seventh-day Adventist, Jehovah's Witness, Hindu, syncretist, and nonreligious) 15.4%.
Major urban areas (1990): Fort-de-France 100,072; Le Lamentin 30,026; Schoelcher 19,825; Sainte-Marie 19,683; Le Robert 17,675.

Vital statistics

Birth rate per 1,000 population (1994): 14.9 (world avg. 25.0); (1992) legitimate 34.1%; illegitimate 65.9%.
Death rate per 1,000 population (1994): 5.8 (world avg. 9.3).
Natural increase rate per 1,000 population (1994): 9.1 (world avg. 15.7).
Total fertility rate (avg. births per childbearing woman; 1993): 1.9.
Marriage rate per 1,000 population (1994): 3.9.
Divorce rate per 1,000 population (1993): 0.9.
Life expectancy at birth (1993): male 74.7 years; female 81.0 years.
Major causes of death per 100,000 population (1990): diseases of the circulatory system 208.0; malignant neoplasms (cancers) 135.5; accidents, poisoning, and violence 54.8; diseases of the digestive system 31.3; endocrine and metabolic disorders 30.7.

National economy

Budget (1994). Revenue: F 1,816,000,000 (general receipts from French central government and local administrative bodies 45.0%; tax receipts 34.0%, of which indirect taxes 19.5%, direct taxes 14.5%). Expenditures: F 1,816,000,000 (health and social assistance 42.0%; wages and salaries 16.7%; other administrative services 7.2%; debt amortization 5.0%).
Public debt (1994): U.S.$186,700,000.
Production (metric tons except as noted). Agriculture, forestry, fishing (1994): bananas 228,000, sugarcane 210,000, pineapples 27,000, plantains 12,000, yams 8,000, cucumbers 3,000, tomatoes 3,000, sweet potatoes 2,000, melons 1,588[1], limes 342[2], pimientos 198[1], flowers and foliage 105[1], avocados 68[1]; livestock (number of live animals) 110,000 sheep, 49,000 pigs, 36,000 cattle; roundwood (1993) 13,000 cu m; fish catch (1993) 4,607. Mining and quarrying (1992): pumice 140,000; sand and gravel for local construction. Manufacturing (1994): cement 230,672; processed pineapples 18,772; sugar 12,748; rum 69,229 hectolitres; other products include clothing, fabricated metals, and yawls and sails. Construction (buildings authorized; 1994): residential permits 6,893; nonresidential 113,279 sq m. Energy production (consumption): electricity (kW-hr; 1994) 865,000,000 (783,000,000); coal, none (none); crude petroleum (barrels; 1993) none (5,571,000); petroleum products (metric tons; 1993) 710,000 (565,000); natural gas, none (none).
Household income and expenditure. Average household size (1990) 3.3; income per household (1989) F 147,150 (U.S.$24,525); sources of income (1989): wages and salaries 80%, other 20%; expenditure (1993): food and beverages 32.1%, transportation and communications 20.7%, housing and energy 10.6%, household durable goods 9.4%, clothing and footwear 8.0%, education and recreation 5.4%, health care 5.2%, other 8.6%.
Tourism (1993): receipts from visitors U.S.$332,000,000; expenditures by nationals abroad, n.a.
Gross domestic product (at current market prices; 1991): U.S.$3,375,000,000 (U.S.$9,210 per capita).

Structure of gross domestic product and labour force

	1991 in value F '000,000	1991 % of total value	1990 labour force	1990 % of labour force
Agriculture, fishing	1,152.2	5.5	8,445	5.2
Mining, manufacturing	1,592.0	7.7	9,706	6.0
Construction	1,078.6	5.2	9,298	5.7
Public utilities	493.7	2.4		
Transportation and communications	1,282.3	6.2	6,673	4.1
Trade, restaurants, hotels	4,556.1	21.9	13,965	8.6
Finance, real estate, insurance	1,017.6	4.9	26,489	16.2
Pub. admin. and defense	305.8	1.5	35,541	21.8
Services	3,424.5	16.4		
Other	5,883.2[3]	28.3[3]	52,900[4]	32.4[4]
TOTAL	20,786	100.0	163,017	100.0

Population economically active (1990): total 164,870[5]; activity rate of total population 45.9% (participation rates: ages 15–64, 68.1%; female 47.5%; unemployed [1994] 26.2%).

Price and earnings indexes (1985 = 100)

	1988	1989	1990	1991	1992	1993	1994
Consumer price index[6]	108.8	112.4	116.8	118.3	126.6	129.3	132.3
Monthly earnings index[7]	108.0	111.0	115.9	118.8	122.9	125.7	127.5

Land use (1993): forested 44.3%; meadows and pastures 17.0%; agricultural and under permanent cultivation 16.0%; other 22.7%.

Foreign trade[8]

Balance of trade (current prices)

	1989	1990	1991	1992	1993	1994
F '000,000	−6,732	−7,970	−7,934	−7,982	−7,744	−7,877
% of total	73.5%	72.7%	78.4%	75.6%	78.0%	76.4%

Imports (1994): F 9,013,493,000 (food products 21.6%, machinery 18.0%, transport equipment 11.0%, chemical products 10.5%, metal manufactures 6.5%). *Major import sources:* France 61.6%; United States 2.7%; Guadeloupe 1.1%; Venezuela 0.7%; other Caribbean 1.9%.
Exports (1994): F 1,013,588,000 (food products 55.6%, refined petroleum 26.7%, machinery 6.9%, chemical products 3.4%). *Major export destinations:* France 47.5%; Guadeloupe 37.4%; French Guiana 3.3%.

Transport and communications

Transport. Railroads: none. Roads (1994): total length 1,299 mi, 2,091 km (paved [1988] 75%). Vehicles (1985): passenger cars 135,269; trucks and buses 7,328. Merchant marine (1992): vessels (100 gross tons and over) 6; total deadweight tonnage 1,121. Air transport (1994): passenger arrivals and departures 1,566,253; cargo unloaded 8,272 metric tons, cargo loaded 5,572 metric tons; airports (1995) with scheduled flights 2.
Communications. Daily newspapers (1992): total number 1; total circulation 32,000; circulation per 1,000 population 86. Radio (1994): total number of receivers 71,000 (1 per 5.4 persons). Television (1994): total number of receivers 65,000 (1 per 5.8 persons). Telephones (main lines; 1993): 149,600 (1 per 2.5 persons).

Education and health

Education (1992–93)

	schools	teachers	students	student/teacher ratio
Primary (age 6–11)	282	2,711	33,170	12.2
Secondary (age 12–18) / Vocational	79	3,830	47,295	12.3
Higher	1	71	3,670	51.7

Educational attainment (1982). Percentage of population age 25 and over having: no formal schooling 9.8%; primary education 62.7%; secondary 21.2%; higher 6.3%. *Literacy* (1982): total population age 15 and over literate 206,807 (92.5%); males literate 97,538 (91.8%); females literate 109,269 (93.2%).
Health (1991): physicians 625 (1 per 584 persons); hospital beds 3,747 (1 per 97 persons); infant mortality rate per 1,000 live births (1993) 4.0.
Food (1992): daily per capita caloric intake 2,829 (vegetable products 75%, animal products 25%); 117% of FAO recommended minimum requirement.

Military

Total active duty personnel (1994): 1,542 French troops.

[1]Production for export only. [2]1993. [3]Includes an estimated F 5,474,000,000 produced in the nonmoney economy. [4]Unemployed. [5]Includes military reserve personnel. [6]Figures are end-of-year unless otherwise footnoted. [7]Based on monthly salaries of employees in commerce, banking, and government services. [8]Imports c.i.f.; exports f.o.b.

Mauritania

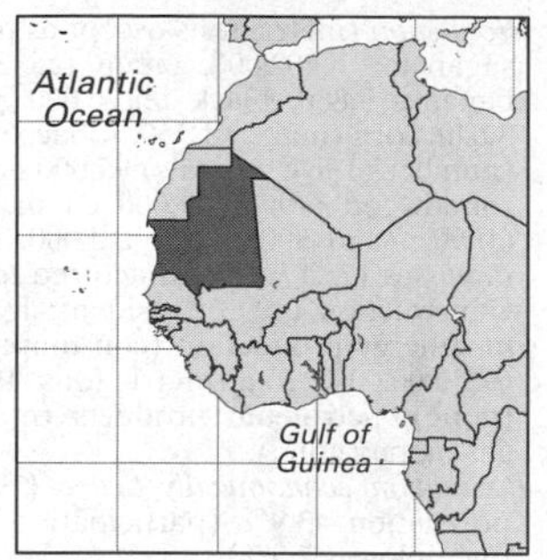

Official name: al-Jumhūrīyah al-Islāmīyah al-Mūrītānīyah (Arabic) (Islamic Republic of Mauritania).
Form of government: unitary multiparty republic with two legislative houses (Senate [56]; National Assembly [79]).
Head of state and government: President.
Capital: Nouakchott.
Official languages: Arabic[1].
Official religion: Islam.
Monetary unit: 1 ouguiya (UM) = 5 khoums; valuation (Oct. 6, 1995) 1 U.S.$ = UM 132.56; 1 £ = UM 209.56.

Area and population

		area		population
Regions	**Capitals**	sq mi	sq km	1992 estimate
el-ʾAçâba	Kiffa	13,900	36,000	185,574
Adrar	Atar	83,100	215,300	62,906
Brakna	Aleg	14,000	37,100	207,590
Dakhlet Nouadhibou	Nouadhibou	11,600	30,000	83,246
Gorgol	Kaédi	5,400	14,000	201,301
Guidimaka	Sélibaby	4,000	10,000	129,797
Hodh ech-Chargui	Néma	64,000	166,000	234,011
Hodh el-Gharbi	ʿAyoûn el-ʾAtroûs	22,000	57,000	175,089
Inchiri	Akjoujt	19,000	49,000	13,630
Tagant	Tidjikdja	36,000	93,000	67,939
Tiris Zemmour	Zouérate	98,600	255,300	37,534
Trarza	Rosso	26,000	67,000	217,867
District				
Nouakchott	Nouakchott	400	1,000	324,037
TOTAL		398,000	1,030,700	1,940,521[2]

Demography

Population (1995): 2,274,000.
Density (1994): persons per sq mi 5.7, persons per sq km 2.2.
Urban-rural (1995): urban 53.8%; rural 46.2%.
Sex distribution (1995): male 49.52%; female 50.48%.
Age breakdown (1995): under 15, 43.1%; 15–29, 27.3%; 30–44, 16.1%; 45–59, 8.3%; 60–74, 4.3%; 75 and over, 0.9%.
Population projection: (2000) 2,580,000; (2010) 3,283,000.
Doubling time: 22 years.
Ethnic composition (1993): Moor 70% (of which about 40% "black" Moor [Ḥarāṭīn, or African Sudanic] and about 30% "white" Moor [Bidan, or Arab-Berber]); other black African 30% (including [1983] Wolof 6.8%, Tukulor 5.3%, Soninke 2.8%, Fulani 1.1%, other 2.5%).
Religious affiliation (1980): Muslim 99.4%; Christian 0.4%; other 0.2%.
Major cities (1992): Nouakchott 480,408; Nouadhibou 72,305; Kaédi 35,241; Kiffa 29,292[3]; Rosso 27,783[3].

Vital statistics

Birth rate per 1,000 population (1994): 48.0 (world avg. 25.0); legitimate, n.a.; illegitimate, n.a.
Death rate per 1,000 population (1994): 16.0 (world avg. 9.3).
Natural increase rate per 1,000 population (1994): 32.0 (world avg. 15.7).
Total fertility rate (avg. births per childbearing woman; 1994): 7.0.
Marriage rate per 1,000 population: n.a.
Divorce rate per 1,000 population: n.a.
Life expectancy at birth (1994): male 45.0 years; female 51.0 years.
Major causes of death per 100,000 population: n.a.; however, mortality and morbidity arise mainly in diseases of the respiratory system, malaria, measles, and diarrhea.

National economy

Budget (1994). Revenue: UM 29,460,000,000 (tax revenue 77.1%; nontax revenue 21.2%; special costs 1.6%). Expenditures: UM 35,200,000,000 (current expenditures 64.8%, of which salaries and wages 19.0%, interest on debt 10.4%, defense 10.3%; capital [development] expenditures 32.9%).
Tourism: receipts from visitors (1991) U.S.$13,000,000; expenditures by nationals abroad (1988) U.S.$27,000,000.
Land use (1993): forested 4.3%; meadows and pastures 38.3%; agricultural and under permanent cultivation 0.2%; desert 57.2%.
Production (metric tons except as noted). Agriculture, forestry, fishing (1994): sorghum 114,000, rice 59,000, dates 22,000, pulses 17,000, vegetables (including melons) 15,000, millet 7,000, corn (maize) 6,000, watermelons 6,000, roots and tubers 5,000; livestock (number of live animals) 4,800,000 sheep, 3,100,000 goats, 1,011,000 cattle, 1,000,000 camels, 155,000 asses, 18,000 horses, 4,000,000 chickens; roundwood (1993) 13,000 cu m; fish catch (metric tons; 1994) 296,627. Mining and quarrying (gross weight; 1994): iron ore 10,342,000; gypsum 4,230; plaster 3,510, gold 1,738 kg. Manufacturing (1994): cow's milk 91,000; goat's milk 77,000; sheep's milk 63,000; meat 61,000, of which fresh beef and veal 18,000, fresh mutton and lamb 12,000, goat meat 8,000; hides and skins 4,318; cheese 1,664; butter 614. Construction (1984): 42,478 sq m. Energy production (consumption): electricity (kW-hr; 1993) 164,593,000 (164,593,000); coal (metric tons; 1993) none (6,000); crude petroleum (barrels; 1993) none (7,315,000); petroleum products (metric tons; 1993) 827,000 (909,000); natural gas, none (n.a.).
Household income and expenditure. Average household size (1980) 5.0; income per household: n.a.; sources of income: n.a.; expenditure (1990): food and beverages 74.5%, housing 9.2%, clothing and footwear 7.6%, health 0.8%, education 0.3%, other 7.6%.
Gross national product (at current market prices; 1993): U.S.$947,000,000 (U.S.$438 per capita).

Structure of gross domestic product and labour force

	1993		1988	
	in value UM '000,000	% of total value	labour force	% of labour force
Agriculture	27,106	23.7	225,238	38.5
Mining	10,447	9.1	6,322	1.1
Manufacturing	12,669	11.1	5,630	1.0
Public utilities } Construction }	7,649	6.7	1,326	0.2
			12,291	2.1
Transportation and communications	7,422	6.5	8,378	1.4
Trade and finance	15,956	13.9	73,451	12.5
Services	7,539	6.6 }	86,807	14.8
Pub. admin., defense	13,191	11.5 }		
Other (indirect taxes net of subsidies)	12,472	10.9	166,366[4]	28.4[4]
TOTAL	114,450[5]	100.0	585,809	100.0

Population economically active (1992): total 654,000; activity rate of total population 30.5% (participation rates: over age 10 [1990] 49.7%; female 13.5%; unemployed [1988] 50.0%).

Price and earnings indexes (1990 = 100)

	1987	1988	1989	1990	1991	1992	1993
Consumer price index	82.0	83.1	93.8	100.0	105.6	116.3	127.2
Monthly earnings index[6]	...	...	100.0	100.0	100.0	114.6	129.2

Public debt (external, outstanding; 1994): U.S.$2,500,000,000.

Foreign trade

Balance of trade (current prices)

	1988	1989	1990	1991	1992	1993
UM '000,000	+4,576	+8,277	+3,838	+1,272	+1,657	+2,163
% of total	6.4%	12.4%	5.8%	1.8%	2.3%	3.2%

Imports (1993[7, 8]): UM 32,436,000,000 (food products 24.8%, petroleum products 9.2%, fishing boats 6.6%, machinery and transport equipment 4.3%). *Major import sources* (1993): France 26.8%; Spain 8.7%; The Netherlands 8.3%; Algeria 7.6%; Belgium and Luxembourg 5.9%; Italy 4.9%; Germany 4.3%; United States 3.8%.
Exports (1993[7]): UM 34,599,000,000 (fish 55.2%, iron ore 39.8%, gold 3.9%). *Major export destinations* (1993)[9]: Japan 25%; Italy 18%; France 15%; Spain 11%; Belgium and Luxembourg 8%; Côte d'Ivoire 6%; United Kingdom 5%; Cameroon 4%.

Transport and communications

Transport. Railroads (1992): route length 416 mi, 670 km; passenger-mi, negligible; passenger-km, negligible; short ton-mi cargo 3,860,000,000, metric ton-km cargo 5,635,000,000. Roads (1995): total length 4,745 mi, 7,636 km (paved 23%). Vehicles (1993): passenger cars 8,000; trucks and buses 5,500. Merchant marine (1992): vessels (100 gross tons and over) 126; total deadweight tonnage 23,875. Air transport (1993)[10]: passenger-mi 129,000,000, passenger-km 207,000,000; short ton-mi cargo 9,000,000, metric ton-km cargo 14,000,000; airports (1995) with scheduled flights 10.
Communications. Daily newspapers (1995): total number 1; total circulation, n.a. Radio (1993): total number of receivers 300,000 (1 per 7.2 persons). Television (1993): total number of receivers 1,100 (1 per 1,974 persons). Telephones (main lines; 1993): 7,600 (1 per 286 persons).

Education and health

Education (1993–94)

	schools	teachers	students	student/ teacher ratio
Primary (age 6–11)	1,635	4,686	248,048	52.9
Secondary (age 12–17)	56[11]	1,776	43,861	24.7
Voc., teacher tr.	5[11]	162	1,949	12.0
Higher	4[11]	248[11]	7,647	...

Educational attainment (1988). Percentage of population age 25 and over having: no formal schooling 60.8%; primary and incomplete secondary 34.1%; secondary 3.8%; higher 1.3%. *Literacy* (1995): percentage of total population age 15 and over literate 37.7%; males literate 49.6%; females literate 26.3%.
Health: physicians (1991) 135 (1 per 14,259 persons); hospital beds (1988) 1,556 (1 per 1,217 persons); infant mortality rate per 1,000 live births (1994) 85.
Food (1992): daily per capita caloric intake 2,685 (vegetable products 82%, animal products 18%); 116% of FAO recommended minimum requirement.

Military

Total active duty personnel (1995): 15,650 (army 95.8%, navy 3.2%, air force 1.0%). *Military expenditure as percentage of GNP* (1993): 2.8% (world 3.3%); per capita expenditure U.S.$17.

[1]The 1991 constitution names Arabic as the official language and the following as national languages: Arabic, Fulani, Soninke, and Wolof. [2]Official population projection based on 1988 census. [3]1988. [4]Mostly unemployed. [5]Detail does not add to total given because of rounding. [6]Statutory minimum wage rate of civil servants. [7]F.o.b. [8]Import figures are not based on customs data but on foreign-exchange records of the central bank and other official sources. [9]Estimated figures. [10]Air Afrique scheduled traffic only. [11]1991–92.

Mauritius

Official name: Republic of Mauritius.
Form of government: republic with one legislative house (Legislative Assembly [70[1]]).
Chief of state: President.
Head of government: Prime Minister.
Capital: Port Louis.
Official language: English.
Official religion: none.
Monetary unit: 1 Mauritian rupee (Mau Re; plural Mau Rs) = 100 cents; valuation (Oct. 6, 1995) 1 U.S.$ = Mau Rs 17.99; 1 £ = Mau Rs 28.43.

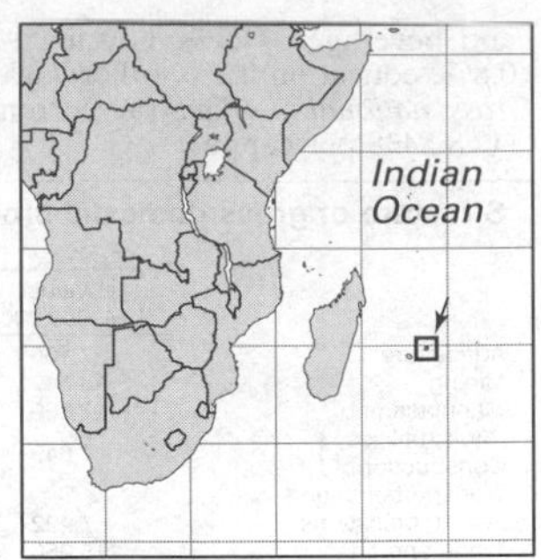

Area and population

Islands Districts/Dependencies	area sq mi	area sq km	population 1993[2] estimate
Mauritius	720	1,865	1,056,741
Black River	100	259	46,716
Flacq	115	298	116,111
Grand Port	100	260	99,676
Moka	89	231	67,721
Pamplemousses	69	179	106,436
Plaines Wilhems	78	203	332,923
Port Louis	17	43	134,516
Rivière du Rempart	57	148	90,071
Savanne	95	245	62,571
Mauritian dependencies			
Agalega[3]; Cargados Carajos Shoals (Saint Brandon)[3]	27	71	170
Rodrigues[4]	40	104	34,493
TOTAL	788[5]	2,040[5]	1,091,404

Demography

Population (1995): 1,128,000.
Density (1995): persons per sq mi 1,431.0, persons per sq km 552.8.
Urban-rural (1991)[6]: urban 40.7%; rural 59.3%.
Sex distribution (1993): male 50.10%; female 49.90%.
Age breakdown (1992)[7]: under 15, 29.3%; 15–29, 28.0%; 30–44, 23.2%; 45–59, 11.2%; 60–74, 6.5%; 75 and over, 1.8%.
Population projection: (2000) 1,183,000; (2010) 1,301,000.
Doubling time: 52 years.
Ethnic composition (1992): Indo-Pakistani 68.0%; Creole (mixed Caucasian, Indo-Pakistani, and African) 27.0%; Chinese 3.0%; white 2.0%.
Religious affiliation (1990): Hindu 50.6%; Roman Catholic 27.2%; Muslim 16.3%; Protestant 5.2%; Buddhist 0.3%; other 0.4%.
Major cities (1992): Port Louis 142,850; Beau Bassin–Rose Hill 94,299; Vacoas-Phoenix 92,072; Curepipe 74,738; Quatre Bornes 71,534.

Vital statistics

Birth rate per 1,000 population (1993): 20.3 (world avg. 25.0); (1985) legitimate 72.8%; illegitimate 27.2%.
Death rate per 1,000 population (1993): 6.8 (world avg. 9.3).
Natural increase rate per 1,000 population (1993): 13.5 (world avg. 15.7).
Total fertility rate (avg. births per childbearing woman; 1992): 2.4.
Marriage rate per 1,000 population (1993): 10.7.
Divorce rate per 1,000 population (1992)[6]: 0.7.
Life expectancy at birth (1989–91): male 65.6 years; female 73.4 years.
Major causes of death per 100,000 population (1992)[6]: diseases of the circulatory system 279.5; diseases of the respiratory system 67.0; malignant neoplasms (cancers) 62.5; homicide, suicide, and accidents 45.5.

National economy

Budget (1993–94). Revenue: Mau Rs 12,860,000,000 (tax revenue 89.0%, of which import and stamp duties 40.6%, income tax 13.2%, sales tax 9.3%). Expenditures: Mau Rs 12,730,000,000 (social services 35.6%, of which education, art, and culture 14.6%, social security 10.9%, health 8.2%; public-debt service 27.7%).
Tourism (1993): receipts from visitors U.S.$301,000,000; expenditures by nationals abroad U.S.$128,000,000.
Public debt (external, outstanding; 1993): U.S.$884,000,000.
Gross national product (at current market prices; 1993): U.S.$3,309,000,000 (U.S.$2,980 per capita).

Structure of gross domestic product and labour force

1994	in value Mau Rs '000,000[8]	% of total value	labour force[9, 10]	% of labour force[9, 10]
Agriculture	4,605	8.7	41,600	14.2
Mining	80	0.1	200	0.1
Manufacturing	12,485	23.7	104,700	35.8
Construction	4,010	7.6	13,400	4.6
Public utilities	1,250	2.4	3,500	1.2
Transportation and communications	6,350	12.0	14,200	4.9
Trade	9,345	17.8	23,300	8.0
Finance	5,745	10.9	...	...
Pub. admin., defense; Services	5,875; 3,000	11.1; 5.7	76,800	26.3
Other	...	...	14,900	5.1
TOTAL	52,745	100.0	292,400	100.0[5]

Production (metric tons except as noted). Agriculture, forestry, fishing (1993): sugarcane 5,402,000, green tea 30,900, potatoes 13,855, tomatoes 13,020, bananas 9,880, black tea 6,000, cabbages 5,515, pineapples 4,050, onions 3,640, corn (maize) 1,750, tobacco 1,015, peanuts (groundnuts) 865; livestock (number of live animals) 95,000 goats, 34,000 cattle, 14,000 pigs, 7,000 sheep; roundwood (1992) 17,000 cu m; fish catch 19,047. Mining and quarrying (1990): sand 800,000, salt 3,000. Manufacturing (1992): raw sugar 643,168; molasses 173,175; manufactured tea 5,845; beer and stout 295,100 hectolitres. Construction (1993): residential 1,179,000 sq m; nonresidential 207,000 sq m. Energy production (consumption): electricity (kW-hr; 1992) 925,000,000 (925,000,000); coal (metric tons; 1992) none (62,000); crude petroleum, none (none); petroleum products (metric tons; 1992) none (388,000); natural gas, none (none).
Population economically active (1992)[6]: total 478,129; activity rate of total population 43.9% (participation rates: ages 15–64, 66.2%; female 33.9%; unemployed 7.9%).

Price and earnings indexes (1990 = 100)

	1988	1989	1990	1991	1992	1993	1994
Consumer price index	78.2	88.1	100.0	107.0	112.0	123.7	132.8
Monthly earnings index[10]	79.9	94.6	100.0	115.8	128.5	135.6	164.2

Household income and expenditure. Average household size (1990) 4.5[6]; income per household (1979) Mau Rs 15,540 (U.S.$2,430); sources of income (1990): salaries and wages 48.4%, entrepreneurial income 41.2%, transfer payments 10.4%; expenditure (1986–87)[11]: food, beverages, and tobacco 49.1%, housing 13.5%, transportation 9.3%, clothing and footwear 8.4%, recreation, entertainment, education and cultural services 6.0%, energy 5.7%, health care 3.0%, other 5.0%.
Land use (1992): forested 28.1%; meadows and pastures 3.4%; agricultural and under permanent cultivation 52.2%; other 16.3%.

Foreign trade[12]

Balance of trade (current prices)

	1988	1989	1990	1991	1992	1993
U.S.$'000,000	−167.8	−211.1	−280.0	−222.6	−170.8	−254.2
% of total	7.7%	9.6%	10.6%	8.4%	6.2%	8.9%

Imports (1993): Mau Rs 30,319,000,000 (manufactured goods classified chiefly by material 36.4%, machinery and transport equipment 22.4%, food 12.3%, mineral fuels and lubricants 6.4%, chemicals 6.3%, inedible crude materials excluding fuels 3.1%, animal and vegetable oils and fats 1.0%). *Major import sources:* South Africa 14.2%; France 12.6%; Japan 7.2%; United Kingdom 5.8%; Hong Kong 4.6%; India 4.4%; Taiwan 4.2%; Germany 4.1%.
Exports (1993): Mau Rs 22,992,000,000 (clothing and textiles 55.3%, sugar 25.1%, yarn 2.5%, pearls and precious stones 1.8%). *Major export destinations:* United Kingdom 32.4%; France 20.5%; United States 17.9%; Germany 7.1%; Italy 4.0%.

Transport and communications

Transport. Railroads: none. Roads (1991): total length 1,138 mi, 1,831 km (paved 93%). Vehicles (1993): passenger cars 33,613; trucks and buses 9,846. Merchant marine (1992): vessels (100 gross tons and over) 35; total deadweight tonnage 152,197. Air transport (1994)[13]: passenger-mi 1,841,057,000, passenger-km 2,962,889,000; short ton-mi cargo 67,359,000, metric ton-km cargo 98,342,000; airports (1995) with scheduled flights 1.
Communications. Daily newspapers (1994): total number 7; total circulation 96,000[14]; circulation per 1,000 population 86[14]. Radio (1994): 380,000 receivers (1 per 2.9 persons). Television (1994) 156,850 receivers (1 per 7.1 persons). Telephones (main lines; 1993): 106,900 (1 per 10 persons).

Education and health

Education (1993)

	schools	teachers[15]	students	student/ teacher ratio[15]
Primary (age 5–12)	281	6,543	125,543	19.8
Secondary (age 12–20)	123	4,050	87,661	20.6
Voc., teacher tr.	19[16]	69[17]	2,052	...
Higher	2	382[18]	2,556	5.7[18]

Educational attainment (1990). Percentage of population age 25 and over having: no formal education 18.3%; incomplete primary 42.6%; primary 6.1%; incomplete secondary 18.0%; secondary 13.1%; higher 1.9%. *Literacy* (1990): percentage of total population age 15 and over literate 79.9%; males literate 85.2%; females literate 74.7%.
Health (1993): physicians 950 (1 per 1,098 persons); hospital beds 3,330 (1 per 351 persons); infant mortality rate per 1,000 live births (1993) 19.6.
Food (1988–90): daily per capita caloric intake 2,897 (vegetable products 87%, animal products 13%); 128% of FAO recommended minimum requirement.

Military

Total active duty personnel: none; however, a special 1,300-person paramilitary force ensures internal security. *Military expenditure as percentage of GNP* (1993): 0.4% (world 3.3%); per capita expenditure U.S.$10.

[1]Includes 8 nonelective seats. [2]January 1. [3]Administered directly from Port Louis. [4]Administered by resident commissioner assisted by local council. [5]Detail does not add to total given because of rounding. [6]Island of Mauritius only. [7]Excludes Agalega and Cargados Carajos Shoals. [8]At factor cost. [9]Employed persons in establishments employing 10 or more persons. [10]March. [11]Current weights of CPI components; Island of Mauritius only. [12]Import figures are f.o.b. in balance of trade and c.i.f. for commodities and trading partners. [13]Air Mauritius only. [14]Circulation for 6 newspapers only. [15]1991. [16]1992. [17]1982. [18]1989.

Mexico

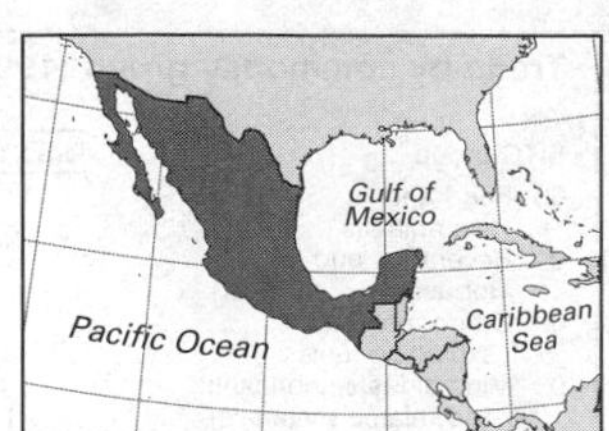

Official name: Estados Unidos Mexicanos (United Mexican States).
Form of government: federal republic with two legislative houses (Senate [128]; Chamber of Deputies [500]).
Chief of state and head of government: President.
Capital: Mexico City.
Official language: Spanish.
Official religion: none.
Monetary unit: 1 new peso[1] (Mex$) = 100 centavos; valuation (Oct. 6, 1995) 1 U.S.$ = Mex$6.54; 1 £ = Mex$10.33.

Area and population

States	Capitals	area sq mi	area sq km	population 1992 estimate
Aguascalientes	Aguascalientes	2,112	5,471	770,972
Baja California Norte	Mexicali	26,997	69,921	1,908,434
Baja California Sur	La Paz	28,369	73,475	351,690
Campeche	Campeche	19,619	50,812	569,417
Chiapas	Tuxtla Gutiérrez	28,653	74,211	3,436,574
Chihuahua	Chihuahua	94,571	244,938	2,503,515
Coahuila	Saltillo	57,908	149,982	2,040,046
Colima	Colima	2,004	5,191	458,607
Durango	Durango	47,560	123,181	1,394,571
Guanajuato	Guanajuato	11,773	30,491	4,170,885
Guerrero	Chilpancingo	24,819	64,281	2,732,699
Hidalgo	Pachuca	8,036	20,813	1,945,514
Jalisco	Guadalajara	31,211	80,836	5,693,177
México	Toluca	8,245	21,355	10,705,862
Michoacán	Morelia	23,138	59,928	3,723,543
Morelos	Cuernavaca	1,911	4,950	1,259,170
Nayarit	Tepic	10,417	26,979	871,710
Nuevo León	Monterrey	25,067	64,924	3,336,044
Oaxaca	Oaxaca	36,275	93,952	3,207,147
Puebla	Puebla	13,090	33,902	4,406,652
Querétaro	Querétaro	4,420	11,449	1,126,143
Quintana Roo	Chetumal	19,387	50,212	577,419
San Luis Potosí	San Luis Potosí	24,351	63,068	2,088,544
Sinaloa	Culiacán	22,521	58,328	2,341,346
Sonora	Hermosillo	70,291	182,052	1,866,757
Tabasco	Villahermosa	9,756	25,267	1,595,487
Tamaulipas	Ciudad Victoria	30,650	79,384	2,351,663
Tlaxcala	Tlaxcala	1,551	4,016	812,749
Veracruz	Jalapa (Xalapa)	27,683	71,699	6,405,478
Yucatán	Mérida	14,827	38,402	1,390,318
Zacatecas	Zacatecas	28,283	73,252	1,309,493
Federal District				
Distrito Federal	—	571	1,479	8,276,345
TOTAL		756,066	1,958,201	85,627,971

Demography

Population (1995): 91,145,000.
Density (1995): persons per sq mi 120.5, persons per sq km 46.5.
Urban-rural (1990): urban 71.3%; rural 28.7%.
Sex distribution (1995): male 49.88%; female 50.12%.
Age breakdown (1995): under 15, 35.9%; 15–29, 30.1%; 30–44, 18.2%; 45–59, 9.5%; 60–74, 4.8%; 75 and over, 1.5%.
Population projection: (2000) 98,881,000; (2010) 112,891,000.
Doubling time: 26 years.
Ethnic composition (1990): mestizo 60.0%; Amerindian 30.0%; Caucasian 9.0%; other 1.0%.
Religious affiliation (1990): Roman Catholic 89.7%; Protestant (including Evangelical) 4.9%; Jewish 0.1%; other 2.1%; none 3.2%.
Major cities (1990): Mexico City 9,815,795; Guadalajara 1,650,042; Ciudad Netzahualcóyotl 1,255,456; Monterrey 1,068,996; Puebla 1,007,170; Juarez 789,522; León 758,279; Tijuana 698,752; Mérida 523,422; Chihuahua 516,153.
Place of birth (1990): 93.1% native-born; 6.9% foreign-born and unknown.
Mobility (1990). Population 5 years and older living in the same state as in 1985: 94.3%; different state 4.9%; unspecified 0.8%.
Households. Total households (1992) 17,152,000; distribution by size (1990): 1 person 1.0%, 2 persons 4.3%, 3 persons 8.9%, 4 persons 14.9%, 5 persons 17.4%, 6 persons 15.3%, 7 or more persons 38.2%. Family households (1990): 17,064,507 (98.4%); nonfamily 1,039,738 (1.3%); unspecified 256,554 (0.3%).
Immigration (1987): permanent immigrants admitted 72,649.
Emigration (1993): legal immigrants into the United States 126,561.

Vital statistics

Birth rate per 1,000 population (1993): 31.5 (world avg. 25.0); (1983) legitimate 72.5%; illegitimate 27.5%.
Death rate per 1,000 population (1993): 4.7 (world avg. 9.3).
Natural increase rate per 1,000 population (1993): 26.8 (world avg. 15.7).
Total fertility rate (avg. births per childbearing woman; 1990): 3.7.
Marriage rate per 1,000 population (1993): 7.7.
Divorce rate per 1,000 population (1993): 0.4.
Life expectancy at birth (1990): male 66.5 years; female 73.1 years.
Major causes of death per 100,000 population (1993): heart diseases 66.5; malignant neoplasms (cancers) 51.1; accidents 42.1; diabetes mellitus 33.7; cerebrovascular diseases 24.5; conditions originating in the perinatal period 23.8; cirrhosis of the liver 23.3; pneumonia and influenza 21.2; homicide 18.3.

Social indicators

Access to services (1992). Proportion of dwellings having: electricity 89.3%; piped water supply 81.0%; drained sewage 66.1%.
Educational attainment (1992). Percentage of population age 15 and over having: no primary education 14.1%; some primary 22.3%; completed primary 20.7%; incomplete secondary 10.4%; complete secondary 24.2%; higher 8.3%.

Distribution of income (1983)
percentage of household income by quintile

1	2	3	4	5 (highest)
4.0	8.8	14.2	22.4	50.6

Quality of working life. Average workweek (1993) 45.0 hours[2]. Annual rate (1992) per 100,000 insured workers for: temporary disability 6,426; indemnification for permanent injury 239; death 18. Labour stoppages (1993): 155, involving 31,708 workers. Average duration of journey to work: n.a. Method of transport: n.a. Rate per 1,000 workers of discouraged (unemployed no longer seeking work): n.a.
Social participation. Eligible voters participating in last national election (1991): *c.* 60%. Population participating in voluntary work: n.a. Trade union membership in total workforce: n.a. Practicing religious population in total affiliated population: national average of weekly attendance (1993) 11%; (1970) weekly 10% of urban dwellers, 25% of rural dwellers; yearly 55% of urban dwellers, 73% of rural dwellers.
Social deviance (1991). Criminal cases tried by local authorities per 100,000 population for: murder 60.3; rape 22.4; other assault 301.0; theft 703.8. Incidence per 100,000 in general population of: alcoholism, n.a.; drug and substance abuse, n.a.[3]; suicide 1.72.
Leisure (1985). Favourite leisure activities (average daily paid attendance): cinema 582,416; sporting events 31,518; live theatre 16,400; museums and archaeological sites 12,169; bullfights 3,049.
Material well-being (1985). Households possessing: radio 96%; television 73%; washing machine 33%; automobile 29%; telephone 27%; refrigerator 23%.

National economy

Gross national product (1993): U.S.$324,951,000,000 (U.S.$3,750 per capita).

Structure of gross domestic product and labour force

	1994 in value Mex$'000,000[1,4]	1994 % of total value	1993 labour force	1993 % of labour force
Agriculture	431.7	7.4	8,842,774	26.3
Mining	197.7	3.4	170,923	0.5
Manufacturing	1,317.0	22.5	5,077,678	15.1
Construction	323.6	5.5	1,879,231	5.6
Public utilities	93.4	1.6	99,123	0.3
Transportation and communications	439.9	7.5	1,362,350	4.0
Trade	1,485.4	25.5	6,892,693	20.5
Finance	674.2	11.5	1,080,051	3.2
Pub. admin., defense Services	998.6	17.0	7,205,262	21.4
Other	104.0[5]	−1.9[5]	1,041,727[6]	3.1
TOTAL	5,857.5	100.0	33,651,812	100.0

Budget (1993). Revenue: Mex$192,826,600,000[1] (petroleum revenues 25.4%). Expenditures: Mex$185,188,800,000[1] (transfers 30.4%, interest on public debt 15.3%, wages and salaries 13.1%).
Public debt (external, outstanding; 1993): U.S.$85,960,000,000.
Tourism (1993): receipts from visitors U.S.$6,167,000,000; expenditures by nationals abroad U.S.$5,562,000,000.

Manufacturing, mining, and construction enterprises (1993)

	no. of enterprises	no. of employees ('000)	yearly wages as a % of avg. of all wages[7]	value added (Mex$'000,000[1,7])
Manufacturing	266,033[8]	3,174.4[8]	97.5[8]	20,950,900[8]
Metal products	46,667	955.6	114.2	6,605,300
Chemicals	7,321	371.2	152.3	4,228,000
Food, beverages, and tobacco	91,894	679.3	86.4	3,378,700
Textiles and apparel	44,071	530.6	80.0	2,414,800
Iron and steel	401	57.4	128.2	1,332,400
Nonmetallic mineral products	24,397	181.8	98.6	1,177,700
Paper and printing	15,022	193.2	100.0	1,127,900
Wood and wood products	31,549	162.6	62.8	497,000
Nonelectrical machinery and transport equipment	[8]	[8]	...[8]	[8]
Electrical machinery	[8]	[8]	...[8]	[8]
Other manufactures	4,711	42.7	...	189,200
Mining	2,845	95.6	161.0	1,643,800
Construction	5,308[7]	342.4[7]	62.1	1,414,800

Production (metric tons except as noted). Agriculture, forestry, fishing (1994): sugarcane 41,106,000, corn (maize) 19,193,000, sorghum 3,869,000, wheat 3,589,000, oranges 2,570,000, bananas 1,700,000, dry beans 1,462,000, mangoes 1,090,000, lemons and limes 760,000, grapes 530,000, apples 522,000, soybeans 430,000, rice 375,000, barley 325,000, pineapples 280,000, cottonseed 154,000, strawberries 65,000, walnuts 23,000; livestock (number of live animals) 30,702,000 cattle, 18,000,000 pigs, 10,450,000 goats, 6,194,000 horses, 6,000,000 turkeys, 5,905,000 sheep, 3,220,000 mules, 3,200,000 asses, 293,000,000 chickens; roundwood (1993) 23,285,000 cu m; fish catch (1993) 1,200,686. Mining and quarrying (metal content of ores; 1994): iron ore 5,458,852; zinc 357,179; copper 303,648; lead 163,507; manganese 109,886; silver 2,314; gold 14.0; (nonmetals; 1994) salt 7,395,152[9]; gypsum 3,568,212; sulfur 873,240; dolomite 588,243; phosphate 541,776; fluorite 333,189. Manufacturing (gross value of production in Mex$'000[1]; 1993): machinery and equipment 74,121,214; food, beverages, and tobacco products 57,872,995; chemical products 44,689,596; metal products 21,770,185; mineral products 15,449,730; paper and paper products 8,673,629; textiles 8,467,903. Construction (gross value of new construction, in Mex$'000,000[1]; 1985): residential 154,835; nonresidential 168,096.

Trade and service enterprises (1993)	no. of establish-ments	no. of employees	yearly wage as a % of avg. of all wages[10]	annual income (Mex$'000,000[1])
Trade	1,208,779	2,969,786	...	565,728,373
Wholesale	68,919	631,802	...	249,597,035
Retail	1,139,860	2,337,984	...	316,131,338
Boutiques (excluding food products)	422,299	922,890	...	108,507,889
Food and tobacco speciality stores	671,050	991,911	...	65,305,180
Automobile, tire, and auto parts dealers	32,138	152,821	...	47,888,576
Small supermarkets and grocery stores	8,719	168,752	...	48,769,283
Gasoline stations	3,042	35,340	...	32,517,091
Other	2,612	66,270	...	13,143,319
Services	711,843	2,766,750	85.2	200,001,682
Professional services	130,475	652,148	77.9	53,533,318
Food and beverage services	677	11,258	...	1,012,369
Transp. and travel agencies	9,967	62,767	133.4	11,858,406
Lodging	9,913	151,445	...	8,960,922
Automotive repair	112,293	252,950	...	7,263,560
Educational services (private)	20,622	247,086	134.3	10,815,238
Medical and social assistance	79,748	203,348	206.4	7,497,794
Amusement services (cinemas and theatres)	4,855	65,608	148.9	9,845,129
Recreation	20,973	65,936	...	3,065,672
Other repair	72,129	104,478	...	2,625,370
Commercial and professional organizations	1,946	11,946	77.9	264,770
Other	248,245	937,780	49.9	83,259,134

Energy production (consumption): electricity (kW-hr; 1992) 131,501,000,000 (120,709,000,000); coal (metric tons; 1992) 6,539,000 (6,932,000); crude petroleum (barrels; 1992) 975,000,000 (968,000,000); petroleum products (metric tons; 1992) 74,844,000 (80,275,000); natural gas (cu m; 1992) 21,826,000,000 (24,109,000,000).

Population economically active (1993): total 33,651,812; activity rate of total population 38.9% (participation rates: ages 15–64, 61.4%; female 31.6%; unemployed 2.4%).

Price and earnings indexes (1990 = 100)	1988	1989	1990	1991	1992	1993	1994
Consumer price index	65.8	79.0	100.0	122.7	141.7	155.5	166.3
Monthly earnings index	57.3	76.6	100.0	129.1	292.9	164.7	174.6

Household income and expenditure. Average household size (1992) 4.8; income per household (1989) Mex$3,461[1] (U.S.$1,384); sources of income (1992): wages and salaries 61.5%, property and entrepreneurship 29.1%, transfer payments 7.8%, other 1.6%; expenditure (1992): food, beverages, and tobacco 36.9%, housing (includes household furnishings) 25.2%, transportation and communications 10.1%, clothing and footwear 8.5%, recreation and entertainment 5.5%, health and medical services 3.5%.

Financial aggregates[1, 11]	1989	1990	1991	1992	1993	1994	1995 (7 mo.)
Exchange rate, Mex$ per:							
U.S. dollar	2.462	2.813	3.018	3.095	3.116	3.375	6.191
£	4.036	5.020	5.114	5.464	4.680	5.164	9.791
SDR	3.471	4.190	4.393	4.284	4.266	7.774	9.495
International reserves (U.S.$)							
Total (excl. gold; '000,000)	6,329	9,863	17,726	18,942	25,110	6,278	14,234
SDRs ('000,000)	383	417	586	548	223	177	1,260
Reserve pos. in IMF ('000,000)	—	—	—	—	—	—	—
Foreign exchange	5,946	9,446	17,140	18,394	24,886	6,101	12,975
Gold ('000,000 fine troy oz)	1.03	0.92	0.92	0.69	0.48	0.43	0.52
% world reserves	0.11	0.10	0.10	0.07	0.05	0.05	0.06
Interest and prices							
Treasury bill rate	45.01	34.76	19.28	15.62	15.03	14.10	40.94
Balance of payments (U.S.$'000,000)							
Balance of visible trade, of which:	−405	−881	−7,279	−15,934	−13,481	−18,465	...
Imports, f.o.b.	−34,766	−41,592	−49,966	−62,130	−65,366	−79,347	...
Exports, f.o.b.	35,171	40,711	42,687	46,196	51,885	60,882	...
Balance of invisibles	−5,420	−8,332	−22,167	−40,376	−36,881	−47,249	...
Balance of payments, current account	−5,825	−7,451	−14,888	−24,442	−23,400	−28,784	...

Land use (1993): forested 25.5%; meadows and pastures 39.0%; agricultural and under permanent cultivation 13.0%; other 22.5%.

Foreign trade

Balance of trade (current prices)	1989	1990	1991	1992	1993	1994
Mex$'000,000,000	−863.8	−7,494.0	−27,746	−57,138	−53,615	−80,166
% of total	6.0%	4.7%	14.4%	25.1%	22.2%	25.6%

Imports (1993): U.S.$65,366,500,000 (manufactured products 94.2%; food and food products 4.2%; minerals and mineral products 0.6%). *Major import sources:* U.S. 68.9%; Japan 5.0%; Germany 4.2%; Brazil 1.8%; Canada 1.7%; Spain 1.7%; France 1.6%; Italy 1.2%.

Exports (1994): U.S.$60,882,000,000 (metallic products, machinery, and equipment 58.0%; crude petroleum 12.2%; metal and metal products 6.3%; processed food, beverages, and tobacco 3.3%). *Major export destinations* (1993): U.S. 83.1%; Canada 3.0%; Spain 1.7%; Japan 1.3%; France 0.8%; Germany 0.8%; Brazil 0.6%; Belgium-Luxembourg 0.5%; Argentina 0.5%.

Trade by commodity group (1993) SITC group	imports U.S.$'000,000	imports %	exports U.S.$'000,000	exports %
00 Food and live animals	3,865	5.9	3,345	6.5
01 Beverages and tobacco	307	0.5	443	0.8
02 Crude materials, excluding fuels	2,623	4.0	1,121	2.2
03 Mineral fuels, lubricants, and related materials	1,596	2.4	7,283	14.1
04 Animal and vegetable oils, fats, and waxes	422	0.6	—	—
05 Chemicals and related products, n.e.s.	5,594	8.6	2,309	4.5
06 Basic manufactures	10,791	16.6	5,534	10.7
07 Machinery and transport equipment	31,816	48.8	25,897	50.1
08 Miscellaneous manufactured articles	8,078	12.4	5,645	10.9
09 Goods not classified by kind	—	—	84	0.2
TOTAL[12]	65,186[13]	100.0[13]	51,644[13]	100.0

Direction of trade (1993)	imports U.S.$'000,000	imports %	exports U.S.$'000,000	exports %
Western Hemisphere	54,306	75.4	51,648	90.8
United States	50,840	70.6	45,778	80.4
Latin America and the Caribbean	2,751	3.8	2,744	4.8
Canada	715	1.0	3,126	5.6
Europe	8,881	12.3	2,957	5.2
EU	8,241	11.4	2,830	5.0
EFTA	438	0.6	74	0.1
Russia	68	0.1	6	—
Other Europe	134	0.2	47	0.1
Asia	7,778	10.8	1,963	3.4
Japan	4,192	5.8	1,218	2.1
Africa	158	0.2	56	0.1
Other	916	1.3	327	0.6
TOTAL	72,039	100.0	56,951	100.0[13]

Transport and communications

Transport. Railroads (1993): route length 12,747 mi, 20,515 km; passenger-mi 2,408,000,000, passenger-km 3,875,000,000; short ton-mi cargo 23,973,000,000, metric ton-km cargo 35,001,000,000. Roads (1994): total length 157,036 mi, 252,725 km (paved 36%[14]). Vehicles (1993): passenger cars 8,014,143; trucks and buses 3,758,034. Merchant marine (1992): vessels (100 gross tons and over) 635; total deadweight tonnage 1,495,311. Air transport (1993): passenger-mi 11,879,344,000, passenger-km 19,117,989,000; short ton-mi cargo 1,248,626,000, metric ton-km cargo 1,822,961,000; airports (1995) 83.

Communications. Daily newspapers (1992): total number 292; total circulation 11,256,000[15]; circulation per 1,000 population 142[15]. Radio (1994): 21,000,000 receivers (1 per 4.3 persons). Television (1992): 13,100,000 receivers (1 per 6.6 persons). Telephones (main lines; 1993): 7,620,900 (1 per 11 persons).

Education and health

Education (1993–94)	schools	teachers	students	student/ teacher ratio
Primary (age 6–12)	85,503	488,139	14,468,700	29.6
Secondary (age 12–18)	20,550	243,877	4,311,800	17.7
Voc., teacher tr.[16]	6,571	77,347	1,076,700	13.9
Higher	13,000	324,148	3,961,000	12.2

Literacy (1992): total population age 15 and over literate 45,050,633 (85.9%); males literate 22,181,999 (88.7%); females literate 22,868,634 (83.5%).

Health (1992): physicians (1993) 149,432 (1 per 885 persons); hospital beds 83,757 (1 per 1,367 persons); infant mortality rate per 1,000 live births 41.0.

Food (1992): daily per capita caloric intake 3,146 (vegetable products 83%, animal products 17%); 135% of FAO recommended minimum requirement.

Military

Total active duty personnel (1995): 175,000 (army 74.3%, navy 21.1%, air force 4.6%). *Military expenditure as percentage of GNP* (1993): 0.5% (world 3.3%); per capita expenditure U.S.$18.

[1]1 new peso = 1,000 (old) pesos; the (old) peso was withdrawn at the beginning of 1995. [2]Manufacturing only. [3]Through 1982, cannabis remained the most abused drug. [4]In constant 1980 prices. [5]Imputed bank service charge. [6]Includes 819,132 unemployed persons. [7]1988. [8]Metal products includes Nonelectrical machinery and transport equipment and Electrical machinery. [9]1992. [10]1984. [11]Exchange rates and treasury bill rates are expressed in period averages; international reserves are expressed in end-of-period rates. [12]Totals include adjustments of unspecified nature. [13]Detail does not add to total given because of rounding. [14]1993. [15]1986. [16]1992–93.

Micronesia, Federated States of

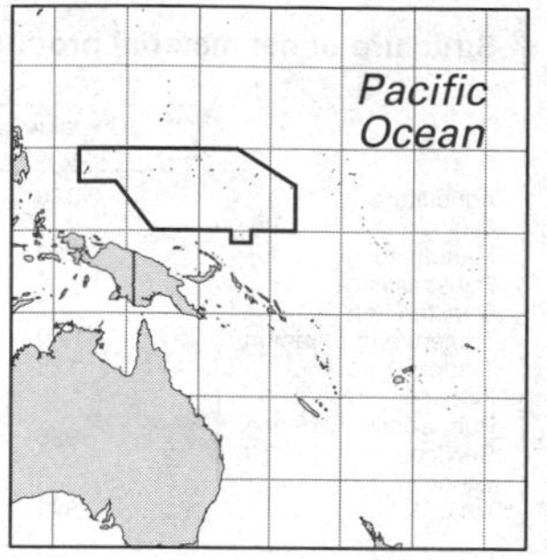

Official name: Federated States of Micronesia.
Political status: federal republic in free association with the United States with one legislative house (National Congress [14])[1].
Head of state and government: President.
Capital: Palikir, on Pohnpei.
Official language: none.
Official religion: none.
Monetary unit: 1 U.S. dollar (U.S.$) = 100 cents; valuation (Oct. 6, 1995) 1 £ = U.S.$1.59.

Area and population

States / Major Islands	area: sq mi	area: sq km	population: 1994 census
Chuuk (Truk)	49.1	127.2	52,870
Weno (Moen) Islands	7.0	18.1	15,253[2]
Kosrae	42.3	109.6	7,354
Kosrae Island	42.3	109.6	7,435[3]
Pohnpei	133.3	345.2	33,372
Pohnpei Island	129.0	334.1	33,372
Yap	45.9	118.9	11,128
Yap Island	38.7	100.2	6,650[4]
TOTAL	270.8[5]	701.4[5]	104,724

Demography

Population (1995): 105,000.
Density (1995): persons per sq mi 387.7, persons per sq km 149.7.
Urban-rural (1992): urban 26.0%; rural 74.0%.
Sex distribution (1994): male 51.09%; female 48.91%.
Age breakdown (1994): under 15, 42.7%; 15–29, 27.4%; 30–44, 17.1%; 45–59, 7.6%; 60 and over, 5.2%.
Population projection: (2000) 110,000; (2010) 120,000.
Doubling time: 24 years.
Ethnic composition (1980): Trukese 41.1%; Pohnpeian 25.9%; Mortlockese 8.3%; Kosraean 7.4%; Yapese 6.0%; Ulithian, or Woleaian, 4.0%; Pingelapese, or Mokilese, 1.2%; Western Trukese 1.0%; Palauan 0.4%; Filipino 0.2%; other 4.5%.
Religious affiliation: Christianity is the predominant religious tradition, with the Kosraeans, Pohnpeians, and Trukese being mostly Protestant and the Yapese mostly Roman Catholic.
Major cities (1989): Weno (Moen) 15,253; Tol 6,705[6]; Kolonia 6,169.

Vital statistics

Birth rate per 1,000 population (1992): 36.7 (world avg. 25.0); legitimate, n.a.; illegitimate, n.a.
Death rate per 1,000 population (1992): 7.8 (world avg. 9.3).
Natural increase rate per 1,000 population (1992): 28.9 (world avg. 15.7).
Total fertility rate (avg. births per childbearing woman; 1994): 5.1.
Marriage rate per 1,000 population: n.a.
Divorce rate per 1,000 population: n.a.
Life expectancy at birth (1991)[7]: male 70.6 years; female 77.3 years.
Major causes of death per 100,000 population (1991)[7]: diseases of the cerebrovascular system 89.6; diseases of the respiratory system 42.8, of which tuberculosis 8.9; malignant neoplasms (cancers) 38.8; homicide, suicide, and accidents 30.8; infectious and parasitic diseases 22.9 (with especially high morbidity rates for tuberculosis and leprosy).

National economy

Budget (1993–94). Revenue: U.S.$159,400,000 (external grants 65.2%; tax revenue 12.5%; fishing rights fees 12.5%). Expenditures: U.S.$168,700,000 (1990; current expenditures 79.4%, of which education 18.2%, health 11.8%, public works 10.2%, transportation 2.7%, public safety 2.6%; capital expenditure 20.6%).
Public debt (external, outstanding; 1994): U.S.$128,800,000.
Production (metric tons except as noted). Agriculture, forestry, fishing: n.a.; however, Micronesia's major crops include coconuts (which provide annually more than 4,000 tons of copra), breadfruit, cassava, sweet potatoes, peppers, and a variety of tropical fruits (including bananas); livestock comprises mostly pigs and poultry; fish catch (1993) 1,555, of which skipjack tuna 450. Mining and quarrying: quarrying of sand and aggregate for local construction only. Manufacturing: n.a.; however, copra and coconut oil, traditionally important products, are being displaced by garment production; the manufacture of handicrafts and personal items (clothing, mats, boats, etc.) by individuals is also important. Construction: n.a. Energy production (consumption): electricity (kW-hr; 1990) 40,000,000 (40,000,000); coal, none (n.a.); crude petroleum, none (n.a.); petroleum products (metric tons; 1992) none (77,000); natural gas, none (n.a.).
Household income and expenditure. Average household size (1988–89) 8.5; annual income per household (1989) U.S.$3,435; sources of income (1994): wages and salaries 51.8%, operating surplus 23.0%, social security 2.1%; expenditure (1985): food and beverages 73.5%.
Land use (1984)[8]: forested 22.5%; meadows and pastures 13.5%; agricultural and under permanent cultivation 33.5%; other 30.5%.

Gross national product (at current market prices; 1989): U.S.$157,400,000 (U.S.$1,595 per capita).

Structure of gross domestic product and labour force

	1983: in value U.S.$'000,000	1983: % of total value	1990: labour force	1990: % of labour force
Agriculture and fishing	44.9	42.2	12,700	41.6
Trade	12.7	11.9	[9]	[9]
Public administration	31.5	29.6	6,300	20.7
Manufacturing	} 17.4	} 16.3	1,600	5.2
Construction			1,900	6.2
Transportation, communications, and public utilities			...	...
Finance			...	...
Services			3,700[9]	12.1[9]
Other			4,400[10]	14.4[10]
TOTAL	106.5	100.0	30,500[5]	100.0[5]

Population economically active (1990): total 30,500; activity rate of total population 60.6% (participation rates: ages 15–64, 60.6%; female 46.9%; unemployed 13.5%).

Price and earnings indexes (1992 = 100)

	1989	1990	1991	1992	1993	1994
Price index	88.5	91.6	95.2	100.0	106.0	110.2
Annual wage index[11]	...	...	...	100.0	109.4	110.3

Tourism (1990): number of visitors 23,171.

Foreign trade

Balance of trade (current prices)

	1988	1989	1990	1991	1992	1993
U.S.$'000,000	−52.7	−55.4	−62.2	−59.9	−57.3	−80.3
% of total	63.7%	61.6%	58.9%	51.0%	40.8%	57.9%

Imports (1993): U.S.$109,486,000 (food, beverages, and tobacco 34.9%; manufactured goods 28.7%; machinery and transport equipment 20.2%; mineral fuels 10.2%; chemicals 3.9%). *Major import sources:* United States (including Guam) 65.3%; Japan 18.0%; Australia 2.9%.
Exports (1993): U.S.$29,169,000 (marine products 86.5%; clothing and textiles 7.4%; agricultural products 5.8%, of which bananas 2.6%, copra 1.8%). *Major export destinations* (1992): Japan 80.0%; United States 9.3%; Guam 8.3%; South Pacific Region 2.4%.

Transport and communications

Transport. Railroads: none. Roads (1990): total length 140 mi, 226 km (paved 17%). Vehicles: passenger cars, trucks, and buses, n.a. Merchant marine (1992): vessels (100 gross tons and over) 17; deadweight tonnage 6,863. Air transport: n.a.; airports (1995) with scheduled flights 6.
Communications. Daily newspapers: there are no private daily newspapers. Radio (1993): total number of receivers 70,000 (1 per 1.5 persons). Television (1993): total number of receivers 7,000 (1 per 15 persons). Telephones (main lines; 1993): 6,015 (1 per 17 persons).

Education and health

Education (1987–88)

	schools	teachers	students	student/teacher ratio
Elementary (age 6–12)	177	1,051[12]	25,139	22.2[12]
Secondary (age 13–18)	16	314[12]	5,305	13.2[12]
College[13]	1	...	[14]	...

Educational attainment (1980). Percentage of population age 25 and over having: no formal schooling 24.8%; some primary education 38.2%; primary 11.7%; some secondary 7.7%; secondary 9.6%; higher 8.0%. *Literacy* (1980): total population age 15 and over literate 30,074 (76.7%); males literate 13,710 (67.0%); females literate 16,364 (87.2%).
Health (1993): physicians 50 (1 per 2,069 persons); hospital beds 325 (1 per 318 persons); infant mortality rate per 1,000 live births (1994) 49.0.
Food: daily per capita caloric intake, n.a.

Military

External security is provided by the United States.

[1]On Nov. 3, 1986, the United States unilaterally terminated the UN trusteeship it held over the Federated States of Micronesia (FSM), thus formally initiating their free-association political status. On Dec. 22, 1990, the United Nations Security Council joined the Trusteeship Council, which had endorsed the termination of the trusteeship in May 1986. [2]1989. [3]1991. [4]1987. [5]Detail does not add to total given because of rounding. [6]1980. [7]Based on registered deaths only. [8]Includes all areas formerly constituting the U.S. Trust Territory of the Pacific Islands. [9]Services includes Trade. [10]Includes 4,100 unemployed. [11]Public sector only. [12]1983–84. [13]In 1985, 1,200 students were enrolled in colleges and universities in the United States. [14]In 1989, fewer than 300 students were enrolled in the College of Micronesia.

Moldova

Official name: Republica Moldova (Republic of Moldova).
Form of government: unitary multiparty republic with a single legislative body (Parliament [104]).
Head of state: President.
Head of government: Prime Minister.
Capital: Chişinău.
Official language: Romanian.
Official religion: none.
Monetary unit[1]: 1 Moldovan leu (plural lei) = 100 bani; valuation (Oct. 6, 1995) free rate, 1 U.S.$ = 4.55 Moldovan lei; 1 £ = 7.19 Moldovan lei.

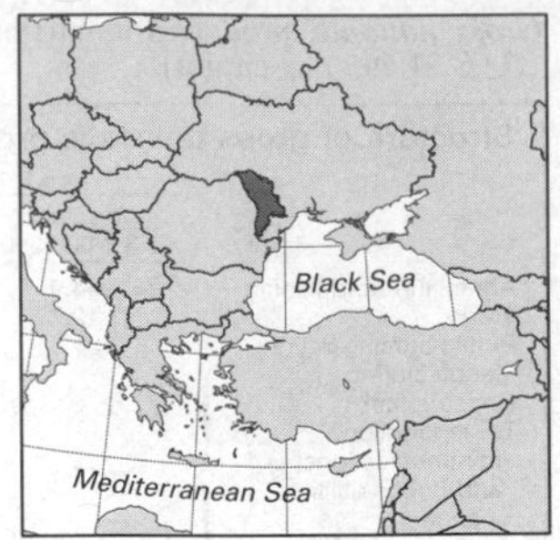

Area

Administrative subdivisions

Cities	area sq km[2]	Rural districts	area sq km[2]	Rural districts	area sq km[2]
Bălţi	...	Anenii Noi	830	Hânceşti (Kotovsk)	1,350
Cahul	...	Basarabeasca	660	Ialoveni	...
Chişinău	160	Brinceni	810	Leova	720
Dubăsari	...	Cahul	800	Nisporeni	760
Orhei	...	Cainari	...	Ocniţa	660
Râbniţa	...	Călăraş	760	Orhei	1,100
Soroca	...	Camenca	820	Râbniţa	850
Tighina (Bendery)	...	Cantemir	860	Rezina	670
Tiraspol	...	Căuşeni	1,120	Rişcani	1,000
Ungheni	...	Ciadâr-Lunga	720	Sângerei	...
		Cimişlia	1,170	Slobozia	960
		Comrat	840	Şoldăneşti	...
		Criuleni	850	Soroca	870
		Donduşeni	890	Ştefan-Vodă (Suvorovo)	1,030
		Drochia	780	Străşeni	760
		Dubăsari	670	Taraclia	...
		Edineţ	860	Teleneşti	860
		Făleşti	1,070	Ungheni	1,070
		Floreşti	830	Vulcăneşti	930
		Glodeni	760	TOTAL	33,700[3]
		Grigoriopol	820		

Demography

Population (1995): 4,350,000.
Density (1995): persons per sq mi 334.3, persons per sq km 129.1.
Urban-rural (1994): urban 46.8%; rural 53.2%.
Sex distribution (1992): male 47.08%; female 52.92%.
Age breakdown (1989): under 15, 27.9%; 15–29, 22.9%; 30–44, 21.0%; 45–59, 15.6%; 60–74, 9.7%; 75 and over, 2.9%.
Population projection: (2000) 4,329,000; (2010) 4,294,000.
Doubling time: not applicable; population is declining.
Ethnic composition (1989): Moldovan 64.5%; Ukrainian 13.8%; Russian 13.0%; Gagauz 3.5%; Jewish 2.0%; Bulgarian 1.5%; other 1.7%.
Religious affiliation: believers are predominantly Moldovan Orthodox.
Major cities (1991): Chişinău 753,500; Tiraspol 186,000; Bălţi 164,900; Tighina (Bendery) 141,500; Râbniţa 62,900.

Vital statistics

Birth rate per 1,000 population (1994): 14.3 (world avg. 25.0); (1992) legitimate 88.4%; illegitimate 11.6%.
Death rate per 1,000 population (1994): 11.9 (world avg. 9.3).
Natural increase rate per 1,000 population (1994): 2.4 (world avg. 15.7).
Total fertility rate (avg. births per childbearing woman; 1993): 2.5.
Marriage rate per 1,000 population (1993): 9.1.
Divorce rate per 1,000 population (1993): 3.3.
Life expectancy at birth (1993): male 67.9 years; female 71.5 years.
Major causes of death per 100,000 population (1993): diseases of the circulatory system 434.5; malignant neoplasms (cancers) 133.1; accidents and violence 105.7; diseases of the digestive system 91.6; diseases of the respiratory system 60.7; infectious and parasitic diseases 11.0.

National economy

Budget (1995). Revenue: 1,947,400,000 lei (enterprise profits tax 22.1%; value-added tax 19.5%; property tax 14.1%; income tax 7.7%; excise duties 5.1%). Expenditures: 2,247,400,000 lei (social welfare, health, and culture 44.3%, of which education 20.0%, health services 14.0%, social insurance 6.0%; capital construction 14.3%; domestic debt service 10.4%; national economy 4.6%; foreign debt service 3.6%).
Production (metric tons except as noted). Agriculture, forestry, fishing (1994): sugar beets 1,534,000, vegetables (except potatoes) 1,477,000, fruit (except grapes) 1,281,000, grain 782,000, grapes 672,000, wheat 640,000, potatoes 435,000; livestock (number of live animals) 1,373,000 sheep, 1,165,000 pigs, 916,000 cattle, 14,000,000 poultry; roundwood (1991) 125,000 cu m; fish catch (1993) 4,700. Mining and quarrying (1993): limestone 1,400,000; clay 350,000; gypsum 250,000. Manufacturing ('000 lei; 1994): food processing 2,173; machinery and metalworking 1,057; textiles 383; clothing 223; fuel and energy 126; wood products 125. Construction (1990): 490,900,000 lei. Energy production (consumption): electricity (kW-hr; 1993) 10,369,000,000 (9,605,000,000); coal (metric tons; 1993) none (2,140,000); crude petroleum (barrels; 1990) none (51,625,000); petroleum products (metric tons; 1993) none (1,774,000); natural gas (cu m; 1993) none (2,775,000,000).
Gross national product (at current market prices; 1993): U.S.$5,140,100,000 (U.S.$1,180 per capita)[4].

Structure of net material product and labour force

	1994 in value '000 lei	% of total value	labour force[5]	% of labour force[5]
Agriculture	2,358	47.7	557,000	42.1
Mining, Manufacturing, Public utilities	1,252	25.3	199,000	15.0
Construction	107	2.2	55,000	4.2
Transp. and commun.	60	1.2	66,000	5.0
Trade	178	3.6	70,000	5.3
Finance, Pub. admin., defense, Services, Other	986	20.0	377,000[6]	28.4[6]
TOTAL	4,941	100.0	1,324,000	100.0

Population economically active (1994): total 1,950,000; activity rate of total population 44.8% (participation rates: ages 16–59 [male], 16–54 [female] 85.2%; female [1989] 50.0%; unemployed 1.2%).
Land use (1993): forested 12.5%; meadows and pastures 12.5%; agricultural and under permanent cultivation 65.1%; other 9.9%.

Price and earnings indexes (1990 = 100)

	1990	1991	1992	1993	1994
Consumer price index	100.0	262.0	3,605	33,780	71,310
Earnings index	100.0	183.0	402.0	353.0	192.0

Household income and expenditure. Average household size (1989) 3.4; income per household (1990) 4,000 rubles; sources of income (1993): wages and salaries 59.8%, social benefits 20.3%, agricultural income 16.0%, other 3.9%; expenditure (1993): food 48.6%, consumer goods 24.7%, services 5.8%, taxes 4.8%, other 16.0%.

Foreign trade

Balance of trade (current prices)

	1987	1988	1989	1990	1991	1992
'000,000 rubles	−287.2	−1,023	−1,155	−284.7	−303.0	−30.2
% of total	2.6%	9.2%	9.6%	2.3%	1.8%	18.9%

Imports (1994): U.S.$745,000,000 (1992; petroleum products 36.1%, food products 14.0%, machinery 12.6%, light-industrial products 10.1%, chemical products 7.4%, wood products 4.2%). *Major import sources* (1993): Russia 32.9%; Ukraine 19.2%; Romania 12.7%; Azerbaijan 5.8%; Belarus 4.8%; Germany 4.4%.
Exports (1994): U.S.$617,000,000 (1992; food products 39.8%, machinery 27.2%, light-industrial products 11.6%, ferrous metals 7.5%, chemical products 3.9%). *Major export destinations* (1993): Russia 33.8%; Romania 23.6%; Ukraine 12.3%; Azerbaijan 6.1%; Bulgaria 3.7%; Belarus 3.4%.

Transport and communications

Transport. Railroads (1991): length 1,150 km; passenger-km 8,875,000,000; metric ton-km cargo 15,007,000,000. Roads (1991): total length 10,300 km (paved 94%). Vehicles (1992): passenger cars 221,883. Air transport (1990): passenger-km 2,352,000,000; metric ton-km cargo 19,000,000; airports (1995) with scheduled flights 1.
Communications. Daily newspapers (1992): total number 5; total circulation 205,000; circulation per 1,000 population 45. Radio (1991): 1,421,000 receivers (1 per 3.1 persons). Television (1991): 1,264,000 receivers (1 per 3.4 persons). Telephones (main lines; 1993): 523,900 (1 per 8.3 persons).

Education and health

Education (1994–95)

	schools	teachers	students	student/ teacher ratio
Primary (age 7–13), Secondary (age 14–17)	1,700	53,000[7]	731,000	13.7[7]
Voc., teacher tr.	64	...	41,800	...
Higher	18	...	49,400	...

Educational attainment (1989). Percentage of population age 15 and over having: no formal schooling or some primary education 24.5%; some secondary 20.4%; secondary or some postsecondary 46.4%; higher 8.7%. *Literacy* (1989): percentage of total population age 15 and over literate 96.4%; males literate 98.6%; females literate 94.4%.
Health (1994): physicians 18,000 (1 per 241 persons); hospital beds 53,000 (1 per 82 persons); infant mortality rate per 1,000 live births (1993) 22.3.

Military

Total active duty personnel (1995): 11,850 (army 89.0%, air force 11.0%). About 7,000 Russian troops remained in Moldova in late 1994. *Military expenditure as percentage of GNP* (1992): 0.8% (world 3.7%); per capita expenditure U.S.$10.

[1]On Sept. 22, 1993, the Moldovan coupon was introduced to permit replacement of the Russian ruble by new national currency, the leu. On Nov. 30, 1993, the leu was introduced at a 1,000-to-1 ratio with the Moldovan coupon and circulates parallel with it. [2]One sq km is equal to approximately 0.3861 sq mi. [3]Total includes 3,190 sq km (1,230 sq mi) not distributable by administrative subdivision. [4]Ruble-area GNP and exchange-rate data are very speculative. [5]Employed labour force only. [6]Includes film, media, forestry, and computer services. [7]1991–92.

Mongolia

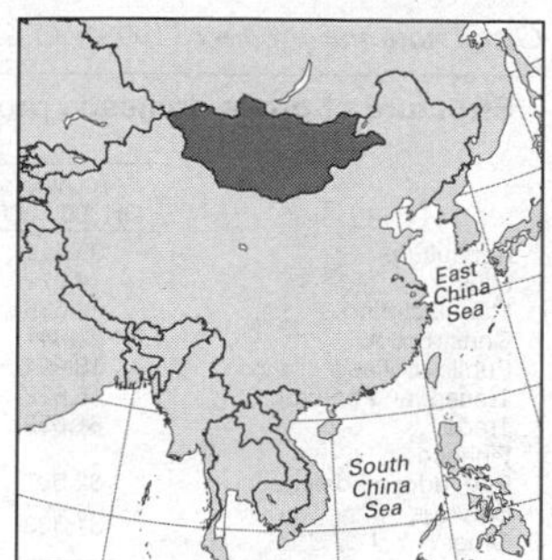

Official name: Mongol Uls (Mongolia).
Form of government: unitary multiparty republic with one legislative house (State Great Hural [76]).
Chief of state: President.
Head of government: Prime Minister.
Capital: Ulaanbaatar (Ulan Bator).
Official language: Khalkha Mongolian.
Official religion: none.
Monetary unit: 1 tugrik (Tug) = 100 möngö; valuation (Oct. 6, 1995) 1 U.S.$ = Tug 449.10; 1 £ = Tug 709.98.

Area and population

Provinces	Capitals	area sq mi	area sq km	population 1991 estimate
Arhangay	Tsetserleg	21,000	55,000	89,200
Bayan-Ölgiy	Ölgiy	18,000	46,000	99,300
Bayanhongor	Bayanhongor	45,000	116,000	78,700
Bulgan	Bulgan	19,000	49,000	56,700
Darhan-Uul	Darhan	100	200	88,600
Dornod	Choybalsan	47,700	123,500	82,600
Dornogovĭ	Saynshand	43,000	111,000	58,600
Dundgovĭ	Mandalgovi	30,000[1]	78,000[1]	51,900[1]
Dzavhan	Uliastay	32,000	82,000	93,600
Govĭ-Altay	Altay	55,000	142,000	65,100
Govĭ-Sümber	Choyr	[1]	[1]	[1]
Hentiy	Öndörhaan	32,000	82,000	76,700
Hovd	Hovd	29,000	76,000	81,100
Hövsgöl	Mörön	39,000	101,000	106,900
Ömnögovĭ	Dalandzadgad	64,000	165,000	43,500
Orhon	Erdenet	300	800	58,200
Övörhangay	Arvayheer	24,000	63,000	100,400
Selenge	Sühbaatar	16,000	42,000	92,000
Sühbaatar	Baruun-Urt	32,000	82,000	53,500
Töv	Dzüünmod	31,000	81,000	105,000
Uvs	Ulaangom	27,000	69,000	91,800
Autonomous municipality				
Ulaanbaatar	—	800	2,000	575,000
TOTAL		604,800[2]	1,566,500	2,149,300

Demography

Population (1995): 2,307,000.
Density (1995): persons per sq mi 3.8, persons per sq km 1.5.
Urban-rural (1994): urban 59.0%; rural 41.0%.
Sex distribution (1993): male 49.70%; female 50.30%.
Age breakdown (1989): under 15, 41.9%; 15–29, 29.2%; 30–44, 14.6%; 45–59, 8.5%; 60–69, 3.3%; 70 and over, 2.5%.
Population projection: (2000) 2,525,000; (2010) 3,025,000.
Doubling time: 44 years.
Ethnic composition (1989): Khalkha Mongol 78.8%; Kazakh 5.9%; Dörbed Mongol 2.7%; Bayad 1.9%; Buryat Mongol 1.7%; Dariganga Mongol 1.4%; other 7.6%.
Religious affiliation: although formal freedom of worship exists, all traditional forms of religious practice (lamaistic Buddhism, shamanism, Islam, and others) have been greatly reduced during the 20th century; reliable data on the current situation do not exist.
Major cities (1994): Ulaanbaatar (Ulan Bator) 680,000; Darhan 85,800; Erdenet 63,000; Choybalsan 46,000; Ölgiy (1991) 29,400.

Vital statistics

Birth rate per 1,000 population (1994): 24.0 (world avg. 25.0); legitimate, n.a.; illegitimate, n.a.
Death rate per 1,000 population (1992): 8.5 (world avg. 9.3).
Natural increase rate per 1,000 population (1994): 15.5 (world avg. 15.7).
Total fertility rate (avg. births per childbearing woman; 1993): 4.6.
Marriage rate per 1,000 population (1989): 7.8.
Divorce rate per 1,000 population (1989): 0.5.
Life expectancy at birth (1994): male 60.0 years; female 63.5 years.
Major causes of death per 100,000 population: n.a.; however, in the early 1990s, major causes of mortality included diseases of the cardiovascular system, diseases of the respiratory system, diseases of the cerebrovascular system, malignant neoplasms (cancers), and injuries, accidents, and poisoning.

National economy

Budget (1994). Revenue: Tug 73,430,000,000 (taxes 92.4%, of which customs duties 36.3%, income tax 31.1%, turnover tax 18.5%, other taxes 6.5%; nontax revenue 7.6%). Expenditures: Tug 128,635,000,000 (social and cultural services 50%, of which education 11.5%, social security 10.3%, health 7.6%; defense 5.3%; administration and other 15.3%).
Public debt (external; 1993): U.S.$10,391,000,000.
Tourism (1994): number of tourists 7,000.
Production (metric tons except as noted). Agriculture, forestry, fishing (1994): cereals 443,000 (of which wheat 417,000), potatoes 54,000, vegetables 22,800; livestock (number of live animals) 13,779,000 sheep, 7,239,100 goats, 3,003,700 cattle, 2,408,400 horses, 366,100 camels, 28,000 pigs; roundwood (1993) 865,000 cu m; fish catch (1993) 130. Mining and quarrying (1994): fluorspar 383,200; copper 343,300; molybdenum 4,396; gold 1,975 kg. Manufacturing (value added by manufacturing in Tug '000,000; 1994): food products 30,802.7; textiles 14,333.7; chemicals 6,900.0; leather and footwear 5,880.0; construction materials 3,381.0; wood products 1,962.0; clothing and apparel 1,432.0; printing and publishing 450.2; glass and ceramics 53.8. Construction (1994): residential 120,400 sq m; nonresidential, n.a. Energy production (consumption): electricity (kW-hr; 1993) 3,200,000,000 (3,260,000,000); coal (metric tons; 1993) 7,425,000 (6,925,000); crude petroleum, none (n.a.); petroleum products (metric tons; 1993) none (583,000).
Gross national product (1993): U.S.$984,800,000 (U.S.$400 per capita).

Structure of gross domestic product and labour force

	1993 in value Tug '000,000	1993 % of total value	1993 labour force	1993 % of labour force
Agriculture	1,293	14.7	299,500	35.5
Manufacturing and mining	2,168	27.4	124,100	14.7
Construction	180	2.1	33,000	3.9
Transp. and commun.	402	4.6	37,500	4.4
Trade	1,619	18.5	61,700	7.3
Services[3]	1,393	15.9	122,700	14.5
Other	1,719[4]	16.8[4]	166,200[5]	19.7[5]
TOTAL	8,774	100.0	844,700	100.0

Population economically active (1993): total 844,700; activity rate of total population 38.4% (participation rates: ages 15–64 [1985] 82.2%; female [1992] 46.0%; unemployed 8.5%).

Price and earnings indexes (1990 = 100)

	1988	1989	1990	1991	1992	1993	1994
Consumer price index	46.4	46.4	100.0	220.2	666.3	2,455	4,605
Monthly earnings index	98.2	96.7	100.0	184.0	260.1	943.1	...

Household income and expenditure. Average family size (1989) 4.8; income per household (1992)[6] Tug 5,500 (U.S.$140); sources of income (1993): wages and salaries 72.1%, transfer payments 9.7%, self-employment 9.5%[7], other 8.7%; expenditure (1991): food 48.6%, clothing 21.9%, housing 10.5%, transportation and communications 6.8%, household goods 4.1%, education and recreation 3.9%, healthcare 0.7%, other 3.5%.
Land use (1993): forested 8.8%; meadows and pastures 79.8%; agricultural and under permanent cultivation 0.9%; other 10.5%.

Foreign trade

Balance of trade (current prices)

	1989	1990	1991	1992	1993	1994
U.S.$'000,000	−963	−496	−101	−29	−21	+106
% of total	37.7%	35.8%	12.7%	3.9%	3.0%	19.5%

Imports (1994): U.S.$218,600,000 (petroleum products 29.0%; industrial technical products 23.4%; raw materials 19.4%; food products 15.5%; consumer products 12.6%). *Major import sources:* Russia 58.7%; China 9.8%; Japan 6.3%; Hong Kong 4.4%; South Korea 4.3%.
Exports (1994): U.S.$324,300,000 (mineral and metal products 48.6%, of which [1993] copper ore 42.4%, smaller quantities of molybdenum and fluorite ores; cashmere products 9.2%; raw materials 4.2%; food products 2.7%. *Major export destinations* (1994): Russia 27.7%; China 19.4%; Japan 13.1%; Kazakhstan 12.6%; Switzerland 6.4%.

Transport and communications

Transport. Railroads (1993): length (1994) 1,294 mi, 2,083 km; passenger-km 788,800,000; metric ton-km cargo 2,150,300. Roads (1988): total length 30,600 mi, 49,200 km (paved 2%). Vehicles (1994): passenger cars 20,663; trucks and buses 33,390. Merchant marine: vessels (100 gross tons and over) none. Air transport (1993): passenger-km 290,000,000; metric ton-km cargo 5,800,000; airports (1995) with scheduled flights 1.
Communications. Daily newspapers (1992): total number 3; total circulation 208,000; circulation per 1,000 population 90. Radio (1992): total number of receivers 275,000 (1 per 7.8 persons). Television (1992): total number of receivers 120,000 (1 per 18 persons). Telephones (main lines; 1993): 66,400 (1 per 36 persons).

Education and health

Education (1994–95)

	schools	teachers	students	student/teacher ratio
Primary and secondary (age 8–18)	659	19,097	381,204	20.0
Vocational	49	2,500[8]	29,900	19.0[8]
Higher	12	1,465[8]	13,800	9.4[8]

Educational attainment (1989). Percentage of population age 10 and over having: primary education 33.7%; some secondary 31.9%; complete secondary 16.9%; vocational secondary 9.4%; some higher and complete higher 8.1%.
Literacy (1988): percentage of total population age 15 and over literate 82.9%; males literate 88.6%; females literate 77.2%.
Health (1991): physicians 6,318 (1 per 340 persons); hospital beds 26,350 (1 per 83 persons); infant mortality rate per 1,000 live births (1994) 47.0.
Food (1992): daily per capita caloric intake 1,899 (vegetable products 56%, animal products 44%); 78% of FAO recommended minimum requirement.

Military

Total active duty personnel (1995): 21,100 (army 94.8%, air force 5.2%). *Military expenditure as percentage of GNP* (1993): 2.4% (world 3.3%); per capita expenditure (1993) U.S.$10.

[1]Dundgovĭ includes Govĭ-Sümber. [2]Detail does not add to total given because of rounding. [3]Services includes finance, public administration, and defense. [4]Other includes depreciation of fixed capital. [5]Includes 71,900 unemployed. [6]Urban households. [7]Includes income from agricultural cooperatives. [8]1990–91.

Morocco

Official name: al-Mamlakah al-Maghribīyah (Kingdom of Morocco).
Form of government: constitutional monarchy with one legislative house (House of Representatives [333]).
Chief of state: King.
Head of government: King assisted by Prime Minister.
Capital: Rabat.
Official language: Arabic.
Official religion: Islam.
Monetary unit: 1 Moroccan dirham (DH) = 100 Moroccan francs; valuation (Oct. 6, 1995) 1 U.S.$ = DH 8.45; 1 £ = DH 13.36.

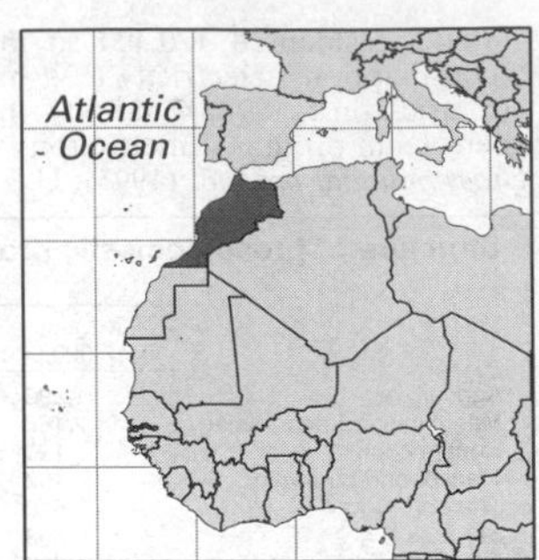

Area and population (1993 est.)

Provinces[1]	area sq km[2]	population	Provinces[1]	area sq km[2]	population
Agadir	5,910	831,000	Safi	7,285	862,000
Azilal	10,050	421,000	Settat	9,750	799,000
Ben Slimane	2,760	206,000	Sidi Kacem	4,060	610,000
Béni Mellal	7,075	966,000	Tan-Tan	17,295	56,000
Boulemane	14,395	158,000	Tangier	1,195	579,000
Chaouen			Taounate	5,585	609,000
(Chefchaouen)	4,350	369,000	Taroudannt	16,460	668,000
Essaouira	6,335	431,000	Tata	25,925	107,000
Fès	5,400	1,051,000	Taza	15,020	724,000
Figuig	55,990	108,000	Tétouan	6,025[3]	878,000[3]
Guelmim	28,750	171,000	Tiznit	6,960	387,000
al-Hoceima	3,550	377,000			
Ifrane	3,310	118,000	**Prefectures**		
el-Jadida	6,000	944,000	Ain Chok–		
el-Kelaa des Sraghna	10,070	694,000	Hay Hassani		470,000
Kénitra	4,745	940,000	Ain Sebaa–		
Khémisset	8,305	480,000	Hay Mohammadi		606,000
Khénifra	12,320	450,000	Ben Msik–	1,615	1,023,000
Khouribga	4,250	558,000	Sidi Othmane		
Larache	[3]	[3]	Casablanca-Anfa		1,081,000
Marrakech	14,755	1,549,000	Mohammadia-		
Meknès	3,995	765,000	Znata		226,000
Nador	6,130	817,000	Rabat		707,000
Ouarzazate	41,550	661,000	Salé	1,275	692,000
Oujda	20,700	992,000	Skhirate-Temara		209,000
er-Rachidia	59,585	511,000	TOTAL	458,730	25,861,000[4]

Demography

Population (1995): 26,980,000.
Density (1995): persons per sq mi 152.3, persons per sq km 58.8.
Urban-rural (1995): urban 48.4%; rural 51.6%.
Sex distribution (1995): male 50.04%; female 49.96%.
Age breakdown (1995): under 15, 36.1%; 15–29, 29.8%; 30–44, 18.9%; 45–59, 9.0%; 60–74, 5.0%; 75 and over, 1.2%.
Population projection: (2000) 29,992,000; (2010) 37,065,000.
Doubling time: 32 years.
Ethnic composition (1986): Arab 70%; Berber 30%; other, less than 1%.
Religious affiliation (1993): Muslim (mostly Sunnī) 98.7%; Christian 1.1%.
Major cities (1993): Casablanca 2,943,000; Rabat 1,220,000; Fès 564,000.

Vital statistics

Birth rate per 1,000 population (1995): 27.9 (world avg. 25.0).
Death rate per 1,000 population (1995): 6.0 (world avg. 9.3).
Natural increase rate per 1,000 population (1995): 21.9 (world avg. 15.7).
Total fertility rate (avg. births per childbearing woman; 1995): 3.7.
Life expectancy at birth (1995): male 67.0 years; female 71.0 years.
Major causes of death (1989)[5]: childhood diseases 22.9%; circulatory diseases 15.4%; accidents 7.3%; infectious and parasitic diseases 6.3%; neoplasms (cancers) 5.6%.

National economy

Budget. Revenue (1994): DH 89,790,000,000 (indirect taxes 26.4%; customs and stamp duties 18.0%). Expenditures (1994): DH 93,380,000,000 (current expenditure 50.4%, debt payments 29.1%, investment expenditure 20.4%).
Public debt (external, outstanding; 1993): U.S.$20,310,000,000.
Land use (1993): forested 20.1%; meadows 46.8%; agricultural 22.2%; built-on, wasteland, and other 10.9%.
Tourism: receipts from visitors (1994) U.S.$1,267,000,000; expenditures by nationals abroad (1993) U.S.$245,000,000.
Production (metric tons except as noted). Agriculture, forestry, fishing (1994): barley 3,720,000, wheat 3,523,000, sugar beets 3,144,000, oranges 955,000, sugarcane 925,000, tomatoes 900,000, potatoes 875,000, olives 560,000, dates 62,000; livestock (number of live animals) 15,594,000 sheep, 4,431,000 goats, 2,431,000 cattle, 91,000,000 chickens; roundwood (1993) 2,009,000 cu m; fish catch (1993) 607,000. Mining and quarrying (value of production in DH '000,000; 1993): phosphate rock 3,551.2; mineral water 217.1; zinc 166.4; copper 137.8; lead 127.4; manganese 75.5; fluorspar 47.2; barite 41.3; iron ore 3.1. Manufacturing (1994): cement 6,324,000; refined sugar 508,000; olive oil 56,000; wine 40,000; passenger automobiles and commercial vehicles 20,150 units[6]. Construction (value added in DH; 1991): 8,821,700. Energy production (consumption): electricity (kW-hr; 1992) 10,325,000,000 (11,257,000,000); coal (metric tons; 1992) 576,000 (1,791,000); crude petroleum (barrels; 1992) 83,600 (47,500,000); petroleum products (metric tons; 1992) 5,111,000 (5,907,000); natural gas (cu m; 1992) 23,987,000 (23,987,000).

Gross national product (1993): U.S.$27,645,000,000 (U.S.$1,030 per capita).

Structure of gross domestic product and labour force

	1993		1982	
	in value DH '000,000	% of total value	labour force	% of labour force
Agriculture	35,419	14.3	2,351,629	39.2
Mining	4,872	2.0	63,360	1.1
Manufacturing	44,636	18.0	930,615	15.5
Construction	11,641	4.7	437,464	7.3
Public utilities	18,994	7.7	22,465	0.4
Transp. and commun.	16,622	6.7	140,981	2.3
Trade	51,659	20.9	498,130	8.3
Finance	...	...		
Pub. admin., defense	32,507	13.1	532,803	8.9
Services	31,333	12.6	474,109	7.9
Other			547,704[7]	9.1[7]
TOTAL	247,683	100.0	5,999,260	100.0

Population economically active (1994): total 8,694,000; activity rate 32.8% (participation rates [1991][8]: over age 15, 49.7%; female 25.5%; unemployed [1993] 16.0%).

Price index (1990 = 100)

	1989	1990	1991	1992	1993	1994	1995[9]
Consumer price index	93.5	100.0	108.0	114.2	120.1	126.3	135.2
Earnings index[10]	79.2	100.0	...	...	...	...	...

Household income and expenditure. Average household size (1982) 5.8; expenditure (1993)[11]: food 45.2%, housing 12.5%, transportation 7.6%, clothing 7.5%.

Foreign trade[12]

Balance of trade (current prices)

	1989	1990	1991	1992	1993	1994
DH '000,000	−14,130	−16,755	−13,576	−23,192	−28,740	−23,353
% of total	20.0%	19.3%	15.4%	25.5%	31.1%	24.1%

Imports (1994): DH 66,119,000,000 (1993; capital goods 27.6%; food, beverages, and tobacco 14.5%, of which wheat 5.3%; consumer goods 10.9%; crude oil 10.8%). *Major import sources* (1993): France 23.0%; Spain 10.5%; U.S. 10.1%; Italy 6.3%; Germany 5.9%; U.K. 2.7%; Iran 2.5%.
Exports (1994): DH 36,815,000,000 (1993; consumer goods 28.8%, of which clothing 11.7%; food 26.1%, of which fresh, canned, and frozen fish 14.4%; minerals 10.2%, of which phosphates 7.0%). *Major export destinations* (1993): France 33.3%; Spain 8.8%; Japan 5.6%; Italy 5.2%; Germany 4.4%; India 3.9%; U.K. 3.6%.

Transport and communications

Transport. Railroads (1994): route length 1,768 km; passenger-km 1,884,000,000; metric ton-km cargo 4,740,000,000. Roads (1992): total length 59,474 km (paved 50%). Vehicles (1993): passenger cars 864,652; trucks and buses 316,941. Merchant marine (1992): vessels (100 gross tons and over) 492; total deadweight tonnage 586,221. Air transport (1994)[13]: passenger-km 4,573,009,000; metric ton-km cargo 49,253,000; airports (1995) 16.
Communications. Daily newspapers (1992): total number 14; total circulation 335,000[13]; circulation per 1,000 population 13[14]. Radio (1994): 5,100,000 receivers (1 per 5.2 persons). Television (1994): 1,210,000 receivers (1 per 21.9 persons). Telephones (main lines; 1993): 820,800 (1 per 32.6 persons).

Education and health

Education (1994–95)

	schools	teachers	students	student/ teacher ratio
Primary (age 7–12)	4,740	102,163	2,895,737	28.3
Secondary (age 13–17)	1,172	73,726	1,247,608	16.9
Vocational[15]	562[16]	2,951	17,585	6.0
Higher[17]	50	6,877	230,012	33.4

Educational attainment (1982). Percentage of population age 25 and over having: no formal education 47.8%; some primary education 47.8%; some secondary 3.8%; higher 0.6%. *Literacy* (1990): total population over age 15 literate 49.5%; males 61.3%; females literate 38.0%.
Health (1993): physicians 7,695 (1 per 3,361 persons); hospital beds 26,273 (1 per 984 persons); infant mortality rate (1995) 45.8.
Food (1992): daily per capita caloric intake 2,984 (vegetable products 93%, animal products 7%); 123% of FAO recommended minimum requirement.

Military

Total active duty personnel (1995): 195,500 (army 89.5%, navy 3.6%, air force 6.9%). *Military expenditure as percentage of GDP* (1994): 4.3% (world 2.6%); per capita expenditure U.S.$44.

[1]Provincial capitals have same name as province. [2]One sq km is approximately equal to 0.3861 sq mi. [3]Tétouan province includes Larache. [4]Detail does not add to total given because of rounding. [5]Registered deaths of urban population only. [6]1992. [7]Unemployed, not previously employed only. [8]Urban labour force only, representing the total urban employed and unemployed. [9]May. [10]Based on minimum hourly wage of workers 18 years of age and older; values reflect adjustments made to the minimum wage during the year. [11]Weights of consumer price index components. [12]Import figures are f.o.b. in balance of trade and c.i.f. for commodities and trading partners. [13]Royal Air Maroc only. [14]Partial data. [15]Excludes teacher training. [16]1991–92. [17]1992–93.

Mozambique

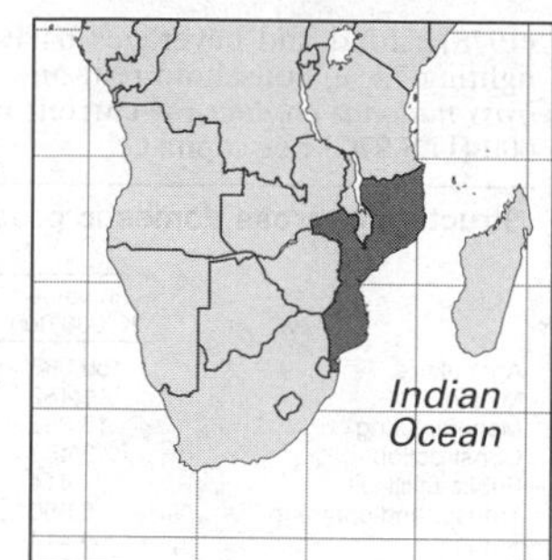

Official name: República de Moçambique (Republic of Mozambique).
Form of government: multiparty republic[1] with a single legislative house (Assembly of the Republic [250]).
Chief of state and head of government: President.
Capital: Maputo.
Official language: Portuguese.
Official religion: none.
Monetary unit: 1 metical (Mt; plural meticais) = 100 centavos; valuation (Oct. 6, 1995) 1 U.S.$ = Mt 9,974; 1 £ = Mt 15,768.

Area and population

		area		population
Provinces	**Capitals**	sq mi	sq km	1991 estimate
Cabo Delgado	Pemba	31,902	82,625	1,202,221
Gaza	Xai-Xai	29,231	75,709	1,401,485
Inhambane	Inhambane	26,492	68,615	1,156,958
Manica	Chimoio	23,807	61,661	609,512
Maputo	Maputo	9,944	25,756	840,757
Nampula	Nampula	31,508	81,606	2,841,416
Niassa	Lichinga	49,828	129,055	686,650
Sofala	Beira	26,262	68,018	1,427,493
Tete	Tete	38,890	100,724	734,561
Zambézia	Quelimane	40,544	105,008	2,619,281
City				
Maputo	—	232	602	931,591
TOTAL LAND AREA		308,642[2]	799,379	
INLAND WATER		5,019	13,000	
TOTAL		313,661	812,379	14,451,925[3]

Demography

Population (1995): 17,889,000.
Density (1995)[4]: persons per sq mi 58.3, persons per sq km 22.4.
Urban-rural (1991): urban 28.1%; rural 71.9%.
Sex distribution (1994): male 48.48%; female 51.52%
Age breakdown (1991): under 15, 46.0%; 15–29, 26.1%, 30–44, 15.3%; 45–59, 8.5%; 60–74, 3.5%; 75 and over, 0.6%.
Population projection: (2000) 20,868,000; (2010) 27,381,000.
Doubling time: 26 years.
Ethnolinguistic composition (1983): Makua 47.3%; Tsonga 23.3%; Malawi 12.0%; Shona 11.3%; Yao 3.8%; Swahili 0.8%, Makonde 0.6%; Portuguese 0.2%; other 0.7%.
Religious affiliation (1980): traditional beliefs 47.8%; Christian 38.9%, of which Roman Catholic 31.4%; Muslim 13.0%; other 0.3%.
Major cities (1991): Maputo 931,591; Beira 298,847; Nampula 250,473.

Vital statistics

Birth rate per 1,000 population (1995): 45.5 (world avg. 25.0).
Death rate per 1,000 population (1995): 18.3 (world avg. 9.3).
Natural increase rate per 1,000 population (1995): 27.2 (world avg. 15.7).
Total fertility rate (avg. births per childbearing woman; 1990–95): 6.5.
Marriage rate per 1,000 population (1974): 0.7.
Divorce rate per 1,000 population (1973): 0.01.
Life expectancy at birth (1990–95): male 44.9 years; female 48.0 years.
Major causes of death per 100,000 population: n.a.; however, major infectious diseases include cholera, malaria, diarrhea, acute respiratory infections, measles, tuberculosis, intestinal parasitoses and infestations, and AIDS.

National economy

Budget (1994). Revenue: Mt 1,525,700,000 (sales tax 48.4%, customs taxes 22.5%, individual income tax 17.9%). Expenditures: Mt 4,096,500,000 (defense and security 18.6%, goods and services 14.7%).
Production (metric tons except as noted). Agriculture, forestry, fishing (1994): cassava 3,294,000, corn (maize) 526,000, coconuts 425,000, sugarcane 230,000, sorghum 164,000, bananas 80,000, peanuts (groundnuts) 74,000; livestock (number of live animals) 1,250,000 cattle, 389,000 goats, 174,000 pigs, 119,000 sheep, 22,000,000 chickens; roundwood (1993) 16,013,000 cu m; fish catch 24,170. Mining and quarrying (1994): marine salt 40,000; bauxite 9,620; copper 133[5, 6]; garnet 3,000 kg; gemstones 6,865 carats. Manufacturing (valued in Mt '000,000; 1994): food processing 263,761.9; beverages and tobacco 137,676.4; textiles 121,243.2; chemical products 92,014.9; nonmetallic mineral products 67,592.8; clothing 48,832.1; machinery and transport equipment 38,956.5; iron and steel products 36,223.3. Construction (value in Mt; 1994) 157,700,000. Energy production (consumption): electricity (kW-hr; 1994) 340,000,000 (728,000,000); coal (metric tons; 1993) 40,000 (60,000); crude petroleum (1993) none (none[7]); petroleum products (metric tons; 1993) none[7] (265,000); natural gas, none (none).
Population economically active (1980): total 5,671,290; activity rate 48.6% (participation rates: over age 15, 87.3%; female 52.4%; unemployed 1.7%).

Price and earnings indexes (1990 = 100)

	1988	1989	1990	1991	1992	1993	1994
Consumer price index	48.5	68.0	100.0	132.9	193.4	275.0	419.2[8]
Monthly earnings index[9]	...	...	100.0	125.8	170.2	242.7	372.7

Public debt (external, outstanding; 1993): U.S.$4,650,000,000.
Household income and expenditure. Average family size (1992–93) 6.7[10]; income per household: n.a.; sources of income (1992–93)[10]: wages and salaries 51.6%, self-employment 12.5%, barter 11.5%, private farming 7.7%; expenditure (1992–93)[10]: food, beverages, and tobacco 74.6%, housing and energy 11.7%, transportation and communications 4.7%, clothing and footwear 3.7%, education and recreation 1.4%, health 0.8%.
Gross national product (at current market prices; 1993): U.S.$1,375,000,000 (U.S.$70 per capita).

Structure of gross domestic product and labour force

	1993		1980	
	in value Mt '000,000	% of total value	labour force	% of labour force
Agriculture	2,454,100	30.8	4,754,831	83.8
Mining	28,900	0.4	73,425	1.3
Manufacturing	642,900	8.1	273,369	4.8
Construction	848,600	10.6	42,121	0.7
Public utilities	162,900	2.0	11	11
Transportation and communications	1,157,200	14.5	77,025	1.4
Finance	...	...	...	...
Trade	826,700	10.4	112,244	2.0
Pub. admin., defense } Services }	1,844,000	23.2	243,449[11]	4.3[11]
Other	...	...	94,826[12]	1.7[12]
TOTAL	7,965,300	100.0	5,671,290	100.0

Tourism: n.a.
Land use (1993): forested 17.9%; meadows and pastures 56.1%; agricultural and under permanent cultivation 4.0%; other 22.0%.

Foreign trade[13]

Balance of trade (current prices)

	1989	1990	1991	1992	1993	1994
U.S.$'000,000	−670	−648	−737	−716	−823	−868
% of total	76.1%	71.8%	69.5%	72.0%	75.7%	71.4%

Imports (1994): U.S.$1,018,000,000 (1990; foodstuffs 28.9%, capital equipment 22.9%, crude petroleum and derivatives 10.9%, machinery and spare parts 9.5%). *Major import sources* (1994): South Africa 35.4%; U.K. 8.4%; France 7.7%; Japan 6.7%; U.S. 6.4%; Portugal 5.0%; Italy 3.0%.
Exports (1994): U.S.$149,500,000 (shrimp 42.3%, cotton 12.6%, petroleum 9.2%, sugar 7.4%, cashew nuts 2.2%). *Major export destinations:* Spain 22.4%; South Africa 14.8%; Japan 13.1%; Portugal 9.9%; United States 9.5%.

Transport and communications

Transport. Railroads (1994): route length 1,946 mi, 3,131 km; passenger-mi 78,900,000, passenger-km 127,000,000; short ton-mi cargo 447,900,000, metric ton-km cargo 654,000,000. Roads (1991): total length 16,955 mi, 27,287 km (paved 17%). Vehicles (1992): passenger cars 35,000; trucks and buses 35,000. Merchant marine (1992): vessels (100 gross tons and over) 107; total deadweight tonnage 31,645. Air transport (1994): passenger-mi 26,967,000, passenger-km 434,000,000; short ton-mi cargo 6,849,000, metric ton-km cargo 10,000,000; airports (1995) with scheduled flights 8.
Communications. Daily newspapers (1994): total number 2; total circulation 81,000; circulation per 1,000 population 4.7. Radio (1994): total number of receivers 620,000 (1 per 28 persons). Television (1994): total number of receivers 35,000 (1 per 496 persons). Telephones (main lines; 1993): 62,100 (1 per 263 persons).

Education and health

Education (1994)

	schools	teachers	students	student/ teacher ratio
Primary (age 5–9)[14]	3,765	22,544	1,301,833	57.7
Secondary (age 10–16)[15]	239	3,889	150,683	38.7
Voc., teacher tr.	31	826	13,816	16.7
Higher	3	877[16]	5,250[16]	6.0[16]

Educational attainment (1980). Percentage of population age 25 and over having: no formal schooling 80.7%; primary education 18.2%; secondary 0.9%; higher 0.2%. *Literacy* (1995): percentage of total population age 15 and over literate 40.1%; males literate 57.7%; females literate 23.3%.
Health (1993): physicians 114 (1 per 143,351 persons); hospital beds 13,280 (1 per 1,231 persons); infant mortality rate per 1,000 live births (1995) 127.7.
Food (1992): daily per capita caloric intake 1,680 (vegetable products 97%, animal products 3%); 72% of FAO recommended minimum requirement.

Military

Total active duty personnel (1995): n.a.[17]. *Military expenditure as percentage of GNP* (1993): 7.6% (world 3.3%); per capita expenditure U.S.$6.

[1]Mozambique adopted a new multiparty constitution that became effective on Nov. 30, 1990; the first multiparty elections took place on Oct. 27–29, 1994. [2]Detail does not add to total given because of rounding. [3]Excludes refugees in neighbouring countries estimated at about 1,200,000 in 1991; most of these refugees were repatriated between June 1993 and the fall of 1994. [4]Based on land area. [5]1990. [6]Metal content only. [7]Internal disorder and a lack of foreign exchange have brought importation of crude petroleum and the production of refined petroleum products practically to a halt. [8]Second quarter. [9]Agricultural workers only. [10]City of Maputo only. [11]Services includes Public utilities. [12]Unemployed. [13]Import figures are c.i.f. [14]Includes initiation classes in which pupils learn Portuguese. [15]Includes the two stages of secondary education and the upper-level primary stage. [16]1993. [17]Under the terms of the 1992 peace agreement, government and Renamo forces are to merge, forming a new army some 30,000 strong.

Myanmar (Burma)

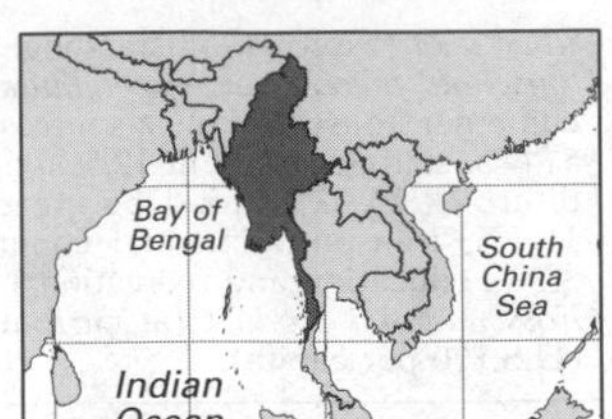

Official name: Pyidaungzu Myanma Naingngandaw (Union of Myanmar).
Form of government: military regime[1].
Head of state and government: Chairman of the State Law and Order Restoration Council.
Capital: Yangôn (Rangoon).
Official language: Burmese.
Official religion: none.
Monetary unit: 1 Myanmar kyat (K) = 100 pyas; valuation (Oct. 6, 1995) 1 U.S.$ = K 5.66; 1 £ = K 8.94.

Area and population

		area		population
				1983
Divisions	**Capitals**	sq mi	sq km	census
Irrawaddy (Ayeyarwady)	Bassein (Pathein)	13,567	35,138	4,994,061
Magwe (Magway)	Magwe (Magway)	17,305	44,820	3,243,166
Mandalay	Mandalay	14,295	37,024	4,577,762
Pegu (Bago)	Pegu (Bago)	15,214	39,404	3,799,791
Sagaing	Sagaing	36,535	94,625	3,862,172
Tenasserim (Tanintharyi)	Tavoy (Dawei)	16,735	43,343	917,247
Yangôn	Yangôn (Rangoon)	3,927	10,171	3,965,916
States				
Chin	Hakha	13,907	36,019	368,949
Kachin	Myitkyinā	34,379	89,041	904,794
Karen	Pa-an (Hpa-an)	11,731	30,383	1,055,359
Kayah	Loi-kaw	4,530	11,733	168,429
Mon	Moulmein (Mawlamyine)	4,748	12,297	1,680,157
Rakhine (Arakan)	Sittwe (Akyab)	14,200	36,778	2,045,559
Shan	Taunggyi	60,155	155,801	3,716,841
TOTAL		261,228	676,577	35,307,913[2]

Demography

Population (1995): 46,527,000.
Density (1995): persons per sq mi 178.1, persons per sq km 68.8.
Urban-rural (1995): urban 26.0%; rural 74.0%.
Sex distribution (1990): male 49.56%; female 50.44%.
Age breakdown (1990): under 15, 36.0%; 15–29, 29.7%; 30–44, 17.8%; 45–59, 10.1%; 60–74, 5.3%; 75 and over, 1.1%.
Population projection: (2000) 51,539,000; (2010) 61,596,000.
Doubling time: 33 years.
Ethnic composition (1983): Burman 69.0%; Shan 8.5%; Karen 6.2%; Rakhine 4.5%; Mon 2.4%; Chin 2.2%; Kachin 1.4%; other 5.8%.
Religious affiliation (1990): Buddhist 89.1%; Christian 4.9%; Muslim 3.8%; other 2.2%.
Major cities (1983): Yangôn (Rangoon) 2,513,023; Mandalay 532,949; Moulmein (Mawlamyine) 219,961; Pegu (Bago) 150,528; Bassein (Pathein) 144,096.

Vital statistics

Birth rate per 1,000 population (1995): 31.0 (world avg. 25.0).
Death rate per 1,000 population (1995): 10.0 (world avg. 9.3).
Natural increase rate per 1,000 population (1995): 21.0 (world avg. 15.7).
Total fertility rate (avg. births per childbearing woman; 1995): 4.0.
Marriage rate per 1,000 population: n.a.
Divorce rate per 1,000 population: n.a.
Life expectancy at birth (1995): male 57.0 years; female 61.0 years.
Major causes of death per 100,000 population (1987): infectious and parasitic diseases 29.5; respiratory diseases 14.8; circulatory diseases 10.0; malignant neoplasms (cancers) 7.9; malnutrition 2.2.

National economy

Budget (1992–93). Revenue: K 20,313,000,000 (revenue from taxes 61.8%, of which taxes on goods and services 31.8%, taxes on international trade 14.4%; nontax revenue 33.8%; capital revenue 4.4%). Expenditures: K 27,931,000,000 (defense 32.7%; education 17.0%; general public service 12.2%; transportation 10.3%; health 7.4%; agriculture 7.1%).
Public debt (external, outstanding; 1993): U.S.$5,135,000,000.
Tourism: receipts from visitors (1993) U.S.$19,000,000; expenditures by nationals abroad (1991) U.S.$1,000,000.
Production (metric tons except as noted). Agriculture, forestry, fishing (1994): rice 19,057,000, sugarcane 2,849,000, pulses 960,000, peanuts (groundnuts) 431,000, corn (maize) 271,000, plantains 265,000, sesame seeds 187,000, potatoes 173,000, onions 160,000, millet 156,000, tobacco leaves 52,000, seed cotton 43,000, jute 25,000; livestock (number of live animals) 9,691,000 cattle, 2,589,000 pigs, 2,130,000 buffalo, 1,417,000 sheep and goats, 4,000,000 ducks, 25,000,000 chickens; roundwood (1993) 22,544,000 cu m; fish catch (1993) 836,878. Mining and quarrying (1994–95): gypsum 28,916; copper concentrates 24,036; refined lead 1,267; tin concentrates 530; jade 258; refined silver 97,350 troy oz. Manufacturing (value of production in '000,000 kyats; 1987–88): food and beverages 23,549.8; clothing and wearing apparel 1,606.6; industrial raw materials 1,468.9; construction materials 1,120.9; transport vehicles 719.0; personal goods 327.8. Construction (units; 1987–88)[3]: residential 1,193; nonresidential 1,483. Energy production (consumption): electricity (kW-hr; 1993) 3,030,000,000 (3,030,000,000); coal (metric tons; 1993) 71,000 (74,000); crude petroleum (barrels; 1993) 5,100,000 (5,285,000); petroleum products (metric tons; 1993) 618,000 (619,000); natural gas (cu m; 1993) 973,000,000 (973,000,000).
Household income and expenditure. Average household size (1983) 5.2; average annual income per household: n.a.; sources of income: n.a.; expenditure (1978)[4]: food and beverages 64.4%, clothing and footwear 8.0%, fuel and lighting 7.8%, household rent and repairs 3.8%, tobacco 3.7%, other 12.3%.
Gross national product (at current market prices; 1992–93): U.S.$30,707,000,000 (U.S.$700 per capita).

Structure of gross domestic product and labour force

	1993–94			
	in value K '000,000	% of total value	labour force[5]	% of labour force[5]
Agriculture	150,068	60.5	11,347,000	68.9
Mining	1,462	0.6	83,000	0.5
Manufacturing	18,683	7.5	1,195,000	7.3
Construction	3,453	1.4	288,000	1.8
Public utilities	414	0.2	17,000	0.1
Transp. and commun.	5,080	2.1	412,000	2.5
Trade	55,414	22.3	1,407,000	8.5
Finance	375	0.2 }	1,238,000	7.5
Public admin., services	13,008	5.2 }		
Other	—	—	482,000	2.9
TOTAL	247,957	100.0	16,469,000	100.0

Population economically active (1990–91): total 15,737,000; activity rate of total population 37.2% (participation rates: ages 15–64 [1983] 64.2%; female [1987–88] 35.3%; unemployed [1987–88] 4.3%).

Price and earnings indexes (1990 = 100)

	1988	1989	1990	1991	1992	1993	1994
Consumer price index	66.8	85.0	100.0	132.3	161.3	212.6	263.8
Monthly earnings index[6]	78.3	107.2	100.0	92.8	129.4	...	...

Land use (1993): forested 49.3%; meadows and pastures 0.5%; agricultural and under permanent cultivation 15.3%; other 34.9%.

Foreign trade[7]

Balance of trade (current prices)

	1989	1990	1991	1992	1993	1994
K '000,000	+274.9	+485.0	−1,055.4	−338.1	−948.4	−195.8
% of total	10.6%	13.5%	16.7%	4.9%	11.6%	2.1%

Imports (1991–92): K 4,059,000,000 (machinery and transport equipment 42.4%; basic manufactures 15.3%; animal and vegetable oils 9.5%; chemicals 9.5%; food, beverages, and tobacco 5.0%). *Major import sources* (1992–93): Singapore 30.3%; China 26.5%; Japan 9.9%; Malaysia 9.2%; South Korea 3.2%; Hong Kong 1.5%.
Exports (1991–92): K 2,633,000,000 (inedible crude materials 47.3%; food, beverages, and tobacco 34.5%; basic manufactures 2.3%). *Major export destinations* (1992–93): China 18.7%; Singapore 14.0%; India 8.0%; Hong Kong 7.0%; Japan 6.8%; United States 5.9%.

Transport and communications

Transport. Railroads (1992–93): track length 2,945 mi, 4,740 km; passenger-mi 2,908,000,000, passenger-km 4,680,000,000; short ton-mi cargo 403,000,000, metric ton-km cargo 648,000,000. Roads (1992–93): total length 15,118 mi, 24,330 km (paved 16%). Vehicles (1993): passenger cars 36,000; trucks and buses 36,000. Merchant marine (1992): vessels (100 gross tons and over) 144; total deadweight tonnage 1,354,005. Air transport (1990–91): passenger-mi 137,700,000, passenger-km 221,600,000; short ton-mi cargo 5,649,000, metric ton-km cargo 8,248,000; airports (1995) with scheduled flights 19.
Communications. Daily newspapers (1993): total number 2; total circulation 414,000; circulation per 1,000 population 9. Radio (1994): total receivers 3,300,000 (1 per 14 persons). Television (1994): total receivers 1,000,000 (1 per 46 persons). Telephones (main lines; 1993): 80,000 (1 per 556 persons).

Education and health

Education (1992–93)

	schools	teachers	students	student/ teacher ratio
Primary (age 5–9)	36,499	198,909	6,518,800	32.8
Secondary (age 10–15)	2,920	67,503	1,633,700	24.2
Voc., teacher tr.	112	2,194	28,200	12.9
Higher	40	6,696	260,300	38.9

Educational attainment (1983). Percentage of population age 25 and over having: no formal schooling 55.8%; primary education 39.4%; secondary 4.6%; religious 0.1%; postsecondary 0.1%. *Literacy* (1983): total population age 15 and over literate 16,472,494 (78.5%); males literate 8,816,031 (85.8%); females literate 7,656,463 (71.6%).
Health (1992–93): physicians 13,353 (1 per 3,306 persons); hospital beds 27,830 (1 per 1,586 persons); infant mortality rate per 1,000 live births (1995) 78.
Food (1992): daily per capita caloric intake 2,598 (vegetable products 96%, animal products 4%); 120% of FAO recommended minimum requirement.

Military

Total active duty personnel (1995): 286,000 (army 92.7%, navy 4.2%, air force 3.1%). *Military expenditure as percentage of GNP* (1992): 3.8% (world 3.7%); per capita expenditure U.S.$37.

[1]The military government has refused to hand over power to the National League for Democracy, which won in the 1990 multiparty elections. [2]Includes 7,710 persons not distributed by area. [3]Construction Corporation activity only. [4]Based on 24 rural townships. [5]Employed only. [6]Wages in manufacturing. [7]Import figures are f.o.b. in balance of trade and c.i.f. in commodities and trading partners.

Namibia

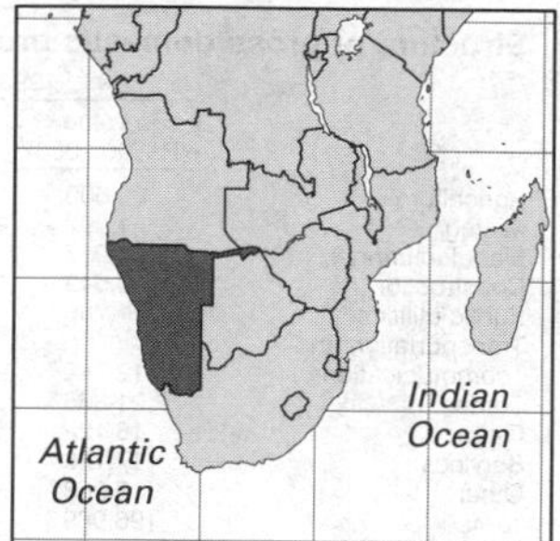

Official name: Republic of Namibia.
Form of government: republic with two legislative houses (National Assembly [72[1]]; National Council[2] [26]).
Head of state and government: President.
Capital: Windhoek.
Official language: English.
Official religion: none.
Monetary unit: 1 Namibian dollar (Nam$) = 100 cents; valuation (Oct. 6, 1995) 1 U.S.$ = Nam$3.66; 1 £ = Nam$5.79.

Area and population[3]

		area		population
Regions	Chief towns	sq mi	sq km	1992 estimate
Erongo[3]	Omaruru	24,602	63,719	98,500
Hardap	Mariental	42,428	109,888	80,000
Karas	Keetmanshoop	62,288	161,324	73,000
Khomas	Windhoek	14,210	36,804	161,000
Kunene	Opuwo	55,697	144,254	58,500
Liambezi	Katima Mulilo	7,541	19,532	92,000
Ohangwena	Oshikango	4,086	10,582	178,000
Okavango	Rundu	16,763	43,417	136,000
Omaheke	Gobabis	32,715	84,731	55,600
Omusati	Ongandjera	5,265	13,637	158,000
Oshana	Oshakati	2,042	5,290	159,000
Oshikoto	Tsumeb	10,273	26,607	176,000
Otjozondjupa	Grootfontein	40,667	105,327	85,000
Other		2	6	1,000
TOTAL		318,580[4]	825,118	1,511,600

Demography

Population (1995): 1,651,000.
Density (1995): persons per sq mi 5.2, persons per sq km 2.0.
Urban-rural (1993): urban 35.2%; rural 64.8%.
Sex distribution (1991): male 49.78%; female 50.22%.
Age breakdown (1990): under 15, 45.7%; 15–29, 25.5%; 30–44, 15.0%; 45–59, 8.6%; 60–74, 4.3%; 75 and over, 0.9%.
Population projection: (2000) 1,957,000; (2010) 2,705,000.
Doubling time: 23 years.
Ethnic composition (1991): Ovambo 47.4%; Kavango 8.8%; Herero 7.1%; Damara 7.1%; white 6.1%; Nama 4.6%; other 18.9%.
Religious affiliation (1981): Lutheran 51.2%; Roman Catholic 19.8%; Dutch Reformed 6.1%; Anglican 5.0%; other 17.9%.
Major cities (1990): Windhoek 125,000; Swakopmund 15,500; Rundu 15,000; Rehoboth 15,000; Keetmanshoop 14,000.

Vital statistics

Birth rate per 1,000 population (1990–95): 41.6 (world avg. 25.0).
Death rate per 1,000 population (1990–95): 10.6 (world avg. 9.3).
Natural increase rate per 1,000 population (1990–95): 31.0 (world avg. 15.7).
Total fertility rate (avg. births per childbearing woman; 1990–95): 5.7.
Life expectancy at birth (1990–95): male 57.5 years; female 60.0 years.
Major causes of death per 100,000 population: n.a., however, tuberculosis has, in the early 1990s, become a serious problem (especially in the southern regions); AIDS cases, while few, are increasing exponentially.

National economy

Budget (1994–95). Revenue: R 3,366,600,000 (customs and excise taxes 26.8%, individual income taxes 16.6%, general sales tax 14.0%, nontax revenues 11.6%, mining taxes 5.2%). Expenditures: R 3,923,000,000 (1993–94; education 23.5%, transportation 18.4%, health and welfare 13.1%, national defense 5.3%, agriculture 5.0%).
Tourism (1992): receipts from visitors U.S.$91,000,000; expenditures by nationals abroad U.S.$81,000,000.
Public debt (external, outstanding; 1993): U.S.$3,180,000.
Production (metric tons except as noted). Agriculture, forestry, fishing (1994): roots and tubers 253,000, cereals 120,000 (of which millet 59,000, corn [maize] 45,000, sorghum 10,000), fruits 10,000, vegetables and melons 8,000, pulses 7,000, wool 3,026, karakul pelts 770,627 units[5]; livestock (number of live animals) 2,620,000 sheep, 2,036,000 cattle, 1,639,000 goats; fish catch (1993) 329,790. Mining and quarrying (1994): diamonds 1,312,000 carats (mostly gem quality); zinc 64,600; copper 29,800; lead 23,800; uranium 2,242; silver 1,993,300 troy oz; gold 78,607 troy oz. Manufacturing (1991): n.a.; products include cut gems (primarily diamonds), fur products (karakul), processed foods (fish, meats, and dairy products), textiles, carved wood products, refined metals (copper and lead). Construction (value of buildings completed in R '000,000; 1990): residential 44.6; nonresidential 92.4. Energy production (consumption): electricity (kW-hr; 1992) 1,714,000,000 (1,714,000,000); coal, none (n.a.); crude petroleum, none (n.a.).
Population economically active: total (1991) 493,580; activity rate of total population, 34.9% (participation rates: ages 15–64, 61.3%; female 43.5%; unemployed 20.1%).

Price and earnings indexes (1990 = 100)

	1988	1989	1990	1991	1992	1993	1994
Consumer price index	77.5	89.3	100.0	111.9	131.7	143.0	158.4
Earnings index	...	...	...	...	...	...	...

Household income and expenditure. Average household size (1981) 4.8; average annual income per household (1980) R 3,223 (U.S.$4,143); sources of income (1992): wages and salaries 69.0%, income from property 25.6%, transfer payments 5.4%; expenditure: n.a.
Gross national product (1993): U.S.$2,598,000,000 (U.S.$1,660 per capita).

Structure of gross domestic product and labour force

	1994		1991	
	in value R '000,000	% of total value	labour force[6]	% of labour force
Agriculture	1,284.9	14.3	189,929	38.5
Mining	1,426.4	15.9	14,686	3.0
Manufacturing	832.5	9.3	22,884	4.6
Construction	243.8	2.7	18,638	3.8
Public utilities	121.6	1.4	2,974	0.6
Transportation and communications	412.1	4.6	9,322	1.9
Trade[7]	902.1	10.1	37,820	7.7
Finance	1,046.9	11.7	8,547	1.7
Services	111.7	1.2	89,541[8]	18.1[8]
Public administration and defense	2,336.1	26.1		
Other	239.4	2.7	99,239	20.1
TOTAL	8,957.5	100.0	493,580	100.0

Land use (1993): forested 21.9%; meadows and pastures 46.2%; agricultural and under permanent cultivation 0.8%; other 31.1%.

Foreign trade

Balance of trade (current prices)

	1989	1990	1991	1992	1993	1994
U.S.$'000,000	...	−28	+102	+79	+122	+165
% of total	...	0.8%	4.3%	3.0%	5.0%	6.6%

Imports (1994): U.S.$1,157,100,000 (1988; chemical and petroleum products 21.5%; food and agricultural products 17.1%; machinery and transport equipment 6.6%; other 46.2%). *Major import source* (1991): South Africa 75–100%.
Exports (1994): U.S.$1,322,200,000 (minerals 50.2%, of which diamonds 31.4%; agricultural products 36.1%, of which cattle 11.0%, karakul pelts 0.2%). *Major export destinations* (1986): United States 25%; South Africa 19%; Japan 15%.

Transport and communications

Transport. Railroads: length (1993) 1,480 mi, 2,382 km; passenger-km 2,008,000,000[9]; metric ton-km 1,097,300. Roads (1994): total length 26,467 mi, 42,594 km (paved 12%). Vehicles (1994): passenger cars 61,269; trucks and buses 60,041. Merchant marine (1992): vessels (100 gross tons and over) 30; total deadweight tonnage 5,874. Air transport (1994)[10]: passenger-km 750,946,000; metric ton-km cargo 25,430,000; airports (1995) with scheduled flights 12.
Communications. Daily newspapers (1994): total number 6; total circulation 43,300; circulation per 1,000 population 54. Radio (1993): 240,000 receivers (1 per 6.4 persons). Television (1993): 39,500 receivers (1 per 39 persons). Telephones (main lines; 1993): 69,800 (1 per 22 persons).

Education and health

Education (1990)

	schools	teachers	students	student/ teacher ratio
Primary (age 6–12)	933	10,912[9]	352,100	32.0[9]
Secondary (age 13–19)	97	2,534[11]	92,136	29.3[11]
Voc., teacher tr.	17	140[12]	1,503	11.9[12]
Higher	7	213[13]	6,523	11.8[13]

Educational attainment (1991). Percentage of population age 25 and over having: no formal schooling 61.8%; primary education 18.8%; secondary 16.6%; higher 1.6%; unknown 1.2%. *Literacy* (1991): total population age 15 and over literate 622,200 (75.8%); males literate 305,800 (77.8%); females literate 316,400 (74.0%).
Health: physicians (1992) 324 (1 per 4,594 persons); hospital beds (1989) 6,997 (1 per 216 persons); infant mortality rate per 1,000 live births (1993) 63.8.
Food (1992): daily per capita caloric intake 2,134 (vegetable products 87%, animal products 13%); 94% of FAO recommended minimum requirement.

Military

Total active duty personnel (1995): 8,100 (army 98.8%, navy 1.2%). *Military expenditure as percentage of GNP* (1993): 2.3% (world 3.3%); per capita expenditure U.S.$37.

[1]72 elected and up to 6 appointed members. [2]Mostly an advisory body. [3]Includes the 434 sq mi (1,124 sq km) district of Walvis Bay (1992 pop. estimate, 23,000) that was jointly administered with South Africa from November 1992 to March 1994. [4]Detail does not add to total given because of rounding. [5]1987. [6]Includes more than 140,000 nonwage (informal) workers. [7]Includes hotels. [8]Unemployed. [9]1992. [10]Namib Air only. [11]1990. [12]1989. [13]1991.

Nepal

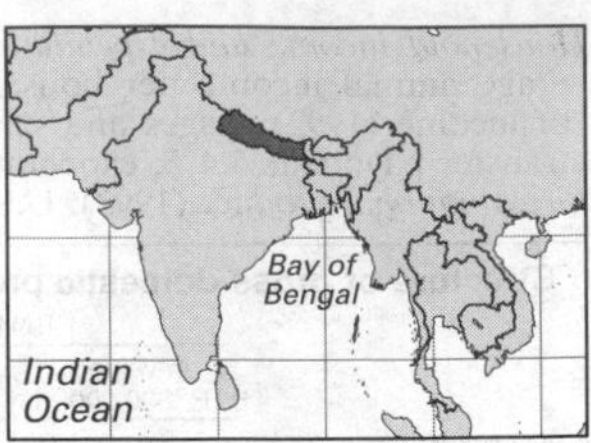

Official name: Nepāl Adhirājya (Kingdom of Nepal).
Form of government: constitutional monarchy with two legislative houses (National Council [60[1]]; House of Representatives [205]).
Chief of state: King.
Head of government: Prime Minister.
Capital: Kāthmāndu.
Official language: Nepālī.
Official religion: Hinduism.
Monetary unit: 1 Nepalese rupee (NRs) = 100 paisa (pice); valuation (Oct. 6, 1995) 1 U.S.$ = NRs 50.39; 1 £ = NRs 79.67.

Area and population

Development regions / Zones	Capitals	area sq mi	area sq km	population 1991 census
Eastern	Dhankūtā	10,987	28,456	4,446,749
Koshī		3,733	9,669	1,728,247
Mechī		3,165	8,196	1,118,210
Sāgarmāthā		4,089	10,591	1,600,292
Central	Kāthmāndu	10,583	27,410	6,183,955
Bāgmatī		3,640	9,428	2,250,805
Janakpur		3,733	9,669	2,061,816
Nārāyanī		3,210	8,313	1,871,334
Western	Pokharā	11,351	29,398	3,770,678
Dhawalāgiri		3,146	8,148	490,877
Gandakī		4,740	12,275	1,266,128
Lumbinī		3,465	8,975	2,013,673
Mid-western	Surkhet	16,362	42,378	2,410,414
Bherī		4,071	10,545	1,103,043
Karnālī		8,244	21,351	260,529
Rāptī		4,047	10,482	1,046,842
Far-western	Dipāyal	7,544	19,539	1,679,301
Mahākālī		2,698	6,989	664,952
Setī		4,846	12,550	1,014,349
TOTAL		56,827	147,181	18,491,097

Demography

Population (1995): 20,093,000.
Density (1994): persons per sq mi 353.6, persons per sq km 136.5.
Urban-rural (1991): urban 9.6%; rural 90.4%.
Sex distribution (1991): male 51.63%; female 48.37%.
Age breakdown (1991): under 15, 42.3%; 15–29, 25.7%; 30–44, 16.7%; 45–59, 9.7%; 60–74, 4.7%; 75 and over, 0.9%.
Population projection: (2000) 22,292,000; (2010) 27,439,000.
Doubling time: 29 years.
Ethnic composition (1991): Nepalese 53.2%; Bihārī (including Maithilī and Bhojpurī) 18.4%; Tharu 4.8%; Tamang 4.7%; Newār 3.4%; Magar 2.2%; Abadhi 1.7%; other 11.6%.
Religious affiliation (1991): Hindu 86.2%; Buddhist 7.8%; Muslim 3.8%; Christian 0.2%; Jain 0.1%; other 1.9%.
Major cities (municipalities; 1991): Kāthmāndu 419,073; Birātnagar 130,129; Lalitpur 117,203; Pokharā 95,311; Birganj 68,764.

Vital statistics

Birth rate per 1,000 population (1994): 37.6 (world avg. 25.0).
Death rate per 1,000 population (1994): 13.3 (world avg. 9.3).
Natural increase rate per 1,000 population (1994): 24.3 (world avg. 15.7).
Total fertility rate (avg. births per childbearing woman; 1994): 5.2.
Marriage rate per 1,000 population: n.a.
Divorce rate per 1,000 population: n.a.
Life expectancy at birth (1994): male 52.4 years; female 52.7 years.
Major causes of death per 100,000 population: n.a.; however, the leading causes of mortality are infectious and parasitic diseases, diseases of the respiratory system, diseases of the nervous system, diseases of the circulatory system, and injuries and poisoning.

National economy

Budget (1993–94). Revenue: NRs 22,412,900,000 (internal revenue 80.7%, foreign grants 19.3%). Expenditures: NRs 35,514,000,000 (development 63.7%, regular 36.3%).
Public debt (external, outstanding; 1993): U.S.$1,938,000,000.
Tourism (1992): receipts from visitors U.S.$110,000,000; expenditures by nationals abroad U.S.$52,000,000.
Production (metric tons except as noted). Agriculture, forestry, fishing (1993): rice 3,100,000, sugarcane 1,366,000, corn (maize) 1,200,000, wheat 765,000, potatoes 733,000, millet 232,000, pulses 206,000, barley 28,000, jute 12,000, tobacco 6,000; livestock (number of live animals) 6,237,000 cattle, 5,452,000 goats, 3,073,000 buffalo, 911,000 sheep, 630,000 pigs; roundwood (1992) 19,591,000 cu m; fish catch (1992) 16,516. Mining and quarrying (1993): limestone 350,000; magnesite 45,000; talc 7,000; garnet 25,000 kg. Manufacturing (value added in NRs '000; 1990–91): cigarettes 1,129,465; carpets and rugs 880,026; wearing apparel 694,640; woven textiles 587,484; structural clay products 498,940. Construction: n.a. Energy production (consumption): electricity (kW-hr; 1992) 931,000,000 (926,000,000); coal (metric tons; 1992) none (92,000); petroleum products (metric tons; 1992) none (298,000); natural gas, none (none).
Gross national product (at current market prices; 1993): U.S.$3,174,000,000 (U.S.$160 per capita).

Structure of gross domestic product and labour force

	1993–94 in value NRs '000,000[2]	1993–94 % of total value	1991 labour force	1991 % of labour force
Agriculture	80,500	40.9	5,961,788	81.2
Mining	1,092	0.6	2,367	—
Manufacturing	17,227	8.7	150,051	2.0
Construction	20,543	10.4	35,658	0.5
Public utilities	1,786	0.9	11,734	0.2
Transportation and communications	12,742	6.5	50,808	0.7
Trade	21,866	11.1	256,012	3.5
Finance	18,122	9.2	20,847	0.3
Services	17,128	8.7	752,019	10.3
Other	5,963[3]	3.0[3]	98,302	1.3
TOTAL	196,969	100.0	7,339,586	100.0

Land use (1992): forested 39.1%; meadows and pastures 14.6%; agricultural and under permanent cultivation 17.2%; other 29.1%.
Population economically active (1991): total 7,339,586; activity rate of total population 39.7% (participation rates: ages 10 years and over, 56.6%; female 40.4%; unemployed [1980] 5.5%).

Price and earnings indexes (1990 = 100)

	1987	1988	1989	1990	1991	1992	1993
Consumer price index	77.9	84.9	92.4	100.0	115.6	135.4	145.5
Earnings index	...	...	...	...	...	...	...

Household income and expenditure (1984–85). Average household size (1991) 5.6; income per household NRs 14,796 (U.S.$853); sources of income: self-employment 63.4%, wages and salaries 25.1%, rent 7.5%, other 4.0%; expenditure: food and beverages 61.2%, housing 17.3%, clothing 11.7%, health care 3.7%, education and recreation 2.9%, transportation and communications 1.2%, other 2.0%.

Foreign trade[4]

Balance of trade (current prices)

	1988	1989	1990	1991	1992	1993
NRs '000,000	−10,780	−10,796	−13,037	−17,059	−16,255	−21,781
% of total	54.6%	56.2%	51.4%	46.5%	33.7%	36.5%

Imports (1992–93): NRs 36,978,500,000 (basic manufactured goods 29.2%; machinery and transport equipment 19.5%; chemicals 12.3%; mineral fuels and lubricants 10.5%; food and live animals, chiefly for food 9.3%; crude materials except fuels 8.5%[5]). *Major import sources* (1991–92): India 40.5%; Singapore 31.8%; Japan 15.6%; West Germany 4.3%; China 3.8%; South Korea 3.7%.
Exports (1992–93): NRs 17,307,400,000 (basic manufactures 59.3%; food and live animals, chiefly for food 11.4%; crude materials except fuels 2.8%; animal and vegetable oils 0.9%). *Major export destinations* (1991–92): West Germany 49.0%; United States 25.9%; India 22.1%; Belgium 2.2%.

Transport and communications

Transport. Railroads (1992–93): route length 33 mi, 53 km; passengers carried 754,000; freight handled 10,000 metric tons. Roads (1993): total length 5,884 mi, 9,470 km (paved 36%). Vehicles (1990–91): passenger cars 4,949; trucks and buses 3,363. Merchant marine: none. Air transport (1991): passenger-mi 439,000,000, passenger-km 706,000,000; short ton-mi cargo 7,500,000, metric ton-km cargo 11,000,000; airports (1995) with scheduled flights 24.
Communications. Daily newspapers (1992): total number 25; total circulation 140,000; circulation per 1,000 population 7.4. Radio (1994): 625,000 receivers (1 per 31 persons). Television (1994): 250,000 receivers (1 per 78 persons). Telephones (main lines; 1993): 72,000 (1 per 286 persons).

Education and health

Education (1992)

	schools	teachers	students	student/ teacher ratio
Primary (age 6–10)	19,498	77,948	3,034,710	38.9
Secondary (age 11–15) / Vocational	6,539	25,357	855,137	33.7
Higher	3	4,925[5]	103,840	22.4[5]

Educational attainment (1981). Percentage of population age 25 and over having: no formal schooling 41.2%; primary education 29.4%; secondary 22.7%; higher 6.8%. *Literacy* (1991): total population age 15 and over literate 4,255,000 (37.7%); males literate 2,975,000 (51.7%); females literate 1,280,000 (23.3%).
Health (1991–92): physicians 1,497 (1 per 12,623 persons); hospital beds 4,848 (1 per 3,898 persons); infant mortality rate per 1,000 live births (1994) 84.
Food (1988–90): daily per capita caloric intake 2,205 (vegetable products 94%, animal products 6%); 100% of FAO recommended minimum requirement.

Military

Total active duty personnel (1994): 35,000 (army 99.4%, air force 0.6%). *Military expenditure as percentage of GNP* (1993): 1.4% (world 3.3%); per capita expenditure U.S.$2.

[1]Includes 10 members nominated by the king. [2]Tentative estimate. [3]Includes indirect taxes. [4]Import figures are f.o.b. in balance of trade and c.i.f. for commodities and trading partners. [5]1991.

Netherlands, The

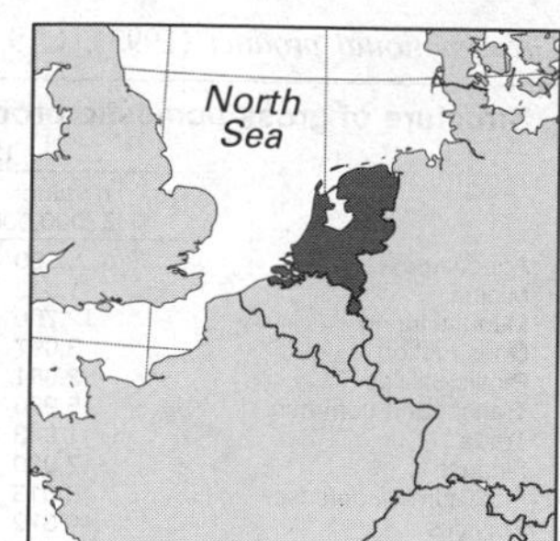

Official name: Koninkrijk der Nederlanden (Kingdom of The Netherlands).
Form of government: constitutional monarchy with a parliament (States General) comprising two legislative houses (First Chamber [75]; Second Chamber [150]).
Chief of state: Monarch.
Head of government: Prime Minister.
Seat of government: The Hague.
Capital: Amsterdam.
Official language: Dutch.
Official religion: none.
Monetary unit: 1 Netherlands guilder (f.) = 100 cents; valuation (Oct. 6, 1995) 1 U.S.$ = f. 1.60; 1 £ = f. 2.53.

Area and population

		area		population
Provinces	Capitals	sq mi	sq km	1994[1] estimate
Drenthe	Assen	1,025	2,655	451,409
Flevoland	Lelystad	545	1,412	253,699
Friesland	Leeuwarden	1,297	3,360	607,016
Gelderland	Arnhem	1,936	5,015	1,851,402
Groningen	Groningen	906	2,347	556,607
Limburg	Maastricht	838	2,170	1,125,187
Noord-Brabant	's-Hertogenbosch	1,910	4,947	2,259,779
Noord-Holland	Haarlem	1,030	2,667	2,457,329
Overijssel	Zwolle	1,290	3,340	1,044,648
Utrecht	Utrecht	525	1,359	1,056,033
Zeeland	Middelburg	693	1,796	363,867
Zuid-Holland	The Hague	1,108	2,871	3,313,103
TOTAL LAND AREA		13,104[2]	33,939	
INLAND WATER		2,929	7,587	
TOTAL		16,033	41,526	15,341,553[3]

Demography

Population (1995): 15,487,000.
Density (1995)[4] : persons per sq mi 1,181.9, persons per sq km 456.3.
Urban-rural (1994[1]): urban 90.4%; rural 9.6%.
Sex distribution (1994[1]): male 49.45%; female 50.55%.
Age breakdown (1994[1]): under 15, 18.4%; 15–29, 22.4%; 30–44, 23.8%; 45–59, 17.8%; 60–74, 12.1%; 75 and over, 5.5%.
Population projection: (2000) 16,121,000; (2010) 16,987,000.
Doubling time: not applicable, vital rates and net migration in near balance.
Ethnic composition (by nationality; 1994[1]): Netherlander 94.9%; Turkish 1.3%; Moroccan 1.1%; German 0.3%; other 2.4%.
Religious affiliation (1993): Roman Catholic 32.0%; Dutch Reformed Church 15.0%; Calvinist 7.0%; Muslim 3.7%; other 2.3%; no religion 40.0%.
Major cities (1994[1]): Amsterdam 724,096; Rotterdam 598,521; The Hague 445,279; Utrecht 234,106; Eindhoven 196,130.

Vital statistics

Birth rate per 1,000 population (1994): 12.7 (world avg. 25.0); (1993) legitimate 87.5%; illegitimate 12.5%.
Death rate per 1,000 population (1994): 8.7 (world avg. 9.3).
Natural increase rate per 1,000 population (1994): 4.0 (world avg. 15.7).
Total fertility rate (avg. births per childbearing woman; 1993): 1.6.
Marriage rate per 1,000 population (1993): 5.8.
Divorce rate per 1,000 population (1993): 2.0.
Life expectancy at birth (1993): male 74.0 years; female 80.0 years.
Major causes of death per 100,000 population (1993): malignant neoplasms (cancers) 238.4, of which lung cancer 56.3; ischemic heart diseases 118.2; cerebrovascular diseases 87.2; accidents, poisoning, and violence 34.1.

National economy

Budget (1993). Revenue: f. 180,373,000,000 (income and corporate taxes 39.0%, social-security contributions 36.8%, value-added taxes 21.0%, property taxes 2.3%). Expenditures: f. 197,158,000,000 (social security and public health 38.0%, education and culture 10.5%, debt service 9.2%, defense 4.2%, transportation 2.9%).
Public debt (1993[5]): U.S.$195,935,000,000.
Tourism (1993): receipts from visitors U.S.$4,690,000,000; expenditures by nationals abroad U.S.$8,974,000,000.
Production (metric tons except as noted). Agriculture, forestry, fishing (1994): potatoes 7,698,600[6], sugar beets 7,478,600[6], wheat 987,700, onions 448,000, barley 235,100; livestock (number of live animals) 14,565,000 pigs, 4,716,000 cattle, 1,766,000 sheep; roundwood (1993) 1,403,000 cu m; fish catch (1993) 486,894. Manufacturing (value added in f. '000,000; 1992): foodstuffs 14,042; chemicals and chemical products 11,403; electrical machinery 9,779; machinery and transport equipment 7,239; publishing and printing 6,629. Construction (buildings completed by value in f. '000,000; 1993): residential 11,300; nonresidential 11,900. Energy production (consumption): electricity (kW-hr; 1992) 77,202,000,000 (85,880,000,000); coal (metric tons; 1992) none (12,140,000); crude petroleum (barrels; 1992) 19,497,000 (393,262,000); petroleum products (metric tons; 1992) 57,813,000 (27,823,000); natural gas (cu m; 1992) 91,013,000,000 (48,934,000,000).
Household income and expenditure (1993). Average household size 2.4; income per household f. 58,478 (U.S.$31,484); sources of income (1992): wages 58.5%, transfer payments 28.9%, self-employment 12.6%; expenditure (1992): rent 18.5%, food, beverages, and tobacco 14.9%, transportation and communications 13.4%, medical care 13.0%, education and recreation 10.1%, household furnishings and appliances 7.0%, clothing and footwear 6.7%, other 16.4%.
Gross national product (at current market price; 1993): U.S.$316,390,000,000 (U.S.$20,710 per capita).

Structure of gross domestic product and labour force

	1993			
	in value f. '000,000	% of total value	labour force	% of labour force
Agriculture	18,509	3.5	232,000	3.6
Mining	15,666	3.0	12,000	0.2
Manufacturing	100,580	19.2	1,064,000	16.6
Construction	29,832	5.7	389,000	6.1
Public utilities	9,722	1.9	41,000	0.6
Transp. and commun.	38,114	7.3	379,000	5.9
Trade	83,945	16.0	958,000	15.0
Finance	7	7	669,000	10.4
Pub. admin., defense	7	7	} 2,097,000	} 32.7
Services	249,245[7]	47.7[7]		
Other	−22,642[8]	−4.3[8]	566,000[9]	8.8[9]
TOTAL	522,971	100.0	6,406,000[2]	100.0[2]

Population economically active (1993): total 6,406,000; activity rate of total population 41.9% (participation rates: ages 15–64, 61.5%; female 37.6%; unemployed 7.5%).

Price and earnings indexes (1990 = 100)

	1988	1989	1990	1991	1992	1993	1994
Consumer price index	96.6	97.6	100.0	103.1	106.4	109.2	112.2
Hourly earnings index	95.9	97.2	100.0	103.7	108.2	111.7	113.8

Land use (1993): forested 10.3%; meadows and pastures 31.0%; agricultural and under permanent cultivation 27.5%; other 31.2%.

Foreign trade

Balance of trade (current prices)

	1989	1990	1991	1992	1993	1994
f. '000,000	19,277	22,345	26,131	22,225	38,995	41,982
% of total	4.4%	4.9%	5.6%	4.7%	8.2%	8.0%

Imports (1993): f. 234,972,000,000 (machinery and transport equipment 28.5%, of which road vehicles 6.5%; foodstuffs, beverages, and tobacco 11.7%; chemicals and chemical products 10.7%; mineral fuels 8.8%, of which petroleum 5.1%; clothing 3.8%). *Major import sources:* Germany 23.5%; Belgium Luxembourg 11.7%; U.K. 9.6%; U.S. 8.0%; France 7.5%.
Exports (1993): f. 258,226,000,000 (machinery and transport equipment 23.6%, of which road vehicles 2.9%; foodstuffs, beverages, and tobacco 19.4%; chemicals and chemical products 15.0%; mineral fuels 8.5%, of which petroleum products 5.5%; iron and steel 2.0%; clothing 1.7%). *Major export destinations:* Germany 29.1%; Belgium-Luxembourg 12.7%; France 10.6%; U.K. 9.4%; Italy 5.7%.

Transport and communications

Transport. Railroads (1993): length 2,757 km; passenger-km 15,245,000,000; metric ton-km cargo 2,681,000,000. Roads (1993): total length 118,943 km (paved 89%). Vehicles (1993): passenger cars 5,755,000; trucks and buses 679,000. Merchant marine (1993): vessels (100 gross tons and over) 399; total deadweight tonnage 2,874,000. Air transport (1993): passenger-km 38,163,000,000; metric ton-km cargo 2,765,900,000; airports (1995) 5.
Communications. Daily newspapers (1994): total number 64; total circulation 4,600,000; circulation per 1,000 population 296. Radio (1993): total number of receivers 13,400,000 (1 per 1.1 persons). Television (1993): total number of receivers 5,675,000 (1 per 2.7 persons). Telephones (main lines; 1993): 7,630,000 (1 per 1.9 persons).

Education and health

Education (1992–93)

	schools	teachers[10]	students	student/teacher ratio[10]
Primary (age 6–12)	9,333	99,031	1,526,000	15.7
Secondary (age 12–18)	1,117	89,370	668,000	7.7
Voc., teacher tr.	747	18,613	498,000	28.0
Higher	206	30,952[11]	389,000	10.2

Educational attainment (1993). Percentage of population ages 15–64 having: primary education 16.4%; secondary 65.8%; higher 17.8%. *Literacy* (1992): virtually 100% literate.
Health (1993[1]): physicians 39,069 (1 per 391 persons); hospital beds 87,025 (1 per 176 persons); infant mortality rate per 1,000 live births 6.3.
Food (1992): daily per capita caloric intake 3,222 (vegetable products 68%, animal products 32%); 120% of FAO recommended minimum requirement.

Military

Total active duty personnel (1994): 70,900 (army 60.9%, navy 20.2%, air force 12.7%, other[12] 6.2%). *Military expenditure as percentage of GNP* (1993): 2.4% (world 3.3%); per capita expenditure U.S.$462.

[1]January 1. [2]Detail does not add to total given because of rounding. [3]Includes 1,384 persons having no fixed municipality of residence. [4]Based on land area only. [5]June. [6]1993. [7]Services includes Finance and Pub. admin., defense. [8]Imputed bank service charge. [9]Includes 481,000 unemployed. [10]1990–91. [11]1985–86. [12]Includes 3,600 military police.

New Zealand

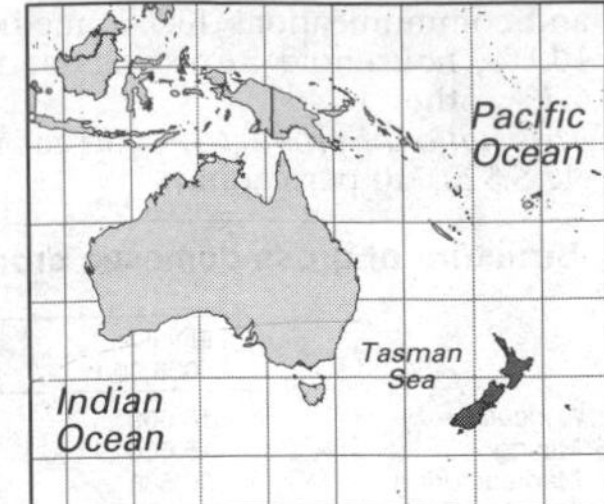

Official name: New Zealand (English); Aotearoa (Maori).
Form of government: constitutional monarchy with one legislative house (House of Representatives [99]).
Chief of state: British Monarch, represented by Governor-General.
Head of government: Prime Minister.
Capital: Wellington.
Official languages: English; Maori.
Official religion: none.
Monetary unit: 1 New Zealand dollar ($NZ) = 100 cents; valuation (Oct. 6, 1995) 1 U.S.$ = $NZ 1.51; 1 £ = $NZ 2.39.

Area and population

Islands / Regional Councils	area sq mi	area sq km	population 1995 estimate[1]
North Island	44,702	115,777	2,678,900
Auckland	...	...	1,027,700
Bay of Plenty	...	...	221,600
Gisborne[2]	...	...	44,500
Hawkes Bay	...	...	141,600
Manawatu-Wanganui	...	...	233,800
Northland	...	...	136,800
Taranaki	...	...	108,200
Waikato	...	...	351,600
Wellington	...	...	413,100
South Island	58,384	151,215	912,700
Canterbury	...	...	466,600
Marlborough	...	...	38,600
Nelson	...	...	41,000
Otago	...	...	191,600
Southland	...	...	102,400
Tasman	...	...	38,700
West Coast	...	...	33,800
Remainder[3, 4]	...	...	800
Offshore islands[5]	322	854	...
Stewart Island[6]	674	1,746	...
Chatham Islands[7]	372	963	...
TOTAL	104,454	270,534	3,592,400

Demography

Population (1995): 3,568,000.
Density (1995): persons per sq mi 34.2, persons per sq km 13.2.
Urban-rural (1994): urban 68.6%; rural 31.4%.
Sex distribution (1994): male 49.33%; female 50.67%.
Age breakdown (1994): under 15, 23.2%; 15–29, 22.8%; 30–44, 22.9%; 45–59, 15.6%; 60–74, 10.8%; 75 and over, 4.7%.
Population projection: (2000) 3,786,000; (2010) 4,097,000.
Doubling time: 81 years.
Ethnic composition (1991): New Zealand European 73.8%; New Zealand Maori 9.6%; Pacific Island Polynesian 3.6%; multiethnic 4.5%; other 8.5%.
Religious affiliation (1991): Anglican 21.4%; Presbyterian 16.0%; Roman Catholic 14.8%; Methodist 4.1%; nonreligious 19.7%; other 24.0%.
Major cities (1995): Auckland 336,500; Christchurch 308,800; Manukau 243,400; North Shore 163,600; Wellington 153,800.

Vital statistics

Birth rate per 1,000 population (1994): 16.3 (world avg. 25.0); legitimate 49.5%; illegitimate 50.5%.
Death rate per 1,000 population (1994): 7.7 (world avg. 9.3).
Natural increase rate per 1,000 population (1994): 8.6 (world avg. 15.7).
Total fertility rate (avg. births per childbearing woman; 1994): 2.0.
Marriage rate per 1,000 population (1994): 6.1.
Divorce rate per 1,000 population (1993): 2.7.
Life expectancy at birth (1994): male 73.4 years; female 79.1 years.
Major causes of death per 100,000 population (1992): diseases of the circulatory system 353.6, of which ischemic heart disease 207.6; malignant neoplasms (cancers) 201.3; diseases of the respiratory system 82.1; accidents 36.5; diabetes mellitus 13.4.

National economy

Budget (1993–94): $NZ 29,598,000,000 (direct taxes 60.8%, indirect taxes 34.5%, interest and profits 4.7%). Expenditures: $NZ 29,174,000,000 (social services 36.1%, education 15.9%, health 14.1%, administration 10.2%).
Public debt (year ending June 30, 1994): $NZ 29,565,000,000.
Tourism (1993): receipts U.S.$1,165,000,000; expenditures U.S.$1,003,000,000.
Production (metric tons except as noted). Agriculture, forestry, fishing (1994): barley 349,000, wheat 181,000, corn (maize) 173,000, peas 80,000, oats 70,000; livestock (number of live animals) 50,135,000 sheep, 8,550,000 cattle, 484,000 goats, 430,000 pigs; roundwood (1993) 15,560,000 cu m; fish catch (1993) 580,874. Mining and quarrying (1993): limestone 4,271,338; iron ore and sand concentrate 2,388,783; serpentine 23,386; silver 25,000 kg; gold 11,000 kg. Manufacturing (1994): wood pulp 1,360,100; chemical fertilizers 1,266,000; yarn 21,072; beer 356,847,000 litres; carbonated soft drinks 230,540,000 litres; footwear 3,406,000 pairs; carpets 9,706,000 sq m. Construction ($NZ '000; 1994–95): residential 3,497,800; nonresidential 2,123,200. Energy production (consumption): electricity (kW-hr; 1992) 31,271,000,000 (31,271,000,000); coal (metric tons; 1992) 2,830,000 (2,430,000); crude petroleum (barrels; 1992) 13,959,000 (32,743,000); petroleum products (metric tons; 1992) 4,635,000 (4,158,000); natural gas (cu m; 1992) 6,877,100,000 (4,605,900,000).

Gross national product (1993): U.S.$44,660,000,000 (U.S.$12,900 per capita).

Structure of gross domestic product and labour force

	1990–91 in value $NZ '000,000	1990–91 % of total value	1994 labour force	1994 % of labour force
Agriculture	5,380	7.4	164,800	9.8
Mining	1,042	1.4	5,200	0.2
Manufacturing	12,790	17.5	292,300	14.7
Construction	3,097	4.2	97,700	4.8
Public utilities	2,081	2.8	10,300	0.7
Transp. and commun.	5,926	8.0	92,300	5.4
Trade	11,943	16.4	343,800	19.0
Finance	17,020	23.2	165,500	9.5
Pub. admin., defense	8,613	11.7	426,300	25.4
Services	2,379	3.2		
Other	3,068[8]	4.2[8]	128,200[9]	10.5[9]
TOTAL	73,339	100.0	1,726,400	100.0

Population economically active (1995[1]): total 1,730,000; activity rate 48.8% (participation rates: over age 15, 64.5%; female 44.2%; unemployed 6.3%).

Price and earnings indexes (1990 = 100)

	1988	1989	1990	1991	1992	1993	1994
Consumer price index	89.2	94.3	100.0	102.6	103.6	105.0	106.8
Weekly earnings index	92.2	95.8	100.0	102.6	104.8	105.5	108.7

Household income and expenditure. Average household size (1995[1]) 3.0; annual income per household (1995) $NZ 42,551 (U.S.$27,497); sources of income (1994–95): wages and salaries 65.8%, transfer payments 15.2%, self-employment 9.8%, other 9.1%; expenditure (1994–95): food 20.0%, housing 19.4%, transportation 17.1%, household durable goods 10.9%, clothing 4.4%.
Land use (1993): forested 27.2%; meadows and pastures 49.8%; agricultural and under permanent cultivation 14.0%; other 9.0%.

Foreign trade

Balance of trade (current prices)

	1989	1990	1991	1992	1993	1994
$NZ '000,000	+1,380.6	+1,349.1	+3,359.6	+2,451.0	+1,673.4	+1,358.2
% of total	4.8%	4.4%	11.2%	7.2%	4.6%	3.6%

Imports (1994): $NZ 18,468,900 (machinery 24.6%; minerals, chemicals, and plastics 22.2%; transport equipment 13.5%; basic manufactures 7.6%; metals and metal products 5.9%; textiles, clothing, and footwear 5.7%). *Major import sources:* Australia 21.5%; U.S. 18.1%; Japan 15.8%; U.K. 6.1%; Germany 4.4%.
Exports (1994): $NZ 19,827,000,100 (food and live animals 46.5%; basic manufactures 25.4%; minerals, chemicals, and plastics 11.5%; metals and metal products 6.5%). *Major export destinations:* Australia 21.0%; Japan 14.6%; U.S. 11.2%; U.K. 6.0%; South Korea 4.7%; Germany 2.5%.

Transport and communications

Transport. Railroads (1993): length 2,469 mi, 3,973 km; passenger-km (1984) 458,160,000; short ton-mi cargo (1992–93) 1,712,000,000, metric ton-km cargo 2,500,000,000. Roads (1992): total length 58,605 mi, 94,315 km (paved 73%). Vehicles (1994): passenger cars 1,600,499; trucks and buses 352,997. Merchant marine (1992): vessels (100 gross tons and over) 139; total deadweight tonnage 279,805. Air transport (1992): passenger-mi 7,798,800,000, passenger-km 12,551,000,000; short ton-mi cargo 1,100,000,000, metric ton-km cargo 1,606,000,000; airports (1995) 36.
Communications. Daily newspapers (1992): total number 31; total circulation 1,050,000; circulation per 1,000 population 304. Radio (1992): 3,215,000 receivers (1 per 1.1 persons). Television (1992): 1,530,000 receivers (1 per 3.1 persons). Telephones (main lines; 1993): 1,593,000 (1 per 2.2 persons).

Education and health

Education (1994)

	schools	teachers	students	student/ teacher ratio
Primary (age 5–12)[10]	2,417	24,099	444,881	18.5
Secondary (age 13–17)	335	17,202	229,694	13.4
Voc., teacher tr.	30	7,379	98,602	13.4
Higher[11]	7	4,308	103,087	23.9

Educational attainment (1991). Percentage of population age 25 and over having: primary and some secondary education 54.9%; secondary 31.1%; higher 6.9%; not specified 6.1%. *Literacy:* virtually 100.0%.
Health (1994): physicians 11,413 (1 per 313 persons); hospital beds (1989) 29,352 (1 per 114 persons); infant mortality rate per 1,000 live births 7.1.
Food (1992): daily per capita caloric intake 3,669 (vegetable products 61%, animal products 39%); 139% of FAO recommended minimum requirement.

Military

Total active duty personnel (1995): 10,050 (army 44.8%, air force 33.3%, navy 21.9%). *Military expenditure as percentage of GNP* (1993): 1.5% (world 3.3%); per capita expenditure U.S.$194.

[1]Provisional; March 31. [2]Reorganized as a unitary authority that is administered by a district council with regional powers. [3]Includes the population of Kermadec Islands and persons on oil rigs. [4]Includes the population of Chatham Islands county and Campbell Island. [5]Excludes islands in Regional Councils. [6]Part of Southland Regional Council. [7]Chatham Islands county remains outside any Regional Council. [8]Includes import duties less imputed bank service charges. [9]Includes 126,000 unemployed. [10]Includes 83 composite schools that provide both primary and secondary education. [11]Universities only.

Nicaragua

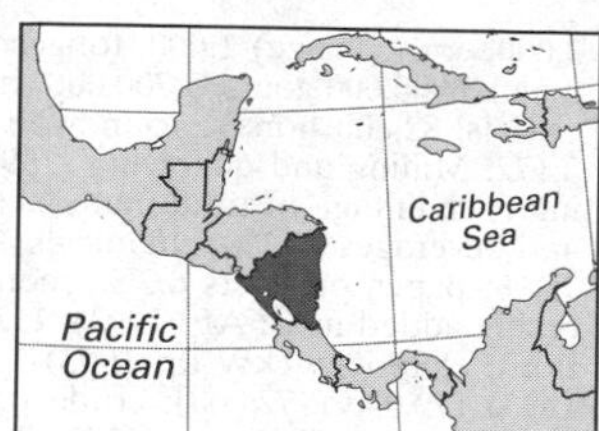

Official name: República de Nicaragua (Republic of Nicaragua).
Form of government: unitary multiparty republic with one legislative house (National Assembly [92[1]]).
Head of state and government: President.
Capital: Managua.
Official language: Spanish.
Official religion: none.
Monetary unit: 1 córdoba oro (C$)[2] = 100 centavos; valuation (Oct. 6, 1995) 1 U.S.$ = C$7.75; 1 £ = C$12.25.

Area and population		area[3]		population
		sq mi	sq km	1993 estimate
Departments	**Capitals**			
Boaco	Boaco	1,639	4,244	129,000
Carazo	Jinotepe	405	1,050	165,200
Chinandega	Chinandega	1,902	4,926	357,700
Chontales	Juigalpa	2,463	6,378	276,600
Estelí	Estelí	902	2,335	181,200
Granada	Granada	359	929	165,200
Jinotega	Jinotega	3,766	9,755	190,100
León	León	1,972	5,107	373,400
Madriz	Somoto	619	1,602	104,400
Managua	Managua	1,418	3,672	1,188,100
Masaya	Masaya	228	590	225,100
Matagalpa	Matagalpa	3,291	8,523	403,700
Nueva Segovia	Ocotal	1,206	3,123	132,000
Río San Juan	San Carlos	2,885	7,473	37,600
Rivas	Rivas	832	2,155	147,800
Autonomous regions				
North Atlantic	...	12,417	32,159	187,700
South Atlantic	Bluefields	10,582	27,407	
TOTAL LAND AREA		46,884[4]	121,428	
INLAND WATER		3,954	10,242	
TOTAL		50,838	131,670	4,264,800

Demography

Population (1995): 4,340,000.
Density (1995)[5]: persons per sq mi 92.6, persons per sq km 35.7.
Urban-rural (1992): urban 61.6%; rural 38.4%.
Sex distribution (1992): male 50.16%; female 49.84%.
Age breakdown (1992): under 15, 45.4%; 15–29, 27.6%; 30–44, 15.3%; 45–59, 7.3%; 60–74, 3.6%; 75 and over, 0.8%.
Population projection: (2000) 4,759,000; (2010) 5,864,000.
Doubling time: 25 years.
Ethnic composition (1991): mestizo (Spanish/Indian) 69.0%; white 17.0%; black 9.0%; Amerindian 5.0%.
Religious affiliation (1992): Roman Catholic 89.3%; other (mostly Baptist, Moravian, and Pentecostal) 10.7%.
Major cities (1992)[6]: Managua 973,759; León 172,042; Masaya 101,878; Chinandega 101,605; Matagalpa 95,268; Granada 91,929.

Vital statistics

Birth rate per 1,000 population (1994): 35.0 (world avg. 25.0).
Death rate per 1,000 population (1994): 7.0 (world avg. 9.3).
Natural increase rate per 1,000 population (1994): 28.0 (world avg. 15.7).
Total fertility rate (avg. births per childbearing woman; 1994): 4.3.
Marriage rate per 1,000 population (1991): 3.3.
Divorce rate per 1,000 population (1991): 0.4.
Life expectancy at birth (1993): male 60.7 years; female 66.4 years.
Major causes of death per 100,000 population (1991)[7]: diseases of the circulatory system 142.0; infectious and parasitic diseases 100.0; accidents and violence 93.0; diseases of the respiratory system 73.0; malignant neoplasms (cancers) 56.0.

National economy

Budget (1994). Revenue: C$2,538,000,000 (indirect taxes 82.9%, direct taxes 11.0%, unspecified 6.1%). Expenditures: C$2,791,000,000 (current expenditure 79.3%, development expenditure 20.7%).
Production (metric tons except as noted). Agriculture, forestry, fishing (1994): sugarcane 2,300,000, corn (maize) 323,000, rice 185,000, sorghum 115,000, dry beans 75,000, oranges 71,000, plantains 54,000, coffee 52,000, cassava 51,000, pineapples 45,000, bananas 43,000, sesame seed 17,000; livestock (number of live animals) 1,650,000 cattle, 535,000 pigs; roundwood (1993) 3,679,000 cu m; fish catch (1993) 8,773, of which crustaceans 5,036. Mining and quarrying (1993): gold 39,900 troy oz. Manufacturing (value of production in C$'000,000; 1991[8]): food 1,579; beverages 945; tobacco products 447; cement, bricks, and tile 236; rubber products 215; textiles 188. Construction (completed; 1991): 569 cu m. Energy production (consumption): electricity (kW-hr; 1993) 1,625,000,000 (1,125,000,000); coal, none (none); crude petroleum (barrels; 1992) none (5,212,000); petroleum products (metric tons; 1992) 635,000 (720,000); natural gas, none (none).
Household income and expenditure. Average household size (1980) 6.9; income per household: n.a.; sources of income: n.a.; expenditure: n.a.
Tourism (1993): receipts from visitors U.S.$30,000,000; expenditures by nationals abroad U.S.$34,000,000.
Population economically active (1991): total 1,386,300; activity rate of total population 34.7% (participation rates: over age 15, 62.0%; female 33.2%; unemployed [1994] more than 60.0%).

Price and earnings indexes (1990 = 100)	1989	1990	1991	1992	1993	1994
Consumer price index	1.32	100.0	2,842	3,418	4,102	4,922
Earnings index	...	...	...	...	...	...

Gross national product (at current market prices; 1993): U.S.$1,421,000,000 (U.S.$360 per capita).

Structure of gross domestic product and labour force	1993		1991	
	in value C$'000,000[9]	% of total value	labour force	% of labour force
Agriculture	3,339	30.3	415,400	30.0
Mining	71	0.7	9,000	0.6
Manufacturing	1,885	17.1	188,200	13.6
Construction	268	2.4	30,200	2.2
Public utilities	132	1.2	10,300	0.7
Transportation and communications	441	4.0	42,600	3.1
Trade	2,700	24.5	195,500	14.1
Finance, real estate	613	5.6	24,700	1.8
Pub. admin., defense	929	8.4	98,100	7.1
Services	637	5.8	183,900	13.3
Other	—	—	188,400[10]	13.6[10]
TOTAL	11,015	100.0	1,386,300	100.0[4]

Public debt (external, outstanding; 1993): U.S.$8,773,000,000.
Land use (1993): forested 27.0%; meadows and pastures 46.3%; agricultural and under permanent cultivation 10.7%; other 16.0%.

Foreign trade[11]

Balance of trade (current prices)	1989	1990	1991	1992	1993	1994
U.S.$'000,000	236.0	200.0	−418.1	−576.2	−411.5	−350.0
% of total	27.6%	26.4%	43.3%	57.0%	43.5%	33.3%

Imports (1993): U.S.$727,700,000 (nondurable consumer goods 29.9%, raw materials for industry 22.1%, capital goods for industry 14.6%, petroleum products 14.6%). *Major import sources*[12]: United States 20.0%; Venezuela 17.0%; Costa Rica 13.0%; Guatemala 10.0%; El Salvador 7.0%.
Exports (1993): U.S.$266,900,000 (fresh and frozen meat 22.8%, nontraditional industrial exports 21.2%, coffee 12.0%, crustaceans 10.0%, gold 9.8%, sugar 6.5%). *Major export destinations*[12]: United States 42.0%; Germany 9.0%; Belgium-Luxembourg 6.0%; El Salvador 5.0%; Mexico 5.0%.

Transport and communications

Transport. Railroads:[13]. Roads (1993): total length 9,499 mi, 15,287 km (paved 10%). Vehicles (1993): passenger cars 31,300; trucks and buses 43,600. Merchant marine (1992): vessels (100 gross tons and over) 25, total deadweight tonnage 1,295. Air transport (1993)[14]: passenger-mi 35,800,000, passenger-km 57,615,000; short ton-mi cargo 1,810,000, metric ton-km cargo 2,643,000; airports (1995) with scheduled flights 4.
Communications. Daily newspapers (1993): total number 3; total circulation 98,602; circulation per 1,000 population 23. Radio (1994): 925,000 receivers (1 per 4.6 persons). Television (1994): 210,000 receivers (1 per 20 persons). Telephones (main lines; 1993): 66,800 (1 per 64 persons).

Education and health

Education (1992)	schools	teachers	students	student/teacher ratio
Primary (age 7–12)	4,571	18,901	766,000[15]	37.2
Secondary (age 13–18)	...	4,465	178,342	39.9
Voc., teacher tr.	...	763	17,765	23.3
Higher[16, 17]	4	1,645	34,984	21.3

Educational attainment: n.a. *Literacy* (1986): total population age 15 and over literate 74.0%.
Health (1994): physicians 3,418 (1 per 1,258 persons); hospital beds 4,968 (1 per 866 persons); infant mortality rate per 1,000 live births 53.0.
Food (1992): daily per capita caloric intake 2,293 (vegetable products 90%, animal products 10%); 102% of FAO recommended minimum requirement.

Military

Total active duty personnel (1994): 15,200 (army 88.8%, navy 3.3%, air force 7.9%). *Military expenditure as percentage of GNP* (1993): 2.6% (world 3.3%); per capita expenditure U.S.$9.

[1]Includes two unsuccessful 1990 presidential candidates meeting special conditions. [2]The córdoba oro (gold cordoba), introduced in August 1990, circulated simultaneously with the new córdoba until April 30, 1991, when the new córdoba ceased to be legal tender; on April 30, 1 córdoba oro equaled 5,000,000 new córdobas. The new córdoba had been introduced in February 1988 at the rate of 1 new córdoba to 1,000 (old) córdobas. [3]Lakes and lagoons are excluded from the areas of departments and autonomous regions. [4]Detail does not add to total given because of rounding. [5]Based on land area. [6]*Municipio* population. [7]Projected rates based on about 45% of total deaths. [8]At prices of 1980. [9]Estimated figures. [10]Unemployed persons previously employed. [11]Imports f.o.b. in balance of trade and c.i.f. in commodities and trading partners. [12]Estimated percentages. [13]Railroad service halted in January 1994 because of insufficient revenue. [14]Nica only. [15]1994. [16]1993. [17]Universities only.

Niger

Official name: République du Niger (Republic of Niger).
Form of government: unitary multiparty republic with one legislative body (National Assembly [83]).
Chief of state: President.
Head of government: Prime Minister.
Capital: Niamey.
Official language: French[1].
Official religion: none.
Monetary unit: 1 CFA franc (CFAF) = 100 centimes; valuation (Oct. 6, 1995) 1 U.S.$ = CFAF 501.49; 1 £ = CFAF 792.78.

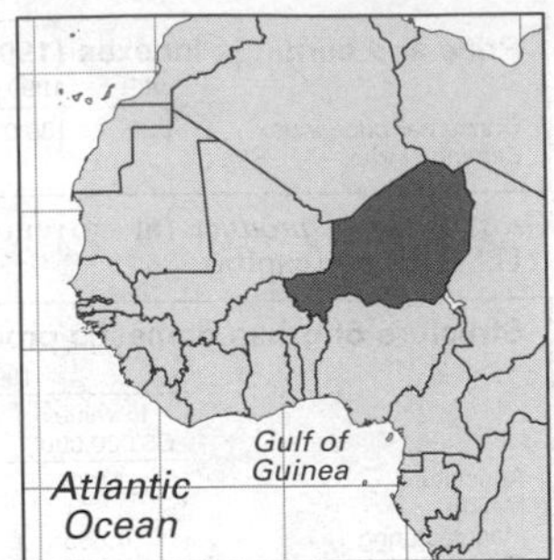

Area and population

		area[2]		population
				1988
Departments	**Capitals**	sq mi	sq km	census[3]
Agadez[4]	Agadez	244,869	634,209	205,232
Diffa	Diffa	54,138	140,216	187,230
Dosso	Dosso	11,970	31,002	1,018,058
Maradi	Maradi	14,896	38,581	1,386,549
Tahoua	Tahoua	41,188	106,677	1,306,948
Tillabéri	Tillabéri	34,863	90,293	1,715,118
Zinder	Zinder	56,151	145,430	1,409,417
TOTAL		458,075	1,186,408	7,228,552

Demography

Population (1995): 9,151,000.
Density (1995)[2]: persons per sq mi 20.0, persons per sq km 7.1.
Urban-rural (1991): urban 20.2%; rural 79.8%.
Sex distribution (1995): male 49.40%; female 50.60%.
Age breakdown (1995): under 15, 48.4%; 15–29, 25.7%; 30–44, 14.4%; 45–59, 7.5%; 60–74, 3.4%; 75 and over, 0.6%.
Population projection: (2000) 10,805,000; (2010) 14,751,000.
Doubling time: 22 years.
Ethnic composition (1988): Hausa 52.8%; Zerma- (Djerma-) Songhai 21.0%; Tuareg 10.6%; Fulani (Peul) 9.8%; Kanuri-Nanga 4.5%; Teda 0.5%; Arab 0.3%; Gurma 0.3%; other 0.2%.
Religious affiliation (1988): Muslim, primarily Sunnī, 98.7%; Christian 0.4%; other, mostly traditional animist beliefs, 0.9%.
Major cities (1988): Niamey 392,165; Zinder 119,838; Maradi 104,386; Tahoua 49,948; Agadez 49,361.

Vital statistics

Birth rate per 1,000 population (1990–95): 52.5 (world avg. 25.0).
Death rate per 1,000 population (1990–95): 18.9 (world avg. 9.3).
Natural increase rate per 1,000 population (1990–95): 33.6 (world avg. 15.7).
Total fertility rate (avg. births per childbearing woman; 1990–95): 7.4.
Marriage rate per 1,000 population: n.a.
Divorce rate per 1,000 population: n.a.
Life expectancy at birth (1990–95): male 44.9 years; female 48.1 years.
Major causes of death (1989): n.a.; however, among selected major causes of infectious disease registered at medical facilities were malaria, measles, diarrhea, meningitis, pneumonia, diphtheria, tetanus, viral hepatitis, and poliomyelitis; malnutrition and shortages of trained medical personnel are widespread.

National economy

Budget (1993). Revenue: CFAF 81,200,000,000 (current revenue 56.7%, of which import duties 17.3%, income taxes 15.9%, external aid and gifts 40.0%). Expenditures: CFAF 105,400,000,000 (current expenditures 76.6%, of which amortization of public debt 10.2%; capital expenditures 23.4%).
Public debt (external, outstanding; 1993): U.S.$1,354,000,000.
Tourism (1993): receipts from visitors U.S.$16,000,000; expenditures by nationals abroad U.S.$43,000,000.
Gross national product (at current market prices; 1993): U.S.$2,279,000,000 (U.S.$270 per capita).

Structure of gross domestic product and labour force

	1993		1988	
	in value CFAF '000,000	% of total value	labour force	% of labour force
Agriculture	233,300	37.1	1,764,049	76.2
Mining	35,100	5.6	5,295	0.2
Manufacturing	43,400	6.9	65,793	2.8
Construction	11,900	1.9	13,742	0.6
Public utilities	14,700	2.3	1,778	0.1
Transportation and communications	27,000	4.3	14,764	0.6
Trade and finance	116,100	18.5	210,354	9.1
Pub. admin., defense	69,300	11.0	59,271	2.6
Services	65,500	10.4	63,991	2.8
Other	12,400	2.0	116,657	5.0
TOTAL	628,700	100.0	2,315,694	100.0

Production (metric tons except as noted). Agriculture, forestry, fishing (1994): millet 1,725,000, pulses 433,000, sorghum 420,000, vegetables and melons 264,000 (of which onions 178,000), roots and tubers 260,000, sugarcane 142,000, rice 70,000, peanuts (groundnuts) 65,000, wheat 5,000, seed cotton 3,000, corn (maize) 1,000, tobacco leaf 1,000; livestock (number of live animals) 5,900,000 goats, 3,700,000 sheep, 1,986,000 cattle, 450,000 asses, 370,000 camels, 82,000 horses; roundwood (1993) 5,467,000 cu m; fish catch (1993) 2,172. Mining and quarrying (1993): salt 3,000, uranium 2,914. Manufacturing (percentage of total manufacturing value added; 1992): food processing and beverages 44.1%; chemicals 31.9%; construction materials 8.9%; textiles 7.1%; paper products 6.3%; metal and wood products 1.1%. Construction (value added in CFAF; 1993): 11,900,000,000. Energy production (consumption): electricity (kW-hr; 1993) 173,000,000 (366,000,000); coal (metric tons; 1993) 172,000 (172,000); crude petroleum, none (n.a.); petroleum products (metric tons; 1993) none (205,000); natural gas, none (n.a.).
Population economically active (1988): total 2,315,694; activity rate of total population 31.9% (participation rates: ages 15–64, 55.2%; female 20.4%; unemployed 1.3%).

Price and earnings indexes (1985 = 100)

	1988	1989	1990	1991	1992	1993	1994
Consumer price index	103.7	100.8	100.0	92.2	88.1	87.0	118.4
Hourly earnings index[5]	100.0	100.0	100.0	100.0	100.0	...	...

Household income and expenditure. Average household size (1988) 6.4; income per household: n.a.; sources of income (1977): self-employment 59.5%, family 30.1%, salary or wages 4.8%, employer 0.7%; expenditure (1987): food and beverages 43.1%, housing 22.8%, clothing 10.0%.
Land use (1993): forested 2.0%; meadows and pastures 7.0%; agricultural and under permanent cultivation 2.8%; other (largely desert) 88.2%.

Foreign trade

Balance of trade (current prices)

	1989	1990	1991	1992	1993	1994
CFAF '000,000,000	−24,900	−36,900	−19,500	+700	−3,100	−10,800
% of total	11.3%	18.0%	10.8%	0.5%	2.7%	4.6%

Imports (1993): CFAF 67,500,000,000 (consumer goods 71.2%, of which grain 8.9%, petroleum products 8.3%; intermediate and capital goods 28.9%).
Major import sources (1993): France 21.8%; Côte d'Ivoire 8.7%; Germany 3.7%; Italy 2.6%; Japan 1.9%.
Exports (1993): CFAF 69,100,000,000 (uranium 45.7%, live animals 10.5%).
Major export destinations (1993): France 55.3%.

Transport and communications

Transport. Railroads (1992): none[6]. Roads (1991): total length 12,244 mi, 19,705 km (paved 22%). Vehicles (1990): passenger cars 31,427; trucks and buses 8,768. Air transport (1994)[7]: passenger-mi 133,440,000, passenger-km 214,745,000; short ton-mi cargo 9,892,000, metric ton-km cargo 14,442,000; airports (1995) with scheduled flights 1.
Communications. Daily newspapers (1992): total number 1; total circulation 5,000; circulation per 1,000 population 0.6. Radio (1994): total number of receivers 440,000 (1 per 20 persons). Television (1994): total number of receivers 25,000 (1 per 352 persons). Telephones (main lines; 1993): 10,500 (1 per 830 persons).

Education and health

Education (1993)

	schools	teachers	students	student/teacher ratio
Primary (age 7–12)	2,656	12,216	414,296	33.9
Secondary (age 13–19)	105[8]	2,219[9]	88,810	35.1[9]
Voc., teacher tr.	7[8]	175[9]	2,110	12.1[9]
Higher	3[8]	341[10, 11]	4,506[8]	11.1[10, 11]

Educational attainment (1988). Percentage of population age 25 and over having: no formal schooling 85.0%; Koranic education 11.2%; primary education 2.5%; secondary 1.1%; higher 0.2%. *Literacy* (1995): percentage of total population age 15 and over literate 13.6%; males literate 20.9%; females literate 6.6%.
Health: physicians (1990) 142 (1 per 54,444 persons); hospital beds (1979) 3,261 (1 per 1,633 persons); infant mortality rate per 1,000 live births (1990–95) 124.0.
Food (1992): daily per capita caloric intake 2,257 (vegetable products 95%, animal products 5%); 95% of FAO recommended minimum requirement.

Military

Total active duty personnel (1995): 5,300 (army 98.1%, air force 1.9%). *Military expenditure as percentage of GNP* (1993): 1.5% (world 3.3%); per capita expenditure U.S.$4.

[1]Hausa, Zerma, and Fulani are national languages. [2]The departmental areas and total shown are obsolete. The total area, according to recent official estimates, is 497,000 sq mi (1,287,000 sq km); but subtotals distributing this total among the departments remain unpublished. [3]De jure. [4]The peace accord signed in October 1994 provided for an eventual limited autonomy for the Tuaregs (a Berber-speaking people), who inhabit Agadez department. [5]Guaranteed minimum wage for professionals. [6]Niger is a cofounder of the Common Benin-Niger Organization (OCBN) for Railroads and Transport, currently maintaining rail operations only in Benin but having the purpose of extending rail services from the sea at Cotonou, Benin, to Dosso and, ultimately, Niamey, Niger; in the interim, freight transported between the two countries is carried by truck. [7]Represents 1/11 of the traffic of Air Afrique, which is operated by 11 West African states. [8]1989. [9]1992. [10]1988. [11]Université de Niamey and École Nationale d'Administration du Niger only.

Nigeria

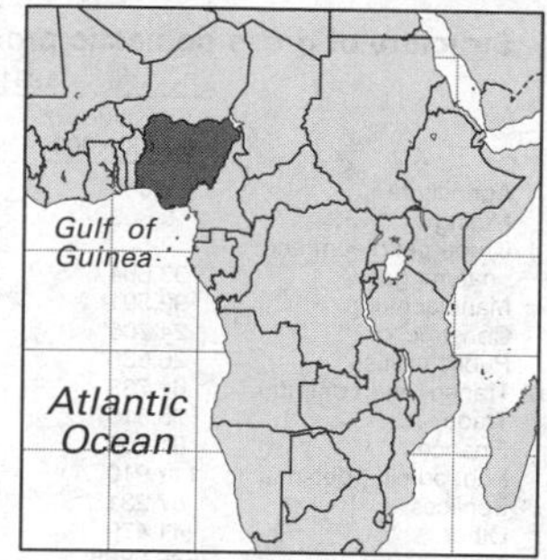

Official name: Federal Republic of Nigeria.
Form of government: military regime[1].
Head of state and government: President assisted by Provisional Council.
Capital: Abuja (Federal Capital Territory)[2].
Official language: English.
Official religion: none.
Monetary unit: 1 Nigerian naira (₦) = 100 kobo; valuation (Oct. 6, 1995) 1 U.S.$ = ₦22.00; 1 £ = ₦34.78.

Area and population

States	Capitals	area sq mi	area sq km	population 1991 census[3]
Abia	Umuahia	[4]	[4]	2,297,978
Adamawa	Yola	35,286[5]	91,390[5]	2,124,049
Akwa Ibom	Uyo	2,734	7,081	2,359,736
Anambra	Awka	6,824[6]	17,675[6]	2,767,903
Bauchi	Bauchi	24,944	64,605	4,294,413
Benue	Makurdi	17,442[7]	45,174[7]	2,780,398
Borno	Maiduguri	44,942[8]	116,400[8]	2,596,589
Cross River	Calabar	7,782	20,156	1,865,604
Delta	Asaba	[9]	[9]	2,570,181
Edo	Benin City	13,707[9]	35,500[9]	2,159,848
Enugu	Enugu	[6]	[6]	3,161,295
Imo	Owerri	4,575[4]	11,850[4]	2,485,499
Jigawa	Dutse	[10]	[10]	2,829,929
Kaduna	Kaduna	17,781	46,053	3,969,252
Kano	Kano	16,712[10]	43,285[10]	5,632,040
Katsina	Katsina	9,341	24,192	3,878,344
Kebbi	Birnin Kebbi	[11]	[11]	2,062,226
Kogi	Lokoja	[7, 12]	[7, 12]	2,099,046
Kwara	Ilorin	25,818[12]	66,869[12]	1,566,469
Lagos	Ikeja	1,292	3,345	5,685,781
Niger	Minna	25,111	65,037	2,482,367
Ogun	Abeokuta	6,472	16,762	2,338,570
Ondo	Akure	8,092	20,959	3,884,485
Osun	Oshogbo	[13]	[13]	2,203,016
Oyo	Ibadan	14,558[13]	37,705[13]	3,488,789
Plateau	Jos	22,405	58,030	3,283,704
Rivers	Port Harcourt	8,436	21,850	3,983,857
Sokoto	Sokoto	39,589[11]	102,535[11]	4,392,391
Taraba	Jalingo	[5]	[5]	1,480,590
Yobe	Damaturu	[8]	[8]	1,411,481
Federal Capital Territory				
Abuja	Abuja	2,824	7,315	378,671
TOTAL		356,660[14]	923,768	88,514,501

Demography

Population (1995): 95,434,000.
Density (1995): persons per sq mi 267.6, persons per sq km 103.3.
Urban-rural (1993): urban 37.7%; rural 62.3%.
Sex distribution (1991): male 50.32%; female 49.68%.
Age breakdown (1990): under 15, 47.4%; 15–29, 26.0%; 30–44, 14.4%; 45–59, 8.0%; 60–74, 3.5%; 75 and over, 0.7%.
Population projection: (2000) 105,885,000; (2010) 130,344,000.
Doubling time: 22 years.
Ethnic composition (1983): Hausa 21.3%; Yoruba 21.3%; Igbo (Ibo) 18.0%; Fulani 11.2%; Ibibio 5.6%; Kanuri 4.2%; Edo 3.4%; Tiv 2.2%; Ijaw 1.8%; Bura 1.7%; Nupe 1.2%; other 8.1%.
Religious affiliation (1980): Christian 49.0%, of which Protestant 26.3%, Roman Catholic 12.1%, African indigenous 10.6%; Muslim 45.0%; other 6.0%.
Major cities (1992): Lagos 1,347,000; Ibadan 1,295,000; Kano 699,900; Ogbomosho 660,600; Oshogbo 441,600; Ilorin 430,600.

Vital statistics

Birth rate per 1,000 population (1990–95): 46.5 (world avg. 25.0).
Death rate per 1,000 population (1990–95): 14.0 (world avg. 9.3).
Natural increase rate per 1,000 population (1990–95): 32.5 (world avg. 15.7).
Total fertility rate (avg. births per childbearing woman; 1990–95): 6.6.
Life expectancy at birth (1993): male 53.5 years; female 55.9 years.

National economy

Budget (1995). Revenue: ₦350,660,000,000 (1992; petroleum royalties and rents 62.0%[15]; petroleum profit tax 12.8%; import duties 11.6%; company income tax 3.9%). Expenditures: ₦351,160,000,000 (1992; recurrent expenditure 64.3%, of which debt service 53.7%, defense 2.9%, education 2.8%, police 2.5%, health 1.4%; capital expenditure 35.7%).
Public debt (external, outstanding; 1994): U.S.$29,496,000,000.
Production (metric tons except as noted). Agriculture, forestry, fishing (1994): yams 22,000,000, cassava 21,000,000, sorghum 4,000,000, rice 3,857,000, millet 3,600,000, plantains and bananas 2,497,000, corn (maize) 2,000,000, taro 1,300,000, peanuts (groundnuts) 1,200,000, green peppers 920,000, sugarcane 900,000; livestock (number of live animals) 25,497,000 goats, 16,717,000 cattle, 14,455,000 sheep; roundwood (1993) 118,052,000 cu m; fish catch (1993) 255,499. Mining and quarrying (1991): limestone 1,435,405; marble 52,379; tin 255[16]. Manufacturing (value added in U.S.$'000,000; 1990): food and beverages 703; textiles 373; chemical products 165; metal products 160; machinery and transport equipment 159; paper products 62; rubber and plastic products 61. Construction (dwellings completed; 1982): 31,038. Energy production (consumption): electricity (kW-hr; 1992) 11,800,000,000 (11,700,000,000); coal (metric tons; 1992) 95,000 (60,000); crude petroleum (barrels; 1992) 669,908,000 (87,780,000); petroleum products (metric tons; 1992) 11,355,000 (11,509,000); natural gas (cu m; 1992) 4,900,000,000 (4,900,000,000).
Tourism (1993): receipts U.S.$31,000,000; expenditures U.S.$234,000,000.
Gross national product (1993): U.S.$32,517,000,000 (U.S.$310 per capita).

Structure of gross domestic product and labour force

	1993 in value ₦'000,000	1993 % of total value	1986 labour force	1986 % of labour force
Agriculture	231,833	33.5	13,259,000	43.1
Mining	246,791	35.7	6,800	0.1
Manufacturing	38,431	5.6	1,263,700	4.1
Construction	8,019	1.2	545,600	1.8
Public utilities	1,601	0.2	130,400	0.4
Transp. and commun.	15,297	2.2	1,111,900	3.6
Trade	102,066	14.8	7,417,400	24.1
Finance	26,247	3.8	120,100	0.4
Pub. admin., defense	19,130	2.8	4,902,100	15.9
Services	2,194	0.3		
Other	...	...	2,008,500[17]	6.5[17]
TOTAL	691,609	100.0[14]	30,765,500	100.0

Population economically active (1986): total 30,765,500; activity rate 31.1% (participation rates: ages 15–64, 58.8%; female 33.3%; unemployed [1992] 4.0%).

Price and earnings indexes (1990 = 100)

	1988	1989	1990	1991	1992	1993	1994
Consumer price index	61.9	93.1	100.0	113.0	163.4	256.8	403.3
Earnings index	...		...	...	...	...	

Household income and expenditure. Avg. household size (1983) 5.0; annual income per household (1981) ₦2,300 (U.S.$3,745)[18]; sources of income (1979): self-employment 49.4%, wages 36.2%, interest 5.4%, rent 4.7%, transfer payments 4.3%; expenditures (1979): food 53.0%, fuel and light 11.4%, clothing 6.0%, transportation 4.7%, household goods 3.8%, other 21.1%.
Land use (1993): forested 12.4%; pastures 43.9%; agricultural 35.6%; other 8.1%.

Foreign trade

Balance of trade (current prices)

	1988	1989	1990	1991	1992	1993
₦'000,000	+8,283	+29,730	+68,587	+40,696	+76,298	+69,145
% of total	14.2%	34.5%	45.4%	20.2%	22.8%	18.8%

Imports (1992): ₦143,151,200,000 (machinery and transport equipment 43.2%; manufactured goods [mostly iron and steel products, textiles, and paper products] 27.8%; chemicals 16.0%; food 8.8%). *Major import sources* (1991): Germany 13.8%; U.K. 13.6%; U.S. 11.8%; France 8.9%.
Exports (1992): ₦205,613,100,000 (crude petroleum 97.9%; cocoa beans 0.6%; rubber 0.4%; fertilizer 0.2%; other exports include cocoa products, textiles, and cashew nuts). *Major export destinations* (1991): U.S. 40.7%; Spain 12.6%; Germany 8.6%; The Netherlands 5.0%; France 5.0%; Italy 4.0%.

Transport and communications

Transport. Railroads (1990): length 3,557 km[19]; passenger-km 453,000,000; metric ton-km cargo 1,870,000,000. Roads (1991): total length 112,140 km (paved 28%). Vehicles (1993): passenger cars 773,000; trucks and buses 606,000. Merchant marine (1992): vessels (100 gross tons and over) 271; total deadweight tonnage 733,329. Air transport (1992): passenger-km 996,000,000; metric ton-km cargo 11,484,000; airports (1995) 12.
Communications. Daily newspapers (1993): total number 23; total circulation 1,140,000[20]; circulation per 1,000 population 12[20]. Radio (1994): 18,000,000 receivers (1 per 5.2 persons). Television (1994): 6,100,000 receivers (1 per 15 persons). Telephones (main lines; 1993): 342,300 (1 per 267 persons).

Education and health

Education (1991–92)

	schools	teachers	students	student/ teacher ratio
Primary (age 6–12)	36,610	384,212	14,805,937	38.5
Secondary (age 12–17)	5,594[21]	141,491	3,600,620	25.4
Voc., teacher tr.	376[21]	15,738[22]	391,583[22]	24.9[22]
Higher[23]	...	19,601	335,824	17.1

Literacy (1990): total population age 15 and over literate 29,537,300 (50.7%); males literate 17,792,300 (62.3%); females literate 11,745,000 (39.5%).
Health (1987): physicians 16,145 (1 per 5,006 persons); hospital beds 95,694 (1 per 844 persons); infant mortality rate (1993) 77.3.
Food (1992): daily per capita caloric intake 2,124 (vegetable products 97%, animal products 3%); 90% of FAO recommended minimum requirement.

Military

Total active duty personnel (1995): 77,100 (army 80.4%, navy 7.3%, air force 12.3%). *Military expenditure as percentage of GNP* (1993): 0.6% (world 3.3%); per capita expenditure U.S.$2.

[1]Assumed control on Sept. 14, 1995. [2]Statutory transfer of capital from Lagos to Abuja took place in December 1991. [3]Preliminary. [4]Imo includes Abia. [5]Adamawa includes Taraba. [6]Anambra includes Enugu. [7]Benue includes part of Kogi. [8]Borno includes Yobe. [9]Edo includes Delta. [10]Kano includes Jigawa. [11]Sokoto includes Kebbi. [12]Kwara includes part of Kogi. [13]Oyo includes Osun. [14]Detail does not add to total given because of rounding. [15]Expected to be 57.2% in 1995. [16]Metal content. [17]Includes 1,263,000 unemployed. [18]Urban households only. [19]1992. [20]For 11 newspapers only. [21]1987–88. [22]1988–89. [23]1989–90.

Norway

Official name: Kongeriket Norge (Kingdom of Norway).
Form of government: constitutional monarchy with one legislative house (Parliament [165]).
Chief of state: King.
Head of government: Prime Minister.
Capital: Oslo.
Official language: Norwegian.
Official religion: Evangelical Lutheran.
Monetary unit: 1 Norwegian krone (NKr) = 100 øre; valuation (Oct. 6, 1995) 1 U.S.$ = NKr 6.31; 1 £ = NKr 9.97.

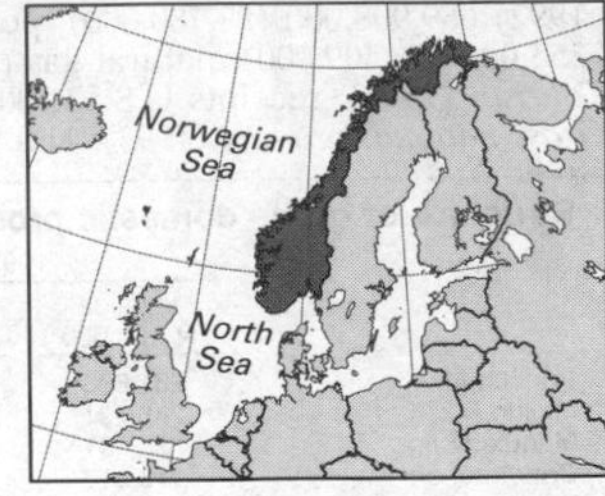

Area and population

Counties	Capitals	area[1] sq mi	area[1] sq km	population 1995[2] estimate
Akershus	—	1,898	4,917	434,544
Aust-Agder	Arendal	3,557	9,212	99,585
Buskerud	Drammen	5,763	14,927	228,506
Finnmark	Vadsø	18,779	48,637	76,668
Hedmark	Hamar	10,575	27,388	186,657
Hordaland	Bergen	6,036	15,634	422,581
Møre og Romsdal	Molde	5,832	15,104	240,215
Nordland	Bodø	14,798	38,327	241,420
Nord-Trøndelag	Steinkjer	8,673	22,463	127,560
Oppland	Lillehammer	9,753	25,260	183,194
Oslo	Oslo	175	454	482,555
Østfold	Moss	1,615	4,183	239,371
Rogaland	Stavanger	3,529	9,141	354,418
Sogn og Fjordane	Leikanger	7,195	18,634	107,612
Sør-Trøndelag	Trondheim	7,271	18,831	256,266
Telemark	Skien	5,913	15,315	163,143
Troms	Tromsø	10,021	25,954	150,606
Vest-Agder	Kristiansand	2,811	7,281	149,563
Vestfold	Tønsberg	856	2,216	203,231
TOTAL		125,050	323,878	4,347,695[3]

Demography

Population (1995): 4,360,000.
Density (1995): persons per sq mi 34.9, persons per sq km 13.5.
Urban-rural (1990): urban 75.0%; rural 25.0%.
Sex distribution (1994): male 49.45%; female 50.55%.
Age breakdown (1994): under 15, 19.3%; 15–29, 22.0%; 30–44, 21.8%; 45–59, 16.6%; 60–74, 13.0%; 75 and over, 7.3%.
Population projection: (2000) 4,426,000; (2010) 4,550,000.
Doubling time: not applicable; doubling time exceeds 100 years.
Ethnic composition (by country of citizenship; 1994): Norway 96.3%; Denmark 0.4%; Sweden 0.3%; United Kingdom 0.3%; Pakistan 0.2%; United States 0.2%; Yugoslavia 0.2%; Iran 0.2%; other 1.9%.
Religious affiliation (1980): Lutheran 87.9%; nonreligious 3.2%; other 8.9%.
Major cities (1995)[4]: Oslo 482,555; Bergen 221,645; Trondheim 142,792; Stavanger 103,496; Baerum 95,612.

Vital statistics

Birth rate per 1,000 population (1993): 13.8 (world avg. 25.0); legitimate 55.6%; illegitimate 44.4%.
Death rate per 1,000 population (1993): 10.9 (world avg. 9.3).
Natural increase rate per 1,000 population (1993): 2.9 (world avg. 15.7).
Total fertility rate (avg. births per childbearing woman; 1994): 1.9.
Marriage rate per 1,000 population (1993): 4.5.
Divorce rate per 1,000 population (1993): 2.5.
Life expectancy at birth (1993): male 74.2 years; female 80.3 years.
Major causes of death per 100,000 population (1992): ischemic heart disease 242.6; malignant neoplasms (cancers) 224.5; cerebrovascular disease 126.1.

National economy

Budget (1995). Revenue: NKr 339,237,000,000 (social-security taxes 24.6%, value-added taxes 24.2%, taxes on interest and dividends 9.2%, taxes on petroleum income and activity 3.1%, ordinary income tax 2.8%). Expenditures: NKr 339,144,000,000 (social security and welfare 25.2%, health 7.9%, debt service 6.0%).
Land use (1992): forested 27.1%; meadows and pastures 0.4%; agricultural and under permanent cultivation 2.9%; built-up and other 69.6%.
Tourism (1993): receipts from visitors U.S.$1,849,000,000; expenditures by nationals abroad U.S.$3,565,000,000.
Production (metric tons except as noted). Agriculture, forestry, fishing (1993): barley 631,000, potatoes 454,000, oats 380,000, wheat 360,000; livestock (number of live animals; 1994) 990,900 sheep[5], 979,600 cattle, 746,700 pigs; roundwood (1992) 10,884,000 cu m; fish catch (1994) 2,329,417, of which herring 535,558, cod 371,957, mackerel 259,765 saithe 187,786. Mining and quarrying (1993)[6]: iron ore 2,162,000, copper 36,000, zinc 29,000, lead 3,200. Manufacturing (value added in NKr '000,000; 1993): machinery and equipment 27,553, of which transport equipment 12,651, electrical equipment 6,478; food products 15,466; paper and paper products 13,055; chemical products 7,858; wood and wood products 2,942. Construction (1994): residential 2,787,000 sq m; nonresidential 2,987,000 sq m. Energy production (consumption): electricity (kW-hr; 1992) 117,682,000,000 (108,938,000,000); coal (metric tons; 1992) 391,000 (703,000); crude petroleum (barrels; 1992) 815,997,000 (105,935,000); petroleum products (metric tons; 1992) 14,109,000 (7,834,000); natural gas (cu m; 1992) 28,036,000,000 (2,032,000,000).
Gross national product (1993): U.S.$113,527,000,000 (U.S.$26,340 per capita).

Structure of gross domestic product and labour force

	1991 in value NKr '000,000	1991 % of total value	1993 labour force	1993 % of labour force
Agriculture	20,052	2.9	115,000	5.4
Mining	3,908	0.6	25,000	1.2
Crude petroleum and natural gas	99,664	14.5	...	...
Manufacturing	92,591	13.5	305,000	14.3
Construction	24,705	3.6	126,000	5.9
Public utilities	26,386	3.8	22,000	1.0
Transp. and commun.	61,738	9.0	162,000	7.6
Trade	75,315[7]	11.0[7]	362,000	17.0
Finance	61,709	9.0	157,000	7.4
Pub. admin., defense	111,910	16.3	793,000	37.2
Services	67,231	9.8		
Other	41,479	6.0	64,000[8]	3.0[8]
TOTAL	686,686[9]	100.0	2,131,000	100.0

Public debt (1990): U.S.$23,430,000,000.
Population economically active (1994): total 2,151,000; activity rate of total population 49.7% (participation rates: ages 16–64, 79.6%; female 47.4%; unemployed 5.4%).

Price and earnings indexes (1990 = 100)

	1988	1989	1990	1991	1992	1993	1994
Consumer price index	91.9	96.0	100.0	103.4	105.8	108.2	109.8
Hourly earnings index	90.1	94.5	100.0	105.1	108.5	...	...

Household income and expenditure. Average household size (1993) 2.2; consumption expenditure per household (1992) NKr 206,908 (U.S.$33,294); sources of income (1991): wages and salaries 58.8%, social security 24.2%, self-employment and property income 16.9%; expenditure (1991): housing 19.4%, food 18.4%, transportation 12.4%, clothing and footwear 6.8%, household furniture and equipment 6.7%, beverages and tobacco 7.0%.

Foreign trade

Balance of trade (current prices)

	1989	1990	1991	1992	1993	1994
NKr '000,000	+27,248	+48,231	+59,565	+61,730	+55,635	+51,512
% of total	7.9%	12.9%	15.9%	16.4%	14.0%	11.8%

Imports (1994): NKr 192,963,300,000 (machinery and transport equipment 34.0%, of which road vehicles 7.7%, ships 4.0%; metals and metal products 11.0%, of which iron and steel 4.3%; food products 4.8%, of which fruits and vegetables 1.6%; petroleum products 2.2%). *Major import sources:* Sweden 14.9%; Germany 13.9%; U.K. 10.3%; Denmark 7.4%.
Exports (1993): NKr 244,475,100,000 (fuels and fuel products 48.8%, of which crude petroleum 37.7%, natural gas 6.8%; machinery and transport equipment 16.4%; metals and metal products 11.4%, of which aluminum 4.9%; food products 8.3%, of which fish 7.7%). *Major export destinations:* U.K. 20.7%; Germany 12.1%; Sweden 9.5%; The Netherlands 9.5%.

Transport and communications

Transport. Railroads (1992): route length 4,026 km; passenger-km 2,312,000,000; metric ton-km cargo 2,300,000,000. Roads (1995): total length 90,174 km (1991; paved 70%). Vehicles (1994): passenger cars 1,653,678; trucks and buses 404,108. Merchant marine (1992): vessels (100 gross tons and over) 2,499; total deadweight tonnage 38,298,755. Air transport (1993): passenger-km 8,083,913,000; metric ton-km cargo 863,880,000; airports (1995) 48.
Communications. Daily newspapers (1994): total number 64; total circulation 2,858,935; circulation per 1,000 population 659. Radio (1994): 3,342,000 receivers (1 per 1.3 persons). Television (1994): 2,000,000 receivers (1 per 2.2 persons). Telephones (main lines; 1993): 2,334,800 (1 per 1.8 persons).

Education and health

Education (1993–94)

	schools	teachers	students	student/teacher ratio
Primary (age 7–12)	3,325	36,196	466,991	12.9
Secondary (age 13–18) and vocational	771	21,780	240,506	11.0
Higher	195	10,213	172,574	16.9

Educational attainment (1993). Percentage of population age 16 and over having: lower secondary education 29.6%; higher secondary 51.6%; higher 18.8%. *Literacy* (1994): virtually 100% literate.
Health: physicians (1994) 14,497 (1 per 299 persons); hospital beds (1993) 22,961 (1 per 183 persons); infant mortality rate per 1,000 live births (1992) 5.9.
Food (1988–90): daily per capita caloric intake 3,221 (vegetable products 65%, animal products 35%); 120% of FAO recommended minimum requirement.

Military

Total active duty personnel (1994): 32,500 (army 55.4%, navy 20.3%, air force 24.3%). *Military expenditure as percentage of GNP* (1993): 3.1% (world avg. 3.3%); per capita expenditure U.S.$752.

[1]Excludes Svalbard and Jan Mayen (24,360 sq mi [63,080 sq km]). [2]January 1. [3]Includes the Norwegian population of Svalbard and Jan Mayen, registered as residents in municipalities on the mainland. [4]Population of municipalities. [5]One year and over. [6]Metal content of ore. [7]Includes hotels. [8]Includes 53,000 unemployed not previously employed. [9]Detail does not add to total given because of rounding.

Oman

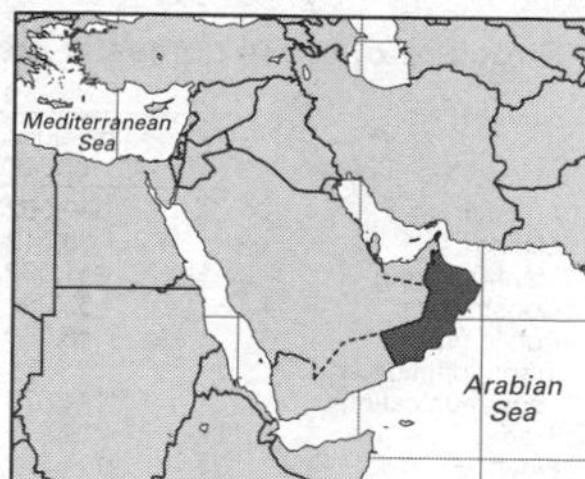

Official name: Salṭanat ʿUmān (Sultanate of Oman).
Form of government: monarchy[1].
Head of state and government: Sultan.
Capital: Muscat.
Official language: Arabic.
Official religion: Islam.
Monetary unit: 1 rial Omani (RO) = 1,000 baizas; valuation (Oct. 6, 1995) 1 RO = U.S.$2.63 = £1.64.

Area and population

		area[2]		population
Regions[3]	Centres[4]	sq mi	sq km	1993 census
al-Bāṭinah	ar-Rustāq; Ṣuḥār	5,320	13,770	538,763
ad-Dākhilīyah	Nizwā; Samā'il	29,770	77,110	220,403
al-Janūbīyah	Salālah	45,370	117,510	174,888
Masqaṭ	Muscat (Masqaṭ)	1,420	3,670	622,506
Musandam	Khaṣab	590	1,530	27,669
ash-Sharqīyah	Ibrā; Sūr	16,190	41,920	247,551
aẓ-Ẓāhirah	al-Buraymī; ʿIbri	19,490	50,490	169,710
TOTAL		118,150	306,000	2,017,591[5]

Demography

Population (1995): 2,163,000.
Density (1995): persons per sq mi 18.3, persons per sq km 7.1.
Urban-rural (1995): urban 13.2%; rural 86.8%.
Sex distribution (1995): male 52.47%; female 47.53%.
Age breakdown (1995): under 15, 47.5%; 15–29, 24.2%; 30–44, 15.8%; 45–59, 8.4%; 60–74, 3.5%; 75 and over, 0.7%.
Population projection: (2000) 2,626,000; (2010) 3,783,000.
Doubling time: 21 years.
Ethnic composition (1990): Omani Arab 73.5%; Pakistani (mostly Baluchi) 21.0%; other 5.5%.
Religious affiliation (1984): Muslim 86%; Hindu 13%; other 1%.
Major cities (1990): Muscat 100,000[6]; Nizwā 62,880; Samā'il 44,721; Salālah 10,000[7].

Vital statistics

Birth rate per 1,000 population (1995): 38.1 (world avg. 25.0).
Death rate per 1,000 population (1995): 5.0 (world avg. 9.3).
Natural increase rate per 1,000 population (1995): 33.1 (world avg. 15.7).
Total fertility rate (avg. births per childbearing woman; 1995): 6.2.
Marriage rate per 1,000 population: n.a.
Divorce rate per 1,000 population: n.a.
Life expectancy at birth (1995): male 68.3 years; female 72.3 years.
Morbidity (reported cases of illness per 100,000 population; 1989): influenza 6,823; malaria 1,235; chicken pox 1,156; mumps 1,048; amebic dysentery 376; measles 294; bacillary dysentery 206; infectious hepatitis 96; tuberculosis 33; brucellosis 15.

National economy

Budget (1995). Revenue: RO 1,847,000,000 (oil revenue 73.2%; other 26.8%). Expenditures: RO 2,139,000,000 (1994; recurrent budget 78.9%, of which defense 43.8%, education 12.0%, general public services 6.8%, fuel and energy 6.8%, health 5.4%; capital development projects and subsidies 21.1%).
Public debt (external, outstanding; 1993): U.S.$2,319,000,000.
Gross national product (at current market prices; 1993): U.S.$9,631,000,000 (U.S.$5,600 per capita).

Structure of gross domestic product and labour force

	1994		1990	
	in value RO '000,000[8]	% of total value	labour force	% of labour force
Agriculture[9]	147.1	3.3	146,400	27.7
Mining	1,717.1	38.4	2,800	0.5
Manufacturing	232.0	5.2	32,800	6.2
Construction	175.0	3.9	104,800	19.8
Public utilities	64.9	1.5	4,100	0.8
Transportation and communications	208.3	4.7	14,500	2.7
Trade	690.0[10]	15.4[10]	87,500	16.5
Finance	188.2[11]	4.2[11]	9,400	1.8
Pub. admin., defense	784.1	17.5	81,000	15.3
Services	526.9[12]	11.8[12]	45,800	8.7
Other	−262.0[13]	−5.9[13]	—	—
TOTAL	4,471.6	100.0	529,100	100.0

Tourism (1993): receipts from visitors U.S.$85,000,000[14]; expenditures by nationals abroad U.S.$47,000,000.
Household income and expenditure. Average household size (1986) 3.7; income per household: n.a.; sources of income: n.a.; expenditure (1990): housing and utilities 27.8%, food, beverages, and tobacco 26.4%, transportation 19.8%, clothing and shoes 7.8%, household goods and furniture 6.1%, education, health services, entertainment, and other 12.1%.
Production (metric tons except as noted). Agriculture, forestry, fishing (1994): vegetables and melons 169,000 (of which watermelons 32,000), dates 139,000, bananas 26,000, mangoes 11,000, onions 9,000, potatoes 6,000, papayas 3,000, tobacco leaf 2,000, wheat 1,000; livestock (number of live animals) 739,000 goats, 149,000 sheep, 144,000 cattle, 96,000 camels, 3,000,000 chickens; fish catch (1994) 118,571. Mining and quarrying (1993): copper 12,000; silver 3,300 kg; gold 90 kg. Manufacturing (value added in RO '000; 1990): textiles and apparel 13,957; metal products 2,303; machinery and equipment 1,797; chemical products 840; food products and beverages 715; wood products 439; paper products 282; other major products include refined petroleum products. Construction (1989): number of residential permits 3,408; nonresidential permits 353. Energy production (consumption): electricity (kW-hr; 1992) 6,237,000,000 (6,237,000,000); coal, none (none); crude petroleum (barrels; 1992) 269,869,000 (21,505,000); petroleum products (metric tons; 1992) 3,043,000 (1,530,000); natural gas (cu m; 1992) 1,839,200,000 (1,839,200,000).
Population economically active (1990)[15]: total 680,850; activity rate of total population 39.9% (participation rates [1988]: ages 15–64, 57.2%; female 6.3%; unemployed, n.a.).

Price and earnings indexes (1990 = 100)

	1989	1990	1991	1992	1993	1994	1995[16]
Consumer price index	99.4	100.0	104.6	105.6	106.9	106.1	103.7
Earnings index	...	...	...	...	...	...	...

Land use (1993): meadows and pastures 4.7%; agricultural and under permanent cultivation 0.3%; other (mostly desert and developed area) 95.0%.

Foreign trade

Balance of trade (current prices)

	1989	1990	1991	1992	1993	1994
RO '000,000	+654	+1,042	+594	+636	+411	+588
% of total	26.4%	32.6%	18.8%	17.5%	11.1%	16.0%

Imports (1994): U.S.$4,739,000,000 (machinery and transport equipment 42.7%, basic manufactured goods 15.1%, food and live animals 13.0%, miscellaneous manufactured articles 9.9%, beverages and tobacco 6.4%, chemicals 5.5%). *Major import sources:* United Arab Emirates 29.1%; Japan 19.9%; United Kingdom 8.8%; United States 6.7%; Germany 4.9%; India 3.1%.
Exports (1994): U.S.$4,831,000,000 (petroleum 76.3%, metals and metal products 1.6%, live animals and products 1.4%, textiles 1.2%). *Major export destinations*[17]: United Arab Emirates 41.9%; Hong Kong 16.9%; Iran 9.1%; Saudi Arabia 4.2%; United States 4.1%; Tanzania 3.6%.

Transport and communications

Transport. Railroads: none. Roads (1994): total length 16,372 mi, 26,349 km (paved 20%). Vehicles (1993): automobiles 180,700, trucks and buses 108,600. Merchant marine (1992): vessels (100 gross tons and over) 26; total deadweight tonnage 11,727. Air transport (1994)[18]: passenger-mi 1,515,300,000, passenger-km 2,438,700,000; short ton-mi cargo 83,636,000, metric ton-km cargo 122,107,000; airports (1995) with scheduled flights 6.
Communications. Daily newspapers (1992): total number 4; total circulation 79,000; circulation per 1,000 population 48. Radio (1994): total number of receivers 900,000 (1 per 2.3 persons). Television (1994): total number of receivers 1,500,000 (1 per 1.4 persons). Telephones (main lines; 1993): 147,800 (1 per 11.6 persons).

Education and health

Education (1992–93)

	schools	teachers	students	student/ teacher ratio
Primary (age 6–14)	416	10,839	280,011	20.7
Secondary (age 15–17)	128[19]	8,112	137,947	17.0
Voc., teacher tr.	25[19]	425	2,814	6.6
Higher	5[19]	433[20]	3,615[21]	...

Educational attainment: n.a. *Literacy* (1990): total population age 6 and over literate 41%; males literate 58%; females literate 24%.
Health (1992): physicians 2,095 (1 per 910 persons); hospital beds 4,472 (1 per 426 persons); infant mortality rate per 1,000 live births (1995) 34.3.
Food: daily per capita caloric intake, n.a.

Military

Total active duty personnel (1995): 39,800 (army 79.2%[22], navy 10.5%, air force 10.3%); foreign troops 3,700. *Military expenditure as percentage of GDP* (1994): 15.9% (world 2.6%); per capita expenditure U.S.$991.

[1]Appointed 80-member Consultative Council is an advisory body only. [2]Approximate; no comprehensive survey of surface area has ever been carried out in Oman. [3]Regions are divided into 59 governorates. [4]Centres of the regions are not administrative capitals. [5]Includes the population (16,101) of al-Wosta, which is not shown separately. [6]1991 estimate. [7]1982. [8]In purchasers' value at current prices. [9]Agriculture includes fishing. [10]Trade includes restaurants and hotels. [11]Finance includes business services. [12]Services include real estate services. [13]Other includes import duties less imputed bank service charges. [14]1992. [15]Non-Omani workers constitute approximately 55–60% of the labour force. [16]Second quarter. [17]Non-oil exports only. [18]One-fourth apportionment of international flights of Gulf Air. [19]1989–90. [20]1990; universities and equivalent institutes. [21]1991–92. [22]Including personnel of Royal Household units not formally part of army table of organization.

Pakistan

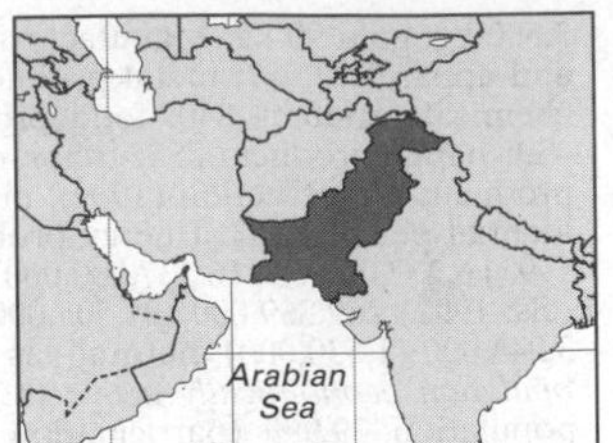

Official name: Islām-ī Jamhūrīya-e Pākistān (Islamic Republic of Pakistan).
Form of government: multiparty, federal Islamic republic with two legislative houses (Senate [87]; National Assembly [217]).
Chief of state: President.
Chief of government: Prime Minister.
Capital: Islāmābād.
Official language: Urdū.
Official religion: Islam.
Monetary unit: 1 Pakistan Rupee (PRs) = 100 paisa; valuation (Oct. 6, 1995) 1 U.S.$ = PRs 31.59; 1 £ = PRs 49.94.

Area and population

		area[1]		population
				1983
Provinces	**Capitals**	sq mi	sq km	estimate[2]
Balochistān	Quetta	134,051	347,190	4,611,000
North-West Frontier	Peshāwar	28,773	74,521	11,658,000
Punjab	Lahore	79,284	205,344	50,460,000
Sindh	Karāchi	54,407	140,914	20,312,000
Federally Administered Tribal Areas	...	10,509	27,220	2,329,000
Federal Capital Area				
Islāmābād	...	350	906	359,000
TOTAL		307,374	796,095	89,729,000

Demography

Population (1995)[2]: 140,497,000.
Density (1995)[3]: persons per sq mi 413.6, persons per sq km 159.7.
Urban-rural (1993): urban 32.0%; rural 68.0%.
Sex distribution (1993): male 52.50%; female 47.50%.
Age breakdown (1988): under 15, 46.3%; 15–29, 24.6%; 30–44, 14.0%; 45–59, 9.0%; 60–74, 4.8%; 75 and over, 1.3%.
Population projection: (2000) 161,827,000; (2010) 210,104,000.
Doubling time: 24 years.
Linguistic composition (1981): Punjābī 48.2%; Pashto 13.1%; Sindhī 11.8%; Saraiki 9.8%; Urdū 7.6%; other 9.5%.
Religious affiliation (1981): Muslim 96.7%; Christian 1.6%; Hindu 1.5%; other 0.2%.
Major cities (1981): Karāchi 5,208,132; Lahore 2,952,689; Faisalābād 1,104,209; Rāwalpindi 794,843; Islāmābād 204,364.

Vital statistics

Birth rate per 1,000 population (1995): 39.0 (world avg. 25.0).
Death rate per 1,000 population (1995): 9.0 (world avg. 9.3).
Natural increase rate per 1,000 population (1995): 30.0 (world avg. 15.7).
Total fertility rate (avg. births per childbearing woman; 1995): 5.9.
Marriage rate per 1,000 population (1975–80): 10.7.
Divorce rate per 1,000 population (1975–80): 0.3.
Life expectancy at birth (1995): male 62.0 years; female 64.0 years.
Major causes of death (percentage of total deaths; 1987): malaria 18.2%; childhood diseases 12.1%; diseases of digestive system 9.8%; diseases of respiratory system 9.2%; infection of intestinal tract 7.7%.

National economy

Budget (1993–94). Revenue: PRs 288,693,000,000 (nontax receipts 27.1%, customs duties 25.7%, excise taxes 14.5%, income taxes 14.0%). Expenditures: PRs 272,455,000,000 (public-debt service 48.1%, defense 32.7%, subsidies 1.8%, law and order 1.7%).
Production (metric tons except as noted). Agriculture, forestry, fishing (1993–94): sugarcane 44,427,000, wheat 15,114,000, rice 3,995,000, corn (maize) 1,215,000, gram 406,000, jowar 212,000, cotton 8,041,000 bales; livestock (number of live animals; 1994) 41,340,000 goats, 28,975,000 sheep, 18,887,000 buffalo, 18,146,000 cattle, 1,121,000 camels, 182,600,000 poultry; roundwood (1993) 27,776,000 cu m; fish catch (1993) 621,695. Mining and quarrying (1993–94): limestone 8,975,000; rock salt 895,000; gypsum 659,000; silica sand 177,000; chromite 10,630. Manufacturing (1993–94): cement 8,200,000; chemical fertilizers 3,875,000, of which urea 3,104,000; refined sugar 2,992,000; cotton yarn 1,288,000; vegetable products 700,000; chemicals 383,000; jute textiles 76,900; paper and paperboard 34,400; cotton textiles 307,000,000 sq m; cigarettes 37,500,000,000 units; motor-vehicle tires 1,594,000 units; bicycles 557,000 units. Construction (value in PRs; 1984): residential 8,490,000,000; nonresidential 14,579,000,000. Energy production (consumption): electricity (kW-hr; 1993) 55,311,000,000 (55,311,000,000); coal (metric tons; 1993) 3,075,000 (4,236,000); crude petroleum (barrels; 1993) 21,900,000 (51,548,000); petroleum products (metric tons; 1993) 6,041,000 (10,914,000); natural gas (cu m; 1993) 14,240,000,000 (14,240,000,000).
Household income and expenditure (1988). Average household size 6.3; income per household PRs 25,572 (U.S.$1,420); sources of income: self-employment 56.0%, wages and salaries 22.0%, other 22.0%; expenditure: food 47.0%, housing 12.0%, clothing and footwear 8.0%, other 33.0%.
Land use (1993): forested 4.5%; meadows and pastures 6.5%; agricultural and under permanent cultivation 27.6%; built-on, wasteland, and other 61.4%.
Gross national product (at current market prices; 1993): U.S.$54,045,000,000 (U.S.$440 per capita).

Structure of gross domestic product and labour force

	1993–94		1992–93	
	in value PRs '000,000	% of total value	labour force	% of labour force
Agriculture	349,592	22.3	15,030,000	44.5
Mining	8,712	0.6	3,920,000	11.6
Manufacturing	241,932	15.5		
Construction	55,081	3.5	2,100,000	6.2
Public utilities	45,665	2.9	260,000	0.8
Transportation and communications	144,870	9.3	1,660,000	4.9
Trade	224,255	14.3	4,200,000	12.4
Finance	114,880	7.3		
Pub. admin., defense	105,215	6.7	4,510,000	13.3
Services	109,172	7.0		
Other	165,600	10.6	2,120,000[4]	6.3[4]
TOTAL	1,564,974	100.0	33,800,000	100.0

Population economically active (1992–93): total 33,800,000; activity rate of total population 28.0% (participation rates: ages 15–64 [1991–92] 50.8%; female [1991–92] 14.2%; unemployed 6.3%).

Price index (1990 = 100)

	1988	1989	1990	1991	1992	1993	1994
Consumer price index	85.0	91.7	100.0	111.8	122.4	133.9	150.6

Tourism (1993): receipts from visitors U.S.$111,000,000; expenditures by nationals abroad U.S.$633,000,000.
Public debt (external, outstanding; 1993): U.S.$20,306,000,000.

Foreign trade[5]

Balance of trade (current prices)

	1989	1990	1991	1992	1993	1994
PRs '000,000	−37,093	−24,896	−28,537	−31,283	−54,352	−22,968
% of total	16.1%	9.3%	8.4%	7.9%	12.6%	4.9%

Imports (1993–94): PRs 258,250,100,000 (petroleum products 16.3%, specialized machinery 9.1%, road vehicles 6.3%, vegetable oil and fats 5.7%, organic chemicals 4.1%, iron and steel manufactures 3.8%, electrical machinery 3.4%, general industrial machinery 3.2%). *Major import sources:* Japan 11.8%; U.S. 10.6%; Malaysia 5.5%; Saudi Arabia 5.4%; Kuwait 5.3%; China 5.1%; U.K. 4.9%; France 4.0%; Germany 3.9%.
Exports (1993–94): PRs 205,499,400,000 (textile fabrics 53.6%, ready-made garments 22.0%, rice 3.6%, leather and leather goods 3.5%, fresh fish 2.3%, cotton 2.1%, sugar and honey 1.8%). *Major export destinations:* U.S. 14.4%; Japan 8.0%; Germany 8.0%; U.K. 7.8%; Dubayy 6.3%; France 4.1%; Saudi Arabia 3.5%; The Netherlands 3.1%.

Transport and communications

Transport. Railroads (1993–94): route length (1992–93) 5,453 mi, 8,775 km; passenger-mi 10,208,000,000, passenger-km 16,428,000,000; short ton-mi cargo 4,011,000,000, metric ton-km cargo 5,856,000,000. Roads (1993): total length 121,119 mi, 194,922 km (paved 54%). Vehicles (1993): passenger cars 732,100; trucks and buses 252,023. Merchant marine (1992): vessels (100 gross tons and over) 73; total deadweight tonnage 513,823. Air transport (1993): passenger-km 9,900,000,000; metric ton-km cargo 417,312,000; airports (1995) with scheduled flights 34.
Communications. Daily newspapers (1992): total number 274; total circulation 809,000; circulation per 1,000 population 6. Radio (1994): total number of receivers 10,200,000 (1 per 13 persons). Television (1994): total number of receivers 2,080,000 (1 per 66 persons). Telephones (main lines; 1993): 1,604,800 (1 per 76 persons).

Education and health

Education (1993–94)

	schools	teachers	students	student/ teacher ratio
Primary (age 5–9)	156,450	383,400	15,532,000	40.5
Secondary (age 10–14)	24,083	294,900	5,199,000	17.6
Voc., teacher tr.	712	6,800	92,000	13.5
Higher	804	29,600	758,000	25.6

Educational attainment (1981). Percentage of population age 25 and over having: no formal schooling 78.9%; some primary education 8.7%; some secondary 10.5%; postsecondary 1.9%. *Literacy* (1993): total population age 15 and over literate 35.0%; males literate 47.3%; females literate 22.3%.
Health (1993): physicians 63,033 (1 per 2,107 persons); hospital beds 78,044 (1 per 1,702 persons); infant mortality rate per 1,000 live births (1995) 83.0.
Food (1992): daily per capita caloric intake 2,315 (vegetable products 86%, animal products 14%); 100% of FAO recommended minimum requirement.

Military

Total active duty personnel (1995): 587,000 (army 88.6%, navy 3.7%, air force 7.7%). *Military expenditure as percentage of GNP* (1993): 6.4% (world 3.3%); per capita expenditure U.S.$23.

[1]Excludes 32,323 sq mi (83,716 sq km) of Jammu and Kashmir, administered, but not claimed, by Pakistan. [2]1983 provincial estimates exclude and 1995 estimate includes Afghan refugees and residents of Pakistani-occupied Jammu and Kashmir. [3]Based on the combined areas of Pakistan and Jammu and Kashmir, 339,697 sq mi (879,811 sq km). [4]Includes unemployed. [5]Import figures are f.o.b. in balance of trade and c.i.f. for commodities and trading partners.

Palau

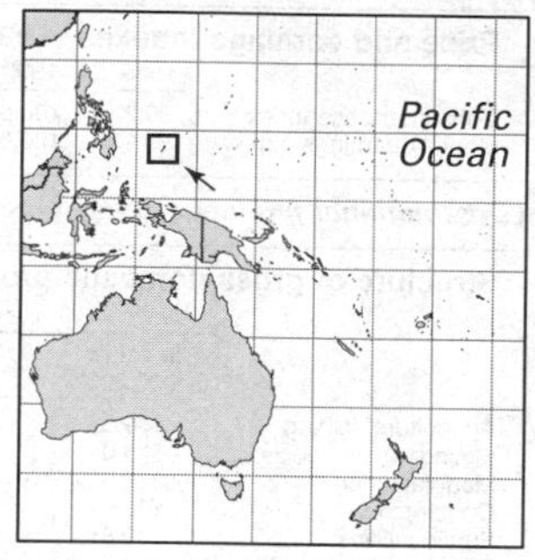

Official name: Belu'u era Belau (Palauan); Republic of Palau (English).
Form of government: unitary republic with a national congress composed of two legislative houses (Senate [14]; House of Delegates [16]).
Head of state and government: President.
Capital: Koror.
Official languages[1]: Palauan; English.
Official religion: none.
Monetary unit: 1 U.S. dollar (U.S.$) = 100 cents; valuation (Oct. 6, 1995) 1 £ = U.S.$1.58.

Area and population

	area		population
States	sq mi	sq km	1990 census
Aimeliik	20	52	439
Airai	17	44	1,234
Angaur	3	8	206
Hatobohei	1	3	22
Kayangel	1	3	137
Koror	7	18	10,501
Melekeok	11	28	244
Ngaraard	14	36	310
Ngarchelong	4	10	354
Ngardmau	18	47	149
Ngatpang	18	47	62
Ngchesar	16	41	287
Ngeremlengui	25	65	281
Ngiwal	10	26	234
Peleliu	5	13	601
Sonsorol	1	3	61
Other			
Rock Islands	18	47	—
TOTAL	188[2]	488	15,122

Demography

Population (1995): 16,900.
Density (1995): persons per sq mi 89.9, persons per sq km 34.7.
Urban-rural (1990): urban 59.6%; rural 40.4%.
Sex distribution (1990): male 53.82%; female 46.18%.
Age breakdown (1990): under 15, 30.3%; 15–29, 27.8%; 30–44, 22.8%; 45–59, 10.5%; 60–74, 6.4%; 75 and over, 2.2%.
Population projection: (2000) 18,500; (2010) 21,900.
Doubling time: 35 years.
Ethnic composition (1990): Palauan 83.2%; Filipino 9.8%; other Micronesian 2.0%; Chinese 1.2%; white 0.8%; other 3.0%.
Religious affiliation (1990): Roman Catholic 40.8%; Protestant 24.8% (includes members of the Modekngei Church); traditional beliefs 24.8%; other 9.6%.
Major cities (1992): Koror 10,500.

Vital statistics

Birth rate per 1,000 population (1995): 22.1 (world avg. 25.0); legitimate, n.a.; illegitimate, n.a.
Death rate per 1,000 population (1995): 6.6 (world avg. 9.3).
Natural increase rate per 1,000 population (1995): 16.0 (world avg. 15.7).
Total fertility rate (avg. births per childbearing woman; 1995): 2.9.
Marriage rate per 1,000 population: n.a.
Divorce rate per 1,000 population: n.a.
Life expectancy at birth (1995): male 69.1 years; female 73.0 years.
Major causes of death per 100,000 population (1993): diseases of the circulatory system 190.9; malignant and benign neoplasms (cancers) 135.5; accidents, poisoning, and violence 110.8; diseases of the respiratory system 43.1; infectious and parasitic diseases 43.1.

National economy

Budget (1992). Revenue: U.S.$45,300,000 (cash grants from the U.S. 38.0%, tax revenue 33.6%). Expenditures: U.S.$45,100,000.
Tourism (1994): total number of visitors 44,073.
Gross national product (at current market prices; 1994)[3]: U.S.$81,800,000 (U.S.$5,000 per capita).

Structure of gross domestic product and labour force

	1985		1990	
	in value U.S.$'000	% of total value	labour force	% of labour force
Agriculture, fisheries	5,453	17.2	445	7.3
Mining } Manufacturing }	130	0.4	14	0.2
			100	1.7
Public utilities	482	1.5	78	1.3
Construction	3,812	12.0	919	15.1
Transportation and communications	1,046	3.3	415	6.8
Trade	6,332	20.0	1,207	19.9
Finance	677	2.1	120	2.0
Public administration, defense	715	2.3	870	14.3
Services	12,075	38.1	1,672	27.6
Other	936[4]	3.0[4]	232	3.8
TOTAL	31,658	100.0[2]	6,072	100.0

Production (metric tons except as noted). Agriculture, forestry, fishing: cash crops (value of sales in U.S.$; 1992) eggs 252,320, fruit and vegetables 122,805, betel nuts 87,284; principal subsistence crops include taro, cassava, sweet potatoes; livestock (number of live animals; 1984) pigs 1,343, cows 82, goats 52, poultry 9,500; roundwood, n.a.; fish catch (1992) 4,068 (major species are parrot fish, snapper, unicorn fish, and rabbitfish). Mining and quarrying: n.a. Manufacturing: includes handicrafts and small items. Construction: Energy production (consumption): electricity (kW-hr; 1990) 22,000,000 (23,288,000); coal, none (n.a.); crude petroleum, none (n.a.); petroleum products, none (n.a.); natural gas, none (n.a.).
Public debt (external, outstanding; 1993): U.S.$100,000,000.
Population economically active (1990): total 6,072; activity rate of total population 40.2% (participation rates: ages 16–64, 64.1%; female 36.9%; unemployed 7.8%).
Land use: n.a.
Household income and expenditure. Average household size (1990) 5.0; income per household (1989) U.S.$8,882; sources of income (1989): wages 63.7%, social security 12.0%, self-employment 7.4%, retirement 5.5%, interest, dividend, or net rental 4.3%, remittance 4.1%, public assistance 1.0%, other 2.0%; expenditure: n.a.

Foreign trade

Imports (1993): U.S.$40,000,000 (1984; food and agricultural raw materials 28.9%, machinery and transport equipment 24.5%, chemicals and related products 4.0%). *Major import sources* (1984): United States 41.8%; Japan 38.2%.
Exports (1989): U.S.$600,000 (1984; food and agricultural raw materials 69.1%, manufactured goods 30.9%). *Major export destinations* (1984): Japan 58.8%; United States 8.0%.

Transport and communications

Transport. Railroads: none. Roads (1993): total length 40 mi, 64 km (paved 59%). Vehicles (1992): passenger cars and trucks 2,945. Merchant marine (1991): vessels (100 gross tons and over) 4; total deadweight tonnage, n.a. Air transport (1992): passenger arrivals 47,582, passenger departures 45,883; airports (1995) with scheduled flights 1.
Communications. Daily newspapers: none. Radio (1994): total number of receivers 9,000 (1 per 1.8 persons). Television (1994): total number of receivers 1,600 (1 per 10.3 persons). Telephones (main lines; 1992): 2,009 (1 per 7.9 persons).

Education and health

Education (1992)

	schools[5]	teachers[5]	students	student/ teacher ratio
Primary (age 6–13)	26	289	2,480	...
Secondary (age 14–18)	6	[6]	981	...
Vocational	1[7]	36[7]	815[8]	...
Higher	...	...	382	...

Educational attainment (1990). Percentage of population age 25 and over having: no formal schooling 1.8%; some primary education 21.8%; completed primary 5.5%; some secondary 13.3%; completed secondary 26.6%; some postsecondary 11.1%; higher 19.9%. *Literacy* (1990): total population age 15 and over literate 10,288 (97.6%); males literate 5,677 (98.3%); females literate 4,611 (96.6%).
Health (1990): physicians[9] 10 (1 per 1,518 persons); hospital beds 70 (1 per 200 persons); infant mortality rate per 1,000 live births (1995) 25.1.
Food: daily per capita caloric intake, n.a.

Military

The United States is responsible for the external security of Palau, as specified in the Compact of Free Association of Oct. 1, 1994.

[1]Sonsorolese-Tobian is also, according to official sources, considered an official language. [2]Detail does not add to total given because of rounding. [3]Gross national product comprises U.S. government spending only. [4]Includes ownership of dwellings. [5]1987. [6]Included with primary. [7]1984. [8]Figure reflects completed requirements for a program. [9]Government-employed health personnel only.

Panama

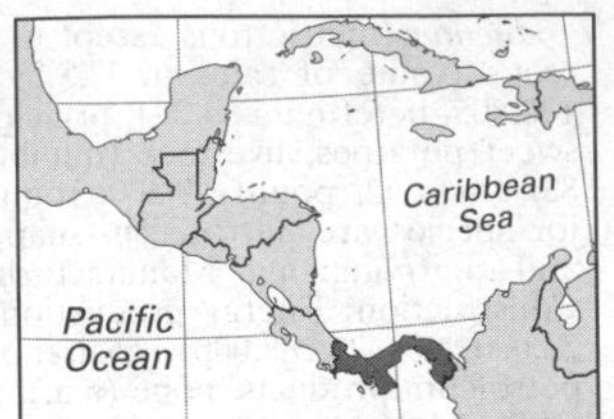

Official name: República de Panamá (Republic of Panama).
Form of government: multiparty republic with one legislative house (Legislative Assembly [72]).
Head of state and government: President assisted by Vice Presidents.
Capital: Panama City.
Official language: Spanish.
Official religion: none.
Monetary unit: 1 balboa (B) = 100 cents; valuation (Oct. 6, 1995)
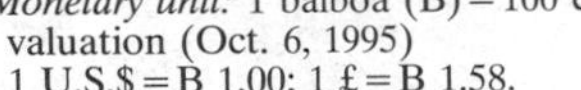
1 U.S.$ = B 1.00; 1 £ = B 1.58.

Area and population

		area		population
				1993
Provinces	Capitals	sq mi	sq km	estimate
Bocas del Toro	Bocas del Toro	3,376	8,745	111,184
Chiriquí	David	3,341	8,653	397,038
Coclé	Penonomé	1,902	4,927	185,027
Colón	Colón	1,888	4,890	219,742[1]
Darién	La Palma	6,437	16,671	51,912
Herrera	Chitré	904	2,341	99,638
Los Santos	Las Tablas	1,470	3,806	79,673
Panamá	Panama City	4,590	11,887	1,174,737
Veraguas	Santiago	4,339	11,239	216,061
Special territory				
Comarca de San Blas	El Porvenir	910	2,357	[1]
TOTAL		29,157	75,517[2]	2,535,012

Demography

Population (1995): 2,631,000.
Density (1995): persons per sq mi 90.2, persons per sq km 34.8.
Urban-rural (1995): urban 53.3%; rural 46.7%.
Sex distribution (1993): male 50.60%; female 49.40%.
Age breakdown (1993): under 15, 34.1%; 15–29, 28.8%; 30–44, 19.0%; 45–59, 10.6%; 60–74, 5.6%; 75 and over, 1.9%.
Population projection: (2000) 2,856,000; (2010) 3,266,000.
Doubling time: 35 years.
Ethnic composition (1992): mestizo 64.0%; black and mulatto 14.0%; white 10.0%; Amerindian 8.0%; Asian (mostly Chinese) 4.0%.
Religious affiliation (1992): Roman Catholic 80.0%; Protestant (mostly evangelical) 10.0%; Muslim 5.0%; Bahā'ī 1.0%; Jewish 0.3%; other 3.7%.
Major cities (1990): Panama City 450,668[3]; San Miguelito 293,564[3, 4]; David 65,763[5]; Colón 54,654; Barú 46,093[5].

Vital statistics

Birth rate per 1,000 population (1994): 25.0 (world avg. 25.0); (1991) legitimate 25.5%; illegitimate 74.5%[6].
Death rate per 1,000 population (1994): 5.0 (world avg. 9.3).
Natural increase rate per 1,000 population (1994): 20.0 (world avg. 15.7).
Total fertility rate (avg. births per childbearing woman; 1994): 2.9.
Marriage rate per 1,000 population (1993): 5.2.
Divorce rate per 1,000 population (1992): 0.8.
Life expectancy at birth (1990–95): male 70.8 years; female 75.0 years.
Major causes of death per 100,000 population (1992)[7]: diseases of the circulatory system 167, of which ischemic heart diseases 71, cerebrovascular disease 61; malignant neoplasms (cancers) 86; accidents 46; homicide, suicide, and violence 32; infectious and parasitic diseases 29.

National economy

Budget (1994). Revenue: B 1,928,600,000 (current revenue 73.4%, of which nontax revenue 25.0%; development revenue 26.6%, of which foreign loans 16.8%). Expenditures: B 1,928,600,000 (current expenditure 80.2%, of which public debt payments 25.6%, current transfers 14.0%, education 11.1%, administration 7.8%, health 7.2%; development expenditure 19.8%).
Public debt (external, outstanding; 1993): U.S.$3,709,000,000.
Production (metric tons except as noted). Agriculture, forestry, fishing (1994): sugarcane 1,650,000, bananas 900,000, rice 200,000, plantains 105,000, corn (maize) 103,000, oranges 28,000, coffee 12,000, tobacco 2,000; livestock (number of live animals) 1,437,000 cattle, 295,000 pigs; roundwood (1993) 1,045,000 cu m; fish catch (value of production in B '000; 1993): shrimps 31,700, fish 21,800. Mining and quarrying (1992): limestone 716,000; gold 8,000 troy oz. Manufacturing (value added in B '000; 1991): food products 133,300; beverages 59,800; paints, soaps, and pharmaceuticals 37,700; wearing apparel 29,800; tobacco products 25,700; cement, bricks, and tiles 24,600. Construction (value of construction in B '000; 1993): residential 295,100; nonresidential 88,300. Energy production (consumption): electricity (kW-hr; 1993) 3,147,000,000 (2,486,000,000); coal (metric tons; 1992) none (67,000); crude petroleum (barrels; 1992) none (12,937,000); petroleum products (metric tons; 1992) 1,731,000 (1,214,000); natural gas (cu m; 1992) none (59,455,000).
Household income and expenditure. Average household size (1990) 4.4; average annual income per household (1990) B 5,450 (U.S.$5,450); sources of income (1983–84)[8]: wages and salaries 60.8%, transfer payments 13.2%, self-employment 12.8%, other 13.2%; expenditure (1983–84)[8]: food and beverages 34.9%, transportation and communications 15.1%, housing and energy 12.6%, education and recreation 11.7%.
Population economically active (1991): total 858,509[9]; activity rate of total population 37.4% (participation rates: ages 15–69, 60.0%; female 33.8%; unemployed [1994] 12.0%).

Price and earnings indexes (1990 = 100)

	1989	1990	1991	1992	1993	1994	1995
Consumer price index	99.2	100.0	101.3	103.1	103.6	104.9	106.1[10]
Monthly earnings index[11]	99.1	100.0	100.3	101.6	...	...	...

Gross national product (1993): U.S.$6,621,000,000 (U.S.$2,610 per capita).

Structure of gross domestic product and labour force

	1993			
	in value B '000,000[12]	% of total value	labour force[9]	% of labour force[9]
Agriculture, fishing	236.8	10.2	192,687	20.5
Mining	5.0	0.2	3,097	0.3
Manufacturing	217.8	9.3	92,620	9.8
Construction	148.6	6.4	57,996	6.2
Public utilities	75.8	3.2	9,774	1.0
Transp. and commun.	593.3[13]	25.4[13]	70,335	7.5
Trade	275.0	11.8	178,988	19.0
Finance, real estate	347.7	14.9	45,272	4.8
Pub. admin.	254.0	10.9	66,024	7.0
Services	225.3	9.7	184,023	19.6
Other	−47.0[14]	−2.0[14]	40,291[15]	4.3[15]
TOTAL	2,332.3	100.0	941,107	100.0

Tourism (1992): receipts from visitors U.S.$207,000,000; expenditures by nationals abroad U.S.$125,000,000.
Land use (1993): forested 43.8%; meadows and pastures 20.0%; agricultural and under permanent cultivation 8.9%; other 27.3%.

Foreign trade[16, 17]

Balance of trade (current prices)

	1989	1990	1991	1992	1993	1994
B '000,000	−453	−894	−1,071	−1,329	−1,426	−1,594
% of total	35.3%	50.1%	54.2%	57.0%	56.3%	57.7%

Imports (1993): B 2,187,000,000 (machinery and apparatus 17.7%, transport equipment 13.2%, mineral fuels 13.2%, chemicals and chemical products 11.1%). *Major import sources:* U.S. 36.5%; Colón Free Zone 16.6%; Japan 7.8%; Ecuador 3.8%; Netherlands Antilles 3.1%; Costa Rica 2.8%.
Exports (1993): B 508,000,000 (bananas 39.6%, shrimps 11.2%, raw sugar 4.3%, clothing 4.2%, fish products 3.7%). *Major export destinations:* U.S. 34.6%; Germany 14.1%; Sweden 9.5%; Costa Rica 6.7%; Italy 5.5%.

Transport and communications

Transport. Railroads (1993): route length 220 mi, 354 km; (1989) passenger-km 600,000; (1992)[18] metric ton-km cargo 673,000. Roads (1993): total length 6,304 mi, 10,146 km (paved 33%). Vehicles: passenger cars (1993) 161,500; trucks and buses 82,800. Merchant marine (1992): vessels (100 gross tons and over) 5,217; total deadweight tonnage 79,255,644. Panama Canal traffic (1994): oceangoing transits 12,478; cargo 170,836,000 metric tons. Air transport (1992): passenger-km 336,000,000; metric ton-km cargo 5,268,000; airports (1995) with scheduled flights 10.
Communications. Daily newspapers (1992): total number 8; total circulation 223,000; circulation per 1,000 population 90. Radio (1994): 527,000 receivers (1 per 4.9 persons). Television (1994): 204,539 receivers (1 per 13 persons). Telephones (main lines; 1993): 261,500 (1 per 9.7 persons).

Education and health

Education (1993)

	schools	teachers	students	student/teacher ratio
Primary (age 6–11)	2,732	14,302	357,402	25.0
Secondary (age 12–17) } Voc., teacher tr.	369	10,730	206,509	19.2
Higher	8	4,029	69,247	17.2

Educational attainment (1990). Percentage of population age 25 and over having: no formal schooling 11.6%; incomplete primary education 20.0%; complete primary 21.6%; secondary 28.7%; incomplete undergraduate 5.4%; complete undergraduate 7.0%; graduate 0.7%; other/unknown 5.0%. *Literacy* (1990): total population age 15 and over literate 1,385,000 (88.1%); males literate 705,000 (88.1%); females literate 680,000 (88.2%).
Health (1993): physicians 3,168 (1 per 800 persons); hospital beds 7,453 (1 per 340 persons); infant mortality rate per 1,000 live births (1994) 17.0.
Food (1992): daily per capita caloric intake 2,242 (vegetable products 80%, animal products 20%); 97% of FAO recommended minimum requirement.

Military

Total active duty personnel (1994): military abolished in 1991 was replaced by an 11,000-member national police force; U.S. forces in former Canal Zone number 7,100.

[1]Colón includes Comarca de San Blas. [2]Detail does not add to total given because of rounding. [3]1993. [4]Population of urban district. [5]Population of the cabecera, the seat, or "head," of the municipality. [6]Includes divorced and widowed mothers as well as mothers separated from the fathers. [7]Projected rates based on about 70% of total deaths. [8]Panama City only. [9]Excludes nonresidents in former Canal Zone and indigenous areas and institutional households. [10]June. [11]Public sector only. [12]At prices of 1970. [13]Includes trans-Panamanian oil pipeline, commission of Panama Canal, and all activities of Colón Free Zone. [14]Net of imputed bank service charges and import fees. [15]All unemployed without previous employment. [16]Import figures are f.o.b. in balance of trade and c.i.f. in commodities and trading partners. [17]Excludes Colón Free Zone (1993 imports f.o.b. B 4,496,000,000; 1993 reexports f.o.b. B 5,151,000,000, of which textiles and clothing 25.8%, nonelectrical and electrical machinery and apparatus 22.3%). [18]Panama Railroad only.

Papua New Guinea

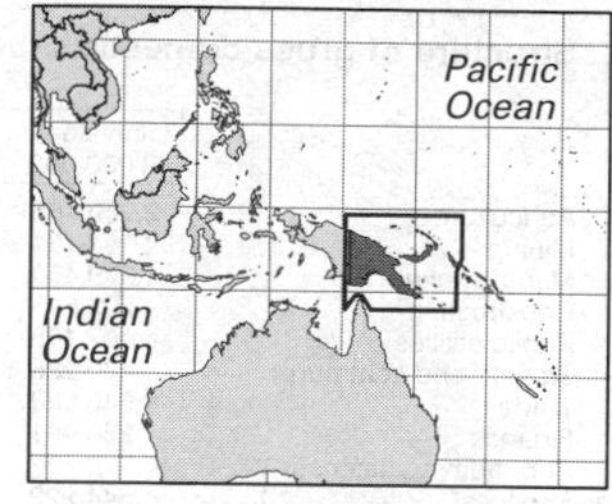

Official name: Independent State of Papua New Guinea.
Form of government: constitutional monarchy with one legislative house (National Parliament [109]).
Chief of state: British Monarch represented by Governor-General.
Head of government: Prime Minister.
Capital: Port Moresby.
Official language: English[1].
Official religion: none.
Monetary unit: 1 Papua New Guinea kina (K) = 100 toea; valuation (Oct. 6, 1995) 1 U.S.$ = K 1.32; 1 £ = K 2.09.

Area and population

Provinces	Administrative centres	area sq mi	area sq km	population 1990 census[2]
Central	Port Moresby (Central)	11,400	29,500	140,584
East New Britain	Rabaul	6,000	15,500	184,408
East Sepik	Wewak	16,550	42,800	248,308
Eastern Highlands	Goroka	4,300	11,200	299,619
Enga	Wabag	4,950	12,800	238,357
Gulf	Kerema	13,300	34,500	68,060
Madang	Madang	11,200	29,000	270,299
Manus	Lorengau	800	2,100	32,830
Milne Bay	Alotau (Samarai)	5,400	14,000	157,288
Morobe	Lae	13,300	34,500	363,535
National Capital District	Port Moresby	100	240	193,242
New Ireland	Kavieng	3,700	9,600	87,194
North Solomons (Bougainville)	Arawa (Buka)	3,600	9,300	[3]
Oro (Northern)	Popondetta	8,800	22,800	96,762
Sandaun (West Sepik)	Vanimo	14,000	36,300	135,185
Simbu (Chimbu)	Kundiawa	2,350	6,100	183,801
Southern Highlands	Mendi	9,200	23,800	302,724
West New Britain	Kimbe	8,100	21,000	127,547
Western	Daru	38,350	99,300	108,705
Western Highlands	Mount Hagen	3,300	8,500	291,090
TOTAL		178,704[4]	462,840	3,529,538[5]

Demography

Population (1995): 4,302,000.
Density (1995): persons per sq mi 24.1, persons per sq km 9.3.
Urban-rural (1995): urban 16.0%; rural 84.0%.
Sex distribution (1990)[2]: male 52.09%; female 47.91%.
Age breakdown (1990): under 15, 40.4%; 15–29, 28.8%; 30–44, 16.9%; 45–59, 9.3%; 60–74, 4.3%; 75 and over, 0.3%.
Population projection: (2000) 4,809,000; (2010) 5,918,000.
Doubling time: 30 years.
Ethnic composition (1983): New Guinea Papuan 84.0%; New Guinea Melanesian 15.0%; other 1.0%.
Religious affiliation (1980): Protestant 58.4%; Roman Catholic 32.8%; Anglican 5.4%; traditional beliefs 2.5%; Bahā'ī 0.6%; other 0.3%.
Major cities (1990)[2]: Port Moresby 193,242; Lae 80,655; Madang 27,057; Wewak 23,224; Goroka 17,855.

Vital statistics

Birth rate per 1,000 population (1995): 33.0 (world avg. 25.0); legitimate, n.a.; illegitimate, n.a.
Death rate per 1,000 population (1995): 10.0 (world avg. 9.3).
Natural increase rate per 1,000 population (1995): 23.0 (world avg. 15.7).
Total fertility rate (avg. births per childbearing woman; 1995): 4.8.
Marriage rate per 1,000 population: n.a.
Life expectancy at birth (1995): male 56.0 years; female 58.0 years.
Major causes of death per 100,000 population (1991): pneumonia 28.7; conditions originating from perinatal period 17.5; malaria 12.7; meningitis 8.5; tuberculosis 7.0; intestinal infections 6.8.

National economy

Budget (1995). Revenue: K 1,571,700,000 (company tax 20.0%, import duties 17.9%, personal income tax 14.6%, nontax revenue 12.8%, foreign grants 12.1%, export tax 10.8%). Expenditures: K 1,629,800,000 (administrative 40.9%, transfers 18.1%, interest payments 13.2%, capital works 11.0%).
Public debt (external, outstanding; 1993): U.S.$1,516,000,000.
Production (metric tons except as noted). Agriculture, forestry, fishing (1994): bananas 1,329,000, coconuts 790,000, sweet potatoes 484,000, sugarcane 300,000, palm oil 225,000, yams 224,000, taro 220,000, cassava 114,000, copra 100,000, palm kernels 66,000, coffee 66,000, cacao 27,000, pineapples 13,000, tea 9,000; livestock (number of live animals) 1,033,000 pigs, 105,000 cattle, 3,000,000 chickens; roundwood (1993) 8,188,000 cu m; fish catch (1993) 26,000. Mining and quarrying (1994): copper 206,329; silver 75,025 kg; gold 57,751 kg. Manufacturing (value added, in K; 1985): food, beverages, and tobacco 162,558,000; metals, metal products, machinery, and equipment 47,493,000; wood products 29,807,000. Construction (value in K; 1986)[6]: residential K 19,369,000; nonresidential K 55,675,000. Energy production (consumption): electricity (kW-hr; 1993) 1,790,000,000 (1,790,000,000); coal (metric tons; 1993) none (1,000); crude petroleum (barrels) none (n.a.); petroleum products (metric tons; 1993) none (732,000).
Tourism: receipts from visitors (1993) U.S.$45,000,000; expenditures by nationals abroad (1990) U.S.$42,000,000.
Gross national product (1993): U.S.$4,646,000,000 (U.S.$1,120 per capita).

Structure of gross domestic product and labour force

	1993 in value K '000,000	1993 % of total value	1980 labour force[7]	1980 % of labour force[7]
Agriculture	1,292.2	26.0	564,500	77.0
Mining	1,439.8	28.9	4,300	0.6
Manufacturing	437.9	8.8	14,000	1.9
Construction	181.7	3.6	21,600	2.9
Public utilities	69.8	1.4	2,800	0.4
Transp. and commun.	212.9	4.3	17,400	2.4
Trade	396.4	8.0	25,100	3.4
Finance	[8]	[8]	4,500	0.6
Pub. admin., defense	713.9	14.3	77,100	10.5
Services	233.9	4.7		
Other	—	—	1,500	0.2
TOTAL	4,978.5	100.0	732,800	100.0[4]

Land use (1993): forested 84.4%; agricultural and under permanent cultivation 0.9%; meadows and pastures 0.2%; other 14.5%.
Population economically active (1980)[7]: total 732,800; activity rate 24.6% (participation rates: over age 10, 35.2%; female 39.8%; unemployed 12.8%[9]).

Price and earnings indexes (1990 = 100)

	1988	1989	1990	1991	1992	1993	1994
Consumer price index	89.5	93.5	100.0	107.0	111.6	117.1	120.5
Weekly earnings index[10]	92.2	96.9	100.0	106.1	110.9	...	...

Household income and expenditure. Average household size (1980) 4.6; income per household (1975–76) K 2,771 (U.S.$3,483); sources of income (1970): wages and salaries 57.3%, transfer payments 1.1%, self-employment and other 41.6%; expenditure (1987)[11]: food and beverages 40.9%, transportation and communications 13.0%, housing 12.5%, clothing and footwear 6.2%, heating and lighting 4.9%, services and other 22.5%.

Foreign trade[12]

Balance of trade (current prices)

	1989	1990	1991	1992	1993	1994
K '000,000	−47.2	+38.5	−52.7	+475.2	+1,318.9	+1,322.8
% of total	2.1%	1.8%	2.0%	15.7%	37.3%	33.1%

Imports (1994): K 1,336,000,000 (1990; machinery and transport equipment 38.7%; basic manufactures 20.4%; food and live animals 17.9%; chemicals 7.5%; mineral fuels, lubricants, and related materials 2.7%). *Major import sources* (1992): Australia 37.1%; Japan 15.0%; Singapore 14.4%; U.S. 6.4%; New Zealand 4.5%; Hong Kong 3.0%; Malaysia 2.2%.
Exports (1994): K 2,662,000,000 (crude oil 26.4%; gold 26.4%; timber 18.1%; copper ore and concentrates 13.8%; coffee 7.7%; palm oil and copra 4.2%; cocoa beans 1.1%). *Major export destinations* (1992): Japan 21.3%; Australia 40.9%; Germany 9.7%; South Korea 7.9%; U.K. 4.3%; Singapore 3.7%.

Transport and communications

Transport. Railroads: none. Roads (1986): total length 12,263 mi, 19,736 km (paved 6%). Vehicles (1993): passenger cars 11,500; trucks and buses 30,800. Merchant marine (1992): vessels (100 gross tons and over) 87; total deadweight tonnage 40,855. Air transport (1993): passenger-mi 458,798,000, passenger-km 738,366,000; short ton-mi cargo 56,418,000, metric ton-km cargo 82,369,000; airports (1995) with scheduled flights 110.
Communications. Daily newspapers (1992): total number 2; total circulation 64,000; circulation per 1,000 population 16. Radio (1994): 260,000 receivers (1 per 16 persons). Television (1994): 10,000 receivers (1 per 421 persons). Telephones (main lines; 1993): 39,800 (1 per 104 persons).

Education and health

Education (1992)

	schools	teachers	students	student/teacher ratio
Primary (age 7–12)	2,821	14,117	443,552	31.4
Secondary (age 13–16)	135[13]	2,415	58,226	24.1
Voc., teacher tr.	117[13]	878	11,370	12.9
Higher	2[13]	902[14]	5,007[13]	7.1[14]

Educational attainment (1990). Percentage of population age 25 and over having: no formal schooling 82.6%; some primary education 8.2%; completed primary 5.0%; some secondary 4.2%. *Literacy* (1990): total population age 15 and over literate 52.0%; males literate 64.9%; females literate 37.8%.
Health: physicians (1990) 301 (1 per 12,874 persons); hospital beds (1989) 15,335 (1 per 234 persons); infant mortality rate (1995) 65.0.
Food (1992): daily per capita caloric intake 2,613 (vegetable products 91%, animal products 9%); 115% of FAO minimum.

Military

Total active duty personnel (1995): 3,800 (army 84.2%, navy 13.2%, air force 2.6%). *Military expenditure as percentage of GNP* (1993): 1.8% (world 3.3%); per capita expenditure U.S.$20.

[1]The national languages are English, Tok Pisin (English Creole), and Motu. [2]Preliminary results. [3]Data unavailable because of civil insurrection. [4]Detail does not add to total given because of rounding. [5]Excludes an estimated population of 160,000 in the North Solomons, 4,500 people in remote areas, and an estimated foreign population of about 20,000–30,000. [6]Completed new buildings. [7]Citizens of Papua New Guinea over age 10 involved in "money-raising activities" only. [8]Included with Services. [9]1977; in six urban centres. [10]Minimum wage of urban labourers. [11]Weights of retail price index components. [12]Import figures are f.o.b. in balance of trade and c.i.f. for commodities and trading partners. [13]1990. [14]1986.

Paraguay

Official name: República del Paraguay (Spanish); Tetä Paraguáype (Guaraní) (Republic of Paraguay).
Form of government: multiparty republic with two legislative houses (Senate [45]; Chamber of Deputies [80]).
Head of state and government: President.
Capital: Asunción.
Official languages: Spanish; Guaraní.
Official religion: none[1].
Monetary unit: 1 Paraguayan Guaraní (₲) = 100 céntimos; valuation (Oct. 6, 1995) 1 U.S.$ = ₲1,963; 1 £ = ₲3,103.

Area and population

Regions / Departments	Capitals	area sq mi	area sq km	population 1992 census
Occidental		95,338	246,925	97,208
Alto Paraguay	Fuerte Olimpo	31,795	82,349	11,816
Boquerón	Filadelfia	35,393	91,669	26,292
Presidente Hayes	Pozo Colorado	28,150	72,907	59,100
Oriental		61,710	159,827	4,026,342
Alto Paraná	Ciudad del Este	5,751	14,895	403,858
Amambay	Pedro Juan Caballero	4,994	12,933	97,158
Asunción[2]	—	45	117	502,426
Caaguazú	Coronel Oviedo	4,430	11,474	383,319
Caazapá	Caazapá	3,666	9,496	128,550
Canindiyú	Salto del Guairá	5,663	14,667	96,826
Central	Asunción	952	2,465	864,540
Concepción	Concepción	6,970	18,051	166,946
Cordillera	Caacupé	1,910	4,948	206,097
Guairá	Villarrica	1,485	3,846	162,244
Itapúa	Encarnación	6,380	16,525	375,748
Misiones	San Juan Bautista	3,690	9,556	88,624
Ñeembucú	Pilar	4,690	12,147	69,884
Paraguarí	Paraguarí	3,361	8,705	203,012
San Pedro	San Pedro	7,723	20,002	277,110
TOTAL		157,048	406,752	4,123,550[3]

Demography

Population (1995): 4,828,000[3].
Density (1995): persons per sq mi 30.7, persons per sq km 11.9.
Urban-rural (1992): urban 50.5%; rural 49.5%.
Sex distribution (1992): male 50.19%; female 49.81%.
Age breakdown (1992): under 15, 40.1%; 15–29, 27.6%; 30–44, 18.7%; 45–59, 8.3%; 60–74, 4.2%; 75 and over, 1.1%.
Population projection: (2000) 5,464,000; (2010) 6,785,000.
Doubling time: 26 years.
Ethnic composition (1980): mestizo (Spanish-Guaraní) 90.8%; Amerindian 3.0%; German 1.7%; other 4.5%.
Religious affiliation (1991): Roman Catholic 93.1%; other 6.9%.
Major cities (1992): Asunción 502,426; Ciudad del Este 133,893; San Lorenzo 133,311; Lambaré 99,681; Fernando de la Mora 95,287.

Vital statistics

Birth rate per 1,000 population (1991): 33.6 (world avg. 25.0); (1985) legitimate 68.7%[4]; illegitimate 31.3%[4].
Death rate per 1,000 population (1991): 6.4 (world avg. 9.3).
Natural increase rate per 1,000 population (1991): 27.2 (world avg. 15.7).
Total fertility rate (avg. births per childbearing woman; 1991): 4.4.
Marriage rate per 1,000 population (1990): 1.8[4].
Life expectancy at birth (1991): male 65.0 years; female 69.4 years.
Major causes of death per 100,000 population (1988)[5]: diseases of the circulatory system 200.9; malignant neoplasms (cancers) 60.8; infectious and parasitic diseases 56.4; diseases of the respiratory system 52.5.

National economy

Budget (1993). Revenue: ₲4,254,817,000,000 (taxes on goods and services 30.7%, income on fixed assets 23.3%, customs duties 11.6%, pension funds 6.2%, documentary tax 3.6%, real estate taxes 2.5%). Expenditures: ₲1,726,216,200,000 (education 19.3%, public works 14.4%, defense 10.5%, public health 7.5%, interior 7.0%, agriculture 5.8%, housing 5.4%).
Public debt (external, outstanding; 1993): U.S.$1,309,000,000.
Production (metric tons except as noted). Agriculture, forestry, fishing (1994): sugarcane 2,799,000, cassava 2,550,000, soybeans 1,796,000, corn (maize) 462,000, seed cotton 380,000, oranges 361,000, bananas 130,000, lint cotton 125,000, sweet potatoes 106,000; livestock (number of live animals) 8,000,000 cattle, 3,300,000 pigs, 13,000,000 chickens; roundwood (1993) 8,538,000 cu m; fish catch (1993) 16,000. Mining and quarrying (1993): limestone 600,000[6]; kaolin 74,000; gypsum 4,500. Manufacturing (value added of production in ₲'000,000; 1992): processed meat 226,295; woven cotton fabric 168,831; soft drinks 116,219; beer 104,427; gasoline 77,512; cement 73,357; sugar 60,276; naphtha 58,583; soybean flour 50,152. Construction (1985): residential 60,800 sq m; nonresidential 163,200 sq m. Energy production (consumption): electricity (kW-hr; 1993) 31,454,000,000 (3,334,000,000); coal, none (none); crude petroleum (barrels; 1993) none (1,840,000); petroleum products (metric tons; 1993) 284,000 (939,000); natural gas, none (none).
Tourism (1993): receipts from visitors U.S.$204,000,000; expenditures by nationals abroad U.S.$138,000,000.
Gross national product (1993): U.S.$6,995,000,000 (U.S.$1,500 per capita).

Structure of gross domestic product and labour force

	1993 in value ₲'000,000	1993 % of total value	1982 labour force	1982 % of labour force
Agriculture	2,939,483	24.5	445,518	42.9
Mining	44,161	0.4	1,406	0.1
Manufacturing	1,979,450	16.5	124,658	12.0
Construction	709,513	5.9	69,900	6.7
Public utilities	407,135	3.4	2,605	0.3
Transp. and commun.	470,236	3.9	30,524	2.9
Trade	3,646,338	30.4	85,961	8.3
Finance	250,481	2.1	18,019	1.7
Pub. admin., defense			174,228	16.8
Services	1,544,922	12.9		
Other			86,444	8.3
TOTAL	11,991,719	100.0	1,039,258[7]	100.0

Population economically active (1982): total 1,039,258; activity rate 51.5% (participation rates: ages 15–64, 57.5%; female 19.7%; unemployed [1989] 9.2%).

Price and earnings indexes (1990 = 100)

	1987	1988	1989	1990	1991	1992	1993
Consumer price index	46.7	57.2	72.4	100.0	124.3	143.1	169.2
Earnings index	...	...	70.3	100.0	115.1	131.8	158.0

Household income and expenditure. Average household size (1992) 4.7; sources of income (1989): wages and salaries 33.9%, transfer payments 2.5%, other 63.6%; expenditure (1980): food 48.7%, housing 16.4%, clothing 9.7%, household durable goods 6.2%, transportation and communications 4.5%.
Land use (1993): forested 32.4%; meadows and pastures 54.6%; agricultural and under permanent cultivation 5.7%; other 7.3%.

Foreign trade

Balance of trade (current prices)

	1988	1989	1990	1991	1992	1993
U.S.$'000,000	+15.1	+363.8	−234.7	−538.3	−580.6	−752.3
% of total	1.5%	21.8%	10.9%	26.7%	30.7%	34.2%

Imports (1994): U.S.$2,140,400,000 (machinery and transport equipment 33.2%, of which transport equipment 12.9%; fuels and lubricants 7.4%; chemicals and pharmaceuticals 6.8%; iron products 5.5%). *Major import sources:* Brazil 31.3%; United States 22.7%; Argentina 11.7%; Hong Kong 8.8%; Japan 4.9%; United Kingdom 2.2%; Chile 1.6%; France 1.3%; Italy 1.3%.
Exports (1994): U.S.$816,833,000 (soybean flour 27.2%; cotton fibres 20.9%; timber 9.6%; vegetable oil 7.7%, of which tung oil 0.6%; hides and skins 7.7%; processed meat 6.9%; perfume oils 1.2%; tobacco 0.8%; oilseed cakes 0.5%). *Major export destinations:* Brazil 39.6%; The Netherlands 19.6%; Argentina 11.1%; United States 7.0%; Italy 3.0%; Germany 1.6%; France 1.5%.

Transport and communications

Transport. Railroads (1993): route length 274 mi, 441 km; passenger-mi 2,900,000, passenger-km 4,600,000; short ton-mi cargo 4,300,000, metric ton-km cargo 6,300,000. Roads (1993): total length 18,217 mi, 29,317 km (paved 10%). Vehicles (1990): passenger cars 117,067; buses 3,375. Merchant marine (1992): vessels (100 gross tons and over) 38; total deadweight tonnage 38,513. Air transport (1993): passenger-mi 791,000,000, passenger-km 1,273,000,000; short ton-mi cargo 16,500,000, metric ton-km cargo 24,100,000; airports (1995) with scheduled flights 3.
Communications. Daily newspapers (1994): total number 5; total circulation 203,000; circulation per 1,000 population 42. Radio (1994): 700,000 receivers (1 per 6.9 persons). Television (1994): 350,000 receivers (1 per 14 persons). Telephones (main lines; 1993): 142,300 (1 per 33 persons).

Education and health

Education (1993–94)

	schools	teachers	students	student/teacher ratio
Primary (age 7–12)	5,172	41,432	792,657	19.1
Secondary (age 13–18)[8]	812	20,793	214,272	10.3
Higher	2[9]	742[10]	42,654	40.9[10]

Educational attainment (1982). Percentage of population age 25 and over having: no formal schooling 13.6%; primary education 64.7%; secondary 15.5%; higher 3.4%; not stated 2.8%. *Literacy* (1995): percentage of total population age 15 and over literate 92.1%; males literate 93%; females literate 90.6%.
Health (1993): physicians 3,341 (1 per 1,406 persons); hospital beds 5,435 (1 per 864 persons); infant mortality rate per 1,000 live births (1990–95) 38.0.
Food (1992): daily per capita caloric intake 2,670 (vegetable products 76%, animal products 24%); 116% of FAO recommended minimum requirement.

Military

Total active duty personnel (1995): 20,300 (army 73.9%, navy 17.7%, air force 8.4%). *Military expenditure as percentage of GNP* (1992): 1.8% (world 3.7%); per capita expenditure U.S.$24.

[1]Roman Catholicism, although not official, enjoys special recognition in the 1992 constitution. [2]Asunción is the capital city, not a department. [3]Preliminary 1992 census figure is not adjusted for undercount. The 1995 population figure is adjusted for estimated undercount. [4]Civil Registry records only. [5]Reporting areas only (constituting about 50 percent of the total population). [6]1992. [7]Detail does not add to total given because of rounding. [8]Includes vocational education and teacher training. [9]1990–91. [10]1992–93.

Peru

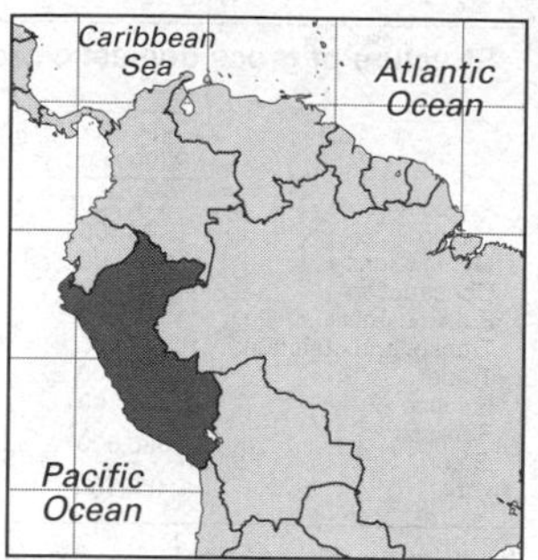

Official name: República del Perú (Spanish) (Republic of Peru).
Form of government[1]: unitary multiparty republic with one legislative house (Congress [120]).
Head of state and government: President.
Capital: Lima.
Official languages: Spanish; Quechua; Aymara.
Official religion: Roman Catholicism.
Monetary unit[2]: 1 nuevo sol (S/.) = 100 céntimos; valuation (Oct. 6, 1995) 1 U.S.$ = S/. 2.25; 1 £ = S/. 3.56.

Area and population

		area		population
Regions[3]	**Capitals**	sq mi	sq km	1993 census
Andres Avelino Cáceres	...	40,707	105,430	2,005,283
Arequipa	...	24,458	63,345	916,806
Chavín	...	15,686	40,627	975,129
Grau	...	15,661	40,562	1,543,785
Inca	...	66,696	172,741	1,300,897
José Carlos Mariátegui	...	40,081	103,809	1,426,949
La Libertad	...	9,873	25,570	1,270,261
Loreto	...	142,414	368,852	687,282
Los Libertadores-Wari	...	34,340	88,939	1,511,462
Nor Oriental del Marañón	...	33,486	86,728	2,517,268
San Martín	...	19,789	51,253	552,387
Ucayali	...	39,541	102,411	314,810
Department				
Lima	...	13,437	34,802	6,386,308
Constitutional Province				
Callao	Callao	57	147	639,729
TOTAL		496,225[4]	1,285,216	22,639,443[5]

Demography

Population (1995): 23,489,000.
Density (1995): persons per sq mi 47.3, persons per sq km 18.3.
Urban-rural (1993): urban 71.8%; rural 28.2%.
Sex distribution (1993): male 50.32%; female 49.68%.
Age breakdown (1993): under 15, 36.4%; 15–29, 29.0%; 30–44, 18.2%; 45–59, 10.2%; 60–74, 5.0%; 75 and over, 1.2%.
Population projection: (2000) 25,573,000; (2010) 29,313,000.
Doubling time: 28 years.
Ethnic composition (1981): Quechua 47.1%; mestizo 32.0%; white 12.0%; Aymara 5.4%; other Amerindian 1.7%; other 1.8%.
Religious affiliation (1989): Roman Catholic 92.5%, Protestant 5.5%.
Major cities (1993): metropolitan Lima 5,706,127; Arequipa 619,156; Callao 615,046; Trujillo 509,312; Chiclayo 411,536.

Vital statistics

Birth rate per 1,000 population (1990–95): 29.0 (world avg. 25.0); (1977) legitimate 57.8%; illegitimate 42.2%.
Death rate per 1,000 population (1990–95): 7.6 (world avg. 9.3).
Natural increase rate per 1,000 population (1990–95): 21.4 (world avg. 15.7).
Total fertility rate (avg. births per childbearing woman, 1990–95): 3.6.
Marriage rate per 1,000 population (1982): 6.0[6].
Life expectancy at birth (1990–95): male 62.7 years; female 66.6 years.
Major causes of death per 100,000 population (1989): diseases of the circulatory system 115.3; respiratory diseases 100.2; infectious diseases 84.5; malignant neoplasms 72.9; accidents, poisoning, and violence 53.6.

National economy

Budget (1993). Revenue: S/. 9,158,076,000 (taxes on goods and services 51.1%; income taxes 15.4%; import duties 10.9%; nontax revenue 13.8%). Expenditures: S/. 12,475,688,000 (current expenditure 64.1%, of which wages and salaries 20.2%, transfer payments 18.9%; capital expenditure 19.4%; public debt amortization 16.5%).
Tourism (1992): receipts U.S.$237,000,000; expenditures U.S.$480,000,000.
Production (metric tons except as noted). Agriculture, forestry, fishing (1994): sugarcane 6,100,000, potatoes 1,745,000, rice 1,391,000, plantains 877,000, corn (maize) 726,000, cassava 500,000, seed cotton 168,000, coffee 91,000; livestock (number of live animals) 11,600,000 sheep, 4,000,000 cattle, 2,405,000 pigs, 68,000,000 chickens; roundwood (1993) 8,329,000 cu m; fish catch (1993) 8,450,600. Mining and quarrying (1993): iron ore 3,398,000; zinc 664,600; copper 375,000; lead 219,000; silver 1,616. Manufacturing (value in S/. '000,000[7]; 1993): processed foods 180.5; base metal products 162.5; industrial chemicals 89.7; wood products 61.6; textiles 56.9; beverages and tobacco 53.4; apparel 36.6. Construction (value in S/. '000,000[7]; 1992): residential 22.4; nonresidential 14.6. Energy production (consumption): electricity (kW-hr; 1992) 13,132,000,000 (13,132,000,000); coal (metric tons; 1992) 90,000 (280,000); crude petroleum (barrels; 1992) 42,000,000 (58,000,000); petroleum products (metric tons; 1992) 7,562,000 (5,988,000); natural gas (cu m; 1992) 1,314,000,000 (525,000,000).
Household income and expenditure. Average household size (1993) 5.1; income per household (1988) I/. 1,086,620[3] (U.S.$2,173); sources of income (1988): business income 65.1%, wages 31.2%, transfers 3.7%; expenditure (1990): food 29.4%, recreation and education 13.2%, household durables 10.1%, clothing and footwear 8.5%, transportation 7.5%, health 7.0%, other 24.3%.
Gross national product (1993): U.S.$33,973,000,000 (U.S.$1,490 per capita).

Structure of gross domestic product and labour force

	1993		1992	
	in value S/. '000,000[7]	% of total value	labour force	% of labour force
Agriculture	487.7	14.1	2,658,000	33.0
Mining	332.0	9.6	198,000	2.4
Manufacturing	782.3	22.6	840,000	10.4
Construction	233.4	6.7	300,000	3.7
Public utilities	54.9	1.6	25,000	0.3
Transp. and commun.	251.1	7.2	355,000	4.4
Trade	586.2	16.9	1,297,000	16.1
Finance	453.7	13.1	192,000	2.4
Services	283.4[8]	8.2[8]	2,199,000[8]	27.3[8]
TOTAL	3,464.7	100.0	8,064,000	100.0

Population economically active (1993): total 7,109,527; activity rate of total population 31.4% (participation rates: over age 15, 51.2%; female 50.9%; unemployed 7.1%).

Price and earnings indexes (1990 = 100)

	1988	1989	1990	1991	1992	1993	1994
Consumer price index	...	...	100	510	884	1,314	1,626
Monthly earnings index[9]	...	...	100	706	1,163	2,059	...

Land use (1993): forest 53.2%; pasture 21.2%; agricultural 2.7%; other 22.9%.
Public debt (external, outstanding; 1993): U.S.$16,123,000,000.

Foreign trade

Balance of trade (current prices)

	1989	1990	1991	1992	1993	1994
U.S.$'000,000	+1,523.9	+585.3	−165.0	−566.7	−623.9	−1,095.2
% of total	27.6%	9.8%	2.4%	7.5%	8.2%	10.8%

Imports (1993): U.S.$3,603,680,000 (raw and intermediate materials 48.2%, machinery and transport equipment 31.4%, consumer goods 20.4%). *Major import sources:* U.S. 27.6%; Japan 7.6%; Argentina 6.4%; Brazil 6.2%; Colombia 5.7%; Germany 4.3%; Chile 4.0%.
Exports (1993): U.S.$3,341,280,000 (copper 17.4%, fish flour 16.3%, zinc 7.9%, gold 6.2%, petroleum and derivatives 4.3%, lead 2.8%, silver 2.2%). *Major export destinations:* U.S. 20.9%; Japan 9.2%; U.K. 8.5%; Germany 6.2%; Italy 4.8%; China 4.2%; Taiwan 3.5%; The Netherlands 3.5%.

Transport and communications

Transport. Railroads (1993): route length 1,318 mi, 2,121 km; passenger-km 165,304,000; metric ton-km cargo 884,352,000. Roads (1993): total length 43,460 mi, 69,942 km (paved 11%). Vehicles (1993): passenger cars 418,648; trucks and buses 275,094. Merchant marine (1992): vessels (100 gross tons and over) 623; total deadweight tonnage 615,582. Air transport (1992): passenger-km 1,292,000,000; metric ton-km cargo 148,000,000; airports (1995) 25.
Communications. Daily newspapers (1992): total number 59; total circulation 1,590,000; circulation per 1,000 population 71. Radio (1994): 5,300,000 receivers (1 per 4.4 persons). Television (1994): 2,000,000 receivers (1 per 12 persons). Telephones (1992): 816,160 (1 per 28 persons).

Education and health

Education (1993)

	schools[10]	teachers	students	student/ teacher ratio
Primary (age 6–11)	54,502	159,022	1,813,666	00.5
Secondary (age 12–16)	7,097	93,277	1,913,163	20.5
Voc., teacher tr.	1,952	11,919	270,668	22.7
Higher	655	46,983	730,987	15.6

Educational attainment (1993). Percentage of population age 15 and over having: no formal schooling 12.3%; less than primary education 0.3%; primary 31.5%; secondary 35.5%; higher 20.4%. *Literacy* (1993): total population age 15 and over literate 12,108,699 (87.2%); males 6,330,056 (92.9%); females 5,778,643 (81.7%).
Health (1992): physicians 20,124 (1 per 1,116 persons); hospital beds 44,100 (1 per 509 persons); infant mortality rate per 1,000 live births (1990–95) 75.8.
Food (1992): daily per capita caloric intake 1,882 (vegetable products 87%, animal products 13%); 80% of FAO recommended minimum requirement.

Military

Total active duty personnel (1994): 115,000 (army 65.2%, navy 21.7%, air force 13.1%). *Military expenditure as percentage of GNP* (1993): 1.8% (world 3.3%); per capita expenditure U.S.$31.

[1]A new constitution promulgated in December 1993 replaced the 1980 constitution, which was suspended in April 1992. [2]A new currency, the nuevo sol, was introduced in January 1991, replacing the inti (abbrev.: I/.) at the rate of one million intis for one nuevo sol. [3]The new regional administrative scheme announced in 1987 was not functioning in late 1994 because of inadequate funding; the regional administrative framework exists, however, alongside the old departmental structure, which was never dismantled. [4]Detail does not add to total given because of rounding. [5]Includes estimated population in the Andean and Pacific coast areas of the country (531,543) and the estimated population of remote indigenous communities in the Amazon (59,544). [6]Excludes Indian jungle population; based on incomplete information. [7]At 1979 prices. [8]Includes public administration and other. [9]Estimate for Lima metropolitan area only. [10]1992.

Philippines

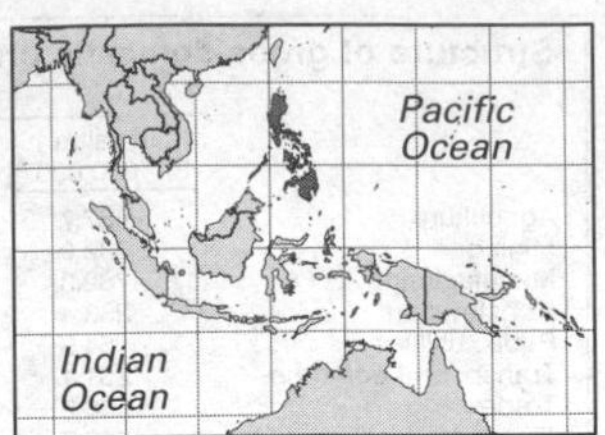

Official name: Republika ng Pilipinas (Pilipino); Republic of the Philippines (English).
Form of government: unitary republic with two legislative houses (Senate [24]; House of Representatives [204]).
Chief of state and head of government: President.
Capital: Manila.
Official languages: Pilipino; English.
Official religion: none.
Monetary unit: 1 Philippine peso (₱) = 100 centavos; valuation (Oct. 6, 1995) 1 U.S.$ = ₱ 25.89; 1 £ = ₱ 40.92.

Area and population

	area		population
	sq mi	sq km	1995 estimate[1]
Regions			
Bicol	6,808	17,633	4,382,000
Cagayan Valley	10,362	26,838	2,656,000
Central Luzon	7,039	18,231	7,178,000
Central Mindanao	5,549	14,373	2,378,000
Central Visayas	5,773	14,951	5,225,000
Eastern Visayas	8,275	21,432	3,401,000
Ilocos	4,958	12,840	3,963,000
National Capital	246	636	9,201,000
Northern Mindanao	10,937	28,328	4,096,000
Southern Mindanao	12,237	31,693	5,242,000
Southern Tagalog	18,117	46,924	9,989,000
Western Mindanao	6,194	16,042	2,848,000
Western Visayas	7,808	20,223	6,047,000
Autonomous Regions			
Cordillera	7,063	18,294	1,304,000
Muslim Mindanao	4,493	11,638	2,103,000
TOTAL	115,860[2]	300,076	70,011,000[2]

Demography

Population (1995): 70,011,000.
Density (1995): persons per sq mi 604.3, persons per sq km 233.3.
Urban-rural (1995): urban 54.0%; rural 46.0%.
Sex distribution (1995): male 50.22%; female 49.78%.
Age breakdown (1991): under 15, 38.2%; 15–29, 28.6%; 30–44, 18.3%; 45–59, 9.4%; 60–74, 4.4%; 75 and over, 1.1%.
Population projection: (2000) 78,414,000; (2010) 94,503,000.
Doubling time: 30 years.
Ethnic composition (by mother tongue of households; 1990): Tagalog 27.9%; Cebuano 24.3%; Ilocano 9.8%; Hiligaynon Ilongo 9.3%; Bicol 5.8%; Waray 4.0%; Pampango 3.1%; Pangasinan 1.9%; other 13.9%.
Religious affiliation (1990): Roman Catholic 82.9%; Protestant 8.3%; Muslim 4.6%; Aglipayan (Philippine Independent Church) 2.6%; other 1.6%.
Major cities (1991): Manila 1,894,667; Quezon City 1,627,890; Davao 867,779; Cebu 641,042; Caloocan 629,473; Zamboanga 453,214.

Vital statistics

Birth rate per 1,000 population (1995): 29.0 (world avg. 25.0); (1982) legitimate 93.9%; illegitimate 6.1%.
Death rate per 1,000 population (1995): 6.0 (world avg. 9.3).
Natural increase rate per 1,000 population (1995): 23.0 (world avg. 15.7).
Total fertility rate (avg. births per childbearing woman; 1995): 3.8.
Marriage rate per 1,000 population (1991): 6.7.
Life expectancy at birth (1995): male 66.0 years; female 69.0 years.
Major causes of death per 100,000 population (1990): heart diseases 74.4; pneumonia 66.3; vascular diseases 54.2; tuberculosis 39.1; malignant neoplasms (cancers) 35.7; diarrhea 12.0; septicemia 9.4; accidents 6.4.

National economy

Budget (1994). Revenue: ₱ 334,488,000,000 (1992; taxes on goods and services 29.1%, international duties 28.5%, income taxes 26.0%, nontax revenues 12.5%). Expenditures: ₱ 309,942,000,000 (1992; debt service 30.7%, education 15.4%, transportation and communications 11.0%, defense 10.2%, general public services 10.0%, agriculture 8.4%, health 4.2%).
Tourism (1993): receipts U.S.$2,122,000,000; expenditures U.S.$130,000,000.
Production. Agriculture, forestry, fishing (value in ₱ '000,000; 1992): rice 43,271, coconuts 22,012, corn (maize) 21,152, sugarcane 13,552, bananas 10,677, pineapples 5,063, mango 4,539, cassava 3,409, tobacco 3,203, coffee 2,655; livestock (number of live animals) 8,022,000 pigs, 2,577,000 buffalo, 2,240,000 goats, 1,658,000 cattle, 63,127,000 chickens; roundwood 38,652,000 cu m; fish catch 25,987. Mining and quarrying (value in ₱ '000,000; 1992): gold 6,602; silver 6,505; copper concentrate 5,909; sand and gravel 2,400; salt 2,194; coal 1,738; nickel ore 566. Manufacturing (gross value added in ₱ '000,000; 1992)[3]: food products 133,274; petroleum and coal products 35,510; industrial chemicals 27,176; footwear and wearing apparel 22,071; beverages 15,849; electrical machinery 13,211; nonmetallic mineral products 10,182. Construction (authorized; 1992): residential 3,862,000 sq m; nonresidential 4,288,000 sq m. Energy production (consumption): electricity (kW-hr; 1992) 25,682,000,000 (25,682,000,000); coal (metric tons; 1992) 1,664,000 (2,321,-000); crude petroleum (barrels; 1992) 3,045,000 (92,126,000); petroleum products (metric tons; 1992) 10,294,000 (11,684,000).
Public debt (external, outstanding; 1993): U.S.$27,471,000,000.
Gross national product (1993): U.S.$54,593,000,000 (U.S.$830 per capita).

Structure of gross domestic product and labour force

	1993			
	in value ₱ '000,000	% of total value	labour force	% of labour force
Agriculture	317,900	21.7	11,194,000	41.7
Mining	16,600	1.1	130,000	0.5
Manufacturing	349,600	23.8	2,454,000	9.1
Construction	80,100	5.5	1,100,000	4.1
Public utilities	36,400	2.5	105,000	0.4
Transp. and commun.	79,000	5.4	1,358,000	5.1
Trade	207,600	14.1	3,415,000	12.7
Finance	58,600	4.0	495,000	1.9
Services }	320,500	21.9	4,174,000	15.6
Other }			2,397,000[4]	8.9[4]
TOTAL	1,466,300	100.0	26,822,000	100.0

Population economically active (1993): total 26,822,000; activity rate 39.7% (participation rates: ages 15–64, 66.2%; female 37.2%; unemployed 8.9%).

Price and earnings index (1990 = 100)

	1988	1989	1990	1991	1992	1993	1994
Consumer price index	78.1	87.6	100.0	118.7	129.3	139.1	151.7
Monthly earnings index[5]	69.2	81.6	100.0	...	...	...	...

Household income and expenditure (1992). Average household size 5.3; income per family ₱ 97,390 (U.S.$3,820); sources of income: wages 45.7%, business profits 42.5%, self-employment 8.4%, transfers 3.4%; expenditure: food, beverages, and tobacco 57.7%, household furnishings and operations 13.5%, transportation 5.0%, fuel and power 4.1%, clothing 3.7%.
Land use (1993): forested 45.6%; meadows and pastures 4.3%; agricultural and under permanent cultivation 30.8%; other 19.3%.

Foreign trade[6]

Balance of trade (current prices)

	1989	1990	1991	1992	1993	1994
₱ '000,000	−57,713	−86,604	−89,465	−121,250	−176,298	−212,086
% of total	14.6%	17.0%	15.6%	19.6%	22.5%	23.2%

Imports (1994): U.S.$22,638,000,000 (machinery and transport equipment 33.5%, basic manufactures 13.9%, chemicals 9.7%, mineral fuels and lubricants 9.5%, food and live animals 6.7%, inedible crude materials 4.3%). *Major import sources:* Japan 24.1%; U.S. 18.5%; Singapore 6.6%; Taiwan 5.7%; South Korea 5.2%; Hong Kong 5.1%; Saudi Arabia 4.4%; Germany 3.5%; Australia 2.8%; Malaysia 1.9%.
Exports (1994): U.S.$13,482,900,000 (machinery and transport equipment 21.6%, food and live animals 9.9%, clothing and accessories 6.7%, basic manufactures 6.5%, animal and vegetable oils and fats 3.6%, inedible crude materials 3.0%). *Major export destinations:* U.S. 36.8%; Japan 15.0%; Singapore 5.3%; Germany 4.9%; Hong Kong 4.8%; U.K. 4.7%; The Netherlands 3.8%; Taiwan 3.4%; Thailand 2.7%.

Transport and communications

Transport. Railroads (1993): route length 658 mi, 1,059 km; passenger-mi 60,000,000, passenger-km 96,000,000; short ton-mi cargo 8,000,000, metric ton-km cargo 12,000,000. Roads (1991): total length 99,813 mi, 160,633 km (paved 14%). Vehicles (1993): passenger cars 1,078,895; trucks and buses 1,024,051. Merchant marine (1992): vessels (100 gross tons and over) 1,499; total deadweight tonnage 13,807,113. Air transport (1994)[7]: passenger-mi 8,679,000,000, passenger-km 13,967,000,000; short ton-mi cargo 260,315,000, metric ton-km cargo 380,053,000; airports (1995) with scheduled flights 21.
Communications. Daily newspapers (1992): total number 43; circulation 3,200,000; circulation per 1,000 population 49. Radio (1994): 8,300,000 receivers (1 per 8.2 persons). Television (1994): 7,000,000 receivers (1 per 9.8 persons). Telephones (main lines; 1993): 859,800 (1 per 76 persons).

Education and health

Education (1993–94)

	schools	teachers	students	student/ teacher ratio
Primary (age 7–12)	35,087	320,634	10,731,453	33.5
Secondary (age 13–16)	5,550[8] }	134,898	4,590,037	34.0
Voc., teacher tr.	1,261[8] }			
Higher	809[8]	56,880[9]	1,582,820	23.7[9]

Educational attainment (1990). Percentage of population age 25 and over having: no grade completed 6.7%; elementary education 46.9%; secondary 24.3%; postsecondary 11.0%; college 10.6%; not stated 0.5%. *Literacy* (1990): total population age 15 and over literate 34,215,672 (93.6%); males literate 17,080,157 (94.0%); females literate 17,135,515 (93.2%).
Health: physicians (1993) 78,445 (1 per 849 persons); hospital beds (1992) 83,330 (1 per 780 persons); infant mortality rate (1995) 40.
Food (1992): daily per capita caloric intake 2,257 (vegetable products 88%, animal products 12%); 100% of FAO recommended minimum requirement.

Military

Total active duty personnel (1995): 106,500 (army 63.8%, navy 21.6%, air force 14.6%). *Military expenditure as percentage of GNP* (1993): 2.2% (world 3.3%); per capita expenditure U.S.$18.

[1]Projection. [2]Detail does not add to total given because of rounding. [3]Manufacturing firms with 10 or more workers. [4]Mostly unemployed. [5]Wages in nonagricultural activities. [6]Import figures are f.o.b. in balance of trade and c.i.f. for commodities and trading partners. [7]Philippines Airlines only. [8]1991–92. [9]1990–91.

Poland

Official name: Rzeczpospolita Polska (Republic of Poland).
Form of government: unitary multiparty republic with two legislative houses (Senate [100]; Diet [460]).
Chief of state: President.
Head of government: Prime Minister.
Capital: Warsaw.
Official language: Polish.
Official religion: none.
Monetary unit: 1 złoty (Zł)[1] = 100 groszy; valuation (Oct. 6, 1995) 1 U.S.$ = Zł 2.44; 1 £ = Zł 3.86.

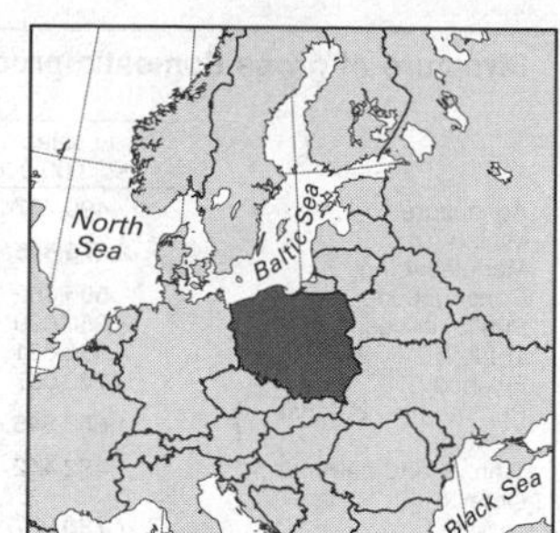

Area and population (1994[2] estimate)

Provinces	area sq km	population	Provinces	area sq km	population
Biała Podlaska	5,348	309,000	Opole	8,535	1,026,700
Białystok	10,055	699,200	Ostrołęka	6,498	405,500
Bielsko-Biała	3,704	911,500	Piła	8,205	489,700
Bydgoszcz	10,349	1,126,500	Piotrków	6,266	644,800
Chełm	3,866	249,600	Płock	5,117	521,000
Ciechanów	6,362	434,800	Poznań	8,151	1,346,600
Częstochowa	6,182	781,800	Przemyśl	4,437	412,600
Elbląg	6,103	488,300	Radom	7,294	761,100
Gdańsk	7,394	1,444,800	Rzeszów	4,397	739,600
Gorzów	8,484	507,900	Siedlce	8,499	659,400
Jelenia Góra	4,379	522,800	Sieradz	4,869	411,900
Kalisz	6,512	719,600	Skierniewice	3,960	423,200
Katowice	6,650	3,954,300	Słupsk	7,453	423,200
Kielce	9,211	1,135,500	Suwałki	10,490	482,000
Konin	5,139	477,200	Szczecin	9,982	984,900
Koszalin	8,470	517,100	Tarnobrzeg	6,283	607,800
Kraków	3,254	1,235,400	Tarnów	4,151	687,100
Krosno	5,702	503,700	Toruń	5,348	667,600
Legnica	4,037	521,500	Wałbrzych	4,168	741,600
Leszno	4,154	394,200	Warszawa	3,788	2,412,700
Łódź	1,523	1,023,800	Włocławek	4,402	433,900
Łomża	6,684	352,900	Wrocław	6,287	1,134,300
Lublin	6,792	1,126,100	Zamość	6,980	493,400
Nowy Sącz	5,576	721,300	Zielona Góra	8,868	669,500
Olsztyn	12,327	765,900	TOTAL	312,685	38,504,700

Demography

Population (1995): 38,641,000.
Density (1993): persons per sq mi 320.1, persons per sq km 123.6.
Urban-rural (1994): urban 61.8%; rural 38.2%.
Sex distribution (1994): male 48.70%; female 51.30%.
Age breakdown (1994): under 15, 23.7%; 15–29, 21.5%; 30–44, 24.0%; 45–59, 15.3%; 60–74, 11.8%; 75 and over, 3.7%.
Population projection: (2000) 39,077,000; (2010) 39,963,000.
Ethnic composition (1990): Polish 98.7%; Ukrainian 0.6%; other 0.7%.
Religious affiliation (1993): Roman Catholic 90.5%; Orthodox 1.5%.
Major cities (1994): Warsaw 1,642,700; Łódź 833,700; Kraków 745,100.

Vital statistics

Birth rate per 1,000 population (1993): 12.8 (world avg. 25.0); (1985) legitimate 95.0%; illegitimate 5.0%.
Death rate per 1,000 population (1993): 10.2 (world avg. 9.3).
Natural increase rate per 1,000 population (1993): 2.6 (world avg. 15.7).
Total fertility rate (avg. births per childbearing woman; 1993): 2.1.
Marriage rate per 1,000 population (1993): 5.4.
Divorce rate per 1,000 population (1993): 0.7.
Life expectancy at birth (1993): male 67.4 years; female 76.0 years.
Major causes of death per 100,000 population (1993): diseases of the circulatory system 529.8; malignant neoplasms 199.4; accidents, poisoning, and violence 73.0; diabetes mellitus 14.9; infectious and parasitic diseases 7.2.

National economy

Budget (1993). Revenue: Zł 459,000,000,000,000 (income tax 39.6%; turnover tax 20.5%). Expenditures: Zł 502,400,000,000,000 (social benefits 20.7%, interest on debts 18.1%).
Public debt (external, outstanding; 1994): U.S.$47,200,000,000.
Gross national product (1993): U.S.$87,272,400,000 (U.S.$2,270 per capita).

Structure of gross domestic product and labour force

	1993			
	in value Zł '000,000,000	% of total value	labour force	% of labour force
Agriculture	105,306	6.8	3,754,100	21.6
Mining and manufacturing	509,361	32.7	3,629,400	20.9
Public utilities	30,314	2.0		
Construction	98,617	6.3	860,800	5.0
Transp. and commun.	81,247	5.2	737,900	4.3
Trade	220,101	14.1	1,947,900	11.2
Finance		223,700		1.3
Public administration	481,053	30.9	330,600	1.9
Services		2,558,900		14.7
Other	31,801[3]	2.0[3]	3,312,700[4]	19.1[4]
TOTAL	1,557,800	100.0	17,356,000	100.0

Production (metric tons except as noted). Agriculture (value of production in Zł '000,000,000; 1993): potatoes 26,237, wheat 19,220, rye 8,243, sugar beets 6,845; livestock (number of live animals; 1993) 22,100,000 pigs, 8,200,000 cattle; roundwood (1993) 18,822,000 cu m; fish catch (1993) 423,029. Mining and quarrying (1993): electrolytic copper 404,000; zinc 150,400; lead 54,000; aluminum 46,900. Manufacturing (value of production in Zł '000,000,000; 1993): food 293,206; machinery and transport equipment 279,797; chemicals 121,030. Construction (1993): 69,741 units, of which residential 36,835. Energy production (consumption): electricity ('000,000 kW-hr; 1993) 133,863 (131,452); coal ('000 metric tons; 1993) 201,682 (178,714); crude petroleum (barrels; 1993) 1,743,000 (103,177,000); petroleum products ('000 metric tons; 1993) 12,086 (13,581); natural gas ('000,000 cu m; 1993) 4,696 (10,993).
Population economically active (1993): total 17,356,000; activity rate of total population 45.1% (participation rates: ages 18–64 [male], 18–59 [female] 61.2%; female [18–59] 53.6%; unemployed 15.0%).

Price and earnings indexes (1985 = 100)

	1988	1989	1990	1991	1992	1993	1994
Consumer price index	4.2	14.6	100.0	170.3	243.0	290.7	468.4
Monthly earnings index	5.6	21.5	100.0	167.1	228.5	320.0	421.4

Household income and expenditure. Average household size (1993) 3.6; average annual income (1993) Zł 104,889,000 (U.S.$4,910); sources of income: wages 76.3%, transfer payments 14.6%, self-employment 2.4%, other 6.7%; expenditure: food 39.1%, housing 19.1%, clothing 7.5%.
Tourism (1993): receipts U.S.$4,500,000,000; expenditures U.S.$181,000,000.
Land use (1993): forest 28.1%; meadow 12.9%; agricultural and under permanent cultivation 46.9%; other 12.1%.

Foreign trade

Balance of trade (current prices)

	1989	1990	1991	1992	1993	1994
Zł '000,000,000	+4,612	+51,935	−6,543	+69,791	−82,615	−98,630
% of total	13.4%	25.1%	2.0%	18.6%	13.8%	11.3%

Imports (1993): Zł 340,183,000,000,000 (machinery and transport equipment 34.4%, chemicals 17.5%, fuel and power 12.6%, light-industrial products 10.0%, food 7.6%). *Major import sources:* Germany 28.0%; Italy 7.8%; Russia 6.8%; U.K. 5.8%; U.S. 5.1%; The Netherlands 4.7%.
Exports (1993): Zł 257,568,000,000,000 (machinery and transport equipment 25.8%, light-industrial products 15.3%, steel products 14.6%, chemicals 9.8%, fuel and power 9.5%, food 9.1%). *Major export destinations:* Germany 36.3%; The Netherlands 5.9%; Italy 5.2%; Russia 4.6%; U.K. 4.3%.

Transport and communications

Transport. Railroads (1993): length 24,926 km; passenger-km 30,865,000,000; metric ton-km cargo 64,359,000,000. Roads (1991): total length 363,116 km (paved 62%). Vehicles (1993): passenger cars 6,771,000; trucks and buses 1,321,000. Merchant marine (1992): vessels (100 gross tons and over) 644; total deadweight tonnage 4,314,308. Air transport (1993): passenger-km 3,653,000,000; metric ton-km cargo 55,000,000; airports (1995) 12.
Communications. Daily newspapers (1992): 72; circulation 6,085,000; circulation per 1,000 population 158. Radio (1993): 10,895,500 (1 per 3.5 persons). Television (1993): 10,087,000 (1 per 3.8 persons). Telephones (main lines; 1993): 4,419,000 (1 per 8.7 persons).

Education and health

Education (1993–94)

	schools	teachers	students	student/teacher ratio
Primary (age 7–14)	20,020	320,400	5,371,841	16.6
Secondary (age 15–18)	1,832	30,300	650,500	21.8
Voc., teacher tr.	9,655	85,600	1,691,000	19.8
Higher	140	65,300	584,000	8.9

Educational attainment (1988). Percentage of population age 15 and over having: no formal schooling or less than full primary education 6.4%; primary 38.8%; secondary 48.3%; higher 6.5%. *Literacy* (1988): 98.7%.
Health (1994): physicians 85,367 (1 per 451 persons); hospital beds 214,786 (1 per 179 persons); infant mortality rate per 1,000 live births 13.3.
Food (1992): daily per capita caloric intake 3,485 (vegetable products 63%, animal products 37%); 133% of FAO recommended minimum.

Military

Total active duty personnel (1993): 283,600 (army 65.5%, navy 6.7%, air force 27.8%). *Military expenditure as percentage of GNP:* 2.5% (world, 3.3); per capita expenditure U.S.$57.

[1]On Jan. 1, 1995, the złoty was redenominated at a rate of 10,000 old złoty to 1 new złoty. [2]January 1. [3]Other material activities. [4]Mostly unemployed.

Portugal

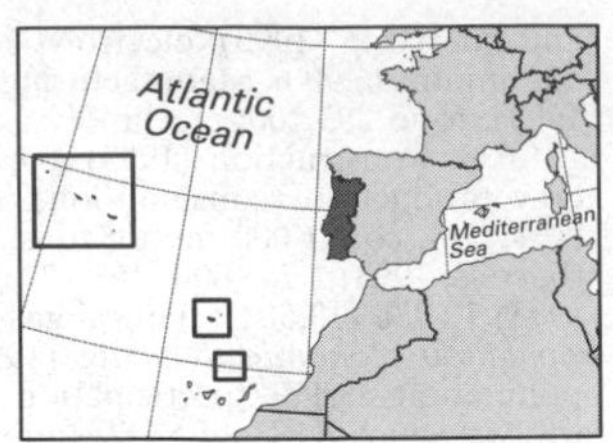

Official name: República Portuguesa (Portuguese Republic).
Form of government: parliamentary state with one legislative house (Assembly of the Republic [230]).
Chief of state: President.
Head of government: Prime Minister.
Capital: Lisbon.
Official language: Portuguese.
Official religion: none.
Monetary unit: 1 escudo (Esc) = 100 centavos; valuation (Oct. 6, 1995) 1 U.S.$ = Esc 150.13; 1 £ = Esc 237.33.

Area and population

		area		population
Continental Portugal				1993[1]
Districts	**Capitals**	sq mi	sq km	estimate
Aveiro	Aveiro	1,081	2,800	658,400
Beja	Beja	3,947	10,223	166,500
Braga	Braga	1,041	2,695	754,700
Bragança	Bragança	2,547	6,597	154,700
Castelo Branco	Castelo Branco	2,555	6,616	211,800
Çoimbra	Çoimbra	1,533	3,971	425,400
Évora	Évora	2,856	7,396	172,400
Faro	Faro	1,925	4,986	342,000
Guarda	Guarda	2,139	5,540	185,400
Leiria	Leiria	1,354	3,508	426,200
Lisboa	Lisbon (Lisboa)	1,065	2,758	2,048,000
Portalegre	Portalegre	2,341	6,064	132,400
Porto	Porto	904	2,341	1,652,000
Santarém	Santarém	2,590	6,707	441,900
Setúbal	Setúbal	1,955	5,064	716,200
Viana do Castelo	Viana do Castelo	853	2,210	248,300
Vila Real	Vila Real	1,662	4,305	233,100
Viseu	Viseu	1,934	5,009	398,800
Azores (Açores) Autonomous Region	Ponta Delgada	868	2,247	237,800
Madeira Autonomous Region	Funchal	306	794	253,800
TOTAL		35,456[2]	91,831[2]	9,859,600[3]

Demography

Population (1995): 9,906,000.
Density (1995): persons per sq mi 279.4, persons per sq km 107.9.
Urban-rural (1993): urban 34.8%; rural 65.2%.
Sex distribution (1994[1]): male 48.16%; female 51.84%.
Age breakdown (1987): under 15, 22.7%; 15–29, 24.6%; 30–44, 18.8%; 45–59, 16.5%; 60–74, 12.6%; 75 and over, 4.8%.
Population projection: (2000) 9,966,000; (2010) 10,089,000.
Nationality (1990): Portuguese 99.5%; Cape Verdean 0.2%; Brazilian 0.1%; Spanish, British, and American 0.1%; other 0.1%.
Religious affiliation (1981): Christian 96.0%, of which Roman Catholic 94.5%, Protestant 0.6%, other Christian (mostly Apostolic Catholic and Jehovah's Witness) 0.9%; nonreligious 3.8%; Jewish 0.1%; Muslim 0.1%.
Major cities (1991): Lisbon 681,063; Porto 309,485; Vila Nova de Gaia 247,499; Amadora 176,137.

Vital statistics

Birth rate per 1,000 population (1993): 11.5 (world avg. 25.0); (1990) legitimate 85.5%; illegitimate 14.5%.
Death rate per 1,000 population (1993): 10.7 (world avg. 9.3).
Natural increase rate per 1,000 population (1993): 0.8 (world avg. 15.7).
Total fertility rate (avg. births per childbearing woman; 1993): 1.6.
Marriage rate per 1,000 population (1993): 6.9.
Divorce rate per 1,000 population (1993): 1.2.
Life expectancy at birth (1992–93): male 70.8 years; female 78.0 years.
Major causes of death per 100,000 population (1993): circulatory diseases 469.1, of which cerebrovascular diseases 250.6, ischemic heart disease 101.1; malignant neoplasms (cancers) 195.5; respiratory diseases 78.9.

National economy

Budget (1993). Revenue: Esc 5,571,100,000,000 (import duties and excise taxes 32.6%, social-security taxes 23.9%, income and inheritance taxes 22.4%). Expenditures: Esc 6,442,200,000,000 (1988; education 12.4%, health 9.8%, defense 6.6%, administration 5.3%, public works 2.8%).
Production (metric tons except as noted). Agriculture, forestry, fishing (1994): potatoes 1,255,000, tomatoes 965,000, corn (maize) 661,000, grapes 660,000, wheat 454,000, olives 215,000, rice 115,000, cork 91,870[4], carrots 83,000, oats 76,000, onions 57,000; livestock (number of live animals) 5,991,000 sheep, 1,487,000 pigs, 1,322,000 cattle; roundwood (1993) 11,584,000 cu m; fish catch (1993) 274,174. Mining and quarrying (1994): salt 556,724; copper 133,630; kaolin 95,900[4]; tin 7,637; zinc 5,675[5]; tungsten 100. Manufacturing (value of production in Esc '000,000; 1989): cotton and synthetic fibres 222,717; refined petroleum 148,274; clothing 138,659; motor vehicles 113,924; knitted fabrics 105,339; dairy products 90,282; iron and steel 70,919; cement 57,720; alcoholic beverages 47,489. Construction (1993): residential 4,793,000 sq m; nonresidential 2,045,167 sq m[6]. Energy production (consumption): electricity (kW-hr; 1993) 31,205,000,000 (31,380,000,000); coal (metric tons; 1993) 197,000 (4,951,000); crude petroleum (barrels; 1993) none (79,530,000); petroleum products (metric tons; 1993) 10,116,000 (10,280,000); natural gas, none (n.a.).
Gross national product (1993): U.S.$77,700,000,000 (U.S.$7,890 per capita).

Structure of gross domestic product and labour force

	1990		1993	
	in value Esc '000,000	% of total value	labour force	% of labour force
Agriculture	490,787	6.3	527,890	10.7
Mining }	2,275,815	29.2	20,630	0.4
Manufacturing }			1,119,680	22.7
Construction	585,382	7.5	384,370	7.8
Public utilities	250,629	3.2	32,860	0.7
Trade	1,352,031	17.4	922,990	18.7
Finance	720,037	9.2	311,970	6.3
Pub. admin., defense } Services }	1,653,845	21.2	1,137,210	23.1
Transp. and commun.	462,412	5.9	215,660	4.4
Other	...	...	257,500[7]	5.2[7]
TOTAL	7,790,937[3]	100.0[3]	4,930,760	100.0

Public debt (1992): U.S.$39,922,000,000.
Tourism (1993): receipts U.S.$4,176,000,000; expenditures U.S.$1,846,000,000.
Population economically active (1993): total 4,930,760; activity rate of total population 49.9% (participation rates: ages 15–64, 69.0%; female 45.6%; unemployed 5.2%).

Price and earnings indexes (1990 = 100)

	1988	1989	1990	1991	1992	1993	1994
Consumer price index	78.3	88.2	100.0	111.4	121.3	129.6	136.0
Daily earnings index	76.0	86.2	100.0	113.5	...	...	...

Household income and expenditure. Average household size (1991) 3.1; income per household: n.a.; sources of income (1993): wages and salaries 46.4%, property and entrepreneurial income 31.8%, transfer payments 21.8%; expenditure (1986): food 34.7%, transportation and communications 15.4%, clothing and footwear 10.3%, cafes and hotels 9.7%, housing 5.0%, health 4.5%, recreation 4.3%, other 16.1%.
Land use (1993): forested 35.9%; meadows and pastures 9.1%; agricultural and under permanent cultivation 34.4%; other 20.6%.

Foreign trade

Balance of trade (current prices)

	1989	1990	1991	1992	1993	1994
Esc '000,000	−705,000	−918,600	−1,067,800	−1,144.6	−1,051.8	−1,099.9
% of total	15.2%	16.4%	18.5%	18.8%	17.5%	15.9%

Imports (1993): Esc 3,883,000,000 (machinery and transport equipment 35.7%, of which road vehicles and parts 15.1%; food and live animals 13.8%; mineral fuels 8.8%; chemicals and chemical products 7.9%; textiles 7.1%; office machines 2.4%). *Major import sources:* Spain 17.8%; Germany 15.0%; France 12.7%; Italy 8.7%; U.K. 7.4%; The Netherlands 4.9%.
Exports (1993): Esc 2,474,000,000 (textiles and wearing apparel 28.4%; machinery and transport equipment 21.3%, of which transport equipment 6.5%; footwear 9.6%; cork and wood products 5.5%; chemicals and chemical products 3.3%). *Major export destinations:* Germany 19.6%; France 15.2%; Spain 14.4%; U.K. 11.4%.

Transport and communications

Transport. Railroads (1993): route length 2,179 mi, 3,507 km; passenger-km 5,397,000,097; metric ton-km cargo 1,867,000,000[4]. Roads (1989): total length 43,605 mi, 70,176 km (paved 86%). Vehicles (1993): passenger cars 4,166,231; trucks and buses 219,696. Merchant marine (1992): vessels (100 gross tons and over) 332; total deadweight tonnage 1,129,382. Air transport (1993): passenger-km 7,896,000,000; metric ton-km cargo 183,990,000; airports (1995) 14.
Communications. Daily newspapers (1992): total number 25; total circulation 465,000; circulation per 1,000 population 47. Radio (1993): 2,475,000 receivers (1 per 4.0 persons). Television (1993): 2,970,892 receivers (1 per 3.3 persons). Telephones (main lines; 1993): 3,260,300 (1 per 3.0 persons).

Education and health

Education (1992–93)

	schools	teachers	students	student/ teacher ratio
Primary (age 5–11)	11,771	71,788	925,936	12.9
Secondary (age 12–19)	1,368	64,479[8]	815,491	14.0[8]
Vocational	220	[8]	84,932	[8]
Higher[9]	250	30,998	214,403	6.9

Educational attainment (1981). Percentage of population age 25 and over having: no formal schooling 33.4%; some primary education 55.1%; some secondary 9.3%; postsecondary 2.2%. *Literacy* (1990): total population age 15 and over literate 6,769,270 (86.8%); males literate 3,208,634 (86.7%); females literate 3,560,636 (86.9%).
Health (1993): physicians 28,769 (1 per 343 persons); hospital beds 41,036 (1 per 241 persons); infant mortality rate per 1,000 live births 8.5.
Food (1992): daily per capita caloric intake 3,634 (vegetable products 74%, animal products 26%); 148% of FAO recommended minimum requirement.

Military

Total active duty personnel (1995): 54,200 (army 54.8%, navy 23.1%, air force 13.5%, paramilitary national guard 8.6%). *Military expenditure as percentage of GNP* (1993): 3.0% (world 3.3%); per capita expenditure U.S.$209.

[1]January 1. [2]Does not include 117 sq mi (304 sq km) of water areas comprising the Tagus and Sado estuaries and the Aveiro Lagoon. [3]Detail does not add to total given because of rounding. [4]1992. [5]1993. [6]1990. [7]Unemployed. [8]Secondary includes Vocational. [9]Includes teacher colleges.

Puerto Rico

Official name: Estado Libre Asociado de Puerto Rico; Commonwealth of Puerto Rico.
Political status: self-governing commonwealth in association with the United States, having two legislative houses (Senate [29[1]]; House of Representatives [53][1]).
Chief of state: President of the United States.
Head of government: Governor.
Capital: San Juan.
Official languages: Spanish; English.
Official religion: none.
Monetary unit: 1 U.S. dollar (U.S.$) = 100 cents; valuation (Oct. 6, 1995) 1 £ = U.S.$1.58.

Population (1992 estimate)

Municipio	population	Municipio	population	Municipio	population
Adjuntas	19,765	Fajardo	37,478	Naguabo	22,986
Aguada	36,492	Florida	8,829	Naranjito	28,365
Aguadilla	60,294	Guánica	20,307	Orocovis	21,500
Agunas Buenas	25,835	Guayama	42,260	Patillas	19,950
Aibonito	25,375	Guayanilla	21,930	Peñuelas	22,879
Añasco	25,642	Guaynabo	94,388	Ponce	190,784
Arecibo	94,895	Gurabo	29,202	Quebradillas	21,771
Arroyo	19,216	Hatillo	33,232	Rincón	12,410
Barceloneta	21,286	Hormigueros	15,458	Río Grande	46,386
Barranquitas	26,019	Humacao	56,096	Sabana Grande	23,212
Bayamón	223,823	Isabela	39,780	Salinas	28,793
Cabo Rojo	39,144	Jayuya	15,778	San Germán	35,527
Caguas	135,605	Juana Díaz	45,929	San Juan	444,822
Camuy	29,385	Juncos	31,107	San Lorenzo	35,732
Canóvanas	37,411	Lajas	23,647	San Sebastián	39,426
Carolina	180,681	Lares	29,484	Santa Isabel	19,630
Cataño	35,146	Las Marías	9,456	Toa Alta	44,814
Cayey	47,306	Las Piedras	28,347	Toa Baja	90,900
Ceiba	17,422	Loíza	29,781	Trujillo Alto	62,108
Ciales	18,376	Luquillo	18,393	Utuado	35,546
Cidra	36,177	Manatí	39,318	Vega Alta	35,118
Coamo	34,384	Maricao	6,306	Vega Baja	56,902
Comerío	20,593	Maunabo	12,547	Vieques	8,741
Corozal	33,630	Mayagüez	101,994	Villalba	23,940
Culebra	1,567	Moca	33,458	Yabucoa	37,073
Dorado	31,256	Morovis	25,697	Yauco	42,738
				TOTAL	3,578,980

Demography

Area: 3,515 sq mi, 9,104 sq km.
Population (1995): 3,725,000.
Density (1995): persons per sq mi 1,059.8, persons per sq km 409.2.
Urban-rural (1990): urban 71.2%; rural 28.8%.
Sex distribution (1992): male 48.43%; female 51.57%.
Age breakdown (1992): under 15, 27.2%; 15–29, 25.1%; 30–44, 20.4%; 45–59, 14.1%; 60–74, 9.2%; 75 and over, 4.0%.
Population projection: (2000) 3,849,000; (2010) 4,199,000.
Doubling time: 69 years.
Ethnic composition (1980): white 80.0%; black 20.0%.
Religious affiliation (1984): Roman Catholic 85.3%; Protestant 4.7%; other 10.0%.
Major cities (1990): San Juan 426,832; Ponce 159,151; Caguas 92,429; Mayagüez 83,010; Arecibo 49,545.

Vital statistics

Birth rate per 1,000 population (1994): 17.9 (world avg. 25.0); (1993) legitimate 59.6%; illegitimate 40.4%.
Death rate per 1,000 population (1994): 7.9 (world avg. 9.3).
Natural increase rate per 1,000 population (1994): 10.0 (world avg. 15.7).
Total fertility rate (avg. births per childbearing woman; 1991): 2.2.
Marriage rate per 1,000 population (1992): 9.6.
Divorce rate per 1,000 population (1992): 4.0.
Life expectancy at birth (1991): male 69.6 years; female 78.5 years.
Major causes of death per 100,000 population (1993): heart disease 142.6; cancers 95.4; diabetes 55.1; cerebrovascular disease 38.0; pneumonia and influenza 29.2.

National economy

Budget. Revenue (1994): U.S.$6,882,200,000 (income taxes 41.8%, excise taxes 18.0%, nontax revenue 6.5%, property taxes 1.0%, other receipts 32.7%). Expenditures (1992): U.S.$5,607,000,000 (education 30.3%, public safety and protection 11.4%, welfare 10.8%, health 10.7%, debt service 6.2%).
Public debt (outstanding; 1994): U.S.$15,257,500,000.
Tourism: receipts from visitors (1994) U.S.$1,736,600,000; expenditures by nationals abroad (1991) U.S.$798,000,000.
Production (in U.S.$'000,000 except as noted). Agriculture, forestry, fishing (gross farm income; 1994): milk 189.7, poultry 93.1, vegetables 71.8, coffee 66.3, beef 42.0, pork 31.2, fruit 31.0, eggs 25.7, sugar 12.0; livestock (number of live animals; 1993) 552,000 cattle, 115,000 pigs; roundwood, n.a.; fish catch (1992) 1,721 metric tons. Mining (value of production in U.S.$'000; 1993): stone 50. Manufacturing (value added in U.S.$'000,000; 1994): chemicals, pharmaceuticals, and allied products 8,174; machinery and metal products 3,049; food products 2,354; clothing 478; printing and publishing 168; stone, clay, and glass products 163. Construction (authorized; 1985): residential 1,798,000 sq m; nonresidential 41,000 sq m. Energy production (consumption): electricity (kW-hr; 1992) 16,434,000,000 (16,434,000,000); coal (metric tons; 1992) none (154,000); crude petroleum (barrels; 1992) none (40,315,-000); petroleum products (metric tons; 1992) 4,945,000 (5,461,000); natural gas, none (none).
Gross national product (1993): U.S.$25,317,000,000 (U.S.$6,700 per capita).

Structure of gross domestic product and labour force

	1994			
	in value U.S.$'000,000	% of total value	labour force	% of labour force
Agriculture	411.2	1.0	34,000	2.8
Manufacturing	16,308.9	41.5	166,000	13.8
Mining }	850.1	2.2	...	...
Construction }			54,000	4.5
Public utilities }	3,092.5	7.9	16,000	1.3
Transp. and commun. }			39,000	3.3
Trade	5,675.8	14.5	201,000	16.7
Finance, real estate	5,085.2	12.9	33,000	2.7
Pub. admin., defense	4,071.2	10.4 }	468,000	38.9
Services	4,249.3	10.8 }		
Other	−479.4[2]	−1.2[2]	192,000[3]	16.0[3]
TOTAL	39,264.8	100.0	1,203,000	100.0

Population economically active (1994): total 1,203,000; activity rate 32.9% (participation rates: ages 16–64, 46.1%; female [1990] 37.1%; unemployed 16.0%).

Price and earnings indexes (1990 = 100)

	1988	1989	1990	1991	1992	1993	1994
Consumer price index	92.9	96.1	100.0	105.3	108.1	111.3	114.5
Hourly earnings index[4]	92.0	95.4	100.0	104.1	...	...	...

Household income and expenditure (1994). Average family size 3.6; income per family U.S.$25,368; sources of income: wages and salaries 53.5%, transfers 29.6%, self-employment 6.6%, rent 4.8%, other 5.5%; expenditure (1994): food and beverages 21.9%, transportation 12.9%, health care 12.9%, housing and energy 12.5%, household furnishings 11.6%, recreation 8.9%, clothing 7.6%, education 3.3%, other 8.4%.
Land use (1992): forested 20.0%; meadows and pastures 37.7%; agricultural and under permanent cultivation 14.0%; other 28.3%.

Foreign trade

Balance of trade (current prices)

	1989	1990	1991	1992	1993	1994
U.S.$'000,000	+2,312	+3,584	+5,419	+5,857	+3,405	+5,098
% of total	7.6%	10.2%	14.6%	16.2%	9.4%	13.3%

Imports (1994): U.S.$16,654,200,000 (chemicals [all forms] 18.7%, electrical machinery 14.7%, food 12.0%, transport equipment 8.9%, nonelectrical machinery 6.8%, petroleum and petroleum products 5.3%, professional and scientific instruments 4.2%). *Major import sources* (1990): U.S. 68.7%; Venezuela 4.4%; Japan 3.2%; Dominican Republic 2.0%; The Bahamas 1.8%; U.K. 1.0%.
Exports (1994): U.S.$21,752,600,000 (chemicals and chemical products 46.7%, food 13.3%, electrical machinery 10.4%, computers 7.4%). *Major export destinations* (1990): U.S. 86.9%; Dominican Republic 2.0%; U.S. Virgin Islands 1.4%; U.K. 0.8%; The Netherlands 0.7%.

Transport and communications

Transport. Railroads (1988)[5]: length 59 mi, 96 km. Roads (1993): total length 14,089 mi, 22,588 km (paved 87%). Vehicles (1993): passenger cars 1,420,000; trucks and buses 227,000. Merchant marine: n.a. Air transport (1990–91): passenger arrivals 4,245,137, passenger departures 4,262,164; cargo loaded and unloaded 222,172 metric tons[6]; airports (1995) with scheduled flights 7.
Communications. Daily newspapers (1993): total number 3; total circulation 506,900; circulation per 1,000 population 140. Radio (1994): 2,480,000 receivers (1 per 1.5 persons). Television (1994): 830,000 receivers (1 per 4.4 persons). Telephones (1992): 1,365,520 (1 per 2.6 persons).

Education and health

Education (1985–86)

	schools	teachers	students	student/ teacher ratio
Primary (age 5–12)	1,542	18,359	427,582	23.3
Secondary (age 13–18)	395	13,612	334,661	24.6
Voc., teacher tr.	52	...	149,191	...
Higher	45	9,045	156,818	17.3

Educational attainment (1990). Percentage of population age 25 and over having: primary education 26.8%; some secondary 23.5%; complete secondary 21.0%; higher 28.7%. *Literacy* (1990): total population age 18 and over literate 2,122,860 (89.7%); males literate 1,001,878 (89.6%); females literate 1,120,982 (89.7%).
Health: physicians (1988) 9,422 (1 per 349 persons); hospital beds (1993–94) 9,598 (1 per 381 persons); infant mortality rate (1993) 13.4.

Military

Total active duty personnel (1992): 3,518 U.S. personnel.

[1]Includes (each house) 2 special at-large seats above usual legally mandated membership of body that were created under a constitutional provision to limit majority party's control of either house to two-thirds. [2]Statistical discrepancy. [3]Unemployed. [4]Manufacturing sector only. [5]Privately owned railway for sugarcane transport only. [6]Handled by the Luis Muñoz Marín International Airport only.

Qatar

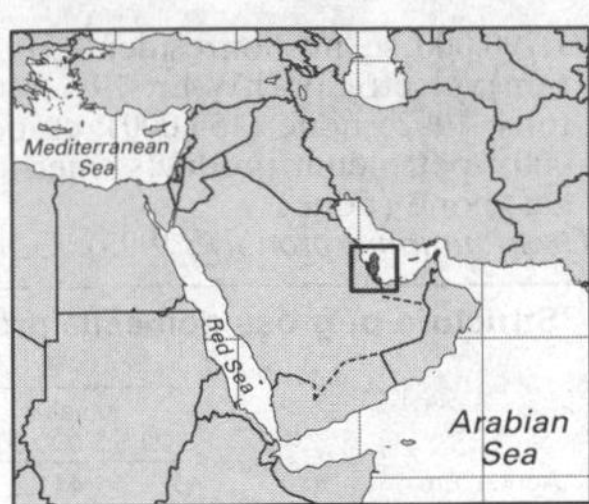

Official name: Dawlat Qaṭar (State of Qatar).
Form of government: monarchy (emirate)[1]; Islamic law is the basis of legislation in the state.
Head of state and government: Emir.
Capital: Doha.
Official language: Arabic.
Official religion: Islam.
Monetary unit: 1 riyal (QR) = 100 dirhams; valuation (Oct. 6, 1995) 1 U.S.$ = QR 3.64; 1 £ = QR 5.76.

Area and population

Municipalities	Capitals	area sq mi	area sq km	population 1992 estimate
ad-Dawḥah (Doha)	—	51	132	313,639
al-Ghuwayrīyah	al-Ghuwayrīyah	241	622	2,349
Jarayān al-Bāṭinah	Jarayān al-Bāṭinah	1,434	3,715	3,932
al-Jumaylīyah	al-Jumaylīyah	990[2]	2,565[2]	10,414
al-Khawr	al-Khawr	385	996	12,982
ar-Rayyān	ar-Rayyān	343	889	132,785
ash-Shamāl	Madinat ash-Shamāl	348	901	6,323
Umm Ṣalāl	Umm Ṣalāl Muḥammad	190	493	16,110
al-Wakrah	al-Wakrah	430	1,114	34,185
TOTAL		4,412	11,427	532,719

Demography

Population (1995): 579,100.
Density (1995): persons per sq mi 131.3, persons per sq km 50.1.
Urban-rural (1990): urban 89.5%; rural 10.5%.
Sex distribution (1992): male 70.65%; female 29.34%.
Age breakdown (1992): under 15, 23.3%; 15–29, 18.8%; 30–44, 43.8%; 45–59, 12.0%; 60–74, 1.8%; 75 and over, 0.3%.
Population projection: (2000) 632,000; (2010) 755,000.
Doubling time: 39 years.
Ethnic composition (1983): South Asian 34%; Qatari 20%; other Arab 25%; Iranian 16%; other 5%.
Religious affiliation (1980): Muslim (mostly Sunnī) 92.4%; Christian 5.9%; Hindu 1.1%; Bahā'ī 0.2%; other 0.4%.
Major cities (1987): Doha 236,131; ar-Rayyān 99,939; al-Wakrah 25,747; Umm Sa'īd 12,111.

Vital statistics

Birth rate per 1,000 population (1993): 19.4 (world avg. 25.0); legitimate, n.a.; illegitimate, n.a.
Death rate per 1,000 population (1993): 1.6 (world avg. 9.3).
Natural increase rate per 1,000 population (1993): 17.8 (world avg. 15.7).
Total fertility rate (avg. births per childbearing woman; 1992): 3.0.
Marriage rate per 1,000 population (1993): 2.8.
Divorce rate per 1,000 population (1993): 0.8.
Life expectancy at birth (1995): male 70.5 years; female 75.5 years.
Major causes of death per 100,000 population (1992): diseases of the circulatory system 56.9; injuries and poisoning 36.0; neoplasms (including benign neoplasms) 21.4; certain conditions originating in the perinatal period 11.1; diseases of the respiratory system 7.5; endocrine, metabolic, and nutritional diseases and immunity disorders 7.3; diseases of the digestive system 3.4; signs, symptoms, and ill-defined conditions 10.9.

National economy

Budget (1994–95). Revenue: QR 8,360,000,000 (1992–93; crude oil 67.3%). Expenditures: QR 11,830,000,000 (wages and salaries 44.4%, state capital-development projects 41.7%, social and health services 8.1%, education 2.7%).
Public debt (external, outstanding; 1993): U.S.$1,500,000,000.
Production (metric tons except as noted). Agriculture, forestry, fishing (value of production in QR '000; 1993): milk and dairy products 131,206, forage 118,809, vegetables and other crops (except cereals) 71,206, beef 44,390, fruits and dates 28,645, poultry meat 25,930, eggs 14,583, cereals 3,710; livestock (number of live animals; 1994) 170,000 sheep, 150,000 goats, 43,000 camels, 12,000 cattle; roundwood, n.a.; fish catch (1993) 6,994. Mining and quarrying (1993): limestone 900,000; sulfur 60,000; gypsum, sand and gravel, and clay are also produced. Manufacturing (value added in QR '000; 1992): chemicals and petroleum products 2,227,000; manufactured products 505,000; paper products 137,000; clothing and footwear 120,000; furniture and wood products 84,000; fabricated metal products 73,000; food, beverages, and tobacco 72,000. Construction (1992): residential 12,420 units; nonresidential 1,416 units. Energy production (consumption): electricity (kW-hr; 1992) 4,740,000,000 (4,740,000,000); coal, none (n.a.); crude petroleum (barrels; 1993) 152,935,000,000 (15,330,000); petroleum products (metric tons; 1992) 4,980,000 (1,744,000); natural gas (cu m; 1993) 11,610,000,000 (11,610,000,000).
Population economically active (1988): total 292,568; activity rate of total population 53.7% (participation rates: ages 15–64, 80.8%; female 11.2%; unemployed [1986] 0.5%).

Price and earnings indexes (1990 = 100)

	1988	1989	1990	1991	1992	1993	1994
Consumer price index	94.0	97.1	100.0	104.4	107.5	110.9	114.2
Earnings index	...	...	...	...	...	...	...

Gross national product (at current market prices; 1993): U.S.$7,871,000,000 (U.S.$15,140 per capita).

Structure of gross domestic product and labour force

	1993 in value QR '000,000	1993 % of total value	1988 labour force	1988 % of labour force
Agriculture	273	1.0	4,544	1.6
Oil sector	8,480	32.4	7,657	2.6
Manufacturing	2,930	11.2	10,627	3.6
Construction	1,290	4.9	64,213	21.9
Public utilities	350	1.3	3,672	1.3
Transportation	880	3.4	11,877	4.1
Trade	1,790	6.8	34,246	11.7
Finance	3,185	12.3	6,172	2.1
Pub. admin., defense; Services; Other	7,005	26.7	149,560	51.1
TOTAL	26,183	100.0	292,568	100.0

Household income and expenditure. Average household size (1986) 6.4; income per household: n.a.; sources of income (1988): wages and salaries 80.8%, rents and royalties 10.6%, self-employment 5.6%, other 3.0%; expenditure (1993): food 28.7%, transportation 19.3%, housing 12.4%, clothing 10.6%, education 7.6%, health 1.2%.
Land use (1993): meadows and pastures 4.7%; agricultural and under permanent cultivation 0.6%; built-up, desert, and other 94.7%.
Tourism (1992): receipts and expenditures, n.a.; total number of tourists staying in hotels 141,000.

Foreign trade

Balance of trade (current prices)

	1988	1989	1990	1991	1992	1993
QR '000,000	+2,253	+4,827	+7,992	+5,423	+6,644	+4,931
% of total	19.8%	33.9%	39.3%	30.2%	31.2%	26.4%

Imports (1993): QR 6,882,000,000 (1992; machinery and transport equipment 44.1%; manufactured goods 31.4%; food and live animals 12.7%; chemicals and chemical products 6.3%; raw materials 3.1%). *Major import sources:* Japan 15.6%; United States 11.4%; United Kingdom 11.2%; Germany 7.3%; Italy 6.6%; France 5.5%; United Arab Emirates 5.0%; Saudi Arabia 3.6%.
Exports (1993): QR 11,813,000,000 (1992; crude petroleum, petroleum products, and liquefied gas 85.7%; non-oil exports 14.3%). *Major export destinations* (1989): Japan 54.4%; Thailand 5.0%; Singapore 4.0%; South Korea 3.6%; United Arab Emirates 3.4%; Italy 2.7%; India 2.7%; Saudi Arabia 2.5%.

Transport and communications

Transport. Railroads: none. Roads (1988): total length 671 mi, 1,080 km (paved 63%). Vehicles (1993): passenger cars 132,144; trucks and buses 55,079. Merchant marine (1992): vessels (100 gross tons and over) 65; total deadweight tonnage 635,580. Air transport (1992)[3]: passenger-mi 1,194,000,000, passenger-km 1,922,000,000; short ton-mi cargo 173,000,000, metric ton-km cargo 252,000,000; airports (1995) with scheduled flights 1.
Communications. Daily newspapers (1992): total number 4; total circulation 70,000; circulation per 1,000 population 155. Radio (1992): total number of receivers 201,000 (1 per 2.6 persons). Television (1992): total number of receivers 205,000 (1 per 2.5 persons). Telephones (main lines; 1993): 111,200 (1 per 4.7 persons).

Education and health

Education (1992–93)[4]

	schools	teachers	students	student/teacher ratio
Primary (age 6–11)	160	4,917	49,059	10.0
Secondary (age 12–17)	36	4,888	34,231	7.0
Vocational	3	128	782	6.1
Higher[5]	1	636	7,351	11.6

Educational attainment (1986). Percentage of population age 25 and over having: no formal education 53.3%, of which illiterates 24.3%; primary 9.8%; preparatory (lower secondary) 10.1%; secondary 13.3%; postsecondary 13.3%; other 0.2%. *Literacy* (1986): total population age 15 and over literate 201,733 (75.7%); males literate 149,980 (76.8%); females literate 51,753 (72.5%).
Health (1992): physicians 758 (1 per 671 persons); hospital beds 1,081 (1 per 481 persons); infant mortality rate per 1,000 live births (1993) 12.8.
Food: daily per capita caloric intake, n.a.

Military

Total active duty personnel (1995): 11,100 (army 76.6%, navy 16.2%, air force 7.2%). *Military expenditure as percentage of GNP* (1993): 4.2% (world 3.3%); per capita expenditure U.S.$610.

[1]Provisional constitution of 1970 provided limited constitutional forms but has not been fully implemented. [2]Includes area of unpopulated Hawar Islands (also claimed by Bahrain). [3]One-fourth apportionment of international flights of Gulf Air. [4]Public schools only; available detail for private schools (1991–92) included 17,728 primary students, 1,695 secondary students, and 1,465 teachers. [5]1993–94.

Réunion

Official name: Département de la Réunion (Department of Réunion).
Political status: overseas department (France) with two legislative houses (General Council [47]; Regional Council [45]).
Chief of state: President of France.
Heads of government: Prefect (for France); President of General Council (for Réunion); President of Regional Council (for Réunion).
Capital: Saint-Denis.
Official language: French.
Official religion: none.
Monetary unit: 1 French franc (F) = 100 centimes; valuation (Oct. 6, 1995) 1 U.S.$ = F 5.01; 1 £ = F 7.93.

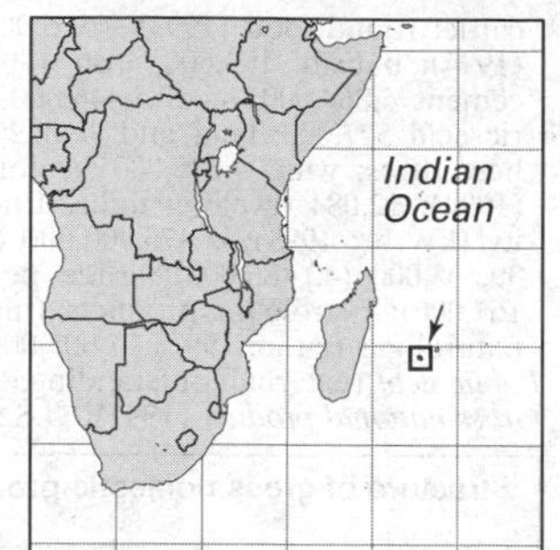

Area and population

		area		population
Arrondissements	Capitals	sq mi	sq km	1990 census
Saint-Benoît	Saint-Benoît	284	736	85,132
Saint-Denis	Saint-Denis	164	423	207,158
Saint-Paul	Saint-Paul	180	467	113,071
Saint-Pierre	Saint-Pierre	339	878	192,462
TOTAL		970[1,2]	2,512[1,2]	597,823

Demography

Population (1995): 660,000.
Density (1995): persons per sq mi 680.4, persons per sq km 262.7.
Urban-rural (1995): urban 67.8%; rural 32.2%.
Sex distribution (1992): male 49.25%; female 50.75%.
Age breakdown (1993): under 15, 29.0%; 15–29, 28.5%; 30–44, 22.0%; 45–59, 11.7%; 60 and over, 8.8%.
Population projection: (2000) 724,000; (2010) 873,000.
Doubling time: 46 years.
Ethnic composition (1983): mixed race 63.5%; East Indian 28.2%; Chinese 2.2%; white 1.9%; East African 1.1%; other 3.1%.
Religious affiliation (1993): Roman Catholic 88.3%; other (mostly Muslim) 11.7%.
Major cities (1990): Saint-Denis 100,926; Le Port 29,190; Le Tampon 27,300; Saint-André 25,237; Saint-Pierre 23,899.

Vital statistics

Birth rate per 1,000 population (1994): 20.6 (world avg. 25.0); (1993) legitimate 46.0%; illegitimate 54.0%.
Death rate per 1,000 population (1994): 5.4 (world avg. 9.3).
Natural increase rate per 1,000 population (1994): 15.2 (world avg. 15.7).
Total fertility rate (avg. births per childbearing woman; 1993): 2.4.
Marriage rate per 1,000 population (1993): 5.5.
Divorce rate per 1,000 population (1993): 1.5.
Life expectancy at birth (1994): male 71.0 years; female 77.0 years.
Major causes of death per 100,000 population (1992): diseases of the circulatory system 173.0; malignant neoplasms (cancers) 87.2; diseases of the digestive system (including all deaths associated with alcoholism) 60.3; diseases of the respiratory system 43.1; homicide and violence 26.6.

National economy

Budget (1993). Revenue: F 4,190,000,000 (receipts from the French central government and local administrative bodies 47.6%, subsidies and related receipts 14.2%, new loans 11.9%). Expenditures: F 4,190,000,000 (current expenditures 66.4%, development expenditures 33.6%).
Public debt (external, outstanding; 1990)[3]: U.S.$61,000,000.
Tourism (1993): receipts U.S.$129,000,000; expenditures, n.a.
Gross national product (at current market prices; 1990): U.S.$1,848,000,000 (U.S.$3,080 per capita).

Structure of gross domestic product and labour force

	1990		1993	
	in value F '000,000	% of total value	labour force	% of labour force
Agriculture, fishing	1,200[4]	4.1[4]	11,513	4.9
Manufacturing	2,600[4]	9.2[4]	10,845	4.6
Construction	1,800	6.2	16,709	7.1
Public utilities	1,400	4.9	...	...
Transportation and communications	1,700[5]	5.9[5]	5,205	2.2
Trade	5,500[5]	19.2[5]	23,491	10.0
Finance, real estate, business services	6,200	21.9	24,662	10.5
Pub. admin., defense, other services	8,100	28.6	67,218	28.7
Other	—	—	74,933[6]	32.0[6]
TOTAL	28,500[7]	100.0	234,576	100.0

Production (metric tons except as noted). Agriculture, forestry, fishing (1994): sugarcane 1,656,000, pe-tsai (Chinese cabbage) and black nightshade 8,291[8], pineapples 5,000, bananas 4,000, mangoes 4,000, tomatoes 4,000, eggplant 3,000, pimento 405[8], ginger 95[8], vanilla 27, tobacco 14[8], geranium essence 2.8; livestock (number of live animals) 86,000 pigs, 32,000 goats, 25,000 cattle; roundwood (1992) 36,000 cu m; fish (value of catch in F '000,000; 1993) lobster 39, other 52. Mining and quarrying: gravel and sand for local use. Manufacturing (value added in F '000,000; 1992): construction materials (mostly cement) 317; sugar, molasses, and related products 220; fabricated metals 196; alcoholic and nonalcoholic beverages (mostly rum) 191; printing and publishing 173. Construction (value of public construction; 1988): residential F 258,200,000; nonresidential F 1,587,000,000. Energy production (consumption): electricity (kW-hr; 1994) 1,206,000,000 (1,056,000,000); coal, none (none); crude petroleum, none (none); petroleum products (metric tons; 1993) none (434,000); natural gas, none (none).
Population economically active (1993): total 234,576; activity rate of total population 36.9% (participation rates: ages 15–64, 56.7%; female 41.7%; unemployed [April 1994–March 1995] 31%).

Price and earnings indexes (December 1992 = 100)[9]

	1989	1990	1991	1992	1993	1994	1995[10]
Consumer price index	90.9	94.4	97.3	100.0	102.4	106.0	108.1
Hourly earnings index[11]	78.7	86.1	91.6	100.0	105.3	107.5	109.7

Household income and expenditure. Average household size (1990) 3.8; income per household (1987) F 89,304 (U.S.$14,858); sources of income (1987): wages and salaries and self-employment 67.5%, transfer payments 29.7%, other 2.8%; expenditure (1986–87): transportation and communications 24.9%, food and beverages 22.4%, housing 11.8%, recreation and education 10.1%, clothing and footwear 7.9%, household furnishings 6.0%, other 16.9%.
Land use (1993): forested 35.2%; meadows and pastures 4.8%; agricultural and under permanent cultivation 19.2%; other 40.8%.

Foreign trade

Balance of trade (current prices)

	1989	1990	1991	1992	1993	1994
F '000,000	−10,067	−10,747	−11,075	−11,542	−10,859	−12,109
% of total	83.1%	84.1%	87.6%	83.9%	84.5%	86.4%

Imports (1994): F 13,062,000,000 (food and agricultural products 19.5%, electrical and nonelectrical machinery 16.9%, transport equipment 14.8%, chemical products 9.9%, mineral fuels 6.1%). *Major import sources:* France 66.8%; other EC countries 12.3%; Bahrain 3.5%.
Exports (1994): F 953,000,000 (food products [mostly sugar; also includes lobster, rum, and geranium essence] 77.3%, electrical and nonelectrical machinery 7.1%, transport equipment 5.8%). *Major export destinations:* France 74.3%; other EC countries 6.0%.

Transport and communications

Transport. Railroads:[12]. Roads (1993): total length 1,684 mi, 2,710 km (paved [1991] 79%). Vehicles (1993): passenger cars 173,200; trucks and buses 61,600. Merchant marine (1992): vessels (100 gross tons and over) 7; total deadweight tonnage 33,476. Air transport (1994): passenger arrivals 528,940, passenger departures 525,605; cargo unloaded 12,959 metric tons, cargo loaded 4,398 metric tons; airports (1995) with scheduled flights 1.
Communications. Daily newspapers (1992): total number 3; total circulation 55,000; circulation per 1,000 population 88. Radio (1994): total number of receivers 170,000 (1 per 3.8 persons). Television (1994): total number of receivers 90,500 (1 per 7.2 persons). Telephones (main lines; 1993): 198,500 (1 per 3.2 persons).

Education and health

Education (1994–95)

	schools	teachers	students	student/ teacher ratio
Primary (age 6–10)	343	...	73,220	...
Secondary (age 11–17) / Voc., teacher tr.	102	...	92,281	...
Higher[13, 14]	1	220	8,300	37.7

Educational attainment (1986–87). Percentage of population age 25 and over having: no formal schooling 18.8%; primary education 44.3%; lower secondary 21.6%; upper secondary 11.0%; higher 4.3%. *Literacy* (1986–87): total population age 15 and over literate 298,965 (78.2%); males literate 141,006 (75.9%); females literate 157,959 (80.3%).
Health (1994): physicians 1,061 (1 per 605 persons); hospital beds 2,858 (1 per 225 persons); infant mortality rate per 1,000 live births 8.0.
Food (1992): daily per capita caloric intake 3,245 (vegetable products 77%, animal products 23%); 143% of FAO recommended minimum requirement.

Military

Total active duty personnel (1994): 4,000 French troops[15].

[1]Includes 3 sq mi (8 sq km) not distributed by arrondissement. [2]Indian Ocean islets administered by France from Réunion are excluded from total. Areas of these islets, which have no permanent population, are: Îles Glorieuses 1.7 sq mi (4.3 sq km), Île Juan de Nova 1.9 sq mi (4.8 sq km), Île Tromelin 0.3 sq mi (0.8 sq km), Bassas da India 0.1 sq mi (0.2 sq km), Île Europa 7.8 sq mi (20.2 sq km). [3]Includes long-term private debt not guaranteed by the government. [4]Manufacturing includes sugarcane production. [5]Transportation and communications includes hotels and restaurants. [6]Includes 497 not adequately defined and 74,436 unemployed. [7]GDP (1992) equals F 33,724,000,000. [8]1992. [9]Indexes refer to December. [10]March. [11]Minimum wage. [12]No public railways; railways in use are for sugar industry. [13]1993–94. [14]University only. [15]Includes troops stationed on Mayotte.

Romania

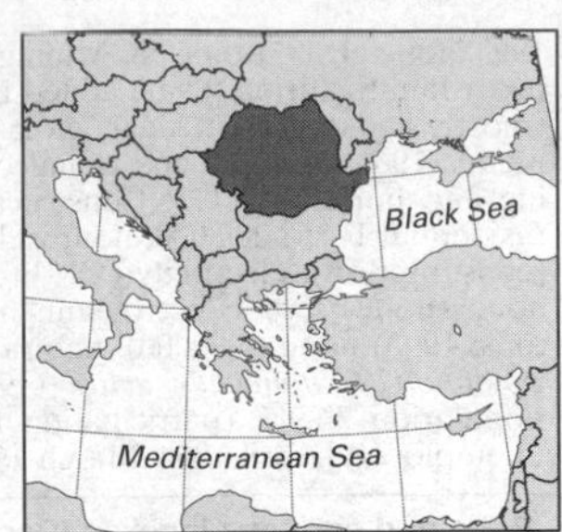

Official name: România (Romania).
Form of government: unitary republic with two legislative houses (Senate [143]; Assembly of Deputies [341[1]]).
Chief of state: President.
Head of government: Prime Minister.
Capital: Bucharest.
Official language: Romanian.
Official religion: none.
Monetary unit: 1 Romanian leu (plural lei) = 100 bani; valuation (Oct. 6, 1995) 1 U.S.$ = 2,192 lei; 1 £ = 3,466 lei.

Area and population		area		population
				1992[2]
		sq mi	sq km	census
Counties	**Capitals**			
Alba	Alba Iulia	2,406	6,231	414,200
Arad	Arad	2,954	7,652	487,400
Arges	Piteşti	2,626	6,801	680,600
Bacău	Bacău	2,551	6,606	736,100
Bihor	Oradea	2,909	7,535	634,100
Bistriţa-Năsăud	Bistriţa	2,048	5,305	327,200
Botoşani	Botoşani	1,917	4,965	458,900
Brăila	Brăila	1,824	4,724	392,100
Braşov	Braşov	2,066	5,351	642,500
Buzău	Buzău	2,344	6,072	516,300
Călăraşi	Călăraşi	1,959	5,074	338,800
Caraş-Severin	Reşiţa	3,283	8,503	375,800
Cluj	Cluj-Napoca	2,568	6,650	735,100
Constanţa	Constanţa	2,724	7,055	748,000
Covasna	Sfântu Gheorghe	1,431	3,705	232,600
Dâmboviţa	Târgovişte	1,559	4,036	559,900
Dolj	Craiova	2,862	7,413	761,100
Galaţi	Galaţi	1,708	4,425	639,900
Giurgiu	Giurgiu	1,356	3,511	313,100
Gorj	Târgu Jiu	2,178	5,641	400,100
Harghita	Miercurea-Ciuc	2,552	6,610	347,700
Hunedoara	Deva	2,709	7,016	548,000
Ialomiţa	Slobozia	1,718	4,449	304,000
Iaşi	Iaşi	2,112	5,469	806,800
Maramureş	Baia Mare	2,400	6,215	538,500
Mehedinţi	Drobeta-Turnu Severin	1,892	4,900	332,100
Mureş	Târgu Mureş	2,585	6,696	607,300
Neamţ	Piatra Neamţ	2,274	5,890	577,600
Olt	Slatina	2,126	5,507	521,000
Prahova	Ploieşti	1,812	4,694	873,200
Sălaj	Zalău	1,486	3,850	266,300
Satu Mare	Satu Mare	1,701	4,405	400,100
Sibiu	Sibiu	2,093	5,422	452,800
Suceava	Suceava	3,303	8,555	700,800
Teleorman	Alexandria	2,224	5,760	482,300
Timiş	Timişoara	3,356	8,692	700,300
Tulcea	Tulcea	3,255	8,430	270,200
Vâlcea	Râmnicu Vâlcea	2,203	5,705	436,300
Vaslui	Vaslui	2,045	5,297	457,800
Vrancea	Focşani	1,878	4,863	392,600
Muncipality				
Bucharest	Bucharest	703	1,820	2,351,000
TOTAL		91,699[3]	237,500	22,760,500

Demography

Population (1995): 22,693,000.
Density (1995): persons per sq mi 247.5, persons per sq km 95.5.
Urban-rural (1993): urban 54.6%; rural 45.4%.
Sex distribution (1995): male 49.27%; female 50.73%.
Age breakdown (1995): under 15, 20.4%; 15–29, 25.0%; 30–44, 20.5%; 45–59, 16.9%; 60–74, 13.6%; 75 and over, 3.6%.
Population projection: (2000) 22,625,000; (2010) 22,490,000.
Ethnic composition (1992): Romanian 89.4%; Hungarian 7.1%; Gypsy (Tigani) 1.8%; German 0.5%; Ukrainian 0.3%; other 0.9%.
Religious affiliation (1992): Romanian Orthodox 86.8%; Roman Catholic 5.0%; Greek Orthodox 3.5%; Pentecostal 1.0%; Muslim 0.2%; other 3.5%.
Major cities (1993): Bucharest 2,066,723; Constanţa 348,985; Iaşi 337,643; Timişoara 325,359; Galaţi 324,234; Braşov 324,104; Cluj-Napoca 321,850.

Vital statistics

Birth rate per 1,000 population (1994): 11.0 (world avg. 25.0).
Death rate per 1,000 population (1994): 11.6 (world avg. 9.3).
Natural increase rate per 1,000 population (1994): −0.6 (world avg. 15.7).
Total fertility rate (avg. births per childbearing woman; 1993): 1.5.
Marriage rate per 1,000 population (1993): 7.1.
Divorce rate per 1,000 population (1990): 1.4.
Life expectancy at birth (1995): male 69.3 years; female 75.4 years.
Major causes of death per 100,000 population (1992): circulatory disease 707.7, cancer 163.4, respiratory disease 94.0, diseases of the digestive system 57.9.

National economy

Budget (1993). Revenue: 3,792,352,000,000 lei (income tax 28.8%; corporate 19.8%; value-added taxes 19.1%; customs duties 7.1%). Expenditures: 4,128,779,000,000 lei (education 14.7%; defense 10.2%; health 8.8%).
Tourism (1993): receipts U.S.$197,000,000; expenditures U.S.$195,000,000.
Production (metric tons except as noted). Agriculture (1994): corn (maize) 9,300,000, wheat 5,991,000, potatoes 3,889,000, sugar beets 3,273,000, barley 1,661,000, apples 1,451,000, grapes 1,349,000, sunflower seeds 932,000; livestock (number of live animals) 11,499,000 sheep, 9,262,000 pigs, 3,597,000 cattle; roundwood (1993) 9,536,000 cu m; fish catch (1993) 34,919. Mining (1994): bauxite 183,600; iron 180,000; zinc 33,240. Manufacturing (1993): cement 6,864,000; steel 5,446,000; fertilizer 1,247,000; pork 804,000; sulfuric acid 527,000; beef and veal 250,000; aluminum 117,000; beer 9,929,000 hectolitres; wine 4,625,000 hectolitres; tires 3,929,000 units. Construction (1994): 12,084 dwelling units. Energy production (consumption): electricity (kW-hr; 1993) 55,476,000,000 (57,349,000,000); coal (metric tons; 1993) 39,603,000 (43,486,000); crude petroleum (barrels; 1993) 50,110,000 (104,167,000); petroleum products (metric tons; 1993) 11,225,000 (10,321,000); natural gas (cu m; 1993) 17,605,000,000 (21,404,000,000).
Public debt (external, outstanding; 1993): U.S.$2,326,000,000.
Gross national product (1993): U.S.$24,810,000,000 (U.S.$1,090 per capita).

Structure of gross domestic product and labour force				
	1992			
	in value '000,000 lei	% of total value	labour force	% of labour force
Agriculture	1,130,200	18.9	2,187,300	20.3
Mining, manufacturing, and public utilities	2,673,900	44.7	4,152,500	38.6
Construction	261,000	4.4	578,500	5.4
Transp. and commun.	382,500	6.4	616,800	5.7
Trade	790,000	13.2	694,200	6.5
Finance	311,700	5.2	57,100	0.5
Pub. admin.	465,700	7.8	1,528,000	14.2
Services	256,900	4.3		
Other	−289,600	−4.8	956,900[4]	8.8[4]
TOTAL	5,982,300	100.0[3]	10,771,300	100.0

Population economically active (1992): total 10,771,300; activity rate 47.4% (participation rates: ages 15–64, 67.2%; female 44.2%; unemployed 8.6%).

Price and earnings indexes (1990 = 100)							
	1989	1990	1991	1992	1993	1994	1995
Consumer price index	96.0	100.0	274.4	854.0	3,033.1	7,181.2	9,238.6[5]
Annual earnings index	90.5	100.0	221.3	597.4	1,804.8	3,779.8[6]	...

Household income and expenditure. Average household size (1992) 3.1; income per household (1989) 73,500 lei (U.S.$4,940); sources of income (1982): wages 62.6%; expenditure (1989): food 51.1%, housing 16.4%, clothing 15.7%.
Land use (1993): forest 29.0%; pasture 21.0%; agricultural 43.2%; other 6.8%.

Foreign trade

Balance of trade (current prices)						
	1989	1990	1991	1992	1993	1994
U.S.$'000,000	+2,050	−3,244	−1,182	−1,420.5	−1,127.8	−411.1
% of total	10.8%	21.7%	12.5%	14.0%	10.3%	3.2%

Imports (1993): 5,087,390,000,000 lei (machinery 41.5%, mineral fuels 26.6%, textiles 9.9%, chemicals 7.5%). *Major import sources:* Germany 15.8%; Russia 12.1%; Iran 9.8%; Italy 9.3%; France 7.6%; U.S. 6.0%.
Exports (1993): 3,775,942,000,000 lei (machinery 34.0%, textiles 16.1%, iron and steel 13.3%, mineral fuels 9.6%, chemicals 6.9%). *Major export destinations:* Germany 14.4%; Italy 8.3%; China 8.1%; Turkey 5.7%; Russia 4.5%.

Transport and communications

Transport. Railroads (1993): length 7,051 mi, 11,348 km; passenger-km 19,404,000,000; metric ton-km cargo 25,176,000,000. Roads (1992): length 95,099 mi, 153,014 km (paved 51%). Vehicles (1992): cars 1,397,118; trucks and buses 332,273. Merchant marine (1992): vessels (100 gross tons and over) 439; total deadweight tonnage 4,845,539. Air transport (1994): passenger-km 2,580,000,000; metric ton-km cargo 19,404,000; airports (1995) 12.
Communications. Daily newspapers (1992): total number 76; total circulation 7,500,000; circulation per 1,000 population 324. Radios (1993): 4,640,000 (1 per 4.9 persons). Televisions (1993): 4,580,000 (1 per 5.0 persons). Telephones (main lines; 1993): 2,623,700 subscribers (1 per 8.7 persons).

Education and health

Education (1992–93)	schools	teachers	students	student/ teacher ratio
Primary (age 6–9)	6,145	57,014	1,201,229	21.1
Secondary (age 10–17)	...	119,460	1,659,362	13.9
Voc., teacher tr.	1,600[7]	45,055	792,262	17.6
Higher	63[7]	18,123	235,669	13.0

Educational attainment (1992). Percentage of population age 25 and over having: no schooling 5.4%; some primary education 24.4%; some secondary 63.2%; postsecondary 6.9%. *Literacy* (1992): total population age 15 and over literate 16,920,000 (96.7%); males literate 8,280,000 (98.5%); females literate 8,640,000 (95.0%).
Health (1992): physicians 48,502 (1 per 469 persons); hospital beds 215,629 (1 per 105 persons); infant mortality rate per 1,000 live births (1993) 23.3.
Food (1992): daily per capita caloric intake 3,051 (vegetable products 76%, animal products 24%); 115% of FAO recommended minimum requirement.

Military

Total active duty personnel (1995): 217,400 (army 59.2%, navy 8.7%, air force 24.8%, paramilitary border guards 7.3%). *Military expenditure as percentage of GNP* (1993): 2.5% (world 3.3%); per capita expenditure U.S.$72.

[1]Includes 13 nonelective seats. [2]Preliminary results of Jan. 7, 1992, census. [3]Detail does not add to total given because of rounding. [4]Unemployed. [5]July. [6]June. [7]1993–94.

Russia

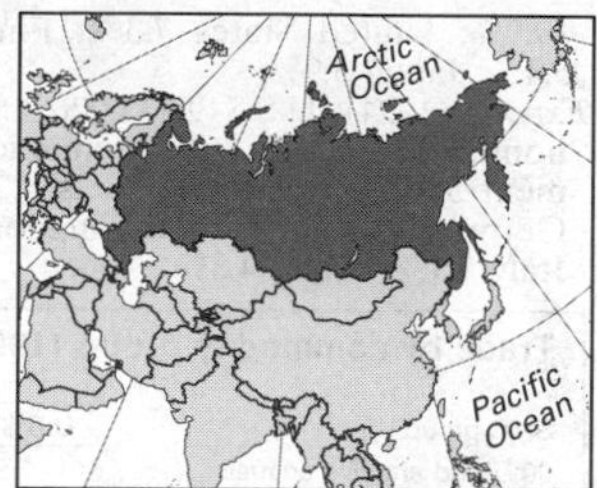

Official name: Rossiyskaya Federatsiya (Russian Federation).
Form of government: federal multiparty republic with a bicameral legislative body (Federal Assembly comprising a Federation Council [178] and a State Duma [450]).
Head of state: President.
Head of government: Prime Minister.
Capital: Moscow.
Official language: Russian.
Official religion: none.
Monetary unit: 1 ruble (Rub) = 100 kopecks; valuation (Oct. 6, 1995) market rate, 1 U.S.$ = Rub 4,496; 1 £ = Rub 7,107.

Area and population

Federal Republics / Other entities	Capitals	area sq mi	area sq km	population 1995[1] estimate
Adygea	Maykop	2,900	7,600	450,000
Bashkortostan	Ufa	55,400	143,600	4,077,000
Buryatia	Ulan-Ude	135,600	351,300	1,052,000
Chechnia (Chechnya)[2, 3]	...	[4]	[4]	[4]
Chuvashia	Cheboksary	7,100	18,300	1,361,000
Dagestan	Makhachkala	19,400	50,300	2,009,000
Gorno-Altay	Gorno-Altaisk	35,700	92,600	200,000
Ingushetia[2, 3]	Grozny	7,400[4]	19,300[4]	1,234,000
Kabardino-Balkaria[5]	Nalchik	4,800	12,500	787,000
Kalmykia (Khalmg Tangch)	Elista	29,400	76,100	320,000
Karachay-Cherkessia	Cherkessk	5,400	14,100	435,000
Karelia	Petrozavodsk	66,600	172,400	789,000
Khakassia	Abakan	23,900	61,900	583,000
Komi	Syktyvkar	160,600	415,900	1,203,000
Mari El	Yoshkar-Ola	9,000	23,200	767,000
Mordvinia	Saransk	10,100	26,200	959,000
North Ossetia	Vladikavkaz	3,100	8,000	604,000
Russia	Moscow	4,709,000[6]	12,198,300	124,527,000
Regions (Oblasts)				
Amur[5]	Blagoveshchensk	140,400	363,700	1,051,000
Arkhangelsk	Arkhangelsk	226,800	587,400	1,537,000
Astrakhan	Astrakhan	17,000	44,100	1,025,000
Belgorod	Belgorod	10,500	27,100	1,456,000
Bryansk	Bryansk	13,500	34,900	1,476,000
Chelyabinsk	Chelyabinsk	33,900	87,900	3,690,000
Chita	Chita	166,600	431,500	1,298,000
Irkutsk	Irkutsk	296,500	767,900	2,803,000
Ivanovo	Ivanovo	9,200	23,900	1,274,000
Kaliningrad[5]	Kaliningrad	5,800	15,100	927,000
Kaluga	Kaluga	11,500	29,900	1,093,000
Kamchatka	Petropavlovsk-Kamchatsky	182,400	472,300	423,000
Kemerovo	Kemerovo	36,900	95,500	3,072,000
Kirov	Kirov	46,600	120,800	1,648,000
Kostroma	Kostroma	23,200	60,100	809,000
Kurgan	Kurgan	27,400	71,000	1,115,000
Kursk	Kursk	11,500	29,800	1,348,000
Leningrad	St. Petersburg	33,200[7]	85,900[7]	1,673,000
Lipetsk	Lipetsk	9,300	24,100	1,251,000
Magadan	Magadan	178,100	461,400	282,000
Moskva (Moscow)	Moscow	18,100[8]	47,000[8]	6,609,000
Murmansk	Murmansk	55,900	144,900	1,075,000
Nizhny Novgorod	Nizhny Novgorod	28,900	74,800	3,734,000
Novgorod	Novgorod	21,400	55,300	745,000
Novosibirsk	Novosibirsk	68,800	178,200	2,740,000
Omsk	Omsk	53,900	139,700	2,175,000
Orenburg	Orenburg	47,900	124,000	2,222,000
Oryol (Orel)	Oryol	9,500	24,700	916,000
Penza	Penza	16,700	43,200	1,562,000
Perm	Perm	62,000	160,600	3,024,000
Pskov	Pskov	21,400	55,300	835,000
Rostov	Rostov-na-Donu	38,900	100,800	4,430,000
Ryazan	Ryazan	15,300	39,600	1,331,000
Sakhalin	Yuzhno-Sakhalinsk	33,600	87,100	681,000
Samara	Samara	20,700	53,600	3,301,000
Saratov	Saratov	38,700	100,200	2,735,000
Smolensk	Smolensk	19,200	49,800	1,171,000
Sverdlovsk[5]	Yekaterinburg	75,200	194,800	4,704,000
Tambov	Tambov	13,200	34,300	1,315,000
Tomsk	Tomsk	122,400	316,900	1,071,000
Tula	Tula	9,900	25,700	1,825,000
Tver	Tver	32,500	84,100	1,650,000
Tyumen	Tyumen	554,100	1,435,200	3,157,000
Ulyanovsk (Simbirsk)	Simbirsk	14,400	37,300	1,491,000
Vladimir	Vladimir	11,200	29,000	1,646,000
Volgograd	Volgograd	44,000	113,900	2,691,000
Vologda[5]	Vologda	56,300	145,700	1,357,000
Voronezh	Voronezh	20,200	52,400	2,502,000
Yaroslavl	Yaroslavl	14,100	36,400	1,455,000
Autonomous Region				
Yevreyskaya (Jewish)	Birobidzhan	13,900	36,000	216,000
Territories (Krays)				
Altay	Barnaul	65,300	169,100	2,695,000
Khabarovsk	Khabarovsk	304,500	788,600	1,601,000
Krasnodar	Krasnodar	29,300	76,000	5,004,000
Krasnoyarsk	Krasnoyarsk	903,400	2,339,700	3,122,000
Primorye (Maritime)[5]	Vladivostok	64,100	165,900	2,278,000
Stavropol	Stavropol	25,700	66,500	2,655,000
Autonomous cities				
Moscow	—	[8]	[8]	8,718,000
St. Petersburg[5]	—	[7]	[7]	4,837,000
Autonomous districts (Okrugs)[9]				
Aga-Buryat	*Aginskoye*	7,300	*19,000*	79,400
Chukchi (Chukotka)	Anadyr	284,800	737,700	99,700
Evenk	*Tura*	296,400	*767,600*	20,800
Khanty-Mansi	*Khanty-Mansiysk*	202,000	*523,100*	1,326,200
Komi-Permyak	*Kudymkar*	12,700	*32,900*	158,800
Koryak	*Palana*	*116,400*	*301,500*	33,800
Nenets	*Naryan-Mar*	*68,100*	*176,400*	49,300
Taymyr	*Dudinka*	*332,900*	*862,100*	47,300
Ust-Orda Buryat	*Ust-Ordynsky*	*8,600*	*22,400*	143,000
Yamalo-Nenets	*Salekhard*	*289,700*	*750,300*	479,700
Sakha (Yakutia)	Yakutsk	1,198,200	3,103,200	1,035,000
Tatarstan	Kazan	26,300	68,000	3,754,000
Tuva (Tyva)	Kyzyl-Orda	65,800	170,500	308,000
Udmurtia	Izhevsk	16,300	42,100	1,641,000
TOTAL		6,592,800	17,075,400	148,155,000

Demography

Population (1995): 147,168,000.
Density (1995): persons per sq mi 22.3, persons per sq km 8.6.
Urban-rural (1994): urban 73.1%; rural 26.9%.
Sex distribution (1994): male 46.96%; female 53.04%.
Age breakdown (1994): under 15, 21.9%; 15–29, 20.4%; 30–44, 24.8%; 45–59, 16.3%; 60–69, 10.1%; 70 and over, 6.5%.
Population projection: (2000) 143,178,000; (2010) 134,816,000.
Doubling time: not applicable; population is declining.
Ethnic composition (1994): Russian 85.0%; Tatar 3.9%; Ukrainian 2.4%; Chuvash 1.2%; Bashkir 1.0%; Belorussian 0.7%; Mordovian 0.7%; German 0.6%; other 4.5%.
Religious affiliation: believers are predominantly Russian Orthodox; there are Catholic, Protestant, Muslim, Old Believer, and Jewish minorities.
Major cities (1994): Moscow 8,570,200; St. Petersburg 4,320,900; Nizhny Novgorod 1,424,600; Novosibirsk 1,418,200; Yekaterinburg 1,347,000; Samara 1,222,500; Omsk 1,161,200; Chelyabinsk 1,124,500; Kazan 1,092,300; Ufa 1,091,800; Perm 1,086,100; Rostov-na-Donu 1,023,200.

Other principal cities (1994)

	population		population		population
Astrakhan	512,400	Krasnoyarsk	914,200	Tolyatti	689,200
Barnaul	596,400	Naberezhnye Chelny	523,700	Tula	535,400
Irkutsk	632,200	Novokuznetsk	592,800	Ulyanovsk (Simbirsk)	669,900
Izhevsk	652,800	Orenburg	557,500	Vladivostok	637,000
Kemerovo	512,700	Penza	551,300	Volgograd	1,000,400
Khabarovsk	609,100	Ryazan	525,900	Voronezh	904,600
Krasnodar	638,000	Saratov	898,600	Yaroslavl	631,000

Mobility (1989). Population living in the same residence as in 1988: 78.8%; different residence, same oblast 11.5%; different republic 9.7%.
Emigration (1994): 339,700.
Households (1989). Total family households 40,246,000; average household size 3.2; 2 persons 34.2%; 3 persons 28.0%; 4 persons 25.2%; 5 persons or more 12.6%. Population in family households: 128,787,000 (87.0%), non-family population 19,254,000 (13.0%).

Vital statistics

Birth rate per 1,000 population (1994): 9.4 (world avg. 25.0); (1992) legitimate 82.9%; illegitimate 17.1%.
Death rate per 1,000 population (1994): 14.5 (world avg. 9.3).
Natural increase rate per 1,000 population (1994): −5.1 (world avg. 15.7).
Total fertility rate (avg. births per childbearing woman; 1993): 1.8.
Marriage rate per 1,000 population (1994): 7.5.
Divorce rate per 1,000 population (1994): 4.5.
Life expectancy at birth (1994): male 57.7 years; female 71.1 years.
Major causes of death per 100,000 population (1994): circulatory diseases 849.5; accidents, poisoning, and violence 230.3, of which suicide 38.6, murder 33.2; malignant neoplasms (cancers) 202.6; respiratory diseases 82.0; digestive diseases 47.4; infectious and parasitic diseases 21.2.

Social indicators

Educational attainment (1994). Percentage of population age 15 and over having: primary or no formal education 10.5%; some secondary 21.1%; secondary and some postsecondary 54.5%; higher and postgraduate 13.9%.
Quality of working life (1990). Average workweek: 40 hours. Annual rate per 100,000 workers of: injury or accident 569; industrial illness 5.3; death 11.2. Proportion of labour force insured for damages or income loss resulting from: injury 100%; permanent disability 100%; death 100%. Average days lost to labour stoppages per 1,000 workdays (1992): 1.1.
Access to services (1990). Proportion of dwellings having access to: electricity, virtually 100%; safe public water supply 94%; public sewage collection 92%; central heating 92%; bathroom 87%; gas 72%; hot water 79%.
Social participation. Eligible voters participating in last national election (1993): 54.8%. Population participating in voluntary work: n.a. Trade union membership in total workforce (1989): 100%. Practicing religious population in total affiliated population (1991): 32%.
Social deviance. Offense rate per 100,000 population (1994) for: murder 14.7; rape 9.5; serious bodily injury 62.8; burglary and housebreaking 125.9; larceny-theft 888.4. Incidence per 100,000 in general population (1992) of: alcoholism 1,727.5; substance abuse 25.1; suicide 26.5.
Material well-being (1993). Goods possessed per 100 households: automobile 20; radio receiver 101; television receiver 112; refrigerator 95; camera 37; motorcycle 22; bicycle 54; tape recorder 59.

National economy

Budget (1996). Revenue: Rub 329,000,000,000,000 (1994; value-added tax 31.8%; foreign activity 24.0%; enterprise profits tax 17.7%; excise taxes 8.1%). Expenditures: Rub 410,800,000,000,000 (current expenditure 74.3%, of which economy 23.3%, defense 20.9%, education 5.8%, health 3.0%, interest on foreign debt 2.4%; development expenditure 25.7%).
Gross national product (1993): U.S.$349,062,000,000 (U.S.$2,350 per capita).

Structure of gross domestic product and labour force				
	1993		1994	
	in value Rub '000,000	% of total value	labour force	% of labour force
Agriculture	1,627,400	9.9	10,350,000	13.9
Mining / Manufacturing / Public utilities	8,045,100	49.0	19,200,000	25.7
Construction	1,253,600	7.7	7,050,000	9.5
Transp. and commun.	1,360,000	8.3	5,300,000	7.1
Trade	1,746,500	10.7	6,450,000	8.7
Finance	1,266,800	7.7	630,000	0.8
Services	1,110,600	6.8	16,500,000	22.1
Pub. admin., defense	414,400	2.5	1,450,000	1.9
Other	−419,900	−2.6	7,660,000	10.3
TOTAL	16,404,500	100.0	74,590,000	100.0

Public debt (external, outstanding; 1995)[10]: U.S.$130,800,000,000.
Production (metric tons except as noted). Agriculture, forestry, fishing (1994): potatoes 33,800,000, wheat 32,100,000, barley 27,100,000, sugar beets 13,900,000, oats 10,800,000, vegetables (other than potatoes) 9,600,000, fodder crops 8,700,000, rye 6,000,000, peas 2,700,000, sunflower seeds 2,600,000, corn (maize) 900,000, buckwheat 781,000, rice 523,000, millet 500,000; livestock (number of live animals; 1994) 48,900,000 cattle, 43,700,000 sheep, 28,600,000 pigs, 2,400,000 horses; roundwood 119,000,000 cu m; fish catch 3,500,000. Mining and quarrying (1993): nickel 243,000,000; chrome ore 120,800,000; iron ore 75,000,000; antimony 6,000,000; tin 5,000,000; molybdenum 4,800,000. Manufacturing (1994): crude steel 48,800,000; cement 37,200,000; pig iron 36,100,000; rolled steel 35,800,000; mineral fertilizers 8,200,000; sulfuric acid 6,300,000; cellulose 3,234,000; paper 2,215,000; synthetic resins and plastics 1,681,000; cardboard 1,192,000; caustic soda 1,138,000; detergents 328,000; synthetic fibres 197,000; cotton fabrics 1,530,000,000 sq m; silk fabrics 250,000,000 sq m; linen fabrics 160,000,000 sq m; wool fabrics 93,000,000 sq m; tableware 341,000,000 pieces; cigarettes 125,000,000,000 units; watches 30,400,000 units; refrigerators 2,631,000 units; television receivers 2,189,000 units; washing machines 2,133,000 units; vacuum cleaners 1,519,000 units; bicycles 875,000 units; passenger cars 798,000 units; tape recorders 720,000 units; cameras 442,000 units; sewing machines 398,000 units; motorcycles 199,000 units; video recorders 82,000 units; forge press machines 3,100 units; leather footwear 75,000,000 pairs; beer 21,500,000 hectolitres; vodka and liquors 12,200,000 hectolitres; champagne 8,600,000 hectolitres; grape wine 6,400,000 hectolitres; brandy 146,000 hectolitres. Construction (value of new construction in Rub '000,000; 1994): residential 29,428; nonresidential 76,809.

Manufacturing, mining, and construction enterprises (1991)				
	no. of enter-prises	no. of employees	monthly wages as a % of avg. of all wages[11]	value added (Rub '000,000)
Manufacturing				
Machinery and metal products	5,429	9,970,000	98.2	3,105
Fuel and energy	1,486	1,378,000	133.3	1,652
Metallurgy	428	1,274,000	124.3	6,321
Chemicals, petrochemicals, pulp, and paper	4,796	2,840,000	94.1	4,977
Light industry	4,725	2,145,000	80.0	...
Food	6,056	1,533,000	100.1	1,041
Other industries[11]	2,729	3,018,000	...	...
Building materials	2,217	7,018,000	108.2	962

Energy production (consumption): electricity (kW-hr; 1993) 956,587,000 (937,130,000); coal (metric tons; 1993) 304,000,000 (315,335,000); crude petroleum (barrels; 1993) 353,905,000 (168,655,000); petroleum products (metric tons; 1993) 193,036,000 (159,221,000); natural gas (cu m; 1993) 514,331,000,000 (369,996,000,000); peat (metric tons; 1993) 2,530,000 (6,765,000); oil shale (metric tons; 1993) 3,300,000 (3,300,000).
Energy production by source (1993): thermal 68.5%, hydroelectric 18.7%, nuclear and other 12.8%.
Population economically active (1994): total 74,590,000; activity rate of total population 50.4% (participation rates: ages 16–59 [male], 16–54 [female] 86.1%; female 48.7%; unemployed [1995] 18.1%).

Price and earnings indexes (1990 = 100)					
	1990	1991	1992	1993	1994
Consumer price index	100.0	192.7	2,800	27,900	112,100
Monthly earnings index	100.0	180.9	1,978	19,361	71,494

Land use (1993): forested *c.* 45.6%; meadows and pastures 4.5%; agricultural and under permanent cultivation 7.8%; other 42.1%.
Household income and expenditure. Average household size (1994) 2.8; income per household: n.a.; sources of income (1994): wages 78.6%, pensions and stipends 11.2%, other 10.2%; expenditure (1992): food 39.8%, clothing 19.4%, taxes and other financial payments 7.5%, furniture and household appliances 7.5%, culture 4.6%, alcoholic beverages 2.8%, housing 0.8%.

Foreign trade

Balance of trade (current prices; non-CIS)					
	1990	1991	1992	1993	1994
U.S.$'000,000	−10,603	+6,438	+4,986	+17,490	+21,800
% of total	6.9%	6.8%	6.7%	24.6%	27.9%

Imports (1994): U.S.$28,135,000,000 (machinery and transport equipment 35.8%, food 29.4%, chemicals 10.6%, textiles 7.4%, fuels and lubricants 4.0%, ferrous and nonferrous metals 3.7%). *Major import sources:* Germany 19.9%; United States 7.3%; Finland 5.8%; The Netherlands 5.7%; Italy 5.4%; Japan 3.9%.
Exports (1994): U.S.$49,935,000,000 (fuels and lubricants 44.0%, ferrous and nonferrous metals 26.3%, chemicals 7.7%, machinery and transport equipment 5.0%, forestry products 4.2%, food 4.2%). *Major export destinations:* Germany 10.6%; United Kingdom 7.3%; United States 6.9%; China 5.7%; Italy 5.5%; Japan 4.3%.

Trade by commodity group (1992)				
	imports		exports	
SITC group	U.S.$'000,000	%	U.S.$'000,000	%
00 Food and live animals	9,300	26.6	1,100	2.2
02 Raw materials, excl. fuels	2,300	6.4	8,100	5.8
03 Mineral fuels, lubricants	1,000	2.6	21,700	62.7
05 Chemicals	3,400	9.8	2,500	6.5
65 Textile yarn, fabrics	3,900	11.2	300	8.8
07 Machinery and transport eqpt.	13,700	39.2	3,700	10.2
08 Misc. manufactured articles	1,300	4.2	2,500	3.8
09 Goods, n.e.s.	...	...	...	...
TOTAL	39,900	100.0	39,900	100.0

Direction of trade (1994)				
	imports		exports	
	U.S.$'000,000	%	U.S.$'000,000	%
Africa	239	0.8	519	1.0
Asia	4,837	17.2	10,303	20.6
Japan	1,104	3.9	2,165	4.3
South America	864	3.1	1,047	2.1
North and Central America	2,239	8.0	3,668	7.3
United States	2,052	7.3	3,442	6.9
Europe	19,655	69.9	34,358	68.9
EU	11,334	40.3	18,561	37.2
EFTA	3,546	12.6	7,426	14.9
other Europe	4,775	17.0	8,371	16.8
Oceania	301	1.0	40	0.1
TOTAL	28,135	100.0	49,935	100.0

Transport and communications

Transport. Railroads (1994): length 152,000 km; passenger-km 227,100,000,000; metric ton-km cargo 1,195,000,000. Roads (1994): total length 942,000 km (paved 79%). Vehicles (1993): passenger cars 10,499,000; trucks and buses 407,000. Merchant marine (1993): vessels (100 gross tons and over) 24; total deadweight tonnage 91,000,000. Air transport (1994): passenger-km 72,300,000,000; metric ton-km cargo 1,500,000,000; airports (1995) 58.

Distribution of traffic (1994)				
	cargo carried ('000,000 tons)	% of national total	passengers carried ('000,000)	% of national total
Intercity transport			25,566	55.3
Road	1,931	48.1	23,438	50.6
Rail	1,058	26.3	2,062	4.5
Sea and river	224	5.6	32	0.1
Air	1	...	34	0.1
Pipeline	801	20.0	—	—
Urban transport			20,717	44.7
Road	—	—	98	0.2
Rail	—	—	20,619	44.5
TOTAL	4,015	100.0	46,283	100.0

Communications. Daily newspapers (1992): total 339; total circulation 57,000,000; circulation per 1,000 population 386. Radio (1992): 48,800,000 receivers (1 per 3 persons). Television (1992): 54,200,000 receivers (1 per 2.7 persons). Telephones (main lines; 1993): 23,397,000 (1 per 6.3 persons).

Education and health

Education (1994–95)	schools	teachers	students	student/ teacher ratio
Primary (age 6–13) / Secondary (age 14–17)	70,000	1,682,000	21,600,000	12.8
Voc., teacher tr.	2,574	...	1,871,000	...
Higher	553	...	2,534,000	...

Health (1994): physicians 674,000 (1 per 220 persons); hospital beds 1,890,000 (1 per 78 persons); infant mortality rate per 1,000 live births (1993) 19.9.
Food (1992): daily per capita caloric intake 2,100 (vegetable products, n.a., animal products, n.a.); 82% of FAO recommended minimum.

Military

Total active duty personnel (1995): 1,520,000 (army 78.2%, navy 13.2%, air force 8.6%). *Military expenditure as percentage of GNP* (1993): 21.5% (world 3.3%); per capita expenditure U.S.$504.

[1]January 1995. [2]The former Chechen-Ingush republic was split into two separate republics June 4, 1992; although both are formally recognized by the Russian Federation, details on final status within the federation remain undetermined. [3]Republic is not signatory to the March 31, 1992, treaty establishing the Russian Federation. [4]Ingushetia's area and population include Chechnia. [5]Entity has formally proclaimed itself a republic; final status remains undetermined. [6]Detail does not add to total given because of rounding. [7]Leningrad region includes area of autonomous city of St. Petersburg. [8]Moskva region includes area of autonomous city of Moscow. [9]With the exception of the Chukchi autonomous district (identified in Roman type), which has formally separated from Magadan region, all autonomous districts are administratively part of another national administrative subdivision, within which their area and population are included. [10]Total as of March 31, 1995; Russia has also assumed responsibility for the governmental and commercial debts of the former U.S.S.R., estimated to constitute a further U.S.$88,000,000,000. [11]1990.

Rwanda

Official name: Repubulika y'u Rwanda (Rwanda); République Rwandaise (French) (Republic of Rwanda).
Form of government: transitional regime with one legislative body (Transitional National Assembly[1] [70]).
Head of state and government: President assisted by Prime Minister and Vice President (Minister of Defense).
Capital: Kigali.
Official languages: Rwanda; French.
Official religion: none.
Monetary unit: 1 Rwanda franc (RF); valuation (Oct. 6, 1995) 1 U.S.$ = RF 302.21; 1 £ = RF 477.76.

Area and population

		area		population
				1991
Prefectures	**Capitals**	sq mi	sq km	census
Butare	Butare	709	1,837	766,839
Byumba	Byumba	1,838	4,761	783,350
Cyangugu	Cyangugu	712	1,845	515,129
Gikongoro	Gikongoro	794	2,057	464,585
Gisenyi	Gisenyi	791	2,050	734,697
Gitarama	Gitarama	845	2,189	851,516
Kibungo	Kibungo	1,562	4,046	655,368
Kibuye	Kibuye	658	1,705	470,747
Kigali	Kigali (city)	1,159	3,002	918,869
Kigali (city)	—	45	116	237,782
Ruhengeri	Ruhengeri	642	1,663	766,112
TOTAL LAND AREA		9,757[2]	25,271	
TOTAL		10,169	26,338	7,164,994[3]

Demography

Population (1995): 6,700,000[4].
Density (1995): persons per sq mi 658.9, persons per sq km 254.4.
Urban-rural (1991): urban 5.4%; rural 94.6%.
Sex distribution (1991): male 48.67%; female 51.33%.
Age breakdown (1995): under 15, 46.0%; 15–29, 28.0%; 30–44, 14.2%; 45–59, 7.7%; 60–74, 3.4%; 75 and over, 0.7%.
Population projection: (2000) 8,855,000; (2010) 11,084,000.
Doubling time: 21 years.
Ethnic composition (1991)[4]: Hutu 85%; Tutsi 14%; Twa 1%.
Religious affiliation: In 1991 the largest organized religion was the Roman Catholic church, representing approximately 44% of the population, followed by Muslims at about 8–9%, with the remainder consisting of indigenous African Protestant churches or traditional animist believers.
Major cities (1991): Kigali 237,782[3]; Ruhengeri 29,578[5]; Butare 28,645[5]; Gisenyi 21,918[5].

Vital statistics

Birth rate per 1,000 population (1990–95): 44.1 (world avg. 25.0); (1978) legitimate 94.9%; illegitimate 5.1%.
Death rate per 1,000 population (1990–95): 16.7 (world avg. 9.3).
Natural increase rate per 1,000 population (1990–95): 27.9 (world avg. 15.7).
Total fertility rate (avg. births per childbearing woman; 1990–95): 6.6.
Marriage rate per 1,000 population (1984)[6]: 2.5.
Divorce rate per 1,000 population: n.a.
Life expectancy at birth (1990–95): male 45.8 years; female 48.9 years.
Major causes of death per 100,000 population: n.a.; however, principal causes in 1991 were malaria, bronchopneumonia, diarrhea, AIDS, pulmonary diseases, cerebrospinal meningitis, kwashiorkor, road accidents, and cirrhosis of the liver. Following the genocide of 1994 (equaling 3 years normal mortality), malnutrition, cholera, and civil violence were also major causes.

National economy

Budget. The civil war of 1994 left Rwanda without a central governmental budget, other than the dispersal of foreign aid.
Production (metric tons except as noted). Agriculture, forestry, fishing (1994): plantains 2,600,000, roots and tubers 1,616,000 (of which sweet potatoes 1,000,000, cassava 350,000, potatoes 200,000), cereals 158,000 (of which sorghum 87,000, corn [maize] 50,000), coffee 20,000, tea 5,000, tobacco 4,000; livestock (number of live animals) 1,100,000 goats, 610,000 cattle, 400,000 sheep, 130,000 pigs; roundwood (1993) 5,660,000 cu m; fish catch (1993) 3,553. Mining and quarrying (1990): cassiterite (tin ore) 730; wolframite (tungsten ore) 175; gold (1992) 15,552 troy oz. Manufacturing (1991): cement 57,000; lye soap 9,000; sugar 2,969[7]; beer 915,000 hectolitres; soft drinks 101,000 hectolitres; footwear 24,000 pairs; blankets 406,876 units[7]; matches 70,942,000 boxes[7]. Construction (1981): residential 59,600 sq m; nonresidential 34,400 sq m. Energy production (consumption): electricity (kW-hr; 1993) 234,000,000 (243,000,000); coal, none (n.a.); petroleum products (metric tons; 1993) none (155,000); natural gas (cu m; 1993) 179,389 (179,389).
Tourism: receipts from visitors (1993) U.S.$2,000,000; expenditures by nationals abroad (1992) U.S.$17,000,000.
Land use (1993): forested 22.3%; meadows and pastures 18.3%; agricultural and under permanent cultivation 47.4%; other 12.0%.
Population economically active (1991): total 3,649,000; activity rate of total population 50.2% (participation rates: ages 14–74 [1989], 46.3%; female 53.5%; unemployed, n.a.).

Price and earnings indexes (1990 = 100)

	1987	1988	1989	1990	1991	1992	1993
Consumer price index	92.3	95.0	96.0	100.0	119.6	131.1	147.3
Earnings index	...	...	...	...	...	...	...

Public debt (external, outstanding; 1993): U.S.$835,800,000.
Gross national product (1993): U.S.$1,499,000,000 (U.S.$200 per capita).

Structure of gross domestic product and labour force

	1991		1989	
	in value RF '000,000[8]	% of total value	labour force	% of labour force
Agriculture	57,151	42.0	2,832,557	90.1
Mining	281	0.2	4,691	0.2
Manufacturing	16,708	12.3	45,089	1.4
Construction	9,660	7.1	38,237	1.2
Public utilities	303	0.2	2,562	0.1
Transportation and communications	9,438	6.9	7,333	0.2
Trade	23,255	17.1	80,026	2.6
Finance	1,947	1.4	3,128	0.1
Pub. admin., defense	11,711	8.6	120,019	3.8
Services	5,684	4.2		
Other	...	...	9,414	0.3
TOTAL	136,138	100.0	3,143,056	100.0

Household income and expenditure. Average household size (1991) 4.7; average annual income per household (1983) RF 122,870 (U.S.$1,300); sources of income (1977): self-employment 71.0%, salaries and wages 16.5%, transfers 9.5%; expenditure (1982)[9]: food 44.2%, housing 13.2%, clothing and footwear 11.4%, transportation 10.3%, household equipment 8.4%.

Foreign trade[10]

Balance of trade (current prices)

	1987	1988	1989	1990	1991	1992
RF '000,000	−10,562	−11,403	−10,918	−6,834	−15,181	−17,729
% of total	37.1%	40.7%	41.7%	27.0%	39.6%	49.9%

Imports (1991): RF 38,474,500,000 (machinery and transport equipment 14.5%, of which machinery 11.1%, transport equipment 3.4%; mineral fuels and lubricants 12.8%; food, beverages, and tobacco 11.4%; construction materials 3.9%). *Major import sources:* Belgium-Luxembourg 17.1%; Kenya 13.4%; France 6.8%; Germany 6.0%; Italy 2.8%; The Netherlands 2.7%; United Kingdom 2.1%; United States 1.0%; Zaire 0.7%.
Exports (1991): RF 11,971,200,000 (coffee 60.2%; tea 23.4%). *Major export destinations:* Germany 21.3%; The Netherlands 18.8%; Belgium-Luxembourg 11.8%; United Kingdom 6.4%; United States 5.8%; Italy 1.7%.

Transport and communications

Transport. Railroads: none. Roads (1993): total length 8,185 mi, 13,173 km (paved 7%). Vehicles (1993): passenger cars 8,000; trucks and buses 2,100. Merchant marine: none. Air transport (1991): passenger arrivals 29,000, passenger departures 30,000; metric ton cargo loaded 2,674, metric ton cargo unloaded 4,794; airports (1995) with scheduled flights 3.
Communications. Daily newspapers (1995): total number, none; total circulation per 1,000 population, n.a. Radio (1992): total number of receivers 650,000 (1 per 12 persons). Television: none. Telephones (main lines; 1993): 11,800 (1 per 634 persons).

Education and health

Education (1991–92)

	schools	teachers	students	student/ teacher ratio
Primary (age 7–15)	1,710	18,937	1,104,902	58.3
Secondary (age 16–19)[11]	...	3,413	94,586	27.7
Higher[12]	3[13]	646	3,389	5.2

Educational attainment (1978). Percentage of population age 25 and over having: no formal schooling 76.9%; some primary education 16.8%; complete primary education 4.0%; some secondary and complete secondary education 2.0%; some postsecondary vocational and higher education 0.3%. *Literacy* (1995): percentage of total population age 15 and over literate 60.5%; males literate 69.8%; females literate 51.6%.
Health: physicians (1989) 272 (1 per 24,697 persons); hospital beds (1984) 9,046 (1 per 649 persons); infant mortality rate (1990–95) 110.0.
Food (1992): daily per capita caloric intake 1,821 (vegetable products 97%, animal products 3%); 78% of FAO recommended minimum requirement.

Military

Total active duty personnel (1994): 5,200[14] (army 96.2%, air force 3.8%). *Military expenditure as percentage of GNP* (1993): 8.0% (world 3.3%); per capita expenditure U.S.$14.

[1]Transitional National Assembly was appointed on Nov. 25, 1994, for an interim period of five years. [2]Detail does not add to total given because of rounding. [3]The population of Kigali decreased to about 100,000–120,000 because of the 1994 civil war. [4]Includes adjustments for (1) the loss of some 2,000,000 refugees to surrounding countries, of whom the majority were Hutu: (2) the death of an estimated 500,000 Tutsi killed during the events of 1994; and (3) the return of 400,000–600,000 Tutsi herdsmen from surrounding countries who had been in exile since 1959. [5]De jure population only. [6]Excludes marriages not registered in court. [7]1990. [8]At factor cost. [9]Weights of consumer price index components. [10]Imports f.o.b. in balance of trade and c.i.f. in commodities and trading partners. [11]Includes vocational and teacher training. [12]1989–90. [13]1985. [14]No reliable information has been received since the civil war ended in 1994.

Saint Kitts and Nevis

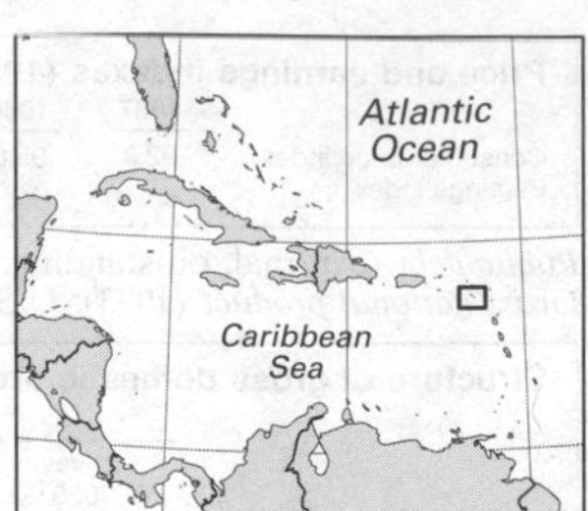

Official name: Federation of Saint Kitts and Nevis[1].
Form of government: constitutional monarchy with one legislative house (National Assembly [15[2]]).
Chief of state: British Monarch represented by Governor-General.
Head of government: Prime Minister.
Capital: Basseterre.
Official language: English.
Official religion: none.
Monetary unit: 1 Eastern Caribbean dollar (EC$) = 100 cents; valuation (Oct. 6, 1995) 1 U.S.$ = EC$2.70; 1 £ = EC$4.27.

Area and population

		area		population
Islands[3]	Capitals	sq mi	sq km	1991 census[4]
Nevis[5]	Charlestown	36.0	93.2	9,130
St. Kitts	Basseterre	68.0	176.2	32,696
TOTAL		104.0	269.4	41,826

Demography

Population (1995): 39,400.
Density (1995): persons per sq mi 378.8, persons per sq km 146.3.
Urban-rural (1995): urban 42.9%; rural 57.1%.
Sex distribution (1990): male 51.56%; female 48.44%.
Age breakdown (1990): under 15, 32.5%; 15–29, 25.6%; 30–44, 18.9%; 45–59, 10.1%; 60–74, 8.9%; 75 and over, 4.0%.
Population projection: (2000) 39,000; (2010) 39,000.
Doubling time: 50 years.
Ethnic composition (1991): black 94.9%; mixed/white/Indo-Pakistani 5.1%.
Religious affiliation (1985): Protestant 76.4%, of which Anglican 36.2%, Methodist 32.3%; Roman Catholic 10.7%; other 12.9%.
Major towns (1995): Basseterre 18,000; Charlestown 1,200[6].

Vital statistics

Birth rate per 1,000 population (1994): 24.0 (world avg. 25.0); (1983) legitimate 19.2%; illegitimate 80.8%.
Death rate per 1,000 population (1994): 10.0 (world avg. 9.3).
Natural increase rate per 1,000 population (1994): 14.0 (world avg. 15.7).
Total fertility rate (avg. births per childbearing woman; 1994): 2.6.
Marriage rate per 1,000 population: n.a.
Divorce rate per 1,000 population: n.a.
Life expectancy at birth (1994): male 63.0 years; female 69.0 years.
Major causes of death per 100,000 population (1985): diseases of the circulatory system 443.2, of which cerebrovascular disease 220.5, diseases of pulmonary circulation and other heart disease 122.7; malignant neoplasms (cancers) 95.5; diseases of the respiratory system 81.8; infectious and parasitic diseases 50.0; ill-defined conditions 102.3.

National economy

Budget (1993). Revenue: EC$131,400,000 (tax revenue 81.2%, of which taxes on international transactions 51.5%, income taxes 16.9%, consumption taxes 11.0%; nontax revenue 16.1%). Expenditures: EC$139,800,000 (current expenditure 83.7%; development expenditure 16.3%).
Tourism (1993): receipts from visitors U.S.$69,400,000; expenditures by nationals abroad U.S.$5,300,000.
Production (metric tons except as noted). Agriculture, forestry, fishing (1994): sugarcane 200,000, coconuts 2,000, potatoes 272[7], tomatoes 123[7], sea island cotton is grown on Nevis; livestock (number of live animals) 14,000 sheep, 10,000 goats, 5,000 cattle; roundwood, n.a.; fish catch (1993) 1,700. Mining and quarrying: excavation of sand for local use. Manufacturing (1991): raw sugar 19,980[8]; molasses 5,700[9]; aerated beverages 47,000 hectolitres; beer 17,200 hectolitres; other manufactures include garments, electronic components, plastics, and ethanol. Construction: n.a. Energy production (consumption): electricity (kW-hr; 1992) 40,000,000 (40,000,000); coal, none (none); crude petroleum, none (none); petroleum products (metric tons; 1992) none (24,000); natural gas, none (none).
Gross national product (at current market prices; 1993): U.S.$185,000,000 (U.S.$4,560 per capita).

Structure of gross domestic product and labour force

	1993		1984	
	in value EC$'000,000[10]	% of total value	labour force[11]	% of labour force[11]
Agriculture	32.7	7.2	4,380	29.6
Mining	1.6	0.4	—	—
Manufacturing	52.5	11.6	2,170	14.7
Construction	54.4	12.0	400	2.7
Public utilities	7.5	1.7	1,030	7.0
Transportation and communications	67.5	14.9	450	3.0
Trade, restaurants	105.9	23.5	940	6.3
Finance, real estate	53.3	11.8	280	1.9
Pub. admin., defense	78.3	17.3	4,700	31.7
Services	19.9	4.4		
Other	−22.0[12]	−4.9[12]	460	3.1
TOTAL	451.3[13]	100.0[13]	14,810	100.0

Household income and expenditure. Average household size (1980) 3.7; income per household: n.a.; sources of income: n.a.; expenditure (1978)[14]: food, beverages, and tobacco 55.6%, household furnishings 9.4%, housing 7.6%, clothing and footwear 7.5%, fuel and light 6.6%, transportation 4.3%, other 9.0%.
Public debt (external, outstanding; 1993): U.S.$39,500,000.
Population economically active (1980): total 17,125; activity rate of total population 39.5% (participation rates: ages 15–64, 69.5%; female 41.0%; unemployed[15]).

Price and earnings indexes (1990 = 100)

	1988	1989	1990	1991	1992	1993	1994
Consumer price index	91.3	95.9	100.0	104.2	107.2	109.1	112.0
Earnings index	...	...	...	...	...	...	...

Land use (1993): forested 17.0%; meadows and pastures 3.0%; agricultural and under permanent cultivation 39.0%; other 41.0%.

Foreign trade[16]

Balance of trade (current prices)

	1989	1990	1991	1992	1993
EC$'000,000	−166.3	−188.4	−183.1	−156.2	−169.4
% of total	51.9%	55.8%	53.7%	50.2%	52.7%

Imports (1993): EC$302,700,000 (basic and miscellaneous manufactures 36.3%, machinery 24.8%, food 16.7%, chemicals and chemical products 7.7%). *Major import sources:* United States 45.0%; Caricom countries 17.6%, of which Trinidad and Tobago 9.7%; United Kingdom 12.2%; Canada 4.4%.
Exports (1993): EC$91,500,000 (electronic goods 39.7%, sugar [all forms] 36.8%, miscellaneous manufactures [mostly garments] 14.6%). *Major export destinations:* United States 48.9%; United Kingdom 25.7%; Caricom countries 10.0%, of which Antigua and Barbuda 2.6%.

Transport and communications

Transport. Railroads (1992)[17]: length 22 mi, 36 km. Roads (1993): total length 186 mi, 300 km (paved 42%). Vehicles (1990): passenger cars 4,000; trucks and buses, n.a. Merchant marine (1992): vessels (100 gross tons and over) 1; total deadweight tonnage 550. Air transport: passenger arrivals (1992) 123,195[18]; passenger departures, n.a.; cargo handled, n.a.; airports (1994) with scheduled flights 2.
Communications (1992). Daily newspapers[19]: none. Radio (1994): total number of receivers 26,000 (1 per 1.5 persons). Television (1994): total number of receivers 9,500 (1 per 4.2 persons). Telephones (main lines; 1993): 12,200 (1 per 3.3 persons).

Education and health

Education (1991–92)

	schools	teachers	students	student/ teacher ratio
Primary (age 5–12)	31	342	6,978	20.4
Secondary (age 13–17)	7	298	4,645	15.6
Voc., teacher tr.	2	35	189	5.4
Higher	1	3	36	12.0

Educational attainment (1980). Percentage of population age 25 and over having: no formal schooling 1.1%; primary education 29.6%; secondary 67.2%; higher 2.1%. *Literacy* (1990): total population age 15 and over literate 25,500 (90.0%); males literate 13,100 (90.0%); females literate 12,400 (90.0%).
Health: physicians (1992) 39 (1 per 1,057 persons); hospital beds (1995) 276 (1 per 142 persons); infant mortality rate per 1,000 live births (1994) 20.0.
Food (1992): daily per capita caloric intake 2,419 (vegetable products 75%, animal products 25%); 101% of FAO recommended minimum requirement.

Military

Total active duty personnel (1994): the 340-member police force includes a 50-member paramilitary unit.

[1]Both Saint Christopher and Nevis and the Federation of Saint Christopher and Nevis are officially acceptable, variant, short- and long-form names of the country. [2]Includes 4 nonelective seats. [3]Parish subdivisions of both islands are for statistical purposes only. [4]Preliminary. [5]Nevis has full internal self-government. The Nevis legislature is subordinate to the National Assembly only with regard to external affairs and defense. [6]1990. [7]1993. [8]1994. [9]1992. [10]At factor cost. [11]Employed persons only. [12]Less imputed bank service charges. [13]Detail does not add to total given because of rounding. [14]Weights of consumer price index components. [15]Official data not available. Unemployment rates were thought to be low in 1993 because of labour shortages in the sugar industry and increased job creation in the construction, manufacturing, and tourism industries. [16]Imports f.o.b. in balance of trade and c.i.f. in commodities and trading partners. [17]Light railway serving the sugar industry on Saint Kitts. [18]Saint Kitts airport only. [19]Total circulation of one weekly newspaper and one twice-weekly newspaper is 9,000.

Saint Lucia

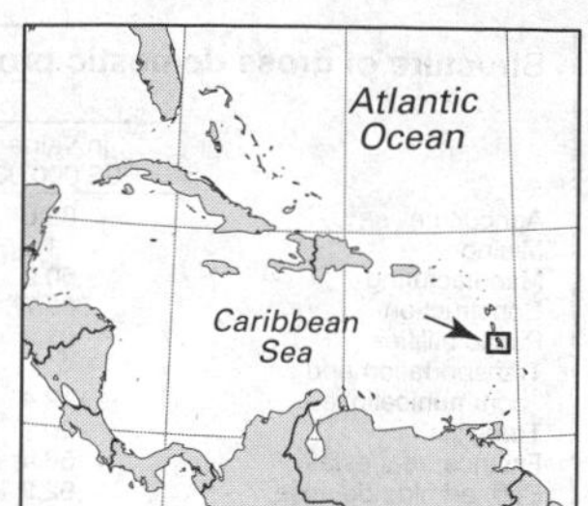

Official name: Saint Lucia.
Form of government: constitutional monarchy with two legislative houses (Senate [11]; House of Assembly [17]).
Chief of state: British Monarch represented by Governor-General.
Head of government: Prime Minister.
Capital: Castries.
Official language: English.
Official religion: none.
Monetary unit: 1 Eastern Caribbean dollar (EC$) = 100 cents; valuation (Oct. 6, 1995) 1 U.S.$ = EC$2.70; 1 £ = EC$4.27.

Area and population

		area		population
Districts	Capitals	sq mi	sq km	1992 estimate
Anse-la-Raye	Anse-la-Raye }	18	47	5,218
Canaries	Canaries }			1,864
Castries	Castries	31	79	53,883
Choiseul	Choiseul	12	31	6,638
Dennery	Dennery	27	70	11,574
Gros Islet	Gros Islet	39	101	13,996
Laborie	Laborie	15	38	7,763
Micoud	Micoud	30	78	15,636
Soufrière	Soufrière	19	51	7,962
Vieux Fort	Vieux Fort	17	44	13,617
TOTAL		238[1]	617[1]	138,151

Demography

Population (1995): 143,000.
Density (1995): persons per sq mi 600.8, persons per sq km 231.8.
Urban-rural (1995): urban 48.1%; rural 51.9%.
Sex distribution (1992): male 48.49%; female 51.51%.
Age breakdown (1992): under 15, 36.7%; 15–29, 29.4%; 30–44, 16.3%; 45–59, 8.8%; 60–74, 6.3%; 75 and over, 2.5%.
Population projection: (2000) 151,000; (2010) 169,000.
Doubling time: 41 years.
Ethnic composition (1990): black 90.5%; mixed 5.5%; East Indian 3.2%; white 0.8%.
Religious affiliation (1991): Roman Catholic 79.0%; Protestant 15.5%, of which Seventh-day Adventist 6.5%, Pentecostal 3.0%; other 5.5%.
Major city (1992): Castries city proper 2,063 (urban area 13,615).

Vital statistics

Birth rate per 1,000 population (1994): 23.0 (world avg. 25.0); legitimate 14.2%; illegitimate 85.8%.
Death rate per 1,000 population (1994): 6.0 (world avg. 9.3).
Natural increase rate per 1,000 population (1994): 17.0 (world avg. 15.7).
Total fertility rate (avg. births per childbearing woman; 1994): 2.5.
Marriage rate per 1,000 population (1992): 3.2.
Divorce rate per 1,000 population (1992): 0.3.
Life expectancy at birth (1994): male 67.0 years; female 72.0 years.
Major causes of death per 100,000 population (1992): diseases of the circulatory system 205.6, of which ischemic heart diseases 133.2, cerebrovascular disease 34.7; malignant neoplasms (cancers) 64.4; diseases of the respiratory system 48.5; infectious and parasitic diseases 31.1; ill-defined conditions 130.3.

National economy

Budget (1993–94). Revenue: EC$378,100,000 (consumption duties on imported goods 25.0%, import duties 22.9%, company taxes 10.4%, taxes on domestic goods and services 10.0%). Expenditures: EC$402,900,000 (current expenditures 62.3%, development expenditures and net lending 37.7%).
Public debt (external, outstanding; 1993): U.S.$96,800,000.
Population economically active (1992): total 57,797; activity rate of total population 41.8% (participation rates: ages 15–64, 72.7%; female 46.5%; unemployed [1994] 25.0%).
Production. Agriculture, forestry, fishing (export value in EC$'000 except as noted; 1992): bananas 116,900[2], copra 2,603[3], breadfruit 713, mangoes 670, cacao beans 404[3], pepper 241, plantains 216, pineapple 189; livestock (number of live animals; 1994) 16,000 sheep, 13,000 pigs, 12,000 cattle, 12,000 goats; roundwood, n.a.; fish catch (1993) 1,114 metric tons. Mining and quarrying: excavation of sand for local construction and pumice. Manufacturing (value of production in EC$'000; 1992): food, beverages, and tobacco 72,379; paper products and cardboard boxes 41,029; garments 10,385; electrical and electronic components 9,501; refined coconut oil 6,981; textiles 4,359. Construction (buildings approved; 1992): residential 91,900 sq m; nonresidential 43,300 sq m. Energy production (consumption): electricity (kW-hr; 1992) 152,100,000 (125,500,000); coal, none (none); crude petroleum, none (none); petroleum products (metric tons; 1992) none (325,000); natural gas, none (none).
Household income and expenditure. Average household size (1991) 4.0; income per household: n.a.; sources of income: n.a.; expenditure (1982)[4]: food 46.8%, housing 13.5%, clothing and footwear 6.5%, transportation and communications 6.3%, household furnishings 5.8%, fuel and light 4.5%, recreation and education 3.2%, beverages and tobacco 2.8%, health care 2.3%, other 8.3%.

Price and earnings indexes (1990 = 100)

	1988	1989	1990	1991	1992	1993	1994
Consumer price index	91.7	95.5	100.0	105.7	111.0	112.0	114.6[5]
Earnings index[6]	94.3	97.1	100.0	103.0	...	...[7]	...

Tourism: receipts from visitors (1993) U.S.$221,000,000; expenditures by nationals abroad (1992) U.S.$21,000,000.
Gross national product (at current market prices; 1993): U.S.$480,000,000 (U.S.$3,040 per capita).

Structure of gross domestic product and labour force

	1993		1992	
	in value EC$'000,000[8]	% of total value[8]	labour force[9]	% of labour force[9]
Agriculture	126.0	12.3	2,824	8.9
Mining	6.9	0.7	...	...
Manufacturing	75.7	7.4	4,360	13.8
Construction	92.2	9.0	2,197	6.9
Public utilities	35.1	3.4	832	2.6
Transportation and communications	185.0	18.1	2,551	8.0
Trade, restaurants	251.3	24.6	8,714	27.5
Finance, real estate	143.1	14.0	3,488	11.0
Pub. admin., defense	134.6	13.2	6,758	21.3
Services	32.7	3.2	...	...
Other	−61.8[10]	−6.1[10]	—	—
TOTAL	1,020.7[11]	100.0[11]	31,724	100.0

Land use (1993): forested 13.0%; meadows and pastures 5.0%; agricultural and under permanent cultivation 30.0%; other 52.0%.

Foreign trade[12]

Balance of trade (current prices)

	1988	1989	1990	1991	1992	1993
U.S.$'000,000	102.2	−104.9	−161.7	−185.3	−190.3	−180.6
% of total	30.0%	42.8%	42.4%	45.7%	43.7%	43.0%

Imports (1993): U.S.$300,300,000 (machinery and transportation equipment 22.8%; food and live animals 20.3%; basic manufactures 19.2%; chemicals and chemical products 9.1%; crude petroleum and petroleum products 7.6%). *Major import sources:* United States 37.3%; United Kingdom 12.5%; Trinidad and Tobago 10.1%; Japan 5.6%; Canada 3.4%.
Exports (1993): U.S.$119,700,000 (food and live animals 50.2%, of which bananas 47.7%; miscellaneous manufactures [primarily clothing] 24.8%; basic manufactures [primarily paper and paperboard] 9.0%). *Major export destinations:* United Kingdom 49.6%; United States 27.0%; Dominica 7.7%; Germany 2.4%; Barbados 1.9%.

Transport and communications

Transport. Railroads: none. Roads (1992): total length 500 mi, 805 km (paved 56%). Vehicles (1993): passenger cars 10,000; trucks and buses 9,200. Merchant marine (1992): vessels (100 gross tons and over) 7; total deadweight tonnage 2,070. Air transport (1993): passenger arrivals and departures 549,569; (1992) cargo unloaded 1,393 metric tons, cargo loaded 3,465 metric tons; airports (1995) with scheduled flights 2.
Communications. Daily newspapers: none[13]. Radio (1994): total number of receivers 98,000 (1 per 1.4 persons). Television (1994): total number of receivers 25,000 (1 per 5.7 persons). Telephones (main lines, 1993): 24,200 (1 per 5.8 persons).

Education and health

Education (1992–93)

	schools	teachers	students	student/teacher ratio
Primary (age 5–11)	84	1,181[14]	32,204	27.4[14]
Secondary (age 12–16)	14	466[14]	7,612	17.5[14]
Voc., teacher tr. } Higher }	1	113[14]	1,125	6.3[14]

Educational attainment (1980). Percentage of population age 25 and over having: no formal schooling 17.5%; primary education 74.4%; secondary 6.8%; higher 1.3%. *Literacy* (1990): about 80%.
Health (1992): physicians 64 (1 per 2,235 persons); hospital beds 435 (1 per 318 persons); infant mortality rate per 1,000 live births (1994) 19.0.
Food (1992): daily per capita caloric intake 2,588 (vegetable products 73%, animal products 27%); 107% of FAO recommended minimum requirement.

Military

Total active duty personnel (1992):[15].

[1]Total includes the uninhabited 30 sq mi (78 sq km) Central Forest Reserve. [2]1994. [3]Value of production. [4]Castries administrative area only. [5]Average of 2nd and 3rd quarters. [6]Public sector only. [7]No wage increases in public sector. [8]At constant prices of 1990. [9]Data exclude workers (all self-employed and many agricultural workers) not making contributions to the national insurance plan and all unemployed. [10]Less imputed bank service charges. [11]Detail does not add to total given because of rounding. [12]Imports c.i.f.; exports f.o.b. [13]In 1993 one newspaper was published twice a week and two others were published weekly. [14]1991–92. [15]The 497-member police force includes a specially trained paramilitary unit and a coast guard unit.

Saint Vincent and the Grenadines

Official name: Saint Vincent and the Grenadines.
Form of government: constitutional monarchy with one legislative house (House of Assembly [21[1]]).
Chief of state: British Monarch represented by Governor-General.
Head of government: Prime Minister.
Capital: Kingstown.
Official language: English.
Official religion: none.
Monetary unit: 1 Eastern Caribbean dollar (EC$) = 100 cents; valuation (Oct. 6, 1995) 1 U.S.$ = EC$2.70; 1 £ = EC$4.27.

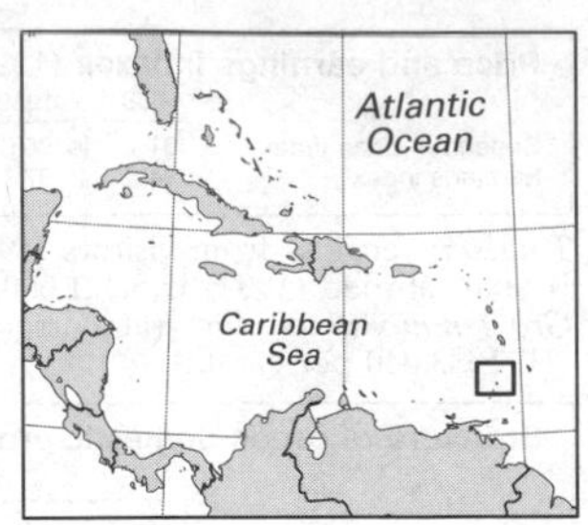

Area and population

Constituencies[2]	area sq mi	area sq km	population 1993[3] estimate
Island of Saint Vincent			
Barrouallie	14.2	36.8	5,319
Bridgetown	7.2	18.6	7,706
Calliaqua	11.8	30.6	20,760
Chateaubelair	30.9	80.0	6,185
Colonarie	13.4	34.7	8,073
Georgetown	22.2	57.5	7,472
Kingstown (city)	1.9	4.9	15,824
Kingstown (suburbs)	6.4	16.6	11,006
Layou	11.1	28.7	6,132
Marriaqua	9.4	24.3	9,069
Sandy Bay	5.3	13.7	2,858
Saint Vincent Grenadines			
Northern Grenadines	9.0	23.3	5,642
Southern Grenadines	7.5	19.4	2,919
TOTAL	150.3	389.3[4]	108,965

Demography

Population (1995): 112,000.
Density (1995): persons per sq mi 745.2, persons per sq km 287.7.
Urban-rural (1991)[5]: urban 24.6%; rural 75.4%.
Sex distribution (1993): male 49.92%; female 50.08%.
Age breakdown (1991): under 15, 37.2%; 15–29, 29.5%; 30–44, 16.1%; 45–59, 8.3%; 60–74, 6.4%; 75 and over, 2.5%.
Population projection: (2000) 119,000; (2010) 133,000.
Doubling time: 39 years.
Ethnic composition (1986): black 65.5%; mulatto 19.0%; East Indian 5.5%; white (mostly Portuguese) 3.5%; Amerindian/black 2.0%; other 4.5%.
Religious affiliation (1985): Protestant 76.0%, of which Anglican 36.0%; Roman Catholic 10.0%; other/nonreligious 14.0%.
Major city (1993[3]): Kingstown 15,824.

Vital statistics

Birth rate per 1,000 population (1992): 24.8 (world avg. 25.0); legitimate, n.a.; illegitimate, n.a.
Death rate per 1,000 population (1992): 6.6 (world avg. 9.3).
Natural increase rate per 1,000 population (1992): 18.2 (world avg. 15.7).
Total fertility rate (avg. births per childbearing woman; 1994): 2.1.
Marriage rate per 1,000 population (1992): 3.7.
Divorce rate per 1,000 population (1992): 0.8.
Life expectancy at birth (1994): male 71.0 years; female 74.0 years.
Major causes of death per 100,000 population (1992): diseases of the circulatory system 222.5, of which hypertensive disease 110.8, diseases of pulmonary circulation and other forms of heart disease 44.3; malignant neoplasms (cancers) 99.7; endocrine and metabolic disorders 55.4; homicide, suicide, and other violence 39.7.

National economy

Budget (1994). Revenue: EC$265,000,000 (current revenue 70.2%; development revenue 29.8%, of which domestic sources 15.8%, foreign loans and grants 14.0%). Expenditures: EC$263,600,000 (current expenditure 70.0%; development expenditure 30.0%).
Land use (1994): forested 36.0%; meadows and pastures 5.0%; agricultural and under permanent cultivation 28.0%; other 31.0%.
Tourism: receipts from visitors (1993) U.S.$55,000,000; expenditures by nationals abroad (1992) U.S.$4,000,000.
Production (metric tons except as noted). Agriculture, forestry, fishing (1994): bananas 30,000, coconuts 23,000, eddoes and dasheens[6] 5,240[7], sweet potatoes 4,000, plantains 3,000, yams 2,000, mangoes 2,000, lemons and limes 1,000, oranges 1,000, ginger 834[7], arrowroot starch 635[8], soursops, guavas, and papaws are other important fruits; livestock (number of live animals) 12,000 sheep, 9,000 pigs, 6,000 cattle; roundwood, n.a.; fish catch (1993) 1,781. Mining and quarrying: sand and gravel for local use. Manufacturing (value added in EC$'000; 1988): beverages and tobacco products 9,686; food products 9,499; textiles, clothing, and footwear 3,872; metal products and electrical machinery 2,510. Construction (gross floor area planned; 1992): 80,800 sq m. Energy production (consumption): electricity (kW-hr; 1993) 61,600,000 (56,400,000); coal, none (none); crude petroleum, none (none); petroleum products (metric tons; 1992) none (27,000); natural gas, none (none).
Gross national product (1993): U.S.$233,000,000 (U.S.$2,130 per capita).

Structure of gross domestic product and labour force

	1993[9] in value EC$'000,000	1993[9] % of total value	1991 labour force	1991 % of labour force
Agriculture	89.6	16.0	8,377	20.1
Mining	1.8	0.3	98	0.2
Manufacturing	50.9	9.1	2,822	6.8
Construction	60.7	10.8	3,535	8.5
Public utilities	27.2	4.9	586	1.4
Transportation and communications	112.4	20.0	2,279	5.5
Trade	90.2	16.1	6,544	15.7
Finance, real estate	56.4	10.1	1,418	3.4
Pub. admin., defense	92.2	16.5	7,696	18.5
Services	10.0	1.8		
Other	–30.8[10]	–5.5[10]	8,327[11]	20.0[11]
TOTAL	560.5[4]	100.0[4]	41,682	100.0[4]

Public debt (external, outstanding; 1993): U.S.$62,400,000.
Population economically active (1991): total 41,682; activity rate of total population 39.1% (participation rates: ages 15–64, 67.5%; female 35.9%; unemployed [1994] 30–40%).

Price and earnings indexes (1990 = 100)

	1989	1990	1991	1992	1993	1994	1995
Consumer price index	92.9	100.0	105.6	109.1	113.8	115.0	116.4[12]
Annual earnings index[13]	100.0	100.0	100.0	100.0	100.0	...	...

Household income and expenditure. Average household size (1991) 3.9; income per household (1988) EC$4,579 (U.S.$1,696); sources of income: n.a.; expenditure (1975–76): food and beverages 59.8%, clothing 7.7%, household furnishings 6.6%, housing 6.3%, energy 6.2%, other 13.4%.

Foreign trade[14]

Balance of trade (current prices)

	1989	1990	1991	1992	1993	1994
EC$'000,000	–111.5	–110.6	–161.2	–113.3	–173.6	–214.0
% of total	21.7%	19.8%	30.7%	21.4%	35.7%	47.9%

Imports (1992): EC$360,600,000 (food products 23.2%; basic manufactures 21.6%; machinery and transport equipment 17.8%). *Major import sources:* United States 35.5%; Trinidad and Tobago 17.6%; United Kingdom 16.9%; Barbados 3.4%; Canada 3.0%.
Exports (1992)[15]: EC$213,000,000 (domestic exports 96.3%, of which bananas 52.7%, flour 11.2%, varieties of taro roots 3.5%, sweet potatoes 2.3%; re-exports 3.7%). *Major export destinations:* United Kingdom 41.2%; Trinidad and Tobago 12.0%; Saint Lucia 10.0%; United States 4.4%; Antigua and Barbuda 4.4%.

Transport and communications

Transport. Railroads: none. Roads (1991): total length 586 mi, 943 km (paved 16%). Vehicles (1993): passenger cars 4,591; trucks and buses 2,878. Merchant marine (1992): vessels (100 gross tons and over) 881; total deadweight tonnage 7,044,189. Air transport (1992): passenger arrivals 112,574, passenger departures 113,699; airports (1995) with scheduled flights 4.
Communications. Daily newspapers: none[16]. Radio (1994): total number of receivers 73,000 (1 per 1.5 persons). Television (1994): total number of receivers 17,700 (1 per 6.3 persons). Telephones (main lines; 1993): 16,500 (1 per 6.6 persons).

Education and health

Education (1991–92)

	schools	teachers	students	student/ teacher ratio
Primary (age 5–11)	60	1,215	24,134	19.9
Secondary (age 12–18)	21	408	7,124	17.5
Voc., teacher tr.	2	...	337	...

Educational attainment (1980). Percentage of population age 25 and over having: no formal schooling 2.4%; primary education 88.0%; secondary 8.2%; higher 1.4%. *Literacy* (1991): total population age 15 and over literate 64,000 (96.0%).
Health (1992): physicians 40 (1 per 2,708 persons); hospital beds (1989) 500 (1 per 209 persons); infant mortality rate per 1,000 live births 17.1.
Food (1992): daily per capita caloric intake 2,347 (vegetable products 84%, animal products 16%); 97% of FAO recommended minimum requirement.

Military

Total active duty personnel (1992): 634-member police force includes a coast guard and paramilitary unit. *Military expenditure as percentage of central government expenditure* (1989–90): 5.6%[17].

[1]Includes 6 nonelective seats; excludes speaker who may be elected from within or from outside of the House of Assembly membership. [2]For statistical purposes and the election of legislative representatives; St. Vincent and the Grenadines has no local administrative authority. [3]January 1. [4]Detail does not add to total given because of rounding. [5]Urban defined as Kingstown and suburbs. [6]Varieties of taro roots. [7]1992. [8]1992–93. [9]At factor cost. [10]Less imputed bank service charges. [11]Unemployed. [12]April. [13]Agriculture and manufacturing sectors only. [14]Imports f.o.b. in balance of trade and c.i.f. in commodities and trading partners. [15]*Exports* (1994): EC$116,300,-000, of which bananas 37.8%. [16]Weekly newspapers (1992): 2. [17]May not agree with military expenditure as percentage of GNP because of different bases used.

San Marino

Official name: Serenissima Repubblica di San Marino (Most Serene Republic of San Marino).
Form of government: unitary multiparty republic with one legislative house (Great and General Council [60]).
Head of state and government: Captains-Regent (2).
Capital: San Marino.
Official language: Italian.
Official religion: none.
Monetary unit: 1 Italian lira (Lit; plural lire) = 100 centesimi; valuation (Oct. 6, 1995) 1 U.S.$ = Lit 1,617; 1 £ = Lit 2,557.

Area and population

		area		population
Castles	Capitals	sq mi	sq km	1995[1] estimate
Acquaviva	Acquaviva	1.88	4.86	1,257
Borgo Maggiore	Borgo	3.48	9.01	5,188
Chiesanuova	Chiesanuova	2.11	5.46	830
Città	San Marino	2.74	7.09	4,327
Domagnano	Domagnano	2.56	6.62	2,215
Faetano	Faetano	2.99	7.75	794
Fiorentino	Fiorentino	2.53	6.56	1,700
Montegiardino	Montegiardino	1.28	3.31	678
Serravalle/Dogano	Serravalle	4.07	10.53	7,758
TOTAL		23.63[2]	61.19	24,747

Demography

Population (1995): 24,900.
Density (1995): persons per sq mi 1,053.7, persons per sq km 406.9.
Urban-rural (1995[1]): urban 89.8%; rural 10.2%.
Sex distribution (1995[1]): male 49.52%; female 50.48%.
Age breakdown (1995[1]): under 15, 14.9%; 15–29, 22.7%; 30–44, 24.2%; 45–59, 18.2%; 60–74, 14.2%; 75 and over, 5.8%.
Population projection: (2000) 26,800; (2010) 31,100.
Doubling time: not applicable; natural population growth is negligible.
Ethnic composition (1995[1]): Sammarinesi 76.8%; Italian 22.0%; other 1.2%.
Religious affiliation (1980): Roman Catholic 95.2%; no religion 3.0%; other 1.8%.
Major cities (1995[1]): Serravalle/Dogano 4,709; Borgo Maggiore 2,367; San Marino 2,315; Murata 1,505; Domagnano 1,046.

Vital statistics

Birth rate per 1,000 population (1990–94): 10.8 (world avg. 25.0); (1985) legitimate 95.2%; illegitimate 4.8%.
Death rate per 1,000 population (1990–94): 7.0 (world avg. 9.3).
Natural increase rate per 1,000 population (1990–94): 3.8 (world avg. 15.7).
Total fertility rate (avg. births per childbearing woman; 1994): 1.5.
Marriage rate per 1,000 population (1990–94): 7.9.
Divorce rate per 1,000 population (1990–94): 0.9.
Life expectancy at birth (1994): male 77.2 years; female 85.3 years.
Major causes of death per 100,000 population (1990–94): diseases of the circulatory system 325.6; malignant neoplasms (cancers) 221.1; accidents, violence, and suicide 45.7; diseases of the respiratory system 13.6.

National economy

Budget (1991). Revenue: Lit 379,337,000,000 (mainly receipts from postage stamp sales, tourism, and customs duties [collected by Italy and paid as a subsidy]). Expenditures: Lit 379,337,000,000 ([3]finance and economic planning 31.0%, internal affairs 11.3%, health and social security 9.0%, education and culture 7.1%, public works 6.3%).
Public debt: n.a.
Tourism: number of tourist arrivals (1994) 3,104,231; receipts from visitors (1983) U.S.$56,454,000; expenditures by nationals abroad, n.a.
Population economically active (1995[1]): total 15,519; activity rate of total population 62.7% (participation rates: ages 15–64 [1992] 72.9%; female 40.6%; unemployed 3.7%).

Price and earnings indexes (1990 = 100)

	1988	1989	1990	1991	1992	1993	1994
Consumer price index	88.4	94.0	100.0	108.0	115.7	121.9	128.0
Earnings index	...	...	...	...	...	...	...

Household income and expenditure. Total number of households (1995[1]) 9,266; average household size 2.7; income per household: n.a.; sources of income: n.a.; expenditure (1991)[4]: food, beverages, and tobacco 22.1%, housing, fuel, and electrical energy 20.9%, transportation and communications 17.6%, clothing and footwear 8.0%, furniture, appliances, and goods and services for the home 7.2%, education 7.1%, health and sanitary services 2.6%, other goods and services 14.5%.
Production (metric tons except as noted). Agriculture, forestry, fishing[3]: wheat *c.* 4,400, grapes *c.* 700, barley *c.* 500; livestock (number of live animals; 1994) 970 cattle, 694 pigs, 13 sheep. Manufacturing (1994): processed meats 364,210 kg, of which beef 269,848 kg, pork 86,345 kg, veal 7,741 kg; cheese 81,860 kg; butter 14,104 kg; milk 1,071,636 litres; yogurt 6,283 litres; other major products include textiles, cement, paper, leather, bricks, pottery, tiles, postage stamps, gold and silver jewelry, paints, synthetic rubber, and furniture. Construction (new units completed; 1994): residential 173; nonresidential 90. Energy production (consumption): all electrical power is imported via electrical grid from Italy (consumption, n.a.); coal, none (n.a.); crude petroleum, none (n.a.); petroleum products, none (n.a.); natural gas, none (n.a.).
Gross national product (at current market prices; 1987): U.S.$188,000,000 (U.S.$8,590 per capita).

Structure of labour force (1995[1])

	labour force	% of labour force
Agriculture	256	1.7
Manufacturing	5,078	32.7
Construction and public utilities	1,291	8.3
Transportation and communications	282	1.8
Trade	2,531	16.3
Finance and insurance	400	2.6
Services	1,322	8.5
Public administration and defense	3,779	24.4
Other	580[5]	3.7[5]
TOTAL	15,519	100.0

Land use (1985): agricultural and under permanent cultivation 74%; meadows and pastures 22%; forested, built-on, wasteland, and other 4%.

Foreign trade

Balance of trade: n.a. San Marino and Italy form a single customs area; separate figures for San Marino are not available.
Imports (1994): manufactured goods of all kinds, oil, and gold. *Major import source:* Italy.
Exports (1994): wine, wheat, woolen goods, furniture, wood, ceramics, building stone, dairy products, meat, and postage stamps. *Major export destination:* Italy.

Transport and communications

Transport. Railroads: none (nearest rail terminal is at Rimini, Italy, 17 mi [27 km] northeast). Roads (1987): total length 147 mi, 237 km. Vehicles (1995[1]): passenger cars 22,945; trucks and buses 3,843. Merchant marine: vessels (100 gross tons and over) none. Air transport: airports with scheduled flights, none; there is, however, a heliport that provides passenger and cargo service between San Marino and Rimini, Italy, during the summer months.
Communications. Daily newspapers (1994): 5; circulation per 1,000 population, n.a. Radio (1994): total number of receivers 12,600 (1 per 1.9 persons). Television (1990): total number of receivers 8,000 (1 per 2.9 persons). Telephones (1988): 15,700 (1 per 1.5 persons).

Education and health

Education (1994–95)

	schools	teachers	students	student/ teacher ratio
Primary (age 6–10)	14	218	1,143	5.2
Secondary (age 11–18)	3	133	775	5.8
Voc., teacher tr.	...	...	408	...
Higher	...	...	...	...

Educational attainment (1995[1]). Percentage of the adult labour force having: basic literacy or primary education 20.2%; secondary 39.7%; some post-secondary 33.6%; higher degree 6.5%. *Literacy* (1986): total population age 15 and over literate 18,135 (98.0%); males literate 8,957 (98.2%); females literate 9,178 (97.7%).
Health (1987): physicians 60 (1 per 375 persons); hospital beds 149 (1 per 151 persons); infant mortality rate per 1,000 live births (1990–94) 7.1.
Food (1992)[6]: daily per capita caloric intake 3,561 (vegetable products 75%, animal products 25%); 141% of FAO recommended minimum requirement.

Military

Total active duty personnel (1995): none[7]. *Military expenditure as percentage of national budget* (1987): 0.9% (world 5.4%); per capita expenditure (1987) U.S.$82.

[1]January 1. [2]Detail does not add to total given because of rounding. [3]Early 1980s. [4]Weighting coefficients for component expenditures are those of the 1991 official Italian consumer price index for the North-Central region of Italy. [5]Unemployed. [6]Figures are for Italy. [7]Defense is provided by a public security force of about 50; all fit males ages 16–55 constitute a militia.

São Tomé and Príncipe

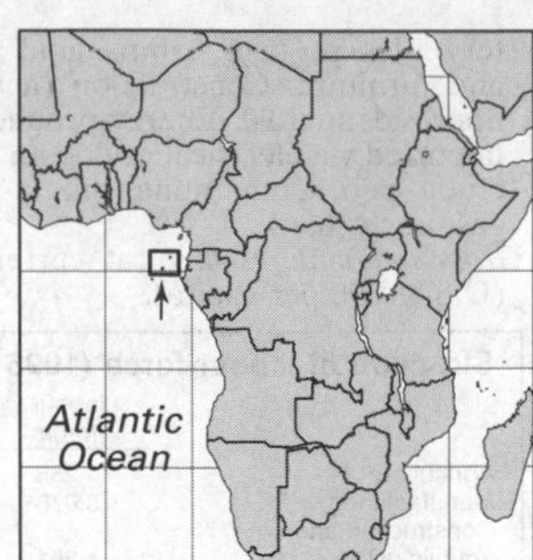

Official name: República democrática de São Tomé e Príncipe (Democratic Republic of São Tomé and Príncipe).
Form of government: Multiparty republic with one legislative house (National Assembly [55]).
Chief of state: President.
Head of government: Prime Minister.
Capital: São Tomé.
Official language: Portuguese.
Official religion: none.
Monetary unit: 1 dobra (Db) = 100 cêntimos; valuation (Oct. 6, 1995) 1 U.S.$ = Db 1,446; 1 £ = Db 2,286.

Area and population

		area		population
Islands / Districts	Capitals	sq mi	sq km	1991 census[1]
São Tomé		332	859	114,507
Aqua Grande	São Tomé	7	17	43,420
Cantagalo	Santana	46	119	11,421
Caué	São João Angolares	103	267	5,541
Lemba	Neves	88	229	9,448
Lobata	Guadalupe	41	105	13,101
Mé-Zóchi	Trindade	47	122	31,576
Autonomous Island		55	142	5,639
Príncipe	Santo António	55	142	5,639
TOTAL		386	1,001	120,146

Demography

Population (1995): 131,000.
Density (1995): persons per sq mi 339.0, persons per sq km 130.7.
Urban-rural (1994): urban 44.1%; rural 55.9%.
Sex distribution (1994): male 49.40%; female 50.60%.
Age breakdown (1990): under 15, 47.6%; 15–29, 25.8%; 30–44, 12.1%; 45–59, 7.3%; 60 and over, 6.4%; not stated, 0.8%.
Population projection: (2000) 146,000; (2010) 182,000.
Doubling time: 23 years.
Ethnolinguistic composition: mestiços, angolares (descendants of Angolan slaves), forros (descendants of freed slaves), serviçais (alien contract labourers), and tongas (children of serviçais) speak Portuguese; non-Portuguese-speaking Europeans speak French and Spanish.
Religious affiliation (1991): Roman Catholic, about 80.8%; remainder mostly Protestant, predominantly Seventh-day Adventist and an indigenous Evangelical Church.
Major cities (1991): São Tomé 43,420; Trindade 11,388[2]; Santana 6,190[2]; Neves 5,919[2]; Santo Amaro 5,878[2].

Vital statistics

Birth rate per 1,000 population (1994): 35.2 (world avg. 25.0); (1977) legitimate 9.8%; illegitimate 90.2%.
Death rate per 1,000 population (1994): 8.9 (world avg. 9.3).
Natural increase rate per 1,000 population (1994): 26.3 (world avg. 15.7).
Total fertility rate (avg. births per childbearing woman; 1994): 4.5.
Marriage rate per 1,000 population: n.a.
Divorce rate per 1,000 population: n.a.
Life expectancy at birth (1994): male 61.5 years; female 65.2 years.
Major causes of death per 100,000 population (1987): malaria 160.6; direct obstetric causes 76.7; pneumonia 74.0; influenza 61.5; anemias 47.3; hypertensive disease 32.1.

National economy

Budget (1994). Revenue: Db 12,329,000,000 (grants 60.9%; indirect taxes 25.2%, of which import taxes 10.3%, sales taxes 10.3%; nontax revenue 9.7%; direct taxes 4.2%). Expenditures: Db 26,421,000,000 (capital 57.3%; recurrent expenditure 42.7%, of which personnel costs 7.1%, goods and services 5.0%; debt service 15.1%).
Public debt (external, outstanding; 1993): U.S.$225,800,000.
Tourism (1990): receipts from visitors U.S.$1,000,000; expenditures by nationals abroad U.S.$2,000,000.
Production (metric tons except as noted). Agriculture, forestry, fishing (1994): coconuts 22,000, vegetables and melons 14,000, bananas 12,000, taro 7,000, cacao 4,000, cereals 4,000, fruits (other than melons) 3,000, palm kernels 3,000, palmetto 3,000[3], cassava 1,000, copra 1,000; livestock (number of live animals) 5,000 goats, 4,000 cattle, 2,000 pigs, 2,000 sheep; roundwood (1993) 9,000 cu m; fish catch (1993) 2,200, principally marine fish and shellfish. Mining and quarrying: some quarrying to support local construction industry. Manufacturing (value in Db; 1994): beer 628,000; clothing 604,000; lumber 328,000; bakery products 325,000; palm oil 182,000; soap 154,000; ceramics 77,000. Construction (1972): buildings authorized 44 (5,561 sq m, of which residential 3,698, mixed residential-commercial 1,361, commercial 502). Energy production (consumption): electricity (kW-hr; 1993) 20,181,000 (12,452,000); coal, none (n.a.); crude petroleum, none (n.a.); petroleum products (metric tons; 1992) none (24,000); natural gas, none (n.a.).
Household income and expenditure. Average household size (1981): 4.0; income per household: n.a.; sources of income: n.a.; expenditure (1990)[4]: food 65.7%, housing, transportation, and communications 14.6%, clothing and other items 11.4%, education and health 4.6%, housing and utilities 3.7%.

Population economically active (1991): total 49,216; activity rate of total population 41.0% (participation rates [1981]: ages 15–64, 61.1%; female 32.4%; unemployed [1994[5]] 22.0%).

Earnings indexes (1990 = 100)

	1989	1990	1991	1992	1993	1994
Consumer price index	70.3	100.0	146.5	195.8	245.8	311.3
Earnings index	...	...	...	...	...	...

Gross national product (at current market prices; 1993): U.S.$41,000,000 (U.S.$370 per capita).

Structure of gross domestic product and labour force

	1993		1991	
	in value Db '000,000	% of total value	labour force	% of labour force
Agriculture	4,663	27.7	13,592	27.6
Mining	...	...	...	...
Manufacturing } Public utilities }	1,326	7.9	1,510	3.1
			269	0.6
Construction	970	5.7	2,866	5.8
Transportation and communications } Trade }	4,642	27.6	2,186	4.4
			4,451	9.0
Finance	...	...	176	0.4
Pub. admin., defense	3,870	23.0	5,592	11.4
Services	1,366	8.1	2,369	4.8
Other	...	...	16,205[6]	32.9[6]
TOTAL	16,837	100.0	49,216	100.0

Land use (1993): meadows and pastures 1.0%; agricultural and under permanent cultivation 38.6%; forest, built-on, wasteland, and other 60.4%.

Foreign trade[7]

Balance of trade (current prices)

	1989	1990	1991	1992	1993	1994
U.S.$'000,000	−27.6	−22.2	−24.6	−22.7	−25.4	−23.9
% of total	70.1%	71.6%	67.2%	67.8%	65.8%	64.8%

Imports (1994): U.S.$30,400,000 (capital goods 40.2%, food and other agricultural products 21.5%, petroleum products 7.2%). *Major import sources* (1994): Portugal 28.3%; France 10.1%; Belgium 7.6%; Japan 5.5%; Angola 4.8%; Germany 2.6%; The Netherlands 2.4%; Gabon 1.8%; Italy 1.7%; United Kingdom 1.1%.
Exports (1994): U.S.$6,500,000 (cocoa 76.9%). *Major export destinations* (1994): The Netherlands 88.2%; Portugal 0.6%.

Transport and communications

Transport. Railroads: none. Roads (1991): total length 149 mi, 240 km (paved 41.7%). Vehicles (1987): passenger cars 2,600; trucks and buses 300. Merchant marine (1992): vessels (100 gross tons and over) 4; total deadweight tonnage 2,277. Air transport (1990): passenger-mi 5,000,000, passenger-km 8,000,000; short ton-mi cargo 700,000, short ton-km cargo 1,000,000; airports (1995) with scheduled flights 2.
Communications. Daily newspapers: none; 2 government weeklies (circulation, n.a.). Radio (1994): total number of receivers 31,000 (1 per 4.1 persons). Television: total number of receivers 21,000 (1 per 6.1 persons). Telephones (main lines; 1993): 2,400 (1 per 52 persons).

Education and health

Education (1989)

	schools	teachers	students	student/ teacher ratio
Primary (age 6–13)	64	559	19,822	35.5
Secondary (age 14–18)	11[8]	318	7,446	23.4
Voc., teacher tr.	2[8]	18[9]	289	...
Higher	...	...	700[10]	...

Educational attainment (1981). Percentage of population age 25 and over having: no formal schooling 56.6%; incomplete primary education 18.0%; primary 19.2%; incomplete secondary 4.6%; complete secondary 1.3%; postsecondary 0.3%. *Literacy* (1981): total population age 15 and over literate 28,114 (54.2%); males literate 17,689 (70.2%); females literate 10,425 (39.1%).
Health: physicians (1989) 61 (1 per 1,881 persons); hospital beds (1983) 640 (1 per 158 persons); infant mortality rate per 1,000 live births (1994) 63.5.
Food (1992): daily per capita caloric intake 2,129 (vegetable products 96%, animal products 4%); 91% of FAO recommended minimum requirement.

Military

Total active duty personnel: a gendarmerie of about 900 men was to be established in the early 1990s. *Military expenditure as percentage of GNP* (1980): 1.6% (world 5.4%); per capita expenditure U.S.$6.

[1]Preliminary. [2]1981. [3]1988. [4]Weights based on CPI components. [5]First 10 months. [6]Includes 15,148 unemployed. [7]Import figures are c.i.f. [8]1984–85. [9]Vocational teachers only. [10]Students abroad, 1982–83.

Saudi Arabia

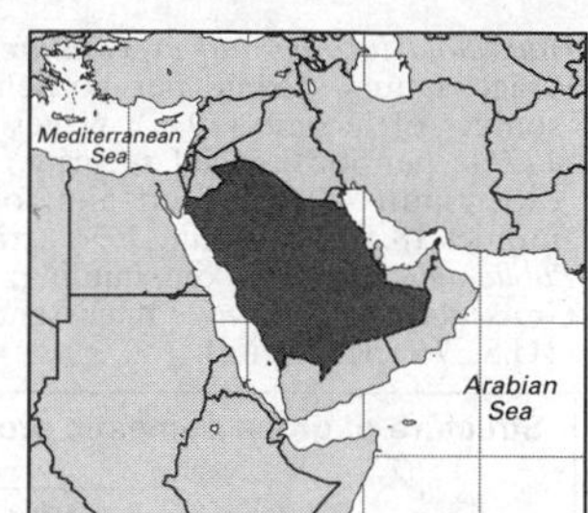

Official name: al-Mamlakah al-ʿArabīyah as-Saʿūdīyah (Kingdom of Saudi Arabia).
Form of government: monarchy[1].
Head of state and government: King.
Capital: Riyadh.
Official language: Arabic.
Official religion: Islam.
Monetary unit: 1 Saudi riyal (SRls) = 100 halalah; valuation (Oct. 6, 1995) 1 U.S.$ = SRls 3.75; 1 £ = SRls 5.93.

Area and population

Geographic Regions / Administrative Regions[2]	Capitals	area sq mi	area sq km	population 1985 estimate
al-Gharbīyah (Western)	—	...	...	3,043,189
al-Bāḥah	al-Bāḥah	...	...	...
al-Madīnah	Medina (al-Madīnah)	...	...	...
Makkah	Mecca (Makkah)	...	...	...
al-Janūbīyah (Southern)	—	...	...	625,017
ʿAsīr	Abha	...	...	...
Jīzān	Jīzān	...	...	...
Najrān	Najrān	...	...	...
ash-Shamālīyah (Northern)	—	...	...	679,476
al-Ḥudūd ash-Shamālīyah (Northern Borders)	ʿArʿar	...	...	...
al-Jawf	Sakākah	...	...	...
Tabūk	Tabūk	...	...	...
ash-Sharqīyah (Eastern)	—	...	...	3,030,765
ash-Sharqīyah (Eastern)	ad-Dammām	...	...	...
al-Wūsṭā (Central)	—	...	...	3,632,092
Ḥā'il	Ḥā'il	...	...	...
al-Qaṣīm	Buraydah	...	...	...
ar-Riyāḍ	Riyadh (ar-Riyāḍ)	...	...	...
TOTAL		865,000	2,240,000	11,010,539[3]

Demography

Population (1995): 17,880,000.
Density (1995): persons per sq mi 20.7, persons per sq km 8.0.
Urban-rural (1995): urban 80.2%; rural 19.8%.
Sex distribution (1995): male 55.72%; female 44.28%.
Age breakdown (1995): under 15, 41.9%; 15–29, 24.5%; 30–44, 19.7%; 45–59, 9.5%; 60–74, 3.6%; 75 and over, 0.8%.
Population projection: (2000) 21,257,000; (2010) 28,880,000.
Doubling time: 24 years.
Ethnic composition (1983): Saudi 82.0%; Yemeni 9.6%; other Arab 3.4%; other 5.0%.
Religious affiliation (1980): Muslim (mostly Sunnī) 98.8%; Christian 0.8%; other 0.4%.
Major cities (1980): Riyadh (ar-Riyāḍ) 1,800,000[4]; Jiddah 1,800,000[4]; Mecca (Makkah) 550,000; aṭ-Ṭāʾif 300,000.

Vital statistics

Birth rate per 1,000 population (1995): 38.8 (world avg. 25.0).
Death rate per 1,000 population (1995): 5.5 (world avg. 9.3).
Natural increase rate per 1,000 population (1995): 33.3 (world avg. 15.7).
Total fertility rate (avg. births per childbearing woman; 1995): 6.5.
Life expectancy at birth (1995): male 66.8 years; female 70.3 years.
Major causes of death per 100,000 population: n.a.; however, principal infectious diseases include malaria, diarrheal diseases, cholera, trachoma, cerebrospinal meningitis, yellow fever, typhoid, tuberculosis, and lung infections. Parasitic infections, motor vehicle accidents, and metabolic disorders are also significant.

National economy

Budget (1994). Revenue: SRls 120,000,000,000 (oil revenues 74.9%). Expenditures: SRls 160,000,000,000 (defense and security 33.5%, education 18.3%, health and social development 7.0%, transportation and communications 4.3%, municipal services 3.3%, economic resource development 2.7%).
Public debt (external, outstanding; 1991): U.S.$2,893,000,000.
Production (metric tons except as noted). Agriculture, forestry, fishing (1994): wheat 2,500,000, barley 1,800,000, dates 564,000, tomatoes 440,000, watermelons 400,000, potatoes 169,000, grapes 115,000, cucumbers and gherkins 113,000, eggplants 69,000, pumpkins, squash, and gourds 69,000, carrots 25,000, millet 11,000; livestock (number of live animals) 7,257,000 sheep, 4,150,000 goats, 415,000 camels, 203,000 cattle, 98,000 asses, 81,000,000 chickens; fish catch (1993) 49,420. Mining and quarrying (1993): gypsum 375,000; gold 7,519 kg. Manufacturing (1993): cement 15,300,000; steel 2,000,000; fuel oils 171,500,000 barrels; diesel oil 165,000,000 barrels; gasoline and naphtha 146,000,000 barrels; jet fuel 40,000,000 barrels; asphalt and related products 35,070,000 barrels[5]. Construction (1991): residential 16,077,677 sq m; nonresidential 2,204,894 sq m. Energy production (consumption): electricity (kW-hr; 1993) 63,331,000,000 (63,331,000,000); coal, n.a. (n.a.); crude petroleum (barrels; 1993) 2,915,000,000 (581,400,000); petroleum products (metric tons; 1993) 89,691,000 (35,680,000); natural gas (cu m; 1993) 35,899,000,000 (35,899,000,000).
Land use (1993): forested 0.8%; meadows and pastures 55.8%; agricultural and under permanent cultivation 1.7%; built-on, waste, and other 41.7%.
Population economically active (1994): total 5,614,000; activity rate of total population 32.2% (participation rates [1988]: ages 15–64, 59.1%; female 3.5%).

Price and earnings indexes (1990 = 100)

	1989	1990	1991	1992	1993	1994	1995[6]
Consumer price index	98.0	100.0	104.9	104.8	105.9	106.5	111.4
Earnings index	...	...	...	...	...	...	...

Gross national product (1994)[7]: U.S.$173,100,000,000 (U.S.$9,510 per capita).

Structure of gross domestic product and labour force

	1992 in value[8] SRls '000,000	1992 % of total value	1990 labour force	1990 % of labour force
Agriculture	28,785	6.3	569,200	9.9
Mining	167,206	36.7	3,500	0.1
Oil sector			46,800	0.8
Manufacturing	38,220	8.4	374,900	6.5
Construction	39,039	8.6	944,100	16.4
Public utilities	701	0.1	126,900	2.2
Transp. and commun.	28,432	6.2	262,300	4.5
Trade	31,239	6.9	898,300	15.6
Finance	25,956[9]	5.7[9]	99,000	1.7
Pub. admin., defense	78,905	17.3	624,800	10.8
Services	12,595	2.8	1,822,000	31.6
Other	4,054[10]	0.9[10]		
TOTAL	455,132	100.0[11]	5,771,800	100.0[11]

Household income and expenditure. Average household size (1986) 6.6; income per household: n.a.; sources of income: n.a.; expenditure (1988)[12]: food 37%, housing 21%, transportation and communications 15%, clothing 8%, household furnishings 7%, education and entertainment 2%.
Tourism: receipts from visitors (1989) U.S.$2,050,000,000; expenditures by nationals abroad (1988) U.S.$2,000,000,000.
Pilgrims to Mecca from abroad (1994): 2,000,000.

Foreign trade[13]

Balance of trade (current prices)

	1989	1990	1991	1992	1993	1994
U.S.$'000,000	+7,230	+20,336	+76,890	+17,014	+14,156	+22,286
% of total	14.6%	29.7%	31.1%	20.1%	20.1%	32.0%

Imports (1994): SRls 87,422,000,000 (1993; machinery and appliances 21.3%, transport equipment 20.8%, metals and metal articles 10.1%, textiles and clothing 7.8%, chemicals 7.2%, vegetables 5.2%, live animals and animal products 3.5%). *Major import sources:* U.S. 21.3%; Japan 11.7%; U.K. 8.5%; Germany 8.3%; Italy 4.7%; France 4.3%; Switzerland 4.2%; S. Korea 2.8%.
Exports (1994): SRls 170,884,300,000 (1993; petroleum 97.0%, other 3.0%). *Major export destinations:* Japan 16.7%; U.S. 16.6%; S. Korea 7.9%; France 5.5%; The Netherlands 3.3%; Italy 2.9%; India 2.9%; U.K. 2.3%; Spain 2.2%.

Transport and communications

Transport. Railroads (1989–90): route length (1991) 864 mi, 1,390 km; passenger-mi 93,800,000, passenger-km 151,000,000; short ton-mi cargo 487,700,000, metric ton-km cargo 712,000,000. Roads (1993): total length 94,157 mi, 151,532 km (paved 40%). Vehicles (1992): passenger cars 2,762,132; trucks and buses 2,286,541. Merchant marine (1992): vessels (100 gross tons and over) 301; total deadweight tonnage 1,381,651. Air transport (1994)[14]: passenger-mi 11,340,000,000, passenger-km 18,249,900,000; short ton-mi cargo 554,500,000, metric ton-km cargo 809,500,000; airports (1995) with scheduled flights 25.
Communications. Daily newspapers (1992): total number 10, total circulation 579,300[15]; circulation per 1,000 population 34[15]. Radio (1994): 3,800,000 receivers (1 per 4.6 persons). Television (1994): 4,700,000 receivers (1 per 3.7 persons). Telephones (main lines; 1993): 1,574,900 (1 per 11.0 persons).

Education and health

Education (1992–93)

	schools	teachers	students	student/teacher ratio
Primary (age 6–12)	10,228	141,930	2,025,948	14.3
Secondary (age 13–18)	4,643[16]	89,171	1,033,521	11.6
Voc., teacher tr.	190[16]	3,804	39,840	10.5
Higher	72[16]	12,669	174,788	13.8

Educational attainment (1986). Percentage of population age 25 and over having: no formal schooling 31.8%; primary, secondary, or higher education 68.2%. *Literacy* (1995): percentage of population age 15 and over literate 62.8%; males literate 71.5%; females literate 50.2%.
Health (1991): physicians 25,543 (1 per 523 persons); hospital beds 40,923 (1 per 359 persons); infant mortality rate per 1,000 live births (1995) 48.9.
Food (1992): daily per capita caloric intake 2,735 (vegetable products 82%, animal products 18%); 113% of FAO recommended minimum requirement.

Military

Total active duty personnel (1995): 105,500 (army 66.4%, navy 12.8%, air force 20.8%). *Military expenditure as percentage of GDP* (1994): 11.2% (world 2.6%); per capita expenditure U.S.$1,109.

[1]The Consultative Council, which consists of 60 appointed members and a speaker, acts as an advisory and reviewing body only. [2]13 administrative regions created September 1993. [3]Preliminary 1992 census total 16,929,294; detail, n.a. [4]1985 estimate. [5]1992. [6]August. [7]Based on purchasing power parity. [8]In purchasers' value at current prices. [9]Finance includes real estate and business services. [10]Other includes import duties. [11]Detail does not add to total given because of rounding. [12]Urban middle-income households only. [13]Import figures are c.i.f. [14]Domestic and international operation of Saudi Arabian Airlines. [15]Circulation for 9 dailies only. [16]1990–91.

Senegal

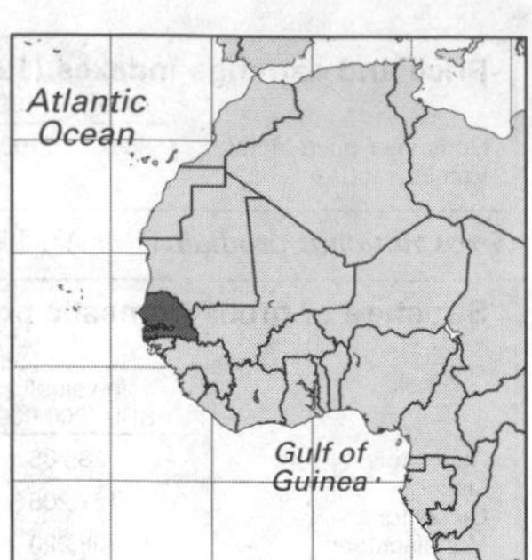

Official name: République du Sénégal (Republic of Senegal).
Form of government: multiparty republic with one legislative house (National Assembly [120]).
Chief of state: President.
Head of government: Prime Minister.
Capital: Dakar.
Official language: French.
Official religion: none.
Monetary unit: 1 CFA franc (CFAF) = 100 centimes; valuation (Oct. 6, 1995) 1 U.S.$ = CFAF 501.49; 1 £ = CFAF 792.78.

Area and population

		area		population
Regions	Capitals	sq mi	sq km	1994 estimate
Dakar	Dakar	212	550	1,869,000
Diourbel	Diourbel	1,683	4,359	750,000
Fatick	Fatick	3,064	7,935	569,000
Kaolack	Kaolack	6,181	16,010	948,000
Kolda	Kolda	8,112	21,011	689,000
Louga	Louga	11,270	29,188	525,000
Saint-Louis	Saint-Louis	17,034	44,117	749,000
Tambacounda	Tambacounda	23,012	59,602	449,000
Thiès	Thiès	2,549	6,601	1,115,000
Ziguinchor	Ziguinchor	2,834	7,339	467,000
TOTAL		75,951	196,712	8,127,000[1]

Demography

Population (1995): 8,312,000.
Density (1995): persons per sq mi 109.4, persons per sq km 42.3.
Urban-rural (1994): urban 41.0%; rural 59.0%.
Sex distribution (1995): male 50.05%; female 49.95%.
Age breakdown (1995): under 15, 44.6%; 15–29, 26.9%; 30–44, 15.5%; 45–59, 8.3%; 60 to 74, 3.9%; 75 and over, 0.8%.
Population projection: (2000) 9,495,000; (2010) 12,241,000.
Doubling time: 26 years.
Ethnic composition (1988): Wolof 43.7%; Peul- (Fulani-) Tukulor 23.2%; Serer 14.0%; Diola 5.5%; Malinke (Mandingo) 4.6%; other 9.0%.
Religious affiliation (1988): Sunnī Muslim 94.0%; Christian, predominantly Roman Catholic, 4.9%; traditional beliefs and other 1.1%.
Major cities (1992): Dakar 1,729,823; Thiès 201,350; Kaolack 179,894; Ziguinchor 148,831; Saint-Louis 125,717.

Vital statistics

Birth rate per 1,000 population (1990–95): 43.0 (world avg. 25.0).
Death rate per 1,000 population (1990–95): 16.0 (world avg. 9.3).
Natural increase rate per 1,000 population (1990–95): 27.0 (world avg. 15.7).
Total fertility rate (avg. births per childbearing woman; 1992–93): 6.0.
Marriage rate per 1,000 population: n.a.
Divorce rate per 1,000 population: n.a.
Life expectancy at birth (1992): male 48.3 years; female 50.3 years.
Major causes of death (percentage of officially confirmed deaths from infectious diseases only; 1988): malaria 44.8%; tetanus 17.8%; meningitis 15.3%; tuberculosis of respiratory system 10.4%.

National economy

Budget (1994). Revenue: CFAF 385,600,000,000 (current revenue 78.2%, of which import duties 32.2%, taxes on goods and services 17.9%, personal and corporate income taxes 15.3%, parafiscal petroleum charges 7.0%; aid, grants, and subsidies 21.8%). Expenditures: CFAF 424,800,000,000 (current expenditures 75.0%, of which wages and salaries 35.0%, debt service 16.8%; capital expenditures 23.6%, of which extrabudgetary 17.4%, budgetary 6.2%).
Production (metric tons except as noted). Agriculture, forestry, fishing (1994): sugarcane 856,000, peanuts (groundnuts) 678,000, millet 548,000, paddy rice 162,000, sorghum 132,000, corn (maize) 108,000, cassava 77,000, seed cotton 37,000; livestock (number of live animals) 4,600,000 sheep, 3,200,000 goats, 2,800,000 cattle, 329,000 pigs; roundwood (1993) 5,022,000 cu m; fish catch (1993) 377,676. Mining and quarrying (1993): calcium phosphate 1,663,100; cement 591,200; aluminum phosphate 32,800; salt 21,900. Manufacturing (1993): paint and varnish 4,229,000; cement 591,200; refined petroleum products 544,300; fertilizers 147,900; wheat flour 138,900; sugar 46,100; soap 35,700; canned fish 22,476; plastic footwear 507,500 pairs. Construction (authorized; 1993)[2]: residential 357,000 sq m; nonresidential 235,000 sq m. Energy production (consumption): electricity (kW-hr; 1992) 762,000,000 (762,000,000); coal, none (n.a.); crude petroleum (barrels; 1992) none (5,935,000); petroleum products (metric tons; 1992) 755,000 (799,000); natural gas, none (n.a.).
Population economically active (1992): total 2,620,000; activity rate of total population 34% (participation rates [1991]: ages 15–64, 63.8%; female 35.9%; unemployed 24.4%).

Price and earnings indexes (1990 = 100)

	1988	1989	1990	1991	1992	1993	1994
Consumer price index	99.2	99.7	100.0	98.2	98.1	97.6	129.1
Hourly earnings index[3]	91.3	95.6	100.0	100.0	100.0	...	...

Household income and expenditure[4]. Average household size (1988) 8.8; average annual income per household (1975) CFAF 1,105,800 (U.S.$5,160); sources of income (1975): wages and salaries 51.6%, remittances and gifts 17.5%, pensions, social security, and related benefits 12.5%, other 18.4%; expenditure (1979): food and tobacco 57.5%, housing, maintenance, and utilities 18.4%, clothing 11.9%, transport 5.4%, other 6.8%.
Public debt (external, outstanding; 1993): U.S.$3,011,000,000.
Gross national product (at current market prices; 1993): U.S.$5,867,000,000 (U.S.$740 per capita).

Structure of gross domestic product and labour force

	1994		1991	
	in value CFAF '000,000,000[5]	% of total value	labour force	% of labour force
Agriculture	332.6	21.8	1,789,467	65.3
Mining }	199.0	13.0	1,998	0.1
Manufacturing }			161,124	5.9
Public utilities	33.1	2.2	...	...
Construction	51.7	3.4	60,935	2.2
Transp. and commun.	145.7	9.5	58,081	2.1
Trade }	321.5	21.1	378,241	13.8
Finance }			4,623	0.2
Services }	443.2	29.0	...	...
Pub. admin., defense }			268,721	9.8
Other	—	—	16,286	0.6
TOTAL	1,526.6[1]	100.0	2,739,476[6]	100.0[6]

Tourism (1993): receipts from visitors U.S.$173,000,000; expenditures by nationals abroad U.S.$106,000,000.
Land use (1993): forested 54.3%; meadows and pastures 16.1%; agricultural and under permanent cultivation 12.2%; other 17.4%.

Foreign trade

Balance of trade (current prices)

	1987	1988	1989	1990	1991	1992
CFAF '000,000,000	−125.4	−145.5	−168.4	−150.3	−134.4	−152.8
% of total	25.6%	29.2%	27.6%	26.6%	25.4%	30.0%

Imports (1992): CFAF 330,900,000,000 (machinery and transportation equipment 20.2%, petroleum products 12.7%, rice 7.4%, dairy products 4.8%, pharmaceutical products 3.6%, paper and paper products 3.5%). *Major import sources* (1992): France 31.2%; Côte d'Ivoire 6.6%; United States 6.4%; Nigeria 6.3%; Italy 5.6%; Thailand 3.7%; Japan 3.5%; Spain 3.4%; Germany 3.4%; Belgium-Luxembourg 3.0%; The Netherlands 2.3%; Canada 2.2%.
Exports (1992): CFAF 178,100,000,000 (petroleum products 12.3%, canned fish 12.2%, phosphates 8.2%, fresh fish 7.5%, peanut oil 7.4%, shellfish 7.3%, cotton 4.1%). *Major export destinations* (1992): France 28.3%; India 14.2%; Mali 6.0%; Italy 5.4%; Iran 3.4%; Côte d'Ivoire 2.9%; The Netherlands 2.5%; Spain 2.3%; Guinea 2.2%; Japan 2.0%; Germany 1.9%.

Transport and communications

Transport. Railroads: (1993) route length 562 mi, 904 km; (1991) passenger-mi 108,000,000, passenger-km 174,000,000; short ton-mi cargo 418,000,000, metric ton-km cargo 610,000,000. Roads (1993): total length 8,873 mi, 14,280 km (paved 28%). Vehicles (1991): passenger cars 97,000; trucks and buses 40,000. Merchant marine (1992): vessels (100 gross tons and over) 183; total deadweight tonnage 27,473. Air transport (1993)[7]: passenger-mi 134,933,000, passenger-km 217,154,000; short ton-mi cargo 8,835,000, metric ton-km cargo 14,218,000; airports (1995) with scheduled flights 2.
Communications. Daily newspapers (1992): total number 1; total circulation 50,000; circulation per 1,000 population 6.5. Radio (1994): total number of receivers 850,000 (1 per 9.5 persons). Television (1994): total number of receivers 61,000 (1 per 133 persons). Telephones (main lines; 1993): 64,100 (1 per 123 persons).

Education and health

Education (1992–93)

	schools	teachers	students	student/ teacher ratio
Primary (age 6–12)	2,454	12,711	738,550	58.1
Secondary (age 13–18)	359	5,509	182,140	33.1
Vocational	19	182	7,301	40.1
Higher	18[8]	770[9]	23,001	19.3[9]

Educational attainment (1988). Percentage of population age 6–34 having: no formal schooling 62.6%; primary education 25.7%; secondary 8.4%; higher 0.8%; other 2.5%. *Literacy* (1988): percentage of total population age 15 and over literate 28.6%; males literate 38.8%; females literate 19.4%.
Health (1992): physicians 520 (1 per 14,817 persons); hospital beds 7,408 (1 per 1,040 persons); infant mortality rate per 1,000 live births (1990–95): 68.0.
Food (1992): daily per capita caloric intake 2,262 (vegetable products 91%, animal products 9%); 95% of FAO recommended minimum requirement.

Military

Total active duty personnel (1995): 13,350 (army 89.9%, navy 5.2%, air force 4.9%). *Military expenditure as percentage of GNP* (1993): 2.4% (world 3.3%); per capita expenditure U.S.$16.

[1]Detail does not add to total given because of rounding. [2]Capital region only. [3]January 1; index refers to the *S.M.I.G.* (*salaire minimum interprofessionnel garanti*), a form of minimum professional wage. [4]Traditional African households in Dakar. [5]At constant 1987 prices. [6]Includes 16,286 positions not adequately defined. [7]Air Afrique only. [8]1990–91. [9]1988.

Seychelles

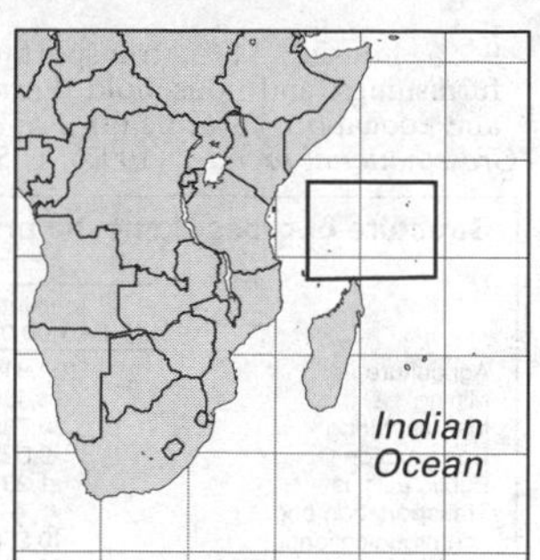

Official name: Repiblik Sesel (Creole); Republic of Seychelles (English); République des Seychelles (French).
Form of government: multiparty republic with one legislative house (National Assembly [33][1]).
Head of state and government: President.
Capital: Victoria.
Official languages: none[2].
Official religion: none.
Monetary unit: 1 Seychelles rupee (SR) = 100 cents; valuation (Oct. 6, 1995) 1 U.S.$ = SR 4.84; 1 £ = SR 7.65.

Area and population

Island Groups	Capital	area sq mi	area sq km	population 1987 census
Central (Granitic) group				
La Digue and satellites	—	6	15	1,926
Mahé and satellites	Victoria	61	158	61,183
Praslin and satellites	—	16	42	5,002
Silhouette	—	8	20	191
Other islands	—	2	4	0
Outer (Coralline) islands	—	83	214	296
TOTAL		176	455[3]	68,598

Demography

Population (1995): 75,000.
Density (1995): persons per sq mi 426.1, persons per sq km 164.8.
Urban-rural (1990): urban 59.3%; rural 40.7%.
Sex distribution (1993): male 49.69%; female 50.31%.
Age breakdown (1993): under 15, 31.5%; 15–29, 29.4%; 30–44, 19.4%; 45–59, 10.0%; 60–74, 6.9%; 75 and over, 2.8%.
Population projection: (2000) 81,000; (2010) 94,000.
Doubling time: 45 years.
Ethnic composition (1983): Seychellois Creole (mixture of Asian, African, and European) 89.1%; Indian 4.7%; Malagasy 3.1%; Chinese 1.6%; English 1.5%.
Religious affiliation (1987): Roman Catholic 88.6%; other Christian (mostly Anglican) 8.5%; Hindu 0.4%; other 2.5%.
Major city (1987): Victoria 24,325.

Vital statistics

Birth rate per 1,000 population (1994): 23.0 (world avg. 25.0); (1993) legitimate 21.6%; illegitimate 78.4%.
Death rate per 1,000 population (1994): 7.6 (world avg. 9.3).
Natural increase rate per 1,000 population (1994): 15.4 (world avg. 15.7).
Total fertility rate (avg. births per childbearing woman; 1993): 2.6.
Marriage rate per 1,000 population (1993): 11.3.
Divorce rate per 1,000 population (1993): 1.1.
Life expectancy at birth (1994): male 66.0 years; female 73.0 years.
Major causes of death per 100,000 population (1993): diseases of the circulatory system 239.4, of which cerebrovascular disease 72.0; malignant neoplasms (cancers) 141.2; diseases of the respiratory system 87.2, of which pneumonia 23.5; infectious and parasitic diseases 49.8; diseases of the digestive system 47.1; accidents and adverse effects 45.7.

National economy

Budget (1995). Revenue: SR 1,170,100,000 (customs taxes and duties 42.4%, transfers from Social Security Fund 16.7%, business taxes 10.9%, administrative fees 5.9%, dividends and interest 4.8%, fees and fines 4.4%, grants 1.9%). Expenditures: SR 1,148,000,000 (debt service 15.2%, education 11.9%, capital projects 10.9%, health 8.2%, social security 6.5%, tourism and transport 6.1%, defense 4.8%).
Tourism (1994): receipts from visitors SR 510,000,000; expenditures by nationals abroad U.S.$16,000,000[4].
Land use (1993): forested 11.1%; agricultural and under permanent cultivation 15.6%; built-on, wasteland, and other 73.3%.
Gross national product (at current market prices; 1993): U.S.$444,000,000 (U.S.$6,370 per capita).

Structure of gross domestic product and labour force

	1993 in value SR '000,000	1993 % of total value	1994 labour force[5]	1994 % of labour force
Agriculture	89.5	3.7	1,959	7.8
Mining, manufacturing, and construction	440.3	18.2	4,711	18.7
Tourism	326.6	13.5	4,721	18.7
Transportation and communications	556.4	23.0	3,793	15.1
Finance	162.1	6.7		
Public admin., defense	343.5	14.2	10,011	39.7
Other	500.8	20.7		
TOTAL	2,419.2	100.0	25,195	100.0

Production (metric tons except as noted). Agriculture, forestry, fishing (1993): coconuts 6,000, bananas 2,000, copra 1,000, cinnamon 677, tea 246; livestock (number of live animals) 18,000 pigs, 5,000 goats, 2,000 cattle, 185,200[6] chickens; fish catch (1993) 5,447, of which (1989) jack 36.9%, snapper 20.8%, mackerel 6.7%, kawakawa 5.3%. Mining and quarrying (1990): guano 6,000. Manufacturing (1993): canned tuna 4,531; soft drinks 70,450 hectolitres; beer and stout 65,230 hectolitres; cigarettes 65,000,000 units. Energy production (consumption): electricity (kW-hr; 1993) 117,600,000 (117,600,000); coal, none (n.a.); crude petroleum, none (n.a.); petroleum products (metric tons; 1992) none (49,000); natural gas, none (n.a.).
Population economically active (1993): total 25,238; activity rate of total population 38.9% (participation rates: ages 15–64 [1989] 74.3%; female [1989] 42.5%; unemployed 11.5%).

Price and earnings indexes (1990 = 100)

	1988	1989	1990	1991	1992	1993	1994
Consumer price index	94.8	96.3	100.0	102.0	105.3	106.7	108.7
Monthly earnings index	...	...	100.0	103.8	123.5	126.0	...

Public debt (external, outstanding; 1993): U.S.$138,100,000.
Household income and expenditure. Average household size (1987) 4.5; average annual income per household (1978) SR 18,480 (U.S.$2,658); sources of income: wages and salaries 77.2%, self-employment 3.8%, transfer payments 3.2%; expenditure (1991–92): food and beverages 47.6%, housing 15.1%, clothing and footwear 8.6%, transportation 8.0%, energy and water 7.4%, recreation 6.7%, household and personal goods 6.6%.

Foreign trade

Balance of trade (current prices)

	1989	1990	1991	1992	1993	1994
SR '000,000	−736.6	−692.3	−652.2	−735.2	−969.8	−780.2
% of total	65.6%	53.4%	55.8%	59.9%	64.7%	59.8%

Imports (1994): SR 1,044,000,000 (manufactured goods 31.1%, of which metal manufactures 9.0%[7], paper products 2.0%[7]; machinery and transport equipment 23.2%, of which vehicles 6.8%, communications equipment 4.0%[7]; food, beverages, and tobacco 20.3%; mineral fuels, lubricants, and related materials 15.6%, of which petroleum products 14.0%[7]; chemicals 6.9%). *Major import sources* (1983): United Kingdom 13.3%; Yemen 13.1%; Singapore 13.1%; South Africa 12.8%; United States 7.7%; France 6.2%; Japan 5.8%; Germany 3.2%; Italy 2.6%; Thailand 2.1%; India 2.1%.
Exports (1994): SR 259,600,000[8] (petroleum products 44.6%[9]; canned tuna 32.4%; other fish 5.2%; buttons 2.8%; cinnamon bark 1.0%; frozen prawns 0.7%; copra 0.1%). *Major export destinations* (1993)[10]: United Kingdom 15.9%; France 4.2%; Réunion 2.6%.

Transport and communications

Transport. Railroads: none. Roads (1994): total length 201 mi, 323 km (paved 72%). Vehicles (1993): passenger cars 5,000; trucks and buses 2,000. Merchant marine (1992): vessels (100 gross tons and over) 9; total deadweight tonnage 3,337. Air transport (1994): passenger arrivals 118,000, passenger departures 118,000; metric ton cargo unloaded 2,876, metric ton cargo loaded 698; airports (1995) with scheduled flights 2.
Communications. Daily newspapers (1992): total number 1; total circulation 3,000; circulation per 1,000 population 44. Radio (1994): total number of receivers 40,000 (1 per 1.8 persons). Television (1994): total number of receivers 13,000 (1 per 5.7 persons). Telephones (main lines; 1993): 11,300 (1 per 6.2 persons).

Education and health

Education (1995)

	schools[11]	teachers	students	student/teacher ratio
Primary (age 6–15)	24	569	9,691	17.0
Secondary (age 16–18)	20	429	6,162	14.4
Voc., teacher tr.	1	155	1,429	9.2

Educational attainment (1987). Percentage of population age 12 and over having: no formal schooling 7.8%; primary education 51.5%; some secondary 12.2%; complete secondary 13.4%; vocational 9.9%; postsecondary 3.1%; unspecified 2.1%. *Literacy* (1987): total population age 15 and over literate 37,984 (84.2%); males literate 18,427 (82.9%); females literate 19,557 (85.7%).
Health (1994): physicians 72 (1 per 997 persons); hospital beds 416 (1 per 173 persons); infant mortality rate per 1,000 live births 8.8.
Food (1992): daily per capita caloric intake 2,287 (vegetable products 85%, animal products 15%); 98% of FAO recommended minimum requirement.

Military

Total active duty personnel (1994): 800[12]. *Military expenditure as percentage of GNP* (1989): 4.2% (world 4.9%); per capita expenditure U.S.$206[13].

[1]Includes 11 nonelective seats (one-half the elected number), which are appointive, allocated according to each party's share of the popular vote. [2]Creole, English, and French are all national languages per 1993 constitution. [3]Detail does not add to total given because of rounding. [4]1992. [5]Excludes self-employed and domestic workers. [6]1986. [7]1993. [8]Includes SR 136,900,000 of reexports. [9]Items reexported. [10]Domestic export only. [11]1994. [12]All services form part of the army. [13]At prices of 1987.

Sierra Leone

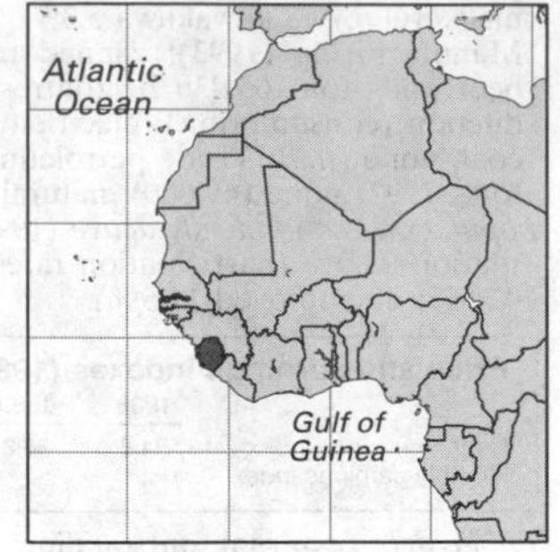

Official name: Republic of Sierra Leone.
Form of government: military regime.
Head of state and government: Chairman, Supreme Council of State.
Capital: Freetown.
Official language: English.
Official religion: none.
Monetary unit: 1 leone (Le) = 100 cents; valuation (Oct. 6, 1995) 1 U.S.$ = Le 756; 1 £ = Le 1,195.

Area and population

Provinces Districts	Capitals	area sq mi	 sq km	population 1985 census[1]
Eastern Province	Kenema	6,005	15,553	960,551
Kailahun	Kailahun	1,490	3,859	233,839
Kenema	Kenema	2,337	6,053	337,055
Kono	Sefadu	2,178	5,641	389,657
Northern Province	Makeni	13,875	35,936	1,259,641
Bombali	Makeni	3,083	7,985	317,729
Kambia	Kambia	1,200	3,108	186,231
Koinaduga	Kabala	4,680	12,121	183,286
Port Loko	Port Loko	2,208	5,719	329,344
Tonkolili	Magburaka	2,704	7,003	243,051
Southern Province	Bo	7,604	19,694	741,377
Bo	Bo	2,015	5,219	268,671
Bonthe (incl. Sherbro)	Bonthe	1,339	3,468	105,007
Moyamba	Moyamba	2,665	6,902	250,514
Pujehun	Pujehun	1,585	4,105	117,185
Western Area[2]	Freetown	215	557	554,243
TOTAL		27,699	71,740	3,515,812

Demography

Population (1995): 4,509,000.
Density (1995): persons per sq mi 162.8, persons per sq km 62.8.
Urban-rural (1993): urban 34.6%; rural 65.4%.
Sex distribution (1995): male 49.10%; female 50.90%.
Age breakdown (1985): under 15, 41.4%; 15–29, 26.1%; 30–44, 17.1%; 45–59, 10.3%; 60–74, 4.5%; 75 and over, 0.6%.
Population projection: (2000) 5,069,000; (2010) 6,366,000.
Doubling time: 26 years.
Ethnic composition (1983): Mende 34.6%; Temne 31.7%; Limba 8.4%; Kono 5.2%; Bullom-Sherbro 3.7%; Fulani 3.7%; Kuranko 3.5%; Yalunka 3.5%; Kissi 2.3%; other 3.4%.
Religious affiliation (1993): Sunnī Muslim 60.0%; traditional beliefs 30.0%; Christian 10.0%[3].
Major cities (1985): Freetown 469,776; Koidu–New Sembehun 80,000; Bo 26,000; Kenema 13,000; Makeni 12,000.

Vital statistics

Birth rate per 1,000 population (1990–95): 48.1 (world avg. 25.0); legitimate, n.a.; illegitimate, n.a.
Death rate per 1,000 population (1990–95): 21.6 (world avg. 9.3).
Natural increase rate per 1,000 population (1990–95): 26.5 (world avg. 15.7).
Total fertility rate (avg. births per childbearing woman; 1990–95): 6.5.
Marriage rate per 1,000 population: n.a.
Divorce rate per 1,000 population: n.a.
Life expectancy at birth (1990–95): male 41.4 years; female 44.6 years.
Major causes of death per 100,000 population: n.a.; however, the major diseases are malaria, tuberculosis, leprosy, whooping cough, measles, tetanus, and diarrhea.

National economy

Budget (1994–95). Revenue: Le 61,869,000,000 (customs duties 41.6%, excise taxes 25.0%, nontax revenue 12.3%, company income tax 8.0%, personal income tax 7.6%). Expenditures: Le 102,279,000,000 (1992–93; debt service 19.8%, education 12.6%, defense 6.9%, health 4.5%, social security 2.8%).
Public debt (external, outstanding; 1994): U.S.$909,000,000.
Tourism (1993): receipts from visitors U.S.$18,000,000; expenditures by nationals abroad U.S.$4,000,000.
Production (metric tons except as noted). Agriculture, forestry, fishing (1994): rice 486,300, cassava 105,800, sugarcane 70,000, pulses 40,000, palm kernels 35,000, plantains 28,000, millet 28,000, sorghum 25,000, coffee 25,000, peanuts (groundnuts) 23,500, tomatoes 22,000, sweet potatoes 14,000, corn (maize) 11,000, cacao beans 10,000; livestock (number of live animals) 362,000 cattle, 302,000 sheep, 168,000 goats, 51,000 pigs, 6,000,000 chickens; roundwood (1993) 3,308,000 cu m; fish catch 65,089. Mining and quarrying (1994–95): bauxite 422,000; rutile and ilmenite (titanium ores) 97,000; diamonds 191,000 carats; gold 3,102 oz. Manufacturing (1994): salt 223,000; beer and stout 33,160 hectolitres; soft drinks 27,800 hectolitres; paint 3,400 hectolitres; cigarettes 457,000,000 units. Construction (value added in Le; 1992–93): 4,972,100,000. Energy production (consumption): electricity (kW-hr; 1992) 230,000,000 (230,000,000); coal, none (n.a.); crude petroleum (barrels; 1992) none (1,554,000); petroleum products (metric tons; 1992) 162,000 (122,000); natural gas, none (n.a.).
Household income and expenditure. Average household size (1985) 6.6; average annual income per household (1984): U.S.$320; sources of income (1984): self-employment 61.6%, wages and salaries 27.9%, other 10.5%; expenditure (1989): food, beverages, and tobacco 66.2%, clothing and footwear 9.9%, housing 5.8%, transportation and communications 4.4%, furniture, furnishings, and household durable goods 4.0%, recreation, entertainment, and education 3.8%, health 3.5%.
Gross national product (1993): U.S.$625,500,000 (U.S.$140 per capita).

Structure of gross domestic product and labour force

	1993–94 in value Le '000,000	 % of total value	1991 labour force	 % of labour force
Agriculture	194,615	41.0	945,000	61.7
Mining	33,489	7.0		
Manufacturing	50,736	10.7	275,000	18.0
Construction	9,023	1.9		
Public utilities	1,297	0.3		
Transportation and communications	40,258	8.5		
Trade	75,406	15.9		
Finance	17,988	3.8	312,000	20.3
Pub. admin., defense	17,884	3.8		
Services	9,769	2.0		
Other	24,020[4]	5.1[4]		
TOTAL	474,485	100.0	1,532,000	100.0

Population economically active (1991): total 1,532,000; activity rate of total population 35.9% (participation rates: ages 10–64, 53.3%; female 32.4%; unemployed [registered; 1986] 9.0%).

Price index (1990 = 100)

	1988	1989	1990	1991	1992	1993	1994
Consumer price index	29.1	47.4	100.0	202.7	335.4	409.9	509.1

Land use (1993): forested 28.5%; meadows and pastures 30.7%; agricultural and under permanent cultivation 7.5%; other 33.3%.

Foreign trade

Balance of trade (current prices)

	1989	1990	1991	1992	1993	1994
Le '000,000	−1,327.9	+1,475.9	+3,903.8	+14,449.7	−7,692.0	−9,511
% of total	7.4%	3.6%	4.6%	10.9%	5.4%	6.5%

Imports (1994–95): Le 84,030,200,000 (food and live animals 42.7%, machinery and transport equipment 26.7%, fuels and lubricants 17.4%, chemicals 7.8%, beverages and tobacco 3.2%, crude minerals 2.2%). *Major import sources* (1990): Nigeria 29.0%; United Kingdom 14.4%; Germany 10.1%; United States 8.2%; The Netherlands 5.6%.
Exports (1994–95): Le 45,216,100,000 (rutile and ilmenite [titanium ores] 36.2%, diamonds 26.6%, bauxite 12.6%, coffee 6.1%, cocoa 3.5%, reexports 2.7%). *Major export destinations* (1993): United States 32.2%; United Kingdom 20.2%; Germany 11.0%; The Netherlands 3.4%.

Transport and communications

Transport. Railroads (1990): length 52 mi, 84 km. Roads (1992): total length 7,254 mi, 11,674 km (paved 11%). Vehicles (1993): passenger cars 32,415; trucks and buses 11,902. Merchant marine (1992): vessels (100 gross tons and over) 62; total deadweight tonnage 18,384. Air transport (1985)[5]: passenger-mi 68,290,000, passenger-km 109,903,000; short ton-mi cargo 1,400,000, metric ton-km cargo 2,044,000; airports (1995) with scheduled flights 1.
Communications. Daily newspapers (1993): total number 1; total circulation 10,000; circulation per 1,000 population 2.3. Radio (1994): 1,000,000 receivers (1 per 4.6 persons). Television (1994): 25,000 receivers (1 per 176 persons). Telephones (main lines; 1993): 14,500 (1 per 296 persons).

Education and health

Education (1991–92)

	schools	teachers	students	student/ teacher ratio
Primary (age 5–11)	1,792	10,051	315,146	31.4
Secondary (age 12–18)	217	3,924	72,516	18.5
Voc., teacher tr.	30	750	6,929	9.2
Higher[6]	2	257	2,571	10.0

Educational attainment (1985). Percentage of population age 5 and over having: no formal schooling 64.1%; primary education 18.7%; secondary 9.7%; higher 1.5%. *Literacy* (1990): total population age 15 and over literate 477,600 (20.7%); males literate 343,800 (30.7%); females literate 133,800 (11.3%).
Health: physicians (1992) 404 (1 per 10,832 persons); hospital beds (1988) 4,025 (1 per 980 persons); infant mortality rate per 1,000 live births (1990–95) 166.
Food (1992): daily per capita caloric intake 1,694 (vegetable products 96%, animal products 4%); 74% of FAO recommended minimum requirement.

Military

Total active duty personnel (1995): 6,200 (army 96.8%, navy 3.2%, air force, none). *Military expenditure as percentage of GNP* (1993): 2.2% (world 3.3%); per capita expenditure U.S.$3.

[1]Preliminary figures exclude adjustment for underenumeration; adjusted total is 3,760,000. [2]Not officially a province; the administration of the Western Area is split among Greater Freetown (the city and its suburbs) and other administrative bodies. [3]Christian (1980) 9.1%, of which Protestant 4.7%, Roman Catholic 2.2%, Anglican 1.2%. [4]Import duties less imputed bank service charges. [5]International flights only. [6]1990–91.

Singapore

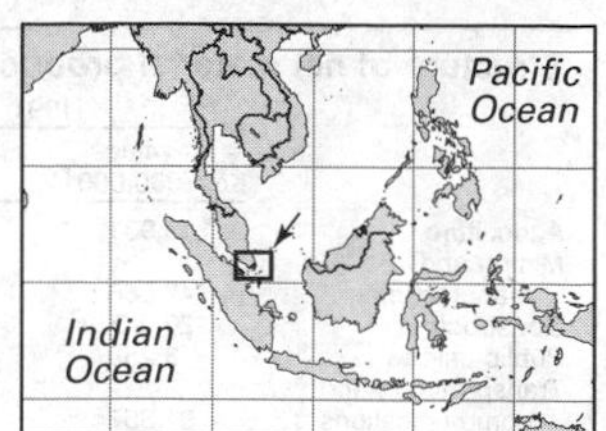

Official name: Hsin-chia-p'o Kung-ho-kuo (Mandarin Chinese); Republik Singapura (Malay); Singapore Kudiyarasu (Tamil); Republic of Singapore (English).
Form of government: unitary multiparty republic with one legislative house (Parliament [87[1]]).
Chief of state: President.
Head of government: Prime Minister.
Capital: Singapore.
Official languages: Chinese; Malay; Tamil; English.
Official religion: none.
Monetary unit: 1 Singapore dollar (S$) = 100 cents; valuation (Oct. 6, 1995) 1 U.S.$ = S$1.43; 1 £ = S$2.26.

Population (1990 census)

Census division[2]	population	Census division[2]	population	Census division[2]	population
Alexandra	27,245	Henderson	18,445	Nee Soon East	58,651
Aljunied	51,669	Hong Kah Central	48,379	Nee Soon South	49,771
Ang Mo Kio	35,814	Hong Kah North	33,265	Pasir Panjang	35,824
Ayer Rajah	44,977	Hong Kah South	37,900	Paya Lebar	41,903
Bedok	22,032	Hougang	36,774	Potong Pasir	32,992
Boon Lay	39,249	Jalan Besar	28,298	Punggol	68,270
Boon Teck	22,652	Jalan Kayu	34,907	Queenstown	19,676
Braddell Heights	47,738	Joo Chiat	35,777	Radin Mas	35,730
Brickworks	10,593	Jurong	74,696	Sembawang	28,039
Bukit Batok	44,918	Kaki Bukit	32,782	Serangoon Gardens	44,702
Bukit Gombak	46,149	Kallang	34,178	Siglap	36,022
Bukit Merah	18,666	Kampong Chai Chee	33,928	Tampines East	41,474
Bukit Panjang	95,827	Kampong Glam	29,481	Tampines North	73,634
Bukit Timah	47,056	Kampong Kembangan	33,510	Tampines West	38,833
Buona Vista	23,873	Kampong Ubi	40,682	Tanah Merah	32,314
Cairnhill	48,445	Kebun Baru	36,878	Tanglin	13,644
Changi	60,003	Kim Keat	20,530	Tanjong Pagar	29,217
Changkat	41,995	Kim Seng	23,683	Teck Ghee	26,622
Cheng San	27,821	Kolam Ayer	22,420	Telok Blangah	29,157
Chong Boon	32,174	Kreta Ayer	29,631	Thomson	71,345
Chong Pang	38,613	Kuo Chuan	26,968	Tiong Bahru	27,468
Chua Chu Kang	43,465	Leng Kee	28,886	Toa Payoh	22,811
Clementi	37,635	Macpherson	23,764	Ulu Pandan	42,923
Eunos	52,976	Marine Parade	31,003	West Coast	46,062
Fengshan	27,285	Moulmein	33,872	Whampoa	18,285
Geylang Serai	36,800	Mountbatten	23,891	Yio Chu Kang	28,589
Geylang West	34,560	Nee Soon Central	47,032	Yuhua	32,733
				TOTAL	3,016,379

Demography

Area: 247.5 sq mi, 641.0 sq km.
Population (1995)[3]: 2,989,000.
Density (1995): persons per sq mi 12,077, persons per sq km 4,663.
Urban-rural: urban 100.0%.
Sex distribution (1994): male 50.38%; female 49.62%.
Age breakdown (1994): under 15, 23.0%; 15–29, 24.0%; 30–44, 28.8%; 45–59, 14.4%; 60–74, 7.3%; 75 and over, 2.5%.
Population projection: (2000) 3,317,000; (2010) 4,072,000.
Doubling time: 60 years.
Ethnic composition (1994): Chinese 77.5%; Malay 14.2%; Indian[4] 7.1%; other 1.2%.
Religious affiliation (1991): Buddhist, Taoist, and other traditional beliefs 53.9%; Muslim 15.4%; Christian 12.6%; Hindu 3.6%; nonreligious 14.5%.
Major cities: Singapore has no separately defined cities within its borders.

Vital statistics

Birth rate per 1,000 population (1994): 16.4 (world avg. 25.0).
Death rate per 1,000 population (1994): 4.7 (world avg. 9.3).
Natural increase rate per 1,000 population (1994): 11.7 (world avg. 15.7).
Total fertility rate (avg. births per childbearing woman; 1994): 1.8.
Marriage rate per 1,000 population (1994): 8.4.
Divorce rate per 1,000 population (1993): 1.4.
Life expectancy at birth (1994): male 74.4 years; female 78.5 years.
Major causes of death per 100,000 population (1993): malignant neoplasms 122.3; cardiovascular diseases 120.7; diseases of the respiratory system 87.6; cerebrovascular diseases 57.3; accidents, poisoning, and violence 21.9.

National economy

Budget (1994). Revenue: S$23,280,200,000 (income tax 36.9%, nontax revenue 15.9%, motor vehicle taxes 8.4%, assets taxes 7.5%, customs and excise duties 6.7%). Expenditures: S$14,118,100,000 (security 34.7%, education 22.5%, general services 7.3%, health 6.6%, communications 6.2%, national development 5.1%).
Tourism (1993): receipts U.S.$5,793,000,000; expenditures U.S.$3,022,000,000.
Production (metric tons except as noted). Agriculture, forestry, fishing (1993): vegetables 4,800, fruits 17; livestock (number of live animals) 1,360,000 chickens, 320,000 ducks; fish catch (1994) 11,280. Mining and quarrying (value added in S$; 1993): granite 50,200,000. Manufacturing (value added in S$; 1993): electronic products 11,566,700,000; transport equipment 2,039,800,000; petroleum products 1,986,200,000; metal products 1,806,900,000; chemical products 1,506,300,000; nonelectrical machinery 1,422,300,000. Construction (1993): residential 3,978,500 sq m; nonresidential 2,873,500 sq m. Energy production (consumption): electricity (kW-hr; 1992) 17,543,000,000 (17,543,000,000); crude petroleum (barrels; 1992) none (354,142,000); petroleum products (metric tons; 1992) 42,070,000 (16,386,000).
Public debt (external, outstanding; 1993): U.S.$11,600,000.
Household income and expenditure. Average household size (1984) 3.9; income per household (1987–88) S$26,560 (U.S.$12,900); sources of income (1987–88): wages 81.2%, self-employment 16.8%, transfer payments and other 2.0%; expenditure (1991): food 18.7%, recreation and education 16.0%, transportation and communications 13.8%, rent and utilities 9.5%, furniture and household equipment 8.9%, clothing and footwear 7.3%, health 4.5%.
Gross national product (1993): U.S.$55,372,000,000 (U.S.$19,310 per capita).

Structure of gross domestic product and labour force

	1994			
	in value S$'000,000[5]	% of total value	labour force[6]	% of labour force[6]
Agriculture	167.3	0.2	...	...
Quarrying	38.9	0.1	...	...
Manufacturing	22,234.8	28.2	422,500	25.6
Construction	5,604.5	7.1	108,800	6.6
Public utilities	1,582.4	2.0	...	...
Transp. and commun.	11,443.8	14.5	174,700	10.6
Trade	13,886.1	17.6	376,900	22.9
Finance	20,935.9	26.6	198,600	12.0
Services	7,741.5	9.8	353,600	21.4
Other	−4,869.8[7]	−6.1[7]	14,100[8]	0.9[8]
TOTAL	78,765.4	100.0	1,649,200	100.0

Population economically active (1993): total 1,635,700; activity rate of total population 56.9% (participation rates: ages 15 and over, 73.9%; female 40.2%; unemployed 2.7%).

Price and earnings indexes (1990 = 100)

	1988	1989	1990	1991	1992	1993	1994
Consumer price index	94.4	96.7	100.0	103.4	105.8	108.3	112.2
Monthly earnings index	83.3	91.5	100.0	109.3	117.4	125.5	...

Land use (1993): forested 4.5%; agricultural 1.1%; built up 49.3%; other 45.1%.

Foreign trade[9]

Balance of trade (current prices)

	1989	1990	1991	1992	1993	1994
S$'000,000	−4,143	−8,559	−5,770	−7,490	−10,338	−216
% of total	2.3%	4.3%	2.7%	3.5%	4.1%	0.1%

Imports (1994): S$156,395,800,000 (office machines 9.7%, telecommunications apparatus 7.2%, crude petroleum 5.7%, electric power machinery 3.9%, petroleum products 3.1%, scientific instruments 3.1%, musical instruments 2.8%). *Major import sources:* Japan 22.0%; Malaysia 16.4%; United States 15.3%; Thailand 4.8%; Taiwan 3.8%; Saudi Arabia 3.6%; Hong Kong 3.4%.
Exports (1994): S$147,327,200,000 (office machines 23.3%, telecommunications apparatus 10.4%, petroleum products 7.7%, optical instruments 2.2%, electrical circuit apparatus 2.1%, clothing 1.6%, industrial machinery 1.5%). *Major export destinations:* Malaysia 19.7%; U.S. 18.8%; Hong Kong 8.7%; Japan 7.0%; Thailand 5.6%; Taiwan 4.0%; Germany 3.5%; U.K. 2.7%.

Transport and communications

Transport. Railroads (1994): length 67 km. Roads (1994): total length 2,989 km (paved 97%). Vehicles (1994): passenger cars 340,647; trucks and buses 134,042. Merchant marine (1992): vessels (100 gross tons and over) 946, total deadweight tonnage 14,929,172. Air transport (1994): passenger-km 44,947,000,000; metric ton-km cargo 3,291,200,000; airports (1995) 1.
Communications. Daily newspapers (1993): total number 8; total circulation 1,004,800; circulation per 1,000 population 350. Radio (1994): 822,000 receivers (1 per 3.6 persons). Television (1994): 650,000 receivers (1 per 4.5 persons). Telephones (main lines; 1993): 1,245,000 (1 per 2.3 persons).

Education and health

Education (1993)

	schools	teachers	students	student/ teacher ratio
Primary (age 6–11)	193	10,711	261,534	24.4
Secondary (age 12–18)	162	9,168	180,729	19.7
Voc., teacher tr.	31	2,972	44,050	14.8
Higher	7	6,295	73,650	11.7

Educational attainment (1990). Percentage of population age 25 and over having: no schooling 64.0%; primary education 31.3%; postsecondary 4.7%.
Literacy (1990): total population age 10 and over literate 90.7%; males literate 95.7%; females literate 85.6%.
Health (1993): physicians 4,146 (1 per 693 persons); hospital beds 10,469 (1 per 275 persons); infant mortality rate per 1,000 live births (1994) 4.3.
Food (1988–90): daily per capita caloric intake 3,121 (vegetable products 76%, animal products 24%); 136% of FAO recommended minimum requirement.

Military

Total active duty personnel (1994): 54,000 (army 83.3%, navy 5.6%, air force 11.1%). *Military expenditure as percentage of GNP* (1993): 4.8% (world 3.3%); per capita expenditure U.S.$940.

[1]Includes 6 nonelected members. [2]The census divisions have no administrative function. [3]De jure population. [4]Includes Sri Lankan. [5]At prices of 1985. [6]Employed only. [7]Imputed bank service charges. [8]Includes agriculture, quarrying, public utilities, and activities not adequately defined. [9]Import figures are f.o.b. in balance of trade and c.i.f. for commodities and trading partners.

Slovakia

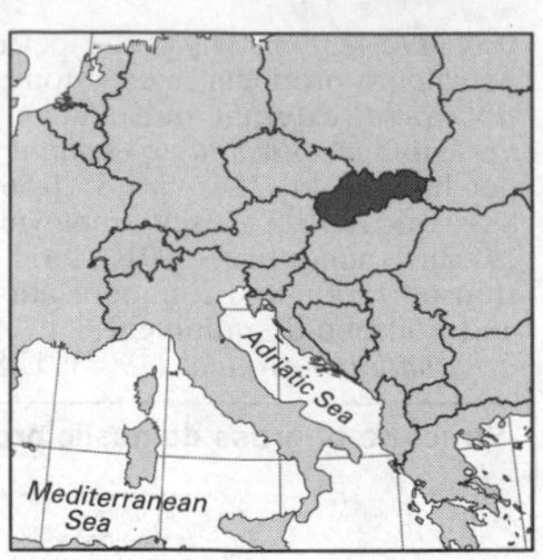

Official name: Slovenská Republika (Slovak Republic).
Form of government: unitary multiparty republic with one legislative house (National Council [150]).
Chief of state: President.
Head of government: Prime Minister.
Capital: Bratislava.
Official language: Slovak.
Official religion: none.
Monetary unit: 1 Slovak koruna[1] (Sk) = 100 halura; valuation (Oct. 6, 1995) 1 U.S.$ = Sk 29.60; 1 £ = Sk 46.80.

Area and population

		area		population
Electoral Regions[3]	**Capitals**	sq mi	sq km	1994[2] estimate
Stredné Slovensko	Banská Bystrica	6,943	17,982	1,630,833
Východné Slovensko	Košice	6,253	16,193	1,534,351
Zapadné Slovensko	Bratislava	5,595	14,492	1,722,486
Capital city				
Bratislava	—	142	368	448,785
TOTAL		18,933	49,036	5,336,455

Demography

Population (1995): 5,355,000.
Density (1995): persons per sq mi 282.8, persons per sq km 109.2.
Urban-rural (1991): urban 56.8%; rural 43.2%.
Sex distribution (1993): male 48.81%; female 51.19%.
Age breakdown (1993): under 15, 24.1%; 15–29, 23.1%; 30–44, 23.0%; 45–59, 14.8%; 60–74, 11.4%; 75 and over, 3.6%.
Population projection: (2000) 5,412,000; (2010) 5,529,000.
Doubling time: not applicable; population growth is negligible.
Ethnic composition (1994[2]): Slovak 85.7%; Hungarian 10.7%; Gypsy 1.6%; Czech 1.1%; Ruthenian 0.3%; Ukrainian 0.3%; German 0.1%; other 0.3%.
Religious affiliation (1991): Roman Catholic 60.3%; nonreligious and atheist 9.7%; Protestant 7.9%, of which Slovak Evangelical 6.2%, Reformed Christian 1.6%; Greek Catholic 3.4%; Eastern Orthodox 0.7%; other 18.0%.
Major cities (1994[2]): Bratislava 448,785; Košice 238,886; Prešov 90,963; Nitra 86,679; Žilina 85,686; Banská Bystrica 84,575.

Vital statistics

Birth rate per 1,000 population (1993): 14.1 (world avg. 25.0); legitimate 90.2%; illegitimate 9.8%.
Death rate per 1,000 population (1993): 10.1 (world avg. 9.3).
Natural increase rate per 1,000 population (1993): 4.0 (world avg. 15.7).
Total fertility rate (avg. births per childbearing woman; 1992): 1.9.
Marriage rate per 1,000 population (1993): 6.4.
Divorce rate per 1,000 population (1993): 1.5.
Life expectancy at birth (1992): male 66.6 years; female 75.4 years.
Major causes of death per 100,000 population (1992): diseases of the circulatory system 521.0; malignant neoplasms (cancers) 200.0; diseases of the respiratory system 77.0; accidents, poisoning, and violence 76.0; diseases of the digestive system 52.0; endocrine and metabolic disorders 19.0.

National economy

Budget (1992). Revenue: Kčs 115,876,000,000[1] (receipts from enterprises 80.6%; taxes 17.2%). Expenditures: Kčs 124,809,000,000[1] (education, health, social welfare, and culture 71.9%; defense 3.5%).
Public debt (external, outstanding; 1993): U.S.$2,059,000,000.
Production (metric tons except as noted). Agriculture, forestry, fishing (1994): cereals 3,730,000 (of which wheat 2,145,000, barley 874,000, corn [maize] 521,000, rye 96,000), sugar beets 1,110,000, potatoes 455,000; livestock (number of live animals) 2,179,000 pigs, 916,000 cattle, 397,000 sheep, 12,000 horses, 12,000,000 poultry; roundwood (1993) 5,250,000 cu m; fish catch (1993) 2,773. Mining and quarrying (1993): iron ore 930,000; lead-zinc ore 320,000; copper ore 290,000. Manufacturing (1993): crude steel 3,922,000; pig iron 3,205,000; cement 2,656,000; flour 419,000; plastic and resins 365,800; nitrogenous fertilizers 149,800; cotton yarn 14,300; beer 3,697,000 hectolitres; refrigerators and freezers 482,102 units; metal-working machines 2,595 units. Construction (1991): residential 1,147,000 sq m. Energy production (consumption): electricity (kW-hr; 1993) 23,811,000,000 (25,898,000,000); coal (metric tons; 1993) 3,547,000 (14,390,000); crude petroleum (barrels; 1993) 491,110 (32,853,000); petroleum products (metric tons; 1993) 3,603,000 (2,323,000); natural gas (cu m; 1993) 211,858,000 (5,037,986,000).
Population economically active (1993): total 2,548,733; activity rate of total population 47.9% (participation rates [1992]: ages 15–64, 74.5%; female 42.8%; unemployed [1995] 15.2%).

Price and earnings indexes (1990 = 100)

	1988	1989	1990	1991	1992	1993	1994
Consumer price index[4]	89.2	90.5	100.0	156.1	171.7	218.5	247.7
Annual earnings index	93.4	95.8	100.0	115.0	136.5	161.1	190.8

Gross national product (at current market prices; 1993): U.S.$10,156,000,000 (U.S.$1,900 per capita).

Structure of net material product and labour force

	1991		1993	
	in value Kčs '000,000[1]	% of total value	labour force	% of labour force
Agriculture	15,931	5.9	259,000	10.2
Mining and manufacturing	147,566	54.6	581,000	22.8
Construction	20,747	7.7	133,000	5.2
Public utilities	3,259	1.2	61,000	2.4
Transportation and communications	21,357	7.9	187,000	7.3
Trade	23,445	8.7	284,000	11.1
Finance	5,102	1.9	188,000	7.4
Pub. admin., defense	7,305	2.7 }	422,000	16.6
Services	25,377	9.4 }		
Other	—	—	433,733	17.0
TOTAL	270,089	100.0	2,548,733	100.0

Land use (1993): forested 40.6%; meadows and pastures 17.0%; agricultural and under permanent cultivation 32.9%; other 9.5%.
Household income and expenditure. Average household size (1991) 3.0; income per household (1991) Kčs 105,227[1, 5] (U.S.$3,595[5]); sources of income (1992): wages and salaries 71.8%, transfer payments 16.3%, other 11.9%; expenditure (1992): food and beverages 26.8%, taxes 14.0%, clothing and footwear 8.9%, housing 7.6%, household durable goods 3.9%, other 42.7%.
Tourism (1993): receipts U.S.$390,000,000; expenditures U.S.$262,000,000.

Foreign trade

Balance of trade (current prices)

	1991	1992	1993
Kčs '000,000[1]	−14,064	−5,158	−33,821
% of total	6.7%	2.4%	9.2%

Imports (1993): Kčs 201,545,000,000[1] (machinery and transport equipment 29.2%; petroleum and petroleum products 21.1%; semimanufactured products 15.0%; chemical products 11.3%; manufactured products 9.0%). *Major import sources:* Czech Republic 35.5%; former U.S.S.R. 23.1%; Germany 11.4%; Austria 6.1%; Italy 3.0%; Poland 1.9%.
Exports (1993): Kčs 167,724,000,000[1] (semimanufactured products 38.8%; machinery and transport equipment 19.4%; manufactured goods 13.4%; chemical products 12.0%; food, beverages, and tobacco 5.5%). *Major export destinations:* Czech Republic 42.4%; Germany 15.2%; former U.S.S.R. 8.3%; Austria 5.0%; Hungary 4.5%; Poland 2.9%.

Transport and communications

Transport. Railroads (1992): length 2,275 mi, 3,661 km; passenger-mi 3,388,000,000, passenger-km 5,543,000,000; short ton-mi cargo 11,437,000,000, metric ton-km cargo 16,697,000,000. Roads (1993): total length 11,021 mi, 17,737 km (paved, n.a.). Vehicles (1992): passenger cars 953,239; trucks and buses 81,350. Merchant marine: n.a. Air transport: passenger-mi 9,496,000,000, passenger-km 15,283,000,000; short ton-mi 855,000,000; metric ton-km 1,376,000,000; airports (1995) with scheduled flights 4.
Communications. Daily newspapers (1992): total number 21; total circulation 378,000; circulation per 1,000 population 71. Radio (1992): total number of receivers 1,068,185 (1 per 5.0 persons). Television (1992): total number of receivers 1,279,101 (1 per 4.1 persons). Telephones (main lines; 1993): 892,800 (1 per 6.0 persons).

Education and health

Education (1993–94)

	schools	teachers	students	student/teacher ratio
Primary (age 6–14)	2,483	38,874	690,189	17.8
Secondary (age 15–18)	175	4,815	68,004	14.1
Voc., teacher tr.	683	14,423	250,129	17.3
Higher	14	7,769	61,257	7.9

Educational attainment (1991). Percentage of adult population having: incomplete primary education 0.5%; primary and incomplete secondary 30.6%; complete secondary 58.6%; higher 9.4%; unknown 0.9%. *Literacy* (1990): total population age 15 and over literate 3,980,202 (100%); males literate 1,916,410 (100%); females literate 2,063,792 (100%).
Health (1992): physicians 15,767 (1 per 336 persons); hospital beds 52,613 (1 per 100 persons); infant mortality rate per 1,000 live births 12.6.
Food (1990): daily per capita caloric intake 3,335 (vegetable products 63%, animal products 37%); 135% of FAO recommended minimum requirement.

Military

Total active duty personnel (1995): 47,000 (army 70.2%, air force 29.8%). *Military expenditure as percentage of GNP* (1993): 2.7% (world 3.3%); per capita expenditure U.S.$50.

[1]The Slovak koruna was introduced Feb. 8, 1993, at par with the former Czechoslovak koruna (Kčs), which it replaced. For settlement of obligations existing prior to February 8 between the Czech and Slovak republics, an interim currency, the clearing koruna (XCS), was introduced. [2]January. [3]Until 1990 Slovakia comprised four regions, subdivided into 38 administrative districts. After 1990 only the districts were retained. In 1995 a new system of administration was under discussion. [4]Cost-of-living index; wage earners only. [5]Worker's household.

Slovenia

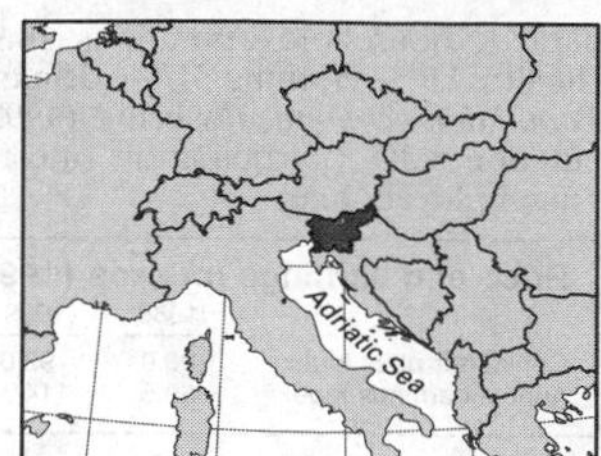

Official name: Republika Slovenija (Republic of Slovenia).
Form of government: multiparty republic with two legislative houses (State Council [40]; State Assembly [90]).
Head of state: President.
Head of government: Prime Minister.
Capital: Ljubljana.
Official language: Slovene.
Official religion: none.
Monetary unit: 1 Slovene tolar (SIT) = 100 stotin; valuation (Oct. 6, 1995) 1 Yugoslav dinar (Din) = 1.11 tolarji; 1 U.S.$ = 122.93 tolarji; 1 £ = 194.34 tolarji.

Area and population (1991 census)

Districts	area sq km[1]	population	Districts	area sq km[1]	population
Ajdovščina	352	22,632	Metlika	108	8,184
Brežice	268	24,724	Mozirje	508	16,533
Celje	230	64,736	Murska Sobota	692	63,744
Çerknica	483	15,020	Nova Gorica	605	59,126
Črnomelj	486	18,374	Novo Mesto	759	58,970
Domžale	240	44,185	Ormož	212	17,570
Dravograd	105	8,507	Pesnica	169	18,083
Gornja Radgona	210	21,315	Piran	45	16,768
Grosuplje	421	28,151	Postojna	492	20,283
Hrastnik	58	11,059	Ptuj	645	68,753
Idrija	425	17,207	Radlje ob Dravi	346	16,929
Ilirska Bistrica	480	14,624	Radovljica	641	34,286
Izola	28	13,770	Ravne na Koroškem	304	27,377
Jesenice	375	31,939	Ribnica	256	12,736
Kamnik	289	28,766	Ruše	200	15,440
Kočevje	766	18,523	Šentjur pri Celju	240	19,101
Koper	273	45,391	Sevnica	293	18,958
Kranj	453	72,185	Şežana	698	23,925
Krško	345	28,576	Škofja Loka	512	38,303
Lasko	250	19,014	Slovenj Gradec	286	20,976
Lenart	204	17,217	Slovenska Bistrica	369	32,516
Lendava	256	26,143	Şlovenske Konjice	222	21,992
Litija	328	18,709	Šmarje pri Jelšah	400	31,888
Ljubljana-Bežigrad	46	58,150	Tolmin	939	20,975
Ljubljana-Center	5	28,351	Trbovlje	58	19,337
Ljubljana-Moste Polje	152	72,081	Trebnje	308	17,722
Ljubljana-Šiška	156	82,845	Tržič	155	14,975
Ljubljana-Vič Rudnik	543	80,180	Velenje	182	42,671
Ljutomer	179	18,744	Vrhnika	169	19,459
Logatec	173	9,764	Zagorje ob Savi	147	16,960
Maribor	359	151,221	Žalec	349	39,340
			TOTAL	20,256	1,965,986

Demography

Population (1995): 1,971,000.
Density (1995): persons per sq mi 252.0, persons per sq km 97.3.
Urban-rural (1991): urban 48.9%; rural 51.1%.
Sex distribution (1993): male 48.50%; female 51.50%.
Age breakdown (1993): under 15, 19.1%; 15–29, 22.3%; 30–44, 23.8%; 45–59, 17.7%; 60–74, 13.0%; 75 and over, 4.1%.
Population projection: (2000) 1,963,000; (2010) 2,003,000.
Doubling time: not applicable; population is declining.
Ethnic composition (1991): Slovene 87.8%; Croat 2.8%; Serb 2.4%; Bosnian 1.4%; Magyar 0.4%; other 5.2%.
Religious affiliation (1991): Roman Catholic 83.6%; other (predominantly Christian adherents of the Slovene Old Catholic Church, a few Protestant denominations, and the Eastern Orthodox Church) 16.4%; there are also small Muslim and Jewish communities.
Major cities (1991): Ljubljana 276,133; Maribor 108,122; Celje 41,279; Kranj 37,318; Velenje 27,665.

Vital statistics

Birth rate per 1,000 population (1993): 9.9 (world avg. 25.0); legitimate 72.0%; illegitimate 28.0%.
Death rate per 1,000 population (1993): 10.0 (world avg. 9.3).
Natural increase rate per 1,000 population (1993): −0.1 (world avg. 15.7).
Total fertility rate (avg. births per childbearing woman; 1993): 1.3.
Marriage rate per 1,000 population (1993): 4.5.
Divorce rate per 1,000 population (1993): 1.0.
Life expectancy at birth (1992–93): male 69.4 years; female 77.3 years.
Major causes of death per 100,000 population (1993): circulatory diseases 455.0; cancers 233.0; accidents 95.2; digestive diseases 64.9; respiratory diseases 60.4; endocrine and metabolic disorders 26.1.

National economy

Budget (1993). Revenue: SIT 335,397,000,000. Expenditures: SIT 332,586,000,-000.
Tourism (1993): receipts U.S.$734,000,000; expenditures U.S.$304,000,000.
Production (metric tons except as noted). Agriculture, forestry, fishing (1994): potatoes 360,000, corn (maize) 200,000, wheat 170,000, sugar beets 133,000, grapes 130,000, plums 6,000; livestock (number of live animals) 620,000 pigs, 504,000 cattle, 21,000 sheep, 12,000,000 poultry; roundwood (1992) 1,168,000 cu m; fish catch 2,969. Mining and quarrying (1992): lead-zinc ore 152,225; alumina 40,000; mercury 7. Manufacturing (1993): cement 707,000; crude steel 355,000; aluminum ingots 82,682; soap and detergents 35,177; cotton yarn 13,346; leather footwear 8,840,000 pairs; refrigerators 665,000 units; bicycles 186,000 units; telephones 172,000 units. Construction (in '000,000 SIT; 1992): residential 2,704; nonresidential 21,690. Energy production (consumption): electricity (kW-hr; 1993) 11,682,000,000 (10,980,000,000); coal (metric tons; 1993) 5,556,000 (5,363,000); crude petroleum (barrels; 1991) 17,584 (3,680,000); petroleum products (metric tons; 1991) 126,000 (1,586,-000); natural gas (cu m; 1991) 19,271,000 (837,000,000).
Gross national product (1993): U.S.$12,576,000,000 (U.S.$6,310 per capita).

Structure of gross material product and labour force

	1991		1993	
	in value SIT '000,000	% of total value	labour force	% of labour force
Agriculture	17,223	6.2	15,014	1.9
Mining Manufacturing }	114,592	40.9	265,118	33.4
Construction	13,015	4.6	33,606	4.2
Public utilities	14,926	5.3	10,337	1.3
Transp. and commun.	22,284	8.0	37,251	4.7
Trade	39,480	14.1	85,558	10.8
Finance	47,385	16.9	13,831	1.7
Pub. admin., defense }			36,613	4.6
Services }	11,520	4.0	165,950	20.9
Other }			131,397	16.5
TOTAL	280,425	100.0	794,675	100.0

Population economically active (1993): total 794,675; activity rate of total population 39.9% (participation rates: ages 18–64, 61.8%; female 48.2%; unemployed 16.2%).

Price and earnings indexes (1990 = 100)

	1988	1989	1990	1991	1992	1993	1994
Consumer price index	1.1	15	100	215	659	867	1,040
Earnings index[2]	1.2	21	100	165	546	826	1,059

Land use (1993): forest 50.4%; pasture 27.6%; agricultural 14.9%; other 7.1%.
Household income and expenditure. Average household size (1991) 3.1; income per household (1993) SIT 1,256,900 (U.S.$9,534); sources of income (1993): wages 53.9%, transfers 21.9%, self-employment 12.9%, other 11.3%; expenditure (1993): food 25.8%, housing 11.8%, transportation 16.3%, clothing 7.5%, health care 6.4%, education and entertainment 6.0%, energy 5.8%, household durable goods 4.7%.

Foreign trade

Balance of trade (current prices)

	1989	1990	1991	1992	1993	1994
U.S.$'000,000	+192	−609	−257	+540	−410	−509
% of total	2.9%	6.9%	3.2%	4.2%	3.3%	3.6%

Imports (1993): SIT 737,409,000,000 (machinery and transport equipment 30.4%, basic manufactures 12.1%, chemicals 11.4%, mineral fuels 10.7%, food 7.7%). *Major import sources:* Germany 25.1%; Italy 16.2%; Croatia 9.1%; Austria 8.5%; France 8.0%.
Exports (1993): SIT 688,842,000,000 (machinery and transport equipment 27.5%, basic manufactures 25.6%, chemicals 9.1%, mineral fuels 5.1%, food 4.6%). *Major export destinations:* Germany 29.5%; Italy 12.4%; Croatia 12.1%; France 8.7%; Austria 4.9%.

Transport and communications

Transport. Railroads (1993): length 746 mi, 1,201 km; passenger-mi 352,-000,000, passenger-km 566,000,000; short ton-mi cargo 1,549,000,000, metric ton-km cargo 2,262,000,000. Roads (1993): total length 9,198 mi, 14,803 km (paved 77%). Vehicles (1993): passenger cars 632,563; trucks and buses 43,824. Merchant marine (1993): vessels (100 gross tons and over) 13; total deadweight tonnage 586,680. Air transport (1993): passenger-mi 295,000,-000, passenger-km 475,000,000; short ton-mi cargo 2,556,000, metric ton-km cargo 3,731,000; airports (1995) 1.
Communications. Daily newspapers (1992): total number 6; total circulation 308,000; circulation per 1,000 population 154. Radio (1989): 687,000 receivers (1 per 2.9 persons). Television (1989): 528,500 receivers (1 per 3.7 persons). Telephones (main lines; 1993): 516,300 (1 per 3.9 persons).

Education[3] and health

Education (1992–93)

	schools	teachers	students	student/ teacher ratio
Primary (age 7–14)	912	15,855	223,104	14.1
Secondary (age 15–18) Voc., teacher tr. }	236	8,926	103,714	11.6
Higher	28	2,783	37,362	13.4

Educational attainment (1991). Percentage of population age 15 and over having: less than full primary education 13.7%; primary 27.9%; secondary 45.6%; postsecondary and higher 12.8%. *Literacy* (1991): virtually 100%.
Health (1993): physicians 2,009 (1 per 990 persons); hospital beds 11,540 (1 per 172 persons); infant mortality rate per 1,000 live births 6.8.

Military

Total active duty personnel (1994): 8,400 (army 100%). *Military expenditure as percentage of GNP:* 1.6% (world 3.3%); per capita expenditure (1993) U.S.$102.

[1]One sq km is equal to approximately 0.3861 sq mi. [2]Based on worker real net personal income. [3]Includes adult education.

Solomon Islands

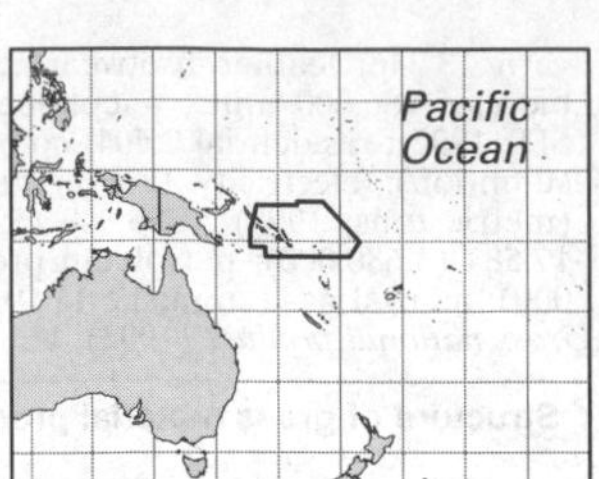

Official name: Solomon Islands.
Form of government: constitutional monarchy with one legislative house (National Parliament [47]).
Chief of state: British Monarch represented by Governor-General.
Head of government: Prime Minister.
Capital: Honiara.
Official language: English.
Official religion: none.
Monetary unit: 1 Solomon Islands dollar (SI$) = 100 cents; valuation (Oct. 6, 1995) 1 U.S.$ = SI$3.40; 1 £ = SI$5.38.

Area and population		area		population
				1986
Provinces	Capitals	sq mi	sq km	census
Central Islands	Tulagi	237	615	16,714
Choiseul	Taro	1,481	3,837	13,597
Guadalcanal	Honiara	2,060	5,336	50,327
Isabel	Buala	1,597	4,136	14,564
Makira	Kira Kira	1,231	3,188	21,646
Malaita	Auki	1,631	4,225	80,183
Rennell and Bellona	Tigoa	259	671	1,808
Temotu	Santa Cruz	334	865	14,683
Western	Gizo	2,114	5,475	41,775
Capital Territory				
Honiara	—	8	22	30,499
TOTAL		10,954[1]	28,370	285,796

Demography

Population (1995): 382,000.
Density (1995): persons per sq mi 34.9, persons per sq km 13.5.
Urban-rural (1995): urban 17.0%; rural 83.0%.
Sex distribution (1991): male 51.73%; female 48.27%.
Age breakdown (1991): under 15, 46.4%; 15–29, 27.2%; 30–44, 14.5%; 45–59, 7.8%; 60–74, 3.5%; 75 and over, 0.6%.
Population projection: (2000) 444,000; (2010) 596,000.
Doubling time: 21 years.
Ethnic composition (1986): Melanesian 94.2%; Polynesian 3.7%; other Pacific Islander 1.4%; European 0.4%; Asian 0.2%; other 0.1%.
Religious affiliation (1986): Christian 96.7%, of which Protestant 77.5%, Roman Catholic 19.2%; Baha'i 0.4%; traditional beliefs 0.2%; other and no religion 2.7%.
Major cities (1986)[2]: Honiara 35,288[3]; Gizo 3,727; Auki 3,262; Kira Kira 2,585; Buala 1,913.

Vital statistics

Birth rate per 1,000 population (1995): 37.0 (world avg. 25.0).
Death rate per 1,000 population (1995): 4.0 (world avg. 9.3).
Natural increase rate per 1,000 population (1995): 33.0 (world avg. 15.7).
Total fertility rate (avg. births per childbearing woman; 1995): 5.2.
Marriage rate per 1,000 population: n.a.
Divorce rate per 1,000 population: n.a.
Life expectancy at birth (1995): male 69.0 years; female 73.0 years.
Major causes of death per 100,000 population (1990): respiratory diseases 22.4; diarrheal diseases 13.6; malaria 10.0.

National economy

Budget (1992). Revenue: SI$228,400,000 (1991; taxes on foreign trade 46.8%, income taxes 29.2%, nontax revenue 14.3%, foreign grants 9.7%). Expenditures: SI$255,900,000 (1991; administrative 33.2%, interest payments 12.6%, capital expenditure 10.7%).
Tourism: receipts from visitors (1993) U.S.$6,000,000; expenditures by nationals abroad (1992) U.S.$11,000,000.
Land use (1993): forested 87.5%; meadows and pastures 1.4%; agricultural and under permanent cultivation 2.0%; other 9.1%.
Gross national product (at current market prices; 1993): U.S.$260,000,000 (U.S.$750 per capita).

Structure of gross domestic product and labour force	1991		1993	
	in value SI$'000[4]	% of total value	labour force[5]	% of labour force
Agriculture	117,600	48.4	8,106	27.4
Mining	−700	−0.3	2,844	9.6
Manufacturing	9,000	3.7		
Construction	10,500	4.3	977	3.3
Public utilities	2,200	0.9	245	0.8
Transportation and communications	17,500	7.2	1,723	5.8
Trade	23,300	9.6	3,390	11.5
Finance	8,000	3.3	1,144	3.9
Pub. admin., defense	55,800	23.0	4,303	14.6
Services			6,845	23.1
Other	44,300	18.2	...	...
TOTAL	243,100[1]	100.0[1]	29,577	100.0

Household income and expenditure. Average household size (1986) 6.4; average annual income per household[6] (1983) SI$1,010 (U.S.$1,160); sources of income (1983): wages and salaries 74.1%, self-employment, remittances, gifts, and other assistance 25.9%; expenditure (1992)[7]: food 46.8%, housing 11.0%, household operations 10.9%, transportation 9.9%, recreation and health 7.9%, clothing 5.7%, drinks and tobacco 5.0%.
Population economically active (1993): total 29,577[5]; activity rate of total population 8.3% (participation rates: ages 15–60 [1986] 98.6%; female 22.6%; unemployed, n.a.).

Price and earnings indexes (1990 = 100)	1988	1989	1990	1991	1992	1993	1994
Consumer price index	80.0	92.0	100.0	115.1	118.3	138.7	157.6
Annual earnings index[5]	89.5	114.7	100.0	121.2	140.5	142.8	...

Production (metric tons except as noted). Agriculture, forestry, fishing (1994): palm oil and kernels 36,920, copra 22,240, cacao beans 3,337, coconut oil 2,827; livestock (number of live animals) 55,000 pigs, 13,000 cattle; roundwood 267,000 cu m; fish catch 39,005. Mining and quarrying (1994): gold 997 troy oz. Manufacturing (1993): processed fish 34,700; sawnwood 16,000 cu m; other major industries include beer brewing, soap and tobacco manufacturing, garment manufacturing, weaving, wood carving, fibreglass products, boatbuilding, and leatherworking. Construction (gross value in SI$ in Honiara; 1994): residential 9,508,000; nonresidential 11,151,000. Energy production (consumption): electricity (kW-hr; 1993) 48,928,000 (43,473,000); coal, none (n.a.); petroleum products (metric tons; 1992) none (52,000); natural gas, none (n.a.).
Public debt (external, outstanding; 1993): U.S.$95,000,000.

Foreign trade[8]

Balance of trade (current prices)	1988	1989	1990	1991	1992	1993
SI$'000	+1,160	−47,300	−21,030	−23,770	+59,150	+33,520
% of total	0.3%	12.1%	5.6%	5.0%	11.0%	5.9%

Imports (1994): SI$437,023,000 (1992; machinery and transport equipment 34.2%, manufactured goods 18.2%, food 14.0%, mineral fuels and lubricants 12.1%). *Major import sources* (1992): Australia 37.6%; Japan 14.7%; Singapore 11.9%; New Zealand 8.5%; United States 6.2%; Germany 3.3%.
Exports (1994): SI$491,664,000 (timber products 56.3%, fish products 20.1%, palm oil products 7.5%, copra 3.7%, cacao beans 2.0%). *Major export destinations* (1992): Japan 34.8%; United Kingdom 19.6%; South Korea 12.2%; The Netherlands 4.0%; Singapore 3.8%; Hong Kong 3.7%.

Transport and communications

Transport. Railroads: none. Roads (1993): total length 840 mi, 1,352 km (paved 35%). Vehicles (1993): passenger cars 2,052; trucks and buses 2,574. Merchant marine (1992): vessels (100 gross tons and over) 33; total deadweight tonnage 4,985. Air transport (1992): passenger-mi 117,100,000, passenger-km 188,400,000; short ton-mi cargo 25,000[9], metric ton-km cargo 37,000[9]; airports (1995) with scheduled flights 30.
Communications. Daily newspapers[10]: none. Radio (1995): total number of receivers 38,000 (1 per 10 persons). Television: none. Telephones (main lines; 1993): 5,300 (1 per 65 persons).

Education and health

Education (1994)	schools	teachers	students	student/teacher ratio
Primary (age 7–12)	520	2,510	73,120	29.1
Secondary (age 13–18)	23	364[11]	7,811	20.2[11]
Voc., teacher tr.[12]	1	...	...	...
Higher[12]	1	...	...	...

Educational attainment (1986)[13]. Percentage of population age 25 and over having: no schooling 44.4%; primary education 46.2%; secondary 6.8%; higher 2.6%. *Literacy* (1976): total population age 15 and over literate 55,500 (54.1%); males 33,600 (62.4%); females 21,900 (44.9%).
Health (1990): physicians 52 (1 per 6,154 persons); hospital beds 265 (1 per 1,208 persons); infant mortality rate per 1,000 live births (1995) 25.0.
Food (1992): daily per capita caloric intake 2,173 (vegetable products 89%, animal products 11%); 95% of FAO recommended minimum requirement.

Military

Total active duty personnel: no military forces are maintained, but a police force of 475 provides internal security.

[1]Detail does not add to total given because of rounding. [2]Ward populations. [3]1990. [4]At 1984 factor cost. [5]Persons employed in the monetary sector only. [6]Public-service earnings. [7]Retail price index components. [8]Import figures are f.o.b. [9]1984. [10]In 1988 there were three weekly newspapers with a combined circulation of 10,000. [11]1993. [12]Vocational and teacher training are carried out at the College of Higher Education. [13]Indigenous population only.

Somalia[1]

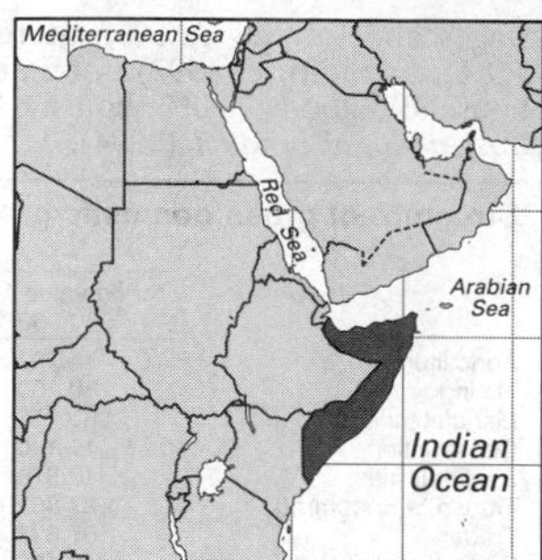

Official name: Soomaaliya (Somali)(Somalia).
Form of government: republic[2, 3].
Head of state and government: [3].
Capital: Mogadishu.
Official languages: Somali; Arabic.
Official religion: Islam.
Monetary unit: 1 Somali shilling (So.Sh.) = 100 cents; valuation (Oct. 6, 1995) 1 U.S.$ = So.Sh. 2,620; 1 £ = So.Sh. 4,142.

Area and population

		area		population
				1980
Regions	Capitals	sq mi	sq km	estimate
Bakool	Xuddur	10,000	27,000	148,700
Banaadir	Mogadishu (Muqdisho)	400	1,000	520,100
Bari	Boosaaso	27,000	70,000	222,300
Bay	Baydhabo	15,000	39,000	451,000
Galguduud	Dhuusamarreeb	17,000	43,000	255,900
Gedo	Garbahaarrey	12,000	32,000	235,000
Hiiraan	Beledweyne	13,000	34,000	219,300
Jubbada Dhexe	Bu'aale	9,000	23,000	147,800
Jubbada Hoose	Kismaayo	24,000	61,000	272,400
Mudug	Gaalkacyo	27,000	70,000	311,200
Nugaal	Garoowe	19,000	50,000	112,200
Sanaag	Ceerigaabo	21,000	54,000	216,500
Shabeellaha Dhexe	Jawhar	8,000	22,000	352,000
Shabeellaha Hoose	Marka	10,000	25,000	570,700
Togdheer	Burao	16,000	41,000	383,900
Woqooyi Galbeed	Hargeysa	17,000	45,000	655,000
TOTAL		246,000[4]	637,000	5,074,000

Demography

Population (1995): 6,734,000[5].
Density (1995): persons per sq mi 27.4, persons per sq km 10.6.
Urban-rural (1991): urban 37.2%; rural 62.8%.
Sex distribution (1995): male 49.50%; female 50.50%.
Age breakdown (1995): under 15, 47.5%; 15–29, 25.9%; 30–44, 14.6%; 45–59, 7.7%; 60–74, 3.6%; 75 and over, 0.7%.
Population projection: (2000) 7,079,000; (2010) 7,823,000.
Doubling time: 22 years.
Ethnic composition (1983): Somali 98.3%[6]; Arab 1.2%; Bantu 0.4%; other 0.1%.
Religious affiliation (1980): Sunnī Muslim 99.8%; Christian 0.1%; other 0.1%.
Major cities (1984): Mogadishu 570,000; Hargeysa 90,000; Kismaayo 86,000; Berbera 83,000; Marka (1981) 60,000.

Vital statistics

Birth rate per 1,000 population (1990–95): 50.2 (world avg. 25.0); legitimate, n.a.; illegitimate, n.a.
Death rate per 1,000 population (1990–95): 18.5 (world avg. 9.3).
Natural increase rate per 1,000 population (1990–95): 31.7 (world avg. 15.7).
Total fertility rate (avg. births per childbearing woman; 1990–95): 7.0.
Marriage rate per 1,000 population: n.a.
Divorce rate per 1,000 population: n.a.
Life expectancy at birth (1990–95): male 45.4 years; female 48.6 years.
Major causes of death per 100,000 population: n.a.; however, major diseases include leprosy, malaria, tetanus, and tuberculosis; civil violence, malnutrition, and poor health services remained epidemic in the mid-1990s.

National economy

Budget (1991). Revenue: So.Sh. 151,453,000,000 (domestic revenue sources, principally indirect taxes and import duties 60.4%; external grants and transfers 39.6%). Expenditures: So.Sh. 141,141,000,000 (general services 46.9%; economic and social services 31.2%; debt service 7.0%).
Public debt (external, outstanding; 1993): U.S.$1,897,000,000.
Production (metric tons except as noted). Agriculture, forestry, fishing (1994): sorghum 252,000, fruits (excluding melons) 207,000, sugarcane 200,000, corn (maize) 150,000, bananas 43,000, sesame seed 22,000, beans 12,000, dates 10,000, seed cotton 6,000, rice 2,000, other forest products include khat, frankincense, and myrrh; livestock (number of live animals) 13,000,000 sheep, 12,000,000 goats, 6,000,000 camels, 5,000,000 cattle; roundwood (1993) 9,047,000 cu m; fish catch (1993) 14,850. Mining and quarrying (1992): sepiolite 2,000 kilograms. Manufacturing (value added in So.Sh. '000,000; 1988): food 794; cigarettes and matches 562; hides and skins 420; paper and printing 328; plastics 320; chemicals 202; beverages 144. Construction (value added in So.Sh.; 1991): 51,100,000,000. Energy production (consumption): electricity (kW-hr; 1993) 258,000,000 (258,000,000); coal, none (n.a.); crude petroleum (barrels; 1991) n.a. (806,000); petroleum products (metric tons; 1991) none (59,000); natural gas, none (n.a.).
Household income and expenditure. Average household size (1980) 4.9; income per household: n.a.; sources of income: n.a.; expenditure (1983)[7]: food and tobacco 62.3%, housing 15.3%, clothing 5.6%, energy 4.3%, other 12.5%.
Tourism: receipts from visitors (1986) U.S.$8,000,000; expenditures by nationals abroad (1983) U.S.$13,000,000.
Population economically active (1991): total 3,215,000; activity rate of total population 40.9% (participation rates [1987]: over age 10, 63.1%; female 48.7%; unemployed, n.a.).

Price and earnings indexes (1985 = 100)

	1983	1984	1985	1986	1987	1988	1989[8]
Consumer price index	38.0	72.6	100.0	135.8	174.0	316.6	707.1
Earnings index	...	...	...	...	...	...	...

Gross national product (at current market prices; 1990): U.S.$946,000,000 (U.S.$150 per capita).

Structure of gross domestic product and labour force

	1991			
	in value So.Sh. '000,000	% of total value	labour force	% of labour force
Agriculture	867,500	64.5	2,275,000	70.8
Mining	2,700	0.2		
Manufacturing	59,200	4.4	336,000	10.4
Construction	51,100	3.8		
Public utilities	9,400	0.7		
Transportation and communications	80,700	6.0		
Trade	125,000	9.3		
Finance	45,700	3.4	604,000	18.8
Pub. admin., defense	80,700	6.0		
Services	30,900	2.3		
Other	−8,100	−0.6		
TOTAL	1,344,900[3]	100.0	3,215,000	100.0

Land use (1993): forested 25.5%; meadows and pastures 68.6%; agricultural and under permanent cultivation 1.6%; other 4.3%.

Foreign trade[9]

Balance of trade (current prices)

	1987	1988	1989	1990	1991	1992
U.S.$'000,000	−382	−373	−299	−274	−274	−305
% of total	64.3%	68.7%	62.4%	61.4%	61.4%	67.0%

Imports (1991): U.S.$360,000,000 (agricultural products 22.1%, of which rice 8.6%; unspecified 77.9%). *Major import sources* (1990): Italy 30.8%; The Netherlands 8.8%; Bahrain 6.0%; United Kingdom 5.9%; Djibouti 5.9%; China 4.9%; Germany 4.7%; Thailand 4.6%.
Exports (1991): U.S.$86,000,000 (agricultural products 46.1%, of which live sheep and goats 23.3%, live camels 7.0%, live cattle 6.4%, bananas 5.8%; fishery products 10.7%; other 43.2%). *Major export destinations* (1990): Italy 28.7%; Saudi Arabia 23.4%; Yemen 19.1%; United Arab Emirates 10.7%.

Transport and communications

Transport. Railroads: none. Roads (1991): total length 13,500 mi, 21,700 km (paved 28%). Vehicles (1993): passenger cars 10,700; trucks and buses 12,000. Merchant marine (1992): vessels (100 gross tons and over) 28; total deadweight tonnage 18,496. Air transport (1991): passenger-mi 81,000,000, passenger-km 131,000,000; short ton-mi cargo 3,000,000, metric ton-km cargo 5,000,000; airports (1995) with scheduled flights 1.
Communications. Daily newspapers (1994): total number 2; total circulation, n.a. Radio (1994): total number of receivers 300,000 (1 per 22 persons). Television (1987): total number of receivers 3,000 (1 per 2,270 persons). Telephones (main lines; 1993): 15,000 (1 per 434 persons).

Education and health

Education (1986–87)

	schools	teachers	students	student/teacher ratio
Primary (age 0–14)	1,125	8,208	171,830	20.9
Secondary (age 15–18)	82	2,109	42,764	20.3
Voc., teacher tr.	21	498	4,809	9.7
Higher	1	262[10]	1,692	...

Educational attainment: n.a. *Literacy* (1990): percentage of total population age 15 and over literate 24.1%; males literate 42.7%; females literate 14.0%.
Health: physicians (1987) 323 (1 per 19,071 persons); hospital beds (1985) 5,536 (1 per 1,053 persons); infant mortality rate per 1,000 live births (1990–95) 122.
Food (1992): daily per capita caloric intake 1,499 (vegetable products 76%, animal products 24%); 65% of FAO recommended minimum requirement.

Military

Total active duty personnel (1995): clan militias and armed gangs have fought for control of the country since the 1991 revolution. *Military expenditure as percentage of GNP* (1986): 3.2% (world 5.5%); per capita expenditure U.S.$6.

[1]Proclamation of the "Republic of Somaliland" by the Somali National Movement in May 1991 on territory corresponding to the former British Somaliland (which unified with the former Italian Trust Territory of Somalia to form Somalia in 1960) has received no international recognition. This entity would represent about a quarter of Somalia's territory and a quarter to a third of its population; a new president was elected in May 1993; a new currency, the Somaliland shilling, was introduced in January 1995. [2]UN operation in Somalia (begun May 1992) ended March 1, 1995. [3]No effective central government exists. [4]Detail does not add to total given because of rounding. [5]Excluding Somali refugees in neighbouring countries, estimated to number about 500,000 in mid-1995. [6]The Somali are divided into six major clans, of which four are predominantly pastoral (representing *c.* 70% of the population) and two are predominantly agricultural (representing *c.* 20% of the population); the remainder are urban dwellers with less clan identification. [7]Capital city only. [8]Third quarter. [9]Imports are c.i.f. [10]1980–81.

South Africa

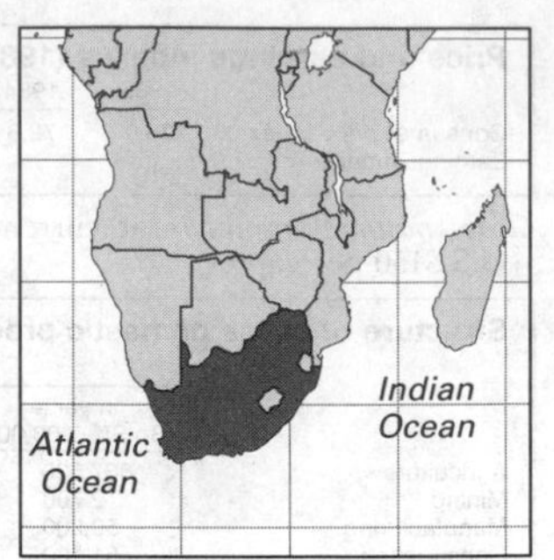

Official name: Republic of South Africa (English).
Form of government: multiparty republic with two legislative houses (Senate [90]; National Assembly [400]).
Head of state and government: President assisted by Executive Deputy Presidents.
Capitals: Pretoria (executive); Bloemfontein (judicial); Cape Town (legislative).
Official languages: [1].
Official religion: none.
Monetary unit: 1 rand (R) = 100 cents; valuation (Oct. 6, 1995) 1 U.S.$ = R 3.66; 1 £ = R 5.79.

Area and population		area		population
				1994[2]
Provinces	Capitals	sq mi	sq km	estimate
Eastern	Bisho	65,483	169,600	6,436,790
Free State	Bloemfontein	49,992	129,480	2,726,840
Gauteng	Johannesburg	7,262	18,810	6,869,103
KwaZulu/Natal	Ulundi	35,591	92,180	8,505,338
Mpumalanga (Eastern Transvaal)	Nelspruit	30,259	78,370	2,921,559
Northern	Pietersburg	47,599	123,280	5,201,630
Northern Cape	Kimberley	139,692	361,800	737,306
North-West	Mafikeng (Mmabatho)	44,861	116,190	3,252,991
Western Cape	Cape Town	49,950	129,370	3,633,077
TOTAL		470,689	1,219,080	40,284,634

Demography

Population (1995): 41,465,000.
Density (1995): persons per sq mi 87.8, persons per sq km 33.9.
Urban-rural (1991): urban 48.8%; rural 51.2%.
Sex distribution (1991): male 49.50%; female 50.50%.
Age breakdown (1995): under 15, 37.3%; 15–29, 27.1%; 30–44, 18.5%; 45–59, 10.4%; 60–74, 5.2%; 75 and over, 1.5%.
Population projection: (2000) 46,215,000; (2010) 56,398,000.
Doubling time: 27 years.
Ethnic composition (1994): black 76.1%, of which Zulu *c.* 22.0%, Xhosa *c.* 18.0%, Pedi *c.* 9.0%, Sotho *c.* 7.0%, Tswana *c.* 7.0%, Tsonga *c.* 3.5%, Swazi *c.* 3.0%, Ndebele *c.* 2.0%, Venda *c.* 2.0%; white 12.8%; Coloured 8.5%, of which Cape Malay 1.0%; Asian 2.6%.
Religious affiliation (1990)[3]: Christian 67.8%, of which black independent churches 22.2%, Afrikaans Reformed 11.8%, Roman Catholic 7.6%, Methodist 5.9%, Anglican 3.8%, Lutheran 2.5%; Hindu 1.3%; Muslim 1.1%; Jewish 0.4%; other/traditional beliefs 29.4%.
Major cities (1991)[4]: Cape Town 2,350,157; Johannesburg 1,916,063[5]; Durban 1,137,378; Pretoria 1,080,187; Port Elizabeth 853,204.

Vital statistics

Birth rate per 1,000 population (1994): 34.0 (world avg. 25.0).
Death rate per 1,000 population (1994): 8.0 (world avg. 9.3).
Natural increase rate per 1,000 population (1994): 26.0 (world avg. 15.7).
Total fertility rate (avg. births per childbearing woman; 1995): 4.1.
Life expectancy at birth (1995): male 63.0 years; female 68.0 years.
Major causes of death per 100,000 population (1993)[6]: accidents and violence 157; diseases of the circulatory system 133; malignant neoplasms 76; infectious and parasitic diseases 67; diseases of the respiratory system 60.

National economy

Budget (1993–94). Revenue: R 88,210,000,000 (income taxes 56.3%, sales and value-added taxes 28.2%, customs duties 5.8%, excise duties 5.5%). Expenditures: R 114,154,000,000 (education 23.9%, interest on debt 19.4%, economic services 14.8%, health 11.3%, defense 9.3%).
Public debt (external, December 1994): U.S.$2,274,000,000.
Production (in R '000,000 except as noted). Agriculture, forestry, fishing (in value of production; 1991–92): poultry and eggs 4,236, beef 2,856, corn (maize) 1,537, temperate fruits 1,373, wheat 1,308, hay 1,237, sugarcane 1,141, milk 1,098, sheep and goat meat 884, grapes 750, citrus fruits 679, tobacco 507; roundwood (1993) 19,811,000 cu m; fish catch (1993) 563,228 metric tons. Mining and quarrying (in value of sales; 1993): gold 22,945; rough diamonds 15,495[7]; coal 9,563; platinum-group metals 2,513; iron ore 1,285; copper 1,023; manganese 561; lime and limestone 535; chrome 296. Manufacturing (in value added; 1992): food products 8,167; soaps, paints, pharmaceuticals, and refined petroleum 8,138; iron and steel 6,658; transport equipment 6,002; metal products 4,594; nonelectrical machinery 4,511; beverages 4,046; industrial chemicals 3,572. Construction (buildings completed in value of construction; 1993): residential 3,920; nonresidential 4,308. Energy production (consumption): electricity (kW-hr; 1993) 155,812,000,000[3] (163,294,000,000[8, 9]); coal (metric tons; 1993) 182,000,000 (140,231,000[9]); crude petroleum (barrels; 1993) none (124,610,000[9]); petroleum products (metric tons; 1993) 16,068,000[9] (16,071,000[9]); natural gas, none (none).
Household income and expenditure[3]. Average household size (1994) 4.6; average annual income per household (1990–91) R 16,814 (U.S.$6,500), of which average black household R 9,348 (U.S.$3,614), average Coloured household R 19,284 (U.S.$7,455), average Asian household R 29,712 (U.S.$11,487), average white household R 56,148 (U.S.$21,707); sources of income (1992): wages and salaries 73.6%, interest, dividends, rent, etc., 21.5%, transfers 4.9%; expenditure (1992): food and beverages 35.8%, transportation 14.7%, household goods 10.0%, housing and energy 9.6%.
Gross national product (1994): U.S.$118,961,000,000 (U.S.$2,930 per capita).

Structure of gross domestic product and labour force	1993		1994	
	in value R '000,000[10]	% of total value	labour force[11]	% of labour force
Agriculture	15,737	4.6	1,227,346	13.3
Mining	30,150	8.7	277,176	2.9
Manufacturing	80,963	23.5	1,614,596	16.7
Construction	11,190	3.2	437,167	4.5
Public utilities	13,874	4.0	95,046	1.0
Transp. and commun.	27,857	8.1	520,789	5.4
Trade	55,323	16.0	1,675,448	17.4
Finance, real estate	43,480	12.6	587,331	6.1
Pub. admin., defense	52,543	15.2	3,055,753	31.7
Services	6,857	2.0		
Other	7,243	2.1	100,320[12]	1.0[12]
TOTAL	345,217	100.0	9,640,972	100.0

Population economically active (1994): total 14,297,048; activity rate of total population 35.3% (participation rates: over age 15, 55.6%; female 44.2%; unemployed 32.6%.

Price and earnings indexes (1990 = 100)	1989	1990	1991	1992	1993	1994	1995[13]
Consumer price index	87.5	100.0	115.3	131.3	144.0	157.1	169.9
Monthly earnings index[14]	86.6	100.0	113.9	132.2	...	...	...

Tourism (1993): receipts U.S.$1,190,000,000; expenditures U.S.$1,598,000,000.
Land use (1993): forest 6.7%; pasture 66.6%; agriculture 10.8%; other 15.9%.

Foreign trade

Balance of trade (current prices)	1989	1990	1991	1992	1993	1994
R '000,000	+13,458	+16,717	+16,146	+13,917	+20,409	+10,786
% of total	13.1%	15.9%	14.3%	11.6%	14.7%	6.3%

Imports (1993): R 59,073,000,000 (machinery and apparatus 29.1%, motor vehicles 15.1%, chemicals and chemical products 11.1%, food 6.5%). *Major import sources* (1994): Germany 16.3%; U.S. 15.7%; U.K. 11.3%; Japan 9.9%; Italy 3.8%; France 3.4%.
Exports (1993): R 79,482,000,000 (gold 28.0%, gem diamonds 12.8%, base metals and metal products 12.5%). *Major export destinations* (1994): Switzerland 6.7%; U.K. 6.6%; U.S. 4.9%; Japan 4.6%; Germany 4.1%.

Transport and communications

Transport. Railroads: route length (1993) 19,955 km; passenger-km (1992–93) 895,000,000[15]; metric ton-km cargo (1992–93) 91,402,000,000. Roads (1991): length 188,309 km (paved 29%). Vehicles (1992): passenger cars 3,488,570; trucks and buses 1,899,721. Merchant marine (1992): vessels 219; total deadweight tonnage 282,533. Air transport (1994)[16]: passenger-km 11,134,000,000; metric ton-km cargo 263,107,000; airports (1995) 27.
Communications. Daily newspapers (1992): total number 20; total circulation 1,248,000; circulation per 1,000 population 32. Radio (1994): 11,200,000 receivers (1 per 3.6 persons). Television (1994): 3,445,000 receivers (1 per 12 persons). Telephones (main lines; 1993): 3,659,900 (1 per 11 persons).

Education and health

Education (1993)	schools	teachers	students	student/ teacher ratio
Primary/Secondary	21,006	337,311	8,681,876	25.7
Voc., teacher tr.	198	15,032	152,962	10.2
Tertiary vocational	15	7,341	137,168	18.7
University	17	32,047	329,892	10.3

Educational attainment (1990). Percentage of all-age population group (black, white, Coloured, Asian) having: no formal schooling (34.4%, 7.8%, 15.5%, 11.4%); primary education (45.2%, 10.3%, 32.6%, 21.8%); secondary (19.8%, 56.4%, 48.9%, 60.3%); technical/teacher training (0.5%, 10.1%, 2.3%, 2.5%); undergraduate (0.06%, 6.7%, 0.3%, 1.7%); graduate (0.05%, 8.7%, 0.4%, 2.3%). *Literacy:* total population age 15 and over literate (1990) n.a.[17]
Health (1993): physicians 25,967 (1 per 1,527 persons); hospital beds 123,355 (1 per 321 persons); infant mortality rate (1994) 47.0[18].
Food (1992): daily per capita caloric intake 2,695 (vegetable products 86%, animal products 14%); 110% of FAO recommended minimum.

Military

Total active duty personnel (1995): 136,900 (army 86.2%, navy 3.3%, air force 6.6%, intraservice medical service 3.9%). *Military expenditure as percentage of GNP* (1993): 2.7% (world 3.3%); per capita expenditure U.S.$73.

[1]Afrikaans; English; Ndebele; Pedi (North Sotho); Sotho (South Sotho); Swazi; Tsonga; Tswana (West Sotho); Venda; Xhosa; Zulu. [2]April 27. [3]Excludes formerly nominally independent Transkei, Venda, Bophuthatswana, and Ciskei (TVBC). [4]Population of urban areas. [5]1991 population of the Witwatersrand (including East Rand [1,378,792] and West Rand [870,066] urban areas) is 4,164,921. [6]Projected rates based on about 63% of total deaths. [7]1994. [8]1992. [9]Includes Botswana, Lesotho, Namibia, and Swaziland. [10]At factor cost. [11]Persons in October 1994 working for pay, profit, or family gain for 5 or more hours during the survey week. [12]All not adequately defined. [13]April. [14]Manufacturing only. [15]Excludes suburban traffic. [16]SAA only. [17]Unofficial estimates range from 65% to less than 50%. [18]Of which black 66.0, white 6.0.

Spain

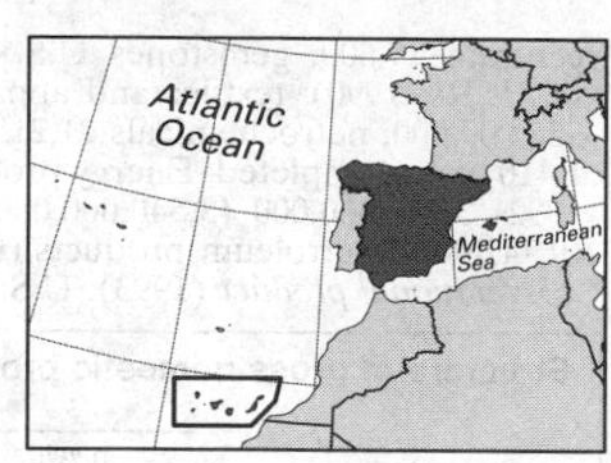

Official name: Reino de España (Kingdom of Spain).
Form of government: constitutional monarchy with two legislative houses (Senate [255[1]]; Congress of Deputies [350]).
Chief of state: King.
Head of government: Prime Minister.
Capital: Madrid.
Official language: Castilian Spanish.
Official religion: none.
Monetary unit: 1 peseta (Pta) = 100 céntimos; valuation (Oct. 6, 1995) 1 U.S.$ = Ptas 123.75; 1 £ = Ptas 195.63.

Area and population

Autonomous communities	Capitals	area sq mi	area sq km	population 1994 estimate
Andalucía	Seville	33,822	87,599	7,053,043
Aragón	Zaragoza	18,425	47,720	1,183,576
Asturias	Oviedo	4,094	10,604	1,083,388
Baleares (Balearic Islands)	Palma de Mallorca	1,927	4,992	736,865
Canarias (Canary Islands)	Santa Cruz de Tenerife	2,875	7,447	1,534,897
Cantabria	Santander	2,054	5,321	526,090
Castilla–La Mancha	Toledo	30,680	79,461	1,656,179
Castilla y León	Valladolid	36,380	94,224	2,504,371
Cataluña	Barcelona	12,399	32,113	6,090,107
Ceuta	—	8	20	68,867
Extremadura	Mérida	16,075	41,634	1,050,590
Galicia	Santiago de Compostela	11,419	29,575	2,720,761
La Rioja	Logroño	1,948	5,045	263,137
Madrid	Madrid	3,100	8,028	5,034,548
Melilla	—	5	12	58,052
Murcia	Murcia	4,368	11,314	1,070,401
Navarra	Pamplona	4,012	10,391	523,614
País Vasco (Basque Country)	Vitoria (Gasteiz)	2,793	7,234	2,075,561
Valencia	Valencia	8,979	23,255	3,909,047
TOTAL		195,364[2, 3]	505,990[3]	39,143,394

Demography

Population (1995): 39,188,000[4].
Density (1995): persons per sq mi 201.1, persons per sq km 77.6.
Urban-rural (1990): urban 78.4%; rural 21.6%.
Sex distribution (1995): male 48.94%, female 51.06%.
Age breakdown (1995): under 15, 16.5%; 15–29, 24.5%; 30–44, 21.7%; 45–59, 16.6%; 60–69, 10.5%; 70 and over, 10.2%.
Population projection: (2000) 39,268,000; (2010) 38,969,000.
Doubling time: not applicable; doubling time exceeds 100 years.
Ethnolinguistic composition (1989): Spanish 72.3%; Catalan 16.3%; Galician 8.1%; Basque 2.3%; other 1.0%.
Religious affiliation (1993): Roman Catholic 94.9%; Muslim 1.2%; Protestant 0.5%; other 3.4%.
Major cities (1991)[5]: Madrid 2,909,792; Barcelona 1,623,542; Valencia 752,909; Seville 659,126; Zaragoza 586,219.

Vital statistics

Birth rate per 1,000 population (1993): 9.7 (world avg. 25.0); (1992) legitimate 89.5%; illegitimate 10.5%.
Death rate per 1,000 population (1993): 8.6 (world avg. 9.3).
Natural increase rate per 1,000 population (1993): 1.1 (world avg. 15.7).
Total fertility rate (avg. births per childbearing woman; 1990–95): 1.2.
Marriage rate per 1,000 population (1993): 5.0.
Divorce rate per 1,000 population (1990): 0.6.
Life expectancy at birth (1995): male 73.2 years; female 81.1 years.
Major causes of death per 100,000 population (1992): circulatory diseases 340.1; malignant neoplasms (cancers) 212.6; respiratory diseases 76.4.

National economy

Budget (1994[6]). Revenue: Ptas 13,217,000,000,000 (direct taxes 45.8%; indirect taxes 37.5%, of which value-added tax on products 9.0%; other taxes on production 16.7%). Expenditures: Ptas 16,514,000,000,000 (current transfers between public administrations 53.2%; interest payments 17.3%; wages 16.0%).
Tourism (1993): receipts U.S.$19,425,000,000; expenditures U.S.$4,706,000,000.
Production (metric tons except as noted). Agriculture, forestry, fishing (1994): sugar beets 8,232,000, barley 7,596,000, wheat 4,312,000, potatoes 4,058,000, grapes 3,167,000, tomatoes 3,066,000, oranges 2,597,000, corn (maize) 2,266,000, onions 1,017,000; livestock (number of live animals) 23,838,000 sheep, 18,188,000 pigs, 5,000,000 cattle, 2,739,000 goats; roundwood (1993) 14,796,000 cu m; fish catch (1993) 1,290,000. Mining and quarrying (metal content in metric tons; 1994): iron ore 2,086,000; zinc 150,000; lead 24,000. Manufacturing (value added in Ptas '000,000; 1990): machinery and transport equipment 2,175,761; food products 1,564,469; chemical products 921,075; paper products 662,993; wood and cork products 379,452; clothing and footwear 338,083; textiles 306,572. Construction (1994): dwellings 298,803. Energy production (consumption): electricity (kW-hr; 1993) 85,962,000,000 (87,229,000,000); coal (metric tons; 1993) 31,504,000 (44,416,000); crude petroleum (barrels; 1993) 6,560,000 (390,777,000); petroleum products (metric tons; 1993) 45,837,000 (38,120,000); natural gas (cu m; 1993) 671,435,000 (6,589,533,000).

Gross national product (1993): U.S.$533,986,000,000 (U.S.$14,230 per capita).

Structure of gross domestic product and labour force

	1994 in value Ptas '000,000	% of total value	labour force	% of labour force
Agriculture	2,244,600	3.5	1,375,300	8.9
Mining }			62,100	0.4
Manufacturing }	14,845,100	22.9	2,802,700	18.1
Public utilities }			92,800	0.6
Construction	5,175,100	8.0	1,474,200	9.5
Transp. and commun.	...	...	769,800	5.0
Trade }			3,273,100	21.2
Finance }			1,088,600	7.1
Services }	38,599,400	59.7	} 3,102,100	20.0
Pub. admin., defense }				
Other	3,808,800[7]	5.9[7]	1,423,100[8]	9.2
TOTAL	64,672,500[2]	100.0	15,468,200[2]	100.0

Public debt (1993[9]): Ptas 34,448,000,000,000 (U.S.$257,000,000,000).
Population economically active (1994): total 15,468,200; activity rate of total population 39.5% (participation rates: ages [1993] 16–64, 60.3%; female 36.7%; unemployed 16.6%).

Price and earnings indexes (1990 = 100)

	1988	1989	1990	1991	1992	1993	1994
Consumer price index	87.7	93.7	100.0	105.9	112.2	117.3	122.9
Monthly earnings index	85.7	92.0	100.0	108.2	116.5	124.4	124.4

Household income and expenditure. Average household size (1991) 3.4; income per household (1993) Ptas 2,663,200 (U.S.$20,900); sources of income (1991): wages and salaries 48.5%, profits and self-employment 27.5%, social security 19.5%; expenditure (1992): housing 24.5%, food 23.6%, transportation 13.3%, clothing and footwear 8.3%, household goods and services 6.2%.
Land use (1993): forested 32.3%; meadows and pastures 20.6%; agricultural and under permanent cultivation 39.4%; other 7.7%.

Foreign trade

Balance of trade (current prices)

	1989	1990	1991	1992	1993	1994
Ptas '000,000	−2,722.0	−2,765.4	−2,724.3	−3,022.5	−1,831.3	−1,853.9
% of total	20.6%	19.7%	19.6%	18.6%	10.2%	8.6%

Imports (1994): Ptas 12,348,734,000,000 (agricultural products 11.6%; machinery 11.0%; energy products 9.4%, of which crude petroleum 9.2%; transportation equipment 8.1%). *Major import sources:* France 17.5%; Germany 14.6%; Italy 8.9%; U.K. 7.8%; Japan 3.6%.
Exports (1994): Ptas 9,796,340,000,000 (transport equipment 21.1%; agricultural products 14.9%; machinery 7.7%). *Major export destinations:* France 20.1%; Germany 14.2%; Italy 9.2%; U.K. 8.2%.

Transport and communications

Transport. Railroads (1993): route length 12,601 km; passenger-km 15,457,000,000; metric ton-km cargo 7,742,000,000. Roads (1991): length 331,961 km (paved 99%). Vehicles (1993): cars 13,440,694; trucks and buses 2,859,438. Merchant marine (1992): vessels 2,190; deadweight tonnage 5,077,275. Air transport (1993): passenger-km 26,738,000,000; metric ton-km cargo 599,016,000; airports (1995) with scheduled flights 25.
Communications. Daily newspapers (1993): total number 119; total circulation 2,516,299[10]; circulation per 1,000 population 64[10]. Radio (1994): 12,000,000 receivers (1 per 3.3 persons). Television (1994): 17,000,000 receivers (1 per 2.3 persons). Telephones (main lines; 1993): (1 per 3.1 persons).

Education and health

Education (1993–94)

	schools	teachers	students	student/teacher ratio
Primary (age 6–11)	16,540	121,353	2,447,859	20.2
Secondary (age 12–18)[11]	25,775[12]	297,697	4,734,401	15.9
Higher[12]	1,415	73,412	1,370,689	18.7

Educational attainment (1986). Percentage of population age 25 and over having: no formal schooling 5.2%; less than primary education 40.3%; primary 29.9%; incomplete secondary 8.9%; completed secondary 8.7%; higher 7.0%.
Literacy (1991): total population age 10 and over literate 33,338,300 (85.4%); males literate 16,458,400 (85.1%); females literate 16,879,900 (84.3%).
Health (1991): physicians 153,306 (1 per 257 persons); hospital beds 168,514 (1 per 234 persons); infant mortality rate (1992) 7.4.
Food (1992): daily per capita caloric intake 3,708 (vegetable products 68%, animal products 32%); 151% of FAO recommended minimum requirement.

Military

Total active duty personnel (1995): 206,000 (army 70.2%, navy 15.5%, air force 14.3%). *Military expenditure as percentage of GNP* (1993): 1.8% (world 3.3%); per capita expenditure U.S.$211.

[1]At the June 1993 elections, 208 seats were directly elected and 47 indirectly elected by the parliaments of the autonomous communities. [2]Detail does not add to total given because of rounding. [3]Includes other enclaves (*plazas de soberanía).*[4]Estimate based on 1991 census. [5]For *municipios,* which may contain rural population. [6]Preliminary. [7]Import taxes and value-added tax on products. [8]Includes 800,300 unemployed persons not previously employed. [9]December. [10]For 51 newspapers only. [11]Includes vocational. [12]1992–93.

Sri Lanka

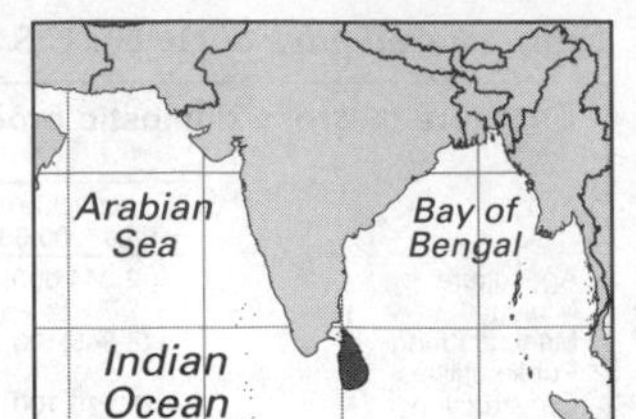

Official name: Sri Lankā Prajathanthrika Samajavadi Janarajaya (Sinhala); Ilangai Jananayaka Socialisa Kudiarasu (Tamil) (Democratic Socialist Republic of Sri Lanka).
Form of government: unitary multiparty republic with one legislative house (Parliament [225]).
Head of state and government: President.
Capitals: Colombo (administrative) and Sri Jayewardenepura Kotte (legislative).
Official languages: Sinhala; Tamil.
Official religion: none.
Monetary unit: 1 Sri Lanka rupee (SL Rs) = 100 cents; valuation (Oct. 6, 1995) 1 U.S.$ = SL Rs 52.10; 1 £ = SL Rs 82.36.

Area and population

		area		population
Districts	Capitals	sq mi	sq km	1993 estimate
Amparai	Amparai	1,705	4,415	501,000
Anuradhapura	Anuradhapura	2,772	7,179	741,000
Badulla	Badulla	1,104	2,861	724,000
Batticaloa	Batticaloa	1,102	2,854	433,000
Colombo	Colombo	270	699	2,026,000
Galle	Galle	638	1,652	971,000
Gampaha	Gampaha	536	1,387	1,555,000
Hambantota	Hambantota	1,007	2,609	531,000
Jaffna	Jaffna	396	1,025	879,000
Kalutara	Kalutara	617	1,598	961,000
Kandy	Kandy	749	1,940	1,269,000
Kegalle	Kegalle	654	1,693	758,000
Kilinochchi	Kilinochchi	494	1,279	107,000
Kurunegala	Kurunegala	1,859	4,816	1,462,000
Mannar	Mannar	771	1,996	137,000
Matale	Matale	770	1,993	429,000
Matara	Matara	495	1,283	797,000
Monaragala	Monaragala	2,177	5,639	361,000
Mullaitivu	Mullaitivu	1,010	2,617	96,000
Nuwara Eliya	Nuwara Eliya	672	1,741	535,000
Polonnaruwa	Polonnaruwa	1,271	3,293	329,000
Puttalam	Puttalam	1,186	3,072	617,000
Ratnapura	Ratnapura	1,264	3,275	960,000
Trincomalee	Trincomalee	1,053	2,727	323,000
Vavuniya	Vavuniya	759	1,967	117,000
TOTAL		25,332	65,610	17,619,000

Demography

Population (1995): 18,090,000.
Density (1995): persons per sq mi 714.1, persons per sq km 275.7.
Urban-rural (1995): urban 22.0%; rural 78.0%.
Sex distribution (1993): male 50.97%; female 49.03%.
Age breakdown (1993): under 15, 35.2%; 15–29, 29.7%; 30–44, 17.9%; 45–59, 10.6%; 60–74, 5.2%; 75 and over, 1.4%.
Population projection: (2000) 19,258,000; (2010) 21,521,000.
Doubling time: 50 years.
Ethnic composition (1991): Sinhalese 82.7%; Tamil 8.9%; Sri Lankan Moor 7.7%; other 0.7%.
Religious affiliation (1981): Buddhist 69.3%; Hindu 15.5%; Muslim 7.6%; Christian 7.5%; other 0.1%.
Major cities (1990): Colombo 615,000; Dehiwala–Mount Lavinia 196,000; Moratuwa 170,000; Jaffna 129,000; Sri Jayewardenepura Kotte 109,000.

Vital statistics

Birth rate per 1,000 population (1995): 20.0 (world avg. 25.0); (1986) legitimate 96.3%; illegitimate 3.7%.
Death rate per 1,000 population (1995): 6.0 (world avg. 9.3).
Natural increase rate per 1,000 population (1995): 14.0 (world avg. 15.7).
Total fertility rate (avg. births per childbearing woman; 1995): 2.4.
Marriage rate per 1,000 population (1990): 8.9.
Divorce rate per 1,000 population (1988): 0.2.
Life expectancy at birth (1995): male 70.0 years; female 75.0 years.
Major causes of death per 100,000 population (1988): violence and poisoning 101.7; diseases of the circulatory system 98.7; diseases of the nervous system 37.0; respiratory diseases 32.1; infectious and parasitic diseases 29.6.

National economy

Budget (1993). Revenue: SL Rs 98,495,000,000 (sales and turnover tax 29.8%, import duties 20.9%, income taxes 12.9%, excise taxes 12.6%, nontax revenue 11.3%). Expenditures: SL Rs 134,728,000,000 (public-debt service 21.5%, transfer payments 15.8%, defense 11.4%, education 10.4%, general public services 8.1%, transport 6.1%, health 5.2%, agriculture 5.1%).
Public debt (external, outstanding; 1993): U.S.$5,936,000,000.
Tourism (1993): receipts U.S.$208,000,000; expenditures U.S.$121,000,000.
Production (metric tons except as noted). Agriculture, forestry, fishing (1994): rice 2,582,000, coconuts 1,704,000, sugarcane 796,000, cassava 310,000, tea 240,000, rubber 102,000, copra 60,000, sweet potatoes 50,000; livestock (number of live animals) 1,600,000 cattle, 870,000 buffalo, 500,000 goats; roundwood (1993) 9,374,000 cu m; fish catch (1993) 220,900. Mining and quarrying (1993): quartz stone 1,133,000; limestone 650,000; titanium concentrate 79,600; gemstones U.S.$60,000,000. Manufacturing (value added, in SL Rs; 1990): textiles and apparel 27,930,000,000; food and tobacco 21,955,000,000; petrochemicals 21,215,000,000. Construction (1992): residential, 1,410 units completed. Energy production (consumption): electricity (kW-hr; 1992) 3,540,000,000 (3,540,000,000); crude petroleum (barrels; 1992) none (9,742,000); petroleum products (metric tons; 1992) 1,227,000 (1,575,000).
Gross national product (1993): U.S.$10,573,000,000 (U.S.$600 per capita).

Structure of gross domestic product and labour force

	1993		1992	
	in value SL Rs '000,000	% of total value	labour force	% of labour force
Agriculture	103,440.5	20.7	2,379,889	40.0
Mining	5,432.8	1.1	52,452	0.9
Manufacturing	85,313.9	17.1	635,457	10.7
Construction	32,794.5	6.5	248,596	4.2
Public utilities	10,362.1	2.1	22,621	0.4
Transp. and commun.	47,339.0	9.5	231,536	3.9
Trade	107,154.5	21.4	530,209	8.9
Finance	32,453.8	6.5	36,091	0.6
Pub. admin., defense	37,429.4	7.5 }	821,449	13.8
Services	14,389.4	2.9 }		
Other	23,527.1	4.7	989,921[1]	16.6[1]
TOTAL	499,637.0	100.0	5,948,221	100.0

Population economically active: total (1992) 5,948,221; activity rate 40.9% (participation rates: ages 15 and over, 56.6%; female 32.6%; unemployed 13.3%).

Price and earnings indexes (1990 = 100)

	1988	1989	1990	1991	1992	1993	1994
Consumer price index	73.8	82.3	100.0	112.2	125.0	139.6	151.4
Average wage index[2]	73.2	84.3	100.0	111.7	128.4	155.4	158.8

Household income and expenditure (1992). Average household size (1981) 5.2; income per household SL Rs 116,100 (U.S.$2,600); sources of income: wages 48.5%, property income and self-employment 41.8%, transfers 9.7%; expenditure: food and beverages 58.6%, transportation 16.0%, clothing 8.4%, housing and energy 4.6%, household furnishings 3.5%.
Land use (1993): forested 32.5%; meadows and pastures 6.8%; agricultural and under permanent cultivation 29.4%; other 31.3%.

Foreign trade

Balance of trade (current prices)

	1989	1990	1991	1992	1993	1994
SL Rs '000,000	−15,135	−17,485	−29,612	−27,128	−36,037	−53,894
% of total	11.9%	9.9%	14.9%	11.0%	11.5%	14.5%

Imports (1993): SL Rs 181,484,000,000 (textile fibres 24.5%, machinery and transport equipment 23.0%, chemical products 10.8%, vegetable products 7.8%, mineral fuels 7.7%). *Major import sources:* Japan 12.1%; India 9.1%; Hong Kong 8.3%; South Korea 7.0%; Taiwan 6.0%; Singapore 5.5%.
Exports (1993): SL Rs 137,286,000,000 (ready-made apparel 45.4%, tea 15.9%, ceramic products 12.3%, pearls 8.0%, natural rubber 4.8%, collectible art 2.0%). *Major export destinations:* U.S. 35.4%; Germany 8.0%; U.K. 7.2%; Belgium 6.2%; Japan 5.2%; The Netherlands 3.8%; France 3.0%.

Transport and communications

Transport. Railroads (1993): route length 1,493 km; passenger-km 3,048,000,000; metric ton-km cargo 156,000,000. Roads (1993): total length 26,004 km (paved 81%). Vehicles (1993): passenger cars 197,300; trucks and buses 165,228. Merchant marine (1992): vessels (100 gross tons and over) 66; total deadweight tonnage 472,625. Air transport (1994): passenger-km 3,684,000,000; metric ton-km cargo 116,172,000; airports (1995) 1.
Communications. Daily newspapers (1992): total number 10; total circulation 480,000; circulation per 1,000 population 27. Radio (1994): 3,300,000 receivers (1 per 5.4 persons). Television (1994): 700,000 receivers (1 per 26 persons). Telephones (main lines; 1993): 157,800 (1 per 111 persons).

Education and health

Education (1991)

	schools	teachers	students	student/ teacher ratio
Primary (age 5–10)	9,590	173,811	2,112,723	12.2
Secondary (age 11–17)	9,041	106,792	2,105,959	19.7
Voc., teacher tr.	23	437	8,908	20.4
Higher	8	1,937	31,447	16.2

Educational attainment (1981). Percentage of population age 25 and over having: no schooling 15.5%; less than complete primary education 12.1%; complete primary 52.3%; postprimary 14.7%; secondary 3.0%; higher 1.1%; unspecified 1.3%. *Literacy* (1991): percentage of population age 10 and over literate 86.9%; males literate 90.1%; females literate 83.8%.
Health (1992): physicians 3,345 (1 per 5,203 persons); hospital beds 48,061 (1 per 362 persons); infant mortality rate per 1,000 live births (1995) 17.0.
Food (1992): daily per capita caloric intake 2,273 (vegetable products 95%, animal products 5%); 102% of FAO recommended minimum.

Military

Total active duty personnel (1994): 126,000 (army 83.3%, navy 8.2%, air force 8.5%). *Military expenditure as percentage of GNP* (1993): 4.8% (world 3.3%); per capita expenditure U.S.$28.

[1]Includes unemployed. [2]Agricultural minimum rates.

Sudan, The

Official name: Jumhūrīyat as-Sūdān (Republic of the Sudan).
Form of government: Islamic military regime with one transitional legislative house (Transitional National Assembly [300][1]).
Head of state and government: President.
Capitals: Khartoum (executive); Omdurman (legislative).
Official language: Arabic.
Official religion: [2].
Monetary unit: 1 Sudanese dinar (Sd)[3]; valuation (Oct. 6, 1995) 1 U.S.$ = Sd 75.00; 1 £ = Sd 118.57.

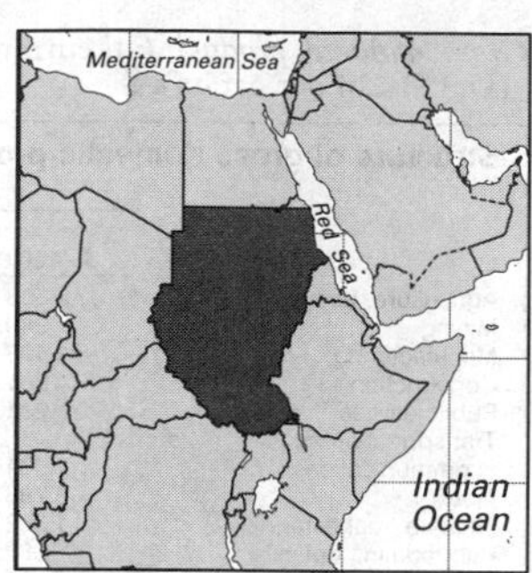

Area and population

		area		population
States[4]	Capitals	sq mi	sq km	1983 census
A'ālī an-Nīl (Upper Nile)	Malakāl	92,198	238,792	1,599,605
Baḥr al-Ghazāl (Bahr el-Ghazal)	Wāw	77,566	200,894	2,265,510
Dārfūr (Darfur)	al-Fāshir	196,404	508,684	3,093,699
al-Istiwā'īyah (Equatoria)	Juba	76,436	197,969	1,406,181
al-Kharṭūm (Khartoum)	Khartoum	10,875	28,165	1,802,299
Kurdufān (Kordofan)	al-Ubayyiḍ	146,817	380,255	3,093,294
ash-Shamālīyah (Northern)	ad-Dāmir	183,800	476,040	1,083,024
ash-Sharqīyah (Eastern)	Kassalā	128,987	334,074	2,208,209
al-Wusṭā (Central)	Wad Madanī	53,675	139,017	4,012,543
TOTAL		966,757[5, 6]	2,503,890[6]	20,564,364[7]

Demography

Population (1995): 28,098,000.
Density (1995): persons per sq mi 29.1, persons per sq km 11.2.
Urban-rural (1991): urban 22.4%; rural 77.6%.
Sex distribution (1995): male 50.20%; female 49.80%.
Age breakdown (1995): under 15, 43.9%; 15–29, 27.0%; 30–44, 15.6%; 45–59, 8.8%; 60–74, 3.9%; 75 and over, 0.8%.
Population projection: (2000) 32,079,000; (2010) 41,534,000.
Doubling time: 23 years.
Ethnic composition (1983): Sudanese Arab 49.1%; Dinka 11.5%; Nuba 8.1%; Beja 6.4%; Nuer 4.9%; Azande 2.7%; Bari 2.5%; Fur 2.1%; Shilluk 1.7%; Lotuko 1.5%; other 9.5%.
Religious affiliation (1992): Sunnī Muslim 74.7%; traditional beliefs 17.1%; Christian 8.2%.
Major cities (1983): Omdurman 526,287[8]; Khartoum 476,218[8]; Khartoum North 341,146[8]; Port Sudan (1990) *c.* 215,000[9]; Wad Madanī (1987) *c.* 145,000.

Vital statistics

Birth rate per 1,000 population (1994): 42.0 (world avg. 25.0).
Death rate per 1,000 population (1994): 12.0 (world avg. 9.3).
Natural increase rate per 1,000 population (1994): 30.0 (world avg. 15.7).
Total fertility rate (avg. births per childbearing woman; 1994): 6.1.
Marriage rate per 1,000 population: n.a.
Divorce rate per 1,000 population: n.a.
Life expectancy at birth (1994): male 53.4 years; female 55.2 years.
Major causes of death per 100,000 population: n.a.; however, principal causes of mortality and morbidity in the early 1990s included malaria, dysentery, tuberculosis, schistosomiasis, trypanosomiasis (sleeping sickness), and AIDS; malnutrition was widespread and amounted, locally, to famine.

National economy

Budget (1993–94). Revenue: LSd 130,800,000,000[3] (taxes on business profits 23.1%, nontax revenue 19.3%, excise taxes 13.5%, import duties 12.9%). Expenditures: LSd 365,350,000,000[3] (interest on debt 45.8%, current expenditure 41.2%, development expenditure 6.9%).
Tourism: receipts from visitors (1993) U.S.$3,000,000; expenditures by nationals abroad (1992) U.S.$21,400,000.
Population economically active (1992): total 8,559,000; activity rate of total population 32.0% (participation rates: ages 15–64 [1983] 57.4%; female 22.3%; unemployed, *c.* 30.0%).

Price and earnings indexes (1990 = 100)

	1988	1989	1990	1991	1992	1993	1994
Consumer price index	36.3	60.5	100.0	223.6	486.6	979.9	2,057[10]
Earnings index	...	...	...	...	...	...	...

Production (metric tons except as noted). Agriculture, forestry, fishing (1994): sugarcane 4,500,000, sorghum 3,498,000, peanuts (groundnuts) 810,000, millet 783,000, wheat 475,000, seed cotton 290,000, sesame seeds 221,000, cottonseed 190,000, yams 126,000, cotton lint 95,000, gum arabic 40,000[11]; livestock (number of live animals) 22,870,000 sheep, 21,751,000 cattle, 16,449,000 goats, 2,856,000 camels; roundwood (1993) 24,781,000 cu m; fish catch (1993) 31,700. Mining and quarrying (1993): salt 75,000; chromite/gross weight 10,000; gold (1994–95) 109,000 troy oz. Manufacturing (1992–93): wheat flour 530,000; raw sugar 515,000; vegetable oils 180,000; cement 170,000; cattlehides and horsehides 38,000[12]; calfskins, goatskins, and sheepskins 18,000[12]; cigarettes 750,000,000 units[12]. Construction: n.a. Energy production (consumption): electricity (kW-hr; 1993) 1,328,000,000 (1,328,000,000); coal, none (none); crude petroleum (barrels; 1993) none (7,513,000); petroleum products (metric tons; 1993) 861,000 (1,041,000); natural gas, none (none).

Land use (1993): forested 18.6%; meadows and pastures 46.3%; agricultural and under permanent cultivation 5.5%; desert and other 29.6%.
Public debt (external, outstanding; 1993): U.S.$8,994,000,000.
Gross national product (1992): U.S.$8,176,000,000 (U.S.$300 per capita).

Structure of gross domestic product and labour force

	1992–93		1983	
	in value LSd '000,000[13]	% of total value	labour force[14]	% of labour force[14]
Agriculture	2,869	35.8	4,028,705	63.5
Mining	12	0.2	6,534	0.1
Manufacturing	851	10.6	266,693	4.2
Construction	412	5.1	139,282	2.2
Public utilities	192	2.4	43,728	0.7
Transportation and communications }	3,022	37.7	215,474	3.4
Trade and finance }			314,676	5.0
Services				
Pub. admin., defense }	656	8.2	550,409	8.7
Other	...	...	777,480[15]	12.2[15]
TOTAL	8,014	100.0	6,342,981	100.0

Household income and expenditure. Average household size (1980) 5.3; income per household: n.a.[16]; sources of income: n.a.; expenditure (1983): food and beverages 63.6%, housing 11.5%, household goods 5.5%, clothing and footwear 5.3%, health care 4.1%, energy 3.8%.

Foreign trade

Balance of trade (current prices)

	1989–90	1990–91	1991–92	1992–93	1993–94
U.S.$'000,000	−592	−1,193	−941	−715	−723
% of total	40.1%	63.6%	57.4%	50.3%	41.8%

Imports (1993–94): U.S.$1,226,000,000 (petroleum products 18.8%; foodstuffs 16.7%, of which wheat flour 4.6%; nonelectrical and electrical machinery 16.5%; transport equipment 10.9%). *Major import sources* (1994): Libya 16.1%; Saudi Arabia 11.6%; U.K. 6.0%; Egypt 5.3%; France 5.0%; U.S. 4.7%.
Exports (1993–94): U.S.$503,000,000 (cotton 19.1%; gum arabic 16.1%; sesame seeds 15.3%; sheep and lambs 15.3%; durra 6.9%; peanuts [groundnuts] 5.1%). *Major export destinations* (1994): Italy 13.0%; Thailand 10.5%; Saudi Arabia 9.9%; China 9.3%; U.S. 6.8%; Japan 6.4%.

Transport and communications

Transport. Railroads (1992): route length 2,960 mi, 4,764 km; passenger-mi 330,000,000[17], passenger-km 531,000,000[17]; short ton-mi cargo 666,000,000, metric ton-km cargo 972,000,000. Roads (1991): total length 12,400 mi, 20,000 km (paved 8%). Vehicles (1992): passenger cars 116,000; trucks and buses 57,000. Merchant marine (1992): vessels (100 gross tons and over) 16; total deadweight tonnage 62,244. Air transport (1994)[18]: passenger-mi 382,136,000, passenger-km 614,990,000; short ton-mi cargo 26,785,000, metric ton-km cargo 39,105,000; airports (1995) with scheduled flights 11.
Communications. Daily newspapers (1992): total number 5; total circulation 620,000; circulation per 1,000 population 25. Radio (1994): 5,755,000 receivers (1 per 4.5 persons). Television (1994): 250,000 receivers (1 per 103 persons). Telephones (main lines; 1993): 64,000 (1 per 416 persons).

Education and health

Education (1991–92)

	schools	teachers	students	student/ teacher ratio
Primary (age 7–12)	8,016	64,227	2,168,180	33.8
Secondary (age 13–18)	2,578	29,208	683,982	23.4
Voc., teacher tr.	67	1,434	34,316	23.9
Higher	24	1,943	54,345	28.0

Educational attainment (1983). Percentage of population age 25 and over having: no formal schooling 76.7%; incomplete primary education 18.6%; incomplete secondary 1.9%; complete secondary 2.0%; higher 0.8%. *Literacy* (1995): total population age 15 and over literate 7,280,000 (46.1%); males 4,540,000 (57.7%); females 2,740,000 (34.6%).
Health: physicians (1990) 2,400 (1 per 10,000 persons); hospital beds (1986) 18,571 (1 per 1,222 persons); infant mortality rate (1994) 80.0.
Food (1992): daily per capita caloric intake 2,706 (vegetable products 89%, animal products 11%); 115% of FAO recommended minimum.

Military

Total active duty personnel (1995): 118,500 (army 97.1%, navy 0.4%, air force 2.5%). *Military expenditure as percentage of GNP* (1992): 17.1% (world 3.7%); per capita expenditure U.S.$36.

[1]Appointed interim legislature. Total number of seats includes seats assigned to southern Sudan (area at war with central government). [2]Islam was being imposed in 1995. [3]A new currency, the Sudanese dinar (introduced May 1992 at a value equal to 10 Sudanese pounds [LSd]), is gradually replacing the Sudanese pound. [4]Local administrative reorganization into 26 new states was officially announced in February 1994; a 27th state was announced in February 1995. [5]Detail does not add to total given because of rounding. [6]Including *c.* 50,000 sq mi (130,000 sq km) of inland water area. [7]Preliminary 1993 census figure was 24,941,000, including an estimated 3,850,000 in the southern Sudan. [8]Khartoum urban agglomeration: 1993 est. (including Omdurman, Khartoum North, squatters, and displaced persons from southern Sudan) *c.* 3,500,000. [9]Excluding about 300,000 refugees from Eritrea. [10]June. [11]1994–95. [12]1992. [13]In constant prices of 1981–82 at factor cost. [14]Excludes nomads, the homeless, and institutionalized persons. [15]Includes 592,759 unemployed not previously employed. [16]Average annual income of paid worker (1992) U.S.$216. [17]1991. [18]Sudan Airways only.

Suriname

Official name: Republiek Suriname (Republic of Suriname).
Form of government: multiparty republic with one legislative house (National Assembly [51]).
Head of state and government: President.
Capital: Paramaribo.
Official language: Dutch.
Official religion: none.
Monetary unit: 1 Suriname guilder (Sf) = 100 cents; valuation (Oct. 6, 1995) 1 U.S.$ = Sf 492.00; 1 £ = Sf 777.80.

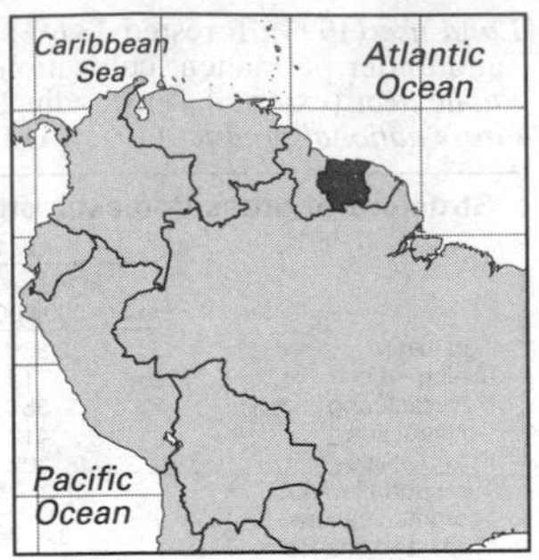

Area and population

Districts	Capitals	area sq mi	area sq km	population 1980 census
Brokopondo	Brokopondo	2,843	7,364	6,621
Commewijne	Nieuw Amsterdam	908	2,353	20,063
Coronie	Totness	1,507	3,902	2,777
Marowijne	Albina	1,786	4,627	16,125
Nickerie	Nieuw Nickerie	2,067	5,353	32,690
Para	Onverwacht	2,082	5,393	12,827
Saramacca	Groningen	1,404	3,636	10,808
Sipaliwini	...	50,412	130,566	23,226
Wanica	Lelydorp	171	443	60,725
Town district				
Paramaribo	Paramaribo	71	183	167,798
TOTAL		63,251[1]	163,820[1]	355,240[2]

Demography

Population (1995): 430,000.
Density (1995): persons per sq mi 6.8, persons per sq km 2.6.
Urban-rural (1993): urban 49.0%; rural 51.0%.
Sex distribution (1994): male 49.28%; female 50.72%.
Age breakdown (1994): under 15, 33.7%; 15–29, 30.0%; 30–44, 18.9%; 45–59, 10.0%; 60–74, 6.0%; 75 and over, 1.4%.
Population projection: (2000) 465,000; (2010) 534,000.
Doubling time: 29 years.
Ethnic composition (1991): Suriname Creole 35.0%; Indo-Pakistani 33.0%; Javanese 16.0%; Bush Negro 10.0%; Amerindian 3.0%; other 3.0%.
Religious affiliation (1983): Hindu 26.0%; Roman Catholic 21.6%; Muslim 18.6%; Protestant (mostly Moravian) 18.0%; other 15.8%.
Major cities (1980): Paramaribo 200,970[3]; Nieuw Nickerie 6,078; Meerzorg 5,355; Marienburg 3,633.

Vital statistics

Birth rate per 1,000 population (1993): 31.0 (world avg. 25.0); legitimate, n.a.; illegitimate, n.a.
Death rate per 1,000 population (1993): 6.5 (world avg. 9.3).
Natural increase rate per 1,000 population (1993): 24.5 (world avg. 15.7).
Total fertility rate (avg. births per childbearing woman; 1993): 2.8.
Marriage rate per 1,000 population (1991): 4.9.
Divorce rate per 1,000 population (1991): 2.5.
Life expectancy at birth (1993): male 66.6 years; female 71.8 years.
Major causes of death per 100,000 population (1987)[4]: diseases of the circulatory system 178.6, of which ischemic heart disease 60.7, diseases of pulmonary circulation and other forms of heart disease 47.2; homicide, suicide, and other violence 68.5; malignant neoplasms (cancers) 57.2; diseases of the respiratory system 33.7; ill-defined conditions 67.6.

National economy

Budget (1993). Revenue: Sf 3,476,800,000 (grants 61.6%; individual income taxes 17.2%; custom duties 5.1%; company profit taxes 4.9%, of which bauxite levy 2.7%; bank profits 4.3%). Expenditures: Sf 4,320,700,000 (current expenditures 91.6%, of which welfare and social services 13.1%, debt service 6.6%, defense 3.8%, health 2.3%, education 1.2%; capital expenditures 8.4%).
Public debt (external, outstanding; 1990): U.S.$138,000,000.
Production (metric tons except as noted). Agriculture, forestry, fishing (1994): rice 225,000, sugarcane 85,000, bananas 50,000, oranges 16,000, plantains 13,000, coconuts 11,000, watermelons 9,000, cucumbers 5,000, cassava 4,000, tomatoes 4,000, palm oil 1,650; livestock (number of live animals) 98,000 cattle, 37,000 pigs; roundwood (1993) 154,000 cu m; fish catch (1993) 9,503. Mining and quarrying (1993): bauxite 3,300,000; gold 9,645 troy oz. Manufacturing (value of production at factor cost in Sf; 1992): food products 417,000,000; beverages 278,000,000; tobacco 153,000,000; wood products 109,000,000; chemical products 103,000,000. Construction (value of buildings authorized; 1985): residential Sf 46,500,000; nonresidential Sf 8,100,000. Energy production (consumption): electricity (kW-hr; 1992) 1,420,000,000 (1,420,000,000); hard coal (metric tons) none (n.a.); crude petroleum (barrels; 1992) 1,730,000 (1,240,000); petroleum products (metric tons; 1992) none (446,000); natural gas, none (none).
Household income and expenditure. Average household size (1980) 3.9; income per household: n.a.; sources of income (1975): wages and salaries 74.6%, transfer payments 3.2%, other 22.2%; expenditure (1968–69): food and beverages 40.0%, household furnishings 12.3%, clothing and footwear 11.0%, transportation and communications 9.5%, recreation and education 8.4%, energy 6.9%, housing 4.4%, other 7.5%.

Gross national product (at current market prices; 1993): U.S.$488,000,000 (U.S.$1,210 per capita).

Structure of gross domestic product and labour force

	1993 in value Sf '000,000	1993 % of total value	1992 labour force	1992 % of labour force
Agriculture, forestry	2,306.8	21.6	29,000	21.0
Mining	249.6	2.3	2,210	1.6
Manufacturing	1,493.8	14.0	8,170	5.9
Construction	561.6	5.3	4,980	3.6
Public utilities	231.5	2.2	850	0.6
Transportation and communications	734.2	6.9	6,650	4.8
Trade	2,786.0	26.1	13,570	9.8
Finance, real estate	1,568.1	14.7	3,180	2.3
Pub. admin., defense	933.6	8.7	41,350	30.0
Services	40.1	0.4		
Other	−232.7[5]	−2.2[5]	28,040[6]	20.3[6]
TOTAL	10,672.5[7]	100.0	138,000	100.0[7]

Population economically active (1992): total 138,000; activity rate of total population 33.6% (participation rates[8]: ages 15–64, 56.0%; female 35.7%; unemployed 13.4%).

Price and earnings indexes (1990 = 100)

	1987	1988	1989	1990	1991	1992	1993
Consumer price index	76.0	81.5	82.1	100.0	126.0	181.0	440.7
Earnings index	...	...	...	...	...	...	...

Tourism (1992): receipts from visitors U.S.$11,000,000; expenditures by nationals abroad U.S.$12,000,000.
Land use (1993): forested 96.2%; meadows and pastures 0.1%; agricultural and under permanent cultivation 0.4%; other 3.3%.

Foreign trade

Balance of trade (current prices)

	1988	1989	1990	1991	1992	1993
U.S.$'000,000	+118.9	+143.5	−7.7	−117.9	−110.8	−77.2
% of total	19.9%	13.1%	0.6%	11.3%	10.2%	8.0%

Imports (1993): U.S.$520,500,000 (machinery and transport equipment 24.4%, fuels and lubricants 13.0%, food and live animals 9.7%, home appliances 4.5%). *Major import sources:* United States 45.2%; The Netherlands 22.6%; Trinidad and Tobago 11.7%; Japan 2.6%; Brazil 1.8%.
Exports (1993): U.S.$443,300,000 (alumina 49.5%, shrimp and fish 11.4%, aluminum 7.9%, rice 6.0%, bananas 1.9%, petroleum 1.2%). *Major export destinations:* Norway 32.3%; The Netherlands 26.4%; United States 12.3%; France 6.5%; Japan 5.9%; Germany 4.4%.

Transport and communications

Transport. Railroads (1991): length 187 mi, 301 km; passengers, not applicable; cargo, n.a. Roads (1990): total length 5,688 mi, 9,153 km (paved 29%). Vehicles (1993): passenger cars 42,561; trucks and buses 15,774. Merchant marine (1992): vessels (100 gross tons and over) 24; total deadweight tonnage 15,721. Air transport (1994)[9]: passenger-mi 336,096,000, passenger-km 540,896,000; short ton-mi cargo 5,402,000, metric ton-km cargo 7,887,000; airports (1995) with scheduled flights 2.
Communications. Daily newspapers (1992): total number 3; total circulation 25,000; circulation per 1,000 population 61. Radio (1993): total number of receivers 290,256 (1 per 1.4 persons). Television (1993): total number of receivers 59,598 (1 per 7.0 persons). Telephones (main lines; 1993): 46,900 (1 per 8.9 persons).

Education and health

Education (1992–93)

	schools	teachers	students	student/teacher ratio
Primary (age 6–11)	301[10]	3,695	79,162	21.4
Secondary (age 12–18)	89[10]	2,487	17,709	12.6
Voc., teacher tr.	64[11]		12,307	
Higher[10]	1	254	2,373	9.3

Educational attainment: n.a. *Literacy* (1990): total population age 15 and over literate 262,700 (94.9%); males literate 128,700 (95.1%); females literate 134,000 (94.7%).
Health: physicians (1990) 299 (1 per 1,348 persons); hospital beds (1989) 1,901 (1 per 212 persons); infant mortality rate per 1,000 live births (1993) 36.5.
Food (1992): daily per capita caloric intake 2,547 (vegetable products 86%, animal products 14%); 113% of FAO recommended minimum requirement.

Military

Total active duty personnel (1995): 1,800[12] (army 77.8%, navy 13.3%, air force 8.9%). *Military expenditure as percentage of GNP* (1993): 1.1% (world 3.3%); per capita expenditure U.S.$181.

[1]Area excludes 6,809 sq mi (17,635 sq km) of territory disputed with Guyana. [2]Detail does not add to total given because of computational discrepancies. [3]1993. [4]Based on 71.6% of total deaths. [5]Indirect taxes less subsidies and imputed bank service charges. [6]Includes 18,460 unemployed. [7]Detail does not add to total given because of rounding. [8]Districts of Wanica and Paramaribo only. [9]SLM (Suriname Airways) only. [10]1991–92. [11]1988–89. [12]All services are part of the army.

Swaziland

Official name: Umbuso weSwatini (Swazi); Kingdom of Swaziland (English).
Form of government[1]: monarchy with two legislative houses (Senate [30[2]]; House of Assembly [65[3]]).
Head of state and government: King, assisted by Prime Minister.
Capitals: Mbabane (administrative); Lobamba (royal and legislative).
Official languages: Swazi; English.
Official religion: none.
Monetary unit: 1 lilangeni[4] (plural emalangeni [E]) = 100 cents; valuation (Oct. 6, 1995) 1 U.S.$ = E 3.66; 1 £ = E 5.79.

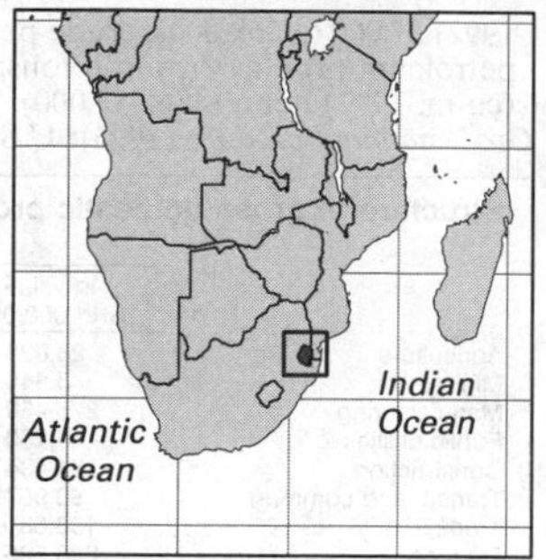

Area and population		area		population
Districts	Capitals	sq mi	sq km	1986 census[5]
Hhohho	Mbabane	1,378	3,569	178,936
Lubombo	Siteki	2,296	5,947	153,958
Manzini	Manzini	1,571	4,068	192,596
Shiselweni	Nhlangano	1,459	3,780	155,569
TOTAL		6,704	17,364	681,059

Demography

Population (1995): 913,000.
Density (1995): persons per sq mi 136.2, persons per sq km 52.6.
Urban-rural (1991): urban 34.3%; rural 65.7%.
Sex distribution (1995): male 47.91%; female 52.09%.
Age breakdown (1995): under 15, 43.4%; 15–29, 29.7%; 30–44, 14.9%; 45–59, 7.9%; 60–74, 3.3%; 75 and over, 0.8%.
Population projection: (2000) 1,047,000; (2010) 1,338,000.
Doubling time: 25 years.
Ethnic composition (1983): Swazi 84.3%; Zulu 9.9%; Tsonga 2.5%; Indian 0.8%; Pakistani 0.8%; Portuguese 0.2%; other 1.5%.
Religious affiliation (1980): Christian 77.0%, of which Protestant 37.3%, African indigenous 28.9%, Roman Catholic 10.8%; traditional beliefs 20.9%; other 2.1%.
Major cities (1986): Manzini 52,000; Mbabane 38,290; Nhlangano 4,107; Piggs Peak 3,223; Siteki 2,271.

Vital statistics

Birth rate per 1,000 population (1990–95): 38.5 (world avg. 25.0); legitimate, n.a.; illegitimate, n.a.
Death rate per 1,000 population (1990–95): 10.7 (world avg. 9.3).
Natural increase rate per 1,000 population (1990–95): 27.8 (world avg. 15.7).
Total fertility rate (avg. births per childbearing woman; 1990–95): 4.9.
Marriage rate per 1,000 population (1989): 4.3.
Divorce rate per 1,000 population: n.a.
Life expectancy at birth (1990–95): male 55.2 years; female 59.8 years.
Major causes of death (1992)[6]: accidents and injuries 15.8%; infectious intestinal diseases 13.3%; tuberculosis 10.3%; malnutrition 6.2%; respiratory diseases 5.3%; circulatory diseases 5.0%; digestive diseases 4.6%.

National economy

Budget (1993–94). Revenue: E 1,240,100,000 (receipts from Customs Union of Southern Africa 45.6%; tax on income and profits 28.6%; sales tax 12.3%; foreign-aid grants 3.2%; property income 2.4%; fees, services, and fines 1.2%). Expenditures: E 1,521,900,000 (recurrent expenditure 61.6%, of which education 18.3%, general administration 13.7%, economic services 9.9%, health 5.9%, justice and police 5.6%, defense 5.3%, public-debt payments 1.8%).
Land use (1993): forested 7.0%; meadows and pastures 62.2%; agricultural and under permanent cultivation 11.1%; other 19.7%.
Tourism (1993): receipts from visitors U.S.$30,000,000; expenditures by nationals abroad U.S.$17,000,000.
Gross national product (at current market prices; 1993): U.S.$933,000,000 (U.S.$1,050 per capita).

Structure of gross domestic product and labour force	1993		1986	
	in value E '000	% of total value	labour force	% of labour force
Agriculture	306,600	10.0	30,197	18.8
Mining	47,600	1.6	5,245	3.3
Manufacturing	888,700	29.0	14,742	9.2
Construction	82,200	2.7	7,661	4.8
Public utilities	36,600	1.2	1,315	0.8
Transp. and commun.	151,400	4.9	7,526	4.7
Trade	209,300	6.8	12,348	7.7
Finance	170,400	5.6	1,931	1.2
Pub. admin., defense	566,400	18.5	32,309	20.1
Services	149,600	4.9		
Other	452,400[7]	14.8[7]	47,081[8]	29.4[8]
TOTAL	3,061,200	100.0	160,355	100.0

Population economically active (1986): total 160,355; activity rate of total population 23.5% (participation rates: ages 15 and over, 44.1%; female 34.2%; unemployed 27.0%).

Price and earnings indexes (1990 = 100)	1988	1989	1990	1991	1992	1993	1994
Consumer price index	83.2	90.1	100.0	110.8	119.9	140.3	160.4
Earnings index	...	...	...	...	...	...	...

Public debt (external, outstanding; 1993): U.S.$217,800,000.
Production (metric tons except as noted). Agriculture, forestry, fishing (1994): sugarcane 3,600,000, corn (maize) 64,000, grapefruit 54,000, seed cotton 50,000, lint cotton 16,000, roots and tubers 8,000 (of which potatoes 6,000, sweet potatoes 2,000), pulses 4,000; livestock (number of live animals) 620,000 cattle, 434,000 goats, 32,000 pigs, 27,000 sheep, 1,000,000 chickens; roundwood (1993) 2,297,000 cu m; fish catch (1993) 110. Mining and quarrying (1994): asbestos 26,720; diamonds 52,800 carats. Manufacturing (value added in E; 1988): food and beverages 290,900,000, of which beverage processing 168,402,000, sugarcane milling 94,934,000; paper and paper products 107,490,000; textiles and garments 17,965,000; wood and wood products 11,453,000; machinery and equipment 10,833,000; nonmetallic mineral products 9,464,000. Construction (value in E; 1993)[9]: residential 38,600,000; nonresidential 3,600,000. Energy production (consumption): electricity (kW-hr; 1991) 387,000,000 (815,000,000); coal (metric tons; 1992) 100,220 (1989; 28,454); crude petroleum, n.a. (n.a.); petroleum products, n.a. (n.a.); natural gas, n.a. (n.a.).
Household income and expenditure. Average household size (1986) 5.7; annual income per household (1985) E 332 (U.S.$151); sources of income (1985): wages and salaries 44.4%, self-employment 22.2%, transfers 12.2%, other 21.2%; expenditure (1985): food and beverages 33.5%, rent and fuel 13.4%, household durable goods 12.8%, transportation and communications 8.8%, clothing and footwear 6.0%, recreation 3.3%.

Foreign trade

Balance of trade (current prices)	1989	1990	1991	1992	1993	1994
E '000,000	−56.7	−77.5	−98.6	−362.7	−406.9	−943.4
% of total	2.1%	2.6%	2.0%	9.1%	8.7%	16.8%

Imports (1993): E 2,971,429,000 (machinery and transport equipment 26.4%; foodstuffs 14.8%; manufactured items 10.6%; minerals, fuels, and lubricants 10.2%; chemical products 9.5%). *Major import sources:* South Africa 81.7%; United Kingdom 2.5%; The Netherlands 0.4%; Switzerland 0.3%; France 0.1%.
Exports (1992): E 1,724,100,000 (sugar 24.6%; canned fruits 5.0%; wood and wood products 4.1%; mineral products 3.9%). *Major export destinations* (1991): South Africa 47.0%; United States 3.6%; United Kingdom 3.3%; Mozambique 2.4%; South Korea 2.2%; Zimbabwe 2.2%.

Transport and communications

Transport. Railroads (1994): length 187 mi, 301 km; passenger-mi 752,000,000[10], passenger-km 1,210,000,000[10]; short ton-mi cargo 1,993,000,000[11], metric ton-km cargo 2,910,000,000[11]. Roads (1992): total length 1,839 mi, 2,960 km (paved 59%). Vehicles (1993): passenger cars 25,946; trucks and buses 7,734. Merchant marine: none (landlocked state). Air transport (1992)[12]: passenger-mi 25,608,000, passenger-km 41,212,000; short ton-mi cargo 101,000, metric ton-km cargo 147,000; airports (1995) with scheduled flights 1.
Communications. Daily newspapers (1995): total number 2; total circulation 36,000; circulation per 1,000 population 41. Radio (1994): total number of receivers 117,000 (1 per 7.5 persons). Television (1994): total number of receivers 12,500 (1 per 71 persons). Telephones (main lines; 1993): 16,000 (1 per 53 persons).

Education and health

Education (1994)	schools	teachers	students	student/teacher ratio
Primary (age 6–13)	535	5,887	192,599	32.7
Secondary (age 14–18)	165	2,872	52,571	18.3
Voc., teacher tr.[13]	5	228	2,958	13.0
Higher[13]	1	190	1,730	9.1

Educational attainment (1986). Percentage of population age 25 and over having: no formal schooling 42.1%; some primary education 23.9%; complete primary 10.5%; some secondary 19.2%; complete secondary and higher 4.3%. *Literacy* (1995): total population age 15 and over literate 76.7%; males literate 78.0%; females literate 75.6%.
Health: physicians (1990) 83 (1 per 9,265 persons); hospital beds (1984) 1,608 (1 per 396 persons); infant mortality rate per 1,000 live births (1990–95) 75.0.
Food (1992): daily per capita caloric intake 2,706 (vegetable products 89%, animal products 11%); 117% of FAO recommended minimum requirement.

Military

Total active duty personnel (1983): 2,657. *Military expenditure as percentage of GNP* (1993): 2.4% (world 3.3%); per capita expenditure U.S.$23.

[1]The government announced on Oct. 9, 1992, that a new constitution would be forthcoming; nonparty legislative elections took place on Sept. 25, 1993, and Oct. 11, 1993. [2]Includes 20 nonelective seats. [3]Includes 10 nonelective seats. [4]The lilangeni is at par with the South African rand. [5]Preliminary. [6]Percentage of deaths of known cause at government, mission, and private hospitals. [7]Includes indirect taxes less imputed bank service charges and subsidies. [8]Includes 43,925 unemployed. [9]Urban areas under the jurisdiction of the Manzini and Mbabane town councils only. [10]1988. [11]1991. [12]Royal Swazi National Airways only; international flights only. [13]1993–94.

Sweden

Official name: Konungariket Sverige (Kingdom of Sweden).
Form of government: constitutional monarchy and parliamentary state with one legislative house (Parliament [349]).
Chief of state: King.
Head of government: Prime Minister.
Capital: Stockholm.
Official language: Swedish.
Official religion: Church of Sweden (Lutheran).
Monetary unit: 1 Swedish krona (SKr) = 100 ore; valuation (Oct. 6, 1995) 1 U.S.$ = SKr 7.03; 1 £ = SKr 11.11.

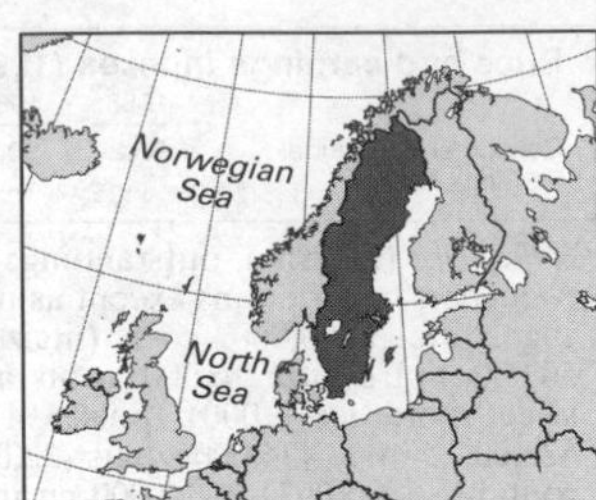

Area and population

Counties	Capitals	area sq mi	area sq km	population 1995[1] estimate
Älvsborg	Vänersborg	4,400	11,395	449,767
Blekinge	Karlskrona	1,136	2,941	153,016
Gävleborg	Gävle	7,024	18,191	289,654
Göteborg och Bohus	Göteborg	1,985	5,141	764,594
Gotland	Visby	1,212	3,140	58,237
Halland	Halmstad	2,106	5,454	268,067
Jämtland	Östersund	19,090	49,443	136,301
Jönköping	Jönköping	3,839	9,944	312,494
Kalmar	Kalmar	4,313	11,170	244,057
Kopparberg	Falun	10,886	28,194	291,203
Kristianstad	Kristianstad	2,350	6,087	294,571
Kronoberg	Växjö	3,266	8,458	180,747
Malmöhus	Malmö	1,907	4,938	811,415
Norrbotten	Luleå	38,191	98,913	267,648
Örebro	Örebro	3,289	8,519	276,828
Östergötland	Linköping	4,078	10,562	415,603
Skaraborg	Mariestad	3,065	7,937	279,921
Södermanland	Nyköping	2,340	6,060	259,793
Stockholm	Stockholm	2,505	6,488	1,708,502
Uppsala	Uppsala	2,698	6,989	286,642
Värmland	Karlstad	6,789	17,584	285,498
Västerbotten	Umeå	21,390	55,401	259,775
Västernorrland	Härnösand	8,370	21,678	260,295
Västmanland	Västerås	2,433	6,302	261,753
TOTAL LAND AREA		158,661[2]	410,929	
INLAND WATER		15,071	39,035	
TOTAL		173,732	449,964	8,816,381

Demography

Population (1995): 8,826,000.
Density (1995)[3]: persons per sq mi 55.6, persons per sq km 21.5.
Urban-rural (1993): urban 83.1%; rural 16.9%.
Sex distribution (1995[1]): male 49.41%; female 50.59%.
Age breakdown (1995[1]): under 15, 18.8%; 15–29, 19.7%; 30–44, 20.4%; 45–59, 19.0%; 60–74, 13.9%; 75 and over, 8.2%.
Population projection: (2000) 9,059,000; (2010) 9,278,000.
Ethnic composition (1994[1]): Swedish 90.1%; Finnish 2.4%; other 7.5%.
Religious affiliation (1993[1]): Church of Sweden 87.3% (nominally; about 30% nonpracticing); Roman Catholic 1.7%; Pentecostal 1.1%; other 9.9%.
Major cities (1995[1]): Stockholm 703,627; Göteborg 444,553; Malmö 242,706; Uppsala 181,191; Linköping 130,489.

Vital statistics

Birth rate per 1,000 population (1994): 12.8 (world avg. 25.0); (1993) legitimate 49.6%; illegitimate 50.4%.
Death rate per 1,000 population (1994): 10.5 (world avg. 9.3).
Natural increase rate per 1,000 population (1994): 2.3 (world avg. 15.7).
Total fertility rate (avg. births per childbearing woman; 1993): 2.0.
Marriage rate per 1,000 population (1994): 3.9.
Divorce rate per 1,000 population (1994): 2.5.
Life expectancy at birth (1989–93): male 75.1 years; female 80.6 years.
Major causes of death per 100,000 population (1992): heart disease 430.6; malignant neoplasms (cancers) 235.0; cerebrovascular disease 119.1.

National economy

Budget (1993–94). Revenue: SKr 343,990,000,000 (value-added and excise taxes 55.4%, social-security contributions 15.8%, income and capital gains taxes 11.2%, nontax revenue 10.5%, property taxes 7.1%). Expenditures: SKr 549,662,000,000 (health and social affairs 23.0%, interest on national debt 17.5%, education and culture 9.9%, defense 7.1%).
Public debt (1994): U.S.$119,370,000,000.
Tourism (1993): receipts from visitors U.S.$2,650,000,000; expenditures by nationals abroad U.S.$4,464,000,000.
Production (metric tons except as noted). Agriculture, forestry, fishing (1994): sugar beets 2,349,800, barley 1,660,900, wheat 1,518,300, oats 990,600, potatoes 762,800; livestock (number of live animals) 2,328,405 pigs, 1,826,489 cattle, 483,428 sheep; roundwood 62,954,000 cu m; fish catch 375,700, of which Baltic herring 53,100. Mining and quarrying (1994): iron ore 12,940,000[4]; copper 293,000; zinc 287,000; lead 153,000. Manufacturing (value added, in SKr '000,000; 1992): machinery and transport equipment 94,898; paper and paper products 32,474; food and beverages 24,216; wood and wood products 11,789; textiles and wearing apparel 3,685. Construction (1993): 35,088 dwellings completed. Energy production (consumption): electricity (kW-hr; 1992) 146,245,000,000 (144,095,000,000); coal (metric tons; 1992) 37,000 (3,368,000); crude petroleum (barrels; 1992) 7,000 (121,713,000); petroleum products (metric tons; 1992) 17,027,000 (16,296,000); natural gas (cu m; 1992) none (486,913,000).
Gross national product (1993): U.S.$216,294,000,000 (U.S.$24,830 per capita).

Structure of gross domestic product and labour force

	1993 in value SKr '000,000	% of total value	labour force	% of labour force
Agriculture	28,829	2.3	137,000	3.2
Mining	3,846	0.3	11,000	0.3
Manufacturing	275,460	21.6	726,000	16.8
Public utilities	44,160	3.5	35,000	0.8
Construction	81,434	6.4	236,000	5.5
Transp. and commun.	88,967	7.0	277,000	6.4
Trade	138,681	10.9	567,000	13.1
Finance	288,595	22.7	368,000	8.5
Pub. admin., defense; Services	371,327	29.2	1,602,000	37.1
Other	−47,989[5]	−3.8[5]	356,000[6]	8.2[6]
TOTAL	1,273,310	100.0[2]	4,320,000[2]	100.0[2]

Population economically active (1993): total 4,320,000; activity rate of total population 49.5% (participation rates: ages 16–64 [1992] 82.0%; female 48.0%; unemployed 8.2%).

Price and earnings indexes (1990 = 100)

	1988	1989	1990	1991	1992	1993	1994
Consumer price index	85.0	90.6	100.0	109.4	118.5	117.1	120.0
Hourly earnings index	83.0	91.0	100.0	105.0	110.0	113.0	118.0

Household income and expenditure. Average household size (1990) 2.1; median income per household SKr 119,000 (U.S.$18,400); sources of income (1992): wages and salaries 58.9%, transfer payments 25.8%, self-employment 15.3%; expenditure (1992): housing and energy 31.4%, food 19.8%, transportation 16.1%, education and recreation 9.8%.
Land use (1993): forested 68.0%; meadows and pastures 1.4%; agricultural and under permanent cultivation 6.8%; other 23.8%.

Foreign trade

Balance of trade (current prices)

	1989	1990	1991	1992	1993	1994
SKr '000,000	23,098	23,272	38,343	42,894	54,010	72,470
% of total	3.6%	3.5%	6.1%	7.0%	7.5%	8.3%

Imports (1994): SKr 399,130,000,000 (machinery and transport equipment 37.9%, of which electrical machinery 11.7%, transport equipment 9.3%; chemicals 11.3%; food 7.5%; clothing 4.9%). *Major import sources:* Germany 18.4%; U.K. 9.7%; U.S. 8.6%; Denmark 6.8%; Finland 6.3%; Norway 6.1%.
Exports (1994): SKr 471,600,000,000 (machinery and transport equipment 45.1%, of which transport equipment 15.2%, electrical machinery 12.0%; paper products 9.5%; chemicals 9.5%; wood and wood pulp 6.3%; iron and steel products 6.2%). *Major export destinations:* Germany 13.3%; U.K. 10.2%; Norway 8.1%; U.S. 8.0%; Denmark 6.9%; Finland 4.8%.

Transport and communications

Transport. Railroads (1993): length 7,012 mi, 11,285 km; passenger-mi 3,712,000,000, passenger-km 5,975,000,000; short ton-mi cargo 12,725,000,000, metric ton-km cargo 18,578,000,000. Roads (1992): total length 84,419 mi, 135,859 km (paved 72%). Vehicles (1993): passenger cars 3,566,040; trucks and buses 315,994. Merchant marine (1993): vessels (100 gross tons and over) 417; total deadweight tonnage 2,339,474. Air transport (1993): passenger-mi 5,096,789,000, passenger-km 8,202,502,000; short ton-mi cargo 123,098,000, metric ton-km cargo 179,720,000; airports (1995) 48.
Communications. Daily newspapers (1993): total number 176; total circulation 4,678,000; circulation per 1,000 population 536. Radio (1993): 7,450,000 receivers (1 per 1.2 persons). Television (1993): 3,750,000 receivers (1 per 2.3 persons). Telephones (main lines; 1993): 5,907,000 (1 per 1.5 persons).

Education and health

Education (1993–94)

	schools	teachers	students	student/ teacher ratio
Primary (age 7–12)	4,826	90,234	893,932	9.9
Secondary (age 13–18)	600	29,539	313,728	10.6
Higher[7]	...	27,523[8]	272,718	9.9

Educational attainment (1990). Percentage of population age 16–64 having: primary education 37.1%; lower secondary education 29.4%; higher secondary 12.2%; some postsecondary 21.3%. *Literacy* (1993): virtually 100%.
Health: physicians (1993) 22,200 (1 per 393 persons); hospital beds (1992) 57,778 (1 per 150 persons); infant mortality rate per 1,000 live births (1994) 3.4.
Food (1992): daily per capita caloric intake 2,972 (vegetable products 62%, animal products 38%); 110% of FAO requirement.

Military

Total active duty personnel (1994): 64,000 (army 68.0%, navy 14.1%, air force 17.9%). *Military expenditure as percentage of GNP* (1993): 2.8% (world 3.3%); per capita expenditure U.S.$574.

[1]January 1. [2]Detail does not add to total given because of rounding. [3]Density based on land area only. [4]Metal content of ore. [5]Includes statistical discrepancies less imputed bank service charges. [6]Unemployed. [7]1989–90. [8]Includes graduate assistants.

Switzerland

Official name: Confédération Suisse (French); Schweizerische Eidgenossenschaft (German); Confederazione Svizzera (Italian) (Swiss Confederation).
Form of government: federal state with two legislative houses (Council of States [46]; National Council [200]).
Head of state and government: President.
Capitals: Bern (administrative); Lausanne (judicial).
Official languages: French; German; Italian.
Official religion: none.
Monetary unit: 1 Swiss Franc (Sw F) = 100 centimes; valuation (Oct. 6, 1995) 1 U.S.$ = Sw F 1.15; 1 £ = Sw F 1.82.

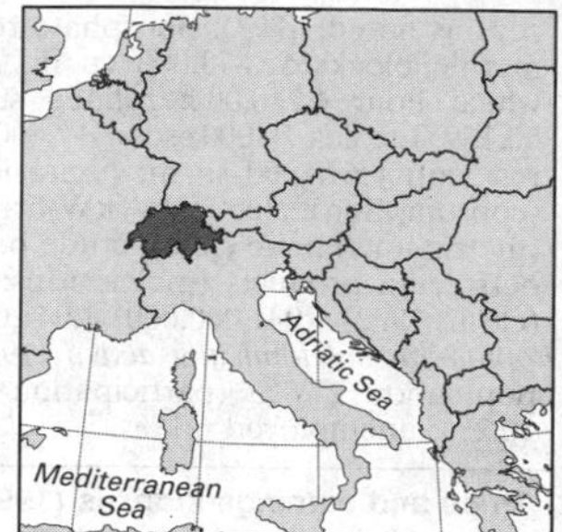

Area and population

Cantons	Capitals	area sq mi	area sq km	population 1994[1] estimate
Aargau	Aarau	542	1,404	518,945
Appenzell Ausser-Rhoden[2]	Herisau	94	243	54,087
Appenzell Inner-Rhoden[2]	Appenzell	67	173	14,680
Basel-Landschaft[2]	Liestal	200	517	234,910
Basel-Stadt[2]	Basel	14	37	197,403
Bern	Bern	2,302	5,961	956,617
Fribourg	Fribourg	645	1,671	218,704
Genève	Geneva	109	282	387,606
Glarus	Glarus	264	685	39,100
Graubünden	Chur	2,743	7,105	181,957
Jura	Delémont	323	836	68,626
Luzern	Luzern	570	1,493	335,385
Neuchâtel	Neuchâtel	310	803	163,884
Nidwalden[2]	Stans	107	276	35,393
Obwalden[2]	Sarnen	189	490	30,837
Sankt Gallen	Sankt Gallen	782	2,026	436,967
Schaffhausen	Schaffhausen	115	299	73,508
Schwyz	Schwyz	351	908	118,528
Solothurn	Solothurn	305	791	236,389
Thurgau	Frauenfeld	383	991	217,129
Ticino	Bellinzona	1,086	2,812	297,955
Uri	Altdorf	416	1,077	35,727
Valais	Sion	2,017	5,225	266,713
Vaud	Lausanne	1,240	3,212	596,736
Zug	Zug	92	239	88,583
Zürich	Zürich	668	1,729	1,162,083
TOTAL		15,940	41,285	6,968,570[3]

Demography

Population (1995): 7,039,000.
Density (1995): persons per sq mi 441.6, persons per sq km 170.5.
Urban-rural (1994): urban 67.9%; rural 32.1%.
Sex distribution (1994): male 48.85%; female 51.15%.
Age breakdown (1994): under 15, 17.6%; 15–29, 20.8%; 30–44, 23.5%; 45–59, 18.7%; 60–74, 12.8%; 75 and over, 6.6%.
Population projection: (2000) 7,279,000; (2010) 7,542,000.
Linguistic composition (1990): German 63.6%; French 19.2%; Italian 7.6%; Spanish 1.7%; Portuguese 1.4%; Romansch 0.6%; other 5.9%.
Religious affiliation (1990): Roman Catholic 46.2%; Protestant 40.0%; Muslim 2.2%; Orthodox Christian 1.0%; Jewish 0.3%; other 10.3%.
Major cities (1994[1]): Zürich 343,045 (940,180[4]); Basel 176,220 (406,391[4]); Geneva 171,744 (424,028[4]); Bern 129,423 (332,494[4]); Lausanne 117,153.

Vital statistics

Birth rate per 1,000 population (1994): 11.9 (world avg. 25.0); (1993) legitimate 93.7%; illegitimate 6.3%.
Death rate per 1,000 population (1994): 8.8 (world avg. 9.3).
Natural increase rate per 1,000 population (1994): 3.1 (world avg. 15.7).
Total fertility rate (avg. births per childbearing woman; 1993): 1.5.
Marriage rate per 1,000 population (1993): 6.2.
Life expectancy at birth (1992–93): male 74.7 years; female 81.4 years.
Major causes of death per 100,000 population (1992): heart disease 264.4, of which ischemic 150.6, other 113.8; malignant neoplasms (cancers) 240.8.

National economy

Budget (1995)[5]. Revenue: Sw F 36,319,000,000 (turnover taxes 29.5%, direct federal taxes 23.8%, motor fuel fees 12.3%). Expenditures: Sw F 42,399,000,000 (social services 25.8%, transportation 15.0%, defense 14.0%).
National debt (end of year; 1994): Sw F 77,774,000,000.
Tourism (1993): receipts from visitors U.S.$7,001,000,000; expenditures by nationals abroad U.S.$5,803,000,000.
Production (metric tons except as noted). Agriculture, forestry, fishing (1993): milk 3,927,000, sugar beets 976,000, potatoes 908,000, wheat 580,000, barley 392,000, apples 243,000, grapes 154,000; livestock (number of live animals) 1,745,000 cattle, 1,692,000 pigs; roundwood 4,338,000 cu m; fish catch (1992) 3,900. Mining (1993): salt 300,000. Manufacturing (value added in Sw F '000,000; 1992): nonelectrical machinery and transport vehicles 13,626; electrical goods, electronics, and optics 11,544; chemical products 11,071; base metals and metal products 8,320. Construction (in Sw F '000,000; 1992): residential 17,010; nonresidential 29,652. Energy production (consumption): electricity (kW-hr; 1993) 58,127,000,000 ([1992] 54,828,000,000); coal (metric tons; 1992) none (263,000); crude petroleum (barrels; 1992) none (30,126,000); petroleum products (metric tons; 1992) 4,115,000 (11,784,000); natural gas (cu m; 1992) 9,607,500 (2,557,000,000).
Gross national product (1993): U.S.$254,066,000,000 (U.S.$36,410 per capita).

Structure of gross domestic product and labour force

	1992 in value Sw F '000,000	1992 % of total value	1993 labour force	1993 % of labour force
Agriculture	9,845	2.9	191,400	5.4
Manufacturing } Mining }	78,299	23.1	800,600	22.5
Public utilities	6,615	1.9 }	24,700	0.7
Construction	25,079	7.4	299,700	8.4
Transp. and commun.	21,523	6.4	212,800	6.0
Trade	59,140	17.5	689,300	19.4
Finance, insurance[6]	83,144	24.5	371,700	10.5
Pub. admin., defense }	70,346	20.8	133,000	3.8
Services }			665,800	18.7
Other	−15,226[7]	−4.5[7]	163,100[8]	4.6[8]
TOTAL	338,765	100.0	3,552,100[9]	100.0

Population economically active (1993): total 3,552,100; activity rate of total population 50.8% (participation rates: age 15 and over 60.8%; female 38.3%; unemployed [February 1994–January 1995] 4.7%).

Price and earnings indexes (1990 = 100)

	1989	1990	1991	1992	1993	1994	1995
Consumer price index	94.9	100.0	105.8	110.1	113.8	114.7	116.7[10]
Annual earnings index	96.2	100.0	106.9	111.9	114.8	116.6	...

Household income and expenditure. Average household size (1993) 2.2; average income per household (1993) Sw F 70,700 (U.S.$47,850); sources of income (1992): wages 63.6%, transfer payments 16.5%, other 19.9%; expenditure (1992): food 19.2%, housing 15.8%, transportation and communications 11.7%, health care 11.1%, beverages and tobacco 7.3%.
Land use (1992): forested 31.7%; meadows and pastures 28.1%; agricultural and under permanent cultivation 11.8%; other 28.4%.

Foreign trade[11]

Balance of trade (current prices)

	1989	1990	1991	1992	1993	1994
Sw F '000,000	−9,998	−7,397	−6,144	+268	+3,721	+3,798
% of total	5.6%	4.0%	3.4%	0.2%	3.2%	2.2%

Imports (1994): Sw F 87,279,000,000 (machinery and electronics 20.5%, chemical products 13.5%, vehicles 9.0%, textiles and clothing 9.0%). *Major import sources:* Germany 34.4%; France 11.4%; Italy 10.5%; U.S. 5.7%; The Netherlands 4.9%.
Exports (1994): Sw F 90,213,000,000 (machinery and electronics 27.3%, chemical products 24.5%, watches 8.3%, base metals and finished products 8.1%). *Major export destinations:* Germany 24.3%; France 9.4%; U.S. 8.7%; Italy 7.7%; U.K. 5.4%.

Transport and communications

Transport. Railroads: length (1992) 3,125 mi, 5,029 km; passenger-km (1993) 12,012,000,000[12]; metric ton-km cargo (1993) 7,332,000,000[12]. Roads (1993): total length 44,201 mi, 71,134 km. Vehicles (1993): passenger cars 3,137,619, trucks and buses 286,501. Merchant marine (1992): vessels (100 gross tons and over) 24; total deadweight tonnage 602,084. Air transport (1994)[13]: passenger-km 18,580,000,000; metric ton-km cargo 1,408,000,000; airports (1995) with scheduled flights 5.
Communications. Daily newspapers (1994): total number 110; total circulation 3,427,801; circulation per 1,000 population 490. Radio (1994): 5,600,000 receivers (1 per 1.2 persons). Television (1994): 2,545,000 receivers (1 per 2.7 persons). Telephones (main lines; 1993): 4,265,800 (1 per 1.6 persons).

Education and health

Education (1993–94)

	schools	teachers	students	student/teacher ratio
Primary (age 7–12)	...	...	423,399	...
Secondary (age 13–19)	...	...	412,385	...
Voc., teacher tr.	...	...	191,344	...
Higher	...	...	144,544	...

Educational attainment (1993). Percentage of resident Swiss and resident alien population age 25–64 having: lower secondary education or less 18%; vocational 50%; upper secondary 11%; higher technical 13%; university 8%.
Health (1992): physicians c. 23,000 (1 per 299 persons); hospital beds 53,349 (1 per 129 persons); infant mortality rate (1994) 5.4.
Food (1988–90): daily per capita caloric intake 3,508 (vegetable products 61%, animal products 39%); 130% of FAO recommended minimum.

Military

Total active duty personnel (1994): 1,800[14]. *Military expenditure as percentage of GNP* (1993): 1.7% (world 3.3%); per capita expenditure U.S.$585.

[1]January 1. [2]Demicanton; functions as a full canton. [3]Includes 1,291,762 resident aliens. [4]1990 population of urban agglomeration. [5]Confederation-level only. [6]Includes consulting services. [7]Import duties less imputed bank charges. [8]Unemployed. [9]Labour force includes 935,300 foreign workers. [10]March. [11]Import figures are f.o.b. in balance of trade and c.i.f. in commodities and trading partners. [12]Swiss Federal Railways. [13]Swissair only. [14]Excludes 565,000 army reservists and 60,000 air corps reservists.

Syria

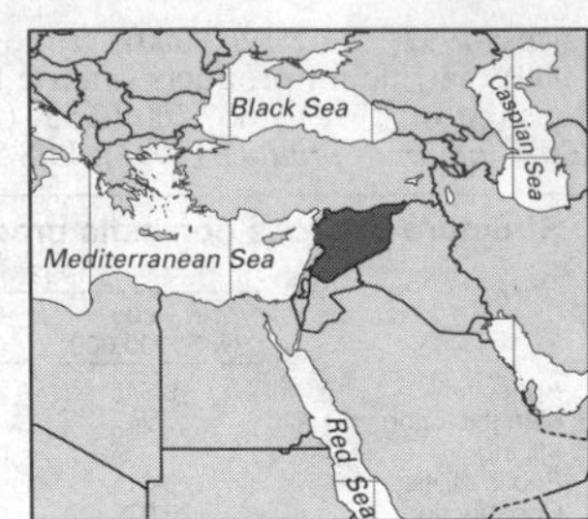

Official name: al-Jumhūrīyah al-ʿArabīyah as-Sūrīyah (Syrian Arab Republic).
Form of government: unitary multiparty[1] republic with one legislative house (People's Council [250]).
Head of state and government: President.
Capital: Damascus.
Official language: Arabic.
Official religion: none[2].
Monetary unit: 1 Syrian pound (LS) = 100 piastres; valuation (nonessential [imports] rate; Oct. 6, 1995) 1 U.S.$ = LS 11.22; 1 £ = LS 17.74[3].

Area and population

Governorates	Capitals	area sq mi	area sq km	population 1994 estimate
Darʿā	Darʿā	1,440	3,730	616,000
Dayr az-Zawr	Dayr az-Zawr	12,765	33,060	599,000
Dimashq	Damascus	6,962	18,032	1,451,000
Ḥalab	Aleppo	7,143	18,500	2,856,000
Ḥamāh	Ḥamāh	3,430	8,883	1,116,000
al-Ḥasakah	al-Ḥasakah	9,009	23,334	1,030,000
Ḥimṣ	Homs	16,302	42,223	1,301,000
Idlib	Idlib	2,354	6,097	937,000
al-Lādhiqīyah	Latakia	887	2,297	834,000
al-Qunayṭirah	al-Qunayṭirah	719[4]	1,861[4]	45,000
ar-Raqqah	ar-Raqqah	7,574	19,616	518,000
as-Suwaydāʾ	as-Suwaydāʾ	2,143	5,550	300,000
Ṭarṭūs	Ṭarṭūs	730	1,892	689,000
Municipality				
Damascus	—	41	105	1,552,000
TOTAL		71,498[4]	185,180[4]	13,844,000

Demography

Population (1995): 14,313,000.
Density (1995): persons per sq mi 200.2, persons per sq km 77.3.
Urban-rural (1995): urban 52.4%; rural 47.6%.
Sex distribution (1994): male 51.08%; female 48.92%.
Age breakdown (1995): under 15, 47.3%; 15–29, 27.5%; 30–44, 14.3%; 45–59, 6.5%; 60–74, 3.6%; 75 and over, 0.8%.
Population projection: (2000) 16,909,000; (2010) 23,019,000.
Doubling time: 28 years.
Ethnic composition (1981): Arab 88.8%; Kurdish 6.3%; other 4.9%.
Religious affiliation (1992): Muslim 86.0%, of which Sunnī 74.0%, ʿAlawite (Shīʿī) 12.0%; Christian 8.9%; Druze 3.0%; other 1.0%.
Major cities (1994): Aleppo 1,591,400; Damascus 1,549,932; Homs 644,204; Latakia 306,535; Ḥamāh 229,000.

Vital statistics

Birth rate per 1,000 population (1994): 28.8 (world avg. 25.0).
Death rate per 1,000 population (1994): 3.3 (world avg. 9.3).
Natural increase rate per 1,000 population (1994): 25.5 (world avg. 15.7).
Total fertility rate (avg. births per childbearing woman; 1993): 5.8.
Marriage rate per 1,000 population (1993)[5]: 8.6.
Divorce rate per 1,000 population (1993)[5]: 0.8.
Life expectancy at birth (1990–95): male 65.2 years; female 69.2 years.
Major causes of death per 100,000 population (1981): diseases of the circulatory system 60.7; accidents 18.3; infectious diseases 15.1.

National economy

Budget (1995). Revenue: LS 125,718,000,000 (current revenues 81.3%, capital [development] revenues 18.7%). Expenditures: LS 162,040,000,000 (current expenditures 54.3%, capital [development] expenditures 45.7%).
Public debt (external, outstanding; 1993): U.S.$16,234,000,000.
Gross national product (1991): U.S.$16,204,000,000 (U.S.$1,170 per capita).

Structure of gross domestic product and labour force

	1993 in value[6] LS '000,000	1993 % of total value	1991 labour force	1991 % of labour force
Agriculture	33,368	18.4	916,952	26.3
Mining	70,593 (Mining and Manufacturing)	38.9 (Mining and Manufacturing)	6,651	0.2
Manufacturing			456,162	13.1
Construction	7,929	4.4	340,779	9.8
Public utilities	...	...	8,422	0.2
Transportation and communications	19,466	10.7	166,965	4.8
Trade	23,704	13.1	378,250	10.9
Finance	5,186	2.8	24,651	0.7
Pub. admin.	17,825	9.8	951,104 (Pub. admin. and Services)	27.3 (Pub. admin. and Services)
Services	3,138	1.7		
Other	142[7]	0.1[7]	235,432[8]	6.8[8]
TOTAL	181,351[9]	100.0[10]	3,485,368	100.0[10]

Production (metric tons except as noted). Agriculture, forestry, fishing (1994): wheat 3,814,000, barley 1,573,000, seed cotton 662,000, tomatoes 437,000, grapes 360,000, apples 240,000, eggplants 150,000; livestock (number of live animals) 12,000,000 sheep, 1,200,000 goats, 770,000 cattle; roundwood (1993) 55,000 cu m; fish catch (1993) 5,600. Mining and quarrying (metric tons except as noted; 1993): phosphate rock 930,000; gypsum 303,000; salt 113,000; marble blocks 52,873,000 cu m. Manufacturing (1993): cement 3,667,000; wheat flour 1,218,000; refined sugar 183,000; fertilizers 89,639; olive oil 60,139; textiles 29,000; soap 17,000; rugs 656,000 sq m. Construction (1993): residential 628,000 sq m; nonresidential 209,000 sq m. Energy production (consumption): electricity (kW-hr; 1993) 12,742,000,000 (12,742,000,000); coal (metric tons) none (n.a.); crude petroleum (barrels; 1993) 222,997,000 (n.a.); petroleum products (metric tons; 1992) 11,148,000 (9,420,000); natural gas (cu m; 1992) 1,941,000,000 (1,941,000,000).
Population economically active (1991): total 3,845,368; activity rate of total population 27.8% (participation rates: ages 15–64 [1986] 46.7%; female 10.2%; unemployed 6.1%).

Price and earnings indexes (1990 = 100)

	1988	1989	1990	1991	1992	1993	1994[11]
Consumer price index	75.2	83.8	100.0	107.7	117.9	131.8	142.8
Earnings index	...	...	...	...	...	...	...

Average household size (1986): 5.7; income per household: n.a.; sources of income: n.a.; expenditure (1987)[12]: food 58.8%, rent, fuel, and light 16.0%, clothing 7.5%, household goods 5.8%, transportation 2.4%, education and recreation 2.1%.
Tourism (1993): receipts from visitors U.S.$700,000,000; expenditures by nationals abroad U.S.$300,000,000.
Land use (1993): steppe and pasture 44.4%; cultivable 32.1%; forested 3.2%; other 20.3%.

Foreign trade[13]

Balance of trade (current prices)

	1988	1989	1990	1991	1992	1993
LS '000,000	−7,879	+12,140	+19,579	+2,835	−1,223	−7,312
% of total	20.7%	21.9%	27.3%	4.2%	1.7%	9.4%

Imports (1993): LS 46,468,900,000 (machinery and equipment 22.3%, food and beverages 15.4%, basic metals industries 13.4%, transportation equipment 11.8%, chemicals and chemical products 10.9%, textiles 8.3%). *Major import sources:* Germany 10.2%; Japan 8.2%; Italy 8.2%; France 7.1%; United States 6.4%; Turkey 5.4%; Romania 4.5%.
Exports (1993): LS 35,318,000,000 (crude petroleum and petroleum products 66.7%, fresh vegetables and fruits 9.3%, raw cotton 5.5%, live animals and meat 3.0%, textiles 2.9%). *Major export destinations:* Italy 30.8%; France 15.3%; Lebanon 10.5%; Spain 7.8%; Saudi Arabia 4.9%; United Kingdom 3.2%.

Transport and communications

Transport. Railroads (1993): route length 2,342 km; passenger-km 1,248,000,000[14]; metric ton-km cargo 1,704,000,000[14]. Roads (1993): total length 36,255 km (paved 77%). Vehicles (1993): passenger cars 117,842; trucks and buses 152,833. Merchant marine (1992): vessels (100 gross tons and over) 94; total deadweight tonnage 210,369. Air transport (1993): passenger-km 801,151,000; metric ton-km cargo 9,481,000; airports (1995) with scheduled flights 5.
Communications. Daily newspapers (1992): total number 11; total circulation 290,000; circulation per 1,000 population 22.4. Radio (1993): 3,000,000 receivers (1 per 4.5 persons). Television (1993): 700,000 receivers (1 per 19.1 persons). Telephones (main lines; 1993): 550,312 (1 per 24.3 persons).

Education and health

Education (1993–94)

	schools	teachers	students	student/teacher ratio
Primary (age 6–11)	10,219	110,580	2,624,594	23.7
Secondary (age 12–18)	2,354	49,951	846,550	16.9
Voc., teacher tr.	289	11,559	76,480	6.6
Higher[15]	47	3,723	173,486	46.6

Educational attainment (1984). Percentage of population age 10 and over having: no schooling 20.1%; knowledge of reading and writing 26.3%; primary education 29.3%; secondary 18.4%; certificate 3.3%; higher 2.7%.
Literacy (1995): percentage of population age 15 and over literate 70.8%; males literate 85.7%; females literate 55.8%.
Health (1993): physicians 13,863 (1 per 966 persons); hospital beds 14,698 (1 per 911 persons); infant mortality rate per 1,000 live births 39.4.
Food (1992): daily per capita caloric intake 3,175 (vegetable products 89%, animal products 11%); 128% of FAO recommended minimum requirement.

Military

Total active duty personnel (1995): 423,000 (army 74.5%, navy 1.9%, air force 23.6%). *Military expenditure as percentage of GNP* (1993): 8.3% (world, 3.3%) per capita expenditure U.S.$178.

[1]Parties ideologically compatible with the Baʿth Party. [2]Islam is required to be the religion of the head of state and is the basis of the legal system. [3]The primary rate used in foreign exchange is 1 U.S.$ = LS 41.95; 1 £ = LS 66.32. [4]Includes territory in the Golan Heights recognized internationally as part of Syria (located between the 1949 Israel-Syria Armistice line [west] and the 1974 UN Disengagement of Forces zone [east]) that has been occupied by Israel since 1967. Israel's unilateral annexation of this territory in December 1981 has received no international recognition. [5]Syrian Arabs only. [6]At prices of 1985. [7]Other productive activities. [8]Unemployed. [9]GDP at current values in 1993 is LS 347,515,000,000. [10]Detail does not add to total given because of rounding. [11]September. [12]Weights of consumer price index components for Damascus only. [13]Import figures are f.o.b. in balance of trade and c.i.f. in commodities and trading partners. [14]1992. [15]University-level institutions only.

Taiwan

Official name: Chung-hua Min-kuo (Republic of China).
Form of government: multiparty republic with a National Assembly (402) and Legislative Yuan (161)[1].
Chief of state: President.
Head of government: Premier.
Capital: Taipei.
Official language: Mandarin Chinese.
Official religion: none.
Monetary unit: 1 New Taiwan dollar (NT$) = 100 cents; valuation (Oct. 6, 1995) 1 U.S.$ = NT$26.90; 1 £ = NT$42.52.

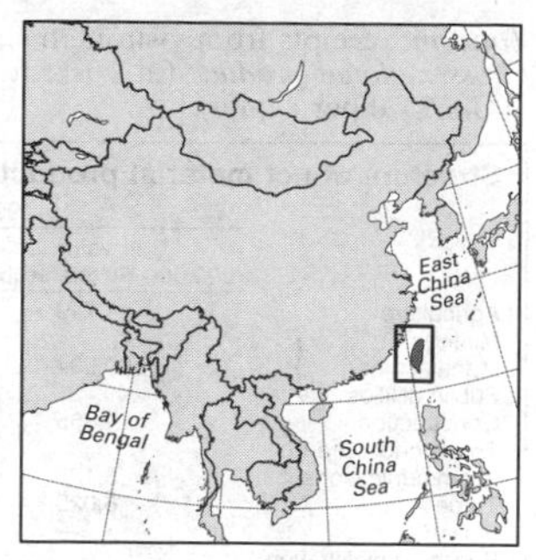

Area and population		area		population
Taiwan area				1995[2]
Counties	**Capitals**	sq mi	sq km	estimate
Chang-hua	Chang-hua	415	1,074	1,282,609
Chia-i	Chia-i	734	1,902	564,050
Hsin-chu	Hsin-chu	551	1,428	402,839
Hua-lien	Hua-lien	1,787	4,629	358,214
I-lan	I-lan	825	2,137	464,178
Kao-hsiung	Feng-shan	1,078	2,793	1,183,660
Miao-li	Miao-li	703	1,820	558,104
Nan-t'ou	Nan-t'ou	1,585	4,106	545,302
P'eng-hu	Ma-kung	49	127	91,867
P'ing-tung	P'ing-tung	1,072	2,776	909,733
T'ai-chung	Feng-yuan	792	2,051	1,386,499
T'ai-nan	Hsin-ying	778	2,016	1,072,166
T'ai-pei	Pan-ch'iao	792	2,052	3,268,287
T'ai-tung	T'ai-tung	1,357	3,515	254,228
T'ao-yüan	T'ao-yüan	471	1,221	1,491,857
Yün-lin	Tou-liu	498	1,291	752,754
Municipalities				
Chia-i	—	23	60	260,756
Chi-lung	—	51	133	365,312
Hsin-chu	—	40	104	338,507
Kao-hsiung	—	59	154	1,416,160
T'ai-chung	—	63	163	836,560
T'ai-nan	—	68	176	702,704
Taipei	—	105	272	2,652,685
non-Taiwan area				
Counties[3]				
Kinmen (Quemoy) Lienchiang (Matsu)	—	69	179	52,292
TOTAL		13,969[4]	36,179	21,211,323

Demography

Population (1995)[5]: 21,268,000.
Density (1995)[5]: persons per sq mi 1,522.5, persons per sq km 587.9.
Urban-rural (1991)[6]: urban 74.7%; rural 25.3%.
Sex distribution (1994)[6]: male 51.54%; female 48.46%.
Age breakdown (1994)[6]: under 15, 24.4%; 15–29, 26.7%; 30–44, 25.5%; 45–59, 12.6%; 60–69, 6.5%; 70 and over, 4.3%.
Population projection: (2000) 22,364,000; (2010) 24,693,000.
Doubling time: 67 years.
Ethnic composition (1986): Taiwanese 84.0%; mainland Chinese 14.0%; aborigine 2.0%.
Religious affiliation (1980): Chinese folk religionist 48.5%; Buddhist 43.0%; Christian 7.4%; Muslim 0.5%; other 0.6%.
Major cities (1994)[6]: Taipei 2,652,685; Kao-hsiung 1,416,160; T'ai-chung 836,560; T'ai-nan 702,704; Chi-lung 365,312.

Vital statistics

Birth rate per 1,000 population (1994): 15.3 (world avg. 25.0); (1993)[6] legitimate 97.7%; illegitimate 2.3%.
Death rate per 1,000 population (1994): 5.4 (world avg. 9.3).
Natural increase rate per 1,000 population (1994): 9.9 (world avg. 15.7).
Total fertility rate (avg. births per childbearing woman; 1993)[6]: 1.8.
Life expectancy at birth (1993): male 71.6 years; female 77.6 years.
Major causes of death per 100,000 population (1993)[6]: malignant neoplasms 107.1; cerebrovascular diseases 65.6; accidents and suicide 63.7; heart disease 60.0; diabetes 25.7; liver diseases 18.0; pneumonia 13.5.

National economy

Budget (1993)[7]. Revenue: NT$1,894,369,000,000 (income taxes 12.6%, land tax 11.7%, business tax 8.9%, surplus of public enterprises 8.9%, commodity tax 7.2%, customs duties 5.3%). Expenditures: NT$1,859,294,000,000 (economic development 29.3%, administration and defense 24.8%, education 18.8%).
Public debt (1993): NT$553,547,000,000.
Production (metric tons except as noted). Agriculture, forestry, fishing (1994): sugarcane 5,275,000, rice 1,679,000, citrus fruits 467,980, corn (maize) 321,322[8], pineapples 252,234, bananas 184,287, sweet potatoes 181,000; livestock (number of live animals) 10,065,552 pigs, 401,197 goats, 164,270 cattle; timber 37,821 cu m; fish catch 1,286,750. Mining and quarrying (1990): silver 3,926 kg. Manufacturing (1994): cement 22,721,650; steel ingots 12,102,257; paperboard 3,045,500; fertilizers 1,975,535; synthetic fibre 1,286,328; polyvinyl chloride plastics 1,113,679; electronic calculators 10,630,627 units; telephones 8,901,497 units. Construction (1994): total residential and nonresidential 49,757,000 sq m. Energy production (consumption): electricity (kW-hr; 1994) 110,276,000,000 (98,561,000,000); coal (metric tons; 1993) 328,000 ([1992] 16,500,000); crude petroleum (barrels; 1993) 400,000 ([1992] 215,400); natural gas (cu m; 1992) 767,000,000 (n.a.).
Gross national product (1994): U.S.$244,650,000,000 (U.S.$11,629 per capita).

Structure of gross domestic product and labour force[6]				
	1994			
	in value NT$'000,000	% of total value	labour force[9]	% of labour force[9]
Agriculture	227,977	3.6	976,000	10.7
Mining	21,001	0.3	18,000	0.2
Manufacturing	1,849,517	29.0	2,485,000	27.4
Construction	340,410	5.3	967,000	10.6
Public utilities	171,706	2.7	36,000	0.4
Transp. and commun.	417,429	6.6	473,000	5.2
Trade	978,857	15.3	1,875,000	20.6
Finance	1,317,214	20.6	504,000	5.6
Pub. admin., defense	677,880	10.6	1,605,000	17.7
Services	469,890	7.4		
Other	−91,682[10]	−1.4[10]	142,000[11]	1.6[11]
TOTAL	6,380,199	100.0	9,081,000	100.0

Tourism (1993): receipts from visitors U.S.$2,943,000,000.
Population economically active (1990): total 10,236,324; activity rate 50.5% (participation rates: age 15–64, 72.5%; female 38.5%; unemployed [1994] 1.6%).

Price and earnings indexes (1990 = 100)[6]							
	1988	1989	1990	1991	1992	1993	1994
Consumer price index	92.0	96.1	100.0	103.6	108.3	111.4	116.0
Monthly earnings index[12]	85.2	93.0	100.0	109.6	113.7	117.4	121.8

Household income and expenditure (1993). Average household size 3.8; income per household NT$840,220 (U.S.$32,200[13]); sources of income: wages 67.7%, self-employment and other 28.8%, transfer payments 3.5%; expenditure: food 26.1%, rent, fuel, and power 19.4%, education 17.3%, transportation 12.5%, health care 7.1%, furniture 5.0%, clothing 4.7%, other 7.9%.
Land use (1980): forested 55.0%; agricultural 25.2%; other 19.8%.

Foreign trade

Balance of trade (current prices)						
	1989	1990	1991	1992	1993	1994
NT$'000,000	359,832	330,980	350,013	231,668	199,604	194,360
% of total	11.5%	10.1%	9.4%	6.0%	4.7%	4.1%

Imports (1994): NT$2,261,651,000,000 (electronic machinery 19.7%, nonelectrical machinery 12.3%, chemicals 10.5%, road motor vehicles 7.1%, iron and steel 6.7%, crude petroleum 3.2%). *Major import sources:* Japan 29.0%; U.S. 21.1%; Germany 5.6%; Korea 3.5%; Singapore 2.8%; Malaysia 2.7%.
Exports (1994): NT$2,456,011,000,000 (electrical machinery 20.3%, nonelectrical machinery 19.7%, plastic articles 6.1%, synthetic fibres 5.5%, transportation equipment 5.2%). *Major export destinations:* U.S. 26.2%; Hong Kong 22.9%; Japan 11.0%; Singapore 3.6%; Germany 3.5%.

Transport and communications

Transport. Railroads (1994): track length 3,879 km; passenger-km 9,505,488,000; metric ton-km cargo 1,947,146,000. Roads (1994): total length 19,038 km (paved 89%). Vehicles (1994): passenger cars 3,798,800; trucks and buses 815,500. Merchant marine (1992): vessels (100 gross tons and over) 649; total deadweight tonnage 9,241,283. Air transport (1994): passenger-km 36,770,240,000; metric ton-km cargo 2,763,330,000; airports (1995) 12.
Communications. Daily newspapers (1988): total number 93; total circulation 4,000,000; circulation per 1,000 population 202. Radio (1994): 8,620,000 receivers (1 per 2.5 persons). Television (1994): 7,000,000 receivers (1 per 3.0 persons). Telephones (main lines; 1993): 7,950,500 (1 per 2.6 persons).

Education and health

Education (1993–94)	schools	teachers	students	student/ teacher ratio
Primary (age 6–12)	2,525	83,480	2,111,037	25.3
Secondary (age 13–18)	906	72,875	1,426,030	19.6
Vocational	209	18,836	515,211	27.4
Higher	125	33,392	689,185	20.6

Educational attainment (1993). Percentage of population age 25 and over having: no formal schooling 10.3%; less than complete primary education 5.9%; primary 25.1%; incomplete secondary 20.2%; secondary 24.2%; some college 8.1%; higher 6.2%. *Literacy* (1993): population age 15 and over literate 14,680,501 (93.4%); males 7,852,192 (97.0%); females 6,828,309 (89.6%).
Health (1993): physicians 25,946 (1 per 804 persons); hospital beds 100,326 (1 per 208 persons); infant mortality rate per 1,000 live births 4.8.
Food: daily per capita caloric intake (1990) 3,020 (1988; vegetable products 77%, animal products 23%); 118% of FAO recommended minimum.

Military

Total active duty personnel (1994): 425,000 (army 68.0%, navy 16.0%, air force 16.0%). *Military expenditure as percentage of GNP* (1993): 4.7% (world 3.3%); per capita expenditure U.S.$494.

[1]National Assembly functions as an electoral college or constituent body; the legislative branch is the formal lawmaking body. [2]End of March. [3]The Nov. 7, 1992, constitutional reforms replaced the military administrations (established in 1949) on Quemoy and Matsu with civilian administrations. [4]Detail does not add to total given because of rounding. [5]Includes Quemoy and Matsu groups. [6]For Taiwan area only, excluding Quemoy and Matsu groups. [7]General government. [8]1991. [9]Civilian employed persons only. [10]Import duties less imputed bank service charge. [11]Unemployed. [12]In manufacturing. [13]Based on the average exchange rate.

Tajikistan

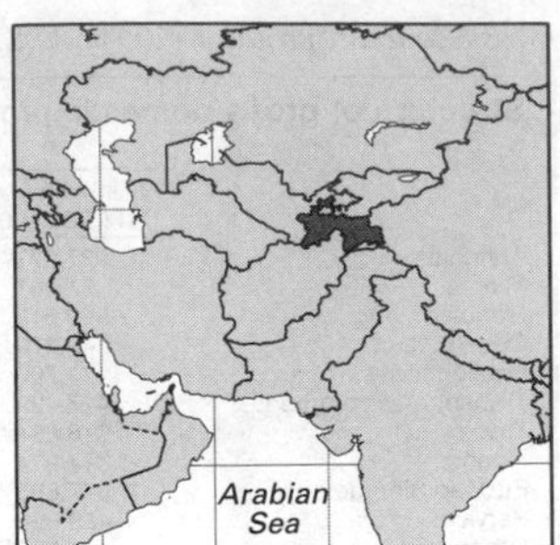

Official name: Jumhurii Tojikistan (Republic of Tajikistan).
Form of government: parliamentary republic with one legislative house (National Assembly [181]).
Chief of state: President of the National Assembly.
Head of government: Chairman of the Council of Ministers (Prime Minister).
Capital: Dushanbe.
Official language: Tajik (Tojik).
Official religion: none.
Monetary unit: 1 Tajik ruble; valuation[1] (Oct. 4, 1995) 1 U.S.$ = 44.90 Tajik rubles; 1 £ = 71.35 Tajik rubles.

Area and population		area		population
		sq mi	sq km	1991 estimate
Autonomous republic	**Capitals**			
Gorno-Badakhshan	Khorugh	24,600	63,700	167,100
Provinces				
Khujand	Khujand	10,100	26,100	1,635,900
Kŭlob	Kŭlob	4,600	12,000	668,100
Qŭrghonteppa	Qŭrghonteppa	4,900	12,600	1,113,500
Regions under republican jurisdiction	—	11,000	28,400	1,181,800
City				
Dushanbe	—	100	300	591,900
TOTAL		55,300	143,100	5,358,300

Demography

Population (1995): 5,832,000.
Density (1995): persons per sq mi 105.5, persons per sq km 40.8.
Urban-rural (1993): urban 30.4%; rural 69.6%.
Sex distribution (1993): male 49.80%; female 50.20%.
Age breakdown (1989): under 15, 42.9%; 15–29, 28.1%; 30–44, 13.8%; 45–59, 9.0%; 60–74, 4.6%; 75 and over, 1.6%.
Population projection: (2000) 6,407,000; (2010) 7,732,000.
Doubling time: 35 years.
Ethnic composition (1991): Tajik 63.8%; Uzbek 24.0%; Russian 6.5%; Tatar 1.4%; Kyrgyz 1.3%; Ukrainian 0.7%; German 0.3%; other 2.0%.
Religious affiliation (1990): believers are predominantly Sunnī Muslim (Ḥanafīyah).
Major cities (1989): Dushanbe 582,400; Khujand (formerly Leninabad) 164,500; Kŭlob 79,300; Qŭrghonteppa 58,400; Urateppa 47,700.

Vital statistics

Birth rate per 1,000 population (1994): 27.2 (world avg. 25.0); (1992) legitimate 92.5%; illegitimate 7.5%.
Death rate per 1,000 population (1994): 7.3 (world avg. 9.3).
Natural increase rate per 1,000 population (1994): 19.9 (world avg. 15.7).
Total fertility rate (avg. births per childbearing woman; 1994): 5.0.
Marriage rate per 1,000 population (1993): 9.6.
Divorce rate per 1,000 population (1993): 0.9.
Life expectancy at birth (1993): male 65.7 years; female 71.5 years.
Major causes of death per 100,000 population (1993): diseases of the circulatory system 222.8; violence, poisoning, and accidents 181.3; diseases of the respiratory system 158.7; infectious and parasitic diseases 128.3; malignant neoplasms (cancers) 40.7; diseases of the digestive system 20.7.

National economy

Production (metric tons except as noted). Agriculture, forestry, fishing (1994): vegetables (except potatoes) 595,000, seed cotton 550,000, fruit (except grapes) 225,000, wheat 165,000, potatoes 140,000, grapes 85,000, barley 34,000, corn (maize) 23,000, rice 20,000; livestock (number of live animals) 2,845,000 sheep and goats, 1,250,000 cattle, 40,000 pigs, 5,000,000 poultry; roundwood, n.a.; fish catch (1993) 37,000. Mining and quarrying (1993): gypsum 400,000; aluminum 300,000; lead 1,600; antimony 1,200. Manufacturing (value of production in '000,000 Russian rubles[1]; 1993): textiles 60,194; ferrous and nonferrous metals 52,877; energy 24,344; food products 15,252; wood products 11,971; machinery 10,199; chemical products 7,266. Energy production (consumption): electricity (kW-hr; 1993) 18,000,000,000 (17,000,000,000); coal (metric tons; 1992) 200,000 (136,000); crude petroleum (barrels; 1992) 733,000 (279,000); petroleum products, n.a. (n.a.); natural gas (cu m; 1992) 99,900,000 (1,771,000,000).
Public debt (external, outstanding): n.a.
Land use (1993): forest 3.8%; pasture 24.8%; agriculture 6.0%; other 65.4%.
Population economically active (1993): total 1,913,000; activity rate of total population 34.4% (participation rates: ages 16–59 [male], 16–54 [female] 67.8%; female [1990] 39.0%; unemployed [1994] 1.7%).

Price and earnings indexes (1990 = 100)	1988	1989	1990	1991	1992	1993	1994
Consumer price index	...	...	100.0	111.6	1,402	32,185	133,762
Monthly earnings index	85.6	90.9	100.0	164.2	922.7	...	...

Tourism: receipts from visitors, n.a.; expenditures by nationals abroad, n.a.
Gross national product (at current market prices; 1993): U.S.$2,671,500,000 (U.S.$470 per capita).

Structure of net material product and labour force	1993		1992	
	in value '000,000 Russian rubles[1]	% of total value	labour force[2]	% of labour force[2]
Agriculture	4,749	5.2	891,500	46.7
Mining, Manufacturing, Public utilities	60,534	66.6	249,800	13.1
Construction	14,885	16.4	132,400	6.9
Transportation and communications	3,126	3.4	83,100	4.4
Trade	6,020	6.6	95,700	5.0
Finance	—	—	6,400	0.3
Public administration, defense	—	—	29,600	1.6
Services	—	—	396,600	20.8
Other	1,586	1.8	22,800	1.2
TOTAL	90,900	100.0	1,907,900	100.0

Budget (1994). Revenue: 773,200,000,000 Russian rubles[1] (value-added tax 30.0%, enterprise profits tax 26.0%, excise tax 13.0%). Expenditures: 948,300,000,000 Russian rubles[1] (national economy 43.0%, social welfare and culture 30.0%, defense 4.0%).
Household income and expenditure. Average household size (1989) 6.1; income per household: n.a.; sources of income (1993): wages and salaries 64.2%, pensions and grants 31.3%, income from agriculture sales 4.4%; expenditure (1993): food and clothing 65.3%, services 9.3%, taxes and other payments 6.6%.

Foreign trade

Balance of trade (current prices)	1991	1992	1993	1994
U.S.$'000,000	−200.0	...	−100.0	−400.0
% of total	25.0%	...	14.3%	33.0%

Imports (1994): U.S.$800,000,000 (food products 46.6%, base metals 40.8%, chemical products 4.4%, machinery 2.8%, textiles 2.5%). *Major import sources:* Poland 41.4%; Austria 35.5%; France 10.0%; United Kingdom 5.5%; Turkey 1.9%.
Exports (1994): U.S.$400,000,000 (base metals 81.8%, textiles 17.4%). *Major export destinations:* Poland 32.8%; Sweden 32.7%; Austria 8.8%; Afghanistan 8.0%; Norway 8.0%; Hungary 5.2%.

Transport and communications

Transport. Railroads (1990): length 553.6 mi, 891.0 km; passenger-mi 6,094,400,000, passenger-km 9,808,000,000; short ton-mi cargo 7,617,000,000, metric ton-km cargo 11,121,000,000. Roads (1990): total length 8,324,000 mi, 13,396,000 km (paved 93%). Vehicles (1988): passenger cars 209,100; trucks and buses, n.a. Merchant marine: vessels (100 gross tons and over) n.a.; total deadweight tonnage, n.a. Air transport (1989): passenger-mi 3,214,600,000, passenger-km 5,173,400,000; short ton-mi cargo 22,124,000, metric ton-km cargo 32,300,000; airports (1995) with scheduled flights 1.
Communications. Daily newspapers (1992): total number 9; total circulation 361,370; circulation per 1,000 population 63.2. Radio (1992): total number of receivers 854,000 (1 per 6.7 persons). Television (1992): total number of receivers 860,000 (1 per 6.6 persons). Telephones (main lines; 1993): 259,600 (1 per 22 persons).

Education and health

Education (1993–94)	schools	teachers	students	student/ teacher ratio
Primary (age 6–13), Secondary (age 14–17)	3,300	97,000	1,227,000	12.6
Voc., teacher tr.	50	...	38,400	...
Higher	22	...	69,000	...

Educational attainment (1989). Percentage of population age 25 and over having: primary education or no formal schooling 16.3%; some secondary 21.1%; completed secondary and some postsecondary 55.1%; higher 7.5%.
Literacy (1989): percentage of total population age 15 and over literate 97.7%; males literate 98.8%; females literate 96.6%.
Health (1994): physicians 13,000 (1 per 447 persons); hospital beds 59,000 (1 per 99 persons); infant mortality rate per 1,000 live births (1993) 47.0.
Food: daily per capita caloric intake 2,760 (vegetable products 60%, animal products 40%); 113% of FAO recommended minimum requirement.

Military

Total active duty personnel (1994): 6,000 (army 100%); about 24,000 Russian troops remained in Tajikistan in late 1994. *Military expenditure as percentage of GNP* (1992): 3.1% (world 3.7%); per capita expenditure U.S.$19.

[1]The Tajik ruble was introduced May 10, 1995, at a rate of 1 Tajik ruble to 100 Russian rubles and circulated in parallel with the Russian ruble; on May 15, 1995, the Tajik ruble became the sole legal tender. [2]State sector only.

Tanzania

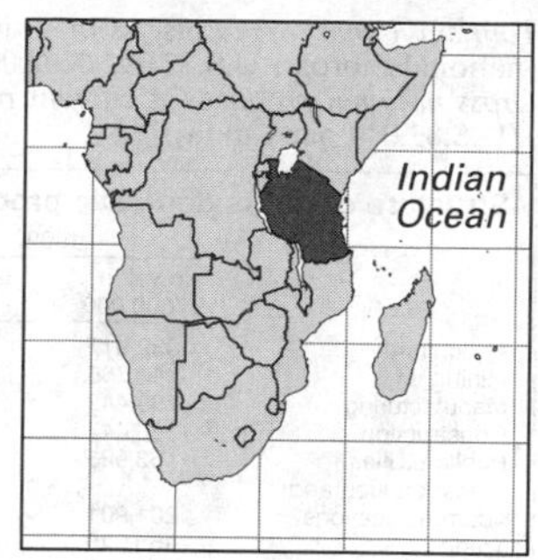

Official name: Jamhuri ya Muungano wa Tanzania (Swahili); United Republic of Tanzania (English).
Form of government: unitary[1] multiparty republic with one legislative house (National Assembly [280]).
Head of state and government: President.
Seat of government: Dar es Salaam[2] (Capital designate, Dodoma).
Official languages: Swahili; English.
Official religion: none.
Monetary unit: 1 Tanzanian shilling (T Sh) = 100 cents; valuation (Oct. 6, 1995) 1 U.S.$ = T Sh 600.00; 1 £ = T Sh 948.54.

Area and population

		area		population
Regions	Capitals	sq mi	sq km	1988 census
Arusha	Arusha	31,778	82,306	1,351,675
Coast	Dar es Salaam	12,512	32,407	638,015
Dar es Salaam	—	538	1,393	1,360,850
Dodoma	Dodoma	15,950	41,311	1,237,819
Iringa	Iringa	21,955	56,864	1,208,914
Kagera	Bukoba	10,961	28,388	1,326,183
Kigoma	Kigoma	14,300	37,037	854,817
Kilimanjaro	Moshi	5,139	13,309	1,108,699
Lindi	Lindi	25,501	66,046	646,550
Mara	Musoma	7,555	19,566	970,942
Mbeya	Mbeya	23,301	60,350	1,476,199
Morogoro	Morogoro	27,336	70,799	1,222,737
Mtwara	Mtwara	6,451	16,707	889,494
Mwanza	Mwanza	7,564	19,592	1,878,271
Pemba North	Wete	222	574	137,399
Pemba South	Chake Chake	128	332	127,640
Rukwa	Sumbawanga	26,500	68,635	694,974
Ruvuma	Songea	24,517	63,498	783,327
Shinyanga	Shinyanga	19,607	50,781	1,772,549
Singida	Singida	19,051	49,341	791,814
Tabora	Tabora	29,402	76,151	1,036,293
Tanga	Tanga	10,351	26,808	1,283,636
Zanzibar North	Mkokotoni	182	470	97,028
Zanzibar South and Central	Koani	330	854	70,184
Zanzibar West	Zanzibar	89	230	208,327
TOTAL LAND AREA		341,217[3]	883,749	
INLAND WATER		22,800	59,050	
TOTAL		364,017	942,799	23,174,336

Demography

Population (1995): 28,072,000[4].
Density (1995)[5]: persons per sq mi 82.3, persons per sq km 31.8.
Urban-rural (1994): urban 23.6%; rural 76.4%.
Sex distribution (1995): male 49.48%; female 50.52%.
Age breakdown (1995): under 15, 45.9%; 15–29, 27.3%; 30–44, 14.6%; 45–59, 8.1%; 60–74, 3.4%; 75 and over, 0.7%.
Population projection: (2000) 32,120,000; (2010) 41,205,000.
Doubling time. 27 years.
Ethnolinguistic composition (1987): Nyamwezi and Sukuma 26.3%, Swahili 8.8%; Haya 5.3%; Hehet and Bena 5.0%; Chagga 4.4%; Gogo 4.4%; Makonde 3.7%; other 42.1%.
Religious affiliation (1984): Muslim 35%; animist 35%; Christian 30%.
Major cities (1988): Dar es Salaam 1,360,850; Mwanza 223,013; Dodoma 203,833; Tanga 187,634; Zanzibar 157,634.

Vital statistics

Birth rate per 1,000 population (1994): 45.5 (world avg. 26.0).
Death rate per 1,000 population (1994): 19.4 (world avg. 9.2).
Natural increase rate per 1,000 population (1994): 26.1 (world avg. 16.8).
Total fertility rate (avg. births per childbearing woman; 1994): 6.0.
Life expectancy at birth (1994): male 41.5 years; female 45.0 years.
Major causes of death per 100,000 population: n.a.; however, the major diseases include malaria, bilharziasis, tuberculosis, and sleeping sickness.

National economy

Budget (1995–96). Revenue: T Sh 627,000,000,000 (1988–89; sales tax 46.3%, income tax 23.2%, customs and excise tax 11.8%). Expenditures: T Sh 627,688,000,000 (1988–89; public administration 17.4%, economic services 15.2%, defense 15.1%, education 5.7%, health 4.9%).
Public debt (external, outstanding; 1993): U.S.$6,746,000,000.
Tourism (1993): receipts from visitors U.S.$147,000,000; expenditures by nationals abroad U.S.$102,000,000.
Production (metric tons except as noted). Agriculture (1994): cassava 7,209,000, corn (maize) 2,159,000, sugarcane 1,530,000, bananas 834,000, plantains 834,000, rice 614,000, sorghum 478,000, coconuts 365,000, sweet potatoes 267,000, potatoes 230,000, millet 218,000; livestock (number of live animals) 13,376,000 cattle, 9,682,000 goats, 3,955,000 sheep, 335,000 pigs, 25,000,000 chickens; roundwood (1993) 36,072,000 cu m; fish catch (1993) 345,000. Mining and quarrying (1993): gemstones (including emeralds, sapphires, and rubies) 32,979 kg; gold 3,370 kg; diamonds 40,847 carats. Manufacturing (1993): cement 540,000[6]; fresh meat and poultry 291,000; sugar 121,000; hides and skins 48,325; wheat flour 3,000[7]; soap 23,900[7]; cotton textiles 38,000,000 sq m[7]. Construction: n.a. Energy production (consumption): electricity (kW-hr; 1993) 907,000,000 (907,000,000); coal (metric tons; 1992) 33,200 (75,000[7]); crude petroleum (barrels; 1993) none (4,237,000); petroleum products (metric tons; 1993) 576,000 (649,000).
Gross national product (1993)[8]: U.S.$2,521,000,000 (U.S.$100 per capita).

Structure of gross domestic product and labour force

	1991			
	in value T Sh '000,000	% of total value	labour force	% of labour force
Agriculture	259,182	57.7	10,540,000	80.3
Mining	4,820	1.1		
Manufacturing	22,953	5.1	614,000	4.7
Construction	13,468	3.0		
Public utilities	7,334	1.6		
Transp. and commun.	39,393	8.8		
Trade	65,596	14.6		
Finance	27,206	6.1	1,969,000	15.0
Pub. admin., defense	18,292	4.1		
Services	17,228	3.8		
Other	−26,463[9]	−5.9[9]	...	...
TOTAL	449,009	100.0	13,123,000	100.0

Population economically active (1994): total 13,852,000; activity rate 48.0% (participation rates: over age 10 [1988] 74.3%; female [1991] 47.6%).

Price index (1990 = 100)

	1988	1989	1990	1991	1992	1993	1994
Consumer price index	58.5	73.6	100.0	128.7	156.8	196.5	263.5

Household income and expenditure. Avg. household size (1988) 5.2; income per household: n.a.; sources of income: n.a.; expenditure (1981): food 54.3%, clothing 10.8%, housing 8.6%, energy 6.6%, transportation 6.4%.
Land use (1993): forested 37.9%; meadows and pastures 39.6%; agricultural and under permanent cultivation 4.0%; other 18.5%.

Foreign trade[10]

Balance of trade (current prices)

	1989	1990	1991	1992	1993	1994
T Sh '000,000	−73,286	−161,606	−213,549	−258,245	−342,654	−385,977
% of total	41.6%	55.6%	58.8%	51.0%	48.6%	42.1%

Imports (1993): T Sh 446,713,000,000 (1988; machinery and transport equipment 45.6%, basic manufactures 16.3%, fuel 10.2%, chemicals 8.8%, metals 5.5%, food 5.4%). *Major import sources* (1991): U.K. 13.1%; Japan 9.9%; Italy 8.3%; Oman 8.1%; Germany 7.4%.
Exports (1993): T Sh 140,088,000,000 (1988; coffee 25.9%, cotton 23.6%, sisal 1.4%). *Major export destinations* (1991): Germany 16.1%; U.K. 8.7%; India 8.5%; The Netherlands 5.8%; Belgium 5.8%; Japan 5.3%.

Transport and communications

Transport. Railroads (1995): length 3,569 km; passenger-km 3,740,000,000[7]; metric ton-km cargo 1,490,000,000[7]. Roads (1994): length 88,000 km (paved 4.2%). Vehicles (1992): passenger cars 50,000; trucks and buses 40,000. Merchant marine (1992): vessels (100 gross tons and over) 43; deadweight tonnage 48,465. Air transport (1994)[11]: passenger-km 152,931,000; metric ton-km 15,674,000; airports (1995) with scheduled flights 11.
Communications. Daily newspapers: total number (1992) 3; total circulation 220,000; circulation per 1,000 population 8.6. Radio (1994): 565,000 receivers (1 per 48 persons). Television (1994): 80,000 receivers (1 per 341 persons). Telephones (main lines; 1993): 85,000 (1 per 312 persons).

Education and health

Education (1993)[12]

	schools	teachers	students	student/ teacher ratio
Primary (age 7–13)	10,892	101,816	3,736,734	36.7
Secondary (age 14–19)	288[13]	9,568	180,899	18.9
Teacher training	63[13]	1,167	15,824	13.6
Higher	4[14]	1,206[14]	6,100[15]	...

Educational attainment (1978). Percentage of population age 10 and over having: no schooling 48.6%; some primary education 40.7%; completed primary 8.7%; secondary and higher 1.9%. *Literacy* (1995): percentage of total population age 15 and over literate 67.8%; males literate 79.4%; females literate 56.8%.
Health: physicians (1990) *c.* 1,200 (1 per 20,300 persons); hospital beds (1986) 22,800 (1 per 924 persons); infant mortality rate (1994) 110.
Food (1992): daily per capita caloric intake 2,018 (vegetable products 93%, animal products 7%); 87% of FAO recommended minimum requirement.

Military

Total active duty personnel (1995): 34,600 (army 86.7%, navy 2.9%, air force 10.4%). *Military expenditure as percentage of GNP* (1993): 3.8% (world 3.3%); per capita expenditure U.S.$3.

[1]Federal governmental structures exist in the Zanzibar constitution and House of Representatives and in 1993 legislation authorizing a similar house in Tanganyika. [2]Government in process of being transferred from Dar es Salaam to Dodoma; legislative branch meets in Dodoma. [3]Detail does not add to total given because of rounding. [4]Data exclude some 750,000 refugees from Rwanda and Burundi. [5]Based on land area. [6]1992. [7]1991. [8]Mainland Tanzania only. [9]Less imputed bank service charges. [10]Import figures are f.o.b. in balance of trade and c.i.f. in commodities and trading partners. [11]Air Tanzania only. [12]Excludes Zanzibar and Pemba. [13]1986–87. [14]1989. [15]1990.

Thailand

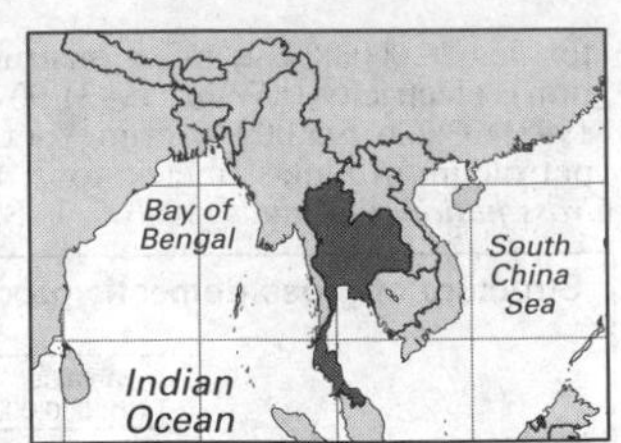

Official name: Muang Thai, or Prathet Thai (Kingdom of Thailand).
Form of government: constitutional monarchy with two legislative houses (Senate [270][1]; House of Representatives [391]).
Chief of state: King.
Head of government: Prime Minister[2].
Capital: Bangkok.
Official language: Thai.
Official religion: Buddhism.
Monetary unit: 1 Thai baht (B) = 100 stangs; valuation (Oct. 6, 1995) 1 U.S.$ = B 25.12; 1 £ = B 39.70.

Area and population	area		population
			1993
Regions[3]	sq mi	sq km	estimate[4]
Bangkok Metropolis	2,995	7,758	8,769,341
Central	6,407	16,594	2,835,662
Eastern	14,094	36,503	3,812,701
Northeastern	65,195	168,854	20,170,986
Northern	65,500	169,644	11,814,337
Southern	27,303	70,715	7,483,789
Western	16,621	43,047	3,449,256
TOTAL	198,115	513,115	58,336,072

Demography

Population (1995): 58,791,000[5].
Density (1995): persons per sq mi 296.8, persons per sq km 114.6.
Urban-rural (1993): urban 17.6%; rural 82.4%.
Sex distribution (1993): male 50.06%; female 49.94%.
Age breakdown (1990): under 20, 44.3%; 20–39, 34.2%; 40–59, 15.4%; 60–69, 3.9%; 70 and over, 2.2%.
Population projection: (2000) 61,909,000; (2010) 67,130,000.
Doubling time: 58 years.
Ethnic composition (1983): Thai 79.5%, of which Siamese 52.6%, Lao 26.9%; Chinese 12.1%; Malay 3.7%; Khmer 2.7%; other 2.0%.
Religious affiliation (1992): Buddhist 94.8%; Muslim 4.0%; Christian 0.6%; other 0.6%.
Major cities (1991)[4]: Bangkok 5,620,591; Nonthaburi 264,201; Nakhon Ratchasima 202,503; Chiang Mai 161,541; Khon Kaen 131,478.

Vital statistics

Birth rate per 1,000 population (1995): 19.0 (world avg. 25.0).
Death rate per 1,000 population (1995): 7.0 (world avg. 9.3).
Natural increase rate per 1,000 population (1995): 12.0 (world avg. 15.7).
Total fertility rate (avg. births per childbearing woman; 1995): 2.1.
Marriage rate per 1,000 population (1993): 8.3.
Divorce rate per 1,000 population (1993): 0.8.
Life expectancy at birth (1995): male 66.0 years; female 71.0 years.
Major causes of death per 100,000 population (1992)[6]: accidents, homicide, and poisonings 13.3; diseases of the heart 11.7; malignant neoplasms (cancers) 9.1; hypertension and cerebrovascular disease 3.5; diseases of the liver and the pancreas 2.8; pneumonia and other lung diseases 2.4%; nephritis and nephrosis 2.0.

National economy

Budget (1993–94). Revenue: B 569,313,000,000 (taxes 90.1%, state enterprises 5.9%, sale of property and services 4.0%). Expenditures: B 504,703,000,000 (1992–93; economic services 26.2%, education 21.1%, defense 17.2%, health 8.1%, general public services 5.7%, internal security 5.5%, external debt service 4.2%, social security 4.0%).
Production (metric tons except as noted). Agriculture, forestry, fishing (1994): sugarcane 37,569,000, rice 18,447,000, corn (maize) 3,800,000, rubber 1,667,000, bananas 1,658,000, coconuts 1,400,000, soybeans 500,000, dry beans 310,000, sorghum 300,000; cabbages 195,000; livestock (number of live animals) 7,593,000 cattle, 4,931,000 pigs, 4,257,000 buffalo, 127,000,000 chickens; roundwood (1993) 38,039,000 cu m; fish catch (1993) 3,348,149. Mining and quarrying (1993): limestone 32,036,000; gypsum 7,455,000; zinc ore 446,000; kaolin clay 397,000; fluorite 48,387; lead ore 14,233; tin concentrates 6,363. Manufacturing (1993): cement 26,300,000; refined sugar 3,650,500; chemical fertilizer 458,103[7]; synthetic fibre 397,700; galvanized iron sheet 249,800; tin plate 222,400; jute products 118,900. Construction (1990): residential 16,343,000 sq m; nonresidential 13,449,000 sq m. Energy production (consumption): electricity (kW-hr; 1992) 59,698,000,000 (60,138,000,000); coal (metric tons; 1992) 15,357,000 (15,567,000); crude petroleum (barrels; 1992) 8,900,000 (102,445,000); petroleum products (metric tons; 1992) 15,995,000 (22,739,000); natural gas (cu m; 1992) 8,078,000,000 (8,078,000,000).
Public debt (external, outstanding; 1993): U.S.$14,562,000,000.
Land use (1993): forested 26.4%; meadows and pastures 1.6%; agricultural and under permanent cultivation 40.7%; other 31.3%.
Population economically active (1993): total 32,845,400; activity rate of total population 56.0% (participation rates: over age 13, 76.0%; female 46.0%; unemployed 2.1%).

Price and earnings indexes (1990 = 100)	1988	1989	1990	1991	1992	1993	1994
Consumer price index	89.6	94.4	100.0	105.7	110.1	114.0	120.1
Monthly earnings index	84.0	87.8	100.0	115.3	...	...	...

Tourism (1993): receipts from visitors U.S.$5,014,000,000; expenditures by nationals abroad U.S.$2,092,000,000.
Gross national product (at current market prices; 1993): U.S.$120,235,000,000 (U.S.$2,040 per capita).

Structure of gross domestic product and labour force	1992		1993	
	in value B '000,000	% of total value	labour force[8]	% of labour force[8]
Agriculture	332,917	11.9	18,244,600	55.5
Mining	41,755	1.5	57,300	0.2
Manufacturing	793,449	28.3	3,961,100	12.0
Construction	186,447	6.6	1,475,000	4.5
Public utilities	63,925	2.3	144,800	0.4
Transportation and communications	201,901	7.2	879,400	2.7
Trade	465,940	16.6	3,704,200	11.3
Finance	250,930	8.9		
Pub. admin., defense	106,291	3.8	3,667,900	11.2
Services	361,380	12.9		
Other	...	...	710,700[9]	2.2[9]
TOTAL	2,804,935	100.0	32,845,000	100.0

Household income and expenditure (1992). Average household size 3.9; average annual income per household B 84,744 (U.S.$3,336); sources of income: wages and salaries 70.1%, self-employment 22.6%, transfer payments 5.8%, other 1.5%; expenditure: food, tobacco, and beverages 39.2%, housing 21.9%, transportation and communications 12.3%, clothing 6.0%, medical and personal care 5.9%, education and recreation 3.9%, other 10.8%.

Foreign trade[10]

Balance of trade (current prices)	1988	1989	1990	1991	1992	1993
B '000,000	−59,529	−71,417	−172,323	−139,742	−107,887	−111,602
% of total	6.9%	6.5%	12.7%	8.8%	6.1%	5.6%

Imports (1993): B 1,170,848,000,000 (nuclear reactors 18.2%, electrical machinery 16.8%, road vehicles 7.9%, iron and steel 7.6%, mineral fuels and lubricants 7.4%, plastics 3.3%, organic chemicals 3.0%). *Major import sources:* Japan 30.2%; U.S. 11.6%; Singapore 6.4%; Germany 5.4%; Taiwan 5.1%; South Korea 4.2%; Malaysia 3.6%; China 2.4%; U.K. 2.3%.
Exports (1993): B 951,360,000,000 (garments 9.4%, precious jewelry 4.4%, plastic articles 4.1%, fresh prawns 4.0%, rice 3.5%, natural rubber 3.1%, canned seafoods 3.0%, footwear 2.9%, integrated circuits 2.8%, furniture 2.1%, tapioca products 2.1%). *Major export destinations:* U.S. 21.3%; Japan 16.8%; Singapore 11.9%; Hong Kong 5.2%; Germany 3.9%; U.K. 3.2%; The Netherlands 3.1%; Malaysia 2.8%; United Arab Emirates 2.2%.

Transport and communications

Transport. Railroads (1993[11]): route length 2,405 mi, 3,870 km; passenger-mi 9,145,000,000, passenger-km 14,718,000,000; short ton-mi cargo 2,095,000,000, metric ton-km cargo 3,059,000,000. Roads (1993): total length 35,358 mi, 56,903 km (paved 78%). Vehicles (1993): passenger cars 1,091,085; trucks and buses 2,472,063. Merchant marine (1992): vessels (100 gross tons and over) 351; total deadweight tonnage 1,194,470. Air transport (1994): passenger-mi 15,688,000,000, passenger-km 25,248,000,000; short ton-mi cargo 872,193,000, metric ton-km cargo 1,273,380,000; airports (1995) with scheduled flights 26.
Communications. Daily newspapers (1992): total number 35; total circulation 4,150,000; circulation per 1,000 population 74. Radio (1994): 10,000,000 receivers (1 per 5.8 persons). Television (1994): 3,300,000 receivers (1 per 17 persons). Telephones (main lines; 1993): 2,184,900 receivers (1 per 27 persons).

Education and health

Education (1992)	schools	teachers	students	student/ teacher ratio
Primary (age 7–12)	34,960	420,401	8,435,245	20.1
Secondary (age 13–18)	2,299	105,225	1,954,062	18.6
Voc., teacher tr.	615	38,548	715,393	18.6
Higher	84	19,747	768,179	38.9

Educational attainment (1991). Percentage of population age 13 and over having: no formal schooling 7.4%; primary education 73.9%; secondary 10.4%; postsecondary 8.3%. *Literacy* (1985): total population age 15 and over literate 28,451,390 (88.8%); males literate 14,877,240 (93.2%); females literate 13,574,150 (84.5%).
Health: physicians (1992) 13,398 (1 per 4,245 persons); hospital beds (1991) 93,852 (1 per 599 persons); infant mortality rate per 1,000 live births (1995) 32.0.
Food (1992): daily per capita caloric intake 2,432 (vegetable products 90%, animal products 10%); 110% of FAO recommended minimum requirement.

Military

Total active duty personnel (1994): 256,000 (army 58.6%, navy 24.6%, air force 16.8%). *Military expenditure as percentage of GNP* (1993): 2.9% (world 3.3%); per capita expenditure U.S.$60.

[1]All members are appointed by the king. [2]The new constitution requires that future prime ministers be elected members of Parliament. [3]Actual local administration is based on 76 provinces. [4]Based on registration records. [5]Based on 1990 census results, which are lower than the 1990 registration records estimate. [6]Percentage distribution. [7]1991. [8]August; economically active persons 13 years and over. [9]Mostly unemployed. [10]Import figures are f.o.b. in balance of trade and c.i.f. for commodities and trading partners. [11]Traffic data refer to fiscal year ending September 30.

Togo

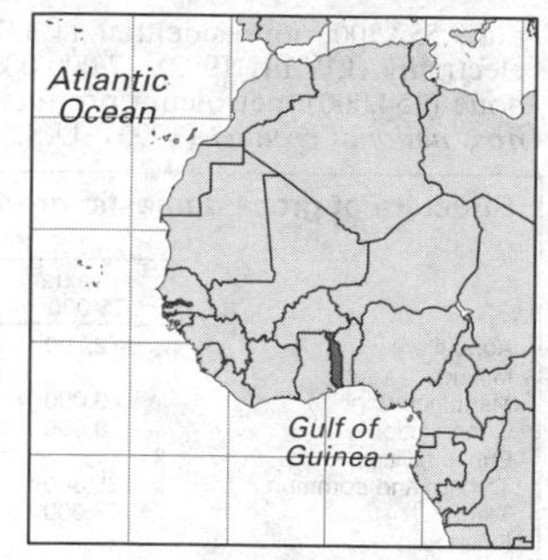

Official name: République Togolaise (Republic of Togo).
Form of government: multiparty republic[1] with one legislative body (National Assembly [81[2]]).
Chief of state: President[1].
Head of government: Prime Minister.
Capital: Lomé.
Official language: French.
Official religion: none.
Monetary unit: 1 CFA franc (CFAF) = 100 centimes; valuation (Oct. 6, 1995) 1 U.S.$ = CFAF 501.49; 1 £ = CFAF 792.78.

Area and population

Regions		area		population
Prefectures	Capitals	sq mi	sq km	1989 estimate
Centrale	Sokodé			339,000
Sotouboua	Sotouboua	2,892	7,491	162,500
Tchamba	Tchamba	1,214	3,143	54,500
Tchaoudjo	Sokodé	984	2,549	122,000
De la Kara	Kara			531,500
Assoli	Bafilo	362	938	41,000
Bassar	Bassar	2,444	6,330	152,000
Binah	Pagouda	180	465	61,000
Doufelgou	Niamtougou	432	1,120	75,000
Kéran	Kandé	419	1,085	49,500
Kozah	Kara	653	1,692	153,000
Des Plateaux	Atakpamé			810,500
Amou	Amlamé	773	2,003	98,500
Haho	Notsé	1,406	3,641	139,000
Kloto	Kpalimé	1,072	2,777	233,500
Ogou	Atakpame	2,349	6,083	204,000
Wawa	Badou	954	2,471	135,500
Des Savanes	Dapaong			410,500
Oti	Sansanné-Mango	1,453	3,762	98,500
Tône	Dapaong	1,869	4,840	312,000
Maritime	Lomé			1,300,000[3]
Golfe	Lomé	133	345	560,000
Lacs	Aného	275	713	172,500
Vo	Vogan	290	750	125,000
Yoto	Tabligbo	483	1,250	187,000
Zio	Tsévié	1,288	3,337	255,000
TOTAL		21,925	56,785	3,391,500

Demography

Population (1995): 4,138,000.
Density (1995): persons per sq mi 188.7, persons per sq km 72.9.
Urban-rural (1991): urban 26.4%; rural 73.6%.
Sex distribution (1995): male 49.54%; female 50.46%.
Age breakdown (1995): under 15, 45.7%; 15–29, 25.9%; 30–44, 14.9%; 45–59, 8.5%; 60–74, 4.1%; 75 and over, 0.9%.
Population projection: (2000) 4,818,000; (2010) 6,427,000.
Doubling time: 22 years.
Ethnic composition (1981): Ewe-Adja 43.1%; Tem-Kabre 26.7%; Gurma 16.1%; Kebu-Akposo 3.8%; Ana-Ife (Yoruba) 3.2%; non-African 0.3%; other 6.8%.
Religious affiliation (1981): traditional beliefs 58.9%; Roman Catholic 21.5%; Muslim 12.1%; Protestant 6.8%; other 0.7%.
Major cities (1983): Lomé 366,476; Sokodé 48,098[4]; Kpalimé 27,669[4].

Vital statistics

Birth rate per 1,000 population (1990–95): 44.5 (world avg. 25.0).
Death rate per 1,000 population (1990–95): 12.8 (world avg. 9.3).
Natural increase rate per 1,000 population (1990–95): 31.7 (world avg. 15.7).
Total fertility rate (avg. births per childbearing woman; 1990–95): 6.6.
Marriage rate per 1,000 population (1979): 2.3.
Life expectancy at birth (1990–95): male 53.2 years; female 56.8 years.
Morbidity (reported cases of illness; 1989): malaria 730,162; injury and trauma 218,949; diarrheal diseases 153,074; diseases of the respiratory system 90,061; intestinal parasites 52,064.

National economy

Budget (1995). Revenue: CFAF 98,920,000,000 (current revenue 86.4%, of which customs duties 38.6%, direct taxes 37.9%; other 14.6%). Expenditures: CFAF 147,780,000,000 (current expenditure 83.1%, of which current operations 66.5%, interest on public debt 16.6%; capital expenditure 16.9%).
Public debt (external, outstanding; 1993): U.S.$1,128,000,000.
Production (metric tons except as noted). Agriculture, forestry, fishing (1994): yams 400,000, cassava 400,000, corn (maize) 280,000, sorghum 130,000, millet 75,000, cottonseed 44,000, pulses 43,000, peanuts (groundnuts) 35,000, rice 35,000, coffee 28,000, bananas 16,000, coconuts 14,000, palm oil 14,000, oranges 12,000, tomatoes 10,000, palm kernels 8,000, cacao beans 7,000; livestock (number of live animals) 2,048,000 goats, 1,250,000 sheep, 934,000 pigs, 250,000 cattle, 6,000,000 chickens; roundwood (1993) 1,295,000 cu m; fish catch (1993) 16,988. Mining and quarrying (1994): phosphate rock 2,149,000; limestone is quarried for cement manufacture; marble production ceased in the early 1990s. Manufacturing (value added in CFAF '000,000,000; 1993): food products, beverages, and tobacco manufactures 15,400; textiles, clothing, and leather 2,700; wood and wood products 1,700; nonmetallic manufactures 1,700; chemical products 1,200; steel 900; paper, printing, and publishing 800. Construction (value added in CFAF; 1993): 5,500,000,000. Energy production (consumption): electricity (kW-hr; 1993) 91,000,000 (403,000,000); coal, none (n.a.); crude petroleum, none (n.a.); petroleum products (metric tons; 1993) none (175,000).
Gross national product (1993): U.S.$1,329,000,000 (U.S.$330 per capita).

Structure of gross domestic product and labour force

	1993		1991	
	in value CFAF '000,000,000	% of total value	labour force	% of labour force
Agriculture	171.8	48.6	991,000	69.2
Mining	13.7	3.9		
Manufacturing	24.7	7.0	161,000	11.2
Construction	5.5	1.6		
Public utilities	19.6	5.5		
Transp. and commun.	13.7	3.9		
Trade and finance	45.4	12.8	280,000	19.6
Pub. admin., defense	34.2	9.7		
Services	25.2	7.1		
TOTAL	353.8	100.0[3]	1,432,000	100.0

Population economically active: total (1992) 1,501,000; activity rate of total population 39.9% (participation rates [1985]: ages 15–64, 69.5%; female 37.5%; unemployed [1994] 16–18%).

Price and earnings indexes (1990 = 100)

	1988	1989	1990	1991	1992	1993	1994
Consumer price index	99.8	99.0	100.0	100.4	101.8	100.8	142.5
Hourly earnings index[5]	100.0	100.0	100.0	100.0	100.0	100.0	...

Household income and expenditure. Average household size (1980) 5.6; average annual income per household CFAF 102,000 (U.S.$452); sources of income: n.a.; expenditure (1970): food and beverages 60.9%, housing 9.9%, transportation 8.2%, clothing 7.7%, household durable goods 3.9%.
Tourism (1993): receipts from visitors U.S.$18,000,000; expenditures by nationals abroad U.S.$30,000,000.
Land use (1993): forested 16.5%; meadows and pastures 3.8%; agricultural and under permanent cultivation 44.7%; other 35.0%.

Foreign trade[6]

Balance of trade (current prices)

	1989	1990	1991	1992	1993	1994
CFAF '000,000,000	−11.2	−29.0	−16.8	−12.5	−10.4	+10.1
% of total	4.4%	11.9%	7.0%	6.4%	7.9%	3.6%

Imports (1994): CFAF 134,500,000,000 (consumer goods 41.1%, capital equipment 27.8%, intermediate goods 16.8%, energy products 8.2%, other 6.1%). *Major import sources* (1990): France 30.5%; W.Ger. 6.0%; U.S. 5.3%; Japan 4.3%; U.K. 3.8%; China 1.5%.
Exports (1994): CFAF 144,600,000,000 (raw materials 57.4%, of which phosphates 31.3%, cotton 19.3%, coffee 4.9%; reexports 27.7%; other 14.9%). *Major export destinations* (1990): Africa 16.2%; France 9.8%; U.S.S.R. 4.7%; W.Ger. 3.7%; U.K. 1.5%; eastern Europe 1.2%.

Transport and communications

Transport. Railroads (1993): route length 326 mi, 525 km; (1991) passenger-km 132,000,000; metric ton-km cargo 17,000,000. Roads (1993): total length 7,545 km (paved 24%). Vehicles (1991): passenger cars 26,000; trucks and buses 16,000. Merchant marine (1992): vessels (100 gross tons and over) 8; total deadweight tonnage 20,633. Air transport (1994)[7]: passenger-km 214,745,000; metric ton-km cargo 14,442,000; airports (1995) with scheduled flights 1.
Communications. Daily newspapers (1992): total number 2; total circulation 12,000; circulation per 1,000 population 3.0. Radio (1994): 720,000 receivers (1 per 5.4 persons). Television (1994): 150,000 receivers (1 per 26.1 persons). Telephones (main lines; 1993): 17,300 (1 per 233 persons).

Education and health

Education (1993)

	schools	teachers	students	student/ teacher ratio
Primary (age 6–11)	2,594	12,487	663,126	53.1
Secondary (age 12–18)	314[8]	2,918	126,335	43.3
Vocational	18[9]	261	8,392	32.2•
Higher[10]	1[9]	276[11]	9,120[12]	26.6[11]

Educational attainment (1981). Percentage of population age 15 and over having: no formal schooling 76.5%; primary education 13.5%; secondary 8.7%; higher 1.3%. *Literacy* (1995): total population age 15 and over literate 51.7%; males 67.0%; females 37.0%.
Health: physicians (1988) 268 (1 per 12,299 persons); hospital beds (1990) 5,307 (1 per 640 persons); infant mortality rate (1990–95) 85.
Food (1992): daily per capita caloric intake 2,242 (vegetable products 95%, animal products 5%); 97% of FAO recommended minimum requirement.

Military

Total active duty personnel (1995): 6,950 (army 93.5%, navy 2.9%, air force 3.6%). *Military expenditure as percentage of GNP* (1993): 2.9% (world 3.3%); per capita expenditure U.S.$12.

[1]Personal military-supported rule from 1967 continues under constitution approved by referendum in September 1992. [2]A total of 34 opposition seats were not occupied for 18 months (February 1994–October 1995) because of a boycott. [3]Detail does not add to total given because of rounding. [4]1981. [5]January 1. [6]Import figures are f.o.b. in total and balance of trade and c.i.f. for commodities and trading partners. [7]Represents 1/11 of the traffic of Air Afrique, which is operated by 11 West African states. [8]1990. [9]1987. [10]Universities only. [11]1988. [12]1989.

Tonga

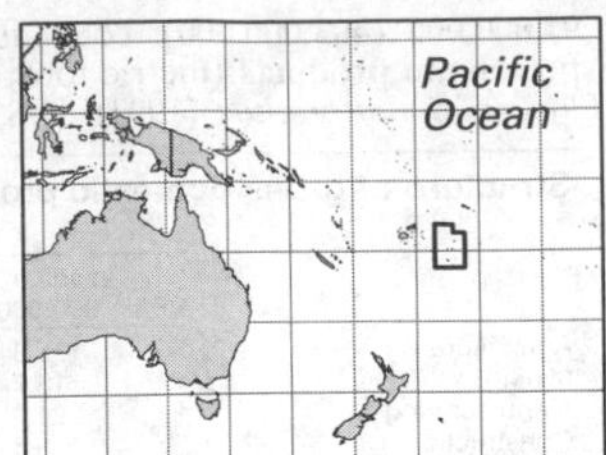

Official name: Pule'anga Fakatu'i 'o Tonga (Tongan); Kingdom of Tonga (English).
Form of government: constitutional monarchy with one legislative house (Legislative Assembly [30[1]]).
Head of state and government: King assisted by Privy Council.
Capital: Nuku'alofa.
Official languages: Tongan; English.
Official religion: none.
Monetary unit: 1 pa'anga[2] (T$) = 100 seniti; valuation (Oct. 6, 1995) 1 U.S.$ = T$1.31; 1 £ = T$2.08.

Area and population

Divisions		area		population
Districts	Capitals	sq mi	sq km	1986 census
'Eua	'Ohonua	33.7	87.4	4,393
'Eua Fo'ou		...	...	1,993
'Eua Motu'a		...	...	2,400
Ha'apai	Pangai	42.5	110.0	8,919
Foa		...	...	1,410
Ha'ano		...	...	891
Lulunga		...	...	1,584
Mu'omu'a		...	...	885
Pangai		...	...	2,850
'Uiha		...	...	1,299
Niuas	Hihifo	27.7	71.7	2,368
Niua Fo'ou		...	...	763
Niua Toputapu		...	...	1,605
Tongatapu	Nuku'alofa	100.6	260.5	63,794
Kolofo'ou		...	...	15,903
Kolomotu'a		...	...	13,115
Kolovai		...	...	4,031
Lapaha		...	...	7,005
Nukunuku		...	...	5,863
Tatakamotonga		...	...	6,773
Vaini		...	...	11,104
Vava'u	Neiafu	46.0	119.2	15,175
Hahake		...	...	2,299
Hihifo		...	...	2,093
Leimatu'a		...	...	2,884
Motu		...	...	1,384
Neiafu		...	...	5,268
Pangaimotu		...	...	1,247
TOTAL LAND AREA		278.1[3]	720.3[3]	
INLAND WATER		11.4	29.6	
TOTAL		289.5	749.9	94,649

Demography

Population (1995): 100,400.
Density (1995)[4]: persons per sq mi 361.0, persons per sq km 139.4.
Urban-rural (1993): urban 38.7%; rural 61.3%.
Sex distribution (1992): male 50.28%; female 49.72%.
Age breakdown (1986): under 15, 40.6%; 15–29, 29.0%; 30–44, 13.8%; 45–59, 10.2%; 60–74, 5.0%; 75 and over, 1.4%.
Population projection: (2000) 103,000; (2010) 105,000.
Doubling time: 39 years.
Ethnic composition (1986): Tongan 95.5%; part Tongan 2.8%; other 1.7%.
Religious affiliation (1986): Free Wesleyan 43.0%; Roman Catholic 16.0%; Mormon 12.1%; Free Church of Tonga 11.0%; Church of Tonga 7.3%; other 10.6%.
Major cities (1986): Nuku'alofa 21,383; Neiafu 3,879; Haveluloto 3,070; Vaini 2,697; Tofoa-Koloua 2,298.

Vital statistics

Birth rate per 1,000 population (1994): 24.8 (world avg. 25.0).
Death rate per 1,000 population (1994): 6.8 (world avg. 9.3).
Natural increase rate per 1,000 population (1994): 18.0 (world avg. 15.7).
Total fertility rate (avg. births per childbearing woman; 1994): 3.6.
Marriage rate per 1,000 population (1992): 8.2.
Divorce rate per 1,000 population (1992): 1.1.
Life expectancy at birth (1994): male 65.6 years; female 70.4 years.
Major causes of death per 100,000 population (1992)[5]: diseases of the circulatory system 158.5; malignant neoplasms 54.9; diseases of the respiratory system 31.5; diseases of the digestive system 18.3; infectious diseases 16.3; nutritional and metabolic disorders 15.2.

National economy

Budget (1994–95). Revenue: T$52,940,000 (foreign-trade taxes 53.8%, government services revenue 15.2%, indirect taxes 12.6%, direct taxes 11.3%, interest and rent 6.3%). Expenditures: T$52,900,000 (general administration 18.1%, education 17.0%, health 12.3%, law and order 11.5%, public works and communications 11.3%, public debt 7.1%, agriculture 5.5%).
Tourism (1993): receipts U.S.$10,000,000; expenditures U.S.$3,000,000.
Production (metric tons except as noted). Agriculture, forestry, fishing (1994): yams 31,000, cassava 30,000, taro 27,000, coconuts 25,000, sweet potatoes 14,000, fruits 13,000, vegetables 8,000, copra 2,000; livestock (number of live animals) 94,000 pigs, 16,000 goats, 11,000 horses, 10,000 cattle; roundwood (1993) 5,000 cu m; fish catch (1993) 2,481. Mining and quarrying (1982): coral 150,000; sand 25,000. Manufacturing (output in T$; 1993): food products and beverages 7,673,000; chemical products 4,674,000; textile and wearing apparel 2,231,000; wood products 1,562,000; paper products 1,294,000; metal products 1,153,000. Construction (value in T$; 1984): residential 9,552,300; nonresidential 11,377,100. Energy production (consumption): electricity (kW-hr; 1992) 27,000,000 (27,000,000); petroleum (barrels; 1989) none (154,000); petroleum products (metric tons; 1992) n.a. (29,000).
Gross national product (1993): U.S.$150,000,000 (U.S.$1,610 per capita).

Structure of gross domestic product and labour force

	1993–94		1990	
	in value T$'000	% of total value	labour force	% of labour force
Agriculture	72,700	33.3	11,682	36.5
Mining	...	... }	4,665	14.6
Manufacturing	9,000	4.1 }		
Construction	8,000	3.7	1,257	3.9
Public utilities	...	...	408	1.3
Transp. and commun.	25,800	11.8	1,821	5.7
Trade	27,000	12.4	2,597	8.1
Finance	...	...	1,188	3.7
Pub. admin., defense } Services	26,900	12.3	7,052	22.0
Other	49,100	22.5	1,343	4.2
TOTAL	218,500	100.0[6]	32,013	100.0

Public debt (external, outstanding; 1993): U.S.$43,700,000.
Population economically active (1990): total 32,013; activity rate 33.6% (participation rates: ages 10 and over, 46.7%; female 33.0%; unemployed 4.2%).

Price and earnings indexes (1990 = 100)

	1988	1989	1990	1991	1992	1993	1994
Consumer price index	87.6	91.1	100.0	110.6	119.4	120.5	121.8
Quarterly earnings index[7]	74.8	100.7	100.0	114.3	124.6	...	...

Household income and expenditure. Average household size (1986) 6.3; income per household: n.a.; sources of income: n.a.; expenditure (1984)[8]: food 49.3%, household operations 13.3%, housing 10.5%, tobacco and beverages 7.0%, transportation 5.8%, clothing and footwear 5.6%.
Land use (1993): forested 11.1%; meadows and pastures 5.6%; agricultural and under permanent cultivation 66.7%; other 16.6%.

Foreign trade[9]

Balance of trade (current prices)

	1989	1990	1991	1992	1993	1994
T$'000,000	−56.7	−64.5	−59.4	−67.7	−61.5	−72.8
% of total	70.9%	69.0%	63.0%	67.1%	56.8%	66.5%

Imports (1994): T$91,210,000 (food and live animals 29.1%, basic manufactures 19.9%, machinery and transport equipment 16.9%, mineral fuels 12.4%, chemicals 8.3%). *Major import sources:* New Zealand 44.8%; Australia 24.4%; U.S. 8.4%; Fiji 7.8%; Japan 6.6%.
Exports (1994): T$17,850,000 (squash 49.0%, fish 17.7%, vanilla beans 14.8%, root crops 3.3%, coconut products 0.4%). *Major export destinations:* Japan 52.0%; U.S. 27.6%; New Zealand 5.3%; Australia 4.1%; Fiji 1.3%.

Transport and communications

Transport. Railroads: none. Roads (1993): total length 386 km (paved 76%). Vehicles (1993): passenger cars 3,400, commercial vehicles 3,900. Merchant marine (1992): vessels (100 gross tons and over) 15; total deadweight tonnage 13,740. Air transport (1994): passenger-km 9,397,000; metric ton-km cargo 16,000; airports (1995) with scheduled flights 5.
Communications. Daily newspapers (1992): 1; total circulation 7,000; circulation per 1,000 population 72. Radio (1994): 52,000 receivers (1 per 1.5 persons). Television (1994)[10]: 2,500 receivers (1 per 40 persons). Telephones (main lines; 1993): 5,900 (1 per 16 persons).

Education and health

Education (1992)

	schools	teachers	students	student/ teacher ratio
Primary (age 6–11)	115	784	16,658	21.2
Secondary (age 12–18)	40	862	15,253	17.7
Voc., teacher tr.	8	65[11]	358	13.4[11]
Higher	1	19	226	11.9

Educational attainment (1986). Percentage of population age 25 and over having: complete primary 38.3%; lower secondary 30.3%; secondary 23.4%; postsecondary 4.9%; higher 1.0%; not stated 2.1%. *Literacy* (1976): total population age 15 and over literate 46,456 (92.8%); males 23,372 (92.9%); females 23,084 (92.8%).
Health (1992): physicians 46 (1 per 2,139 persons); hospital beds 307 (1 per 320 persons); infant mortality rate per 1,000 live births (1994) 20.8.
Food (1992): daily per capita caloric intake 2,946 (vegetable products 82%, animal products 18%); 129% of FAO recommended minimum requirement.

Military

Total active duty personnel (1991): Tonga has a national police (defense) force of about 300. *Military expenditure as percentage of GNP* (1989): 4.9% (world 4.9%); per capita expenditure U.S.$21.

[1]Includes 12 nonelective seats and 9 nobles elected by the 33 hereditary nobles of Tonga. [2]The pa'anga was pegged at par to the Australian dollar through Feb. 8, 1991, but beginning Feb. 11, 1991, it was linked to a weighted basket of foreign currencies. [3]Total includes 27.6 sq mi (71.5 sq km) of uninhabited islands. [4]Density is based on land area. [5]Reported inpatient deaths at all hospitals. [6]Detail does not add to total given because of rounding. [7]In manufacturing. [8]Current weight of consumer price index components. [9]Import data used in computing balance of trade is c.i.f. [10]Tonga has no authorized television service, but a "pirate" station began transmitting in mid-1984. [11]1990.

Trinidad and Tobago

Official name: Republic of Trinidad and Tobago.
Form of government: multiparty republic with two legislative houses (Senate [31]; House of Representatives [36[1]]).
Chief of state: President.
Head of government: Prime Minister.
Capital: Port of Spain.
Official language: English.
Official religion: none.
Monetary unit: 1 Trinidad and Tobago dollar (TT$) = 100 cents; valuation (Oct. 6, 1995) 1 U.S.$ = TT$5.70; 1 £ = TT$9.02.

Area and population

		area		population
				1990
Counties	Capitals	sq mi	sq km	census
Caroni	Chaguanas	191.0	494.7	120,508
Nariva/Mayaro	Rio Claro	349.0	903.9	36,781
St. Andrew/St. David	Sangre Grande	360.0	932.4	62,944
St. George	Tunapuna	354.0	916.9	445,620
St. Patrick	Siparia	252.0	652.7	120,129
Victoria	Princes Town	315.0	815.9	210,833
Unitary State				
Tobago	Scarborough	116.0	300.4	50,282
Cities				
Port of Spain	—	4.0	10.4	50,878
San Fernando	—	3.0	7.8	30,092
Boroughs				
Arima	—	4.0	10.4	29,695
Chaguanas	—	23.0	59.6	56,601
Point Fortin	—	9.0	23.3	20,025
TOTAL		1,980.1[2]	5,128.4	1,234,388

Demography

Population (1995): 1,265,000.
Density (1995): persons per sq mi 638.9, persons per sq km 246.7.
Urban-rural (1994): urban 71.3%; rural 28.7%.
Sex distribution (1995): male 49.46%; female 50.54%.
Age breakdown (1995): under 15, 31.7%; 15–29, 26.6%; 30–44, 22.1%; 45–59, 11.5%; 60–74, 6.0%; 75 and over, 2.1%.
Population projection: (2000) 1,303,000; (2010) 1,384,000.
Doubling time: 64 years.
Ethnic composition (1990): East Indian 40.3%; black 39.6%; mixed 18.4%; white 0.6%; Chinese 0.4%; other/not stated 0.7%.
Religious affiliation (1990): six largest Protestant bodies 29.7%, of which Anglican 10.9%, Pentecostal 7.5%; Roman Catholic 29.4%; Hindu 23.7%; Muslim 5.9%; other 11.3%.
Major cities (1990): Chaguanas 56,601; Port of Spain 50,878; San Fernando 30,092; Arima 29,695; Point Fortin 20,025; Scarborough 4,000.

Vital statistics

Birth rate per 1,000 population (1993): 17.4 (world avg. 25.0).
Death rate per 1,000 population (1993): 6.5 (world avg. 9.3).
Natural increase rate per 1,000 population (1993): 10.9 (world avg. 15.7).
Total fertility rate (avg. births per childbearing woman; 1994): 2.3.
Marriage rate per 1,000 population (1993): 5.6.
Divorce rate per 1,000 population (1993): 0.9.
Life expectancy at birth (1993): male 68.0 years; female 73.2 years.
Major causes of death per 100,000 population (1991): diseases of the circulatory system 260.0, of which ischemic heart diseases 113.5, cerebrovascular disease 75.9; malignant neoplasms (cancers) 83.4; diabetes mellitus 83.3.

National economy

Budget (1994). Revenue: TT$7,501,000,000 (corporate taxes 21.3%, of which petroleum sector 13.4%; individual income taxes 19.3%; value-added taxes 16.8%; nontax revenues 10.8%; import duties 7.7%). Expenditures: TT$7,473,000,000 (current expenditures 93.7%; development expenditures 6.3%).
Tourism (1993): receipts from visitors U.S.$80,000,000; expenditures by nationals abroad U.S.$115,000,000.
Production (metric tons except as noted). Agriculture, forestry, fishing (1994): sugarcane 1,422,000, coconuts 52,000, rice 16,200[3], oranges 8,000, bananas 6,000, corn (maize) 5,000, grapefruit 4,000, cucumbers 2,509[3], cocoa 1,556[3], coffee 859[3]; livestock (number of live animals) 55,000 cattle, 52,000 goats, 48,000 pigs; roundwood (1993) 48,000 cu m; fish catch (1993) 10,565. Mining and quarrying (1994): natural asphalt 16,700. Manufacturing (1994): anhydrous ammonia and urea (nitrogenous fertilizers) 2,452,700; methanol 1,019,500; steel billets 630,200; cement 582,900; steel wire rods 521,100; raw sugar 131,100; beer and stout 452,000 hectolitres; rum 107,300 hectolitres. Construction (authorized; 1991): residential 207,400 sq m; nonresidential 32,700 sq m. Energy production (consumption): electricity (kW-hr; 1993) 3,816,000,000 ([1992] 3,945,000,000); coal, none (none); crude petroleum (barrels; 1994) 47,945,000 ([1992] 40,903,000); petroleum products (metric tons; 1993) 5,261,000 ([1992] 1,924,000); natural gas (cu m; 1994) 7,690,000,000 ([1993] 4,878,000,000).
Land use (1993): forested 45.8%; meadows and pastures 2.2%; agricultural and under permanent cultivation 23.7%; other 28.3%.
Public debt (external, outstanding; 1993): U.S.$1,704,000,000.

Gross national product (at current market prices; 1993): U.S.$4,776,000,000 (U.S.$3,730 per capita).

Structure of gross domestic product and labour force

	1994		1993	
	in value TT$'000,000	% of total value	labour force	% of labour force
Agriculture	685	2.4	50,700	10.1
Petroleum[4], natural gas, quarrying	7,548	26.6	18,900	3.7
Manufacturing[5]	2,461	8.7	50,100	9.9
Construction	2,122	7.5	79,400	15.7
Public utilities	522	1.8	7,800	1.5
Transp. and commun.	2,536	8.9	33,800	6.7
Trade	4,058	14.3	87,000	17.3
Finance, real estate	3,583	12.6	32,200	6.4
Pub. admin., defense	2,866	10.1	143,900	28.5
Services	1,693	6.0		
Other	316[6]	1.1[6]	500	0.1
TOTAL	28,390	100.0	504,500[2]	100.0[2]

Population economically active (1993): total 504,500; activity rate of total population 40.5% (participation rates: ages 15–64, 63.2%; female 37.0%; unemployed 19.8%).

Price and earnings indexes (1990 = 100)

	1989	1990	1991	1992	1993	1994	1995
Consumer price index	90.1	100.0	103.9	110.6	122.4	133.2	137.7[7]
Weekly earnings index[8]	94.5	100.0	100.1	103.0	104.6	101.1[9]	...

Household income and expenditure. Average household size (1990) 4.1; income per household (1988) TT$17,083 (U.S.$4,444); sources of income: n.a.; expenditure (1993): food, beverages, and tobacco 25.5%, housing 21.6%, transportation 15.2%, household furnishings 14.3%, clothing and footwear 10.4%, other 13.0%.

Foreign trade[10]

Balance of trade (current prices)

	1989	1990	1991	1992	1993	1994
TT$'000,000	+1,517	+3,480	+1,352	+1,842	+1,306	+4,354
% of total	12.7%	24.5%	8.7%	13.1%	8.0%	24.4%

Imports (1993): TT$7,495,000,000 (capital goods 25.4%; nondurable consumer goods 18.6%, of which food 11.9%; mineral fuels and lubricants 15.9%; chemical products [mostly medicines and plastics] 11.0%). *Major import sources* (1993): United States 38.9%; EC 19.3%, of which United Kingdom 8.1%; Venezuela 16.8%; Canada 4.9%; Japan 3.8%.
Exports (1993): TT$8,801,000,000 (refined petroleum 33.3%; crude petroleum 21.8%; anhydrous ammonia and urea 8.9%; steel wire rods 6.7%; food 5.7%, of which raw sugar 1.6%). *Major export destinations* (1993): United States 45.6%; Caricom 20.2%, of which Barbados 4.4%, Jamaica 4.4%; Guyana 3.6%; EC 4.7%.

Transport and communications

Transport. Railroads: none. Roads (1991): total length 4,970 mi, 8,000 km (paved 50%). Vehicles (1993): passenger cars 122,201; trucks and buses 23,828. Merchant marine (1992): vessels (100 gross tons and over) 53; total deadweight tonnage 17,533. Air transport: (1992) passenger-mi 2,030,000,000, passenger-km 3,267,000,000; (1991) short ton-mi cargo 10,100,000, metric ton-km cargo 14,800,000; airports (1995) with scheduled flights 2.
Communications. Daily newspapers (1993): total number 3; total circulation 96,000; circulation per 1,000 population 76. Radio (1993): 700,000 receivers (1 per 1.8 persons). Television (1993): 250,000 receivers (1 per 5.0 persons). Telephones (main lines; 1993): 192,500 (1 per 6.5 persons).

Education and health

Education (1991–92)

	schools	teachers	students	student/ teacher ratio
Primary (age 5–11)	471	7,511	196,848[11]	26.1
Secondary (age 12–16)	101	4,844	103,922[11]	19.4
Higher[12, 13]	1	438	5,191	11.9

Educational attainment (1990). Percentage of population age 25 and over having: no formal schooling 4.5%; primary education 56.4%; secondary 32.1%; higher 3.4%; other/not stated 3.6%. *Literacy* (1990): total population age 15 and over literate 810,000 (96.9%).
Health (1993): physicians 1,051 (1 per 1,191 persons); hospital beds[14] 4,216 (1 per 297 persons); infant mortality rate per 1,000 live births (1994) 17.0.
Food (1992): daily per capita caloric intake 2,585 (vegetable products 85%, animal products 15%); 107% of FAO recommended minimum requirement.

Military

Total active duty personnel (1994): 2,600 (army 76.9%, coast guard 23.1%). *Military expenditure as percentage of GNP* (1993): 1.8% (world 3.3%); per capita expenditure U.S.$63.

[1]Excludes speaker, who may be elected from outside the House of Representatives. [2]Detail does not add to total given because of rounding. [3]1993. [4]Includes refined petroleum. [5]Excludes refined petroleum. [6]Net of value-added taxes less imputed bank service charges. [7]March. [8]Manufacturing sector only. [9]Average of first three quarters only. [10]Exports f.o.b.; imports c.i.f. [11]1992–93. [12]University of the West Indies, St. Augustine campus. [13]1993–94. [14]Includes nursing homes.

Tunisia

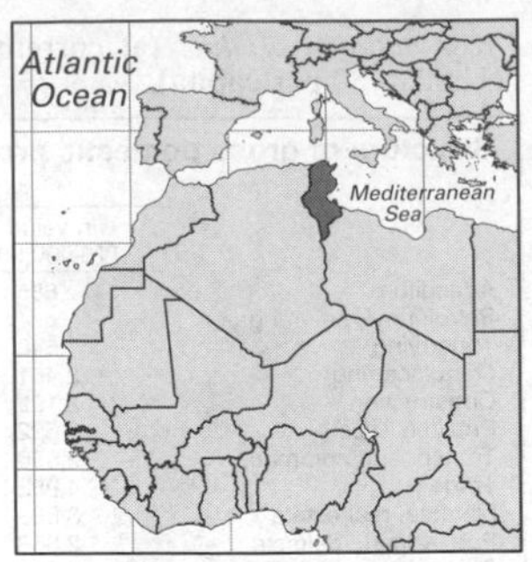

Official name: al-Jumhūrīyah at-Tūnisīyah (Republic of Tunisia).
Form of government: multiparty republic with one legislative house (Chamber of Deputies [163]).
Chief of state: President.
Head of government: Prime Minister.
Capital: Tunis.
Official language: Arabic.
Official religion: Islam.
Monetary unit: 1 dinar (D) = 1,000 millimes; valuation (Oct. 6, 1995) D 1.00 = U.S.$1.05 = £0.67.

Area and population

Governorates	Capitals	area sq mi	area sq km	population 1994 census[1]
al-Ariānah	al-Ariānah	602	1,558	566,247
Bājah	Bājah	1,374	3,558	301,898
Banzart	Bizerte (Banzart)	1,423	3,685	475,053
Bin ʿArūs	Bin ʿArūs	294	761	369,552
Jundūbah	Jundūbah	1,198	3,102	402,487
al-Kāf	al-Kāf	1,917	4,965	270,996
Madanīn	Madanīn	3,316	8,588	382,699
al-Mahdīyah	al-Mahdīyah	1,145	2,966	334,208
al-Munastīr	al-Munastīr	393	1,019	363,126
Nābul	Nābul	1,076	2,788	577,813
Qābis	Qābis	2,770	7,175	310,643
Qafṣah	Qafṣah	3,471	8,990	304,665
al-Qaṣrayn	al-Qaṣrayn	3,114	8,066	385,450
al-Qayrawān	al-Qayrawān	2,591	6,712	528,899
Qibilī	Qibilī	8,527	22,084	131,661
Ṣafāqis	Ṣafāqis	2,913	7,545	732,471
Sīdī Bū Zayd	Sīdī Bū Zayd	2,700	6,994	374,835
Siliānah	Siliānah	1,788	4,631	243,536
Sūsah	Sūsah	1,012	2,621	432,312
Tatāuīn	Tatāuīn	15,015	38,889	133,676
Tawzar	Tawzar	1,822	4,719	89,088
Tūnis	Tunis (Tūnis)	134	346	881,560
Zaghwān	Zaghwān	1,069	2,768	143,010
TOTAL		63,378[2]	164,150[2]	8,735,885

Demography

Population (1995): 8,896,000.
Density (1995): persons per sq mi 140.4, persons per sq km 54.1.
Urban-rural (1985): urban 53.0%; rural 47.0%.
Sex distribution (1994): male 50.62%; female 49.38%.
Age breakdown (1992): under 15, 36.6%; 15–29, 28.9%; 30–44, 16.9%; 45–59, 10.1%; 60–74, 5.9%; 75 and over, 1.6%.
Population projection: (2000) 9,694,000; (2010) 11,209,000.
Doubling time: 39 years.
Ethnic composition (1983): Arab 98.2%; Berber 1.2%; French 0.2%; Italian 0.1%; other 0.3%.
Religious affiliation (1980): Sunnī Muslim 99.4%; Christian 0.3%; Jewish 0.1%; other 0.2%.
Major cities (commune; 1994): Tunis 674,100; Ṣafāqis 230,900; Aryānah 152,700; Ettadhamen 149,200; Sūsah 125,000.

Vital statistics

Birth rate per 1,000 population (1993): 24.1 (world avg. 25.0); (1974) legitimate 99.8%; illegitimate 0.2%.
Death rate per 1,000 population (1993): 6.3 (world avg. 9.3).
Natural increase rate per 1,000 population (1993): 17.8 (world avg. 15.7).
Total fertility rate (avg. births per childbearing woman; 1990–95): 3.2.
Marriage rate per 1,000 population (1993): 6.3.
Divorce rate per 1,000 population (1992): 1.5.
Life expectancy at birth (1990–95): male 66.9 years; female 68.7 years.
Major causes of death per 100,000 population: n.a.; however, of approximately 12,000 deaths[3] for which a cause was reported in 1992, complications of pregnancy and childbirth represented 31.6%, circulatory diseases 22.4%, accidents and poisoning 14.9%, respiratory diseases 7.2%, endocrine and metabolic disorders 5.2%, infectious and parasitic diseases 4.8%.

National economy

Budget (1992). Revenue: D 4,925,400,000 (indirect taxes 42.2%, direct taxes 11.4%, investment 9.4%). Expenditures: D 5,662,800,000 (finance 17.9%, education 12.4%, interior affairs 5.8%, national economy 4.9%, health 4.9%).
Land use (1993): forested 4.3%; meadows and pastures 19.9%; agricultural and under permanent cultivation 31.7%; other 44.1%.
Production (metric tons except as noted). Agriculture, forestry, fishing (1994): olives 665,000, wheat 503,000, tomatoes 470,000, sugar beets 350,000, watermelons 280,000, potatoes 220,000, oranges 156,000, grapes 121,000, dates 86,000; livestock (number of live animals) 7,100,000 sheep, 1,420,000 goats, 660,000 cattle; roundwood (1993) 3,373,000 cu m; fish catch (1993) 83,762. Mining and quarrying (1994): phosphate rock 5,564,000; iron ore 235,000; zinc 23,400. Manufacturing (1994): cement 4,240,000; phosphoric acid 986,100; flour 654,400; crude steel 192,000[4]. Construction (1982): residential building authorized 2,679,000 sq m. Energy production (consumption): electricity (kW-hr; 1993) 6,416,000 (6,406,000); coal (metric tons; 1993) none (14,000); crude petroleum (barrels; 1993) 35,754,000 (12,687,000); petroleum products (metric tons; 1993) 1,584,000 (3,884,000); natural gas (cu m; 1993) 277,500,000 (1,080,700,000).
Gross national product (1993): U.S.$15,332,000,000 (U.S.$1,780 per capita).

Structure of gross domestic product and labour force

	1994 in value D '000,000	1994 % of total value	1989 labour force	1989 % of labour force
Agriculture	2,070.4	13.0	543,100	23.0
Mining	698.3	4.4	36,600	1.6
Public utilities	293.4	1.8		
Manufacturing	2,827.5	17.7	422,300	17.9
Construction	647.8	4.1	295,200	12.5
Transp. and commun.	1,267.2	8.0		
Trade	4,355.0	27.3	349,000	14.8
Finance				
Pub. admin., defense	2,165.0	13.6	465,400	19.7
Services				
Other	1,603.6	10.1	249,000[5]	10.5[5]
TOTAL	15,928.2	100.0	2,360,600	100.0

Public debt (external, outstanding; 1993): U.S.$7,627,000,000.
Population economically active (1989): total 2,360,000, activity rate of total population 28.8% (participation rates: ages 15–64, 42.2%; female 20.9%; unemployed 13.4%).

Price and earnings indexes (1990 = 100)

	1988	1989	1990	1991	1992	1993	1994
Consumer price index	87.2	93.9	100.0	107.8	113.8	118.7	124.7
Hourly earnings index[6]	89.9	92.2	100.0	101.6	105.5	113.3	...

Household income and expenditure. Average household size (1994) 5.1; income per household: n.a.; sources of income: n.a.; expenditure (1985): food and beverages 39.0%, household durable goods 11.2%, housing 10.7%, transportation 9.0%, recreation 7.1%, clothing and footwear 6.0%, energy 5.1%, health care 3.0%, education 1.8%, other 7.1%.
Tourism (1993): receipts U.S.$1,114,000,000; expenditures U.S.$203,000,000.

Foreign trade

Balance of trade (current prices)

	1989	1990	1991	1992	1993	1994
D '000,000	−1,089.8	−1,439.7	−1,037.5	−1,726.1	−1,999.2	−1,504.2
% of total	16.3%	18.9%	13.1%	24.2%	20.7%	13.8%

Imports (1994): D 6,647,300,000 (textiles 23.0%, machinery and electrical equipment 20.0%, petroleum and petroleum products 6.9%, transportation equipment 6.5%, iron and steel products 4.6%, plastics and plastic products 3.2%, pharmaceutical products 2.0%). *Major import sources:* France 27.4%; Italy 15.4%; Germany 12.2%; U.S. 6.6%; Belgium 4.3%; Spain 3.6%; United Kingdom 2.2%.
Exports (1994): D 4,696,600,000 (clothing and accessories 43.3%, petroleum and petroleum products 9.4%, olive oil 6.5%, machinery and electrical products 6.5%, chemical products 4.9%). *Major export destinations:* France 27.2%; Italy 19.6%; Germany 15.5%; Belgium 6.5%; Spain 4.7%.

Transport and communications

Transport. Railroads (1993): route length 1,404 mi, 2,260 km; passenger-mi 657,000,000, passenger-km 1,057,000,000; short ton-mi cargo 1,378,000,000, metric ton-km cargo 2,012,000,000. Roads (1989): total length 18,133 mi, 29,183 km (paved 60%). Vehicles (1993): passenger cars 320,000; trucks and buses 180,500. Merchant marine (1992): vessels (100 gross tons and over) 77; total deadweight tonnage 443,290. Air transport (1993)[7]: passenger-mi 1,226,774,000, passenger-km 1,974,306,000; short ton-mi cargo 11,865,000, metric ton-km cargo 17,323,000; airports (1995) 5.
Communications. Daily newspapers (1994): total number 7; total circulation 190,000[8]; circulation per 1,000 population 22[8]. Radio (1994): 1,700,000 receivers (1 per 5.1 persons). Television (1994): 650,000 receivers (1 per 13 persons). Telephones (main lines; 1993): 421,400 (1 per 20 persons).

Education and health

Education (1994–95)

	schools	teachers	students	student/ teacher ratio
Primary (age 6–11)	4,286	58,279	1,472,844	25.3
Secondary (age 12–18)	712	27,785	662,222	23.8
Teacher tr.[9, 10]	...	237	3,839	16.2
Higher[11]	...	5,655	96,101	17.0

Educational attainment (1989). Percentage of population age 25 and over having: no formal schooling 54.9%; primary 26.9%; secondary 14.3%; higher 3.4%; unspecified 0.5%. *Literacy* (1995): total population age 15 and over literate 66.7%; males literate 78.6%; females literate 54.6%.
Health (1992): physicians 4,670 (1 per 1,799 persons); hospital beds 16,116 (1 per 521 persons); infant mortality rate (1990–95) 43.0.
Food (1992): daily per capita caloric intake 3,330 (vegetable products 92%, animal products 8%); 139% of FAO recommended minimum requirement.

Military

Total active duty personnel (1995): 35,500 (army 76.0%, navy 14.1%, air force 9.9%). *Military expenditure as percentage of GNP* (1993): 3.4% (world 3.3%); per capita expenditure U.S.$60.

[1]Preliminary. [2]Total includes 3,714 sq mi (9,620 sq km) of territory in southwestern Tunisia that is not distributed by governorate. [3]Recorded deaths from urban areas only, including complete figures for Tunis. [4]1989. [5]Includes 218,300 unemployed. [6]Year-end; index refers to the *S.M.I.G.* (*salaire minimum interprofessionel garanti*), a form of minimum professional wage. [7]Tunis Air only. [8]Circulation for four dailies only. [9]1987–88. [10]Teacher training only. [11]1993–94.

Turkey

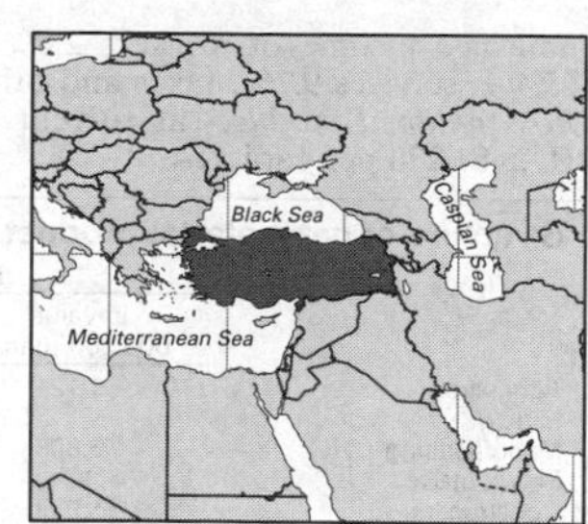

Official name: Türkiye Cumhuriyeti (Republic of Turkey).
Form of government: multiparty republic with one legislative house (Turkish Grand National Assembly [450]).
Chief of state: President.
Head of government: Prime Minister.
Capital: Ankara.
Official language: Turkish.
Official religion: none.
Monetary unit: 1 Turkish lira (LT) = 100 kurush; valuation (Oct. 6, 1995) 1 U.S.$ = LT 50,093; 1 £ = LT 79,189.

Area and population

	area		population
Geographic regions[1]	sq mi	sq km	1990 census
Akdeniz kıyısı (Mediterranean Coast)	22,933	59,395	5,443,867
Batı Anadolu (West Anatolia)	29,742	77,031	3,864,661
Doğu Anadolu (East Anatolia)	68,074	180,180	6,867,415
Güneydoğu Anadolu (Southeast Anatolia)	15,347	35,880	2,699,776
İç Anadolu (Central Anatolia)	91,254	236,347	13,096,179
Karadeniz kıyısı (Black Sea Coast)	31,388	81,295	6,827,304
Marmara ve Ege kıyıları (Marmara and Aegean coasts)	33,035	85,560	11,698,384
Trakya (Thrace)	9,175	23,764	5,975,449
TOTAL	300,948	779,452	56,473,035

Demography

Population (1995): 62,526,000.
Density (1995): persons per sq mi 207.8, persons per sq km 80.2.
Urban-rural (1993): urban 65.6%; rural 34.4%.
Sex distribution (1990): male 50.66%; female 49.34%.
Age breakdown (1993): under 15, 32.9%; 15–29, 28.0%; 30–44, 18.2%; 45–59, 11.7%; 60–74, 7.5%; 75 and over, 1.7%.
Population projection: (2000) 69,694,000; (2010) 80,120,000.
Doubling time: 35 years.
Ethnolinguistic composition (1992)[2]: Turkish 92.0%; Kurdish 6.2%; Arabic 1.4%; other 0.4%.
Religious affiliation (1992): Sunnī Muslim *c.* 80.0%; Alevi (nonorthodox Shīʿi sect) *c.* 19.8%; Christian *c.* 0.2%.
Major cities (1993): Istanbul 7,331,927; Ankara 2,719,981; İzmir 1,920,807; Adana 1,010,363; Bursa 949,810; Gaziantep 683,557; Konya 558,308.

Vital statistics

Birth rate per 1,000 population (1994): 26.0 (world avg. 25.0).
Death rate per 1,000 population (1994): 6.0 (world avg. 9.3).
Natural increase rate per 1,000 population (1994): 20.0 (world avg. 15.7).
Total fertility rate (avg. births per childbearing woman; 1992): 2.7.
Marriage rate per 1,000 population (1991): 8.0.
Divorce rate per 1,000 population (1991): 0.5.
Life expectancy at birth (1994): male 69.0 years; female 73.0 years.
Major causes of death per 100,000 population (1990)[3]: diseases of the circulatory system 344; malignant neoplasms (cancers) 75; infectious and parasitic diseases 27; ill-defined conditions 87.

National economy

Budget (1994). Revenue: LT 753,440,000,000,000 (indirect taxes 40.4%, direct taxes 37.7%, nontax revenue 20.6%). Expenditures: LT 899,375,000,000,000 (interest payments 33.2%, personnel 30.3%, investments 8.5%).
Tourism (1994): receipts from visitors U.S.$4,321,000,000; expenditures by nationals abroad U.S.$866,000,000.
Production (in '000 metric tons except as noted). Agriculture, forestry, fishing (1994): wheat 17,500, sugar beets 12,736, barley 7,000, potatoes 4,350, grapes 3,450, apples 2,095, corn (maize) 1,850, olives 1,400, cottonseed 1,006, oranges 920, sunflower seeds 740, cotton (lint) 632, lentils 610, hazelnuts 490, lemons 470, tobacco 242, oats 230, sultana raisins 176, attar of roses 800 kg[4]; livestock (number of live animals; 1993) 37,541,000 sheep, 11,910,000 cattle; roundwood (1993) 13,940,000 cu m; fish catch (1993) 556,000. Mining (1993): boron (concentrate) 1,124; pumice 1,045; chromite 533; celestite (concentrate) 44. Manufacturing (1991)[5]: refined petroleum 19,048; textiles 14,125; food products 13,722; electrical machinery 7,648; motor vehicles 7,632; iron and steel 7,478. Construction (completed; 1994): residential 45,714,000 sq m; nonresidential 11,610,000 sq m. Energy production (consumption): electricity (kW-hr; 1994) 78,261,000,000 ([1993] 73,432,000,000); coal (metric tons; 1994) 52,523,000 ([1993] 55,987,000); crude petroleum (barrels; 1994) 26,355,000 ([1993] 186,332,000); petroleum products (metric tons; 1993) 22,360,000 (23,379,000); natural gas (cu m; 1994) 199,500,000 ([1993] 4,771,000,000).
Land use (1993): forested 26.2%; meadows and pastures 16.1%; agricultural and under permanent cultivation 35.8%; other 21.9%.
Household income and expenditure. Average household size (1993) 4.5; income per household (1987) LT 3,680,500 (U.S.$4,294); sources of income (1987): self-employment 51.4%, wages and salaries 24.1%, rent and interest 13.7%, transfers 10.8%; expenditure (1987): food and beverages 33.1%, housing 14.7%, clothing 12.3%, household furnishings 11.5%.
Gross national product (at current market prices; 1993): U.S.$126,330,000,000 (U.S.$2,120 per capita).

Structure of gross domestic product and labour force

	1994		1993	
	in value LT '000,000'000[6]	% of total value	labour force[7]	% of labour force[7]
Agriculture	577,548	16.3	8,436,936	40.2
Mining	46,936	1.3	150,586	0.7
Manufacturing	713,852	20.1	2,902,730	13.8
Construction	241,117	6.8	1,136,636	5.4
Public utilities	108,088	3.1	110,679	0.5
Transportation and communications	516,238	14.6	954,137	4.6
Trade	657,575	18.5	2,476,805	11.8
Finance, real estate	199,229	5.6	470,802	2.2
Pub. admin., defense	344,530	9.7 }	2,698,603	12.9
Services	141,750	4.0 }		
Other	—	—	1,658,788[8]	7.9[8]
TOTAL	3,546,863	100.0	20,996,702	100.0

Population economically active (1993)[7]: total 20,996,702; activity rate of total population 35.3% (participation rates: ages 15–64, 57.2%; female 30.8%; unemployed [1994] 8.4%).

Price and earnings indexes (1990 = 100)

	1989	1990	1991	1992	1993	1994	1995
Consumer price index	62.4	100.0	166.0	282.3	468.8	967.0	1,740[9]
Daily earnings index[10]	...	100.0	202.1	395.2	666.0	1,007	...

Public debt (external, outstanding; December 1994): U.S.$52,625,000,000.

Foreign trade[11]

Balance of trade (current prices)

	1989	1990	1991	1992	1993	1994
U.S.$'000,000	−4,167	−9,343	−7,454	−8,156	−14,080	−5,164
% of total	15.2%	26.5%	21.6%	21.7%	31.4%	12.5%

Imports (1994): U.S.$23,270,000,000 (nonelectrical machinery 16.0%; mineral fuels 12.2%; iron and steel 10.3%; road vehicles 9.2%; electrical and electronic equipment 7.7%). *Major import sources:* Germany 15.7%; United States 10.4%; Italy 8.6%; former U.S.S.R. 7.9%; France 6.3%; Saudi Arabia 5.3%.
Exports (1994): U.S.$18,106,000,000 (textiles 34.7%; iron and steel products 13.1%; edible fruits 6.1%; electrical and electronic machinery 3.8%). *Major export destinations:* Germany 21.7%; United States 8.4%; former U.S.S.R. 7.9%; Italy 5.7%; United Kingdom 4.9%; France 4.7%.

Transport and communications

Transport. Railroads: (1993) route length 6,470 mi, 10,413 km; (1994) passenger-mi 3,967,000,000, passenger-km 6,385,000,000; (1994) short ton-mi cargo 5,654,000,000, metric ton km cargo 8,254,000,000. Roads (1992): total length 240,286 mi, 386,704 km (paved 15%). Vehicles (1994): passenger cars 2,862,000; trucks and buses 942,000. Merchant marine (1992): vessels (100 gross tons and over) 880; total deadweight tonnage 7,114,289. Air transport (1994)[12]: passenger-mi 5,675,000,000, passenger-km 9,133,000,000; short ton-mi cargo 143,736,000, metric ton-km cargo 209,851,000; airports (1995) with scheduled flights 24.
Communications. Daily newspapers (1991)[13]: total number 31; total circulation 4,054,000; circulation per 1,000 population 71. Radio (1994): total number of receivers 8,800,000 (1 per 7.0 persons). Television (1994): total number of receivers 10,530,000 (1 per 5.8 persons). Telephones (1994)[14]: 12,318,969 (1 per 5.0 persons).

Education and health

Education (1991–92)

	schools	teachers	students	student/ teacher ratio
Primary (age 6–10)	50,701	234,961	6,878,923	29.3
Secondary (age 11–16)	8,064	117,702	3,010,672	25.6
Voc., teacher tr.	2,971	57,425	977,010	17.0
Higher	424	35,132	759,047	21.6

Educational attainment (1993). Percentage of population age 25 and over having: no formal schooling 30.5%; incomplete primary education 6.6%; complete primary 40.4%; incomplete secondary 3.1%; complete secondary or higher 19.1%; unknown 0.3%. *Literacy* (1995): total population age 15 and over literate 33,605,000 (82.3%); males literate 19,191,000 (91.7%); females literate 14,414,000 (72.4%).
Health: physicians (1990) 50,639 (1 per 1,108 persons); hospital beds (1992) 139,606 (1 per 420 persons); infant mortality rate per 1,000 live births (1994) 49.0.
Food (1992): daily per capita caloric intake 3,429 (vegetable products 88%, animal products 12%); 136% of FAO recommended minimum requirement.

Military

Total active duty personnel (1995): 507,800 (army 78.8%, navy 10.0%, air force 11.2%). *Military expenditure as percentage of GNP* (1993): 5.8% (world 3.3%); per capita expenditure U.S.$118.

[1]Administratively divided into 76 provinces. [2]Official data based on mother tongue. Unofficially, Kurds as an ethnic group are estimated to constitute about 20% of the population. [3]Projected rates based on about 35% of total deaths. [4]1993. [5]Value added in LT '000,000,000. [6]At factor cost. [7]Civilian population only. [8]Unemployed. [9]May. [10]Based on June average. [11]Imports c.i.f.; exports f.o.b. [12]Turkish Airlines only. [13]Principal daily newspapers in Istanbul, Ankara, and five other large cities. [14]Number of lines.

Turkmenistan

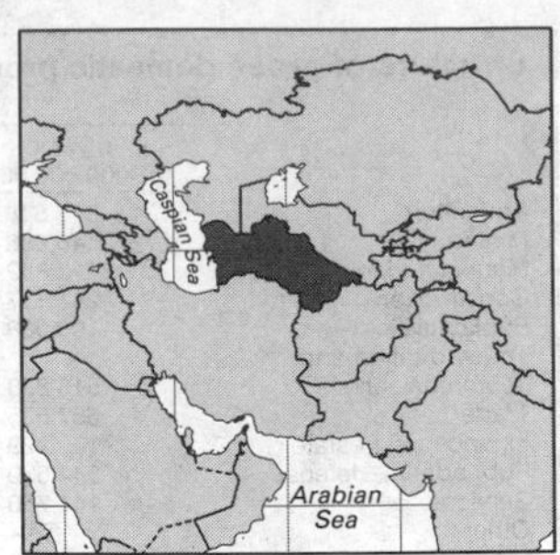

Official name: Türkmenistan Jumhuriyäti (Republic of Turkmenistan).
Form of government: republic with one legislative body (Majlis [50]).
Head of state and government: President.
Capital: Ashgabat.
Official language: Turkmen.
Official religion: none.
Monetary unit: manat; valuation (Oct. 4, 1995) 1 U.S.$ = 200.00 manat; 1 £ = 316.18 manat.

Area and population

		area		population
				1991
Provinces	**Capitals**	sq mi	sq km	estimate
Balkan	Nebitdag	90,300	233,900	925,500
Dashhovuse	Dashhovuse	28,400	73,600	738,000
Leban	Leban	36,200	93,800	774,700
Mariy	Mariy	33,500	86,800	859,500
City				
Ashkhabad	—	...	...	416,400
TOTAL		188,500[1]	488,100	3,714,100

Demography

Population (1995): 4,081,000.
Density (1995): persons per sq mi 21.7, persons per sq km 8.4.
Urban-rural (1992): urban 45.1%; rural 54.9%.
Sex distribution (1992): male 49.32%; female 50.68%.
Age breakdown (1989): under 15, 40.5%; 15–29, 28.8%; 30–44, 15.5%; 45–59, 9.1%; 60–74, 4.7%; 75 and over, 1.4%.
Population projection: (2000) 4,474,000; (2010) 5,277,000.
Doubling time: 27 years.
Ethnic composition (1992): Turkmen 73.3%; Russian 9.8%; Uzbek 9.0%; Kazakh 2.0%; Tatar 0.9%; other 5.0%.
Religious affiliation: believers are predominantly Sunnī Muslim (Ṣūfī).
Major cities (1991): Ashkhabad 416,400; Chardzhou 166,400; Dashovuse 117,000; Mariy 94,900; Nebit-Dag 89,100.

Vital statistics

Birth rate per 1,000 population (1993): 33.1 (world avg. 25.0); (1992) legitimate 96.5%; illegitimate 3.5%.
Death rate per 1,000 population (1992): 7.9 (world avg. 9.3).
Natural increase rate per 1,000 population (1992): 25.2 (world avg. 15.7).
Total fertility rate (avg. births per childbearing woman; 1993): 3.8.
Marriage rate per 1,000 population (1993): 10.7.
Divorce rate per 1,000 population (1993): 1.4.
Life expectancy at birth (1993): male 61.4 years; female 68.6 years.
Major causes of death per 100,000 population (1992): diseases of the circulatory system 333.8; diseases of the respiratory system 140.7; infectious and parasitic diseases 75.2; accidents, poisoning, and violence 62.7; malignant neoplasms (cancers) 62.3; diseases of the digestive system 28.2; diseases of the nervous system (1989) 9.1; endocrine and metabolic disorders (1989) 8.0.

National economy

Budget (1992). Revenue: 62,719,000,000 rubles (tax revenue 52.5%, of which turnover tax 26.3%, company profit tax 19.6%, individual income tax 4.8%, excise tax 1.9%; nontax revenue 47.5%). Expenditures: 94,882,000,000 rubles (1991; social and cultural affairs 56.9%, of which social security 26.7%, education and science 19.7%, health 9.4%; national economy 39.0%; government administration 2.7%).
Public debt (external, outstanding; 1992): U.S.$650,000,000.
Production (metric tons except as noted). Agriculture, forestry, fishing (1994): seed cotton 1,300,000, vegetables 672,000, grain 360,000, fruit 249,000; livestock (number of live animals) 6,314,000 sheep and goats, 1,104,000 cattle, 159,000 pigs, 7,000,000 poultry; roundwood (1990) 4,000,000 cu m; fish catch (1993) 37,000. Mining and quarrying (1993): sulfur 200,000; sodium sulphate 200,000. Manufacturing (value of production in '000,000 manat; 1993): textiles 1,999; petroleum products 950; food products 764; construction materials 327; clothing 311; chemical products 129; wood products 58; machine-building equipment 56. Construction (1992): 20,754,000 sq m. Energy production (consumption): electricity (kW-hr; 1992) 13,100,000,000 (13,100,000,000); coal (metric tons; 1992) none (269,000); crude petroleum (barrels; 1992) 35,184,000 (43,386,000); petroleum products (metric tons; 1991) 500,000 (500,000); natural gas (cu m; 1992) 60,107,000,000 (11,197,000,000).
Population economically active (1992): total: 1,572,900; activity rate of total population 40.8% (participation rates: ages 16–59 [male], 16–54 [female] 81.0%; female 50.5%; unemployed [1991] 20–25%).

Price and earnings indexes (1990 = 100)

	1988	1989	1990	1991	1992	1993	1994
Consumer price index	85.6	89.9	100	185.7	1,922	6,153	c. 25,570
Monthly earnings index	85.5	90.8	100	190.0	1,642	...	...

Household income and expenditure. Average household size (1989) 5.6; income per household: n.a.; sources of income (1992): wages and salaries 73.5%, pensions and grants 17.3%, income from agriculture sales 6.6%, nonwage income of workers 2.6%; expenditure (1992): food and clothing 65.4%, services 9.7%, taxes and other payments 8.6%.
Gross national product (at current market prices; 1993): U.S.$4,898,390,000 (U.S.$1,270 per capita)[2].

Structure of net material product and labour force

	1993		1992	
	in value '000,000 manat	% of total value	labour force	% of labour force
Agriculture	1,121	11.3	695,200	44.2
Mining / Manufacturing / Public utilities	6,898	69.3	154,300	9.8
Construction	1,098	11.0	163,500	10.4
Transportation and communications	299	3.0	56,400	3.6
Trade	—	—	88,500	5.6
Finance	—	—	...	...
Public administration, defense	—	—	49,800	3.2
Services	—	—	338,700	21.5
Other	534	5.4	26,500	1.7
TOTAL	9,950	100.0	1,572,900	100.0

Tourism: n.a.
Land use (1993): forested 8.2%; meadows and pastures 63.1%; agricultural and under permanent cultivation 3.1%; other 25.6%.

Foreign trade

Balance of trade (current prices)

	1987	1988	1989	1990	1991	1992
'000,000 rubles	−477	−284	−676	−971	+898	+2,409
% of total	8.9%	5.1%	11.3%	15.5%	6.1%	17.9%

Imports (1992): 5,497,000,000 rubles (machinery and transport equipment 30.3%, manufactured items 21.8%, food 17.1%, chemicals 6.5%). *Major import sources:* Russia 35.1%; Kazakhstan 11.8%; Azerbaijan 8.5%; Uzbekistan 8.1%; Ukraine 4.6%.
Exports (1992): 7,906,000,000 (fuels and lubricants 42.3%, manufactured items 38.1%, chemicals 5.5%, food 4.0%). *Major export destinations:* Russia 20.1%; Ukraine 17.5%; Uzbekistan 17.0%; Kazakhstan 8.1%; Georgia 6.7%;

Transport and communications

Transport. Railroads (1991): length 1,317 mi, 2,120 km; passengers transported 5,900,000; short ton cargo 20,700,000, metric ton cargo 22,800,000. Roads (1990): total length 8,300 mi, 13,400 km (paved 86%). Vehicles (1988): passenger cars 170,600; trucks and buses, n.a. Merchant marine: vessels (100 gross tons and over) n.a.; total deadweight tonnage, n.a. Air transport (1989): passenger-mi 2,021,000,000, passenger-km 3,253,000,000; short ton-mi cargo 222,000,000, metric ton-km cargo 324,200,000; airports (1995) with scheduled flights 1.
Communications. Daily newspapers (1989): total number 66; total circulation 1,141,000; circulation per 1,000 population 319. Radio (1991): 823,000 receivers (1 per 5.2 persons). Televisions (1991): 705,000 receivers (1 per 6.1 persons). Telephones (main lines; 1993): 265,100 (1 per 14.9 persons).

Education and health

Education (1991–92)

	schools	teachers	students	student/ teacher ratio
Primary (age 6–13) / Secondary (age 14–17)	1,791	60,000	842,000	14.0
Voc., teacher tr.	41	...	33,700	...
Higher	9	...	41,700	...

Educational attainment (1989). Percentage of population age 25 and over having: primary education or no formal schooling 13.6%; some secondary 21.3%; completed secondary and some postsecondary 56.8%; higher 8.3%.
Literacy (1989): total population age 15 and over literate 3,453,000 (97.7%); males literate 1,714,000 (98.8%); females literate 1,739,000 (96.6%).
Health (1994): physicians 14,000 (1 per 285 persons); hospital beds 47,000 (1 per 85 persons); infant mortality rate per 1,000 live births 45.9.

Military

Total active duty personnel (1995): CIS joint-control forces 25,000 (100% army). *Military expenditure as a percentage of GNP* (1993): 1.5% (world 3.3%); per capita expenditure U.S.$18.

[1]Detail does not add to total given because of rounding. [2]Ruble-area GNP and exchange-rate data are very speculative.

Tuvalu

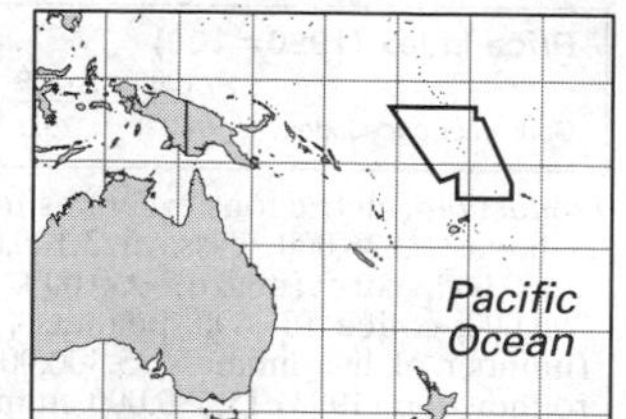

Official name: Tuvalu.
Form of government: constitutional monarchy with one legislative house (Parliament [12]).
Chief of state: British Monarch, represented by Governor-General.
Head of government: Prime Minister.
Capital: Fongafale, on Funafuti atoll.
Official language: none.
Official religion: none.
Monetary units[1]: 1 Tuvalu dollar = 1 Australian dollar ($T = $A) = 100 Tuvalu and Australian cents; valuation (Oct. 6, 1995) 1 U.S.$ = $A 1.31; 1 £ = $A 2.08.

Area and population

	area		population
Islands[2]	sq mi	sq km	1987 estimate
Funafuti	0.91	2.36	2,718
Nanumaga	1.00	2.59	717
Nanumea	1.38	3.57	965
Niulakita	0.16	0.41	75
Niutao	0.82	2.12	867
Nui	1.27	3.29	622
Nukufetau	1.18	3.06	722
Nukulaelae	0.64	1.66	335
Vaitupu	1.89	4.90	1,437
TOTAL	9.25[3]	23.96[3]	8,458[4, 5]

Demography

Population (1995): 9,400.
Density (1995): persons per sq mi 1,000.0, persons per sq km 385.2.
Urban-rural (1995): urban 46.0%; rural 54.0%.
Sex distribution (1991): male 48.39%; female 51.61%.
Age breakdown (1991): under 15, 34.7%; 15–64, 59.4%; 65 and over, 5.9%.
Population projection: (2000) 9,900; (2010) 10,900.
Doubling time: 43 years.
Ethnic composition (1979): Tuvaluan (Polynesian) 91.2%; mixed (Polynesian/Micronesian/other) 7.2%; European 1.0%; other 0.6%.
Religious affiliation (1979): Church of Tuvalu (Congregational) 96.9%; Seventh-day Adventist 1.4%; Bahā'ī 1.0%; Roman Catholic 0.2%; other 0.5%.
Major locality (1990): Fongafale, on Funafuti atoll, 3,432.

Vital statistics

Birth rate per 1,000 population (1993): 25.5 (world avg. 25.0); (1989) legitimate 82.2%; illegitimate 17.8%.
Death rate per 1,000 population (1993): 9.1 (world avg. 9.3).
Natural increase rate per 1,000 population (1993): 16.4 (world avg. 15.7).
Total fertility rate (avg. births per childbearing woman; 1993): 3.0.
Marriage rate per 1,000 population: n.a.
Divorce rate per 1,000 population: n.a.
Life expectancy at birth (1991): male 67.2 years; female 64.0 years.
Major causes of death per 100,000 population (1985): diseases of the digestive system 170.0; diseases of the circulatory system 150.0; diseases of the respiratory system 120.0; diseases of the nervous system 120.0; malignant neoplasms (cancers) 70.0; infectious and parasitic diseases 40.0; endocrine and metabolic disorders 20.0; ill-defined conditions 430.0; in 1992 the leading causes of death included liver diseases, meningitis, tuberculosis, and still and perinatal deaths; other health problems included acute respiratory infections, diarrhea, filariasis, conjunctivitis, fish poisoning, diabetes, rheumatism, and hypertension.

National economy

Budget (1990). Recurrent revenue: $A 5,301,000 (local sources [including fisheries licenses, import duties, sales tax, and income and company taxes] 77.4%; Tuvalu Trust Fund[6] 22.6%). Expenditures: $A 10,826,000[7] (1987; capital [development] expenditures 68.9%, of which marine transport 20.7%, education 13.0%, fisheries 5.6%, health 3.1%; current expenditures 31.1%).
Gross domestic product (at current market prices; 1990): U.S.$8,750,000 (U.S.$967 per capita).

Structure of gross domestic product and labour force

	1993		1991	
	in value[8] $A	% of total value	labour force	% of labour force
Agriculture, fishing, forestry	2,805,000	22.2	4,020	68.0
Mining	282,000	2.2	—	—
Manufacturing[9]	402,000	3.2	60	1.0
Construction	1,731,000	13.7	240	4.0
Public utilities	296,000	2.4	—	—
Transportation and communications	504,000	4.0	60	1.0
Trade, hotels, and restaurants	1,784,000	14.1	240	4.0
Finance	1,260,000	10.0	—	—
Pub. admin., defense } Services }	3,559,000	28.2	1,290	22.0
TOTAL	12,623,000	100.0	5,910	100.0

Production (metric tons except as noted). Agriculture[10], forestry, fishing (1994): coconuts 2,000, fruits 1,000, hens' eggs 13, other agricultural products include breadfruit, pulaka (taro), bananas, pandanus fruit, sweet potatoes, and pawpaws; livestock (number of live animals) 13,000 pigs[11]; forestry, n.a.; fish catch (1993) 1,460, of which tuna 15.0%. Mining and quarrying: n.a.[12]. Manufacturing (1988): copra 90 metric tons; handicrafts and baked goods are also important. Construction: n.a.; however, the main areas of construction activity are roadworks, coastal protection, government facilities, and water-related infrastructure projects. Energy production (consumption): electricity (kW-hr; 1992) 1,300,000 (1,300,000); coal, none (none); crude petroleum, none (n.a.); petroleum products, none (n.a.); natural gas, none (none).
Public debt: n.a.
Tourism (1993): receipts from visitors U.S.$300,000; expenditures by nationals abroad, n.a.
Population economically active (1991): total 5,910; activity rate of total population 65.3% (participation rates: ages 15–64, 85.5%; female [1979] 51.3%; unemployed [1979] 4.0%).

Price and earnings indexes (1990 = 100)

	1987	1988	1989	1990	1991	1992	1993
Consumer price index	86.5	93.8	96.4	100.0	106.2	100.0	102.1
Earnings index[13]	91.1	93.3	97.8	100.0	...	...	...

Household income and expenditure. Average household size (1979) 6.4; average annual income per household $A 2,575; sources of income (1987): agriculture and other 45.0%, cash economy only 38.0%, overseas remittances 17.3%; expenditure (1992)[14]: food 45.5%, housing and household operations 11.5%, transportation 10.5%, alcohol and tobacco 10.5%, clothing 7.5%, other 14.5%.
Land use (1987): agricultural and under permanent cultivation 73.6%[15]; scrub 16.1%; other 10.3%.

Foreign trade

Balance of trade (current prices)

	1984	1985	1986	1987	1988	1989
$A '000	–3,637	–3,969	–4,076	–4,946	–6,780	–5,158
% of total	85.4%	92.7%	99.9%	99.9%	99.7%	99.6%

Imports (1992): U.S.$6,700,000 (1989; food 29.3%, manufactured goods 28.2%, petroleum and petroleum products 12.8%, machinery and transport equipment 12.2%, chemicals 7.1%, beverages and tobacco 3.9%). *Major import sources:* United States 35.8%; Australia 26.9%; New Zealand 11.9%; Japan 11.9%; United Kingdom 4.5%.
Exports (1992): U.S.$5,200,000 (1989; clothing and footwear 29.5%, copra 21.5%, fruits and vegetables 8.0%). *Major export destinations:* United States 55.8%; Yugoslavia 32.7%; Germany 3.8%.

Transport and communications

Transport. Railroads: none. Roads (1985): total length 5 mi, 8 km (paved, none). Vehicles[16]: passenger cars, n.a.; trucks and buses, n.a. Merchant marine (1992): vessels (100 gross tons and over) 6; total deadweight tonnage 16,005. Air transport (1977): passenger arrivals (Funafuti) 1,443; cargo, n.a.; airports (1995) with scheduled flights 1.
Communications. Daily newspapers: none. Radio (1994): total number of receivers 3,000 (1 per 3.1 persons). Television: none. Telephones (main lines; 1993): 120 (1 per 77 persons).

Education and health

Education (1990)

	schools	teachers	students	student/teacher ratio
Primary (age 5–11)	9	72	1,485	20.6
Secondary (age 12–18)	1	21	314	15.0
Vocational	1	10	31	3.1
Higher	—	—	—	—

Educational attainment (1979). Percentage of population age 25 and over having: no formal schooling 0.4%; primary education 93.0%; secondary 6.1%; higher 0.5%. *Literacy* (1990): total population literate in Tuvaluan 8,593 (95.0%); literacy in English estimated at 45.0%.
Health (1993): physicians 8 (1 per 1,152 persons); hospital beds (1990) 30 (1 per 302 persons); infant mortality rate per 1,000 live births 73.6.
Food: daily per capita caloric intake, n.a.

Military

Total active duty personnel (1987): there is a police force numbering 32.

[1]The value of the Tuvalu dollar is pegged to the value of the Australian Dollar, which is also legal currency in Tuvalu. [2]Local government councils have been established on all islands except Niulakita. [3]A recent survey puts the area at 9.4 sq mi (24.4 sq km). [4]De facto population. [5]1991 census total is 9,043. [6]The Tuvalu Trust Fund was capitalized in 1987 with $A 27,700,000 to replace recurrent grant aid from the United Kingdom; the fund was valued at $A 36,000,000 in late 1991. [7]Figure includes $A 5,200,000 of capital expenditures, paid for primarily by foreign-aid contributions that are not part of recurrent revenue. [8]At 1988 factor cost. [9]Including cottage industry. [10]Because of poor soil quality, only limited subsistence agriculture is possible on the islands. [11]Other livestock include goats. [12]Research into the mineral potential of Tuvalu's maritime exclusive economic zone (289,500 sq mi [750,000 sq km] of the Pacific Ocean) is currently being conducted by the South Pacific Geo Science Commission. [13]Average minimum wage. [14]Weights of consumer price index components. [15]Capable of supporting coconut palms, pandanus, and breadfruit. [16]There are several cars, tractors, trailers, and light trucks on Funafuti; a few motorcycles are in use on most islands.

Uganda

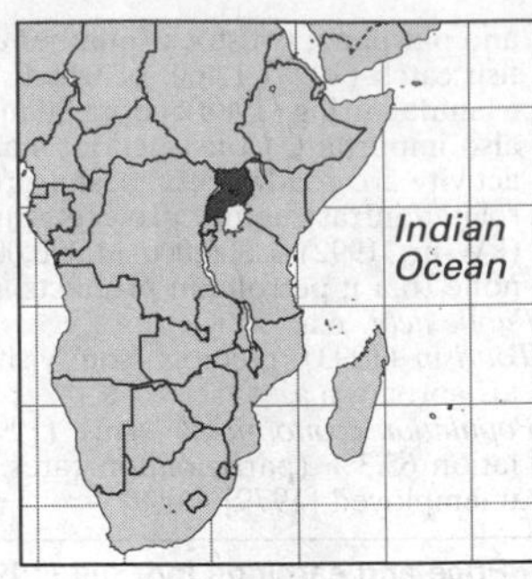

Official name: Republic of Uganda.
Form of government: transitional military regime with a constituent assembly (Constituent Assembly [214[1][2]).
Head of state and government: President assisted by Prime Minister.
Capital: Kampala.
Official languages: English; Swahili.
Official religion: none.
Monetary unit: 1 Uganda shilling (U Sh) = 100 cents; valuation (Oct. 6, 1995) 1 U.S.$ = U Sh 995; 1 £ = U Sh 1,573.

Area and population

Regions / Districts	Capitals	area sq mi	area sq km	population 1991 census[3]
Central				
Kalangala	...	...	...	16,400
Kampala	Kampala	70	180	773,500
Kiboga	...	...	...	140,800
Luwero	Luwero	3,550	9,200	449,200
Masaka	Kasawa Bukoto	6,310	16,330	831,300
Mpigi	Mpigi	2,400	6,220	915,400
Mubende	Bageza	3,980	10,310	497,500
Mukono	Kawuga Mukono	5,500	14,240	816,200
Rakai	Byakabanda	1,920	4,970	382,000
Eastern				
Iganga	Bulamogi	5,060	13,110	944,000
Jinja	Jinja	280	730	284,900
Kamuli	Namwendwa	1,680	4,350	480,700
Kapchorwa	Kaptanya	670	1,740	116,300
Kumi	Kumi	1,100	2,860	237,000
Mbale	Bunkoko	980	2,550	706,600
Pallisa	...	...	...	355,000
Soroti	Soroti	3,880	10,060	430,900
Tororo	Sukulu	1,780	4,550	554,000
Northern				
Apac	Apac	2,510	6,490	460,700
Arua	Olaki	3,020	7,830	624,600
Gulu	Bungatira	4,530	11,740	338,700
Kitgum	Labongo	8,230	16,140	350,300
Kotido	Kotido	5,100	13,210	190,700
Lira	Lira	2,800	7,250	498,300
Moroto	Katikekile	5,450	14,110	171,500
Moyo	Moyo	1,930	5,010	178,500
Nebbi	Nebbi	1,120	2,890	315,900
Western				
Bundibugyo	Busaru	900	2,340	116,000
Bushenyi	Bumbaire	2,080	5,400	734,800
Hoima	Hoima	3,820	9,900	197,800
Kabale	Rubale	960	2,490	412,800
Kabarole	Karambe	3,230	8,360	741,400
Kasese	Rukoki	1,240	3,200	343,000
Kibaale	...	...	...	219,300
Kisoro	...	...	...	184,900
Masindi	Nyangeya	3,720	9,640	253,500
Mbarara	Kakika	4,190	10,840	929,600
Rukungiri	Kagunga	1,060	2,750	388,000
TOTAL LAND AREA		76,080	197,040	
INLAND WATER[4]		16,990	44,000	
TOTAL		93,070[5]	241,040[5]	16,582,700[5]

Demography

Population (1995): 18,659,000.
Density (1995)[6]: persons per sq mi 245.2, persons per sq km 94.7.
Urban-rural (1993): urban 12.0%; rural 88.0%.
Sex distribution (1991): male 49.00%; female 51.00%.
Age breakdown (1990): under 15, 49.6%; 15–29, 25.4%; 30–44, 13.9%; 45–59, 7.1%; 60 and over, 4.0%.
Population projection: (2000) 21,168,000; (2010) 27,244,000.
Doubling time: 19 years.
Ethnic composition (1983): Ganda 17.8%; Teso 8.9%; Nkole 8.2%; Soga 8.2%; Gisu 7.2%; Chiga 6.8%; Lango 6.0%; Rwanda 5.8%; other 31.1%.
Religious affiliation (1980): Roman Catholic 49.6%; Protestant 28.7%; Muslim 6.6%; other 15.1%.
Major cities (1991): Kampala 773,000; Jinja 61,000; Mbale 54,000.

Vital statistics

Birth rate per 1,000 population (1990–95): 51.5 (world avg. 25.0).
Death rate per 1,000 population (1990–95): 14.1 (world avg. 9.3).
Natural increase rate per 1,000 population (1990–95): 37.4 (world avg. 15.7).
Total fertility rate (avg. births per childbearing woman; 1993): 7.2.
Life expectancy at birth (1990–95): male 51.4 years; female 54.7 years.

National economy

Budget (1993–94). Revenue: U Sh 651,423,000,000 (taxes 52.0%, of which customs duties 23.4%, sales taxes 11.6%, income taxes 8.1%; grants 44.2%). Expenditures: U Sh 816,773,000,000 (current expenditures 47.8%, of which security 11.1%, education 5.8%, health 2.3%; capital expenditures 52.2%).
Tourism (1993): receipts from visitors U.S.$50,000,000; expenditures by nationals abroad U.S.$40,000,000.
Land use (1993): forested 27.6%; pastures 9.0%; agricultural 33.9%; other 29.5%.
Population economically active (1991): total 8,365,000; activity rate of total population 49.6% (participation rates: ages 15–64, 78.9%[7]; female 35.2%).

Price index (1990 = 100)

	1988	1989	1990	1991	1992	1993	1994
Consumer price index	47.0	75.0	100.0	128.0	195.0	207.0	227.0

Production (metric tons except as noted). Agriculture, forestry, fishing (1994): bananas 8,836,000, cassava 3,100,000, sweet potatoes 2,129,000, sugarcane 1,080,000, corn (maize) 900,000, millet 610,000, pulses 495,000, sorghum 390,000, coffee 166,600, peanuts (groundnuts) 161,000, tea 12,300; livestock (number of live animals) 5,400,000 goats, 4,900,000 cattle, 1,300,000 sheep; roundwood (1993) 15,580,000 cu m; fish catch 206,000. Mining and quarrying (1993): tungsten (wolfram) 60.0; tin ore 30.0; gold 57,900 troy oz. Manufacturing (1993): cement 52,000; sugar 49,300; soap 47,600; metal products 14,300; footwear 326,000 pairs; fabrics 7,500,000 sq m; beer 239,000 hectolitres. Energy production (consumption): electricity (kW-hr; 1992) 786,000,000 (674,000,000); petroleum products (metric tons; 1992) none (303,000).
Gross national product (1993): U.S.$3,425,000,000 (U.S.$190 per capita).

Structure of gross domestic product and labour force

	1993–94 in value U Sh '000,000	1993–94 % of total value	1991 labour force	1991 % of labour force
Agriculture	2,020,304	49.1	6,724,000	80.4
Mining	12,844	0.3	478,000	5.7
Manufacturing	279,713	6.8		
Construction	235,177	5.7		
Public utilities	63,417	1.5		
Transp. and commun.	153,884	3.7	1,163,000	13.9
Trade	496,597	12.1		
Finance	245,713	6.0		
Pub. admin., defense / Services	453,929	11.0		
Other	158,021	3.8	...	...
TOTAL	4,119,599	100.0	8,365,000	100.0

Household size. Average household size (1983) 4.8; income per household: n.a.; expenditure (1989–90)[8]: food 57.1%, rent, education, and health 15.7%, fuel and lighting 7.3%, transportation 5.9%, clothing 5.5%.
Public debt (external, outstanding; 1992): U.S.$2,495,000,000.

Foreign trade

Balance of trade (current prices)

	1989	1990	1991	1992	1993	1994
U.S.$'000,000	−23,471	−374.7	−369.6	−278.6	−416.1	−463.8
% of total	17.4%	47.2%	51.3%	44.7%	57.0%	47.7%

Imports (1994): U.S.$717,700,000 (1992; machinery and transport equipment 32.2%; minerals, fuel, and electricity 13.4%; chemicals 8.4%; food and live animals 4.0%). *Major import sources* (1991): Kenya 23.3%; U.K. 15.0%; Japan 9.3%; Germany 6.9%.
Exports (1994): U.S.$253,900,000 (unroasted coffee 67.9%; tea 3.5%; cotton 1.7%). *Major export destinations* (1991): The Netherlands 21.5%; France 16.2%; U.S. 11.9%; Spain 11.1%; Germany 10.9%; Italy 7.9%.

Transport and communications

Transport. Railroads (1991): route length 1,241 km; passenger-km 330,000,000; metric ton-km cargo 87,000,000. Roads (1991): total length 28,660 km (paved 16%). Vehicles (1993): passenger cars 17,804; trucks and buses 25,246. Merchant marine (1992): vessels (100 gross tons and over) 2; total deadweight tonnage 8,600[9]. Air transport (1993)[10]: passenger-km 24,089,000; metric ton-km cargo 62,000; airports (1995) 1.
Communications. Daily newspapers (1992): total number 4; total circulation 55,000; circulation per 1,000 population 3.2. Radio (1993): 3,500,000 receivers (1 per 5.1 persons). Television (1994): 115,000 receivers (1 per 158 persons). Telephones (main lines; 1993): 20,800 (1 per 853 persons).

Education and health

Education (1994)

	schools[11]	teachers	students	student/teacher ratio
Primary (age 5–11)	7,905	102,126	2,496,139	24.4
Secondary (age 12–15)	774	16,245	244,248	15.0
Voc., teacher tr.	136	2,766	46,238	16.7
Higher	9	941	8,966	9.5

Educational attainment (1991). Percentage of population age 25 and over having: no formal schooling or less than one full year 46.9%; primary education 42.1%; secondary 10.5%; higher 0.5%. *Literacy* (1990): population age 15 and over literate 4,586,000 (48.3%); males literate 2,900,000 (62.2%); females literate 1,686,000 (34.9%).
Health (1989): physicians 774 (1 per 20,720 persons); hospital beds 20,136 (1 per 817 persons); infant mortality rate (1990–95) 94.0.
Food (1992): daily per capita caloric intake 2,159 (vegetable products 93%, animal products 7%); 93% of FAO recommended minimum requirement.

Military

Total active duty personnel (1995): 50,000 (army 97.6%, navy 0.8%, air force 1.6%). *Military expenditure as percentage of GNP* (1993): 1.4% (world 3.3%); per capita U.S.$3.

[1]Elective seats only. [2]Body was elected and appointed in 1994 and promulgated a new constitution in October 1995. [3]Preliminary. [4]Includes swamps; excludes 30,960 sq km of Uganda's Lake Victoria territorial waters. [5]Detail does not add to total given because of rounding. [6]Based on land area. [7]1985. [8]Kampala and Entebbe only. [9]1988. [10]Uganda Airlines only. [11]1989.

Ukraine

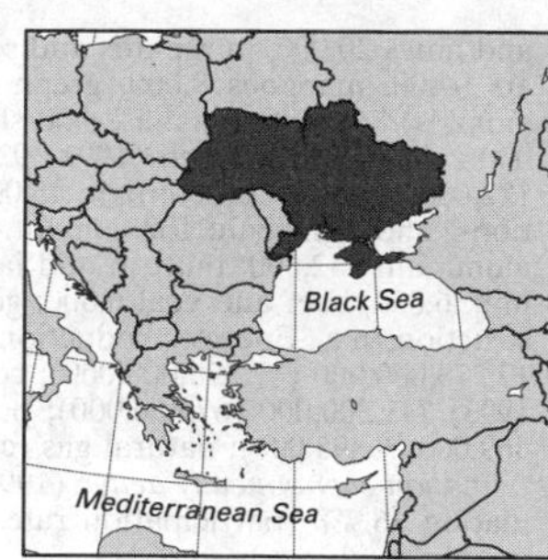

Official name: Ukrayina (Ukraine).
Form of government: unitary multiparty republic with a single legislative body (Supreme Council [450]).
Head of state: President.
Head of government: Prime Minister.
Capital: Kiev (Kyyiv).
Official language: Ukrainian.
Official religion: none.
Monetary unit: karbovanets[1] (no decimal unit); valuation (Oct. 6, 1995) free rate, 1 U.S.$ = 172,000 karbovantsy; 1 £ = 271,915 karbovantsy.

Area and population

		area		population
		sq mi	sq km	1994[2] estimate
Autonomous republic	**Capitals**			
Crimea (Krym)	Simferopol	10,400	27,000	2,651,700
Provinces				
Cherkasy	Cherkasy	8,100	20,900	1,530,000
Chernihiv	Chernihiv	12,300	31,900	1,384,800
Chernivtsi	Chernivtsi	3,100	8,100	946,800
Dnipropetrovsk	Dnipropetrovsk	12,300	31,900	3,923,700
Donetsk	Donetsk	10,200	26,500	5,331,500
Ivano-Frankivsk	Ivano-Frankivsk	5,400	13,900	1,465,600
Kharkiv	Kharkiv	12,100	31,400	3,158,200
Kherson	Kherson	11,000	28,500	1,282,200
Khmelnytsky	Khmelnytsky	8,000	20,600	1,525,500
Kirovohrad	Kirovohrad	9,500	24,600	1,246,300
Kyyiv (Kiev)	Kiev	11,200	28,900	4,581,100
Luhansk	Luhansk	10,300	26,700	2,867,100
Lviv	Lviv	8,400	21,800	2,778,300
Mykolayiv	Mykolayiv	9,500	24,600	1,360,800
Odessa	Odessa	12,900	33,300	2,627,600
Poltava	Poltava	11,100	28,800	1,765,600
Rivne	Rivne	7,800	20,100	1,194,300
Sumy	Sumy	9,200	23,800	1,424,700
Ternopil	Ternopil	5,300	13,800	1,180,300
Vinnytsya	Vinnytsya	10,200	26,500	1,904,800
Volyn	Volodymyr-Volynsky	7,800	20,200	1,080,700
Zakarpatska	Uzhhorod	4,900	12,800	1,286,700
Zaporizhzhya	Zaporizhzhya	10,500	27,200	2,110,200
Zhytomyr	Zhytomyr	11,600	29,900	1,505,900
TOTAL		233,100	603,700	52,114,400

Demography

Population (1995): 52,003,000.
Density (1995): persons per sq mi 223.1, persons per sq km 86.1.
Urban-rural (1994): urban 67.9%; rural 32.1%.
Sex distribution (1994): male 46.45%; female 53.55%.
Age breakdown (1993[2]): under 15, 21.0%; 15–29, 20.6%; 30–44, 22.2%; 45–59, 17.5%; 60–69, 11.0%; 70 and over, 7.7%.
Population projection: (2000) 51,634,000; (2010) 50,903,000.
Ethnic composition (1991): Ukrainian 72.6%; Russian 22.2%; Belarusian 0.9%; Jewish 0.7%; Moldovan 0.6%; Tatar 0.4%; other 2.6%.
Religious affiliation: believers are predominantly Ukrainian Orthodox; there is a Ukrainian Catholic minority.
Major cities (1994[2]): Kiev 2,645,000; Kharkiv 1,599,000; Dnipropetrovsk 1,176,000; Donetsk 1,114,000; Odessa 1,073,000.

Vital statistics

Birth rate per 1,000 population (1993): 10.7 (world avg. 25.0); (1992) legitimate 87.9%; illegitimate 12.1%.
Death rate per 1,000 population (1993): 14.2 (world avg. 9.3).
Natural increase rate per 1,000 population (1993): −3.5 (world avg. 15.7).
Total fertility rate (avg. births per childbearing woman; 1993): 1.8.
Marriage rate per 1,000 population (1993): 8.2.
Divorce rate per 1,000 population (1993): 4.2.
Life expectancy at birth (1993): male 65.3 years; female 74.7 years.
Major causes of death per 100,000 population (1993): circulatory diseases 783.0; cancers 201.0; accidents 131.0; respiratory diseases 81.0; diseases of the digestive system (1992) 36.4; infectious diseases (1992) 13.1.

National economy

Budget (1995). Revenue: 2,100,000,000,000,000 karbovantsy (1993; tax revenue 87.6%, of which value-added tax 24.5%, corporate tax 16.6%, foreign trade tax 12.4%; nontax revenue 12.4%). Expenditures: 2,400,000,000,000,000 karbovantsy (1993; current expenditure 92.4%, of which social safety net 20.3%, national economy 14.6%, education 13.6%, health care 11.4%; capital expenditure 7.6%).
Public debt (external; 1994): U.S.$7,100,000,000.
Production (metric tons except as noted). Agriculture, forestry, fishing (1994): sugar beets 28,138,000, potatoes 16,102,000, wheat 13,857,000, sunflower seeds 1,569,000, corn (maize) 1,539,000, grapes 395,000; livestock (number of live animals) 21,607,000 cattle, 15,298,000 pigs, 6,863,000 sheep and goats; roundwood (1993) 4,888,200 cu m; fish catch (1993) 371,343. Mining and quarrying (1993): iron ore 65,000,000; manganese 5,000,000. Manufacturing (value in karbovantsy '000,000; 1993): machine and metalworking equipment 54,960; food products 21,307; light industrial products 16,191; metallurgy 12,406; chemical products 6,079; construction materials 5,017; wood products 4,847. Construction (1993): residential 12,300,000 sq m. Energy production (consumption): electricity (kW-hr; 1992) 252,400,000,000 (246,800,000,000); coal (metric tons; 1992) 133,600,000 (138,900,000,000); crude petroleum (barrels; 1992) 32,800,000 (298,500,000); petroleum products 32,500,000 (28,800,000); natural gas (cu m; 1992) 18,200,000,000 (96,900,000,000).
Gross national product (1993)[3]: U.S.$99,589,000,000 (U.S.$1,910 per capita).

Structure of gross domestic product and labour force

	1991		1993	
	in value '000,000 karbovantsy	% of total value	labour force	% of labour force
Agriculture	51,373	22.3	4,900,000	20.5
Mining / Manufacturing	98,266	42.5	7,000,000	29.3
Public utilities	4,386	1.9	800,000	3.4
Construction	23,176	10.0	1,800,000	7.5
Transp. and commun.	18,908	8.2	1,600,000	6.7
Trade	15,187	6.6	1,700,000	7.1
Finance	6,536	2.8	200,000	0.8
Pub. admin., defense	10,090	4.4	600,000	2.5
Services	32,365	14.0	4,200,000	17.6
Other	−29,416[4]	−12.7[4]	1,100,000	4.6
TOTAL	230,871	100.0	23,900,000	100.0

Population economically active (1993): total 23,900,000; activity rate of total population 45.9% (participation rates: ages 16–59 [male], 16–54 [female] 82.4%; female [1991] 54.5%; unemployed [1994] 14.2%).

Price and earnings indexes (1990 = 100)

	1987	1988	1989	1990	1991	1992	1993
Consumer price index	70.3	76.3	85.5	100.0	203.2	687.5	965.4
Monthly earnings index	71.3	78.0	86.3	100.0	190.8	2,677	...

Land use (1993): forested 17.1%; meadows and pastures 12.4%; agricultural and under permanent cultivation 57.0%; other 13.5%.
Household income and expenditure (1992). Average household size 3.0; income per household 12,825 karbovantsy[1]; sources of income (1993): wages 58.5%, pensions 22.5%, sales of agricultural products 4.0%, other 15.0%; expenditure (1991): food and nonalcoholic beverages 39.2%, consumer goods 32.2% (of which furniture and household appliances 6.8%), entertainment and culture 6.3%, alcoholic beverages 2.1%, housing 1.7%.

Foreign trade

Balance of trade (current prices)

	1990	1991	1992	1993
'000,000,000 karbovantsy	−8.5	+7.3	+96.6	−548.7
% of total	8.5%	6.4%	4.2%	0.1%

Imports (1994): U.S.$9,767,862,000 (crude petroleum and natural gas 62.9%, machinery and metalworking equipment 12.3%, chemical products 6.4%, other manufactured products 3.7%, nonferrous metals 3.1%). *Major import sources:* Russia 59.2%; Turkmenistan 7.0%; Germany 5.8%; Belarus 3.4%.
Exports (1994): U.S.$9,882,560,000 (ferrous metals 35.7%, machinery and metalworking equipment 20.7%, chemical products 15.7%, food products 14.1%, other manufactured products 6.3%). *Major export destinations:* Russia 38.8%; Belarus 5.4%; China 5.1%; U.S. 3.4%; Switzerland 3.3%.

Transport and communications

Transport. Railroads (1993): length 23,350 km; passenger-km 75,900,000,000; metric ton-km cargo (1992) 338,000,000,000. Roads (1993): total length 273,700 km (paved 86%). Vehicles (1988): passenger cars 2,920,000. Air transport (1993): passenger-km 3,200,000,000; metric ton-km cargo (1992) 100,000,000; airports (1995) with scheduled flights 20.
Communications (1992). Daily newspapers: total number 90; total circulation 6,083,000; circulation per 1,000 population 52. Radio (1991): 14,520,000 receivers (1 per 4.1 persons). Television (1991): 17,024,000 receivers (1 per 3.0 persons). Telephones (main lines; 1993): 2,225,000 (1 per 6.7 persons).

Education and health

Education (1993–94)

	schools	teachers	students	student/ teacher ratio
Primary (age 6–13) / Secondary (age 14–17)	21,694	574,000	6,937,000	12.1
Voc., teacher tr.	754	...	680,700	...
Higher	159	...	829,200	...

Educational attainment (1989). Percentage of population age 15 and over having: some primary education 6.8%; completed primary 13.8%; some secondary 18.4%; completed secondary 31.1%; some postsecondary 19.5%; higher 10.4%. *Literacy* (1989): percentage of total population age 15 and over literate 98.4%; males literate 99.5%; females literate 97.4%.
Health (1993): physicians 230,000 (1 per 226 persons); hospital beds 678,700 (1 per 75 persons); infant mortality rate per 1,000 live births 14.9.

Military

Total active duty personnel (1994): 517,000 (army 59.6%, air force and air defense 40.4%). *Military expenditure as percentage of GNP* (1993) 3.9% (world 3.3%). The Black Sea Fleet of the former U.S.S.R. remained to be divided with Russia and Georgia at year-end. Commonwealth of Independent States- (CIS-) controlled Strategic Nuclear Forces constituted a third military establishment during a two-year transition period.

[1]On Nov. 12, 1992, Ukraine replaced the Russian ruble with the karbovanets, or Ukrainian coupon, a temporary national currency; a prospective permanent national currency, the hryvnya, had not been issued as of October 1995. [2]January 1. [3]Ruble-area GNP and exchange-rate data are very speculative. [4]Less imputed bank service charges, net indirect taxes, and taxes on production.

United Arab Emirates

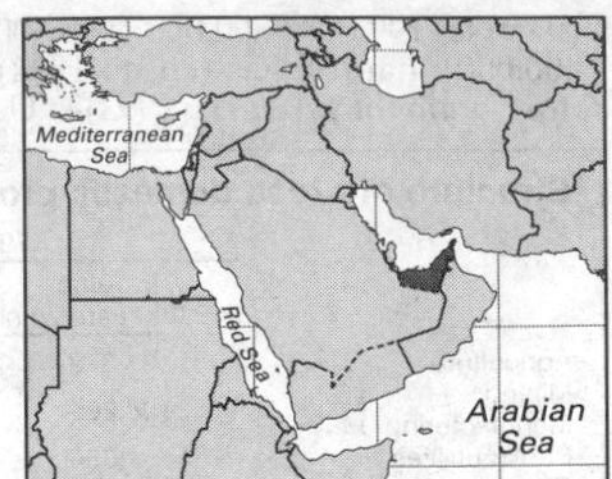

Official name: al-Imārāt al-ʿArabīyah al-Muttaḥidah (United Arab Emirates).
Form of government: federation of seven emirates with one appointive advisory body (Federal National Council [40[1]]).
Chief of state: President.
Head of government: Prime Minister.
Capital: Abu Dhabi.
Official language: Arabic.
Official religion: Islam.
Monetary unit: 1 U.A.E. dirham (Dh) = 100 fils; valuation (Oct. 6, 1995) 1 U.S.$ = Dh 3.67; 1 £ = Dh 5.81.

Area and population

		area		population
Emirates	Capitals	sq mi	sq km	1991 estimate
Abu Dhabi (Abū Ẓaby)	Abu Dhabi	28,210[2]	73,060[2]	798,000
ʿAjmān (Ajman)	ʿAjmān	100	260	76,000
Dubayy (Dubai)	Dubayy	1,510	3,900	501,000
al-Fujayrah (Fujairah)	al-Fujayrah	500	1,300	63,000
Ra's al-Khaymah (Ras al-Khaimah)	Ra's al-Khaymah	660	1,700	130,000
ash-Shāriqah (Sharjah)	ash-Shāriqah	1,000	2,600	314,000
Umm al-Qaywayn (Umm al-Qaiwain)	Umm al-Qaywayn	300	780	27,000
TOTAL		32,280	83,600	1,909,000

Demography

Population (1995): 2,195,000.
Density (1995): persons per sq mi 68.0, persons per sq km 26.3.
Urban-rural (1995): urban 84.0%; rural 16.0%.
Sex distribution (1995): male 63.87%; female 36.13%.
Age breakdown (1995): under 15, 31.3%; 15–29, 18.5%; 30–44, 31.4%; 45–59, 15.6%; 60–74, 2.8%; 75 and over, 0.5%.
Population projection: (2000) 2,429,000; (2010) 2,882,000.
Doubling time: 24 years.
Ethnic composition (1993): expatriates of Bangladesh, India, Pakistan, and Sri Lanka 45%; Arabs 25%, of which non-UAE Arabs (primarily Egyptians) 13%, UAE Arabs 12%; Iranians 17%; other Asians and Africans 8%; Europeans and North Americans 5%.
Religious affiliation (1980): Muslim 94.9% (Sunnī 80%, Shīʿī 20%); Christian 3.8%; other 1.3%.
Major cities (1989): Dubayy 585,189; Abu Dhabi 363,432; al-ʿAyn 176,411; ash-Shāriqah 125,000[3]; Ra's al-Khaymah 42,000[3].

Vital statistics

Birth rate per 1,000 population (1995): 27.0 (world avg. 25.0); legitimate, n.a.; illegitimate, n.a.
Death rate per 1,000 population (1995): 3.0 (world avg. 9.3).
Natural increase rate per 1,000 population (1995): 24.0 (world avg. 15.7).
Total fertility rate (avg. births per childbearing woman; 1995): 4.5.
Marriage rate per 1,000 population (1990): 2.6.
Divorce rate per 1,000 population (1990): 0.9.
Life expectancy at birth (1995): male 70.4 years; female 74.7 years.
Major causes of death per 100,000 population (1989)[4]: accidents and poisoning 43.7; diseases of the circulatory system 34.3; malignant neoplasms (cancers) 13.7; respiratory diseases 8.1.

National economy

Budget (1994). Revenue: Dh 16,200,000,000 (1993; current [domestic] grants 83.5%; other sources 16.5%, of which nontax revenue 12.5%, tax revenue 4.0%). Expenditures: Dh 17,600,000,000 (1993; current expenditures 96.2%, of which defense 37.8%, education 16.7%, public safety 13.1%, health 7.4%, economic services 4.5%; cultural and religious affairs 3.3%).
Gross national product (at current market prices; 1993): U.S.$38,720,000,000 (U.S.$22,470 per capita).

Structure of gross domestic product and labour force

	1994		1990	
	in value Dh '000,000[5]	% of total value	labour force	% of labour force
Agriculture	3,400	2.5	43,100	6.3
Petroleum	45,040	33.4	10,000	1.5
Manufacturing	11,160	8.3	63,400	9.2
Construction	13,210	9.8	119,200	17.3
Public utilities	3,100	2.3	20,600	3.0
Transportation and communications	8,530	6.3	71,700	10.4
Trade	14,870	11.0	101,400	14.7
Finance, real estate	16,830	12.5	18,800	2.7
Pub. admin., defense	16,280	12.1	} 241,300	} 35.0
Services	4,460[6]	3.3[6]		
Other	−2,080[7]	−1.5[7]	—	—
TOTAL	134,800	100.0	689,500	100.0[8]

Public debt (external, outstanding; 1991): U.S.$1,067,000,000.
Tourism (1992): total number of tourist arrivals 50,000.
Production (metric tons except as noted). Agriculture, forestry, fishing (1994): tomatoes 243,000, dates 240,000, cabbages 107,000, eggplants 67,000, lemons and limes 20,000, pumpkins and squash 17,000, cucumbers 13,000, cauliflowers 9,000, mangoes 9,000, green peppers 6,000; livestock (number of live animals) 861,000 goats, 333,000 sheep, 148,000 camels, 65,000 cattle, 8,000,000 chickens; fish catch (1991) 92,300. Mining and quarrying (1993): sulfur 122,000; gypsum 95,000; lime 45,000; also marble, shale for ceramic applications, and aggregate for cement. Manufacturing (1993): cement 3,500,000; aluminum 242,300; mutton and lamb meat 24,000; goat's milk 19,000; cow's milk 6,000; beef and veal 6,000; goat meat 5,000; butter and ghee 261. Construction: n.a. Energy production (consumption): electricity (kW-hr; 1993) 17,578,000,000 (17,578,000,000); coal, none (n.a.); crude petroleum (barrels; 1993) 741,300,000 (67,350,000); petroleum products (metric tons; 1993) 13,469,000 (6,495,000); natural gas (cu m; 1993) 22,929,000,000 (19,521,000,000).
Population economically active (1992): total 733,500; activity rate of total population 36.9% (participation rates [1986]: ages 15–64, 76.7%; female 6.6%; unemployed, n.a.).

Price and earnings indexes (1990 = 100)

	1986	1987	1988	1989	1990	1991	1992
Consumer price index[9]	91.2	93.9	95.0	98.8	100.0	105.5	102.1
Earnings index	...	...	...	...	...	...	...

Household income and expenditure. Average household size (1986) 6.8; income per household: n.a.; sources of income: n.a.; expenditure (1991): rent, fuel, and light 23.9%, food 22.7%, transportation and communications 14.1%, durable household goods 11.6%, education, recreation, and entertainment 8.6%.
Land use (1993): forested, virtually none; meadows and pastures 2.4%; agricultural and under permanent cultivation 0.5%; built-on, wasteland, and other 97.1%.

Foreign trade

Balance of trade (current prices)

	1989	1990	1991	1992	1993	1994
U.S.$'000,000	+6,917	+10,200	+9,341	+4,460	+903	−2,977
% of total	26.6%	30.8%	25.3%	11.3%	2.3%	6.6%

Imports (1994): U.S.$23,883,000,000 (1991; machinery and transport equipment 42.4%, basic manufactures 21.4%, food and live animals 13.5%, chemicals 8.8%, crude minerals 1.3%, mineral fuels 1.1%). *Major import sources:* Japan 10.4%; United Kingdom 7.8%; Germany 7.5%; United States 7.3%; Italy 6.7%; South Korea 5.4%; India 4.9%; Hong Kong 4.5%; China 4.0%; France 3.9%; Singapore 3.7%; Taiwan 2.8%; Malaysia 2.3%; Saudi Arabia 2.0%; The Netherlands 1.8%.
Exports (1994): U.S.$20,906,000,000 (1989; crude petroleum 65.6%, nonpetroleum exports and reexports 34.4%). *Major export destinations:* Japan 39.7%; India 5.3%; Oman 4.9%; South Korea 4.7%; Iran 4.6%; Singapore 3.8%; Thailand 2.7%; Hong Kong 2.4%; United States 2.1%; United Kingdom 1.5%; Pakistan 1.3%; Kenya 1.2%; Taiwan 1.1%; Turkey 1.0%.

Transport and communications

Transport. Railroads: none. Roads (1994): total length 2,830 mi, 4,555 km (paved 38.5%). Vehicles (1993): passenger cars 297,128; trucks and buses 72,824. Merchant marine (1992): vessels (100 gross tons and over) 276; total deadweight tonnage 1,491,728. Air transport (1994)[10]: passenger-mi 3,975,022,000, passenger-km 6,397,190,000; short ton-mi cargo 233,981,000, metric ton-km cargo 341,607,000; airports (1995) with scheduled flights 4.
Communications. Daily newspapers (1992): total number 11; total circulation 335,000[11]; circulation per 1,000 population 189[11]. Radio (1994): total number of receivers 490,000 (1 per 4.4 persons). Television (1994): total number of receivers 170,000 (1 per 12.6 persons). Telephones (main lines; 1993): 623,800 (1 per 2.8 persons).

Education and health

Education (1993–94)

	schools	teachers	students	student/teacher ratio
Primary (age 6–11)	} 354[12]	14,754	251,182	17.0
Secondary (age 12–18)		} 11,637	145,143	} 12.6
Vocational	9[13]		1,143	
Higher	1	510[14]	9,793[14]	19.2[14]

Educational attainment (1975). Percentage of population age 25 and over having: no formal schooling 72.2%; primary education 5.2%; secondary 16.6%; higher 6.0%. *Literacy* (1995): total population age 15 and over literate 79.2%; males literate 78.9%; females literate 79.8%.
Health (1993): physicians 3,000 (1 per 694 persons); hospital beds 4,314 (1 per 483 persons); infant mortality rate per 1,000 live births (1995) 21.0.
Food (1992): daily per capita caloric intake 3,384 (vegetable products 75%, animal products 25%); 140% of FAO recommended minimum requirement.

Military

Total active duty personnel (1995): 70,000 (army 92.8%, navy 2.1%, air force 5.1%). *Military expenditure as percentage of GDP* (1994): 5.7% (world 2.6%); per capita expenditure U.S.$1,149.

[1]All appointed seats. [2]Approximate, based on reported total and on reported partial areas for smaller emirates. [3]1980. [4]Registered; Abu Dhabi Emirate only. [5]At factor cost. [6]Services include domestic help. [7]Less imputed bank service charges. [8]Detail does not add to total given because of rounding. [9]City of Abu Dhabi only. [10]Emirates Airlines only. [11]Partial circulation only. [12]1987–88. [13]1985–86. [14]1992–93.

United Kingdom

Official name: United Kingdom of Great Britain and Northern Ireland.
Form of government: constitutional monarchy with two legislative houses (House of Lords [1,198]; House of Commons [651]).
Chief of state: Sovereign.
Head of government: Prime Minister.
Capital: London.
Official language: English.
Official religion: Churches of England and Scotland "established" (protected by the state, but not "official") in their respective countries; no established church in Northern Ireland or Wales.
Monetary unit: 1 pound sterling (£) = 100 new pence; valuation (Oct. 6, 1995) 1 £ = U.S.$1.58; 1 U.S.$ = £0.63.

Area and population

Countries	Capitals	area sq mi	area sq km	population 1993 estimate
England	London	50,363	130,439	48,532,700
Counties				
Avon	Bristol	520	1,346	973,300
Bedfordshire	Bedford	477	1,235	539,400
Berkshire	Reading	486	1,259	763,700
Buckinghamshire	Aylesbury	727	1,883	651,700
Cambridgeshire	Cambridge	1,316	3,409	682,600
Cheshire	Chester	800	2,083	971,900
Cleveland	Middlesbrough	225	583	559,500
Cornwall[1]	Truro	1,376	3,564	477,000
Cumbria	Carlisle	2,629	6,810	490,200
Derbyshire	Matlock	1,016	2,631	950,900
Devon	Exeter	2,591	6,711	1,049,200
Dorset	Dorchester	1,025	2,654	667,500
Durham	Durham	941	2,436	607,500
East Sussex	Lewes	693	1,795	722,200
Essex	Chelmsford	1,418	3,672	1,560,300
Gloucestershire	Gloucester	1,020	2,643	543,900
Greater London[2]	London	610	1,579	6,933,000
Greater Manchester[2]	Manchester	497	1,287	2,578,900
Hampshire	Winchester	1,458	3,777	1,593,700
Hereford & Worcester	Worcester	1,516	3,927	694,800
Hertfordshire	Hertford	631	1,634	999,700
Humberside	Hull	1,356	3,512	884,400
Isle of Wight	Newport	147	381	124,800
Kent	Maidstone	1,441	3,731	1,539,700
Lancashire	Preston	1,183	3,064	1,420,700
Leicestershire	Leicester	986	2,553	910,300
Lincolnshire	Lincoln	2,284	5,915	601,400
Merseyside[2]	Liverpool	252	652	1,440,900
Norfolk	Norwich	2,073	5,368	765,100
North Yorkshire	Northallerton	3,208	8,309	721,800
Northamptonshire	Northampton	914	2,367	591,900
Northumberland	Newcastle upon Tyne	1,943	5,032	307,200
Nottinghamshire	Nottingham	836	2,164	1,028,400
Oxfordshire	Oxford	1,007	2,608	585,800
Shropshire	Shrewsbury	1,347	3,490	413,900
Somerset	Taunton	1,332	3,451	474,100
South Yorkshire[2]	Barnsley	602	1,560	1,306,200
Staffordshire	Stafford	1,049	2,716	1,053,600
Suffolk	Ipswich	1,466	3,797	646,200
Surrey	Kingston upon Thames	648	1,079	1,037,900
Tyne and Wear[2]	Newcastle upon Tyne	208	540	1,137,900
Warwickshire	Warwick	765	1,981	493,600
West Midlands[2]	Birmingham	347	899	2,633,700
West Sussex	Chichester	768	1,989	717,700
West Yorkshire[2]	Wakefield	787	2,039	2,101,600
Wiltshire	Trowbridge	1,344	3,480	583,000
Northern Ireland[3]	Belfast	5,452	14,120	1,631,800
Scotland	Edinburgh	30,418	78,783	5,120,200
Regions				
Borders	Newton Saint Boswells	1,814	4,698	105,300
Central	Stirling	1,042	2,700	272,900
Dumfries and Galloway	Dumfries	2,481	6,425	147,900
Fife	Glenrothes	509	1,319	351,200
Grampian	Aberdeen	3,379	8,752	528,100
Highland	Inverness	10,092	26,137	206,900
Lothian	Edinburgh	683	1,770	753,900
Strathclyde	Glasgow	5,318	13,773	2,286,800
Tayside	Dundee	2,951	7,643	395,200
Island areas[4] (TOTAL)	—	2,149	5,566	72,000
Wales	Cardiff	8,019	20,768	2,906,500
Counties				
Clwyd	Mold	937	2,427	415,900
Dyfed	Carmarthen	2,227	5,768	351,500
Gwent	Newport	531	1,376	450,300
Gwynedd	Caernarvon	1,494	3,869	240,200
Mid Glamorgan	Cardiff	393	1,018	544,300
Powys	Llandrindod Wells	1,960	5,077	119,900
South Glamorgan	Cardiff	161	416	413,200
West Glamorgan	Swansea	316	817	371,200
TOTAL		94,251	244,110	58,191,200

Demography

Population (1995): 58,586,000.
Density (1995): persons per sq mi 621.6, persons per sq km 240.0.
Urban-rural (1993): urban 89.3%; rural 10.7%.
Sex distribution (1993): male 48.93%; female 51.07%.
Age breakdown (1993): under 15, 19.4%; 15–29, 21.4%; 30–44, 21.2%; 45–59, 17.3%; 60–74, 13.8%; 75 and over, 6.9%.
Population projection: (2000) 59,595,000; (2010) 61,127,000.
Doubling time: not applicable; doubling time exceeds 100 years.
Ethnic composition (1991)[5]: white 94.5%; Asian Indian 1.5%; Pakistani 0.9%; West Indian 0.8%; African 0.3%; Chinese 0.3%; Bangladeshi 0.2%; Arab 0.1%; other and not stated 1.8%.
Religious affiliation (religious participation of about 8,400,000 active members only; 1990): Christian *c.* 80%, of which Roman Catholic *c.* 21%, Anglican *c.* 20%, Presbyterian *c.* 14%, Methodist *c.* 5%, Baptist *c.* 3%; Muslim *c.* 11%; Sikh *c.* 4%; Hindu *c.* 2%; Jewish *c.* 1%; other *c.* 2%.
Major cities (1993): Greater London 6,933,000; Birmingham 1,012,400; Leeds 724,500; Glasgow 681,500; Sheffield 531,900; Bradford 488,000; Liverpool 477,000; Edinburgh 441,600; Manchester 432,000; Bristol 397,600.
Place of birth (1991): native-born 93.2% (52,721,000); foreign-born 6.8%, of which India 1.5%, Ireland 1.1%, Caribbean 0.9%, Pakistan 0.9.%, other 2.2%.
Mobility (1991[5]). Population living in the same residence as 1990: 90.1%; different residence, same country (of Great Britain) 8.1%; different residence, different country within Great Britain 1.2%; from outside Great Britain 0.6%.
Households (1990–91)[5, 6]. Average household size 2.5 (3.1); 1 person 26% (20%), 2 persons 34% (26%), 3 persons 17% (16%), 4 persons 16% (17%), 5 persons 6% (10%), 6 or more persons 2% (11%). Family households (1987): 17,836,500 (77.4%), nonfamily 5,208,500 (22.6%, of which 1-person 9.9%).
Immigration (annual average; 1991–93): permanent residents 231,670, from United States 11.0%, Australia 10.7%, Bangladesh, India, and Sri Lanka 4.9%, Pakistan 3.9%, New Zealand 3.8%, South Africa 2.9%.

Vital statistics

Birth rate per 1,000 population (1993): 13.1 (world avg. 25.0); legitimate 68.2%; illegitimate 31.8%.
Death rate per 1,000 population (1993): 11.3 (world avg. 9.3).
Natural increase rate per 1,000 population (1993): 1.8 (world avg. 15.7).
Total fertility rate (avg. births per childbearing woman; 1993): 1.8.
Marriage rate per 1,000 population (1992): 6.1.
Divorce rate per 1,000 population (1992): 3.0.
Life expectancy at birth (1996): male 74.4 years; female 79.7 years.
Major causes of death per 100,000 population (1992): diseases of the circulatory system 501.0, of which ischemic heart disease 287.5, cerebrovascular disease 130.8; malignant neoplasms (cancers) 280.8; diseases of the respiratory system 120.4, of which pneumonia 54.4; diseases of the digestive system 36.7; accidents and violence 34.2; diseases of the endocrine system 19.5, of which diabetes mellitus 14.8; diseases of the genitourinary system 11.1.

Social indicators

Educational attainment (1981). Percentage of population age 25 and over having: primary or secondary education only 89.7%; some postsecondary 4.8%; bachelor's or equivalent degree 4.9%; higher university degree 0.6%.

Distribution of disposable income (1993)

percentage of household income by quintile

1	2	3	4	5 (highest)
7.9	12.1	16.3	22.9	40.8

Quality of working life (1992). Average workweek (hours): male 43.3, female 30.2 (overtime [1986]: male 8.6%, female 2.1%). Annual rate per 100,000 workers for: injury or accident 752.6; industrial diseases 0.3[7]; death 1.5. Proportion of labour force (employed persons) insured for damages or income loss resulting from: injury 100%; permanent disability 100%; death 100%. Average days lost to labour stoppages per 1,000 employee workdays 1993: 0.1. Principal means of transport to work (1991; London only): public transportation 81%, private automobile 15%, motor or pedal cycle 2%, other 2%.
Access to services (1990)[5]. Proportion of households having access to: bath or shower 98%; toilet 99%; central heating 80%.
Social participation. Eligible voters participating in last national election (April 1992): 76.9%. Population age 16 and over participating in voluntary work (1987)[5]: 22%. Trade union membership in total workforce (1990) 34.9%.
Social deviance (1994)[8]. Offense rate per 100,000 population for: theft and handling stolen goods 4,382.8; burglary 2,154.6; violence against the person 375.6; fraud and forgery 249.7; robbery 102.4; sexual offense 55.7. Incidence per 100,000 population of: registered drug addicts 36.5; suicide 7.9.
Leisure (1994). Favourite leisure activities (hours weekly): watching television 17.1; listening to radio 10.3; reading 8.8, of which books 3.8, newspapers 3.3; gardening 2.1.
Material well-being (1993). Households possessing: automobile 68.6%, telephone 89.6%, television receiver 98.3% (colour 95%), refrigerator 99.1%, central heating 82.5%, washing machine 89.3%, videocassette recorder 73.4%.

National economy

Budget (1994–95). Revenue: £222,105,000,000 (income tax 35.8%, taxes on expenditures 18.7%, social-security contributions 17.9%). Expenditures: £260,762,000,000 (social-security benefits 32.0%, national health service 13.0%, education and science 12.0%, defense 8.0%, debt interest 7.0%).
Production (metric tons except as noted). Agriculture, forestry, fishing (1994): wheat 13,100,000, sugar beets 8,125,000, potatoes 7,065,000, barley 5,900,000, rapeseed 1,323,000, carrots 769,000, cabbage 633,000, oats 605,000; livestock (number of live animals) 29,300,000 sheep, 11,735,000 cattle, 7,869,000 pigs; roundwood (1993) 6,195,000 cu m; fish catch (1993) 898,121. Mining (1991): limestone 119,200,000; iron 7,920[9]; tin 1,640; lead 1,200. Manufacturing (value added in £'000,000; 1994): food and beverages 16,749; electrical and optical equipment 14,912; paper, printing, and publishing 14,293; chemicals and chemical products 13,697; metals and metal products 12,483; transport

equipment 12,707. Construction (value in £; 1993)[5]: residential 6,628,000,000; nonresidential 11,384,000,000, of which commercial 5,131,000,000, industrial 2,208,000,000.

Gross national product (1993): U.S.$1,042,700,000,000 (U.S.$17,920 per capita).

Structure of gross domestic product and labour force

	1994		1993	
	in value £'000,000	% of total value	labour force	% of labour force
Agriculture	11,548	2.0	522,000	1.8
Mining	13,078	2.2	149,000	0.5
Manufacturing	121,272	20.9	5,334,000	18.9
Construction	31,035	5.4	1,679,000	5.9
Public utilities	15,458	2.7	292,000	1.0
Transp. and commun.	49,039	8.5	1,626,000	5.8
Trade	83,472	14.4	5,031,000	17.8
Finance	154,550	26.7	3,210,000	11.4
Pub. admin., defense	107,913	18.6	7,214,000	25.5
Services	22,044	3.8		
Other	−30,269[10]	−5.2[10]	3,214,000[11]	11.4[11]
TOTAL	579,140	100.0	28,271,000	100.0

Total national debt (March 1993): £223,877,000,000.

Financial aggregates

	1989	1990	1991	1992	1993	1994	1995[12]
Exchange rate:							
U.S. dollar per £	1.64	1.78	1.77	1.76	1.50	1.53	1.57
SDRs per £	1.22	1.36	1.31	1.10	1.08	1.07	1.04
International reserves (U.S.$)							
Total (excl. gold; '000,000,000)	34.77	35.85	41.89	36.64	36.78	41.01	42.62[13]
SDRs ('000,000,000)	1.14	1.25	1.31	0.54	0.29	0.49	0.36
Reserve pos. in IMF ('000,000,000)	1.64	1.68	1.85	2.01	1.86	1.99	2.33
Foreign exchange ('000,000,000)	31.99	32.93	38.73	34.09	34.63	38.53	39.84[13]
Gold ('000,000 fine troy oz)	18.99	18.97	18.89	18.61	18.45	18.44	18.44[13]
% world reserves	2.0	2.0	2.0	2.0	2.0	2.0	2.0[13]
Interest and prices							
Central bank discount (%)	...	...	...	...	...	...	...
Govt. bond yield (%) long term	9.58	11.08	9.92	9.15	7.87	7.83	7.98
Industrial share prices (1990 = 100)	101.9	100.0	109.8	114.7	131.7	141.5	147.4[14]
Balance of payments (U.S.$'000,000)							
Balance of visible trade,	−39,157	−32,400	−17,990	−24,618	−20,570	−16,127	...
Imports, f.o.b.	190,898	214,693	201,081	212,058	201,802	222,263	...
Exports, f.o.b.	151,741	182,293	183,091	187,440	181,232	206,136	...
Balance of invisibles	3,570	3,010	6,768	3,904	4,179	13,736	...
Balance of payments, current account	−35,587	−29,390	−11,222	−20,714	−16,391	−2,391	...

Tourism (1993): receipts from visitors U.S.$13,451,000,000; expenditures by nationals abroad U.S.$17,431,000,000.

Manufacturing, mining, and construction enterprises (1992)

	no. of enter-prises[15]	no. of employees	annual wages as a % of avg. of all wages[16]	annual value added (£'000,000)
Manufacturing				
Food, beverages, and tobacco	8,916	564,000	103.0	15,616
Paper and paper products; printing and publishing	21,495	438,000	133.8	13,023
Mechanical engineering	23,322	521,000	108.4	12,491
Chemical engineering	3,137	278,000	118.1	11,894
Transport equipment	4,233	468,000	...	11,832
Electrical and data-processing equipment	9,644	504,000	96.8	11,389
Rubber and plastics	4,785	224,000	118.1	5,510
Clothing and footwear	11,207	258,000	85.6	3,405
Timber and wood products	13,794	186,000	98.1	3,137
Textiles	4,466	172,000	79.2	2,956
Metal manufacturing	1,188	112,000	102.8	2,943
Mineral-oil processing	123	13,000	118.1	1,434
Mining				
Extraction of coal, mineral oil, and natural gas	...	80,000	118.1	9,267
Extraction of minerals other than fuels	793	7,000	103.1	309
Construction	185,854	1,016,000	...	17,642

Land use (1993): forested 10.1%; meadows and pastures 45.7%; agricultural and under permanent cultivation 25.4%; other 18.8%.

Retail trade enterprises (1992)

	no. of enter-prises	no. of employees	weekly wage as a % of all wages	annual turnover (£'000,000)[17]
Food and grocery,	60,119	854,000	...	51,462
of which				
large grocery	71	579,000	...	40,837
other grocery	18,557	95,000	...	4,086
meats	12,149	58,000	...	2,523
Household goods,	45,532	299,000	...	20,881
of which				
electrical and musical goods	10,887	87,000	...	7,270
furniture	11,927	60,000	...	4,575
Drink, confectionery, and tobacco,	46,671	254,000	...	13,810
of which				
tobacco and confectionery	41,502	215,000	...	10,880
Clothing and footwear,	24,923	264,000	...	12,428
of which				
women's, girls', and infants' wear	13,624	102,000	...	4,771
footwear	3,098	67,000	...	2,589
men's and boys' wear	3,751	37,000	...	2,063
Pharmaceuticals	7,560	87,000	...	5,231
Mail order	129	33,000	...	4,076

Energy production (consumption): electricity (kW-hr; 1993) 323,029,000,000 (339,745,000,000); coal (metric tons; 1993) 74,604,000 (94,191,000); crude petroleum (barrels; 1993) 701,420,000 (626,110,000); petroleum products (metric tons; 1993) 88,796,000 (76,657,000); natural gas (cu m; 1993) 71,899,000,000 (76,310,000,000).

Population economically active (1993): total 28,271,000; activity rate of total population 48.6% (participation rates: ages 15–64, 76.2%; female 43.8%; unemployed 10.2%).

Price and earnings indexes (1990 = 100)

	1988	1989	1990	1991	1992	1993	1994
Consumer price index	84.7	91.3	100.0	105.9	109.8	111.5	114.3
Monthly earnings index	83.5	91.1	100.0	108.0	114.6	118.5	123.3

Household income and expenditure (1993). Average household size 2.4; average annual disposable income per household £14,913 (U.S.$22,400); sources of income: wages and salaries 64.7%, social-security benefits 13.8%, rent, dividends, and interest 11.3%, income from self-employment 8.3%; expenditure: food and beverages 22.4%, housing 16.2%, transport and vehicles 15.6%, household goods 8.3%, clothing 6.3%, energy 4.8%.

Foreign trade

Balance of trade (current prices)

	1989	1990	1991	1992	1993	1994
£'000,000	−39,157	−31,131	−17,990	−24,618	−20,570	−12,029
% of total	11.4%	7.8%	4.7%	6.2%	5.4%	4.3%

Imports (1994): £145,059,000,000 (machinery and transport equipment 40.7%, of which electrical equipment 18.0%, road vehicles 10.9%; chemicals and chemical products 9.8%, of which plastics 2.5%, organic chemicals 2.4%; food and live animals 8.3%, of which vegetables and fruits 2.3%, meat and meat preparations 1.3%; petroleum and petroleum products 3.1%; textile yarn and fabrics 3.0%; paper and paperboard 2.8%; nonferrous metals 2.0%; iron and steel products 2.0%). *Major import sources:* Germany 15.3%; U.S. 12.2%; France 10.6%; The Netherlands 6.8%; Japan 6.1%; Italy 5.0%; Belgium-Luxembourg 4.9%; Ireland 3.9%; Switzerland 3.3%; Norway 2.6%.

Exports (1994): £134,465,000,000 (machinery and transport equipment 41.4%, of which electrical equipment 18.6%, road vehicles 7.0%; chemicals and chemical products 14.0%, of which organic chemicals 3.5%; petroleum and petroleum products 6.4%; professional, scientific, and controlling instruments 4.0%; iron and steel products 2.7%; clothing and footwear 2.4%). *Major export destinations:* Germany 13.0%; U.S. 12.5%; France 10.0%; The Netherlands 7.2%; Belgium-Luxembourg 5.7%; Italy 5.1%; Ireland 4.9%; Spain 3.7%; Sweden 2.5%; Japan 2.2%; Switzerland 1.8%.

Transport and communications

Transport. Railroads (1993–94)[18]: length 23,518 mi[19], 37,849 km[19]; passenger-mi 18,867,000,000, passenger-km 30,362,000,000; short ton-mi cargo 9,428,000,000, metric ton-km cargo 13,764,000,000. Roads (1993): total length 241,535 mi, 388,714 km (paved 100%). Vehicles (1993)[5]: passenger cars 20,344,000; trucks and buses 2,753,000. Merchant marine (1992): vessels (100 gross tons and over) 1,631; total deadweight tonnage 4,355,063. Air transport (1993): passenger-mi 58,825,000,000, passenger-km 94,670,000,000; short ton-mi cargo 1,999,753,000, metric ton-km cargo 2,919,591,000; airports (1995) with scheduled flights 53.

Communications. Daily newspapers (1992): total number 101; total circulation 22,100,000; circulation per 1,000 population 381. Radio (1993): 70,000,000 receivers (1 per 0.8 person). Television (1994): 20,413,000 licenses (1 per 2.9 persons). Telephones (main lines; 1993): 28,680,900 receivers (1 per 2.0 persons).

Education and health

Education (1992–93)[20]

	schools	teachers	students	student/ teacher ratio
Primary (age 5–10)	23,829	224,400	4,923,000	21.9
Secondary (age 11–19)	4,648	233,600	3,605,800	15.4
Voc., teacher tr.	724[21]	93,000[22]	586,000	...
Higher[23]	70	33,447	435,617	13.0

Literacy (1990): total population literate, virtually 100%[24].

Health (1993)[5]: physicians 92,474 (1 per 629 persons); hospital beds 283,814 (1 per 205 persons); infant mortality rate (1994) 6.1.

Food (1992): daily per capita caloric intake 3,317 (vegetable products 68%, animal products 32%); 132% of FAO recommended minimum requirement.

Military

Total active duty personnel (1995): 236,900 (army 49.0%, navy 21.3%, air force 29.7%). *Military expenditure as percentage of GNP* (1993): 3.6% (world 3.3%); per capita expenditure U.S.$587.

[1]Includes separately administered Isles of Scilly (area 6 sq mi [16 sq km]; pop. 2,000). [2]Geographic entity only; since April 1, 1986, the administrative functions of the former metropolitan county councils have been dispersed among other local authorities. [3]Comprises 26 local government districts not shown separately. [4]Includes three separately administered island groups (Orkney 377 sq mi [976 sq km], pop. 19,800; Shetland 553 sq mi [1,432 sq km], pop. 22,800; Western Isles 1,119 sq mi [2,898 sq km], pop. 29,400). [5]Great Britain only. [6]Figures in parentheses are for Northern Ireland (1984). [7]1982. [8]England and Wales only. [9]1992. [10]Plus rent; less imputed bank service charges. [11]Includes 2,732,000 unemployed not distributed by sector. [12]August. [13]May. [14]June. [15]1988. [16]1984. [17]Includes value-added taxes. [18]British Rail only. [19]1990. [20]Public sector only. [21]1987–88. [22]1984–85. [23]Universities only. [24]A survey in 1986–87, however, put the number of functional illiterates at 9–12% of the adult population.

United States

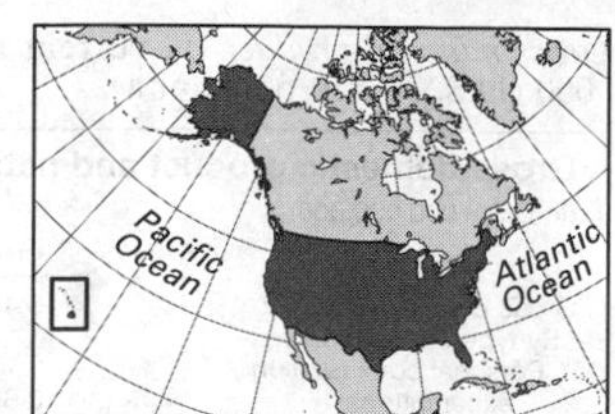

Official name: United States of America.
Form of government: federal republic with two legislative houses (Senate [100]; House of Representatives [435[1]]).
Head of state and government: President.
Capital: Washington, D.C.
Official language: none.
Official religion: none.
Monetary unit: 1 dollar (U.S.$) = 100 cents; valuation (Oct. 6, 1995) 1 U.S.$ = £0.63; 1 £ = U.S.$1.58.

Area and population

		area[2]		population
States	Capitals	sq mi	sq km	1995 estimate
Alabama	Montgomery	51,705	133,915	4,274,000
Alaska	Juneau	591,004	1,530,693	634,000
Arizona	Phoenix	114,000	295,259	4,072,000
Arkansas	Little Rock	53,187	137,754	2,468,000
California	Sacramento	158,706	411,407	32,398,000
Colorado	Denver	104,091	269,594	3,710,000
Connecticut	Hartford	5,018	12,997	3,274,000
Delaware	Dover	2,045	5,294	718,000
Florida	Tallahassee	58,664	151,939	14,210,000
Georgia	Atlanta	58,910	152,576	7,102,000
Hawaii	Honolulu	6,471	16,760	1,221,000
Idaho	Boise	83,564	216,430	1,156,000
Illinois	Springfield	57,871	149,885	11,853,000
Indiana	Indianapolis	36,413	94,309	5,820,000
Iowa	Des Moines	56,275	145,752	2,861,000
Kansas	Topeka	82,277	213,096	2,601,000
Kentucky	Frankfort	40,410	104,659	3,851,000
Louisiana	Baton Rouge	47,752	123,677	4,359,000
Maine	Augusta	33,265	86,156	1,236,000
Maryland	Annapolis	10,460	27,091	5,078,000
Massachusetts	Boston	8,284	21,455	5,976,000
Michigan	Lansing	97,102	251,493	9,575,000
Minnesota	St. Paul	86,614	224,329	4,619,000
Mississippi	Jackson	47,689	123,514	2,666,000
Missouri	Jefferson City	69,697	180,514	5,286,000
Montana	Helena	147,046	380,847	862,000
Nebraska	Lincoln	77,355	200,349	1,644,000
Nevada	Carson City	110,561	286,352	1,477,000
New Hampshire	Concord	9,279	24,032	1,132,000
New Jersey	Trenton	7,787	20,168	7,931,000
New Mexico	Santa Fe	121,593	314,924	1,676,000
New York	Albany	52,735	136,583	18,178,000
North Carolina	Raleigh	52,669	136,412	7,150,000
North Dakota	Bismarck	70,702	183,117	637,000
Ohio	Columbus	44,787	115,998	11,203,000
Oklahoma	Oklahoma City	69,956	181,185	3,271,000
Oregon	Salem	97,073	251,418	3,141,000
Pennsylvania	Harrisburg	46,043	119,251	12,134,000
Rhode Island	Providence	1,212	3,139	1,001,000
South Carolina	Columbia	31,113	80,582	3,732,000
South Dakota	Pierre	77,116	199,730	735,000
Tennessee	Nashville	42,144	109,152	5,228,000
Texas	Austin	266,807	691,027	18,592,000
Utah	Salt Lake City	84,899	219,887	1,944,000
Vermont	Montpelier	9,614	24,900	579,000
Virginia	Richmond	40,767	105,586	6,646,000
Washington	Olympia	68,139	176,479	5,497,000
West Virginia	Charleston	24,232	62,758	1,824,000
Wisconsin	Madison	66,215	171,496	5,159,000
Wyoming	Cheyenne	97,809	253,324	487,000
District				
Dist. of Columbia	—	69	179	559,000
TOTAL		3,679,192[3]	9,529,063	263,434,000[3]

Demography

Population (1995)[4]: 263,057,000.
Density (1995)[4]: persons per sq mi 71.5, persons per sq km 27.6.
Urban-rural (1993): urban 75.8%; rural 24.2%.
Sex distribution (1994): male 48.81%; female 51.19%.
Age breakdown (1994): under 15, 22.0%; 15–29, 21.2%; 30–44, 24.5%; 45–59, 15.7%; 60–74, 11.1%; 75 and over, 5.5%.
Population projection: (2000) 276,052,000; (2010) 300,226,000.
Doubling time: not applicable; doubling time exceeds 100 years.
Population by race and Hispanic[5] origin (1994): non-Hispanic white 74.0%; non-Hispanic black 12.0%; Hispanic 10.0%; Asian and Pacific Islander 3.3%; American Indian and Eskimo 0.7%.
Religious affiliation (1995): Christian 85.3%, of which Protestant 57.9%, Roman Catholic 21.0%, other Christian 6.4%; Jewish 2.1%; Muslim 1.9%; nonreligious 8.7%; other 2.0%.
Mobility (1993). Population living in the same residence as in 1992: 83.0%; different residence, same county 11.0%; different county, same state 3.0%; different state 3.0%; moved from abroad 1.0%.
Households (1994). Total households 97,107,000 (married-couple families 53,171,000 [54.8%]). Average household size 2.7; 1 person 24.3%, 2 persons 32.2%, 3 persons 17.4%, 4 persons 15.5%, 5 or more persons 10.6%. Family households: 68,490,000 (70.5%); nonfamily 28,617,000 (29.5%), of which 1-person 82.5%.
Immigration (1993[6]): permanent immigrants admitted 904,000, from Mexico 14.0%, China 7.2%, Vietnam 7.0%, Philippines 7.0%, former U.S.S.R. 6.5%, Dominican Republic 5.0%, India 4.4%, El Salvador 3.0%, Poland 3.0%, United Kingdom 2.1%, Ukraine 2.0%, South Korea 2.0%, Jamaica 1.9%, Canada 1.9%, Iran 1.6%, Taiwan 1.6%, Ireland 1.5%. Refugee arrivals (1993[6]): 127,343.
Major cities (1994): New York 7,333,253; Los Angeles 3,448,613; Chicago 2,731,743; Houston 1,702,086; Philadelphia 1,524,249; San Diego 1,151,977; Phoenix 1,048,949; Dallas 1,022,830; San Antonio 998,905; Detroit 992,038.

Other principal cities (1994)

	population		population		population
Akron	221,886	Fort Worth	451,814	Omaha	345,033
Albuquerque	411,994	Fresno	386,551	Pittsburgh	358,883
Anaheim	282,133	Honolulu	385,881	Portland (Ore.)	450,777
Anchorage	253,649	Indianapolis	752,279	Raleigh	236,707
Arlington (Tex.)	290,827	Jacksonville	665,070	Riverside	241,644
Atlanta	396,052	Kansas City (Mo.)	443,878	Rochester (N.Y.)	231,171
Aurora (Colo.)	250,717	Las Vegas	327,878	Sacramento	373,964
Austin	514,013	Lexington (Ky.)	237,612	St. Louis	368,215
Baltimore	702,979	Long Beach	433,852	St. Paul	262,071
Baton Rouge	227,022	Louisville	270,308	St. Petersburg	238,585
Birmingham	264,527	Memphis	614,289	San Francisco	734,676
Boston	547,725	Mesa	313,649	San Jose	816,884
Buffalo	312,965	Miami	373,024	Santa Ana	290,827
Charlotte	437,797	Milwaukee	617,044	Seattle	520,947
Cincinnati	358,170	Minneapolis	354,590	Tampa	285,523
Cleveland	492,901	Nashville	504,505	Toledo	322,550
Colorado Springs	316,480	New Orleans	484,149	Tucson	434,726
Columbus	635,913	Newark	258,751	Tulsa	374,851
Corpus Christi	275,419	Norfolk	241,426	Virginia Beach	430,295
Denver	492,901	Oakland	366,926	Washington, D.C.	567,094
El Paso	579,307	Oklahoma City	463,201	Wichita	310,236

Place of birth (1990): native-born 227,078,000 (91.3%); foreign-born 21,632,000 (8.7%), of which Mexico 4,447,000, Germany (East and West) 1,163,000, Philippines 998,000, Canada 871,000, United Kingdom 765,000, Cuba 751,000, South Korea 663,000, Italy 640,000, Vietnam 556,000, China 543,000, India 463,000, Japan 422,000, Poland 397,000, U.S.S.R. 337,000, Portugal 219,000, Greece 189,000, other 8,208,000.

Vital statistics

Birth rate per 1,000 population (1994): 14.1 (world avg. 25.0); (1992) legitimate 69.8%; illegitimate 30.2%.
Death rate per 1,000 population (1994): 8.5 (world avg. 9.3).
Natural increase rate per 1,000 population (1994): 5.6 (world avg. 15.7).
Total fertility rate (avg. births per childbearing woman; 1994): 2.1.
Marriage rate per 1,000 population (1994): 7.8; median age at first marriage (1991): men 26.3 years, women 24.1 years.
Divorce rate per 1,000 population (1994): 4.7.
Life expectancy at birth (1993): white male 73.0 years, black and other male 67.4 years; white female 79.5 years, black and other female 75.5 years.
Major causes of death per 100,000 population (1993): cardiovascular diseases 366.3, of which ischemic heart disease 190.0, cerebrovascular diseases 57.4, atherosclerosis 5.3; malignant neoplasms (cancers) 205.8; diseases of the respiratory system 70.9, of which pneumonia 31.3; accidents and adverse effects 34.4, of which motor-vehicle accidents 15.9; diabetes mellitus 21.4; AIDS 13.7; suicide 12.1; chronic liver disease and cirrhosis 9.6.
Morbidity rates of infectious diseases per 100,000 population (1993): gonorrhea 170.1; chicken pox 52.2; AIDS 40.2; syphilis 39.1; salmonellosis 16.1; shigellosis 12.5; tuberculosis 9.8; hepatitis A (infectious) 9.4; hepatitis B (serum) 5.2; aseptic meningitis 5.0; mumps 0.7.
Incidence of chronic health conditions per 1,000 population (1993): chronic sinusitus 144.5; arthritis 126.5; deformities or orthopedic impairments 120.8; hypertension 106.7; hearing impairment 93.5; hay fever 92.0; heart conditions 82.3; chronic bronchitis 53.5; asthma 50.6; migraine 42.7.

Social indicators

Educational attainment (1991). Percentage of population age 25 and over having: incomplete primary education 6.2%; primary 4.4%; incomplete secondary 11.0%; secondary 38.6%; some postsecondary 18.4%; 4-year higher degree or more 21.4%. Number of earned degrees (1993): bachelor's degree 1,145,000; master's degree 364,000; doctor's degree 42,000; first-professional degrees (in fields such as medicine, theology, and law) 74,000.

Distribution of income (1993)

percentage of disposable household income by quintile				
1	2	3	4	5 (highest)
4.2	10.1	15.2	23.6	46.2

Quality of working life (1994). Average workweek: 39.1 hours. Annual rate per 100,000 workers for (1993): injury or accident 2,700; death 6.4. Proportion of labour force insured for damages or income loss resulting from: injury, permanent disability, and death (1988) 56.6%. Average days per 1,000 workdays lost to labour stoppages (1994): 0.2. Average duration of journey to work (1990): 22.4 minutes (private automobile 94.7%, of which drive alone 80.0%, carpool 14.7%; public transportation 5.3%). Rate per 1,000 employed workers of discouraged workers (unemployed no longer seeking work; 1992): 6.9.
Access to services (1991). Proportion of occupied dwellings having access to: electricity, virtually 100.0%; safe public water supply 98.2% (12.6% from wells); public sewage collection 76.9%; septic tanks 23.0%.
Social participation. Eligible voters participating in last presidential election (1992): 54.0%. Population age 18 and over participating in voluntary work (1993): 47.7%. Trade-union membership in total workforce (1994): 15.5%. Practicing religious population in total affiliated population (church attendance; 1987): once a week 47%; once in six months 67%; once a year 74%.
Social deviance (1993). Offense rate per 100,000 population for: murder 9.5; rape 40.7; robbery 255.7; aggravated assault 439.7; motor-vehicle theft 604.8; burglary and housebreaking 1,098.3; larceny-theft 3,030.0; drug-abuse

violation 309.2[7]; drunkenness 260.1[7]. Drug and substance users (population age 26 and over; 1993): alcohol 52.1%; tobacco (cigarettes) 25.3%; marijuana 3.0%; cocaine 0.5%; analgesics 0.5%; tranquilizers 0.2%; stimulants 0.2%; hallucinogens 0.1%[7]; heroin, n.a. Rate per 100,000 population of suicide (1993): 12.2.

Crime rates per 100,000 population in metropolitan areas[8] (1993)

	violent crime				
	total	murder	rape	robbery	assault
Atlanta	4,041	50.4	122.1	1,501	2,368
Baltimore	2,994	48.2	91.1	1,689	1,166
Boston	1,958	17.7	86.7	737	1,117
Chicago	...	30.3	...	1,262	1,425
Dallas	1,743	30.4	95.9	712	905
Detroit	...	56.8	...	1,332	1,274
Houston	1,454	25.9	64.3	625	739
Los Angeles	2,374	30.5	50.3	1,090	1,204
Miami	3,893	34.1	54.8	1,901	1,903
Minneapolis	...	15.8	...	867	744
New York	2,090	26.5	38.4	1,171	854
Philadelphia	1,255	28.1	50.3	739	437
Pittsburgh	1,216	21.7	61.3	756	377
St. Louis	3,875	69.0	82.4	1,608	2,116
San Francisco	1,815	17.5	49.0	1,148	600
Washington, D.C.	2,922	78.5	56.1	1,230	1,558

	property crime			
	total	burglary	larceny	auto theft
Atlanta	13,313	3,269	7,757	2,288
Baltimore	9,547	2,442	5,655	1,449
Boston	8,073	1,441	4,477	2,154
Chicago	7,437	1,637	4,350	1,450
Dallas	8,884	2,012	5,197	1,657
Detroit	9,212	2,264	4,198	2,751
Houston	6,734	1,567	3,571	1,596
Los Angeles	6,498	1,425	3,378	1,695
Miami	14,852	3,296	8,556	3,001
Minneapolis	9,268	2,552	5,442	1,274
New York	6,081	1,350	3,200	1,531
Philadelphia	5,007	969	2,512	1,525
Pittsburgh	6,550	1,251	3,533	1,766
St. Louis	12,773	3,204	6,969	2,600
San Francisco	7,709	1,515	4,693	1,501
Washington, D.C.	8,834	1,995	5,444	1,395

Leisure (1992). Favourite leisure activities (percentage of total population age 18 and over that undertook activity at least once in the previous year): movie 59.0%, amusement park 50.0%, sports event 37.0%, live theatre 31.0%, art museum 27.0%; exercising 60.0%, reading literature 54.0%, playing sports 39.0%.
Material well-being (1992). Occupied dwellings with householder possessing: automobile 84.9%[9]; telephone 93.9%; radio receiver 99.0%; television receiver 98.3%; air conditioner 69.9%[10]; washing machine 76.3%[10]; videocassette recorder 72.5%; cable television 60.2%.
Recreational expenditures (1993): U.S.$339,900,000,000 (television and radio receivers 19.3%; nondurable toys and sports equipment 11.0%; sports supplies 10.2%; magazines and newspapers 7.9%; golfing, bowling, and other participatory activities 7.2%; books and maps 4.9%; spectator amusements 3.7%, of which spectator sports 1.2%, theatre and opera 1.2%, movies 1.2%; flowers, seeds, and potted plants 3.1%).

National economy

Budget (1995). Revenue: U.S.$1,346,400,000,000 (individual income tax 43.7%, social-insurance taxes and contributions 35.9%, corporation income tax 11.2%, other 9.2%). Expenditures: U.S.$1,538,900,000,000 (social security and medicare 32.0%, defense 17.6%, interest on debt 15.2%, income security 14.5%, health 7.5%, other 13.2%).
Total national debt (Oct. 17, 1994): U.S.$4,613,524,000,000.

Manufacturing, mining, and construction enterprises (1995)

	no. of enterprises[11]	no. of employees	hourly wage as a % of all wages	value added (U.S.$'000,000)[12]
Manufacturing				
Chemical and related products	12,109	1,046,900	135.2	165,135
Transportation equipment	10,500	1,721,300	144.7	161,058
Food and related products	20,624	1,716,400	104.0	156,843
Machinery, except electrical	52,135	2,040,100	114.9	132,144
Electric and electronic machinery	15,962	1,615,900	101.1	121,950
Instruments and related products	10,326	843,800	111.2	89,806
Fabricated metal products	36,105	1,419,700	105.3	83,871
Paper and related products	6,342	691,200	125.5	59,923
Rubber and plastic products	14,515	958,300	95.8	58,477
Primary metals	6,771	706,700	127.8	51,816
Apparel and related products	22,872	892,500	66.3	36,357
Stone, clay, and glass products	16,166	549,400	108.4	34,558
Lumber and wood	33,982	762,200	88.9	33,352
Textile-mill products	6,412	646,400	81.8	29,862
Tobacco products	138	36,200	191.6	27,167
Petroleum and coal products	2,254	146,900	167.5	23,797
Furniture and fixtures	11,613	484,700	85.6	22,821
Leather and leather products	2,193	102,200	69.7	4,517
Miscellaneous manufacturing industries	16,544	385,700	87.2	19,999
Mining				
Oil and gas extraction	22,910	318,800	127.9	79,700
Coal mining	3,905	106,800	159.9	17,283
Nonmetallic, except fuels	5,775	108,900	117.3	9,619
Metal mining	1,027	52,800	145.5	7,180
Construction				
Special trade contractors	367,800[12]	3,453,000	134.6	122,422
Heavy construction contractors	37,300[12]	807,200	129.5	49,066
General contractors and operative builders	168,200[12]	1,295,600	123.4	63,743

Gross national product (at current market prices; 1994): U.S.$6,738,400,000,000 (U.S.$25,850 per capita).

Gross domestic product and national income
(in U.S.$'000,000,000)

	1990	1991	1992	1993	1994
Gross domestic product	5,465.1	5,677.5	6,038.6	6,377.9	6,738.4
By type of expenditure					
Personal consumption expenditures	3,657.3	3,887.7	4,139.9	4,391.8	4,628.4
Durable goods	480.3	446.1	497.3	537.9	591.5
Nondurable goods	1,193.7	1,251.5	1,300.9	1,350.0	1,394.3
Services	1,983.3	2,190.1	2,341.6	2,503.9	2,642.7
Gross private domestic investment	741.0	721.1	796.5	891.7	1,032.9
Fixed investment	746.1	731.3	789.1	876.1	980.7
Changes in business inventories	−5.0	−10.2	7.3	15.6	52.2
Net exports of goods and services	−71.4	−19.9	−30.3	−65.3	−98.2
Exports	557.1	601.1	638.1	659.1	718.7
Imports	628.5	620.9	668.4	724.3	816.9
Government purchases of goods and services	1,098.1	1,090.5	1,131.8	1,158.1	1,175.3
Federal	424.0	447.3	448.8	443.4	437.3
State and local	674.1	643.2	313.8	714.6	738.0
By major type of product					
Goods output	2,143.3	2,182.5	2,312.8	2,421.9	2,584.7
Durable goods	928.0	888.4	977.9	1,047.9	1,153.6
Nondurable goods	1,215.2	1,294.1	1,334.9	1,374.0	1,431.1
Services	2,864.2	3,030.3	3,221.1	3,410.5	3,576.2
Structures	457.4	464.7	504.6	545.5	577.6
National income (incl. capital consumption adjustment)	4,418.4	4,544.2	4,836.6	5,140.3	5,458.4
By type of income					
Compensation of employees	3,244.2	3,390.8	3,582.0	3,772.2	4,004.6
Proprietors' income	402.5	368.0	414.3	321.0	473.7
Rental income of persons	6.9	−10.4	−8.9	12.6	27.7
Corporate profits	298.3	346.3	407.2	466.6	542.7
Net interest	466.7	449.5	442.0	445.6	409.7
By industry division (excl. capital consumption adjustment)					
Agriculture, forestry, fishing	103.4	90.9	100.9	105.3	101.9
Mining and construction	267.3	246.8	251.3	268.1	278.5
Manufacturing	806.5	841.0	895.3	929.0	979.7
Durable	461.5	464.2	501.7	523.0	562.4
Nondurable	345.0	376.8	393.6	406.1	417.3
Transportation	144.0	140.8	151.0	161.8	177.5
Communications	92.8	95.3	103.7	107.4	113.4
Public utilities	92.0	99.0	101.5	106.9	116.5
Wholesale and retail trade	638.8	669.3	700.3	742.8	785.8
Finance, insurance, real estate	647.5	685.0	748.9	815.6	894.2
Services	963.4	1,002.5	1,085.8	1,171.0	1,254.4
Government and government enterprise	648.4	699.5	734.5	765.3	793.4
Other	41.7	17.4	7.3	0.2	−11.4

Structure of gross domestic product and labour force

	1992		1994	
	in value U.S.$'000,000,000	% of total value	labour force[13]	% of labour force[13]
Agriculture	116	1.9	3,409,000	2.6
Mining	85	1.4	669,000	0.5
Manufacturing	1,063	17.6	20,157,000	15.4
Construction	222	3.7	7,493,000	5.7
Public utilities	173	2.9	8,692,000	6.6
Transp. and commun.	356	5.9		
Trade	952	15.8	25,699,000	19.6
Finance	1,106	18.4	8,141,000	6.2
Public administration, defense	756	12.6	48,800,000	37.2
Services	1,183	19.6		
Other	9[14]	0.2[14]	7,996,000[15]	6.1[15]
TOTAL	6,020[3]	100.0	131,056,000	100.0[3]

Business activity (1991): number of businesses 20,499,000 (sole proprietorships 74.1%, active corporations 18.5%, active partnerships 7.4%), of which services 8,964,000, wholesaling and retailing 3,893,000; business receipts $12,214,000,000,000 (active corporations 89.8%, sole proprietorships 5.8%, active partnerships 4.4%), of which wholesaling and retailing $3,637,000,000,000, services $1,180,000,000,000; net profit $508,000,000,000 (active corporations 67.9%, sole proprietorships 28.0%, partnerships 4.1%), of which services $125,000,000,000, wholesaling and retailing $46,000,000,000. New business concerns and business failures (1994): total number of new incorporations 705,537[16]; total failures 71,520, of which commercial service 20,595, retail trade 12,575; failure rate per 10,000 concerns 74.0; current liabilities of failed concerns $29,357,000,000; average liability $410,500. Business expenditures for new plant and equipment (1994): total $638,400,000,000, of which trade, services, and communications $336,900,000,000, manufacturing businesses $192,600,000,000 (nondurable goods 51.8%, durable goods 48.2%), public utilities $76,500,000,000, transportation $21,200,000,000, mining $11,200,000,000.
Production. Agriculture, forestry, fishing (value of production/catch in U.S.$'000,000 except as noted; 1993): corn (maize) 16,032, soybeans 11,950, hay 10,957, wheat 7,645, cotton lint 4,521, tobacco 2,831, potatoes 2,641, grapes 2,007, oranges 1,582, lettuce 1,464, apples 1,361, rice 1,246, sorghum 1,234, tomatoes 1,127, peanuts (groundnuts) 1,031, almonds 911, sugar beets 886, sugarcane 886, onions 813, barley 812, cottonseed 714, dry beans 539, bell peppers 437, peaches 395, walnuts 364, sunflower seeds 326, cantaloupe 297, carrots 295, oats 291, cabbage 284, broccoli 277, watermelon 262, celery 260, lemons 238, pears 232, pecans 213, avocados 211, cranberries 198; livestock (number of live animals; 1994) 100,988,000 cattle, 57,904,000 pigs, 9,600,000 sheep, 3,860,000 horses, 1,530,000,000 chickens; roundwood 495,800,000 cu m; fish and shellfish catch 3,471, of which fish

1,884 (including salmon 423, Alaska pollack 358), shellfish 1,587 (including crabs 510, shrimp 413). Mining (metal content in metric tons except as noted; 1994): iron 36,670,000; copper 1,790,000; zinc 556,000; lead 363,000; molybdenum 40,000; vanadium 2,700; mercury 400; silver 3,400,000 kg; gold 500,000 kg; helium 96,000,000 cu m. Quarrying (metric tons; 1993): crushed stone 1,195,000,000; sand and gravel 949,000,000; cement 83,600,000; clay 42,300,000; phosphate rock 41,000,000; common salt 38,000,000; lime 17,400,000; gypsum 17,400,000. Manufacturing (metric tons except as noted; 1993): crude steel 87,343,000; paper and paperboard 76,688,000; wood pulp 57,189,000; pig iron 48,275,000; sulfuric acid 40,153,000; coke 21,237,000[12]; phosphoric acid 10,474,000; cheese 5,877,000; newsprint 5,833,000; aerospace vehicles (sales) U.S.$121,852,000,000[12]; machine tools (new orders for metal-cutting-type tools) U.S.$2,322,400,000; cotton fabric 4,402,000,000 sq m; carpets and rugs 1,134,300,000 sq m[12]; footwear 167,803,000 pairs[12]; motor-vehicle tires 237,448,000 units; major household appliances 51,277,000 units, of which 8,109,000 refrigerators, 7,703,000 microwave ovens, 6,793,000 washing machines, 5,074,000 clothes driers; television receivers 21,304,000 units[12]; radio receivers 18,405,000 units; new passenger cars (factory sales) 5,955,000 units; new trucks and buses (factory sales) 4,786,000 units. Construction (completed; 1994): private U.S.$377,784,000,000, of which residential U.S.$237,944,000,000, nonresidential U.S.$97,795,000,000; public U.S.$129,180,000,000.

Retail and wholesale trade and services (1995)

	no. of establish-ments[12]	no. of employees	hourly wage as a % of all wages	annual sales or receipts (U.S.$'000,000)[17]
Retail trade	1,564,200	20,988,000	66.9	2,237,000
Automotive dealers	202,800	2,228,300	91.4	526,300
Food stores	190,300	3,376,600	70.5	397,800
General merchandise group stores	36,300	2,466,200	65.8	282,500
Eating and drinking places	430,100	7,432,500	46.6[18]	228,400
Gasoline service stations	100,100	647,100	60.5	142,200
Building materials, hardware, garden supply, and mobile home dealers	69,600	888,800	79.4	122,500
Furniture, home furnishings, equipment stores	113,100	937,900	88.4	119,600
Apparel and accessory stores	146,600	1,085,700	65.4	109,600
Drugstores and proprietary stores	48,700	607,800	77.5	81,500
Liquor stores	30,300	112,200	...	21,800
Wholesale trade	495,500	6,367,000	107.7	2,072,500
Durable goods	313,500	3,693,000	111.5	1,089,500
Machinery, equipment, and supplies	73,900	774,300	112.5	180,400
Motor vehicles, automotive equipment	47,300	408,000	98.1	201,200
Professional and commercial equipment	46,800	768,700	133.5	165,200
Electrical goods	39,300	477,400	116.2	147,400
Metals and minerals, except petroleum	11,200	140,300	110.5	95,500
Lumber and other construction materials	19,500	242,700	102.5	76,800
Hardware, plumbing, heating equipment and supplies	24,700	290,600	105.8	63,300
Furniture and home furnishings	16,500	149,600	97.7	36,000
Miscellaneous durable goods	34,300	327,200	88.5	150,400
Nondurable goods	182,000	2,674,000	102.3	983,000
Groceries and related products	42,900	890,700	105.4	286,500
Petroleum and petroleum products	16,100	166,400	96.6	138,300
Farm-products raw materials	11,600	109,000	78.1	95,800
Drugs, drug proprietaries, and druggists' sundries	6,100	197,100	128.2	78,400
Apparel and accessories	19,600	212,700	100.4	73,400
Paper and paper products	19,700	262,700	106.7	64,900
Beer, wine, and distilled alcoholic beverages	5,300	155,900	116.3	53,000
Chemicals and allied products	14,200	140,100	116.4	42,200
Miscellaneous nondurable goods	43,700	539,800	84.5	150,000
Services[19]	2,217,700	33,106,000	98.4	1,299,400
Health	464,900	9,280,900	108.0	285,000
Business, except computer services	306,500	6,628,100	92.9	201,900
Computer and data-processing services	54,700	1,043,300	154.0	100,700
Legal services	153,600	946,200	140.0	96,200
Automotive repair, services, garages	167,300	1,031,200	86.4	79,500
Management and public relations	49,500	813,200	125.5	70,000
Hotels and motels	42,700	1,724,400	68.1	62,100
Engineering services	39,200	579,000	154.7	61,500
Personal services	198,100	1,115,000	65.6	59,100
Amusement and recreation	84,300	1,720,600	73.2	51,100
Motion pictures	40,700	601,700	121.8	43,800

Energy production (consumption): electricity (kW-hr; 1993) 3,145,892,000,000 (3,174,638,000,000); coal (metric tons; 1993) 857,675,000 (799,412,000); crude petroleum (barrels; 1993) 2,532,000,000 (4,974,000,000); petroleum products (metric tons; 1993) 710,675,000 (737,826,000); natural gas (cu m; 1993) 520,851,000,000 (582,138,000,000). Domestic production of energy by source (1993): natural gas 32.5%, coal 31.1%, crude petroleum 22.0%, other[20] 14.4%.

Energy consumption by source (1993): petroleum and petroleum products 40.2%, natural gas 24.8%, coal 23.4%, other[20] 11.6%; by end use: industrial 36.7%, residential and commercial 36.1%, transportation 27.2%.

Household income and expenditure. Average household size (1993) 2.6; average (mean) annual income per household U.S.$41,428, of which average white household U.S.$43,285, average Hispanic[5] household U.S.$30,291, average black household U.S.$27,229; sources of income: wages and salaries 57.3%, transfer payments 17.0%, self-employment 7.4%, other 18.3%; expenditure: transportation 17.8%, housing 17.6%, food 14.3%, fuel and utilities 6.9%, wearing apparel 5.5%, recreation 5.8%, health 5.8%, expenditures in restaurants and hotels 5.4%, household furnishings 4.0%, education 1.5%, other 15.4%.

Selected household characteristics (1994). Total number of households 97,107,000, of which (by race) white 84.8%, black 11.6%, other 3.6%; in central cities 31.4%, in suburbs 46.3%, outside metropolitan areas 22.3%; (by tenure) owned 62,374,000 (64.2%), rented 34,732,000 (35.8%); family households 68,490,000, of which married couple 77.6%, female head with own children[21] under age 18, 11.2%, female head without own children[21] under 18, 6.9%; nonfamily households 28,617,000, of which female living alone 49.5%, male living alone 33.0%, other 17.5%.

Financial aggregates

	1989	1990	1991	1992	1993	1994	1995[22]
Exchange rate, U.S.$ per:							
£[23]	1.64	1.78	1.77	1.76	1.50	1.53	1.55
SDR[23]	1.28	1.36	1.37	1.41	1.40	1.43	1.51
International reserves (U.S.$)[24]							
Total (excl. gold; '000,000,000)	63.55	72.26	66.66	60.27	62.35	63.28	80.48[25]
SDRs ('000,000,000)	9.95	10.99	11.24	8.50	9.02	10.04	11.15
Reserve pos. in IMF ('000,000,000)	9.05	9.08	9.49	11.76	11.80	12.03	14.47
Foreign exchange ('000,000,000)	44.55	52.19	45.93	40.01	41.53	41.22	54.23[25]
Gold ('000,000 fine troy oz)	261.93	261.91	261.91	261.84	261.79	261.73	261.78
% world reserves	27.78	27.84	27.86	28.13	28.67	28.70	29.02
Interest and prices							
Central bank discount (%)[24]	7.0	6.5	3.5	3.0	3.0	4.75	5.25
Govt. bond yield (%)[23]	8.56	8.25	6.81	5.31	4.44	6.26	6.10
Industrial share prices[23] (1990=100)	94.7	100.0	114.1	125.5	132.3	138.0	170.0
Balance of payments (U.S.$'000,000,000)							
Balance of visible trade	−115.71	−108.84	−73.44	−96.14	−112.74	−164.33	...
Imports, f.o.b.	−477.38	−497.55	−489.40	−536.28	580.51	−668.87	...
Exports, f.o.b.	361.67	388.71	415.96	440.14	467.77	504.54	...
Balance of invisibles	14.51	18.38	69.75	29.84	3.40	162.83	...
Balance of payments, current account	−101.20	−90.46	−3.69	−66.30	−109.25	−1.50	

Population economically active (1994): total 131,056,000[13]; activity rate of total population 50.3% (participation rates: ages 15–64, 76.5%; female 46.0%; unemployed 6.1%).

Price and earnings indexes (1990 = 100)

	1989	1990	1991	1992	1993	1994	1995[26]
Consumer price index	94.9	100.0	104.2	107.4	110.6	113.4	116.7
Hourly earnings index[27]	96.8	100.0	103.3	105.8	108.5	111.4	113.7

Average employee earnings

	average hourly earnings in U.S.$		average weekly earnings in U.S.$	
	July 1994	July 1995	July 1994	July 1995
Manufacturing				
Durable goods	12.63	12.90	531.70	532.77
Lumber and wood products	9.87	10.22	404.67	407.78
Furniture and fixtures	9.57	9.83	383.76	380.42
Stone, clay, and glass products	12.16	12.46	533.82	538.27
Primary metal industries	14.39	14.68	637.48	628.30
Fabricated metal products	11.88	12.10	500.15	[illegible]
Machinery, except electrical	12.95	13.20	558.15	568.08
Electrical and electronic equipment	11.58	11.73	479.41	476.24
Transportation equipment	16.42	16.63	696.21	700.12
Instruments and related products	12.46	12.78	515.84	521.42
Miscellaneous manufacturing	9.58	10.02	378.41	388.78
Nondurable goods	11.29	11.67	460.63	467.97
Food and kindred products	10.70	10.93	445.12	450.32
Tobacco manufactures	20.38	22.02	772.40	865.39
Textile mill products	9.12	9.57	375.74	381.84
Apparel and other textile products	7.30	7.62	272.29	278.13
Paper and allied products	11.83	14.42	516.97	618.62
Printing and publishing	12.13	12.32	465.79	465.70
Chemicals and allied products	15.21	15.70	655.55	675.10
Petroleum and coal products	18.94	19.25	829.57	847.00
Rubber and miscellaneous plastics products	10.74	11.01	446.78	443.70
Leather and leather products	7.96	8.01	300.89	293.17
Nonmanufacturing				
Metal mining	16.03	15.33	708.53	682.19
Coal mining	17.54	18.37	747.20	771.54
Oil and gas extraction	13.92	14.70	623.62	649.74
Nonmetallic minerals, except fuels	13.14	13.48	632.03	648.39
Construction	14.72	15.10	585.86	604.00
Transportation and public utilities	13.82	14.23	556.95	570.62
Wholesale trade	11.99	12.42	460.42	476.93
Retail trade	7.44	7.66	220.97	227.50
Finance, insurance, and real estate	11.71	12.32	418.05	447.22
Hotels, motels, and tourist courts	7.58	7.72	239.53	248.58
Health services	12.12	12.41	398.75	409.53
Legal services	15.61	16.24	540.11	574.90
Miscellaneous services	14.55	15.90	568.91	567.63

Tourism (1994): receipts from visitors U.S.$77,653,000,000; expenditures by nationals abroad U.S.$55,618,000,000; number of foreign visitors 45,504,000 (14,970,000 from Canada, 11,325,000 from Mexico, 8,509,000 from Europe); number of nationals traveling abroad 46,426,000 (15,759,000 to Mexico, 12,543,000 to Canada).

Land use (1993): forested 29.9%; meadows and pastures 25.0%; agricultural and under permanent cultivation 19.6%; other 25.5%.

Foreign trade

Balance of trade (current prices)

	1988	1989	1990	1991	1992	1993	1994
U.S.$'000,000,000	−118.5	−109.4	−101.7	−99.2	−84.5	−115.7	−151.3
% of total	15.5%	13.1%	11.4%	9.8%	8.6%	11.1%	12.9%

Imports (1994): U.S.$683,830,000,000 (machinery and transport equipment 46.4%, of which motor vehicles and parts 15.6%; office and data-processing machines 7.8%; petroleum and petroleum products 7.4%; wearing apparel 7.3%; chemicals and related products 3.4%; food and live animals 3.1%). *Major import sources:* Canada 19.4%; Japan 17.9%; Mexico 7.5%; China 5.8%; Germany 4.8%; Taiwan 4.0%; United Kingdom 3.8%; South Korea 3.0%; France 2.5%; Singapore 2.3%; Italy 2.2%; Malaysia 2.1%; Thailand 1.6%; Hong Kong 1.5%; Brazil 1.3%.

Exports (1994): U.S.$512,416,000,000 (machinery and transport 49.2%, of which motor vehicles and parts 15.3%; electrical machinery 10.3%; chemicals and related products 10.2%; food and live animals 6.4%; scientific and precision equipment 4.3%). *Major export destinations:* Canada 22.3%; Japan 10.4%; Mexico 9.9%; United Kingdom 5.2%; Germany 3.8%; South Korea 3.5%; Taiwan 3.3%; France 2.6%; The Netherlands 2.6%; Singapore 2.5%; Hong Kong 2.2%; Belgium 2.1%.

Trade by commodity group (1993)

	imports		exports	
SITC Group	U.S.$'000,000	%	U.S.$'000,000	%
00 Food and live animals	22,984	4.0	32,895	7.1
01 Beverages and tobacco	5,512	0.9	6,503	1.4
02 Crude materials, excluding fuels	15,374	2.6	24,341	5.2
03 Mineral fuels, lubricants, and related materials	55,582	9.6	9,736	2.1
04 Animal and vegetable oils, fat, and waxes	1,000	0.2	1,461	0.3
05 Chemicals and related products, n.e.s.	29,166	5.0	45,066	9.7
06 Basic manufactures	66,168	11.4	36,609	7.9
07 Machinery and transport equipment	259,975	44.8	208,986	45.0
08 Miscellaneous manufactured articles	104,485	18.0	50,630	10.9
09 Goods not classified by kind	20,398	3.5	48,540	10.4
TOTAL	580,644	100.0	464,767	100.0

Direction of trade (1994)

	imports		exports	
	U.S.$'000,000	%	U.S.$'000,000	%
Africa	15,101	2.2	9,203	1.8
South Africa	2,131	0.3	2,173	0.4
Other Africa	12,970	1.9	7,030	1.4
Americas	219,884	31.8[3]	206,847	40.4
Canada	128,948	18.7	114,258	22.3
Caribbean countries and Central America	10,924	1.6	12,269	2.4
Mexico	49,493	7.2	50,840	9.9
South America	30,519	4.4	29,480	5.8
Asia	305,142	44.3	161,368	31.5
Japan	122,470	17.8	53,481	10.4
Other Asia	182,672	26.5	107,887	21.1
Europe	141,850	20.6	123,073	24.0
EU	115,046	16.7	102,820	20.1
EFTA	11,489	1.7	6,231	1.2
Russia	3,437	0.5	2,579	0.5
Other Europe	11,878	1.7	11,443	2.2
Oceania	5,147	0.8	11,413	2.2
Australia	3,447	0.5	9,781	1.9
Other Oceania	1,700	0.3	1,632	0.3
Other	2,186	0.3	493	0.1
TOTAL	689,310	100.0	512,397	100.0

Transport and communications

Transport. Railroads (1993): length 136,000 mi[12], 219,000 km[12]; passenger-mi 14,000,000,000, passenger-km 22,500,000,000; short ton-mi cargo 1,183,000,000,000, metric ton-km cargo 1,727,000,000,000. Roads (1993): total length 3,904,721 mi, 6,284,051 km (paved 88.7%). Vehicles (1993): passenger cars 146,314,000; trucks and buses 59,227,000. Merchant marine (1993): vessels (1,000 gross tons and over) 603; total deadweight tonnage 20,419,000. Air transport (1993): passenger-mi 480,463,000,000, passenger-km 773,232,000,000; short ton-mi cargo 13,320,000,000, metric ton-km cargo 19,447,000,000; localities (1995) with scheduled flights 834[28]. Certified route passenger/cargo air carriers (1992) 77; operating revenue (U.S.$'000,000; 1991) 74,942, of which domestic 56,119, international 18,823; operating expenses 76,669, of which domestic 56,596, international 20,073.

Intercity passenger and freight traffic by mode of transportation (1993)

	cargo traffic ('000,000,000 ton-mi)	% of nat'l total	passenger traffic ('000,000,000 passenger-mi)	% of nat'l total
Rail	1,183	38.1	14	0.7
Road	871	28.0	1,718	81.7
Inland water	467	15.1	—	—
Air	12	0.4	370	17.6
Petroleum pipeline	572	18.4	—	—
TOTAL	3,105	100.0	2,102	100.0

Communications. Daily newspapers (1995): total number 1,710; total circulation 62,600,000; circulation per 1,000 population 238. Radio (1993[29]): total number of receivers 538,000,000 (1 per 0.5 persons). Television (1994[29]): total number of receivers 211,000,000 (1 per 1.2 persons). Telephones (access lines; 1993): 147,000,000 (1 per 1.8 persons).

Other communications media (1994)

	titles		titles
Print		Home economics	90
Books (new)	40,584	Industrial arts	106
of which		Journalism and communications	90
Agriculture	401	Labour and industrial relations	70
Art	1,131	Law	273
Biography	1,758	Library and information sciences	118
Business	1,294	Literature and language	158
Education	1,041	Mathematics and science	238
Fiction	4,765	Medicine	182
General works	1,666	Philosophy and religion	130
History	1,899	Physical education and recreation	151
Home economics	768	Political science	136
Juvenile	4,271	Psychology	138
Language	544	Sociology and anthropology	149
Law	836	Zoology	94
Literature	1,854		
Medicine	2,515	**Cinema**[16]	
Music	271	Feature films	430
Philosophy, psychology	1,445		
Poetry, drama	766		traffic
Religion	2,148	**Cellular telephones**	
Science	2,234	Number of subscribers	24,134,000
Sociology, economics	6,232		
Sports, recreation	882		(pieces of mail)
Technology	1,523	**Post**	
Travel	340	Mail	177,062,000,000
Periodicals[9]	3,731	Domestic	176,202,000,000
of which		International	860,000,000
Agriculture	153		
Business and economics	262		
Chemistry and physics	170		
Children's periodicals	78		
Education	203		
Engineering	265		
Fine and applied arts	145		
General interest	181		
History	151		

Education and health

Education (1993–94)

	schools	teachers	students	student/teacher ratio
Primary (age 5–13)[30]	84,578[31]	1,771,000	35,654,000	20.1
Secondary and vocational (age 14–17)		1,100,000	13,170,000	12.0
Higher, including teacher-training colleges	5,758[31]	842,000	14,600,000	17.3

Literacy: studies in the late 1980s indicated that adult "functional" literacy may not exceed 85%.

Health (1993): doctors of medicine 670,300[32] (1 per 391 persons), of which office-based practice 398,800 (including specialties in internal medicine 16.9%, general and family practice 14.6%, pediatrics 7.7%, obstetrics and gynecology 6.9%, general surgery 6.1%, psychiatry 5.6%, anesthesiology 5.2%, orthopedics 4.1%, ophthalmology 4.0%); doctors of osteopathy 33,400; nurses 1,853,024 (1 per 138 persons)[12]; dentists 154,000 (1 per 1,676 persons); hospital beds 1,158,000 (1 per 223 persons), of which nonfederal 92.4% (community hospitals 79.1%, psychiatric 11.3%, long-term general and special 1.8%), federal 7.4%; infant mortality rate per 1,000 live births (1994) 8.3.

Food (1992): daily per capita caloric intake 3,732 (vegetable products 67%, animal products 33%); 141% of FAO recommended minimum requirement. Per capita consumption of major food groups (pounds annually; 1993): milk 226.6; cereal products 189.2; sweeteners 147.1; potatoes 135.7; fresh vegetables 113.0; red meat 111.9; fresh fruits 99.9; fats and oils 65.0; poultry products 61.1; fish and shellfish 14.9.

Military

Total active duty personnel (1995): 1,547,300 (army 33.9%, navy 28.6%, air force 26.4%, marines 11.1%). *Military expenditure as percentage of GNP* (1993): 4.7% (world 3.3%); per capita expenditure U.S.$1,153. *Military aid* (1993): total $4,143,000,000 (Middle East 76.2%, of which Israel 43.4%, Egypt 31.4%; Europe 20.8%, of which Turkey 10.9%; Latin America 1.8%).

[1]Excludes 4 delegates having only committee voting privileges. [2]Total area excluding U.S. share of Great Lakes is 3,618,770 sq mi (9,372,571 sq km). [3]Detail does not add to total given because of rounding. [4]Includes military personnel residing overseas. [5]Persons of Hispanic origin may be of any race. [6]Fiscal year ending September 30. [7]1991. [8]Estimated crime rates include unreported crimes. [9]1988. [10]1990. [11]1987. [12]1992. [13]Excludes military personnel overseas. [14]Statistical discrepancy. [15]Unemployed. [16]1993. [17]1994. [18]Excludes tips. [19]Annual receipts for 1992. [20]Includes hydroelectric, nuclear, and geothermal power. [21]"Own children" includes adopted children and stepchildren. [22]August. [23]Period average. [24]End-of-year. [25]July. [26]June. [27]Manufacturing sector only. [28]Includes 292 localities in Alaska. [29]January 1. [30]Primary includes kindergarten. [31]1992–93. [32]578,100 professionally active.

Uruguay

Official name: República Oriental del Uruguay (Oriental Republic of Uruguay).
Form of government: republic with two legislative houses (Senate [31][1]; Chamber of Representatives [99]).
Head of state and government: President.
Capital: Montevideo.
Official language: Spanish.
Official religion: none.
Monetary unit: 1 peso uruguayo (Uruguayan peso)[2]; valuation (Oct. 6, 1995) 1 U.S.$ = Ur$6.60; 1 £ = Ur$10.43.

Area and population

		area		population
Departments	**Capitals**	sq mi	sq km	1985 census
Artigas	Artigas	4,605	11,928	69,145
Canelones	Canelones	1,751	4,536	364,248
Cerro Largo	Melo	5,270	13,648	78,416
Colonia	Colonia del Sacramento	2,358	6,106	112,717
Durazno	Durazno	4,495	11,643	55,077
Flores	Trinidad	1,986	5,144	24,739
Florida	Florida	4,022	10,417	66,474
Lavalleja	Minas	3,867	10,016	61,466
Maldonado	Maldonado	1,851	4,793	94,314
Montevideo	Montevideo	205	530	1,311,976
Paysandú	Paysandú	5,375	13,922	103,763
Río Negro	Fray Bentos	3,584	9,282	48,644
Rivera	Rivera	3,618	9,370	89,475
Rocha	Rocha	4,074	10,551	66,601
Salto	Salto	5,468	14,163	108,487
San José	San José de Mayo	1,927	4,992	89,893
Soriano	Mercedes	3,478	9,008	79,439
Tacuarembó	Tacuarembó	5,961	15,438	83,498
Treinta y Tres	Treinta y Tres	3,679	9,529	46,869
TOTAL LAND AREA		67,574	175,016	
INLAND WATER		463	1,199	
TOTAL		68,037	176,215	2,955,241

Demography

Population (1995): 3,186,000.
Density (1995): persons per sq mi 46.8, persons per sq km 18.1.
Urban-rural (1993): urban 89.6%; rural 10.4%.
Sex distribution (1993): male 48.74%; female 51.26%.
Age breakdown (1990): under 15, 25.8%; 15–29, 23.0%; 30–44, 18.9%; 45–59, 15.8%; 60–74, 11.9%; 75 and over, 4.6%.
Population projection: (2000) 3,274,000; (2010) 3,453,000.
Doubling time: 90 years.
Ethnic composition (1990): white (mostly Spanish, Italian, or mixed Spanish-Italian) 86.0%; mestizo 8.0%; mulatto or black 6.0%.
Religious affiliation (1988): Roman Catholic 66.0%; Protestant 2.0%; Jewish 0.8%; nonreligious and atheist 31.2%.
Major cities (1985): Montevideo 1,311,976; Salto 80,823; Paysandú 76,191; Las Piedras 58,288; Rivera 57,316.

Vital statistics

Birth rate per 1,000 population (1994): 17.7 (world avg. 25.0); (1983) legitimate 73.8%; illegitimate 26.2%.
Death rate per 1,000 population (1994): 9.4 (world avg. 9.3).
Natural increase rate per 1,000 population (1994): 8.3 (world avg. 15.7).
Total fertility rate (avg. births per childbearing woman; 1994): 2.4.
Marriage rate per 1,000 population (1992): 6.2.
Divorce rate per 1,000 population (1991): 3.1.
Life expectancy at birth (1994): male 70.9 years; female 77.5 years.
Major causes of death per 100,000 population (1990): diseases of the circulatory system 378.4; malignant neoplasms (cancers) 222.8; respiratory diseases 76.3; accidents 47.0; diseases of the digestive system 39.1.

National economy

Budget (1994). Revenue: Ur$15,319,966,000 (direct taxes 77.6%, receipts from foreign trade 6.9%). Expenditures: Ur$17,031,645,000 (social security and welfare 60.0%, general public services 14.1%, capital investments 8.7%, interest on public debt 6.1%, subsidies 4.0%).
Public debt (external, outstanding; 1993): U.S.$4,629,000,000.
Production (metric tons except as noted). Agriculture, forestry, fishing (1993): rice 700,000, sugarcane 350,000, wheat 300,000, barley 170,000, corn (maize) 128,000, sugar beets 40,000; livestock (number of live animals) 25,702,000 sheep, 10,093,000 cattle, 477,000 horses; roundwood 4,087,000 cu m; fish catch (1994) 117,230. Mining and quarrying (1992): hydraulic cement 500,000; gypsum 145,000. Manufacturing (value added in NUr$'000,000[2]; 1988): food products (excluding beverages) 128,600; petroleum products 69,873; chemicals and chemical products 68,178; textiles 63,459; beverages 51,012; transport equipment 46,570; tobacco products 31,004; leather products 28,155; paper and paper products 25,002. Construction (approvals; 1993): residential 338,674 sq m; nonresidential 153,040 sq m. Energy production (consumption): electricity (kW-hr; 1992) 8,898,000,000 (5,514,000,000); coal (metric tons; 1992) none (1,000); crude petroleum (barrels; 1992) none (9,727,000); petroleum products (metric tons; 1992) 1,073,000 (1,402,000); natural gas, none (n.a.).
Gross national product (1993): U.S.$12,314,000,000 (U.S.$3,910 per capita).

Structure of gross domestic product and labour force

	1994		1992	
	in value Ur$'000	% of total value	labour force	% of labour force
Agriculture	6,548,765	8.3	56,200	4.5
Mining	159,750	0.2	1,700	0.1
Manufacturing	13,731,566	17.5	261,200	20.7
Construction	4,150,291	5.3	85,700	6.8
Public utilities	2,229,648	2.8	16,700	1.3
Transp. and commun.	5,575,432	7.1	68,100	5.4
Trade	11,378,328	14.5	223,500	17.8
Finance	7,570,015	9.6	67,500	5.4
Pub. admin., defense	7,415,989	9.5	446,300	35.4
Services	9,086,393	11.6		
Other	10,670,692[3]	13.6[3]	32,300[4]	2.6[4]
TOTAL	78,516,869	100.0	1,259,200	100.0

Population economically active (1992): total 1,259,200; activity rate 45.0% (participation rates: ages 14 and over, 57.6%; female 42.4%; unemployed 2.5%).

Price and earnings indexes (1990 = 100)

	1988	1989	1990	1991	1992	1993	1994
Consumer price index	26.1	47.1	100.0	202.0	340.2	524.3	758.9
Monthly earnings index[5]	28.5	51.3	100.0	212.0	363.7	588.1	858.3

Household income and expenditure. Avg. household size (1985) 3.3; avg. annual income per household (1985) NUr$266,261[2] (U.S.$2,625); sources of income[6]: wages 53.5%, self-employment 17.0%, transfer payments and other 29.5%; expenditure (1982–83)[7]: food 39.9%, housing 17.6%, transportation and communications 10.4%, health care 9.3%, clothing 7.0%, durable goods 6.3%, recreation 3.1%, education 1.3%, personal effects and other 5.1%.
Tourism (1993): receipts U.S.$447,000,000; expenditures U.S.$129,000,000.
Land use (1992): forested 3.8%; meadows and pastures 77.3%; agricultural and under permanent cultivation 7.5%; other 11.4%.

Foreign trade[8]

Balance of trade (current prices)

	1989	1990	1991	1992	1993	1994
U.S.$'000,000	+478.8	+435.4	+44.9	−248.9	−536.7	−732.2
% of total	17.6%	14.8%	1.4%	6.8%	14.0%	16.1%

Imports (1994): U.S.$2,772,600,000 (machinery and appliances 21.1%; transport equipment 15.5%; chemical products 11.5%; mineral products 10.2%; synthetic plastics, resins, and rubber 6.0%; textile products 6.0%; base metals and products 5.3%). *Major import sources:* Brazil 25.6%; Argentina 23.5%; United States 9.4%; Italy 4.9%; Spain 4.4%; Germany 3.6%.
Exports (1994): U.S.$1,913,400,000 (live animals and live-animal products 25.6%; textiles and textile products 20.5%; vegetable products 13.0%; hides and skins 11.1%; synthetic plastics, resins, and rubber 3.3%; processed foods 3.0%). *Major export destinations:* Brazil 25.7%; Argentina 20.0%; United States 6.8%; Germany 6.3%, United Kingdom 3.8%; Italy 3.2%.

Transport and communications

Transport. Railroads[9]: route length (1993) 3,004 km; passenger-km (1987) 140,600,000; metric ton-km cargo (1991) 203,200,000. Roads (1985): length 52,000 km (paved 23%). Vehicles (1993): passenger cars 310,833; trucks and buses 148,644. Merchant marine (1992): vessels (100 gross tons and over) 93; deadweight tonnage 172,520. Air transport (1991): passenger-km 471,000,000; metric ton-km cargo 2,600,000; airports (1995) 1.
Communications. Daily newspapers (1992): total number 32; total circulation 750,000; circulation per 1,000 population 240. Radio (1994): total receivers 1,850,000 (1 per 1.7 persons). Television (1994): total receivers 600,000 (1 per 5.3 persons). Telephones (main lines; 1993): 530,000 (1 per 5.9 persons).

Education and health

Education (1993)

	schools	teachers	students	student/ teacher ratio
Primary (age 6–11)	2,422	16,392	338,204	20.6
Secondary (age 12–17)	335	17,750	201,805	11.4
Vocational	105	...	54,839	...
Higher	2	7,016	62,893	9.0

Educational attainment (1985). Percentage of population age 25 and over having: no formal schooling 7.5%; less than primary education 26.6%; primary 31.2%; secondary 19.9%; higher 14.8%. *Literacy* (1985): population age 15 and over literate 95.0%; males 975,200 (94.5%); females 1,074,300 (95.4%).
Health: physicians (1993) 11,021 (1 per 286 persons); hospital beds (1987) 14,133 (1 per 215 persons); infant mortality rate per 1,000 live births (1992) 18.7.
Food (1988–90): daily per capita caloric intake 2,668 (vegetable products 65%, animal products 35%); 100% of FAO recommended minimum requirement.

Military

Total active duty personnel (1994): 25,600 (army 67.2%, navy 21.1%, air force 11.7%). *Military expenditure as percentage of GNP* (1993): 2.0% (world 3.3%); per capita expenditure U.S.$81.

[1]Includes the vice president, who serves as ex officio presiding officer. [2]The peso uruguayo (Uruguayan peso [Ur$]) replaced the new Uruguayan peso (Nur$) on March 1, 1993, at the rate of 1 Uruguayan peso = 1,000 new Uruguayan pesos. [3]Includes indirect taxes less subsidies. [4]Includes unemployed not previously employed. [5]From urban areas only. [6]Salaried employees only. [7]Weights of consumer price index components in Montevideo. [8]Import figures are f.o.b. in balance of trade and c.i.f. for commodities and trading partners. [9]Passenger service ceased in 1988.

Uzbekistan

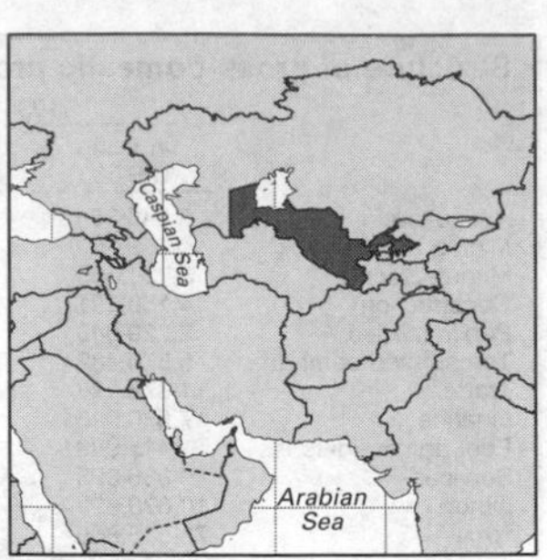

Official name: Ozbekistan Jumhuriyäti (Republic of Uzbekistan).
Form of government: multiparty republic with a single legislative body (Supreme Soviet [250]).
Head of state: President.
Head of government: Prime Minister.
Capital: Tashkent (Toshkent).
Official language: Uzbek.
Official religion: none.
Monetary unit: sum[1] (plural sumy); valuation (Oct. 4, 1995) 1 U.S.$ = 33.80 sumy; 1 £=53.72 sumy.

Area and population

Autonomous Republic	Administrative centres	area sq mi	area sq km	population 1992 estimate
Qoraqalpoghiston	Nuqus	63,700	164,900	1,311,000
Provinces				
Andijon	Andijon	1,600	4,200	1,839,000
Bukhoro	Bukhara (Bukhoro)	54,900	142,100	1,232,000
Farghona	Fergana (Farghona)	2,700	7,100	2,282,000
Jizzakh	Jizzakh	7,900	20,500	806,000
Khorazm	Urganch	2,400	6,300	1,100,000
Namangan	Namangan	3,100	7,900	1,604,000
Qashqadaryo	Qarshi	11,000	28,400	1,756,000
Samarqand	Samarkand (Samarqand)	9,500	24,500	2,265,000
Sirdaryo	Guliston	2,000	5,100	587,000
Surkhondaryo	Termiz	8,000	20,800	1,385,000
Toshkent	Tashkent (Toshkent)	6,000	15,600	4,331,000
TOTAL		172,700[2]	447,400	20,498,000

Demography

Population (1995): 22,886,000.
Density (1995): persons per sq mi 132.5, persons per sq km 51.2.
Urban-rural (1993): urban 39.29%; rural 60.71%.
Sex distribution (1993): male 49.51%; female 50.49%.
Age breakdown (1989): under 15, 40.8%; 15–29, 28.4%; 30–44, 15.0%; 45–59, 9.3%; 60–74, 4.7%; 75 and over, 1.8%.
Population projection: (2000) 25,383,000; (2010) 30,703,000.
Doubling time: 28 years.
Ethnic composition (1991): Uzbek 73.0%; Russian 7.7%; Tajik 4.8%; Tatar 2.3%; Kyrgyz 0.9%; Ukrainian 0.7%; Turkmen 0.6%; other 10.0%.
Religious affiliation (1993): believers are predominantly Sunnī Muslim (Ḥanafīyah).
Major cities (1992): Tashkent 2,119,900; Samarkand 372,000; Namangan 333,000; Andijon 302,000; Bukhara 235,000.

Vital statistics

Birth rate per 1,000 population (1993): 31.5 (world avg. 25.0); (1992) legitimate 95.8%; illegitimate 3.4%.
Death rate per 1,000 population (1993): 6.6 (world avg. 9.3).
Natural increase rate per 1,000 population (1993): 24.9 (world avg. 15.7).
Total fertility rate (avg. births per childbearing woman; 1993): 3.8.
Marriage rate per 1,000 population (1993): 10.3.
Divorce rate per 1,000 population (1993): 1.2.
Life expectancy at birth (1990): male 65.1 years; female 71.8 years.
Major causes of death per 100,000 population (1993): diseases of the circulatory system 300.3; diseases of the respiratory system 113.8; accidents, poisoning, and violence 49.5; malignant neoplasms (cancers) 48.2; infectious and parasitic diseases 38.0; diseases of the digestive system 31.4; diseases of the nervous system (1989) 9.1; endocrine and metabolic disorders (1989) 6.5.

National economy

Budget (1994). Revenue: 1,603,800,000,000 rubles (value-added tax 30.6%; corporate income tax 20.6%; individual income tax 8.7%; excise tax 2.5%). Expenditures: 1,805,000,000,000 rubles (social and cultural affairs 38.4%, of which education 24.5%, health care 10.9%; subsidies 20.0%; defense 11.5%; national economy 10.1%; administration 2.6%).
Household income and expenditure (1992). Average household size (1989) 5.5; income per household 2,343 rubles; sources of income: wages and salaries 61.8%, subsidies, grants, and nonwage income 22.8%, other 15.4%; expenditure: food and consumer goods 72.4%, other 27.6%.
Public debt (external, outstanding; 1992): U.S.$123,000,000.
Production (metric tons except as noted). Agriculture, forestry, fishing (1994): seed cotton 3,935,000, vegetables 3,737,000, fruit (except grapes) and berries 1,005,000, potatoes 562,000, rice 544,000, grapes 450,000, barley 340,000, corn (maize) 200,000, rye 12,000; livestock (number of live animals) 9,400,000 sheep, 5,300,000 cattle, 530,000 pigs, 33,000,000 chickens; roundwood (1990) 15,000 cu m; fish catch (1993) 23,401. Mining and quarrying (1993): copper 100,000; lead 40,000; gold 85. Manufacturing (value of production in '000,000 sumy; 1993): textiles 1,999; petroleum products 950; food products 764; construction materials 327; clothing 311; chemical products 129; wood products 58; machine-building equipment 56. Construction (1992): residential 7,000,000,000 sq m. Energy production (consumption): electricity (kW-hr; 1993) 49,149,000,000 (49,018,000,000); coal (metric tons; 1993) 3,807,000 (4,259,000); crude petroleum (barrels; 1993) 17,621,000 (46,714,000); petroleum products (metric tons; 1993) 7,337,000 (7,907,000); natural gas (cu m; 1993) 39,181,000,000 (37,954,000,000).
Gross national product (1993): U.S.$21,030,000,000 (U.S.$960 per capita).

Structure of gross domestic product and labour force

	1993 in value '000,000 rubles	1993 % of total value	1992 labour force	1992 % of labour force
Agriculture	1,017,383	25.5	3,577,000	43.4
Mining } Manufacturing } Public utilities }	1,177,544	29.6	1,135,000	13.8
Public utilities			182,000	2.2
Construction	416,146	10.4	622,000	7.5
Transp. and commun.	247,000	6.2	360,000	4.4
Trade	346,271	8.7	462,000	5.6
Finance } Pub. admin., defense } Services }	754,889	19.0		
Finance			25,000	0.3
Pub. admin., defense			96,000	1.2
Services			1,664,000	20.2
Other	25,405	0.6	119,800	1.4
TOTAL	3,984,638	100.0	8,242,800	100.0

Population economically active (1992): total 8,242,800; activity rate of total population 39.0% (participation rates: ages 16–59 [male], 16–54 [female] 79.7%; female 43.8%; unemployed 1.1%).

Price and earnings indexes (1990 = 100)

	1990	1991	1992	1993	1994
Consumer price index	100.0	205.0	1,527	9,683	79,689
Earnings index	...	...	...	...	...

Land use (1993): forested 2.9%; meadows and pastures 46.5%; agricultural and under permanent cultivation 10.1%; other 40.5%.

Foreign trade

Balance of trade (current prices)

	1987	1988	1989	1990	1991	1992
'000,000,000 rubles	−3.9	−1.2	−3.5	−3.7	−0.6	−4.1
% of total	20.8%	8.5%	17.0%	18.4%	1.5%	12.0%

Imports (1992): 191,885,000,000 Russian rubles (petroleum products 18.1%, food products 14.0%, ferrous and nonferrous metal products 13.7%, chemical products 11.1%, machinery 10.5%, light industrial products 7.1%). *Major import sources:* Russia 52.9%; Ukraine 13.6%; Kazakhstan 12.2%; Turkmenistan 7.0%; Belarus 5.8%.
Exports (1992): 150,635,000,000 Russian rubles (light industrial products 47.9%, machinery 15.1%, ferrous and nonferrous metal products 11.9%, petroleum products 11.3%, chemical products 7.6%). *Major export destinations:* Russia 53.1%; Ukraine 14.0%; Kazakhstan 11.2%; Turkmenistan 5.3%; Kyrgyzstan 3.7%.

Transport and communications

Transport. Railroads (1991): length 4,225 mi, 6,800 km; passenger-mi 3,231,000,000, passenger-km 5,200,000,000; short ton-mi cargo 48,357,000,000, metric ton-km cargo 70,600,000,000. Roads (1990): total length 55,431 mi, 89,207 km (paved 83%). Vehicles (1988): passenger cars 790,800; trucks and buses, n.a. Merchant marine: vessels (100 gross tons and over) n.a.; total deadweight tonnage, n.a. Air transport (1991): passenger-mi 6,524,000,000, passenger-km 10,500,000,000; short ton-mi cargo 60,754,000,000; metric ton-km cargo 88,700,000,000; airports (1995) with scheduled flights 2.
Communications. Daily newspapers (1992): total number 12; total circulation 452,000; circulation per 1,000 population 21. Radio (1991): total number of receivers 3,677,000 (1 per 5.6 persons). Television (1991): total number of receivers 3,308,000 (1 per 6.3 persons). Telephones (main lines; 1993): 1,451,500 (1 per 15.1 persons).

Education and health

Education (1992–93)

	schools	teachers	students	student/ teacher ratio
Primary (age 6–13) } Secondary (age 14–17) }	8,500			
Primary (age 6–13)		91,500	1,852,841	20.3
Secondary (age 14–17)		300,800	2,893,058	9.6
Voc., teacher tr.	440	22,164	242,793	11.0
Higher	53	...	321,682	...

Educational attainment (1989). Percentage of population age 25 and over having: primary education or no formal schooling 13.3%; some secondary 19.8%; completed secondary and some postsecondary 57.7%; higher 9.2%.
Literacy: (1989): percentage of total population age 15 and over literate 97.2%; males literate 98.5%; females literate 96.0%.
Health (1994): physicians 79,000 (1 per 284 persons); hospital beds 190,000 (1 per 118 persons); infant mortality rate per 1,000 live births 32.0.

Military

Total active duty personnel (1995): 25,000[3] (army 84.0%, air force 16.0%). *Military expenditure as percentage of GNP* (1993): 0.2%; per capita expenditure U.S.$15.

[1]The sum was introduced on July 1, 1994, to replace the sum-coupon (an interim currency introduced in November 1993 to replace the Russian ruble) at a rate of 1 sum to 1,000 sum-coupons. The Russian ruble was banned from circulation in Uzbekistan from mid-April 1994. [2]Detail does not add to total given because of rounding. [3]Includes CIS centrally controlled units. About 5,000 Russian troops remained in Uzbekistan in late 1994.

Vanuatu

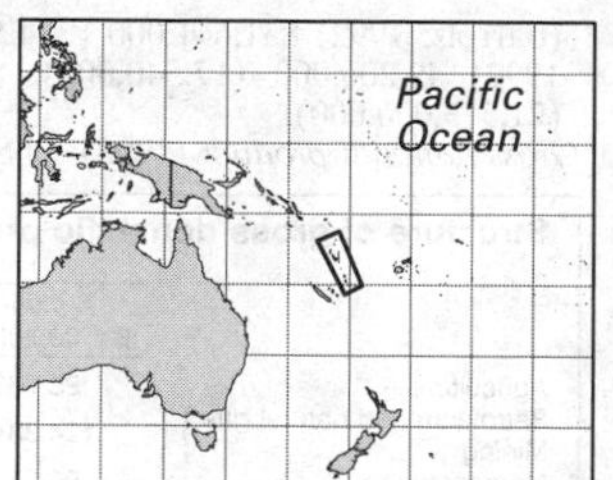

Official name: Ripablik blong Vanuatu (Bislama); République de Vanuatu (French); Republic of Vanuatu (English).
Form of government: republic with a single legislative house (Parliament [46]).
Chief of state: President.
Head of government: Prime Minister.
Capital: Vila.
Official languages: Bislama; French; English.
Official religion: none.
Monetary unit: vatu (VT); valuation (Oct. 6, 1995) 1 U.S.$ = VT 112.30; 1 £ = VT 172.53.

Area and population

Local Government Regions	Capitals	area sq mi	area sq km	population 1989 census
Ambae/Maéwo	Longana	270	699	10,958
Ambrym	Eas	257	666	7,191
Banks/Torres	Sola	341	882	5,985
Éfaté	Vila	356	923	30,868
Épi	Ringdove	172	446	3,628
Malekula	Lakatoro	793	2,053	19,298
Paama	Liro	23	60	1,696
Pentecost	Loltong	193	499	11,341
Santo/Malo	Luganville	1,640	4,248	25,581
Shepherd	Morua	33	86	3,975
Taféa	Isangel	629	1,628	22,423
TOTAL		4,707	12,190	142,944

Demography

Population (1995): 168,000.
Density (1995): persons per sq mi 35.7, persons per sq km 13.8.
Urban-rural (1995): urban 19.0%[1]; rural 81.0%.
Sex distribution (1989): male 51.60%; female 48.40%.
Age breakdown (1989)[2]: under 15, 45.5%; 15–29, 26.6%; 30–44, 15.2%; 45–59, 8.4%; 60–74, 3.7%; 75 and over, 0.6%.
Population projection: (2000) 189,000; (2010) 231,000.
Doubling time: 26 years.
Ethnic composition (1989): Ni-Vanuatu 97.9%; European 1.0%; other Pacific Islanders 0.4%; other 0.7%.
Religious affiliation (1989): Christian 77.2%, of which Presbyterian 35.8%, Roman Catholic 14.5%, Anglican 14.0%, Seventh-day Adventist 8.2%; Custom 4.6%; nonreligious 1.7%; unknown 4.0%; other 12.5%.
Major towns (1989): Vila (Port-Vila) 19,400; Luganville (Santo) 6,900; Port Olry 884[3]; Isangel 752[3].

Vital statistics

Birth rate per 1,000 population (1995): 34.0 (world avg. 25.0).
Death rate per 1,000 population (1995): 7.0 (world avg. 9.3).
Natural increase rate per 1,000 population (1995): 28.0 (world avg. 15.7).
Total fertility rate (avg. births per childbearing woman; 1995): 4.5.
Marriage rate per 1,000 population (1985): c. 7.4.
Divorce rate per 1,000 population (1985): less than 0.7.
Life expectancy at birth (1995): male 65.0 years; female 68.0 years.
Major causes of death per 100,000 population (1994)[4]: diseases of the circulatory system 39.0; diseases of the respiratory system 30.4; malignant neoplasms (cancers) 29.2; infectious and parasitic diseases 25.0; diseases of the digestive system 9.7.

National economy

Budget (1994). Revenue: VT 5,475,000,000 (taxes on international trade 53.8%, nontax revenue 20.7%, taxes on goods and services 18.2%). Expenditures: VT 8,554,000,000 (economic affairs and services 22.6%, general public services 20.4%, education 14.3%, health 7.2%, public order and safety 5.5%).
Public debt (external, outstanding; 1993): U.S.$39,400,000.
Tourism (1993): receipts from visitors U.S.$30,000,000; expenditures by nationals abroad U.S.$1,000,000.
Production (metric tons except as noted). Agriculture, forestry, fishing (1994): coconuts 259,000, roots and tubers 51,000, copra 30,000, bananas 13,000, vegetables and melons 8,000, cacao beans 2,000, peanuts (groundnuts) 2,000, corn (maize) 1,000; livestock (number of live animals) 132,000 cattle, 59,000 pigs, 11,000 goats; roundwood (1993) 63,000 cu m; fish catch (1993) 2,925. Mining and quarrying: small quantities of coral-reef limestone, crushed stone, sand, and gravel. Manufacturing (value added in '000,000 VT; 1993): food, beverages, and tobacco 568; wood products 287; fabricated metal products 153; chemical, rubber, plastic, and nonmetallic products 118; paper products 68; textiles, clothing, and leather 48. Construction (approvals in Vila and Luganville; 1992): residential 20,386 sq m; nonresidential 19,876 sq m. Energy production (consumption): electricity (kW-hr; 1992) 28,681,000 (28,681,000); coal, none (none); crude petroleum, none (none); petroleum products (metric tons; 1991) none (26,000); natural gas, none (none).
Land use (1993): forested 75.0%; meadows and pastures 2.0%; agricultural 11.8%; other 11.2%.
Population economically active (1989): total 66,957; activity rate of total population 47.0% (participation rates: ages 15–64, 85.0%; female 46.3%; unemployed 0.5%).

Price and earnings indexes (1990 = 100)

	1988	1989	1990	1991	1992	1993	1994
Consumer price index	88.6	95.5	100.0	106.5	108.8	114.7	117.4
Earnings index	...	...	...	...	...	...	...

Gross national product (at current market prices; 1993): U.S.$198,000,000 (U.S.$1,230 per capita).

Structure of gross domestic product and labour force

	1993 in value VT '000,000[5]	1993 % of total value	1989 labour force	1989 % of labour force
Agriculture	2,783	20.8	49,811	74.4
Mining	...	...	1	—
Manufacturing	863	6.5	891	1.3
Construction	697	5.2	1,302	1.9
Public utilities	326	2.4	109	0.2
Transportation and communications	939	7.0	1,031	1.5
Trade	4,128	30.9	2,713	4.1
Finance	1,465	11.0	646	1.0
Pub. admin., defense	1,597	11.9	7,892	11.8
Services	899	6.7		
Other	−331[6]	−2.5[6]	2,561	3.8
TOTAL	13,365[7]	100.0[7]	66,957	100.0

Household income and expenditure (1985)[1]. Average household size (1989) 5.1; income per household U.S.$11,299; sources of income: wages and salaries 59.0%, self-employment 33.7%; expenditure (1990)[1,8]: food and nonalcoholic beverages 30.5%, housing 20.7%, transportation 13.2%, health and recreation 12.3%, tobacco and alcohol 10.4%.

Foreign trade[9]

Balance of trade (current prices)

	1988	1989	1990	1991	1992	1993
VT '000,000	−5,000	−5,319	−8,566	−7,364	−6,689	−6,409
% of total	54.8%	50.9%	66.0%	67.0%	56.8%	53.7%

Imports (1993): VT 9,167,000,000 (1992; machinery and transport equipment 27.5%; food and live animals 17.4%; basic manufactures 14.9%; mineral fuels 9.0%; chemical products 6.6%; beverages and tobacco 4.1%). *Major import sources* (1992): Australia 38.7%; New Zealand 10.0%; Japan 9.1%; France 7.9%; New Caledonia 6.3%; Fiji 5.2%; Hong Kong 3.5%; Singapore 2.8%.
Exports (1993): VT 2,758,000,000 (domestic exports 77.6%, of which copra 25.6%, beef and veal 16.6%, timber 9.7%, cacao beans and preparations 5.6%; reexports 22.4%). *Major export destinations*[10]: European Union 32.0%; Japan 29.0%; Australia 11.0%; New Caledonia 7.0%.

Transport and communications

Transport. Railroads: none. Roads (1993): total length 702 mi, 1,130 km (paved 21%). Vehicles (1993): passenger cars 4,000; trucks and buses 2,200. Merchant marine (1992): vessels (100 gross tons and over) 280; total deadweight tonnage 3,259,594. Air transport (1992): international passenger arrivals 52,188, international passenger departures 52,837; international cargo unloaded 571 metric tons, international cargo loaded 188 metric tons; airports (1995) with scheduled flights 29.
Communications. Daily newspapers: none. Radio (1994): total number of receivers 55,000 (1 per 3.0 persons). Television (1992): total number of receivers 2,000 (1 per 78 persons). Telephones (main lines, 1993): 4,100 (1 per 40 persons).

Education and health

Education (1992)

	schools	teachers	students	student/ teacher ratio
Primary (age 6–11)[11]	272	852	26,267	30.8
Secondary (age 11–18)	21[12]	220	4,269	19.4
Voc., teacher tr.	...	...	444	...
Higher	1	...	124[13]	...

Educational attainment (1989). Percentage of population age 6 and over having: no formal schooling or less than one year 22.3%; some primary education 52.6%; lower-level secondary 18.3%; upper-level secondary and higher 4.8%; not stated 2.0%. *Literacy* (1979): total population age 15 and over literate 32,120 (52.9%); males 18,550 (57.3%); females 13,570 (47.8%).
Health (1995): physicians 12 (1 per 14,025 persons); hospital beds 374 (1 per 450 persons); infant mortality rate per 1,000 live births (1994) 44.0.
Food (1992): daily per capita caloric intake 2,739 (vegetable products 85%, animal products 15%); 120% of FAO recommended minimum requirement.

Military

Total active duty personnel: Vanuatu has a paramilitary force of about 300.

[1]Vila and Luganville only. [2]For indigenous population only. [3]1979. [4]Deaths reported to the Ministry of Health only. [5]At 1983 prices. [6]Imputed bank service charges. [7]Detail does not add to total given because of rounding. [8]Weights of consumer price index components. [9]Imports c.i.f.; exports f.o.b. [10]Destination of domestic exports only. [11]Excludes independent private schools. [12]1986. [13]1991.

Venezuela

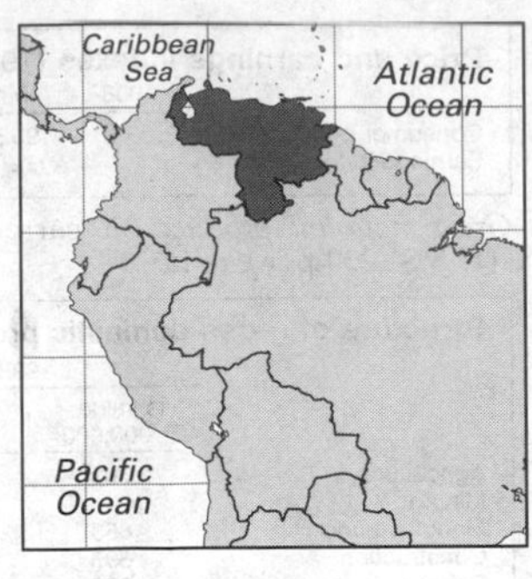

Official name: República de Venezuela (Republic of Venezuela).
Form of government: federal multiparty republic with two legislative houses (Senate [53[1]]; Chamber of Deputies [199]).
Head of state and government: President.
Capital: Caracas.
Official language: Spanish.
Official religion: none.
Monetary unit: 1 bolívar (B, plural Bs) = 100 céntimos; valuation[2] (Oct. 6, 1995) 1 U.S.$ = Bs 170.00; 1 £ = Bs 268.75.

Area and population

		area		population
States	Capitals	sq mi	sq km	1995 estimate
Amazonas	Puerto Ayacucho	67,900	175,750	66,668
Anzoátegui	Barcelona	16,700	43,300	1,028,097
Apure	San Fernando de Apure	29,500	76,500	376,220
Aragua	Maracay	2,700	7,014	1,335,303
Barinas	Barinas	13,600	35,200	516,789
Bolívar	Ciudad Bolívar	91,900	238,000	1,122,975
Carabobo	Valencia	1,795	4,650	1,807,542
Cojedes	San Carlos	5,700	14,800	226,684
Delta Amacuro	Tucupita	15,500	40,200	110,838
Falcón	Coro	9,600	24,800	684,062
Guárico	San Juan de Los Morros	25,091	64,986	585,418
Lara	Barquisimeto	7,600	19,800	1,423,683
Mérida	Mérida	4,400	11,300	686,709
Miranda	Los Teques	3,070	7,950	2,326,143
Monagas	Maturín	11,200	28,900	551,015
Nueva Esparta	La Asunción	440	1,150	325,909
Portuguesa	Guanare	5,900	15,200	719,473
Sucre	Cumaná	4,600	11,800	771,580
Táchira	San Cristóbal	4,300	11,100	944,259
Trujillo	Trujillo	2,900	7,400	549,878
Yaracuy	San Felipe	2,700	7,100	463,911
Zulia	Maracaibo	24,400	63,100	2,752,431
Other federal entities				
Dependencias Federales	—	50	120	...
Distrito Federal	Caracas	745	1,930	2,268,534
TOTAL		352,144[3]	912,050	21,644,121

Demography

Population (1995): 21,844,000.
Density (1995): persons per sq mi 62.0, persons per sq km 24.0.
Urban-rural (1992): urban 84.6%; rural 15.4%.
Sex distribution (1994): male 50.40%; female 49.60%.
Age breakdown (1992): under 15, 37.4%; 15–29, 28.0%; 30–44, 19.0%; 45–59, 9.7%; 60 and over, 5.9%.
Population projection: (2000) 24,170,000; (2010) 28,716,000.
Doubling time: 33 years.
Ethnic composition (1993): mestizo 67%; white 21%; black 10%; Indian 2%.
Religious affiliation (1991): Roman Catholic 92.1%; other 7.1%.
Major cities (1990): Caracas 1,822,465; Maracaibo 1,249,670; Valencia 903,621; Barquisimeto 625,450; Ciudad Guayana 453,047.

Vital statistics

Birth rate per 1,000 population (1994): 25.7 (world avg. 25.0); (1974) legitimate 47.0%; illegitimate 53.0%.
Death rate per 1,000 population (1994): 4.6 (world avg. 9.3).
Natural increase rate per 1,000 population (1994): 21.1 (world avg. 15.7).
Total fertility rate (avg. births per childbearing woman; 1994): 3.1.
Marriage rate per 1,000 population (1992): 5.4.
Divorce rate per 1,000 population (1992): 0.9.
Life expectancy at birth (1994): male 70.1 years; female 76.0 years.
Major causes of death per 100,000 population (1992): heart diseases 79.9; malignant neoplasms (cancers) 53.7; accidents 43.6; perinatal problems 33.0; cerebrovascular diseases 29.7; pneumonia 17.3.

National economy

Budget (1993). Revenue: Bs 961,495,000,000 (tax revenues 41.4%, oil revenues 38.3%, nontax revenues 20.3%). Expenditures: Bs 1,192,848,000,000 (subsidies 29.8%, goods and services 28.9%, capital transfers 17.6%, interest payments 16.6%).
Public debt (external, outstanding; 1993): U.S.$26,856,000,000.
Tourism (1992): receipts U.S.$432,000,000; expenditures U.S.$1,428,000,000.
Production (metric tons except as noted). Agriculture, forestry, fishing (1994): sugarcane 6,880,000, bananas 936,000, corn (maize) 884,000, rice 738,000, plantains 546,000, sorghum 446,000, cassava 285,000, coffee 79,000, cacao 19,000; livestock (number of live animals) 15,071,000 cattle, 2,250,000 pigs, 1,850,000 goats, 90,000,000 chickens; roundwood (1993) 2,245,000 cu m; fish catch (1993) 390,333. Mining and quarrying (1994): iron ore 18,309,000; bauxite 4,667,000; aluminum ore 635,000; gold 9,944 kg; diamonds 558,000 carats. Manufacturing (value added in Bs '000; 1990): base metals 60,320,000; food products 56,737,000; chemicals 51,838,000; beverages 27,350,000; metal products 15,770,000; textiles 13,658,000; paper and paper products 12,982,000; tobacco 12,826,000; electrical machinery 11,506,000. Construction (in Bs; 1992): residential 77,648,000,000; nonresidential 356,982,000,000. Energy production (consumption): electricity (kW-hr; 1992) 69,460,000,000 (69,100,000,000); coal (metric tons; 1992) 2,427,000 (350,000); crude petroleum (barrels; 1992) 851,641,000 (334,574,000); petroleum products (metric tons; 1992) 49,206,000 (17,540,000); natural gas (cu m; 1992) 21,573,000,000 (21,573,000,000).
Gross national product (1993): U.S.$58,916,000,000 (U.S.$2,840 per capita).

Structure of gross domestic product and labour force

	1993			
	in value Bs '000,000[4]	% of total value	labour force	% of labour force
Agriculture	25,738	4.6	749,700	9.9
Petroleum and natural gas / Mining	124,334	22.4	69,700	0.9
Manufacturing	90,655	16.3	1,080,700	14.3
Construction	40,037	7.2	653,800	8.7
Public utilities	9,329	1.7	52,100	0.7
Transp. and commun.	29,409	5.3	452,300	6.0
Trade	75,527	13.6	1,596,600	21.2
Finance	[5]	[5]	463,600	6.1
Pub. admin., defense	46,940	8.5	1,944,000	25.8
Services	103,705	18.7		
Other	9,569	1.7	483,700[6]	6.4[6]
TOTAL	555,243	100.0	7,546,200	100.0

Population economically active (1993): total 7,546,200; activity rate 36.3% (participation rates: over age 15, 57.9%; female 31.2%; unemployed 6.3%).

Price and earnings indexes (1990 = 100)

	1988	1989	1990	1991	1992	1993	1994
Consumer price index	38.5	71.1	100.0	134.2	176.4	243.6	391.8
Monthly earnings index[7]	45.0	67.1	100.0	...	...	...	...

Household income and expenditure. Average household size (1990) 5.1; average annual income per household (1981) Bs 42,492 (U.S.$9,899); sources of income: n.a.; expenditure (1990): food 37.1%, rent and utilities 9.4%, clothing 8.3%, transportation and communications 5.1%, education and recreation 4.9%, household furnishings and maintenance 2.8%.
Land use (1993): forested 34.0%; meadows and pastures 20.2%; agricultural and under permanent cultivation 4.4%; other 41.4%.

Foreign trade

Balance of trade (current prices)

	1989	1990	1991	1992	1993	1994
Bs '000,000	+232,261	+529,115	+286,500	+154,700	+274,600	+1,159,400
% of total	33.5%	46.7%	20.1%	9.3%	12.1%	32.7%

Imports (1993): Bs 997,499,600,000 (machinery 32.8%, transport equipment 17.9%, chemicals 12.0%, basic metal manufactures 6.6%, textile products 3.8%, cereals and preparations 3.6%, precision and photographic equipment 2.7%). *Major import sources:* U.S. 46.2%; Japan 7.6%; Germany 5.6%; Italy 4.7%; Colombia 4.2%; Brazil 3.5%; Canada 3.2%; France 2.9%.
Exports (1993): Bs 1,306,300,000,000 (crude petroleum and petroleum products 77.5%, basic metal manufactures 8.2%). *Major export destinations:* U.S. 56.4%; Netherlands Antilles 9.0%; Colombia 6.1%; Brazil 2.5%; Germany 2.3%; The Netherlands 2.2%; Mexico 1.5%; Japan 1.5%.

Transport and communications

Transport. Railroads (1992): route length 226 mi, 363 km; passenger-km 46,670,000; metric ton-km cargo 36,240,000. Roads (1993): total length 58,081 mi, 93,472 km (paved 32%). Vehicles (1993): passenger cars 1,507,309; trucks and buses 474,466. Merchant marine (1992): vessels (100 gross tons and over) 271; total deadweight tonnage 1,355,419. Air transport (1993): passenger-km 6,708,000,000; metric ton-km cargo 149,000,000; airports (1995) with scheduled flights 24.
Communications. Daily newspapers (1992): total number 82; total circulation 4,200,000; circulation per 1,000 population 208. Radio (1994): 8,300,000 receivers (1 per 2.6 persons). Television (1994): 3,700,000 receivers (1 per 5.7 persons). Telephones (main lines; 1993): 2,082,800 (1 per 10 persons).

Education and health

Education (1991–92)

	schools	teachers	students	student/teacher ratio
Primary (age 7–12)	15,800	183,298	4,190,047	22.9
Secondary (age 13–17)[8]	1,621	32,572	289,430	8.9
Higher	99[9]	43,833	550,783	12.6

Educational attainment (1990). Percentage of population age 25 and over having: no formal schooling 23.5%; primary education or less 47.2%; some secondary and secondary 22.3%; postsecondary 7.0%. *Literacy* (1990): total population age 15 and over literate 13,371,743 (92.2%); males 6,742,992 (93.5%); females 6,628,751 (91.1%).
Health (1992): physicians (1989) 32,616 (1 per 576 persons); hospital beds 52,786 (1 per 382 persons); infant mortality rate (1994) 27.7.
Food (1992): daily per capita caloric intake 2,618 (vegetable products 85%, animal products 15%); 106% of FAO recommended minimum.

Military

Total active duty personnel (1994): 79,000 (army 72.1%, navy 19.0%, air force 8.9%). *Military expenditure as percentage of GNP* (1993): 1.8% (world 3.3%); per capita expenditure U.S.$50.

[1]In addition, four former presidents hold lifetime membership. [2]Fixed exchange rate to U.S.$ introduced July 1994. [3]Detail does not add to total given because of rounding. [4]At 1984 prices. [5]Included with Services. [6]Mostly unemployed. [7]Blue-collar workers. [8]Includes vocational and teacher training. [9]1990–91.

Vietnam

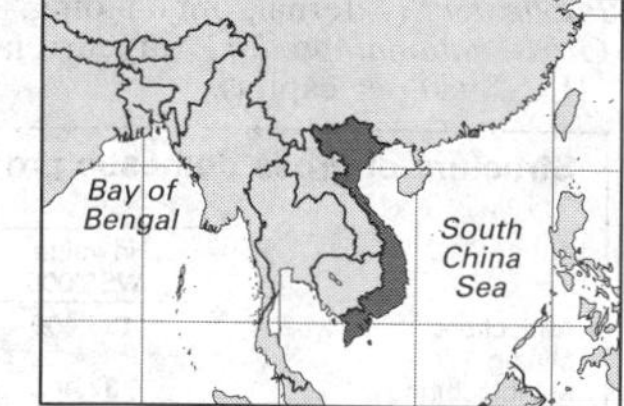

Official name: Cong Hoa Xa Hoi Chu Nghia Viet Nam (Socialist Republic of Vietnam).
Form of government: socialist republic with one legislative house (National Assembly [395]).
Chief of state: President.
Head of government: Prime Minister.
Capital: Hanoi.
Official language: Vietnamese.
Official religion: none.
Monetary unit: 1 dong (D) = 10 hao = 100 xu; valuation (Oct. 6, 1995) 1 U.S.$ = D 11,014; 1 £ = D 17,412.

Area and population

Regions / Provinces	Capitals	area sq mi	area sq km	population 1993 estimate
Dong bang song Cuu Long		15,280	39,575[1]	15,531,600
An Giang	Long Xuyen	1,322	3,424	1,933,800
Ben Tre	Ben Tre	868	2,247	1,309,400
Can Tho	Can Tho	1,179	3,054	1,780,600
Dong Thap	Cao Lanh	1,265	3,276	1,462,900
Kien Giang	Rach Gia	2,410	6,243	1,326,600
Long An	Tan An	1,675	4,338	1,224,800
Minh Hai	Ca Mau	2,969	7,689	1,719,100
Soc Trang	Soc Trang	1,200	3,107	1,172,600
Tien Giang	My Tho	903	2,339	1,622,000
Tra Vinh	Tra Vinh	915	2,369	938,500
Vinh Long	Vinh Long	574	1,487	1,041,300
Dong bang song Hong		4,810[1]	12,457[1]	13,808,800
Ha Tay	Ha Dong	831	2,153	2,217,800
Hai Hung	Hai Duong	985	2,552	2,658,000
Haiphong (MUNICIPALITY)	—	580	1,503	1,583,900
Hanoi (CAPITAL)	—	355	920	2,154,900
Nam Ha	Nam Dinh	934	2,419	2,585,900
Ninh Binh	Ninh Binh	536	1,387	[illegible]
Thai Binh	Thai Binh	588	1,524	1,768,400
Dong Nam Bo		9,066[1]	23,481	8,692,900
Ba Ria–Vung Tau	Vung Tau	756	1,957	657,100
Dong Nai	Bien Hoa	2,264	5,864	1,762,900
Ho Chi Minh City (MUNICIPALITY)	—	807	2,090	4,322,300
Song Be	Thu Dau Mot	3,686	9,546	1,081,700
Tay Ninh	Tay Ninh	1,554	4,024	868,900
Duyen hai mien trung		17,692[1]	45,823	7,374,700
Binh Dinh	Quy Nhon	2,346	6,076	1,373,100
Binh Thuan	Phan Thiet	3,086	7,992	858,700
Khanh Hoa	Nha Trang	2,030	5,258	923,700
Ninh Thuan	Phan Rang Thap Cham	1,324	3,430	449,100
Phu Yen	Tuy Hoa	2,017	5,223	708,900
Quang Nam–Da Nang	Da Nang	4,029	11,988	1,911,700
Quang Ngai	Quang Ngai	2,261	5,856	1,149,500
Khu Bon cu		19,763	51,107	9,516,900
Ha Tinh	Ha Tinh	2,337	6,054	1,293,600
Nghe An	Vinh	6,325	16,381	2,680,600
Quang Binh	Dong Hoi	3,082	7,983	736,700
Quang Tri	Dong Ha	1,773	4,592	520,900
Thanh Hoa	Thanh Hoa	4,312	11,168	3,311,900
Thua Thien–Hue	Hue	1,934	5,009	973,200
Mien nui va trung du		39,749[1]	102,949	12,109,300
Bac Thai	Thai Nguyen	2,511	6,503	1,144,500
Cao Bang	Cao Bang	3,261	8,445	624,700
Ha Bac	Bac Giang	1,781	4,614	2,262,800
Ha Giang	Ha Giang	3,024	7,831	520,400
Hoa Binh	Hoa Binh	1,701	4,612	712,900
Lai Chau	Lai Chau	6,618	17,110	501,200
Lang Son	Lang Son	3,153	8,167	671,900
Lao Cai	Lao Cai	3,108	8,049	535,400
Quang Ninh	Hong Gai	2,293	5,939	889,600
Son La	Son La	5,487	14,210	776,000
Tuyen Quang	Tuyen Quang	2,240	5,801	628,500
Vinh Phu	Viet Tri	1,867	4,836	2,203,200
Yen Bai	Yen Bai	2,626	6,802	638,200
Tay Nguyen		21,455[1]	55,569	2,903,500
Dac Lac	Buon Ma Thuot	7,645	19,800	1,173,300
Gia Lai	Play Ku	6,047	15,662	737,700
Kon Tum	Kon Tum	3,835	9,934	249,600
Lam Dong	Da Lat	3,929	10,173	742,900
TOTAL		127,816[1]	331,041	70,982,500[2]

Demography

Population (1995): 74,545,000.
Density (1995): persons per sq mi 583.2, persons per sq km 225.2.
Urban-rural (1995): urban 20.8%; rural 79.2%.
Sex distribution (1995): male 49.24%; female 50.76%.
Age breakdown (1995): under 15, 37.5%; 15–29, 28.8%; 30–44, 18.5%; 45–59, 7.9%; 60–74, 5.8%; 75 and over, 1.5%.
Population projection: (2000) 82,648,000; (2010) 98,448,000.
Ethnic composition (1989): Vietnamese 87.1%; Tho (Tay) 1.8%; Chinese (Hoa) 1.5%; Tai 1.5%; Khmer 1.4%; Muong 1.4%; Nung 1.1%; other 4.2%.
Religious affiliation (1992): Buddhist *c.* 67.0%; Roman Catholic *c.* 8.0%.
Major cities (1993): Ho Chi Minh City 4,322,300; Hanoi 2,154,900.

Vital statistics

Birth rate per 1,000 population (1995): 26.3 (world avg. 25.0).
Death rate per 1,000 population (1995): 7.6 (world avg. 9.3).
Natural increase rate per 1,000 population (1995): 18.7 (world avg. 15.7).
Total fertility rate (avg. births per childbearing woman; 1995): 3.2.
Life expectancy at birth (1995): male 63.7 years; female 67.9 years.
Morbidity (cases of reportable infectious disease per 100,000 population; 1990): malaria 2,564; trachoma 241; diarrhea 183.

National economy

Budget (1995). Revenue: D 51,570,000,000 (transfers from state enterprises 39.1%; taxes 29.6%; nontax revenues 13.1%). Expenditures: D 55,970,000,000 (current expenditures 73.4%, of which social services 31.7%).
Public debt (external, outstanding; 1994): U.S.$24,700,000,000.
Gross national product (1993): U.S.$11,997,000,000[3] (U.S.$170 per capita[3]).

Structure of gross domestic product and labour force

	1994 in value D '000,000,000	% of total value	labour force	% of labour force
Agriculture, forestry, fishing	48,865	28.7	24,587,000	73.0
Mining, manufacturing }	50,481	29.6	3,595,000	10.7
Construction			875,000	2.6
Transp. and commun.	6,924	4.1	568,000	1.7
Trade and restaurants	23,072	13.6	1,825,000	5.4
Finance, insurance	3,450	2.0 }	1,290,000	3.8
Pub. admin. } Services	18,270	10.7 }		
Other	19,196[4]	11.3[4]	929,000	2.8
TOTAL	170,258	100.0	33,669,000	100.0

Tourism (1993): receipts from visitors U.S.$350,000,000.
Production (metric tons except as noted). Agriculture, forestry, fishing (1994): rice 22,500,000, sugarcane 6,000,000, cassava 2,631,000; livestock (number of live animals) 15,043,000 pigs, 3,438,000 cattle, 3,009,000 buffalo; roundwood (1993) 33,483,000 cu m; fish catch (1993) 1,100,000. Mining and quarrying (1993): phosphate rock 250,000; gold 10,000 kg. Manufacturing (1994): cement 5,161,000; fish sauce 131,700,000 litres[5]. Energy production (consumption): electricity (kW-hr; 1993) 10,854,000,000 (10,854,000,000); coal (metric tons; 1993) 5,899,000 (3,965,000); crude petroleum (barrels; 1993) 44,702,000 (283,300); petroleum products (metric tons; 1993) 38,000 (3,452,000).
Population economically active (1989): total 30,521,019; activity rate 47.4% (participation rates: ages 15–64, 79.9%; female 51.7%; unemployed 5.8%).
Household income and expenditure. Average household size (1989) 4.8; income per household (1990)[6] D 577,008 (U.S.$93); expenditure (1990): food 62.4%, clothing 5.0%, household goods 4.6%, education 2.9%, housing 2.5%.
Land use (1993): forest 29.6%; pasture 1.0%; agricultural 20.6%; other 48.8%.

Foreign trade[7]

Balance of trade (current prices)

	1989	1990	1991	1992	1993	1994
U.S.$'000,000	−350	−41	−63	−60	−655	−900
% of total	11.7%	1.2%	1.5%	1.2%	10.3%	11.1%

Imports (1994): U.S.$4,500,000,000 (machinery and spare parts 18.2%, petroleum products 14.0%, fertilizers 5.0%, steel 3.0%). *Major import sources:* Singapore 25.5%; North and South Korea 14.6%; Japan 12.6%.
Exports (1994): U.S.$3,600,000,000 (crude petroleum 24.1%, fish and fish products 13.6%, agricultural and forestry products 13.3%, rice 11.9%). *Major export destinations:* Japan 29.7%; Singapore 15.9%; Taiwan 5.9%.

Transport and communications

Transport. Railroads (1993): length 2,605 km; passenger-km 1,833,700,000; metric ton-km cargo 965,000,000. Roads (1993): total length 105,000 km (paved 10%). Vehicles (1976): passenger cars 100,000; trucks and buses 200,000. Merchant marine (1992): vessels (100 gross tons and over) 230; total deadweight tonnage 872,752. Air transport (1990): passenger-km 87,000,000; metric ton-km cargo 1,000,000; airports (1995) with scheduled flights 12.
Communications. Daily newspapers (1994): 5. Radio (1994): 7,000,000 receivers. Television (1994): 2,500,000 receivers. Telephones (main lines; 1993): 260,000 (1 per 270 persons).

Education and health

Education (1993–94)

	schools	teachers	students	student/teacher ratio
Primary (age 7–12)	13,092[8]	275,640	9,725,095	35.3
Secondary (age 13–18)[9]	6,298	166,968	3,815,852	22.9
Vocational	451	12,197	137,405	11.3
Higher	104	20,648	118,589	5.7

Educational attainment (1989). Percentage of population 25 and over having: no formal education (illiterate) 16.6%; some primary 46.6%; complete primary 23.5%; secondary 6.5%; postsecondary and higher 6.8%. *Literacy* (1991): persons 15 and over literate 88.0%; males 93.0%; females 84.0%.
Health (1993): physicians 28,500 (1 per 2,502 persons); hospital beds 194,700 (1 per 366 persons); infant mortality rate (1995) 44.6.
Food (1992): daily per capita caloric intake 2,250; 104% of FAO recommended minimum requirement.

Military

Total active duty personnel (1995): 572,000 (army 87.4%, navy 7.3%, air force 5.3%). *Military expenditure as percentage of GNP* (1994): 5.7%.

[1]Detail does not add to total given because of rounding. [2]Total includes 1,044,800 persons in special enumeration groups not distributed in province and region estimates. [3]Figure indicates the World Bank's nominal assessment of the Vietnamese economy. [4]Includes housing and tourism. [5]1992. [6]Wage workers and government officials only. [7]Data reflects trade with the convertible currency area; import figures are f.o.b. [8]Includes 2,955 institutions that provide primary and first cycle of secondary education. [9]Includes first and second cycles of secondary education.

Western Samoa

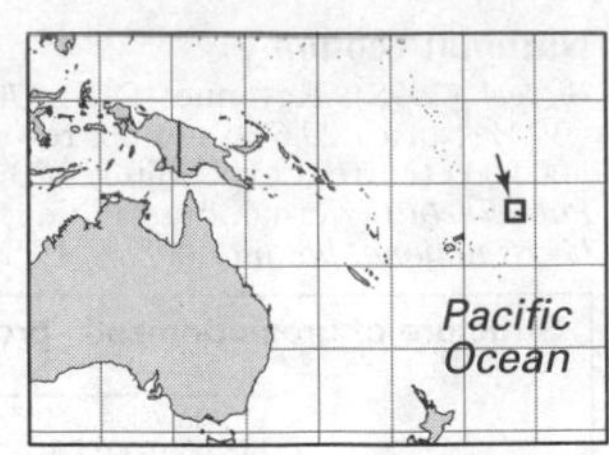

Official name: Malo Sa'oloto Tuto'atasi o Samoa i Sisifo (Samoan); Independent State of Western Samoa (English).
Form of government: constitutional monarchy[1] with one legislative house (Legislative Assembly [49]).
Chief of state: Head of State[2].
Head of government: Prime Minister.
Capital: Apia.
Official languages: Samoan; English.
Official religion: none.
Monetary unit: 1 tala (WS$, plural tala) = 100 sene; valuation (Oct. 6, 1995) 1 U.S.$ = WS$2.50; 1 £ = WS$3.95.

Area and population

Islands / Political Districts	area sq mi	area sq km	population 1986 census
Savaii	659	1,707	44,930
Fa'aseleleaga			...
Gaga'emauga			...
Gaga'ifomauga			...
Palauli			...
Satupa'itea			...
Vaisigano			...
Upolu	432	1,119	112,228
A'ana			...
Aiga-i-le-Tai			...
Atua			...
Tuamasaga			...
Vaa-o-Fonoti			...
TOTAL	1,093[3]	2,831[3]	157,158[4]

Demography

Population (1995): 166,000.
Density (1995): persons per sq mi 151.9, persons per sq km 58.6.
Urban-rural (1995): urban 21.0%; rural 79.0%.
Sex distribution (1991): male 52.45%; female 47.55%.
Age breakdown (1991): under 15, 40.6%; 15–29, 29.9%; 30–44, 14.6%; 45–59, 8.8%; 60–74, 5.0%; 75 and over, 1.1%.
Population projection: (2000) 174,000; (2010) 192,000.
Doubling time: 23 years.
Ethnic composition (1982): Samoan (Polynesian) *c.* 88%; Euronesian *c.* 10%; European *c.* 2%.
Religious affiliation (1986): Congregational 47.2%; Roman Catholic 22.3%; Methodist 15.1%; Mormon 8.6%; other 6.8%.
Major city (1991): Apia 34,126.

Vital statistics

Birth rate per 1,000 population (1995): 36.0 (world avg. 25.0); (1978) legitimate 43.5%; illegitimate 56.5%.
Death rate per 1,000 population (1995): 6.0 (world avg. 9.3).
Natural increase rate per 1,000 population (1995): 30.0 (world avg. 15.7).
Total fertility rate (avg. births per childbearing woman; 1995): 4.3.
Marriage rate per 1,000 population (1989)[5]: 5.3.
Divorce rate per 1,000 population (1989)[5]: 0.2.
Life expectancy at birth (1992): male 63.8 years; female 70.0 years.
Major causes of death per 100,000 population (percentage distribution; 1990)[5]: congestive heart failure 18.7%; cerebrovascular diseases 11.0%; pneumonia 10.0%; suicide 6.6%; chronic liver diseases 5.9%; acute myocardial infarction 4.5%; septicemia 4.2%; diabetes mellitus 3.5%.

National economy

Budget (1994–95). Revenue: WS$178,949,000 (tax revenue 84.2%, of which taxes on international trade 35.8%, taxes on goods and services 22.1%, income tax 16.0%; nontax revenue 15.8%, of which departmental enterprises 7.7%, rents, royalties, and interest 4.2%). Expenditures: WS$250,669,000 (development expenditure 49.6%; current expenditure 43.3%, of which administration 14.0%, education 7.1%, health 5.7%, public works 4.8%; net lending 7.1%).
Production (metric tons except as noted). Agriculture, forestry, fishing (1994): coconuts 130,000, taro 37,000, copra 11,000, bananas 10,000, papayas 10,000, pineapples 6,000, mangoes 5,000, avocados 2,000, cow's milk 1,000; livestock (number of live animals) 179,000 pigs, 26,000 cattle; roundwood (1993) 131,000 cu m; fish catch (1993) 1,608. Mining and quarrying: n.a. Manufacturing (in WS$'000; 1990): beer 8,708; cigarettes 6,551; coconut cream 5,576; sawn wood 3,662; coconut oil 3,442; corned meat 2,905; soap 1,487; paints 1,457. Construction (permits issued in WS$; 1993): residential 12,415,000; commercial, industrial, and other 19,346,000. Energy production (consumption): electricity (kW-hr; 1993) 50,000,000 (50,000,000); coal, none (n.a.); crude petroleum, none (n.a.); petroleum products (metric tons; 1993) none (42,000).
Household income and expenditure. Average household size (1981) 5.1; income per household (1972) WS$1,518 (U.S.$2,200); sources of income (1972): wages 49.4%, self-employment 22.8%, remittances, gifts, and other assistance 18.0%, land rent 8.7%, other 1.1%; expenditure (1987)[6]: food 58.8%, transportation 9.0%, housing and furnishings 5.1%, fuel and lighting 5.0%, clothing 4.2%, other goods and services 1.9%, other 16.0%.

Public debt (external, outstanding; 1993): U.S.$139,200,000.
Gross national product (at current market prices; 1993): U.S.$160,000,000 (U.S.$980 per capita).

Structure of gross domestic product and labour force

	1993 in value WS$'000	1993 % of total value	1986 labour force	1986 % of labour force
Agriculture	133,400	42.9	29,023	63.6
Mining	...	... }	1,587	3.5
Manufacturing	37,400	12.0 }		
Construction	9,700	3.1	62	0.1
Public utilities	19,800	6.4	855	1.9
Transp. and commun.	9,100	2.9	1,491	3.3
Trade	25,800	8.3	1,710	3.7
Finance	...	...	842	1.8
Pub. admin., defense	44,800	14.4 }	9,436	20.7
Services	30,900	9.9 }		
Other	...	...	629	1.4
TOTAL	310,900	100.0[7]	45,635	100.0

Population economically active (1994): total 47,207; activity rate of total population 28.7% (participation rates: ages 15–64 [1981] 48.6%; female [1986] 18.8%).

Price and earnings indexes (1990 = 100)

	1988	1989	1990	1991	1992	1993	1994
Consumer price index	81.5	86.8	100.0	98.2	107.0	108.9	128.9
Earnings index	...	...	...	...	...	...	...

Tourism: receipts from visitors (1993) U.S.$21,000,000; expenditures by nationals abroad (1992) U.S.$2,000,000.
Land use (1993): forested 47.3%; meadows and pastures 0.4%; agricultural and under permanent cultivation 43.1%; other 9.2%.

Foreign trade[8]

Balance of trade (current prices)

	1989	1990	1991	1992	1993	1994
WS$'000	–109,249	–137,300	–196,994	–238,965	–228,318	–178,638
% of total	65.4%	77.0%	83.9%	89.3%	87.4%	90.7%

Imports (1993): WS$269,079,000 (industrial supplies 32.3%, food 23.4%, machinery 18.4%, petroleum products 10.8%, consumer goods 9.9%, transportation equipment 5.1%). *Major import sources:* New Zealand 38.9%; Australia 16.4%; United States 11.5%; Japan 10.7%; Fiji 9.6%; Germany 2.0%; Singapore 1.3%.
Exports (1993): WS$16,522,000 (taro 57.6%, coconut cream 21.0%, beer 7.9%, cigarettes 4.8%). *Major export destinations:* New Zealand 51.6%; American Samoa 17.4%; United States 12.6%; Australia 12.1%.

Transport and communications

Transport. Railroads: none. Roads (1987): total length[9] 1,296 mi, 2,085 km (paved 19%). Vehicles (1993): passenger cars 962; trucks and buses 863. Merchant marine (1992): vessels (100 gross tons and over) 7; total deadweight tonnage 6,501. Air transport: passengers, n.a.; cargo, n.a.; airports (1995) with scheduled flights 2.
Communications. Daily newspapers: none. Radio (1994): 75,000 receivers (1 per 2.2 persons). Television (1990): 9,000 receivers (1 per 18 persons). Telephones (main lines; 1993): 6,500 (1 per 25 persons).

Education and health

Education (1986–87)

	schools	teachers	students	student/teacher ratio
Primary (age 5–11)	164[10]	1,511[11]	40,755	27.0
Secondary (age 12–18)	38[12]	492	11,395	23.2
Voc., teacher tr.	4[10]	37	228	6.2
Higher[10]	6	25	271	10.8

Educational attainment (1981). Percentage of population age 25 and over having: some primary education 16.5%; complete primary 24.5%; some secondary 52.1%; complete secondary 3.1%; higher 2.0%; unknown 1.8%.
Literacy (1981): virtually 100%.
Health: physicians (1990) 50 (1 per 3,183 persons); hospital beds (1991) 863 (1 per 255 persons); infant mortality rate per 1,000 live births (1994) 21.0.
Food (1992): daily per capita caloric intake 2,828 (vegetable products 74%, animal products 26%); 124% of FAO recommended minimum requirement.

Military

No military forces are maintained; New Zealand is responsible for defense.

[1]According to the constitution, the current Head of State, paramount chief HH Malietoa Tanumafili II, will hold office for life. Upon his death, the monarchy will functionally cease, and future Heads of State will be elected by the Legislative Assembly. [2]Official title is O le Ao o le Malo. [3]Total includes 2 sq mi (5 sq km) of uninhabited islands. [4]The provisional total for the 1991 census is 159,862. [5]Registered only. [6]Consumer price index components. [7]Detail does not add to total given because of rounding. [8]Import figures are f.o.b. in balance of trade and c.i.f. in commodities and trading partners. [9]Total length includes 733 mi (1,180 km) of plantation roads. [10]1983. [11]Includes some secondary teachers. [12]1982.

Yemen

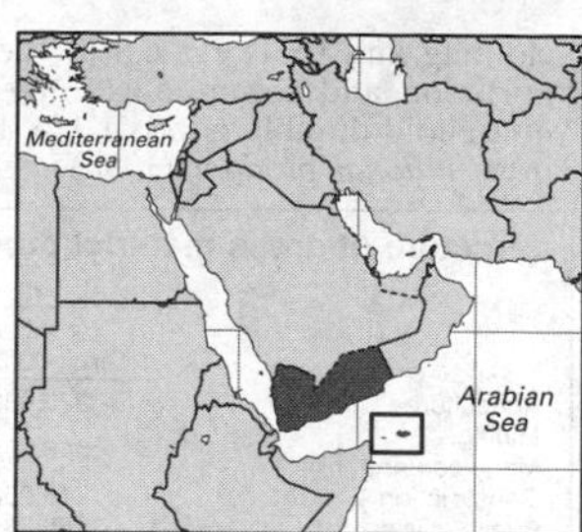

Official name: al-Jumhūrīyah al-Yamanīyah (Republic of Yemen).
Form of government: multiparty republic with one legislative house (Council of Representatives [301]).
Head of state: President[1].
Head of government: Prime Minister.
Capital: Ṣanʿāʾ.
Official language: Arabic.
Official religion: Islam.
Monetary unit: 1 Yemen rial (YRls) = 100 fils; valuation (Oct. 6, 1995): official rate (pegged to U.S.$) 1 U.S.$ = YRls 50.00, 1 £ = YRls 79.04; free market rate 1 U.S.$ = YRls 140.00, 1 £ = 221.32 YRls.

Area and population

Governorates	Capitals	area sq mi	area sq km	population 1987 estimate
North Yemen				
al-Bayḍāʾ	al-Bayḍāʾ	4,310	11,170	318,980
Dhamār	Dhamār	3,430	8,870	794,210
Ḥajjah	Ḥajjah	3,700	9,590	890,950
al-Ḥudaydah	al-Ḥudaydah	5,240	13,580	1,087,510
Ibb	Ibb	2,480	6,430	1,328,660
al-Jawf	al-Jawf	...	...	83,020
al-Maḥwīt	al-Maḥwīt	830	2,160	296,210
Maʾrib	Maʾrib	15,400	39,890	110,270
Ṣaʿdah	Ṣaʿdah	4,950	12,810	336,500
Ṣanʿāʾ	Ṣanʿāʾ	7,840	20,310	1,756,970
Taʿizz	Taʿizz	4,020	10,420	1,553,720
South Yemen				
Abyān	Zinjibār	8,297	21,489	416,000
ʿAdan	Aden	2,695	6,980	417,000
Ḥaḍramawt	al-Mukallā	59,991	155,376	704,000
Lahij	Lahij	4,928	12,700	392,000
al-Mahrah	al-Ghayḍah	25,618	66,350	87,000
Shabwah	ʿAtāq	28,536	73,908	232,000
TOTAL		182,278[2, 3]	472,099[2]	10,835,000

Demography

Population (1995): 13,058,000.
Density (1994)[4]: persons per sq mi 63.6, persons per sq km 24.6.
Urban-rural (1994): urban 25.3%; rural 74.7%.
Sex distribution (1995): male 49.39%; female 50.61%.
Age breakdown (1992): under 15, 50.6%; 15–29, 22.9%; 30–44, 13.6%; 45–59, 7.7%; 60–74, 4.0%; 75 and over, 1.2%.
Population projection: (2000) 15,164,000; (2010) 19,975,000.
Doubling time: 19 years.
Ethnic composition (1986): predominantly Arab.
Religious affiliation (1980): Muslim 99.9%, of which Sunnī 53.0%, Shīʿī 46.9%; other 0.1%.
Major cities (1986): Ṣanʿāʾ 427,150; Aden 318,000[5]; Taʿizz 178,043; al-Ḥudaydah 155,110; al-Mukallā 59,100[5].

Vital statistics

Birth rate per 1,000 population (1995): 44.9 (world avg. 25.0).
Death rate per 1,000 population (1995): 8.0 (world avg. 9.3).
Natural increase rate per 1,000 population (1995): 36.9 (world avg. 15.7).
Total fertility rate (avg. births per childbearing woman; 1995): 7.2.
Marriage rate per 1,000 population: n.a.
Life expectancy at birth (1995): male 61.6 years; female 63.5 years.
Major causes of death per 100,000 population: n.a.; however, major diseases include malaria, tuberculosis, leprosy, and intestinal infections.

National economy

Budget (1995). Revenue: YRls 87,000,000,000 (1992; excise tax 30.2%, taxes on income and profits 29.3%, import duties 29.1%). Expenditures: YRls 124,100,000,000 (1992; defense 21.9%, education 14.3%, general public services 6.3%, health 3.5%).
Production (metric tons except as noted). Agriculture, forestry, fishing (1994): sorghum 444,000, tomatoes 182,000, potatoes 181,000, wheat 171,000, grapes 146,000, watermelons 101,000, bananas 74,000, onions 57,000, papayas 55,000, millet 54,000; livestock (number of live animals) 3,715,000 sheep, 3,232,000 goats, 1,128,000 cattle, 500,000 asses, 173,000 camels, 3,000 horses, 22,000,000 chickens; roundwood (1993) 324,000 cu m; fish catch (1993) 86,811. Mining and quarrying (1993): salt 280,000; gypsum 80,000. Manufacturing (1988)[6]: flour 23,700; wheat bran 10,500; canned tomatoes 1,265; cotton lint 800; foam rubber 715; soft drinks 49,000,000 bottles; beer 5,200,000 litres; textiles 2,600,000 m; cigarettes 1,166,000,000 units. Construction: n.a. Energy production (consumption): electricity (kW-hr; 1993) 1,850,000,000 (1,850,000,000); coal, none (n.a.); crude petroleum (barrels; 1993) 87,497,000 (42,734,000); petroleum products (metric tons; 1993) 5,535,000 (2,855,000).
Population economically active (1986): total 2,043,237; activity rate of total population 19.6% (participation rates: 15–64, 41.2%; female [1992] 14.0%; unemployed [1994] *c.* 50%).

Price index (1990 = 100)

	1989	1990	1991	1992	1993	1994
Consumer price index	73.1	100.0	144.9	218.2	354.2	619.8

Gross national product (at current market prices; 1993): U.S.$6,864,000,000 (U.S.$520 per capita).

Structure of gross domestic product and labour force

	1992 in value YRls '000,000[7]	1992 % of total value	1986 labour force	1986 % of labour force
Agriculture	24,144	19.9	1,151,348	56.3
Mining	6,623	5.5	11,771	0.6
Manufacturing	11,738	9.7	94,913	4.6
Public utilities	1,694	1.4	160,952	7.9
Construction	6,098	5.0	32,852	1.6
Transp. and commun.	9,240	7.6	107,611	5.3
Trade	15,794	13.0	248,979	12.2
Finance	7,085	5.8	8,757	0.4
Pub. admin., defense	30,452	25.1	226,054	11.1
Services	1,023	0.8	...	...
Other	7,450[8]	6.1[8]	...	...
TOTAL	121,341	100.0[3]	2,043,237	100.0

Household income and expenditure. Average household size (1986) 5.6; income per household: n.a.; sources of income: n.a.; expenditure: n.a.
Tourism: receipts from visitors (1993) U.S.$45,000,000; expenditures by nationals abroad (1989) U.S.$81,000,000.
Public debt (external, outstanding; 1991): U.S.$8,198,000.
Land use (1993): forested 3.8%; meadows and pastures 30.4%; agricultural and under permanent cultivation 2.8%; other 63.0%.

Foreign trade[9]

Balance of trade

	1989	1990	1991	1992	1993	1994
YRls '000,000	−10,839	−13,797	−8,582	−18,238	−25,382	−29,389
% of total	44.5%	49.4%	37.7%	60.0%	69.0%	76.6%

Imports (1991): YRls 15,667,000,000 (food and live animals 23.8%; machinery and transport equipment 11.9%; basic manufactured goods 10.9%; chemical products 6.2%; raw materials 1.6%; beverages and tobacco 1.5%). *Major import sources:* United States 11.1%; Japan 7.4%; U.K. 6.7%; Germany 5.7%; Thailand 5.1%; France 4.7%; Saudi Arabia 4.7%.
Exports (1991): YRls 7,084,700,000 (food and live animals 73.9%, of which fish 64.9%, coffee 5.8%, fruit and vegetables 2.0%; raw materials 16.5%; petroleum products 8.2%). *Major export destinations:* Germany 27.8%; Japan 12.9%; France 10.7%; United States 9.8%; Taiwan 5.1%.

Transport and communications

Transport. Railroads: none. Roads (1993): total length 51,709 km (paved 9.5%). Vehicles (1993): passenger cars 186,172; trucks and buses 254,355. Merchant marine (1992): vessels (100 gross tons and over) 40; deadweight tonnage 13,653. Air transport (1992): passenger-km 1,124,000,000; metric ton-km cargo 114,000,000; airports (1995) with scheduled flights 11.
Communications. Daily newspapers (1992): total number 4; total circulation 236,000; circulation per 1,000 population 19. Radio (1993): 325,000 receivers (1 per 39 persons). Television (1992): 350,000 receivers (1 per 34 persons). Telephones (main lines; 1993): 162,100 (1 per 83 persons).

Education and health

Education (1990–91)[10]

	schools	teachers	students	student/ teacher ratio
Primary (age 7–12)	7,313[11]	35,350	1,291,372	36.5
Secondary (age 13–18)	942[12]	12,106	394,578	32.6
Voc., teacher tr.	73[12]	1,247	26,119	20.9
Higher[11]	1	470	23,457	49.9

Educational attainment (1986)[10]. Percentage of population age 10 and over having: no formal schooling 74.2%; reading and writing ability 19.8%; primary education 4.0%; secondary education 0.6%; higher 0.6%; not specified 0.8%. *Literacy* (1994): percentage of total population age 15 and over literate 43.2%; males literate 68.6%; females literate 23.1%.
Health (1990): physicians 2,640 (1 per 4,254 persons); hospital beds 10,485 (1 per 995 persons); infant mortality rate per 1,000 live births (1994) 83.
Food (1992): daily per capita caloric intake 2,203 (vegetable products 95%, animal products 5%); 91% of FAO recommended minimum requirement.

Military

Total active duty personnel (1995): 39,500 (army 93.7%, navy 3.8%, air force 2.5%). *Military expenditure as percentage of GNP* (1991): 15.7% (world 5.0%); per capita expenditure (1993) U.S.$25.

[1]Presidential Council assisting the President was abolished by a constitutional amendment of September 1994. [2]Former North Yemeni territorial claims with regard to alignment of the long-undemarcated eastern boundary with Saudi Arabia (which increased Yemen's claimed total area to 205,356 sq mi [531,869 sq km]) were under negotiation with Saudi Arabia in 1995. [3]Detail does not add to total given because of rounding. [4]Based on the higher total area estimate of 205,356 sq mi (531,869 sq km). [5]1984. [6]Democratic Republic of Yemen only. [7]In purchasers' value at current prices. [8]Includes import duties of 7.9 million Yemeni rials less imputed bank service charges. [9]Imports are f.o.b. [10]Yemen Arab Republic only. [11]1988–89. [12]1985–86.

Yugoslavia

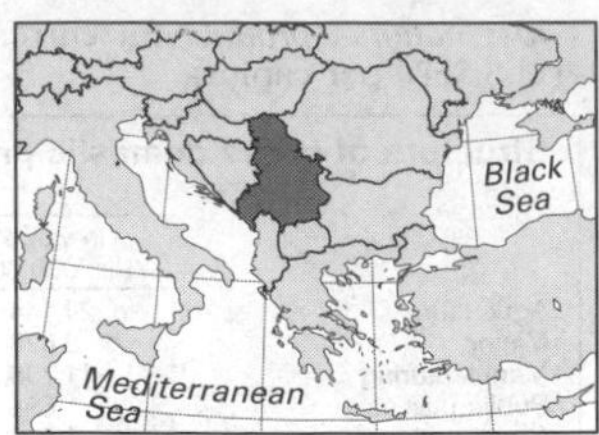

Official name: Savezna Republika Jugoslavija (Federal Republic of Yugoslavia).
Form of government: federal multiparty republic with two legislative houses (Chamber of Republics [40]; Chamber of Citizens [138]).
Chief of state: Federal President.
Head of government: Prime Minister.
Capital: Belgrade.
Official language: Serbo-Croatian.
Official religion: none.
Monetary unit[1]: 1 new dinar (second) = 100 paras; valuation (Oct. 6, 1995) 1 U.S.$ = 1.42 new dinars; 1 £ = 2.25 new dinars.

Area and population

		area		population
Republics	**Capitals**	sq mi	sq km	1994 estimate
Montenegro	Podgorica	5,333	13,812	631,000
Serbia	Belgrade	21,609	55,968	5,808,000
Autonomous provinces[2]				
Kosovo and Metohia	Priština	4,203	10,887	2,079,000
Vojvodina	Novi Sad	8,304	21,506	1,996,000
TOTAL		39,449	102,173	10,514,000

Demography

Population (1995): 10,555,000.
Density (1995): persons per sq mi 267.6, persons per sq km 103.3.
Urban-rural (1991): urban 52.0%; rural 48.0%.
Sex distribution (1991): male 49.6%; female 50.4%.
Age breakdown (1991): under 15, 22.8%; 15–29, 21.6%; 30–44, 21.7%; 45–59, 17.1%; 60–74, 12.2%; 75 and over, 3.5%; unknown, 1.1%.
Population projection: (2000) 10,406,000; (2010) 10,785,000.
Doubling time: not applicable; doubling time exceeds 100 years.
Ethnic composition (1991): Serb 62.3%; Albanian 16.6%; Montenegrin 5.0%; Yugoslav 3.3%; Hungarian 3.3%; Muslim 3.1%; Croat 1.1%; other 5.3%.
Religious affiliation (1991): most believers are affiliated with the Serbian Orthodox Church; there are also Muslim, Roman Catholic, and Protestant minorities.
Major cities (1994): Belgrade 1,168,454; Novi Sad 179,626; Niš 175,391; Kragujevac 147,305; Subotica 100,386.

Vital statistics

Birth rate per 1,000 population (1993): 13.5 (world avg. 25.0).
Death rate per 1,000 population (1993): 10.2 (world avg. 9.3).
Natural increase rate per 1,000 population (1993): 3.3 (world avg. 15.7).
Total fertility rate (avg. births per childbearing woman; 1991): 2.1.
Marriage rate per 1,000 population (1993): 5.9.
Divorce rate per 1,000 population (1993): 0.7.
Life expectancy at birth (1992): male 68.6 years; female 74.4 years.
Major causes of death per 100,000 population (1992): diseases of the circulatory system 528.3; malignant neoplasms (cancers) 154.7; accidents, violence, and poisoning 56.6; diseases of the respiratory system 47.2; diseases of the digestive system 26.4.

National economy

Budget (1993). Revenue: Din 30,353,000,000[3] (social security tax 50.9%, turnover tax 20.9%, income tax 9.7%). Expenditure[4]: Din 30,353,000,000[3] (social security 50.9%, current transfers 46.6%).
Land use (1992): forested 26.4%; meadows and pastures 19.6%; agricultural and under permanent cultivation 37.7%; other 16.3%.
Production (metric tons except as noted). Agriculture, forestry, fishing (1994): corn (maize) 4,676,000, wheat 3,249,000, potatoes 763,000, grapes 458,000, plums 436,000; livestock (number of live animals) 4,192,000 pigs, 2,672,000 sheep, 1,950,000 cattle, 25,590,000 poultry; roundwood (1993) 1,755,000 cu m; fish catch (1994) 6,465. Mining and quarrying (1994): copper ore 17,935,000; lead-zinc ore 272,000; magnesite 68,000; salt 32,000; asbestos ore 7,000; aluminum and ingots 6,800; refined silver 18,300 kg. Manufacturing (1994): wheat flour 773,000; nitric acid 156,000; crude steel 137,000; electrolytic copper 72,200; canned fruit 60,000; sulfuric acid 24,000; rolled copper 13,500; medicines 12,000; rolled aluminum 11,600; canned meat 10,000; cotton yarn 10,000; welded pipes 7,000; linoleum flooring 5,000; refined lead 4,500; knitted clothing 3,000; woolen fabrics 14,585,000 sq m; parquet flooring 635,000 cu m; liquor 25,359,000 hectolitres; hosiery 24,248,000 pairs; leather footwear 8,796,000 pairs; furniture 822,000 units; kitchen ranges 94,000 units; refrigerators 47,000 units; television receivers 40,000 units; bicycles 31,000 units; gasoline engines 21,000 units; automobiles 8,000 units; tractors 5,000 units; telephones 3,000 units; trucks 696 units; radios 301 units; railway-goods cars 63 units. Construction (residential units constructed; 1993): 20,013. Energy production (consumption): electricity (kW-hr; 1993) 34,156,000,000 (34,556,000,000); coal (metric tons; 1993) 37,433,000 (37,493,000); crude petroleum (barrels; 1993) 8,516,000,000 (12,225,000); petroleum products (metric tons; 1993) 888,000 (988,000); natural gas (cu m; 1993) 919,000,000 (1,946,000,000).
Household income and expenditure. Average household size (1993) 3.9; income per household (1992) Din 1,155,094[3] (U.S.$1,540); sources of income (1993): wages and salaries 47.8%, self-employment 12.7%, transfer payments 9.0%, other 30.5%; expenditure (1993): food 54.3%, beverages and tobacco 6.9%, clothing and footwear 6.8%, fuel and light 5.3%, health care 5.0%, transportation and communications 4.0%, education and entertainment 1.9%, household durable goods 1.1%, housing 1.0%.
Gross national product (1990)[5]: U.S.$31,867,000,000 (U.S.$3,093 per capita).

Structure of gross material product and labour force

	1992		1994	
	in value Din '000,000[3]	% of total value	labour force	% of labour force
Agriculture	1,220,080	19.5	116,000	3.7
Mining Manufacturing	2,548,855	40.7	891,000	28.4
Construction	443,988	7.1	148,000	4.7
Public utilities	65,739	1.0	53,000	1.7
Transp. and commun.	339,443	5.4	146,000	4.7
Trade	1,414,012	22.5	304,000	9.7
Finance	235,714	3.8	81,000	2.6
Pub. admin., defense			90,000	2.9
Services			342,000	10.9
Other			961,000[6]	30.7[6]
TOTAL	6,267,831	100.0	3,132,000	100.0

Population economically active (1994): total 3,132,000; activity rate 29.8% (participation rates: ages 15–64, 61.9%; female [1992] 45.3%; unemployed [1993] 23.0%).

Price and earnings indexes (1990 = 100)

	1987	1988	1989	1990[3]	1991[3]	1992[3]	1993
Consumer price index	0.2	0.9	13	100	324	29,800	...
Monthly earnings index[7]	0.4	1	19	100	195	295	412

Tourism (1993): receipts from visitors U.S.$23,000,000; expenditures, n.a.

Foreign trade

Balance of trade (current prices)

	1987	1988	1989	1990	1991	1992
Din '000,000[3]	−1,431	−1,027	−1,716	−2,647	−1,356	−2,105
% of total	8.9%	6.3%	9.3%	12.2%	8.0%	20.8%

Imports (1992): Din 6,119,000,000[3] (1991; machinery and transport equipment 22.7%, of which road vehicles 6.8%; mineral fuels and lubricants 19.0%; chemicals 13.7%; manufactured goods 10.4%, of which textiles 3.2%; food and live animals 8.4%, of which beverages 0.8%). *Major import sources* (1991): Germany 20.2%; former U.S.S.R. 12.6%; Italy 10.6%; U.S. 4.1%.
Exports (1992): Din 4,014,000,000[3] (1991; manufactured goods 49.9%, of which clothing 14.2%, iron and steel 5.4%, textile products 4.3%; machinery and transport equipment 19.6%; food and live animals 11.8%, of which fruits and vegetables 3.7%; chemicals 9.1%). *Major export destinations* (1991): Germany 23.1%; former U.S.S.R. 17.8%; Italy 14.0%; U.S. 4.4%.

Transport and communications

Transport. Railroads (1994): length (1993) 2,460 mi, 3,960 km; passenger-mi 1,570,000,000; passenger-km 2,525,000,000; short ton-mi cargo 950,000,000, metric ton-km cargo 1,387,000,000. Roads (1992): total length 29,771 mi, 47,912 km (paved 59%). Vehicles (1993): passenger cars 58,873; trucks and buses 6,435. Merchant marine (1992): fishing vessels 12. Air transport (1994): passenger-mi 93,000,000, passenger-km 150,000,000; short ton-mi cargo 92,000,000, metric ton-km cargo 134,000,000; airports (1995) 5.
Communications. Daily newspapers (1990)[5]: total number 12; total circulation 1,006,000; circulation per 1,000 population 98. Radio (1993): 2,692,000 receivers (1 per 3.9 persons). Television (1989): 1,642,522 receivers (1 per 4.8 persons). Telephones (main lines; 1993): 1,922,600 (1 per 5.5 persons).

Education and health

Education (1993–94)

	schools	teachers	students	student/ teacher ratio
Primary (age 7–14)	4,421	51,801	922,939	17.8
Secondary (age 15–18)	538	25,596	348,132	13.6
Higher	144	11,513[8]	141,587[8]	12.3

Educational attainment (1981)[5]. Percentage of population age 15 and over having: less than full primary education 44.6%; primary 24.4%; secondary 24.7%; postsecondary and higher 5.7%. *Literacy* (1981)[5]: total population age 10 and over literate 7,411,500 (89.2%); males literate 4,236,900 (95.4%; females literate 3,174,600 (83.2%).
Health (1993): physicians 24,968 (1 per 420 persons); hospital beds 57,307 (1 per 183 persons); infant mortality rate per 1,000 live births 21.9.
Food (1990)[5]: daily per capita caloric intake 3,545 (1988–90; vegetable products 93%, animal products 7%); 140% of FAO recommended minimum.

Military

Total active duty personnel (1995): 126,500 (army 71.2%, air force 22.9%, navy 5.9%). *Military expenditure as percentage of government expenditure:* 76.6%.

[1]Yugoslavia experienced extreme hyperinflation between early 1993 and January 1994. The new dinar (second), or "super dinar," introduced on Jan. 24, 1994, was pegged to the German Mark at a rate of one-to-one and equaled 13,000,000,000,000,000,000 new dinars. The new dinar had been introduced Jan. 1, 1990, at the rate of 1 new dinar = 10,000 (old) dinars. Inflation was close to zero between January 1994 and September 1994. [2]The autonomous provinces are administratively part of the Republic of Serbia. [3]In new dinars before extreme hyperinflation. [4]External analysts estimate defense expenditure at 76.7% of government expenditure. [5]Data refer to Yugoslavia as constituted prior to 1991. [6]Includes 236,000 workers in the private sector. [7]Based on worker nominal net personal income. [8]Number of teachers and students is reduced because of a boycott of Serbian schools by Albanians.

Zaire

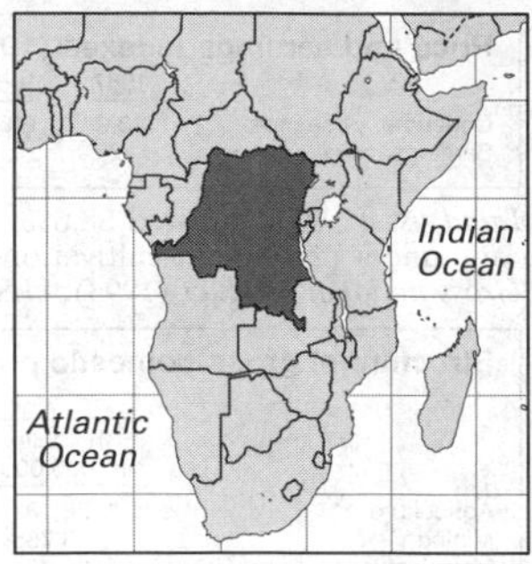

Official name: République du Zaïre (Republic of Zaire).
Form of government: Transitional regime with one legislative body (High Council of the Republic–Parliament of Transition [738])[1].
Chief of state: President[1].
Head of government: Prime Minister[1].
Capital: Kinshasa.
Official language: French.
Official religion: none.
Monetary unit: new zaïre (NZ)[2]; valuation (Oct. 6, 1995) 1 U.S.$ = NZ 5,422; 1 £ = NZ 8,572.

Area and population		area		population
		sq mi	sq km	1994 estimate
Regions	**Capitals**			
Bandundu	Bandundu	114,154	295,658	4,907,000
Bas-Zaïre	Matadi	20,819	53,920	2,578,000
Equateur	Mbandaka	155,712	403,292	4,789,000
Haute-Zaïre	Kisangani	194,302	503,239	5,432,000
Kasai-Occidental	Kananga	59,746	154,742	3,117,000
Kasai-Oriental	Mbuji-Mayi	65,754	170,302	3,778,000
Kinshasa	—	3,848	9,965	4,655,000
Maniema	Kindu	51,062	132,250	1,048,000[3]
Nord-Kivu	Goma	22,967	59,483	3,546,000[3]
Shaba	Lubumbashi	191,845	496,877	5,602,000
Sud-Kivu	Bukavu	25,147	65,130	3,093,000[3]
TOTAL		905,354[4]	2,344,858	42,545,000[3]

Demography

Population (1995): 43,901,000.
Density (1995): persons per sq mi 48.5, persons per sq km 18.7.
Urban-rural (1985): urban 39.5%; rural 60.5%.
Sex distribution (1995): male 49.41%; female 50.59%.
Age breakdown (1995): under 15, 47.3%; 15–29, 25.9%; 30–44, 14.1%; 45–59, 8.1%; 60–74, 3.8%; 75 and over, 0.8%.
Population projection: (2000) 51,136,000; (2010) 68,876,000.
Doubling time: 22 years.
Ethnic composition (1983): Luba 18.0%; Kongo 16.1%; Mongo 13.5%; Rwanda 10.3%; Azande 6.1%; Bangi and Ngale 5.8%; Rundi 3.8%; Teke 2.7%; Boa 2.3%; Chokwe 1.8%; Lugbara 1.6%; Banda 1.4%; other 16.6%.
Religious affiliation (1980): Roman Catholic 48.4%; Protestant 29.0%; indigenous Christian 17.1%; traditional beliefs 3.4%; Muslim 1.4%; other 0.7%.
Major cities (1994): Kinshasa 4,655,313; Lubumbashi 851,381; Mbuji-Mayi 806,475; Kisangani 417,517; Kananga 393,030.

Vital statistics

Birth rate per 1,000 population (1990–95): 47.5 (world avg. 25.0).
Death rate per 1,000 population (1990–95): 14.5 (world avg. 9.3).
Natural increase rate per 1,000 population (1990–95): 33.0 (world avg. 15.7).
Total fertility rate (avg. births per childbearing woman; 1990–95): 6.7.
Marriage rate per 1,000 population: n.a.
Divorce rate per 1,000 population: n.a.
Life expectancy at birth (1990–95): male 50.4 years; female 53.7 years.
Major causes of death per 100,000 population: n.a.; however, major causes in the early 1990s included malaria, measles, diarrhea, acute respiratory infections, and AIDS; malnutrition, parasitic diseases, and influenza were major causes of morbidity.

National economy

Budget (1993). Revenue: NZ 1,104,000,000[2] (current revenue 83.1%, of which external trade taxes 32.6%, excise taxes 22.2%, corporate taxes 20.2%; nontax revenues 16.9%). Expenditures: NZ 4,689,000,000[2] (general administration 54.5%, of which defense 26.8%, economic affairs 5.9%, roads and highways 5.5%).
Public debt (external, outstanding; 1993): U.S.$8,769,000,000.
Tourism (1993): receipts U.S.$6,000,000; expenditures U.S.$16,000,000.
Production (metric tons except as noted). Agriculture, forestry, fishing (1994): cassava 19,600,000, plantains 2,300,000, sugarcane 1,350,000, corn (maize) 1,250,000, peanuts (groundnuts) 550,000, rice 450,000, bananas 406,000, sweet potatoes 386,000, yams 322,000, mangoes 214,000, papayas 211,000, palm oil 181,000, oranges 157,000, pineapples 146,000, dry beans 124,000, coffee 88,000, seed cotton 77,000, palm kernels 72,000, natural rubber 9,000; livestock (number of live animals) 4,317,000 goats, 1,696,000 cattle, 1,185,000 pigs, 1,012,000 sheep, 37,000,000 chickens; roundwood (1993) 44,532,000 cu m; fish catch (1993) 147,250. Mining and quarrying (1994): copper (metal content) 33,725; cobalt (metal content) 3,631; zinc (metal content) 2,515; gold 780 kg; diamonds 16,252,000 carats. Manufacturing (1990): cement 154,400[5], sulfuric acid 164,000; sugar 70,000; soap 47,109; iron and steel products 5,875; printed fabrics 44,370,000 sq m; cigarettes 5,236,000,000 units; tires 102,000 units; beer 4,590,000 hectolitres; leather shoes 2,954,000 pairs. Construction (1985): residential 20,000 sq m; nonresidential 39,000 sq m. Energy production (consumption): electricity (kW-hr; 1993) 6,189,000,000 (5,996,000,000); coal (metric tons; 1993) 92,000 (134,000); crude petroleum (barrels; 1994) 8,972,000 ([1993] 2,770,000); petroleum products (metric tons; 1993) 343,000 (1,012,000); natural gas, none (none).
Household income and expenditure. Average household size (1982) 6.0; average annual income per household Z 1,200 (U.S.$209); sources of income: n.a.; expenditure (1985): food 61.7%, housing and energy 11.5%, clothing and footwear 9.7%, transportation 5.9%, furniture and utensils 4.9%.
Gross national product (1991): U.S.$8,123,000,000 (U.S.$220 per capita).

Structure of gross domestic product and labour force	1991			
	in value Z '000,000[2]	% of total value	labour force	% of labour force
Agriculture	197,903	31.4	9,021,000	65.1
Mining	152,327	24.2		
Manufacturing	8,636	1.4		
Construction	34,874	5.5	2,200,000	15.9
Public utilities	394	0.1		
Transp. and commun.	5,047	0.8		
Trade	110,356	17.5		
Finance	18,316	2.9		
Pub. admin., defense	60,830	9.7	2,627,000	19.0
Services	42,019	6.7		
Other	−1,328	−0.2		
TOTAL	629,374	100.0	13,848,000	100.0

Population economically active (1991): total 13,848,000; activity rate 35.9% (participation rates [1987]: over age 10, 57.4%; female 40.8%; unemployed, n.a.).

Price and earnings indexes (1990 = 1)	1989	1990	1991	1992	1993	1994
Consumer price index	0.55	1	23	953	19,897	477,800,000
Earnings index	...	...	...	...	...	...

Land use (1993): forested 76.7%; meadows and pastures 6.6%; agricultural and under permanent cultivation 3.5%; other 13.2%.

Foreign trade

Balance of trade (current prices)	1989	1990	1991	1992	1993	1994
U.S.$'000,000	+521	+234	+217	+64	+47	+90
% of total	26.2%	13.3%	15.0%	0.1%	0.0%	13.1%

Imports (1990): NZ 368,800 (machinery and transport equipment 31.7%, basic manufactures 21.1%, food and live animals 19.6%, chemicals 10.2%, mineral fuels 7.5%). *Major import sources* (1991): Belgium-Luxembourg 21.2%; France 12.4%; Germany 11.6%; China 7.0%; U.S. 6.8%; The Netherlands 4.9%; Italy 4.5%.
Exports (1990): NZ 512,400 (copper 47.6%, diamonds 11.4%, crude petroleum 10.8%, coffee 5.7%). *Major export destinations* (1991): Belgium-Luxembourg 44.7%; U.S. 18.3%; Germany 8.4%; Italy 5.8%; Japan 5.5%; France 2.6%; Canada 2.2%.

Transport and communications

Transport. Railroads (1991)[6]: length 3,162 mi, 5,088 km; passenger-mi 360,000,000, passenger-km 580,000,000; short ton-mi cargo 1,258,000,000, metric ton-km cargo 1,836,000,000. Roads (1991): total length 91,200 mi, 146,800 km (paved 2%). Vehicles (1992): passenger cars 105,000; trucks and buses 95,000. Merchant marine (1992): vessels (100 gross tons and over) 27; total deadweight tonnage 30,692. Air transport (1991)[7]: passenger-mi 89,627,000, passenger-km 144,242,000; short ton-mi cargo 14,415,000, metric ton-km cargo 21,046,000; airports (1995) with scheduled flights 12.
Communications. Daily newspapers (1992): total number 9; total circulation 112,000; circulation per 1,000 population 2.7. Radio (1994): 3,480,000 receivers (1 per 13 persons). Television (1994): 22,000 receivers (1 per 1,990 persons). Telephones (main lines; 1993): 36,000 (1 per 1,140 persons).

Education and health

Education (1993)	schools	teachers	students	student/ teacher ratio
Primary (age 6–11)	12,987	112,041	4,939,297	44.1
Secondary (age 12–17)	4,276[8]	59,325[8]	640,298	22.6[8]
Voc., teacher tr.	[8]	[8]	701,148	[8]
Higher[9]	...	3,873	61,422	15.9

Educational attainment: n.a. *Literacy* (1995): percentage of total population age 15 and over literate 77.3%; males literate 86.6%; females literate 67.7%.
Health: physicians (1990) 2,469 (1 per 15,584 persons); hospital beds (1986) 68,508 (1 per 487 persons); infant mortality rate per 1,000 live births (1990–95) 93.
Food (1992): daily per capita caloric intake 2,060 (vegetable products 97%, animal products 3%); 89% of FAO recommended minimum requirement.

Military

Total active duty personnel (1995): 28,100 (army 89.0%, navy 4.6%, air force 6.4%). *Military expenditure as percentage of GNP* (1988): 2.8% (world 4.9%); per capita expenditure U.S.$8.

[1]Transitional government was established April 9, 1994, according to the terms of the Transitional Constitutional Act; the term of the transition was extended by the Zairian Supreme Court beyond its original date of July 9, 1995, to one year from July 10, 1995. [2]The new zaïre (NZ) replaced the (old) zaïre (Z) at a rate of 3,000,000 (old) zaïres to 1 NZ on Oct. 22, 1993. [3]Estimated to account for division of former Kivu province. [4]Detail does not add to total given because of rounding. [5]1994. [6]Traffic statistics are for services operated by the Zaire National Railways (SNCZ), which controls more than 90% of the country's total rail facility. [7]Air Zaire only; declared bankrupt 1995. [8]Secondary includes Voc., teacher tr. [9]1989.

Zambia

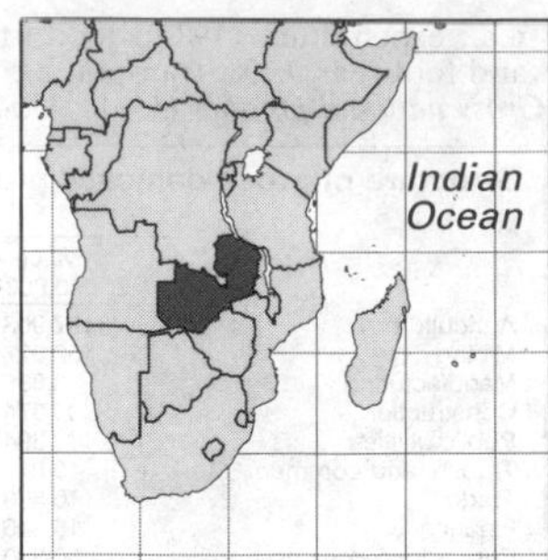

Official name: Republic of Zambia.
Form of government: multiparty republic with one legislative house (National Assembly [151[1]]).
Head of state and government: President.
Capital: Lusaka.
Official language: English.
Official religion: none.
Monetary unit: 1 Zambian kwacha (K) = 100 ngwee; valuation (Oct. 6, 1995) 1 U.S.$ = K 941; 1 £ = K 1,489.

Area and population

		area		population
Provinces	**Capitals**	sq mi	sq km	1990 census
Central	Kabwe	36,446	94,395	725,611
Copperbelt	Ndola	12,096	31,328	1,579,542
Eastern	Chipata	26,682	69,106	973,818
Luapula	Mansa	19,524	50,567	526,705
Lusaka	Lusaka	8,454	21,896	1,207,980
Northern	Kasama	57,076	147,826	867,795
North-Western	Solwezi	48,582	125,827	383,146
Southern	Livingstone	32,928	85,283	946,353
Western	Mongu	48,798	126,386	607,497
TOTAL		290,586	752,614	7,818,447

Demography

Population (1995): 9,456,000.
Density (1995): persons per sq mi 32.5, persons per sq km 12.6.
Urban-rural (1993): urban 42.4%; rural 57.6%.
Sex distribution (1990): male 49.16%; female 50.84%.
Age breakdown (1990): under 15, 48.4%; 15–29, 27.2%; 30–44, 13.7%; 45–59, 7.0%; 60–74, 3.1%; 75 and over, 0.6%.
Population projection: (2000) 10,754,000; (2010) 13,657,000.
Doubling time: 19 years.
Ethnolinguistic composition (1980): Bemba peoples 36.2%; Maravi (Nyanja) peoples 17.6%; Tonga peoples 15.1%; North-Western peoples 10.1%; Barotze peoples 8.2%; Mambwe peoples 4.6%; Tumbuka peoples 4.6%; other 3.6%.
Religious affiliation (1980): Christian 72.0%, of which Protestant 34.2%, Roman Catholic 26.2%, African Christian 8.3%; traditional beliefs 27.0%; Muslim 0.3%; other 0.7%.
Major cities (1990): Lusaka 982,362; Ndola 376,311; Kitwe 348,571; Mufulira 175,025.

Vital statistics

Birth rate per 1,000 population (1990–95): 50.3 (world avg. 25.0); legitimate, n.a.; however, marriage is both early and universal, suggesting that legitimate births are a relatively high proportion of all births.
Death rate per 1,000 population (1990–95): 12.4 (world avg. 9.3).
Natural increase rate per 1,000 population (1990–95): 37.9 (world avg. 15.7).
Total fertility rate (avg. births per childbearing woman; 1993): 5.9.
Marriage rate per 1,000 population: n.a.
Divorce rate per 1,000 population: n.a.
Life expectancy at birth (1993): male 45.0 years; female 46.2 years.
Major causes of death per 100,000 population: n.a.; however, the major causes of morbidity are respiratory infections, diarrheal diseases, malaria, malnutrition, measles, AIDS, and accidents.

National economy

Budget (1993). Revenue: K 353,506,000,000 (grants 33.4%; income taxes 23.0%, of which company 11.1%, personal 9.9%; customs duties 22.1%; excise taxes 19.1%). Expenditures: K 436,456,000,000 (current expenditures 80.8%, of which debt service 41.8%, defense 5.3%; capital expenditures 19.2%).
Production (metric tons except as noted). Agriculture, forestry, fishing (1994): sugarcane 1,311,000, corn (maize) 1,021,000, cassava 580,000, fruits and vegetables 372,000 (of which onions 27,000, tomatoes 27,000, oranges 4,000), millet 63,000, sweet potatoes 57,000, wheat 43,000, sorghum 35,000, peanuts (groundnuts) 27,000, seed cotton 26,000, soybeans 25,000, sunflower seeds 10,000, tobacco 7,000; livestock (number of live animals) 3,300,000 cattle, 620,000 goats, 295,000 pigs, 69,000 sheep, 22,000,000 chickens; roundwood (1993) 13,804,000 cu m; fish catch (1993) 65,307. Mining and quarrying (1994): copper 510,606; cobalt 3,705; zinc 3,446; lead 2,002; silver 18,800 kg; gold 8,037 troy oz. Manufacturing (1993): smelter copper 435,400; refined copper 424,800; cement 376,000[2]; raw sugar 147,000; wheat flour 50,400[3]; refined zinc 7,320; refined lead 2,400; cigarettes 1,500,000,000 units[2]. Construction (value in K; 1985): buildings 151,100,000; other construction 43,200,000. Energy production (consumption): electricity (kW-hr; 1992) 7,780,000,000 (6,300,000,000); coal (metric tons; 1992) 395,000 (674,000); crude petroleum (barrels; 1992) none (3,995,000); petroleum products (metric tons; 1992) 502,000 (440,000); natural gas, none (n.a.).
Household income and expenditure. Average household size (1981) 5.8; average annual income per household (1981) K 1,041 (U.S.$908); sources of income (1981): wages and salaries 94.0%, other 6.0%; expenditure (1977): food 37.7%, housing 11.0%, clothing 8.3%, transportation 4.3%, education 2.1%, health 1.0%.
Population economically active (1993): total 2,918,000; activity rate of total population 32.7% (participation rates: ages 15–64, 60.1%[4]; female 28.2%[4]; unemployed 17.4%[5]).

Price and earnings indexes (1990 = 100)

	1987	1988	1989	1990	1991	1992	1993
Consumer price index	13.0	20.2	46.0	100.0	192.6	572.8	1,655.4
Earnings index	...	...	86.1	100.0	120.6	110.9	74.8

Land use (1993): forested 38.6%; meadows and pastures 40.4%; agricultural and under permanent cultivation 7.1%; other 13.9%.
Gross national product (1993): U.S.$3,155,000,000 (U.S.$370 per capita).

Structure of gross domestic product and labour force

	1991		1990	
	in value K '000,000	% of total value	labour force	% of labour force
Agriculture	28,132	12.9	1,872,000	68.9
Mining	33,755	15.5	56,800	2.1
Manufacturing	61,725	28.4	50,900	1.9
Construction	10,911	5.0	29,100	1.1
Public utilities	1,909	0.9	8,900	0.3
Transportation and communications	15,812	7.3	25,600	0.9
Trade	24,021	11.0	30,700	1.1
Finance	24,832	11.4	24,200	0.9
Public admin., defense } Services }	19,254	8.8	111,600	4.1
Other	−2,726[6]	−1.2[6]	506,100	18.6
TOTAL	217,625	100.0	2,716,000[7]	100.0[7]

Public debt (external, outstanding; 1993): U.S.$6,219,000,000.
Tourism (1993): receipts from visitors U.S.$44,000,000; expenditures by nationals abroad U.S.$56,000,000[8].

Foreign trade

Balance of trade (current prices)

	1988	1989	1990	1991	1992	1993
U.S.$'000,000	+502	+566	−257	+420	−85	+202
% of total	26.8%	26.8%	9.3%	21.8%	5.3%	12.6%

Imports (1993): U.S.$702,000,000 (1988; machinery and transport equipment 38.3%; basic manufactures 19.8%; chemicals 16.9%; mineral fuels, lubricants, and electricity 12.3%; food 3.8%). *Major import sources:* South Africa 43.2%; United Kingdom 10.7%; Saudi Arabia 7.3%; Zimbabwe 6.7%; Germany 4.7%; Japan 4.3%; U.A.E. 3.4%; United States 2.8%.
Exports (1993): U.S.$904,000,000 (copper 86.4%; cobalt 12.7%; zinc 0.8%; lead 0.1%). *Major export destinations:* The Netherlands 18.5%; Japan 11.6%; Germany 9.1%; Saudi Arabia 7.6%; Belgium-Luxembourg 7.3%; Pakistan 7.1%.

Transport and communications

Transport. Railroads (1993): length 791 mi, 1,273 km; passenger-mi 166,690,000[3], passenger-km 268,262,000[3]; short ton-mi cargo 735,600,000, metric ton-km cargo 1,074,000. Roads (1994): total length 23,214 mi, 37,359 km (paved 18%). Vehicles (1993): passenger cars 96,000; trucks and buses 68,000. Merchant marine: vessels (100 gross tons and over) none. Air transport (1993): passenger-mi 191,595,000, passenger-km 308,343,000; short ton-mi cargo 6,771,000, metric ton-km cargo 9,886,000; airports (1995) with scheduled flights 8.
Communications. Daily newspapers (1990): total number 2; total circulation 105,000; circulation per 1,000 population 13. Radio (1994): total number of receivers 1,660,380 (1 per 5.5 persons). Television (1994): total number of receivers 200,000 (1 per 46 persons). Telephones (main lines; 1993): 78,000 (1 per 112 persons).

Education and health

Education (1989)

	schools	teachers	students	student/ teacher ratio
Primary (age 7–13)	3,489	32,348[9]	1,446,847	44.1[9]
Secondary (age 14–18)	480	5,786[9]	161,349[9]	27.9[9]
Voc., teacher tr.	26	846	8,218	9.7
Higher	2	320	6,247	19.5

Educational attainment (1980). Percentage of population age 25 and over having: no formal schooling 54.7%; some primary education 34.4%; some secondary 10.5%; higher 0.4%. *Literacy* (1990): population age 15 and over literate 3,131,000 (72.8%); males literate 1,676,000 (80.8%); females literate 1,455,000 (65.3%).
Health: physicians (1985) 986 (1 per 6,959 persons); hospital beds (1989) 22,461 (1 per 349 persons); infant mortality rate per 1,000 live births (1990–95) 72.0.
Food (1992): daily per capita caloric intake 1,931 (vegetable products 95%, animal products 5%); 83% of FAO recommended minimum requirement.

Military

Total active duty personnel (1995): 21,600 (army 92.6%; navy, none; air force 7.4%). *Military expenditure as percentage of GNP* (1990): 2.7% (world 4.4%); per capita expenditure U.S.$10.

[1]President may appoint a maximum of 8 additional members. [2]1991. [3]1990. [4]1985. [5]1987. [6]Less imputed bank service charge. [7]Detail does not add to total given because of rounding. [8]1992. [9]1988.

Zimbabwe

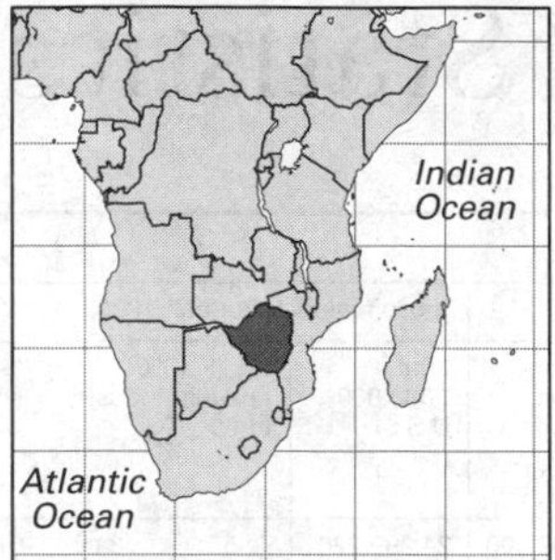

Official name: Republic of Zimbabwe.
Form of government: multiparty republic with one legislative house (House of Assembly [150[1]]).
Head of state and government: President.
Capital: Harare.
Official language: English.
Official religion: none.
Monetary unit: 1 Zimbabwe dollar (Z$) = 100 cents; valuation (Oct. 6, 1995) 1 U.S.$ = Z$8.85; 1 £ = Z$14.00.

Area and population

		area		population
Provinces	Capitals	sq mi	sq km	1992 census[2]
Bulawayo	—	185	479	620,936
Harare	—	337	872	1,478,810
Manicaland	Mutare	14,077	36,459	1,537,676
Mashonaland Central	Bindura	10,945	28,347	857,318
Mashonaland East	Marondera	12,444	32,230	1,033,336
Mashonaland West	Chinhoyi	22,178	57,441	1,116,928
Masvingo	Masvingo	21,840	56,566	1,221,845
Matabeleland North	...	28,967	75,025	640,957
Matabeleland South	Gwanda	20,916	54,172	591,747
Midlands	Gweru	18,983	49,166	1,302,214
TOTAL		150,872	390,757	10,401,767

Demography

Population (1995): 11,261,000.
Density (1995): persons per sq mi 74.6, persons per sq km 28.8.
Urban-rural (1988): urban 26.4%; rural 73.6%.
Sex distribution (1992): male 48.80%; female 51.20%.
Age breakdown (1990): under 15, 45.5%; 15–29, 28.3%; 30–44, 15.1%; 45–59, 7.2%; 60–74, 3.1%; 75 and over, 0.8%.
Population projection: (2000) 12,514,000; (2010) 15,260,000.
Doubling time: 28 years.
Ethnolinguistic composition (1982): African 97.6%, of which Shona-speaking Bantu 70.8%, Ndebele-speaking Bantu 15.8%; European 2.0%; Asian 0.1%; other 0.3%.
Religious affiliation (1980): Christian 44.8%, of which Protestant (including Anglican) 17.5%, African indigenous 13.6%, Roman Catholic 11.7%; animist 40.4%; other 14.8%.
Major cities (1992): Harare 1,184,169; Bulawayo 620,936; Chitungwiza 274,035; Mutare 131,808; Gweru 124,735.

Vital statistics

Birth rate per 1,000 population (1992): 34.5 (world avg. 25.0).
Death rate per 1,000 population (1992): 9.5 (world avg. 9.3).
Natural increase rate per 1,000 population (1992): 25.0 (world avg. 15.7).
Total fertility rate (avg. births per childbearing woman; 1992): 4.4.
Marriage rate per 1,000 population: n.a.
Divorce rate per 1,000 population: n.a.
Life expectancy at birth (1992): male 58.0 years; female 62.0 years.
Major causes of death per 100,000 population (1990): infectious and parasitic diseases 64.7; accidents and poisoning 44.4, diseases of the circulatory system 40.9; diseases of the respiratory system 39.5; malignant neoplasms (cancers) 28.4; diseases of the digestive system 12.1; diseases of the nervous system 9.4; endocrine and metabolic disorders 4.9.

National economy

Budget (1993–94). Revenue: Z$13,300,000,000 (income tax 45.6%; customs duties 16.2%; sales tax 15.3%; revenue from investments and property 6.5%; international grants 5.3%; excise tax 3.8%). Expenditures: Z$14,684,870,000 (recurrent expenditures 78.7%, of which goods and services 48.7%, transfer payments 29.9%).
Population economically active (1986–87): total 3,260,000; activity rate of total population 38.3% (participation rates: over age 15, 76.5%; female 36.6%; unemployed 7.2%[3]).

Price and earnings indexes (1990 = 100)

	1988	1989	1990	1991	1992	1993	1994
Consumer price index	75.5	85.2	100.0	123.3	175.2	223.6	273.3
Earnings index	...	...	...	...	...	...	...

Production (metric tons except as noted). Agriculture, forestry, fishing (1994): sugarcane 4,060,000, corn (maize) 2,300,000, wheat 270,000, tobacco leaves 182,000, soybeans 150,000, vegetables (including melons) 143,000, cottonseed 98,000, sorghum 90,000, peanuts (groundnuts) 70,000; livestock (number of live animals) 4,500,000 cattle, 2,530,000 goats, 550,000 sheep, 280,000 pigs, 13,000,000 chickens; roundwood (1993) 8,065,000 cu m; fish catch (1993) 21,800 metric tons. Mining and quarrying (value of production in Z$; 1994): gold 1,393,300,000; asbestos 475,800,000; coal 387,500,000; nickel 369,000,000; copper 87,800,000; chrome 54,300,000. Manufacturing (value in Z$; 1992): foodstuffs 5,123,200,000; metals and metal products 4,674,700,000; chemicals and petroleum products 2,822,800,000; beverages and tobacco 2,073,100,000; textiles 1,772,300,000; transport equipment 1,315,400,000; clothing and footwear 1,175,800,000; paper, printing, and publishing 1,020,200,000; nonmetallic mineral products 640,100,000; wood and furniture 570,100,000; other manufactured goods 230,200,000. Construction (Z$; 1994): residential 635,657,000; commercial 155,129,000; industrial 190,172,000. Energy production (consumption): electricity (kW-hr; 1993) 7,643,000,000 (9,561,000,000); coal (metric tons; 1993) 5,266,000 (5,385,000); crude petroleum, none (none); petroleum products (metric tons; 1993) none (1,023,000); natural gas, none (none).
Public debt (external, outstanding; 1993): U.S.$3,021,000,000.
Household income and expenditure. Average household size (1992) 4.8; income per household Z$1,689 (U.S.$2,628); sources of income: n.a.; expenditure (1987): food, beverages, and tobacco 30.1%, household durable goods 11.1%, clothing, footwear, and textiles 10.3%, energy 7.3%, housing 6.5%, transportation 6.1%, education 6.0%, health service 3.8%, recreation 0.6%.
Gross national product (1993): U.S.$5,756,000,000 (U.S.$540 per capita).

Structure of gross domestic product and labour force

	1994		1993	
	in value Z$'000,000	% of total value	labour force[4]	% of labour force[4]
Agriculture	4,004	10.1	324,100	26.1
Mining	2,739	6.9	47,700	3.9
Manufacturing	16,300	41.0	187,700	15.1
Construction	865	2.2	90,500	7.3
Public utilities	2,455	6.2	7,900	0.6
Transp. and commun.	2,125	5.3	49,800	4.0
Trade	4,357	10.9	95,900	7.7
Finance	1,973	5.0	20,200	1.6
Pub. admin., defense	902	2.3 }	416,500	33.7
Services	2,670	6.7 }		
Other	1,385[5]	3.4[5]	...	...
TOTAL	39,775	100.0	1,240,300	100.0

Land use (1993): forested 22.7%; meadows and pastures 12.6%; agricultural and under permanent cultivation 7.4%; other 57.3%.
Tourism (1993): receipts U.S.$103,000,000; expenditures U.S.$97,000,000.

Foreign trade

Balance of trade (current prices)

	1987	1988	1989	1990	1991	1992
Z$'000,000	629.7	896.5	...	−296.8	−1,867.4	−2,475.6
% of total	15.3%	17.8%	...	3.4%	14.4%	14.4%

Imports (1993): Z$11,798,400,000 (machinery and transport equipment 35.1%, of which transport equipment 7.9%; fuels 14.7%, of which petroleum products 14.6%; chemicals 13.9%; manufactured goods 13.5%, of which textiles 2.0%, paper and paperboard 1.5%). *Major import sources:* South Africa 27.0%; United Kingdom 10.1%; United States 8.9%; Japan 6.0%; Germany 4.9%; The Netherlands 2.6%; France 2.5%; Switzerland 1.9%; Italy 1.5%.
Exports (1993): Z$10,164,200,000 (domestic exports 84.3%, of which tobacco 24.3%; gold sales 15.1%; ferroalloys 6.4%; asbestos 3.6%; nickel metal 3.4%; cut flowers 1.7%; cotton 1.5%; corn [maize] 1.2%). *Major export destinations*[6]: South Africa 12.0%; United Kingdom 9.3%; Germany 5.0%; Botswana 4.7%; Zambia 4.3%; Mozambique 3.4%; Italy 3.1%; The Netherlands 3.0%; Switzerland 2.8%; Malaŵi 2.7%.

Transport and communications

Transport. Railroads (1991): route length 1,714 mi, 2,759 km; passenger-mi 355,057,000, passenger-km 571,410,000; short ton-mi cargo 3,695,000, metric ton-km cargo 5,394,000. Roads (1992): total length 56,593 mi, 91,078 km (paved 16%). Vehicles (1992): passenger cars 310,412; trucks and buses 30,182. Merchant marine: none. Air transport (1994)[7]: passenger-mi 514,000,000, passenger-km 828,000,000; short ton-mi cargo 27,000,000, metric ton-km cargo 40,000,000; airports (1995) with scheduled flights 5.
Communications. Daily newspapers (1994): total number 2; total circulation 195,342; circulation per 1,000 population 18. Radio (1994): 801,000 receivers (1 per 14 persons). Television (1994): 137,090 receivers (1 per 80 persons). Telephones (main lines; 1993): 128,100 (1 per 84 persons).

Education and health

Education (1993)

	schools	teachers	students	student/teacher ratio
Primary (age 7–13)	4,578	52,415	2,376,048	45.3
Secondary (age 14–19)	1,518[8]	21,403	639,559	29.9
Voc., teacher tr.[8]	25	1,479	27,431	18.5
Higher[8, 9]	28	2,414	39,406	16.3

Educational attainment (1986–87). Percentage of employed population age 15 and over having: no formal schooling 24.5%; primary 42.9%; secondary and tertiary 31.7%. *Literacy* (1995): percentage of total population age 15 and over literate 85.1%; males literate 90.4%; females literate 79.9%.
Health: physicians (1993) 1,551 (1 per 6,909 persons); hospital beds (1994) 19,866 (1 per 554 persons); infant mortality rate per 1,000 live births (1992) 61.
Food (1992): daily per capita caloric intake 1,985 (vegetable products 92%, animal products 8%); 95% of FAO recommended minimum requirement.

Military

Total active duty personnel (1995): 45,000 (army 91.1%, air force 8.9%). *Military expenditure as percentage of GNP* (1993): 4.3% (world 3.3%); per capita expenditure U.S.$21.

[1]Includes 30 nonelective seats. [2]Preliminary results. [3]Does not take into consideration seasonal unemployment of communal workers. [4]Wage-earning workers only. [5]Less imputed bank service charges. [6]Excludes gold sales and reexports. [7]Air Zimbabwe only. [8]1992. [9]Includes postsecondary vocational and teacher training at the higher level.

Comparative National Statistics

World and regional summaries

region/bloc	area and population, 1995						gross national product, 1993						labour force, 1990		
	area		population			population projection, 2010	total ('000,000 U.S.$)	% agricul-ture	% industry	% ser-vices	growth rate, 1985–93	GNP per capita (U.S.$)	total ('000)	% male	% female
	square miles	square kilometres	total	per sq mi	per sq km										
World	52,513,240	136,008,690	5,670,327,000	108.0	41.7	6,939,492,000	24,299,220	5	34	61	1.7	4,380	2,353,806	63.8	36.2
Africa	11,724,320	30,365,720	699,164,000	59.6	23.0	1,006,581,000	442,190	18	35	47	−0.6	650	242,784	65.6	34.4
Central Africa	2,553,070	6,612,400	82,467,000	32.3	12.5	126,942,000	36,380	23	37	40	−3.2	470	26,428	64.7	35.3
East Africa	2,471,320	6,400,640	220,884,000	89.4	34.5	327,312,000	44,630	34	21	45	0.2	210	85,082	58.8	41.2
North Africa	3,287,810	8,515,370	157,233,000	47.8	18.5	212,078,000	161,790	15	35	50	0.1	1,080	40,016	84.6	15.4
Southern Africa	1,033,890	2,667,770	47,628,000	46.1	17.8	65,771,000	126,460	4	42	54	−1.2	2,720	14,532	64.3	35.7
West Africa	2,378,230	6,159,540	190,952,000	80.3	31.0	274,478,000	72,930	35	30	35	0.3	370	76,726	63.8	36.2
Americas	16,311,500	42,246,630	764,837,000	46.9	18.1	913,920,000	8,344,720	3	30	67	1.0	11,140	293,723	66.5	33.5
Anglo-America[3]	8,368,970	21,675,560	292,643,000	35.0	13.5	334,305,000	6,965,320	2	29	69	1.1	24,350	135,438	58.7	41.3
Canada	3,849,670	9,970,610	29,463,000	7.7	3.0	33,946,000	574,880	2	33	65	1.7	20,670	13,360	60.2	39.8
United States	3,679,190	9,529,060	263,057,000	71.5	27.6	300,226,000	6,387,690	2	29	69	1.2	24,750	122,005	58.6	41.4
Latin America	7,942,530	20,571,070	472,194,000	59.5	23.0	579,615,000	1,379,400	9	34	57	0.4	2,980	158,285	73.1	26.9
Caribbean	90,650	234,750	35,331,000	389.8	150.5	41,424,000	76,240	8	35	57	−1.0	2,190	13,813	66.9	33.1
Central America	202,190	523,680	32,432,000	160.4	61.9	45,459,000	37,120	17	22	61	0.5	1,200	9,520	78.5	21.5
Mexico	756,070	1,958,200	91,145,000	120.6	46.5	112,891,000	324,950	8	29	63	0.9	3,750	30,487	72.9	27.1
South America	6,893,620	17,854,440	313,286,000	45.4	17.5	379,841,000	941,090	10	35	55	0.3	3,030	104,465	73.6	26.4
Andean Group	2,110,450	5,466,100	113,516,000	53.8	20.8	143,126,000	204,210	10	38	52	1.2	1,830	34,715	75.6	24.4
Brazil	3,300,170	8,547,400	155,822,000	47.2	18.2	184,157,000	471,980	11	37	52	−0.6	3,020	55,026	72.6	27.4
Other South America	1,483,000	3,840,940	43,948,000	29.6	11.4	52,558,000	264,900	7	30	63	1.5	6,210	14,724	72.4	27.6
Asia	12,325,400	31,922,550	3,449,731,000	279.9	108.1	4,251,231,000	6,734,550	7	42	51	3.6	2,010	1,464,452	64.5	35.5
Eastern Asia	4,546,940	11,776,500	1,430,491,000	314.6	121.5	1,616,318,000	5,205,890	4	44	52	4.3	3,700	775,590	57.4	42.6
China	3,696,120	9,572,900	1,206,600,000	326.5	126.0	1,371,580,000	581,110	19	48	33	6.5	490	669,693	56.7	43.3
Japan	145,870	377,800	125,362,000	859.4	331.8	130,344,000	3,926,670	2	44	54	3.6	31,450	62,202	62.1	37.9
South Korea	38,330	99,270	44,834,000	1,169.7	451.6	49,683,000	338,060	8	44	48	8.1	7,670	18,664	66.2	33.8
Other Eastern Asia	666,620	1,726,530	53,695,000	80.5	31.1	64,711,000	360,050	4	35	61	5.7	6,860	25,031	58.8	41.2
South Asia	1,971,180	5,105,300	1,253,715,000	636.0	245.6	1,640,642,000	361,170	31	26	43	2.5	300	411,136	77.4	22.6
India	1,222,240	3,165,600	935,744,000	765.6	295.6	1,189,082,000	262,810	32	27	41	3.0	290	322,944	74.8	25.2
Pakistan	339,700	879,810	140,497,000	413.6	159.7	210,104,000	53,250	25	25	50	1.5	430	33,698	87.5	12.5
Other South Asia	409,240	1,059,890	177,474,000	433.7	167.4	241,456,000	45,110	32	22	46	1.0	260	54,494	86.2	13.8
Southeast Asia	1,735,800	4,495,710	482,875,000	278.2	107.4	609,811,000	458,010	16	38	47	5.3	990	189,297	63.0	37.0
ASEAN	1,312,900	3,400,410	421,858,000	321.3	124.1	527,342,000	444,960	14	39	47	5.4	1,100	164,976	63.2	36.8
Non-ASEAN	422,900	1,095,300	61,017,000	144.3	55.7	82,469,000	13,050	61	10	29	1.1	220	24,321	62.2	37.8
Southwest Asia	4,071,470	10,545,040	282,650,000	69.4	26.8	384,460,000	709,480	14	37	49	−1.1	2,550	88,429	69.4	30.6
Central Asia	1,542,250	3,994,400	53,951,000	35.0	13.5	67,231,000	58,830	28	38	34	−3.4	1,100	20,728	54.8	45.2
Gulf Cooperation Council	1,026,850	2,659,540	25,087,000	24.4	9.4	39,572,000	223,040	4	54	42	−0.3	9,670	6,511	91.7	8.3
Iran	632,460	1,638,060	61,271,000	96.9	37.4	84,005,000	141,240	23	28	49	−0.7	2,200	15,253	82.0	18.0
Other Southwest Asia	869,910	2,253,040	142,341,000	163.6	63.2	193,652,000	286,370	15	27	58	−1.2	2,080	45,936	68.7	31.3
Europe	8,868,210	22,968,610	728,102,000	82.1	31.7	733,522,000	8,410,400	4	33	63	1.3	11,470	340,666	57.1	42.9
Eastern Europe	7,437,180	19,262,210	343,219,000	46.1	17.8	331,496,000	743,960	16	44	40	−3.9	2,120	171,080	50.6	49.4
Russia	6,592,850	17,075,400	147,168,000	22.3	8.6	134,816,000	348,410	16	45	39	−5.0	2,350	72,286	47.6	52.4
Ukraine	233,090	603,700	52,003,000	223.1	86.1	50,903,000	99,680	35	47	18	−3.9	1,710	25,401	48.0	52.0
Other Eastern Europe	611,240	1,583,110	144,048,000	235.7	91.0	145,777,000	295,870	11	41	48	−2.3	2,050	73,393	54.4	45.6
Western Europe	1,431,030	3,706,400	384,883,000	269.0	103.8	402,026,000	7,666,440	3	32	65	2.0	20,060	169,586	63.6	36.4
European Union (EU)	1,249,130	3,235,230	372,406,000	298.1	115.1	388,829,000	7,280,990	3	32	65	2.0	19,680	163,771	63.6	36.4
France	210,030	543,970	58,172,000	277.0	106.9	62,649,000	1,289,240	3	28	70	1.8	23,360	25,404	60.1	39.9
Germany	137,830	356,970	81,912,000	594.3	229.5	89,822,000	1,903,000	1	37	62	2.7	23,560	38,981	60.7	39.3
Italy	116,330	301,300	57,386,000	493.3	190.5	56,180,000	1,134,980	3	31	66	1.9	19,620	23,339	68.1	31.9
Spain	194,900	504,780	39,188,000	201.1	77.6	38,969,000	533,990	4	32	64	3.1	13,650	14,456	75.5	24.5
United Kingdom	94,250	244,110	58,586,000	621.6	240.0	61,127,000	1,042,700	2	33	65	1.3	17,970	27,766	61.4	38.6
Other EU	495,790	1,284,100	77,162,000	155.6	60.1	80,082,000	1,377,080	4	31	65	1.7	18,010	33,825	63.4	36.6
Non-EU	181,900	471,170	12,477,000	68.6	26.5	13,197,000	385,450	3	34	63	0.7	31,230	5,815	61.9	38.1
Oceania	3,283,800	8,505,080	28,493,000	8.7	3.4	34,238,000	367,360	4	29	67	1.0	13,230	12,181	63.0	37.0
Australia	2,966,150	7,682,300	18,025,000	6.1	2.3	20,778,000	309,970	3	30	67	1.1	17,510	7,963	61.9	38.1
Pacific Ocean Islands	317,650	822,780	10,468,000	33.0	12.7	13,460,000	57,390	9	26	65	0.5	5,700	4,218	65.0	35.0

[1]Refers only to the long-term external public and publicly guaranteed debt of the 137 countries that report under the World Bank's Debtor Reporting System (DRS). [2]World total contains

Africa

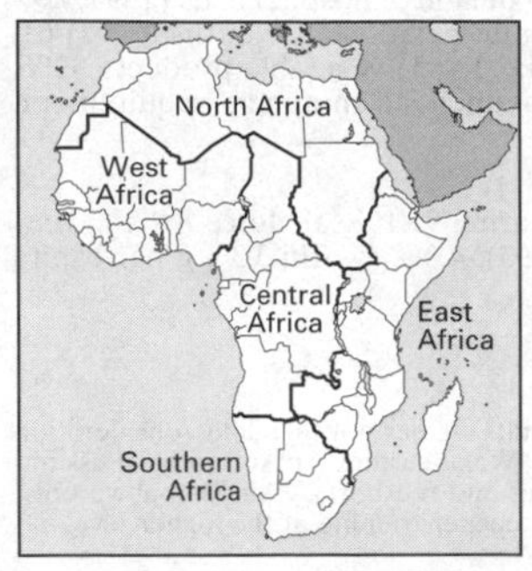

Americas

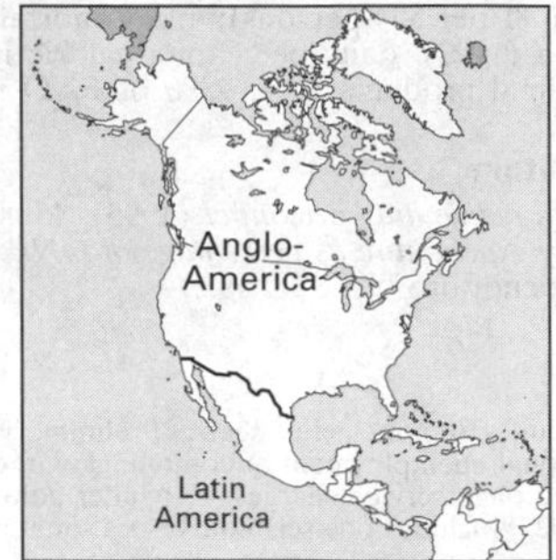

Asia

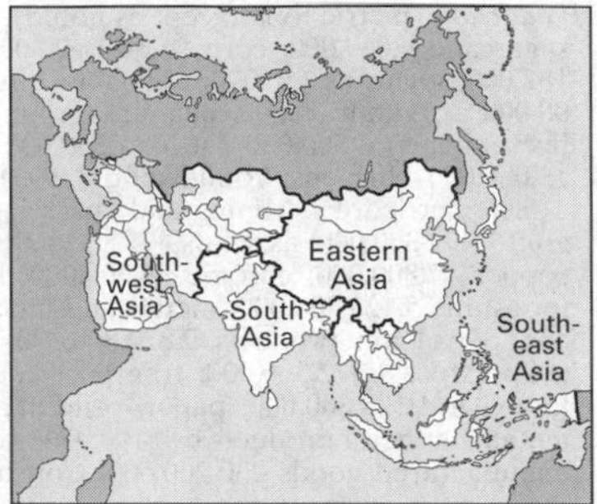

economic indicators							social indicators (latest)								region/bloc
pop. per 1,000 ha of arable land, 1993	electricity consump-tion (kW-hr per capita), 1993	trade ('000,000 U.S.$), 1994			debt ('000,000 U.S.$), 1993[1]		life expec-tancy (years)		health			food (% FAO recom-mended minimum), 1992	literacy (%)		
		imports (c.i.f.)	exports[2] (f.o.b.)	balance[2]	total	% of GNP	male	female	pop. per doctor	infant mor-tality per 1,000 births	pop. having safe water (%)		male	female	
4,110	2,216	4,318,300	4,184,600[2]	−133,700[2]	1,206,894	26.8	64.2	68.4	720	63.1	76	115	83.8	71.3	World
3,940	493	115,100	96,610	−18,490	232,264	79.5	53.4	56.5	2,820	92.8	50	97	66.7	46.6	Africa
3,530	158	5,450	4,670	−780	30,864	84.8	49.7	53.0	12,770	97.0	42	89	77.5	56.2	Central Africa
4,790	131	17,950	14,050	−3,900	41,932	100.5	47.4	50.4	12,700	108.9	40	81	67.7	47.7	East Africa
4,090	661	45,390	40,200	−5,190	97,918	72.4	63.4	66.4	980	64.0	73	123	64.9	40.2	North Africa
3,260	3,830	23,740	17,810	−5,940	1,356	23.3	61.6	67.3	1,680	50.2	56	109	81.6	79.9	Southern Africa
3,460	118	22,570	19,880	−2,690	60,194	82.6	51.3	54.2	6,820	96.1	46	94	58.2	37.1	West Africa
2,100	5,835	1,065,570	1,036,580	−28,980	336,360	25.4	68.3	74.5	520	33.5	88	126	91.2	89.9	Americas
1,240	12,812	845,830	820,500	−25,330	—	—	72.4	79.2	390	8.3	100	139	95.8	95.4	Anglo-America[3]
630	17,347	155,310	152,550	−2,760	—	—	74.7	81.7	460	6.3	100	116	96.6	96.6	Canada
1,390	12,308	689,310	666,010	−23,300	—	—	72.1	78.9	390	8.5	100	141	95.7	95.3	United States
3,720	1,532	219,730	216,080	−3,650	336,360	25.4	65.7	71.6	660	43.1	80	116	87.8	85.6	Latin America
7,580	1,324	20,040	18,640	−1,400	10,416	48.1	63.7	68.2	480	58.0	75	106	83.7	82.7	Caribbean
5,440	582	15,200	24,630	+9,430	23,460	63.2	64.3	69.5	1,190	45.1	64	107	73.6	68.4	Central America
3,800	1,486	75,430	71,670	−3,750	74,450	22.9	66.5	73.1	580	27.1	84	135	91.8	87.4	Mexico
3,400	1,664	109,070	101,140	−7,930	228,034	24.3	65.9	71.7	690	47.6	81	113	88.5	87.0	South America
5,990	1,459	45,320	40,480	−4,830	78,330	38.4	68.0	72.5	870	38.8	78	103	92.6	88.7	Andean Group
3,610	1,783	36,740	32,390	−4,350	86,650	18.4	63.0	70.4	720	60.0	87	118	83.3	83.2	Brazil
1,480	1,753	27,010	28,260	+1,250	63,054	23.9	67.8	74.3	410	30.7	67	120	96.0	95.7	Other South America
7,050	983	1,227,040	1,131,700	−95,340	441,192	21.5	64.6	67.5	980	63.7	73	113	81.1	63.8	Asia
13,760	1,534	744,370	683,280	−61,090	94,935	10.3	69.7	73.6	630	24.2	73	117	91.4	77.0	Eastern Asia
12,830	719	115,630	121,390	+5,760	70,024	12.1	69.1	72.4	630	26.0	69	116	89.9	72.7	China
30,980	7,281	274,120	245,230	−28,890	—	—	76.6	83.0	570	4.5	97	124	100.0	100.0	Japan
23,470	3,704	102,350	89,370	−12,980	24,567	7.3	68.0	76.0	860	15.0	93	140	99.3	96.7	South Korea
13,080	5,817	252,270	227,290	−24,980	344	36.5	70.1	75.8	520	17.8	99	121	95.7	91.3	Other Eastern Asia
5,800	355	45,590	44,600	−990	122,408	34.4	60.0	60.9	2,350	90.6	77	104	62.4	35.5	South Asia
5,430	397	25,530	26,730	+1,200	80,985	30.8	60.4	61.2	2,140	[illegible]	79	108	65.5	37.7	India
6,390	416	8,880	9,130	+250	20,306	38.1	62.0	64.0	2,110	83.0	68	100	50.0	24.4	Pakistan
8,180	90	11,180	8,740	−2,440	21,117	52.6	56.4	56.8	5,740	108.9	70	87	53.3	30.8	Other South Asia
7,590	467	284,110	259,400	−24,720	137,223	34.6	61.0	65.2	2,690	66.5	54	116	91.9	83.6	Southeast Asia
8,380	525	280,960	256,530	−24,430	129,901	33.8	61.0	66.1	2,550	63.2	57	116	92.6	85.0	ASEAN
4,590	60	3,150	2,870	−290	7,322	56.1	55.2	59.0	4,160	86.2	33	114	86.7	73.3	Non-ASEAN
2,640	1,994	152,970	144,420	−8,540	86,625	22.8	64.9	69.6	590	50.2	86	120	86.1	72.7	Southwest Asia
1,260	3,345	7,190	6,720	−480	2,586	4.4	64.2	71.8	290	32.9	100	...	98.8	96.2	Central Asia
6,400	4,882	64,820	65,180	+370	2,319	24.1	69.6	72.7	570	22.9	95	115	72.5	53.1	Gulf Cooperation Council
3,500	1,122	12,060	10,870	−1,190	8,880	6.3	65.0	67.0	1,600	60.0	89	119	78.4	65.8	Iran
3,380	1,372	68,900	61,650	−7,240	72,840	42.6	64.1	69.3	690	56.5	78	122	87.0	69.1	Other Southwest Asia
2,480	5,624	1,840,140	1,791,670	−48,470	195,017	23.8	68.5	76.7	290	11.5	99	133	99.0	97.5	Europe
1,600	4,029	154,120	144,970	−9,150	169,746	23.0	67.8	77.2	280	10.0	[illegible]	123	99.2	96.7	Eastern Europe
1,140	6,342	38,400	41,300	+2,900	72,769	20.9	57.7	71.1	240	18.6	100	...	99.5	96.8	Russia
1,560	4,430	11,520	10,480	−1,050	3,457	3.5	65.3	74.7	230	14.0	100	...	99.5	97.4	Ukraine
2,770	3,426	104,200	93,200	−11,000	93,520	32.1	67.1	74.8	370	16.4	97	123	98.9	96.3	Other Eastern Europe
4,900	6,349	1,686,020	1,646,690	−39,330	25,301	31.5	73.5	79.9	300	6.8	100	135	98.9	98.2	Western Europe
4,820	6,090	1,584,640	1,540,050	−44,600	25,173	32.4	73.4	79.9	300	6.9	100	136	98.8	98.1	European Union (EU)
3,160	7,126	228,320	220,350	−7,970	—	—	73.1	81.3	370	7.3	100	144	98.9	98.7	France
6,950	6,513	369,600	358,820	−10,780	—	—	72.5	79.0	310	5.8	100	126	100.0	100.0	Germany
6,320	4,588	167,700	150,340	−17,360	—	—	73.6	80.2	190	8.3	100	141	97.8	96.4	Italy
2,610	4,037	92,180	85,830	−6,360	—	—	74.6	80.5	250	7.4	100	151	97.5	94.2	Spain
9,570	5,843	226,010	220,460	−5,550	—	—	74.4	79.7	450	6.6	100	132	100.0	100.0	United Kingdom
4,580	7,225	500,840	504,260	+3,430	25,173	32.4	73.1	79.3	340	6.6	100	133	98.1	97.4	Other EU
9,380	14,278	101,380	106,650	+5,270	128	4.9	74.5	80.9	310	5.7	100	124	99.9	99.9	Non-EU
560	7,215	70,450	64,110	−6,350	2,033	28.9	70.5	76.2	520	24.7	88	122	96.1	93.9	Oceania
380	9,284	53,610	49,020	−4,580	—	—	74.5	80.8	450	5.8	100	120	99.5	99.5	Australia
3,530	3,611	16,850	15,080	−1,770	2,033	28.9	63.8	68.0	740	42.6	67	126	89.1	82.1	Pacific Ocean Islands

U.S.$63,930,000,000 undistributable by continent or region. [3]Anglo-America includes Canada, the United States, Greenland, Bermuda, and St. Pierre and Miquelon.

Europe

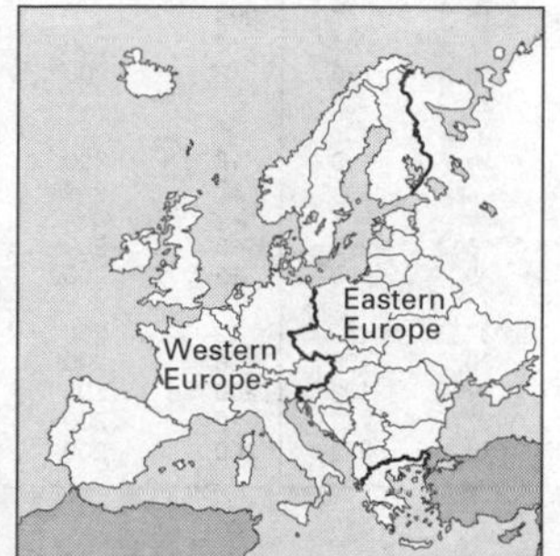

Eastern Europe

Oceania

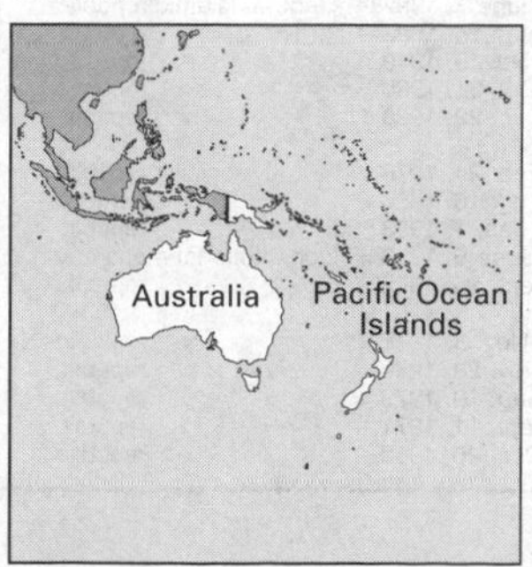

Government and international organizations

This table summarizes principal facts about the governments of the countries of the world, their branches and organs, the topmost layers of local government constituting each country's chief administrative subdivisions, and the participation of their central governments in the principal intergovernmental organizations of the world.

In this table "date of independence" may refer to a variety of circumstances. In the case of the newest countries, those that attained full independence after World War II, the date given is usually just what is implied by the heading—the date when the country, within its present borders, attained full sovereignty over both its internal and external affairs. In the case of longer established countries, the choice of a single date may be somewhat more complicated, and grounds for the use of several different dates often exist. The reader should refer to *Macropædia* and *Micropædia* articles on national histories and relevant historical acts. In cases of territorial annexation or dissolution, the date given here refers either to the final act of union of a state composed of smaller entities or to the final act of separation from a larger whole (*e.g.,* the separation of Bangladesh from Pakistan in 1971).

The date of the current, or last, constitution is in some ways a less complicated question, but governments sometimes do not, upon taking power, either adhere to existing constitutional forms or trouble to terminate the previous document and legitimize themselves by the installation of new constitutional forms. Often, however, the desire to legitimize extraconstitutional political activity by associating it with existing forms of long precedent leads to partial or incomplete modification, suspension, or abrogation of a constitution, so that the actual day-to-day conduct of government may be largely unrelated to the provisions of a constitution still theoretically in force. When a date in this column is given in italics, it refers to a document that has been suspended, abolished by extraconstitutional action, or modified extensively.

The characterizations adopted under "type of government" represent a compromise between the forms provided for by the national constitution and the more pragmatic language that a political scientist might adopt to describe these same systems. For an explanation of the application of these terms in the Britannica World Data, *see* the Glossary at page 541.

The positions denoted by the terms "chief of state" and "head of government" are usually those identified with those functions by the constitution. The duties of the chief of state may range from largely ceremonial responsibilities, with little or no authority over the day-to-day conduct of government, to complete executive authority as the effective head of government. In certain countries, an official of a political party or a revolutionary figure outside the constitutional structure may exercise the powers of both positions.

Membership in the legislative house(s) of each country as given here includes all elected or appointed members, as well as ex officio members (those who by virtue of some other office or title are members of the body), whether voting or nonvoting. The legislature of a country with a unicameral system is shown as the upper house in this table.

The number of administrative subdivisions for each country is listed down to the second level. A single country may, depending on its size, complexity, and historical antecedents, have as many as five levels of administrative subordination or it may have none at all. Each level of subordination may have several kinds of subdivisions.

Government and international organizations

country	date of independence[a]	date of current or last constitution[b]	type of government	executive branch[c]		legislative branch[d]		admin. subdivisions		seaward claims	
				chief of state	head of government	upper house (members)	lower house (members)	first-order (number)	second-order (number)	territorial (nautical miles)	fishing/economic (nautical miles)
Afghanistan	Aug. 19, 1919	[1]	republic	president	prime minister	...	...	...	...	—	—
Albania	Nov. 28, 1912	April 29, 1991[2]	republic	president	prime minister	140	—	26	*c.* 200	12	[3]
Algeria	July 5, 1962	*Feb. 23, 1989*	republic[5]	president	prime minister	200[6, 7]	—	48	1,541	12	12
American Samoa	—	July 1, 1967	territory (U.S.)	U.S. president	governor	18	21[8]	3	14	12	200
Andorra	Dec. 6, 1288	May 4, 1993	parl. coprincipality	[9]	head of the govt.	28	—	7	...	—	—
Angola	Nov. 11, 1975	Aug. 27, 1992	republic	president[10]		220	—	18	163	20	200
Antigua and Barbuda	Nov. 1, 1981	Nov. 1, 1981	constitutional monarchy	British monarch	prime minister	17	17	30	—	12[11]	200[11]
Argentina	July 9, 1816	Aug. 24, 1994[12]	federal republic	president		72	257	24	1,617	12	200
Armenia	Sept. 23, 1991	July 5, 1995[13]	republic	president	prime minister	190	—	40	...	—	—
Aruba	—	Jan. 1, 1986	overseas territory (Neth.)	Dutch monarch	[14]	21	—	...	...	12	200
Australia	Jan. 1, 1901	July 9, 1900	federal parl. state[16]	British monarch	prime minister	76	147	8	*c.* 900	12	200
Austria	Oct. 30, 1918	Oct. 1, 1920	federal republic	president	chancellor	63	183	9	99	—	—
Azerbaijan	Aug. 30, 1991	Nov. 12, 1995[13]	republic	president	prime minister	125	—	2	64	...	...
Bahamas, The	July 10, 1973	July 10, 1973	constitutional monarchy	British monarch	prime minister	16	49	—	21	3	200
Bahrain	Aug. 15, 1971	June 1973	monarchy (emirate)	emir	prime minister	30[6]	—	1	—	12	[18]
Bangladesh	March 26, 1971	Dec. 16, 1972	republic	president	prime minister	330	—	5	64	12	200
Barbados	Nov. 30, 1966	Nov. 30, 1966	constitutional monarchy	British monarch	prime minister	21	28	—	—	12	200
Belarus	Aug. 25, 1991	March 30, 1994	republic	president		260	—	6	118	—	—
Belgium	Oct. 4, 1830	May 5, 1993	fed. const. monarchy	monarch	prime minister	71	150	[19]	589	12	[18]
Belize	Sept. 21, 1981	Sept. 21, 1981	constitutional monarchy	British monarch	prime minister	9	29	6	...	12[20]	200
Benin	Aug. 1, 1960	Dec. 2, 1990	republic	president		83	—	6	77	200	200
Bermuda	—	June 8, 1968	colony (U.K.)	British monarch	[21]	11	40	11	—	12	200
Bhutan	March 24, 1910	—	[22]	king		152	—	4	18	—	—
Bolivia	Aug. 6, 1825	Feb. 2, 1967	republic	president		27	130	9	112	—	—
Bosnia and Herzegovina	March 3, 1992	Nov. 21, 1995[23]	republic[24]	president	prime minister	240[7]	—	...	...	...	...
Botswana	Sept. 30, 1966	Sept. 30, 1966	republic	president		15[6]	46	21	...	—	—
Brazil	Sept. 7, 1822	Oct. 5, 1988	federal republic	president		81	513	27	4,491	12	200
Brunei	Jan. 1, 1984	*Sept. 29, 1959*	monarchy (sultanate)	sultan		21[6]	—	4	...	12	200
Bulgaria	Oct. 5, 1908	July 12, 1991	republic	president	prime minister	240	—	9	328	12	200
Burkina Faso	Aug. 5, 1960	June 11, 1991	republic	president	prime minister	107	—	30	109	—	—
Burundi	July 1, 1962	March 13, 1992[2]	republic[5]	president[25]		81	—	15	122	—	—
Cambodia	Nov. 9, 1953	Sept. 24, 1993	constitutional monarchy	king	[26]	120	—	21	...	12	200
Cameroon	Jan. 1, 1960	June 2, 1972	republic	president	prime minister	180	—	10	58	50	[3]
Canada	July 1, 1867	April 17, 1982	federal parl. state[16]	Canadian GG[27]	prime minister	104	295	12	...	12	200
Cape Verde	July 5, 1975	Sept. 25, 1992	republic	president	prime minister	79	—	14	31	12[11]	200[11]
Central African Republic	Aug. 13, 1960	Jan. 14, 1995	republic	president	prime minister	85	—	17	66	—	—
Chad	Aug. 11, 1960	April 6, 1993[2]	republic	president	prime minister	57	—	15	53	—	—
Chile	Sept. 18, 1810	March 11, 1981	republic	president		47	120	13	51	12	200
China	1523 BC	Dec. 4, 1982	people's republic	president	premier SC	2,978	—	30	335	12	[3]
Colombia	July 20, 1810	July 5, 1991	republic	president		102	163	33	1,011	12	200
Comoros	July 6, 1975	June 7, 1992[13]	federal Islamic republic	president	prime minister	42	—	3	7	12[11]	200[11]
Congo	Aug. 15, 1960	March 15, 1992[13]	republic	president	prime minister	60	125	15	47	200	[3]
Costa Rica	Sept. 15, 1821	Nov. 9, 1949	republic	president		57	—	7	81	12	200
Côte d'Ivoire	Aug. 7, 1960	Oct. 31, 1960	republic	president	prime minister	175	—	10	50	12	200
Croatia	June 25, 1991	Dec. 22, 1990	republic	president	prime minister	68	127	21	...	...	...
Cuba	May 20, 1902	Feb. 24, 1976	socialist republic	president		589	—	15	169	12	200
Cyprus[29]	Aug. 16, 1960	Aug. 16, 1960	republic	president		80[7]	—	...	...	12	[3]
Czech Republic	Jan. 1, 1993	Jan. 1, 1993	republic	president	prime minister	[30]	200	75	...	—	—
Denmark	*c.* 800	June 5, 1953	constitutional monarchy	monarch	prime minister	179	—	16	275	3	200
Djibouti	June 27, 1977	Sept. 15, 1992	republic	president		65	—	5	9	12	200
Dominica	Nov. 3, 1978	Nov. 3, 1978	republic	president	prime minister	31	—	37	—	12	200
Dominican Republic	Feb. 27, 1844	Nov. 28, 1966	republic	president		30	120	30	136	6	200
Ecuador	May 24, 1822	Aug. 10, 1979	republic	president		77	—	21	193	200	200
Egypt	Feb. 28, 1922	Sept. 11, 1971	republic	president	prime minister	454	—	27	...	12[31]	200[31]
El Salvador	Jan. 30, 1841	Dec. 20, 1983	republic	president		84	—	14	262	200	200

Finally, in the second half of the table are listed the memberships each country maintains in the principal international intergovernmental organizations of the world. This part of the table may also be utilized to provide a complete membership list for each of these organizations as of Dec. 1, 1995.

Notes for the column headings

a. The date may also be either that of the organization of the present form of government or the inception of the present administrative structure (federation, confederation, union, etc.).
b. Constitutions whose dates are in italic type had been wholly or substantially suspended or abolished as of late 1995.
c. For abbreviations used in this column see the list on the facing page.
d. When a legislative body has been adjourned or otherwise suspended, figures in parentheses indicate the number of members in the legislative body as provided for in constitution or law.
e. Vatican City also a member.
f. States contributing funds to or receiving aid from UNICEF in 1995.
g. Palestine (Liberation Organization) also a member.

International organizations, conventions

ACP	African, Caribbean, and Pacific (Lomé IV) convention
ADB	Asian Development Bank
APEC	Asia-Pacific Economic Cooperation Council
CARICOM	Caribbean Community and Common Market
EU	The European Union
ECOWAS	Economic Community of West African States
EEC	European Economic Community
FAO	Food and Agriculture Org.
GATT (WTO)	General Agreement on Tariffs and Trade (World Trade Org. as of January 1995)
GCC	Gulf Cooperation Council
I-ADB	Inter-American Development Bank
IAEA	International Atomic Energy Agency
IBRD	International Bank for Reconstruction and Development
ICAO	International Civil Aviation Org.
ICJ	International Court of Justice
IDA	International Development Assn.
IDB	Islamic Development Bank
IFC	International Finance Corporation
ILO	International Labour Org.
IMF	International Monetary Fund
IMO	International Maritime Org.
ITU	International Telecommunication Union
LAS	League of Arab States
OAS	Organization of American States
OAU	Organization of African Unity
OPEC	Organization of Petroleum Exporting Countries
SPC	South Pacific Commission
UNCTAD	United Nations Conference on Trade and Development
UNESCO	United Nations Educational Scientific and Cultural Org.
UNICEF	United Nations Children's Fund
UNIDO	United Nations Industrial Development Org.
UPU	Universal Postal Union
WHO	World Health Org.
WIPO	World Intellectual Property Org.
WMO	World Meteorological Org.

Abbreviations used in the executive-branch column

AFPRC	Armed Forces Provisional Ruling Council
CS	Council of State
FC	Federal Council
GG	Governor-General
GPC	General People's Committee
NA	National Assembly
PC	Provisional Council
PNA	Palestine National Authority
PRC	Provisional Ruling Council
SC	State Council
SLORC	State Law and Order Restoration Council
SCS	Supreme Council of State

membership in international organizations

United Nations (date of admission)	UN organs★ and affiliated intergovernmental organizations																				Commonwealth of Nations	regional multipurpose						economic									country
	UNCTAD★[e]	UNICEF★[f]	CJ★	FAO	GATT (WTO)	IAEA[e]	IBRD	ICAO	IDA	IFC	ILO	IMF	IMO	ITU[e]	UNESCO	UNIDO	UPU[e]	WHO	WIPO[e]	WMO		EU	GCC	LAS[g]	OAS	OAU	SPC	ACP	ADB	APEC	CARICOM	ECOWAS	EEC	I-ADB	IDB[g]	OPEC	
1946	●	●	●	●		●	●	●	●	●	●	●		●	●	●	●	●		●									●						●		Afghanistan
1955	●	●	●	●	●[4]	●	●	●	●	●	●	●	●	●	●	●	●	●	●	●															●		Albania
1962	●	●	●	●	●	●	●	●	●	●	●	●	●	●	●	●	●	●	●	●				●		●									●	●	Algeria
—																	●										●										American Samoa
1993	●													●	●				●																		Andorra
1976	●	●	●	●	●		●	●	●	●	●	●	●	●	●	●	●	●	●	●						●		●									Angola
1981	●	●	●	●	●		●	●		●	●	●	●	●	●		●	●		●	●				●			●			●						Antigua and Barbuda
1945	●	●	●	●	●	●	●	●	●	●	●	●	●	●	●	●	●	●	●	●					●									●			Argentina
1992	●	●		●	●[4]		●	●	●		●	●		●	●	●	●	●	●	●																	Armenia
—															●[15]		●																				Aruba
1945	●	●	●	●	●	●	●	●	●	●	●	●	●	●	●	●	●	●	●	●	●						●		●	●							Australia
1955	●	●	●	●	●	●	●	●	●	●	●	●	●	●	●	●	●	●	●	●		●							●				●	●			Austria
1992	●	●			●[4]		●	●			●	●		●	●	●	●	●																	●		Azerbaijan
1973	●	●	●	●	●[17]		●	●		●	●	●	●	●	●	●	●	●	●	●	●				●			●			●			●			Bahamas, The
1971	●	●	●	●	●		●	●		●	●	●	●	●	●	●	●	●		●			●	●											●		Bahrain
1974	●	●	●	●	●	●	●	●	●	●	●	●	●	●	●	●	●	●	●	●	●								●						●		Bangladesh
1966	●	●	●	●	●		●	●		●	●	●	●	●	●	●	●	●	●	●	●				●			●			●			●			Barbados
1945	●				●[4]	●	●	●		●	●	●		●	●	●	●	●	●	●																	Belarus
1945	●	●	●	●	●	●	●	●	●	●	●	●	●	●	●	●	●	●	●	●		●							●				●	●			Belgium
1981	●	●	●	●	●		●	●	●	●	●	●	●	●	●	●	●	●		●	●				●			●			●			●			Belize
1960	●	●	●	●	●		●	●	●	●	●	●	●	●	●	●	●	●	●	●						●		●				●			●		Benin
—																	●																				Bermuda
1971	●	●	●	●			●	●	●			●		●	●	●	●	●	●										●								Bhutan
1945	●	●	●	●	●	●	●	●	●	●	●	●	●	●	●	●	●	●	●	●					●									●			Bolivia
1992	●			●			●[17]	●			●		●	●	●	●	●	●	●																		Bosnia and Herzegovina
1966	●	●	●	●	●		●	●	●	●	●	●		●	●	●	●	●		●	●					●		●									Botswana
1945	●	●	●	●	●	●	●	●	●	●	●	●	●	●	●	●	●	●	●	●					●									●			Brazil
1984	●	●	●		●			●					●	●			●	●	●	●	●									●					●		Brunei
1955	●	●	●	●	●[4]	●	●	●	●	●	●	●	●	●	●	●	●	●	●	●																	Bulgaria
1960	●	●	●	●	●		●	●	●	●	●	●		●	●	●	●	●	●	●						●		●				●			●		Burkina Faso
1962	●	●	●	●	●		●	●	●	●	●	●		●	●	●	●	●	●	●						●		●									Burundi
1955	●	●	●	●	●[17]	●	●	●	●		●	●	●	●	●		●	●		●									●								Cambodia
1960	●	●	●	●	●	●	●	●	●	●	●	●	●	●	●	●	●	●	●	●	●					●		●							●		Cameroon
1945	●	●	●	●	●	●	●	●	●	●	●	●	●	●	●	●	●	●	●	●	●				●				●	●				●			Canada
1975	●	●	●	●	●[17]		●	●	●	●	●	●	●	●	●	●	●	●		●						●		●				●					Cape Verde
1960	●	●	●	●	●		●	●	●	●	●	●		●	●	●	●	●	●	●						●		●									Central African Republic
1960	●	●	●	●	●		●	●	●		●	●		●	●	●	●	●	●	●						●		●							●		Chad
1945	●	●	●	●	●	●	●	●	●	●	●	●	●	●	●	●	●	●	●	●					●					●				●			Chile
1945	●	●	●	●		●	●	●	●	●	●	●	●	●	●	●	●	●	●	●									●	●							China
1945	●	●	●	●	●	●	●	●	●	●	●	●	●	●	●	●	●	●	●	●					●									●			Colombia
1975	●	●	●	●	●[17]		●	●	●		●	●	●	●	●	●	●	●		●				●		●		●							●		Comoros
1960	●	●	●	●	●		●	●	●	●	●	●	●	●	●	●	●	●	●	●						●		●									Congo
1945	●	●	●	●	●	●	●	●	●	●	●	●	●	●	●	●	●	●	●	●					●									●			Costa Rica
1960	●	●	●	●	●	●	●	●	●	●	●	●	●	●	●	●	●	●	●	●						●		●				●					Côte d'Ivoire
1992	●	●		●	●[4]	●	●	●	●	●	●	●	●	●	●	●	●	●	●	●														●			Croatia
1945	●	●	●	●	●	●		●			●		●	●	●	●	●	●	●	●					●[28]												Cuba
1960	●	●	●	●	●	●	●	●	●	●	●	●	●	●	●	●	●	●	●	●	●												●[15]				Cyprus[29]
1993	●	●		●	●	●	●	●	●	●	●	●	●	●	●	●	●	●	●	●																	Czech Republic
1945	●	●	●	●	●	●	●	●	●	●	●	●	●	●	●	●	●	●	●	●		●							●				●	●			Denmark
1977	●	●	●	●	●[17]		●	●	●	●	●	●	●	●	●	●	●	●		●				●		●		●							●		Djibouti
1978	●	●	●	●	●		●		●	●	●	●	●		●	●	●	●		●	●				●			●			●						Dominica
1945	●	●	●	●	●	●	●	●	●	●	●	●	●	●	●	●	●	●		●					●			●			●[4]			●			Dominican Republic
1945	●	●	●	●	●[4]	●	●	●	●	●	●	●	●	●	●	●	●	●	●	●					●									●			Ecuador
1945	●	●	●	●	●	●	●	●	●	●	●	●	●	●	●	●	●	●	●	●				●		●									●		Egypt
1945	●	●	●	●	●	●	●	●	●	●	●	●	●	●	●	●	●	●	●	●					●									●			El Salvador

Government and international organizations (continued)

country	date of independence[a]	date of current or last constitution[b]	type of government	executive branch[c]: chief of state	executive branch[c]: head of government	legislative branch[d]: upper house (members)	legislative branch[d]: lower house (members)	admin. subdivisions: first-order (number)	admin. subdivisions: second-order (number)	seaward claims: territorial (nautical miles)	seaward claims: fishing/economic (nautical miles)
Equatorial Guinea	Oct. 12, 1968	Nov. 16, 1991[13]	republic[5]	president	prime minister	80	—	7	18	12	200
Eritrea	May 24, 1993	May 1993[32]	republic[5]	——president——		150[33]	—	6[33]	...	...	...
Estonia	Aug. 20, 1991	July 3, 1992	republic	president	prime minister	101	—	15	198	12	...
Ethiopia	c. 1000 BC	Aug. 22, 1995[34]	republic	president	prime minister	117	548	10	...	—	—
Faroe Islands	—	April 1, 1948	part of Danish realm	Danish monarch	[35]	32	—	7	50	3	200
Fiji	Oct. 10, 1970	July 25, 1990	republic	president	prime minister	34	70	4	15	12[11]	200[11]
Finland	Dec. 6, 1917	July 17, 1919	republic	president	prime minister	200	—	12	455	4	12
France	August 843	Oct. 4, 1958	republic	president	prime minister	321	577	22	96	12	200
French Guiana	—	Feb. 28, 1983	overseas dept. (Fr.)	French president	[36]	19	31	2	21	12	200
French Polynesia	—	Sept. 6, 1984	overseas territory (Fr.)	French president	[37]	41	—	5	48	12	200
Gabon	Aug. 17, 1960	March 26, 1991	republic	president	prime minister	120	—	9	37	12	200
Gambia, The	Feb. 18, 1965	*April 24, 1970*	republic	——chairman AFPRC——		—	—	7	35	12	200
Gaza Strip	—	May 4, 1994[38]	interim authority	——chairman PNA——		—	—	—	—	...	...
Georgia	April 9, 1991	Aug. 24, 1995[39]	republic	president	prime minister	235	—	13	...	...	...
Germany	May 5, 1955	May 23, 1949	federal republic	president	chancellor	68	672	16	29	[40]	200
Ghana	March 6, 1957	Jan. 7, 1993	republic	——president——		200	—	110	...	12	200
Gibraltar	—	May 23, 1969	colony (U.K.)	British monarch	governor	18	—	—	—	...	...
Greece	Feb. 3, 1830	June 11, 1975	republic	president	prime minister	300	—	13	53	6/10	[3]
Greenland	—	May 1, 1979	part of Danish realm	Danish monarch	[35]	31	—	3	18	3	200
Grenada	Feb. 7, 1974	Feb. 7, 1974	constitutional monarchy	British monarch	prime minister	13	15	9	...	12	200
Guadeloupe	—	Feb. 28, 1983	overseas dept. (Fr.)	French president	[36]	42	41	3	34	12	200
Guam	—	Aug. 1, 1950	territory (U.S.)	U.S. president	governor	21	—	19	—	12	200
Guatemala	Sept. 15, 1821	Jan. 14, 1986	republic	——president——		80	—	22	330	12	200
Guernsey	—	Jan. 1, 1949[41]	crown dependency (U.K.)	British monarch[42]	bailiff	60	—	1	2	...	...
Guinea	Oct. 2, 1958	Dec. 23, 1990[2]	republic	——president——		114	—	31	175	12	200
Guinea-Bissau	Sept. 10, 1974	May 11, 1991	republic	president	prime minister	100	—	9	37	12	200
Guyana	May 26, 1966	Oct. 6, 1980	cooperative republic	——president——		65	—	10	71	12	200
Haiti	Jan. 1, 1804	March 29, 1987	republic	president	prime minister	27	83	9	82	12	200
Honduras	Nov. 5, 1838	Jan. 20, 1982	republic	——president——		128	—	18	292	12	200
Hong Kong	—	[41]	crown colony (U.K.)	British monarch	governor	60	—	...	18	12	[3]
Hungary	Nov. 16, 1918	Oct. 18, 1989[2]	republic	president	prime minister	394	—	20	184	—	—
Iceland	June 17, 1944	June 17, 1944	republic	president	prime minister	63	—	8	196	12	200
India	Aug. 15, 1947	Jan. 26, 1950	federal republic	president	prime minister	245	545	32	477	12	200
Indonesia	Aug. 17, 1945	Aug. 17, 1945	republic	——president——		1,000	500	27	303	12[11]	200[11]
Iran	Oct. 7, 1906	Dec. 2–3, 1979	Islamic republic	——president[43]——		270	—	25	229	12	50[44]
Iraq	Oct. 3, 1932	Sept. 22, 1968[45]	republic	——president——		250	—	16[46]	96	12	[3]
Ireland	Dec. 6, 1921	Dec. 29, 1937	republic	president	prime minister	60	166	32	86	12	200
Isle of Man	—	1961[41]	crown dependency (U.K.)	British monarch[42]	chief minister	10	24	...	—	12[47]	...
Israel	May 14, 1948	June 1950[41]	republic	president	prime minister	120	—	6	15	12	[3]
Italy	March 17, 1861	Jan. 1, 1948	republic	president	prime minister	326	630	20	102	12	[3]
Jamaica	Aug. 6, 1962	Aug. 6, 1962	constitutional monarchy	British monarch	prime minister	21	60	13	—	12	200
Japan	c. 660 BC	May 3, 1947	constitutional monarchy	emperor	prime minister	252	511	47	3,260	12[48]	200
Jersey	—	Jan. 1, 1949[41]	crown dependency (U.K.)	British monarch[42]	bailiff	58	—	—	—	3	...
Jordan	May 25, 1946	Jan. 8, 1952	constitutional monarchy	——king[25]——		40	80	12	...	3	[3]
Kazakhstan	Dec. 16, 1991	Aug. 30, 1995[13]	republic	president	prime minister	[49]	[49]	19	218	—	—
Kenya	Dec. 12, 1963	Dec. 12, 1963	republic	——president——		202	—	8	40	12	200
Kiribati	July 12, 1979	July 12, 1979	republic	——president——		41	—	21	—	12[11]	200[11]
Korea, North	Sept. 9, 1948	Dec. 27, 1972	socialist republic	president	premier	687	—	13	172	12	200
Korea, South	Aug. 15, 1948	Feb. 25, 1988	republic	president	prime minister	299	—	15	204	12[50]	12
Kuwait	June 19, 1961	Nov. 16, 1962	const. mon. (emirate)	——emir[25]——		50	—	—	—	12	[3]
Kyrgyzstan	Aug. 31, 1991	May 5, 1993	republic	president	prime minister	70	35	7	89	—	—
Laos	Oct. 23, 1953	Aug. 15, 1991	republic	president	prime minister	85	—	17	114	—	—
Latvia	Aug. 21, 1991	Nov. 7, 1922	republic	president	prime minister	100	—	33	49	12	...
Lebanon	Nov. 26, 1941	Sept. 21, 1990	republic	president	prime minister	128	—	...	...	12	[3]
Lesotho	Oct. 4, 1966	April 2, 1993	constitutional monarchy	king	prime minister	33[6]	65	10	...	—	—
Liberia	July 26, 1847	Aug. 20, 1995[23]	republic[5]	——chairman CS——		35	—	...	...	200	[3]
Libya	Dec. 24, 1951	March 2, 1977	socialist state[51]	rev. leader	sec. GPC	750	—	13	c. 1,500	12[52]	[3]
Liechtenstein	July 12, 1806	Oct. 5, 1921	constitutional monarchy	prince	head of govt.	25	—	11	—	—	—
Lithuania	Sept. 6, 1991	Nov. 6, 1992	republic	president	prime minister	141	—	10[53]	...	12	...
Luxembourg	May 10, 1867	Oct. 17, 1868	constitutional monarchy	grand duke	prime minister	21[6]	60	3	12	—	—
Macau	—	May 10, 1990	special terr. (Port.)	——governor——		23	—	...	...	6	12
Macedonia	April 1992	Nov. 17, 1991	republic	president	prime minister	120	—	34	...	—	—
Madagascar	June 26, 1960	Sept. 21, 1992	republic	president	prime minister	138	—	6	113	12	200
Malawi	July 6, 1964	May 18, 1994	republic	——president——		177	—	3	24	—	—
Malaysia	Aug. 31, 1957	Aug. 31, 1957	fed. const. monarchy	paramount ruler	prime minister	69	192	15	144	12	200
Maldives	July 26, 1965	Nov. 11, 1968	republic	——president——		48	—	21	201	12[11]	[31]
Mali	Sept. 22, 1960	Jan. 5, 1992	republic	president	prime minister	116	—	9	46	—	—
Malta	Sept. 21, 1964	Dec. 13, 1974	republic	president	prime minister	65	—	...	—	12	25
Marshall Islands	Dec. 22, 1990	May 1, 1979	republic	——president——		12[6]	33	24	—	12[11]	200
Martinique	—	Feb. 28, 1983	overseas dept. (Fr.)	French president	[36]	45	41	3	34	12	200
Mauritania	Nov. 28, 1960	July 21, 1991	republic	——president——		56	79	13	53	12	200
Mauritius	March 12, 1968	March 12, 1992	republic	president	prime minister	70	—	11	105	12	200
Mayotte	—	Dec. 24, 1976	terr. collectivity (Fr.)	French president	[54]	17	—	17	—	12	200
Mexico	Sept. 16, 1810	Feb. 5, 1917	federal republic	——president——		128	500	32	2,378	12	200
Micronesia	Dec. 22, 1990	May 10, 1979	federal republic	——president——		14	—	4	...	12	200
Moldova	Aug. 27, 1991	Aug. 27, 1994	republic	president	prime minister	104	—	50	...	—	—
Monaco	Feb. 2, 1861	Dec. 17, 1962	constitutional monarchy	prince	min. of state	18	—	—	—	12	[3]
Mongolia	March 13, 1921	Feb. 12, 1992	republic	president	prime minister	76	—	21	299	—	—
Morocco	March 2, 1956	Oct. 9, 1992	constitutional monarchy	——king[25]——		333	—	...	...	12	200
Mozambique	June 25, 1975	Nov. 30, 1990	republic	——president——		250	—	11	112	12	200
Myanmar (Burma)	Jan. 4, 1948	*Jan. 4, 1974*	republic	——chairman SLORC——		(492)	—	14	317	12	200
Namibia	March 21, 1990	March 21, 1990	republic	——president——		26	72	13	—	12	200
Nauru	Jan. 31, 1968	Jan. 31, 1968	republic	——president——		18	—	1	—	12	200
Nepal	Nov. 13, 1769	Nov. 9, 1990	constitutional monarchy	king	prime minister	60	205	14	75	—	—
Netherlands, The	March 30, 1814	Feb. 17, 1983	constitutional monarchy	monarch	prime minister	75	150	12	646	12	200

membership in international organizations																																					country
United Nations (date of admission)	UN organs★ and affiliated intergovernmental organizations																				Commonwealth of Nations	regional multipurpose						economic									
	UNCTAD★e	UNICEF★f	ICJ★	FAO	GATT (WTO)	IAEAe	IBRD	ICAO	IDA	IFC	ILO	IMF	IMO	ITUe	UNESCO	UNIDO	UPUe	WHO	WIPOe	WMO		EU	GCC	LASg	OAS	OAU	SPC	ACP	ADB	APEC	CARICOM	ECOWAS	EEC	I-ADB	IDBg	OPEC	
1968	●	●	●	●	●[17]		●	●	●	●	●	●	●	●	●	●	●	●								●		●									Equatorial Guinea
1993	●	●		●			●	●	●		●	●	●	●	●		●	●		●				●[17]		●											Eritrea
1991	●	●		●	●[4]	●	●	●		●	●	●	●	●	●		●	●	●	●																	Estonia
1945	●	●	●	●		●	●	●	●	●	●	●	●	●	●	●	●	●		●						●		●									Ethiopia
—																	●																				Faroe Islands
1970	●	●	●	●	●		●	●	●	●	●	●	●	●	●	●	●	●	●	●							●	●	●								Fiji
1955	●	●	●	●	●	●	●	●	●	●	●	●	●	●	●	●	●	●	●	●		●							●				●	●			Finland
1945	●	●	●	●	●	●	●	●	●	●	●	●	●	●	●	●	●	●	●	●		●					●		●				●	●			France
—																	●																				French Guiana
—																	●			●							●										French Polynesia
1960	●	●	●	●	●	●	●	●	●	●	●	●	●	●	●	●	●	●	●	●						●		●							●	●	Gabon
1965	●	●	●	●	●		●	●	●	●		●	●	●	●	●	●	●	●	●	●					●		●				●			●		Gambia, The
—																																					Gaza Strip
1992	●	●					●	●	●		●	●	●	●	●	●	●	●																			Georgia
1973	●	●	●	●	●	●	●	●	●	●	●	●	●	●	●	●	●	●	●	●		●							●				●	●			Germany
1957	●	●	●	●	●	●	●	●	●	●	●	●	●	●	●	●	●	●	●	●	●					●		●				●					Ghana
—		●															●																				Gibraltar
1945	●	●	●	●	●	●	●	●	●	●	●	●	●	●	●	●	●	●	●	●		●											●				Greece
—																	●																				Greenland
1974	●	●	●	●	●		●	●	●	●	●	●		●	●	●	●	●			●				●			●			●						Grenada
—																	●																				Guadeloupe
—																	●										●										Guam
1945	●	●	●	●	●	●	●	●	●	●	●	●	●	●	●	●	●	●	●	●					●									●			Guatemala
—																	●																				Guernsey
1958	●	●	●	●	●		●	●	●	●	●	●	●	●	●	●	●	●	●	●						●		●				●			●		Guinea
1974	●	●	●	●	●		●	●	●	●	●	●	●	●	●	●	●	●	●	●						●		●				●			●		Guinea-Bissau
1966	●	●	●	●	●		●	●	●	●	●	●	●	●	●	●	●	●	●	●	●				●			●			●			●			Guyana
1945	●	●	●	●	●	●	●	●	●	●	●	●	●	●	●	●	●	●	●	●					●			●			●[4]			●			Haiti
1945	●	●	●	●	●		●	●	●	●	●	●	●	●	●	●	●	●	●	●					●									●			Honduras
—		●			●								●[15]				●			●									●	●							Hong Kong
1955	●	●	●	●	●	●	●	●	●	●	●	●	●	●	●	●	●	●	●	●																	Hungary
1946	●	●	●	●	●	●	●	●	●	●	●	●	●	●	●	●	●	●	●	●																	Iceland
1945	●	●	●	●	●	●	●	●	●	●	●	●	●	●	●	●	●	●	●	●	●								●								India
1950	●	●	●	●	●	●	●	●	●	●	●	●	●	●	●	●	●	●	●	●									●	●					●	●	Indonesia
1945	●	●	●	●	●[4]	●	●	●	●	●	●	●	●	●	●	●	●	●	●	●															●	●	Iran
1945	●	●	●	●		●	●	●	●	●	●	●	●	●	●	●	●	●	●	●				●											●	●	Iraq
1955	●	●	●	●	●	●	●	●	●	●	●	●	●	●	●	●	●	●	●	●		●											●				Ireland
—																	●																				Isle of Man
1949	●	●	●	●	●	●	●	●	●	●	●	●	●	●	●	●	●	●	●	●														●			Israel
1955	●	●	●	●	●	●	●	●	●	●	●	●	●	●	●	●	●	●	●	●		●							●				●	●			Italy
1962	●	●	●	●	●	●	●	●	●	●	●	●	●	●	●	●	●	●	●	●	●				●			●			●			●			Jamaica
1956	●	●	●	●	●	●	●	●	●	●	●	●	●	●	●	●	●	●	●	●									●	●				●			Japan
—																	●																				Jersey
1955	●	●	●	●	●[4]	●	●	●	●	●	●	●	●	●	●	●	●	●	●	●				●											●		Jordan
1992	●	●			●[4]	●	●	●	●	●	●	●	●	●	●		●	●	●	●									●								Kazakhstan
1963	●	●	●	●	●	●	●	●	●	●	●	●	●	●	●	●	●	●	●	●	●					●		●									Kenya
—		●			●[17]		●	●	●	●		●		●	●		●	●			●						●	●	●								Kiribati
1991	●	●		●		●		●					●	●	●	●	●	●	●	●																	Korea, North
1991	●	●		●	●	●	●	●	●	●	●	●	●	●	●	●	●	●	●	●									●	●							Korea, South
1963	●	●	●	●	●	●	●	●	●	●	●	●	●	●	●	●	●	●		●			●	●											●	●	Kuwait
1992	●	●		●	●[4]		●	●	●	●	●	●			●	●	●	●	●										●							●	Kyrgyzstan
1955	●	●	●	●			●	●	●	●	●	●		●	●	●	●	●	●	●									●								Laos
1991	●			●	●[4]		●	●	●	●	●	●	●	●	●		●	●	●	●																	Latvia
1945	●	●	●	●		●	●	●	●	●	●	●	●	●	●	●	●	●	●	●				●											●		Lebanon
1966	●	●	●	●	●		●	●	●	●	●	●		●	●	●	●	●	●	●	●					●		●									Lesotho
1945	●	●	●	●		●	●	●	●	●	●	●	●	●	●	●	●	●	●	●						●		●				●					Liberia
1955	●	●	●	●		●	●	●	●	●	●	●	●	●	●	●	●	●	●	●				●		●									●	●	Libya
1990	●	●	●		●	●								●			●	●[4]	●																		Liechtenstein
1991	●			●	●[4]	●	●	●		●	●	●		●	●	●	●	●	●	●		●[15]															Lithuania
1945	●	●	●	●	●	●	●	●	●	●	●	●	●	●	●	●	●	●	●	●		●											●				Luxembourg
—				●	●								●[15]				●																				Macau
1993	●			●	●[4]	●	●[17]	●	●	●	●	●	●	●	●	●	●	●	●	●																	Macedonia
1960	●	●	●	●	●		●	●	●	●	●	●	●	●	●	●	●	●	●	●						●		●									Madagascar
1964	●	●	●	●	●		●	●	●	●	●	●	●	●	●	●	●	●	●	●	●					●		●									Malaŵi
1957	●	●	●	●	●	●	●	●	●	●	●	●	●	●	●	●	●	●	●	●	●								●	●					●		Malaysia
1965	●	●	●	●	●		●	●	●	●		●	●	●	●	●	●	●		●	●								●						●		Maldives
1960	●	●	●	●	●	●	●	●	●	●	●	●		●	●	●	●	●	●	●						●		●				●			●		Mali
1964	●	●	●	●	●		●	●			●	●	●	●	●	●	●	●	●	●	●												●[15]				Malta
1991	●	●					●	●	●	●		●					●[17]	●									●		●								Marshall Islands
—																	●																				Martinique
1961	●	●	●	●	●		●	●	●	●	●	●	●	●	●	●	●	●	●	●				●		●		●				●			●		Mauritania
1968	●	●	●	●	●	●	●	●	●	●	●	●	●	●	●	●	●	●	●	●	●					●		●									Mauritius
—																	●																				Mayotte
1945	●	●	●	●	●	●	●	●	●	●	●	●	●	●	●	●	●	●	●	●					●					●	●[4]			●			Mexico
1991	●	●					●	●	●	●		●		●			●[17]	●									●		●								Micronesia
1992	●				●[4]		●	●	●		●	●		●	●	●	●	●	●																		Moldova
1993	●	●				●		●				●	●	●	●		●	●	●																		Monaco
1961	●	●	●	●	●[4]	●	●	●	●	●	●	●		●	●	●	●	●	●	●									●								Mongolia
1956	●	●	●	●	●	●	●	●	●	●	●	●	●	●	●	●	●	●	●	●				●											●		Morocco
1975	●	●	●	●	●		●	●	●	●	●	●	●	●	●	●	●	●		●	●					●		●									Mozambique
1948	●	●	●	●	●	●	●	●	●	●	●	●	●	●	●	●	●	●		●									●								Myanmar (Burma)
1990	●	●		●	●	●	●	●	●[17]	●	●	●		●	●	●		●	●	●	●					●		●									Namibia
—								●						●			●	●			●[55]						●		●								Nauru
1955	●	●	●	●	●[4]		●	●	●	●	●	●	●	●	●	●	●	●		●									●								Nepal
1945	●	●	●	●	●	●	●	●	●	●	●	●	●	●	●	●	●	●	●	●		●							●				●	●			Netherlands, The

Government and international organizations (continued)

country	date of independence[a]	date of current or last constitution[b]	type of government	executive branch[c]		legislative branch[d]		admin. subdivisions		seaward claims	
				chief of state	head of government	upper house (members)	lower house (members)	first-order (number)	second-order (number)	territorial (nautical miles)	fishing/economic (nautical miles)
Netherlands Antilles	—	Dec. 29, 1954	overseas territory (Neth.)	Dutch monarch	[14]	22	—	5	—	12	200
New Caledonia	—	Nov. 9, 1988	overseas territory (Fr.)	French president	[56]	54	—	3	32	12	200
New Zealand	Sept. 26, 1907	June 30, 1852[41]	constitutional monarchy	British monarch	prime minister	99	—	12	74	12	200
Nicaragua	April 30, 1838	Jan. 9, 1987	republic	president		92	—	17	143	200	200
Niger	Aug. 3, 1960	Dec. 26, 1992[13]	republic	president	prime minister	83	—	7	38	—	—
Nigeria	Oct. 1, 1960	*Oct. 1, 1979*	federal republic	president PC		(91)	(593)	31	589	30	200
Northern Mariana Is.	—	Jan. 9, 1978	commonwealth (U.S.)	U.S. president	governor	9	18	4	—	12	200
Norway	June 7, 1905	May 17, 1814	constitutional monarchy	king	prime minister	165	—	19	435	4	200
Oman	Dec. 20, 1951	—	monarchy (sultanate)	sultan		80[6]	—	8	59	12	200
Pakistan	Aug. 14, 1947	Aug. 14, 1973	federal Islamic republic	president	prime minister	87	217	16[57]	...	12	200
Palau	Oct. 1, 1994	Jan. 1, 1981	republic	president		14	16	16	—	...	...
Panama	Nov. 3, 1903	May 20, 1983[58]	republic	president[59]		72	—	10	67	200	[3]
Papua New Guinea	Sept. 16, 1975	Sept. 16, 1975	constitutional monarchy	British monarch	prime minister	109	—	[60]	...	12[11]	200[11]
Paraguay	May 14, 1811	June 22, 1992	republic	president		45	80	18	217	—	—
Peru	July 28, 1821	Dec. 29, 1993	republic	president		120	—	25[61]	...	200	200
Philippines	July 4, 1946	Feb. 11, 1987	republic	president		24	204	15	90	[30]	200[11]
Poland	Nov. 10, 1918	Dec. 8, 1992[62]	republic	president	prime minister	100	460	49	2,465	12	[63]
Portugal	c. 1140	April 25, 1976	parliamentary state	president	prime minister	230	—	20	305	12	200
Puerto Rico	—	July 25, 1952	commonwealth (U.S.)	U.S. president	governor	29	53	78	...	12	200
Qatar	Sept. 3, 1971	July 1970[45]	monarchy	emir		35[6]	—	9	—	12	[64]
Réunion	—	Feb. 28, 1983	overseas dept. (Fr.)	French president	[36]	47	45	4	24	12	200
Romania	May 21, 1877	Dec. 13, 1991	republic	president	prime minister	143	341	41	...	12[31]	200[31]
Russia	Dec. 8, 1991	Dec. 24, 1993	federal republic	president	prime minister	178	450	89	1,863	12	...
Rwanda	July 1, 1962	May 5, 1995[65]	republic[5]	president	prime minister	70	—	11	...	—	—
St. Kitts and Nevis	Sept. 19, 1983	Sept. 19, 1983	constitutional monarchy	British monarch	prime minister	15	—	1	—	12	200
St. Lucia	Feb. 22, 1979	Feb. 22, 1979	constitutional monarchy	British monarch	prime minister	11	17	10	—	12	200
St. Vincent	Oct. 27, 1979	Oct. 27, 1979	constitutional monarchy	British monarch	prime minister	21	—	—	—	12	200
San Marino	855	Oct. 8, 1600	republic	captains-regent (2)		60	—	9	—	—	—
São Tomé and Príncipe	July 12, 1975	Sept. 10, 1990	republic	president	prime minister	55	—	1	6	12[11]	200[11]
Saudi Arabia	Sept. 23, 1932	[66]	monarchy	king		61[6]	—	13	...	12	[3]
Senegal	Aug. 20, 1960	March 7, 1963	republic	president	prime minister	120	—	10	31	12[31]	200[31]
Seychelles	June 29, 1976	June 18, 1993	republic	president		33	—	...	...	12	200
Sierra Leone	April 27, 1961	*Oct. 1, 1991*	republic	chairman SCS		(127)	—	4	12	200	[3]
Singapore	Aug. 9, 1965	June 3, 1959[41]	republic	president	prime minister	87	—	—	—	3	12
Slovakia	Jan. 1, 1993	Jan. 1, 1993	republic	president	prime minister	150	—	...	...	—	—
Slovenia	June 25, 1991	Dec. 23, 1991	republic	president	prime minister	40	90	62	...	...	...
Solomon Islands	July 7, 1978	July 7, 1978	constitutional monarchy	British monarch	prime minister	47	—	10	...	12[11]	200[11]
Somalia	July 1, 1960	July 1, 1960	republic[67]	[68]		...	—	...	...	200	200
South Africa	May 31, 1910	April 27, 1994[2]	republic	president[69]		90	400	9	349	12	200
Spain	1492	Dec. 29, 1978	constitutional monarchy	king	prime minister	255	350	19	50	12	200
Sri Lanka	Feb. 4, 1948	Sept. 7, 1978	republic	president		225	—	...	...	12	200
Sudan, The	Jan. 1, 1956	*Oct. 10, 1985*	Islamic military regime	president		300	—	27[70]	...	12	[3]
Suriname	Nov. 25, 1975	Nov. 25, 1987	republic	president		51	—	10	—	12	200
Swaziland	Sept. 6, 1968	*Sept. 6, 1968*	monarchy	king[25]		30	65	4	40	—	—
Sweden	before 836	Jan. 1, 1975	constitutional monarchy	king	prime minister	349	—	24	286	12	[18]
Switzerland	Sept. 22, 1499	May 29, 1874	federal state	president FC		46	200	26	2,915	—	—
Syria	April 17, 1946	March 14, 1973	republic	president		250	—	14	59	35	[3]
Taiwan	Oct. 25, 1945	Dec. 25, 1947[41]	republic	president	premier	402[71]	164	2	25	24	200
Tajikistan	Sept. 9, 1991	Nov. 6, 1994	republic	president NA	prime minister	181	—	5	...	—	—
Tanzania	Dec. 9, 1961	April 25, 1977	republic	president		280	—	25	99	12	200
Thailand	1350	Dec. 9, 1991	constitutional monarchy	king	prime minister	270	391	73	711	12	200
Togo	April 27, 1960	Sept. 27, 1992[13]	republic	president	prime minister	81	—	5	21	30	200
Tonga	June 4, 1970	Nov. 4, 1875	constitutional monarchy	monarch[72]		30	—	5	23	12	200
Trinidad and Tobago	Aug. 31, 1962	July 27, 1976	republic	president	prime minister	31	36	12	...	12[11]	200[11]
Tunisia	March 20, 1956	June 1, 1959	republic	president	prime minister	163	—	23	257	12	[3]
Turkey	Oct. 29, 1923	Nov. 7, 1982	republic	president	prime minister	450	—	76	829	12[73]	[18]
Turkmenistan	Oct. 27, 1991	May 18, 1992	republic	president		50	—	5	...	—	—
Tuvalu	Oct. 1, 1978	Sept. 15, 1986	constitutional monarchy	British monarch	prime minister	12	—	8	—	12[11]	200[11]
Uganda	Oct. 9, 1962	Oct. 8, 1995[74]	republic[5]	president[25]		214[75]	—	38	...	—	—
Ukraine	Aug. 24, 1991	April 20, 1978	republic	president	prime minister	450	—	25	485	12	200
United Arab Emirates	Dec. 2, 1971	Dec. 2, 1971[45]	federation of emirates	president	prime minister	40[6]	—	7	—	12	200
United Kingdom	Oct. 14, 1066	[76]	constitutional monarchy	monarch	prime minister	1,198	651	...	...	12[47]	200
United States	July 4, 1776	March 4, 1789	federal republic	president		100	435	51	3,043[77]	12	200
Uruguay	Aug. 25, 1828	Feb. 15, 1967	republic	president		31	99	19	...	200	200
Uzbekistan	Aug. 31, 1991	Dec. 8, 1992	republic	president	prime minister	250	—	13	...	...	...
Vanuatu	July 30, 1980	July 30, 1980	republic	president	prime minister	46	—	6	...	12[11]	200[11]
Venezuela	July 5, 1811	Jan. 23, 1961	federal republic	president		53	199	24	202	12	200
Vietnam	Sept. 2, 1945	April 15, 1992	socialist republic	president	prime minister	395	—	53	467	12	200
Virgin Islands (U.S.)	—	July 22, 1954	territory (U.S.)	U.S. president	governor	15	—	1	—	12	200
West Bank	—	—	Israeli military[78]	—	area commander	—	—	...	—	—	—
Western Sahara	—	—	annexture of Morocco	—	—	—	—	5	...	12	200
Western Samoa	Jan. 1, 1962	Oct. 28, 1960	[80]	head of state	prime minister	49	—	330[81]	—	12	200
Yemen	December 1918	Sept. 29, 1994[82]	republic	president	prime minister	301	—	17	...	12	200
Yugoslavia	Dec. 1, 1918	April 27, 1992	federal republic	federal president	prime minister	40	138	2	...	12	...
Zaire	June 30, 1960	April 9, 1994[84]	republic[5]	president	prime minister	738	—	11	...	12	200
Zambia	Oct. 24, 1964	Aug. 30, 1991	republic	president		159	—	9	57	—	—
Zimbabwe	April 18, 1980	April 18, 1980	republic	president		150	—	10	80	—	—

[1]No effective constitution because of multifactional warfare. [2]Transitional constitution. [3]Territorial sea claim assumed to claim fishing/economic rights within the same zone. [4]Observer status. [5]Transitional government. [6]Body with limited or no legislative authority. [7]Includes unoccupied seats. [8]Includes nonvoting delegate. [9]President of France and Bishop of Urgell, Spain. [10]Assisted by two vice presidents pending implementation of November 1994 Lusaka Protocol. [11]Measured from claimed archipelagic baselines. [12]Promulgation date of significant amendments to July 9, 1853, constitution. [13]Date of referendum approving new constitution. [14]Executive responsibilities divided between (for The Netherlands) the governor and (locally) the prime minister. [15]Associate member. [16]Formally a constitutional monarchy. [17]Full membership pending. [18]Defined by equidistant line. [19]Five region/community councils; 10 provincial councils. [20]3 nautical miles from mouth of Sarstoon River (southern boundary with Guatemala) to Ranguana Caye. [21]Executive responsibilities divided between (for the U.K.) the governor and (locally) the premier of the cabinet. [22]Resembles a constitutional monarchy without a formal constitution. [23]Date of peace accord. [24]Peace accord to establish two political entities (a Bosnian-Muslim–Bosnian-Croat federation and a Bosnian Serb republic). [25]Assisted by the prime minister. [26]First prime minister assisted by second prime minister. [27]Governor-general can exercise all the powers of the reigning monarch of the Commonwealth. [28]Suspended membership. [29]Republic of Cyprus only. [30]First elections scheduled for 1996. [31]Zone defined by geographic coordinates. [32]Official proclamations organizing government. [33]Being created in 1995 per official announcement. [34]Date new republic was formally established. [35]Executive responsibilities divided between (for Denmark) the high commissioner and (locally) the prime minister. [36]Executive responsibilities divided among (for France) the prefect and (locally) the president of the General Council and the president of the Regional Council. [37]Executive responsibilities divided between (for France) the high commissioner and (locally) the president of the territorial government. [38]Date of agreement providing for Palestinian self-rule. [39]Approval date by national legislature. [40]3 nautical miles in Baltic Sea, 16 nautical miles in North Sea. [41]Evolving body of constitutional law. [42]Represented by the lieutenant governor. [43]Shares coexecutive authority with

membership in international organizations																																					country
United Nations (date of admission)	UN organs★ and affiliated intergovernmental organizations																				Commonwealth of Nations	regional multipurpose						economic									
	UNCTAD★[e]	UNICEF★[f]	ICJ★	FAO	GATT (WTO)	IAEA[e]	IBRD	ICAO	IDA	IFC	ILO	IMF	IMO	ITU[e]	UNESCO	UNIDO	UPU[e]	WHO	WIPO[e]	WMO		EU	GCC	LAS[g]	OAS	OAU	SPC	ACP	ADB	APEC	CARICOM	ECOWAS	EEC	I-ADB	IDB[g]	OPEC	
—															•[15]		•			•											•[4]						Netherlands Antilles
—																	•			•							•										New Caledonia
1945	•	•	•	•	•	•	•	•	•	•	•	•	•	•	•	•	•	•	•	•	•						•			•							New Zealand
1945	•	•	•	•	•	•	•	•	•	•	•	•	•	•	•	•	•	•	•	•					•									•			Nicaragua
1960	•	•	•	•	•	•	•	•	•	•	•	•	•	•	•	•	•	•	•	•						•		•				•			•		Niger
1960	•	•	•	•	•	•	•	•	•	•	•	•	•	•	•	•	•	•	•	•	•[28]					•		•				•				•	Nigeria
—																	•										•										Northern Mariana Is.
1945	•	•	•	•	•	•	•	•	•	•	•	•	•	•	•	•	•	•	•	•									•					•			Norway
1971	•	•	•	•			•	•	•	•	•	•	•	•	•	•	•	•		•			•	•											•		Oman
1947	•	•	•	•	•	•	•	•	•	•	•	•	•	•	•	•	•	•	•	•	•								•						•		Pakistan
1994		•															•										•										Palau
1945	•	•	•	•	•[4]	•	•	•	•	•	•	•	•	•	•	•	•	•	•	•					•									•			Panama
1975	•	•	•	•	•[17]		•	•	•	•	•	•	•	•	•	•	•	•		•	•						•	•	•	•							Papua New Guinea
1945	•	•	•	•	•	•	•	•	•	•	•	•	•	•	•	•	•	•	•	•					•									•			Paraguay
1945	•	•	•	•	•	•	•	•	•	•	•	•	•	•	•	•	•	•	•	•					•									•			Peru
1945	•	•	•	•	•	•	•	•	•	•	•	•	•	•	•	•	•	•	•	•									•	•							Philippines
1945	•	•	•	•	•	•	•	•	•	•	•	•	•	•	•	•	•	•	•	•																	Poland
1955	•	•	•	•	•	•	•	•	•	•	•	•	•	•	•	•	•	•	•	•		•											•	•			Portugal
—				•													•	•[15]													•[4]						Puerto Rico
1971	•	•	•	•	•	•	•	•			•	•	•	•	•	•	•	•	•	•			•	•											•	•	Qatar
—																	•																				Réunion
1955	•	•	•	•	•	•	•	•	•	•	•	•	•	•	•	•	•	•	•	•																	Romania
1991	•	•			•[4]	•	•	•	•	•	•	•	•	•	•	•	•	•	•	•																	Russia
1962	•	•	•	•	•		•	•	•	•	•	•		•	•	•	•	•	•	•						•		•									Rwanda
1983	•	•	•	•	•		•		•			•			•	•	•	•			•				•			•			•						St. Kitts and Nevis
1979	•	•	•	•	•		•	•	•	•	•	•	•		•	•	•	•	•	•	•				•			•			•						St. Lucia
1980	•	•	•	•	•		•	•	•			•	•	•	•	•	•	•		•	•				•			•			•						St. Vincent
1992	•		•					•			•	•		•	•		•	•	•	•																	San Marino
1975	•	•	•	•	•[17]		•	•	•		•	•	•	•	•	•	•	•		•						•		•									São Tomé and Príncipe
1945	•	•	•	•	•[4]	•	•	•	•	•	•	•	•	•	•	•	•	•	•	•			•	•											•	•	Saudi Arabia
1960	•	•	•	•	•	•	•	•	•	•	•	•	•	•	•	•	•	•	•	•						•		•				•			•		Senegal
1976	•	•	•	•	•[17]		•	•		•	•	•	•	•	•	•	•	•		•	•					•		•									Seychelles
1961	•	•	•	•	•	•	•	•	•	•	•	•	•	•	•	•	•	•	•	•	•					•		•				•			•		Sierra Leone
1965	•	•	•		•	•	•	•		•	•	•	•	•			•	•	•	•	•								•	•							Singapore
1993	•	•		•	•	•	•	•	•	•	•	•	•	•	•	•	•	•	•	•																	Slovakia
1992	•	•		•	•	•	•	•	•	•	•	•	•	•	•	•	•	•	•	•														•			Slovenia
1978	•	•	•	•	•[17]		•	•	•	•	•	•	•	•	•		•	•		•	•						•	•	•								Solomon Islands
1960	•	•	•	•			•	•	•	•	•	•	•	•	•	•	•	•	•	•				•		•		•							•		Somalia
1945	•	•	•	•	•	•	•	•	•	•		•		•	•		•	•	•	•	•					•											South Africa
1955	•	•	•	•	•	•	•	•	•	•	•	•	•	•	•	•	•	•	•	•		•							•				•	•			Spain
1955	•	•	•	•	•	•	•	•	•	•	•	•	•	•	•	•	•	•	•	•	•								•								Sri Lanka
1956	•	•	•	•		•	•	•	•	•	•	•	•	•	•	•	•	•	•	•				•		•		•							•		Sudan, The
1975	•	•	•	•	•		•	•			•	•	•	•	•	•	•	•		•					•			•			•[4]			•			Suriname
1968	•	•	•	•	•		•	•	•	•	•	•		•	•	•	•	•	•	•	•					•		•									Swaziland
1946	•	•	•	•	•	•	•	•	•	•	•	•	•	•	•	•	•	•	•	•		•							•				•	•			Sweden
—	•	•	•	•	•	•	•	•	•	•	•	•	•	•	•	•	•	•	•	•									•					•			Switzerland
1945	•	•	•	•		•	•	•	•	•	•	•	•	•	•	•	•	•	•	•				•											•		Syria
—					•[4]																								•	•							Taiwan
1992	•	•					•	•	•		•	•			•	•	•	•	•	•																	Tajikistan
1961	•	•	•	•	•	•	•	•	•	•	•	•	•	•	•	•	•	•	•	•	•					•		•									Tanzania
1946	•	•	•	•	•	•	•	•	•	•	•	•	•	•	•	•	•	•	•	•									•	•							Thailand
1960	•	•	•	•	•		•	•	•	•	•	•	•	•	•	•	•	•	•	•						•		•				•					Togo
—	•	•		•	•[17]		•	•	•	•		•		•	•	•	•	•		•	•						•	•	•								Tonga
1962	•	•	•	•	•		•	•	•	•	•	•	•	•	•	•	•	•	•	•	•				•			•			•			•			Trinidad and Tobago
1956	•	•	•	•	•	•	•	•	•	•	•	•	•	•	•	•	•	•	•	•				•		•									•		Tunisia
1945	•	•	•	•	•	•	•	•	•	•	•	•	•	•	•	•	•	•	•	•									•				•[15]		•		Turkey
1992	•	•			•[4]		•	•	•[17]		•	•	•	•	•		•	•		•															•		Turkmenistan
—		•			•[17]										•		•	•			•[55]						•	•	•								Tuvalu
1962	•	•	•	•	•	•	•	•	•	•	•	•	•	•	•	•	•	•	•	•	•					•		•							•		Uganda
1945	•				•[4]	•	•	•	•[17]		•	•	•	•	•	•	•	•	•	•																	Ukraine
1971	•	•	•	•	•	•	•	•	•	•	•	•	•	•	•	•	•	•	•	•			•	•											•	•	United Arab Emirates
1945	•	•	•	•	•	•	•	•	•	•	•	•	•	•	•[4]	•	•	•	•	•	•	•					•		•				•	•			United Kingdom
1945	•	•	•	•	•	•	•	•	•	•	•	•	•	•	•[4]	•	•	•	•	•					•		•		•	•				•			United States
1945	•	•	•	•	•	•	•	•	•	•	•	•	•	•	•	•	•	•	•	•					•									•			Uruguay
1992	•	•			•[4]	•	•	•	•	•	•	•	•	•	•	•	•	•	•	•																	Uzbekistan
1981	•	•	•	•			•	•	•	•		•	•	•	•	•	•	•		•	•						•	•	•								Vanuatu
1945	•	•	•	•	•	•	•	•	•	•	•	•	•	•	•	•	•	•	•	•					•						•[4]			•		•	Venezuela
1977	•	•	•	•	•[4]	•	•	•	•	•	•	•	•	•	•	•	•	•	•	•									•								Vietnam
—																	•														•						Virgin Islands (U.S.)
—																																					West Bank
—																										•[79]											Western Sahara
1976	•	•	•	•			•		•	•		•		•	•		•	•			•						•	•	•								Western Samoa
1947	•	•	•	•	•[17]		•	•	•	•	•	•	•	•	•	•	•	•	•	•				•											•		Yemen
1945[83]	•	•	•	•	•	•	•[17]	•[17]	•[17]	•	•	•	•	•	•	•	•	•	•	•																	Yugoslavia
1960	•	•	•	•	•	•	•	•	•	•	•	28	•	•	•	•	•	•	•	•						•		•									Zaire
1964	•	•	•	•	•	•	•	•	•	•	•	•		•	•	•	•	•	•	•	•					•		•									Zambia
1980	•	•	•	•	•	•	•	•	•	•	•	•		•	•	•	•	•	•	•	•					•		•									Zimbabwe

spiritual leader. [44]Sea of Oman only; median line boundaries in the Persian Gulf. [45]Provisional constitution. [46]De facto administration. [47]Median line between the Isle of Man and the United Kingdom. [48]3 nautical miles in 5 straits. [49]Bicameral elections planned for December 1995. [50]3 nautical miles in Korea Strait. [51]Formally a *jamahiriya*, translated as "the masses of people." [52]Based on Gulf of Sidra closing line (32° 30′ N), in part. [53]Created in 1995. [54]Executive responsibilities divided between (for France) the prefect and (locally) the president of the General Council. [55]Special member. [56]Executive responsibilities divided between (for France) the high commissioner and (locally) the president of the General Council. [57]Includes 11 federally administered tribal areas; excludes Jammu and Kashmir. [58]Effective date of significant amendments to Oct. 11, 1972, constitution. [59]Assisted by vice presidents. [60]New local administrative arrangement as of August 1995. [61]Administrative units of still functioning old administrative scheme. [62]"Little constitution." [63]Defined by international treaties. [64]Limits of continental shelf or median line boundaries. [65]Date constitution adopted by transitional legislature. [66]Royal decrees since March 1, 1992, provide a formal description of how the king has decided to develop his governance. [67]Somaliland (the former colonially administered area of British Somaliland in northern Somalia) declared its unilateral independence from Somalia in May 1991. [68]No effective central government. [69]Assisted by executive deputy presidents. [70]Per official announcements. [71]Occupied seats mid-1994. [72]Assisted by Privy Council. [73]Black Sea and Mediterranean Sea; 6 nautical miles in Aegean Sea. [74]Constituent assembly promulgated new constitution. [75]Elective seats only of constituent assembly. [76]Based on evolving body of statutes and common law. [77]County (parish in Louisiana) governments. [78]Jericho and 6 other large towns under Palestine National Authority. [79]Membership held by Sahrawi Arab Democratic Republic. [80]Mixed political system approximating a constitutional monarchy. [81]Number of villages. [82]Date of significant amendments. [83]Suspended from participation in UN proceedings from September 1992, however, Yugoslavia is permitted to participate in the work of UN organs other than General Assembly bodies. [84]Date of Transitional Constitutional Act.

Area and population

This table provides the area and population for each of the countries of the world and for all but the smallest political dependencies having a permanent civilian population. The data represent the latest published and unpublished data for both the surveyed area of the countries and their populations, the latter both as of a single year (1995) to provide the best comparability and as of the most recent census to provide the fullest comparison of certain demographic measures that are not always available between successive national censuses. The 1995 midyear estimates represent a combination of national, United Nations (UN) or other international organizations, and *Encyclopædia Britannica* estimates so as to give the best fit to available published series, to take account of unpublished information received in correspondence, and to incorporate the results of very recent censuses for which published analyses are not yet available.

One principal point to bear in mind when studying these statistics is that all of them, whatever degree of precision may be implied by the exactness of the numbers, are estimates—all of varying, and some of suspect, accuracy—even when they *contain* a very full enumeration. The United States—which has a long tradition both of census taking and of the use of the most sophisticated analytical tools in processing the data—is unable to determine within 2.1% (the estimated 1990 undercount) its total population nationally. And that is an *average* underenumeration. In states and larger cities, where enumeration of particular populations, both legal and illegal, is most difficult, the accuracy of the enumerated count may be off as much as 4% at a state level and as much as 10% for a single city. The high accuracy attained by census operations in China may approach 0.25% of rigorously maintained civil population registers. Other national census operations not so based, however, are inherently less accurate. For example, Ethiopia's first-ever census in 1984 resulted in figures that were 30% or more above prevailing estimates; Nigeria's 1991 census corrected decades of miscounts and was well below prevailing estimates. An undercount of 2–8% is more typical, but even census operations offering results of 30% or more above or below prevailing estimates can still represent well-founded benchmarks from which future planning may proceed. The editors have tried to take account of the range of variation and accuracy in published data, but it is difficult to establish a value for many sources of inaccuracy unless some country or agency has made a conscientious effort to establish both the relative accuracy (precision) of its estimate and the absolute magnitude of the quantity it is trying to measure—for example, the number of people in Cambodia who died at the hands of the Khmer Rouge. If a figure of 1,000,000 is adopted, what is its accuracy: ± 1%, 10%, 50%? Are the original data documentary or evidentiary, complete or incomplete, analytically biased or unbiased, in good agreement with other published data?

Many similar problems exist and in endless variations: What is the extent of southern European immigration to western Europe in search of jobs? How many refugees from Afghanistan, Liberia, Rwanda, or Burundi are there in surrounding countries? How many undocumented aliens are there in the United States? How many Palestinians are there in the Middle East (they are politically inconvenient to enumerate everywhere)? How many Amerindians exist (remain, preserving their original language and a mode of life unassimilated by the larger national culture) in the countries of South America? How many people have died or emigrated as a result of the civil violence in Central America?

Still, much information is accurate, well founded, and updated regularly.

Area and population

country	area			population (latest estimate)					population (latest census)				
	square miles	square kilometres	rank	total midyear 1995	rank	density per sq mi	density per sq km	% annual growth rate 1990–95	census year	total	male (%)	female (%)	urban (%)
Afghanistan	251,825	652,225	41	18,129,000	48	72.0	27.8	3.4	1979	13,051,358[1]	51.4	48.6	15.1
Albania	11,100	28,748	142	3,412,000	125	307.4	118.7	0.9	1989	3,182,417	51.5	48.5	35.7
Algeria	919,595	2,381,741	11	27,939,000	36	30.4	11.7	2.2	1987	23,038,942	49.9	50.1	49.7
American Samoa	77	199	205	57,000	206	740.3	286.4	3.8	1990	46,773	51.4	48.6	33.4
Andorra	181	468	193	62,900	203	347.5	134.4	3.6	1992[2]	61,599	53.1	46.9	66.2[3]
Angola	481,354	1,246,700	24	11,558,000	62	24.0	9.3	2.9	1970	5,673,046	52.1	47.9	14.2
Antigua and Barbuda	171	442	195	63,900	202	373.7	144.6	0.0	1991	60,089	48.2	51.8	31.0
Argentina	1,073,518	2,780,400	8	34,587,000	31	32.2	12.4	1.2	1991	32,615,528	48.9	51.1	87.2
Armenia	11,500	29,800	141	3,548,000	122	308.5	119.1	1.2	1989	3,287,677	49.3	50.7	67.8
Aruba	75	193	206	72,700	198	969.3	376.7	2.9	1991	66,687	49.2	50.8	...
Australia	2,966,200	7,682,300	6	18,025,000	50	6.1	2.3	1.1	1991	17,284,036	49.6	50.4	85.4[4]
Austria	32,378	83,858	115	8,063,000	84	249.0	96.2	0.9	1991	7,795,786	48.2	51.8	64.5
Azerbaijan	33,400	86,600	113	7,525,000	87	225.3	86.9	1.1	1989	7,037,867	48.7	51.3	53.8
Bahamas, The	5,382	13,939	158	276,000	174	51.3	19.8	1.5	1990	255,095	49.0	51.0	64.3
Bahrain	268	694	186	579,000	162	2,160.4	834.3	3.6	1991	508,037	57.9	42.1	88.4
Bangladesh	56,977	147,570	93	120,093,000	9	2,107.7	813.8	2.1	1991	111,455,185	51.4	48.6	20.2
Barbados	166	430	196	265,000	176	1,596.4	616.3	0.4	1990[5]	257,083	47.7	52.3	37.9[6]
Belarus	80,153	207,595	85	10,332,000	70	128.9	49.8	0.1	1989	10,199,709	46.9	53.1	65.5
Belgium	11,787	30,528	139	10,064,000	73	853.8	329.7	0.2	1991	9,978,681	48.9	51.1	96.6[3]
Belize	8,867	22,965	150	216,000	180	24.4	9.4	2.8	1991	189,392	50.9	49.1	47.5
Benin	43,500	112,680	101	5,409,000	100	124.3	48.0	3.1	1992	4,855,349	48.7	51.3	39.6
Bermuda	21	54	212	61,000	204	2,904.8	1,129.6	0.6	1991[5]	58,460	48.5	51.5	100.0
Bhutan	18,150	47,000	131	816,000	154	45.0	17.4	2.1	...	...	50.6[6]	49.4[6]	5.3[6]
Bolivia	424,164	1,098,581	28	7,414,000	88	17.5	6.7	2.4	1992	6,420,792	49.4	50.6	57.5
Bosnia and Herzegovina	19,741	51,129	127	3,459,000	124	175.2	67.7	−4.3	1991	4,365,639	49.7[7]	50.3[7]	36.2[7]
Botswana	224,607	581,730	47	1,549,000	145	6.9	2.7	3.9	1991	1,326,796	47.8	52.2	23.9
Brazil	3,300,171	8,547,404	5	155,822,000	5	47.2	18.2	1.5	1991	146,825,475	49.4	50.6	75.6
Brunei	2,226	5,765	167	291,000	173	130.7	50.5	2.8	1991	260,482	52.8	47.2	59.4[7]
Bulgaria	42,855	110,994	103	8,406,000	82	196.1	75.7	−0.7	1992	8,487,317	49.1	50.9	67.2
Burkina Faso	105,946	274,400	73	10,324,000	71	97.4	37.6	2.8	1985[5]	7,964,705	48.1	51.9	11.7
Burundi	10,740	27,816	145	5,936,000	95	552.7	213.4	2.4	1990[5]	5,292,793	48.6	51.4	6.3
Cambodia	70,238	181,916	89	9,608,000	76	136.8	52.8	2.3	1981	6,682,000	46.3[8]	53.7[8]	10.3[8]
Cameroon	183,569	475,442	53	13,233,000	60	72.1	27.8	2.8	1987	10,516,232	49.0	51.0	38.3
Canada	3,849,674	9,970,610	2	29,463,000	32	7.7	3.0	1.2	1991	27,296,859	49.3	50.7	76.6
Cape Verde	1,557	4,033	169	392,000	169	251.8	97.2	2.8	1990	341,491	47.3	52.7	44.1
Central African Republic	240,324	622,436	43	3,141,000	128	13.1	5.0	2.4	1988	2,688,426	49.1	50.9	36.5
Chad	495,755	1,284,000	22	6,361,000	93	12.8	5.0	2.8	1993	6,279,931	49.3[6]	50.7[6]	30.0[6]
Chile	292,135	756,626	38	14,210,000	59	48.6	18.8	1.6	1992	13,231,803	49.1	50.9	85.1[9]
China	3,696,100	9,572,900	3	1,206,600,000	1	326.5	126.0	1.3	1990	1,133,682,501	51.6	48.4	26.4
Colombia	440,762	1,141,568	26	35,099,000	30	79.6	30.7	1.7	1985	30,062,193	49.5	50.5	67.2[10]
Comoros	719	1,862	175	545,000	163	758.0	292.7	3.3	1991	446,817	50.6[6]	49.4[6]	27.8[6]
Congo	132,047	342,000	63	2,590,000	132	19.6	7.6	3.0	1984[5]	1,909,248	48.7	51.3	52.0
Costa Rica	19,730	51,100	128	3,344,000	126	169.5	65.4	2.2	1984	2,416,809	50.0	50.0	43.9
Côte d'Ivoire	124,504	322,463	68	14,253,000	58	114.5	44.2	3.5	1988	10,815,694	51.1	48.9	39.0
Croatia	21,829	56,538	126	4,495,000	109	205.9	79.5	−1.2	1991	4,784,265	48.5	51.5	54.3
Cuba	42,804	110,861	104	11,068,000	65	258.6	99.8	0.8	1993	10,900,000	50.3	49.7	72.8[6]
Cyprus[11]	3,572	9,251	164	806,000	155	225.6	87.1	1.3	1992[5, 12]	615,013	49.8	50.2	67.7
Czech Republic	30,450	78,864	117	10,346,000	69	339.8	131.2	0.1	1991	10,302,215	48.5	51.5	...
Denmark	16,639	43,094	133	5,223,000	104	313.9	121.2	0.3	1994[2]	5,196,642	49.3	50.7	84.9[9]
Djibouti	8,950	23,200	149	586,000	160	65.5	25.3	3.0	1960–61	81,200	...	...	80.7[6]
Dominica	290	750	184	72,100	199	248.6	96.1	0.1	1991	71,183	49.8	50.2	...
Dominican Republic	18,704	48,443	130	7,823,000	86	418.3	161.5	1.9	1993	7,089,000	50.1[7]	49.9[7]	52.0[7]
Ecuador	105,037	272,045	74	11,460,000	63	109.1	42.1	2.2	1990	9,648,189	49.7	50.3	55.4
Egypt	385,229	997,739	30	59,695,000	17	155.0	59.8	2.3	1986	48,205,049	51.1	48.9	43.9
El Salvador	8,124	21,041	151	5,768,000	97	710.0	274.1	2.2	1992	5,047,925	48.0	52.0	50.0

The sources of these data are censuses; national population registers (cumulated periodically); registration of migration, births, deaths, and so on; sample surveys to establish demographic conditions; and the like.

The statistics provided for area and population by country are ranked, and the population densities based on those values are also provided. The population densities, for purposes of comparison within this table, are calculated on the bases of the 1995 midyear population estimate as shown and of total area of the country. Elsewhere in individual country presentations the reader may find densities calculated on more specific population figures and more specialized area bases: land area for Finland (because of its many lakes) or ice-free area for Greenland (most of which is ice cap). The data in this section conclude with the estimated average annual growth rate for the country (including both natural growth and net migration) during the five-year period, 1990–95.

In the section containing census data, information supplied includes the census total (usually de facto, the population actually present, rather than de jure, the population legally resident, who might be anywhere); the male-female breakdown; the proportion that is urban (according to the country's own definition of the term "urban," which differs very much from country to country); and finally an analysis of the age structure of the population by 15-year age groups. This last analysis may be particularly useful in distinguishing the type of population being recorded—young, fast-growing nations show a high proportion of people under 30 (most countries in sub-Saharan Africa and the Middle East have nearly one-half of their population under 15 years), while other nations (for example Sweden, which suffered no age-group losses in World War II) exhibit quite uniform proportions.

Finally, a section is provided giving the population of each country at 10-year intervals from 1940 to 2010. The data for years past represent the best available analysis of the published data by the country itself, by the demographers of the United Nations, or by the editors of Britannica. The projections for 2000 and 2010 similarly represent the best fit of available data through the mid-1990s with projected population structure and growth rates during the next two decades. The evidence of the last 25 years with respect to similar estimates published about 1970, however, shows how cloudy is the glass through which these numbers are read. In 1970 no respectable Western analyst would have imagined proposing that mainland China could achieve the degree of birth control that it apparently has since then (as evidenced by the results of 1982 and 1990 censuses); on the other hand, even the Chinese admit that their methods have been somewhat Draconian and that they have already seen some backlash in terms of higher birth rates among those who have so far postponed larger families. How much is "some" by 2000? Compound that problem with all the social, economic, political, and biological factors that can affect 216 countries' populations, and the difficulty facing the prospective compiler of such projections may be appreciated.

Specific data about the vital rates affecting the data in this table may be found in great detail in both the country statistical boxes in "The Nations of the World" section and in the *Vital statistics, marriage, family* table, beginning at page 786.

Percentages in this table for male and female population will always total 100.0, but percentages by age group may not, for reasons such as nonresponse on census forms, "don't know" responses (which are common in countries with poor birth registration systems), and the like.

age distribution (%)						population (by decade, '000s)								country
0–14	15–29	30–44	45–59	60–74	75 and over	1940	1950	1960	1970	1980	1990	2000 projection	2010 projection	
44.5	26.9	15.8	8.6	3.6	0.6	...	8,150	9,829	12,431	14,985	15,332	25,725	32,889	Afghanistan
33.0	28.9	18.5	11.7	5.9	1.9	1,088	1,215	1,607	2,136	2,671	3,256	3,610	4,016	Albania
40.9	28.0	13.9	8.4	4.2	1.6	7,688	8,956	10,800	14,330	18,666	25,012	31,158	37,489	Algeria
38.1	29.0	18.1	9.4	4.3	1.1	13	19	20	27	33	47	67	86	American Samoa
16.3	27.7	27.2	15.1	9.9	3.8	5	6	8	19	33	53	66	71	Andorra
41.7	23.2	17.0	7.4	3.8	1.0	3,738	4,131	4,816	5,588	7,722	10,020	13,400	18,082	Angola
30.5	27.8	20.5	10.2	7.7	3.4	34	45	55	66	69	64	64	64	Antigua and Barbuda
30.6	23.3	19.3	13.9	9.6	3.3	14,169	17,150	20,616	23,962	28,114	32,547	36,648	40,755	Argentina
30.3	25.7	20.8	13.6	6.4	3.2	1,320	1,354	1,867	2,520	3,067	3,335	3,685	3,854	Armenia
24.4	22.0	27.0	16.1	7.2	3.0	31	51	57	61	60	63	76	83	Aruba
22.1	24.2	23.4	15.0	11.1	4.4	7,079	8,219	10,315	12,552	14,741	17,065	18,974	20,778	Australia
17.4	23.7	21.6	17.2	13.4	6.7	6,684	6,935	7,048	7,447	7,549	7,718	8,246	8,350	Austria
32.8	29.7	16.8	12.8	5.7	2.2	3,274	2,896	3,895	5,172	6,165	7,134	7,937	8,832	Azerbaijan
32.2	30.8	19.7	10.6	5.0	1.8	70	79	110	170	210	256	295	332	Bahamas, The
31.7	28.4	28.2	8.0	3.1	0.6	90	127	162	215	342	484	650	778	Bahrain
41.5	25.2	16.2	8.1	4.3	1.1	41,259	45,482	54,699	68,171	88,821	108,118	133,324	158,162	Bangladesh
24.1	27.1	22.1	11.4	9.9	5.4	179	209	232	236	249	261	269	278	Barbados
23.0	22.4	20.6	18.0	11.5	4.5	9,046	7,745	8,190	9,040	9,650	10,260	10,239	10,056	Belarus
18.2	21.8	22.5	16.9	14.1	6.6	8,301	8,639	9,153	9,690	9,859	9,967	10,050	10,040	Belgium
43.9	27.9	14.9	7.2	4.4	1.6	56	68	90	120	146	189	245	304	Belize
46.6[6]	25.7[6]	14.7[6]	8.4[6]	3.8[6]	0.8[6]	...	2,046	2,273	2,693	3,459	4,633	6,266	8,300	Benin
19.5	24.0	26.8	16.4	—13.3—		31	37	43	53	55	59	63	67	Bermuda
40.6[6]	26.5[6]	17.1[6]	10.4[6]	4.6[6]	0.8[6]	...	...	...	...	600	737	900	1,100	Bhutan
41.2	26.2	16.8	8.9	—6.5—		2,508	2,714	3,351	4,212	5,355	6,573	8,329	10,229	Bolivia
27.5[7]	29.0[7]	19.2[7]	15.8[7]	6.3[7]	2.0[7]	...	2,662	3,240	3,703	4,107	4,308	4,330	4,420	Bosnia and Herzegovina
42.8	27.3	14.3	7.3	4.1	2.2	278	407	490	581	905	1,276	1,789	2,318	Botswana
34.7	28.1	19.3	10.6	5.7	1.6	41,525	53,444	72,594	95,847	118,563	144,723	165,715	184,157	Brazil
34.5	29.3	24.2	7.9	—4.1—		36	48	84	129	185	253	334	432	Brunei
20.5	19.2	—39.8—		—20.5—		6,344	7,251	7,867	8,490	8,862	8,718	8,221	7,900	Bulgaria
48.3	23.4	13.4	8.7	4.7	1.4	3,036	3,584	4,350	5,412	6,599	9,012	11,884	15,549	Burkina Faso
46.4	25.3	15.4	7.0	4.0	1.7	1,887	2,435	2,908	3,350	4,120	5,280	6,674	8,437	Burundi
44.2[8]	28.2[8]	14.7[8]	8.4[8]	4.0[8]	0.5[8]	3,400	4,346	5,433	6,938	6,400	8,592	10,907	13,685	Cambodia
46.4	24.5	14.6	8.7	4.1	1.6	...	4,466	5,296	6,612	8,655	11,526	15,245	20,163	Cameroon
20.9	22.7	25.1	15.3	11.3	4.7	11,693	13,737	17,909	21,324	24,593	27,791	31,029	33,946	Canada
45.0	27.3	11.4	8.0	5.5	2.9	181	146	196	267	289	341	448	565	Cape Verde
43.2	27.5	15.0	9.2	4.1	0.8	991	1,311	1,500	1,793	2,257	2,793	3,528	4,449	Central African Republic
43.3[6]	25.8[6]	15.6[6]	9.6[6]	4.8[6]	0.9[6]	2,351	2,658	3,064	3,652	4,477	5,553	7,307	9,319	Chad
30.6[9]	27.0[9]	21.2[9]	12.2[9]	6.8[9]	2.2[9]	5,063	6,082	7,608	9,496	11,147	13,100	15,211	17,010	Chile
27.7	31.0	20.7	12.1	6.9	1.7	530,000	556,613	667,070	818,316	981,242	1,133,683	1,268,970	1,371,580	China
36.1	31.2	17.2	9.5	4.6	1.4	9,097	11,268	15,321	20,884	26,906	32,300	37,822	42,959	Colombia
48.3[6]	26.3[6]	13.8[6]	7.7[6]	3.3[6]	0.6[6]	119	148	177	245	333	464	640	883	Comoros
44.7	27.2	13.3	9.1	4.6	0.7	...	808	988	1,263	1,669	2,232	2,970	3,853	Congo
37.9	31.5	15.8	9.2	4.4	1.2	619	862	1,236	1,731	2,246	2,994	3,709	4,428	Costa Rica
46.8	27.3	15.0	7.5	2.8	0.6	2,350	2,776	3,799	5,515	8,194	11,974	16,761	23,058	Côte d'Ivoire
19.4	20.7	22.7	18.3	12.9	4.5	...	3,851	4,140	4,411	4,588	4,770	4,433	4,373	Croatia
22.8[6]	31.6[6]	19.7[6]	14.0[6]	8.3[6]	3.5[6]	4,566	5,752	7,019	8,565	9,724	10,631	11,502	12,181	Cuba
25.4	22.0	22.3	15.4	10.2	4.7	413	494	573	615	631	757	878	1,046	Cyprus[11]
21.0	21.8	22.6	16.8	12.7	5.1	...	8,925	9,539	9,830	10,292	10,298	10,393	10,489	Czech Republic
17.1	21.7	21.8	19.4	13.0	7.0	3,832	4,271	4,581	4,929	5,123	5,141	5,278	5,320	Denmark
45.2[6]	24.9[6]	16.1[6]	9.0[6]	—4.8[6]—		44	60	78	158	355	505	680	916	Djibouti
33.3	28.3	16.3	9.7	—11.8—		45	51	60	70	75	72	73	74	Dominica
40.6[7]	30.1[7]	15.1[7]	8.7[7]	—5.5[7]—		1,759	2,353	3,231	4,423	5,697	7,110	8,495	9,708	Dominican Republic
38.8	28.5	17.3	9.0	4.7	1.7	2,546	3,307	4,421	5,958	8,123	10,264	12,646	14,899	Ecuador
39.5	26.4	16.9	10.6	5.2	1.0	16,942	20,461	26,085	33,329	40,546	53,153	66,091	75,751	Egypt
44.4[6]	27.6[6]	13.4[6]	8.9[6]	4.6[6]	1.1[6]	1,550	1,931	2,527	3,534	4,525	5,172	6,425	7,772	El Salvador

Area and population (continued)

country	area			population (latest estimate)					population (latest census)				
	square miles	square kilo-metres	rank	total midyear 1995	rank	density per sq mi	density per sq km	% annual growth rate 1990–95	census year	total	male (%)	female (%)	urban (%)
Equatorial Guinea	10,831	28,051	144	396,000	168	36.6	14.1	2.5	1983	300,000	48.3	51.7	28.2
Eritrea	45,300	117,400	100	3,531,000	123	77.9	30.1	2.8	1984	2,703,998	49.9	50.1	15.1
Estonia	17,462	45,227	132	1,487,000	146	85.2	32.9	−1.1	1989	1,572,916	46.9	53.1	71.6
Ethiopia	437,794	1,133,882	27	55,053,000	22	125.8	48.6	3.0	1984	39,480,954	50.0	50.0	9.9
Faroe Islands	540	1,399	177	43,700	209	80.9	31.2	−1.7	1995[2]	43,694	51.8	48.2	...
Fiji	7,055	18,272	155	791,000	156	112.1	43.3	1.6	1986	715,375	50.7	49.3	38.7
Finland	130,559	338,145	64	5,101,000	105	39.1	15.1	0.5	1990	4,998,478	48.5	51.5	79.7
France	210,026	543,965	48	58,172,000	20	277.0	106.9	0.5	1990	56,625,026	48.7	51.3	74.3[6]
French Guiana	33,399	86,504	114	145,000	186	4.3	1.7	4.4	1990	114,808	52.1	47.9	73.4[13]
French Polynesia	1,544	4,000	170	220,000	178	142.5	55.0	2.2	1988	188,814	52.1	47.9	55.0
Gabon	103,347	267,667	76	1,156,000	149	11.2	4.3	1.4	1993	1,014,976	48.0	52.0	73.0
Gambia, The	4,127	10,689	162	1,115,000	151	270.2	104.3	4.0	1993	1,025,867	50.2	49.8	21.2[14]
Gaza Strip	140	363	199	790,000	157	5,642.9	2,176.3	4.7	1993[2]	716,200	50.2	49.8	...
Georgia	26,900	69,700	121	5,514,000	98	205.0	79.1	0.2	1989	5,443,359	47.2	52.8	55.7
Germany	137,828	356,974	62	81,912,000	12	594.3	229.5	0.6	1987[15]	61,077,042	48.0	52.0	85.3[6]
Ghana	92,098	238,533	81	16,472,000	54	178.9	69.1	2.6	1984	12,296,081	49.3	50.7	32.0
Gibraltar	2.2	5.8	216	28,100	213	12,772.7	4,844.8	−1.8	1991[16]	26,703	51.0	49.0	...
Greece	50,949	131,957	96	10,493,000	68	206.0	79.5	0.6	1991	10,264,156	49.3	50.7	58.9
Greenland	840,000	2,175,600	14	55,800	208	0.1	0.0	0.1	1995[2]	55,732	53.3	46.7	80.6[17]
Grenada	133	344	201	92,000	194	691.7	267.4	0.2	1991	91,158	49.4	50.6	32.2
Guadeloupe	687	1,780	176	434,000	164	631.7	243.8	2.2	1990	387,034	48.9	51.1	48.4
Guam	209	541	190	149,000	185	712.9	275.4	2.3	1990	133,152	53.3	46.7	38.2
Guatemala	42,042	108,889	105	10,621,000	66	252.6	97.5	2.9	1981[5]	6,043,559	49.8	50.2	34.3
Guernsey	30	78	210	65,000	201	2,166.7	833.3	1.2	1991[19]	58,867	48.1	51.9	...
Guinea	94,926	245,857	78	6,700,000	91	70.6	27.3	3.1	1983	5,781,014	48.6	51.4	26.0
Guinea-Bissau	13,948	36,125	137	1,073,000	152	76.9	29.7	2.2	1991	983,367	49.2[6]	50.8[6]	20.3[3]
Guyana	83,044	215,083	84	770,000	158	9.3	3.6	0.4	1980	758,619	49.5	50.5	30.5[8]
Haiti	10,695	27,700	146	6,589,000	92	616.1	237.9	1.7	1982	5,053,792	48.5	51.5	20.6
Honduras	43,433	112,492	102	5,512,000	99	126.9	49.0	3.3	1988	4,376,839	49.6	50.4	43.7[6]
Hong Kong	415	1,075	179	6,205,000	94	14,952.7	5,773.3	1.7	1991[5]	5,674,114	51.1	48.9	93.1[4]
Hungary	35,920	93,033	110	10,231,000	72	284.8	110.0	−0.3	1990	10,375,323	48.1	51.9	61.8
Iceland	39,699	102,819	106	269,000	175	6.8	2.6	1.1	1994[2]	266,786	50.2	49.8	91.4
India	1,222,243	3,165,596	7	935,744,000	2	765.6	295.6	1.9	1991	846,302,688	51.9	48.1	25.7
Indonesia	741,052	1,919,317	16	195,283,000	4	265.3	101.7	1.8	1990	179,378,946	49.9	50.1	30.9
Iran	632,457	1,638,057	18	61,271,000	16	96.9	37.4	2.5	1991[5]	55,473,187	51.5	48.5	57.3
Iraq	167,975	435,052	58	20,413,000	44	121.5	46.9	2.8	1987	16,335,199	51.4	48.6	70.2
Ireland	27,137	70,285	120	3,590,000	120	132.3	51.1	0.4	1991	3,525,719	49.7	50.3	57.0
Isle of Man	221	572	189	69,600	200	314.9	121.7	0.2	1991[5]	69,788	48.3	51.7	51.1
Israel[20, 21]	7,876	20,400	152	5,386,000	102	673.9	260.2	3.1	1983[5, 22]	4,037,620	49.8	50.2	86.9
Italy	116,336	301,309	71	57,386,000	21	493.3	190.5	0.2	1991	57,103,833	48.6	51.4	67.1
Jamaica	4,244	10,991	161	2,520,000	133	593.8	229.3	1.0	1991	2,391,700	48.9	51.1	50.2
Japan	145,883	377,835	61	125,362,000	8	859.4	331.8	0.3	1990	123,611,167	49.1	50.9	77.4
Jersey	45	116	209	87,600	195	1,946.7	755.2	1.0	1991	84,082	48.6	51.4	...
Jordan[23]	34,458	89,246	112	4,187,000	115	121.9	47.1	5.1	1994	4,095,579	51.5[6]	48.5[6]	68.0[6]
Kazakhstan	1,049,200	2,717,300	9	16,669,000	53	15.9	6.1	−0.1	1989	16,536,511	48.5	51.5	57.2
Kenya	224,961	582,646	46	28,626,000	33	127.2	49.1	3.6	1989	21,443,636	49.6	50.4	23.6[6]
Kiribati	313	811	181	80,400	196	256.9	99.1	2.3	1990	72,335	49.2	50.8	35.1
Korea, North	47,399	122,762	98	23,487,000	39	495.5	191.3	1.9	[24]	[24]	49.0[6]	51.0[6]	59.8[6]
Korea, South	38,330	99,274	108	44,834,000	25	1,169.7	451.6	0.9	1990[5]	43,410,899	50.2	49.8	74.4
Kuwait	6,880	17,818	156	1,691,000	143	245.8	94.9	−4.6	1985	1,697,301	56.9	43.1	100.0
Kyrgyzstan	76,600	198,500	86	4,483,000	110	58.5	22.6	0.4	1989	4,290,442	48.9	51.1	38.2
Laos	91,429	236,800	83	4,882,000	106	53.4	20.6	3.0	1990	4,201,660	49.1	50.9	18.6[6]
Latvia	24,946	64,610	124	2,515,000	134	100.8	38.9	−1.3	1989	2,680,029	46.6	53.4	71.1
Lebanon	3,950	10,230	163	3,009,000	129	761.8	294.1	3.3	1970	2,126,325	50.8	49.2	60.1
Lesotho	11,720	30,355	140	2,050,000	141	174.9	67.5	2.7	1986[5]	1,577,536	48.2	51.8	16.0
Liberia	38,250	99,067	109	2,380,000	135	62.2	24.0	0.1	1984	2,101,628	50.6	49.4	38.8
Libya	678,400	1,757,000	17	5,407,000	101	8.0	3.1	3.5	1984	3,637,488	53.6	46.4	64.5[10]
Liechtenstein	62	160	208	30,900	211	498.4	193.1	1.5	1980	25,215	49.6	50.4	...
Lithuania	25,213	65,301	123	3,700,000	119	146.7	56.7	−0.2	1989	3,689,779	47.4	52.6	68.0
Luxembourg	999	2,586	172	409,000	167	409.4	158.2	1.4	1991	384,634	49.0	51.0	85.9[3]
Macau	7.5	19.3	215	428,000	166	57,066.7	22,176.2	5.2	1991	339,464	48.5	51.5	97.0
Macedonia	9,928	25,713	148	2,104,000	140	211.9	81.8	0.8	1994	1,936,877	50.4	49.6	58.7
Madagascar	226,658	587,041	45	14,763,000	56	65.1	25.1	3.3	1993[5]	12,092,157	49.5	50.5	21.9[6]
Malawi	45,747	118,484	99	9,939,000	74	217.3	83.9	1.4	1987	7,988,507	48.4	51.6	10.7
Malaysia	127,584	330,442	66	19,948,000	46	156.4	60.4	2.4	1991	17,566,982	50.4	49.6	50.6
Maldives	115	298	203	253,000	177	2,200.0	849.0	3.5	1990	213,215	51.3	48.7	25.9
Mali	482,077	1,248,574	23	9,008,000	79	18.7	7.2	2.1	1987	7,696,348	48.9	51.1	22.0
Malta	122	316	202	370,000	172	3,032.8	1,170.9	0.9	1985	345,418	49.2	50.8	85.3
Marshall Islands	70	181	207	56,200	207	802.9	310.5	4.0	1988	43,380	51.1	48.9	64.5
Martinique	436	1,128	178	388,000	170	889.9	344.0	1.5	1990	359,579	48.4	51.6	80.5
Mauritania	398,000	1,030,700	29	2,274,000	137	5.7	2.2	2.6	1988	1,864,236	49.5	50.5	39.1
Mauritius	788	2,040	174	1,128,000	150	1,431.5	552.9	1.0	1990	1,056,827	49.9	50.1	39.3
Mayotte	144	373	198	116,000	189	805.6	311.0	5.4	1991	94,385	52.0	48.0	59.7[25]
Mexico	756,066	1,958,201	15	91,145,000	11	120.6	46.5	1.8	1990	81,249,645	49.1	50.9	71.3
Micronesia	271	701	185	105,000	191	387.5	149.8	1.0	1994	104,724	51.1[26]	48.9[26]	19.4[26]
Moldova	13,000	33,700	138	4,346,000	112	334.3	129.0	−0.1	1989	4,337,592	47.5	52.5	46.9
Monaco	0.75	1.95	217	30,400	212	40,533.3	15,589.7	0.3	1990	29,972	47.5	52.5	100.0
Mongolia	604,800	1,566,500	19	2,307,000	136	3.8	1.5	1.7	1989	2,043,100	48.9	51.1	57.1
Morocco	177,117	458,730	55	26,980,000	37	152.3	58.8	2.1	1994	26,073,593[27]	50.1[13]	49.9[13]	42.7[13]
Mozambique	313,661	812,379	36	17,889,000	51	57.0	22.0	4.4	1980	12,130,000	48.7	51.3	13.2
Myanmar (Burma)	261,228	676,577	40	46,527,000	24	178.1	68.8	2.2	1983	35,313,905	49.6	50.4	24.0
Namibia	318,580	825,118	35	1,651,000	144	5.2	2.0	3.5	1991	1,401,711	48.6	51.4	32.8
Nauru	8.2	21.2	214	10,400	216	1,268.3	490.6	2.0	1992	9,919	51.2	48.8	100.0
Nepal	56,827	147,181	94	20,093,000	45	353.6	136.5	2.1	1991	18,491,097	49.9	50.1	9.6
Netherlands, The	16,033	41,526	134	15,487,000	55	965.9	372.9	0.7	1994[2]	15,341,553	49.4	50.6	90.4

age distribution (%) 0–14	15–29	30–44	45–59	60–74	75 and over	population (by decade, '000s) 1940	1950	1960	1970	1980	1990	2000 projection	2010 projection	country
41.7	25.1	15.7	11.2	5.3	1.0	...	211	244	291	255	350	448	573	Equatorial Guinea
46.1	23.0	15.9	8.9	4.4	1.6	...	1,140	1,420	1,831	2,382	3,082	4,025	5,153	Eritrea
22.2	21.4	21.0	18.5	11.7	5.1	1,054	1,101	1,216	1,365	1,473	1,571	1,441	1,352	Estonia
46.6	22.7	15.6	8.9	4.5	1.7	...	18,434	22,771	28,791	36,368	47,423	63,785	85,078	Ethiopia
24.0	——58.2——			——17.8——		27	31	35	39	43	48	44	44	Faroe Islands
38.2	29.5	17.8	9.6	3.8	0.8	218	289	394	520	634	732	855	999	Fiji
19.3	20.5	24.6	17.1	12.9	5.7	3,698	4,009	4,430	4,606	4,780	4,986	5,160	5,226	Finland
19.1	22.6	22.8	15.6	12.8	7.1	41,300	41,736	45,684	50,770	53,880	56,735	59,628	62,649	France
33.4	27.3	23.2	10.2	4.4	1.5	30	27	33	49	68	117	163	206	French Guiana
36.0	29.7	18.9	10.4	4.1	0.9	50	62	84	109	151	197	246	296	French Polynesia
33.0[6]	29.3[6]	15.8[6]	12.9[6]	7.3[6]	1.7[6]	442	469	486	504	808	1,078	1,244	1,445	Gabon
43.8[14]	26.5[14]	15.7[14]	7.3[14]	——5.7[14]——		193	232	357	458	632	917	1,288	1,607	Gambia, The
51.2	——38.7——		——10.1——			...	...	...	370	456	630	926	1,272	Gaza Strip
24.8	24.1	19.2	17.5	10.8	3.6	3,612	3,527	4,160	4,708	5,075	5,460	5,569	5,680	Georgia
14.6	24.0	20.1	20.6	13.6	7.2	57,400	68,373	72,673	77,772	78,289	79,433	84,468	89,822	Germany
45.0	26.4	14.6	8.1	4.1	1.8	3,636	5,297	6,958	8,789	11,222	14,470	18,749	24,293	Ghana
19.6	21.3	22.6	18.2	12.9	5.3	14	23	24	26	30	31	28	28	Gibraltar
19.3	22.2	20.3	18.3	14.1	5.9	7,319	7,566	8,327	8,793	9,643	10,161	10,616	10,500	Greece
27.6	23.4	27.1	14.6	——7.2——		19	23	33	41	50	56	57	59	Greenland
35.9[18]	28.5[18]	14.2[18]	8.5[18]	——11.3[18]——		71	76	90	95	89	91	93	95	Grenada
24.9	29.5	21.4	12.5	8.3	3.4	180	206	265	320	327	390	473	541	Guadeloupe
30.0	30.0	22.6	10.8	5.5	1.1	22	59	67	85	107	133	167	198	Guam
44.9	26.8	14.8	8.5	3.9	1.1	2,201	2,969	3,964	5,246	6,917	9,197	12,222	15,827	Guatemala
17.0	23.3	22.2	16.8	13.5	7.2	44	44	45	51	55	61	69	78	Guernsey
46.3[10]	26.1[10]	14.9[10]	8.4[10]	3.7[10]	0.6[10]	...	2,550	3,136	3,900	4,461	5,755	7,759	10,301	Guinea
41.0[6]	24.9[6]	16.7[6]	10.9[6]	5.6[6]	1.0[6]	341	505	542	525	795	964	1,192	1,473	Guinea-Bissau
40.0	00.5	14.0	0.0	4.4	1.2	344	423	560	702	759	754	788	823	Guyana
39.2	26.9	15.6	10.0	5.4	2.9	2,827	3,097	3,723	4,605	5,473	6,052	7,102	8,121	Haiti
44.6[6]	28.3[6]	14.4[6]	7.8[6]	3.9[6]	1.1[6]	1,146	1,390	1,873	2,553	3,316	4,681	6,323	7,998	Honduras
23.0	25.0	26.2	——25.8——			1,786	1,974	3,074	3,942	5,063	5,705	6,796	8,152	Hong Kong
21.3	19.4	22.5	17.9	13.4	5.6	9,280	9,338	9,984	10,337	10,693	10,365	10,170	9,951	Hungary
24.8	23.7	22.7	13.9	10.2	4.7	121	143	176	204	228	255	282	307	Iceland
36.0[6]	27.7[6]	18.0[6]	11.2[6]	5.9[6]	1.2[6]	317,000	357,561	442,344	554,911	688,856	850,638	1,022,021	1,189,082	India
36.6	28.3	18.1	10.6	5.2	1.1	70,500	75,449	92,701	119,467	146,449	178,302	210,249	236,806	Indonesia
44.3	26.6	15.1	8.2	4.8	0.8	14,000	16,913	21,554	28,359	38,783	54,051	67,304	84,005	Iran
45.2	27.2	14.2	7.0	3.7	1.4	3,745	5,180	6,847	9,356	13,043	17,751	23,631	30,565	Iraq
26.7	24.1	20.2	13.8	10.6	4.6	2,958	2,969	2,834	2,954	3,421	3,526	3,672	3,841	Ireland
17.3	20.7	20.4	17.0	15.0	9.2	52	55	49	52	64	69	70	72	Isle of Man
32.6	26.4	18.0	12.3	9.4	3.1	...	...	2,114	2,958	3,862	4,613	5,881	6,713	Israel[20, 21]
17.3[6]	24.2[6]	20.2[6]	18.5[6]	13.7[6]	6.1[6]	43,840	47,104	50,200	53,822	56,434	56,749	57,453	56,180	Italy
32.5[9]	30.9[9]	17.3[9]	9.3[9]	——10.0[9]——		1,212	1,403	1,629	1,891	2,133	2,403	2,619	2,925	Jamaica
18.2	21.7	22.2	20.1	12.6	4.8	73,075	83,200	93,419	103,720	116,807	123,478	127,287	130,344	Japan
15.5	24.9	23.9	17.0	11.9	6.8	61	67	63	71	70	04	92	101	Jersey
43.6[6]	31.6[6]	12.0[6]	8.3[6]	3.4[6]	1.1[6]	...	1,095	1,384	1,795	2,174	3,271	4,932	6,590	Jordan[23]
31.9	26.3	19.4	13.2	6.9	2.3	6,148	6,703	9,996	13,110	14,940	16,742	17,237	18,828	Kazakhstan
47.8	27.6	13.1	6.6	3.4	1.5	4,470	6,018	8,115	11,225	16,667	24,000	32,997	44,114	Kenya
40.3	27.5	17.3	9.2	4.8	0.9	29	33	41	49	57	72	88	106	Kiribati
28.6[6]	34.6[6]	19.8[6]	10.5[6]	5.2[6]	1.3[6]	...	9,740	10,568	14,388	17,999	21,412	25,491	28,491	Korea, North
25.7	30.4	22.9	13.4	6.1	1.5	...	21,147	25,142	32,976	38,124	42,869	46,789	49,683	Korea, South
36.8	28.3	24.1	8.0	1.8	0.4	...	145	292	748	1,358	2,141	1,987	2,494	Kuwait
37.5	27.0	16.3	10.9	6.2	2.1	1,528	1,740	2,173	2,965	3,631	4,395	4,551	4,691	Kyrgyzstan
44.2[25]	25.2[25]	14.4[26]	9.9[25]	4.9[25]	1.4[25]	1,075	1,755	2,177	2,713	3,205	4,202	5,602	7,188	Laos
21.4	21.7	20.3	19.2	12.0	5.3	1,886	1,949	2,129	2,374	2,544	2,684	2,356	2,068	Latvia
42.6	23.8	16.7	9.1	——7.7——		965	1,443	1,857	2,469	2,669	2,555	3,289	3,742	Lebanon
40.7	25.1	16.6	10.7	5.6	1.3	566	734	870	1,064	1,339	1,792	2,338	3,012	Lesotho
43.2	28.2	14.7	7.7	4.4	1.8	...	758	1,004	1,393	1,879	2,365	2,760	3,660	Liberia
46.4[10]	25.0[10]	16.2[10]	8.6[10]	3.3[10]	0.6[10]	900	1,029	1,349	1,986	3,043	4,545	6,387	8,724	Libya
23.0	26.5	24.1	14.1	9.2	3.1	11	14	16	21	26	29	33	39	Liechtenstein
22.6	23.8	20.0	17.9	10.9	4.8	2,925	2,567	2,779	3,148	3,439	3,737	3,692	3,736	Lithuania
17.3	21.5	23.8	17.5	12.8	7.1	296	296	314	339	364	382	428	443	Luxembourg
24.1	27.2	29.4	9.6	7.3	2.3	375	188	169	221	243	332	481	568	Macau
24.8	24.1	22.3	15.8	10.6	2.4	...	1,229	1,392	1,629	1,900	2,024	2,185	2,356	Macedonia
45.6[6]	26.7[6]	15.0[6]	7.7[6]	——5.0[6]——		4,034	4,229	5,367	6,874	9,063	12,571	17,259	23,326	Madagascar
46.1	25.4	14.5	8.0	——6.0——		1,696	3,033	3,481	4,511	6,128	9,289	11,405	13,233	Malawi
38.1[6]	28.1[6]	18.4[6]	9.6[6]	4.5[6]	1.2[6]	...	6,187	7,908	10,466	13,764	17,756	22,087	25,989	Malaysia
46.9	26.7	12.3	9.0	4.0	0.8	81	82	106	128	155	213	286	345	Maldives
46.1	23.9	15.0	8.9	4.9	1.2	3,388	3,426	4,224	5,690	6,816	8,130	9,980	12,252	Mali
24.1	23.2	23.0	15.4	10.5	3.8	270	308	329	326	324	354	378	394	Malta
51.0	24.5	14.6	5.5	3.6	0.8	...	11	15	22	32	46	68	100	Marshall Islands
23.1	28.9	20.5	13.5	9.7	4.3	200	222	252	287	326	361	415	458	Martinique
44.1	26.6	15.0	8.1	4.7	1.4	666	825	991	1,221	1,551	2,003	2,580	3,283	Mauritania
29.7	28.9	22.3	10.9	6.6	1.6	428	479	662	824	957	1,075	1,183	1,301	Mauritius
47.0	27.4	15.0	6.5	3.0	1.2	16	17	25	35	52	89	150	250	Mayotte
38.3	29.4	16.6	8.9	4.5	1.7	19,815	27,737	36,945	50,596	67,570	83,226	98,881	112,891	Mexico
46.4[26]	26.8[26]	12.6[26]	8.5[26]	4.5[26]	1.1[26]	...	30	40	57	73	101	110	120	Micronesia
27.9	22.9	21.0	15.6	9.7	2.9	2,468	2,341	3,004	3,595	4,002	4,364	4,329	4,294	Moldova
12.3	16.7	21.2	20.4	17.9	10.8	20	22	23	24	27	30	31	31	Monaco
41.9	29.2	14.6	8.5	——5.8——		750	747	931	1,248	1,663	2,122	2,525	3,025	Mongolia
42.2[13]	28.3[13]	14.1[13]	9.2[13]	4.8[13]	1.5[13]	7,750	8,953	11,640	15,126	19,177	24,294	29,992	37,065	Morocco
44.4	26.7	15.9	8.7	3.6	0.7	...	6,458	7,584	9,390	12,103	14,438	20,868	27,381	Mozambique
40.7	27.7	15.0	10.5	——6.1——		...	17,832	21,746	27,102	33,821	41,813	51,539	61,596	Myanmar (Burma)
44.4[6]	25.8[6]	15.2[6]	8.6[6]	5.0[6]	1.0[6]	336	405	522	761	1,002	1,387	1,957	2,705	Namibia
41.8	25.0	20.7	8.2	——2.8——		3	4	5	7	8	9	11	13	Nauru
42.3	25.7	16.7	9.7	4.7	0.9	7,000	8,000	9,180	11,232	14,634	18,111	22,292	27,439	Nepal
18.4	22.4	23.8	17.8	12.1	5.5	8,834	10,027	11,417	12,958	14,150	14,952	16,121	16,987	Netherlands, The

Area and population (continued)

country	area			population (latest estimate)					population (latest census)				
	square miles	square kilo-metres	rank	total midyear 1995	rank	density per sq mi	density per sq km	% annual growth rate 1990–95	census year	total	male (%)	female (%)	urban (%)
Netherlands Antilles	308	800	182	201,000	181	652.6	251.3	1.4	1992	189,474	47.9	52.1	...
New Caledonia	7,172	18,576	154	187,000	182	26.1	10.1	2.1	1989	164,173	51.1	48.9	59.4
New Zealand	104,454	270,534	75	3,568,000	121	34.2	13.2	1.2	1991	3,434,950	49.3	50.7	75.9
Nicaragua	50,838	131,670	97	4,340,000	113	85.4	33.0	2.3	1971	1,877,952	48.3	51.7	48.0
Niger	496,900	1,287,000	20	9,151,000	78	18.4	7.1	3.4	1988[5]	7,228,552	49.5	50.5	15.3
Nigeria	356,669	923,768	32	95,434,000	10	267.6	103.3	2.1	1991	88,514,501	50.3	49.7	35.2[6]
Northern Mariana Islands	184	477	192	57,900	205	314.7	121.4	5.4	1990	43,345	52.6	47.4	28.0
Norway	125,050	323,878	67	4,355,000	111	34.8	13.4	0.5	1990	4,247,546	49.4	50.6	75.0[6]
Oman	118,150	306,000	70	2,163,000	139	18.3	7.1	4.3	1993	2,017,591	51.0[28]	49.0[28]	10.6[6]
Pakistan	339,697	879,811	34	140,497,000	7	413.6	159.7	2.9	1981[29]	84,253,644	52.5	47.5	28.3
Palau	188	488	191	16,900	215	89.9	34.6	2.2	1990	15,122	53.8	46.2	69.4
Panama	29,157	75,517	118	2,631,000	131	90.2	34.8	1.9	1990	2,329,329	50.6	49.4	53.7
Papua New Guinea	178,704	462,840	54	4,302,000	114	24.1	9.3	2.3	1990[30]	3,607,954	52.7	47.3	15.2
Paraguay	157,048	406,752	59	4,828,000	107	30.7	11.9	2.7	1992	4,123,550	50.2	49.8	50.5
Peru	496,225	1,285,216	21	23,489,000	38	47.3	18.3	1.7	1993	22,639,443	49.7	50.3	70.1
Philippines	115,860	300,076	72	70,011,000	14	604.3	233.3	2.4	1990	60,684,887	50.3	49.7	48.6
Poland	120,728	312,685	69	38,641,000	29	320.1	123.6	0.3	1988	37,878,641	48.7	51.3	61.2
Portugal	35,574	92,135	111	9,906,000	75	278.5	107.5	0.0	1991	9,862,540	48.2	51.8	29.7[7]
Puerto Rico	3,515	9,104	165	3,725,000	118	1,059.7	409.2	1.1	1990	3,522,037	48.4	51.6	71.2
Qatar	4,412	11,427	160	579,000	161	131.2	50.7	3.7	1986	369,079	67.2	32.8	88.0[10]
Réunion	970	2,512	173	660,000	159	680.4	262.7	1.9	1990	597,828	49.2	50.8	73.4
Romania	91,699	237,500	82	22,693,000	41	247.5	95.5	−0.4	1992	22,760,449	49.1	50.9	54.4
Russia	6,592,800	17,075,400	1	147,168,000	6	22.3	8.6	−0.2	1989	147,400,537	46.9	53.1	73.6
Rwanda	10,169	26,338	147	7,855,000	85	772.4	298.2	2.6	1991	7,164,994	48.7	51.3	5.4
St. Kitts and Nevis	104	269	204	39,400	210	378.8	146.5	−1.2	1991	41,826	51.6[6]	48.4[6]	48.9[6]
St. Lucia	238	617	188	143,000	187	600.8	231.8	1.3	1991	133,308	48.5	51.5	44.1[6]
St. Vincent and the Grenadines	150	389	197	112,000	190	746.7	287.9	1.3	1991	106,499	49.9	50.1	24.6
San Marino	24	61	211	24,900	214	1,053.7	406.9	1.5	1976	19,149	50.4	49.6	90.1[3]
São Tomé and Príncipe	386	1,001	180	131,000	188	339.4	130.9	2.2	1991	120,146	49.4	50.6	44.1[9]
Saudi Arabia	865,000	2,240,000	13	17,880,000	52	20.7	8.0	2.2	1992	16,929,294	55.9	44.1	77.3[6]
Senegal	75,951	196,712	87	8,312,000	83	109.4	42.3	2.6	1988	6,928,405	48.7	51.3	38.6
Seychelles	176	455	194	75,000	197	426.1	164.8	1.5	1987	68,598	49.7	50.3	35.5
Sierra Leone	27,699	71,740	119	4,509,000	108	162.8	62.9	2.4	1985	3,517,530	49.6	50.4	31.8
Singapore	247	641	187	2,989,000	130	12,077.2	4,663.0	2.0	1990[5]	2,705,115	50.6	49.4	100.0
Slovakia	18,933	49,035	129	5,355,000	103	282.8	109.2	0.2	1991	5,268,935	48.9	51.1	56.8
Slovenia	7,821	20,256	153	1,971,000	142	252.0	97.3	−0.3	1991	1,974,839	48.5	51.5	48.9
Solomon Islands	10,954	28,370	143	382,000	171	34.9	13.5	3.6	1986	285,176	51.9	48.1	15.7
Somalia	246,000	637,000	42	6,734,000	90	27.4	10.6	−0.1	1975	4,089,203	50.1	49.9	25.4
South Africa[31]	472,281	1,223,201	25	41,465,000	27	87.8	33.9	2.3	1991[32]	26,504,191	48.8	51.2	60.3
Spain	194,898	504,783	51	39,188,000	28	201.1	77.6	0.2	1991	38,999,181	49.1	50.9	75.3
Sri Lanka	25,332	65,610	122	18,090,000	49	714.1	275.7	1.3	1981	14,848,364	50.8	49.2	21.5
Sudan, The	966,757	2,503,890	10	28,098,000	34	29.1	11.2	2.7	1993	24,940,683	50.2[6]	49.8[6]	22.5[6]
Suriname	63,251	163,820	92	430,000	165	6.8	2.6	1.3	1980	354,860	49.5	50.5	44.8[8]
Swaziland	6,704	17,364	157	913,000	153	136.2	52.6	3.5	1986	681,059	47.2	52.8	22.8
Sweden	173,732	449,964	56	8,826,000	81	50.8	19.6	0.6	1993[2]	8,745,109	49.4	50.6	84.3[9]
Switzerland	15,940	41,284	135	7,039,000	89	441.6	170.5	1.0	1990[33]	6,873,687	49.3	50.7	59.7[3]
Syria	71,498	185,180	88	14,313,000	57	200.2	77.3	3.4	1981	9,052,628	51.1	48.9	47.1
Taiwan	13,969	36,179	136	21,268,000	43	1,522.5	587.9	1.0	1990[5]	20,393,628	52.1	47.9	74.5
Tajikistan	55,300	143,100	95	5,832,000	96	105.5	40.8	1.9	1989	5,108,576	49.7	50.3	32.6
Tanzania	364,017	942,799	31	28,072,000	35	77.1	29.8	2.8	1988	23,174,336	48.9	51.1	32.8[6]
Thailand	198,115	513,115	50	58,791,000	18	296.8	114.6	1.1	1990	54,532,300	49.6	50.4	18.7
Togo	21,925	56,785	125	4,138,000	116	188.7	72.9	3.2	1981	2,719,567	48.7	51.3	15.2
Tonga	290	750	183	100,000	192	344.8	133.3	0.7	1986[5]	94,649	50.3	49.7	30.7
Trinidad and Tobago	1,980	5,128	168	1,265,000	148	638.9	246.7	0.6	1990	1,234,388	50.1	49.9	64.8
Tunisia	63,378	164,150	91	8,896,000	80	140.4	54.2	2.0	1994	8,785,364	50.6	49.4	61.0
Turkey	300,948	779,452	37	62,526,000	15	207.8	80.2	2.2	1990	56,473,035	50.7	49.3	59.0
Turkmenistan	188,500	488,100	52	4,081,000	117	21.6	8.4	2.2	1995	4,000,460	49.6	50.3	46.0
Tuvalu	9.4	24.4	213	9,400	217	1,000.0	385.2	1.0	1991	9,043	48.4	51.6	42.5
Uganda	93,070	241,040	80	18,659,000	47	200.5	77.4	2.6	1991	16,671,705	49.1	50.9	11.3
Ukraine	233,100	603,700	44	52,003,000	23	223.1	86.1	0.0	1989	51,706,746	46.3	53.7	66.9
United Arab Emirates	32,280	83,600	116	2,195,000	138	68.0	26.3	3.5	1985	1,622,464	64.9	35.1	76.9[10]
United Kingdom	94,251	244,110	79	58,586,000	19	621.6	240.0	0.4	1991[2]	56,467,000	48.4	51.6	89.1[6]
United States	3,679,192	9,529,063	4	263,057,000	3	71.5	27.6	1.0	1990[36]	248,709,873	48.7	51.3	75.2
Uruguay	68,037	176,215	90	3,186,000	127	46.8	18.1	0.6	1985	2,955,241	48.7	51.3	86.2
Uzbekistan	172,700	447,400	57	22,886,000	40	132.5	51.2	2.2	1989	19,905,158	49.3	50.7	40.7
Vanuatu	4,707	12,190	159	168,000	183	35.7	13.8	2.7	1989	142,630	51.6	48.4	17.7
Venezuela	352,144	912,050	33	21,844,000	42	62.0	24.0	2.3	1990	19,405,429	49.7	50.3	84.0
Vietnam	127,816	331,041	65	74,545,000	13	583.2	225.2	2.3	1989	64,411,713	48.7	51.3	20.1
Virgin Islands (U.S.)	136	352	200	97,800	193	719.1	277.8	−0.8	1990	101,809	48.3	51.7	37.2
West Bank[37]	2,270	5,900	166	1,266,000	147	557.7	214.6	4.6	1993[2]	1,051,300	50.4	49.6	...
Western Sahara	97,344	252,120	77	218,000	179	2.2	0.9	2.4	1970	76,425	...	...	...
Western Samoa	1,093	2,831	171	166,000	184	151.9	58.6	0.8	1991	161,298	52.5	47.5	21.2
Yemen	205,356	531,869	49	13,058,000	61	63.6	24.6	3.1	1994	14,561,330	49.7[9]	50.3[9]	29.3[6]
Yugoslavia	39,449	102,173	107	10,555,000	67	267.6	103.3	0.0	1991	10,394,026	49.6	50.4	46.8[7]
Zaire	905,446	2,345,095	12	43,901,000	26	48.5	18.7	3.2	1984	29,671,407	49.2	50.8	36.6[10]
Zambia	290,586	752,614	39	9,456,000	77	32.5	12.6	3.0	1990	7,818,447	49.2	50.8	42.0
Zimbabwe	150,872	390,757	60	11,261,000	64	74.6	28.8	2.6	1992	10,401,767	48.8	51.2	23.0[13]

[1]Settled population only. [2]Civil register; not a census. [3]1991 estimate. [4]1986 census. [5]Data are for de jure population. [6]1990 estimate. [7]1981 census. [8]1980 estimate. [9]1992 estimate. [10]1985 estimate. [11]Except census, data are for the island of Cyprus. [12]Republic of Cyprus only. [13]1982 census. [14]1983 census. [15]Former West Germany only. [16]Excludes visitors, transients, and family members of British servicemen. [17]1994 estimate. [18]1988 estimate. [19]Data exclude Alderney (population 2,297) and Sark (population 604). [20]Area figures exclude the West Bank, East Jerusalem, Gaza Strip, and Golan Heights. [21]Population figures include the Golan Heights and East Jerusalem, and exclude Israelis in the West Bank and Gaza Strip. [22]Includes East Jerusalem and Israelis in the West

age distribution (%) 0–14	15–29	30–44	45–59	60–74	75 and over	population (by decade, '000s) 1940	1950	1960	1970	1980	1990	2000 projection	2010 projection	country
26.0	23.9	25.5	14.3	7.3	3.0	77	112	136	163	174	188	214	243	Netherlands Antilles
32.6	28.6	19.8	12.1	5.4	1.6	53	59	79	110	140	168	204	238	New Caledonia
23.2	24.6	22.4	14.4	10.9	4.5	1,637	1,909	2,377	2,820	3,144	3,363	3,786	4,097	New Zealand
48.1	25.6	14.1	7.4	3.8	1.1	825	1,109	1,472	1,972	2,771	3,871	4,459	5,864	Nicaragua
48.7	24.8	14.6	6.8	3.6	1.5	1,700	2,400	3,028	4,165	5,586	7,731	10,805	14,751	Niger
47.4[6]	26.0[6]	14.4[6]	8.0[6]	3.5[6]	0.6[6]	...	33,320	42,366	56,346	69,875	86,015	105,885	130,344	Nigeria
23.8	33.5	30.7	9.1	2.3	0.5	48	6	9	10	17	45	65	83	Northern Mariana Islands
18.8	22.9	22.1	15.1	13.9	7.2	2,973	3,265	3,581	3,877	4,086	4,241	4,426	4,550	Norway
46.7[6]	23.6[6]	17.2[6]	8.3[6]	3.5[6]	0.7[6]	...	456	558	723	1,101	1,751	2,626	3,783	Oman
44.5	23.9	15.4	9.3	5.3	1.6	28,300	39,513	49,955	65,706	85,299	121,933	161,827	210,104	Pakistan
30.3	27.8	22.8	10.5	—8.6—		25	6	9	10	12	15	19	22	Palau
34.8	29.2	18.2	10.2	5.5	2.0	620	893	1,148	1,531	1,950	2,398	2,856	3,266	Panama
41.9	28.5	16.6	8.7	—3.2—		1,308	1,613	1,920	2,422	3,086	3,839	4,809	5,918	Papua New Guinea
40.1	27.6	18.7	8.3	4.2	1.1	1,111	1,351	1,774	2,351	3,136	4,220	5,464	6,785	Paraguay
37.0	28.6	17.7	9.8	—7.0—		6,784	7,632	9,931	13,193	17,295	21,550	25,573	29,313	Peru
39.6	28.7	17.3	9.2	4.2	1.1	16,459	20,988	27,561	36,850	48,287	62,049	78,414	94,503	Philippines
25.4	21.2	23.3	15.5	10.4	4.2	31,500	24,824	29,561	32,526	35,578	38,111	39,077	39,963	Poland
25.5[7]	23.5[7]	18.0[7]	17.2[7]	11.9[7]	3.9[7]	7,696	8,405	8,826	9,040	9,766	9,896	9,967	10,089	Portugal
27.2	25.1	20.4	14.1	9.2	4.0	1,878	2,218	2,360	2,721	3,204	3,528	3,934	4,386	Puerto Rico
27.8	29.3	32.3	8.6	1.6	0.4	...	47	59	151	229	484	632	755	Qatar
29.5	29.8	20.3	11.7	6.5	2.1	221	244	338	447	507	601	724	873	Réunion
22.4	22.9	20.8	17.1	—16.8—		15,907	16,311	18,403	20,253	22,201	23,201	22,625	22,490	Romania
23.1	22.0	21.9	17.6	11.2	4.2	110,098	105,018	119,906	130,392	138,914	148,292	143,178	134,816	Russia
45.6	28.6	12.4	8.4	3.9	0.9	1,910	2,120	2,742	3,728	5,113	6,925	8,855	11,084	Rwanda
32.5[6]	25.6[6]	18.9[6]	10.1[6]	8.9[6]	4.0[6]	43	49	51	46	43	42	39	39	St. Kitts and Nevis
36.8	29.4	16.3	8.7	6.3	2.5	70	79	86	101	122	134	151	169	St. Lucia
37.4[10]	32.7[10]	14.9[10]	7.5[10]	5.6[10]	1.9[10]	61	67	80	86	99	105	118	133	St. Vincent and the Grenadines
24.4	23.0	19.9	17.4	11.4	3.9	10	13	15	19	21	23	27	31	San Marino
47.6[6]	25.8[6]	12.1[6]	7.3[6]	—6.4[6]—		60	60	64	74	94	117	146	182	São Tomé and Príncipe
42.9[6]	24.6[6]	19.9[6]	8.1[6]	3.4[6]	0.7[6]	...	3,201	4,075	5,745	9,604	16,048	21,257	28,880	Saudi Arabia
47.5	26.1	13.6	7.8	—5.0—		1,857	2,500	3,187	4,158	5,538	7,327	9,495	12,241	Senegal
33.6	30.3	15.3	10.7	7.1	2.9	32	34	42	54	63	70	81	94	Seychelles
43.9[10]	25.6[10]	15.7[10]	9.6[10]	4.5[10]	0.7[10]	1,700	1,944	2,241	2,656	3,236	3,999	5,069	6,366	Sierra Leone
23.2	27.3	27.7	12.7	6.9	2.2	751	1,022	1,639	2,075	2,282	2,705	3,303	4,034	Singapore
25.0	22.7	22.8	14.6	10.7	4.2	3,553	3,463	3,994	4,528	4,984	5,298	5,412	5,529	Slovakia
20.0	22.4	23.7	17.4	11.9	4.6	1,450	1,467	1,580	1,727	1,901	1,998	1,963	2,003	Slovenia
47.3	25.7	13.9	8.1	—4.9—		94	104	125	163	230	320	444	596	Solomon Islands
45.6	24.9	15.5	7.4	—5.4—		...	2,438	2,956	3,667	5,799	6,753	7,079	7,823	Somalia
32.1	29.4	20.7	10.5	5.7	1.6	10,353	13,683	17,396	22,458	29,170	37,066	46,215	56,398	South Africa[31]
18.4[9]	25.1[9]	20.6[9]	—35.9[9]—			25,757	27,868	30,303	33,779	37,636	38,798	39,268	38,969	Spain
35.3	29.0	17.9	10.6	5.2	1.4	5,972	7,678	9,889	12,514	14,747	16,993	19,258	21,521	Sri Lanka
45.2[6]	26.1[6]	15.5[6]	8.7[6]	3.9[6]	0.7[6]	8,500	9,190	11,165	13,859	18,681	24,585	32,079	41,534	Sudan, The
39.3	29.5	13.8	10.0	4.5	2.8	193	215	247	292	355	403	465	634	Suriname
47.3	26.6	13.4	7.4	3.4	1.3	154	253	320	409	550	769	1,047	1,338	Swaziland
18.7	20.0	20.3	18.7	14.1	8.2	6,371	7,041	7,498	8,081	8,310	8,559	9,059	9,278	Sweden
16.8	22.8	23.2	18.0	12.5	6.7	4,234	4,715	5,429	6,270	6,362	6,712	7,279	7,452	Switzerland
48.5	25.8	12.5	8.3	3.7	1.2	2,597	3,495	4,561	6,305	8,704	12,116	16,909	23,019	Syria
27.1	27.8	23.1	12.3	7.9	1.8	5,987	7,619	10,668	14,583	17,705	20,279	22,306	24,536	Taiwan
42.9	28.1	13.8	9.0	4.6	1.6	1,525	1,532	2,083	2,942	3,968	5,303	6,407	7,732	Tajikistan
47.2[6]	26.7[6]	14.2[6]	7.8[6]	3.3[6]	0.7[6]	...	7,892	10,073	13,273	18,441	24,403	32,120	41,205	Tanzania
28.8	30.4	21.2	12.3	5.7	1.6	15,296	20,010	26,392	35,745	46,718	55,583	61,909	67,130	Thailand
49.8	24.8	13.1	6.8	3.3	2.0	834	1,329	1,514	2,020	2,615	3,531	4,818	6,427	Togo
10.0	[illegible]	10.0	10.1	5.0	1.4	37	50	65	80	92	97	103	105	Tonga
31.3[6]	26.9[6]	21.5[6]	12.2[6]	8.1[6]		500	668	828	941	1,082	1,227	1,303	1,384	Trinidad and Tobago
39.7[34]	28.8[34]	14.2[34]	10.7[34]	5.4[34]	1.2[34]	2,887	3,530	4,221	5,137	6,392	8,074	9,694	11,209	Tunisia
35.0	28.6	18.4	10.9	—7.1—		17,723	20,809	27,509	35,321	44,438	56,098	69,694	80,120	Turkey
40.5[35]	28.8[35]	15.5[35]	9.1[35]	4.7[35]	1.4[35]	1,302	1,211	1,594	2,189	2,860	3,668	4,474	5,277	Turkmenistan
34.6	24.0	20.7	11.3	—9.2—		4	5	5	6	8	9	10	11	Tuvalu
48.3[6]	26.6[6]	13.9[6]	7.2[6]	3.4[6]	0.7[6]	4,233	5,969	7,551	9,806	12,779	16,447	21,168	27,244	Uganda
21.5	21.0	20.6	18.5	10.7	7.7	41,340	36,906	42,783	47,317	50,034	51,892	51,634	50,903	Ukraine
31.9[10]	24.9[10]	32.1[10]	8.7[10]	1.9[10]	0.5[10]	...	70	90	223	1,015	1,844	2,429	2,882	United Arab Emirates
19.1	21.9	21.2	16.7	14.1	7.0	48,226	50,290	52,372	55,632	56,330	57,561	59,595	61,127	United Kingdom
21.5	23.4	23.9	14.4	11.5	5.3	132,594	152,271	180,671	204,879	227,726	249,911	276,052	300,226	United States
26.6	22.8	18.3	16.5	11.4	4.3	1,974	2,194	2,531	2,824	2,914	3,094	3,274	3,453	Uruguay
40.8	28.4	15.0	9.3	4.7	1.8	6,551	6,314	8,559	11,973	15,977	20,515	25,383	30,703	Uzbekistan
45.5	26.6	15.2	8.4	3.7	0.6	43	52	65	86	115	148	189	231	Vanuatu
38.3	28.1	18.6	9.3	4.5	1.2	3,740	5,094	7,579	10,721	15,091	19,502	24,170	28,716	Venezuela
39.0	28.7	16.0	9.1	5.6	1.6	...	29,954	34,743	42,729	53,711	66,689	82,648	98,448	Vietnam
28.9	23.7	22.0	16.0	7.3	2.2	25	27	32	75	97	102	99	107	Virgin Islands (U.S.)
48.3	—40.4—		—11.3—			...	...	...	608	733	1,011	1,533	2,244	West Bank[37]
42.9	27.2	16.3	7.4	4.4	1.8	...	14	32	76	155	193	244	306	Western Sahara
40.5	30.0	14.6	8.7	—6.0—		61	82	111	143	155	159	174	192	Western Samoa
50.6[9]	22.9[9]	13.6[9]	7.7[9]	4.0[9]	1.2[9]	...	4,316	5,247	6,332	8,219	11,230	15,164	19,975	Yemen
22.8	21.6	21.7	17.1	12.2	3.5	...	7,131	8,050	8,910	9,842	10,529	10,406	10,781	Yugoslavia
45.2[10]	25.9[10]	15.5[10]	8.7[10]	3.9[10]	0.7[10]	10,370	13,055	16,151	21,368	27,009	37,436	51,136	68,876	Zaire
48.4[6]	27.2[6]	13.7[6]	7.0[6]	3.1[6]	0.7[6]	1,484	2,440	3,141	4,189	5,738	8,150	10,754	13,657	Zambia
51.0[13]	26.3[13]	13.4[13]	6.5[13]	1.2[13]	1.6[13]	1,940	2,730	3,812	5,260	7,126	9,903	12,514	15,260	Zimbabwe

Bank, Gaza Strip, and Golan Heights. [23]Excludes the West Bank. [24]No census ever taken. [25]1985 census. [26]1980 census. [27]Includes Western Sahara. [28]Omani nationals only. [29]Excludes Afghan refugees and residents of Pakistani-occupied Jammu and Kashmir. [30]Excludes an estimated 155,000 persons in North Solomons province and five remote census districts. [31]Includes the former black independent states of Bophuthatswana, Ciskei, Transkei, and Venda. [32]Excludes the former black independent states of Bophuthatswana, Ciskei, Transkei, and Venda. [33]Includes resident aliens; excludes seasonal workers. [34]1984 census. [35]1989 census. [36]Excludes 515,000 armed forces overseas. [37]Excludes East Jerusalem.

Major cities and national capitals

The following table lists the principal cities or municipalities (those exceeding 100,000 in population [50,000 for Anglo-America]) of the countries of the world, together with figures for each national capital (indicated by a ★), regardless of size.

Most of the populations given refer to a so-called city proper, that is, a legally defined, incorporated, or chartered area defined by administrative boundaries and by national or state law. Some data, however, refer to the municipality, or commune, similar to the medieval city-state in that the city is governed together with its immediately adjoining, economically dependent areas, whether urban or rural in nature. Some countries define no other demographic or legal entities within such communes or municipalities, but many identify a centre, seat, head (*cabecera*), or locality that corresponds to the most densely populated, compact, contiguous core of the municipality. Because the amount of work involved in carefully defining these "centres" may be considerable, the necessary resources usually exist only at the time of a national census (generally 5 or 10 years apart). Between censuses, therefore, it may be possible only to track the growth of the municipality as a whole. Thus, in order to provide the most up-to-date data for cities in this table, figures referring to municipalities or communes may be given (identified by the abbreviation "MU"), even though the country itself may define a smaller, more closely knit city proper. Specific identification of municipalities is provided in this table *only* when the country also publishes data for a more narrowly defined city proper; it is *not* provided when the sole published figure is the municipality, whether or not this is the proper local administrative term for the entity.

Problems also exist in the identification of cities in terms of named legal entities. There is, for example, a single municipality (*commune*) named Brussel (Brussels) at the centre of the Brussels agglomeration in Belgium; the *commune* numbers only about 136,000 population, while the agglomeration, which is understood by most people to constitute the city, numbers nearly a million. Both are shown so as to apprise the reader of the existence of a problem.

For certain countries, more than one form of the name of the city is given, usually to permit recognition of recent place name changes or of *forms* of the place name likely to be encountered in press stories if the title of the city's entry in the *Encyclopædia Britannica* is spelled according to a different romanization or spelling policy. Chinese names, for example, are given first in their Wade-Giles spelling (the scholarly system used by Britannica) and then, parenthetically, in their Pinyin spelling, the official Chinese system now encountered in press reports, official documents, and maps.

Sources for this data were usually the national census and statistical abstracts of the countries concerned, supplemented by correspondence with most national statistical offices to solicit unpublished data.

Major cities and national capitals

country city	population
Afghanistan (1988 est.)	
Herāt	177,300
★ Kābul	700,000[1]
Kandahār (Qandahār)	225,500
Mazār-e Sharīf	130,600
Albania (1991 est.)	
★ Tiranë	300,000
Algeria (1987)	
★ Algiers	1,507,241
Annaba	222,518
Batna	181,601
Béchar	107,311
Bejaïa	114,534
Biskra	128,280
Blida (el-Boulaida)	127,284
Constantine (Qacentina)	440,842
Mostaganem	114,037
Oran (Wahran)	609,823
Sétif	170,182
Sidi bel Abbès	152,778
Skikda	128,747
Tébessa	107,559
Tlemcen (Tilimsen)	107,632
American Samoa (1990)	
★ Fagatogo (legislative and judicial)	2,323[2]
★ Utulei (executive)	930[2]
Andorra (1993 est.)	
★ Andorra la Vella	22,387
Angola (1993 est.)	
Huambo	400,000
★ Luanda	2,000,000
Lubango	105,000[3]
Antigua and Barbuda (1991)	
★ Saint John's	21,514
Argentina (1991)	
Avellaneda	346,620[4]
Bahía Blanca	255,145
★ Buenos Aires	2,960,976[4]
Catamarca	110,269
Comodoro Rivadavia	123,672
Concordia	116,491
Córdoba	1,148,305
Corrientes	257,766
Formosa	153,855
General San Martín	407,506[4]
La Matanza	1,111,811
La Plata	520,647
La Rioja	104,494
Lanús	466,755[4]
Lomas de Zamora	572,769[4]
Mar del Plata	519,707
Mendoza	121,739
Morón	641,541[4]
Neuquén	167,078
Paraná	206,848
Posadas	201,943
Quilmes	509,445[4]
Resistencia	228,199
Río Cuarto	133,741
Rosario	894,645
Salta	367,099
San Fernando	141,496
San Isidro	299,022[4]
San Juan	119,492
San Miguel de Tucumán	470,604
San Nicolás	114,752
San Salvador de Jujuy	181,318
Santa Fe	342,796
Vicente López	289,142[4]
Armenia (1994 est.)	
Gyumri (Kumayri; Leninakan)	120,000[5]
★ Yerevan	1,226,000
Aruba (1991)	
★ Oranjestad	20,046
Australia (1994 est.)	
Adelaide	1,076,400[6]
Bankstown	162,600
Blacktown	228,400
Brisbane	786,442
Campbelltown	149,100
★ Canberra	278,904
Canterbury	134,500
Fairfield	186,100
Geelong	152,200[7]
Gold Coast-Tweed	314,000[7]
Gosford	142,150
Hobart	194,200[6]
Keilor	114,639
Knox	132,686
Lake Macquarie	175,510
Liverpool	106,750
Melbourne	3,198,200[6]
Moorabbin	100,389
Newcastle	460,200[7]
Parramatta	137,450
Penrith	163,500
Perth	1,239,400[6]
Randwick	117,600
Stirling	178,734[1]
Sydney	3,738,500[6]
Wanneroo	190,965[1]
Wollongong	182,560
Austria (1991)	
Graz	237,810
Innsbruck	118,112
Linz	203,044
Salzburg	143,978
★ Vienna	1,539,848
Azerbaijan (1991 est.)	
★ Baku (Baky)	1,087,000[8]
Gäncä (Gyandzha)	282,200
Sumqayıt (Sumgait)	236,200
Bahamas, The (1990)	
★ Nassau	172,196[9]
Bahrain (1992 est.)	
★ al-Manāmah	140,401
Bangladesh (1991)	
Barisāl	180,014
Brāhmanbāria	114,297
Chittagong	1,566,070
Comilla	164,509
★ Dhākā (Dacca)	3,637,892
Dinājpur	136,657
Gāzipur	100,690
Jamālpur	108,416
Jessore	176,398
Khulna	601,051
Mymensingh	198,662
Naogaon	109,156
Nārāyanganj	288,008
Narsinghdi	100,120
Nawābganj	131,260
Pābna	113,146
Rājshāhi	324,532
Rangpur	220,849
Saidpur	110,494
Sirājganj	100,003
Sylhet	114,284
Tangail	111,783
Tongi	165,099
Barbados (1990)	
★ Bridgetown	6,070
Belarus (1992 est.)	
Baranovichi	169,000
Bobruysk	224,000
Borisov	152,000
Brest	284,000
Gomel	517,000
Grodno	291,000
★ Minsk	1,666,000[8]
Mogilyov	364,000
Mozyr	104,000
Orsha	140,000
Pinsk	127,000
Vitebsk	373,000
Belgium (1994 est.)	
Antwerp	462,880
Brugge (Bruges)	116,724
★ Brussels	136,424[10]
Agglomeration	949,070
Charleroi	206,898
Ghent	228,490
Liège (Luik)	195,389
Namur	104,610
Belize (1993 est.)	
★ Belmopan	3,852
Benin (1992)	
Abomey-Calavi	125,565
★ Cotonou (official)	533,212
Djougou	132,192
Parakou	106,708
★ Porto-Novo (de facto)	177,660
Bermuda (1994 est.)	
★ Hamilton	1,100
Bhutan (1993 est.)	
★ Paro (administrative)	3,000[11]
★ Thimphu (official)	30,340
Bolivia (1992)	
Cochabamba	407,825
El Alto	405,492
★ La Paz (administrative)	713,378
Oruro	183,422
Potosí	112,078
Santa Cruz	697,278
★ Sucre (judicial)	131,769
Bosnia and Herzegovina (1991; MU)	
Banja Luka	195,139
Doboj	102,546
Mostar	126,067
Prijedor	112,470
★ Sarajevo	300,000[1]
Tuzla	131,861
Zenica	145,577
Botswana (1992 est.)	
★ Gaborone	138,000
Brazil (1991)	
Alvorada	132,582
Americana	153,592
Anápolis	222,400
Aracaju	401,676
Araçatuba	145,751
Arapiraca	124,790
Araraquara	101,302
Barra Mansa	145,112
Bauru	254,211
Belém	765,476
Belo Horizonte	1,529,566
Betim	152,846
Blumenau	185,200
Boa Vista	118,928
★ Brasília	1,492,542
Cachoeiro de Itapemirim	112,099
Campina Grande	298,331
Campinas	748,076
Campo Grande	516,403
Campos	275,508
Canoas	269,234
Carapicuíba	207,264
Caruaru	180,654
Cascavel	175,294
Caxias do Sul	262,983
Colombo	105,464
Contagem	195,705
Cuiabá	252,784
Curitiba	841,882
Diadema	305,068
Divinópolis	141,984
Dourados	116,754
Duque de Caxias	325,903
Embu	155,851
Feira de Santana	340,034
Florianópolis	191,664
Fortaleza	743,335
Foz do Iguaçu	186,362
Franca	227,613
Goiânia	912,136
Governador Valadares	210,396
Gravataí	166,954
Guarapuava	107,046
Guarulhos	544,698
Ilhéus	135,117
Imperatriz	209,970
Ipatinga	120,025
Itabuna	170,434
Itajaí	114,558
Itapevi	107,983
Itaquaquecetuba	164,665
Jaboatão	217,905
Jacareí	143,468
Jequié	114,542
João Pessoa	497,306
Joinville	326,208
Juàzeiro do Norte	163,527
Juiz de Fora	377,538
Jundiaí	253,177
Lages	137,169
Limeira	177,016
Londrina	355,062
Luziânia	194,128
Macapá	146,523
Maceió	554,727
Manaus	1,005,634
Marabá	102,364
Maracanaú	133,206
Marília	144,906
Maringá	225,516
Mauá	294,631
Mogi das Cruzes	125,992
Montes Claros	223,046
Mossoró	117,020
Natal	459,827
Nilópolis	104,671
Niterói	400,586
Nova Friburgo	111,020
Nova Iguaçu	562,062
Novo Hamburgo	199,479
Olinda	341,059
Osasco	566,949
Parnaíba	105,131
Passo Fundo	135,158
Pelotas	260,510
Petrolina	123,857
Petrópolis	164,849
Piracicaba	223,170
Poços de Caldas	104,800
Ponta Grossa	219,648
Porto Alegre	1,237,223
Porto Velho	226,198
Presidente Prudente	157,618
Recife	1,296,995
Ribeirão Prêto	416,186
Rio Branco	167,457
Rio Claro	130,364
Rio de Janeiro	5,473,909
Rio Grande	157,608
Salvador	2,070,296
Santa Bárbara d'Oeste	140,208
Santa Maria	193,294
Santarém	168,153
Santo André	518,272
Santos	415,554
São Bernardo do Campo	550,030
São Caetano do Sul	149,203
São Carlos	100,502
São Gonçalo	296,021
São João de Meriti	220,742
São José do Rio Prêto	263,454
São José dos Campos	385,879
São Leopoldo	160,228
São Luís	164,334
São Paulo	9,393,753
São Vicente	268,467
Sapucaia do Sul	104,626
Sete Lagoas	137,537
Sorocaba	348,952
Susano (Suzano)	110,414
Taboão da Serra	159,894
Taubaté	185,790
Teresina	556,073
Uberaba	198,565
Uberlândia	354,710
Uruguaiana	103,160
Vila Velha	263,897
Vitória	258,243
Vitória da Conquista	179,868
Volta Redonda	219,988
Brunei (1991)	
★ Bandar Seri Begawan	21,484
Bulgaria (1994 est.)	
Burgas	198,439
Dobrich	104,668
Pleven	130,354
Plovdiv	345,205
Ruse	170,209
Sliven	106,958
★ Sofia	1,113,674
Stara Zagora	150,926
Varna	307,200
Burkina Faso (1991 est.)	
Bobo Dioulasso	268,926
★ Ouagadougou	634,479
Burundi (1994 est.)	
★ Bujumbura	300,000
Gitega	101,827[12]

country city	population
Cambodia (1994 est.)	
★ Phnom Penh	920,000
Cameroon (1987)	
Bafoussam	112,920
Bamenda	110,690
Douala	810,490
Garoua	142,170
Maroua	123,450
★ Yaoundé	650,540
Canada (1991)	
Barrie	62,728
Beauport	69,158
Brampton	234,445
Brantford	81,997
Brossard	64,793
Burlington	129,575
Burnaby	158,858
Calgary	710,677
Cambridge	92,772
Charlesbourg	70,788
Chicoutimi	62,670
Dartmouth	67,798
Delta	88,978
East York	102,696
Edmonton	616,741
Etobicoke	309,993
Guelph	87,976
Halifax	114,455
Hamilton	318,499
Hull	60,707
Jonquiere	57,933
Kamloops	67,057
Kelowna	75,950
Kingston	56,597
Kitchener	168,282
Laval	314,000
Lethbridge	60,974
London	303,165
Longueuil	129,874
Markham	153,811
Mississauga	463,388
Moncton	57,010
Montreal	1,017,666
Montreal-Nord	85,516
Nanaimo	60,129
Niagara Falls	75,399
North Bay	55,405
North York	562,564
Oakville	114,670
Oshawa	129,344
★ Ottawa	313,987
Peterborough	68,371
Prince George	69,653
Quebec	167,517
Red Deer	58,134
Regina	179,178
Richmond	126,624
Saint Catharines	129,300
Saint-Hubert	74,027
Saint John	74,969
Saint John's	95,770
Saint-Laurent	72,402
Sainte-Foy	71,133
Sarnia-Clearwater	74,167
Saskatoon	186,058
Sault Sainte Marie	81,476
Scarborough	524,598
Sherbrooke	76,429
Sudbury	92,884
Surrey	245,173
Thunder Bay	113,746
Toronto	635,395
Vancouver	471,844
Verdun	61,307
Victoria	71,228
Waterloo	71,181
Windsor	191,435
Winnipeg	616,790
York	140,525
Cape Verde (1990)	
★ Praia	61,797
Central African Republic (1990 est.)	
★ Bangui	706,000[13]
Chad (1993)	
Abéché	187,757
Bongor	194,992
Doba	185,477
Moundou	281,477
★ N'Djamena	529,555
Sarh	198,113
Chile (1993 est.; MU)	
Antofagasta	227,985
Arica	206,600
Calama	120,602
Chillán	166,669
Concepción	318,140
Copiapó	100,946[14]
Coquimbo	122,872[14]
Curicó	103,919[14]
Iquique	161,914
La Serena	123,552
Los Angeles	142,136[14]
Osorno	140,370
Puente Alto	220,039
Puerto Montt	128,537
Punta Arenas	132,396
Quilpué	115,782
Rancagua	210,473
San Bernardo	217,154
★ Santiago (administrative)	4,628,320
Talca	190,255
Talcahuano	257,767
Temuco	262,624
Valdivia	125,067
★ Valparaíso (legislative)	301,677
Viña del Mar	319,440
China (1990 est.)[15]	
A-ch'eng (Acheng)	197,595
A-k'o-su (Aksu)	164,092
An-ch'ing (Anqing)	250,718
An-k'ang (Ankang)	142,170
An-shan (Anshan)	1,203,986
An-shun (Anshun)	174,142
An-ta (Anda)	136,446
An-yang (Anyang)	420,332
Canton (Guangzhou)	2,914,281
Chan-chiang (Zhanjiang)	400,997
Ch'ang-chi (Changji)	132,260
Chang-chia-k'ou (Zhangjiakou)	529,136
Ch'ang-chih (Changzhi)	317,144
Ch'ang-chou (Changzhou)	531,470
Chang-chou (Zhangzhou)	181,424
Ch'ang-ch'un (Changchun)	1,679,270
Ch'ang-sha (Changsha)	1,113,212
Ch'ang-shu (Changshu)	181,805
Ch'ang-te (Changde)	301,276
Chao-ch'ing (Zhaoqing)	194,784
Ch'ao-chou (Chaozhou)	313,469
Ch'ao-hsien (Chaoxian)	120,070
Chao-tung (Zhaodong)	179,976
Ch'ao-yang (Chaoyang)	222,394
Chen-chiang (Zhenjiang)	368,316
Cheng-chou (Zhengzhou)	1,159,679
Ch'eng-te (Chengde)	246,799
Ch'eng-tu (Chengdu)	1,713,255
Chi-an (Ji'an)	148,583
Chi-hsi (Jixi)	683,885
Chi-lin (Jilin)	1,036,858
Chi-nan (Jinan)	1,480,915
Chi-ning (Jining) (*Inner Mongolia*)	163,552
Chi-ning (Jining) (*Shantung*)	265,248
Ch'i-t'ai-ho (Qitaihe)	214,957
Ch'i-tung (Qidong)	126,872
Chia-hsing (Jiaxing)	211,526
Chia-mu-ssu (Jiamusi)	493,409
Chiang-men (Jiangmen)	230,587
Chiang-yin (Jiangyin)	213,659
Chiang-yu (Jiangyou)	175,753
Chiao-hsien (Jiaoxian)	153,364
Chiao-nan (Jiaonan)	121,397
Chiao-tso (Jiaozuo)	409,100
Ch'ien-chiang (Qianjiang)	205,504
Ch'ih-feng (Chifeng)	350,077
Chin-ch'ang (Jinchang)	105,287
Chin-ch'eng (Jincheng)	136,396
Chin-chou (Jinzhou)	569,518
Ch'in-chou (Qinzhou)	114,586
Chin-hsi (Jinxi)	357,052
Chin-hua (Jinhua)	144,280
Ch'in-huang-tao (Qinhuangdao)	364,972
Ch'ing-chou (Qingzhou)	128,258
Ch'ing-tao (Qingdao)	1,459,195
Ching-te-chen (Jingdezhen)	281,183
Ch'ing-yüan (Qingyuan)	164,641
Chiu-chiang (Jiujiang)	291,187
Chiu-t'ai (Jiutai)	180,130
Chou-k'ou (Zhoukou)	146,288
Chou-shan (Zhoushan)	156,317
Chu-ch'eng (Zhucheng)	102,134
Ch'ü-ching (Qujing)	178,669
Ch'ü-chou (Quzhou)	112,373
Chu-chou (Zhuzhou)	409,924
Chu-hai (Zhuhai)	164,747
Ch'u-hsien (Chuxian)	125,341
Chu-ma-tien (Zhumadian)	123,232
Ch'üan-chou (Quanzhou)	185,154
Chung-shan (Zhongshan)	278,829
Chungking (Chongqing)	2,266,772
Feng-ch'eng (Fengcheng)	193,784
Fo-shan (Foshan)	303,160
Fu-chin (Fujin)	103,104
Fu-chou (Fuzhou) (*Fukien*)	874,809
Fu-chou (Fuzhou) (*Kiangsi*)	121,949
Fu-hsin (Fuxin)	635,473
Fu-ling (Fuling)	173,878
Fu-shun (Fushun)	1,202,388
Fu-yang (Fuyang)	179,572
Fu-yü (Fuyu)	192,981
Ha-mi (Hami)	161,315
Hai-ch'eng (Haicheng)	205,560
Hai-k'ou (Haikou)	280,153
Hai-la-erh (Hailar)	180,650
Hai-lun (Hailun)	133,565
Hai-ning (Haining)	100,478
Han-chung (Hanzhong)	169,930
Han-tan (Handan)	837,552
Hang-chou (Hangzhou)	1,099,660
Harbin	2,443,398
Heng-shui (Hengshui)	104,269
Heng-yang (Hengyang)	487,148
Ho-fei (Hefei)	733,278
Ho-kang (Hegang)	522,747
Ho-pi (Hebi)	212,976
Ho-tse (Heze)	189,293
Ho-yuan (Heyuan)	120,101
Hsi-ch'ang (Xichang)	134,110
Hsi-ning (Xining)	551,776
Hsia-men (Xiamen)	368,786
Hsiang-fan (Xiangfan)	410,407
Hsiang-t'an (Xiangtan)	441,968
Hsiao-kan (Xiaogan)	166,280
Hsiao-shan (Xiaoshan)	162,930
Hsien-ning (Xianning)	136,811
Hsien-t'ao (Xiantao)	222,884
Hsien-yang (Xianyang)	352,125
Hsin-hsiang (Xinxiang)	473,762
Hsin-t'ai (Xintai)	281,248
Hsin-yang (Xinyang)	192,509
Hsin-yu (Xinyu)	173,524
Hsing-ch'eng (Xingcheng)	102,384
Hsing-hua (Xinghua)	161,910
Hsing-t'ai (Xingtai)	302,789
Hsü-ch'ang (Xuchang)	208,815
Hsü-chou (Xuzhou)	805,695
Hsuan-ch'eng (Xuancheng)	112,673
Hu-chou (Huzhou)	218,071
Hu-ho-hao-t'e (Hohhot)	652,534
Hua-tien (Huadian)	175,073
Huai-an (Huai'an)	131,110
Huai-hua (Huaihua)	126,785
Huai-nan (Huainan)	703,934
Huai-pei (Huaibei)	366,549
Huai-yin (Huaiyin)	239,675
Huang-shan (Huangshan)	102,628
Huang-shih (Huangshi)	457,601
Hui-chou (Huizhou)	161,023
Hun-chiang (Hunjiang)	482,043
Hung-hu (Honghu)	190,772
I-ch'ang (Yichang)	371,601
I-cheng (Yizheng)	109,268
I-ch'un (Yichun)	795,789
I-ch'un (Yichun) (*Kiangsi*)	151,585
I-hsing (Yixing)	200,824
I-ning (Yining)	177,193
I-pin (Yibin)	241,019
I-yang (Yiyang)	185,818
Jen-ch'iu (Renqiu)	114,256
Jih-chao (Rizhao)	185,048
Jui-an (Rui'an)	156,468
K'ai-feng (Kaifeng)	507,763
K'ai-li (Kaili)	113,958
K'ai-yuan (Kaiyuan)	124,219
Kan-chou (Ganzhou)	220,129
Kashgar (Kashi)	174,570
Ko-chiu (Gejiu)	214,294
K'o-la-ma-i (Karamay)	197,602
K'u-erh-le (Korla)	159,344
Kuang-shui (Guangshui)	102,770
Kuang-yüan (Guangyuan)	182,241
Kuei-hsien (Guixian)	114,025
Kuei-lin (Guilin)	364,130
K'uei-t'un (Kuitun)	118,553
Kuei-yang (Guiyang)	1,018,619
K'un-ming (Kunming)	1,127,411
K'un-shan (Kunshan)	102,052
Kung-chu-ling (Gongzhuling)	226,569
Lai-chou (Laizhou)	198,664
Lai-wu (Laiwu)	246,833
Lai-yang (Laiyang)	137,080
Lan-chou (Lanzhou)	1,194,640
Lang-fang (Langfang)	148,105
Lao-ho-k'ou (Laohekou)	123,366
Le-shan (Leshan)	341,128
Lei-yang (Leiyang)	130,115
Leng-shui-chiang (Lengshuijiang)	137,994
Lhasa	106,885
Li-ling (Liling)	108,504
Li-yang (Liyang)	109,520
Liang-ch'eng (Liangcheng)	156,307
Liao-ch'eng (Liaocheng)	207,844
Liao-yang (Liaoyang)	492,559
Liao-yüan (Liaoyuan)	354,141
Lien-yüan (Lianyuan)	118,858
Lien-yün-kang (Lianyungang)	354,139
Lin-ch'ing (Linqing)	123,958
Lin-fen (Linfen)	187,309
Lin-ho (Linhe)	133,183
Lin-i (Linyi)	324,720
Liu-chou (Liuzhou)	609,320
Liu-p'an-shui (Liupanshui)	363,954
Lo-ho (Luohe)	126,438
Lo-yang (Luoyang)	759,752
Long-yen (Longyan)	134,481
Lou-ti (Loudi)	128,418
Lu-an (Lu'an)	144,248
Lu-chou (Luzhou)	262,892
Lung-ching (Longjing)	139,417
Lung-k'ou (Longkou)	148,362
Ma-an-shan (Ma'anshan)	305,421
Man-chou-li (Manzhouli)	120,023
Mao-ming (Maoming)	178,683
Mei-ho-k'ou (Meihekou)	209,038
Mei-hsien (Meixian)	132,156
Mi-shan (Mishan)	132,744
Mien-yang (Mianyang)	262,947
Mu-tan-chiang (Mudanjiang)	571,705
Nan-ch'ang (Nanchang)	1,086,124
Nan-ch'ung (Nanchong)	180,273
Nan-ning (Nanning)	721,877
Nan-p'ing (Nanping)	195,064
Nan-t'ung (Nantong)	343,341
Nan-yang (Nanyang)	243,303
Nanking (Nanjing)	2,090,204
Nei-chiang (Neijiang)	256,012
Ning-po (Ningbo)	552,540
O-ch'eng (Echeng)	190,123
Pai-ch'eng (Baicheng)	217,987
Pai-yin (Baiyin)	204,970
P'an-chih-hua (Panzhihua) (Tu-k'ou [Dukou])	415,466
P'an-shan (Panshan)	362,773
Pang-pu (Bengbu)	449,245
Pao-chi (Baoji)	337,765
Pao-ting (Baoding)	483,155
Pao-t'ou (Baotou)	983,508
Pei-an (Bei'an)	204,899
Pei-hai (Beihai)	112,673
Pei-p'iao (Beipiao)	194,301
★ Peking (Beijing)	5,769,607
Pen-hsi (Benxi)	768,778
Pin-chou (Binzhou)	133,555
P'ing-hsiang (Pingxiang)	425,579
P'ing-ting-shan (Pingdingshan)	410,775
P'ing-tu (Pingdu)	150,123
Po-chou (Bozhou)	106,346
P'u-ch'i (Puqi)	117,264
P'u-yang (Puyang)	175,988
San-men-hsia (Sanmenxia)	120,523
San-ming (Sanming)	160,691
San-ya (Sanya)	102,820
Sha-shih (Shashi)	281,352
Shan-t'ou (Shantou)	578,630
Shan-wei (Shanwei)	107,847
Shao-hsing (Shaoxing)	179,818
Shao-kuan (Shaoguan)	350,043
Shao-yang (Shaoyang)	247,227
Shang-chih (Shangzhi)	215,373
Shang-ch'iu (Shangqiu)	164,880
Shang-jao (Shangrao)	132,455
Shanghai	7,496,509
Shen-chen (Shenzhen)	350,727
Shen-yang (Shenyang)	3,603,712
Shih-chia-chuang (Shijiazhuang)	1,068,439
Shih-ho-tzu (Shihezi)	299,676
Shih-shou (Shishou)	104,571
Shih-tsui-shan (Shizuishan)	257,862
Shih-yen (Shiyan)	273,786
Shuang-ch'eng (Shuangcheng)	142,659
Shuang-ya-shan (Shuangyashan)	386,081
Sian (Xi'an)	1,959,044
Ssu-p'ing (Siping)	317,223
Su-ch'ien (Suqian)	105,021
Su-chou (Suzhou) (*Anhwei*)	151,862
Su-chou (Suzhou) (*Kiangsu*)	706,459
Sui-hua (Suihua)	227,881
Sui-ning (Suining)	146,086
Ta-an (Da'an)	138,963
Ta-ch'ing (Daqing)	657,297
Ta-hsien (Daxian)	188,101
Ta-li (Dali)	136,554
Ta-lien (Dalian)	1,723,302
Ta-t'ung (Datong)	798,319
T'ai-an (Tai'an)	350,696
T'ai-chou (Taizhou)	152,442
T'ai-yüan (Taiyuan)	1,533,884
Tan-chiang (Danjiang)	103,211
Tan-tung (Dandong)	523,699
Tan-yang (Danyang)	169,603
T'ang-shan (Tangshan)	1,044,194
T'ao-nan (Taonan)	150,168
Te-chou (Dezhou)	195,485
Te-yang (Deyang)	182,488
T'eng-hsien (Tengxian)	315,083
T'ieh-fa (Tiefa)	131,807
T'ieh-li (Tieli)	265,683
T'ieh-ling (Tieling)	254,842
T'ien-men (Tianmen)	186,332
T'ien-shui (Tianshui)	244,974
Tientsin (Tianjin)	4,574,689
Tsa-lan-t'un (Zalantun)	130,031
Ts'ang-chou (Cangzhou)	242,708
Tsao-chuang (Zaozhuang)	380,846
Tsao-yang (Zaoyang)	162,198
Tsitsihar (Qiqihar)	1,070,051
Tsun-i (Zunyi)	261,862
Tu-chiang-yen (Dujiangyan)	123,357
Tu-yun (Duyun)	132,971
Tun-hua (Dunhua)	235,100
T'ung-ch'uan (Tongchuan)	280,657
T'ung-hua (Tonghua)	324,600
Tung-kuan (Dongguan)	308,669
T'ung-liao (Tongliao)	255,129
T'ung-ling (Tongling)	228,017
Tung-t'ai (Dongtai)	192,247
Tung-ying (Dongying)	281,728
Tz'u-hsi (Cixi)	107,329
Tzu-hsing (Zixing)	110,048
Tzu-kung (Zigong)	393,184
Tzu-po (Zibo)	1,138,074
Wa-fang-tien (Wafangdian)	251,733
Wan-hsien (Wanxian)	156,823
Wei-fang (Weifang)	428,522
Wei-hai (Weihai)	128,888
Wei-nan (Weinan)	140,169
Wen-chou (Wenzhou)	401,871
Wen-teng (Wendeng)	133,910
Wu-chou (Wuzhou)	210,452
Wu-hai (Wuhai)	264,081
Wu-han (Wuhan)	3,284,229
Wu-hsi (Wuxi)	826,833
Wu-hu (Wuhu)	425,740
Wu-lan-hao-t'e (Ulanhot)	159,538
Wu-lu-mu-ch'i (Ürümqi)	1,046,898
Wu-wei (Wuwei)	133,101
Ya-k'o-she (Yakeshi)	377,869
Yang-chiang (Yangjiang)	215,196
Yang-chou (Yangzhou)	312,892
Yang-ch'üan (Yangquan)	362,268
Yen-an (Yan'an)	113,277
Yen-ch'eng (Yancheng)	296,831
Yen-chi (Yanji)	230,892
Yen-t'ai (Yantai)	452,127
Yin-ch'uan (Yinchuan)	356,652
Ying-k'ou (Yingkou)	421,589
Yü-lin (Yulin)	144,467
Yü-men (Yumen)	109,234
Yü-shu (Yushu)	131,861
Yü-tz'u (Yuci)	191,356
Yu-yao (Yuyao)	114,065
Yüan-chiang (Yuanjiang)	107,004

Major cities and national capitals (continued)

country / city	population
Yüeh-yang (Yueyang)	302,800
Yun-ch'eng (Yuncheng)	108,359
Yung-an (Yong'an)	111,762
Colombia (1995 est.)	
Armenia	220,303
Barrancabermeja	180,653
Barranquilla	1,064,255
Bello	304,819
Bucaramanga	351,737
Buenaventura	266,988
Cali	1,718,871
Cartagena	745,689
Cartago	117,166
Ciénaga	144,340
Cúcuta	479,309
Dosquebradas	163,599
Envigado	109,240
Florencia	118,027
Floridablanca	246,834
Ibagué	346,632
Itagüí	169,374
Magangué	104,496
Medellín	1,621,356
Montería	276,074
Neiva	248,178
Palmira	256,823
Pasto	325,540
Pereira	352,530
Popayán	223,128
Quibdó	130,921
Ríohacha	142,455
Santa Marta	309,372
★ Santafé de Bogotá, D.C.	5,025,989
Sincelejo	180,076
Soacha	266,817
Soledad	264,583
Tuluá	138,124
Tumaco	114,802
Tunja	120,210
Turbo	127,045
Valledupar	265,505
Villavicencio	252,711
Comoros (1990 est.)	
★ Moroni	23,432
Congo (1992 est.)	
★ Brazzaville	937,579
Pointe-Noire	576,206
Costa Rica (1994 est.)	
★ San José	315,909[16]
Côte d'Ivoire (1988)	
★ Abidjan	2,797,000[17]
Bouaké	329,850
Daloa	121,842
Korhogo	109,445
Yamoussoukro	106,786
Croatia (1991)	
Osijek	129,792
Rijeka	167,964
Split	200,459
★ Zagreb	867,865
Cuba (1994 est.)	
Bayamo	137,663
Camagüey	293,961
Cienfuegos	132,038
Guantánamo	207,796
★ Havana	2,241,000[17]
Holguín	242,085
Las Tunas	126,930
Manzanillo	107,650[18]
Matanzas	123,843
Pinar del Río	128,570
Santa Clara	205,400
Santiago de Cuba	440,084
Cyprus (1993 est.)	
Limassol	137,000
★ Nicosia (Lefkosia)	177,000[19]
Czech Republic (1994 est.)	
Brno	390,100
Hradec Králové	100,900
Liberec	101,000
Olomouc	105,900
Ostrava	326,200
Plzen	172,300
★ Prague	1,225,000[17]
Denmark (1994 est.; MU)	
Ålborg	158,141
Århus	274,535
★ Copenhagen	1,339,395[13, 20]
Odense	181,824
Djibouti (1991 est.)	
★ Djibouti	317,000
Dominica (1991)	
★ Roseau	15,853
Dominican Republic (1993)	
La Romana	136,000[21]
La Vega	189,000[21]
San Francisco de Macorís	162,000[21]
San Pedro de Macorís	137,000[21]
Santiago de los Caballeros	690,000
★ Santo Domingo	2,100,000
Ecuador (1990)	
Ambato	124,166
Cuenca	194,981
Guayaquil	1,508,444
Machala	144,197
Manta	125,505
Portoviejo	132,937
★ Quito	1,100,847
Santo Domingo	114,422
Egypt (1992 est.)	
Alexandria	3,382,000[8]
Aswān	220,000
Asyūṭ	321,000
Banhā	136,000
Banī Suwayf	179,000
Būr Sa'īd (Port Said)	460,000[8]
★ Cairo	6,849,000[8]
Damanhūr	222,000
al-Fayyūm	250,000
Hulwan (Helwan)	352,300[22]
al-Ismā'īlīyah	255,000
al-Jīzah (Giza)	2,144,000
Kafr ad-Dawwar	226,000
Kafr ash-Shaykh	102,910[23]
al-Maḥallah al-Kubrā	408,000
al-Manṣūrah	371,000
al-Minyā	208,000
Qinā	141,000
Sawhāj	156,000
Shibīn al-Kawm	158,000
Shubrā al-Khaymah	834,000
as-Suways (Suez)	388,000
Ṭanṭā	380,000
al-Uqṣur (Luxor)	155,000[8]
az-Zaqāzīq	287,000
El Salvador (1992; MU)	
Mejicanos	145,000
Nueva San Salvador	116,575
San Miguel	182,817
★ San Salvador	422,570
Santa Ana	202,337
Soyapango	104,470[21]
Equatorial Guinea (1991 est.)	
★ Malabo	58,040
Eritrea (1991 est.)	
★ Asmera	367,300
Estonia (1994 est.)	
★ Tallinn	442,679
Tartu	105,844
Ethiopia (1993 est.)	
★ Addis Ababa	2,200,186
Bahir Dar	102,700
Dese	106,710
Dire Dawa	173,588
Gonder	146,777
Harer	162,645
Jima	106,842
Mekele	107,671
Nazret	131,585
Faroe Islands (1994 est.)	
★ Tórshavn	16,200
Fiji (1990 est.)	
★ Suva	200,000[13]
Finland (1995 est.)	
Espoo	186,507
★ Helsinki	515,765
Oulu	106,419
Tampere	179,251
Turku	162,370
Vantaa	164,376
France (1990)	
Aix-en-Provence	126,854
Amiens	136,234
Angers	146,163
Besançon	119,194
Bordeaux	213,274
Boulogne-Billancourt	101,971
Brest	153,099
Caen	115,624
Clermont-Ferrand	140,167
Dijon	151,636
Grenoble	153,973
Le Havre	197,219
Le Mans	148,465
Lille	178,301
Limoges	136,407
Lyon	422,444
Marseille	807,726
Metz	123,920
Montpellier	210,866
Mulhouse	109,905
Nancy	102,410
Nantes	252,029
Nice	345,674
Nîmes	133,607
Orléans	107,965
★ Paris	2,175,200
Perpignan	108,049
Reims	185,164
Rennes	203,533
Rouen	105,470
Saint-Étienne	201,569
Strasbourg	255,937
Toulon	170,167
Toulouse	365,933
Tours	133,403
Villeurbanne	119,848
French Guiana (1990)	
★ Cayenne	41,659
French Polynesia (1988)	
★ Papeete	23,555
Gabon (1993)	
★ Libreville	419,596
Gambia, The (1986 est.)	
★ Banjul	44,188[24]
Serekunda	102,600
Gaza Strip (1988 est.)	
Gaza (Ghazzah)	57,000
Georgia (1991 est.)	
Batumi	137,500
Kutaisi	238,200
Rustavi	161,900
Sukhumi	120,000
★ Tbilisi	1,279,000
Germany (1994 est.)	
Aachen	246,671
Augsburg	264,764
Bergisch Gladbach	104,991
Berlin	3,475,392
Bielefeld	324,674
Bochum	401,058
★ Bonn	296,859
Bottrop	119,676
Braunschweig	256,267
Bremen	551,604
Bremerhaven	131,492
Chemnitz	279,520
Cologne (Köln)	962,517
Cottbus	128,121
Darmstadt	139,754
Dortmund	601,966
Dresden	479,273
Duisburg	536,797
Düsseldorf	574,936
Erfurt	200,799
Erlangen	102,383
Essen	622,380
Frankfurt am Main	659,803
Freiburg im Breisgau	197,384
Fürth	108,097
Gelsenkirchen	295,037
Gera	122,974
Göttingen	128,419
Hagen	214,877
Halle	295,372
Hamburg	1,702,887
Hamm	182,390
Hannover	524,823
Heidelberg	139,429
Heilbronn	122,396
Herne	180,539
Hildesheim	106,303
Ingolstadt	109,666
Jena	100,093
Kaiserslautern	102,370
Karlsruhe	277,998
Kassel	202,158
Kiel	248,931
Koblenz	109,807
Krefeld	249,565
Leipzig	490,851
Leverkusen	161,761
Lübeck	217,269
Ludwigshafen	168,130
Magdeburg	270,546
Mainz	185,487
Mannheim	318,025
Moers	106,631
Mönchengladbach	265,312
Mülheim an der Ruhr	177,175
Munich (München)	1,255,623
Münster	267,367
Neuss	148,560
Nürnberg	498,945
Oberhausen	226,254
Offenbach am Main	116,870
Oldenburg	147,701
Osnabrück	168,078
Paderborn	130,130
Pforzheim	117,450
Potsdam	139,262
Recklingshausen	127,150
Regensburg	125,337
Remscheid	123,610
Reutlingen	107,607
Rostock	237,307
Saarbrücken	190,902
Salzgitter	117,684
Schwerin	122,189
Siegen	111,845
Solingen	166,064
Stuttgart	594,406
Ulm	114,839
Wiesbaden	270,873
Witten	105,807
Wolfsburg	128,032
Wuppertal	386,625
Würzburg	128,875
Zwickau	107,988
Ghana (1988 est.)	
★ Accra	1,781,100[13, 18]
Kumasi	385,192
Sekondi-Takoradi	103,653
Tamale	151,069
Tema	109,975
Gibraltar (1995 est.)	
★ Gibraltar	28,000[25]
Greece (1991)	
★ Athens	748,110
Iráklion	117,167
Kallithéa	110,738
Larissa	113,426
Pátrai (Patras)	155,180
Peristérion	145,854
Piraiévs (Piraeus)	169,622
Thessaloníki	377,951
Greenland (1995 est.)	
★ Nuuk (Godthåb)	12,723
Grenada (1991)	
★ Saint George's	4,439
Guadeloupe (1990)	
★ Basse-Terre	14,107
Guam (1990)	
★ Agana	1,139
Guatemala (1994 est.; MU)	
★ Guatemala City	1,150,452
Mixco	413,002
Villa Nueva	154,508
Guernsey (1991)	
★ St. Peter Port	16,648
Guinea (1995 est.)	
★ Conakry	1,508,000
Guinea-Bissau (1991 est.)	
★ Bissau	200,000
Guyana (1992 est.)	
★ Georgetown	248,500
Haiti (1992 est.)	
Carrefour	241,223
Delmas	200,251
★ Port-au-Prince	752,600
Honduras (1993 est.; MU)	
San Pedro Sula	353,800
★ Tegucigalpa	738,500[26]
Hong Kong (1995 est.)	
Hong Kong	6,205,300[25]
Hungary (1994 est.)	
★ Budapest	1,996,000
Debrecen	218,000
Györ	131,000
Kecskemét	106,000
Miskolc	190,000
Nyíregyháza	115,000
Pécs	173,000
Szeged	180,000
Székesfehérvár	110,000
Iceland (1994 est.)	
★ Reykjavík	103,036
India (1991)	
Abohar	107,016
Ādoni	135,718
Agartala	157,636
Āgra	899,195
Ahmadābād	2,872,865
Ahmadnagar	181,015
Āizawl	154,343
Ajmer	401,930
Akola	327,946
Alandur	125,009
Alīgarh	479,978
Allahābād	806,447
Alleppey	174,606
Alwar	206,107
Ambāla	119,535
Ambattur	223,332
Amrāvati	433,746
Amritsar	709,456
Amroha	136,893
Anand	110,144
Anantapur	174,792
Āra (Arrah)	156,871
Āsānsol	261,836
Aurangābād (Shambājinagar)	572,634
Āvadi	180,291
Baharampur	115,036
Bahraich	135,352
Bally	181,978
Bālurghāt	119,829
Bangalore	2,650,659
Bānkura	114,927
Barāhanagar	223,770
Bārāsat	107,365
Barddhamān (Burdwān)	244,789
Bareilly	583,473
Barrackpore	133,429
Basīrhāt	101,652
Bathinda (Bhatinda)	159,144
Beāwar	105,357
Belgaum	325,639
Bellary	245,758
Bhāgalpur	254,993
Bharatpur	148,506
Bharūch (Broach)	132,312
Bhātpāra	304,298
Bhāvnagar	400,636
Bhilainagar	389,601
Bhīlwāra	183,791
Bhīmavaram	125,495
Bhind	109,731
Bhiwandi	378,546
Bhiwāni	121,449
Bhopāl	1,063,662
Bhubaneshwar	411,542
Bhusāwal	144,804
Bīd (Bhīr)	112,351
Bīdar	107,542
Bihār Sharīf	200,976
Bijāpur	186,846
Bīkaner	415,355
Bilāspur	190,911
Bokāro	350,540
Bombay (Mumbāi)	9,909,547[13]
Brahmapur	210,585
Budaun	116,706
Bulandshahr	126,737
Burhānpur	172,809
Burnpur	174,704
Calcutta	4,388,262
Calicut (Kozhikode)	419,531
Chandannagar	122,351
Chandīgarh	502,992
Chandrapur	225,841
Chhapra	136,824
Chittoor	133,233
Cochin	564,038
Coimbatore	853,402
Cuddalore	143,774
Cuddapah	121,422
Cuttack	402,390
Darbhanga	218,274
Dāvangere	265,971
Dehra Dūn	270,028
Delhi	7,174,755
Dewās	163,699
Dhānbād	151,334
Dhūle (Dhūlia)	277,957
Dibrugarh	118,374
Dindigul	182,293
Durg	150,513
Durgāpur	415,986
Elūru	212,918
Erode	158,774
Etāwah	124,032
Faizābād	125,012
Farīdābād	613,828
Farrukhābād-cum-Fatehgarh	193,624
Fatehpur	117,203
Fīrozābād	215,089
Gadag-Betigeri	133,918
Gāndhīdhām	104,392
Gāndhīnagar	121,746
Gangānagar	161,377
Gaya	291,220
Ghāziābād	460,949
Gonda	106,078
Gondia	109,271
Gorakhpur	489,850
Gudivāda	101,635
Gulbarga	303,139
Guna	100,389
Guntakal	107,560
Guntūr	471,020
Gurgaon	120,790
Guwāhāti (Gauhāti)	577,591
Gwalior	692,982
Hābra	100,142
Haldia	100,109
Haldwāni-cum-Kāthgodam	102,744
Hālisahar	113,670
Hāpur	146,591
Haridwār (Hardwār)	148,882
Hāthras	113,653
Hindupur	104,635
Hisār (Hissār)	172,873
Hoshiārpur	122,528
Howrah (Hāora)	946,732
Hubli-Dhārwād	647,640
Hugli-Chunchura	142,388
Hyderābād	2,991,884
Ichalkaranji	214,835
Imphāl	196,268
Indore	1,086,673
Ingrāj Bāzār	139,018

country city	population
Jabalpur	739,961
Jaipur	1,454,678
Jalandhar (Jullundur)	519,530
Jalgaon	241,603
Jālna	174,958
Jammu	206,135[11]
Jāmnagar	325,475
Jamshedpur	461,212
Jaunpur	136,287
Jhānsi	301,304
Jodhpur	648,621
Jūnāgadh	130,132
Kākināda	279,875
Kalyān	1,014,062
Kāmārhāti	266,625
Kānchipuram	145,028
Kānchrāpāra	100,059
Kānpur	1,958,282
Karīmnagar	148,349
Karnāl	173,742
Katihār	135,348
Khammam	127,812
Khandwa	145,111
Kharagpur	189,010
Kolhāpur	405,118
Kota	536,444
Krishnanagar	120,918
Kukatpalle	185,378
Kulti-Barākar	108,930
Kumbakonam	139,449
Kurnool	236,313
Lātūr	197,164
Lucknow	1,592,010
Ludhiāna	1,012,062
Machilīpatnam (Masulipatam)	159,007
Madras	3,795,028
Madurai	951,696
Mahbūbnagar	116,775
Mālegaon	342,431
Mālkājgiri	126,066
Mandya	119,970
Mangalore	272,819
Māngo	110,024
Mathura	226,850
Maunāth Bhanjan	136,447
Medinīpur (Midnāpore)	125,098
Meerut	752,078
Miraj	121,564
Mirzāpur-cum-Vindhyāchal	169,368
Modinagar	102,307
Moga	108,213
Morādābād	416,836
Morena	147,095
Munger (Monghyr)	150,042
Murwāra (Katni)	163,699
Muzaffarnagar	240,057
Muzaffarpur	240,450
Mysore	480,006
Nadiād	166,852
Nāgercoil	189,482
Nāgpur	1,622,225
Naihāti	102,032
Nānded (Nānder)	274,626
Nandyāl	120,171
Nāshik (Nāsik)	646,896
Navadwīp	125,247
Navsāri	125,980
Nellore	316,445
★ New Delhi	294,149
Neyveli	117,471
Nizāmābād	240,924
Noida	167,440
North Barrackpore	100,513
North Dum Dum	151,298
Ongole	100,544
Pālghāt	122,964
Pāli	136,797
Pallavaram	111,194
Pānihāti	275,359
Pānīpat	191,010
Parbhani	190,235
Pathānkot	142,862
Patiāla	253,341
Patna	916,980
Pīlībhīt	106,329
Pimpri-Chinchwad	515,962
Pondicherry	202,648
Porbandar	116,546
Proddatūr	133,860
Pune	1,559,558
Puri	124,835
Pūsa	122,086
Quilon	139,717
Qutubullapur	105,380
Rāe Bareli	130,101
Rāichūr	157,477
Rāiganj	151,454
Raipur	437,887
Rāj Nāndgaon	125,394
Rājahmundry	326,071
Rājapālaiyam	114,042
Rājkot	556,137
Rāmagundam	213,962
Rāmpur	242,752
Rānchi	598,498
Ratlām	183,370
Raurkela Steel Township	215,489
Rewa	128,918
Rishra	102,649
Rohtak	215,844
Sāgar	195,106
Sahāranpur	373,904
Salem	363,934
Sambalpur	130,766
Sambhal	150,012
Sāngli	193,181
Satna	156,321
Shāhjahānpur	237,663
Shāntipur	109,911
Shiliguri (Silīguri)	226,677
Shillong	130,691
Shimoga	178,882
Shivpuri	108,271
Sholāpur (Solapur)	603,870
Shrīrāmpur	137,087
Sīkar	148,235
Silchar	115,045
Sirsa	112,542
Sitāpur	120,595
Sonīpat	142,992
South Dum Dum	230,507
Srīnagar	586,038[11]
Sūrat	1,496,943
Surendranagar	105,973
Tāmbaram	106,690
Tellicherry	103,577
Tenāli	143,836
Thāne (Thāna)	796,620
Thanjāvūr	200,216
Tiruchchirāppalli	386,628
Tirunelveli	135,762
Tirupati	174,393
Tirupper (Tiruppūr)	235,076
Tiruvannāmalai	100,291
Tiruvottiyūr	167,851
Titāgarh	113,831
Tonk	100,020
Trivandrum	523,733
Tumkūr	138,598
Tuticorin	205,105
Udaipur	307,682
Ujjain	366,787
Ulhāsnagar	368,822
Uluberia	155,188
Unnāo	107,246
Uttarpāra-Kotrung	100,867
Vadodara (Baroda)	1,021,084
Vārānasi (Benares)	925,962
Vellore	172,467
Vijayawāda	701,351
Vishākhapatnam	750,024
Vizianagaram	159,461
Warangal	446,760
Wardha	102,974
Yamunanagar	144,250
Yavatmāl (Yeotmāl)	108,591
Indonesia (1990)	
Ambon	206,260
Balikpapan	309,492
Banda Aceh	143,409
Bandar Lampung	458,215
Bandung	2,026,893
Banjarmasin	443,738
Bengkulu	146,439
Binjai	127,222
Blitar	113,064
Bogor	271,711
Cilacap	113,893[27]
Cimahi	105,940[27]
Cirebon	245,307
Denpasar	261,263[27]
★ Jakarta	8,259,266
Jambi	301,359
Jayapura	149,618[27]
Jember	140,105[27]
Kediri	235,602
Madiun	165,999
Magelang	123,213
Malang	650,295
Manado	275,374
Mataram	141,387[27]
Medan	1,685,972
Padang	477,344
Palembang	1,084,483
Pangkal Pinang	108,411
Pasuruan	134,019
Pekalongan	227,535
Pekanbaru	341,328
Pontianak	387,112
Probolinggo	131,291
Purwokerto	105,395[27]
Samarinda	335,016
Semarang	1,005,316
Sukabumi	119,981
Sumba	355,073[27]
Surabaya	2,421,016
Surakarta	504,176
Tanjung Balai	102,095
Tanjung Karang-Telukbetung	284,275[27]
Tasikmalaya	165,297[27]
Tebing Tinggi	116,767
Tegal	225,770
Ujung Pandang	913,196
Yogyakarta	412,392
Iran (1991)	
Ahvāz	724,653
Āmol	139,923
Arāk	331,354
Ardabīl	311,022
Bābol	137,348
Bākhtarān	624,084
Bandar 'Abbās	249,504
Bandar-e Būshehr	132,824
Bīrjand	101,177
Bojnūrd	112,426
Borūjerd	201,016
Dezfūl	181,309
Eşfahān (Isfahan)	1,127,030
Gorgān	162,468
Hamadān	349,653
Īlām	116,428
Islāmshahr (Eslāmshahr)	230,183
Karaj	442,387
Kāshān	155,188
Kermān	311,643
Khomeynīshahr	118,348
Khorramābād	249,258
Khvoy	137,885
Malāyer	130,458
Marāgheh	117,388
Mashhad (Meshed)	1,559,155
Masjed-e Soleymān	107,539
Najafābād	160,004
Neyshābūr	135,681
Orūmīyeh	357,399
Qā'emshahr	123,684
Qazvin	278,826
Qom	681,253
Rājaishahr	160,362
Rasht	340,637
Sabzevār	148,065
Sanandaj	244,039
Sārī	167,602
Shīrāz	965,117
Sīrjān	107,887
Tabrīz	1,088,985
★ Tehrān	11,000,000[8]
Yazd	275,298
Zāhedān	361,623
Zanjān	254,100
Iraq (1985 est.)	
al-'Amārah	131,758
★ Baghdad	4,044,000[18]
Ba'qūbah	114,516
Basra	616,700
al-Ḥillah	215,249
Irbīl	333,903
Karbalā'	184,574
Kirkūk	570,000[28]
Mosul	570,926
an-Najaf	242,603
an-Nāṣirīyah	138,842
ar-Ramādī	137,388
as-Sulaymānīyah	279,424
Ireland (1991)	
Cork	127,000[29]
★ Dublin	478,389[29]
Isle of Man (1991)	
★ Douglas	22,214
Israel (1994 est.)	
Ashdod	110,300
Bat Yam	143,200
Beersheba (Be'er Sheva')	141,400
Bene Beraq	125,000
Haifa (Ḥefa)	246,500
Holon	162,800
★ Jerusalem (Yerushalayim, Al-Quds)	567,100
Netanya	142,700
Petaḥ Tiqwa	151,100
Ramat Gan	122,800
Rishon le-Ẕiyyon	154,300
Tel Aviv–Yafo	357,400
Italy (1994 est.; MU)	
Ancona	100,597
Bari	338,949
Bergamo	115,889
Bologna	394,969
Brescia	191,875
Cagliari	178,063
Catania	327,163
Ferrara	137,384
Florence (Firenze)	392,800
Foggia	155,892
Forlì	108,693
Genoa (Genova)	659,754
Latina	108,819
Lecce	100,474
Livorno	165,536
Messina	233,845
Milan (Milano)	1,334,171
Modena	176,588
Monza	120,882
Naples (Napoli)	1,061,583
Novara	102,768
Padua (Padova)	212,589
Palermo	694,749
Parma	169,299
Perugia	147,489
Pescara	120,613
Piacenza	101,692
Prato	166,305
Ravenna	133,604
Reggio di Calabria	178,736
Reggio nell'Emilia	134,169
Rimini	130,006
★ Rome (Roma)	2,687,881
Salerno	146,546
Sassari	122,010
Siracusa (Syracuse)	127,496
Taranto	213,933
Terni	108,294
Trento	103,063
Trieste	226,707
Turin (Torino)	945,551
Venice (Venezia)	306,439
Verona	256,756
Vicenza	108,013
Jamaica (1991)	
★ Kingston	103,771
Japan (1994 est.)	
Abiko	124,065
Ageo	206,368
Aizuwakamatsu	120,251
Akashi	282,912
Akishima	108,121
Akita	310,219
Amagasaki	493,158
Anjō	148,988
Aomori	289,920
Asahikawa	362,908
Asaka	108,268
Ashikaga	166,903
Atsugi	207,146
Beppu	129,387
Chiba	853,853
Chigasaki	211,878
Chōfu	198,180
Daitō	127,232
Ebetsu	111,099
Ebina	112,514
Fuchu	215,597
Fuji	229,267
Fujieda	124,578
Fujinomiya	120,455
Fujisawa	365,250
Fukaya	100,097
Fukui	255,084
Fukuoka	1,275,165
Fukushima	284,250
Fukuyama	373,685
Funabashi	540,306
Gifu	409,063
Habikino	117,554
Hachinohe	241,588
Hachiōji	495,053
Hadano	163,244
Hakodate	302,135
Hamamatsu	562,156
Handa	106,096
Higashi-Hiroshima	107,963
Higashi-Kurume	112,829
Higashi-Murayama	136,045
Higashi-Ōsaka	513,876
Hikone	102,656
Himeji	465,941
Hino	167,307
Hirakata	397,183
Hiratsuka	253,485
Hirosaki	175,781
Hiroshima	1,106,367
Hitachi	201,116
Hōfu	119,178
Ibaraki	255,586
Ichihara	275,129
Ichikawa	444,468
Ichinomiya	267,136
Iida	107,021
Ikeda	103,377
Ikoma	104,939
Imabari	120,371
Iruma	143,017
Ise	103,047
Isesaki	120,208
Ishinomaki	121,164
Itami	189,375
Iwaki	360,111
Iwakuni	108,529
Iwatsuki	109,660
Izumi	152,284
Joetsu	131,974
Kadoma	141,473
Kagoshima	542,932
Kakamigahara	132,378
Kakogawa	251,735
Kamakura	171,815
Kanazawa	447,733
Kariya	125,568
Kashihara	120,621
Kashiwa	319,321
Kasugai	275,728
Kasukabe	199,498
Katsuta	114,685
Kawachi-Nagano	115,777
Kawagoe	320,639
Kawaguchi	452,381
Kawanishi	143,321
Kawasaki	1,202,069
Kiryū	121,858
Kisarazu	125,510
Kishiwada	191,872
Kita-Kyūshū	1,019,372
Kitami	109,405
Kobe	1,518,982
Kochi	320,498
Kodaira	170,720
Kofu	199,347
Koganei	107,766
Kokubunji	105,066
Komaki	135,763
Komatsu	106,817
Koriyama	324,321
Koshigaya	297,131
Kumagaya	156,734
Kumamoto	642,847
Kurashiki	419,528
Kure	210,884
Kurume	233,829
Kushiro	201,150
Kuwana	101,975
Kyōto	1,448,377
Machida	360,200
Maebashi	287,145
Matsubara	133,803
Matsudo	463,973
Matsue	145,885
Matsumoto	204,879
Matsusaka	120,740
Matsuyama	457,497
Minō	124,801
Misato	133,070
Mishima	107,021
Mitaka	165,328
Mito	247,281
Miyakonojō	131,319
Miyazaki	296,201
Moriguchi	155,081
Morioka	284,906
Muroran	113,008
Musashino	135,508
Nagano	354,532
Nagaoka	189,876
Nagareyama	146,554
Nagasaki	439,471
Nagoya	2,153,293
Naha	299,898
Nara	357,720
Narashino	154,329
Neyagawa	257,521
Niigata	492,009
Niihama	128,439
Niiza	143,280
Nishinomiya	424,328
Nobeoka	127,610
Noda	118,896
Numazu	213,304
Obihiro	171,099
Odawara	199,165
Ōgaki	148,701
Ōita	424,160
Okayama	608,115
Okazaki	322,162
Okinawa	111,665
Ōme	136,480
Ōmiya	427,519
Ōmuta	146,184
Ōsaka	2,575,042
Ōta	143,562
Otaru	159,993
Ōtsu	272,668
Oyama	148,438
Saga	170,294
Sagamihara	567,058
Sakai	803,640
Sakata	100,663
Sakura	159,839
Sapporo	1,744,806
Sasebo	245,015
Sayama	163,053
Sendai	958,705
Seto	128,961
Shimizu	241,575
Shimonoseki	259,581
Shizuoka	473,859
Sōka	216,022
Suita	338,079
Suzuka	179,540
Tachikawa	156,254
Tajimi	100,237
Takamatsu	330,707
Takaoka	175,202
Takarazuka	206,140
Takasaki	238,425
Takatsuki	361,494
Tama	148,438
Tokorozawa	318,714
Tokushima	265,670
Tokuyama	109,671
★ Tokyo	8,021,943
Tomakomai	168,349
Tondabayashi	119,363
Tottori	145,672

Major cities and national capitals (continued)

country / city	population
Toyama	324,638
Toyohashi	351,702
Toyokawa	114,405
Toyonaka	399,988
Toyota	342,968
Tsu	163,167
Tsuchiura	131,813
Tsukuba	153,767
Tsuruoka	100,083
Ube	175,234
Ueda	121,776
Uji	183,880
Urawa	447,281
Urayasu	123,376
Utsunomiya	434,860
Wakayama	395,491
Yachiyo	155,309
Yaizu	115,521
Yamagata	252,716
Yamaguchi	134,077
Yamato	203,718
Yao	275,865
Yatsushiro	107,438
Yokkaichi	284,052
Yokohama	3,300,513
Yokosuka	435,158
Yonago	133,496
Zama	118,147
Jersey (1991)	
★ St. Helier	28,123
Jordan (1994)	
★ Amman	963,490
Irbid	208,201
al-Mafraq	109,841[13]
ar-Ruṣayfah	131,130
as-Salṭ	187,014[13]
az-Zarqāʾ	344,524
Kazakhstan (1991 est.)	
Aktau (Aqtaū; (Shevchenko)	169,000
★ Almaty (Alma-Ata)	1,164,000[8]
Aqmola (Akmola; Tselinograd)	286,000
Aqtöbe (Aktyubinsk)	266,600
Atyraū (Guryev)	156,700
Auliye-Ata (Dzhambul)	312,300
Ekibastuz	138,900
Kökshetaū (Kokchetav)	143,300
Oral (Uralsk)	214,000
Öskemen (Ust-Kamenogorsk)	332,900
Pavlodar	342,500
Petropavl (Petropavlovsk)	248,300
Qaraghandy (Karaganda)	608,600
Qostanay (Kustanay)	233,900
Qyzylord (Kzyl-Orda)	158,200
Rūdny	128,800
Semey (Semipalatinsk)	344,700
Shymkent (Shimkent; Chimkent)	438,800
Taldyqorghan (Taldy-Kurgan)	136,100
Temirtaū	213,100
Zhezqazghan (Zhezkazgan; Dzhezkazgan)	111,100
Kenya (1991 est.)	
Kisumu	201,100
Mombasa	600,000
★ Nairobi	2,000,000
Nakuru	124,200
Kiribati (1990)	
★ Bairiki	2,226
Korea, North (1987 est.)	
Anju	186,000
Ch'ŏngjin	520,000
Haeju	195,000
Hamhŭng-Hungnam	701,000
Hŭich'ŏn	163,000
Kaesŏng	120,000
Kanggye	211,000
Kimch'aek (Songjin)	179,000
Kusŏng	177,000
Namp'o	370,000
★ P'yŏngyang	2,355,000
Sinp'o	158,000
Sinŭiju	289,000
Sunch'ŏn	356,000
Tanch'ŏn	284,000
Tŏkch'ŏn	217,000
Wŏnsan	274,000
Korea, South (1990)	
Andong	116,958
Ansan	252,418
Anyang	481,291
Ch'angwŏn	323,223
Cheju	232,643
Chinhae	120,212
Chinju	255,695
Ch'ŏnan	211,363
Ch'ŏngju	477,783
Chŏnju	517,059
Ch'unch'ŏn	174,224
Ch'ungju	128,425
Hanam	101,325
Inch'ŏn	1,817,919
Iri	203,382
Kangnŭng	152,678
Kimhae	106,206
Kumi	206,121
Kunp'o	100,059
Kunsan	218,205
Kuri	109,374
Kwangju	1,139,003
Kwangmyŏng	328,593
Kyŏngju	141,896
Masan	493,731
Mokp'o	243,064
P'ohang	317,768
Puch'ŏn	667,993
Pusan	3,798,113
★ Seoul (Sŏul)	10,612,577
Shihŭng	107,176
Sŏngnam	540,754
Sunch'ŏn	167,214
Suwŏn	644,805
Taegu	2,229,040
Taejŏn	1,049,578
Ŭijŏngbu	212,352
Ulsan	682,411
Wŏnju	162,415
Yŏsu	173,169
Kuwait (1993 est.)	
al-Jahra	139,476
★ Kuwait (al-Kuwayt)	31,241
as-Sālimīyah	116,104
Kyrgyzstan (1994 est.)	
★ Bishkek (Frunze)	597,000
Osh	238,200[30]
Laos (1990 est.; MU)	
★ Vientiane (Viangchan)	442,000
Latvia (1993 est.)	
Daugavpils	125,000
Liepāja	108,000
★ Rīga	874,000
Lebanon (1991 est.)	
★ Beirut (Bayrūt)	1,100,000[13]
Jūniyah	100,000
an-Nabaṭīyah	100,000[31]
Sidon (Ṣaydā)	100,000[31]
Tripoli (Ṭarābulus)	240,000
Zaḥlah	200,000[31]
Lesotho (1990 est.)	
★ Maseru	170,000[13]
Liberia (1990 est.)	
★ Monrovia	668,000[13]
Libya (1988 est.)	
Banghāzī	446,250
Misrātah	121,669
★ Tripoli (Ṭarābulus)	591,062
Liechtenstein (1994 est.)	
★ Vaduz	5,072
Lithuania (1993 est.)	
Kaunas	429,000
Klaipėda	206,400
Panevėžys	132,000
Šiauliai	147,800
★ Vilnius	590,100
Luxembourg (1991)	
★ Luxembourg	75,622
Macau (1991)	
★ Macau (Santo Nome de Deus)	326,460
Macedonia (1991; MU)	
Bitola	124,003
Giostivar	116,065
Kumanovo	135,482
★ Skopje (Skopije)	563,102
Tetovo	180,605
Madagascar (1993)	
★ Antananarivo	1,052,835
Antsirabe	120,239
Mahajanga	100,807
Toamasina	127,441
Malaŵi (1993 est.)	
Blantyre	399,263
★ Lilongwe	267,659
Malaysia (1991)	
Alor Setar	125,026
George Town (Pinang)	219,376
Ipoh	382,633
Johor Baharu	328,646
Kelang	243,698
Kota Baharu	219,713
Kota Kinabalu	208,484
★ Kuala Lumpur	1,145,075
Kuala Terengganu	228,659
Kuantan	198,356
Kuching	147,729
Melaka	295,999
Petaling Jaya	254,849
Port Kelang	192,080
Sandakan	223,432
Seloyang Baru	124,606
Seremban	182,584
Shah Alam	101,733
Sibu	126,384
Taiping	183,165
Tawai	244,765
Maldives (1990)	
★ Male'	55,130
Mali (1992 est.)	
★ Bamako	745,787
Malta (1994 est.)	
★ Valletta	9,144
Marshall Is. (1990 est.)	
★ Majuro	20,000
Martinique (1990)	
★ Fort-de-France	101,540
Mauritania (1992)	
★ Nouakchott	480,408
Mauritius (1993 est.)	
★ Port Louis	134,516
Mayotte (1991; MU)	
★ Mamoudzou	20,274
★ Dzaoudzi	8,268
Mexico (1990)	
Acapulco	515,374
Aguascalientes	440,425
Atizapán de Zaragoza (Ciudad López Mateos)	315,059
Campeche	150,518
Cancún	167,730
Celaya	214,856
Chihuahua	516,153
Ciudad Apodaca	103,364
Ciudad Madero	160,331
Ciudad Obregón	219,980
Ciudad Santa Catarina	162,707
Ciudad Victoria	194,996
Coatzacoalcos	198,817
Colima	106,967
Córdoba	130,695
Cuautla	110,242
Cuernavaca	279,187
Culiacán	415,046
Durango	348,036
Ensenada	169,426
Gómez Palacio	164,092
Guadalajara	1,650,042
Guadalupe	535,332
Hermosillo	406,417
Heroica Nogales	105,873
Irapuato	265,042
Juárez	789,522
La Paz	137,641
León	758,279
Los Mochis	162,659
Matamoros	266,055
Mazatlán	262,705
Mérida	523,422
Mexicali	438,377
★ Mexico City	9,815,795
Minatitlán	142,060
Monclova	177,792
Monterrey	1,068,996
Morelia	428,486
Nezahualcóyotl	1,255,456
Nuevo Laredo	218,413
Oaxaca	212,818
Orizaba	114,216
Pachuca	174,013
Poza Rica	151,739
Puebla	1,007,170
Querétaro	385,503
Reynosa	265,663
Salamanca	123,190
Saltillo	420,947
San Luis Potosí	488,238
San Nicolás de los Garza	436,603
San Pedro Garza García	113,017
Soledad de Graciano Sanchez	123,943
Tampico	272,690
Tapachula	138,858
Tehuacán	139,450
Tepic	206,967
Tijuana	698,752
Tlaquepaque	328,031
Toluca	327,865
Tonala	151,190
Torreón	439,436
Tuxtla	289,626
Uruapan	187,623
Veracruz	438,821
Villahermosa	261,231
Xalapa (Jalapa) Enríquez	279,451
Zacatecas	100,051
Zamora de Hidalgo	109,751
Zapopan	668,323
Micronesia	
★ Palikir	—
Moldova (1991 est.)	
Bălţi (Beltsy)	164,900
★ Chişinău (Kishinyov)	662,000[8]
Tighina (Bendery)	141,500
Tiraspol	186,000
Monaco (1995 est.)	
★ Monaco	30,400[25]
Mongolia (1993 est.)	
★ Ulaanbaatar (Ulan Bator)	619,000
Morocco (1993 est.)	
Agadir	137,000
Beni-Mellal	139,000
Casablanca (Dar el-Beida)	2,943,000
Fès (Fez)	564,000
el-Jadida (Mazagan)	125,000
Kenitra	234,000
Khouribga	190,000
Marrakech	602,000
Meknès	401,000
Mohammedia	156,000
Oujda	331,000
★ Rabat	1,220,000
Safi	278,000
Salé	521,000
Tanger	307,000
Tétouan	272,000
Mozambique (1991 est.)	
Beira	298,847
Chimoio	108,818
★ Maputo (Lourenço Marques)	931,591
Matala	337,239
Nacala	125,208
Nampula	250,473
Quelimane	146,206
Tete	112,221
Myanmar (Burma) (1983)	
Bassein (Pathein)	144,096
Mandalay	532,949
Monywa	106,843
Moulmein (Mawlamyine)	219,961
Pegu (Bago)	150,528
Sittwe (Akyab)	107,621
Taunggye	108,231
★ Yangôn (Rangoon)	3,851,000[17]
Namibia (1992 est.)	
★ Windhoek	161,000
Nauru (1983)	
★ Yaren	559
Nepal (1993 est.; MU)	
Bhaktapur (Bhādgāon)	130,000
Birātnagar	132,000
★ Kāthmāndu	535,000
Lalitpur (Patan)	190,000
Netherlands, The (1994 est.)	
Amersfoort	110,117
★ Amsterdam (capital)	724,096
Apeldoorn	149,449
Arnhem	133,670
Breda	129,125
Dordrecht	113,394
Eindhoven	196,130
Enschede	147,624
Groningen	170,535
Haarlem	150,213
Haarlemmermeer	103,684
Leiden	114,892
Maastricht	118,102
Nijmegen	147,018
Rotterdam	598,521
★ The Hague (seat of government)	445,279
Tilburg	163,383
Utrecht	234,106
Zaanstad	132,508
Zoetermeer	103,420
Netherlands Antilles (1993 est.)	
★ Willemstad	197,019[13]
New Caledonia (1989)	
★ Nouméa	65,110
New Zealand (1995 est.)	
Auckland	336,500
Christchurch	308,800
Dunedin	121,100
Hamilton	106,700
Manukau	243,400
North Shore	163,600
Waitakere	147,500
★ Wellington	153,800
Nicaragua (1992 est.; MU)	
Chinandega	101,605
León	172,042
★ Managua	1,195,000[17]
Masaya	101,878
Niger (1988)	
Maradi	112,965
★ Niamey	398,265
Zinder	120,892
Nigeria (1995 est.)[32]	
Aba	291,600
Abeokuta	416,800
★ Abuja (capital designate)	339,100[33]
Ado-Ekiti	350,500
Agege	100,300
Akure	158,200
Awka	108,400
Benin City	223,900
Bida	122,500
Calabar	170,000
Deba Habe	135,400
Ede	299,500
Effon-Alaiye	149,300
Ejigbo	103,300
Enugu	308,200
Gombe	105,200
Gusau	154,000
Ibadan	1,365,000
Ife	289,500
Igboho	104,100
Ijebu-Ode	152,500
Ikare	137,300
Ikerre	238,500
Ikire	120,200
Ikirun	177,000
Ikorodu	180,300
Ila	257,400
Ilawe-Ekiti	179,900
Ilesha	369,000
Ilobu	194,400
Ilorin	464,000
Inisa	116,800
Ise-Ekiti	127,100
Iseyin	211,800
Iwo	353,000
Jos	201,200
Kaduna	333,600
Kano	657,300
Katsina	201,500
Kumo	144,400
Lafia	119,500
★ Lagos	1,484,000
Maiduguri	312,100
Makurdi	120,100
Minna	133,600
Mushin	324,900
Offa	192,300
Ogbomosho	711,900
Oka	139,600
Ondo	165,400
Onitsha	362,700
Oshogbo	465,000
Owo	178,900
Oyo	250,100
Port Harcourt	399,700
Sapele	135,800
Shagamu	114,300
Shaki	169,700
Shomolu	144,100
Sokoto	199,900
Ugep	100,000
Warri	122,900
Zaria	369,800
Northern Mariana Is. (1990)	
★ Saipan	38,896
Norway (1995 est.; MU)	
Bergen	221,645
★ Oslo	482,555
Stavanger	103,496
Trondheim	142,792
Oman (1991 est.)	
★ Muscat	100,000[13]
Pakistan (1981)	
Bahāwalpur	180,263
Chiniot	105,559
Dera Ghāzi Khān	102,007
Faisalābād (Lyallpur)	1,875,000[17]
Gujrānwāla	1,663,000[17]
Gujrāt	155,058
Hyderābād	1,107,000[17]
★ Islamābād	204,364
Jhang	195,558
Jhelum	106,462
Karāchi	9,863,000[17]
Kasūr	155,523
Lahore	5,085,000[17]
Lahore Cantonment	237,000
Lārkāna	123,890
Mardān	147,977
Mīrpur Khās	124,371
Multān	1,257,000[17]
Nawābshāh	102,139
Okāra	153,483
Peshāwar	1,676,000[17]
Quetta	285,719
Rahīm Yār Khān	119,036
Rāwalpindi	1,290,000[17]
Sāhīwāl	150,954
Sargodha	291,362
Sheikhūpura	141,168
Siālkot	302,009
Sukkur	190,551
Wāh Cantonment	122,335

country / city	population
Palau (1990)	
Koror	10,501
Panama (1993 est.)	
Colón	137,825[20]
★ Panama City	450,668
San Miguelito	293,564
Papua New Guinea (1990)	
★ Port Moresby (National Capital District)	193,242
Paraguay (1992)	
★ Asunción	502,426
Ciudad del Este	133,893
San Lorenzo	133,311
Peru (1993)	
Arequipa	619,156
Ayacucho	105,918
Callao	615,046
Chiclayo	411,536
Chimbote	268,979
Chincha Alta	110,016
Cuzco	255,568
Huancayo	258,209
Huánuco	118,814
Ica	161,406
Iquitos	274,759
Juliaca	142,576
★ Lima	421,570[18]
Metro Lima-Callao	5,706,127
Piura	277,964
Pucallpa	172,286
Sullana	147,361
Tacna	174,336
Trujillo	509,312
Philippines (1990)	
Angeles	237,000
Bacolod	364,000
Bago	124,000
Baguio	183,000
Batangas	185,000
Butuan	228,000
Cabanatuan	173,000
Cadiz	120,000
Cagayan de Oro	340,000
Calbayog	115,000
Caloocan	761,000
Cebu	610,000
Cotabato	127,000
Dagupan	122,000
Davao	850,000
General Santos	250,000
Iligan	227,000
Iloilo	310,000
Lapu-Lapu	146,000
Las Piñas	286,000
Legaspi	121,000
Lipa	160,000
Lucena	151,000
Makati	453,000
Malabon	277,000
Mandaluyong	247,000
Mandaue	180,000
★ Manila	1,599,000
Metro Manila	7,832,000
Marikina	000,000
Muntilupa	278,000
Naga	115,000
Navotas	187,000
Olongapo	193,000
Ormoc	129,000
Pagadian	106,000
Parañaque	308,000
Pasay	367,000
Pasig	395,000
Quezon City	1,667,000
Roxas	103,000
San Carlos (*Negros Occidental*)	106,000
San Carlos (*Pangasinan*)	124,000
San Juan del Monte	127,000
San Pablo	161,000
Surigao	100,000
Tacloban	138,000
Tagig	267,000
Toledo	120,000
Valenzuela	340,000
Zamboanga	442,000
Poland (1994 est.)	
Białystok	276,100
Bielsko-Biała	181,000
Bydgoszcz	384,800
Bytom	229,600
Chorzów	127,000
Czestochowa	259,900
Dąbrowa Górnicza	132,800
Elbląg	127,800
Gdańsk	463,100
Gdynia	250,600
Gliwice	214,500
Gorzów Wielkopolski	125,000
Grudziadz	103,700
Jastrzębie-Zdrój	103,600
Kalisz	106,700
Katowice	359,400
Kielce	214,100
Koszalin	111,100
Kraków	745,100
Legnica	107,100
Łódź	833,700
Lublin	351,600
Olsztyn	166,200
Opole	130,000
Płock	125,900
Poznań	582,800
Radom	231,600
Ruda Śląska	168,000
Rybnik	143,800
Rzeszów	158,500
Słupsk	102,400
Sosnowiec	250,400
Szczecin	417,700
Tarnów	122,200
Toruń	203,100
Tychy	136,800
Wałbrzych	140,300
★ Warsaw (Warszawa)	1,642,700
Włocławek	122,900
Wrocław	642,300
Zabrze	204,000
Zielona Góra	115,600
Portugal (1991)	
★ Lisbon	677,790
Porto	310,600
Puerto Rico (1990)	
Bayamón	202,103
Carolina	162,404
Ponce	159,151
★ San Juan	426,832
Qatar (1992 est.)	
★ Doha	313,639[13]
Réunion (1990)	
★ Saint-Denis	100,926
Romania (1992)	
Arad	190,088
Bacău	204,495
Baia Mare	148,815
Botoşani	126,204
Brăila	234,706
Braşov	323,835
★ Bucharest	2,064,474
Buzău	148,247
Cluj-Napoca	328,008
Constanţa	350,476
Craiova	303,520
Drobeta-Turnu Severin	115,526
Focşani	101,296
Galaţi	325,788
Iaşi	342,994
Oradea	220,848
Piatra Neamţ	123,175
Piteşti	179,479
Ploieşti	252,073
Râmnicu Vâlcea	113,356
Satu Mare	131,859
Sibiu	169,696
Suceava	114,355
Timişoara	334,278
Tîrgu Mureş	163,625
Russia (1994 est.)	
Abakan	159,100
Achinsk	122,400
Almetyevsk	137,500
Angarsk	267,200
Anzhero-Sudzhensk	105,700
Arkhangelsk	407,100
Armavir	163,200
Arzamas	111,800
Astrakhan	512,000
Balakovo	206,000
Balashikha	136,200
Barnaul	596,400
Belgorod	317,900
Berezniki	196,000
Biysk	232,900
Blagoveshchensk	213,600
Bratsk	257,600
Bryansk	460,000
Cheboksary	446,200
Chelyabinsk	1,124,500
Cherepovets	319,300
Cherkessk	119,100
Chita	367,000
Dimitrovgrad	132,700
Dzerzhinsk	285,500
Elektrostal	151,000
Engels	184,400
Glazov	107,000
Grozny	364,000[1]
Irkutsk	632,200
Ivanovo	475,600
Izhevsk	652,800
Kaliningrad	415,100
Kaliningrad (*Moscow oblast*)	134,700
Kaluga	344,600
Kamensk-Uralsky	206,700
Kamyshin	127,200
Kansk	109,700
Kazan	1,092,300
Kemerovo	512,700
Khabarovsk	609,100
Khimki	134,900
Kineshma	103,400
Kirov	491,100
Kirovo-Chepetsk	100,400
Kiselyovsk	124,800
Kislovodsk	118,900
Kolomna	162,100
Kolpino	143,200
Komsomolsk-na-Amure	311,100
Kostroma	283,000
Kovrov	161,100
Krasnodar	638,000
Krasnoyarsk	914,200
Kurgan	361,600
Kursk	438,900
Kuznetsk	100,700
Leninsk-Kuznetsky	130,700
Lipetsk	469,800
Lyubertsy	164,700
Magadan	135,200
Magnitogorsk	439,000
Makhachkala	327,300
Maykop	163,600
Mezhdurechensk	107,400
Miass	171,000
Michurinsk	108,400
★ Moscow	8,792,000
Murmansk	443,500
Murom	126,600
Mytishchi	152,000
Naberezhnye Chelny (Brezhnev)	523,700
Nakhodka	163,800
Nalchik	239,300
Nevinnomyssk	128,600
Nikolo Boryozovka (Neftekamsk)	116,100
Nizhnekamsk	206,500
Nizhnevartovsk	240,800
Nizhny Novgorod (Gorky)	1,424,600
Nizhny Tagil	429,100
Noginsk	120,300
Norilsk	163,400
Novgorod	232,800
Novocheboksarsk	121,800
Novocherkassk	188,700
Novokuybyshevsk	114,300
Novokuznetsk	592,800
Novomoskovsk (*Tula oblast*)	144,400
Novorossiysk	193,700
Novoshakhtinsk	106,700
Novosibirsk	1,418,200
Novotroitsk	108,800
Obninsk	106,600
Odintsovo	129,700
Oktyabrsky	108,500
Omsk	1,161,200
Orekhovo-Zuyevo	133,600
Orenburg	557,500
Orsk	274,000
Oryol	346,300
Penza	551,300
Perm	1,086,100
Pervouralsk	143,300
Petropavlovsk-Kamchatsky	256,400
Petrozavodsk	278,700
Podolsk	204,100
Prokopyevsk	266,100
Pskov	207,400
Pyatigorsk	132,200
Rostov-na-Donu	1,023,200
Rubtsovsk	170,800
Ryazan	525,900
Rybinsk (Andropov)	249,300
Saint Petersburg (Leningrad)	4,882,600
Salavat	155,000
Samara (Kuybyshev)	1,222,500
Saransk	320,300
Sarapul	109,900
Saratov	898,600
Sergiev Posad (Zagorsk)	114,400
Serov	101,900
Serpukhov	139,100
Severodvinsk	242,600
Shakhty	228,500
Shchyolkovo	108,400
Simbirsk (Ulyanovsk)	669,900
Smolensk	352,600
Sochi	353,300
Solikamsk	108,600
Stary Oskol	192,600
Stavropol	336,600
Sterlitamak	256,200
Surgut	259,200
Syktyvkar	227,100
Syzran	176,000
Taganrog	291,000
Tambov	313,200
Tolyatti	689,200
Tomsk	495,500
Tula	535,400
Tver (Kalinin)	454,000
Tyumen	491,300
Ufa	1,091,800
Ukhta	109,000
Ulan-Ude	364,500
Usolye-Sibirskoye	106,400
Ussuriysk	161,800
Ust-Ilimsk	111,100
Velikiye Luki	116,200
Vladikavkaz (Ordzhonikidze)	310,800
Vladimir	338,000
Vladivostok	637,000
Volgodonsk	182,200
Volgograd	1,000,400
Vologda	296,000
Volzhsky	285,600
Vorkuta	109,100
Voronezh	904,600
Votkinsk	104,200
Yakutsk	194,400
Yaroslavl	631,000
Yekaterinburg (Sverdlovsk)	1,347,000
Yelets	118,900
Yoshkar-Ola	247,900
Yuzhno-Sakhalinsk	162,400
Zelenograd	182,500
Zhukovsky	100,000
Zlatoust	205,800
Rwanda (1991)	
★ Kigali	232,733
St. Kitts and Nevis (1990 est.)	
★ Basseterre	15,000
St. Lucia (1992 est.)	
★ Castries	13,615[34]
St. Vincent and The Grenadines (1991)	
★ Kingstown	15,466
San Marino (1995 est.)	
★ San Marino	2,015
São Tomé and Príncipe (1990 est.)	
★ São Tomé	43,420
Saudi Arabia (1980 est.)	
ad Dammām	200,000
Jiddah	1,800,000[31]
Mecca (Makkah)	550,000
Medina (al-Madīnah)	290,000
★ Riyadh (ar-Riyad)	1,800,000[31]
aṭ-Ṭā'if	300,000
Senegal (1994 est.)	
★ Dakar	1,729,823
Kaolack	193,115
Mboure	106,046
Rufisque	138,837
St.-Louis	132,444
Thiès	216,381
Ziquinchor	161,680
Seychelles (1993 est.)	
★ Victoria	25,000
Sierra Leone (1990 est.)	
★ Freetown	669,000[13]
Singapore (1995 est.)[21]	
★ Singapore	2,989,300
Slovakia (1993 est.)	
★ Bratislava	446,655
Košice	237,336
Slovenia (1994 est.)	
★ Ljubljana	270,759
Maribor	103,512
Solomon Islands (1990 est.)	
★ Honiara	35,288
Somalia (1990 est.)	
★ Mogadishu	900,000
South Africa (1991)	
Alexandria	124,586
Benoni	113,501
★ Bloemfontein (judicial)	126,867
Boksburg	119,890
Botshabelo	177,926
★ Cape Town (legislative)	854,616
Dareyton	151,659
Diepmeadow	241,099
Durban	715,669
East London	102,325
Evaton	201,026
Germiston	134,005
Ibhayi	257,054
Johannesburg	712,507
Kathlehong (Katlehong)	201,785
Kempton Park	106,606
Khayelitsa	189,586
Kwamashu (Kwa Mashu)	156,679
Lekoa	217,582
Manguang (Mangaung)	125,545
Mdantsane	242,823
Ntuzuma	102,310
Pietermaritzburg	156,473
Port Elizabeth	303,353
★ Pretoria (executive)	525,583
Roodepoort	162,632
Sandton	101,197
Soweto	596,632
Tembisa	209,238
Umlazi	299,275
Spain (1994 est.; MU)	
Albacete	141,179
Alcalá de Henares	159,355[10]
Alcorcón	139,641[10]
Algeciras	101,063[10]
Alicante	274,964
Almería	167,361
Badajoz	130,153
Badalona	206,585[10]
Baracaldo	104,883[10]
Barcelona	1,630,867
Bilbao	371,787
Burgos	166,251
Cádiz	155,438
Cartagena	166,736[10]
Castellón de la Plana	139,094
Córdoba	315,948
Coruña, La	255,087
Donostia (San Sebastián)	177,929
Elche	181,658[10]
Fuenlabrada	144,723[10]
Getafe	138,704[10]
Gijón	259,054[10]
Granada	271,180
Hospitalet de Llobregat	268,241[10]
Huelva	145,049
Jaén	112,772
Jerez de la Frontera	182,939[10]
La Laguna	109,485[10]
Leganés	171,400[10]
León	147,311
Lleida (Lérida)	114,234
Logroño	124,823
★ Madrid	3,041,101
Málaga	531,443
Mataró	101,501[10]
Móstoles	192,018[10]
Murcia	341,531
Ourense (Orense)	108,547
Oviedo	201,712
Palma (de Mallorca)	322,008
Palmas de Gran Canaria, Las (Is. Canarias)	371,787
Pamplona	182,465
Sabadell	184,460[10]
Salamanca	167,382
Santa Coloma de Gramanet	132,173[10]
Santa Cruz de Tenerife	203,929
Santander	194,822
Sevilla (Seville)	714,148
Tarragona	114,630
Terrassa	154,300[10]
Valencia	764,293
Valladolid	336,917
Vigo	274,629[10]
Vitoria (Gasteiz)	214,148
Zaragoza (Saragossa)	606,620
Sri Lanka (1990 est.)	
★ Colombo (administrative)	615,000
Dehiwala-Mount Lavinia	196,000
Jaffna	129,000
Kandy	104,000
Moratuwa	170,000
★ Sri Jayawardenepura Kotte (legislative and judicial)	109,000[35]
Sudan, The (1993)	
Juba	114,980
Kassalā	234,270
★ Khartoum (executive)	924,505
Khartoum North	879,105
Nyala	228,778
★ Omdurman (legislative)	1,267,077
Port Sudan	305,385
al-Qaḍārif	189,384
al-Ubayyiḍ	228,096
Wad Madanī	218,714
Wāw	116,000[36]
Suriname (1993 est.)	
★ Paramaribo	200,970
Swaziland (1990 est.)	
★ Mbabane	47,000
Sweden (1995 est.; MU)	
Göteborg	444,553
Helsingborg	113,411
Jönköping	114,811
Linköping	130,489

Major cities and national capitals (continued)

country city	population
Malmö	242,706
Norrköping	123,240
Örebro	118,606
★ Stockholm	703,627
Uppsala	181,191
Västerås	122,998
Switzerland (1994 est.)	
Basel (Bâle)	176,220
★ Bern (Berne)	129,423
Geneva (Genève)	171,744
Lausanne	117,153
Zürich	343,045
Syria (1994 est.)	
Aleppo (Ḥalab)	1,591,400
★ Damascus (Dimashq)	1,549,932
Dar'ā	180,093
Dayr az-Zawr	174,085
Dūmā	131,158
Ḥamāh	229,000[20]
al-Ḥasakah	106,000[20]
Homs (Ḥims)	644,204
Jaramānah	138,469
Latakia (al-Ladhiqiyah)	306,535
al-Qāmishlī	151,000[20]
ar-Raqqah	219,016
Ṭarṭūs	136,812
Taiwan (1995 est.)	
Chang-hua	221,090[8]
Chi-lung (Keelung)	365,312
Chia-i	260,756
Chung-ho	387,264
Chung-li	289,054[8]
Feng-shan (Kao-hsiung-hsien)	298,059[8]
Fêng-yüan	156,906[8]
Hsin-chu	338,507
Hsin-chuang	321,970[8]
Hsin-tien	245,897[8]
Hua-lien	107,441[8]
Kao-hsiung	1,416,160
Pan-ch'iao (T'ai-pei-hsien)	544,067[8]
P'ing-tung	214,304[8]
San-chu'ung	383,943[8]
T'ai-chung	836,560
T'ai-nan	702,704
T'ai-tung	108,606[8]
★ Taipei (T'ai-pei)	2,652,685
T'ao-yuan	256,612[8]
Yung-ho	245,743[8]
Tajikistan (1994 est.)	
★ Dushanbe	524,000
Khujand (Khudzhand; Leninabad)	164,500[30]
Tanzania (1988)	
★ Dar es Salaam	1,360,850
Dodoma (capital designate)	203,833
Mbeya	194,000[33]
Mwanza	223,013
Tabora	214,000[33]
Tanga	187,634
Zanzibar	157,634
Thailand (1993 est.)	
★ Bangkok	5,572,712
Chiang Mai	170,397
Hat Yai	148,632
Nakhon Ratchasima	188,171
Nonthanburi	261,335
Ubon Ratchathani	105,936
Togo (1990 est.)	
★ Lomé	513,000[13]
Tonga (1990 est.)	
★ Nuku'alofa	34,000
Trinidad and Tobago (1992 est.)	
★ Port-of-Spain	52,451
Tunisia (1990 est.)	
Aryānah	137,000
Ettadhamen	111,793[21]
Ṣafāqis (Sfax)	227,000
Sūsah	104,000
★ Tunis	1,826,652[37]
Turkey (1993 est.)	
Adana	1,010,363
Adapazari	181,869
Adıyaman	100,045[12]
★ Ankara	2,719,981
Antakya	123,871[12]
Antalya	461,645
Aydın	107,011[12]
Balıkesir	182,821
Batman	172,414
Bursa	949,810
Çorum	116,810[12]
Denizli	225,851
Diyarbakır	428,993
Edirne	102,345[12]
Elazığ	217,715
Erzurum	247,987
Eskişehir	440,380
Gaziantep	683,557
Gebze	159,116[12]
Hatay	133,474
İçel	422,357[12]
İskenderun	156,286
Isparta	118,461
Istanbul	7,331,927
İzmir	1,920,807
İzmit	270,519
Kahramanmaraş	238,297
Karabük	105,373[12]
Kayseri	444,923
Kırıkkale	174,310
Kocaeli	256,882[12]
Konya	558,308
Kütahya	138,001
Malatya	308,972
Manisa	179,302
Mersin	493,556
Ordu	102,107[12]
Osmaniye	133,579
Samsun	320,515
Sivas	234,946
Tarsus	214,136
Trabzon	144,992
Urfa (Şanlıurfa)	333,738
Uşak	105,270[12]
Van	182,347
Zonguldak	116,109
Turkmenistan (1994 est.)	
★ Ashkhabad (Ashgabat)	518,000
Chärjew (Chardzhev; Chardzhou)	166,400[30]
Dashhowuz (Dashkhovuz; Tashauz)	117,000[30]
Tuvalu (1991)	
★ Funafuti	3,839
Uganda (1991)	
★ Kampala	773,463
Ukraine (1994 est.)	
Alchevsk	128,000
Berdyansk	137,000
Bila Tserkva (Belaya Tserkov)	216,000
Cherkasy (Cherkassy)	313,000
Chernihiv (Chernigov)	315,000
Chernivtsi (Chernovtsy)	263,000
Dniprodzerzhynsk (Dneprodzerzhinsk)	287,000
Dnipropetrovsk (Dnepropetrovsk)	1,176,000
Donetsk	1,114,000
Horlivka (Gorlovka)	332,000
Ivano-Frankivsk (Ivano-Frankovsk)	236,000
Kamyanets-Podilsky (Kamenets-Podolsky)	108,000
Kerch	182,000
Kharkiv (Kharkov)	1,599,000
Kherson	369,000
Khmelnytsky (Khmelnitsky)	256,000
★ Kiev (Kyyiv)	2,645,000
Kirovohrad	280,000
Konotop	100,000
Kostyantynivka (Konstantinovka)	105,000
Kramatorsk	203,000
Krasny Luch	114,000
Kremenchuk (Kremenchug)	249,000
Kryvy Rih (Krivoy Rog)	735,000
Luhansk (Voroshilovgrad)	500,000
Lutsk	218,000
Lviv (Lvov)	809,000
Lysychansk (Lisichansk)	126,000
Makiyivka (Makeyevka)	422,000
Mariupol (Zhdanov)	521,000
Melitopol	178,000
Mykolayiv (Nikolayev)	517,000
Nikopol	161,000
Odesa (Odessa)	1,073,000
Oleksandriya (Aleksandriya)	106,000
Pavlohrad	137,000
Poltava	325,000
Rivne (Rovno)	246,000
Sevastopol	374,000
Severodonetsk	135,000
Simferopol	356,000
Slovyansk (Slavyansk)	137,000
Stakhanov	113,000
Sumy	307,000
Ternopil (Ternopol)	232,000
Uzhhorod	126,000
Vinnytsya (Vinnitsa)	387,000
Yenakiyeve (Yenakiyevo)	118,000
Yevpatoriya	115,000
Zaporizhzhya (Zaporozhye)	895,000
Zhytomyr (Zhitomir)	303,000
United Arab Emirates (1989 est.)	
★ Abu Dhabi (Abū Ẓaby)	363,432
Al-'Ayn	176,441
Dubai (Dubayy)	585,189
Sharjah (ash-Shāriqah)	125,123[23]
United Kingdom (1992 est.)[38]	
Aberdeen	218,220[1]
Barnsley	224,800
Belfast	296,700[1]
Birmingham	1,009,100
Blackburn	136,612[10]
Blackpool	146,069[10]
Bolton	263,800
Bournemouth	151,302[10]
Bradford	477,500
Brighton	143,582[10]
Bristol	396,600
Cardiff	295,600
Coventry	304,600
Derby	227,100
Doncaster	293,500
Dudley	311,000
Dundee	170,120[1]
Edinburgh	439,880
Gateshead	203,100
Glasgow	681,470[1]
Gloucester	101,608[10]
Huddersfield	148,544[39]
Ipswich	116,956[10]
Kingston upon Hull	268,500
Kirklees	383,200
Leeds	721,800
Leicester	285,400
Liverpool	479,000
★ London	6,679,699[10]
Luton	171,671[10]
Manchester	434,600
Middlesbrough	140,849
Newcastle upon Tyne	281,700
Newport	133,311[10]
Northampton	180,567[10]
Norwich	120,895[10]
Nottingham	282,500
Ogwr	132,442[10]
Oldbury/Smethwick	153,461[39]
Oldham	220,200
Oxford	110,103[10]
Peterborough	153,166[10]
Plymouth	257,500
Poole	133,050[10]
Portsmouth	174,697[10]
Preston	126,082[10]
Reading	128,877[10]
Renfrew	201,150[1]
Rochdale	205,700
Rotherham	255,100[10]
St. Helens	178,764[10]
Salford	230,300
Sandwell	294,100
Sefton	294,900
Sheffield	531,000
Slough	101,066[10]
Solihull	200,900
Southampton	208,100
Southend-on-Sea	158,517
Stockport	288,800
Stoke-on-Trent	252,900
Sunderland	297,100
Sutton Coldfield	103,097[39]
Swansea	181,906[10]
Swindon	128,493
Tameside	221,000
Trafford	215,900
Wakefield	317,100
Walsall	263,400
West Bromwich	154,531
Wigan	312,400
Wirral	335,300
Wolverhampton	247,500
United States (1994 est.)	
Abilene (*Texas*)	110,034
Akron (*Ohio*)	221,886
Alameda (*Calif.*)	78,672
Albany (*Ga.*)	81,062
Albany (*N.Y.*)	104,828
Albuquerque (*N.M.*)	411,994
Alexandria (*Va.*)	112,879
Alhambra (*Calif.*)	84,411
Allentown (*Pa.*)	105,339
Altoona (*Pa.*)	52,531
Amarillo (*Texas*)	165,036
Anaheim (*Calif.*)	282,133
Anchorage (*Alaska*)	253,649
Anderson (*Ind.*)	60,846
Ann Arbor (*Mich.*)	108,817
Antioch (*Calif.*)	73,019
Apple Valley (*Calif.*)	51,994
Appleton (*Wis.*)	69,594
Arcadia (*Calif.*)	50,654
Arlington (*Texas*)	286,922
Arlington (*Va.*)	174,603[40]
Arlington Heights (*Ill.*)	77,438
Arvada (*Colo.*)	95,446
Asheville (*N.C.*)	64,261
Atlanta (*Ga.*)	396,052
Aurora (*Colo.*)	250,717
Aurora (*Ill.*)	112,313
Austin (*Texas*)	514,013
Bakersfield (*Calif.*)	191,060
Baldwin Park (*Calif.*)	72,763
Baltimore (*Md.*)	702,979
Baton Rouge (*La.*)	227,482
Battle Creek (*Mich.*)	55,053
Bayonne (*N.J.*)	62,270
Baytown (*Texas*)	67,454
Beaumont (*Texas*)	115,022
Beaverton (*Ore.*)	59,367
Bellevue (*Wash.*)	84,239
Bellflower (*Calif.*)	66,667
Bellingham (*Wash.*)	57,119
Berkeley (*Calif.*)	99,830
Bethlehem (*Pa.*)	72,821
Billings (*Mont.*)	86,578
Binghamton (*N.Y.*)	51,144
Birmingham (*Ala.*)	264,527
Bismarck (*N.D.*)	52,592
Bloomington (*Ill.*)	55,570
Bloomington (*Ind.*)	62,560
Bloomington (*Minn.*)	85,185
Boca Raton (*Fla.*)	66,422
Boise City (*Idaho*)	145,987
Bossier City (*La.*)	54,419
Boston (*Mass.*)	547,725
Boulder (*Colo.*)	85,613
Boynton Beach (*Fla.*)	51,230
Bridgeport (*Conn.*)	132,919
Bristol (*Conn.*)	60,647
Brockton (*Mass.*)	87,411
Broken Arrow (*Okla.*)	65,679
Brooklyn Park (*Minn.*)	58,786
Brownsville (*Texas*)	112,904
Bryan (*Texas*)	60,756
Buena Park (*Calif.*)	72,671
Buffalo (*N.Y.*)	312,965
Burbank (*Calif.*)	99,665
Burnsville (*Minn.*)	55,081
Camarillo (*Calif.*)	56,734
Cambridge (*Mass.*)	99,890
Camden (*N.J.*)	82,866
Canton (*Ohio*)	84,188
Cape Coral (*Fla.*)	84,968
Carlsbad (*Calif.*)	65,461
Carrollton (*Texas*)	94,261
Carson (*Calif.*)	90,025
Cary (*N.C.*)	60,775
Cedar Rapids (*Iowa*)	113,438
Cerritos (*Calif.*)	54,786
Champaign (*Ill.*)	66,888
Chandler (*Ariz.*)	119,227
Charleston (*S.C.*)	76,854
Charleston (*W.V.*)	56,553
Charlotte (*N.C.*)	437,797
Chattanooga (*Tenn.*)	152,259
Chesapeake (*Va.*)	180,577
Cheyenne (*Wyo.*)	53,559
Chicago (*Ill.*)	2,731,743
Chicopee (*Mass.*)	55,024
Chino (*Calif.*)	64,781
Chula Vista (*Calif.*)	149,255
Cicero (*Ill.*)	74,823
Cincinnati (*Ohio*)	358,170
Clarksville (*Tenn.*)	92,116
Clearwater (*Fla.*)	99,838
Cleveland (*Ohio*)	492,901
Cleveland Heights (*Ohio*)	51,477
Clifton (*N.J.*)	74,002
Clovis (*Calif.*)	60,281
College Station (*Texas*)	57,273
Colorado Springs (*Colo.*)	316,480
Columbia (*Mo.*)	74,072
Columbia (*S.C.*)	104,101
Columbus (*Ga.*)	186,470
Columbus (*Ohio*)	635,913
Compton (*Calif.*)	96,477
Concord (*Calif.*)	111,889
Coon Rapids (*Minn.*)	62,324
Coral Springs (*Fla.*)	92,612
Corona (*Calif.*)	92,898
Corpus Christi (*Texas*)	275,419
Costa Mesa (*Calif.*)	98,427
Council Bluffs (*Iowa*)	54,850
Cranston (*R.I.*)	77,323
Dallas (*Texas*)	1,022,830
Daly City (*Calif.*)	94,036
Danbury (*Conn.*)	64,675
Danville (*Va.*)	54,227
Davenport (*Iowa*)	96,964
Davie (*Fla.*)	57,156
Dayton (*Ohio*)	178,540
Daytona Beach (*Fla.*)	64,644
Dearborn (*Mich.*)	86,187
Dearborn Heights (*Mich.*)	58,288
Decatur (*Ala.*)	52,465
Decatur (*Ill.*)	83,105
Delray Beach (*Fla.*)	51,026
Denton (*Texas*)	69,210
Denver (*Colo.*)	493,559
Des Moines (*Iowa*)	193,965
Des Plaines (*Ill.*)	52,896
Detroit (*Mich.*)	992,038
Diamond Bar (*Calif.*)	58,828
Dothan (*Ala.*)	55,792
Downers Grove (*Ill.*)	50,622
Downey (*Calif.*)	99,889
Dubuque (*Iowa*)	59,084
Duluth (*Minn.*)	83,990
Durham (*N.C.*)	143,439
Eagan (*Minn.*)	56,992
East Lansing (*Mich.*)	50,322
East Orange (*N.J.*)	72,847
East Providence (*R.I.*)	50,059
Eau Claire (*Wis.*)	58,476
Edmond (*Okla.*)	61,224
El Cajon (*Calif.*)	92,658
El Monte (*Calif.*)	104,661
El Paso (*Texas*)	579,307
Elgin (*Ill.*)	85,339
Elizabeth (*N.J.*)	106,298
Elyria (*Ohio*)	57,119
Encinitas (*Calif.*)	57,029
Erie (*Pa.*)	108,398
Escondido (*Calif.*)	116,349
Euclid (*Ohio*)	53,251
Eugene (*Ore.*)	118,122
Evanston (*Ill.*)	73,433
Evansville (*Ind.*)	129,452
Everett (*Wash.*)	76,685
Fairfield (*Calif.*)	83,776
Fall River (*Mass.*)	89,425
Fargo (*N.D.*)	79,715
Farmington Hills (*Mich.*)	79,144
Fayetteville (*N.C.*)	83,999
Federal Way (*Wash.*)	72,802
Flagstaff (*Ariz.*)	50,708
Flint (*Mich.*)	138,164
Florissant (*Mo.*)	51,398
Fontana (*Calif.*)	103,737
Fort Collins (*Colo.*)	98,954
Fort Lauderdale (*Fla.*)	162,842
Fort Myers (*Fla.*)	50,489
Fort Smith (*Ark.*)	74,480
Fort Wayne (*Ind.*)	183,359
Fort Worth (*Texas*)	451,814
Fountain Valley (*Calif.*)	55,467
Fremont (*Calif.*)	183,575
Fresno (*Calif.*)	386,551
Fullerton (*Calif.*)	116,863
Gainesville (*Fla.*)	87,806
Galveston (*Texas*)	59,224
Garden Grove (*Calif.*)	147,958
Gardena (*Calif.*)	53,479
Garland (*Texas*)	194,218
Gary (*Ind.*)	114,256
Gastonia (*N.C.*)	59,093
Gilbert (*Ariz.*)	51,074
Glendale (*Ariz.*)	168,439
Glendale (*Calif.*)	178,481
Glendora (*Calif.*)	51,957
Grand Forks (*N.D.*)	50,168
Grand Prairie (*Texas*)	108,908
Grand Rapids (*Mich.*)	190,395
Great Falls (*Mont.*)	58,202
Greeley (*Colo.*)	64,189
Green Bay (*Wis.*)	102,708
Greensboro (*N.C.*)	196,167
Greenville (*S.C.*)	59,808
Gresham (*Ore.*)	78,594
Hamilton (*Ohio*)	64,912
Hammond (*Ind.*)	82,837
Hampton (*Va.*)	139,628
Harlingen (*Texas*)	55,522
Harrisburg (*Pa.*)	54,328
Hartford (*Conn.*)	124,196
Haverhill (*Mass.*)	52,962
Hawthorne (*Calif.*)	75,329
Hayward (*Calif.*)	115,590
Henderson (*Nev.*)	101,997
Hesperia (*Calif.*)	59,131
Hialeah (*Fla.*)	194,120
High Point (*N.C.*)	72,208
Hollywood (*Fla.*)	124,992
Honolulu (*Ha.*)	385,881
Houston (*Texas*)	1,702,086
Huntington (*W.V.*)	53,789
Huntington Beach (*Calif.*)	189,220
Huntington Park (*Calif.*)	55,712
Huntsville (*Ala.*)	160,325
Independence (*Mo.*)	111,669
Indianapolis (*Ind.*)	752,279

[1]1993 estimate. [2]Eight villages, including Fagatogo, Utulei, and Pago Pago, are collectively known as Pago Pago (1990 census pop. 10,559). [3]1984 estimate. [4]Population of municipality. [5]1989 census. [6]Population of the statistical division containing the city. [7]Statistical district. [8]1994 estimate. [9]Population cited is for New Providence Island. [10]1991 census. [11]1982 estimate. [12]1990 census. [13]Population refers to widest officially defined agglomeration or metropolitan area. [14]1992 census. [15]Excludes the agricultural population of the named civil division. [16]San José canton. [17]1995 estimate. [18]1990 estimate. [19]Excludes population of Lefkosia (Turkish-occupied Nicosia), estimated at 37,400 in 1985. [20]1992 estimate. [21]1989 estimate. [22]1986 estimate. [23]1986 census.

country city	population
Inglewood (*Calif.*)	110,085
Iowa City (*Iowa*)	60,655
Irvine (*Calif.*)	125,624
Irving (*Texas*)	164,917
Jackson (*Miss.*)	193,097
Jackson (*Tenn.*)	52,343
Jacksonville (*Fla.*)	665,070
Jacksonville (*N.C.*)	79,494
Janesville (*Wis.*)	56,862
Jersey City (*N.J.*)	226,022
Johnson City (*Tenn.*)	51,573
Joliet (*Ill.*)	79,492
Jonesboro (*Ark.*)	50,209
Kalamazoo (*Mich.*)	81,644
Kansas City (*Kan.*)	142,630
Kansas City (*Mo.*)	443,878
Kenner (*La.*)	72,891
Kenosha (*Wis.*)	85,122
Kettering (*Ohio*)	59,357
Killeen (*Texas*)	82,856
Knoxville (*Tenn.*)	169,311
La Crosse (*Wis.*)	50,877
La Habra (*Calif.*)	53,664
La Mesa (*Calif.*)	54,316
Lafayette (*La.*)	102,281
Laguna Niguel (*Calif.*)	56,681
Lake Charles (*La.*)	72,424
Lake Forest (*Calif.*)	59,894
Lakeland (*Fla.*)	71,255
Lakewood (*Calif.*)	79,416
Lakewood (*Colo.*)	126,031
Lakewood (*Ohio*)	57,063
Lancaster (*Calif.*)	119,186
Lancaster (*Pa.*)	57,721
Lansing (*Mich.*)	119,590
Laredo (*Texas*)	149,914
Largo (*Fla.*)	67,721
Las Cruces (*N.M.*)	71,043
Las Vegas (*Nev.*)	327,878
Lauderhill (*Fla.*)	52,023
Lawrence (*Kan.*)	71,721
Lawrence (*Mass.*)	63,117
Lawton (*Okla.*)	86,078
Lewisville (*Texas*)	51,143
Lexington-Fayette (*Ky.*)	237,612
Lincoln (*Neb.*)	203,076
Little Rock (*Ark.*)	178,136
Livermore (*Calif.*)	63,362
Livonia (*Mich.*)	100,415
Lodi (*Calif.*)	52,123
Long Beach (*Calif.*)	433,852
Longmont (*Colo.*)	56,264
Longview (*Texas*)	73,265
Lorain (*Ohio*)	70,919
Los Angeles (*Calif.*)	3,448,613
Louisville (*Ky.*)	270,308
Lowell (*Mass.*)	96,054
Lubbock (*Texas*)	194,467
Lynchburg (*Va.*)	66,491
Lynn (*Mass.*)	78,312
Lynwood (*Calif.*)	64,809
McAllen (*Texas*)	95,299
Macon (*Ga.*)	109,191
Madison (*Wis.*)	194,586
Malden (*Mass.*)	51,803
Manchester (*N.H.*)	96,640
Mansfield (*Ohio*)	53,192
Marietta (*Ga.*)	50,290
Medford (*Mass.*)	55,671
Medford (*Ore.*)	52,611
Melbourne (*Fla.*)	68,024
Memphis (*Tenn.*)	614,289
Mentor (*Ohio*)	50,058
Merced (*Calif.*)	60,348
Meriden (*Conn.*)	56,928
Mesa (*Ariz.*)	313,649
Mesquite (*Texas*)	113,631
Miami (*Fla.*)	373,024
Miami Beach (*Fla.*)	90,153
Midland (*Texas*)	96,163
Midwest City (*Okla.*)	53,473
Milpitas (*Calif.*)	55,927
Milwaukee (*Wis.*)	617,044
Minneapolis (*Minn.*)	354,590
Minnetonka (*Minn.*)	50,778
Mission Viejo (*Calif.*)	83,813
Mobile (*Ala.*)	204,490
Modesto (*Calif.*)	176,357
Monroe (*La.*)	57,049
Montebello (*Calif.*)	61,519
Monterey Park (*Calif.*)	57,921
Montgomery (*Ala.*)	195,471
Moreno Valley (*Calif.*)	139,311
Mount Prospect (*Ill.*)	53,605
Mount Vernon (*N.Y.*)	65,862
Mountain View (*Calif.*)	65,812
Muncie (*Ind.*)	71,407
Murfreesboro (*Tenn.*)	56,194
Napa (*Calif.*)	63,444
Naperville (*Ill.*)	101,163
Nashua (*N.H.*)	79,631
Nashville-Davidson (*Tenn.*)	504,505
National City (*Calif.*)	57,538
New Bedford (*Mass.*)	94,623
New Britain (*Conn.*)	69,887
New Haven (*Conn.*)	119,604
New Orleans (*La.*)	484,149
New Rochelle (*N.Y.*)	66,764
New York City (*N.Y.*)	7,333,253
Newark (*N.J.*)	258,751
Newport Beach (*Calif.*)	70,668
Newport News (*Va.*)	179,127
Newton (*Mass.*)	85,358
Niagara Falls (*N.Y.*)	60,517
Norfolk (*Va.*)	241,426
Norman (*Okla.*)	87,290
North Charleston (*S.C.*)	67,720
North Las Vegas (*Nev.*)	64,536
North Little Rock (*Ark.*)	62,197
North Miami (*Fla.*)	53,504
North Richland Hills (*Texas*)	55,471
Norwalk (*Calif.*)	100,744
Norwalk (*Conn.*)	78,710
Oak Lawn (*Ill.*)	56,690
Oak Park (*Ill.*)	54,385
Oakland (*Calif.*)	366,926
Ocala (*Fla.*)	53,225
Oceanside (*Calif.*)	146,229
Odessa (*Texas*)	94,763
Ogden (*Utah*)	67,763
Oklahoma City (*Okla.*)	463,201
Olathe (*Kan.*)	72,455
Omaha (*Neb.*)	345,033
Ontario (*Calif.*)	134,825
Orange (*Calif.*)	116,785
Orem (*Utah*)	74,402
Orlando (*Fla.*)	176,948
Oshkosh (*Wis.*)	56,229
Overland Park (*Kan.*)	125,225
Owensboro (*Ky.*)	53,645
Oxnard (*Calif.*)	145,863
Palm Bay (*Fla.*)	75,139
Palmdale (*Calif.*)	103,423
Palo Alto (*Calif.*)	50,925
Paramount (*Calif.*)	52,209
Parma (*Ohio*)	85,792
Pasadena (*Calif.*)	134,170
Pasadena (*Texas*)	129,292
Passaic (*N.J.*)	56,042
Paterson (*N.J.*)	138,290
Pawtucket (*R.I.*)	69,002
Pembroke Pines (*Fla.*)	81,498
Pensacola (*Fla.*)	60,025
Peoria (*Ariz.*)	70,139
Peoria (*Ill.*)	112,878
Philadelphia (*Pa.*)	1,524,249
Phoenix (*Ariz.*)	1,048,949
Pico Rivera (*Calif.*)	[illegible]
Pine Bluff (*Ark.*)	57,971
Pittsburg (*Calif.*)	52,036
Pittsburgh (*Pa.*)	358,883
Plano (*Texas*)	157,394
Plantation (*Fla.*)	74,748
Pleasanton (*Calif.*)	57,682
Plymouth (*Minn.*)	60,143
Pomona (*Calif.*)	143,870
Pompano Beach (*Fla.*)	75,719
Pontiac (*Mich.*)	66,708
Port Arthur (*Texas*)	58,795
Port St. Lucie (*Fla.*)	70,399
Portland (*Maine*)	61,982
Portland (*Ore.*)	450,777
Portsmouth (*Va.*)	103,464
Providence (*R.I.*)	150,639
Provo (*Utah*)	88,519
Pueblo (*Colo.*)	100,471
Quincy (*Mass.*)	84,040
Racine (*Wis.*)	86,014
Raleigh (*N.C.*)	236,707
Rancho Cucamonga (*Calif.*)	114,799
Rapid City (*S.D.*)	57,609
Reading (*Pa.*)	78,246
Redding (*Calif.*)	72,906
Redlands (*Calif.*)	64,526
Redondo Beach (*Calif.*)	64,236
Redwood City (*Calif.*)	67,786
Reno (*Nev.*)	145,029
Rialto (*Calif.*)	83,519
Richardson (*Texas*)	78,989
Richmond (*Calif.*)	87,944
Richmond (*Va.*)	201,108
Riverside (*Calif.*)	241,644
Roanoke (*Va.*)	96,643
Rochester (*Minn.*)	75,769
Rochester (*N.Y.*)	231,170
Rochester Hills (*Mich.*)	66,267
Rockford (*Ill.*)	143,263
Rocky Mount (*N.C.*)	51,941
Rosemead (*Calif.*)	52,024
Roseville (*Calif.*)	53,019
Roseville (*Mich.*)	51,592
Rosewell (*Ga.*)	54,908
Royal Oak (*Mich.*)	68,431
Sacramento (*Calif.*)	373,964
Saginaw (*Mich.*)	70,607
St. Charles (*Mo.*)	56,339
St. Clair Shores (*Mich.*)	63,834
St. Cloud (*Minn.*)	50,785
St. Joseph (*Mo.*)	71,711
St. Louis (*Mo.*)	368,215
St. Paul (*Minn.*)	262,071
St. Petersburg (*Fla.*)	238,585
Salem (*Ore.*)	115,912
Salinas (*Calif.*)	119,814
Salt Lake City (*Utah*)	171,849
San Angelo (*Texas*)	88,726
San Antonio (*Texas*)	998,905
San Bernardino (*Calif.*)	181,718
San Buenaventura (Ventura) (*Calif.*)	[illegible]
San Diego (*Calif.*)	1,151,977
San Francisco (*Calif.*)	734,676
San Jose (*Calif.*)	816,884
San Leandro (*Calif.*)	69,490
San Mateo (*Calif.*)	87,836
Sandy (*Utah*)	85,406
Santa Ana (*Calif.*)	290,827
Santa Barbara (*Calif.*)	85,626
Santa Clara (*Calif.*)	94,562
Santa Clarita (*Calif.*)	123,676
Santa Fe (*N.M.*)	62,514
Santa Maria (*Calif.*)	65,932
Santa Monica (*Calif.*)	87,047
Santa Rosa (*Calif.*)	116,962
Santee (*Calif.*)	55,222
Sarasota (*Fla.*)	54,411
Savannah (*Ga.*)	140,597
Schaumburg (*Ill.*)	73,521
Schenectady (*N.Y.*)	64,274
Scottsdale (*Ariz.*)	152,439
Scranton (*Pa.*)	77,964
Seattle (*Wash.*)	520,947
Sheboygan (*Wis.*)	50,368
Shreveport (*La.*)	196,982
Simi Valley (*Calif.*)	106,949
Sioux City (*Iowa*)	82,735
Sioux Falls (*S.D.*)	109,174
Skokie (*Ill.*)	58,980
Somerville (*Mass.*)	68,940
South Bend (*Ind.*)	105,092
South Gate (*Calif.*)	91,907
South San Francisco (*Calif.*)	56,576
Southfield (*Mich.*)	79,789
Sparks (*Nev.*)	60,238
Spokane (*Wash.*)	192,781
Springfield (*Ill.*)	105,938
Springfield (*Mass.*)	149,164
Springfield (*Mo.*)	149,727
Springfield (*Ohio*)	70,388
Stamford (*Conn.*)	107,199
Sterling Heights (*Mich.*)	119,505
Stockton (*Calif.*)	222,633
Suffolk (*Va.*)	54,922
Sunnyvale (*Calif.*)	119,584
Sunrise (*Fla.*)	75,038
Syracuse (*N.Y.*)	159,895
Tacoma (*Wash.*)	183,060
Tallahassee (*Fla.*)	133,718
Tampa (*Fla.*)	285,523
Taunton (*Mass.*)	51,624
Taylor (*Mich.*)	68,541
Tempe (*Ariz.*)	144,289
Temple (*Texas*)	52,087
Terre Haute (*Ind.*)	60,200
Thornton (*Colo.*)	63,079
Thousand Oaks (*Calif.*)	110,981
Toledo (*Ohio*)	322,550
Topeka (*Kan.*)	120,646
Torrance (*Calif.*)	138,219
Trenton (*N.J.*)	84,441
Troy (*Mich.*)	79,029
Troy (*N.Y.*)	52,606
Tucson (*Ariz.*)	434,726
Tulsa (*Okla.*)	374,851
Tuscaloosa (*Ala.*)	79,797
Tustin (*Calif.*)	58,480
Tyler (*Texas*)	80,194
Union City (*Calif.*)	55,383
Union City (*N.J.*)	56,308
Upland (*Calif.*)	61,827
Utica (*N.Y.*)	64,095
Vacaville (*Calif.*)	83,008
Vallejo (*Calif.*)	111,484
Vancouver (*Wash.*)	51,847
Victoria (*Texas*)	60,584
Victorville (*Calif.*)	50,123
Vineland (*N.J.*)	54,673
Virginia Beach (*Va.*)	430,295
Visalia (*Calif.*)	85,073
Vista (*Calif.*)	79,816
Waco (*Texas*)	105,892
Walnut Creek (*Calif.*)	62,030
Waltham (*Mass.*)	54,791
Warren (*Mich.*)	142,625
Warren (*Ohio*)	50,343
Warwick (*R.I.*)	86,006
★ Washington, D.C.	567,094
Waterbury (*Conn.*)	103,523
Waterloo (*Iowa*)	66,537
Waukegan (*Ill.*)	67,751
Waukesha (*Wis.*)	60,138
West Allis (*Wis.*)	61,259
West Covina (*Calif.*)	103,290
West Haven (*Conn.*)	52,848
West Palm Beach (*Fla.*)	75,456
West Valley City (*Utah*)	94,663
Westland (*Mich.*)	85,221
Westminster (*Calif.*)	79,751
Westminster (*Colo.*)	87,045
Wheaton (*Ill.*)	54,298
Whittier (*Calif.*)	79,813
Wichita (*Kan.*)	310,236
Wichita Falls (*Texas*)	97,766
Wilmington (*Del.*)	72,799
Wilmington (*N.C.*)	62,651
Winston-Salem (*N.C.*)	155,128
Worcester (*Mass.*)	105,387
Wyoming (*Mich.*)	[illegible]
Yakima (*Wash.*)	61,976
Yonkers (*N.Y.*)	183,400
Yorba Linda (*Calif.*)	61,497
Youngstown (*Ohio*)	91,775
Yuma (*Ariz.*)	67,185
Uruguay (1992 est.)	
★ Montevideo	1,383,660
Uzbekistan (1992 est.)	
Andijon (Andizhan)	302,000
Angren	133,000
Bukhoro (Bukhara)	235,000
Chirchiq (Chirchik)	158,000
Farghona (Fergana)	100,000
Jizzakh (Dzhizak)	115,000
Marghilon (Margilan)	128,000
Namangan	333,000
Nawoiy (Navoi)	113,000
Nukus	182,000
Olmaliq (Almalyk)	116,000
Qarshi (Karshi)	175,000
Quqon (Kokand)	177,000
Samarqand (Samarkand)	372,000
★ Tashkent (Toshkent)	2,106,000[8]
Urganch (Urgench)	132,000
Vanuatu (1993 est.)	
★ Vila	26,100
Venezuela (1990)	
Acarigua	116,551
Barcelona	221,792
Barinas	153,630
Barquisimeto	625,450
Baruta	182,941[13]
Cabimas	165,755[13]
★ Caracas	1,822,465
Catia la Mar	100,104
Ciudad Bolívar	225,340
Ciudad Guayana (San Felix de Guayana)	453,047
Cumaná	212,432
Guacara	100,766
Guarenas	134,158
Los Teques	140,617
Maracaibo	1,249,670
Maracay	354,196
Maturín	206,654
Mérida	170,902
Petare	338,417
Puerto Cabello	128,825
Puerto La Cruz	155,731
San Cristóbal	220,675
Santa Ana de Coro	124,506
Turmero	174,280
Valencia	903,621
Vietnam (1989)	
Bien Hoa	273,879
Cam Pha	105,336
Cam Rahn	114,041
Can Tho	208,078
Da Lat	102,583
Da Nang	369,734
Haiphong	449,747
★ Hanoi	2,099,600[20]
Ho Chi Minh City (Saigon)	4,181,600[20]
Hong Gai	123,102
Hue	211,718
Long Xuyen	128,817
My Tho	104,724
Nam Dinh	165,629
Nha Trang	213,460
Phan Thiet	114,236
Qui Nhon	159,852
Rach Gia	137,784
Thai Nguyen	124,871
Vinh	110,793
Vung Tau	123,528
Virgin Islands (U.S.) (1990)	
★ Charlotte Amalie	12,331
West Bank (1987 est.)	
Nābulus	106,944
★ —	—
Western Sahara (1982)	
★ El Aaiún (Laayoune)	93,875
Western Samoa (1991)	
★ Apia	32,859
Yemen (1986)	
Aden	318,000[3]
Al-Hudaydah	155,110
★ Ṣan‘ā’	500,000[18]
Ta‘izz	178,430
Yugoslavia (1994 est.)	
★ Belgrade (Beograd)	1,168,454
Kragujevac	147,305
Niš	175,391
Novi Sad	179,626
Podgorica (Titograd)	117,875
Priština	155,499
Subotica	100,386
Zaire (1994 est.)	
Boma	135,284
Bukavu	201,569
Butembo	109,406
Goma	109,094
Kalemi	101,309
Kananga	393,030
Kikwit	182,142
★ Kinshasa	4,655,313
Kisangani	417,517
Kolwezi	417,810
Likasi	299,118
Lubumbashi	851,381
Matadi	172,730
Mbandaka	169,841
Mbuji-Mayi	806,475
Mwene-Ditu	137,459
Tshikapa	180,860
Uvira	115,590
Zambia (1990)	
Chingola	167,954
Kabwe	166,519
Kitwe	338,207
Luanshya	146,275
★ Lusaka	982,362
Mufulira	152,944
Ndola	376,311
Zimbabwe (1992)	
Bulawayo	620,936
Chitungwiza	274,035
Gweru	124,735
★ Harare	1,184,169
Mount Darwin	164,362
Mutare	131,808

[24]1983 census. [25]No separate areas within the state are distinguished administratively as cities. [26]Population includes Comayagüela. [27]1980 census, adjusted for consistent bounding of localities. [28]1901 estimate. [29]County borough. [30]1991 estimate. [31]1985 estimate. [32]Projections based on a repudiated census taken in 1963. [33]Federal Capital territory. [34]Urban area. [35]Population refers to Kotte only. [36]1980 estimate. [37]1994 census. [38]Population of local authority areas. [39]1981 census. [40]Census-designated place (CDP).

Language

This table presents estimated data on the principal language communities of the countries of the world. The countries, and the principal languages (occasionally, language families) represented in each, are listed alphabetically. A bullet (●) indicates those languages that are official in each country. The sum of the estimates equals the 1995 population of the country given in the "Area and population" table.

The estimates represent, so far as national data collection systems permit, the distribution of mother tongues (a mother tongue being the language spoken first and, usually, most fluently by an individual). Many countries do not collect any official data whatever on language use, and published estimates not based on census or survey data usually span a substantial range of uncertainty. The editors have adopted the best-founded distribution in the published literature (indicating uncertainty by the degree of rounding shown) but have also adjusted or interpolated using data not part of the base estimate(s). Such adjustments have not been made to account for large-scale refugee movements, as these are of a temporary nature.

A variety of approaches have been used to approximate mother-tongue distribution when census data were unavailable. Some countries collect data on ethnic or "national" groups only; for such countries ethnic distribution often had to be assumed to conform roughly to the distribution of language communities. This approach, however, should be viewed with caution, because a minority population is not always free to educate its children in its own language and because better economic opportunities often draw minority group members into the majority-language community. For some countries, a given individual may be visible in national statistics only as a passport-holder of a foreign country, however long he may remain resident. Such persons, often guest workers, have sometimes had to be assumed to be speakers of the principal language of their home country. For other countries, the language mosaic may be so complex, the language communities so minute in size, scholarly study so inadequate, or the census base so obsolete that it was possible only to assign percentages to entire groups, or families, of related languages, despite their mutual unintelligibility (Papuan and Melanesian languages in Papua New Guinea, for instance). For some countries in the Americas, so few speakers of any single indigenous language remain that it was necessary to combine these groups as *Amerindian* so as to give a fair impression of their aggregate size within their respective countries.

No systematic attempt has been made to account for populations that may legitimately be described as bilingual, unless the country itself collects data on that basis, as does Bolivia or the Comoros, for example. Where a nonindigenous official or excolonial language constitutes a lingua franca of the country, however, speakers of the language as a second tongue are shown in italics, even though very few may speak it as a mother tongue. No comprehensive effort has been made to distinguish between dialect communities *usually* classified as belonging to the same language, though such distinctions were possible for some countries—*e.g.,* between French and Occitan (the dialect of southern France) or among the various dialects of Chinese.

In giving the names of Bantu languages, grammatical particles specific to a language's autonym (name for itself) have been omitted (the form *Rwanda* is used here, for example, rather than *kinyaRwanda,* and *Tswana* instead of *seTswana*). Parenthetical alternatives are given for a number of languages that differ markedly from the name of the people speaking them (such as Kurukh, spoken by the Oraon tribes of India) or that may be combined with other groups sometimes distinguishable in national data but appearing here under the name of the largest member—*e.g.,* "Tamil (and other Indian languages)" combining data on South Asian Indian populations in Singapore. The term *creole* as used here refers to distinguishable dialectal communities related to a national, official, or former colonial language (such as the French creole that survives in Mauritius from the end of French rule in 1810).

Language

Major languages by country	Number of speakers
Afghanistan[1]	
Indo-Aryan languages	
Pashai	110,000
Iranian languages	
Balochi	170,000
● Dari (Persian)	
Chahar Aimak	510,000
Hazāra	1,600,000
Tajik	3,700,000
Nūristāni group	140,000
Pamir group	110,000
● Pashto	9,500,000
Turkic languages	
Turkmen	350,000
Uzbek	1,600,000
Other	350,000
Albania[1]	
● Albanian	3,342,000
Greek	63,000
Macedonian	5,000
Other	1,000
Algeria	
● Arabic	23,190,000
Berber	4,710,000
French	*13,000,000*
Other	40,000
American Samoa	
● English	2,000
English (lingua franca)	*56,000*
● Samoan	52,000
Tongan	2,000
Other	2,000
Andorra[2]	
● Catalan (Andorran)	18,000
English	1,000
French	5,000
Portuguese	7,000
Spanish	29,000
Other	3,000
Angola[1]	
Ambo (Ovambo)	280,000
Chokwe	490,000
Herero	80,000
Kongo	1,520,000
Luchazi	280,000
Luimbe-Nganguela	620,000
Lunda	140,000
Luvale (Luena)	420,000
Mbunda	130,000
Mbundu	2,490,000
Nyaneka-Humbe	620,000
Ovimbundu (Umbundu)	4,300,000
● Portuguese	*4,000,000*
Other	180,000
Antigua and Barbuda	
● English	...
English/English Creole	61,000
Other	3,000
Argentina	
Amerindian languages	100,000
Italian	610,000
● Spanish	33,490,000
Other	380,000
Armenia	
● Armenian	3,310,000
Azerbaijani	90,000
Other	140,000
Aruba	
● Dutch	4,000
English	6,000
Papiamento	56,000
Spanish	5,000
Other	1,000
Australia	
Aboriginal languages	50,000
Arabic	180,000
Cantonese	180,000
Dutch	52,000
● English	15,316,000
English (lingua franca)	*17,400,000*
Filipino languages	65,000
French	50,000
German	124,000
Greek	315,000
Hindī	25,000
Hungarian	32,000
Indonesian Malay	32,000
Italian	461,000
Japanese	23,000
Korean	22,000
Macedonian	70,000
Mandarin	59,000
Maltese	58,000
Polish	74,000
Portuguese	29,000
Russian	27,000
Serbo-Croatian	97,000
Spanish	99,000
Turkish	47,000
Vietnamese	121,000
Other	413,000
Austria	
Czech	19,000
● German	7,418,000
Hungarian	34,000
Polish	19,000
Romanian	17,000
Serbo-Croatian	175,000
Slovene	30,000
Turkish	123,000
Other	229,000
Azerbaijan	
Armenian	350,000
● Azerbaijani	6,200,000
Lezgian	170,000
Russian	570,000
Other	240,000
Bahamas, The	
● English	...
English/English Creole	220,000
French (Haitian) Creole	50,000
Bahrain[2]	
● Arabic	420,000
English	*410,000*
Other	160,000
Bangladesh[1]	
● Bengali	117,370,000
Chakmā	440,000
● English	*3,100,000*
Gāro	110,000
Khāsī	100,000
Marma (Magh)	230,000
Mro	40,000
Santhālī	80,000
Tripurī	80,000
Other	1,650,000
Barbados	
Bajan (English Creole)	238,000
● English	27,000
Belarus	
● Belarusian	6,780,000
Polish	60,000
Russian	3,300,000
Ukrainian	130,000
Other	60,000
Belgium[2, 3]	
Arabic	160,000
● Dutch	5,970,000
● French	3,290,000
● German	90,000
Italian	240,000
Spanish	50,000
Turkish	90,000
Other	170,000
Belize	
Black Carib (Garífuna)	14,000
● English	109,000
English Creole (lingua franca)	*170,000*
German	3,000
Mayan languages	21,000
Spanish	68,000
Spanish (lingua franca)	*120,000*
Benin[1]	
Adja	590,000
Bariba	460,000
Dendi	120,000
Djougou	160,000
Fon	2,120,000
● French	*840,000*
Fulani (Peul)	300,000
Houéda (Péda)	460,000
Somba (Otamary)	350,000
Yoruba (Nago)	650,000
Other	200,000
Bermuda	
● English	61,000
Bhutan[1]	
Assamese	120,000
● Dzongkha (Bhutiā)	410,000
Nepālī (Hindī)	290,000
Bolivia	
● Aymara	240,000
Guaraní	10,000
● Quechua	600,000
● Spanish	3,090,000
Spanish-Amerindian (multilingual)	3,410,000
Spanish-Aymara	1,470,000
Spanish-Guaraní	30,000
Spanish-Quechua	1,920,000
Other	60,000
Bosnia and Herzegovina	
● Serbo-Croatian	3,430,000
Other	30,000
Botswana[1]	
● English (lingua franca)	*620,000*
Khoikhoin (Hottentot)	38,000
Ndebele	20,000
San (Bushmen)	54,000
Shona	192,000
Tswana	1,169,000
Tswana (lingua franca)	*1,240,000*
Other	75,000
Brazil[1]	
Amerindian languages	260,000
German	860,000
Italian	650,000
Japanese	750,000
● Portuguese	151,850,000
Other	1,450,000
Brunei	
Chinese	27,000
English	10,000
● Malay	132,000
Malay-Chinese	2,000
Malay-English	84,000
English-Chinese	6,000
Malay-Chinese-English	12,000
Other	15,000
Bulgaria[1]	
● Bulgarian	6,690,000
French	*230,000*
Macedonian	210,000
Romany	310,000
Turkish	790,000
Other	100,000
Burkina Faso[1, 4]	
● French	30,000
French (lingua franca)	*610,000*
Fulani	1,000,000
Kru languages	
Siamou (Seme)	20,000
Mande languages	
Bisa (Busansi)	370,000
Dyula	270,000
Marka	170,000
Samo	240,000
Tamashek (Tuareg)	90,000
Voltaic (Gur) languages	
Bobo group	
Bobo	230,000
Bwamu	220,000
Dogon	30,000
Gouin (Cerma)	60,000
Gurunsi (Grusi) group	
Ko	20,000
Lyele	250,000
Nuni	120,000
Sissala	10,000
Lobi	200,000
Mossi group	
Dagara	320,000
Gurma	590,000
Kusaal	10,000
Mossi	5,180,000
Senufo group	
Minianka	—
Senufo	150,000
Other	740,000
Burundi[1]	
● French	*550,000*
● Rundi	5,780,000
Hutu	4,860,000
Tutsi	800,000
Twa	60,000
Other[5]	160,000
Cambodia[1]	
Cham	220,000
Chinese	300,000
● Khmer	8,510,000
Vietnamese	530,000
Other[6]	50,000
Cameroon[1]	
Chadic languages	
Buwal	260,000
Hausa	160,000
Kotoko	140,000
Mandara (Wandala)	750,000
Masana (Masa)	520,000
● English	...
● French	*1,990,000*
Niger-Congo languages	
Adamawa-Eastern languages	
Baya (Gbaya)	160,000
Chamba	320,000
Mbum	170,000

Major languages by country	Number of speakers
Benue-Congo languages	
Bamileke (Medumba)-Widikum (Mogha-mo)-Bamum (Mum)	2,450,000
Basa (Bassa)	140,000
Duala	1,440,000
Fang (Pangwe)-Beti-Bulu	2,600,000
Ibibio (Efik)	20,000
Jukun	90,000
Lundu	360,000
Maka	650,000
Tikar	980,000
Tiv	350,000
Wute	40,000
Kwa languages	
Igbo	70,000
West Atlantic languages	
Fulani	1,270,000
Saharan languages	
Kanuri	40,000
Semitic languages	
Arabic	130,000
Other	100,000
Canada	
● English	17,916,000
● French	7,071,000
English-French	236,000
English-other	436,000
French-other	50,000
English-French-other	32,000
Aboriginal (Amerindian and Eskimo [Inuktitut]) languages	212,000
Arabic	47,000
Chinese	309,000
Czech	27,000
Danish	24,000
Dutch	144,000
Filipino (Pilipino)	50,000
Finnish	29,000
German	510,000
Greek	130,000
Hungarian	80,000
Italian	530,000
Polish	144,000
Portuguese	180,000
Punjābī	74,000
Russian	29,000
Serbo-Croatian	47,000
Spanish	97,000
Ukrainian	242,000
Vietnamese	47,000
Yiddish	27,000
Other	742,000
Cape Verde	
Crioulo (Portuguese Creole)	392,000
● Portuguese	...
Central African Republic	
Banda	770,000
Baya (Gbaya)	740,000
● French	*360,000*
Manjia	460,000
Mbum	200,000
Ngbaka	240,000
Nzakara	50,000
● Sango (lingua franca)	*2,800,000*
Sara	200,000
Zande (Azande)	60,000
Other	450,000
Chad[1]	
● Arabic	1,660,000
Dagu	150,000
● French	*830,000*
Hausa	150,000
Kanuri	150,000
Kotoko	130,000
Masa	150,000
Masalit, Maba, and Mimi	400,000
Mbum	410,000
Mubi	270,000
Sara, Bagirmi, and Kreish	1,940,000
Tama	400,000
Teda (Tubu)	460,000
Other	110,000
Chile[1]	
Araucanian (Mapuche)	1,370,000
Aymara	70,000
Rapa Nui	33,000
● Spanish	12,740,000
China[1]	
Achang	30,000
Bulang (Blang)	90,000
Ch'iang (Qiang)	210,000
Chinese (Han)	1,109,530,000
Cantonese (Yüeh [Yue])	*55,000,000*
Hakka	*41,000,000*
Hsiang (Xiang)	*53,000,000*
Kan (Gan)	*27,000,000*
● Mandarin	*793,000,000*
Min	*45,000,000*
Wu	*94,000,000*
Ching-p'o (Jingpo)	130,000
Chuang (Zhuang)	16,490,000
Daghur (Daur)	130,000
Evenk (Ewenki)	30,000
Gelo	470,000
Hani (Woni)	1,330,000
Hui	9,160,000
Kazakh	1,180,000
Korean	2,040,000
Kyrgyz	150,000
Lahu	440,000
Li	1,180,000
Lisu	610,000
Manchu	10,450,000
Maonan	80,000
Miao	7,870,000
Mongol	5,120,000
Mulam	170,000
Nakhi (Naxi)	300,000
Nu	30,000
Pai (Bai)	1,700,000
Pumi	30,000
Puyi (Chung-chia)	2,710,000
Salar	90,000
She	670,000
Shui	370,000
Sibo (Xibe)	180,000
Tai (Dai)	1,090,000
Tajik	40,000
Tibetan	4,890,000
Tu	200,000
T'u-chia (Tujia)	6,070,000
Tung (Dong)	2,680,000
Tung hsiang (Dongxiang)	400,000
Uighur	7,680,000
Wa (Va)	370,000
Yao	2,270,000
Yi	6,990,000
Other	950,000
Colombia[1]	
Amerindian languages	300,000
Arawakan	40,000
Cariban	20,000
Chibchan	150,000
Other	90,000
English Creole	50,000
● Spanish	34,760,000
Comoros	
● Arabic	...
● Comorian	409,000
Comorian-French	70,000
Comorian-Malagasy	30,000
Comorian-Arabic	9,000
Comorian-Swahili	3,000
Comorian-French-other	21,000
● French	*30,000*
Other	3,000
Congo[1]	
Bubangi	30,000
● French	*760,000*
Kongo	1,330,000
Kota	20,000
Lingala (lingua franca)	...
Maka	50,000
Mbete	130,000
Mboshi	300,000
Monokutuba (lingua franca)	*1,600,000*
Punu	80,000
Sango	70,000
Teke	450,000
Other	130,000
Costa Rica	
Chibchan languages	10,000
Bribrí	6,000
Cabécar	4,000
Chinese	6,000
English Creole	67,000
● Spanish	3,261,000
Côte d'Ivoire[1]	
Akan (including Baule and Anyi)	4,280,000
● French	*5,000,000*
Kru (including Bete)	1,630,000
Malinke (including Dyula and Bambara)	1,630,000
Southern Mande (including Dan and Guro)	1,100,000
Voltaic ([Gur] including Senufo and Lobi)	1,670,000
Other (non-Ivoirian population)	4,080,000
Croatia	
● Serbo-Croatian	4,320,000
Other	180,000
Cuba	
● Spanish	11,068,000
Cyprus[1]	
● Greek	630,000
● Turkish	150,000
Other	30,000
Czech Republic[1]	
Bulgarian	3,000
● Czech	8,399,000
German	49,000
Greek	3,000
Hungarian	20,000
Moravian	1,332,000
Polish	60,000
Romanian	1,000
Romany	33,000
Russian	5,000
Ruthenian	2,000
Silesian	44,000
Slovak	317,000
Ukrainian	8,000
Other	70,000
Denmark[2]	
● Danish	5,033,000
English	19,000
German	10,000
Iranian languages	8,000
Norwegian	11,000
South Slavic languages	12,000
Swedish	9,000
Turkish	35,000
Other	88,000
Djibouti[1]	
Afar	120,000
● Arabic	40,000
● French	*50,000*
Somali	360,000
Gadaboursi	90,000
Issa	200,000
Issaq	80,000
Other	70,000
Dominica	
● English	3,000
French Creole	50,000
French Creole-English	19,000
Dominican Republic	
French (Haitian) Creole	160,000
● Spanish	7,670,000
Ecuador	
Quechua (and other Indian languages)	800,000
● Spanish	10,660,000
Egypt[1]	
● Arabic	58,980,000
French	*270,000*
Other	720,000
El Salvador	
● Spanish	5,768,000
Equatorial Guinea[1]	
Bubi	40,000
Fang	330,000
French	...
Krio (English Creole)	...
● Spanish	...
Other	30,000
Eritrea	
Cushitic languages	
Afar	150,000
Bilin (Agew [Awngi])	110,000
Hadareb (Beja)	140,000
Saho	110,000
Nilotic languages	
Kunama	100,000
Nara	70,000
Semitic languages	
Amharic	60,000
● Arabic (Rashaida)	10,000
Tigré	1,120,000
● Tigrinya	1,730,000
Estonia	
● Estonian	920,000
Russian	520,000
Other	50,000
Ethiopia[1]	
● Amharic	16,540,000
Gurage	2,580,000
Oromo (Oromifa)	17,070,000
Sidamo	1,760,000
Somali	2,230,000
Tigrinya	3,960,000
Walaita (Welayta)	1,520,000
Other	9,390,000
Faroe Islands	
● Danish	...
● Faroese	44,000
Fiji[1]	
● English	*160,000*
Fijian	398,000
Hindī	350,000
Other	43,000
Finland	
● Finnish	4,744,000
● Swedish	295,000
Other	61,000
France	
Arabic[7]	1,470,000
English[7]	80,000
● French[7, 8, 9]	54,480,000
Basque	*80,000*
Breton	*580,000*
Catalan (Rousillonais)	*210,000*
Corsican	*170,000*
Dutch (Flemish)	*110,000*
German (Alsatian)	*1,320,000*
Occitan	*1,580,000*
Italian[7]	260,000
Polish[7]	50,000
Portuguese[7]	670,000
Spanish[7]	220,000
Turkish[7]	200,000
Other[7]	740,000
French Guiana	
Amerindian languages	4,000
English Creole	2,000
● French	...
French Creoles	132,000
Other	7,000
French Polynesia[10]	
Chinese	12,000
● French	177,000
Polynesian languages	201,000
Other	43,000
Gabon[1]	
Fang	410,000
● French	*300,000*
Kota	40,000
Mbete	160,000
Mpongwe (Myene)	170,000
Punu, Sira, Nzebi	190,000
Teke	20,000
Other	160,000
Gambia, The	
● English	...
Gambians	
Aku (Krio)	7,000
Mande languages	
Bambara	8,000
Malinke	380,000
Soninke	86,000
West Atlantic languages	
Dyola	102,000
Fulani	181,000
Manjak	18,000
Serer	27,000
Wolof	110,000
Other	14,000
non-Gambians	154,000
Gaza Strip	
Arabic	785,000
Hebrew	5,000
Georgia	
Abkhaz	90,000
Armenian	380,000
Azerbaijani	310,000
● Georgian	3,940,000
Ossetian	130,000
Russian	490,000
Other	170,000
Germany[2]	
● German	77,390,000
Greek	350,000
Italian	560,000
Polish	290,000
Portuguese	100,000
South Slavic languages	1,030,000
Spanish	140,000
Turkish	1,880,000
Kurdish	*400,000*
Other	180,000
Ghana[1]	
Akan	8,640,000
● English	...
Ewe	1,960,000
Ga-Adangme	1,280,000
Gurma	550,000
Hausa (lingua franca)	*9,900,000*
Mole-Dagbani (Mossi)	2,610,000
Yoruba	220,000
Other	1,220,000
Gibraltar[2]	
Arabic	2,000
● English	25,000
Spanish	...
Other	1,000
Greece[1]	
Albanian	60,000
● Greek	10,020,000
Macedonian	160,000
Turkish	100,000
Other	150,000
Greenland[2]	
● Danish	7,000
● Greenlandic	48,000
Grenada	
● English	...
English/English Creole	92,000
Guadeloupe	
French Creole/French	413,000
● French	...
Other	21,000
Guam	
● Chamorro	44,000
Chinese	2,000
Chuukese (Trukese)	2,000
● English	56,000
English (lingua franca)	*148,000*
Japanese	3,000
Korean	5,000
Palauan	2,000
Philippine languages	30,000
Other	0,000
Guatemala	
Black Carib (Garifuna)	20,000
Mayan languages	3,720,000
Cakchiquel	950,000
Kekchí	520,000
Mam	290,000
Quiché	1,080,000
● Spanish	6,870,000
Guernsey	
English	65,000
French	...
Guinea[1]	
● French	*570,000*
Mande languages	
Kpelle	310,000
Loma	160,000
Malinke	1,550,000
Susu	740,000
Yalunka	190,000
Other	460,000
West Atlantic languages	
Basari-Koniagi	80,000
Fulani (Peul)	2,590,000
Kissi	400,000
Other	210,000
Other	10,000
Guinea-Bissau	
Balante	156,000
Crioulo (Portuguese Creole)	46,000
Crioulo-Portuguese	24,000
Crioulo-other (except Portuguese)	321,000
Fulani	178,000
Malinke	74,000
Mandyako	53,000
Pepel	30,000
● Portuguese	—
Portuguese-other (except Crioulo)	87,000
Other	105,000
Guyana	
Amerindian languages	
Arawakan	11,000
Cariban	11,000
● English	...
English/English Creoles	748,000
Haiti	
● French	60,000
French-Haitian (French) Creole	800,000
● Haitian (French) Creole	5,740,000
Honduras	
Black Carib (Garifuna)	75,000
English Creole	12,000
Miskito	10,000
● Spanish	5,413,000
Other	2,000
Hong Kong	
Chinese	
● Cantonese	5,502,000
Cantonese (lingua franca)	*5,940,000*

Language (continued)

Major languages by country	Number of speakers
Chiu Chau	87,000
Fukien (Min)	118,000
Hakka	99,000
Putonghua (Mandarin)	69,000
Putonghua (lingua franca)	*1,120,000*
Sze Yap	25,000
● English	137,000
English (lingua franca)	*1,960,000*
Filipino (Pilipino)	6,000
Japanese	12,000
Other	150,000
Hungary	
German	40,000
● Hungarian	10,080,000
Romanian	10,000
Romany	50,000
Serbo-Croatian	20,000
Slovak	10,000
Other	20,000
Iceland[2]	
● Icelandic	252,000
Other	17,000
India	
Austro-Asiatic languages	
Ho	1,100,000
Khaṛiā	270,000
Khāsī	870,000
Korkū	500,000
Muṇḍā	480,000
Muṇḍārī	1,030,000
Santhālī	5,780,000
Savara (Sora)	320,000
Dravidian languages	
Goṇḍī	2,680,000
Kannaḍa	36,920,000
Khond	280,000
Koyā	330,000
Kui	700,000
Kurukh (Oraon)	1,740,000
Malayālam	35,640,000
Tamil	61,430,000
Telugu	74,470,000
Tuḷu	1,890,000
English	320,000
● English (lingua franca)	*30,000,000*
Indo-Iranian (Indo-Aryan) languages	
Assamese	15,320,000
Bengali	70,730,000
Bhīlī (Bhilodī)	6,110,000
Barel	*400,000*
Bhilalī	*400,000*
Dogrī	2,090,000
Gujarātī	45,580,000
Halabī	720,000
● Hindī	362,800,000
Aṅga (Aṅgikā)	*700,000*
Baghelkhaṇḍī	*400,000*
Bāgrī	*1,800,000*
Banjārī	*800,000*
Bhojpurī	*24,500,000*
Bundelkhaṇḍī	*600,000*
Chhattīsgaṛhī	*11,400,000*
Gaṛhwālī	*2,200,000*
Gojrī	*600,000*
Hāṛautī	*600,000*
Khorthā (Khottā)	*900,000*
Kumaunī	*2,100,000*
Lamanī (Banjārī)	*2,100,000*
Magahī (Magadhī)	*11,300,000*
Maithilī	*10,500,000*
Mālvī	*1,100,000*
Maṇḍealī	*400,000*
Māṛwāṛī	*8,100,000*
Mewārī	*1,400,000*
Nagpurī	*600,000*
Nīmāḍī	*1,400,000*
Pahāṛī	*2,200,000*
Rājasthānī	*3,600,000*
Sadānī (Sadrī)	*1,400,000*
Surgujiā	*900,000*
Hindī (lingua franca)	*421,000,000*
Kashmīrī	4,360,000
Khandeshī	1,630,000
Kiṣan	210,000
Koṅkanī	2,180,000
Marāṭhī	68,150,000
Nepālī (Gorkhalī)	1,720,000
Oṛiyā	31,420,000
Punjābī	25,530,000
Sindhī	2,670,000
Kachchhī	*800,000*
Urdū	48,510,000
Sino-Tibetan languages	
Ādi	160,000
Āo	150,000
Gāro	560,000
Lushai (Mizo)	530,000
Meithei (Manipurī)	1,240,000
Nissī	190,000
Tripurī	670,000
Other	15,760,000
Indonesia	
Balinese	3,240,000
Banjarese	3,420,000
Batak	4,340,000
Buginese	4,300,000
● Indonesian Malay	23,650,000
Javanese	77,000,000
Madurese	8,460,000
Minang	4,610,000
Sundanese	30,800,000
Other	35,480,000
Iran[1]	
Armenian	290,000
Iranian languages	
Bakhtyārī (Lurī)	1,030,000
Balochi	1,400,000
● Farsī (Persian)	27,960,000
Farsī (lingua franca)	*50,700,000*
Gīlakī	3,240,000
Kurdish	5,590,000
Lurī	2,650,000
Māzandarānī	2,210,000
Other	1,330,000
Semitic languages	
Arabic	1,320,000
Other	150,000
Turkic languages	
Afshari	690,000
Azerbaijani	10,300,000
Qashqa'i	780,000
Shahsavani	370,000
Turkish (mostly Pishagchi, Bayat, and Qajar)	440,000
Turkmen	960,000
Other	120,000
Other	450,000
Iraq[1]	
● Arabic	15,740,000
Assyrian	170,000
Azerbaijani	350,000
Kurdish	3,870,000
Persian	170,000
Other	120,000
Ireland	
● English	3,340,000
● Irish	180,000
Isle of Man	
● English	70,000
Israel[11]	
● Arabic	990,000
English	65,000
French	44,000
German	36,000
● Hebrew	3,704,000
Hungarian	30,000
Romanian	84,000
Russian	93,000
Spanish	46,000
Yiddish	115,000
Other	179,000
Italy[1]	
Albanian	120,000
Catalan	30,000
French	300,000
German	300,000
Greek	40,000
● Italian	53,980,000
Rhaetian	730,000
Friulian	710,000
Ladin	20,000
Sardinian	1,520,000
Slovene	120,000
Other	130,000
Jamaica	
● English	...
English/English Creoles	2,370,000
Hindī and other Indian languages	50,000
Other	100,000
Japan[2]	
Ainu	25,000
Chinese	200,000
English	70,000
● Japanese	124,230,000
Korean	690,000
Philippine languages	60,000
Other	90,000
Jersey	
English	88,000
● French	...
Jersey Norman French	*6,000*
Jordan[1]	
● Arabic	4,150,000
Other	30,000
Kazakhstan	
German	530,000
● Kazakh	6,550,000
Russian	7,890,000
Tatar	230,000
Uighur	180,000
Ukrainian	330,000
Uzbek	320,000
Other	640,000
Kenya[1]	
Bantu languages	
Bajun (Rajun)	70,000
Basuba	110,000
Embu	340,000
Gusii (Kisii)	1,760,000
Kamba	3,220,000
Kikuyu	5,980,000
Kuria	170,000
Luhya	3,960,000
Mbere	110,000
Meru	1,570,000
Nyika (Mijikenda)	1,370,000
Pokomo	70,000
Swahili	10,000
● Swahili (lingua franca)	*19,000,000*
Taita	290,000
Cushitic languages	
Oromo languages	
Boran	130,000
Gabbra	60,000
Gurreh	150,000
Orma	60,000
Somali languages	
Degodia	170,000
Ogaden	50,000
Somali	290,000
English (lingua franca)	*2,200,000*
Nilotic languages	
Kalenjin	3,090,000
Luo	3,650,000
Masai	450,000
Sambur	140,000
Teso	250,000
Turkana	390,000
Semitic languages	
Arabic	70,000
Other	640,000
Kiribati[1]	
● English	...
Kiribati (Gilbertese)	79,500
Tuvaluan (Ellice)	400
Other	500
Korea, North[1]	
Chinese	40,000
● Korean	23,450,000
Korea, South[1]	
Chinese	40,000
● Korean	44,780,000
Kuwait[2]	
● Arabic	1,640,000
Other	50,000
Kyrgyzstan	
● Kyrgyz	2,360,000
Russian	1,150,000
Uzbek	570,000
Other	410,000
Laos[1]	
● Lao-Lum (Lao)	3,270,000
Lao-Soung (Miao [Hmong] and Man [Yao])	260,000
Lao-Tai (Tai)	380,000
Lao-Theung (Mon-Khmer)	810,000
Other[12]	170,000
Latvia	
● Latvian	1,310,000
Russian	1,060,000
Other	150,000
Lebanon[1]	
● Arabic	2,800,000
Armenian	180,000
French	*720,000*
Other	30,000
Lesotho[1]	
● English	...
● Sotho	1,740,000
Zulu	310,000
Liberia[1]	
● English	*480,000*
Krio (English Creole)	*2,100,000*
Kwa (Kru) languages	
Bassa	330,000
Belle (Bellleh)	12,000
De (Dey)	9,000
Grebo	213,000
Krahn	90,000
Kru	174,000
Mande (Northern) languages	
Gbandi	67,000
Kpelle	462,000
Loma	134,000
Malinke (Mandingo)	121,000
Mende	19,000
Vai	85,000
Mande (Southern) languages	
Gio (Dan)	187,000
Mano	169,000
West Atlantic (Mel) languages	
Gola	94,000
Kissi	96,000
Other	118,000
Libya[1]	
● Arabic	5,190,000
Berber	160,000
Other[13]	50,000
Liechtenstein[2]	
● German	27,200
Italian	900
Turkish	800
Other	2,100
Lithuania	
● Lithuanian	2,970,000
Polish	220,000
Russian	430,000
Other	80,000
Luxembourg[2]	
Belgian	11,000
Danish	2,000
Dutch	4,000
English	4,000
French	14,000
German	9,000
Greek	1,000
Italian	20,000
Luxemburgian	287,000
Portuguese	42,000
Spanish	3,000
Other	13,000
Macau	
Chinese	
● Cantonese	370,000
Mandarin	5,000
Other Chinese languages	40,000
English	2,000
● Portuguese	10,000
Other	5,000
Macedonia	
Albanian	450,000
● Macedonian	1,450,000
Turkish	70,000
Other	140,000
Madagascar[1]	
● French	*1,500,000*
● Malagasy	14,610,000
Other	160,000
Malaŵi[1]	
Chewa (Maravi)	5,800,000
● English	*500,000*
Lomwe	1,820,000
Ngoni	660,000
Yao	1,310,000
Other	340,000
Malaysia	
Bajau	130,000
Chinese	1,150,000
Chinese-others	650,000
Dusun	210,000
English	100,000
English-others	220,000
English (lingua franca)	*6,100,000*
Iban	470,000
Iban-others	80,000
● Malay	8,600,000
Malay-others	3,060,000
Tamil	770,000
Tamil-others	10,000
Other	4,490,000
Maldives	
● Divehi (Maldivian)	253,000
Mali[1]	
Afro-Asiatic languages	
Berber languages	
Tamashek (Tuareg)	660,000
Semitic languages	
Arabic (Mauri)	140,000
● French	*710,000*
Niger-Congo languages	
Mande languages	
Bambara	2,870,000
Bambara (lingua franca)	*5,400,000*
Bobo Fing	10,000
Dyula	260,000
Malinke, Khasonke, and Wasulunka	600,000
Samo (Duun)	60,000
Soninke	790,000
Voltaic (Gur) languages	
Bwa (Bobo)	220,000
Dogon	360,000
Mossi	40,000
Senufo and Minianka	1,080,000
West Atlantic languages	
Fulani and Tukulor	1,260,000
Nilo-Saharan languages	
Songhai	650,000
Other	20,000
Malta[1]	
● English	8,000
● Maltese	354,000
Other	8,000
Marshall Islands[2]	
● English	...
● Marshallese	54,400
Other	1,800
Martinique	
French Creole/French	375,000
● French	...
Other	13,000
Mauritania[1]	
● Arabic	...
French	*130,000*
Fulani	30,000
Ḥassānīyah Arabic	1,850,000
Soninke	60,000
Tukulor	120,000
Wolof	150,000
Zenaga	30,000
Other	30,000
Mauritius	
Bhojpurī	215,000
Bhojpurī-other	23,000
Chinese	4,000
● English	2,000
French	39,000
French Creole	696,000
French Creole-other	100,000
Hindī	14,000
Marāṭhī	8,000
Tamil	9,000
Telugu	7,000
Urdū	7,000
Other	3,000
Mayotte[14]	
● Arabic	...
Mahorais (local dialect of Comorian Swahili)	102,000
Other Comorian Swahili dialects	45,000
Malagasy	39,000
● French	49,000
Other	7,000
Mexico	
Amerindian languages	7,190,000
Amuzgo	40,000
Aztec (Nahuatl)	1,630,000
Chatino	40,000
Chinantec	150,000
Chocho	20,000
Chol	180,000
Chontal	50,000
Cora	20,000
Cuicatec	20,000
Huastec	170,000
Huave	20,000
Huichol	30,000
Kanjobal	20,000
Mame	20,000
Mayo	50,000
Mazahua	180,000
Mazatec	220,000
Mixe	130,000
Mixtec	520,000
Otomí	390,000
Popoluca	40,000
Purepecha	130,000
Tarahumara	70,000
Tepehua	10,000
Tepehuan	30,000
Tlapanec	90,000
Tojolabal	50,000
Totonac	280,000
Triqui	20,000
Tzeltal	360,000
Tzotzil	320,000
Yaqui	10,000

Major languages by country	Number of speakers
Yucatec (Mayan)	970,000
Zapotec	530,000
Zoque	60,000
Other	320,000
● Spanish	83,950,000
Spanish-Amerindian languages	*5,850,000*
Micronesia	
Chuukese (Trukese)	43,700
● English	500
Kosraean	7,700
Mortlockese	8,000
Palauan	400
Pohnpeian	24,900
Woleaian	3,900
Yapese	6,100
Other	9,900
Moldova	
Bulgarian	70,000
Gagauz	140,000
● Romanian (Moldovan)	2,690,000
Russian	1,010,000
Ukrainian	370,000
Other	60,000
Monaco[2]	
English	2,000
● French	12,000
Italian	5,000
Monegasque	5,000
Other	6,000
Mongolia[1]	
Bayad	44,000
Buryat	39,000
Darhat	16,000
Dariganga	32,000
Dörbed	62,000
Dzakhchin	25,000
Kazakh	136,000
● Khalkha (Mongolian)	1,818,000
Ould	9,000
Torgut	12,000
Uryankhai	23,000
Other	90,000
Morocco	
● Arabic	17,540,000
Berber	8,900,000
Other[15]	540,000
Mozambique	
Chopi	510,000
Chuabo	1,020,000
Koti	60,000
Kunda	10,000
Lomwe	1,400,000
Makonde	350,000
Makua	4,970,000
Marendje	620,000
Mwani	80,000
Ngulu	20,000
Nsenga	40,000
Nyanja	590,000
Nyungwe	400,000
Phimbi	20,000
● Portuguese	220,000
Ronga	650,000
Sena	1,670,000
Shona	1,170,000
Swahili	10,000
Swazi	20,000
Tonga	350,000
Tsonga	2,220,000
Tswa	1,070,000
Yao	300,000
Zulu	10,000
Other	120,000
Myanmar (Burma)[1]	
● Burmese	32,090,000
Burmese (lingua franca)	*37,200,000*
Chin	1,010,000
Kachin (Ching-p'o)	630,000
Karen	2,890,000
Kayah	190,000
Mon	1,130,000
Rakhine (Arakanese)	2,090,000
Shan	3,940,000
Other	2,550,000
Namibia	
Afrikaans	156,000
Caprivi	77,000
● English	13,000
English (lingua franca)	*138,000*
German	15,000
Herero	132,000
Kavango (Okavango)	160,000
Nama	206,000
Ovambo (Ambo [Kwanyama])	836,000
San (Bushmen)	32,000
Tswana	7,000
Other	17,000
Nauru	
Chinese	900
English	800
English (lingua franca)	*10,300*
Kiribati (Gilbertese)	1,800
● Nauruan	6,000
Tuvaluan (Ellice)	900
Nepal	
Austro-Asiatic (Munda) languages	
Santhālī	30,000
Indo-Aryan languages	
Bengali	20,000
Bhojpurī	1,330,000
Dhanwar	20,000
Hindī	170,000
Hindī (Awadhī dialect)	340,000
Maithilī	2,380,000
● Nepālī (Eastern Pahāṛī)	10,690,000
Rājbanśī	90,000
Tharu	970,000
Urdū	210,000
Tibeto-Burman languages	
Bhutiā (Sherpa)	120,000
Chepang	20,000
Gurung	230,000
Limbū	260,000
Magar	450,000
Newārī	690,000
Rai and Kirāntī	390,000
Tamāng	940,000
Thakali	10,000
Thami	10,000
Other	710,000
Netherlands, The[2]	
Arabic	167,000
● Dutch	14,737,000
Dutch and Frisian	*580,000*
Turkish	220,000
Other	362,000
Netherlands Antilles	
● Dutch	...
English	16,000
Papiamento	173,000
Other	12,000
New Caledonia[1]	
● French	63,000
Melanesian languages	[illegible]
Polynesian languages (mostly Wallisian)	22,000
Other	17,000
New Zealand	
● English	3,244,000
English-Maori	152,000
● Maori	51,000
Other	121,000
Nicaragua	
English Creole	43,000
Misumalpan languages	
Miskito	171,000
Sumo	10,000
● Spanish	4,112,000
Other	4,000
Niger[1]	
Berber languages	
Tamashek (Tuareg)	950,000
Chadic languages	
Hausa	4,850,000
Hausa (lingua franca)	*6,410,000*
● French	*1,370,000*
Saharan languages	
Kanuri	410,000
Teda (Tubu)	40,000
Semitic languages	
Arabic	30,000
Songhai and Zerma	1,940,000
Voltaic (Gur) languages	
Gurma	30,000
West Atlantic languages	
Fulani (Fulfulde)	890,000
Other	10,000
Nigeria[1]	
Arabic	300,000
Bura	1,500,000
Edo	3,200,000
● English (lingua franca)	*14,000,000*
English Creole (lingua franca)[16]	*33,000,000*
Fulani	10,700,000
Hausa	20,400,000
Hausa (lingua franca)	*48,000,000*
Ibibio	5,400,000
Igbo (Ibo)	17,100,000
Ijo (Ijaw)	1,700,000
Kanuri	4,000,000
Nupe	1,200,000
Tiv	2,100,000
Yoruba	20,400,000
Other	7,500,000
Northern Mariana Islands	
Carolinian	2,800
Chamorro	17,300
Chinese	4,100
Chuukese (Trukese)	1,300
● English	2,800
English (lingua franca)	*52,400*
Japanese	1,100
Korean	3,800
Palauan	2,000
Philippine languages	19,800
Other	2,900
Norway[2]	
Danish	18,000
English	24,000
● Norwegian	4,204,000
Swedish	12,000
Other	97,000
Oman	
● Arabic (Omani)	1,590,000
Balochī	410,000
Farsi (Persian)	60,000
Swahili	40,000
Urdū	50,000
Other	20,000
Pakistan	
Balochī	4,230,000
Brāhūī	1,090,000
English (lingua franca)	*16,000,000*
Pashto	18,460,000
Punjābī	
Punjābī	67,680,000
Hindko	3,410,000
Sindhī	
Sindhī	16,540,000
Siraikī	13,810,000
● Urdū	10,680,000
Other	4,000,000
Palau	
Chinese	300
● English	500
English (lingua franca)	*16,800*
● Palauan	13,900
Philippine languages	1,600
Other	600
Panama	
Amerindian languages	219,000
Bokotá	4,000
Chibchan	195,000
Cuna	53,000
Guaymí	140,000
Teribe	2,000
Chocó	20,000
Embera	17,000
Waunama	3,000
Chinese	8,000
English	...
English Creoles	368,000
● Spanish	2,036,000
Papua New Guinea[1]	
● English	*60,000*
Melanesian languages	860,000
Motu	*140,000*
Papuan languages	3,360,000
Tok Pisin (English Creole)	*2,850,000*
Other	90,000
Paraguay	
German	43,000
● Guaraní	1,990,000
Guaraní-Spanish	2,412,000
Portuguese	157,000
● Spanish	322,000
Other	36,000
Peru	
Amerindian languages	4,560,000
Aymara	540,000
● Quechua	3,870,000
Other	160,000
● Spanish	18,740,000
Other	190,000
Philippines	
Aklanon	460,000
Bicol	4,070,000
Bilaan	130,000
Binisaya	160,000
Cebuano	17,010,000
Chavacano	340,000
Cuyonon	140,000
Davaweno	170,000
● English (lingua franca)	*36,410,000*
● Filipino (Pilipino; Tagalog)	19,550,000
Hiligaynon	6,540,000
Ibaloi (Nabaloi)	130,000
Ibanag	360,000
Ifugao	190,000
Ilocano	6,850,000
Itawit	140,000
Kalinga	110,000
Kankanai	250,000
Kinaray-a (Hamtikanon)	620,000
Maguindanao	890,000
Manobo	180,000
Maranao	900,000
Masbateño	400,000
Pampango	2,190,000
Pangasinan	1,350,000
Romblon	150,000
Samal	290,000
Sambal	130,000
Subanon	160,000
Surigaonon	400,000
Tau Sug	750,000
Waray-Waray	2,820,000
Yakan	120,000
Other	2,060,000
Poland	
Belarusian	190,000
German	500,000
● Polish	37,710,000
Ukrainian	230,000
Portugal[2]	
● Portuguese	9,810,000
Other	100,000
Puerto Rico	
English	19,000
● Spanish	1,912,000
Spanish-English	1,746,000
Other	48,000
Qatar[2]	
● Arabic	230,000
Other[17]	350,000
Réunion	
● French	*200,000*
French Creole	600,000
Other[18]	60,000
Romania	
Bulgarian	9,000
Czech	5,000
German	98,000
Hungarian	1,631,000
Polish	3,000
● Romanian	20,577,000
Romany (Tigani)	166,000
Russian	31,000
Serbo-Croatian	33,000
Slovak	18,000
Tatar	23,000
Turkish	27,000
Ukrainian	63,000
Other	8,000
Russia	
Adyghian	120,000
Armenian	360,000
Avar	530,000
Azerbaijani	280,000
Bashkir	980,000
Belarusian	440,000
Buryat	360,000
Chechen	890,000
Chuvash	1,380,000
Dargin	350,000
Georgian	90,000
German	350,000
Ingush	210,000
Kabardinian	380,000
Kalmyk	150,000
Karachay	150,000
Kazakh	560,000
Komi	240,000
Komi-Permyak	100,000
Kumyk	270,000
Lak	100,000
Lezgian	240,000
Mari	530,000
Mordovinian	740,000
Ossetian	380,000
Romanian	120,000
Romany	130,000
● Russian	127,430,000
Tabasaran	90,000
Tatar	4,730,000
Tuvinian	200,000
Udmurt	510,000
Ukrainian	1,870,000
Uzbek	100,000
Yakut	360,000
Other	1,450,000
Rwanda	
● French	*540,000*
● Rwanda	7,860,000
St. Kitts and Nevis	
● English	...
English/English Creole	39,000
St. Lucia	
● English	29,000
English/French Creole	114,000
St. Vincent and the Grenadines	
● English	...
English/English Creole	111,000
Other	1,000
San Marino[1]	
● Italian	25,000
São Tomé and Príncipe	
Crioulo (Portuguese Creole)	113,000
● Portuguese	...
Other	18,000
Saudi Arabia[1]	
● Arabic	16,990,000
Other	890,000
Senegal	
● French	*420,000*
Senegalese	
Diola (Dyola)	410,000
Fulani (Peul)-Tukulor	1,800,000
Malinke (Mandingo)	310,000
Serer	1,040,000
Soninke	110,000
Wolof	4,000,000
Wolof (lingua franca)	*6,600,000*
Other	450,000
non-Senegalese	190,000
Seychelles	
English	2,000
French	1,000
● Seselwa (French Creole)	69,000
Other	3,000
Sierra Leone[1]	
● English	*700,000*
Krio (English Creole [lingua franca])	*4,300,000*
Mande languages	
Kono-Vai	230,000
Kuranko	160,000
Mende	1,560,000
Susu	60,000
Yalunka	160,000
West Atlantic languages	
Bullom-Sherbro	170,000
Fulani	170,000
Kissi	100,000
Limba	380,000
Temne	1,430,000
Other	80,000
Singapore[1]	
Chinese	2,318,000
● English	*1,118,000*
● Malay	424,000
● Mandarin Chinese	...
● Tamil (and other Indian languages)	212,000
Other	35,000
Slovakia[1]	
Czech, Moravian, and Silesian	59,000
German	5,000
Hungarian	572,000
Polish	3,000
Romany	81,000
Russian	2,000
Ruthenian and Ukrainian	31,000
● Slovak	4,587,000
Other	13,000
Slovenia	
Hungarian	9,000
Serbo-Croatian	155,000
● Slovene	1,732,000
Other	75,000
Solomon Islands[1]	
● English	...
Melanesian languages	327,000
Papuan languages	32,000
Polynesian languages	14,000
Other[19]	8,000
Somalia[1]	
● Arabic	...
English	...
● Somali	6,620,000
Other	110,000
South Africa[20]	
● Afrikaans	6,490,000
● English	3,600,000
Nguni	
● Ndebele	840,000
● Swazi	970,000

Language (continued)

Major languages by country	Number of speakers
● Xhosa	7,230,000
● Zulu	8,960,000
Sotho	
● North Sotho (Pedi)	3,610,000
● South Sotho	2,780,000
● Tswana (Western Sotho)	3,780,000
● Tsonga	1,410,000
● Venda	800,000
Other	990,000
Spain[2]	
Basque (Euskera)	590,000
● Castilian Spanish	31,530,000
Catalan (Català)	5,120,000
English	100,000
Galician (Gallego)	1,570,000
Other	270,000
Sri Lanka	
English	10,000
English-Sinhala	990,000
English-Sinhala-Tamil	650,000
English-Tamil	210,000
● Sinhala	10,920,000
Sinhala-Tamil	1,690,000
● Tamil	3,550,000
Other	60,000
Sudan, The[1]	
● Arabic	13,870,000
Azande (Zande)	760,000
Bari	690,000
Beja	1,790,000
Dinka	3,240,000
Fur	580,000
Lotuko	410,000
Nubian languages	2,280,000
Nuer	1,380,000
Shilluk	480,000
Other	2,610,000
Suriname	
● Dutch	...
English	...
Sranantonga	170,000
Sranantonga-other	170,000
Other (mostly Hindī, Javanese, and Saramacca)	90,000
Swaziland[1]	
● English	...
● Swazi	820,000
Zulu	20,000
Other	70,000
Sweden[2]	
Arabic	67,000
Danish	41,000
English	32,000
Finnish	208,000
German	45,000
Iranian languages	49,000
Norwegian	46,000
Polish	39,000
South Slavic languages	116,000
Spanish	55,000
● Swedish	7,903,000
Turkish	29,000
Other	196,000
Switzerland	
● French	1,350,000
● German	4,480,000
● Italian	540,000
Romansch	40,000
Other	630,000
Syria[1]	
● Arabic	12,710,000
Armenian	400,000
Kurdish	900,000
Other	300,000
Taiwan	
Austronesian languages	
Ami	127,000
Atayal	81,000
Bunun	39,000
Paiwan	62,000
Puyuma	8,000
Rukai	8,000
Saisiyat	4,000
Tsou	6,000
Yami	4,000
Chinese	
Hakka	2,160,000
● Mandarin	2,800,000
Min (South Fukien)	15,950,000
Other	20,000
Tajikistan	
Russian	570,000
● Tajik	3,630,000
Uzbek	1,350,000
Other	290,000
Tanzania[1]	
Chaga (Chagga), Pare	1,380,000
● English	*900,000*
Gogo	1,100,000
Ha	970,000
Haya	1,650,000
Hehet	1,930,000
Iramba	800,000
Luguru	1,380,000
Luo	230,000
Makonde	1,650,000
Masai	280,000
Ngoni	370,000
Nyakyusa	1,520,000
Nyamwezi (Sukuma)	5,920,000
Shambala	1,200,000
● Swahili	2,480,000
Swahili (lingua franca)	*25,000,000*
Tatoga	210,000
Yao	690,000
Other	4,320,000
Thailand[1]	
Chinese	7,130,000
Karen	210,000
Malay	2,140,000
Mon-Khmer languages	
Khmer	750,000
Kuy	630,000
Other	210,000
Thai languages	
Lao	15,810,000
● Thai (Siamese)	30,910,000
Other	410,000
Other	610,000
Togo[1]	
● French	*710,000*
Chadic languages	
Hausa	11,000
Kwa languages	
Adja-Ewe group	
Adja	129,000
Ane (Mina)	234,000
Anlo	3,000
Ewe	960,000
Fon	41,000
Hwe	5,000
Kpessi	4,000
Peda-Hula (Pla)	17,000
Watyi (Ouatchi)	426,000
Ana-Ife group	
Ahlo	7,000
Ana (Ana-Ife)	104,000
Anyana	8,000
Nago	11,000
Yoruba	8,000
Kebu-Akposo group	
Adele	8,000
Akposo	111,000
Kebu	47,000
Voltaic (Gur) languages	
Kabre-Tem group	
Kabre	571,000
Kotokoli (Tem)	238,000
Namba (Lamba)	126,000
Naudemba (Losso)	170,000
para-Gurma group	
Basari	73,000
Chekossi (Akan)	49,000
Chamba	40,000
Dye (Gangam)	39,000
Gurma	140,000
Konkomba	58,000
Moba	222,000
Mossi	11,000
Tamberma	23,000
Yanga	12,000
West Atlantic (Mel) languages	
Fulani (Peul)	56,000
Other	175,000
Tonga	
● English	...
● Tongan	98,000
Other	2,000
Trinidad and Tobago	
● English	...
English Creole[21]	36,000
Hindī	44,000
Trinidad English	1,182,000
Other	3,000
Tunisia	
● Arabic	6,220,000
Arabic-French	2,330,000
Arabic-French-English	280,000
Arabic-other	10,000
Other-no Arabic	20,000
Other	30,000
Turkey[1]	
Arabic	850,000
Kurdish[22]	6,630,000
● Turkish	54,760,000
Other	290,000
Turkmenistan	
Russian	490,000
● Turkmenian	2,940,000
Uzbek	350,000
Other	310,000
Tuvalu	
● English	...
Kiribati (Gilbertese)	700
Tuvaluan (Ellice)	8,700
Uganda[1]	
Bantu languages	
Ganda (Luganda)	3,320,000
Gisu	1,340,000
Gwere	540,000
Kiga (Chiga)	1,280,000
Konjo	260,000
Nkole	1,530,000
Nyoro	610,000
Rundi	570,000
Rwanda	1,080,000
Soga	1,530,000
Swahili (lingua franca)	*6,500,000*
Toro	600,000
Central Sudanic languages	
Lugbara	710,000
Madi	260,000
English	*190,000*
Nilotic languages	
Acholi	870,000
Alur	320,000
Karamojong	380,000
Kuman	190,000
Lango	1,120,000
Padhola	310,000
Teso	1,660,000
Other	180,000
Ukraine	
Belarusian	160,000
Bulgarian	160,000
Hungarian	160,000
Polish	30,000
Romanian	340,000
Russian	17,080,000
● Ukrainian	33,630,000
Other	450,000
United Arab Emirates[2]	
● Arabic	920,000
Other[17]	1,270,000
United Kingdom	
● English	56,990,000
Scots-Gaelic	80,000
Welsh	560,000
Other	950,000
United States	
Amharic	40,000
Arabic	410,000
Armenian	170,000
Bengali	40,000
Cajun	40,000
Chinese (including Formosan)	1,480,000
Czech	110,000
Danish	40,000
Dutch	160,000
● English	226,710,000
English (lingua franca)	*255,440,000*
Finnish	60,000
French	1,940,000
French Creole (mostly Haitian)	210,000
German	1,770,000
Greek	440,000
Gujarātī	120,000
Hebrew	160,000
Hindī (including Urdū)	380,000
Hungarian	170,000
Ilocano	50,000
Italian	1,490,000
Japanese	490,000
Korean	720,000
Kru (Gullah)	80,000
Lithuanian	60,000
Malayālam	40,000
Miao (Hmong)	90,000
Mon-Khmer (mostly Cambodian)	150,000
Navajo	170,000
Norwegian	90,000
Pennsylvania Dutch	100,000
Persian	230,000
Polish	830,000
Portuguese	490,000
Punjābī	60,000
Romanian	70,000
Russian	280,000
Samoan	40,000
Serbo-Croatian	130,000
Slovak	90,000
Spanish	19,790,000
Swedish	90,000
Syriac	40,000
Tagalog	960,000
Thai (including Laotian)	240,000
Turkish	50,000
Ukrainian	110,000
Vietnamese	580,000
Yiddish	240,000
Other	780,000
Uruguay	
● Spanish	3,080,000
Other	110,000
Uzbekistan	
Crimean Tatar	200,000
Karakalpak	450,000
Kazakh	870,000
Korean	120,000
Kyrgyz	160,000
Russian	2,490,000
Tajik	1,010,000
Tatar	420,000
Turkish	120,000
Turkmenian	130,000
Ukrainian	90,000
● Uzbek	16,320,000
Other	510,000
Vanuatu[23]	
● Bislama (English Creole)	110,000
● English	50,000
● French	30,000
Other	2,000
Venezuela	
● Amerindian languages	
Goajiro	80,000
Warrau (Warao)	30,000
Other	100,000
● Spanish	21,160,000
Other	470,000
Vietnam[1]	
Bahnar	160,000
Cham	110,000
Chinese (Hoa)	1,040,000
Hre	110,000
Jarai	280,000
Khmer	1,040,000
Ko'ho	100,000
Man (Mien, or Yao)	550,000
Miao (Meo, or Hmong)	650,000
Mnong	70,000
Muong	1,060,000
Nung	820,000
Rhadé	220,000
Roglai	80,000
San Chay (Cao Lan)	130,000
San Diu	110,000
Sedang	110,000
Stieng	60,000
Tai	1,210,000
Tho (Tay)	1,380,000
● Vietnamese	64,730,000
Other	510,000
Virgin Islands (U.S.)	
● English	79,000
French	3,000
Spanish	13,000
Other	3,000
West Bank[24]	
Arabic	1,150,000
Hebrew	120,000
Western Sahara	
Arabic	218,000
Western Samoa	
● English	1,000
● Samoan	79,000
Samoan-English	86,000
Yemen[1]	
● Arabic	12,800,000
Other	260,000
Yugoslavia	
Albanian	1,440,000
Hungarian	400,000
Romanian	60,000
Romany	100,000
● Serbo-Croatian	8,150,000
Slovak	70,000
Vlach	140,000
Other	200,000
Zaire[1]	
Azande (Zande)	2,680,000
Boa	1,030,000
Chokwe	800,000
● French	*3,400,000*
Kongo	7,050,000
Kongo (lingua franca)	*13,000,000*
Lingala (lingua franca)	*30,000,000*
Luba	7,890,000
Lugbara	710,000
Mongo	5,920,000
Ngala and Bangi	2,540,000
Rundi	1,690,000
Rwanda	4,510,000
Swahili (lingua franca)	*22,000,000*
Teke	1,200,000
Other	7,890,000
Zambia[25]	
Bemba group	
Aushi (Ushi)	160,000
Bemba	2,360,000
Bisa	140,000
Lala	270,000
Lamba	220,000
Other	280,000
● English	*800,000*
Lozi (Barotse) group	
Lozi (Barotse)	570,000
Luyi (Luyana)	140,000
Nkoya	50,000
Other	10,000
Mambwe group	
Lungu	90,000
Mambwe	150,000
Mwanga (Winawanga)	170,000
Other	20,000
North-Western group	
Chokwe	60,000
Kaonde	260,000
Luchazi	60,000
Lunda	240,000
Luvale (Luena)	190,000
Mbunda	140,000
Nyanja (Maravi) group	
Chewa	500,000
Ngoni	190,000
Nsenga	430,000
Nyanja (Maravi)	490,000
Other	50,000
Tonga (Ila-Tonga) group	
Ila	80,000
Lenje	170,000
Soli	70,000
Tonga	1,030,000
Other	80,000
Tumbuka group	
Senga	80,000
Tumbuka	350,000
Other	340,000
Zimbabwe	
● English	250,000
Ndebele (Nguni)	1,830,000
Nyanja	250,000
Shona	8,120,000
Other	810,000

[1]Figures given represent ethnolinguistic groups. [2]Data refer to nationality (usually resident aliens holding foreign passports). [3]Data are partly based on place of residence. [4]Majority of population speak Moré (language of the Mossi); Dyula is language of commerce. [5]Swahili also spoken. [6]English and French also spoken. [7]Based on "nationality" at 1982 census. [8]Includes naturalized citizens. [9]French is the universal language throughout France; traditional dialects and minority languages are retained regionally in the approximate numbers shown, however. [10]Data reflect multilingualism; 1995 population estimate is 220,000. [11]Includes the population of the Golan Heights and East Jerusalem; excludes the Israeli population in the West Bank and Gaza Strip. [12]English and French also spoken. [13]English and Italian also spoken. [14]Data reflect ability to speak the language, not mother tongue; 1995 population estimate is 116,000. [15]French also spoken. [16]Includes speakers of standard English. [17]Mostly Pakistanis, Indians, and Iranians. [18]Gujarātī and Chinese also spoken. [19]Solomon Islands Pidgin (English) is the lingua franca. [20]Includes the former Black independent states of Bophuthatswana, Ciskei, Transkei, and Venda. [21]Spoken on Tobago only. [22]Other estimates of the Kurdish population range from 6 percent to 20–25 percent. [23]Data reflect multilingualism; 1995 population is 168,000. [24]Excludes East Jerusalem. [25]Groups are officially defined geographic divisions; elements comprising them are named by language.

Religion

The following table presents statistics on religious affiliation for each of the countries of the world. An assessment was made for each country of the available data on distribution of religious communities within the total population; the best available figures, whether originating as census data, membership figures of the churches concerned, or estimates by external analysts in the absence of reliable local data, were applied as percentages to the estimated 1995 midyear population of the country to obtain the data shown below.

Several concepts govern the nature of the available data, each useful separately but none the basis of any standard of international practice in the collection of such data. The word "affiliation" was used above to describe the nature of the relationship joining the religious bodies named and the populations shown. This term implies some sort of formal, usually documentary, connection between the religion and the individual (a baptismal certificate, a child being assigned the religion of its parents on a census form, maintenance of one's name on the tax rolls of a state religion, etc.) but says nothing about the nature of the individual's personal religious practice, in that the individual may have lapsed, never been confirmed as an adult, joined another religion, or may have joined an organization that is formally atheist.

The user of these statistics should be careful to note that not only does the nature of the affiliation (with an organized religion) differ greatly from country to country, but the social context of religious practice does also. A country in which a single religion has long been predominant will often show more than 90% of its population to be *affiliated,* while in actual fact, no more than 10% may actually *practice* that religion on a regular basis. Such a situation often leads to undercounting of minority religions (where someone [head of household, communicant, child] is counted at all), blurring of distinctions seen to be significant elsewhere (a Hindu country may not distinguish Protestant [or even Christian] denominations; a Christian country may not distinguish among its Muslim or Buddhist citizens), or double-counting in countries where an individual may conscientiously practice more than one "religion" at a time.

Until 1989 communist countries had for long consciously attempted to ignore, suppress, or render invisible religious practice within their borders. Countries with large numbers of adherents of traditional, often animist, religions and belief systems usually have little or no formal methodology for defining the nature of local religious practice. On the other hand, countries with strong missionary traditions, or good census organizations, or few religious sensitivities may have very good, detailed, and meaningful data.

The most comprehensive work available is DAVID B. BARRETT (ed.), *World Christian Encyclopedia* (1982); it examines both the theoretical and practical problems of collecting and analyzing religious statistics, assembles a mine of national detail, and establishes a basis for further study.

Religion

Religious affiliation	1995 population
Afghanistan	
Sunnī Muslim	15,230,000
Shīʿī Muslim	2,720,000
other	180,000
Albania	
Muslim	2,390,000
Albanian Orthodox	680,000
Roman Catholic	340,000
Algeria	
Sunnī Muslim	27,800,000
Ibāḍīyah Muslim	110,000
other	30,000
American Samoa	
Congregational	32,000
Roman Catholic	12,000
other	13,000
Andorra	
Roman Catholic	58,000
other	5,000
Angola	
Roman Catholic	7,940,000
Protestant	2,290,000
traditional beliefs	1,100,000
other	230,000
Antigua and Barbuda	
Anglican	21,000
Protestant	18,000
Roman Catholic	7,000
other	18,000
Argentina	
Roman Catholic	31,680,000
other	2,910,000
Armenia	
Armenian Apostolic (Orthodox)	3,340,000
other (mostly Roman Catholic and Muslim)	210,000
Aruba	
Roman Catholic	64,000
other	9,000
Australia	
Roman Catholic	4,700,000
Anglican	4,300,000
Uniting Church and Methodist	1,370,000
Presbyterian	650,000
other Protestant	1,110,000
Orthodox	490,000
nonreligious	2,290,000
other	3,120,000
Austria	
Roman Catholic	6,290,000
Evangelical Lutheran	390,000
atheist and nonreligious	690,000
other	690,000
Azerbaijan	
Muslim (mostly Shīʿī)	7,030,000
Russian Orthodox	190,000
Armenian Apostolic (Orthodox)	170,000
other	130,000
Bahamas, The	
Anglican	87,000
Protestant	79,000
Roman Catholic	52,000
other	58,000
Bahrain	
Shīʿī Muslim	330,000
Sunnī Muslim	140,000
other	110,000
Bangladesh	
Muslim	106,050,000
Hindu	12,630,000
other	1,410,000
Barbados	
Anglican	87,000
Protestant	79,000
Roman Catholic	12,000
other	87,000
Belarus	
Believers are predominantly Belarusian Orthodox; Roman Catholic and Jewish minorities.	
Belgium	
Roman Catholic	8,690,000
other	1,380,000
Belize	
Roman Catholic	125,000
Protestant	59,000
Anglican	15,000
other	17,000
Benin	
traditional beliefs	3,350,000
Roman Catholic	1,140,000
Muslim	650,000
other	270,000
Bermuda	
Anglican	23,000
Methodist	10,000
Roman Catholic	8,000
other	20,000
Bhutan	
Buddhist	610,000
Hindu	200,000
Bolivia	
Roman Catholic	5,880,000
Evangelical Protestant	750,000
other	780,000
Bosnia and Herzegovina	
Sunnī Muslim	1,380,000
Serbian Orthodox	1,070,000
Roman Catholic	520,000
Protestant	140,000
other	350,000
Botswana	
traditional beliefs	760,000
Protestant	410,000
African Christian	180,000
Roman Catholic	150,000
other	40,000
Brazil	
Roman Catholic (including syncretic Afro-Catholic cults having Spiritist beliefs and rituals)	109,000,000
Evangelical Protestant	30,000,000
other	17,000,000
Brunei	
Muslim	195,000
other	96,000
Bulgaria	
Christian (mostly Bulgarian Orthodox)	7,280,000
Muslim (mostly Sunnī)	1,100,000
other	30,000
Burkina Faso	
traditional beliefs	6,070,000
Muslim	3,170,000
Christian	1,090,000
Burundi	
Roman Catholic	3,860,000
nonreligious	1,110,000
other (mostly Protestant)	960,000
Cambodia	
Buddhist	9,130,000
Muslim	210,000
other	270,000
Cameroon	
Roman Catholic	4,600,000
traditional beliefs	3,440,000
Muslim	2,880,000
Protestant	2,310,000
Canada	
Roman Catholic	13,320,000
Protestant	8,370,000
Anglican	2,390,000
Eastern Orthodox	440,000
Jewish	350,000
Muslim	120,000
Hindu	90,000
Sikh	80,000
nonreligious	3,650,000
other	650,000
Cape Verde	
Roman Catholic	364,000
Protestant	28,000
Central African Republic	
Protestant	790,000
Roman Catholic	790,000
traditional beliefs	750,000
Muslim	470,000
other	350,000
Chad	
Muslim	3,430,000
Roman Catholic	1,290,000
Protestant	920,000
traditional beliefs	470,000
other	250,000
Chile	
Roman Catholic	10,900,000
Evangelical Protestant	1,760,000
other	1,650,000
China	
nonreligious	689,000,000
Chinese folk-religionist	243,000,000
atheist	145,000,000
Buddhist	102,000,000
Muslim	17,000,000
Christian	9,000,000
traditional beliefs	1,000,000
Colombia	
Roman Catholic	32,680,000
other	2,420,000
Comoros	
Sunnī Muslim	541,000
Christian	4,000
Congo	
traditional beliefs	1,240,000
Roman Catholic	1,020,000
Protestant	280,000
Muslim	50,000
Costa Rica	
Roman Catholic	2,720,000
other	630,000
Côte d'Ivoire	
Muslim	5,510,000
Roman Catholic	2,960,000
traditional beliefs	2,430,000
nonreligious	1,910,000
Protestant	950,000
other	490,000
Croatia	
Roman Catholic	3,440,000
Serbian Orthodox	500,000
Sunnī Muslim	50,000
Protestant	20,000
other	490,000
Cuba	
Roman Catholic	4,380,000
nonreligious	5,390,000
atheist	710,000
other	590,000
Cyprus	
Greek Orthodox	620,000
Muslim (mostly Sunnī)	160,000
other (mostly Christian)	30,000
Czech Republic	
Roman Catholic	4,040,000
Evangelical Church of Czech Brethren	200,000
Czechoslovak Hussite	180,000
Silesian Evangelical	30,000
Eastern Orthodox	20,000
atheist and nonreligious	4,130,000
other	1,750,000
Denmark	
Evangelical Lutheran	4,608,000
other	615,000
Djibouti	
Sunnī Muslim	551,000
Christian[1]	35,000
Dominica	
Roman Catholic	51,000
Protestant	12,000
other	9,000
Dominican Republic	
Roman Catholic	7,130,000
other	690,000
Ecuador	
Roman Catholic	10,660,000
other	800,000
Egypt	
Sunnī Muslim	53,730,000
Christian (mostly Coptic[2])	5,970,000
El Salvador	
Roman Catholic	4,330,000
other (mostly Protestant)	1,440,000
Equatorial Guinea	
Roman Catholic	390,000
other	10,000
Eritrea	
Christian (mostly Ethiopian Orthodox)	1,770,000
Muslim	1,770,000
Estonia	
Believers are predominantly affiliated with the Evangelical Lutheran Church of Estonia; Russian Orthodox and Protestant minorities.	
Ethiopia	
Ethiopian Orthodox	29,000,000
Muslim (mostly Sunnī)	16,570,000

Religion (continued)

Religious affiliation	1995 population
traditional beliefs	6,720,000
other	2,760,000
Faroe Islands	
Evangelical Lutheran	33,000
other	12,000
Fiji	
Christian (mostly Methodist and Roman Catholic)	418,000
Hindu	302,000
Muslim	62,000
other	9,000
Finland	
Evangelical Lutheran	4,408,000
other	693,000
France	
Roman Catholic	42,990,000
nonreligious	7,100,000
Muslim	3,200,000
atheist	1,980,000
Protestant	1,160,000
Jewish	640,000
other	1,740,000
French Guiana	
Roman Catholic	106,000
other	39,000
French Polynesia	
Protestant	103,000
Roman Catholic	87,000
other	30,000
Gabon	
Roman Catholic	610,000
traditional beliefs	400,000
African Christian	110,000
other	30,000
Gambia, The	
Muslim (mostly Sunnī)	1,060,000
other	60,000
Gaza Strip	
Muslim (mostly Sunnī)	780,000
other	11,000
Georgia	
Georgian Orthodox	3,580,000
Sunnī Muslim	610,000
Russian Orthodox	550,000
Armenian Apostolic (Orthodox)	440,000
other (mostly nonreligious)	330,000
Germany	
Protestant (mostly Evangelical Lutheran)	36,860,000
Roman Catholic	30,310,000
Muslim	1,750,000
other (mostly nonreligious or unaffiliated)	13,000,000
Ghana	
traditional beliefs	6,260,000
Muslim	4,940,000
Roman Catholic	1,990,000
Protestant	810,000
African Christian	810,000
Anglican	350,000
other	1,320,000
Gibraltar	
Roman Catholic	22,000
other	7,000
Greece	
Greek Orthodox	10,280,000
Muslim	140,000
other	70,000
Greenland	
Evangelical Lutheran	55,000
other	1,000
Grenada	
Roman Catholic	49,000
Anglican	13,000
other	30,000
Guadeloupe	
Roman Catholic	390,000
other	40,000
Guam	
Roman Catholic	118,000
Protestant	23,000
other	8,000
Guatemala	
Roman Catholic	7,970,000
Evangelical Protestant	2,660,000
Guernsey	
Anglican	42,000
other	23,000
Guinea	
Muslim	5,700,000
Christian	540,000
traditional beliefs	470,000
Guinea-Bissau	
traditional beliefs	700,000
Muslim	320,000
Christian	50,000
Guyana	
Hindu	262,000
Roman Catholic	140,000
Protestant	133,000
Anglican	127,000
Muslim	69,000
other	39,000
Haiti	
Roman Catholic	5,290,000
Baptist	640,000
Pentecostal	240,000
other	420,000
Honduras	
Roman Catholic	4,690,000
Evangelical Protestant	550,000
other	280,000
Hong Kong	
Buddhist and Taoist	4,580,000
Protestant	270,000
Roman Catholic	260,000
other	1,090,000
Hungary	
Roman Catholic	6,940,000
Protestant	2,570,000
nonreligious and atheist	490,000
other	230,000
Iceland	
Evangelical Lutheran	247,000
other	22,000
India	
Hindu	751,000,000
Sunnī Muslim	77,000,000
Shīʿī Muslim	26,000,000
Sikh	18,000,000
Roman Catholic	13,000,000
Protestant	9,000,000
Buddhist	7,000,000
Jain	5,000,000
Zoroastrian (Parsi)	130,000
other	29,000,000
Indonesia	
Muslim	170,310,000
Protestant	11,800,000
Roman Catholic	6,990,000
Hindu	3,570,000
Buddhist	2,010,000
other	600,000
Iran	
Shīʿī Muslim	57,330,000
Sunnī Muslim	3,460,000
other	480,000
Iraq	
Shīʿī Muslim	12,760,000
Sunnī Muslim	7,040,000
other (mostly Christian)	610,000
Ireland	
Roman Catholic	3,290,000
other	300,000
Isle of Man	
Anglican	43,000
other	27,000
Israel	
Jewish[3]	4,390,000
Muslim (mostly Sunnī)	760,000
other	240,000
Italy	
Roman Catholic	47,690,000
Muslim	700,000
other (mostly nonreligious and atheist)	9,000,000
Jamaica	
Protestant	1,230,000
Anglican	180,000
Roman Catholic	120,000
other	990,000
Japan	
Shintoist[4]	119,210,000
Buddhist[4]	89,650,000
Christian	1,520,000
other	11,230,000
Jersey	
Anglican	54,000
Roman Catholic	20,000
other	13,000
Jordan	
Sunnī Muslim	3,850,000
other	330,000
Kazakhstan	
Muslim (mostly Sunnī)	7,830,000
Russian Orthodox	7,330,000
Protestant	330,000
other (mostly nonreligious)	1,160,000
Kenya	
Roman Catholic	7,560,000
Protestant	5,520,000
traditional beliefs	5,410,000
African Christian	5,040,000
Anglican	2,060,000
Muslim	1,720,000
other	1,320,000
Kiribati	
Roman Catholic	43,000
Congregational	31,000
other	6,000
Korea, North	
atheist and nonreligious	15,950,000
traditional beliefs	3,660,000
Ch'ŏndogyo	3,260,000
other	610,000
Korea, South	
nonreligious	22,460,000
Buddhist	10,920,000
Protestant	8,140,000
Roman Catholic	2,640,000
Confucian	180,000
Wonbulgyo	130,000
Ch'ŏndogyo	40,000
other	310,000
Kuwait	
Sunnī Muslim	760,000
Shīʿī Muslim	510,000
other Muslim	170,000
other	250,000
Kyrgyzstan	
Muslim (mostly Sunnī)	3,140,000
other (mostly nonreligious and Russian Orthodox)	1,340,000
Laos	
Buddhist	2,820,000
traditional beliefs	1,640,000
other	430,000
Latvia	
Believers are predominantly affiliated with the Latvian Evangelical Lutheran Church; Russian Orthodox, Roman Catholic, and Protestant minorities.	
Lebanon	
Shīʿī Muslim	1,090,000
Sunnī Muslim	710,000
Maronite Christian	600,000
Druze	200,000
Greek Orthodox	170,000
Greek Catholic	110,000
Armenian Christian	110,000
other	30,000
Lesotho	
Roman Catholic	890,000
Protestant	610,000
other	550,000
Liberia	
Christian	1,610,000
traditional beliefs	440,000
Muslim	330,000
Libya	
Sunnī Muslim	5,240,000
other	160,000
Liechtenstein	
Roman Catholic	25,000
other	6,000
Lithuania	
Roman Catholic	2,960,000
other (mostly Russian Orthodox, Old Believer, Evangelical Lutheran, and nonreligious)	740,000
Luxembourg	
Roman Catholic	388,000
other	21,000
Macau	
nonreligious	260,000
Buddhist	72,000
other	96,000
Macedonia	
Serbian (Macedonian) Orthodox	1,410,000
Sunnī Muslim	630,000
other	60,000
Madagascar	
traditional beliefs	8,120,000
Protestant	2,950,000
Roman Catholic	2,950,000
Muslim	740,000
Malaŵi	
Protestant (mostly Presbyterian)	4,970,000
Roman Catholic	1,990,000
Muslim	1,990,000
traditional beliefs	990,000
Malaysia	
Muslim	10,550,000
Buddhist	3,450,000
Chinese folk-religionist	2,310,000
Hindu	1,400,000
Christian	1,280,000
other	960,000
Maldives	
Sunnī Muslim	253,000
Mali	
Muslim	8,110,000
traditional beliefs	810,000
Christian	90,000
Malta	
Roman Catholic	365,000
other	5,000
Marshall Islands	
Believers are predominantly Protestant (mainly Congregational); Roman Catholic minority.	
Martinique	
Roman Catholic	340,000
other	50,000
Mauritania	
Sunnī Muslim	2,260,000
other	10,000
Mauritius	
Hindu	570,000
Roman Catholic	310,000
Muslim	180,000
other	70,000
Mayotte	
Sunnī Muslim	112,000
Christian	3,000
Mexico	
Roman Catholic	81,750,000
Protestant and Evangelical Catholic	4,460,000
nonreligious	2,950,000
other	1,990,000
Micronesia	
Believers are about equally Roman Catholic and Protestant (mainly Congregational).	
Moldova	
Russian (Moldovan) Orthodox	4,330,000
other	20,000
Monaco	
Roman Catholic	28,000
other	3,000
Mongolia	
Tantric Buddhist (Lamaist)	2,170,000
Muslim	140,000
Morocco	
Muslim (mostly Sunnī)	26,900,000
other	80,000
Mozambique	
traditional beliefs	8,550,000
Roman Catholic	5,620,000
Muslim	2,330,000
other	1,390,000
Myanmar (Burma)	
Buddhist	41,610,000
Christian	2,280,000
Muslim	1,780,000
traditional beliefs	540,000
Hindu	240,000
other	70,000
Namibia	
Lutheran	845,000
Roman Catholic	327,000
Dutch Reformed	101,000
Anglican	83,000
other	296,000
Nauru	
Congregational	5,700
other	4,800
Nepal	
Hindu	17,380,000
Buddhist	1,560,000
Muslim	710,000
other	440,000
Netherlands, The	
Roman Catholic	5,110,000
Dutch Reformed Church (NHK)	2,320,000
Reformed Churches	1,240,000
Muslim	490,000
nonreligious	6,040,000
other	290,000
Netherlands Antilles	
Roman Catholic	149,000
other	52,000
New Caledonia	
Roman Catholic	113,000
other	73,000
New Zealand	
Anglican	770,000
Presbyterian	570,000
Roman Catholic	530,000
Methodist	150,000
Baptist	70,000
Ratana	50,000
Mormon	50,000
nonreligious	710,000
other	670,000
Nicaragua	
Roman Catholic	3,880,000
other (mostly Protestant)	460,000

Religious affiliation	1995 population
Niger	
Sunnī Muslim	9,030,000
other	130,000
Nigeria	
Muslim	47,720,000
Protestant	20,490,000
Roman Catholic	9,430,000
African Christian	8,260,000
traditional beliefs	9,540,000
Northern Mariana Islands	
Roman Catholic	51,000
other	6,000
Norway	
Evangelical Lutheran (Church of Norway)	3,827,000
other	528,000
Oman	
Ibāḍīyah Muslim	1,220,000
Sunnī Muslim	410,000
Hindu	540,000
Pakistan	
Muslim (mostly Sunnī)	136,000,000
Christian	2,190,000
Hindu	2,120,000
other	180,000
Palau	
Roman Catholic	7,000
traditional beliefs	5,000
Protestant	4,000
other	1,000
Panama	
Roman Catholic	2,110,000
Protestant	260,000
other	260,000
Papua New Guinea	
Protestant	2,510,000
Roman Catholic	1,410,000
Anglican	230,000
other	150,000
Paraguay	
Roman Catholic	4,500,000
other (mostly Protestant)	330,000
Peru	
Roman Catholic	20,810,000
Evangelical Protestant	1,690,000
nonreligious	330,000
other	660,000
Philippines	
Roman Catholic	58,060,000
Protestant	3,770,000
Muslim	3,200,000
Aglipayan	1,840,000
Church of Christ (Iglesia ni Cristo)	1,640,000
other	1,510,000
Poland	
Roman Catholic	35,550,000
nonreligious	2,160,000
Polish Orthodox	580,000
other	350,000
Portugal	
Roman Catholic	9,360,000
other	550,000
Puerto Rico	
Roman Catholic	3,000,000
other	720,000
Qatar	
Muslim (mostly Sunnī)	550,000
other	29,000
Réunion	
Roman Catholic	580,000
other (mostly Muslim)	80,000
Romania	
Romanian Orthodox	19,700,000
Roman Catholic	1,140,000
other	1,850,000
Russia	
Believers are predominantly affiliated with the Russian Orthodox Church; Roman Catholic, Protestant, Muslim, Jewish, and Buddhist minorities.	
Rwanda	
Roman Catholic	5,110,000
traditional beliefs	1,960,000
Protestant	710,000
Muslim	80,000
St. Kitts and Nevis	
Anglican	13,000
Methodist	11,000
other	15,000
St. Lucia	
Roman Catholic	113,000
other	30,000
St. Vincent and the Grenadines	
Anglican	47,000
Methodist	23,000
Roman Catholic	13,000
other	29,000
San Marino	
Roman Catholic	24,000
other	1,000
São Tomé and Príncipe	
Roman Catholic	110,000
Protestant	20,000
Saudi Arabia	
Sunnī Muslim	17,070,000
Shīʿī Muslim	600,000
other	210,000
Senegal	
Sunnī Muslim	7,810,000
Christian	410,000
other	90,000
Seychelles	
Roman Catholic	66,000
other	9,000
Sierra Leone	
Sunnī Muslim	2,710,000
traditional beliefs	1,350,000
Christian	450,000
Singapore	
Buddhist and Taoist	1,611,000
Muslim	459,000
Protestant	233,000
Roman Catholic	145,000
Hindu	106,000
nonreligious	418,000
other	16,000
Slovakia	
Roman Catholic	3,230,000
Slovak Evangelical	330,000
atheist	520,000
other	1,270,000
Slovenia	
Roman Catholic	1,850,000
other	120,000
Solomon Islands	
Protestant	160,000
Anglican	129,000
Roman Catholic	73,000
other	20,000
Somalia	
Sunnī Muslim	6,720,000
other	10,000
South Africa[5]	
Christian	22,340,000
Protestant	11,010,000
Dutch (Afrikaans) Reformed Churches	3,950,000
Nederduitse Gereformeerde	3,490,000
Gereformeerde	170,000
Nederduitsch Hervormde	290,000
other Protestant	7,060,000
Methodist	1,970,000
Presbyterian	440,000
United Congregational	420,000
Lutheran	840,000
Apostolic Faith Mission of South Africa	440,000
New Apostolic Church	160,000
other Apostolic	460,000
Baptist	270,000
Pentecostal Protestant	80,000
African Protestant Church	30,000
Full Gospel	220,000
Pentecostal	20,000
Salvation Army	40,000
Seventh-day Adventist	90,000
Swiss	50,000
Assemblies of God	160,000
other	1,380,000
Roman Catholic	2,540,000
Anglican	1,270,000
Greek Orthodox	30,000
black independent churches	7,470,000
Zion Christian Church	1,650,000
other	5,820,000
Mormon	10,000
Hindu	420,000
Muslim	370,000
Jewish	70,000
other beliefs	30,000
nonreligious	400,000
not stated	9,990,000
Spain	
Roman Catholic	37,190,000
Muslim	450,000
other	1,550,000
Sri Lanka	
Buddhist	12,540,000
Hindu	2,800,000
Muslim	1,370,000
Roman Catholic	1,250,000
other	140,000
Sudan, The	
Sunnī Muslim	20,510,000
traditional beliefs	4,690,000
Christian[1]	2,560,000
other	340,000
Suriname	
Hindu	118,000
Roman Catholic	98,000
Muslim	84,000
Protestant	81,000
other	49,000
Swaziland	
Christian[1]	700,000
traditional beliefs	190,000
other	20,000
Sweden	
Church of Sweden (Lutheran)	7,702,000
other	1,124,000
Switzerland	
Roman Catholic	3,250,000
Protestant	2,810,000
other	980,000
Syria	
Sunnī Muslim	10,590,000
Shīʿī Muslim	2,150,000
Christian	1,290,000
other	280,000
Taiwan	
Chinese folk-religionist	10,310,000
Buddhist	9,150,000
Christian[1]	1,570,000
other	240,000
Tajikistan	
Sunnī Muslim	4,670,000
Shīʿī Muslim	290,000
other (mostly nonreligious)	870,000
Tanzania	
Muslim	9,830,000
traditional beliefs	9,830,000
Christian	8,420,000
Thailand	
Buddhist	55,480,000
Muslim	2,320,000
Christian	310,000
other	680,000
Togo	
traditional beliefs	2,430,000
Roman Catholic	890,000
Sunnī Muslim	500,000
Protestant	280,000
other	30,000
Tonga	
Free Wesleyan	43,000
Roman Catholic	16,000
other	41,000
Trinidad and Tobago	
Roman Catholic	372,000
Hindu	300,000
Protestant	238,000
Anglican	138,000
Muslim	74,000
other	138,000
Tunisia	
Sunnī Muslim	8,850,000
other	50,000
Turkey	
Muslim (mostly Sunnī)	62,410,000
other	120,000
Turkmenistan	
Muslim (mostly Sunnī)	3,550,000
Russian Orthodox	450,000
other	80,000
Tuvalu	
Congregational	9,100
other	300
Uganda	
Roman Catholic	8,850,000
Anglican	4,890,000
traditional beliefs	2,350,000
Muslim (mostly Sunnī)	1,230,000
other	930,000
Ukraine	
Believers are predominantly affiliated with the Ukrainian Orthodox Church; Ukrainian Autocephalous Orthodox and Ukrainian Catholic (Uniate) minorities.	
United Arab Emirates	
Sunnī Muslim	1,760,000
Shīʿī Muslim	350,000
other	90,000
United Kingdom	
Christian[1]	51,060,000
Church of England	33,420,000
Protestant	8,790,000
Roman Catholic	7,680,000
Eastern Orthodox	350,000
other Christian	820,000
Muslim	820,000
Hindu	410,000
Jewish	320,000
Sikh	230,000
nonreligious and atheist	5,570,000
other	180,000
United States	
Christian (professing)	224,457,000
Christian (affiliated)	180,494,000
Protestant	105,939,000
Roman Catholic	55,259,000
Eastern Orthodox	5,631,000
Anglican	2,350,000
other Christian	11,315,000
Christian (unaffiliated)	43,963,000
nonreligious	22,928,000
Jewish	5,602,000
Muslim	5,100,000
New-Religionist	947,000
Hindu	910,000
atheist	870,000
Buddhist	780,000
Baha'i	300,000
Sikh	190,000
other	1,164,000
Uruguay	
Roman Catholic	2,100,000
other	1,090,000
Uzbekistan	
Muslim (mostly Sunnī)	20,140,000
Russian Orthodox	2,060,000
other (mostly nonreligious)	690,000
Vanuatu	
Presbyterian	60,000
Roman Catholic	21,000
Anglican	24,000
other	60,000
Venezuela	
Roman Catholic	20,120,000
other	1,720,000
Vietnam	
Buddhist	49,690,000
Roman Catholic	6,300,000
New-Religionist	
Cao Dai	2,020,000
Hoa Hao	1,570,000
other	14,360,000
Virgin Islands (U.S.)	
Protestant	45,000
Roman Catholic	33,000
other	20,000
West Bank	
Muslim (mostly Sunnī)	1,050,000
Jewish[6]	110,000
Christian and other	100,000
Western Sahara	
Sunnī Muslim	218,000
Western Samoa	
Congregational	79,000
Roman Catholic	36,000
other	51,000
Yemen	
Muslim (mostly Sunnī)	13,040,000
other	20,000
Yugoslavia	
Serbian Orthodox	6,860,000
Sunnī Muslim	2,010,000
Roman Catholic	420,000
Protestant	110,000
other	1,160,000
Zaire	
Roman Catholic	21,250,000
Protestant	12,730,000
African Christian	7,510,000
traditional beliefs	1,490,000
Muslim	610,000
other	310,000
Zambia	
Christian[1]	6,810,000
traditional beliefs	2,550,000
other	100,000
Zimbabwe	
Christian[1]	6,530,000
traditional beliefs	4,560,000
other	170,000

[1]Includes affiliated and nominal Christians. [2]Official 1986 census figure is 5.9 percent. [3]Includes the Golan Heights and East Jerusalem; excludes the West Bank and Gaza Strip. [4]Many Japanese practice both Shintoism and Buddhism. [5]Excludes the former black independent states of Bophuthatswana, Ciskei, Transkei, and Venda, in which there are about 5,800,000 Christians and 2,100,000 practicers of traditional beliefs. [6]Excludes East Jerusalem.

Vital statistics, marriage, family

This table provides some of the basic measures of the factors that influence the size, direction, and rates of population change within a country. The accuracy of these data depends on the effectiveness of each respective national system for registering vital and civil events (birth, death, marriage, etc.) and on the sophistication of the analysis that can be brought to bear upon the data so compiled.

Data on birth rates, for example, depend not only on the completeness of registration of births in a particular country but also on the conditions under which those data are collected: Do all births take place in a hospital? Are the births reported comparably in all parts of the country? Are the records of the births tabulated at a central location in a timely way with an effort to eliminate inconsistent reporting of birth events, perinatal mortality, etc.? Similar difficulties attach to death rates but with the added need to identify "cause of death." Even in a developed country such identifications are often left to nonmedical personnel, and in a developing country with, say, only one physician for every 10,000 population, there will be too few physicians to perform autopsies to assess accurately the cause of death after the fact and also too few to provide ongoing care at a level where records would permit inference about cause of death based on prior condition or diagnosis.

Calculating natural increase, which at its most basic is simply the difference between the birth and death rates, may be affected by the differing degrees of completeness of birth and death registration for a given country. The total fertility rate may be understood as the average number of children that would be borne per woman if all childbearing women lived to the end of their childbearing years and bore children at each age at the average rate for that age. Calculating a meaningful fertility rate requires analysis of changing age structure of the female population over time, changing mortality rates among mothers and their infants, and changing medical practice at births, each improvement of natural survivorship or medical support leading to greater numbers of live-born children and greater numbers of children who survive their first year (the basis for measurement of infant mortality, another basic indicator of demographic conditions and trends within a population).

As indicated above, data for causes of death are not only particularly difficult to obtain, since many countries are not well equipped to collect the data, but also difficult to assess, as their accuracy may be suspect and their meaning may be subject to varying interpretation. Take the case of a citizen of a less developed country who dies of what is clearly a lung infection: Was the death complicated by chronic malnutrition, itself complicated by a parasitic infestation, these last two together so weakening the subject that he died of an infection that he might have survived had his general health been better? Similarly, in a developed country: Someone may die from what is identified in an autopsy as a cerebrovascular accident, but if that accident occurred in a vascular system that was weakened by diabetes, what was the actual cause of death? Statistics on causes of death seek to identify the "underlying" cause (that which sets the final train of events leading to death in motion) but often must settle for the most proximate cause or symptom. Even this kind of analysis may be misleading for those charged with interpreting the data with a view to ordering health-care priorities for a particular country. The eight groups of causes of death utilized here include most, but not all, of the detailed

Vital statistics, marriage, family

country	vital rates						causes of death (rate per 100,000 population)								
	year	birth rate per 1,000 population	death rate per 1,000 population	infant mortality rate per 1,000 live births	rate of natural increase per 1,000 population	total fertility rate	year	infectious and parasitic diseases	malignant neoplasms (cancers)	endocrine and metabolic disorders	diseases of the nervous system	diseases of the circulatory system	diseases of the respiratory system	diseases of the digestive system	accidents, poisoning, and violence
Afghanistan	1993	51.0	22.0	161.0	29.0	6.7	...	...	...	...	...	...	...	...	...
Albania	1991	23.8	5.5	32.9	18.3	2.9[2]	1992	7.1	53.5	4.7	15.8	187.9	75.0	17.2	31.7
Algeria	1992	30.3	6.1	52.0[3]	24.2	3.8[3]	...	...	...	...	...	...	...	...	...
American Samoa	1991	35.7	4.3	11.0	31.4	5.4	1990	16.4[5]	46.8	16.4[6]	...	131.1[7]	65.6[8]	...	58.5
Andorra	1993	11.9	3.5	6.4[9]	8.4	1.7[3]	...	...	...	...	...	...	...	...	...
Angola	1990–95	51.3	19.2	124	32.1	7.2	...	...	...	...	...	...	...	...	...
Antigua and Barbuda	1993	17.5	5.5	19.2	12.0	1.7	1988	14.0	44.5	25.4	7.6	237.5	44.5	15.2	5.1
Argentina	1994	19.6	8.6	29.4	11.0	2.7	1991	27.3	143.0	26.3	13.7	337.3	49.0	33.5	51.6
Armenia	1994	13.5	6.5	17.1[12]	7.0	3.3[12]	1992	15.4	102.8	21.6	4.9	383.9	48.8	25.7	73.8
Aruba	1992	18.1	5.8	9.6[13]	12.3	1.8[14]	1991	9.8	124.9	47.7	4.2	189.5	30.9	23.9	11.2
Australia	1994	14.5	7.1	5.8	7.4	1.9[12]	1992	5.0	179.9	13.5	14.9	307.8	56.8	22.0	40.3
Austria	1994	11.6	10.1	7.4[15]	1.5	1.6[15]	1993	2.8	244.3	23.1	15.0	544.5	48.2	50.9	63.4
Azerbaijan	1995	21.0	6.0	27.0	15.0	2.4	1989	42.1	72.1	8.6	9.7	292.4	88.9	25.6	42.1
Bahamas, The	1992	25.6	5.0	23.8[2]	20.6	2.1	1990	18.0	80.4	72.2	11.0	126.3	52.2	29.0	40.8
Bahrain	1992	29.8	4.8	25.1	25.0	3.9	1991	2.8	32.3	16.8	3.8	86.6	27.7	10.2	19.0
Bangladesh	1995	34.0	11.0	109.2[12]	23.0	4.1	...	...	...	...	...	...	...	...	...
Barbados	1993	13.9	9.1	11.0	4.8	1.8[15]	1992	19.0	178.5	120.2	17.1	366.8	39.9	28.9	40.3
Belarus	1994	12.0	11.0	12.0	1.0	1.7	1993	8.0	184.5	9.0[16]	14.7	624.7	69.7	8.9	132.6
Belgium	1993	12.1	10.8	8.0	1.3	1.6[17]	1990	11.1	270.1	23.1	38.0	398.9	88.1	38.8	65.1
Belize	1993	35.7	6.1	36.5	29.6	4.5	1990	...	52.4	37.0[6]	...	164.0	57.1	32.8	92.6[18]
Benin	1994	47.7	14.4	110.1	33.3	6.8	...	...	...	...	...	...	...	...	...
Bermuda	1992	15.1	7.4	8.8	7.7	1.8[13]	1990	...	181.5	...	...	344.4	25.2	...	38.6
Bhutan	1994	39.3	15.9	121.0	23.4	5.4	...	...	...	...	...	...	...	...	...
Bolivia	1994	34.4	9.6	75.0	24.8	4.8	...	...	...	...	...	...	...	...	...
Bosnia and Herzegovina	1994	14.0	7.0	15.2	7.0	1.6	1989	9.9	122.6[20]	12.6	11.9	344.1	29.0	29.2	47.1
Botswana	1990–95	37.1	6.6	43.0	30.5	4.8	...	...	...	...	...	...	...	...	...
Brazil	1994	21.0	9.0	60.0	12.0	2.4	1990[22]	*37*	*75*	*31*[16]	*8*	*206*	*64*	*28*	*91*
Brunei	1992	27.2	3.3	9.6	23.9	3.5	1986	5.3	27.0	...	...	80.0	23.4	...	39.8
Bulgaria	1993	10.0	12.9	16.9	−2.9	1.6[15]	1993	7.5	183.9	20.7	6.9	810.4	63.3	38.1	65.3
Burkina Faso	1990–95	46.8	18.2	130	28.6	6.5	...	...	...	...	...	...	...	...	...
Burundi	1991	47.0	15.0	111.0	32.0	6.9	...	...	...	...	...	...	...	...	...
Cambodia	1994	45.1	16.4	110.6	28.7	5.8	...	...	...	...	...	...	...	...	...
Cameroon	1990–95	40.7	12.2	63.0	28.5	5.7	...	...	...	...	...	...	...	...	...
Canada	1993	13.4	7.1	6.3	6.3	1.7	1993	10.9	196.7	22.2	19.9	274.4	62.8	26.3	47.2
Cape Verde	1995	45.3	8.7	55.9	36.6	6.2	1980	153.7	43.8	20.6	16.5	135.8	72.3	27.7	30.1
Central African Republic	1994	42.3	20.7	137.2	21.6	5.4	...	...	...	...	...	...	...	...	...
Chad	1990–95	43.7	18.0	122.0	25.7	5.9	...	...	...	...	...	...	...	...	...
Chile	1993	21.0	5.5	13.1	15.5	2.6	1993	15.1	111.5	16.2	8.0	157.4	64.9	34.2	66.1
China	1994	17.7	6.5	26.0[12]	11.2	2.0[12]	1992[23]	17.9	115.9	8.4[16]	3.9	199.4	131.9	26.9	55.6
Colombia	1990–95	24.0	6.0	37.0	19.9	2.5	1991	18.3	62.9	12.5	7.4	144.7	37.9	16.7	132.3
Comoros	1994	46.0	11.0	80.0	35.0	6.8	...	...	...	...	...	...	...	...	...
Congo	1990–95	44.7	14.9	83.0	29.8	6.3	...	...	...	...	...	...	...	...	...
Costa Rica	1993	26.1	3.6	11.6	22.5	3.1	1991	10.5	74.6	13.6	8.2	111.3	38.5	19.9	39.7
Côte d'Ivoire	1990–95	49.9	15.1	92.0	34.8	7.4	...	...	...	...	...	...	...	...	...
Croatia	1992	9.8	10.8	11.6	−1.0	1.7[2]	1991	10.8	226.1[20]	14.9[16]	6.9	571.8	29.5	53.2	91.8
Cuba	1993	14.0	7.2	9.4[3]	6.8	1.8[19]	1990	9.4	128.7	23.3	10.6	294.7	58.0	26.3	79.9
Cyprus	1994	16.4	7.8	9.0	8.6	2.2	...	...	...	...	...	...	...	...	...
Czech Republic	1993	11.7	11.5	8.5	0.2	1.9[19]	1993	3.0	270.5	15.4	9.1	638.9	46.6	40.2	82.3
Denmark	1993	13.0	12.1	5.6	0.9	1.7	1993	10.2	298.5	24.2	14.0	513.9	98.9	43.3	74.1
Djibouti	1990–95	38.1	16.1	115.0	22.0	5.8	...	...	...	...	...	...	...	...	...
Dominica	1994	20.5	5.0	10.3	15.5	2.0	1990	37.5	116.6	51.4	9.7	273.5	43.0	20.8	18.0
Dominican Republic	1993	30.0	8.0	66.0	22.0	2.8	1985	51.4	27.4	12.3	8.6	100.3	35.4	22.3	33.7
Ecuador	1993	26.5	5.8	36.9	20.7	3.2	1992	52.0	50.0	11.8[6]	1.9[26]	93.1	40.6	13.2	66.7
Egypt	1993	28.2	6.9	59.0[15]	21.3	4.2[15]	1987	98.9	22.0	9.1	13.6	314.4	140.7	45.8	39.1
El Salvador	1994	33.0	6.0	41.0	27.0	3.8	1990[22]	*52*	*43*	*17*	*12*	*120*	*49*	*38*	*137*

causes classified by the World Health Organization and would not, thus, aggregate to the country's crude death rate for the same year. Among the lesser causes excluded by the present classification are: benign neoplasms; nutritional disorders; anemias; mental disorders; kidney and genitourinary diseases not classifiable under the main groups; maternal deaths (for which data *are* provided, however, in the "Health services" table); diseases of the skin and musculoskeletal systems; congenital and perinatal conditions; and general senility and other ill-defined (ill-diagnosed) conditions, a kind of "other" category.

Expectation of life is probably the most accurate single measure of the quality of life in a given society. It summarizes in a single number all of the natural and social stresses that operate upon individuals in that society. The number may range from as few as 40 years of life in the least developed countries to as much as 80 years for women in the most developed nations. The lost potential in the years separating those two numbers is prodigious, regardless of how the loss arises—wars and civil violence, poor public health services, or poor individual health practice in matters of nutrition, exercise, stress management, and so on.

Data on marriages and marriage rates probably are less meaningful in terms of international comparisons than some of the measures mentioned above because the number, timing, and kinds of social relationships that substitute for marriage depend on many kinds of social variables—income, degree of social control, heterogeneity of the society (race, class, language communities), or level of development of civil administration (if one must travel for a day or more to obtain a legal civil ceremony, one may forgo it). Nevertheless, the data for a single country say specific things about local practice in terms of the age at which a man or woman typically marries, and the overall rate will at least define the number of legal civil marriages, though it cannot say anything about other, less formal arrangements (here the figure for the legitimacy rate for children in the next section may identify some of the societies in which economics or social constraints may operate to limit the number of marriages that are actually confirmed on civil registers). The available data usually include both first marriages and remarriages after annulment, divorce, widowhood, or the like.

The data for families provide information about the average size of a family unit (individuals related by blood or civil register) and the average number of children under a specified age (set here at 15 to provide a consistent measure of social minority internationally, though legal minority depends on the laws of each country). When well-defined family data are not collected as part of a country's national census or vital statistics surveys, data for households are substituted on the assumption that most households worldwide represent families in some conventional sense. In the older countries of Europe and North America, increasing numbers of households are composed of unrelated individuals (unmarried heterosexual couples, aged [or younger] groups sharing limited [often fixed] incomes for reasons of economy, or homosexual couples); such arrangements are not yet so common in the rest of the world that they represent great numbers overall. Very few census programs, even in developed countries, make adequate provision for distinguishing these households.

expectation of life at birth (latest year)		nuptiality, family, and family planning															country
		marriages			age at marriage (latest)						families (F), households (H) (latest)						
		year	total number	rate per 1,000 population	groom (percent)			bride (percent)			families (households)		children		induced abortions		
male	female				19 and under	20–29	30 and over	19 and under	20–29	30 and over	total ('000)	size	number under age 15	percent legitimate	number	ratio per 100 live births	
44.0	43.0	...	...	...	...	...	...	...	...	...	H 2,110	H 6.2	H 2.8[1]	...	...	...	Afghanistan
69.3	75.4	1991	24,853	7.6	1.5	80.4	18.1	24.0	71.4	4.6	F 675	F 4.7	F 1.6	...	...	...	Albania
67.0	69.0	1990	139,930	5.9	0.7[4]	67.1[4]	32.2[4]	29.8[4]	61.4[4]	8.8[4]	H 3,322	H 6.9	H 3.0	...	...	...	Algeria
69.0	74.0	1990	370	7.8	...	...		...	...	...	H 7	H 7.0	H 2.7	72.0	...	...	American Samoa
76.0	82.0	1992	135	2.2	...	...	...	...	...	...	...	...	...	...	...	...	Andorra
44.9	48.1	...	...	...	...	...	...	...	...	...	...	H 4.8	...	...	...	...	Angola
70.8	74.9	1988	382	4.9	1.0[10]	37.4[11]	61.6	3.7[10]	52.4[11]	43.9	H 20	H 3.5	H 1.2	23.4	...	...	Antigua and Barbuda
68.1	74.8	1983	177,010	6.0	5.6	71.5	22.9	26.0	58.6	15.4	H 10,097	H 3.2	H 1.0	67.6	...	...	Argentina
68.4	75.4	1994	17,300	4.6	0.7[2]	75.4[2]	20.9[2]	38.0[2]	50.6[2]	11.4[2]	H 550	H 4.7	H 1.8	87.7	27,174	34.9	Armenia
71.1	77.1	1992	566	7.9	...	...	...	...	...	...	H 19	H 3.6	...	63.2	...	...	Aruba
74.5	80.8	1992	114,752	6.6	1.1[2]	58.0[2]	40.9[2]	5.4[2]	65.1[2]	29.5[2]	H 5,853	H 3.0	H 0.6	77.0	...	...	Australia
72.9	79.4	1993	44,786	5.6	1.7[15]	59.8[15]	38.5[15]	6.3[15]	67.6[15]	26.1[15]	H 3,021	H 2.6	H 0.5	75.2	...	...	Austria
66.7	74.6	1993	60,028	8.3	1.2[13]	80.4[13]	18.4[13]	24.8[13]	63.9[13]	11.3[13]	H 1,381	H 4.8	H 1.7	97.5	42,134	23.2	Azerbaijan
68.0	75.0	1992	2,407	9.1	19.0	53.0	27.7	34.0	48.3	17.1	H 68	H 3.8	...	41.2	...	...	Bahamas, The
68.7	72.8	1992	3,048	5.9	2.2[2]	72.1[2]	24.6[2]	29.4[2]	58.6[2]	10.5[2]	H 67	H 6.5	H 2.2	...	...	...	Bahrain
57.0	57.0	1992	1,200,000	10.7	...	...	...	...	...		H 19,700	H 5.3	...	...	...	...	Bangladesh
72.9	77.0	1990	2,310	8.5	0.1	40.2	59.7	1.4	53.6	44.9	H 67	H 3.7	H 1.5	26.9	723	19.6	Barbados
66.0	75.7	1993	82,326	7.9	5.5[2]	73.0[2]	21.5[2]	30.1[2]	51.9[2]	18.0[2]	H 2,796	H 3.2	H 0.9	91.0	161,100	76.6	Belarus
73.0	79.8	1992	61,110	5.4	0.7	64.9	34.4	4.9	69.5	25.6	F 3,613	F 2.7	F 0.5	90.9	...	...	Belgium
66.0	70.0	1992	1,241	6.0	0.7	66.8	32.5	29.7	49.6	20.7	H 38	H 4.9	H 2.2	42.5	822	12.1	Belize
49.9	53.7	1980–85	...	12.8	...	...	...	...	...	...	...	H 5.4	...	...	...	...	Benin
73.0	79.0	1992	909	15.1	0.2[19]	37.4[19]	62.4[19]	1.5[19]	49.4[19]	49.1[19]	H 22	H 2.6	H 0.5	63.9	92	11.0	Bermuda
50.7	49.6	...	...	...	...	...	...	...	...	...	...	H 5.4	...	...	...	...	Bhutan
57.7	61.0	1980	26,990	4.8	8.3	75.1	16.6	26.1	55.4	18.5	H 1,655	H 3.8	H 1.6	80.9	...	...	Bolivia
72.1	77.7	1990	31,449	7.0	2.3[13]	76.0[13]	21.7[13]	28.5[13]	59.3[13]	12.2[13]	H 1,203	H 3.6	H 1.1[21]	...	...	...	Bosnia and Herzegovina
63.0	66.7	1986	1,638	1.5	—	33.0	67.0	5.0	69.2	25.8	H 125	H 5.7	H 2.0	28.8	17	0.1	Botswana
57.0	67.0	1991	743,416	4.9	7.7	71.7	20.6	33.4	54.5	12.1	F 31,888	F 4.2	...	...	...	...	Brazil
69.5	72.8	1992	1,795	6.7	10.6	50.1	39.3	11.4	54.7	33.9	H 45	H 5.8	H 2.0	99.6	...	...	Brunei
69.6	76.3	1993	41,973	5.0	5.9[19]	76.6[19]	17.5[19]	38.0[19]	51.8[19]	10.2[19]	F 2,627	F 3.3	F 0.7	88.0	144,644	137.5	Bulgaria
45.8	49.0	...	...	...	...	...	...	...	...	...	...	H 6.2	...	...	...	...	Burkina Faso
50.0	54.0	...	...	...	...	...	...	...	...	...	...	H 4.6	...	...	...	...	Burundi
49.0	52.0	...	...	...	...	...	...	...	...	...	...	H 5.6	...	...	...	...	Cambodia
54.5	57.5	...	...	...	...	...	...	...	...	...	...	H 5.2	...	...	...	...	Cameroon
74.9	81.0	1993	159,316	5.5	0.9	52.1	47.0	3.9	60.2	35.9	H 10,018	H 2.7	H 0.6	83.8	99,971	25.7	Canada
61.1	65.0	1988	1,040	3.2	2.3	62.4	35.3	17.0	61.1	21.9	F 59	F 5.1	...	55.2	...	...	Cape Verde
44.7	49.4	...	...	...	...	...	...	...	...	...	...	H 4.7	...	...	...	...	Central African Republic
45.9	49.1	...	...	...	...	...	...	...	...	...	...	H 3.9	...	...	...	...	Chad
72.0	77.9	1993	92,821	6.7	5.5	70.2	24.3	20.1	63.4	16.5	H 3,261	H 4.1	H 1.2	65.7	29	—	Chile
69.1	72.4	1993	9,545,047	7.7	...	...	...	...	...	...	H 278.6[24]	H 4.1	H 1.1	...	10,500,000	47.7	China
69.3	72.3	1986	70,350	2.3	4.0	64.1	31.5	22.3	58.5	19.0	F 4,772	F 5.4	F 2.5	75.2	...	...	Colombia
56.0	60.0	...	...	...	...	...	...	...	...	...	...	H 5.6	...	...	...	...	Comoros
48.9	53.8	...	...	...	...	...	...	...	...	...	H 326	H 4.7	H 2.0	...	...	...	Congo
71.9	77.5	1993	21,715	6.8	7.5[19]	65.6[19]	26.9[19]	27.8[19]	54.6[19]	17.6[19]	H 752.5	H 4.2	...	62.8	...	...	Costa Rica
49.7	52.4	...	...	...	...	...	...	...	...	...	...	H 5.4	...	...	...	...	Côte d'Ivoire
66.8	74.8	1992	22,169	4.6	1.2[13]	72.4[13]	26.4[13]	19.5[13]	64.8[13]	15.7[13]	H 1,544	H 3.1	H 0.6	...	...	...	Croatia
73.9	77.6	1991	161,160	15	7.5[19]	56.0[19]	36.3[19]	22.3[19]	50.4[19]	27.2[19]	F 2,860	F 3.7	H 1.6	...	147,530	79.0	Cuba
74.6	79.1	1994	6,097	9.6	0.6	61.0	38.4	11.0	64.7	24.3	H 160	H 3.5	H 1.1	99.6	...	...	Cyprus
68.5	76.1	1993	66,033	6.4	9.1[2]	67.0[2]	23.8[2]	33.2[2]	50.4[2]	16.3[2]	H 3,984	H 2.7	H 0.5	90.3	126,055	96.2	Czech Republic
72.5	77.8	1993	31,638	6.1	0.5	56.3	43.2	1.8	70.2	28.0	H 2,339	H 2.2	...	53.2	19,729	30.7	Denmark
47.4	50.7	...	...	...	...	...	...	...	...	...	...	H 5.6	...	96.8	...	...	Djibouti
74.1	79.9	1990	228	3.3	—	41.2	58.8	3.1	58.3	38.6	H 18	H 4.3	H 2.2	...	...	...	Dominica
60.0	64.0	1987	15,642	2.3	8.0[25]	63.0[25]	29.0[25]	29.7[25]	51.0[25]	19.3[25]	H 753	H 5.1	H 2.5	32.8	562	0.5	Dominican Republic
65.7	72.6	1992	68,337	6.4	13.0[2]	64.4[2]	22.6[2]	34.2[2]	52.0[2]	13.8[2]	...	H 4.1	...	67.9	...	...	Ecuador
62.4	64.8	1993	479,000	8.3	5.9[4]	61.8[4]	32.3[4]	40.4[4]	49.2[4]	10.4[4]	H 9,733	H 4.9	H 2.1	100.0	...	...	Egypt
64.0	70.0	1991	22,658	4.3	6.5	54.7	38.8	21.8	51.0	27.2	H 1,046	H 4.9	H 2.4	30.6	...	...	El Salvador

Vital statistics, marriage, family (continued)

country	vital rates						causes of death (rate per 100,000 population)								
	year	birth rate per 1,000 population	death rate per 1,000 population	infant mortality rate per 1,000 live births	rate of natural increase per 1,000 population	total fertility rate	year	infectious and parasitic diseases	malignant neoplasms (cancers)	endocrine and metabolic disorders	diseases of the nervous system	diseases of the circulatory system	diseases of the respiratory system	diseases of the digestive system	accidents, poisoning, and violence
Equatorial Guinea	1994	40.7	14.7	102.6	26.0	5.3	...	...	...	...	...	...	...	...	...
Eritrea[27]	1990–95	43.0	15.2	105	27.8	5.8	...	...	...	...	...	...	...	...	...
Estonia	1994	9.5	14.8	14.5	−5.3	1.4	1994	11.4	218.1	10.1	13.6	816.0	44.3	34.5	233.2
Ethiopia[27]	1990–95	48.5	18.0	119.0	30.5	7.0	...	...	...	...	...	...	...	...	...
Faroe Islands	1992	16.8	8.4	8.5[2]	8.4	2.7[19]	1992	4.3	191.3	14.9[6]	—	352.8	59.5	14.9	57.4
Fiji	1994	24.7	5.4	27.0[14]	19.3	3.1[19]	1987	18.2	35.5	27.3[6]	2.4[26]	153.4	31.7	15.5	32.2
Finland	1994	13.0	9.4	4.4	3.6	1.8[12]	1993	6.7	198.9	13.4	20.6	485.2	85.6	37.5	85.2
France	1993	12.3	9.2	7.3	5.0	1.8[2]	1992	12.2	245.7	26.0	19.6	298.2	65.8	45.5	81.1
French Guiana	1990	31.5	5.2	15.8	26.3	3.7[2]	1989	61.7	58.1	16.3	10.9	114.3	20.9	13.6	98.0
French Polynesia	1990	27.4	4.6	10.4	22.8	3.9	1985–89	25.0	78.0	12.0	10.0	121.0	29.0	11.0	89.0
Gabon	1990–95	37.3	15.5	94.0	21.8	5.7	...	...	...	...	...	...	...	...	...
Gambia, The	1990–95	43.7	18.8	132.0	24.9	5.2	...	...	...	...	...	...	...	...	...
Gaza Strip	1994	56.0	6.0	43.0	50.0	7.7	...	...	...	...	...	...	...	...	...
Georgia	1994	17.0	9.0	16.0	8.0	2.2	1989	13.5	98.6	12.0	4.1	553.2	51.4	32.1	58.2
Germany	1993	9.4	10.8	5.8	−1.4	1.3[3]	1992	7.0	263.7	35.0	16.8	543.1	65.2	52.1	52.6
Ghana	1990–95	41.7	11.7	81.0	30.0	6.0	...	...	...	...	...	...	...	...	...
Gibraltar	1993	18.5	9.8	5.7[2]	8.7	2.8[2]	1987	17.0	203.9	—	—	601.4	34.0	23.8	3.4
Greece	1994	9.8	9.3	8.6	0.5	1.5[17]	1993	6.5	202.3	12.4	13.1	460.2	53.9	27.1	41.5
Greenland	1993	30.8	6.5	12.7	24.4	2.9[15]	1993	27.1	186.3	...	...	188.2	47.0	12.7	152.0
Grenada	1994	30.0	6.0	12.0	24.0	3.9	1984	13.5	90.5	62.9	11.4	290.3	54.1	39.5	47.9
Guadeloupe	1992	17.8	5.6	10.4	12.2	2.2[17]	1990	20.8[14]	121.2	23.0[14]	12.3[14]	186.8	30.5	29.7	72.9
Guam	1995	24.0	4.0	8.0	20.0	3.1	1992	4.9	65.2	29.5[6]	9.8	123.4	14.7[30]	11.2	68.7
Guatemala	1993	36.2	7.7	55.6	28.5	4.9	1984	211.5	29.8	29.6	9.0	57.2	145.7	21.7	52.0
Guernsey	1993	10.7	9.5	1.3[19]	1.2	1.6[13]	1990	8.4	314.3	11.8	15.1	430.3	112.6	30.3	20.2
Guinea	1994	46.0	21.0	147.0	25.0	6.0	...	...	...	...	...	...	...	...	...
Guinea-Bissau	1994	43.0	21.0	140.0	22.0	5.8	...	...	...	...	...	...	...	...	...
Guyana	1994	20.0	7.0	49.0	13.0	2.3	1984	19.3	37.1	33.3	11.6	202.5	39.8	74.0	56.5
Haiti	1994	40.0	19.0	109.0	21.0	4.7[15]	...	...	...	...	...	...	...	...	...
Honduras	1993	35.8	6.4	47.2	29.4	4.9	1983	46.6	12.4	5.3	7.8	48.4	26.3	16.7	42.2
Hong Kong	1994	11.9	4.9	4.8	7.0	1.2[19]	1993	8.4	174.5	8.0	4.1	141.1	94.7	23.0	28.6
Hungary	1994	11.0	14.8	11.5	−3.8	1.8[15]	1993	9.1	312.8	19.2	11.6	751.7	68.8	116.3	119.5
Iceland	1994	16.7	6.5	3.2	10.2	4.6[12]	1993	4.1	171.0	12.1	13.6	294.6	89.5	14.0	38.3
India	1991	29.3	9.8	88.0[17]	19.5	3.9[15]	...	...	...	...	...	...	...	...	...
Indonesia	1991	32.2	11.7	90.0	20.5	3.7	...	...	...	...	...	...	...	...	...
Iran	1994	42.0	8.0	60.0	34.0	5.5[12]	...	...	...	...	...	...	...	...	...
Iraq	1994	44.0	7.0	67.0	37.0	6.7	...	...	...	...	...	...	...	...	...
Ireland	1993	13.9	8.9	6.0	5.0	2.1[17]	1992	4.8	211.2	17.9	16.3	393.3	116.7	23.6	38.5
Isle of Man	1993	12.3	14.5	5.7	−2.2	1.8[13]	1993	8.6	337.8	4.3[6]	—	701.6	258.8	18.7	50.3
Israel	1993	21.3	6.3	7.8	15.0	2.9[19]	1992	14.6	130.5	23.2	9.7	268.4	44.1	18.6	38.4
Italy	1993	9.4	9.5	8.3[15]	−0.1	7.4	1991	3.4	260.6	34.2	18.2	425.3	59.6	50.1	53.2
Jamaica	1994	23.7	5.4	27.0[13]	18.3	2.8	1991	8.1	84.1	51.3	7.5	189.5	30.2	14.1	8.4
Japan	1994	10.1	7.0	4.5[15]	3.1	1.5[15]	1993	11.2	189.1	10.3	5.8	253.4	93.6	32.0	47.3
Jersey	1991	12.5	9.9	6.0[13]	2.6	1.3[13]	...	...	...	...	...	...	...	...	...
Jordan	1992	37.8	5.2	33.8	32.6	5.9	...	...	...	...	...	...	...	...	...
Kazakhstan	1994	20.0	8.0	27.0	12.0	2.5	1993	26.5	135.2	9.6	8.7	425.1	85.5	29.3	133.0
Kenya	1990–95	44.5	11.7	69.0	32.8	6.3	...	...	...	...	...	...	...	...	...
Kiribati	1994	31.6	12.3	98.4	19.3	3.8	...	...	...	...	...	...	...	...	...
Korea, North	1993	23.0	5.0	24.0	18.0	2.4	1986	19.4	69.0	3.0[16]	6.5	224.9	46.7	51.6	38.2
Korea, South	1993	16.7	5.6	15.0	11.1	1.8	1993	12.6	105.6	16.9	6.7	149.0	24.0	40.5	73.0
Kuwait	1993	25.6	2.4	11.2	23.5	5.3	1993	9.6	27.4	6.6	5.7	82.1	13.7	4.3	41.3
Kyrgyzstan	1994	24.6	8.3	29.1	16.3	3.1	1994	32.7	67.9	8.0	8.9	330.8	131.5	34.3	95.7
Laos	1995	43.0	14.0	92.0	29.0	6.4	...	...	...	...	...	...	...	...	...
Latvia	1994	9.5	16.4	15.5	6.9	1.4	1993	15.4	211.3	11.8	7.8	503.8	41.7	35.3	212.3
Lebanon	1992	25.2	4.5	28.0	20.7	2.9	...	...	...	...	...	...	...	...	...
Lesotho	1990–95	36.9	10.0	79.0	26.9	5.2	...	...	...	...	...	...	...	...	...
Liberia	1990–95	47.3	14.2	126.0	33.1	6.8	...	...	...	...	...	...	...	...	...
Libya	1990–95	41.9	8.1	68	33.8	6.4	...	...	...	...	...	...	...	...	...
Liechtenstein	1994	11.7	6.7	5.3	5.0	1.5	1994	...	133.9	...	...	326.4	35.9	...	35.9
Lithuania	1993	12.5	12.4	16.0	0.1	2.0[13]	1993	13.2	200.8	7.9	9.7	670.2	48.2	27.3	167.2
Luxembourg	1993	13.4	9.9	6.0	3.5	1.7	1992	8.0	254.5	22.6	16.1	416.5	69.3	47.0	67.6
Macau	1994	15.2	3.3	6.2	11.9	1.6[2]	1994	9.5	81.4	7.2	2.6	128.6	39.9	11.3	23.2
Macedonia	1994	16.0	7.0	24.5	9.0	1.9	1993	12.9	6.2	16.4	4.7	385.8	34.5	14.8	35.3
Madagascar	1990–95	43.9	11.8	93.0	32.1	6.1	...	...	...	...	...	...	...	...	...
Malaŵi	1990–95	50.5	20.0	143	30.5	7.2	1986[32]	*711*	*27*	*25*	*60*	*50*	*265*	*34*	*78*
Malaysia	1992	28.6	4.5	11.7	24.1	3.3	1992	13.2	21.0	4.4	6.4[16]	54.1	7.5	1.9	28.5
Maldives	1993	32.6	5.5	34.0	27.1	6.1	1988	31.3	—	—	—	170.1	66.2	—	9.9
Mali	1994	51.8	20.4	106.2	31.4	7.3	...	...	...	...	...	...	...	...	...
Malta	1993	14.0	7.3	10.3[15]	6.7	2.1[15]	1993	9.6	173.8	30.7	9.0	354.5	58.4	26.9	21.9
Marshall Islands	1993	46.6	7.9	53.0	38.7	7.0	1991	102.0	29.1	...	—	74.9	52.0	41.6	35.4
Martinique	1993	15.8	6.0	6.2[15]	9.8	1.9	1990	22.0	135.5	30.7	10.7[25]	208.0	34.2	31.3	54.8
Mauritania	1994	46.0	18.0	117.0	28.0	6.5	...	...	...	...	...	...	...	...	...
Mauritius	1994	19.6	6.7	18.1	12.9	2.3	1994	13.7	64.0	23.3	3.8	297.1	68.6	32.1	44.7
Mayotte	1991	43.7	6.0	38.0	37.7	6.8[13]	...	...	...	...	...	...	...	...	...
Mexico	1992	31.7	4.6	27.1	27.1	3.7[19]	1992	28.5	50.6	42.6	6.8	101.2	45.9	40.6	69.5
Micronesia	1995	37.0	8.0	23.0	29.0	4.3	1984	20.4	27.1	6.8	4.5	53.2	47.5	5.7	23.8
Moldova	1994	16.0	10.0	19.0	6.0	2.1	1989	12.4	131.6	8.3	8.2	452.2	64.2	85.4	105.3
Monaco	1988	22.9	18.5	9.0[13]	4.4	1.2[13]	...	...	...	...	...	...	...	...	...
Mongolia	1994	34.0	7.7	48	26.3	4.5	...	...	...	...	...	...	...	...	...
Morocco	1992	22.7	3.7	68.0[17]	19.0	4.4[17]	1992	10.2	14.0	12.2	4.9	35.5	9.5	7.9	19.2
Mozambique	1990–95	45.2	18.5	148.0	26.7	6.5	...	...	...	...	...	...	...	...	...
Myanmar (Burma)	1995	31.0	10.0	78.0	21.10	4.0	...	...	...	...	...	...	...	...	...
Namibia	1990–95	32.5	11.1	84.0	21.4	4.2	...	...	...	...	...	...	...	...	...
Nauru	1995	24.0	5.0	26.0	19.0	2.5[13]	1976–81[33]	33.0	38.0	24.0	13.0	89.0	16.0	53.0	116.0
Nepal	1994	37.6	13.3	84.0	24.3	5.2	...	...	...	...	...	...	...	...	...
Netherlands, The	1994	12.1	8.7	6.3[12]	3.4	1.6[15]	1992	6.1	236.8	28.3	17.7	339.6	64.8	32.5	35.7

expectation of life at birth (latest year)		nuptiality, family, and family planning: marriages			age at marriage (latest): groom (percent)			bride (percent)			families (F), households (H) (latest): families (households)		children		induced abortions		country
male	female	year	total number	rate per 1,000 population	19 and under	20–29	30 and over	19 and under	20–29	30 and over	total ('000)	size	number under age 15	percent legitimate	number	ratio per 100 live births	
50.0	54.3	...	...	...	...	...	...	...	...	...	...	H 4.5	...	...	...	...	Equatorial Guinea
48.9	52.1	...	...	...	...	...	...	...	...	...	...	...	...	...	...	...	Eritrea[27]
62.6	74.1	1994	7,378	4.9	5.3	53.7	41.0	17.2	47.8	35.0	H 427	H 3.1	H 0.8	66.1	19,784	139.5	Estonia
45.9	49.1	...	...	...	...	...	...	...	...	...	...	H 4.5	...	...	...	...	Ethiopia[27]
72.8	79.6	1990	203	4.3	1.0[28]	68.8[28]	30.2[28]	8.8[28]	70.7[28]	20.5[28]	F 14	F 3.0	F 0.9	57.5	26	3.3	Faroe Islands
61.0	65.0	1988	6,892	9.6	6.6[28]	68.7[28]	24.7[28]	31.0[28]	55.8[28]	13.2[28]	F 97	F 6.0	F 2.5	82.7	...	...	Fiji
71.7	79.4	1993	23,681	4.7	1.2[19]	58.9[19]	39.9[19]	4.7[19]	66.7[19]	28.6[19]	H 2,218	H 2.3	H 0.4	71.1	12,232	18.7	Finland
72.9	81.1	1992	269,940	4.7	0.4[10]	61.7	37.9	3.3[10]	69.5	27.2	H 20,899	H 2.6	H 1.0	68.1	161,129	21.2	France
63.4	69.7	1990	465	4.1	...	...	...	...	...	...	H 33	H 3.4	H 1.2	20.3	388	16.8	French Guiana
66.1	71.3	1992	1,468	10.5	11.3[28, 29]	75.8[28, 29]	12.9[28, 29]	41.5[28, 29]	52.5[28, 29]	6.0[28, 29]	H 40	H 4.7	H 1.7	41.5	...	...	French Polynesia
51.9	55.2	...	...	...	...	...	...	...	...	...	H 136	H 4.0	...	...	...	...	Gabon
43.4	46.6	...	...	...	...	...	...	...	...	...	...	H 8.3	...	...	...	...	Gambia, The
66.5	69.2	...	...	...	...	...	...	...	...	...	...	...	...	...	...	...	Gaza Strip
68.9	76.5	1993	24,105	4.9	5.7[13]	66.2[13]	28.1[13]	27.8[13]	55.7[13]	16.5[13]	H 1,244	H 4.1	H 1.1	82.3	68,883	75.6	Georgia
73.2	79.8	1993	441,261	5.4	0.8[2]	55.9[2]	43.3[2]	4.6[2]	65.8[2]	29.9[2]	H 34,827	H 2.3	H 0.3	85.1	118,609	14.7	Germany
53.3	57.2	...	...	...	...	...	...	...	...	...	H 2,355	H 4.9	H 2.2	...	...	...	Ghana
73.4	80.4	1993	758	8.2	...	...	...	...	...	...	H 8	H 3.2	H 0.7	97.1	...	...	Gibraltar
74.6	79.8	1992	48,631	4.7	1.2	55.7	43.1	13.7	65.5	20.8	H 2,990	H 3.3	H 0.7	96.1	11,109	10.8	Greece
60.7	68.4	1991	451	8.1	1.1	44.6	54.3	2.7	59.6	37.7	F 31	F 1.8	F 0.5	28.0	962	80.7	Greenland
68.0	73.0	...	...	...	...	...	...	...	...	...	H 24	H 3.7	H 2.2	...	...	...	Grenada
70.0	77.0	1992	1,880	4.7	0.5[2]	51.4[2]	48.0[2]	7.2[2]	61.4[2]	31.4[2]	H 112	H 3.4	H 0.9	39.3	561	8.7	Guadeloupe
73.0	79.0	1992	1,477	10.6	3.0	55.5	41.5	9.2	59.3	31.5	H 31	H 4.0	H 1.3	67.8	...	...	Guam
61.5	66.7	1988	46,155	5.4	15.9	55.7	28.4	41.5	38.0	20.5	H 1,611	H 5.4	H 5.4	34.8	...	...	Guatemala
...	...	1990	403	6.8	...	...	...	...	...	...	H 21	H 2.6	H 0.5	80.2	...	...	Guernsey
44.0	45.0	...	...	...	...	...	...	...	...	...	H 1,064	H 4.7	...	...	...	...	Guinea
41.9	45.1	...	...	...	...	...	...	...	...	...	H 124	H 4.1	H 2.8	11.3	...	...	Guinea-Bissau
62.0	68.0	...	...	...	...	...	...	...	...	...	H 150	H 5.1	H 2.1	...	...	...	Guyana
43.0	47.0	...	...	...	...	...	...	...	...	...	H 1,147	H 4.4	H 1.0	...	...	...	Haiti
61.8	60.2	1990	19,875	4.9	7.7	65.1	27.2	27.9	58.5	13.6	H 463	H 5.7	H 2.8	...	...	...	Honduras
75.4	81.0	1992	45,702	7.9	0.8	48.2	51.0	3.6	69.2	27.2	H 1,582	H 3.4	H 0.7	94.5	17,600	25.2	Hong Kong
64.6	73.7	1992	57,005	5.5	5.6	70.6	23.8	27.2	56.4	16.4	F 3,058	F 2.9	F 0.8	81.5	87,065	71.5	Hungary
76.8	80.7	1993	1,219	4.6	0.7	47.7	51.6	6.8	62.3	30.9	H 85	H 2.9	H 1.3	41.7	743	16.1	Iceland
60.4	61.2	...	...	...	...	...	...	...	...	...	H 119,231	H 5.6	H 2.4	...	596,345	2.4	India
58.2	61.9	1991–92[31]	1,358,616	7.9	...	...	...	...	...	...	H 39,695	H 4.5	H 1.8	...	...	...	Indonesia
65.0	67.0	1991	448,851	8.1	...	...	...	...	...	...	H 9,759	H 6.1	H 2.2	...	...	...	Iran
46.0	57.0	1990	143,518	8.1	...	...	...	...	...	...	H 1,873	H 8.9	H 4.1	...	...	...	Iraq
71.0	76.7	1993	15,728	4.4	0.9[2]	69.4[2]	29.6[2]	3.2[2]	78.5[2]	18.1[2]	H 726	H 3.9	H 1.3	80.5	...	...	Ireland
...	...	1993	417	6.0	0.7	55.9	43.4	4.6	61.6	33.8	...	...	...	73.5	...	...	Isle of Man
75.1	78.5	1993	32,572	6.2	3.5[2]	73.1[2]	23.3[2]	22.5[2]	66.3[2]	11.0[2]	H 1,355	H 3.7	H 1.1	98.5	16,379	14.9	Israel
73.6	80.2	1993	272,200	4.8	0.8[19]	67.3[19]	31.9[19]	8.1[19]	75.9[19]	16.0[19]	F 19,766	F 2.8	F 0.5	93.7	146,639	26.1	Italy
66.7	70.2	1994	15,171	6.1	...	...	...	...	...	...	H 554	H 4.2	H 1.4	14.9	...	...	Jamaica
76.1	82.2	1993	792,648	6.4	1.3[15]	61.9[15]	36.8[15]	3.3[15]	79.0[15]	17.7[15]	H 40,670	H 3.0	...	99.0	413,032	34.2	Japan
...	...	...	...	...	...	...	...	...	...	...	H 29	H 2.6	H 0.4	88.1	313	29.2	Jersey
70.0	73.0	1991	35,926	8.1	5.0	74.0	21.0	40.3	53.8	5.9	H 679	H 6.0	H 3.4	...	...	...	Jordan
63.2	72.7	1993	146,161	8.6	6.0[15]	73.4[15]	20.6[15]	31.0[15]	53.6[15]	15.4[15]	H 3,824	H 4.0	H 1.4	87.6	296,586	87.6	Kazakhstan
54.2	57.3	...	...	...	...	...	...	...	...	...	H 1,938	H 6.2	H 2.7	...	...	...	Kenya
52.6	55.8	1988	352	5.2	...	...	...	...	...	...	H 11	H 6.6	H 2.5	...	...	...	Kiribati
68.0	74.0	1987	188,007	9.3	...	...	...	...	...	...	H 4,054	H 4.8	H 1.7	...	...	...	Korea, North
67.7	75.7	1993	397,750	9.0	0.3	70.2	29.5	2.3	87.4	10.3	H 11,355	H 3.8	H 1.0	99.5	...	...	Korea, South
71.8	73.3	1993	11,418	7.8	3.2[13]	69.5[13]	27.3[13]	31.2[13]	57.3[13]	11.5[13]	H 246	H 7.4	H 1.6	100.0	...	...	Kuwait
64.2	72.2	1994	26,097	5.8	6.3	79.3	14.4	40.6	50.1	[illegible]	H [illegible]	H 4.2	H 1.9	83.2	49,325	44.8	Kyrgyzstan
51.0	54.0	...	...	...	...	...	...	...	...	...	...	H 6.0	...	...	...	...	Laos
61.6	70.0	1994	11,572	4.5	6.5	64.9	28.8	19.8	56.1	24.1	H 732	H 3.1	H 0.8	81.6	26,795	110.5	Latvia
72.5	77.9	...	...	...	...	...	...	...	...	...	H 405	H 5.3	H 2.2	...	...	...	Lebanon
58.0	63.0	...	...	...	...	...	...	...	...	...	H 330	H 4.8	H 2.0	...	...	...	Lesotho
54.0	57.0	...	...	...	...	...	...	...	...	...	H 474	H 5.0	...	...	...	...	Liberia
61.6	65.0	...	...	...	...	...	...	...	...	...	F 383	F 5.4	F 2.9	...	...	...	Libya
66.5	79.5	1994	202	13.1	—	54.5	44.5	0.0	66.3	29.2	H 8	H 3.0	H 0.7	85.3	...	...	Liechtenstein
65.3	76.1	1993	23,709	6.4	8.8[15]	69.9[15]	21.3[15]	27.7[15]	54.3[15]	18.0[15]	H 1,000	H 3.2	H 0.8	93.3	48,400	90.3	Lithuania
72.6	79.1	1992	2,512	6.4	1.0	55.2	43.8	3.9	64.9	31.2	H 145	H 2.8	H 0.5	87.3	...	...	Luxembourg
68.1	71.8	1994	2,742	6.8	0.6	38.5	60.9	2.6	62.4	35.0	H 99	H 3.5	H 0.9	99.3	...	...	Macau
70.1	74.4	1993	15,080	7.3	5.6	79.3	15.1	30.1	63.0	6.9	H 435	H 4.4	H 1.3	...	18,754	57.9	Macedonia
55.0	58.0	...	...	...	...	...	...	...	...	...	H 1,709	H 4.7	H 2.0	...	...	...	Madagascar
45.0	46.2	...	...	...	...	...	...	...	...	...	...	H 4.3	...	...	...	...	Malawi
69.1	73.8	...	...	...	...	...	...	...	...	...	H 3,580	H 4.9	...	...	...	...	Malaysia
65.0	62.0	1993	2,778	11.7	13.7	58.2	29.1	...	...	...	...	H 7.1	...	...	...	...	Maldives
54.7	58.2	1987	33,646	4.4	...	...	...	...	...	...	H 1,364	H 5.6	...	...	...	...	Mali
73.0	77.8	1993	2,476	6.8	2.5	73.1	23.8	9.9	76.9	13.2	H 76	H 3.6	H 1.2	97.7	...	...	Malta
61.9	65.0	...	...	...	...	...	...	...	...	...	H 5	H 8.7	...	...	...	...	Marshall Islands
74.7	81.0	1993	1,555	4.2	0.1[14]	46.8[14]	53.1[14]	3.3[14]	61.5[14]	35.2[14]	H 107	H 3.3	H 0.8	34.1	1,753	30.6	Martinique
45.0	51.0	...	...	...	...	...	...	...	...	...	H 246	H 5.0	...	...	...	...	Mauritania
66.4	73.7	1994	11,414	10.3	1.9	59.9	38.2	25.5	55.9	18.6	F 155	F 5.3	F 2.0	72.8	...	...	Mauritius
54.0	58.0	...	...	...	...	...	...	...	...	...	H 19	H 4.9	H 2.3	89.2	...	...	Mayotte
66.5	73.1	1992	667,598	7.6	16.9	64.7	18.4	36.4	52.4	11.2	H 17,152	H 5.1	H 2.0	72.5	...	...	Mexico
71.0	71.0	...	...	...	...	...	...	...	...	...	H 11	H 7.0	...	...	...	...	Micronesia
67.9	71.5	1993	39,469	9.1	5.9[2]	74.6[2]	19.5[2]	37.6[2]	46.9[2]	15.5[2]	H 1,144	H 3.4	H 1.1	89.6	52,003	74.7	Moldova
72.0	80.0	1987	...	7.5	...	...	...	...	...	...	H 14	H 2.2	H 0.3	96.8	...	...	Monaco
63.0	65.0	1989	16,100	7.8	...	...	...	...	...	...	F 428	F 4.8	...	...	...	...	Mongolia
65.8	68.7	...	...	...	...	...	...	...	...	...	H 2,819	H 5.8	H 2.5	...	...	...	Morocco
44.9	48.0	...	...	...	...	...	...	...	...	...	F 1,860	F 4.4	F 2.0	73.1	...	...	Mozambique
57.0	61.0	...	...	...	...	...	...	...	...	...	...	H 5.2	...	...	...	...	Myanmar (Burma)
57.5	60.0	...	...	...	...	...	...	...	...	...	...	H 4.8	...	...	...	...	Namibia
64.0	69.0	1976	43	6.1	...	...	...	...	...	...	H 1	H 8.0	H 2.6	...	...	...	Nauru
52.4	52.7	...	...	...	...	...	...	...	...	...	H 3,345	H 5.5	H 2.3	...	...	...	Nepal
74.3	80.3	1992	93,638	6.2	0.4	53.0	46.6	2.1	65.6	32.3	H 6,185	H 2.4	H 0.4	87.5	18,384	9.3	Netherlands, The

Vital statistics, marriage, family (continued)

country	vital rates						causes of death (rate per 100,000 population)								
	year	birth rate per 1,000 population	death rate per 1,000 population	infant mortality rate per 1,000 live births	rate of natural increase per 1,000 population	total fertility rate	year	infectious and parasitic diseases	malignant neoplasms (cancers)	endocrine and metabolic disorders	diseases of the nervous system	diseases of the circulatory system	diseases of the respiratory system	diseases of the digestive system	accidents, poisoning, and violence
Netherlands Antilles	1991	18.3	5.8	6.3[13]	12.5	2.2[15]	1995[34]	16.7	149.0	61.7	9.9	71.6	40.8	21.4	47.6
New Caledonia	1994	25.0	5.0	21.0	20.0	2.9	1992	19.3	129.0	10.8	9.1	115.3	45.4	15.3	80.7
New Zealand	1994	16.3	7.7	7.1	8.6	2.0	1992	5.9	199.9	17.8	12.7	351.1	81.7	23.2	52.6
Nicaragua	1994	35.0	7.0	53.0	28.0	4.3	1991[35]	*100*	*56*	*18*	*13*	*142*	*73*	*34*	*93*
Niger	1990–95	52.5	18.9	124.0	33.6	7.4	...	...	...	...	...	...	...	...	...
Nigeria	1990–95	45.4	15.4	84.0	30.0	6.5	...	...	...	...	...	...	...	...	...
Northern Mariana Islands	1992	29.0	3.0	9.0[2]	26.0	2.4[19]	1987	18.7	70.2[20]	23.4	14.0	135.7	70.2	9.4	145.1
Norway	1993	13.8	10.9	5.9[15]	2.9	1.9	1992	6.6	228.4	16.8	18.4	482.9	106.7	28.3	57.0
Oman	1992	61.3	4.5	24.2	56.8	7.9	...	...	...	...	...	...	...	...	...
Pakistan	1995	39.0	9.0	83.0	30.0	5.9	...	...	...	...	...	...	...	...	...
Palau	1995	22.1	6.6	25.1	15.5	2.9	...	...	...	...	...	...	...	...	...
Panama	1994	25.0	5.0	17.0	20.0	2.9	1992[37]	*28.7*	*85.7*	*18.4*[6]	*1.6*[26]	*167.0*	*26.9*	*11.3*	*78.7*
Papua New Guinea	1995	33.0	10.0	65.0	23.0	4.8	...	...	...	...	...	...	...	...	...
Paraguay	1991	33.6	6.4	39.0[17]	27.2	4.4	1988[38]	*56*	*61*	*23*	*11*	*201*	*53*	*21*	*49*
Peru	1995	26.2	6.6	50.0	19.6	3.2	1989[35]	*85*	*73*	*19*	*11*	*115*	*100*	*36*	*67*
Philippines	1994	30.0	7.0	39.0	23.0	3.8	1991	65.9	35.2	17.9	124.9	82.2	20.5	20.5	71.8
Poland	1993	12.8	10.2	13.3	2.6	2.1[2]	1993	7.2	196.8	15.8	8.1	529.7	35.8	32.3	73.0
Portugal	1993	11.5	10.7	8.6	0.8	1.5	1993	10.4	195.5	37.3	9.8	469.1	78.9	50.4	61.2
Puerto Rico	1993	18.0	7.9	13.4	10.1	2.1	1993	59.4	122.2	66.7	19.2	242.3	80.5	43.9	34.1
Qatar	1992	19.6	1.8	15.8	17.8	4.8	1992	3.4	21.4[20]	7.3[19]	2.6	59.9	7.5	3.4	36.0
Réunion	1994	20.6	5.4	8.0	15.2	2.4[12]	1992	14.7	87.2	21.8[2]	22.6	173.0	43.1	60.3[40]	58.0
Romania	1993	10.9	11.6	23.4	−0.7	2.2[13]	1992	12.4	163.4	11.7	8.2	707.7	94.0	57.9	74.3
Russia	1994	9.6	15.7	18.6	−6.1	37.6	1994	19.9	203.4	11.0	10.9	832.6	80.3	43.9	249.3
Rwanda	1990–95	44.1	16.7	110.0	27.4	6.5	...	...	...	...	...	...	...	...	...
St. Kitts and Nevis	1994	24.0	10.0	20.0	14.0	2.6	1985	50.0	95.5	20.5[6]	11.4	443.2	81.8	25.0	29.5
St. Lucia	1994	23.0	6.0	19.0	17.0	2.5	1992	31.1	64.4	22.4	5.8	205.6	48.5	21.0	34.7
St. Vincent and the Grenadines	1992	24.8	6.6	17.1	18.2	2.1	1992	17.5	99.7	55.4	13.9	222.5	33.2	25.9	62.8
San Marino	1990–94	10.8	7.0	7.1	3.8	1.5[3]	1990–94	...	221.1	2.6[6]	...	325.6	13.6	...	45.7
São Tomé and Príncipe	1994	35.2	8.9	63.5	26.3	4.5	1987	240.7	19.6	5.3[6]	2.7[26]	143.5	86.5	15.2	14.3
Saudi Arabia	1992	42.7	4.6	23.6	38.1	7.0	...	...	...	...	...	...	...	...	...
Senegal	1990–95	43.0	16.0	68	27.0	6.1	...	...	...	...	...	...	...	...	...
Seychelles	1994	23.0	7.6	8.8	15.4	2.6	1994	43.3	128.6	16.2	16.2	288.4	98.8	39.3	43.3
Sierra Leone	1990–95	49.1	25.2	166.0	23.9	6.5	...	...	...	...	...	...	...	...	...
Singapore	1994	16.4	4.7	4.3	11.7	1.8	1994	12.3	128.0	12.8	2.4	185.3	86.9	13.3	32.5
Slovakia	1993	14.1	10.1	12.6	4.0	1.9[15]	1992	4.0	200.0[20]	19.0	8.0	521.0	77.0	52.0	76.0
Slovenia	1993	9.9	10.0	8.9[15]	−0.1	1.3[15]	1993	5.0	228.9	26.0	9.3	454.7	60.3	64.9	95.1
Solomon Islands	1995	37.0	4.0	26.0[15]	33.0	5.2	...	...	...	...	...	...	...	...	...
Somalia	1990–95	50.2	18.5	122.0	31.7	7.0	...	...	...	...	...	...	...	...	...
South Africa	1994	34.0	8.0	47.0	26.0	3.2[12]	1993	42.4	48.0	19.1	7.7	91.2	38.2	12.4	99.3
Spain	1993	9.7	8.6	7.4[15]	1.1	1.4[17]	1991	10.3	202.1	33.6	12.8	353.2	80.7	48.4	47.6
Sri Lanka	1993	19.9	5.6	24.0	15.4	2.5	1989	26.0	26.7	8.4	36.9	101.4	31.1	17.4	135.7
Sudan, The	1994	42.0	12.0	80.0	30.0	6.1	...	...	...	...	...	...	...	...	...
Suriname	1990–95	25.3	5.8	28.0	19.5	2.7	1987[37]	*35*	*57*	*42*	*10*	*179*	*34*	*25*	*69*
Swaziland	1990–95	38.5	10.7	75	27.8	4.9	...	...	...	...	...	...	...	...	...
Sweden	1994	12.8	10.5	3.4	2.3	2.0	1992	8.2	235.0	22.2	13.2	549.7	82.9	36.8	52.9
Switzerland	1994	11.9	8.8	5.4	3.1	1.5[12]	1993	16.0	236.1	24.1[16]	17.6	390.8	68.2	27.3	68.7
Syria	1990–95	41.1	5.8	39.0	35.3	5.4	1981[22]	*22*	*12*	*7*	*13*	*86*	*19*	*8*	*27*
Taiwan	1994	15.3	5.4	4.8[12]	9.9	1.8[12]	1992	...	101.5	23.7[6]	...	140.1[12]	24.3[37]	18.2[41]	63.7[41]
Tajikistan	1994	35.0	6.0	40.0	29.0	4.5	1991	85.6	48.3	8.8[16]	7.9	185.8	125.4	18.2	43.5
Tanzania	1995	45.3	19.8	109.0	25.5	6.1	...	...	...	...	...	...	...	...	...
Thailand	1995	19.0	7.0	32.0	12.0	2.1	1991	...	162.0	...	...	250.0	55.0	73.0	104.0
Togo	1995	46.8	11.0	86.5	35.8	6.8	...	...	...	...	...	...	...	...	...
Tonga	1993	25.2	6.8	21.4	18.4	3.7	1992	16.3	54.9	15.2	6.1	158.5	31.5	18.3	4.1
Trinidad and Tobago	1993	17.4	6.5	17.0[3]	10.9	2.3[3]	1991	22.5	83.4	83.3[6]	2.4[26]	260.0	31.1	13.7	51.4
Tunisia	1992	25.3	6.2	43.0[17]	19.1	3.4[17]	...	...	...	...	...	...	...	...	...
Turkey	1994	26.0	6.0	49.0	20.0	3.2	1990[41]	*23*	*79*	*9*[6]	*3*[26]	*358*	*29*	*12*	*28*
Turkmenistan	1994	33.0	7.0	45.0	26.0	4.1	1989	79.3	65.1	8.0	9.1	275.3	160.6	32.2	62.4
Tuvalu	1993	25.5	9.1	73.6	16.4	3.0	1985	40.0	70.0	20.0	120.0	150.0	120.0	170.0	...
Uganda	1990–95	51.8	19.2	115	32.6	7.3	...	...	...	...	...	...	...	...	...
Ukraine	1994	12.0	13.0	14.0	−0.2	1.7	1992	13.2	201.8	8.2[16]	8.9	915.5	74.0	36.5	128.8
United Arab Emirates	1990–95	23.2	2.7	19.0	20.5	4.2	...	...	...	...	...	...	...	...	...
United Kingdom	1992	13.5	10.9	6.6	2.6	1.8	1992	5.1	280.8	19.5	21.8	501.0	120.4	36.7	34.2
United States	1993	15.7	8.5	8.5[15]	7.2	2.0[2]	1993	27.5[42]	206.0	21.3[6]	0.3[26]	364.7	70.1[30]	15.2	54.9
Uruguay	1994	17.7	9.4	18.7[9]	8.3	2.4	1990	16.0	222.8	25.5	16.2	378.4	76.3	39.1	61.7
Uzbekistan	1994	33.0	6.0	35.0	27.0	4.0	1992	40.7	51.5	9.4	8.9	283.4	119.2	28.2	52.9
Vanuatu	1995	34.0	7.0	43.0	27.0	4.5	1994[43]	25.0	29.2	9.1	5.5	39.0	30.4	9.7	9.1
Venezuela	1994	25.7	4.6	27.7	21.1	3.1	1989	30.0	51.1	18.6	7.4	115.0	29.0	18.8	61.4
Vietnam	1995	29.0	8.0	40.0	21.0	3.7	1979	48.0	54.0	...	...	123.8	...	...	...
Virgin Islands (U.S.)	1988	22.0	5.0	13.1	17.0	2.6[13]	1989	10.8	78.9	36.5[5]	—	232.7	14.8[30]	12.8	56.2
West Bank	1994	46.0	7.0	40.0	39.0	5.7	...	...	...	...	...	...	...	...	...
Western Sahara	1995	46.9	18.5	149.0	28.4	6.9	...	...	...	...	...	...	...	...	...
Western Samoa	1993	29.8	7.0	30.0	22.8	4.8	1992	3.1	11.2	9.9	3.1	24.2	9.9	6.8	2.5
Yemen	1992	48.7	14.2	114.8	34.5	8.4	...	...	...	...	...	...	...	...	...
Yugoslavia	1993	13.5	10.2	21.9	3.3	2.1[2]	1991	9.3	155.8[20]	21.6	8.2	528.3	47.5	26.6	57.0
Zaire	1990–95	47.5	14.5	93.0	33.0	6.7	...	...	...	...	...	...	...	...	...
Zambia	1990–95	44.6	15.1	104	29.5	6.0	...	...	...	...	...	...	...	...	...
Zimbabwe	1992	34.5	9.5	61.0	25.0	4.4	1990	64.7	28.4	4.9	9.4	40.8	39.5	12.1	44.9

[1]Excludes nomadic tribes. [2]1991. [3]1994. [4]1986. [5]Septicemia only. [6]Diabetes mellitus only. [7]Cerebrovascular disease and heart disease only. [8]Chronic obstructive pulmonary diseases, pneumonia, and influenza only. [9]1991–92 average. [10]Under 21 years of age. [11]21–29 years of age. [12]1993. [13]1989. [14]1988. [15]1992. [16]Includes nutritional disorders. [17]1990–95. [18]Accidents only. [19]1990. [20]Includes benign neoplasms. [21]1981. [22]Rates based on about 75 percent of total deaths. [23]Results based on a sample population of about 100,000. [24]Millions of households. [25]1985. [26]Meningitis only. [27]Ethiopia includes Eritrea. [28]1987. [29]First marriages only. [30]Bronchitis, pneumonia, and influenza. [31]Muslims only.

expectation of life at birth (latest year)		nuptiality, family, and family planning															country
		marriages			age at marriage (latest)						families (F), households (H) (latest)						
					groom (percent)			bride (percent)			families (households)		children		induced abortions		
male	female	year	total number	rate per 1,000 population	19 and under	20–29	30 and over	19 and under	20–29	30 and over	total ('000)	size	number under age 15	percent legitimate	number	ratio per 100 live births	
71.1	75.8	1993	1,223	6.3	...	...	...	...	...	...	H 41	H 3.7	H 2.1	51.6	...	...	Netherlands Antilles
69.0	76.0	1993	896	5.0	0.5[28]	54.5[28]	45.0[28]	10.2[28]	61.9[28]	27.9[28]	...	H 4.1	...	48.1	...	...	New Caledonia
72.9	78.7	1994	21,858	6.2	0.8	50.6	48.6	3.2	60.8	36.0	H 1,178	H 2.9	H 0.7	63.3	11,725	20.4	New Zealand
60.7	66.4	1991	13,122	3.3	18.1[10, 25]	—81.9[25, 36]—		48.2[10, 25]	—51.8[25, 36]—		...	H 6.9	...	...	...	...	Nicaragua
44.9	48.1	...	...	...	...	...	...	...	...	...	H 1,130	H 6.4	...	...	...	...	Niger
48.8	52.0	...	...	...	...	...	...	...	...	...	H 14,441	H 5.0	...	...	...	...	Nigeria
59.0	64.0	1987	685	31.2	2.5	50.2	47.3	5.7	70.4	23.9	H 7	H 4.6	H 1.5	53.9	...	...	Northern Mariana Islands
74.2	80.3	1993	19,464	4.5	0.6[15]	53.7[15]	45.7[15]	3.2[15]	67.6[15]	29.2[15]	F 1,983	F 2.2	F 0.4	55.6	15,164	25.2	Norway
69.8	72.7	...	...	...	...	...	...	...	...	...	H 350	H 3.7	...	...	...	...	Oman
62.0	64.0	...	...	...	...	...	...	...	...	...	...	H 6.3	...	...	...	...	Pakistan
69.1	73.0	...	...	...	...	...	...	...	...	...	...	...	...	...	...	...	Palau
70.8	75.0	1993	13,280	5.2	2.7[15]	52.4[15]	43.8[15]	12.3[15]	55.2[15]	31.1[15]	H 524	H 4.4	H 1.5	25.5	...	...	Panama
56.0	58.0	...	...	...	...	...	...	...	...	...	H 674	H 4.6	...	...	...	...	Papua New Guinea
65.0	69.4	1987	17,741	4.5	3.8	64.4	31.8	34.0	46.5	19.5	H 868	H 4.7	1.9	68.7	...	...	Paraguay
65.2	70.0	1988	90,973	4.4	5.5[39]	60.4[39]	34.1[39]	25.9[39]	51.4[39]	22.6[39]	H 3,099	H 5.1	...	57.8	...	...	Peru
63.6	68.8	1991	445,526	14.0	5.5	68.1	26.4	19.5	64.3	16.2	F 9,566	F 5.7	F 2.4	93.9	2,315	...	Philippines
66.7	75.7	1991	233,206	6.1	4.4	76.6	19.0	21.8	65.0	13.2	F 9,435	F 3.6	F 0.9	95.0	30,878	5.7	Poland
70.8	78.0	1993	68,176	6.9	4.0	79.0	17.0	18.0	71.0	11.0	H 2,954	H 3.8	H 0.8	85.5	...	...	Portugal
69.6	78.5	1993	33,262	12.6	10.1	54.7	35.2	21.1	50.1	28.8	H 1,005	H 3.6	H 1.0	63.2	...	...	Puerto Rico
69.7	74.2	1992	1,578	3.0	4.8	71.7	23.5	34.0	56.9	9.1	H 61	H 6.4	...	...	...	...	Qatar
71.0	77.0	1993	3,503	5.5	1.2[19]	65.2[19]	33.6[19]	12.5[19]	66.8[19]	20.7[19]	H 158	H 3.8	H 1.1	46.0	4,302	31.7	Réunion
66.5	72.4	1993	161,600	7.1	3.3[15]	77.2[15]	19.5[15]	31.0[15]	57.1[15]	11.9[15]	H 7,115	H 3.1	...	...	691,863	265.7	Romania
57.3	71.1	1994	1,080,600	7.4	9.7	79.4	10.9	41.0	51.6	7.4	H 40,426	H 3.2	H 0.8	85.4	6,084,122	339.0	Russia
45.8	48.9	1982	14,313	2.6	...	...	...	...	...	...	H 1,509	H 4.7	2.3	94.9	...	...	Rwanda
63.0	69.0	...	...	...	...	...	...	...	...	...	H 12	H 3.7	H 1.4	19.2	...	...	St. Kitts and Nevis
67.0	72.0	1992	136	3.0	0.0[13]	34.4[13]	61.8[13]	3.5[13]	45.1[13]	51.4[13]	H 33	H 4.0	H 2.0	14.2	...	...	St. Lucia
71.0	74.0	1992	404	3.7	1.0	37.0	62.0	4.8	46.3	48.9	H 27	H 3.9	H 2.0	...	...	...	St. Vincent and the Grenadines
77.2	85.3	1989	169	7.4	0.6	75.1	24.3	5.3	85.3	9.5	H 9	H 2.7	H 0.1	05.2	...	...	San Marino
01.5	05.2	...	...	...	...	...	...	...	...	...	...	...	...	9.8	...	...	São Tomé and Príncipe
68.9	72.3	...	...	...	...	...	...	...	...	...	H 1,513	H 6.6	...	...	...	...	Saudi Arabia
54.0	56.0	...	...	...	...	...	...	...	...	...	...	H 8.8	...	...	...	...	Senegal
69.0	74.3	1994	937	12.7	2.0	45.8	42.2	11.2	51.5	29.6	H 13	H 4.8	H 1.9	27.2	387	22.8	Seychelles
37.5	40.6	...	...	...	...	...	...	...	...	...	H 749	H 4.7	...	...	...	...	Sierra Leone
74.0	79.0	1994	24,654	8.4	0.6	56.3	43.1	3.7	74.9	21.4	H 510	H 3.9	H 1.3	...	17,073	34.5	Singapore
66.6	75.4	1992	33,880	6.4	8.3[2]	77.5[2]	14.2[2]	35.9[2]	55.0[2]	9.1[2]	H 1,778	H 3.0	H 0.7	00.2	45,919	01.5	Slovakia
69.4	77.3	1993	9,022	4.5	0.8	66.3	32.9	8.8	71.8	19.4	H 641	H 3.1	H 0.6	...	13,263	66.4	Slovenia
69.0	73.0	...	...	...	...	...	...	...	...	...	F 41	F 5.6	F 2.3	...	...	...	Solomon Islands
45.4	48.6	...	...	...	...	...	...	...	...	...	...	H 4.9	...	...	...	...	Somalia
62.0	68.0	1993	120,159	3.0	...	...	...	...	...	...	8,688	H 4.6	...	75.9	...	...	South Africa
74.6	80.5	1993	196,304	5.0	1.8[2]	71.5[2]	26.7[2]	8.2[2]	76.7[2]	15.1[2]	F 10,005	F 3.5	...	92.0	...	...	Spain
69.5	74.2	1992	152,154	8.7	0.6	67.0	32.4	15.7	70.9	13.4	H 2,721	H 6.2	H 1.9	94.0	...	...	Sri Lanka
53.4	55.2	...	...	...	...	...	...	...	...	...	H 3,471	H 5.3	...	...	...	...	Sudan, The
67.8	72.8	1991	1,974	4.6	...	...	...	...	...	...	...	H 3.9	...	...	...	...	Suriname
55.2	59.8	...	...	...	...	...	...	...	...	...	H 122	H 5.7	...	...	1,145	...	Swaziland
74.8	80.5	1992	37,173	4.3	0.4	40.8	52.8	2.2	53.2	37.3	H 3,670	H 2.2	H 0.5	50.5	34,849	28.4	Sweden
74.7	81.4	1993	43,257	6.2	0.2	50.0	49.8	2.3	64.3	33.4	H 3,250	H 2.2	0.4	93.7	...	...	Switzerland
65.2	69.2	1988	101,946	7.5	...	...	...	...	...	...	F 1,151	H 6.2	F 2.4	...	...	...	Syria
71.6	77.6	1990	143,886	7.1	1.5	62.3	36.2	6.0	77.7	16.3	H 5,485	H 3.8	H 1.0	97.7	...	...	Taiwan
65.7	71.5	1993	53,946	9.6	2.1	86.8	11.1	39.0	54.3	6.7	H 799	H 6.1	H 2.7	93.0	54,494	27.2	Tajikistan
40.9	44.2	...	...	...	...	...	...	...	...	...	H 3,435	H 5.1	H 2.3	...	...	...	Tanzania
66.0	71.0	1992	449,913	8.3	...	...				...	H 10,110	H 6.0	H 1.3	...	...	...	Thailand
55.3	59.6	...	...	...	...	...	...	...	...		H 479	H 5.6	...	...	...	...	Togo
65.5	70.2	1992	806	8.2	...	...	...	...	...	...	F 15	F 6.1	F 2.7	80.6	...	...	Tonga
68.0	73.2	1993	7,012	5.6	5.9[2]	61.0[2]	33.1[2]	25.5[2]	52.6[2]	21.9[2]	H 301	H 4.1	H 1.3	...	9	—	Trinidad and Tobago
66.9	68.7	1992	64,694	7.7	0.4[13]	63.6[13]	36.0[13]	21.5[13]	66.8[13]	11.7[13]	H 1,703	H 5.1	H 1.9	99.8	23,300	10.9	Tunisia
69.0	73.0	1991	459,624	8.0	8.5[14]	75.9[14]	15.6[14]	36.1[14]	56.5[14]	7.4[14]	...	H 4.5	...	...	...	...	Turkey
61.4	68.6	1993	42,106	10.7	3.0[13]	87.4[13]	9.6[13]	16.1[13]	77.1[13]	6.8[13]	H 598	H 5.6	H 2.4	96.5	39,068	31.3	Turkmenistan
67.2	64.0	...	...	...	...	...	...	...	...	...	H 1	H 6.4	H 2.2	82.2	...	...	Tuvalu
43.6	46.2	...	...	...	...	...	...	...	...	...	H 2,766	H 4.8	...	...	...	...	Uganda
65.3	74.7	1993	427,882	8.2	7.0[15]	70.5[15]	22.5[15]	37.3[15]	44.2[15]	18.5[15]	H 14,507	H 3.2	H 0.8	89.2	957,022	159.5	Ukraine
72.9	75.3	...	...	...	...	...	...	...	...	...	H 247	H 6.8	...	...	...	...	United Arab Emirates
73.2	78.6	1991	349,739	6.1	1.6	58.1	40.3	5.8	63.9	30.3	H 21,672	H 2.7	H 1.7	69.1	171,260	21.9	United Kingdom
72.0	78.9	1993	2,334,000	9.0	4.5[14]	54.1[14]	41.4[14]	11.8[14]	55.7[14]	32.5[14]	H 96,391	H 2.6	F 1.0	70.5	1,354,000	35.5	United States
70.9	77.5	1992	54,754	6.2	7.2[19]	59.8[19]	33.0[19]	23.6[19]	52.3[19]	24.1[19]	H 863	H 3.3	H 0.9	73.8	...	...	Uruguay
65.1	71.8	1993	225,451	10.3	2.3	87.4	10.3	37.9	55.2	6.9	H 3,415	H 5.5	H 2.4	95.8	226,276	33.8	Uzbekistan
65.0	68.0	1989	49,460	34.0	...	...	...	...	...	...	H 28	H 5.1	H 2.2	...	113	2.4	Vanuatu
70.1	76.0	1992	108,955	5.4	10.7[2]	61.3[2]	28.0[2]	30.4[2]	51.7[2]	17.9[2]	H 2,707	H 5.3	H 2.2	47.0	...	...	Venezuela
64.0	68.0	...	...	...	...	...	...	...	...	...	H 12,958[44]	H 4.8[44]	H 1.9[44]	...	...	...	Vietnam
66.7	70.7	1987	1,906	18.0	4.5	50.9	44.6	1.0	38.4	60.6	H 32	H 3.1	H 1.0	38.4	...	...	Virgin Islands (U.S.)
68.0	71.0	...	...	...	...	...	...	...	...	...	...	...	...	...	...	...	West Bank
45.3	47.6	...	...	...	...	...	...	...	...	...	...	...	...	...	...	...	Western Sahara
63.5	65.5	1993	759	4.7	0.5	51.0	48.5	8.0	65.0	27.0	F 20	F 7.8	F 3.8	43.5	...	...	Western Samoa
53.3	55.5	...	...	...	...	...	...	...	...	...	H 1,848	H 5.6	...	...	...	...	Yemen
68.6	74.4	1993	...	5.9	2.4[15]	66.7[15]	30.9[15]	22.4[15]	60.6[15]	17.0[15]	H 2,870	H 3.6	H 0.9	...	...	...	Yugoslavia
50.4	53.7	...	...	...	...	...	...	...	...	...	...	H 6.0	...	...	...	...	Zaire
48.0	49.7	...	...	...	...	...	...	...	...	...	H 1,370	H 4.4	H 2.1	...	...	...	Zambia
52.4	55.1	...	...	...	...	...	...	...	...	...	H 2,166	H 4.8	1.1	95.8	...	...	Zimbabwe

[32]Projected rates based on about 10 percent of total deaths. [33]Average annual rates for the period. [34]Includes Aruba. [35]Projected rates based on about 45 percent of total deaths. [36]Over 21 years of age. [37]Projected rates based on about 70 percent of total deaths. [38]Reporting areas only (constituting about 50 percent of the total population). [39]1982. [40]Includes all deaths associated with alcoholism. [41]Projected rates based on about 35 percent of total deaths. [42]Of which AIDS, 14.3. [43]Registered events only. [44]Private households only.

National product and accounts

This table furnishes, for most of the countries of the world, breakdowns of (1) gross national product (GNP)—its global and per capita values, purchasing power parity (PPP), and growth rates (1985–93), (2) principal industrial and accounting components of gross domestic product (GDP), and (3) principal elements of each country's balance of payments, including international goods trade, invisibles, and tourism payments.

Measures of national output. The two most commonly used measures of national output (except for the accounting systems of centrally planned economies) are GDP and GNP. Each of these measures represents an aggregate value of goods and services produced by a specific country. The GDP, the more basic of these, is a measure of the total value of goods and services produced entirely within a given country. The GNP, the more comprehensive value, is composed of both domestic production (GDP) and the net income from current (short-term) transactions with other countries. When the income received from other countries is greater than payments to them, a country's GNP is greater than its GDP. In theory, if all national accounts could be equilibrated, the global summation of GDP would equal GNP.

In the first section of the table, data are provided for the nominal and real GNP. ("Nominal" refers to value in current prices for the year indicated and is distinguished from a "real" valuation, which is one adjusted to eliminate the effect of recent inflation [most often] or, occasionally, of deflation between two given dates.) Both the total and per capita values of this product are denominated in U.S. dollars for ease of comparison, as is a new value for GNP per capita adjusted for purchasing power parity. The latter is a concept that provides a better approximation of the ability of equivalent values of two (or more) national currencies to purchase comparable quantities of goods and services in their respective domestic markets and may differ substantially from two otherwise equal GNP per capita values based solely on currency exchange rates. Beside these are given figures for average annual growth of total and per capita real GNP. GNP per capita provides a rough measure of annual national income per person, but values should be compared cautiously, as they are subject to a number of distortions, notably of exchange rate, but also of purchasing power parity and in the existence of elements of national production that do not enter the monetary economy in such a way as to be visible to fiscal authorities (*e.g.,* food, clothing, or housing produced and consumed within families or communal groups or services exchanged).

In a decreasing number of countries with centrally planned economies, the conventional concept for the aggregated national income/product is net material product (NMP), which includes only material goods and "productive" services. These NMP accounts are not directly comparable to the GDP values presented in this table for market economies. The GDP value is more comprehensive and includes a number of sectors (especially personal and financial services) excluded from the NMP value. Estimated GNPs have been supplied for most countries (including the centrally planned), based either on the country's own, or on external, analysis.

The internal structure of the national product. GDP/GNP values allow comparison of the relative size of national economies, but further information is provided when these aggregates are analyzed according to

National product and accounts

country	gross national product (GNP), 1993						origin of gross domestic product (GDP) by economic sector, 1992 (%)									
	nominal, ('000,000 U.S.$)	per capita		average annual growth rates, 1993			primary		secondary			tertiary				
		nominal (U.S.$)	purchasing power parity (PPP; U.S.$)	real GNP (%)	population (%)	real GNP per capita (%)	agriculture	mining	manufacturing	construction	public utilities	transp., communications	trade	financial svcs.	other svcs.	government
Afghanistan	4,956	280	...	...	2.5	...	52[1]	2	26[1,2]	7[1]	2	4[1]	9[1]		—2[1]—	
Albania	1,167	340	...	−5.2	1.8	−7.0	40[3]	4		—13[3,4]—		—		—47[3]—		
Algeria	44,347	1,650	4,390	0.4	2.6	−2.2	12	26	10	12	1		—26—			13
American Samoa	128[7]	2,600[7]	...	...	3.8	...	...	...	...	...	...	...	...	...	...	...
Andorra	760[6]	14,000[6]	...	...	4.6	...	...	...	...	...	...	...	...	...	...	...
Angola	7,210	700	...	2.0	2.9	−0.9	10[7]	58[7]	3[7]	2[7]	—	2[7]	6[7]	1[7]	—18[7]—	
Antigua and Barbuda	425	6,390	...	3.1	0.7	2.4	4	2	3	10	4	20	23	15	7	17
Argentina	244,013	7,290	9,130	2.6	1.2	1.4	6	2	22	5	2	5	15	17	—26—	
Armenia	2,471	660	2,080	−10.3	1.4	−11.7	40	2	46[2]	5	2	2	6		—1—	
Aruba	1,200	17,400	...	...	0.4	...	...	...	...	...	...	...	...	...	...	...
Australia	309,967	17,510	18,490	2.6	1.5	1.1	3	4	15	7	3	7	17	24	17	4
Austria	183,530	23,120	18,800	2.8	0.7	2.1	2	4	26[4]	8	3	6	16	17	4	14
Azerbaijan	5,424	730	2,230	−8.0	1.4	−9.4	33[9]	2	48[2,9]	10[9]	2	3[9]	1[9]		—5[9]—	
Bahamas, The	3,059	11,500	16,820	1.6	1.8	−0.2	3	4	3[4]	3	3	7	23	20	17	6
Bahrain	4,283	7,870	13,480	2.1	3.1	−1.0	1	18	17	6	2	13	11	17	5	20
Bangladesh	25,882	220	1,290	4.0	2.2	1.8	33	—	9	6	2	12	8	2	23	5
Barbados	1,620	6,240	10,940	−0.1	0.3	−0.4	5	1	6	3	3	8	26	14	3	15
Belarus	29,290	2,840	6,360	0.2	0.4	−0.2	29[9]	2	44[2,9]	12[9]	2	5[9]	6[9]		—4[9]—	
Belgium	213,435	21,210	18,490	2.7	0.3	2.4	2[3]	—	23[3]	5[3]	3[3]	8[3]	14[3]	20[3]	17[3]	10[3]
Belize	499	2,440	...	8.3	2.6	5.7	20	1	15	7	2	14	18	10	7	9
Benin	2,189	420	1,630	2.1	3.2	−1.1	39[7]	4[7]	4[7]	6[7]	1[7]	18[7]	19[7]	—1[7]—		8[7]
Bermuda	1,713	28,510	...	...	1.3	...	...	...	...	...	...	...	...	...	...	...
Bhutan	253	170	...	6.7	2.2	4.5	41	3	9	7	7	7	7	7	—9—	
Bolivia	5,472	770	2,400	3.7	2.3	1.4	17[3]	8[3]	16[3]	5[3]	1[3]	11[3]	10[3]	9[3]	—16[3]—	
Bosnia and Herzegovina	14,000[7]	3,200[7]	...	...	0.1	...	11[5,11]	4	58[4,5,11]	7[5,11]	1[5,11]	6[5,11]	14[5,11]		—3[5,11]—	
Botswana	3,630	2,590	4,650	9.1	3.4	5.7	5	37	5	5	2	4	15	5	3	20
Brazil	471,978	3,020	5,470	1.3	1.9	−0.6	11	2	23	7	4	6	7[12]	25	14[12]	10
Brunei	5,688	20,760	...	...	3.2	...	3	4	42[4]	5	1	5	12	7	—28—	
Bulgaria	9,773	1,160	3,730	−3.6	−0.8	−2.8	11	3	39[3]	5	3	6	8		—32—	
Burkina Faso	2,928	300	800	2.8	2.8	0.0	31	1	15	6	1	4	15	2	—22—	
Burundi	1,102	180	660	3.5	2.9	0.6	51[7]	1[7]	12[7]	4[7]	1[7]	3[7]	11[7]	—2[7]—		15[7]
Cambodia	1,940	200	...	...	3.2	...	...	...	...	...	...	...	...	...	...	...
Cameroon	9,663	770	2,060	−4.3	3.0	−7.3	24[7]	13[7]	14[7]	5[7]	1[7]	6[7]	25[7]	—2[7]—		10[7]
Canada	574,884	20,670	20,410	1.7	1.3	0.4	2	4	18	7	4	9	12	16	23	7
Cape Verde	347	870	1,830	4.7	2.6	2.1	21[7]	—	6[7]	20[7]	3[7]	12[7]	28[7]	—1[7]—		9[7]
Central African Republic	1,263	390	1,060	−0.3	2.7	−3.0	43[7]	3[7]	7[7]	3[7]	1[7]	5[7]	27[7]	—1[7]—		12[7]
Chad	1,248	200	710	3.0	2.5	0.5	44[7]	—	9[7]	2[7]	1[7]	2[7]	31[7]	—1[7]—		10[7]
Chile	42,454	3,070	8,380	7.7	1.6	6.1	8	8	18	5	3	8	16		—33—	
China	581,109	490	2,120	7.9	1.4	6.5	21[3]	2	45[2,3]	7[3]	2	6[3]	6[3]		—15[3]—	
Colombia	50,119	1,400	5,630	3.9	1.6	2.3	16	8	20	5	3	10	11		—28—	
Comoros	272	520	1,320	1.5	3.7	−2.2	40	...	4	6	2	4	26		—18—	
Congo	2,318	920	2,430	1.4	3.3	−1.9	15[7]	21[7]	9[7]	1[7]	2[7]	11[7]	13[7]	—10[7]—		17[7]
Costa Rica	7,041	2,160	5,580	5.3	2.7	2.6	15[3]	—	19[3]	2[3]	4[3]	6[3]	21[3]	11[3]	7[3]	14[3]
Côte d'Ivoire	8,397	630	1,420	−1.4	3.8	−5.2	34[3]	—	6[3]	2[3]	6[3]	8[3]	7[3]	—9[3]—		13[3]
Croatia	21,800[6]	4,500[6]	...	...	0.4	...	14	2	44[2]	7	1	9	20	3	—1—	
Cuba	12,753	1,170	...	...	1.0	...	16[5,13]	4[5,13]	39[5,13]	9[5,13]	3[5,13]	8[5,13]	20[5,13]		—15[5,13,14]—	
Cyprus[15]	7,539	10,380	15,470	6.3	1.1	5.2	6	—	14	10	2	8	21	16	6	12
Czech Republic	28,192	2,730	7,700	−2.0	0.0	−2.0	6[7]	2	44[2,7]	6[7]	2	4[7]	10[7]	10[7]	5[7]	7[7]
Denmark	137,610	26,510	18,940	1.3	0.2	1.1	4	1	19	6	2	9	14	20	6	22
Djibouti	448	780	...	...	4.9	...	3[7]	—	5[7]	6[7]	5[7]	13[7]	35[7]	—3[7]—		29[7]
Dominica	193	2,680	...	4.5	−0.3	4.8	23	1	7	8	3	18	14	16	1	18
Dominican Republic	8,039	1,080	3,240	2.2	1.9	0.3	16	3	18	10	2	10	15	12	5	10
Ecuador	13,217	1,170	4,260	3.2	2.4	0.8	15	9	20	4	—	11	21	10	5	6
Egypt	36,679	660	3,530	3.0	2.3	0.7	17[3]	10[3]	17[3]	4[3]	2[3]	11[3]	18[3]	5[3]	—7[3]—	
El Salvador	7,233	1,320	2.360	3.0	1.8	1.2	10	—	19	3	2	5	35	8	10	7

their industrial sectors of origin, component kinds of expenditure, and cost components.

The distribution of GDP for ten industrial sectors is aggregated into three major industrial groups:

1. The primary sector, composed of agriculture (including forestry and fishing) and mineral production (including fossil fuels).
2. The secondary sector, composed of manufacturing, construction, and public utilities.
3. The tertiary sector, which includes transportation and communications, trade (wholesale and retail), restaurants and hotels, financial services (including banking, real estate, insurance, and business services), other services (community, social, and personal), and government services.

Percentages in this section of the table may not add to 100 because the value of each economic sector is calculated as a percentage of the total GDP, which may contain adjustments such as import duties and bank service charges that are not distributed by sector.

There are three major domestic components of GDP expenditure: private consumption (analyzed in greater detail in the "Household budgets and consumption" table), government spending, and gross domestic investment. The fourth, nondomestic, component of GDP expenditure is net foreign trade; values are given for both exports (a positive value) and imports (a negative value, representing obligations to other countries). The sum of these five percentages, excluding statistical discrepancies and rounding, should be 100% of the GDP.

The structure of GDP as accounted by cost components here comprises four general categories: indirect taxes (excise or value-added taxes), net of subsidies; consumption of fixed capital (depreciation); and two income categories: (a) compensation of employees (salaries, wages, etc.) and (b) net operating surplus ("profits," interests, rent, etc.).

Balance of payments (external account transactions). The external account records the sum (net) of all economic transactions of a current nature between one country and the rest of the world. The account shows a country's net of overseas receipts and obligations, including not only the trade of goods and merchandise but also such invisible items as services, interest and dividends, short- and long-term investments, tourism, transfers to or from overseas residents, etc. Each transaction gives rise either to a foreign claim for payment, recorded as a deficit (*e.g.,* from imports, capital outflows), or a foreign obligation to pay, recorded as a surplus (*e.g.,* from exports, capital inflows) or a domestic claim on another country. Any international transaction automatically creates a deficit in the balance of payments of one country and a surplus in that of another. Values are given in U.S. dollars for comparability.

Tourist trade. Net income or expenditure from tourism (in U.S. dollars for comparability) is often a significant element in a country's balance of payments. Receipts from foreign nationals reflect payments for goods and services from foreign currency resources by tourists in the given country. Expenditures by nationals abroad are also payments for goods and services, but in this case made by the residents of the given country as tourists abroad.

gross domestic product (GDP) by type of expenditure, 1992(%)					cost components of gross domestic product (GDP), 1992 (%)				balance of payments, 1993 (current external transactions; '000,000 U.S.$)			tourist trade, 1993 ('000,000 U.S.$)		country
consumption		gross domestic invest-ment	foreign trade		indirect taxes net of subsides	consump-tion of fixed capital	compen-sation of employ-ees	net operating surplus	net transfers		current balance of payments	receipts from foreign nationals	expendi-tures by nationals abroad	
private	govern-ment		exports	imports					goods, merchan-dise	invisibles				
...	...	...	...	...	...	...	...	...	...	...	...	1[1]	1[1]	Afghanistan
—170[3]—		10[3]	12[3]	−92[3]	...	13[1]	62[1]	25[1]	...	...	...	8	5	Albania
53	17	29	27	−26	18[5]	8[5]	39[5]	35[5]	2,002	−1,641	361	55	163[6]	Algeria
...	...	...	...	...	...	...	...	...	...	...	...	10[7]	...	American Samoa
...	...	...	...	...	...	...	...	...	...	...	...	...	...	Andorra
61[7]	20[7]	8[7]	29[7]	−26[7]	7[1]	8	39[1]	54[1,8]	...	...	...	20	75[6]	Angola
48	18	35	91	−92	15	—85—			−229	209	−20	372	23[6]	Antigua and Barbuda
—85—		17	7	−8	...	...	...	...	−2,428	−5,024	−7,452	3,614	2,445	Argentina
91[3]	22[3]	14[3]	−27[3]	...	...	...	...	...	...	...	...	...	...	Armenia
...	...	...	...	...	...	...	...	...	−311	388	77	464	57	Aruba
63	18	19	10	−19	11	15	50	23	−123	−10,246	−10,369	4,655	4,100	Australia
55	18	25	39	−38	13	12	53	21	−7,825	6,950	−875	13,566	8,180	Austria
54[3]	20[3]	14[3]	—12[3]—		...	...	...	...	...	...	...	...	...	Azerbaijan
74	15	21	46	−55	14	8	52	34	−824	751	−73	1,304	195	Bahamas, The
36[1]	26[1]	31[1]	119[1]	−102[1]	3[1]	16[1]	47[1]	35[1]	−313[6]	−680[6]	−993[6]	177[6]	141[6]	Bahrain
79	14	13	11	−17	7	—93—			−1,283	1,480	197	15	153	Bangladesh
67	19	16	47	−50	...	...	...	...	−359	423	64	502	41[8]	Barbados
51	15	32	60	−58	12	17	42	30	...	...	...	...	...	Belarus
63	15	19	70	67	9	10	55	26	3,933[10]	8,655[10]	12,588[10]	4,017	6,363	Belgium
60	18	30	60	−68	15	6	—78—		−119	70	49	73	21	Belize
85[3]	11[3]	15[3]	22[3]	−33[3]	4[5]	8	20[5]	70[5,9]	−239	187	−52	38	13	Benin
71	13	14	59	−56	...	...	...	...	−480	486	6	505	139	Bermuda
59	19	47	— −25 —		3	9	—88—		−31	43	12	3	...	Bhutan
81[3]	13[3]	15[3]	17[3]	−26[3]	...	...	...	...	−432[6]	−101[6]	−533[6]	115	151	Bolivia
...	...	...	...	...	...	...	...	...	...	...	...	...	...	Bosnia and Herzegovina
46[7]	33[7]	24[7]	44[7]	−47[7]	...	...	...	...	180	−50	130	79[7]	40[7]	Botswana
60	16	20	10	−7	12[1]	—88[1]—			13,072	−13,709	−637	1,449	1,842	Brazil
...	...	...	...	...	...	...	...	...	...	...	...	32[5]	...	Brunei
78	10	21	— −9 —		8	13	51	27	...	...	...	307	257	Bulgaria
83	16	21	11	−31	4	8	27	69[8]	−367	249	−118	8	35	Burkina Faso
83	16	22	9	−29	11[1]	5[1]	22[1]	62[1]	−98	72	−26	3	20	Burundi
...	...	...	...	...	...	...	...	...	...	...	...	48	4	Cambodia
69	14	16	15	−14	...	...	...	...	217	−959	−742	47	225	Cameroon
61	22	18	26	−27	12	12	58	17	7,612	−31,481	−23,869	5,897	10,629	Canada
89	12	42	11	−54	...	...	...	...	−148	138	−10	...	...	Cape Verde
89[3]	10[3]	9[3]	15[3]	−23[3]	...	...	...	...	−42[6]	−15[6]	−57[6]	9[1]	41[1]	Central African Republic
88	23	10	12	−33	...	...	...	...	−66	−18	−84	23	12	Chad
64	10	24	31	−29	...	...	...	...	−982	−1,114	−2,096	824	568	Chile
51[3]	9[3]	41[3]	24[3]	−25[3]	...	...	...	...	−10,654	−955	−11,609	4,683	812[6]	China
70	11	17	18	−16	10	8	39	51[8]	1,233[6]	−321[6]	912[6]	705[6]	641[6]	Colombia
92[7]	23[7]	10[7]	9[7]	−34[7]	...	...	...	...	−30	−9	−39	8[6]	6[6]	Comoros
73	14	15	40	−42	14[5]	19[5]	32[5]	35[5]	617	−1,125	−508	2	81	Congo
60	16	29	38	−43	13[7]	3[3]	47[7]	37[7]	−666	196	−470	577	267	Costa Rica
66[3]	18[3]	9[3]	34[3]	−27[3]	...	...	...	...	1,072	−2,301	1,229	64	199	Côte d'Ivoire
...	...	...	...	...	11[1]	13[1]	62[1]	14[1]	...	...	...	...	...	Croatia
95[5,9]	9[5,9]	18[5,9]	— −21[5,9] —		...	...	...	...	...	...	...	720	...	Cuba
66	14	28	51	−56	8	11	—81—		−2,087[6]	1,845[6]	−242[6]	1,396	133	Cyprus[15]
55[3]	23[3]	18[3]	57[3]	−53[3]	...	...	...	...	...	...	...	...	...	Czech Republic
52	26	15	36	−29	14	9	55	23	7,812	−3,101	4,711	3,052	3,214	Denmark
80[7]	30[7]	16[7]	41[7]	−67[7]	...	...	...	...	−191	103	−88	13	7	Djibouti
68	20	31	49	−68	16	—84—			−51	28	−23	29	5	Dominica
81	5	21	24	−31	5[7]	6[7]	—89[7]—		−1,607	1,446	−161	1,234	118	Dominican Republic
68	7	21	32	−28	12	8	13	75	578	−938	360	230	190	Ecuador
73	10	20	29	−32	8[7]	—92[7]—			−6,680	8,979	2,299	1,332	1,048	Egypt
89	11	16	11	−28	6	4	—90—		−1,035	917	−118	121	61	El Salvador

National product and accounts

country	gross national product (GNP), 1993						origin of gross domestic product (GDP) by economic sector, 1992 (%)									
	nominal, ('000,000 U.S.$)	per capita		average annual growth rates, 1993			primary		secondary			tertiary				
		nominal (U.S.$)	purchasing power parity (PPP; U.S.$)	real GNP (%)	population (%)	real GNP per capita (%)	agriculture	mining	manufacturing	construction	public utilities	transp., communications	trade	financial svcs.	other svcs.	government
Equatorial Guinea	161	360	...	3.8	2.3	1.5	50[7]	[4]	1[4,7]	3[7]	3[7]	2[7]	7[7]	2[7]	13[7]	14[7]
Eritrea	363	110	...	...	3.5	...	19[16]	—	12[16]	5[16]	1[16]	13[16]	30[16]	4[16]	5[16]	11[16]
Estonia	4,307	3,040	6,860	−5.1	0.1	−5.2	12	2	28	5	4	12	14	4	10	2
Ethiopia	5,190	100	380	1.2	3.0	−1.8	50	[4]	9[4]	3	1	5	10	3	8	7
Faroe Islands	635[6,17]	13,500[6,17]	...	...	0.1	...	15[3]	—	13[3]	4[3]	1[3]	9[3]	11[3]	7[3]	24[3]	16[3]
Fiji	1,626	2,140	5,220	3.4	0.9	2.5	21	—	12	6	1	14	19	13	—17—	
Finland	96,220	18,970	15,230	0.1	0.4	−0.3	5	—	22	6	3	9	12	18	3	22
France	1,289,235	22,360	19,440	2.4	0.6	1.8	3	1	20	5	2	6	15	4	24	16
French Guiana	891[5,17]	8,020[5,17]	...	...	5.9	...	11[5]	[4]	7[4,5]	13[5]	[5]	7[5]	12[5]	12[5]	12[5]	25[5]
French Polynesia	3,007[1,17]	15,260[1,17]	...	...	2.7	...	5[1]	—	7[1]	6[1]	[21]	[18]	23[1]	—29[1,18]—		29[1]
Gabon	5,004	4,050	...	1.0	2.7	−1.7	9[7]	31[7]	7[7]	9[7]	3[7]	6[7]	10[7]	—27—		16[7]
Gambia, The	372	360	1,280	4.7	3.7	1.0	19	—	6	6	1	16	19	6	3	10
Gaza Strip	974[6]	1,390[6]	...	...	4.4	...	17	[4]	12[4]	21	[19]	—49[19]—				
Georgia	3,071	560	1,410	−16.0	0.4	−16.4	52	[4]	18[4]	6	2	4	3	6	5	3
Germany	1,902,995	23,560	20,980	2.5	0.6	1.9	1	3[20]	28	6	[20]	5	8	13	19	10
Ghana	7,036	430	2,160	4.5	3.2	1.3	49	2	9	3	2	4	18	4	2	7
Gibraltar	465	17,090	...	...	0.1	...	...	...	...	...	...	...	...	...	...	...
Greece	76,698	7,390	8,360	1.8	0.5	1.3	15	1	15	7	3	7	13	4	9	19
Greenland	987[1]	17,780[1]	...	...	0.5	...	...	—	...	...	...	...	...	...	...	...
Grenada	219	2,410	...	4.0	−0.1	4.1	14	—	6	10	3	15	21	10	3	22
Guadeloupe	2,900[7,17]	8,400[7,17]	...	...	1.7	...	9[5]	[2]	6[2,5]	7[5]	[2]	[18]	17[5]	—67[5,18]—		
Guam	2,000[7]	14,000[7]	...	...	2.0	...	...	...	...	...	...	...	...	...	...	...
Guatemala	11,092	1,110	3,390	3.7	2.9	0.8	26	—	15	2	3	8	24	9	6	7
Guernsey[21]	1,531[6]	26,000[6]	...	...	1.2	...	...	...	...	...	...	...	...	...	...	...
Guinea	3,170	510	...	4.2	2.9	1.3	23[7]	22[7]	4[7]	6[7]	—	5[7]	29[7]	—27—		9[7]
Guinea-Bissau	233	220	790	3.7	2.1	1.6	44[7]	—	5[7]	7[7]	1[7]	1[7]	27[7]	—6[7]—		8[7]
Guyana	285	350	1,710	0.3	0.3	0.0	50	12	10[22]	3	[22]	6	5	9	2	9
Haiti	2,553	370[4]	...	−1.5	1.9	−3.4	37	—	11	5	1	2	16	7	4	17
Honduras	3,220	580	1,890	3.6	3.0	0.5	22	2	17	7	3	6	11	14	10	7
Hong Kong	104,731	17,860	21,670	6.2	0.9	5.3	—	—	12	5	2	9	25	25	—15—	
Hungary	34,254	3,330	6,260	−0.5	−0.5	0.0	7	[4]	23[4]	5	4	7	16	9	—15—	
Iceland	6,236	23,620	17,160	1.3	1.2	0.1	17[7]	—	12[7]	9[7]	4[7]	8[7]	14[7]	18[7]	6[7]	15[7]
India	262,810	290	1,250	5.1	2.1	3.0	32	2	17	6	2	8	13	8	6	6
Indonesia	136,991	730	3,140	6.6	1.8	4.8	19	13	21	6	1	7	17	7	3	7
Iran	141,240	2,200	...	...	3.6	...	23	9	14	4	1	8	17	12	2	10
Iraq	29,250	1,500	...	...	3.2	...	28[7]	—	4[7]	3[7]	—	13[7]	20[7]	16[7]	—24[7]—	
Ireland	44,906	12,580	11,850	4.8	0.0	4.8	9	[23]	39[23]	[23]	[23]	—18—		—28—		7
Isle of Man	904[7]	13,050[7]	...	...	1.0	...	2[7]	—	12[7]	8[7]	3[7]	9[7]	[24]	27[7]	33[7,24]	6[7]
Israel	72,662	13,760	14,890	5.2	2.9	2.3	3	[4]	22[4]	8	2	8	10	25	4	23
Italy	1,134,980	19,620	18,070	2.1	0.2	1.9	3	[4]	20[4]	6	5	6	18	13	14	13
Jamaica	3,362	1,390	3,000	3.9	0.8	3.1	8	9	20	13	3	8	25	12	5	6
Japan	3,926,668	31,450	21,090	4.0	0.4	3.6	2	—	31	9	4	6	14[12]	16	19[12]	3
Jersey	2,884[7]	34,200[7]	...	...	1.0	...	5[1]	—	—21[1]—			—93[1]—				
Jordan	4,893	1,190	4,010	0.0	5.9	−5.9	7	4	15	5	3	15	10	19	4	20
Kazakhstan	26,490	1,540	3,770	−3.6	1.0	−4.6	21	[4]	28[4]	5	1	6	4	14	5	1
Kenya	6,743	270	1,310	3.3	3.0	0.3	29[3]	—	10[3]	6[3]	1[3]	8[3]	14[3]	17[3]	1[3]	15[3]
Kiribati	54	710	...	0.7	2.0	−1.3	24	—	2	5	2	15	14	7	—26—	
Korea, North	22,310	970	...	...	1.9	...	...	...	...	...	...	...	...	...	...	...
Korea, South	338,062	7,670	9,810	9.1	1.0	8.1	8	—	27	15	2	7	10	17	7	8
Kuwait	34,120	23,350	...	−2.1	−2.9	0.8	—	42	14	2	−1	2	8	3	—30—	
Kyrgyzstan	3,752	830	2,420	−0.5	1.6	−2.1	37	[2]	34[2]	3	[2]	3	5	4	4	9
Laos	1,295	290	...	5.0	2.9	2.1	58	—	13	3	1	5	7	8	—5—	
Latvia	5,257	2,030	5,170	−4.6	−0.1	−4.5	16	—	26	5	1	17	14	6	2	6
Lebanon	6,020	2,150	...	...	2.3	...	9	5[6]	13	3	[6]	4	28	17	11	10
Lesotho	1,254	660	1,800	3.4	2.6	0.8	9	—	13	23	2	2	9	10	10	7
Liberia	1,260	450	...	...	0.9	...	34[5]	10[5]	7[5]	2[5]	2[5]	7[5]	5[5]	12[5]	3[5]	12[5]
Libya	26,550	5,310	...	...	3.6	...	8[7]	26[7]	8[7]	12[7]	2[7]	6[7]	9[7]	11[7]	7[7]	11[7]
Liechtenstein	978[7]	33,510[7]	...	...	1.4	...	...	...	...	...	...	...	...	...	...	...
Lithuania	4,891	1,310	3,160	−5.7	0.7	−6.4	26	[4]	19[4]	9	9	13	14	1	10	8
Luxembourg	14,233	35,850	29,510	3.7	1.0	2.7	1[7]	—	24[7]	7[7]	2[7]	7[7]	16[7]	14[7]	15[7]	15[7]
Macau	5,834[17]	15,030[17]	...	...	3.2	...	...	...	...	...	...	...	...	...	...	...
Macedonia	1,709	780	...	...	1.0	...	18	—	12	1	2	16	11	2	17	6
Madagascar	3,039	240	700	1.4	3.1	−1.7	33[7]	—	12[7]	1[7]	2[7]	16[7]	11[7]	2[7]	17[7]	6[7]
Malawi	2,034	220	780	3.7	3.3	0.4	28	...	15	4	3	6	13	12	5	16
Malaysia	60,061	3,160	8,630	8.1	2.4	5.7	16[3]	8[3]	30[3]	4[3]	2[3]	7[3]	12[3]	11[3]	2[3]	10[3]
Maldives	194	820	...	...	3.3	...	24	2	6[22]	9	[22]	6	18	—36—		
Mali	2,744	300	530	−1.5	2.8	−4.3	42[3]	2[3]	9[3]	4[3,25]	[25]	5[3]	17[3]	—7[3]—		8[3]
Malta	2,628	7,280	...	...	0.7	...	3[7]	[26]	26[7]	4[7,26]	[27]	6[7]	14[7]	14[7]	9[7]	23[7,27]
Marshall Islands	85[17]	1,640[17]	...	...	3.9	...	...	...	...	...	...	...	...	...	...	...
Martinique	3,300[7,17]	9,500[7,17]	...	...	1.0	...	6[5]	[4]	7[4,5]	5[5]	3[5]	6[5]	19[5]	9[5]	18[5]	26[5]
Mauritania	1,087	510	1,590	2.6	2.7	−0.1	26	11	9	—6—		6	—14—		6	12
Mauritius	3,309	2,980	12,450	6.9	1.1	5.8	10	—	23	7	2	12	17	12	5	10
Mayotte	54[17]	600[17]	...	...	5.7	...	...	...	...	...	...	...	...	...	...	...
Mexico	324,951	3,750	7,100	2.7	1.8	0.9	7[3]	3[3]	22[3]	5[3]	2[3]	7[3]	26[3]	11[3]	—17[3]—	
Micronesia	116	980	...	...	2.4	...	...	...	...	...	...	...	...	...	...	...
Moldova	5,160	1,180	3,210	−4.9	0.5	−5.4	43[9]	[2]	33[2,9]	9[9]	[2]	5[9]	9[9]	—1[9]—		
Monaco	475[7]	16,000[7]	...	...	0.9	...	...	...	...	...	...	...	...	...	...	...
Mongolia	943	400	...	2.5	2.8	−0.3	36[9]	[2]	39[2,9]	2[9]	[2]	5[9]	15[9]	—3[9]—		
Morocco	27,645	1,030	3,270	3.3	2.4	0.9	14[3]	2[3]	18[3]	5[3]	8[3]	7[3]	21[3]	...	13[3]	13[3]
Mozambique	1,375	80	380	4.5	2.6	1.9	39[7]	—	25[7]	13[7]	4[7]	10[7]	5[7]	—	—37—	
Myanmar (Burma)	9,812	220	...	...	2.2	...	59	1	7	2	—	2	22	—	—6—	
Namibia	2,594	1,660	3,930	5.3	3.0	2.3	11[7]	32[7]	4[7]	2[7]	1[7]	7[7]	11[7]	7[7]	5[7]	20[7]
Nauru	90[5]	10,000[5]	...	...	2.0	...	...	...	...	...	...	...	...	...	...	...
Nepal	3,174	160	1,150	4.4	2.6	1.8	46	—	8	8	1	7	6	9	—8—	
Netherlands, The	316,404	20,710	18,050	2.7	0.7	2.0	4	3	20	6	2	7	16	—46—		

gross domestic product (GDP) by type of expenditure, 1992 (%)					cost components of gross domestic product (GDP), 1992 (%)				balance of payments, 1993 (current external transactions; '000,000 U.S.$)			tourist trade, 1993 ('000,000 U.S.$)		country
consumption		gross domestic investment	foreign trade		indirect taxes net of subsides	consumption of fixed capital	compensation of employees	net operating surplus	net transfers		current balance of payments	receipts from foreign nationals	expenditures by nationals abroad	
private	government		exports	imports					goods, merchandise	invisibles				
76[7]	14[7]	16[7]	28[7]	−35[7]	...	...	...	...	−24[7]	−1[7]	−25[7]	...	...	Equatorial Guinea
...	...	...	...	...	...	...	...	...	...	...	...	...	...	Eritrea
59	12	26	55	−54	9	4	42	44	−97	135	38	51	26	Estonia
87	10	9	5	−11	...	...	...	...	−507	453	−54	20	10[6]	Ethiopia
53[5]	25[5]	19[5]	34[5]	−31[5]	...	...	...	...	...	...	...	...	...	Faroe Islands
66	19	13	55	−53	11[5]	7[5]	41[5]	41[5]	−231	218	−13	236	39	Fiji
57	25	17	27	−26	12	17	57	14	6,392	−7,372	−980	1,239	1,617	Finland
60	19	20	23	−21	12	13	53	22	6,997	3,204	10,201	23,410	12,800	France
68[5]	36[5]	46[5]	71[5]	−120[5]	10[5]	[8]	65[5]	25[5, 8]	...	...	...	...	...	French Guiana
60[1]	40[1]	21[1]	9[1]	−31[1]	...	...	...	...	...	...	...	182	...	French Polynesia
47	15	27	39	−28	18[5]	14[5]	35[5]	34[5]	1,305	−1,574	−269	5	132	Gabon
74[3]	18[3]	20[3]	53[3]	−65[3]	18[7]	10[7]	—72[7]—		−31[6]	68[6]	37[6]	26	13[6]	Gambia, The
149	16	41	19	−84	...	...	...	...	...	...	...	...	...	Gaza Strip
89[3]	9[3]	32[3]	36[3]	−66[3]	...	...	...	...	...	...	...	...	...	Georgia
54	18	26	33	−31	11	13	55	21	45,290	−60,050	−14,760	10,509	37,514	Germany
85	13	13	16	−27	...	...	...	...	−470[6]	92[6]	−378[6]	206	17[6]	Ghana
...	...	...	...	...	...	...	...	...	...	...	...	82[6]	...	Gibraltar
72[3]	19[3]	19[3]	23[3]	−33[3]	15	9	37	39	−10,557	9,810	−747	3,293	1,003	Greece
...	...	...	...	...	...	...	...	...	...	...	...	...	...	Greenland
66	20	35	39	−59	18		—82—		−91	63	−28	45	4[6]	Grenada
89[5]	32[5]	30[5]	6[5]	−57[5]	12[5]	[8]	72[5]	16[5, 8]	...	...	...	370	...	Guadeloupe
...	...	...	...	...	...	...	...	...	...	...	...	950	...	Guam
85	6	18	18	−27	6[1]	2[1]	—92[1]—		−1,021	319	−702	265	116	Guatemala
...	...	...	...	...	...	...	...	...	...	...	...	146	...	Guernsey[21]
78	10	18	24	−30	...	...	...	...	−22	92	70	6	28	Guinea
111	11	27	8	−56	...	...	...	...	−38	9	−29	...	...	Guinea-Bissau
51[3]	13[3]	52[3]	91[3]	−107[3]	14		—86—		...	...	...	36	...	Guyana
—97—		8	7	−12	10[1]	2[1]	—88[1]—		−185	107	−78	46	33[7]	Haiti
67	12	26	32	−36	11[1]	7[1]	43[1]	39[1]	−98	−158	−256	32	39	Honduras
60	9	29	143	−142	5[1]	0	50[1]	45[1, 8]	...	...	...	7,562	...	Hong Kong
69	12	20	33	−34	13[7]	8[7]	59[7]	20[7]	−4,021	−241	−4,262	1,181	741	Hungary
63	20	17	30	−31	18	13	53	16	181	−186	−5	132	264	Iceland
61	11	25	—3—		7	7	—86—		−6,110[1]	−716[1]	−6,826[1]	1,487	393[1]	India
52	10	36	29	−27	7	5	—88—		8,231	−6,215	2,016	3,988	1,539	Indonesia
60	10	34	14	−18	2[1]	15[1]	—83[1]—		−3,406[6]	−3,098[6]	−6,504[6]	39	1,109[6]	Iran
48[7]	35[7]	19[7]	3[7]	−5[7]	−7[7]	10[7]	45[7]	52[7]	...	...	...	55[1]	...	Iraq
59	16	15	62	−52	11	10	51	29	8,172	−4,526	3,646	1,639	1,256	Ireland
...	...	...	...	...	...	...	...	...	...	...	...	...	...	Isle of Man
61	28	24	31	−45	18	14	48	22	−5,607	4,234	−1,373	2,110	2,313	Israel
63	18	19	18	−18	9	12	45	34	32,825	−21,763	11,062	20,521	13,053	Italy
60	9	29	70	−68	15[5]	8[5]	44[5]	33[5]	−814	588	−226	942	64	Jamaica
57	9	31	10	−8	7	16	56	20	141,570	−10,060	131,510	3,557	26,860	Japan
...	...	...	...	...	...	...	...	...	...	...	...	526[1]	...	Jersey
76	23	35	52	−85	15	11	37	38	−1,899	1,270	−629	563	345	Jordan
62[3]	28[3]	31[3]	— −11[3] —		...	...	...	...	−414	−24	−438	...	...	Kazakhstan
66	16	17	27	−27	14	[8]	36	50[8]	−307	460	153	413	48	Kenya
70[5]	45[5]	31[5]	22[5]	−70[5]	...	...	...	...	...	...	...	1	2[7]	Kiribati
...	...	...	...	...	...	...	...	...	...	...	...	...	...	Korea, North
54	11	37	29	−30	12	10	47	31	1,860	−1,476	384	3,510	4,105	Korea, South
55	41	19	43	−57	...	...	...	...	3,499	−1,087	2,412	83	1,888	Kuwait
51	10	54	34	−46	—	16[5]	50[5]	34[5]	...	...	...	...	...	Kyrgyzstan
...	...	...	...	...	...	...	...	...	...	...	...	...	...	Laos
39	12	41	80	−73	6	1	37	55	...	...	...	...	...	Latvia
110[1]	44[1]	10[1]	32[1]	−96[1]	...	...	...	...	...	...	...	...	...	Lebanon
131	19	70	19	−139	21		—79—		−778	800	22	17	7	Lesotho
58[1]	13[1]	10[1]	42[1]	−23[1]	...	...	...	...	...	...	...	...	...	Liberia
34[7]	27[7]	22[7]	46[7]	−28[7]	...	...	...	...	3,777	−1,576[1]	2,201[1]	5	154[6]	Libya
...	...	...	...	...	...	...	...	...	...	...	...	...	...	Liechtenstein
68	13	10	32	−23	10	2	39	50	305[6]	6[6]	311[6]	...	...	Lithuania
56	17	30	89	−93	16	11	66	8	[10]	[10]	[10]	290[1]	...	Luxembourg
30[3]	8[3]	31[3]	74[3]	−43[3]	...	...	...	...	...	...	...	2,500	71	Macau
...	...	...	...	...	...	...	...	...	...	...	...	11[6]	...	Macedonia
89	8	11	17	−25	...	...	...	...	−138[6]	2[6]	−136[6]	41	37[6]	Madagascar
80	19	19	22	−39	9		—91—		—	−96	−96	13[7]	13[1]	Malaŵi
51	13	34	78	−76	14		—86—		3,183	−5,649	−2,466	1,876	1,960	Malaysia
49[1]	22[1]	19[1]	62[1]	−53[1]	...	...	...	...	−139	91	−48	146	29	Maldives
83	14	18	12	−27	...	...	...	...	−120	17	−103	11	61	Mali
61	19	28	92[1]	−99	12[7]	5[7]	44[7]	39[7]	−602	534	−68	653	211	Malta
...	...	...	...	...	4[7]	4[7]	70[7]	22[7]	...	...	...	3	...	Marshall Islands
84[5]	30[5]	25[5]	8[5]	−47[5]	11[5]	[8]	70[5]	19[5, 8]	...	...	...	332	...	Martinique
54	15	18	35	−22	...	...	...	...	−55[6]	−62[6]	−117[6]	15[1]	31[1]	Mauritania
63	11	29	62	−65	16[7]	[8]	40[7]	44[7, 8]	−254	160	−94	301	128	Mauritius
47[1]	92[1]	3[1]	— −42[1] —		...	...	...	...	...	...	...	...	...	Mayotte
72	10	23	13	−18	10	11	27	53	−18,891	−4,500	−23,391	6,167	5,562	Mexico
...	...	...	...	...	...	...	...	...	...	...	...	...	...	Micronesia
—104[3]—		7[3]	31[3]	−42[3]	...	...	...	...	−37[6]	2[6]	−35[6]	...	...	Moldova
...	...	...	...	...	...	...	...	...	...	...	...	...	...	Monaco
66[3]	18[3]	19[3]	63[3]	−66[3]	[28]	22[1]	39[1]	40[1, 28]	−807	−31[7]	−111[7]	...	...	Mongolia
65	16	24	23	−28	...	...	...	...	−2,380	1,855	−525	1,243	245	Morocco
68	19	64	24	−75	...	...	...	...	−659[6]	278[6]	−381[6]	...	...	Mozambique
—87—		14	1	−2	3	4	43	49	...	...	...	19	1[7]	Myanmar (Burma)
63	36	11	58	−69	15	5	50	30	110[6]	32[6]	142[6]	91[6]	81[6]	Namibia
...	...	...	...	...	...	...	...	...	...	...	...	...	...	Nauru
81	8	21	16	−26	7		—93—		−462	239	−223	157	93	Nepal
60	14	21	52	−48	10	12	53	25	12,915	−3,544	9,371	4,690	8,974	Netherlands, The

National product and accounts

country	gross national product (GNP), 1993						origin of gross domestic product (GDP) by economic sector, 1992 (%)									
	nominal, ('000,000 U.S.$)	per capita		average annual growth rates, 1993			primary		secondary			tertiary				
		nominal (U.S.$)	purchasing power parity (PPP; U.S.$)	real GNP (%)	population (%)	real GNP per capita (%)	agriculture	mining	manufacturing	construction	public utilities	transp., communications	trade	financial svcs.	other svcs.	government
Netherlands Antilles	1,800[17]	9,700[17]	...	...	0.9	...	...	...	...	...	...	...	...	...	...	...
New Caledonia	1,000[7]	6,000[7]	...	...	2.0	...	2[1]	4[1]	13[1]	6[1]	3[1]	6[1]	23[1]	—20[1]—		25[1]
New Zealand	44,674	12,900	15,390	1.0	0.8	0.2	7[7]	1[7]	17[7]	4[7]	3[7]	8[7]	16[7]	23[7]	3[7]	12[7]
Nicaragua	1,421	360	2,070	−3.6	2.6	−6.2	24	1	22	3	3	5	18	3	9	11
Niger	2,313	270	810	1.1	3.2	−2.1	37[7]	5[7]	7[7]	2[7]	2[7]	4[7]	18[7]	—22[7]—		
Nigeria	32,988	310	1,480	6.1	2.9	3.2	31[7]	38[7]	6[7]	2[7]	—	2[7]	13[7]	6[7]	—	3[7]
Northern Mariana Is.	541[6]	12,080[6]	...	...	6.4	...	...	...	...	...	...	...	...	...	...	...
Norway	113,527	26,340	19,130	1.0	0.5	0.5	3[7]	15[7]	13[7]	4[7]	4[7]	9[7]	11[7]	9[7]	10[7]	16[7]
Oman	9,631	5,600	10,720	5.1	3.9	1.2	4	43	4	4	2	4	14	—10—		17
Pakistan	53,250	430	2,110	4.6	3.1	1.5	22	1	15	4	3	9	14	7	7	7
Palau	...	...	...	...	...	...	...	...	...	...	...	...	...	...	...	...
Panama	6,621	2,580	5,940	1.3	2.0	−0.7	11	—	9	5	4	25	12	15	9	13
Papua New Guinea	4,637	1,120	2,470	3.4	2.3	1.1	26	20	9	5	2	7	10	1	—21—	
Paraguay	6,995	1,500	3,490	4.2	2.9	1.3	24	—	17	6	3	4	30	2	—13—	
Peru	34,030	1,490	3,130	−1.4	2.1	−3.5	14[3]	10[3]	23[3]	7[3]	2[3]	7[3]	17[3]	13[3]	—8[3]—	
Philippines	54,609	830	2,660	3.9	2.3	1.6	22	1	24	5	3	6	14	4	—22—	
Poland	87,315	2,270	5,010	−1.4	0.4	−1.8	7	[4]	38[4]	9	2	6	14	—22—		
Portugal	77,749	7,890	9,890	4.1	−0.6	4.7	6[1]	[4]	29[1,4]	8[1]	3[1]	6[1]	17[1]	9[1]	8[1]	13[1]
Puerto Rico	25,317	7,020	...	2.6	0.8	1.8	1	[26]	39	2[26]	[29]	8[29]	15	13	10	11
Qatar	7,871	15,140	22,910	4.6	5.3	−0.7	1	36	13	4	1	3	7	11	—25—	
Réunion	6,225[6,17]	9,980[6,17]	...	...	1.5	...	6[1]	...	12[1]	8[1]	7[1]	—67[1]—				
Romania	25,427	1,120	2,910	−6.5	0.0	−6.5	19	[2]	45[2]	4	[2]	6	13	5	4	8
Russia	348,413	2,350	5,240	−4.6	0.4	−5.0	16[7]	[2]	36[2,7]	9[7]	[2]	7[7]	—26[7]—			
Rwanda	1,499	200	640	−0.6	2.9	−3.5	42[7]	—	12[7]	7[7]	—	7[7]	17[7]	1[7]	4[7]	9[7]
St. Kitts	185	4,470	...	4.8	−0.4	5.2	7	—	12	12	2	15	23	12	5	17
St. Lucia	480	3,040	...	6.1	1.8	4.3	13	1	8	8	4	17	25	14	3	13
St. Vincent	233	2,130	...	5.5	0.9	4.6	19	—	10	10	5	20	15	10	2	16
San Marino	370[6,17]	16,000[6,17]	...	...	1.0	...	...	...	...	...	...	...	...	...	...	...
São Tomé and Príncipe	41	330	...	0.6	2.4	−1.8	28	—	7[22]	6	[22]	—27—			—32—	
Saudi Arabia	128,421	7,510	...	3.5	4.4	−0.9	6	36	7	9	—	6	7	6	2	19
Senegal	5,876	730	1,640	2.7	3.0	−0.3	22	1	15	3	2	11	27	—19—		
Seychelles	444	6,370	...	4.9	0.9	4.0	4	[23]	17[23]	[23]	[23]	23	17	8	18	13
Sierra Leone	647	140	770	2.0	2.6	−0.6	27	13	11	1	—	10	20	11	—	5
Singapore	55,372	19,310	20,470	8.0	1.9	6.1	—	—	28	7	2	15	17	26	—10—	
Slovakia	10,145	1,900	6,450	−2.2	0.4	−2.6	6[7]	[2]	53[2,7]	7[7]	[2]	8[7]	10[7]	2[7]	12[7]	3[7]
Slovenia	12,566	6,310	...	...	0.6	...	5	2	30	4	2	7	13	14	4	13
Solomon Islands	261	750	...	5.4	2.9	2.5	31[1]	—	—7[1]—		[29]	8[1,29]	—13[1]—		—23[1]—	
Somalia	1,350	150	...	0.8	3.1	−2.3	65[7]	—	4[7]	4[7]	1[7]	6[7]	9[7]	3[7]	2[7]	6[7]
South Africa	118,057	2,900	...	0.9	2.4	−1.5	4	10	25	3	4	8	14	12	2	16
Spain	533,986	13,650	13,310	3.3	0.2	3.1	4	[2]	23[2]	9	[2]	—58—				
Sri Lanka	10,658	600	3,030	3.9	1.3	2.6	21	1	17	7	2	10	21	6	3	7
Sudan, The	11,172	420	...	2.6	2.8	−0.2	34	—	9	5	2	—39—				11
Suriname	488	1,210	3,670	2.2	0.0	2.2	15	2	11	8	3	6	23	20	1	18
Swaziland	933	1,050	1,690	7.6	3.8	3.8	13[7]	1[7]	27[7]	2[7]	2[7]	5[7]	9[7]	10[7]	2[7]	14[7]
Sweden	216,294	24,830	17,560	0.7	0.6	0.1	2	—	20	7	3	7	11	25	—30—	
Switzerland	254,066	36,410	23,620	1.7	1.0	0.7	3[1]	[4]	24[1,4]	8[1]	2[1]	6[1]	18[1]	21[1]	—20[1]—	
Syria	15,892	1,160	...	1.2	3.3	−2.1	30	13	6	4	—	9	23	4	2	10
Taiwan	226,243	10,850	...	8.3	1.2	7.1	4	1	33	5	3	6	16	19	7	11
Tajikistan	2,686	470	1,430	−5.0	2.8	−7.8	15[9]	[2]	60[2,9]	11[9]	[2]	4[9]	7[9]	—2[9]—		
Tanzania	2,521	100	...	4.4	3.0	1.4	58[7]	1[7]	5[7]	3[7]	2[7]	9[7]	15[7]	6[7]	4[7]	4[7]
Thailand	120,235	2,040	6,390	10.0	1.6	8.4	12	2	28	7	2	7	17	9	13	4
Togo	1,325	330	1,040	0.2	3.6	−3.4	35[7]	10[7]	7[7]	4[7]	4[7]	7[7]	17[7]	4[7]	3[7]	9[7]
Tonga	150	1,610	...	1.2	−0.3	1.5	36[3]	...	4[3]	4[3]	...	13[3]	13[3]	—11[3]—		
Trinidad and Tobago	4,776	3,740	8,850	−1.4	1.3	−2.7	3	23	9	8	2	9	15	12	7	12
Tunisia	15,332	1,780	5,070	4.3	2.1	2.2	18	6	17	4	2	7	25		—13—	
Turkey	126,330	2,120	5,550	5.1	2.1	3.0	15[3]	1[3]	19[3]	7[3]	3[3]	13[3]	18[3]	7[3]	4[3]	12[3]
Turkmenistan	4,797	1,230	...	0.9	2.5	−1.6	46[7,9]	[2]	20[2,7,9]	18[7,9]	[2]	7[7,9]	—9[7,9]—			
Tuvalu	6	650	...	...	1.8	...	24[1]	3[1]	3[1]	15[1]	2[1]	4[1]	15[1]	9[1]	—26[1]—	
Uganda	3,486	190	840	5.1	3.2	1.9	51[7]	—	4[7]	6[7]	1[7]	8[7]	12[7]	7[7]	7[7]	3[7]
Ukraine	99,677	1,910	4,030	−3.6	0.3	−3.9	29[7,9]	[2]	43[2,7,9]	14[7,9]	[2]	4[7,9]	6[7,9]	—4[7,9]—		
United Arab Emirates	38,720	22,470	23,390	3.7	3.2	0.5	2	41	8	9	2	6	10	11	3	11
United Kingdom	1,042,700	17,970	17,750	1.6	0.3	1.3	2	2	22	6	3	8	14	24	6	17
United States	6,387,686	24,750	24,750	2.1	0.9	1.2	2[5]	2[5]	19[5]	5[5]	3[5]	6[5]	16[5]	17[5]	19[5]	12[5]
Uruguay	12,314	3,910	6,350	3.6	0.6	3.0	11	—	22	5	2	6	13	10	26	10
Uzbekistan	21,100	960	2,580	0.8	2.4	−1.6	36	[2]	29[2]	13	[2]	—22—				
Vanuatu	198	1,230	...	3.0	2.8	0.2	21[3]	—	6[3]	5[3]	2[3]	7[3]	31[3]	17[3]	1[3]	12[3]
Venezuela	58,916	2,840	8,130	3.5	2.5	1.0	5	17	21	7	2	5	14	14	6	9
Vietnam	11,997	170	1,040	7.2	2.4	4.8	41[7]	[2]	20[2,7]	3[7]	[2]	4[7]	12[7]	11[7]	—9[7]—	
Virgin Islands (U.S.)	1,246[17,30]	11,740[17,30]	...	...	−1.1	...	...	...	...	...	...	...	...	...	...	...
West Bank	2,518[6]	2,240[6]	...	...	4.2	...	...	...	...	...	...	...	...	...	...	...
Western Sahara	60[7,17]	300[7,17]	...	...	1.9	...	...	...	...	...	...	...	...	...	...	...
Western Samoa	159	980	...	0.4	0.5	−0.1	43[3]	...	12[3]	3[3]	6[3]	3[3]	8[3]	...	10[3]	14[3]
Yemen	6,864	520	...	...	4.4	...	20	5	10	5	1	8	13	6	1	25
Yugoslavia	10,000[17]	1,000[17]	...	...	0.8	...	9	...	45	6	—	3	33	—5—		
Zaire	9,476	230	...	2.5	3.3	−0.8	31[7]	24[7]	1[7]	6[7]	—	1[7]	18[7]	3[7]	7[7]	10[7]
Zambia	3,152	370	1,170	4.9	3.1	1.8	13[7]	15[7]	28[7]	5[7]	1[7]	7[7]	11[7]	11[7]	—9[7]—	
Zimbabwe	5,756	540	1,900	2.0	3.1	−1.1	22	5	30	2	3	7	8	5	10	5

[1]1990. [2]Manufacturing includes mining and public utilities. [3]1993. [4]Manufacturing includes mining. [5]1989. [6]1992. [7]1991. [8]Net operating surplus includes consumption of fixed capital. [9]Net material product (NMP). [10]Data refer to the Belgium-Luxembourg Economic Union (BLEU). [11]Gross material product. [12]Services includes restaurants and hotels. [13]Global social product. [14]Activities in the material sphere not elsewhere specified. [15]Republic of Cyprus only, except GNP section. [16]1994. [17]Gross domestic product (GDP). [18]Services includes transportation,

gross domestic product (GDP) by type of expenditure, 1992 (%): consumption		gross domestic investment	foreign trade		cost components of gross domestic product (GDP), 1992 (%)				balance of payments, 1993 (current external transactions; '000,000 U.S.$): net transfers			tourist trade, 1993 ('000,000 U.S.$)		country
private	government		exports	imports	indirect taxes net of subsides	consumption of fixed capital	compensation of employees	net operating surplus	goods, merchandise	invisibles	current balance of payments	receipts from foreign nationals	expenditures by nationals abroad	
...	...	...	...	...	...	...	...	...	−904	888	−16	721	...	Netherlands Antilles
45[5]	31[5]	20[5]	32[5]	−29[5]	6[5]	11[5]	44[5]	40[5]	...	...	...	95	...	New Caledonia
61	17	19	31	−29	14	9	43	33	1,714	−2,646	−932	1,165	1,003	New Zealand
95	19	17	16	−48	...	...	...	...	−392	−252	−644	30	34	Nicaragua
82[3]	17[3]	6[3]	13[3]	−18[3]	...	...	...	...	−6	−23	−29	16	29	Niger
74	4	11	36	−24	1[7]	5[7]	14[7]	80[7]	4,611[6]	−2,343[6]	2,268[6]	31	234	Nigeria
...	...	...	...	...	...	...	...	...	...	...	...	515	...	Northern Mariana Is.
52	22	18	43	−36	11	15	53	22	8,016	−5,563	2,453	1,849	3,565	Norway
33	39	17	49	−38	[28]	[8]	33	67[8, 28]	1,336	−2,405	−1,069	85[6]	47	Oman
70	13	20	17	−20	10	6	—83—		−2,552	−384	−2,936	111	633	Pakistan
...	...	...	...	...	...	...	...	...	...	...	...	...	...	Palau
60	17	23	39	−38	9	8	46	36	−853	855	2	222[6]	120[6]	Panama
58	22	24	45	−49	11[7]	12[7]	37[7]	40[7]	1,370	−816	554	45	42[5]	Papua New Guinea
79	6	23	22	−30	7	8	30	56	−1,019	416	−603	204	138	Paraguay
80	7	17	10	−13	7[7]	4[7]	20[7]	69[7]	−580	−1,220	−1,800	268	304	Peru
75	10	21	29	−34	10	8	35	47	−6,222	2,933	−3,289	2,122	130	Philippines
67	9	24	20	−20	...	...	...	...	−3,316	−2,049	−5,365	4,500	181	Poland
66	19	28	25	−37	13	[8]	46	41	−6,886	7,833	947	4,176	1,846	Portugal
63	14	17	69	−63	5	6	43	47	1,730[7]	−5,131[7]	−3,401[7]	1,629	774	Puerto Rico
31	33	19	51	−34	...	...	...	...	...	...	...	...	...	Qatar
79	29	27	4	−39	11[5]	[8]	60[5]	30[5, 8]	...	...	...	157[6]	...	Réunion
71	6	31	27	−35	—	5	42	53	−1,128	−34	−1,162	197	195	Romania
52[3]	15[3]	26[3]	39[3]	−32[3]	...	...	...	...	−4,300[6]	—	−4,300[6]	...	...	Russia
77	25	15	7	−24	7[5]	8[5]	25[5]	61[5]	−712[6]	87[6]	−85[6]	2	17[6]	Rwanda
56	17	40	62	−76	13	—87—			−57	36	−21	69	5	St. Kitts
72	15	24	67	−77	16	—84—			−144	102	−42	221	21[6]	St. Lucia
68	20	27	54	−68	15	—85—			−80	18	−42	55	4[6]	St. Vincent
...	...	...	...	...	...	...	...	...	...	...	...	...	...	San Marino
75	50	29	—	−54	...	...	...	...	−6[1]	−2[1]	−8[1]	1[1]	2[2]	São Tomé and Príncipe
40	33	24	43	−40	−0.2[5]	[8]	46[5]	54[5, 8]	19,020	−33,238	14,210	1,884[1]	...	Saudi Arabia
80[3]	12[3]	14[3]	22[3]	−28[3]	...	...	...	...	−383	78	−305	173	106	Senegal
51	30	21	46	−48	22[7]	11[7]	38[7]	29[7]	−143[6]	141[6]	−2[6]	116	16[6]	Seychelles
84[3]	11[3]	9[3]	22[3]	−26[3]	8[1]	6[1]	14[1]	73[1]	11[7]	−1[7]	10[7]	18	4	Sierra Leone
43	9	40	—7—		...	...	...	...	−8,065	10,104	2,039	5,793	3,022	Singapore
54	25	25	93	−87	13[7]	14[7]	48[7]	25[7]	...	...	...	390	262	Slovakia
56[3]	23[3]	20[3]	63[3]	−62[3]	12	20	64	4	−154	347	193	734	304	Slovenia
69[5]	31[5]	33[5]	52[5]	−85[5]	...	...	...	...	14[6]	16[6]	−2[6]	6	11[6]	Solomon Islands
75[1]	9[1]	20[1]	1[1]	−5[1]	...	...	...	...	...	...	...	...	...	Somalia
60	20	16	23	−19	10	15	55	20	5,781	−3,976	1,805	1,190	1,598	South Africa
63	17	23	18	−20	9	11	46	34	−15,718	11,078	−4,640	19,425	4,706	Spain
75	10	24	32	−41	14	5	45	36	−742	361	−381	208	121	Sri Lanka
71[7]	18[7]	17[7]	5[7]	−10[7]	...	...	...	...	−597[6]	91[6]	506[6]	3	33[6]	Sudan, The
52	25	23	10	−13	7	11	45	36	60[6]	−57[6]	11[6]	11	11[6]	Suriname
79[5]	20[5]	19[5]	60[5]	−78[5]	...	...	...	...	−125	88	−37	30	17	Swaziland
54	28	17	28	−26	11	14	61	14	7,669	−11,814	−4,057	2,650	4,464	Sweden
58	15	23	36	−33	4	10	64	21	2,237	14,459	16,696	7,001	5,803	Switzerland
72	16	24	26	−38	−4	3	—101—		−322	−285	−607	700	300	Syria
56	17	25	43	−41	11	5	58	26	11,587	−4,873	6,714	2,934	7,585	Taiwan
...	...	...	...	...	...	...	...	...	...	...	...	...	...	Tajikistan
85	11	42	21	−59	17[7]	2[7]	9[7]	72[7]	−838	429	−409	147	102	Tanzania
66	10	40	36	−41	13[7]	9[7]	24[7]	53[7]	−4,146	−2,782	−6,928	5,014	2,092	Thailand
86[3]	17[3]	6[3]	23[3]	−32[3]	...	...	...	...	−34	61	60	18	30	Togo
...	...	...	...	...	...	...	...	...	−38	42	1	10	3	Tonga
59	18	12	11	00	3	10	54	28	524	−422	102	80	115	Trinidad and Tobago
62	16	30	39	−46	12[5]	11[5]	—78[5]—		−2,068	1,156	−912	1,114	203	Tunisia
64	13	22	16	−18	9	5	49	37	−14,162	7,782	−6,380	3,959	934	Turkey
44[3]	23[3]	46[3]	—−13[3]—		...	...	...	...	194[6]	1[6]	195[6]	...	...	Turkmenistan
...	...	...	...	...	...	...	...	...	...	...	...	0.3	...	Tuvalu
89[3]	14[3]	15[3]	5[3]	−23[3]	...	...	...	...	−278	171	−107	50	40	Uganda
80[3]	13[3]	8[3]	17[3]	−18[3]	−5[7]	15[7]	77[7]	13[7]	...	...	...	...	...	Ukraine
45	18	24	69	−57	−1[1]	13[1]	23[1]	66[1]	...	...	...	...	...	United Arab Emirates
64	22	15	24	−25	13	11	57	18	−20,146	2,370	−17,776	13,451	17,431	United Kingdom
69	16	16	11	−11	8	13	60	19	−132,570	28,640	−103,930	56,501	41,260	United States
73	13	14	22	−22	19	[8]	44	37[8]	−387	160	−227	447	129	Uruguay
44[3]	22[3]	29[3]	—5[3]—		...	...	...	...	−61[6]	4[6]	57[6]	...	...	Uzbekistan
63[1]	28[1]	44[1]	46[1]	−77[1]	20[5]	[8]	41[5]	38[5, 8]	−47	46	−1	30	1	Vanuatu
73	9	19	26	−27	4	8	34	54	2,902	−5,125	−2,223	432[6]	−1,428[6]	Venezuela
—84[3]—		21[3]	28[3]	−33[3]	11[5]	7[5]	59[5]	22[5]	...	...	...	85[1]	...	Vietnam
...	...	...	...	...	...	...	...	...	...	...	...	921	...	Virgin Islands (U.S.)
...	...	...	...	...	...	...	...	...	...	...	...	...	...	West Bank
...	...	...	...	...	...	...	...	...	...	...	...	...	...	Western Sahara
...	...	...	...	...	...	...	...	...	−81	42	−39	21	2[6]	Western Samoa
68[3]	29[3]	20[3]	15[3]	−32[3]	9[1]	5[1]	—86[1]—		...	...	...	45	81[5]	Yemen
...	...	...	...	...	...	...	...	...	...	...	...	23	...	Yugoslavia
69	22	7	22	−19	...	...	...	...	600[1]	−1,243[1]	−643[1]	7[1]	16[1]	Zaire
74	15	14	32	−35	7[1]	9[1]	57[1]	26[1]	420[7]	−727[7]	−307[7]	44	56[6]	Zambia
64[3]	19[3]	22[3]	34[3]	−39[3]	14[1]	—86[1]—			122	−238	−116	103	97	Zimbabwe

communications. [19]Services includes public utilities. [20]Mining includes public utilities. [21]Excludes Alderney and Sark. [22]Manufacturing includes public utilities. [23]Manufacturing includes mining, construction, and public utilities. [24]Services includes trade. [25]Construction includes public utilities. [26]Construction includes mining. [27]Government includes public utilities. [28]Net operating surplus includes indirect taxes net of subsidies. [29]Transportation includes public utilities. [30]1987.

Employment and labour

This table provides international comparisons of the world's national labour forces—giving their size; composition by demographic component and employment status; and structure by industry.

The table focuses on the concept of "economically active population," which the International Labour Organisation (ILO) defines as persons of all ages who are either employed or looking for work. In general, "economically active population" does not include students, persons occupied solely in domestic duties, retired persons, persons living entirely on their own means, and persons wholly dependent on others. Persons engaged in illegal economic activities—smugglers, prostitutes, drug dealers, bootleggers, black marketeers, and others—also fall outside the purview of the ILO definition. Countries differ markedly in their treatment, as part of the labour force, of such groups as members of the armed forces, inmates of institutions, the unemployed (both persons seeking their first job and those previously employed), seasonal and international migrant workers, and persons engaged in informal, subsistence, or part-time economic activities. Some countries include all or most of these groups among the economically active, while others may treat the same groups as inactive.

Three principal structural comparisons of the economically active total are given in the first part of the table: (1) participation rate, or the proportion of the economically active who possess some particular characteristic, is given for women and for those of working age (usually ages 15 to 64), (2) activity rate, the proportion of the total population who *are* economically active, is given for both sexes and as a total, and (3) employment status, usually (and here) grouped as employers, self-employed, employees, family workers (usually unpaid), and others.

Each of these measures indicates certain characteristics in a given national labour market; none should be interpreted in isolation, however, as the meaning of each is influenced by a variety of factors—demographic structure and change, social or religious customs, educational opportunity, sexual differentiation in employment patterns, degree of technological development, and the like. Participation and activity rates, for example, may be high in a particular country because it possesses an older population with few children, hence a higher proportion of working age, or because, despite a young population with many below working age, the economy attracts eligible immigrant workers, themselves almost exclusively of working age. At the same time, low activity and participation rates might be characteristic of a country having a young population with poor employment possibilities or of a country with a good job market distorted by the presence of large numbers of "guest" or contract workers who are not part of the domestic labour force. An illiterate woman in a strongly sex-differentiated labour force is likely to begin and end as a family or

Employment and labour

country	year	economically active population										distribution by economic sector			
		total ('000)	participation rate (%)		activity rate (%)			employment status (%)				agriculture, forestry, fishing		manufacturing; mining, quarrying; public utilities	
			female	ages 15–64	total	male	female	employers, self-employed	employees	unpaid family workers	other	number ('000)	% of econ. active	number ('000)	% of econ. active
Afghanistan	1979	3,941	7.9	49.1	30.3	54.2	4.9	...	...	...	...	2,369	60.1	494	12.5
Albania	1994	1,340	47.0[3]	92.0[3, 4]	57.4[3]	60.8[3]	54.0[3]	...	...	...	...	534	39.9	84[5]	6.3[5]
Algeria	1987	5,341	9.2	44.3	23.6	42.4	4.4	16.8	61.7	2.6	18.9	725	13.6	622	11.6
American Samoa	1990	14.2	41.1	52.6[8]	30.4	34.8	25.7	2.1	92.6	0.2	5.1	0.3	2.3	4.8	33.7
Andorra	1989	25	45.6	74.3	55.1	...	...	...	...	...	...	0.3	1.2	2.7	11.0
Angola	1991	4,166	38.4	60.1[10]	40.3	50.4	30.4	...	...	...	...	2,892	69.4	438[11]	10.5[11]
Antigua and Barbuda	1991	26.8	45.6	69.7	45.1	50.9	39.6	12.1	82.8	0.7	4.4	1.0	3.9	1.9	7.3
Argentina	1991	13,202	36.2	56.7[13]	40.5	52.9	28.7	28.0	60.4	5.0	6.6	1,201[14]	12.0[14]	2,136[14]	21.3[14]
Armenia	1993	1,633	...	75.6[16]	43.6	...	...	...	...	...	...	493	30.2	380	23.3
Aruba	1991	31.1	42.5	67.1	46.7	54.5	39.0	7.0	86.4	0.3	6.3	0.2	0.5	2.3	7.3
Australia	1993[18]	8,537	42.0	72.8	49.0	57.0	41.1	14.3	74.2	0.8	10.7	433	5.1	1,358	15.9
Austria	1992[18]	3,679	41.6	69.1	46.7	56.6	37.5	9.8	87.0	3.2	—	253	6.9	1,011	27.5
Azerbaijan	1990	3,242	42.6[20]	71.8[16]	45.4	52.1	38.8	...	...	...	...	...	...	...	...
Bahamas, The	1993	137	47.5	...	51.1	54.8	47.5	76.5[20]	11.1[20]	0.3[20]	12.1[20]	6.4	4.7	6.7	4.9
Bahrain	1991	226	17.5	66.8	44.6	63.5	18.5	5.1	88.5	0.1	6.3	5	2.3	33	14.6
Bangladesh	1989	50,744	41.4	79.9	46.9	53.2	40.2	29.3	9.4	45.2	16.1	32,569	64.2	7,081	14.0
Barbados	1993[18]	126	48.4	77.3[22]	50.2[22]	54.4[22]	46.4[22]	8.8[23]	76.4[23]	0.2[23]	14.6[23]	5.3	4.2	11.3	8.9
Belarus	1993	4,826	...	78.5[16]	46.9	...	...	...	...	...	...	958	19.9	1,425	29.5
Belgium	1992	4,237	42.3	51.5[24]	42.2	49.8	34.9	12.7	72.4	3.4	11.5	95	2.2	788	18.6
Belize	1993	66.1	30.8	55.7[13]	33.1	45.9	20.3	26.2	59.2	4.9	9.8	18.3[25]	31.4[25]	7.0[25]	12.0[25]
Benin	1992	2,085	42.6	73.4	43.0	50.6	35.7	58.4	5.3	30.5	5.8	1,148	55.0	162	7.8
Bermuda	1993	33.4	48.2[26]	63.5[25]	60.2[25]	65.8[25]	55.0[25]	7.7[14]	88.6[14]	0.5[14]	3.2[14]	0.4	1.2	1.7	5.0
Bhutan	...	...	...	...	...	...	...	...	...	...	...	...	...	...	...
Bolivia	1992	2,530	38.2	64.0	39.4	48.7	30.4	41.2	31.5	7.1	20.2	984	38.9	281	11.1
Bosnia and Herzegovina	1990[5]	1,026	36.9	...	22.7	...	...	...	...	...	...	39	3.8	519	50.5
Botswana	1991[18]	441	38.5	59.4	33.3	42.8	24.5	6.5	62.5	17.1	13.9	98	22.1	47	10.7
Brazil	1990[18]	64,468	35.5	63.6[24]	43.8	57.5	30.5	26.3	62.3	7.7	3.7	14,181	22.0	10,217	15.9
Brunei	1991	112	32.9	67.6	43.0	54.6	30.0	3.5	91.4	0.4	4.7	2.2	1.9	11.6	10.4
Bulgaria	1992	3,932	48.4	68.8	46.3	48.7	44.1	...	...	...	...	471	12.0	1,099	27.9
Burkina Faso	1991	4,679	48.7	78.1[10, 27]	50.9	53.5	48.5	...	...	...	...	4,294	91.8	58	1.2
Burundi	1990	2,780	52.6	91.4	52.5	51.2	53.8	62.8	5.1	30.3	1.8	2,574	92.6	37	1.3
Cambodia	1992	3,964	55.7	91.2[28]	43.1	41.2	44.7	...	...	...	...	2,454[14]	74.4[14]	220[11, 14]	6.7[11, 14]
Cameroon	1991	4,740	33.2	58.9[10]	40.0	53.9	26.3	60.2[23]	14.6[23]	18.0[23]	7.1[23]	2,856	60.3	628[11]	13.2[11]
Canada	1993[18]	13,946	45.2	74.9	51.7	57.2	46.3	9.6	89.0	0.5	0.9	481	3.4	2,343	16.8
Cape Verde	1990	121	37.1	64.3	35.3	46.9	24.9	24.7	53.7	2.0	19.6	29.9	24.8	6.8	5.7
Central African Republic	1988	1,187	46.8	78.3	48.2	52.2	44.3	75.3	8.0	8.1	8.6	881	74.2	31	2.6
Chad	1991	2,016	18.2	51.6[10]	35.3	56.5	14.7	...	...	...	...	1,489	73.9	149[11]	7.4[11]
Chile	1993[18]	5,219	32.5	59.8	38.6	53.3	24.6	25.9	66.5	3.1	4.5	825	15.8	954	18.3
China	1987[18]	584,569	44.5	76.8[24]	54.7	59.6	49.7	...	...	...	...	414,740	71.0	95,977	16.4
Colombia	1985	9,558	32.8	49.4[29]	34.3	46.6	22.3	...	...	...	...	2,412[14]	28.5[14]	1,231[14]	14.5[14]
Comoros	1991	215	40.0	57.8[10]	44.4	53.7	35.2	47.6[14]	25.6[14]	— 26.8[14] —		171	79.4	14[11]	6.5[11]
Congo	1984	563	45.6	54.0	29.5	33.0	26.2	64.3	31.4	1.2	3.1	294	52.2	50	8.8
Costa Rica	1993	1,143	29.9	56.5[24]	38.1	53.5	22.7	20.1	72.3	3.4	4.2	257	22.5	223	19.5
Côte d'Ivoire	1991	5,131	34.2	64.1[10]	39.0	50.5	27.0	...	...	...	...	2,815	54.9	560[11]	10.9[11]
Croatia	1991	2,040	42.9	65.2	45.3	53.9	37.4	12.7	73.7	2.0	11.6	341	16.7	571	28.0
Cuba	...	...	...	...	...	...	...	...	...	...	...	...	...	...	...
Cyprus[30, 31]	1992	287	38.7	70.5	46.3	57.0	35.7	18.7	73.1	6.1	2.1	35	12.2	50	17.5
Czech Republic	1991	5,421	47.6	77.9	52.6	56.8	48.7	2.2	88.7	7.6	1.5	628	11.6	2,021	37.3
Denmark	1993	2,910	46.5	79.6[32]	56.2	61.0	51.6	8.4[25]	89.5[25]	1.7[25]	0.4[25]	140	4.8	502	17.3
Djibouti	1991	282	40.8	70.4[10]	61.5	74.1	50.3	...	...	...	...	212	75.2	31[11]	11.0[11]
Dominica	1989	30.6	41.8	62.3	37.5	47.1	29.3	29.2	50.6	1.9	18.3	7.7	25.2	3.6	11.8
Dominican Republic	1981	1,915	28.9	53.6	33.9	48.1	19.7	36.5	51.3	3.3	8.9	420	22.0	243	12.7
Ecuador	1990	3,360	26.4	55.7	34.8	51.5	18.3	45.7	42.5	4.4	7.4	1,036	30.8	404	12.0
Egypt	1991[18]	15,964	23.7	47.9	29.2	44.0	13.8	19.6	58.6	12.2	9.6	4,332	28.3	2,300	15.0
El Salvador	1980[18]	1,593	34.8	62.4	35.4	47.5	24.0	28.2	59.2	10.9	1.7	637	40.0	262	16.4
Equatorial Guinea	1983	103	35.7	66.7	39.2	52.5	26.9	29.0	16.0	29.9	25.1	59.4	57.9	1.8	1.8
Eritrea[34]	...	...	...	...	...	...	...	...	...	...	...	...	...	...	...
Estonia	1989	856	50.0	79.7	54.7	58.5	51.3	...	...	...	...	100	11.7	270	31.5
Ethiopia[34]	1992	23,518	41.1	70.1	41.3	48.5	34.1	58.5[35]	6.5[35]	34.0[35]	1.0[35]	16,101[35]	88.3[35]	312[35]	1.7[35]
Faroe Islands	1977	17.6	27.2	64.0	41.9	58.2	23.9	11.9	86.1	...	2.0	3.3	18.8	3.9	21.9

traditional agricultural worker. Loss of working-age men to war, civil violence, or emigration for job opportunities may also affect the structure of a particular labour market.

The distribution of the economically active population by employment status reveals that a large percentage of economically active persons in some less developed countries falls under the heading "employers, self-employed." This occurs because the countries involved have poor, largely agrarian economies in which the average worker is a farmer who tills his own small plot of land. In countries with well-developed economies, "employees" will usually constitute the largest portion of the economically active.

Caution should be exercised when using the economically active data to make intercountry comparisons, as countries often differ in their choices of classification schemes, definitions, and coverage of groups and in their methods of collection and tabulation of data. The population base containing the economically active population, for example, may range, in developing countries, from age 9 or 10 with no upper limit to, in developed countries, age 18 or 19 upward to a usual retirement age of from 55 to 65, with sometimes a different range for each sex. Data on female labour-force participation, in particular, often lack comparability. In many less developed countries, particularly those dominated by the Islamic faith, a cultural bias favouring traditional roles for women results in the undercounting of economically active women. In other less developed countries, particularly those in which subsistence workers are deemed economically active, the role of women may be overstated.

The second major section of the table provides data on the distribution by economic (also conventionally called industrial) sector of the "economically active population." The data usually include such groups as unpaid family workers, members of the armed forces, and the unemployed, the last distributed by industry as far as possible.

The categorization of industrial sectors is based on the divisions listed in the *International Standard Industrial Classification of All Economic Activities.* The "other" category includes persons whose activities were not adequately defined and the unemployed who were not distributable by industrial sector.

A substantial part of the data presented in this table is summarized from various issues of the ILO's *Year Book of Labour Statistics,* which compiles its statistics both from official publications and from information submitted directly by national census and labour authorities. The editors have supplemented and updated ILO statistical data with information from Britannica's holdings of relevant official publications and from direct correspondence with national authorities.

construction		transportation, communications		trade, hotels, restaurants		finance, real estate		public administration, defense		services		other		country
number ('000)	% of econ. active	number ('000)	% of econ. active	number ('000)	% of econ. active	number ('000)	% of econ. active	number ('000)	% of econ. active	number ('000)	% of econ. active	number ('000)	% of econ. active	
61	1.3	66	1.6	138	3.5	[1]	[1]	[1]	[1]	749[1]	19.0[1]	78[2]	2.0[2]	Afghanistan
33[5]	2.5[5]	19[5]	1.4[5]	3[5]	0.2[5]	3[5]	0.2[5]	16[5]	1.2[5]	145[5]	10.8[5]	505[6]	37.7[6]	Albania
690	12.9	216	4.1	391	7.3	143	2.7	[7]	[7]	1,180[7]	22.1[7]	1,374	25.7	Algeria
1.2	8.3	0.8	5.5	1.8	13.0	0.3	2.1	1.4	10.0	2.8	19.8	0.7[9]	5.1[9]	American Samoa
2.9	11.8	...	...	6.0	24.2	1.3	5.4	2.6	10.3	4.1	16.7	0.1	0.5	Andorra
[11]	[11]	[12]	[12]	[12]	[12]	[12]	[12]	[12]	[12]	836[12]	20.1[12]	—	—	Angola
3.1	11.6	2.4	9.0	8.5	31.9	1.5	5.4	[7]	[7]	6.4[7]	23.9[7]	1.0	7.0	Antigua and Barbuda
1,003[14]	10.0[14]	400[14]	4.6[14]	1,702[14]	17.0[14]	396[14]	3.9[14]	[7]	[7]	2,399[7, 14]	23.9[7, 14]	736[14, 15]	7.3[14, 15]	Argentina
122	7.5	60	3.7	69	4.2	22	1.3	29	1.8	331	20.3	127[17]	7.8[17]	Armenia
3.2	10.4	2.3	7.5	11.0	35.1	2.4	7.8	[7]	[7]	8.6[7]	27.7[7]	1.1[17]	3.5[17]	Aruba
604	7.1	511	6.0	2,062[19]	24.2[19]	886	10.4	[7]	[7]	2,217[7, 19]	26.0[7, 19]	467[15]	5.5[15]	Australia
304	8.3	238	6.5	694	18.9	269	7.3	[7]	[7]	862[7]	23.4[7]	49	1.3	Austria
...	...	...	...	...	...	...	...	...	...	...	...	...	...	Azerbaijan
7.7	5.6	9.1	6.6	36.7	26.8	11.2	8.2	[7]	[7]	40.5[7]	20.6[7]	18.5[17]	13.5[17]	Bahamas, The
27	11.8	14	6.1	30	13.2	17	7.6	41	18.1	43	19.0	16[17]	7.3[17]	Bahrain
661	1.3	1,278	2.5	4,130	8.1	238	0.5	[7]	[7]	3,439[7]	6.8[7]	1,341[21]	2.6[21]	Bangladesh
6.9	5.5	4.5	3.6	14.5	11.5	5.5	4.4	[7]	[7]	38.1[7]	30.2[7]	40.2[17]	31.8[17]	Barbados
415	8.6	338	7.0	366	7.6	98	2.0	76	1.6	943	19.5	207[21]	4.3[21]	Belarus
245	5.8	257	6.1	634	15.0	342	8.1	[7]	[7]	1,393[7]	32.9[7]	484[17]	11.4[17]	Belgium
4.1[25]	7.0[25]	2.9[25]	5.0[25]	10.0[25]	17.2[25]	1.8[25]	3.1[25]	5.4[25]	9.2[25]	6.0[25]	10.3[25]	2.8[25]	4.8[25]	Belize
52	2.5	53	2.5	433	20.7	3	0.1	[7]	[7]	165[7]	7.9[7]	71[21]	3.4[21]	Benin
1.7	5.2	2.3	7.0	10.7	32.1	5.4	16.2	[7]	[7]	11.2[7]	33.4[7]	—	—	Bermuda
...	...	...	...	...	...	...	...	...	...	...	...	...	...	Bhutan
129	5.1	117	4.6	232	9.2	54	2.1	59	2.2	660	10.0	323[15]	12.7[15]	Bolivia
73	7.3	69	6.7	131	12.8	39	3.8	[7]	[7]	155[7]	15.1[7]		—	Bosnia and Herzegovina
58	13.2	11	2.6	35	8.0	13	3.0	[7]	[7]	107[7]	24.2[7]	72[17]	16.2[17]	Botswana
3,823	5.9	2,440	3.6	7,976	12.4	1,716	2.7	[7]	[7]	21,694[7]	33.7[7]	2,367[9]	3.7[9]	Brazil
14.1	12.6	5.4	4.8	15.4	13.8	5.8	5.2	[7]	[7]	52.1[7]	46.6[7]	5.3[17]	4.7[17]	Brunei
207	5.3	248	6.3	401	10.2	38	1.0	[7]	[7]	821[7]	20.9[7]	647[17]	16.4[17]	Bulgaria
11	0.2	1.5	0.3	120	2.6	2	—	[7]	[7]	112[7]	2.4[7]	67[17]	1.4[17]	Burkina Faso
20	0.7	9	0.3	26	0.9	2.0	0.1	[7]	[7]	85[7]	3.1[7]	27[17]	1.0[17]	Burundi
[11]	[11]	[12]	[12]	[12]	[12]	[12]	[12]	[12]	[12]	625[12, 14]	18.9[12, 14]	—	—	Cambodia
[11]	[11]	[12]	[12]	[12]	[12]	[12]	[12]	[12]	[12]	1,256[12]	26.5[12]	—	—	Cameroon
851	6.1	992	7.1	2,391	17.1	817	5.9	[7]	[7]	5,949[7]	42.7[7]	122[9]	0.9[9]	Canada
22.7	18.8	6.1	5.1	12.7	10.6	0.8	0.7	[7]	[7]	17.4[7]	14.4[7]	24.1	20.0	Cape Verde
6	0.5	7	0.6	92	7.8	0.7	0.1	[7]	[7]	70[7]	5.9[7]	100[17]	8.5[17]	Central African Republic
[11]	[11]	[12]	[12]	[12]	[12]	[12]	[12]	[12]	[12]	377[12]	18.7[12]	—	—	Chad
403	7.7	355	6.8	926	17.7	289	5.5	[7]	[7]	1,233[7]	23.6[7]	234[17]	4.5[17]	Chile
13,298	2.3	10,898	1.9	20,785	3.6	1,268	0.2	9,704	1.7	17,414	3.0	487	0.1	China
242[14]	2.9[14]	353[14]	4.2[14]	1,262[14]	14.9[14]	278[14]	3.3[14]	[7]	[7]	1,998[7, 14]	23.6[7, 14]	691[14, 15]	8.2[14, 15]	Colombia
[11]	[11]	[12]	[12]	[12]	[12]	[12]	[12]	[12]	[12]	30[12]	14.1[12]	—	—	Comoros
25	4.5	29	5.1	67	11.8	3	0.5	[7]	[7]	85[7]	15.1[7]	10	2.0	Congo
71	6.2	53	4.7	204	17.8	47	4.2	[7]	[7]	268[7]	23.4[7]	21[15]	1.8[15]	Costa Rica
[11]	[11]	[12]	[12]	[12]	[12]	[12]	[12]	[12]	[12]	1,756[12]	34.2[12]	—	—	Côte d'Ivoire
93	4.5	112	5.5	223	10.9	58	2.8	104	5.1	204	10.0	329[17]	16.1[17]	Croatia
...	...	...	...	...	...	...	...	...	...	...	...	...	...	Cuba
24	8.4	16	5.6	67	23.2	18	6.4	[7]	[7]	56[7]	19.7[7]	20[21]	7.0[21]	Cyprus[30, 31]
412	7.6	366	6.8	544	10.0	86	1.6	238	4.4	957	17.7	169	3.1	Czech Republic
148	5.1	187	6.4	433	14.9	233	8.0	[7]	[7]	944[7]	32.5[7]	322[17]	11.1[17]	Denmark
[11]	[11]	[12]	[12]	[12]	[12]	[12]	[12]	[12]	[12]	39[12]	13.8[12]	—	—	Djibouti
2.6	8.5	1.6	5.2	2.9	9.5	0.7	2.3	[7]	[7]	5.7[7]	18.6[7]	5.4[21]	17.6[21]	Dominica
81	4.3	40	2.1	192	10.0	22	1.2	[7]	[7]	363[7]	18.9[7]	553[15]	28.9[15]	Dominican Republic
197	5.9	131	3.9	477	14.2	81	2.4	[7]	[7]	838[7]	24.9[7]	196[15]	5.8[15]	Ecuador
1,135	7.4	1,085	7.1	1,478	9.7	422	2.8	[7]	[7]	3,074[7]	20.1[7]	1,466[17]	9.6[17]	Egypt
80	5.0	66	4.1	256	16.1	16	1.0	[7]	[7]	250[7]	15.7[7]	27[33]	1.7[33]	El Salvador
1.9	1.9	1.8	1.7	3.1	3.0	0.4	0.4	[7]	[7]	8.4[7]	8.2[7]	25.8[17]	25.2[17]	Equatorial Guinea
...	...	...	...	...	...	...	...	...	...	...	...	...	...	Eritrea[34]
73	8.5	73	8.5	75	8.8	4	0.5	19	2.2	182	21.3	60	7.0	Estonia
46[35]	0.3[35]	77[35]	0.4[35]	696[35]	3.8[35]	15[35]	0.1[35]	[7]	[7]	933[7, 35]	5.1[7, 35]	56[2, 35]	0.3[2, 35]	Ethiopia[34]
2.0	11.1	1.9	11.1	2.1	11.9	0.3	1.9	[7]	[7]	3.5[7]	20.1[7]	0.6	3.2	Faroe Islands

Employment and labour (continued)

country	year	economically active population						employment status (%)				distribution by economic sector			
		total ('000)	participation rate (%)		activity rate (%)							agriculture, forestry, fishing		manufacturing; mining, quarrying; public utilities	
			female	ages 15–64	total	male	female	employers, self-employed	employees	unpaid family workers	other	number ('000)	% of econ. active	number ('000)	% of econ. active
Fiji	1986	241	21.2	56.0	33.7	52.4	14.5	33.6	42.2	16.3	7.9	106	44.1	22	9.0
Finland	1993	2,508	46.9	73.5	49.5	54.0	45.2	12.6	83.7	0.7	3.0	193	7.7	502	20.0
France	1993[18]	25,756	44.7	67.6	44.8	50.8	39.0	10.6	77.8	...	11.6	1,102	4.4	4,585	18.2
French Guiana	1990	48.8	38.2	67.3	42.5	50.5	33.9	10.6	62.7	2.5	24.2	4.2	8.6	3.1	6.4
French Polynesia	1988	75	37.1	64.8	39.9	48.2	30.9	13.0	55.0	4.0	28.0	7.6	10.0	5.4	7.2
Gabon	1991	504	36.9	56.0[10]	43.9	53.9	30.7	...	...	...	...	338	67.1	71[11]	14.1[11]
Gambia, The	1983	326	46.3	78.2	47.3	51.1	43.6	0.5	78.0	14.3	7.1	240	73.7	9	2.9
Gaza Strip	1993	120	2.7	34.2[24]	16.1	32.0	0.9	...	...	...	...	21.1	17.6	12.2[36]	10.1[36]
Georgia	1991	2,514	45.9[20]	90.1[16, 20]	46.4	...	...	...	...	...	...	682	27.1	488	19.4
Germany	1992	40,126	42.6	72.4	49.9	59.2	41.2	7.6	91.1	1.3	—	1,241	3.2	10,978	28.0
Ghana	1984	5,580	51.2	82.5[24]	45.4	44.9	45.8	67.7	15.7	12.2	4.4	3,311	59.3	631	11.3
Gibraltar	1991	14.8	33.4	66.9[24]	53.8	71.9	35.4	6.6[38]	89.7[38]	...	3.6[38]	—	—	1.1	7.5
Greece	1992[18]	4,034	37.0	63.9	40.6	52.7	29.1	32.5	51.6	11.1	4.8	812	20.1	815	20.2
Greenland	1976	21.4	33.4	63.5[24]	43.1	53.0	31.4	12.6	82.5	0.4	4.5	3.2	15.1	3.3	15.3
Grenada	1988	38.9	48.6	72.7[39]	39.9	42.9	37.2	...	...	...	...	5.6	14.3	3.3	8.6
Guadeloupe	1990	172	45.5	66.4	44.5	49.6	39.7	13.2	53.7	2.0	31.1	8.4	4.9	9.6	5.6
Guam	1990	66.1	37.4	75.7[8]	49.7	58.4	39.7	2.4	94.4	0.1	3.1	0.5	0.8	3.5	5.3
Guatemala	1989[18]	2,898	25.5	59.1	33.5	50.8	16.7	32.7	47.6	16.2	3.5	1,416	48.9	405	14.0
Guernsey[40]	1991	30.2	43.2	74.2	51.2	60.6	42.6	13.7	86.3	—	—	2.4	7.8	2.4	7.9
Guinea	1983	1,823	39.4	63.5	39.1	48.7	30.1	36.2	15.6	37.6	10.6	1,424	78.1	27	1.5
Guinea-Bissau	1991	464	40.5	67.1[10]	45.9	56.2	36.1	...	...	...	...	362	78.0	21[11]	4.5[11]
Guyana	1987[41]	270	29.9	60.4	35.7	50.9	21.0	14.3[14]	63.8[14]	1.9[14]	20.0[14]	50[14]	20.4[14]	41[14]	16.8[14]
Haiti	1990	2,679	40.0	64.8	41.1	50.3	32.3	59.1	16.5	10.4	14.0	1,535	57.3	178	6.6
Honduras	1992[18]	1,729	31.2	58.3[24]	34.8	49.0	21.2	36.5	48.7	10.7	4.1	640	37.0	264	15.3
Hong Kong	1993[18]	2,873	36.9	69.3	49.9	62.1	37.4	10.3	86.9	0.8	2.0	18	0.6	620	21.6
Hungary	1993	5,015	48.5	82.8[16]	48.6	52.3	45.3	...	...	...	...	431	8.6	1,304	26.0
Iceland	1994	146	47.3	84.3[43]	54.6	57.3	51.8	...	...	...	...	12.2	8.4	25.8	17.7
India	1991	314,131	28.6	60.7[24, 38]	37.5	51.6	22.3	8.8[38]	16.3[38]	3.6[38]	71.3[38]	191,341	60.9	30,423	9.7
Indonesia	1992	79,451	38.2	67.0	42.9	53.1	32.7	43.2	28.7	25.7	2.4	42,048	52.9	8,816	11.1
Iran	1986	12,855	10.3	46.8	26.0	45.6	5.5	36.9	41.5	3.9	17.7	3,209	25.0	1,584	12.3
Iraq	1988	4,127	12.0	45.3	24.7	42.3	6.1	25.4[44]	59.5[44]	11.4[44]	3.7[44]	477	11.6	439	10.6
Ireland	1991	1,334	32.2	59.7	37.8	51.4	24.3	18.2	77.8	1.4	2.6	155	11.6	246	18.4
Isle of Man	1991	33.2	42.3	73.2	47.6	56.9	38.9	15.8	80.1	—	4.1	1.2	3.7	3.9	11.6
Israel	1993[18]	1,946	42.0	59.3	36.9	43.2	30.7	14.6	74.5	0.8	10.1	65	3.4	410	21.1
Italy	1991[18]	24,245	37.1	65.1[45]	42.5	54.9	30.7	21.6	63.8	3.7	10.9	1,823	7.5	4,958	20.4
Jamaica	1994	1,091	47.3	71.6[26, 46]	43.7	46.1	41.3	32.7	49.5	2.0	15.8	218	20.0	107	9.8
Japan	1993	66,150	40.5	71.3	53.1	64.3	42.2	12.3	78.6	6.3	2.8	3,830	5.8	15,710	23.7
Jersey	1991	47.5	43.2	66.9[24]	56.5	66.1	47.5	12.6	84.0	...	3.4	2.2	4.7	3.8	8.0
Jordan	1988	644	11.4	43.2	22.8	39.3	5.3	22.8[47]	67.2[47]	0.8[47]	9.2[47]	33	5.1	55	8.6
Kazakhstan	1992	7,390	54.0[20]	76.8[16]	43.7	...	...	...	...	...	...	1,794	24.3	1,490	20.2
Kenya	1991	10,260	39.4	64.4[10]	39.0	47.4	30.7	...	...	...	...	7,857	76.6	816[11]	8.0[11]
Kiribati	1990	32.6	46.4	75.6[24]	45.1	48.9	41.4	71.9	25.3	...	2.8	23.1	71.0	0.9	2.8
Korea, North	1985	9,084	46.0	75.3	44.6	48.6	40.6	...	...	...	...	3,726[23]	44.1[23]	2,790[11, 23]	33.0[11, 23]
Korea, South	1993[18]	19,754	39.9	63.7[22]	45.4[22]	54.0[22]	36.6[22]	27.6	59.2	10.4	2.8	2,845	14.4	4,702	23.8
Kuwait	1988	730	24.3	61.5	38.9	53.5	21.0	3.9	94.1	0.1	1.9	9	1.3	69	9.4
Kyrgyzstan	1992	1,836	48.6[20]	78.8[16]	41.2	...	...	...	...	...	...	701	38.2	300	16.3
Laos	1985	2,014	45.3	84.2	48.9	53.1	44.6	...	...	...	...	1,393[14]	75.7[14]	130[11, 14]	7.1[11, 14]
Latvia	1991	1,462	50.0[20]	80.0[20]	55.1[20]	59.3[20]	51.5[20]	—95.5—		—4.5—		248	17.0	371	25.4
Lebanon	1988	904	16.6	44.0	26.5	43.9	8.9	...	...	...	...	132[48]	19.1[48]	131[48]	18.9[48]
Lesotho	1986	504	27.0	44.0	31.6	47.3	16.7	16.8	55.7	20.5	7.0	131	25.9	142	28.2
Liberia	1984	704	41.0	56.3	33.5	39.1	27.8	59.1	21.6	14.4	5.0	481	68.3	31	4.4
Libya	1991	1,169	9.3	37.1[10]	24.8	42.9	4.9	...	...	...	...	129	11.0	372[11]	31.8[11]
Liechtenstein	1994	15.1	38.1	70.0	49.3	62.8	36.5	6.2	91.3	0.1	2.4	0.3	2.2	4.8	32.1
Lithuania	1993	1,808	48.9[20]	79.4[16]	48.5	...	...	...	...	...	...	399	22.1	457	25.3
Luxembourg	1991[49]	168	36.5	62.5	43.5	56.4	31.2	9.2	85.3	1.1	4.4	5	3.2	26	15.8
Macau	1992[18]	173	41.7	62.2	45.4	54.6	36.8	10.5	85.7	1.6	2.2	0.3	0.2	49	28.4
Macedonia	1993	937	...	...	45.2	...	...	...	...	...	...	215	22.9	168	17.9
Madagascar	1991	5,311	39.3	63.9[10]	42.8	52.4	33.0	...	...	...	...	4,043	76.1	632[11]	11.9[11]
Malawi	1987	3,458	51.0	89.4	43.3	43.9	42.8	4.9	16.2	77.6	1.3	2,968	85.8	114	3.3
Malaysia	1990[18]	6,685	35.5	63.5	37.6	48.2	26.9	23.6	66.0	10.4	—	1,738	26.0	1,416	21.2
Maldives	1990	56	19.9	50.2	26.5	41.3	10.8	39.7	49.3	4.5	6.5	14.1	25.0	9.4	16.6
Mali	1987	3,438	37.4	67.4	44.7	57.2	32.7	35.4	5.2	57.6	1.8	2,803	81.5	191	5.6
Malta	1990	132	25.4	47.4[13]	37.2	56.1	18.7	14.1[52]	77.4[52]	...	8.5[52]	3	2.5	38	28.8
Marshall Islands	1988	11.5	30.1	54.1[24]	26.5	37.7	14.8	21.6	58.9	7.1	12.5	2.2	18.7	1.0	9.0
Martinique	1990	165	47.5	68.1	45.9	49.8	42.2	9.5	56.9	1.5	32.1	8.4	5.1	9.7	5.9
Mauritania	1991	638	22.3	45.5[10]	30.8	48.1	13.8	...	...	...	...	410	64.3	70[11]	11.0[11]
Mauritius[53]	1991	463	35.2	68.0	44.5	57.9	31.2	12.2[26]	80.1[26]	1.9[26]	5.9[26]	81	17.5	146	31.5
Mayotte	1991	27.3	29.4	56.4	28.9	39.2	17.7	12.0	42.9	7.3	37.8	3.1	11.4	1.3	4.7
Mexico	1993	33,652	30.9	61.4	38.9	54.6	23.6	30.1	53.8	13.6	2.6	8,843	26.3	5,348	15.9
Micronesia	1990	30.5	29.8[14]	60.6	30.3	...	...	2.7[14]	74.4[14]	0.1[14]	22.7[14]	12.7	41.5	1.6	5.2
Moldova	1992	2,050	50.0[20]	80.2[16]	47.1	...	...	...	...	...	...	749	36.5	415	20.2
Monaco	1990	12.6	39.7	...	42.0	53.2	31.8	17.4	75.1	0.3	7.2	—	0.3	2.7	21.8
Mongolia	1990	694	45.5[55]	82.2[55]	46.9[55]	50.9[55]	42.8[55]	...	...	...	...	192	27.6	123	17.8
Morocco	1982	5,999	19.7	48.9	29.3	47.1	11.6	27.1	40.5	17.6	14.8	2,352	39.2	1,016	16.9
Mozambique	1980	5,671	52.4	87.3[24]	48.6	47.6	49.5	...	...	...	...	4,755	83.8	347	6.1
Myanmar (Burma)	1991–92[18]	16,510	35.3[52]	64.2[52]	40.2[52]	52.4[52]	28.2[52]	...	...	...	...	11,076	67.1	1,220	7.4
Namibia	1991	494	43.6	61.3	35.2	39.9	30.5	17.8	49.1	17.9	15.2	190	38.5	41	8.2
Nauru	1977	2.2	...	...	30.5	...	...	...	...	...	...	...	...	...	...
Nepal	1990	8,585	34.7	82.5[48]	45.4	57.5	32.6	86.2[38]	9.1[38]	2.5[38]	2.2[38]	6,244[38]	91.1[38]	37[38]	0.5[38]
Netherlands, The	1993	6,406	37.6	61.5	42.1	53.1	31.3	9.4	82.1	0.9	7.6	232	3.6	1,117	17.4
Netherlands Antilles	1992	87.8	45.1	68.6	46.3	53.1	40.1	...	...	...	...	0.5	0.6	8.4	9.6
New Caledonia	1989	66	37.5	70.7[45]	40.2	49.1	30.8	16.3	64.3	1.6	17.8	7.8	11.8	6.2	9.3
New Zealand	1993[18]	1,653	43.6	73.0	48.7	55.7	41.9	18.2	71.3	1.0	9.5	158	9.5	270	16.3
Nicaragua	1993	1,490	33.2[25]	51.6[10]	34.7[25]	47.8[25]	22.3[25]	...	...	...	...	430	28.8	183	12.3
Niger	1988[56]	2,316	20.4	55.2	31.9	51.1	13.0	51.4	5.0	40.3	3.3	1,764	76.2	73	3.1

construction		transportation, communications		trade, hotels, restaurants		finance, real estate		public administration, defense		services		other		country
number ('000)	% of econ. active	number ('000)	% of econ. active	number ('000)	% of econ. active	number ('000)	% of econ. active	number ('000)	% of econ. active	number ('000)	% of econ. active	number ('000)	% of econ. active	
12	4.9	13	5.5	26	10.8	6	2.5	[7]	[7]	37[7]	15.2[7]	20[17]	8.2[17]	Fiji
193	7.7	176	7.0	356	14.2	203	8.1	127	5.1	671	26.8	87[33]	3.5[33]	Finland
1,495	5.9	1,401	5.6	3,659	14.5	2,222	8.8	[7]	[7]	7,559[7]	30.1[7]	3,131[17]	12.4[17]	France
4.4	9.1	1.9	3.8	4.2	8.5	1.7	3.5	[7]	[7]	17.5[7]	35.9[7]	11.8[9]	24.2[9]	French Guiana
5.5	7.4	2.8	3.7	10.3	13.7	1.2	1.5	[7]	[7]	21.5[7]	28.6[7]	21.1[17]	28.0[17]	French Polynesia
[11]	[11]	[12]	[12]	[12]	[12]	[12]	[12]	[12]	[12]	95[12]	18.8[12]	—	—	Gabon
4	1.3	8	2.5	17	5.1	5	1.4	8	2.5	9	2.9	25	7.7	Gambia, The
36.4	30.3	7.1	5.9	18.4	15.3	[36]	[36]	[7]	[7]	14.0[7]	11.6[7]	11.1[21, 36]	9.2[21, 36]	Gaza Strip
225	8.9	104	4.1	[37]	[37]	12	0.5	48	1.9	955[37]	38.8[37]	—	—	Georgia
2,603	6.6	2,215	5.7	5,728	14.6	2,905	7.4	[7]	[7]	10,319[7]	26.3[7]	3,205[9]	8.2[9]	Germany
65	1.2	123	2.2	792	14.2	27	0.5	98	1.7	376	6.7	158[9]	2.8[9]	Ghana
2.8	19.0	0.7	4.6	3.0	20.0	1.5	10.1	2.6	17.3	3.2	21.6	—	—	Gibraltar
261	6.5	262	6.5	722	17.9	205	5.1	[7]	[7]	762[7]	18.9[7]	194[33]	4.8[33]	Greece
3.1	14.6	1.8	8.6	2.7	12.6	0.3	1.6	[7]	[7]	6.3[7]	29.5[7]	0.6	2.8	Greenland
3.5	9.1	1.7	4.4	5.4	13.9	0.8	2.0	[7]	[7]	5.9[7]	15.3[7]	12.7[17]	32.5[17]	Grenada
14.0	8.1	7.0	4.0	15.0	8.7	2.8	1.6	[7]	[7]	60.8[7]	35.2[7]	54.9[17]	31.8[17]	Guadeloupe
8.0	12.1	4.5	6.8	11.5	17.5	3.9	6.0	17.7	26.7	14.5	21.9	2.0[9]	3.1[9]	Guam
114	3.9	72	2.5	375	12.9	38	1.3	[7]	[7]	417[7]	14.4[7]	60[17]	2.1[17]	Guatemala
3.2	10.5	1.4	4.5	7.4	24.6	5.8	19.3	1.9	6.4	5.3	17.7	0.4	1.3	Guernsey[40]
9	0.5	29	1.6	37	2.0	4	0.2	[7]	[7]	138[7]	7.5[7]	156	8.5	Guinea
[11]	[11]	[12]	[12]	[12]	[12]	[12]	[12]	[12]	[12]	81[12]	17.5[12]	—	—	Guinea-Bissau
7[14]	2.8[14]	9[14]	3.8[14]	15[14]	6.2[14]	3[14]	1.2[14]	30[14]	12.1[14]	29[14]	11.9[14]	61[14, 17]	24.7[14, 17]	Guyana
28	1.0	21	0.8	353	13.2	5	0.2	[7]	[7]	155[7]	5.8[7]	404[17]	15.1[17]	Haiti
72	4.2	52	3.0	282	16.3	30	1.7	[7]	[7]	334[7]	19.3[7]	55[17]	3.2[17]	Honduras
224	7.8	318	11.1	800	27.9	269	9.4	[7]	[7]	560[7]	19.8[7]	57[9]	2.0[9]	Hong Kong
271	5.4	369	7.4	654	13.0	[42]	[42]	274	5.5	1,049[42]	20.9[42]	663[9]	13.2[9]	Hungary
11.1	7.6	8.6	5.9	22.8	15.7	12.4	8.5	6.0	4.1	39.8	27.3	6.9[9]	4.8[9]	Iceland
5,543	1.8	8,108	2.6	21,296	6.8	[1]	[1]	[1]	[1]	29,312[1]	9.3[1]	28,199	9.0	India
2,414	3.0	2,566	3.2	11,650	14.7	527	0.7	[7]	[7]	9,402[7]	11.9[7]	1,937[17]	2.4[17]	Indonesia
1,207	9.4	631	4.9	876	6.8	114	0.9	[7]	[7]	3,051[7]	23.7[7]	2,183[17]	17.0[17]	Iran
461	11.2	266	6.4	282	6.8	42	1.0	[7]	[7]	2,160[7]	52.3[7]	—	—	Iraq
80	6.0	65	4.9	201	15.0	95	7.1	[7]	[7]	286[7]	21.5[7]	209[33]	15.7[33]	Ireland
3.4	10.3	2.4	7.3	6.1	18.4	4.4	13.1	[7]	[7]	10.4[7]	31.4[7]	1.4[9]	4.1[9]	Isle of Man
131	6.7	110	5.7	270	13.9	192	9.9	[7]	[7]	652[7]	33.5[7]	115[33]	5.9[33]	Israel
1,957	8.1	1,149	4.7	4,660	19.2	1,003	4.1	[7]	[7]	6,042[7]	24.9[7]	2,652[9]	10.9[9]	Italy
66	6.1	40	3.7	196	17.9	47	4.3	[7]	[7]	237[7]	21.7[7]	180[17]	16.5[17]	Jamaica
6,400	9.7	3,940	6.0	14,180	21.0	5,470	8.3	[7]	[7]	14,380[7]	21.7[7]	1,930[17]	2.9[17]	Japan
4.4	9.3	2.4	5.0	6.8	14.4	7.4	15.6	3.1	6.5	15.7	33.1	1.6[17]	3.4[17]	Jersey
51	7.9	52	8.1	76	11.8	18	2.8	[7]	[7]	358[7]	55.6[7]	—	—	Jordan
740	10.0	664	9.0	533	7.2	329	4.5	184	2.5	1,490	20.2	166[21]	2.2[21]	Kazakhstan
[11]	[11]	[12]	[12]	[12]	[12]	[12]	[12]	[12]	[12]	1,587[12]	15.5[12]	—	—	Kenya
0.3	1.0	0.9	2.8	1.3	4.1	0.4	1.4	2.1	6.5	2.3	7.0	1.1[17]	3.4[17]	Kiribati
[11]	[11]	[12]	[12]	[12]	[12]	[12]	[12]	[12]	[12]	1,939[12, 23]	22.9[12, 23]	—	—	Korea, North
1,680	8.5	1,007	5.1	4,830	24.5	1,355	6.9	[7]	[7]	2,783[7]	14.1[7]	551[9]	2.8[9]	Korea, South
115	15.7	38	5.2	83	11.4	22	3.0	[7]	[7]	384[7]	52.6[7]	11[2]	1.5[2]	Kuwait
114	6.2	94	5.1	107	5.8	50	2.7	54	2.9	376	20.5	40	2.2	Kyrgyzstan
[11]	[11]	[12]	[12]	[12]	[12]	[12]	[12]	[12]	[12]	316[12, 14]	17.2[12, 14]	—	—	Laos
130	8.9	107	7.3	178	12.2	85	5.8	24	1.6	254	17.4	65	4.5	Latvia
43[48]	6.2[48]	48[48]	7.0[48]	115[48]	10.5[48]	24[48]	3.5[48]	[7]	[7]	200[7, 48]	28.8[7, 48]	—	—	Lebanon
28	5.5	8	1.6	24	4.7	2	0.5	[7]	[7]	157[7]	31.1[7]	13	2.6	Lesotho
4	0.6	14	2.0	47	6.7	[1]	[1]	[1]	[1]	00[1]	9.0[1]	64[17]	9.1[17]	Liberia
[11]	[11]	[12]	[12]	[12]	[12]	[12]	[12]	[12]	[12]	668[12]	67.1[12]		—	Libya
1.2	7.7	0.5	3.2	2.1	13.8	1.1	7.4	0.9	6.0	3.7	24.2	0.5[17]	3.5[17]	Liechtenstein
127	7.0	100	5.5	191	10.6	61	3.4	57	3.2	386	21.3	30[9]	1.7[9]	Lithuania
14	8.4	11	6.3	29	17.5	15	9.2	21	12.8	31	18.7	14[21]	8.1[21]	Luxembourg
16	9.1	10	5.5	41	23.8	9	5.2	[7]	[7]	44[7]	25.3[7]	4[17]	2.4[17]	Macau
37	3.9	21	2.3	54	5.8	20	2.2	15	1.6	69	7.4	338[50]	36.1[50]	Macedonia
[11]	[11]	[12]	[12]	[12]	[12]	[12]	[12]	[12]	[12]	636[12]	12.0[12]	—	—	Madagascar
46	1.4	25	0.7	94	2.7	6	0.2	[7]	[7]	147[7]	4.3[7]	57	1.7	Malaŵi
424	6.3	302	4.5	1,218	18.2	259	3.9	[7]	[7]	1,329[7]	19.9[7]	—	—	Malaysia
3.2	5.6	5.3	9.4	8.9	15.7	1.1	1.9	[7]	[7]	11.8[7]	21.0[7]	2.7[51]	4.7[51]	Maldives
13	0.4	6	0.2	159	4.6	0.3	—	75	2.2	84	2.4	107	3.1	Mali
6	4.4	9	6.9	13	9.8	5	3.7	[7]	[7]	53[7]	40.0[7]	5[9]	3.8[9]	Malta
1.1	9.4	0.5	4.7	1.4	12.1	0.8	7.3	[7]	[7]	3.1[7]	26.4[7]	1.4[17]	12.5[17]	Marshall Islands
9.3	5.6	6.7	4.0	14.0	8.5	3.0	1.8	[7]	[7]	59.1[7]	35.8[7]	54.8[17]	33.2[17]	Martinique
[11]	[11]	[12]	[12]	[12]	[12]	[12]	[12]	[12]	[12]	158[12]	24.8[12]	—	—	Mauritania
24	5.2	32	6.9	61	13.2	11	2.4	[7]	[7]	94[7]	20.3[7]	14[17]	3.1[17]	Mauritius[53]
3.1	11.4	1.5	5.4	2.0	7.2	0.1	0.4	[7]	[7]	5.7[7]	21.0[7]	10.5[17]	38.4[17]	Mayotte
1,879	5.6	1,362	4.0	6,893	20.5	1,080	3.2	[7]	[7]	7,205[7]	21.4[7]	1,041[17]	3.1[17]	Mexico
1.8	6.1	[54]	[54]	[54]	[54]	[54]	[54]	6.3	20.8	3.7[54]	12.1[54]	4.1[9]	13.5[9]	Micronesia
146	7.1	105	5.1	132	6.4	75	3.7	35	1.7	371	18.1	22	1.1	Moldova
0.7	5.3	...	...	2.5	20.2	1.0	8.0	2.8	22.4	1.9	14.9	0.9[21]	7.1[21]	Monaco
45	6.4	55	7.9	49	7.1	[1]	[1]	[1]	[1]	184[1]	26.5[1]	47[17]	6.7[17]	Mongolia
437	7.3	141	2.3	498	8.3	[42]	[42]	533	8.9	474[42]	7.9[42]	548[2]	9.1[2]	Morocco
42	0.7	7.7	1.4	112	2.0	[1]	[1]	[1]	[1]	243[1]	4.3[1]	95[9]	1.7[9]	Mozambique
283	1.7	394	2.4	1,355	8.2	1,205	7.3	[7]	[7]	474[7]	2.9[7]	503[9]	3.0[9]	Myanmar (Burma)
19	3.8	9	1.9	38	7.7	9	1.7	[7]	[7]	6[7]	1.2[7]	183[17]	37.1[17]	Namibia
...	...	...	...	...	...	...	...	...	...	...	...	...	...	Nauru
2[38]	—	7[38]	0.1[38]	109[38]	1.6[38]	10[38]	0.1[38]	[7]	[7]	314[7, 38]	4.6[7, 38]	127[38]	1.9[38]	Nepal
389	6.1	379	5.9	958	15.0	669	10.4	[7]	[7]	2,097[7]	32.7[7]	566[17]	8.8[17]	Netherlands, The
6.5	7.4	5.0	5.7	20.9	23.8	8.2	9.3	[7]	[7]	24.8[7]	28.2[7]	13.4[9]	15.3[9]	Netherlands Antilles
4.5	6.8	3.1	4.7	9.5	14.3	2.5	3.8	[7]	[7]	22.0[7]	33.4[7]	13.5[9]	16.0[9]	New Caledonia
81	4.9	91	5.5	316	19.1	149	9.0	[7]	[7]	429[7]	26.0[7]	160[17]	9.7[17]	New Zealand
30	2.0	33	2.2	195	13.1	19	1.3	86	5.7	190	12.7	325[9]	21.8[9]	Nicaragua
14	0.6	15	0.6	209	9.0	2	0.1	[7]	[7]	123[7]	5.3[7]	117[21]	5.0[21]	Niger

Employment and labour (continued)

country	year	economically active population										distribution by economic sector			
		total ('000)	participation rate (%)		activity rate (%)			employment status (%)				agriculture, forestry, fishing		manufacturing; mining, quarrying; public utilities	
			female	ages 15–64	total	male	female	employers, self-employed	employees	unpaid family workers	other	number ('000)	% of econ. active	number ('000)	% of econ. active
Nigeria	1986[18]	30,766	33.3	58.8	31.1	41.1	20.9	64.6	18.8	10.7	5.9	13,259	43.1	1,401	4.6
Northern Mariana Islands	1990	26.6	43.2	83.6[8]	61.3	66.2	55.9	1.4	96.1	0.2	2.3	0.6	2.3	6.0	22.5
Norway	1993	2,131	45.4	79.6[45]	49.4	54.5	44.4	8.3	84.4	1.1	6.2	115	5.4	352	16.5
Oman	1988	644	6.3	57.2	38.2	60.7	5.9	...	...	...	...	399	62.0	33	5.1
Pakistan	1992–93[18]	33,829	14.2	50.8	28.0	46.4	8.2	41.2	32.4	20.2	6.2	15,034	44.5	4,190	12.4
Palau	1990	6.1	36.9	64.1[8]	40.2	47.1	32.1	2.5	89.5	0.2	7.8	0.4	7.1	0.2	3.0
Panama	1991[18]	859	33.8	60.0[57]	37.4	48.9	25.6	28.4	61.0	4.4	6.2	196	22.9	91	10.6
Papua New Guinea	1980[58]	733	39.8	35.2[10]	24.6	28.3	20.5	72.7	26.4	—	0.9	564	77.0	21	2.9
Paraguay	1982	1,039	19.7	57.5	34.3	54.8	13.6	43.1	37.7	9.2	9.9	446	42.9	129	12.4
Peru	1993	8,293	38.3[59]	56.9[24]	36.2	...	...	39.8[38]	41.8[38]	8.4[38]	10.0[38]	2,693	32.5	1,091	13.2
Philippines	1993[18]	26,822	37.2	66.2	39.7	49.7	29.7	36.6	40.6	14.0	8.8	11,194	41.7	2,691	10.0
Poland	1993[18]	17,367	46.1	69.0	45.1	50.0	40.5	21.9	68.7	6.0	3.4	3,988	23.0	4,348	25.0
Portugal	1993[18]	4,715	44.7	67.5	47.9	55.2	41.2	23.1	74.2	1.8	0.9	528	11.2	1,173	24.9
Puerto Rico	1993[18]	1,211	39.1	53.7[8]	33.5	42.3	24.1	14.0	84.1	0.7	1.2	35	2.9	217	17.9
Qatar	1988	293	11.2	80.8	53.7	77.3	22.2	1.8[48]	97.7[48]	—	0.5[48]	4.5	1.6	22.0	7.5
Réunion	1990[18]	234	41.1	60.3	39.1	46.8	31.6	8.4	53.1	1.1	37.4	11	4.8	11	4.8
Romania	1992	10,465	44.7	68.3	45.9	51.6	40.4	13.9	79.7	2.0	4.4	2,417	23.1	4,016	38.4
Russia	1992	72,610	48.5[20]	86.7[16]	49.0	...	...	...	...	...	...	10,336	14.2	21,324	29.4
Rwanda	1991	3,649	47.5	79.1[10]	50.2	53.3	47.2	...	...	...	...	3,313	90.8	129[11]	3.5[11]
St. Kitts and Nevis	1980	17.1	41.0	69.5	39.5	48.4	31.2	9.7	78.5	0.4	11.4	4.5	26.1	3.8	22.3
St. Lucia	1980	42.2	39.1	69.9	37.2	47.1	28.0	21.0	55.8	1.6	21.6	10.7	25.5	3.7	8.7
St. Vincent	1991	41.7	35.9	67.5	39.1	50.3	28.0	18.2	59.6	2.1	20.1	8.4	20.1	3.5	8.4
San Marino	1993	14.9	40.8	74.8	55.4	63.5	46.8	22.2	77.3	0.5	—	0.3	2.0	4.7	31.9
São Tomé and Príncipe	1981	31	32.4	61.1	31.7	43.1	20.4	15.8	79.4	0.1	4.7	16	53.9	1.9	6.2
Saudi Arabia	1988	5,369	3.6	59.1	36.3	54.9	3.6	...	...	...	...	192	3.6	595	11.1
Senegal	1991	3,249	39.1	64.2[10]	42.6	52.6	32.9	...	...	...	...	2,543	78.3	228[11]	7.0[11]
Seychelles	1993[60]	28.1	...	...	38.9	...	...	...	...	...	...	2.2	7.7	4.6[11]	16.4[11]
Sierra Leone	1991	1,532	32.4	53.3[10]	35.9	49.4	22.8	...	...	...	...	945	61.7	275[11]	18.0[11]
Singapore	1993[18]	1,636	40.2	68.7	49.6	58.7	40.3	12.3	84.1	0.9	2.7	4	0.2	437	26.7
Slovakia	1993[18]	2,509	46.1	71.9	47.2	52.2	42.5	5.7	90.0	0.1	4.2	226	9.0	691	27.5
Slovenia	1991	946	46.7	66.7	48.1	52.9	43.6	2.2	88.8	1.9	7.1	121	12.8	335	35.4
Solomon Islands	1992[61]	26.8	25.6[48]	24.9[13, 48]	13.7[48]	19.7[48]	7.3[48]	29.6[48]	68.6[48]	—	1.8[48]	6.4	23.7	2.5	9.0
Somalia	1991	3,215	40.5	64.3[10]	40.9	51.1	31.0	...	...	...	...	2,275	70.8	336[11]	10.5[11]
South Africa[62]	1991	11,624	39.4	69.3[45]	37.5	45.5	29.5	7.0	74.8	...	18.2	1,224	10.5	2,361	20.3
Spain	1993[18]	15,319	36.8	60.3[8]	39.4	51.1	28.3	17.1	71.0	3.6	8.3	1,410	9.2	3,060	20.0
Sri Lanka	1993	6,066	33.9	56.7[24]	41.0	54.9	27.5	27.0	52.5	6.7	13.8	2,011	33.2	833	13.7
Sudan, The	1983[56]	6,343	29.1	57.4	35.1	50.0	20.4	...	...	...	...	4,029	63.5	317	5.0
Suriname	1992[63]	107	37.8	56.0	48.2	61.4	35.7	...	...	...	...	3.8	3.5	11.2	10.5
Swaziland	1991	326	39.0	62.3[10]	39.8	49.5	30.3	...	...	...	...	215	66.0	39[11]	12.0[11]
Sweden	1993	4,320	48.1	79.1[8]	49.4	51.9	46.9	9.5	81.8	0.5	8.2	136	3.1	772	17.9
Switzerland	1993	3,552	38.3	60.8[24]	50.8	64.0	38.2	9.7[14]	90.3[14]	...	...	191	5.4	825	23.2
Syria	1991[18]	3,485	18.0	46.7[48]	27.8	44.6	10.2	31.0	49.3	13.0	6.7	917	26.3	471	13.5
Taiwan	1994[18]	9,081	38.4	59.0[24]	43.0	51.4	34.0	22.2	67.8	8.4	1.6	976	10.7	2,539	28.0
Tajikistan	1991	1,969	39.0[26]	76.3[16]	36.9	...	...	...	...	...	...	881	44.7	257	13.1
Tanzania	1991	13,123	40.0	87.8[10]	46.0	48.9	43.2	...	...	...	...	10,540	80.3	614[11]	4.7[11]
Thailand	1993[18, 64]	31,636	44.7	77.3[24]	54.3	60.0	48.7	30.3	37.7	24.3	7.7	15,530[65]	49.1[65]	4,601	14.5
Togo	1991	1,432	36.2	58.8[10]	40.0	51.8	28.5	70.3[38]	10.4[38]	11.3[38]	8.0[38]	991	69.2	161[11]	11.2[11]
Tonga	1990	32.0	33.0	57.0	33.6	45.2	22.0	33.7	45.4	16.8	4.1	11.7	36.5	5.1	15.8
Trinidad and Tobago	1993	505	37.0	63.2	40.5	50.5	30.2	18.3	77.4	3.1	1.2	51	10.0	77	15.2
Tunisia	1989	2,361	20.9	52.8	29.8	46.5	12.7	20.9	54.9	7.4	16.8	510	21.6	418	17.7
Turkey	1993[18]	20,997	30.8	57.2	35.3	48.5	21.9	27.6	41.5	27.7	3.2	8,437	40.2	3,164	15.1
Turkmenistan	1992	1,573	52.2[26]	77.8[16]	40.9	...	...	...	...	...	...	695	44.2	154	9.8
Tuvalu	1991	5.9	51.3[47]	85.5	65.3	...	...	0.3[47]	22.2[47]	—77.5[47]—		4.2	68.0	0.1	2.0
Uganda	1991	8,365	40.8	67.3[10]	43.6	52.2	35.2	...	...	...	...	6,724	80.4	478[11]	5.7[11]
Ukraine	1992	24,028	49.2[20]	83.3[16]	46.2	...	...	...	...	...	...	4,989	20.8	7,401	30.8
United Arab Emirates	1990	690	10.4[27]	69.0[27]	47.0[27]	67.6[27]	12.9[27]	6.8[14]	92.7[14]	0.1[14]	0.5[14]	43	6.3	94	13.6
United Kingdom	1993	28,271	43.8	76.2	49.4	56.8	42.3	11.2	76.7	0.5	11.6	522	1.8	5,775	20.4
United States	1993[66]	129,525	45.2	73.6	49.9	56.0	44.1	8.2	90.9	0.3	0.7	3,509	2.7	23,401	18.1
Uruguay	1992	1,259	42.4	68.3[46]	45.0	55.4	35.9	22.9	72.3	2.3	2.5	56	4.5	280	22.2
Uzbekistan	1992	8,273	43.8[25]	80.0[16]	39.2	...	...	...	...	...	...	3,595	43.5	1,147	13.9
Vanuatu	1989	67.0	46.3	85.0	47.0	49.0	44.9	...	...	...	...	49.8	74.4	1.0	1.5
Venezuela	1993[18]	7,546	31.2	60.0	36.3	49.5	22.8	30.2	61.8	1.7	6.3	750	9.9	1,203	15.9
Vietnam	1989	30,521	51.7	79.9	47.4	47.0	47.7	...	...	...	...	20,471	67.1	3,390	11.1
Virgin Islands (U.S.)	1990[18]	47.4	47.8	70.3	46.6	50.3	43.1	7.6	85.5	0.2	6.7	0.6	1.2	3.7	7.8
West Bank	1993	218	11.5	40.2[24]	20.1	35.4	4.7	...	...	...	...	41.0	18.8	28.1[36]	12.9[36]
Western Sahara	...	...	...	...	...	...	...	...	...	...	...	...	...	...	...
Western Samoa	1986	45.6	18.8	48.6[38]	29.0	44.5	11.6	21.1[38]	43.5[38]	35.0[38]	0.4[38]	29.0	63.6	2.4	5.4
Yemen	1988	3,029	31.6	52.6	26.4	36.8	16.4	...	...	...	...	2,152	71.1	129	4.3
Yugoslavia	1994	3,132	41.6[22]	61.9[24]	29.8	...	...	...	...	...	...	116	3.7	944	30.1
Zaire	1991	13,848	35.2	64.2[10]	36.1	47.2	25.2	...	...	...	...	9,021	65.1	2,200[11]	15.9[11]
Zambia	1991	2,928	29.6	52.6[10]	33.4	47.4	19.6	22.9[14]	42.5[14]	3.6[14]	31.0[14]	2,010	68.6	333[11]	11.4[11]
Zimbabwe	1986–87	3,260	47.8	76.5[24]	42.1	44.8	39.6	...	...	...	...	2,110	64.7	179	5.5

[1]Services includes finance, real estate and public administration, defense. [2]Unemployed, not previously employed only. [3]Includes emigrant workers (352,000). [4]Ages 15–59 (male) and 15–54 (female). [5]State sector only. [6]Includes nonagricultural private sector (241,000) and unemployed (261,000). [7]Services includes public administration, defense. [8]Ages 16–64. [9]Unemployed only. [10]Over age 10. [11]Manufacturing; mining, quarrying; public utilities includes construction. [12]Services includes transportation, communications; trade, hotels, restaurants; finance, real estate; and public administration, defense. [13]Over age 14. [14]1980. [15]Includes unemployed, not previously employed. [16]Ages 16–59 (male) and 16–54 (female). [17]Mostly unemployed. [18]Excludes all or some classes or elements of the military. [19]Services includes restaurants, hotels. [20]1989. [21]Includes unemployed. [22]1992. [23]1982. [24]Over age 15. [25]1991. [26]1990. [27]1988. [28]Ages 16–60. [29]Over age 12. [30]Republic of Cyprus only. [31]1993 population economically active for Turkish Republic of Northern Cyprus is 75,947. [32]Ages 16–66. [33]Mostly unemployed, not previously employed. [34]Ethiopia includes Eritrea. [35]1984. [36]Other includes public utilities and finance, real estate. [37]Services includes trade, hotels, restaurants. [38]1981. [39]Ages 15–65. [40]Excludes Alderney and Sark. [41]Data are

construction		transportation, communications		trade, hotels, restaurants		finance, real estate		public administration, defense		services		other		country
number ('000)	% of econ. active	number ('000)	% of econ. active	number ('000)	% of econ. active	number ('000)	% of econ. active	number ('000)	% of econ. active	number ('000)	% of econ. active	number ('000)	% of econ. active	
546	1.8	1,112	3.6	7,417	24.1	120	0.4	[7]	[7]	4,902[7]	15.9[7]	2,009[17]	6.5[17]	Nigeria
5.8	21.7	1.4	5.3	5.3	19.8	1.0	3.8	1.4	5.3	4.5	16.9	0.6[9]	2.3[9]	Northern Mariana Islands
126	5.9	162	7.6	362	17.0	157	7.4	146	6.9	647	30.4	64[33]	3.0[33]	Norway
52	8.0	26	4.0	23	3.6	1	0.2	[7]	[7]	110[7]	17.1[7]	—	—	Oman
2,099	6.2	1,663	4.9	4,198	12.4	283	0.8	[7]	[7]	4,207[7]	12.4[7]	2,146[17]	6.3[17]	Pakistan
0.9	14.2	0.4	6.6	1.1	18.7	0.2	2.9	0.8	13.7	1.6	26.1	0.5[9]	7.8[9]	Palau
34	3.9	54	6.3	167	19.5	34	4.0	[7]	[7]	227[7]	26.4[7]	54[33]	6.3[33]	Panama
22	2.9	1.7	2.4	25	3.4	4	0.6	[7]	[7]	77[7]	10.5[7]	2	0.2	Papua New Guinea
70	6.7	31	2.9	86	8.3	18	1.7	[7]	[7]	174[7]	16.8[7]	86[15]	8.3[15]	Paraguay
308	3.7	364	4.4	1,352	16.3	197	2.4	[7]	[7]	2,287[7]	27.6[7]	—	—	Peru
1,102	4.1	1,359	5.1	3,415	12.7	496	1.8	[7]	[7]	4,174[7]	15.6[7]	2,392[17]	8.9[17]	Philippines
1,160	6.7	921	5.3	2,028	11.7	248	1.4	331	1.9	3,756	21.6	586[33]	3.4[33]	Poland
384	8.2	216	4.6	923	19.6	312	6.6	[7]	[7]	1,137[7]	24.1[7]	42[2]	0.9[2]	Portugal
92	7.6	44	3.6	258	21.3	37	3.1	[7]	[7]	513[7]	42.4[7]	15[2]	1.2[2]	Puerto Rico
64.2	22.0	11.9	4.1	34.2	11.7	6.2	2.1	[7]	[7]	149.6[7]	51.1[7]	—	—	Qatar
17	7.1	7	3.1	18	7.7	3	1.3	[7]	[7]	79[7]	33.9[7]	87[17]	37.4[17]	Réunion
583	5.6	634	6.1	779	7.4	306	2.9	[7]	[7]	1,244[7]	11.9[7]	486[33]	4.6[33]	Romania
7,887	10.9	5,632	7.8	5,679	7.8	3,482	4.8	1,480	2.0	14,173	19.5	2,617[21]	3.6[21]	Russia
[11]	[11]	[12]	[12]	[12]	[12]	[12]	[12]	[12]	[12]	207[12]	5.7[12]	—	—	Rwanda
0.4	2.5	0.3	1.6	1.3	7.3	0.8	4.7	1.0	5.7	2.9	17.0	2.2[17]	12.8[17]	St. Kitts and Nevis
2.6	6.3	1.5	3.5	2.8	6.5	0.5	1.1	2.4	5.6	7.9	18.8	10.1[17]	24.0[17]	St. Lucia
3.5	8.5	2.3	5.5	6.5	15.7	1.4	3.4	[7]	[7]	7.7[7]	18.5[7]	8.3[9]	20.0[9]	St. Vincent
1.2	8.0	0.3	1.9	2.5	16.8	0.4	2.6	3.6	24.4	1.2	8.3	0.6[9]	4.1[9]	San Marino
1.8	5.9	1.0	3.4	2.0	6.5	0.2	0.5	2.4	7.8	3.5	11.3	1.4[9]	4.6[9]	São Tomé and Príncipe
1,181	22.0	321	6.0	964	18.0	151	2.8	[7]	[7]	1,965[7]	36.6[7]	—	—	Saudi Arabia
[11]	[11]	[12]	[12]	[12]	[12]	[12]	[12]	[12]	[12]	477[12]	14.7[12]	—	—	Senegal
[11]	[11]	3.4	12.2	5.2	18.6	1.0	3.4	2.6	9.1	5.6	20.0	3.6[17]	12.6[17]	Seychelles
[11]	[11]	[12]	[12]	[12]	[12]	[12]	[12]	[12]	[12]	312[12]	20.4[12]	—	—	Sierra Leone
102	6.2	167	10.2	364	22.2	173	10.6	[7]	[7]	344[7]	21.0[7]	45[17]	2.7[17]	Singapore
194	7.7	172	6.8	266	10.6	21	0.9	85	3.4	385	15.4	486[21]	18.7[21]	Slovakia
42	4.4	53	5.6	103	10.9	44	4.7	[7]	[7]	177[7]	18.7[7]	71[17]	7.5[17]	Slovenia
1.1	4.1	1.4	5.3	3.2	11.9	1.2	4.5	4.3	15.9	6.9	25.6	—	—	Solomon Islands
[11]	[11]	[12]	[12]	[12]	[12]	[12]	[12]	[12]	[12]	604[12]	18.8[12]	—	—	Somalia
526	4.5	497	4.3	1,358	11.7	504	4.3	[7]	[7]	2,641[7]	22.7[7]	2,513[17]	21.6[17]	South Africa[62]
1,530	10.0	787	5.1	3,185	20.8	1,081	7.1	[7]	[7]	3,066[7]	20.0[7]	1,200[33]	7.8[33]	Spain
259	4.3	216	3.6	574	9.5	74	1.2	[7]	[7]	1,094[7]	18.0[7]	1,005[17]	16.6[17]	Sri Lanka
139	2.2	215	3.4	294	4.6	21	0.3	[7]	[7]	550[7]	8.7[7]	777[33]	12.3[33]	Sudan, The
5.0	4.7	6.6	6.2	13.6	12.7	3.2	3.0	[7]	[7]	41.3[7]	38.6[7]	22.4[17]	20.9[17]	Suriname
[11]	[11]	[12]	[12]	[12]	[12]	[12]	[12]	[12]	[12]	72[12]	20.1[12]	—	—	Swaziland
236	5.5	277	6.4	567	13.1	368	8.5	[7]	[7]	1,602[7]	37.1[7]	362[17]	8.4[17]	Sweden
300	8.4	213	6.0	689	19.4	372	10.5	133	3.8	600	18.7	163[9]	4.6[9]	Switzerland
341	9.8	167	4.8	378	10.0	25	0.7	[7]	[7]	951[7]	27.3[7]	235[9]	6.8[9]	Syria
967	10.6	473	5.2	1,875	20.6	504	5.6	317	3.5	1,288	14.2	142[9]	1.6[9]	Taiwan
148	7.5	93	4.7	109	5.5	22	1.1	41	2.1	389	19.8	29	1.5	Tajikistan
[11]	[11]	[12]	[12]	[12]	[12]	[12]	[12]	[12]	[12]	1,969[12]	15.0[12]	—	—	Tanzania
1,755	5.5	939	3.0	3,909	12.4	[1]	[1]	[1]	[1]	3,685[1]	11.6[1]	1,215[17]	3.8[17]	Thailand
[11]	[11]	[12]	[12]	[12]	[12]	[12]	[12]	[12]	[12]	280[12]	19.6[12]	—	—	Togo
1.3	3.9	1.8	5.7	2.6	8.1	1.2	3.7	[7]	[7]	7.1[7]	22.0[7]	1.3[9]	4.2[9]	Tonga
79	15.7	34	6.7	87	17.2	32	6.4	[7]	[7]	144[7]	28.5[7]	1	0.1	Trinidad and Tobago
248	10.5	96	4.1	217	9.2	16	0.7	[7]	[7]	444[7]	18.8[7]	412[17]	17.5[17]	Tunisia
1,137	5.4	954	4.5	2,477	11.8	471	2.2	[7]	[7]	2,055[7]	12.9[7]	1,659[9]	7.9[9]	Turkey
164	10.4	56	3.6	89	5.6	38	2.4	74	4.7	276	17.5	27	1.7	Turkmenistan
0.2	4.0	0.1	1.0	0.2	4.0	—	—	[7]	[7]	1.3[7]	22.0[7]	—	—	Tuvalu
[11]	[11]	[12]	[12]	[12]	[12]	[12]	[12]	[12]	[12]	1,163[12]	13.9[12]	—	—	Uganda
1,910	7.9	1,623	6.8	1,751	7.3	144	0.6	562	2.3	5,298	22.0	351[21]	1.5[21]	Ukraine
119	17.3	72	10.4	101	14.7	19	2.7	[7]	[7]	241[7]	35.0[7]	—	—	United Arab Emirates
1,679	5.9	1,626	5.8	5,031	17.8	3,210	11.4	[7]	[7]	7,214[7]	25.5[7]	3,214[17]	11.4[17]	United Kingdom
8,170	6.3	7,233	5.6	26,736[67]	20.6[67]	13,789	10.6	[7]	[7]	45,684[7, 67]	35.3[7, 67]	1,003[33]	0.8[33]	United States
86	6.8	68	5.4	224	17.7	68	5.4	[7]	[7]	446[7]	35.4[7]	32[33]	2.5[33]	Uruguay
598	7.2	368	4.4	452	5.5	25	0.3	104	1.3	1,802	21.8	182	2.2	Uzbekistan
1.3	1.9	1.0	1.5	2.7	4.1	0.6	1.0	[7]	[7]	7.9[7]	11.8[7]	2.6	3.8	Vanuatu
654	8.7	452	6.0	1,597	21.2	464	6.1	[7]	[7]	1,944[7]	25.8[7]	484[17]	6.4[17]	Venezuela
581	1.9	576	1.9	1,880	6.2	90	0.3	305	1.0	1,374	4.5	1,854[17]	6.1[17]	Vietnam
5.7	12.0	3.7	7.8	10.3	21.8	3.6	7.7	5.1	10.8	7.8	16.4	6.9	14.6	Virgin Islands (U.S.)
58.9	27.0	11.1	5.1	27.7	12.7	[36]	[36]	[7]	[7]	23.9[7]	11.0[7]	27.5[17, 36]	12.6[17, 36]	West Bank
...	...	...	...	...	...	...	...	...	...	...	...	...	...	Western Sahara
0.1	0.1	1.5	3.3	1.7	3.7	0.8	1.8	[7]	[7]	9.4[7]	20.7[7]	0.6	1.4	Western Samoa
178	5.9	90	3.0	84	2.8	4	0.1	[7]	[7]	391[7]	12.9[7]	—	—	Yemen
148	4.7	146	4.7	304	9.7	81	2.6	90	2.9	342	10.9	961[68]	30.7[68]	Yugoslavia
[11]	[11]	[12]	[12]	[12]	[12]	[12]	[12]	[12]	[12]	2,627[12]	19.0[12]	—	—	Zaire
[11]	[11]	[12]	[12]	[12]	[12]	[12]	[12]	[12]	[12]	585[12]	20.0[12]	—	—	Zambia
51	1.6	76	2.3	128	3.9	24	0.7	[7]	[7]	397[7]	12.2[7]	277[17]	8.5[17]	Zimbabwe

for the economically active population ages 15–64 only. [42]Services includes finance, real estate. [43]Ages 16–69. [44]1977. [45]Ages 20–64. [46]Ages 14–64. [47]1979. [48]1986. [49]Excludes about 30,000 foreign border workers. [50]Includes unemployed, emigrant workers, and employees in private nonagricultural sector. [51]Includes unemployed, previously employed. [52]1983. [53]Island of Mauritius only. [54]Services includes transportation, communications; trade, hotels, restaurants; and finance, real estate. [55]1985. [56]Excludes nomadic population. [57]Ages 15–69. [58]Citizens over age 10 involved in money-raising activities only. [59]1985–86. [60]Excludes domestic workers (private households), self-employed, and family workers. [61]Wage earners only. [62]Excludes the former black independent states of Bophuthatswana, Ciskei, Transkei, and Venda. [63]Districts of Wanica and Paramaribo only. [64]February survey. [65]Includes seasonally inactive labour force (1,236,000). [66]Excludes armed forces overseas. [67]Services includes hotels. [68]Private sector 7.5%, unemployed 23.2%.

Agriculture and land use

This table provides data on the structure of national agricultural sectors from the perspective of farms and farmland use. The data are taken mainly from national agricultural censuses and surveys, supplemented by reports of the United Nations Food and Agriculture Organization's (FAO's) *World Census of Agriculture*. Many of these national censuses, of course, are taken under guidelines established by the FAO for the *World Census of Agriculture* programs (the 1990 census is the fifth and will include national censuses taken during the decade 1986–95). It represents a cooperative effort by FAO member countries to collect agricultural data within a general framework that permits international harmonization of concepts and definitions; transfer of technical expertise; and increased effectiveness in the collection, analysis, publication, and policy-related use of such statistics. More than 100 countries were expected to participate in the 1990 census.

All agricultural statistics are subject to quality-control problems, including errors or biases arising from such factors as incomplete or inaccurate lists of holdings, ambiguous questions, respondents who inadvertently or willfully give inaccurate information, failure to record data for all parts of fragmented holdings, respondents' misunderstandings of the definitions of land use and cropping methods, or a failure to report livestock temporarily absent from the holding on public or common pasture land or in transit. Frequently, subjects studied, classificational schemes, and definitions vary from the FAO guidelines (economic planners need different information about a commercial, high-technology, multicrop agricultural sector than they do for a family-subsistence, low-technology, one-crop sector). When a complete census of agriculture is impossible, a sample survey may be taken. This is a limited census of a predetermined number of carefully screened holdings. From these results, nationwide projections may be prepared.

With respect to the first section of the table, number and size of farms, many countries impose a minimum size limit for holdings that may be covered in their census reports, and this cutoff, if not sufficiently low, can result in a substantial undercount of smaller holdings; conversely Soviet-bloc nations formerly published statistics only on state collective or cooperative farms and excluded production from privately held plots of land, even though these often represented a significant fraction of agricultural output.

The land tenure statistics classify farms (a single parcel of land, or holding, or a group of holdings operated as a single farm) according to the rights under which the farmer holds the land or operates the enterprise represented by the farm. Owner-operated includes two types of ownership: outright ownership in which the holder has title and has the right to determine use and transfer of the land; and ownerlike possession in which the holder lacks the legal title but uses it under perpetual lease, hereditary tenure, or leases of 30 years or more with nominal, or no, rent. Farms classed as owner-operated are divided into individual and family, corporate or state, and socialized or collective proprietorships. Rented includes

Agriculture and land use

country	farms (latest census of agriculture)[a]										tenure (% of farms)					
	year	number of farms ('000)	size of holding								owner-operated			rented (including share-croppers)	tribal/ communal	other[b]
			average (ha)	size class (%)												
				under 1 ha	1–5 ha	5–10 ha	10–20 ha	20–50 ha	50–200 ha	over 200 ha	individual/ family	corporate/ state	socialized/ collective			
Afghanistan	1981	126[1]	3.5[1]	44.8[1]	35.2[1]			20.0[1]			55.1[1]	—	—	25.1[1]	—	19.8[1]
Albania	1990	0.5[2]	1,182[2, 3]	...	...	...	...	...	...	...	97.0[4]	3.0[4]		—	—	—
Algeria	1987	899[7]	6.2[7]	1.1[7]	12.7[7]	15.8[7]	21.7[7]	25.6[7]	18.0[7]	5.1[7]	...	...	...	...	...	...
American Samoa	1990	1.1	2.9	44.7[9]	40.0[10]	13.8[11]			1.6[12]		93.9	—	—	2.2	—	3.9
Andorra	—	...	...	...	...	...	...	...	...	...	...	...	...	...	...	...
Angola	1970–71	1,067	3.9	3.3	13.5	9.3	11.3	13.7	19.2	29.7	80.5	1.1	—	—	18.2	0.2
Antigua and Barbuda	1984	2.3	2.1	61.7	33.8	2.9	0.6	0.6	0.4	—	32.1[14]	22.9[14]		40.5[14]	—	4.5[14]
Argentina	1988	421	469	15.1		8.4	14.0[15]	12.0[16]	25.1	25.5	85.1[14]	—	—	8.3[14]	—	6.6[14]
Armenia	1993	243[18, 19]	2[18]	...	...	...	...	...	...	...	...	...	...	...	...	...
Aruba	...	...	...	...	...	...	...	...	...	...	...	...	...	...	...	...
Australia	1993–94	123	3,710[8]			15.7			9.2[20]	75.1[21]	...	...	...	...	...	...
Austria	1993	267	26.4[26]	3.3[26]	32.2[26]	17.8[26]	20.0[26]	21.5[26]	4.6[26]	0.7[26]	38.9[26]	1.5[26]	—	59.5[26]	—	0.1[26]
Azerbaijan	1993	0.2[18, 19]	39[18]	...	...	...	...	...	...	...	...	...	...	...	...	...
Bahamas, The	1994	4.2	8.5	55.2[9]	30.1[10]	12.3[11]		1.1[27]	0.4[28]	1.0[29]	74.9	0.6	—	4.0	—	20.5
Bahrain	1980	0.8	4.4	19.4	52.9	17.4	8.2	2.0	0.1		37.9	0.1	—	62.0	—	—
Bangladesh	1983–84	10,045	0.9	70.3	27.0[30]	2.5[31]		0.2[32]			62.8	...	...	1.4	...	35.8
Barbados	1989	17.2	95.8[35]	95.0	3.9	0.3	0.2	0.1	0.3	0.2	70.1[14]	—	—	6.9[14]	23.0[14]	
Belarus	1993	5.2[18]	21[18]	...	...	...	...	...	...	...	52.1	13.1	34.8	—	—	—
Belgium	1991	84	16.5	13.9	24.1	14.8	19.1	22.1	6.0		33.4[14]	...	...	65.7[14]	—	0.9[14]
Belize	1984–85	11.0	26.7[17]	9.3	15.2		56.3		19.1		43.6[17]	56.4[17]	—	—	—	—
Benin	1992	408	...	...	...	...	...	...	...	...	...	...	...	...	...	...
Bermuda	1990	0.08[37]	3.1[37]	...	...	...	...	...	...	...	...	...	...	...	...	...
Bhutan	1984	160	0.8	51.3[9, 38]	42.9[10, 38]			5.8[38, 39]			...	...	...	...	...	...
Bolivia	1984	315	72.1	25.3	42.1	12.1	6.8	6.1	4.9	2.8	70.3	...	...	2.0	4.3	23.3
Bosnia and Herzegovina[18]	1981	540	...	33.4	48.9	13.7	2.3		0.6		100.0	—	—	—	—	—
Botswana	1990	90.3[40]	5.0	9.1	56.1	26.9		7.9			—	0.4	—	—	99.6	—
Brazil	1985	5,835	64.5	11.1	28.6	13.2	14.0	15.6	12.4	4.9	63.2	—	—	17.9	—	18.4[42]
Brunei	1964	6.3	2.6	44.1[9]	40.4[10]			15.5[39]			52.3	1.0	—	22.0	—	24.7
Bulgaria	1991	2.2[6, 44]	2,467[6, 44]	...	...	...	...	...	...	...	—	84.6[6, 44]	—	15.4[6]	—	—
Burkina Faso	1984	1,860	4.8	...	...	...	...	...	...	...	...	...	...	...	...	...
Burundi	1983	...	...	...	...	...	...	...	...	...	...	...	...	...	...	...
Cambodia	1962[45]	840	3.6	30.7	54.9	10.4	3.4		0.6		...	...	...	...	...	...
Cameroon	1973	926	1.6	42.7	53.8	3.2	0.3	—	—	—	2.4	—	—	5.2	59.5	32.9
Canada	1991	280	242	1.4[9]	3.5[10]		24.2[46]		70.9[47]			63.5[14]		36.5[14]	—	—
Cape Verde	1988	32.2	...	...	...	...	...	...	...	...	...	...	...	...	...	...
Central African Republic	1974	283	1.7	32.2	65.2	2.5	—	—	—	—	0.3[14]	—	—	0.1[14]	98.6[14]	1.2[14]
Chad	1973	366	2.6	19.7	69.5	10.0	0.8		—	—	...	...	...	...	...	...
Chile	1975–76	306	94.1	16.0	32.5	13.4	12.3	11.8	9.2	4.8		84.0		7.2	8.8	
China	1987	1,650[50]	...	...	...	...	...	...	...	...	—	10.0[51]	90.0[51]	—	—	—
Colombia	1988	1,548	26.3[51]	22.8[51]	36.7[51]	13.6[51]	10.0[51]	8.5[51]	6.3[51]	2.1[51]	77.6	—	—	5.6	3.7	13.1
Comoros	1982	...	...	...	...	...	...	...	...	...	...	...	...	...	...	...
Congo	1986	143[7]	1.4[7]	37.3[7]	62.2[7]	0.5[7]	—	—	—	—	91.7[14]	8.3[14]	—	—	—	—
Costa Rica	1973	82	38.3	23.3	25.5	11.2	10.8	15.2	10.7	3.3	97.9	1.7	—	0.1	—	0.3
Côte d'Ivoire	1975	550	5.0	9.5	54.4	24.9	9.4	1.7	0.1	—	...	...	...	...	...	...
Croatia[52]	1981	569	...	30.7	51.1	14.7	2.3		0.3		100.0	—	—	—	—	—
Cuba	1988	1.8[44]	1,047[44]	...	...	...	...	...	...	...	...	...	...	...	...	...
Cyprus	1985	48.0	3.8	24.4	56.8	15.0	2.9		0.9			79.0		9.4	—	11.6[53]
Czech Republic[54]	1980	1,391	8.1	89.9[55]		9.9[56]			0.2[57]		6.0[14]	30.8[14]	63.2[14]	—	0.6	—
Denmark	1993[59]	73.8	35.9[60]	2.7		15.9	23.1	36.1	22.2			64.4[2]			35.6[2]	
Djibouti	1988–89	1.2	0.4	*c. 100*	...	...	...	...	...	...	...	...	...	...	...	...
Dominica	1986–88	1.9	...	89[61]		9[62]			2		33	...	...	15	...	52
Dominican Republic	1981	385	6.3	16.0	65.7	8.5	5.4	2.6	1.5	0.3	53.2	18.5	4.5	1.6	—	17.4
Ecuador	1974	517	15.4	27.8	38.8	10.6	8.0	8.2	5.6	0.9	70.3	0.3	—	7.7	7.4	14.3
Egypt	1990	3,896	0.7[37]	95.8[63]	2.3[64]			1.9[65]			...	...	...	...	...	...
El Salvador	1970–71	271	5.4	48.9	37.9	5.8	3.4	2.6	1.2	0.2	41.5	—	—	28.2	6.3	24.1

sharecropping; communal/tribal includes types of customary or traditional arrangements in which title or goods do not change hands. "Other" usually includes farms operated on several parcels of land and held under multiple forms of tenure.

Statistics on types of farms by commodities produced refer to FAO categories. The terms "mainly crops" and "mainly livestock" indicate that more than half of the for-sale production was that indicated.

The section on technology provides some measures of the role modern technology plays in the farm activities of each country (although, of course, irrigation may employ technology developed in ancient times). Ratios referred to area mean area of "arable" (cultivated and cultivable) land, roughly "cropland," less area of permanent crops (see below).

The classification of farmland by economic use is also subject to differing treatment internationally. For purposes of this table, "cropland" comprises: (1) land under temporary crops (those requiring replanting after each harvest), (2) land under permanent crops (those *not* requiring replanting, including tree, bush and shrub, and vine crops), and (3) land temporarily (less than five years) fallow (unused, but capable of being returned to cultivation with no special preparation). "Meadows and pastures" includes land (both permanent and temporary use) whose principal purpose is the raising of animal fodder or forage. "Woodland and forest" includes both natural and planted tracts of timber (*e.g.,* plantings of Christmas trees), whether harvested or not. "Other" comprises: (1) mixed and multiple use lands, (2) residue of farmland holdings not classifiable according to categories listed above (including areas of farm buildings, roads, ornamental gardens, watercourses and flooded land, wasteland, etc.), (3) land not classified by respondents in census, or (4) detail not distinguishable as one of the categories above by reason of its summarization in a published source. When "cropland" is indicated to compose 100 percent of farmland, it should usually be understood to mean only that woodland, pasture, etc., were not part of the published data, rather than that those classes of land use do not exist.

Measurements of area are given in hectares (ha; 1 hectare is equal to 2.471 acres). A kilogram (kg) is equal to 2.205 pounds (1 kg/ha = 0.89 lb/ac). The following notes further define the column headings:

a. All properties used wholly or partly for agricultural production. A property need not have agricultural land to be considered a farm; piggeries, hatcheries, and poultry batteries are farms because they engage in agricultural production, *i.e.,* raise livestock and produce livestock products.

b. All forms of tenure not included in the preceding categories. Includes land operated by schools, religious bodies, squatters, seasonally by nomads, and built-on, waste, and similar types of alienation.

... Not available, or no agricultural census or survey ever taken.

— None, less than half the smallest unit shown, or not applicable.

farmland use																	country
activity (% of farms)			technology (latest)				land in farms		land use (%)								
									cropland								
mainly crops	mainly livestock	mixed/other	tractors (per 1,000 ha)	electricity (% of farms having)	irrigation (% of land irrig.)	artificial fertilizer (kg/ha)	total ('000 ha)	% of total land area	permanent crops	temporary crops	fallow	total cropland	meadows and pastures	woodland and forest	other		
...	...	...	0.1	...	38	7	39,810	61.0	1.8	46.3	51.9	19.9	75.4	4.8	—		Afghanistan
57.9[5]	36.2[5]	5.9[5]	15.7	...	59	158	1,111[6]	40.0[6]	17.8	—82.2—		64.3[6]	35.7[6]	...	...		Albania
...	...	...	12.5	...	8	13	39,814[8]	16.7[8]	6.9[8]	55.2[8]	37.9[8]	20.4[8]	77.2[8]	—	2.4[8]		Algeria
55.7[5]	44.3[5]	—	15	38.5	...	...	3.2	16.4	—88.7—		11.3	71.4	5.3	...	23.3		American Samoa
...	...	...	...	...	...	...	...	2.0	...	...	...	2.8	69.4	27.8	...		Andorra
...			3.4	...	80[13]	7	4,180	3.4	36.8	63.2	—	1.7	82.0	...	16.2		Angola
32.9	44.1	23.0	30.0	...	...	...	2.5	9.0	26.0	57.1	16.9	62.6	36.0	—1.4—			Antigua and Barbuda
10.6[17]	78.9[17]	10.5[17]	11.2	...	7	4	177,437	64.8	4.8	71.5	23.7	15.4	56.4	21.3	6.9		Argentina
...	...	...	33.4	...	59	...	1,300	40.1	12.6	84.3	3.1	30.8	61.5	—	7.7		Armenia
...	...	...	...	...	...	...	...	...	...	...	...	...	...	...	...		Aruba
27.8[22]	61.7	17.5[23]	0.8	...	5	28	460,000[24]	59.9[24]	1.1	—98.9—		3.5	6.6	...	89.9[25]		Australia
59.8[26]	—	40.2[26]	242	...	0.3	201	7,530	91.0	5.3	93.5	1.2	20.0	26.0	43.0	11.0		Austria
	...	...	20.6	...	62	...	4,300	49.6	28.9	63.9	7.2	37.2	53.5	—	9.3		Azerbaijan
...	...	...	10.0	...	10[13]	...	15.0	1.5	23.3	59.9	16.8	23.3	6.9	25.7	44.0		Bahamas, The
...	...	...	...	21.3	100	333	3.5	5.2	50.7	49.3	—	45.9	...	...	54.1		Bahrain
91.3[33]	8.7[33]	—	0.6	...	33	98	9,137[34]	70.2[34]	—88.2[34]—		11.8[34]	89.5[34]	—10.5[34]—				Bangladesh
...	...	...	38.0	...	...	91	21.6	50.2	3.0	82.9	14.1	78.7	8.9	0.6	11.8		Barbados
79.1	19.4	1.5	20.2	...	2	...	9,400	45.1	...	...	...	65.3	—34.7—				Belarus
...	2.5[36]	...	145.3	...	0.1	496	1,392	45.6	1.2	98.4	0.4	51.9	45.2	0.5	2.4		Belgium
...	...	...	25.6	...	4	88	233[17]	10.0[17]	13.1[17]	81.1[17]	5.8[17]	36.5[17]	15.9[17]	36.1[17]	11.6[17]		Belize
...	...	...	0.1	...	0.7	2	3,300	29.3	...	...	...	100.0	—	—	—		Benin
...	...	...	12.5	...	...	...	2.4	4.1	18.6	72.9	8.5	91.1	8.9		...		Bermuda
...	...	...	...	...	30	1	156	3.4	11.7	—88.3—		100.0	—	—	—		Bhutan
			2.6	...	0	3	22,670	20.6	—55.0—		45.0	6.9	47.7	39.0	6.4		Bolivia
...	...	...	214	...	0.3	...	2,525[26]	49.4[26]	8.9[26]	70.9[26]	20.2[26]	44.2[26]	55.4[26]	—	0.4[26]		Bosnia and Herzegovina[18]
13.6[37]	27.9[37]	58.5[37]	14.3	...	0.5	1	343[41]	5.9[41]	—	100.0[41]	—	83.5[41]	...	...	...		Botswana
80.0[43]	16.2[43]	3.8[43]	17.5	4.1[43]	7	43	376,287	44.5	18.2[41]	66.9[41]	14.9[41]	15.8[41]	47.8[41]	24.2[41]	12.2[41]		Brazil
...	...	...	24.0	...	33	57	16.4	2.8	78.0	22.0	—	54.8	0.1	16.4	28.7		Brunei
43.9[4]	56.1[4]	—	11.7	...	30	195	6,159[4]	55.7[4]	6.3[4]	—93.7[4]—		75.4[4]	24.6[4]	...	...		Bulgaria
...	...	...	0.04	...	0.6	6	8,919	32.6	...	...	...	...	...	...	...		Burkina Faso
...	...	...	0.1	...	1.2	4	2,388	85.8	—73.8—		26.2	56.7	37.7	5.6	...		Burundi
...	...	...	0.6	...	4	1	2,984	16.5	94.0	3.5	1.6	96.1	—	3.9	—		Cambodia
...	...	...	0.1	...	0.3	6[2]	1,490	3.3	...	...	...	100.0	—	—	—		Cameroon
43.9	42.9	13.2	16.3	...	1.6	47	67,754	7.3	—80.9—		19.1	61.1	6.1	—32.7—			Canada
...	...	...	0.4	...	7	—	41	10.2	20.8[48]	79.1[48]	...	100.0[48]	—	—	—		Cape Verde
...	...	...	0.1	...	...	2	491	0.8	11.8	88.2	—	100.0	—	—	—		Central African Republic
...	...	...	0.05	...	0.4	2	23,877[49]	45.8[49]	50.0[49]	—50.0[49]—		23.7[49]	76.3[49]	...	...		Chad
...	...	...	10.5	...	32	69	8,746[19]	11.7[19]	26.5[19]	59.5[19]	14.0[19]	15.3[19]	52.4[19]	...	32.3[19]		Chile
...	...	...	8.0	...	54	261	166,902	17.4	4.1	—95.9—		100.0	—	—	—		China
...	...	...	9.3	...	13	101	36,034	34.7	47.3	34.6	18.1	14.7	48.5	14.0	22.8		Colombia
...	...	...	...	...	...	...	83	44.3	56.4	—43.6—		100.0	—	—	—		Comoros
6.2[5]	93.8[5]	—	4.9	...	0.7	3	226	0.7	14.8	85.2	—	100.0	—	—	—		Congo
...	...	...	24.6	...	42	203	3,122	60.0	42.2	57.8	—	15.7	49.9	22.9	11.4		Costa Rica
...	...	...	1.5	...	3	11	2,753	8.6	65.9	34.1	—	100.0	—	—	—		Côte d'Ivoire
...	...	...	3.4	...	0.3	...	3,220	57.0	8.8	81.8	9.4	50.4	48.5	—	1.1		Croatia[52]
...	...	...	30.0	...	35	199	8,679	78.3	...	...	...	33.9	32.1	31.9	2.1		Cuba
72.7	27.3	—	125	...	35	144	210	35.6	34.7	54.3	11.0	74.9	—	—25.1—			Cyprus
45.0[5, 58]	55.0[5, 58]	—	24.6[58]	100.0	0.8	314	4,282[58]	54.3[58]	2.9[58]	—97.1[58]—		74.7[58]	20.4[58]	—4.9[58]—			Czech Republic[54]
49.7	22.4	27.9	61.4	...	17	255	2,739	64.5	...	92.7	7.3	78.4	21.6	...	...		Denmark
...	...	...	...	...	...	...	1	0.5	...	6.8	...	100.0	—	—	—		Djibouti
...	...	...	12.9	...	...	259	20	26.3	...	...	...	...	...	...	...		Dominica
44.0	56.0	—	2.4	60.0	23	50	2,412	49.8	38.0	40.2	21.8	34.1	51.6	13.0	0.9		Dominican Republic
67.8	12.4	19.8	5.5	...	34	29	7,954[32]	30.5[32]	50.1[32]	20.7[32]	29.2[32]	34.7[32]	62.0[32]	—3.2[32]—			Ecuador
...	...	...	24.9	...	132	384	5,216[3, 4]	5.2[3, 4]	7.3[4]	92.7[4]	...	100.0[4]	—	—	—		Egypt
95.3	4.7	—	6.1	...	21	106	1,452	69.0	25.1	58.6	16.4	44.9	38.2	11.6	5.3		El Salvador

Agriculture and land use (continued)

country	farms (latest census of agriculture)[a]															
	year	number of farms ('000)	size of holding								tenure (% of farms)					
			average (ha)	size class (%)							owner-operated			rented (including share-croppers)	tribal/ com-munal	other[b]
				under 1 ha	1–5 ha	5–10 ha	10–20 ha	20–50 ha	50–200 ha	over 200 ha	individual/ family	corporate/ state	socialized/ collective			
Equatorial Guinea	...	...	...	...	...	...	...	...	...	...	...	...	...	...	...	...
Eritrea[66]	—	...	...	...	...	...	...	...	...	...	...	...	...	...	...	...
Estonia[52]	1994	10.4	...	8.0[4]		12.8[4]	27.8[4]	42.2[4]	9.2[4]		93.5[4]	6.5[4]		...	...	...
Ethiopia[66]	1989–92[68]	6,092[68]	1.3[68]	49.9[33]	46.5[33]	3.4[33]	0.2[33]	—	—	—	98.4[33]	1.6[33]	—	—	—	—
Faroe Islands	...	...	...	...	...	...	...	...	...	...	...	...	...	...	...	...
Fiji	1991	95	4.2[69]	43.3	31.4	13.3	6.6	3.3	1.5[20]	0.6[21]	15.8	0.4	—	49.5	32.2	2.1
Finland	1993[71]	192	12.8[26]	—	34.1	21.0	23.2	18.9	2.8		84.5			15.5	—	—
France	1993	801	26.6[41]	37.3			27.8[72]	10.7[73]	24.1		65.2[51]	—	—	33.5[51]	—	1.2[51]
French Guiana	1989	4.5	4.6	16.5	73.6	6.0	1.5	2.4			17.0[3]	—	—	57.2[3]	—	25.8[3]
French Polynesia	1987	5.6	...	37.7	62.3						36.5	...	...	6.3	...	57.1
Gabon	1975	71	1.0	68.0	32.0		—	—	—	—	81.8	—	—	0.3	5.3	12.5
Gambia, The	1989–90	...	...	...	...	...	...	...	...	...	...	...	...	...	...	...
Gaza Strip	1968	...	...	...	...	...	...	...	...	...	...	...	...	...	...	...
Georgia	1990	17.0[18, 19]	...	...	...	...	...	...	...	...	...	...	...	...	...	...
Germany	1993[3, 71]	593	28.0[19]	12.4[19, 61]	17.1[19, 75]	16.4[19]	19.5[19]	24.5[19]	10.1[19]		89.8	—	—	10.2	—	...
Ghana	1970	805	3.2	36.6	48.7	9.0	3.9	1.8	—	—	...	...	...	...	...	...
Gibraltar	—	...	...	...	...	...	...	...	...	...	...	...	...	...	...	...
Greece	1991	862	3.5[76]	25.7[77]	50.6	14.4	6.2	2.0			...	...	...	...	...	...
Greenland	—	...	...	...	...	...	...	...	...	...	...	...	...	...	...	...
Grenada	1981	8	1.7	88.3[61]	6.9[78]	3.3[79]	0.7	0.4[27]	0.3[80]		73.2			14.1	—	12.7
Guadeloupe	1988–89	17	2.8	32.1	58.3	7.0	1.6	0.9			57.7[3, 14]	—	—	18.8[3, 14]	—	23.5[3, 14]
Guam	1992	0.2	4.0	58.8[9]	17.6[10]	19.6[11]		4.0[12]			53.8	—	—	30.1	—	16.1[81]
Guatemala	1979	600	6.8	39.7[82]	49.8[83]	8.2[84]			2.2[85]		74.0[86]			6.3[86]	5.8[86]	13.9[86]
Guernsey	1993	0.089	16.2[60]	6.7[17]	24.0[17]	23.1[17]	46.1[17]		—	—	32.4[2, 14]	—	—	67.6[2, 14]	—	—
Guinea	1989[3]	431	2.4[50]	...	...	...	...	...	...	...	...	...	...	...	...	...
Guinea-Bissau	1988	84	3.0[1]	13.4[1]	73.3[1]	10.0[1]	3.0[1]	0.3[1]	—	—	...	...	...	...	...	...
Guyana	1964	...	...	...	...	...	...	...	...	...	...	90.0	...	...	...	10.0
Haiti	1987	667	1.4[51]	61.8	36.6	1.5	0.1	—	—	—	93.4	—	—	5.9	—	0.7
Honduras	1992–93	318	13.5	25.2	46.5	11.0	7.2	6.3	3.1	0.6	39.9	23.1	—	16.6	—	20.4
Hong Kong	1986	11	0.3	97.5	2.3	0.1	0.1		—	—	9.0			77.0	—	14.0
Hungary	1993	3.2[87]	...	90[60]	9.9[60]		0.1[60]				6.8[76]	13.3[76]	74.5[76]	—	—	—
Iceland	1981	7.0	...	15.7	9.3	11.7	23.7	35.8	3.7		...	...	...	...	...	...
India	1985–86	97,700	1.7	58.1	31.9[30]	8.1[79]	1.9				94.1	—	—	0.5	—	5.4
Indonesia	1993	21,737	1.0	70.8	27.8	1.2	0.2				74.8[6]	—[7]	—[7]	3.2[7]	—[7]	22.1[7]
Iran	1988	3,330	...	...	...	...	...	...	...	...	...	...	...	...	...	...
Iraq	1979	470	13.3	25.9[90]	27.6[91]	23.2[92]	11.5[93]	9.4	1.9[94]	0.5[95]	52.5[13]	—	—	40.9[13]	—	6.6[13]
Ireland	1986	279[43]	25.0[17]	2.7[43]	37.8[43]		52.4[43]		7.1[43]	—	...	...	...	...	...	...
Isle of Man	1992	0.8	59.7	26.7[96]			16.2[97]	17.0[27]	12.4[28]	27.9[29]	72.4[6]	—	—	27.6[6]	—	—
Israel	1981	52	11.3	26.5	57.6	8.3	4.0	2.0	1.8		84.0	—	1.4	—	—	14.6
Italy	1990	2,941	7.5[34]	33.0[34]	43.0[34]	11.7[34]	6.7[34]	3.8[34]	1.8[34]		81.5[43]	—	—	6.7[43]	—	11.8[43]
Jamaica	1978–79	184	2.9	32.5[98]	60.7[99]	4.8[79]	0.9	0.4[27]	0.3[28]	0.4[29]	99.5[35]	0.2[35]	—	—	—	0.3[35]
Japan	1993	2,835	1.4	56.9	41.0	2.1					79.4[43]	...	...	...	...	20.6[43]
Jersey	1990	0.6	11.1	45.0[100]		16.4[101]	19.7[102]	19.0[103]			31.4[38]	—	—	68.6[38]	—	—
Jordan	1983	57	6.3	25.3	44.6	15.6	8.6	4.5	1.3	0.1	80.5	—	—	13.1	0.3	6.1
Kazakhstan	1993	8.5[18, 19]	412[18, 19]	...	...	...	...	...	...	...	...	...	...	...	...	...
Kenya	1976–79[107]	2,750	2.5	65.5	27.3	2.7[108]	4.4[109]				...	...	...	...	...	...
Kiribati	...	...	...	...	...	...	...	...	...	...	...	...	...	...	...	...
Korea, North	...	...	...	...	...	...	...	...	...	...	...	...	...	...	...	...
Korea, South	1990[3]	1,767	1.2	60.8[2]	39.2[2]						82.5[42]	—	—	17.4[43]	—	0.1[43]
Kuwait	1992–93	2.3[8]	2.4[110]	48.6[43]	25.4[43]	10.2[43]	8.7[43]	4.0[43]	3.1[43]	—	95.3[8]	...	...	...	...	4.7[8]
Kyrgyzstan	1993	8.6[18, 19]	44[18, 19]	...	...	...	...	...	...	...	...	...	...	...	...	...
Laos	1983	...	...	...	...	...	...	...	...	...	...	...	...	...	...	...
Latvia	1993	57.5[18, 19]	16.5[18, 19]	...	...	...	...	...	...	...	...	...	...	...	...	...
Lebanon	1970	143	4.3	47.7	44.5		6.5		1.2	0.1	...	...	...	...	...	...
Lesotho	1989–90	207[111]	2.0[43]	27.0[43]	67.5[43]	5.5[43]		—	—	—	...	...	...	...	...	...
Liberia	1971[112]	122	3.0	52.8	31.0	12.0	3.7		0.5		40.0[14]	—	—	—	43.3[14]	16.7[14]
Libya	1974	144	14.0	12.7	34.1	20.6	17.4	12.0	3.2		...	...	...	...	...	...
Liechtenstein	1990	0.42	8.7	33.8	25.7	10.3	10.8	18.7	0.7		31.7	—	—	24.5	—	43.8
Lithuania	1994	5.9[18, 19]	16[18, 19]	...	...	...	...	...	...	...	57.2[4]			42.8[4]		
Luxembourg	1994	3.3	38	14.6[61]	11.9	8.3	8.3	21.1	35.8		45.4[4, 14]	...	...	...	...	...
Macau	—	...	...	...	...	...	...	...	...	...	...	...	...	...	...	...
Macedonia[52]	1981	176	...	44.7	43.0	6.7	1.2	0.2			100.0	—	—	—	—	—
Madagascar	1984–85	1,453	1.3	54.8	44.2	1.0	0.2	0.1	0.1		87.3[14]			4.9[14]	...	7.4[14]
Malawi	1980–81[107]	1,136	1.2	54.9	40.1[114]	5.0[115]					...	...	...	...	...	...
Malaysia	1980[107, 116]	920	2.2	...	...	...	...	...	...	...	53.2[43]	18.2[43]	...	19.6[43]	...	9.0[43]
Maldives	1985	...	...	...	...	...	...	...	...	...	...	...	...	...	...	...
Mali	1982–83	562	4.0	20.1	54.1	17.4	8.4			—	96.8[118]	3.2	—	...	—	—
Malta	1983	12	1.1	67.8	30.0	2.0	0.2				16.0	—	—	70.4	—	13.6[53]
Marshall Islands	—	...	...	...	...	...	...	...	...	...	...	...	...	...	...	...
Martinique[3]	1988–89	16.0	2.3	64.9	28.2	4.0	1.6	1.4			48.3[14]	...	...	16.7[14]	...	35.0[14]
Mauritania	1984–85	100	2.0	49.2	41.0[30]	7.0[79]	2.0	0.5[27]	0.3[80]		68.4	...	...	4.4	10.4	17.0
Mauritius	1980	32.5	1.1	61.3	36.2	1.9	0.3	0.2	0.1		95.8	—	—	4.2	—	—
Mayotte	1987	5.9[76]	1.7[104]	...	...	...	...	...	...	...	...	...	...	...	...	...
Mexico	1970[119]	2,848	49	23.5	39.4	21.1	8.8	2.7	2.9	1.5	97.6			1.0	—	1.5
Micronesia	...	...	...	...	...	...	...	...	...	...	...	...	...	...	...	...
Moldova	1991	0.5[18, 19]	3[18, 19]	...	...	...	...	...	...	...	—	30.8	55.2	—	—	14.0
Monaco	...	...	...	...	...	...	...	...	...	...	...	...	...	...	...	...
Mongolia	1985	0.3	385,000	...	...	...	...	...	...	...	—	16.0	84.0	—	—	—
Morocco	1985–86	1,900[104]	3.9[104]	29.8[7]	44.0[7]	14.9[7]	7.7[7]	3.0[7]	0.7[7]		...	...	...	...	...	...
Mozambique	1973	1,605	3.1	...	...	...	...	...	...	...	0.2	0.1	—	—	99.7	—
Myanmar (Burma)	1987–88	4,308[120]	2.3[120]	61.2[61, 120]	24.7[78, 120]	11.5[120, 121]	2.5[97, 120]	0.8[12, 120]			...	...	...	...	...	...
Namibia	1989	6.3[122]	...	...	...	...	...	...	...	...	45.0	—	—	55.0	—	—
Nauru	...	...	...	...	...	...	...	...	...	...	...	...	...	...	...	...
Nepal	1992	2,736	1.1[38]	66.7[38]	29.9[38]	2.7[38]	0.7[38]				82.6	—	—	1.8	—	15.6
Netherlands, The	1994[59]	116[123]	15.5[36]	9.6	24.1	16.1	18.6	25.8	5.8		31.5[14, 36]		—	12.2[14, 36]	—	56.4[14, 36]

activity (% of farms)			technology (latest)				farmland use									country
							land in farms		land use (%)							
									cropland							
mainly crops	mainly livestock	mixed/ other	tractors (per 1,000 ha)	electricity (% of farms having)	irrigation (% of land irrig.)	artificial fertilizer (kg/ha)	total ('000 ha)	% of total land area	permanent crops	temporary crops	fallow	total cropland	meadows and pastures	woodland and forest	other	
...	...	...	0.8	...	...	...	...	...	...	...	...	...	...	...	...	Equatorial Guinea
...	...	...	0.7	...	2	...	...	...	...	...	...	...	...	...	...	Eritrea[66]
...	...	...	13.3	...	...	...	252.3[67]	22.7[67]	...	...	...	44.0[67]	10.0[67]	34.0[67]	12.0[67]	Estonia[52]
16.5[68]	2.0[68]	81.5[68]	0.3	...	2	7	7,042[68]	6.4[68]	6.9[68]	82.0[68]	11.1[68]	87.0[68]	8.7[68]	0.8[68]	3.5[68]	Ethiopia[66]
...	...	...	...	...	...	...	...	...	...	...	...	...	...	...	...	Faroe Islands
26.5	29.3	44.2[70]	39.4[69]	...	1[69]	96[69]	277[69]	15.2[69]	...	...	...	37.8	34.0	19.1	9.1	Fiji
52.3	—47.6—		89.9	100.0	3	210	14,535	47.7	1.4[67]	78.5[67]	20.1[67]	17.8[67]	0.7[67]	61.3[67]	20.2[67]	Finland
36.6[26, 74]	38.0[26]	25.4[26]	80.0	...	8	319	30,223	55.0	7.2	81.8	11.0	55.1	35.6	—9.3—		France
...	...	...	32.5	...	20	64	21.7[19]	0.3[19]	22.8[3]	76.3[3]	0.9[3]	57.6[3]	42.4[3]	...	...	French Guiana
...	...	...	31.2	...	19.4	33	36.8	10.4	90.0	7.1	2.9	62.0	8.5	1.9	27.6	French Polynesia
...	...	...	5.1	...	1	3	73.0	0.3	...	...	...	...	...	...	...	Gabon
...	...	...	0.2	...	8	11	176.4	16.5	...	100.0	...	100.0	...	...	...	Gambia, The
...	...	...	83.3	...	133	...	16.5[19]	50.0[19]	68.8[19]	31.2[19]	...	100.0	—	—	—	Gaza Strip
...	...	...	28.6	...	57	...	3,200	45.7	24.6	—75.4—		32.6	62.5	—	4.9	Georgia
...	...	...	111.3	...	4	384	19,185[60]	54.9[60]	1.8[60]	—98.2[60]—		61.3[60]	27.4[60]	8.0[60]	3.3[60]	Germany
...	...	...	1.5	...	0.2	3	2,574	10.8	61.4	38.6	—	100.0	—	—	—	Ghana
...	...	...	...	...	...	4	...	...	...	...	...	...	...	...	...	Gibraltar
69.2	1.1	29.7	89.3	...	54	175	3,351	26.0	32.5	63.5	4.0	90.1	9.9	...	...	Greece
...	c. 100	...	...	...	...	...	...	...	...	...	...	...	...	...	...	Greenland
...	...	...	6.0	...	...	...	13.9	40.2	...	...	...	...	...	...	...	Grenada
...	...	...	34.8	...	13	307	46.7[19]	35.3[19]	14.5[19]	39.1[19]	46.5[19]	56.7[19]	43.3[19]	...	...	Guadeloupe
38.2	29.6	32.2	181.5	...	20.7	...	0.8	1.4	—51.0—		49.0	71.6	9.5	6.5	12.4	Guam
...	...	...	3.2	...	9	66	4,147	38.1	27.6	—72.4—		42.0	27.3	27.2	3.4	Guatemala
...	71.9	...	...	...	...	...	2	27.6	—	100.0	—	12.3	87.7	...	...	Guernsey
...	...	...	0.5	...	15	1	1,600[26]	6.5	...	...	...	...	...	...	...	Guinea
...	...	...	0.1	...	6	3	96[3]	3.4	...	...	...	...	...	...	...	Guinea-Bissau
...	...	...	7.6	...	27	33	10,652	26.2	...	...	...	8.4	91.6	...	...	Guyana
...	...	...	0.4	...	13	4	1,579	57.0	...	...	...	33.5	18.0	1.5	47.0	Haiti
...	...	...	2.9	...	4	18	3,337	29.8	23.9	33.7	42.5	41.7	45.9	10.9	1.5	Honduras
56.3	37.3	6.4	0.7	...	33	100.0[37]	7.3	6.8	7.4	37.0	55.6	100.0	—	—	—	Hong Kong
43.4[5, 19]	44.3[5, 19]	12.3[5, 19]	8.2	...	4	231	7,956[67]	85.5[67]	5.5[67]	94.5[67]	—	59.6[67]	14.4[67]	22.2[67]	3.8[67]	Hungary
...	...	...	1,809	87.0[48]	...	2,529	...	...	...	...	...	...	...	...	...	Iceland
...	...	...	7.2	...	29	75	172,900[88]	52.6[88]	—84.4[89]—		15.6[89]	97.9[89]		—2.1[89]—		India
86.8[7]	—[7]	13.2[7]	1.9	...	24	110	48,583[6]	25.3[6]	27.0[6]	45.2[6]	27.8[6]	60.7[6]	5.1[6]	18.9[6]	15.3[6]	Indonesia
...	...	...	7.1	...	56	80	104,900[38]	63.8[38]	4.9[38]	62.0[38]	33.2[38]	14.2[38]	85.8[38]	...	...	Iran
87.9	11.2	0.8	6.1	...	49	39	5,732	13.1	3.0	62.4	34.6	87.2	0.7	0.2	11.9	Iraq
...	...	...	182	...	...	741	5,692	82.6	0.5	99.5	...	9.5	69.5	—21.0—		Ireland
...	...	...	...	...	...	...	47	81.4	3.4	—96.6—		11.3	88.7	...	...	Isle of Man
...	...	...	72.6	...	51	252	435[4]	21.2[4]	25.0[19]	—75.0[19]—		81.5[19]		—18.5[19]—		Israel
81.2	13.2	5.6	158	...	30	151	22,702	75.3	25.5	—74.5—		48.1	18.2	24.7	9.0	Italy
...	...	...	19.9	...	23	116	603[35]	54.8[35]	22.2[35]	72.2[35]	5.6[35]	41.3[35]	21.6[35]	13.5[35]	23.6[35]	Jamaica
80.8[41]	—19.2[41]—		507	...	69	414	5,124[3]	13.7[3]	9.1	—90.9—		95.6	—	—	4.4	Japan
85.1[104]	14.9[104]	—	...	...	...	...	6.5	56.2	—98.9—		1.1	63.4		—36.6—		Jersey
58.2[105, 106]	14.9[105, 106]	26.9[105, 106]	18.4	1.5	20	63	364	4.1	13.3	63.0	23.7	87.7	1.0	0.3	11.0	Jordan
...	...	...	5.2	...	6	...	181,300	66.7	1.5	86.4	12.1	19.1	80.6	—	0.3	Kazakhstan
...	...	...	3.5	...	2	48	6,922	11.9	11.5	—88.5—		71.0	23.8	1.9	3.3	Kenya
...	...	...	...	...	...	...	...	...	...	...	...	...	...	...	...	Kiribati
...	...	...	44.2	...	86	407	...	...	...	...	...	...	...	...	...	Korea, North
82.3[5]	17.7[5]	—	40.9	...	71	454	2,109	21.2	6.7	—93.3—		100.0	—	—	—	Korea, South
38.9[8]	61.1[8]	—	20.0	100.0	40	167	7.9	0.4	20.6[8]	79.4[8]	—	70.0[8]		—30.0[8]—		Kuwait
...	...	...	10.4		64		10,100	50.0	0.1	50.9	3.0	13.9	86.1	—	—	Kyrgyzstan
...	...	...	1.1	...	16	2	1,680	7.1	2.3	97.7		52.4	47.6	...	...	Laos
...	...	...	31.0	...	...	...	2,500	38.5	...	...	...	68.0[19]		—32.0[19]—		Latvia
77.0[105]	8.1[105]	14.9[105]	13.9	...	40	79	275[41]	27.0[41]	36.7[41]	39.7[41]	23.6[41]	100.0[41]	—	—	—	Lebanon
37.3[111]	—	62.7[111]	5.8	...	0.9	14	372[43]	12.3[43]	—	89.6[43]	10.4[43]	98.8[43]	...	...	1.2[43]	Lesotho
...	...	...	2.6	...	2	7	370[76]	3.8[76]	66.2[76]	33.8[76]	—	98.3[76]	...	1.7[76]	...	Liberia
...	...	...	19.0	...	26	39	8,800[76]	5.1[76]	—33.3[76]—		66.7[76]	20.5[76]	79.5[76]	...	...	Libya
23.9[37]	61.6[37]	14.5[37]	112	...	...	...	3.9	24.2	1.1	—98.9—		39.9	57.5	1.1	1.5	Liechtenstein
...	...	...	20.0	...	...	...	3,519	53.9	38.3	60.9	0.8	76.2	13.5	—10.3—		Lithuania
24.5[113]	59.8	15.7	143	...	...	...	137	53.3	—96.6—		3.4	41.7	49.5	6.6	2.2	Luxembourg
...	...	...	...	...	...	...	...	...	...	...	...	...	...	...	...	Macau
...	...	...	83.8	...	14	...	1,320	51.3	9.3	65.4	25.3	46.4	53.4	—	1.2	Macedonia[52]
...	...	...	1.1	...	42	2	2,044	3.5	15.4	84.6	—	100.0	—	—	—	Madagascar
22.1	...	77.9	0.8	...	2	23	1,332	14.1	0.2	99.8	—	94.8	...	5.2	...	Malaŵi
...	...	...	12.0[117]	...	33[117]	170[117]	4,100[38]	31.2[38]	84.8[38]	15.2[38]	—	100.0[38]	...	...	...	Malaysia
...	...	...	...	...	...	...	19	63.5	...	...	...	...	...	...	...	Maldives
...	...	...	0.3	...	3	9	2,277	1.8	—	100.0	—	100.0	—	—	—	Mali
...	...	...	37.5	...	8	39	13.0	41.2	5.0	—95.0—		87.5		—12.5—		Malta
...	...	...	...	...	...	...	...	...	...	...	...	...	...	...	...	Marshall Islands
...	...	...	115	...	50	945	37.2[19]	39.0[19]	46.6[19]	50.7[19]	2.7[19]	52.1[19]	47.9[19]	...	—	Martinique[3]
...	...	...	1.6	...	24	12	196[36]	0.2[36]	—	56.2	43.8	100.0	—	—	—	Mauritania
...	...	...	3.7	...	17	304	100[111]	53.8[111]	4.2[111]	95.8[111]	—	90.0[111]		—10.0[111]—		Mauritius
...	...	...	...	...	...	...	14.6	39.0	33.3	66.7	—	100.0	—	—	—	Mayotte
83.9	12.9	3.2	7.4	...	26	70	139,868	72.7	6.3	58.1	35.6	16.5	53.3	14.2	16.0	Mexico
61.4[5]	15.7[5]	22.9[5]	7.4	45	0	...	5.8	12.2	—9.3—		90.7	32.9	30.2	—36.9—		Micronesia
...	...	...	31.0	...	18	...	2,500[19]	73.5[19]	26.5[19]	—73.5[19]—		68.0[19]	12.0[19]	—	20.0[19]	Moldova
...	...	...	...	...	...	...	...	...	...	...	...	...	...	...	...	Monaco
...	...	...	8.4	...	6	12	124,587	79.6	—	66.8	33.2	0.9	99.1	...	...	Mongolia
...	...	...	4.5	...	14	36	9,256[24, 61]	20.7[24, 61]	7.2[24, 61]	63.8[24, 61]	29.0[24, 61]	100.0[24, 61]	—	—	—	Morocco
...	...	...	1.9	...	4	1	13,626	17.8	—44.9—		55.1	55.0	45.0	...	...	Mozambique
...	...	...	1.1	...	11	8	12,560	18.6	3.0	79.5	17.5	97.0	3.0	...	...	Myanmar (Burma)
1.3[5]	94.4[5]	4.3[5]	4.8	...	0.9	...	662	0.8	0.3	—99.7—		100.0	—	—	—	Namibia
...	...	...	...	...	...	...	...	...	...	...	...	...	...	...	...	Nauru
...	...	...	2.0	...	37	25	2,599	19.0	1.7	97.1	1.2	90.6	1.4	4.2	3.8	Nepal
31.7	57.5	10.8	201	...	62	628	1,971	58.1	—98.4—		1.6	46.7	53.3	—	—	Netherlands, The

Agriculture and land use (continued)

country	year	number of farms ('000)	average (ha)	size class (%) under 1 ha	1–5 ha	5–10 ha	10–20 ha	20–50 ha	50–200 ha	over 200 ha	tenure (% of farms) owner-operated individual/ family	corporate/ state	socialized/ collective	rented (including share-croppers)	tribal/ com-munal	other[b]
	farms (latest census of agriculture)[a]		size of holding													
Netherlands Antilles	...	...	...	...	...	...	...	...	...	...	...	...	...	...	...	...
New Caledonia	1991	10.3	23[124]	71.2[61, 124]	13.8[75, 124]	3.7[124]	2.3[124]	2.5[124]	3.8[124]	2.8[124]	...	...	...	...	84.5	15.5
New Zealand	1993	81.2	217[60]	—13.3—		11.6	9.9	—44.7—		20.5	85.7[37]	10.9[37]	...	—	—	3.4[37]
Nicaragua	1991	...	...	—26.2[50]—				—30.6[50]—		43.3[50]	64.4[14, 38]	—35.6[14, 38]—		—	—	—
Niger	1980[3]	699	4.9	3.8	54.1	37.8	—4.3—				...	...	...	...	...	...
Nigeria	1971	...	...	92.0	7.8	0.2	—	—	—	—	...	...	...	...	...	...
Northern Mariana Is.	1990	0.1	49.1	26.1[127]	35.3[128]	—24.4[11]—		—14.3—			56.3	...	...	23.5	...	20.2
Norway	1994[59]	85.7[129]	10.2[2]	—29.6—		24.7	28.9	15.3	—1.5—		—65.4[2]—			34.6[2]	—	—
Oman	1992–93	95	1.6	71.0	24.3	3.8	0.5	0.3	0.1	—	99.3	—	—	0.4	—	0.3
Pakistan	1990	5,071	...	27.0	54.0	12.2	4.7	—2.1—			68.8	—	—	18.8	—12.4[130]—	
Palau[131]	1989	0.3	...	...	...	...	...	...	...	...	79.1[14]	—	—	12.7[14]	8.2[14]	—
Panama	1991	214	13.8	46.7	24.8	7.6	7.1	7.7	5.3	0.8	28.6	—	—	1.4	—	70.0[42]
Papua New Guinea	1985[132]	0.8	483	—26.8[59]—					28.3[84]	44.9[84]	26.9[14, 84]	71.0[14, 84]	—	2.1[14, 84]	—	—
Paraguay	1986	307	88[76]	8.6[76]	27.4[76]	19.9[76]	22.7[76]	14.5[76]	4.4[76]	2.5[76]	51.0[3]	—	—	7.2[3]	—	41.8[42]
Peru	1984	1,574	9.5	24.1	47.7	13.2	6.7	5.5	—2.8—		75.5	—	—	0.8	6.8	16.9
Philippines	1980	3,420	2.6	22.7	63.3	10.5	—3.5—				58.3	—	—	27.4	—	14.3
Poland[18]	1994	2,026	7.0[110]	21.6[61]	32.7[75]	26.8	11.1[133]	—7.8[134]—			78.3[4, 14]	13.9[4, 14]	3.3[4, 14]	—	—	4.5[4, 14]
Portugal	1993	489	10.5	24.9	53.2	—17.0—		3.0	—1.9—		92.0	—	—	—8.0—		
Puerto Rico	1992	22	14.5	—5.1[135]—		7.5[136]	14.3[137]	14.2[138]	—58.9[80]—		—79.5—		—	10.6	—	9.9
Qatar	1990	0.8	7.0	20.5	41.8	18.0	12.6	5.8	—1.4—		...	...	...	...	...	...
Réunion[3]	1989	15	4.1	35.6	47.9	12.5	2.7	—1.3—			46.1[7]	—	—	22.5[7]	—	31.4[7]
Romania	1993	3.6[44]	3,900[44]	...	...	...	...	...	...	...	69.9[14]	...	...	...	...	30.1[14]
Russia	1994	28.1	7,068[44, 60]	...	...	...	...	...	...	...	...	...	...	...	...	...
Rwanda	1984	1,112	1.2	56.8	26.8[139]	—16.4[140]—					50.9	—	—	1.4	—	47.7[53]
St. Kitts and Nevis	1987	3.4	...	...	...	...	...	...	...	...	82.0[14]	—	—	7.7[14]	—	10.3[42]
St. Lucia	1986	12	2.0	75.9[61]	10.3[78]	4.9[79]	0.9	0.3[27]	0.2[28]	0.4[29]	72.0	—	—	15.5	—	12.5
St. Vincent	1988	9	1.8[141]	48.0[98, 141]	40.7[141, 142]	8.5[78, 141]	2.4[11, 141]	—0.5[12, 141]—			53.8	—	—	12.3	—	33.9[42]
San Marino	1975	0.7	7.0	21.3	47.8	—24.7—		5.1	—1.1—		39.9[14]	15.5[14]	—	29.9[14]	—	14.7[14]
São Tomé and Príncipe	1989	13.8	8.7[143]	88.5[143]	9.8[143]	0.7[143]	0.2[143]	0.2[143]	0.2[143]	0.4[143]	77.2[143]	—	—	20.5[143]	—	2.3[143]
Saudi Arabia	1982–83	212	10.1	36.6	35.8	11.3	8.2	5.0	2.6	0.5	85.9	—	—	2.6	—	11.5
Senegal	1976	362	7.0	—99.4—					—0.6—		...	...	0.6	...	...	99.4
Seychelles	1993	0.9[144]	...	...	...	...	...	...	...	...	98.9	—1.1—		—	—	—
Sierra Leone	1971	286	1.8	38.8	55.0	—6.1—		—0.1—			93.6	—	—	6.4	—	—
Singapore	1973	16	0.8	77.4	22.2	0.3	—0.1—				7.4	—	—	88.8	—	3.8
Slovakia	1991	...	...	...	...	...	...	...	...	...	...	...	...	...	...	...
Slovenia[52]	1991	157	...	28.4	36.0	18.0	—17.6—				100.0	—	—	—	—	—
Solomon Islands	1975[107]	92	1.0	...	...	...	...	...	...	...	—	—	—	—	100.0	—
Somalia	1984	198	3.6	...	...	...	...	...	...	...	99.9	0.1	—	—	—	—
South Africa[147]	1992	62[148]	1,319	—0.8[100]—		1.5	1.9	6.4	13.7	75.7	89.6[81]	...	...	...	...	10.4
Spain	1989	2,285	19.0	27.7	36.6	13.2	9.5	6.8	3.9	2.3	72.5	...	...	19.8	—7.7—	
Sri Lanka	1982	1,817	1.1	77.5[9]	—22.2[150]—		0.1[151]	0.1[27]	—0.1[80]—		59.0[152]	27.2[152]	—	8.2[152]	—	5.6[152]
Sudan, The	1982	...	...	...	...	...	...	...	...	...	22.3	2.2	—	28.0	42.0	5.5
Suriname	1981	22	7.5	21.9[35]	61.2[35]	11.1[35]	3.6[35]	1.6[35]	0.3[35]	0.3[35]	20.2[35]	0.9[35]	—	49.5[35]	—	29.4[35]
Swaziland[153]	1992–93	0.4	51	41.2	29.5	10.3	6.1	—12.9—			84.4[34]	—	—	—15.6[34]—		
Sweden	1994	90	29.5[26]	...	15.2	19.8	21.2	26.6	16.3	1.0	48.0	—	—	15.0	—	37.0[53]
Switzerland	1990	108	9.9	21.7	19.0	17.4	29.1	12.3	0.6	—	36.2[41]	—	0.8[41]	58.5[41]	—	4.5[41]
Syria	1988	444	8.9	16.7	36.8[30]	22.8[79]	13.1	8.5	2.0[155]	0.2[156]	65.8[14, 118]	1.8[14]	32.5[14]	...	—	—
Taiwan	1993	723[2]	1.2[2]	72.6[2]	27.4[2]	...	...	...	...	...	83.0	—	—	4.0	—	13.0
Tajikistan	1993	...	...	...	...	...	...	...	...	...	...	...	...	...	...	...
Tanzania	1986–87	3,626	0.9[3]	70.1	28.8	1.0	—0.1—				87.3[141]	—	—	3.6[141]	—	9.1[141]
Thailand	1988	4,877	3.7	14.3	72.0[157]	—13.1[158]—		—0.5[159]—			87.0	—	—	3.6	—	9.3
Togo	1982–83	263	1.5	48.8	38.6[114]	—12.7[115]—					70.7[14]	—	—	21.1[14]	8.2[14]	—
Tonga	1985	10.1	3.3	18.9	67.9	12.7	—	0.5	—	—	—97.2—			—	—	2.8
Trinidad and Tobago	1982	30.6	4.3	35.1	50.7	9.6	4.1	—	0.4	0.1	52.1	—	—	36.5	—	11.4
Tunisia	1988	376	13.6	—45.7—		20.6	17.9	11.4	—4.4—		...	...	...	...	...	...
Turkey	1991	4,068	...	16.0[26]	51.1[26]	18.0[26]	9.7[26]	4.4[26]	—0.8[26]—		95.9	—	—	1.1	—	3.0
Turkmenistan	1993	0.1[18, 19]	10[18, 19]	...	...	...	...	...	...	...	...	...	...	...	...	...
Tuvalu	1976	1.5	1.7	...	...	...	...	...	...	...	99.9	...	...	...	0.1	—
Uganda	1991	1,704	3.9	20.7[143]	59.8[143]	11.2[143]	—8.3[143]—				78.8	—	—	—	17.3	3.9
Ukraine	1993	14.4[18, 19]	20[18, 19]	...	...	...	...	...	...	...	...	...	...	...	...	...
United Arab Emirates	1986–87	17.9	2.3	45.4	38.8[161]	—15.9[162]—					...	...	...	...	...	...
United Kingdom	1993	242[19]	107.3[19, 163]	5.6[19, 61]	8.4[19, 62]	11.9[19]	15.2[19]	24.7[19]	28.0[19]	6.2[19]	—74.3[164]—		—	25.7[164]	—	—
United States	1992	2,073[165]	190[165]	—8.6[99]—		—20.1[11]—		30.3[166]	22.2[167]	18.7[168]	57.7	...	—	11.3	—	31.0[81]
Uruguay	1990	55	280.5[111]	—	8.2	12.1	13.2	16.5	23.3	26.7	—59.1[41]—		—	17.3[41]	—	23.6[41]
Uzbekistan	1993	5.9[18, 19]	7[18, 19]	...	...	...	...	...	...	...	...	...	...	...	...	...
Vanuatu[169]	1993	22	6.9[124]	...	...	...	...	...	...	...	65.3[41]	34.7[41]	—	...	...	...
Venezuela	1984–85	381	82.0	8.3	36.3	15.7	13.0	10.4	9.3	7.1	61.5[51]	...	—	6.1[51]	...	31.3[19, 51]
Vietnam	1991	31[44]	28.0[3]	...	...	...	...	...	...	...	—	—100—		—	—	—
Virgin Islands (U.S.)	1992	0.3[6]	27.0[6]	30.0[6, 170]	30.3[6, 171]	12.0[6]	13.9[6]	6.0[6]	3.7[6, 172]	4.1[6, 173]	75.3[6]	...	—	8.6[6]	—	16.1[6]
West Bank	1965	55	3.4	49.8	34.4	10.6	4.0	1.0	0.2	0.0	7.16	—	—	6.4	—	22.0
Western Sahara	1983	...	...	...	...	...	...	...	...	...	...	...	...	...	...	...
Western Samoa	1989	11	6.1	...	...	...	...	...	...	...	0.1	...	...	2.6[14]	94.2[14]	3.1[14]
Yemen[174]	1977–83	591	2.3	57.5	30.9	7.4	3.3	0.8	0.1	—	90.3[14]	—	—	9.4[14]	—	0.3[14]
Yugoslavia	1981	1,198	...	24.7	48.8	19.9	4.4	—0.7—			83.0[60]	—17.0[60]—		—	—	—
Zaire	1970	2,538	2.3	41.6	57.3	1.0	0.2	—	—	—	4.2	0.1	—	...	95.6	0.1
Zambia	1990	520	3.1[51]	50.5[51]	45.2[51]	—3.8[51]—		—0.5[51]—			99.9	0.1	—	—	—	—
Zimbabwe	1994	1,079[177]	38.7[17]	—16.7[17, 96]—			—82.6[17, 178]—		—0.7[17, 21]—		—2.0[17]—		—	—	98.0[17]	—

[1]1967. [2]1989. [3]Cultivated area only. [4]1993. [5]Based on value of output by sector. [6]1987. [7]1973. [8]1991–92. [9]Less than 1.6 ha. [10]1.6 to 4.0 ha. [11]4.0 to 20 ha. [12]20 ha or more. [13]Percentage of farms having irrigation. [14]Based on area, not number, of holdings. [15]10 to 25 ha. [16]25 to 50 ha. [17]1974. [18]Private farms only. [19]1992. [20]50 to 100 ha. [21]100 ha or more. [22]Includes fruits and vegetables. [23]Includes houseplants and cut flowers. [24]1992–93. [25]Includes fallow and grazing lands. [26]1990. [27]20 to 40 ha. [28]40 to 61 ha. [29]61 ha or more. [30]1.0 to 4.0 ha. [31]4.0 to 10.1 ha. [32]10.1 ha or more. [33]1977. [34]1990–91. [35]1969. [36]1988. [37]1985. [38]1982. [39]4.0 ha or more. [40]Includes about 21,000 farms without land; distribution by size refers to traditional farms with land only. [41]1980. [42]More than one-half squatters. [43]1970. [44]State farms and cooperatives only. [45]Precollectivization. [46]4.0 to 52.2 ha. [47]52.2 ha and over. [48]Irrigated land only. [49]1968. [50]1984. [51]1971. [52]Holdings and tenure refer to private plots only; size and tenure 1990. [53]Owned and rented holdings. [54]Data for Czech Republic include Slovakia unless otherwise noted. [55]Less than 0.5 ha. [56]0.5 to 50 ha. [57]50 to 1,000 ha. [58]Excludes Slovakia; 1994. [59]Arable area only. [60]1991. [61]Less than 2.0 ha. [62]2.0 to 20 ha. [63]2.1 ha or less. [64]2.1 to 4.2 ha. [65]4.2 ha or more. [66]Data for Ethiopia include Eritrea, unless otherwise staed. [67]1994. [68]Excludes Eritrea. [69]1978–79. [70]Includes 28 percent under forests. [71]Excludes holdings of less than 1.0 ha. [72]10 to 35 ha. [73]35 to 50 ha. [74]Includes fruit-growing and viticulture. [75]2.0 to 5.0 ha. [76]1981. [77]Excludes 1.1 percent of holdings with no agricultural land. [78]2.0 to 4.0 ha. [79]4.0 to 10 ha. [80]40 ha or more. [81]Includes part-owners. [82]Less than 0.7 ha. [83]0.7 to 7.1 ha. [84]7.1 to 45 ha. [85]45 ha or more. [86]Excludes holdings of 0.04 ha (500 sq m) or less. [87]Agricultural cooperatives only. [88]1987–88. [89]1986–87. [90]Less than 2.5 ha. [91]2.5 to 7.5 ha. [92]7.5 to 12.5 ha. [93]12.5 to 20 ha. [94]50 to 250 ha. [95]250 ha or more. [96]Less than 8.0 ha. [97]8.0 to 20 ha. [98]Less than 0.4 ha. [99]0.4 to 4.0 ha. [100]Less than 4.5 ha. [101]4.5 to 9.0 ha. [102]9.0 to 18 ha. [103]18 ha or more. [104]1978. [105]Commercial farms only. [106]1975.

activity (% of farms)			technology (latest)				farmland use									country
							land in farms		land use (%)							
									cropland				meadows and pastures	woodland and forest	other	
mainly crops	mainly livestock	mixed/other	tractors (per 1,000 ha)	electricity (% of farms having)	irrigation (% of land irrig.)	artificial fertilizer (kg/ha)	total ('000 ha)	% of total land area	permanent crops	temporary crops	fallow	total cropland				
...	...	...	2.5	...	...	...	...	...	...	...	...	...	...	...	...	Netherlands Antilles
...	...	...	200	...	...	60	314	17.2	39.9	—60.1—		4.8	68.2	10.6	16.4	New Caledonia
13.1[22]	67.5	19.4	197	...	74	741	17,335	64.7	—85.5[19]—		14.5[19]	2.8[19]	78.1[19]	7.7[125]	11.4[126]	New Zealand
...	...	...	2.4	...	8	28	5,651	47.7	...	...	...	...	...	...	...	Nicaragua
...	...	...	0.05	...	2	1	3,806[111]	3.0[111]	...	...	...	...	...	...	...	Niger
...	...	...	0.4	...	3	12	34,290	37.1	—20.0—		80.0	31.4	27.5	41.1	...	Nigeria
64.3[5]	35.7[5]	...	22	45	...	...	5.8	12.2	...	...	...	32.9	30.2	—36.9—		Northern Mariana Is.
24.3[5]	70.6[5]	3.9[5]	175	...	11	242	1,019	3.3	—95.7—		4.3	42.7	—57.3—			Norway
28.0	34.0	38.0	9.4	...	92	83	106	0.4	68.5	31.5	—	59.1	—40.9—			Oman
...	...	...	13.6	...	82	91	21,350	27.7	—76.5—		23.5	98.9	—1.1—			Pakistan
...	...	...	2.2	...	...	...	...	...	—78.5—		21.5	43.3	—56.7—			Palau[131]
88.1	11.9	—	10.1	0.5[51]	6	58	2,942	39.0	23.7	41.3	35.0	22.2	50.0	24.1	3.6	Panama
...	...	...	28.5	...	...	40	386	0.8	100.0	—	—	33.7	26.4	...	39.9	Papua New Guinea
33.0[76]	—67.0[76]—		7.5	...	3	9	23,818	59.9	1.9	85.5	12.6	19.1	43.1	32.8	5.0	Paraguay
4.9	93.0	2.1	4.9	6.5	38	41	14,893	11.6	24.1	75.9	—	27.1	47.5	19.8	5.6	Peru
98.2	1.5	0.3	2.1	...	29	67	9,034	30.1	57.5	42.5	—	86.3	6.8	—6.9—		Philippines
53.8[5]	46.2[5]	—	80.8	...	0.7	219	18,648	59.6	1.9	—98.1—		78.3	21.7	...	...	Poland[18]
66.7	19.4	13.9	55.5	...	27	73	4,822	52.4	28.0	50.1	21.9	56.0	18.9	18.3	6.8	Portugal
61.0[5]	33.4[5]	5.6[5]	61.5	...	60	...	325	36.7	—78.9—		21.1	33.3	50.1	9.4	7.2	Puerto Rico
50.4[5]	49.6[5]	—	9.9	...	114	200	5.7	0.5	25.2	74.8	—	100.0	—	—	—	Qatar
...	...	...	37.2	...	14	282	60.2	24.1	7.8[4]	88.7[4]	3.5[4]	79.4[4]	20.6[4]	...	...	Réunion[3]
...	...	...	15.7	...	33	133	14,793	64.2	6.0	94.0	—	67.2	32.8	—	—	Romania
...	...	...	9.3	...	3	...	210,100	12.3	—87.0[4]—		13.0[4]	61.6[4]	36.3[4]	—	2.1[4]	Russia
...	...	...	0.1	...	0.5	1	1,350	51.3	—85.6—		14.4	63.7	10.6	5.2	20.5	Rwanda
...	...	...	27.0	...	...	...	8.9	24.7	17.3	70.7	12.0	65.5	18.3	10.9	5.3	St. Kitts and Nevis
25.0[17]	—75.0[17]—		17.4	...	20	...	23	38.0	60.5[17]	—31.5[17]—		57.9[17]	10.2[17]	26.4[17]	5.5[17]	St. Lucia
...	...	...	20.0	...	25	...	12	30.8	64.3	16.1	19.6	84.2	...	12.3	3.5	St. Vincent
...	...	...	...	...	...	...	4.7	76.5	60.9	6.5	32.6	69.2	6	0.2	10.4	San Marino
...	...	...	62.5	...	...	...	76	79.2	94.9	—5.1—		54.0	—45.7—			São Tomé and Príncipe
...	...	...	0.6	...	27	398	2,135	1.0	4.1	18.7	77.2	88.5	—11.5—			Saudi Arabia
...	...	...	0.2	...	8	2	11,338	59.1	0.1	—99.9—		22.4	77.6	...	...	Senegal
1.8[145]	32.4	65.8[146]	40.0	...	...	...	7.5	27.8	89.6	—10.4—		100.0	—	—	—	Seychelles
50.3	—49.7—		1.1	...	6	1	2,732	38.1	20.7	—79.3—		19.3	80.7	...	...	Sierra Leone
12.5	6.2	81.3	65.0	...	100	5,600	5.6[50]	9.0[50]	75.0	25.0	—	66.7	...	33.3	...	Singapore
...	...	...	22.2[19]	...	5.4	98[19]	2,447[19]	49.9[19]	3.2	92.1	4.7	60.7[19]	34.0[19]	—5.3[10]—		Slovakia
50.7	11.9	37.4	204	...	0.8	...	862	42.6	18.8	—81.2—		35.0	64.7	—	0.3	Slovenia[52]
43.4	—56.6—		...	...	...	...	00	0.4	40.0	45.2	14.8	100.0	—		—	Solomon Islands
20.0	60.0	20.0	2.1	...	18	3	...	...	...	...	...	...	...	...	...	Somalia
26.2	52.5	21.3[149]	9.8	...	10	59	81,236	66.5	...	...	...	12.5[36]	83.7[36]	2.1[36]	1.7[36]	South Africa[147]
...	...	...	51.7	...	23	101	24,740	57.6	—79.4—		20.0	40.9	34.3	16.8	—	Spain
...	...	...	35.5	...	59	111	2,009	30.6	56.4	43.6	—	86.0	1.0	2.7	8.8	Sri Lanka
...	...	...	0.8	...	15	4	31,500	13.3	0.0	88.7	10.5	23.8	76.2	...	...	Sudan, The
33.0[35]	12.5[35]	54.5[35]	23.3	...	105	26	165	1.0	15.0	53.0	32.0	40.4	23.1	19.1	17.4	Suriname
45.8[124]	25.3[124]	28.9[124, 125]	24.1	...	36	46	527	30.6	6.3	70.8	22.9	10.2	57.2	17.9	14.7	Swaziland[153]
14.0	42.0	44.0[154]	59.3	...	4	127	7,856	19.1	—98.1—		1.9	35.4	4.3	50.2	10.1	Sweden
58.0	—42.0—		288	...	6	430	1,071	27.1	6.2	93.8	—	31.2	68.1	—	0.7	Switzerland
...	...	...	13.9	...	18	46	6,065	32.8	—77.3—		22.7	91.7	...	...	8.3	Syria
41.9[2]	30.3[2]	27.8[2]	...	...	38	400[104]	2,827	78.5	27.5[2]	72.5[2]	—	31.7[2]	...	65.7[2]	2.4[2]	Taiwan
...	...	...	37.0	...	79	...	4,300	30.1	43.1	56.6	0.3	20.9	76.7	—	2.4	Tajikistan
44.1	4.7	51.2	2.2	...	5	9	7,545[141]	8.5[141]	19.1[141]	72.5[141]	8.4[141]	49.8[141]	10.2[141]	24.7[141]	15.3[141]	Tanzania
...	...	...	9.6	...	26	36	17,464	34.2	13.5	86.5		90.0	0.9	2.1	3.2	Thailand
...	...	...	0.2	...	0.3	8	406	7.1	17.3[33]	—82.7[33]—		71.0[33]	20.0[33]	...	...	Togo
...	—	...	0.0	...	...	2	33	44.5	—62.7—		37.3	81.2	0.7	10.1	1.9	Tonga
63.7[160]	—36.0[160]—		35.3	40.7	29	57	132	25.8	55.9	—44.1—		62.3	4.4	6.1	27.2	Trinidad and Tobago
...	...	...	9.2	...	13	20	10,040[19]	64.6[19]	—87.1[19]—		12.9[19]	74.5[19]	25.5[19]	...	...	Tunisia
—	3.6[26]	96.4[26]	30.5	...	15	64	23,451	30.5	9.0	76.1	14.9	91.5	3.9	0.8	3.8	Turkey
...	...	...	37.4	...	93	...	32,300	66.2	48.3	—51.7—		4.3	95.4	—	0.3	Turkmenistan
...	...	...	...	...	...	...	...	...	...	...	...	...	...	...	...	Tuvalu
...	...	...	0.9	...	0.2	...	3,683	18.4	29.8[143]	70.2[143]	—	100.0[143]	—	—	—	Uganda
...	...	...	12.8	...	8	...	40,400	69.7	7.7	88.2	4.1	80.9	16.3	—	2.8	Ukraine
...	...	...	6.4	...	17	120	17.5[104]	0.2[104]	64.8[104]	18.2[104]	17.1[104]	97.6[104]	...	1.3[104]	1.1[104]	United Arab Emirates
...	...	...	82.2	...	2	376	18,530	76.9	0.7	98.3	1.0	33.1	61.2	—5.7—		United Kingdom
44.8	55.2	—	25.9	68.8	11	99	393,471[165]	41.1[165]	—88.5—		11.5	46.0	43.5	7.8	2.7	United States
37.1[41]	58.7[41]	4.2[41]	26.2	...	11	54	15,682	89.7	6.6	—93.4—		4.3	—95.7—			Uruguay
...	...	...	41.5	...	98	...	25,500	57.0	43.9	55.6	0.5	16.1	82.0	—	1.9	Uzbekistan
92.2[124]	7.2[124]	0.6[124]	3.8	...	...	...	183	15.0	62.5[124]	3.0[124]	34.5[124]	84.9[124]	15.1[124]	...	...	Vanuatu[169]
27.6	9.0	63.4	15.2	...	6	138	31,278	34.3	19.0[51]	59.0[51]	22.0[51]	13.2[51]	57.0[51]	22.8[51]	7.0[51]	Venezuela
74.5[5]	25.5[5]	—	6.7	...	34	82	9,060	27.4	7.4	—92.6—		100.0	...	...	...	Vietnam
48.3[6]	40.8[6]	10.9[6]	15.6	15.6	...	...	7.2	20.9	18.3[6]	13.7[6]	68.0[6]	10.7[6]	75.3[6]	10.3[6]	3.7[6]	Virgin Islands (U.S.)
...	...	...	14.1[38]	...	5	...	185[41]	31.4[41]	62.2[41]	37.8[41]	—	100.0[41]	—	—	—	West Bank
...	...	...	...	...	...	...	5,002	18.8	—	—	—	—	100.0	...	...	Western Sahara
...	...	...	1.4	...	...	...	67	23.7	71.2[106]	28.8[106]	—	93.8[106]	6.2[106]	...	...	Western Samoa
35.5[14, 175]	56.9[14, 175]	7.6[14, 175]	4.0	...	26	12	1,351	0.1	6.7	69.7	23.6	98.8	...	...	1.2	Yemen[174]
12.7[35, 176]	—87.3[35, 176]—		108	...	2	115	6,228[60]	61.1[60]	8.6[60]	88.8[60]	2.6[60]	65.4[60]	33.9[60]	—	0.7[60]	Yugoslavia
92.3	—9.7—		0.3	...	0.1	1	5,897	2.6	7.7	—92.3—		70.6	20.1	2.0	7.3	Zaire
15.8[51]	9.7[51]	74.5[51]	1.1	...	0.9	15	938	1.3	4.5[51]	—95.5—		14.2[51]	38.1[51]	...	47.7[51]	Zambia
1.8[14, 104]	26.7[14, 104]	71.5[14, 104]	5.9	...	7	53	29,620	76.6	2.5[17]	—97.5—		34.5[17]	65.7[17]	...	...	Zimbabwe

[107]Excludes large commercial farms. [108]5.0 to 8.0 ha. [109]8.0 ha or more. [110]1985–86. [111]1986. [112]Excludes temporary rangeland available for agricultural use to subsistence farms. [113]Two-fifths under horticulture and viticulture. [114]1.0 to 3.0 ha. [115]3.0 ha or more. [116]West Malaysia except as noted. [117]Malaysia. [118]Includes some rented farms. [119]Preliminary 1991 census reported 4,310,000 farms and an average size of 50 ha. [120]Family farms only. [121]4.0 to 8.0 ha. [122]Commercial farms owned mostly by whites. [123]Includes agricultural and horticultural farms. [124]1983–84. [125]Includes timber plantations. [126]Includes conservation planting and plantations of native trees. [127]Less than 0.8 ha. [128]0.8 to 4.0 ha. [129]Excludes holdings of less than 0.5 ha. [130]Excludes 149 government holdings. [131]Partial data. [132]Large holdings only. [133]10 to 15 ha. [134]15 ha or more. [135]1.0 to 3.9 ha. [136]3.9 to 7.5 ha. [137]7.5 to 19.3 ha. [138]19.3 to 39 ha. [139]1.0 to 2.0 ha. [140]2.0 ha or more. [141]1972. [142]0.4 to 2.0 ha. [143]1964. [144]Includes 700 part-time farmers. [145]Includes root crops. [146]Includes fruits, vegetables, coconuts, and cinnamon. [147]Data excludes Transkei, Bophuthatswana, Venda, and Ciskei states. [148]Total indicates white commercial farmers, of which 60 percent have viable farming units. [149]Includes horticulture. [150]1.2 to 12 ha. [151]12 to 20 ha. [152]1988–89. [153]Includes individual-tenured farms and large estates. [154]Includes 36 percent of small farms not identified by activity. [155]50 to 300 ha. [156]300 ha or more. [157]1.0 to 6.4 ha. [158]6.4 to 22.4 ha. [159]22.4 ha or more. [160]1963. [161]1.0 to 7.5 ha. [162]7.5 ha or more. [163]Full-time operations only. [164]Excludes Northern Ireland. [165]July 1995. [166]20 to 72 ha. [167]72 to 202 ha. [168]202 ha or more. [169]Tanna Island only. [170]Less than 3.0 ha. [171]3.0 to 10 ha. [172]100 to 260 ha. [173]260 ha or more. [174]Former Yemen Arab Republic only. [175]1976. [176]Data refer to Yugoslavia as constituted prior to 1991. [177]Includes resettlement schemes and commercial land holdings. [178]8.0 to 100 ha.

Crops and livestock

This table provides comparative data for selected categories of agricultural production for the countries of the world. The data are taken mainly from the United Nations Food and Agriculture Organization's (FAO) annual *Production Yearbook.*

The FAO depends largely on questionnaires supplied to each country for its statistics, but, where no official or semiofficial responses are returned, the FAO makes estimates, using incomplete, unofficial, or other similarly limited data. And, although the FAO provides standardized guidelines upon which many nations have organized their data collection systems and methods, persistent, often traditional, variations in standards of coverage, methodology, and reporting periods reduce the comparability of statistics that *can* be supplied on such forms. FAO data are based on calendar-year periods; that is, data for any particular crop refer to the calendar year in which the harvest (or the bulk of the harvest) occurred.

In spite of the often tragic food shortages in a number of countries in recent years, worldwide agricultural production is probably more often underreported than overreported. Many countries do not report complete domestic production. Some countries, for example, report only crops that are sold commercially and ignore subsistence crops produced for family or communal consumption, or barter; others may limit reporting to production for export only, to holdings above a certain size, or represent a sampling only.

Methodological problems attach to much smaller elements of the agricultural whole, however. The FAO's cereals statistics relate, ideally, to weight or volume of crops harvested for dry grain (excluding cereal crops used for grazing, harvested for hay, or harvested green for food, feed, or silage). Some countries, however, collect the basic data they report to the FAO on sown or cultivated areas instead and calculate production statistics from estimates of yield. Millet and sorghum, which in many European and North American countries are used primarily as livestock or poultry feed, may be reportable by such countries as animal fodder only, while elsewhere many nations use the same grains for human consumption and report them as cereals. Statistics for tropical fruits are frequently not compiled by producing countries, and coverage is not uniform, with some countries reporting only commercial fruits and others including those consumed for subsistence as well. Figures on wild fruits and berries are seldom included

Crops and livestock

country	crops															
	grains				roots and tubers[a]				pulses[b]				fruits[c]		vegetables[d]	
	production ('000 metric tons)		yield (kg/hectare)		production ('000 metric tons)		yield (kg/hectare)		production ('000 metric tons)		yield (kg/hectare)		production ('000 metric tons)		production ('000 metric tons)	
	1979–81 average	1994	1979–81 average	1994	1979–81 average	1994	1979–81 average	1994	1979–81 average	1994	1979–81 average	1994	1979–81 average	1994	1979–81 average	1994
Afghanistan	4,060	2,662	1,337	1,179	265	228	14,881	16,889	41	35	989	946	807	614	516	492
Albania	916	692	2,500	2,601	112	100	6,967	10,000	23	25	512	948	154	97	333	352
Algeria	1,958	2,195	656	756	540	1,200	6,878	10,000	52	48	431	409	1,197	1,241	824	1,958
American Samoa	...	...	...	...	3	2	4,116	3,361	...	...	...	...	2	1	...	1
Andorra	...	...	...	...	...	...	...	...	...	...	...	...	...	...	...	...
Angola	379	274	533	245	1,464	1,203	4,028	2,798	42	34	385	252	430	417	231	249
Antigua and Barbuda	—	—	1,809	1,832	—	—	4,673	5,318	...	...	...	...	9	9	1	3
Argentina	24,457	24,668	2,183	2,785	2,328	2,550	14,087	18,613	239	277	918	1,340	6,184	6,766	2,280	2,882
Armenia	270	240	1,783	1,324	240	400	12,213	13,333	...	2	...	1,077	407	275	468	424
Aruba	...	...	...	...	...	...	...	...	...	...	...	...	...	...	...	...
Australia	21,150	14,462	1,321	1,250	843	1,158	23,413	29,245	192	1,252	912	651	2,121	2,803	1,044	1,618
Austria	4,388	4,681	4,131	5,699	1,356	750	25,387	25,220	23	114	2,876	3,458	950	788	666	440
Azerbaijan	1,105	1,012	2,253	1,614	142	150	7,359	7,500	2,167	...	9	...	1,647	1,282	852	813
Bahamas, The	1	1	1,142	1,250	2	2	8,998	9,162	1	1	1,238	1,312	12	13	28	28
Bahrain	...	...	...	...	—	—	19,048	13,125	—	—	917	909	35	24	15	15
Bangladesh	20,983	28,741	1,938	2,721	1,705	1,865	10,062	10,596	637	517	646	724	1,303	1,379	1,066	1,459
Barbados	2	2	2,538	2,500	11	3	11,653	11,237	1	1	1,209	1,254	3	3	10	9
Belarus	4,108	5,930	1,438	2,253	12,672	8,241	16,085	10,988	101	140	496	1,400	510	298	799	981
Belgium[1]	2,069	2,273	4,861	6,585	1,468	2,080	39,246	39,942	7	31	3,080	4,396	386	766	980	1,885
Belize	27	26	1,924	1,544	3	4	20,000	22,093	1	2	526	630	72	167	3	5
Benin	366	646	698	953	1,363	2,510	7,449	9,448	34	71	445	635	142	162	121	257
Bermuda	...	...	...	...	1	1	9,041	23,941	...	...	...	...	1	1	2	3
Bhutan	159	106	1,439	1,088	40	56	6,767	10,750	2	2	592	800	29	64	11	10
Bolivia	663	1,047	1,183	1,522	1,063	1,371	5,185	6,652	18	29	1,014	1,058	547	878	317	429
Bosnia and Herzegovina	...	1,110	...	3,013	...	180	...	4,000	...	16	...	929	...	102	...	59
Botswana	35	50	203	389	7	9	5,513	6,000	19	13	622	433	9	11	16	16
Brazil	30,805	45,930	1,496	2,284	27,265	27,274	11,570	13,043	2,206	3,307	464	600	18,607	32,515	4,089	6,181
Brunei	3	1	1,640	1,625	1	1	1,470	2,813	...	...	...	...	5	5	8	8
Bulgaria	8,130	6,424	3,853	2,814	376	476	10,175	10,068	68	43	984	914	1,975	845	2,022	1,293
Burkina Faso	1,166	2,509	575	853	126	86	8,927	5,904	46	63	1,004	861	56	74	155	254
Burundi	219	213	1,081	1,224	1,036	1,124	6,775	6,135	317	287	959	883	1,243	1,349	151	210
Cambodia	1,334	1,864	1,025	1,066	178	233	6,569	8,133	14	14	526	583	125	269	368	488
Cameroon	866	985	849	1,213	1,663	1,967	3,866	5,854	105	78	542	566	1,715	1,138	370	466
Canada	42,726	47,054	2,173	2,598	2,626	3,518	23,818	26,650	199	2,028	1,577	1,712	697	720	1,747	2,017
Cape Verde	6	6	465	300	10	8	3,901	5,915	4	—	353	200	12	16	1	9
Central African Republic	103	92	529	807	1,106	901	3,270	3,877	7	16	556	1,032	165	208	44	65
Chad	508	963	587	650	424	534	4,505	4,472	47	34	413	584	94	100	59	74
Chile	1,742	2,619	2,124	4,489	901	907	10,262	15,240	171	91	843	1,223	1,657	3,086	1,760	2,660
China	286,456	397,212	3,027	4,500	144,354	150,098	13,594	14,968	6,658	6,078	1,223	1,338	8,814	37,298	83,196	128,811
Colombia	3,339	3,703	2,452	2,501	4,144	5,139	11,043	12,933	128	194	604	818	3,905	5,935	1,362	1,264
Comoros	18	19	1,058	1,194	48	63	5,556	5,676	5	8	1,237	833	36	60	3	4
Congo	15	27	825	922	679	703	6,685	6,629	5	9	572	789	126	188	33	44
Costa Rica	337	215	2,498	3,308	45	146	5,764	24,283	12	35	498	565	1,362	2,518	58	175
Côte d'Ivoire	866	1,359	867	1,048	3,414	4,761	5,154	5,786	8	8	667	667	1,549	1,788	317	454
Croatia	...	2,595	...	4,138	...	563	...	8,478	...	24	...	1,055	...	495	...	300
Cuba	551	277	2,458	1,776	997	744	6,092	4,914	12	26	306	344	810	1,324	466	484
Cyprus	87	148	1,793	2,129	182	154	23,108	20,329	6	2	1,047	1,310	358	320	102	123
Czech Republic	...	6,777	...	4,097	...	1,231	...	16,056	...	163	...	2,306	...	476	...	522
Denmark	7,346	7,885	4,040	5,584	913	1,826	26,904	38,530	14	454	3,420	3,765	124	118	263	316
Djibouti	—	—	833	1,625	...	...	...	...	...	...	...	...	...	...	13	22
Dominica	—	—	1,427	1,333	26	23	10,241	9,293	—	—	467	450	46	90	7	6
Dominican Republic	447	610	3,004	4,131	214	249	5,783	6,422	73	90	958	922	1,333	1,767	209	239
Ecuador	686	1,937	1,633	2,410	552	513	9,595	6,472	39	39	547	453	3,769	6,053	243	376
Egypt	8,134	14,766	4,053	6,097	1,330	1,859	18,336	22,231	283	380	2,000	2,130	2,310	4,628	7,345	9,402
El Salvador	719	943	1,702	1,907	27	51	12,350	18,149	41	57	850	722	257	322	96	128
Equatorial Guinea	...	...	...	...	53	84	2,926	2,596	...	...	...	...	11	17	...	...
Eritrea	...	72	...	715	...	109	...	2,804	...	13	...	368	...	4	...	25
Estonia	796	661	1,862	1,836	1,031	700	14,257	14,286	1	...	1,333	1,375	46	49	117	83
Ethiopia	...	6,734	...	1,355	...	2,018	...	3,679	...	800	...	899	...	227	...	565
Faroe Islands	...	...	...	...	1	2	13,684	13,502	...	...	...	...	...	...	...	...

in national reports at all. FAO vegetable statistics include vegetables and melons grown for human consumption only. Some countries do not make this distinction in their reports, and some exclude the production of kitchen gardens and small family plots, although in certain countries, such small-scale production may account for 20 to 40 percent of total output.

Livestock statistics may be distorted by the timing of country reports. Ireland, for example, takes a livestock enumeration in December that is reported the following year and that appears low against data for otherwise comparable countries because of the slaughter and export of animals at the close of the grazing season. It balances this, however, with a June enumeration, when numbers tend to be high. Milk production as defined by the FAO includes whole fresh milk, excluding milk sucked by young animals but including amounts fed by farmers or ranchers to livestock, but national practices vary. Certain countries do not distinguish between milk cows and other cattle, so that yield per dairy cow must be estimated. Some countries do not report egg production statistics (here given in metric tons), and external estimates must be based on the numbers of chickens and reported or assumed egg-laying rates. Other countries report egg production by number, and this must be converted to weight, using conversion factors specific to the makeup by species of national poultry flocks.

Metric system units used in the table may be converted to English system units as follows:

metric tons × 1.1023 = short tons
kilograms × 2.2046 = pounds
kilograms per hectare × 0.8922 = pounds per acre.

The notes that follow, keyed by references in the table headings, provide further definitional information.

a. Includes such crops as potatoes and cassava.
b. Includes beans and peas harvested for dry grain only. Does not include green beans and green peas.
c. Excludes melons.
d. Includes melons, green beans, and green peas.
e. From milk cows only.
f. From chickens only.

livestock														country
cattle		sheep		hogs		chickens		milk[e]				eggs[f]		
stock ('000 head)		stock ('000 head)		stock ('000 head)		stock ('000 head)		production ('000 metric tons)		yield (kg/animal)		production (metric tons)		
1979–81 average	1994	1979–81 average	1994	1979–81 average	1994	1979–81 average	1994	1979–81 average	1994	1979–81 average	1994	1979–81 average	1994	
3,723	1,500	18,667	14,200	...	...	0,000	7,000	552	500	491	395	14,000	14,600	Afghanistan
606	630	1,232	1,900	174	86	3,000	3,000	296	520	1,326	1,600	9,333	13,200	Albania
1,356	1,370	13,111	17,850	4	6	24,000	78,000	514	595	975	952	24,550	150,000	Algeria
...	...	...	...	10	11	...	...	—	—	800	800	34	30	American Samoa
...	...	...	...	...	...	...	...	...	...	...	...	...	...	Andorra
3,083	3,280	225	255	600	820	5,000	6,000	153	160	497	488	3,650	3,900	Angola
14	16	12	13	4	4	...	...	6	6	959	969	138	120	Antigua and Barbuda
55,620	50,000	31,473	20,000	3,751	2,200	38,000	59,000	5,311	7,868	1,746	2,622	253,731	344,800	Argentina
766	502	2,242	720	231	80	9,000	3,000	501	200	1,677	741	25,367	10,600	Armenia
...	...	...	...	...	...	...	...	...	...	...		...	...	Aruba
26,161	24,732	134,871	132,609	2,416	2,740	46,000	65,000	5,598	8,326	2,994	4,725	197,870	162,000	Australia
2,553	2,430	193	324	3,906	3,800	15,000	13,000	3,434	3,200	3,509	3,902	96,804	95,000	Austria
1,765	1,621	5,128	4,339	179	115	17,000	23,000	800	650	1,208	929	40,200	48,000	Azerbaijan
4	6	35	40	14	15	1,000	2,000	1	2	1,000	1,000	356	620	Bahamas, The
6	16	7	29	...	...	...	1,000	6	20	2,703	2,600	3,200	3,400	Bahrain
25,053	24,130	750	1,070	...	...	59,000	116,000	833	774	221	206	39,716	76,800	Bangladesh
18	25	50	41	35	30	2,000	3,000	7	15	1,495	1,783	1,489	1,300	Barbados
6,760	5,851	525	289	4,520	4,175	35,000	45,000	6,082	5,300	2,215	2,356	166,267	186,100	Belarus
3,104	3,289	110	160	5,083	6,948	29,000	35,000	4,042	3,533	3,876	4,667	200,655	182,856	Belgium[1]
50	59	3	4	16	26	...	1,000	4	7	1,021	1,015	1,034	1,500	Belize
810	1,223	972	940	400	555	11,000	20,000	12	16	120	130	7,860	19,260	Benin
1	1	...	...	2	1	...	...	2	1	2,836	2,400	435	350	Bermuda
299	435	10	59	55	75	...	...	26	29	257	257	159	365	Bhutan
4,570	6,012	8,967	7,789	1,553	2,331	17,000	36,000	71	139	1,396	1,401	22,500	58,500	Bolivia
...	390	...	600	...	223	...	7,000	...	476	...	1,453	...	16,500	Bosnia and Herzegovina
2,906	2,800	147	344	5	17	1,000	3,000	90	88	760	250	700	1,000	Botswana
116,645	151,600	18,414	20,500	34,102	30,450	426,000	680,000	11,378	15,774	712	789	765,117	1,400,000	Brazil
0	1	...	...	11	14	1,000	2,000	...	...	...	...	1,787	0,000	Brunei
1,782	750	10,358	3,763	3,803	2,071	39,000	15,000	1,843	1,135	2,638	2,714	131,679	83,916	Bulgaria
2,760	4,261	3,200	5,686	198	551	11,000	19,000	81	125	175	175	7,448	16,800	Burkina Faso
614	380	301	350	44	80	3,000	4,000	42	29	350	350	2,356	2,888	Burundi
809	2,589	...	...	162	2,154	3,000	11,000	14	19	170	170	5,400	10,400	Cambodia
3,521	4,867	2,167	3,770	1,139	1,380	8,000	20,000	88	122	500	500	8,400	13,000	Cameroon
12,096	12,306	480	691	9,548	11,200	96,000	96,000	7,354	7,700	4,137	6,077	330,863	320,000	Canada
12	18	1	7	40	111	...	1,000	1	1	500	524	200	737	Cape Verde
1,662	2,800	84	152	243	480	2,000	3,000	23	50	200	222	966	1,407	Central African Republic
4,360	4,621	2,620	2,152	9	17	3,000	4,000	118	125	270	270	2,850	3,960	Chad
3,650	3,692	6,059	4,649	1,068	1,407	26,000	58,000	1,111	1,730	1,561	1,922	66,046	106,942	Chile
52,567	90,906	101,864	111,649	313,660	402,846	906,000	2,692,000	1,143	5,600	1,802	1,545	2,325,749	10,060,000	China
24,110	25,700	2,399	2,540	2,013	2,635	30,000	75,000	2,187	4,690	965	998	176,972	293,400	Colombia
70	50	8	15	...	...	...	...	3	4	500	500	564	640	Comoros
64	68	69	111	28	56	1,000	2,000	1	1	500	500	825	1,230	Congo
2,183	1,694	2	3	223	252	5,000	15,000	318	482	1,067	1,488	16,760	24,000	Costa Rica
664	1,232	1,020	1,251	315	404	17,000	27,000	12	20	110	94	10,253	17,577	Côte d'Ivoire
...	519	...	444	...	1,347	...	13,000	...	600	...	1,818	...	46,600	Croatia
5,166	4,500	356	310	1,443	1,503	24,000	25,000	1,045	700	1,579	1,458	98,936	70,000	Cuba
22	61	290	285	162	370	2,000	3,000	33	125	4,305	4,874	5,309	7,900	Cyprus
...	2,113	...	196	...	4,071	...	24,000	...	3,231	...	4,087	...	149,953	Czech Republic
2,970	2,082	55	82	9,699	10,864	15,000	19,000	5,126	4,442	4,920	6,195	77,130	89,200	Denmark
47	190	417	470	...	...	...	...	2	7	350	350	...	...	Djibouti
7	9	6	8	8	5	...	...	3	5	1,000	1,000	177	158	Dominica
1,918	2,450	65	134	298	900	19,000	34,000	427	385	1,742	1,704	19,267	43,893	Dominican Republic
2,987	4,963	1,148	1,728	3,417	2,540	33,000	59,000	924	1,832	1,446	2,207	43,056	52,500	Ecuador
1,906	3,070	1,791	3,382	21	27	28,000	38,000	648	995	674	675	78,100	130,000	Egypt
1,234	1,256	4	5	455	325	5,000	4,000	268	280	958	903	36,822	52,500	El Salvador
4	5	33	36	4	5	...	...	...	...	...	...	116	195	Equatorial Guinea
...	1,550	...	1,510	...	...	...	4,000	...	36	...	194	...	5,934	Eritrea
821	463	164	83	1,038	424	6,000	3,000	1,149	812	3,633	3,587	29,267	25,000	Estonia
...	29,450	...	21,700	...	20	...	54,000	...	738	...	209	...	73,370	Ethiopia
2	2	67	69	...	...	...	...	...	...	...	...	...	...	Faroe Islands

Crops and livestock (continued)

country	crops															
	grains				roots and tubers[a]				pulses[b]				fruits[c]		vegetables[d]	
	production ('000 metric tons)		yield (kg/hectare)		production ('000 metric tons)		yield (kg/hectare)		production ('000 metric tons)		yield (kg/hectare)		production ('000 metric tons)		production ('000 metric tons)	
	1979–81 average	1994	1979–81 average	1994	1979–81 average	1994	1979–81 average	1994	1979–81 average	1994	1979–81 average	1994	1979–81 average	1994	1979–81 average	1994
Fiji	19	32	2,004	2,001	22	64	11,634	13,878	—	1	540	1,251	11	12	6	13
Finland	2,993	3,400	2,511	3,599	629	726	15,578	19,879	13	14	2,182	2,242	107	90	130	201
France	46,078	53,641	4,700	6,554	6,735	5,456	28,465	32,728	340	3,450	3,304	5,011	14,124	10,649	6,999	7,223
French Guiana	1	25	1,159	3,333	13	37	10,842	13,806	...	...	...	...	2	8	3	8
French Polynesia	...	...	...	...	17	13	13,874	12,547	...	...	...	...	4	8	6	6
Gabon	11	24	1,718	1,740	372	374	5,209	5,409	—	—	528	667	181	266	22	31
Gambia, The	78	109	1,189	1,239	6	6	3,000	3,000	4	4	267	267	4	4	7	8
Gaza Strip	5	1	2,793	529	5	27	18,333	24,364	...	...	3,071	...	200	125	61	160
Georgia	573	353	1,942	1,342	412	229	12,400	11,450	10	...	711	...	1,678	1,265	960	1,130
Germany	32,044	36,353	4,166	5,721	19,465	9,257	23,587	31,551	116	204	1,902	2,703	4,448	4,342	3,206	3,630
Ghana	726	1,450	807	1,213	3,183	6,650	6,721	6,585	14	20	101	100	966	1,468	299	473
Gibraltar	...	...	...	...	...	...	...	...	...	...	...	...	...	...	...	...
Greece	4,951	4,896	3,090	3,794	1,041	1,002	16,378	20,000	94	45	1,262	1,489	3,437	4,395	3,636	3,870
Greenland	...	...	...	...	...	...	...	...	...	...	...	...	...	...	...	...
Grenada	—	—	949	1,000	3	4	4,582	5,138	1	1	1,607	1,132	29	23	2	2
Guadeloupe	...	...	...	...	22	22	8,459	10,995	—	—	514	600	115	166	17	27
Guam	—	—	3,000	1,894	2	2	13,756	14,870	...	...	...	...	2	2	2	5
Guatemala	1,122	1,507	1,578	1,872	52	63	3,535	4,953	77	113	840	810	734	852	277	386
Guernsey	...	...	...	...	...	...	...	...	...	...	...	...	...	...	...	...
Guinea	678	1,172	958	825	644	1,203	7,116	7,212	42	60	646	857	664	1,054	410	420
Guinea-Bissau	102	201	711	1,587	47	65	5,986	7,308	2	3	971	625	45	67	21	20
Guyana	267	343	2,907	3,522	16	32	6,626	7,341	1	1	487	591	41	73	9	12
Haiti	419	380	1,009	927	689	789	3,778	3,875	90	89	471	685	1,007	883	281	219
Honduras	492	639	1,170	1,364	18	30	5,842	10,168	38	41	517	542	1,647	1,331	95	241
Hong Kong	—	—	1,712	—	—	—	25,407	19,500	...	...	...	...	3	5	189	92
Hungary	13,001	11,911	4,519	4,027	1,507	826	15,894	14,268	127	119	1,547	1,827	2,389	1,748	1,841	1,584
Iceland	...	...	...	...	11	8	11,858	10,000	...	...	...	...	...	...	1	2
India	138,182	212,482	1,324	2,107	16,777	21,490	12,926	15,658	10,509	14,536	461	607	20,409	33,235	43,866	65,137
Indonesia	33,605	52,862	2,837	3,863	16,153	17,914	9,054	11,313	352	504	882	1,269	4,941	7,125	2,434	5,280
Iran	8,855	17,522	1,108	1,830	1,284	2,850	14,324	17,484	247	730	799	723	3,234	9,021	4,966	10,050
Iraq	1,803	2,520	832	833	96	410	18,464	17,447	36	38	802	1,147	1,161	1,629	1,992	2,799
Ireland	2,009	1,700	4,733	6,443	822	600	20,799	27,273	—	7	3,444	4,705	22	19	283	218
Isle of Man	...	...	...	...	...	...	...	...	...	...	...	...	...	...	...	...
Israel	239	157	1,840	1,724	201	241	36,551	31,854	8	6	955	1,006	1,913	1,516	762	1,287
Italy	18,025	18,918	3,548	4,679	2,962	1,984	18,274	22,847	321	184	1,335	1,732	20,661	17,972	13,401	13,629
Jamaica	7	6	1,667	1,315	230	232	11,666	13,473	8	7	882	1,051	332	377	104	151
Japan	14,318	15,787	5,252	6,449	5,342	5,244	22,838	25,858	108	113	1,258	1,579	6,330	4,564	15,230	13,870
Jersey	...	...	...	...	...	...	...	...	...	...	...	...	...	...	...	...
Jordan	91	119	516	1,067	9	70	16,866	23,330	8	8	588	1,439	90	295	437	883
Kazakhstan	26,790	16,395	1,063	793	1,918	1,950	10,220	9,142	...	80	...	800	379	177	1,185	1,065
Kenya	2,281	3,481	1,364	1,876	1,257	1,752	7,993	8,122	185	200	430	286	650	974	490	655
Kiribati	...	...	...	...	9	8	8,011	7,813	...	...	...	...	5	5	4	5
Korea, North	5,536	4,525	3,405	3,237	1,909	2,266	12,486	12,473	280	293	849	821	851	1,393	2,630	3,988
Korea, South	8,452	7,588	4,986	5,808	1,653	721	17,787	20,031	56	35	940	1,193	994	2,024	9,070	10,503
Kuwait	—	2	3,087	5,473	—	1	16,934	19,659	...	...	...	...	1	1	36	89
Kyrgyzstan	1,413	1,047	2,452	1,907	272	288	12,348	11,520	2	...	1,000	...	247	132	396	328
Laos	1,056	1,730	1,402	2,557	184	221	10,114	8,717	17	43	1,728	1,950	89	152	26	154
Latvia	859	799	1,278	1,932	1,371	944	12,979	14,255	7	6	1,167	1,735	106	78	229	232
Lebanon	41	67	1,307	1,833	130	296	16,923	20,686	10	38	940	1,941	704	1,402	354	964
Lesotho	198	258	977	1,720	6	8	15,526	15,000	8	3	536	508	16	18	21	26
Liberia	254	50	1,251	1,111	346	441	6,894	7,939	3	3	500	500	121	130	64	71
Libya	225	263	430	614	97	130	6,671	7,303	9	12	1,079	1,120	203	247	527	614
Liechtenstein	...	...	...	...	11	12[2]	18,742	17,974[2]	...	...	...	...	...	...	...	...
Lithuania	1,742	2,412	1,642	2,047	1,832	1,200	13,022	10,000	110	30	...	1,322	202	133	333	280
Luxembourg[1]	...	...	...	...	...	...	...	...	...	...	...	...	...	...	...	...
Macau	...	...	...	...	4	8	11,174	13,417	...	1	...	...	...	...	2	1
Macedonia	...	656	...	2,712	...	134	...	10,212	...	26	...	1,712	...	338	...	448
Madagascar	2,178	2,517	1,664	1,875	2,267	3,210	5,704	6,539	53	60	852	828	719	760	283	333
Malaŵi	1,341	1,110	1,161	901	562	550	4,458	3,254	204	268	609	583	376	507	212	265
Malaysia	2,061	2,080	2,828	3,032	468	543	8,951	9,775	...	...	...	...	931	1,206	314	396
Maldives	—	—	806	1,011	7	8	5,176	4,876	—	—	600	642	8	10	15	19
Mali	1,064	2,705	790	960	123	145	8,349	8,529	47	65	338	215	13	16	173	271
Malta	8	9	3,252	3,430	21	25	8,948	21,167	1	1	2,333	2,295	11	12	47	54
Marshall Islands	...	...	...	...	...	...	...	...	...	...	...	...	...	...	...	...
Martinique	...	...	...	...	22	21	10,464	10,660	...	...	...	...	178	269	27	23
Mauritania	48	188	384	757	7	5	2,888	2,000	29	17	407	321	15	25	7	9
Mauritius	1	2	2,536	4,339	12	20	17,368	17,845	1	2	491	714	6	11	26	57
Mayotte	...	...	...	...	...	...	...	...	...	...	...	...	...	...	...	...
Mexico	20,692	27,412	2,152	2,678	1,120	1,348	12,906	17,160	1,265	1,702	715	756	7,316	9,547	3,947	6,078
Micronesia	...	...	...	...	...	...	...	...	...	...	...	...	...	...	...	...
Moldova	2,565	1,423	3,221	2,005	324	435	7,969	6,816	53	86	1,463	1,311	1,994	1,281	1,609	1,477
Monaco	...	...	...	...	...	...	...	...	...	...	...	...	...	...	...	...
Mongolia	320	443	573	999	50	64	7,878	9,636	—	3	292	806	3	...	26	15
Morocco	3,583	9,789	811	1,606	504	887	14,221	17,749	229	261	571	760	1,623	2,377	1,320	3,102
Mozambique	649	819	603	538	3,679	3,426	4,157	3,710	59	99	381	302	327	292	184	114
Myanmar (Burma)	12,984	19,607	2,521	2,795	167	265	8,087	9,233	365	960	588	641	838	1,020	1,872	2,217
Namibia	73	120	626	924	203	253	9,242	8,228	6	7	944	1,062	8	10	6	8
Nauru	...	...	...	...	...	...	...	...	...	...	...	...	...	...	...	...
Nepal	3,640	5,929	1,615	1,926	349	891	5,455	7,540	140	197	536	612	135	587	517	1,252
Netherlands, The	1,280	1,355	5,696	7,146	6,329	7,748	37,752	45,049	24	28	3,145	4,000	535	873	2,527	3,561
Netherlands Antilles	...	...	...	...	...	...	...	...	...	...	...	...	...	...	...	...
New Caledonia	3	1	2,134	1,438	21	22	5,692	6,034	—	—	772	567	9	4	3	3
New Zealand	785	779	4,077	5,230	220	276	26,301	25,593	63	85	2,882	2,537	364	933	382	590
Nicaragua	392	623	1,475	1,620	28	79	9,107	12,122	39	75	576	678	313	236	47	57
Niger	1,702	2,221	440	307	212	260	7,210	7,429	292	433	269	170	37	47	142	264

livestock														country
cattle		sheep		hogs		chickens		milk[e]				eggs[f]		
stock ('000 head)		stock ('000 head)		stock ('000 head)		stock ('000 head)		production ('000 metric tons)		yield (kg/animal)		production (metric tons)		
1979–81 average	1994	1979–81 average	1994	1979–81 average	1994	1979–81 average	1994	1979–81 average	1994	1979–81 average	1994	1979–81 average	1994	
212	334	...	6	64	115	1,000	3,000	54	66	1,701	1,703	1,976	2,900	Fiji
1,747	1,230	107	79	1,430	1,300	9,000	6,000	3,236	2,512	4,572	6,087	77,967	71,700	Finland
23,825	20,112	12,133	10,452	11,472	13,383	177,000	217,000	27,084	24,935	3,707	5,314	849,667	982,000	France
6	10	3	4	6	10	...	...	—	—	2,080	2,545	292	600	French Guiana
8	8	2	...	24	38	...	...	2	2	2,771	2,135	923	1,700	French Polynesia
5	38	105	170	126	165	2,000	3,000	...	1	250	250	1,050	1,500	Gabon
293	414	136	121	10	11	...	1,000	5	7	175	175	402	932	Gambia, The
5	3	15	24	...	...	1,000	3,000	11	8	4,185	4,100	2,265	6,000	Gaza Strip
1,552	1,050	1,961	1,300	926	650	17,000	17,000	643	350	1,055	753	35,900	30,000	Georgia
20,672	15,891	3,148	2,360	34,768	26,044	137,000	96,000	31,725	28,200	4,178	5,320	1,123,573	1,100,000	Germany
804	1,680	1,942	3,288	379	595	11,000	12,000	16	23	130	130	12,203	15,428	Ghana
...	...	...	...	...	...	...	...	...	...	...	...	...	...	Gibraltar
929	608	8,040	9,604	944	1,143	30,000	27,000	666	797	1,867	3,644	122,540	121,200	Greece
...	...	20	22	...	...	...	...	...	...	...	...	...	...	Greenland
7	4	14	12	2	3	...	...	1	1	769	887	948	920	Grenada
91	56	3	4	44	30	...	...	1	1	507	500	778	2,000	Guadeloupe
1	...	...	...	13	4	...	...	...	...	...	...	1,071	700	Guam
1,886	2,210	615	440	640	720	14,000	16,000	263	273	749	77	40,590	71,600	Guatemala
...	...	...	...	...	...	...	...	9	...	4,202	...	...	...	Guernsey
1,500	1,658	436	435	39	33	7,000	14,000	41	48	185	185	7,420	14,910	Guinea
290	494	177	263	256	312	...	1,000	9	13	170	170	300	632	Guinea-Bissau
193	190	115	131	90	50	11,000	11,000	13	28	832	933	8,033	8,300	Guyana
1,000	800	88	85	1,533	200	5,000	5,000	20	22	229	252	2,943	3,300	Haiti
1,980	2,286	5	14	410	000	6,000	12,000	224	390	538	967	19,093	32,300	Honduras
7	2	...	...	520	97	6,000	4,000	4	—	3,022	2,405	2,737	1,130	Hong Kong
1,936	1,002	2,960	1,280	8,232	5,002	62,000	31,000	2,550	1,006	3,727	4,537	250,000	211,100	Hungary
60	77	838	500	11	22	...	...	121	101	3,635	3,483	3,000	2,500	Iceland
186,500	192,980	44,987	44,809	9,433	11,780	160,000	467,000	13,420	30,000	530	984	568,333	1,446,000	India
6,502	11,595	4,124	6,411	3,234	8,720	168,000	640,000	79	425	762	1,184	177,767	436,600	Indonesia
5,450	7,100	31,672	45,400	17	...	97,000	182,000	1,125	1,930	700	760	155,333	350,000	Iran
1,690	1,100	10,842	6,320	...	...	26,000	24,000	290	200	750	702	48,362	42,000	Iraq
6,043	6,308	2,374	5,991	1,122	1,487	8,000	11,000	4,729	5,523	3,178	3,741	35,000	31,500	Ireland
...	...	...	...	...	...	...	...	...	...	...	...	...	...	Isle of Man
299	362	243	330	96	100	25,000	23,000	702	1,105	6,817	9,389	91,675	116,290	Israel
8,697	7,683	9,120	10,370	8,885	8,200	138,000	137,000	10,546	10,300	3,478	3,887	659,163	720,900	Italy
279	335	4	2	208	180	5,000	8,000	48	54	1,000	1,000	15,500	29,800	Jamaica
4,201	4,080	13	25	9,851	10,621	284,000	324,000	6,526	8,365	4,526	6,044	1,998,041	2,562,000	Japan
...	...	...	...	...	...	...	...	...	...	...	...	...	...	Jersey
29	42	950	2,100	...	...	28,000	77,000	18	93	1,000	3,000	19,000	56,000	Jordan
8,349	9,347	34,102	33,621	3,017	2,445	44,000	55,000	4,490	5,000	1,546	1,683	187,867	185,000	Kazakhstan
10,418	11,000	5,100	5,500	75	107	17,000	26,000	958	1,905	460	493	19,896	42,720	Kenya
...	...	...	...	10	9	...	...	...	...	...	...	105	132	Kiribati
945	1,330	292	396	2,100	3,368	18,000	23,000	55	90	2,244	2,310	103,833	151,200	Korea, North
1,634	3,200	6	4	2,153	6,300	41,000	74,000	449	1,986	4,864	6,829	255,786	457,000	Korea, South
17	12	250	150	...	...	9,000	14,000	24	14	2,653	3,550	8,573	4,000	Kuwait
968	1,061	9,853	7,077	320	165	9,000	12,000	676	750	1,803	1,705	23,283	30,600	Kyrgyzstan
437	1,107	...	...	1,117	1,605	5,000	9,000	6	12	200	200	22,167	37,000	Laos
1,413	995	207	133	1,623	737	10,000	4,000	1,668	937	2,898	1,787	40,407	18,600	Latvia
60	80	152	258	18	41	19,000	24,000	85	139	2,290	2,770	41,275	62,000	Lebanon
581	663	1,062	1,691	75	78	1,000	1,000	20	24	200	200	789	830	Lesotho
39	36	200	210	103	120	2,000	4,000	1	1	130	130	2,336	3,600	Liberia
164	50	5,380	3,500	...	...	6,000	15,000	63	55	1,499	1,375	16,233	22,000	Libya
6	6	2	3	3	3	...	...	9	12	3,310	4,444	...	...	Liechtenstein
2,195	1,650	61	48	2,568	1,200	13,600	7,000	2,565	2,400	2,955	3,265	54,000	55,000	Lithuania
...	...	...	...	...	...	...	...	...	...	...	...	...	...	Luxembourg[1]
...	...	...	...	3	1	...	...	...	...	...	...	575	645	Macau
...	276	...	2,444	...	181	...	4,000	...	120	...	1,345	...	19,260	Macedonia
10,147	10,288	695	740	1,175	1,558	18,000	23,000	440	481	255	275	12,717	18,200	Madagascar
817	980	84	196	192	245	8,000	9,000	35	42	458	460	10,503	11,500	Malawi
539	686	65	336	1,869	3,098	51,000	98,000	25	34	549	559	131,100	373,800	Malaysia
...	...	...	...	...	...	...	...	...	...	...	...	...	...	Maldives
5,670	5,554	6,247	5,173	48	63	12,000	23,000	139	139	245	245	6,720	12,060	Mali
13	20	5	6	12	111	1,000	1,000	29	24	4,111	3,810	6,256	6,800	Malta
...	...	...	...	...	...	...	...	...	...	...	...	...	...	Marshall Islands
57	36	77	110	37	49	...	...	5	2	754	613	1,500	1,510	Martinique
1,262	1,011	5,166	4,800	...	...	3,000	4,000	85	91	350	350	2,720	4,590	Mauritania
27	34	10	7	7	17	2,000	3,000	25	25	2,500	2,500	2,800	4,500	Mauritius
...	...	...	...	...	...	...	...	...	...	...	...	...	...	Mayotte
27,706	30,702	6,484	5,905	16,895	18,000	177,000	293,000	6,949	7,547	1,284	1,165	636,256	1,246,223	Mexico
...	...	...	...	...	...	...	...	...	...	...	...	...	...	Micronesia
1,138	916	1,208	1,373	2,020	1,165	16,000	14,000	1,189	846	2,780	2,061	48,633	45,000	Moldova
...	...	...	...	...	...	...	...	...	...	...	...	...	...	Monaco
2,452	2,779	14,261	14,392	32	49	...	...	210	251	355	316	983	1,200	Mongolia
3,362	2,431	15,228	15,594	7	10	24,000	91,000	753	820	640	571	72,900	207,000	Morocco
1,400	1,250	106	119	120	174	17,000	22,000	64	57	170	170	8,733	11,600	Mozambique
8,565	9,691	235	304	2,263	2,589	23,000	25,000	283	441	245	368	31,435	40,495	Myanmar (Burma)
2,318	2,036	4,084	2,620	15	18	1,000	2,000	68	71	412	410	900	1,500	Namibia
...	...	...	...	2	3	...	...	...	...	...	...	8	16	Nauru
6,893	6,546	730	914	375	612	6,000	8,000	190	278	325	376	14,300	18,000	Nepal
5,071	4,629	856	2,174	10,058	13,991	81,000	110,000	11,832	10,755	5,025	6,289	540,409	606,000	Netherlands, The
2	1	8	7	7	3	...	...	1	—	1,262	1,250	517	510	Netherlands Antilles
113	125	4	4	16	39	...	1,000	3	4	600	600	887	1,400	New Caledonia
8,063	8,550	67,393	50,135	433	430	7,000	10,000	6,586	8,379	3,016	2,940	56,855	49,000	New Zealand
2,373	1,650	3	4	625	535	5,000	7,000	234	194	814	688	28,833	27,500	Nicaragua
3,343	1,986	3,007	3,700	31	39	10,000	20,000	97	154	200	400	6,800	9,180	Niger

…ps and livestock (continued)

…untry	crops															
	grains				roots and tubers[a]				pulses[b]				fruits[c]		vegetables[d]	
	production ('000 metric tons)		yield (kg/hectare)		production ('000 metric tons)		yield (kg/hectare)		production ('000 metric tons)		yield (kg/hectare)		production ('000 metric tons)		production ('000 metric tons)	
	1979–81 average	1994	1979–81 average	1994	1979–81 average	1994	1979–81 average	1994	1979–81 average	1994	1979–81 average	1994	1979–81 average	1994	1979–81 average	1994
Nigeria	7,480	13,517	1,264	1,247	18,789	44,415	8,794	10,424	647	1,750	444	825	6,238	7,911	3,355	5,670
Northern Mariana Islands	...	...	...	...	...	...	...	...	...	...	...	...	...	...	...	...
Norway	1,129	1,268	3,634	3,661	524	471	25,884	25,480	...	...	...	...	117	118	189	166
Oman	2	3	982	1,762	1	6	13,663	23,024	...	...	...	...	111	210	105	169
Pakistan	17,200	22,256	1,608	1,842	537	1,460	11,060	13,881	595	621	397	411	2,552	4,428	1,962	4,029
Palau	...	...	...	...	...	...	...	...	...	...	...	...	...	...	...	...
Panama	253	327	1,524	1,817	76	72	7,796	5,783	5	10	443	426	1,208	1,076	44	75
Papua New Guinea	4	3	2,087	1,692	1,125	1,303	7,087	7,205	2	2	500	511	1,327	1,833	286	383
Paraguay	659	941	1,538	2,167	2,080	2,658	13,100	14,230	69	56	803	722	826	717	229	253
Peru	1,429	2,396	1,944	2,864	2,477	2,672	7,574	8,733	111	114	856	934	1,487	1,945	720	1,037
Philippines	10,942	15,550	1,611	2,397	3,100	2,777	6,632	6,826	37	37	652	786	6,816	6,799	3,470	4,440
Poland	18,466	21,763	2,345	2,566	39,508	23,058	16,808	13,585	216	624	1,232	1,914	1,584	2,111	4,573	5,313
Portugal	1,210	1,546	1,102	2,203	1,141	1,278	8,947	14,452	76	62	228	293	2,055	1,409	1,529	2,047
Puerto Rico	6	—	8,925	4,600	39	13	6,470	6,280	6	1	829	539	296	218	28	37
Qatar	1	5	2,623	3,028	—	—	13,367	10,909	...	...	...	...	6	12	18	38
Réunion	12	15	5,064	6,180	11	17	13,295	11,429	1	1	2,626	1,500	23	32	15	56
Romania	18,109	17,512	2,854	2,767	4,317	3,889	14,728	15,621	115	76	258	1,142	2,952	3,930	4,202	3,755
Russia	82,466	78,709	1,147	1,449	37,632	33,780	9,962	9,935	2,659	3,000	815	1,500	3,075	3,026	12,696	10,190
Rwanda	271	158	1,134	1,003	1,743	1,616	8,809	6,396	221	142	727	631	2,162	2,655	169	120
St. Kitts and Nevis	...	...	...	...	2	1	3,649	3,372	—	—	1,000	1,000	1	2	1	1
St. Lucia	—	—	703	715	10	12	4,250	4,139	—	—	2,187	1,968	90	199	1	1
St. Vincent and the Grenadines	1	1	3,294	3,659	24	18	8,049	4,613	—	—	913	1,001	35	98	2	3
San Marino	...	...	...	...	...	...	...	...	...	...	...	...	...	...	...	...
São Tomé and Príncipe	—	4	1,505	2,263	14	10	8,953	6,494	...	...	...	...	4	14	3	3
Saudi Arabia	303	4,509	820	4,206	4	169	9,931	17,979	6	7	1,813	1,850	499	919	682	2,138
Senegal	850	952	690	753	43	91	4,344	2,861	21	18	398	242	75	132	82	115
Seychelles	...	...	...	...	—	—	5,000	5,000	...	...	...	...	2	2	1	2
Sierra Leone	542	515	1,249	1,129	124	115	3,315	4,046	31	40	579	666	128	157	153	182
Singapore	...	...	...	...	2	—	11,330	10,000	...	...	...	...	9	...	39	5
Slovakia	...	3,730	...	4,296	...	455	...	10,322	...	165	...	2,805	...	270	...	499
Slovenia	...	409	...	3,504	...	360	...	12,414	...	5	...	943	...	260	...	67
Solomon Islands	13	—	3,513	—	87	110	15,039	17,896	2	2	840	1,000	11	14	5	6
Somalia	305	405	474	410	39	39	10,863	10,000	10	12	494	225	182	207	27	72
South Africa	14,036	14,422	2,117	2,391	793	1,564	12,002	22,532	110	94	1,051	1,045	3,140	3,670	1,662	1,980
Spain	14,709	15,341	1,986	2,332	5,670	4,084	15,986	19,663	365	211	704	683	12,603	11,648	8,547	10,680
Sri Lanka	2,130	2,620	2,462	3,032	717	485	9,685	9,327	47	39	845	750	1,717	762	385	685
Sudan, The	2,962	4,805	659	504	296	157	3,329	2,941	99	116	1,260	1,067	754	804	789	922
Suriname	258	225	3,972	3,747	3	4	5,301	12,406	—	—	849	765	52	82	6	35
Swaziland	92	67	1,345	1,098	13	8	1,993	1,930	3	4	576	614	121	149	12	12
Sweden	5,407	4,571	3,595	3,896	1,191	991	28,914	30,038	32	67	2,248	2,428	207	96	228	238
Switzerland	843	1,218	4,883	5,901	924	800	37,834	43,956	1	10	3,354	3,636	724	579	306	298
Syria	3,069	5,660	1,156	1,605	279	377	15,302	17,613	180	174	799	805	733	1,426	2,973	1,806
Taiwan	...	...	...	...	...	...	...	...	...	...	...	...	...	...	...	...
Tajikistan	285	254	1,295	966	152	140	16,926	10,769	6	6	792	600	431	225	495	595
Tanzania	3,010	3,534	1,063	1,169	6,158	7,716	9,491	8,270	315	302	454	483	1,953	2,228	973	1,001
Thailand	20,316	22,576	1,911	2,285	15,512	19,309	14,226	13,757	342	441	685	836	6,051	6,338	2,711	2,603
Togo	301	526	729	784	922	848	8,722	7,250	23	43	238	227	41	49	65	170
Tonga	...	...	...	...	91	102	5,970	6,654	...	...	...	...	14	13	7	8
Trinidad and Tobago	13	21	3,167	3,000	20	12	12,206	10,222	4	2	1,638	1,662	57	65	30	18
Tunisia	1,146	660	828	893	127	200	12,905	13,750	89	65	560	736	518	871	1,044	1,550
Turkey	25,232	27,001	1,869	1,961	2,958	4,352	16,664	22,640	817	1,752	1,140	986	7,682	9,700	13,338	19,354
Turkmenistan	281	1,573	2,142	2,578	16	30	7,833	10,000	...	...	...	...	90	249	279	672
Tuvalu	...	...	...	...	...	...	...	...	...	...	...	...	...	1	...	...
Uganda	1,171	2,036	1,555	1,572	3,548	5,923	5,802	6,567	236	572	638	786	6,300	9,239	290	413
Ukraine	33,181	32,862	2,208	2,726	18,429	16,102	11,017	10,545	1,551	2,636	1,238	2,213	3,973	1,548	7,773	5,506
United Arab Emirates	3	7	5,608	7,504	2	4	14,558	20,374	...	...	...	...	62	297	130	576
United Kingdom	18,840	19,670	4,791	6,451	6,601	7,065	32,891	41,437	240	743	3,168	3,285	524	477	3,762	3,791
United States	301,405	357,377	4,150	5,572	15,487	21,432	28,795	36,320	1,466	1,552	1,614	1,762	26,531	25,854	25,476	36,443
Uruguay	1,012	1,428	1,644	2,586	197	226	5,497	9,487	5	6	909	981	273	458	153	136
Uzbekistan	2,597	2,306	2,208	1,508	264	562	10,409	12,489	7	...	952	...	1,284	1,005	2,718	3,737
Vanuatu	1	1	513	517	32	51	19,630	9,500	...	...	...	...	11	20	6	8
Venezuela	1,550	2,069	1,904	2,870	599	655	8,058	8,802	37	50	509	653	2,029	2,494	402	739
Vietnam	12,222	23,455	2,049	3,335	6,284	5,431	6,592	7,717	117	217	558	706	2,584	4,067	2,504	4,028
Virgin Islands (U.S.)	...	...	...	...	...	...	...	...	...	...	...	...	...	...	...	...
West Bank	...	...	...	...	...	...	...	...	...	...	...	...	...	...	...	...
Western Sahara	...	...	...	...	...	...	...	...	...	...	...	...	...	...	...	...
Western Samoa	...	...	...	...	39	41	6,929	6,152	...	...	...	...	53	43	...	1
Yemen	903	802	1,045	1,092	133	181	11,992	13,689	80	69	1,087	1,320	173	361	335	460
Yugoslavia	...	8,910	...	3,559	...	700	...	6,481	...	91	...	1,416	...	1,424	...	883
Zaire	900	1,798	807	910	13,595	20,447	6,901	7,946	155	198	604	626	2,624	3,569	479	583
Zambia	990	1,168	1,676	1,845	333	648	5,458	5,396	7	23	340	477	76	103	209	269
Zimbabwe	2,273	2,764	1,359	1,503	76	163	3,823	4,561	23	49	566	668	109	157	136	143

livestock														country
cattle		sheep		hogs		chickens		milk[e]				eggs[f]		
stock ('000 head)		stock ('000 head)		stock ('000 head)		stock ('000 head)		production ('000 metric tons)		yield (kg/animal)		production (metric tons)		
1979–81 average	1994	1979–81 average	1994	1979–81 average	1994	1979–81 average	1994	1979–81 average	1994	1979–81 average	1994	1979–81 average	1994	
12,066	16,717	8,022	14,455	1,000	6,926	80,000	122,000	289	389	239	233	198,333	315,000	Nigeria
...	...	...	...	...	...	...	...	...	...	...	...	...	...	Northern Mariana Islands
989	1,003	2,033	2,316	675	745	4,000	4,000	1,926	1,863	5,125	5,533	44,665	50,779	Norway
141	144	114	149	...	...	...	3,000	18	19	420	420	710	6,700	Oman
15,268	18,146	22,580	28,975	...	...	44,000	98,000	2,189	4,100	864	891	96,367	234,000	Pakistan
...	...	...	...	...	...	...	...	...	...	...	...	...	...	Palau
1,425	1,437	...	...	205	295	5,000	9,000	94	163	988	1,265	14,553	13,500	Panama
130	105	2	4	870	1,033	2,000	3,000	—	—	228	96	1,810	3,600	Papua New Guinea
5,966	8,000	387	386	1,090	3,300	12,000	13,000	163	250	1,903	1,894	26,025	42,000	Paraguay
4,276	4,000	13,767	11,600	2,116	2,405	40,000	68,000	796	830	1,298	1,496	59,700	109,800	Peru
1,885	1,825	30	30	7,712	8,227	53,000	68,000	13	14	994	1,037	201,285	275,100	Philippines
12,494	7,696	4,105	870	20,343	19,466	77,000	44,000	16,250	12,218	2,778	3,161	488,642	301,408	Poland
1,332	1,322	4,440	5,991	3,367	1,487	18,000	22,000	750	1,500	2,123	1,177	62,008	105,000	Portugal
407	429	6	8	225	196	7,000	13,000	420	359	2,324	4,088	21,902	20,221	Puerto Rico
9	12	48	170	...	...	1,000	3,000	4	4	1,561	1,510	281	3,350	Qatar
20	25	2	2	61	86	3,000	8,000	5	5	526	520	3,040	5,000	Réunion
6,351	3,597	15,766	11,499	10,926	9,262	92,000	77,000	3,987	3,600	1,914	2,000	323,833	313,700	Romania
58,414	48,900	63,566	41,078	36,218	28,600	507,000	600,000	46,953	44,000	2,113	2,200	2,193,000	2,184,000	Russia
625	610	303	400	124	130	1,000	1,000	61	85	510	607	860	2,000	Rwanda
5	5	14	14	2	2	...	...	...	...	...	...	297	350	St. Kitts and Nevis
10	12	13	16	10	13	...	...	1	1	1,390	1,527	497	541	St. Lucia
8	6	13	12	6	9	...	...	1	1	1,362	1,340	530	648	St. Vincent and the Grenadines
...	...	...	...	...	...	...	...	...	...	...	...	...	...	San Marino
3	4	2	2	2	2	...	...	—	—	170	170	148	280	São Tomé and Príncipe
374	203	4,040	7,257			19,000	81,000	04	045	443	6,832	40,791	127,000	Saudi Arabia
2,424	2,800	1,966	4,600	180	329	8,000	38,000	87	106	357	360	6,353	30,000	Senegal
3	2	...	...	10	18	...	...	1	...	519	529	811	1,600	Seychelles
349	362	208	302	36	51	4,000	6,000	18	17	250	250	4,669	7,130	Sierra Leone
1	...	...	...	1,017	150	14,000	2,000	...	...	...	...	26,870	15,500	Singapore
...	916	...	397	...	2,179	...	12,000	...	1,155	...	3,122	...	52,637	Slovakia
...	504	...	21	...	620	...	11,000	...	380	...	1,652	...	25,500	Slovenia
23	13	...	...	45	55	...	...	1	1	600	860	284	280	Solomon Islands
4,437	5,000	10,467	13,000	9	9	3,000	3,000	477	550	414	407	2,320	2,400	Somalia
13,647	12,584	31,625	29,134	1,339	1,511	30,000	42,000	2,553	2,350	2,809	2,554	159,952	231,000	South Africa
4,608	5,000	14,721	23,838	10,392	18,188	51,000	51,000	5,984	5,751	3,255	4,295	665,560	669,000	Spain
1,662	1,600	27	19	71	90	6,000	9,000	182	227	448	353	28,857	50,900	Sri Lanka
18,376	21,751	17,628	22,870	...	...	27,000	35,000	1,352	2,610	500	480	31,745	38,000	Sudan, The
40	98	3	9	19	37	5,000	6,000	7	17	1,209	1,753	2,638	3,100	Suriname
658	020	32	27	17	32	1,000	1,000	36	43	252	273	272	340	Swaziland
1,928	1,830	392	483	2,711	2,168	13,000	13,000	3,452	3,357	5,257	6,590	113,633	103,112	Sweden
2,008	1,700	350	425	2,113	1,680	6,000	6,000	3,653	3,900	4,194	5,000	43,186	35,000	Switzerland
778	770	9,311	12,000	...	1	15,000	19,000	504	750	1,353	2,344	68,759	102,500	Syria
135	164	...	...	5,021	10,066	41,411	97,827	47	289	4,127	4,802	...	...	Taiwan
1,177	1,250	2,377	2,000	130	40	6,000	5,000	452	450	1,025	968	19,000	16,000	Tajikistan
12,616	13,376	3,754	3,955	160	335	18,000	25,000	374	471	160	160	35,302	50,050	Tanzania
4,228	7,593	25	98	3,344	4,931	60,000	127,000	19	265	1,950	2,144	145,500	403,200	Thailand
229	250	592	1,250	231	934	2,000	6,000	7	10	225	225	1,677	6,670	Togo
10	10	...	...	105	94	...	...	—	—	2,106	1,500	220	260	Tonga
77	55	10	14	59	48	7,000	11,000	6	11	1,169	1,618	7,433	9,500	Trinidad and Tobago
583	660	4,651	7,100	4	6	24,000	39,000	216	450	878	1,698	36,383	55,000	Tunisia
15,467	11,910	46,100	37,541	10	9	55,000	178,000	7,737	8,950	1,300	1,459	217,164	515,000	Turkey
606	1,104	4,277	0,000	159	159	5,000	7,000	311	204	1,372	816	13,550	14,500	Turkmenistan
...	...	...	...	6	13	...	...	...	...	...	...	11	13	Tuvalu
4,919	5,100	1,319	1,980	187	880	13,000	20,000	344	446	350	350	10,587	16,400	Uganda
25,433	21,607	8,912	6,118	20,197	15,298	209,000	159,000	21,044	17,933	2,272	2,241	850,167	500,038	Ukraine
26	65	132	333	...	...	2,000	8,000	4	6	446	201	2,533	11,955	United Arab Emirates
13,321	11,735	21,643	29,300	7,856	7,910	116,000	126,000	15,917	15,005	4,755	5,506	834,000	625,832	United Kingdom
112,152	100,988	12,670	9,600	64,045	57,904	1,068,000	1,530,000	58,139	69,682	5,377	7,277	4,116,200	4,374,000	United States
10,965	10,316	19,219	23,441	308	230	6,000	10,000	811	1,188	1,442	1,759	16,903	22,700	Uruguay
3,391	5,291	7,949	8,600	441	391	22,000	30,000	2,123	2,600	1,627	1,529	81,567	88,000	Uzbekistan
94	132	...	...	68	59	...	...	2	3	201	261	237	282	Vanuatu
10,527	15,071	333	550	2,241	2,250	42,000	90,000	1,356	1,611	1,163	1,268	128,745	138,800	Venezuela
1,646	3,438	...	...	9,396	15,043	55,000	85,000	26	42	800	800	55,317	118,900	Vietnam
8	8	4	3	5	3	...	...	3	2	3,477	2,738	196	160	Virgin Islands (U.S.)
...	...	...	...	...	...	...	...	...	...	...	...	...	...	West Bank
...	...	...	...	...	...	...	...	...	...	...	...	...	...	Western Sahara
26	26	...	...	71	179	...	...	1	1	1,000	1,000	152	204	Western Samoa
973	1,128	3,002	3,715	...	...	5,000	22,000	70	150	361	600	7,083	18,100	Yemen
...	1,809	...	2,752	...	4,000	...	21,000	...	1,500	...	1,500	...	60,000	Yugoslavia
1,159	1,696	726	1,012	685	1,185	14,000	37,000	6	8	827	849	7,247	8,500	Zaire
2,238	3,300	29	69	217	295	18,000	22,000	60	89	300	300	27,880	35,200	Zambia
5,378	4,500	481	550	155	280	8,000	13,000	455	495	431	450	10,400	16,800	Zimbabwe

[1]Belgium includes Luxembourg.

Extractive industries

Extractive industries are generally defined as those exploiting in situ natural resources and include such activities as mining, forestry, fisheries, and agriculture; the definition is often confined, however, to nonrenewable resources only. For the purposes of this table, agriculture is excluded; it is covered in the two tables immediately preceding.

Extractive industries are divided here into three parts: mining, forestry, and fisheries. These major headings are each divided into two main subheadings, one that treats production and one that treats foreign trade. The production sections are presented in terms of volume except for mining, and the trade sections are presented in terms of U.S. dollars. Volume of production data usually imply output of primary (unprocessed) raw materials only, but, because of the way national statistical information is reported, the data may occasionally include some processed and manufactured materials as well, since these are often indistinguishably associated with the extractive process (sulfur from petroleum extraction, cured or treated lumber, or "processed" fish). This is also the case in the trade sections, where individual national trade nomenclatures may not distinguish some processed and manufactured goods from unprocessed raw materials.

Mining. In the absence of a single international source publication or standard of practice for reporting volume or value of mineral production, single-country sources predominantly have been used to compile mining production figures, supplemented by U.S. Bureau of Mines data, by the United Nations' *National Accounts Statistics* (annual; 2 parts), and by industry sources, especially *Mining Journal*'s *Mining Annual Review*. Each country has its own methods of classifying mining data, which do not always accord with the principal mineral production categories adopted in this table—namely, "metals," "nonmetals," and "energy." The available data have therefore been adjusted to accord better with the definition of each group. Included in the "metal" category are all ferrous and nonferrous metallic ores, concentrates, and scrap; the "nonmetal" group includes all nonmetallic minerals (stone, clay, precious gems, etc.) except the mineral fuels; the last group, "energy," is composed predominantly of the natural hydrocarbon fuels, though it may also include manufactured gas.

The contribution (value) of each national mineral sector to its country's gross domestic product is given, as is the distribution by group of that contribution (to gross domestic product and to foreign trade), although statistics regarding the value of mineral production are less readily available in country sources than those regarding trade or volume of minerals produced. Figures for value added by mineral output, though not always available, were sought first, as they provide the most consistent standard to compare the importance of minerals both within a particular national economy and among national mineral sectors worldwide. Where value added to the gross domestic product was not available, gross value of production or sales was substituted and the exception footnoted. Figures for value of production are reported here in millions of U.S. dollars to permit comparisons to be made from country to country. Comparisons can also be made as to the relative importance of each mineral group within a given country.

Extractive industries

country	mining														
	% of GDP, 1993	mineral production (value added)					trade (value)								
		year	total ('000,000 U.S.$)	by kind (%)			year	exports				imports			
				metals[a]	non-metals[b]	energy[c]		total ('000,000 U.S.$)	by kind (%)			total ('000,000 U.S.$)	by kind (%)		
									metals[a]	non-metals[b]	energy[c]		metals[a]	non-metals[b]	energy[c]
Afghanistan	...	1988[1]	16.2	—	17.7	82.3	1992	5.4	72.6	27.4	—	0.1	—	100.0	—
Albania	...	1994[1]	81.4	46.1	0.8	53.1	1992	162.6	30.1	0.6	69.3	—	—	—	—
Algeria	21.7	1994	9,880.5	—0.6—		99.4	1992	8,481.4	0.1	0.3	99.6	117.3	32.3	23.5	44.2
American Samoa	...	1993	...	—	100.0	—	1989	0.1	100.0	—	—	0.1	—	—	100.0
Andorra	...	...	...	...	...	...	1992	0.3	—	100.0	—	7.8	—	100.0	—
Angola	58.2[2]	1989	[1]2,609.0	—	4.9	95.1	1991	3,340.4	—	6.4	93.6	—	—	—	—
Antigua and Barbuda	1.3	1993	6.1	—	100.0	—	...	...	...	...	...	...	...	...	...
Argentina	1.8[3]	1992	4,108.1	2.7[4]	3.9[4]	93.4[4]	1993	599.8	0.4	0.7	98.9	364.2	47.9	10.7	41.4
Armenia	...	...	...	...	...	...	1993	5.4	—	100.0	—	...	...	...	...
Aruba	...	1993	...	—	100.0	—	1989	—	100.0	—	—	0.8	—	—	100.0
Australia	4.3	1992–93	12,253.8	37.5[5]	7.1[5]	55.4[5]	1993	10,364.2[3]	30.5[3]	5.9[3]	63.6[3]	1,916.3	4.5	9.7	85.8
Austria	0.2[3]	1992	385.0	5.3[4]	30.8[4]	63.9[4]	1993	328.3	39.0	60.8	0.2	2,254.5	14.5	10.2	75.3
Azerbaijan	...	...	...	...	...	...	1993	18.9	100.0	—	—	...	...	...	...
Bahamas, The	...	1993	...	—	100.0	—	1991	25.0	—	100.0	—	8.4	—	—	100.0
Bahrain	17.9[3]	1992	779.8	—	1.2[6]	98.8[6]	1993	188.4[3]	2.2[3]	32.1[3]	65.7[3]	1,431.6	1.9	2.3	95.8
Bangladesh	...	1993	...	—	—100.0[7]—		1992	—	—	—	—	432.0	0.2	2.7	97.1
Barbados	...	1993	...	—	—100.0[8]—		1993	—	—	—	—	5.2	—	18.4	81.6
Belarus	0.1[3]	1992	2.0	—	—100.0—		1993	11.2	99.9	0.1	—	...	...	...	...
Belgium	0.2	1993	433.6	—	—100.0—		1992[9]	8,793.5	5.2	93.6	1.2	16,622.2	13.0	49.6	37.4
Belize	0.5[10]	1994	2.3	—	100.0	—	1993	—	—	—	—	2.9	—	27.9	72.1
Benin	0.6	1993	13.1[11]	—	—100.0[11]—		1990	22.5	—	—	100.0	...	...	...	...
Bermuda	...	...	...	...	...	...	1993	72.2	—	100.0	—	31.4	—	1.3	98.7[12, 13]
Bhutan	1.3	1993	2.9	—	100.0	—	1987	1.5	13.8	85.9	0.3[12, 13]	0.9	—	9.7	90.3[12, 13]
Bolivia	9.6	1993	576.1	—58.1—		41.9	1993	289.8	65.4	1.3	33.3	19.1	82.4	17.6	—
Bosnia and Herzegovina	...	...	...	...	...	...	...	...	...	...	...	...	...	...	...
Botswana	38.1	1993	1,234.1[1]	11.1[1]	88.1[1]	0.8[1]	[14]	...	...	...	...	...	...	...	...
Brazil	1.6[3]	1992	5,738.7	...	...	...	1993	2,739.1	91.3	8.7	—	3,883.2	11.0	3.6	85.4
Brunei	36.1[15]	1991	1,476.0[8]	...	...	...	1993	1,591.9	—	—	100.0	13.0	—	100.0	—
Bulgaria	0.4[15]	1991[1]	582.1	24.6	28.2	47.2	1993	68.0[3]	73.8[3]	26.2[3]	—	1,395.3	4.1	1.5	94.4
Burkina Faso	0.9	1992	28.4	—100.0—		—	1990	—	—	—	—	3.2	—	100.0	—
Burundi	0.5[2]	1991	4.7	...	...	...	1992	—	—	—	—	1.1	—	100.0	—
Cambodia	...	1993	...	—	100.0	—	...	...	...	...	...	...	...	...	...
Cameroon	13.1[2]	1991	1,441.0[11]	...	...	...	1991	1,371.9	—	—	100.0	143.0	90.7	9.3	—
Canada	4.2	1990	25,411.4	24.6	6.4	69.0	1993	15,769.0	16.8	4.3	78.9	6,100.1	27.5	8.1	64.4
Cape Verde	0.3[2]	1991	0.8	—	100.0	—	1990	—	—	—	—	1.3	—	—	100.0
Central African Republic	3.9	1993	49.1[16]	—100.0[16]—		—	1989	60.7	—	100.0	—	1.0	—	100.0	—
Chad	0.5[2]	1991	5.0	—	100.0	—	1989–90[17]	2.9	100.0	—	—	...	...	...	...
Chile	8.2[3]	1992	2,066.4	...	...	...	1993	1,177.9	94.5	5.5	—	938.3	—	3.0	97.0
China	2.7[2]	1991	9,885.2	10.7	11.8	77.5	1993	3,961.6	2.5	18.9	78.6	4,860.6	42.4	5.8	51.8
Colombia	7.6[3]	1992	2,952.4	...	...	...	1993	2,024.1	0.2	20.0	79.8	84.3	33.0	67.0	—
Comoros	—	1993	...	—	100.0	—	...	...	...	...	...	...	...	...	...
Congo	21.0[2]	1991	586.2[11]	...	...	...	1993	784.0	—	32.2	67.8	3.8[6]	—	100.0[6]	—
Costa Rica	...	1990	3.8	12.8	87.2	—	1992	—	—	—	—	89.1	—	10.4	89.6
Côte d'Ivoire	2.5[2]	1991	248.1[11]	...	...	...	1989–90[2]	87.4	—	100.0	—	...	...	...	...
Croatia	...	1991	119.7	1.3	71.3	27.4	1993	50.1	19.3	24.8	55.9	499.0	6.2	9.1	84.7
Cuba	...	...	...	...	...	...	1989	485.3	99.3	0.7	—	1,799.4	—	2.1	97.9
Cyprus	0.3[19]	1992[19]	17.2	1.1	98.9	—	1993[19]	8.1	64.9	35.1	—	104.7	—	18.5	81.5
Czech Republic	...	1991[1]	2,225.4	—8.4—		91.6	1990[20]	627.2[13, 21]	2.5[21]	12.1[21]	85.4[13, 21]	1,282.7	24.0	8.6	67.4
Denmark	0.8	1992	1,232.1	—	14.5	85.5	1992	847.4	15.2	8.7	76.1	881.8	3.9	14.4	81.7
Djibouti	—	1993	...	—	100.0	—	1989	—	—	—	—	14.6[13]	0.2	9.7	90.1[13]
Dominica	0.6	1993	1.3	—	100.0	—	1991	0.2	—	100.0	—	1.6	—	21.1	78.9
Dominican Republic	2.7[3]	1992	141.0	...	...	...	1991	261.6	99.6	0.4	—	...	...	...	...
Ecuador	9.0[3]	1991	882.6	0.6	0.2	99.2	1993	1,159.3	0.1	0.1	99.8	26.8	—	25.0	75.0
Egypt	10.1	1988	1,960.0	0.4	6.7	92.9	1993	1,333.3	0.6	0.7	98.7	578.3	79.7	4.3	16.0
El Salvador	0.2[3]	1992	10.8	100.0	—	—	1992	—	—	—	—	162.2	—	3.5	96.5

Since the data for value of mineral production are obtained mostly from country sources, there is some variation (from a standard calendar year) in the time periods to which the data refer. In addition, the time period for which production data are available does not always correspond with the year for which mineral trade data are available.

The Standard International Trade Classification (SITC), Revision 3, was used to determine the commodity groupings for foreign trade statistics. The actual trade data for these groups is taken largely from the United Nations' *International Trade Statistics Yearbook* (2 vol.) and national sources.

Forestry. Data for the production and trade sections of forestry are based on the Food and Agriculture Organization (FAO) of the United Nations' *Yearbook of Forest Products.* Production of roundwood (all wood obtained in removals from forests) is the principal indicator of the volume of each country's forestry sector; this total is broken down further (as percentages of the roundwood total) into its principal components: fuelwood and charcoal, and industrial roundwood. The latter group was further divided to show its principal component, sawlogs and veneer; lesser categories of industrial roundwood could not be shown for reasons of space. These included pitprops (used in mining, a principal consumer of wood) and pulpwood (used in papermaking and plastics). Value of trade in forest products is given for both imports and exports, although exports alone tend to be the significant indicator for producing countries, while imports of wood are rarely a significant fraction of the trade of most importing countries.

Fisheries. Data for nominal (live weight) catches of fish, crustaceans, mollusks, etc., in all fishing areas (marine areas and inland waters) are taken from the FAO *Yearbook of Fishery Statistics* (*Catches and Landings*). Total catch figures are given in metric tons; the catches in inland waters and marine areas are given as percentages of the total catch, as are the main kinds of catch—fish, crustaceans, and mollusks. The total catch figures exclude marine mammals, such as whales and seals; and such aquatic animal products as corals, sponges, and pearls; but include frogs, turtles, and jellyfish. The subtotals by kind of catch, however, exclude the last group, which do not belong taxonomically to the fish, crustaceans, or mollusks.

Figures for trade in fishery products (including processed products and preparations like oils, meals, and animal feeding stuffs) are taken from the FAO's *Yearbook of Fishery Statistics* (*Fishery Commodities*). Value figures for trade in fish products are given for both imports and exports.

The following notes further define the column headings:

a. Includes ferrous and nonferrous metallic ores, concentrates, and scraps, such as iron ore, bauxite and alumina, copper, zinc, gold (except unwrought or semimanufactured), lead, or uranium.

b. Includes natural fertilizers; stone, sand, and aggregate; and pearls, precious and semiprecious stones, worked and unworked.

c. Includes hydrocarbon solids, liquids, and gases.

1 cubic metre = 35.3147 cubic feet

1 metric ton = 1.1023 short tons

forestry, 1993						fisheries, 1993									country
production of roundwood				trade (value, '000 U.S.$)		catch (nominal)							trade (value, '000 U.S.$)		
total ('000 cubic metres)	fuelwood, charcoal (%)	industrial roundwood (%)		exports	imports	total ('000 metric tons)	by source (%)		by kind of catch (%)				exports	imports	
		total	sawlogs, veneer				marine	inland	fish	crusta-ceans	mollusks				
7,817	78.2	21.8	11.0	401	1,550	1.2	—	100.0	100.0	—	—		...	...	Afghanistan
2,556	60.9	39.1	39.1	620	3,307	3.5	59.7	40.3	87.9	0.5	11.6		2,590	420	Albania
2,367	87.0	13.0	1.9	302	187,251	90.6	99.5	0.5	96.7	2.4	0.9		2,320	1,210	Algeria
...	...	...	...	663	377	0.1	100.0	—	100.0	—	—		...	...	American Samoa
...	...	...	...	116	6,000	—	—	100.0	100.0	—	—		...	...	Andorra
6,583	85.9	14.1	1.0	644	4,147	80.7	91.3	8.7	97.8	1.9	0.3		15,120	13,400	Angola
...	...	...	...	33	9,093	2.4	100.0	—	87.5	12.5	—		420	1,840	Antigua and Barbuda
11,865	36.1	63.9	29.0	148,584	460,040	930.6	98.6	1.4	77.0	2.0	21.0		709,292	44,763	Argentina
...	...	...	...	13	12	4.3	—	100.0	100.0	—	—		...	...	Armenia
...	...	...	...	6	6,638	0.0	100.0	—	100.0	—	—		190	5,450	Aruba
20,531	14.1	85.9	43.0	467,944	1,471,306	218.3	97.8	2.2	65.2	20.2	19.2		670,432	360,421	Australia
12,857	24.5	75.5	53.7	2,813,226	1,215,687	4.6	—	100.0	99.9	0.1	—		4,451	157,688	Austria
...	...	...	...	21[3]	...	36.0	—	100.0	100.0	—	—		...	...	Azerbaijan
117	—	100.0	12.8	557	19,881	10.1	100.0	—	16.3	78.5	5.2		47,124	7,000	Bahamas, The
—	—	—	—	51	17,081	9.0	100.0	—	64.7	33.8	1.5		3,769	5,506	Bahrain
32,513	97.7	2.3	0.9	253	25,765	1,047.2	29.9	70.1	89.7	10.2	—		168,290	160	Bangladesh
5	—	100.0	100.0	500	17,253	2.9	100.0	—	100.0	—	—		253	6,466	Barbados
10,031	8.2	91.8	30.1	97,010	1,285	14.0	—	100.0	100.0	—	—		5,885	3,670	Belarus
4,240[9]	13.0[9]	87.0[9]	61.8[9]	1,742,214[9]	2,992,743[9]	36.4	97.7	2.3	93.4	4.6	2.0		228,837[9]	730,459[9]	Belgium
188	67.0	33.0	33.0	1,995	3,051	2.1	99.9	0.1	18.3	70.8	10.9		12,452	780	Belize
5,538	94.5	5.5	0.9	265	1,604	39.0	23.1	76.9	81.5	18.5	—		165	8,110	Benin
...	...	...	...	845	5,066	0.4	100.0	—	97.4	2.6	—		—	8,600	Bermuda
1,497	91.5	8.5	6.0	23	245	0.4	—	100.0	100.0	—	—		...	...	Bhutan
1,555	90.5	9.5	4.5	54,110	19,863	6.2	—	100.0	100.0	—	—		341	1,481	Bolivia
5,379[4]	...	...	...	3,586	2,297	2.5	—	100.0	100.0	—	—		...	4,630	Bosnia and Herzegovina
1,440	93.8	6.2	—	...	...	2.0	—	100.0	100.0	—	—		31	5,599	Botswana
272,078	71.4	28.6	15.1	1,994,730	308,471	780.0	72.4	27.6	89.1	10.1	0.8		191,633	200,567	Brazil
295	26.8	73.2	69.8	73	1,010	1.8	96.4	3.6	78.3	19.7	2.0		510	6,380	Brunei
3,565	48.5	51.5	22.5	42,163	29,342	21.6	55.7	44.3	95.1	—	4.9		8,009	5,333	Bulgaria
9,520	95.5	4.5	—	126	2,036	7.0	—	100.0	100.0	—	—		—	4,292	Burkina Faso
4,613	98.8	1.2	0.1	95	546	22.0	—	100.0	100.0	—	—		243	726	Burundi
7,025	83.7	16.3	7.3	102,143	871	108.9	30.4	69.6	92.4	6.3	1.3		...	...	Cambodia
14,741	79.9	20.1	14.3	319,564	18,450	80.0	75.0	25.0	81.2	18.8	—		1,430	20,100	Cameroon
179,967	3.8	96.2	76.2	19,295,376	2,082,219	1,171.6	96.9	3.1	75.4	12.3	12.2		2,055,438	821,404	Canada
...	...	...	...	3	2,008	7.1	100.0	—	98.8	1.1	—		2,715	180	Cape Verde
3,701	87.8	12.2	4.5	10,208	271	13.5	—	100.0	100.0	—	—		—	870	Central African Republic
4,283	85.6	14.4	0.3	4	691	80.0	—	100.0	100.0	—	—		...	...	Chad
32,241	29.9	70.1	28.7	1,134,024	152,259	6,038.0	99.7	0.3	97.1	0.5	1.8		1,124,679	18,505	Chile
300,668[18]	66.5[18]	33.5[18]	17.2[18]	1,120,806[18]	4,648,253[18]	17,567.9	57.3	42.7	73.7	8.9	16.6		1,542,426	575,930	China
20,903	82.4	17.6	12.8	18,480	182,741	146.4	67.8	32.2	92.3	7.3	0.4		161,209	71,925	Colombia
...	...	...	...	426	3,947	7.0	100.0	—	99.4	0.6	—		—	1,160	Comoros
3,561	62.3	37.7	17.8	113,185	1,080	41.5	53.5	46.5	99.0	1.0	—		6,200	32,120	Congo
4,315	74.4	25.6	20.2	2,454	111,408	17.7	87.2	12.8	70.5	29.2	0.3		63,730	13,175	Costa Rica
13,694	79.5	20.5	14.3	304,051	26,936	70.2	78.9	21.1	98.3	1.7	—		116,944	110,420	Côte d'Ivoire
2,131	33.3	66.7	51.9	248,262	136,770	30.3	85.3	14.7	91.8	2.2	6.0		49,357	23,422	Croatia
3,146	80.6	19.4	6.1	316	8,635	93.4	81.3	18.7	78.4	16.7	4.5		73,332	18,921	Cuba
50	36.0	64.0	46.0	1,813	84,597	2.9	96.9	3.1	84.2	0.1	15.7		3,474	28,283	Cyprus
10,306	9.8	90.2	43.7	351,171	168,130	24.4	—	100.0	100.0	—	—		22,132	52,498	Czech Republic
2,192	24.3	75.7	39.2	231,331	1,107,672	1,534.1	97.7	2.3	97.4	0.7	1.9		2,150,665	1,094,253	Denmark
...	...	...	...	32	786	0.3	100.0	—	100.0	—	—		80	1,150	Djibouti
...	...	...	...	9	4,320	0.8	99.9	0.1	99.9	0.1	—		—	1,420	Dominica
982	99.4	0.6	0.4	225	106,752	14.1	77.5	22.5	70.0	11.2	18.8		940	34,990	Dominican Republic
7,499	56.4	43.6	37.2	27,656	111,531	330.7	98.4	1.6	68.3	30.9	0.8		573,775	3,723	Ecuador
2,404	95.3	4.7	—	6,784	413,837	302.8	31.5	68.5	97.0	2.6	0.4		5,277	50,158	Egypt
6,493	97.8	2.2	1.4	104	45,121	13.0	64.7	35.3	57.3	36.3	6.4		21,699	4,615	El Salvador

Extractive industries (continued)

country	mining						trade (value)								
	% of GDP, 1993	mineral production (value added)					year	exports				imports			
		year	total ('000,000 U.S.$)	by kind (%)				total ('000,000 U.S.$)	by kind (%)			total ('000,000 U.S.$)	by kind (%)		
				metals[a]	non-metals[b]	energy[c]			metals[a]	non-metals[b]	energy[c]		metals[a]	non-metals[b]	energy[c]
Equatorial Guinea	...	1993	...	—	—	100.0	1990	...	...	...	...	2.1	—	100.0	—
Eritrea	—	...	...	...	...	...		...	...	...	...	...	...	...	...
Estonia	1.9	1993	31.0	...	——100.0——			...	...	...	...	...	...	...	...
Ethiopia	0.3[3]	1992	11.1	——100.0——		—	1991	...	...	...	...	29.4	—	0.8	99.2
Faroe Islands	0.1[15]	1988	1.2	—	—	100.0	1993	—	—	—	—	0.2	—	100.0	—
Fiji	0.2	1990	11.2	95.2	4.8	—	1992	—	—	—	—	2.9	—	100.0	—
Finland	0.4	1992	374.6	21.2	78.8	—	1993	149.8	42.2	52.3	5.5	2,269.9	21.1	10.5	68.4
France	0.8[3]	1992	6,233.7	3.0	21.2	75.8	1993	2,059.6	47.0	36.3	16.7	15,331.5	8.2	7.0	84.8
French Guiana	...	1993	...	——100.0——		—	1990	—	—	—	—	2.0	—	—	100.0
French Polynesia	...	...	...	...	...	...	1993	117.9	—	100.0	—	3.9[15]	—	25.5[15]	74.5[15]
Gabon	30.6[2]	1991	1,055.9	20.1[22]	—	79.9[22]	1993	2,123.6	7.6	—	92.4	...	...	...	...
Gambia, The	—	1993	...	—	100.0	—	1986	3.3	100.0	—	—	...	...	...	...
Gaza Strip	...	...	...	...	...	...		...	...	...	...	...	...	...	...
Georgia	...	...	...	...	...	...	1990	275.2	74.7	9.9	15.4	547.0	55.8	12.4	31.8
Germany	3.4[22, 23]	1989[23]	11,803.2	0.6	20.0	79.4	1993	3,421.1	45.7	33.5	20.8	24,409.1	13.9	6.8	79.3
Ghana	1.9[3]	1992	130.7	——100.0——		—	1993	289.5	16.4	83.6	—	...	...	...	...
Gibraltar	...	...	...	...	...	...	1986	1.0	—	100.0	—	0.3	—	100.0	—
Greece	1.3[3]	1990	666.2	13.6	34.6	51.8	1993	150.9	40.0	29.1	30.9	1,843.1	1.9	1.3	96.8
Greenland	—	1993	—	—	—	—	1993	—	—	—	—	1.1	—	100.0	—
Grenada	0.5	1993	1.1	—	100.0	—	1991	—	—	—	—	1.6	—	11.2	88.8
Guadeloupe	...	1993	...	—	100.0	—	1992	0.7	100.0	—	—	3.5	—	—	100.0
Guam	...	1987[1]	2.3	—	100.0	—	1986[24]	—	100.0	—	—	...	...	...	...
Guatemala	0.2	...	...	...	...	...	1992	20.0	—	—	100.0	155.6	—	4.1	95.9
Guernsey	...	...	...	...	...	...		...	...	...	...	...	...	...	...
Guinea	22.0[2]	1991	592.8[26]	——100.0[26]——		—	1993	310.2	84.3	15.7	—	...	...	...	...
Guinea-Bissau	—	1993	...	—	100.0	—	1986	1.0	—	100.0	—	...	...	...	...
Guyana	20.7	1993	81.1	——100.0——		—	1991	79.3	100.0	—	—	1.1[6]	—	100.0[6]	—
Haiti	0.1[3]	1992	1.2	—	100.0	—	1993	—	—	—	—	...	...	...	...
Honduras	2.0	1993	52.3	——100.0——		—	1992	19.1	100.0	—	—	51.4	—	21.3	78.7
Hong Kong	—	1993	25.4	—	100.0	—	1993	1,573.0	19.2	79.3	1.5	3,630.6	6.5	80.4	13.1
Hungary	...	1989	939.5	4.8	4.3	90.9	1993	167.2	91.0	0.5	8.5	88.1	28.1	53.9	18.0
Iceland	...	1993	...	—	100.0	—	1993	7.8	—	100.0	—	46.4	71.2	19.4	9.4
India	2.4[27]	1991–92	4,827.9	9.6	11.2	79.2	1992	3,858.1	14.2	85.7	0.1	8,521.8	8.7	36.9	54.4
Indonesia	10.2	1993	14,733.1	——6.5[21]——		93.5[21]	1993	10,476.1	8.6	1.0	90.4	1,620.2	31.1	10.9	58.0
Iran	18.1	1993–94	11,264.3	——3.9——		97.1	1993	13,943.9	0.2	0.2	99.6	149.0	66.4	33.6	—
Iraq	0.7[2]	1991	480.6	...	...	...	1993	292.9	—	—	100.0	—	—	—	—
Ireland	...	1989	512.1[28]	30.3	68.7	1.0[28]	1993	461.0	64.8	23.0	12.2	651.7	20.9	9.2	69.9
Isle of Man	...	1993	...	—	100.0	—		...	...	...	...	...	...	...	...
Israel	...	1990	352.6	...	...	...	1993	4,311.6	0.2	97.9	1.9	5,003.2	0.1	73.0	26.9
Italy	...	1989	2,554.5	3.4	25.2	71.4	1993	637.7	25.0	64.9	10.1	13,734.1	14.9	8.6	76.5
Jamaica	7.3	1993	279.0	99.2[2]	0.8[2]	—	1991	658.6	99.8	0.2	—	138.0	0.1	—	99.9
Japan	0.3[3]	1992	10,509.3	7.5[15]	36.6[15]	55.9[15]	1993	697.3	44.1	55.3	0.6	54,869.1	12.8	8.0	79.2
Jersey	...	...	...	...	...	...		...	...	...	...	...	...	...	...
Jordan	3.3	1993	145.2	—	100.0	—	1993	275.2	2.1	97.9	—	371.0	1.0	4.5	94.5
Kazakhstan	...	...	...	...	...	...	1993	55.3	64.5	3.5	32.0	0.4	100.0	—	—
Kenya	0.3	1993	12.1	——100.0——		—	1993	4.4	—	100.0	—	332.6	0.2	—	99.8
Kiribati	—	1993	—	—	—	—	1991	0.3	100.0	—	—	...	...	...	...
Korea, North	...	...	...	...	...	...		...	...	...	...	...	...	...	...
Korea, South	0.4	1990	1,384.7	3.9	41.3	54.8	1993	182.3	23.6	65.2	11.2	15,358.0	16.7	3.5	79.8
Kuwait	43.4	1993	9,840.7	—	—	100.0	1992	5,202.6	0.4	—	99.6	2.9	—	100.0	—
Kyrgyzstan	...	...	...	...	...	...	...	...	...	...	...	...	...	...	...
Laos	0.2	1993	1.8	——100.0——		—	...	...	...	...	...	...	...	...	...
Latvia	0.1	1991	30.9	—	——100.0——		1993	66.7	84.8	—	15.2	...	...	...	...
Lebanon	—[3]	...	...	...	...	...	1986	45.8	28.3	71.7	—	28.9	2.2	78.3	19.5
Lesotho	0.2[2]	1991	1.1	—	100.0	—	[14]	...	...	...	...	...	...	...	...
Liberia	3.0[4]	1989	122.3[29]	——100.0[29]——		—	1989–90[17]	129.0	85.9	8.5	5.6	...	...	...	...
Libya	26.3[2]	1991	9,988.9[8]	—	——100.0[8]——		1993	8,855.0	—	—	100.0	13.6	—	100.0	—
Liechtenstein	...	...	...	...	...	...		...	...	...	...	...	...	...	...
Lithuania	...	...	...	...	...	...	1992	3.6	—	100.0	—	324.8	—	3.5	96.5
Luxembourg	0.3[2]	1991	29.2	—	100.0	—	[9]	...	...	...	...	...	...	...	...
Macau	...	1991	1.8	—	100.0	—	1993	—	—	—	—	87.4	—	89.1	10.9
Macedonia	...	...	...	...	...	...		...	...	...	...	...	...	...	...
Madagascar	0.3[2]	1991	8.1	——100.0——		—	1991	19.5	48.5	51.5	—	26.4	—	—	100.0
Malawi	...	1986	0.1	—	100.0	—	1989	—	—	—	—	5.8	—	96.4	3.6
Malaysia	8.0	1990	5,542.9	2.1	2.4	95.5	1992	5,031.1	2.7	2.2	95.1	900.5	34.7	30.4	34.9
Maldives	1.8	1993	1.9	—	100.0	—	1990	0.05	100.0	—	—	24.2[13]	0.1	10.3	89.6[13]
Mali	1.5[2]	1991	40.1	——100.0——		—	1992	35.0	—	100.0	—	0.3	—	100.0	—
Malta	...	1988	3.1	—	100.0	—	1992	3.0	74.9	25.1	—	19.7	—	53.5	46.5
Marshall Islands	0.3[10]	1994	0.2	—	100.0	—	1994	—	—	—	—	...	...	...	...
Martinique	...	1993	...	—	100.0	—	1993	2.1	—	—	100.0	104.1	—	—	100.0
Mauritania	9.1	1993	86.5	——100.0——		—	1993	239.9	100.0	—	—	0.3[6]	—	100.0[6]	—
Mauritius	0.1	1993	3.1	—	100.0	—	1992	22.5	—	100.0	—	36.4	—	70.8	29.2
Mayotte	...	...	...	...	...	...		...	...	...	...	...	...	...	...
Mexico	3.5	1991	5,946.9[13]	18.9	27.9	53.2[13]	1993	7,026.4	3.6	2.7	93.7	710.0	30.8	25.6	43.6
Micronesia	—	—	—	—	—	—		...	...	...	...	...	...	...	...
Moldova	...	1993	...	—	100.0	—	1993	0.8	—	—	100.0	...	...	...	...
Monaco	...	...	...	...	...	...		...	...	...	...	...	...	...	...
Mongolia	...	...	...	...	...	...		...	...	...	...	...	...	...	...
Morocco	2.2[3]	1992	629.0	——93.6[15]——		6.4[15]	1993	386.8	22.7	87.3	—	1,028.6	1.4	13.7	84.9
Mozambique	0.2[2]	1991	2.4	0.4[1, 21]	79.7[1, 21]	19.9[1, 21]	1993	1.1	—	—	100.0	...	...	...	...
Myanmar (Burma)	0.6[31]	1992–93	223.0[8]	...	...	...	1991	39.2	17.7	82.3	—	...	...	...	...
Namibia	16.3	1993	319.0	——100.0——		—	[14]	...	...	...	...	...	...	...	...
Nauru	...	1993	...	—	100.0	—	1993	99.6	—	100.0	—	...	...	...	...
Nepal	0.6[27]	1993–94	22.3	——100.0——		—	1990	—	—	100.0	—	5.0	43.8	0.1	56.1
Netherlands, The	3.0	1992	9,396.1	—	5.5	94.5	1993	6,030.6	22.8	7.2	70.0	10,370.9	11.6	7.2	81.2

forestry, 1993						fisheries, 1993								country
production of roundwood				trade (value, '000 U.S.$)		catch (nominal)						trade (value, '000 U.S.$)		
total ('000 cubic metres)	fuelwood, charcoal (%)	industrial roundwood (%)		exports	imports	total ('000 metric tons)	by source (%)		by kind of catch (%)			exports	imports	
		total	sawlogs, veneer				marine	inland	fish	crusta-ceans	mollusks			
638	70.1	29.9	29.9	33,134	72	3.8	89.5	10.5	83.7	11.3	3.7	—	1,850	Equatorial Guinea
...	...	...	...	...	...	2.5	80.0	20.0	100.0	—	—	...	...	Eritrea
2,439	43.0	57.0	23.0	52,304	6,251	146.9	98.2	1.8	99.1	—	0.9	49,778	2,609	Estonia
46,969	96.3	3.7	—	63	4,518	4.2	—	100.0	100.0	—	—	—	140	Ethiopia
...	...	...	...	362	6,043	261.6	100.0	—	94.9	3.8	1.3	312,338	10,845	Faroe Islands
307	12.1	87.9	86.6	23,501	8,924	31.4	90.2	9.8	83.5	1.8	13.7	28,143	37,080	Fiji
39,644	10.5	89.5	43.3	7,411,113	475,111	152.5	63.8	36.2	99.8	0.2	—	13,364	102,624	Finland
44,069	23.7	76.3	43.9	3,996,581	4,962,172	830.0	93.2	6.8	64.8	2.7	32.5	857,752	2,556,151	France
254	26.0	74.0	70.5	1,147	3,735	7.0	98.9	1.1	47.4	52.6	—	30,504	3,898	French Guiana
...	...	...	...	37	15,480	8.1	99.9	0.1	99.1	0.9	—	748	8,243	French Polynesia
4,436	63.2	36.8	36.8	345,334	5,660	28.3	91.2	8.8	96.2	3.6	0.2	6,360	13,280	Gabon
958	97.8	2.2	1.5	57	920	20.5	88.3	11.7	96.9	3.1	—	2,538	470	Gambia, The
...	...	...	...	...	...	...	...	...	...	...	...	...	...	Gaza Strip
...	...	...	...	923	164	37.0	92.2	7.8	99.9	—	0.1	...	...	Georgia
36,156	10.5	89.5	48.5	5,751,002	9,502,076	316.4	84.4	15.6	87.5	4.3	8.2	654,212	1,883,684	Germany
17,192	90.2	9.8	8.9	154,222	10,514	371.2	86.0	14.0	99.0	0.5	0.5	20,164	16,403	Ghana
...	...	...	...	50	1,218	—	100.0	—	100.0	—	—	...	...	Gibraltar
2,779	54.7	45.3	23.4	47,012	401,580	199.6	93.4	6.6	80.7	2.9	16.4	132,065	162,957	Greece
—	—	—	—	125	9,802	113.6	100.0	—	30.6	68.0	1.4	290,037	4,270	Greenland
...	...	...	...	27[3]	3,175	2.1	100.0	—	97.7	1.2	0.5	130	2,250	Grenada
22	68.2	31.8	31.8	127	42,809	8.0	99.5	0.5	90.2	3.5	6.0	268	21,199	Guadeloupe
...	...	...	...	64[3]	1,365	0.6	70.2	29.8	96.9	3.1	—	...	...	Guam
11,200	90.9	1.1	1.0	3,634	66,910	8.1	41.2	50.0	67.3	32.5	0.2	23,940	4,010	Guatemala
...	...	...	...	...	...	[25]	[25]	[25]	[25]	[25]	[25]	...	...	Guernsey
4,549	87.2	12.8	3.1	2,094	2,860	40.0	90.0	10.0	96.2	1.3	2.5	4,390	5,070	Guinea
574	73.5	26.5	7.0	1,211	518	5.4	95.3	4.7	79.6	20.2	0.2	960	430	Guinea-Bissau
180	7.8	92.2	83.9	5,632	1,813	40.0	98.0	2.0	91.5	8.5	—	17,222	—	Guyana
6,171	96.1	3.9	3.6	18	5,161	5.6	89.3	10.7	75.9	17.0	7.1	1,920	3,960	Haiti
6,454	90.5	9.5	9.2	29,306	39,913	24.4	98.8	1.2	24.2	52.6	23.2	76,129	6,407	Honduras
193	100.0	—	—	1,044,231	2,218,545	226.8	97.5	2.5	87.9	4.4	7.7	561,573	1,376,856	Hong Kong
4,660	50.2	49.8	22.0	135,935	279,654	23.4	—	100.0	100.0	—	—	4,745	31,372	Hungary
—	—	—	—	372	54,205	1,718.5	99.9	0.1	95.9	3.4	0.7	1,137,638	23,374	Iceland
287,449	91.4	8.6	6.4	16,799	262,381	4,324.2	57.5	42.5	91.2	7.4	1.4	810,645	4,497	India
188,118	79.2	20.8	19.0	5,157,973	555,961	3,637.7	75.1	24.9	87.1	10.5	2.0	1,419,492	99,820	Indonesia
7,647	33.8	66.2	5.5	274	102,443	343.9	71.8	28.2	97.3	2.0	0.7	23,190	33,700	Iran
155	67.7	32.3	12.9	9	581	23.5	19.1	80.9	100.0	—	—	...	...	Iraq
1,750	2.8	97.2	70.7	108,081	400,050	305.0	99.7	0.3	88.4	3.4	8.2	271,885	75,609	Ireland
...	...	...	...	...	...	4.0	100.0	—	22.1	3.7	74.2	...	...	Isle of Man
113	11.5	88.5	31.9	21,296	520,138	18.7	17.7	82.3	98.9	0.8	0.3	7,180	101,790	Israel
0,060	10.7	60.0	00.6	0,000,006	6,616,070	660.0	00.0	10.0	60.1	1.6	00.0	001,007	0,101,101	Italy
495	71.7	28.3	16.2	89	76,969	11.0	68.2	31.8	98.2	1.6	0.2	8,250	25,490	Jamaica
32,570	1.1	98.9	53.9	1,683,688	16,767,431	8,128.1	97.8	2.2	78.1	1.9	18.7	766,952	14,187,149	Japan
...	...	...	...	...	...	2.9[25]	100.0[25]	—[25]	19.2[25]	77.7[25]	3.1[25]	...	...	Jersey
11	63.6	36.4	—	7,293	166,742	0.1	3.2	96.8	100.0	—	—	845	19,690	Jordan
...	...	...	...	6,024	1,254	75.0	—	100.0	100.0	—	—	3,911	...	Kazakhstan
38,554	95.2	4.8	1.2	961	15,476	185.4	2.6	97.4	99.7	0.2	0.1	38,440	905	Kenya
...	...	...	...	...	363	29.3	100.0	—	85.3	0.7	14.0	550	280	Kiribati
4,830	87.6	12.4	12.4	9,008	32,837	1,780.0	93.7	6.3	96.2	0.7	3.1	65,815	1,700	Korea, North
6,485	69.3	30.7	16.4	570,113	3,125,851	2,649.0	98.9	1.1	59.0	4.6	35.3	1,335,419	545,518	Korea, South
...	...	...	...	10	00,100	0.0	100.0		00.1	00.0		7,200	15,500	Kuwait
...	...	...	...	544	667	1.1	—	100.0	100.0	—	—	410	...	Kyrgyzstan
4,906	86.7	13.3	10.9	67,906	740	30.5	—	100.0	100.0	—	—	—	210	Laos
4,558	15.4	84.6	48.5	84,414	4,003	142.2	99.4	0.6	96.7	0.1	3.2	30,686	3,232	Latvia
496	98.6	1.4	1.4	1,228	74,320	2.2	90.9	9.1	97.8	1.1	1.1	...	...	Lebanon
651	100.0	—	—	...	...	—	—	100.0	100.0	—	—	[14]	[14]	Lesotho
6,183	82.8	17.2	14.4	3,415	454	7.8	48.6	51.4	96.7	3.0	0.2	1,440	2,030	Liberia
648	82.7	17.3	9.7	279	55,475	8.8	99.1	0.9	99.5	0.5	—	21,900	19,520	Libya
...	...	...	...	...	...	—	—	100.0	100.0	—	—	[30]	[30]	Liechtenstein
...	...	...	...	28,959	2,153	119.9	98.6	1.4	87.3	—	12.7	8,651	6,292	Lithuania
[9]	[9]	[9]	[9]	[9]	[9]	—	—	100.0	100.0	—	—	[9]	[9]	Luxembourg
...	...	...	...	3,714	18,773	1.9	100.0	—	63.2	35.7	1.1	5,963	15,091	Macau
756[3]	...	...	...	13,316	21,835	1.4	—	100.0	100.0	—	—	398	6,696	Macedonia
8,858	90.9	9.1	5.3	2,249	1,955	115.0	73.9	26.1	89.4	9.7	0.5	50,388	300	Madagascar
10,075	94.7	5.3	1.3	10	4,537	65.0	—	100.0	100.0	—	—	360	800	Malaŵi
54,332	17.3	82.7	80.2	4,189,778	411,173	680.0	97.1	2.9	72.0	12.1	14.6	306,845	265,032	Malaysia
...	...	...	...	431	11	90.0	100.0	—	99.9	—	—	28,685	—	Maldives
6,145	93.6	6.4	0.2	123	2,337	64.4	—	100.0	100.0	—	—	514	3,700	Mali
...	...	...	...	202	38,526	5.6	100.0	—	99.8	0.1	0.1	2,290	17,870	Malta
...	...	...	...	...	...	0.3	100.0	—	100.0	—	—	625	230	Marshall Islands
13	76.9	23.1	23.1	64	30,001	4.6	97.7	2.3	96.1	3.5	—	261	31,406	Martinique
13	61.5	38.5	7.7	100	1,201	92.8	94.6	5.4	48.0	0.3	51.7	121,859	1,000	Mauritania
15	13.3	86.7	53.3	179	4,194	21.1	99.7	0.3	97.5	0.4	2.1	23,108	19,698	Mauritius
...	...	...	...	...	...	0.4	100.0	—	100.0	—	—	2	...	Mayotte
23,285	67.7	32.3	23.5	276,214	1,187,089	1,200.7	86.3	13.7	86.0	8.1	5.8	430,774	128,026	Mexico
...	...	...	...	...	...	1.6	99.7	0.3	98.1	1.0	0.6	430	1,140	Micronesia
...	...	...	...	364	315	4.7	—	100.0	100.0	—	—	...	...	Moldova
...	...	...	...	...	...	—	100.0	—	100.0	—	—	...	...	Monaco
865	51.4	48.6	48.6	7,511	274	0.1	—	100.0	100.0	—	—	—	1,820	Mongolia
2,009	71.2	27.9	3.9	63,580	286,780	622.4	99.7	0.3	84.1	1.1	14.8	538,688	7,775	Morocco
16,013	93.8	6.2	0.3	5,648	1,255	30.2	84.5	15.5	59.0	40.2	0.8	70,887	11,280	Mozambique
22,544	85.0	15.0	9.1	294,153	1,903	836.9	74.7	25.3	99.1	0.9	—	46,362	—	Myanmar (Burma)
[32]	[32]	[32]	[32]	[32]	[32]	329.8	99.7	0.3	99.9	—	—	[14]	[14]	Namibia
...	...	...	...	23	257	0.5	100.0	—	100.0	—	—	...	...	Nauru
20,060	96.9	3.1	3.1	208	523	16.9	—	100.0	100.0	—	—	...	...	Nepal
1,403	11.9	88.1	29.2	1,921,199	4,250,307	486.9	99.7	0.3	83.8	2.0	14.2	1,289,136	802,444	Netherlands, The

ustries (continued)

	mining															
	% of GDP, 1993	mineral production (value added)					trade (value)									
		year	total ('000,000 U.S.$)	by kind (%)			year	exports				imports				
				metals[a]	non-metals[b]	energy[c]		total ('000,000 U.S.$)	by kind (%)			total ('000,000 U.S.$)	by kind (%)			
									metals[a]	non-metals[b]	energy[c]		metals[a]	non-metals[b]	energy[c]	
Netherlands Antilles	...	1988	7.4	—	100.0	—	1992	112.2	—	9.0	91.0	986.4	—	—	100.0	
New Caledonia	10.4[4]	1990	262.4	100.0	—	—	1993	106.1[33]	100.0[33]	—	—	7.7[3]	—	—	100.0[3]	
New Zealand	1.0[34]	1990–91	552.8	—17.3—		82.7	1993	253.8	12.9	6.4	80.7	706.1	19.7	14.5	65.8	
Nicaragua	0.6	1991	16.5	82.2	17.8	—	1992	0.6	100.0	—	—	115.5	—	1.1	98.9	
Niger	5.6	1993	124.0	—100.0—		—	1993	376.2[35]	100.0[35]	—	—	—	—	—	—	
Nigeria	37.6[2]	1991	12,196.0	—	0.6	99.4	1993	10,559.2	0.1	—	99.9	18.0	8.6	91.4	—	
Northern Mariana Islands	—	—	—	—	—	—	...	...	...	...	...	...	...	...	...	
Norway	15.1[2]	1991	13,949.0	0.4	1.2	98.4	1993	15,260.0	1.0	1.4	97.6	1,488.8	67.6	11.6	20.8	
Oman	38.5	1993	4,382.1	—	0.7	99.3	1993	4,054.0	0.3	—	99.7	51.2	73.0	27.0	—	
Pakistan	0.6[31]	1992–93	301.5	...	...	...	1993	73.7	3.7	20.1	76.2	736.9	18.8	4.4	76.8	
Palau	...	...	...	...	...	...	...	...	...	...	...	...	...	...	...	
Panama	0.2	1993	5.0	—100.0—		—	1993	87.0	1.6	98.4	—	212.3	1.4	—	98.6	
Papua New Guinea	28.9	1993	1,471.6	100.0	—	—	1990	583.6	100.0	—	—	3.8	—	100.0	—	
Paraguay	0.4[3]	1992	24.2	—	100.0	—	1993	—	—	—	—	63.0	5.8	—	94.2	
Peru	9.6	1991	1,098.1	—52.9[37]—		47.1	1993	470.0	99.5	0.5	—	164.7	5.2	—	94.8	
Philippines	1.2[3]	1992	637.5	67.3	29.1	3.6	1993	333.1	60.1	2.3	37.6	1,893.5	12.9	3.9	83.2	
Poland	...	1990	1,903.5	17.9	17.6	64.5	1992	1,456.0	20.4	16.0	63.6	2,515.9	10.2	5.9	83.9	
Portugal	...	1986	129.2	14.4	77.7	7.9	1993	142.5	82.0	18.0	—	1,474.5	1.2	1.8	97.0	
Puerto Rico	0.1[31]	1992–93	31.0	—	100.0	—	1986[24]	50.7	2.4	95.9	1.7	52.1	0.4	28.8	70.8	
Qatar	35.8[3]	1992	2,678.6[8]	...	...	...	1992	2,887.6	—	0.1	99.9	45.5	72.4	27.6	—	
Réunion	...	1993	...	—	100.0	—	1993	0.2	100.0	—	—	10.3	—	—	100.0	
Romania	...	1991	1,315.6	1.7	7.8	90.5	1993	16.0	7.2	92.8	—	1,622.2	7.6	4.2	88.2	
Russia	...	1989[1,39]	90,630.0	21.6	12.4	65.8	1993	14,698.3	7.6	6.2	86.2	135.4	100.0	—	—	
Rwanda	0.2[2]	1991	2.2	...	...	...	1990	5.1	100.0	—	—	5.7	—	100.0	—	
St. Kitts and Nevis	0.4[3]	1992	0.5	—	100.0	—	1988	—	—	—	—	0.6	—	—	100.0	
St. Lucia	0.7	1993	2.6	—	100.0	—	1991	—	—	—	—	5.0	—	61.5	38.5	
St. Vincent	0.3	1993	0.7	—	100.0	—	1990	—	—	—	—	1.4	—	—	100.0	
San Marino	...	...	...	...	...	...	...	...	...	...	...	...	...	...	...	
São Tomé and Príncipe	0.1[2]	1992	—	—	100.0	—	...	...	...	...	...	...	...	...	...	
Saudi Arabia	35.7[3]	1992	42,456.4	—1.4[4]—		98.6[4]	1990	17,504.1	0.2	0.3	99.5	236.8	36.4	63.6	—	
Senegal	0.7[3]	1992	42.3	—	100.0	—	1991	57.7	3.1	96.9	—	95.3	—	4.0	96.0	
Seychelles	...	1993	—	—	100.0	—	1991	—	—	—	—	37.8[13]	—	0.4	99.6[13]	
Sierra Leone	13.1[31]	1992–93	84.2	—100.0—		—	1993	99.0	27.1	72.9	—	3.3	—	100.0	—	
Singapore	0.1	1994	25.5	—	100.0	—	1993	467.2	33.2	42.8	24.0	6,947.3	1.3	6.3	92.4	
Slovakia	...	...	...	...	...	...	...	...	...	...	...	...	...	...	...	
Slovenia	...	1991	207.7	0.7	15.2	84.1	1993	234.2	0.8	0.2	99.0	468.8	13.6	8.9	77.5	
Solomon Islands	−0.3[2]	1991	−0.5	—100.0—		—	1988	0.7[41]	100.0[41]	—	—	0.7	—	51.1	48.9	
Somalia	0.2[2]	1991	1.0	—	100.0	—	1989–90[17]	—	—	—	—	...	...	...	...	
South Africa	8.7	1989	9,012.6	—86.6—		13.4	1992[14]	4,867.3[28]	21.5	49.6	28.9[28]	273.2[28]	27.9	59.5	12.6[28]	
Spain	...	1990	3,786.9	8.6	32.3	59.1	1993	452.2	43.8	56.2	—	8,693.9	15.0	4.2	80.8	
Sri Lanka	1.1	1993	112.4[42]	—100.0[42]—		—	1992	179.6	4.0	96.0	—	261.4	2.2	36.0	61.8	
Sudan, The	—[27]	1991	17.1	—100.0—		—	1992	1.3	100.0	—	—	...	...	...	...	
Suriname	2.3	1993	85.0[43]	...	...	...	1990	355.5	98.3	—	1.7	7.0	23.9	76.1	—	
Swaziland	1.1[2]	1991	8.9	...	...	...	[14]	...	...	...	...	...	...	...	...	
Sweden	0.3[3]	1992	560.5	55.2	44.8	—	1993	818.9	83.5	12.7	3.8	3,058.0	12.1	7.2	80.7	
Switzerland	...	1993	...	—	100.0	—	1993	3,064.2	4.8	95.2	—	4,153.5	2.5	73.8	23.7	
Syria	11.1[3]	1992	3,657.1[11]	—	—100.0[11]—		1992	1,895.5	—	2.4	97.6	54.5	23.2	15.3	61.5	
Taiwan	0.5	1993	1,194.1	—	85.6	14.4	1993	606.3	...	...	...	6,416.4	—36.2—		63.8	
Tajikistan	...	...	...	...	...	...	...	...	...	...	...	...	...	...	...	
Tanzania	1.1[2]	1991	22.0	...	...	...	1988	8.4	—	100.0	—	113.5	—	24.1	75.9	
Thailand	1.5[3]	1991	1,541.4	1.3	36.2	62.5	1993	1,187.8	1.0	89.8	9.2	3,222.3	12.8	29.8	57.4	
Togo	9.6[2]	1991	146.8	—	100.0	—	1991	124.7	—	100.0	—	3.1	—	100.0	—	
Tonga	0.3	1993–94	0.4	—	100.0	—	1992	—	—	—	—	0.8	—	44.9	55.1	
Trinidad and Tobago	13.5[3]	1992	706.6	—	1.2[15]	98.8[15]	1993	399.4	—	0.2	99.8	247.7	6.6	2.2	91.2	
Tunisia	5.7[3]	1992	889.9	—9.1[6]—		90.9[6]	1993	417.9	1.7	9.7	88.6	270.0	0.8	36.4	62.8	
Turkey	1.1	1990	2,077.0	10.6	19.9	69.5	1993	262.3	19.7	76.7	3.6	4,403.9	20.2	2.1	77.7	
Turkmenistan	...	...	...	...	...	...	...	...	...	...	...	...	...	...	...	
Tuvalu	—	1993	—	—	—	—	1986	—	—	—	—	—	—	—	100.0	
Uganda	0.3	1993–94	11.8	—100.0—		—	1992	—	—	—	—	8.0	—	100.0	—	
Ukraine	...	...	...	...	...	...	1993	317.2	30.1	1.2	68.7	...	...	...	...	
United Arab Emirates	39.3	1993	14,088.5	—	0.5	99.5	1991	12,247.5	0.3	0.3	99.4	219.7	74.7	25.3	—	
United Kingdom	1.9[3]	1992	17,376.1	—	5.0[1,22]	95.0[1,22]	1993	11,247.1	8.0	19.8	72.2	15,025.8	12.4	32.5	55.1	
United States	1.6[2]	1991	93,200.0	6.2	7.7	86.1	1993	10,311.5	32.4	31.6	36.0	56,772.9	5.8	12.7	81.5	
Uruguay	0.2	1994	31.6	—	100.0	—	1993	2.9	—	100.0	—	49.5	0.7	17.7	81.6	
Uzbekistan	...	...	...	...	...	...	...	...	...	...	...	...	...	...	...	
Vanuatu	...	1993	—	—	100.0	—	1986	—	—	—	—	0.5	—	38.0	62.0	
Venezuela	14.8[3]	1992	8,942.5	3.0	1.5	95.5	1993	7,548.7	1.1	0.3	98.6	151.8	48.7	42.3	9.0	
Vietnam	...	1989	1,062.9	...	...	...	1993	896.6	1.0	1.0	98.0	90.1	0.1	9.5	90.4	
Virgin Islands (U.S.)	...	1987[1]	2.7	—	100.0	—	1986[24]	0.3	18.3	81.7	—	966.5	—	0.2	99.8	
West Bank	...	...	...	...	...	...	...	...	...	...	...	...	...	...	...	
Western Sahara	...	...	...	...	[44]	...	...	...	...	...	...	...	...	...	...	
Western Samoa	—	1993	—	—	—	—	...	...	...	...	...	...	...	...	...	
Yemen	5.5[3]	1992	551.5	—	—100.0—		...	...	...	...	...	...	...	...	...	
Yugoslavia	3.2[2,45]	1991[45]	2,205.9	33.6	8.5	57.9	1990[45]	369.7	90.5	6.5	3.0	3,313.8	8.7	5.3	86.0	
Zaire	24.2[2]	1991	708.0	...	...	...	1993	167.9	5.1	66.5	28.4	...	...	...	...	
Zambia	15.3[2]	1991	546.8	96.1[21]	3.9[21]	—	1993	24.5	—	100.0	—	1.2	—	100.0	—	
Zimbabwe	7.2	1993	290.5	...	...	...	1992	95.5	10.0	89.4	0.6	17.3	24.9	75.1	—	

[1]Gross value of production (output). [2]1991. [3]1992. [4]1990. [5]1988–89. [6]1986. [7]Mostly natural gas. [8]Mostly crude petroleum and natural gas. [9]Belgium includes Luxembourg. [10]1994. [11]Mostly crude petroleum. [12]Includes coke and briquettes. [13]Includes petroleum products. [14]South Africa includes Botswana, Lesotho, Namibia, and Swaziland. [15]1988. [16]Mostly diamonds, some gold. [17]Average for the two-year period. [18]China includes Taiwan. [19]Republic of Cyprus only. [20]Data refer to former Czechoslovakia. [21]1987. [22]1989. [23]Data refer to former West Germany only. [24]Trade with the United States only. [25]Jersey includes Guernsey. [26]Mostly bauxite and diamonds. [27]1993–94. [28]Excludes crude petroleum and natural gas. [29]Mostly iron ore. [30]Switzerland

forestry, 1993: production of roundwood: total ('000 cubic metres)	fuelwood, charcoal (%)	industrial roundwood (%): total	industrial roundwood (%): sawlogs, veneer	trade (value, '000 U.S.$): exports	trade (value, '000 U.S.$): imports	fisheries, 1993: catch (nominal): total ('000 metric tons)	by source (%): marine	by source (%): inland	by kind of catch (%): fish	crusta-ceans	mollusks	trade (value, '000 U.S.$): exports	trade (value, '000 U.S.$): imports	country
...	...	...	...	36	21,893	1.2	100.0	—	100.0	—	—	260	8,250	Netherlands Antilles
6	—	100.0	66.7	11	8,181	3.5	100.0	—	55.7	19.2	2.8	7,121	5,497	New Caledonia
15,948	0.3	99.7	66.7	1,309,577	273,426	470.4	99.7	0.3	82.2	0.9	16.7	648,254	36,107	New Zealand
3,697	91.9	8.1	6.8	523	6,115	8.8	93.7	6.3	41.7	57.4	0.9	28,545	1,460	Nicaragua
5,467	93.8	6.2	—	406	714	2.2	—	100.0	100.0	—	—	340	1,130	Niger
118,052	93.0	7.0	5.1	19,916	76,502	255.5	56.2	43.8	93.1	6.9	—	31,690	154,240	Nigeria
...	...	...	...	...	...	0.1	100.0	—	99.2	0.8	—	30	...	Northern Mariana Islands
10,134	9.2	90.8	43.7	1,267,761	642,123	2,561.8	100.0	—	97.6	2.0	0.4	2,302,346	310,352	Norway
...	...	...	...	750	52,396	116.5	100.0	—	97.4	0.9	1.7	51,462	3,563	Oman
27,776	90.1	9.9	7.3	882	162,767	621.7	80.3	19.7	93.2	5.8	1.0	184,591	185	Pakistan
...	...	...	...	...	...	1.5	100.0	—	99.0	0.9	—	...	190	Palau
1,045	88.7	11.3	5.6	3,658	67,514	158.2	99.7	0.3	90.9	7.9	1.2	93,220[36]	11,951[36]	Panama
8,188	67.6	32.4	30.3	463,528	4,597	26.0	48.1	51.9	90.5	6.0	—	13,880	47,800	Papua New Guinea
8,538	63.6	36.4	31.5	61,868	32,026	16.0	—	100.0	100.0	—	—	24	1,605	Paraguay
8,329	86.9	13.1	12.0	12,194	104,312	8,450.6	99.5	0.5	98.4	0.1	1.5	685,004	818	Peru
39,576	90.9	9.1	1.7	96,597	330,312	2,263.8	74.6	25.4	80.9	7.9	11.1	478,086	94,601	Philippines
18,822	15.2	84.8	46.9	387,757	259,555	423.0	88.2	11.8	93.8	3.8	2.4	70,312	128,633	Poland
11,584	5.2	94.8	33.8	734,021	527,698	274.2	99.5	0.5	90.5	0.9	8.6	210,426	627,713	Portugal
...	...	...	...	...	...	1.9	79.8	20.2	74.4	18.8	6.8	[38]	[38]	Puerto Rico
...	...	...	...	11	8,871	7.0	100.0	—	98.1	1.2	0.7	50	2,620	Qatar
36	86.1	13.9	11.1	202	58,898	2.7	99.9	0.1	84.6	15.0	—	7,995	34,922	Réunion
9,536	18.8	81.2	36.8	44,668	29,120	34.9	15.1	84.9	99.9	—	0.1	653	14,813	Romania
207,452	23.6	76.4	34.6	1,835,583	93,865	4,461.4	93.1	6.9	96.3	1.4	2.2	1,471,446	19,074	Russia
5,660	95.3	4.7	1.1	250	734	3.6	—	100.0	100.0	—	—	—	355	Rwanda
...	...	...	...	33	1,730	1.7	100.0	—	88.2	11.8	—	180[40]	1,200[40]	St. Kitts and Nevis
...	...	...	...	8[3]	10,252	1.1	100.0	—	98.7	1.3	—	8	3,290	St. Lucia
...	...	...	...	10	4,821	1.8	100.0	—	93.8	—	6.2	1,494	900	St. Vincent
...	...	...	...	...	...	—	—	100.0	100.0	—	—	...	...	San Marino
9	—	100.0	100.0	28[3]	160	2.2	100.0	—	99.2	0.1	0.7	...	390	São Tomé and Príncipe
...	...	...	...	1,081	634,352	49.4	95.6	4.4	95.6	4.3	0.1	4,520	77,060	Saudi Arabia
5,022	86.3	13.7	0.8	103	12,960	377.7	92.7	7.3	94.7	1.0	4.3	147,680	24,918	Senegal
...	...	...	...	99	324	7.0	100.0	—	99.0	0.3	0.6	14,323	6,987	Seychelles
3,308	96.4	3.6	—	1,248	1,268	62.0	77.4	22.6	97.9	0.5	1.6	16,750	1,800	Sierra Leone
120	100.0	—	—	441,570	799,049	11.7	99.8	0.2	70.4	13.6	16.0	482,312	566,502	Singapore
5,250	9.3	90.7	31.6	108,154	32,229	2.8	—	100.0	100.0	—	—	...	...	Slovakia
1,168	9.2	90.8	55.2	348,994	238,335	3.0	69.1	30.9	100.0	—	—	5,914	19,653	Slovenia
468	29.5	70.5	70.5	83,080	321	45.4	100.0	—	98.7	—	0.2	33,760	185	Solomon Islands
9,047	98.8	1.2	0.3	19	80	14.9	98.3	1.7	95.9	2.4	1.7	7,170	270	Somalia
19,811[32]	36.4[32]	63.6[32]	24.2[32]	566,433[32]	327,477[32]	563.2	99.6	0.4	97.8	0.5	1.7	199,030[14]	90,038[14]	South Africa
14,796	13.4	86.6	40.4	1,031,518	2,479,093	1,290.0	97.6	2.4	81.4	2.5	16.1	813,750	2,629,799	Spain
9,374	92.8	7.2	0.4	2,346	31,446	220.9	91.9	8.1	96.5	3.4	0.1	31,378	34,463	Sri Lanka
24,781	90.7	9.3	—	76	9,500	31.7	4.7	95.3	100.0	—	—	172	2,500	Sudan, The
154	12.3	87.7	70.8	1,491	2,352	9.5	98.0	2.0	99.3	0.7	—	3,440	520	Suriname
2,297	24.4	75.6	13.9	74,516[3]	...	0.1	—	100.0	100.0	—	—	[14]	[14]	Swaziland
62,954	7.0	93.0	41.0	7,483,051	845,224	347.8	98.5	1.5	98.9	0.9	0.2	122,586	371,756	Sweden
4,553	18.6	81.4	64.1	1,239,577	1,926,107	3.2	—	100.0	100.0	—	—	5,426[30]	353,668[30]	Switzerland
55	36.4	63.6	29.1	234	59,934	5.6	28.6	71.4	98.6	1.4	—	60	1,560	Syria
61	22.7	77.3		...	...	1,415.8	87.5	12.5	...	...	...	...	...	Taiwan
...	...	...	...	24	100	3.7	—	100.0	100.0	—	—	...	...	Tajikistan
36,072	94.2	5.8	0.9	3,709	3,620	315.0	13.0	87.0	99.1	0.5	0.1	6,435	226	Tanzania
38,039	92.8	7.2	0.2	205,371	1,378,566	3,348.1	91.5	8.5	77.1	11.9	18.1	3,404,268	830,480	Thailand
1,295	84.7	15.3	0.5	486	1,068	17.0	96.9	3.1	99.8	—	0.2	2,700	12,833	Togo
5	—	100.0	100.0	87[3]	1,699	2.5	100.0	—	96.8	3.2	—	1,630	350	Tonga
48	45.8	54.2	50.0	1,174	53,939	10.6	100.0	—	87.7	12.3	—	6,128	4,219	Trinidad and Tobago
3,373	95.9	4.1	0.2	7,185	102,415	83.8	100.0	—	83.3	2.9	13.8	85,857	2,238	Tunisia
15,350	63.5	36.5	21.5	38,071	833,692	550.6	90.9	9.1	90.6	0.9	8.2	29,067	18,490	Turkey
...	...	...	...	85	223	37.0	—	100.0	100.0	—	—	2,118	...	Turkmenistan
...	...	...	...	1[3]	98	1.5	100.0	—	100.0	—	—	...	...	Tuvalu
15,580	86.6	13.4	1.0	41	2,011	219.8	—	100.0	100.0	—	—	15,794	...	Uganda
...	...	...	...	12,712	11,498	371.3	78.7	21.3	95.5	1.6	2.9	11,387	46,812	Ukraine
...	...	...	...	31,296	213,401	92.5	100.0	—	99.9	0.1	—	19,450	23,700	United Arab Emirates
6,195	4.1	95.9	56.3	1,931,674	8,191,864	898.1	98.3	1.7	89.1	4.5	6.4	1,036,916	1,628,852	United Kingdom
495,800	18.8	81.2	48.7	13,400,614	16,872,624	5,939.3	94.2	5.8	77.2	8.2	14.0	3,179,474[38]	6,290,233[38]	United States
4,087	74.5	25.5	19.2	30,838	48,206	118.8	99.5	0.5	96.4	0.2	3.4	74,476	6,028	Uruguay
...	...	...	...	12	2,381	23.4	—	100.0	100.0	—	—	...	...	Uzbekistan
63	38.1	61.9	61.9	1,839	291	2.9	100.0	—	63.8	13.5	21.3	55	1,140	Vanuatu
2,245	46.0	54.0	51.8	41,112	208,471	390.3	93.7	6.3	86.2	5.0	8.8	89,150	16,768	Venezuela
33,483	86.6	13.4	7.7	84,061	32,125	1,100.0	75.0	25.0	66.8	27.8	5.4	368,435	—	Vietnam
...	...	...	...	...	...	0.9	100.0	—	87.4	8.4	4.2	...	...	Virgin Islands (U.S.)
...	...	...	...	...	...	...	...	...	...	...	...	...	...	West Bank
...	...	...	...	...	...	—	100.0	—	—	—	—	...	...	Western Sahara
131	53.4	46.6	44.3	19	1,964	1.6	100.0	—	98.1	0.4	1.5	25	3,960	Western Samoa
324	100.0	—	—	1	40,402	86.8	99.0	1.0	95.3	2.1	2.5	10,600	3,600	Yemen
3,056	...	...	...	22,866	28,115	6.5	4.4	95.6	99.4	0.2	0.4	2,600	24,140	Yugoslavia
44,532	92.7	7.3	0.9	49,915	4,622	147.3	1.5	98.5	100.0	—	—	—	28,850	Zaire
13,804	93.8	6.2	2.5	18	893	65.3	—	100.0	100.0	—	—	250	2,080	Zambia
8,065	77.7	22.3	6.5	5,603	6,022	21.8	—	100.0	100.0	—	—	250	2,900	Zimbabwe

includes Liechtenstein. [31]1992–93. [32]South Africa includes Namibia. [33]Mostly nickel. [34]1990–91. [35]Radioactive materials only. [36]Excludes the Free Zone of Colón and the Canal Zone. [37]Includes coal mining. [38]United States includes Puerto Rico. [39]Data refer to the former U.S.S.R. [40]Includes Anguilla. [41]Gold only. [42]Mostly precious and semiprecious stones. [43]Mostly bauxite. [44]Accounts for 8–9% of 1993 phosphate production of Morocco. [45]Data refer to former Socialist Federal Republic of Yugoslavia only.

Manufacturing industries

This table provides a summary of manufacturing activity by industrial sector for the countries of the world, providing figures for total manufacturing value added, as well as the percentage contribution of 29 major branches of manufacturing activity to the gross domestic product. U.S. dollar figures for total value added by manufacturing are given but should be used with caution because of uncertainties with respect to national accounting methods, purchasing power parities, price structures and preferments, exchange rates, and so on, especially for countries having nonconvertible currencies.

Manufacturing activity is classified here according to a modification of the International Standard Industrial Classification (ISIC), revision 2, published by the United Nations. A summary of the 2-, 3-, and 4-digit ISIC codes (groups) defining these 29 sectors follows, providing definitional detail beyond that possible in the column headings.

The collection and publication of national manufacturing data is usually carried out by one of three methods: a full census of manufacturing (usually done every 5 to 10 years for a given country), a periodic survey of manufacturing (usually taken at annual or other regular intervals between censuses), and the onetime sample survey (often limited in geographic, sectoral, or size of enterprise coverage). The full census is, naturally, the most complete, but, since up to 10 years may elapse between such censuses, it is sometimes necessary to substitute a survey of more recent date but less complete coverage. In other instances, data published by the United Nations Industrial Development Organization (UNIDO), especially its *International Yearbook of Industrial Statistics;* occasional publications of the International Monetary Fund (IMF); and other sources have been used.

ISIC code(s)		Products manufactured
31		Food, beverages, and tobacco
	311+312	food including prepared animal feeds
	313	alcoholic and nonalcoholic beverages
	314	tobacco manufactures
32		Textiles, wearing apparel, and leather goods
	321	spinning of textile fibres, weaving and finishing of textiles, knitted articles, carpets, rope, etc.
	322	wearing apparel (including leather clothing; excluding knitted articles and footwear)
	323+324	leather products (including footwear; excluding wearing apparel), leather substitutes, and fur products

Manufacturing industries

country	year	total manufacturing value added ('000,000 U.S.$)	(31) food (311+312)	beverages (313)	tobacco manufactures (314)	(32) textiles (exc. wearing apparel) (321)	wearing apparel (322)	leather and fur products (323+324)	(33) wood products (exc. furniture) (331)	wood furniture (332)	(34) paper, paper products (341)	printing and publishing (342)	(35) industrial chemicals (351)	paints, soaps, etc. (352 exc. 3522)	drugs and medicines (3522)
Afghanistan	1988–89[1]	435	18.3	1.9	—	8.0	0.4	16.7	—0.5—		0.9	4.9	4.8	0.2	2.7
Albania	1992[1, 2]	290	—51.5—		3.9	9.1	12.8	4.3	—1.3—		0.3	...	1.5[3]	[3]	[3]
Algeria	1990	5,739	14.2	3.0	3.8	7.3	6.4	3.5	3.3	1.6	3.9	0.4	0.4	—3.0—	
American Samoa	1993[2, 6]	326	99.5[7]	...	...	...	...	...	...	...	...	...	...	...	...
Andorra	1992[8]	38	2.3	9.0	0.1	0.3	30.2	0.9	—0.6—		2.6	5.9	1.0	1.8	0.1
Angola	1989	319	20.0	—12.2—		—11.6—			—3.7—		—0.3—		9.1[9]	[9]	[9]
Antigua and Barbuda	1992[11]	9.9	...	...	...	...	...	...	...	...	...	...	...	...	...
Argentina	1990	31,156	15.1	3.0	1.5	7.1	1.6	1.7	0.8	0.8	2.8	2.2	5.9	—5.7—	
Armenia	1991[12]	1,348[13]	6.4	19.9	2.3	15.6	21.5	8.6	2.7	...	0.3	0.4	−1.3	—	0.8
Aruba	...	...	...	...	...	...	...	...	...	...	...	...	...	...	...
Australia	1991–92[11]	40,244	14.5	3.4	0.7	3.1	2.2	0.6	3.2	1.4	2.6	6.6	3.0	3.0	1.1
Austria	1991[12]	31,872	7.6	2.7	4.5	4.0	1.6	0.9	2.7	3.7	4.1	3.9	3.8	1.7	1.9
Azerbaijan	1990[2, 14]	12,166[15]	—38.0—		...	—18.4—			...	...	1.7	...	5.9[9]	[9]	[9]
Bahamas, The	1991[2, 11]	96	8.0	49.3	—	0.6	2.6	—	—	3.1	—8.7—		—13.3—		
Bahrain	1992	720	...	...	...	...	...	...	...	...	...	...	...	...	...
Bangladesh	1989–90[11, 16]	1,819	15.0	0.2	8.7	24.9	9.0	3.6	0.8	0.3	3.0	1.3	7.6	3.4	6.0
Barbados	1992	50[17]	28.1[17]	—15.1—		—	7.1	—	—0.8—		—15.2—		15.6[18]	—4.1—	
Belarus	1989[2, 14]	39,976[15]	—14.3—		...	—18.1—			—4.7—		...	...	8.7[9]	[9]	[9]
Belgium	1990	42,392	14.2	1.7	0.6	4.2	2.3	0.6	1.1	3.6	2.6	3.9	10.6	—2.8—	
Belize	1992[12]	59	45.9	7.5	3.9	—3.8—			5.5	2.7	1.1	1.5	—14.1—		
Benin	1986	56	—62.5—			—8.8—			—3.4—		—4.0—		—5.5—		
Bermuda	1990	173	...	...	...	...	...	...	...	...	...	...	...	...	...
Bhutan	1989[12]	21	6.0	10.1	—	—5.6—			18.1	2.7	0.4	1.0	21.5	—1.7—	
Bolivia	1991[12, 21]	697	7.7	12.1	0.9	2.1	0.3	0.8	1.6	0.1	0.2	1.8	0.3	—2.1—	
Bosnia and Herzegovina	1989	4,252	8.3	0.9	1.1	3.5	10.5	6.5	—12.0—		3.3	1.0	7.3[22]	[22]	[22]
Botswana	1990	148	38.8	19.0	—	9.5	1.4	0.7	0.7	0.7	2.7	0.7	0.7	—0.7—	
Brazil	1993[2, 11]	94,932[23]	12.4	2.1	1.3	4.5	—3.8—		1.1	1.0	3.5	2.7	12.5	1.0	2.6
Brunei	1990	582	...	...	...	...	...	...	...	...	...	...	...	...	...
Bulgaria	1992[14]	8,082	16.6	3.8	5.7	4.9	1.9	1.7	1.4	1.1	1.5	0.5	5.9	—4.5—	
Burkina Faso	1992	97	25.6	25.0	...	—26.0—		...	...	...	...	...	...	7.2	...
Burundi	1990	109	52.3	23.4	6.5	2.8	3.7	—	—	—	—	0.9	2.8	—0.9—	
Cambodia	1993	137	...	...	...	...	...	...	...	...	...	...	...	...	...
Cameroon	1990	826	22.4	35.6	2.8	−10.5	−3.3	1.0	7.4	3.1	1.3	0.7	2.1	—2.5—	
Canada	1992[12]	102,962	13.0	3.3	1.0	2.7	2.3	0.4	4.5	1.8	6.1	6.9	3.7	3.6	2.5
Cape Verde	1986[2]	24	—45.5—		8.3	—	...	...	—20.8—		—	...	—	...	...
Central African Republic	1990	48	27.1	12.5	20.8	2.1	—	—	18.8	2.1	—	4.2	2.1	—4.2—	
Chad	1991	99	...	...	...	...	—	—	—	—	—	—	—	...	—
Chile	1991[12, 27]	8,870	18.3	5.1	4.6	3.8	2.1	1.8	3.0	0.6	6.8	2.9	2.9	5.2	2.6
China	1993	188,215	6.3	2.6	3.9	8.8	3.0	1.4	0.9	0.5	1.4	1.1	—7.7—		2.1
Colombia	1991	6,714	15.7	12.9	2.1	8.6	2.9	2.1	—1.2—		4.2	2.4	6.9	5.6	3.4
Comoros	1993	11	...	...	—	...	...	...	...	...	—	—	—	—	—
Congo	1990	104	22.3	23.3	8.7	1.9	1.0	1.9	6.8	3.9	1.0	1.0	7.8	—3.9—	
Costa Rica	1992[12]	1,159	28.5	14.6	3.5	2.6	4.0	1.3	2.0	1.7	4.2	3.4	3.9	4.0	2.1
Côte d'Ivoire	1990	1,409	24.1	4.8	4.2	11.5	0.6	1.3	2.3	0.8	0.7	0.9	1.3	—5.7—	
Croatia	1992	5,066	16.8	3.5	3.3	5.2	5.0	2.2	3.5	2.6	2.2	3.2	3.5	—7.4—	
Cuba	1990[23]	5,990	17.2	6.0	43.9	1.8	1.5	1.2	0.9	0.7	0.2	1.4	1.1	—4.8—	
Cyprus[28]	1992	924	13.5	9.3	6.5	4.2	13.6	4.4	5.1	4.6	2.1	4.9	0.4	3.1	0.9
Czech Republic	1993[2, 14]	22,520	—26.7—			—6.3—		2.1	—1.7—		—3.6—		—5.8—		
Denmark	1991[11, 21]	23,588	18.7	3.5	1.2	2.5	1.1	0.5	2.1	2.8	2.8	6.6	4.7	2.1	4.6
Djibouti	1991	11	...	...	—	—	...	...	...	...	—	—	...	...	—
Dominica	1992[11]	13	...	...	—	—	...	—	...	...	—	—	—	...	—
Dominican Republic	1990	1,298	31.9	13.8	5.2	3.5	1.2	3.0	0.2	1.5	2.9	1.7	1.6	—3.4—	
Ecuador	1990[12, 16]	1,196	19.1	2.8	0.1	7.9	0.9	0.8	1.3	0.8	2.9	2.2	1.5	5.6	0.7
Egypt	1989–90[11, 30]	7,012	13.6	1.4	2.6	21.4	0.5	0.7	0.2	0.2	1.4	1.6	4.1	2.6	2.2
El Salvador	1992[2]	1,209	37.0	14.2	4.4	6.3	4.6	1.5	1.5	2.3[31]	1.6	1.6	—5.5—		
Equatorial Guinea	1990[3]	1.9	27.6	4.1	...	...	2.6	...	...	49.3	...	1.2	...	—13.8—	
Eritrea	1983–84	151	17.1	19.4	2.0	7.6	0.3	2.2	—	0.1	0.6	1.3	0.1	3.1	—
Estonia	1993[14]	908	38.2[32]	7.4	[32]	5.5	4.6	1.8	4.2	6.0	0.4	3.6	8.1[33]	[33]	[33]
Ethiopia[34]	1991–92[14]	507	23.2	17.7	7.2	14.5	2.5	13.5	—1.0—		—6.8—		—	2.0	—
Faroe Islands	1990[2, 11]	120	69.3[35]	...	...	...	...	...	...	...	...	...	...	...	...

ISIC code(s)	Products manufactured
33	Wood and wood products
331	sawlogs, wood products (excluding furniture), cane products, and cork products
332	wood furniture
34	Paper and paper products, printing and publishing
341	wood pulp, paper, and paper products
342	printing, publishing, and bookbinding
35	Chemicals and chemical, petroleum, coal, rubber, and plastic products
351	basic industrial chemicals (including fertilizers, pesticides, and synthetic fibres)
352 minus 3522	chemical products not elsewhere specified (including paints, varnishes, and soaps and other toiletries)
3522	drugs and medicines
353+354	refined petroleum and derivatives of petroleum and coal
355	rubber products
356	plastic products (excluding synthetic fibres)
36	Glass, ceramic, and nonmetallic mineral products
361+362	pottery, china, glass, and glass products
369	bricks, tiles, cement, cement products, plaster products, etc.

ISIC code(s)	Products manufactured
37	Basic metals
371	iron and steel
372	nonferrous basic metals and processed nickel and cobalt
38	Fabricated metal products, machinery and equipment
381	fabricated metal products (including cutlery, hand tools, fixtures, and structural metal products)
382 minus 3825	nonelectrical machinery and apparatus not elsewhere specified
3825	office, computing, and accounting machinery
383 minus 3832	electrical machinery and apparatus not elsewhere specified
3832	radio, television, and communications equipment (including electronic parts)
384 minus 3843	transport equipment not elsewhere specified
3843	motor vehicles (excluding motorcycles)
385	professional and scientific equipment; photographic and optical goods; watches and clocks
39	Other manufactured goods
390	jewelry, musical instruments, sporting goods, artists' equipment, toys, etc.

			(36)		(37)		(38)								(39)	
refined petroleum and products	rubber products	plastic products	pottery, china, and glass	bricks, tiles, cement, etc.	iron and steel	non-ferrous metals	fabricated metal products	nonelectrical machinery	office equip., computers	electrical equip.	radio, television	transport equip. exc. motor vehicles	motor vehicles	professional equip.	jewelry, musical instruments	country
(353+354)	(355)	(356)	(361+362)	(369)	(371)	(372)	(381)	(382 exc. 3825)	(3825)	(383 exc. 3832)	(3832)	(384 exc. 3843)	(3843)	(385)	(390)	
—	—	2.1	1.1		0.4	—	—	—		—	—	—	0.1		37.1	Afghanistan
6.1[4]	[3]	...	...	4.1	1.0[5]	...	[5]	3.4							...	Albania
2.9	0.4	1.0	1.2	8.9	10.0	0.6	10.0	1.6		4.6		5.5		1.2	1.3	Algeria
...	...	...	...	...	...	...	...	...	...	...	...	...	...	...	...	American Samoa
—	0.3	0.4	0.6	0.3	1.7	0.2	0.5	3.8		4.3		—	21.1	9.1	2.9	Andorra
20.0	[9]	[9]	11.3		1.9		5.0					4.7		[10]	0.3[10]	Angola
...	...	...	...	...	...	...	...	...	...	...	...	...	...	...	...	Antigua and Barbuda
19.9	1.2	1.4	1.3	3.0	5.3	1.0	5.2	2.7		3.3		6.9		0.4	0.3	Argentina
...	0.3	1.4	0.6	...	0.3	4.4	...	...	...	15.5		—	0.4	...	...	Armenia
...	...	...	...	...	...	...	...	...	...	...	...	...	...	...	...	Aruba
3.7	0.9	3.4	1.2	3.6	4.7	8.8	7.2	3.6		3.3	2.9	3.3	6.1	1.0	0.8	Australia
1.6	1.0	1.9	2.0	5.0	5.7	1.4	7.8	10.8		10.0	2.5	1.1	4.6	0.8	0.8	Austria
9.2	[9]	[9]	...	2.7	3.4		18.7								...	Azerbaijan
...	...	...	6.8		2.3	—	—	—		...	...	—	—	...		Bahamas, The
...	...	...	...	...	...	...	...	...	...	...	...	...	...	...	...	Bahrain
0.6	0.3	0.8	1.0	1.8	2.4	—	1.3	0.4	—	2.2	1.3	1.0	2.1	—	1.0	Bangladesh
[18]	[18]	[18]	4.6		—	—	5.4	1.6				1.8			0.5	Barbados
4.5	[9]	[9]	...	4.0	...	...	38.7								...	Belarus
0.9	0.7	5.2	2.2	2.1	5.9	2.7	6.7	8.7		6.9		7.5		0.6	1.8	Belgium
—	0.3[19]		[19]	6.2	—	—	2.0	—	—	0.1		4.2		—	1.1	Belize
			10.1		—	—	5.0								0.7	Benin
...	...	...	...	...	...	...	...	...	...	...	...	...	...	...	...	Bermuda
...	0.7	2.2	29.0		...	...	1.0[20]								[20]	Bhutan
61.0	0.2	1.0	0.4	4.0	...	1.7	1.0	0.1		0.2		0.2		0.1	0.1	Bolivia
0.7	0.2	[22]	2.4		5.8	7.0	11.6	5.8		6.3		7.1		...	0.3	Bosnia and Herzegovina
—	0.7	—	—	—	—	—	7.5	0.7		0.7		0.7		—	14.3	Botswana
...	1.1	2.3	4.4		11.0[24]		[24]	11.8		7.0		9.3		...	...	Brazil
...	...	...	...	...	...	...	...	...	...	...	...	...	...	...	...	Brunei
9.6	1.4	1.5	1.4	2.5	4.6	2.8	4.3	6.3[25]		6.0		4.1		[25]	5.9	Bulgaria
0.8	3.5	2.1	...	...	...	...	1.9		...	3.5	...	4.3	...	...	...	Burkina Faso
—	—	—	—	1.9	—	—	4.7	—	—	—	—	—	—	—	—	Burundi
...	...	...	...	...	...	...	...	...	...	...	...	...	...	...	...	Cambodia
13.8	0.1	3.0	1.7	1.9	3.6	2.8	2.1	3.9		1.1		0.4		—	0.7	Cameroon
1.9	1.6	2.8	0.6	2.0	2.9	2.7	5.0	5.5	0.8	2.5	4.2	3.9	9.4	0.8	1.5	Canada
—	—	—	...	...	...	—	[26]	—	—	—	—	10.8[26]	—	—	—	Cape Verde
—	—	—	—	—	—	—	—	—		—	—	4.2		—	2.1	Central African Republic
—	—	—	—	—	—	—	—	...	—	—	—	...	—	—	...	Chad
6.4	0.9	1.9	0.7	3.0	3.0	16.0	3.6	1.8	—	1.1	0.1	0.6	0.9	0.1	0.2	Chile
3.2	1.2	1.9	8.3		11.8	2.4	3.7	9.7		4.9	3.3	6.4		1.1	2.4	China
2.2	1.9	3.4	2.2	4.0	3.3	0.6	3.3	1.8	—	2.6	0.6	0.9	3.3	1.0	0.9	Colombia
—	—	—	—	—	—	—	—	—	—	—	—	—	—	—	—	Comoros
1.9	1.0	1.0	1.0	—	—	—	4.9	1.9		1.9		2.9		—	—	Congo
3.4	1.4	3.8	1.3	3.2	...	0.1	2.2	1.5		1.3	3.5	1.0	1.1	...	0.4	Costa Rica
16.5	0.3	—	0.1	1.8	0.2	0.1	4.0	0.1		1.1		15.8		—	1.6	Côte d'Ivoire
4.9	0.4	1.6	1.5	3.7	2.6	1.0	4.6	5.7		6.8		8.1		0.4	0.3	Croatia
...	1.4	1.2	0.4	1.9	0.6	1.1	1.3	2.9		0.9		3.8		0.2	3.6	Cuba
1.0	0.4	3.4	0.5	8.3	—	—	6.5	3.0		1.4	—	0.3	0.6	—	1.9	Cyprus[28]
5.7	2.1		4.5		16.8[24]		[24]	8.6		4.3[29]		8.5		...	...	Czech Republic
1.5	0.5	2.7	0.7	3.8	1.1	0.3	8.1	12.4	0.6	2.5	2.6	4.1	1.1	2.6	2.3	Denmark
—	—	...	—	...	—	—	—	—	—	—	—	—	—	—	...	Djibouti
—	—	—	—	...	—	—	...	—	—	...	—	—	—	—	...	Dominica
16.2	0.8	1.6	0.7	3.5	1.8	0.2	3.7	0.5		0.8		0.1		0.2	0.2	Dominican Republic
31.6	1.4	3.5	1.3	5.0	1.6	0.2	3.7	0.2		2.3	0.4	—	1.8	0.2	0.3	Ecuador
18.2	0.4	1.0	1.5	5.0	5.3	3.0	4.1	2.7	—	2.5	0.2	1.3	1.8	0.3	0.1	Egypt
6.0	0.7	...	5.2		2.7		0.9	0.7		1.7		0.3		...	...	El Salvador
...	...	...	...	0.8	...	...	0.6	...	...	...	...	...	...	...	...	Equatorial Guinea
38.4	—	3.0	1.0	1.6	0.8	—	1.2	—	0.1	—	—	—	—	—	—	Eritrea
[33]	1.1		4.5		...	...	3.2	2.8		1.8	0.6	4.8		1.0	0.3	Estonia
—	1.7	1.5	0.2	5.2	—	—	3.1	—	—	—	—	—	—	—	—	Ethiopia[34]
...	...	...	...	...	...	...	...	...	...	...	...	...	...	...	...	Faroe Islands

Manufacturing industries (continued)

country	year	total manufacturing value added ('000,000 U.S.$)	(31) food (311+312)	beverages (313)	tobacco manufactures (314)	(32) textiles (exc. wearing apparel) (321)	wearing apparel (322)	leather and fur products (323+324)	(33) wood products (exc. furniture) (331)	wood furniture (332)	(34) paper, paper products (341)	printing and publishing (342)	(35) industrial chemicals (351)	paints, soaps, etc. (352 exc. 3522)	drugs and medicines (3522)
Fiji	1990	142	42.5	—9.8—		—11.3—		0.6	7.6	2.2	3.6	4.4	—	5.2	—
Finland	1992[11]	20,321	11.1	2.6	0.6	1.5	1.1	0.5	5.0	1.7	14.7	7.5	4.6	1.2	1.5
France	1992[12]	270,288	10.8	2.1	0.8	2.8	2.3	1.0	1.6	1.7	2.5	5.6	3.3	—5.5—	
French Guiana	1991[16]	45	...	...	...	—[37]—			—38.2[37]—		...	...	...	...	...
French Polynesia	1990[2]	213	—27.4—		—	...	...	—	...	...	—	—	—	...	—
Gabon	1990	268	9.7	7.5	6.3	1.1	1.9	0.7	19.8	2.6	0.7	1.5	2.6	—1.1—	
Gambia, The	1990	13	45.5	18.2	—	—	—	—	—	9.1	—	—	—	—	—
Gaza Strip	1991	71	...	...	...	...	...	...	...	...	...	...	...	...	...
Georgia	1988[2, 14]	11,879[15]	—36.7—		...	—21.9—			—3.5—		...	...	4.0[9]	[9]	[9]
Germany[39]	1992[12, 21]	606,940	5.8	2.3	2.3	2.0	1.0	0.4	1.3	1.7	2.6	2.0	5.6	3.4	2.2
Ghana	1990	620	12.2	14.0	11.2	8.0	0.2	0.3	9.0	1.1	0.6	1.6	0.8	—4.3—	
Gibraltar	...	...	...	...	...	...	...	...	...	...	...	...	...	...	...
Greece	1992[11, 16]	10,660	17.0	5.9	3.6	10.2	5.3	1.7	1.8	1.0	3.0	3.2	2.2	4.9	2.4
Greenland	1991	27	...	...	...	...	...	...	...	...	...	...	...	...	...
Grenada	1992[11]	14	...	...	...	—	...	—	...	...	—	—	—	...	...
Guadeloupe	1991[16]	95	...	...	—	—[37]—			—25.8[37]—		...	...	...	...	...
Guam	1986	9.1	...	—	—	...	—	—	...	—	...	...	—	—	—
Guatemala	1988[12, 41]	842	24.1	5.3	2.5	6.5	3.2	2.7	1.2	0.6	1.4	4.8	4.9	9.1	6.8
Guernsey	1993[6]	61	—5.1—		—	—1.5—		—	...	...	—	17.6	—	—	7.8
Guinea	1993	123	...	...	...	...	...	...	...	...	...	...	...	...	...
Guinea-Bissau	1991[11]	13	...	...	...	...	...	...	...	...	...	...	...	...	...
Guyana	1993[42]	50	...	...	...	...	...	...	...	...	...	...	—	...	...
Haiti	1993–94[2, 43]	21	...	...	...	11.6	56.8	1.7	...	...	...	...	...	...	...
Honduras	1989	589	31.0	9.9	4.6	4.1	2.8	0.9	6.2	1.7	3.3	2.7	0.6	4.1	1.5
Hong Kong	1992	12,570	3.9	1.4	1.9	15.2	20.1	0.5	0.3	0.4	2.6	8.0	—2.0—		
Hungary	1993[14]	18,725	23.2	2.7[45]	1.2	3.2	2.0	2.3	1.6	1.5	2.0	3.1	5.6	1.2	4.1
Iceland	1991[12]	817	41.3	2.8	...	2.1	1.6	1.1	0.1	5.6	1.3	11.7	2.1	2.1	—
India	1990–91[11, 46]	23,350	8.8	1.0	1.9	13.0	1.3	0.9	0.4	—	2.3	1.3	7.3	3.5	3.0
Indonesia	1990	12,268	10.5	0.7	9.4	11.2	2.2	0.9	10.0	0.4	2.2	1.3	3.9	—4.0—	
Iran	1991–92[11, 16]	65,639[47]	10.4	1.5	1.8	14.8	0.6	1.4	1.0	0.4	1.8	1.2	2.6	—3.8—	
Iraq	1991[11, 48]	2,128[47]	10.5	9.6	1.4	7.0	4.1	5.8	—0.6—		—3.1—		—44.6—		
Ireland	1990[49]	14,780	20.5	5.4	1.1	2.3	1.4	0.3	1.2	0.6	1.3	3.8	2.8	1.4	12.6
Isle of Man	1990–91[2, 11]	98	—15.7—		...	...	...	...	...	...	...	...	...	...	...
Israel	1991[12, 41]	11,034	11.2	1.5	0.3	3.9	4.2	0.7	1.3	1.2	2.2	4.6	6.4[50]	—3.9—	
Italy	1991[21]	146,179	7.4	1.3	0.4	7.2	3.8	2.5	1.1	2.1	2.7	4.4	3.6	2.8	—
Jamaica	1990	734	16.6	12.3	11.5	0.7	3.8	2.3	0.6	1.9	1.4	3.6	7.6	—1.4—	
Japan	1992[51]	1,050,825	8.2	1.1	0.3	3.0	1.4	0.4	1.5	0.9	2.4	5.5	4.3	2.6	2.8
Jersey	1991	45	...	...	...	...	...	...	...	...	...	...	...	...	...
Jordan	1992[11]	905	12.9	2.6	0.2	2.9	1.2	0.6	1.3	2.8	2.8	3.2	5.1	—9.8—	
Kazakhstan	1994[2, 14]	1,157	—11.5—		...	—5.9—			—1.2[52]—		[52]	...	7.1[9]	[9]	[9]
Kenya	1991[11, 21]	897	28.8	10.2	1.4	5.8	1.7	1.4	1.8	1.2[31]	4.4	3.0	1.9	5.5	1.6
Kiribati	1992	0.68	...	...	—	—	—	—	...	—	—	—	—	...	—
Korea, North	...	...	...	...	...	...	...	...	...	...	...	...	...	...	...
Korea, South	1992[12, 41]	122,969	—8.3—		2.2	7.5	3.1	2.7	0.9	[53]	2.4	2.4	—9.6—		
Kuwait	1992	3,177	—4.0—			—3.0—			—1.9—		—2.5—		3.8[9]	[9]	[9]
Kyrgyzstan	1992[14]	113,902[13]	15.5	1.5	4.1	25.9	3.3	1.2	0.4	0.6	0.1	0.1	—	—0.3—	
Laos	1990[14]	66	4.5	7.4	16.3	—	5.1	0.3	40.1	5.0	—	1.2	—4.0—		
Latvia	1991[14]	24,420[13]	25.5	1.4	0.4	15.4	4.9	3.2	2.4	1.7	2.0	1.4	2.4	4.5	1.1
Lebanon	1992	481	...	...	...	...	...	...	...	...	...	...	...	...	...
Lesotho	1992[2]	75	—39.5—		...	—49.9—			—1.6—		...	1.7	...	—1.9—	
Liberia	1985[12, 14, 21]	64	10.8	42.7	...	—	—	0.3	—	4.5	0.6	1.3	0.4	—7.2—	
Libya	1990	1,211	5.5	2.8	10.8	2.7	0.7	7.1	0.9	0.7	0.4	0.3	7.2	—5.8—	
Liechtenstein	...	...	...	...	...	...	...	...	...	...	...	...	...	...	...
Lithuania	1993[14]	1,726	—38.7—		0.6	11.3	2.7	2.2	1.7	[53]	1.2	0.7	—5.3—		
Luxembourg	1991	2,334	3.2	—6.6—		—4.7—			—0.4—		—4.0—		—5.7—		
Macau	1992[12]	485	1.2	0.6	—	21.8	55.6	1.9	0.2	0.9	0.7	2.8	—	0.5	0.3
Macedonia	1992	...	12.5	2.8	9.3	10.6	10.8	6.5	0.6	2.3	1.3	2.4	6.3	—2.5—	
Madagascar	1990	147	15.3	11.1	0.7	41.7	2.8	2.8	—	—	3.5	0.7	—	—6.2—	
Malawi	1990	133	20.2	9.0	6.7	13.4	1.5	3.0	1.5	0.7	0.7	6.7	3.7	—15.7—	
Malaysia	1991[11]	11,323	8.1	1.4	1.1	3.5	2.7	0.2	5.7	1.0	1.6	2.7	9.6	2.3	0.3
Maldives	1993	10[42]	...	...	—	—	...	—	—	...	—	...	—	...	—
Mali	1990	122	13.9	1.6	10.7	41.8	10.7	—	—	—	—	0.8	0.8	—0.8—	
Malta	1991[2]	533	11.1	8.1	1.8	2.9	14.2	3.0	—5.4—		...	9.1	—3.5—		
Marshall Islands	1993[2]	0.60[56]	...	...	...	...	...	...	...	...	...	...	...	...	...
Martinique	1991[16]	191	...	...	...	—[37]—			—16.8[37]—		...	...	...	...	...
Mauritania	1992[2]	82	58.5[35]	...	...	...	...	...	...	...	...	...	...	...	...
Mauritius	1991[12]	502	16.1	5.9	0.5	6.4	42.6	1.6	0.7	1.1	0.7	2.6	3.2	1.8	0.1
Mayotte	1992	...	...	...	—	—	—	—	—	—	—	—	—	—	—
Mexico	1988[12, 57]	30,308	12.4	4.3	2.4	5.3	1.5	1.3	0.9	0.8	2.9	2.2	6.9	3.6	2.7
Micronesia	1992	2.2[6]	[58]	...	...	...	91.0	...	...	...	...	...	...	1.6[58]	...
Moldova	1992[14]	198,637[13]	37.0	7.0	1.7	14.1	3.0	2.7	0.6	1.8	0.8	0.3	0.1	—0.7—	
Monaco	...	...	...	...	...	...	...	...	...	...	...	...	...	...	...
Mongolia	1993[2, 14]	602	—17.1—		...	7.0	1.1	5.4	—1.5—		...	0.3	—	—	—
Morocco	1992[2, 16]	4,227	6.6	—18.9—		9.4	7.1	1.6	—1.9—		3.3	1.2	14.0	—0.7—	
Mozambique	1988	292	28.6	9.2	5.4	18.2	4.1	1.4	1.3	0.8	2.9	2.2	0.5	—5.1—	
Myanmar (Burma)	1984–85[2]	731	—38.8—			—9.4—			...	...	...	3.4	...	...	...
Namibia	1991[2]	110	11.0[35]	...	...	...	...	...	...	...	...	...	...	...	...
Nauru	1989	—	—	—	—	—	—	—	—	—	—	—	—	—	—
Nepal	1991–92[12, 16]	341	14.3	6.1	10.2	29.9	8.4	1.3	2.0	1.4	0.7	0.7	—2.8—		0.8
Netherlands, The	1992	47,960	—22.5—			2.1	0.5	0.3	—2.1—		3.5	7.9	—13.5—		
Netherlands Antilles	1990	120	...	...	...	...	...	...	...	...	...	...	...	...	...
New Caledonia	1989[2]	371	...	...	...	...	...	...	...	...	...	...	...	...	...
New Zealand	1990–91	7,352	22.8	—9.2—		3.2	—4.1—		—6.1—		7.5	7.3	3.4	—2.9—	
Nicaragua	1991[2]	426	36.9	22.1	10.4	4.4	0.5	1.1	2.1	0.6	0.5	1.8	—4.1—		
Niger	1991	156	...	...	...	...	...	...	...	...	...	...	...	...	...

			(36)		(37)		(38)								(39)	country
refined petroleum and products	rubber products	plastic products	pottery, china, and glass	bricks, tiles, cement, etc.	iron and steel	non-ferrous metals	fabricated metal products	nonelectrical machinery	office equip., computers	electrical equip.	radio, television	transport equip. exc. motor vehicles	motor vehicles	professional equip.	jewelry, musical instruments	
(353+354)	(355)	(356)	(361+362)	(369)	(371)	(372)	(381)	(382 exc. 3825)	(3825)	(383 exc. 3832)	(3832)	(384 exc. 3843)	(3843)	(385)	(390)	
—	0.6	2.4	—	3.6[36]	[36]	—	3.9	0.9				0.5	0.2	—	0.8	Fiji
2.3	0.5	2.6	0.9	2.6	4.5	1.5	4.6	10.6	1.0	4.0	3.3	3.4	1.6	1.6	1.3	Finland
6.4	1.4	2.9	1.2	2.8	2.6	1.7	8.0	8.6		10.3		10.9		1.6	1.7	France
...	...	...	61.8[38]		[38]		[38]								...	French Guiana
—	...	...	...	...	—	—	42.5								...	French Polynesia
11.6	—	—	1.1	6.3	1.5	1.5	7.5	1.1		4.5		6.3		0.4	2.6	Gabon
—	—	—	—	—	—	—	—	—	—	—	—	—	—	—	27.3	Gambia, The
...	...	...	...	...	...	...	...	...	...	...	...	...	...	...	...	Gaza Strip
...	[9]	[9]	...	5.2	...	...	15.7								...	Georgia
4.4	1.1	3.4	1.2	2.5	3.0	1.3	7.6	12.8	1.9	6.6	6.6	1.6	11.4	1.5	0.5	Germany[39]
7.2	0.8	0.5	0.2	3.7	0.5	19.4	2.2	0.3		0.8		0.6		0.2	0.2	Ghana
...	...	...	...	...	...	...	...	...	...	...	...	...	...	...	...	Gibraltar
5.5	0.7	3.1	1.0	6.0	1.9	2.7	4.7	1.6	—	3.4	1.6	3.8	1.2	0.2	0.5	Greece
...	...	...	...	...	...	...	...	...	...	...	...	...	...	...	...	Greenland
—	...	—	—	—	—	—	—	—	—	...	...	—	—	—	...	Grenada
—	...	...	[40]		[40]		64.1[40]	10.0							...	Guadeloupe
—	—	...	...	...	—	—	—	—	—	—	—	...	—	...	...	Guam
1.1	2.3	3.6	3.4	5.9	3.1	0.1	2.8	0.7	0.1	2.4	0.4	0.1	0.2	0.2	0.5	Guatemala
—	—	10.9	—	1.9	—	—	—	7.4		—	40.3	3.0	—	—	4.6	Guernsey
...	...	...	...	...	...	...	...	...	...	...	...	...	...	...	...	Guinea
...	...	...	...	...	...	...	...	...	...	...	...	...	...	...	...	Guinea-Bissau
—	—	—	—	—	—	—	—	...	—	...	—	—	—	—	...	Guyana
...	2.7		...	...	...	...	...	...	...	4.6	...	...	...	...	5.8[11]	Haiti
1.9	2.2	4.3	0.2	7.0	0.9	0.2	5.0	0.9	—	1.1	0.5	0.2	0.3	0.2	1.6	Honduras
0.1	0.1	4.9	0.9		0.7		6.3	6.9	4.6	1.3	0.9	3.5		4.1	3.4	Hong Kong
9.4	0.7	2.3	1.5	2.5	4.0	1.5	5.3	4.9	0.5	4.7	1.9	0.6	4.8	1.3	0.4	Hungary
—	—	3.4	0.6	4.7	0.6	2.2	10.7		—	—	—	2.7	—	—	3.4	Iceland
4.9	2.3	1.2	0.6	4.5	10.2	2.6	2.4	7.4	0.6	6.0	2.0	4.0	5.5	0.7	0.4	India
13.0	4.2	1.2	0.9	1.9	6.0	—	6.0	0.9		2.4		6.3		0.1	0.5	Indonesia
0.6	1.4	1.7	2.0	8.5	9.5	3.8	4.2	10.1		2.6		13.4		0.4	0.5	Iran
——			2.8		1.1		4.6	2.3		1.9		0.5		—	—	Iraq
0.2	0.8	2.2	1.2	3.8	0.6	0.1	3.2	2.6	11.2	2.9	9.5	1.5	0.6	4.1	0.9	Ireland
...	...	...	...	...	...	...	...	...	...	...	...	...	...	...	...	Isle of Man
[50]	0.8	5.0	0.8	3.7	1.4	0.6	11.7	2.5		22.2		7.5		1.4	1.1	Israel
1.8	1.6	3.4	3.1	3.1	4.9	1.2	5.9	13.0	1.0	7.5	2.9	3.1	6.1	1.2	1.0	Italy
11.0	2.1	3.3	1.6	3.7	1.2	—	2.6	1.8		1.9		6.0		—	1.1	Jamaica
1.2	1.3	3.7	1.2	3.1	5.1	1.2	7.5	10.2	3.3	6.6	7.7	1.5	9.0	1.3	1.7	Japan
...	...	...	...	...	...	...	...	...	...	...	...	...	...	...	...	Jersey
4.2	0.4	4.3	33.3		1.8	0.4	6.2	1.8		1.1		0.3		0.6	0.2	Jordan
...	[9]	[9]	...	5.2	29.7	22.8	8.6								...	Kazakhstan
0.8	3.6	2.8	0.6	4.5	0.2		6.9	0.6		5.2		2.8	1.4	—	1.9	Kenya
—	—	—	—	—	—	—	...	—	—	—	—	...	—	—	...	Kiribati
...	...	...	...	...	...	...	...	...	...	...	...	...	...	...	...	Korea, North
3.4	3.8		5.7		7.4		4.4	7.9	0.6	3.3	9.2	3.6	7.7	1.0	2.8[53]	Korea, South
75.7	[9]	[9]	3.2		0.5		4.9								0.6	Kuwait
0.1	0.1	0.1	0.9	4.3	—	5.9	34.6								1.0	Kyrgyzstan
—	0.5		0.1	3.8	—	—	10.8	0.5		0.2		—	—	—	0.1	Laos
0.1	0.7	0.7	1.4	2.9	0.7	0.1	1.7	5.9	0.1	2.7	6.7	2.9	1.6	0.2	5.3	Latvia
...	...		...	...	...	...	...	...	...	...	...	...	...	...	...	Lebanon
...	...	...	2.9		1.1	...	...		...	...	...			...	...	Lesotho
—	—	0.6	0.2	20.7	—		0.5	0.3		0.7		—	—	—	—	Liberia
30.9	0.1	0.8	0.1	18.3	—	—	1.7	—	—	—	—	—	—	—	3.2	Libya
...	...	...	...	...	...	...	...	...	...	...	...	...	...	...	...	Liechtenstein
6.1	0.4		5.0		0.5		1.2	7.2	0.2	1.9	6.6	1.4	0.5	1.2	3.4[53]	Lithuania
...	12.9		9.7		26.3	2.3	7.2	9.5	6.9[54]			0.6		[54]	0.1	Luxembourg
—	—	1.3	0.3	0.6	—	—	1.7	0.1	—	1.2	—	0.9	—	0.8	6.5	Macau
0.9	—	1.4	1.5	0.9	5.1	1.6	4.9	2.6		6.9		5.3		0.2	0.8	Macedonia
6.2	0.7	0.7	0.7	2.1	—	—	2.8	—	—	1.4		0.7		—	—	Madagascar
—	—	3.7	—	6.0	—	—	3.7	2.2		0.7		0.7		—	—	Malawi
2.2	5.2	3.0	1.1	4.5	2.9	0.6	3.7	4.0	0.8	3.4	19.9	1.8	3.9	1.4	1.4	Malaysia
—	—	...	—	...	—	—	...	—	—	—	—	...	—	—	...	Maldives
0.8	—	—	—	0.8	—	—	4.1	1.6		1.6		9.8		—	—	Mali
...	[55]	2.1	0.5	3.7	—	—	5.2	12.0				7.9[55]		...	...	Malta
...	...	...	...	...	...	...	...	...	...	...	...	...	...	...	...	Marshall Islands
52.2	...	...	[40]		[40]		28.8[40]	2.2							...	Martinique
...	...	...	...	...	...	...	...	...	...	...	...	...	...	...	...	Mauritania
—	0.4	1.7	0.1	2.5	0.7		2.4	0.8		1.1	0.3	0.9	0.1	2.2	3.5	Mauritius
—	—	—	—	...	—	—	—	—	—	—	—	—	—	—	—	Mayotte
7.3	1.5	2.5	2.8	2.9	4.5	1.5	4.7	2.9	1.0	5.3	2.3	0.5	12.3	0.3	0.6	Mexico
...	...	...	...	...	...	...	...	...	...	...	...	...	...	...	7.4	Micronesia
0.5	—	0.3	1.1	3.8	5.2	—	3.1	8.7		2.6		0.5		—	4.4	Moldova
...	...	...	...	...	...	...	...	...	...	...	...	...	...	...	...	Monaco
...	—	—	—	1.5	...	52.9	0.4	...	...	...	...	...	...	...	...	Mongolia
...	2.7		10.0		1.7		5.3	...	...	2.9		3.5		0.2	0.1	Morocco
0.8	2.5	1.2	0.9	2.9	0.8	0.4	2.7	0.8		4.3		2.6		0.1	0.1	Mozambique
...	...	...	...	10.0	...	...	...	1.4		1.1		5.3		...	...	Myanmar (Burma)
...	...	...	...	...	...	...	...	...	...	...	...	...	...	...	...	Namibia
—	—	—	—	—	—	—	—	—	—	—	—	—	—	—	—	Nauru
—	0.9	1.6	—	11.9	2.7	—	2.3	—	—	1.1	0.3	—	—	—	0.4	Nepal
2.1	3.7		3.8		3.4		7.6	8.6		11.6		5.6		0.8	0.4	Netherlands, The
...	...	...	...	...	...	...	...	...	...	...	...	...	...	...	...	Netherlands Antilles
...	...	...	...	...	...	80.8	7.1								...	New Caledonia
2.0	0.8	3.1	3.6		3.4		6.5	4.6		3.5		4.4		0.3	1.2	New Zealand
0.1	5.0	...	5.5		...	—	2.3	0.8				0.1		—	...	Nicaragua
...	...	...	...	...	...	...	...	...	...	...	...	...	...	...	...	Niger

Manufacturing industries (continued)

country	year	total manufacturing value added ('000,000 U.S.$)	(31) food (311+312)	beverages (313)	tobacco manufactures (314)	(32) textiles (exc. wearing apparel) (321)	wearing apparel (322)	leather and fur products (323+324)	(33) wood products (exc. furniture) (331)	wood furniture (332)	(34) paper, paper products (341)	printing and publishing (342)	(35) industrial chemicals (351)	paints, soaps, etc. (352 exc. 3522)	drugs and medicines (3522)
Nigeria	1990	3,606	14.0	12.0	2.0	12.4	0.1	3.0	0.7	0.9	3.2	3.0	0.5	12.8	
Northern Mariana Islands	1987[1,2]	58		3.3		26.0	62.7[59]		...	...	...	1.3	...	...	...
Norway	1993[16]	12,531	13.0	9.5		1.4	0.5	0.2	3.3	[53]	4.4	10.0	5.4	3.4	
Oman	1993[2]	598	...	...	...	...	...	...	...	...	...	...	...	...	...
Pakistan	1990	4,299	16.1	1.8	10.2	18.4	1.7	1.3	0.3	0.1	1.1	0.9	6.5	7.2	
Palau	1983	0.13	...	...	...	...	...	...	...	...	...	...	...	...	...
Panama	1991	454	29.4	13.2	5.7	1.2	6.6	1.9	1.8	2.2	5.2	3.0	0.7	8.3	
Papua New Guinea	1989	451	48.4	13.1	4.9	—	0.4	—	11.6	2.0	1.1	2.4	1.1	1.1	
Paraguay	1990	633	35.4	8.7	1.4	6.5	0.5	5.1	14.5	1.4	0.2	5.1	0.3	0.9	
Peru	1991	3,130	22.4	9.2		8.9	5.2	1.2	4.9		1.0	2.6	2.8	3.7	1.6
Philippines	1992	12,076	40.7	4.8	2.7	2.9	6.8		1.8	1.5	0.9	1.3	8.3[22]	[22]	[22]
Poland	1993	21,138		29.2		3.5	4.9	1.6	5.9		1.2	1.5		10.6 —	
Portugal	1990	11,680	11.6	3.5	1.9	14.9	4.2	3.3	2.5	1.2	5.9	2.8	5.2	4.6	
Puerto Rico	1992[2]	22,737	4.6	11.6	...	0.5	4.0	1.0	...	0.5	0.8	1.4	2.7	1.9	43.9
Qatar	1991	917	1.9	0.4	...	—	2.4		1.2	0.2	—	1.4	35.7	0.3	
Réunion	1992[2]	348	31.4	10.4	—	0.5		—	2.3		4.6[61]	9.4	[62]	3.4	
Romania	1991	9,217	13.2	4.7	1.4	9.0	3.3	2.7	3.3	2.7	1.7	0.6	2.5	3.9	
Russia[63]	1990	502,639[64]	17.1	1.7	0.5	7.4	4.8	1.6	1.3	1.1	0.8	0.8	3.9	1.9	
Rwanda	1990	180	32.6	19.3	8.8	...	...	...	4.4	0.6	1.1	1.1	7.7	—	—
St. Kitts and Nevis	1992[2,11]	19	17.4[65]	...	...	...	...	...	...	...	...	...	...	...	...
St. Lucia	1991[14,66]	42	44.7		...	3.4	11.6	...	...	...	30.2	...	0.5	...	...
St. Vincent	1988[2,11]	14	24.9	25.4			10.1		1.9		5.3		...	...	...
San Marino	...	...	...	...	...	...	...	...	...	...	...	...	...	...	...
São Tomé and Príncipe	1991[11]	3.0	...	...	—	—	...	—	...	...	—	—	—	...	—
Saudi Arabia	1990	5,387	5.9	0.8	0.6	0.4	0.1	0.1	0.2	0.7	2.0	1.1	35.4	3.1	
Senegal	1990	639	36.4	3.0	0.9	1.6	0.6	—	0.8	0.9	3.0	4.1	10.3	4.1	
Seychelles	1989	26		79.6			0.6		2.1		6.0			4.1 —	
Sierra Leone	1985–86[16]	43		60.6			0.5		15.8		0.5			4.1 —	
Singapore	1993[16]	17,522	2.4	1.0	0.7	0.4	1.5	0.2	0.2	0.8	1.3	4.8	3.0	5.3	
Slovakia	1992[14,69]	9,860		17.0		5.3		2.4	2.2		5.1		10.0		
Slovenia	1992	3,838	8.9	3.1	4.3	11.7	—	4.0	3.1	3.3	3.0	4.5	3.5	6.4	
Solomon Islands	1991	7.1	...	...	...	—	...	—	...	...	—	...	—	—	—
Somalia	1988	18	26.5	4.8	18.7	3.3	0.4	14.0	—	0.1	10.9		6.7		
South Africa	1991[11,71]	24,151	10.6	4.8	0.4	3.4	3.1	1.6	1.5	1.2	5.0	3.7	4.9	11.6[72]	
Spain	1991[11,41]	91,087	12.1	4.5	1.2	3.6	2.7	1.5	2.3	1.9	2.3	5.2	3.7	3.6	3.0
Sri Lanka	1990[12,41]	1,005	17.4	4.4	15.5	8.2	16.9	2.0	0.9	—	1.7	1.5	1.1	3.0	0.2
Sudan, The	1988	354	44.1	2.3	12.7	9.3	0.3	2.5	0.3	0.3	1.7	2.3	0.8	4.0	
Suriname	1992[11,14,66]	700	33.4	22.3	12.3	...	1.5	1.6	8.7	1.4	0.7	1.6	...	8.3	
Swaziland	1990[11]	252	29.3	40.0	—		7.7		2.4		15.9			0.8 —	
Sweden	1992[11,16]	37,464	9.0	1.4	0.6	1.4	0.3	0.2	4.7	1.1	8.2	7.2	3.7	1.9	4.5
Switzerland	1990	58,051	10.3	1.7	0.5	3.0	2.0	0.8	3.9	2.5	2.4	7.3	7.2	7.8	
Syria	1991[11,30]	1,902		24.9			29.0		4.6		0.8			17.9 —	
Taiwan	1993	67,740	7.6		1.6	6.6	3.3	1.0	0.9	1.1	2.0	1.4	5.2	2.6	
Tajikistan	1993[14]	207,055[73]	13.2		...	44.0	2.1	0.7	1.4[74]		[74]			3.4 —	
Tanzania	1990	87	12.5	5.7	10.2	17.0	1.1	2.3	2.3	1.1	3.4	2.3	13.6	2.3	
Thailand	1991[2,12,16]	65,413	4.1	2.3	2.9	3.1	5.0	1.4	0.6	0.4	0.2	...	1.5	0.7	0.6
Togo	1991[2]	168		47.5			14.8		11.2		3.8			5.7 —	
Tonga	1992[12,14]	16		39.0		2.3	8.7	3.8	1.4	[75]	[75]	4.5	—	22.2	
Trinidad and Tobago	1991[2]	758		29.9			2.3		1.7[52]		[52]	5.1	28.0[76]	[76]	[76]
Tunisia	1990	1,612	7.4	5.8	2.2	5.1	7.6	3.0	1.3	1.0	2.1	1.6	2.7	8.7	
Turkey	1991[12,77]	31,369	10.5	3.6	4.8	10.8	3.3	0.5	0.6	0.3	1.8	1.4	4.2	2.3	2.9
Turkmenistan	1990[2,14]	4,550[13]	15.4		...	38.4	6.2		...	...	1.4	...	4.2[9]	[9]	[9]
Tuvalu	1990	0.3	...	—	—	—	...	—	—	...	—	—	—	...	—
Uganda	1982	406	33.9	11.7	9.4	27.1	2.3	1.3	2.1	0.8	—	—	—	2.5	
Ukraine	1992[11,14]	4,334,000[13]	19.8	1.5	0.5	5.4	2.2	1.6	0.7	1.3	0.7	0.2	6.1	1.4	
United Arab Emirates	1993[11,23]	2,967	...	...	...	...	...	...	...	...	...	...	...	...	...
United Kingdom	1992[11]	192,962	10.3	2.8	1.2	2.7	2.4	0.6	1.2	1.7	3.3	8.6	5.1	2.2	4.0
United States	1991	1,313,829	9.0	2.0	1.9	2.0	2.5	0.3	2.1	1.6	4.4	7.9	5.3	3.2	3.3
Uruguay	1990[12,41]	2,379	19.9	7.6	3.8	9.9	4.7	3.7	0.8	0.6	2.1	3.4	2.8	6.8	
Uzbekistan	1994[2,14,78]	271	21.9		...		21.9		1.8[74]		[74]			5.3 —	
Vanuatu	1993[2]	10		44.5			3.8		22.5		5.3	...		9.2[79] —	
Venezuela	1992[2,41]	12,505	12.1	6.2	3.3	2.2	1.8	1.3	0.4	0.8	2.4	2.0	5.0	5.4	2.0
Vietnam	1992[2,14]	3,706		36.5		8.4	1.5	0.5	3.4	...	2.0	0.7	8.1[3]	[3]	[3]
Virgin Islands (U.S.)	...[81]	...	...	...	...	...	...	...	...	...	...	...	...	...	...
West Bank	1991	100	...	...	...	...	...	...	...	...	...	...	...	...	...
Western Sahara	...	...	...	...	...	...	...	...	...	...	...	...	...	...	...
Western Samoa	1990	15	36.0	25.5	19.2	—	...	—	10.7	—	—	—	—	8.6	...
Yemen[82]	1986	540		51.9			8.7		3.9		0.5			9.2 —	
Yugoslavia	1991[2]	1,998	11.5	2.5	1.7	3.5	10.6	2.8	1.0	2.8	1.2	2.0	3.9	7.6	
Zaire	1990	96	5.1	28.9	15.5	5.1	2.1	5.1	2.1	—	—	1.0	8.2	—	—
Zambia	1990	1,028	8.5	23.0	9.4	6.0	4.5	3.4	2.7	2.0	1.1	2.3	3.6	7.1	
Zimbabwe	1991–92[11]	2,110	13.7	12.8	5.1	9.6	4.1	2.9	1.8	1.2	2.7	3.5	2.8[50]	5.5	

[1]Gross output in value of sales. [2]Complete ISIC detail is not available. [3]351 includes 352 and 355. [4]Includes petroleum extraction. [5]371 includes 381. [6]Value of manufactured exports. [7]Canned tuna and salmon. [8]Value of manufactured exports (excluding duty-free reexports). [9]351 includes 352, 355, and 356. [10]390 includes 385. [11]In factor values. [12]In producer's prices. [13]Rubles of former U.S.S.R. [14]Gross output of production. [15]Constant rubles of 1982 of the former U.S.S.R. [16]Establishments employing 10 or more persons. [17]Excludes sugar refining. [18]351 includes 353 + 354, 355, and 356. [19]355 and 356 include 361 + 362. [20]38 includes 39. [21]Establishments employing 20 or more persons. [22]351 includes 352 and 356. [23]Excludes petroleum refining. [24]37 includes 381. [25]382 includes 385. [26]384 minus 3843 includes 381. [27]Establishments employing 50 or more persons. [28]Republic of Cyprus only. [29]Includes optical goods. [30]Private establishments employing 10 or more persons, and all public establishments. [31]Includes metal furniture. [32]311 + 312 includes 314. [33]351 includes 352, 353, and 354. [34]Ethiopia includes Eritrea. [35]Processed fish only. [36]369 includes 371. [37]33 includes 32. [38]36 includes 37 and 38. [39]Former West Germany only. [40]381 includes 36 and 37. [41]Establishments employing five or more persons. [42]Includes public utilities. [43]Value added of assembled exports only. [44]Sporting goods only. [45]Alcoholic beverages only. [46]Establishments with electric power and 10 or more employees,

refined petroleum and products	rubber products	plastic products	(36) pottery, china, and glass	bricks, tiles, cement, etc.	(37) iron and steel	non-ferrous metals	(38) fabricated metal products	nonelectrical machinery	office equip., computers	electrical equip.	radio, television	transport equip. exc. motor vehicles	motor vehicles	professional equip.	(39) jewelry, musical instruments	country
(353+354)	(355)	(356)	(361+362)	(369)	(371)	(372)	(381)	(382 exc. 3825)	(3825)	(383 exc. 3832)	(3832)	(384 exc. 3843)	(3843)	(385)	(390)	
1.2	1.8	3.0	0.5	6.3	0.7	2.0	5.6	—1.2—		—2.2—		—10.7—		—	0.3	Nigeria
...	59	59	—4.9—		...		...		...		...		...	...	...	Northern Mariana Islands
2.0	—1.9—		—3.1—		—6.8—		4.4	6.7	0.3	3.7	1.7	13.0	1.1	1.6	2.8[53]	Norway
16.6[60]	...	...	...	...	...	...	...	...	...	...	...	...	...	...	...	Oman
6.9	0.9	0.5	1.1	7.9	6.8	—	1.0	—1.8—		—3.2—		—3.6—		0.3	0.4	Pakistan
...	...	...	...	...	...	...	...	...	...	...	...	...	...	...	...	Palau
3.8	0.3	3.9	0.9	5.4	0.7	0.6	3.6	—0.1—		—0.5—		—0.2—		0.4	0.6	Panama
—	—	0.4	0.7	1.6	...	...	6.7	—1.3—		—0.7—		—2.4—		...	...	Papua New Guinea
9.8	—	1.9	0.3	4.1	—	0.3	1.9	—0.2—		—	—	—0.9—		...	0.5	Paraguay
1.0	—1.9—		—5.1—		2.1	18.4	1.5	—0.9—		—2.1—		—2.1—		10	1.5[10]	Peru
10.8	1.3	22	—3.1—		—2.5—		2.4	—1.1—		—4.0—		—1.2—		10	1.8[10]	Philippines
——			1.3	3.9	3.9	2.8	6.9	—6.1—		—5.2—		—8.6—		1.8	1.0	Poland
2.9	0.9	2.4	4.0	6.1	2.7	0.5	4.7	—2.6—		—6.9—		—4.1—		0.4	0.2	Portugal
0.5	0.1	1.0	0.3	1.1	...	...	1.4	1.1	2.1	3.2	4.3	—	0.4	5.7	0.9	Puerto Rico
40.5	0.1	0.5	—3.0—		9.6	...	—2.6—								0.1	Qatar
—	—	61	3.2[62]	17.2	—	—	10.6	...	...	...	2.4	...	...	...	—	Réunion
3.6	1.3	2.5	6.3	0.3	6.0	1.4	5.1	—11.2[25]—		—6.0—		—6.2—		25	1.2	Romania
4.2	1.1	0.6	1.0	3.5	3.1	1.6	2.3	—26.1—		—3.0—		—3.8—		3.2	3.7	Russia[63]
—	—	—	—	13.3	—	—	9.4	—0.6—		—0.6—		—0.6—		—	...	Rwanda
...	...	...	...	...	...	...	...	...	...	...	...	...	...	...	...	St. Kitts and Nevis
...	...	2.1	...	...	...	...	...	...	...	—7.5—		...	...	...	...	St. Lucia
...	...	0.4	...	...	...	...	6.6[67]	...	...	67	67	...	...	...	...	St. Vincent
...	...	...	...	...	...	...	...	...	...	...	...	...	...	...	...	San Marino
—	...	—	...	...	—	—	—	...	—	—	—	—	—	—	—	São Tomé and Príncipe
17.1	0.1	2.7	0.9	12.6	6.4	0.3	5.0	—1.1—		—2.0—		—0.6—		0.1	0.7	Saudi Arabia
10.3	—	—	—	8.0	—	—	6.7	—2.7—		—1.1—		—5.5—		—	—	Senegal
——			—5.2—		—	—	—2.4—								—	Seychelles
——			—6.8[68]—		—68—		—4.1—								7.7	Sierra Leone
7.0	0.3	2.3	0.3	1.5	0.8	0.3	6.4	—5.0—		3.8	40.9	—7.2—		1.8	0.7	Singapore
9.1	—3.7—		—4.6—		—17.5[24]—		24	—10.0—		—5.2[70]—		—5.1—		70	2.7	Slovakia
1.0	2.6	1.7	—4.2—		1.7	1.5	6.6	—7.9—		—10.1—		—5.3—		0.4	1.1	Slovenia
—	—		—	—	—	—	—	—	—	—	—	...	—	—	—	Solomon Islands
—	—	10.7	—	2.1	—	0.3	1.5	—	—	—	—	—	—	—	—	Somalia
72	1.6	2.6	1.4	3.2	8.8	3.6	6.4	—6.1—		—4.3—		1.6	6.0	0.8	1.7	South Africa
1.9	1.7	3.0	1.7	5.1	3.7	1.1	6.4	6.2	0.6	4.0	2.3	2.6	10.7	0.5	1.0	Spain
10.6	5.0	0.9	1.1	2.8	0.8	0.3	1.5	0.9	—	0.6	0.1	1.7	...	—	1.0	Sri Lanka
2.0	2.0	1.1	0.3	1.1	—	4.5	4.0	—	—	—2.5—		—1.7—		—	0.3	Sudan, The
...	0.7	0.6	—5.3—		...	...	...	...	...	...	...	—0.9—		0.2	0.5	Suriname
——			—1.0—		—	—	2.0	—0.9—					—	—	—	Swaziland
1.3	0.7	1.7	0.7	2.4	3.4	1.4	8.3	12.6	1.4	3.9	4.6	3.8	6.6	2.6	0.4	Sweden
2.9	1.2	3.2	1.1	1.6	2.0	1.7	0.7	—13.2—		—10.0—		—1.8—		4.8	0.2	Switzerland
——			—9.0—		—1.6—		—12.0—							—	0.2	Syria
7.4	1.4	6.0	—5.2—		—7.2—		6.9	—5.1—		—16.3—		—7.6—		1.0	2.6	Taiwan
——			...	2.0	—27.2—		—6.1—								...	Tajikistan
3.4	1.1	1.1	—	4.6	2.3	1.1	4.6	—1.1—		—1.1—		—5.7—		—	—	Tanzania
...	1.6	0.3	0.9	3.5	1.7	0.5	1.7	10.3	0.1	1.5	5.6	0.2	5.8	0.2	1.5	Thailand
——			—10.4—		1.3	...	4.6	...	...	...	...	...	...	...	...	Togo
—	—	—	—2.2—		—	—	5.6	—0.3—				—2.2—		—	7.8[75]	Tonga
16.9	76	76	—76—		...	...	—14.2—								...	Trinidad and Tobago
0.9	1.2	2.2	1.6	15.2	8.9	0.7	9.4	—0.2—		—5.3—		—5.3—		0.1	0.6	Tunisia
15.7	1.6	1.2	2.9	4.1	5.7	1.3	3.1	4.4	—	2.6	0.2	0.9	5.8	0.3	0.2	Turkey
21.7	0	3	...	6.3	...	...	—5.4—								...	Turkmenistan
—	—	—	—	...	—	—	—	—	—	—	...	—	—	—	...	Tuvalu
—	—	—	0.7	6.8	1.5	—	—	—	—	—	—	—	—	—	—	Uganda
13.3	1.5	0.3	0.9	5.0	20.5	1.8	0.8	—7.5—		—2.7—		—3.4—		0.8	...	Ukraine
...	...	...	...	...	...	...	...	...	...	...	...	...	...	...	...	United Arab Emirates
1.3	1.3	3.8	1.6	2.3	1.9	0.8	5.2	11.4	1.6	3.9	4.9	5.4	5.4	1.7	1.3	United Kingdom
1.8	1.2	2.7	0.9	1.6	2.1	1.4	5.8	7.4	2.1	3.3	4.8	6.0	5.6	6.3	1.5	United States
10.1	2.5	2.7	1.7	1.8	1.3	0.1	3.1	—0.9—		—2.9—		—5.4—		0.8	0.6	Uruguay
——			...	6.7	—9.1—		—10.9—								...	Uzbekistan
——			—79—		—12.0[24]—		24	...	...	...	...	...	...	...	...	Vanuatu
25.1	1.2	2.0	1.6	3.0	6.0	2.5	3.5	2.0	0.1	1.9	0.2	0.4	4.6	0.4	0.5	Venezuela
17.7[80]	3	...	1.2	7.9	—2.5—		1.9	—3.8—		—1.9—		...	...	...	...	Vietnam
...	...	...	...	...	...	...	...	...	...	...	...	...	...	...	...	Virgin Islands (U.S.)
...	...	...	...	...	...	...	...	...	...	...	...	...	...	...	...	West Bank
...	...	...	...	...	...	...	...	...	...	...	...	...	...	...	...	Western Sahara
—	—	—	—	—	—	—	—	—	—	—	—	...	—	—	—	Western Samoa
——			—15.3—		—	—	8.7	—	—	—	—	—	—	—	1.8	Yemen[82]
1.9	2.2	...	...	4.3	3.0	1.8	9.0	—6.7—		—4.8—		—10.8—		...	...	Yugoslavia
1.0	—	—	—	2.1	2.1	1.0	3.1	—3.1—		—2.1—		—3.1—		—	9.3	Zaire
0.9	2.2	1.2	0.5	5.3	0.7	0.1	8.0	—1.9—		—1.7—		—3.8—		—	0.1	Zambia
50	1.0	2.3	0.6	3.0	8.8	0.6	6.4	—1.1—		3.4	0.5	0.4	5.6	0.1	0.5	Zimbabwe

or without electric power and with 20 or more employees. [47]Conversion to U.S. dollars based on official exchange rate. [48]Establishments employing 30 or more persons. [49]Establishments employing three or more persons. [50]351 includes 353 + 354. [51]Establishments employing four or more persons. [52]33 includes 341. [53]39 includes 332. [54]3825 and 383 include 385. [55]384 includes 355. [56]Handicrafts 63.4%, processed copra products −154.7%, other manufactures 191.3%. [57]Includes production of *maquiladores* (foreign-owned assembly plants). [58]Coconut soap includes coconut oil. [59]322 and 323 + 324 includes 355 + 356. [60]Refined petroleum only. [61]341 includes 356. [62]361 + 362 includes 351. [63]Data refer to former U.S.S.R. [64]In constant U.S.$ of 1980. [65]Refined sugar only. [66]Selected industries only. [67]381 includes 383. [68]36 includes 37. [69]Establishments employing 25 or more persons. [70]383 includes 385. [71]Excludes formerly nominally independent republics of Bophuthatswana, Ciskei, Venda, and Transkei. [72]352 includes 353 + 354. [73]Rubles of former U.S.S.R. in constant prices of January 1993. [74]33 includes 34. [75]39 includes 332 and 341. [76]351 includes 352, 355, 356, and 36. [77]Private establishments employing 25 or more persons, and all public establishments. [78]January through September only. [79]35 includes 36. [80]Includes crude petroleum production. [81]Data withheld for reasons of confidentiality. [82]Former Yemen Arab Republic only.

Energy

This table provides data about the commercial energy supplies (reserves, production, consumption, and trade) of the various countries of the world, together with data about oil pipeline networks and traffic. Many of the data and concepts used in this table are adapted from the United Nations' *Energy Statistics Yearbook*.

Electricity. Total installed electrical power capacity comprises the sum of the rated power capacities of all main and auxiliary generators in a country. "Total installed capacity" (kW) is multiplied by 8,760 hours per year to yield "Total production capacity" (kW-hr).

Production of electricity comprises the total gross production of electricity by publicly or privately owned enterprises and also that generated by industrial establishments for their own use, but usually excludes consumption by the utility itself. Measured in millions of kilowatt-hours (kW-hr), annual production of electricity ranges generally between 50% and 60% of total production capacity. The data are further analyzed by type of generation: fossil fuels, hydroelectric power, and nuclear fuel.

The great majority of the world's electrical and other energy needs are met by the burning of fossil hydrocarbon solids, liquids, and gases, either for thermal generation of electricity or in internal combustion engines. Many renewable and nontraditional sources of energy are being developed worldwide (wood, biogenic gases and liquids, tidal, wave, and wind power, geothermal and photothermal [solar] energy, and so on), but collectively these sources are still negligible in the world's total energy consumption. For this reason only hydroelectric and nuclear generation are considered here separately with fossil fuels.

Trade in electrical energy refers to the transfer of generated electrical output via an international grid. Total electricity consumption (residential and nonresidential) is equal to total electricity requirements less transformation and distribution losses.

Coal. The term coal, as used in the table, comprises all grades of anthracite, bituminous, subbituminous, and lignite that have acquired or may in the future, by reason of new technology or changed market prices, acquire an economic value. These types of coal may be differentiated according to heat content (density) and content of impurities. Most coal reserve data are based on proven recoverable reserves only, of all grades of coal. Exceptions are footnoted, with proven in-place reserves reported only when recoverable reserves are unknown. Production figures include deposits removed from both surface and underground workings as well as quantities used by the producers themselves or issued to the miners. Wastes recovered from mines or nearby preparation plants are excluded from production figures.

Natural gas. This term refers to any combustible gas (usually chiefly methane) of natural origin from underground sources. The data for production cover, to the extent possible, gas obtained from gas fields, petroleum fields, or coal mines that is actually collected and marketed. (Much natural gas in Middle Eastern and North African oil fields is

Energy

country	electricity												coal		
	installed capacity, 1993 ('000 kW)	production, 1993		power source, 1993			trade, 1993		consumption				reserves, latest ('000,000 metric tons)	production, 1993 ('000 metric tons)	consumption, 1993 ('000 metric tons)
		capacity ('000,000 kW-hr)	amount ('000,000 kW-hr)	fossil fuel (%)	hydropower (%)	nuclear fuel (%)	exports ('000,000 kW-hr)	imports ('000,000 kW-hr)	amount, 1993 ('000,000 kW-hr)	per capita, 1993 (kW-hr)	residential, 1990 (%)	nonresidential, 1990 (%)			
Afghanistan	494	4,327	695	31.7	68.3	—	—	130	825	47	...	...	66	7	7
Albania	1,892	16,574	3,450	3.5	96.5	—	570	—	2,880	850	...	...	15[1]	430	630
Algeria	5,813	50,922	19,415	98.2	1.8	—	1,324	83	18,174	680	...	...	43	20	1,420
American Samoa	33	289	90	100.0	—	—	—	—	90	1,765	27.5[3]	72.5[3]	—	—	...
Andorra	...	...	...	...	...	...	...	...	...	...	...	...	—	—	...
Angola	617	5,405	1,855	25.9	74.1	—	—	—	1,855	181	27.5[2]	72.5[2]	...	—	—
Antigua and Barbuda	26	228	95	100.0	—	—	—	—	95	1,462	42.4[4]	57.6[4]	...	...	...
Argentina	18,035	157,987	63,038	49.4	38.3	12.3	23	1,265	64,280	1,903	45.9	54.1	130	167	1,133
Armenia	4,200	36,792	6,300	52.4	47.6	—	...	...	6,300	1,803	...	...	...	...	8
Aruba	90	788	352	100.0	—	—	—	—	352	5,101	...	...	...	...	...
Australia	37,206	325,925	163,557	89.9	10.1	—	—	—	163,557	9,284	30.1[2]	69.9[2]	90,940	224,175	99,573
Austria	33,016	290,885	52,675	27.8	72.2	—	8,805	8,072	51,942	6,606	23.1[2]	83.4[2]	59	1,691	4,374
Azerbaijan	4,919	43,090	19,051	87.3	12.7	...	9	12	19,054	2,580	...	...	...	...	13
Bahamas, The	401	3,513	980	100.0	—	—	—	—	980	3,657	33.6[4]	66.4[4]	...	—	—
Bahrain	1,050	9,198	4,330	100.0	—	—	—	—	4,330	8,093	...	...	...	...	...
Bangladesh	2,738	23,985	9,685	92.0	8.0	—	—	—	9,685	84	43.8	56.2	1,054[1]	—	380
Barbados	140	1,226	548	100.0	—	—	—	—	548	2,108	33.7	66.3	...	—	—
Belarus	7,205	63,116	33,369	99.9	0.1	...	128	6,133	39,374	3,865	...	...	...	—	1,608
Belgium	14,053	123,104	69,845	38.5	1.5	60.0	5,359	7,590	72,076	7,175	26.9[9]	73.1[9]	410	862	13,036
Belize	23	201	110	100.0	—	—	—	—	110	539	...	...	...	...	...
Benin	15	131	5	100.0	—	—	—	240	245	48	...	...	...	...	...
Bermuda	140	1,226	518	100.0	—	—	—	—	518	8,222	39.6	60.4	...	—	—
Bhutan	361	3,162	1,627	0.4	99.6	—	1,445	3	185	116	29.2[3]	69.8[3]	...	2	19
Bolivia	745	6,526	2,445	43.8	56.2	—	3	15	2,457	348	76.1	23.9	...	—	—
Bosnia and Herzegovina	3,400	29,784	11,000	63.6	36.4	—	502	577	11,075	2,988	21.8	78.2	...	15,000[6]	15,000[6]
Botswana	[11]	[11]	522[11, 12]	[11]	[11]	[11]	[11]	82[11, 12]	[11]	[11]	...	...	3,500	[11]	[11]
Brazil	56,212	492,417	251,484	6.5	93.3	0.2	11	27,570	279,043	1,783	46.2	53.8	2,359	4,595	15,811
Brunei	492	4,310	1,285	100.0	—	—	—	—	1,285	4,690	55.3[4]	44.7[4]	...	—	—
Bulgaria	12,087	105,882	37,997	58.1	5.1	36.8	1,520	1,630	38,107	4,296	41.2[3]	58.8[3]	3,730	29,032	33,958
Burkina Faso	65	569	196	100.0	—	—	—	—	196	20	...	...	...	...	...
Burundi	43	377	117	1.7	98.3	—	—	24	141	23	...	...	...	...	...
Cambodia	35	307	180	61.1	38.9	—	—	—	180	19	...	...	...	—	—
Cameroon	627	5,493	2,726	2.9	97.1	—	—	—	2,726	218	...	...	...	1	1
Canada	110,554	968,453	527,316	20.6	61.4	18.0	34,967	7,551	499,900	17,347	28.8[4]	71.2[4]	8,623	69,016	49,675
Cape Verde	7	61	37	100.0	—	—	—	—	37	100	...	...	...	—	—
Central African Republic	43	377	97	19.6	80.4	—	—	—	97	31	...	...	4	...	...
Chad	29	254	87	100.0	—	—	—	—	87	14	...	...	...	...	...
Chile	4,809	42,127	24,004	26.5	73.5	—	—	—	24,004	1,737	32.7	67.3	1,181	1,397	2,709
China	175,194	1,534,699	839,453	81.6	18.1	0.3	—	5,200	844,653	719	7.7	92.3	114,500	1,149,745	1,129,095
Colombia	10,361	90,762	40,298	30.6	69.4	—	—	302	40,600	1,195	69.8	30.2	4,539	21,713	5,113
Comoros	5	44	16	87.5	12.5	—	—	—	16	26	...	...	...	...	...
Congo	118	1,034	431	0.7	99.3	—	—	110	541	221	...	...	...	...	...
Costa Rica	1,044	9,145	4,386	9.7	90.3	—	81	78	4,383	1,340	72.1	27.9	...	...	...
Côte d'Ivoire	1,173	10,275	1,910	42.5	57.5	—	—	—	1,910	143	29.6	70.4	...	...	...
Croatia	3,494	30,607	9,359	53.6	46.4	—	1,198	3,636	11,797	2,615	50.6	49.4	...	116	1,012
Cuba	3,988	34,935	11,054	99.0	1.0	—	—	—	11,054	1,016	56.0	44.0	...	—	152
Cyprus	666	5,834	2,581	100.0	—	—	—	—	2,581	3,555	77.3	22.7	...	—	31
Czech Republic	14,227	124,629	58,882	75.8	2.7	21.5	8,056	5,952	56,778	5,515	23.6[3, 13]	76.4[3, 13]	5,370[13]	85,239	72,693
Denmark	10,355	90,535	33,738	96.9	0.1	3.0[14]	5,095	6,280	34,923	6,761	32.5[9]	67.5[9]	63[5]	—	11,898
Djibouti	85	745	182	100.0	—	—	—	—	182	327	...	...	...	...	...
Dominica	8	70	31	48.4	51.6	—	—	—	31	437	53.5[4]	46.5[4]	...	...	...
Dominican Republic	1,447	12,676	5,874	70.0	30.0	—	—	—	5,874	779	...	...	...	—	120
Ecuador	2,295	20,104	7,447	21.2	78.8	—	—	—	7,447	678	68.2	31.8	24	...	...
Egypt	11,854	103,841	47,470	82.1	17.9	—	—	—	47,470	787	29.6	70.4	53	—	1,500
El Salvador	751	6,579	2,858	23.0	63.0	14.0[14]	11	90	2,937	532	68.8	31.2	...	...	...

flared [burned] because it is often not economical to capture and market it.) Manufactured gas is generally a by-product of industrial operations such as gasworks, coke ovens, and blast furnaces. It is usually burned at the point of production and rarely enters the marketplace. Production of manufactured gas is, therefore, only reported as a percentage of domestic gas consumption.

Crude petroleum. Crude petroleum is the liquid product obtained from oil wells; the term also includes shale oil, tar sand extract, and field or lease condensate. Production and consumption data in the table refer, so far as possible, to the same year so that the relationship between national production and consumption patterns can be clearly seen; both are given in barrels.

Proven reserves are that oil remaining underground in known fields whose existence has been "proved" by the evaluation of nearby producing wells or by seismic tests in sedimentary strata known to contain crude petroleum, and that is judged recoverable within the limits of present technology and economic conditions (prices). The published proven reserve figures do not necessarily reflect the true reserves of a country, because government authorities or corporations often have political or economic motives for withholding or altering such data.

The estimated exhaustion rate of petroleum reserves is an extrapolated ratio of published proven reserves to the current rate of withdrawal/production. Present world published proven reserves will last about 40 to 45 years at the present rate of withdrawal, but there are large country-to-country variations above or below the average.

Data on petroleum and refined product pipelines are provided because of the great importance to both domestic and international energy markets of this means of bringing these energy sources from their production or transportation points to refineries, intermediate consumption and distribution points, and final consumers. Their traffic may represent a very significant fraction of the total movement of goods within a country. Available data for petroleum pipelines are often incomplete and their basis varies internationally, some countries reporting only international shipments, others reporting domestic shipments of 50 kilometres or more, and so on.

For data in the hydrocarbons portions of the table (coal, natural gas, and petroleum), extensive use has been made of a variety of international sources, such as those of the United Nations, the International Energy Agency (of the Organization for Economic Cooperation and Development), the World Energy Conference (in its *Survey of Energy Resources* [triennial]); the U.S. Department of Energy (especially its *International Energy Annual*); and of various industry surveys, such as those published by the *International Petroleum Encyclopedia,* the *Oil and Gas Journal,* and *World Oil.*

natural gas						crude petroleum							country
published proven reserves, 1995 ('000,000,000 cu m)	production		consumption			reserves, 1995		production, 1994 ('000,000 barrels)	consumption, 1993 ('000,000 barrels)	refining capacity, 1995 ('000 barrels per day)	pipelines (latest)		
	natural gas, 1994 ('000,000 cu m)	manufactured gas, 1993 (% of total gas consumption)	amount, 1993 ('000,000 cu m)	residential, 1990 (%)	non-residential, 1990 (%)	published proven ('000,000 barrels)	years to exhaust proven reserves				length (km)	traffic ('000,000 metric ton-km)	
99	300	...	183	...	...	...	...	—	—	—	...	...	Afghanistan
2	136	...	90	...	...	165	41	4	5	40	200	...	Albania
3,625	50,376	30.7	18,546	26.8[2]	73.2[2]	9,200	34	272	169	465	6,910	...	Algeria
...	...	...	...	...	...	...	...	—	—	—	—	...	American Samoa
...	...	...	...	...	...	...	...	—	—	—	—	—	Andorra
51	561	10.9	168	...	...	5,412	27	198	11	32	179	...	Angola
...	...	...	...	...	...	...	...	—	—	—	—	—	Antigua and Barbuda
517	17,136	10.0	20,002	49.2	50.8	2,217	9	240	186	665	6,990		Argentina
...	170[5]	...	701	...	...	...	...	—	2	—	...	...	Armenia
...	...	...	...	...	...	...	...	—	2	...	—	—	Aruba
555	28,025	28.7	18,308	...	...	1,615	8	194	193	705	3,000	...	Australia
22	1,328	12.4	7,246	25.7[2]	74.3[2]	101	13	8	61	210	725	6,701	Austria
170[6]	5,921[7]	28.9	8,115	...	...	3,300[6]	38[6]	75[7]	82	442	1,760	1,705	Azerbaijan
...	—	—	...	...	...	...	...	—	—	—	—	—	Bahamas, The
150	5,193	4.9	6,517	...	...	210	6	38	90	250	72	...	Bahrain
714	6,315	0.2	5,960	34.2	65.8	4	10	0.4	8	31	—	—	Bangladesh
0.1	16	6.2	26	62.6	37.4	3	6	0.5	2	3	—	—	Barbados
...	210[8]	1.6	15,124	...	...	...	...	15[7]	105	835	2,570	...	Belarus
	14[6]	18.8	13,752	43.4[9]	56.6[9]	...	...	—	204[10]	614	1,328	1,168	Belgium
...	...	...	...	...	...	...	...	—	—	—	—	—	Belize
—	...		...	...	...	27	25	1.1	—	—	—	—	Benin
...	...	...	...	...	...	...	...	—	—	—	—	—	Bermuda
...	...	...	...	...	...	...	...	—	—	—	—	—	Bhutan
126	3,231	26.5	695	—	100.0	139	15	9	9	45	2,380	...	Bolivia
...	—	7.4[6]	380	...	...	...	...	—	15[6]	...	174	—	Bosnia and Herzegovina
...	...	[11]	...	...	...	—	...	—	[11]	—	—	—	Botswana
137	2,965	61.2	3,958	—	100.0	3,797	15	246	431	1,253	5,804	...	Brazil
396	9,042	0.9	1,867	...	...	1,350	23	59	2	9	553	...	Brunei
7	11	17.2	4,532	...	...	15	50	0.3	65	300	718	259	Bulgaria
...	...	...	...	...	...	...	...	—	—	—	—	—	Burkina Faso
...	...	...	...	...	...	...	...	—	—	—	—	—	Burundi
...	...	...	...	...	...	...	...	—	—	—	—	—	Cambodia
110	—	100.0	...	...	...	400	9	40	5	42	—	—	Cameroon
2,244	166,011	23.5	74,077	20.6[2]	79.4[2]	5,038	8	636	516	1,908	23,564	99,908	Canada
...	...	...	...	...	...	...	...	—	—	—	—	—	Cape Verde
...	...	...	...	...	...	...	...	—	—	—	—	—	Central African Republic
...	...	...	...	...	...	...	...	—	—	—	—	—	Chad
110	1,138	35.9	1,802	23.4	76.6	300	75	4	51	165	1,540	...	Chile
1,671	16,605	49.3	16,933	12.2	87.8	24,000	22	1,077	1,012	2,867	10,800	...	China
223	4,797	25.6	4,314	12.8	87.2	3,393	20	166	92	249	4,935	...	Colombia
...	...	...	...	...	...	...	...	—	—	—	—	—	Comoros
76	2[8]	61.7	3	...	...	830	12	69	5	21	25	...	Congo
...	—	9.4	—	—	—	...	...	—	4	15	176	...	Costa Rica
14	—	60.7	—	—	—	50	250	0.2	24	64	—	—	Côte d'Ivoire
35	1,897	24.4	2,373	...	...	150	11	14	36	294	690	89	Croatia
3	31[5]	85.5	38	3.4	96.6	100	13	8	37	280	—	—	Cuba
—	—	64.1	—	—	—	...	...	—	6	22	—	—	Cyprus
13[13]	699[13]	25.8	7,513	...	...	15[13]	13	1.2[13]	42	307	...	...	Czech Republic
121	4,565	16.5	2,659	...	...	736	11	67	64	188	688	2,212	Denmark
...	...	...	...	...	...	...	...	—	—	—	—	—	Djibouti
...	...	...	...	...	...	—	—	—	—	—	—	—	Dominica
—	—	11.6	...	...	...	...	...	—	14	48	104	...	Dominican Republic
108	102	43.5	100	—	—	2,014	15	138	47	148	2,158	...	Ecuador
546	8,427	12.2	9,643	5.3	94.7	3,260	10	326	185	532	1,767	...	Egypt
—	—	50.0	—	—	—	...	...	—	7	19	—	—	El Salvador

Energy (continued)

country	electricity												coal		
	installed capacity, 1993 ('000 kW)	production, 1993		power source, 1993			trade, 1993		consumption				reserves, latest ('000,000 metric tons)	production, 1993 ('000 metric tons)	consumption, 1993 ('000 metric tons)
		capacity ('000,000 kW-hr)	amount ('000,000 kW-hr)	fossil fuel (%)	hydropower (%)	nuclear fuel (%)	exports ('000,000 kW-hr)	imports ('000,000 kW-hr)	amount, 1993 ('000,000 kW-hr)	per capita, 1993 (kW-hr)	residential, 1990 (%)	nonresidential, 1990 (%)			
Equatorial Guinea	5	44	19	89.5	10.5	—	—	—	19	50	...	...	...	...	...
Eritrea	...	...	...	...	...	...	...	...	...	...	...	...	...	...	...
Estonia	3,332	29,188	9,118	99.9	0.1	...	1,596	...	7,522	4,847	...	...	...	14,915	16,604
Ethiopia	464	4,065	1,293	7.0	87.8	5.2[14]	—	—	1,293	25	...	...	11	—	—
Faroe Islands	91	797	199	57.8	42.2	—	—	—	199	4,234	...	...	...	—	—
Fiji	200	1,752	465	17.2	82.8	—	—	—	465	613	10.5	89.5	...	—	20
Finland	14,077	123,315	61,172	45.3	22.2	32.5	429	8,013	68,756	13,594	18.6[2]	81.3[2]	...	—	6,002
France	143,559[15]	1,257,577[15]	471,448[15]	7.5[15]	14.4[15]	78.1[15]	65,093[15]	3,663[15]	410,018[15]	7,126[15]	30.3[9]	69.7[9]	210	10,248[15]	22,723[15]
French Guiana	165	1,445	446	100.0	—	—	—	—	446	3,304	...	58.7[2, 16]	...	...	...
French Polynesia	79	692	323	76.8	23.2	—	—	—	323	1,531	...	...	...	...	...
Gabon	310	2,716	922	23.0	77.0	—	—	—	922	739	55.1	44.9	...	...	...
Gambia, The	29	254	73	100.0	—	—	—	—	73	70	...	...	...	...	...
Gaza Strip	...	...	...	...	...	...	...	...	...	...	...	...	...	...	...
Georgia	4,000	35,040	9,700	33.0	67.0	...	...	311	10,011	1,838	...	...	...	—	156
Germany	114,294	1,001,215	525,721	66.7	4.1	29.2	32,758	33,628	526,591	6,513	26.3[9, 17]	73.7[9, 17]	80,069	285,976	303,970
Ghana	1,187	10,398	6,154	0.6	99.4	—	288	4	5,870	357	...	...	...	—	3
Gibraltar	33	289	88	100.0	—	—	5	—	83	2,964	...	...	...	—	—
Greece	8,790	77,000	38,396	93.3	6.6	0.1	284	1,093	39,205	3,778	30.6[9]	69.4[9]	3,000	54,800	56,618
Greenland	105	920	252	100.0	—	—	—	—	252	4,421	35.3[18]	64.7[18]	183	...	...
Grenada	9	79	65	100.0	—	—	—	—	65	707	46.8[4]	53.2[4]	...	...	...
Guadeloupe	388	3,399	960	100.0	—	—	—	—	960	2,324	...	32.9[16, 18]	...	...	...
Guam	302	2,646	800	100.0	—	—	—	—	800	5,556	39.7	60.3	...	...	...
Guatemala	696	6,097	3,084	37.7	62.3	—	—	—	3,084	308	27.0[2]	73.0[2]	...	...	...
Guernsey	...	...	227[6]	100.0[6]	...	...	...	...	227[6]	4,997[6]	...	...	...	...	...
Guinea	176	1,542	536	64.9	35.1	—	—	—	536	85	...	...	...	...	...
Guinea-Bissau	11	96	42	100.0	—	—	—	—	42	41	...	...	...	...	...
Guyana	114	999	240	97.9	2.1	—	—	12	252	309	...	...	...	...	...
Haiti	153	1,340	394	58.1	41.9	—	—	—	394	57	...	...	13[1]	...	10
Honduras	290	2,540	2,464	8.1	91.9	—	5[6]	16	2,480	465	51.7	48.3	21[1]	...	...
Hong Kong	9,037	79,164	36,394	100.0	—	—	4,500	—	31,894	5,490	70.8	29.2	...	—	11,828
Hungary	6,727	58,929	32,784	57.4	0.5	42.1	756	3,230	35,258	3,453	30.7[3]	69.3[3]	4,461	14,616	16,765
Iceland	1,076	9,426	4,727	0.1	94.4	5.5[14]	—	—	4,727	17,973	20.9[2]	79.1[2]	...	—	53
India	85,314	747,351	356,519	78.3	19.8	1.9	160	1,400	357,759	397	45.8	54.2	62,548	263,198	267,639
Indonesia	15,915	139,415	58,888	77.6	20.5	1.9[14]	—	—	58,888	307	55.0	45.0	32,063	27,584	9,003
Iran	20,874	182,856	71,980	84.7	15.3	—	—	—	71,980	1,122	21.1[12]	78.9[12]	193	1,460	7,567
Iraq	7,260	63,598	26,300	97.7	2.3	—	—	—	26,300	1,352	...	...	...	—	—
Ireland	3,933	34,453	16,416	93.7	6.2	0.1[14]	—	—	16,416	4,658	41.4[9]	58.6[9]	14	1	2,932
Isle of Man	...	...	188[4]	100.0	—	—	—	—	172[3]	2,530[3]	48.1[9]	51.9[9]	...	...	...
Israel	4,280	37,493	26,000	99.9	0.1	—	320	—	25,680	4,888	68.4	31.6	...	—	5,653
Italy	63,486[19]	556,137[19]	222,788[19]	74.4[19]	20.0[19]	1.6[4, 19]	677[19]	40,109[19]	262,220[19]	4,588[19]	25.0[9]	75.0[9]	34	1,005[19]	16,034[19]
Jamaica	732	6,412	2,298	96.1	3.9	—	—	—	2,298	953	25.6	74.4	...	—	55
Japan	212,913	1,865,118	906,705	60.7	11.6	27.7	—	—	906,705	7,281	20.8[2]	79.2[2]	844	7,232	118,900
Jersey	...	...	440[6]	...	...	...	...	...	440[6]	6,579[6]	...	...	...	...	...
Jordan	1,006	8,813	4,761	99.5	0.5	—	—	...	4,761	965	60.0	40.0	...	...	...
Kazakhstan	15,910	139,372	77,444	90.1	9.9	...	52,953	64,659	89,150	5,259	...	...	25,000	116,543	85,195
Kenya	805	7,052	3,396	3.9	88.1	8.0[14]	—	273	3,669	139	35.1	64.9	...	—	131
Kiribati	2	18	7	100.0	—	—	—	—	7	92	...	...	...	...	...
Korea, North	9,500	83,220	38,000	36.8	63.2	—	—	—	38,000	1,649	...	...	600	99,000	100,950
Korea, South	30,519	267,346	163,449	60.8	3.7	35.5	—	—	163,449	3,704	34.0	66.0	203	9,443	42,419
Kuwait	6,988	61,215	18,200	100.0	—	—	—	—	18,200	10,254	92.1	7.9	...	...	...
Kyrgyzstan	3,485	30,529	11,091	19.7	80.3	...	6,641	5,800	10,250	2,233	...	...	...	1,721	2,136
Laos	256	2,243	900	4.8	95.2	—	632	25	293	64	...	...	...	1	1
Latvia	2,424	21,234	3,924	26.7	73.3	...	170	2,672	6,426	2,461	...	...	...	—	599
Lebanon	1,220	10,687	3,950	90.9	9.1	—	—	50	4,000	1,426	...	...	...	—	—
Lesotho	[11]	[11]	[11]	[11]	[11]	[11]	[11]	[11]	[11]	[11]	...	...	...	[11]	[11]
Liberia	332	2,908	480	63.5	36.5	—	—	—	480	169	...	...	...	...	...
Libya	4,600	40,296	17,000	100.0	—	—	—	—	17,000	3,368	...	...	—	—	4
Liechtenstein	[21]	[21]	[21]	[21]	[21]	[21]	[21]	[21]	[21]	[21]	...	...	...	—	[21]
Lithuania	5,448	47,724	14,122	10.4	2.8	86.8	8,467	5,736	11,391	3,069	...	...	...	...	664
Luxembourg	1,238	10,845	1,067	56.6	43.4	—	394	4,445	5,118	12,957	15.3[9]	84.7[9]	...	—	277
Macau	260	2,278	1,190	100.0	—	—	—	118	1,308	3,406	75.0[4]	25.0[4]	...	—	—
Macedonia	1,370	12,001	5,980	84.9	15.1	—	300	550	6,230	2,940	27.4	72.6	...	7,300	7,450
Madagascar	220	1,927	599	42.1	57.9	—	—	—	599	43	...	...	1,075[1]	—	14
Malaŵi	185	1,621	795	2.0	98.0	—	—	—	795	76	52.8	47.2	12	—	15
Malaysia	6,857	60,067	35,579	86.2	13.8	—	195	170	35,554	1,847	51.6	48.4	4	260	2,081
Maldives	14	123	40	100.0	—	—	—	—	40	168	50.9[3]	49.1[3]	...	...	...
Mali	87	762	330	35.8	64.2	—	—	—	330	33	...	...	—	...	...
Malta	250	2,190	1,500	100.0	—	—	—	—	1,500	4,155	25.1[12]	74.9[12]	...	—	300
Marshall Islands	99[8]	867[8]	...	...	...	...	...	...	...	...	...	...	...	...	...
Martinique	115	1,007	792	100.0	—	—	—	—	792	2,135	...	40.9[16, 18]	...	...	...
Mauritania	105	920	146	82.2	17.8	—	—	—	146	68	...	...	...	—	6
Mauritius	361	3,162	988	89.5	10.5	—	—	—	988	906	...	...	...	—	58
Mayotte	10	88	22	100.0	...	...	...	...	22	211	...	...	...	...	...
Mexico	33,228	291,077	134,925	72.3	19.3	8.4[14]	2,015	909	133,819	1,486	17.4[12]	82.6[12]	1,720	7,630	7,663
Micronesia	...	...	...	...	...	...	...	...	...	...	...	...	...	...	...
Moldova	3,046	26,683	10,369	96.4	3.6	...	849	85	9,605	2,179	...	...	...	—	2,140
Monaco	[15]	[15]	[15]	[15]	[15]	[15]	[15]	[15]	[15]	[15]	...	...	...	[15]	[15]
Mongolia	901	7,893	3,200	100.0	—	—	—	60	3,260	1,406	29.8[3]	70.2[3]	24,000[1]	7,425	6,925
Morocco	2,722	23,845	9,917	95.5	4.5	—	—	1,000	10,917	421	66.6	33.4	45	604	1,640
Mozambique	2,358	20,656	490	89.8	10.2	—	—	325	815	54	...	...	240	40	60
Myanmar (Burma)	1,151	10,083	3,030	52.1	47.9	—	—	—	3,030	68	...	59.1[2, 16]	3	71	74
Namibia	[11]	[11]	[11]	[11]	[11]	[11]	[11]	[11]	[11]	[11]	...	...	...	[11]	[11]
Nauru	10	88	30	100.0	—	—	—	—	30	3,000	...	...	...	...	...
Nepal	277	2,427	936	6.5	93.5	—	87	85	934	45	67.3	32.7	...	—	100
Netherlands, The	17,599	154,167	76,992	94.5	0.1	5.4	269	10,572	87,295	5,711	25.0[4]	75.0[4]	497	—	13,124

natural gas						crude petroleum							country
published proven reserves, 1995 ('000,000,000 cu m)	production		consumption			reserves, 1995		production, 1994 ('000,000 barrels)	consumption, 1993 ('000,000 barrels)	refining capacity, 1995 ('000 barrels per day)	pipelines (latest)		
	natural gas, 1994 ('000,000 cu m)	manufactured gas, 1993 (% of total gas consumption)	amount, 1993 ('000,000 cu m)	residential, 1990 (%)	non-residential, 1990 (%)	published proven ('000,000 barrels)	years to exhaust proven reserves				length (km)	traffic ('000,000 metric ton-km)	
37	...	...	...	...	...	12	6	1.9	...	—	—	—	Equatorial Guinea
...	...	...	...	...	...	...	...	...	...	18	...	...	Eritrea
...	...	4.1	385	...	...	...	...	...	...	...	...	...	Estonia
23	—	100.0	—	...	...	...	...	—	5	—	—	—	Ethiopia
...	...	...	...	...	...	...	...	—	—	—	—	—	Faroe Islands
...	—	...	—	—	—	...	...	—	—	—	—	—	Fiji
—	—	31.2	3,104	0.6[9]	99.4[9]	...	...	—	57	200	—	—	Finland
36	3,574	20.2[15]	34,859[14]	32.4[9]	67.6[9]	152	7	21	571[15]	1,768	7,546	22,501	France
...	...	...	...	...	...	...	...	—	—	—	—	—	French Guiana
...	...	...	...	...	...	...	...	—	—	—	—	—	French Polynesia
14	102	8.8	98	19.7	80.3	1,340	11	120	7	17	284	...	Gabon
...	...	...	...	...	...	...	...	—	—	—	—	—	Gambia, The
...	...	...	...	...	...	...	...	—	—	—	—	—	Gaza Strip
...	45[8]	...	3,256	...	...	...	...	0.9[7]	2	106	670	...	Georgia
303	18,304	17.9	90,957	36.6[9, 17]	63.4[9, 17]	368	18	21	746	2,317	7,590	13,872	Germany
23	—	100.0	—	—	—	0.5	0.25	2	7	25	—	—	Ghana
...	...	...	...	...	...	...	...	—	...	—	—	—	Gibraltar
8	139	91.5	109	...	...	41	10	4	80	401	573	...	Greece
...	...	...	...	...	...	...	...	—	—	—	—	—	Greenland
...	...	...	...	...	...	...	...	—	—	—	—	—	Grenada
...	...	...	...	...	...	...	...	—	—	—	—	—	Guadeloupe
...	—	100.0[5]	—	—	—	...	...	—	—	—	...	...	Guam
0.3	8	8.9	9	...	...	488	163	3	5	20	275	...	Guatemala
...	...	...	...	...	...	...	...	—	—	—	—	—	Guernsey
24[6]	...		...	...	...	...	...	—	—	—	—	—	Guinea
...	...	...	...	...	...	...	...	—	—	—	—	—	Guinea-Bissau
...	...	...	...	...	...	...	...		—	—	—	—	Guyana
...	...	...	...	...	...	...	...	—	—	—	—	—	Haiti
—	—	30.7[6]	—	—	—	...	...	—	3[6]	14	—	—	Honduras
...	—	76.2	—	—	—	...	...	—	—	—	—	—	Hong Kong
98	5,992	8.1	9,650	14.0[9]	86.0[9]	132	5	26	52	242	1,204	2,607	Hungary
...	...	...	...	...	...	...	...	—	—	—	—	—	Iceland
707	17,024	20.4	12,214	53.7	46.3	5,776	25	227	428	1,086	5,200	...	India
1,823	55,252	42.5	21,051	—	100.0	5,779	12	485	309	805	2,961	...	Indonesia
21,000	28,025	13.4	26,343	—	100.0[4]	89,250	68	1,304	341	1,184	9,800	...	Iran
3,101	2,917	33.9	2,550	...	...	100,000	526	190	186	348	5,075	...	Iraq
15	2,500	2.9	2,522	13.9[9]	86.1[9]	...	...	—	14	53	—	—	Ireland
...	—	...	...	...	...	...	...	...	...	—	—	—	Isle of Man
0.4	20	111.6	22	—	100.0	3	30	0.1	86	220	998	...	Israel
374	20,337	14.1[19]	51,239[19]	45.6[9]	54.4[9]	621	19	32	660[10]	2,286	3,851	11,348	Italy
—	—	30.2	—	—	—	...	...	—	5	36	10	...	Jamaica
27	2,180	40.8	54,187	61.3[9]	38.7[9]	49	8	6	1,534	4,847	406	...	Japan
...	...	...	...	...	...	...	...	—	—	—	—	—	Jersey
6	229	81.4	—	—	—	0.3	3	0.1	21	100	209	...	Jordan
...	3,349	...	13,662	...	...	...	...	142	118	394	4,350	22,300	Kazakhstan
—	—	103.9	—	—	—	...	...	—	17	90	483	...	Kenya
...	...	...	...	...	...	...	...	—	—	—	—	—	Kiribati
...	...	...	...	...	...	...	...	—	17	42	37	...	Korea, North
—	—	30.9	6,140	...	...	...	...	—	545	1,170	455	...	Korea, South
1,498	4,664	97.9	4,470	25.0	75.0	96,500	130	711	102	735	917	...	Kuwait
...	68[6]	...	1,206	...	...	...	...	0.9[6]	0.2	...	...	...	Kyrgyzstan
...	...	...	...	...	...	...	...	—	—	—	136	...	Laos
...	...	...	1,219	...	...	...	...	—	...	...	1,530	...	Latvia
—	—	2.7	...	...	...	...	...	—	3	38	72	...	Lebanon
—	—	[11]	—	...	...	...	...	—	[11]	—	—	—	Lesotho
—	—	50.5[20]	—	...	...	...	...	—	—	15	—	—	Liberia
1,297	6,402	12.2	4,760	...	...	22,800	46	499	113	348	4,826	...	Libya
—	—	[21]	[21]	...	...	...	...	—	[21]	—	—	—	Liechtenstein
...	...	9.5	1,858	...	...	...	...	...	38	267	105	...	Lithuania
...	—	38.1	565	48.0[9]	52.0[9]	...	...	—	[10]	—	48	...	Luxembourg
...	...	...	...	...	...	...	...	—	—	—	—	—	Macau
...	—	100.0	269	...	...	...	...	—	8	51	—	—	Macedonia
2	—	33.6	—	...	...	...	...	—	1.2	16	—	—	Madagascar
...	—	—	—	—	—	...	...	—	—	—	—	—	Malaŵi
1,926	24,687	17.2	6,150	6.6	93.4	4,300	18	235	82	286	1,307	...	Malaysia
...	...	...	...	...	...	...	...	—	—	—	—	—	Maldives
...	...	...	...	...	...	...	...	—	—	—	—	—	Mali
—	...	—	...	...	...	...	...	—	—	—	—	—	Malta
...	...	...	...	...	...	...	...	—	—	...	—	—	Marshall Islands
—	—	163.7	...	...	...	...	...	—	6	16	—	—	Martinique
...	...	87.8	...	...	...	...	...	—	7	—	—		Mauritania
...	...	...	...	...	...	...	...	—	—	—	—	—	Mauritius
...	...	...	...	...	...	...	...	—	—	—	—	—	Mayotte
1,973	37,514	28.7	23,057	3.9[12]	96.1[12]	50,776	52	980	477	1,524	38,350	...	Mexico
...	...	...	...	...	...	...	...	—	—	...	—	—	Micronesia
...	—	...	2,775	...	...	...	...	—	52[5]	...	...	...	Moldova
...	...	[15]	[15]	...	...	...	...	—	[15]	—	—	—	Monaco
...	...	...	...	...	...	...	...	—	—	—	—	—	Mongolia
1.5	25	33.4	24	—	100.0	1.7	17	0.1	48	155	362	...	Morocco
77	—	—	—	...	...	...	...	—	—	...	595	...	Mozambique
278	1,102	0.5	973	—	100.0[4]	50	8	6	5	32	1,343	...	Myanmar (Burma)
57	—	[11]	—	...	...	...	...	—	[11]	—	—	—	Namibia
...	...	...	...	...	...	...	...	—	—	—	—	—	Nauru
...	—	—	—	—	—	...	...	—	—	—	—	—	Nepal
1,875	83,000	17.2	50,190	46.8[4]	53.4[4]	113	4	26	360	1,187	1,383	5,503	Netherlands, The

Energy (continued)

country	electricity													coal		
	installed capacity, 1993 ('000 kW)	production, 1993		power source, 1993			trade, 1993		consumption				reserves, latest ('000,000 metric tons)	production, 1993 ('000 metric tons)	consumption, 1993 ('000 metric tons)
		capacity ('000,000 kW-hr)	amount ('000,000 kW-hr)	fossil fuel (%)	hydropower (%)	nuclear fuel (%)	exports ('000,000 kW-hr)	imports ('000,000 kW-hr)	amount, 1993 ('000,000 kW-hr)	per capita, 1993 (kW-hr)	residential, 1990 (%)	nonresidential, 1990 (%)			
Netherlands Antilles	200	1,752	877	100.0	—	—	—	—	877	4,497	...	...	...	...	...
New Caledonia	253	2,216	1,170	70.5	29.5	—	—	—	1,170	6,686	...	...	2	—	170
New Zealand	7,520	65,875	31,248	26.8	68.1	5.1[14]	—	—	31,248	8,966	37.5[4]	62.5[4]	117	3,101	2,290
Nicaragua	457	4,003	1,683	51.1	18.3	30.6[14]	—	—	1,683	409	67.1	32.9	...	...	...
Niger	63	552	173	100.0	—	—	—	193	366	43	50.0	50.0	70	172	172
Nigeria	4,574	40,068	11,800	72.9	27.1	—	100	—	11,700	111	80.4	19.6	190	95	60
Northern Mariana Islands	114[6]	999[6]	...	...	...	...	...	...	...	...	...	...	...	...	...
Norway	27,333	239,437	120,001	0.4	99.6	—	8,379	595	112,217	26,079	27.0[2]	73.0[2]	13	267	821
Oman	1,539	13,482	7,048	100.0	—	—	—	—	7,048	3,538	...	...	...	...	...
Pakistan	10,550	92,418	55,311	60.3	38.9	0.8	—	—	55,311	416	64.5	35.5	524	3,075	4,236
Palau	62	543	203	85.2	14.8	—	—	—	203	879	...	...	—	—	—
Panama	959	8,401	3,286	30.2	69.8	—	102	192	3,376	1,330	26.8[12]	73.2[12]	...	—	58
Papua New Guinea	490	4,292	1,790	74.3	25.7	—	—	—	1,790	436	27.5	72.5	...	...	1
Paraguay	6,533	57,229	31,454	0.1	99.9	—	28,121	1	3,334	709	...	...	...	...	...
Peru	4,187	36,678	14,326	20.3	79.7	—	—	—	14,326	626	35.8	64.2	1,060	83	233
Philippines	6,793	59,507	21,885	54.3	19.5	26.2[14]	—	—	21,885	338	53.0	47.0	262	1,678	2,368
Poland	29,187	255,678	133,867	97.3	2.7	—	8,011	5,600	131,456	3,432	33.5[3]	66.5[3]	41,200	198,584	177,805
Portugal	8,733	76,501	31,205	72.0	28.0	—	1,902	2,077	31,380	3,190	36.4[2]	63.6[2]	36	197	4,951
Puerto Rico	4,230	37,055	16,540	98.1	1.9	—	—	—	16,540	4,572	31.0[12]	69.0[12]	...	—	160
Qatar	1,110	9,724	5,560	100.0	—	—	—	—	5,560	10,510	83.0	17.0	...	...	...
Réunion	299	2,619	1,130	55.9	44.1	—	—	—	1,130	1,782	...	...	...	...	...
Romania	22,262	195,015	55,476	77.0	23.0	—	1,118	2,991	57,349	2,491	23.6[3]	76.4[3]	3,118	39,751	43,816
Russia	213,421	1,869,568	956,587	69.2	18.3	12.5	44,138	24,681	937,130	6,342	21.6[3, 22]	78.4[3, 22]	241,000[22]	304,110	315,335
Rwanda	64	561	234	1.7	98.3	—	3	12	243	32	...	...	...	...	...
St. Kitts and Nevis	15	131	42	100.0	—	—	—	—	42	1,000	...	...	...	...	...
St. Lucia	22	193	107	100.0	—	—	—	—	107	770	26.6[3]	73.4[3]	...	...	...
St. Vincent and the Grenadines	14	123	52	23.1	76.9	—	—	—	52	473	45.3[4]	54.7[4]	...	...	...
San Marino	[19]	[19]	[19]	[19]	[19]	[19]	[19]	[19]	[19]	[19]	...	...	...	[19]	[19]
São Tomé and Príncipe	6	53	15	46.7	53.3	—	—	—	15	118	...	...	...	...	...
Saudi Arabia	18,436	161,499	63,331	100.0	—	—	—	—	63,331	3,699	69.3[18]	30.7[18]	...	...	...
Senegal	231	2,024	765	100.0	—	—	—	—	765	97	...	...	...	...	...
Seychelles	28	245	110	100.0	—	—	—	—	110	1,528	...	...	...	...	...
Sierra Leone	126	1,104	233	100.0	—	—	—	—	233	54	...	...	...	—	—
Singapore	3,575	31,317	18,962	100.0	—	—	52	—	18,910	6,770	48.0	52.0	...	—	1
Slovakia	7,115	62,327	23,881	41.3	12.7	46.0	2,280	4,297	25,898	4,874	...	...	...	3,547	14,390
Slovenia	2,481	21,734	11,692	40.3	25.8	33.9	2,124	706	10,274	5,304	18.0	82.0	...	5,121	5,569
Solomon Islands	12	105	30	100.0	—	—	—	—	30	85	69.4	30.6	...	...	...
Somalia	70	613	258	100.0	—	—	—	—	258	29	...	...	...	...	...
South Africa	26,739[11]	234,234[11]	175,910[11]	95.4[11]	0.5[11]	4.1[11]	2,602[11]	100	173,408[11]	3,830[11]	...	...	55,333	182,881[11]	140,231[11]
Spain	43,892	384,494	156,529	47.7	16.5	35.8	3,339	4,606	157,796	4,037	16.7[2]	83.2[2]	1,450	31,504	44,416
Sri Lanka	1,409	12,343	3,979	4.6	95.4	—	—	—	3,979	222	65.1	34.9	...	—	1[6]
Sudan, The	500	4,380	1,328	29.3	70.7	—	—	—	1,328	50	...	...	...	—	—
Suriname	415	3,635	1,392	18.9	81.1	—	—	—	1,392	3,362	...	...	...	—	—
Swaziland	[11]	[11]	[11]	[11]	[11]	[11]	[11]	[11]	[11]	[11]	...	...	999	[11]	[11]
Sweden	37,179	325,688	144,311	5.2	52.2	42.6	8,566	7,977	143,722	16,531	26.4[2]	73.6[2]	1	4	3,380
Switzerland	15,550[21]	136,218[21]	61,070[21]	1.8[21]	60.0[21]	38.2[21]	26,719[21]	19,520[21]	53,871[21]	7,602[21]	26.6[9]	73.4[9]	...	—	220[21]
Syria	4,157	36,415	12,638	46.9	53.1	—	—	—	12,638	923	21.2[9]	78.8[9]	...	—	—
Taiwan	19,355	169,550	101,784	61.0	6.6	32.4	—	—	92,085	4,397	31.9	68.1	100	328	...
Tajikistan	4,443	38,921	17,741	3.5	96.5	...	6,386	5,214	16,569	2,873	...	...	...	200	176
Tanzania	439	3,846	907	31.1	68.9	—	—	—	907	32	...	...	200	4	4
Thailand	13,861	121,422	66,305	94.4	5.6	—	49	645	66,901	1,162	51.0	49.0	999	15,546	15,773
Togo	34	298	91	94.5	5.5	—	—	312	403	104	...	...	...	...	...
Tonga	7	61	27	100.0	—	—	—	—	27	276	...	...	...	...	...
Trinidad and Tobago	1,150	10,074	3,817	100.0	—	—	—	—	3,817	2,987	41.0	59.0	...	—	—
Tunisia	1,414	12,387	6,416	99.0	1.0	—	140	130	6,406	747	42.8	57.2	—	—	14
Turkey	20,335	178,135	73,808	53.9	46.0	0.1[14]	589	213	73,432	1,232	14.2[12]	85.8[12]	7,148	48,161	55,987
Turkmenistan	3,950	34,602	12,637	99.8	0.2	...	...	...	12,637	3,223	...	...	...	...	135
Tuvalu	...	...	...	...	...	...	...	...	...	...	...	...	...	...	...
Uganda	162	1,419	788	0.9	99.1	—	114	—	674	34	...	...	...	...	...
Ukraine	54,261	475,326	229,907	62.4	4.9	32.7	17,317	15,773	228,363	4,430	...	...	...	115,713	120,517
United Arab Emirates	4,756	41,663	17,578	100.0	—	—	—	—	17,578	9,680	...	...	...	...	...
United Kingdom	68,455	599,666	323,029	70.5	1.8	27.7	5	16,721	339,745	5,843	35.4[9]	64.6[9]	3,800	68,199	87,370
United States	760,427	6,661,341	3,145,892	71.1	8.8	20.1	8,146	36,892	3,174,638	12,308	34.9[9]	65.1[9]	240,116	857,675	799,412
Uruguay	2,065	18,089	7,989	8.6	91.4	—	2,328	14	5,675	1,802	60.6	39.4	...	—	—
Uzbekistan	17,625	154,395	49,149	85.0	15.0	...	131	...	49,018	2,242	...	...	...	3,807	4,259
Vanuatu	11	96	29	100.0	—	—	—	—	29	180	...	...	...	...	...
Venezuela	18,775	164,469	71,388	33.5	66.5	—	300	—	71,088	3,399	42.0	58.0	417	3,891	291
Vietnam	3,478	30,467	10,854	17.9	76.5	5.6[14]	—	—	10,854	152	36.4[3]	63.6[3]	150	5,899	3,965
Virgin Islands (U.S.)	316	2,768	1,040	100.0	—	—	—	—	1,040	10,000	40.2[4]	59.8[4]	...	—	230
West Bank	...	...	...	...	...	...	...	...	...	...	...	...	...	...	...
Western Sahara	56	491	85	100.0	—	—	—	—	85	326	...	...	...	...	...
Western Samoa	19	166	50	60.0	40.0	—	—	—	50	299	...	...	...	...	...
Yemen	810	7,096	1,850	100.0	—	—	—	—	1,850	140	...	...	1[5]	...	...
Yugoslavia	10,424	91,314	34,156	70.7	29.3	—	100	500	34,556	3,253	26.0	74.0	16,570[23]	37,433	37,493
Zaire	2,831	24,800	6,189	2.7	97.3	—	195	2	5,996	145	...	89.1[2, 16]	600	92	134
Zambia	2,436	21,339	7,785	0.5	99.5	—	1,500	20	6,305	706	31.8	68.2	55	400	395
Zimbabwe	2,148	18,816	7,643	77.8	22.2	—	3	1,921	9,561	890	44.2	55.8	734	5,266	5,385

natural gas						crude petroleum							country
published proven reserves, 1995 ('000,000,000 cu m)	production		consumption			reserves, 1995		production, 1994 ('000,000 barrels)	consumption, 1993 ('000,000 barrels)	refining capacity, 1995 ('000 barrels per day)	pipelines (latest)		
	natural gas, 1994 ('000,000 cu m)	manufactured gas, 1993 (% of total gas consumption)	amount, 1993 ('000,000 cu m)	residential, 1990 (%)	nonresidential, 1990 (%)	published proven ('000,000 barrels)	years to exhaust proven reserves				length (km)	traffic ('000,000 metric ton-km)	
—	—	128.9	...	...	...	...	...	—	99	490	—	—	Netherlands Antilles
...	...	...	...	...	...	...	...	—	—	—	—	—	New Caledonia
85	4,933	7.8	4,769	4.8[4]	95.2[4]	137	9	16	35	89	310	...	New Zealand
—	—	100.0	—	—	—	...	...	—	5	17	56	...	Nicaragua
...	—	—	—	—	—	...	...	—	—	—	—	—	Niger
3,398	4,582	1.4	4,900	—	100.0	17,900	25	704	88	433	5,042	...	Nigeria
...	...	...	...	...	...	...	...	—	...	—	—	—	Northern Mariana Islands
2,008	26,570	40.7	2,897	...	...	9,416	10	912	105	285	53	11,019	Norway
630	3,752	8.3	2,517	...	...	4,828	16	293	18	85	1,300	...	Oman
779	16,316	1.4	14,240	41.5	58.5	203	10	21	52	139	1,135	...	Pakistan
—	—	...	...	...	...	—	—	—	...	...	...	—	Palau
—	—	28.2	60	—	—	...	...	—	13	40	130	...	Panama
425	93	...	—	—	—	229	5	44	—	—	—	—	Papua New Guinea
—	—	3.2	...	...	...	...	...	—	2	8	—	—	Paraguay
199	1,303	32.5	524	61.4	38.6	800	17	48	58	184	800	...	Peru
98	—	57.5	—	—	—	239	133	1.8	99	280	357	...	Philippines
155	4,686	29.8	10,935	...	...	35	21	1.7	99	352	2,346	11,932	Poland
—	—	54.9	...	...	...	...	...	—	79	304	80	...	Portugal
—	—	100.0	...	...	...	...	...	—	41	127	—	—	Puerto Rico
7,079	12,224	10.1	13,500	—	100.0	3,700	25	148	18	58	235	...	Qatar
...	...	...	...	...	...	...	...	—	...	—	—	—	Réunion
348	18,746	8.7	21,404	...	...	1,606	32	50	107	651	4,229	2,558	Romania
48,677	643,000[6]	4.2	369,996	...	...	156,700	60	2,595[7]	1,689	6,527	63,000	883,621	Russia
57	0.2[8]	—	0.2	...	...	...	...	—	—	—	—	—	Rwanda
...	...	...	...	...	...	...	...	—	—	—	—	—	St. Kitts and Nevis
...	...	...	...	...	...	...	...	—	—	—	—	—	St. Lucia
...	...	...	...	...	...	...	...	—	—	—	—	—	St. Vincent and the Grenadines
...	...	19	19	...	...	...	...	—	19	—	—	—	San Marino
...	...	...	...	...	...	...	...	—	—	—	—	—	São Tomé and Príncipe
5,264	35,510	49.7	35,899	9.8[9]	90.2[9]	261,203	89	2,924	581	1,661	6,550	...	Saudi Arabia
—	—	14.3	...	...	...	...	...	—	6	17	—	—	Senegal
...	...	...	...	...	...	...	...	—	—	—	—	—	Seychelles
—	...	...	...	...	...	...	...	—	2	10	—	—	Sierra Leone
—	—	365.3	—	—	—	...	...	—	380	1,091	—	—	Singapore
8	313[8]	8.4	5,038	...	...	7	14	0.5[6]	33	193	...	...	Slovakia
...	24[5]	...	628	...	...	...	...	0.02[5]	4	11	290	128	Slovenia
...	—	—	—	—	—	...	...	—	—	—	—	—	Solomon Islands
6	—	...	...	...	...	...	...	—	...	10	15	...	Somalia
27	—	100.0[11]	—	...	...	40	10	4	125[11]	401	2,679	...	South Africa
19	600	38.2	6,590	...	...	20	3	6	391	1,283	2,059	5,266	Spain
—	—	60.2	—	—	—	...	...	—	14	50	62	...	Sri Lanka
85	—	54.5	...	...	...	300	429	0.7	8	22	815	...	Sudan, The
—	...	...	...	...	...	82	41	2	1.4	—	—	—	Suriname
...	...	11	...	...	...	...	...	...	11	—	—	—	Swaziland
—	—	37.9	836	...	...	...	...	—	130	428	—	—	Sweden
—	—	14.6[21]	2,466[21]	38.3[9]	61.7[9]	...	...	...	33[21]	132	314	1,265	Switzerland
198	4,151	11.9	1,950	...	...	2,500	12	208	85	242	1,819	...	Syria
68	827	...	...	...	...	4	10	0.4	...	543	615	...	Taiwan
...	49[7]	...	1,438	...	...	...	...	0.3[7]	1	...	...	...	Tajikistan
116	—	100.0		...	...	...	...		4	17	000	...	Tanzania
174	9,330	14.8	9,107	—	100.0	218	11	20	118	347	67	...	Thailand
—	...	...	...	...	...	...	...	...	...	—	—	—	Togo
...	...	...	...	...	...	...	...	...	...	—	—	—	Tonga
240	6,054	4.0	5,194	1.8	98.2	488	10	47	38	245	1,051	...	Trinidad and Tobago
30	235	10.0	1,081	9.1	90.9	416	13	33	13	34	883	...	Tunisia
11	195	31.2	4,771	...	...	488	19	26	182	713	4,059	2,994	Turkey
326[6]	84,300[8]	...	9,874	...	...	740[6]	17	32[7]	36	234	250	...	Turkmenistan
...	...	...	...	...	...	...	...	...	...	—	—	—	Tuvalu
...	...	...	...	...	...	...	...	...	...	—	—	—	Uganda
...	19,502[7]	0.8	99,183	...	...	...	...	31[7]	175	1,259	3,930	38,402	Ukraine
5,794	23,948	17.6	19,521	...	...	98,100	121	814	67	193	830	...	United Arab Emirates
630	76,294	12.6	76,310	52.7[9]	47.3[9]	4,517	5	914	626	1,869	3,926	10,388	United Kingdom
4,599	558,978	17.4	582,138	33.4[12]	66.6[12]	22,957	9	2,424	4,975	15,319	276,000	843,586	United States
—	—	40.6	—	—	—	...	...	...	3	35	—	—	Uruguay
...	40,226	...	37,954	...	...	...	...	40	47	175	290	200	Uzbekistan
...	...	...	...	...	...	...	...	...	...	—	—	—	Vanuatu
3,693	23,591	18.8	23,229	9.1	90.9	64,477	72	899	341	1,167	6,850	...	Venezuela
105	697	...	3	...	...	500	10	49	0.3	—	150	...	Vietnam
—	—	97.6	...	...	...	...	...	...	115	545	—	—	Virgin Islands (U.S.)
...	...	...	...	...	...	...	...	...	...	—	—	—	West Bank
...	...	...	...	...	...	...	...	...	...	—	—	—	Western Sahara
...	...	...	...	...	...	...	...	...	...	—	—	—	Western Samoa
425	...	38.7	...	...	...	4,000	32	126	43	120	676	—	Yemen
45	765	0.7	1,946	...	...	78	10	8	12	168	545	...	Yugoslavia
1.4	—	7.8	—	—	—	187	21	9	3	17	390	...	Zaire
—	—	100.0	—	—	—	...	...	...	4	24	1,724	...	Zambia
...	—	89.9	—	—	—	...	...	...	...	—	212	...	Zimbabwe

[1]Estimated reserves in place. [2]1981. [3]1985. [4]1984. [5]1990. [6]1992. [7]1993. [8]1991. [9]1983. [10]Belgium includes Luxembourg. [11]South Africa includes Botswana, Lesotho, Namibia, and Swaziland. [12]1982. [13]Data refer to former Czechoslovakia. [14]Geothermally generated electricity. [15]France includes Monaco. [16]Transportation and industry only; excludes agricultural, commercial, and public-service sectors. [17]Data refer to former West Germany only. [18]1988. [19]Italy includes San Marino. [20]1989. [21]Switzerland includes Liechtenstein. [22]Data refer to former U.S.S.R. [23]Data refer to Yugoslavia as constituted prior to 1991.

Transportation

This table presents data on the transportation infrastructure of the various countries and dependencies of the world and on their commercial passenger and cargo traffic. Most states have roads and airports, with services corresponding to the prevailing level of economic development. A number of states, however, lack railroads or inland waterways because of either geographic constraints or lack of development capital and technical expertise. Pipelines, one of the oldest means of bulk transport if aqueducts are considered, are today among the most narrowly developed transportation modes worldwide for shipment of bulk materials. Because the principal contemporary application of pipeline technology is to facilitate the shipment of hydrocarbon liquids and gases, coverage of pipelines will be found in the "Energy" table. It is, however, also true that pipelines now find increasing application for slurries of coal or other raw materials.

While the United Nations' *Statistical Yearbook* and *Monthly Bulletin of Statistics* provide much data on infrastructure and traffic and have established basic definitions and classifications for transportation statistics, the number of countries covered is limited. Several commercial publications maintain substantial databases and publishing programs for their particular areas of interest: highway and vehicle statistics are provided by the International Road Federation's annual *World Road Statistics;* the International Union of Railways' *International Railway Statistics* and Jane's *World Railways* provide similar data for railways; Lloyd's *Register of Shipping Statistical Tables* summarizes the world's merchant marine; the *Official Airline Guide,* the International Civil Aviation Organization's *Digest of Statistics: Commercial Air Carriers,* and the International Air Transport Association's *World Air Transport Statistics* have also been used to supplement and update data collected by the UN. Because several of these agencies are commercially or insurance-oriented, their data tend to be more complete, accurate, and timely than those of intergovernmental organizations, which depend on periodic responses to questionnaires or publication of results in official sources. All of these international sources have been extensively supplemented by national statistical sources to provide additional data. Such diversity of sources, however, imposes limitations on the comparability of the statistics from country to country because the basis and completeness of data collection and the frequency and timeliness of analysis and publication may vary greatly. Data shown in italic are from 1990 or earlier.

The categories adopted in the table also have special problems of comparability. Total road length is subject to wide international variation of interpretation, as "roads" can mean anything from mere tracks to highly developed highways. Each country also has individual classifications that differ according to climate, availability of road-building materials, traffic patterns, administrative responsibility, and so on. "Paved roads," by contrast, is a much more tightly definable category, but the proportion of paved to total roads may be distorted by the less comparable total road statistics. Automobile and truck and bus fleet statistics, which are usually

Transportation

country	roads and motor vehicles (latest)								railroads (latest)					
	roads			motor vehicles			cargo		track length		traffic			
	length		paved (per-cent)	auto-mobiles	trucks and buses	persons per vehicle	short ton-mi ('000,-000)	metric ton-km ('000,-000)	mi	km	passengers		cargo	
	mi	km									passen-ger-mi ('000,000)	passen-ger-km ('000,000)	short ton-mi ('000,000)	metric ton-km ('000,000)
Afghanistan	*11,930*	*19,200*	*47*	31,000	25,000	295	*1,993*	*2,910*	16	25	...	...	...	...
Albania	*4,629*	*7,450*	*38*	16,000	32,900	68	818.5	1,195	447	720	*484.2*	*779.2*	*400*	*584*
Algeria	59,388	95,576	66	725,000	480,000	22	9,589	14,000	2,965[2]	4,772[2]	1,720	2,768	1,569	2,291
American Samoa	217	350	43	5,000	1,800	7.8	...	...	—	—	—	—	—	—
Andorra	167	269	74	36,660	4,362	1.5	...	...	—	—	—	—	—	—
Angola	45,128	72,626	25	122,000	42,200	65	...	...	*1,739*[2]	*2,798*[2]	*203*	*326*	*1,178*	*1,720*
Antigua and Barbuda	721	1,161	33	14,300	3,800	3.5	...	...	—	—	—	—	—	—
Argentina	133,954	215,578	29	4,856,000	1,664,000	5.2	...	...	*21,198*[2]	*34,115*[2]	*6,618*	*10,651*	*5,790*	*8,453*
Armenia	4,800	7,700	99	*230,100*	...	...	46.6	68.0	511	823	270	435	308	450
Aruba	*236*	*380*	*100*	32,060	814	2.1	...	...	—	—	—	—	—	—
Australia	*503,474*	*810,264*	*36*	8,280,211	2,225,659	1.7	60,416	88,206	23,174[2, 7]	37,295[2, 7]	7,152	11,510	61,000	89,000
Austria	68,400	110,000	100	3,367,626	745,987	1.9	6,232	9,099	3,480	5,600	5,988[7]	9,636[7]	8,080[7]	11,796[7]
Azerbaijan	38,972	62,720	94	251,192	104,006	21	3,549	5,181	1,322	2,127	3,025	4,869	9,439	13,781
Bahamas, The	1,491	2,400	56	69,000	14,000	3.2	...	...	—	—	—	—	—	—
Bahrain	1,719	2,767	79	114,045	26,771	3.8	...	...	—	—	—	—	—	—
Bangladesh	*120,100*	*193,283*	*4*	75,409	96,853	655	...	...	1,706[2]	2,746[2]	3,323	5,348	492	718
Barbados	*977*	*1,573*	*95*	43,077	8,479	5.1	...	...	—	—	—	—	—	—
Belarus	31,390	50,518	98	773,582	10,279	13	15,321	22,369	3,410	5,488	11,195	18,017	38,659	56,441
Belgium	*85,672*	*137,876*	*97*	4,109,601	389,812	2.2	18,833	27,495	2,119[2]	3,410[2]	4,159	6,694	5,184	7,568
Belize	1,684	2,710	18	9,989	6,294	12	...	...	—	—	—	—	—	—
Benin	3,770	6,070	20	22,000	12,200	149	...	...	359	578	39.4	63.4	111.3	162.5
Bermuda	120	193	100	20,148	3,300	2.6	...	...	—	—	—	—	—	—
Bhutan	1,502	2,418	79	*2,590*	*1,367*	*348*	...	...	—	—	—	—	—	—
Bolivia	26,370	42,438	4	340,365	185,922	13	*1,133*	*1,654*	2,295[2]	3,694[2]	216.8	348.9	521.9	761.9
Bosnia and Herzegovina	13,153	21,168	54	*438,080*	*50,578*	*8.9*	*2,708*	*3,954*	*646*	*1,039*	...	...	...	...
Botswana	11,933	19,204	13	20,785	42,136	22	...	...	551	887	160	257	867	1,266
Brazil	1,031,693	1,660,352	9	12,974,991	1,371,127	11	*178,359*	*260,400*	18,877[2]	30,379[2]	8,723	14,038	85,439	124,738
Brunei	1,502	2,417	51	122,104	13,658	2.0	...	...	12[13]	19[13]	—	—	...	...
Bulgaria	22,942	36,922	92	1,358,976	130,000	5.8	2,384	3,480	4,044	6,508	3,144	5,059	5,325	7,774
Burkina Faso	8,161	13,134	*12*	11,000	13,300	402	...	...	*308*[2]	*495*[2]	*422*	*680*	*322*	*470*
Burundi	8,993	14,473	7	14,483	14,914	188	...	...	—	—	—	—	—	—
Cambodia	8,296	13,351	20	28,919	9,247	240	7.7	11.3	380	612	*33.6*	*54.0*	*6.9*	*10.0*
Cameroon	30,074	48,400	8	90,000	79,000	74	*175*	*255*	686[2]	1,104[2]	247	398	405	592
Canada	527,794	849,404	37	13,477,896	3,712,486	1.7	*29,033*	*42,388*	53,166	85,563	852	1,371	166,057	242,439
Cape Verde	680	1,095	78	6,479	2,099	43	...	...	—	—	—	—	—	—
Central African Republic	14,750	23,738	2	14,000	6,300	148	62	90	—	—	—	—	—	—
Chad	*24,855*	*40,000*	*1*	9,500	7,200	361	...	...	—	—	—	—	—	—
Chile	49,270	79,293	16	826,794	437,520	11	...	...	4,076[2]	6,560[2]	582	937	1,732	2,528
China	673,239	1,083,476	89	2,859,800	5,010,000	150	278,806	407,050	43,131	69,412	225,990	363,700	853,576	1,246,200
Colombia	66,721	107,377	12	854,160	430,611	26	*4,265*	*6,227*	2,007[2]	3,230[2]	9.6	15.5	166.4	242.9
Comoros	466	750	28	2,000	5,000	68	...	...	—	—	—	—	—	—
Congo	7,919	12,745	10	26,000	20,100	53	*46*	*67*	494	795	340	547	273	399
Costa Rica	22,084	35,541	17	220,142	114,911	9.6	1,536	2,243	590[2]	950[2]	3.6	5.9	45.8	66.8
Côte d'Ivoire	42,250	68,000	8	155,300	90,300	54	...	...	410[2]	660[2]	752[15]	1,210[15]	466[15]	680[15]
Croatia	16,732	26,928	81	646,210	43,513	6.5	603	880	1,676	2,699	610	981	1,212	1,770
Cuba	*28,928*	*46,555*	*27*	*241,300*	*208,400*	*23*	*2,482*	*3,623*	3,033	4,881	1,880	3,025	937	1,368
Cyprus	6,746	10,857	54	203,610	90,209	2.7	...	...	—	—	—	—	—	—
Czech Republic	34,742	55,912	...	2,693,905	354,690	3.4	5,569[17]	8,131[17]	5,866	9,441	5,311	8,548	17,520	25,579
Denmark	44,186	71,111	100	1,674,939	260,833	2.7	7,404	10,809	1,763	2,838	2,793	4,495	1,231	1,797
Djibouti	1,789	2,879	13	13,500	3,000	33	...	...	*66*	*106*	*182*	*293*	*81.7*	*119.3*
Dominica	466	750	66	4,700	5,500	7.0	...	...	—	—	—	—	—	—
Dominican Republic	7,100	11,400	51	117,800	78,900	38	...	...	*65*	*104*	...	...	...	...
Ecuador	28,200	45,400	14	191,746	292,830	23	2,147	3,135	594[2]	956[2]	29.9	48.2	3.6	5.3
Egypt	29,445[19]	47,387[19]	73[19]	1,119,727	466,650	36	21,480	31,361	5,274	8,487	29,821	47,992	1,597	2,332
El Salvador	7,791	12,539	16	95,670	150,385	22	...	...	374[2]	602[2]	3.8	6.1	24.2	35.4

based upon registration, are relatively accurate, though some countries round off figures, and unregistered vehicles may cause substantial undercount. There is also inconsistent classification of vehicle types; in some countries a vehicle may serve variously as an automobile, a truck, or a bus, or even as all three on certain occasions. Relatively few countries collect and maintain commercial road traffic statistics.

Data on national railway systems are generally given for railway track length rather than the length of routes, which may be multitracked. Siding tracks usually are not included, but some countries fail to distinguish them. The United States data include only class 1 railways, which account for about 94 percent of total track length. Passenger traffic is usually calculated from tickets sold to fare-paying passengers. Such statistics are subject to distortion if there are large numbers of nonpaying passengers, such as military personnel, or if season tickets are sold and not all the allowed journeys are utilized. Railway cargo traffic is calculated by weight hauled multiplied by the length of the journey. Changes in freight load during the journey should be accounted for but sometimes are not, leading to discrepancies.

Merchant fleet and tonnage statistics collected by Lloyd's registry service for vessels over 100 gross tons are quite accurate. Cargo statistics, however, reflect the port and customs requirements of each country and the reporting rules of each country's merchant marine authority (although these, increasingly, reflect the recommendations of the International Maritime Organization); often, however, they are only estimates based on customs declarations and the count of vessels entered and cleared. Even when these elements are reported consistently, further uncertainties may be introduced because of ballast, bunkers, ships' stores, or transshipped goods included in the data.

Airport data are based on scheduled flights reported in the commercial *Official Airline Guide* and are both reliable and current. The comparability of civil air traffic statistics suffers from differing characteristics of the air transportation systems of different countries; data for an entire country may be two to three years behind those for a single airport.

Outside of Europe, where standardization of data on inland waterways is necessitated by the volume of international traffic, comparability of national data declines markedly. Calculations as to both the length of a country's waterway system (or route length of river, lake, and coastal traffic) and the makeup of its stock of commercially significant vessels (those for which data will be collected) are largely determined by the nature and use of the country's hydrographic net—its seasonality, relief profile, depth, access to potential markets—and inevitably differ widely from country to country. Data for coastal or island states may refer to scheduled coastwise or interisland traffic.

merchant marine				air					canals and inland waterways (latest)				country
fleet, 1992 (vessels over 100 gross tons)	total dead-weight tonnage, 1992 ('000)	international cargo (latest)		airports with sched-uled flights, 1995	traffic (latest)				length		cargo		
					passengers		cargo						
		loaded metric tons ('000)	off-loaded metric tons ('000)		passenger-mi ('000,000)	passenger-km ('000,000)	short ton-mi ('000,000)	metric ton-km ('000,000)	mi	km	short ton-mi ('000,000)	metric ton-km ('000,000)	
—	—	—	—	3	127[1]	205[1]	5.5[1]	8.0[1]	750	1,200	...	...	Afghanistan
24	81.0	*1,065*	*664*	1	...	...	...	...	27	43	21	35	Albania
149	1,093.4	*57,607*	*14,284*	28	2,010[3]	3,234[3]	13.8[3]	20.2[3]	...	...	...	...	Algeria
3	0.1	*380*	*733*	3	...	...	...	...	...	...	...	...	American Samoa
—	—	—	—	—	—	—	...	...	—	—	—	—	Andorra
113	123.5	23,288	1,261	17	771[4]	1,241[4]	28.8[4]	42.0[4]	805	1,295	...	...	Angola
292	997.4	*28*	*113*	2	121	195	0.1	0.2	...	...	...	...	Antigua and Barbuda
423	1,173.1	36,792	6,864	42	4,816[5]	7,751[5]	120.8[5]	176.4[5]	6,800	11,000	*19,326*	*28,215*	Argentina
...	...	...	...	2	138.1	222.2	17.6	25.7	...	...	...	...	Armenia
[6]	[6]		...	1	...	...	...	...	...	...	...	...	Aruba
695	3,857.3	332,124	40,284	428	25,649	41,270	1,766	2,578	5,200	8,368	*66,439*	*97,000*	Australia
26	208.6	1,267	4,419	6	4,552	7,325	94.6	138.1	277	446	4,299	6,276	Austria
...	...	...	...	1	*3,025*	*4,869*	...	...	...	...	3,775	5,512	Azerbaijan
1,061	33,081.7	*5,920*	*5,705*	24	215	346	0.2	0.3	...	...	...	...	Bahamas, The
87	192.5	*13,285*	*3,512*	1	1,515[8]	2,439[8]	73.4[8]	107.1[8]	...	...	...	...	Bahrain
301	566.8	1,740	9,000	8	1,588	2,556	190	278	5,000	8,046	...	...	Bangladesh
37	84.0	*206*	*538*	1	*93*[9]	*149*[9]	*0.8*[10]	*1.1*[10]	...	...	...	...	Barbados
...	18,373.0	...	...	1	3,487	5,611	23	34	...	...	678	990	Belarus
232	218.5	57,168	88,908	2	4,658	7,497	289.1	422.1	1,269	2,043	3,482	5,083	Belgium
32	45.7	*178*	*241*	9	...	...	...	...	513	825	...	...	Belize
12	0.2	246	1,489	1	106.0[11]	217.2[11]	23.4[11]	34.2[11]	...	...	...	...	Benin
94	5,206.5	*130*	*470*	1		...	...	...	...	...	...	...	Bermuda
—	—	—	—	1	*2.7*	*4.4*	...	...	—	—	—	—	Bhutan
1	15.8	...	...	21	729	1,173	108.5	158.4	6,214	10,000	*90*	*132*	Bolivia
...	...	...	...	1	...	...	...	...	...	...	...	...	Bosnia and Herzegovina
—	—	—	—	4	36.3[12]	58.4[12]	0.3[12]	0.4[12]	...	...	...	...	Botswana
635	9,348.3	*168,026*	*52,570*	139	20,264	32,612	1,452	2,120	31,069	50,000	*56,030*	*81,803*	Brazil
51	349.7	*13,554*	*1,325*	1	1,261	2,029	64.7	94.4	130	209	...	...	Brunei
222	1,938.2	5,290	20,080	3	2,239	3,604	32.2	47.0	292	470	573	837	Bulgaria
—	—	—	—	2	146	235	11.0	16.0	...	...	...	...	Burkina Faso
1	*0.4*	35	188	1	...	...	...	...	...	...	...	...	Burundi
3	3.8	*11*	*95*	6	...	...	...	...	2,300	3,700	5	8	Cambodia
47	39.8	1,260	2,328	5	187	301	6.8	10.0	1,299	2,090	...	...	Cameroon
1,185	2,896.8	153,795	69,080	244	25,633	41,253	856	1,250	1,860	3,000	...	...	Canada
42	30.9	87	580	9	106	171	13.2	19.2	...	...	...	...	Cape Verde
—	—	*53*	*126*	1	134[11]	216[11]	11.0[11]	16.0[11]	500	800	61	89	Central African Republic
—	—	—	—	4	131	211	11	16	1,240	2,000	...	...	Chad
392	854.9	21,768	13,464	18	2,750	4,425	422	616	450	725	*5,629*	*8,218*	Chile
2,390	20,658.0	105,852	101,688	108	33,100	53,300	1,336	1,950	86,100	138,600	949,386	1,386,080	China
101	403.0	22,332	11,268	70	3,280	5,278	619	904	8,900	14,300	*7,038*	*10,276*	Colombia
6	3.6	12	107	4	*1.9*	*3.0*	...	...	...	...	...	...	Comoros
22	10.8	*8,987*	*736*	3	157	253	12	17	696	1,120	...	...	Congo
24	8.4	*1,605*	*1,892*	13	999[14]	1,607[14]	29.7[14]	43.4[14]	454	730	...	...	Costa Rica
51	98.6	3,853	5,936	7	178[16]	286[16]	11.0[16]	16.0[16]	609	980	...	...	Côte d'Ivoire
203	140.9	4,140	6,252	4	196	316	1.8	2.6	488	785	99	144	Croatia
393	924.6	*8,092*	*15,440*	14	1,908	3,070	23.8	34.8	149	240	*2,085*	*3,044*	Cuba
1,416	36,198.1	2,184	4,968	2	1,903	3,063	24.5	35.8	...	...	...	...	Cyprus
22[17]	446.2[17]	...	...	4	1,588	2,555	46.7	68.2	295	475	864	1,261	Czech Republic
456	7,569.1	17,508	34,368	13	2,714[18]	4,368[18]	91.2[18]	133.2[18]	259	417	1,100	1,600	Denmark
10	4.1	*414*	*958*	1	...	...	...	...	...	...	...	...	Djibouti
7	3.2	103	181	2	...	...	...	...	...	...	...	...	Dominica
28	10.4	*2,550*	*4,182*	5	174	280	1.9	2.8	...	...	...	...	Dominican Republic
154	504.1	*11,783*	*1,958*	14	780	1,255	44.0	64.2	932	1,500	...	...	Ecuador
444	1,685.2	14,808	22,860	14	3,437	5,531	68.8	100.5	2,175	3,500	844	1,232	Egypt
15	...	*221*	*1,023*	1	801[20]	1,289[20]	4.8[20]	7.0[20]	...	...	...	...	El Salvador

Transportation (continued)

country	roads and motor vehicles (latest)								railroads (latest)					
	roads			motor vehicles			cargo		track length		traffic			
	length		paved (per-cent)	auto-mobiles	trucks and buses	persons per vehicle	short ton-mi ('000,-000)	metric ton-km ('000,-000)	mi	km	passengers		cargo	
	mi	km									passen-ger-mi ('000,000)	passen-ger-km ('000,000)	short ton-mi ('000,000)	metric ton-km ('000,000)
Equatorial Guinea	1,667	2,682	19	6,200	4,100	37	...	...	—	—	—	—	—	—
Eritrea	621	1,000	...	...	...	...	...	...	...	...	...	...	...	...
Estonia	9,178	14,771	55	317,400	82,800	3.8	723	1,056	636	1,024	449	722	2,844	4,152
Ethiopia	17,381	27,972	15	37,799	20,939	856	...	...	*486*[21]	*782*[21]	172	277	86	126
Faroe Islands	269	433	...	11,844	3,920	2.9	...	...	—	—	—	—	—	—
Fiji	2,996	4,821	13	43,979	30,899	10	...	...	370[13]	595[13]	...	...	...	...
Finland	47,763	76,868	63	1,872,933	261,364	2.4	17,000	25,000	3,657[2]	5,885[2]	1,514	2,436	6,345	9,264
France	504,055	811,200	*92*	24,385,000	5,065,000	2.0	100,000	146,000	21,173[2]	34,074[2]	36,276	58,380	31,414	45,864
French Guiana	*706*	*1,137*	*40*	*25,000*	*9,000*	*3.4*	...	...	—	—	—	—	—	—
French Polynesia	584	940	42	37,800	15,300	4.0	...	...	—	—	—	—	—	—
Gabon	4,671	7,518	8	24,000	17,500	27	...	...	414	668	*21*	*34*	*126*	*184*
Gambia, The	*1,483*	*2,386*	*32*	7,300	3,100	99	...	...	—	—	—	—	—	—
Gaza Strip	...	...	...	21,206	4,639	29	...	...	—	—	—	—	—	—
Georgia	*21,000*	*33,900*	*87*	*427,400*	...	...	4,168	6,085	*976*	*1,570*	*10.6*	*17.0*	...	...
Germany	395,367	636,282	99	39,086,000	2,923,000	1.9	138,975	202,900	56,813	91,432	35,567	57,240	46,254	72,848
Ghana	22,800	36,700	32	90,000	44,200	117	*873*	*1,275*	592[2]	953[2]	73.1	117.7	93.9	137.1
Gibraltar	27	43	100	18,404	1,064	1.4	...	...	—	—	—	—	—	—
Greece	72,170	116,150	92	2,807,447	848,903	2.8	6,682	9,756	1,552[2]	2,497[2]	1,072	1,726	358	523
Greenland	50	80	...	2,023	1,484	16	...	...	—	—	—	—	—	—
Grenada	650	1,046	66	*4,784*	*981*	*16*	...	...	—	—	—	—	—	—
Guadeloupe	1,480	2,384	*80*	*86,000*	*34,000*	*3.2*	...	...	—	—	—	—	—	—
Guam	419	674	100	61,300	23,800	1.7	...	...	—	—	—	—	—	—
Guatemala	7,363	11,849	26	98,700	95,000	52	...	...	708[2]	1,139[2]	*6.3*	*10.1*	92.5	135.1
Guernsey	...	...	...	33,037	7,522	1.6	...	...	—	—	—	—	—	—
Guinea	9,974	16,051	9	24,000	13,500	168	...	...	411[2]	662[2]	...	...	...	...
Guinea-Bissau	2,579	4,150	9	3,700	2,600	163	...	...	—	—	—	—	—	—
Guyana	4,474	7,200	10	24,000	9,000	23	...	...	116[13]	187[13]	...	...	...	...
Haiti	2,485	4,000	15	32,000	21,000	120	...	...	—	—	—	—	—	—
Honduras	8,825	14,203	18	67,777	128,264	26	...	...	614	988	*4.8*	*7.7*	*20.7*	*30.2*
Hong Kong	1,010	1,625	100	311,929	158,107	13	...	...	21	34	1,971	3,172	75	109
Hungary	98,618	158,711	44	2,058,334	288,914	4.4	2,314	3,379	8,200	13,200	5,706	9,183	6,860	10,015
Iceland	7,008	11,279	24	116,195	15,644	2.0	*318*	*464*	—	—	—	—	—	—
India	1,342,000	2,160,000	46	3,330,000	1,980,000	170	*144,000*	*210,000*	38,189[2]	61,459[2]	195,926	315,313	171,213	249,966
Indonesia	196,016	315,458	43	1,676,781	1,554,582	59	*17,000*	*25,000*	4,090	6,583	7,690	12,376	2,803	4,092
Iran	94,130	151,488	*34*	1,557,000	584,100	27	*46,750*	*68,250*	3,014[2]	4,851[2]	2,848	4,584	5,277	7,704
Iraq	*28,305*	*45,554*	*84*	672,000	368,000	18	...	...	1,493[2]	2,403[2]	572	920	79	115
Ireland	57,369	92,327	94	891,027	146,204	3.4	3,519	5,138	1,749	2,814	665.5	1,071	393.6	574.6
Isle of Man	357	574	58	43,450	4,753	1.4	...	...	37[2]	59[2]	...	...	...	...
Israel	8,620	13,872	100	988,176	222,108	4.3	...	...	356[2]	573[2]	134	215	734	1,072
Italy	188,597	303,518	100	29,600,000	2,745,500	1.8	125,171	182,746	12,176	19,595	30,050	48,361	15,091	22,033
Jamaica	10,212	16,435	29	73,015	30,548	24	...	...	129[2]	208[2]	12.1	19.5	1.7	2.5
Japan	702,702	1,130,892	72	40,772,407	22,493,773	2.0	192,879	281,599	23,690	38,125	250,242	402,727	17,420	25,433
Jersey	...	...	...	58,491	9,922	1.3	...	...	—	—	—	—	—	—
Jordan	3,958	6,370	100	162,000	91,600	15	*19,133*	*27,934*	490[2]	788[2]	*3.7*	*6.0*	542	791
Kazakhstan	102,500	164,900	69	*734,800*	...	...	20.0	29.2	13,200	21,200	12,100	19,400	256.3	374.2
Kenya	39,400	63,400	14	157,166	133,968	88	*134*	*196*	1,885[2]	3,034[2]	288	464	899	1,312
Kiribati	398	640	5	*307*	*130*	*147*	...	...	—	—	—	—	—	—
Korea, North	18,600	30,000	8	*248,000*	...	...	...	...	*5,302*	*8,533*	*2,100*	*3,400*	*6,200*	*9,100*
Korea, South	38,087	61,296	85	4,271,253	2,002,755	7.0	33,475	48,873	4,049	6,517	18,775	30,216	9,633	14,064
Kuwait	*2,655*	*4,273*	*100*	530,000	144,300	2.2	...	...	—	—	—	—	—	—
Kyrgyzstan	*11,900*	*19,100*	*86*	*173,800*	...	...	3.0	4.4	*490*	*789*	81.5	131.2	1,088	1,589
Laos	8,780	14,130	16	20,233	12,987	135	36.2	52.8	—	—	—	—	—	—
Latvia	37,421	60,224	55	351,000	85,000	5.9	1,200	1,700	1,499	2,413	1,484	2,388	6,732	9,828
Lebanon	*4,579*	*7,370*	*85*	*473,372*	*49,560*	*5.0*	...	...	138	222	*5.3*	*8.6*	29	*42*
Lesotho	3,308	5,324	15	5,944	17,785	82	...	...	1.6	2.6	...	...	...	...
Liberia	3,787	6,095	39	8,000	3,100	214	...	...	*304*[2]	*490*[2]	...	...	*1,746*[13]	*2,549*[13]
Libya	12,000	19,300	56	448,000	322,000	6.3	...	...	—	—	—	—	—	—
Liechtenstein	201	323	...	17,767	1,817	1.5	...	...	12	19	...	...	...	...
Lithuania	34,550	55,603	76	597,735	93,920	5.4	4,730	6,906	1,862	2,996	547	880	7,555	11,030
Luxembourg	3,190	5,134	99	217,754	25,050	1.7	*164*	*239*	171[2]	275[2]	176	284	443	647
Macau	*60*	*97*	*100*	29,894	5,692	11	...	...	—	—	—	—	—	—
Macedonia	5,223	8,406	60	279,861	25,574	6.7	975	1,424	573	922	64	103	395	577
Madagascar	21,586	34,739	15	47,000	33,300	172	*220*	*321*	640[2]	1,030[2]	152	245	90	132
Malaŵi	*7,590*	*12,215*	22	15,000	18,900	315	—	—	495[2]	797[2]	28.3	45.5	29.0	42.3
Malaysia	57,505	92,545	75	2,147,974	472,414	7.1	...	...	1,381	2,222	1,148[29]	1,848[29]	945[29]	1,380[29]
Maldives	...	...	...	823	869	141	...	...	—	—	—	—	—	—
Mali	*11,185*	*18,000*	*8*	21,000	8,400	294	...	...	*399*[2]	*642*[2]	*304.2*	*489.5*	*187.2*	*273.3*
Malta	988	1,588	92	120,320	27,978	2.4	...	...	—	—	—	—	—	—
Marshall Islands	...	...	...	1,418	193	34	...	...	—	—	—	—	—	—
Martinique	1,286	2,069	*75*	*135,269*	*7,328*	*2.3*	...	...	—	—	—	—	—	—
Mauritania	4,683	7,536	24	8,000	5,500	160	...	...	416[2]	670[2]	*4.4*	*7.0*	3,860	5,635
Mauritius	1,138	1,831	93	33,613	9,846	25	...	...	—	—	—	—	—	—
Mayotte	*143*	*230*	*49*	——*1,528*——		*40*	...	...	—	—	—	—	—	—
Mexico	157,036	252,725	36	8,014,143	3,758,034	7.4	96,049	140,229	12,784[2]	20,515[2]	2,408	3,875	23,973	35,001
Micronesia	*140*	*226*	*17*	...	...	...	...	...	—	—	—	—	—	—
Moldova	6,400	10,300	94	221,883	20,409	18	2,587	3,777	715	1,150	5,515	8,875	10,279	15,007
Monaco	31	50	100	17,000	3,700	1.5	...	...	1	2	...	...	...	...
Mongolia	*30,600*	*49,200*	2	*5,660*	*29,794*	*58*	183.8	268.4	1,445	2,325	361.9	582.5	1,734	2,531
Morocco	36,955	59,474	50	864,652	316,941	22	*830*	*1,212*	1,099[2]	1,768[2]	1,186	1,908	3,025	4,416
Mozambique	16,955	27,287	17	35,000	35,000	224	...	...	1,946	3,131	16.2	26.0	421.9	616.0
Myanmar (Burma)	15,118	24,330	16	36,000	36,000	619	*71*	*103.7*	2,945	4,740	2,908	4,680	444	648
Namibia	26,024	41,882	11	54,000	59,000	14	...	...	1,481	2,383	1,248	2,008	840	1,226
Nauru	17	27	78	——*1,448*——		*6.3*	...	...	3[13]	5[13]	...	...	*4.7*	*6.8*
Nepal	5,884	9,470	36	4,949	3,363	2,259	*984*	*1,437*	33[2]	53[2]	...	...	...	...
Netherlands, The	73,908	118,943	89	5,755,000	679,000	2.4	17,553	25,627	1,713	2,757	9,472	15,245	1,836	2,681

merchant marine				air					canals and inland waterways (latest)				country
fleet, 1992 (vessels over 100 gross tons)	total dead-weight tonnage, 1992 ('000)	international cargo (latest)		airports with sched-uled flights, 1995	traffic (latest)				length		cargo		
		loaded metric tons ('000)	off-loaded metric tons ('000)		passengers		cargo		mi	km	short ton-mi ('000,000)	metric ton-km ('000,000)	
					passenger-mi ('000,000)	passenger-km ('000,000)	short ton-mi ('000,000)	metric ton-km ('000,000)					
3	6.7	100	60	1	4	7	0.7	1.0	...	...	...	...	Equatorial Guinea
...	...	...	...	2	...	...	...	...	...	...	...	...	Eritrea
234	680.4	7,068	4,308	2	141.8	228.2	0.3	0.4	311	500	0.3	0.4	Estonia
27	84.3	592	3,120	25	998	1,607	75.5	110.3	...	...	...	...	Ethiopia
191	59.8	190	350	1	...	...	...	...	...	...	...	...	Faroe Islands
64	60.4	568	625	13	671	1,080	38.2	55.8	126	203	...	...	Fiji
263	989.3	35,604	38,640	25	5,142	8,275	115.4	168.5	4,148	6,675	2,055	3,000	Finland
729	4,981.0	61,200	182,400	63	33,012[22]	53,128[22]	6,230[22]	9,096[22]	9,278	14,932	4,110	6,000	France
7	0.7	73	638	8	...	...	...	...	286	460	...	...	French Guiana
41	16.5	15	666	36	...	...	...	...	...	...	...	...	French Polynesia
29	30.2	12,828	212	16	276.7	445.3	17.9	26.1	994	1,600	...	...	Gabon
11	2.0	169	212	1	...	...	...	...	250	400	...	...	Gambia, The
—	—	...	...	—	...	...	...	...	—	—	...	...	Gaza Strip
...	...	...	...	1	3,291	5,296	...	...	...	...	...	...	Georgia
1,375	6,832.3	64,980	124,824	40	60,997	98,166	9,725	14,198	4,686	7,541	37,877	55,300	Germany
155	131.0	1,810	2,842	1	296.7	477.5	16.3	23.8	803	1,293	75	110	Ghana
49	1,136.1	5	400	1	...	...	...	...	—	—	...	...	Gibraltar
1,872	45,276.6	18,465	32,429	31	4,908	7,899	87.0	127.0	50	80	585	854	Greece
82	17.2	298	288	5	16.3	26.3	0.23	0.34	...	...	...	...	Greenland
3	0.5	25	190	2	...	...	...	...	...	...	...	...	Grenada
20	4.4	423	2,178	6	...	...	...	...	...	...	...	...	Guadeloupe
5	0.1	195	1,524	1	...	...	...	...	...	...	...	...	Guam
8	0.4	1,818	3,025	2	239	384	14	21	162	260	...	...	Guatemala
—	—	...	...	1	...	...	...	...	...	...	...	...	Guernsey
23	1.7	12,210	712	2	17.9	28.8	1.7	2.5	805	1,295	...	...	Guinea
19	1.8	40	315	2	6	9	0.7	1.0	...	...	...	...	Guinea-Bissau
82	13.5	1,730	673	1	200	322	1.9	2.8	3,700	6,000	...	...	Guyana
4	0.4	170	704	2	...	...	...	...	60	100	...	...	Haiti
966	1,437.3	1,316	1,002	8	321[23]	516[23]	2.0[23]	3.0[23]	289	465	...	...	Honduras
387	11,688.6	34,272[24]	76,668[24]	1	...	...	...	...	...	...	...	...	Hong Kong
15	134.5	...	...	1	1,027	1,653	12.1	17.7	1,008	1,622	3,540	5,169	Hungary
394	114.9	927	1,633	24	1,474	2,372	28.8	42.0	...	...	58	84	Iceland
888	10,365.9	53,220	75,000	66	10,878	17,506	379.7	554.3	10,054	16,180	...	...	India
2,014	3,130.2	226,980	36,252	122	12,273	19,751	458.4	669.3	13,409	21,579	17,000	25,000	Indonesia
403	8,345.3	113,207	16,719	20	3,121	5,023	54.0	78.8	562	904	...	...	Iran
131	1,578.8	97,830	8,638	...	976	1,570	37.4	54.6	631	1,015	...	...	Iraq
189	208.6	6,367	17,637	10	2,660	4,281	69.3	101.2	...	...	...	...	Ireland
101	2,836.5	6	203	1	115.5	185.9	0.2	0.3	...	...	...	...	Isle of Man
58	723.4	8,448	20,964	7	5,930[25]	9,544[25]	654.4[25]	955.4[25]	...	...	...	...	Israel
1,030	10,940.1	51,420	222,060	32	18,429[26]	29,659[26]	914.3[26]	1,335[26]	1,500	2,400	59	86	Italy
12	16.2	8,802	5,285	4	934.8	1,504	107.2	156.6	...	...	...	...	Jamaica
10,001	67,015.0	111,160	751,404	74	69,346	111,602	3,697	5,308	1,100	1,770	169,867	248,002	Japan
—	—	...	...	1	...	...	...	...	...	...	...	...	Jersey
5	113.6	8,868	6,168	2	1,455	2,342	81.9	119.5	...	...	19,202	28,035	Jordan
...	...	...	...	6	7,800	12,600	48.0	70.0	...	...	175	255	Kazakhstan
29	11.6	1,596	4,884	14	1,079[27]	1,737[27]	39.2[27]	57.2[27]	...	...	...	...	Kenya
7	2.7	15	26	18	5.3	8.6	0.5	0.8	3	5	...	...	Kiribati
100	951.2	635	5,520	1	...	...	...	...	1,400	2,253	...	...	Korea, North
2,138	11,724.9	74,736	273,672	14	24,395	39,260	3,306	4,826	1,000	1,609	26,552	38,765	Korea, South
209	3,188.5	51,400	4,522	1	2,805	4,514	195.1	284.8	...	...	...	...	Kuwait
...	...	...	...	1	1,602	2,578	158.8	231.9	...	...	10	15	Kyrgyzstan
1	1.3	—	—	11	27	44	3.0	5.0	2,850	4,587	24	35	Laos
261	1,136.0	22,540	3,904	1	1,863	2,999	15.1	22.0	186	300	0.7	1	Latvia
163	400.2	152	1,150	1	987	1,588	26.3	38.4	...	...	...	...	Lebanon
—	—	—	—	1	4.8	7.7	0.2	0.3	—	—	—	—	Lesotho
1,672	97,374.0	14,900	1,520	2	4.3	7.0	0.7	1.0	...	...	...	...	Liberia
150	1,223.6	67,000	12,200	12	264.2[28]	425.2[28]	0.2[28]	0.3[28]	—	—	...	...	Libya
—	—	—	—	—	—	—	—	—	...	...	...	...	Liechtenstein
52	373.9	11,736	2,784	3	135.1	217.5	0.8	1.1	373	600	34	50	Lithuania
54	2,603.6	—	—	1	79.5	232	338	886.1	23	37	232	338	Luxembourg
6	0.1	755	3,935	—	—	—	—	—	...	...	...	...	Macau
...	...	...	...	1	181.7	292.4	...	...	...	...	...	...	Macedonia
85	82.1	540	984	18	268.2	431.7	45.2	66.1	...	...	...	...	Madagascar
1	0.3	...	...	6	165.2	265.9	10.1	14.8	891	1,434	6.7	9.8	Malawi
552	2,916.3	66,025	35,760	38	10,853	17,466	524.6	765.9	4,534	7,296	...	...	Malaysia
44	79.0	27	78	1	1.9	3.0	...	...	...	...	...	...	Maldives
—	—	—	—	1	134.9	217.2	23.4	34.2	1,128	1,815	18	27	Mali
889	17,073.2	90	2,458	1	777	1,250	5.0	7.3	...	...	...	...	Malta
35	4,182.4	29	123	23	32	52	2.4	3.5	...	...	...	...	Marshall Islands
6	1.1	516	1,440	2	...	...	...	...	...	...	...	...	Martinique
126	23.9	10,037	674	10	171	275	28	41	...	...	...	...	Mauritania
35	152.2	956	2,232	1	1,841	2,963	67.4	98.3	...	...	...	...	Mauritius
1	1.1	—	—	1	...	...	...	...	...	...	...	...	Mayotte
635	1,495.3	129,696	52,716	83	11,879[30]	19,118[30]	1,249[30]	1,823[30]	1,800	2,900	...	...	Mexico
17	6.9	...	...	4	...	...	...	...	...	...	...	...	Micronesia
...	...	...	...	1	1,461	2,352	13.0	19.0	...	...	18	27	Moldova
1	...	...	...	1	—	—	...	...	...	...	...	...	Monaco
—	—	—	—	1	179.9	289.6	4.0	5.8	247	397	2.9	4.3	Mongolia
492	586.2	19,476	21,120	16	2,731	4,395	36.5	53.3	...	...	2,622	3,828	Morocco
107	31.6	2,800	3,400	8	253	407	7.1	10.3	2,330	3,750	...	...	Mozambique
144	1,354.0	1,343	1,284	19	137.7	221.6	5.6	8.2	7,954	12,800	236.5	345.3	Myanmar (Burma)
30	5.9	483	260	12	332	535	40	59	...	...	...	...	Namibia
2	5.8	1,650	59	1	148[31]	238[31]	1.1[31]	1.6[31]	...	...	...	...	Nauru
—	—	—	—	24	439	706	7.5	11.0	...	...	...	...	Nepal
1,076	4,191.0	88,476	277,008	5	23,713	38,163	1,895	2,766	3,939	6,340	4,032	5,886	Netherlands, The

Transportation (continued)

country	roads and motor vehicles (latest)								railroads (latest)					
	roads			motor vehicles			cargo		track length		traffic			
	length		paved (per-cent)	auto-mobiles	trucks and buses	persons per vehicle	short ton-mi ('000,-000)	metric ton-km ('000,-000)	mi	km	passengers		cargo	
	mi	km									passen-ger-mi ('000,000)	passen-ger-km ('000,000)	short ton-mi ('000,000)	metric ton-km ('000,000)
Netherlands Antilles	368	592	51	66,327	14,057	2.4	...	...	—	—	—	—	—	—
New Caledonia	3,580	5,762	22	56,700	21,200	2.3	...	...	—	—	—	—	—	—
New Zealand	58,605	94,315	73	1,600,499	352,997	1.8	...	...	2,469	3,973	*285*	*458*	1,700	2,500
Nicaragua	9,499	15,287	10	31,300	43,600	57	...	...	186[2]	300[2]	*15.8*	*25.5*	*46.6*	*68.0*
Niger	12,244	19,705	22	*31,427*	*8,768*	*192*	*1,044*	*1,524*	—	—	—	—	—	—
Nigeria	69,680	112,140	28	773,000	606,000	66	...	...	*2,210*	*3,557*	281	453	1,281	1,870
Northern Mariana Islands	307	494	27	12,000	6,300	3.0	...	...	—	—	—	—	—	—
Norway	56,031	90,174	70	1,653,678	404,108	2.1	5,179	7,561	2,502[2]	4,026[2]	1,437	2,312	1,575	2,300
Oman	16,372	26,349	20	180,700	108,600	6.9	...	...	—	—	—	—	—	—
Pakistan	121,119	194,922	54	732,100	252,023	135	260	379	5,453[2]	8,775[2]	10,208	16,428	4,011	5,856
Palau	...	...	...	...	...	...	...	...	...	...	...	...	...	...
Panama	6,304	10,146	33	161,500	82,800	10	...	...	220[2]	354[2]	*0.3*	*0.6*	0.5	0.7
Papua New Guinea	*12,263*	*19,736*	*6*	11,500	30,800	97	...	...	—	—	—	—	—	—
Paraguay	18,217	29,317	10	*117,067*	*3,375*	*36*	...	...	274[2]	441[2]	2.9	4.6	4.3	6.3
Peru	43,460	69,942	11	418,648	275,094	33	...	...	1,318[2]	2,121[2]	102.7	165.3	605.8	884.4
Philippines	99,860	160,709	16	1,078,895	1,024,051	32	...	...	658[2]	1,059[2]	75.2	121.1	3.5	5.1
Poland	225,629	363,116	62	6,771,000	1,321,000	4.8	39,110	57,100	15,488	24,926	19,179	30,865	44,082	64,359
Portugal	*43,605*	*70,176*	*86*	2,210,000	759,100	3.3	7,258	10,597	2,066[2]	3,325[2]	3,538	5,694	1,279	1,867
Puerto Rico	14,089	22,673	87	1,420,000	227,000	2.2	...	...	—	—	—	—	—	—
Qatar	*671*	*1,080*	*63*	123,200	59,000	3.1	...	...	—	—	—	—	—	—
Réunion	1,684	2,710	79	173,200	61,600	2.7	...	...	—	—	—	—	—	—
Romania	95,099	153,014	51	1,793,054	342,492	11	9,955	14,534	7,051	11,348	12,057	19,404	17,244	25,176
Russia	585,000	942,000	79	10,499,000	407,000	14	26,000	38,000	94,400	152,000	141,100	227,100	819	1,195
Rwanda	8,283	13,330	6	7,868	2,048	697	*140*	*200*	—	—	—	—	—	—
St. Kitts and Nevis	186	300	42	*4,000*	*700*	*10*	...	...	—	—	—	—	—	—
St. Lucia	500	805	56	10,000	9,200	7.3	...	...	—	—	—	—	—	—
St. Vincent and the Grenadines	586	943	16	4,591	2,878	15	...	...	—	—	—	—	—	—
San Marino	*147*	*237*	...	22,945	3,843	0.9	...	...	—	—	—	—	—	—
São Tomé and Príncipe	149	240	42	*2,600*	*300*	*39*	...	...	—	—	—	—	—	—
Saudi Arabia	94,157	151,532	40	2,762,132	2,286,541	3.3	...	...	864[2]	1,390[2]	94	151	523	763
Senegal	9,625	15,490	27	102,000	46,000	53	*375*	*547*	562	904	108	174	418	610
Seychelles	201	323	72	5,000	2,000	10	...	...	—	—	—	—	—	—
Sierra Leone	7,254	11,674	11	32,415	11,902	97	*36*	*53*	*52*	*84*	...	...	...	...
Singapore	1,857	2,989	97	340,647	134,042	6.2	...	...	42	67	...	...	...	...
Slovakia	11,110	17,880	...	994,933	160,328	4.6	...	...	2,275	3,661	3,444	5,543	11,436	16,697
Slovenia	9,198	14,803	77	632,563	43,824	2.9	3.9	5.7	746	1,201	352	566	1,549	2,262
Solomon Islands	840	1,352	35	2,052	2,574	75	...	...	—	—	—	—	—	—
Somalia	13,500	21,700	28	10,700	12,000	287	...	...	—	—	—	—	—	—
South Africa	117,010	188,309	29	3,488,570	1,899,721	7.4	*1,053*	*1,538*	12,399[2]	19,955[2]	556	895	62,605	91,402
Spain	206,271	331,961	99	13,440,694	2,859,438	2.4	105,824	154,500	7,830[2]	12,601[2]	9,605	15,457	5,303	7,742
Sri Lanka	16,158	26,004	81	197,300	165,228	49	*3,373*	*4,925*	928[2]	1,493[2]	1,894	3,048	106.9	156.0
Sudan, The	12,400	20,000	8	116,000	57,000	143	...	...	2,960[2]	4,764[2]	330	531	666	972
Suriname	*5,687*	*9,153*	*29*	42,509	15,742	7.1	...	...	187	301	...	...	...	...
Swaziland	1,839	2,960	59	25,946	7,734	25	...	...	199	320	752	1,210	1,993	2,910
Sweden	84,419	135,859	72	3,566,040	315,994	2.2	20,000	29,000	7,012	11,285	3,712	5,975	12,725	18,578
Switzerland	44,201	71,134	96	3,137,619	286,501	2.0	6,863	10,020	3,125	5,029	7,464	12,012	5,022	7,332
Syria	22,528	36,255	77	125,807	186,366	43	*1,075*	*1,570*	1,405[2]	2,261[2]	775	1,248	1,167	1,704
Taiwan	11,830	19,038	89	3,798,800	815,500	4.6	8,967	13,091	2,410	3,879	5,906	9,505	1,334	1,947
Tajikistan	*8,324*	*13,396*	*93*	*209,100*	...	...	*3,518*	*5,136*	*554*	*891*	*6,094*	*9,808*	*7,617*	*11,121*
Tanzania	55,000	88,000	4	44,000	57,200	262	...	...	1,600	2,600	2,324	3,740	1,021	1,490
Thailand	35,358	56,903	78	1,091,085	2,472,063	16	...	...	2,405[2]	3,870[2]	9,145	14,718	2,095	3,059
Togo	4,688	7,545	24	25,000	16,100	95	...	...	326	525	82	132	12	17
Tonga	240	386	76	3,400	3,900	14	...	...	—	—	—	—	—	—
Trinidad and Tobago	4,970	8,000	50	122,201	23,828	8.6	...	...	—	—	—	—	—	—
Tunisia	*18,133*	*29,183*	*60*	320,000	180,500	17	*678*	*990*	1,404[2]	2,260[2]	670	1,078	1,380	2,015
Turkey	240,286	386,704	15	2,862,000	942,000	16	67,017	97,843	6,470[2]	10,413[2]	3,967	6,385	5,654	8,254
Turkmenistan	*8,300*	*13,400*	*86*	*170,600*	...	...	*3,283*	*4,793*	1,317	2,120	...	...	...	...
Tuvalu	*5*	*8*	—	...	...	...	...	...	—	—	—	—	—	—
Uganda	17,808	28,660	16	17,804	25,246	402	...	...	*770*[2]	*1,240*[2]	205	330	60	87
Ukraine	170,069	273,700	86	*2,920,000*	...	...	35,079	51,215	14,509	23,350	47,200	75,900	232,000	338,000
United Arab Emirates	2,830	4,555	100	297,128	72,824	5.6	...	...	—	—	—	—	—	—
United Kingdom	240,241	386,631	100	20,479,000	2,733,000	2.5	86,600	126,500	23,518[43]	37,849[43]	19,693	31,693	10,623	15,509
United States	3,904,721	6,283,868	89	146,314,000	59,227,000	1.3	815,014	1,189,900	136,000	219,000	14,000	23,000	1,183,000	1,727,000
Uruguay	*32,311*	*52,000*	*23*	310,833	148,644	6.8	*500*	*730*	1,867[2]	3,004[2]	*87.4*	*140.6*	139.2	203.2
Uzbekistan	*55,431*	*89,207*	*83*	*790,800*	...	...	*15,037*	*21,954*	4,200	6,800	3,300	5,200	48,400	70,600
Vanuatu	702	1,130	21	4,000	2,200	26	...	...	—	—	—	—	—	—
Venezuela	58,081	93,472	32	1,507,309	474,466	11	...	...	226[2]	363[2]	29.0	46.7	24.8	36.2
Vietnam	65,200	105,000	10	...	...	...	*1,845*	*2,693*	1,619	2,605	1,140	1,834	661	965
Virgin Islands (U.S.)	532	856	100	51,000	13,300	1.5	...	...	—	—	—	—	—	—
West Bank	...	...	...	69,200	20,723	13	...	...	...	...	...	...	...	...
Western Sahara	*3,900*	*6,200*	*23*	*6,284*	*424*	*20*	...	...	—	—	—	—	—	—
Western Samoa	*1,296*	2,085	*19*	962	863	89	...	...	—	—	—	—	—	—
Yemen	32,130	51,709	10	214,561	269,819	25	...	...	—	—	—	—	—	—
Yugoslavia	29,771	47,912	59	*1,406,000*	*132,100*	*6.8*	*14,929*[46]	*21,796*[46]	2,461	3,960	1,569	2,525	950	1,387
Zaire	91,200	146,800	2	94,000	86,000	229	...	...	3,162	5,088	360[47]	580[47]	1,258[47]	1,836[47]
Zambia	23,214	37,359	18	96,000	68,000	54	...	...	791	1,273	166.7	268.3	735.6	1,074
Zimbabwe	56,593	91,078	16	310,412	30,182	30	...	...	1,714[2]	2,759[2]	355.1	571.4	3.7	5.4

[1]Ariana Afghan Airlines only. [2]Route length. [3]Air Algérie international flights only. [4]TAAG airline only. [5]Aerolineas Argentinas only. [6]Included in Netherlands Antilles. [7]Government railways only. [8]Including Gulf Air international traffic. [9]Caribbean Airways only. [10]Caribbean Air Cargo only. [11]Air Afrique only. [12]Air Botswana only. [13]For industrial purposes only. [14]LASCA only. [15]Traffic between Ouagadougou, Burkina Faso, and Abidjan, Côte d'Ivoire. [16]Air Ivoire only. [17]Data refer to former Czechoslovakia. [18]Including SAS international and domestic traffic. [19]National roads only. [20]TACA airlines only. [21]Includes 62 mi (100 km) of the Chemin de Fer Djibouti-Ethiopien (CDE) in Djibouti. [22]Air France and UTA only. [23]TAN and SAHSA airlines only. [24]Includes

merchant marine				air					canals and inland waterways (latest)				country
fleet, 1992 (vessels over 100 gross tons)	total dead-weight tonnage, 1992 ('000)	international cargo (latest)		airports with sched-uled flights, 1995	traffic (latest)				length		cargo		
		loaded metric tons ('000)	off-loaded metric tons ('000)		passengers		cargo		mi	km	short ton-mi ('000,000)	metric ton-km ('000,000)	
					passenger-mi ('000,000)	passenger-km ('000,000)	short ton-mi ('000,000)	metric ton-km ('000,000)					
154[32]	1,053.6[32]	18,560	18,715	5	234[33]	377[33]	1.2[33]	1.8[33]	...	...	...	...	Netherlands Antilles
17	18.1	1,040	930	10	92.9[34]	149.6[34]	1.2[34]	1.7[34]	...	...	...	...	New Caledonia
139	279.8	17,748	10,776	36	7,799	12,551	1,100	1,606	1,000	1,609	1,503	2,195	New Zealand
25	1.3	320	1,629	4	35.8	57.6	1.8	2.6	1,379	2,220	...	...	Nicaragua
—	—	—	—	1	126	203	11.0	16.0	186	300	...	...	Niger
271	733.3	80,607	10,812	12	619	996	7.9	11.5	5,328	8,575	...	...	Nigeria
2	0.9	...	...	3	...	...	...	...	...	...	...	...	Northern Mariana Islands
1,630	2,143.3	125,184	22,116	48	5,023[18]	8,084[18]	591.7[18]	863.9[18]	980	1,577	6,091	8,893	Norway
26	11.7	33,843	2,492	6	1,194[8]	1,922[8]	47.8[8]	69.8[8]	...	...	...	...	Oman
73	513.8	5,976	24,684	34	6,152	9,900	285.8	417.3	...	...	...	...	Pakistan
...	...	...	...	...	...	...	...	...	...	...	...	...	Palau
5,217	79,255.6	105,744	70,572	10	209	336	3.6	5.3	497	800	...	...	Panama
87	40.9	2,463	1,784	110	458.8	738.4	56.4	82.4	6,798	10,940	...	...	Papua New Guinea
38	38.5	...	...	3	791	1,273	16.5	24.1	1,900	3,100	...	...	Paraguay
623	615.6	10,197	5,077	25	803	1,292	101	148	5,300	8,600	...	...	Peru
1,499	13,807.1	12,864	34,128	21	8,679[35]	13,967[35]	260.3[35]	380.1[35]	2,000	3,219	...	...	Philippines
644	4,314.3	33,984	13,524	12	2,270	3,653	37.7	55.0	2,484	3,997	452	660	Poland
326	1,129.3	4,068	16,044	14	4,745	7,637	123	180	510	820	...	...	Portugal
13	...	...	...	7	...	...	...	...	...	...	...	...	Puerto Rico
65	635.6	18,145	2,588	1	1,042[8]	1,676[8]	35.1[8]	51.2[8]	...	...	...	...	Qatar
7	33.5	399	1,975	1	...	...	...	...	...	...	...	...	Réunion
439	4,845.5	13,164	18,144	16	1,171	1,884	11.4	16.7	1,071	1,724	1,091	1,593	Romania
4,543	16,592.3	25,476	1,896	58	44,900	72,300	1,027	1,500	63,380	100,000	59,600	87,000	Russia
—	—	...	...	3	...	...	...	...	...	...	...	...	Rwanda
1	0.6	24	36	2	...	...	...	...	...	...	...	...	St. Kitts and Nevis
7	2.1	150	234	2	...	...	...	...	...	...	...	...	St. Lucia
881	7,044.2	80	140	4	...	...	...	...	...	...	...	...	St. Vincent and the Grenadines
—	—	—	—	—	—	—	—	—	—	—	—	—	San Marino
4	2.3	15	26	2	5.0	8.0	0.7	1.0	...	...	...	...	São Tomé and Príncipe
301	1,381.7	214,070	46,437	25	11,540	18,572	492	718	...	...	...	...	Saudi Arabia
183	27.5	2,591	2,477	5	138[28]	222[28]	25[28]	36[28]	557	897	...	...	Senegal
9	3.3	11	348	2	388.9	625.8	47.7	69.6	...	...	...	...	Seychelles
62	18.4	1,802	533	1	68.3[36]	109.9[36]	1.4[36]	2.0[36]	500	800	447	652	Sierra Leone
946	14,929.2	114,768	164,400	1	27,929	44,947	2,254	3,291	...	...	...	...	Singapore
...	...	...	...	4	9.5	15.3	0.9	1.4	...	...	...	...	Slovakia
22	596.9	...	...	1	295	475	2,556	3,731	...	...	2	3	Slovenia
33	5.0	278	349	30	40.5[37]	65.1[37]	0.9[37]	1.3[37]	...	...	...	...	Solomon Islands
28	18.5	324	1,007	...	81	131	3.0	5.0	...	...	...	...	Somalia
219	282.5	95,904	13,560	27	6,588[38]	10,602[38]	863[38]	1,260[38]	...	...	...	...	South Africa
2,190	5,077.3	40,836	133,956	25	16,614	26,738	410	599	649	1,045	21,030[39]	31,880[39]	Spain
66	472.6	5,220	8,796	1	2,289	3,684	79.6	116.2	267	430	...	...	Sri Lanka
16	[illegible]	1,193	3,467	11	382.1[40]	615.0[40]	26.8[40]	[illegible][40]	3,300	5,310	...	...	Sudan, The
24	15.7	5,776	1,286	2	336[41]	541[41]	18.2[41]	26.6[41]	746	1,200	...	...	Suriname
—	—	—	—	1	25.6	41.2	0.1	0.1	—	—	—	—	Swaziland
664	3,327.7	48,048	56,976	48	5,097[18]	8,203[18]	123.1[18]	179.7[18]	1,275	2,052	5,300	7,800	Sweden
24	602.8	...	...	5	11,545	18,580	964.4	1,408	40	65	34	50	Switzerland
94	210.4	17,868	5,676	5	521	838	7.9	11.5	541	870	...	...	Syria
649	9,241.3	140,705	243,019	12	22,848	36,770	1,892	2,763	...	...	...	...	Taiwan
...	...	...	...	1	3,214	5,173	22.1	32.3	...	...	...	...	Tajikistan
43	48.5	1,249	2,721	12	94	151	1.3	1.9	...	...	...	...	Tanzania
351	1,194.5	21,192	40,152	26	15,688	25,248	872.2	1,273	2,300	3,701	...	...	Thailand
0	20.0	2,362	1,050	1	135	217	23.4	34.2	31	50	...	...	Togo
15	13.7	15	104	5	5.8	9.4	0.01	0.01	...	...	...	...	Tonga
53	17.5	9,622	10,961	2	2,030	3,267	10.1	14.8	...	...	...	...	Trinidad and Tobago
77	443.3	6,060	10,200	5	1,227	1,974	11.8	17.3	...	...	...	...	Tunisia
880	7,114.3	22,956	61,728	24	5,675[42]	9,133[42]	143.7[42]	209.9[42]	750	1,200	209	305	Turkey
...	...	...	...	1	2,021	3,253	222	324	...	...	...	...	Turkmenistan
6	16.0	...	...	1	...	...	...	...	...	...	...	...	Tuvalu
2	...	...	...	1	15.0	24.1	0.1	0.1	...	...	...	...	Uganda
...	...	34,200	...	20	1,988	3,200	68	100	1,039	1,672	3,851	5,622	Ukraine
276	1,491.7	88,153	9,595	4	3,470[8]	5,584[8]	190[8]	277[8]	...	...	...	...	United Arab Emirates
1,631	4,687.3	68,076	117,804	54	58,825	94,670	2,000	2,920	1,424	2,291	37,740	55,100	United Kingdom
5,710	25,646.4	340,344[44]	598,116[44]	834	480,463	773,232	13,320	19,447	25,482	41,009	454,008	662,840	United States
93	172.5	710[45]	1,450[45]	1	293	471	1.8	2.6	1,000	1,600	...	...	Uruguay
...	...	...	...	1	6,500	10,500	60,800	88,700	...	...	...	...	Uzbekistan
280	3,259.6	80	55	29	...	...	—	—	...	...	...	...	Vanuatu
271	1,355.4	101,435	17,932	24	4,168	6,708	102	149	4,400	7,100	...	...	Venezuela
230	872.8	303	1,510	12	54	87	0.7	1.0	11,000	17,702	...	...	Vietnam
1	...	105.5	648.3	4	...	...	...	...	...	...	...	...	Virgin Islands (U.S.)
—	—	...	...	—	—	—	—	—	...	...	...	...	West Bank
—	—	40	15	1	...	...	...	...	...	...	...	...	Western Sahara
7	6.5	12	192	2	...	...	...	...	...	...	...	...	Western Samoa
40	13.7	1,936	7,829	11	698	1,124	78	114	...	...	...	...	Yemen
462[46]	5,173.1[46]	8,520[46]	10,176[46]	5	93	150	92	134	1,616[46]	2,600[46]	3,430[46]	5,007[46]	Yugoslavia
27	30.7	2,395	1,453	11	183[48]	295[48]	38[48]	56[48]	9,300	15,000	678	990	Zaire
—	—	—	—	8	313	504	11.4	16.7	1,398	2,250	...	...	Zambia
—	—	—	—	5	514	828	27	40	...	...	...	...	Zimbabwe

transshipments. [25]El Al only. [26]Alitalia only. [27]Kenya Airways only. [28]International traffic only. [29]Peninsular Malaysia and Singapore. [30]Aeronaves de Mexico and Mexicana only. [31]Air Nauru only. [32]Includes Aruba. [33]Antillean Airlines only. [34]Air Caledonie only. [35]Philippines Air Lines only. [36]Sierra Leone Airlines international traffic only. [37]Solair only. [38]SAA only. [39]Coastal shipping only. [40]Sudan Airways only. [41]Suriname Airways only. [42]Turkish Airlines only. [43]British Railways only; excludes Northern Ireland. [44]Includes Puerto Rico. [45]Port of Montevideo only. [46]Data refer to Yugoslavia as constituted prior to 1991. [47]Zaire National Railways only. [48]Air Zaire only.

Communications

Virtually all the states of the world have a variety of communications media and services available to their citizens: book publishing and newspapers (although only daily papers are included in this table); postal services; radio and television broadcast systems; telephones; and cinema. Unfortunately, the availability of information about the structure and volume of these national services and sectors often runs behind the capabilities of the services themselves. Certain countries publish no official information; others publish data analyzed according to a variety of fiscal, calendar, religious, or other years; still others, while they possess such data almost simultaneously with the end of the business year, may not see them published except in company or parastatal reports of limited distribution. Even when such data are published in national statistical summaries, it may be only after a delay of up to several years. Figures in italics are from 1989 or earlier.

The data also differ in their completeness and reliability. Figures for book production, for example, generally include all works published in separate bindings except advertising works, timetables, telephone directories, price lists, catalogs of businesses or exhibitions, musical scores, maps, atlases, and the like. The figures include government publications, school texts, theses, offprints, series works, and illustrated works, even those consisting principally of illustrations. Figures refer to works actually published during the year of survey, usually by a registered publisher, and deposited for copyright. A book is defined as a work of 49 or more pages, a pamphlet as a work of from 5 to 48 pages. A work published simultaneously in more than one country is counted as having been published in each. Newspaper statistics are especially difficult to collect and compare. Newspapers continually are founded, cease publication, merge, or change frequency of publication. Data on circulation, sales, and readership are often incomplete, slow to be aggregated at the national level, or regarded as proprietary. In some countries circulation data are virtually nonexistent. In others no daily newspaper exists.

Post office statistics are compiled mainly from the Universal Postal Union's annual summary *Statistique des services postaux*. Postal services, unlike the other media discussed earlier, tend most often to be operated by a single national service, to cover a country completely, and to record traffic data according to broadly similar schemes (although the details of *classes* of mail handled may differ). Some countries do not enumerate

Communications

country	publishing (latest)								daily newspapers (latest)		
	number of titles				number of copies ('000)						
	books		periodicals	pamphlets	books		periodicals	pamphlets	number	total circulation ('000)	circulation per 1,000 population
	total	school textbooks			total	school textbooks					
Afghanistan	1,776	150	*105*	1,019	...	...	...	...	16	206	11
Albania	363	190	*143*	18	3,498	3,110	*3,477*	270	4	165	50
Algeria	454	15	48	52	...	...	803	...	5	1,000	38
American Samoa	...	...	...	...	...	...	...	...	—	—	—
Andorra	56	5	...	...	...	...	*15*	...	3	4	83
Angola	*14*	...	...	...	*130*	...	...	...	4	116	12
Antigua and Barbuda	...	...	...	...	...	...	...	...	—	—	—
Argentina	5,628	436	...	...	49,293	4,720	...	...	190	3,940	144
Armenia	817[7]	...	40	[7]	10,100[7]	...	5,064	[7]	7	84	23
Aruba	...	...	...	...	...	...	...	...	*5*	...	...
Australia	*6,800*	*487*	...	*3,923*	...	...	...	...	69	4,300	261
Austria	3,786	...	2,524	...	...	...	...	...	27	3,108	400
Azerbaijan	530	29	49	69	7,961	2,276	801	993	6	427	58
Bahamas, The	15	...	...	—	16	...	...	—	3	35	133
Bahrain	...	...	...	...	...	...	...	...	3	43	81
Bangladesh	*1,209*	...	*41*	...	...	...	*163*	...	51	710	6
Barbados	17	...	52	60	...	...	...	...	2	41	160
Belarus	1,666	101	155	698	61,690	7,698	3,765	10,250	10	1,899	184
Belgium	13,913[7]	...	13,706	[7]	...	...	...	...	33	3,100	310
Belize	43	—	...	91	43	—	...	76	—	—	—
Benin	647	6	...	...	874	9	...	...	1	12	2
Bermuda	...	...	...	...	...	...	...	...	1	16	258
Bhutan	...	...	...	...	...	...	...	...	—	—	—
Bolivia	*365*	...	...	*82*	*365*	...	...	*46*	16	390	52
Bosnia and Herzegovina	966	...	92	...	7,540	...	1,887	...	2	518	53
Botswana	97	4	14	61	...	...	177	...	1	40	30
Brazil	*13,973*	...	*3,782*	*3,675*	...	...	*980*	...	373	8,500	55
Brunei	25	6	15	...	56	22	132	...	1	20	74
Bulgaria	4,045	990	745	728	47,374	11,766	3,097	6,303	46	1,464	164
Burkina Faso	*4*	...	37	...	*9*	...	24	...	1	3	0.3
Burundi	*37*	*9*	...	*17*	*274*	*229*	...	*174*	1	20	3
Cambodia	...	...	...	...	...	...	...	...	1	20	3
Cameroon	...	...	*58*	...	...	...	*127*	...	1	50	4
Canada	12,750	...	1,400	...	...	...	37,108	...	106	5,815	215
Cape Verde	*9*	—	...	*1*	9	—	...	1	—	—	—
Central African Republic	...	...	...	...	...	...	...	...	1	2	1
Chad	...	...	*10*	...	...	...	...	...	1	2	0.4
Chile	1,493	148	417	327	...	...	3,450	...	45	6,000	445
China	73,923	11,107	6,486	...	5,387,020	2,657,140	205,060	...	74	...	...
Colombia	1,481	44	...	...	11,314	700	...	...	46	2,100	63
Comoros	...	...	...	...	...	...	...	...	—	—	—
Congo	...	...	3	...	...	...	34	...	6	19	8
Costa Rica	230	1	...	14	...	...	...	...	4	322	101
Côte d'Ivoire	...	...	...	...	...	...	...	...	1	90	7
Croatia	2,239	...	352	...	12,220	...	6,357	...	9	636	133
Cuba	736[18]	156	160	281[18]	18,900[18]	8,158	2,458[18]	2,797	17	1,315	122
Cyprus	534	54	48	366	688	282	244	671	9	77	108
Czech Republic	6,743[7]	269	2,898	[7]	...	...	...	...	55	5,000	485
Denmark	8,132	869	285	3,629	...	...	7,838	...	42	1,710	332
Djibouti	...	...	*7*	...	...	...	*6*	...	1	4	8
Dominica	...	...	...	...	...	...	...	...	—	—	—
Dominican Republic	...	...	*277*	...	...	...	...	...	11	265	35
Ecuador	717[7]	...	...	[7]	...	...	...	...	36	688	62
Egypt	*1,311*	*256*	266	*140*	*20,096*	*14,267*	1,815	*2,967*	16	2,426	44
El Salvador	*15*	*6*	...	—	*63*	*21*	...	—	8	485	90
Equatorial Guinea	...	*17*	...	...	...	*17*	...	...	1	1	3
Eritrea[19]	...	...	...	...	...	...	...	...	...	...	...
Estonia	1,557	75	250	435	12,052	996	2,044	3,908	15	...	...
Ethiopia[19]	147	23	*3*	93	426	69	*14*	248	4	70	1
Faroe Islands	*148*	...	...	...	...	...	...	...	—	—	—

domestic traffic or may record only international traffic requiring handling charges.

Data for some kinds of communications apparatus and traffic are relatively easy to collect; telephones, for example, must be installed, and service recorded so that it may be charged. But in most countries radios may be purchased by anyone and turned on whenever desired; car radios are seldom enumerated or licensed separately. As a result, data on distribution and use of radio and television apparatus may be collected in a variety of ways—on the basis of numbers of subscribers, licenses issued, periodic sample surveys, census or housing surveys, or private consumer surveys. Statistics on commercial cinema attendance (usually those of the United Nations Educational, Scientific and Cultural Organization [Unesco] or national data) may refer to a variety of screening facilities, including fixed, mobile, or drive-in facilities.

The *Statistical Yearbook* of Unesco contains extensive data on book publishing, newspapers, radio and television, and cinema that have been collected from standardized questionnaires. The quality and recency of its data, however, depend on the completion and timely return of each questionnaire by national authorities, and response rates depend on a variety of factors. In general, however, response rates for inquiries by international organizations in communications are better than in other fields because these organizations and the responsible authorities in each country must conduct day-to-day business and, hence, have a better ongoing relationship. The commercially published annual *World Radio TV Handbook* (Andrew G. Sennitt, editor) is a valuable source of information on broadcast media and has complete and timely coverage. It depends on data received from broadcasters, but, because some do not respond, local correspondents and monitors are used in many countries, and some unconfirmed or unofficial data are included as estimates. The statistics on telephones are derived mainly from the UN-affiliated International Telecommunication Union's *World Telecommunication Indicators* (annual) and refer to "main lines," or telephone lines that connect the subscriber's apparatus to the public, switched net.

... Not available.

—None, nil, or not applicable.

post offices, 1993				radio, 1994		television, 1994		telephones, 1993		cinema (latest)		country
number	persons per office	pieces of mail handled ('000)	pieces of mail handled per capita	receivers (all types; '000)	persons per receiver	receivers (all types; '000)	persons per receiver	main lines		annual attendance		
								receivers ('000)	persons per receiver	number ('000,000)	per 1,000 population	
358[1]	41,400[1]	36,981[1, 2]	2.5[1, 2]	1,670	10	100	169	29	770	...	...	Afghanistan
615	5,430	7,936[3]	2.4[3]	550	6.1	246[4]	13[4]	49	70	*6.9*	*2,160*	Albania
2,077[4]	8,910[4]	417,362[4]	18[4]	3,500	7.8	2,000	14	1,068	25	*21.0*	*880*	Algeria
...	...	...	...	20	2.9	8.0	6.9	6.0	6.5	...	...	American Samoa
...	...	3,483[5]	90[5]	10	6.2	6.0[1]	8.6[1]	29	2.4	...	...	Andorra
76	145,000	2,063	0.2	450	25	51	220	53	190	*3.2*	*370*	Angola
...	...	...	...	75	0.9	28	2.3	19	3.5	...	...	Antigua and Barbuda
5,489	6,150	326,111[6]	9.8[6]	21,500	1.6	7,165	4.8	4,115	8.1	18.0	550	Argentina
898[8]	3,840[8]	49,000[9]	14[9]	642[4]	5.6[4]	722[4]	5.0[4]	584	6.4	13.4	4,020	Armenia
...	...	...	...	40	1.8	19	3.8	20	3.3	...	...	Aruba
4,233[10]	4,130[10]	4,131,260[10]	240[10]	21,000	0.9	8,000	2.2	8,540	2.1	*39.8*	*2,360*	Australia
2,670[10, 11]	2,950[10, 11]	3,313,573	420	4,710	1.7	2,706	3.0	3,579	2.2	10.5	1,340	Austria
1,821[8]	3,970[8]	538,885	75	3,682[12]	1.9[12]	1,522[4]	4.7[4]	647	11	31.0	4,290	Azerbaijan
136	1,990	59,365	220	134	2.0	60	4.5	80	3.3	...	...	Bahamas, The
13	41,500	48,730[3]	90[3]	320	1.7	270	2.1	124	4.3	*0.6*	*1,230*	Bahrain
7,985[1]	13,100[1]	197,363[4]	1.8[4]	4,650	25	350	336	268	440	*302.3*	*3,000*	Bangladesh
17	15,300	12,788	49	224	1.2	69	3.8	83	3.2	...	...	Barbados
4,002	2,590	240,412[3, 10]	23[3, 10]	3,140[4]	3.3[4]	3,500[1]	2.9[1]	1,814	5.7	94.0	9,120	Belarus
1,756	5,700	3,441,741	344	7,640	1.3	4,200	2.4	4,396	2.3	*16.1*	*1,630*	Belgium
112[13]	1,520[13]	3,096[13]	18[13]	106	2.0	27	7.6	29	7.1	...	...	Belize
180	29,000	6,088	1.2	400	13	20	262	20	260	*1.3*	*330*	Benin
14	4,290	22,700	380	80	0.8	30	2.0	42	1.5	*0.2*	*3,630*	Bermuda
83[10]	19,400[10]	1,817	1.2	23	35	0.2[5]	6,180[5]	3.8	400	...	...	Bhutan
133	53,200	8,879	1.3	4,250	1.7	50	144	234	33	4.6	650	Bolivia
656[4]	6,630[4]	128,886[4]	30[4]	733[14]	5.9[14]	629[14]	6.9[14]	600[14]	7.3[14]	4.3	1,000	Bosnia and Herzegovina
167	8,620	37,387	26	140	11	14	106	44	32	...	...	Botswana
12,766	11,900	3,908,203[6]	26[6]	55,000	3.0	30,000	5.3	11,744	13	*91.3*	*680*	Brazil
6	46,600	15,839[3]	57[3]	60	1.7	70	4.0	55	5.1	*2.3*	*11,900*	Brunei
3,119	2,880	254,813[3]	28[3]	3,920	2.2	3,127	2.7	2,000	3.8	25.7	2,860	Bulgaria
66	121,200	13,689	1.7	225	45	46	218	22	460	*6.0*	*720*	Burkina Faso
68	87,600	6,300	1.1	300	19	4.5	1,289	16	390	*0.1*	*24*	Burundi
...	...	...	...	860	11	70	134	5.9	1,670	...	...	Cambodia
259	48,500	22,590[3, 10]	1.9[3, 10]	1,500	8.6	15	858	57	220	...	...	Cameroon
19,102	1,500	10,714,615[15]	372[15]	26,878	1.1	17,400	1.7	16,471	1.7	76.3	2,750	Canada
63	6,190	1,997	5.1	57	6.7	5.0[16]	65[16]	15	26	...	...	Cape Verde
52	62,700	...	...	180	17	7.5	409	6.7	480	...	...	Central African Republic
36	35,700	4,270	0.7	1,310	4.7	5.0[16]	1,050[16]	4.6	1,430	...	...	Chad
602	22,900	297,526	22	4,400	3.2	2,000	7.0	1,520	9.1	9.7	740	Chile
52,969	22,800	6,753,807[15]	5.6[15]	206,000	5.8	227,880	5.2	17,332	68	*16,878*	*15,300*	China
3,806	8,920	220,456[14]	6.7[14]	5,400	6.4	5,500	6.3	3,828	8.9	*41.0*	*1,290*	Colombia
36	16,900	900,700[17]	15[17]	61	8.6	0.2[4]	2,310[4]	4.0	130	...	...	Comoros
114	21,400	3,240	1.3	240	11	8.5	296	19	130	...	...	Congo
276	11,590	26,093	8.2	760	4.3	340	9.6	364	11	*0.2*	*76*	Costa Rica
386	34,700	39,791	3.0	1,600	8.9	810	18	94	140	...	...	Côte d'Ivoire
1,082	4,400	206,702	43	2,000	2.3	750	6.0	1,027	4.5	3.1	640	Croatia
1,546	7,050	27,868	2.6	3,608	3.1	2,500	4.4	344	31	29.9	2,790	Cuba
774	930	53,000	74	200	4.0	235	3.4	311	2.0	...	...	Cyprus
3,504	2,970	1,188,226	114	9,100	1.1	3,185[10]	3.2[10]	1,961	5.3	36.4	3,530	Czech Republic
1,293	4,010	1,846,000	356	5,000	1.0	2,700	1.9	3,060	1.7	9.2	1,790	Denmark
9	53,300	9,904	21	35	16	17	34	7.3	78	...	...	Djibouti
63[5]	1,210[5]	2,051[5]	27[5]	45	1.6	5.2	14	14	5.3	...	...	Dominica
206	36,942	9,800[14]	1.3[14]	1,180	6.6	728	11	552	13	...	...	Dominican Republic
332	33,072	17,310	1.6	3,240	3.5	900	13	598	19	6.8	650	Ecuador
7,106	7,940	114,874	2.0	16,450	3.6	5,000	12	2,375	24	*26.9*	*520*	Egypt
307[10]	18,400[10]	18,572[10]	3.3[10]	2,080	2.7	501	11	174	26	...	...	El Salvador
20[1]	17,100[1]	...	...	128	3.0	2.5	154	1.3[16]	330[16]	...	...	Equatorial Guinea
...	...	...	...	...	...	...	...	20	170	...	...	Eritrea[19]
590	2,580	22,939	15	926[1]	1.7[1]	600	2.5	358	4.3	7.3	4,640	Estonia
561	101,000	27,078	0.5	9,000	5.9	100	534	133	400	...	...	Ethiopia[19]
43	1,160	8,613	170	21	2.1	14	3.2	23	2.0	...	500	Faroe Islands

Communications (continued)

country	publishing (latest)								daily newspapers (latest)		
	number of titles				number of copies ('000)						
	books		periodicals	pamphlets	books		periodicals	pamphlets	number	total circulation ('000)	circulation per 1,000 population
	total	school textbooks			total	school textbooks					
Fiji	*10*	*6*	...	*3*	*20*	*12*	...	*6*	1	27	37
Finland	8,228	462	5,711	2,805	...	...	...	...	58	2,578	515
France	45,379[7]	971	2,672	[7]	...	...	120,018	...	77	11,695	205
French Guiana	...	...	...	...	...	...	...	...	1	2	15
French Polynesia	...	...	...	...	...	...	...	...	4	24	116
Gabon	...	...	...	...	...	...	...	...	1	20	16
Gambia, The	15	*2*	10	6	6	*22*	885	1	2	2	2
Gaza Strip	...	...	...	...	...	...	...	...	—	—	—
Georgia	1,659[7]	...	75	[7]	20,100[7]	...	29,700	[7]	*147*	*3,677*	*671*
Germany	67,277	3,084	7,831	...	...	...	309,041	...	355	26,425	331
Ghana	*338*	*27*	121	*12*	...	...	774	...	4	280	18
Gibraltar	...	...	*15*	...	...	...	*4*	...	2	3	135
Greece	4,066[7]	...	*309*	[7]	...	...	...	...	145	*1,400*	137
Greenland	...	...	...	...	...	...	...	...	—	—	—
Grenada	...	...	...	...	...	...	...	...	—	—	—
Guadeloupe	...	...	...	...	...	...	...	...	1	35	88
Guam	...	...	...	...	...	...	...	...	1	25	179
Guatemala	...	...	...	...	...	...	...	...	5	180	18
Guernsey	...	...	...	...	...	...	...	...	1	16	277
Guinea	...	...	3	...	...	...	5	...	—	—	—
Guinea-Bissau	...	...	...	...	...	...	...	...	1	6	6
Guyana	*9*	—	...	*37*	...	—	...	...	2	80	99
Haiti	*188*	17	...	*83*	...	...	...	...	4	50	7
Honduras	...	...	...	...	...	...	...	...	4	159	29
Hong Kong	*3,642*	*538*	598	*2,039*	*27,483*	*7,771*	...	*16,829*	49	4,750	819
Hungary	7,629	1,187	1,203	907	80,988	24,309	14,927	7,109	28	2,896	275
Iceland	1,036	141	598	566	...	...	...	...	5	135	519
India	11,170	269	...	3,268	...	...	...	...	2,300	19,804	31
Indonesia	6,128	715	117	175	...	...	3,985	...	68	4,591	24
Iran	5,018	...	318	...	24,310	...	6,166	...	13	1,250	20
Iraq	...	...	...	...	...	...	...	...	6	660	34
Ireland	*628*	...	*257*	*2,051*	...	...	*2,975*	...	8	652	187
Isle of Man	...	...	...	...	...	...	...	...	—	—	—
Israel	*2,038*	*291*	*807*	*176*	*8,872*	*3,961*	...	...	31	1,240	242
Italy	26,620	1,912	10,064	2,731	204,308	50,373	85,071	19,347	78	6,068	105
Jamaica	*23*	*3*	...	*48*	...	...	...	...	3	160	65
Japan	42,345[7]	*1,657*	3,918	[7]	466,100[7]	*2,117*	...	[7]	121	71,690	580
Jersey	...	...	...	...	...	...	...	...	1	24	300
Jordan	790	...	31	...	...	...	43	...	4	250	58
Kazakhstan	1,226	...	88	...	30,500[7]	...	33,300	[7]	456	8,622	512
Kenya	239	...	...	5	452	...	...	9	5	354	14
Kiribati	...	...	...	...	...	...	...	...	—	—	—
Korea, North	...	...	...	...	...	...	...	...	11	5,000	221
Korea, South	25,017	3,008	...	2,872	122,006	93,391	...	14,386	63	18,000	407
Kuwait	187	...	*73*	9	...	...	*257*	...	9	480	244
Kyrgyzstan	936[7]	...	50	[7]	9,700[7]	...	34,400	[7]	128	1,622	367
Laos	79	9	...	30	423	180	...	143	3	14	3
Latvia	1,509	77	170	354	17,451	1,006	1,912	4,529	17	517	193
Lebanon	...	...	...	...	...	...	...	...	16	500	176
Lesotho	...	...	...	...	...	...	...	...	2	14	8
Liberia	...	...	...	...	...	...	...	...	8	35	13
Libya	*121*	*20*	...	...	*553*	*180*	...	...	4	71	15
Liechtenstein	...	...	*79*	...	...	...	*220*	...	2	20	700
Lithuania	1,524	146	237	837	21,424	3,743	2,602	9,530	18	836	223
Luxembourg	*362*	*13*	508	*158*	...	...	...	...	5	145	384
Macau	...	...	16	...	...	...	...	...	9	250	510
Macedonia	492	178	74	67	1,537	810	347	146	2	55	27
Madagascar	46	1	63	39	183	3	191	219	7	48	4
Malaŵi	*66*	*5*	*14*	*75*	...	...	*124*	...	1	25	2
Malaysia	3,682	772	*1,631*	66	13,449	6,028	*1,689*	171	39	2,200	117
Maldives	...	...	*64*	...	...	...	*70*	...	2	3	13
Mali	*160*	*76*	...	...	*92*	*56*	...	...	2	41	4
Malta	283	10	359	112	...	...	...	...	3	54	150
Marshall Islands	...	...	...	...	...	...	...	...	—	—	—
Martinique	...	...	...	...	...	...	...	...	1	32	86
Mauritania	...	...	...	...	...	...	...	...	1	1	0.5
Mauritius	56	19	62	24	85	58	...	14	6	80	73
Mayotte	...	...	...	...	...	...	...	...	*1*	*12*	*160*
Mexico	2,587	101	182	21	...	...	28,016	...	292	10,231	116
Micronesia	...	...	...	...	...	...	...	...	—	—	—
Moldova	685	66	68	117	361	20	351	2	5	205	45
Monaco	41[7]	...	3	[7]	722[7]	...	38	[7]	1	8	296
Mongolia	193	45	45	524	6,397[7]	...	6,361	[7]	3	208	90
Morocco	...	...	...	...	...	...	...	...	14	335	14
Mozambique	*29*	...	*3*	*37*	*3,130*	...	*1,828*	*360*	2	81	5
Myanmar (Burma)	*673*	...	...	...	...	...	...	...	2	324	7
Namibia	131	41	...	62	...	...	...	...	4	209	136
Nauru	...	...	...	...	...	...	...	...	—	—	—
Nepal	...	*122*	...	...	...	*7,243*	...	...	25	140	7
Netherlands, The	11,844	2,196	367	...	...	...	19,283	...	*86*	*4,592*	*311*
Netherlands Antilles	...	...	...	...	...	...	...	...	6	53	301
New Caledonia	*11*	...	...	*3*	...	...	...	...	3	23	133
New Zealand	*1,601*	*14*	*5,788*	*1,851*	...	...	...	...	31	1,050	304
Nicaragua	*27*	—	...	*14*	*271*	—	...	*192*	3	90	23
Niger	5	—	...	—	11	—	...	—	1	5	1

post offices, 1993				radio, 1994		television, 1994		telephones, 1993		cinema (latest)		country
number	persons per office	pieces of mail handled ('000)	pieces of mail handled per capita	receivers (all types; '000)	persons per receiver	receivers (all types; '000)	persons per receiver	main lines		annual attendance		
								receivers ('000)	persons per receiver	number ('000,000)	per 1,000 population	
139	5,400	23,562[3]	31[3]	450	1.7	10[14]	73[14]	54	11	...	...	Fiji
2,073	2,430	779,000	153	4,950	1.0	1,900	2.7	2,761	1.8	6.0	1,450	Finland
16,877[20]	3,416[20]	25,176,530[20]	436[20]	50,000	1.2	29,300	2.0	30,900	1.9	117.5	2,060	France
...	...	...	...	44[13]	2.1[13]	6.5	22	39	3.4	...	...	French Guiana
95[10]	2,210[10]	20,439[10]	97[10]	105	2.1	27	8.0	45	4.7	*0.4*	*2,190*	French Polynesia
52[14]	22,500[14]	19,190	19	155	7.3	40	28	30	41	*0.1*	*95*	Gabon
...	...	...	...	140	7.7	...	...	16	63	...	...	Gambia, The
...	...	...	...	...	...	...	...	...	...	...	...	Gaza Strip
...	...	138,000[9, 14]	25[9, 14]	...	...	...	...	571	9.6	47.0	8,680	Georgia
22,043[10]	3,660[10]	19,200,413	240	30,000	2.7	30,500	2.7	36,900	2.2	119.9	1,500	Germany
1,011[10]	15,200[10]	145,576[10]	9.5[10]	4,300	3.7	250	64	49	333	*3.9*	*340*	Ghana
4[10]	7,750[10]	12,280[10]	400[10]	35	0.8	7.5	3.7	14	2.1	*0.17*	*5,830*	Gibraltar
1,262	8,200	455,549[10]	44[10]	4,200	2.5	2,300	4.6	4,744	2.2	...	...	Greece
53	780	3,310	55	22	2.5	21	2.6	18	3.2	...	...	Greenland
19[14, 11]	450[4, 11]	...	...	53	1.7	30	3.1	20	4.5	...	...	Grenada
...	...	...	...	85	5.0	150	2.8	149	2.7	...	...	Guadeloupe
...	...	...	...	274	0.5	75	2.0	66	2.2	...	...	Guam
540	18,600	173,047	17	570	18	475	22	231	43	*7.7*	*910*	Guatemala
15	4,000	14,458[18]	240[18]	...	...	...	...	38	1.6	...	...	Guernsey
75[4]	84,100[4]	6,688	1	230	28	65	100	12	560	3.9	780	Guinea
24[10]	41,700[10]	410[2, 17, 21]	0.4[2, 17, 21]	40	26	...	...	8.6	120	...	...	Guinea-Bissau
91	9,700	4,582[2, 3]	5.6[2, 3]	386	1.9	15	49	41	20	*13.0*	*17,200*	Guyana
132	52,300	398,873	57	270	24	25	260	45[12]	150[12]	*2.1*	*380*	Haiti
...	...	...	...	1,910	2.8	160	33	117	48	...	...	Honduras
123	49,300	1,049,305[22]	180[22]	3,700	1.6	1,749	3.5	2,992	2.0	58.5	10,290	Hong Kong
3,208	3,210	1,487,375	150	6,250	1.6	4,262	2.4	1,498	6.9	21.6	2,070	Hungary
120	2,170	64,877	250	197	1.4	76	3.5	144	1.8	*1.3*	5,160	Iceland
152,382	5,880	13,314,660[10]	16[10]	65,000	14	20,000	46	8,037	110	4,297.3	5,010	India
26,291[10]	7,000[10]	545,972[10]	3.0[10]	26,000	7.3	11,000	17	1,713	110	*133.2*	*770*	Indonesia
8,053	7,890	313,151	5.0	13,000	4.6	7,000	8.5	3,598	17	66.6	1,200	Iran
343	57,100	48,807[10, 17]	2.5[10, 17]	3,700	5.4	1,000	20	675	29	...	...	Iraq
3,250	1,095	473,450[3]	130[3]	2,150	1.8	1,000	3.5	1,170	3.1	*11.6*	*3,290*	Ireland
32	2,190	19,640	280	...	...	...	...	...	...	...	...	Isle of Man
692	7,600	456,000[22]	87[22]	2,250	2.3	1,500	3.5	1,958	2.7	...	...	Israel
14,447	3,940	6,929,647	120	43,350	1.3	17,000	3.4	24,176	2.4	88.6	1,550	Italy
728	3,430	81,086	32	955	2.6	484	5.2	255	9.5	...	...	Jamaica
24,359	5,130	24,283,947	190	110,000	1.1	100,000	1.3	58,459	2.1	*143.6*	*1,170*	Japan
23	3,650	49,900[3]	590[3]	...	...	...	...	56	1.5	...	...	Jersey
916	4,850	136,740	31	980	4.1	250	16	288	14	*0.9*	*290*	Jordan
4,591	3,681	1,602,917[4]	95[4]	4,188[4]	4.0[4]	4,795[4]	3.5[4]	1,559	11	150.0	8,890	Kazakhstan
1,102	25,500	377,356	13	2,200	13	260	106	215	120	...	...	Kenya
24[10]	3,010[10]	707[10]	0.7[10]	16	5.2	...	...	1.8	43	...	...	Kiribati
...	...	...	...	2,500	9.2	2,000	11	1,089	21	*187.4*	*9,560*	Korea, North
3,309	13,300	2,966,731[18]	67[18]	42,570	1.0	10,403	4.3	16,633	2.7	*55.3*	*1,300*	Korea, South
89	16,100	98,888	69	1,000	1.6	800	2.0	358	4.1	*0.9*	*480*	Kuwait
1,020[8]	4,350[8]	355,300[4]	80[4]	825[4]	5.4[4]	875[4]	5.1[4]	367	12	32.0	7,190	Kyrgyzstan
127	36,200	3,809	0.8	500	9.5	80	59	8.6	530	1.0	229	Laos
1,048	2,470	16,912[2]	6.5[2]	2,000	1.3	1,200	2.1	694	3.7	19.7	7,340	Latvia
...	...	...	...	2,247	1.3	1,100	2.7	350	11	...	...	Lebanon
140[14]	12,600[14]	77,615[14]	44[14]	118	17	50	40	10.5	179	...	...	Lesotho
44[12]	55,400[12]	98,455	40	600	4.0	45	53	4.5[16]	530[16]	...	...	Liberia
373	12,600	21,679[3]	0.7[3]	1,000	5.0	500	10	240	21	...	...	Libya
12	2,500	17,192[18]	580[18]	11[23]	2.8[23]	11[23]	0.0[23]	19	1.6	...	...	Liechtenstein
1,037	3,600	40,865	11	1,420	2.6	1,400	2.7	858	4.4	13.9	3,690	Lithuania
106	3,580	151,000	400	240	1.7	101	4.0	215	1.9	*0.5*	*1,330*	Luxembourg
15	27,900	63,426	163	115	3.5	70	5.8	135	2.9	*2.7*	*6,400*	Macau
263	7,600	16,644	8.3	365[14]	5.5[14]	331[14]	6.1[14]	324	6.8	2.1	1,060	Macedonia
921	14,400	29,048	2.2	2,300	6.2	130	110	35	370	0.4	32	Madagascar
263[24]	28,000[24]	113,975[24]	15[24]	2,000	5.5	...	...	33	290	...	...	Malaŵi
1,970	9,770	1,011,206	53	7,460	2.6	2,000	9.8	2,411	7.9	*41.6*	*2,400*	Malaysia
40	6,000	1,962[2]	8.2[2]	25	9.8	4.8	51	10	24	...	...	Maldives
127	79,800	2,040	200	350	25	10	882	14	670	...	...	Mali
50[4]	7,140[4]	47,240[4]	130[4]	90	4.1	133	2.8	158	2.3	0.3	860	Malta
...	...	...	...	...	...	...	...	2.3	23	...	...	Marshall Islands
...	...	...	...	71	5.4	65	5.9	150	2.5	*1.1*	*3,150*	Martinique
60[4]	33,700[4]	...	...	300	6.9	1.1	1,881	7.6	290	...	...	Mauritania
105	10,400	40,448	37	380	2.9	157	7.1	107	10	0.6	550	Mauritius
...	...	...	...	50	2.2	3.5	31	4.0	25	...	...	Mayotte
7,275	12,500	889,827	10	21,000	4.3	56,000	1.6	7,621	11	*351.0*	*4,500*	Mexico
...	...	...	...	70	1.5	7.0	15	6.1	18	...	...	Micronesia
1,320	3,300	122,879	28	1,421[4]	3.1[4]	1,264[4]	3.5[4]	524	8.3	30.0	6,880	Moldova
...	...	...	...	30	1.0	20	1.5	14	2.1	0.1	3,390	Monaco
420	5,640	1,016[3]	0.4[3]	280	8.1	120	19	66	36	*20.1*	*9,720*	Mongolia
1,329	19,600	235,783	9.0	5,100	5.2	1,210	22	281	32	*30.2*	*1,240*	Morocco
627	24,900	8,573	0.6	620	28	35	495	62	270	*4.1*	*300*	Mozambique
1,152[10]	36,200[10]	70,499[10]	1.7[10]	3,300	14	1,000	46	80[12]	560[12]	...	...	Myanmar (Burma)
87	18,200	89,743	64	230	6.9	39	41	70	22	...	...	Namibia
3	3,000	168[24]	20[24]	6.0	1.7	...	...	1.2[12]	8.3[12]	...	...	Nauru
2,461	8,570	327,905	16	625	32	250	79	72	290	...	...	Nepal
3,567[11]	4,265[11]	6,105,000[1]	410[1]	13,400	1.2	6,500	2.4	7,630	2.0	14.7	975	Netherlands, The
16[1]	11,800[1]	17,427[1]	92[1]	206	1.0	35	5.7	50[1]	3.9[1]	...	...	Netherlands Antilles
274[10]	616[10]	22,257[17]	132[17]	92	2.0	36	5.1	39	4.6	*0.2*	*1,260*	New Caledonia
1,242[13]	2,670[13]	838,656[13, 17]	250[13, 17]	3,350	1.1	1,100	3.2	1,593	2.2	...	...	New Zealand
...	...	...	...	925	4.7	210	21	67	60	*5.0*	*1,750*	Nicaragua
64	131,000	4,647	0.6	440	20	25	352	11	830	...	...	Niger

Communications (continued)

country	publishing (latest)								daily newspapers (latest)		
	number of titles				number of copies ('000)						
	books		periodicals	pamphlets	books		periodicals	pamphlets	number	total circulation ('000)	circulation per 1,000 population
	total	school textbooks			total	school textbooks					
Nigeria	1,022	340	*92*	540	...	...	*495*	...	26	1,800	16
Northern Mariana Islands	...	...	...	...	...	...	...	...	—	—	—
Norway	4,079	...	7,010	802	...	...	...	...	82	2,600	606
Oman	24	...	15	...	25	...	...	...	4	79	48
Pakistan	70	10	*282*	...	317	252	*7,674*	...	274	809	6
Palau	...	...	...	...	...	...	...	...	—	—	—
Panama	...	...	*8*	...	...	...	*18*	...	8	223	89
Papua New Guinea	58	3	...	64	...	...	...	...	2	64	16
Paraguay	...	...	...	...	...	...	...	...	5	168	37
Peru	761	36	*45*	302	...	...	*90*	...	59	1,590	71
Philippines	763	323	1,570	62	...	...	9,468	...	43	3,200	49
Poland	9,172	501	2,950	1,555	107,414	34,362	54,703	18,406	72	6,085	158
Portugal	6,430[7]	1,545	937	[7]	24,928[7]	11,458	6,359	[7]	25	465	47
Puerto Rico	...	...	...	...	...	...	...	...	3	507	141
Qatar	372	200	190	...	...	...	120	...	4	70	155
Réunion	50	1	...	19	...	...	...	...	3	55	88
Romania	3,662[7]	...	1,379	[7]	66,598[7]	...	...	[7]	76	7,500	322
Russia	22,028	629	2,592	6,688	1,084,579	189,621	918,218	228,385	339	57,367	386
Rwanda	*131*	*42*	15	*76*	*746*	*552*	101	*2,109*	1	0.5	0.1
St. Kitts and Nevis	—	—	9	*3*	—	—	43	*3*	—	—	—
St. Lucia	*44*	*25*	...	*19*	*89*	*84*	...	*7*	—	—	—
St. Vincent	...	...	...	...	...	...	...	...	—	—	—
San Marino	...	...	18	...	...	...	10	...	6	2	87
São Tomé and Príncipe	...	...	...	...	...	...	...	...	—	—	—
Saudi Arabia	...	...	*58*	...	...	...	...	...	13	729	46
Senegal	...	...	*123*	...	...	...	*381*	...	1	50	6
Seychelles	...	...	*2*	...	...	...	*2*	...	1	3	44
Sierra Leone	...	*16*	...	...	...	...	...	...	1	10	2
Singapore	...	...	*1,786*	...	...	...	...	...	10	930	336
Slovakia	3,078	701	424	230	10,560	2,040	8,725	2,698	21	1,680	317
Slovenia	1,728	410	482	408	6,267	...	7,194	...	6	308	154
Solomon Islands	...	...	...	...	...	...	...	...	—	—	—
Somalia	...	...	...	...	...	...	...	...	1	9	2
South Africa	3,123	302	11	1,615	32,268	16,714	2,149	10,667	20	1,248	31
Spain	37,325	2,338	*1,998*	4,491	172,281	25,908	...	22,504	148	4,100	105
Sri Lanka	1,398	85	*170*	2,827	11,200	7,718	*1,770*	15,577	10	480	27
Sudan, The	...	...	*10*	...	...	...	*136*	...	5	620	23
Suriname	...	...	...	...	...	...	...	...	3	43	98
Swaziland	...	...	...	...	...	...	...	...	3	12	15
Sweden	9,902	487	*46*	2,911	...	...	*4,947*	...	124	4,419	511
Switzerland	14,663[7]	344	*3,079*	[7]	...	...	...	...	83	2,635	387
Syria	598	*1*	...	...	*553*	...	...	...	11	290	22
Taiwan	16,156	...	4,134	...	...	...	...	...	*93*	*4,000*	*202*
Tajikistan	787[7]	...	26	[7]	12,000[7]	...	18,841	[7]	9	...	...
Tanzania	127	23	...	45	275	46	...	89	3	220	8
Thailand	7,565	640	1,293	61	...	...	...	...	35	4,150	74
Togo	...	...	...	...	...	...	...	...	2	12	3
Tonga	...	...	...	...	...	...	...	...	1	7	72
Trinidad and Tobago	...	...	...	...	...	...	...	...	4	175	138
Tunisia	1,165	—	...	—	94	—	...	—	9	410	49
Turkey	5,854	503	1,325	695	...	...	1,325	...	399	4,000	71
Turkmenistan	386	27	33	179	4,435	1,678	12,800	2,169	66	1,141	319
Tuvalu	...	...	...	...	...	...	...	...	—	—	—
Uganda	...	...	26	...	...	...	158	...	6	80	4
Ukraine	3,550	177	321	860	102,832	23,268	3,491	25,639	90	6,083	117
United Arab Emirates	...	270	80	...	...	5,490	922	...	11	335	201
United Kingdom	80,787	2,773	*6,408*	5,786	...	...	...	...	101	22,100	383
United States	49,276	...	*11,593*	...	...	...	...	...	1,586	60,700	240
Uruguay	790	48	*465*	353	1,391	110	...	579	32	750	240
Uzbekistan	2,080[7]	...	61	[7]	51,000[7]	...	1,598	[7]	12	452	21
Vanuatu	...	...	...	...	...	...	...	...	—	—	—
Venezuela	3,366	...	...	513	...	...	...	...	82	4,200	208
Vietnam	...	...	...	...	...	...	...	...	4	570	8
Virgin Islands (U.S)	...	...	...	...	...	...	...	...	2	21	206
West Bank	...	...	...	...	...	...	...	...	—	—	—
Western Sahara	...	...	...	...	...	...	...	...	—	—	—
Western Samoa	...	...	...	...	...	...	...	...	—	—	—
Yemen	...	...	...	...	...	...	...	...	4	236	19
Yugoslavia	2,365	334	397	253	10,750	6,274	747	601	10	544	52
Zaire	...	...	*68*	...	...	...	...	...	9	112	3
Zambia	...	...	...	...	...	...	...	...	2	70	8
Zimbabwe	151	6	28	81	...	...	680	...	2	195	18

post offices, 1993				radio, 1994		television, 1994		telephones, 1993		cinema (latest)		country
number	persons per office	pieces of mail handled ('000)	pieces of mail handled per capita	receivers (all types; '000)	persons per receiver	receivers (all types; '000)	persons per receiver	main lines		annual attendance		
								receivers ('000)	persons per receiver	number ('000,000)	per 1,000 population	
3,619[11]	32,900[11]	681,977	5.7	18,000	5.2	6,100	15	342	300	*4.6*	*51*	Nigeria
...	...	...	...	10.5	5.4	4.1	14	14	3.3	...	...	Northern Mariana Islands
2,541	1,760	2,164,233	500	3,342	1.3	2,000	2.2	2,335	1.8	10.7	2,510	Norway
76[4]	19,700[4]	34,292[15]	20[15]	900	2.3	1,500	1.4	148	8.6	...	...	Oman
13,196	9,310	722,293[6]	5.9[6]	10,200	14	2,080	66	1,605	76	*25.3*	*230*	Pakistan
...	...	...	...	9	67	1.6	9.4	...	...	...	...	Palau
231	11,000	14,456	5.7	527	4.9	205	13	262	9.8	...	...	Panama
108[4]	34,800[4]	38,686[2, 4]	10[2, 4]	260	16	10	421	40	100	...	...	Papua New Guinea
321	14,500	7,333	1.6	700	6.9	350	14	142	33	...	...	Paraguay
1,373	16,400	37,751	1.7	5,300	4.4	2,000	11	670	34	*33.0*	*1,910*	Peru
2,147	30,600	986,027	15	8,300	8.2	7,000	9.8	860	76	...	...	Philippines
7,119	5,400	1,188,495[22]	31[22]	16,300	2.4	10,000	3.9	4,419	8.7	20.9	550	Poland
7,272	1,360	907,170[6]	92[6]	2,220	4.5	1,687	5.9	3,260	3.2	9.6	974	Portugal
...	...	...	...	2,480	1.5	830	4.4	1,207	3.0	...	...	Puerto Rico
28	20,000	27,051[2]	48[2]	180	3.2	251	2.3	111	4.7	*0.3*	*710*	Qatar
...	...	...	...	170	3.8	91	7.1	199	3.1	...	...	Réunion
4,884	4,660	250,509	11	4,500	5.1	4,000	5.7	2,624	8.7	*203.4*	*8,790*	Romania
48,061	3,100	10,390,706	700	90,000	1.6	54,200[4]	2.7[4]	23,397	6.3	750	5,040	Russia
43	169,000	9,972[4]	1.3[4]	650	12	...	...	12	630	*0.3*	*56*	Rwanda
8	5,000	1,906	48	26	1.5	9.5	4.2	12	3.4	...	...	St. Kitts and Nevis
62	2,300	5,095[10]	34[10]	98	1.4	25	5.7	24	6.5	...	...	St. Lucia
103	1,070	526[2, 4]	4.9[2, 4]	73	1.5	18	6.2	17	6.7	...	...	St. Vincent
10	2,000	...	...	13	1.9	8.0[14]	2.9[14]	14	1.6	0.03	1,300	San Marino
11	10,900	101,525[10]	860[10]	31	4.1	21	6.1	2.4	52	...	...	São Tomé and Príncipe
1,754	9,540	365,522[3]	21[3]	3,800	4.6	4,700	3.7	1,575	11[4]	...	...	Saudi Arabia
139	55,700	15,150	2.0	850	9.5	61	132	64	130		...	Senegal
5	14,000	4,502	64	40	1.9	13	5.7	11	6.2	...	...	Seychelles
71	63,200	2,018	0.5	900	4.9	25	176	15	310	...	...	Sierra Leone
998	2,880	577,419	200	822	3.6	650	8.2	1,246	2.3	*30.7*	*20,600*	Singapore
1,744	3,050	85,620[15]	16[15]	2,806	0.7	1,279	1.6	893	6.0	13.8	2,630	Slovakia
504	3,970	218,625	110	601[14]	3.3[14]	445[14]	4.4[14]	516	3.9	2.8	1,440	Slovenia
117[4]	2,900[4]	4,289	12	38	9.6	...	...	5.3	65	...	...	Solomon Islands
...	...	...	...	300	22	3.0[16]	2,270[16]	15	560	...	...	Somalia
...	...	...	...	11,200	3.6	3,445	12	3,660	11	26.0	680	South Africa
5,894[14]	6,610[14]	4,318,678	110	12,000	3.3	17,000	2.3	14,254	2.7	79.1	2,080	Spain
4,043	4,360	350,748	20	3,300	5.5	700	26	158	111	*37.2*	*2,270*	Sri Lanka
619	45,400	5,309	0.2	5,755	4.8	250	109	64	440	*13.0*	*600*	Sudan, The
...	...	...	...	262	1.6	43	9.8	47	8.6	...	...	Suriname
69	11,700	20,085	25	117	7.5	13	68	16	56	...	...	Swaziland
1,836	4,800	8,418,751	062	7,450	1.2	3,750	2.3	5,903	1.5	15.6	1,810	Sweden
3,733	1,860	4,234,907	614	5,600	1.3	2,545	2.8	4,266	1.6	15.4	2,270	Switzerland
626	21,300	17,974	1.4	2,000	1.0	700	20	330	24	6.9	590	Syria
13,233[4]	1,550[4]	1,754,119[4]	86[4]	8,620	2.4	7,000	3.0	7,951	2.6	*64.2*	*3,200*	Taiwan
785[4, 8]	6,920[4, 8]	320,049[4]	59[4]	854[10]	6.4[10]	860[10]	6.3[10]	260	22	30.0	5,520	Tajikistan
885	32,500	82,171	2.9	565	48	80	341	85	313	1.8	72	Tanzania
4,265	13,700	904,878	16	10,000	5.8	3,300	18	2,185	27	...	...	Thailand
43	90,200	3,511	0.9	720	5.6	150	27	17	230	...	...	Togo
108	93	4,014	400	52	1.9	3.0	33	5.9	16	...	...	Tonga
232[10]	5,300[10]	23,288[10]	19[10]	580	2.2	250	5.0	193	6.7	...	...	Trinidad and Tobago
906	9,470	144,522[10]	17[10]	1,700	5.2	650	14	421	20	...	...	Tunisia
42,541	1,420	1,651,700	27	8,800	7.0	10,530	5.8	10,936	5.4	16.5	287	Turkey
580[4, 8]	6,490[4, 8]	344,027[4]	[illegible]	[illegible]	4.0[1]	705[1]	5.5[1]	[illegible]	15	46.0	12,200	Turkmenistan
9[12]	970[12]	88[2, 12]	10[2, 12]	3.0	3.1	...	...	0.12	77	...	...	Tuvalu
319	51,700	17,239	1	1,800	10	115	150	21	830	...	...	Uganda
16,500	3,160	1,506,173	29	15,000[14]	3.5[14]	17,200[14]	3.0[14]	2,225	6.7	415.8	8,000	Ukraine
161	10,600	249,058	145	490	4.4	170	13	624	2.6	...	...	United Arab Emirates
19,782	2,920	16,651,000[6]	290[6]	65,400	0.9	20,000	2.9	28,681	2.0	102	1,770	United Kingdom
51,193	5,130	170,544,202	662	524,200	0.5	215,000	1.2	148,084	1.7	981.9	3,890	United States
167	18,800	15,370	4.9	1,850	1.7	600	5.2	530	5.9	*6.2*	*2,110*	Uruguay
3,800[4, 8]	5,520[4, 8]	1,537,874[4]	73[4]	3,677[4]	5.7[4]	3,308[4]	6.3[4]	1,452	15	126.0	6,010	Uzbekistan
...	...	...	...	55	3.0	1.0[14]	148[14]	4.1	39	...	...	Vanuatu
556[10]	35,500[10]	94,854[10]	4.8[10]	8,300	2.6	3,701	5.8	2,083	10	18	1,590	Venezuela
...	...	...	...	7,000	10	2,500	29	260	270	*239.9*	*3,760*	Vietnam
9	1,670	3,779[2]	252[2]	100	1.0	32	3.1	59	1.7	...	...	Virgin Islands (U.S.)
...	...	...	...	...	...	...	...	...	...	...	...	West Bank
...	...	...	...	...	...	...	...	...	...	...	...	Western Sahara
40	4,000	1,089	6.8	75	2.2	5.0	32	6.5	25	...	...	Western Samoa
217[14]	51,800[14]	9,999[14]	0.9[14]	665	19	100	126	162	83	...	...	Yemen
1,569	6,780	210[3]	—	2,692[23]	3.9[23]	1,643[1]	6.4[1]	1,923	5.6	2.9	280	Yugoslavia
304	135,400	45,394[14]	1.3[14]	3,480	12	22	1,934	36[12]	1,110[12]	...	...	Zaire
421	21,100	48,868	5.5	603	15	200	46	78	110	...	...	Zambia
202	54,000	321,825	30	801	14	137	80	128[4]	83[4]	*5.6*	*690*	Zimbabwe

[1]1989. [2]Foreign-dispatched only. [3]Letters only. [4]1991. [5]1983. [6]Domestic and foreign-dispatched only. [7]Books includes pamphlets. [8]Includes telephone and telegraph offices. [9]Letters dispatched only. [10]1992. [11]Permanent post offices only. [12]1988. [13]1986. [14]1990. [15]Domestic only. [16]1987. [17]Excludes postcards. [18]Data refer only to titles published by the Ministry of Culture. [19]Ethiopia includes Eritrea. [20]Includes overseas departments and Monaco. [21]Excludes printed matter. [22]Excludes small packets. [23]1993. [24]1985.

Trade: external

The following table presents comparative data on the international, or foreign, trade of the countries of the world. The table analyzes data for both imports and exports in two ways: (1) into several major commodity groups defined in accordance with the United Nations system called the Standard International Trade Classification (SITC) and (2) by direction of trade for each country with major world trading blocs and partners. These commodity groupings are defined by the SITC code numbers beneath the column headings. The single-digit numbers represent broad SITC categories (in the SITC, called "sections"); the double-digit numbers represent subcategories ("divisions") of the single-digit categories (27 is a subcategory of 2); the three-digit number is a subcategory ("group") of the double-digit (667 is a subcategory of 66). Where a plus or minus sign is used before one of these SITC numbers, the SITC category or subcategory is being added to or subtracted from the aggregate implied by the total of the preceding sections. The SITC commodity aggregations used here are listed in the table at the end of this headnote. The full SITC commodity breakdown—some 3,118 basic headings—is presented in the 1986 United Nations publication *Standard International Trade Classification, Revision 3.*

The SITC was developed by the United Nations through its Statistical Commission as an outgrowth of the need for a standard system of aggregating commodities of external trade to provide international comparability of foreign trade statistics. The United Nations Statistical Commission has defined external merchandise trade as "all goods whose movement into or out of the customs area of a country compiling the statistics adds to or subtracts from the material resources of the country." Goods passing through a country for transport only are excluded, but goods entering for reexport, or deposited (as in a bonded warehouse, or free trade area) for reimport, are included. Statistics in this table refer only to goods and exclude purely financial transactions that are covered in the "Finance" and "National product and accounts" tables. Gold for fabrication (*e.g.,* as jewelry) is included; monetary and reserve gold are excluded.

For purposes of comparability of data, total value of imports and exports is given in this table in U.S. dollars. Conversions from currencies other than U.S. dollars are determined according to the average market rates for the year for which data are supplied; these are mainly as calculated by the International Monetary Fund (IMF) or other official sources. The commodity categories are given in terms of percentages of the total value of the country's import or export trade (with the exclusions noted above). Value is based on transaction value: for imports, the value at which the goods were purchased by the importer plus the cost of transportation and insurance to the frontier of the importing country (c.i.f. [cost, insurance,

Trade: external

country	year	imports												
		total value ('000,000 U.S.$)	Standard International Trade Classification (SITC) categories (%)							direction of trade (%)				
			food and agricultural raw materials (0+1+2 −27−28 +4)	mineral ores and concen-trates (27+28 +667)	fuels and other energy (3)	manufactured goods				from European Union (EU)[b]	from United States	from Eastern Europe[c]	from Japan	from all other[d]
						total[a] (5+6 −667 +7+8 +9)	of which chemicals and related products (5)	of which machinery and transport equipment (7)	of which other[a] (6−667 +8+9)					
Afghanistan	1991[1]	936.4	15.0	—[2]	0.4	84.6[3]	2.1	48.2	34.3[3]	4.8[4]	0.2[4]	59.9[4,5]	7.9[4]	27.2[4]
Albania	1990	446.5	25.7	—24.5—		49.8	9.3	31.0	9.5	41.3[6]	2.2[4]	27.9[5]	0.1	28.6[4]
Algeria	1992	8,647.8	31.4	0.8	1.4	66.4	10.9	30.7	24.9	66.5	11.0	1.2	4.5	16.8
American Samoa	1991	371.9	—6.3[2]—		15.9	77.8[3]	1.2	3.4	73.3[3,7]	—	28.7	—	3.8	67.5
Andorra	1992	1,136.8	—28.3[2,8]—		3.7[8]	68.0[3,8]	7.3[8]	19.9[8]	40.8[8]	80.1[6]	1.4[4]	...	6.7	11.8[4]
Angola	1991	1,347.0	—32.4[2,9]—		0.7[9]	66.9[3,9]	10.6[9]	25.0[9]	31.3[3,9]	66.8[4]	10.5	0.2[4]	7.8	14.7[4]
Antigua and Barbuda	1987	247.0	—17.8[2]—		9.9	72.3[3]	6.2	26.8	39.4[3]	41.3	29.5	—	—	29.2
Argentina	1993	16,772.9	7.4	1.3	2.4	89.0	14.1	50.5	24.4	25.8	23.0	0.7	4.0	46.5
Armenia	1993	310.0	—57.1[2]—		21.6	21.6[3]	1.9	11.3	8.4[3]	23.2[4]	27.4[4]	27.9	—[4]	21.5[4]
Aruba	1988	334.2	22.3	0.1	7.6	70.0	8.0	19.7	42.3	22.9	40.7	0.1[5]	3.7	32.7
Australia	1994	53,425.0	—7.3[2]—		4.8	88.0[3]	10.8	46.1	31.0[3]	26.4	21.8	0.2	17.8	33.8
Austria	1994	55,058.5	8.4	1.2	4.4	85.9	10.4	38.0	37.5	68.4	4.4	7.5	4.3	15.5
Azerbaijan	1992	929.9	—31.9[2]—		5.1	63.0[3]	12.1	22.7	28.2[3]	11.5	2.6	58.4	—	27.5
Bahamas, The	1990	2,919.9	8.6	—	65.2	26.2	5.3	8.3	12.7	5.9	36.2	0.2[5]	0.5	57.3
Bahrain	1993	3,858.0	11.0	0.3	41.1	47.6	9.8	18.0	19.9	21.0[4]	18.6[4]	...	6.5[4]	53.8[4]
Bangladesh	1993[11]	2,708.8	40.6	4.6	9.6	45.3	9.2	13.6	22.5	11.1	5.2	1.3	6.7	75.8
Barbados	1993	574.0	22.4	0.2	9.7	67.7	12.7	22.9	32.1	17.0	38.2	0.1	5.4	39.3
Belarus	1992	3,499.0	—37.3[2]—		11.1	51.6[3]	10.0	31.7	10.0[3]	7.7	2.6	76.2	0.2	13.2
Belgium[12]	1993	111,063.8	13.0	9.6	7.5	69.9	13.0	25.2	31.7	76.1	5.4	1.8	2.8	14.0
Belize	1993	280.9	18.3	0.3	11.1	70.3	11.4	26.4	32.5	14.0	56.9	0.1	1.3	27.7
Benin	1989	207.3	—31.0[2]—		15.3	53.7[3]	7.1	14.5	32.1[3]	41.3	7.3	2.4[5]	2.7	46.3
Bermuda	1993	588.9	20.5	0.1[2]	5.8	73.6[3]	13.9	23.3	36.3[3]	10.1[6]	70.2	—	5.4	14.3
Bhutan	1990	78.1	24.0	0.5	13.1	62.4	5.5	26.0	30.9	4.2	1.3	—	5.4	89.1[14]
Bolivia	1993	1,249.6	10.6	1.6	4.7	83.2	11.2	47.7	24.3	21.0	22.6	1.3	10.9	44.1
Bosnia and Herzegovina	1993	422.2[4]	...	...	31.6[9]	...	...	...	...	28.0[4]	4.0[4]	11.7[4]	—[4]	56.3[4]
Botswana	1991	1,946.5	15.5	2.5	6.3	75.7	7.1	33.0	35.6	6.7	1.2	—	0.3	91.7[17]
Brazil	1993	27,712.3	13.8	2.0	20.2	63.9	15.9	34.0	14.0	23.6	23.4	1.5	6.0	45.4
Brunei	1991	1,111.2	16.1	0.7	0.6	82.6	6.3	38.3	38.0	23.9	13.7	—	15.8	46.7
Bulgaria	1993	4,233.3	13.8[4]	1.9[2]	35.7	48.7[3,4]	12.1[4]	23.6[4]	12.9[3,4]	34.3	3.4	40.3	1.3	20.7
Burkina Faso	1990	539.6	23.1	0.6	11.2	65.1	13.7	24.7	26.7	48.1[4]	3.0[4]	0.2[4]	4.0[4]	44.7[4]
Burundi	1992	229.5	11.2	0.5	12.2	76.2	14.1	27.5	34.5	47.9	4.3	0.5	8.1	39.3
Cambodia	1993	403.9	17.2[19]	...	11.7	...	6.5[19]	17.0[19]	...	9.2[4]	4.5[4]	2.5[4]	12.2[4]	71.6[4]
Cameroon	1991	2,306.2	16.8	6.2	3.4	73.6	14.7	27.1	31.7	64.6	6.6	0.4[5]	2.9	25.4
Canada	1994	147,851.0	7.6	1.7	3.5	87.3	7.9	51.6	27.8	9.7	67.6	0.4	5.6	16.7
Cape Verde	1990	136.3	30.7	—	7.5	61.8	6.1	30.7	24.9	68.7	2.4	3.0[5]	3.8	22.1
Central African Republic	1989	159.1	20.1	0.7	6.7	72.6	14.0	33.2	25.3	56.7	1.3	0.3	7.6	34.2
Chad	1991	296.6	15.9[23]	0.6[23]	14.2[23]	69.3[23]	16.4[23]	28.8[23]	24.1[23]	38.8[4]	5.1[4]	...	1.7[4]	54.3[4]
Chile	1994	11,149.1	8.7	0.8	9.8	80.7	12.1	42.6	26.0	21.1	23.7	0.7	9.0	45.5
China	1994	115,613.6	8.8	2.2	3.5	85.5	10.5	44.5	30.5	16.1	12.0	4.3	22.8	44.9
Colombia	1993	9,840.8	10.1	0.9	3.8	85.2	16.2	39.5	29.5	18.9	33.3	0.7	11.1	36.0
Comoros	1993	59.4	25.9[19]	...	10.7	63.5	2.0[19]	9.0[19]	...	66.0[4]	—[4]	1.0[4]	2.0[4]	31.0[4]
Congo	1990	594.5	18.9[24]	0.7[24]	1.7[24]	78.7[24]	9.1[24]	35.3[24]	34.3[24]	66.9	11.1	0.6[5]	4.0	17.4
Costa Rica	1992	2,789.1	8.9	0.3	8.7	82.0	16.3	25.5	40.3	11.0	49.7	0.3[5]	6.1	33.0
Côte d'Ivoire	1989	2,185.3	—23.7—		21.3	55.0	14.8	16.4	23.8	53.9	4.3	1.0[5]	2.7	38.2
Croatia	1993	4,666.4	11.0	1.6	9.9	77.5	12.4	24.2	41.0	56.4	2.7	10.6	0.9	29.5
Cuba	1989	8,122.1	14.9	0.5[2]	32.4	52.2[3]	6.2	27.5	18.5[3]	10.9	—	76.5[5]	0.6	12.0
Cyprus	1994	3,014.1	19.5	0.8	8.4	71.3	8.4	27.3	35.6	52.7	10.3	5.9	6.8	24.2
Czech Republic	1993	12,566.8	—12.7[2]—		11.4	75.9[3]	12.0	35.8	28.0[3]	51.9	3.0	32.7	1.7	10.7
Denmark	1994	33,937.2	16.3	0.5	4.3	78.8	11.3	32.5	35.0	65.8	5.1	3.6	3.4	22.2
Djibouti	1991	214.4	38.3	0.2	9.1	52.3	6.0	15.5	30.8	46.6	3.7	0.7[5]	7.2	41.8
Dominica	1991	109.6	27.6	0.3	7.9	64.2	12.0	21.6	30.5	21.2	31.4	0.3	5.6	41.5
Dominican Republic	1991	1,988.1	13.7[27]	0.3[27]	35.2[27]	50.7[27]	11.7[27]	23.2[27]	15.9[27]	14.6[4]	45.7[4]	—[4]	5.2[4]	34.5[4]
Ecuador	1993	2,552.7	7.4	0.3	1.7	90.6	15.5	49.1	26.1	24.3	31.7	1.2	13.5	29.2
Egypt	1993	8,187.8	26.0	5.9	1.7	66.4	13.0	31.0	22.4	45.4	15.0	5.0	4.5	30.1
El Salvador	1993	1,858.3	14.7	0.4	11.3	73.6	17.0	31.3	25.2	9.0	42.5	0.3	5.3	42.9

and freight] valuation); for exports, the value at which the goods were sold by the exporter, including the cost of transportation and insurance to bring the goods onto the transporting vehicle at the frontier of the exporting country (f.o.b. [free-on-board] valuation).

The largest part of the information presented here comes from the United Nations' *Commodity Trade Statistics* (including microfiche format) and *International Trade Statistics Yearbook*. These publications, however, cannot always provide the most recent data for all countries listed in this table and must be supplemented by national and regional sources. In some cases where the original data were only available for an alternative trade classification, an approximation has been made of the SITC commodity groupings.

a. Also includes any unallocated commodities.
b. EU of 15 countries (Austria, Belgium, Denmark, Finland, France, Germany, Greece, Ireland, Italy, Luxembourg, The Netherlands, Portugal, Spain, Sweden, and the United Kingdom). Austria, Finland, and Sweden joined Jan. 1, 1995; figures for these countries are included for all years.
c. Includes Albania, Bulgaria, Czech Republic, Hungary, Poland, Romania, Slovakia, and European republics of the former U.S.S.R. (Belarus, Estonia, Latvia, Lithuania, Moldova, Russia, and Ukraine).
d. May include value of trade shown as not available (...) in any of the four preceding columns. May include any unspecified areas or countries.
... Not available.
— None, less than 0.05%, or not applicable.

Detail may not add to 100.0 or indicated subtotals because of rounding.

SITC category codes

0		food and live animals
1		beverages and tobacco
2		crude materials, inedible, except fuels
	27	crude fertilizers and crude minerals (excluding coal, petroleum, and precious stones)
	28	metalliferous ores and metal scrap
3		mineral fuels, lubricants, and related materials (including coal, petroleum, natural gas, and electric current)
4		animal and vegetable oils, fats, and waxes
5		chemicals and related products not elsewhere specified
6		manufactured goods classified chiefly by material
	667	pearls, precious and semiprecious stones, unworked or worked
7		machinery and transport equipment
8		miscellaneous manufactured articles
9		commodities and transactions not classified elsewhere

exports													country
total value ('000,000 U.S.$)	Standard International Trade Classification (SITC) categories (%)							direction of trade (%)					
	food and agricultural raw materials (0+1+2 −27−28 +4)	mineral ores and concentrates (27+28 +667)	fuels and other energy (3)	manufactured goods				to European Union (EU)[b]	to United States	to Eastern Europe[c]	to Japan	to all other[d]	
				total[a] (5+6 −667 +7+8 +9)	of which chemicals and related products (5)	of which machinery and transport equipment (7)	of which other[a] (6−667 +8+9)						
235.1	——63.0[2]——		...	37.0[3]	...	...	...	7.3[4]	0.5[4]	70.2[4, 5]	0.3[4]	21.8[4]	Afghanistan
267.4	37.9	——46.8——		15.3	1.5	0.8	13.0	30.5[6]	1.1[4]	38.2[5]	2.1	28.1[4]	Albania
11,136.8	0.7	0.3	96.6	2.4	0.6	0.8	0.9	72.8	13.9	1.8	0.7	10.7	Algeria
326.9	65.9		—	34.1[7]	—	—	34.1[7]	—	100.0	—	—	—	American Samoa
41.1	——29.6[2, 8]——		—[8]	70.4[3, 8]	7.2[8]	10.9[8]	52.4[3, 8]	98.0[6]	0.2[4]	...	—[4]	2.0[4]	Andorra
3,409.7	0.3	4.9	94.8	—	—	—	—	26.9	61.4	0.4[5]	—	11.3	Angola
19.4	——7.4[2]——		17.8	74.7[3]	9.5	24.0	41.3[3]	15.0	15.4	—	—	69.5	Antigua and Barbuda
13,090.5	57.5	0.1	9.3	33.0	5.4	11.0	16.6	28.2	9.7	1.4	3.6	57.1	Argentina
108.0	——7.4[2]——		—	92.6[3]	6.5	25.9	60.2[3]	—	—	62.1	—	37.9	Armenia
30.6	54.0	1.2	0.2	44.5	7.1	7.9	29.5	5.6	22.3	—	—	72.1	Aruba
47,548.1	——41.9[2]——		16.6	41.5[3]	3.8	11.7	26.0[3]	11.7	7.1	0.6	24.6	55.9	Australia
44,870.9	7.2	0.8	1.3	90.7	9.1	39.0	42.5	64.8	3.4	10.9	1.6	19.4	Austria
1,449.8	——16.2[2]——		8.7	75.1[3]	45.2[10]	16.9	13.0[3]	15.4	2.8	38.0	0.1	42.9	Azerbaijan
2,592.6	——4.9——		73.5	21.5	19.9	0.6	1.0	2.6	93.8	—	0.6	3.0	Bahamas, The
3,710.1	1.9	0.3	72.1	25.7	2.5	0.9	22.3	4.8[4]	2.7[4]	...	9.4[4]	83.2[4]	Bahrain
2,137.6	16.0	0.1	0.9	83.1	2.4	0.1	80.6	37.4	35.0	1.6	2.6	23.4	Bangladesh
181.0	29.2	0.4	16.1	54.3	14.4	18.0	21.8	18.1	18.6	—	0.6	62.6	Barbados
3,558.8	——14.1[2]——		2.1	83.7[3]	19.0	45.9	18.8[3]	9.3	1.2	68.1	0.2	21.2	Belarus
120,686.6	12.1	7.8	3.4	76.7	15.6	27.4	33.8	75.6	4.7	1.7	1.1	16.9	Belgium[12]
126.6	74.4	—	2.2	23.4	0.8	3.3	19.2	36.3	42.4	—	0.5	20.8	Belize
97.5	——71.4[2]——		21.3	7.3[3]	0.4	2.0	4.9[3]	27.3	21.3	—	0.2	51.2	Benin
35.3	...	...	...	...	71.1	...	...	27.0[13]	62.3[13]	—[13]	—[13]	10.6[13]	Bermuda
68.1	35.0	3.9	32.6[15]	28.4	16.6	0.1	11.8	0.2	—	—	—	99.8[16]	Bhutan
808.9	23.1	24.0	12.7	40.2	0.7	2.0	37.5	33.6	26.1	—	0.3	40.0	Bolivia
70.3[4]	...	...	...	...	9.4[9]	20.8[9]	...	46.6[4]	10.3[4]	15.1[4]	0.1[4]	27.8[4]	Bosnia and Herzegovina
1,853.5	6.7	86.6	—	6.7	1.0	2.4	3.3	3.0	0.3	—	—	96.8[18]	Botswana
38,700.9	28.3	7.1	1.7	62.9	6.0	20.9	35.9	26.4	20.7	1.2	6.0	45.7	Brazil
2,466.5	0.5	—	96.7	2.7	0.1	1.3	1.3	0.5	1.1	—	62.6	35.8	Brunei
3,369.9	28.2[4]	1.5[2]	7.9	62.5[3, 4]	16.7[4]	16.0[4]	29.8[3, 4]	29.8	3.3	23.6	0.4	42.8	Bulgaria
151.1	74.3	—	—	25.7	0.1	0.8	24.8	23.1	0.8[4]	—	1.3	74.8[4]	Burkina Faso
74.7	82.3	—	—	17.7	—	—	17.7	75.3[4]	7.6[4]	—[4]	2.7[4]	14.4[4]	Burundi
219.1[20]	88.9[21]	...	...	...	...	...	...	15.5[4]	0.5[4]	0.5[4]	37.6[4]	45.9[4]	Cambodia
2,892.5	35.3	—	47.5	17.2	0.7	7.5	9.0	61.3	0.4	0.3[5]	0.3	37.6	Cameroon
165,836.8	16.6	2.1	9.7	71.6	5.4	40.0	26.1	5.4	81.7	0.2	4.3	8.4	Canada
28.6	——18.4——		65.1	16.5	0.9	11.1	4.5	11.4	—	—	—	88.5[22]	Cape Verde
140.3	54.3	43.2	—	2.5	0.2	0.2	2.0	89.9	0.6	—	—	9.5	Central African Republic
193.9	——85.6[2]——		11.0	3.4[3]	0.7	0.7	2.1[3]	29.1[4]	0.1[4]	...	4.8[4]	66.0[4]	Chad
11,368.7	38.2	13.4	0.2	48.2	4.6	2.7	40.8	23.8	16.4	0.5	17.3	42.0	Chile
121,006.3	12.2	1.0	3.4	83.4	5.2	18.1	60.2	12.7	17.7	2.2	17.8	49.5	China
7,454.9	——39.9——		25.3	34.8	5.6	5.8	23.4	23.6	40.4	0.1[6]	3.2	32.7	Colombia
21.9	81.8[19]	—	...	18.2	13.3[19]	...	...	50.1[6]	46.2	—[4]	—[4]	3.7[4]	Comoros
977.7	15.3	1.3[25]	70.8	12.5[26]	—	1.0	11.5[26]	60.8[4]	36.3	0.1[5]	—	2.8[4]	Congo
1,833.7	65.3	0.1	0.5	34.0	5.6	3.3	25.1	24.8	48.4	0.2	0.7	25.9	Costa Rica
2,931.2	——75.4——		9.6	14.9	3.4	2.9	8.7	62.2	6.6	5.0[5]	1.3	24.8	Côte d'Ivoire
3,903.8	17.7	0.6	9.7	72.1	14.5	14.2	43.5	57.5	2.1	7.7	—	32.6	Croatia
5,392.0	——91.7[2]——		...	8.3[3]	1.2	0.8	6.3[3]	14.5	—	70.1[5]	1.9	13.5	Cuba
961.2	43.7	2.3	3.9	50.0	6.8	12.3	30.9	36.8	1.6	20.0	0.2	41.3	Cyprus
12,770.6	——14.0[2]——		6.2	79.9[3]	9.3	27.4	43.1[3]	50.9	15.8	30.9	0.5	15.8	Czech Republic
39,834.6	29.2	0.6	2.6	67.6	9.6	25.8	32.2	58.7	4.9	3.7	3.7	29.0	Denmark
17.3	32.5	—	—	67.5	0.4	8.3	58.7	62.6	0.8	—	0.9	35.7	Djibouti
54.2	67.2	0.4	—	32.4	23.7	4.2	4.4	61.2	5.2	—	—	33.6	Dominica
658.3	49.1	39.7[2]	0.1	11.2[3]	0.7	2.0	8.5[3]	21.9	63.7	—	3.6	10.8	Dominican Republic
3,020.0	49.3	0.1	41.4	9.3	1.1	2.3	5.9	16.3	46.3	1.8	1.7	33.9	Ecuador
3,110.0	12.3	0.4	49.8	37.5	3.6	0.9	33.0	40.1	13.9	3.6	1.8	40.7	Egypt
716.3	51.0	0.1	0.2	48.8	12.2	3.3	33.2	16.5	29.7	—	2.0	51.8	El Salvador

Trade: external (continued)

country	year	imports												
		total value ('000,000 U.S.$)	Standard International Trade Classification (SITC) categories (%)							direction of trade (%)				
			food and agricultural raw materials (0+1+2 −27−28 +4)	mineral ores and concen-trates (27+28 +667)	fuels and other energy (3)	manufactured goods				from European Union (EU)[b]	from United States	from Eastern Europe[c]	from Japan	from all other[d]
						total[a] (5+6 −667 +7+8 +9)	of which chemicals and related products (5)	of which machinery and transport equipment (7)	of which other[a] (6−667 +8+9)					
Equatorial Guinea	1990	61.6	13.5	3.4	7.7	75.4	3.9	58.2	13.3	31.5	39.9	—	0.3[4]	28.3
Eritrea	1992	138.5	———33.0———			67.0	9.0	...	58.0	8.0[6]	...	...	...	92.0[29]
Estonia	1994	1,660.4	23.1	0.6	13.8	62.5	10.5	28.3	23.7	63.2	2.5	25.1	2.9	6.2
Ethiopia	1991	471.8	6.5	0.2	10.6	82.6	15.4	44.6	22.6	40.3	13.1	1.9[5]	9.6	35.0
Faroe Islands	1993	249.8	30.4	0.6	15.5	53.5	9.5	15.3	28.7	66.6	3.0	3.2	1.6	25.5
Fiji	1994	830.5	15.9	0.3	11.2	72.5	7.3	30.9	34.3	3.9	14.8	0.1	8.0	73.3
Finland	1994	23,017.6	9.8	3.6	11.6	75.0	12.8	35.9	26.3	55.2	7.6	12.0	6.5	18.8
France[30]	1994	229,334.2	13.5	1.1	7.7	77.6	12.0	35.3	30.4	62.5	8.5	2.3	3.7	23.0
French Guiana	1994	673.4	18.3	0.1	6.8	74.8	7.4	41.5	25.8	77.9	2.9	—	1.7	17.5
French Polynesia	1988	808.3	20.4	0.2	5.4	74.1	6.4	35.9	31.8	65.5	11.3	0.1	4.4	18.6
Gabon	1990	772.0	—12.1[2, 4]—		1.9[4]	86.0[3, 4]	8.3[4]	42.0[4]	35.7[3, 4]	69.9	6.4[4]	0.1[4]	4.9	18.7[4]
Gambia, The	1992	234.2	—39.6[2]—		8.0	52.4[3]	5.8	19.9	26.7[4]	41.3[4]	2.9[4]	2.6[4, 5]	2.9[4]	50.4[4]
Gaza Strip	1993	353.1	...	...	...	...	...	...	...	...	...	...	...	100.0[32]
Georgia	1992	216.0[4]	—21.4[2]—		61.2	17.4[3]	2.1	4.2	11.1[3]	5.1[4]	7.4[4]	34.7[4]	2.3[4]	50.5[4]
Germany	1994	377,992.3	12.5	1.6	7.0	79.0	8.8	33.7	36.5	55.5	7.3	7.2	5.6	24.5
Ghana	1990	1,412.3	—11.8[2]—		27.6	60.6[3]	9.6	26.7	24.3[3]	51.2	10.8	0.8[5]	5.5	31.7
Gibraltar	1993	401.9[34]	—24.4[2, 35]—		20.7[35]	54.9[3, 35]	4.3[35]	21.4[35]	29.2[3, 35]	66.5	2.2[4]	...	3.2	28.2
Greece	1993	22,802.6	16.0	0.5	10.6	72.8	11.0	35.2	26.6	62.9	3.7	4.6	6.8	21.9
Greenland	1993	346.6	17.6	0.3	11.2	70.8	4.4	22.5	44.0	83.9	4.0	0.7	3.6	7.7
Grenada	1991	117.2	28.4	0.2	7.4	64.1	8.5	24.2	31.3	19.8	32.2	0.1	7.1	40.8
Guadeloupe	1994	1,537.9	24.3	0.2	1.7	73.8	10.2	30.5	33.1	81.4	3.1	0.2	2.4	12.9
Guam	1983	610.7	16.9	0.1	46.9	36.2	2.3	19.1	14.8	...	23.4	...	19.9	56.6
Guatemala	1992	2,462.8	12.4	0.3	13.8	73.4	17.8	31.8	23.8	12.4	45.4	0.4[5]	6.0	35.9
Guernsey[37]	...	...	...	...	...	...	...	...	...	...	...	...	...	...
Guinea	1990	699.0	—12.8[2, 35]—		13.7[35]	73.5[3, 35]	...	17.0[35]	56.5[3, 35]	60.7[4]	9.0	...	3.6[4]	26.7[4]
Guinea-Bissau	1990	85.7	20.1[38]	2.2[38]	6.2[38]	71.5[38]	5.6[38]	36.4[38]	29.5[38]	57.8[4]	1.0[4]	3.1[4]	10.6[4]	27.5[4]
Guyana	1991	306.6	—4.2—		21.9	73.9	1.1	48.1	24.7	25.1[4]	30.7[4]	0.7[4]	5.5[4]	38.0[4]
Haiti	1992[39]	278.0	—47.9—		22.0	30.1	8.0	6.6	15.6	16.7[4]	54.1[4]	0.1[4]	0.6[4]	28.5[4]
Honduras	1992	667.8	13.1	1.2	14.2	71.5	21.3	23.7	26.5	7.5	54.2	0.3	4.8	33.2
Hong Kong	1994	165,940.0	7.3	2.3	1.9	88.5	6.6	34.6	47.4	10.3	7.5	0.3	15.2	66.6
Hungary	1994	14,553.7	9.5	0.8[2]	11.8	77.9[3]	12.7	34.1	31.2[3]	61.1	3.1	21.8	2.7	11.3
Iceland	1994	1,472.4	13.1	3.0	8.3	75.7	9.2	31.5	34.9	58.3	8.9	3.3	4.0	25.4
India	1994[1]	23,304.1	6.5	14.5	27.1	51.9	12.9	18.6	20.4	30.2	11.5	2.2	6.5	49.5
Indonesia	1994	31,983.5	13.4	1.8	7.6	77.2	15.2	42.1	20.0	20.7	11.2	1.1[5]	24.2	42.8
Iran	1991[1]	18,869.3	—17.4[2]—		2.3	80.3[3]	15.4	33.5	31.5[3]	52.6	2.7[4]	3.2[5]	12.6	28.9
Iraq	1990	6,525.5	17.6[40]	0.2[40]	0.3[40]	81.9[40]	7.5[40]	39.8[40]	34.6[40]	45.7[4]	10.8[4]	3.0[4]	4.6[4]	35.9[4]
Ireland	1993	21,677.4	11.2	0.9	4.8	83.1	12.4	36.9	33.8	58.5	17.1	0.7	6.5	17.1
Isle of Man[37]	...	...	...	...	...	...	...	...	...	...	...	...	...	...
Israel	1994	24,242.0	8.4	18.0	6.0	67.6	8.9	34.6	24.0	53.5	18.0	1.4	4.1	23.1
Italy[41]	1993	156,958.7	18.0	2.1	9.3	70.6	12.4	28.4	29.7	59.5	5.3	5.1	2.6	27.6
Jamaica	1992	1,692.8	16.7	0.1	17.4	65.8	12.7	21.7	31.4	10.0	52.3	0.2	5.0	32.5
Japan	1994	274,742.0	24.1	4.3	17.4	54.2	7.4	19.9	27.0	14.1	22.8	1.5	—	61.6
Jersey	1980	537.1	23.9	0.4	9.3	66.5	6.5	24.8	35.2	84.9[42]	...	...	...	15.1
Jordan	1993	3,560.7	21.5	0.7	12.8	65.0	10.1	26.9	28.0	33.2	12.7	5.8	5.0	43.3
Kazakhstan	1993	4,107.0	—19.2[2, 9]—		9.9[9]	71.0[3, 9]	9.7[9]	30.9[9]	30.4[3, 9]	4.0	0.9	75.7	0.1	19.3
Kenya	1992	1,793.0	18.8	0.9	25.2	55.1	15.4	23.9	15.8	33.2	8.2	0.5	7.1	51.1
Kiribati	1992	36.7	27.5	—	7.8	64.7	3.5	47.3	13.9	10.5	2.9	—	22.7	64.0
Korea, North	1994	1,407.0[4]	...	...	...	...	...	...	...	26.4[4]	—[4]	...	13.4[4]	60.2[4]
Korea, South	1993	83,794.0	12.3	3.7	18.0	66.0	9.8	33.9	22.3	13.3	21.4	1.4	23.9	40.1
Kuwait	1993	7,042.1	15.9	0.4	0.4	83.2	6.2	42.5	34.5	39.0	14.9	0.8[5]	12.7	32.6
Kyrgyzstan	1992	396.0	—20.5[2]—		26.5	53.0[3]	11.9	21.7	19.4[3]	3.0	5.8	51.3	—	39.9
Laos	1993	353.0	—35.0[4]—		10.0[4]	55.0[4]	...	25.0[4]	30.0[4]	6.0[4]	1.4[4]	0.6[4]	11.6[4]	80.5[4]
Latvia	1994	1,241.5	11.5	0.4	28.8	59.3	11.2	22.9	25.2	40.7	2.0	42.9	1.2	13.2
Lebanon	1994	5,039.0	—17.3[2, 44]—		3.6[44]	79.1[3, 44]	7.8[44]	29.3[44]	42.0[3, 44]	57.3[4]	9.7[4]	3.3[4]	2.7[4]	27.0[4]
Lesotho	1992	977.0	23.2[24]	0.4[24]	8.7[24]	67.8[24]	7.4[24]	16.7[24]	43.7[24]	1.3[31]	0.3[4, 31]	—[4, 31]	—[4, 31]	98.4[31, 46]
Liberia	1988	272.3	—19.8[2]—		20.3	59.9[3]	5.6	30.2	24.1[3]	42.3	21.2	2.6	4.4	29.5
Libya	1991	5,357.5	25.7	0.3	0.4	73.7	7.6	33.8	32.2	62.6	1.3	0.9[5]	3.3	31.9
Liechtenstein	1993	678.6	3.2	0.3[2]	1.1	95.3[3]	6.3	31.5	57.5[3]	...	...	...	...	...
Lithuania	1994	2,353.4	15.4	1.3	31.6	51.8	11.2	22.5	18.1	32.3	2.0	55.3	0.2	10.2
Luxembourg	1993	7,545.0	12.1	—12.3[2]—		75.6[3]	13.2	30.2	32.3[3]	88.2	6.6	...	1.1	4.1
Macau	1994	2,089.2	16.4	0.9	4.7	78.1	4.5	20.3	53.3	15.5	6.8	0.4	12.8	64.5
Macedonia	1993	1,199.4	23.8	1.8	15.9	58.5	15.5	16.6	26.4	34.4	2.2	27.1	0.8	35.5
Madagascar	1991	402.5	12.5	0.1	12.2	75.2	11.1	41.1	22.9	57.7	6.3	1.2[5]	7.1	27.8
Malaŵi	1989	508.3	11.6	1.1	10.9	76.4	20.4	30.7	25.4	33.3	3.4	0.2	6.3	56.8
Malaysia	1993	45,610.0	7.1	1.6	3.6	87.7	7.5	55.7	24.4	12.7	16.9	0.4[5]	27.5	42.5
Maldives	1993	191.4	31.5	2.8	12.8	52.9	7.5	22.2	23.2	7.9	1.0	0.4	3.9	86.9
Mali	1990	601.8	26.2	0.9	19.5	53.5	10.7	22.2	20.6	46.8	4.8	1.3[5]	4.3	42.9
Malta	1993	2,173.4	10.8	0.4	4.7	84.1	6.8	50.1	27.2	72.5	8.7	1.3	2.7	14.8
Marshall Islands	1991	56.4	39.9	1.0[4]	11.1	48.0	2.7	16.3	29.0	—	83.7	—	9.6	6.6
Martinique	1994	1,639.2	22.4	0.3	7.8	69.6	10.6	27.5	31.5	76.2	2.8	0.3	2.1	18.6
Mauritania	1991	486.0[4]	30.6[35]	...	7.0[35]	62.4[35]	...	51.0[35]	11.4[35]	65.0[4]	4.9[4]	2.5[4]	1.4[4]	26.1[4]
Mauritius	1993	1,919.1	16.7	1.8	7.0	74.5	7.3	22.5	44.8	34.0	2.4	0.3	5.9	57.4
Mayotte	1994	97.2	—25.2—		5.2	69.6	11.1	33.7	24.8	74.0[13, 47]	...	...	3.3[13]	22.7[13]
Mexico	1994	80,170.3	10.4	0.6	1.8	87.2	9.0	39.4	38.9	11.2	69.2	0.4	6.0	13.2
Micronesia	1991	88.6	—36.6[2]—		13.2	50.2[3]	4.1	14.1	31.9[3]	...	40.4	...	19.3	40.3
Moldova	1992	905.0	—17.2[2]—		44.1	38.7[3]	7.5	11.8	19.3[3]	2.2[4]	1.0[4]	79.7[4]	—[4]	17.1[4]
Monaco[30]	...	...	...	...	...	...	...	...	...	...	...	...	...	...
Mongolia	1990	488.0	8.8	—27.2[25]—		64.0[26]	5.3	31.1	27.6[26]	5.0[6]	—	87.4[5]	1.1	6.6
Morocco	1994	7,194.0	20.5	2.1	15.5	62.0	12.2	27.1	22.7	56.5	8.6	3.9	1.7	29.3
Mozambique	1991	899.0	—37.3[2, 35]—		8.5[35]	54.2[3, 35]	6.5[35]	33.4[35]	14.3[3, 35]	34.5[4]	12.3[4]	...	4.8[4]	48.4[4]
Myanmar (Burma)	1992[1]	845.2	—11.2[2]—		3.5	85.3[3]	7.2	32.2	45.8[3]	12.8[4]	2.7[4]	1.1[5]	21.1	62.2[4]
Namibia	1991	1,167.1	—24.1[2]—		9.3	66.6[3]	7.9	28.5	30.2[3]	...	2.7[4]	...	—[4]	97.3[48]
Nauru	1991[49]	17.8	—24.2[2]—		4.8	70.9[3]	2.1	23.4[19]	45.4[3]	...	...	...	...	...
Nepal	1993[11]	696.0	17.9	2.4	11.8	67.8	12.0	16.6	39.3	7.3	0.7	3.0	8.0	80.9
Netherlands, The	1994	130,511.7	17.5	1.5	8.2	72.8	12.3	31.3	29.1	62.0	7.9	2.3	3.6	24.1

exports													country
total value ('000,000 U.S.$)	Standard International Trade Classification (SITC) categories (%)							direction of trade (%)					
	food and agricultural raw materials (0+1+2 −27−28 +4)	mineral ores and concentrates (27+28 +667)	fuels and other energy (3)	manufactured goods: total[a] (5+6 −667 +7+8 +9)	of which chemicals and related products (5)	of which machinery and transport equipment (7)	of which other[a] (6−667 +8+9)	to European Union (EU)[b]	to United States	to Eastern Europe[c]	to Japan	to all other[d]	
61.7	48.6	—	—	51.4	0.1	39.8[28]	11.5	47.2	—	—	—	52.8	Equatorial Guinea
17.4		89.0		11.0	1.0	...	10.0	8.0[5]	...	...	...	92.0[29]	Eritrea
1,305.9	36.0	1.5	7.1	55.4	8.1	16.9	30.4	47.8	1.8	43.7	0.5	6.2	Estonia
188.6	84.4	—	1.0	14.7	1.2	—	13.4	59.1	4.3	0.5[5]	20.3	15.7	Ethiopia
377.8	95.8	—	—	4.2	0.1	3.9	0.2	86.8	2.5	0.3	2.6	7.9	Faroe Islands
544.5	49.3	0.1	7.4	43.2	1.0	8.0	34.3	20.3	17.9	—	6.8	55.0	Fiji
29,457.9	12.7	0.6	2.3	84.4	6.6	31.8	46.0	58.4	7.2	11.8	2.1	20.6	Finland
234,352.8	16.3	0.8	2.4	80.4	14.5	39.4	26.6	63.3	7.0	1.8	2.0	25.9	France[30]
149.2	31.2	—	—	68.7	0.9	25.3	42.6	77.3	5.0	—	—	17.7	French Guiana
74.7	5.9	31.3	—	62.8	1.6	38.6	22.6	40.0	18.9	—	22.5	18.6	French Polynesia
2,463.8	11.7	10.6[2, 25]	74.2	3.6[3, 26]	1.7	0.2	1.7[3, 26]	46.1	29.7	0.4[5]	4.1	19.7	Gabon
63.7	62.8[31]	—[31]	—[31]	37.2[31]	—[31]	—[31]	37.2[31]	76.3[4]	0.4[4]	0.2[4]	14.4[4]	8.7[4]	Gambia, The
62.6	...	...	...	...	...	...	...	...	...	...	...	100.0[33]	Gaza Strip
121.0[4]	16.3[2]		1.2	82.6[3]	2.4	11.9	68.3[3]	28.1[4]	6.6[4]	47.1[4]	0.8[4]	17.4[4]	Georgia
423,994.8	6.4	0.8	1.1	91.8	13.4	49.1	29.3	57.7	7.9	6.8	2.6	24.9	Germany
1,072.3	52.1	21.2[2, 25]	3.4	23.3[3, 26]	0.1	0.3	22.9[3, 26]	63.5[4]	13.1[4]	4.4[4, 5]	5.0[4]	14.0[4]	Ghana
93.6[34]	8.2[2, 35]		51.5[35]	40.3[3, 35]	2.8[35]	18.1[35]	19.4[3, 35]	22.2[6, 35]	...	...	...	77.8[36]	Gibraltar
8,783.7	33.1	2.3	7.8	56.8	4.7	6.3	45.9	58.9	4.5	10.5	0.9	25.2	Greece
312.3	92.7	—	1.2	6.1	—	1.6	4.5	80.9	1.9	—	13.1	4.1	Greenland
20.1	77.0	—	—	23.0	4.5	2.1	16.4	44.1	14.2	—	2.6	39.2	Grenada
152.0	61.4	0.6	0.1	37.9	1.0	29.9	6.9	79.9	2.3	—	—	17.8	Guadeloupe
39.2	23.5	2.7	3.5	70.3	5.6	11.5	53.2	...	24.9	...	4.8	70.4	Guam
1,295.3	67.8	0.3	2.0	30.0	11.1	1.5	17.4	11.8	35.4	0.5[5]	1.7	50.6	Guatemala
...	...	...	...	...	...	...	...	...	...	...	...	...	Guernsey[37]
671.2	6.3	86.5	—	7.2	—	—	7.2	87.3[4]	23.0	...	1.1[4]	18.6[4]	Guinea
19.3	87.1[38]	0.3[38]	—[38]	12.6[38]	0.3[38]	—[38]	12.3[38]	27.9[4]	0.4[4]	—[4]	0.6[4]	71.1[4]	Guinea-Bissau
265.9	40.9	28.6[2, 25]	—	30.4[3, 26]	3.6	7.2	19.6[3, 26]	47.0[4]	34.2[4]	1.9[4]	6.4[4]	10.5[4]	Guyana
77.7	14.5[9]	0.2[9, 25]	—[9]	85.4[9, 26]	2.0[9]	13.6[9]	69.8[9, 26]	20.6[4]	75.7[4]	0.1[4]	0.7[4]	2.9[4]	Haiti
515.7	84.3	2.8	0.5	12.4	2.1	0.3	10.0	31.5	52.5	0.6[5]	2.5	13.0	Honduras
151,478.4	4.4	1.2	0.8	93.6	5.6	31.3	56.7	15.2	23.2	0.5	5.6	55.5	Hong Kong
10,700.8	23.3	1.4[2]	4.0	71.4[3]	11.2	25.6	34.6[3]	63.7	4.0	18.3	0.9	13.2	Hungary
1,626.7	79.7	1.2	0.1	19.0	0.1	4.1	14.8	61.6	14.5	0.8	14.1	9.0	Iceland
22,236.9	18.7	20.0	2.2	59.0	6.9	6.8	45.3	27.1	18.0	4.4	7.8	42.6	India
40,053.4	17.6	3.2	26.3	52.9	2.5	7.6	42.8	14.9	14.6	0.7[5]	27.3	42.6	Indonesia
14,619.0	3.4	0.3[25]	92.5	3.8[26]	—	0.1	3.7[26]	46.9[4]	1.9[4]	3.4[4, 5]	16.1[4]	31.7[4]	Iran
6,659.0	0.8	0.3[25]	96.8	2.1[26]	1.2	0.2	0.7[26]	26.6[4]	33.6[4]	6.8[4, 5]	9.5[4]	23.5[4]	Iraq
28,881.9	23.2	1.5	0.6	74.7	19.3	28.8	26.6	71.1	9.1	0.7	3.7	15.4	Ireland
...	...	...	...	...	...	...	...	...	...	...	...	...	Isle of Man[37]
16,884.0	7.0	30.2	0.6	62.2	14.5	30.5	17.2	29.2	31.1	2.6	5.8	31.3	Israel
178,937.3	7.5	0.3	2.2	90.0	7.4	36.7	45.9	57.0	7.7	3.9	1.9	29.5	Italy[41]
1,052.8	23.8	53.3	1.0	22.0	2.5	1.9	17.6	26.1	36.5	0.4	1.4	35.5	Jamaica
395,600.0	1.1	0.1	0.6	98.2	6.0	71.5	20.8	15.5	29.7	0.5	—	54.3	Japan
209.2	27.6	4.3[43]	—	68.0	1.2	31.1	35.7	67.3[42]	...	...	...	32.7	Jersey
1,255.7	18.8	21.9	—	59.2	24.9	12.5	21.9	8.7	3.1	3.8	1.1	83.3	Jordan
3,449.0	27.8[2, 9]		14.3[9]	58.0[3, 9]	11.6[9]	8.4[9]	38.0[3, 9]	15.7	4.2	52.0	1.1	27.1	Kazakhstan
1,361.7	48.4	2.3	11.2	38.1	3.3	1.5	33.3	33.4	2.9	—	1.1	62.6	Kenya
4.7	82.5	—	—	17.5	—	—	17.5	6.0	12.3	—	—	81.7	Kiribati
1,703.0[4]	...	...	...	...			...	14.3[4]	—[4]	...	17.4[4]	68.3[4]	Korea, North
82,232.2	3.8	0.2	2.3	93.7	6.0	44.9	42.8	12.1	22.2	1.5	14.1	50.2	Korea, South
10,536.5	0.3	0.3	95.1	4.3	1.0	2.1	1.3	17.7[4]	17.3[4]	[4]	14.6[4]	50.4[4]	Kuwait
285.0	9.1[2]		6.7	84.2[3]	2.1	35.4	46.7[3]	10.2	—	45.0	1.1	43.8	Kyrgyzstan
203.1	14.3[19]		8.4[19]	77.3	...	21.0[19]	56.2	24.6[4]	3.9[4]	3.4[4]	5.4[4]	62.0[4]	Laos
989.7	29.8	0.4	1.8	68.0	7.8	20.3	39.8	39.3	1.2	49.6	0.4	9.5	Latvia
825.0	30.5[45]	55.8[25, 45]	0.2[45]	13.4[26, 45]	0.5[45]	9.0[45]	3.9[26, 45]	13.6[4]	2.9[4]	3.0[4]	0.4[4]	80.1[4]	Lebanon
109.1	14.8	1.3	—	83.9	0.5	10.2	73.2	21.1[4]	23.0[4]	—	—	55.9[4]	Lesotho
396.3	39.4	57.7	0.5	2.4	—	0.5	1.9	67.6	18.8	—	1.2	12.3	Liberia
11,211.7	0.7	—	95.4	3.9	3.4	—	0.5	86.2	—	1.6	—	12.2	Libya
1,371.8	3.6	—[2]	0.1	96.2[3]	10.7	44.6	40.9[3]	41.6[6]	...	...	...	58.4	Liechtenstein
2,028.8	31.5	1.2	15.9	51.4	12.0	15.7	23.7	30.1	0.6	59.7	0.1	9.4	Lithuania
5,942.4	7.7	1.1[2]		91.2[3]	18.3	21.3	51.6[3]	84.8	4.2	...	0.5	10.5	Luxembourg
1,872.2	5.9	—	—	94.1	1.2	4.2	88.7	31.9	36.4	0.1	1.3	30.2	Macau
1,055.3	24.9	1.8	0.2	73.1	4.5	16.2	52.4	35.3	5.8	26.0	1.0	31.8	Macedonia
291.7	72.4	8.0	0.5	19.1	2.8	2.3	14.1	50.7	14.6	6.1[5]	8.9	19.7	Madagascar
266.9	92.8	—	—	7.2	0.5	1.8	4.9	50.7	12.6	—	12.6	24.1	Malaŵi
47,099.0	18.2	0.5	10.3	71.1	2.2	48.5	20.4	14.9	20.3	0.2[5]	13.0	51.6	Malaysia
34.4	83.7	0.2	—	16.1	0.1	—	16.0	31.3	11.3	—	4.1	53.3	Maldives
330.3	98.4	—	—	1.6	—	0.9	0.8	26.0	0.6[4]	—	0.9[4]	72.5	Mali
1,355.4	3.3	0.2	2.2	94.2	2.5	57.1	34.5	72.0	7.5	1.8	0.6	18.1	Malta
2.9	99.9	—	—	0.1	—	—	0.1	—	100.0	—	—	—	Marshall Islands
218.0	53.2	0.8	28.8	17.2	2.4	10.3	4.5	51.1	1.1	—	—	47.8	Martinique
451.4	47.2	49.5[2, 25]	2.0	1.3[3, 26]	—	0.2	1.1[3, 26]	58.3	2.3	10.7[5]	19.5	9.2	Mauritania
1,467.1	29.9	2.0	—	68.1	1.0	1.0	66.1	71.5	17.9	—	0.4	10.2	Mauritius
3.9	23.5[21]	—[21]	—[21]	76.5[21]	76.4[21]	—[21]	0.1[21]	70.0[13, 47]	...	...	...	30.0[13]	Mayotte
61,964.3	8.2	1.0	11.9	78.9	4.5	53.6	20.8	4.3	85.2	—	1.6	8.9	Mexico
11.0	94.7	—	—	5.3	...	...	...	...	1.1	...	88.1	10.8	Micronesia
868.0	45.7[2]		2.0	52.2[3]	3.2	28.1	20.9[3]	3.7[4]	1.2[4]	72.8[4]	—[4]	22.4[4]	Moldova
...	...	...	...	...	...	...	...	...	...	...	...	...	Monaco[30]
349.0	27.3	48.1[25]		24.6[26]	...	...	...	4.0[6]	0.1	90.7[5]	1.2	4.0	Mongolia
4,033.9	31.8	11.1	2.1	55.0	20.2	4.1	30.7	64.0	3.5	1.2	6.6	24.7	Morocco
162.0	65.5	13.0[2, 25]	1.2	20.4[3, 26]	—	2.5	17.9[3, 26]	50.0[4]	13.6[4]	2.5[4]	12.3[4]	21.6[4]	Mozambique
464.3	73.5[2]		0.2	26.3[3]	0.1	—	26.2[3]	3.5[4]	0.4[4]	—	6.5	89.6[4]	Myanmar (Burma)
1,244.4	35.9	59.2	0.1	4.8	—	—	4.8	...	3.0[4]	...	—[4]	97.0[4]	Namibia
28.9	—	99.4	—	0.6	—	—	0.6	...	...	...	...	...	Nauru
354.6	12.2	0.1	—	87.6	0.6	—	87.0	54.9	21.4	0.1	0.5	23.2	Nepal
145,825.3	25.3	1.1	7.6	66.0	15.3	24.9	25.9	70.8	3.7	2.5	0.9	22.1	Netherlands, The

Trade: external (continued)

country	year	imports: total value ('000,000 U.S.$)	SITC categories (%): food and agricultural raw materials (0+1+2 −27−28 +4)	mineral ores and concentrates (27+28 +667)	fuels and other energy (3)	manufactured goods: total[a] (5+6 −667 +7+8 +9)	of which chemicals and related products (5)	of which machinery and transport equipment (7)	of which other[a] (6−667 +8+9)	direction of trade (%): from European Union (EU)[b]	from United States	from Eastern Europe[c]	from Japan	from all other[d]
Netherlands Antilles	1992	1,868.3	9.1	0.1	58.8	32.0	3.7	13.7	14.7	11.7	17.0	0.1	2.2	69.0
New Caledonia	1992	927.3	—19.8[2]—		8.9	71.3[3]	7.0	31.4[19]	33.0[3]	62.0	5.3	0.1	6.3	26.3
New Zealand	1994	11,901.4	8.7	2.1	5.6	83.6	13.1	41.8	28.8	20.1	19.2	0.2	15.3	45.2
Nicaragua	1993	755.1	22.3	0.2	13.9	63.6	15.4	26.1	22.0	8.6	26.6	1.1[5]	8.0	55.7
Niger	1990	388.8	—32.1[2]—		12.9	55.0[3]	10.2	22.3	22.5[3]	49.2[4]	3.3[4]	—[4]	3.5[4]	44.0[4]
Nigeria	1991	9,031.0	—10.6[2]—		0.7	88.7[3]	18.0	43.0	27.7[3]	56.0	10.4	1.3[5]	7.4	24.9
Northern Mariana Islands	1991	392.2	19.3	—	20.9	59.8	2.3	22.2	35.3	...	18.2	...	16.6	65.2
Norway	1994	27,357.4	9.3	5.0	3.4	82.4	9.6	37.0	35.7	68.9	7.4	3.6	6.0	14.1
Oman	1993	4,114.0	19.1	1.2	3.0	76.7	6.0	43.2	27.4	22.1	8.1	0.1	20.9	48.8
Pakistan	1994	8,897.0	22.6	1.6	18.3	57.6	16.4	28.5	12.7	25.8	9.8	2.4	9.4	52.7
Palau	1984	25.1[50]	28.9	0.1[2]	0.9[50]	70.0[3]	4.0	24.5	41.5[3]	—	41.8	—	38.2	20.0
Panama	1993	2,187.4	10.2	0.4	12.8	76.6	13.0	31.4	32.2	7.8	36.8	0.7[5]	7.8	46.9
Papua New Guinea	1992	1,485.0	18.8[9]	0.3[9]	6.8[9]	74.1[9]	7.0[9]	38.3[9]	28.8[9]	6.5[4]	5.5[4]	...	12.9[4]	75.1[4]
Paraguay	1993	1,688.0	11.6	0.4	12.1	75.9	11.0	41.8	23.1	11.8	14.1	0.3[5]	12.1	61.7
Peru	1993	4,901.3	21.6	0.2	8.1	70.0	14.1	36.0	20.0	14.4	29.6	0.9	7.8	47.3
Philippines	1993	18,772.7	10.1	1.7	11.5	76.7	9.7	32.7	34.3	10.9	20.0	1.2	22.8	45.0
Poland	1993	18,783.2	13.7	2.1	12.5	71.7	13.3	29.6	28.7	64.8	5.1	12.9	1.8	15.5
Portugal	1993	24,244.3	16.5	0.7	8.8	74.0	9.6	35.6	28.8	74.5	3.2	1.1	3.2	18.0
Puerto Rico	1988[11]	11,859.1	19.7	0.6	10.7	69.0	15.6	23.7	29.7	6.9	66.8	0.1	4.9	21.3
Qatar	1993	1,890.7	15.5	1.7	0.6	82.2	7.8	42.4	32.0	32.3	11.6	0.9	16.4	38.7
Réunion	1994	2,356.5	20.6	0.2	4.9	74.2	10.5	31.5	32.3	79.2	1.9	0.1	1.8	17.0
Romania	1993	6,521.7	17.3	3.0	25.8	54.0	9.0	22.3	22.6	45.3	5.7	20.3	0.9	27.7
Russia	1992	45,840.0	—14.4[2, 9]—		7.0[9]	78.7[3, 9]	8.0[9]	47.5[9]	23.1[3, 9]	34.8[4]	6.3[4]	22.3[4]	3.7[4]	33.0[4]
Rwanda	1990	291.1	18.2	1.9	15.3	64.6	10.2	16.1	38.3	44.6	1.2	1.4[5]	7.7	45.1
St. Kitts and Nevis	1990	110.7	21.2	0.1	5.0	73.7	7.3	29.4	37.0	13.5[6]	43.6	—	3.7	39.2
St. Lucia	1993	300.3	—26.8[2]—		7.6	65.6[3]	9.1	22.8	33.6[3]	19.1	37.3	—	5.6	38.0
St. Vincent and the Grenadines	1992	132.1	28.3	0.7[2]	7.7	63.3[3]	12.6	18.0	32.7[3]	23.0	36.1	0.1	2.8	38.0
San Marino[41]	...	...	...	...	...	...	...	...	...	...	...	...	...	...
São Tomé and Príncipe	1993	28.1	23.5[19]	...	11.0	65.5	...	32.0	33.5	86.0[4]	8.0[4]	...	—[4]	6.0[4]
Saudi Arabia	1994	23,343.5	14.0	0.9	0.2	84.8	8.7	40.1	36.1	34.7	21.3	0.6	11.7	31.6
Senegal	1991	1,097.0	31.7	0.3	11.0	57.0	14.1	22.7	20.2	56.9	7.2	1.6[5]	3.0	31.3
Seychelles	1993	241.6	21.3	0.1	14.2	64.4	6.6	25.1	32.8	30.5	7.7	—	5.8	56.0
Sierra Leone	1994	149.9	—41.7[2]—		18.5	39.8[3]	7.3	18.0	14.5[3]	47.0[4]	10.0[4]	2.2[4]	5.6[4]	35.2[4]
Singapore	1994	102,286.7	6.1	0.5	8.8	84.6	6.5	56.5	21.6	13.1	15.3	0.4	22.0	49.2
Slovakia[7]	1993	6,655.0	—14.2[2]—		21.1	64.7[3]	11.3	29.2	24.1[3]	27.9	1.8	62.1[5]	1.1	7.1
Slovenia	1993	6,500.9	11.9	1.6	10.9	75.6	11.1	30.2	34.2	65.6	2.9	8.8	1.9	20.8
Solomon Islands	1992	133.9	—18.9[2]—		12.1	69.1[3]	4.8	34.2	30.1[3]	5.9	6.2	—	14.7	73.2
Somalia	1990	394.0[4]	30.3[24]	0.2[24]	4.6[24]	64.9[24]	5.1[24]	37.1[24]	22.7[24]	51.1[4]	3.1[4]	—[4]	2.3[4]	43.5[4]
South Africa[53]	1993	20,042.6	8.4	3.1	9.1[4]	79.4	12.9	44.5	21.9[4]	41.7	13.3	0.5	12.6	31.9
Spain	1994	92,057.9	16.3	2.3	9.4	72.0	11.7	35.3	25.0	64.1	7.3	2.0	3.6	23.0
Sri Lanka	1994	4,483.6	17.7	3.4	6.2	72.7	8.7	23.4	40.6	17.9	6.3	0.7	11.7	63.2
Sudan, The	1992	820.9	15.2	0.7	28.0	56.2	6.6	30.6	19.1	23.8	7.9	2.6	3.5	62.3
Suriname	1990	472.0	11.8	1.5	18.0	68.7	21.4	24.7	22.6	29.4	41.1	—	2.8	26.7
Swaziland	1990	666.0	18.3	1.0	15.8	64.9	10.0	23.8	31.2	5.0	0.3	...	0.8	94.0[56]
Sweden	1994	51,778.3	9.9	1.4	7.6	81.1	11.3	37.8	31.9	62.5	8.6	3.9	4.7	20.2
Switzerland[57]	1994	66,653.1	8.9	4.3	3.4	83.5	14.1	30.8	38.6	79.4	6.6	1.3	3.4	9.3
Syria	1992	3,490.3	21.2	0.6	3.9	74.3	12.8	31.3	30.2	39.1	6.2	14.1	9.9	30.6
Taiwan	1994	85,474.3	10.6	3.4	6.9	79.1	13.3	39.1	26.6	15.1	21.1	2.1	29.0	32.6
Tajikistan	1993	733.8	—58.0[2, 13, 25]—		15.1[13]	26.9[3, 13, 26]	11.3[13]	7.0[13]	8.6[3, 13, 26]	42.6	4.6	19.7	0.3	32.9
Tanzania	1990	1,021.5	5.4	1.5	10.3	82.8	9.8	45.6	27.4	58.2	1.6	0.8[5]	7.7	31.8
Thailand	1993	46,239.3	8.8	3.0	7.4	80.8	10.2	45.0	25.5	16.6	11.6	2.2	30.2	39.3
Togo	1991	443.9	24.4	0.7	9.8	65.1	11.9	28.3	25.0	56.0	6.4	0.1	6.7	30.8
Tonga	1992	62.6	29.9	0.5	12.8	56.8	6.2	19.3	31.4	2.6	8.3	—	12.5	76.6
Trinidad and Tobago	1993	1,462.9	16.3	1.5	15.9	66.3	11.0	32.9	22.4	20.0	39.6	0.1	3.8	36.5
Tunisia	1993	6,214.2	11.4	1.6	7.8	79.1	8.3	32.0	38.8	74.1	5.8	3.0	2.3	14.8
Turkey	1993	29,429.3	10.5	3.4	13.5	72.6	12.1	38.2	22.4	47.1	11.4	10.3	5.5	25.7
Turkmenistan	1992	1,009.0	—41.8[2]—		8.2	50.0[3]	10.2	22.3	17.4[3]	4.8[4, 31]	0.5[4, 31]	56.4[4, 31]	0.5[4, 31]	37.8[4, 31]
Tuvalu	1991	4.8	36.1	0.1[2]	14.6	49.2[3]	6.8	13.9	28.5[3]	1.8[6]	0.5	...	6.6	91.1
Uganda	1992	524.4	13.0	1.5[2]	13.4	72.0[3]	8.3	32.2	31.5[3]	29.7	4.8	—	9.9	55.6
Ukraine	1992	7,098.9	—11.3[2]—		32.1	56.6[3]	6.4	12.8	37.4[3]	10.2	1.4	67.8	0.6	20.0
United Arab Emirates	1991	13,921.2	—14.6[2]—		2.1	83.3[3]	6.8	34.6	42.0[3]	30.3	9.9	0.6[5]	15.5	43.6
United Kingdom[37]	1994	227,228.6	12.9	2.8	4.0	80.3	9.7	40.7	29.9	55.5	11.9	1.8	6.0	24.9
United States[59]	1994	689,030.0	7.1	1.6	8.7	82.6	5.1	45.7	31.8	18.0	—	0.9	17.8	63.4
Uruguay	1994	2,707.2	13.9	0.4	8.2	77.5	15.0	37.1	25.3	19.0	9.7	1.6	2.9	66.8
Uzbekistan	1992	1,756.0	—59.8[2, 25]—		14.2	26.0[3, 26]	7.6	8.3	10.1[3, 26]	6.4	1.2	37.1	0.3	55.0
Vanuatu	1992	81.8	—24.4[2]—		9.7	65.9[3]	6.6	29.3	30.1[3]	8.0[47]	1.9[4]	—	9.4	80.7[4]
Venezuela	1993	11,266.6	13.8	1.2	1.2	83.8	12.3	50.6	20.9	22.0	46.2	0.3[5]	7.6	24.0
Vietnam	1991	2,338.0	—9.4[2]—		22.9	67.8[3]	16.3	26.1	25.4[3]	11.3	—	17.8[5]	6.2	64.7
Virgin Islands (U.S.)	1992	3,550.8	...	...	71.4	...	...	...	...	...	49.8	...	...	...
West Bank	1993	80.8[61]	...	...	...	...	...	...	...	...	...	...	...	...
Western Sahara	...	...	...	...	...	...	...	...	...	...	...	...	...	...
Western Samoa	1991	98.9	24.3[44]	0.3[44]	17.5[44]	57.9[44]	7.4[44]	22.9[44]	27.6[44]	4.0[4]	10.0[4]	—[4]	9.0[4]	77.0[4]
Yemen	1992	2,589.6	35.2	0.6[2]	6.1	58.2[3]	6.6	21.8	29.7[3]	28.8	9.2	1.9[5]	7.0	53.1
Yugoslavia	1991	5,548.6	12.4	1.3	19.0	67.4	13.7	22.7	31.0	46.5[4]	4.2	24.5[5]	2.3	22.6
Zaire	1991	711.0	—20.0[8]—		13.8[8]	66.2[8]	4.4[8]	45.5[8]	16.3[8]	58.7[4]	6.5[4]	0.1[4]	4.2[4]	30.5[4]
Zambia	1990	1,237.7	3.7	1.1[2]	15.2	79.9[3]	12.6	47.0	20.3[3]	38.7	10.1	0.1	6.7	44.4
Zimbabwe	1992	2,213.3	19.8	0.8	11.8	67.6	11.7	36.4	19.5	29.0	9.0	0.2	5.9	55.9

[1]Year ending March. [2]Excluding precious stones, etc. (667). [3]Including precious stones, etc. (667). [4]Estimate. [5]Including also Asian republics of the former U.S.S.R. [6]Main countries only. [7]Includes special transactions: imports 51.0%, exports 34.1%. [8]1987. [9]1990. [10]Includes petrochemicals. [11]Year ending June 30. [12]Figures for Belgium-Luxembourg Economic Union (Luxembourg is also shown separately). [13]1992. [14]Includes 83.6% from India. [15]Mainly electricity. [16]Includes 84.8% to India. [17]Includes 83.8% from South Africa and Namibia. [18]Includes 78.3% to Switzerland. [19]Main items only. [20]Includes 82.8% for reexports. [21]Domestic exports only. [22]Includes ships' bunkers and stores. [23]1975. [24]1986. [25]Including metals. [26]Excluding metals. [27]1985. [28]Includes 38.7% for ships and boats. [29]Includes the following percentages for Ethiopia and main Middle East countries: imports 76.0%, exports 88.0%. [30]Figures for France include Monaco. [31]1991. [32]Includes 88.2% from Israel. [33]Includes 76.7% to Israel and 23.0% to Jordan. [34]Excluding petroleum products. [35]1988. [36]Includes 51.5% for ships' bunkers. [37]Figures for United Kingdom include Guernsey, Isle of Man, and Jersey (the latter is also shown separately). [38]1980. [39]Year ending September 30. [40]1986; commercial imports only (excluding oil

exports: total value ('000,000 U.S.$)	SITC: food and agricultural raw materials (0+1+2−27−28+4)	SITC: mineral ores and concentrates (27+28+667)	SITC: fuels and other energy (3)	manufactured goods: total[a] (5+6−667+7+8+9)	manufactured goods: of which chemicals and related products (5)	manufactured goods: of which machinery and transport equipment (7)	manufactured goods: of which other[a] (6−667+8+9)	direction of trade: to European Union (EU)[b]	to United States	to Eastern Europe[c]	to Japan	to all other[d]	country
1,558.9	3.0	0.8	91.2	5.0	0.9	3.0	1.0	8.1	25.0	—	3.1	63.8	Netherlands Antilles
409.5	5.0[4]	33.4	0.2[4]	61.4	1.0[4]	7.0[4]	53.4	52.3	3.6	—	23.5	20.6	New Caledonia
12,185.5	61.2	0.5	2.0	36.4	7.7	8.2	20.5	16.0	11.0	1.0	15.2	56.8	New Zealand
267.5	73.1	1.0	1.7	24.2	1.6	0.8	21.7	16.6	43.8	0.6[5]	0.5	38.5	Nicaragua
282.6	—92.0[2]—		1.1	7.0[3]	0.1	1.0	5.9[3]	76.1[4]	15.3[4]	—[4]	—[4]	8.6[4]	Niger
12,265.0	—3.4[2]—		94.4	2.2[3]	0.4	0.1	1.7	39.5	45.3	0.1[5]	—	15.0	Nigeria
263.0				100.0	—	—	100.0		100.0				Northern Mariana Islands
34,814.2	10.7	1.2	49.7	38.5	6.6	12.2	19.7	77.8	6.7	1.8	1.9	11.8	Norway
5,299.0	4.7	0.2	78.9	16.2	0.5	11.7	4.0	2.6[4]	5.2[4]	—	26.7[4]	65.4[4]	Oman
7,370.2	12.0	0.2	0.8	87.0	0.6	0.5	85.9	32.5	15.8	0.5	7.3	44.0	Pakistan
0.5	69.1	—	—	30.9	—	—	30.9	—	8.0	—	58.8	33.2	Palau
507.6	80.5	0.3	2.0	17.2	4.4	0.3	12.6	37.7	37.2	—	0.1	25.0	Panama
1,931.1	21.4	21.0[4]	16.8[4]	40.8	0.1[4]	5.5	35.1[51]	15.4[4]	3.5[4]	0.9[5]	20.2	60.0[4]	Papua New Guinea
725.2	82.9	0.2	0.2	16.7	2.0	0.6	14.1	34.2	7.3	0.1[5]	0.1	58.2	Paraguay
3,496.5	31.4	14.0	6.0	48.6	2.1	1.0	45.4	29.3	21.4	0.5	8.7	40.1	Peru
11,374.8	16.8	1.9	2.0	79.2	2.3	18.6	58.3	17.7	38.5	0.2	16.1	27.5	Philippines
14,142.5	14.4	2.2	9.7	73.7	6.8	21.0	45.9	69.2	2.9	12.4	0.3	15.2	Poland
15,417.4	11.1	2.4	3.4	83.2	4.4	21.2	57.6	80.1	4.4	0.7	0.8	14.0	Portugal
13,952.8	16.9	1.0	2.2	79.9	39.8	19.7	20.4	3.4	88.0	—	0.1	8.5	Puerto Rico
3,245.4	0.4	0.1	81.4	18.1	8.8	1.3	8.0	1.8[4]	2.0[4]	0.2[4]	59.4[4]	36.6[4]	Qatar
170.8	77.3	0.3	0.2	22.1	1.5	12.5	8.1	80.3	0.2	—	6.2	13.2	Réunion
4,892.2	9.9	0.6	10.0	79.5	8.0	17.1	54.5	41.4	1.4	13.9	1.1	42.2	Romania
54,230.0	—6.5[2,9]—		35.2[9]	58.3[3,9]	7.0[9]	32.7[9]	18.6[3,9]	37.3[4]	1.3[4]	27.4[4]	2.9[4]	31.2[4]	Russia
131.9	72.8	3.9	—	23.3[52]	—	—	23.3[52]	64.1[4]	6.1[4]	—[4]	1.9[4]	27.9[4]	Rwanda
27.7	32.8	—	—	67.2	0.0	40.2	20.7	20.9	50.9	—	—	20.2	St. Kitts and Nevis
119.7	56.4	—	—	43.6	1.3	8.6	33.8	53.2	27.0	—	0.1	19.7	St. Lucia
78.1	85.5	—	—	14.4	0.4	4.3	9.7	53.6	4.4	—	—	42.0	St. Vincent and the Grenadines
...	...	...	...	...	...	...	...	...	...	...	...	...	San Marino[41]
5.0	78.0[19]	...	...	...	...	...	...	71.0[4]	14.0[4]	...	—[4]	15.0[4]	São Tomé and Príncipe
45,630.0[4]	1.0[31]	0.2[31]	91.4[31]	7.4[31]	5.0[31]	0.9[31]	1.5[31]	21.5[4]	16.6[4]	—[4]	16.7[4]	45.3[4]	Saudi Arabia
652.2	54.0	8.8	16.0	21.1	14.6	2.1	4.4	51.1	1.0	—	1.8	46.0	Senegal
51.6	30.4	—	55.1	14.5	0.3	7.8	6.4	28.7	7.0	—	—	64.3	Seychelles
115.8	4.8	84.2	...	11.0	...	...	...	50.6[4]	28.1[4]	1.1[4]	1.7[4]	18.5[4]	Sierra Leone
90,375.9	5.8	0.4	9.6	84.4	5.7	64.0	14.7	13.5	18.8	1.0	7.0	59.7	Singapore
5,450.9	—11.4[2]—		4.9	83.7[3]	12.0	19.4	52.3[3]	29.5	1.1	58.9[5]	0.1	10.3	Slovakia[7]
6,082.9	6.6	—	5.2	88.3	8.9	27.3	52.0	63.2	3.6	10.1	0.4	22.7	Slovenia
102.9	—94.5[2]—		—	5.5[3]	—	—	5.5[3]	28.9	1.3	—	34.8	35.0	Solomon Islands
81.0	97.2	1.1[2,25]	0.2	1.5[3,26]	—	0.6	0.9[3,26]	61.0	0.3[4]	—	0.5	38.2[4]	Somalia
24,353.7	10.8	6.0	7.9	75.4	5.4	8.0	62.0[54]	20.9	7.2	1.1	5.5	65.3[55]	South Africa[53]
73,031.4	17.2	0.7	2.2	79.9	8.1	42.1	29.7	70.7	4.9	1.7	1.3	21.4	Spain
3,210.1	24.8	7.6	0.7	66.9	0.9	2.6	63.4	31.9	34.7	1.8	5.1	26.5	Sri Lanka
319.3	87.4	5.3	—	7.2	—	—	7.2	29.1	1.2	—	5.0	64.6	Sudan, The
472.6	15.7	74.0	1.2	9.0	—	0.3	8.7	36.9	11.4	—	6.8	44.9	Suriname
566.2	80.9[21]	3.2[21]	0.9[21]	14.9[21]	0.2[21]	2.1[21]	12.6[21]	24.3[21]	6.9[21]	—[21]	0.7[21]	68.0[21]	Swaziland
61,359.6	8.8	1.3	2.5	87.4	9.5	45.0	32.8	59.1	8.0	3.4	2.7	26.8	Sweden
68,903.5	3.7	3.9	0.1	92.3	25.0	29.6	37.6	62.1	9.2	2.3	3.9	22.6	Switzerland[57]
3,093.1	19.7	1.5	69.6	9.2	0.2	0.3	8.7	63.2	0.8	5.7	0.3	30.0	Syria
92,819.8	11.6	0.3	0.6	87.5	8.7	45.8	33.0	12.9	26.2	0.5	11.0	49.5	Taiwan
426.7	—67.4[2,13,25]—		1.3[13]	31.3[3,13,26]	2.5[13]	14.6[13]	14.2[3,13,26]	48.2	5.7	25.8	5.1	15.2	Tajikistan
416.1	82.0	1.0	2.0	15.1	1.0	2.2	11.8	40.5	6.8	0.7[5]	3.9	48.2	Tanzania
07,100.9	23.8	2.9	1.1	70.2	2.9	29.7	37.7	17.4	21.5	2.1	17.0	42.0	Thailand
253.2	42.0	49.2	2.3	6.5	1.1	1.0	4.4	29.5	0.1	5.5[5]	—	64.9	Togo
12.8	83.4	—		16.6	—	4.0	12.7	0.7[4]	17.7	—	51.2	30.5	Tonga
1,662.1	7.9	0.1	57.6	34.4	16.9	2.8	14.7	4.8	47.7	—	1.1	46.4	Trinidad and Tobago
3,804.5	11.9	1.3	11.5	75.3	11.1	9.6	54.6	79.4	0.8	1.0	0.2	18.5	Tunisia
15,348.9	24.4	1.6	1.1	72.8	4.0	8.4	60.4	49.5	6.4	7.7	1.0	35.3	Turkey
2,149.0	—19.9[2]—		77.9	2.3[3]	1.1	0.2	1.0[3]	3.3[4,31]	0.1[4,31]	57.3[4,31]	0.3[4,31]	39.0[4,31]	Turkmenistan
0.2[45]	92.2[45]	—[45]	—[45]	7.8[45]	—[45]	—[45]	7.8[45]	—	—	—	—	100.0[45,58]	Tuvalu
171.4	95.2	—	3.0	1.8	—	0.9	0.9	63.8	8.1	—	0.6	27.5	Uganda
8,044.7	—6.4[2]—		9.5	84.1[3]	9.8	16.1	58.1[3]	7.2	0.3	58.2	1.2	33.0	Ukraine
24,436.0	3.3	0.2[2]	80.1	16.4[3]	0.8	6.0	9.6[3]	8.7[4]	2.9[4]	0.3[4]	39.1[4]	49.1[4]	United Arab Emirates
205,020.7	8.5	2.9	6.7	81.9	14.0	41.3	26.5	56.9	12.5	1.8	2.2	26.5	United Kingdom[37]
512,337.0	13.1	1.5	1.8	83.7	10.2	49.3	24.2	21.0	—	0.9	10.4	67.6	United States[59]
1,918.2	56.2	0.4	—	43.4	5.3	11.7	26.4	20.9	6.8	0.8	1.1	70.4	Uruguay
1,497.0	—12.0[2,25]—		7.7	80.3[26]	5.5	8.6	66.3[3,26]	28.8	2.5	39.8	0.3	28.5	Uzbekistan
23.6	82.3[21]	—[21]	—[21]	17.7[21]	...	...	...	49.8[21]	...	—[21]	18.7[21]	31.4[21]	Vanuatu
15,208.1	3.0	0.8	78.4	17.8	2.8	2.8	12.2	8.4	55.7	—	1.5	34.4	Venezuela
2,087.0	—48.9[2]—		35.6	15.5[3]	0.7	0.1	14.7[3]	3.2	—	10.4[5]	35.1	51.3	Vietnam
2,303.5	...	...	84.2[60]	...	...	...	...	...	94.1	...	...	...	Virgin Islands (U.S.)
41.6[62]	...	...	...	...	...	...	...	...	...	...	...	...	West Bank
...	...	...	...	...	...	...	...	...	...	...	...	...	Western Sahara
7.6	74.8	—	—	25.2	—	—	25.2	0.1[4]	7.1	...	...	92.8[4]	Western Samoa
474.4	20.5[21]	2.7[21]	74.4[21]	2.4[21]	1.5[21]	0.1[21]	0.8[21]	23.0[21]	35.3[21]	—[21]	16.9[21]	24.7[21]	Yemen
4,704.1	15.9	0.6	4.4	79.1	9.1	19.6	50.3	54.6[4]	4.5	29.1[5]	0.2	11.6	Yugoslavia
853.0	13.2	55.9[2,25]	12.7	18.1[3,26]	0.1	0.7	17.3[3,26]	54.8[4]	19.8[4]	1.2[4]	7.4[4]	16.8[4]	Zaire
1,350.2	5.3[45]	83.4[2,25,45]	0.1[45]	11.3[3,26,45]	0.1[45]	0.3[45]	10.9[3,26,45]	30.6	1.6	—	31.0	36.8	Zambia
1,248.9	47.4	7.7	0.4	44.6	3.0	3.0	38.6	34.7	6.4	1.3	6.6	51.0	Zimbabwe

companies' imports). [41]Figures for Italy include San Marino. [42]United Kingdom only. [43]Including coins. [44]1983. [45]1989. [46]Includes 94.1% from rest of Customs Union of Southern Africa. [47]France only. [48]Includes 89.7% from South Africa. [49]Based on trade with Australia and New Zealand only. [50]Excluding bulk imports of fuels. [51]Includes 33.5% for nonmonetary gold. [52]Includes 19.8% for nonmonetary gold. [53]Figures for South Africa refer to the Customs Union of Southern Africa (includes South Africa, Botswana, Lesotho, Namibia, and Swaziland, also shown separately). [54]Includes gold (included in "special transactions" accounting for 34.7%). [55]Including unspecified destinations of 34.7%. [56]Includes 90.1% from South Africa; this includes imports passing through South Africa in transit, which may have had their origin from other countries. [57]Figures for Switzerland include Liechtenstein also shown separately. [58]All to the South Pacific region in 1985. [59]Figures for United States include American Samoa, Guam, Puerto Rico, and Virgin Islands (U.S.), also shown separately. [60]Exports of refined petroleum to United States only. [61]Excluding imports from Israel ($580.7 million in 1987). [62]Excluding exports to Israel ($160.5 million in 1987).

Trade: domestic

The following table presents data relating to domestic wholesale and retail trade for the countries of the world. The section on wholesale trade is based for the most part on establishments (service points from which a business enterprise operates [*see* note a]) engaged primarily in selling goods to retailers and distributors for resale or to purchasers who buy for business and farm uses. The retail trade section is based on businesses engaged in selling merchandise for personal or household consumption; restaurants are, when possible, included, hotels excluded.

The data presented here are based on information from a variety of country and international sources. The country sources include statistical abstracts, correspondence, annual reports, and censuses of business and trade.

Because there is no single published source or common international methodology for the compilation of data on wholesale and retail trade, nor a single current year on which, by common agreement, the various national reports would be based, allowance must be made for variations in the meaning and recency of the information provided for any single country and for its comparability internationally. Variations occur in part because of the ways in which countries define wholesale and retail trade; the conventional free-enterprise distinction between wholesale and retail activity (of a single enterprise or an entire national trade sector) may not exist in the business practice of some countries. Variations also exist in the kind and level of detail reported. For example, countries may design surveys differently according to the size (number of employees, sales, surface area) of establishments surveyed, their profitability, or other less direct criteria, such as ownership or location. The depth of analysis to which the data are subjected may also vary. The structure of a national trade sector is also affected by the degree of government involvement, which may range from total control of wholesale distribution in some socialist countries to partial involvement in some strategic sectors, or to relative noninvolvement in fully private trade sectors of capitalist countries. In some smaller countries data may refer to a single trading enterprise.

At the table's extreme left, preceding the year to which the trade data refer, the combined value of the country's wholesale and retail trade as a percentage of gross domestic product or net material product is given. Unless otherwise noted, GDP data include restaurants and exclude hotels.

Both the wholesale and retail sections of the table provide similar detail: establishments or outlets, employees, sales, and certain derived values for relationships among these measures; the retail section provides an additional breakdown of sales by an end-use classification of retail sales outlets.

Although all sales figures are given in U.S. dollars, the comparability of these dollar figures may differ considerably; for instance, the purchasing power of various national currencies in domestic transactions may bear only a distant relationship to the exchange rate of the same currency in international transactions, especially for countries having nonconvertible currencies. The price of goods may also vary, depending on the degree to which they are subject to direct subsidies and artificial cost controls such as tax, investment, or free-trade preferences by a central government seeking to influence social or economic conditions.

Trade: domestic

country	domestic trade as percentage of GDP, 1992	year	wholesale trade					retail trade		
			establishments[a]	employees[b]	sales[c] (U.S.$'000,000)	employees per establishment	sales per establishment (U.S.$'000)	outlets[a]	employees[b]	sales[c] (U.S.$'000,000)
Afghanistan	7.9[1, 2]	1981–82	...	[3]	...	...	...	...	126,100[3]	...
Albania	4.6[4]	1990	...	[3]	...	...	...	11,741[5]	62,000[3]	1,570[5]
Algeria	17.8[6]	1986	...	[3]	...	...	...	3,600[7, 8]	390,990[1, 3, 9]	16,200
American Samoa	...	1990	177	255	...	1.4	...	583	1,495	...
Andorra	24.2[6]	1988	...	...	...	...	...	592[10]	7,227	...
Angola	6.1[11]	1973	[3]	...	...	...	...	29,138[3]	...	...
Antigua and Barbuda	25.6[1, 11]	1980	25	350	...	14.0	...	199	1,000	23[12]
Argentina	15.4	1985	54,452	351,087[13]	1,113	6.4[13]	20,435	500,342	1,055,071[13]	1,003
Armenia	5.7	1990	...	[3]	...	...	...	...	88,100[3]	...
Aruba	37.2[1, 14]	1990	...	723	...	...	...	...	5,700	[15]
Australia	17.4[16]	1991–92	15,514	153,092	44,553	9.9	2,872	209,909	1,290,173	107,230
Austria	16.4[1]	1993	17,149[6]	188,000	75,378	10.2[6]	3,526[6]	33,601[6]	250,000	40,432
Azerbaijan	2.2[17]	...	...	...	...	...	...	...	...	...
Bahamas, The[18]	23.0	1980	23	1,066	143	46.3	6,235	132	4,059	460[19]
Bahrain	10.6[1]	1983	[3]	[3]	...	[3]	...	255[3]	12,551[3]	1,601
Bangladesh	8.1[1, 16]	1985	...	[3]	...	...	...	271,000	3,610,000[3]	5,500[19]
Barbados	26.5[1, 17]	1990	...	[3]	...	...	...	1,911[20]	20,800[3]	264[12]
Belarus	6.5	1991	[3]	[3]	[3]	...	...	22,300[3]	299,900[3]	19,900[3]
Belgium	14.1[17]	1984	60,589	160,600	65,110	2.6	1,075	135,534	193,500	20,957
Belize	17.7[1]	1983	...	[3]	...	...	...	...	4,558[3]	33[19]
Benin	19.5[1, 6]	1979	...	...	...	...	...	170[7]	1,910[13, 19]	150[12]
Bermuda	32.8[21]	1985	60[21]	820	...	...	...	310[7, 21]	4,342[13]	116[22, 23]
Bhutan	7.6[1, 11]	1982	...	[3]	...	...	...	...	9,000[3, 5, 13]	...
Bolivia	10.1[17]	1989	...	[3]	...	...	...	...	244,907[3, 5]	1,570[19]
Bosnia and Herzegovina	13.9[6]	1990	...	[3]	18,469[6]	...	...	...	130,914[3]	18,065[6]
Botswana	15.2[24]	1983–84	205	3,500	494[12]	...	...	1,660	10,700	165[12]
Brazil	6.8[15]	1990	45,278	652,054	22,706	14.1	501	680,634	4,102,638	39,312
Brunei	12.3[1]	1986	[3]	[3]	...	[3]	...	833[3, 25]	4,261[3, 25]	...
Bulgaria	10.5[1, 4, 26]	1987	...	7,700[27]	...	...	...	41,339[22]	79,820[22]	34,700[22]
Burkina Faso	15.3	1975	...	[3]	...	...	...	...	19,354[3, 13]	...
Burundi	9.1[11]	1986	...	...	...	...	...	...	...	210
Cambodia	16.8[17]	...	...	...	...	...	...	...	...	...
Cameroon	11.7[11]	1980	...	...	...	...	...	1,312[7]	13,776[13, 19]	1,430[19]
Canada	12.1[17]	1993	...	[3]	232,900[6]	...	...	...	2,428,000[3, 4]	150,200
Cape Verde	28.4[6]	1980	...	[3]	...	...	...	...	3,930[3]	...
Central African Republic	23.5[11]	1989	113	302	...	2.7	...	14,543	23,078	230
Chad	29.5[6]	1983	...	[3]	[3]	...	...	...	1,661[3, 7, 28]	497[3]
Chile	15.6	1983	561[7]	15,300[7]	2,312[7]	27.2[7]	4,121[7]	1,125[19, 22]	21,700[19, 22]	1,403[19, 22]
China	5.9	1993	33,779	2,357,000[13]	161,031	69.8[13]	4,767	74,567[13]	3,766,000	235,910
Colombia	11.0[11]	1985	...	...	...	...	...	1,110[30]	49,000[30]	8,600[19]
Comoros	28.0[1, 17]	1980	...	[3]	...	...	...	...	1,873[3, 7]	...
Congo	12.3[11]	1984	...	[3]	...	...	...	...	13,240[3]	...
Costa Rica	21.3[17]	1975	332[31]	4,073[31]	35[31]	12.3[31]	104[31]	9,713	26,486	475[32]
Côte d'Ivoire	12.9[6]	1981	...	...	...	...	...	2,023[7]	16,720[7]	1,800[19]
Croatia	20.2	1992	...	27,376	38,117[6]	...	...	17,969	78,287	39,231[6]
Cuba	20.1[6, 26]	1989	...	...	15,174	...	...	56,916[27]	230,000[9, 13]	8,124
Cyprus	19.3[1, 17]	1993	1,559[24]	14,137	443	5.3[23]	720[23]	8,474[23]	39,676	1,102
Czech Republic[33]	12.9[11]	1990	63,110[27]	251,000[27]	40,083[27]	4.0[27]	635[27]	62,667[6]	258,127	21,235
Denmark	14.4	1992	32,432	176,205	73,937	5.4	2,280	40,733	210,015	32,145
Djibouti	16.3[11]	1985	28	371[14]	...	...	...	431	1,877[14]	...
Dominica	13.6[1]	1989	...	[3]	...	...	...	...	3,700[3]	790[19]
Dominican Republic	15.2	1983	670	...	3,136	...	4,681	11,220[14]	...	1,259[14]
Ecuador	20.8	1990	426	18,014	139	42.3	326	554	20,168	102
Egypt	18.4[16]	1983–84	2,552	45,500[13]	4,492	18.0[13]	1,760	2,545	55,800[13]	29,700[19]
El Salvador	35.3	1983	396	6,400	1,038	16.2	2,621	1,416	10,700	485

The data on distribution of retail sales by kind of consumer goods may have their origin in several different types of data or analysis. One country may aggregate sales data by kind of establishment only (this may be perfectly satisfactory in a country of small, independent outlets); another may aggregate data directly by kind of goods (most easily done in a country with well-developed statistical, tax-reporting, and commercial systems). Other countries may find it impolitic to publish data that reflect the poverty of their distribution network or their supply of consumer goods and may aggregate or publish data for only a few sectors: food or nonfood goods, for example. For countries with only a few trading enterprises in a particular sector, detail must often be withheld to preserve the confidentiality of individual businesses.

The notes that follow further define the column headings.

a. The number of establishments or outlets refers to economic units that operate at a single physical location in one principal kind of activity, whether singly owned or part of a multiunit firm. Such units are not necessarily identical with a company or enterprise.
b. Number of employees refers to full-time and part-time paid workers, including salaried managers and officers; it usually excludes owner-operators, partners, vendors, and unpaid relatives.
c. Total sales (also called turnover) includes the value of merchandise sold for cash or credit; amounts received from customers for layaway purchases; receipts from rental or leasing of vehicles, equipment, tools, instruments, etc.; receipts for delivery, installation, maintenance, repair, alteration, storage, and other services.
d. Outlets engaged primarily in the sale of food and nonalcoholic beverages, such as grocery stores, meat and fish markets, and bakeries.
e. Outlets engaged primarily in the sale of clothing and shoes; also includes outlets that sell accessory items, such as millinery, furs, and leather goods.
f. Outlets engaged primarily in the sale of home furnishings, including furniture, draperies, floor coverings, household appliances, and home entertainment equipment.
g. Outlets that primarily serve food and drink, including restaurants, lunchrooms, cafeterias, social caterers, refreshment places, contract feeders, ice cream parlors, and bars and taverns.
h. Outlets engaged primarily in the sale of pharmaceuticals, cosmetics, and perfumes.
i. Outlets engaged primarily in the sale of building materials, hardware, garden supplies, paint, electrical supplies, and farm equipment.
j. Outlets engaged primarily in the sale of motor vehicles, motorcycles, bicycles, and tires, batteries, and other automotive supplies and parts; includes service stations.
k. Outlets engaged in the sale of multiple lines of merchandise, such as department stores, variety stores, and rural general stores.
l. Miscellaneous specialized outlets such as those engaged primarily in the sale of liquors, sporting goods, books, jewelry, photographic and optical goods, gifts, flowers, tobacco products, home fuels, and newspapers.

retail trade (continued)												country
percentage breakdown of sales									employees per outlet	sales per outlet (U.S.$'000)	population per outlet	
food[d]	clothing, shoes[e]	home furnishings[f]	eating, drinking[g]	drugs, pharmaceuticals[h]	building materials[i]	automobile parts[j]	general merchandise[k]	other[l]				
...	...	...	...	...	...	...	...	...	...	...	...	Afghanistan
62.4				37.6					...	134[5]	277[5]	Albania
...	...	...	...	...	...	...	...	...	5.0[7,8]	...	5,146[7,8]	Algeria
...	...	...	...	...	...	...	...	...	...	...	81	American Samoa
...	...	...	...	...	...	...	...	...	3.8[10]	...	39[10]	Andorra
...	...	...	...	...	...	...	...	...	...	...	...	Angola
...	...	...	...	...	...	...	...	...	5.0	100	378	Antigua and Barbuda
15.5	13.3	7.1	5.4	4.3	7.8	13.7	10.1	22.8	2.1[13]	2,004	61	Argentina
...	...	...	...	...	...	...	...	...	...	...	...	Armenia
...	...	...	...	...	...	...	...	...	...	...	...	Aruba
28.9	3.6	8.0	3.7	2.9	2.4	31.9	7.9	10.7	6.1	511	82.8	Australia
31.0	12.2	6.9	...	6.7	1.9	17.3	4.3	19.7	7.1[6]	857[6]	227[6]	Austria
...	...	...	...	...	...	...	...	...	...	...	...	Azerbaijan
24.4[14]	7.7[14]	7.1[14]	—	3.7[14]	8.4[14]	30.1[14]	7.6[14]	11.0[14]	30.8	1,881	1,026	Bahamas, The[18]
...	...	...	...	...	...	...	...	...	49.2[3]	...	1,507[3]	Bahrain
...	...	...	...	...	...	...	...	...	...	...	...	Bangladesh
...	...	...	...	...	...	...	...	...	...	...	130[20]	Barbados
...	...	...	...	...	...	...	...	...	13.4[3]	892[3]	460[3]	Belarus
35.1				64.9					1.4	155	73	Belgium
...	...	...	...	...	...	...	...	...	...	...	...	Belize
...	...	...	...	...	...	...	...	...	11.3[13,19]	...	19,871[19]	Benin
...	...	...	...	...	...	...	...	...	11.0[12,22]	...	178[7,21]	Bermuda
...	...	...	...	...	...	...	...	...	...	...	...	Bhutan
...	...	...	...	...	...	...	...	...	...	...	...	Bolivia
...	...	...	...	...	...	...	...	...	...	...	...	Bosnia and Herzegovina
...	...	...	...	...	...	...	...	...	6.4	99	604	Botswana
11.1	12.1	...	...	4.2	8.4	31.4	15.4	17.4	6.0	55	213	Brazil
...	...	...	...	...	...	...	...	...	5.1[3,25]	...	279[3,25]	Brunei
50.9	10.9	3.4	...	5.9	...	...	0.2	28.7	1.9[22]	839[22]	217[22]	Bulgaria
...	...	...	...	...	...	...	...	...	...	...	...	Burkina Faso
...	...	...	...	...	...	...	...	...	...	...	...	Burundi
...	...	...	...	...	...	...	...	...	...	...	...	Cambodia
...	...	...	...	...	...	...	...	...	10.5[7,13]	...	6,481[7]	Cameroon
26.1	5.8	5.5	...	6.1	...	34.3	10.8	11.4	...	...	...	Canada
...	...	...	...	...	...	...	...	...	...	...	...	Cape Verde
...	...	...	...	...	...	...	...	...	1.6	16	187	Central African Republic
...	...	...	...	...	...	...	...	...	...	...	...	Chad
28.3[14]	[29]	5.0[14]	1.6[14]	5.4[14]	4.7[14]	18.0[14]	17.1[14,29]	19.9[14]	19.3[19,22]	1,247[19,22]	10,210[19,22]	Chile
54.9	16.3	...	...	4.6	...	2.9	13.8	7.5	50.5[13]	3,163	15,804	China
...	...	...	...	...	...	...	...	...	44.1[30]	1,522[30]	...	Colombia
...	...	...	...	...	...	...	...	...	...	...	...	Comoros
...	...	...	...	...	...	...	...	...	...	...	...	Congo
37.7	13.5	6.9	...	8.2	7.0	15.1	5.9	5.7	2.7	59	202	Costa Rica
...	...	...	...	...	...	...	...	...	8.3[7]	...	4,257[7]	Côte d'Ivoire
23.8	6.1	3.2	...	...	5.8	19.8	32.0	9.3	4.4	1,973[6]	266	Croatia
35.8	17.2	9.9	...	5.3	0.8	5.1	...	25.9	4.0[9,13]	184[27]	177[27]	Cuba
10.2	8.2	...	43.7	2.4	3.1	14.9	...	17.5	1.0[23]	124[23]	77[23]	Cyprus
42.9	15.1	12.8	...	3.6	2.9	10.0	...	12.7	4.2[6]	362[6]	249[6]	Czech Republic[33]
47.1	5.6	3.4	...	3.2	3.1	17.7	1.4	18.5	5.2	789	127	Denmark
...	...	...	...	...	...	...	...	...	...	...	998	Djibouti
...	...	...	...	...	...	...	...	...	...	...	...	Dominica
...	...	...	...	...	...	...	...	...	...	112[14]	519[14]	Dominican Republic
26.3	2.0	11.5	3.9	1.6	7.2	38.2	6.2	3.1	36.4	184	18,520	Ecuador
...	...	...	...	...	...	...	...	...	21.9[13]	1,278	17,756	Egypt
11.9[8,34]	7.6[8,34]	16.2[8,34]	...	7.9[8,34]	6.3[8,34]	12.4[8,34]	28.2[8,34]	9.5[8,34]	7.6	342	3,336	El Salvador

Trade: domestic (continued)

country	domestic trade as percentage of GDP, 1992	year	wholesale trade: establishments[a]	wholesale trade: employees[b]	wholesale trade: sales[c] (U.S.$'000,000)	wholesale trade: employees per establishment	wholesale trade: sales per establishment (U.S.$'000)	retail trade: outlets[a]	retail trade: employees[b]	retail trade: sales[c] (U.S.$'000,000)
Equatorial Guinea	7.1[11]	1983	...	36	...	...	...	...	2,701	...
Eritrea[35]	...	...	...	...	...	...	...	...	...	...
Estonia	14.5	1993	...	...	5,445	...	...	...	70,000[4]	2,981
Ethiopia[35]	10.2[1, 24]	1984	375[7, 36]	3,200[7, 36]	...	8.5[7, 36]	...	7,416[7, 36]	17,100[7, 36]	273
Faroe Islands	13.1	1987	78	[3]	19	...	241	430	1,484[1, 3, 32]	38
Fiji	19.0[1]	1991	342	3,245	388	9.5	1,134	1,188	8,158	556
Finland	12.2[1]	1992	9,367[37]	80,394[37]	46,334[37]	8.6[37]	4,946[37]	37,303	137,609	35,052
France	15.0	1992	88,371	912,131	399,844	10.3	4,525	363,701	1,615,700	320,274
French Guiana	12.2[6]	1991	175	905	1,798	5.2	10,274	820	2,522	1,984
French Polynesia	22.7[4]	1986	[3]	[3]	...	...	...	947[3]	5,038[3]	...
Gabon	9.6[11]	1982	...	[3]	...	...	...	...	12,683[3, 13, 21]	...
Gambia, The	19.5[16]	1983	...	[3]	...	...	...	...	16,551[3]	...
Gaza Strip	...	1986	...	[3]	...	...	...	...	13,400[3]	...
Georgia	3.3	1988	...	[3]	...	...	...	...	172,400[3]	...
Germany	8.1[17]	1991	...	1,336,200	624,396	...	...	147,974	2,313,400	404,296
Ghana	11.3	1983	460[39]	1,100[39]	115[39]	2.4[39]	250[39]	1,500	16,000	252[19]
Gibraltar	...	1991	...	737	...	...	...	...	1,835	...
Greece	13.1[1]	1988	31,032	115,979	...	3.7	...	184,821	388,132	12,263[40]
Greenland	8.0[20]	1992	...	[3]	139	...	...	...	2,214[3, 9]	211
Grenada	20.6[1]	1988	...	[3]	[3]	...	...	...	5,421[3]	6[3, 12]
Guadeloupe	19.6[1, 6]	1991	736	4,053	1,066	5.5	145	4,005	11,754	1,306
Guam	51.5[14]	1992	169	2,045	[3]	12.1	[3]	768	12,060	1,400[3]
Guatemala	24.0	1989	...	[3]	...	...	...	88,200[14]	374,690[3]	1,200[19]
Guernsey	...	1991	...	642	...	...	...	...	2,573	...
Guinea	23.8[11]	1979	...	[3]	...	...	...	...	12,808[3, 39]	...
Guinea-Bissau	27.5[1, 6]	1979	[3]	[3]	...	...	...	685[3, 39]	5,085[3]	44[3, 25]
Guyana	4.9[17]	1980	...	[3]	...	...	...	147[7]	14,690[3]	93[12]
Haiti	16.2	1983	...	[3]	...	...	...	653[7, 41]	303,353[3]	500[19]
Honduras	11.0	1991	...	[3]	...	...	...	...	156,500[3]	401[12]
Hong Kong	24.9	1992	23,160	84,446	20,604	3.6	890	70,941	432,756	35,312
Hungary	8.6	1993	206[14]	122,600[14]	13,121[21]	595[21]	...	200,049	652,300[11]	21,400
Iceland	13.7[11]	1992	1,509[12, 43]	5,132[21]	598[32, 43]	...	...	1,680	7,774[44]	825
India	12.7[16]	1980	[3]	[3]	...	...	...	3,132,000[3, 22]	3,615,000[3, 22]	108,300[12]
Indonesia	16.6	1980	[3]	[3]	[3]	[3]	[3]	54,632[3]	85,400[3]	3,451[3]
Iran	17.1[16]	1986–87	118,698	[3]	2,429[46]	...	133[46]	634,084	521,708[3, 47]	37,350
Iraq	15.6[11]	1987–88[25]	1,942	3,902	130	2.0	67	108,460	165,594	7,077
Ireland	11.2[1, 9]	1988	3,972	39,101	11,420	9.8	2,875	31,699	89,680	10,952
Isle of Man	12.0[12]	1981	...	775	...	...	...	...	3,146	...
Israel	9.4[11]	1988	17,967	67,300	16,875	3.8	939	43,844	103,100	10,763
Italy	18.4[1]	1983	...	[3]	...	...	...	1,033,725	1,369,200[3]	122,978
Jamaica	23.7[1, 17]	1991	...	[3]	...	...	...	10,150[32]	173,500[3]	1,457[12]
Japan	14.0	1991	475,967	4,773,000[13]	4,253,448	10.0[13]	8,963	1,591,186[22]	6,936,000[13, 22]	1,043,976[22]
Jersey	...	1986	...	855	...	...	...	...	7,046	...
Jordan	9.3[17]	1991	488	2,862	147	5.9	301	34,086	69,393	1,002
Kazakhstan	1.4	1991	...	...	...	...	...	42,168	484,800	...
Kenya	14.1[17]	1990	2,097	21,266	...	10.1	...	4,316	36,300	...
Kiribati	14.1	1987	...	[3]	...	...	...	30	1,127[3, 27]	3.8
Korea, North	...	...	...	...	...	...	...	...	...	...
Korea, South	12.7[17]	1993	114,444	558,880	81,194	4.9	709	1,147,734	2,399,883	90,756
Kuwait	5.5[17]	1989	2,982	25,897	65	8.7	22	14,521	54,588	145
Kyrgyzstan	3.0	1992	...	[3]	...	...	...	...	92,900[3, 37]	138
Laos	7.2	1990	...	...	...	...	...	15,000	...	576
Latvia	13.6[4]	1991	...	...	...	...	...	7,214	95,300	20,425
Lebanon	7.7	1986	...	[3]	...	...	...	...	114,706[3]	1,662[13]
Lesotho	7.7[11]	...	...	...	...	...	...	...	...	...
Liberia	5.3[6]	1984	...	[3]	...	...	...	...	46,850[3]	115[19]
Libya	8.8[11]	1973	1,126	4,148[13]	...	3.7[13]	...	26,825	44,605[13]	9,205[12]
Liechtenstein	...	1975	67	216	...	3.2	...	228	740	...
Lithuania	13.5	1992	...	[3]	...	...	...	6,425	127,400[3]	236
Luxembourg	16.4[11]	1992	1,880	11,645	7,390	6.2	3,931	3,438	19,462	4,603
Macau	...	1991	...	[3]	...	...	...	...	47,706[3]	...
Macedonia	19.8	1990	...	[3]	9,522[6]	...	...	...	65,593[6]	9,238[6]
Madagascar	10.9[11]	1976	1,104	...	...	...	...	1,570	...	696[21]
Malaŵi	11.0[17]	1984	439	23,000	522	52	1,189	500	8,600	127
Malaysia	12.3[17]	1980	19,663	116,200	15,461	5.9	786	95,993	73,000	8,200[19]
Maldives	17.9[1]	1990	...	[3]	...	...	...	...	8,884[3]	5[19]
Mali	15.5[1, 11]	1979	...	[3]	...	...	...	...	5,200[3]	...
Malta	14.3[1, 11]	1983	3	[3]	1.0	...	333	4[20]	11,936[3, 7]	2.3
Marshall Islands	83.7[1, 21]	1988	...	[3]	...	...	...	...	1,394[3]	...
Martinique	20.7[1, 6]	1991	740	[3]	...	...	...	5,489	12,399[3, 19]	234[12]
Mauritania	19.1[1, 6]	1971[7]	23	100	102	4.3	4,445	59	700	103
Mauritius	17.4[1, 17]	1986	[3]	[3]	...	[3]	...	207[1, 3, 7]	10,107[1, 3, 7]	164[1, 3, 7]
Mayotte	...	1983	[3]	[3]	[3]	...	[3]	41[3]	597[3, 9]	27[3]
Mexico	25.6[17]	1988	36,512	[3]	23,506	...	644	713,315	3,875,100[3, 4]	39,810
Micronesia	11.9[12]	1980	...	348[13]	...	...	...	...	489[1, 13]	...
Moldova	9.4[11]	1990	...	[3]	...	...	...	...	148,000[3]	...
Monaco	...	1975	...	273	...	...	...	...	1,439	...
Mongolia	21.7[6]	1983[3, 49]	...	...	...	...	...	4,828	21,100	1,235[27]
Morocco	20.9[17]	1972	...	...	...	...	...	4,000[7]	20,000[7]	5,750[19]
Mozambique	4.9[11]	1980	...	[3]	...	...	...	...	63,058[3]	...
Myanmar (Burma)	22.5[16]	1983	...	[3]	...	...	...	...	1,405,000[2, 3]	2,116
Namibia	11.5[11]	1977	222	5,035	377	22.7	1,698	1,248	7,569	254
Nauru	...	...	...	...	...	...	...	...	...	...
Nepal	6.0[1, 16]	1983	...	[3]	...	...	...	...	119,000[3, 13, 21]	736
Netherlands, The	16.2	1992	50,600	344,000	211,658	6.8	4,183	81,500	482,500	65,626

retail trade (continued)												country
percentage breakdown of sales									employees per outlet	sales per outlet (U.S.$'000)	population per outlet	
food[d]	clothing, shoes[e]	home furnishings[f]	eating, drinking[g]	drugs, pharma-ceuticals[h]	building materials[i]	automobile parts[j]	general merchandise[k]	other[l]				
...	...	...	...	...	...	...	...	...	...	...	...	Equatorial Guinea
...	...	...	...	...	...	...	...	...	...	...	...	Eritrea[35]
38.9	7.4	...	9.1	...	...	11.7	...	32.9	...	...	...	Estonia
15.9	45.2	...	...	...	7.9	9.8	10.5	10.7	2.3[7, 36]	27[7, 36]	55,200[7, 36]	Ethiopia[35]
...	...	...	...	...	...	...	...	...	...	89	109	Faroe Islands
11.9	10.2	7.6	8.5	2.6	12.3	9.6	36.1	1.2	6.9	468	625	Fiji
30.0	6.1	2.3	...	3.8	9.4	24.2	11.7	12.5	3.7	940	135	Finland
38.2	15.7	17.6	...	6.4	...	6.1	6.3	9.7	4.4	881	158	France
...	...	...	...	...	...	...	...	...	3.1	2,419	155	French Guiana
...	...	...	...	...	...	...	...	...	5.3[3]	...	188[3]	French Polynesia
50.5	9.6	...	...	...	33.8	6.1	...	...	...	...	...	Gabon
...	...	...	...	...	...	...	...	...	...	...	...	Gambia, The
...	...	...	...	...	...	...	...	...	...	...	...	Gaza Strip
...	...	...	...	...	...	...	...	...	...	...	...	Georgia
27.0	12.3	4.7	...	6.1	2.5	19.6	[39]	27.8[38]	15.6	2,732	540	Germany
...	...	...	...	...	...	...	...	...	1.1	108[39]	7,993	Ghana
...	...	...	...	...	...	...	...	...	...	...	...	Gibraltar
60.0[40]	18.1[40]	9.5[40]	...	...	...	...	...	12.4[40]	2.1	...	54	Greece
...	...	...	...	...	...	...	...	...	...	...	...	Greenland
...	...	...	...	...	...	...	...	...	...	...	...	Grenada
44.8	13.4	19.6	...	7.1	...	...	...	15.1	2.9	326	91	Guadeloupe
11.6[9]	10.9[9]	4.9[9]	8.0[9]	0.3[9]	5.2[9]	26.9[9]	3.3[9]	28.9[9]	15.7	1,494[3]	181	Guam
...	...	...	...	...	...	...	...	...	...	...	83[14]	Guatemala
...	...	...	...	...	...	...	...	...	...	...	...	Guernsey
...	...	...	...	...	...	...	...	...	...	...	...	Guinea
...	...	...	...	...	...	...	...	...	0.8[3, 39]	...	1,080[3, 39]	Guinea-Bissau
9.7	18.9	13.8	4.5	2.8	17.7	18.6	...	14.0	...	743	5,884	Guyana
...	...	...	...	...	...	...	...	...	...	...	7,034[7, 41]	Haiti
...	...	...	...	...	...	...	...	...	...	...	...	Honduras
13.1	11.8	...	20.5	...	...	3.2	...	51.4[42]	6.1	489	82	Hong Kong
28.0	7.6	...	11.3	2.9	21.5	14.8	2.6	11.3	4.2[11]	107	51	Hungary
62.6[45]	8.8	...	...	...	...	...	[45]	28.6	4.6[44]	825	155	Iceland
...	...	...	...	...	...	...	...	...	1.2[3, 22]	...	219[3, 22]	India
...	...	...	...	...	...	...	...	...	1.6[3]	63[3]	2,681[3]	Indonesia
...	...	...	...	...	...	...	...	...	...	59	78	Iran
...	...	...	...	...	...	...	...	...	1.5	20	158	Iraq
40.6	9.1	1.4	10.4	2.9	5.1	21.6	2.8	6.1	2.8	345	112	Ireland
...	...	...	...	...	...	...	...	...	...	...	...	Isle of Man
35.4	12.2	20.0	...	...	...	...	6.2	26.2	2.4	245	103	Israel
50.8	15.1	...	...	3.4	...	...	...	30.7	...	119	55	Italy
...	...	...	...	...	...	...	...	...	...	...	214[32]	Jamaica
29.5	10.6	8.5	—	2.8	...	13.5	14.1	21.0	4.4[13, 22]	656[22]	77.9[22]	Japan
...	...	...	...	...	...	...	...	...	...	...	...	Jersey
28.9	12.1	6.6	...	1.6	7.4	22.6	9.5	11.3	2.0	29	108	Jordan
...	...	...	...	...	...	...	...	...	11.5	...	400	Kazakhstan
...	...	...	...	...	...	...	...	...	8.4	...	6,003	Kenya
...	...	...	...	...	...	...	...	...	...	127	2,226	Kiribati
...	...	...	...	...	...	...	...	...	...	...	...	Korea, North
29.4[20]	13.1[20]	8.9[20]	18.9[20]	5.0[20]	2.4[20]	5.4[20]	1.2[20]	15.6[20]	2.1	79	38	Korea, South
18.4[45]	14.5	17.3	...	2.6	6.5	16.4	[45]	24.3	3.8	10	138	Kuwait
...	...	...	...	...	...	...	...	...	...	...	...	Kyrgyzstan
...	...	...	...	...	...	...	...	...	...	38	270	Laos
...	...	...	...	...	...	...	...	...	13.2	2,831	373	Latvia
...	...	...	...	...	...	...	...	...	...	...	...	Lebanon
...	...	...	...	...	...	...	...	...	...	...	...	Lesotho
...	...	...	...	...	...	...	...	...	...	...	...	Liberia
...	...	...	...	...	...	...	...	...	1.7[13]	...	84	Libya
...	...	...	...	...	...	...	...	...	3.2	...	105	Liechtenstein
59.2	10.9	3.7	...	...	1.3	0.8	...	24.1	19.8[3]	38	584	Lithuania
26.8	10.5	9.9	...	3.8	...	30.9	...	18.1	5.7	1,339	113	Luxembourg
...	...	...	...	...	...	...	...	...	...	...	...	Macau
...	...	...	...	...	...	...	...	...	...	...	...	Macedonia
...	...	...	...	...	...	...	...	...	...	...	4,977	Madagascar
...	...	...	...	...	...	...	...	...	17.2	254	14,196	Malaŵi
32.9[48]	7.3[48]	10.8[48]	...	2.5[48]	1.1[48]	33.3[48]	4.4[48]	7.7[48]	0.8	64	143	Malaysia
...	...	...	...	...	...	...	...	...	...	...	...	Maldives
...	...	...	...	...	...	...	...	...	...	...	...	Mali
...	...	...	...	...	...	...	...	...	...	578[7]	83,378[7]	Malta
...	...	...	...	...	...	...	...	...	...	...	...	Marshall Islands
...	...	...	...	...	...	...	...	...	...	...	68	Martinique
...	...	...	...	...	...	...	...	...	11.9	1,742	20,300	Mauritania
...	...	...	...	...	...	...	...	...	48.8[1, 3, 7]	792[1, 3, 7]	4,976[1, 3, 7]	Mauritius
...	...	...	...	...	...	...	...	...	...	652[3]	1,477[3]	Mayotte
33.8	...	...	...	...	37.0	23.7	...	5.8	...	59	113	Mexico
...	...	...	...	...	...	...	...	...	...	...	...	Micronesia
...	...	...	...	...	...	...	...	...	...	...	...	Moldova
...	...	...	...	...	...	...	...	...	...	...	...	Monaco
...	...	...	...	...	...	...	...	...	4.3	225	372	Mongolia
...	...	...	...	...	...	...	...	...	5.0[7]	...	*c.* 4,000[7]	Morocco
...	...	...	...	...	...	...	...	...	...	...	...	Mozambique
...	...	...	...	...	...	...	...	...	...	...	...	Myanmar (Burma)
31.4	11.9	5.3	...	2.8	1.7	...	41.9	5.0	5.9	196	713	Namibia
...	...	...	...	...	...	...	...	...	...	...	...	Nauru
...	...	...	...	...	...	...	...	...	...	...	...	Nepal
40.2	11.8	11.1	...	2.3	4.6	5.8	2.8	21.4	5.9	805	186	Netherlands, The

Trade: domestic (continued)

country	domestic trade as percentage of GDP, 1992	year	wholesale trade					retail trade		
			establishments[a]	employees[b]	sales[c] (U.S.$'000,000)	employees per establishment	sales per establishment (U.S.$'000)	outlets[a]	employees[b]	sales[c] (U.S.$'000,000)
Netherlands Antilles	21.8[4]	1988	...	[3]	...	...	...	...	15,890[3]	149[13, 15]
New Caledonia	31.0[4]	1991	...	[3]	...	...	...	1,023	4,995[3]	...
New Zealand	16.4[1, 51]	1994	8,263[51]	76,664[51]	16,295[51]	9.3[51]	1,972[51]	29,961[22, 51]	116,301[22, 51]	17,055
Nicaragua	18.5	1987	...	[3]	...	...	...	20,610[14]	94,600[3]	790[19]
Niger	13.2[1, 6]	...	...	...	...	...	...	...	...	...
Nigeria	13.1[11]	1983[7]	154	16,000	2,220	104	14,415	421	20,000	2,202
Northern Mariana Islands	...	1987	28	187	49	6.7	1,777	383	2,304	155
Norway	11.0[1, 11]	1992	18,390	101,385[44]	56,056	5.5[44]	3,048	40,154	121,677[44]	31,264
Oman	13.9	1990	[3]	[3]	...	...	...	25,840[1, 3, 6]	87,500[3]	2,449[12]
Pakistan	14.5[1, 16]	1983	...	...	...	...	...	276,701[41]	501,773[13, 41]	12,848
Palau	19.0[27]	1984	...	124	...	...	...	...	133	...
Panama	11.8	1982[54]	560	13,115	1,491	23.4	2,662	7,561	15,765[7]	1,334
Papua New Guinea	9.6	1985	...	[3]	...	...	...	...	25,100[3, 32]	669[1]
Paraguay	30.3[1]	1982	...	[3]	...	...	...	...	85,961[3]	2,645[19]
Peru	12.4	1973	4,210	34,100	2,163	8.1	514	103,010	72,200	8,500[19]
Philippines	13.7	1981	20,642	122,717	4,538	5.9	220	279,968	241,872	4,836
Poland	14.4	1993	...	119,600[28, 45]	15,945	...	...	785,000	943,179	53,382
Portugal	17.4[4]	1983	4,522	135,400[13]	9,260	29.9[13]	2,048	4,889	74,400[13]	3,057
Puerto Rico	14.7	1991	1,876	34,571	7,365[27]	18.4	3,165[27]	9,164	106,239	7,206[27]
Qatar	6.7	1990	134	3,801	85	28.4	636	4,956	18,238	1,048[37]
Réunion	19.2[4]	1992	1,313	6,732	2,664	5.1	203	3,506	12,927	2,114
Romania	8.5[1, 11]	1989	...	...	...	...	...	82,035	465,200	19,926
Russia	15.1[4]	1992	...	...	...	...	...	319,500	3,135,000	18,771
Rwanda	17.1[1, 11]	1978	...	[3]	...	...	...	...	8,014[1, 3]	350[19]
St. Kitts and Nevis	22.4[1, 11]	1984	...	[3]	...	...	...	...	940[3]	...
St. Lucia	24.6[17]	1980	...	[3]	...	...	...	...	4,770[1, 3, 13]	...
St. Vincent	13.2[1]	...	...	...	...	...	...	...	...	...
San Marino	...	1994	209	[3]	...	...	...	1,126	2,531[3]	...
São Tomé and Príncipe	10.0[6]	1981	...	[3]	...	...	...	...	1,994[3]	...
Saudi Arabia	6.9	1991[22]	4,460	31,481[13]	1,354	7.1[13]	304	80,266	174,187[13]	2,292
Senegal	27.4	1987	97[7]	1,843[7]	...	19[7]	...	289[7]	4,964[7]	664[12]
Seychelles	11.3[4]	1985	[3]	[3]	...	[3]	...	131[3]	1,298[3]	...
Sierra Leone	20.0[16]	1983–84	...	[3]	...	...	...	...	7,211[3]	177[12]
Singapore	17.9[1, 17]	1992	24,820	158,993	132,480	6.4	5,338	17,798[22]	78,152[22]	12,058[22]
Slovakia	8.9[11, 26]	1992	...	...	...	...	...	5,590	24,638	1,313
Slovenia	14.1[11]	1993	714	19,149	4,189	26.8	5,867	6,896	35,002	4,271
Solomon Islands	9.6[11]	1991	...	[3]	...	...	...	405[19]	2,849[3]	139[19]
Somalia	9.3[11]	...	...	...	...	...	...	...	...	...
South Africa	13.7	1991	...	...	46,541	...	...	58,100[32]	373,200[32]	35,592
Spain	20.5[1, 28]	1984	40,000[20]	...	...	...	...	710,865[20]	1,400,000[20]	54,777
Sri Lanka	20.4[1, 11]	1983[7]	190	15,000	[3]	78.9	...	1,348	44,300	1,116[3, 23]
Sudan, The	12.8[6]	1981	...	...	...	...	...	...	...	3,278
Suriname	23.5	1985	...	[3]	...	...	...	13,000[53]	12,840[3]	110[19]
Swaziland	8.7[1, 11]	1984	67	1,000	...	14.9	...	656	3,700	23[20]
Sweden	10.9	1992	31,960[23]	167,800[23]	37,518[23]	5.2[23]	1,174[23]	70,467	248,208	59,250
Switzerland	18.0[4]	1985	15,019	143,470	...	9.6	...	53,465	259,674	23,620[23]
Syria	22.8	1983	2,827[41]	...	...	...	...	75,865[41]	110,000[13, 41]	7,330[19]
Taiwan	16.5[1, 17]	1987	55,654[12]	169,100	7,572[28]	2.9[12]	101[12]	355,760[12]	181,200	14,291[27]
Tajikistan	17.0[6]	...	...	[3]	...	...	...	...	145,400[3]	...
Tanzania	14.6[1, 11]	1983	...	...	...	...	...	1,620[7]	16,524[7]	3,975[19]
Thailand	17.0[11]	1988	16,740	139,252	14,535	8.3	868	260,030	280,886	13,683
Togo	17.4[11]	1980	...	...	...	...	...	181[7]	1,815[7]	112
Tonga	12.6[16]	1976	...	14[13]	...	...	...	...	654[13]	...
Trinidad and Tobago	15.5[1, 16]	1977	124	6,786	509	54.7	4,102	370	15,986	1,670[19]
Tunisia	24.7[1]	1984	...	[3]	...	...	...	...	153,860[3, 27]	2,814
Turkey	18.3[17]	1990	54,567	225,427	68,961	4.1	1,264	445,365	560,796	73,834
Turkmenistan	...	1990	...	[3]	...	...	...	...	90,000[3]	4,150
Tuvalu	14.9[1]	1979	...	[3]	...	...	...	...	113[3, 13]	...
Uganda	12.3[11]	1977	226	4,100	...	18.1	...	251	3,200	5,285[22]
Ukraine	5.7[11]	1991	...	[3]	...	...	...	...	1,753,000[3, 4]	70,800
United Arab Emirates	10.2[17]	1983	[3]	[3]	...	[3]	...	13,906[1, 3, 39]	121,278[3, 39]	5,910[19]
United Kingdom	14.1	1992[57]	126,729	861,000	395,078	6.8	3,118	318,751	2,324,000	242,802
United States	15.8[11]	1993	478,000[11]	6,113,000	1,922,600	12.7[11]	3,686[11]	1,547,000[11]	19,743,000	2,081,600
Uruguay	13.0	1988	...	[3]	...	...	...	52,954[1, 3]	161,285[1, 3]	5,397[22, 23]
Uzbekistan	6.5	1991	...	[3]	...	...	...	...	462,000[3]	...
Vanuatu	32.2[4]	1983[47]	18	187[13]	...	10.4[13]	...	256	1,439[13]	...
Venezuela	14.3	1979	...	...	...	...	...	...	161,596	12,345[19]
Vietnam	22.8[17]	1990	...	...	...	...	...	25,723	419,400	4,414
Virgin Islands (U.S.)	...	1987	84	1,322	211	15.7	2,509	1,311	8,529	703
West Bank	...	1986	...	[3]	...	...	...	...	23,000[3]	...
Western Sahara	...	...	...	...	...	...	...	...	...	...
Western Samoa	10.3[6]	1986	...	[3]	...	...	...	...	842[3]	...
Yemen[58]	13.0	1986	...	[3]	...	...	...	...	201,606[3]	2,195[12]
Yugoslavia	22.5	1992	5,723	17,693	8,671	3.1	1,515	51,159	125,348	8,958
Zaire	17.5[11]	1981	...	...	...	...	...	3,036[7]	33,398[7]	3,300[12]
Zambia	10.9[11]	1974	494[7]	15,500[7]	977[7]	31.4[7]	1,978[7]	1,636[7]	13,700[7]	768[12]
Zimbabwe	8.3	1990	...	[3]	...	...	...	...	95,400[3]	693[27]

[1]Includes hotels. [2]1989–90. [3]Retail-trade data include wholesale trade. [4]1990. [5]Excludes retail-trade network of the agricultural cooperatives. [6]1989. [7]Data refer to larger establishments only. [8]1971. [9]1987. [10]1972. [11]1991. [12]1983. [13]All persons engaged, including proprietors. [14]1982. [15]Netherlands Antilles. [16]1992–93. [17]1993. [18]Data refer to New Providence Island only. [19]1986. [20]1979. [21]1981. [22]Excludes restaurants (eating and drinking establishments). [23]1984. [24]1991–92. [25]Privately owned establishments only. [26]Percentage of net material product. [27]1985. [28]1976. [29]General merchandise includes clothing and shoes. [30]For major cities only. [31]Wholesale selling directly to the public only. [32]1980. [33]Data refer to former Czechoslovakia. [34]Selected outlets in urban areas only. [35]Ethiopia includes Eritrea. [36]Excludes Addis Ababa and Asmera. [37]1988. [38]Other includes general merchandise. [39]1977. [40]1978. [41]1975. [42]Includes home

retail trade (continued)												country
percentage breakdown of sales									employees per outlet	sales per outlet (U.S.$'000)	population per outlet	
food[d]	clothing, shoes[e]	home furnishings[f]	eating, drinking[g]	drugs, pharma-ceuticals[h]	building materials[i]	automobile parts[j]	general merchandise[k]	other[l]				
...	...	...	...	...	...	...	...	...	...	...	...	Netherlands Antilles
...	...	...	...	...	...	...	...	...	...	...	169	New Caledonia
22.1	5.4	7.4	14.4	3.2	2.4	32.1	4.6	8.4	3.9[22, 51]	346[22, 51]	106[22, 51]	New Zealand
...	...	...	...	...	...	...	...	...	...	...	143[14]	Nicaragua
...	...	...	...	...	...	...	...	...	...	...	...	Niger
...	...	...	...	...	...	...	...	...	47.5	5,230	226,615	Nigeria
27.0	[52]	2.3	8.8	...	7.2	[52]	4.7	50.0[52]	6.0	406	56	Northern Mariana Islands
34.9	9.9	7.3	...	...	4.8	27.0	4.0	12.1	3.0[44]	779	107	Norway
...	...	...	...	...	...	...	...	...	...	...	56[1, 3, 6]	Oman
64.0	12.0	4.0	...	...	...	...	...	20.0	1.8[13, 41]	...	273[41]	Pakistan
...	...	...	...	...	...	...	...	...	...	...	...	Palau
...	...	...	...	...	...	...	...	...	13.9[7]	176	270	Panama
...	...	...	7.1[1]	...	...	26.0	...	66.9	...	...	...	Papua New Guinea
...	...	...	...	...	...	...	...	...	...	...	...	Paraguay
...	...	...	...	...	...	...	...	...	0.7	20	145	Peru
25.4	12.3	6.7	...	...	11.3	29.5	...	14.8	0.9	17	177	Philippines
39.3	8.3	3.0	...	...	...	24.3	...	25.1	1.2	68	49	Poland
21.5[40]	14.1[40]	11.2[40]	...	3.3[40]	5.6[40]	35.2[40]	——9.1[40]——		15.3[13]	625	2,047	Portugal
30.5[14]	9.9[14]	4.5[14]	7.5[14]	4.3[14]	5.9[14]	23.2[14]	8.9[14]	5.3[14]	11.6	201[27]	387	Puerto Rico
9.0[37]	9.6[37]	13.2[37]	...	2.7[37]	7.2[37]	29.7[37]	9.1[37]	19.5[37]	3.7	177[10]	98	Qatar
54.4	11.5	17.8	...	6.9	...	...	...	9.4	3.7	603	178	Réunion
30.0[32]	10.0[32]	5.9[32]	25.0[32]	1.6[32]	0.8[32]	...	...	26.7[32]	5.7	243	282	Romania
...	...	...	...	...	...	...	...	...	9.8	59	563	Russia
...	...	...	...	...	...	...	...	...	...	...	...	Rwanda
...	...	...	...	...	...	...	...	...	...	...	...	St. Kitts and Nevis
...	...	...	...	...	...	...	...	...	...	...	...	St. Lucia
...	...	...	...	...	...	...	...	...	...	...	...	St. Vincent
...	...	...	...	...	...	...	...	...	2.2[3]	...	21.8[3]	San Marino
...	...	...	...	...	...	...	...	...	...	...	...	São Tomé and Príncipe
...	...	...	...	...	...	...	...	...	2.2[13]	29	201	Saudi Arabia
...	...	...	...	...	...	...	...	...	17.2[7]	...	23,430[7]	Senegal
...	...	...	...	...	...	...	...	...	9.9[3]	...	498[3]	Seychelles
...	...	...	...	...	...	...	...	...	...	...	...	Sierra Leone
17.7[45]	20.4	11.6	...	...	...	24.2	[45]	26.1	4.4	677	158	Singapore
42.1	7.7	9.3	...	1.9	0.8	3.7	1.7	32.8	1.4	235	948	Slovakia
31.8	6.6	1.1	...	4.0	[55]	8.4[55]	34.4	11.5	5.1	619	289	Slovenia
...	...	...	...	...	...	...	...	...	...	...	...	Solomon Islands
...	...	...	...	...	...	...	...	...	...	...	...	Somalia
35.0	13.9	8.1	...	3.3	...	18.7	4.5	16.5	6.4[32]	383[32]	c. 540[32]	South Africa
39.2	10.5	16.7	...	...	...	4.2	...	29.4	2.0[20]	119[20]	52[20]	Spain
...	...	...	...	...	...	...	...	...	32.9	...	11,436	Sri Lanka
...	...	...	...	...	...	...	...	...	...	...	...	Sudan, The
...	...	...	...	...	...	...	...	...	...	...	...	Suriname
52.5[20]	25.1[19]	22.4[19]	...	...	...	...	...	...	5.6	...	969	Swaziland
35.5	——9.3——		...	...	...	...	...	55.2	3.5	841	123	Sweden
46.4[23]	13.5[23]	...	...	4.0[23]	...	...	...	36.1[23]	4.9	...	122[23]	Switzerland
16.0	2.5	...	...	3.5	12.3	39.5[56]	3.5	22.7	1.4[13, 41]	...	97[41]	Syria
21.5[21]	3.2[21]	8.8[21]	...	4.1[21]	3.1[21]	8.7[21]	3.1[21]	47.5[21]	0.3[12]	33[12]	52[12]	Taiwan
...	...	...	...	...	...	...	...	...	...	...	...	Tajikistan
...	...	...	...	...	...	...	...	...	10.0[7]	...	12,000[7]	Tanzania
10.5	3.4	4.6	...	1.0	7.2	43.2	12.4	17.7	1.1	53	209	Thailand
...	...	...	...	...	...	...	...	...	10.0[7]	...	15,000[7]	Togo
...	...	...	...	...	...	...	...	...	...	...	...	Tonga
18.6	...	0.5	2.7	...	10.7	28.2	15.3	15.9	43.2	1,467	2,798	Trinidad and Tobago
...	...	...	...	...	...	...	...	...	...	...	...	Tunisia
15.0	10.6	15.5	3.8	2.8	2.9	27.3	10.6	11.5	1.3	166	126	Turkey
...	...	...	...	...	...	...	...	...	...	...	...	Turkmenistan
...	...	...	...	...	...	...	...	...	...	...	...	Tuvalu
...	...	...	...	...	...	...	...	...	12.7	...	47,200	Uganda
...	...	...	...	...	...	...	...	...	...	...	...	Ukraine
...	...	...	...	...	...	...	...	...	...	...	49[1, 3, 39]	United Arab Emirates
37.4	9.0	5.1	10.0	3.8	10.1	...	14.0	10.6	7.3	761	169	United Kingdom
18.8	5.1	5.5	10.1	3.9	5.6	28.2	12.8	10.0	12.5[11]	1,177[11]	163[11]	United States
...	...	...	...	...	...	...	...	...	3.0[1, 3]	...	...	Uruguay
...	...	...	...	...	...	...	...	...	...	...	...	Uzbekistan
...	...	...	...	...	...	...	...	...	5.6[13]	...	484	Vanuatu
50.2	10.1	7.6	...	...	...	5.0	...	27.1	...	...	...	Venezuela
...	...	...	...	...	...	...	...	...	16.6	171	2,575	Vietnam
17.6	7.9	6.4	12.0	2.3	4.8	11.4	1.9	35.7	6.5	536	81	Virgin Islands (U.S.)
...	...	...	...	...	...	...	...	...	...	...	...	West Bank
...	...	...	...	...	...	...	...	...	...	...	...	Western Sahara
...	...	...	...	...	...	...	...	...	...	...	...	Western Samoa
...	...	...	...	...	...	...	...	...	...	...	...	Yemen[58]
...	...	...	...	...	...	...	...	...	2.5	175	205	Yugoslavia
...	...	...	...	...	...	...	...	...	11.0[7]	...	9,676[7]	Zaire
...	...	...	...	...	...	...	...	...	8.4[7]	359[7]	2,873[7]	Zambia
...	...	...	...	...	...	...	...	...	...	...	...	Zimbabwe

furnishings, building materials, and general merchandise. [43]Excludes fuels, automobiles, alcohol and tobacco, building materials. [44]Full-time equivalents. [45]Food includes general merchandise. [46]1972–73. [47]Urban establishments only. [48]Peninsular Malaysia only. [49]State- and cooperative-owned establishments, including public catering. [50]1990–91. [51]1982–83. [52]Other includes clothing, shoes, and automobile parts. [53]1973. [54]Excludes Colón Free Zone. [55]Automobile parts includes building materials. [56]Includes machinery, transport equipment, and petroleum products. [57]Great Britain only. [58]Data refer to former Yemen Arab Republic only.

Finance

This table presents major statistical aggregates comprising national financial structure or constituting a basis for certain international financial comparisons. It includes such data as international reserves, money supply, central banking activity and discount rates, commercial (or "deposit money") banking activity, and external indebtedness of the central government. The country models are broadly similar and permit comparison of internal structure and external position at a high level of generalization.

One of the principal financial criteria of the relative economic position of a country is the size of its international reserves. International reserves as represented in this table comprise the sum of a country's (1) reserve position in the International Monetary Fund (IMF), a quota subscribed in the country's own currency, constituting a level up to which transactions may be effected within the IMF system, (2) holdings of foreign exchange, (3) holdings of gold, and (4) holdings of Special Drawing Rights (SDRs; an unconditional credit allocation, within a quota system set by the IMF, of currency needed by a country to maintain stability of foreign exchange transactions or markets). At appropriate accounting intervals these four elements are valued in a single unit of account (the SDR) and summed. The portion of this reserve total comprised by foreign exchange is very significant as an indication of the country's international liquidity (ability to pay its debts immediately in hard, or convertible, currencies). The ratio of external debt to total reserves, however, is less susceptible of interpretation in isolation: a low ratio, for example, may characterize the situation of a country with little need to borrow or of one with substantial debt but also the means to repay it. Much higher ratios, on the other hand, may be manageable, despite small reserves, if a country's export earnings are also high.

The section on money supply for the country, both as a total and as a per capita amount, refers to one particular measure of money in circulation: M1, the sum of money in private sector demand deposit accounts and outside banks in circulation; it is distinguished from a broader measure of supply, M2, which is roughly M1 plus "quasi-money" (the time, savings, and foreign-currency deposits of residents).

The section of the table outlining banking activity and the principal monetary aggregates encompasses both central bank authorities and commercial (deposit) banks. For both, the principal component aggregates are grouped under assets and liabilities. For certain countries, the four principal aggregates under assets and liabilities do not comprise the entire total, and the percentages shown, therefore, may add to less than 100% (occasionally more, when the net of other liabilities [capital, reserves, undistributed profits, checks, and other transit items] is negative, reducing the total against which these percentages are calculated). The items excluded by the choice of categories are the least significant worldwide but may be important locally; they include such items as quasi-money, money seasonally adjusted, unused bank overdrafts, and so on. In the case of the central bank authority, data are also provided for the central bank discount

Finance

country	international reserves, 1995[a]			money supply, 1994[b]		central bank authority, 1994[b]								
						assets (%)				liabilities (%)				
	total ('000,000 SDRs)	% foreign exchange	ratio of external debt to total reserves, 1993[b]	stock ('000,000,000 national currency)	M1 per capita	claims on government	claims on private sector	claims on banks	claims on foreign assets	reserve money	government deposits	foreign liabilities	capital accounts	central bank discount rate, 1995[a]
Afghanistan	...	...	...	...	...	...	...	...	...	...	...	...	...	...
Albania	...	...	...	...	...	...	...	...	...	...	...	...	...	...
Algeria	1,640	86.8	14.1	505.7	18,300	59.9	—	11.8	28.2	55.6	2.2	16.3	—	...
American Samoa	...	...	...	...	...	...	...	...	...	...	...	...	...	...
Andorra	...	...	...	...	...	...	...	...	...	...	...	...	...	...
Angola	...	...	...	...	...	...	...	...	...	...	...	...	...	...
Antigua and Barbuda	27	100.0	...	0.222	3,480	23.8	—	0.8	75.4	100.0	—	—	—	7.0[3]
Argentina	7,747	93.6	4.0	15.119[5]	440[5]	22.6[5]	—	46.3[5]	31.2[5]	30.2[5]	2.7[5]	7.4[5]	14.3[5]	19[6]
Armenia	...	...	...	...	...	...	...	...	...	...	...	...	...	...
Aruba	127	97.6	...	0.418	5,780	—	—	—	100.0	64.2	19.8	—	15.9	9.5
Australia	8,197	92.1	...	79.134	4,410	42.6	—	—	57.4	74.4	3.1	0.7	—	5.75
Austria	14,004	92.8	...	334.7	41,600	3.3	—	21.4	75.2	74.1	0.1	—	30.5	4.5
Azerbaijan	...	...	...	...	...	...	...	...	...	...	...	...	...	...
Bahamas, The	125	95.2	...	0.411	1,500	45.3	—	1.0	53.7	70.5	6.4	—	27.9	6.5
Bahrain	894	93.4	...	0.345	610	—	—	—	100.0	32.8	34.6	—	43.8	6.5[7]
Bangladesh	2,191	98.1	5.4	120.020	1,010	3.6[2]	—	22.4	74.0	67.1	2.8	18.6	10.8	5.0
Barbados	124	100.0	2.3	0.516	1,950	32.7	—	1.5	65.8	47.4	31.5	27.5	5.3	9.5
Belarus	...	...	...	...	...	...	...	...	...	...	...	...	...	20.0[1]
Belgium	11,308	85.6	...	1,432.9[5]	142,000[5]	6.6[1]	—	—	93.4[1]	54.9[1]	—	—	—	4.0
Belize	17	82.4	4.2	0.144	680	49.5	—	—	50.5	75.1	13.1	9.1	13.0	12.0
Benin	168	98.2	5.8	185.0	34,700	17.0	—	—	83.0	65.9	10.8	24.1	—	9.0
Bermuda	...	...	...	...	...	...	...	...	...	...	...	...	...	...
Bhutan	74	98.6	1.1[1]	1.044	1,290	—	—	2.1[1]	97.9[1]	60.7[1]	1.0[1]	—	—	8.0[6]
Bolivia	364	83.0	13.8	3.216	440	48.3[2]	—	21.4	30.2	22.1	21.1	14.6	13.7	15.8[6, 8]
Bosnia and Herzegovina	...	...	...	...	...	...	...	...	...	...	...	...	...	...
Botswana	3,027	98.5	0.2	0.774	510	—	—	—	100.0	12.5	63.8	—	27.8	13.6[8]
Brazil	24,398	99.5	2.8	...	...	32.1[2]	—	24.9	43.0	42.0	14.7	9.3	1.2	65
Brunei	...	...	...	...	...	...	...	...	...	...	...	...	...	...
Bulgaria	...	...	...	...	...	...	...	...	...	...	...	...	...	...
Burkina Faso	158	91.8	2.9	170.3	16,700	26.1	—	0.2	73.7	70.0	11.3	19.5	—	9.0
Burundi	147	95.9	6.1	...	...	13.1[2]	0.6	4.8	81.5	33.5	11.6	15.9	18.4	...
Cambodia	...	...	...	...	...	...	...	...	...	...	...	...	...	...
Cameroon	12[5]	8.3[5]	329.8	361.3	27,700	90.8	—	7.2	2.0	48.2	12.0	92.5	0.8	12.5[8]
Canada	9,509	81.0	...	121.8	4,160	43.1	—	—	56.9	94.6	—	—	—	8.0
Cape Verde	...	...	...	10.811	28,000	44.3[2]	10.5	5.7	39.5	78.2	0.2	0.6	25.8	4.0[6, 8]
Central African Republic	144[8]	100.0[8]	7.1	103.4	33,300	26.8	—	—	73.2	61.7	1.2	14.2	0.7	12.5[8]
Chad	58[8]	98.3[8]	17.7	59.8	9,530	52.7	—	0.5	46.7	51.4	3.9	25.3	1.1	12.5[8]
Chile	8,895	99.3	0.9	1.186[5]	85,300[5]	33.9[2, 5]	1.5[5]	22.5[5]	42.2[5]	53.3[5]	12.2[5]	9.9[5]	8.0[5]	12.95[6]
China	38,478	96.5	3.0	1,424.4[5]	1,200[5]	11.6[5]	7.0[5]	70.7[5]	10.7[5]	92.1[5]	3.6[5]	—	7.1[5]	...
Colombia	5,236	95.8	1.7	6,695.0	192,000	10.6[4]	—	4.9	84.5	69.8	5.8	3.9	16.9	42.2
Comoros	20[1]	95.0[1]	6.1	11.575[5]	22,300[5]	25.0[1]	—	—	75.0[1]	58.6[1]	6.6[1]	5.0[1]	29.7[1]	...
Congo	35[8]	97.1[8]	2,982.7	134.5	52,700	71.5	—	1.4	27.0	79.6	20.7	10.6	1.6	12.5[8]
Costa Rica	585	98.3	3.1	161.6	48,900	30.0[2]	—	20.8	49.2	85.2	2.9	70.9	8.5	43.0
Côte d'Ivoire	225	98.2	3,840.6	798.8	57,000	63.9	—	19.6	16.1	68.3	6.8	26.0	—	9.0
Croatia	...	...	...	...	...	...	...	...	...	...	...	...	...	...
Cuba	...	...	...	...	...	...	...	...	...	...	...	...	...	...
Cyprus[10]	843	95.0	...	0.577	900	35.7	—	1.1	63.2	78.1	15.7	2.4	—	6.5
Czech Republic	5,310	98.7	1.4	403.973	39,100	12.7[2]	—	23.4	63.9	69.8	16.2	15.7	5.3	8.5
Denmark	5,986	91.5	...	279.0	53,500	11.9	1.7	48.9	37.5	37.5	33.8	0.9	—	6.0
Djibouti	50	100.0	2.5	37.608	65,100	—	—	0.3	99.7	84.8	5.5	—	9.9	...
Dominica	5	100.0	4.4	0.074	1,030	37.4	—	2.9	59.7	90.4	—	9.6	—	6.4[3]
Dominican Republic	175	99.4	5.8	13.742	1,770	23.8[2]	—	24.3	51.8	190.3	—	180.7	−6.3	...
Ecuador	1,078	96.9	7.1	1,860.2[1]	171,000[1]	66.6[2]	0.4	0.3	32.8	20.2	13.6	71.4	5.7	71.1
Egypt	9,085	97.8	2.8	38.275	650	40.9[2]	—	11.3	47.8	37.8	26.6	34.1	—	14.0
El Salvador	415	95.9	3.4	7.802	1,370	39.1[2]	—	14.3	46.6	67.1	12.5	8.7	13.9	15.21[6]

rate, generally the controlling interest rate for banking and commercial activity in the country.

The largest share of assets in the case of both central and commercial banks is usually either claims on government and government agencies or foreign assets and holdings, though some of the latter, such as the large outstanding loans to socialist and less developed countries, have become the chief liabilities. The chief liability of a central bank is usually reserve money (the currency and notes issued by the bank). When government deposits represent a substantial share, budgetary surpluses have usually been deposited by the central government. Large foreign liabilities imply extensive foreign investment. Among the deposit money banks, loans to the private sector normally represent the largest share of assets and savings deposits the largest share of liabilities.

Because the majority of the world's countries are in the less developed bloc, and because their principal financial concern is often external debt and its service, data are given for outstanding external public and publicly guaranteed long-term debt rather than for total public debt, which is the major concern in the developed countries. For comparability, the data are given in U.S. dollars. The volume of debt by itself does not create external payment problems. If the country's external debt service (interest payments plus principal repayment) needs can be met by a strong, dependable export market, by export of services, or, occasionally, by direct remittances from abroad (by residents working abroad and sending wages home in foreign currencies, for example), no debt problem need exist. Countries whose debt service ratio (total debt service as a percent of exports of goods and services) is relatively high, however, must often base their external borrowing policy on maintenance of domestic conditions of strict efficiency and, sometimes, austerity. The failure to adhere to such policies may lead to eventual crises of financial liquidity, deflation, and slower growth.

Ideally, the data presented here should be obtained by utilizing a single international methodology to provide a universally comparable set of international statistics. No international agency, however, can collect such data for all countries because of differences, both overall and in detail, in national definitions of financial aggregates, in accounting methodology, and in the completeness with which it is possible to survey a country's financial activity. The greater part of the data presented in the table comes from the IMF's *International Financial Statistics* and the World Bank's *World Debt Tables.* These sources are supplemented by other recent data from national, regional, or other international sources. In a few cases the desired data are negligible or unavailable, as noted.

Detailed percentages may not add to 100.0 because of rounding, statistical discrepancy, or nonaccounting of negligible quantities.

— None, less than half the last significant figure, or not applicable.

... Not available.

a. Latest month.

b. Year-end.

deposit money banks, 1994[b]									external public debt outstanding (long-term, disbursed only), 1993							country
assets (%)				liabilities					total ('000,000 U.S.$)	creditors (%)		debt service				
loans to govern-ment	loans to private sector	re-serves	foreign assets	deposits ('000,000,000 national currency)	composition (%)					offi cial	private	total ('000,000 U.S.$)	repayment (%)		debt service ratio (%)	
					demand depos.	savings depos.	govt. depos.	foreign liabilities					princi-pal	inter-est		
...	...	...	...	...	...	...	...	...	...	...	...	...	...	...	...	Afghanistan
...	...	...	...	...	...	...	...	...	173.9	56.6	43.4	0.3	—	100.0	0.8[1]	Albania
70.2[2]	20.5	1.3	8.0	561.6	35.0	44.1	9.3	32.1	24,587	26.7	73.7	8,739	80.5	19.5	73.5	Algeria
...	...	...	...	...	...	...	...	...	...	...	...	...	...	...	...	American Samoa
...	...	...	...	...	...	...	...	...	...	...	...	...	...	...	...	Andorra
...	...	...	...	...	...	...	...	...	7,727	40.8	59.2	87	69.0	31.0	3.0	Angola
12.5[2]	59.2	9.0	19.4	1.078	14.3	60.2[4]	5.0	15.2	...	...	...	...	...	...	...	Antigua and Barbuda
15.7[2]	69.4	7.2	7.7	73.7	8.2	48.7[4]	4.7	14.8	55,415	28.2	71.8	6,522	48.3	51.7	39.1	Argentina
...	...	...	...	...	...	...	...	...	140.0	100.0	—	2.0	30.0	70.0	0.9	Armenia
4.4	60.6	9.6	25.3	1.530	21.4	48.9	2.4	17.8	...	...	...	...	...	...	...	Aruba
8.5[2]	65.5	1.4	4.0	374.409	16.2	52.7	0.8	13.5	...	...	...	...	...	...	...	Australia
30.7[2]	44.8	2.1	22.3	3,826.7	5.3	45.0	1.9	24.2	...	...	...	...	...	...	...	Austria
...	...	...	...	...	...	...	...	...	35.5	100.0	—	—	—	—	...	Azerbaijan
19.9[2]	87.0	6.6	−13.6	1.852	15.6	66.8[4]	1.6	—	...	...	...	...	...	...	...	Bahamas, The
5.8	31.7	2.8	59.7	2.353	10.2	40.9	19.4	26.8	...	...	...	...	...	...	...	Bahrain
23.4[2]	55.7	14.3	6.7	422.134	14.9	64.6	8.9	2.6	13.048	98.9	1.1	427	64.2	35.8	10.8	Bangladesh
25.2	59.5	4.8	10.6	2.398	12.9	63.2	7.2	14.4	346.5	57.2	42.8	100.4	71.8	28.2	11.1[1]	Barbados
...	...	...	...	...	...	...	...	...	864.4	68.5	31.5	12.6	15.9	84.1	0.6	Belarus
...	...	...	...	...	...	...	...	...	...	...	...	...	...	...	...	Belgium
51.5[2]	39.4	4.4	4.7	1.029	8.4	30.7[4]	4.3	7.5	162.2	81.9	18.1	17.1	68.4	31.6	6.2	Belize
19.4	33.3	13.5	33.7	228.2	46.6	29.0	15.3	7.1	1,409	99.7	0.3	32	56.2	43.8	6.8	Benin
...	...	...	...	8.356[5]	...	...	...	...	...	...	...	...	...	...	...	Bermuda
31.6[1,2]	10.0[1]	57.0[1]	0.5[1]	2.240[1]	22.1[1]	33.3[1,4]	8.9[1]	15.9[1]	83.3	86.4	13.6	6.6	70.5	28.0	6.9[1]	Bhutan
—	88.7	8.7	2.6	13.774	10.1	55.1[1]	—	16.0	3,687	97.3	2.7	413	72.9	27.1	50.2	Bolivia
...	...	...	...	...	...	...	...	...	...	...	...	...	...	...	...	Bosnia and Herzegovina
5.8[2]	65.0	25.1	4.1	2.606	19.8	53.2	—	5.3	665.8	92.5	7.5	87.4	62.7	37.3	3.6[9]	Botswana
...	...	...	...	...	...	...	...	...	86,650	30.3	69.7	4,979	60.4	39.6	11.3	Brazil
...	...	...	...	...	...	...	...	...	...	...	...	...	...	...	...	Brunei
...	...	...	...	...	...	...	...	...	9,746	23.1	76.9	238	17.6	82.4	4.6	Bulgaria
16.8	34.5	10.0	38.6	209.9	33.3	29.8	28.1	10.1	1,093	99.6	0.4	32	51.6	48.4	6.6	Burkina Faso
16.4[2]	69.5	4.4	9.7	49.168	38.8	30.4	0.2	6.4	999	99.7	0.3	31	61.3	38.7	35.2	Burundi
...	...	...	...	...	...	...	...	...	239.4	99.8	0.2	—	—	—	—	Cambodia
31.5[2]	52.4	6.0	10.1	714.2	31.2	46.2	13.6	3.7	5,436	85.0	15.0	277	53.4	46.6	13.6	Cameroon
14.6[2]	72.0	0.8	12.5	625.3	15.6	52.3[4]	0.4	16.9	...	...	...	...	...	...	...	Canada
32.4[2]	30.7	24.0	12.9	20.292	36.8	50.9[4]	5.0	1.4	148.7	98.5	1.5	5.3	71.7	28.3	4.6	Cape Verde
24.9[2]	42.7	18.5	14.0	43.8	16.6	11.8	4.5	8.1	797.2	97.3	2.7	5.2	32.7	67.3	2.7	Central African Republic
29.7[2]	46.6	12.1	11.6	51.0	36.8	5.6	9.6	23.4	704.6	99.0	1.0	9.7	21.6	78.4	5.8	Chad
2.2[2, 5]	89.8[5]	5.8[5]	2.3[5]	9,962.1[5]	6.1[5]	57.5[4, 5]	4.3[5]	16.4[5]	8,868	57.6	42.4	1,574	56.0	44.0	12.8	Chile
—	77.5[5]	18.3[5]	4.1[5]	3,622.4[5]	21.2[5]	42.0[5]	—	3.5[5]	70,024	34.8	65.2	9,296	71.9	28.1	9.9	China
9.0[2]	70.0	18.3	2.7	15,725.6	24.0	39.4[4]	4.7	9.8	12,861	56.3	43.7	2,760	68.4	31.6	25.4	Colombia
—	78.1[1]	12.5[1]	9.4[1]	12.795[1]	30.2[1]	44.7[1]	—	10.2[1]	169.4	100.0	—	3.0	81.7	18.3	5.9	Comoros
27.0[2]	50.4	8.0	14.6	151.4	40.0	16.4	4.0	17.7	4,097	69.7	30.3	95	78.9	21.1	8.0	Congo
7.5[2]	45.1	40.8	6.6	499.7	17.3	71.1[4]	3.4	8.3	3,139	79.9	20.1	451	64.7	35.3	14.6	Costa Rica
23.8	63.0	5.0	8.2	1,323.5	30.5	31.1	12.9	12.1	10,551	75.4	24.6	441	51.5	48.5	13.7	Côte d'Ivoire
...	...	...	...	...	...	...	...	...	870	88.0	12.0	170	53.5	46.5	...	Croatia
...	...	...	...	...	...	...	...	...	...	...	...	...	...	...	...	Cuba
11.7	56.8	12.6	18.8	4.845	6.7	57.7	0.8	26.3	...	...	...	...	...	...	...	Cyprus[10]
27.1[2]	58.3	6.9	7.7	1,170.867	26.3	36.4[4]	4.4	5.9	5,392	21.0	79.0	1,080	77.5	22.5	7.6[1]	Czech Republic
14.3	46.5	3.7	35.5	873.4	28.4	30.0	—	21.0	...	...	...	...	...	...	...	Denmark
0.6[2]	46.0	1.6	51.8	72.543	30.1	31.7	2.9	21.7	192.6	99.9	0.1	7.3	72.6	27.4	2.0	Djibouti
18.6[2]	60.9	6.5	14.0	0.514	9.7	50.6[4]	10.8	20.7	85.5	100.0	—	6.5	67.7	32.3	4.1[1]	Dominica
6.0[2]	68.5	20.1	5.4	33.549	17.9	59.5	5.2	7.6	3,763	75.8	24.2	274	58.4	41.6	10.9[1]	Dominican Republic
0.6[1]	73.6[1]	19.3[1]	6.5[1]	3,339.7[1]	28.5[1]	39.6[1]	—	4.3[1]	9,935	45.6	54.4	762	60.8	39.2	21.4	Ecuador
38.8[2]	26.8	13.6	20.8	186.680	8.5	58.8[4]	4.2	2.7	36,603	91.0	9.0	2,058	45.2	54.8	13.0	Egypt
4.6	65.7	28.0	1.7	29.887	12.7	70.5[4]	2.9	3.9	1,897	90.2	9.8	284	58.8	41.2	14.8	El Salvador

Finance (continued)

country	international reserves, 1995[a]			money supply, 1994[b]		central bank authority, 1994[b]								central bank discount rate, 1995[a]
						assets (%)				liabilities (%)				
	total ('000,000 SDRs)	% foreign exchange	ratio of external debt to total reserves, 1993[b]	stock ('000,000,000 national currency)	M1 per capita	claims on government	claims on private sector	claims on banks	claims on foreign assets	reserve money	government deposits	foreign liabilities	capital accounts	
Equatorial Guinea	—	—	15.9[1]	6.0	15,300	98.8	—	—	1.2	24.3	0.3	85.2	1.6	12.5[8]
Eritrea	...	...	...	...	...	...	...	...	...	...	...	...	...	6[6, 8]
Estonia	...	...	...	6.380	4,270	0.2[2]	0.1	8.0	91.6	71.8	—	15.1	30.3	5.3[11]
Ethiopia	407	97.3	9.8	9.027	170	68.3	—	3.8	28.0	57.3	14.4	10.5	5.9	12.0
Faroe Islands	...	...	...	...	...	...	...	...	...	...	...	...	...	...
Fiji	161	88.8	0.7	0.345	440	—	—	—	100.0	58.1	3.8	—	11.9	6.0
Finland	6,821	93.5	...	155.995	30,600	3.0	6.6	2.9	87.6	95.4	0.2	0.2	11.2	5.25
France	20,677	75.2	...	1,623.0[5]	28,100[5]	11.1	0.6	30.9	57.3	43.9	19.0	9.6	31.1	9.5
French Guiana	...	...	...	6.175	43,100	...	...	...	...	...	...	...	...	...
French Polynesia	...	...	...	55.347	254,000	...	...	...	...	...	...	...	...	...
Gabon	36[8]	97.2[8]	2,103.2	195.0	170,000	49.8	—	0.1	50.1	69.6	9.6	25.1	0.8	12.5[8]
Gambia, The	62	96.8	3.7[1]	0.408	370	24.1[2]	—	—	75.9	24.9	48.4	27.7	6.1	13.5
Gaza Strip	...	...	...	...	...	...	...	...	...	...	...	...	...	...
Georgia	...	...	...	...	...	...	...	...	...	...	...	...	...	...
Germany	55,135	86.0	...	732.0	8,960	7.1	—	58.4	34.5	82.6	0.1	5.3	—	4.0
Ghana	428	92.1	7.9	695.6	42,800	69.8[2, 5]	—	0.5[5]	29.6[5]	20.1[5]	3.7[5]	62.4[5]	6.8[5]	33.0[8]
Gibraltar	...	...	...	...	...	...	...	...	...	...	...	...	...	...
Greece	10,191	97.7	...	2,644.4[5]	254,000[5]	51.2	—	3.8	45.0	35.2	2.1	35.6	—	20.5
Greenland	...	...	...	...	...	...	...	...	...	...	...	...	...	...
Grenada	18	100.0	3.5	0.143	1,560	22.4	—	0.2	77.4	98.8	1.2	—	—	6.5[3]
Guadeloupe	...	...	...	6.605	15,400	...	...	...	...	...	...	...	...	...
Guam	...	...	...	...	...	...	...	...	...	...	...	...	...	...
Guatemala	427	95.8	2.6	7.074	680	23.6[2]	—	16.0	60.4	353.1	100.6	24.1	8.7	6.9[6]
Guernsey	...	...	...	...	...	...	...	...	...	...	...	...	...	...
Guinea	...	...	...	252.582	38,300	57.0[2]	—	2.1	40.8	43.9	37.6	18.9	14.3	17.0
Guinea-Bissau	...	...	46.1	319.3	301,000	29.8[2]	2.5	33.7	34.0	41.3	17.4	87.4	8.4	27.0
Guyana	157	100.0	7.0	13.115	18,000	77.0	—	—	23.0	10.6	14.5	68.9	1.5	19.8
Haiti	...	...	...	...	...	82.9[2]	—	13.0	4.1	96.6	8.3	9.4	4.0	...
Honduras	117	99.1	35.7	3.929	720	33.1[2]	—	26.3	40.6	59.6	14.2	135.9	29.8	11.0[6, 8]
Hong Kong	...	...	...	185.337	30,100	...	...	...	...	...	...	...	...	...
Hungary	4,757	98.5	3.0	...	...	...	...	...	...	...	...	...	...	28.0
Iceland	218	94.5	...	35.121	131,000	51.8	0.7	4.0	43.5	28.9	21.8	38.6	—	6.4
India	13,727	94.7	7.5	1,653.2	1,780	54.4	—	7.7	37.9	81.2	—	6.7	8.1	12.0
Indonesia	7,947	95.9	4.6	28,801.0[1]	154,000[1]	13.6[1, 2]	1.6[1]	25.1[1]	59.7[1]	26.6[1]	30.5[1]	6.1[1]	10.3[1]	...
Iran	...	...	...	18,305.4[5]	311,000[5]	61.8[2, 5]	—	12.3[5]	25.9[5]	54.1[5]	16.3[5]	9.6[5]	2.6[5]	...
Iraq	...	...	...	...	...	...	...	...	...	...	...	...	...	...
Ireland	4,291	93.5	...	3.996[5]	1,140[5]	6.9[5]	—	—	93.1[5]	54.0[5]	31.0[5]	—	29.7[5]	7.25
Isle of Man	...	...	...	...	...	...	...	...	...	...	...	...	...	...
Israel	6,044	99.9	...	14.523	5,450	21.7	—	33.8	44.5	56.8	37.9	2.0	—	15.8
Italy	19,931	81.0	...	596,610.0	10,411,000	67.8[5]	—	0.8[5]	31.4[5]	72.9[5]	—	0.4[5]	—	8.25
Jamaica	529	99.2	11.4[1]	21.252	8,470	23.4	—	—	76.6	78.1	83.0	39.0	6.2	22.19[3]
Japan	99,646	91.3	...	151,670.0	1,212,000	56.4	—	33.2	10.4	126.9	12.9	—	...	1.0
Jersey	...	...	...	...	...	...	...	...	...	...	...	...	...	...
Jordan	1,090	97.4	4.1	1.742	420	32.2	—	—	67.8	83.6	8.0	—	—	8.5
Kazakhstan	...	...	...	...	...	...	...	...	...	...	...	...	...	...
Kenya	350	95.4	12.5	59.322[5]	2,200[5]	58.8[5]	—	—	41.2[5]	56.8[5]	45.7[5]	29.7[5]	0.9[5]	18.0
Kiribati	...	...	...	...	...	...	...	...	...	...	...	...	...	...
Korea, North	...	...	...	...	...	...	...	...	...	...	...	...	...	...
Korea, South	17,341	97.3	1.2	32,511.0	728,000	5.5[2]	—	55.0	39.5	47.8	12.3	0.1	—	5.0
Kuwait	2,142	86.6	...	1.065	650	5.0	—	—	95.0	41.0	30.0	—	17.0	4.0
Kyrgyzstan	...	...	...	...	...	...	...	...	...	...	...	...	...	...
Laos	...	...	...	...	...	...	...	...	...	...	...	...	...	...
Latvia	...	...	...	...	...	...	...	...	...	...	...	...	...	...
Lebanon	2,612	86.5	0.1	1,436.8	485,000	0.3	0.6	1.3	97.8	30.6	19.1	0.4	0.7	18.3
Lesotho	268	98.5	1.9	0.487	240	15.1	—	—	84.8	15.8	71.9	9.5	5.2	13.5
Liberia	...	...	...	0.457	190	94.7[2]	1.1	3.8	0.4	39.0	5.4	45.7	4.3	6.3[6, 8]
Libya	4,622[1]	84.4[1]	...	4.987[1]	1,110[1]	71.0[1]	0.1[1]	—	28.9[1]	61.5[1]	12.4[1]	—	—	...
Liechtenstein	...	...	...	...	...	...	...	...	...	...	...	...	...	...
Lithuania	...	...	...	...	...	...	...	...	...	...	...	...	...	...
Luxembourg	...	...	...	81.8[1]	209,000[1]	39.0	—	0.7	60.3	39.0	24.1	7.1	29.8	5.0[6]
Macau	...	...	...	20.603[5]	53,100[5]	...	...	...	...	...	...	...	...	...
Macedonia	...	...	...	...	...	...	...	...	...	...	...	...	...	...
Madagascar	42	100.0	...	1,601.3	110,000	77.6[2]	—	7.4	15.1	48.8	15.5	39.3	4.2	...
Malawi	24	79.2	29.9	1.535	160	69.9[2]	—	—	30.1	61.1	17.1	57.7	—	45.0
Malaysia	16,108	97.0	0.5	56.175	2,850	1.3	2.1	6.8	89.8	50.7	11.2	—	—	5.52
Maldives	26	96.2	4.3	0.851	3,410	72.4[2]	—	0.5	27.1	71.9	2.3	13.7	6.5	5.0[7, 8]
Mali	146	93.8	7.5	177.2	19,900	33.2	—	—	66.8	67.1	5.5	35.6	—	9.0
Malta	1,151	94.4	0.1	0.464	1,260	5.3	—	—	94.7	79.2	3.0	—	—	5.5[8]
Marshall Islands	...	...	...	...	...	...	...	...	...	...	...	...	...	...
Martinique	...	...	...	6.778	17,600	...	...	...	...	...	...	...	...	...
Mauritania	35	97.1	43.2	20.938[5]	9,500[5]	67.6[2, 5]	1.8[5]	8.5[5]	22.1[5]	81.0[5]	26.9[5]	94.0[5]	17.6[5]	11[8]
Mauritius	449	93.1	0.9	8.864	7,900	11.3	—	1.9	86.8	57.2	—	0.2	2.9	11.6
Mayotte	...	...	...	1.092	9,740	...	...	...	...	...	...	...	...	...
Mexico	5,741	94.7	3.0	145.429	1,610	–105.6	—	155.7	49.9	92.9	—	31.9	3.5	46.75[7]
Micronesia	...	...	...	...	...	...	...	...	...	...	...	...	...	...
Moldova	127	89.8	...	0.487	110	62.0	—	9.8	28.2	19.8	52.4	25.3	0.9	...
Monaco	...	...	...	...	...	...	...	...	...	...	...	...	...	...
Mongolia	...	...	...	43.422	19,000	21.9	—	15.3	62.8	43.2	3.6	51.3	4.9	435.0
Morocco	2,514	97.5	5.5	128.091	4,800	14.3	14.5	0.9	70.4	87.1	1.1	3.0	—	7.0
Mozambique	...	...	...	...	...	...	...	...	...	...	...	...	...	...
Myanmar (Burma)	351	97.4	16.3	...	...	...	...	...	...	...	...	...	...	9.0[5, 6]
Namibia	...	...	...	1.683	1,040	49.8	—	—	50.2	25.8	20.1	49.2	—	16.5
Nauru	...	...	...	...	...	...	...	...	...	...	...	...	...	...
Nepal	467	97.6	3.0	25.320[5]	1,300[5]	36.0[5]	1.0[5]	1.0[5]	61.9[5]	48.8[5]	14.9[5]	8.3[5]	20.1[5]	11.0[7]
Netherlands, The	24,826	89.2	...	152.2	9,850	4.7	—	9.4	85.9	67.8	10.9	—	—	4.36[7]

deposit money banks, 1994[b]									external public debt outstanding (long-term, disbursed only), 1993							country
assets (%)				liabilities					total ('000,000 U.S.$)	creditors (%)		debt service				
				deposits ('000,000,000 national currency)	composition (%)							total ('000,000 U.S.$)	repayment (%)		debt service ratio (%)	
loans to govern-ment	loans to private sector	re-serves	foreign assets		demand depos.	savings depos.	govt. depos.	foreign liabilities		offi-cial	private		princi-pal	inter-est		
13.7[2]	32.6	9.0	44.7	6.9	32.4	25.5	6.7	20.7	218.7	93.1	6.9	1.1	45.5	54.5	1.8	Equatorial Guinea
...	...	...	...	...	...	...	...	...	...	...	...	...	...	...	...	Eritrea
8.3[2]	45.5	13.2	32.9	9.169	35.4	19.8[4]	18.7	7.6	85.8	69.1	30.9	13.5	73.3	26.7	1.6	Estonia
49.0[2,5]	17.6[5]	19.4[5]	14.0[5]	8.439[5]	31.7[5]	38.5[5]	4.9[5]	5.4[5]	4,530	89.3	10.7	63	55.6	44.4	8.2	Ethiopia
...	...	...	...	...	...	...	...	...	...	...	...	...	...	...	...	Faroe Islands
14.6[2]	69.9	9.8	5.7	1.547	14.8	69.2	2.6	6.0	199.4	98.5	1.5	52.8	72.0	28.0	5.8	Fiji
3.0	68.3	8.8	19.9	529.147	27.1	27.5	2.1	27.2	...	...	...	...	...	...	...	Finland
7.0[5]	60.8[5]	0.3[5]	31.9[5]	10,777.0[5]	12.7[5]	25.6[5]	0.5[5]	28.6[5]	...	...	...	...	...	...	...	France
...	...	...	...	...	...	...	...	...	...	...	...	...	...	...	...	French Guiana
...	...	...	...	...	...	...	...	...	...	...	...	...	...	...	...	French Polynesia
40.8[2]	36.8	12.7	9.8	449.1	26.3	29.2	7.2	4.9	2,889	79.5	20.5	61	47.5	52.5	2.5	Gabon
16.3[2]	62.4	15.7	5.6	0.618	32.4	63.7	—	4.7	348.8	98.6	1.4	24.7	76.1	23.9	10.9[1]	Gambia, The
...	...	...	...	...	...	...	...	...	...	...	...	...	...	...	...	Gaza Strip
...	...	...	...	...	...	...	...	...	568.0	86.3	13.7	13.1	35.9	64.1	2.7	Georgia
18.4[2]	65.0	1.7	14.9	5,045.5	10.0	27.1	4.9	11.6	...	...	...	...	...	...	...	Germany
2.6[2]	20.6	39.8	37.0	1,151.9	27.9	23.9	6.0	20.6	3,341	95.0	5.0	167	57.5	42.5	13.7	Ghana
—18.1[5]—		0.1[5]	—	6.198[5]	—52.3[5]—			—	...	...	...	...	...	...	...	Gibraltar
41.2[2,5]	20.6[5]	17.9[5]	10.3[5]	13,009.8[5]	6.9[5]	48.0[5]	—	26.2[5]	...	...	...	...	...	...	...	Greece
...	...	...	...	...	...	...	...	...	...	...	...	...	...	...	...	Greenland
7.5[2]	63.0	8.4	21.1	0.665	13.5	61.5[4]	3.7	16.1	96.2	89.2	10.8	6.9	76.1	23.9	5.6	Grenada
...	...	...	...	...	...	...	...	...	...	...	...	...	...	...	...	Guadeloupe
...	...	...	...	1.378[5]	...	...	...	...	...	...	...	...	...	...	...	Guam
20.1	64.0	15.2	0.7	14.302	23.3	52.1	0.5	14.7	2,301	85.3	14.7	224	61.6	38.4	10.9	Guatemala
...	...	...	...	...	...	...	...	...	...	...	...	...	...	...	...	Guernsey
5.1[2]	56.1	6.0	32.8	257.640	36.7	20.3[4]	6.6	20.0	2,675	96.1	3.9	78	52.6	47.4	11.9	Guinea
5.5[2]	44.1	23.1	27.3	680.470	17.7	30.6[4]	0.4	16.3	633.6	95.7	4.3	3.0	36.7	63.3	8.3	Guinea-Bissau
30.2[2]	33.6	10.7	8.6	41.469	11.9	69.4	7.8	7.1	1,727	97.6	2.4	81	56.2	43.8	30.2[9]	Guyana
...	...	...	...	...	...	...	...	...	617.6	92.6	7.4	—	—	—	—	Haiti
14.1[2]	70.0	7.3	8.7	9.150	19.2	46.9[4]	3.3	7.1	3,479	92.8	7.2	320	57.4	42.6	20.0	Honduras
...	...	...	...	7,332.4	...	...	...	...	...	...	...	...	...	...	...	Hong Kong
...	...	...	...	...	...	...	...	...	20,357	19.2	80.8	3,895	66.3	33.7	35.8	Hungary
9.5	82.2	4.9	3.4	235.797	12.9	56.4	—	13.3	...	...	...	...	...	...	...	Iceland
29.4	55.3	15.3	—	4,073.8	16.4	72.0	—	—	80,985	68.9	31.1	7,778	49.1	50.9	24.7	India
7.5[1,2]	75.2[1]	9.5[1]	7.8[1]	166,401.0[1]	10.2[1]	54.2[1,4]	3.9[1]	9.7[1]	52,451	84.6	15.4	8,139	64.6	35.4	19.9	Indonesia
3.4[5]	60.6[5]	29.0[5]	7.0[5]	36,517.6[5]	33.3[5]	63.5[5]	—	16.4[5]	8,880	3.3	96.7	562	69.4	30.6	3.2	Iran
...	...	...	...	...	...	...	...	...	...	...	...	...	...	...	...	Iraq
12.9	61.3	2.5	23.3	23.092	10.7	56.9	0.8	20.3		...	...	...	...	...	...	Ireland
...	...	...	...	...	...	...	...	...	...	...	...	...	...	...	...	Isle of Man
24.1	56.0	7.5	12.4	275.526	3.2	50.8	8.4	14.3	...	...	...	...	...	...	...	Israel
13.9[1]	63.3[1]	11.8[1]	11.0[1]	1,144,340.0[1]	39.0[1]	31.3[1]		22.2[1]	...	...	...	...	...	...	...	Italy
21.3[2]	38.9	22.2	17.7	84.551	16.7	52.4	7.7	15.4	3,604	87.4	12.6	377	55.2	44.8	15.3	Jamaica
9.9[2]	79.0	1.0	10.1	708,710.0	15.4	54.0	...	10.2	...	...	...	...	...	...	...	Japan
...	...	...	...	...	...	...	...	...	...	...	...	...	...	...	...	Jersey
4.9	43.7	24.9	26.6	6.329	10.5	44.0	7.9	27.9	6,825	68.5	31.5	517	59.8	40.2	13.2	Jordan
...	...	...	...	...	...	...	...	...	1,552.2	91.1	8.9	7.9	5.1	94.9	...	Kazakhstan
18.6[2,5]	48.4[5]	15.4[5]	17.6[5]	135.391[5]	24.9[5]	47.5[4,5]	3.5[5]	2.5[5]	5,121	79.2	20.8	429	64.3	35.7	18.4	Kenya
...	...	...	...	...	...	...	...	...	...	...	...	...	...	...	...	Kiribati
...	...	...	...	...	...	...	...	...	...	...	...	...	...	...	...	Korea, North
2.3	79.2	11.1	26.4	222,874.0	8.8	45.2[4]	5.1	7.5	24,567	38.4	61.6	6,214	74.3	25.7	6.3	Korea, South
52.0	21.7	1.1	25.2	6.299	11.1	77.2	1.4	10.9	...	...	...	...	...	...	...	Kuwait
...	...	...	...	...	...	...	...	...	248.1	100.0	—	0.4	—	100.0	...	Kyrgyzstan
...	...	...	...	...	...	...	...	...	1,948	100.0	—	28	83.3	16.7	9.5	Laos
...	...	...	...	...	...	...	...	...	118.8	90.1	9.9	8.0	55.6	44.4	...	Latvia
29.1	32.8	11.7	26.4	23,764.1	2.1	76.6[6]	1.1	10.9	376	76.0	24.0	67	65.7	34.3	3.2	Lebanon
11.4[2]	58.9	15.2	14.5	1.187	36.6	46.4	3.3	3.1	471.9	95.3	4.7	31.7	63.7	36.3	5.5	Lesotho
13.3[2]	43.2	41.7	1.8	0.516	29.9	62.9	6.8	9.0	1,070	81.3	18.7	20	60.0	40.0	...	Liberia
—	59.6[1]	37.5[1]	2.9[1]	4.764[1]	56.5[1]	26.4[1]	3.8[1]	4.4[1]	...	...	...	...	...	...	...	Libya
...	...	...	...	...	...	...	...	...	...	...	...	...	...	...	...	Liechtenstein
...	...	...	...	...	...	...	...	...	163.5	81.6	18.4	0.5	—	100.0	...	Lithuania
—	4.4[1]	—	95.6[1]	13,070.8[1]	0.8[1]	10.6[1]	—	81.4[1]	...	...	...	...	...	...	...	Luxembourg
...	...	...	...	98.544	...	...	...	...	...	...	...	...	...	...	...	Macau
...	...	...	...	...	...	...	...	...	528	63.6	36.4	8	62.5	37.5	...	Macedonia
10.1	54.0	11.3	24.6	2,478.8	39.8	26.6	5.8	5.8	3,920	93.9	6.1	51	54.9	45.1	10.5	Madagascar
16.6[2]	46.0	22.5	14.9	2.627	34.1	42.6	—	15.9	1,724	98.2	1.8	67	59.7	40.3	19.9	Malawi
5.7	80.7	8.2	5.4	193.907	16.4	56.2	1.4	8.8	13,863	32.7	67.3	3,331	75.1	24.9	6.3	Malaysia
10.9[2]	40.2	39.5	9.5	1.264	28.2	34.0	2.5	12.7	111.6	93.5	6.5	8.1	70.4	29.6	3.7	Maldives
13.9	42.1	12.5	31.5	201.6	41.2	31.3	19.5	9.1	2,506	99.9	0.1	14	50.0	50.0	3.3	Mali
8.9	51.3	12.8	27.0	1.523	4.7	72.6	—	6.2	127.9	100.0	—	13.8	64.1	35.9	0.7[1]	Malta
...	...	...	...	...	...	...	...	...	...	...	...	...	...	...	...	Marshall Islands
...	...	...	...	...	...	...	...	...	...	...	...	...	...	...	...	Martinique
2.2[2,5]	73.0[5]	19.1[5]	5.7[5]	56.440[5]	20.4[5]	11.8[5]	2.3[5]	23.4[5]	1,960	99.0	1.0	115	63.5	36.5	25.0	Mauritania
22.2	61.5	9.5	6.8	46.661	9.5	78.8	—	1.5	717	85.4	14.6	106	60.8	39.2	5.0	Mauritius
...	...	...	...	...	...	...	...	...	...	...	...	...	...	...	...	Mayotte
3.9[2]	90.1	1.4	4.6	671.010	13.6	41.2[4]	5.7	19.1	74,450	35.1	64.9	10,360	54.6	45.4	16.2	Mexico
...	...	...	...	...	...	...	...	...	...	...	...	...	...	...	...	Micronesia
...	...	...	...	...	...	...	...	...	201.6	100.0	—	1.0	75.0	25.0	0.2	Moldova
...	...	...	...	...	...	...	...	...	...	...	...	...	...	...	...	Monaco
15.9[2]	50.1	12.7	21.2	81.284	17.4	54.0[4]	10.4	6.1	344.4	64.6	35.4	13.8	60.1	39.9	3.5	Mongolia
36.8	52.1	6.2	4.9	137.910	57.4	33.3	—	4.4	20,310	76.9	23.1	2,376	57.2	42.8	27.9	Morocco
...	...	...	...	...	...	...	...	...	4,650	97.6	2.4	64	35.9	64.1	17.2	Mozambique
...	...	...	...	...	...	...	...	...	5,135	94.5	5.5	115	21.7	78.3	11.0[9]	Myanmar (Burma)
5.8	85.7	3.8	4.7	4.132	35.5	50.5[4]	2.0	9.5	...	...	...	...	...	...	...	Namibia
...	...	...	...	...	...	...	...	...	...	...	...	...	...	...	...	Nauru
25.4[2,5]	50.2[5]	11.7[5]	12.8[5]	50.010[5]	13.2[5]	72.4[5]	—	6.8[5]	1,938	96.4	3.6	65	59.2	40.8	11.2[1]	Nepal
12.4[2]	53.8	0.3	33.5	1,039.0	11.0	34.1[4]	—	31.1	...	...	...	...	...	...	...	Netherlands, The

Finance (continued)

country	international reserves, 1995[a]: total ('000,000 SDRs)	international reserves, 1995[a]: % foreign exchange	international reserves, 1995[a]: ratio of external debt to total reserves, 1993[b]	money supply, 1994[b]: stock ('000,000,000 national currency)	money supply, 1994[b]: M1 per capita	central bank authority, 1994[b]: assets (%): claims on government	assets (%): claims on private sector	assets (%): claims on banks	assets (%): claims on foreign assets	liabilities (%): reserve money	liabilities (%): government deposits	liabilities (%): foreign liabilities	liabilities (%): capital accounts	central bank discount rate, 1995[a]
Netherlands Antilles	122	84.4	...	0.893	4,470	11.7	—	—	88.3	75.7	2.6	—	13.3	5.0
New Caledonia	...	...	...	60.229	326,000	...	...	...	...	...	...	...	...	...
New Zealand	2,628	96.1	...	28.974	8,170	32.5	—	3.3	64.2	21.0	58.0	—	—	10.0
Nicaragua	...	...	...	1.097	250	87.9	3.1	4.5	4.6	5.7	1.2	93.1	0.8	10.5
Niger	88	88.6	7.0	92.3	10,300	44.0	—	1.0	54.9	56.9	14.0	32.3	—	9.0
Nigeria	1,102	97.5	20.1	...	...	...	...	...	...	...	...	...	...	13.5[8]
Northern Mariana Islands	...	...	...	...	...	...	...	...	...	...	...	...	...	...
Norway	14,474	93.8	...	340.1[5]	78,600[5]	8.4	—	3.6	88.0	27.0	53.5	—	—	6.75
Oman	664	92.2	2.5	0.473	220	13.3	—	—	86.7	40.5	2.0	0.1	32.1	4.34[6, 8]
Pakistan	1,715	95.2	15.7	435.388	3,140	49.7	—	21.9	28.4	69.4	9.3	11.9	—	11.73[7]
Palau	...	...	...	...	...	...	...	...	...	...	...	...	...	...
Panama	480	97.5	6.2	0.804	310	50.2[2]	14.9	—	34.9	12.0	85.0	21.1	11.3	6.57[6, 8]
Papua New Guinea	23	100.0	10.5	0.614	140	87.3	—	—	12.7	24.9	74.6	4.6	15.8	6.38[8]
Paraguay	697[8]	88.1[8]	2.0	1,370.3	280,000	37.3[2]	0.2	3.3	59.2	52.9	12.2	3.3	9.7	18.0
Peru	4,545	99.1	4.6	5.495	240	3.7[2]	—	−1.2	97.5	44.0	22.4	21.3	2.3	19.6
Philippines	3,674	93.8	5.7	159.9	2,310	56.1[2]	—	2.6	41.3	45.6	25.9	19.5	6.3	9.18
Poland	5,661	98.3	10.1	27.450	710	46.0[2]	—	17.5	36.4	46.2	6.5	17.4	0.7	31.0
Portugal	10,280	91.8	1.5	3,949.1	399,000	7.0[2]	—	13.5	79.5	30.2	12.3	0.3	9.6	10.5
Puerto Rico	...	...	...	...	...	...	...	...	...	...	...	...	...	...
Qatar	481	94.6	...	3.910	6,810	—	—	8.7	91.3	67.9	6.7	—	8.4	4.5[6, 8]
Réunion	...	...	...	11.626	17,800	...	...	...	...	...	...	...	...	...
Romania	1,298	91.0	1.9	4,892.4	215,000	25.7	—	33.8	40.5	67.2	19.6	35.4	—	...
Russia	...	...	...	...	...	...	...	...	...	...	...	...	...	...
Rwanda	35[5]	65.7[5]	17.4	25.041[5]	3,250[5]	69.8[2, 5]	0.3[5]	2.3[5]	27.6[5]	33.8[5]	18.0[5]	14.4[5]	20.7[5]	11.0[5]
St. Kitts and Nevis	19	100.0	1.4	0.073	1,830	5.3	—	3.7	91.0	100.0	—	—	—	6.5[3]
St. Lucia	32	96.9	1.6	0.234	1,650	5.8	—	—	94.2	96.4	3.6	—	—	7.0[3]
St. Vincent and the Grenadines	16	100.0	2.0	0.109	970	10.1	—	—	89.9	99.9	0.1	—	—	6.5[3]
San Marino	...	...	...	...	...	...	...	...	...	...	...	...	...	...
São Tomé and Príncipe	...	...	...	...	...	...	...	...	...	...	...	...	...	...
Saudi Arabia	5,350	78.2	...	125.6	7,110	...	...	...	...	...	...	...	...	...
Senegal	132	97.7	548.0	302.3	36,800	71.1	—	3.2	25.7	50.8	3.4	63.6	—	9.0
Seychelles	20	95.0	3.9	0.327	4,450	77.9	—	1.0	21.1	83.5	4.6	—	2.0	12.48[3]
Sierra Leone	27	77.8	22.1	38.542	8,650	16.8	—	—	83.2	85.7	16.2	865.4	—	11.11[3]
Singapore	39,294	99.5	...	23,411	7,910	—	—	—	100.0	18.3	41.9	—	—	2.0[7]
Slovakia	...	...	...	123.820	23,100	32.7[2]	—	25.3	42.1	33.9	8.2	43.7	5.6	11.0
Slovenia	...	...	...	140.6	71,100	6.6	—	12.7	80.6	34.2	11.6	0.4	12.3	10.0
Solomon Islands	15[8]	100.0[8]	4.6	0.163	440	54.3[2]	—	—	45.7	48.6	8.6	1.1	45.4	11.25[3]
Somalia	...	...	...	...	...	...	...	...	...	...	...	...	...	...
South Africa	946	82.1	...	...	...	34.4[5]	—	24.2[5]	41.4[5]	63.9[5]	47.4[5]	35.1[5]	—	14.0
Spain	21,544	92.0	...	18,593.0	475,000	20.2	—	40.4	39.4	58.4	13.9	—	7.9	8.5
Sri Lanka	1,191[5]	97.9[5]	3.6	70.462	3,920	27.6	—	2.4	69.9	49.5	2.0	33.3	14.4	17.0
Sudan, The	50	100.0	242.5	242.8	8,750	86.5[2]	—	1.4	12.1	78.6	—	521.4	0.9	...
Suriname	2	—	...	6.043[5]	14,400[5]	18.4	—	—	81.5	60.1	2.9	25.6	0.2	...
Swaziland	210	95.7	0.8	0.312	350	4.4	—	0.6	95.0	32.7	42.0	12.4	4.4	13.75
Sweden	15,888	94.4	...	...	...	33.0	—	0.5	67.0	75.6	—	0.1	—	7.0
Switzerland	22,684	83.5	...	98.9	14,100	7.7	—	2.0	90.3	59.2	1.1	—	—	3.0
Syria	...	...	...	181.979[1]	13,800[1]	58.8[1, 2]	—	22.4[1]	18.9[1]	64.9[1]	24.9[1]	18.8[1]	0.2[1]	...
Taiwan	63,746	99.3	...	3,148.5	149,000	0.1	—	12.1	87.9	53.4	4.3	—	—	5.8
Tajikistan	...	...	...	...	...	...	...	...	...	...	...	...	...	...
Tanzania	220	95.5	33.1	237.9[5]	8,840[5]	72.5[5]	—	0.6[5]	26.9[5]	42.1[5]	—	124.2[5]	—	65.3
Thailand	19,598	97.9	0.6	346.4	5,920	3.9	—	5.7	90.4	39.3	28.1	—	34.6	9.5[8]
Togo	59	100.0	7.2	94.6	23,200	45.8	—	7.8	46.4	58.1	8.5	42.9	—	9.0
Tonga	18	88.9	1.2	0.028	280	17.9	—	—	82.1	38.9	4.0	—	5.5	4.67[6]
Trinidad and Tobago	220	98.6	8.2	3.748	2,930	23.1	—	7.9	69.0	49.0	11.7	13.0	39.7	13.0
Tunisia	991	99.1	8.6	3.317	380	3.9	—	34.9	61.2	63.6	8.4	13.6	5.0	8.81[7]
Turkey	7,440	97.8	6.7	228,413.0	3,693,000	48.9	—	2.7	48.5	36.8	2.9	51.8	1.8	66.98[7]
Turkmenistan	...	...	...	...	...	...	...	...	...	...	...	...	...	...
Tuvalu	...	...	...	...	...	...	...	...	...	...	...	...	...	...
Uganda	209	99.0	17.8	269.945[5]	15,000[5]	81.6[2, 5]	0.4[5]	0.6[5]	17.3[5]	18.2[5]	55.3[5]	38.1[5]	6.2[5]	12.0
Ukraine	...	...	...	...	...	...	...	...	...	...	...	...	...	...
United Arab Emirates	4,726	95.2	...	18.174[5]	8,640[5]	—	—	0.2[5]	99.8[5]	56.1[5]	29.0[5]	1.3[5]	7.2[5]	...
United Kingdom	27,933	91.7	...	252.2[5]	4,320[5]	29.6[5]	—	0.7[5]	69.6[5]	56.7[5]	—	55.9[5]	—	5.25[7]
United States	57,678	56.3	...	1,231.4	4,700	83.7	—	—	16.3	95.1	6.4	0.1	—	5.25
Uruguay	697	89.1	5.5	5.678	1,790	46.5[2]	0.5	17.1	35.8	46.1	33.1	24.6	—	200.9
Uzbekistan	...	...	...	...	...	...	...	...	...	...	...	...	...	...
Vanuatu	28	92.9	0.8	5.728	34,500	1.5	—	—	98.5	56.1	42.8	0.5	14.8	6.0[7, 8]
Venezuela	5,373	83.9	2.7	991.4	45,900	39.9[2]	—	0.6	59.5	21.7	8.9	29.0	5.5	43.5
Vietnam	...	...	...	...	...	...	...	...	...	...	...	...	...	...
Virgin Islands (U.S.)	...	...	...	...	...	...	...	...	...	...	...	...	...	...
West Bank	...	...	...	...	...	...	...	...	...	...	...	...	...	...
Western Sahara	...	...	...	...	...	...	...	...	...	...	...	...	...	...
Western Samoa	31	93.5	2.7	0.047	290	0.1	—	5.4	94.5	52.0	42.4	—	—	5.5[6]
Yemen	173[8]	79.2[8]	36.0	...	...	98.7[2, 5]	—	—	1.3[5]	79.2[5]	11.9[5]	1.4[5]	0.8[5]	...
Yugoslavia	...	...	...	...	...	...	...	...	...	...	...	...	...	...
Zaire	79	98.7	187.8	373.0	8,630	24.0[2]	0.4	2.4	73.2	33.4	4.3	350.3	58.5	145.0
Zambia	...	...	...	...	...	...	...	...	...	...	...	...	...	33.1
Zimbabwe	340	95.6	6.6	7.333	660	63.5[2]	—	—	36.5	31.9	29.1	33.3	—	29.5

deposit money banks, 1994[b]									external public debt outstanding (long-term, disbursed only), 1993							country
assets (%)				liabilities					total ('000,000 U.S.$)	creditors (%)		debt service				
loans to govern-ment	loans to private sector	re-serves	foreign assets	deposits ('000,000,000 national currency)	composition (%)					offi-cial	private	total ('000,000 U.S.$)	repayment (%)		debt service ratio (%)	
					demand depos.	savings depos.	govt. depos.	foreign liabilities					princi-pal	inter-est		
3.5[2]	56.1	3.5	36.9	3.628	15.5	44.2[4]	1.0	35.5	...	...	...	...	...	...	...	Netherlands Antilles
...	...	...	...	...	...	...	...	...	...	...	...	...	...	...	...	New Caledonia
7.4	86.6	3.5	2.5	82.046	33.6	42.7[4]	—	23.4	...	...	...	...	...	...	...	New Zealand
0.9[2]	77.2	14.7	7.2	5.277	7.7	47.4[4]	10.2	4.3	8,773	78.4	21.6	110	47.7	52.3	27.8	Nicaragua
11.5	61.5	8.3	18.7	116.2	34.6	32.0	18.1	22.9	1,354	99.9	0.1	50	70.0	30.0	16.8	Niger
5.9[1]	46.8[1]	27.3[1]	20.0[1]	99.264[1]	31.3[1]	41.7[1]	3.6[1]	1.3[1]	28,237	64.6	35.4	1,769	28.2	71.8	29.0[1]	Nigeria
...	...	...	...	...	...	...	...	...	...	...	...	...	...	...	...	Northern Mariana Islands
6.2[2]	84.9	0.7	8.2	577.0	44.7	25.9[4]	1.1	10.6	...	...	...	...	...	...	...	Norway
5.7	71.8	3.0	19.4	1.709	13.3	54.5	8.7	5.4	2,319	25.2	74.8	583	72.9	27.1	8.4[1]	Oman
32.3	49.5	12.0	6.3	778.624	30.2	35.8	5.3	11.0	20,306	93.8	6.2	1,911	64.3	35.7	19.2	Pakistan
...	...	...	...	...	...	...	...	...	...	...	...	...	...	...	...	Palau
0.8	23.0	—	76.2	21.810	3.3	17.6	—	68.1	3,709	35.2	64.8	217	62.4	37.6	8.9	Panama
22.7	64.7	2.1	10.5	1.967	22.0	53.4	3.7	7.2	1,516	80.8	19.2	265	69.4	30.6	9.7	Papua New Guinea
0.0[2]	67.6	20.2	12.2	4,700.5	10.6	56.7	9.2	5.1	1,283	88.6	11.4	270	70.7	29.3	14.0	Paraguay
8.7[2]	57.5	23.1	10.7	23.029	13.5	60.4[4]	10.3	5.5	16,123	74.8	25.2	1,711	56.1	43.9	39.3	Peru
17.5[2]	54.1	13.0	15.4	955.2	5.8	64.2	2.8	11.9	27,471	77.1	22.9	4,243	60.9	39.1	22.1	Philippines
44.9[2]	25.6	10.4	19.2	98.407	15.4	50.7[4]	3.7	3.8	41,426	78.4	21.6	1,315	37.4	62.6	8.2	Poland
24.5[2]	46.6	11.3	17.6	19,007.9	16.4	40.4	2.7	26.5	25,173	19.7	80.3	4,799	66.1	33.9	15.9[1]	Portugal
...	...	...	...	...	...	...	...	...	...	...	...	...	...	...	...	Puerto Rico
—	72.2	2.4	25.4	28.625	8.9	50.7	6.6	0.5	...	...	...	...	...	...	...	Qatar
...	...	...	...	...	...	...	...	...	...	...	...	...	...	...	...	Réunion
4.1	65.8	11.1	19.0	14,421.5	19.9	39.8[4]	9.0	8.4	2,080	69.9	30.1	203	63.1	36.9	3.6	Romania
...	...	...	...	...	...	...	...	...	72,769	36.1	63.9	2,200	70.8	29.2	...	Russia
15.5[2, 5]	53.4[5]	17.3[5]	13.9[5]	33.464[5]	38.5[5]	39.9[5]	8.5[5]	2.7[5]	835.8	99.8	0.2	5.8	44.8	55.2	4.9	Rwanda
14.3[2]	53.0	8.4	24.3	0.785	5.7	43.2[4]	18.0	25.2	39.5	99.0	1.0	3.8	67.1	32.9	2.1[1]	St. Kitts and Nevis
10.0[2]	74.7	9.1	6.3	1.075	15.2	54.1[4]	14.7	12.1	96.8	99.9	0.1	10.9	55.0	45.0	3.4[1]	St. Lucia
15.0[2]	52.4	10.7	21.0	0.581	13.6	50.3[4]	19.7	12.9	62.4	100.0	—	4.7	61.7	38.3	3.5[1]	St. Vincent and the Grenadines
...	...	...	...	...	...	...	...	...	...	...	...	...	...	...	...	San Marino
...	...	...	...	...	...	...	...	...	225.8	99.5	0.5	1.0	47.2	52.8	15.0	São Tomé and Príncipe
25.0[2]	37.7	3.9	32.7	300.5	26.9	35.8[4]		13.0	...	...	...	...	...	...	...	Saudi Arabia
11.3	68.7	6.2	13.7	511.1	30.4	31.6	26.7	14.0	3,011	96.4	3.6	68	70.6	29.4	5.2	Senegal
69.4[2]	14.2	28.9	1.7	1.470	12.5	52.3	8.1	2.2	138.1	84.3	15.7	17.3	66.5	33.5	6.1	Seychelles
22.5[2]	37.3	16.9	23.3	44.479	33.1	38.1	—	4.0	728	92.7	7.3	4	62.5	37.5	2.4	Sierra Leone
8.0	54.6	3.6	33.7	169.049	8.3	41.7	3.9	35.4	...	...	...	...	...	...	...	Singapore
45.4[2]	34.3	6.2	14.1	316.626	30.0	55.1[4]	2.8	4.9	2,058	25.8	74.2	551	77.0	23.0	7.4	Slovakia
...	...	...	...	...	...	...	...	...	1,256	57.5	42.5	187	55.6	44.4	...	Slovenia
53.8[2]	37.6	4.4	4.2	0.284	39.6	52.6	1.8	5.6	95.0	90.0	10.0	9.9	73.2	26.8	5.0[1]	Solomon Islands
...	...	...	...	...	...	...	...	...	1,897	98.2	1.8	—	—	—	—	Somalia
...	...	...	...	...	...	...	...	...	...	...	...	...	...	...	...	South Africa
24.0[2]	54.2	5.0	16.8	86,778.0	13.2	30.6	1.7	15.3	...	...	...	...	...	...	...	Spain
12.7[2]	62.1	11.2	14.1	226.870	13.8	53.4	4.1	17.6	5,936	91.8	8.2	372	63.2	36.8	8.8	Sri Lanka
0.8	34.7	21.9	42.5	254.1	37.3	52.8	0.0	6.0	6,004	89.8	10.2	17	52.9	47.1	5.1[1]	Sudan, The
3.2[5]	38.2[5]	34.0[5]	20.7[5]	0.225[5]	39.8[5]	38.7[5]	1.3[5]	8.2[5]	...	...	...	...	...	...	...	Suriname
2.9	68.3	17.2	11.7	1.323	18.3	63.0	6.9	4.8	217.8	99.1	0.9	23.5	69.4	30.6	3.8	Swaziland
12.4	65.3	0.7	21.6	1,305.6	—49.0[4]—		—	38.6	...	...	...	...	...	...	...	Sweden
4.0	67.3	0.9	27.9	883.5	5.4	38.9	—	25.4	...	...	...	...	...	...	...	Switzerland
58.9[2, 5]	18.4[5]	10.3[5]	12.4[5]	240.683[5]	26.6[5]	26.8[5]	2.8[5]	2.3[5]	16,234	92.7	7.3	174	58.6	41.4	3.3	Syria
12.4[2]	74.9	9.4	3.4	12,496.2	21.1	60.7	5.6	4.1	...	...	...	...	...	...	...	Taiwan
...	...	...	...	...	...	...	...	...	41.2	100.0	—	—	—	—	—	Tajikistan
54.3[2, 5]	30.0[5]	10.0[5]	5.6[5]	349.400[5]	33.0[5]	33.3[5]	1.5[5]	16.4[5]	6,734	94.4	5.6	144	54.2	45.8	23.3	Tanzania
3.4[2]	90.2	2.1	4.4	3,840.8	2.5	64.6	3.2	20.4	14,562	64.1	35.9	2,165	66.7	33.3	4.4	Thailand
6.6	54.3	8.0	31.1	188.4	26.2	36.0	20.7	11.0	1,120	95.6	4.4	14	42.9	57.1	4.3	Togo
6.0[2]	47.9	46.0	—	0.106	17.5	40.1	14.4	—	43.7	100.0		1.7	70.0	29.4	3.2	Tonga
9.9[2]	58.8	17.9	13.5	12.970	21.6	66.7	0.8	2.3	1,704	48.0	51.2	420	76.2	23.8	18.7[1]	Trinidad and Tobago
5.5	86.1	3.0	5.4	9.880	19.8	40.5	—	17.3	7,424	84.3	15.7	1,219	66.2	33.8	18.2	Tunisia
21.3[2]	41.3	13.1	24.3	1,379,826.0	9.1	31.5	6.6	9.1	43,321	38.6	61.4	6,909	57.2	42.8	22.7	Turkey
...	...	...	...	...	...	...	...	...	9.0	100.0	—	—	—	—	—	Turkmenistan
...	...	...	...	...	...	...	...	...	...	...	...	...	...	...	...	Tuvalu
14.9[2, 5]	43.0[5]	11.1[5]	31.0[5]	332.767[5]	38.1[5]	30.0[5]	3.4[5]	26.7[5]	2,617	96.3	3.7	287	82.9	17.1	115.3	Uganda
...	...	...	...	...	...	...	...	...	3,456.7	84.7	15.3	161.0	67.3	32.7	1.0	Ukraine
10.1[5]	40.6[5]	5.0[5]	44.2[5]	149.352[5]	8.4[5]	33.6[5]	10.1[5]	17.8[5]	...	...	...	...	...	...	...	United Arab Emirates
2.2[2, 5]	49.6[5]	0.5[5]	47.8[5]	1,428.1[5]	16.4[5]	25.3[4, 5]	—	49.5[5]	...	...	...	...	...	...	...	United Kingdom
11.3[2]	80.3	2.0	6.4	5,436.6	16.0	51.3	0.4	5.4	...	...	...	...	...	...	...	United States
8.1[2]	38.0	14.1	39.8	51.393	4.6	43.4[4]	2.9	36.3	4,629	28.6	71.4	621	49.9	50.1	37.8	Uruguay
...	...	...	...	...	...	...	...	...	735.9	87.3	12.7	34.2	79.2	20.8	...	Uzbekistan
2.2[2]	30.2	4.9	62.6	28.397	15.3	68.5[4]	1.0	10.5	39.4	98.0	2.0	1.4	64.3	35.7	1.4	Vanuatu
23.5[2]	34.9	33.6	8.0	2,329.8	28.5	70.7[4]	2.0	1.9	26,856	14.2	85.8	2,301	33.9	66.1	13.3	Venezuela
...	...	...	...	...	...	...	...	...	21,554	94.2	5.8	341	77.4	22.6	9.3	Vietnam
...	...	...	...	...	...	...	...	...	...	...	...	...	...	...	...	Virgin Islands (U.S.)
...	...	...	...	...	...	...	...	...	...	...	...	...	...	...	...	West Bank
...	...	...	...	...	...	...	...	...	...	...	...	...	...	...	...	Western Sahara
4.8[2]	53.6	30.7	10.9	0.141	21.6	64.5	1.6	5.0	139.2	99.6	0.4	4.1	68.3	31.7	5.0[1]	Western Samoa
...	...	...	...	...	...	...	...	...	5,341	67.9	32.1	99	78.8	21.2	6.2	Yemen
...	...	...	...	...	...	...	...	...	8,199	49.6	50.4	14	85.7	14.3	...	Yugoslavia
6.7[2]	18.1	6.7	68.4	368.000	23.8	36.5[4]	—	26.4	8,769	90.5	9.5	12	37.5	62.5	...	Zaire
22.2[5]	30.4[5]	15.5[5]	31.9[5]	321.958[5]	17.3[5]	32.0[5]	1.8[5]	2.6[5]	4,666	92.9	7.1	217	55.5	44.5	20.4	Zambia
8.1[2]	58.4	20.1	13.3	20.199	25.5	26.7	4.5	24.1	3,021	76.4	23.6	483	69.4	30.6	24.9	Zimbabwe

[1]1992. [2]Includes claims on nonfinancial government (public) enterprises and/or local governments. [3]Treasury bill rate. [4]Includes foreign currency deposits. [5]1993. [6]Short-term deposit rate. [7]Money market rate. [8]1994. [9]1991. [10]Republic of Cyprus only. [11]Interbank rate.

Housing and construction

The present table summarizes data about the housing stock and the construction industries of the countries of the world. The principal focus is on the elements that are most comparable internationally: the age of the housing (by decade, so far as possible), the legal tenure of the householder, construction of exterior walls, principal physical amenities, sanitary arrangements, and the amount of space both absolutely (total area of the average dwelling in square metres [1 square metre equals 1.20 square yards, or 10.76 square feet]) and relatively (persons per room). The data on construction characterize the industry in terms of: (1) the portion of national gross domestic product (GDP) represented by each country's construction industry, (2) the number of new dwelling units constructed annually, their area, and the rate (in years) required to replace the total national stock of dwellings shown on the extreme left of the table, and (3) for nonresidential construction, the number of buildings or portions of buildings built for nonresidential purposes and their area in square metres.

Because housing patterns differ greatly from country to country, the portion of each country's housing stock for which data are compared was defined as specifically as possible. In general, the numbers refer to permanent, private dwelling units that are usually occupied year-round, whether or not actually occupied on the date of the housing census or survey. That definition implies the exclusion of certain housing that is often part of national housing censuses: vacation homes, second homes occupied less than half the year, collective or communal dwellings, and so on. The housing unit to which the data on tenure refer may be either the individual dwelling or the household, according to the reporting practice of the country concerned.

The data are collected mostly from national housing censuses and surveys. The majority of countries combine the housing census with the population census at five- to ten-year intervals. Some countries, however, can conduct a meaningful housing census only in the capital city or in the few largest cities; others may be able to collect and process data for only a few of the most important housing characteristics even when national coverage is complete. These choices may be dictated by the lack of funding to collect data for the entire country or by the perception, particularly in a tropical, rural country where adequate dwellings can be built by hand, that no urgent housing problem exists. These choices may be complex, however, as

Housing and construction

country	housing stock														
	year	dwelling units[a]	median age[b] (years)	decade built (percent)					tenure[c] (percent)			construction of exterior walls (percent)			
				1949 or earlier	1950–59	1960–69	1970–79	1980 or later	owned	rented	collective, vacant, other	traditional materials	sawn/framed wood	masonry or cement	other
Afghanistan	1979	3,940,000[1]	...	...	...	...	...	...	55.2	23.5	21.3	...	...	...	...
Albania	1989	385,769[4]	22.6	14.0[5]	20.3[6]	19.0[7]	24.3[8]	22.4[9]	91.2	8.8	—	...	...	...	...
Algeria	1987	3,050,812	...	—51.4[13]—		6.4[14]	18.6	23.6	63.0[15]	24.6[15]	12.4[15]	...	...	...	...
American Samoa	1990	6,959	13.9	4.4	7.5	21.9	22.7	43.5	78.1	21.9	—	4.1[17]	56.3[17]	34.9[17]	4.7[17]
Andorra	1990	...	18.1	18.0	5.7	20.8	—55.5—		...	...	...	...	...	...	...
Angola	...	...	...	...	...	...	...	...	...	...	...	...	...	...	...
Antigua and Barbuda	1991	18,476	18.1	—39.6—		11.3	16.3	32.8	64.6	29.3	6.1	...	49.6	49.2	1.2
Argentina	1991	8,515,441[21]	21.6[17]	24.0[17]	17.3[17]	22.0[17]	18.3[17]	18.4[17]	78.0	16.0	6.0	6.1[17]	6.7[17]	84.2[17]	3.0[17]
Armenia	1989	559,000[24]	...	...	...	...	...	...	...	...	...	...	...	...	...
Aruba	1991	19,224	27.7	17.0[26]	25.8[27]	12.1	16.8	28.3	70.6	26.7	2.7	—	7.7	90.6	1.7
Australia	1991	5,852,517[22]	26.1[28]	37.9[28]	10.4[28]	18.6[28]	—33.1[28]—		67.1	26.7	6.2	...	...	...	...
Austria	1991	3,393,271	33.8	33.0[5]	14.7[6]	18.1[7]	18.5[8]	15.7[9]	50.0	38.7	11.3	—	5.1[4]	81.9[4]	13.0[4]
Azerbaijan	1989	1,381,000[24]	...	...	...	...	...	...	...	...	...	...	...	...	...
Bahamas, The	1980	54,308	30.7	—54.7—		25.6	—19.7—		51.4	37.4	11.2	4.0[34]	32.3	54.7	9.0
Bahrain	1991	83,470	15.2[28]	58.3[28]	14.5[28]	—27.2[28]—			48.2[28]	33.6[28]	18.2[28]	—	—	93.6[28]	6.4[28]
Bangladesh	1991	19,020,489	...	...	...	...	...	...	86.3	6.5	7.2	78.9	2.4	8.0	10.7
Barbados	1990	75,211	19.1	—48.6—			22.9	28.5	76.1	20.4	3.5	0.2	61.2[35]	35.4	3.2
Belarus	1989	2,796,000[24]	...	...	...	...	...	...	...	...	...	...	...	...	...
Belgium	1991	3,748,165	...	37.0[5]	21.5[36]	13.1[37]	18.5[8]	9.9[9]	64.5	34.2	1.3	...	...	...	...
Belize	1991	37,658	...	—26.3—			17.8	55.9	65.9	22.8	11.3	5.1	65.6	24.8	4.5
Benin	1979	612,041	...	...	...	...	...	...	76.8	10.1	13.1	...	...	...	...
Bermuda	1991	22,061	...	—56.0—		15.8	12.0	16.2	43.4	52.4	4.2	—	1.7[17,35]	95.1[17]	3.2[17]
Bhutan	...	...	...	...	...	...	...	...	...	...	...	...	...	...	...
Bolivia	1992	1,444,817	...	...	...	...	...	...	65.5	19.8	14.7	72.3[40]	2.3[40]	21.1[40]	4.2[40]
Bosnia and Herzegovina	1989	...	...	...	...	...	...	...	...	...	...	...	...	...	...
Botswana	1991	276,209	...	...	...	...	...	...	59.2	22.9	17.9	48.7	—	49.3	2.0
Brazil	1990	35,578,857	...	...	...	...	...	...	67.0	17.7	15.3	...	...	...	...
Brunei	1981	28,676	...	...	...	...	...	...	83.8	11.8	4.4	0.2	54.8	36.5	8.5
Bulgaria	1975	3,396,000[42]	17.9	—81.9—		11.1	—7.0—		77.3	22.7	—	...	...	...	...
Burkina Faso	1985	1,274,546[24]	...	...	...	...	...	...	...	...	...	...	...	...	...
Burundi	1979	938,000[45]	...	...	...	...	...	...	98.7	1.1	0.2	...	...	...	...
Cambodia	1987	1,787,835	...	...	...	...	...	...	74.0	18.0	8.0	4.0	13.0	17.0	66.0
Cameroon	1976	1,390,896[21]	...	...	...	...	...	...	83.4	11.2	5.4	75.5	13.9	9.5	1.1
Canada	1986	10,079,442[12]	10.5	20.3[5]	20.0[6]	19.4[7]	—40.3[47]—		62.1	37.5	0.5	...	...	...	...
Cape Verde	1990	67,619	...	—73.6—				26.4	...	15.4[17]	...	36.1	—	60.1	3.8
Central African Republic	1975	519,314[40]	...	...	...	...	...	...	...	...	...	82.2	7.1	2.5	8.2
Chad	...	...	...	...	...	...	...	...	...	...	...	...	...	...	...
Chile	1992	3,369,849	20.4[46]	—46.2[46]—		21.1[46]	—32.7[46]—		68.3	24.6	7.1	14.0	53.1	31.9	1.0
China	1990	276,947,962	...	...	...	...	...	...	18.5[2,46]	81.5[2,46]	—	...	...	...	...
Colombia	1985	5,824,857	20.6[49]	54.6[49]	26.2[49]	19.2[49]	—	—	67.6	23.6	8.8	16.7	7.0	75.6	0.7
Comoros	1980	81,791	...	5.3	7.7	21.3	—63.7—		87.4	3.1	9.5	73.5	1.8	16.9	7.8
Congo	1984	363,140[24]	...	...	...	...	...	...	61.4	24.1	14.5	10.5	15.9	54.9	18.7
Costa Rica	1984	500,788	...	...	...	...	...	...	65.8	20.7	13.5	1.1	60.1	35.6	3.2
Côte d'Ivoire	1985	1,146,370[50]	...	...	...	...	...	...	...	...	...	...	...	...	...
Croatia	1991	1,575,644	...	...	...	...	...	...	64.0	35.4	0.6	...	...	...	...
Cuba	1981	2,363,364	24.6	23.2[51]	21.3[52]	21.6	—25.6—		...	...	...	3.8	33.2	61.5	1.4
Cyprus	1982	168,588	22.8	—39.9—		15.4	—44.7—		60.0	16.5	23.5	11.9	—	87.6	0.5
Czech Republic	1991	3,705,691	42.4	41.7[5]	10.2[6]	14.5[7]	19.6[8]	14.0[9]	44.7[17]	41.7[17]	13.6[17]	—	32.0[53]	67.1	0.9
Denmark	1991	2,374,970	36.6	44.3	10.0	16.4	18.1	11.2	53.8	44.5	1.7	...	...	...	...
Djibouti	1982	25,000[48]	27.6	...	...	...	...	...	...	...	...	—	73.0[54]	22.5	4.5
Dominica	1991	19,374[24]	18.6	—36.2—		11.6	12.8	31.8	71.9	19.7	8.4	—	50.5	48.4	1.1
Dominican Republic	1981	1,125,785[21]	...	...	...	...	...	...	72.0	17.0	11.0	31.1	31.3	31.4	6.2
Ecuador	1990	2,111,121	...	...	...	...	...	...	68.1	22.6	9.3	32.2	9.3	57.7	0.8
Egypt	1986	9,732,728	...	—37.1[2]—		—62.9[2]—			64.0	27.2	8.8	...	...	...	...
El Salvador	1992	1,236,866	...	...	...	...	...	...	69.6	17.9	12.5	39.8	2.9	52.6	4.7
Equatorial Guinea	...	...	...	...	...	...	...	...	...	...	...	...	...	...	...
Eritrea	...	...	...	...	...	...	...	...	...	...	...	...	...	...	...
Estonia	1989	663,708	19.1	18.5[56]	11.8[57]	22.5[7]	27.0[8]	20.2[9]	18.3	81.5	0.2	—	18.2	77.4	4.4
Ethiopia	1984	9,300,000	...	...	...	...	...	...	48.8[2]	47.2[2]	4.0[2]	89.5	...	5.9	4.6
Faroe Islands	1977	11,172[15]	32.5	—60.1—		21.8	—15.0—		84.5	9.9	5.6	—	43.9	53.5	2.6
Fiji	1986	124,098	...	...	...	...	...	...	75.5	11.1	13.4	9.0	26.4	29.8	34.8
Finland	1990	2,152,938	17.1	—29.6—		16.5	26.4	27.5	71.5	20.5	8.0	14.0[4,15]	81.8[4,15]	—4.2[4,15]—	
France	1990	21,535,677	19.1[20]	—43.5[20,60]—		11.6[20,61]	27.3[20,62]	17.7[20,63]	54.4	39.6	6.0	...	...	...	...
French Guiana	1990	38,324	...	—38.7[64]—			21.5[65]	39.8[66]	41.3	—58.7—		29.4	—70.6—		
French Polynesia	1988	39,513	10.8	—11.3—		16.0	27.6	45.1	68.5	21.2	10.3	36.9	15.8	45.2	2.2

planners are always aware that much housing is physically inadequate to protect dwellers from the elements, is disadvantageously placed in relation to tainted or disease-infested water supply or to the outfall of unprocessed sewage, or is built of materials (mud, skins, thatch, etc.) that may harbour pests or disease. In the developed countries, median age and the distribution of physical amenities provide strong indicators of the quality and availability of housing.

The data for the construction industry refer to the most recent year in which a broad range of countries could be surveyed.

The broadest indication of total activity in a national construction industry is its contribution to the national gross domestic product, since that figure, in addition to construction of buildings, also includes civil engineering projects, such as dams, roads and other transportation infrastructure, recreational facilities, irrigation and land reclamation works, and the like. The scope of the data relating to construction of buildings may be limited in several respects. It may be confined to activity capable of being surveyed in the modern or urban sectors only, may be limited to private new construction only or to government and government-financed activity only, or may refer to construction mortgaged or financed through certain organizations only. Depending on national data-collection systems, it usually excludes remodeling of old premises but may include extensions or enlargements of existing buildings. The data for new construction are usually of two principal types: authorized new construction or certification after construction that newly built structures meet building and fire codes and the like. Data for construction completed are naturally more meaningful but are not available for every country, necessitating the substitution of authorized construction data, which are usually available only for areas regulated by certain types of governmental authorities.

The following notes further define the column headings:

a. Data refer to permanent, private dwelling units that are usually occupied year-round, whether or not occupied on the census date.
b. Data are estimates unless specifically provided by a country source.
c. Data may be either for dwellings or for households, depending on country reporting practice.
d. Data may be either for construction completed or for construction authorized, depending on country reporting practice.

									construction industry (1992)						country
physical amenities (percent)			sewage disposal (percent)			space[b]			percent of GDP	new residential[d]			new nonresidential[d]		
piped water	electricity	inside toilet or WC	closed public sewer or septic tank	open public sewer	other	average area (sq m)	rooms per dwelling unit	persons per room		total no. of dwellings	floor area ('000 sq m)	years to replace nat'l stock	number of units	floor area ('000 sq m)	
25.3[2]	66.5[2]	5.5[2]	5.5	77.9	16.6	...	5.5	2.1	5.8[3]	...	...	...	...	...	Afghanistan
33.0	...	21.3	...	...	...	35.7	1.8	2.6	6.4[10, 11]	12,428[12]	...	37.4[12]	...	...	Albania
87.4	72.7	68.9	52.4	19.1	28.5	...	2.9	2.6	11.9	71,433[16]	...	42.6[16]	...	...	Algeria
96.2	94.4	93.4	68.5	—31.5—		...	4.5	1.6	...	218[18]	...	21.5[18]	...	...	American Samoa
—	...	—	...	—	...	...	...	...	19.9[11]	90[4, 19, 20]	84[19, 20]	...	[19, 20]	[19, 20]	Andorra
...	...	...	...	...	...	...	...	...	1.9[12]	...	585[17]	...	210[17]	104.5[17]	Angola
91.5	...	...	53.0	—47.0—		...	3.6	0.9	10.2[12]	764[18]	...	20.2[18]	...	...	Antigua and Barbuda
77.4	86.8[17]	95.1[17]	77.1[17]	—22.9[17]—		...	3.9[17]	1.3[17]	5.3	67,528[22]	1,968[19]	105.2[23]	...	[19]	Argentina
...	...	...	...	...	...	...	...	...	5.3	...	1,910[12, 25]	...	...	...	Armenia
97.9	98.7[28]	89.2[28]	...	...	...	...	5.2	0.7	8.2	126	...	94.5[12]	50	...	Aruba
97.1[29]	98.4[30]	92.2[28]	99.0[28]	—1.0[28]—		...	5.1[28]	0.6[28]	7.0[31]	146,900[31]	11,170[32]	43.9	23,340[15]	13,727[32]	Australia
95.0[28]	...	88.7	94.3[28]	—	5.7[28]	85.0	4.3[18]	0.6[18]	7.6	36,553[11]	3,981[12]	92.8[11]	500[15]	100[15]	Austria
...	...	...	...	...	...	...	...	...	13.7[10, 33]	...	2,600[19]	...	...	[19]	Azerbaijan
83.0[33]	77.9	...	63.2	2.2	34.6	...	4.0	1.2	3.0	733[4, 19]	...	52.9[16]	[19]	...	Bahamas, The
92.8	97.1	78.2	99.8	...	0.2	...	4.2	1.4	5.6	1,919[18]	...	27.5[18]	1,444[10]	...	Bahrain
56.8[28]	14.3	12.5	1.5[28]	—98.5[28]—		...	2.0[20]	2.9[20]	5.8[31]	300,900[22]	...	49.1	...	...	Bangladesh
94.0	92.6	66.2	66.8	0.4	32.8	...	4.3	0.8	3.5[33]	2,116[11]	...	...	...	...	Barbados
...	...	...	...	...	...	...	...	...	12.0[10]	...	5,395[12, 19]	...	...	[19]	Belarus
99.6	100.0	91.9	62.5[38]	—37.5[38]—		86.3	4.0	0.0	5.4[33]	28,136[33]	27,096[33]	129.0[12]	8,612	35,592[33]	Belgium
54.9	67.2	34.7	34.7	—65.3—		...	...	...	9.6[33]	...	6,185[20]	...	...	...	Belize
...	...	...	...	...	...	...	...	...	3.4[12]	...	...	...	...	...	Benin
97.4[17]	...	96.7[17]	96.7[17]	—3.3[17]—		...	3.2[17]	0.7[17]	4.9[39]	556[23]	268	36.6[23]	...	...	Bermuda
...	...	...	...	...	...	...	...	...	8.4[12]	...	...	...	...	...	Bhutan
57.5	55.5	42.8	22.5[40]	—77.5[40]—		...	...	...	5.1[33]	24,980[23]	...	52.8[23]	...	...	Bolivia
66.2	94.2	53.2	...	...	...	56.0	...	...	7.1[10, 23]	26,568[12]	...	...	...	...	Bosnia and Herzegovina
77.0	5.4[28]	25.4[28]	8.6[28]	20.4[28]	71.0[28]	...	2.5	1.9	5.1[41]	...	96[16]	...	472[15]	132[16]	Botswana
73.4	87.8	...	60.1[18]	—39.9[18]—		...	5.1[17]	0.9[17]	7.3	...	20,090[2, 16]	...	5,017[15]	8,180[2, 16]	Brazil
90.3	64.2	94.2	57.4	—42.6—		...	4.2	1.6	4.9	195[4, 20]	...	147.0	5[20]	...	Brunei
74.6	99.8	33.2	33.2	—66.8—		16.0[42]	2.5[11]	1.1[11]	5.4[10, 40]	17,996	1,384	53.0[23]	...	...	Bulgaria
...	...	...	...	...	...	...	...	...	5.5	...	...	...	...	...	Burkina Faso
11.0	0.6	...	1.6	—98.4—		37.2[46]	2.4[46]	0.6[46]	4.1[12]	...	...	...	...	...	Burundi
11.0	...	7.0	...	...	...	...	...	1.2	8.2[33]	...	...	...	...	...	Cambodia
22.0	5.9	2.2	2.2	70.4	27.6	...	4.1	1.2	5.3[12]	...	230[1]	...	53[1]	51.1[1]	Cameroon
99.8[40]	100.0	99.4[40]	98.9[28]	—1.1—		...	5.7	0.5	5.3[33]	160,020[12]	...	44.0[23]	14,846[15]	...	Canada
16.2	24.9	25.1	—3.4[17]—		96.6[17]	...	1.8[17]	2.8[17]	10.8[40]	...	31[46]	...	3[46]	0.5[46]	Cape Verde
...	...	...	...	...	...	...	...	...	2.8[12]	...	10[48]	...	11[11, 48]	82[48]	Central African Republic
...	...	...	...	...	...	...	...	...	1.9[12]	...	...	...	...	...	Chad
88.2	90.2	...	70.3	—29.7—		59.9[40, 43]	4.4	1.0	5.4	117,384[33]	7,056[33]	32.1[23]	...	2,916[33]	Chile
89.4[2, 16]	...	25.2[2, 16]	47.0[2, 16]	—53.0[2, 16]—		37.0[16]	2.2[16]	1.8[16]	6.0	...	850,170	...	...	297,830	China
70.5	78.5	77.9	69.6	—30.4—		...	3.3	1.6	5.0	11,052[33]	9,436	70.2[16]	...	2,181	Colombia
12.9	5.7	...	2.1	—97.9—		33.7	2.5	2.1	5.6[33]	...	...	...	...	...	Comoros
30.5	8.8	16.6	—86.2[2]—		13.8[2]	...	3.7[2]	1.7[2]	1.4[12]	...	...	...	...	...	Congo
86.9	97.3	...	66.5	—33.5—		...	4.0	1.4	2.5[33]	...	1,914[23]	...	2,868[15]	178[15]	Costa Rica
23.0	39.6	23.9	—68.5—		31.5	...	...	...	2.2[20]	...	...	...	...	...	Côte d'Ivoire
86.2	98.6	80.3	80.8	—19.2—		70.4	2.8	1.1	6.6	12,623[12]	623	...	477[12]	1,081	Croatia
74.1	82.9	45.2	60.9	9.3	30.1	71.0[43]	4.1	1.0	9.3[10, 23]	25,344[40]	1,800[40]	93.2[40]	469[15]	1,803[15]	Cuba
100.0	98.1	74.5	95.6	—4.4—		...	4.6	0.8	10.0[33]	6,639[16]	4,728[33]	25.4[16]	1,103[15]	1,572[33]	Cyprus
96.9	100.0	88.5	98.1	—1.9—		70.5	2.7	1.0	6.3[12]	69,300[12]	2,212	53.4[12]	...	...	Czech Republic
100.0	100.0	99.2[23]	98.6[28]	—1.4[28]—		107.8	3.8	0.6	5.6	13,668[33]	1,224[33]	149.5	3,312[33]	4,195	Denmark
45.0	58.0	82.0	26.0	23.0	51.0	...	1.9	6.9	4.8[12]	...	54[23]	...	26[16]	13.7[16]	Djibouti
87.4	...	36.8	36.8	—63.2—		...	3.3	1.1	7.6	...	...	...	...	...	Dominica
64.4	36.7[38]	14.1	52.1[38]	22.6[38]	25.3[38]	...	2.8[38]	1.5[38]	10.5	...	648[16]	...	856[16]	508[16]	Dominican Republic
62.7[21]	77.7[21]	49.6[21]	39.5[21]	25.1[21]	35.4[21]	...	2.8	1.7	3.6	...	3,825[15]	...	596[15]	412.7[15]	Ecuador
73.1	87.0	...	...	...	...	...	3.3	1.5	6.3[31]	160,613[32]	...	53.0[23]	...	...	Egypt
46.4	69.3	39.7	39.7	—60.3—		...	1.5[55]	3.3[55]	2.9	694	341[15]	...	271	0.7[15]	El Salvador
...	...	...	...	...	...	...	...	...	2.8[12]	...	...	...	...	...	Equatorial Guinea
...	...	...	...	...	...	...	...	...	...	...	...	...	...	...	Eritrea
92.7	99.9	...	...	...	...	34.5	2.5	0.9	4.6	...	329[12, 19]	...	...	[19]	Estonia
67.9[2]	...	55.2[2]	...	...	...	...	1.9	2.4	2.8[41]	...	260[58]	...	92[1]	63.3[58]	Ethiopia
99.7	99.5	95.0	89.7	8.1	2.2	...	5.5	1.1	10.6	223[42]	...	37.5[16]	...	...	Faroe Islands
73.7	48.5	56.0	35.4[59]	—64.6[59]—		...	3.3	1.8	4.7[33]	1,344[33]	64[33]	72[33]	105[16]	48[33]	Fiji
95.1	95.9[4, 15]	92.7	96.4	—3.6—		74.2	3.5	0.6	6.3	30,412[33]	13,830[25]	41.6[11]	32,886[29]	23,310[25]	Finland
99.7[40]	...	93.5	73.8[50]	—26.2[50]—		77.0[55]	3.9	0.7	5.3	248,400	...	83.2[12]	...	42,950[12]	France
77.0	86.7	62.0	34.3[46]	—65.7[46]—		...	2.8	1.2	9.3[23]	1,209	195	35.7[11]	...	28.5[15]	French Guiana
92.5	91.0	78.9	2.0[1]	67.0[1]	31.0[1]	...	3.8	1.3	6.1[11]	700[16]	85[19]	59.3[16]	156[16]	[19]	French Polynesia

Housing and construction (continued)

country	housing stock														
	year	dwelling units[a]	median age[b] (years)	decade built (percent)					tenure[c] (percent)			construction of exterior walls (percent)			
				1949 or earlier	1950–59	1960–69	1970–79	1980 or later	owned	rented	collective, vacant, other	traditional materials	sawn/ framed wood	masonry or cement	other
Gabon	1967	15,886[48]	...	...	...	...	...	...	—87.0—		13.0	...	...	...	
Gambia, The	1983	202,199	...	...	...	...	...	...	63.9	21.9	14.2	82.9	—	12.9	4.2
Gaza Strip	1992	66,819[67]	23.0	4.7	31.2	14.3	25.8	23.9	89.1[15,68]	7.6[15,68]	3.3[15,68]	—	—	96.0	4.0
Georgia	1989	1,244,000[24]	...	...	...	...	...	...	...	...	...	...	...	...	...
Germany	1987[69]	34,547,348[37]	...	30.6[60]	15.2[70]	23.6[71]	19.8[72]	10.8[73]	39.0	60.3	0.7	...	...	...	...
Ghana	1984	1,216,677	...	...	...	...	...	...	47.7[50]	25.3[50]	27.0[50]	...	...	...	...
Gibraltar	1991	7,604[21]	25.0	37.3[75]	16.7[76]	15.6[77]	23.0[78]	7.4[79]	15.2	84.8	...	...	...	...	...
Greece	1981	3,999,332	29.2	30.2[5]	27.4[6]	20.7[7]	—21.5—		73.1[80]	26.9[80]	—	...	...	...	...
Greenland	1989	18,401	10.2	11.9[29]	18.8[29]	46.5[29]	—22.8[29]—		39.3[15]	—60.7[15]—		...	...	...	...
Grenada	1981	21,017	18.3[38]	48.0[38]	29.0[38]	22.2[38]	—0.8[38]—		74.5	14.4	11.1	—	80.3	13.2	6.5
Guadeloupe	1990	112,478	...			8.1[80]			62.6	—37.4—		29.5	—70.5—		
Guam	1990	35,223	15.8	2.3	7.1	19.2	41.5	29.9	45.6	54.4	—	0.0	5.1	85.8	9.1
Guatemala	1981	1,259,598	12.5	—62.0—		10.0	—28.0—		64.7	11.3	24.0	55.6	21.1	19.3	4.0
Guernsey	1991	21,215[21]	...	...	...	...	...	...	68.4	31.6	—	...	...	...	...
Guinea	1983	716,378	...	...	...	...	...	...	81.3	10.6	8.1	26.2	...	12.7	61.1
Guinea-Bissau	1979	123,936	...	...	...	...	...	...	...	...	...	95.7	0.1	2.3	1.9
Guyana	1980	149,734[24]	17.6	—43.5—		19.4	—37.1—		57.2	27.3	15.5	1.8	85.6	6.6	6.0
Haiti	1987	1,164,136	...	—75.9—			—24.1—		73.2	4.5	22.3	37.0	57.4	5.4	0.2
Honduras	1988	809,263	12.1[80]	—38.9[80]—		37.8[72,80]	—23.3[80]—		71.8[80]	16.5[80]	12.7[80]	61.0[80]	26.4[80]	11.7[80]	0.9[80]
Hong Kong	1991	1,580,072	...	—48.1[28]—		13.6[28]	—38.3[28]—		42.6	53.0	4.4	...	...	...	...
Hungary	1990	3,817,000	16.4	32.9[5]	11.8[52]	14.9	23.2	17.2	75.9	23.7	0.4	21.8	14.6	63.6	—
Iceland	1984	70,777	25.6	—46.0—		—54.1—			70.3[82]	—29.7[82]—		...	...	71.9[82]	...
India	1991	195,024,357	...	...	...	...	...	...	86.3	11.8	1.9	87.7	1.5	2.0	8.7
Indonesia	1989	38,881,106[24]	...	...	...	...	...	...	87.0[30]	5.0[30]	8.0[30]	...	...	...	...
Iran	1986	8,211,375	...	—82.5[29]—			—17.5[29]—		77.0	12.2	9.8	28.8	0.7	69.2	1.3
Iraq	1956	741,000	...	...	...	...	...	...	83.0	12.8	4.2	...	...	...	...
Ireland	1981	1,038,000[12]	47.2	—60.0—		12.8	—26.2—		67.9	20.9	11.2	...	...	...	...
Isle of Man	1991	27,316	...	...	...	...	...	...	66.5	32.5	1.0	...	...	...	...
Israel	1983	1,104,270	...	9.5[83]	—90.5[84]—				74.3	23.1	2.6	...	...	...	...
Italy	1991	19,509,362[24]	32.2	30.8[5]	19.7[36]	27.5[85]	—22.0[47]—		58.9[28]	35.5[28]	5.6[28]	...	...	...	...
Jamaica	1982	517,297[24]	17.0	—33.6—		28.8	—39.6—		46.7	32.6	20.7	7.1	28.4	54.4	10.1
Japan	1993	40,835,000	16.5	5.4[87]	10.9[88]	13.4[7]	31.5[8]	38.8[9]	59.8	38.5	1.7	—	68.1	—31.9—	
Jersey	1991	32,463	...	...	...	...	...	...	49.6	48.0	2.4	...	...	...	...
Jordan	1979	378,815	...	...	...	...	...	...	62.6	30.8	6.6	...	...	...	...
Kazakhstan	1989	3,824,000[24]	...	...	...	...	...	...	...	...	...	...	...	...	...
Kenya	1979	2,956,369[24]	...	...	...	...	...	...	...	...	...	...	...	...	...
Kiribati	1990	11,301[24]	...	...	...	...	...	...	68.2[55]	17.9[55]	13.9[55]	64.4[55]	—35.6[55]—		
Korea, North	1987	4,054,027[24]	...	...	...	...	...	...	...	...	...	...	...	...	...
Korea, South	1990	11,301,006	13.1	13.2	6.6	12.7	23.7	43.8	79.0	17.7	3.3	7.8	18.9	73.0	0.3
Kuwait	1985	228,781	14.5[17]	—12.2[17]—		38.8[17]	—34.5[17]—		38.2	53.6	8.2	46.5[4]	—	36.5[4]	17.0[4]
Kyrgyzstan	1989	856,000[24]	...	...	...	...	...	...	...	...	...	...	...	...	...
Laos	...	...	...	...	...	...	...	...	...	...	...	...	...	...	...
Latvia	1989	732,000[24]	...	...	...	...	...	...	...	...	...	...	...	...	...
Lebanon	1970	483,908[21]	...	30.1[89]	40.2[90]	—29.4—			...	...	...	...	...	...	...
Lesotho	1986	317,161[21]	...	...	...	...	...	...	...	...	...	...	...	...	...
Liberia	1974[48]	263,333	...	...	...	...	...	...	...	...	...	...	...	...	...
Libya	1984	569,679	...	...	...	...	...	...	62.5[49]	28.0[49]	9.5[49]	...	...	...	...
Liechtenstein	1980	10,386[11,21]	29.4	27.1[89]	15.0[90]	27.1	—30.8—		53.6	41.7	4.7	...	...	...	...
Lithuania	1993	1,203,800	...	...	...	...	...	...	83.5	—16.5—		...	...	...	...
Luxembourg	1991	144,683	33.1	34.5[5]	17.6[6]	12.5[7]	17.8[8]	17.6[9]	66.1	28.3	5.6	...	...	...	...
Macau	1991	89,193	...	...	...	...	...	...	65.9	32.0	2.1	—	0.5[38]	99.3[38]	0.2[38]
Macedonia	1989	...	...	...	...	...	...	...	...	...	...	...	...	...	...
Madagascar	1975	1,671,473[24]	...	...	...	...	...	...	...	...	...	...	...	...	...
Malaŵi	1987	1,859,572	...	...	...	...	...	...	39.6	—60.4—		51.6	3.1	44.4	0.9
Malaysia	1991	3,447,597	...	...	...	...	...	...	63.4[17]	25.0[17]	11.6[17]	...	...	...	...
Maldives	1990	37,114	11.6	15.1	7.9	13.7	21.7	41.6	96.4	3.6	—	53.8	2.7	41.1	2.4
Mali	1987	1,364,079	...	...	...	...	...	...	84.2	8.5	7.3	75.9	8.5	10.3	5.3
Malta	1985	101,509	...	—81.8[92]—		—18.2[93]—			53.9	43.0	3.1	93.0[67]	...	92.9[67]	0.21[67]
Marshall Islands	1980[94]	4,923[40]	...	6.4	13.3	24.7	—55.5—		60.0	33.0	7.0	10.7	63.5	15.9	9.9
Martinique	1990	123,317	19.0	—54.5[64]—		17.9[63]	—27.6[79]—		60.9	32.5	6.6	20.4[46]	—79.6[46]—		
Mauritania	1977	246,462[24]	...	...	...	...	...	...	...	...	...	...	...	...	...
Mauritius	1990	223,821	...	—19.7[1]—		24.3[1,96]	—56.0[1,97]—		75.9	15.2	8.9	—	4.2[1]	66.8[1]	28.9[1]
Mayotte	1991	19,227	...	...	...	...	...	...	77.8	14.8	7.3	50.4	—48.2—		1.4
Mexico	1990	16,197,802	...	—51.4[17]—		15.4[17]	—33.2[17]—		77.9	14.6	7.5	19.0	8.1	69.5	3.4
Micronesia	1980	11,562	...	3.8	5.2	21.3	—69.7—		51.8	39.2	9.0	6.0	41.8	14.6	37.6
Moldova	1989	1,144,000[24]	...	...	...	...	...	...	...	...	...	...	...	...	...
Monaco	1990	16,122	30.0	—39.5[60]—		13.0[61]	19.7[62]	27.8[65]	23.3	60.5	16.2	...	...	...	...
Mongolia	1969	242,000	...	...	...	...	...	...	100.0	—	—	...	...	...	...
Morocco	1982	3,419,282[24]	...	...	...	...	...	...	41.2[2]	43.3[2]	15.5[2]	24.5	—	73.5	1.8
Mozambique	1980	2,712,439[24]	...	...	...	...	...	...	...	...	...	86.5	2.3	8.3	2.9
Myanmar (Burma)	1983	6,750,884	...	...	...	...	...	...	...	...	...	80.3	14.8	3.2	1.7
Namibia	...	...	...	...	...	...	...	...	...	...	...	...	...	...	...
Nauru	1977	508[98]	...	—88.6[98]—			—11.4[98]—		11.0[99]	80.6[99]	8.4[99]	...	...	...	...
Nepal	1981	2,585,154[24]	...	...	...	...	...	...	75.3[99]	10.7[99]	14.0[99]	...	...	...	...
Netherlands, The	1990	5,802,400	25.4	28.2	11.8	18.0	21.7	20.3	43.2[15]	56.8[15]	...	...	...	...	...
Netherlands Antilles	1992	57,608	14.0	—28.4—		13.6	21.3	36.7	64.8[28]	35.2[28]	—	—	18.3[28]	78.8[28]	2.9[28]
New Caledonia	1989	44,047	...	—19.3—		—80.7—			56.4	29.7	13.9	6.4	11.7	61.7	20.2
New Zealand	1991	1,185,396	...	—64.1[28]—		19.2[28]	—16.2[28]—		72.4	22.7	4.9	...	...	...	...
Nicaragua	1971	330,422	...	...	...	...	...	...	64.4	20.3	15.3	30.8	45.6	21.8	1.8
Niger	1988	1,163,424[24]	...	...	...	...	...	...	...	...	...	66.5	...	...	...
Nigeria	1982[100]	...	...	...	...	...	...	...	37.0	46.0	17.0	29.0	—	71.0	—
Northern Mariana Islands	1990	8,210	...	1.0	2.5	6.4	13.3	76.8	39.5	56.6	3.9	0.0	13.5	66.5	20.0
Norway	1990	1,769,000	25.3	44.1[5]	20.6[6]	17.8[7]	20.7[8]	16.0[9]	80.3	—19.7—		...	...	...	...
Oman	1989	2,469[46]	...	...	...	...	...	...	70.2	19.8	20.8	...	...	...	...
Pakistan[101]	1980	12,597,000	17.2	17.1[89]	36.7[102]	24.9[103]	—21.3[104]—		78.4	7.7	13.9	49.2	2.4	41.4	7.1

physical amenities (percent)			sewage disposal (percent)			space[b]			construction industry (1992)						country
									percent of GDP	new residential[d]			new nonresidential[d]		
piped water	electricity	inside toilet or WC	closed public sewer or septic tank	open public sewer	other	average area (sq m)	rooms per dwelling unit	persons per room		total no. of dwellings	floor area ('000 sq m)	years to replace nat'l stock	number of units	floor area ('000 sq m)	
...	50.5	...	...	...	...	...	3.0	1.3	9.3[12]	...	216[50]	...	75[50]	119.4[50]	Gabon
21.9	...	...	...	...	...	...	2.0	2.0	6.0[31]	...	...	...	14[50]	...	Gambia, The
97.2[15]	97.6	98.4	...	...	...	144.3[43]	2.6[15]	2.5[15]	18.2[12]	1,247[16]	180[16]	53.6[16]	...	31.1[16]	Gaza Strip
...	...	...	...	...	...	...	...	...	7.8	...	1,005[17]	...	...	...	Georgia
100.0	99.7	98.3	97.1[17]	—2.9[17]—		82.1[12]	4.3[12]	0.6[12]	6.0[33]	431,991[33]	34,400	92.2	50,331	33,508	Germany
34.0[74]	...	...	...	...	...	...	...	...	3.5	...	...	...	...	...	Ghana
96.7[28]	100.0[28]	99.2	100.0[28]	—	—	...	3.3	1.1	...	...	...	...	...	...	Gibraltar
81.3[81]	89.0[81]	93.0[81]	...	...	...	138.4[18]	3.3[18]	0.9[18]	6.7	100,332[12]	46,434[11, 25]	37.4[40]	11,471[29]	12,536[11, 25]	Greece
62.7[29]	84.2[29]	39.1[29]	39.1[29]	—60.9[29]—		72.0[43]	2.8	1.1	8.5	325[12]	26[12]	71.1[23]	...	387	Greenland
86.5[81]	...	23.0[81]	23.0[81]	—77.0[38]—		...	2.9	1.6	10.5	...	...	...	...	...	Grenada
83.2	89.4	78.2	24.6[46]	—75.4[46]—		...	3.3	1.0	7.4[17]	676[23]	358	126.7[23]	...	160	Guadeloupe
99.2	98.4	97.0	97.0	—3.0—		...	5.0	0.8	7.9[46]	417[16]	...	67.4[16]	500[16]	...	Guam
52.0	37.0	14.3	20.1	3.4	76.5	...	2.4	2.2	2.0	...	495[19, 23]	...	...	[19]	Guatemala
96.5[29]	...	98.8	65.9	—34.1—		...	5.8[18]	0.5[18]	...	148	...	128.6[23]	...	...	Guernsey
11.9	12.5	...	...	...	...	...	...	...	6.0[12]	...	...	...	...	...	Guinea
3.7	3.9	...	4.2	—95.8—		...	1.4	4.5	6.4[23]	...	...	...	...	...	Guinea-Bissau
38.1	69.0	29.0	10.4	—89.6—		...	2.9	1.8	3.6[33]	...	...	...	56[22]	...	Guyana
5.8	21.9	45.8	2.0[46]	—98.0[46]—		...	2.3	2.1	4.5	...	...	...	...	...	Haiti
55.0[17]	25.0[17]	13.0[17]	14.4[17]	—85.6[17]—		...	2.4[17]	2.3[17]	6.6	1,442[20]	214[18]	...	148[18]	98[18]	Honduras
85.7[28]	...	69.2[49]	65.4[49]	—34.6[49]—		53.2[30]	3.1[49]	2.8[49]	4.8	67,579[16]	1,428[33]	25.5[16]	303[16]	1,656[33]	Hong Kong
90.1	98.8[20]	75.9	85.5	—14.5—		52.3	2.6	1.0	5.3	20,925[33]	4,353[23]	78.3[40]	3,433[15]	21,886[15, 25]	Hungary
99.1[81]	94.6[81]	93.6[81]	86.5[81]	—13.5[81]—		...	4.8[82]	0.9[82]	8.6[12]	1,594[12]	568[25]	...	552[12]	729[12, 25]	Iceland
32.3	42.4	23.7	...	...	...	...	2.2	2.7	5.5[31]	...	...	...	13,908[20]	...	India
12.9	44.0	26.6[17]	22.8[30]	—77.2[30]—		59.0	3.3	1.7[30]	6.0	...	...	...	...	...	Indonesia
74.6	84.1	43.6	...	...	...	60.0[29]	2.8	1.8	4.0[31]	124,891[15]	15,818[32]	65.0[15]	5,235[15]	853[35]	Iran
20.8	17.1	...	...	...	...	...	2.4	...	2.8[12]	...	4,558[12]	...	11,799[15]	410[12]	Iraq
94.8	94.7[30]	93.0	72.3[30]	—27.7[30]—		...	3.7[15]	1.0[15]	5.0[16]	21,306[33]	2,046	44.0	...	2,067	Ireland
...	...	99.5	...	...	...	...	...	0.4[28]	9.8[16]	168[16]	...	161.0[16]	...	...	Isle of Man
96.5[30]	96.5[30]	98.8	99.0[80]	—1.0[80]—		149.8[43]	3.0	1.2	7.6[12]	42,336[33]	5,340[33]	25.9[12]	...	1,884[33]	Israel
98.7[28]	99.0[28]	94.0[28]	95.7[81]	—4.3[29]—		85.3[28]	4.0[15]	0.8[28]	5.8	197,978[12]	93,214[25]	98.5[12]	29,235[23]	103,628[25]	Italy
76.9	48.6	35.2	...	...	...	...	2.4[38]	4.3	12.9	5,286	...	136.4[12]	...	6,989[86]	Jamaica
94.0[1]	...	74.7	61.2[1]	—38.8[1]—		89.2[40]	4.9[40]	0.7[40]	8.8	1,603,632[33]	144,120[33]	28.7[12]	...	86,544[33]	Japan
94.0[81]	...	93.0[29]	96.0[81]	...	...	...	5.0	0.5	...	354[16]	...	82.5[16]	...	...	Jersey
77.2	77.3	55.4[81]	15.7	—84.3—		...	...	...	5.9[33]	4,200[33]	4,206[10, 33]	60.2[19]	820[18]	[19]	Jordan
50.0	...	...	...	—41.0—		...	...	...	6.0	...	6,125[12]	...	...	...	Kazakhstan
...	...	...	...	...	...	...	...	...	5.6[33]	...	828[12, 19]	...	85[18]	[19]	Kenya
33.1	23.7[55]	53.3	...	...	...	...	...	...	5.0	...	...	...	...	...	Kiribati
...	...	...	...	...	...	...	...	...	...	...	...	...	...	...	Korea, North
74.1	49.9[81]	51.3	...	...	...	80.6	2.3	1.5	11.5[33]	750,000[23]	69,300[33]	9.8[23]	36,801[16]	48,487[33]	Korea, South
53.9[17]	99.5[17]	...	35.9[17]	—64.1[17]—		...	4.0[17]	1.8[17]	3.2[33]	9,735[18, 45]	4,716[33]	23.5[16, 45]	370[16]	408[33]	Kuwait
...	...	...	...	...	...	...	...	...	5.9	...	1,232	...	...	...	Kyrgyzstan
...	...	...	...	...	...	...	...	...	3.0	...	...	...	...	...	Laos
...	...	...	...	...	...	...	...	...	6.3[10]	...	312	...	...	...	Latvia
...	93.4	82.9	...	...	...	...	...	...	3.3	...	4,938[16, 19]	...	...	[19]	Lebanon
...	...	...	...	...	...	...	...	...	18.9[12]	...	...	...	52[18]	...	Lesotho
...	...	...	...	...	...	...	2.3[15]	1.7	2.2[23]	...	...	...	...	...	Liberia
70.1[49]	72.1[49]	40.6[49]	40.6[49]	—59.4[49]—		...	3.3[49]	1.8[49]	11.8[12]	...	...	...	...	...	Libya
96.5	96.6	86.7	90.2	—9.8—		102.0	4.5[11]	0.6[11]	...	6,858[11]	299[25]	...	...	193[25]	Liechtenstein
95.7	...	...	...	...	...	58.5	...	...	8.9	8,200[33]	610[33]	147[33]	...	...	Lithuania
99.4	...	99.4	93.0[38]	—7.0[38]—		114.2	5.4[17]	0.5[17]	7.5[12]	4,020[33]	2,352[25, 33]	53.6[12]	91	1,184[25, 33]	Luxembourg
98.0	99.8	97.9	...	...	...	...	3.1	1.3	...	15,668[33]	1,427[33]	20.2	1,003[11]	495[33]	Macau
72.0	96.4	56.3	...	...	...	68.6	...	...	6.6	6,583	...	...	953	...	Macedonia
...	...	...	...	...	...	...	...	...	1.2[12]	...	24[16, 48]	...	...	8.9[16, 48]	Madagascar
23.6	22.8[17]	33.4[17]	33.0[67]	67.0[67]		...	1.9	1.7	3.8[33]	...	...	...	...	...	Malawi
65.0[17]	64.4[17]	...	66.4[17]	4.4[17]	29.2[17]	...	2.3[38, 81]	2.6[38, 81]	4.0[33]	...	8,809[18]	...	...	960[18]	Malaysia
...	53.4[15]	...	43.2	—56.8—		...	4.4	1.5	8.9	680[16]	...	54.6[16]	...	...	Maldives
3.8	3.6	1.3	...	...	...	...	2.6	2.2	4.0[12]	10,025[22]	...	...	...	...	Mali
98.0	98.0	98.8	98.0	15.4[67]	6.1[67]	...	3.2[67]	1.3[67]	...	4,605[33]	...	22.5[33]	2,024[33]	...	Malta
49.8[40]	56.0[40]	43.7[40]	28.6	—71.4—		...	...	...	10.4[95]	...	...	...	...	...	Marshall Islands
94.1	90.2	89.0	41.8[46]	—58.2[46]—		...	3.2	0.9	4.9[23]	1,528[12]	...	55.8[12]	...	56.2[28]	Martinique
...	...	...	...	...	...	...	...	...	7.9[20]	...	42[19, 20]	...	...	[19]	Mauritania
94.7	96.2	63.3	63.3	—36.7—		...	3.6[1]	1.4[1]	7.8[33]	4,592[22]	921[12]	48.7	552[10]	297[12]	Mauritius
42.5	32.2	6.7	54.4	—45.6—		...	2.2	2.2	...	616[18]	...	21.3[18]	...	...	Mayotte
79.4	87.5	45.0[17]	60.9	2.7	36.4	...	3.4	1.5	5.4[33]	...	...	...	61,386[28]	...	Mexico
40.0	28.3	...	8.0	—92.0—		...	...	...	...	...	...	...	...	...	Micronesia
...	...	...	...	...	...	...	...	...	6.9[12]	...	1,594[11]	...	...	...	Moldova
100.0	100.0	96.2	98.4[50]	—1.6[50]—		...	2.8	0.8	...	...	...	...	...	...	Monaco
0.3	47.5	...	...	...	...	...	...	...	5.8[23]	...	112[12]	...	...	176[18]	Mongolia
30.5[2]	37.2[2]	50.2[2]	...	...	...	...	2.7	2.2	4.7[33]	51,911[18]	2,156[15]	65.9[18]	1,014[15]	457[15]	Morocco
12.7	4.2	...	...	...	...	...	...	...	13.2[12]	...	247[80]	...	...	121[80]	Mozambique
...	...	...	...	...	...	...	...	...	1.5[31]	1,193[58]	...	...	1,483[58]	...	Myanmar (Burma)
...	...	...	...	...	...	...	...	...	1.8[12]	...	...	...	...	...	Namibia
...	49.2	...	...	...	...	...	3.6[99]	1.6[99]	...	...	...	...	...	...	Nauru
47.7	30.2	6.1	...	...	...	...	3.7	2.0	8.2[31]	...	...	...	...	...	Nepal
100.0	98.0	100.0	90.0[16]	—10.0[16]—		...	4.1[15]	0.7[15]	5.9	87,696[33]	35,616[17, 25]	70.0[11]	15,091[23]	49,968[23, 25]	Netherlands, The
79.6[28]	96.9[28]	82.0[28]	...	...	...	...	4.2[28]	1.0[28]	9.5[40]	547[12]	...	150.2[12]	361[33]	...	Netherlands Antilles
90.1	85.3	70.9	76.7	—23.3—		...	3.3	1.2	4.9[40]	772	46[18]	57.1	1[20]	...	New Caledonia
92.7[30]	...	97.1[30]	...	...	...	126.3[16, 43]	5.6	0.5	4.2[32]	12,937[95]	1,396[95]	61.2[23]	...	2,568[95]	New Zealand
27.9	40.9	19.3	19.2	—80.8—		...	2.2	2.1	3.1	...	569[12, 19]	...	...	[19]	Nicaragua
...	...	...	...	...	...	...	...	...	2.3[12]	...	...	...	...	...	Niger
...	81.3	7.0	...	...	...	...	1.4	3.0	1.5[12]	31,038[46]	...	...	1,592[17]	...	Nigeria
91.0	94.1[17]	79.5	81.7	—18.3—		...	3.6	1.1	...	...	...	...	...	...	Northern Mariana Islands
97.5[38]	...	94.6	86.8[38]	—13.2[17]—		103.5	4.1	0.6	3.6[12]	17,748[95]	2,388[33]	82.2[12]	4,954[15]	2,272[33]	Norway
...	...	...	...	...	...	...	...	...	4.0	1,043[18]	...	...	266[18]	...	Oman
20.3	30.6	25.1	...	...	...	...	1.9	3.3	3.8[31]	...	...	...	...	...	Pakistan[101]

Housing and construction (continued)

country	housing stock														
	year	dwelling units[a]	median age[b] (years)	decade built (percent)					tenure[c] (percent)			construction of exterior walls (percent)			
				1949 or earlier	1950–59	1960–69	1970–79	1980 or later	owned	rented	collective, vacant, other	traditional materials	sawn/framed wood	masonry or cement	other
Palau	1990	3,312	12.8	2.1	6.0	16.8	30.6	44.5	76.4	23.6	—	0.0	27.9	26.5	45.6
Panama	1990[105]	524,284[21]	18.0[17]	47.4[17]	12.8[17]	18.1[17]	—21.7[17]—		75.5	15.7	8.8	16.9	—	81.2	1.9
Papua New Guinea	1980	556,519[24]	...	...	...	...	...	...	40.0[50]	—60.0[50]—		...	...	...	...
Paraguay	1982	868,284[42]	21.1	—56.0—		17.0	—27.0—		80.4	10.5	9.1	21.5	29.7	47.6	1.2
Peru	1993	4,427,517	...	—30.9[28]—		—69.1[28]—			82.0	11.0	7.0	55.7	7.0	35.7	1.6
Philippines	1990	11,380,000[24]	...	—78.5[38]—		—21.5[38]—			83.0	8.0	9.0	35.3	27.3	33.5	3.9
Poland	1988	11,967,021	...	35.0[87]	—33.7[107]—		—31.3[47]—		35.2	64.3	0.9	—14.1[55]—		—85.9[55]—	
Portugal	1981	4,188,655[12]	33.7	—53.3—		17.5	—29.2—		56.7	38.8	4.6	—	0.7	61.0	38.3
Puerto Rico	1990	1,188,985	18.0	9.0	12.8	22.9	29.5	25.8	72.1	27.9	—	—	15.1	83.6	1.3
Qatar	1986	64,543	...	...	...	...	...	...	21.9	72.0	6.1	...	...	...	...
Réunion	1990	157,853	14.3	—47.6[64]—		19.9[63]	—32.5[79]—		56.3	35.7	8.0	40.0	—	41.0	19.0
Romania	1992	7,632,000	...	...	...	...	...	...	78.6	20.8	0.6	...	...	...	...
Russia	1989	40,246,000[24]	...	...	...	...	...	...	...	...	...	...	...	...	...
Rwanda	1978	1,055,950[24]	...	...	...	...	...	...	95.3	1.7	3.0	88.6	7.9	1.3	2.2
St. Kitts and Nevis	1980	11,615[24]	24.2	—63.5—		17.9	—14.7—		54.7	29.5	15.8	—	76.2	21.3	2.5
St. Lucia	1991	33,079	13.5	—17.0—		12.4	26.0	44.6	72.4	26.8	0.8	—	53.4	46.1	0.5
St. Vincent and the Grenadines	1980	27,110	...	—	...	...	...	...	72.1	16.0	11.9	—	53.8	42.9	3.3
San Marino	1979	8,384[11]	...	...	...	...	...	...	73.5	21.9	4.6	...	...	...	...
São Tomé and Príncipe	1981	30,056	...	...	...	...	...	...	...	...	...	2.2	29.8	67.2	0.8
Saudi Arabia	...	...	...	...	...	...	...	...	...	...	...	...	...	...	...
Senegal	1955[48, 109]	13,000	...	...	...	...	...	...	—84.6—		15.4	...	...	...	...
Seychelles	1987	15,050	...	...	...	...	...	...	63.7	25.1	11.2	1.0	40.0	52.0	7.0
Sierra Leone	...	...	...	...	...	...	...	...	...	...	...	...	...	...	...
Singapore	1980	513,224	...	—63.2—		—36.8—			55.0	39.6	5.4	4.7	—95.3—		
Slovakia	1991	1,617,829	26.9	17.1[5]	17.3[6]	20.3[7]	25.4[8]	19.9[9]	...	...	...	—	38.0[53]	61.4	0.6
Slovenia	1992	664,505	...	...	...	...	...	...	...	...	...	...	...	...	...
Solomon Islands	1986	43,842[24]	...	...	...	...	...	...	27.4[29]	43.0[29]	29.6[29]	...	...	...	...
Somalia	...	...	...	...	...	...	...	...	...	...	...	...	...	...	...
South Africa	1991	3,599,518[110]	18.6[38]	40.6[38]	24.2[38]	35.2[38]	—	—	54.5	34.0	11.5	...	...	...	...
Spain	1991	11,824,851[21]	39.4[17]	39.2[17, 111]	23.4[17, 112]	18.5[7, 113]	—18.9[17, 47]—		67.5	14.9	17.6	...	...	...	...
Sri Lanka	1981	2,811,406	...	...	...	...	...	...	69.4	10.1	20.5	...	...	...	...
Sudan, The	1983	...	...	...	...	...	...	...	86.2	8.1	5.7	76.5	4.4	16.7	2.4
Suriname	1980	77,744	...	—52.4—		—47.6—			...	...	...	38.9[114]	—61.1[114]—		
Swaziland	1986	122,369	...	...	...	...	...	...	...	...	...	65.9	—34.1—		
Sweden	1990	3,830,037	20.0	33.2	14.2	22.4	22.2	10.6	55.9	40.0	4.1	...	...	...	...
Switzerland	1990	2,800,953	28.5	33.2[89]	15.9[90]	19.4[7]	17.2[8]	14.3[9]	31.3	66.5	2.2	...	...	...	...
Syria	1987	1,836,195	...	—91.3[38]—		—8.7[38]—			81.6[38]	15.5[38]	2.8[38]	...	...	...	...
Taiwan	1990	4,237,174[21]	17.2	6.1[5]	6.7[6]	15.8[7]	42.6[8]	28.8[9]	78.5	12.8	8.7	...	...	...	...
Tajikistan	1989	799,000[24]	...	...	...	...	...	...	...	...	...	...	...	...	...
Tanzania	1978	3,554,793	...	—17.0—		—83.0—			75.4	19.4	5.2	83.0	—	16.3	0.7
Thailand	1990	12,305,197[24]	...	22.0[38]	25.0[38]	53.0[38]	—	—	86.0	11.2	2.8	8.4	68.2	22.3	1.1
Togo	1981	462,694	...	...	...	...	...	...	...	...	...	...	...	...	...
Tonga	1986	15,091	22.5	—59.4[115]—		20.3[116]	—20.3[117]—		82.0	3.5	14.5	35.1[29]	45.4[29]	15.3[29]	4.2[29]
Trinidad and Tobago	1980	314,739[11]	...	—56.3—		14.5	—29.2—		64.6	34.0	1.4	3.3	32.6	53.8	10.3[35]
Tunisia	1984	1,703,279[94]	...	...	...	...	...	...	78.9	12.6	8.5	...	...	...	...
Turkey	1986	10,855,495	8.4	16.2[115]	6.2[119]	19.6[103]	—58.0[105]—		77.2	12.0	10.8	—28.8—		—71.2—	
Turkmenistan	1989	598,000[24]	...	...	...	...	...	...	...	...	...	...	...	...	...
Tuvalu	1979	1,079	...	...	...	...	...	...	81.6	12.1	6.6	64.9	4.2	31.0	—
Uganda	...	...	...	...	...	...	...	...	...	...	...	...	...	...	...
Ukraine	1989	14,057,000[24]	...	...	...	...	...	...	...	...	...	...	...	...	...
United Arab Emirates	1980	153,009	15.0	0.8	1.3	11.4	—86.5—		36.2	45.2	18.6	2.9	7.3	87.3	2.5
United Kingdom[121]	1991	21,897,322	32.6[28]	54.0[28]	13.0[28]	16.6[28]	—16.4[28]—		66.4	33.6	—	...	...	...	...
United States	1990	102,263,678	25.0	32.9[15]	14.0[15]	16.6[15]	—36.5[15]—		64.2	35.8	—	...	...	...	...
Uruguay	1985	852,400	...	...	...	...	...	...	57.6	23.2	19.2	...	...	...	...
Uzbekistan	1989	3,415,000[24]	...	...	...	...	...	...	...	...	...	...	...	...	...
Vanuatu	1979	28,252[23, 24]	...	...	...	...	...	...	40.9[48]	25.7[48]	33.4[48]	61.4	7.7	13.6	17.2
Venezuela	1990	3,534,507	...	...	...	...	...	...	75.8	13.9	10.3	14.6	0.5	84.9	—
Vietnam	1989	12,958,041[24]	...	...	...	...	...	...	...	...	...	...	...	...	...
Virgin Islands (U.S.)	1990	39,290	14.7	10.0[17]	8.9[17]	42.7[17]	—38.4[17]—		44.6	55.4	—	...	...	...	...
West Bank	1992	119,165[67]	12.2	8.0	12.7	24.6	26.2	28.6	86.2[68]	11.5[68]	2.3[68]	23.0	—	75.3	1.7
Western Sahara	1982	19,559	...	...	...	...	...	...	32.2[51]	62.3[51]	5.5[51]	...	...	...	...
Western Samoa	1981	33,402	...	...	...	...	...	...	80.1	2.0	17.9	62.3	24.4	8.6	4.7
Yemen[122]	1988[123]	1,701,203	...	...	...	...	...	...	83.9	5.2	10.9	...	...	...	...
Yugoslavia	1981[124]	3,074,000[42]	...	31.1	12.7	26.8	—29.4—		67.1	25.0	7.9	...	—82.6—		17.4
Zaire	1984	5,669,600[24]	...	...	...	...	...	...	47.4[48, 67]	38.3[48, 67]	14.3[48, 67]	52.4[48]	—45.5[48]—		2.1[48]
Zambia	1980	1,128,356	...	...	...	...	...	...	78.8[125]	21.1[125]	...	...	...	...	...
Zimbabwe	1992	2,165,744[24]	...	...	...	...	...	...	65.1[110, 125]	32.6[110, 125]	2.3[110, 125]	55.9[125, 126]	—44.1[125, 126]—		

[1]1983. [2]Urban only. [3]1989–90. [4]Data refer to buildings. [5]1945 or earlier. [6]1946–60. [7]1961–70. [8]1971–80. [9]1981 or later. [10]Percentage of net material product. [11]1990. [12]1991. [13]1962 or earlier. [14]1963–69. [15]1985. [16]1987. [17]1980. [18]1986. [19]Residential includes nonresidential. [20]1984. [21]Occupied dwellings only. [22]Average annual gain in housing stock during intercensal interval. [23]1989. [24]Data refer to households. [25]Volume in cubic metres. [26]1939 or earlier. [27]1940–59. [28]1981. [29]1976. [30]1971. [31]1992–93. [32]1990–91. [33]1993. [34]Stucco. [35]Includes wood and brick, and wood and concrete. [36]1946–61. [37]1962–70. [38]1970. [39]1983–85 average. [40]1988. [41]1991–92. [42]1992. [43]Average size of dwelling unit in year to which new dwellings and floor area data refer. [44]1986–87. [45]Data refer to compound dwellings. [46]1982. [47]1971 or later. [48]Capital city only. [49]1973. [50]1975. [51]1934–45. [52]1946–59. [53]Includes prefabricated units. [54]Includes corrugated steel. [55]1978. [56]1950 or earlier. [57]1951–60. [58]1987–88. [59]1977. [60]1948 or earlier. [61]1949–61. [62]1962–74. [63]1975–81. [64]1974 or earlier. [65]1975–82. [66]1983 or later. [67]1967. [68]Excludes refugee camps. [69]Former West Germany. [70]1949–57. [71]1958–68. [72]1969–78. [73]1979 or later. [74]1979. [75]1952 or earlier. [76]1953–62. [77]1963–72. [78]1973–81.

physical amenities (percent)			sewage disposal (percent)			spaceb			construction industry (1992)						country
									percent of GDP	new residentiald			new nonresidentiald		
piped water	electricity	inside toilet or WC	closed public sewer or septic tank	open public sewer	other	average area (sq m)	rooms per dwelling unit	persons per room		total no. of dwellings	floor area ('000 sq m)	years to replace nat'l stock	number of units	floor area ('000 sq m)	
87.9	75.7[17]	75.2	44.3	—55.7—		...	2.6	1.8	11.0[15]	...	...	...	...	...	Palau
80.7	65.7[17]	74.3[17]	44.2	—55.8—		...	2.8	1.6	5.3	2,496[42]	492[42]	34.6[16]	90[15]	276[42]	Panama
50.0	56.0	40.0	...	...	...	...	...	...	5.3	587[18]	...	...	...	...	Papua New Guinea
...	...	26.4	...	...	...	...	2.2[106]	2.4[106]	5.8	...	61[15]	...	2,715[16]	365[16]	Paraguay
46.7	54.9	35.7	40.0	22.2	37.8	42.4[28]	2.6[28]	2.0[28]	6.6	...	952[18]	...	...	...	Peru
38.8	55.1	35.0[17]	67.6	14.4	18.0	...	2.4[106]	2.3[106]	5.1	...	3,862	...	2,807[15]	4,288	Philippines
84.3	96.2[55]	68.9	67.0[55]	—33.0[55]—		55.6[20]	3.2	1.0	8.6	129,492[12]	13,856[16]	56.9[23]	38,600	...	Poland
99.1[12]	99.4[12]	78.1[12]	75.5	—24.5—		75.4[23, 43]	5.0[35]	0.8	7.5	63,199[33]	6,156[42]	62.5[12]	4,292[33]	1,772[42]	Portugal
95.6	97.4[81]	94.7	95.7	—4.3—		...	4.8[17]	0.8[17]	2.1[40]	10,212[42]	1,872[42]	82.8[16]	900[15]	41.0[15]	Puerto Rico
...	93.2	...	—50.5—		49.5	...	4.1	1.3	4.1	12,240	391[18]	58.9[16]	1,416	168[18]	Qatar
81.0	95.0	70.0	52.4[46]	—47.6[46]—		...	3.9	1.0	6.1[11]	7,272[33]	...	17.6[11]	...	...	Réunion
...	48.6[108]	...	12.2[108]	—87.8[108]—		89.6[43]	2.6	1.4	5.0[12]	60,400[23]	5,409[23]	98.6[23]	...	...	Romania
...	...	...	...	...	...	...	...	...	9.1[12]	...	31,500	...	...	...	Russia
...	...	...	...	...	...	...	...	...	7.1[12]	435[20]	60[28]	...	63[20]	34[28]	Rwanda
46.3	57.5	33.5	31.8[25]	—68.2[25]—		...	3.0	1.1	13.5[12]	171[22]	...	68.0[22]	...	...	St. Kitts and Nevis
64.7	72.9	35.7	35.7	—64.3—		...	3.4	1.2	9.0[33]	471[4, 16]	92	57.2[4, 16]	121[18]	43	St. Lucia
95.0[1]	...	...	22.0[1]	—78.0[1]—		...	2.8	1.8	10.4	465[16, 19]	81[19]	...	[19]	[19]	St. Vincent and the Grenadines
99.8	100.0	98.3	98.3	—1.7—		...	4.5	0.8	...	161[33]	...	64.0	102[33]	...	San Marino
...	22.0	9.2	9.8	...	...	...	...	...	6.2	...	...	...	...	...	São Tomé and Príncipe
...	...	...	...	...	...	...	...	...	8.5	...	16,078[12]	...	2,205[12]	...	Saudi Arabia
87.7	95.9	...	...	...	...	...	2.3	1.5	3.2	...	257[16]	...	34[16]	33[16]	Senegal
77.0	75.8	95.0	33.1[59]	—66.9[59]—		...	4.1	1.1	4.2[11]	4,802[19, 59]	...	...	46[18]	[19]	Seychelles
...	...	...	...	...	...	...	...	...	1.4[33]	...	...	...	...	...	Sierra Leone
90.6[38]	98.3	63.6[38]	63.6[38]	—36.4[38]—		...	1.8[38]	2.5[38]	6.7[33]	18,948[33]	4,222	36.2[11]	1,991[12]	2,730	Singapore
91.8	...	80.1	87.6	—12.4—		71.7	2.9	1.1	7.7[12]	...	1,147[12]	...	...	...	Slovakia
97.4	99.5	86.8	...	...	...	69.0	3.0	1.0	4.6[12]	6,492	646	102	...	18[12]	Slovenia
92.7[29]	79.6[29]	89.2	89.2[29]	—10.8[29]—		10.8[29]	2.3[29]	2.0[29]	4.0[12]	...	...	...	...	...	Solomon Islands
...	...	...	...	...	...	...	...	...	3.8[12]	...	...	...	...	...	Somalia
...	...	...	...	...	...	117.6[43]	3.4[38]	...	3.0	39,266[23]	4,619[23]	34.5[23]	...	1,316[23]	South Africa
98.7	00.2	07.1	07.9[17]	—12.1[17]—		86.6	4.4[38]	...	8.2[33]	237,637[33]	...	43.9[12]	...	...	Spain
18.2	14.9	4.7	4.7	—95.3—		18.6[38]	2.5	2.1	7.1[12]	59,637[18]	...	47.2[18]	...	...	Sri Lanka
29.4	9.9	70.2[2, 108]	2.6[2, 108]	–97.4[2, 108]–		...	2.2[108]	2.5[108]	5.4[41]	...	...	...	...	...	Sudan, The
62.9	82.0	40.4	19.6[114]	—80.4[114]—		...	2.1	1.9	7.5	...	355[15, 25]	...	161[15]	...	Suriname
42.5	11.6	21.4	...	...	...	...	...	...	2.4[12]	...	...	...	28[20]	...	Swaziland
99.0[15]	96.2[17]	98.0	96.3[17]	—3.7[17]—		...	3.4	0.6	6.7	57,319	...	57.3[12]	...	3,818[20]	Sweden
100.0[17]	...	93.3[17]	92.2[18]	—	7.8[17]	93.0	3.7	0.6	8.4[11]	35,422	...	84.6[12]	8,109[18]	...	Switzerland
40.2[1]	41.7[1]	...	36.0[1]	—64.0[1]—		93.0	3.0	2.0	3.9	18,960[40]	2,390[40]	33.0[16]	...	339[40]	Syria
79.4[17]	99.7[17]	94.2[17]	69.3[17]	...	...	30.5	4.1	1.2	5.5[33]	...	47,533[19, 33]	...	...	[19]	Taiwan
...	...	...	...	...	...	...	...	...	14.7[11]	...	400	...	...	...	Tajikistan
37.2	6.3	...	...	...	...	...	2.5	1.9	3.0[12]	...	...	...	...	...	Tanzania
29.7	89.7	40.9[81]	40.9[29]	9.8[29]	49.3[29]	...	1.6	2.7	6.8[12]	...	16,343[12]	...	...	13,499[12]	Thailand
4.1[82]	10.3[82]	...	—	—100.0[82]—		...	1.8	3.4	3.5[12]	...	...	...	...	...	Togo
01.0[00]	20.9[00]	42.3[20]	11.2[25]	—88.8[29]—		...	...	...	4.3[118]	...	...	...	...	...	Tonga
64.3	83.3	41.1	41.0	—59.0—		...	3.3	1.4	7.7[33]	...	211[12]	...	69[18]	27.2[12]	Trinidad and Tobago
26.4	63.4	43.3	69.2[23]	—30.8[23]—		...	1.9	2.4	3.9	34,566[16]	...	43.8[16]	...	...	Tunisia
68.0	56.8	70.6	42.0	52.0	6.0	110.5[43]	2.4[15]	2.2[38]	7.2[33]	232,018[11]	33,169[11]	43.3[23]	3,933[18]	16,165[12]	Turkey
...	...	...	...	...	...	...	...	...	22.7[12]	...	20,754[19, 42]	...	...	[19]	Turkmenistan
65.4	7.4	37.3	...	...	...	...	...	...	14.6[11]	...	...	...	...	...	Tuvalu
...	...	...	...	...	...	...	...	...	6.4[12]	...	...	...	65[106]	26.8[106]	Uganda
...	...	...	...	...	...	...	...	...	13.8[12]	...	14,454[12]	...	...	...	Ukraine
30.9[120]	24.2[120]	84.5	...	...	...	...	2.8	1.8	8.8[33]	...	...	...	133[20]	...	United Arab Emirates
...	...	99.8	...	...	...	...	5.0	0.5	6.2	172,908[33]	...	122.2[12]	...	...	United Kingdom[121]
00.5	90.9	90.9	99.2	—0.8—		147.1	5.2	0.5	3.9[12]	1,284,000[33]	214,900[18]	78.2	...	140,100[18]	United States
89.2	81.7	73.0	...	92.0	...	...	3.4	1.7	4.5	...	160[15]	...	105[15]	21.4[15]	Uruguay
...	...	...	...	...	...	...	...	...	8.3	...	7,000	...	...	...	Uzbekistan
39.2[23]	14.2	27.5[23]	...	...	...	...	...	...	5.8[11]	...	5.7[18]	...	...	15.3[18]	Vanuatu
86.2	89.8	84.4[28]	80.2	—19.8—		53.5[43]	4.2	1.3	7.3	91,666[18]	4,904[18]	29.5[18]	678[18]	1,067[18]	Venezuela
...	...	...	...	...	...	...	...	...	6.8[33]	...	...	...	53[20]	59.3[20]	Vietnam
96.3[17]	98.1[17]	86.0[17]	93.6[17]	—6.4[17]—		...	4.3	0.6	...	...	...	...	262[17]	...	Virgin Islands (U.S.)
75.2[15]	75.3	98.4	...	...	...	127.2[43]	2.4[15]	2.7[15]	14.1[16]	5,740[12]	730[12]	20.8[12]	...	175.8[12]	West Bank
78.5	95.3	...	...	...	...	...	4.5	1.2	4.4[23]	...	...	...	...	...	Western Sahara
80.7	37.7	71.0	16.6	—83.4—		...	3.9[29, 109]	1.5[29, 109]	1.9[23]	132[15]	...	...	118[15]	...	Western Samoa
5.7[50]	4.6[50]	...	...	...	...	...	2.0[50]	2.8[50]	5.0	...	1,988[15]	...	...	...	Yemen[122]
67.8	95.7	53.3	...	...	...	67.2[42]	2.9[42]	1.2[42]	7.1	20,013	...	51.3[12]	2,805[12]	2,073[25]	Yugoslavia
...	...	...	...	...	...	...	...	...	5.5[12]	...	20[15]	...	73[15]	39[15]	Zaire
12.4[125]	27.5[82]	15.1[125]	...	...	82.3[125]	...	1.9[125]	2.6[125]	5.0[12]	...	...	...	...	...	Zambia
...	9.3[125, 126]	...	...	...	...	...	2.8[125]	1.9[125]	1.9	...	...	...	...	...	Zimbabwe

[79]1982 or later. [80]1974. [81]Minimum. [82]1960. [83]1947 or earlier. [84]1948–83. [85]1961–71. [86]Factory space only. [87]1944 or earlier. [88]1945–60. [89]1946 or earlier. [90]1947–60. [91]Peninsular Malaysia only. [92]1957 or earlier. [93]1958–67. [94]Includes second residences. [95]1994. [96]1960–68. [97]1969 or later. [98]Dwellings of indigenous population only. [99]1961. [100]Lagos only. [101]Excludes Islāmābad, North-West Frontier, and federally administered tribal lands. [102]1947–65. [103]1966–75. [104]1976 or later. [105]Excludes areas under U.S. military control in the provinces of Panama and Colón. [106]1972. [107]1945–70. [108]1966. [109]European-style dwellings only. [110]White, Coloured, and Asian dwellings only; excludes Bantu. [111]1940 or earlier. [112]1941–60. [113]1988–89. [114]1964. [115]1955 or earlier. [116]1956–66. [117]1967 or later. [118]1993–94. [119]1956–65. [120]1968. [121]Excludes Northern Ireland. [122]Former Yemen Arab Republic only. [123]Combined from 1986 and 1988 census data. [124]Data refer to Yugoslavia as constituted prior to 1991. [125]1969. [126]Bantu dwellings only.

Household budgets and consumption

This table provides international data on household income, on the consumption expenditure of households for goods and services, and on the principal object of such expenditure (in most countries), food consumption (by kind). For purposes of this compilation, income comprises pretax monetary payments and payment in kind. The first part of the table provides data on distribution of income by households and by sources of income; the second part analyzes the largest portion of income use—consumption expenditure. Such expenditure is defined as the purchase of goods and services to satisfy current wants and needs. This definition excludes income expended on taxes, debts, savings and investments, and insurance policies. The third and last part of the table focuses on food, which usually, and often by a wide margin, represents the largest share of consumer spending worldwide. The data provided include daily available calories per capita and consumption of major food groups.

For both sources of income and consumption expenditure, the primary basis of analysis for most countries is the household, an economic unit that can be as small as a single person or as large as an extended family. For some of the countries that do not compile information by household, the table provides data on personal income and personal expenditure—*i.e.*, the income and expenditure of all the individuals constituting a society's households. When no expenditure data at all is available, the table reports the weights of each major class of goods and services making up a given country's consumer (or retail) price index (CPI). The weighting of the components of the CPI usually reflects household spending patterns within the country or its principal urban or rural areas.

The data on distribution of income show, collectively for an entire country, the proportion of total income earned (occasionally, expended) by households constituting the lowest quintile and highest decile (poorest 20% and wealthiest 10%) within the country. These figures show the degree to which either group represents a disproportionate share of poverty or wealth.

The data on sources of income illuminate patterns of economic structure in the gaining of an income. They indicate, for example, that in poor, agrarian countries income often derives largely from self-employment (usually farming) or that in industrial countries, with well-developed systems of salaried employment and social welfare, income derives mainly from wages and salaries and secondarily from transfer payments (*see* note a). Because household sizes and numbers of income earners vary so greatly internationally, and because the frequency and methodology of household and CPI surveys do not permit single-year comparisons for more than a few countries at once, no summary of total *household* income or expenditure was possible. Instead, U.S. dollar figures are supplied for *per capita* private final consumption expenditure (for a single, recent year) that are more comparable internationally and refer to the same date. The figures on distribution of consumption expenditure by end use reveal patterns of personal and family use of disposable income and indicate, inter alia, that in developing countries food may absorb 50% or more of disposable income, while in the larger household budgets of the developed countries, by contrast, food purchases may account for only 20–30% of spending. Each category of expenditure betrays similar complexities of local habit, necessity, and aspiration.

The reader should exercise caution when using these data to make inter-country comparisons. Most of the information comes from single-country surveys, which often differ markedly in their coverage of economically or demographically stratified groups, in sample design, or in the methods

Household budgets and consumption

country	income (latest)						consumption expenditure						
	percent received by		by source (percent)				per capita private final, U.S.$ 1993	by kind or end use (percent of household or personal budget; latest)					
	lowest 20% of households	highest 10% of households	wages, salaries	self-employment	transfer payments[a]	other[b]		food[c]	housing[d]	clothing[e]	health care	energy, water	education
Afghanistan	...	...	20.7	28.0	8.2	43.1	...	33.9	3.0	...	1.1	0.7	...
Albania	...	...	...	...	...	...	680[1]	...	...	...	...	...	...
Algeria	6.9	31.7	...	...	...	...	800	52.3	6.7[2]	8.6	2.8	[2]	[3]
American Samoa	...	...	...	...	...	...	1,880[4]	44.3	23.4[5]	5.8	...	...	...
Andorra	...	...	...	...	...	...	...	...	...	...	...	...	...
Angola	...	...	...	...	...	...	420[6]	...	...	...	...	...	...
Antigua and Barbuda	...	...	...	...	...	...	2,170[7]	*42.9*	*23.3*	*7.5*	...	5.5	...
Argentina	*4.4*	*35.2*	53.9	31.5	1.5	12.7	6,310	38.2	9.3	8.0	7.9	9.0	2.6
Armenia	...	...	65.6	—	34.4	—	500	47.3	...	17.4	...	...	...
Aruba	...	...	...	...	...	...	...	26.9	9.9	8.4	2.9	8.5	1.9
Australia	4.8	28.1	59.7	15.8	16.3	8.2	10,130	18.7	18.5	5.6	7.1	2.2	1.6
Austria	*4.0*	*28.7*	55.7	[8]	24.4	19.9[8]	12,520	18.8	11.8	8.5	4.5	5.1	0.3
Azerbaijan	...	...	81.0	—	19.0	—	380	...	...	...	...	...	...
Bahamas, The	3.6	32.1	...	...	...	...	3,950[6]	19.8	19.2	7.2	3.4	4.3	7.8
Bahrain	...	...	...	...	...	...	2,800[1]	32.4	21.2	5.9	2.3	2.2	2.3
Bangladesh	9.5[9]	24.6[9]	26.1	50.8	0.5	22.6	170	63.3	8.8	5.9	1.1	8.4	1.2
Barbados	*7.0*	*44.0*[10]	...	...	...	...	4,540[11]	*43.2*	*13.1*	*5.1*	...	*6.2*	...
Belarus	...	...	63.4	11.1	24.5	1.0	1,400	29.0	2.7	...	...	...	...
Belgium	*7.9*[12]	*21.5*[12]	47.2	14.5	24.2	14.1	13,060	18.3	11.4	7.0	10.5	6.2	[3]
Belize	...	...	*84.1*	—	*15.9*	—	1,350[11]	51.5[13]	2.3	11.1	3.4	6.0	1.5
Benin	*8.0*	*39.0*	26.3	—	73.7	—	360	37.0	10.0	14.0	5.0	2.0	4.0
Bermuda	7.2	24.7	72.2	6.7	2.4	18.7	12,690[14]	14.6	27.7	4.9	7.6	3.3	3.8
Bhutan	...	...	...	...	...	...	220	*72.3*	...	*21.2*	...	*3.7*	...
Bolivia	5.6[9]	31.7[9]	...	...	...	...	620	39.4	7.8	5.1	2.1	4.6	0.3
Bosnia and Herzegovina	...	...	53.2	12.0	18.2	16.6	1,890[1]	44.7	1.6	8.3	3.4	7.8	[3]
Botswana	3.7	42.9	73.3	15.4	10.8	0.4	1,290[6]	39.5[13]	13.3[2]	5.6	2.3	[2]	[3]
Brazil	2.1[15]	51.3[15]	...	...	...	...	2,250	35.0	9.0	10.0	6.0	2.0	5.0
Brunei	...	...	...	...	...	...	...	*45.1*	*5.0*[2]	*6.1*	...	[2]	[3]
Bulgaria	10.4[15]	21.9[15]	58.3	3.8	27.3	10.6	760	43.4	1.1	4.7	6.7	4.4	[16]
Burkina Faso	...	...	...	...	...	...	220	38.7[17]	5.1[17]	4.4[17]	5.2[17]	13.7[17]	[3]
Burundi	...	...	...	...	...	...	130	59.6[17]	4.4[17]	11.1[17]	...	5.8[17]	...
Cambodia	...	...	...	...	...	...	...	...	...	...	...	...	...
Cameroon	...	...	41.4	52.6	3.0	3.0	620	24.0	13.0	7.0	12.0	3.0	9.0
Canada	5.7	24.1	63.9	6.7	17.7	11.7	10,040	13.4	24.5[2]	5.3	4.7	[2]	3.1
Cape Verde	...	...	...	...	...	...	880[1]	60.0	8.5	2.5	0.5	4.9	[16]
Central African Republic	...	...	...	...	...	...	350	70.5[17]	0.6[17]	9.5[17]	1.0[17]	6.5[17]	...
Chad	*8.0*	*30.0*	...	...	...	...	180	45.3[17]	...	3.5[17]	11.9[17]	5.8[17]	...
Chile	3.7[15]	48.9[15]	*40.8*	...	*8.0*	*51.2*	2,060	27.9	15.2	22.5	...	...	...
China	6.4[15]	24.6[15]	79.8[19]	—	20.2[19]	—	180	53.8[13, 19]	2.3[19]	13.7[19]	2.2[19]	3.7[19]	2.3[19]
Colombia	3.6[15]	39.5[15]	45.1	35.4	14.2	5.3	1,050	38.9	11.2	[6]	5.6	1.3	1.6
Comoros	...	...	*25.6*	*64.5*	*8.7*	*1.2*	430[1]	56.0	...	10.0	5.0	14.4	...
Congo	*7.0*	*43.5*	...	...	...	...	835	37.0	6.0	6.0	6.0	3.0	8.0
Costa Rica	4.0[15]	34.1[15]	61.0	22.6	9.6	6.8	1,490	39.1	12.1[2]	9.4	3.7	[2]	[3]
Côte d'Ivoire	7.3[9]	26.9[9]	44.9	49.9	— 5.2	—	390	39.0	4.0	9.0	9.0	1.0	6.0
Croatia	...	...	40.2	40.8	12.1	6.9	5,050[1]	37.8	2.9	8.6	4.3	7.6	[3]
Cuba	...	...	57.3	...	...	42.7	1,510[6]	26.7	...	...	...	2.5	...
Cyprus	*7.9*[19]	...	76.3	5.9	14.4	3.4	6,500[11]	22.7	5.5	10.0	3.1	1.3	1.4
Czech Republic	10.0[20]	21.8[20]	49.8	...	27.4	22.8[8]	1,710	26.1	5.5[2]	7.3	[21]	[2]	...
Denmark	3.5	25.6	61.0	14.1	24.9	...	12,230	18.4	22.7	5.3	2.3	5.5	2.2
Djibouti	...	...	*51.6*	*36.0*	*10.5*	*1.9*	1,030[1]	50.3	6.4	1.7	2.4	13.1	...
Dominica	...	...	...	...	...	...	1,800[6]	43.1	16.1	6.5	...	5.4	...
Dominican Republic	4.2[15]	39.6[15]	*41.7*	*31.8*	*1.5*	*25.0*	840	46.0	10.0	3.0	8.0	5.0	3.0
Ecuador	*2.9*	*51.5*	15.4	76.1	5.2	3.3	930	36.7	3.7	9.6	4.6	1.2	[16]
Egypt	*5.8*	*33.2*	...	...	...	...	510	49.0	6.0	11.0	3.0	3.0	6.0
El Salvador	*5.5*[12]	*29.5*[12]	...	...	...	...	1,120	37.0[19]	12.1[19]	6.7[19]	4.2[19]	3.6[19]	3.7[19]

employed for collection, classification, and tabulation of data. Further, the reference period of the data varies greatly; while a significant portion of the data is from 1980 or later, information for some countries dates from the 1970s. This older information is typeset in italic. Finally, intercountry comparisons of annual personal consumption expenditure may be misleading because of the distortions of price and purchasing power present when converting a national currency unit into U.S. dollars.

The table's food consumption data include total daily available calories per capita (food supply), which amounts to domestic production and imports minus exports, animal feed, and nonfood uses, and a percentage breakdown of the major food groups that make up food supply.

The data for daily available calories per capita provide a measure of the nutritional adequacy of each nation's food supply. The following list, based on estimates from the United Nations Food and Agriculture Organization (FAO), indicates the regional variation in recommended daily minimum nutritional requirements, which are defined by factors such as climatic ambience, physical activity, and average body weight: Africa (2,320 calories), formerly Centrally Planned Asia (2,300 calories), Far East (2,240 calories), Latin America (2,360 calories), Near East (2,440 calories).

The breakdown of diet by food groups describes the character of a nation's food supply. A typical breakdown for a low-income country might show a diet with heavy intake of vegetable foods, such as cereals, potatoes, or cassava. In the high-income countries, a relatively larger portion of total calories derives from animal products (meat, eggs, and milk). The reader should note that these data refer to total national *supply* and often do not reflect the differences that may exist within a single country.

In compiling this table, Britannica editors rely on both numerous national reports and principal secondary sources such as the World Bank's *World Development Report* (annual), the International Labour Organisation's *Statistical Sources and Methods, vol. 1 Consumer Price Indices* (2nd ed.), the UN's *Yearbook of National Accounts Statistics* (annual) and *National Accounts Statistics: Compendium of Income Distribution Statistics,* and the FAO's *Food Balance Sheets 1988–90* and *Compendium of Food Consumption Statistics from Household Surveys in Developing Countries* (2 vol.).

The following terms further define the column headings:

a. Includes pensions, family allowances, unemployment payments, remittances from abroad, and social security and related benefits.
b. Includes interest and dividends, rents and royalties, and all other income not reported under the three preceding categories.
c. Includes alcoholic and nonalcoholic beverages and meals away from home when identifiable. Excludes tobacco except as noted.
d. Rent, maintenance of dwellings, and taxes only; excludes energy and water (heat, light, power, and water) and household durables (furniture, appliances, utensils, and household operations), shown separately.
e. Includes footwear.
f. Furniture, appliances, and utensils; usually includes expenditure on household operation.
g. Includes expenditure on cultural activities other than education.
h. May include data not shown separately in preceding categories, including meals away from home (*see* note c).
i. Represents pure fats and oils only.
j. Consists mainly of peas, beans, and lentils; spices; stimulants; alcoholic beverages (when combined with "other"); sugars and honey; and nuts and oilseeds.

transpor-tation, com-munications	household durable goods[f]	recrea-tion[g]	personal effects, other[h]	food consumption: daily available calories per capita (1988–90)	percent of total calories (latest) derived from: cereals	potatoes, cassava	meat, poultry	fish	eggs, milk	fruits, vegeta-bles	fats, oils[i]	other[j]	country
...	...	...	61.3	1,764	75.5	1.2	4.8	—	3.3	2.8	7.9	4.5	Afghanistan
...	...	...	...	2,585	63.4	1.6	5.3	0.2	7.4	3.5	7.7	10.9	Albania
12.0	4.5	4.6[3]	8.5	2,945	55.0	2.5	1.7	0.4	6.5	4.3	14.7	14.9	Algeria
14.9	[5]	...	11.6	...	...	...	...	...	...	...	...	...	American Samoa
...	...	...	...	*3,567*	*23.8*	*5.5*	*18.0*	*1.5*	*9.4*	*6.7*	*15.9*	*19.1*	Andorra
...	...	...	...	1,000	32.5	32.4	4.4	3.0	2.8	3.6	9.9	11.2	Angola
10.0	...	...	*10.8*	2,307	20.9	1.0	16.7	3.0	11.0	7.2	13.0	21.2	Antigua and Barbuda
11.6	...	7.5	5.9	3,068	30.9	5.5	18.1	0.3	9.0	4.1	12.8	19.4	Argentina
...	6.6	...	28.7	...	...	...	...	...	...	...	...	...	Armenia
15.5	0.1	0.1	11.9	...	...	...	...	...	...	...	...	...	Aruba
15.1	7.0	7.5	16.7	3,302	24.3	3.0	19.9	0.8	11.1	4.9	13.6	22.4	Australia
18.5	8.0	7.2	17.3	3,486	19.8	3.3	13.7	0.6	10.5	6.6	22.2	23.2	Austria
...	...	...	...	...	...	...	...	...	...	...	...	...	Azerbaijan
18.9	10.2	5.3	3.9	2,776	25.2	1.9	17.4	1.3	7.6	9.6	9.3	27.6	Bahamas, The
8.5	9.8	6.4	9.0	...	...	...	...	...	...	...	...	...	Bahrain
0.9	...	...	10.4	2,038	82.9	1.3	0.5	0.6	1.2	1.1	5.4	6.9	Bangladesh
4.6	*0.6*	...	*16.2*	3,217	28.1	3.9	13.7	2.5	7.4	3.3	13.4	27.7	Barbados
...	...	...	68.3	...	...	...	...	...	...	...	...	...	Belarus
13.4	10.6	6.8[3]	15.8	[illegible]	10.0	4.7	10.0	1.0	9.1	5.6	21.3	20.7	Belgium
6.5	10.1	2.2	5.4	2,575	32.9	1.9	8.7	0.4	10.9	0.2	11.7	27.3	Belize
14.0	5.0	...	9.0	2,383	35.0	39.0	2.3	0.8	0.9	2.9	7.8	11.3	Benin
7.3	16.6	10.8	3.4	2,960	20.5	2.3	19.7	2.7	8.9	9.5	13.4	23.0	Bermuda
...	*0.7*	...	*2.1*	...	*85.2*	*2.4*	*0.4*	*0.1*	*0.6*	*1.4*	*5.3*	*4.6*	Bhutan
17.7	9.7	2.7	10.6	2,012	41.2	11.2	9.7	0.1	2.5	8.4	9.2	17.6	Bolivia
6.0	4.1	3.5[3]	2.3	...	...	...	...	...	...	...	...	...	Bosnia and Herzegovina
13.1	14.0	8.3[3]	3.9	2,260	62.7	0.8	4.0	0.3	7.1	1.4	5.5	18.2	Botswana
8.0	8.0	...	17.0	2,730	34.4	6.4	6.8	0.4	6.4	5.0	15.0	25.5	Brazil
17.2	*8.3*	*8.9*[3]	*9.4*	2,859	47.6	1.0	11.9	1.6	5.7	4.0	7.0	21.1	Brunei
8.3	3.2	[16]	28.2[16]	3,695	39.6	1.5	10.3	0.4	8.8	5.1	15.2	19.2	Bulgaria
18.6[17]	3.0[17]	2.3[3, 17]	9.0[17]	2,218	71.8	1.4	2.3	0.2	1.4	0.8	4.1	17.6	Burkina Faso
...	6.0[17]	...	13.1[17, 18]	1,947	21.1	29.0	1.0	0.2	0.8	9.6	2.6	35.8	Burundi
...	...	...	...	2,122	83.4	3.1	3.2	0.8	0.4	3.2	1.2	4.8	Cambodia
12.0	3.0	...	17.0	2,208	38.9	15.9	3.5	1.1	1.6	11.8	8.6	18.6	Cameroon
14.3	8.8	8.0	17.9	3,242	22.6	3.4	15.1	1.4	9.9	6.4	18.5	22.7	Canada
8.8	6.9	[16]	7.9[16]	2,780	51.5	5.0	3.7	0.9	3.0	2.4	13.9	19.6	Cape Verde
4.1[17]	0.8[17]	1.3[17]	5.7[17]	1,847	25.6	33.4	7.3	0.5	1.2	5.7	7.3	19.2	Central African Republic
...	...	...	33.5[17]	1,733	50.2	16.3	3.5	1.8	2.8	2.8	5.0	17.3	Chad
6.4	...	...	28.0	2,484	45.7	4.3	8.3	1.4	6.5	5.5	8.6	19.7	Chile
1.4[19]	...	6.0[19]	14.6[19]	2,642	69.7	5.8	8.0	0.6	1.4	2.6	4.7	7.1	China
13.1	5.7	4.5	12.1	2,453	31.4	8.1	7.4	0.2	6.6	9.1	9.9	27.2	Colombia
6.6	...	3.0	5.0	1,760	44.9	17.8	1.7	1.5	1.6	8.9	7.3	16.3	Comoros
15.0	4.0	...	15.0	2,295	18.6	43.9	2.7	3.2	1.0	7.4	11.6	11.6	Congo
11.6	10.9	4.4[3]	8.8	2,711	35.7	0.8	5.1	0.3	8.8	4.9	13.0	31.3	Costa Rica
10.0	3.0	...	19.0	2,565	36.7	27.2	2.5	1.2	1.4	9.4	9.9	11.6	Côte d'Ivoire
9.3	4.5	4.1[3]	1.5	...	...	...	...	...	...	...	...	...	Croatia
5.4	...	...	65.4	3,129	32.9	4.8	6.5	1.1	7.9	3.8	14.1	29.0	Cuba
15.6	10.5	6.3	23.6	...	*40.0*	*2.5*	*13.7*	*0.4*	*7.9*	*7.0*	*10.1*	*18.4*	Cyprus
3.1	4.5	0.8[21]	52.7	3,574[22]	29.9[22]	4.2[22]	13.0[22]	0.5[22]	9.5[22]	4.2[22]	17.5[22]	21.2[22]	Czech Republic
15.3	6.2	8.0	14.1	3,639	20.4	3.6	23.7	2.0	8.7	3.9	17.7	20.1	Denmark
...	1.5	...	24.6	2,363	53.5	0.6	4.1	0.3	6.0	2.8	11.9	20.9	Djibouti
11.6	6.0	...	11.3	2,911	27.9	8.5	8.9	1.0	9.2	9.6	9.3	25.6	Dominica
4.0	8.0	...	13.0	2,310	32.7	3.5	5.2	0.3	5.2	15.2	14.1	23.7	Dominican Republic
12.6	7.1	[16]	24.5[16]	2,399	33.4	3.2	4.8	1.0	6.9	11.1	20.7	19.0	Ecuador
4.0	3.0	...	15.0	3,310	63.2	1.8	2.8	0.4	1.8	6.3	11.1	12.6	Egypt
10.2[19]	5.7[19]	4.3[19]	12.5[19]	2,331	53.8	0.8	2.3	0.1	6.2	4.5	8.3	24.0	El Salvador

Household budgets and consumption (continued)

country	income (latest): percent received by: lowest 20% of households	income (latest): percent received by: highest 10% of households	income (latest): by source (percent): wages, salaries	by source (percent): self-employment	by source (percent): transfer payments[a]	by source (percent): other[b]	consumption expenditure: per capita private final, U.S.$ 1993	by kind or end use (percent of household or personal budget; latest): food[c]	housing[d]	clothing[e]	health care	energy, water	education
Equatorial Guinea	...	...	57.0[17]	42.0[17]	—	1.0[17]	380[1]	62.0[17]	...	10.0[17]	6.0[17]	...	...
Eritrea[23]	...	...	...	...	...	...		...	...	...	...	...	...
Estonia	5.0	27.0	61.4	13.9	23.6	1.1	1,450	43.1	5.0	8.0	[21]	7.2	2.5
Ethiopia[23]	8.6[9]	27.5[9]	0.2	79.5	—	20.3	95	49.0	7.0	6.0	3.0	7.0	4.0
Faroe Islands	...	...	...	...	...	...	...	40.9	11.0	8.0	...	18.9	...
Fiji	*3.7*	*37.8*	*81.5*	*9.1*	—	*9.4*	1,280[1]	34.7	15.6[2]	9.3	2.4	[2]	[3]
Finland	3.7	26.9	56.5	10.0	27.1	6.4	8,450	22.5	16.9	5.0	4.8	4.6	[3]
France	5.6	26.1	51.1	14.1	27.5	7.3	13,400	17.4	16.2	6.1	9.8	3.8	0.7
French Guiana	...	...	74.6		—25.4—		...	30.0[13]	16.1[2]	6.7	4.4	[2]	[3]
French Polynesia	...	...	63.7	[8]	14.8	21.5[8]	4,310[24]	32.1	...	6.3	1.0	8.1	[3]
Gabon	*3.3*	*54.4*	...	...	...	...	2,600	54.7[13, 17, 25]	13.0[17, 25]	17.5[17, 25]	1.9[17, 25]	...	...
Gambia, The	...	...	...	...	...	...	220	58.0[26]	5.1[26]	17.5[26]	...	5.4[26]	...
Gaza Strip	...	...	...	...	...	...	910[7]	...	...	...	...	...	...
Georgia	...	...	76.5		—23.5—		530	38.3	...	14.8	...	0.3	...
Germany	7.0[27]	24.4[27]	57.9	[8]	21.3	20.8[8]	13,680	19.0	16.9	7.9	3.5	4.1	[3]
Ghana	7.0[9]	29.0[9]	41.6[28]	47.1[28]	—	11.3[28]	340	*57.4*	*11.5*[2]	*14.3*	*1.3*	[2]	[3]
Gibraltar	...	...	...	...	...	...		39.1[13]	12.6	11.0	...	...	...
Greece	...	...	37.6	[8]	16.7	45.7[8]	4,490	29.9	14.1	6.5	3.1	3.3	0.5
Greenland	...	...	...	...	...	...	...	29.5	8.9	7.6	...	7.1	...
Grenada	...	...	...	...	...	...	1,610[11]	40.7[13]	11.9	5.2	[29]	3.9	[3]
Guadeloupe			78.9	13.7	7.4	—	4,080[7]	31.6[13]	11.3[2]	9.3	4.6	[2]	[3]
Guam	...	...	...	...	...	...	...	*24.1*	*28.6*	*10.6*	*4.8*	...	...
Guatemala	2.1[15]	46.6[15]	...	...	...	...	960	64.4	16.0[2]	3.1	0.6	[2]	0.3
Guernsey	...	...	...	...	...	...	...	23.7	12.1	7.5	...	8.2	...
Guinea	...	...	...	...	...	...	440	*61.5*	*7.3*[2]	*7.9*	*11.1*	[2]	...
Guinea-Bissau	2.1[9]	42.4[9]	...	...	...	...	220	...	...	...	...	...	...
Guyana	4.0	40.0[10]	*73.0*	...	*6.3*	*20.7*	240[11]	*42.5*[13]	*21.4*	*8.6*	...	*5.2*	[3]
Haiti	...	...	...	...	...	...	370[10]	51.1[13]	4.3	8.7	2.2	...	[3]
Honduras	2.7[15]	47.9[15]	58.3	[8]	1.8	39.9[8]	400	44.4	22.4[2]	9.1	7.0	[2]	[3]
Hong Kong	5.4[20]	31.3[20]	...	...	...	...	9,000	15.1	15.7[2]	21.3	5.0	[2]	0.5
Hungary	10.9[15]	20.8[15]	46.1	11.9	22.4	19.6	2,360	38.1	5.7	7.4	1.5	6.1	0.7
Iceland	4.7	27.3	74.4	3.0	16.6	6.0	15,550[11]	23.7	14.3	7.2	1.5	3.0	0.8
India	8.8[9]	27.1[9]	42.2	39.7	...	18.1	170	52.2	6.1[30]	10.0	2.4	4.7[30]	1.8
Indonesia	8.7[9]	27.9[9]	*42.1*	*41.5*	*2.5*	*13.9*	460	47.5[19]	20.1[2, 19]	5.5[19]	...	[2]	...
Iran	*3.8*	*41.7*	37.4[19]	30.5[19]	—32.1[19]—		920	42.6[13]	24.9[2]	11.8	3.9	[2]	[3]
Iraq	*2.1*	...	23.9	33.9	23.0	18.6	1,710[12]	50.2	19.9[2]	10.6	1.6	[2]	[3]
Ireland	4.6	26.5	58.6	13.3	19.9	8.2	6,010	30.5	7.1	7.4	3.2	6.1	2.4
Isle of Man	6.4	26.6	64.1	6.6	16.9	12.4	...	31.0	7.9	7.0	...	11.0	...
Israel	8.4	23.1	86.9[19, 25]	2.4[19, 25]	—10.6[19, 25]—		8,230	23.8	19.8	5.3	6.2	2.4	2.9
Italy	6.8	25.3	41.7	25.9	20.3	12.1	10,790	19.5	10.0	9.8	6.7	3.8	0.7
Jamaica	6.0[9]	32.6[9]	63.6	13.9	14.0	8.5	1,200	35.7	5.7	4.6	2.8	4.9	0.2
Japan	10.9	31.6[10]	59.3	11.1	19.5	10.1	19,700	23.9	5.3	6.8	2.7	5.4	4.5
Jersey	...	...	...	...	...	...		*28.3*	*14.9*	*8.3*	...	*6.5*	...
Jordan	6.5[9]	32.6[9]	47.0	24.7	5.9	22.4	1,000	40.6	15.8	6.7	2.2	5.0	3.5
Kazakhstan	...	...	82.3		—17.7—		900	29.6	2.6	...	...	...	...
Kenya	3.4	47.9	...	...	...	...	120	46.5	10.0	7.7	2.2	2.6	1.0
Kiribati	...	...	*69.7*	*21.4*	*6.0*	*2.9*	370[4]	50.0[13]	7.5[2, 5]	8.0	...	[2]	...
Korea, North	...	...	...	...	...	...	...	46.5[31]	0.6[31]	29.9[31]	...	3.3[31]	...
Korea, South	7.4	27.6	53.8	25.1	13.1	8.0	4,060	34.1[13]	9.9[2]	4.3	7.8	[2]	[3]
Kuwait	...	...	*53.8*	*20.8*	—*25.4*—		4,140	28.1[13]	15.5	8.1	0.7	9.6	[3]
Kyrgyzstan	3.0	57.0[10]	67.3		—32.7—		410	33.5	2.2	...	...	...	...
Laos	...	...	...	...	...	...	140[6]	...	...	...	...	...	...
Latvia	...	...	58.0	21.8	18.1	2.1	870	45.2	...	...	...	...	...
Lebanon	*5.0*	*45.0*	*27.9*	...	*3.0*	*69.1*	780[4]	*42.8*[17]	*16.8*[17]	*8.6*[17]	*7.2*[17]	*4.5*[17]	*3.9*[17]
Lesotho	2.9[9]	43.6[9]	22.4	27.8	44.7	5.1	320	48.0[13]	10.1	16.4	...	...	...
Liberia	5.0	73.0[10]	...	...	...	...	330[6]	*34.4*[17]	*14.9*[17]	*13.8*[17]	...	*5.0*[17]	...
Libya	*10.1*	...	...	...	...	...	2,330[6]	*37.2*[13]	*32.2*[2]	*6.9*	*3.3*	[2]	[3]
Liechtenstein	...	...	92.9[32]	7.1[32]	...	...	...	21.3[13]	18.0	6.6	7.7	4.4	[3]
Lithuania	...	...	66.4	9.7	18.7	5.2	820	50.3	...	...	...	...	...
Luxembourg	10.0	34.0[10]	88.6	9.1	2.3	—	13,880[11]	12.8	13.7	5.9	7.3	6.1	[3]
Macau	...	...	65.0	18.1	7.0	9.9	4,160[11]	39.2[12]	17.5	6.8	4.0	5.2	[3]
Macedonia	...	...	57.7	17.2	16.2	9.0	1,800[1]	40.6	1.9	7.8	3.0	7.8	[3]
Madagascar	*5.2*	...	*58.8*[17, 33]	*14.1*[17, 33]	—	*27.1*[17, 33]	200	59.0	6.0	6.0	2.0	6.0	4.0
Malawi	*10.4*	*40.1*	83.3	6.0	—	11.7	130	30.0	4.0	9.0	4.0	5.0	10.0
Malaysia	4.6[15]	37.9[15]	...	...	...	...	1,660	28.7	10.2[2]	4.3	2.5	[2]	0.6
Maldives	...	...	...	...	...	...	270[6]	57.4	1.6	8.0	2.5	...	[3]
Mali	...	...	...	...	...	...	220	57.0	2.0	6.0	2.0	6.0	4.0
Malta	...	...	62.4	20.1	—	17.5	4,100[1]	31.2	3.5	7.6	3.5	2.0	0.4
Marshall Islands	...	...	...	...	...	...	...	57.7	15.6[2, 5]	12.0	...	[2]	...
Martinique	...	...	80.0	...	...	20.0	4,840[7]	32.1[13]	10.6[2]	8.0	5.2	[2]	[3]
Mauritania	3.5[9]	30.2[9]	...	...	...	...	340	51.2	2.3	7.7	1.4	7.9	0.3
Mauritius	4.0	46.7	51.7	29.0	11.2	8.1	1,810	41.9	8.8	8.4	3.0	6.4	2.9
Mayotte	...	...	...	...	...	...		42.2	...	31.5	...	6.8	...
Mexico	4.0	38.2	61.5	29.1	7.8	1.6	2,860	36.6[13]	13.3[2]	8.4	3.4	[2]	[3]
Micronesia	...	...	67.2	18.0	...	14.8	...	73.5	...	...	...	...	...
Moldova	...	...	59.8	16.0	20.3	3.9	790	...	...	...	...	...	...
Monaco	...	...	...	...	...	...	...	...	...	...	...	...	...
Mongolia	...	...	72.1	9.5	9.6	8.8	180	39.1	5.9[2]	23.4	0.5	[2]	2.9
Morocco	6.6[9]	30.5[9]	...	...	...	...	670	38.0	7.0	11.0	5.0	2.0	8.0
Mozambique	...	...	...	...	...	...	87	...	...	...	...	...	...
Myanmar (Burma)	*8.0*	40.0[10]	...	...	...	...	750[34]	*49.1*[17]	*10.4*[17]	*15.3*[17]	*2.4*[17]	*4.0*[17]	*5.9*[17]
Namibia	...	...	67.1	27.5	5.4	...	1,300	...	...	...	...	...	...
Nauru	...	...	...	...	...	...	...	...	...	...	...	...	...
Nepal	9.1[9]	25.0[9]	25.1	63.4	—11.5—		135	61.2	17.3	11.7	3.7	...	[3]
Netherlands, The	8.2	21.9	48.2	10.7	29.1	12.0	12,570	13.6	14.9	7.1	12.9	3.1	0.7

transportation, communications	household durable goods[f]	recreation[g]	personal effects, other[h]	food consumption: daily available calories per capita (1988–90)	percent of total calories (latest) derived from: cereals	potatoes, cassava	meat, poultry	fish	eggs, milk	fruits, vegetables	fats, oils[i]	other[j]	country
...	...	...	22.0[17]	...	...	...	...	...	...	...	...	...	Equatorial Guinea
...	...	...	...	...	...	...	...	...	...	...	...	...	Eritrea[23]
9.2	5.6	5.0[21]	14.4	...	...	...	...	...	...	...	...	...	Estonia
8.0	2.0	...	14.0	1,699	71.5	4.1	3.1	—	2.4	0.8	3.6	14.5	Ethiopia[23]
...	6.6	...	14.6	...	*29.3*	*5.5*	*15.8*	*3.9*	*7.0*	*3.3*	*18.0*	*17.2*	Faroe Islands
13.8	9.3	4.3[3]	10.6	2,768	38.7	6.1	3.9	3.1	4.6	1.5	14.1	27.9	Fiji
14.8	6.3	9.5[3]	15.6	3,066	23.4	4.9	16.7	1.9	15.4	4.9	12.8	20.0	Finland
16.1	7.7	6.9	15.3	3,593	23.9	3.7	16.0	1.2	12.5	4.9	18.9	18.9	France
17.5	7.9	6.2[3]	11.2	2,805	29.1	4.3	17.0	3.0	7.7	8.7	8.0	22.1	French Guiana
12.2	12.3	6.9[3]	21.1	2,765	36.5	5.2	12.4	2.4	5.1	4.3	11.5	22.7	French Polynesia
6.3[17, 25]	...	...	6.6[17, 25]	2,442	24.4	25.5	6.3	2.1	1.4	14.7	7.9	17.7	Gabon
...	...	...	14.0[26]	2,290	67.2	1.0	2.4	1.3	1.7	1.1	9.7	15.5	Gambia, The
...	...	...	...	...	*50.4*	*1.6*	*4.2*	*0.2*	*4.9*	*9.0*	*13.8*	*15.9*	Gaza Strip
...	5.9	...	40.7	...	...	...	...	...	...	...	...	...	Georgia
17.8	9.4	10.6[3]	10.8	3,522	22.3	4.8	13.9	0.8	10.1	6.0	18.8	23.3	Germany
3.3	*3.8*	*3.9*[3]	*4.5*	2,141	29.0	39.3	1.9	2.5	0.3	8.5	8.6	9.9	Ghana
13.3	10.0	...	14.0	...	...	...	...	...	...	...	...	...	Gibraltar
17.5	6.9	5.2	13.0	3,775	27.7	3.9	12.2	0.8	10.1	9.5	18.4	17.3	Greece
7.7	9.3	12.4	17.5	...	...	...	...	...	...	...	...	...	Greenland
9.1	13.7	4.6[3]	10.9[29]	2,400	26.5	2.4	7.6	2.4	12.3	8.3	10.0	30.6	Grenada
20.5	9.3	4.7[3]	8.7	2,777	34.4	3.3	11.2	3.2	7.5	8.0	11.2	21.3	Guadeloupe
18.0	...	*5.1*	*8.8*	...	...	...	...	...	...	...	...	...	Guam
7.0	5.0	0.9	2.7	2,254	60.5	0.4	1.4	—	2.9	2.1	7.2	25.4	Guatemala
15.7	8.3	...	24.7	...	...	...	...	...	...	...	...	...	Guernsey
5.1	*2.9*	*4.1*	*0.1*	2,243	48.2	13.2	1.5	0.7	1.2	14.4	12.0	8.7	Guinea
...	...	...	...	2,235	63.6	6.1	4.6	0.3	1.5	4.2	13.0	6.7	Guinea-Bissau
1.8	*0.9*	*0.4*[3]	*8.2*	2,495	48.4	2.1	4.5	3.0	5.6	5.0	6.9	24.6	Guyana
7.6	9.2	5.3[3]	11.6	2,005	37.4	12.4	3.5	0.3	1.7	9.8	6.1	28.7	Haiti
3.0	8.3	2.4[3]	3.1	2,211	50.9	0.5	2.3	0.3	6.1	6.8	10.0	20.9	Honduras
8.4	17.5	8.1	8.4	2,860	35.4	1.0	16.2	3.0	4.8	4.5	16.2	18.8	Hong Kong
15.2	8.8	5.9	10.6	3,608	29.1	2.8	12.6	0.3	8.8	4.5	20.8	21.1	Hungary
17.6	9.3	10.4	12.2	3,473	27.5	2.7	12.5	5.0	15.8	3.3	10.3	22.9	Iceland
10.6	3.1	1.8	5.7	2,229	63.1	1.8	0.7	0.3	4.8	3.2	7.2	18.9	India
...	2.9[19]	...	24.0	2,605	66.5	6.2	1.3	1.2	0.6	2.3	7.7	14.3	Indonesia
5.0	6.4	1.7[3]	3.7	3,022	62.8	2.1	3.3	0.3	3.2	7.1	10.8	10.3	Iran
6.5	6.7	0.8[3]	3.7	3,092	61.5	0.5	3.5	0.1	3.0	6.4	12.7	12.4	Iraq
14.0	7.2	8.9[3]	13.1	3,951	24.3	6.0	14.8	0.8	14.5	3.6	17.4	18.7	Ireland
14.9	*6.7*	...	*22.5*	...	...	...	...	...	...	...	...	...	Isle of Man
12.9	10.8	4.3	11.6	3,220	31.3	1.9	8.1	1.1	9.6	9.0	19.1	19.9	Israel
13.2	9.5	8.4	18.4	3,498	32.1	2.1	11.0	1.1	8.6	7.4	21.7	15.9	Italy
12.4	5.5	2.1	26.1	2,558	32.6	7.3	6.5	1.4	6.1	7.0	11.5	27.7	Jamaica
9.0	1.4	9.5	31.5	2,921	39.7	2.6	5.6	6.0	6.2	4.4	11.2	23.3	Japan
13.9	*7.1*	...	*31.0*	...	...	...	...	...	...	...	...	...	Jersey
11.2	6.1	4.0	4.9	2,710	51.8	1.0	6.2	0.2	4.6	4.6	11.0	20.9	Jordan
...	...	...	67.8	...	...	...	...	...	...	...	...	...	Kazakhstan
8.4	9.4	3.1	9.1	2,064	52.0	7.4	4.1	0.5	8.4	3.2	6.4	17.9	Kenya
8.0	[5]	...	26.5	2,516	39.0	10.9	3.7	5.7	1.2	5.8	8.2	25.5	Kiribati
...	3.8[31]	...	15.9	2,843	62.1	5.7	3.4	2.6	1.1	5.8	3.3	16.0	Korea, North
11.9	6.2	12.5[3]	13.3	2,826	52.5	0.7	5.2	3.5	2.2	6.9	9.1	19.8	Korea, South
13.7	11.2	5.2[3]	7.9	3,057	36.0	1.2	10.7	0.7	9.5	8.1	15.8	17.9	Kuwait
...	...	...	64.3	...	...	...	...	...	...	...	...	...	Kyrgyzstan
...	...	...	...	2,465	74.7	1.6	7.0	0.4	1.7	2.5	1.9	7.2	Laos
...	...	...	54.8	2,490	...	...	...	...	...	...	...	...	Latvia
5.4[17]	*2.6*[17]	*1.9*[17]	*6.3*[17]	3,142	37.6	3.1	6.0	—	5.9	11.4	15.7	20.3	Lebanon
4.7	11.9	...	8.8	2,121	75.3	0.6	4.2	0.2	1.5	1.7	3.9	12.5	Lesotho
...	*6.1*[17]	...	*25.8*[17]	2,264	46.7	22.6	2.0	1.1	0.5	4.9	14.4	7.7	Liberia
9.4	*4.6*	*8.5*[3]	*2.5*	3,293	45.4	1.7	5.6	0.2	6.7	7.5	16.5	16.3	Libya
13.3	5.8	16.3[3]	6.6	...	...	...	...	...	...	...	...	...	Liechtenstein
...	...	...	49.7	2,110	...	...	...	...	...	...	...	...	Lithuania
19.1	10.8	4.2[3]	20.1	3,925	19.0	4.7	18.6	1.0	9.1	5.6	21.3	20.7	Luxembourg
8.2	3.0	8.8[3]	7.3	2,295	42.7	2.0	16.0	1.4	4.6	5.3	12.8	15.3	Macau
6.5	4.2	3.3[3]	1.8	...	...	...	...	...	...	...	...	...	Macedonia
4.0	1.0	...	12.0	2,156	55.8	19.2	6.2	0.7	3.3	4.2	3.5	7.1	Madagascar
10.0	3.0	...	25.0	2,048	68.8	4.0	1.5	0.9	0.7	4.6	1.7	17.9	Malawi
20.9	7.7	11.0	14.1	2,671	40.3	3.4	7.3	1.7	4.9	3.4	19.2	19.7	Malaysia
2.6	17.0	5.9[3]	5.0	2,400	52.6	3.9	0.6	12.6	—	4.2	4.8	21.4	Maldives
10.0	1.0	...	12.0	2,259	72.7	1.9	3.3	0.6	4.2	0.8	7.8	8.6	Mali
16.4	9.9	7.1	18.4	3,169	30.1	1.5	10.7	1.0	11.3	6.6	15.9	22.9	Malta
...	[5]	...	14.7	...	...	...	...	...	...	...	...	...	Marshall Islands
20.7	9.4	5.4[3]	8.6	2,768	31.2	3.7	11.3	2.7	7.7	10.9	11.2	21.2	Martinique
2.0	1.9	0.5	24.8	2,447	54.8	0.4	4.0	0.6	12.5	1.6	8.3	17.9	Mauritania
10.0	6.4	—	12.2	2,897	50.0	1.2	3.7	1.4	6.4	1.5	12.2	23.5	Mauritius
5.1	8.8	...	5.6	...	...	...	...	...	...	...	...	...	Mayotte
10.0	11.8	5.5[3]	11.0	3,061	46.7	0.7	8.5	0.6	5.8	3.3	12.5	21.8	Mexico
...	...	...	26.5	...	...	...	...	...	...	...	...	...	Micronesia
...	...	...	...	...	...	...	...	...	...	...	...	...	Moldova
...	...	...	...	3,593	23.9	3.7	16.0	1.2	12.5	4.9	18.9	18.9	Monaco
3.5	8.0	0.4	16.2	2,361	46.5	2.0	24.1	0.1	6.4	0.8	6.2	13.8	Mongolia
8.0	5.0	...	16.0	3,031	54.5	1.7	2.1	0.6	1.8	4.4	10.9	24.0	Morocco
...	...	...	...	1,804	32.0	43.3	1.5	0.3	0.7	1.8	12.7	7.7	Mozambique
3.8[17]	*0.5*[17]	*1.1*[17]	*7.5*[17]	2,453	79.5	0.4	1.8	1.0	1.0	2.5	6.3	7.5	Myanmar (Burma)
...	...	...	...	1,968	55.0	15.5	8.1	0.7	3.0	1.7	7.1	8.9	Namibia
...	...	...	...	...	...	...	...	...	...	...	...	...	Nauru
1.2	...	2.9[3]	2.0	2,206	80.9	3.0	1.2	—	4.1	0.9	4.4	5.4	Nepal
13.3	7.1	9.7	17.6	3,078	17.8	5.3	12.2	0.6	13.1	6.1	20.2	24.6	Netherlands, The

Household budgets and consumption (continued)

country	income (latest)						consumption expenditure						
	percent received by		by source (percent)				per capita private final, U.S.$ 1993	by kind or end use (percent of household or personal budget; latest)					
	lowest 20% of households	highest 10% of households	wages, salaries	self-employment	transfer payments[a]	other[b]		food[c]	housing[d]	clothing[e]	health care	energy, water	education
Netherlands Antilles	...	...	...	...	...	...	4,110[14]	19.6	16.9[2]	8.8	1.3	[2]	[3]
New Caledonia	...	...	52.6	23.8	23.6	...	5,410[35]	25.7	21.5[2, 5]	4.7	[22]	[2]	...
New Zealand	5.1[20]	28.7[20]	52.1	5.6	21.0	21.3	8,740	16.1	20.0	5.2	6.4	2.4	[3]
Nicaragua	4.0[36]	55[10]	...	...	...	...	410	...	...	...	...	...	...
Niger	...	...	...	...	...	...	160	50.5	19.1[5]	7.3	...	...	...
Nigeria	5.0	49.0[10]	30.2[19]	46.3[19]	0.9[19]	22.6[19]	190	48.0	3.0	5.0	3.0	1.0	4.0
Northern Mariana Islands	...	...	...	...	...	...	...	49.2[13]	19.5[2, 5]	9.1	[21]	[2]	...
Norway	2.6	26.6	58.8	9.9	24.2	7.1	13,400	23.5	13.7	7.0	5.4	6.2	0.6
Oman	...	...	...	...	...	...	1,990	40.6	24.6	5.1	2.4	3.2	[3]
Pakistan	8.4[9]	25.2[9]	22.0	56.0	...	22.0	280	37.0	11.0	6.0	1.0	5.0	1.0
Palau	...	...	...	...	...	...	...	...	...	...	...	...	...
Panama	2.0[15]	42.1[15]	60.8[17]	12.8[17]	13.2[17]	13.2[17]	1,290	34.9	12.6[2]	5.1	3.5	[2]	[3]
Papua New Guinea	...	...	*57.3*	[8]	*1.1*	*41.6*[8]	650	40.9	12.5[5]	6.2	...	4.9	...
Paraguay	6.0	46.0[10]	35.0	[8]	4.3	60.7[8]	1,050	48.7	16.4	9.7	3.4	—	1.5
Peru	4.9[9]	35.4[9]	31.2	65.1	3.7	...	1,400	44.1[13]	6.8[2]	10.1	2.7	[2]	[3]
Philippines	6.5[9]	32.1[9]	45.7	42.5	3.4	8.4	640	56.8	4.1[2]	3.9	...	[2]	...
Poland	9.2[15]	21.6[15]	34.0	4.3	20.7	41.0	1,470	41.2	2.8	10.9	8.1	1.0	[3]
Portugal	*5.2*	*33.4*	42.6	25.0	21.3	11.1	5,570	34.8	2.0	10.3	4.5	3.0	1.4
Puerto Rico	*3.2*	*34.7*	54.1	6.8	29.8	9.3	5,640	20.6	11.8[2]	7.4	11.6	[2]	3.1
Qatar	...	...	80.8	5.6	...	13.6	3,600[4]	24.5	35.1[5]	9.1	1.0	1.9	4.3
Réunion	*3.1*[20]	*51.4*[20]	—67.5—		29.7	2.8	4,820[35]	22.4	11.8	7.9	2.2	2.2	[3]
Romania	...	...	62.6		—37.4—		740	51.1	16.4[2, 5]	15.7	1.2	[2]	[3]
Russia	5.3	46.3[10]	68.5	6.4	15.7	12.1	1,150	34.8	2.7	22.3	...	...	...
Rwanda	9.7[9]	24.6[9]	10.4[36]	47.7[36]	13.9[36]	28.0[36]	150	32.1[36]	13.1[36]	9.4[36]	1.3[36]	1.2[36]	[2, 36]
St. Kitts and Nevis	...	...	...	...	...	...	2,580[1]	*55.6*[13]	*7.6*	*7.5*	...	*6.6*	...
St. Lucia	...	...	...	...	...	...	...	49.6[13]	13.5	6.5	2.3	4.5	[3]
St. Vincent and the Grenadines	...	...	...	...	...	...	1,240[1]	59.8	6.3	7.7	...	6.2	...
San Marino	...	...	...	...	...	...	...	22.1[12]	20.9[2]	8.0	2.6	[2]	[3]
São Tomé and Príncipe	...	...	...	...	...	...	400[1]	...	...	...	...	...	...
Saudi Arabia	...	...	...	...	...	...	2,860	52.2[19, 38]	17.2[19, 38]	6.6[19, 38]	2.1[19, 38]	1.8[19, 38]	1.1[19, 38]
Senegal	3.5	42.2	51.6[17]		—48.4[17]—		580	49.0	7.0	11.0	2.0	4.0	6.0
Seychelles	4.1	35.6	*77.2*	*3.8*	*3.2*	*15.8*	3,110[1]	53.9	13.6	4.2	0.4	9.1	...
Sierra Leone	*5.6*	*37.8*	27.9	61.6	...	10.5	140	63.8	5.8[2]	10.0	3.5	[2]	[3]
Singapore	5.1	33.5	81.2	16.8	—2.0—		7,900	16.9	10.2[2]	7.1	4.6	[2]	1.4
Slovakia	17.0	22.0[10]	71.8	[8]	16.3	11.9[8]	1,200	26.8	7.6[2]	8.9	...	[2]	...
Slovenia	...	...	59.4	14.5	17.5	8.6	2,890	30.8	18.3	8.5	5.0	7.3	[3]
Solomon Islands	...	...	74.1		—25.9—		820[4]	46.8	21.9[2, 5]	5.7	[21]	[2]	...
Somalia	...	...	...	...	...	...	17[1]	62.3[12, 17]	15.3[17]	5.6[17]	...	4.3[18]	...
South Africa	3.0	63.0[10]	73.6	[8]	4.9	21.5[8]	1,580	29.3	12.6[2]	7.5	4.5	[2]	1.4
Spain	8.3[12]	21.8[12]	47.8	23.8	20.3	8.1	7,730	21.6[13]	12.6[2]	8.6	4.7	[2]	[3]
Sri Lanka	8.9[9]	25.2[9]	48.5	[8]	9.7	41.8[8]	390	48.0	1.9	10.1	1.8	3.3	0.8
Sudan, The	*4.0*	*34.6*	...	...	...	...	760[1]	63.6	11.5	5.3	4.1	3.8	[3]
Suriname	*9.3*	...	*74.6*	...	*3.2*	*22.2*	2,260[1]	*39.9*[17]	*4.4*[17]	*11.0*[17]	*3.6*[17]	*6.9*[17]	*2.6*[17]
Swaziland	*2.8*	*54.5*	44.4	22.2	12.2	21.2	650[1]	33.5[13]	13.4[2]	6.0	1.8	[2]	[3]
Sweden	5.3	18.6	58.9	9.7	25.8	5.6	10,190	21.3	19.9	8.6	3.2	4.9	0.1
Switzerland	6.0[39]	27.0[39]	63.6	[8]	16.5	19.9[8]	19,570	27.0[13]	13.1	4.4	9.9	7.7	[3]
Syria	*6.0*	...	40.7	...	25.1	34.2	1,630	58.8[13]	16.0[2]	7.5	...	[2]	[3]
Taiwan	7.5	38.6[10]	68.3	[8]	3.6	28.1[8]	4,670	27.2	19.3[2]	4.6	5.3	[2]	[3]
Tajikistan	...	...	64.2	4.4	31.3	0.1	440[34]	...	...	...	...	...	...
Tanzania	2.4[9]	46.5[9]	28.1	34.2	3.5	34.2	61	54.3	8.6	10.8	4.5	6.6	0.8
Thailand	6.1[9]	35.3[9]	36.4	45.0	0.9	17.7	1,200	29.0	6.3	11.6	8.0	1.7	0.5
Togo	*8.0*	*30.5*	...	...	...	...	270	42.5[17]	13.4[17]	11.5[17]	5.0[17]	[2, 17]	[3, 17]
Tonga	...	...	...	...	...	...	...	49.3	10.5	5.6	0.3	2.7	...
Trinidad and Tobago	*2.6*	*33.6*	...	...	...	...	2,960	25.5[13]	21.6	10.4	[16]	...	1.5
Tunisia	5.9[9]	30.7[9]	...	...	...	...	890	39.0	10.7	6.0	3.0	5.1	1.8
Turkey	*3.5*[12]	*41.5*[12]	24.1	51.4	10.8	13.7	1,690	33.1	14.7	12.3	2.6	6.1	1.6
Turkmenistan	...	...	73.5	6.6	17.3	2.6	570	...	...	...	...	...	...
Tuvalu	...	...	*17.9*	*76.1*	...	*6.0*	...	45.5	11.5[5]	7.5	...	...	...
Uganda	8.5[9]	27.2[9]	...	...	...	...	190	57.1[13, 17]	...	5.5[17]	...	7.3[17]	...
Ukraine	...	...	58.5	4.0	22.5	15.0	1,680	41.3	1.7	...	...	...	[3]
United Arab Emirates	...	...	...	...	...	...	8,560	24.1	23.7	9.1	1.1	1.2	3.9
United Kingdom	4.6[12]	27.8[12]	59.6	13.6	14.3	12.5	9,040	19.1	14.3	6.8	1.5	4.5	1.0
United States	3.8	46.9[10, 40]	57.8	8.1	16.7	17.4	16,500	10.8	15.5	7.0	6.7	8.0	1.7
Uruguay	6.0[12, 16]	29.3[12, 16]	53.5	17.0	—29.5—		3,150	39.9	17.6[2]	7.0	9.3	[2]	1.3
Uzbekistan	...	...	59.8	18.5	21.7	...	410	...	...	...	...	...	...
Vanuatu	...	...	56.7	[8]	7.7	35.6[8]	660[1]	30.5[13]	29.0[2, 5]	4.7	[21]	[2]	...
Venezuela	4.8[15]	33.2[15]	...	...	...	...	2,090	30.4	11.5	10.6	2.9	3.0	0.8
Vietnam	8.0	44.0[10]	17.2	64.6	17.6	0.5	150	62.4	2.5	5.0	...	...	2.9
Virgin Islands (U.S.)	...	...	65.7	2.6	13.0	12.7	...	25.3[41]	*24.9*[41]	*5.4*[41]	...	*6.5*[41]	...
West Bank	...	...	...	...	...	...	1,380[7]	...	...	...	...	...	...
Western Sahara	...	...	...	...	...	...	...	...	...	...	...	...	...
Western Samoa	...	...	*49.4*	*22.8*	...	*27.8*	710[1]	58.8	5.1[5]	4.2	...	5.0	...
Yemen	...	...	...	...	...	...	630	61.0[42]	13.2[42]	...	1.1[42]	6.1[42]	...
Yugoslavia	5.3[15, 43]	27.4[15, 43]	53.1	9.3	15.3	22.3	2,480[11]	48.0	2.5	8.5	4.5	9.1	[3]
Zaire	...	...	...	...	...	...	190	61.7	11.5[2]	9.7	2.6	[2]	[3]
Zambia	5.6[9]	34.2[9]	79.9	17.8	1.3	1.0	310	36.0	7.0	10.0	8.0	4.0	14.0
Zimbabwe	4.0	46.9	92.0	1.0	...	7.0	290	30.1[12]	6.5	10.3	7.1	8.9	6.0

[1]1990. [2]Housing includes energy, water. [3]Recreation includes education. [4]1988. [5]Housing includes household durable goods. [6]1989. [7]1986. [8]Other includes self-employment. [9]1990. [10]Highest 20%. [11]1991. [12]Based on posttax income. [13]Includes tobacco. [14]1985. [15]Data refer to income shares by fractiles of persons. [16]Personal effects, other includes education and recreation. [17]Capital city only. [18]Includes wage taxes. [19]Urban areas only. [20]Based on posttax per capita income. [21]Recreation includes health care. [22]Data refer to former Czechoslovakia. [23]Ethiopia includes Eritrea. [24]1984. [25]Wage earners only. [26]Low-income population in Banjul and Kombo St. Mary only. [27]Former West Germany only. [28]Urban areas of Eastern Region only.

transpor-tation, com-munications	household durable goods[f]	recrea-tion[g]	personal effects, other[h]	food consumption: daily available calories per capita (1988–90)	percent of total calories (latest) derived from: cereals	potatoes, cassava	meat, poultry	fish	eggs, milk	fruits, vegeta-bles	fats, oils[i]	other[j]	country
16.3	11.5	7.1[3]	18.5	2,681	33.5	3.3	16.0	1.9	9.3	6.6	11.4	18.1	Netherlands Antilles
24.0	[5]	11.6	12.5	2,909	40.2	6.4	10.0	1.2	5.7	4.5	13.1	18.9	New Caledonia
15.7	6.9	7.8[3]	19.4	3,460	22.3	2.8	16.8	1.6	10.8	6.3	16.4	23.0	New Zealand
...	...	...	...	2,234	51.1	1.6	2.1	—	4.7	2.9	8.3	29.3	Nicaragua
...	[5]	...	23.1	2,240	73.9	3.6	2.1	—	2.1	1.1	3.0	14.2	Niger
3.0	6.0	...	27.0	2,199	36.8	34.2	1.3	0.4	0.5	3.3	11.8	11.6	Nigeria
8.3	[5]	13.9[21]	—	...	...	...	...	...	...	...	...	...	Northern Mariana Islands
12.8	6.9	8.8	15.1	3,221	27.0	5.3	10.6	4.2	13.2	4.9	16.9	18.0	Norway
8.9	7.1	4.1[3]	4.0	...	...	...	...	...	...	...	...	...	Oman
13.0	5.0	...	21.0	2,283	58.9	0.4	2.2	0.1	7.3	2.6	13.8	14.6	Pakistan
...	...	...	...	...	...	...	...	...	...	...	...	...	Palau
15.1	8.4	11.7[3]	8.7	2,269	37.7	3.1	7.5	1.3	7.0	6.6	13.8	23.0	Panama
13.0	[5]	...	22.5	2,589	23.0	26.5	5.9	1.9	0.8	24.8	4.8	12.1	Papua New Guinea
4.5	6.2	2.3	7.3	2,684	29.2	17.0	11.7	0.2	4.2	8.0	10.7	19.0	Paraguay
7.3	7.5	7.6[3]	13.9	2,035	42.9	9.3	5.2	1.7	5.2	4.9	7.2	23.7	Peru
5.0	12.8	...	17.3	2,343	56.3	4.5	5.3	3.2	1.9	7.3	5.8	15.7	Philippines
8.9	8.3	15.0[3]	3.8	3,426	33.3	5.8	12.1	0.9	10.8	3.3	15.4	18.4	Poland
15.4	8.6	4.4	15.6	3,342	30.8	5.5	11.9	2.6	6.6	5.8	17.1	19.6	Portugal
11.8	11.2	7.9	14.7	...	...	...	...	...	...	...	...	...	Puerto Rico
13.0	[5]	11.1		...	...	...	...	...	...	...	...	...	Qatar
24.9	6.0	10.1[3]	12.5	3,083	47.8	2.3	10.5	1.5	5.3	5.1	10.3	17.2	Réunion
6.6	[5]	4.5[3]	4.5	3,081	44.1	4.0	8.3	0.7	7.9	5.3	13.6	16.0	Romania
...	9.4	...	30.8	3,380[37]	36.8[37]	5.3[37]	10.6[37]	2.1[37]	8.8[37]	3.4[37]	13.2[37]	19.8[37]	Russia
1.7[36]	5.3[36]	0.4	35.5[36]	1,915	18.0	31.0	1.0	—	1.4	16.0	2.5	30.1	Rwanda
4.3	*9.4*	...	*9.0*	2,435	18.7	3.8	11.3	3.4	7.9	4.2	18.6	32.1	St. Kitts and Nevis
6.3	5.8	3.2[3]	8.3	2,424	26.7	5.7	14.0	1.3	7.7	9.8	11.0	23.8	St. Lucia
3.7	6.6	...	9.7	2,460	34.6	10.6	8.8	0.4	5.2	4.1	7.4	28.9	St. Vincent and the Grenadines
17.6	7.2	7.1[3]	14.5	3,498	32.1	2.1	11.0	1.1	8.6	7.4	21.7	15.9	San Marino
...	...	...	...	2,153	31.3	13.9	1.3	2.5	1.2	2.9	16.4	30.5	São Tomé and Príncipe
4.5[19, 38]	5.9[19, 38]	...	8.6[19, 38]	2,932	49.5	0.8	6.9	0.5	6.7	10.5	11.4	13.6	Saudi Arabia
5.0	2.0	...	12.0	2,323	63.3	1.3	3.7	1.9	2.6	1.2	12.4	13.6	Senegal
6.4	6.6	1.4	4.4	2,356	48.9	1.1	5.3	2.4	5.9	3.5	11.6	21.3	Seychelles
4.4	3.9	3.8[3]	4.8	1,899	52.7	5.8	1.1	1.4	0.8	3.6	21.7	13.0	Sierra Leone
14.5	8.9	13.1	23.3	3,121	41.4	2.3	15.0	1.8	4.8	7.2	5.7	21.9	Singapore
...	3.9	...	26.2	...	...	...	...	...	...	...	...	...	Slovakia
12.7	3.3	6.1[3]	8.0	...	...	...	...	...	...	...	...	...	Slovenia
9.9	[5]	...[21]	15.7	2,277	25.3	36.6	3.6	5.4	0.7	2.9	8.7	16.8	Solomon Islands
...	...	...	12.1[17]	1,873	52.8	0.9	6.6	0.3	21.2	2.2	8.6	7.4	Somalia
16.7	10.0	6.3	11.7	3,134	53.9	1.7	7.6	0.7	4.0	2.4	9.5	20.3	South Africa
15.3	7.1	7.0[3]	23.1	3,472	21.3	5.2	20.0	1.6	8.6	7.3	17.5	10.5	Spain
17.0	3.9	2.4	10.8	2,246	57.5	3.1	0.4	1.4	2.8	4.7	3.8	26.1	Sri Lanka
1.5	5.5	0.7[3]	4.0	2,042	56.0	0.8	4.2	0.1	11.3	3.0	10.6	14.0	Sudan, The
9.5[17]	*12.3[17]*	*5.8[17]*	*4.0[17]*	2,436	52.1	2.0	6.5	0.5	6.2	4.1	9.9	18.8	Suriname
8.8	12.8	3.3[3]	20.4	2,634	53.9	1.1	4.7	—	3.7	3.6	7.5	25.5	Swaziland
15.7	6.6	10.9	8.8	2,976	21.1	4.4	10.1	2.3	15.3	5.5	20.1	21.3	Sweden
12.9	5.1	9.8[3]	10.1	3,508	20.3	2.4	17.6	0.7	12.9	5.8	18.3	22.0	Switzerland
2.4	5.8	2.1[3]	7.4	3,121	53.1	1.4	3.0	—	6.3	7.2	13.1	15.8	Syria
13.2	5.1	17.2[3]	8.1	2,872	36.8	2.5	14.3	1.9	3.1	8.3	14.4	18.7	Taiwan
...	...	...	...	...	...	...	...	...	...	...	...	...	Tajikistan
6.4	6.3	1.6	0.1	2,195	40.5	22.6	2.3	1.2	1.7	6.0	5.0	12.6	Tanzania
12.9	10.9	4.2	14.9	2,280	58.7	1.1	5.0	1.6	1.4	5.6	5.3	21.4	Thailand
9.5[17]	4.4[17]	5.1[3, 17]	8.6[17]	2,269	47.7	29.0	2.3	1.2	0.6	1.8	9.2	8.0	Togo
5.8	10.6	0.5	14.7	2,967	15.7	35.1	12.2	2.0	2.1	4.5	8.0	20.5	Tonga
15.2	14.3	[10]	6.2[16]	2,769	42.1	2.5	5.0	0.5	6.5	3.4	13.1	26.9	Trinidad and Tobago
9.0	11.2	7.1	7.1	3,123	53.0	1.3	2.7	0.6	4.7	5.5	17.6	14.5	Tunisia
8.6	11.5	3.0	6.5	3,197	48.4	3.7	2.5	0.4	2.9	8.5	15.8	18.0	Turkey
...	...	...		...	...	...	...	...	...	...	...	...	Turkmenistan
10.5	[5]	...	25.0	...	...	...	...	...	...	...	...	...	Tuvalu
5.9[17]	...	...	24.2[17]	2,179	23.5	30.8	2.4	1.1	1.7	17.3	1.8	21.3	Uganda
...	6.8	6.3[3]	43.9	...	...	...	...	...	...	...	...	...	Ukraine
14.1	11.6	4.7	6.5	3,286	34.6	1.3	11.5	1.4	9.3	14.6	10.8	16.4	United Arab Emirates
17.1	7.0	9.6	19.1	3,270	22.1	6.1	14.7	0.9	11.8	4.5	17.8	22.1	United Kingdom
21.4	4.8	6.8	13.5	3,642	21.7	2.7	14.7	0.8	11.4	5.6	18.1	25.0	United States
10.4	6.3	3.1	5.1	2,668	36.8	3.9	18.3	0.2	13.0	3.7	9.6	14.4	Uruguay
...	...	...	...	...	...	...	...	...	...	...	...	...	Uzbekistan
13.2	[5]	12.3[21]	10.3	2,736	21.7	24.5	12.2	2.2	1.8	3.3	10.4	23.9	Vanuatu
7.1	4.5	2.7	26.4	2,440	36.4	2.0	5.9	1.2	7.4	7.3	16.1	23.6	Venezuela
...	4.6	...	22.6	2,216	72.7	7.5	6.0	0.9	0.5	4.3	1.8	6.2	Vietnam
11.7[41]	*4.3[41]*	...	*21.9[41]*	...	...	...	...	...	...	...	...	...	Virgin Islands (U.S.)
...	...	...	...	...	*44.4*	*1.9*	*6.1*	*0.1*	*6.2*	*11.0*	*12.5*	*17.8*	West Bank
...	...	...	...	...	...	...	...	...	...	...	...	...	Western Sahara
9.0	[5]	...	17.9	*2,469*	*20.1*	*19.1*	*12.0*	*3.6*	*1.2*	*13.2*	*8.4*	*22.4*	Western Samoa
1.9[42]	3.0[42]	...	13.7[42]	2,231	66.9	1.0	3.5	0.4	3.7	3.5	6.5	14.4	Yemen
8.7	3.3	4.6[3]	10.8	3,545[43]	43.2[43]	2.3[43]	8.2[43]	0.2[43]	7.9[43]	3.7[43]	16.9[43]	17.7[43]	Yugoslavia
5.9	4.8	3.8[3]	—	2,129	16.4	55.8	1.8	0.7	0.1	7.7	7.0	10.4	Zaire
5.0	1.0	...	15.0	2,016	75.0	4.8	2.4	0.7	1.3	1.6	3.2	11.0	Zambia
1.1	12.9	0.6	16.5	2,256	59.4	1.4	2.5	0.2	1.5	1.1	9.6	24.3	Zimbabwe

[29]Personal effects, other includes health care. [30]Housing includes water. [31]Workers and clerical workers only. [32]Earned income only. [33]Malagasy households only. [34]1992. [35]1987. [36]Rural areas only. [37]Data refer to former U.S.S.R. [38]Middle-income population only. [39]Excludes transfer payments and property income. [40]Income of highest 5% of households is 18.6%. [41]St. Thomas only. [42]Data refer to former Yemen Arab Republic. [43]Data refer to former Socialist Federal Republic of Yugoslavia.

Health services

The provision of health services in most countries is both a principal determinant of the quality of life and a large and growing sector of the national economy. This table summarizes the basic indicators of health personnel; hospitals, by kind and utilization; mortality rates that are most indicative of general health services; external controls on health (adequacy of food supply and availability of safe drinking water); and sources and amounts of expenditure on health care. Each datum refers more or less directly to the availability or use of a particular health service in a country, and, while each may be an accurate measure at a national level, each may also conceal considerable differences in availability of the particular service to different segments of a population or regions of a country. In the United States, for example, the availability of physicians ranges from about one per 769 persons in the least well-served states to one per 299 in the best-served, with a rate of one per 150 in the national capital. Such disparities are even more pronounced in most other countries, unless the government has made some special effort to achieve a more uniform distribution of personnel and facilities. In addition, even when trained personnel exist and facilities have been created, the country may lose health professionals via the "brain drain" to foreign countries; or low levels of financial support at the national level may leave facilities underserved; or lack of good transportation may prevent those most in need from reaching a clinic or hospital that could help them.

Definitions and limits of data have been made as specific as possible in the compilation of this table. For example, despite wide variation worldwide in the nature of the qualifying or certifying process that permits an individual to represent himself as a physician, organizations such as the World Health Organization (WHO) try to maintain more consistent international standards for training and qualification. International statistics presented here for "physicians" refer to persons qualified according to WHO standards and exclude traditional health practitioners, whatever the local custom with regard to the designation "doctor." Statistics for health personnel in this table uniformly include all those actually working in the health service field, whether in the actual provision of services or in teaching, administration, research, or other tasks. One group of practitioners for whom this type of guideline works less well is that of midwives, whose training and qualifications vary enormously from country to country but who must be included, as they represent, after nurses, perhaps the largest and most important category of health auxiliary worldwide. The statistics here refer to those midwives working in some kind of institutional setting (a hospital, clinic, community health-care centre, or the like) and exclude rural noninstitutional midwives and traditional birth attendants.

Hospitals also differ considerably worldwide in terms of staffing and services. In this tabulation, the term hospital refers generally to a permanent facility offering inpatient services and/or nursing care and staffed by at least one physician. Establishments offering only outpatient or custodial care are excluded. These statistics are broken down into data for general hospitals (those providing care in more than one specialty), specialized facilities (with care in only one specialty), local medical centres, and rural health-care centres; the last two generally refer to institutions that provide a more limited range of medical or nursing care, often less than full-time. Hospital data are further analyzed into three categories of administrative classification: public, private nonprofit, and private for profit. Statistics on number of beds refer to beds that are maintained and staffed on a full-time basis for a succession of inpatients to whom care is provided.

Data on hospital utilization refer to institutions defined as above. Admission and discharge, the two principal points at which statistics are normally

Health services

country	health personnel							hospitals									
	year	physicians	dentists	nurses	pharmacists	midwives	population per physician	year	number	kinds (%)				ownership (%)			hospital beds per 10,000 pop.
										general	specialized	medical centres	rural	government	private nonprofit	private for profit	
Afghanistan	1989–91	2,233	267	1,451	510	338	7,414	1988–93	...	...	...	...	...	...	...	...	3
Albania	1990	4,467	1,099	...	772[1]	9,936[1]	729	1989	895	—17.9—		—82.1—		100.0	—	—	57
Algeria	1992	25,304	7,563[2]	...	2,575[2]	...	1,014	1992	284[3, 4]	...	...	...	...	...	...	...	22
American Samoa	1989	34	7	140	2	1	1,384	1990	1	100.0	—	—	—	100.0	—	—	27
Andorra	1992	110	...	...	...	...	548	1992	1	100.0	—	—	—	100.0	—	—	20
Angola	1990	662	10	9,334	...	...	15,136	1990	58	...	...	...	...	...	...	...	12
Antigua and Barbuda	1991	59	13	179	13	...	1,085	1991	2	50.0	50.0	—	—	100.0	—	—	65
Argentina	1992	88,800	21,900[2]	18,000[5]	...	...	373	1992	...	...	...	...	...	...	...	...	44
Armenia	1994	14,000[7]	[7]	34,000[8, 9]	...	[8]	263[7]	1994	183	...	...	...	...	100.0	...	...	83
Aruba	1992	74	19	515[2]	13	3	936	1992	2	50.0	—	50.0	—	100.0	—	—	44
Australia	1991	38,800	6,700	188,600[8]	10,637[10]	[8]	445	1990	1,071[6]	...	...	...	...	65.5[6]	—34.5[6]—		50
Austria	1993	26,121	3,517	35,533	2,043[11]	967	307	1993	324	39.2	60.8	—	—	...	...	...	92
Azerbaijan	1994	29,000[7]	[7]	72,200[8, 9]	...	[8]	256[7]	1994	749[2]	...	...	...	...	100.0[2]	...	...	105
Bahamas, The	1992	357	58	682[4]	52[4]	...	714	1991	5	60.0	20.0	20.0	—	60.0	—40.0—		40
Bahrain	1991	542	38	1,607	121	...	953	1991	12	58.3	42.7	—	—	75.0	16.7	8.3	23
Bangladesh	1992	21,749	702	10,607	7,485[4]	9,363	5,184	1992	891	...	...	...	...	68.6	—31.4—		3
Barbados	1992	312	38	889	138	377	842	1992	10	70.0	30.0	—	—	80.0	—	20.0	75
Belarus	1994	45,000[7]	[7]	115,700[8, 9]	...	[8]	233[7]	1994	868[2]	...	...	...	...	100.0[2]	...	...	122
Belgium	1994	37,792	7,070	...	13,657	...	267	1993	363	80.4	19.6	—	—	38.6	61.4	—	76
Belize	1992	110	12	303	16	233	1,809	1992	7	...	...	...	...	100.0	—	—	29
Benin	1989	323	16	1,384	86	453	13,879	...	...	...	...	...	...	...	...	...	...
Bermuda	1993	91	23	534	28	...	662	1993	2	50.0	50.0	—	—	...	...	...	42
Bhutan	1990	141	9	233	5	70	5,226	1993	27	...	...	...	...	...	...	...	12
Bolivia	1993	3,392	1,643[9]	1,869	...	...	2,083	1995	336	10.7	8.9	23.5	56.8	...	...	...	15[2]
Bosnia and Herzegovina	1989	6,929	1,368	...	781	...	624	1989	...	...	...	...	...	...	...	...	46
Botswana	1988	240	21	2,488	40	...	4,964	1990	30	...	...	...	...	80.0	10.0	10.0	25
Brazil	1992	208,966	118,609	...	57,047	...	715	1990	35,701	—18.3—		—81.7—		66.8	—33.2—		37[12]
Brunei	1992	197	27	1,228	10	254	1,359	1992	10	90.0	—	—	10.0	90.0	—10.0—		36
Bulgaria	1993	28,457	5,727	52,038	2,376	6,903	298	1993	287	71.8	28.2	—	—	...	...	...	106
Burkina Faso	1991[13]	341	19	2,627	113	339	27,158	1993	78	—14.1—		85.9	—	100.0	—	—	5[2]
Burundi	1990	317	9	670[13]	55	97[13]	16,657	1988	264	—12.5—		—87.5—		87.5	—12.5—		19[4]
Cambodia	1990	600	36[9]	7,271[12]	262[9]	2,232[12]	14,300	1988	188[3]	...	...	...	...	100.0	—	—	16
Cameroon	1989	945	55	6,053	206	...	11,848	1988	629	—27.0—		—73.0—		72.3	—27.7—		27
Canada	1991	60,559	14,621	262,288	22,121	...	464	1989	1,079	81.8	16.6	1.6	—	95.8	—	4.2	50[15]
Cape Verde	1988	112	...	205	9	...	2,931	1987	75	6.7	—	93.3	—	100.0	—	—	15
Central African Republic	1990	170	8	1,353	22	166	16,447	1988	133	—21.1—		—78.9—		79.7	—20.3—		15
Chad	1993	217	5[5]	239	10	130	27,765	1993	...	...	...	...	...	...	...	...	7
Chile	1993	15,015	5,200	5,653	230[13]	1,924[13]	920	1992	217	...	...	...	...	82.9	—17.1—		32
China	1993	1,832,000[16]	...	1,056,000	413,000	55,000	633[16]	1993	60,784	17.7	6.5	—75.8—		100.0	—	—	24
Colombia	1992	36,551	13,815	46,376	...	...	914	1989	947	...	...	...	...	...	...	...	14
Comoros	1990	57	6	155	6	86	8,135	1989	...	...	...	...	...	...	...	...	25
Congo	1990	613	35	1,624	175	498	4,028	1990	...	...	...	...	...	...	...	...	33
Costa Rica	1993	4,027	1,200	7,021	1,152	...	792	1993	33	...	...	...	...	87.9	—	12.1	21
Côte d'Ivoire	1990	2,020	219	3,691	135	1,533	5,931	1989	...	...	...	...	...	...	...	...	8
Croatia	1993	9,280	1,940	...	1,696[9]	...	486	1992	98	32.7	61.3	—	—	...	...	...	61
Cuba	1992	46,860	8,057	73,943	650[10]	...	231	1993	244	...	...	...	...	100.0	—	—	61[2]
Cyprus[17]	1993	1,441	498	2,536	423	120	433	1993[18]	110	39.1	58.2	—	2.7	10.0	0.9	89.1	18[3]
Czech Republic	1993	31,897	6,015	...	...	...	324	1993	287	65.9	34.1	—	—	88.9	—11.1—		98
Denmark	1994	14,497	5,088	63,841	1,498[12]	915[14]	358	1992	163	42.9	57.1	—	—	42.9	57.1	—	35
Djibouti	1989	97	10	...	14	...	5,258	1993	8	—25.0—		—75.0—		100.0	...	...	27[5]

collected, are the basis for the data on the amount and distribution of care by kind of facility. The data on numbers of patients exclude babies born during a maternal confinement but include persons who die before being discharged. The bed-occupancy and average length-of-stay statistics depend on the concept of a "patient-day," which is the annual total of daily censuses of inpatients. The bed-occupancy rate is the ratio of total patient-days to potential days based on the number of beds; the average length-of-stay rate is the ratio of total patient-days to total admissions. Bed-occupancy rates may exceed 100% because stays of partial days are counted as full days.

Two measures that give health planners and policy makers an excellent indication of the level of ordinary health care are those for mortality of children under age five and for maternal mortality. The former reflects the probability of a newborn infant dying before age five. The latter refers to deaths attributable to delivery or complications of pregnancy, childbirth, the puerperium (the period immediately following birth), or abortion.

Levels of nutrition and access to safe drinking water are two of the most basic limitations imposed by the physical environment in which health-care activities take place. The nutritional data are based on recommendations of the United Nations' Food and Agriculture Organization for the necessary daily intake (in calories) for a moderately active person of average size in a climate of a particular kind (fewer calories are needed in a hot climate) to remain in average *good* health. Excess intake in the many developed countries ranges to more than 40% above the minimum required to maintain health (the excess usually being construed to diminish, rather than raise, health). The range of deficiency is less dramatic numerically but far more critical to the countries in which deficiencies are chronic, because the deficiencies lead to overall poor health (raising health service needs and costs), to decreased productivity in nearly every area of national economic life, and to the loss of social and economic potential through early mortality. By "safe" water is meant only water that has no substantial quantities of chemical or biological pollutants—*i.e.,* quantities sufficient to cause "immediate" health problems.

The data on health care expenditure represent a joint effort by the WHO and the World Bank to create better analytical tools by which the interrelations among health policy, health care delivery systems, and human health might be examined against the more general frameworks of government operations, resource allocation, and development process. First published in the World Bank's *World Development Report 1993: Investing in Health* and, the following year, in the World Health Organization's *Global Comparative Assessments in the Health Sector* (edited by C.J.L. Murray and A.D. Lopez), the database and underlying methodology are expected to provide a continuing basis for international comparisons and policy analysis.

Expenditures were tabulated for direct preventative and curative activities and for public health and public education programs having direct impact on health status—family planning, nutrition, and health education—but not more indirect programs like environmental, waste removal, or relief activities. Public, parastatal (semipublic, *e.g.,* social security institutions), international aid, and household expenditure reports and surveys were utilized to build up a comprehensive picture of national, regional, and world patterns of health care expenditures and investment that could not have been assembled from any single type of source. For reasons of space, public and parastatal are combined as the former.

admissions or discharges					bed occupancy rate (%)	average length of stay (days)	mortality		population with access to safe water (latest) (%)	food supply (% of FAO requirement) 1992	total health expenditures, 1990					country
rate per 10,000 pop.	by kinds of hospital (%)						under age 5 per 1,000 live newborn 1993	maternal mortality per 100,000 live births (latest)			as percent of GDP	per capita (U.S.$)	by source (percent)			
	general	specialized	medical centres	rural									public	private	international aid	
...	...	...	...	...	...	...	257	640	23	62	...	...	...	...	...	Afghanistan
...	...	...	...	...	...	...	41	43.1	100	108	4.00	26	84.0	16.0	—	Albania
...	...	...	...	...	...	...	68	140	68	121	6.95	149	76.9	23.0	0.1	Algeria
965	100.0	—	—	—	38.4	4	11[5]	0.0	62	...	...	...	...	...	...	American Samoa
...	...	...	...	...	...	...	...	...	100	...	...	...	...	...	...	Andorra
238	...	...	...	...	44.5[6]	16[6]	292	900	41	78	...	...	...	...	...	Angola
636		...	...	...	[illegible]	[illegible]	24	...	100	105	4.55	241	59.1	37.3	3.6	Antigua and Barbuda
520	...	...	...	...	51.9[3]	8[3]	27	52.0	71	123	4.21	137	60.1	39.7	0.2	Argentina
...	...	...	...	...	...	...	33	12.8	...	...	4.17	152	59.8	40.2	—	Armenia
...	...	...	...	...	92.2	...	...	...	...	...	...	...	...	...	...	Aruba
...	...	...	...	...	...	...	8	3.4	100	120	7.67	1,294	69.6	30.4	—	Australia
2,619	...	...	...	...	77.3	11	8	4.2	100	132	8.38	1,711	66.4	33.6	—	Austria
...	...	...	...	...	...	...	52	28.6	...	...	4.27	99	61.2	38.8	—	Azerbaijan
822[3]	...	...	...	...	83.7[3]	8[3]	29	69.3	100	108	...	...	...	...	...	Bahamas, The
1,274[12]	...	...	...	...	80.0[12]	7[12]	22	7.9	100	...	4.62	324	63.0	36.9	0.1	Bahrain
853[1]	...	...	...	...	...	...	122	600	84	87	3.19	6	24.8	50.7	18.5	Bangladesh
810	[illegible]	6.5			[illegible]	[illegible]	10	26.7	100	133	5.04	323	64.3	33.8	1.9	Barbados
...	...	...	...	...	...	...	22	21.1	...	...	3.19	157	68.7	31.3	—	Belarus
1,963	96.0	4.0	—	—	84.4	12	10	6.6	100	139	7.50	1,449	82.5	17.5	—	Belgium
...	...	...	...	...	...	...	42	...	75	118	5.88	23	40.4	41.0	10.7	Belize
...	...	...	...	...	...	...	144	160	51	110	4.32	19	26.3	36.4	37.3	Benin
1,319	97.2	2.8	—	—	76.4	9	9[4]	...	...	106	...	...	...	...	...	Bermuda
...	...	...	...	...	...	...	197	1,310	34	...	5.05	10	41.1	30.4	28.5	Bhutan
252[2]	...	...	...	...	45.9[2]	5[2]	114	600	54	88	4.01	25	39.9	39.6	20.5	Bolivia
529[6]	...	...	...	...	82.4[6]	11[6]	15	56.0	...	...	...	...	...	...	...	Bosnia and Herzegovina
...	...	...	...	...	93.1[5]	...	56	250	89	98	6.19	139	61.8	21.6	16.5	Botswana
1,277	...	...	...	...	...	7[5]	63	64.7	87	118	4.20	146	65.7	33.9	0.4	Brazil
...	...	...	...	...	...	...	10	...	100	123	...	...	...	...	...	Brunei
...	...	...	...	...	...	...	19	21.3	100	113	5.36	121	81.4	18.6	—	Bulgaria
...	...	...	...	...	...	...	175	810	56	101	8.46	7	9.8	17.9	72.3	Burkina Faso
109[14]	...	...	...	...	...	...	178	800	57	83	3.28	30	42.4	48.3	9.3	Burundi
...	...	...	...	...	...	...	181	500	36	91	...	...	...	...	...	Cambodia
...	...	...	...	...	...	...	113	430	50	85	2.62	27	26.4	61.7	11.9	Cameroon
...	...	...	...	...	...	14	8	2.9	100	116	9.05	1,945	74.1	25.9	—	Canada
...	...	...	...	...	...	...	73	...	71	119	6.32	64	20.7	25.5	53.7	Cape Verde
...	...	...	...	...	...	...	177	600	24	75	4.19	18	26.5	37.5	36.0	Central African Republic
...	...	...	...	...	...	...	206	960	57	84	6.22	12	27.6	24.7	47.7	Chad
1,041[2]	...	...	...	...	64.9[2]	7[2]	17	40.5	86	106	4.73	100	70.1	29.1	0.7	Chile
418	—61.3—		—38.7—		71.1	16	43	95	69	116	3.51	11	58.5	40.9	0.6	China
614	41.4	16.7	—41.9—		57.2	6	19	69.2	86	115	3.98	51	44.0	54.4	1.6	Colombia
...	...	...	...	...	...	...	128	500	63	81	5.40	28	46.3	29.2	24.5	Comoros
...	...	...	...	...	...	...	109	900	38	103	3.99	50	47.1	40.7	12.1	Congo
958[2]	...	...	...	...	78.2[2]	6[2]	16	34.5	93	129	6.51	132	73.6	25.2	1.2	Costa Rica
...	...	...	...	...	...	...	120	680	76	108	3.35	28	48.7	47.9	3.4	Côte d'Ivoire
1,172	80.1	19.9	—	—	78.9	15	11	3.6	...	...	...	...	...	...	...	Croatia
1,376[2]	...	...	...	...	...	...	10	41.8	98	123	...	...	...	...	...	Cuba
747[3]	...	...	...	...	75.7[3]	7[3]	10	10	100	152	3.96	64	62.9	26.8	10.3	Cyprus[17]
1,938	96.6	3.4	—	—	73.8	14	10	11.6	100	...	5.94[19]	169[19]	84.9[19]	15.1[19]	—	Czech Republic
1,253	92.9	7.1	—	—	80.4	8	7	7.4	100	136	6.30	1,588	84.2	15.8	—	Denmark
...	...	...	...	...	...	...	158	740	45	101	...	...	...	...	...	Djibouti

Health services (continued)

country	health personnel							hospitals									
	year	physicians	dentists	nurses	pharma-cists	midwives	population per physician	year	number	kinds (%)				ownership (%)			hospital beds per 10,000 pop.
										general	specialized	medical centres	rural	government	private non-profit	private for profit	
Dominica	1991	38	4[4]	218[9]	12[4]	...	1,889	1994	53	1.9	—	—	98.1	100.0	—	—	25
Dominican Republic	1992	11,130	1,898	6,035	129[10]	...	671	1992	103[1]	—44.7[1]—		—55.3[1]—		...	...	...	20
Ecuador	1992	12,853	1,826	4,215	...	667	836	1992	429	16.1	6.1	—77.8—		...	...	...	16
Egypt	1992	101,500	15,150	...	34,700	...	552	1991	6,418	5.1	—94.9—			...	...	...	20
El Salvador	1993	4,525	1,182	5,094	...	1,940[2]	1,219	1993	78	...	...	...	...	61.5	1.3	37.2	17
Equatorial Guinea	1990	99	...	154	...	55	3,532	1988	...	...	...	...	...	...	...	...	29
Eritrea	1993	68	...	488	...	33	49,200	1986–87	...	...	...	...	...	...	...	...	9
Estonia	1994	4,680	820	7,302	930[2]	710	319	1994	115[15]	...	...	...	...	98.8[20]	—1.2[20]—		84
Ethiopia	1988	1,466	...	3,496	364	...	30,195	1986–87	86	...	...	...	...	...	...	...	3
Faroe Islands	1992	81	42	301	10[2]	17	581	1992	3	33.3	—	—	66.7	100.0	—	—	57
Fiji	1994	426	40	1,631	...	...	1,829	1994	25	...	...	...	...	...	...	...	22
Finland	1993	13,344	4,602	123,456	579[11]	956	380	1992[6]	317	100.0	—	—	—	...	...	...	90
France	1992	155,896	38,451	313,374	51,613	11,205	367	1992	3,834	—91.7—			8.3	26.9	—73.1—		120
French Guiana	1992	200	32	489	33	31	644	1991	6[1]	50.0[1]	—	—	50.0[1]	50.0[1]	—50.0[1]—		66
French Polynesia	1991	323	85	599	42	41	624	1991	34	...	...	...	...	...	...	...	58
Gabon	1989	448	32	759	71	240	2,504	1988	27	...	...	...	...	...	...	...	51
Gambia, The	1991	61	...	430[5]	...	...	14,536	1994	13	15.4	—	—84.6—		...	...	...	7[3]
Gaza Strip	1984	250	...	...	...	...	2,000	1993	6	...	...	...	...	83.3	—16.7—		13
Georgia	1994	30,000[7]	[7]	64,100[4, 8]	...	[8]	183[7]	1994	422[4]	...	...	...	...	100.0[4]	...	...	105
Germany	1993	259,981	58,194	708,000[8, 9]	42,887	[8]	312	1992	2,381	...	...	...	...	50.2	35.5	14.3	80
Ghana	1989[13]	628	39	11,808	67	1,736	22,452	1991	121	90.9	9.1	—	—	60.3	—39.7—		13
Gibraltar	1993	29	2[12]	302[2]	3[12]	8[12]	981	1993	2	50.0	50.0	—	—	100.0	...	...	86
Greece	1993	40,116	10,731	34,314[21]	7,948[11]	1,916[21]	259	1992	372	46.5	53.5	—	—	...	...	...	50
Greenland	1993	78	30	356[2]	10[2]	17[2]	709	1990	16	6.3	—	—	93.7	100.0	—	—	75
Grenada	1993	47	7	347	28[4]	36[4]	1,949	1991[6]	3	100.0	—	—	—	100.0	—	—	38
Guadeloupe	1991	590	119	1,476	192	107	680	1991	30[5]	...	...	...	...	56.7[5]	—43.3[5]—		80
Guam	1986	147	...	594[8]	...	[8]	823	...	...	...	...	...	...	...	...	...	...
Guatemala	1992	7,601	1,065[1]	14,401	...	...	1,282	1985	...	...	...	...	...	...	...	...	16[5]
Guernsey	1993	79	...	...	...	...	804	1993	1	100.0	—	—	—	100.0	—	—	...
Guinea	1990	773	22[12]	243[12]	261[12]	343[12]	7,445	1988	38	—100.0—		...	...	100.0	—	—	6
Guinea-Bissau	1986	274	13	674[14]	12	111[14]	3,245	1993	16	...	...	...	...	62.5	—37.5—		13
Guyana	1992	138	15[5]	708	29[5]	172[5]	5,314	1989	...	...	...	...	...	...	...	...	33
Haiti	1992	564	81	2,489	...	...	11,113	1992	87[5]	...	...	...	...	...	...	...	8
Honduras	1993	3,803	622	6,288	792[12]	...	1,358	1993	86	...	...	...	...	34.9	—65.1—		12
Hong Kong	1994[22]	7,670	1,615	32,876	951	981[9]	790	1993	81	...	...	...	...	84.0	—16.0—		45
Hungary	1993	36,643	4,754	54,472[9]	4,806[9]	2,704[9]	248	1993	148	76.1[20]	14.6[20]	—9.3[20]—		...	...	...	98
Iceland	1990	726	219	1,793	132	202	353	1991	26	88.5	11.5	—	—	...	...	...	111
India	1992[22]	405,253	11,300	340,208[2]	...	181,323[1]	2,140	1991	15,067	...	...	...	...	55.0	—45.0—		8
Indonesia	1992	25,135	3,821[12]	118,555[8]	3,520[11]	[8]	7,402	1992	971	...	...	...	...	...	...	...	6
Iran	1994	37,000	4,770[9]	48,639[2, 8]	...	[8]	1,600	1995	609[12]	...	...	...	...	...	...	...	15
Iraq	1991	9,366	1,577	13,206	1,552	...	1,922	1990	177	72.9	27.1	—	—	...	...	...	18
Ireland	1992	6,036[23]	1,205[12]	23,127[12]	...	...	588[23]	1992[3, 6]	63	100.0	—	—	—	100.0	—	—	34
Isle of Man	1988	86	...	...	...	...	745	1986	3	33.3	33.3	—	33.3	100.0	—	—	...
Israel	1993	24,344	6,956	...	4,127	...	214	1994	244	19.7	80.3	—	—	12.7	50.0	37.3	63
Italy	1992	296,385	10,814[5]	170,409[5]	53,948[5]	...	193	1992	1,926	71.2	28.8	—	—	59.3	—40.7—		68
Jamaica	1992	1,589	270	1,687	65[13]	340[13]	1,541	1992	30	80.0	20.0	—	—	80.0	—20.0—		22[3]
Japan	1992	219,704	77,416	795,810	162,021	22,690	566	1992	9,963	89.1	10.9	—	—	71.7	—28.3—		136
Jersey	1992	88	...	...	...	...	967	1990	6	16.7	83.3	—	—	100.0	—	—	88
Jordan	1991	6,395	1,477	6,466	2,220	513[4]	574	1992	53[4]	...	...	...	...	52.8[4]	—47.2[4]—		11
Kazakhstan	1994	66,000[7]	[7]	229,600[8, 9]	...	[8]	256[7]	1994	1,805[2]	...	...	...	...	100.0[2]	...	...	134
Kenya	1993	3,794	664	27,143	605	...	7,022	1993	877	—35.1—		—64.9—		...	...	...	14
Kiribati	1993	10	1[14]	147	3[14]	...	7,687	1990	...	...	...	...	...	...	...	...	40
Korea, North	1989	57,690	...	...	...	...	370	1989	...	...	...	...	...	...	...	...	135
Korea, South	1993	51,518	12,180	107,883	40,779	8,150	855	1993[21]	...	...	...	...	...	...	...	...	29
Kuwait	1994[13]	2,717	399	7,406	903	...	596	1994	22	63.6	36.4	—	—	63.6	—	36.4	26[3]
Kyrgyzstan	1994	14,674	226	41,939	1,122	3,414	305	1994	396	89.1	—	10.9	—	100.0	—	—	99
Laos	1990	1,173	...	6,753[8, 14]	...	[8]	3,555	1990	1,074	0.7	—99.3—			100.0	—	—	25
Latvia	1994	7,714	968	12,559	292	981	330	1994	170	51.2	4.1	28.8	15.9	97.6	2.4	—	121
Lebanon	1989–91	6,638	1,015	1,248	1,390	153	407	1993	...	...	...	...	...	...	...	...	50
Lesotho	1993	136	...	874[4]	60[4]	...	14,306	1987	22	90.9	9.1	—	—	54.5	45.5	—	15
Liberia	1985	89	5	908	...	443	24,600	1988	92	—37.0—		—63.0—		...	...	...	...
Libya	1989–91	4,749	686	13,849	...	...	690	1990	...	...	...	...	...	...	...	...	41
Liechtenstein	1993	32	12	...	2	...	957	1989	1	...	...	...	...	...	...	...	35
Lithuania	1993	14,670	1,952	29,179	...	1,830	255	1993	198	...	...	...	...	100.0	...	...	117
Luxembourg	1993	848	203	...	336	143	473	1993	34	50.0	50.0	—	—	...	...	...	115
Macau	1993	467	27	883	44	...	831	1993	43	4.7	—	95.3	—	37.2	—62.8—		28
Macedonia	1993	4,528	1,078	5,638	358	1,436	458	1993	61	27.9	41.0	16.4	14.8	100.0	—	—	52
Madagascar	1990	1,392	89	3,124	19	1,703	8,628	1990	...	...	...	...	...	...	...	...	9
Malawi	1989	186	...	284	5	...	49,118	1987	395	12.2	0.8	—87.0—		59.2	—40.8—		16
Malaysia	1990	7,012	1,288[12]	36,076[5]	1,084[12]	...	2,475	1989	264	...	...	...	...	38.6	—61.4—		22
Maldives	1993	45	1[4]	153	...	...	5,297	1993	5	20.0	—	80.0	—	100.0	—	—	8
Mali	1988	435	13	1,509	57	321	18,046	1987	...	...	...	...	...	...	...	...	4
Malta	1995	900	115	4,100	600	290	409	1995	7	...	...	...	...	...	...	...	58
Marshall Islands	1991	20	...	130	...	4	2,402	1985	2	100.0	—	—	—	100.0	—	—	14
Martinique	1992	625	121	1,567	199	130	590	1991	...	...	...	...	...	...	...	...	103
Mauritania	1991	135	20	819	6	141	14,259	1990	16	...	...	...	...	100.0	—	—	7
Mauritius	1994	941	148	2,575[8, 13]	206	[8]	1,187	1994	23	73.9	17.4	8.7	—	60.9	4.3	34.8	28[3]
Mayotte	1985	9	1	51	1	2	7,427	1991	2	100.0	—	—	—	100.0	—	—	11
Mexico	1992	149,432	4,730[13]	141,404[2, 13]	...	...	578	1993	1,539	...	...	...	...	53.9	—46.1—		10
Micronesia	1993	50	7	230	7	...	2,069	1993	4	100.0	—	—	—	100.0	—	—	31
Moldova	1994	18,000[7]	[7]	48,600[8, 9]	...	[8]	241[7]	1994	335[2]	...	...	...	...	100.0[2]	...	...	122
Monaco	1993	112	31[5]	293[5]	64[5]	8[5]	270	1992	1	100.0	—	—	—	100.0	...	...	168
Mongolia	1993	5,911	299	9,183	1,113	...	376	1993	475	...	...	...	...	...	...	...	105
Morocco	1993	7,695	1,132	13,358	2,214	87[4]	3,361	1990[25]	203	31.0	—	69.0	—	100.0	—	—	11
Mozambique	1989	388	17	2,847	332[12]	1,089	36,428	1990	238	4.2	0.8	—95.0—		100.0	—	—	9[12]

admissions or discharges: rate per 10,000 pop.	by kinds of hospital (%): general	special-ized	medical centres	rural	bed occu-pancy rate (%)	aver-age length of stay (days)	mortality: under age 5 per 1,000 live newborn 1993	maternal mortality per 100,000 live births (latest)	popu-lation with access to safe water (latest) (%)	food supply (% of FAO require-ment) 1992	total health expenditures, 1990: as percent of GDP	per capita (U.S.$)	by source (percent): public	private	inter-national aid	country
1,026	...	...	...	...	94.6	8	22	...	77	115	8.06	192	65.1	20.4	14.5	Dominica
470[3]	...	...	...	...	55.3[1]	4[1]	48	...	59	101	3.72	38	52.7	43.3	4.0	Dominican Republic
518	...	...	...	...	57.5	7	57	152.2	55	113	4.14	44	55.9	37.3	6.8	Ecuador
...	...	...	...	...	...	...	59	65.2	90	133	2.61	28	30.3	62.0	7.7	Egypt
...	...	...	...	...	54.9[3, 9]	6[3, 9]	60	37.4	47	116	5.86	58	29.7	55.6	14.7	El Salvador
...	...	...	...	...	...	...	180	800	...	...	7.60	28	36.6	20.7	42.7	Equatorial Guinea
...	...	...	...	...	...	...	204	...	...	...	...	...	...	...	...	Eritrea
1,773	76.7	21.5	—	1.8	83.9	14	23	33.0	...	...	3.62	228	53.0	47.0	—	Estonia
...	...	...	...	...	...	...	204	560	25	69	3.80	4	41.3	39.9	18.8	Ethiopia
1,812[10]	76.6[10]	—	—	24.3[10]	61.7	11[10]	...	...	...	...	...	...	...	...	...	Faroe Islands
886[10]	...	...	...	...	72.6[10]	7[10]	28	41.1	80	135	3.76	70	54.9	38.3	6.9	Fiji
2,276	100.0	—	—	—	91.5	13	5	3.1	100	111	7.82	2,046	83.3	16.7	—	Finland
2,318[4]	...	...	...	...	83.0[12]	16[12]	9	12.9	100	144	9.40	1,869	74.2	25.8	—	France
1,903	...	...	...	...	75.1	10	...	...	...	128	...	...	...	...	...	French Guiana
...	...	...	...	...	...	...	...	0.0	...	124	...	...	...	...	...	French Polynesia
...	...	...	...	...	...	...	154	190	68	107	4.10	164	52.7	40.9	6.4	Gabon
...	...	...	...	...	...	...	216	1,000	77	99	7.53	22	28.3	20.7	51.0	Gambia, The
1,375	...	...	...	...	97.9	3	...	...	...	...	...	...	...	...	...	Gaza Strip
...	...	...	...	...	...	...	28	54.9	...	...	4.45	152	62.5	37.5	—	Georgia
1,843	...	...	...	...	83.9	13	7	5.5	100	126	8.73	1,511	72.7	27.3	—	Germany
...	...	...	...	...	...	...	170	1,000	52	96	3.50	15	35.0	51.8	13.2	Ghana
1,474[2]	...	...	...	...	41.4[2]	8[2]	...	...	...	...	...	...	...	...	...	Gibraltar
1,367	78.7	21.3	—	—	69.8	9	10	2.9	100	143	5.39	359	76.0	24.0	—	Greece
2,450	29.2	—	—	70.8	69.4	8	21[9]	...	...	...	...	...	...	...	...	Greenland
910	100.0	—	—	—	45.6	8	35	65.4	85	99	5.96	133	68.8	27.8	3.5	Grenada
2,136	...	...	...	...	82.3	11		...	...	111	...	...	...	...	...	Guadeloupe
...	...	...	...	...	...	...	15[5]	...	100	...	...	...	...	...	...	Guam
284	...	...	...	...	57.7	9	73	92.3	62	103	3.70	27	44.2	43.2	12.6	Guatemala
1,100	100.0	—	—		...	...	...	...	...	...	...	...	...	...	...	Guernsey
...	...	...	...	...		...	226	800	55	103	3.90	17	39.7	40.3	20.0	Guinea
...	...	...	...	...	...	...	235	700	41	111	8.15	16	31.3	18.9	49.8	Guinea-Bissau
...	...	...	...	...	...	...	63	200	61	105	10.37	42	40.7	15.1	44.2	Guyana
...	...	...	...	...	...	...	130	600	39	75	6.99	27	26.3	54.8	19.0	Haiti
503[9]	...	...	...	...	...	...	56	220	68	102	4.54	52	56.7	35.7	7.7	Honduras
1,613	...	...	...	...	...	...	7	5.9	100	137	5.69	687	19.5	80.5	0.0	Hong Kong
2,234	...	...	...	...	73.9	12	15	9.9	100	133	5.95	185	84.4	15.6	—	Hungary
2,781	95.4	4.6	—	—	87.8	13	6	0.0	100	116	8.31	1,004	87.5	12.5	—	Iceland
...	...	...	...	...	...	...	122	460	79	108	6.00	21	20.0	78.4	1.6	India
...	...	...	...	...	...	...	111	450	51	127	2.01	12	25.6	66.7	7.7	Indonesia
...	...	...	...	...	...	...	54	120	89	119	2.54	244	56.9	43.1	0.0	Iran
645	...	...	...	...	42.4	4	71	120	77	88	...	...	...	...		Iraq
1,448	100.0			—	77.7	7	7	7.6	100	153	7.22	876	81.1	18.0		Ireland
...	...	...	...	...	...	...	4[9]	...	...	...	...	...	...	...	...	Isle of Man
1,935	...	...	...	...	91.2	11	9	8.5	100	119	4.20	480	49.3	50.6	0.1	Israel
1,554	90.5	9.5	—	—	69.8	11	9	4.8	100	141	7.54	1,449	77.7	22.3	—	Italy
550[3]	81.7[3]	18.3[3]	—	—	63.8[3, 6]	6[3, 6]	13	120	100	116	5.04	83	57.4	33.2	9.5	Jamaica
...	...	...	...	...	...	...	6	9.2	97	124	6.45	1,538	74.5	25.5	—	Japan
1,718	84.0	16.0	—	—	...	...	...	...	...	...	...	...	...	...	...	Jersey
408[3]	...	...	...	...	68.7[3]	3[3]	27	48	99	123	3.77	55	36.9	52.3	10.8	Jordan
...	...	...	...	...	...	...	49	49.6	...	...	4.44	154	62.3	37.7		Kazakhstan
...	...	...	...	...	...	...	90	170	49	89	4.33	10	40.0	37.9	22.1	Kenya
...	...	...	...	...	...	...	80	225	44	116	...	...	...	...	...	Kiribati
			...	...	...	...	32	41	100	121	...	...	...	...	...	Korea, North
620	97.8	2.2	—	—	75.1	13	9	13.7	93	140	6.61	365	40.9	58.9	0.2	Korea, South
950[3]	72.2[3]	27.8[3]	—	—	64.9[3]	7[3]	13	1.9	100	104	4.06	541	64.2	35.6	0.1	Kuwait
1,775	95.5	—	4.5	—	75.6	15	58	62.9	...	...	4.97	118	66.7	33.3	—	Kyrgyzstan
...	...	...	...	...	...	...	141	300	36	102	2.53	5	17.4	60.7	21.9	Laos
2,106	78.4	4.6	13.8	3.2	78.7	16	26	29.9	...	...	3.87	220	56.1	43.9	—	Latvia
...	...	...	...	...	...	...	40	200	92	134	...	...	...	...	...	Lebanon
221[6]	...	...	...	...	...	...	156	350	47	97	8.32	26	38.3	26.5	35.2	Lesotho
...	...	...	...	...	...	...	217	600	50	71	8.24	4	19.9	11.8	68.3	Liberia
...	...	...	...	...	...	...	100	70	97	140	...	...	...	...	...	Libya
...	...	...	...	...	...	...	5[4]	...	...	...	...	...	...	...	...	Liechtenstein
1,966	...	...	...	...	...	...	20	20.5	...	...	3.58	159	72.0	28.0	—	Lithuania
1,956	94.6	5.4	—	—	73.4	16	10	0.0	100	139	6.56	1,662	91.4	8.6	—	Luxembourg
449	...	...	...	...	50.6	11	10[4]	30.0	...	99	...	...	...	...	...	Macau
913	66.6	27.9	3.7	1.8	84.2	18	33	6.2	...	...	...	...	...	...	...	Macedonia
...	...	...	...	...	...	...	164	570	23	94	2.56	7	29.0	49.6	21.4	Madagascar
436[14]	...	...	...	...	90.6[14]	8[14]	223	400	56	79	4.98	11	35.0	41.7	23.3	Malaŵi
717[3]	...	...	...	...	...	...	17	59	78	130	2.96	71	44.0	55.8	0.2	Malaysia
256[24]	...	...	...	...	71.4[24]	4[24]	78	313.4	95	117	...	...	...	...	...	Maldives
...	...	...	...	...	...	...	217	2,000	41	97	5.19	15	24.9	46.7	28.4	Mali
...	...	...	...	...	...	...	12	0.0	100	141	5.38	349	68.3	31.7	0.0	Malta
...	...	...	...	...	...	...	92	...	...	...	...	...	...	...	...	Marshall Islands
2,139	...	...	...	...	61.0	11	...	94.8	...	117	...	...	...	...	...	Martinique
...	...	...	...	...	...	...	202	800	66	116	3.80	18	28.5	41.5	30.0	Mauritania
1,440[3]	...	...	...	...	74.6[3]	5[3]	22	99.2	97	119	4.40	100	47.8	39.0	13.3	Mauritius
778[14]	100.0[14]	—	—	—	74.8[14]	6[14]	...	...	...	...	...	...	...	...	...	Mayotte
403[2, 3]	...	...	...	...	64.7[2, 3]	5[2, 3]	32	51.3	84	135	3.17	89	49.3	49.8	0.9	Mexico
2,171[14]	100.0[14]	—	—	—	...	...	29	...	...	...	...	...	...	...	...	Micronesia
...	...	...	...	...	...	...	36	34.1	...	...	3.91	143	74.4	25.6	—	Moldova
...	...	...	...	...	...	...	...	...	100	...	...	...	...	...	...	Monaco
...	...	...	...	...	...	...	78	200	80	78	6.63	58	83.0	15.1	1.9	Mongolia
238	93.6[20]	—	6.4[20]	—	52.9	9	59	300	54	123	2.55	26	33.6	63.3	3.1	Morocco
...	...	...	...	...	...	...	282	300	22	72	5.86	5	21.0	25.7	53.3	Mozambique

Health services (continued)

country	health personnel							hospitals									
	year	physicians	dentists	nurses	pharma-cists	midwives	population per physician	year	number	kinds (%)				ownership (%)			hospital beds per 10,000 pop.
										general	spe-cialized	medical centres	rural	govern-ment	private non-profit	private for profit	
Myanmar (Burma)	1994	12,245	1,062	9,064	...	8,615	3,721	1994	717	...	...	...	...	...	...	...	6
Namibia	1992	324	51	4,471	91[2]	...	4,594	1992	47	...	...	...	...	91.5	—8.5—		45[2]
Nauru	...	...	...	...	...	...	...	...	...	...	...	...	...	...	...	...	...
Nepal	1992	1,497	...	2,781	427[10]	2,379[4]	12,623	1992	114	...	...	...	...	...	...	...	3
Netherlands, The	1993	39,069	7,900[2]	121,000[5]	2,464	1,142	391	1993	236	65.3	34.7	—	—	...	...	...	57
Netherlands Antilles	1994	291	63	998[9]	31	11	677	1994	11	36.4	36.4	27.2	—	...	...	...	73
New Caledonia	1993	370	98	...	58	63	485	1990	8	12.5	12.5	75.0	—	62.5	—37.5—		62
New Zealand	1994	11,413	1,916	44,670[8]	3,483	[8]	309	1994	330	...	...	...	...	38.2	—61.8—		77
Nicaragua	1993	2,554	332	1,753	...	...	1,668	1993	56	46.4	7.1	46.4	—	...	...	...	12
Niger	1990	142	5	2,036	29	457	54,472	1987	...	...	...	...	...	...	...	...	5
Nigeria	1989	17,954	1,088	64,503	5,318	52,378	4,692	1985	11,588	6.6	0.5	—92.9—		81.4	—18.6—		12[1]
Northern Mariana Islands	1986	23	4	103	2	2	1,324	1988	1	100.0	—	—	—	100.0	—	—	19
Norway	1994	14,497	5,088	61,367	...	...	298	1993	350	19.1	80.9	—	—	...	...	...	53
Oman	1992	2,095	142	5,567	350	...	910	1989	180	—28.3—		—71.7—		100.0	—	—	23[9]
Pakistan	1993	63,033	2,401	20,245	3,772[9]	18,641	2,107	1992	10,905	—7.1—		—92.9—		...	...	...	6
Palau	1990	10	...	84	...	...	1,518	1986	1	...	...	...	...	...	...	...	50
Panama	1993	3,168	570	2,692	115[5]	...	800	1993	60	...	...	...	...	86.7[20]	—13.3[20]—		29
Papua New Guinea	1990	301	...	2,447	...	...	12,874	1989	...	...	...	...	...	...	...	...	40
Paraguay	1992	2,924	1,160	4,558	...	...	1,522	1992	...	...	...	...	...	...	...	...	12
Peru	1992	23,771	7,945	15,026	5,940[2]	3,520[2]	944	1992	427	...	...	...	...	56.7	—43.3—		17
Philippines	1993	78,445	1,614[13]	14,853[13]	730[12, 13]	12,339[13]	849	1992	1,723	96.5	3.1	0.5	—	36.4	—63.6—		11
Poland	1994	87,706	17,296	208,641	19,208	24,255	440	1994	752	93.6	6.4	—	—	...	...	...	63
Portugal	1993	24,499	1,509	30,975	5,950	824[14]	403	1993	335	43.0	18.8	38.2	—	74.3	14.7	11.0	42
Puerto Rico	1989	6,269	902	19,666	2,111	120	558	1994	72	83.3	8.3	8.3	—	36.1	30.6	33.3	26
Qatar	1992	758	114	1,829[13]	175[13]	...	671	1992	3	33.3	66.7	—	—	100.0	—	—	20
Réunion	1994	1,061	308	2,520	248[11]	166	605	1993	...	...	...	...	...	70.4[20]	—29.6[20]—		44
Romania	1992[13]	42,808	6,414	...	6,432[5]	...	531	1992	...	...	...	...	...	...	...	...	95
Russia	1994	612,400	47,100	1,008,800	7,300	117,200	241	1994	12,265	37.4	17.2	—	45.4	99.8	—0.2—		119
Rwanda	1989	272	7	835	25	...	24,697	1985[3]	220	—13.6—		—86.4—		100.0	—	—	9[5]
St. Kitts and Nevis	1992	39	8	260	14	...	1,057	1992	4	50.0	—50.0—			...	...	...	67
St. Lucia	1992	64	6	256	...	...	2,235	1992	4	25.0	25.0	—	50.0	...	...	...	37
St. Vincent	1992	40	6	224	27[2]	...	2,708	1992	9	...	...	...	...	77.8	—22.2—		44
San Marino	1987	60	...	...	...	...	375	1987	...	...	...	...	...	...	...	...	66
São Tomé and Príncipe	1989	61	5	223	1	54	1,881	...	...	...	...	...	...	...	...	...	...
Saudi Arabia	1991	25,543	1,967	48,066	1,811	...	523	1990	229	...	...	...	...	71.2	—28.8—		21
Senegal	1992	520	58[12]	934[12]	200[12]	474[12]	14,817	1992	...	...	...	...	...	...	...	...	10
Seychelles	1994	72	11	344	5	...	1,026	1994	7	14.3	14.3	71.4	—	100.0	—	—	56
Sierra Leone	1992	404	...	...	...	...	10,832	1988	219	—25.6—		—74.4—		...	...	...	10
Singapore	1994	4,301	767	11,688	773	506	681	1994	22	...	...	...	...	50.0	9.1	40.9	36
Slovakia	1992	15,767	2,444	...	499	...	336	1991	111	72.1	27.9	—	—	100.0	—	—	91
Slovenia	1990	4,086	1,148	...	1,019	...	489	1993	24	54.2	45.8	—	—	...	...	...	58
Solomon Islands	1990	52	...	447	...	...	6,154	1986	8	100.0	—	—	—	75.0	25.0	—	53
Somalia	1986	450	2	1,834	180	556	13,315	1988	...	...	...	...	...	...	...	...	7
South Africa[28]	1993	25,967	4,024	157,497	9,388	...	1,527	1992	834	...	...	...	...	...	...	...	39
Spain	1993	159,291	12,247	167,894	39,608	6,210	246	1991	813	...	...	...	...	42.4	—57.6—		42
Sri Lanka	1992[13]	3,345	333[5]	11,214	520[5]	5,030[5]	5,203	1992[3]	422	...	...	...	...	100.0	—	—	28
Sudan, The	1990[13]	2,400	...	...	...	...	10,000	1986	...	...	...	...	...	...	...	...	8
Suriname	1992	329	...	995	...	...	1,247	1989	...	...	...	...	...	...	...	...	47
Swaziland	1990	83	7	1,264	13	...	9,265	1986	24	—41.7—		—58.3—		...	...	...	...
Sweden	1993	22,200	4,900	92,300[8]	5,603	[8]	393	1992	...	...	...	...	...	...	...	...	52
Switzerland	1992	23,000	4,400	...	1,547[11]	...	299	1992	...	...	...	...	...	...	...	...	78
Syria	1991	11,808	4,495	11,957	4,041	4,443	1,061	1988	213	80.3	19.7	—	—	23.0	—77.0—		12
Taiwan	1994	27,288	7,095	53,734	18,762	1,004	772	1993	810	...	...	...	...	11.6	—88.4—		48
Tajikistan	1994	13,084	926	38,852	709	1,027	439	1994	449	...	...	...	...	98.2	—1.8—		88
Tanzania	1984	1,065	...	...	...	...	19,775	1988	...	...	...	...	...	...	...	...	11
Thailand	1992	13,398	2,669	87,868	4,609	19,526	4,245	1992	1,097	92.9	7.1	—	—	73.7	—26.3—		17
Togo	1991	319	22	1,187	65	222	11,270	1990	...	...	...	...	...	...	...	...	16
Tonga	1992	46	11	285	2[5]	37[5]	2,139	1992	4	...	...	...	...	...	...	...	31
Trinidad and Tobago	1993	1,051	136	2,260[8]	529	[8]	1,191	1992	31[14]	...	...	...	...	...	...	...	33
Tunisia	1992	4,670	836	12,143	1,596	...	1,799	1991[3]	138	5.8	3.6	—90.6—		100.0	—	—	20
Turkey	1990	50,639	10,514	44,904	15,792	30,415	1,108	1990	857	74.9	8.5	—16.6—		85.4	—14.6—		24[9]
Turkmenistan	1994	14,000[7]	[7]	40,600[8, 9]	...	[8]	286[7]	1994	368	...	...	...	...	100.0	...	...	115
Tuvalu	1993	8	2[1]	39	...	...	1,152	1985	8	11.1	—	—	88.9	100.0	—	—	36
Uganda	1989	774	...	2.332	...	...	20,720	1989	89	...	...	...	...	...	...	...	12[12]
Ukraine	1994	230,000[7]	[7]	618,000[8, 9]	...	[8]	226[7]	1994	3,900	...	...	...	...	100.0	...	...	130
United Arab Emirates	1991	3,090	388[4]	7,130[4]	...	...	618	1993	35	...	...	...	...	82.9	—17.1—		21
United Kingdom	1992	87,000[23]	...	284,578[5]	37,832[4]	24,801[5]	667[23]	1988	2,423[14]	...	...	...	...	100.0	—	—	54[9, 23]
United States	1993	670,300	187,000	1,956,000	182,000	3,000	385	1993	6,580	82.1	17.9	—	—	31.1	51.2	17.7	46
Uruguay	1993	11,201	3,712	2,047	948	581	286	1993	112	...	...	...	...	61.6	—38.4—		45
Uzbekistan	1994	79,000[7]	[7]	247,000[8, 9]	...	[8]	286[7]	1994	1,388[2]	...	...	...	...	100.0[2]	...	...	85
Vanuatu	1995	12	3	259	6	33	14,025	1995	90	5.6	—	21.1	73.3	100.0	—	—	22
Venezuela	1992	32,616	7,945	52,260	5,615	...	626	1992	610	...	...	...	...	37.0	—63.0—		26
Vietnam	1993	28,500	...	53,700	6,500	12,000	2,490	1993	12,500	...	...	...	...	...	...	...	27
Virgin Islands (U.S.)	1985	167	...	...	...	...	622	1985	...	...	...	...	...	...	...	...	49
West Bank	1984	510	...	...	...	...	1,535	1993	17	...	...	...	...	52.9	—47.1—		12
Western Sahara	...	...	...	...	...	...	...	...	...	...	...	...	...	...	...	...	...
Western Samoa	1992	50[4]	7	298	6	...	3,183[4]	1992	36	2.8	—	—	97.2	100.0	—	—	34
Yemen	1992	3,065	163	6,430[4]	231	199[4]	3,900	1992	75	...	...	...	...	...	...	...	8
Yugoslavia	1993	24,698	4,478[9]	...	2,209	...	420	1993	...	...	...	...	...	...	...	...	55
Zaire	1990	2,469	41	27,601	59	...	15,584	1986	400	...	...	...	...	52.5	—47.5—		21
Zambia	1990	713	26	1,503	24	311	11,414	1987	965	8.2	0.3	19.0	72.5	80.9	19.1	—	29[5]
Zimbabwe	1993	1,551	194	22,590	411	2,894	6,909	1993[3]	1,378	0.9	2.6	83.7	12.7	100.0	—	—	15

[1]1987. [2]1991. [3]Government hospitals only. [4]1990. [5]1989. [6]General hospitals only. [7]Physicians includes dentists. [8]Nurses includes midwives. [9]1992. [10]1986. [11]Number of pharmacies. [12]1988. [13]Government-employed health personnel only. [14]1985. [15]1993. [16]Includes physicians practicing dentistry and doctors of traditional Chinese medicine (358,000 in 1993). [17]Republic of Cyprus only. [18]Excludes psychiatric hospitals. [19]Data refer to former Czechoslovakia. [20]Based on bed ownership. [21]General and specialized hospitals only. [22]Registered personnel; all may not be present and

admissions or discharges					bed occupancy rate (%)	average length of stay (days)	mortality		population with access to safe water (latest) (%)	food supply (% of FAO requirement) 1992	total health expenditures, 1990					country
rate per 10,000 pop.	by kinds of hospital (%)						under age 5 per 1,000 live newborn 1993	maternal mortality per 100,000 live births (latest)			as percent of GDP	per capita (U.S.$)	by source (percent)			
	general	specialized	medical centres	rural									public	private	international aid	
...	...	...	...	...	...	...	111	460	32	120	...	...	...	...	...	Myanmar (Burma)
...	...	...	...	...	...	...	79	370	52	94	3.92	45	47.8	41.3	10.9	Namibia
...	...	...	...	...	...	...	...	...	...	...	...	...	...	...	...	Nauru
54[12]	...	...	...	...	...	...	128	830	42	89	4.54	7	23.0	51.7	25.4	Nepal
1,057	97.4	2.6	—	—	78.5	15	8	7.1	100	120	8.03	1,501	72.6	27.4	—	Netherlands, The
...	...	...	...	...	...	...	...	...	...	107	...	...	...	...	...	Netherlands Antilles
1,165[6]	...	...	...	...	84.8[6]	8[6]	...	...	...	124	...	...	...	...	...	New Caledonia
1,374[3, 15]	...	...	...	...	93.3[3, 15]	8[3, 15]	9	8.4	100	139	7.37	925	81.7	18.3	—	New Zealand
596	——87.6——		12.4	—	...	...	72	61.2	54	102	8.61	34	56.9	22.5	20.6	Nicaragua
...	...	...	...	...	...	...	320	700	59	96	4.98	16	24.5	31.3	34.1	Niger
...	...	...	...	...	...	...	191	800	36	90	2.72	10	36.5	57.4	6.1	Nigeria
1,550	100.0	—	—	—	54.7	4	...	...	...	...	...	...	...	...	...	Northern Mariana Islands
1,569	90.7	9.3	—	—	83.1	10	8	5.8	100	121	7.35	1,835	95.7	4.3	—	Norway
1,226	...	...	...	...	83.0[6]	5[6]	29	220	84	...	4.22	209	59.5	40.1	0.5	Oman
...	...	...	...	...	...	...	137	500	68	100	3.48	12	47.4	47.1	5.5	Pakistan
...	...	...	...	...	...	...	...	...	...	...	...	...	...	...	...	Palau
773	...	...	...	...	58.4	8	20	62.6	84	97	7.13	142	72.6	23.1	4.3	Panama
253[6, 12]	...	...	...	...	...	...	95	900	33	115	4.44	37	59.1	36.1	4.8	Papua New Guinea
...	...	...	...	...	...	...	34	280.3	35	116	2.97	35	35.1	58.2	6.7	Paraguay
...	...	...	...	...	...	...	62	300	72	80	3.21	61	56.1	41.7	2.2	Peru
538	...	...	...	...	62.1	5	59	100	82	100	2.15	16	46.7	46.4	6.9	Philippines
1,288[9]	96.0[9]	4.0[9]	—	—	72.5[9]	14[9]	15	11.8	100	126	5.07	84	80.3	19.7	—	Poland
1,146	86.3	10.5	3.2	—	74.5	10	11	6.1	100	148	6.99	383	61.7	38.3	—	Portugal
1,101	94.0	4.3	1.7	—	63.1	5	16[5]	20.1	...	...	...	...	...	...	...	Puerto Rico
...	...	...	...	...	71.7[26]	7[26]	25	...	100	...	4.73	630	63.0	36.9	0.0	Qatar
2,160	...	...	...	...	82.7	6	...	...	...	143	...	...	...	...	...	Réunion
...	...	...	...	...	...	...	29	60.3	100	115	3.87	58	61.4	38.6	—	Romania
2,150	...	...	...	...	83.2	17	31	50.8	...	...	3.02	159	66.8	33.2	—	Russia
85[21]	...	...	...	...	42.8[21]	7[21]	141	210	66	78	3.44	10	15.0	45.2	39.8	Rwanda
1,068[6]	...	...	...	...	49.3[6]	9[6]	41	...	100	100	5.99	212	58.1	27.8	14.1	St. Kitts and Nevis
890[21]	...	...	...	...	...	...	22	...	67	107	7.18	169	75.6	23.0	1.4	St. Lucia
776[6]	...	...	...	...	67.9[6]	6[6]	24	...	75	97	5.69	102	68.5	28.8	2.7	St. Vincent
...	...	...	...	...	...	...	...	...	...	...	...	...	...	...	...	San Marino
...	...	...	...	...	...	...	84	76.7	52	91	9.22	38	28.8	17.0	54.2	São Tomé and Príncipe
...	...	...	...	...	...	...	38	41	95	113	4.76	260	64.3	35.7	0.0	Saudi Arabia
...	...	...	...	...	...	...	120	600	48	95	3.66	29	45.1	38.0	16.9	Senegal
1,605[27]	...	...	...	...	75.2[27]	6[27]	20	...	100	98	6.03	289	50.2	28.0	21.9	Seychelles
...	...	...	...	...	...	...	284	450	37	74	2.43	4	19.6	30.9	49.5	Sierra Leone
1,174	85.8	14.2	—	—	73.1	8	6	4.1	100	...	1.87	215	58.3	41.6	0.1	Singapore
1,679	94.9	5.1	—	—	73.2	14	10	...	100	...	...	...	...	...	...	Slovakia
1,579	...	...	...	...	82.7	11	10	5.1	...	...	...	...	...	...	...	Slovenia
...	...	...	...	...	...	...	33	10	82	95	2.10	117	43.2	50.5	6.3	Solomon Islands
...	...	...	...	...	...	...	211	1,100	37	65	1.51	8	7.3	41.1	51.6	Somalia
...	...	...	...	...	...	...	69	84	...	110	5.56	77	57.5	42.5	0.0	South Africa[28]
997	...	...	...	...	76.7	12	9	5.5	100	151	6.59	831	78.4	21.6	—	Spain
1,464[4]	...	...	...	...	...	...	19	46.5	60	102	3.74	18	40.4	51.1	8.6	Sri Lanka
...	...	...	...	...	...	...	128	550	48	94	3.33	34	11.0	84.5	4.5	Sudan, The
766[29]	...	...	...	...	68.8[29]	10[29]	34	31.1	68	113	2.88	93	37.9	58.0	4.1	Suriname
...	...	...	...	...	...	...	107	400	30	117	7.22	64	43.6	22.2	31.2	Swaziland
1,881	...	...	...	...	78.0	8	6	0.0	100	110	8.79	2,343	89.3	10.7	—	Sweden
...	...	...	...	...	...	...	8	4.6	100	126	7.52	2,520	68.5	31.5	—	Switzerland
474					67.0	5	00	140	74	128	2.07	41	16.6	79.4	4.0	Syria
...	...	...	...	...	...	...	8	7.8	...	...	4.00	020	53.0	47.0	0.0	Taiwan
1,492	...	...	...	...	70.2	15	83	53.2	...	...	5.98	100	72.6	27.4	—	Tajikistan
...	...	...	...	...	...	...	167	340	50	87	4.73	4	14.4	31.6	54.0	Tanzania
...	...	...	...	...	...	...	33	50	77	110	4.98	72	20.4	78.7	0.9	Thailand
...	...	...	...	...	...	...	135	420	60	97	4.10	18	40.4	38.5	21.2	Togo
622	...	...	...	...	56.2	10	25	...	75	129	6.46	63	60.3	25.0	14.8	Tonga
1,114[3, 6]	...	...	...	...	70.7[3, 6]	6[3, 6]	21	49.2	97	107	4.54	180	62.4	36.9	0.6	Trinidad and Tobago
...	...	...	...	...	...	...	36	70	99	139	4.91	76	63.8	33.3	3.0	Tunisia
568	...	...	...	...	...	...	60	150	78	136	3.94	76	36.2	63.3	0.5	Turkey
...	...	...	...	...	...	...	89	55.2	...	...	4.99	125	66.4	33.2	0.4	Turkmenistan
1,368	40.9	—	—	59.1	51.5[6]	12.2[6]	56	...	...	...	2.66	472	34.0	66.0	0.1	Tuvalu
...	...	...	...	...	...	...	185	550	31	93	3.40	8	13.3	53.0	33.7	Uganda
...	...	...	...	...	...	...	25	31.3	...	...	3.30	131	69.7	30.3	—	Ukraine
...	...	...	...	...	...	...	21	130	95	140	2.66	472	34.0	66.0	0.1	United Arab Emirates
1,434	...	...	...	...	80.6[10]	15[10]	8	6.7	100	132	6.11	1,039	84.9	15.1	—	United Kingdom
1,191[30]	...	...	...	...	64.6[30]	7[30]	10	8.2	100	141	12.71	2,765	44.1	55.9	—	United States
401[3]	...	...	...	...	69.1[3]	15[3]	21	15.9	75	103	4.62	123	53.8	44.8	1.4	Uruguay
...	...	...	...	...	...	...	66	30.1	...	...	5.90	116	72.1	27.9	—	Uzbekistan
567	...	...	...	...	41.9	6	58	...	100	120	5.68	67	51.5	25.7	22.8	Vanuatu
601[3]	...	...	...	...	69.7[3]	6[3]	24	64.1	89	106	3.60	88	54.2	45.6	0.1	Venezuela
...	...	...	...	...	...	...	48	120	24	104	2.11	3	39.3	47.4	13.3	Vietnam
...	...	...	...	...	...	...	16[12]	...	...	...	...	...	...	...	...	Virgin Islands (U.S.)
809	...	...	...	...	81.0	4	...	...	...	...	...	...	...	...	...	West Bank
...	...	...	...	...	...	...	...	...	...	...	...	...	...	...	...	Western Sahara
894	70.8	—	—	29.2	32.9	5	57	...	83	124	2.94	20	6.1	54.2	39.7	Western Samoa
...	...	...	...	...	...	...	137	800	36	91	3.19	20	34.7	54.1	11.3	Yemen
1,060	...	...	...	...	71.6	13	...	...	...	...	5.11[31]	264[31]	80.4[31]	19.6[31]	—	Yugoslavia
...	...	...	...	...	...	...	187	800	39	93	2.38	5	8.5	64.8	26.7	Zaire
1,249	——75.7——		——24.3——		68.5	7	203	150	53	84	3.16	17	65.4	30.6	4.1	Zambia
546	...	...	...	...	69.8	7	83	330	84	83	6.23	39	40.3	48.7	11.0	Zimbabwe

working in the country. [23]OECD estimate. [24]Central Hospital only. [25]Public sector only. [26]Hamad General Hospital only. [27]Victoria Hospital only. [28]Data exclude the former Black independent states of Bophuthatswana, Ciskei, Transkei, and Venda. [29]Paramaribo hospitals (1,213 beds) only. [30]5,261 community hospitals only. [31]Data refer to former Socialist Federal Republic of Yugoslavia.

Social protection

This table summarizes three principal areas of social protective activity for the countries of the world: social security, crime and law enforcement, and military affairs. Because the administrative structure, financing, manning, and scope of institutions and programmed tasks in these fields vary so greatly from country to country, no well-accepted or well-documented body of statistical comparisons exists in international convention to permit objective assessment of any of these subjects, either from the perspective of a single country or internationally. The data provided within any single subject area do, however, represent the most consistent approach to problems of international comparison found in the published literature for that field.

The provision of social security programs to answer specific social needs, for example, is summarized simply in terms of the existence or nonexistence of a specific type of benefit program because of the great complexity of national programs in terms of eligibility, coverage, term, age limits, financing, payments, and so on. Activities connected with a particular type of benefit often take place at more than one governmental level, through more than one agency at the same level, or through a mixture of public and private institutions. The data shown here are summarized from the U.S. Social Security Administration's *Social Security Programs Throughout the World* (biennial). A bullet symbol (●) indicates that a country has at least one program within the defined area; in some cases it may have several. A blank space indicates that no program existed providing the benefit shown; ellipses [...] indicate that no information was available as to whether a program existed.

Data given for social security expenditure as a percentage of total central governmental expenditure are taken from the International Monetary Fund's *Government Finance Statistics Yearbook,* which provides the most comparable analytic series on the consolidated accounts of central governments, governmentally administered social security funds, and independent national agencies, all usually separate accounting entities, through which these services may be provided in a given country.

Data on the finances of social security programs are taken in large part from the International Labour Office's *The Cost of Social Security* (triennial), supplemented by national data sources.

Figures for criminal offenses known to police, usually excluding civil offenses and minor traffic violations, are taken in part from Interpol's *International Crime Statistics* (biennial) and a variety of national sources. Statistics are usually based on the number of offenses reported to police, not the number of offenders apprehended or tried in courts. Attempted offenses are counted as the offense that was attempted. A person identified as having committed multiple offenses is counted only under the most serious offense. Murder refers to all acts involving the voluntary taking of life, including infanticide, but excluding abortion, or involuntary acts such as those normally classified as manslaughter. Assault includes "serious," or aggravated, assault—that involving injury, endangering life, or perpetrated with the use of a dangerous instrument. Burglary involves theft from the premises of another; although Interpol statistics are reported as "breaking and entering," national data may not always distinguish cases of forcible

Social protection

country	social security															
	programs available, 1995					expenditures, 1992 (% of total central govt.)	finances									
							year	receipts					expenditures			
	old-age, invalidity, death[a]	sickness and maternity[b]	work injury[c]	unemployment[d]	family allowances[e]			total ('000,000 natl. cur.)	insured persons (%)	employers (%)	government (%)	other (%)	total ('000,000 natl. cur.)	benefits (%)	administration (%)	other (%)
Afghanistan	●	●	●		●	...	...	...	...	...	...	...	...	...	...	...
Albania	●	●	●	●	●	...	1990	967.0	—	—	88.8	11.2	1,440.0	99.5	—0.5—	
Algeria	●	●	●		●	...	1990	27,700.0	...	...	...	...	28,748.0	61.8	30.6	7.6
American Samoa	●	...	...	...	...	...	1990	...	...	...	...	...	13.0	100.0	—	—
Andorra	...	...	...	...	...	...	1993	11,832.2	...	...	...	...	7,937.2	90.2	4.6	5.2
Angola	...	...	...	...	...	...	...	...	...	...	...	...	...	...	...	...
Antigua and Barbuda	●	●				...	1983	13.0	29.2	48.7	—	22.1	4.2	66.1	33.9	—
Argentina	●	●	●	●	●	35.3[5]	1986	4,994.5	31.3	45.6	19.5	3.6	4,500.2	97.4	2.3	0.3
Armenia	●	●	●	●	●	...	...	...	...	...	...	...	...	...	...	...
Aruba	●	...	●	...	...	[11]	1992	66.3	...	...	...	...	60.4	...	...	...
Australia	●	●	●	●	●	29.6	1986	24,310.5	1.8	12.5	84.8	0.9	23,896.9	98.8	1.2	—
Austria	●	●	●	●	●	44.6[12]	1986	368,562.0	29.5	46.8	21.2	2.5	361,191.0	96.2	2.4	1.4
Azerbaijan	●	●	●	●	●	...	...	...	...	...	...	...	...	...	...	...
Bahamas, The	●	●	●			9.3[9]	1986	73.6	26.8	40.7	1.3	31.2	31.8	75.6	23.2	1.2
Bahrain	●		●			2.6[12]	1986	35.8	21.1	42.2	—	36.7	7.6	73.2	19.7	7.1
Bangladesh		●	●	●		9.8[12, 14]	1986	154.3	37.4	41.8	1.4	19.4	57.9	95.8	4.2	—
Barbados	●	●	●	●		19.8[5]	1986	148.0	37.7	39.4	5.6	17.3	129.5	92.9	5.2	1.9
Belarus	●	●	●	●	●	11.0	1986	3,199.0	—	—	93.2	6.8	3,199.0	100.0	—	—
Belgium	●	●	●	●	●	41.3[5]	1986	1,347,070.0	24.4	39.7	31.6	4.3	1,322,636.0	94.5	4.3	1.2
Belize	●	●	●			3.3	1986	11.2	9.4	56.4	—	34.2	2.4	52.1	46.2	1.7
Benin	●		●		●	8.7[12, 15]	1986	4,539.2	15.9	78.4	—	5.7	3,906.3	65.5	3.0	1.0
Bermuda	●		●			...	...	...	...	...	...	...	...	...	...	...
Bhutan	...	...	...	...	...	0.5	1990	...	...	...	...	...	26.0[12]	...	...	...
Bolivia	●	●	●		●	12.0	1986	70,737,008.0	25.6	39.4	23.4	11.5	52,958.650.0	82.0	12.0	0.4
Bosnia and Herzegovina	●	●	●	●	●	...	...	...	...	...	...	...	...	...	...	...
Botswana			●			0.6[12, 13]	1988	—	...	...	...	...	33.0[12]	...	...	...
Brazil	●	●	●	●	●	27.7	1986	201,807,600.0	38.5	53.5	3.8	4.2	184,814,900.0	91.7	6.4	1.9
Brunei	●	...	...	...	...	...	1984	...	...	...	...	...	39.5	...	...	...
Bulgaria	●	●	●	●	●	32.3[16]	1986	3,707.4	—	17.8	0.4	—	3,593.0	99.8	0.2	—
Burkina Faso	●		●		●	8.4[9, 12]	1986	8,057.5	15.6	64.3	—	20.1	2,060.4	99.2	—	0.8
Burundi	●		●		●	0.7[18]	1986	1,368.9	30.9	51.1	—	18.0	933.1	82.2	14.8	3.0
Cambodia	...	...	●	...	●	...	...	...	...	...	...	...	...	...	...	...
Cameroon	●		●		●	6.5[5, 12]	1986	56,770.0	14.0	68.2	—	17.8	19,869.0	100.0	—	—
Canada	●	●	●	●	●	32.1[13]	1986	87,538.9	11.7	16.6	61.2	10.5	77,122.0	96.2	2.7	1.1
Cape Verde	●	●	●		●	...	1986	499.9	27.5	62.5	1.5	8.5	210.3	62.3	14.7	23.0
Central African Republic	●		●		●	6.2[4, 12]	1986	4,549.0	9.8	88.5	—	1.7	5,550.0	45.7	13.6	40.7
Chad	●		●		●	1.9[19]	1986	1,221.9	26.3	65.9[12]	—	7.8	841.4	41.4	55.3	3.3
Chile	●	●	●	●	●	31.1	1986	588,205.0	30.1	2.0	48.9	19.0	425,099.0	92.0	7.4	0.6
China	●	●	●	●		...	...	...	...	...	...	...	...	...	...	...
Colombia	●	●	●		●	16.4[9]	1986	169,872.0	21.5	56.5	1.7	20.2	133,837.0	51.6	42.3	6.1
Comoros	...	...	...	...	...	...	1983	40.7	100.0	—	—	—	54.3	17.4	62.3	20.3
Congo	●		●		●	0.4[22]	1983	15,272.8	12.1	80.2	—	7.7	7,256.7	66.6	21.3	12.1
Costa Rica	●	●	●		●	11.5[12]	1986	23,387.4	25.5	49.2	2.7	22.6	18,080.1	81.8	3.8	14.4
Côte d'Ivoire	●		●		●	3.6[4]	1986	40,277.4	13.6	53.1	—	33.3	22,866.5	79.6	14.1	6.3
Croatia	●	●	●	●	●	2.3	...	...	...	...	...	...	...	...	...	...
Cuba	●	●	●			...	1986	1,887.7	—	41.8	58.2	—	1,887.7	96.4	—	3.6
Cyprus[23]	●	●	●	●	●	19.6	1986	141.6	29.4	39.9	17.2	13.5	81.7	98.5	1.4	0.1
Czech Republic[24]	●	●	●	●	●	25.6	1986	120,692.0	—	3.7	94.5	1.8	120,692.0	99.7	0.3	—
Denmark	●	●	●	●	●	38.5[13]	1986	178,991.9	3.5	8.0	85.7	2.8	174,349.8	97.1	2.9	—
Djibouti	●	...	...	...	●	6.2[12, 25]	1979	1,352.2	...	...	...	...	1,115.7	...	...	...
Dominica	●	●	●			1.4[15]	1986	12.3	22.6	50.9	—	26.5	4.4	68.0	32.0	—
Dominican Republic	●	●	●			4.7[3]	1986	77.9	20.1	72.9	—	6.8	74.3	75.9	24.1	—
Ecuador	●	●	●	●		1.9[3]	1986	101,137.5	16.4	24.3	11.0	48.3	41,625.0	88.1	11.9	—
Egypt	●	●	●	●		9.1	1988	2,633.0	38.6	61.4	—	—	2,596.0	...	...	...
El Salvador	●	●	●			2.4	1986	287.4	23.2	54.0	—	22.8	210.9	75.0	25.0	—

entry. Automobile theft excludes brief use of a car without the owner's permission, "joyriding," and implies intent to deprive the owner of the vehicle permanently. Criminal offense data for certain countries refer to cases disposed of in court, rather than to complaints. Police manpower figures refer, for the most part, to full-time, paid professional staff, excluding clerical support and volunteer staff. Personnel in military service who perform police functions are presumed to be employed in their principal activity, military service.

The figures for military manpower refer to full-time, active-duty military service and exclude reserve, militia, paramilitary, and similar organizations. Because of the difficulties attached to the analysis of data on military manpower and budgets (including problems such as data withheld on national security grounds, or the publication of budgetary data specifically intended to hide actual expenditure, or the complexity of long-term financing of purchases of military matériel [how much was actually spent as opposed to what was committed, offset by nonmilitary transfers, etc.]), extensive use is made of the principal international analytic tools: publications such as those of the International Institute for Strategic Studies (*The Military Balance* and *Strategic Survey*) and the U.S. Arms Control and Disarmament Agency (*World Military Expenditures and Arms Transfers*), both annuals.

The data on military expenditures are from the sources identified above, as well as from the IMF's *Government Finance Statistics Yearbook* and country statistical publications.

The following notes further define the column headings:

a. Programs providing cash payments for *each* of the three types of long-term benefit indicated to persons (1) exceeding a specified working age (usually 50–65, often 5 years earlier for women) who are qualified by a term of covered employment, (2) partially or fully incapacitated for their usual employment by injury or illness, and (3) qualified by their status as spouse, cohabitant, or dependent minor of a qualified person who dies.
b. Programs providing cash payments (jointly, or alternatively, medical services as well) to occupationally qualified persons for *both* of the short-term benefits indicated: (1) illness and (2) maternity.
c. Programs providing cash or medical services to employment-qualified persons who become temporarily or permanently incapacitated (fully or partially) by work-related injury or illness.
d. Programs providing term-limited cash compensation (usually 40–75% of average earnings) to persons qualified by previous employment (of six months minimum, typically) for periods of involuntary unemployment.
e. Programs providing cash payments to families or mothers to mitigate the cost of raising children and to encourage the formation of larger families.
f. A police officer is a full-time, paid professional, performing domestic security functions. Data include administrative staff but exclude clerical employees, volunteers, and members of paramilitary groups.
g. Includes all active-duty personnel, regular and conscript, performing national security functions. Excludes reserves, paramilitary forces, border patrols, and gendarmeries.

crime and law enforcement (latest)						military protection								country
offenses reported to the police per 100,000 population					population per police officer[f]	manpower, 1995[g]		expenditure, 1993				arms trade, 1993 ('000,000 U.S.$)		
total	personal		property			total ('000)	per 1,000 population	total '000,000	per capita	% of central government expenditure	% of GDP or GNP	imports	exports	
	murder	assault	burglary	automobile theft										
...	...	...	...	...	540[1]	[2]	[2]	408[3]	24[4]	64.4[4]	9.1[4]	0	0	Afghanistan
...	...	...	...	...	550	73.0	21.4	157[5]	56[5]	11.3[5]	4.1[5]	0	0	Albania
584	1.0	19.7	39.7	8.5	840	121.7	4.4	1,360	50	5.9[6]	3.0	10	0	Algeria
3,448	11.8	579.6	1,060.9	21.6	460	—	[7]	—	—	—	—	...	...	American Samoa
7,000	2.0	46.0	1,204.0	150.0	220	—	—	...	...	...	...	...	...	Andorra
250	7.7	1.8	...	...	14[8]	82.0	7.1	1,127[9]	161[9]	28.8[10]	23.9[9]	100	0	Angola
4,977	4.7	475.0	1,984.4	35.9	120	0.2	2.3	...	...	...	...	...	...	Antigua and Barbuda
84	0.1	0.3	—	9.8	1,270	67.3	1.9	4,251	127	24.8	1.7	10	10	Argentina
437	9.7	6.0	11.6	14.7	...	60.0	16.9	...	...	...	...	0	0	Armenia
6,268	38.5	453.8	1,363.1	101.5	...	—	[7]	—	—	—	—	...	...	Aruba
5,319	7.1	369.6	1,062.8	1,005.5	450	50.1	3.1	7,441	417	9.5	2.6	300	40	Australia
6,421	2.6	2.5	1,307.3	42.4	470	55.8	6.9	1,730	219	2.5[13]	1.0	10	0	Austria
305	9.6	10.9	8.7	8.7	...	86.7	11.5	...	...	...	...	10	...	Azerbaijan
6,752	17.6	115.7	1,336.5	...	125	0.9	3.1	9[4]	40[4]	2.5[4]	0.5[4]	...	...	Bahamas, The
3,457	0.8	...	...	...	180	10.7	18.5	245	430	15.3[6]	6.1	40	0	Bahrain
64	2.2	3.7	4.9	0.4	2,560	115.5	1.0	355	3	8.4[6]	1.5	10	0	Bangladesh
4,958	7.4	159.1	388.7	43.6	280	0.6	2.3	8[6]	34[6]	1.7[6]	0.6[6]	0	0	Barbados
650	2.9	7.0	...	...	...	98.4	9.5	...	...	...	...	0	0	Belarus
3,591	2.7	117.9	752.1	312.5	640	47.2	4.7	3,740	373	3.7[6]	1.8	290	50	Belgium
2,781	34.6	629.8	819.5	...	290	1.1	4.9	6	27	3.2	1.1	0	0	Belize
125	0.9	37.9	3.4	1.3	3,250	4.8	0.9	26[6]	5[6]	19.4[5]	1.3[6]	0	0	Benin
8,871	5.1	221.7	1,949.2	...	370	—	[7]	—			—	...	...	Bermuda
...	...	...	...	...	...	4.0[14]	3.1[14]	...	...	...	...	0	0	Bhutan
...	...	...	...	...	...	33.5	4.5	126	17	7.6	2.4	5	0	Bolivia
558	...	...	...	...	...	92.0	26.6	...	...	...	...	0	0	Bosnia and Herzegovina
8,758	29.2	519.2	2.1	...	750	7.5	4.8	196	148	10.8	5.9	10	0	Botswana
116	...	...	...	...	...	295.0	1.9	5,852	37	4.9[13]	1.1	60	50	Brazil
520	0.1	85.0	96.2	28.5	100	4.9	16.8	302[3]	1,297[3]	20.9[5]	8.4[3]	0	0	Brunei
2,255	9.5	8.4	1,202.5	136.7	...	101.9	12.1	1,010	114	7.5[6]	3.2	0	10	Bulgaria
41	0.2	4.1	—	—	...	10.0	1.0	60	6	17.5[17]	2.2	13	3	Burkina Faso
87	3.3	7.4	...	...	...	14.6	2.5	28[13]	5[13]	13.4[13]	2.4[13]	0	0	Burundi
...	...	...	...	...	1,980	88.5	9.2	74	7	...	3.3	5	0	Cambodia
108	0.7	0.2	4.8	1.3	1,170	23.6	1.8	181	14	8.6	2.1	0	0	Cameroon
13,296.6	2.7	159.7	1,674	556.7	8,640	70.5	2.4	10,300	371	8.1	2.0	210	200	Canada
...	...	...	...	...	110	1.1	2.8	3[6]	8[6]	2.8[13]	1.0[6]	0	0	Cape Verde
135	1.6	22.8	2.7	...	2,740[1]	5.0	1.6	26[6]	9[6]	6.6[5]	2.1[6]	0	0	Central African Republic
...	...	...	...	...	990	30.4	4.8	31[6]	6[6]	8.3[6]	2.7[6]	10	0	Chad
1,125	5.0	93.3	...	15.2	470	99.0	7.0	1,002	73	9.2	2.4	40	0	Chile
201	1.9	4.1	17.5	...	1,360[20]	2,930.0	2.4	56,170	48	16.2	2.7	440	950	China
641	81.9	110.5	...	32.4	420	146.4	4.2	1,232	35	13.9[6]	2.6	20	0	Colombia
...	...	...	...	...	960	—	[21]	...	...	...	...	...	...	Comoros
32	1.5	4.7	0.2	0.2	870	10.0	3.9	123[6]	54[6]	11.1[3]	5.8[6]	0	0	Congo
868	5.3	11.1	232.4	23.1	480	7.5	2.2	20[13]	6[13]	1.4[13]	0.4[13]	0	0	Costa Rica
67	2.5	73.1	19.5	11.9	4,640	8.4	0.6	134[6]	10[6]	...	1.7[6]	0	0	Côte d'Ivoire
1,087	...	...	...	...	...	105.0	23.5	...	...	...	...	20	...	Croatia
...	...	...	...	...	650	105.0	9.5	426	39	...	2.0	100	0	Cuba
667	1.4	9.9	195.6	3.9	180	10.0	15.4	234	324	8.8	3.6	10	0	Cyprus[23]
1,911	2.0	89.4	621.5	95.7	640	86.4	8.4	2,040	196	6.8	2.6	5	130	Czech Republic[24]
10,399	4.6	169.2	2,381.0	619.7	600	33.1	6.3	2,682	518	4.8	2.0	50	10	Denmark
402	4.4	12.4	40.0	16.0	...	9.6	16.4	28	69	19.2[13]	6.0	0	0	Djibouti
1,956	4.2	25.2	1,078.1	33.6	300	[26]	[26]	...	...	...	...	...	...	Dominica
946	11.9	30.8	154.0	24.8	580	24.5	3.1	108	14	6.9	1.4	0	0	Dominican Republic
278	6.2	7.9	17.6	7.3	260	57.1	5.0	150	14	7.8	1.1	20	0	Ecuador
3,693	1.6	0.7	...	3.1	580	436.0	7.3	1,670	28	9.6	4.3	1,100	10	Egypt
...	...	...	...	...	1,000	30.5	5.3	100	18	10.1	1.3	30	0	El Salvador

Social protection (continued)

country	social security: programs available, 1995: old-age, invalidity, death[a]	sickness and maternity[b]	work injury[c]	unemployment[d]	family allowances[e]	expenditures, 1992 (% of total central govt.)	finances: year	receipts: total ('000,000 natl. cur.)	insured persons (%)	employers (%)	government (%)	other (%)	expenditures: total ('000,000 natl. cur.)	benefits (%)	administration (%)	other (%)
Equatorial Guinea	•	•	•	...	•	...	1983	43.0	4.7	95.3	—	—	20.0	30.0	70.0	—
Eritrea[28]	...	...	...	...	...	...	...	...	...	...	...	...	...	...	...	...
Estonia	•	•	•	•	•	33.5[12]	...	90.1	...	...	...	...	...	...	...	...
Ethiopia[28]	•	...	•	...	...	3.9[3]	1986	162.1	32.5	63.2	—	4.2	116.3	98.2	1.8	—
Faroe Islands	•	...	...	...	...	...	...	...	...	...	...	...	...	...	...	...
Fiji	•		•			4.0	1986	111.6	26.5	26.5	—	47.0	34.4	94.8	5.2	—
Finland	•	•	•	•	•	49.4[12]	1986	90,413.3	8.3	39.7	44.7	7.3	82,164.8	96.8	3.2	—
France	•	•	•	•	•	34.2[13]	1986	1,431,025.0	23.4	50.6	23.0	3.0	1,439,788.7	95.1	4.0	0.9
French Guiana	•	...	•	...	•	...	1991	1,071.5	...	...	...	...	997.1	...	...	...
French Polynesia	•	...	•	...	•	...	1990	19,268.0	...	...	...	...	17,832.0	...	...	...
Gabon	•	•	•		•	...	1986	37,788.0	8.3	84.8	—	6.9	42,326.0	80.7	15.1	4.2
Gambia, The	•		•			3.5[31]	1982	—	...	...	...	...	5.6	...	...	...
Gaza Strip	...	...	...	...	...	—	...	...	...	...	...	...	...	...	...	...
Georgia	•	•	•	•	•	...	...	...	...	...	...	...	...	...	...	...
Germany	•	•	•	•	•	48.5[5, 12]	1986[32]	459,340.0	36.6	35.0	25.8	2.6	451,885.0	97.2	2.8	—
Ghana	•		•			6.2	...	—	...	...	...	...	...	...	...	...
Gibraltar	•	•	...	•	•	...	...	...	...	...	...	...	...	...	...	...
Greece	•	•	•	•	•	12.2	1986	872,503.0	29.4	42.5	21.4	6.7	898,814.0	93.7	6.3	—
Greenland	•	...	...	...	•	...	...	...	...	...	...	...	...	...	...	...
Grenada	•	•				5.0[12, 18]	1986	15.2	27.7	57.9	—	14.4	6.0	91.0	9.0	—
Guadeloupe	•	...	...	...	•	...	1991	2,733.1	...	...	...	...	4,719.6	...	...	...
Guam	•	...	...	...	•	...	1989	...	...	...	...	...	7.3	...	...	...
Guatemala	•	•	•			5.2[5, 12]	1986	209.0	26.9	55.9	—	17.2	134.4	86.0	10.9	3.1
Guernsey	...	...	...	...	...	...	1993	66,369	——44.3——		45.5	10.2	62,458	94.2	5.8	...
Guinea	•	•	•		•	...	1986	269.2	3.0	90.9	—	6.1	268.7	85.2	1.8	13.0
Guinea-Bissau	...	...	...	...	...	8.8[12]	1986	138.0	22.8	63.4	10.3	3.8	61.9	59.6	40.4	—
Guyana	•	•	•			3.7[10]	1986	200.2	17.3	21.4	0.7	60.6	62.1	80.2	18.2	1.6
Haiti	•		•			5.1[4]	1977	60.5	——26.6——		69.9	3.5	52.4	92.7	7.3	—
Honduras	•	•	•			4.5[15]	1986	166.2	23.9	40.8	3.3	32.0	76.8	84.6	15.4	—
Hong Kong	•	•	•	•	•	...	1993–94	...	...	...	...	...	8,780.7	74.7	25.3	—
Hungary	•	•	•	•	•	27.7[3]	1986	149,400.0	21.1	78.9	—	—	142,939.0	99.3	0.7	—
Iceland	•	•	•	•	34	19.6	1991	14,406.0	—	54.3	45.7	—	69,255.0	98.1	1.9	—
India	•	•	•			...	1986	87,807.7	9.8	66.9	9.6	13.7	40,362.2	98.4	1.6	—
Indonesia	•	•	•			—	1986	97.9	17.3	58.1	—	24.6	92.2	12.5	19.4	68.1
Iran	•	•	•	•	•	11.0[16]	1986	346,460.0	83.2	0.1	8.2	8.5	167,879.0	43.4	6.3	50.0
Iraq	•	•	•			...	1977	107.8	9.9	55.6	21.9	12.6	71.0	94.0	2.4	3.6
Ireland	•	•	•	•	•	26.9[16]	1986	4,299.6	13.0	24.4	61.7	0.9	4,302.2	95.2	4.7	0.1
Isle of Man	•	•	•	•	•	37.0[35]	1985	...	...	...	...	...	14.4	...	...	...
Israel	•	•	•	•	•	20.9	1986	6,723.0	23.9	37.3	30.7	8.1	6,146.8	89.9	5.4	4.7
Italy	•	•	•	•	•	28.5[17]	1986	90,646.0	19.5	51.7	17.6	11.2	100,251.0	89.3	2.0	8.7
Jamaica	•		•			3.2[18]	1986	330.4	11.8	14.3	36.1	37.8	171.5	93.4	6.0	0.6
Japan	•	•	•	•	•	...	1986	50,525,725.0	27.2	30.6	26.8	15.4	40,145,652.0	94.6	1.7	3.7
Jersey	•	•	•	...	•	9.5	1991	60.9	——63.8——		23.4	12.8	52.8	...	...	...
Jordan	•		•			8.7	1986	53.6	28.7	55.3	—	16.0	9.5	77.4	14.0	8.6
Kazakhstan	•	•	•	•	•	...	...	...	...	...	...	...	...	...	...	...
Kenya	•		•			0.1	1986	1,660.0	27.7	27.7	1.2	43.4	268.0	85.1	14.9	—
Kiribati	•		•			...	...	...	...	...	...	...	...	...	...	...
Korea, North	...	...	...	...	...	...	...	...	...	...	...	...	...	...	...	...
Korea, South	•		•			8.1	1993	3,994,000.0	—	31.4	—	—	4,800,900.0	...	...	...
Kuwait	•					7.4	1986	385.8	6.3	12.4	54.6	26.7	169.5	96.3	3.7	—
Kyrgyzstan	•	•	•	•	•	...	...	...	...	...	...	...	...	...	...	...
Laos	...	...	•	...	...	...	...	...	...	...	...	...	...	...	...	...
Latvia	•	•	•	•	•	...	...	...	...	...	...	...	...	...	...	...
Lebanon	•	•	•	...	•	...	...	...	...	...	...	...	...	...	...	...
Lesotho	...	...	...	...	...	1.5[12, 13]	1988	—	...	...	...	...	5.3	...	...	...
Liberia	•		•			1.0[17]	1983	2.9	—	69.0	13.8	17.2	2.6	54.4	45.6	—
Libya	•	•	•			...	1977	192.9	9.1	28.7	58.7	3.5	128.2	96.2	3.2	0.5
Liechtenstein	•	•	•	•	•	...	...	...	...	...	...	...	...	...	...	...
Lithuania	•	•	•	•	•	33.6	...	...	...	...	...	...	24,981.7	...	...	...
Luxembourg	•	•	•	•	•	46.5	1986	59,427.9	24.7	34.2	34.5	6.6	51,643.0	96.8	2.7	0.5
Macau	•	...	...	...	•	...	1993	118.4	...	...	...	...	114.8	...	...	...
Macedonia	•	•	•	•	•	...	...	...	...	...	...	...	...	...	...	...
Madagascar	•		•		•	1.5[12, 13]	1986	10,288.2	22.2	77.8	—	—	10,075.3	87.0	13.0	—
Malaŵi			•			1.0[9]	1986	—	...	...	...	...	5.4	...	...	...
Malaysia	•		•			5.6[12]	1986	6,304.0	21.6	40.5	2.5	35.4	1,589.3	93.9	6.1	—
Maldives	...	...	...	...	...	1.0[13]	1989	—	...	...	...	...	6.4	...	...	...
Mali	•	•	•		•	3.0[17]	1986	8,128.8	16.6	74.3	—	9.1	7,924.6	63.7	34.7	1.6
Malta	•	•	•	•	•	34.7	1986	71.6	26.8	33.5	39.7	—	94.0	94.4	5.6	—
Marshall Islands	•					...	...	...	...	...	...	...	...	...	...	...
Martinique	•	...	...	...	•	...	1991	2,958.8	...	...	...	...	4,873.3	...	...	...
Mauritania	•		•		•	3.7[15]	1986	584.6	6.3	87.7	—	6.0	583.3	81.8	18.2	—
Mauritius	•		•		•	15.3[12]	1986	993.8	9.6	35.0	37.7	17.7	654.1	95.1	4.1	0.8
Mayotte	...	...	...	...	...	...	...	...	...	...	...	...	...	...	...	...
Mexico	•	•	•			12.3[3]	1986	2,463,649.0	19.6	63.1	5.0	12.3	2,115,574.0	73.6	17.3	9.1
Micronesia	•					...	...	...	...	...	...	...	...	...	...	...
Moldova	•	•	•	•	•	...	...	...	...	...	...	...	...	...	...	...
Monaco	...	...	...	...	...	...	...	...	...	...	...	...	...	...	...	...
Mongolia	•	•	•	...	•	25.6	...	...	...	...	...	...	...	...	...	...
Morocco	•	•	•		•	5.4[3, 12]	1986	3,660.7	27.6	41.2	—	31.2	2,506.5	94.5	3.5	1.9
Mozambique	•	...	...	...	...	...	1986	228.2	—	86.2	13.7	0.1	145.0	100.0	—	—
Myanmar (Burma)		•	•			0.4	1986	44.3	19.9	59.6	18.5	2.0	35.9	51.5	15.6	32.9
Namibia	•		•			6.8[13]	...	...	...	...	...	...	...	...	...	...
Nauru	•	•	•	...	•	...	...	...	...	...	...	...	...	...	...	...
Nepal	•		•			0.7[14]	1985	—	...	...	...	...	59.3	...	...	...
Netherlands, The	•	•	•	•	•	33.6	1986	140,734.0	38.0	33.4	15.6	13.0	122,791.0	97.0	3.0	—

crime and law enforcement (latest)						military protection								country
offenses reported to the police per 100,000 population					population per police officer[f]	manpower, 1995[g]		expenditure, 1993				arms trade, 1993 ('000,000 U.S.$)		
total	personal		property			total ('000)	per 1,000 population	total '000,000	per capita	% of central government expenditure	% of GDP or GNP	imports	exports	
	murder	assault	burglary	automobile theft										
...	...	...	...	...	190	1.3	3.3	2[27]	9[27]	21.0[27]	...	0	0	Equatorial Guinea
...	...	...	...	...	...	[29]	[29]	...	...	...	...	...	...	Eritrea[28]
2,750.3	15.9	25.1	399.7	116.3	...	3.5	2.4	471	293	10.2[6]	4.4	20	0	Estonia
94	6.7	24.8	1.9	...	1,100	[30]	[30]	151	3	10.9	4.4	0	0	Ethiopia[28]
...	...	...	...	...	...	—	[7]	—	—	—	—	...	...	Faroe Islands
2,374	4.2	41.3	453.0	69.9	440	3.9	4.9	26	34	5.5	1.6	0	0	Fiji
8,388	0.6	38.8	1,921.9	79.6	640	31.1	6.1	1,710	339	5.5[6]	2.2	290	0	Finland
6,660	4.7	96.7	804.0	648.5	630	409.0	7.0	42,590	740	7.6	3.4	50	675	France
8,936	27.2	178.7	1,367.3	150.6	...	—	[7]	—	—	—	—	...	...	French Guiana
1,799	0.9	98.9	232.7	...	...	—	[7]	—	—	—	—	...	...	French Polynesia
114	1.4	17.9	2.3	7.5	1,290	4.7	4.1	142[3]	144[3]	13.7[6]	3.4[3]	0	0	Gabon
...	...	...	...	...	3,310	0.8	0.7	3	3	2.0[4]	0.8	0	0	Gambia, The
4,355	...	...	...	...	...	—	—	...	...	...	...	...	...	Gaza Strip
...	...	...	...	...	...	—	—	...	...	...	...	0	0	Georgia
7,838	4.1	104.8	2,039.4	215.6	...	339.9	4.1	36,650	454	6.3[6]	2.2	250	1,100	Germany
864	2.0	95.9	4.7	...	620	7.0	0.4	35	2	5.0	0.7	0	0	Ghana
12,581	—	1,761	...	...	170	—	[7]	—	—	—	—	...	...	Gibraltar
3,699	2.5	66.4	301.9	83.2	380	171.3	16.3	4,070	389	13.5[6]	5.5	725	10	Greece
9,360	18.1	845.0	1,883.5	...	340	—	[7]	—	—	—	—	...	...	Greenland
2,679	10.0	880.0	153.0	...	230	[26]	[26]	...	...	...	...	...	...	Grenada
4,533	10.2	154.8	554.5	146.9	...	—	[7]	—	—	—	—	...	...	Guadeloupe
10,080	7.9	169.3	634.2	333.6	...	—	[7]	—	—	—	—	...	...	Guam
510	27.4	77.1	27.9	58.1	670	44.2	4.2	113	11	9.5	1.0	5	0	Guatemala
...	...	...	...	...	...	—	[7]	—	—	—	—	...	...	Guernsey
18.4	0.5	0.7	0.7	0.1	1,140	9.7	1.4	43[6]	7[6]	5.1[3]	1.5[6]	0	0	Guinea
128	0.8	8.7	4.0	0.2	...	9.2	8.6	7	7	7.6	3.3	0	0	Guinea-Bissau
1,980	15.6	28.1	434.7	...	190	1.6	2.1	5	7	2.8	2.0	0	0	Guyana
701	...	...	...	...	400	[33]	[33]	30	5	13.4[6]	1.5[6]	0	0	Haiti
...	9.4	7.7	...	3.3	1,040	18.8	3.4	44	8	7.0	1.4	10	0	Honduras
1,446	2.2	116.8	233.9	51.7	221	—	[7]	—	—	—	—	...	...	Hong Kong
4,326	4.1	77.7	889.6	62.3	710	70.5	6.9	1,261	122	5.7	2.0	875	10	Hungary
1,550	0.9	64.3	704.8	112.8	940	—	—	—	—	—	—	0	0	Iceland
594	4.6	...	15.6	...	820	1,145.0	1.2	8,471	9	18.8	3.3	10	5	India
113	0.8	5.0	1.8	7.4	1,340	274.5	1.4	2,031	10	6.7	1.5	160	20	Indonesia
76.6	0.5	47.7	...	...	...	513.0	8.4	4,857	78	12.4	3.6	1,000	5	Iran
197	7.1	34.7	...	...	140	382.0	18.7	9,007[13]	528[13]	50.8[31]	74.9[13]	0	0	Iraq
2,710	0.7	18.0	913.3	67.3	310	12.9	3.7	514	146	3.1	1.3	0	0	Iroland
3,488	...	...	892.4	...	...	—	[7]	—	—	—	—	...	...	Isle of Man
5,982	1.8	229.4	1,008.1	410.5	210	172.0	31.9	0,290	1,279	21.3	9.1	850	200	Israel
4,165	5.8	36.2	...	566.6	680	328.7	5.7	20,570	354	4.0[6]	2.1	50	400	Italy
2,006	25.6	18.2	252.2	13.9	430	3.3	1.3	10	10	0.4[13]	1.1	0	0	Jamaica
1,166	1.0	15.2	107.0	27.9	480	239.5	1.9	41,730	335	6.2	1.0	340	10	Japan
...	...	...	...	...	...	—	[7]	—	—	—	—	...	...	Jersey
751	2.0	19.1	43.4	28.5	630	98.6	23.5	438	115	23.5	9.0	20	0	Jordan
815	...	...	...	...	...	[36]	[36]	298	17	...	0.5	0	0	Kazakhstan
484	6.4	54.1	76.9	9.7	1,500	24.2	0.8	179	7	8.7	3.5	5	0	Kenya
285	12.4	5.5	73.3	...	330	—	—	...	...	...	...	...	...	Kiribati
...	...	...	...	...	460	1,128.0	48.0	5,500	253	40.7[17]	25.0	0	30	Korea, North
414	1.4	43.2	11.5	83.5	420	633.0	14.1	11,930	267	18.1	3.6	875	50	Korea, South
709	10.2[37]	92.2	66.8	17.1	80	10.0	9.8	3,545	2,088	27.3	13.3	650	0	Kuwait
987	10.4[37]	12.6	482.4		...	7.0	1.0	51	11	...	0.5	0	0	Kyrgyzstan
...	...	...	...	...	280	37.0	7.6	105	23	21.3[4]	7.0	80	0	Laos
1,571	8.0	...	18.3	...	...	7.0	2.8	122	45	2.7[6]	0.9	0	0	Latvia
366	13.2	14.7	65.7	67.3	530	44.3	14.7	274	77	15.4	3.4	10	0	Lebanon
1,885	33.9	170.6	221.5	...	1,130	2.0	1.0	37[6]	20[6]	17.1[3]	3.3[6]	0	0	Lesotho
...	...	...	...	...	1,570	[38]	[38]	58[5]	23[5]	13.3[5]	4.8[5]	0	0	Liberia
907	3.0	4.9	...	...	...	80.0	14.8	1,599	328	28.0[5]	5.1	0	0	Libya
...	...	114.3	614.3	153.6	660	—	[39]	—	—	—	—	...	...	Liechtenstein
1,199	6.9	9.1	325.2	28.1	...	8.9	2.4	651	170	5.5	3.8	10	0	Lithuania
7,044	1.3	131.1	731.5	275.5	730	0.8	1.9	108	271	2.4[13]	0.8	5	0	Luxembourg
4,432	1.8	76.2	74.8	215.3	...	—	[7]	...	...	...	...	...	...	Macau
686	...	...	...	...	...	10.4	4.9	...	...	...	...	0	0	Macedonia
231	1.3	23.2	1.9	0.7	2,900	21.0	1.4	36	3	7.5[13]	1.1	0	0	Madagascar
1,094	2.6	100.9	16.7	...	1,670	8.0	0.8	21	2	4.4[13]	1.0	20	0	Malawi
447	2.4	14.9	107.8	14.3	760	114.5	5.7	2,642	140	15.5	4.3	80	0	Malaysia
2,353	1.9	3.3	36.1	...	35,710	—	—	...	...	...	...	...	...	Maldives
33	—	1.1	3.9	—	160	7.4	0.8	58	6	9.4[6]	2.2	0	0	Mali
2,697	14.4	64.7	1,668.7	385.5	230	1.9	5.0	21	59	2.2	0.9[6]	0	0	Malta
2,273	...	...	...	...	400	—	[40]	—	—	—	—	...	...	Marshall Islands
3,924	7.9	156.4	689.0	102.6	...	—	[7]	—	—	—	—	...	...	Martinique
225	1.8	38	2.5	9.1	710	15.7	6.9	37	18	15.9[5]	41	0	0	Mauritania
3,219	3.3	13.6	66.0	...	240	—	—	11	10	1.6	0.4	5	0	Mauritius
...	...	...	...	...	...	—	[7]	—	—	—	—	...	...	Mayotte
108	7.3	30.2	...	...	...	175.0	1.9	1,656	18	2.8	0.5	10	20	Mexico
...	...	...	...	...	...	—	[40]	—	—	—	—	...	...	Micronesia
...	...	...	...	...	...	11.9	2.7	...	...	...	...	0	0	Moldova
4,277	...	63.4	407.1	126.8	...	—	—	...	...	...	...	...	...	Monaco
453	0.7	41.9	17.0	...	120	21.1	9.1	132[13]	62[13]	9.0[13]	4.2[13]	0	0	Mongolia
366	1.4	6.7	...	...	840	195.5	7.2	1,193	43	19.5	4.5	20	0	Morocco
166	4.2	9.2	45.9	...	...	[41]	[41]	91	6	40.7[17]	7.6	0	0	Mozambique
309	4.1	31.2	0.1	0.1	650	286.0	6.1	1,510	35	29.1[13]	3.8[6]	120	0	Myanmar (Burma)
...	...	...	...	...	...	8.1	3.1	...	...	—	—	0	0	Namibia
...	25.0	400.0	100.0	...	110	—	—	...	...	...	...	...	...	Nauru
13	2.6	1.5	0.2	...	1,000	35.0	1.7	40	2	5.5	1.4	0	0	Nepal
10,181	24.9	191.8	3,803.0	316.8	510	74.4	4.8	7,055	465	4.6[6]	2.4	100	240	Netherlands, The

Social protection (continued)

country	social security: programs available, 1995: old-age, invalid-ity, death[a]	sickness and mater-nity[b]	work injury[c]	unem-ploy-ment[d]	family allow-ances[e]	expendi-tures, 1992 (% of total central govt.)	finances: year	receipts: total ('000,000 natl. cur.)	insured persons (%)	em-ployers (%)	govern-ment (%)	other (%)	expenditures: total ('000,000 natl. cur.)	benefits (%)	admin-istration (%)	other (%)
Netherlands Antilles	●	...	●	●	...	34.1[11]	1992	139.2	100.0	—	—	—	142.0	...	...	...
New Caledonia	...	...	...	...	●	...	1987	15,834.0	...	...	...	...	14,598.0	...	...	...
New Zealand	●	●	●	●	●	36.2	1986	9,645.5	1.6	3.1	92.5	2.9	9,534.5	97.4	2.4	0.2
Nicaragua	●	●	●		●	14.4	1983	832.9	20.4	53.5	10.4	15.7	427.5	65.5	28.5	6.0
Niger	●		●		●	1.7[12, 27]	1986	12,890.6	12.3	39.2	37.8	10.7	10,032.1	49.0	32.4	18.6
Nigeria	●		●			2.5[44]	1986	108.4	17.9	24.4	—	57.7	17.5	44.7	55.3	—
Northern Mariana Islands	●	...	...	...	...	...	...	...	...	...	...	...	...	...	...	...
Norway	●	●	●	●	●	38.0[3, 12]	1986	157,853.7	17.5	24.6	55.7	2.2	153,249.6	99.0	1.0	—
Oman	●	...	●	...	...	4.8[12]	1990	—	...	...	...	...	38.0[12]	...	...	...
Pakistan	●	●	●			0.2[9]	1986	5,134.8	1.0	10.1	83.6	5.3	4,629.5	98.4	1.2	0.4
Palau	●					...	...	...	...	...	...	...	...	...	...	...
Panama	●	●	●			18.9	1986	500.5	30.0	44.9	3.4	21.7	425.9	94.3	5.5	0.2
Papua New Guinea	●		●			6.1	1983	45.0	40.5	32.1	8.0	19.4	9.4	82.3	9.7	8.0
Paraguay	●	●	●			15.7	1988	49,272.0	...	...	...	...	40,588.0	...	...	...
Peru	●	●	●			0.2[10]	1986	7,041,677.0	31.1	68.9	—	—	6,136,672.0	39.5	51.6	8.9
Philippines	●	●	●			1.8	1986	10,705.0	18.6	26.5	—	54.9	4,244.8	86.9	13.1	—
Poland	●	●	●	●	●	...	1986	2,242,443.0	2.6	60.7	35.3	1.4	1,830,162.0	99.2	0.8	—
Portugal	●	●	●	●	●	27.3[3, 12]	1986	494,527.0	24.6	66.0	7.0	2.4	459,353.8	95.4	4.6	—
Puerto Rico	●	●	●	●	●	...	1980	...	...	...	...	...	1,041.3	100.0	—	—
Qatar	...	...	...	...	...	...	1986	80.0	—	—	100.0	—	80.0	100.0	—	—
Réunion	...	...	...	...	...	...	...	...	...	...	...	...	8,470.4	...	...	...
Romania	●	●	●	●	●	22.8	1983	72,064.9	—	54.0	46.0	—	63,927.5	100.0	—	—
Russia	●	●	●	●	●	...	...	...	...	...	...	...	...	...	...	...
Rwanda	●		●			2.9[31]	1986	2,123.8	24.5	41.0	—	34.5	585.9	65.0	35.0	—
St. Kitts and Nevis	●	●	●			9.4[12, 45]	1989	14.3	...	...	...	...	7.9	...	...	...
St. Lucia	●	●	●			...	1986	14.6	28.6	28.6	—	42.8	3.4	61.4	38.6	—
St. Vincent and the Grenadines	●	●	●			2.3[12]	1989	—	...	...	...	...	—	...	...	...
San Marino	●	...	...	●	...	...	1983	51,673.0	12.0	48.7	36.1	3.2	46,179.0	95.7	3.7	0.6
São Tomé and Príncipe	●	●	●			...	1986	46.4	37.7	56.3	—	6.0	23.7	100.0	—	—
Saudi Arabia	●		●			...	...	...	...	...	...	...	...	...	...	...
Senegal	●		●		●	2.6[3, 13]	1986	22,094.0	21.2	69.9	—	8.7	18,827.0	84.8	15.3	—
Seychelles	●	●	●			5.3[18]	1983	69.1	30.1	60.2	—	9.7	42.7	69.6	4.9	25.5
Sierra Leone			●			1.9[3]	1977	10.5	——26.7——		73.3	—	10.0	100.0	—	—
Singapore	●		●			2.0	1986	6,691.0	51.0	23.2	0.1	25.7	5,601.2	71.9	0.4	27.7
Slovakia	●	●	●	●	●	...	1992	28,013	13.9	85.3	...	0.8	13,823	...	...	...
Slovenia	●	●	●	●	●	...	...	...	...	...	...	...	...	...	...	...
Solomon Islands	●		●			0.6[17]	1986	13.7	27.9	41.8	—	30.3	6.8	40.8	11.5	47.7
Somalia			●			1.7[12, 44]	...	—	...	...	...	...	...	...	...	...
South Africa	●	●	●	●		...	1987	976.0	—	100.0	—	—	668.0	...	...	...
Spain	●	●	●	●	●	36.7[13]	1986	5,893,481.0	16.4	54.0	27.1	2.5	5,801,152.0	95.0	2.7	2.3
Sri Lanka	●		●			16.2[13]	1986	10,432.8	20.9	24.2	32.2	22.7	4,022.6	98.8	1.1	0.1
Sudan, The	●		●			0.4[5]	1986	42.1	14.3	28.7	—	57.0	8.5	49.4	50.6	—
Suriname	●	...	...	...	●	6.0[9]	1983	125.8	35.8	26.5	36.6	1.1	106.3	98.1	1.9	—
Swaziland	●		●			0.4[12]	1986	10.7	31.4	31.4	—	37.2	3.9	45.8	54.2	—
Sweden	●	●	●	●	●	46.4	1986	318,641.9	1.8	38.5	49.2	10.5	291,962.1	95.9	4.1	—
Switzerland	●	●	●	●	●	49.9[4]	1986	37,602.7	45.1	23.2	26.3	5.4	35,691.2	91.5	2.8	5.7
Syria	●		●			1.4	1989	—	...	...	...	...	1,150.0	...	...	...
Taiwan	●	●	●			13.8[3]	...	...	...	...	...	...	...	...	...	...
Tajikistan	●	●	●	●	●	...	...	...	...	...	...	...	...	...	...	...
Tanzania	●		●			0.5[14]	1986	1,286.6	26.9	33.7	2.0	37.4	487.7	41.4	55.3	3.3
Thailand		●	●			3.8	1986	284.8	—	100.0	—	—	246.0	88.8	11.2	—
Togo	●		●		●	6.5[45]	1986	9,588.0	9.3	70.9	—	19.8	4,671.0	70.7	29.3	—
Tonga	...	...	...	...	...	0.8[13]	...	...	...	...	...	...	...	...	...	...
Trinidad and Tobago	●	●	●			5.3[25]	1986	505.4	15.7	31.5	34.9	17.9	383.2	77.1	11.8	11.1
Tunisia	●	●	●	●	●	12.2	1989	325.3	36.9	63.1	—	—	358.3	90.0[18]	6.1[18]	3.9[18]
Turkey	●	●	●			0.7	1986	1,753,294.0	28.2	32.5	15.9	23.4	1,417,940.0	97.1	2.6	0.3
Turkmenistan	●	●	●	●	●	...	...	...	...	...	...	...	...	...	...	...
Tuvalu	●	...	...	...	...	...	1981	...	...	...	...	...	0.1	67.6	32.4	—
Uganda	●		●			2.1[9]	1986	75.1	44.6	44.6	—	10.8	0.5	100.0	—	—
Ukraine	●	●	●	●	●	...	1986	16,835.0	—	—	94.7	5.3	16,835.0	100.0	—	—
United Arab Emirates	...	...	...	...	...	3.4[12]	1989	42.0	...	...	...	...	420.0[12]	...	...	...
United Kingdom	●	●	●	●	●	29.6	1986	78,737.0	18.3	23.4	55.1	3.2	76,059.0	95.4	2.9	1.7
United States	●		●	●		22.2	1986	644,464.0	24.5	33.7	30.2	11.6	525,855.0	95.9	3.2	0.9
Uruguay	●	●	●	●	●	55.7[12]	1986	92,849.0	33.3	37.2	24.0	5.4	93,379.0	92.7	6.0	1.3
Uzbekistan	●	●	●	●	●	...	...	...	...	...	...	...	...	...	...	...
Vanuatu	●					0.9[9]	...	—	...	...	...	...	—	...	...	...
Venezuela	●	●	●	●		6.9[9]	1986	7,457.6	21.3	40.7	12.7	25.3	6,355.7	86.1	14.9	—
Vietnam	●	●	●			...	...	...	...	...	...	...	...	...	...	...
Virgin Islands (U.S.)	●	...	...	●	●	...	...	...	...	...	...	...	...	...	...	...
West Bank	...	...	...	...	...	...	...	...	...	...	...	...	...	...	...	...
Western Sahara	...	...	...	...	...	...	...	...	...	...	...	...	...	...	...	...
Western Samoa	●		●			—	...	—	...	...	...	...	—	...	...	...
Yemen	●	...	●	...	...	—	...	—	...	...	...	...	—	...	...	...
Yugoslavia	●	●	●	●	●	6.0[52]	1986[52]	2,777,651.0	63.3	32.2	3.4	1.1	2,732,679.0	90.3	1.9	7.8
Zaire	●		●		●	0.4	1986	1,238.3	28.6	60.2	—	11.2	1,044.2	27.9	72.1	—
Zambia	●		●			1.5[5]	1986	179.2	28.4	28.4	—	43.2	67.7	40.6	59.4	—
Zimbabwe	●		●			2.5[5]	1983	167.0	25.9	7.6	64.2	2.3	112.2	93.7	6.2	0.1

[1]Rural areas only. [2]The bulk of the national armed forces disintegrated after the fall of the central government in April 1992, with only the northern corps retaining its integrity. [3]1990. [4]1984. [5]1989. [6]1992. [7]Political dependency; defense is the responsibility of the administering country. [8]Includes civilian militia. [9]1986. [10]1983. [11]Netherlands Antilles includes Aruba. [12]Includes welfare. [13]1991. [14]1985. [15]1979. [16]1993. [17]1988. [18]1977. [19]1976. [20]Local officers only. [21]Military defense is the responsibility of France. [22]1971. [23]Republic of Cyprus only. [24]Data refer to former Czechoslovakia, except military manpower, 1994. [25]1981. [26]Paramilitary unit of a country participating in the U.S.-sponsored Regional Security System, a defense pact among eastern Caribbean states. [27]1980. [28]Ethiopia includes Eritrea. [29]Demobilization of some Eritrean forces began in late 1993. Estimated strength of these forces is currently about 55,000. [30]Following the declaration of independence by Eritrea in April 1993, estimated strength of Ethiopian forces was some 120,000. [31]1982. [32]Former West Germany. [33]In 1994 the military government of Haiti was replaced by

crime and law enforcement (latest)							military protection								country
offenses reported to the police per 100,000 population						population per police officer[f]	manpower, 1995[9]		expenditure, 1993				arms trade, 1993 ('000,000 U.S.$)		
total	personal		property				total ('000)	per 1,000 population	total '000,000	per capita	% of central government expenditure	% of GDP or GNP	imports	exports	
	murder	assault	burglary	automobile theft											
4,750[42]	...	350	...	...	330	—	[7]	—	—	—	—	...	...	Netherlands Antilles
...	...	...	...	...	...	—	[7]	—	—	—	—	...	...	New Caledonia
14,496	4.0	313.6	2,942.3	905.4	630	10.5	2.9	650	193	4.5	1.5	60	0	New Zealand
772	18.3	140.0	110.7	...	90[8]	12.0	2.8	37	9	10.5[6]	2.6	5	0	Nicaragua
32	0.2	2.5	1.0	0.1	2,350[43]	5.3	0.6	32	4	7.0[6]	1.5	0	0	Niger
312	...	...	...	...	1,140	77.1	0.8	210	2	2.7	0.6	50	0	Nigeria
245	3.8	92.6	73.7	20.8	...	—	[7]	—	—	—	—	...	...	Northern Mariana Islands
5,466	2.6	53.8	89.0	474.1	660	30.0	6.9	3,232	752	6.2	3.1	90	50	Norway
162	...	...	...	...	430	43.5	20.1	1,638	997	35.3[6]	21.5	60	0	Oman
221	5.6	0.1	9.1	4.1	720	587.0	4.2	3,111	25	26.3	6.4	430	5	Pakistan
...	...	...	323.0	...	...	—	[40]	—	—	—	—	...	...	Palau
703	6.1	18.9	...	125.1	180	11.8	4.5	—	—	—	—	0	0	Panama
766	8.6	66.7	63	22.0	720	3.2	0.7	82	20	5.4	1.8	0	0	Papua New Guinea
816	3.0	27.8	105.1	93.4	310	20.3	4.2	116	24	8.3	1.8	5	0	Paraguay
1,178	9.3	104.3	87.0	22.7	730	115.0	4.9	696	30	13.3	1.8	10	0	Peru
230	30.1	41.8	...	1.2	1,160	106.5	1.5	1,200	17	11.6	2.2	40	0	Philippines
2,020	3.0	56.5	764.2	...	370	278.6	7.2	4,334	113	7.1	2.3	0	10	Poland
900	4.0	6.3	52.8	178.8	660	54.2	5.5	2,192	209	6.4	3.0	130	5	Portugal
3,350	26.2	188.4	931.2	487.0	380	—	[7]	—	—	—	—	...	...	Puerto Rico
301	2.4	9.7	...	4.2	...	11.1	19.2	608[27]	2,638[27]	20.1[45]	9.3[45]	0	0	Qatar
2,097	7.8	123.1	181.3	137.9	220	—	[7]	—	—	—	—	...	...	Réunion
636	3.6	3.7	6.8	6.0	...	217.4	9.6	1,676	72	11.4	2.5	0	0	Romania
1,857	15.5[37]	50.4	860.1	23.5	...	1,520.0	10.3	113,800	762	28.1[6]	14.6	0	0	Russia
346	15.6	66.6	4.0	...	4,650	40.0	5.1	114	14	24.1	8.0	5	0	Rwanda
15,468	...	...	...	...	300	[26]	[26]	...	...	...	...	...	...	St. Kitts and Nevis
4,000	17.0	1,193.0	778.0	...	430	[26]	[26]	...	...	...	...	...	...	St. Lucia
3,977	10.3	986.9	...	...	250	[26]	[26]	...	...	...	...	...	...	St. Vincent and the Grenadines
...	4.1	...	...	...	...	—	—	...	...	...	...	...	...	San Marino
558	4.0	...	...	...	400	—	—	1[27]	7[27]	2.5[27]	1.6[27]	0	0	São Tomé and Príncipe
114	0.6	19.2	...	16.9	280	105.5	5.9	20,480	1,163	41.0	15.8	5,100	0	Saudi Arabia
295	1.8	61.1	6.7	...	730	13.4	1.6	134	16	13.7[6]	2.4	0	0	Senegal
5,267	5.7	741.9	1,640.7	...	120	0.3	4.0	8[4]	124[4]	7.4[4]	5.6[4]	...	...	Seychelles
...	...	...	...	...	600	6.2	1.4	14	3	12.5[6]	2.2	0	0	Sierra Leone
1,560	1.5	6.7	107.8	15.2	230	53.9	18.0	2,700	955	26.1	4.8	60	20	Singapore
1,982	2.2	84.2	...	...	...	47.0	8.8	843	157	5.2	2.4	150	...	Slovakia
2,739	5.2	21.3	479.8	21.8	...	8.4	4.3	195	99	3.7	1.3	0	0	Slovenia
...	...	...	...	...	620	—	—	...	...	...		0	0	Solomon Islands
144	1.5	8.0	31.2	...	540	[46]	[46]	8	1	30.0[9]	0.9	0	0	Somalia
...	...	...			870	136.9	3.3	2,806	68	8.2	2.7	0	140	South Africa
2,402	2.3	23.8	1,096.8	285.3	580	206.0	5.3	8,280	211	5.0	1.8	190	150	Spain
280	8.2	10.8	54.7		860	125.3	6.9	407	23	10.0[6]	4.0	20	0	Sri Lanka
1,565	4.2	40.5	0.4	3.4	740	110.5	4.2	882[6]	32[6]	175.4[13]	17.1[6]	5	0	Sudan, The
17,819	7.6	1,824.4	...	...	...	1.8	4.2	75	181	5.3[3]	1.1	0	0	Suriname
4,955.3	71.6	630.6	934.9	...	610	—	—	21	23	4.1	2.4	0	0	Swaziland
13,750	8.4	42.5	1,801.5	748.0	330	64.0	7.3	5,011	574	5.6[6]	2.8	90	10	Sweden
5,457	2.6	53.6	1,018.0	1,520[47]	640	3.4	0.5	4,061	581	19.4[13]	1.7	40	60	Switzerland
89	1.4	7.0	21.2	2.9	1,970	423.0	29.6	4,526[13]	342[13]	60.3[13]	17.9[13]	120	0	Syria
672	7.7	...	...	101.4	720	376.0	17.8	10,420	494	20.0	4.7	480	10	Taiwan
317	2.5	4.6	...	...	...	—	—	...	...	...	...	0	0	Tajikistan
1,250	6.4	0.5	97.3	0.9	1,330	34.6	1.2	90	3	12.3[6]	3.8	0	0	Tanzania
356	0.9	41.9	11.7	17.0	530	259.0	4.4	3,611	62	10.0	2.9	50	0	Thailand
11	...	...	...	...	1,970	7.0	1.7	48	12	11.7[13]	3.0	0	0	Togo
2,100	...	...	...	...	330	—	[48]	—	—	—	—	...	...	Tonga
3,170	8.7	177.4	633.9	...	280	2.1	1.7	79	60	4.9	1.8	0	0	Trinidad and Tobago
1,240	2.1	134.0	143.6	11.1	340	35.5	4.0	492	57	7.2	3.4	10	0	Tunisia
209	3.2	21.3	...	11.1	1,570	507.8	8.1	7,075	116	19.5	5.8	975	20	Turkey
...	...	...	...	...	...	[49]	[49]	207[6]	55[6]	5.3[6]	1.8[6]	0	0	Turkmenistan
...	...	...	...	—	290	—	—	...	...	...	...	...	...	Tuvalu
140	9.5	15.6	15.1	5.3	1,090	50.0	2.7	54	3	8.8	1.4	0	0	Uganda
781	5.6	24.5	...	36.0	...	452.5	8.6	...	...	...	...	0	50	Ukraine
1,496	1.1	1.7	10.5	...	140	70.0	31.9	1,771	666	36.9	4.8	380	0	United Arab Emirates
10,403[50]	2.5[50]	362.1[50]	2,404.4[50]	1,147.3[50]	420	236.9	4.0	34,020	587	9.4	3.6	150	4,300	United Kingdom
5,482	9.5	440.1	1,099.2	605.3	318	1,547.3	5.9	297,600	1,153	20.1	4.7	1,400	10,300	United States
6,806	4.1	169.6	56.9	...	170	25.6	8.0	256	81	7.8	2.0	0	0	Uruguay
420	5.1	15.6	...	...	...	25.0	1.1	...	...	...	...	0	0	Uzbekistan
...	...	...	...	...	450	—	—	...	...	...	...	...	...	Vanuatu
1,221	16.6	175.2	330.1	212.7	320	79.0	3.6	1,029	51	7.8	1.8	60	0	Venezuela
...	...	...	...	...	...	572.0	7.7	720[13]	11[13]	40.0[13]	4.8[13]	10	0	Vietnam
10,441	22.3	1,943.2	3,183.7	954	240	—	[7]	—	—	—	—	...	...	Virgin Islands (U.S.)
2,226	...	...	...	...	...	—	—	...	...	...	...	...	...	West Bank
...	...	...	...	...	...	—	[7]	—	—	—	—	...	...	Western Sahara
...	...	...	...	...	...	—	[48]	—	—	—	—	...	...	Western Samoa
170[51]	...	...	...	...	1,940	39.5	3.0	1,068[6, 51]	105[6, 51]	19.6[6, 51]	10.4[6, 51]	520	0	Yemen
1,135[52]	5.4[52]	35.5[52]	...	...	140[48]	126.5	12.0	3,608[13, 52]	158[13, 52]	55.0[3, 52]	3.9[13, 52]	0	80	Yugoslavia
...	...	...	...	...	910	49.1	1.1	49[17]	1[17]	1.6[17]	0.8[17]	10	0	Zaire
666	9.8	9.5	153.5	9.6	540	21.6	2.3	56	6	14.4[5]	2.4[5]	0	0	Zambia
4,653	17.4	203.3	418.7	23.6	750	45.0	4.0	231	21	15.0	4.3	10	0	Zimbabwe

a civilian administration. Both the armed forces and police have been disbanded. [34]Coverage is through tax system. [35]1988–89. [36]Russian-controlled forces in Kazakhstan territory, estimated at about 40,000. [37]Includes attempted murders. [38]As a result of civil war, the armed forces of Liberia, with a combat strength of about 2,000 to 3,000, are now confined to Monrovia, the capital. [39]Military defense is the responsibility of Switzerland. [40]Military defense is the responsibility of the United States. [41]Under the terms of 1992 peace accord, government and Renamo forces are to merge to form a new National Army some 30,000 strong. [42]Curaçao only. [43]Includes paramilitary forces. [44]1978. [45]1987. [46]Following the 1991 revolution, no national armed forces have yet been formed. [47]Includes bicycles and motorcycles. [48]Military defense is the responsibility of New Zealand. [49]Forces under joint Turkmenistan/Russian control. [50]England and Wales. [51]Former Yemen Arab Republic. [52]Data refer to Yugoslavia as constituted prior to 1991.

Education

This table presents international data on education analyzed to provide maximum comparability among the different educational systems in use among the nations of the world. The principal data are, naturally, numbers of schools, teachers, and students, arranged by four principal levels of education—the first (primary); general second level (secondary); vocational second level; and third level (higher). Whenever possible, data referring to preprimary education programs have been excluded from this compilation. The ratio of students to teachers is calculated for each level. These data are supplemented at each level by a figure for enrollment ratio, an indicator of each country's achieved capability to educate the total number of children potentially educable in the age group usually represented by that level. At the first and second levels this is given as a net enrollment ratio and at the third level as a gross enrollment ratio. Two additional comparative measures are given at the third level: students per 100,000 population and proportion (percentage) of adults age 25 and over who have achieved some level of higher or postsecondary education. Data in this last group are confined as far as possible to those who have completed their educations and are no longer in school. No enrollment ratio is provided for vocational training at the second level because of the great variation worldwide in the academic level at which vocational training takes place, in the need of countries to encourage or direct students into vocational programs (to support national development), and, most particularly, in the age range of students who normally constitute a national vocational system (some will be as young as 14, having just completed a primary cycle; others will be much older).

At each level of education, differences in national statistical practice, in national educational structure, public-private institutional mix, training and deployment of teachers, and timing of cycles of enrollment or completion of particular grades or standards all contribute to the problems of comparability among national educational systems.

Reporting the number of schools in a country is not simply a matter of counting permanent red-brick buildings with classrooms in them. Often the resources of a less developed country are such that temporary or outdoor facilities are all that can be afforded, while in a developed but sparsely settled country students might have to travel 80 km (50 mi) a day to find a classroom with 20 students of the same age, leading to the institution of measures such as traveling teachers, radio or televisual instruction at home under the supervision of parents, or similar systems. According to UNESCO definitions, therefore, a "school" is defined only as "a body of students . . . organized to receive instruction."

Such difficulties also limit the comparability of statistics on numbers of teachers, with the further complications that many at any level must work part-time, or that the institutions in which they work may perform a mixture of functions that do not break down into the tidy categories required by a table of this sort. In certain countries teacher training is confined to higher education, in others as a vocational form of secondary training, and so on. For purposes of this table, teacher training at the secondary level has been treated as vocational education. At the higher level, teacher training is classified as one more specialization in higher education itself.

The number of students may conceal great variation in what each country defines as a particular educational "level." Many countries do, indeed, have a primary system composed of grades 1 through 6 (or 1 through 8) that passes students on to some kind of postprimary education. But the age of intake, the ability of parents to send their children or to permit

Education

country	year	first level (primary)					general second level (secondary)					vocational second level[a]	
		schools	teachers[c]	students[d]	student/ teacher ratio	net enroll- ment ratio[b]	schools	teachers[c]	students[d]	student/ teacher ratio	net enroll- ment ratio[b]	schools	teachers[c]
Afghanistan	1989	553	16,756	586,014	35.0	29	819	5,715	271,000	47.4	...	33	556
Albania	1993	1,777	32,098	535,713	16.7	...	47[1]	4,149	73,259	17.7	...	466[1]	7,390[1]
Algeria	1993	13,970	153,793	4,436,363	28.8	94	3,402[2]	135,730[2]	2,305,196[2]	17.0[2]	55	[2]	[2]
American Samoa	1991	30	524	7,884	15.0	...	7[3]	245	3,483	14.2	...	1	21
Andorra	1993	12[5]	...	5,519[5]	...	...	6[6]	...	1,659[6]	...	...	...	...
Angola	1991	6,308[7]	31,062	990,155	31.9	...	5,276[7]	5,138[1]	166,812	30.2[1]	...	...	566[1]
Antigua and Barbuda	1992	43	549	10,770	19.6	...	12	353	4,373	12.5	...	1	45
Argentina	1992	24,511	306,372	5,041,090	16.5	95	7,224[2, 3]	283,583[2]	2,262,378[2]	8.0[2]	59	[2]	[2]
Armenia	1994	1,374[9]	54,000[9, 10]	574,500[9]	11.0[9, 10]	...	[9]	[9]	[9]	[9]	...	69	...
Aruba	1993	32	331	7,139	21.6	...	10	183	3,247	17.7	...	14	225
Australia	1993	9,865[9]	98,526	1,816,066	18.4	98	[9]	103,385	1,282,309	12.4	81	...	...
Austria	1994	3,684	36,208	401,147	11.1	90	1,899	54,822	457,970	8.4	91	1,028	24,752
Azerbaijan	1995	4,500[9]	139,000[9, 10]	1,462,000[9]	9.9[9, 10]	...	[9]	[9]	[9]	[9]	...	78	...
Bahamas, The	1993	227[9, 10]	3,161[9, 10]	61,464[9]	19.0[9, 10]	95	[9]	[9]	[9]	[9]	87	...	...
Bahrain	1993	114	3,312	68,898	20.8	100	35[4]	2,309	45,020	19.5	85	9[4]	823
Bangladesh	1992	49,964	208,271	13,717,000	65.9	70	9,892	116,336	4,009,000	34.5	17	153	1,722
Barbados	1992	106	1,553	26,662	17.2	78	33[1]	1,406[1]	21,259[1]	15.1[1]	75	8[4]	79[4]
Belarus	1994	4,900[9]	122,700[9]	1,628,500[9]	13.3[9]	...	[9]	[9]	[9]	[9]	...	147	...
Belgium	1993	4,450	72,589[13]	735,670	...	96	1,962	110,599	790,377	6.9	88	304	14,548[4]
Belize	1993	237[13]	1,804[13]	48,612[14]	26.2[13]	96	30	643[14]	9,457	11.4	36	8[10, 15]	...
Benin	1991	2,904	13,422	534,810	39.8	53	151[4]	2,178	76,672	35.2	...	13[4]	687[4]
Bermuda	1990	24	310	5,472	17.7	...	12	331	3,555	10.7	...	...	...
Bhutan	1990	156	1,757	52,029	29.6	...	31	662	15,984	24.1	...	8	149
Bolivia	1991	9,758[8]	51,763	1,278,775	24.7	91	724[8]	12,434[2]	219,232[2]	17.6[2]	29	47[8]	[2]
Bosnia and Herzegovina	1991	2,205	23,369	539,875	23.1	...	238	9,030	172,063	19.1	...	...	...
Botswana	1994	781	9,552	301,370	31.6	97	199	5,192	99,560	19.2	42	45	856
Brazil	1993	195,544	1,346,285	30,520,748	22.7	90	12,603	275,845	4,208,766	15.3	19	...	...
Brunei	1992	161	3,047	50,434	16.6	89	23	1,939	25,309	13.1	61	6	340
Bulgaria	1995	3,359[9]	70,487[9]	980,491[9]	13.9[9]	82	[9]	[9]	[9]	[9]	57	513	18,885
Burkina Faso	1992	2,587	8,565	530,002	61.9	31	173	2,419	60,629	25.1	7	22	537
Burundi	1992	1,342[16]	9,582	631,039	65.9	...	113[16]	2,026[16]	46,508	21.8[16]	5	...	...
Cambodia	1993	4,539	42,405	1,465,958	34.6	...	440	19,540	239,363	12.2	...	65	2,618
Cameroon	1991	6,709	38,430	1,964,146	51.1	76	388[8]	11,400[1]	409,729	32.2[1]	...	220[8]	6,267[1]
Canada	1994	16,231[9]	300,797[9]	5,360,900[9]	17.8[9]	98	[9]	[9]	[9]	[9]	90	...	...
Cape Verde	1990	367	2,028	67,761	33.4	100	16[8]	238	7,114	29.9	12	3[8]	56[17]
Central African Republic	1991	930	4,004	308,409	77.0	58	46[2]	845[2]	46,989[2]	55.6[2]	...	[2]	[2]
Chad	1991	2,544	9,238	591,417	64.0	...	66[3]	2,062	72,641	35.2	...	25[8]	285[3]
Chile	1991	8,626	81,742	2,033,862	36.0	87	1,694[4]	...	436,892	...	53	1,262[4]	...
China	1993	861,878	6,388,000	149,737,000	23.4	96	82,795	3,167,000	47,391,000	15.0	...	13,945	501,000
Colombia	1992	44,139	162,445	4,525,929	27.9	85	6,134[2, 4]	130,514[2]	2,686,515[2]	20.6[2]	41	[2]	[2]
Comoros	1992	255	1,894	75,577	39.9	51	...	613	15,647	25.5	...	...	11
Congo	1993	1,623	6,891	505,925	73.4	...	238[4]	6,048	192,229	31.8	...	60[4]	1,813
Costa Rica	1993	3,442	15,107	484,958	32.1	91	179[1]	5,281[10]	117,975[10]	22.3[10]	41	77[1]	2,360[10]
Côte d'Ivoire	1993	7,249	39,691	1,553,540	39.1	52	...	9,644	445,505	46.2	...	...	...
Croatia	1993	1,930	24,067	441,837	18.4	80	...	3,636	48,083	13.2	66	...	11,329
Cuba	1993	9,368	76,161	942,431	12.4	100	2,175[1]	57,455	520,290	9.1	58	618[1]	35,358
Cyprus[18]	1994	381	3,424	64,907	19.0	97	103	3,714	50,870	13.7	91	11	501
Czech Republic	1994	4,199	63,767	1,061,396	16.6	...	324	8,456	122,171	14.4	...	821	16,854
Denmark	1993	2,668[20]	56,323[20]	589,123[20]	10.5[20]	98	153[6]	7,500[6, 10]	72,704[6]	9.9[6, 10]	87	204[10]	...
Djibouti	1993	56	787	33,005	41.9	30	...	367[2, 21]	10,384	...	11	...	[2]

them to finish that level, or the need to withdraw the children seasonally for agricultural work all make even a simple enrollment figure difficult to assess in isolation. All of these difficulties are compounded when a country has instruction in more than one language or when its educational establishment is so small that higher, sometimes even secondary, education cannot take place within the country. Enrollment figures in this table may, therefore, include students enrolled outside the country.

Student-teacher ratio, however, usually provides a good measure of the ratio of trained educators to the enrolled educable. In general, at each level of education both students and teachers have been counted on the basis of full-time enrollment or employment, or full-time equivalent when country statistics permit. At the primary and secondary levels, net enrollment ratio is the ratio of the number of children within the usual age group for a particular level who are actually enrolled to the total number of children in that age group (× 100). This ratio is usually less than (occasionally, equal to) 100 and is the most accurate measure of the completeness of enrollment at that particular level. It is not always, however, the best indication of utilization of teaching staff and facilities. Utilization, provided here for higher education only, is best seen in a gross enrollment ratio, which compares total enrollment (of all ages) to the population within the normal age limits for that level. For a country with substantial adult literacy or general educational programs, the difference may be striking: typically, for a less developed country, even one with a good net enrollment ratio of 90 to 95, the gross enrollment ratio may be 20%, 25%, even 30% higher, indicating the heavy use made by the country of facilities and teachers at that level.

Literacy data provided here have been compiled as far as possible from data for the population age 15 and over for the best comparability internationally. Standards as to what constitutes literacy may also differ markedly; sometimes completion of a certain number of years of school is taken to constitute literacy; elsewhere it may mean only the ability to read or write at a minimal level testable by a census taker; in other countries studies have been undertaken to distinguish among degrees of functional literacy. When a country reports an official 100% (or near) literacy rate, it should usually be viewed with caution, as separate studies of "functional" literacy for such a country may indicate 10%, 20%, or even higher rates of inability to read, or write, effectively. Substantial use has been made of UNESCO literacy estimates, both for some of the least-developed countries (where the statistical base is poorest) and for some of the most fully developed, where literacy is no longer perceived as a problem, thus no longer in need of monitoring.

Finally, the data provided for public expenditure on education are complete in that they include all levels of public expenditure (national, state, local) but are incomplete for certain countries in that they do not include data for private expenditure; in some countries this fraction of the educational establishment may be of significant size. Occasionally data for external aid to education may be included in addition to domestic expenditure.

The following notes further define the column headings:

a. Usually includes teacher training at the second level.
b. Latest.
c. Full-time.
d. Full-time; may include students registered in foreign schools.

		third level (higher)							literacy[b]				public expenditure on education (percent of GNP)[b]	country
students[d]	student/ teacher ratio	institutions	teachers[c]	students[d]	student/ teacher ratio	gross enroll-ment ratio[b]	students per 100,000 popula-tion[b]	percent of population age 25 and over with post-secondary education[b]	over age	total (%)	male (%)	female (%)		
8,507	15.4	5	198	1,419	7.5	1.7	162	...	15	31.5	47.2	15.0	...	Afghanistan
138,000[1]	18.7[1]	8[1]	1,774	30,185	17.0	9.5	891	...	15	100.0	100.0	100.0	...	Albania
[2]	[2]	...	14,379	243,397	16.9	11.4	1,160	...	15	61.5	73.9	49.0	5.7	Algeria
160	7.6	2	...	909[4]	...	...	...	...	15	95.9	95.6	96.3	...	American Samoa
...	...	—	—	—	—	...	...	...	15	100.0	100.0	100.0	...	Andorra
19,687	...	1[7]	439	6,534	14.9	0.7	66	...	15	41.7	55.6	28.5	...	Angola
590	13.1	...	...	...	...	...	...	...	15	90.0	...	...	...	Antigua and Barbuda
[2]	[2]	1,540[8]	89,609	1,077,212	12.0	40.5	3,323	12.0	15	96.2	96.2	96.2	0.0	Argentina
46,500	...	14	...	46,500	...	48.9	3,711	...	15	98.8	99.4	98.1	7.3	Armenia
2,594	11.5	1	16	88	5.5	...	...	...	15	95.0	...	...	...	Aruba
...	...	95[3]	27,780[11]	575,617[11]	20.7[11]	41.9	3,267	...	15	99.5	...	...	5.5	Australia
299,323	12.1	44	15,576	219,204	14.1	43.2	2,893	...	15	100.0	100.0	100.0	5.8	Austria
30,400	...	23	...	89,100	...	25.7	2,323	...	15	97.3	98.9	95.9	6.5	Azerbaijan
...	...	1[12]	300[12]	3,201[12]	10.7[12]	...	1,945	13.5	15	98.2	98.5	98.0	3.9	Bahamas, The
6,393	7.8	4[4]	582	7,763	13.3	20.1	1,493	10.3	15	85.2	89.1	79.4	5.0	Bahrain
31,275	18.2	1,046	25,195	853,343	33.9	3.8	382	...	15	38.1	49.4	26.1	2.3	Bangladesh
996[4]	12.6[4]	1[1]	153[1]	1,314[1]	8.6[1]	17.6	1,647	...	15	97.4	98.0	96.8	7.5	Barbados
126,400	...	38	16,900	178,016	10.5	44.1	3,062	...	15	97.9	99.4	96.6	5.3	Belarus
155,102	...	21	10,517[4]	123,320	...	40.2	2,772	...	...	100.0	100.0	100.0	5.1	Belgium
1,191[10, 15]	...	[15]	...	[15]	...	—	...	6.6	14	70.3	70.3	70.3	5.7	Belize
6,879[4]	10.0[4]	13[4]	956[1]	10,873[1]	11.4[1]	2.7	235	...	15	37.0	48.7	25.8	...	Benin
...	...	1	56	498	8.9	...	...	18.4	15	96.9	96.7	97.0	...	Bermuda
1,822	12.2	2	57	519	9.1	...	18	...	15	42.2	56.2	28.1	3.4	Bhutan
[2]	[2]	10[8]	4,261[10]	109,503[10]	25.7[10]	22.6	2,214	9.9	15	83.1	90.5	76.0	2.7	Bolivia
...	...	44	2,801	37,541	13.4	...	...	...	10	85.5	96.5	76.7	...	Bosnia and Herzegovina
9,570	11.2	1	475	4,533	9.5	3.0	294	...	15	69.8	80.5	59.9	8.2	Botswana
...	...	873	150,823	1,594,668	10.6	11.5	1,080	...	15	83.3	83.3	83.2	4.6	Brazil
1,756	5.2	4	289	1,372	4.7	6.0	516	...	15	88.2	92.6	83.4	4.6	Brunei
212,401	11.2	88	24,185	221,207	9.2	32.2	2,324	15.0	15	97.9	98.7	97.1	5.8	Bulgaria
8,022	14.9	9	437	7,387	16.9	0.7	60	...	15	19.2	29.5	9.2	1.6	Burkina Faso
...	...	8[16]	492	3,830	7.8	0.8	73	...	15	35.3	49.3	22.5	3.7	Burundi
15,537	5.9	9	268	22,182	82.8	...	158	...	15	74.3	85.0	65.0	...	Cambodia
90,543	14.8[1]	5[8]	1,086	33,177	30.5	3.2	288	...	15	63.4	75.0	52.1	3.0	Cameroon
...	...	272	64,100	921,300	14.4	102.9	6,980	21.4	15	96.6	...	...	7.6	Canada
752	...	...	...	...	...	...	...	...	15	71.6	81.4	63.8	4.4	Cape Verde
[2]	[2]	1[11]	139[11]	3,783[11]	27.2[11]	1.7	150	...	15	60.0	68.5	52.4	2.8	Central African Republic
3,819[3]	15.1[3]	4[3]	59[3]	2,969[3]	50.3[3]	1.2	103	...	15	48.1	62.1	34.7	2.6	Chad
262,563	...	201[4]	...	286,962	...	26.7	2,369	...	15	95.2	95.4	95.0	2.7	Chile
6,446,000	12.9	1,065	388,000	2,536,000	6.5	3.8	377	2.0	15	81.5	89.9	72.7	1.9	China
[2]	[2]	235[8]	54,164	510,649	9.4	15.5	1,554	...	15	91.3	91.2	91.4	3.5	Colombia
129	11.7	—	32[1]	223	7.8[1]	0.5	47	...	15	57.3	64.2	50.4	4.2	Comoros
20,621	11.4	12[4]	656[10]	13,806[10]	21.0[10]	...	582	...	15	74.9	83.1	67.2	8.6	Congo
33,538[10]	14.2[10]	6[11]	7,969[11]	65,625[11]	8.2[11]	30.3	2,767	...	15	94.8	94.7	95.0	4.6	Costa Rica
...	...	...	...	23,642[7]	...	3.1	204	...	15	40.1	49.9	30.0	...	Côte d'Ivoire
158,930	14.0	54[16]	6,429	82,361	12.8	27.2	1,826	...	15	96.7	98.8	94.8	...	Croatia
299,422	9.1	35[1]	25,264	198,474	7.9	18.1	1,840	...	15	95.7	96.2	95.3	6.6	Cuba
3,867	7.7	30	568	6,732	11.9	15.0	927	14.0[19]	15	95.2	97.8	92.8	4.3	Cyprus[18]
219,249	13.0	23	13,463	127,137	9.4	15.5	1,257	8.5	15	100.0	100.0	100.0	5.8	Czech Republic
153,987	...	235[10]	...	165,559	...	40.9	3,045	19.6	...	100.0	100.0	100.0	7.4	Denmark
[2]	...	1[16]	13[16]	106[16]	8.2[16]	0.1	10	...	15	46.2	60.3	32.7	3.8	Djibouti

Education (continued)

country	year	first level (primary)					general second level (secondary)					vocational second level[a]	
		schools	teachers[c]	students[d]	student/ teacher ratio	net enroll-ment ratio[b]	schools	teachers[c]	students[d]	student/ teacher ratio	net enroll-ment ratio[b]	schools	teachers[c]
Dominica	1993	65[14]	608[9]	12,795	31.2[9]	...	13[14]	[9]	6,169	[9]	...	...	...
Dominican Republic	1993	5,686[21]	22,365[21]	989,012[21]	44.2[21]	81	...	5,392[21]	144,372[21]	26.8[21]	24	...	...
Ecuador	1991	16,146[8]	61,039	1,846,338	30.2	...	2,027[2, 8]	60,126[2]	785,844[2]	13.1[2]	...	[2]	[2]
Egypt	1993	14,654[22]	273,055[10, 22]	6,333,703[22]	24.9[10, 22]	89	7,307[22]	201,040[10, 22]	4,071,936[22]	...	65	1,351	77,951[10]
El Salvador	1992	3,806	23,339[21]	1,028,877	38.0[21]	70	...	...	28,032	...	15	...	...
Equatorial Guinea	1988	703	1,065	61,009	57.3	...	9	319	9,226	28.9	...	1	52
Eritrea	1994	491	5,272	207,099	39.3	26	86[23]	1,933	65,537	32.9	11	4[23]	102
Estonia	1994	724[9]	15,298[9]	215,400[9]	14.1[9]	79	[9]	[9]	[9]	[9]	73	83	1,073
Ethiopia	1992	8,120	69,743	1,855,894	26.6	...	1,209[7]	21,970	712,489	32.4	...	...	602
Faroe Islands	1991	66[9]	600[9]	5,212	13.7[9]	...	[9]	[9]	2,975	[9]	...	10	...
Fiji	1992	693	4,644	145,630	31.4	99	142	3,045	60,237	19.8	...	45	625
Finland	1993	4,734[24]	41,222[24]	584,749[24]	14.2[24]	...	448[25]	6,322[25]	121,516[25]	19.2[25]	93	570	...
France	1994	41,656	218,100	4,060,607	18.6	99	11,325[2, 16]	454,000[2]	5,737,422[2]	12.6[2]	90	[2]	[2]
French Guiana	1993	110[13]	...	16,024	...	...	22[16]	...	10,685	...	...	8[4]	...
French Polynesia	1992	176	1,741	29,132	16.7	100	32[2]	1,276	18,636	14.6	61	[2]	316
Gabon	1991	1,024	4,782	210,000	43.9	...	...	1,356	42,871	31.6	...	...	476
Gambia, The	1992	245	3,193	97,262	30.5	55	32[1]	1,054[1]	25,929[1]	24.6[1]	18	[1]	[1]
Gaza Strip	1993	397[9]	5,226[9]	221,133[9]	42.3[9]	...	[9]	[9]	[9]	[9]	...	...	...
Georgia	1994	3,808[9]	90,171[9]	807,687[9]	9.0[9]	...	[9]	[9]	[9]	[9]	...	...	...
Germany	1993	18,867	225,068	3,524,219	15.7	81	...	408,663	5,532,012	13.5	85	...	112,647
Ghana	1992	11,056	66,068	1,796,490	27.2	...	5,513	43,349[1]	861,630[1]	19.9[1]	...	57	422[1]
Gibraltar	1991	21[9]	92[3]	5,308[9]	31.9[3]	...	[9]	124[3]	[9]	...	...	1	29[3]
Greece	1993	7,634[21]	37,549[21]	745,666[21]	19.9[21]	94	2,988	45,794	700,488	15.3	88	695	14,349
Greenland	1994	88[9]	955[9]	8,344	10.5[9]	...	[9]	[9]	1,636	[9]	...	8[8]	110[8]
Grenada	1994	57	781	21,311	27.3	...	19	352	6,939	19.7	...	...	...
Guadeloupe	1993	340	3,135	39,075	12.5	...	78[2]	3,813[2]	49,295[2]	12.9[2]	...	[2]	[2]
Guam	1990	36	850	16,819	19.8	...	24	736	15,733	21.4	...	3	370
Guatemala	1991	9,362	36,757	1,249,413	34.0	...	1,274	13,588	207,935	15.3	...	626	7,129
Guernsey	1992	22	231	4,469	19.3	...	8	286	3,521	12.3	...	...	...
Guinea	1993	2,849	9,718	471,792	48.5	40	225[4]	3,417	97,533	28.5	9	35[4]	1,302
Guinea-Bissau	1988	632[8]	3,065[8]	79,035	24.6[8]	45	12[7]	824[7]	5,505	7.5[7]	...	4[8]	107
Guyana	1990	423	4,010[3]	118,015[3]	29.4[3]	...	93	...	72,096[3]	...	...	8	176
Haiti	1993	7,306[16]	27,607	787,553	28.5	26	...	10,174[2]	193,624[2]	19.0[2]	...	...	[2]
Honduras	1993	8,054	27,056	990,352	36.6	90	661	10,303	151,196	14.7	21	5[3]	581[3]
Hong Kong	1995	884	19,122	476,847	25.4	...	488	21,391	471,121	22.1	...	9	2,488[4]
Hungary	1993	3,959	96,223	1,092,563	11.8	92	876	26,335	335,153	12.7	75	343	6,624
Iceland	1993	...	...	27,500	...	...	...	...	17,888	...	...	...	...
India	1994	572,923	1,703,164	108,200,539	63.5	...	241,129	2,485,160	60,817,397	24.5	...	...	...
Indonesia	1993[28]	147,683[16]	1,276,217	29,598,790	23.2	97	27,664[16]	594,000[16]	9,433,778[16]	13.6[16]	37	3,557[16]	103,000[16]
Iran	1993	61,323	311,839	9,937,369	31.9	97	18,445[1]	211,711	5,995,051	28.3	...	1,006[1]	20,947
Iraq	1993	8,003	131,271	2,857,467	21.8	79	2,746[10]	48,496	992,617	20.5	37	296[10]	10,621
Ireland	1993[29]	3,405	20,761	521,531	25.1	90	467	12,250	221,167	18.1	82	323	7,630
Isle of Man	1989	32	...	5,458	...	...	7	...	4,908	...	...	1	...
Israel	1994	1,844	52,135	677,404	12.8	...	838	34,956	341,929	9.8	...	383	19,479
Italy	1994	21,378	172,777	2,863,003	16.6	...	9,721	101,800	1,996,677	19.6	...	7,774	129,821
Jamaica	1994[21]	...	10,417	311,146	29.9	100	126	7,848	216,285	27.6	64	18	897
Japan	1994	24,635	435,000	8,583,000	19.7	100	16,786	556,000	9,544,000	17.2	96	6,679[16]	53,000[16]
Jersey	1990	32	294[8]	5,794	19.2[8]	...	14	372[8]	4,405	12.3[8]	...	1	...
Jordan	1993	2,441	45,871	1,014,295	22.1	89	662	6,915	86,475	12.5	36	49	2,107
Kazakhstan	1992	8,841[9]	262,600[9]	3,226,400[9]	12.3[9]	...	[9]	[9]	[9]	[9]	...	3,115	...
Kenya	1993	15,804	173,002	5,428,600	31.4	...	2,639	31,657	517,577	16.3	...	63	1,332[4]
Kiribati	1993	92	537	16,316	30.4	...	9[1]	179	3,152	17.6	...	6[1]	43[10]
Korea, North	1987	6,122	138,945	1,543,000	11.1	...	...	111,000	2,468,000	22.2	...	473[7]	...
Korea, South	1994	5,900	139,096	4,099,395	29.5	96	3,691	155,528	3,717,987	23.9	92	738	41,311
Kuwait	1995	246	8,815	132,204	15.0	45	391	18,072	200,828	11.1	45	34	683
Kyrgyzstan	1993	1,862	76,300[9]	954,700[9]	12.5[9]	...	1,472	[9]	[9]	[9]	...	37	...
Laos	1992	7,140	21,036	580,792	27.6	68	750[1]	8,936	117,504	13.1	18	139[3]	1,262
Latvia	1993	921	12,758	133,846	10.5	81	...	8,344	187,332	10.2	77	57	6,691
Lebanon	1992	2,100	...	345,662	...	...	...	...	241,964[3]	...	...	...	4,240
Lesotho	1994	1,201	7,292	354,275	48.6	65	187	2,526	55,312	21.9	17	9[10]	225[10]
Liberia	1987	...	...	80,048[7]	...	...	...	...	...	...	...	...	...
Libya	1992	...	99,623	1,238,986	12.4	97	...	11,429	138,860	12.1	...	...	7,072
Liechtenstein	1994	14	122	1,986	16.3	...	8	124	1,587	12.8	...	1	40
Lithuania	1994	2,317[9]	41,052[9]	511,000[9]	12.4[9]	...	[9]	[9]	[9]	[9]	...	168	5,035
Luxembourg	1994	...	1,911[21]	27,595[21]	14.1[21]	85	...	1,948[2]	8,712[23]	...	60	...	[2]
Macau	1992	70	1,262	37,719	29.9	...	20	949	18,652	19.7	...	2	11
Macedonia	1993	1,050	13,102	260,659	19.9	84	90[16]	4,520[2]	74,583[2]	16.5[2]	...	...	[2]
Madagascar	1993	13,624	37,676	1,504,668	39.9	...	1,142[3]	15,118	298,241	19.7	...	61[4]	1,484[16]
Malawi	1992	3,118	26,333	1,795,451	68.2	52	94[1]	1,096[1]	36,550	26.8[1]	2	...	...
Malaysia	1992	6,891	125,916	2,641,000	21.0	...	1,336	77,149	1,400,000	18.1	...	75	3,489
Maldives	1986	243	1,138	41,812	36.7	...	9	291	3,581	12.3	...	10	52
Mali	1992	1,514	7,963	375,131	47.1	19	307	5,883[16]	88,529	19.8[16]	5	...	...
Malta	1993	168[10]	1,478	35,488	24.0	100	46[10]	1,746	23,528	13.5	83	31[10]	690
Marshall Islands	1994	104	833	13,565	16.3	...	11	138	2,483	18.0	...	...	...
Martinique	1993	282	2,711	33,170	12.2	...	79[2]	3,830[2]	47,295[2]	12.3[2]	...	[2]	[2]
Mauritania	1993	1,635	4,686	248,048	52.9	...	56[10]	1,776	43,861	24.7	...	5[10]	162
Mauritius	1993	281	6,543[16]	125,543	19.8[16]	94	123	4,050[16]	87,661	20.6[16]	...	19[10]	...
Mayotte	1993	88[1]	555	21,579	38.9	...	5	246	3,973	16.2	...	2[1]	17[1]
Mexico	1994	85,503	488,139	14,468,700	29.6	99	20,550	243,877	4,311,800	17.7	46	6,571[23]	77,347[23]
Micronesia	1988	177	...	25,139	...	...	16	...	5,385	...	...	...	...
Moldova	1995	1,700[9]	53,000[9, 10]	731,000	13.6[9, 10]	...	[9]	[9]	[9]	[9]	...	64	...
Monaco	1990	6[8]	735[9]	5,523[9]	7.5[9]	...	3[8]	[9]	[9]	[9]	...	...	...
Mongolia	1991	638[1]	20,600[9]	440,900[9]	21.4[9]	...	...	[9]	[9]	[9]	...	75	2,500
Morocco	1995	4,740	102,163	2,895,737	28.3	63	1,172	73,726	1,247,608	16.9	29	562[10, 17]	2,951[17]
Mozambique	1993	3,466	22,396	1,227,341	54.8	41	...	3,924	147,201	37.5	7	32[4]	885

		third level (higher)							literacy[b]				public expenditure on education (percent of GNP)[b]	country
students[d]	student/ teacher ratio	institutions	teachers[c]	students[d]	student/ teacher ratio	gross enroll- ment ratio[b]	students per 100,000 popula- tion[b]	percent of population age 25 and over with post- secondary education[b]	over age	total (%)	male (%)	female (%)		
...	...	2[14]	40[10]	658[10]	16.5[10]	...	...	...	15	90.0	...	...	5.8	Dominica
...	...	7[11]	5,041[11]	68,301[11]	13.5[11]	...	1,929	...	15	82.1	82.0	82.2	1.7	Dominican Republic
[2]	[2]	21[8]	12,856[1]	206,541[1]	16.1[1]	20.0	2,012	12.7	15	90.1	92.0	88.2	3.0	Ecuador
1,464,836	...	12[11]	36,609[11, 22]	542,602[11]	...	17.1	1,560	4.6	15	51.4	63.6	38.8	5.0	Egypt
77,061	...	6[11, 23]	2,850[11, 23]	56,868[11, 23]	20.0[11, 23]	15.4	1,598	...	15	74.1	77.4	71.3	1.6	El Salvador
882	17.0	4	81	660	8.1	1.8	164	...	15	78.5	89.6	68.1	1.8	Equatorial Guinea
787	7.7	1[23]	144[23]	2,032[23]	14.1[23]	...	...	...	...	20.0	...	...	...	Eritrea
28,200	26.3	22	...	23,214	...	37.8	1,566	13.7	15	99.7	99.9	99.6	5.9	Estonia
8,290	13.8	...	1,697[16]	26,218[16]	15.4[16]	0.6	54	...	15	35.5	45.5	25.3	6.4	Ethiopia
1,417	...	1	20	91	4.6	...	...	...	15	99.0	99.0	99.0	...	Faroe Islands
7,283	11.6	5[16]	277[16]	7,908[16]	28.5[16]	11.9	1,076	4.5	15	91.6	93.8	89.3	5.6	Fiji
197,894	...	20	7,917	121,736	15.4	63.2	3,902	15.4	15	100.0	100.0	100.0	7.2	Finland
[2]	[2]	1,062[3]	57,429[10]	1,700,800[10]	29.6[10]	49.5	3,607	...	...	98.8	98.9	98.7	5.8	France
3,778[4]	...	1	...	324	...	...	...	...	15	83.0	83.6	82.3	...	French Guiana
3,730	11.8	4[3]	70[3]	701[3]	10.0[3]	1.1	114	...	15	95.0	94.9	95.0	...	French Polynesia
8,477	11.8	1	299	3,000	10.0	...	373	...	15	63.2	73.7	53.3	2.9	Gabon
[1]	[1]	...	...	...	...	—	...	...	15	38.6	52.8	24.9	2.7	Gambia, The
...	...	...	...	...	...	...	...	...	...	...	...	...	...	Gaza Strip
...	...	19[1]	...	103,900[16]	...	36.9	2,710	...	15	99.0	99.5	98.5	...	Georgia
2,264,244	20.1	314	171,025[10]	1,875,099	10.7[16]	35.6	3,051	19.9[26]	15	100.0	100.0	100.0	4.0[26]	Germany
13,232[1]	31.4[1]	16	700[1]	9,274[1]	13.2[1]	1.4	126	...	15	64.5	75.9	53.5	3.1	Ghana
772	14.1[7]	—	—	—	—	...	...	...	15	99.0	99.0	99.0	...	Gibraltar
190,443	13.3	17[10]	9,124[10]	115,284[10]	12.6[10]	25.9	1,906	8.7	15	95.2	97.7	93.0	3.1	Greece
650[8]	5.9[8]	2[8]	35[8]	200[8]	5.7[8]	...	...	...	15	100.0	100.0	100.0	...	Greenland
...	...	1	66	651	9.9	...	...	...	15	85.0	...	...	...	Grenada
[2]	[2]	1	310	4,296	13.9	...	...	...	15	90.1	89.7	90.5	...	Guadeloupe
3,788	10.2	1	192	2,385	12.4	...	...	39.9	15	99.0	99.0	99.0	...	Guam
94,485	13.3	5[3]	4,346[3]	69,532[3]	16.0[3]	...	741	...	15	55.6	62.6	48.6	1.6	Guatemala
...	...	—	—	—	—	...	...	...	15	100.0	100.0	100.0	...	Guernsey
9,278	7.1	10[4]	805[10, 11]	6,245[10, 11]	7.8[10, 11]	1.1	93	...	15	35.9	49.9	21.9	2.2	Guinea
825	7.7	...	...	404	...	0.5	...	...	15	54.9	68.0	42.5	2.8	Guinea-Bissau
5,388	30.6	1[11, 14]	220[11, 14]	3,607[11, 14]	16.4[11, 14]	9.3	1,012	...	15	98.1	98.6	97.5	7.8	Guyana
[2]	[2]	2[27]	554[27]	6,678[27]	12.1[27]	...	107	0.7	15	45.0	48.0	42.2	1.4	Haiti
65,539	13.7[3]	10	3,758	48,468	12.9	8.6	852	...	15	72.7	72.6	72.7	4.1	Honduras
47,900	18.5[4]	10	1,422[4]	73,167	32.4[4]	20.7	1,540	10.6	15	92.2	96.0	88.2	...	Hong Kong
212,932	32.2	91	17,743	119,828	6.8	16.9	1,312	10.1	15	98.9	99.2	98.6	6.7	Hungary
...	...	5[16]	...	5,672	...	29.6	2,393	...	15	100.0	100.0	100.0	5.6	Iceland
...	...	7,958	215,234	4,804,773	22.3	7.8	755	...	15	52.0	65.5	37.7	3.7	India
1,429,657	13.1[16]	1,000[16]	135,462	1,973,094	11.6	10.2	1,045	...	15	83.8	89.6	78.0	2.2	Indonesia
327,937	15.7	...	25,208[10]	724,000	25.2[10]	15.1	1,400	...	15	72.1	78.4	65.8	5.4	Iran
152,321	14.3	20[10]	10,520[10]	197,786[10]	18.8[10]	12.6	1,240	...	15	58.0	70.7	45.0	5.1	Iraq
138,022	18.1	26	4,535	[illegible]	17.7	34.2	3,087	...	15	100.0	100.0	100.0	6.2	Ireland
425[16]	...	...	...	...	...	...	...	...	...	...	...	...	...	Isle of Man
122,721	6.3	7	6,150[10]	91,480	...	35.3	3,208	...	15	94.9	97.1	92.7	5.8	Israel
2,718,958	20.9	50[11, 23]	56,723[11, 23]	1,538,606[11, 23]	27.1[11, 23]	37.3	2,944	...	15	97.1	97.8	96.4	5.4	Italy
15,776	17.6	15[3]	1,047[4]	23,834	17.9[4]	5.9	658	...	15	85.0	81.8	89.1	6.2	Jamaica
1,242,000[16]	23.4[16]	1,207	160,000	3,059,000	19.1	30.4	2,340	21.2	15	100.0	100.0	100.0	4.7	Japan
283[8]	...	...	...	...	...	...	...	...	15	100.0	100.0	100.0	...	Jersey
27,435	13.0	55[3]	4,014	88,506	22.0	19.4	1,741	...	15	86.6	93.4	79.4	4.0	Jordan
1,091,600		61	...	288,000	...	41.6	3,443	12.4	15	97.5	99.1	96.1	5.4	Kazakhstan
29,593	13.4[4]	14	4,392[11, 16]	88,180	8.1[11, 16]	1.6	110	...	15	70.1	[illegible]	70.0	6.7	Kenya
288[10]	6.7[10]	—	—	—	—			...	15	90.0	...	...	7.4	Kiribati
220,000	...	281	27,000	390,000	14.4	...	...	...	15	95.0	...	...	...	Korea, North
851,495	20.6	645	51,196	1,767,517	34.2	50.8	4,756	13.4	15	98.0	99.3	96.7	4.2	Korea, South
2,936	4.3	1	927[1]	11,284[23]	15.2[3]	16.3	1,370	12.7	15	78.6	82.2	74.9	6.1	Kuwait
40,922	...	12	...	53,670	...	20.6	1,837	...	15	97.0	98.6	95.5	3.6	Kyrgyzstan
8,198	6.5	9[1]	698[1]	4,730[1]	6.8[1]	2.1	193	...	15	56.6	69.4	44.4	2.3	Laos
55,312	8.3	14	4,478	41,138	9.2	38.8	2,627	13.4	15	99.5	99.8	99.2	6.7	Latvia
37,403	8.8	...	5,400	85,495	15.8	28.9	3,275	...	15	92.4	94.7	90.3	1.9	Lebanon
2,326[10]	10.3[10]	...	492	4,001	8.1	2.3	206	...	15	71.3	81.1	62.3	4.9	Lesotho
...	...	...	472	5,095	10.8	2.5	...	...	15	38.3	53.9	22.4	...	Liberia
76,648	10.8	10[3]	...	72,899	...	16.4	1,548	...	15	76.2	87.9	63.0	9.6	Libya
197	4.9	...	...	...	...	...	...	...	15	100.0	100.0	100.0	...	Liechtenstein
69,000	13.7	14	9,003[4]	53,000	7.3[4]	39.1	2,802	12.6	15	98.4	99.2	97.8	4.4	Lithuania
12,662	6.5	...	...	4,957[16]	...	...	...	...	15	100.0	100.0	100.0	4.3	Luxembourg
365	33.2	11	584	7,055	12.1	...	...	5.9	15	89.5	94.1	85.3	...	Macau
[2]	[2]	27[16]	2,320	27,340	11.8	16.1	1,290	...	10	89.1	94.2	83.8	5.0	Macedonia
17,419[16]	11.7[16]	5[3]	855[10]	42,681[10]	49.9[10]	3.5	318	...	15	80.2	87.7	72.9	1.5	Madagascar
863	...	4[1]	309[11]	3,684[11]	11.9[11]	0.9	78	0.4	15	56.4	71.9	41.8	3.4	Malawi
33,000	9.5	54	11,471[16]	136,000[16]	11.9[16]	7.2	679	...	15	83.5	89.1	78.1	5.1	Malaysia
462	8.9	—	—	—	—	...	...	...	15	93.2	93.3	93.0	8.1	Maldives
...	...	7[16]	701	6,703	9.6	0.8	73	...	15	31.0	39.4	23.1	2.1	Mali
6,200	9.0	1	284	3,679	13.0	18.6	1,300	...	15	96.0	96.2	95.9	4.6	Malta
...	...	...	...	...	...	...	...	...	15	91.2	92.4	90.0	...	Marshall Islands
[2]	[2]	1	71	3,670	51.7	...	...	...	15	92.5	91.8	93.2	...	Martinique
1,949	12.0	4[10]	266[10]	8,495[10]	31.9[10]	4.1	393	1.3	15	37.7	49.6	26.3	...	Mauritania
2,052[10]	...	2	382[3]	2,556	5.7[3]	4.1	378	1.9	15	82.9	87.1	78.8	3.7	Mauritius
839	23.1[1]	—	—	—	—	...	...	...	15	91.9	...	...	...	Mayotte
1,076,700[23]	13.9[23]	13,000	324,148	3,961,000	12.2	13.8	1,509	...	15	89.6	91.8	87.4	6.0	Mexico
...	...	...	...	920[8]	...	...	...	...	15	76.7	67.0	87.2	...	Micronesia
41,800	...	18	...	49,400	...	34.8	2,665	11.3	15	96.4	98.6	94.4	6.5	Moldova
...	...	...	...	...	...	...	...	...	...	...	...	...	...	Monaco
47,600	19.0	9	1,465	13,829	9.4	14.4	1,267	...	15	82.9	88.6	77.2	8.5	Mongolia
17,585[17]	6.0[17]	50[23]	6,877[23]	230,012[23]	33.4[23]	10.3	1,040	...	15	43.7	56.6	31.0	5.8	Morocco
16,546	18.7	2[4]	877	5,250	6.0	0.4	35	...	15	40.1	57.7	23.3	6.2	Mozambique

Education (continued)

country	year	first level (primary)					general second level (secondary)					vocational second level[a]	
		schools	teachers[c]	students[d]	student/ teacher ratio	net enroll-ment ratio[b]	schools	teachers[c]	students[d]	student/ teacher ratio	net enroll-ment ratio[b]	schools	teachers[c]
Myanmar (Burma)	1993	36,499	198,909	6,518,800	32.8	...	2,920	67,503	1,633,700	24.2	...	112	2,194
Namibia	1993	933	10,912[10]	352,100	32.0[10]	89	97	2,534[1]	92,136	29.3[1]	30	17	140[3]
Nauru	1989	3	61	1,367	22.4	...	2	34	629	18.5	...	1	3
Nepal	1992	19,498	77,948	3,034,710	38.9	...	6,539[2]	25,357[2]	855,137[2]	33.7[2]	...	[2]	[2]
Netherlands, The	1993	9,333	99,031[16]	1,526,000	15.7[16]	94	1,117	89,370[16]	668,000	7.7[16]	86	747	18,613[16]
Netherlands Antilles	1992	86	1,077	22,410	20.8	...	25	591	8,682	14.7	...	42	431
New Caledonia	1992	280	1,758	34,591	19.7	98	46	1,669[2, 16]	15,664	13.1[2, 16]	72	16	[2]
New Zealand	1994	2,417[30]	24,099[30]	444,881[30]	18.5[30]	99	335	17,202	229,694	13.4	88	30	7,379
Nicaragua	1992	4,571	18,901	766,000[14]	37.2	80	...	4,465	178,342	39.9	26	...	763
Niger	1993	2,656	12,216	414,296	33.9	25	105[3]	2,219[10]	88,810	35.1[10]	6	7[3]	175[10]
Nigeria	1992	36,610	384,212	14,805,937	38.5	...	5,594[4]	141,491	3,600,620	25.4	...	376[4]	15,738[3]
Northern Mariana Islands	1989	18	240	4,882	20.3	...	9[2]	163[2]	2,075[2]	12.7[2]	...	[2]	[2]
Norway	1994	3,325	36,196	466,991	12.9	99	771[2]	21,780[2]	240,506[2]	11.0[2]	92	[2]	[2]
Oman	1993	416	10,839	289,911	26.7	73	128[1]	8,112	137,947	17.0	52	25[1]	425
Pakistan	1994	156,450	383,400	15,532,000	40.5	...	24,083	294,900	5,199,000	17.6	...	712	6,800
Palau	1992	26[8]	289[8, 9]	2,480	...	...	6[8]	[9]	981	...	...	...	...
Panama	1993	2,732	14,302	357,402	25.0	91	369[2]	10,730[2]	206,509[2]	19.2[2]	51	[2]	[2]
Papua New Guinea	1992	2,821	14,117	443,552	31.4	73	135[1]	2,415	58,226	24.1	...	117[1]	878
Paraguay	1994	4,649[10]	41,432	792,657	19.1	96	...	20,793[2]	195,677	10.3[2]	32	...	[2]
Peru	1993	54,502[10]	159,022	4,843,666	30.5	88	7,097[10]	93,277	1,913,163	20.5	46	1,952[10]	11,919
Philippines	1994	35,087	320,634	10,731,453	33.5	99	5,550[10]	134,898[2]	4,590,037[2]	34.0[2]	59	1,261[10]	[2]
Poland	1994	20,326	323,400	5,371,841	16.6	96	1,832	30,300	659,500	21.8	78	9,655	85,600
Portugal	1993	11,771	71,788	925,936	12.9	100	1,368	64,479	815,491	12.6	...	220	...
Puerto Rico	1986	1,542	18,359	427,582	23.3	...	395	13,612	334,661	24.6	...	52	...
Qatar	1993	158	5,656	52,016	9.2	81	...	3,695	35,518	9.6	69	...	128
Réunion	1995	343	...	73,220	...	...	102[2]	...	92,281[2]	...	...	[2]	...
Romania	1992	6,145	57,014	1,201,229	21.1	77	...	119,460	1,659,362	13.9	72	...	45,851
Russia	1993	66,235	395,000	7,738,000	19.6	94	...	1,070,000	12,424,000	11.6	...	...	...
Rwanda	1992	1,724	18,937	1,104,903	58.3	71	192[2]	4,054[2]	62,701[2]	15.5[2]	8	[2]	[2]
St. Kitts and Nevis	1992	31	342	6,978	20.4	...	7	298	4,645	15.6	...	2	35
St. Lucia	1993	84	1,181[10]	32,204	27.4[10]	...	14	466[10]	7,612	17.5[10]	...	1[15]	113[10]
St. Vincent and the Grenadines	1992	60	1,215	24,134	19.9	...	21	408	7,124	17.5	...	2	...
San Marino	1995	14	218	1,143	5.2	...	3	133	775	5.8	...	...	...
São Tomé and Príncipe	1989	64	559	19,822	35.5	...	...	318	7,446	23.4	...	...	...
Saudi Arabia	1993	10,228	141,930	2,025,948	14.3	61	4,643[16]	89,171	1,033,521	11.6	34	190[16]	3,804
Senegal	1993	2,454	12,711	738,550	58.1	48	359	5,509	182,140	33.1	12	19	182
Seychelles	1995	24[14]	569	9,691	17.0	...	20[14]	429	6,129	14.4	...	1[14]	155
Sierra Leone	1992	1,792	10,051	315,146	31.4	...	217	3,924	72,516	18.5	...	30	750
Singapore	1993	193	10,711	261,534	24.4	100	162	9,168	180,729	19.7	...	31	2,972
Slovakia	1994	2,483	15,433	345,594	22.4	...	...	28,256	412,575	14.6	...	...	14,423
Slovenia	1993	912	15,855	223,104	14.1	...	236[2]	8,926[2]	103,714[2]	11.6[2]	...	[2]	[2]
Solomon Islands	1994	520	2,510	73,120	29.1	...	23	364[23]	7,351[23]	20.2[23]	...	...	...
Somalia	1987	1,125	8,208	171,830	20.9	...	82	2,109	42,764	20.3	3	21	498
South Africa	1993	21,006[9]	337,311[9]	8,681,876[9]	25.7[9]	92	[9]	[9]	[9]	[9]	46	198	15,032
Spain	1993	38,512[13]	267,725[13]	4,474,775[13]	16.7[13]	100	23,107	170,144	2,558,717	15.0	90	2,668[3]	63,236[3]
Sri Lanka	1991	9,590	173,811	2,112,723	12.2	...	9,041	106,792	2,105,959	19.7	...	23	437
Sudan, The	1992	8,016	64,227	2,168,180	33.8	...	2,578	29,208	683,982	23.4	...	67	1,434
Suriname	1993	301[10]	3,695	76,162	21.4	...	89[10]	2,487[2]	17,709	12.6[2]	...	64[3]	[2]
Swaziland	1993	520	5,696	186,271	32.7	93	153[16]	2,824	50,304	17.8	...	8[16]	280[16]
Sweden	1994	4,826	90,234	893,932	9.9	99	600[2]	29,539[2]	313,728[2]	10.6[2]	93	[2]	[2]
Switzerland	1994	...	...	423,399	...	94	...	...	412,385	...	79	...	...
Syria	1994	10,219	110,580	2,624,594	23.7	95	...	49,951	846,550	16.9	42	...	11,559
Taiwan	1994	2,525	83,480	2,111,037	25.3	...	906	72,875	1,426,030	19.6	...	209	18,836
Tajikistan	1994	3,300[9]	97,000[9]	1,227,000[9]	12.6[9]	...	[9]	[9]	[9]	[9]	...	50	...
Tanzania	1993[31]	10,892	101,816	3,736,734	36.7	50	...	9,568	180,899	18.9	...	...	1,167
Thailand	1992	34,960	420,401	8,435,245	20.1	...	2,299	105,225	1,954,062	18.6	...	615	38,548
Togo	1993	2,594	12,487	663,126	53.1	69	...	2,918	126,335	43.3	18	18[8]	261[1]
Tonga	1992	115	784	16,658	21.2	...	40	862	15,253	17.7	...	8	65[1]
Trinidad and Tobago	1992	471	7,511	196,838[23]	26.1	88	101	4,844	103,922[23]	19.4	65	...	...
Tunisia	1994	4,201	56,154	1,476,329	26.3	98	...	38,891[2]	688,004[2]	17.7[2]	43	...	[2]
Turkey	1992	50,701	234,961	6,878,923	29.3	93	8,064	117,702	3,010,672	25.6	54	2,971	57,425
Turkmenistan	1992	1,791[9]	60,000[9]	842,000[9]	14.0[9]	...	[9]	[9]	[9]	[9]	...	41	...
Tuvalu	1990	9	72	1,485	20.6	...	1	21	314	15.0	...	1	10
Uganda	1994	7,905[3]	102,126	2,496,139	24.4	...	774[3]	16,245	244,248	15.0	...	136[3]	2,766
Ukraine	1994	21,694[9]	574,000[9]	6,937,000[9]	12.1[9]	...	[9]	[9]	[9]	[9]	...	754	...
United Arab Emirates	1994	354[4, 9]	14,754	251,182	17.0	100	[9]	11,637[2]	145,143	12.6[2]	79	...	[2]
United Kingdom	1993	23,829[13]	256,500[13]	5,023,200[13]	19.6[13]	96	4,730[10]	288,000	3,951,000	13.7	85	...	...
United States	1994	84,578[16, 32]	1,771,000[32]	35,654,000[32]	20.1[32]	100	...	1,100,000[2]	13,170,000[2]	12.0[2]	90	...	[2]
Uruguay	1993	2,422	16,392	338,204	20.6	94	335	17,750	201,805	11.4	...	105	...
Uzbekistan	1993	...	91,500	1,852,841	20.2	...	...	300,800	2,893,058	9.6	...	243[10]	22,164
Vanuatu	1992	272	852	26,267	30.8	74	...	220	4,269	19.4	17	...	...
Venezuela	1992	15,800	183,298	4,190,047	22.9	88	1,621[2]	32,572[2]	289,430[2]	8.9[2]	20	[2]	[2]
Vietnam	1994	13,092	275,640	9,725,095	35.3	...	6,298	166,968	3,815,852	22.9	...	451	12,197
Virgin Islands (U.S.)	1991[21]	57	777	15,256	19.6	...	...	541	9,263	17.2	...	...	...
West Bank[33]	1993	1,406[9]	11,872[9]	383,386[9]	32.3[9]	...	[9]	[9]	[9]	[9]	...	...	...
Western Sahara	1989[21]	27	596	14,794	24.8	...	18	577	9,218	16.0	...	...	...
Western Samoa	1989	...	...	37,833	...	...	...	...	...	...	...	...	...
Yemen[34]	1991	7,313[3]	35,350	1,291,372	36.5	...	942[7]	12,106	394,578	32.6	...	73[7]	1,247
Yugoslavia	1994	4,421	51,801	922,939	17.8	69	538	25,596	348,132	13.6	62	...	...
Zaire	1993	12,987	112,041	4,939,297	44.1	54	...	59,325[2]	640,298	22.6[2]	17	...	[2]
Zambia	1989	3,489	32,348[4]	1,446,847	44.1[4]	81	480	5,786[4]	161,349[4]	27.9[4]	16	26	846
Zimbabwe	1992	4,578[23]	52,415[23]	2,376,048[23]	45.3[23]	...	1,518	23,233	657,344	28.3	...	25	1,479

[1]1990. [2]General second level includes vocational second level. [3]1989. [4]1988. [5]Includes lower second level. [6]Upper second level only. [7]1986. [8]1987. [9]First level includes general second level. [10]1992. [11]Universities only. [12]College of the Bahamas only. [13]Includes preschool. [14]1994. [15]Vocational second level includes third level. [16]1991. [17]Excludes teacher training. [18]Republic of Cyprus only. [19]Over age 20. [20]Includes preschool, primary, and lower second level (to age 15). [21]Public schools only. [22]Data exclude the al-Azhar education system. [23]1993.

		third level (higher)							literacy[b]				public expenditure on education (percent of GNP)[b]	country
students[d]	student/ teacher ratio	institutions	teachers[c]	students[d]	student/ teacher ratio	gross enroll-ment ratio[b]	students per 100,000 popula-tion[b]	percent of population age 25 and over with post-secondary education[b]	over age	total (%)	male (%)	female (%)		
28,200	12.9	40	6,696	260,300	38.9	4.8	...	...	15	83.1	88.7	77.7	2.4	Myanmar (Burma)
1,503	11.9[3]	7	213[16]	6,523	11.8[16]	3.3	300	...	15	75.8	77.8	74.0	8.6	Namibia
30	10.0	1	...	200	...	...	...	...	15	99.0	...	...	...	Nauru
[2]	[2]	3	4,925[16]	103,840	22.4[16]	5.6	558	...	15	27.5	40.9	14.0	2.9	Nepal
498,000	28.0[16]	206	30,952[7]	389,000	...	44.8	3,339	...	15	100.0	100.0	100.0	5.9	Netherlands, The
6,354	14.7	1	53	620	11.7	...	...	...	15	93.8	94.2	93.4	...	Netherlands Antilles
7,543	[2]	6	141[3]	1,207[1]	9.9[3]	...	...	...	15	57.9	57.4	58.3	...	New Caledonia
98,602	13.4	7[11]	4,308[11]	103,087[11]	23.9[11]	57.5	4,675	39.1	15	100.0	100.0	100.0	7.3	New Zealand
17,765	23.3	4	1,645	34,984	21.3	8.7	809	...	15	65.7	64.6	66.6	4.1	Nicaragua
2,110[10]	12.1[10]	3[4]	341[4]	4,506[3]	11.1[54]	1.0	81	...	15	13.6	20.9	6.6	3.1	Niger
391,583[3]	24.9[3]	...	19,601[1]	335,824[1]	17.1[1]	4.0	360	...	15	57.1	67.3	47.3	1.7	Nigeria
[2]	[2]	1	102	1,097	10.8	...	...	...	15	96.3	96.9	95.6	...	Northern Mariana Islands
[2]	[2]	195	10,213	172,574	16.9	54.4	4,111	17.9	15	100.0	100.0	100.0	8.4	Norway
2,814	6.6	5[1]	433[1]	3,615[10]	7.0[1]	4.9	400	...	6	41.0	58.0	24.0	5.8	Oman
92,000	13.5	804	29,600	758,000	25.6	2.6	247	2.5	15	37.8	50.0	24.4	2.7	Pakistan
...	...	...	...	382	...	...	...	...	15	97.6	98.3	96.6	...	Palau
[2]	[2]	8	4,029	69,247	17.2	23.4	2,398	16.8	15	90.8	91.4	90.2	5.6	Panama
11,370	12.9	2[1]	902[7]	5,007[1]	7.1[7]	...	...	...	15	72.2	81.0	62.7	...	Papua New Guinea
18,595	[2]	2[16]	742[23]	30,373[23]	40.9[23]	9.9	907	...	15	92.1	93.5	90.6	2.8	Paraguay
270,668	22.7	655[10]	46,963	730,987	15.6	40.1	4,188	...	15	88.7	94.5	83.0	1.5	Peru
[2]	[2]	809[10]	56,880[16]	1,582,820	23.7[16]	26.2	2,654	...	15	94.6	95.0	94.3	2.4	Philippines
1,691,000	19.8	140	65,300	584,000	8.9	25.5	1,812	7.9	15	98.7	99.2	98.3	5.5	Poland
84,932	...	250	30,998	214,403	6.9	23.4	1,936	...	15	86.8	86.7	86.9	5.0	Portugal
149,191	...	45	9,045	156,818	17.3	...	...	...	18	89.7	89.6	89.7	...	Puerto Rico
774	6.0	1	637	7,351	11.5	27.3	1,389	13.3	15	79.4	79.2	79.9	3.5	Qatar
[2]	...	1[11]	220[11, 14]	8,300[11, 14]	37.7[11, 14]	...	...	...	15	78.2	75.9	80.3	...	Réunion
792,262	17.3	...	18,123	235,669	13.0	11.8	1,019	6.9	15	96.7	98.5	95.0	3.6	Romania
1,308,000	...	...	363,508	4,587,045	12.6	45.3	3,017	14.1	15	98.0	99.5	96.8	4.4	Russia
[2]	[2]	...	646[1]	3,454	5.2[1]	0.6	50	...	15	60.5	69.8	51.6	3.8	Rwanda
189	5.4	1	3	36	12.0	...	...	...	15	90.0	90.0	90.0	3.3	St. Kitts and Nevis
1,125[15]	6.3[1]	[15]	...	[15]	...	...	...	...	15	80.0	...	...	5.5	St. Lucia
337	...	...	...	...	...	...	...	...	15	96.0	...	...	6.7	St. Vincent and the Grenadines
408	...	...	...	...	...	...	...	...	15	98.0	98.2	97.7	...	San Marino
289	...	...	...	...	...	...	...	...	15	54.2	70.2	39.1	4.3	São Tomé and Príncipe
39,840	10.5	72[16]	12,669	174,788	13.8	13.7	1,145	...	15	62.8	71.5	50.2	6.4	Saudi Arabia
7,301	40.1	18[16]	965[10, 11]	23,001[10, 11]	23.8[10, 11]	3.4	298	...	15	33.1	43.0	23.2	4.2	Senegal
1,429	9.2	...	...	...	...	...	...	...	15	84.2	82.9	85.7	8.5	Seychelles
6,929	9.2	2[1]	257[16]	2,571[16]	10.0[16]	1.3	129	...	15	31.4	45.4	18.2	1.4	Sierra Leone
44,050	14.8	7	6,295	73,650	11.7	...	...	4.7	15	91.1	95.9	86.3	3.4	Singapore
245,653	17.0	...	8,392[11]	71,916[11]	8.6[11]	17.1	1,369	9.5	15	100.0	100.0	100.0	5.7	Slovakia
[2]	[2]	28	2,783	37,362	13.4	28.1	2,077	10.4	10	99.2	99.3	99.1	6.2	Slovenia
...	...	1	...	...	...	...	...	...	15	54.1	62.4	44.9	4.2	Solomon Islands
4,809	9.7	1	...	1,692	...	...	...	...	10	54.8	60.9	47.9	0.4	Somalia
152,962	10.2	32	39,388	467,060	11.9	13.4	1,264	...	15	81.8	81.9	81.7	7.0	South Africa
1,234,045[3]	19.5[3]	1,415	67,166[3]	1,261,012	...	41.1	3,474	7.0	15	95.8	97.5	94.2	4.6	Spain
8,908	20.4	8	1,937	31,447	16.2	6.1	504	...	15	90.2	93.4	87.2	3.1	Sri Lanka
34,316	23.9	24	1,943	54,345	28.0	3.0	266	...	15	46.1	57.7	34.6	...	Sudan, The
12,307	[2]	1[10]	254[10]	2,373[10]	9.3[10]	...	1,079	...	15	93.0	95.1	91.0	7.3	Suriname
772[16]	2.8[16]	...	452[10]	3,224[16]	7.1[16]	3.6	384	...	15	76.7	78.0	75.6	6.8	Swaziland
[2]	[2]	...	...	226,830[10]	...	38.3	2,100	...	15	100.0	100.0	100.0	8.3	Sweden
191,344	...	...	...	144,544	...	30.6	2,107		15	100.0	100.0	100.0	5.5	Switzerland
76,480	6.6	...	5,997[11]	178,526[11]	29.8[11]	17.6	1,700	...	15	70.8	85.7	55.8	4.2	Syria
515,211	27.4	125	33,392	689,185	20.6	...	...	...	15	93.4	97.0	89.6	3.6	Taiwan
38,400		22	...	69,000	...	24.8	2,298	...	15	97.7	98.8	96.6	11.2	Tajikistan
15,824	13.6	4[3]	1,206[3]	6,100[1]	4.4[3]	...	21	...	15	67.8	79.4	56.8	5.0	Tanzania
715,393	18.6	84	19,747	768,179	38.9	18.7	2,029	...	15	93.8	96.0	91.6	4.0	Thailand
8,392[1]	32.2[1]	1[11]	276[4, 11]	9,120[11]	...	2.7	235	...	15	51.7	67.0	37.0	6.7	Togo
358	13.4[1]	1	19	226	11.9	...	...	...	15	92.8	92.9	92.8	4.8	Tonga
...	...	1	438[14]	5,191[14]	11.9[14]	7.6	673	...	15	97.9	98.8	97.0	4.0	Trinidad and Tobago
[2]	[2]	...	5,655	96,101	17.0	11.4	1,121	...	15	66.7	78.6	54.6	6.4	Tunisia
977,010	17.0	424	35,132	759,047	21.6	15.7	1,918	...	15	82.3	91.7	72.4	4.0	Turkey
33,700	...	9	...	41,700	...	21.8	2,078	...	15	97.7	98.8	96.6	7.9	Turkmenistan
31	3.1	—	—	—	—	...	...	...	15	95.5	95.5	95.5	...	Tuvalu
46,238	16.7	9[3]	941	8,966	9.5	1.3	121	...	15	61.8	73.7	50.2	2.0	Uganda
680,700	...	159	...	829,200	...	45.9	3,152	...	15	98.4	99.5	97.4	6.1	Ukraine
1,143	[2]	1	510[23]	9,793[23]	19.2[23]	10.5	601	...	15	79.2	78.9	79.8	2.0	United Arab Emirates
586,000	...	...	92,067	1,528,389	16.6	37.4	2,646	...	15	100.0	100.0	100.0	5.2	United Kingdom
[2]	[2]	5,758	842,000	14,600,000	17.3	80.6	5,611	45.2	15	95.5	95.7	95.3	5.3	United States
54,839	...	2	7,016	62,893	9.0	30.0	2,396	8.1	15	97.3	96.9	97.7	2.8	Uruguay
242,793	11.0	52[10]	...	337,400[10]	...	32.9	3,054	...	15	97.2	98.5	96.0	11.0	Uzbekistan
444	...	1	...	124[16]	...	—	...	...	15	52.9	57.3	47.8	4.5	Vanuatu
[2]	[2]	99[16]	43,833	550,783	12.6	28.5	2,757	11.8	15	91.1	91.8	90.3	5.3	Venezuela
137,405	11.3	104	20,648	118,589	5.7	1.5	147	...	15	93.7	96.5	91.2	...	Vietnam
...	...	1	240	2,924	12.2	...	...	...	...	...	...	...	...	Virgin Islands (U.S.)
...	...	...	988[3]	14,434[3]	15.1[3]	...	...	...	...	...	...	...	...	West Bank[33]
...	...	...	...	...	...	...	...	...	...	...	...	...	...	Western Sahara
...	...	...	...	...	...	...	...	...	15	100.0	100.0	100.0	4.2	Western Samoa
26,119	20.9	1[3]	470[3]	23,457[3]	49.9[3]	2.9	447	...	15	38.5	53.3	26.3	4.6	Yemen[34]
...	...	144	11,513	141,587	12.3	18.9	1,370	...	15	93.3	97.6	89.2	...	Yugoslavia
701,148	[2]	...	3,873[3]	61,422[3]	15.9[3]	1.9	176	...	15	77.3	86.6	67.7	1.0	Zaire
8,218	9.7	2	320	6,247	19.5	2.0	183	...	15	78.2	85.6	71.3	2.6	Zambia
27,431	18.5	28	2,414	39,406	16.3	6.1	588	...	15	85.1	90.4	79.9	8.3	Zimbabwe

[24]Includes lower second level students at all-age schools. [25]Excludes lower second level students at all-age schools. [26]Former West Germany only. [27]Port-au-Prince universities only. [28]Department of Education and Culture schools only. [29]National schools only. [30]Includes schools that provide both first and second level education. [31]Mainland Tanzania only. [32]Primary includes kindergarten. [33]Excludes East Jerusalem. [34]Former Yemen Arab Republic only.

BIBLIOGRAPHY AND SOURCES

The following list indicates the principal documentary sources used in the compilation of *Britannica World Data.* It is by no means a complete list, either for international or for national sources, but is indicative only of the range of materials to which reference has been made in preparing this compilation. For example, in addition to the kinds of works cited below, reference has also been made to the constitution of each country, to the publications of its central or commercial banks, and to unpublished information received in correspondence from the countries. Reference is made to an organization's or country's Internet resources when these have been used, but no reference to telephone, fax, or other more informal sources.

International Statistical Sources

Asian Development Bank. *Asian Development Outlook* (annual); *Key Indicators of Developing Member Countries of ADB* (annual, with supplements).

Billboard Ltd. *World Radio TV Handbook* (annual).

Caribbean Development Bank. *Annual Report.*

Comité Monétaire de la Zone Franc. *La Zone Franc: Rapport* (annual).

Commonwealth of Independent States. *Demographic Yearbook; Sodruzhestvo Nezavizimykh Gosudarstv v 19** godu; Strany-Chleny SNG: Statistichesky Yezhegodnik* (*Member States of the CIS: Statistical Yearbook*).

Eastern Caribbean Central Bank. *Report and Statement of Accounts* (annual).

Europa Publications Ltd. *Africa South of the Sahara* (annual); *The Europa Year Book* (2 vol.); *The Far East and Australasia* (annual); *The Middle East and North Africa* (annual).

Food and Agriculture Organization. *Food Balance Sheets; Production Yearbook; Trade Yearbook; World Census of Agriculture* (decennial); *Yearbook of Fishery Statistics* (2 vol.); *Yearbook of Forest Products;* its Internet resources.

FT Caribbean. *The Caribbean Handbook* (annual).

Her Majesty's Stationery Office. *The Commonwealth Yearbook.*

Instituts d'Émission d'Outre-Mer et des Départements d'Outre-Mer (France). *Bulletin trimestriel* (quarterly); *Rapport annuel.*

Inter-American Development Bank. *Economic and Social Progress in Latin America* (annual); its Internet resources.

Inter-Parliamentary Union. *Chronicle of Parliamentary Elections and Developments* (annual); *World Directory of Parliaments* (annual).

International Air Transport Association. *World Air Transport Statistics* (annual).

International Bank for Reconstruction and Development/The World Bank. *Statistical Handbook 19**: States of the Former USSR* (annual); *World Bank Atlas* (annual); *World Debt Tables* (annual); *World Development Report* (annual).

International Civil Aviation Organization. *Civil Aviation Statistics of the World* (annual); *Digest of Statistics.*

International Institute for Strategic Studies. *The Military Balance* (annual).

International Labour Organisation. *Year Book of Labour Statistics; The Cost of Social Security: Basic Tables* (triennial).

International Monetary Fund. *Annual Report on Exchange Arrangements and Exchange Restrictions; Direction of Trade Statistics Yearbook; Government Finance Statistics Yearbook; IMF Economic Reviews* (irreg.); *IMF Staff Country Reports* (irreg.); *International Financial Statistics* (monthly, with yearbook).

International Road Federation. *World Road Statistics* (annual).

International Telecommunication Union. *World Telecommunication Indicators* (annual).

Jane's Publishing Co., Ltd. *Jane's World Railways* (annual).

Lloyd's Register of Shipping. *Lloyd's Register of Shipping: Statistical Tables* (annual).

Longman Group U.K. Ltd. *Keesing's Record of World Events* (monthly).

Macmillan Press Ltd. *The Statesman's Year-Book.*

Middle East Economic Digest Ltd. *Africa Economic Digest* (semimonthly); *Middle East Economic Digest* (semimonthly).

Mining Journal. *Mining Annual Review* (2 vol.).

Nordic Council. *Yearbook of Nordic Statistics.*

Official Airline Guides, Inc. *Official Airline Guide* (monthly).

Organization of Eastern Caribbean States. *Statistical Pocket Digest.*

Organization for Economic Cooperation and Development. *Economic Surveys* (annual); *Financing and External Debt of Developing Countries* (annual).

Oxford University Press. *World Christian Encyclopedia* (David B. Barrett, ed. [1982]).

Pan American Health Organization. *Health Conditions in the Americas* (2 vol.; quadrennial); its Internet resources.

PennWell Publishing Co. *International Petroleum Encyclopedia* (annual).

René Moreux et Cie. *Marchés tropicaux & Méditerranéens* (weekly).

South Pacific Commission. *Key Economic Indicators* (irreg.); *South Pacific Economies: Statistical Summary* (biennial).

United Nations (UN). *Demographic Yearbook; International Trade Statistics Yearbook* (2 vol.); *Energy Statistics Yearbook; Monthly Bulletin of Statistics; Population Studies* (irreg.); *National Accounts Statistics* (3 vol.; annual); *Population and Vital Statistics Report* (quarterly); *Statistical Yearbook; World Population Prospects 19*** (biennial).

UN: Conference on Trade and Development. *Handbook of International Trade and Development Statistics* (annual).

UN: Economic Commission for Africa. *African Socio-Economic Indicators* (annual); *African Statistical Yearbook* (2 vol. in 4 parts); *Demographic and Related Socio-Economic Data Sheets for ECA Member States* (irreg.); *Survey of Economic and Social Conditions in Africa* (annual).

UN: Economic Commission for Europe. *Annual Bulletin of Housing and Building Statistics for Europe; Annual Bulletin of Transport Statistics for Europe.*

UN: Economic Commission for Latin America. *Economic Survey of Latin America and the Caribbean* (annual); *Statistical Yearbook for Latin America and the Caribbean.*

UN: Economic and Social Commission for Asia and the Pacific. *Foreign Trade Statistics of Asia and the Pacific* (annual); *Statistical Indicators for Asia and the Pacific* (quarterly); *Statistical Yearbook for Asia and the Pacific.*

UN: Economic and Social Commission for Western Asia. *Demographic and Related Socio-Economic Data Sheets* (irreg.); *National Accounts Studies of the ESCWA Region* (irreg.); *Population Bulletin* (irreg.); *The Population Situation in the ESCWA Region* (irreg.); *Prices and Financial Statistics in the ESCWA Region* (irreg.); *Statistical Abstract of the Region of the Economic and Social Commission for Western Asia* (annual).

UN: Educational, Scientific, and Cultural Organization. *Statistical Yearbook.*

United Nations Development Programme. *Human Development Report* (annual).

United Nations Industrial Development Organization. *Industrial Development Review Series* (irreg.); *Industry and Development: Global Report* (annual); *International Yearbook of Industrial Statistics.*

United States: Central Intelligence Agency, *The World Factbook* (annual); Dept. of Commerce, *World Population Profile* (irreg.); Dept. of Energy, *International Energy Annual;* Dept. of Health and Human Services, *Social Security Programs Throughout the World* (biennial); Dept. of Interior, *Minerals Yearbook* (3 vol. in 8); Dept. of State, *Background Notes* (irreg.).

Vatican (Central Statistics Office of the Church). *Statistical Yearbook of the Church.*

World Energy Conference. *Survey of Energy Resources* (triennial).

World Health Organization. *World Health Statistics Annual; World Health Statistics Quarterly.*

World Tourism Organization. *World Tourism Statistics* (2 vol.; annual).

National Statistical Sources

Afghanistan. *First Seven-Year Economic and Social Development Plan, 1355–1361* (*March 1976–March 1983*)*; Preliminary Results of the First Afghan Population Census, 1979*).

Albania. *IMF Economic Reviews: Albania* (1994); *Population and Housing Census 1989; Statistical Yearbook of Albania.*

Algeria. *Annuaire statistique; Recensement général de la population et de l'habitat, 1987.*

American Samoa. *American Samoa Statistical Digest* (annual); *1990 Census of Population and Housing* (U.S.).

Andorra. *Estadístiques* (annual); *Recull Estadístic General de la Població Andorra 90.*

Angola. *Angola: An Introductory Economic Review* (A World Bank Country Study [1991]); *Informação Estatìstica* (annual); *Perfil estatìstico de Angola* (annual).

Antigua. *Statistical Yearbook; 1991 Population and Housing Census.*

Argentina. *Anuario estadístico de la República Argentina; Censo nacional de población y vivienda, 1991; Encuesta permanente de hogares* (irreg.); its Internet resources.

Armenia. *Economic Reviews: Armenia* (IMF [annual]); *Statisticheskii Yezhegodnik Armenii* (Statistical Yearbook of Armenia).

Aruba. *Statistical Yearbook; Third Population and Housing Census October 6, 1991.*

Australia. *Census of Manufacturing Establishments: Summary of Operations by Industry Subdivision, Australia* (annual); *Foreign Trade Australia: Comparative and Summary Tables* (annual); *Monthly Summary of Statistics, Australia; National Income and Expenditure* (annual); *Social Indicators* (irreg.); *Year Book Australia; 1991 Census of Population and Housing.*

Austria. *Grosszählung 1991* (General Census 1991). *Österreichisches Jahrbuch* (annual); *Sozialstatistische Daten* (irreg.); *Statistisches Jahrbuch für die Republik Österreich.*

Azerbaijan. *A World Bank Country Study: Azerbaijan, from Crisis to Sustained Growth* (1993); *Economic Reviews: Azerbaijan* (IMF [annual]); *Narodnoye Khozyaystvo Azerbaydzhanskoy SSR* (National Economy of the Azerbaijan S.S.R. [annual]).

Bahamas, The. *Census of Population and Housing 1990; Quarterly Statistical Summary; Statistical Abstract* (annual); *Vital Statistics Report* (annual).

Bahrain. *Statistical Abstract* (annual); *The Population, Housing, Buildings and Establishments Census—1991.*

Bangladesh. *Bangladesh Population Census, 1991; Population of Bangladesh* (ESCAP; Country Monograph Series No. 8 [1981]); *Statistical Yearbook of Bangladesh.*

Barbados. *Barbados Economic Report* (annual); *Monthly Digest of Statistics; 1993–2000 Development Plan.*

Belarus. *Economic Reviews: Belarus* (IMF [annual]); *Narodnoye Kozyaystvo Belorusskoy S.S.R.* (National Economy of the Belorussian S.S.R. [annual]).

Belgium. *Annuaire statistique de la Belgique; Recensement de la population et des logements au 1*[er] *mars 1991.*

Belize. *Abstract of Statistics* (annual); *Belize Economic Survey* (annual); *Belize Today: Development Plan 1990–94; Labour Force Survey* (*1993*); *1991 Population Census: Major Findings.*

Benin. *Annuaire statistique; Recensement des Entreprises 1980* (2 parts); *Recensement général de la population et de l'habitation* (1992).

Bermuda. *Bermuda Digest of Statistics* (annual); *Report of the Manpower Survey* (annual); *The 1991 Census of Population and Housing.*

Bhutan. *Bhutan: Development Planning in a Unique Environment* (A World Bank Country Study [1988]); *Statistical Yearbook of Bhutan.*

Bolivia. *Anuario Estadístico; Censo Nacional de población y vivienda 1992; Compendio Estadístico* (annual); *Estadísticas Socio-económicas* (annual); *Estrategia de Desarrollo Económico y Social 1989–2000; Resumen estadístico* (annual).

Botswana. *National Development Plan 7, 1991–1997; 1991 Population and Housing Census.*

Brazil. *Anuário Estatístico do Brasil; Censo Demografico 1991; Comercio Exterior do Brasil* (2 vol.; annual).

Brunei. *Brunei Statistical Yearbook; Population Survey 1986: Demographic Report; Report on the Census of Population, 1981.*

Bulgaria. *Prebroyavaneto na naselenieto kŭm 4.12.1985 godina* (Census of Population of Dec. 4, 1985); *Statisticheskii godishnikna Republika Bŭlgariya* (Statistical Yearbook of the Republic of Bulgaria).

Burkina Faso. *Annuaire Statistique; Recensement général de la population du 10 au 20 decembre 1985.*

Burundi. *Annuaire statistique; Recensement général de la population, 1990.*

Cambodia. *Cambodia: A Country Study* (1990); *Intersectoral Basic Needs Assessment Mission to Cambodia* (Unesco; 1991); *Report of the Kampuchea Needs Assessment Study* (UNDP; 1989).

Cameroon. *Note annuelle de statistique; Recensement général de la population et de l'habitat 1987.*

Canada. *Canada Year Book* (biennial); *Census Canada 1991: Population.*

Cape Verde. *Boletím Anual de Estatística; I.º Recenseamento Geral da População e Habitação—1990.*

Central African Republic. *Annuaire statistique; Economic and Social Development Plan 1986–90; Recensement général de la population 1988.*

Chad. *Annuaire statistique; Chad: a Country Study* (1990); *Chad—Background Issues and Statistical Update* (*IMF Staff Country Report* [1995]).

Chile. *Chile XVI censo nacional de población y V de vivienda, 22 de abril 1992; Compendio estadístico* (annual); *Plan nacional indicativo de desarrollo* (quinquennial).

China, People's Republic of. *China: A Statistics Survey in 19**** (annual); *People's Republic of China Year-Book; Statistical Yearbook of China; 10 Percent Sampling Tabulation on the 1990 Population Census of the People's Republic of China.*

Colombia. *Colombia estadística* (2 vol.; annual); *XV Censo nacional de población y IV de vivienda* (1985).

Comoros. *Plan interimaire de développement économique et sociale* (*1983–1986*); *Recensement général de la population et de l'habitat 15 septembre 1980.*

Congo. *Annuaire statistique; Recensement Général de la Population et de l'Habitat de 1984.*

Costa Rica. *Anuario estadístico; Censo de Población 1984; Plan Nacional de Desarrollo, 1986–90* (2 vol.).

Côte d'Ivoire. *Annuaire statistique; La Côte d'Ivoire en chiffres* (irreg.); *L'Économie Ivoirienne* (irreg.); *Enquête permanente aupres des menages: resultats provisoires 1985; Recensement général de la population et de l'habitat 1988.*

Croatia. *Census of Population, Households, Dwellings and Farms 31st March 1991; Statistical Yearbook.*

Cuba. *Anuario estadístico; Censo de población y viviendas, 1981; Compendio estadístico de Cuba* (annual); *Cuba Half-Yearly Economic Report.*

Cyprus. *Census of Industrial Production* (annual); *Census of Population 1992; Economic Report* (annual); *Statistical Abstract* (annual).

Czech Republic. *Statistická ročenka České Republiky* (Statistical Yearbook of the Czech Republic).

Denmark. *Folke- og boligtaellingen, 1981* (Population and Housing Census); *Statistisk årbog* (Statistical Yearbook).

Djibouti. *Annuaire statistique de Djibouti.*

Dominica. *Population and Housing Census 1991; Statistical Digest* (irreg.).

Dominican Republic. *República Dominicana en cifras* (annual); *VI Censo nacional de población y vivienda, 1981.*

Ecuador. *Serie estadística* (quinquennial); *Censo de población* (*V*) *y de vivienda* (*IV*) *1990.*

Egypt. *Population, Housing, and Establishment Census, 1986; Statistical Yearbook.*

El Salvador. *Anuario estadístico* (8 vol.); *Censos Nacionales: V Censo de Población y IV de Vivienda* (*1992*); *El Salvador en cifras* (annual); *Indicadores Económicos y Sociales* (annual); *Plan de Desarrollo Economico y Social 1989–1994.*

Equatorial Guinea. *Censos Nacionales, I de Población y I de Vivienda—4 al 17 de Julio de 1983; Guinea en cifras* (irreg.).

Eritrea. *Eritrea—Recent Economic Developments* (*IMF Staff Country Report* [1995]); *Ethiopia and Eritrea: A Documentary Study* (1993).

Estonia. *Eesti Statistika Aastaraamat* (Estonia Statistical Yearbook); *Estonia: The Transition to a Market Economy* (1993); *Estonian Human Development Report* (1995).

Ethiopia. *Ethiopia 1984 Population and Housing Census; Ethiopia Statistical Abstract* (annual).

Faroe Islands. *Arbog for Færøerne* (Yearbook for the Faroe Islands); *Rigsombudsmanden på Færøerne: Beretning* (annual).

Fiji. *Annual Employment Survey; Census of Industries* (annual); *Current Economic Statistics* (quarterly); *1986 Census of the Population.*

Finland. *Annual Statistics of Agriculture; Economic Survey* (annual); *Population Census 1990; Statistical Yearbook of Finland.*

France. *Annuaire statistique de la France; Données sociales* (triennial); *Recensement général de la population de 1990; Tableaux de l'Economie Française* (annual).

French Guiana. *Recensement général de la population de 1990: logements-population-emplois, 973: Guyane; Tableaux economiques regionaux: Guyane* (biennial).

French Polynesia. *Résultats du Recensement Général de la Population de la Polynésie Française, du 6 Septembre 1988; Tableaux de l'economie polynesienne* (irreg.); *Te avei'a: Bulletin d'information statistique* (monthly).

Gabon. *Situation économique, financière et sociale de la République Gabonaise* (annual).

Gambia, The. *Statistical Abstract* (annual?).

Gaza Strip. *Judaea, Samaria, and Gaza Area Statistics Quarterly; Palestinian Statistical Abstract* (annual).

Georgia. *Economic Reviews: Georgia* (IMF [annual]); *Narodnoye Khozyaystvo Gruzinskoy SSR* (National Economy of the Georgian S.S.R. [annual]).

Germany. *Statistisches Jahrbuch für die Bundesrepublik Deutschland; Volkszählung vom 25. Mai 1987* (Census of Population).

Ghana. *Population Census of Ghana, 1984, Quarterly Digest of Statistics.*

Gibraltar. *Abstract of Statistics* (annual); *Census of Gibraltar, 1991.*

Greece. *Recensement de la population et des habitations, 1991; Statistical Yearbook of Greece.*

Greenland. *Grønland* (annual); *Grønlands befolkning* (Greenland Population [annual]).

Grenada. *Abstract of Statistics* (annual); *1991 Population and Housing Census.*

Guadeloupe. *Recensement général de la population de 1990: logements-population-emplois, 971: Guadeloupe; Tableaux economiques regionaux: Guadeloupe* (biennial).

Guam. *Guam Annual Economic Review; Census '90: Guam.*

Guatemala. *Anuario Estadística; Censos nacionales, 1981: IX de población—IV de habitación.*

Guernsey. *Guernsey Census 1991; Statistical Digest* (annual).

Guinea. *Situation Économique et Conjoncturelle au 31 decembre 1985 et éléments sur la mise en oeuvre de la réform économique au cours du première trimestre 1986; Guinea—Statistical Annex* (*IMF Staff Country Report* [1995]).

Guinea-Bissau. *Boletim Trimestral de Estatística; Recenseamento Geral da População e da Habitação, 16 de Abril de 1979.*

Guyana. *Annual Statistical Abstract; Guyana: From Economic Recovery to Sustained Growth* (1993); *Guyana and Belize: Country Studies* (*1993*).

Haiti. *Bulletin trimestriel de statistique; Dominican Republic and Haiti: Country Studies* (1991); *Résultats préliminaires du recensement général* (*Septembre 1982*).

Honduras. *Anuario estadístico; Censo nacional de Población y Vivienda, 1988; Honduras en cifras* (annual); *Plan nacional de desarrollo, 1987–90.*

Hong Kong. *Annual Digest of Statistics; Hong Kong* (annual); *Hong Kong 1991 Population Census; Hong Kong in Figures* (annual); *Hong Kong Social and Economic Trends* (biennial).

Hungary. *Statisztikai évkönyv* (Statistical Yearbook); *1990, Évi népszámlálás* (Census of Population).

Iceland. *Hagtidhindi* (monthly); *Landshagir* (Statistical Yearbook of Iceland [annual]); *Verslunarskýrslur* (External Trade [annual]).

India. *Census of India, 1991; Economic Survey* (annual); *India: A Reference Annual; Statistical Abstract* (annual).

Indonesia. *Indonesia: An Official Handbook* (irreg.); *Hasil Sensus penduduk Indonesia, 1990* (Census of Population); *Statistical Yearbook of Indonesia.*

Iran. *National Census of Population and Housing, October 1986; A Statistical Reflection of the Islamic Republic of Iran* (annual); *Iran Statistical Yearbook.*

Iraq. *Iraq: A Country Study* (1990); *Annual Abstract of Statistics.*

Ireland. *Census of Population of Ireland, 1991; National Income and Expenditure* (annual); *Statistical Abstract* (annual).

Isle of Man. *Census Report 1991; Isle of Man Digest of Economic and Social Statistics* (annual).

Israel. *1983 Census of Population and Housing; Statistical Abstract* (annual).

Italy. *Annuario di statistica agraria: Annuario di statistiche demografiche; Annuario di statistiche industriali; Annuario statistico dell'istruzione; Annuario statistico Italiano; 13° Censimento generale della popolazione e delle Abitazioni 20 Ottobre 1991.*

Jamaica. *Economic and Social Survey* (annual); *Statistical Abstract* (annual); *Statistical Yearbook of Jamaica.*

Japan. *Japan Statistical Yearbook; Statistical Indicators on Social Life* (annual); *1990 Population Census of Japan.*

Jersey. *Report of the Census for 1991; Statistical Digest* (annual).

Jordan. *Population and Housing Census 1994; Family Expenditure Survey* (1980); *National Accounts* (irreg.); *Statistical Yearbook.*

Kazakhstan. *Economic Reviews: Kazakhstan* (IMF [annual]); *Statistichesky Yezhegodnik* (Statistical Yearbook).

Kenya. *Economic Survey* (annual); *Statistical Abstract* (annual).

Kiribati. *Annual Abstract of Statistics; Kiribati Population Census 1990; Sixth National Development Plan, 1987–1991.*

Korea, North. *North Korea: A Country Study* (1994); *The Population of North Korea* (1990).

Korea, South. *Korea Statistical Yearbook; Social Indicators in Korea* (irreg.); *Social Indicators in Korea* (annual); *1990 Population and Housing Census.*

Kuwait. *Annual Statistical Abstract; Economic Report* (annual); *General Census of Population and Housing and Buildings 1985.*

Kyrgyzstan. *Economic Reviews: Kyrgyz Republic* (IMF [annual]); *Statistichesky Yezhegodnik Kyrgyzstana* (Statistical Yearbook of Kyrgyzstan).

Laos. *Lao People's Democratic Republic: Industrial Transition* (UNIDO; 1994).

Latvia. *Latvia: The Transition to a Market Economy* (1993); *Statistical Yearbook of Latvia.*

Lebanon. *Lebanon: A Country Study* (1989).

Lesotho. *Statistical Yearbook; 1986 Population Census.*

Liberia. *Economic Survey* (annual); *1974 Census of Population and Housing.*

Libya. *The Five-Year Development Plan 1981–85; Libya Population Census, 1973; Statistical Abstract for Libya* (annual).

Liechtenstein. *Statistisches Jahrbuch; Volkszählung, 2 Dezember 1980* (Census of Population).

Lithuania. *Lithuania: The Transition to a Market Economy* (1993); *Lithuania's Statistics Yearbook.*

Luxembourg. *Annuaire statistique; Bulletin du STATEC* (monthly); *Recensement général de la population du 31 mars 1991.*

Macau. *Anuário Estatístico; Inquerito Industrial* (annual); *XIII Recenseamento Geral da População, 1991.*

Macedonia. *Basic Statistical Data* (annual); *Former Yugoslav Republic of Macedonia—Recent Economic Developments* (*IMF Staff Country Report* [1995]).

Madagascar. *Recensement général de la population et de l'habitat, aout 1993; Situation économique* (annual).

Malaŵi. *Malaŵi Population and Housing Census, 1987; Malawi Statistical Yearbook; Malawi Yearbook.*

Malaysia. *Fifth Malaysia Plan, 1986–1990; Malaysia Official Year Book; Malaysian Annual Statistical Bulletin; Population and Housing Census of Malaysia 1991.*

Maldives. *National Development Plan 1991–1993; Population and Housing Census of Maldives 1990; Statistical Year Book of Maldives.*

Mali. *Annuaire statistique du Mali; Comptes Economiques du Mali* (annual); *Recensement general de la population et de l'habitat* (*du 1*[er] *au 14 avril 1987*).

Malta. *Annual Abstract of Statistics; Census of Industrial Production Report for 19*** (annual); *Malta Year Book* (annual).
Marshall Islands. *Marshall Islands Statistical Abstract* (annual).
Martinique. *Bulletin de statistique* (quarterly); *Recensement de la population de 1990: logements-population-emplois, 972: Martinique; Tableaux economiques regionaux: Martinique* (biennial).
Mauritania. *Annuaire Statistique; Mauritania: A Country Study* (1990).
Mauritius. *Annual Digest of Statistics; 1990 Housing and Population Census of Mauritius.*
Mayotte. *Recensement général de la population de la Collectivité territoriale de Mayotte: août 1991.*
Mexico. *Anuario estadístico; XI Censo general de población y vivienda, 1990; La Economia Mexicana en Cifras* (1990); *Informe de Gobierno: Estadístico* (annual).
Micronesia. *Second National Development Plan 1992–1996.*
Moldova. *Economic Reviews: Moldova* (IMF [annual]); *Republica Moldova in Cifre* (annual).
Monaco. *Annuaire Officiel.*
Mongolia. *Mongolia—Background Paper (IMF Staff Country Report* [1995]); *National Economy of the MPR, 1921–86* (1986; quinquennial?); *The Mongolian People's Republic: Towards a Market Economy* (1991).
Morocco. *Annuaire statistique du Maroc; Economic and Social Development Report, 1981; Recensement général de la population et de l'habitat de 1982.*
Mozambique. *Anuário Estatístico; 1º Recenseamento Geral da População, 1980.*
Myanmar (Burma). *Report to the Pyithu Hluttaw on the Financial, Social, and Economic Conditions for 19*** (annual); *1983 Population Census.*
Namibia. *Budget 19**–19*** (annual); *Population Census 1981; Statistical/Economic Review* (annual).
Nepal. *Census of Manufacturing Establishments of Nepal, 1986–87; Economic Survey* (annual); *Population Monograph of Nepal* (1987); *The Seventh Plan (1985–90); Statistical Pocket Book* (irreg.); *Statistical Yearbook of Nepal.*
Netherlands, The. *Statistical Yearbook of the Netherlands; 14e Algemene volkstelling, 28 februari 1971* (14th General Population Census).
Netherlands Antilles. *Tweede Algemene Volks- en Woningtelling Nederlandse Antillen: toestand per 1 Februari 1981; Statistical Yearbook of the Netherlands Antilles.*
New Caledonia. *Annuaire statistique; Enquête socio-économique, 1980–1981; Recensement de la population de la Nouvelle-Calédonie au 4 avril 1989; Tableaux de l'economie Caledonienne* (annual).
New Zealand. *1991 New Zealand Census of Population and Dwellings; New Zealand Official Yearbook.*
Nicaragua. *Compendio Estadístico* (annual); *Nicaragua: A Country Study* (1982); *Plan Económico, 1987* (irreg.).
Niger. *Annuaire statistique; Les comptes economiques de la nation* (triennial); *Plan de developpement economique et social du Niger 1987–91; 2ème Recensement général de la population 1988.*
Nigeria. *Annual Abstract of Statistics; Fourth National Development Plan* (1981); *Nigeria: A Country Study* (1992).
Norway. *Folke- og boligtelling 1990* (Population and Housing Census); *Industristatistikk* (annual); *Statistisk årbok* (Statistical Yearbook).
Oman. *Statistical Year Book; Fourth Five-Year Development Plan (1991–1995).*
Pakistan. *Economic Survey* (annual); *Pakistan Statistical Yearbook; Population Census of Pakistan, 1981; Some Socio-Economic Trends* (annual).
Palau. *Abstract of Statistics* (annual); *Census '90.*
Panama. *Indicadores económicos y sociales* (annual); *Censos nacionales de 1990: IX de población y V de vivienda, 13 de mayo de 1990; Panama en cifras* (annual); *Situación económica: Cuentas nacionales* (annual); *Situación económica: Industria* (annual).
Papua New Guinea. *Abstract of Statistics* (quarterly); *National Accounts Statistics—Statistical Bulletin* (quarterly); *Social Indicators of Papua New Guinea, 1980–85; Summary of Statistics* (annual); *1990 National Population Census.*
Paraguay. *Anuario estadístico del Paraguay; Censo nacional de población y viviendas, 1992.*
Peru. *Censos nacionales; IX de población: IV de vivienda, 11 de julio de 1993; Compendio estadístico* (3 vol.; annual); *Informe estadístico* (annual).
Philippines. *Philippine Statistical Yearbook; Philippine Yearbook; 1990 Census of Population and Housing.*
Poland. *Narodowy spis powszechny 1988* (Census of Population); *Rocznik statystyczny* (Statistical Yearbook).
Portugal. *Anuário Estatístico; Estatísticas Agricolas* (annual); *Estatísticas do Comercio Externo* (annual); *Estatísticas Demograficas* (annual); *Estatísticas Industriais* (2 vol.; annual); *Recenseamento Agricola, 1979; XIII Recenseamento Geral da População: III Recenseamento Geral da Habitação, 1991.*
Puerto Rico. *Anuario estadístico; Estadísticas socio-economicas* (annual); *Informe económico al gobernador* (Economic Report to the Governor [annual]); *1990 Census of Population and Housing* (U.S.).
Qatar. *Annual Statistical Abstract; Economic Survey of Qatar* (annual); *Qatar Year Book.*
Réunion. *Recensement général de la population de 1990: logements-population-emploi, 974; Réunion; Tableau Economique de la Réunion* (biennial).
Romania. *Anuarul statistic al României; Population and Housing Census January 7, 1992; Romania Yearbook.*
Russia. *Economic Reviews: Russian Federation* (IMF [annual]); *Rossiysky Statistichesky Yezhegodnik* (Russian Statistical Yearbook).
Rwanda. *Bulletin de Statistique: Supplement Annuel; IIIème Plan de Developpement Economique, Social et Culturel 1982–86; Recensement General de la Population et de l'Habitat 1991.*
St. Kitts and Nevis. *Annual Digest of Statistics; St. Christopher and Nevis: Economic Report* (World Bank Country Study) (1985).
St. Lucia. *Annual Statistical Digest.*
St. Vincent and the Grenadines. *Digest of Statistics* (annual); *Population and Housing Census 1991.*
San Marino. *Annuario statistico, 1981–84* (4 vol.?; irreg.); *3 Censimento generale dell agricoltura* (1977); *5 Censimento generale della popolazione* (1979).
São Tomé and Príncipe. *1° Recenseamento Geral da População e da Habitação 1981.*
Saudi Arabia. *The Statistical Indicator* (annual); *Statistical Summary* (Saudi Arabian Monetary Agency [annual]); Statistical Year Book.
Senegal. *Le Sénégal en chiffres* (irreg.); *Recensement de la Population et de l'Habitat 1988; Situation économique du Senegal* (annual).
Seychelles. *National Development Plan, 1990–94;* (2 vol.); *Statistical Abstract* (annual); *1987 Census Report.*
Sierra Leone. *Sierra Leone: 12 Years of Economic Achievement and Political Consolidation under the APC and Dr. Siaka Stevens, 1968–80.*
Singapore. *Census of Population, 1990; Report on the Census of Industrial Production* (annual); *Singapore Yearbook; Yearbook of Statistics Singapore.*
Slovakia. *Sčítanie L'udu, Domov a Bytov 1991* (Census of Population, Housing, and Families 1991); *Statistical Yearbook of the Slovak Republic.*
Slovenia. *Statistični Letopis Republike Slovenija* (Statistical Yearbook of the Republic of Slovenia).
Solomon Islands. *Solomon Islands 1986 Population Census; Statistical Bulletin* (irreg.).
Somalia. *Statistical Abstract* (annual).
South Africa. *1991 Population Census; South Africa: Official Yearbook of the Republic of South Africa; South African Statistics* (biennial).
Spain. *Anuario estadístico; Censo de población de 1991.*
Sri Lanka. *Census of Population and Housing, 1981; Sri Lanka Year Book; Statistical Pocketbook of the Democratic Socialist Republic of Sri Lanka* (annual).
Sudan, The. *Third Population Census, 1983.*
Suriname. *General Population Census 1980; Statistisch Jaarboek van Suriname.*
Swaziland. *Annual Statistical Bulletin; Fourth Five-Year Development Plan (1986/87–90/91 Fiscal Years); Report on the 1986 Swaziland Population Census.*
Sweden. *Folk- och bostadsräkningen, 1990* (Population and Housing Census); *Statistisk årsbok för Sverige* (Statistical Abstract of Sweden [annual]).
Switzerland. *Recensement fédéral de la population, 1990; Statistisches Jahrbuch* (Statistical Yearbook).
Syria. *General Census of Housing and Inhabitants, 1981; Statistical Abstract* (annual).
Taiwan. *Industry of Free China* (monthly); *Social Indicators of the Republic of China* (annual); *Statistical Abstract* (annual); *Statistical Yearbook of the Republic of China; Taiwan Statistical Data Book* (annual); *Yearbook of Labor Statistics; 1990 Census of Population and Housing.*
Tajikistan. *Economic Reviews: Tajikistan* (IMF [annual]); *Narodnoye Khozyaystvo Tadzhikskoy SSR* (National Economy of the Tadzhik S.S.R. [annual]).
Tanzania. *Tanzania Statistical Abstract* (irreg.); *1978 Population Census.*
Thailand. *Report of the Survey of Business Trade and Services* (biennial); *Foreign Trade Statistics* (monthly); *Report of the Industrial Survey, Whole Kingdom* (biennial); *Report of the Labor Force Survey: Whole Kingdom* (quarterly); *Statistical Handbook of Thailand* (annual); *Statistical Yearbook; 1990 Population and Housing Census.*
Togo. *Annuaire statistique du Togo; Eurostat Country Profile: Togo* (1991); *Plan de développement économique & social, 1981–1985; Recensement Général de la Population et de l'Habitat 1981.*
Tonga. *Population Census, 1986; Sixth Development Plan 1991–95; Statistical Abstract* (irreg.).
Trinidad and Tobago. *Annual Statistical Digest; 1990 Population and Housing Census.*
Tunisia. *Annuaire statistique de la Tunisie; Recensement général de la population et des logements, 30 mars 1984.*
Turkey. *Diş Ticaret İstatistikleri* (Annual Foreign Trade Statistics); *1990 Genel Nüfus Sayımı* (1990 Census of Population); *İnşaat İstatistikleni* (Construction Statistics [annual]); *Türkiye İstatistik Yilliği* (Statistical Yearbook of Turkey).
Turkmenistan. *Economic Reviews: Turkmenistan* (IMF [annual]); *Narodnoye Khozyaystvo Turkmenskoy SSR* (National Economy of the Turkmen S.S.R. [annual]).
Tuvalu. *1992–94 Medium-Term Economic Framework Programme.*
Uganda. *Uganda: A Country Study; Uganda—Background Paper (IMF Staff Country Report* [1995]).
Ukraine. *Economic Reviews: Ukraine* (IMF [annual]); *Narodne Hospodarstvo Ukrayini u 19** rotsi* (National Economy of Ukraine in the Year 19** [annual]).
United Arab Emirates. *Statistical Yearbook* (Abu Dhabi).
United Kingdom. *Annual Abstract of Statistics; Britain: An Official Handbook* (annual); *Census 1991; Report on the Census of Production: Summary Tables* (annual); *United Kingdom National Accounts.*
United States. *Agricultural Statistics* (annual); *Annual Energy Review; Current Population Reports* (Series P-20, P-23, P-25, P-26, P-27, P-28, P-60); *Digest of Education Statistics* (annual); *Minerals Yearbook* (3 vol.; annual); *National Transportation Statistics* (annual); *Statistical Abstract* (annual); *U.S. Exports: SIC-Based Products* (annual); *U.S. Imports: SIC-Based Products* (annual); *Vital and Health Statistics* (series 1–20); *1992 Census of Agriculture; 1992 Census of Construction Industries; 1992 Census of Manufacturing; 1992 Census of Retail Trade; 1992 Census of Service Industries; 1992 Census of Wholesale Trade; 1990 Census of Population and Housing;* its Internet resources.
Uruguay. *Anuario Estadístico; Censo General: VI de población: IV de viviendas, Octubre 1985. Encuesta Nacional de Hogares* (annual).
Uzbekistan. *Economic Reviews: Uzbekistan* (IMF [annual]); *Narodnoye Khozyaystvo Respubliki Uzbekistan v 19** g.* (National Economy of Uzbekistan in the Year 19** [annual]).
Vanuatu. *National Population Census 1989; Second National Development Plan 1987–1991* (2 vol.); *Vanuatu Statistical Yearbook.*
Venezuela. *Anuario estadístico; Censo General de la Población y Vivienda 1990; Encuesta de hogares por muestreo* (annual); *Encuesta industrial* (annual).
Vietnam. *IMF Economic Reviews: Vietnam* (1994); *Nien Giam Thong Ke* (Statistical Yearbook); *Tong Dieu Tra Dan So Viet Nam—1989* (*Vietnam Population Census—1989*); *Vietnam: A Country Study* (1989).
Virgin Islands of the United States. *Annual Report; 1990 Census of Population and Housing* (U.S.).
West Bank. *Judaea, Samaria, and Gaza Area Statistics Quarterly; Palestinian Statistical Abstract* (annual).
Western Sahara. *Recensement General de la Population et de l'Habitat* (1982 [Morocco]).
Western Samoa. *Annual Statistical Abstract; Census of Population and Housing,* 1981; *Seventh Development Plan 1992–1994.*
Yemen. *Country Presentation: Republic of Yemen* (1990); *The Yemens: Country Studies* (1986).
Yugoslavia. *Popis stanovištva, domaćinstava, stanova i poljoprivrednih gazdinstava 1991 godine* (Census of Population, Households, Housing, and Agricultural Holdings 1991); *Statistički godišnjak Jugoslavije* (Statistical Yearbook of Yugoslavia).
Zaire. *Annuaire statistique* (irreg.); Conjoncture Economique (semiannual); *Recensement Scientifique de la Population du 1er juillet 1984.*
Zambia. *Country Profile: Zambia 1985; Monthly Digest of Statistics; National Development Plan, 1989–93; 1990 Census of Population, Housing, Agriculture.*
Zimbabwe. *Population Census 1991; Statistical Yearbook* (irreg.).

Index

This index covers both *Britannica Book of the Year* (cumulative for ten years) and *Britannica World Data*.

Entries in dark type are titles of articles in the ***Book of the Year;*** **an accompanying year in dark type gives the year the reference appears, and the accompanying page number in light type shows where the article appears. References for previous years are preceded by the year in dark type. For example, "Archaeology 96:**114; **95:**101; **94:**95; **93:**96; **92:**95; **91:**125; **90:**143; **89:**125; **88:**125; **87:**141**" indicates that the article "Archaeology" appeared every year from 1987 through 1996. Other references that appear with a page number but without a year refer to references from the current yearbook.**

Indented entries in light type that follow dark type article titles refer by page number to other places in the text where the subject of the article is discussed. Light type entries that are not indented refer by page number to subjects that are not themselves article titles. Names of people covered in biographies and obituaries are followed by the abbreviation "(biog.)" or "(obit.)" with the year in dark type and a page number in light type, *e.g.*, Eisenstaedt, Alfred (obit.) **96:**80, or Clinton, William (Bill) Jefferson (biogs.) **94:**37; **93:**37. In cases where a person has both a biography and an obituary, the words appear as subentries under the main entry and are alphabetized accordingly, *e.g.*:

Rabin, Yitzhak
  biography **93:**47
  obituary **96:**93

References to illustrations are by page number and are preceded by the abbreviation *il.*

The index uses word-by-word alphabetization (treating a word as one or more characters separated by a space from the next word). Names beginning with "Mc" and "Mac" are alphabetized as "Mac"; "St." is treated as "Saint."

A

References with dark type numbers refer to the previous years, *e.g.,* 95:264 for the 1995 edition, page 264.

B

D

References with dark type numbers refer to the previous years, *e.g.,* **95**:264 for the 1995 edition, page 264.

F

References with dark type numbers refer to the previous years, *e.g.*, **95**:264 for the 1995 edition, page 264.

G

H

I

References with dark type numbers refer to the previous years, *e.g.*, **95:264** for the 1995 edition, page 264.

J

K

L

References with dark type numbers refer to the previous years, *e.g.*, **95:264** for the 1995 edition, page 264.

M

References giving only a page number in light type are for the current edition.

References with dark type numbers refer to the previous years, *e.g.,* **95**:264 for the 1995 edition, page 264.

References with dark type numbers refer to the previous years, *e.g.*, **95**:264 for the 1995 edition, page 264.

References with dark type numbers refer to the previous years, *e.g.*, **95**:264 for the 1995 edition, page 264.

T

V

References with dark type numbers refer to the previous years, *e.g.,* **95**:264 for the 1995 edition, page 264.